PRONUNCIATION SYMBOLS

ə					
banana	**mitten**	capital	cotton	suppose	perplex
bun	**lunch**	putty	color	supper	pup
burn	**learnt**	pert	curl	serpent	purple

[in the words in the first line above, ə (called *schwa* \'shwä\) is spoken with very weak force; in the words in the second and third lines ə is spoken with stronger force]

a ax, map
ā age, vacation, day
ä father, cot, cart
ȧ [a sound between \a\ and \ä\, as in an eastern New England pronunciation of aunt, half]
aů out, now
b baby, rib
ch chin, match, nature \'nā-chər\
d did, ladder
e less
ē seaweed, any, serial, cereal
f fifty, cuff, phone
g gift, pig, bigger
h hat, ahead
i trip
ī life, buy, my
j job, gem, edge
k kin, cook, chasm
l lily, pool, mortal
m murmur
n nine, cotton
ng sing, singer, finger, ink
ō low, bone, cooperate
ȯ moth, law, sort, all
ȯi coin, destroy
p pepper, lip
r rarity
s spice, less
sh shy, dish, machine, mission, special
t tight, latter
th thin, ether
th this, either
ü boot, rule
ů foot, pull
v give, vivid
w we, away
y you, yet
yü few, union, mule, youth
yů furious
z zone, raise
zh vision, beige

\ \ slant lines used in pairs to mark the beginning and end of a pronunciation: \'pen\
' mark at the beginning of a syllable that has primary (strongest) stress: \'pen-mən-ˌship\
ˌ mark at the beginning of a syllable that has secondary (next-strongest) stress: \'pen-mən-ˌship\
\- mark of syllable division in pronunciations [the mark of syllable division in boldface entry words is a centered dot • and the position of the two kinds of division often does not agree, as in **build•ing** \'bil-diŋ\, **spe•cial** \'spesh-əl\, **ca•ter** \'kāt-ər\]
( ) parentheses indicate that what is between is present in some utterances but not in others: at *factory*, \'fak-t(ə-)rē\ = \'fak-tə-rē, 'fak-trē\ or \'fak-trē, 'fak-tə-rē\

WEBSTER'S INTERMEDIATE DICTIONARY

A NEW SCHOOL DICTIONARY

A Merriam-Webster®

AMERICAN BOOK COMPANY

New York Cincinnati Atlanta Dallas M

Registered User of the Trademarks in Canada

Library of Congress Cataloging in Publication Data
Main entry under title:

Webster's intermediate dictionary.

SUMMARY: Provides definitions, pronunciation, etymology, part of speech designation, and other appropriate information for 58,000 entries.
"A Merriam-Webster."
1. English language – Dictionaries, juvenile.
[1. English language – Dictionaries]
PE1628.W55674 1972 423 77-38973
ISBN 0-278-45972-2 Regular
0-278-45974-9 TAE

MADE IN THE UNITED STATES OF AMERICA

CONTENTS

PREFACE

WEBSTER'S INTERMEDIATE DICTIONARY is a new work in the Merriam-Webster series of dictionaries. It is a school dictionary edited for use either as the middle dictionary in a three-dictionary progression, being preceded by *Webster's New Elementary Dictionary* and followed by *Webster's New Students Dictionary,* or as the first of a two-dictionary progression, preceding *Webster's New Students Dictionary.*

The vocabulary entries in WEBSTER'S INTERMEDIATE DICTIONARY have been selected chiefly on the basis of their occurrence in textbooks and supplementary reading in all subjects of the school curriculum. The definers have had before them this firsthand evidence as well as the millions of examples of usage that underlie *Webster's Third New International Dictionary* and *Webster's Seventh New Collegiate Dictionary.* This method of editing ensures the coverage of today's school vocabularies, especially in mathematics, science, and social studies, and at the same time makes certain that the current literary and general vocabulary is not neglected.

This dictionary includes several features of more advanced Merriam-Webster dictionaries. The etymologies, in square brackets, give students a substantial basis for the fascinating study of word origins. The synonymy paragraphs, at the end of definitions, discriminate between words of similar meaning (as *error, mistake,* and *blunder*), and antonyms are provided where appropriate. There are more than 700 pictorial illustrations and numerous useful tables (as of the metric system and the Morse code). The back matter includes in columnar form the names with pronunciations of the presidents and vice-presidents of the United States, the states and state capitals of the United States, the provinces of Canada, and the nations of the world.

A section on the use of the dictionary comes immediately after this preface. It contains a large number of questions to be answered from information available in the dictionary as well as several sets of written exercises designed to teach the student how to use the dictionary intelligently. This section, in fact, lends itself to a variety of classroom lessons that can be assigned according to the needs of the class.

The plans for this dictionary were jointly agreed on by the American Book Company and G. & C. Merriam Company. The reading and checking, the defining and editing, and the proofreading have been carried out by the permanent Merriam-Webster editorial staff. The front matter on "Using Your Dictionary" was prepared chiefly by the editorial staff of the American Book Company.

G. & C. MERRIAM COMPANY

USING YOUR DICTIONARY

If a younger brother or sister should ask you what a dictionary is, what would you say? Would you be able to tell all the different ways in which a dictionary can help you? Try writing your own definition. Then turn to the word *dictionary* in this book and see what further information you can find there. After that, check yourself on what you already know. As you answer the questions below, use your dictionary.

WHAT DO YOU ALREADY KNOW ABOUT THE DICTIONARY?

1. Between what two entries do you find the word *dictionary* listed (see page 6a for "Using alphabetical order")?
2. What is the purpose of the two words at the top of the page (see page 6a for "Using guide words")?
3. How can you divide the word *dictionary* at the end of a line in writing (see page 7a for "Understanding the centered period")?
4. What is the plural form of the word *dictionary* (see page 25a for "Using the dictionary for finding the plurals of nouns")?
5. How many spoken syllables are there in the word *dictionary* (see page 20a for "Understanding the purpose of the hyphen in pronunciations")?
6. Upon which syllable of *dictionary* do you place the greatest stress in speaking (see page 20a for "Interpreting the purpose and position of stress marks")?
7. Which syllable of *dictionary* do you say with medium stress (see page 20a for "Interpreting the purpose and position of stress marks")?
8. Where are the marks which show stress in the word *dictionary* (see page 20a for "Interpreting the purpose and position of stress marks")?
9. How may the word *dictionary* be used in a sentence (see page 25a for "Recognizing the labels which indicate the function of a word")?
10. How many meanings are given for the word *dictionary*? Which meaning fits this book (see page 33a for "Understanding the different senses of the entry")?

FINDING A WORD QUICKLY

Using alphabetical order. To help you find a word quickly, the words in this dictionary follow one another in alphabetical order letter by letter. For example, *poll tax* follows *pollster* as if it were printed *polltax* without space between the words. Words with hyphens also follow as if printed solid:

opening
open–minded
openmouthed
open secret

To find a word quickly, you may need to look at the second letter, or the third, or the fourth, or even beyond. Study the list of words given above. What part is the same in all of them? Which letter determines the listing of *open-minded* after *opening?* of *openmouthed* after *open-minded?*

Words containing an arabic numeral are listed alphabetically as if they were spelled out:

four–footed
4–H (four-H)
four–o'clock

Dividing the dictionary into thirds. If you divided the dictionary into three almost equal parts, or thirds, you would have targets for finding words quickly. In the front you would find words beginning with *a, b, c, d, e,* and *f.* In the middle you would see words beginning with *g, h, i, j, k, l, m, n, o,* and *p.* In the back you would find words beginning with *q, r, s, t, u, v, w, x, y,* and *z.* Through practice you can quickly find any letter by opening your dictionary at approximately the right place.

Using guide words. Every dictionary page except page 1 and those pages on which a new letter of the alphabet is the first entry has at the top two words printed in colored boldface type:

faddist 266 **fake**

These words, called guide words, are the first and the last of the words entered in alphabetical order on one page of the dictionary. Guide words are in alphabetical order from page to page.

CHECKUP

1. Between what two entries do you find these entries?

   3-D made-up wolf spider

2. What are the guide words for the page on which these words appear?

   bird dog hide-and-seek reciprocate
   AWOL Neptune zucchini

CAN YOU FIND A WORD QUICKLY?

1. Between what two entries are these words listed:

   daddy longlegs BB half-moon Mars

2. What are the guide words for the page where each word is entered:

   Fourth of July edit go-getter jukebox

UNDERSTANDING ENTRY WORDS

Recognizing the main entry. A letter or a combination of letters printed in boldface type at the extreme left of each column on the page is a main entry, or entry word. The main entry shows the actual spelling of the word.

All the information which follows each boldface entry explains the main entry. The boldface entry plus all the added information is also called an entry.

For the present, consider only the main entries, which may be many different kinds as these examples show:

i (single letter
-ial (word part called a suffix)
Icelandic (capitalized proper noun)
ice–skate (word with a hyphen)
IOU (capital-letter combination)
imaginary number (compound idea with space)
in-(word part called a prefix)
inalienable (word with both a prefix and a suffix)

CHECKUP

Find these entries, alphabetize them, and write their correct forms. Check to see if they are written as one word, with a hyphen, or with dividing space.

faultfinder
faroff
farflung
featherweight
fedup
fallowdeer
facecard
farmhouse

Understanding the centered period. In many entry words you see boldface periods centered between word parts. These show points in the word where you may use a hyphen at the end of a line in writing. For example, the word *in•ter•plan•e•tary* may be divided in writing as follows:

	in-
terplanetary	inter-
planetary	
	interplan-
etary	
	interplane-
tary	

Notice that your dictionary shows no centered period between *r* and *y* in this word. Therefore, you should not break the word at this point in writing. It is not good practice in writing or printing to separate one letter only from the rest of the word. A single letter at the beginning of a word should not be separated either. For that reason, words such as *about* and *April* do not have centered periods in this dictionary.

Distinguishing between entries which are spelled alike. You will sometimes find that one entry has the same spelling as another entry or entries which follow it. Words alike in spelling but different in origin or meaning are called "homographs". Before each homograph you will see a small number placed high and to the left:

^{1}**cap** . . . **1:** a head covering
^{2}**cap** . . . **1:** to provide with a cap

These two words are related in meaning. The first *cap* is the name of a familiar object. The second *cap* is something you do with the first *cap*.

Homographs may differ in meaning:

[1]**cape** . . . : a point of land jutting out into water
[2]**cape** . . . : a sleeveless garment or part of a garment . . .

In this dictionary homographs are listed and numbered in the order in which they came into the English language. The word *cape* meaning a landform was used before *cape* meaning wearing apparel.

CHECKUP

Find the entries below to determine which are homographs and how many homographs there are for each.

fair	input	pike
brass	nap	sinew
dress	down	top

Using entries with different spellings or forms. An entry may be followed by the word *or* and another spelling or form. The two spellings or forms are called "variants". When the spellings or forms are in alphabetical order, the two variants are equally good. The first is probably used more than the other by educated writers:

cook•ie *or* **cooky** (two spellings)
graph•ic . . . *or* **graph•i•cal** (two forms)

If the variants joined by *or* are not in alphabetical order, they are still both equally good. The first is generally more common than the other:

glam•our *or* **glam•or** (two spellings)
beg•gar's–lice . . . *or* **beg•gar–lice** (two forms)

Sometimes a spelling or form may be joined to the first entry by the word *also.* It is good, but it is not used as often as the first one:

gel•a•tin . . . *also* **gel•a•tine** (two spellings)
rel•e•vance . . . *also* **rel•e•van•cy** (two forms)

Some variants which are not shown with an *or* or *also* after the main entry are listed separately in alphabetical order. When variants are entered separately, the abbreviation *var* for "variant" follows. Some variants may have a label as *Brit* for *British.* To learn the meaning and the pronunciation of some entries you must refer to the more common spelling or form at its alphabetical place in the dictionary:

mus•tache *var of* MOUSTACHE
nought \'nȯt, 'nät\ *var of* NAUGHT
offence *chiefly Brit var of* OFFENSE

A few entries represent an abbreviated form without the label *var of.* You must refer directly to the more complete form or spelling of the entry at its alphabetical place in your dictionary:

B complex . . . : VITAMIN B COMPLEX

For a more common spelling or for a complete form you are sent, or *referred,* to other entries. Those words printed in small capitals are "cross-references".

CHECKUP

Each word below has two spellings. Write each one and underline the spelling most commonly used.

judgment	catalogue
loth	briar
licence	kerosene

Using different kinds of cross-references. A word in small capitals signals you to refer to a main entry at its own alphabetical place. Besides the cross-references preceded by the abbreviation *var of*, you will find many examples like the following:

[1]**best** . . . *superlative of* GOOD
geese *pl of* GOOSE
taught *past of* TEACH
been *past part of* BE

Sometimes a cross-reference follows a light dash (—) within the entry and begins with either *see* or *compare*. Such a cross-reference never stands for a definition, but it often appears in connection with one. For example:

im- — see IN-
mil·lion . . . **1** — see NUMBER table
daf·fo·dil . . . — compare JONQUIL

CHECKUP

Find the cross-references at the following entries:

flyer	him	argon
sprung	Genesis	tuber

Determining capitalization of the main entry. A capital letter at the beginning of a word indicates that the word is usually capitalized. The entire entry may be capitalized or only certain words. For example:

Al·ba·ni·an
April Fools' Day
Ar·i·es
Bun·sen burner
California poppy
Ches·a·peake Bay retriever

Some entries are capitalized when used in a special way or when they have a special meaning. Labels will guide you in handling words of this kind:

braille . . . *often cap*
[2]**continental** . . . **1 a** *often cap*
plaster of par·is . . . *often cap 2d P*

Words which are trademarks protected by law are capitalized:

Le·vi's . . . *trademark*
Roque·fort . . . *trademark*

CHECKUP

Use your dictionary to determine the capitalization of the following:

sweet william	black-eyed susan
yom kippur	t-shirt
great dane	adam's apple

Using entries which are parts of words. Many entries in your dictionary are not whole words but parts of words. These entries may appear *before* or *after* the root, or main part, of a word. Word parts before a root are called "prefixes" or "combining forms".

A word part preceding the root of a word is listed in your dictionary like this:

bi- *prefix*
pre- *prefix*
astro- *comb form*
tele- *or* **tel-** *comb form*

In the word parts above, the position of the hyphen indicates that something else will follow in a full word. Each prefix and combining form is defined in your dictionary.

Word parts that follow the root of a word are called "suffixes" or "combining forms". For example:

-a•ble *also* **-i•ble** . . . *adj suffix*
-ence . . . *n suffix*
-gram . . . *n comb form*
-graph . . . *n comb form*

In the word parts above, the position of the hyphen indicates that something else will come before the ending. Each suffix and combining form is defined.

CHECKUP

Find the parts listed below and make five words from each form. Use your dictionary if you need help.

dis-	-ment
hydr- *or* hydro-	-phone

Locating run-on entries. At the end of the definitions for a main entry you may often find boldface entries after a light dash (—). Such entries are called "run-on" entries as these examples show:

fluffy . . . — **fluff·i·ness** . . .
glad . . . — **glad·ly** . . .

Notice that the run-on entries contain the main entry words *fluffy* and *glad.* If you were unsure about the meaning of the run-ons, you would look up the meaning of each suffix: *-ly* and *-ness.*

Other run-on entries are commonly used phrases. They, too, appear after the definitions. For example:

[1]**far** . . . — **by far** : GREATLY
[1]**talk** . . . — **talk back** : to answer impertinently

WHAT HAVE YOU LEARNED ABOUT ENTRIES?

1. See how quickly you can find the entries listed below. Write each word on a piece of paper and beside it write the guide words for the page on which you found it.

biscuit	DDT	-ion	forest ranger
revolution	french fry	Old Glory	post-

2. Find each entry, list those which are homographs and write the number of times each homograph appears.

eager	put	take	double
halter	gauze	lagoon	better

3. Write these headings on your paper: "Words with Cross-references" and "Words with Run-on Entries". Find each entry and list it under the proper heading.

brought	fiord	[1]find	[2]keep
Venus	apogee	men	[1]run

PRONUNCIATION SYMBOLS

ə						
	banana	mitten	capital	cotton	suppose	perplex
	bun	lunch	putty	color	supper	pup
	burn	learnt	pert	curl	serpent	purple

[in the words in the first line above, ə (called *schwa* \ˈshwä\) is spoken with very weak force; in the words in the second and third lines ə is spoken with stronger force]

a	ax, map	**n**	nine, cotton
ā	age, vacation, day	**ng**	sing, singer, finger, ink
ä	father, cot, cart	**ō**	low, bone, cooperate
ȧ	[a sound between \a\ and \ä\, as in an eastern New England pronunciation of **aunt, half**]	**ȯ**	moth, law, sort, all
		ȯi	coin, destroy
		p	pepper, lip
au̇	out, now	**r**	rarity
b	baby, rib	**s**	spice, less
ch	chin, match, nature \ˈnā-chər\	**sh**	shy, dish, machine, mission, special
d	did, ladder	**t**	tight, latter
e	less	**th**	thin, ether
ē	seaweed, any, serial, cereal	**t͟h**	this, either
f	fifty, cuff, phone	**ü**	boot, rule
g	gift, pig, bigger	**u̇**	foot, pull
h	hat, ahead	**v**	give, vivid
i	trip	**w**	we, away
ī	life, buy, my	**y**	you, yet
j	job, gem, edge	**yü**	few, union, mule, youth
k	kin, cook, chasm	**yu̇**	furious
l	lily, pool, mortal	**z**	zone, raise
m	murmur	**zh**	vision, beige

\ \ slant lines used in pairs to mark the beginning and end of a pronunciation: \ˈpen\

ˈ mark at the beginning of a syllable that has primary (strongest) stress: \ˈpen-mən-ˌship\

ˌ mark at the beginning of a syllable that has secondary (next-strongest) stress: \ˈpen-mən-ˌship\

\- mark of syllable division in pronunciations [the mark of syllable division in boldface entry words is a centered dot • and the position of the two kinds of division often does not agree, as in **build•ing** \ˈbil-diŋ\, **spe•cial** \ˈspesh-əl\, **ca•ter** \ˈkāt-ər\]

( ) parentheses indicate that what is between is present in some utterances but not in others: at *factory*, \ˈfak-t(ə-)rē\ = \ˈfak-tə-rē, ˈfak-trē\ or \ˈfak-trē, ˈfak-tə-rē\

PRONUNCIATION SYMBOLS AND LETTERS

The difference between symbols and letters. Most of the symbols on the preceding page look like familiar letters of the alphabet. True, they have the shape of letters, but they are not letters.

The symbol \a\, for example, is the symbol of a single sound, the sound of the vowel in *mat, map,* and *add.*

The letter *a,* on the other hand, represents not only the sound of the vowel in *map,* but also the very different vowel sounds found in *made, father,* and *sofa.*

Whereas many of the letters of the alphabet may be used to represent any of several sounds, each pronunciation symbol represents only one sound.

Symbol names. In naming symbols we use the terms *bar, one-dot, two-dot,* and *plain;* thus **ā** is "bar a", **t͟h** is "bar t-h", **ȯ** is "one-dot o", **ü** is "two-dot u", **a** is "plain a", **th** is "plain t-h". Call **i** "plain i" because the dot is not a diacritical mark. **ə** is called *schwa* \'shwä\.

The value of pronunciation symbols. If the sign $ makes you think of nothing but a capital S with two lines drawn through it, you do not recognize it as a symbol. But if $ immediately makes you think of dollars, you have learned to use this sign as a symbol.

So it is with all the pronunciation symbols. If you look at \ə\ and think, "That's the letter *e* upside down", \ə\ has no value for you as a symbol of pronunciation. But if you think instantaneously of the schwa sound, the most frequently used vowel sound in our language, then \ə\ has meaning for you as a symbol.

The letter *s* is pronounced in several different ways, and in some words is not pronounced at all. For instance, in each of the words *sun, easy, sure,* and *vision,* the letter *s* has a different pronunciation, and in *island* it has no sound at all. The pronunciation symbol \s\ and the letter *s* have the same form. If the symbol makes you think only of the letter, it does not have value for you as a symbol. But if the symbol \s\ makes you think immediately of the sound of the *s* in *school* \'skül\, of the *sc* in *science* \'sī-ən(t)s\, of the *c* in *cell* \'sel\ and *rice* \'rīs\, and of the last sound in *tax* \'taks\ and *quartz* \'kwȯrts\, then \s\ does have value for you — a single value — as a pronunciation symbol.

The pronunciation symbols include those representing consonant sounds and those representing vowel sounds. Each symbol is treated more fully in the pages which follow.

Locating the pronunciation symbols. The pronunciation symbols on the preceding page are also listed for your convenience on the inside front and back covers of this dictionary and (in part) in the key lines at the foot of each left-hand page within the vocabulary pages.

After you have used this dictionary for a while, you should not have to glance at the key lines or turn to the front or back of your book to see what a symbol stands for. You should become so familiar with each symbol that you instantly think of the sound it represents.

CAN YOU USE THE HELPS ON THE PAGE OF PRONUNCIATION SYMBOLS?

1. What is the name of the symbol for which most examples are given? In what two ways may this symbol be spoken?
2. How can you recognize in the examples the letters for which the symbol stands?
3. What do slant lines used in pairs mark?
4. How is primary, or strong, stress shown?
5. How is secondary, or medium, stress shown?
6. How is syllabic division shown in pronunciations?
7. What do parentheses within a pronunciation indicate?

THE CONSONANT SYMBOLS

\b The sound represented by the symbol \b\ is spelled with the letter *b* as in *boy, cab,* and *able,* or with *bb* as in *robber.* In the spelling of certain words, such as *climb* and *debt,* the *b* is silent.

\ch This is really a \t\ sound quickly followed by an \sh\ sound. The \ch\ sound is usually spelled by several letter combinations: *ch* as in *church, tch* as in *watch, ti* as in *question,* or *si* as in *pension.* The sound \ch\ is heard in *factual* but cannot be referred to the *t* alone.

\d The sound represented by the symbol \d\ is spelled with the letter *d* as in *dad,* with *dd* as in *daddy,* and with *ed* as in *stayed* and *manned.* Refer to the entry **-ed** at its alphabetical place for an explanation of its pronunciation as \d\.

In rapid speech the sound \d\ is often heard for the letter *t.* Thus *latter* is often spoken the same as *ladder* and *waited* the same as *waded.*

\f This sound may be spelled with the letter *f* as in *fan,* with *ff* as in *offer,* with *ph* as in *telephone,* or with *gh* as in *cough.*

\g The sound represented by \g\ may be spelled with the letter *g* as in *go,* with *gg* as in *egg,* with *gh* as in *ghost,* or with *gu* as in *guard;* and \g\ is the first of the two sounds \gz\ spelled with *x* as in *exact.*

CHECKUP

Write the proper consonant symbol in place of the question mark:

pasture \'pas-?ər\	cobbler \'kä?-lər\
failed \'fāl?\	ghastly \'?ast-lē\
cough \'kȯ?\	watched \'wä?t\
example \i?-'zam-pəl\	phony \'?ō-nē\

\h This sound is spelled with the letter *h* as in *hat.* The sound occurs only at the beginning of syllables, even when the spelling is *wh,* as in *whale* \'hwāl\. The pronunciation \hw\ is shown for most words like *whale,* but some speakers have no \h\ sound in these words, pronouncing *whale* the same as *wail.*

\j This is really a \d\ sound quickly followed by a \zh\ sound. The sound \j\ may be spelled with the letter *j* as in *jam* and *reject,* with *g* as in *gem,* with *ge* as in *page,* with *dge* as in *fudge,* with *dg* as in *judgment,* or with *di* as in *soldier.* The sound \j\ is heard in *graduation* but cannot be referred to the *d* alone.

\k This sound may be spelled with the letter *k* as in *kite,* with *c* as in *cat,* with *ck* as in *pick,* with *ch* as in *chemist,* with *che* as in *ache,* with *q* as in *quite,* with *qu* as in *antique;* and \k\ is the first of two sounds \ks\ spelled with *x* as in *tax.*

\l The sound represented by the symbol \l\ is spelled with the letter *l* as in *lap* and *pal,* or with *ll* as in *pull.* This sound may be heard at the beginning of a syllable as in *along* or at the end of a syllable as in *brittle* and *annual.*

\m The sound represented by the symbol \m\ may be spelled with the letter *m* as in *made, dismay,* and *him,* with *mm* as in *accommodate* and *trimmer,* with *mn* as in *autumn* and *column,* or with *mb* as in *bomb* and *climb.*

CHECKUP

Write the proper consonant symbol in place of the question mark:

quit \'?wit\	hymn \'hi?\
soldier \'sōl-?ər\	change \'chān?\
chic \'shē?\	whole \'?ōl\
grudge \'grə?\	petal \'pet-ə?\
called \'?ȯld\	comb \'kō?\

\n The sound represented by \n\ may be spelled with the letter *n* as in *net* and *ten,* with *nn* as in *winner,* with *gn* as in *gnaw,* with *kn* as in *knight,* or with *pn* as in *pneumonia.* This sound is often heard at the end of a syllable as in *prison, happen,* and *puritan.*

\ng The sound \ng\ may be spelled with the letters *ng* as in *sing* and *singer,* and in both syllables of *ringing,* or with *n* as in *finger, longer, rink, lynx, anchor, uncle,* and *conquer.* Although the sound occurs in both *singer* and *finger,* the two words are usually not pronounced as rhymes, the *-inger* of *finger* having one more sound than the *-inger* of *singer.* In this dictionary the pronunciation of *finger* is shown as \'fiŋ-gər\, while the pronunciation of *singer* is shown as \'siŋ-ər\.

\p The sound represented by the symbol \p\ is spelled with the letter *p* as in *pan* and *nap* or with *pp* as in *happen.*

\r The sound \r\ is spelled with the letter *r* as in *rat, brass, parade,* and *deer,* with *rr* as in *merry,* with *rh* as in *rhubarb,* or *wr* as in *write.* This sound may occur before a vowel as in *rat,* may follow a vowel as in *deer* and *water,* or may occur between vowels as in *parade* and *merry.*

Most Americans and Canadians have as many \r\ sounds in their pronunciation of a word as there are letters *r* or letter groups *rr* in the spelling. Such speakers may be called *r*-retainers. But speakers in southeastern United States, in eastern New England, in New York City, and in southern England frequently do not have \r\ sounds before consonants or pauses. Such speakers are called *r*-droppers. The pronunciations used by *r*-droppers are as correct as those used by *r*-retainers.

R-droppers do one of several things: (1) they simply omit the \r\, saying \'ban-ə\ instead of \'ban-ər\ for *banner* and saying \'fȯm-yə-lə\ instead of \'fȯrm-yə-lə\ for *formula;* (2) they use \ə\ instead of \r\, saying \'pōət-ə-bəl\ instead of \'pōrt-ə-bəl\ for *portable;* (3) they omit the \r\ but prolong the vowel that precedes in *r*-retainers' speech, saying \'fää\ instead of \'fär\ for *far* (the doubled symbol shows a longer lasting sound than the same symbol used singly); or (4) they use instead of vowel plus \r\ a single vowel different in quality from the vowel of *r*-retainers, saying \'fȧ\ instead of \'fär\ for *far*.

Even *r*-retainers sometimes drop an *r* when a word contains one or more other *r*'s. An *r* that even an *r*-retainer may drop is shown in parentheses.

\s This sound may be spelled with the letter *s* as in *say,* with *ss* as in *miss,* with *sc* as in *scene,* with *ps* as in *psychology,* with *c* as in *cent,* or with *z* as in *quartz;* and it is the second of the two sounds \ks\ spelled with *x* as in *tax*.

The letter *s* is used to spell four different sounds: \sh\ as in *sure,* \zh\ as in *vision,* \s\ as in *yes, quits,* and \z\ as in *days, wins*. Refer to the entry **-s** at its alphabetical place for an explanation of its different pronunciations. The letter *s* may also be silent as in *isle;* and *si* after *n* often spells the sound \ch\ as in *pension* and *dimension*.

CHECKUP

Write the proper consonant symbol in place of the question mark:

rhythm \'?it͟h-əm\	knight \'?īt\
arrival \ə-'?ī-vəl\	explode \ik-'s?lōd\
scent \'?ent\	practice \'prak-tə?\
hunger \'hə?-gər\	shakes \'shāk?\

\sh The sound represented by \sh\ may be spelled with the letters *sh* as in *ship, fish,* with *s* as in *sure,* with *ssi* as in *mission,* with *ci* as in *special,* with *ti* as in *nation,* or with *ch* as in *machine*. This sound is not a combination of \s\ and \h\, but a single sound, different from both \s\ and \h\.

\t The sound \t\ may be spelled with the letter *t* as in *tap* and *sat,* with *tt* as in *attack,* or with *ed* as in *walked*. Refer to the entry **-ed** for an explanation of its pronunciation as \t\.

\th\ \t͟h The sound represented by \th\, called plain t-h, is the sound spelled with the letters *th* in *thing* and *breath*. The sound represented by \t͟h\, called bar t-h, is the sound spelled with the letters *th* in *these* and *breathe*. Both the \th\ and \t͟h\ sounds are single sounds, quite different from either the \t\ or the \h\ sound. The \t͟h\ is voiced (uttered with the vocal cords close together and vibrating) whereas \th\ is voiceless (uttered with the vocal cords wide apart and not vibrating).

\v The sound represented by the symbol \v\ is spelled with the letter *v* as in *very, save, never,* with *f* as in *of,* or with *ph* as in *Stephen*.

\w The consonant sound \w\ may be spelled with the letter *w* as in *wait* and *twist*, with *u* as in *queer* and *persuade*, or with *o* as in *choir*. This sound occurs only before vowels.

Many words have a latter *w* in the spelling but no corresponding \w\ sound in the pronunciation — for example, *write* and *snow*. In many words *ow* is pronounced \au̇\ as in *how*, where the letter *w* represents the second vowel of the diphthong \au̇\. The letter combination *ew* often represents the \yü\ or \ü\ sounds. After some consonants only \yü\ is acceptable, as in *few*. After other consonants either \ü\ or \yü\ is acceptable, as in *new*. After \l\, \r\, \s\, and \z\ the \yü\ sound is seldom heard in American speech, and so only \ü\ is given in this dictionary.

The sound spoken for *wh* at the beginning of a word is not the same in all words. In *who, whose, whom, whole*, and often in *whoop* the *w* is not heard. In most other words beginning with *wh* both letters are pronounced by most Americans but in an order, \hw\, that is the opposite of the order in the spelling.

\y The consonant sound \y\ may be spelled with the letter *y* as in *yes* or with *i* as in *onion*. This sound is also the first of two sounds with *ue* in *cue*, with *ew* in *few*, and with *eu* in *feud*. Often the single letter *u* represents two sounds: \yü\ as in *use*, \yu̇\ as in *furious*, or \yə\ as in *January*.

\z The sound \z\ may be spelled with the letter *z* as in *zone, wizard, whiz*, with *zz* as in *buzz*, or with *s* as in *wise, busy, wins*. Refer to the entry **-s** for an explanation of its pronunciation as \z\.

\zh The sound \zh\ may be spelled with the letters *si* as in *vision* or with *ge* as in *rouge*. The sound \zh\ is heard in *azure* and *leisure* but cannot be referred to the *z* or *s* alone. The \zh\ sound is a single sound, different from either \z\ or \h\.

CHECKUP

Write the proper consonant symbol in place of the question mark:

mother \'mə?-ər\	thistle \'?is-əl\
union \'?ü-n?ən\	business \'bi?-nəs\
sugar \'?u̇g-ər\	explosion \ik-'splō-?ən\
revise \ri-'?ī?\	stopped \'stäp?\

CAN YOU RECOGNIZE THE CONSONANT SOUNDS?

Each line below contains a consonant symbol followed by four words which may or may not contain the sound represented by the symbol. Say each word to yourself. Write each symbol and the words in each line that contain the sound. Then check with your dictionary.

\b\	dumb	possible	cupboard	subtlety
\ch\	nature	mansion	chaperon	question
\d\	stopped	handsome	declared	handkerchief
\f\	of	laugh	phone	conference
\g\	gnaw	guide	raged	exactly
\h\	wholly	honest	Utah	elephant
\j\	judge	soldier	adjective	gesture

\k\	quick	headache	exist	exercise
\l\	half	you'll	talkative	article
\m\	bomb	hymn	stomach	criticism
\n\	gnat	autumn	autumnal	knowledge
\ng\	uncle	conquer	singe	hungry
\p\	spirit	hiccough	spherical	pneumonia
\r\	parade	ferry	tolerant	granite
\s\	island	relax	ranches	psychology
\sh\	action	chic	unsure	television
\t\	listen	rapped	rotten	dodged
\th\	thin	then	wreath	wreathed
\t͟h\	cloth	clothing	whether	weather
\v\	off	various	evening	recover
\w\	sword	whole	quiet	liquid
\y\	billion	united	feudal	merry
\z\	fuse	quartz	checkers	business
\zh\	rogue	exposure	erosion	measure

THE VOWEL SYMBOLS

\ə One of the most frequent sounds in English is the sound called schwa, represented by the symbol \ə\. When stressed, this sound may be spelled with the letter *u* as in *cut* and *hurt,* with *e* as in *herd,* with *i* as in *bird,* with *oo* as in *blood,* or with *o* as in *front* and *word.* When unstressed, schwa may be spelled with any of the vowel letters, as in *about* \ə-'bau̇t\, *silent* \'sī-lənt\, *capital* \'kap-ət-əl\, *collect* \kə-'lekt\, and *suppose* \sə-'pōz\. In some words like *chasm, rhythm,* nothing in the spelling corresponds to schwa.

\a\ \ā\ \ä\ \ȧ The four "a" symbols are: \a\, called plain a, which represents the sound of the *a* in *fat* and *carry;* \ā\, called bar a, which represents the sound of the *a* in *age*, the *ai* in *main,* the *ei* in *vein,* the *ea* in *break,* the *ay* in *day,* the *ey* in *prey,* and the *au* in *gauge;* \ä\, called two-dot a, which represents the sound of the *o* in *cot* and *bother,* and also the sound used by most American speakers for the *a* in *cart* and *father;* and \ȧ\, called one-dot a, which represents the vowel sound used by some speakers in *aunt* and *cart* and in the first syllable of *father*.

\e\ \ē The symbol \e\, called plain e, represents the vowel sound in *met, said, says, death, friend,* and *berry.*

The symbol \ē\, called bar e, stands for the vowel sound in *he, feed, seat, field, key,* and *eve,* in the stressed syllable of *people, deceive,* and *machine,* and in the unstressed syllable of *react* and *city.*

Many words which contain the letter *e* do not contain either the \e\ sound or the \ē\ sound. In such words as *excite* and *examine,* the sound of the initial vowel is usually \i\. In such words as *magnet, perplex,* and *element,* the unstressed *e*'s are usually \ə\.

> **CHECKUP**
>
> Copy these words, writing the symbol for the sound of the boldface letter or letters in each:
>
> | | | |
> |---|---|---|
> | c**a**mel | w**ei**ght | m**ai**nly |
> | exc**ee**d | st**o**pper | sugg**e**st |
> | serg**ea**nt | m**o**dest | br**ea**kf**a**st |
> | heartl**e**ss | che**a**ted | far**a**way |

\i\ \ī\ The symbol \i\, called plain i, represents the vowel sound in *sit, build, hymn,* and *sieve,* and in the stressed syllable of *busy* and *women.* The first vowel in *excite, exaggerate,* and *encourage* is usually pronounced \i\.

The symbol \ī\, called bar i, stands for the vowel sound in *light, height, try, buy, bite,* and *aisle.*

Many words that contain the letter *i* do not contain either the \i\ sound or the \ī\ sound. In such words as *possible, vanity, policy,* and *animal* the letter *i* is usually pronounced \ə\.

\ō\ \ȯ\ The symbol \ō\, called bar o, represents the sound of the vowel letter or letters in *go, coat, though,* and *beau,* of the *o* in *cone,* of the *ew* in *sew,* and of the *ow* in *bowl.*

The symbol \ȯ\ called one-dot o, stands for the vowel sound in *soft, corn, saw, all, caught, fought,* and *broad.* Speakers in some parts of the country make no consistent distinction between \ȯ\ and \ä\, and this lack of distinction may be correct for your speech.

Many words that contain the letter *o* do not contain either the \ō\ sound or the \ȯ\ sound. In such words as *cot, lock,* and *rod* the usual vowel sound is \ä\. In such words as *color* and *comfort* the vowel sound in the stressed syllable is \ə\. In such words as *confirm* and *baron,* the vowel sound in the unstressed syllable is \ə\.

\ü\ \u̇\ The two "u" symbols are: \ü\, called two-dot u, which stands for the vowel sound in *flu, school, blue, youth, rule,* and *crew;* and \u̇\, called one-dot u, which represents the vowel sound in *pull, wood,* and *sugar.* In a word such as *few,* the \ü\ sound is preceded by the consonant sound \y\: \fyü\. In a word such as *security,* the \u̇\ sound is preceded by the consonant sound \y\: \si-ˈkyu̇r-ət-ē\.

In words in which *u, ue, eu,* or *ew* in a stressed syllable is immediately preceded by *t, d, n,* or *th,* pronunciation is not uniform in the United States. Both \ü\ and \yü\ occur in the following words: *tune, due, neutral, enthuse, news.* The pronunciation with \y\ is especially common in the South.

Many words that contain the letter *u* do not have either of these sounds. The vowel sound in *cut,* for example, is \ə\. The letter *u* in an unstressed syllable frequently has the \ə\ sound, as in *cactus* \ˈkak-təs\.

\au̇\ \ȯi\ In the word *out* \ˈau̇t\ two vowel sounds occur in succession as part of a single syllable. Such a succession of two vowel sounds is called a diphthong.

This dictionary uses two diphthong symbols: \aů\, representing the vowel sounds of *cow* and *sound* and of both *au*'s in *sauerkraut;* and \ȯi\, representing the vowel sounds of *join* and *boy*.

The sound of the words *eye* and *I*, represented by \ī\ in this dictionary, is really a diphthong, too, consisting of \ä\ and \i\ or of \ȧ\ and \i\.

CHECKUP

Copy the following words and write the sound symbols for the boldface letters:

coin	lawyer	broadcloth
soul	thought	woodwind
cowl	gym	schoolroom
bowl	excite	royal

ARE YOU SURE OF THE VOWEL SOUNDS?

Each line below contains a vowel symbol followed by four words which may or may not contain the sound represented by the symbol. Say each word to yourself. Write each symbol and the words in each line that contain the sound. Then check with your dictionary.

\a\	grab	grapple	behave	barrier
\ā\	there	gauze	taped	restrain
\ä\	sober	spotted	father	farther
\ȧ\	aunt	taunt	half	married
\aů\	mower	bound	vowel	ought
\e\	chair	fearless	person	weather
\ē\	queer	every	meringue	fatigue
\i\	expire	merely	rhyme	rhythm
\ī\	entire	height	ravine	divine
\ō\	scowl	bureau	sewing	thought
\ȯ\	scorn	recall	worthy	taught
\ȯi\	coinage	coincide	choir	employee
\ü\	cruise	gradual	foolish	tout
\ů\	fooling	woolen	insure	wolf
\ə\	sir	density	supple	confide

Locating the pronunciation at the entry. Two slanted lines mark the beginning and end of a pronunciation, which usually appears just after the main entry word.

ant \'ant\

As in the case of the word *ant*, the pronunciation may sometimes look very much like the entry word. Usually, however, the pronunciation looks more or less different.

bug \'bəg\

As you have learned in your language study, many words have more than one form, depending upon the way they are used. When the spelling and pronunciation of these different forms do not follow a so-called "regular" pattern, your dictionary gives you help. For example:

[1]**fly** \'flī\ . . . **flew** \'flü\; **flown** \'flōn\; **fly·ing**
[1]**knife** \'nīf\ . . . *pl* **knives** \'nīvz\

In addition to the pronunciation help at the main entry word, you may often find full or partial pronunciations for run-on entries:

dumb \'dəm\ . . . — **dumb·ly** \'dəm-lē\ . . .
ecol·o·gy \i-'käl-ə-jē\ . . . — **eco·log·ic** \ˌē-kə-'läj-ik, ˌek-ə-\ *or* **eco·log·i·cal** \-'läj-i-kəl\ . . . — **eco·log·i·cal·ly** \-'läj-i-k(ə-)lē\ . . . — **ecol·o·gist** \i-'käl-ə-jəst\ . . .

Understanding the purpose of the hyphen in pronunciations. Many words have more than one of the units of pronunciation called "syllables". In the pronunciation of such words the syllables are separated by hyphens. The hyphen shows syllable division in saying a word, not in writing the word.

The syllables in the pronunciation and the divisions shown by the centered periods in the boldface entry spelling may correspond:

chop·stick \'chäp-ˌstik\
in·struct \in-'strəkt\
mus·tard \'məs-tərd\

Often, however, the divisions are not the same, and the hyphens do not correspond with the centered periods in the entry. For example:

[1]**bor·der** \'bȯrd-ər\
fran·tic \'frant-ik\
[1]**po·si·tion** \pə-'zish-ən\

CHECKUP

Compare the divisions for writing and the syllables for pronunciation. Which correspond?

restless	advice	creeper
vision	begin	talkative
journal	qualify	optician

Interpreting the purpose and position of stress marks. Some syllables of a word are spoken with greater force, emphasis, or loudness than others. Your dictionary calls this relative loudness "stress" and shows vertical marks *before* the syllable to alert you to the pronunciation of that syllable. Three degrees of stress are shown in this book: primary (or strong), secondary (or medium), and weak.

Primary stress is indicated by a high vertical mark at the beginning of the syllable:

[1]**vote** \'vōt\
clip·per \'klip-ər\ (primary \'klip-\)
re·cite \ri-'sīt\ (primary \-'sīt\)

This dictionary shows primary stress before one-syllable words to indicate that they may be stressed in speech. As you say this sentence, notice the stress you give to *vote:* It is the duty of each citizen to vote.

Secondary stress is indicated by a low vertical mark at the beginning of the syllable:

lip·stick \'lip-ˌstik\ (secondary \-ˌstik\)
shop·keeper \'shäp-ˌkē-pər\ (secondary \-ˌkē-\)

A syllable without either of these marks in front of it has weak stress:

hes·i·tate \'hez-ə-ˌtāt\ (weak\-ə-\)

CHECKUP

Which syllables have the strongest stress (primary), medium stress (secondary), and the weakest stress in these pronunciations?

\'rat-əl-ˌsnāk\	\'in-di-ˌgō\
\ˌmak-ə-'rō-nē\	\'bī-bəl\
\ˌred-ē-'mād\	\ri-'bel\
\'bī-ˌsik-əl\	\'rāl-ˌrōd\
\'fel-ō-ˌship\	\'lȯng-ˌplā-ing\

Using variant pronunciations given in full or in part. Different pronunciations may be given at some words to show that not all educated speakers pronounce them the same way. *All* pronunciations are correct. The one given first is probably heard more often than a second or others following. Pronunciations vary because of personal preference, regional practice, and other speech habits.

A second pronunciation may be given in full, as in these entries:

sloth \'slȯth, 'slōth\
ha•rass \hə-'ras, 'har-əs\

A variant pronunciation may not be shown in full. In a long word the difference between two pronunciations may be confined to only a part of the word. For such words the second pronunciation may be indicated for only the part of the word where the difference is. The rest of the second pronunciation is the same as that for the first pronunciation, as in these entries:

en•force \in-'fōrs, -'fȯrs\
goose•ber•ry \'güs-ˌber-ē, 'güz-\
pla•nar•ia \plə-'nar-ē-ə, -'ner-\

The full second pronunciations for these words are:

\in-'fȯrs\ \'güz-ˌber-ē\ \plə-'ner-ē-ə\

In such partial second pronunciations only whole syllables are recorded and there is always at least one hyphen. A hyphen at the beginning of a partial pronunciation means that the first part is missing and is to be supplied from the pronunciation that precedes within the same slant lines. The hyphen before \'fȯrs\ means that there is something that goes ahead of it: \in\. Other examples are:

mer•can•tile \'mər-kən-ˌtēl, -ˌtīl\
par•a•dise \'par-ə-ˌdīs, -ˌdīz\

A hyphen at both the beginning and the end of a partial pronunciation means that both the first and the last parts of the pronunciation are missing. The missing parts are to be supplied from a pronunciation that precedes within the same slant lines. The hyphens with \-'ner-\ after *pla•nar•ia* tell you that something goes ahead of this syllable and something comes after it.

When one syllable of a word can be pronounced two ways and another syllable can also be pronounced two ways, the total number of possible pronunciations is four. Thus *washroom* \'wȯsh-ˌrüm, 'wäsh-, -ˌru̇m\ may be pronounced \'wȯsh-ˌrüm, 'wäsh-ˌrüm, 'wȯsh-ˌru̇m, 'wäsh-ˌru̇m\.

CHECKUP

Write in full the variant pronunciation for each entry:

¹route	¹water	archipelago
absorb	liaison	ratio
evangelical	apparatus	centrifugal
¹direct	statute	tactile

Using variant pronunciations indicated by parentheses. A variant pronunciation is not always given in full or by syllable omission. Instead, a symbol, symbols, or stress mark may be enclosed within parentheses ( ) to save space. The sound or stress within the parentheses may be used by some speakers and not used by others. Or it may be said at one time and not at another by the same speaker.

A sound symbol is enclosed within parentheses in the following:

dense \'den(t)s\ (pronounced \'dens\ or \'dents\)
[1]**fire** \'fī(ə)r\ (pronounced \'fīr\ or \'fīər\)

A stress mark is enclosed within parentheses in the following:

in·for·mal \(')in-'fȯr-məl\ (pronounced \in-'fȯr-məl\ or \'in-'fȯr-məl\)
in·dus·try \'in-(ˌ)dəs-trē\ (pronounced \'in-dəs-trē\ or \'in-ˌdəs-trē\)

In the pronunciation of the main entry or of another form of the same entry a variation in the number of syllables is indicated by schwa and a hyphen within parentheses:

[1]**ad·e·noid** \'ad-(ə-)ˌnȯid\ (pronounced \'ad-ə-ˌnȯid\ or \'ad-ˌnȯid\)
nes·tle \'nes-əl\ . . . **nes·tling** \-(ə-)ling\ (**nes-tling** pronounced \'nes-ə-ling\ or \'nes-ling\)

CHECKUP

Write in full all possible pronunciations for these entries:

homemade	factory	outwear
excellent	fortunate	recipe
altitude	[1]garage	[1]substitute

Using variant pronunciations in special context or usage. Some words may have special pronunciations which are shown by italicized, or slanted-type, labels or notes within slanted lines. Sometimes such a pronunciation is used for a particular definition, or sense, within the entry, as follows:

gon·do·la \'gän-də-lə (*usual for sense 1*), gän-'dō-\ . . . **1** : a long narrow boat with a high prow and stern used on the canals of Venice
[2]**con·tract** \kən-'trakt, *oftenest for 2* 'kän-ˌ\ . . . **2** : to undertake by contract . . .

A variant pronunciation may show how a word is pronounced in a certain region of the United States. For example:

great \'grāt, *in South also* 'gre(ə)t\

Occasionally a pronunciation which is heard more often in a part of the English-speaking world other than the United States is shown. In this example *Brit* stands for *British:*

[1]**prog·ress** \'präg-rəs,-ˌres, *chiefly Brit* 'prō-ˌgres\

Pronouncing words without pronunciations or with other kinds of partial pronunciations. The pronunciation of many run-on entries is not given because you can easily determine it for yourself. Use the pronunciation at the main entry and look up the pronunciation of the one or more suffixes if you need help in saying the run-on entries.

eat \'ēt\ . . . — **eat·er** . . .
[1]**safe** \'sāf\ . . . — **safe·ly** . . . — **safe-ness** . . .
tape–re·cord . . . — **tape recorder** . . . — **tape recording** . . .
[2]**worship** . . . — **wor·ship·er** *or* **wor·ship-per** . . .

You have learned that variant pronunciations are often partial. You will also find partial pronunciations at many run-on entries:

healthy \\'hel-thē\\ . . . — **health•i•ly** \\-thə-lē\\ . . . **health•i•ness** \\-thē-nəs\\ . . .

In a few cases a part of an entry may not be a separate entry with pronunciation. You will find a pronunciation for that part, as in the following examples:

Green•wich time \\'grin-ij-, 'gren-, -ich-\\
Gre•go•ri•an calendar \\gri-ˌgōr-ē-ən-, -ˌgȯr-\\

Some entry words with full pronunciations may be followed by other entry words with only partial pronunciations. The examples below show that there is an identically spelled, identically pronounced word part common to the first entry:

rain•mak•ing \\'rān-ˌmā-king\\
rain•proof \\-ˌprüf\\
rain•storm \\-ˌstȯrm\\

Some entries whose parts are separated by one or more spaces may have no pronunciation given. If you cannot pronounce any one of the parts of such entries, you should refer to that word at its alphabetical place in your dictionary:

graph paper
gross national product

Usually no pronunciation is given at run-on phrases. Any word in the phrase can be found at its alphabetical place:

[1]**fall** \\'fȯl\\ . . . — **fall flat** . . . — **fall for** . . . — **fall from grace** . . . — **fall on** *or* **fall upon** . . . — **fall short** . . .

CHECKUP

1. Write the pronunciations for:
   depot gallant conjure
2. Write the pronunciations for:
   clumsily clumsiness
3. Write the pronunciations for:
   homespun mainstay rabble-rouser
4. Write the pronunciations for:
   club moss leaf bud screw cap

The pronunciation of most homographs is given only for the first entry if their pronunciations and boldface divisions are the same:

[1]**com•ment** \\'käm-ˌent\\ . . . **1** : an expression of opinion . . .
[2]**comment** . . . : to make a comment . . .

Using homographs whose pronunciations differ. Not all homographs are pronounced the same way. When you encounter such homographs in your reading, the context often helps you with pronunciation and meaning. When there are differences in the pronunciation of homographs, your dictionary shows these differences:

[1]**do** \\(')dü\\ . . . **1 a** : to engage in or carry out . . .
[2]**do** \\'dō\\ . . . : the 1st note of the diatonic scale

CHECKUP

Which of these homographs have differing pronunciations?

combine earnest row
collect forward transit

DO YOU UNDERSTAND DICTIONARY PRONUNCIATIONS?

1. In the following quotations, the pronunciation of each word is shown to provide you with practice in reading the symbols of this dictionary. Write the quotations in their ordinary spelling.

\'if ət 'fərst yü 'dōnt sək-'sēd, 'trī, 'trī ə-'gen\

\'ər-lē tə 'bed ən 'ər-lē tə 'rīz 'māks ə 'man 'hel-thē, 'wel-thē, ən 'wīz\

\'dü 'ən-tü 'ət̲h̲-ərz əz yü wəd hav 't̲h̲em dü 'ən-tə 'yü\

\ə 'pen-ē 'sāvd iz ə 'pen-ē 'ərnd\

\ən 'aủn(t)s əv pri-'ven-chən iz 'wərth ə 'paủnd əv 'kyủər\

\'tü 'rȯngz dōnt 'māk ə 'rīt\

\'hē t̲h̲ət 'fȯlz in 'ləv wit̲h̲ im-'self wil 'hav nō 'rī-vəlz\

2. As a check upon your understanding of stress say each word below, write it on your paper, and place stress marks where you think they belong. Compare your work with the dictionary entries.

as tro naut	de tec tive	guar an tee	ob li ga tion
but ter fly	fi nal ize	mar su pi al	pro nun ci a tion

3. Find the entry for each word below. List only the words for which variant pronunciations are given. Write these pronunciations on your paper and underline the one you use.

adult	module	exquisite	ominous
tomato	roof	gravity	kilometer

4. Each of the following words is one of a set of two or more homographs. List each one on your paper under the correct heading: "Same Pronunciation" or "Different Pronunciation".

console	desert	monitor	contract
debate	tear	rebel	telescope

5. Find the entry for each word below and write it on your paper. Next, write the kind of entry it is. Finally, write in full the pronunciation for each entry.

clothes tree	kingbird	nonresistant	overgraze
huskiness	run riot	hail from	worthily

FUNCTION AND FORMS OF WORDS

Recognizing the labels which indicate the function of a word. The main entry is usually followed by an abbreviation which signals the function of the word when used as explained by the definitions. Such an abbreviation is called a "part-of-speech label".

Eight part-of-speech labels are regularly used in this dictionary:

able . . . *adj* (adjective)
ably . . . *adv* (adverb)
al·though . . . *conj* (conjunction)
alas . . . *interj* (interjection)
ab·a·cus . . . *n* (noun)
[1]**in** . . . *prep* (preposition)
he . . . *pron* (pronoun)
[1]**beat** . . . *vb* (verb)

Some entries have a double part-of-speech label:

abeam . . . *adv or adj*

Recognizing other italicized labels. The function of the main entry may be indicated by other labels, some of which are shown with the pronunciation and the part of speech while others are not. Some entries are homographs with different functions and occasionally variant spellings. Examples of these entries follow:

astro- *comb form* (combining form)
-gram \ˌgram\ *n comb form* (noun combining form)
ab- *prefix*
-less \ləs\ *adj suffix* (adjective suffix)
[1]**-an** *or* **-ian** *also* **-ean** *n suffix* (noun suffix)
[2]**-an** *or* **-ian** *also* **-ean** *adj suffix*
-dom \dəm\ *n suffix*
gee \ˈjē\ *imperative verb*

In other instances the main entry may be followed by the label *abbr* for *abbreviation,* a shortened form of a word or phrase. Abbreviated entries appear in their alphabetical place. Since the use of periods varies widely, most abbreviations are shown without them. Some abbreviations have pronunciations while others do not:

FD *abbr* fire department (no definition, just the expanded, or full, form)
DC *abbr* **1** da capo **2** direct current **3** District of Columbia (more than one expanded form)
hf *abbr* **1** half **2** high frequency (lowercase, more than one expanded form)
P.I. *abbr* Philippine Islands (expanded form with periods)
TNT \ˌtē-ˌen-ˈtē\ *n* : a high explosive (pronunciation, a part-of-speech label, and a definition)

Locating function labels. As you have seen from the examples above, function labels usually follow closely the main entry. You will also find such labels at run-on entries. For example:

[2]**dainty** *adj* . . . — **dain·ti·ly** . . . *adv* — **dain·ti·ness** . . . *n*
[1]**ob·jec·tive** . . . *adj* . . . — **ob·jec·tive·ly** *adv* — **ob·jec·tiv·i·ty** . . . *n*

CHECKUP

What labels do you find for these entries?

FBI	legend	because
ahoy	crew cut	ltd
-ic	-ation	pre-
occur	DDS	practical

Using the dictionary for finding the plurals of nouns. Most nouns in the English language have their plural forms made by simple addition of the letters *-s* or *-es* to an unchanged singular. For example: *boy, boys; house, houses; lunch, lunches.* The plurals of such nouns are said to be "regular" and therefore easy to spell and to pronounce. They are not shown in this dictionary unless there is a chance they might be mistaken or misspelled, as in these examples:

val•ley . . . *n, pl* **valleys** (not *vallies*)
jour•ney . . . *n, pl* **journeys** (not *journies*)

Nouns which form their plurals in any other way than by the addition of *-s* or *-es* to an unchanged singular are said to be "irregular". Such plurals are always given in your dictionary. For example:

alum•nus . . . *n, pl* **-ni** (Latin plural)
cri•sis . . . *n, pl* **cri•ses** (Greek plural)
dai•sy . . . *n, pl* **daisies** (change *-y* to *-i* before *-es*)
[1]**knife** . . . *n, pl* **knives** (change *-f-* to *-v-* before *-s*)
[1]**man** . . . *n, pl* **men** (root change)
moth•er–in–law . . . *n, pl* **moth•ers–in–law** (first part adds *-s*)

Understanding nouns with more than one plural. Some nouns, like *hippopotamus,* may have more than one plural. Others, like *fish,* may be used collectively or have a regular plural.

If the plurals are joined by *or,* they are equally common in usage. If the plurals are joined by *also,* the second form is less common than the first. Study these examples:

[1]**bass** . . . *n, pl* **bass** *or* **bass•es** (fish)
bus . . . *n, pl* **bus•es** *or* **bus•ses**
[1]**dwarf** . . . *n, pl* **dwarfs** . . . *also* **dwarves**

Words that come into English from a foreign language may have both an English and a foreign plural spelling. Usage may vary, and the plural forms may be shown in full or in part. For example:

cri•te•ri•on . . . *n, pl* **-ria** . . . *also* **-rions**
pla•teau . . . *n, pl* **plateaus** *or* **plateaux**
se•nor *or* **se•ñor** . . . *n, pl* **senors** *or* **se•ño•res** . . .
stra•tum . . . *n, pl* **stra•ta** . . . *also* **stratums**

Understanding nouns with special kinds of plurals. Some nouns have the same form in both the singular and plural:

corps . . . *n, pl* **corps** (*corps* is and *corps* are)
sheep . . . *n, pl* **sheep** (*sheep* is and *sheep* are)

Still other nouns are used only in the plural and are followed by a plural verb:

en•vi•rons . . . *n pl* (*environs* are)
over•alls . . . *n pl* (*overalls* are)

Finally, other plural nouns are not always used in plural construction. The word *news,* for instance, takes a singular verb. Others, like *politics,* are used in both the singular and the plural. Such nouns are labeled in the dictionary as follows:

ath•let•ics . . . *n sing or pl*
dy•nam•ics . . . *n sing or pl*

Locating irregular plural forms in alphabetical order. Irregular plural forms are entered in their own alphabetical places if they fall more than a column away from the main entry. You will find *teeth,* for example, listed between *teeterboard* and *teethe,* as well as at *tooth.* You will not find *oxen* in its alphabetical place because it is not more than a column away from the word *ox.*

Other examples of irregular plurals entered in their alphabetical places cross-refer you to another main entry, as follows:

mice *pl of* MOUSE
geese *pl of* GOOSE

CHECKUP

Use your dictionary to find the plurals for:

cargo	fungus	cello
buffalo	scarf	bacillus

RULES FOR FORMING PLURALS

You will find the rules which follow most helpful in writing the plurals of nouns correctly:

1. -s. Most nouns simply add *-s:*

bag	bags	violet	violets

2. Silent -e. Nouns ending in *-e* that is silent regularly add *-s:*

college	colleges	race	races

3. -es. Nouns ending in *-s, -z, -x, -ch,* or *-sh* regularly add *-es:*

gas	gases	buzz	buzzes
fox	foxes	torch	torches
dash	dashes		

4. Consonant + -y. Nouns ending in *-y* preceded by a consonant regularly change *-y* to *-i-* and add *-es:*

courtesy	courtesies	sky	skies

Proper names add only *-s:*

Germany	Germanys	Mary	Marys

5. Vowel + -y. Nouns ending in *-y* preceded by a vowel (except those ending in *-quy*) regularly add *-s:*

bay	bays	boy	boys
guy	guys	key	keys

6. Vowel + -o. Nouns ending in *-o* preceded by a vowel regularly add *-s:*

duo	duos	embryo	embryos

7. Consonant + -o. Most nouns ending in *-o* preceded by a consonant add *-s:*

alto	altos	ego	egos
piano	pianos	two	twos

but other nouns ending in *-o* preceded by a consonant add *-es:*

tomato	tomatoes	potato	potatoes

and a few nouns add either *-s* or *-es:*

cargo	cargoes *or* cargos
zero	zeros *or* zeroes

8. -oo. Nouns ending in *-oo* regularly add *-s:*

zoo	zoos	cuckoo	cuckoos
tattoo	tattoos	kangaroo	kangaroos

9. -i. Most nouns ending in *-i* add *-s:*

rabbi	rabbis	ski	skis

but a few add either *-s* or *-es:*

taxi	taxis *or* taxies

10. -f. A few nouns ending in *-f* change the *-f* to *-v-* and add *-es:*

leaf	leaves	self	selves
thief	thieves	wolf	wolves

but some of these also add *-s* without consonant change:

calf	calves *or* calfs
wharf	wharves *or* wharfs

11. -fe. A few nouns ending in *-fe* change *-f-* to *-v-* and add *-s:*

knife	knives	life	lives

12. Single letters, numbers, figures, and signs. These add apostrophe and *-s* or just *-s:*

A	A's *or* As
1920	1920's *or* 1920s
4	4's *or* 4s
#	#'s *or* #s

13. Nouns formed from abbreviations. Abbreviations used as nouns add either apostrophe and *-s* or more often just *-s:*

IOU	IOU's *or* IOUs
IQ	IQ's *or* IQs

14. Abbreviations formed by cutting off part of a word or contracting. These usually add *-s* without apostrophe:

apt	apts	bbl	bbls
cap	caps	mt	mts

but some may become plural without any change:

1 hr	4 hr *or* 4 hrs	1 mo	4 mo *or* 4 mos
1 yd	4 yd *or* 4 yds		

and some single-letter abbreviations double the letter:

p.	pp. (pages)	v.	vv. (verses)
l.	ll. (lines)		

15. -en. One noun usually adds *-en:*

ox	oxen

Another changes the stem and adds *-en:*

child	children

One sometimes changes the stem and adds *-en:*

brother	brethren

16. Vowel change. Six nouns change the middle vowel:

foot	feet	goose	geese
louse	lice	man	men
mouse	mice	tooth	teeth

Compounds in which one of these is the final element likewise change:

dormouse	dormice	forefoot	forefeet
Englishman	Englishmen	woman	women
eyetooth	eyeteeth		

17. Foreign endings. Many nouns of foreign origin retain the foreign plural. Most of them have also a regular English *-s* or *-es* plural, which is often preferred:

formula	formulas *or* formulae
tableau	tableaus *or* tableaux

but sometimes a foreign plural signals a difference in meaning (compare *stadia* and *stadiums*).

Latin. Most of these common anglicized foreign plurals come from Latin:

alga	algae	alumnus	alumni
index	indices	medium	media
opus	opera	series	series

Greek. The second largest group of anglicized foreign plurals comes from Greek:

analysis	analyses	ellipsis	ellipses
criterion	criteria	phalanx	phalanges

Other languages:

cherub	cherubim (Hebrew)
fellah	fellahin (Arabic)
señor	señores (Spanish)

18. Compounds. Two-word compounds consisting of noun plus adjective hyphened or open usually pluralize the noun:

heir apparent	heirs apparent

but sometimes the adjective is considered a noun and a suffix may be added to it:

court-martial	courts-martial *or* court-martials

In similar-appearing compounds in which the second word is a noun, a regular suffix is added at the end:

brigadier general	brigadier generals

Three-word compounds consisting of noun plus prepositional phrase hyphened or open usually pluralize the noun:

brother-in-law	brothers-in-law
man-of-war	men-of-war
rule of thumb	rules of thumb

19. Animals. Many names of fishes, birds, and mammals have both a plural with a suffix and a plural that is identical with the singular. A plural form like the singular is called a "zero" plural. Some words have one or the other.

Some that form a plural with a suffix (except occasionally when modified by an adjective like *wild, native, sea, mountain*) are:

bird	crow	dog	eagle
hen	rat	shark	swallow

The following have both plurals of which the zero plural is likely to be preferred by those who hunt or fish:

antelope	bear	doe	duck
flounder	hare	pheasant	rabbit
raccoon	squirrel		

The following have both plurals of which the zero plural is the commoner:

bass cod elk pike quail

but the plural with a suffix is used to signify diversity in kind or species

trouts *of the Rocky mountains*
fishes *of the Atlantic*

The following customarily prefer the zero plural:

cattle deer moose sheep swine

20. Numbers. A small number of general terms for numbers or quantities have both a plural form with suffix and a zero plural used in some constructions:

dozen	dozens *or* dozen
hundred	hundreds *or* hundred
score	scores *or* score

21. -ese. Most names derived from a place name and ending in *-ese* have only a zero plural, as in the examples that follow:

Burmese Siamese Chinese Japanese

CHECKUP

Use the rules for plurals to write the plurals of the following:

match	journey	radio
tally	1975	beef
5 mo	axis	Frenchman

Using the dictionary for finding the forms of verbs. Most verbs in the English language are said to be "regular". Such verbs have *-ed* added to an unchanged plain form, or present tense, to form the past form, or tense, as *look, looked.* Verbs are regular, too, if the final *-e* of the plain form is dropped before adding *-ed*, as *race, raced.* In regular verbs the *-ing* form, or present participle, is formed in a way similar to the past. Since the inflected forms of regular verbs are usually easy to spell and pronounce, they are generally not shown in this dictionary.

Verbs which do not add *-ed* to form the past are said to have irregular forms, as *do, did.* So are verbs in which the final consonant of the plain form is doubled to show the past, as *stop, stopped,* and others which present spelling problems.

The examples which follow show how inflected forms of irregular verbs are entered in your dictionary. The main entry represents the plain form. It is followed by the past form, or past tense, by the participle form if it differs from the past form, and by the *-ing* form, or present participle.

bring . . . *vb* **brought** . . . **bring·ing**
[1]**ᴅɪe** . . . *vb* **died; dy·ing**
[1]**go** . . . *vb* **went** . . . **gone** . . . **go·ing**
[2]**picnic** *vb* **pic·nicked; pic·nick·ing**
[2]**volley** *vb* **vol·leyed; vol·ley·ing**

Locating variant inflected forms. Some verbs may have variant forms for the past or for the participles. These forms are shown both in full and in part, joined by *or* or by *also*. For example:

[1]**burn** *vb* **burned** . . . *or* **burnt** . . . **burn-ing**
learn . . . *vb* **learned** . . . *also* **learnt** . . . **learn·ing**
[1]**show** . . . *vb* **showed; shown** . . . *or* **showed; show·ing**
[1]**trav·el** . . . *vb* **-eled** *or* **-elled; -el·ing** *or* **-el·ling**

Understanding partial entries of inflected forms. Some English words are a combination of elements, one of which is irregular, as the verb *undergo*. For verbs such as *undergo* the inflected forms are cut back to show only the forms of the final element. Some verbs of this type have variant inflected forms. Examples follow:

for·get . . . *vb* **-got** . . . ; **-got·ten** . . . *or* **-got; get·ting**
out·spread . . . *vb* **-spread; -spreading**
over·see . . . *vb* **-saw** . . . **-seen** . . . **-see·ing**

For other verbs like *outlive* in which the final element is regular, the inflected forms are not given:

over·haul . . . *vb* **post·date** . . . *vb*

Locating irregular verb forms in alphabetical order. Irregular verb forms are entered in their own alphabetical places if they fall alphabetically more than a column away from the main entry. For example:

am *pres 1st sing of* BE
[1]**are** *pres 2d sing or pres pl of* BE
sought *past of* SEEK
swum *past part of* SWIM

CHECKUP

Use your dictionary to help you write the inflected forms for these verbs:

do	signal	panic
fall	break	wake
build	clothe	overcome
sleep	rebel	seek
bear	sing	outrun

Using the dictionary for finding the forms of adjectives and adverbs. Many adjectives and some adverbs in the English language add *-er* and *-est* without any change in the simple form to show different levels of whatever the simple form expresses; for example, *tall, taller, tallest; cold, colder, coldest*. The addition of *-er* and *-est* to the simple form is called the "comparison" of the adjective or adverb. The *-er* makes the comparative form, and the *-est* makes the superlative form.

Adjectives and adverbs may also be compared by the use of *more* or *less* for the comparative, as *more dangerous* and *less dangerous*. The superlative form may be expressed by the use of *most* or *least,* as *most dangerous* and *least dangerous*. The comparison of longer adjectives and adverbs is usually formed in this way, although the same method is equally good for shorter words.

The comparison of the adjectives and adverbs just described is said to be regular. Since the forms are easy to spell and pronounce, they are generally not shown in this dictionary.

bright . . . *adj*
[2]**slow** *adv*

Adjectives and adverbs with comparative and superlative forms made otherwise than by simple addition of *-er* and *-est* to the unchanged root have these forms shown in full or in part in this dictionary:

[1]**good** . . . *adj* **bet·ter** . . . **best**
hap·py . . . *adj* **hap·pi·er; -est** (changes *-y* to *-i-* before endings)
[2]**much** *adv* **more; most**
[1]**no·ble** . . . *adj* **no·bler** . . . **no·blest** (drops final *-e* before endings)
sad . . . *adj* **sad·der; sad·dest** (doubles final consonant before endings)
[3]**well** *adv* **bet·ter** . . . **best**

Locating the comparative and superlative forms of adverbs which are homographs. Some adverbs may have the same form as adjectives, and therefore they are homographs. A comparison may be shown for the adjective but it is usually not repeated for an adverb which follows in the vocabulary listing:

[1]**free** . . . *adj* **fre·er** . . . **fre·est**
[2]**free** *adv*

Determining the comparative and superlative forms of compound adjectives. Compound adjectives which include a form to which *-er* and *-est* may be added do not have the comparatives and superlatives shown in this dictionary. You will not find forms for a word such as *kindhearted.* You may say or write *kinderhearted, kindesthearted* or *more (less) kindhearted, most (least) kindhearted.*

CHECKUP

1. Write the comparative form of these adjectives in two different ways:

steady	thin	mad
able	gentle	hungry

2. Write the superlative form of these adjectives in two different ways:

greedy	close	clever
fat	wise	big

DO YOU UNDERSTAND THE FUNCTION AND FORMS OF WORDS?

1. Your dictionary shows only one part-of-speech label for the words below. Write each word on your paper and write out in full the label which tells the function of the word.

ouch	piston	everybody	with
and	inflect	therefore	congenial

2. Write on your paper each main entry listed below and all the run-ons listed for each one. Then write out in full the label which tells the function of each word.

astronaut	fearful	[1]material	[2]reel
campaign	hazy	[1]pirate	tradition

3. List on your paper the plurals of these nouns in four columns under these heads: "Regular", "Same as Singular", "Irregular", and "Two Plurals". Use your dictionary.

gas	series	torch	loaf
calf	hobby	index	radius
mouse	handful	cattle	child

4. Find each entry and list on your paper those which function in the plural only.

knickers	alms	mathematics	physics
spareribs	calisthenics	scissors	headwaters

5. Find each verb listed below. Then write its inflected forms.

foresee	bite	frolic	blow
beseech	grub	fly	take

6. On your paper write the comparative or superlative form of the adjective or adverb in each sentence.

The sun rose ______ (early) today than yesterday.
A Great Dane was the ______ (good) dog in the show.
Tom thought he was the ______ (lonely) cowboy on the ranch.
Are you ______ (thin) than you were a year ago?

FINDING THE RIGHT MEANING

Locating the definitions. After the main entry, its pronunciation, and its forms (if given) your dictionary lists the meaning or meanings for the word. The dictionary term for meaning is "definition", or "sense".

This dictionary uses a boldface colon (:) as a joining symbol between the main entry and a definition. This boldface colon tells you that the material just after it is a definition, or meaning, of the word you are looking up.

Here are examples of simple definitions called "phrase definitions". The labels *also* and *esp* for *especially* may precede a phrase definition:

beef·steak . . . *n* **:** a slice of beef suitable for broiling or frying
beet . . . *n* **:** a garden plant with thick long-stalked edible leaves and a swollen root used as a vegetable, as a source of sugar, or for forage; *also* **:** this root
blink·er . . . *n* **:** one that blinks; *esp* **:** a blinking light used as a warning . . .

Sometimes the boldface colon may be followed by a word or several words in lightface small capitals. For example:

by·path . . . *n* **:** BYWAY

These small capital definitions are called "synonymous cross-references". They are synonyms, or words similar in meaning to the entry word. They also send, or refer, you to the main boldface entry for the word or words in small capitals. The definition or definitions you find there may be substituted at the entry where the synonymous cross-reference appears. For the entry *bypath* you may substitute the definition of *byway* and read the definition like this:

by·path . . . *n* : a little-traveled side road

A synonymous cross-reference may sometimes refer you to a numbered homograph:

^{1}**cas·tle** . . . *n* . . . **2 :** ^{3}ROOK
dril·ling . . . *n* **:** ^{5}DRILL
^{2}**ere** *conj* **:** ^{3}BEFORE

A synonymous cross-reference may also refer you to a word with a single sense number after it or to a sense number followed by a letter to indicate a further division into senses:

weath·er·cock . . . *n* **:** VANE 1
de·mise . . . *n* **:** DEATH 1
English daisy *n* **:** DAISY 1a

CHECKUP

Find these entries and tell whether the definition is a phrase or a cross-reference:

day coach	meteorite	pelf
asthma	daybreak	ninny
prankster	run-in	snobby

Understanding the different senses of the entry. Unlike the word *bypath* most words in the dictionary have more than one definition, or sense. Boldface numerals separate the different meanings, or senses, of the entry. Each numeral is followed by the boldface colon which signals a phrase definition, or a synonymous cross-reference, or a combination of both. For example:

ar·chery . . . *n* **1 :** the art, practice, or skill of shooting with bow and arrow **2 :** a body of archers
art·ful . . . *adj* **1 :** performed with or showing art or skill **2 :** CRAFTY, WILY
astir . . . *adj* **1 :** being in a state of activity **:** STIRRING **2 :** out of bed **:** UP

A numbered sense may be further divided into senses. These subsenses are set off by small boldface letters:

day . . . *n* **1 a :** the time of light between one night and the next **b :** DAYLIGHT **2 :** the time the earth takes to make one turn on its axis
^{2}**blossom** *vb* **1 :** BLOOM **2 a :** to flourish and prosper markedly **b :** DEVELOP, EXPAND

Sometimes an unnumbered sense is divided into subsenses:

fight·er . . . *n* **:** one that fights: **a :** WARRIOR, SOLDIER **b :** BOXER **c :** a fast maneuverable airplane
^{2}**else** *adj* **:** OTHER **: a :** being different in identity . . . **b :** being in addition . . .

In some entries a definition introduced by letters is still further subdivided. These smallest subdivisions are shown by lightface numerals in parentheses:

^{2}**compass** *n* **1** . . . **c** (1) **:** RANGE, SCOPE (2) **:** the range of pitch lying within the capacity of a voice or instrument
^{3}**down** *adj* . . . **2** . . . **b** (1) **:** DEPRESSED, DEJECTED (2) **:** SICK . . . (3) **:** having a low opinion or dislike . . .

Understanding the order of the definitions. In this dictionary the senses, or meanings, of a word are listed in historical order. This means the order in time in which the different meanings came into use in the English language. The one known to have been used first in English is entered first. This order does not mean that each meaning developed from the one that precedes it. The following entry shows how meanings evolve:

bas•ket . . . **1 a :** a woven container (as of straw, cane, or strips of wood) **b :** the contents of a basket **2 :** something that resembles a basket in shape or use **3 a :** a net open at the bottom and suspended from a metal ring that constitutes the goal in basketball **b :** a score made in basketball . . .

CHECKUP

Compare the first and last meanings of these words:

chute	gridiron	wring
[1]train	[1]print	[1]shell
[1]roll	abroad	estate

Using verbal illustrations as aids to meaning. Your dictionary helps you understand meanings by giving phrases or sentences which show the appropriate use of the entry word. Such examples of usage are called "verbal illustrations" and they are enclosed within angle brackets ⟨ ⟩. The word being illustrated appears in italic type, as follows:

con•fuse . . . **1 a :** to make mentally unclear or uncertain : PERPLEX ⟨a complicated problem *confuses* him⟩ **b :** DISCONCERT ⟨heckling *confused* the speaker⟩ **2 :** to make indistinct : BLUR ⟨stop *confusing* the issue⟩ **3 :** to mix up : JUMBLE ⟨his motives were hopelessly *confused*⟩ **4 :** to fail to distinguish between ⟨teachers always *confused* the twins⟩

Using illustrations and tables as aids to meaning. The illustrations accompanying some of the entry words were selected to help you visualize the unfamiliar and to develop new concepts. For example, the picture at *ovenbird* not only shows you what the bird looks like but also shows the curious nest it builds.

At other entries you will find diagrams as at *leaf*. You may also find cross-references to such diagrams at other entries:

ra•chis . . . *n* . . . — see LEAF illustration

You will also find the tables in this dictionary very helpful. Material following a lightface dash refers you to the tables:

dram . . . *n* **1 a** — see MEASURE table
gram . . . *n* . . . — see METRIC SYSTEM table

Using special labels and phrases as aids to meaning. For many entries italicized labels identify the kind of context in which the word or the sense is usually found. Some of the labels are:

archaic (used only in special contexts after 1755)
slang (informal speech not used in formal writing)
chiefly dial (dialect, or a regional variety of language)
chiefly Brit (or another country or region)

The following examples illustrate the use of these special labels:

[1]**even** . . . *n, archaic* : EVENING
[1]**buck** . . . *n* . . . **3** *slang* : DOLLAR 3b
em•met . . . *n, chiefly dial* : ANT
lor•ry . . . *n* . . . *Brit* : a large open truck
kirk . . . *n, chiefly Scot* : CHURCH

An italicized phrase, or "guide phrase", may appear before a definition to indicate a special meaning for the entry:

[1]**rare** . . . *adj* . . . *of meat* :
[2]**reflex** *adj* . . . **3** *of an angle* :

CHECKUP

1. Find the numbered definition for each word italicized in these verbal illustrations:

set a watch
the motor *died*
they *exhausted* all possibilities
three *times* at bat

2. At each of these entries find the special label and give the meaning associated with it:

[1]dig [5]pen sugar orchard
bonny petrol eftsoons

Understanding special meanings of plural forms. Sometimes a noun has a sense in which it is always or generally used in the plural and which differs in meaning from any of its meanings in the singular.

Your dictionary shows these special plural meanings preceded by the abbreviation *pl* at the sense. It also indicates which plural applies if there is more than one plural form for the entry. For example:

cher•ub . . . *n* **1** *pl* **cher•u•bim** . . . an angel of high rank **2** *pl* **cher•ubs** . . . **a** : a painting or drawing of a beautiful child usu. with wings . . .
[1]**cus•tom** . . . *n* . . . **2** *pl* **:** duties or taxes imposed by law on imports or exports . . .
pha•lanx . . . *n, pl* **pha•lanx•es** *or* **pha•lan•ges** . . . **2** *pl phalanges* **:** one of the bones of a finger or toe

Understanding special meanings of capitalized words. Some English words have special meanings when capitalized that they do not have when written with a small letter. Your dictionary shows the use of the capital with such entries by the abbreviations *cap* or *often cap* at the proper sense:

com•mu•nism . . . *n* . . . **2** *cap* **:** a system of government in which a single party controls state-owned means of production with the aim of establishing a stateless society— **com•mu•nist** . . . *n or adj, often cap* . . .

Occasionally, some words that are almost always capitalized in their usual meanings have special meanings in which they are not capitalized. Your dictionary shows the abbreviations *not cap* or *often not cap* at the proper sense:

[1]**Ro•man** . . . *n* . . . **3** *not cap* **:** roman letters or type
Re•nais•sance . . . *n* . . . **2** *often not cap* **:** a movement or period marked by . . .

CHECKUP

1. Find the sense number and the special meaning of these nouns in the plural:

[1]damage goose [1]horse
manner grocery [1]order

2. Find the sense number and the special meaning of these words when they are capitalized:

pilgrim [2]right continent
[3]west dipper capitol

Understanding usage notes as aids to meaning. For some entries a note beginning "used as", "used in", or "used to" may stand in place of a definition. The note is preceded by a light dash and not a boldface colon. You often find usage notes at words whose function becomes clear only in context or at other words like cries, calls, signals, and so on.

Usage notes may be found immediately following an entry, as follows:

ah . . . *interj* — used to express delight, relief, regret, or contempt
ahoy . . . *interj* — used in hailing ⟨ship *ahoy*⟩
at . . . *prep* — used to indicate (1) location in space or time . . . (2) a goal . . . (3) a condition . . . (4) how or why . . . (5) rate, degree, or position in a scale or series . . .

A usage note preceded by a light dash may also be found at the end of a particular definition, explaining usage in that sense only. Such a note may give help in grammatical construction, plural usage, or other matters:

cal·i·per *or* **cal·li·per** . . . *n* : a measuring instrument . . . — usu. used in pl. ⟨a pair of *calipers*⟩
a tem·po . . . *adv or adj* : in time — used as a direction in music to return to the original speed
[1]**gob·ble** . . . *vb* . . . **2** : to take eagerly : GRAB — usu. used with *up*

Finding the right meaning among homographs. Since many English words are spelled alike, you must select a definition which fits your needs. As you may have noted earlier, each homograph is numbered, and the sense or senses differ for each homograph:

[1]**brown** . . . *adj* : of the color brown . . .
[2]**brown** *n* : a color like that of coffee or chocolate that is a blend of red and yellow darkened by black
[3]**brown** *vb* : to make or become brown

Suppose you wondered about the meaning of *brown* in this sentence: You should *brown* the meat before putting it in the oven. You would know that *brown* is used as a verb. Therefore you would disregard the meanings of the first and second homographs and study the entry labeled *vb*.

CHECKUP

1. What usage notes do you find at the following entries or within their definitions?

[1]in	[2]gill	and
[1]jump	hey	amen

2. Give the number of the homograph and the sense which applies to the italicized word:

He will *chop* down that tree.
She has an *iron* will.
Did you see the *tug* in the harbor?

Using synonyms as aids to meaning. You are already familiar with the synonymous cross-references which appear in small capitals at various senses:

[2]**percent** *n* . . . **1** : one part in a hundred : HUNDREDTH **2** : PERCENTAGE

At some entries the italic boldface abbreviation ***syn*** for *synonym* introduces a paragraph of explanation at the end of the definitions. Such a paragraph is called a "synonymy paragraph" and it explains the relation of words similar in meaning to the main entry. Study this paragraph at *give:*

[1]**give** . . . *vb* . . . **1** : to make a present of or to **2 a** : . . .
syn GIVE, PRESENT, DONATE can mean to pass over freely to another. GIVE applies to delivering in any manner; PRESENT suggests more ceremony or formality; DONATE implies a free contribution (as to a charity)

The boldface abbreviation ***syn*** followed by the word "see" at the end of the definitions directs you to look elsewhere. You are referred to *give* by the directions at the end of the definitions for the synonyms explained in the synonymy paragraph at *give:*

do·nate . . . *vb* : to make a gift of : CONTRIBUTE . . . ***syn*** see GIVE
[2]**pre·sent** . . . *vb* **1 a** : to bring or introduce into the presence of someone **b** : . . . ***syn*** see GIVE

Using antonyms as aids to meaning. The italic boldface abbreviation ***ant*** for *antonym* following a synonymy paragraph or a "***syn*** see" direction introduces a word or words opposite in meaning to the main entry:

fru·gal . . . *adj* : characterized by or reflecting economy in the expenditure of resources . . .
syn FRUGAL, THRIFTY, ECONOMICAL mean in common careful with money and other resources . . . ***ant*** wasteful

fee·ble . . . *adj* . . . ***syn*** see WEAK ***ant*** robust, sturdy . . .

Using run-on phrases as aids to meaning. The boldface entries which follow a light dash at the end of the definitions are commonly used phrases called "idioms". An idiom is an expression that cannot be understood from the meanings of its separate words but must be learned as a whole. Study some idioms at the verb *go:*

[1]**go** . . . *vb* . . . — **go back on** : BETRAY — **go for 1** : to pass for or serve as **2** : to have an interest in or liking for : FAVOR — **go in for** : to take part in out of interest or liking ⟨*go in for* stamp collecting⟩ — **go one better** : OUTDO, SURPASS — **go over 1** : STUDY, REVIEW **2** : REVISE — **go places** : to be on the way to success — **go steady** : to date one person exclusively and frequently

Now study the idioms at the noun *go:*

[2]**go** *n* . . . — **no go** : to no avail : USELESS — **on the go** : constantly or restlessly active

CHECKUP

1. To what entry do the following refer you for a synonymy paragraph?

infirm	[2]rule	customary
rectify	motive	voluble

2. Find antonyms for:

danger	[1]easy	fresh

3. What run-on phrases are found at these entries?

[1]hand	[1]do	[1]grain
[1]point	[1]hold	mourning

Using etymologies as aids to meaning. Each word in the English language has an interesting history. The origin and history of that word is called its "etymology". The present use of some words is just the same as in the original language. More often than not, however, the word has passed through various stages of development with the result that its form today is quite different from the original source.

Locating the etymologies. In this dictionary the etymologies are shown in boldface brackets [ ] just before the boldface colon which precedes the definition. Most etymologies begin with the word *from.* If a word has entered the language with little or no change, the etymology may show only the language of origin, a slightly different original form, or a brief explanation. Study the following examples:

dai·sy . . . *n* [from Old English *dægesēage,* meaning literally "day's eye"]
ka·ra·te . . . *n* [from Japanese, meaning literally "empty hand"]
lei . . . *n* [from Hawaiian]
shek·el . . . *n* [from Hebrew *sheqel*]

In ordinary conversation many of our words might be called "native words", for they have been used with little or no change for many centuries. Other words have a long earlier history. Study these examples:

drag·on . . . *n* [from Old French, from Latin *dracon-,* stem of *draco* "serpent", "dragon", from Greek *drakōn* "serpent" . . .]
cof·fee . . . *n* [from Turkish *kahve,* from Arabic *qahwah*]
church . . . *n* [from Old English *cirice,* from Greek *kyriakon,* "house of the Lord", from *kyrios* "lord"]

Many English words have meanings quite different from their source. The "story" behind the development of such words makes the study of our language most interesting. Compare the original and final meaning of these entries:

can·di·date . . . *n* [from Latin *candidātus,* literally "one clothed in white", from *candidus* "white"; so called from the white toga worn by a candidate for office in ancient Rome]
bou·le·vard . . . *n* [from French, from medieval Dutch *bolwerc* "bulwark"; so called because the first boulevards followed the lines of abandoned city fortifications]

CHECKUP

What is the etymology for each of the following words?

calculate	wassail	muscle
secure	knight	foreign
least	digit	acrobat

Studying the etymologies of "new" words in the English language. When we need new words to express new ideas, we may borrow words from other languages. English contains words borrowed from every corner of the globe. Other languages, in turn, borrow from English. The following examples illustrate some interesting borrowed words and their origins:

ba·bush·ka . . . *n* [from the Russian word for "grandmother" . .]
ban·shee . . . *n* [from Scottish Gaelic *bean-sìth,* literally "woman of fairyland"]
mael·strom . . . *n* [from obsolete Dutch, from *malen* "to grind" and *strom* "stream"]
orang·u·tan . . . *n* [from Malay *orang hutan,* meaning literally "man of the forest"]
ro·bot . . . *n* [from Czech, from *robota* "forced labor"]
som·bre·ro . . . *n* [from Spanish, from *sombra* "shade"]
[2]**trek** . . . *n* [from South African Dutch, from Dutch *trekken* "to pull", "haul", "migrate"]

A second interesting way to get new words is using an older word in a new sense. These "new" words may be cut back from longer words, or they may be names of people or places or even references in literature:

frank·furt·er . . . *n* [from German *Frankfurter* "coming from Frankfurt", from *Frankfurt,* a city in Germany]
od·ys·sey . . . *n* [from the *Odyssey,* Greek epic poem attributed to Homer recounting the ten-year wanderings of Odysseus, king of Ithaca]
prom . . . *n* [short for *promenade*]
watt . . . *n* [named in honor of James *Watt* (1736-1819), Scottish engineer]

A third way of getting new words is to add prefixes or suffixes to an older word. (See "Using entries which are parts of words", page 9a.) In a similar way we may combine two or more older words to make a new word, as *raincoat* and *merry-go-round*. We may also make a new word by combining words or forms belonging to a foreign language, as *phonograph* and *xylophone*. In quite recent times some words have been formed by putting together just the first letter or letters of several older words. One such word is *scuba,* which like others so formed is called an "acronym". Study these examples:

> **ab•nor•mal•i•ty** . . . *n* (prefix + root + suffix)
>
> **pen•knife** . . . *n* [so called from its original use for making and mending quill pens]
>
> **¹pho•to•graph** . . . *n* [from Greek *phōt-*, stem of *phōs* "light" and *graphein* "to write", "record"]
>
> **ra•dar** . . . *n* [from the beginning letters of *ra*dio *d*etecting *a*nd *r*anging]

The fact that English has so often borrowed words from other languages descended from the same common parent language means that English may often have two or more words derived by different routes from the same remote source. Because of independent changes in form and meaning the ultimate relationship may not be obvious. Thus both *friar* and *pal* can be traced back to the same source as *brother,* the first through Latin *frater* and French *frère,* the second through Sanskrit *bhrātr* and Romany *phral* or *phal.* Attention is often called to such remote kinships by the phrase "from the same source as" in the etymologies.

Using etymologies to build vocabulary. A study of foreign forms in the etymologies, particularly Latin and Greek, will help you with the meaning of many English words. Note carefully the etymology of this entry:

> **ag•gres•sion** . . . *n* [from Latin *aggress-*, past participle stem of *aggredi* "to attack", from *ad-* "to" and *gradi* "to step", from the same root as Latin *gradus* "step", from which comes English *grade*]

Among the many words derived from Latin *gradi* are *ingredient, degree, congress, egress, progress,* and so on.

CHECKUP

How did these words come into the English language?

polka	spaghetti	motel
boycott	Siamese twin	etch

DO YOU UNDERSTAND HOW TO FIND THE RIGHT MEANING?

1. Refer to your dictionary to find out which of these entries have phrase definitions, which have synonymous cross-references, and which have both:

bairn	indicate	convene	wisdom
by-line	gym	groove	hit or miss

2. For each entry study the order of the definitions and decide how the later meanings may have developed:

¹face	magazine	¹print	corduroy
tablet	¹rasp	¹water	formula

3. Find the numbered definition for each italicized word in the verbal illustrations below and determine its meaning:

air safety	hand it *over*	*watch* a game
finish on a new car	*stretch* the truth	*minds* her parents
dash off a letter	*green* with envy	*new* lands

4. Find the sense number and the special meaning of these nouns when they are used in the plural:

[1]honor	jean	[1]British	[1]horse
[1]way	notion	[1]glass	[1]ground

5. Find the special meaning or meanings for each of the following entries when it is capitalized:

right	mercury	law	south

6. On your paper write the usage note which appears at or within the definitions of the following entries:

caliper	[1]out	senor	[1]but
dame	[1]father	gentleman	[2]forte

7. Give the number of the homograph and the sense which applies to the italicized word in each sentence below:

Don't you hate to get *gum* on your shoe?
The referee said that the batter was *out*.
Joe certainly did not feel *right* today.
That airline will *fly* passengers at a reduced rate.

8. Find and study the synonymy paragraph to which you are referred by each entry listed below:

[1]keen	chide	[1]combine	habitual
appease	inborn	admit	gaunt

9. Find the definition of each prefix and suffix and then write on your paper five words containing each one:

bi-	-ion	re-	un-	-able

10. Find the etymology for each entry listed below:

tycoon	isotope	opossum	[1]electric
foolscap	bishop	[1]focus	salaam

SPELLING AND WRITING

Depending upon the dictionary as a spelling aid. Three marks of a good speller are: (1) he knows when he is sure that a word is spelled right; (2) he knows when he is not sure; and (3) he turns to his dictionary for help when he needs it. A good speller likes to have a dictionary beside him as he writes. A poor speller is on his way to becoming a good speller if he checks with his dictionary every time he writes.

Before dictionaries were published, people had to remember how to spell, or put down some combination of letters that seemed right. Written language attempts to represent by letters the sounds which make up our spoken words. The spelling of these words would be easy if each letter of the alphabet represented a single sound, but that is not the case. So our language has many pairs of words like *hair* and *hare,* which are spelled differently but pronounced alike, and words such as *cough, rough, bough, through,* and *though,* which look alike but have several different sounds.

English spelling is difficult. A writer is therefore dependent upon a reliable and up-to-date dictionary.

Checking the spelling of a word. What should you do if you are uncertain about how a word begins? What should you do if *any* part of a word gives you trouble when you try to spell or write it? Refer immediately to the pronunciation symbols on page 11a. Study the key words carefully to see what letter or letters represent the sound with which you are having difficulty. For added help find the difficult letter or letters in the more detailed explanation for each symbol (see pages 13a-19a).

For example, three common spellings for the sound \k\ when it is the first sound in a word are *k, c,* and *ch.* Suppose you need help with the word *chalcedony,* which you heard spoken in a science discussion but have never seen written or printed. You might try the *k* listings first. Then the *c* listings. You will find the word *chalcedony* in the *ch* section. What other words do you know which begin with this same sound and spelling? What key word at **k** on page 11a helps you to spell the word? A knowledge of sounds and the letters which stand for them is very important in developing skill in spelling.

Using the dictionary for spelling and writing correctly. In the section titled "Understanding Entry Words", which begins on page 7a, you have learned that the boldface main entry gives you the actual spelling of the word. The centered periods show you where you may break a word at the end of a line in writing. You are reminded never to separate just one letter from the rest of the word.

You know, also, that words may have variant spellings and forms. What spelling will you use if more than one is given? Remember, the first spelling may be more common than the other or others, but they are all correct. Choose one spelling and use it consistently in writing.

Study these entries to review the use of centered periods and variant spellings or forms:

a cap•pel•la *also* **a ca•pel•la**
af•ter•ward . . . *or* **af•ter•wards**
guer•ril•la *or* **gue• ril•la**
co•sy . . . *var of* COZY

RULES FOR SPELLING

Your dictionary is always the final authority on the spelling of words. Whenever you write, keep your dictionary handy to help you spell words correctly.

You will also want to familiarize yourself with the most useful spelling rules — those which apply to many words.

1. Words ending in -x are unchanged before any suffix:

coax	coaxed	coaxing
six	sixteen	sixty

2. Words ending in -c remain unchanged before *a, o, u,* or a consonant:

tropic	tropical	frolic	frolicsome

Before *e* or *i* they usually add *k* if the pronunciation of the *c* remains hard:

picnic	picnicked	picnicking

but add nothing if the pronunciation of the *c* becomes soft:

critic	criticism	criticize

3. Words ending in consonant plus -c usually remain unchanged before any suffix:

disc	disced	discing

4. Words ending in a single consonant except x or c immediately preceded by two or more vowels in the same syllable remain unchanged before any suffix:

air	aired	airing	airy
brief	briefed	briefer	briefly
cloud	clouded	cloudless	cloudy
suit	suitable	suited	suitor

5. Words ending in a single consonant immediately preceded by a single vowel bearing primary stress double the consonant before a suffix beginning with a vowel:

abet	abetted	abetting	abettor
bag	baggage	bagged	bagging

They do not double the consonant before a suffix beginning with a consonant:

drop	droplet	fit	fitness
glad	gladly	win	winsome

EXCEPTIONS (among others):

chagrin	chagrined	chagrining
prefer	preferable	preference

6. Words ending in a single consonant immediately preceded by a single vowel bearing secondary stress vary greatly in their derivatives:

a. Some always double the consonant:

handicap	handicapped	handicapping

b. Some have a single consonant only:

chaperon	chaperoned	chaperoning

c. Some have both forms:

kidnap	kidnapped *or* kidnaped
	kidnapping *or* kidnaping

7. Words ending in a single consonant immediately preceded by one or more vowels without stress remain unchanged before any suffix:

credit	credited	crediting	creditor
solid	solider	solidest	solidify

EXCEPTIONS: A large group of words doubles a final consonant; in British use such doubling is the regular practice; in

U.S. use it is usually an accepted alternative:

travel	traveled *or* travelled
	traveling *or* travelling

8. Words ending in two or more consonants the last of which is not c remain unchanged before any suffix:

attach	attached	attachment
length	lengthen	lengthy

EXCEPTIONS: Words ending in *-ll:*

a. The second *l* of final *-ll* always disappears before a suffix beginning with *l:*

dull	dully	full	fully

b. The second *l* of final *-ll* may disappear before *-less,* but hyphened forms retaining all three *l*'s are more frequent:

hull	hull-less	skill	skill-less

c. The hyphened form retaining all three *l*'s is usually used with *-like:*

bell	bell-like	scroll	scroll-like

9. Words ending in silent -e drop the vowel before a suffix beginning with a vowel:

curve	curvature	curved	curving

They remain unchanged before a suffix beginning with a consonant:

bone	boneless	curve	curvesome

EXCEPTIONS: The final *-e* is retained in some instances:

a. Proper names ending in single *-e* preceded by one or more consonants usually keep the *-e* before the suffix *-an:*

Europe	European

b. mile mileage

c. Words ending in *-le* usually drop the *-le* before the suffix *-ly:*

gentle	gently	subtle	subtly

d. Words ending in *-ce* or *-ge* usually retain the *-e* before any suffix beginning with a vowel other than *e, i,* or *y,* thus preserving the softness of the *c* or *g:*

change	changeable
peace	peaceable

A *d* preceding *g* may in a few cases act as a preserver of the soft sound and permit the dropping of the *-e:*

judge	judgment

e. Although final *-e* regularly drops before the suffix *-able,* some adjectives in *-able* have alternatives retaining the *-e:*

like	likable *or* likeable

f. Usage varies greatly with regard to dropping or retaining final *-e* before the suffix *-y.*

Many words have both the *-ey* and the *-y:*

stone	stony *or* stoney

Some words have only one form in common usage:

rose	rosy	shade	shady

g. In some present participles the silent *-e* remains to distinguish them from the corresponding forms of other verbs:

dye	dyeing *(in contrast to* dying*)*
singe	singeing *(in contrast to* singing*)*

10. Words ending in -e preceded by a vowel drop the final *-e* before *-a-* or *-e-* in the suffix:

argue	argued		
blue	blued	bluer	bluest
lie	liar		

EXCEPTIONS: The ending is sometimes unchanged:

a. Words ending in *-ee* usually retain both *e*'s before *-a-* and always before *-i-* in the suffix:

agree agreeable agreeing

b. In an accented syllable *-ie* becomes *-y* before *-i-* in the suffix:

die dying

c. Final *-oe* remains unchanged before *-i-* in the suffix:

canoe canoeing hoe hoeing

d. Final *-ue* usually drops *-e* before *-i-* in the suffix:

argue arguing true truism

e. Final *-ye* alternatively keeps or drops *-e* before *-i-* in the suffix:

eye eyeing *or* eying

f. Adjectives with the suffix *-y* retain *-e:*

glue gluey

g. A double vowel usually remains unchanged before a suffix beginning with a consonant:

agree	agreement	blue	blueness
woe	woeful *or* woful		

11. Words ending in -y preceded by a consonant usually change the *-y* to *-i-* before any letter in the suffix except *i* and the possessive sign *'s:*

beauty	beautiful	beautify
defy	defiant	defying
everybody	everybody's	

EXCEPTIONS: The *-y* is not always changed to *-i-:*

a. One-syllable words usually retain *-y* before *-ly* and *-ness:*

dry dryly dryness

b. Comparatives and superlatives of one-syllable adjectives alternatively retain *-y* or replace it with *-i-:*

dry drier *or* dryer driest *or* dryest

c. Before *-er* alternative uses of *-y* and *-i-* occur:

fly flier *or* flyer

d. Before *-like* and *-ship* and in derivatives of *baby* the *-y* remains unchanged:

lady	ladylike	ladyship
baby	babyhood	

e. When separated by one or more syllables from the primary stress of the base word, the *-y* may be lost completely before *-i-* in a suffix:

accompany	accompanist	
military	militarist	militarize

12. Words ending in -y preceded by a vowel usually remain unchanged before any suffix:

alloy	alloys	attorney	attorneys	
play	played	playing	player	playful

EXCEPTIONS: The *-y* is sometimes changed to *-i-:*

a. A few words ending in *-ay* change *-y* to *-i-:*

day	daily	lay	laid
say	saith	slay	slain

b. A few words alternatively retain *-y* or replace it with *-i-:*

gay	gaiety *or* gayety	gaily *or* gayly
stay	stayed *or* staid	

c. Comparatives and superlatives of adjectives ending in *-ey* replace these two letters with *-i-:*

gluey	gluier	gluiest
phoney	phonier	phoniest

d. Adjectives ending in *-wy* change the *-y* to *-i-* before any suffix:

showy showier showiest showily showiness

13. Verbs ending in a vowel except e or y, when adding a suffix beginning with a vowel, remain unchanged before their inflectional suffixes:

radio	radioed	radioing	
ski	skied	skiing	skier

EXCEPTIONS: Verbs ending in single *-o* usually insert *e* before adding *-s* for the third person singular:

echo echoes lasso lassoes

14. Nouns ending in a vowel when adding one of the suffixes -esque, -ism, -ist usually remain unchanged especially if the base word is short and the final vowel is essential to its recognition:

solo soloist Zola Zolaesque

15. Geographical and personal names ending in -a regularly drop the *-a* before the suffix *-an* or *-ian:*

America American Canada Canadian

16. Some geographical names ending in -o drop the *-o* before *-an* or *-ian:*

Mexico Mexican Ontario Ontarian

17. Scientific terms of Greek or Latin origin ending in -a regularly drop the *-a* before a suffix beginning with a vowel:

pleura pleural

18. Geographical and personal names ending in -o or a combination of letters pronounced \ō often insert *n* or *v* before *-an* or *-ian:*

Buffalo Buffalonian Marlowe Marlovian

19. When a prefix is added that forms a new word, a base word usually remains unchanged:

act	enact	call	recall
change	exchange	prove	disprove

20. Two or more words joining to form a compound usually retain the full spelling of both component words:

billfold makeup sidestep widespread

CHECKUP

Use the rules for spelling to write the past form of:

beg	gain	attack
box	fancy	benefit
dye	delay	imagine
alibi	frolic	handicap

CAN YOU USE THE DICTIONARY FOR WRITING AND SPELLING?

1. Write each of these words, hyphenating the points (if any) at which it may be divided at the end of a line. After each word put the number of *spoken* syllables it has.

area	usual	ebony	anybody	blessed	naughty
oral	arena	utopia	athletic	dressing	blotched
idea	usurp	utensil	business	obituary	wretched

2. Which of the following spellings are correct?

fish, fishes	buses, busses	allied, allyed	indices, indexes
draft, draught	dwelled, dwelt	potatos, potatoes	drought, drouth
defying, defiing	sining, sinning	canoeing, canoing	picnicer, picnicker
prettiest, prettyest	repeated, repeatted	traveler, traveller	destroied, destroyed
travelogue, travelog	analyses, analysises	pianoes, pianos	top-mast, topmast

3. To the following words add the suffixes given in parentheses. Check with the dictionary if you are not sure.

stone(-y)	radio(-ed)	courage(-ous)	care(-ful, -ing)
lie(-ing)	music(-al)	state(-ment)	defy(-ant, -ing)
dye(-ing)	lady(-like)	decorate(-ive)	encourage(-ing)
drop(-ed)	grace(-ful)	sun(-y)	carry(-age, -ing)
true(-ly)	baby(-hood)	fit(-ing, -ly)	arrive(-al, -ing)
begin(-er)	elevate(-or)	credit(-ed, -or)	glad(-en, -est, -ly)

THE HISTORY OF YOUR DICTIONARY

This dictionary, which bears the distinguished label *A Merriam-Webster,* has a proud history that goes back well over a hundred years. The first of its line appeared at a time when the United States was a young nation, rejoicing in the success of the American Revolution.

This dictionary which you are now using developed from the work of America's first lexicographer, Noah Webster. A zealous patriot, Webster felt that the people of the United States needed a dictionary of their language — not a dictionary of English as it was spoken or spelled in Great Britain. In patriotic fervor Webster argued against continuing dependence upon Great Britain: "We have thrown off the shackles of her government, why not her language also?"

With devoted singleness of purpose Webster spent most of his life making two dictionaries. His goal was the recording of American language for Americans. He had no assistants to lighten his laborious task and no assurance of financial reward for years of hard work.

NOAH WEBSTER AND HIS DICTIONARIES

Noah Webster was born in West Hartford, Connecticut, October 16, 1758. Although he attended the village school, tutored privately, and graduated from Yale, Webster was largely a self-taught man. He studied all his life, devoting his energies to language — its origins, its spelling, its sounds, its meanings.

As a young man Noah Webster lived through the exciting days of the Revolution. He even went with the militia toward Saratoga but turned back when word came that the fighting was over. Perhaps more than others of his day Webster was carried away with enthusiasm for America and all things American. He disliked the British then and, in a sense, continued to fight them and their language all his life.

During the few years that he taught school, Webster found that the textbooks were not adequate for young American scholars. Since nearly all books were shipped from England, the content of the texts centered around British life with references to the king, parliament, and other objectionable or inappropriate subjects. Then, too, books were hard to obtain, for trade with England diminished greatly just after the Revolution.

Webster recognized the need for American schoolbooks and set about to fill that need. In 1783 he found a publisher for a spelling book — later called the *Blue-Backed Speller*. This little book treated the letters and their sounds as used by Americans and emphasized patriotic and moral virtues. So famous did this speller become that every peddler carried it in his pack, every store stocked it along with food staples, and every family bought it for their simple home library. The *Blue-Backed Speller* is still sold today.

In the years immediately following the publication of his speller, Noah Webster pursued many interests. He fought for uniform copyright laws. He began giving lectures — something he enjoyed doing all his life. He published pamphlets which revealed a vast knowledge of government and statesmanship. He continued in law, the profession for which he had studied, and he even served as an editor of several newspapers in New York. His interest in science produced a two-volume work remarkable for its time: *A Brief History of Epidemic and Pestilential Diseases*.

During a prolonged stay in Philadelphia Webster frequently talked with Benjamin Franklin, who was also interested in the language as spoken and written by Americans. The two men agreed that a reform in English spelling was highly desirable.

Noah Webster was well equipped to write the first dictionary of the American language. He always took notes on words he met in his reading and failed to find in English dictionaries. He traveled through the colonies by stage, by boat, and on horseback, listening to people talk and noting the words they used, how they used them, and how they said them.

In 1806 Webster's first dictionary, a work of some 400 pages, was published. It bore the awesome title *A Compendious Dictionary of the English Language*. Noteworthy because it was the first dictionary in the United States, it still was only a start toward the great publication that was to come.

After publishing a grammar in 1807, Webster began the task that was to consume his time and efforts for the next twenty years — the making of his *American Dictionary of the English Language*, 1828. Noah Webster worked diligently to make his *American Dictionary* more useful to Americans than the most authoritative work of English origin: Dr. Samuel Johnson's dictionary published in 1755.

Webster observed that the language was constantly changing and believed that those changes should be recorded. He states: "The process of a living language is like the motion of a broad river, which flows with a slow, silent, irresistible current". He also argued that "a living language must keep pace with improvements in knowledge and with the multiplication of ideas".

Webster prepared his dictionary for the plain reader. He considered it to be a vast schoolbook. His goal was to write a book that would make all other books of its class unnecessary. Above everything else Webster made good the title of the dictionary by eliminating many references applicable only in Great Britain and by constantly emphasizing American usage.

The *American Dictionary* was widely acclaimed on its publication. It was America's first work of impressive scholarship. It became a chief factor in unifying the language of a new nation.

Noah Webster read the final proofs of his great dictionary at the age of 70. During these years he had supported himself and his family largely on royalties from the sale of the *Blue-Backed Speller*. He lived to be 84, continuing his literary and lexicographical interests to the very end.

CHECKUP

1. How does Noah Webster's life reflect his patriotism?
2. Why is the adjective *versatile* frequently used to describe Noah Webster?
3. What contributions did Noah Webster make toward the education of young people?
4. How did Noah Webster collect evidence for his dictionary entries?

NOAH WEBSTER AND AMERICAN ENGLISH

Noah Webster influenced for all time the English language as used by Americans. He brought order to spelling and usage in the early days of the United States. He contributed much to the homogeneous quality of American English today — an English that is fairly uniform and not broken up into many provincial dialects.

The changes in spelling and usage which Webster effected in his *American Dictionary* are interesting to observe:

1. The letter *k* was dropped from such words as *public* and *music* (not *publick, musick*).
2. The letter *u* was omitted from such words as *honor* and *favor* (not *honour, favour*).
3. The letters *er* were substituted for letters *re* in such words as *center* and *sepulcher* (not *centre, sepulchre*).
4. The final consonant of verbs having the accent on the first syllable or on a syllable preceding the last was not doubled before endings: *travel, traveler, traveling* (not *traveller, travelling*).
5. New words which had appeared in American English were included: *applesauce, moccasin, scow, skunk,* and many others. None of these words had previously been entered in Dr. Johnson's English dictionary.

In addition to the Americanization of many entries Noah Webster made two other great contributions to lexicography. Perhaps his greatest distinction lies in the completeness and accuracy of his definitions. His strength is said to derive from the fact that he was "a born definer".

Another contribution to lexicography was Webster's inclusion of detailed etymologies — the histories of words. Webster claimed to have "mastered twenty languages" in order to substantiate his etymologies. Be that as it may, he surrounded himself with dictionaries in various languages and attempted for the first time to write scholarly etymologies.

As for the new words which Webster added to his dictionary, he himself enumerates the words under five heads:

1. Words of common use, formerly omitted from Dr. Johnson's literature-centered dictionary
2. Participles of verbs
3. Terms of frequent occurrence in historical works
4. Legal terms
5. Terms in the arts and sciences

In summary, then, Noah Webster may be credited with the following contributions which made his *American Dictionary* superior to the highly regarded English dictionary of Dr. Johnson:

more words
American spelling and pronunciation
American usage
more exact definitions
fuller etymologies

CHECKUP

1. In what way are users of American English indebted to Noah Webster?
2. Name three spelling changes that appeared in the *American Dictionary*.
3. What were Noah Webster's greatest contributions to lexicography?
4. What kinds of new words appeared in the *American Dictionary?*

THE MERRIAM-WEBSTER DICTIONARIES

The name *Webster* is immortalized by the man's scholarly efforts to produce a dictionary for American usage. The name *Merriam* became associated with the name *Webster* in 1843. In that year the Merriam brothers, George and Charles, owners of a printing office and bookstore in Springfield, Massachusetts, arranged to revise and print the 1841 edition of the *American Dictionary*. After acquiring all rights from Webster's heirs and an Amherst company, G. & C. Merriam Company gathered together a well-trained staff of editors and produced their first product: *An American Dictionary of the English Language*, 1847.

Today as in those early days G. & C. Merriam Company insists upon scholarship. It states decisively the function of dictionary makers: to record the language as it is used by the majority of its users, not to create it or legislate concerning it.

In place of one dedicated man, Noah Webster, who jotted down what he saw and heard, a large staff reads widely in all areas of written communication and listens to all forms of oral communication.

This Merriam-Webster editorial staff is comprised of scholars from every part of the United States, representing many different universities and cultural backgrounds. Former college professors now contribute their scholarship to dictionary making. Included on the staff are specialists in varied fields: linguistics, pronunciation, dialect, etymology, sports, science, religion, music, and so on.

The vast amount of information acquired by the editorial staff is recorded on cards which make up a unique "citation file" insured for over a million dollars. A citation is the quotation of a passage *exactly* as it was written or spoken, with source and date.

General readers and specialists read everything available printed in the English language: fiction and nonfiction, journals, magazines, reviews, reports, mail-order catalogs, menus, schoolbooks, word lists supplied by school systems and testing bureaus. The staff draws upon its own editorial library, university libraries, and public libraries including the Springfield (Massachusetts) City Library.

Similarly, pronunciation editors listen attentively to the words spoken by educated people. They record radio, television, and live speeches for evidence in the citation files.

Each word entered in this very dictionary has traveled a long, arduous route. First, it was marked in various contexts by readers who wanted to determine (1) what kinds of matter included the word; (2) how the word was used; (3) by whom the word was used; and (4) when the word was used. Next, the word in the marked material was sent to assistants for photographing or typing on citation slips. File clerks then sorted the citation slips and filed them for future analysis. Such accumulated evidence helps the editors decide which words ought to be included in the dictionary and how they should be defined.

Then came the time for an editor to define the word. He first drew the citation slips from the files and studied the word to determine many things: scope of meaning, currency of use, level of use, etymology, pronunciation, variant spellings, usage, part of speech. Then the editor assembled the complete entry. His work passed on to a reviewing editor, to a supervisory editor, to a copyreader, and finally to a printer.

The editors recognize, as did Noah Webster, that the vocabulary is constantly changing in meaning and acquiring new senses. The scholarly editing of the Merriam-Webster staff keeps the dictionary up to date by:

1. Inclusion of new words in the language
2. Recording of shifts of meaning in established words
3. Indication of transference of application from one subject to another, as certain senses now used in both radio and television

From this brief account of dictionary making today, you can readily see how the goals toward which Noah Webster aspired have been realized. Today, Merriam-Webster dictionaries are used in law courts, international councils, universities, and schools everywhere.

CHECKUP

1. Why is the name *Merriam* associated with the name *Webster?*
2. How was evidence for each word in your dictionary collected?
3. How do staff lexicographers use the citation files at G. & C. Merriam?
4. How is your dictionary kept up to date?
5. What significance lies in the label *A Merriam-Webster?*

A DICTIONARY OF THE ENGLISH LANGUAGE

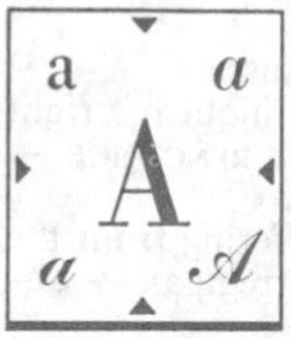

[1]a \'ā\ *n, often cap* **1 :** the 1st letter of the English alphabet **2 :** the musical tone A **3 :** a grade rating a student's work as superior

[2]a \ə, (')ā\ *indefinite article* **1 :** some one unspecified ⟨*a* man overboard⟩ ⟨*a* dozen⟩ **2 :** ONE : the same ⟨two of *a* kind⟩ ⟨birds of *a* feather⟩ **3 :** ANY ⟨*a* man who is sick can't work⟩ **4 :** in each : to each : for each ⟨twice *a* week⟩ — used in all senses before words beginning with a consonant sound; compare [1]AN

[1]a- \ə\ *prefix* **1 :** on : in : at ⟨*a*bed⟩ **2 :** in a specified state or condition ⟨*a*fire⟩ **3 :** in (such) a manner ⟨*a*loud⟩ **4 :** in the act or process of ⟨gone *a*-hunting⟩

[2]a- *or* **an-** *prefix* : not : without ⟨*a*sexual⟩ — *a-* before consonants other than *h* and sometimes before *h*, *an-* before vowels and usu. before *h* ⟨*an*hydrate⟩

a *abbr* **1** acre **2** alto

Å *abbr* **1** ace **2** assist

Å *abbr* angstrom

aard·vark \'ärd-ˌvärk\ *n* [from Afrikaans (South African Dutch), meaning literally "earth pig"] : a large burrowing ant-eating African mammal with a long sticky tongue

aardvark (2 ft. high at shoulder)

AAU *abbr* Amateur Athletic Union

ab- *prefix* : from : away : off ⟨*ab*normal⟩

AB *abbr* **1** at bat **2** bachelor of arts

ABA *abbr* American Bar Association

aback \ə-'bak\ *adv* **1** *archaic* : BACK, BACKWARD **2 :** by surprise : UNAWARES ⟨taken *aback* by the turn of events⟩

ab·a·cus \'ab-ə-kəs\ *n, pl* **-ci** \-ˌsī, -ˌkē\ *or* **-cus·es** \-kə-səz\ : an instrument for making calculations by sliding counters along rods or in grooves

[1]abaft \ə-'baft\ *adv* : toward the stern : at the stern : AFT

[2]abaft *prep* : to the rear of; *esp* : toward the stern from

ab·a·lo·ne \ˌab-ə-'lō-nē\ *n* : a mollusk with a flattened slightly spiral shell perforated along the edge and lined with mother-of-pearl

[1]aban·don \ə-'ban-dən\ *vb* **1 :** to give up completely **2 :** to withdraw from often in the face of danger ⟨*abandon* ship⟩ **3:** to withdraw protection, support, or help from **4 :** to give oneself over completely to an emotion — **aban·don·ment** \-mənt\ *n*

syn ABANDON, DESERT, FORSAKE mean in common to leave behind. ABANDON is likely to stress a complete giving up in the face of need or trouble; DESERT often implies shirking responsibilities; FORSAKE generally applies to leaving someone or something (as a familiar place) held dear ***ant*** reclaim

[2]abandon *n* **1 :** a complete yielding to natural impulses **2 :** ENTHUSIASM, EXUBERANCE

aban·doned \ə-'ban-dənd\ *adj* **1 :** DESERTED, FORSAKEN ⟨an *abandoned* house⟩ **2 :** wholly given up to wickedness or vice ⟨an *abandoned* criminal⟩

abase \ə-'bās\ *vb* : to lower in rank or position : HUMBLE, DEGRADE — **abase·ment** \-mənt\ *n*

abash \ə-'bash\ *vb* : to destroy the self-possession or self-confidence of ***syn*** see EMBARRASS ***ant*** reassure — **abash·ment** \-mənt\ *n*

abate \ə-'bāt\ *vb* : to decrease in degree, amount, or intensity : DIMINISH ⟨the wind *abated*⟩ ⟨the excitement has *abated*⟩ — **abat·er** *n*

abate·ment \ə-'bāt-mənt\ *n* **1 :** the act or process of abating : the state of being abated **2 :** an amount abated; *esp* : a deduction from the full amount of a tax

ab·at·toir \'ab-ə-ˌtwär\ *n* : SLAUGHTERHOUSE

ab·bess \'ab-əs\ *n* : a woman who is the superior of a convent of nuns

ab·bey \'ab-ē\ *n, pl* **abbeys 1 a :** a monastery governed by an abbot **b :** a convent governed by an abbess **2 :** a church that once belonged to an abbey ⟨Westminster *Abbey*⟩

ab·bot \'ab-ət\ *n* : the superior of a monastery

ab·bre·vi·ate \ə-'brē-vē-ˌāt\ *vb* : to make briefer : SHORTEN; *esp* : to reduce (as a word) to a shorter form intended to stand for the whole

ab·bre·vi·a·tion \ə-ˌbrē-vē-'ā-shən\ *n* **1 :** the act or result of abbreviating : ABRIDGMENT **2 :** a shortened form of a word or phrase used for brevity esp. in writing

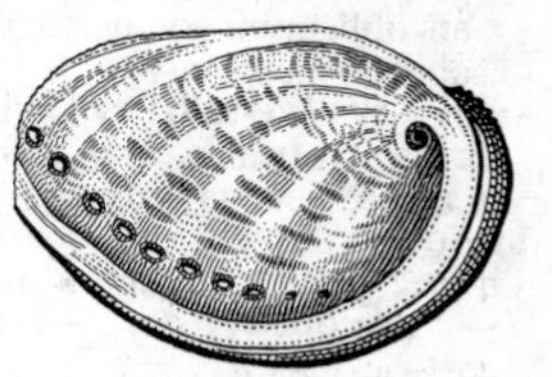

abalone

ABC *abbr* American Broadcasting Company

ab·di·cate \'ab-di-ˌkāt\ *vb* : to relinquish sovereign power, office, or responsibility formally — **ab·di·ca·tion** \ˌab-di-'kā-shən\ *n*

ab·do·men \'ab-də-mən, ab-'dō-mən\ *n* **1 :** the part of the body between the chest and the pelvis; *also* : the body cavity containing the chief digestive organs **2** : the hind portion of the body behind the thorax in an arthropod — see INSECT illustration — **ab·dom·i·nal** \ab-'däm-ə-nəl\ *adj* — **ab·dom·i·nal·ly** \-ē\ *adv*

ab·duct \ab-'dəkt\ *vb* **1** : to carry a person off by force **2** : to draw (a part of the body) away from the median axis of the body — **ab·duc·tion** \-'dək-shən\ *n*

ab·duc·tor \-'dək-tər\ *n* : one that abducts; *esp* : a muscle that draws a body part away from the median axis

abeam \ə-'bēm\ *adv or adj* : at right angles to a ship's keel

abed \ə-'bed\ *adv or adj* : in bed

Ab·er·deen An·gus \ˌab-ər-ˌdēn-'ang-gəs\ *n* : any of a breed of black hornless beef cattle originating in Scotland

ab·er·rant \a-'ber-ənt\ *adj* : deviating from the usual or natural type

ab·er·ra·tion \ˌab-ə-'rā-shən\ *n* **1** : the act of deviating esp. from a moral standard or normal state **2** : unsoundness or disorder of the mind **3** : a small periodic change of apparent position in heavenly bodies due to the combined effect of the motion of light and the motion of the observer

abet \ə-'bet\ *vb* **abet·ted**; **abet·ting** : to encourage or aid esp. in doing wrong — **abet·ment** \-'bet-mənt\ *n* — **abet·tor** *or* **abet·ter** \-'bet-ər\ *n*

abey·ance \ə-'bā-ən(t)s\ *n* : a temporary suspension of activity ⟨plans held in *abeyance*⟩

ab·hor \ab-'hȯ(ə)r, əb-\ *vb* **ab·horred**; **ab·hor·ring** : to shrink from in disgust : LOATHE ***syn*** see HATE ***ant*** admire (*as persons or their acts*), enjoy (*things that are a matter of taste*) — **ab·hor·rence** \-'hȯr-ən(t)s, -'här-\ *n* — **ab·hor·rer** \-'hȯr-ər\ *n*

ab·hor·rent \-'hȯr-ənt, -'här-\ *adj* : DETESTABLE — **ab·hor·rent·ly** *adv*

abide \ə-'bīd\ *vb* **abode** \-'bōd\ *or* **abid·ed**; **abid·ing** **1** *archaic* : to wait for **2** : to bear patiently : TOLERATE **3** : LAST, ENDURE ⟨an *abiding* friendship⟩ **4** : DWELL — **abid·ance** \ə-'bīd-ən(t)s\ *n* — **abid·er** *n* — **abide by** : to accept the terms of : be obedient to ⟨*abide by* the rules⟩

abil·i·ty \ə-'bil-ət-ē\ *n, pl* **-ties** **1 a** : the quality or state of being able : power to do something **b** : competence in doing : SKILL **2** : natural talent
syn ABILITY, APTITUDE, TALENT mean unusual capacity for doing or accomplishing. ABILITY is likely to stress an innate power of effective accomplishment; APTITUDE implies both a quickness to learn and a natural liking usually for a particular field or activity; TALENT tends to suggest such great or creative ability as constitutes an obligation for use and development ***ant*** inability, incapacity

-abil·i·ty *also* **-ibil·i·ty** \ə-'bil-ət-ē\ *n suffix, pl* **-ties** : capacity, fitness, or tendency to act or be acted on in a specified way ⟨read*ability*⟩

ab·ject \'ab-ˌjekt, ab-'\ *adj* : very low in spirit or hope : WRETCHED ⟨*abject* misery⟩ ⟨an *abject* coward⟩ — **ab·ject·ly** *adv* — **ab·ject·ness** \-ˌjek(t)-nəs, -'jek(t)-\ *n*

ab·jure \ab-'ju̇(ə)r\ *vb* : to renounce solemnly ⟨*abjure* allegiance⟩

ab·la·tion \a-'blā-shən\ *n* **1** : surgical cutting and removal **2** : the vaporization of an outer covering (as of a spacecraft) to keep an inner part cool

ablaze \ə-'blāz\ *adj* **1** : being on fire **2** : radiant with light or bright color

able \'ā-bəl\ *adj* **abler** \-b(ə-)lər\; **ablest** \-b(ə-)ləst\ **1 a** : having enough power, skill, or resources to do something ⟨*able* to swim⟩ **b** : not prevented ⟨*able* to vote⟩ **2** : COMPETENT, SKILLFUL ⟨an *able* editor⟩

-a·ble *also* **-i·ble** \ə-bəl\ *adj suffix* **1** : capable of, fit for, or worthy of being ⟨break*able*⟩ ⟨collect*ible*⟩ **2** : tending, given, or liable to ⟨peace*able*⟩ ⟨perish*able*⟩

able–bod·ied \ˌā-bəl-'bäd-ēd\ *adj* : having a sound strong body : physically fit

abloom \ə-'blüm\ *adj* : BLOOMING

ab·lu·tion \a-'blü-shən, ə-'blü-\ *n* : washing oneself esp. as a religious rite

ably \'ā-blē\ *adv* : in an able manner

ABM \ˌā-(ˌ)bē-'em\ *n* : ANTIBALLISTIC MISSILE

ab·ne·gate \'ab-ni-ˌgāt\ *vb* **1** : to relinquish a right or privilege **2** : to deny to oneself : RENOUNCE — **ab·ne·ga·tion** \ˌab-ni-'gā-shən\ *n*

ab·nor·mal \(')ab-'nȯr-məl\ *adj* : differing from the normal or average; *esp* : markedly irregular — **ab·nor·mal·ly** \-mə-lē\ *adv*

ab·nor·mal·i·ty \ˌab-nȯr-'mal-ət-ē\ *n, pl* **-ties** **1** : the state of being abnormal **2** : something abnormal

[1]**aboard** \ə-'bōrd, -'bȯrd\ *adv* : on, onto, or within a ship, railway car, or vehicle

[2]**aboard** *prep* : on or into esp. for passage ⟨go *aboard* ship⟩

abode \ə-'bōd\ *n* : dwelling place : RESIDENCE

abol·ish \ə-'bäl-ish\ *vb* : to do away with completely : put an end to — **abol·ish·a·ble** \-ə-bəl\ *adj* — **abol·ish·er** *n* — **abol·ish·ment** \-ish-mənt\ *n*

ab·o·li·tion \ˌab-ə-'lish-ən\ *n* **1** : the act of abolishing : the state of being abolished **2** : the abolishing of slavery

ab·o·li·tion·ist \-'lish-(ə-)nəst\ *n* : a person who is in favor of abolition esp. of Negro slavery — **ab·o·li·tion·ism** \-'lish-ə-ˌniz-əm\ *n*

A–bomb \'ā-ˌbäm\ *n* : ATOM BOMB

abom·i·na·ble \ə-'bäm-(ə-)nə-bəl\ *adj* **1** : HATEFUL, DETESTABLE ⟨*abominable* behavior⟩ **2** : quite disagreeable ⟨*abominable* weather⟩ — **abom·i·na·bly** \-blē\ *adv*

abominable snow·man \-'snōmən, -ˌman\ *n, often cap A&S* : a creature thought to exist in the Himalayas and held to be a subhuman, an ape, or more commonly a bear

abom·i·nate \ə-'bäm-ə-ˌnāt\ *vb* : HATE, LOATHE — **abom·i·na·tor** \-ˌnāt-ər\ *n*

abom·i·na·tion \ə-ˌbäm-ə-'nā-shən\ *n* **1** : something detestable **2** : extreme disgust and hatred : LOATHING

ab·o·rig·i·nal \ˌab-ə-'rij-(ə-)nəl\ *adj* **1** : NATIVE, ORIGINAL **2** : of, relating to, or being aborigines ***syn*** see NATIVE ***ant*** immigrant — **ab·o·rig·i·nal·ly** \-ē\ *adv*

ab·o·rig·i·ne \ˌab-ə-'rij-ə-(ˌ)nē\ *n* : an original inhabitant esp. as contrasted with an invading or colonizing people : NATIVE

abort \ə-'bȯrt\ *vb* **1** : to bring forth premature or stillborn offspring **2** : to become checked in development **3** : to terminate prematurely ⟨*abort* a project⟩

abor·tion \ə-'bȯr-shən\ *n* **1** : a premature birth occurring before the fetus can survive — compare MISCARRIAGE **2** : failure of a project or action to reach full development; *also* : a result of such failure

ə abut	ər further	a back	ā bake
ä cot, cart	au̇ out	ch chin	e less
ē easy	g gift	i trip	ī life
j joke	ng sing	ō flow	ȯ flaw
ȯi coin	th thin	t͟h this	ü loot
u̇ foot	y yet	yü few	yu̇ furious
zh vision			

abor·tion·ist \-sh(ə-)nəst\ *n* : a producer of illegal abortions

abor·tive \ə-'bȯrt-iv\ *adj* **1** : failing to achieve the desired end : UNSUCCESSFUL ⟨an *abortive* attempt⟩ **2** : imperfectly formed or developed : RUDIMENTARY — **abor·tive·ly** *adv* — **abor·tive·ness** *n*

abound \ə-'bau̇nd\ *vb* **1** : to be present in large numbers or in great quantity **2** : to be filled or abundantly supplied ⟨a stream *abounding* in fish⟩

[1]**about** \ə-'bau̇t\ *adv* **1** : on all sides : AROUND ⟨wander *about*⟩ ⟨people standing *about*⟩ **2** : APPROXIMATELY, NEARLY ⟨*about* three years⟩ ⟨*about* ready to go⟩ **3** : in succession : ALTERNATELY ⟨turn *about* is fair play⟩ **4** : in the opposite direction ⟨face *about*⟩

[2]**about** *prep* **1** : on every side of : AROUND **2 a** : NEAR **b** : on or near the person of ⟨has no knife *about* him⟩ **c** : at the command of ⟨keeps his wits *about* him⟩ **3 a** : engaged in ⟨do it well while you're *about* it⟩ **b** : on the point of ⟨*about* to join the army⟩ **4** : CONCERNING ⟨told me *about* it⟩ **5** : over or in different parts of ⟨traveled *about* the country⟩ **6** : in connection with ⟨something strange *about* him⟩

about–face \ə-'bau̇t-'fās\ *n* **1** : a reversal of direction **2** : a reversal of attitude or point of view — **about–face** *vb*

[1]**above** \ə-'bəv\ *adv* **1** : in or to a higher place : OVERHEAD **2** : higher on the same or a preceding page **3** : in or to a higher rank or number

[2]**above** *prep* **1** : in or to a higher place than : OVER **2** : superior to ⟨a captain is *above* a lieutenant⟩ ⟨*above* criticism⟩ **3** : too proud or honorable to stoop to ⟨*above* such mean tricks⟩ **4** : exceeding in number, quantity, or size ⟨*above* the average⟩

[3]**above** *adj* : written above

above·board \ə-'bəv-,bōrd, -,bȯrd\ *adv or adj* : without concealment or deceit

ab·ra·ca·dab·ra \,ab-rə-kə-'dab-rə\ *n* **1** : a magical charm or incantation against calamity **2** : unintelligible language : JARGON

abrade \ə-'brād\ *vb* **1** : to rub or wear away esp. by friction **2** : to irritate or roughen by rubbing — **abrad·er** *n*

abra·sion \ə-'brā-zhən\ *n* **1** : a rubbing or wearing away ⟨protect the surface from *abrasion*⟩ **2** : a place where the surface has been rubbed or scraped off ⟨an *abrasion* on his knee⟩

[1]**abra·sive** \ə-'brā-siv, -ziv\ *adj* : having the effect of abrading

[2]**abrasive** *n* : a substance (as emery) used for grinding, smoothing, or polishing

abreast \ə-'brest\ *adv or adj* **1** : side by side with bodies in line **2** : up to a standard or level ⟨keep *abreast* of the times⟩

abridge \ə-'brij\ *vb* [from medieval French *abregier*, from Latin *abbreviare*, the source of English *abbreviate*, from *ab-* "off" and *brevis* "short", the source of English *brief*] **1** : to make less : DIMINISH ⟨forbidden to *abridge* the rights of citizens⟩ **2** : to shorten in duration or extent **3** : to shorten by omission of words : CONDENSE — **abridg·er** *n*

abridg·ment *or* **abridge·ment** \ə-'brij-mənt\ *n* **1 a** : the action of abridging **b** : the state of being abridged **2** : a shortened form of a written work

abroad \ə-'brȯd\ *adv or adj* **1** : over a wide area **2 a** : outside of an implied place ⟨doesn't go *abroad* at night⟩ **b** : in the open **3** : in or to foreign countries ⟨travel *abroad*⟩ **4** : in wide circulation ⟨rumors were *abroad*⟩

ab·ro·gate \'ab-rə-,gāt\ *vb* : to annul or repeal by authority ⟨*abrogate* a law⟩ — **ab·ro·ga·tion** \,ab-rə-'gā-shən\ *n*

abrupt \ə-'brəpt\ *adj* [from Latin *abruptus*, meaning "broken off", the past participle of *abrumpere* "to break off", from *ab* "off" and *rumpere* "to break"] **1 a** : SUDDEN ⟨*abrupt* change in the weather⟩ **b** : rudely brief : CURT ⟨*abrupt* manner⟩ **2** : STEEP ⟨a high *abrupt* bank bounded the stream⟩ — **abrupt·ly** *adv* — **abrupt·ness** \ə-'brəp(t)-nəs\ *n*

abs *abbr* absolute

ab·scess \'ab-,ses\ *n* : a collection of pus surrounded by inflamed tissue at some point in the body — **ab·scessed** \-,sest\ *adj*

ab·scis·sa \ab-'sis-ə\ *n* **1** : the distance of a point on a graph to the right or to the left of the axis labeled *y* **2** : the horizontal coordinate on a graph

ab·scis·sion \ab-'sizh-ən\ *n* **1** : the act or process of cutting off **2** : the natural separation of flowers, fruit, or leaves from plants

abscission layer *n* : a distinct plant layer at which abscission takes place and which consists of small cells containing abundant starch and dense cytoplasm

ab·scond \ab-'skänd\ *vb* : to depart secretly and hide oneself — **ab·scond·er** *n*

ab·sence \'ab-sən(t)s\ *n* **1** : the state of being absent **2** : WANT, LACK

[1]**ab·sent** \'ab-sənt\ *adj* **1** : not present or attending : MISSING **2** : not existing : LACKING **3** : INATTENTIVE — **ab·sent·ly** *adv*

[2]**ab·sent** \ab-'sent\ *vb* : to keep oneself away

ab·sen·tee \,ab-sən-'tē\ *n* : a person who is absent

ab·sent·mind·ed \,ab-sənt-'mīn-dəd\ *adj* : lost in thought and unaware of one's surroundings or action — **ab·sent·mind·ed·ly** *adv* — **ab·sent·mind·ed·ness** *n*

ab·sinthe *or* **ab·sinth** \'ab-,sin(t)th\ *n* : a green liqueur flavored with aromatics (as wormwood and anise)

ab·so·lute \'ab-sə-,lüt, ,ab-sə-'\ *adj* **1 a** : COMPLETE, PERFECT **b** : free from mixture : PURE ⟨*absolute* alcohol⟩ **2** : free from restraint or limitation ⟨*absolute* power⟩ ⟨an *absolute* monarch⟩ **3** : without exception : UNQUALIFIED ⟨an *absolute* requirement⟩ ⟨*absolute* freedom⟩ **4** : free from doubt : CERTAIN ⟨*absolute* proof⟩ **5 a** : independent of arbitrary standards of measurement : ACTUAL ⟨*absolute* brightness of a star⟩ ⟨*absolute* motion⟩ **b** : relating to or derived from the fundamental units of length, mass, and time ⟨*absolute* electric units⟩ **c** : relating to the absolute-temperature scale ⟨10° *absolute*⟩ — **ab·so·lute·ly** *adv* — **ab·so·lute·ness** *n*

absolute error *n* : the difference between the true value of a quantity and the value determined by experiment

absolute music *n* : music that is free of any associations or ideas (as a plot or narrative) outside the music itself ⟨a fugue is an example of *absolute music*⟩

absolute temperature *n* : temperature measured on a scale that has absolute zero as the zero point

absolute value *n* : the numerical value of a number without regard to whether it is positive or negative

absolute zero *n* : a hypothetical temperature characterized by complete absence of heat and equivalent to approximately −273.16°C or −459.69°F that is the point at which all motion of the molecules ceases

ab·so·lu·tion \,ab-sə-'lü-shən\ *n* : the act of absolving; *esp* : a forgiving of sins

ab·solve \əb-'sälv, -'zälv, -'sȯlv, -'zȯlv\ *vb* : to set free from an obligation or from the consequences of guilt — **ab·solv·er** *n*

ab·sorb \əb-'sȯrb, -'zȯrb\ *vb* **1** : to take in or suck or swallow up ⟨a sponge *absorbs* water⟩ **2** : to hold the

interest of : ENGROSS ⟨*absorbed* in thought⟩ **3** : to receive without giving back ⟨a sound-*absorbing* surface⟩ — **ab·sorb·a·bil·i·ty** \-ˌsȯr-bə-ˈbil-ət-ē, -ˌzȯr-\ *n* — **ab·sorb·a·ble** \-ˈsȯr-bə-bəl, -ˈzȯr-\ *adj* — **ab·sorb·er** *n*
ab·sorb·ent \-ˈsȯr-bənt, -ˈzȯr-\ *adj* : able to absorb — **ab·sorb·en·cy** \əb-ˈsȯr-bən-sē, -ˈzȯr-\ *n* — **absorbent** *n*
absorbent cotton *n* : cotton made absorbent by chemically freeing it from its fatty matter
ab·sorp·tion \əb-ˈsȯrp-shən, -ˈzȯrp-\ *n* **1** : the process of absorbing or being absorbed: as **a** : the passing of digested food through the intestinal wall into the blood or lymph **b** : interception esp. of light or sound waves **2** : entire occupation of the mind — **ab·sorp·tive** \-ˈsȯrp-tiv, -ˈzȯrp-\ *adj*
ab·stain \əb-ˈstān\ *vb* : to refrain voluntarily ⟨*abstain* from voting⟩ — **ab·stain·er** *n*
ab·ste·mi·ous \ab-ˈstē-mē-əs\ *adj* : sparing esp. in eating and drinking — **ab·ste·mi·ous·ly** *adv*
ab·sten·tion \əb-ˈsten-chən\ *n* : the act or practice of abstaining; *esp* : a formal refusal to vote ⟨3 ayes, 5 nays, and 2 *abstentions*⟩
ab·sti·nence \ˈab-stə-nən(t)s\ *n* : an abstaining esp. from drinking alcoholic beverages — **ab·sti·nent** \-nənt\ *adj* — **ab·sti·nent·ly** *adv*
abstr *abbr* abstract
1**ab·stract** \ˈab-ˌstrakt, ab-ˈ\ *adj* **1** : expressing a quality or idea without reference to an actual person or thing that possesses it ⟨*honesty* is an *abstract* word⟩ **2** : difficult to understand : HARD ⟨*abstract* problems⟩ **3** : having only intrinsic form with little or no attempt at pictorial representation ⟨*abstract* art⟩ — **ab·stract·ly** *adv* — **ab·stract·ness** \-ˌstrak(t)-nəs, -ˈstrak(t)-\ *n*
2**ab·stract** \ˈab-ˌstrakt\ *n* : a brief statement of the main points or facts : SUMMARY
3**ab·stract** \ab-ˈstrakt, ˈab-ˌ, *in sense 3 usu* ˈab-ˌ\ *vb* **1** : REMOVE, SEPARATE **2** : to consider apart from application to a particular instance ⟨*abstract* the idea of roundness from a ball⟩ **3** : to make an abstract of : SUMMARIZE **4** : to draw away the attention of — **ab·strac·tor** *or* **ab·stract·er** \-ˈstrak-tər, -ˌstrak-\ *n*
ab·stract·ed \ab-ˈstrak-təd, ˈab-ˌ\ *adj* : PREOCCUPIED, ABSENTMINDED — **ab·stract·ed·ly** *adv* — **ab·stract·ed·ness** *n*
ab·strac·tion \ab-ˈstrak-shən\ *n* **1 a** : the act or process of abstracting : the state of being abstracted **b** : an abstract idea or term **c** : a purely imaginary or visionary idea **2** : a state of not paying attention to nearby persons or things : ABSENTMINDEDNESS **3** : an artistic composition or creation characterized by designs that do not represent actual objects — **ab·strac·tive** \-ˈstrak-tiv\ *adj*
ab·struse \ab-ˈstrüs, əb-\ *adj* : hard to understand : ABSTRACT — **ab·struse·ly** *adv* — **ab·struse·ness** *n*
ab·surd \əb-ˈsərd, -ˈzərd\ *adj* : ridiculously unreasonable, unsound, or incongruous — **ab·sur·di·ty** \-ˈsərd-ət-ē, -ˈzərd-\ *n* — **ab·surd·ly** *adv* — **ab·surd·ness** *n*
abun·dance \ə-ˈbən-dən(t)s\ *n* **1** : an ample or overflowing quantity : PROFUSION **2** : AFFLUENCE, WEALTH

ə abut	ər further	a back	ā bake
ä cot, cart	au̇ out	ch chin	e less	ē easy
g gift	i trip	ī life	j joke	ng sing	ō flow
ȯ flaw	ȯi coin	th thin	th this	ü loot
u̇ foot	y yet	yü few	yu̇ furious	zh vision

abun·dant \-dənt\ *adj* [from Latin *abundant-*, stem of present participle of *abundare* "to abound", literally "to overflow", from *ab-* "off" and *unda* "wave"] : existing in or possessing abundance : ABOUNDING — **abun·dant·ly** *adv*
1**abuse** \ə-ˈbyüz\ *vb* **1** : to attack in words : REVILE **2** : to treat cruelly : MISTREAT ⟨*abuse* a dog⟩ **3** : to put to an improper use : MISUSE ⟨*abuse* a privilege⟩ **4** : to use so as to injure or damage : MALTREAT ⟨*abused* his car⟩ — **abus·er** *n*
2**abuse** \ə-ˈbyüs\ *n* **1** : a corrupt practice or custom ⟨election *abuses* such as buying votes⟩ **2** : improper use or treatment : MISUSE ⟨*abuse* of privileges⟩ **3** : abusive language **4** : physical maltreatment
abu·sive \ə-ˈbyü-siv, -ziv\ *adj* **1** : using or characterized by harsh insulting language **2** : physically harmful — **abu·sive·ly** *adv* — **abu·sive·ness** *n*
abut \ə-ˈbət\ *vb* **abut·ted**; **abut·ting** : to touch along an edge : BORDER ⟨the farm *abuts* on the road⟩ ⟨stores *abut* the sidewalk⟩ — **abut·ter** *n*
abut·ment \ə-ˈbət-mənt\ *n* **1** : the action or place of abutting **2** : something against which another thing rests or pushes ⟨*abutments* that support a bridge⟩
abys·mal \ə-ˈbiz-məl\ *adj* **1** : resembling an abyss : immeasurably deep ⟨*abysmal* ignorance⟩ **2** : of or relating to the lowest depths of the ocean — **abys·mal·ly** \-mə-lē\ *adv*
abyss \ə-ˈbis\ *n* : an immeasurably deep gulf or great space
abys·sal \ə-ˈbis-əl\ *adj* : of or relating to the bottom waters of the ocean depths
Ab·ys·sin·i·an \ˌab-ə-ˈsin-ē-ən, -ˈsin-yən\ *adj* : of, relating to, or characteristic of Abyssinia or its people — **Abyssinian** *n*
ac- — see AD-
AC *abbr* **1** alternating current **2** area code
aca·cia \ə-ˈkā-shə\ *n* **1** : any of numerous woody legumes with ball-shaped white or yellow flower clusters and often fernlike leaves **2** : GUM ARABIC
acad *abbr* academy
ac·a·dem·ic \ˌak-ə-ˈdem-ik\ *adj* **1** : of or relating to school or college **2** : literary or general rather than technical ⟨took the *academic* course⟩ **3** : having no practical significance : THEORETICAL ⟨an *academic* question⟩ — **ac·a·dem·i·cal·ly** \-ˈdem-i-k(ə-)lē\ *adv*
acad·e·my \ə-ˈkad-ə-mē\ *n, pl* **-mies** [from Greek *Akadēmeia*, the name of the school established in the suburbs of Athens by the Greek philosopher Plato in the 4th century B.C., originally the name of a grove in which the school met, sacred to the worship of a local demigod *Akadēmos*] **1 a** : SCHOOL; *esp* : a private high school **b** : an institution for training in special subjects or skills ⟨military *academy*⟩ **2** : a society of scholars united to advance art, science, or literature
a cap·pel·la *also* **a ca·pel·la** \ˌäk-ə-ˈpel-ə\ *adv or adj* : without instrumental accompaniment ⟨sing *a cappella*⟩
acc *abbr* accusative
ac·cede \ak-ˈsēd\ *vb* **1** : to give consent : AGREE ⟨*accede* to a proposed plan⟩ **2** : to enter upon an office or dignity ⟨*acceded* to the throne in 1838⟩
accel *abbr* accelerando
ac·ce·le·ran·do \(ˌ)ä-ˌchel-ə-ˈrän-dō\ *adv or adj* : gradually faster — used as a direction in music
ac·cel·er·ate \ik-ˈsel-ə-ˌrāt, ak-\ *vb* **1** : to bring about earlier : HASTEN ⟨*accelerated* his departure⟩ **2** : to move or cause to move faster; *esp* : to move with constantly increasing speed — **ac·cel·er·a·tive** \-ˌrāt-iv\ *adj*
ac·cel·er·a·tion \-ˌsel-ə-ˈrā-shən\ *n* **1** : the act or

process of accelerating : the state of being accelerated **2** : the rate of change of velocity

acceleration of gravity : the acceleration of a freely falling body under the influence of gravity that is expressed as the rate of increase of velocity per unit of time and that amounts to a value of about 980.616 centimeters per second per second

ac·cel·er·a·tor \ik-'sel-ə-ˌrāt-ər, ak-\ *n* **1** : one that accelerates **2** : a pedal in an automobile used to control the speed of the motor **3** : an apparatus for imparting high velocities to charged particles (as electrons and protons)

ac·cel·er·om·e·ter \ik-ˌsel-ə-'räm-ət-ər, ak-\ *n* : an instrument for measuring acceleration or vibrations

¹ac·cent \'ak-ˌsent\ *n* **1** : a peculiar or characteristic manner of speech ⟨a foreign *accent*⟩ **2** : special prominence given to a syllable of a word in speaking ⟨*before* has the *accent* on the last syllable⟩ **3** : a mark (as ' or ˌ) identifying a syllable that is accented in speaking **4** : greater stress given to a beat in music

²ac·cent \ak-'sent, 'ak-ˌ\ *vb* : ACCENTUATE

accent mark *n* **1** : ACCENT 3 **2** : one of several symbols used to indicate musical stress

ac·cen·tu·ate \ak-'sen-chə-ˌwāt\ *vb* **1** : to pronounce or mark with an accent **2** : EMPHASIZE — **ac·cen·tu·a·tion** \ak-ˌsen-chə-'wā-shən\ *n*

ac·cept \ik-'sept, ak-\ *vb* **1** : to receive with consent or approval ⟨*accept* a gift⟩ ⟨*accepted* him as a member⟩ **2 a** : to receive as true ⟨*accept* new ideas⟩ **b** : to regard as proper, normal, or inevitable ⟨*accept* a wage cut⟩ **3 a** : to make an affirmative response to ⟨*accept* an offer⟩ **b** : to undertake the responsibility of ⟨*accept* a job⟩ **4** : to assume an obligation to pay ⟨*accept* a bill⟩ — **ac·cept·er** *or* **ac·cep·tor** \-'sep-tər\ *n*

ac·cept·a·ble \ik-'sep-tə-bəl, ak-\ *adj* **1** : capable or worthy of being accepted : SATISFACTORY ⟨an *acceptable* excuse⟩ **2** : barely adequate ⟨plays an *acceptable* game⟩ — **ac·cept·a·bil·i·ty** \-ˌsep-tə-'bil-ət-ē\ *n* — **ac·cept·a·bly** \-'sep-tə-blē\ *adv*

ac·cept·ance \ik-'sep-tən(t)s, ak-\ *n* **1** : the act of accepting **2** : the quality or state of being accepted or acceptable

ac·cep·ta·tion \ˌak-ˌsep-'tā-shən\ *n* : the generally understood meaning of a word or expression

ac·cess \'ak-ˌses\ *n* **1** : permission or power to enter, approach, or make use of ⟨*access* to the president⟩ **2** : a way or means of approach ⟨a nation's *access* to the sea⟩

ac·ces·si·ble \ak-'ses-ə-bəl, ik-\ *adj* **1** : easy to reach ⟨*accessible* by train⟩ **2** : OBTAINABLE ⟨*accessible* information⟩ — **ac·ces·si·bil·i·ty** \-ˌses-ə-'bil-ət-ē\ *n* — **ac·ces·si·bly** \-blē\ *adv*

ac·ces·sion \ak-'sesh-ən, ik-\ *n* **1** : something added : ACQUISITION **2** : increase by something added **3** : the act of agreeing ⟨*accession* to a proposal⟩ **4** : the act of coming to office or power ⟨the *accession* of a king⟩

¹ac·ces·so·ry \ak-'ses-(ə-)rē, ik-\ *n, pl* **-ries** **1** : something (as an object or device) that is not essential in itself but adds to the beauty, convenience, or effectiveness of something else **2** : a person who aids another in doing wrong or in an attempt to escape justice

²accessory *adj* : aiding or contributing in a secondary way : SUPPLEMENTARY

accessory fruit *n* : a fruit (as the strawberry, apple, or fig) of which a conspicuous part consists of tissue other than that of the ripened ovary

ac·ci·dent \'ak-səd-ənt, -sə-ˌdent\ *n* **1 a** : an event occurring by chance or from unknown causes **b** : CHANCE **2** : an unintended and usu. sudden and unexpected event resulting in loss or injury ⟨an automobile *accident*⟩

¹ac·ci·den·tal \ˌak-sə-'dent-əl\ *adj* **1** : happening unexpectedly or by chance ⟨an *accidental* discovery of oil⟩ **2** : not intended ⟨an *accidental* shooting⟩ — **ac·ci·den·tal·ly** \-'dent-(ə-)lē\ *adv*

²accidental *n* : a chromatically altered note (as a sharp or flat) foreign to a key indicated by a signature

ac·cip·i·ter \ak-'sip-ət-ər\ *n* : any of various low-flying hawks that have short wings and long legs

¹ac·claim \ə-'klām\ *vb* **1** : to welcome with applause or great praise ⟨a novel *acclaimed* by the critics⟩ **2** : to proclaim by or as if by acclamation — **ac·claim·er** *n*

²acclaim *n* **1** : the act of acclaiming **2** : APPLAUSE, PRAISE

ac·cla·ma·tion \ˌak-lə-'mā-shən\ *n* **1** : a loud eager expression of approval, praise, or assent **2** : an overwhelming affirmative vote by voice ⟨elected by *acclamation*⟩

ac·cli·mate \ə-'klī-mət, 'ak-lə-ˌmāt\ *vb* : ACCLIMATIZE — **ac·cli·ma·tion** \ˌak-ˌlī-'mā-shən, ˌak-lə-\ *n*

ac·cli·ma·tize \ə-'klī-mə-ˌtīz\ *vb* : to adapt to a new climate or environment — **ac·cli·ma·ti·za·tion** \ə-ˌklī-mət-ə-'zā-shən\ *n*

ac·co·lade \'ak-ə-ˌlād\ *n* **1** : a formal salute (as a tap on the shoulder with the blade of a sword) that marks the conferring of knighthood **2** : a mark of recognition of merit : PRAISE

ac·com·mo·date \ə-'käm-ə-ˌdāt\ *vb* **1** : ADAPT **2** : to undergo accommodation **3** : OBLIGE 2 ⟨*accommodated* me with a ride⟩ **4 a** : to provide with lodgings **b** : to make or have room for ⟨the table *accommodates* 12 comfortably⟩ — **ac·com·mo·da·tive** \-ˌdāt-iv\ *adj* — **ac·com·mo·da·tive·ness** *n*

ac·com·mo·dat·ing *adj* : disposed to help : OBLIGING

ac·com·mo·da·tion \ə-ˌkäm-ə-'dā-shən\ *n* **1 a** : something supplied for convenience or to satisfy a need **b** *pl* : hotel lodging and services **2** : the act of accommodating : the state of being accommodated **3** : the automatic adjustment of the eye for seeing at different distances **4** : an adjustment of differences : SETTLEMENT — **ac·com·mo·da·tion·al** \-sh(ə-)nəl\ *adj*

accomp *abbr* accompaniment

ac·com·pa·ni·ment \ə-'kəmp-(ə-)nē-mənt\ *n* **1** : music to support or complement a principal voice or instrument **2** : an accompanying object, situation, or event

ac·com·pa·nist \ə-'kəmp-(ə-)nəst\ *n* : a musician who plays an accompaniment

ac·com·pa·ny \ə-'kəmp-(ə-)nē\ *vb* **-nied; -ny·ing** **1** : to go with or attend as a companion **2** : to perform an accompaniment to or for **3** : to occur at the same time as or along with ⟨a thunder storm *accompanied* by high winds⟩

syn ACCOMPANY, ATTEND, ESCORT mean to go in the company of. ACCOMPANY stresses closeness of association and usually equality of status; ATTEND usually implies waiting upon another in a subordinate status; ESCORT is likely to stress protection or control or courtesy as a reason for accompanying or attending

ac·com·plice \ə-'käm-pləs, -'kəm-\ *n* : one associated with another in wrongdoing

ac·com·plish \ə-'käm-plish, -'kəm-\ *vb* : to bring to

a successful finish : PERFORM — **ac·com·plish·a·ble** \-ə-bəl\ *adj*

syn ACCOMPLISH, ACHIEVE, EFFECT means to attain some end. ACCOMPLISH may refer to any successful completion; ACHIEVE usually suggests accomplishment of an important task or with effort; EFFECT is likely to imply accomplishment by overcoming resistance or obstacles ***ant*** undo

ac·com·plished *adj* **1** : COMPLETED, DONE ⟨an *accomplished* fact⟩ **2 a** : skilled or polished through practice or training : EXPERT ⟨an *accomplished* pianist⟩ **b** : having many accomplishments ⟨a very *accomplished* young lady⟩

ac·com·plish·ment \ə-'käm-plish-mənt, -'kəm-\ *n* **1** : the act of accomplishing : COMPLETION **2** : something accomplished : ACHIEVEMENT **3** : an ability, social quality, or skill acquired by training or practice

1**ac·cord** \ə-'kȯrd\ *vb* **1** : to grant as suitable or proper ⟨rights not *accorded* to foreigners⟩ **2** : to be in harmony : AGREE

2**accord** *n* **1 a** : AGREEMENT, HARMONY **b** : an agreement between parties ⟨reach an *accord*⟩ **2** : WILLINGNESS ⟨went of his own *accord*⟩

ac·cord·ance \ə-'kȯrd-ən(t)s\ *n* : AGREEMENT, CONFORMITY ⟨in *accordance* with a rule⟩

ac·cord·ing as *conj* **1** : in accord with the way in which **2** : depending on how or whether

ac·cord·ing·ly \ə-'kȯrd-ing-lē\ *adv* **1** : in accordance : CORRESPONDINGLY **2** : CONSEQUENTLY, SO

according to *prep* **1** : in agreement or conformity with ⟨stood *according to* height⟩ **2** : as stated by ⟨*according to* the broadcast⟩ **3** : depending on

1**ac·cor·di·on** \ə-'kȯrd-ē-ən\ *n* : a portable keyboard instrument in which wind is forced past metal reeds by a bellows — **ac·cor·di·on·ist** \-ē-ə-nəst\ *n*

accordion

2**accordion** *adj* : creased to fold like an accordion ⟨*accordion* pleats⟩

ac·cost \ə-'kȯst\ *vb* : to approach and speak first to often in a challenging or aggressive way

1**ac·count** \ə-'kaůnt\ *n* **1** : a record of money paid and received **2 a** : a periodic reckoning listing purchases and credits : BILL **b** : the transactions between a business and a customer **3 a** : VALUE ⟨a man of little *account*⟩ **b** : ESTEEM ⟨held in high *account*⟩ **4** : PROFIT, ADVANTAGE ⟨labored to no *account*⟩ **5 a** : a statement of reasons, causes, or motives ⟨gave an *account* of his actions⟩ **b** : a statement of facts : RELATION ⟨*accounts* of the game⟩ **6** : a sum of money deposited in a bank ***syn*** see NARRATIVE — **on account of** : for the sake of : by reason of : because of — **on no account** : in no circumstances

2**account** *vb* **1** : to think of as ⟨*accounts* himself lucky⟩ **2** : to give an analysis or explanation ⟨*account* for his expenditures⟩ **3 a** : to be the cause ⟨illness *accounts* for so many absences⟩ **b** : to bring about the capture or destruction of something ⟨*accounted* for two rabbits⟩

ac·count·a·ble \ə-'kaůnt-ə-bəl\ *adj* **1** : responsible for giving an account of one's acts ⟨*accountable* to his superiors⟩ **2** : capable of being accounted for : EXPLAINABLE — **ac·count·a·bil·i·ty** \-ˌkaůnt-ə-'bil-ət-ē\ *n* — **ac·count·a·bly** \-'kaůnt-ə-blē\ *adv*

ac·count·ant \ə-'kaůnt-ənt\ *n* : a person professionally trained in accounting

ac·count·ing \ə-'kaůnt-ing\ *n* : the skill, system, or practice of recording money transactions of a person or business

ac·cou·ter *or* **ac·cou·tre** \ə-'küt-ər\ *vb* **-cou·tered** *or* **-cou·tred**; **-cou·ter·ing** *or* **-cou·tring** \-'küt- ə-ring, -'kü-tring\ : to furnish with equipment : OUTFIT

ac·cou·ter·ment *or* **ac·cou·tre·ment** \ə-'kü-trə-mənt, -'küt-ər-mənt\ *n* **1** : the act of equipping : the state of being equipped **2** : EQUIPMENT; *esp* : a soldier's outfit other than clothes and weapons

ac·cred·it \ə-'kred-ət\ *vb* **1** : to send with credentials and authority to act as representative ⟨*accredit* an ambassador to France⟩ **2** : to certify as in conformity with a standard ⟨an *accredited* school⟩ **3** : CREDIT, BELIEVE — **ac·cred·i·ta·tion** \ə-ˌkred-ə-'tā-shən\ *n*

ac·cre·tion \ə-'krē-shən\ *n* **1** : the process of growth or enlargement; *esp* : increase by external addition or accumulation **2** : a product or result of accretion

ac·crue \ə-'krü\ *vb* **1** : to come by increase or addition ⟨benefits *accrue* to society from free education⟩ **2** : to accumulate over a period of time ⟨*accrued* interest⟩ — **ac·cru·al** \-'krü-əl\ *n*

acct *abbr* account

ac·cu·mu·late \ə-'kyü-myə-ˌlāt\ *vb* [from Latin *accumulare*, from *ad-* "to" and *cumulus* "heap", "pile"] **1** : to pile up : AMASS ⟨*accumulate* a fortune⟩ **2** : COLLECT, GATHER ⟨a closet that seems to *accumulate* junk⟩ **3** : to increase in quantity, number, or amount ⟨rubbish *accumulates* quickly⟩

ac·cu·mu·la·tion \ə-ˌkyü-myə-'lā-shən\ *n* **1** : a collecting together : AMASSING **2** : increase or growth by addition ⟨*accumulation* of interest⟩ **3** : something accumulated : COLLECTION

ac·cu·ra·cy \'ak-yə-rə-sē\ *n, pl* **-cies** **1** : freedom from error : CORRECTNESS **2** : conformity to a standard : EXACTNESS

ac·cu·rate \'ak-yə-rət\ *adj* **1** : free from mistakes esp. as the result of care **2** : conforming exactly to truth or to a standard : EXACT ***syn*** see CORRECT ***ant*** inaccurate — **ac·cu·rate·ly** *adv* — **ac·cu·rate·ness** *n*

ac·cursed \ə-'kər-səd, -'kərst\ *or* **ac·curst** \ə-'kərst\ *adj* **1** : being under a curse **2** : DAMNABLE, DETESTABLE — **ac·curs·ed·ly** \-'kər-səd-lē\ *adv* — **ac·curs·ed·ness** \-'kər-səd-nəs\ *n*

ac·cu·sa·tion \ˌak-yə-'zā-shən\ *n* **1** : the act of accusing : the fact of being accused **2** : a charge of wrongdoing

ac·cu·sa·tive \ə-'kyü-zət-iv\ *adj* : of, relating to, or constituting the grammatical case that marks the direct object of a verb or the object of a preposition

ac·cuse \ə-'kyüz\ *vb* : to charge with a fault and esp. with a crime — **ac·cus·er** *n* — **ac·cus·ing·ly** \-'kyü-zing-lē\ *adv*

ac·cused \ə-'kyüzd\ *n, pl* **accused** : one charged with an offense; *esp* : the defendant in a criminal case

ac·cus·tom \ə-'kəs-təm\ *vb* : to make familiar

ac·cus·tomed *adj* **1** : CUSTOMARY ⟨*accustomed* lunch hour⟩ **2** : familiar with : USED ⟨*accustomed* to hard luck⟩ ***syn*** see USUAL ***ant*** unaccustomed

[1]**ace** \'ās\ *n* **1 :** a dice face or a card marked with one spot or design **2 :** a very small amount or degree ⟨within an *ace* of winning⟩ **3 a :** a combat pilot who has brought down at least five enemy airplanes **b :** one that excels at something

[2]**ace** *adj* **:** of first or high rank or quality

acel·lu·lar \(')ā-'sel-yə-lər\ *adj* **:** not made up of cells

-a·ceous \'ā-shəs\ *adj suffix* **:** consisting of ⟨carbon*aceous*⟩ **:** having the nature or form of ⟨herb*aceous*⟩

ac·e·tab·u·lar·i·a \ˌas-ə-ˌtab-yə-'ler-ē-ə\ *n* **:** any of a genus of delicate green algae native to the warmer seas and resembling small mushrooms

ac·e·tate \'as-ə-ˌtāt\ *n* **1 :** a salt or ester of acetic acid **2 a :** a textile fiber made from cellulose and acetate **b :** a fabric or plastic made of this fiber

ace·tic \ə-'sēt-ik\ *adj* **:** of, relating to, or producing acetic acid or vinegar

acetic acid *n* **:** a colorless pungent liquid acid that gives the sour taste to vinegar and that is used esp. in synthesis (as of plastics)

ac·e·tone \'as-ə-ˌtōn\ *n* **:** a volatile fragrant flammable liquid compound used chiefly as a solvent

ace·tyl·cho·line \ə-ˌsēt-əl-'kō-ˌlēn\ *n* **:** a compound released at autonomic nerve endings that functions in the transmission of the nerve impulse

acet·y·lene \ə-'set-ə-lən, -ˌlēn\ *n* **:** a colorless gas used chiefly in welding and soldering

ace·tyl·sal·i·cyl·ic acid \ə-'sēt-əl-ˌsal-ə-ˌsil-ik-\ *n* **:** ASPIRIN 1

[1]**ache** \'āk\ *vb* **1 :** to suffer a dull persistent pain **2 :** to long earnestly **:** YEARN ⟨*aches* for her return⟩

[2]**ache** *n* **:** a dull persistent pain — **achy** \'ā-kē\ *adj*

achene \ə-'kēn\ *n* **:** a small dry one-seeded fruit (as of the buttercup) that ripens without bursting — **ache·ni·al** \ə-'kē-nē-əl\ *adj*

achieve \ə-'chēv\ *vb* [from French *achever*, literally "to bring to a head", from *a* "to" and *chief* "head"] **1 :** ACCOMPLISH ⟨*achieved* his purpose⟩ **2 :** to get by effort **:** WIN ⟨*achieve* greatness⟩ ***syn*** see ACCOMPLISH ***ant*** fail (*in, to do*) — **achiev·a·ble** \-'chē-və-bəl\ *adj*

achieve·ment \ə-'chēv-mənt\ *n* **1 :** the act of achieving **2 :** something achieved ⟨heroic *achievements* of the settlers⟩

Achil·les tendon \ə-ˌkil-ēz-\ *n* **:** the strong tendon joining the muscles in the calf of the leg to the bone of the heel

ach·ro·mat·ic \ˌak-rə-'mat-ik\ *adj* **1 :** giving an image practically free from colors not in the object ⟨*achromatic* lens⟩ **2 :** being black, gray, or white **:** COLORLESS

[1]**ac·id** \'as-əd\ *adj* **1 :** sour, sharp, or biting to the taste **:** resembling vinegar in taste **2 :** sour in temper **:** CROSS ⟨*acid* remarks⟩ **3 :** of, relating to, or having the characteristics of an acid ⟨*acid* soil⟩ ⟨*acid* indigestion⟩ — **ac·id·ly** *adv* — **ac·id·ness** *n*

[2]**acid** *n* **1 :** a sour substance **2 :** a usu. water-soluble compound that has a sour taste, reacts with a base to form a salt, and turns litmus paper red **3 :** LSD

ac·id–fast \'as-əd-ˌfast\ *adj* **:** not easily decolorized by acids

ac·id·head \-ˌhed\ *n* **:** a person who uses LSD

acid·ic \ə-'sid-ik\ *adj* **1 :** acid-forming **2 :** ACID

acid·i·fy \ə-'sid-ə-ˌfī\ *vb* **-fied; -fy·ing 1 :** to make or become acid **2 :** to change into an acid — **acid·i·fi·ca·tion** \ə-ˌsid-ə-fə-'kā-shən\ *n*

acid·i·ty \ə-'sid-ət-ē\ *n, pl* **-ties 1 :** the quality, state, or degree of being acid **:** TARTNESS **2 :** HYPERACIDITY

ac·knowl·edge \ik-'näl-ij, ak-\ *vb* **1 :** to admit the truth or existence of ⟨*acknowledged* his mistake⟩ **2 :** to recognize the rights or authority of **3 :** to make known that something has been received or noticed ⟨*acknowledge* a letter⟩ — **ac·knowl·edge·a·ble** \-ə-bəl\ *adj*

syn ACKNOWLEDGE, ADMIT, CONFESS mean to disclose against one's will or inclination. ACKNOWLEDGE implies making known what has been or might have been kept secret; ADMIT is likely to suggest pressure from without and reluctance to acknowledge or concede; CONFESS implies an admitting of weakness, failure, or guilt ***ant*** deny

ac·knowl·edged \-ijd\ *adj* **:** generally recognized or accepted ⟨the *acknowledged* leader⟩

ac·knowl·edg·ment \ik-'näl-ij-mənt, ak-\ *n* **1 a :** the act of acknowledging **b :** recognition or favorable notice of an act or achievement **2 :** a thing done or given in recognition of something received

ac·me \'ak-mē\ *n* **:** the highest point **:** PEAK ⟨the *acme* of perfection⟩

ac·ne \'ak-nē\ *n* **:** a disorder of the skin caused by inflammation of skin glands and hair follicles and marked by pimples esp. on the face

ac·o·lyte \'ak-ə-ˌlīt\ *n* **:** a man or boy who assists the clergyman in a service

ac·o·nite \'ak-ə-ˌnīt\ *n* **1 :** any of a genus of poisonous usu. blue-flowered or purple-flowered plants related to the buttercups **2 :** a drug obtained from the common Old World monkshood

acorn \'ā-ˌkórn, -kərn\ *n* **:** the nut of the oak tree

acous·tic \ə-'kü-stik\ *adj* **:** of or relating to the sense or organs of hearing, to sound, or to the science of sounds: as **a :** deadening sound **b :** operated by or utilizing sound waves — **acous·ti·cal** \-sti-kəl\ *adj* — **acous·ti·cal·ly** \-sti-k(ə-)lē\ *adv*

acoustical engineering *n* **:** engineering that deals with acoustics and esp. with applications (as to soundproofing and to the effective distribution of sound in buildings) — **acoustical engineer** *n*

acous·tics \ə-'kü-stiks\ *n sing or pl* **1 :** the science dealing with sound **2** *also* **acous·tic** \-stik\ **:** the qualities in a room or hall that make it easy or hard for a person in it to hear distinctly ⟨the *acoustics* of the hall permitted the faintest sound to be heard⟩ — **acous·ti·cian** \ˌa-ˌkü-'stish-ən, ə-ˌkü-\ *n*

ac·quaint \ə-'kwānt\ *vb* **1 :** to cause to know socially ⟨became *acquainted* through mutual friends⟩ **2 :** to cause to know firsthand **:** INFORM ⟨*acquaint* him with his duties⟩

ac·quaint·ance \ə-'kwānt-ən(t)s\ *n* **1 :** knowledge gained by personal experience ⟨had some *acquaintance* with the subject⟩ **2 :** a person one knows but not familiarly — **ac·quaint·ance·ship** \-ˌship\ *n*

ac·qui·esce \ˌak-wē-'es\ *vb* **:** to accept, agree, or give consent by keeping silent or by not raising objections — **ac·qui·es·cence** \-'es-ən(t)s\ *n*

ac·qui·es·cent \-'es-ənt\ *adj* **:** acquiescing or disposed to acquiesce — **ac·qui·es·cent·ly** *adv*

ac·quire \ə-'kwī(ə)r\ *vb* **:** to come to have often by one's own efforts **:** GAIN ⟨*acquired* great wealth⟩ — **ac·quir·a·ble** \-'kwī-rə-bəl\ *adj*

ac·quired *adj* **1 :** gained by or as a result of effort or experience **2 :** caused by environmental forces (as use and disuse) and not subject to hereditary transmission from parent to offspring ⟨*acquired* heart disease⟩ ⟨*acquired* characteristics⟩

acquired immunity *n* **:** immunity that is taken on following an attack of disease or induced by injection

ac·quire·ment \ə-'kwī(ə)r-mənt\ *n* **1 :** the act of acquiring **2 :** an attainment usu. resulting from continued endeavor **:** ACCOMPLISHMENT

ac·qui·si·tion \ˌak-wə-'zish-ən\ *n* **1 :** the act of ac-

quiring **2 :** something acquired
ac·quis·i·tive \ə-'kwiz-ət-iv\ *adj* **:** strongly desirous of acquiring **:** GRASPING — **ac·quis·i·tive·ness** *n*
ac·quit \ə-'kwit\ *vb* **ac·quit·ted; ac·quit·ting** **1 :** to set free (as from an accusation) ⟨the court *acquitted* the prisoner⟩ **2 :** CONDUCT, BEHAVE ⟨*acquitted* themselves like veterans⟩
ac·quit·tal \ə-'kwit-əl\ *n* **:** the freeing of a person from a charge by legal process
acre \'ā-kər\ *n* [from Old English *acer*, meaning originally "a piece of cultivated land", "a field", and then "as much land as a yoke of oxen could plow in a day"; it is from the same prehistoric source as Latin *ager* "field", from which was derived English *agriculture*] **1** *pl* **:** LANDS, ESTATE **2 :** a unit of area equal to 160 square rods — see MEASURE table
acre·age \'ā-k(ə-)rij\ *n* **:** area in acres **:** ACRES
acre–foot *n* **:** the volume (as of irrigation water) that would cover one acre to a depth of one foot
ac·rid \'ak-rəd\ *adj* **1 :** sharp and harsh or unpleasantly pungent in taste or odor **:** IRRITATING, CORROSIVE **2 :** bitterly irritating to the feelings ⟨an *acrid* remark⟩ — **ac·rid·ly** *adv* — **ac·rid·ness** *n*
ac·ri·mo·ny \'ak-rə-ˌmō-nē\ *n, pl* **-nies :** harsh or biting sharpness esp. of words, manner, or disposition — **ac·ri·mo·ni·ous** \ˌak-rə-'mō-nē-əs\ *adj* — **ac·ri·mo·ni·ous·ly** *adv* — **ac·ri·mo·ni·ous·ness** *n*
ac·ro·bat \'ak-rə-ˌbat\ *n* [from Greek *akrobatēs* "tightrope walker", from *akron* "high place" and *bainein* "to step", "go"] **:** one that performs gymnastic feats requiring skillful control of the body — **ac·ro·bat·ic** \ˌak-rə-'bat-ik\ *adj*
ac·ro·bat·ics \ˌak-rə-'bat-iks\ *n sing or pl* **1 :** the art or performance of an acrobat **2 :** a striking performance involving great agility or maneuverability ⟨airplane *acrobatics*⟩
ac·ro·nym \'ak-rə-ˌnim\ *n* **:** a word (as *radar*) formed from the initial letter or letters of each of the successive parts or major parts of a compound term
acrop·o·lis \ə-'kräp-ə-ləs\ *n* **:** the upper fortified part of an ancient Greek city
¹**across** \ə-'krȯs\ *adv* **1 :** so as to reach or pass from one side to the other ⟨boards sawed directly *across*⟩ **2 :** to or on the opposite side ⟨got *across* in a boat⟩
²**across** *prep* **1 :** to or on the opposite side of ⟨*across* the street⟩ **2 :** so as to intersect or pass at an angle ⟨lay one stick *across* another⟩ **3 :** into an accidental meeting with ⟨ran *across* an old friend⟩
acryl·ic resin \ə-ˌkril-ik-\ *n* **:** a glassy synthetic organic plastic used for cast and molded parts or as coatings and adhesives
¹**act** \'akt\ *n* **1 :** something that is done **:** DEED ⟨an *act* of kindness⟩ **2 :** the doing of something ⟨caught in the *act* of stealing⟩ **3 :** a law made by a governing body (as a legislature) ⟨an *act* of Congress⟩ **4 a :** one of the main divisions of a play or opera **b :** one of the successive parts of a variety show or circus
²**act** *vb* **1 :** to perform by action esp. on the stage **2 :** to play the part of ⟨*act* the man of the world⟩ **3 a :** to behave in a manner suitable to ⟨*act* your age⟩ **b :** to conduct oneself ⟨*act* like a fool⟩ **4 :** to take action **:** MOVE ⟨think before you *act*⟩ **5 a :** to perform a function **:** SERVE ⟨*act* as mayor⟩ **b :** to produce an effect **:** WORK ⟨wait for a medicine to *act*⟩
act *abbr* active
act·ing \'ak-ting\ *adj* **:** serving temporarily or in place of another ⟨*acting* chairman⟩
ac·ti·nism \'ak-tə-ˌniz-əm\ *n* **:** the property of radiant energy by which chemical changes are produced — **ac·tin·ic** \ak-'tin-ik\ *adj*
ac·tin·i·um \ak-'tin-ē-əm\ *n* **:** a radioactive metallic element found esp. in pitchblende — see ELEMENT table
ac·tion \'ak-shən\ *n* **1 :** a legal proceeding in a court by which one demands one's right or the redress of a wrong **2 :** the working of one thing on another so as to produce a change ⟨the *action* of acids on metals⟩ **3 :** the process or manner of acting or functioning **:** PERFORMANCE **4 a :** a thing done **:** DEED **b** *pl* **:** BEHAVIOR, CONDUCT **5 :** combat in war **:** BATTLE **6 :** the plot of a drama or work of fiction
ac·ti·vate \'ak-tə-ˌvāt\ *vb* **1 :** to make active **2 :** to make (as molecules) reactive **3 :** to make (a substance) radioactive **4 :** to treat (as carbon or alumina) so as to improve adsorptive properties **5 :** to aerate (sewage) so as to favor the growth of organisms that cause decomposition **6 :** to place on active duty ⟨*activate* the reserves⟩ — **ac·ti·va·tion** \ˌak-tə-'vā-shən\ *n* — **ac·ti·va·tor** \'ak-tə-ˌvāt-ər\ *n*
ac·tive \'ak-tiv\ *adj* **1 :** producing or involving action or movement ⟨an *active* sport⟩ **2 :** representing the subject as performing the action expressed by the verb ⟨*hits* in "he hits the ball" is an *active* verb⟩ **3 :** quick in movement **:** LIVELY **4 a :** disposed to action **:** ENERGETIC **b :** engaged in an action or activity **:** PARTICIPATING ⟨an *active* member⟩ **c :** erupting or likely to erupt ⟨an *active* volcano⟩ **5 :** engaged in or requiring full-time service esp. in the armed forces ⟨*active* duty⟩ **6 :** marked by present action or use ⟨*active* account⟩ ⟨a student's *active* vocabulary⟩ **7 a :** capable of acting or reacting **b :** tending to progress or increase ⟨*active* tuberculosis⟩ — **active·ly** *adv* — **ac·tive·ness** *n*
active immunity *n* **:** immunity produced by the individual when exposed to an antigen — compare PASSIVE IMMUNITY
active transport *n* **:** the movement (as across a cell membrane) of substances from regions of lower concentration to regions of higher concentration by the use of metabolic energy
ac·tiv·i·ty \ak-'tiv-ət-ē\ *n, pl* **-ties** **1 :** the quality or state of being active **2 :** vigorous or energetic action **3 :** natural, normal, or assigned function **4 a :** a process that an organism carries on or participates in by virtue of being alive **b :** a similar process actually or potentially involving mental function **5 :** an educational procedure designed to stimulate learning by firsthand experience **6 :** an active force ⟨solar *activity*⟩ **7 a :** PURSUIT 2 **b :** a form of organized, supervised, extracurricular recreation
ac·tor \'ak-tər\ *n* **:** one that acts; *esp* **:** a theatrical performer — **ac·tress** \'-trəs\ *n*
Acts \'ak(t)s\ *or* **Acts of the Apostles** — see BIBLE table
ac·tu·al \'ak-ch(ə-w)əl, 'aksh-wəl\ *adj* **:** existing in fact and not merely as a possibility **:** REAL — **ac·tu·al·i·ty** \ˌak-chə-'wal-ət-ē\ *n* — **ac·tu·al·ize** \-ˌīz\ *vb* — **ac·tu·al·ly** \-ē\ *adv*
ac·tu·ary \'ak-chə-ˌwer-ē\ *n, pl* **-ar·ies :** one who calculates insurance premiums and dividends — **ac·tu·ar·i·al** \ˌak-chə-'wer-ē-əl\ *adj*
ac·tu·ate \'ak-chə-ˌwāt\ *vb* **1 :** to put into action ⟨the windmill *actuates* the pump⟩ **2 :** to arouse to

action ⟨*actuated* by the hope of winning⟩
act up *vb* : to act in an unruly way : MISBEHAVE
acu·ity \ə-ˈkyü-ət-ē\ *n* : keenness of perception
acu·men \ə-ˈkyü-mən\ *n* : keenness of mind : SHREWDNESS
acute \ə-ˈkyüt\ *adj* **1** : measuring less than a right angle ⟨*acute* angle⟩ **2 a** : KEEN, SHREWD **b** : having sharp perceptions : OBSERVANT **3** : SHARP, SEVERE ⟨*acute* pain⟩ **4** : HIGH, SHRILL ⟨an *acute* sound⟩ **5 a** : having a sudden onset and short duration ⟨*acute* disease⟩ **b** : being at or near a turning point : CRITICAL ⟨an *acute* situation that may lead to war⟩ ***syn*** see SHARP ***ant*** obtuse — **acute·ly** *adv* — **acute·ness** *n*
ad \ˈad\ *n* : ADVERTISEMENT 2
ad- *or* **ac-** *or* **ag-** *or* **al-** *or* **ap-** *or* **as-** *or* **at-** *prefix* **1** : to : toward — usu. *ac-* before *c*, *k*, or *q* and *ag-* before *g* and *al-* before *l* and *ap-* before *p* and *as-* before *s* and *at-* before *t* and *ad-* before other sounds but sometimes *ad-* even before one of the listed consonants **2** : near : adjacent to — in this sense always in the form *ad-* ⟨*ad*renal⟩
AD *abbr* anno Domini
ad·age \ˈad-ij\ *n* : a saying embodying common observation : PROVERB
¹**ada·gio** \ə-ˈdäj-ō, -ˈdäj-ē-ˌō, -ˈdäzh-\ *adv or adj* : in an easy graceful manner : SLOWLY — used as a direction in music
²**adagio** *n* **1** : a musical composition or movement in adagio tempo **2** : a ballet duet or trio displaying difficult feats of balance, lifting, or spinning
¹**ad·a·mant** \ˈad-ə-mənt, -ˌmant\ *n* **1** : an imaginary stone of great hardness **2** : an extremely hard substance
²**adamant** *adj* : IMMOVABLE, UNYIELDING — **ad·a·mant·ly** *adv*
ad·a·man·tine \ˌad-ə-ˈman-ˌtēn, -ˌtīn\ *adj* **1** : made of or having the quality of adamant **2** : ADAMANT
Ad·am's apple \ˌad-əmz-\ *n* : the projection in the front of the neck formed by the largest cartilage of the larynx
adapt \ə-ˈdapt\ *vb* : to make or become suitable; *esp* : to change so as to fit a new or specific use or situation ⟨*adapt* to life in a new school⟩ ⟨*adapt* the novel for children⟩ — **adapt·a·bil·i·ty** \-ˌdap-tə-ˈbil-ət-ē\ *n* — **adapt·a·ble** \-ˈdap-tə-bəl\ *adj*
ad·ap·ta·tion \ˌad-ˌap-ˈtā-shən\ *n* **1 a** : the act or process of adapting **b** : the state of being adapted **2** : adjustment to environmental conditions: as **a** : adjustment of a sense organ to the intensity or quality of stimulation **b** : change in an organism or its parts that fits it better for the conditions of its environment; *also* : a structure resulting from this change **3** : something that is adapted; *esp* : a composition rewritten into a new form — **ad·ap·ta·tion·al** \-sh(ə-)nəl\ *adj* — **ad·ap·ta·tion·al·ly** \-ē\ *adv*
adapt·ed \ə-ˈdap-təd\ *adj* : suited by nature or design to a particular use, purpose, or situation
adapt·er *also* **adap·tor** \ə-ˈdap-tər\ *n* **1** : someone or something that adapts **2 a** : a device for connecting two parts (as of different diameters) of an apparatus **b** : an attachment for adapting apparatus for uses not originally intended
ADC *abbr* aide-de-camp
add \ˈad\ *vb* **1 a** : to join or unite to a thing so as to enlarge or increase it ⟨*add* a wing to the house⟩ **b** : to unite in a single whole **2** : to put or say something more ⟨*add* one cup of sugar⟩ ⟨*add* to his remarks⟩ **3** : to combine mathematical quantities (as numbers) into a single sum — **add·a·ble** *or* **add·i·ble** \ˈad-ə-bəl\ *adj*
ad·dend \ˈad-ˌend\ *n* : a number that is to be added to another
ad·den·dum \ə-ˈden-dəm\ *n, pl* **-den·da** \-ˈden-də\ : something added; *esp* : a supplement to a book
¹**ad·der** \ˈad-ər\ *n* **1** : a poisonous European viper; *also* : any of several related snakes **2** : any of several harmless No. American snakes (as the hognose snakes)
²**add·er** \ˈad-ər\ *n* : one that adds
ad·der's–tongue \ˈad-ərz-ˌtəŋ\ *n* **1** : a fern whose fruiting spike resembles a serpent's tongue **2** : DOGTOOTH VIOLET
¹**ad·dict** \ə-ˈdikt\ *vb* **1** : to devote or surrender oneself to something habitually ⟨*addicts* himself to science⟩ **2** : to cause (a person) to make habitual use of a drug ⟨a pusher tries to *addict* others⟩
²**ad·dict** \ˈad-(ˌ)ikt\ *n* : one who is addicted (as to a drug)
ad·dic·tion \ə-ˈdik-shən\ *n* : the quality or state of being addicted; *esp* : uncontrollable use of habit-forming drugs
ad·dic·tive \ə-ˈdik-tiv\ *adj* : causing or characterized by addiction
ad·di·tion \ə-ˈdish-ən\ *n* **1** : the result of adding : INCREASE **2** : the act, process, or operation of adding **3** : a part added (as to a building) — **in addition** : BESIDES — **in addition to** : over and above
ad·di·tion·al \-ˈdish-(ə-)nəl\ *adj* : ADDED, EXTRA ⟨an *additional* charge⟩ — **ad·di·tion·al·ly** \-ē\ *adv*
¹**ad·di·tive** \ˈad-ət-iv\ *adj* : relating to or produced by addition — **ad·di·tive·ly** *adv*
²**additive** *n* : a substance added to another in relatively small amounts to impart or improve desirable properties or suppress undesirable properties ⟨a gasoline *additive* intended to improve engine performance⟩
additive identity element *n* : an element (as zero in the set of real numbers) of a mathematical set that leaves every element of the set unchanged when added to it
additive inverse *n* : a number of opposite sign with respect to a given number so that addition of the two numbers gives zero ⟨the *additive inverse* of 4 is −4⟩
ad·dle \ˈad-əl\ *vb* **ad·dled**; **ad·dling** \ˈad-(ə-)liŋ\ **1** : to make or become confused **2** : to become rotten ⟨*addled* eggs⟩
addn *abbr* addition
¹**ad·dress** \ə-ˈdres\ *vb* **1** : to direct the attention of oneself ⟨*addressed* himself to his work⟩ **2 a** : to communicate directly ⟨*address* a petition to the governor⟩ **b** : to deliver a formal speech to ⟨*address* the convention⟩ **3** : to mark directions for delivery on ⟨*address* a letter⟩ **4** : to greet by a prescribed form — **ad·dress·er** *n*
²**ad·dress** \ə-ˈdres, ˈad-ˌres\ *n* **1** : manner of speaking : DELIVERY **2** : a formal speech **3 a** : a place where a person or organization may be found or communicated with **b** : directions for delivery on a letter or package
ad·dress·ee \ˌad-ˌres-ˈē, ə-ˌdres-ˈē\ *n* : one to whom mail is addressed
ad·duce \ə-ˈd(y)üs\ *vb* : to offer as example, reason, or proof
ad·duct \ə-ˈdəkt\ *vb* : to draw (a part of the body) toward or past the median axis of the body
ad·duc·tor \ə-ˈdək-tər\ *n* : a muscle that draws a body part toward the median axis
ad·e·nine \ˈad-ə-ˌnēn\ *n* : a base regularly present in DNA and RNA
¹**ad·e·noid** \ˈad-(ə-)ˌnȯid\ *or* **ad·e·noi·dal** \ˌad-ə-ˈnȯid-əl\ *adj* **1** : of, relating to, or resembling glands

or glandular or lymphoid tissue **2** : of or relating to adenoids or adenoid disorder

[2]**adenoid** *n* : an abnormally enlarged mass of tissue at the back of the pharynx characteristically obstructing breathing — usu. used in pl.

aden·o·sine di·phos·phate \ə-'den-ə-ˌsēn-dī-'fäs-ˌfāt\ *n* : ADP

adenosine tri·phos·phate \-trī-'fäs-ˌfāt\ *n* : ATP

[1]**ad·ept** \'ad-ˌept\ *n* : a highly skilled or well-trained individual : EXPERT

[2]**adept** \ə-'dept\ *adj* : thoroughly proficient : EXPERT — **adept·ly** *adv* — **adept·ness** \-'dep(t)-nəs\ *n*

ad·e·quate \'ad-i-kwət\ *adj* **1** : suitable or sufficient for a requirement **2** : barely sufficient — **ad·e·qua·cy** \-kwə-sē\ *n* — **ad·e·quate·ly** *adv* — **ad·e·quate·ness** *n*

ad·here \ad-'hi(ə)r, əd-\ *vb* **1** : to give support or maintain loyalty (as to a cause or belief) **2** : to stick by or as if by gluing : CLING **3** : to agree to accept as binding ⟨*adhere* to a treaty⟩

ad·her·ence \-'hir-ən(t)s\ *n* **1** : the action or quality of adhering **2** : steady or faithful attachment : FIDELITY ⟨*adherence* to a cause⟩

syn ADHERENCE, ADHESION mean a sticking to or sticking together. ADHERENCE may be preferred when referring to mental or moral attachment; ADHESION is usually restricted to physical attachment

[1]**ad·her·ent** \-'hir-ənt\ *adj* : able or tending to adhere

[2]**adherent** *n* : a follower of a leader, belief, or group

ad·he·sion \ad-'hē-zhən, əd-\ *n* **1** : steady or firm attachment; *esp* : a sticking together **2** : abnormal union of tissues following inflammation (as after surgery) **3** : the molecular attraction exerted between the surfaces of bodies in contact *syn* see ADHERENCE

[1]**ad·he·sive** \ad-'hē-siv, əd-, -ziv\ *adj* : tending to adhere : prepared for adhering : STICKY — **ad·he·sive·ness** *n*

[2]**adhesive** *n* : an adhesive substance (as glue or cement)

adhesive plaster *n* : material that resembles adhesive tape and that is sometimes made up in flat sheets

adhesive tape *n* : tape that is coated on one side with an adhesive and is used esp. for medical purposes

ad·i·a·bat·ic \ˌad-ē-ə-'bat-ik, ˌā-ˌdī-ə-\ *adj* : occurring without loss or gain of heat ⟨*adiabatic* expansion⟩ — **ad·i·a·bat·i·cal·ly** \-'bat-i-k(ə-)lē\ *adv*

adieu \ə-'d(y)ü\ *n, pl* **adieus** *or* **adieux** \-'d(y)üz\ [from French, from *a Dieu* "to God", meaning that the speaker commits the person addressed to the protection of God] : FAREWELL — often used interjectionally

adi·os \ˌad-ē-'ōs, ˌäd-\ *interj* — used to express farewell

ad·i·pose \'ad-ə-ˌpōs\ *adj* : of or relating to animal fat : FATTY — **ad·i·pos·i·ty** \ˌad-ə-'päs-ət-ē\ *n*

adj *abbr* **1** adjective **2** adjutant

ad·ja·cent \ə-'jās-ənt\ *adj* **1** : lying next or near : having a common border ⟨a field *adjacent* to the road⟩ **2** : having a common vertex and side ⟨*adjacent* angles⟩ — **ad·ja·cent·ly** *adv*

ə abut	ər further	a back	ā bake	
ä cot, cart	aü out	ch chin	e less	ē easy
g gift	i trip	ī life	j joke	ng sing	ō flow
ȯ flaw	ȯi coin	th thin	th this	ü loot
u̇ foot	y yet	yü few	yu̇ furious	zh vision

ad·jec·tive \'aj-ik-tiv\ *n* : a word modifying a noun by denoting a quality of the thing named, indicating its quantity or extent, or specifying a thing as distinct from something else — **adjective** *adj* — **ad·jec·ti·val** \ˌaj-ik-'tī-vəl\ *adj or n* — **ad·jec·ti·val·ly** \-və-lē\ *adv*

ad·join \ə-'jȯin\ *vb* **1** : to add or attach by joining **2** : to lie next to or in contact with

ad·journ \ə-'jərn\ *vb* : to suspend proceedings for an indefinite or stated period ⟨Congress *adjourned*⟩ ⟨*adjourn* a meeting⟩ — **ad·journ·ment** \-mənt\ *n*

ad·judge \ə-'jəj\ *vb* **1** : ADJUDICATE **2** : to hold or pronounce to be : DEEM

ad·ju·di·cate \ə-'jüd-i-ˌkāt\ *vb* : to decide, award, or sentence judicially ⟨*adjudicate* a claim⟩ — **ad·ju·di·ca·tion** \-ˌjüd-i-'kā-shən\ *n*

ad·junct \'aj-ˌəng(k)t\ *n* : ACCESSORY 1

ad·jure \ə-'ju̇(ə)r\ *vb* : to charge or command solemnly as if under oath — **ad·ju·ra·tion** \ˌaj-ə-'rā-shən\ *n*

ad·just \ə-'jəst\ *vb* **1** : to bring to a more satisfactory state : set right ⟨*adjust* conflicts⟩ ⟨*adjust* the error⟩ **2** : to move the parts of an instrument or a piece of machinery until they fit together in the best working order : REGULATE ⟨*adjust* a watch⟩ **3** : to determine the amount of an insurance claim **4** : to accommodate oneself to conditions — **ad·just·a·ble** \-'jəs-tə-bəl\ *adj* — **ad·just·er** *also* **ad·jus·tor** \-'jəs-tər\ *n*

ad·just·ment \ə-'jəs(t)-mənt\ *n* **1** : the act or process of adjusting **2** : a settlement of a claim or debt **3** : the state of being adjusted **4** : a means of adjusting one part (as in a machine) to another ⟨an *adjustment* for focusing a microscope⟩

ad·ju·tant \'aj-ət-ənt\ *n* **1** : a staff officer (as in the army) assisting the commanding officer in clerical work **2** : ASSISTANT

ad lib \(ˈ)ad-'lib\ *adv* [shortened from *ad libitum*] : without restraint or limit

[1]**ad–lib** \(ˈ)ad-'lib\ *adj* : spoken, composed, or performed without preparation

[2]**ad–lib** *vb* **ad–libbed**; **ad–lib·bing** : to improvise lines, or a speech, or music

ad li·bi·tum \(ˈ)ad-'lib-ət-əm\ *adv* [from modern Latin, meaning "at pleasure"] : freely as one wishes — used as a direction in music

adm *abbr* admiral

admin *abbr* administration

ad·min·is·ter \əd-'min-ə-stər\ *vb* **ad·min·is·tered**; **ad·min·is·ter·ing** \-st(ə-)ring\ **1** : to direct the affairs of : MANAGE ⟨*administer* a government⟩ **2** : SETTLE 6a ⟨*administer* an estate⟩ **3** : to mete out : DISPENSE ⟨*administer* justice⟩ **4** : to give ritually ⟨*administer* the sacraments⟩ **5** : to give as a remedy ⟨*administer* a drug⟩

ad·min·is·tra·tion \əd-ˌmin-ə-'strā-shən, ad-\ *n* **1** : the act or process of administering **2** : performance of executive duties : MANAGEMENT **3** : the execution of public policy as distinguished from making it **4** : a body of persons who administer; *esp, cap* : the executive branch of a government

ad·min·is·tra·tive \əd-'min-ə-ˌstrāt-iv\ *adj* : of or relating to administration

ad·min·is·tra·tor \əd-'min-ə-ˌstrāt-ər\ *n* : one that administers; *esp* : a person legally appointed to administer an estate — **ad·min·is·tra·trix** \-ˌmin-ə-'strā-triks\ *n*

ad·mi·ra·ble \ˌad-mə-rə-bəl, -mrə-bəl\ *adj* : deserving to be admired : EXCELLENT — **ad·mi·ra·ble·ness** *n* — **ad·mi·ra·bly** \-blē\ *adv*

ad·mi·ral \'ad-mə-rəl, -mrəl\ *n* [from medieval French *amiral*, from Arabic *amīr-al-baḥr* "commander of the sea"] **1 a** : a naval officer of flag rank **b** : a commissioned officer in the navy ranking next below a fleet admiral **2** : any of several brightly colored butterflies

ad·mi·ral·ty \'ad-mə-rəl-tē, -mrəl-\ *adj* : MARITIME ⟨*admiralty* court⟩ ⟨*admiralty* law⟩

Admiralty *n* : the body of officials having jurisdiction over the British navy

ad·mi·ra·tion \ˌad-mə-'rā-shən\ *n* **1** : an object of admiring esteem **2** : delighted or astonished approval

ad·mire \əd-'mī(ə)r\ *vb* [from Latin *admirari* "to wonder at", from *ad-* "at" and *mirari* "to wonder", the source of English *miracle*] **1** : to look at with admiration ⟨*admire* the scenery⟩ **2** : to esteem highly ⟨*admired* his courage⟩ — **ad·mir·er** \-'mīr-ər\ *n*

ad·mis·si·ble \əd-'mis-ə-bəl\ *adj* : that can be or is worthy to be admitted : ALLOWABLE ⟨*admissible* evidence⟩ — **ad·mis·si·bil·i·ty** \-ˌmis-ə-'bil-ət-ē\ *n* — **ad·mis·si·bly** \-'mis-ə-blē\ *adv*

ad·mis·sion \əd-'mish-ən\ *n* **1** : the act of admitting **2** : the right or permission to enter ⟨standards of *admission* to a school⟩ **3** : the price of entrance **4** : a granting of something that has not been proved ⟨an *admission* of guilt⟩ ***syn*** see ADMITTANCE — **ad·mis·sive** \-'mis-iv\ *adj*

ad·mit \əd-'mit\ *vb* **ad·mit·ted**; **ad·mit·ting** **1 a** : to allow scope for : PERMIT **b** : to concede to be true **2** : to allow entry : let in ⟨*admit* a state to the Union⟩ **3** : to confess to : make acknowledgment ⟨*admit* guilt⟩ ***syn*** see ACKNOWLEDGE — **ad·mit·ted·ly** \-'mit-əd-lē\ *adv*

ad·mit·tance \əd-'mit-ən(t)s\ *n* : permission to enter : ENTRANCE

syn ADMITTANCE, ADMISSION mean permitted entrance. ADMITTANCE implies mere physical entrance (as into a building); ADMISSION can imply formal acceptance that carries with it rights (as of membership or participation)

ad·mix·ture \ad-'miks-chər\ *n* **1** : MIXTURE **2** : something mixed into another thing

ad·mon·ish \ad-'män-ish\ *vb* **1** : to reprove gently but seriously : warn of a fault **2** : to give friendly advice or encouragement to ***syn*** see REBUKE ***ant*** commend — **ad·mon·ish·ment** \-mənt\ *n*

ad·mo·ni·tion \ˌad-mə-'nish-ən\ *n* : a friendly reproof or warning

ad·mon·i·to·ry \ad-'män-ə-ˌtōr-ē, -ˌtȯr-\ *adj* : expressing admonition : WARNING

ado \ə-'dü\ *n* : FUSS, TROUBLE ⟨much *ado* about nothing⟩

ado·be \ə-'dō-bē\ *n* [from Spanish, from Arabic *aṭ-ṭub* "the brick"] **1** : a brick made of clay dried in the sun **2** : a building made of adobe bricks

ad·o·les·cence \ˌad-ə-'les-ən(t)s\ *n* [from Latin *adolescentia*, from *adolescent-*, stem of *adolescens* "adolescent", from present participle of *adolescere* "to be growing up"] : the state or process of growing up; *also* : the period of life from puberty to maturity — **ad·o·les·cent** \-ənt\ *adj or n*

adopt \ə-'däpt\ *vb* **1** : to take legally as one's own child ⟨*adopt* an orphan⟩ **2** : to take up as one's own ⟨*adopt* a point of view⟩ **3** : to accept formally ⟨the assembly *adopted* a constitution⟩ — **adopt·able** \-'däp-tə-bəl\ *adj* — **adopt·er** *n* — **adop·tion** \ə-'däp-shən\ *n*

adop·tive \ə-'däp-tiv\ *adj* : acquired by adoption

ador·a·ble \ə-'dōr-ə-bəl, -'dȯr-\ *adj* **1** : deserving to be adored **2** : CHARMING, LOVELY ⟨an *adorable* child⟩ — **ador·a·bly** \-blē\ *adv*

adore \ə-'dō(ə)r, -'dȯ(ə)r\ *vb* [from Latin *adorare*, from *ad-* "to" and *orare* "to pray"] **1** : WORSHIP **2** : to be extremely fond of — **ad·o·ra·tion** \ˌad-ə-'rā-shən\ *n* — **ador·er** \ə-'dōr-ər, -'dȯr-\ *n*

adorn \ə-'dȯrn\ *vb* : to decorate with ornaments : BEAUTIFY

adorn·ment \-mənt\ *n* **1** : the action of adorning : the state of being adorned **2** : something that adorns

ADP \ˌā-ˌdē-'pē, ā-'dē-ˌpē\ *n* : a compound formed in living cells that reacts to form ATP

1**ad·re·nal** \ə-'drē-nəl\ *adj* **1** : adjacent to the kidneys **2** : of, relating to, or derived from adrenal glands or secretion

2**adrenal** *n* : ADRENAL GLAND

adrenal gland *n* : either of a pair of complex endocrine glands that are located near the kidney and produce the hormone epinephrine

adren·a·line \ə-'dren-ə-lən\ *n* : EPINEPHRINE

adrift \ə-'drift\ *adv or adj* **1** : without motive power, anchor, or mooring ⟨a ship *adrift* in the storm⟩ **2** : without guidance or purpose

adroit \ə-'drȯit\ *adj* **1** : skillful with the hands **2** : SHREWD, RESOURCEFUL — **adroit·ly** *adv* — **adroit·ness** *n*

ad·sorb \ad-'sȯrb, -'zȯrb\ *vb* : to take up and hold by adsorption — **ad·sorb·ent** \-'sȯr-bənt, -'zȯr-\ *adj or n*

ad·sorp·tion \-'sȯrp-shən, -'zȯrp-\ *n* : the adhesion in an extremely thin layer of molecules (as of gases, solutes, or liquids) to the surfaces of solid bodies or liquids with which they are in contact — **ad·sorp·tive** \-'sȯrp-tiv, -'zȯrp-\ *adj*

ad·u·late \'aj-ə-ˌlāt\ *vb* : to flatter or admire excessively or slavishly — **ad·u·la·tion** \ˌaj-ə-'lā-shən\ *n* — **ad·u·la·tor** \'aj-ə-ˌlāt-ər\ *n* — **ad·u·la·to·ry** \'aj-ə-lə-ˌtōr-ē, -ˌtȯr-\ *adj*

1**adult** \ə-'dəlt, 'ad-ˌəlt\ *adj* [from Latin *adultus* "having grown up", past participle of *adolescere* "to be growing up"] **1** : fully developed and mature **2** : of, relating to, or characteristic of adults — **adult·hood** \ə-'dəlt-ˌhu̇d\ *n* — **adult·ness** \ə-'dəlt-nəs, 'ad-ˌəlt-\ *n*

2**adult** *n* : a fully grown person, animal, or plant

adul·ter·ant \ə-'dəl-tə-rənt\ *n* : something used to adulterate another thing

adul·ter·ate \ə-'dəl-tə-ˌrāt\ *vb* : to make impure or weaker by adding a foreign or inferior substance; *esp* : to prepare for sale by using in whole or in part a substance that reduces quality or strength — **adul·ter·a·tion** \ə-ˌdəl-tə-'rā-shən\ *n* — **adul·ter·a·tor** \ə-'dəl-tə-ˌrāt-ər\ *n*

adul·tery \ə-'dəl-t(ə-)rē\ *n, pl* **-ter·ies** : voluntary sexual intercourse between a married person and someone other than his or her spouse — **adul·ter·er** \-tər-ər\ *n* — **adul·ter·ess** \-t(ə-)rəs\ *n* — **adul·ter·ous** \-t(ə-)rəs\ *adj*

adv *abbr* **1** adverb **2** adverbial **3** advertisement

1**ad·vance** \əd-'van(t)s\ *vb* **1** : to move forward or upward ⟨*advance* a few yards⟩ ⟨prices *advanced*⟩ **2** : to further the progress of ⟨sacrifices that *advance* the cause of freedom⟩ **3** : to raise to a higher rank or position : PROMOTE **4** : to supply in expectation of repayment ⟨*advance* a loan⟩ **5** : to bring forward : PROPOSE ⟨*advance* a new plan⟩ **6** : to raise or rise in rate or price : INCREASE ⟨gasoline *advanced* another two cents⟩ — **ad·vance·ment** \-mənt\ *n* — **ad·vanc·er** *n*

2**advance** *n* **1** : a forward movement **2** : progress in development : IMPROVEMENT **3** : a rise in price, value, or amount **4** : a first approach : OFFER **5 a** : a provision of something (as money) before a return is received ⟨an *advance* on his salary⟩ **b** : the money or goods supplied — **in advance** : BEFORE,

BEFOREHAND ⟨knew of the change two weeks *in advance*⟩ — **in advance of** : ahead of

3**advance** *adj* **1** : made, sent, or furnished ahead of time ⟨*advance* payment⟩ **2** : going or situated before ⟨*advance* guard⟩

ad·vanced \əd-'van(t)st\ *adj* **1** : being beyond the elementary or introductory ⟨*advanced* mathematics⟩ **2** : being far along in progress or development ⟨an *advanced* civilization⟩ ⟨*advanced* paralysis⟩ **3** : having altered from a more primitive ancestral state ⟨*advanced* insects like the wasps and bees⟩

ad·van·tage \əd-'vant-ij\ *n* [from French *avantage*, literally "getting in front", from *avant* "ahead", "in front", from Latin *abante*, literally "from before"] **1** : superiority of position or condition ⟨gain the *advantage*⟩ **2** : BENEFIT, GAIN **3** : something that helps its possessor ⟨speed is an *advantage* in sport⟩ — **to advantage** : so as to produce a favorable impression or effect

ad·van·ta·geous \ˌad-vən-'tā-jəs, -ˌvan-\ *adj* : giving an advantage : HELPFUL, FAVORABLE ***syn*** see BENEFICIAL ***ant*** disadvantageous — **ad·van·ta·geous·ly** *adv* — **ad·van·ta·geous·ness** *n*

ad·vent \'ad-ˌvent\ *n* **1** *cap* : the season beginning four Sundays before Christmas **2** : COMING, ARRIVAL ⟨the *advent* of spring⟩

ad·ven·ti·tious \ˌad-vən-'tish-əs\ *adj* **1** : added externally and not becoming an essential part : ACCIDENTAL **2** : appearing out of the usual or normal place ⟨*adventitious* buds⟩ — **ad·ven·ti·tious·ly** *adv* — **ad·ven·ti·tious·ness** *n*

1**ad·ven·ture** \əd-'ven-chər\ *n* **1** : an undertaking involving unknown or extraordinary dangers **2** : the encountering of risks

2**adventure** *vb* **-ven·tured; -ven·tur·ing** \-'vench-(ə-)riŋ\ : RISK, VENTURE

ad·ven·tur·er \-'ven-chər-ər\ *n* **1** : a person who seeks out adventures **2** : a person who seeks position or wealth by trickery — **ad·ven·tur·ess** \-chə-rəs\ *n*

ad·ven·ture·some \-'ven-chər-səm\ *adj* : ADVENTUROUS 1

ad·ven·tur·ous \əd-'vench-(ə-)rəs\ *adj* **1** : ready to take risks or to cope with the new and unknown **2** : characterized by unknown dangers and risks — **ad·ven·tur·ous·ly** *adv* — **ad·ven·tur·ous·ness** *n*

syn ADVENTUROUS, VENTURESOME, DARING can mean exposing oneself to risks beyond the demands of need or courage. ADVENTUROUS implies an inclination to adventure in spite of possible dangers; VENTURESOME may stress a tendency to take chances; DARING heightens the implication of fearlessness and a disregard for or even courting of risks ***ant*** cautious

ad·verb \'ad-ˌvərb\ *n* : a word used to modify a verb, an adjective, another adverb, a preposition, a phrase, a clause, or a sentence and often used to show degree, manner, place, or time — **adverb** *adj* — **ad·ver·bi·al** \ad-'vər-bē-əl\ *adj or n* — **ad·ver·bi·al·ly** \-bē-ə-lē\ *adv*

ad·ver·sary \'ad-və(r)-ˌser-ē\ *n, pl* **-sar·ies** : someone or something that contends with, opposes, or resists

ad·verse \ad-'vərs, 'ad-ˌ\ *adj* **1** : acting in a contrary direction ⟨*adverse* winds⟩ **2** : actively opposed : ANTAGONISTIC ⟨a mind *adverse* to compromise⟩ **3** : having a harmful or hindering effect : UNFAVORABLE ⟨*adverse* circumstances⟩ — **ad·verse·ly** *adv* — **ad·verse·ness** *n*

ad·ver·si·ty \ad-'vər-sət-ē\ *n, pl* **-ties** : serious or continued misfortune

ad·vert \ad-'vərt\ *vb* : to direct attention : REFER ⟨*advert* to a remark of the previous speaker⟩

ad·ver·tise \'ad-vər-ˌtīz\ *vb* **1** : to announce publicly esp. by a printed notice or a broadcast ⟨*advertise* a sale⟩ **2** : to call public attention to esp. by emphasizing desirable qualities so as to arouse a desire to buy or patronize ⟨*advertise* a cereal⟩ **3** : to issue or sponsor advertising ⟨*advertise* for a lost dog⟩ — **ad·ver·tis·er** *n*

ad·ver·tise·ment \ˌad-vər-'tīz-mənt, əd-'vərt-əz-\ *n* **1** : the act or process of advertising **2** : a public notice; *esp* : one published or broadcast

ad·vice \əd-'vīs\ *n* **1** : recommendation regarding a decision or course of conduct : COUNSEL **2** : information or notice given : NEWS — usu. used in pl.

ad·vis·a·ble \əd-'vī-zə-bəl\ *adj* : reasonable or proper under the circumstances : WISE, PRUDENT ⟨not *advisable* to swim after a meal⟩ — **ad·vis·a·bil·i·ty** \-ˌvī-zə-'bil-ət-ē\ *n* — **ad·vis·a·bly** \-'vī-zə-blē\ *adv*

ad·vise \əd-'vīz\ *vb* **1 a** : to give advice to : COUNSEL **b** : RECOMMEND **2** : INFORM **3** : to take counsel : CONSULT — **ad·vis·er** *or* **ad·vi·sor** \-'vī-zər\ *n*

ad·vised \-'vīzd\ *adj* : thought out : CONSIDERED ⟨well *advised* conduct⟩ — **ad·vis·ed·ly** \-'vī-zəd-lē\ *adv*

ad·vise·ment \əd-'vīz-mənt\ *n* : careful consideration ⟨take a matter under *advisement*⟩

ad·vi·so·ry \əd-'vīz-(ə-)rē\ *adj* **1** : having the power or right to advise ⟨an *advisory* committee⟩ **2** : giving or containing advice ⟨an *advisory* opinion⟩

1**ad·vo·cate** \'ad-və-kət, -ˌkāt\ *n* **1** : one that pleads the cause of another esp. before a judicial tribunal **2** : one that argues for, recommends, or supports a cause or policy

2**ad·vo·cate** \-ˌkāt\ *vb* : to speak in favor of : support or recommend openly ⟨*advocate* a new plan⟩ — **ad·vo·ca·cy** \'ad-və-kə-sē\ *n*

advt *abbr* advertisement

adz *or* **adze** \'adz\ *n* : a cutting tool with a thin arched blade set at right angles to the handle and used for shaping wood

AEC *abbr* Atomic Energy Commission

aë·des \ā-'ēd-ēz\ *n, pl* **aëdes** [from scientific Latin, from Greek *aēdēs* "unpleasant", from *a-* "not" and *ēdos* "pleasure", which come from the same prehistoric sources as English *un-* and *sweet* respectively] : any of a genus of mosquitoes including carriers of disease (as yellow fever)

AEF *abbr* American Expeditionary Force

ae·gis \'ē-jəs\ *n* **1** : PROTECTION **2** : PATRONAGE, SPONSORSHIP

ae·on \'ē-ən, 'ē-ˌän\ *n* : a vast period of time : AGE

aer- *or* **aero-** *comb form* **1 a** : air : atmosphere ⟨*aer*ate⟩ **b** : aerial and ⟨*aero*marine⟩ **2** : gas ⟨*aero*sol⟩ **3** : aviation ⟨*aero*drome⟩

aer·ate \'a(-ə)r-ˌāt, 'e(-ə)r-\ *vb* **1** : to supply (blood) with oxygen by respiration **2 a** : to supply or impregnate (as soil) with air **b** : to expose to air (as for purification or ventilation) **3** : to combine or charge with gas — **aer·a·tion** \ˌa(-ə)r-'ā-shən, ˌe(-ə)r-\ *n* — **aer·a·tor** \'a(-ə)r-ˌāt-ər, 'e(-ə)r-\ *n*

1**aer·i·al** \'ar-ē-əl, 'er-; ā-'ir-ē-əl\ *adj* **1 a** : of, relating to, or occurring in the air or atmosphere **b** : living or growing in the air rather than on the ground or in

A

water **c** : operating or operated overhead on elevated cables or rails ⟨an *aerial* tramway⟩ **2 a** : lacking substance : THIN **b** : IMAGINARY, ETHEREAL **3 a** : of or relating to aircraft **b** : designed for use in, taken from, or operating from aircraft ⟨*aerial* photograph⟩ — **aer·i·al·ly** \-ē-ə-lē\ *adv*

²**aer·i·al** \'ar-ē-əl, 'er-\ *n* **1** : ANTENNA 2 **2** : FORWARD PASS

aerial root *n* : a root (as for clinging to a wall) that does not enter the soil

aer·ie \'a(ə)r-ē, 'e(ə)r-, 'i(ə)r-\ *n* **1** : the nest of a bird on a cliff or a mountaintop **2** : a dwelling on a height

aer·o·bat·ics \ˌar-ə-'bat-iks, ˌer-\ *n sing or pl* : performance of stunts with an aircraft

aer·o·bic \ˌa-(ə-)'rō-bik, ˌe-\ *adj* **1** : living or active only in the presence of oxygen **2** : of, relating to, or caused by aerobic organisms (as bacteria) — **aer·o·bi·cal·ly** \-bi-k(ə-)lē\ *adv*

aer·o·drome \'ar-ə-ˌdrōm, 'er-\ *n, Brit* : AIRFIELD, AIRPORT

aero·dy·nam·ics \ˌar-ō-dī-'nam-iks, ˌer-\ *n* : a science that deals with the motion of gaseous fluids (as air) and with the forces acting on bodies exposed to such fluids — **aero·dy·nam·ic** \-ik\ *adj*

aer·ol·o·gy \ˌa-(ə-)'räl-ə-jē, ˌe-\ *n* **1** : METEOROLOGY **2** : a branch of meteorology that deals esp. with the air at some distance above the earth — **aer·o·log·i·cal** \ˌar-ə-'läj-i-kəl, ˌer-\ *adj* — **aer·ol·o·gist** \ˌa-(ə-)'räl-ə-jəst, ˌe-\ *n*

aero·med·i·cine \ˌar-ō-'med-ə-sən, ˌer-\ *n* : a branch of medicine that deals with the diseases and disturbances arising from flying — **aero·med·i·cal** \-'med-i-kəl\ *adj*

aer·o·naut \'ar-ə-ˌnȯt, 'er-\ *n* : one that operates or travels in an airship or balloon

aeronautical engineering *n* : engineering that deals with aeronautics and flight control — **aeronautical engineer** *n*

aer·o·nau·tics \ˌar-ə-'nȯt-iks, ˌer-\ *n* : a science dealing with the operation of aircraft or with aircraft design and manufacture — **aer·o·nau·ti·cal** \-'nȯt-i-kəl\ *adj*

aero·pause \'ar-ō-ˌpȯz, 'er-\ *n* : the level above the earth's surface where the atmosphere becomes ineffective for human and aircraft functions

aero·plane \'ar-ə-ˌplān, 'er-\ *chiefly Brit var of* AIRPLANE

aero·sol \-ˌsȯl, -ˌsäl\ *n* : a suspension of fine solid or liquid particles (as of smoke, fog, or an insecticide) in gas

aerosol bomb *n* : a small container from which an aerosol can be released in the form of a mist or a fine spray

aero·space \'ar-ō-ˌspās, 'er-\ *n* : the earth's atmosphere and the space beyond

aes·thet·ic \es-'thet-ik\ *adj* **1** : of or relating to beauty or what is beautiful **2** : appreciative of what is beautiful — **aes·thet·i·cal·ly** \-i-k(ə-)lē\ *adv*

aes·thet·ics \es-'thet-iks\ *n* : the philosophy of the principles and forms of beauty esp. in art and literature

aes·ti·vate \'es-tə-ˌvāt\ *vb* : to pass the summer in a state of torpor — **aes·ti·va·tion** \ˌes-tə-'vā-shən\ *n*

AF *abbr* air force

afar \ə-'fär\ *adv* : to or at a great distance

af·fa·ble \'af-ə-bəl\ *adj* : characterized by ease and friendliness esp. in conversation — **af·fa·bil·i·ty** \ˌaf-ə-'bil-ət-ē\ *n* — **af·fa·bly** \'af-ə-blē\ *adv*

af·fair \ə-'fa(ə)r, -'fe(ə)r\ *n* **1 a** *pl* : commercial, professional, or public business ⟨government *affairs*⟩ **b** : MATTER, CONCERN ⟨not your *affair* at all⟩ **2 a** : EVENT, ACTIVITY ⟨a social *affair*⟩ **b** : PRODUCT, THING ⟨a flimsy *affair* of ropes bridging the river⟩ **3** : a brief romantic relationship

¹**af·fect** \ə-'fekt, a-\ *vb* **1** : to be given to : FANCY ⟨*affect* flashy clothes⟩ **2** : to put on a pretense of : FEIGN ⟨*affect* indifference⟩

²**affect** *vb* **1** : to produce a usu. deleterious effect (as of disease) upon ⟨lungs *affected* by cancer⟩ ⟨a situation that *affected* his mind⟩ **2** : to produce a material change in ⟨rainfall *affects* plant growth⟩ **3** : to make an impression on ⟨deeply *affected* by the death of her parents⟩ ***syn*** see CONCERN

af·fec·ta·tion \ˌaf-ˌek-'tā-shən\ *n* : an unnatural form of behaving intended to impress others

af·fect·ed \ə-'fek-təd, a-\ *adj* : not natural or genuine ⟨an *affected* interest in music⟩ ⟨a man with *affected* manners⟩ — **af·fect·ed·ly** *adv* — **af·fect·ed·ness** *n*

af·fect·ing \-ting\ *adj* : arousing pity, sympathy, or sorrow ⟨an *affecting* story⟩ — **af·fect·ing·ly** \-ting-lē\ *adv*

¹**af·fec·tion** \ə-'fek-shən\ *n* : a feeling of attachment : FONDNESS

²**af·fec·tion** *n* : DISEASE, DISORDER ⟨an *affection* of the brain⟩

af·fec·tion·ate \ə-'fek-sh(ə-)nət\ *adj* : feeling or showing affection : LOVING — **af·fec·tion·ate·ly** *adv*

af·fer·ent \'af-ə-rənt, 'af-ˌer-ənt\ *adj* : bearing or conducting inward; *esp* : conveying impulses toward a nerve center — **af·fer·ent·ly** *adv*

af·fi·ance \ə-'fī-ən(t)s\ *vb* : to solemnly promise in marriage : ENGAGE ⟨the *affianced* couple⟩

af·fi·da·vit \ˌaf-ə-'dā-vət\ *n* : a sworn written statement; *esp* : one made under oath before an authorized official

¹**af·fil·i·ate** \ə-'fil-ē-ˌāt\ *vb* : to connect closely often as a member, branch, or associate ⟨*affiliated* himself with a political party⟩ — **af·fil·i·a·tion** \-ˌfil-ē-'ā-shən\ *n*

²**af·fil·i·ate** \ə-'fil-ē-ət\ *n* : an affiliated person or organization

af·fin·i·ty \ə-'fin-ət-ē\ *n, pl* **-ties** **1** : RELATIONSHIP, KINSHIP **2** : ATTRACTION; *esp* : an attractive force between substances or particles that causes them to enter into and remain in chemical combination

af·firm \ə-'fərm\ *vb* : to state positively or with confidence : ASSERT — **af·fir·ma·tion** \ˌaf-ər-'mā-shən\ *n*

¹**af·firm·a·tive** \ə-'fər-mət-iv\ *adj* **1** : asserting that the fact is so **2** : POSITIVE ⟨take an *affirmative* approach⟩ — **af·firm·a·tive·ly** *adv*

²**affirmative** *n* **1** : an expression (as the word *yes*) of affirmation or assent **2** : an affirmative statement **3** : the affirmative side in a debate or vote

¹**af·fix** \ə-'fiks\ *vb* **1** : to attach physically : FASTEN ⟨*affix* a stamp to a letter⟩ **2** : to add as an associated part (as to a document) ⟨*affixed* his signature⟩

²**af·fix** \'af-ˌiks\ *n* : one or more sounds or letters attached to the beginning or end of a word and serving to produce a derivative word or an inflectional form

af·flict \ə-'flikt\ *vb* : to cause suffering or unhappiness to ⟨*afflicted* with pain⟩

af·flic·tion \ə-'flik-shən\ *n* **1** : the state of being afflicted : SORROW, SUFFERING **2** : the cause of continued pain or distress

af·flu·ence \'af-ˌlü-ən(t)s; a-'flü-, ə-\ *n* : abundance of wealth or property

af·flu·ent \-ənt\ *adj* **1** : ABUNDANT, COPIOUS **2** : WEALTHY, RICH — **af·flu·ent·ly** *adv*

af·ford \ə-ˈfōrd, -ˈfȯrd\ *vb* **1** : to have resources enough to pay for ⟨unable to *afford* a new car⟩ **2** : to be able to do or to bear without serious harm ⟨no one can *afford* to waste his strength⟩ **3** : PROVIDE, FURNISH ⟨playing tennis *affords* healthful exercise⟩
af·fray \ə-ˈfrā\ *n* : a noisy quarrel or fight : BRAWL
af·fright \ə-ˈfrīt\ *vb* : FRIGHTEN, ALARM
¹af·front \ə-ˈfrənt\ *vb* : to insult esp. to the face : OFFEND
²affront *n* : a deliberately offensive act or utterance : INSULT
Af·ghan \ˈaf-gən, -ˌgan\ *n* **1** : a native or inhabitant of Afghanistan **2** *not cap* : a blanket or shawl of knitted or crocheted colored wool — **Afghan** *adj*
Afghan hound *n* : a tall slim swift hunting dog native to the Near East with a coat of silky thick hair and a long silky topknot
afield \ə-ˈfēld\ *adv* **1** : to, in, or on the field **2** : away from home **3** : out of one's regular course : ASTRAY
afire \ə-ˈfī(ə)r\ *adj* : on fire : BURNING
aflame \ə-ˈflām\ *adj* : FLAMING, GLOWING
AFL–CIO *abbr* American Federation of Labor and Congress of Industrial Organizations
afloat \ə-ˈflōt\ *adv or adj* **1 a** : borne on or as if on the water **b** : at sea **2** : circulating about : RUMORED ⟨the story was *afloat* that he was ill⟩ **3** : FLOODED, AWASH ⟨the decks were *afloat*⟩
aflut·ter \ə-ˈflət-ər\ *adj* **1** : FLUTTERING **2** : nervously excited
afoot \ə-ˈfu̇t\ *adv or adj* **1** : on foot ⟨travels *afoot*⟩ **2 a** : on the move : ASTIR ⟨trouble *afoot*⟩ **b** : in progress ⟨projects *afoot*⟩
afore \ə-ˈfō(ə)r, -ˈfȯ(ə)r\ *adv or conj or prep, chiefly dial* : BEFORE
afore·men·tioned \-ˌmen-chənd\ *adj* : mentioned previously
afore·said \-ˌsed\ *adj* : said or named previously
afore·thought \-ˌthȯt\ *adj* : thought of, deliberated, or planned beforehand : PREMEDITATED ⟨with malice *aforethought*⟩
afoul \ə-ˈfau̇l\ *adj* : FOULED, TANGLED
afoul of *prep* **1** : in or into collision or entanglement with **2** : in or into conflict with
Afr *abbr* **1** Africa **2** African
afraid \ə-ˈfrād, *South also* -ˈfre(ə)d\ *adj* **1** : filled with fear or apprehension ⟨*afraid* of snakes⟩ **2** : filled with concern or regret ⟨*afraid* he might be late⟩ **3** : DISINCLINED, RELUCTANT ⟨not *afraid* to talk straight⟩
afresh \ə-ˈfresh\ *adv* : from a new start : AGAIN
Af·ri·can \ˈaf-ri-kən\ *n* **1** : a native or inhabitant of Africa **2** : a person of African descent; *esp* : NEGRO — **African** *adj*
African elephant *n* : the tall large-eared elephant of tropical Africa
African sleeping sickness *n* : SLEEPING SICKNESS 1
African violet *n* : a tropical African plant widely grown as a houseplant for its velvety fleshy leaves and showy purple, pink, or white flowers
Af·ri·kaans \ˌaf-ri-ˈkän(t)s, -ˈkänz\ *n* : a language developed from 17th century Dutch that is one of the official languages of the Republic of South Africa
Af·ri·ka·ner \-ˈkän-ər\ *n* : a native South African of European descent; *esp* : an Afrikaans-speaking descendant of the 17th century Dutch settlers

ə abut	ər further	a back	ā bake
ä cot, cart	au̇ out	ch chin	e less	ē easy
g gift	i trip	ī life	j joke	ng sing	ō flow
ȯ flaw	ȯi coin	th thin	t͟h this	ü loot
u̇ foot	y yet	yü few	yu̇ furious	zh vision

¹Af·ro \ˈaf-rō\ *adj* : of or relating to African or Afro-American fashion or culture ⟨an *Afro* wig⟩
²Afro *n* : an Afro haircut
Af·ro–Amer·i·can \ˌaf-rō-ə-ˈmer-ə-kən\ *or* **Af·ra·mer·i·can** \ˌaf-rə-ˈmer-ə-kən\ *adj* : of or relating to Americans of African and esp. of negroid descent — **Afro–American** *n*

Afro

aft \ˈaft\ *adv* : near, toward, or in the stern of a ship or the tail of an aircraft
¹af·ter \ˈaf-tər\ *adv* : following in time or place : AFTERWARD, BEHIND
²after *prep* **1 a** : behind in place ⟨following *after* him⟩ **b** : later in time than ⟨*after* dinner⟩ **c** : below in rank or order ⟨the highest mountain *after* Everest⟩ **2** : in search of ⟨go *after* gold⟩ ⟨thirsting *after* fame⟩ **3 a** : in accordance with ⟨*after* an old custom⟩ **b** : with the name of or a name derived from that of ⟨named *after* his father⟩ **c** : in imitation or resemblance of ⟨patterned *after* a Gothic cathedral⟩
³after *conj* : later than the time when
⁴after *adj* **1** : later in time ⟨in *after* years⟩ **2** : located aft
af·ter·birth \ˈaf-tər-ˌbərth\ *n* : the placenta and fetal membranes that are expelled after delivery
af·ter·burn·er \ˌ-bər-nər\ *n* : an auxiliary burner attached to the tail pipe of a turbojet engine for injecting fuel into the hot exhaust gases and burning it to provide extra thrust
af·ter·ef·fect \-ə-ˌfekt\ *n* : an effect that arises after the first or immediate effect has subsided ⟨a medicine with no noticeable *aftereffects*⟩
af·ter·glow \-ˌglō\ *n* : a glow remaining (as in the sky after sunsets) where a light has disappeared
af·ter·im·age \-ˌim-ij\ *n* : a usu. visual sensation continuing after the stimulus causing it has ended
af·ter·life \-ˌlīf\ *n* : an existence after death
af·ter·math \ˈaf-tər-ˌmath\ *n* [originally meaning a second growth of hay after the mowing, from *after* and *math*, a word now found only in dialect, meaning "mowing", from Old English *mæth*] : CONSEQUENCE, RESULT
af·ter·noon \ˌaf-tər-ˈnün\ *n* : the part of day between noon and sunset — **afternoon** *adj*
af·ter·taste \ˈaf-tər-ˌtāst\ *n* : a sensation (as of flavor) continuing after the stimulus causing it has ended
af·ter·thought \-ˌthȯt\ *n* : a later thought about something one has done or said
af·ter·ward \ˈaf-tə(r)-wərd\ *or* **af·ter·wards** \-wərdz\ *adv* : at a later time
ag- — see AD-
again \ə-ˈgen\ *adv* **1** : in return ⟨bring us word *again*⟩ **2** : another time : ANEW ⟨come see us *again*⟩ **3** : in addition ⟨half as much *again*⟩ **4** : on the other hand ⟨he may, and *again* he may not⟩ **5** : FURTHER, MOREOVER ⟨*again*, there is another matter to consider⟩
against \ə-ˈgen(t)st\ *prep* **1** : OPPOSITE, FACING ⟨over *against* the park⟩ **2 a** : opposed to ⟨campaign

against the enemy⟩ **b** : as a protection from ⟨a shield *against* aggression⟩ **3** : in preparation for ⟨storing food *against* the winter⟩ **4** : in or into contact with ⟨ran *against* a tree⟩ ⟨leaning *against* the wall⟩ **5** : in a direction opposite to ⟨*against* the wind⟩ **6** : before the background of ⟨green trees *against* the blue sky⟩

agape \ə-'gāp, ə-'gap\ *adj* : having the mouth open in wonder or surprise : GAPING ⟨the crowd stood *agape* at the speaker⟩

agar \'äg-ˌär\ *or* **agar–agar** \ˌäg-ˌär-'äg-ˌär\ *n* **1** : a jellylike colloidal substance obtained from a red alga and used esp. in culture media or as a stabilizing agent in foods **2** : a culture medium containing agar

ag·ate \'ag-ət\ *n* **1** : a fine-grained quartz having its colors arranged in stripes or cloudy masses **2** : a playing marble of agate or glass

aga·ve \ə-'gäv-ē\ *n* : any of a genus of plants (as the century plant) related to the amaryllis that have spiny-edged leaves and flowers in tall branched clusters and include some cultivated for fiber or for ornament

agave (stalk may reach 40 ft.)

agcy *abbr* agency

[1]age \'āj\ *n* **1 a** : the time from birth to a specified date ⟨a boy six years of *age*⟩ **b** : the time of life when a person attains some right or capacity ⟨*age* of reason⟩; *esp* : MAJORITY ⟨come of *age*⟩ **c** : normal lifetime **d** : the later part of life ⟨youth and *age*⟩ **2** : a period of time characterized by some distinguishing feature ⟨machine *age*⟩ ⟨*Age* of Discovery⟩ ⟨*Age* of Reptiles⟩ **3** : a long period of time ⟨graduated *ages* ago⟩

[2]age *vb* **aged**; **ag·ing** *or* **age·ing** **1** : to become or cause to become old or old in appearance **2** : to become or cause to become mellow or mature : RIPEN

-age \ij\ *n suffix* **1** : aggregate : collection ⟨track*age*⟩ **2 a** : action : process ⟨haul*age*⟩ **b** : result of ⟨break*age*⟩ **c** : rate of ⟨dos*age*⟩ **3** : house or place of ⟨orphan*age*⟩ **4** : state : rank ⟨vassal*age*⟩ **5** : fee : charge ⟨post*age*⟩

aged *adj* **1** \'ā-jəd\ : of an advanced age **2** \'ājd\ : having reached a specified age ⟨a man *aged* forty years⟩ ***syn*** see OLD ***ant*** youthful — **ag·ed·ness** \'ā-jəd-nəs\ *n*

age·less \'āj-ləs\ *adj* **1** : not growing old or showing the effects of age **2** : TIMELESS, ETERNAL ⟨an *ageless* story⟩ — **age·less·ly** *adv*

agen·cy \'ā-jən-sē\ *n, pl* **-cies** **1** : a person or thing through which power is exerted or an end is achieved : MEANS **2** : the office or function of an agent **3** : an establishment doing business for another ⟨automobile *agency*⟩ **4** : an administrative division (as of a government) ⟨Central Intelligence *Agency*⟩

agen·da \ə-'jen-də\ *n* : a list of items of business to be considered (as at a meeting)

agent \'ā-jənt\ *n* **1 a** : something that produces an effect ⟨a cleansing *agent*⟩ **b** : a chemically, physically, or biologically active principle **2** : one who acts or does business for another ⟨government *agent*⟩ ⟨real estate *agent*⟩

Age of Fishes : DEVONIAN

Age of Mammals : CENOZOIC

Age of Reptiles : MESOZOIC

age–old \'āj-'ōld\ *adj* : having existed for ages : ANCIENT

ag·er·a·tum \ˌaj-ə-'rāt-əm\ *n* : any of a large genus of tropical American herbs related to the daisies and often cultivated for their small showy heads of blue or white flowers

[1]ag·glom·er·ate \ə-'gläm-ə-ˌrāt\ *vb* : to gather into a ball, mass, or cluster

[2]ag·glom·er·ate \-rət\ *n* **1** : a jumbled mass or collection **2** : a rock composed of volcanic fragments of various sizes

ag·glom·er·a·tion \ə-ˌgläm-ə-'rā-shən\ *n* **1** : the action or process of collecting in a mass **2** : a heap or cluster of dissimilar elements — **ag·glom·er·a·tive** \-'gläm-ə-ˌrāt-iv\ *adj*

ag·glu·ti·nate \ə-'glüt-ə-ˌnāt\ *vb* **1** : to cause to adhere : FASTEN **2** : to cause to clump or undergo agglutination **3** : to unite into a group or gather into a mass

ag·glu·ti·na·tion \ə-ˌglüt-ə-'nā-shən\ *n* **1** : the action or process of agglutinating **2** : a mass or group formed by the union of separate elements **3** : a reaction in which particles (as red blood cells or bacteria) suspended in a liquid collect into clumps usu. as a response to a specific antibody — **ag·glu·ti·na·tive** \-'glüt-ə-ˌnāt-iv\ *adj*

ag·glu·ti·nin \ə-'glüt-ə-nən\ *n* : an antibody causing agglutination

ag·glu·tin·o·gen \ˌag-lü-'tin-ə-jən\ *n* : an antigen whose presence results in the formation of an agglutinin

ag·gran·dize \ə-'gran-ˌdīz, 'ag-rən-\ *vb* : to make great or greater (as in power, rank, size, or resources) — **ag·gran·dize·ment** \ə-'gran-dəz-mənt, -ˌdīz-; ˌag-rən-'dīz-mənt\ *n* — **ag·gran·diz·er** *n*

ag·gra·vate \'ag-rə-ˌvāt\ *vb* [from Latin *aggravare* "to add to the weight of", from *ad-* "to" and *gravis* "heavy", the source of English *gravity*] **1** : to make more serious or severe ⟨*aggravate* an injury⟩ **2** : EXASPERATE, ANNOY

ag·gra·va·tion \ˌag-rə-'vā-shən\ *n* **1** : the act of making something worse or more severe : an increase in severity ⟨the treatment caused an *aggravation* of the pain⟩ **2** : something that aggravates ⟨the cold winter was an *aggravation* of their misery⟩ **3** : IRRITATION, PROVOCATION

[1]ag·gre·gate \'ag-ri-gət\ *adj* **1** : formed by the collection together of units or particles : COMBINED ⟨*aggregate* expenses⟩ **2** : clustered in a dense mass or head ⟨an *aggregate* flower⟩

[2]ag·gre·gate \-ˌgāt\ *vb* **1** : to collect or gather into a mass or whole **2** : to amount to as a whole

[3]ag·gre·gate \-gət\ *n* **1** : a collection or sum of units or parts **2** : a clustered mass of individual soil particles considered the basic structural unit of soil

aggregate fruit *n* : a compound fruit (as a raspberry) made up of the several separate ripened ovaries of a single flower

ag·gre·ga·tion \ˌag-ri-'gā-shən\ *n* **1** : the collecting of units or parts into a mass or whole **2** : a group, body, or mass composed of many distinct parts

ag·gres·sion \ə-'gresh-ən\ *n* [from Latin *aggress-*, past participle stem of *aggredi* "to attack", from *ad-* "to" and *gradi* "to step", from the same root as Latin *gradus* "step", from which comes English *grade*] **1** : an unprovoked attack **2** : the practice of making attacks

ag·gres·sive \ə-'gres-iv\ *adj* **1 a** : showing readiness to attack ⟨an *aggressive* dog⟩ **b** : practicing aggression ⟨*aggressive* nation⟩ **2** : ENERGETIC, FORCE-

FUL ⟨an *aggressive* fund-raising campaign⟩ — **ag·gres·sive·ly** *adv* — **ag·gres·sive·ness** *n*

ag·gres·sor \ə-ˈgres-ər\ *n* : a person or country that makes an unprovoked attack

ag·grieved \ə-ˈgrēvd\ *adj* **1** : troubled or distressed in spirit **2** : having a grievance; *esp* : suffering from injury or loss

aghast \ə-ˈgast\ *adj* : struck with terror, amazement, or horror : SHOCKED

ag·ile \ˈaj-əl\ *adj* **1** : able to move quickly and easily : NIMBLE **2** : mentally quick ⟨an *agile* thinker⟩ — **ag·ile·ly** \-ə(l)-lē\ *adv* — **agil·i·ty** \ə-ˈjil-ət-ē\ *n*

aging *pres part of* AGE

ag·i·tate \ˈaj-ə-ˌtāt\ *vb* **1** : to shake jerkily : set in violent irregular motion ⟨water *agitated* by wind⟩ **2** : to stir up : EXCITE, DISTURB ⟨*agitated* by bad news⟩ **3** : to attempt to arouse public interest esp. by discussion or appeals ⟨*agitate* for better schools⟩ — **ag·i·tat·ed·ly** \-ˌtāt-əd-lē\ *adv* — **ag·i·ta·tion** \ˌaj-ə-ˈtā-shən\ *n*

ag·i·ta·tor \ˈaj-ə-ˌtāt-ər\ *n* **1** : one who stirs up public feeling on a controversial issue **2** : a device for stirring or shaking

agleam \ə-ˈglēm\ *adj* : GLEAMING

aglit·ter \ə-ˈglit-ər\ *adj* : GLITTERING

aglow \ə-ˈglō\ *adj* : GLOWING

ag·nos·tic \ag-ˈnäs-tik, əg-\ *n* [from Greek *agnōstos* "unknown", from *a-* "not", "un-" and *gnō-* the root of *gignōskein* "to know", which comes from the same source as English *know*] : a person who holds that whether God exists is not known and probably cannot be known — **agnostic** *adj* — **ag·nos·ti·cism** \-ˈnäs-tə-ˌsiz-əm\ *n*

ago \ə-ˈgō\ *adj or adv* : earlier than the present time

agog \ə-ˈgäg\ *adj* : full of intense interest or excitement

ag·o·nize \ˈag-ə-ˌnīz\ *vb* **1** : to suffer or cause to suffer extreme pain or anguish of body or mind **2** : to strive desperately : STRUGGLE — **ag·o·niz·ing·ly** \-ˌnī-zing-lē\ *adv*

ag·o·ny \ˈag-ə-nē\ *n, pl* **-nies** [from Greek *agōnia*, from *agōn*, meaning at first "a gathering of people", then especially one at which athletic contests were held, then the contest itself, and finally the struggle of the contestant] **1 a** : intense pain of mind or body **b** : the throes of death **2** : a strong sudden display of emotion : OUTBURST

ag·o·ra \ˈag-ə-rə\ *n, pl* **agoras** \-rəz\ *or* **ag·o·rae** \-ˌrē, -ˌrī\ : the marketplace or place of assembly in an ancient Greek city

agou·ti \ə-ˈgüt-ē\ *n* **1** : a tropical American rodent about the size of a rabbit **2** : a grizzled color of fur resulting from the barring of each hair in several alternate dark and light bands

agrar·i·an \ə-ˈgrer-ē-ən\ *adj* **1** : of or relating to the land or its ownership ⟨*agrarian* reforms⟩ **2** : of, relating to, or concerned with farmers or farming interests ⟨an *agrarian* political party⟩ **3** : AGRICULTURAL 2 ⟨an *agrarian* country⟩

agree \ə-ˈgrē\ *vb* **agreed**; **agree·ing** **1** : to give one's approval : CONSENT ⟨*agree* to a plan⟩ **2** : ADMIT, CONCEDE ⟨all *agreed* he was a good man⟩ **3** : to be alike : CORRESPOND **4** : to get on well together **5** : to come to an understanding ⟨*agree* on a price⟩ **6** : to be fitting, pleasing, or healthful : SUIT ⟨climate *agrees* with him⟩ **7** : to be alike or correspond grammatically in gender, number, case, or person

agree·a·ble \ə-ˈgrē-ə-bəl\ *adj* **1** : pleasing to the mind or senses : PLEASANT **2** : ready or willing to agree **3** : being in harmony : CONSONANT — **agree·a·ble·ness** *n* — **agree·a·bly** \-blē\ *adv*

agreed \ə-ˈgrēd\ *adj* : settled by agreement

agree·ment \ə-ˈgrē-mənt\ *n* **1 a** : the act of agreeing **b** : harmony of opinion, action, or character : CONCORD **2 a** : a mutual arrangement or understanding (as a contract or treaty) **b** : a written record of such an agreement **3** : the fact of agreeing grammatically

syn AGREEMENT, CONTRACT, BARGAIN can mean an arrangement between parties on a matter of common interest. AGREEMENT implies mutual understanding arrived at by discussion. CONTRACT applies to a formal often written agreement ⟨they came to an *agreement* on the repairs and drew up a *contract* for the work⟩; BARGAIN applies to a firm agreement esp. concerning purchase and sale

agric *abbr* **1** agricultural **2** agriculture

ag·ri·cul·tur·al \ˌag-ri-ˈkəlch-(ə-)rəl\ *adj* **1** : of, relating to, or used in agriculture **2** : engaged in or concerned with agriculture ⟨an *agricultural* society⟩ — **ag·ri·cul·tur·al·ly** \-ē\ *adv*

ag·ri·cul·ture \ˈag-ri-ˌkəl-chər\ *n* : the science or occupation of cultivating the soil, producing crops, and raising livestock : FARMING — **ag·ri·cul·tur·ist** \ˌag-ri-ˈkəlch-(ə-)rəst\ *or* **ag·ri·cul·tur·al·ist** \-(ə-)rə-ləst\ *n*

ag·ro·bi·ol·o·gy \ˌag-rō-bī-ˈäl-ə-jē\ *n* : the study of plant nutrition and growth and crop production in relation to soil management — **ag·ro·bi·o·log·ic** \-ˌbī-ə-ˈläj-ik\ *or* **ag·ro·bi·o·log·i·cal** \-ˈläj-i-kəl\ *adj* — **ag·ro·bi·o·log·i·cal·ly** \-i-k(ə-)lē\ *adv*

agrol·o·gy \ə-ˈgräl-ə-jē\ *n* : a branch of agriculture dealing with soils esp. in relation to crops

agron·o·my \ə-ˈgrän-ə-mē\ *n* : a branch of agriculture that deals with the raising of crops and the care of the soil — **agron·o·mist** \-məst\ *n*

aground \ə-ˈgraůnd\ *adv or adj* : on or onto the shore or the bottom : STRANDED ⟨ship ran *aground*⟩

agt *abbr* agent

ague \ˈā-gyü\ *n* **1** : a fever (as malaria) marked by outbreaks of chills, fever, and sweating that recur at regular intervals **2** : a fit of shivering : CHILL

ah \ˈä\ *interj* — used to express delight, relief, regret, or contempt

aha \ä-ˈhä\ *interj* — used to express surprise, triumph, or scorn

ahead \ə-ˈhed\ *adv* **1** : in or toward the front ⟨the man *ahead*⟩ ⟨go *ahead*⟩ **2** : in, into, or for the future ⟨think *ahead*⟩ **3** : in or toward a more advantageous position ⟨$10 *ahead*⟩ **4** : in advance ⟨make payments *ahead*⟩ — **ahead** *adj*

ahead of *prep* : in front or advance of ⟨*ahead* of schedule⟩

A–ho·ri·zon \ˈā-hə-ˌrī-zən\ *n* : the outer dark-colored light-textured layer of soil consisting usu. of soil rich in organic debris in various stages of disintegration

ahoy \ə-ˈhȯi\ *interj* — used in hailing ⟨ship *ahoy*⟩

¹aid \ˈād\ *vb* : to provide with what is useful or necessary : ASSIST — **aid·er** *n*

²aid *n* **1** : the act of helping or the help given : ASSISTANCE **2** : ASSISTANT **3** : something that is of help or assistance

aide \ˈād\ *n* **1** : a military or naval officer acting as assistant to a superior **2** : ASSISTANT

aide–de–camp \ˌād-di-ˈkamp, -ˈkän\ *n, pl* **aides–de–camp** \ˌādz-di-\ : AIDE 1

A

ai·grette \ā-'gret, 'ā-,\ *n* : a plume or decorative tuft for the head

ail \'āl\ *vb* **1** : to be the matter with : TROUBLE ⟨what *ails* you?⟩ **2** : to have something the matter; *esp* : to suffer ill health

ai·lan·thus \ā-'lan(t)-thəs\ *n* : a widely grown quick-growing Asiatic tree with fernlike leaves and terminal clusters of ill-scented greenish flowers

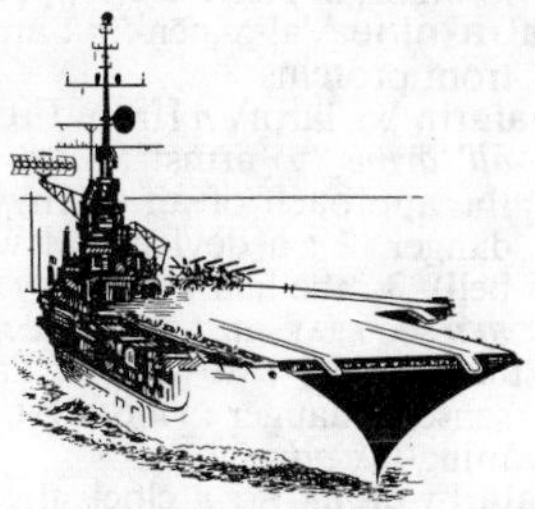
aircraft carrier

ai·le·ron \'ā-lə-,rän\ *n* : a movable part (as a flap) of an airplane wing

ail·ment \'āl-mənt\ *n* : a bodily disorder : SICKNESS

[1]**aim** \'ām\ *vb* **1** : to point a weapon **2** : ASPIRE, INTEND ⟨*aims* to please⟩ **3** : to direct to or toward an object or goal ⟨*aim* a camera⟩

[2]**aim** *n* **1** : the directing of a weapon or a missile at a mark **2** : GOAL, PURPOSE

aim·less \'ām-ləs\ *adj* : lacking a goal or purpose ⟨*aimless* wandering⟩ — **aim·less·ly** *adv* — **aim·less·ness** *n*

ain't \(')ānt\ **1 a** : are not **b** : is not **c** : am not — used orally in most parts of the U.S. by many educated speakers esp. in the phrase *ain't I* but disapproved by many and more common in less educated speech **2** *substand* **a** : have not **b** : has not

[1]**air** \'a(ə)r, 'e(ə)r\ *n* **1 a** : the invisible mixture of odorless tasteless gases (as nitrogen and oxygen) that surrounds the earth **b** : a light breeze **2** : COMPRESSED AIR ⟨*air* sprayer⟩ **3 a** : AIRCRAFT ⟨*air* attack⟩ **b** : AVIATION ⟨*air* safety⟩ **4 a** : the medium of transmission of radio waves **b** : RADIO, TELEVISION ⟨went on the *air*⟩ **5 a** : outward appearance : apparent nature ⟨an *air* of mystery⟩ **b** *pl* : an artificial or affected manner ⟨put on *airs*⟩ **6** : TUNE, MELODY

[2]**air** *vb* **1** : to place in the air for cooling, refreshing, or cleaning ⟨*air* blankets⟩ **2** : to make known in public

air base *n* : a base of operations for military aircraft

air bladder *n* **1** : a sac in a fish containing gas and esp. air and serving in respiration or the regulation of buoyancy **2** : a hollow vesicle found in various algae that contains gases and serves to buoy up the plant

air·borne \-,bōrn, -,bȯrn\ *adj* : supported or transported by air ⟨*airborne* troops⟩

air brake *n* **1** : a brake operated by a piston driven by compressed air **2** : a surface that may be projected into the air for lowering the speed of an airplane

air·brush \-,brəsh\ *n* : an atomizer for applying by compressed air a fine spray (as of paint or a protective coating) — **airbrush** *vb*

air–con·di·tion \,a(ə)r-kən-'dish-ən, ,e(ə)r-\ *vb* : to equip with an apparatus for cleaning air and controlling its humidity and temperature; *also* : to subject (air) to these processes — **air con·di·tion·er** \-'dish-(ə-)nər\ *n*

air–cool \'a(ə)r-'kül, 'e(ə)r-\ *vb* : to cool (as an internal-combustion engine) by air

air·craft \-,kraft\ *n, pl* **aircraft** : a machine (as an airplane, glider, or helicopter) for navigation of the air that is supported either by its own buoyancy or by the action of the air against its surfaces

aircraft carrier *n* : a warship with a deck on which airplanes can be launched and landed

air·drome \-,drōm\ *n* : AIRPORT

air·drop \-,dräp\ *n* : delivery of cargo or personnel by parachute from an airplane — **air–drop** \-,dräp\ *vb*

Aire·dale \'a(ə)r- ,dāl, 'e(ə)r-\ *n* : any of a breed of large terriers with a hard wiry coat

air·field \'a(ə)r-,fēld, 'e(ə)r-\ *n* **1** : the landing field of an airport **2** : AIRPORT

air·foil \-,fȯil\ *n* : an airplane surface (as a wing or rudder) designed to produce reaction from the air through which it moves

air force *n* : the military organization of a nation for air warfare

air·frame \-,frām\ *n* : the structure of an airplane or rocket without the power plant

air gun *n* **1** : a pistol-shaped hand tool that works by compressed air **2** : AIRBRUSH

air lane *n* : an airway that is customarily followed by airplanes

air·less \'a(ə)r-ləs, 'e(ə)r-\ *adj* : lacking air, fresh air, or movement of air

air letter *n* **1** : an airmail letter **2** : a sheet of paper designed for folding and sealing so as to form an envelope for a message written on the inside and sometimes bearing a stamp for airmail delivery

air·lift \'a(ə)r-,lift, 'e(ə)r-\ *n* : a supply line operated by aircraft — **airlift** *vb*

air·line \-,līn\ *n* **1 a** : a system of transportation by airplanes **b** : the organization operating an airline **2** : a regular airline route

air·lin·er \-,lī-nər\ *n* : a large passenger airplane operating over an airline

air lock *n* : an air space with two airtight doors that permits movement between two spaces with different pressures or different atmospheres

air·mail \'a(ə)r-'māl, 'e(ə)r-, -,māl\ *n* **1** : the system of transporting mail by airplanes **2** : mail transported by air — **airmail** *vb*

air·man \-mən\ *n* **1** : an enlisted man in the air force; *esp* : one of any of four ranks below a staff sergeant **2** : PILOT, AVIATOR

air map *n* : a map made up of a series of photographs taken from an aircraft

air mass *n* : a body of air extending hundreds or thousands of miles horizontally and sometimes as high as the stratosphere and having nearly uniform conditions of temperature and humidity at any given level

air mass weather *n* : weather within an air mass that is different from weather occurring at its front

air–mind·ed \'a(ə)r-'mīn-dəd, 'e(ə)r-\ *adj* : interested in aviation or in air travel — **air–mind·ed·ness** *n*

air·plane \-,plān\ *n* : a fixed-wing aircraft heavier than air that is driven by a screw propeller or by a rearward jet and supported by the reaction of the air against its wings

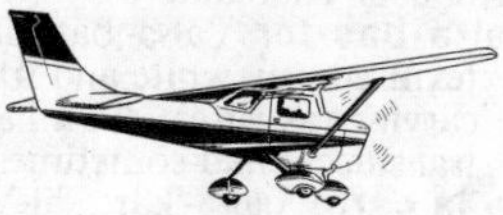
airplane

air plant *n* **1** : EPIPHYTE **2** : BRYOPHYLLUM

air pocket *n* : a condition of the atmosphere that causes an airplane to drop suddenly

air·port \'a(ə)r-,pōrt, 'e(ə)r-, -,pȯrt\ *n* : a tract of land or water where airplanes may land to receive and discharge passengers or cargo and that usu. has facilities for the shelter, supply, and repair of planes

air pressure *n* : the pressure resulting from the weight of the atmosphere

air pump *n* : a pump for removing air from a closed space or for compressing air or forcing it through other apparatus

air raid *n* : an attack by airplanes (as bombers) on a surface target

air sac *n* **1** : one of the air-filled spaces connected with the lungs of a bird **2** : one of the thin-walled microscopic pouches in which gases are exchanged in the lungs

air·ship \'a(ə)r-ˌship, 'e(ə)r-\ *n* : a lighter-than-air aircraft (as a dirigible) having propulsion and steering systems

air·sick \-ˌsik\ *adj* : affected with motion sickness associated with flying — **air·sick·ness** *n*

air·speed \-ˌspēd\ *n* : the speed of an airplane with relation to the air as distinguished from its speed relative to the earth

air·strip \-ˌstrip\ *n* : a runway without normal air base or airport facilities

air·tight \-'tīt\ *adj* **1** : so tightly sealed that no air can get in or out **2** : leaving no opening for attack ⟨an *airtight* argument⟩

air·wave \-ˌwāv\ *n* : AIR 4 — usu. used in pl.

air·way \-ˌwā\ *n* **1** : a passage for a current of air **2** : a regular route for aircraft; *esp* : one equipped with navigational aids

air·wor·thy \-ˌwər-t͟hē\ *adj* : fit or safe for operation in the air — **air·wor·thi·ness** *n*

airy \'a(ə)r-ē, 'e(ə)r-\ *adj* **air·i·er**; **-est** **1** : of, relating to, or living in the air : AERIAL ⟨*airy* spirits⟩ **2** : open to the air : BREEZY ⟨an *airy* room⟩ **3** : resembling air in lightness : DELICATE, ETHEREAL **4** : lacking a sound or solid basis — **air·i·ly** \'ar-ə-lē, 'er-\ *adv* — **air·i·ness** \'ar-ē-nəs, 'er-\ *n*

aisle \'īl\ *n* : a passage between sections of seats (as in a church or theater)

1**ajar** \ə-'jär\ *adv or adj* : slightly open ⟨the door was *ajar*⟩

2**ajar** *adj* : DISCORDANT

AK *abbr* Alaska

akim·bo \ə-'kim-bō\ *adv or adj* : with the hand on the hip and the elbow turned outward

akin \ə-'kin\ *adj* **1** : related by blood **2** : essentially similar or related : ALIKE

Ak·ka·di·an \ə-'kād-ē-ən\ *n* **1** : one of a Semitic people invading and settling central Mesopotamia north of the Sumerians (3000–1900 B.C.) **2** : an ancient Semitic language of Mesopotamia used from about the 28th to the 1st century B.C. — **Akkadian** *adj*

al- — see AD-

1**-al** \əl\ *adj suffix* : of, relating to, or characterized by ⟨direction*al*⟩ ⟨fiction*al*⟩

2**-al** *n suffix* : action : process ⟨rehears*al*⟩

AL *abbr* **1** Alabama **2** American League **3** American Legion

Ala *abbr* Alabama

al·a·bas·ter \'al-ə-ˌbas-tər\ *n* **1** : a compact fine-textured usu. white and translucent gypsum used for carving (as vases) **2** : a hard compact calcite that is translucent and sometimes banded

a la carte \ˌal-ə-'kärt, ˌäl-\ *adv or adj* : with a separate price for each item on the menu

alac·ri·ty \ə-'lak-rət-ē\ *n* : a cheerful readiness to do something — **alac·ri·tous** \-rət-əs\ *adj*

a la mode \ˌal-ə-'mōd, ˌäl-\ *adj* [from French *à la mode*, literally "according to the fashion"] **1** : FASHIONABLE, STYLISH **2** : topped with ice cream

al·a·nine \'al-ə-ˌnēn\ *n* : an amino acid formed esp. from proteins

1**alarm** \ə-'lärm\ *n* [from French *alarme*, from Italian *all' arme* "to arms!", a cry used to warn citizens of the approach of an enemy force] **1** : a warning of danger **2** : a device that warns or signals (as by a bell) **3** : the fear caused by a sudden sense of danger ***syn*** see FEAR ***ant*** assurance, composure

2**alarm** *vb* **1** : to warn of danger **2** : to arouse to a sense of danger : FRIGHTEN — **alarm·ing·ly** \ə-'lär-ming-lē\ *adv*

alarm clock *n* : a clock that can be set to sound an alarm at any desired time

alarm·ist \ə-'lär-məst\ *n* : a person who is given to alarming others esp. needlessly — **alarm·ism** \-ˌmiz-əm\ *n*

alas \ə-'las\ *interj* — used to express unhappiness, pity, or concern

Alas·kan malamute \ə-ˌlas-kən-\ *n* : any of a breed of powerful heavy-coated deep-chested dogs of Alaskan origin with erect ears, heavily cushioned feet, and a plumy tail

alb \'alb\ *n* : a full-length white linen vestment worn by priests at the Eucharist

Alb *abbr* Albanian

al·ba·core \'al-bə-ˌkō(ə)r, -ˌkȯ(ə)r\ *n, pl* **-core** *or* **-cores** : a large tuna with long pectoral fins and white flesh used esp. for canning

Al·ba·ni·an \al-'bā-nē-ən, -nyən\ *n* **1** : a native or inhabitant of Albania **2** : the Indo-European language of the Albanian people — **Albanian** *adj*

al·ba·tross \'al-bə-ˌtrȯs, -ˌträs\ *n, pl* **-tross** *or* **-tross·es** : any of various large web-footed seabirds that are related to the petrels and include the largest birds of the sea

albatross
(wingspread 11 ft. 6 in.)

al·be·it \ȯl-'bē-ət, al-\ *conj* : even though : ALTHOUGH

al·bi·no \al-'bī-nō\ *n, pl* **-nos** : an organism deficient in coloring matter; *esp* : a human being or lower animal that has an hereditary deficiency in pigment and usu. a milky skin, white or colorless hair, and eyes with pink or blue iris and deep red pupil — **al·bi·nism** \'al-bə-ˌniz-əm, al-'bī-\ *n* — **albino** *adj*

al·bite \'al-ˌbīt\ *n* : a usu. white feldspar containing sodium

al·bum \'al-bəm\ *n* **1** : a book with blank pages for autographs, stamps, or photographs **2** : a container with envelopes for phonograph records **3** : one or more phonograph records or tape recordings carrying a major work or a group of selections **4** : a collection usu. in book form of literary selections, musical compositions, or pictures

al·bu·men \al-'byü-mən\ *n* **1** : the white of an egg **2** : ALBUMIN

al·bu·min \al-'byü-mən\ *n* : any of numerous water-soluble proteins found esp. in blood, the whites of eggs, and various animal and plant tissues

al·bu·mi·nous \al-'byü-mə-nəs\ *adj* : relating to, containing, or having the properties of albumen or albumin

alc *abbr* alcohol

ə abut   ər further   a back   ā bake
ä cot, cart   au̇ out   ch chin   e less   ē easy
g gift   i trip   ī life   j joke   ng sing   ō flow
ȯ flaw   ȯi coin   th thin   t͟h this   ü loot
u̇ foot   y yet   yü few   yu̇ furious   zh vision

al·che·my \'al-kə-mē\ *n* : a medieval chemistry aiming to change base metals into gold and to discover a single cure for all diseases — **al·che·mist** \-məst\ *n*

al·co·hol \'al-kə-ˌhȯl\ *n* **1 a** : a colorless volatile flammable liquid that is the intoxicating agent in fermented and distilled liquors (as beer, wine, whiskey) **b** : any of various carbon compounds that are similar to ethyl alcohol in having at least one hydroxyl group **2 a** : a liquor (as beer, wine, or whiskey) containing alcohol **b** : alcoholic beverages ⟨he never touches *alcohol*⟩

1**al·co·hol·ic** \ˌal-kə-'hȯl-ik, -'häl-\ *adj* **1** : of, relating to, or containing alcohol **2** : affected with alcoholism — **al·co·hol·i·cal·ly** \-i-k(ə-)lē\ *adv*

2**alcoholic** *n* : one affected with alcoholism

al·co·hol·ism \'al-kə-ˌhȯl-ˌiz-əm\ *n* : an abnormal state associated with excessive use of alcoholic drinks

al·cove \'al-ˌkōv\ *n* **1** : a small room opening off a larger room **2** : a niche or arched opening (as in a wall)

ald *abbr* alderman

al·der \'ȯl-dər\ *n* : any of a genus of toothed-leaved trees or shrubs related to the birches

al·der·man \'ȯl-dər-mən\ *n* : a member of a legislative body in a U.S. city — **al·der·man·ic** \ˌȯl-dər-'man-ik\ *adj*

al·drin \'ȯl-drən\ *n* : a long-acting insecticide that is a chlorinated derivative of naphthalene

ale \'āl\ *n* : an alcoholic drink made from malt and flavored with hops and usu. heavier bodied and more bitter than beer

alee \ə-'lē\ *adv or adj* : on or toward the lee

1**alert** \ə-'lərt\ *adj* **1 a** : being watchful and prompt to meet danger **b** : quick to perceive and act **2** : ACTIVE, BRISK — **alert·ly** *adv* — **alert·ness** *n*

2**alert** *n* **1** : a signal of danger **2** : the period during which an alert is in effect — **on the alert** : on the lookout for danger

3**alert** *vb* : to call to alertness : WARN ⟨sirens to *alert* the public in case of attack⟩

ale·wife \'āl-ˌwīf\ *n* : a food fish of the herring family abundant on the Atlantic coast

al·fal·fa \al-'fal-fə\ *n* : a deep-rooted European leguminous plant with purple flowers and leaves like clover that is widely grown for hay and forage

alg *abbr* algebra

al·ga \'al-gə\ *n, pl* **al·gae** \'al-(ˌ)jē\ : any plant (as a seaweed) of a group that forms the lowest division of the plant kingdom and includes forms mostly growing in water, lacking a vascular system, and having chlorophyll often masked by brown or red coloring matter — **al·gal** \'al-gəl\ *adj*

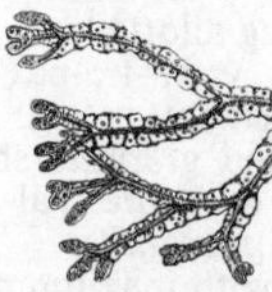

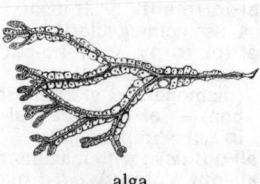

alga (about 1 ft. long)

al·ge·bra \'al-jə-brə\ *n* : a branch of mathematics which generalizes arithmetic relations and explores them using letters or other symbols to represent numbers or other mathematical entities — **al·ge·bra·ic** \ˌal-jə-'brā-ik\ *adj* — **al·ge·bra·i·cal·ly** \-'brā-ə-k(ə-)lē\ *adv*

Al·ge·ri·an \al-'jir-ē-ən\ *adj* : of, relating to, or characteristic of Algeria or its people — **Algerian** *n*

Al·gon·qui·an \al-'gän-kwē-ən, -'gäŋ-\ *n* **1** : a stock of Indian languages spoken from Labrador to the Carolinas and westward to the Great Plains **2** : a member of any of the Amerindian peoples speaking Algonquian languages

al·go·rithm \'al-gə-ˌrith-əm\ *n* : a rule of procedure for solving a recurrent mathematical problem

1**ali·as** \'ā-lē-əs, 'āl-yəs\ *adv* [from Latin, meaning simply "otherwise", from *alius* "other"] : otherwise called : otherwise known as ⟨John Doe *alias* Richard Roe⟩

2**alias** *n* : an assumed name

1**al·i·bi** \'al-ə-ˌbī\ *n, pl* **-bis** \-ˌbīz\ **1** : the plea made by a person accused of a crime that he was at another place when the crime occurred **2** : a plausible excuse

2**alibi** *vb* **-bied**; **-bi·ing** : to offer an alibi

1**alien** \'ā-lē-ən, 'āl-yən\ *adj* **1** : relating or belonging to another country : FOREIGN ⟨*alien* residents⟩ **2** : wholly different in nature or character ⟨opinions *alien* to his outlook⟩

2**alien** *n* : a foreign-born resident who is a subject or citizen of a foreign country

alien·ate \'ā-lē-ə-ˌnāt, 'āl-yə-ˌnāt\ *vb* **1** : to transfer (as a title, property, or right) to another **2** : to cause a loss of feelings of love, loyalty, or attachment ⟨*alienated* her affections⟩ — **alien·a·tion** \ˌā-lē-ə-'nā-shən, ˌāl-yə-'nā-\ *n*

alien·ist \'ā-lē-ə-nəst, 'āl-yə-nəst\ *n* : PSYCHIATRIST; *esp* : one who testifies in a legal proceeding

1**alight** \ə-'līt\ *vb* **alight·ed** \-'līt-əd\ *also* **alit** \ə-'lit\; **alight·ing** **1** : to get down : DISMOUNT **2** : to descend from the air and settle : LAND

2**alight** *adj* : LIGHTED, AFLAME

align *also* **aline** \ə-'līn\ *vb* **1** : to bring into or be in line or alignment **2** : to array on the side of or against a cause — **align·er** *n*

align·ment *also* **aline·ment** \ə-'līn-mənt\ *n* **1 a** : the act of aligning : the state of being aligned **b** : the proper adjustment of parts in relation to each other **2** : an arrangement of groups or forces ⟨a new political *alignment*⟩

1**alike** \ə-'līk\ *adj* : LIKE — **alike·ness** *n*

2**alike** *adv* : in the same manner, form, or degree

al·i·ment \'al-ə-mənt\ *n* : FOOD, NUTRIMENT; *also* : SUSTENANCE

al·i·men·ta·ry \ˌal-ə-'ment-ə-rē, -'men-trē\ *adj* : of or relating to nourishment or nutrition

alimentary canal *n* : the tube that extends from mouth to anus and functions in direction and absorption of food and in elimination of waste

al·i·mo·ny \'al-ə-ˌmō-nē\ *n* : money paid by a man to a woman for her support during or after divorce or separation

alive \ə-'līv\ *adj* **1** : LIVING ⟨proudest boy *alive*⟩ **2** : still in existence, force, or operation : ACTIVE ⟨kept hope *alive*⟩ **3** : knowingly aware or conscious : SENSITIVE ⟨*alive* to the beauty of life⟩ **4** : marked by much life, animation, or activity : SWARMING ⟨blossoms *alive* with bees⟩ — **alive·ness** *n*

aliz·a·rin \ə-'liz-ə-rən\ *n* : an orange or red crystalline compound made synthetically and used as a red dye and in making red pigments

alk *abbr* alkaline

al·ka·li \'al-kə-ˌlī\ *n, pl* **-lies** *or* **-lis** **1** : a substance (as a hydroxide) that has a bitter taste and neutralizes acids **2** : ALKALI METAL **3** : a soluble salt or a mixture of soluble salts present in some soils of arid regions

alkali metal *n* : any of the metals in the group that consists of lithium, sodium, potassium, rubidium, cesium, and francium

al·ka·line \'al-kə-ˌlīn, -lən\ *adj* : of, relating to, or having the properties of an alkali — **al·ka·lin·i·ty** \ˌal-kə-'lin-ət-ē\ *n*

alkaline earth *n* **1 :** an oxide of any of several strongly basic metals comprising calcium, strontium, and barium and sometimes magnesium, radium, or beryllium **2 :** ALKALINE-EARTH METAL
alkaline–earth metal *n* **:** any of the metals whose oxides are the alkaline earths
al·kyd \'al-kəd\ *n* **:** any of numerous synthetic resins used esp. for protective coatings
[1]**all** \'ȯl\ *adj* **1 a :** the whole of ⟨sat up *all* night⟩ **b :** as much as possible ⟨told in *all* seriousness⟩ **2 :** every one of ⟨*all* men will go⟩ **3 :** any whatever ⟨beyond *all* doubt⟩
[2]**all** *adv* **1 :** WHOLLY, ALTOGETHER ⟨sat *all* alone⟩ ⟨*all* across the country⟩ **2 :** so much ⟨*all* the better for it⟩ **3 :** for each side **:** APIECE ⟨the score is two *all*⟩
[3]**all** *pron* **1 :** EVERYONE, EACH ⟨*all* of us⟩ ⟨known to *all*⟩ **2 :** EVERYTHING ⟨*all* that I have⟩ ⟨sacrificed *all* for love⟩
allarg *abbr* allargando
al·lar·gan·do \,äl-,är-'gän-dō\ *adv or adj* **:** gradually slower with crescendo — used as a direction in music
all–around \,ȯl-ə-'raůnd\ *adj* **1 :** competent in many fields **2 :** having general utility
al·lay \ə-'lā\ *vb* **-layed**; **-lay·ing 1 :** to make less severe **:** RELIEVE ⟨*allay* pain⟩ **2 :** to make quiet **:** CALM ⟨*allay* anxiety⟩
al·le·ga·tion \,al-i-'gā-shən\ *n* **1 :** the act of alleging **2 :** something alleged; *esp* **:** an assertion unsupported by proof or evidence
al·lege \ə-'lej\ *vb* **1 :** to state positively without offering proof ⟨*allege* a person's guilt⟩ **2 :** to offer as a reason or excuse ⟨*allege* illness to avoid work⟩ — **al·leg·ed·ly** \ə-'lej-əd-lē\ *adv*
al·le·giance \ə-'lē-jən(t)s\ *n* **1 :** the obligation of fidelity and obedience owed by a subject or citizen to his sovereign or government **2 :** devotion or loyalty to a person, group, or cause ***syn*** see LOYALTY ***ant*** treachery, treason
al·le·go·ry \'al-ə-,gōr-ē, -,gȯr-\ *n, pl* **-ries :** a story in which the characters and events are symbols expressing truths about human life — **al·le·gor·i·cal** \,al-ə-'gȯr-i-kəl, -'gär-\ *adj* — **al·le·gor·i·cal·ly** \-i-k(ə-)lē\ *adv*
al·le·gret·to \,al-ə-'gret-ō\ *adv or adj* **:** faster than andante but not so fast as allegro — used as a direction in music
[1]**al·le·gro** \ə-'leg-rō, -'lā-grō\ *adv or adj* **:** in a brisk lively manner — used as a direction in music
[2]**allegro** *n, pl* **-gros :** a piece or movement in allegro tempo
al·lele \ə-'lēl\ *n* **1 :** either of a pair of characters inherited alternatively **2 :** one of several forms of a gene that occur at one locus and determine alternate forms of one or more genetic traits — **al·le·lic** \-'lē-lik, -'lel-ik\ *adj*
al·le·lu·ia \,al-ə-'lü-yə\ *interj* **:** HALLELUJAH
al·ler·gen \'al-ər-jən\ *n* **:** a substance that induces allergy — **al·ler·gen·ic** \,al-ər-'jen-ik\ *adj*
al·ler·gic \ə-'lər-jik\ *adj* **1 :** of, relating to, or inducing allergy ⟨an *allergic* reaction⟩ **2 :** disagreeably sensitive **:** ANTIPATHETIC ⟨*allergic* to hard work⟩
al·ler·gist \'al-ər-jəst\ *n* **:** a specialist in allergy
al·ler·gy \'al-ər-jē\ *n, pl* **-gies 1 a :** altered bodily reactivity (as to antigens) **b :** exaggerated or abnormal reaction (as by sneezing, itching, or rashes) to substances, situations, or physical states that are harmless to most people **2 :** a feeling of dislike
al·le·vi·ate \ə-'lē-vē-,āt\ *vb* **:** to make easier to be endured **:** RELIEVE ⟨*alleviate* pain⟩ — **al·le·vi·a·tion** \-,lē-vē-'ā-shən\ *n*
[1]**al·ley** \'al-ē\ *n, pl* **al·leys 1 :** a garden or park walk bordered by trees or bushes **2 :** a place for bowling or skittles **3 :** a narrow street or passageway; *esp* **:** one giving access to the rear of buildings
al·ley·way \'al-ē-,wā\ *n* **:** ALLEY 3
All Fools' Day *n* **:** APRIL FOOLS' DAY
all fours *n pl* **:** all four legs of a four-legged animal or the two legs and two arms of a person
All·hal·lows \ȯl-'hal-ōz, -əz\ *n* **:** ALL SAINTS' DAY
al·li·ance \ə-'lī-ən(t)s\ *n* **1 :** the state of being allied **2 a :** a union between persons, families, or parties **b :** a union between nations for their mutual assistance and protection **3 :** a treaty of alliance
al·lied \ə-'līd, 'al-,īd\ *adj* **1 :** RELATED, CONNECTED ⟨chemistry and *allied* subjects⟩ **2 :** joined in alliance ⟨*allied* nations⟩
al·li·ga·tor \'al-ə-,gāt-ər\ *n* [from Spanish *el lagarto* "the lizard"] **1 :** either of two large short-legged reptiles resembling crocodiles but having a shorter and broader snout **2 :** leather made from alligator's hide
alligator gar *n* **:** a large freshwater gar of the central U.S. that grows to a length of 7 feet and weighs as much as 150 pounds

alligator
(up to 16 ft. long)

alligator pear *n* **:** AVOCADO
al·lit·er·a·tion \ə-,lit-ə-'rā-shən\ *n* **:** the repetition of a sound at the beginning of two or more neighboring words (as in *wild and woolly* or *a babbling brook*) — **al·lit·er·a·tive** \-'lit-ə-,rāt-iv\ *adj* — **al·lit·er·a·tive·ly** *adv*
al·lo·cate \'al-ə-,kāt\ *vb* **1 :** APPORTION, DISTRIBUTE ⟨*allocate* funds among charities⟩ **2 :** to set apart and designate **:** ASSIGN ⟨*allocate* materials for a project⟩ — **al·lo·ca·tion** \,al-ə-'kā-shən\ *n*
al·lot \ə-'lät\ *vb* **al·lot·ted**; **al·lot·ting :** ASSIGN, ALLOCATE ⟨each in his *allotted* place⟩
al·lot·ment \ə-'lät-mənt\ *n* **1 :** the act of allotting **2 :** something allotted
al·lot·ro·py \ə-'lä-trə-pē\ *n* **:** the existence of a chemical element in two or more different forms ⟨diamond and graphite show the *allotropy* of carbon⟩ — **al·lo·trope** \'al-ə-,trōp\ *n* — **al·lo·trop·ic** \,al-ə-'träp-ik\ *adj*
all out *adv* **:** with maximum effort
all–out \'ȯl-'aůt\ *adj* **:** made with maximum effort **:** EXTREME
all over *adv* **:** EVERYWHERE
all·over \'ȯl-,ō-vər\ *adj* **:** covering the whole surface of something
al·low \ə-'laů\ *vb* **1 a :** to assign as a share or suitable amount (as of time or money) **b :** to allot as a deduction or an addition ⟨*allow* a gallon for leakage⟩ **2 :** ADMIT, CONCEDE ⟨*allowed* that the situation was serious⟩ **3 :** PERMIT ⟨gaps *allow* passage⟩ ⟨*allow* smoking⟩ **4 :** to make allowance ⟨*allow* for growth⟩ — **al·low·a·ble** \ə-'laů-ə-bəl\ *adj*
al·low·ance \ə-'laů-ən(t)s\ *n* **1 a :** a share or portion allotted or granted **b :** a sum granted ⟨gets a

weekly *allowance*〉 〈*allowance* for expenses〉 **c** : a reduction from a list price or stated price 〈a trade-in *allowance*〉 **2** : an allowed difference between mating parts of a machine **3** : the act of allowing : PERMISSION **4** : the taking into account of things that may be partial excuses 〈make *allowances* for his age〉

[1]**al·loy** \'al-ˌȯi, ə-'lȯi\ *n* **1** : a substance composed of two or more metals or of a metal and a nonmetal united usu. by being melted together **2** : a metal mixed with a more valuable metal to give a desired quality (as durability)

[2]**al·loy** \ə-'lȯi, 'al-ˌȯi\ *vb* **1** : to reduce the purity of by mixing with a less valuable metal **2** : to mix so as to form an alloy **3** : to debase by admixture

[1]**all right** *adv* **1** : SATISFACTORILY 〈does *all right* in school〉 **2** : YES 〈*all right*, I'll come〉 **3** : beyond doubt : CERTAINLY 〈that's him *all right*〉

[2]**all right** *adj* **1** : SATISFACTORY, CORRECT **2** : SAFE, WELL

all–round \'ȯl-'raund\ *var of* ALL-AROUND

All Saints' Day *n* : November 1 observed as a church festival in honor of the saints

All Souls' Day *n* : November 2 observed in some churches as a day of prayer for the souls in purgatory

all·spice \'ȯl-ˌspīs\ *n* **1** : the berry of a West Indian tree related to the myrtle **2** : a mildly pungent and aromatic spice prepared from the allspice

al·lude \ə-'lüd\ *vb* : to make indirect reference 〈*alluding* to a recent scandal〉 — **al·lu·sion** \-'lü-zhən\ *n* — **al·lu·sive** \-'lü-siv, -ziv\ *adj* — **al·lu·sive·ly** *adv* — **al·lu·sive·ness** *n*

al·lure \ə-'lu̇(ə)r\ *n* : ATTRACTION, CHARM — **allure** *vb* — **al·lure·ment** \-mənt\ *n*

al·lu·vi·al \ə-'lü-vē-əl\ *adj* : relating to, composed of, or found in alluvium

al·lu·vi·um \-vē-əm\ *n, pl* **-vi·ums** *or* **-via** \-vē-ə\ : soil material (as clay, silt, sand, or gravel) deposited by running water

[1]**al·ly** \ə-'lī, 'al-ˌī\ *vb* **al·lied**; **al·ly·ing** [from French *allier*, from Latin *alligare*, from *ad-* "to" and *ligare* "to bind", the source also of English *ligament* and *ligature*] : to form a connection between : UNITE; *esp* : to join in an alliance

[2]**al·ly** \'al-ˌī, ə-'lī\ *n, pl* **al·lies** **1** : a plant or animal linked to another by genetic or evolutionary relationship 〈ferns and their *allies*〉 **2** : one associated or united with another for some common purpose; *esp* : a nation that has joined an alliance

-al·ly \(ə-)lē\ *adv suffix* : [2]-LY 〈terrific*ally*〉

al·ma ma·ter \ˌal-mə-'mät-ər\ *n* [from Latin, meaning "a foster mother", from *almus* "nourishing", from *alere* "to nourish", the source of English *alimentary* and *alimony*] : a school, college, or university that one has attended

al·ma·nac \'ȯl-mə-ˌnak, 'al-\ *n* : a publication containing astronomical and meteorological data arranged according to the days, weeks, and months of the year and often including a miscellany of other information

al·man·dine \'al-mən-ˌdēn\ *n* : ALMANDITE

al·man·dite \-ˌdīt\ *n* : a deep red garnet containing iron and aluminum

al·mighty \ȯl-'mīt-ē\ *adj, often cap* : having unlimited power 〈*Almighty* God〉

Almighty *n* : [2]GOD — used with *the*

al·mond \'äm-ənd, 'am-; 'al-mənd\ *n* : a small tree having flowers like those of a peach tree; *also* : the edible kernel of its fruit used as a nut

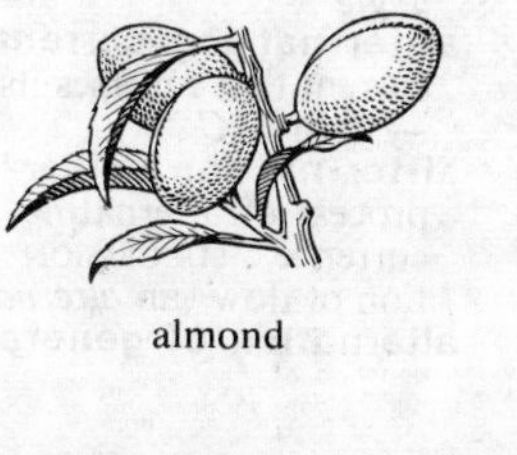
almond

al·most \'ȯl-ˌmōst, ȯl-'\ *adv* : only a little less than : NEARLY

alms \'ämz, 'älmz\ *n, pl* **alms** [from Old English *ælmesse*, from Greek *eleēmosynē* meaning first "mercy", and then, among Christians, "alms", regarded as an expression of the Christian virtue of charity; from the Greek verb *eleein* "to have mercy", heard in the ritual appeal *kyrie eleison* "Lord have mercy"] : something and esp. money given to help the poor : CHARITY — **alms·giv·er** \-ˌgiv-ər\ *n* — **alms·giv·ing** \-ˌgiv-iŋ\ *n*

alms·house \-ˌhau̇s\ *n* : POORHOUSE

al·ni·co \'al-ni-ˌkō\ *n* : a powerful permanent-magnet alloy containing iron, nickel, aluminum, and one or more of the elements cobalt, copper, and titanium

al·oe \'al-ō\ *n* : any of a large genus of chiefly southern African plants related to lilies and having spikes of often showy flowers; *also* : the dried bitter juice of the leaves of an aloe used as a purgative and tonic — usu. used in pl.

aloft \ə-'lȯft\ *adv or adj* **1** : in the air; *esp* : in flight **2** : at, on, or to the higher rigging

alo·ha \ə-'lō-ə, ä-'lō-ˌhä\ *interj* — used to express greeting or farewell

[1]**alone** \ə-'lōn\ *adj* **1** : separated from others : ISOLATED **2** : exclusive of anyone or anything else

[2]**alone** *adv* **1** : SOLELY, EXCLUSIVELY 〈the proof rests on that statement *alone*〉 **2** : without company, aid, or support 〈did it *alone*〉

[1]**along** \ə-'lȯŋ\ *prep* **1** : lengthwise of : parallel with the length of 〈walk *along* the beach〉 〈lined up *along* the wall〉 **2** : at a point on 〈stopped *along* the way〉

[2]**along** *adv* **1** : FORWARD, ON 〈move *along*〉 **2** : as a companion or associate 〈brought his wife *along*〉 **3** : throughout the time 〈knew the truth all *along*〉 **4** : at or on hand 〈had his gun *along*〉

along·shore \-ˌshō(ə)r, -ˌshȯ(ə)r\ *adv or adj* : along the shore or coast

[1]**along·side** \-ˌsīd\ *adv* : along or close at the side : in parallel position

[2]**alongside** *prep* : side by side with; *esp* : parallel to

[1]**aloof** \ə-'lüf\ *adv* : at a distance : out of involvement 〈stood *aloof* from their quarrels〉

[2]**aloof** *adj* : removed or distant in interest or feeling : RESERVED 〈a shy, *aloof* manner〉 — **aloof·ly** *adv* — **aloof·ness** *n*

aloud \ə-'lau̇d\ *adv* : so as to be clearly heard

alp \'alp\ *n* : a high rugged mountain

al·paca \al-'pak-ə\ *n* **1** : a mammal with fine long woolly hair domesticated in Peru and related to the llama **2** : wool of the alpaca or a cloth made of it; *also* : a rayon or cotton imitation of this cloth

alpaca
(3 ft. 8 in. at shoulder)

al·pen·stock \'al-pən-ˌstäk\ *n* : a long iron-pointed staff used in mountain climbing

al·pha \'al-fə\ *n* **1** : the 1st letter of the Greek alphabet — Α or α **2** : something first : BEGINNING

al·pha·bet \'al-fə-ˌbet, -bət\ *n* [from Greek *alphabētos*, from *alpha* and *bēta*, the names of the first two letters of the Greek alphabet, borrowed from their names in the unknown Semitic alphabet from which the Greek alphabet was derived, preserved also in the names of the corresponding letters *aleph* and *beth* of the Hebrew alphabet, derived from the same source] **1 :** the letters of a language arranged in their customary order **2 :** a system of signs or signals that serve as equivalents for letters

ALPHABET TABLE

Showing the letters of three non-Roman alphabets and the transliterations used in the etymologies

HEBREW[1,3]			GREEK[4]			RUSSIAN	
א	aleph	' [2]	Α α	alpha	a	А а	a
ב	beth	b, bh	Β β	beta	b	Б б	b
ג	gimel	g, gh	Γ γ	gamma	g, n	В в	v
ד	daleth	d, dh	Δ δ	delta	d	Г г	g
ה	he	h	Ε ε	epsilon	e	Д д	d
ו	waw	w	Ζ ζ	zeta	z	Е е	e
ז	zayin	z	Η η	eta	ē	Ж ж	zh
ח	heth	ḥ	Θ θ	theta	th	З з	z
ט	teth	ṭ	Ι ι	iota	i	И и Й й	i, ĭ
י	yod	y	Κ κ	kappa	k	К к	k
כ ך	kaph	k, kh	Λ λ	lambda	l	Л л	l
ל	lamed	l	Μ μ	mu	m	М м	m
מ ם	mem	m	Ν ν	nu	n	Н н	n
נ ן	nun	n	Ξ ξ	xi	x	О о	o
ס	samekh	s	Ο ο	omicron	o	П п	p
ע	ayin	ʻ	Π π	pi	p	Р р	r
פ ף	pe	p, ph	Ρ ρ	rho	r, rh	С с	s
צ ץ	sadhe	ṣ	Σ σ ς	sigma	s	Т т	t
ק	qoph	q	Τ τ	tau	t	У у	u
ר	resh	r	Υ υ	upsilon	y, u	Ф ф	f
שׂ	sin	ś	Φ φ	phi	ph	Х х	kh
שׁ	shin	sh	Χ χ	chi	ch	Ц ц	ts
ת	taw	t, th	Ψ ψ	psi	ps	Ч ч	ch
			Ω ω	omega	ō	Ш ш	sh
						Щ щ	shch
						Ъ ъ[5]	"
						Ы ы	y
						Ь ь[5]	'
						Э э	e
						Ю ю	yu
						Я я	ya

[1]Where two forms of a letter are given, the one at the right is the form used at the end of a word.
[2]Not represented in transliteration when initial.
[3]Hebrew is written from right to left. The Hebrew letters are all primarily consonants; a few of them are also used to represent certain vowels, but full writing of vowels in Hebrew, when given at all, is by means of a system of dots or strokes adjacent to the consonantal characters.
[4]See ALPHA, BETA, GAMMA, etc., in the vocabulary. The letter gamma is transliterated *n* before gamma, kappa, xi, and chi; the letter upsilon is transliterated *u* only as the final element in diphthongs.
[5]This sign represents a silent letter that affects the quality of the immediately preceding consonant.

ə abut	ər further	a back	ā bake	
ä cot, cart	aů out	ch chin	e less	ē easy
g gift	i trip	ī life	j joke	ŋ sing	ō flow
ȯ flaw	ȯi coin	th thin	th this	ü loot
ů foot	y yet	yü few	yů furious	zh vision

al·pha·bet·ic \ˌal-fə-ˈbet-ik\ *adj* **:** arranged in the order of the letters of the alphabet — **al·pha·bet·i·cal** \-ˈbet-i-kəl\ *adj* — **al·pha·bet·i·cal·ly** \-i-k(ə-)lē\ *adv*

al·pha·bet·ize \ˈal-fə-bə-ˌtīz\ *vb* **:** to arrange in alphabetic order — **al·pha·bet·i·za·tion** \ˌal-fə-ˌbet-ə-ˈzā-shən\ *n*

alpha particle *n* **:** a positively charged particle that is identical with the nucleus of a helium atom, consists of 2 protons and 2 neutrons, and is ejected at high speed in various radioactive transformations

alpha ray *n* **1 :** an alpha particle moving at high speed **2 :** a stream of alpha particles — called also *alpha radiation*

al·pine \ˈal-ˌpīn\ *adj, often cap* **1 :** relating to or resembling mountains and esp. the Alps **2 :** of, relating to, or growing on upland slopes above timberline

al·ready \ȯl-ˈred-ē, ˈȯl-ˌ\ *adv* **:** before a time **:** PREVIOUSLY ⟨when the firemen arrived the fire was *already* out⟩

al·right \ȯl-ˈrīt\ *adv or adj* **:** all right

Al·sa·tian \al-ˈsā-shən\ *n* **:** GERMAN SHEPHERD

al·sike clover \ˌal-ˌsak-, -ˌsīk-\ *n* **:** a European perennial clover widely grown as a forage plant

al·so \ˈȯl-sō\ *adv* **1 :** LIKEWISE **2 :** in addition **:** TOO

al·so–ran \-ˌran\ *n* **1 :** a horse or dog that finishes out of the money in a race **2 :** a contestant that does not win

alt *abbr* **1** alternate **2** altitude

Alta *abbr* Alberta

al·tar \ˈȯl-tər\ *n* **1 :** a raised place on which sacrifices are offered in worship **2 :** a table used in consecrating the eucharistic elements or as a center of worship

al·ter \ˈȯl-tər\ *vb* **1 :** to change partly but usu. not completely ⟨*alter* a dress⟩ ⟨my opinion has never *altered*⟩ **2 :** CASTRATE, SPAY — **al·ter·a·ble** \ˈȯl-tə-rə-bəl\ *adj*

al·ter·ation \ˌȯl-tə-ˈrā-shən\ *n* **1 a :** the act or process of altering **b :** the state of being altered **2 :** the result of altering **:** MODIFICATION

al·ter·ca·tion \ˌȯl-tər-ˈkā-shən\ *n* **:** a noisy or angry dispute **:** WRANGLE

¹al·ter·nate \ˈȯl-tər-nət, ˈal-\ *adj* **1 :** occurring or succeeding by turns ⟨*alternate* sunshine and rain⟩ **2 a :** occurring first on one side and then on the other at different levels along an axis ⟨leaves *alternate*⟩ **b :** arranged one above, beside, or next to another in regular sequence ⟨*alternate* layers of cake and filling⟩ **3 :** every other **:** every second ⟨delivery on *alternate* days⟩ **4 :** ALTERNATIVE, SUBSTITUTE — **al·ter·nate·ly** *adv*

²al·ter·nate \-ˌnāt\ *vb* **1 :** to do, occur, or act by turns **2 :** to cause to alternate ***syn*** see ROTATE

³al·ter·nate \-nət\ *n* **:** a person named to take the place of another **:** SUBSTITUTE

alternate angle *n* **1 :** one of a pair of angles on opposite sides of a transversal at its intersections with two other lines and within the two intersected lines — called also *alternate interior angle* **2 :** one of a pair of angles on opposite sides of a transversal at its intersections with two other lines and outside the two intersected lines — called also *alternate exterior angle*

al·ter·nat·ing current \-ˌnāt-iŋ-\ *n* **:** an electric current that reverses its direction at regular intervals — abbr. *AC*

al·ter·na·tion \ˌȯl-tər-ˈnā-shən, ˌal-\ *n* **1 :** the act or process of alternating **2 :** alternate position or occurrence **:** SUCCESSION **3 :** regular reversal in direction of flow ⟨an *alternation* of an electric current⟩

alternation of generations : the alternate occur-

A

rence of two or more forms and esp. of a sexual and an asexual generation in the life cycle of a plant or animal

¹**al·ter·na·tive** \ȯl-ˈtər-nət-iv, al-\ *adj* **1** : offering or expressing a choice ⟨*alternative* plans⟩ **2** : ALTERNATE — **al·ter·na·tive·ly** *adv* — **al·ter·na·tive·ness** *n*

²**alternative** *n* **1** : a chance to choose between two things ⟨the *alternative* of going by bus or car⟩ **2** : one of the things between which a choice is to be made

al·ter·na·tor \ˈȯl-tər-ˌnāt-ər, ˈal-\ *n* : an electric generator for producing alternating current

alt·horn \ˈalt-ˌhȯrn\ *n* : an alto horn often used in bands in place of the French horn

al·though *also* **al·tho** \ȯl-ˈt͟hō\ *conj* : in spite of the fact that : THOUGH

al·tim·e·ter \al-ˈtim-ət-ər, ˈal-tə-ˌmēt-ər\ *n* : an instrument for measuring altitude; *esp* : an aneroid barometer that registers changes in atmospheric pressure accompanying changes in altitude

al·ti·tude \ˈal-tə-ˌt(y)üd\ *n* **1 a** : the angular height of a celestial object above the horizon **b** : the vertical distance of an object above a given level (as sea level) **c** : the perpendicular distance in a geometric figure from the vertex to the base, from the vertex of an angle to the side opposite, or from the base to a parallel side or face **2** : an elevated region : EMINENCE — usu. used in pl. ***syn*** see HEIGHT

al·to \ˈal-tō\ *n, pl* **altos** **1 a** : CONTRALTO **b** : the second highest of the four voice parts of a mixed chorus **2** : the second highest member of a family of musical instruments; *esp* : ALTHORN

al·to·cu·mu·lus \ˌal-tō-ˈkyü-myə-ləs\ *n* : a fleecy cloud formation consisting of large whitish globular cloudlets with shaded portions

al·to·geth·er \ˌȯl-tə-ˈget͟h-ər\ *adv* **1** : WHOLLY, THOROUGHLY **2** : on the whole

al·to·stra·tus \ˌal-tō-ˈstrāt-əs, -ˈstrat-\ *n* : a cloud formation similar to cirrostratus but darker and at a lower level

al·tru·ism \ˈal-trü-ˌiz-əm\ *n* : unselfish interest in the welfare of others — **al·tru·ist** \-trü-əst\ *n* — **al·tru·is·tic** \ˌal-trü-ˈis-tik\ *adj* — **al·tru·is·ti·cal·ly** \-ˈis-ti-k(ə-)lē\ *adv*

al·um \ˈal-əm\ *n* **1** : either of two colorless crystalline compounds containing aluminum that have a sweetish-sourish taste and a puckering effect on the mouth and are used in medicine (as to check local sweating or to stop bleeding) **2** : an aluminum compound made from bauxite and used in paper manufacture, dyeing, and sewage treatment

alu·mi·na \ə-ˈlü-mə-nə\ *n* : the oxide of aluminum that occurs native as corundum and in bauxite and is used as a source of aluminum, as an abrasive, and as an absorbent

al·u·min·i·um \ˌal-yə-ˈmin-ē-əm\ *n, chiefly Brit* : ALUMINUM

alu·mi·nize \ə-ˈlü-mə-ˌnīz\ *vb* : to treat or coat with aluminum

alu·mi·num \ə-ˈlü-mə-nəm\ *n* : a silver-white malleable light element with good electrical and thermal conductivity and resistance to oxidation that is the most abundant metal in the earth's crust — see ELEMENT table

aluminum oxide *n* : ALUMINA

alum·na \ə-ˈləm-nə\ *n, pl* **-nae** \-(ˌ)nē\ : a girl or woman who has attended or graduated from a school, college, or university

alum·nus \ə-ˈləm-nəs\ *n, pl* **-ni** \-ˌnī\ [from Latin "foster son", from *alere* "to nourish"; compare ALMA MATER] : a graduate or former pupil of a school, college, or university

al·ve·o·lar \al-ˈvē-ə-lər\ *adj* : of, relating to, resembling, or having alveoli

al·ve·o·lus \al-ˈvē-ə-ləs\ *n, pl* **-li** \-ˌlī, -(ˌ)lē\ : a small cavity or pit; *esp* : an air cell of the lungs

al·ways \ˈȯl-wēz, -wəz, -ˌwāz\ *adv* **1** : at all times : INVARIABLY **2** : FOREVER, PERPETUALLY

aly *abbr* alley

am *pres 1st sing of* BE

a.m. *abbr* ante meridiem

Am *abbr* **1** America **2** American

AM *abbr* **1** amplitude modulation **2** master of arts

amain \ə-ˈmān\ *adv* **1** : with all one's might **2 a** : at full speed **b** : in great haste

amal·gam \ə-ˈmal-gəm\ *n* **1** : an alloy of mercury with some other metal or metals that is used esp. for tooth filling **2** : a combination or mixture of different elements

amal·gam·ate \ə-ˈmal-gə-ˌmāt\ *vb* **1** : to unite in an amalgam **2** : to combine into a single body

amal·gam·a·tion \ə-ˌmal-gə-ˈmā-shən\ *n* **1 a** : the act or process of amalgamating ⟨made by the *amalgamation* of mercury with silver⟩ **b** : the state of being amalgamated **2** : the result of amalgamating; *esp* : a combination of different elements (as business corporations) into a single body

am·a·ni·ta \ˌam-ə-ˈnīt-ə, -ˈnēt-\ *n* : any of various mostly poisonous white-spored fungi with a bulbous sac about the base of the stem

aman·u·en·sis \ə-ˌman-yə-ˈwen(t)-səs\ *n, pl* **aman·u·en·ses** \-ˈwen(t)-sēz\ : a person employed to write from dictation or to copy manuscript: SECRETARY

am·a·ranth \ˈam-ə-ˌran(t)th\ *n* **1** *archaic* : an imaginary flower that never fades **2** : any of a large genus of coarse herbs having alternate leaves and small flowers and sometimes cultivated for color

am·a·ran·thine \ˌam-ə-ˈran(t)-thən, -ˈran-ˌthīn\ *adj* **1** : of the color of an amaranth **2** : UNDYING

am·a·ryl·lis \ˌam-ə-ˈril-əs\ *n* : any of various plants of a group related to the lilies; *esp* : any of several African bulbous herbs grown for their clusters of large showy flowers

amass \ə-ˈmas\ *vb* : to collect into a mass : ACCUMULATE — **amass·er** *n*

am·a·teur \ˈam-ə-ˌtər, -ət-ər, -ə-ˌt(y)u̇(ə)r\ *n* [from French, "lover (of something)", "devotee", from Latin *amator* "lover", from *amare* "to love"] **1** : a person who takes part in sports or pursuits for pleasure and not for pay **2** : a person who engages in something without experience or competence ⟨mistakes made only by an *amateur*⟩ — **amateur** *adj* — **am·a·teur·ish** \ˌam-ə-ˈtər-ish, -ˈt(y)u̇(ə)r-ish\ *adj* — **am·a·teur·ish·ly** *adv* — **am·a·teur·ish·ness** *n*

am·a·to·ry \ˈam-ə-ˌtōr-ē, -ˌtȯr-\ *adj* : of, relating to, or expressing sexual love

amaze \ə-ˈmāz\ *vb* : to surprise or astonish greatly : fill with wonder : ASTOUND — **amaz·ing·ly** \-ˈmā-zing-lē\ *adv*

amaze·ment \ə-ˈmāz-mənt\ *n* : great surprise or astonishment

am·a·zon \ˈam-ə-ˌzän, -ə-zən\ *n* **1** *cap* : a member of a race of female warriors of ancient Greek mythology **2** : a tall strong masculine woman

Am·a·zo·ni·an \ˌam-ə-ˈzō-nē-ən, -ˈzō-nyən\ *adj* **1** : of or resembling an Amazon : WARLIKE **2** : of or relating to the Amazon river or its valley

amb *abbr* ambassador

am·bas·sa·dor \am-ˈbas-əd-ər\ *n* **1** : an official envoy; *esp* : a diplomatic agent of the highest rank who is the resident representative of his own government or is appointed for a special temporary assignment **2 :** an authorized representative or messenger — **am·bas·sa·do·ri·al** \(,)am-,bas-ə-'dōr-ē-əl, -'dȯr-\ *adj* — **am·bas·sa·dor·ship** \am-'bas-əd-ər-,ship\ *n*

am·ber \'am-bər\ *n* **1 :** a hard yellowish translucent resin from trees long dead that takes a fine polish and is used mostly for jewelry **2 :** a dark orange yellow — **amber** *adj*

am·ber·gris \'am-bər-,gris, -,grēs\ *n* **:** a waxy substance from the sperm whale used in the manufacture of perfumes

am·bi·dex·trous \,am-bi-'dek-strəs\ *adj* **:** using both hands with equal ease — **am·bi·dex·trous·ly** *adv*

am·bi·ent \'am-bē-ənt\ *adj* **:** surrounding on all sides **:** ENCOMPASSING

am·bi·gu·i·ty \,am-bə-'gyü-ət-ē\ *n, pl* **-ties** **1 :** uncertainty or confusion of meaning (as of a word or phrase) **2 :** an ambiguous word or passage

am·big·u·ous \am-'big-yə-wəs\ *adj* **:** not clear in meaning because able to be understood in more than one way **:** EQUIVOCAL — **am·big·u·ous·ly** *adv* — **am·big·u·ous·ness** *n*

am·bi·tion \am-'bish-ən\ *n* [from Latin *ambition-*, stem of *ambitio* "campaign for votes", literally "going around", from "*ambire*" to go around, from *ambi-* "around" and *ire* "to go"] **1 a :** an ardent desire for status, fame, or power **b :** desire to achieve a particular end **:** ASPIRATION **2 :** the object of ambition

am·bi·tious \am-'bish-əs\ *adj* **1 :** stirred by or possessing ambition ⟨*ambitious* to be captain of the team⟩ **2 :** showing ambition ⟨an *ambitious* plan⟩ — **am·bi·tious·ly** *adv*

amble *n* **1 :** an easy gait of a horse in which the legs on the same side of the body move together **2 :** a gentle easy gait — **amble** *vb* — **am·bler** \-b(ə-)lər\ *n*

am·bro·sia \am-'brō-zh(ē-)ə\ *n* **1 :** the food of the Greek and Roman gods **2 :** something extremely pleasing to taste or smell — **am·bro·sial** \-zh(ē-)əl\ *adj*

am·bu·lance \'am-byə-lən(t)s\ *n* **:** a vehicle equipped for transporting the injured or the sick

am·bu·la·to·ry \'am-byə-lə-,tōr-ē, -,tȯr-\ *adj* **1 :** of or relating to walking **2 :** able to walk about ⟨*ambulatory* patients in a hospital⟩

am·bus·cade \'am-bə-,skād\ *n* **:** AMBUSH — **ambuscade** *vb* — **am·bus·cad·er** *n*

[1]**am·bush** \'am-,bu̇sh\ *vb* **1 :** to station in ambush **2 :** to attack from an ambush **:** WAYLAY

[2]**ambush** *n* **:** a trap in which concealed persons lie in wait to attack by surprise

amdt *abbr* amendment

ame·ba \ə-'mē-bə\ *n, pl* **amebas** \-bəz\ *or* **amebae** \-(,)bē\ **:** any of numerous protozoans that have lobed and separate pseudopodia and no permanent cell organs or supporting structures and are widespread in fresh and salt water and in moist soils — **ame·bic** \-bik\ *adj*

am·e·bi·a·sis \,am-i-'bī-ə-səs\ *n, pl* **-bi·a·ses** \-'bī-ə-,sēz\ **:** infection with or disease caused by amebas

amebic dysentery *n* **:** acute intestinal amebiasis of man marked by dysentery, griping pain, and injury to the intestinal wall

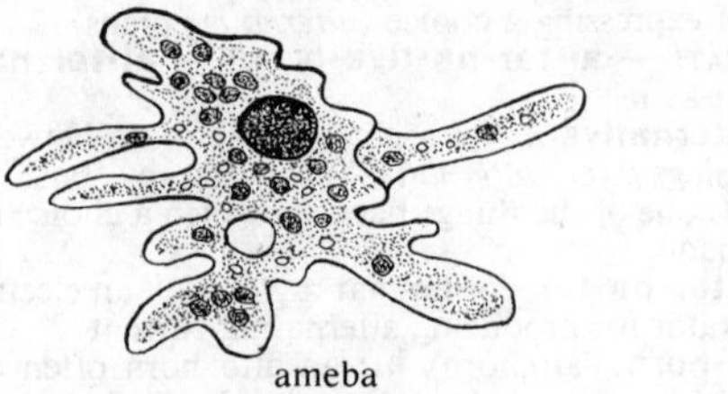
ameba
(magnified 150 times)

ame·boid \ə-'mē-,bȯid\ *adj* **:** resembling an ameba esp. in moving or changing in shape by means of protoplasmic flow

ame·lio·rate \ə-'mēl-yə-,rāt\ *vb* **:** to make or grow better or more tolerable — **ame·lio·ra·tion** \-,mēl-yə-'rā-shən\ *n* — **ame·lio·ra·tive** \-'mēl-yə-,rāt-iv\ *adj*

amen \(')ā-'men, (')ä-; *in singing*, 'ä-\ *interj* — used to express solemn agreement or hearty approval

ame·na·ble \ə-'mē-nə-bəl, -'men-ə-\ *adj* **1 :** liable to be called to account ⟨*amenable* to the law⟩ **2 :** easily influenced or managed **:** RESPONSIVE ⟨*amenable* to discipline⟩ — **ame·na·bil·i·ty** \-,mē-nə-'bil-ət-ē, -,men-ə-\ *n* — **ame·na·bly** \-'mē-nə-blē, -'men-ə-\ *adv*

amend \ə-'mend\ *vb* **1 :** to change for the better **:** IMPROVE **2 :** ALTER; *esp* **:** to alter formally by modification, deletion, or addition ⟨*amend* a legislative bill⟩ *syn* see CORRECT — **amend·a·ble** \-'men-də-bəl\ *adj* — **amend·er** *n*

amend·ment \ə-'men(d)-mənt\ *n* **1 :** the act or process of amending esp. for the better **2 :** a modification, addition, or deletion made or proposed ⟨a constitutional *amendment*⟩

amends \ə-'men(d)z\ *n sing or pl* **:** something done or given by a person to make up for a loss or injury he has caused ⟨make *amends* for an unkindness⟩

amen·i·ty \ə-'men-ət-ē, -'mē-nət-\ *n, pl* **-ties** **1 :** the quality of being pleasant or agreeable **2 :** something (as a social gesture) that makes life pleasant and agreeable — usu. used in pl.

am·ent \'am-ənt, 'ā-mənt\ *n* **:** a flower cluster in which flowers all of one sex and without petals grow in close circular rows on a slender stalk (as in the alder, willow, birch, and poplar) **:** CATKIN

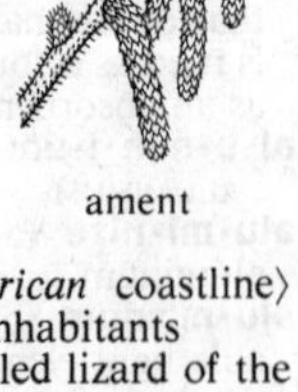
ament

Amer *abbr* **1** America **2** American

[1]**Amer·i·can** \ə-'mer-ə-kən\ *n* **:** a native or inhabitant of No. America or So. America; *esp* **:** a citizen of the U.S.

[2]**American** *adj* **1 :** of or relating to America or its inhabitants ⟨*American* coastline⟩ **2 :** of or relating to the U.S. or its inhabitants

American chameleon *n* **:** a long-tailed lizard of the southeastern U.S. that can change its color

American elm *n* **:** a large ornamental tree common in the eastern U.S.

American Indian *n* **:** INDIAN 2a

Amer·i·can·ism \ə-'mer-ə-kə-,niz-əm\ *n* **1 :** a characteristic feature of English as used in the U.S. **2 :** attachment or loyalty to the traditions, interests, or ideals of the U.S. **3 :** a custom or trait peculiar to Americans

amer·i·can·ize \-kə-,nīz\ *vb, often cap* **:** to make or

ə abut	ər further	a back	ā bake	
ä cot, cart	au̇ out	ch chin	e less	ē easy
g gift	i trip	ī life	j joke	ng sing	ō flow
ȯ flaw	ȯi coin	th thin	t͟h this	ü loot
u̇ foot	y yet	yü few	yu̇ furious	zh vision

become American (as in customs, habits, dress, or speech) — **amer·i·can·i·za·tion** \ə-ˌmer-ə-kə-nə-ˈzā-shən\ *n, often cap*

American plan *n* : a hotel rate whereby guests are charged a fixed sum for room and meals combined

American Standard Version *n* : an American revision of the Authorized Version of the Bible published in 1901 — called also *American Revised Version*

am·er·i·ci·um \ˌam-ə-ˈris(h)-ē-əm\ *n* : a radioactive metallic element produced by bombardment of uranium with high-energy helium nuclei — see ELEMENT table

AmerInd *abbr* American Indian

Am·er·in·di·an \ˌam-ə-ˈrin-dē-ən\ *adj* : of, relating to, or characteristic of an American Indian or Eskimo — **Am·er·ind** \ˈam-ə-ˌrind\ *n*

am·e·thyst \ˈam-ə-thəst\ *n* **1** : a clear purple or bluish violet variety of crystallized quartz used as a jeweler's stone **2** : a moderate purple

ami·a·ble \ˈā-mē-ə-bəl\ *adj* : generally agreeable : having a friendly, sociable, and congenial disposition — **ami·a·bil·i·ty** \ˌā-mē-ə-ˈbil-ət-ē\ *n* — **ami·a·ble·ness** \ˈā-mē-ə-bəl-nəs\ *n* — **ami·a·bly** \-blē\ *adv*

am·i·ca·ble \ˈam-i-kə-bəl\ *adj* : characterized by friendship and goodwill : PEACEABLE ⟨an *amicable* settlement of differences⟩ — **am·i·ca·bil·i·ty** \ˌam-i-kə-ˈbil-ət-ē\ *n* — **am·i·ca·bly** \ˈam-i-kə-blē\ *adv*

amicable number *n* : either of a pair of numbers (as 220 and 284) each of which is equal to the sum of all the exact divisors of the other

am·ice \ˈam-əs\ *n* : a white linen cloth worn about the neck and shoulders under other vestments by a priest at Mass

amid \ə-ˈmid\ *or* **amidst** \-ˈmidst\ *prep* : in or into the middle of : AMONG

amid·ships \ə-ˈmid-ˌships\ *adv* : in or near the middle of a ship

ami·no acid \ə-ˈmē-nō-\ *n* : any of numerous organic acids that include some which are the building blocks of proteins and are synthesized by living cells or are obtained in the diet

¹**amiss** \ə-ˈmis\ *adv* : WRONGLY

²**amiss** *adj* : WRONG, FAULTY, IMPROPER ⟨something is *amiss* here⟩

am·i·ty \ˈam-ət-ē\ *n, pl* **-ties** : FRIENDSHIP; *esp* : friendly relations between nations

am·me·ter \ˈam-ˌēt-ər\ *n* : an instrument for measuring electric current in amperes

am·mo·nia \ə-ˈmō-nyə\ *n* **[**from Latin *sal ammoniacus* "ammonium chloride," literally "salt of Ammon," named after the Egyptian god *Ammon* near whose temple the salt was produced**]** **1** : a colorless gas that is a compound of nitrogen and hydrogen, has a sharp smell and taste, is very soluble in water, can be easily liquefied by cold and pressure, is used in the manufacture of ice, fertilizers, and explosives, and is the chief nitrogenous waste product of many aquatic organisms **2** : a solution of ammonia in water — **am·mo·ni·a·cal** \ˌam-ə-ˈnī-ə-kəl\ *adj*

am·mo·nite \ˈam-ə-ˌnīt\ *n* : any of numerous flat spiral fossil shells of mollusks similar to the nautilus that are esp. abundant in the Mesozoic — **am·mo·nit·ic** \ˌam-ə-ˈnit-ik\ *adj*

am·mo·ni·um \ə-ˈmō-nē-əm\ *n* : an ion or radical derived from ammonia by combination with a hydrogen ion or atom and known in compounds (as ammonium chloride)

ammonium chloride *n* : a white crystalline volatile salt used in dry cells and as an expectorant

ammonium cy·a·nate \-ˈsī-ə-ˌnāt\ *n* : a white crystalline salt that changes into urea on standing or on heating in an aqueous solution

ammonium di·chro·mate \-dī-ˈkrō-ˌmāt\ *n* : an orange salt used esp. as a reagent and in making explosives

ammonium hydroxide *n* : a compound that is formed when ammonia dissolves in water and that exists only in solution

ammonium nitrate *n* : a colorless crystalline salt used in explosives and fertilizers

ammonium sulfate *n* : a colorless crystalline salt used chiefly as a fertilizer

am·mu·ni·tion \ˌam-yə-ˈnish-ən\ *n* **1** : something (as a bullet, shell, grenade, or bomb) that can be hurled at a target **2** : material that may be used in attack or defense

am·ne·sia \am-ˈnē-zhə\ *n* : severe loss of memory — **am·ne·si·ac** \-z(h)ē-ˌak\ *adj or n*

am·nes·ty \ˈam-nə-stē\ *n, pl* **-ties** : a general pardon granted by a ruler or government to a large group of persons guilty of a political offense (as treason or rebellion)

amoe·ba \ə-ˈmē-bə\, **amoe·bic**, **amoe·boid** *var of* AMEBA, AMEBIC, AMEBOID

amok \ə-ˈmək, -ˈmäk\ *adv* : in a murderously or violently frenzied state ⟨run *amok*⟩ — **amok** *adj*

among \ə-ˈməng\ *also* **amongst** \-ˈməng(k)st\ *prep* **1** : in or through the midst of ⟨*among* the crowd⟩ **2** : in company with ⟨living *among* artists⟩ **3** : through all or most of ⟨discontent *among* the poor⟩ **4** : in the class of ⟨wittiest *among* poets⟩ **5** : in shares to each of ⟨divided *among* the heirs⟩ **6** : through the joint action of ⟨quarrel *among* themselves⟩ ⟨made a fortune *among* themselves⟩

am·o·rous \ˈam-(ə-)rəs\ *adj* **1** : inclined to love : easily falling in love ⟨an *amorous* nature⟩ **2** : of, relating to, or caused by love ⟨an *amorous* glance⟩ — **am·o·rous·ly** *adv* — **am·o·rous·ness** *n*

amor·phous \ə-ˈmȯr-fəs\ *adj* **1** : having no determinate form : SHAPELESS **2** : UNCRYSTALLIZED — **amor·phous·ly** *adv* — **amor·phous·ness** *n*

¹**amount** \ə-ˈmau̇nt\ *vb* **1** : to add up ⟨the bill *amounted* to $10⟩ **2** : to be equivalent ⟨acts that *amount* to treason⟩

²**amount** *n* **1** : the total number or quantity : AGGREGATE **2** : a principal sum and the interest on it

amour \ə-ˈmu̇(ə)r, a-, ä-\ *n* : a love affair; *esp* : a secret love affair

amp *abbr* ampere

am·per·age \ˈam-pə-rij, -ˌpi(ə)r-ij\ *n* : the strength of a current of electricity expressed in amperes

am·pere \ˈam-ˌpi(ə)r\ *n* : a unit for measuring the strength of an electric current

am·per·sand \ˈam-pər-ˌsand\ *n* **[**from older *and per se and*, spoken form of the phrase *& per se and*, which followed *Z* in early lists of letters of the alphabet, and meant "(the character) & by itself (stands for) *and*"**]** : a character & standing for the word *and*

am·phet·amine \am-ˈfet-ə-ˌmēn, -mən\ *n* : a compound used esp. in the treatment of head colds and hay fever and as a stimulant of the central nervous system

am·phib·ia \am-ˈfib-ē-ə\ *n pl* : AMPHIBIANS

am·phib·i·an \-ē-ən\ *n* **1** : any organism that is able to live both on land and in water; *esp* : any of a class of cold-blooded vertebrate animals (as frogs and newts) intermediate in many respects between fishes and reptiles **2** : an airplane designed to take off from and land on either land or water **3** : a vehicle that operates on both land and water — **amphibian** *adj*

am·phib·i·ous \-ē-əs\ *adj* [from Greek *amphibios*, from *amphi-* "on both sides" and *bios* "life"] **1 :** able to live both on land and in water ⟨*amphibious* plants⟩ **2 a :** relating to or adapted for both land and water ⟨*amphibious* vehicles⟩ **b :** trained or organized for invasion from the sea; *also* : executed by amphibious forces ⟨*amphibious* assault⟩ — **am·phib·i·ous·ly** *adv* — **am·phib·i·ous·ness** *n*

am·phi·bole \'am(p)-fə-,bōl\ *n* : any of a group of white, gray, green, or black rock-forming minerals that contain calcium, magnesium, iron, aluminum, and sodium combined with silica

am·phi·ox·us \,am(p)-fē-'äk-səs\ *n, pl* **-oxi** \-'äk-,sī\ *or* **-ox·us·es** : LANCELET

am·phi·pod \'am(p)-fi-,päd\ *n* : any of a large group of crustaceans comprising the sand fleas and related forms — **amphipod** *adj*

am·phi·the·a·ter \'am(p)-fə-,thē-ət-ər\ *n* **1 :** a building with seats rising in curved rows around an open space on which games and plays take place **2 :** something (as a piece of level ground surrounded by hills) that resembles an amphitheater

am·ple \'am-pəl\ *adj* **1 :** generous in size, scope, or capacity : COPIOUS **2 :** enough to satisfy : ABUNDANT — **am·ple·ness** *n* — **am·ply** \-plē\ *adv*

am·pli·fi·ca·tion \,am-plə-fə-'kā-shən\ *n* **1 :** an act, example, or product of amplifying **2 a :** matter by which a statement is expanded **b :** an expanded statement

am·pli·fi·er \'am-plə-,fī(-ə)r\ *n* : one that amplifies; *esp* : a device usu. employing electron tubes or transistors to obtain amplification of voltage, current, or power

am·pli·fy \'am-plə-,fī\ *vb* **-fied; -fy·ing 1 :** ENLARGE; *esp* : to expand by clarifying details or illustration ⟨*amplify* a statement⟩ **2 :** to increase (voltage, current, or power) in magnitude or strength **3 :** to make louder ⟨*amplify* the voice by using a megaphone⟩

am·pli·tude \'am-plə-,t(y)üd\ *n* **1 :** the quality or state of being ample : FULLNESS **2 :** EXTENT, RANGE **3 a :** the extent of a vibratory movement (as of a pendulum) measured from the mean position to an extreme **b :** the up-and-down extent of the vibration of a wave (as of alternating current)

amplitude modulation *n* **1 :** modulation of the amplitude of a radio carrier wave in accordance with the strength of the signal **2 :** a broadcasting system using amplitude modulation — abbr. *AM* — **amplitude modulated** *adj*

am·pu·tate \'am-pyə-,tāt\ *vb* : to cut off; *esp* : to cut a limb from the body — **am·pu·ta·tion** \,am-pyə-'tā-shən\ *n*

am·pu·tee \,am-pyə-'tē\ *n* : one that has had a limb amputated

amt *abbr* amount

amuck \ə-'mək\ *var of* AMOK

am·u·let \'am-yə-lət\ *n* : a small object worn as a charm against evil

amuse \ə-'myüz\ *vb* **1 :** to occupy with something pleasant : DIVERT ⟨*amuse* a child with a toy⟩ **2 :** to please the sense of humor of ⟨his story *amused* everyone⟩ — **amus·ing·ly** \-'myü-zing-lē\ *adv*

amuse·ment \ə-'myüz-mənt\ *n* **1 :** the condition of being amused **2 :** pleasant diversion **3 :** something that amuses

am·y·lase \'am-ə-,lās\ *n* : an enzyme that accelerates the digestion of starch or glycogen

an \ən, (')an\ *indefinite article* : [2]A — in standard speech and writing used (1) before words beginning with a vowel letter and sound ⟨*an* oak⟩; (2) before *h*-initial words in which the *h* is always silent ⟨*an* honor⟩; (3) frequently before *h*-initial words which have in an initial unstressed syllable an \h\ sound often lost after the *an* ⟨*an* historian⟩

an- — see A-

[1]**-an** *or* **-ian** *also* **-ean** *n suffix* **1 :** one that belongs to ⟨Americ*an*⟩ ⟨Boston*ian*⟩ **2 :** one skilled in or specializing in ⟨diagnostic*ian*⟩

[2]**-an** *or* **-ian** *also* **-ean** *adj suffix* **1 :** of or belonging to ⟨Americ*an*⟩ ⟨Florid*ian*⟩ **2 :** characteristic of : resembling ⟨Mozart*ean*⟩

ana- *or* **an-** *prefix* : up : upward ⟨*ana*bolism⟩

anab·o·lism \ə-'nab-ə-,liz-əm\ *n* : the part of metabolism concerned with the building up of the substance of plants and animals — **an·a·bol·ic** \,an-ə-'bäl-ik\ *adj*

anach·ro·nism \ə-'nak-rə-,niz-əm\ *n* **1 :** the placing of persons, events, objects, or customs in times to which they do not belong ⟨the *anachronism* of describing Lincoln riding in a plane⟩ **2 :** a person or a thing out of place in the present — **anach·ro·nis·tic** \ə-,nak-rə-'nis-tik\ *adj* — **anach·ro·nis·ti·cal·ly** \-ti-k(ə-)lē\ *adv*

an·a·con·da \,an-ə-'kän-də\ *n* : a large So. American snake that crushes its prey in its coils; *also* : a large constricting snake

anae·mia \ə-'nē-mē-ə\ *var of* ANEMIA

an·aer·o·bic \,an-ə-'rō-bik; ,an-,a-(ə-)'rō-, -,e-(ə-)'rō-\ *adj* : living, active, or occurring in the absence of free oxygen — **an·aer·obe** \'an-ə-,rōb; (')an-'a(-ə)r-,ōb, -'e(-ə)r-\ *n* — **an·aer·o·bi·cal·ly** \,an-ə-'rō-bi-k(ə-)lē; ,an-,a-(ə-)'rō-, -,e-(ə-)'ro-\ *adv*

an·aes·the·sia \,an-əs-'thē-zhə\, **an·aes·thet·ic** *var of* ANESTHESIA, ANESTHETIC

an·a·gram \'an-ə-,gram\ *n* : a word or phrase made out of another by changing the order of the letters ⟨*rebate* is an *anagram* of *beater*⟩

anal \'ā-nəl\ *adj* : of, relating to, or situated near the anus — **anal·ly** \-nə-lē\ *adv*

anal fin *n* : an unpaired median fin located behind the vent of a fish

an·al·ge·sia \,an-əl-'jē-zhə\ *n* : insensibility to pain without loss of consciousness — **an·al·ge·sic** \-'jē-zik, -sik\ *adj or n*

analog computer *n* : a calculating machine that operates with numbers represented by directly measurable quantities (as voltages or resistances) — compare DIGITAL COMPUTER

anal·o·gous \ə-'nal-ə-gəs\ *adj* **1 :** showing analogy : SIMILAR **2 :** related by analogy — **anal·o·gous·ly** *adv* — **anal·o·gous·ness** *n*

an·a·logue *or* **an·a·log** \'an-ə-,lȯg\ *n* **1 :** something that is analogous to something else **2 :** an organ similar in function to an organ of another animal or plant but different in structure and origin

anal·o·gy \ə-'nal-ə-jē\ *n, pl* **-gies 1 :** resemblance in some particulars between things otherwise unlike : SIMILARITY **2 :** correspondence in function between anatomical parts of different structure and origin — **an·a·log·i·cal** \,an-ə-'läj-i-kəl\ *adj* — **an·a·log·i·cal·ly** \-k(ə-)lē\ *adv*

anal·y·sis \ə-'nal-ə-səs\ *n, pl* **anal·y·ses** \-'nal-ə-,sēz\ [from Greek, meaning "a breaking up into parts", from *analyein* "to break up", from *ana* "up" and *lyein* "to loosen"] **1 a :** an examination of a whole to discover its elements and their relations b : a statement of such an analysis **2** : an interpretation of the nature and significance of something ⟨*analysis* of the news⟩ **3** : the identification or separation of ingredients of a substance **4** : PSYCHOANALYSIS

an·a·lyst \'an-ə-ləst\ *n* **1** : a person who analyzes or who is skilled in analysis ⟨news *analyst*⟩ **2** : PSYCHOANALYST

an·a·lyt·ic \ˌan-ə-'lit-ik\ *adj* **1 a** : of or relating to analysis **b** : separating something into component parts or constituent elements **2** : skilled in or prone to using analysis ⟨a keenly *analytic* man⟩ — **an·a·lyt·i·cal** \-i-kəl\ *adj* — **an·a·lyt·i·cal·ly** \-k(ə-)lē\ *adv*

analytical balance *n* : a very precise balance used esp. for weighing quantitative analysis samples

an·a·lyze \'an-ə-ˌlīz\ *vb* : to make an analysis of; *esp* : to study or determine the nature and relationship of the parts of by analysis ⟨*analyze* a traffic pattern⟩ — **an·a·lyz·a·ble** \-ˌlī-zə-bəl\ *adj*

an·a·pest \'an-ə-ˌpest\ *n* : a metrical foot consisting of two unaccented syllables followed by one accented syllable (as in *the accused*) — **an·a·pes·tic** \ˌan-ə-'pes-tik\ *adj*

ana·phase \'an-ə-ˌfāz\ *n* : a stage of mitosis or meiosis in which the chromosomes move toward the poles of the spindle

an·ar·chic \a-'när-kik\ *adj* : of, relating to, or tending toward anarchy : LAWLESS — **an·ar·chi·cal** \-ki-kəl\ *adj* — **an·ar·chi·cal·ly** \-ki-k(ə-)lē\ *adv*

an·ar·chism \'an-ər-ˌkiz-əm\ *n* **1** : a political theory holding government to be unnecessary and advocating a society based on voluntary cooperation **2** : the advocacy or practice of anarchy

an·ar·chist \'an-ər-kəst\ *n* **1** : one who rebels against any authority, established order, or ruling power **2** : one who believes in, advocates, or promotes anarchism; *esp* : one who uses violent means to overthrow the established order — **anarchist** *or* **an·ar·chis·tic** \ˌan-ər-'kis-tik\ *adj*

an·ar·chy \'an-ər-kē\ *n* **1** : the condition of a society without a government **2** : a state of lawlessness, confusion, or disorder

anas·to·mose \ə-'nas-tə-ˌmōz, -ˌmōs\ *vb* : to connect or communicate by anastomosis

anas·to·mo·sis \ə-ˌnas-tə-'mō-səs\ *n, pl* **-mo·ses** \-'mō-ˌsēz\ : the union of parts or branches (as of streams or blood vessels) so as to intercommunicate; *also* : NETWORK, MESH

anat *abbr* anatomy

anath·e·ma \ə-'nath-ə-mə\ *n* **1 a** : a solemn curse pronounced by ecclesiastical authority and accompanied by excommunication **b** : a vigorous denunciation : CURSE **2** : a person or thing that is cursed or intensely disliked

anath·e·ma·tize \-ˌtīz\ *vb* : to pronounce an anathema upon : CURSE

anat·o·mize \ə-'nat-ə-ˌmīz\ *vb* **1** : to dissect so as to show or to examine the structure and use of the parts **2** : ANALYZE

anat·o·my \ə-'nat-ə-mē\ *n, pl* **-mies** **1** : a branch of knowledge that deals with the structure of organisms; *also* : a book on bodily structure **2** : structural makeup esp. of an organism or any of its parts — **an·a·tom·ic** \ˌan-ə-'täm-ik\ *or* **an·a·tom·i·cal** \-'täm-i-kəl\ *adj* — **an·a·tom·i·cal·ly** \-k(ə-)lē\ *adv* — **anat·o·mist** \ə-'nat-ə-məst\ *n*

anc *abbr* ancient

-ance \ən(t)s\ *n suffix* **1** : action or process ⟨further*ance*⟩ ⟨perform*ance*⟩ **2** : quality or state : instance of a quality or state ⟨protuber*ance*⟩ **3** : amount or degree ⟨conduct*ance*⟩

an·ces·tor \'an-ˌses-tər\ *n* [from Old French *ancestre*, from Latin *antecessor* "one who goes before", from *ante-* and *cess-*, past participle stem of *cedere* "to go"] **1** : one from whom an individual, group, or species is descended **2** : FORERUNNER, PROTOTYPE — **an·ces·tress** \-trəs\ *n*

an·ces·tral \an-'ses-trəl\ *adj* : of, relating to, or derived from an ancestor ⟨*ancestral* home⟩ ⟨*ancestral* portraits⟩ — **an·ces·tral·ly** \-trə-lē\ *adv*

an·ces·try \'an-ˌses-trē\ *n* **1** : line of descent : LINEAGE **2** : a series of ancestors

1an·chor \'ang-kər\ *n* **1** : a heavy iron or steel device attached to a boat or ship by a cable or chain and so made that when thrown overboard it digs into the earth and holds the boat or ship in place **2** : something that secures or steadies or that gives a feeling of stability ⟨the *anchor* of a bridge⟩ **3** : ANCHOR MAN 1

2anchor *vb* **an·chored**; **an·chor·ing** \-k(ə-)ring\ **1** : to hold in place by means of an anchor ⟨*anchor* a ship⟩ **2** : to fasten securely to a firm foundation ⟨*anchor* the cables of a bridge⟩ **3** : to drop anchor : become anchored ⟨the boat *anchored* in the harbor⟩

an·chor·age \'ang-k(ə-)rij\ *n* **1** : a place where boats may be anchored **2** : a secure hold to resist a strong pull **3** : a means of security : REFUGE

an·cho·rite \'ang-kə-ˌrīt\ *n* : HERMIT 1

anchor man *n* **1** : one who competes or is placed last **2** : a news broadcaster who coordinates the activities of other broadcasters (as at a political convention)

an·cho·vy \'an-ˌchō-vē, an-'\ *n, pl* **-vies** *or* **-vy** : any of numerous small fishes resembling herrings; *esp* : a common Mediterranean fish used esp. for sauces and relishes

1an·cient \'ān-shənt, -chənt; 'āng(k)-shənt\ *adj* **1** : having existed for many years ⟨*ancient* customs⟩ **2** : of or relating to a period of time long past; *esp* : of or relating to the period preceding the fall of Rome A.D. 476 **3 a** : AGED, VENERABLE **b** : OLD-FASHIONED, ANTIQUE — **an·cient·ness** *n*

2ancient *n* **1** : an aged person **2** *pl* : the civilized peoples of ancient times and esp. of Greece and Rome

an·cient·ly \-lē\ *adv* : in ancient times

-an·cy \ən-sē\ *n suffix, pl* **-ancies** : quality or state ⟨piqu*ancy*⟩

and \ən(d), (')an(d)\ *conj* **1** : added to ⟨2 *and* 2 make 4⟩ **2** : as well as ⟨you *and* I⟩ — used as a function word to join words or word groups of the same grammatical rank or function (as two nouns that are subjects of the same verb or two clauses modifying the same noun)

1an·dan·te \än-'dän-ˌtā, an-'dant-ē\ *adv or adj* : moderately slow — used as a direction in music

2andante *n* : a musical piece or movement in andante tempo

and·iron \'an-ˌdī(-ə)rn\ *n* : one of a pair of metal supports for firewood in a fireplace

an·dra·dite \an-'dräd-ˌīt\ *n* : a garnet ranging from yellow and green to brown and black and containing calcium and iron

an·ec·dote \'an-ik-ˌdōt\ *n* : a short narrative of an interesting, amusing, or biographical incident — **an·ec·dot·al** \ˌan-ik-'dōt-əl\ *adj* — **an·ec·dot·al·ly** \-ə-lē\ *adv*

ane·mia \ə-'nē-mē-ə\ *n* **1** : a condition in which the blood is deficient in red blood cells, in hemoglobin, or in total volume and which is usu. marked by pale skin, shortness of breath, and irregular heart action **2** : lack of vitality — **ane·mic** \-mik\ *adj*

an·e·mom·e·ter \ˌan-ə-ˈmäm-ət-ər\ *n* : an instrument for measuring the force or speed of the wind

anem·o·ne \ə-ˈnem-ə-nē\ *n* **1** : any of a large genus of herbs related to the buttercups that have showy flowers without petals but with conspicuous often colored sepals **2** : SEA ANEMONE

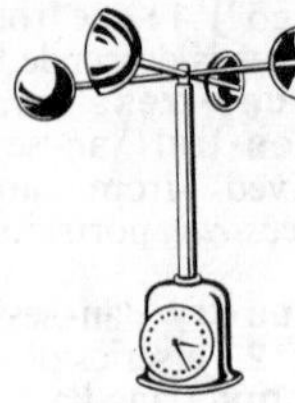

anemometer

an·er·oid barometer \ˌan-ə-ˌrȯid-\ *n* : an instrument in which the atmospheric pressure in bending a metallic surface is made to move a pointer

an·es·the·sia \ˌan-əs-ˈthē-zhə\ *n* : loss of bodily sensation with or without loss of consciousness

1**an·es·thet·ic** \ˌan-əs-ˈthet-ik\ *adj* : of, relating to, or capable of producing anesthesia — **an·es·thet·i·cal·ly** \-ˈthet-i-k(ə-)lē\ *adv*

2**anesthetic** *n* : a substance that produces either local or general anesthesia

anes·the·tist \ə-ˈnes-thət-əst\ *n* : one who administers anesthetics

anes·the·tize \ə-ˈnes-thə-ˌtīz\ *vb* : to make insensible to pain esp. by the use of an anesthetic

anew \ə-ˈn(y)ü\ *adv* **1** : over again : AFRESH ⟨begin *anew*⟩ **2** : in a new or different form

an·gel \ˈān-jəl\ *n* [from Greek *angelos*, literally "messenger"] **1** : a spiritual being serving God esp. as a messenger or as a guardian of men **2** : an attendant spirit **3** : MESSENGER, HARBINGER ⟨*angel* of death⟩ **4** : a person as pure, lovely, or good as an angel **5** : a financial backer of a theatrical venture or other enterprise — **an·gel·ic** \an-ˈjel-ik\ *or* **an·gel·i·cal** \-i-kəl\ *adj* — **an·gel·i·cal·ly** \-i-k(ə-)lē\ *adv*

an·gel·fish \ˈān-jəl-ˌfish\ *n* : any of several compressed bright-colored bony fishes of warm seas; *esp* : SCALARE

1**an·ger** \ˈang-gər\ *n* : a strong feeling of displeasure and usu. of antagonism

2**anger** *vb* **an·gered**; **an·ger·ing** \-g(ə-)ring\ : to make angry

an·gi·na \an-ˈjī-nə, ˈan-jə-nə\ *n* : a disorder marked by spasmodic attacks of intense pain; *esp* : ANGINA PECTORIS — **an·gi·nal** \-nəl\ *adj*

angina pec·to·ris \an-ˌjī-nə-ˈpek-t(ə-)rəs, ˌan-jə-nə-\ *n* : a heart disorder marked by brief recurrent attacks of intense chest pain

an·gio·sperm \ˈan-jē-ə-ˌspərm\ *n* : any of a class of vascular plants with the seeds in a closed ovary : FLOWERING PLANT — **an·gio·sper·mous** \ˌan-jē-ə-ˈspər-məs\ *adj*

1**an·gle** \ˈang-gəl\ *n* **1** : the figure formed by two lines extending from the same point **2** : a measure of the amount of turning that would be required to bring one line of an angle over to meet the other at all points **3** : a sharp projecting corner **4** : POINT OF VIEW, ASPECT ⟨consider a problem from a new *angle*⟩ **5** : an abruptly diverging course or direction — **an·gled** \-gəld\ *adj*

2**angle** *vb* **an·gled**; **an·gling** \-g(ə-)ling\ **1** : to turn, move, or direct at an angle **2** : to present (as a news story) from a particular often biased point of view : SLANT

3**angle** *vb* **an·gled**; **an·gling** \-g(ə-)ling\ **1** : to fish with hook and line **2** : to use sly means to get what one wants

angle bracket *n* : BRACKET 3b

angle of incidence : the angle that a line (as a ray of light) falling on a surface makes with a perpendicular to the surface at the point of incidence

angle of reflection : the angle between a reflected ray and the perpendicular to a reflecting surface drawn at the point of incidence

an·gler \ˈang-glər\ *n* **1** : FISHERMAN; *esp* : one who fishes for sport **2** : a bottom-dwelling marine fish that has a large flat head with projections that lure other fish within reach of its broad mouth

an·gle·worm \ˈang-gəl-ˌwərm\ *n* : EARTHWORM

an·gli·cize \ˈang-glə-ˌsīz\ *vb, often cap* : to make English (as in habits, speech, character, or outlook)

an·gling \ˈang-gling\ *n* : the act of fishing with hook and line usu. for sport

Anglo- *comb form* **1** : English ⟨*Anglo*-Norman⟩ **2** : English and ⟨*Anglo*-Japanese⟩

An·glo–Sax·on \ˌang-glō-ˈsak-sən\ *n* **1** : a member of the Germanic people conquering England in the 5th century A.D. **2** : ENGLISHMAN **3** : a person of English ancestry **4 a** : OLD ENGLISH **b** : direct plain English — **Anglo–Saxon** *adj*

an·go·ra \ang-ˈgōr-ə, an-, -ˈgȯr-\ *n* : yarn or cloth made from the hair of the Angora goat or the Angora rabbit

Angora cat *n* : a long-haired domestic cat

Angora goat *n* : any of a breed or variety of the domestic goat raised for its long silky hair which is used to make true mohair fabrics

Angora rabbit *n* : a usu. white rabbit raised for its long fine soft hair

an·gry \ˈang-grē\ *adj* **an·gri·er**; **-est** **1 a** : stirred by anger : ENRAGED ⟨*angry* at the insult⟩ **b** : showing or arising from anger ⟨*angry* words⟩ **c** : threatening as if in anger ⟨an *angry* sky⟩ **2** : painfully inflamed ⟨an *angry* rash⟩ — **an·gri·ly** \-grə-lē\ *adv* — **an·gri·ness** \-grē-nəs\ *n*

ang·strom \ˈang-strəm\ *n* : a unit of length used esp. of wavelengths (as of light) and equal to one ten-billionth of a meter — abbr. Å

an·guish \ˈang-gwish\ *n* : extreme pain or distress of body or mind — **an·guished** \-gwisht\ *adj*

an·gu·lar \ˈang-gyə-lər\ *adj* **1** : having one or more angles : sharp-cornered : POINTED ⟨an *angular* mountain peak⟩ **2** : measured by an angle ⟨*angular* distance⟩ **3** : being lean and bony ⟨his *angular* figure⟩ — **an·gu·lar·i·ty** \ˌang-gyə-ˈlar-ət-ē\ *n* — **an·gu·lar·ly** \ˈang-gyə-lər-lē\ *adv*

An·gus \ˈang-gəs\ *n* : ABERDEEN ANGUS

an·hy·drite \(ˈ)an-ˈhī-ˌdrīt\ *n* : a mineral consisting of an anhydrous calcium sulfate

an·hy·drous \-ˈhī-drəs\ *adj* : free from water

an·i·line \ˈan-ə-lən\ *n* : an oily poisonous fluid used in making dyes

an·i·mad·ver·sion \ˌan-ə-ˌmad-ˈvər-zhən\ *n* **1** : a critical remark or comment **2** : hostile criticism

an·i·mad·vert \-ˈvərt\ *vb* : to make a critical remark : comment unfavorably

1**an·i·mal** \ˈan-ə-məl\ *n* **1** : any of a kingdom of living beings typically differing from plants in capacity for active movement, in rapid response to stimulation, and in lack of cellulose cell walls **2 a** : one of the lower animals as distinguished from man **b** : MAMMAL

2**animal** *adj* **1** : of, relating to, or derived from animals **2** : of or relating to the body as contrasted with the mind; *esp* : SENSUOUS ⟨man's *animal* appetites⟩

an·i·mal·cule \ˌan-ə-'mal-kyül\ *n* : a very small animal that is invisible or nearly invisible to the naked eye — **an·i·mal·cu·lar** \-'mal-kyə-lər\ *adj*

animal heat *n* : heat produced in the body of a living animal by its chemical and physical activity

animal husbandry *n* : a branch of agriculture concerned with the production and care of domestic animals

[1]**an·i·mate** \'an-ə-mət\ *adj* **1** : having life : ALIVE **2** : ANIMATED, LIVELY — **an·i·mate·ly** *adv* — **an·i·mate·ness** *n*

[2]**an·i·mate** \'an-ə-ˌmāt\ *vb* **1** : to give life to : make alive **2** : to give spirit and vigor to : ENLIVEN ⟨jokes *animated* the talk⟩ **3** : to make appear to move ⟨*animate* a cartoon⟩ — **an·i·mat·ed** \-ˌmāt-əd\ *adj* — **an·i·mat·ed·ly** *adv*

an·i·ma·tion \ˌan-ə-'mā-shən\ *n* **1** : SPIRIT, LIVELINESS **2 a** : a film made by photographing successive positions of inanimate objects (as puppets) **b** : an animated cartoon **3** : the preparation of animations

an·i·mos·i·ty \ˌan-ə-'mäs-ət-ē\ *n, pl* **-ties** : ILL WILL, HOSTILITY

an·i·mus \'an-ə-məs\ *n* **1** : basic attitude : DISPOSITION **2** : deep-seated hostility : ANTAGONISM

an·ion \'an-ˌī-ən, -ˌī-ˌän\ *n* : a negatively charged ion

an·ise \'an-əs\ *n* : an herb with aromatic seeds that is related to the carrot; *also* : ANISEED

ani·seed \'an-ə(s)-ˌsēd\ *n* : the seed of anise often used as a flavoring

an·kle \'ang-kəl\ *n* : the joint between the foot and the leg; *also* : the region of this joint

an·kle·bone \-'bōn, -ˌbōn\ *n* : the bone that in man bears the weight of the body and with the tibia and fibula forms the ankle joint

an·klet \'ang-klət\ *n* **1** : something (as an ornament) worn around the ankle **2** : a short sock reaching slightly above the ankle

ann *abbr* annual

an·nal·ist \'an-ə-ləst\ *n* : a writer of annals : HISTORIAN — **an·nal·is·tic** \ˌan-ə-'lis-tik\ *adj*

an·nals \'an-əlz\ *n pl* **1** : a record of events arranged in yearly sequence **2** : historical records : CHRONICLES

an·nat·to \ə-'nät-ō\ *n, pl* **-tos** : a yellowish red dyestuff made from the pulp around the seeds of a tropical tree

an·neal \ə-'nēl\ *vb* : to heat and then cool so as to toughen and make less brittle : TEMPER

an·ne·lid \'an-ə-ləd\ *n* : any of a phylum of long segmented invertebrate animals having a body cavity and including the earthworms, leeches, and related forms — **annelid** *adj*

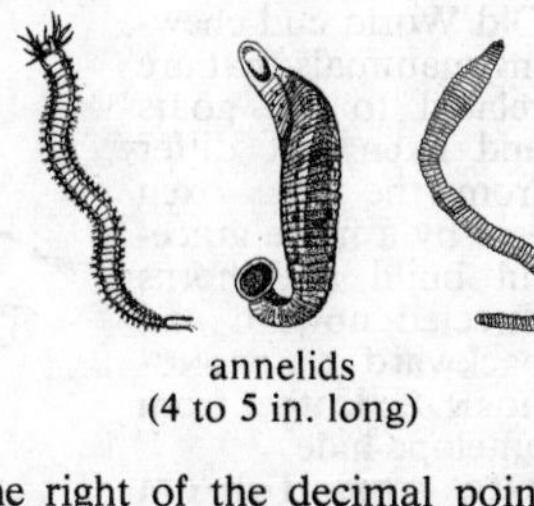

annelids
(4 to 5 in. long)

[1]**an·nex** \ə-'neks, 'an-ˌeks\ *vb* **1** : to attach as an addition : APPEND ⟨*annexed* zeros to the right of the decimal point⟩ **2** : to incorporate (a territory) within one's own domain ⟨the United States *annexed* Texas in 1845⟩ — **an·nex·a·tion** \ˌan-ˌek-'sā-shən\ *n* — **an·nex·a·tion·ist** \-sh(ə-)nəst\ *n*

[2]**an·nex** \'an-ˌeks, 'an-iks\ *n* : something annexed; *esp* : an added part of a building : WING

an·ni·hi·late \ə-'nī-ə-ˌlāt\ *vb* : to destroy completely ⟨*annihilate* an entire army⟩ — **an·ni·hi·la·tion** \-ˌnī-ə-'lā-shən\ *n* — **an·ni·hi·la·tor** \-'nī-ə-ˌlāt-ər\ *n*

an·ni·ver·sa·ry \ˌan-ə-'vərs-(ə-)rē\ *n, pl* **-ries** **1** : the annual recurrence of the date of a notable event **2** : the celebration of an anniversary

an·no Do·mi·ni \ˌan-ō-'däm-ə-nē, -'dō-mə-, -ˌnī\ *adv, often cap A* [a medieval Latin phrase meaning "in the year of the Lord"] — used to indicate that a time division falls within the Christian era

an·no·tate \'an-ə-ˌtāt\ *vb* : to make or furnish critical or explanatory notes — **an·no·ta·tor** \-ˌtāt-ər\ *n*

an·no·ta·tion \ˌan-ə-'tā-shən\ *n* **1** : the act of annotating **2** : a note added by way of comment or explanation

an·nounce \ə-'naủn(t)s\ *vb* **1** : to make known publicly : PROCLAIM **2** : to give notice of the coming, arrival, or presence of **3** : to serve as an announcer

an·nounce·ment \-mənt\ *n* **1** : the act of announcing **2** : a public notice announcing something

an·nounc·er \ə-'naủn(t)-sər\ *n* : one that announces; *esp* : one that introduces television or radio programs and gives the news and station identification

an·noy \ə-'nỏi\ *vb* : to disturb or irritate esp. by repeated disagreeable acts : VEX — **an·noy·er** *n* — **an·noy·ing·ly** \-'nỏi-ing-lē\ *adv*

an·noy·ance \ə-'nỏi-ən(t)s\ *n* **1 a** : the act of annoying **b** : the feeling of being annoyed : VEXATION **2** : a source of annoyance : NUISANCE

[1]**an·nu·al** \'an-y(ə-w)əl\ *adj* **1** : covering the period of a year **2** : occurring or performed once a year : YEARLY **3** : completing the life cycle in one growing season — **an·nu·al·ly** \-ē\ *adv*

[2]**annual** *n* **1** : a publication appearing yearly **2** : an annual plant

annual ring *n* : the layer of wood produced by a single year's growth of a woody plant

an·nu·i·ty \ə-'n(y)ü-ət-ē\ *n, pl* **-ties** **1** : a sum of money paid at regular intervals (as every year) **2** : an insurance contract providing for the payment of an annuity ⟨buy an *annuity*⟩

an·nul \ə-'nəl\ *vb* **an·nulled**; **an·nul·ling** **1** : to make ineffective or inoperative : NEUTRALIZE, CANCEL ⟨*annul* the drug's effect⟩ **2** : to make legally void ⟨*annul* a marriage⟩ — **an·nul·ment** \ə-'nəl-mənt\ *n*

an·nu·lar \'an-yə-lər\ *adj* : of, relating to, or forming a ring — **an·nu·lar·i·ty** \ˌan-yə-'lar-ət-ē\ *n* — **an·nu·lar·ly** \'an-yə-lər-lē\ *adv*

annular eclipse *n* : an eclipse in which a thin outer ring of the sun's disk is not covered by the apparently smaller dark disk of the moon

an·nu·lus \'an-yə-ləs\ *n, pl* **-li** \-ˌlī, -ˌlē\ *also* **-luses** : RING; *esp* : a part, structure, or marking resembling a ring

An·nun·ci·a·tion \ə-ˌnən(t)-sē-'ā-shən\ *n* : the announcement of the Incarnation to the Virgin Mary; *also* : March 25 observed as a church festival in commemoration of the Annunciation

an·ode \'an-ˌōd\ *n* **1** : the positive electrode of an electrolytic cell to which the negative ions are attracted — compare CATHODE **2** : the negative terminal of a battery **3** : the electron-collecting electrode of an electron tube — **an·od·ic** \a-'näd-ik\ *adj*

an·o·dize \'an-ə-ˌdīz\ *vb* : to subject (a metal) to electrolytic action as the anode of a cell in order to coat with a protective or decorative film

anoint \ə-'nỏint\ *vb* **1** : to rub over with oil or an oily substance **2** : to consecrate with or as if with oil — **anoint·er** *n* — **anoint·ment** \-'nỏint-mənt\ *n*

anom·a·lous \ə-'näm-ə-ləs\ *adj* : deviating from a

general rule or method : ABNORMAL ⟨an *anomalous* procedure⟩ — **anom·a·lous·ly** *adv* — **anom·a·lous·ness** *n*

anom·a·ly \ə-ˈnäm-ə-lē\ *n, pl* **-lies** **1** : deviation from the common rule **2** : something anomalous

anon \ə-ˈnän\ *adv* : SOON; *also* : LATER

anon *abbr* anonymous

an·o·nym·i·ty \ˌan-ə-ˈnim-ət-ē\ *n, pl* **-ties** : the quality or state of being anonymous

anon·y·mous \ə-ˈnän-ə-məs\ *adj* **1** : having or giving no name ⟨*anonymous* author⟩ **2** : of unknown or unnamed origin ⟨*anonymous* gifts⟩ ⟨an *anonymous* letter⟩ — **anon·y·mous·ly** *adv* — **anon·y·mous·ness** *n*

anoph·e·les \ə-ˈnäf-ə-ˌlēz\ *n* : any of a genus of mosquitoes that includes all mosquitoes which transmit malaria to man — **anoph·e·line** \-ˌlīn\ *adj or n*

an·or·thite \ə-ˈnȯr-ˌthīt\ *n* : a white, grayish, or reddish calcium-containing feldspar

[1]**an·oth·er** \ə-ˈnəth-ər\ *adj* **1** : some other : LATER ⟨at *another* time⟩ ⟨from *another* angle⟩ **2** : being one more in addition ⟨bring *another* cup⟩

[2]**another** *pron* **1** : one more ⟨has one pen in his pocket and *another* at home⟩ **2** : something different ⟨horseplay is one thing but destruction *another*⟩

an·ox·ia \a-ˈnäk-sē-ə\ *n* : a condition in which too little oxygen (as at high altitudes) reaches the tissues

ans *abbr* answer

[1]**an·swer** \ˈan(t)-sər\ *n* **1 a** : something spoken or written in reply esp. to a question **b** : a correct response; *esp* : SOLUTION ⟨the *answer* to the problem⟩ **2** : a reply to an accusation : DEFENSE **3** : an act done in response

[2]**answer** *vb* **an·swered**; **an·swer·ing** \ˈan(t)s-(ə-)riŋ\ **1** : to speak or write in or by way of reply **2** : to be or make oneself responsible or accountable ⟨*answered* for the children's safety⟩ **3** : CONFORM, CORRESPOND ⟨*answered* to the description⟩ **4** : to act in response ⟨the ship *answers* to the helm⟩ **5** : to be adequate : SERVE ⟨*answer* the purpose⟩ **6** : to offer a solution for; *esp* : SOLVE — **an·swer·er** \ˈan(t)-sər-ər\ *n*

an·swer·a·ble \ˈan(t)s-(ə-)rə-bəl\ *adj* **1** : liable to be called to account : RESPONSIBLE ⟨*answerable* for one's actions⟩ **2** : capable of being answered; *esp* : capable of being proved wrong ⟨an *answerable* argument⟩

ant \ˈant\ *n* : any of a family of colonial insects that are related to the wasps and bees and have various castes performing special duties

ant- — see ANTI-

[1]**-ant** \ənt\ *n suffix* **1** : one that performs or promotes a specified action ⟨cool*ant*⟩ **2** : thing that is acted upon in a specified manner ⟨inhal*ant*⟩

[2]**-ant** *adj suffix* **1** : performing a specified action or being in a specified condition ⟨propell*ant*⟩ **2** : promoting a specified action or process ⟨expector*ant*⟩

ant *abbr* antonym

ant·ac·id \(ˈ)ant-ˈas-əd\ *adj* : tending to prevent or neutralize acidity ⟨*antacid* tablets⟩ — **antacid** *n*

an·tag·o·nism \an-ˈtag-ə-ˌniz-əm\ *n* : active opposition or hostility

an·tag·o·nist \-nəst\ *n* : one that opposes another esp. in combat : ADVERSARY

an·tag·o·nis·tic \(ˌ)an-ˌtag-ə-ˈnis-tik\ *adj* : showing antagonism : HOSTILE — **an·tag·o·nis·ti·cal·ly** \-ti-k(ə-)lē\ *adv*

an·tag·o·nize \an-ˈtag-ə-ˌnīz\ *vb* : to incur the hostility of : arouse dislike

ant·arc·tic \(ˈ)ant-ˈärk-tik, -ˈärt-ik\ *adj, often cap* : of or relating to the south pole or to the region near it

antarctic circle *n, often cap A&C* : a circle of the earth parallel to the equator approximately 23° from the south pole

ant bear *n* : a large So. American anteater with shaggy gray fur, a black band across the breast, and a white shoulder stripe

ant bear
(2 ft. high at shoulder)

ant cow *n* : an aphid from which ants obtain honeydew

ante- *prefix* **1** : prior : earlier ⟨*ante*nuptial⟩ ⟨*ante*date⟩ **2** : in front of ⟨*ante*room⟩

ant·eat·er \ˈant-ˌēt-ər\ *n* : any of several mammals (as an echidna or aardvark) that feed on ants

an·te·bel·lum \ˌant-i-ˈbel-əm\ *adj* : existing before a war; *esp* : existing before the Civil War

[1]**an·te·ce·dent** \ˌant-ə-ˈsēd-ənt\ *n* **1** : a noun, pronoun, phrase, or clause referred to by a pronoun ⟨in "the house that Jack built", *house* is the *antecedent* of *that*⟩ **2** : a preceding event or cause ⟨the *antecedents* of the war⟩ **3** *pl* : ANCESTORS, PARENTS

[2]**antecedent** *adj* : coming earlier in time or order — **an·te·ce·dent·ly** *adv*

an·te·cham·ber \ˈant-i-ˌchām-bər\ *n* : ANTEROOM

an·te·date \ˈant-i-ˌdāt\ *vb* **1** : to date with a date prior to that of actual writing ⟨*antedate* a check⟩ **2** : to precede in time ⟨automobiles *antedate* airplanes⟩

an·te·di·lu·vi·an \ˌant-i-də-ˈlü-vē-ən, -dī-\ *adj* **1** : of or relating to the period before the Flood described in the Bible **2** : very old or old-fashioned : ANTIQUATED — **antediluvian** *n*

an·te·lope \ˈant-ə-ˌlōp\ *n, pl* **-lope** *or* **-lopes** **1 a** : any of various Old World cud-chewing mammals that are related to the goats and oxen but differ from the true oxen esp. by a more graceful build and horns directed upward and backward **b** : PRONGHORN **2** : leather from antelope hide

antelope 1a
(3 ft. at shoulder)

an·te me·ri·di·em \ˌant-i-mə-ˈrid-ē-əm\ *adj* [a Latin prepositional phrase, from *ante* "before" and *meridiem* accusative of *meridies* "noon", from *meri-* (an alteration of *medi-* "mid-") and *dies* "day"] : being before noon — abbr. *a.m.*

an·ten·na \an-ˈten-ə\ *n, pl* **-ten·nae** \-ˈten-(ˌ)ē\ *or* **-tennas** [from Latin, meaning "the yard of a sailing

ə abut	ər further	a back	ā bake
ä cot, cart	au̇ out	ch chin	e less
ē easy	g gift	i trip	ī life
j joke	ŋ sing	ō flow	ȯ flaw
ȯi coin	th thin	t͟h this	ü loot
u̇ foot	y yet	yü few	yu̇ furious
zh vision			

vessel"] **1** : any of one or two pairs of long slender segmented sensory organs on the head of an arthropod (as an insect or a crab) **2** *pl usu antennas* : a usu. metal device (as a rod or wire) for radiating or receiving radio waves

an·ten·nule \an-'ten-yül\ *n* : a small antenna (as of a crayfish)

an·te·pe·nult \ˌant-i-'pē-ˌnəlt\ *n* : the 3d syllable of a word counting from the end ⟨*-cu-* is the *antepenult* in *accumulate*⟩ — **an·te·pen·ul·ti·mate** \-pi-'nəl-tə-mət\ *adj or n*

an·te·ri·or \an-'tir-ē-ər\ *adj* **1** : situated before or toward the front **2** : coming before in time — **an·te·ri·or·ly** *adv*

an·te·room \'ant-i-ˌrüm, -ˌrum\ *n* : a room used as an entrance to another

an·them \'an(t)-thəm\ *n* **1** : a sacred composition with words usu. from the Scriptures **2** : a song of praise or gladness

an·ther \'an(t)-thər\ *n* : the part of a flower that produces and contains pollen and is usu. borne on a stalk

ant·hill \'ant-ˌhil\ *n* : a mound thrown up by ants in digging their nest

an·tho·cy·a·nin \ˌan(t)-thə-'sī-ə-nən\ *n* : any of various soluble pigments producing blue to red coloring in flowers and plants

an·thol·o·gy \an-'thäl-ə-jē\ *n, pl* **-gies** : a collection of literary pieces or passages — **an·thol·o·gist** \-jəst\ *n*

an·thra·cite \'an(t)-thrə-ˌsīt\ *n* : a hard glossy coal that burns without much smoke or flame

an·thrax \'an-ˌthraks\ *n* : an infectious and usu. fatal bacterial disease of warm-blooded animals (as cattle and sheep); *also* : a bacterium causing anthrax

anthrop *abbr* anthropology

1**an·thro·poid** \'an(t)-thrə-ˌpȯid\ *adj* **1** : resembling man **2** : resembling an ape ⟨*anthropoid* mobsters⟩

2**anthropoid** *n* : any of several large tailless apes (as a gorilla or chimpanzee) — **an·thro·poi·dal** \ˌan(t)-thrə-'pȯid-əl\ *adj*

an·thro·pol·o·gy \ˌan(t)-thrə-'päl-ə-jē\ *n* : the science of man and esp. of his physical characteristics, his origin and the distribution of races, his environment and social relations, and his culture — **an·thro·po·log·i·cal** \-pə-'läj-i-kəl\ *adj* — **an·thro·pol·o·gist** \-'päl-ə-jəst\ *n*

anti- \ˌant-i, ˌant-ē, ˌan-ˌtī\ *or* **ant-** *or* **anth-** *prefix* **1** : opposite in kind, position, or action ⟨*anti*climax⟩ ⟨*anti*histamine⟩ **2** : hostile toward ⟨*anti*slavery⟩

an·ti·air·craft \ˌant-ē-'a(ə)r-ˌkraft, -'e(ə)r-\ *adj* : designed or used for defense against aircraft ⟨an *antiaircraft* gun⟩ — **antiaircraft** *n*

an·ti·bac·te·ri·al \ˌant-ē-ˌbak-'tir-ē-əl, ˌan-ˌtī-ˌbak-\ *adj* : directed or effective against bacteria

an·ti·bal·lis·tic missile \ˌant-i-bə-ˌlis-tik-\ *n* : a missile for intercepting and destroying ballistic missiles

an·ti·ber·i·beri \ˌant-i-ˌber-ē-'ber-ē, ˌan-ˌti-\ *adj* : tending to prevent or cure beriberi

an·ti·bi·ot·ic \ˌant-i-bī-'ät-ik, ˌan-ˌtī-,-bē-\ *n* : a substance produced by an organism (as a fungus or bacterium) that in dilute solution inhibits or kills a harmful microorganism — **antibiotic** *adj*

an·ti·body \'ant-i-ˌbäd-ē\ *n* : a substance produced by the body that interacts with an antigen and counteracts the effects of a disease-producing microorganism or its poisons

1**an·tic** \'ant-ik\ *n* : a grotesquely ludicrous act or action : CAPER

2**antic** *adj* : whimsically gay : FROLICSOME

an·tic·i·pate \an-'tis-ə-ˌpāt\ *vb* **1** : to be before in doing or acting **2** : FORESTALL ⟨*anticipate* an opponent's objections⟩ **3** : to see and perform beforehand ⟨*anticipate* a person's wishes⟩ **4** : to expect esp. with pleasure : look forward to ⟨*anticipate* the pleasure of your visit next week⟩ — **an·tic·i·pa·tor** \-ˌpāt-ər\ *n*

an·tic·i·pa·tion \(ˌ)an-ˌtis-ə-'pā-shən\ *n* **1** : a prior action that takes into account or forestalls a later action **2** : EXPECTATION; *esp* : pleasurable expectation **3** : the act of providing for an expected event or state — **an·tic·i·pa·to·ry** \an-'tis-ə-pə-ˌtōr-ē, -ˌtȯr-\ *adj*

an·ti·cli·max \ˌant-i-'klī-ˌmaks\ *n* **1** : the transition in writing or speaking from a significant idea to a trivial or ludicrous idea; *also* : an instance of this transition **2** : an event esp. closing a series that is strikingly less important than what has preceded it — **an·ti·cli·mac·tic** \-klī-'mak-tik\ *adj*

an·ti·cline \'ant-i-ˌklīn\ *n* : an arch of stratified rock in which the layers bend downward in opposite directions from the crest — compare SYNCLINE

an·ti·cy·clone \ˌant-i-'sī-ˌklōn\ *n* : a system of winds that rotates about a center of high atmospheric pressure clockwise in the northern hemisphere, that usu. advances at 20 to 30 miles per hour, and that usu. has a diameter of 1500 to 2500 miles — **an·ti·cy·clon·ic** \-sī-'klän-ik\ *adj*

an·ti·dote \'ant-i-ˌdōt\ *n* [from Greek *antidotos*, from an adjective meaning "given in opposition", from *anti-* "against"] **1** : a remedy to counteract the effects of poison **2** : something that relieves, prevents, or counteracts — **an·ti·dot·al** \ˌant-i-'dōt-əl\ *adj* — **an·ti·dot·al·ly** \-ə-lē\ *adv*

an·ti·elec·tron \ˌant-ē-ə-'lek-ˌträn, ˌan-ˌtī-\ *n* : POSITRON

an·ti·freeze \'ant-i-ˌfrēz\ *n* : a substance added to the liquid in an automobile radiator to prevent freezing

an·ti·gen \'ant-i-jən\ *n* : a substance (as a toxin or enzyme) that when introduced into the body stimulates the production of an antibody — **an·ti·gen·ic** \ˌant-i-'jen-ik\ *adj*

an·ti·his·ta·mine \ˌant-i-'his-tə-ˌmēn, -mən\ *n* : any of various drugs used for treating allergic reactions and cold symptoms

an·ti–in·tel·lec·tu·al·ism \ˌant-i-ˌint-ə-'lek-chə(-wə)-ˌliz-əm, ˌan-ˌtī-\ *n* : hostility toward or suspicion of intellectuals or intellectual traits and activities

an·ti·knock \ˌant-ē-'näk\ *n* : a substance that when added to the fuel of an internal-combustion engine helps to prevent knocking

an·ti·mag·net·ic \ˌant-i-mag-'net-ik, ˌan-ˌtī-\ *adj* : having a balance unit composed of alloys that will not remain magnetized ⟨an *antimagnetic* watch⟩

an·ti·ma·lar·i·al \-mə-'ler-ē-əl\ *adj* : serving to prevent, check, or cure malaria — **antimalarial** *n*

an·ti·mat·ter \'ant-i-ˌmat-ər\ *n* : matter held to be composed of the counterparts of ordinary matter

an·ti·me·tab·o·lite \ˌant-i-mə-'tab-ə-ˌlīt, ˌan-ˌtī-\ *n* : a substance that inhibits the use of or is used instead of another substance essential for metabolism

an·ti·mo·ny \'ant-ə-ˌmō-nē\ *n* : a metallic silvery white crystalline and brittle element that is used esp. as a constituent of alloys and in medicine — see ELEMENT table

an·ti·neu·tron \ˌant-i-'n(y)ü-ˌträn, ˌan-ˌtī-\ *n* : the uncharged antiparticle of the neutron

an·ti·ox·i·dant \ˌant-ē-'äk-səd-ənt, ˌan-ˌtī-\ *n* : a substance that opposes oxidation or inhibits reactions promoted by oxygen

an·ti·par·ti·cle \'ant-i-ˌpärt-i-kəl, 'an-ˌtī-\ *n* : an elementary particle identical to another elementary

particle in mass but opposite to it in electric or magnetic properties
an·tip·a·thy \an-'tip-ə-thē\ *n, pl* **-thies 1 :** strong and deep-seated dislike **2 :** a person or thing that arouses strong dislike — **an·ti·pa·thet·ic** \ˌant-i-pə-'thet-ik\ *adj*
an·ti·pode \'ant-ə-ˌpōd\ *n, pl* **an·tip·o·des** \an-'tip-ə-ˌdēz\ **1 :** the parts of the earth diametrically opposite — usu. used in pl. **2 :** the exact opposite or contrary — **an·tip·o·dal** \an-'tip-əd-əl\ *adj* — **an·tip·o·de·an** \(ˌ)an-tip-ə-'dē-ən\ *adj*
an·ti·pov·er·ty \ˌant-i-'päv-ərt-ē, ˌan-ˌtī-\ *adj* **:** of or relating to legislation designed to relieve poverty ⟨*antipoverty* program⟩
an·ti·pro·ton \-'prō-ˌtän\ *n* **:** the antiparticle of the proton
1**an·ti·quar·i·an** \ˌant-ə-'kwer-ē-ən\ *n* **:** ANTIQUARY
2**antiquarian** *adj* **:** of or relating to antiquaries or antiquities
an·ti·quary \'ant-ə-ˌkwer-ē\ *n, pl* **-quar·ies :** a person who collects or studies antiquities
an·ti·quate \'ant-ə-ˌkwāt\ *vb* **:** to make old or obsolete
1**an·tique** \an-'tēk\ *adj* **1 :** belonging to antiquity **2 :** belonging to earlier periods ⟨*antique* furniture⟩ **3 :** belonging to or resembling a former style or fashion **:** OLD-FASHIONED ⟨silver of an *antique* design⟩
2**antique** *n* **:** an object of an earlier period; *esp* **:** a work of art, piece of furniture, or decorative object made at an earlier period
an·tiq·ui·ty \an-'tik-wət-ē\ *n, pl* **-ties 1 :** ancient times; *esp* **:** those before the Middle Ages **2 :** very great age **3** *pl* **:** relics or monuments of ancient times
an·ti·sep·tic \ˌant-ə-'sep-tik\ *adj* **1 :** killing or making harmless germs that cause disease or decay **2 :** relating to or characterized by the use of antiseptic substances ⟨*antiseptic* surgery⟩ — **antiseptic** *n* — **an·ti·sep·ti·cal·ly** \-ti-k(ə-)lē\ *adv*
an·ti·se·rum \'ant-i-ˌsir-əm, 'an-ˌtī-\ *n* **:** a serum containing antibodies
an·ti·so·cial \ˌant-i-'sō-shəl, ˌan-ˌtī-\ *adj* **1 :** hostile to the well-being of society ⟨crime is *antisocial*⟩ **2 :** disliking the society of others **:** MISANTHROPIC
an·ti·tank \ˌant-i-'tangk\ *adj* **:** designed to destroy or stop tanks
an·tith·e·sis \an-'tith-ə-səs\ *n, pl* **-tith·e·ses** \-'tith-ə-ˌsēz\ **1 :** the rhetorical contrast of ideas by means of parallel arrangements of words, clauses, or sentences **2 :** OPPOSITION, CONTRAST **3 :** the direct opposite **:** CONTRARY — **an·ti·thet·i·cal** \ˌant-ə-'thet-i-kəl\ *adj*
an·ti·tox·in \ˌant-i-'täk-sən\ *n* **:** any of various specific antibodies that are formed in response to a foreign and usu. poisonous substance introduced into the body and that can often be produced commercially in lower animals for use in treating human diseases by injection — **an·ti·tox·ic** \-sik\ *adj*
an·ti·ven·in \ˌant-i-'ven-ən, ˌan-ˌtī-\ *n* **:** a serum containing an antitoxin to a venom (as of a snake)
ant·ler \'ant-lər\ *n* **:** the solid often branched deciduous horn of a deer or one of its close relatives; *also* **:** a branch of such horn — **ant·lered** \-lərd\ *adj*
ant lion *n* **:** a 4-winged insect that when a larva digs a conical pit in which it lies in wait to catch insects (as ants) on which it feeds

ə abut	ər further	a back	ā bake
ä cot, cart	aù out	ch chin	e less	ē easy
g gift	i trip	ī life	j joke	ng sing	ō flow
ȯ flaw	ȯi coin	th thin	th this	ü loot
ù foot	y yet	yü few	yù furious	zh vision

an·to·nym \'an-tə-ˌnim\ *n* **:** a word of opposite meaning ⟨*hot* and *cold* are *antonyms*⟩ — **an·ton·y·mous** \an-'tän-ə-məs\ *adj*
anus \'ā-nəs\ *n* **:** the posterior opening of the alimentary canal
an·vil \'an-vəl\ *n* **1 :** a heavy iron block on which metal is shaped **2 :** the middle of a chain of three small bones in the ear of a mammal
anx·i·e·ty \ang-'zī-ət-ē\ *n, pl* **-ties 1 :** painful or apprehensive uneasiness of mind usu. over an anticipated misfortune **2 :** solicitous concern or interest
anx·ious \'ang(k)-shəs\ *adj* **1 :** fearful of what may happen **:** WORRIED ⟨*anxious* about her son's health⟩ **2 :** desiring earnestly ⟨a boy *anxious* to make good⟩ — **anx·ious·ly** *adv* — **anx·ious·ness** *n*
1**any** \'en-ē\ *adj* **1 :** one taken at random ⟨*any* man you meet⟩ **2 :** EVERY ⟨a poem *any* child knows⟩ **3 :** of whatever quantity, number, or extent ⟨have you *any* money⟩ ⟨give me *any* letters you find⟩
2**any** *pron* **1 :** any person or persons ⟨*any* of you can go⟩ **2 a :** any thing or things **b :** any part, quantity, or number ⟨is there *any* left⟩
3**any** *adv* **:** to any extent or degree **:** at all ⟨can't go *any* farther⟩
any·body \'en-ē-ˌbäd-ē\ *pron* **:** ANYONE
any·how \'en-ē-ˌhaù\ *adv* **1 :** in any way, manner, or order **2 :** at any rate **:** in any case
any·more \ˌen-ē-'mō(ə)r, -'mȯ(ə)r\ *adv* **:** at the present time **:** NOWADAYS ⟨never see him *anymore*⟩
any·one \'en-ē-(ˌ)wən\ *pron* **:** any person at all
any·place \'en-ē-ˌplās\ *adv* **:** ANYWHERE
any·thing \'en-ē-ˌthing\ *pron* **:** any thing at all
any·way \'en-ē-ˌwā\ *adv* **:** ANYHOW
any·where \'en-ē-ˌhwe(ə)r, -ˌhwa(ə)r\ *adv* **:** in, at, or to any place
any·wise \'en-ē-ˌwīz\ *adv* **:** in any way whatever **:** at all
A-OK \ˌā-ō-'kā\ *adj* **:** working or going well **:** FINE
A1 \'ā-'wən\ *adj* **:** of the finest quality **:** FIRST-RATE
aor·ta \ā-'ȯrt-ə\ *n, pl* **aortas** *or* **aor·tae** \-'ȯrt-ē\ **:** the main artery that carries blood from the heart to be distributed by branch arteries through the body — **aor·tic** \-'ȯrt-ik\ *adj*
aortic arch *n* **:** one of the paired branches of the aorta in fish and the embryos of higher vertebrates that are reduced in the adult of amphibians and reptiles to a single pair and in the adult of birds and mammals to a single arch
aou·dad \'aù-ˌdad\ *n* **:** a wild sheep of No. Africa
1**ap-** — see AD-
2**ap-** — see APO-
AP *abbr* Associated Press
apace \ə-'pās\ *adv* **:** at a quick pace **:** SWIFTLY
Apache \ə-'pach-ē\ *n* **:** a member of an Amerindian people of the American Southwest
ap·a·nage *var of* APPANAGE
1**apart** \ə-'pärt\ *adv* **1 :** at a distance in space or time ⟨towns five miles *apart*⟩ **2 :** as a separate unit **:** INDEPENDENTLY ⟨considered *apart* from other points⟩ **3 :** ASIDE ⟨joking *apart*⟩ **4 :** into two or more parts **:** to pieces ⟨tear a book *apart*⟩
2**apart** *adj* **1 :** SEPARATE, ISOLATED **2 :** DIVIDED — **apart·ness** *n*
apart·ment \ə-'pärt-mənt\ *n* **1 :** a room or set of rooms used as a dwelling **2 :** APARTMENT BUILDING
apartment building *n* **:** a building divided into apartments — called also *apartment house*
ap·a·thet·ic \ˌap-ə-'thet-ik\ *adj* **:** having little or no interest or concern **:** INDIFFERENT — **ap·a·thet·i·cal·ly** \-'thet-i-k(ə-)lē\ *adv*
ap·a·thy \'ap-ə-thē\ *n, pl* **-thies 1 :** lack of feeling

or emotion **2 :** lack of interest or concern : INDIFFERENCE

ap·a·tite \'ap-ə-,tīt\ *n* : any of a group of minerals of variable color that are phosphates of calcium usu. with some fluorine and that are used as a source of phosphorus and its compounds

APB *abbr* all points bulletin

[1]**ape** \'āp\ *n* **1 a :** MONKEY; *esp* : one of the larger tailless or short-tailed forms **b :** any of a family of large primates (as the chimpanzee or gorilla) **2 :** MIMIC

[2]**ape** *vb* : to copy slavishly ***syn*** see IMITATE — **aper** *n*

ape hanger *n* : a very high handlebar esp. on a motorcycle

ape–man \'āp-'man, -,man\ *n* : a primate (as pithecanthropus) intermediate in character between true man and the higher apes

ape·ri·ent \ə-'pir-ē-ənt\ *adj* : gently moving the bowels : LAXATIVE — **aperient** *n*

ap·er·ture \'ap-ə-(r)-,chů(ə)r, -chər\ *n* : an opening or open space : HOLE

apex \'ā-,peks\ *n, pl* **apex·es** *or* **api·ces** \'ā-pə-,sēz, 'ap-ə-\ **1 :** the uppermost point : TOP ⟨*apex* of a mountain⟩ **2 :** TIP ⟨*apex* of the tongue⟩ **3 :** the highest point : PEAK ⟨*apex* of development⟩

aph·elion \a-'fēl-yən\ *n, pl* **aph·elia** \-yə\ : the point of a planet's or comet's orbit most distant from the sun

aphid \'ā-fəd, 'af-əd\ *n* : any of numerous small sluggish insects that suck the juices of plants

aphis \'ā-fəs, 'af-əs\ *n, pl* **aphi·des** \'ā-fə-,dēz, 'af-ə-\ : APHID

aphis lion *n* : any of several insect larvae (as a lacewing or ladybug larva) that feed on aphids

aph·o·rism \'af-ə-,riz-əm\ *n* : a short sentence stating a general truth or practical observation — **aph·o·ris·tic** \,af-ə-'ris-tik\ *adj* — **aph·o·ris·ti·cal·ly** \-ti-k(ə-)lē\ *adv*

api·ary \'ā-pē-,er-ē\ *n, pl* **-ar·ies** : a place where bees are kept; *esp* : a collection of beehives — **api·a·rist** \'ā-pē-ə-rəst\ *n*

apiece \ə-'pēs\ *adv* : for each one : INDIVIDUALLY ⟨selling for 10 cents *apiece*⟩

ap·ish \'ā-pish\ *adj* : given to slavish imitation — **ap·ish·ly** *adv* — **ap·ish·ness** *n*

aplomb \ə-'pläm, -'pləm\ *n* : SELF-CONFIDENCE, POISE

apo- *or* **ap-** *prefix* : away from : off ⟨*ap*helion⟩

apoc·ry·pha \ə-'päk-rə-fə\ *n sing or pl* — see BIBLE table

apo·gee \'ap-ə-(,)jē\ *n* : the point farthest from the center of a celestial body (as the earth or the moon) reached by an object (as a satellite or vehicle) orbiting it — compare PERIGEE

apogee

apol·o·get·ic \ə-,päl-ə-'jet-ik\ *adj* **1 :** offered by way of apology **2 :** expressing or seeming to express apology ⟨an *apologetic* expression⟩ — **apol·o·get·i·cal·ly** \-'jet-i-k(ə-)lē\ *adv*

apol·o·gist \ə-'päl-ə-jəst\ *n* : one who speaks or writes in defense of a faith, cause, or institution

apol·o·gize \ə-'päl-ə-,jīz\ *vb* : to make an apology : express regret for something one has done — **apol·o·giz·er** *n*

apol·o·gy \-jē\ *n, pl* **-gies 1 :** an admission of error or discourtesy accompanied by an expression of regret **2 :** a poor substitute

ap·o·plec·tic \,ap-ə-'plek-tik\ *adj* **1 :** of, relating to, or caused by apoplexy ⟨*apoplectic* symptoms⟩ **2 a :** affected with or inclined to apoplexy ⟨*apoplectic* patients⟩ **b :** highly excited or excitable

ap·o·plexy \'ap-ə-,plek-sē\ *n, pl* **-plex·ies** : sudden weakening or loss of consciousness or the power to feel or move caused by breaking of a blood vessel in the brain or by the cutting off of the supply of blood to the brain by a clot in a blood vessel

aport \ə-'pōrt, -'pȯrt\ *adv or adj* : on or toward the left side of a ship

apos·ta·sy \ə-'päs-tə-sē\ *n, pl* **-sies** : renunciation of a religious faith or of a previous loyalty

apos·tate \ə-'päs-,tāt, -tət\ *n* : one who commits apostasy — **apostate** *adj*

apos·tle \ə-'päs-əl\ *n* **1 a :** one of a group made up of Christ's twelve original disciples and Paul **b :** the first Christian missionary to a region **2 :** the first advocate of a viewpoint or reform — **apos·tle·ship** \-,ship\ *n*

ap·os·tol·ic \,ap-ə-'stäl-ik\ *adj* **1 :** of, relating to, or derived from an apostle or the apostles or their mission **2 :** PAPAL

[1]**apos·tro·phe** \ə-'päs-trə-(,)fē\ *n* : the rhetorical addressing of an absent person as if present or of an abstract idea or inanimate object as if capable of understanding (as in "O grave, where is thy victory?")

[2]**apostrophe** *n* : a mark ' used to show the omission of letters or figures (as in *can't* for *cannot* or *'76* for *1776*), the possessive case (as in *James's*), or the plural of letters or figures (as in *cross your t's*)

apoth·e·car·ies' measure \ə-'päth-ə-,ker-ēz-\ *n* : a measure of capacity — see MEASURE table

apothecaries' weight *n* — see MEASURE table

apoth·e·cary \ə-'päth-ə-,ker-ē\ *n, pl* **-car·ies** : DRUGGIST

app *abbr* **1** apparatus **2** appendix

ap·pall \ə-'pȯl\ *vb* : to overcome with fear or dread

ap·pall·ing *adj* : inspiring horror or dismay : SHOCKING — **ap·pall·ing·ly** \-'pȯ-ling-lē\ *adv*

Ap·pa·loo·sa \,ap-ə-'lü-sə\ *n* : one of a breed of rugged saddle horses of western No. America with a spotted skin, vertically striped hoofs, and a patch of white hair over the rump and loins

ap·pa·nage \'ap-ə-nij\ *n* **1 a :** a grant (as of land) made by a sovereign to a member of the royal family **b :** a customary right or privilege **2 :** a natural accompaniment or endowment

ap·pa·rat·us \,ap-ə-'rat-əs, -'rāt-\ *n, pl* **-us·es** \-ə-səz\ *or* **-us** \-əs, -,üs\ **1 a :** the equipment used to do a particular kind of work ⟨gymnasium *apparatus*⟩ ⟨the digestive *apparatus*⟩ **b :** a complex instrument or device **2 :** MEANS, INSTRUMENT

[1]**ap·par·el** \ə-'par-əl\ *vb* **-eled** *or* **-elled**; **-el·ing** *or* **-el·ling** : CLOTHE, DRESS

[2]**apparel** *n* : personal attire : CLOTHING

ap·par·ent \ə-'par-ənt, -'per-\ *adj* **1 :** open to view : VISIBLE **2 :** clear to the understanding ⟨*apparent* that the road was little used⟩ **3 :** appearing to be true or real ⟨the *apparent* conclusion to be drawn⟩ — **ap·par·ent·ly** *adv*

ap·pa·ri·tion \,ap-ə-'rish-ən\ *n* **1 :** an unusual or unexpected sight **2 :** GHOST

[1]**ap·peal** \ə-'pēl\ *n* **1 :** a legal proceeding by which a case is brought from a lower to a higher court for review **2 :** an earnest request : PLEA **3 :** the power of arousing interest : ATTRACTION

[2]**appeal** *vb* **1 :** to make a legal appeal **2 :** to call upon another for corroboration or vindication **3 :** to make an earnest request **4 :** to arouse a sympathetic response

ap·pear \ə-ˈpi(ə)r\ *vb* **1 :** to come into sight **:** become evident **:** SHOW ⟨stars *appeared* in the sky⟩ **2 :** to present oneself formally (as to answer a charge) ⟨*appear* in court⟩ **3 :** to become clear to the mind **4 a :** to come out in printed form ⟨the book *appeared* last month⟩ **b :** to come before the public on stage or screen ⟨*appears* on television⟩ **5 :** SEEM, LOOK ⟨*appear* to be tired⟩

ap·pear·ance \ə-ˈpir-ən(t)s\ *n* **1 :** the act, process, or an instance of appearing **2 a :** outward aspect **:** LOOK **b :** mere external show **:** SEMBLANCE **3 :** something that appears

ap·pease \ə-ˈpēz\ *vb* **1 :** to make calm or quiet **:** ALLAY **2 :** to make concessions to usu. at the sacrifice of principles in order to avoid war ⟨*appease* an aggressor⟩ ***syn*** see PACIFY ***ant*** aggravate — **ap·pease·ment** \-mənt\ *n* — **ap·peas·er** *n*

[1]**ap·pel·lant** \ə-ˈpel-ənt\ *adj* **:** making an appeal

[2]**appellant** *n* **:** one that appeals; *esp* **:** one that appeals a judicial decision

ap·pel·late \ə-ˈpel-ət\ *adj* **:** of or relating to appeals; *esp* **:** having the power to review the decisions of a lower court ⟨an *appellate* court⟩

ap·pel·la·tion \ˌap-ə-ˈlā-shən\ *n* **:** an identifying or descriptive name or title **:** DESIGNATION

ap·pel·lee \ˌap-ə-ˈlē\ *n* **:** one against whom an appeal is taken

ap·pend \ə-ˈpend\ *vb* **:** to add as a supplement ⟨*append* a postscript to a letter⟩

ap·pend·age \ə-ˈpen-dij\ *n* **1 :** something attached to a larger or more important thing **2 :** a subordinate or derivative body part; *esp* **:** a limb or an analogous part

ap·pen·dec·to·my \ˌap-ən-ˈdek-tə-mē\ *n, pl* **-mies :** surgical removal of the human appendix

ap·pen·di·ci·tis \ə-ˌpen-də-ˈsīt-əs\ *n* **:** inflammation of the appendix

ap·pen·dix \ə-ˈpen-diks\ *n, pl* **-dix·es** *or* **-di·ces** \-də-ˌsēz\ **1 :** supplementary material attached at the end of a piece of writing **2 :** a bodily outgrowth or process; *esp* **:** a small tubular outgrowth from the cecum of the intestine

ap·per·tain \ˌap-ər-ˈtān\ *vb* **:** to belong or be connected as a possession, part, or right **:** PERTAIN ⟨duties that *appertain* to the office of governor⟩

ap·pe·tite \ˈap-ə-ˌtīt\ *n* **1 :** the desire to eat or drink **2 :** TASTE, PREFERENCE ⟨an *appetite* for adventure⟩

ap·pe·tiz·er \-ˌtī-zər\ *n* **:** a food or drink that stimulates the appetite and is usu. served before a meal

ap·pe·tiz·ing \-ˌtī-zing\ *adj* **:** appealing to the appetite — **ap·pe·tiz·ing·ly** \-zing-lē\ *adv*

ap·plaud \ə-ˈplȯd\ *vb* **1 :** PRAISE, APPROVE **2 :** to show approval esp. by clapping the hands — **ap·plaud·a·ble** \-ə-bəl\ *adj* — **ap·plaud·er** *n*

ap·plause \ə-ˈplȯz\ *n* **:** approval publicly expressed (as by clapping the hands)

ap·ple \ˈap-əl\ *n* **:** a rounded fruit with a red, yellow, or green skin, firm white flesh and a seedy core; *also* **:** the tree related to the roses that bears this fruit

ap·ple·sauce \-ˌsȯs\ *n* **:** a sauce made of sweetened stewed apples

ap·pli·ance \ə-ˈplī-ən(t)s\ *n* **1 :** a piece of equipment for adapting a tool or machine to a special purpose **2 :** a device designed for a particular use ⟨a fire-fighting *appliance*⟩ ⟨an *appliance* serving as an artificial arm⟩ **3 :** a piece (as a stove or iron) of household or office equipment that is operated by gas or electricity

ap·pli·ca·ble \ˈap-li-kə-bəl, ə-ˈplik-ə-\ *adj* **:** capable of being or suitable to be applied **:** APPROPRIATE — **ap·pli·ca·bil·i·ty** \ˌap-li-kə-ˈbil-ət-ē, ə-ˌplik-ə-\ *n*

ap·pli·cant \ˈap-li-kənt\ *n* **:** one who applies for something ⟨an *applicant* for work⟩

ap·pli·ca·tion \ˌap-lə-ˈkā-shən\ *n* **1 :** the act or an instance of applying ⟨*application* of paint to a house⟩ **2 :** something put or spread on a surface ⟨hot *applications* on a sprained ankle⟩ **3 :** ability to fix one's attention on a task **4 a :** a request made personally or in writing ⟨an *application* for a job⟩ **b :** an application form **5 :** capacity for practical use

ap·pli·ca·tor \ˈap-lə-ˌkāt-ər\ *n* **:** a device for applying a substance (as medicine or polish)

ap·plied \ə-ˈplīd\ *adj* **:** put to practical use; *esp* **:** applying general principles to solve definite problems ⟨*applied* sciences⟩

ap·ply \ə-ˈplī\ *vb* **ap·plied; ap·ply·ing 1 a :** to put to use ⟨*apply* knowledge⟩ **b :** to lay or spread on ⟨*apply* a coat of paint⟩ **c :** to place in contact ⟨*apply* heat⟩ **d :** to put into operation or effect ⟨*apply* a law⟩ **2 :** to employ diligently ⟨*applied* himself to the work⟩ **3 :** to have relevance ⟨this law *applies* to everyone⟩ **4 :** to make an application **:** make a request ⟨*apply* for a job⟩ — **ap·pli·er** \-ˈplī(ə)r\ *n*

appnt *abbr* appointment

ap·point \ə-ˈpȯint\ *vb* **1 :** to fix or set officially ⟨*appoint* a day for a meeting⟩ **2 :** to name officially esp. to an office or position ⟨the president *appoints* the members of his cabinet⟩

ap·point·ed *adj* **:** FURNISHED, EQUIPPED ⟨a well-*appointed* house⟩

ap·poin·tee \ə-ˌpȯin-ˈtē, ˌa-ˌpȯin-\ *n* **:** a person appointed to a position or an office

ap·point·ive \ə-ˈpȯint-iv\ *adj* **:** of, relating to, or filled by appointment ⟨an *appointive* office⟩

ap·point·ment \ə-ˈpȯint-mənt\ *n* **1 :** the act or an instance of appointing **:** DESIGNATION ⟨holds office by *appointment*⟩ **2 :** a position or office to which a person is named but not elected ⟨received an *appointment* from the president⟩ **3 :** an agreement to meet at a fixed time ⟨an *appointment* with the dentist⟩ **4 :** EQUIPMENT, FURNISHINGS — usu. used in pl.

ap·por·tion \ə-ˈpōr-shən, -ˈpȯr-\ *vb* **-tioned; -tion·ing** \-sh(ə-)ning\ **:** to divide and distribute proportionately ⟨*apportioned* his time well⟩ — **ap·por·tion·ment** \-shən-mənt\ *n*

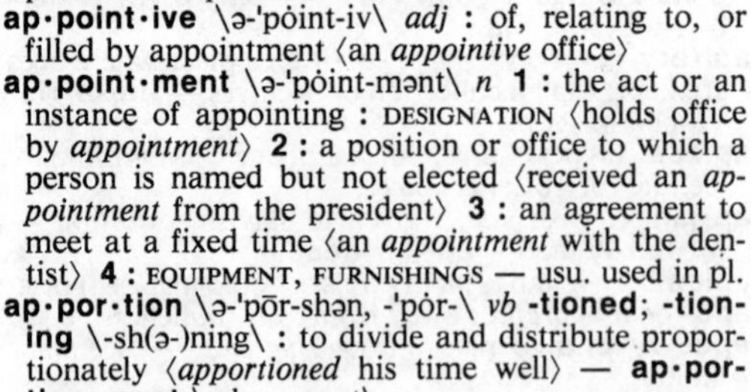

apples

ap·po·site \ˈap-ə-zət\ *adj* **:** highly pertinent or appropriate

ap·po·si·tion \ˌap-ə-ˈzish-ən\ *n* **1 :** a grammatical construction in which a noun or noun equivalent is followed by another that explains it (as *the poet* and *Burns* in "a biography of the poet Burns") **2 :** the relation of words in apposition

[1]**ap·pos·i·tive** \ə-ˈpäz-ət-iv, a-\ *adj* **:** of, relating to, or standing in apposition — **ap·pos·i·tive·ly** *adv*

ə abut	ər further	a back	ā bake	
ä cot, cart	au̇ out	ch chin	e less	ē easy
g gift	i trip	ī life	j joke	ng sing	ō flow
ȯ flaw	ȯi coin	th thin	t͟h this	ü loot
u̇ foot	y yet	yü few	yu̇ furious	zh vision

2**appositive** *n* : the second of a pair of nouns or noun equivalents in apposition

ap·prais·al \ə-'prā-zəl\ *n* **1** : an act or instance of appraising **2** : the value determined by appraisal

ap·praise \ə-'prāz\ *vb* : to set a value on; *esp* : to determine the money value of ⟨a house *appraised* at $29,000⟩ — **ap·praise·ment** \-mənt\ *n*

ap·prais·er \ə-'prā-zər\ *n* : one that appraises; *esp* : an official who appraises real estate and personal property for purposes of taxation

ap·pre·cia·ble \ə-'prē-shə-bəl\ *adj* : large enough to be recognized and measured or to be felt ⟨an *appreciable* difference in temperature⟩ — **ap·pre·cia·bly** \-blē\ *adv*

ap·pre·ci·ate \ə-'prē-shē-,āt\ *vb* **1** : to see the worth, quality, or significance of **2** : to enjoy intelligently ⟨*appreciate* good art⟩ **3** : to be fully aware of **4** : to recognize with gratitude ⟨*appreciate* a kindness⟩ **5** : to increase in number or value — **ap·pre·ci·a·tion** \ə-,prē-shē-'ā-shən\ *n* — **ap·pre·cia·tive** \ə-'prē-shət-iv\ *adj* — **ap·pre·cia·tive·ly** *adv* — **ap·pre·cia·tive·ness** *n*

ap·pre·hend \,ap-ri-'hend\ *vb* **1** : ARREST, SEIZE ⟨*apprehend* a suspect⟩ **2** : to expect with anxiety or dread **3** : to grasp with the understanding : UNDERSTAND

ap·pre·hen·sion \,ap-ri-'hen-chən\ *n* **1** : CAPTURE, ARREST ⟨*apprehension* of a burglar⟩ **2** : UNDERSTANDING **3** : fear of what may be coming : dread of the future

ap·pre·hen·sive \,ap-ri-'hen(t)-siv\ *adj* : fearful of what may be coming — **ap·pre·hen·sive·ly** *adv* — **ap·pre·hen·sive·ness** *n*

1**ap·pren·tice** \ə-'prent-əs\ *n* : one who is learning a trade, art, or calling by practical experience under a skilled worker — **ap·pren·tice·ship** \-,ship\ *n*

2**apprentice** *vb* : to bind by contract or set at work as an apprentice

ap·prise *also* **ap·prize** \ə-'prīz\ *vb* : to give notice to : INFORM

1**ap·proach** \ə-'prōch\ *vb* **1** : to come near or nearer **2** : to take preliminary steps toward

2**approach** *n* **1** : an act or instance of approaching **2** : a preliminary step **3** : manner of advance **4** : a means of access : AVENUE

ap·proach·a·ble \ə-'prō-chə-bəl\ *adj* : capable of being approached : ACCESSIBLE; *esp* : easy to meet or deal with — **ap·proach·a·bil·i·ty** \-,prō-chə-'bil-ət-ē\ *n*

ap·pro·ba·tion \,ap-rə-'bā-shən\ *n* : APPROVAL, COMMENDATION

1**ap·pro·pri·ate** \ə-'prō-prē-,āt\ *vb* **1** : to take for one's own often without right : ANNEX **2** : to set apart for a particular purpose or use ⟨*appropriate* funds for research⟩

2**ap·pro·pri·ate** \-prē-ət\ *adj* : especially suitable or fitting : PROPER *syn* see FIT *ant* inappropriate — **ap·pro·pri·ate·ly** *adv* — **ap·pro·pri·ate·ness** *n*

ap·pro·pri·a·tion \ə-,prō-prē-'ā-shən\ *n* **1** : an act or instance of appropriating **2** : something that has been appropriated; *esp* : a sum of money formally set aside for a specific use

ap·prov·al \ə-'prü-vəl\ *n* : an act or instance of approving — **on approval** : subject to a prospective buyer's acceptance or refusal ⟨goods sent *on approval*⟩

ap·prove \ə-'prüv\ *vb* **1** : to have or express a favorable judgment : take a favorable view **2** : to accept as satisfactory esp. formally ⟨the school board *approved* the plans for the new school⟩ — **ap·prov·ing·ly** \-'prü-ving-lē\ *adv*

approx *abbr* approximate

1**ap·prox·i·mate** \ə-'präk-sə-mət\ *adj* : nearly correct or exact ⟨the *approximate* cost⟩ — **ap·prox·i·mate·ly** *adv*

2**ap·prox·i·mate** \-,māt\ *vb* : to bring or come near or close ⟨this sketch *approximates* the right dimensions⟩

ap·prox·i·ma·tion \ə-,präk-sə-'mā-shən\ *n* **1** : the act or process of approximating **2** : the quality or state of being close esp. in value **3** : something approximate; *esp* : a nearly exact estimate of a value

ap·pur·te·nance \ə-'pərt-(ə-)nən(t)s\ *n* : something that belongs to or goes along with another usu. larger and more important thing ⟨a house with all *appurtenances*⟩

Apr *abbr* April

ap·ri·cot \'ap-rə-,kät, 'ā-prə-\ *n* : an oval orange-colored fruit resembling the related peach and plum in flavor; *also* : a tree that bears apricots

April \'ā-prəl\ *n* [from Latin *Aprilis*] : the 4th month of the year

April fool *n* : one who is tricked on April Fools' Day

April Fools' Day *n* : April 1 characteristically marked by the playing of practical jokes

apron \'ā-prən, -pərn\ *n* [from Middle English *napron* (the phrase *a napron* being misunderstood as *an apron*), borrowed from medieval French *naperon*, diminutive of *nape* "tablecloth", the source also of English *napkin*] **1** : a garment worn on the front of the body to protect the clothing **2** : something resembling an apron in shape, position, or use: as **a** : the part of the stage in front of the proscenium arch **b** : the extensive paved part of an airport immediately adjacent to the terminal area or hangars

1**ap·ro·pos** \,ap-rə-'pō, 'ap-rə-,\ *adv* : at the right time : SEASONABLY

2**apropos** *adj* : being to the point : PERTINENT

apropos of *prep* : with regard to : CONCERNING

apse \'aps\ *n* : a usu. semicircular projection on the end of a building (as a church)

apt \'apt\ *adj* **1** : suited to a purpose; *specif* : being to the point : APPOSITE ⟨an *apt* remark⟩ **2** : INCLINED, LIKELY ⟨*apt* to become angry over trifles⟩ **3** : quick to learn ⟨*apt* in arithmetic⟩ *syn* see FIT *ant* inapt, inept — **apt·ly** *adv* — **apt·ness** \'ap(t)-nəs\ *n*

apt *abbr* apartment

ap·ti·tude \'ap-tə-,t(y)üd\ *n* **1** : capacity for learning : APTNESS **2** : a natural ability : TALENT ⟨an *aptitude* for mathematics⟩ *syn* see ABILITY

aq *abbr* aqueous

aq·ua·cade \'ak-wə-,kād, 'äk-\ *n* : an elaborate water spectacle consisting of exhibitions of swimming, diving, and acrobatics accompanied by music

aq·ua·lung·er \'ak-wə-,ləng-ər, 'äk-\ *n* : an underwater swimmer who uses a breathing device consisting of one or more cylinders of compressed air and a watertight face mask

aq·ua·ma·rine \,ak-wə-mə-'rēn, ,äk-\ *n* **1** : a transparent semiprecious bluish or greenish stone **2** : a pale blue to light greenish blue

aq·ua·naut \'ak-wə-,nȯt, 'äk-\ *n* : OCEANAUT

aq·ua·plane \'ak-wə-,plān, 'äk-\ *n* : a board which is towed behind a motorboat and on which a person rides — **aquaplane** *vb* — **aq·ua·plan·er** *n*

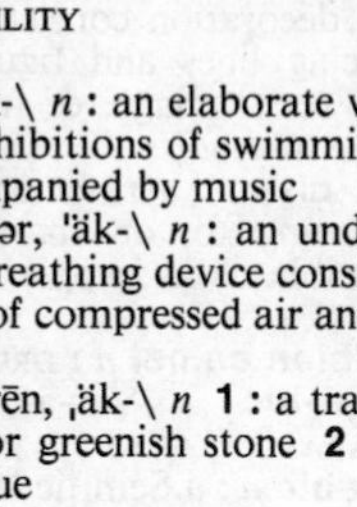
aquaplane

aq·ua re·gia \,ak-wə-'rē-j(ē-)ə, ,äk-\ *n* : a mixture of nitric and hydrochloric acids that dissolves gold or platinum

aq·ua·relle \,ak-wə-'rel,

ˌäk-\ *n* : a drawing in watercolor and esp. transparent watercolor — **aq·ua·rell·ist** \-ˈrel-əst\ *n*

aquar·ist \ə-ˈkwer-əst, -ˈkwar-\ *n* : one who keeps an aquarium

aquar·i·um \ə-ˈkwer-ē-əm, -ˈkwar-\ *n, pl* **-i·ums** *or* **-ia** \-ē-ə\ : a container (as a glass tank) in which living water animals or plants are kept; *also* : an establishment where such aquatic collections are kept and shown

Aquar·i·us \ə-ˈkwar-ē-əs, -ˈkwer-\ *n* — see ZODIAC table

[1]**aquat·ic** \ə-ˈkwät-ik, -ˈkwat-\ *adj* **1** : growing or living in or frequenting water **2** : performed in or on water

[2]**aquatic** *n* : an aquatic animal or plant

aq·ua·tint \ˈak-wə-ˌtint, ˈäk-\ *n* : an etching in which spaces are eaten in with nitric acid to produce an effect resembling a drawing in watercolors or india ink — **aquatint** *vb*

aq·ue·duct \ˈak-wə-ˌdəkt\ *n* : an artificial channel for carrying flowing water from place to place; *esp* : a structure that carries the water of a canal across a river or hollow

aque·ous \ˈā-kwē-əs, ˈak-wē-\ *adj* **1 a** : of, relating to, or resembling water **b** : made of, by, or with water ⟨an *aqueous* solution⟩ **2** : of or relating to the aqueous humor

aqueous humor *n* : a clear fluid between the lens and the cornea of the eye

aq·ui·fer \ˈak-wə-fer, ˈäk-\ *n* : a water-bearing stratum of permeable rock, sand, or gravel — **aquif·er·ous** \a-ˈkwif-ə-rəs, ä-\ *adj*

aq·ui·line \ˈak-wə-ˌlīn, -lən\ *adj* **1** : of or resembling an eagle **2** : curving like an eagle's beak — **aq·ui·lin·i·ty** \ˌak-wə-ˈlin-ət-ē\ *n*

-ar \ər\ *adj suffix* : of or relating to ⟨molecul*ar*⟩ : being ⟨spectacul*ar*⟩ : resembling ⟨oracul*ar*⟩

ar *abbr* **1** arrive **2** arrives

AR *abbr* Arkansas

Ar·ab \ˈar-əb\ *n* **1 a** : a member of the Semitic people of the Arabian peninsula **b** : a member of an Arabic-speaking people **2** : a horse of the stock used by the natives of Arabia and adjacent regions; *esp* : one of a breed noted for graceful build, speed, intelligence, and spirit — **Arab** *adj*

Arab *abbr* **1** Arabian **2** Arabic

ar·a·besque \ˌar-ə-ˈbesk\ *n* : an ornament or a style of decoration consisting of interlacing lines and figures usu. of flowers, foliage, or fruit — **arabesque** *adj*

arabesque

Ara·bi·an \ə-ˈrā-bē-ən\ *adj* : of, relating to, or characteristic of Arabia or its people — **Arabian** *n*

Arabian camel *n* : DROMEDARY 2

[1]**Ar·a·bic** \ˈar-ə-bik\ *adj* : ARABIAN, ARAB

[2]**Arabic** *n* : a Semitic language of Arabia spoken also in Jordan, Lebanon, Syria, Iraq, and northern Africa

arabic numeral *n, often cap A* : one of the number symbols 1, 2, 3, 4, 5, 6, 7, 8, 9, and 0

ar·a·ble \ˈar-ə-bəl\ *adj* : fit for or cultivated by plowing : suitable for producing crops

arach·nid \ə-ˈrak-nəd\ *n* : any of a class of arthropods including the spiders, scorpions, mites, and ticks and having a segmented body divided into two regions of which the anterior bears four pairs of legs but no antennae — **arachnid** *adj*

arag·o·nite \ə-ˈrag-ə-ˌnīt, ˈar-ə-gə-\ *n* : a mineral that is chemically the same as calcite but is denser and takes a different crystalline form

Ar·a·mae·an \ˌar-ə-ˈmē-ən\ *n* **1** : a member of a Semitic people of the 2d millennium B.C. in Syria and Upper Mesopotamia **2** : ARAMAIC — **Aramaean** *adj*

Ar·a·ma·ic \ˌar-ə-ˈmā-ik\ *n* : a Semitic language of the Aramaeans later used extensively in southwest Asia (as by the Jews after the Babylonian exile)

Arap·a·ho *or* **Arap·a·hoe** \ə-ˈrap-ə-ˌhō\ *n* : a member of an Algonquian Amerindian people of the plains region of the U.S. and Canada

ar·bi·ter \ˈär-bət-ər\ *n* **1** : ARBITRATOR **2** : a person having absolute authority to judge and decide what is right or proper ⟨an *arbiter* of taste⟩

ar·bit·ra·ment \är-ˈbi-trə-mənt\ *n* **1** : the settling of a dispute by an arbiter : ARBITRATION **2** : a decision or award made by an arbiter

ar·bi·trary \ˈär-bə-ˌtrer-ē\ *adj* **1** : depending on choice or discretion **2** : arising from or guided by personal preference or impulse ⟨an *arbitrary* ruler⟩ **3** : selected at random — **ar·bi·trar·i·ly** \ˌär-bə-ˈtrer-ə-lē\ *adv* — **ar·bi·trar·i·ness** \ˈär-bə-ˌtrer-ē-nəs\ *n*

ar·bi·trate \ˈär-bə-ˌtrāt\ *vb* **1** : to settle a dispute after considering the arguments of both sides ⟨a committee to *arbitrate* between the company and the union⟩ **2** : to refer a dispute to others for settlement : submit to arbitration ⟨agreed to *arbitrate* their differences⟩

ar·bi·tra·tion \ˌär-bə-ˈtrā-shən\ *n* : the act of arbitrating; *esp* : the settling of a dispute in which both parties agree beforehand to abide by the decision of an arbitrator or body of arbitrators

ar·bi·tra·tor \ˈär-bə-ˌtrāt-ər\ *n* : a person chosen to settle differences between two parties in controversy

ar·bor \ˈär-bər\ *n* : a bower covered with climbing shrubs or vines

Arbor Day *n* : a day appointed for planting trees

ar·bo·re·al \är-ˈbōr-ē-əl, -ˈbȯr-\ *adj* **1** : of, relating to, or resembling a tree **2** : living in or frequenting trees

ar·bo·re·tum \ˌär-bə-ˈrēt-əm\ *n, pl* **-retums** *or* **-re·ta** \-ˈrēt-ə\ : a place where trees and plants are grown for scientific and educational purposes

ar·bo·rist \ˈär-bə-rəst\ *n* : a specialist in the care of trees

ar·bor·vi·tae \ˌär-bər-ˈvīt-ē\ *n* : any of various evergreen trees with closely overlapping scale leaves that are often grown for ornament and hedges

ar·bu·tus \är-ˈbyüt-əs\ *n* : any of a genus of shrubs and trees related to the heath and having white or pink flowers and scarlet berries; *also* : a related trailing plant of eastern No. America with fragrant pinkish flowers borne in early spring

[1]**arc** \ˈärk\ *n* **1** : something curved **2** : a luminous discharge of electricity across a gap in a circuit or between electrodes **3** : a continuous portion of a circle or curve

[2]**arc** *vb* **1** : to form an electric arc **2** : to follow an arc-shaped course

arc *abbr* arcade

ar·cade \är-ˈkād\ *n* **1** : a row of arches with the columns that support them **2** : an arched or covered passageway; *esp* : one lined with shops — **ar·cad·ed** \-ˈkād-əd\ *adj*

ə abut	ər further	a back	ā bake
ä cot, cart	aù out	ch chin	e less
ē easy	g gift	i trip	ī life
j joke	ng sing	ō flow	ȯ flaw
ȯi coin	th thin	th this	ü loot
ù foot	y yet	yü few	yù furious
zh vision			

1arch \ärch\ *n* **1** : a usu. curved structural member spanning an opening and serving as a support **2** : something resembling an arch in form or function; *esp* : either of two portions of the bony structure of the foot that give it elasticity **3** : ARCHWAY

2arch *vb* **1** : to cover or provide with an arch **2** : to form or bend into an arch **3** : to move in an arch : ARC

3arch \ärch\ *adj* **1** : PRINCIPAL, CHIEF ⟨an *arch*-villain⟩ **2** : playfully saucy : ROGUISH

arch- *prefix* : chief : principal ⟨*arch*enemy⟩

ar·chae·ol·o·gy *or* **ar·che·ol·o·gy** \ˌär-kē-ˈäl-ə-jē\ *n* : the science that deals with past human life as shown by fossil relics and the monuments and artifacts left by ancient peoples — **ar·chae·o·log·i·cal** \-kē-ə-ˈläj-i-kəl\ *adj* — **ar·chae·ol·o·gist** \-kē-ˈäl-ə-jəst\ *n*

ar·chae·op·ter·yx \ˌär-kē-ˈäp-tə-riks\ *n* : a primitive extinct Mesozoic European bird with reptilian characteristics

ar·cha·ic \är-ˈkā-ik\ *adj* : of, relating to, characteristic of, or surviving from an earlier time; *esp* : no longer in general use ⟨the *archaic* words *methinks* and *saith*⟩

ar·cha·ism \ˈär-kē-ˌiz-əm, -kā-\ *n* **1** : the use of archaic words **2** : an archaic word or expression

arch·an·gel \ˈärk-ˌān-jəl\ *n* : an angel of high rank — **arch·an·gel·ic** \ˌärk-ˌan-ˈjel-ik\ *adj*

arch·bish·op \(ˈ)ärch-ˈbish-əp\ *n* : the bishop of highest rank in a group of dioceses — **arch·bish·op·ric** \-ˈbish-ə-(ˌ)prik\ *n*

arch·dea·con \(ˈ)ärch-ˈdē-kən\ *n* : an ecclesiastical dignitary usu. ranking below a bishop — **arch·dea·con·ate** \-kə-nət\ *n* — **arch·dea·con·ry** \-kən-rē\ *n*

arch·di·o·cese \(ˈ)ärch-ˈdī-ə-səs, -ˌsēz, -ˌsēs\ *n* : the diocese of an archbishop

arch·duke \-ˈd(y)ük\ *n* : a sovereign prince; *esp* : a prince of the imperial family of Austria — **arch·du·cal** \-ˈd(y)ü-kəl\ *adj* — **arch·duch·ess** \-ˈdəch-əs\ *n* — **arch·duchy** \-ˈdəch-ē\ *n* — **arch·duke·dom** \-dəm\ *n*

arch·en·e·my \(ˈ)ärch-ˈen-ə-mē\ *n* : a principal enemy

Ar·cheo·zo·ic \ˌär-kē-ə-ˈzō-ik\ *n* : the earliest of the five eras of geologic history; *also* : the corresponding system of rocks — see GEOLOGIC TIME table — **Archeozoic** *adj*

ar·cher \ˈär-chər\ *n* : one who uses a bow and arrow — called also *bowman*

ar·chery \ˈärch-(ə-)rē\ *n* **1** : the art, practice, or skill of shooting with bow and arrow **2** : a body of archers

ar·che·type \ˈär-ki-ˌtīp\ *n* : the original pattern or model from which something is copied — **ar·che·typ·al** \ˌär-ki-ˈtī-pəl\ *or* **ar·che·typ·i·cal** \-ˈtip-i-kəl\ *adj*

ar·chi·epis·co·pal \ˌär-kē-ə-ˈpis-kə-pəl\ *adj* : of or relating to an archbishop

Ar·chi·me·des principle \ˌär-kə-ˈmēd-ēz-\ *n* : a law of fluid mechanics: a body immersed in a fluid is buoyed up with a force equal to the weight of the displaced fluid

ar·chi·pel·a·go \ˌär-kə-ˈpel-ə-ˌgō, ˌär-chə-\ *n, pl* **-goes** *or* **-gos** : a body of water with many scattered islands; *also* : a group of islands in an archipelago

ar·chi·tect \ˈär-kə-ˌtekt\ *n* : a person who designs buildings and oversees their construction

ar·chi·tec·ture \ˈär-kə-ˌtek-chər\ *n* **1** : the art of making plans for buildings **2** : the style of building that architects produce or imitate ⟨a church of modern *architecture*⟩ **3** : architectural work : BUILDINGS — **ar·chi·tec·tur·al** \ˌär-kə-ˈtek-chə-rəl\ *adj* — **ar·chi·tec·tur·al·ly** \-rə-lē\ *adv*

ar·chi·trave \ˈär-kə-ˌtrāv\ *n* : the line of stones resting immediately on the capital of the column in an ancient Greek or Roman building

ar·chive \ˈär-ˌkīv\ *n* : a place in which public records or historical documents are preserved; *also* : the material preserved — usu. used in pl.

ar·chi·vist \ˈär-kə-vəst, -ˌkī-\ *n* : a person in charge of archives

arch·ly \ˈärch-lē\ *adv* : in an arch manner : ROGUISHLY, MISCHIEVOUSLY

arch·ness *n* : the quality of being arch

arch·way \ˈärch-ˌwā\ *n* : a passage under an arch

-ar·chy \ˌär-kē, *in some words also* ər-kē\ *n comb form, pl* **-archies** : rule : government ⟨squire*archy*⟩

arc lamp *n* : a lamp whose light is produced when an electric current passes between two hot electrodes surrounded by gas — called also *arc light*

1arc·tic \ˈärk-tik, ˈärt-ik\ *adj* [from Greek *arktikos*, from *Arktos* "the Bear", name of the most conspicuous constellation near the north pole of the sky] **1** *often cap* : of or relating to the north pole or the region around it **2** : very cold : FRIGID

2arc·tic \ˈärt-ik, ˈärk-tik\ *n* : a rubber overshoe reaching to the ankle or above

arctic circle *n, often cap A&C* : a small circle of the earth parallel to its equator approximately 23° from the north pole

arctic cotton *n* : a sedge that is found esp. in bogs and that has a stalked fruiting spike resembling a cotton ball

arctic fox *n* : a small fox of arctic regions having a valuable fur that is blue-gray or brownish in summer and white in winter

arctic hare *n* : a large hare of arctic America that is almost completely white in winter

arctic tern *n* : a tern breeding in arctic regions of both the Old and New World and migrating to So. America and Africa

ar·dent \ˈärd-ənt\ *adj* **1** : characterized by warmth of feeling : PASSIONATE **2** : FIERY, HOT **3** : GLOWING, SHINING — **ar·den·cy** \-ən-sē\ *n* — **ar·dent·ly** *adv*

ar·dor \ˈärd-ər\ *n* **1** : a warmth of feeling or sentiment **2** : ZEAL, EAGERNESS

ar·du·ous \ˈärj-(ə-)wəs\ *adj* : extremely difficult : LABORIOUS ⟨an *arduous* climb⟩ — **ar·du·ous·ly** *adv* — **ar·du·ous·ness** *n*

1are *pres 2d sing or pres pl of* BE

2are \ˈa(ə)r, ˈe(ə)r, ˈär\ *n* — see METRIC SYSTEM table

ar·ea \ˈar-ē-ə, ˈer-\ *n* **1** : a flat surface; *esp* : a level piece of ground **2** : the amount of surface within a closed figure; *esp* : the number of unit squares equal in measure to the included surface ⟨a circle with *area* of 2000 square feet⟩ **3 a** : REGION ⟨a farming *area*⟩ **b** : a field of activity **4** : a part of the brain having a particular function (as vision or hearing)

area code *n* : a 3-digit code that identifies a geographic area and that is used in addition to a telephone number in making direct long-distance calls

area·way \-ē-ə-ˌwā\ *n* : a sunken space affording access, air, and light to a basement

are·na \ə-ˈrē-nə\ *n* **1** : an enclosed area used for public entertainment **2** : a building containing an arena **3** : a sphere of interest or activity

aren't \(ˈ)ärnt, ˈär-ənt\ : are not

are·o·la \ə-ˈrē-ə-lə\ *n, pl* **-lae** \-ˌlē\ *or* **-las** : a colored ring (as about the nipple) — **are·o·lar** \-lər\ *adj*

arête \ə-ˈrāt\ *n* : a sharp-crested ridge in rugged mountains

ar·gent \ˈär-jənt\ *adj* : SILVERY, WHITE

Ar·gen·tine \ˈär-jən-ˌtēn\ *adj* : of, relating to, or characteristic of Argentina or its people — **Argentine** *n* — **Ar·gen·tin·e·an** *or* **Ar·gen·tin·i·an** \ˌär-jən-ˈtin-ē-ən\ *adj or n*

ar·gen·tite \ˈär-jən-ˌtīt\ *n* : a dark gray mineral that is a sulfide of silver and an ore of silver

ar·gen·tum \är-ˈjent-əm\ *n* : SILVER

ar·gil·la·ceous \ˌär-jə-ˈlā-shəs\ *adj* : of, relating to, or containing clay or the minerals of clay

ar·gi·nine \ˈär-jə-ˌnēn\ *n* : an amino acid that is found in various proteins

ar·gon \ˈär-ˌgän\ *n* : a colorless odorless gaseous element found in the air and in volcanic gases and used esp. as a filler for electric bulbs — see ELEMENT table

ar·go·naut \ˈär-gə-ˌnȯt\ *n* : NAUTILUS 2

ar·go·sy \ˈär-gə-sē\ *n, pl* **-sies** : a large merchant ship

ar·got \ˈär-gət, -gō\ *n* : the language of a particular group or class esp. of the underworld

ar·gue \ˈär-gyü\ *vb* **1** : to give reasons for or against ⟨*argue* in favor of lowering taxes⟩ **2** : to debate or discuss some matter : DISPUTE ⟨*argue* about politics⟩ **3** : to persuade by giving reasons ⟨tried to *argue* his father into getting a new car⟩ *syn* see DISCUSS — **ar·gu·er** *n*

ar·gu·ment \ˈär-gyə-mənt\ *n* **1 a** : a reason for or against something **b** : a discussion in which arguments are presented : DISPUTE, DEBATE **2** : a heated dispute : QUARREL **3** : the subject matter (as of a book) or a summary of the subject matter

ar·gu·men·ta·tion \ˌär-gyə-mən-ˈtā-shən, -ˌmen-\ *n* **1** : the act or process of forming reasons and of drawing conclusions and applying them to a case under discussion **2** : DEBATE, DISCUSSION

ar·gu·men·ta·tive \ˌär-gyə-ˈment-ət-iv\ *adj* : marked by or given to argument : DISPUTATIOUS — **ar·gu·men·ta·tive·ly** *adv*

aria \ˈär-ē-ə\ *n* : AIR, MELODY; *esp* : an accompanied elaborate solo in an opera

ar·id \ˈar-əd\ *adj* : very dry : BARREN — **arid·i·ty** \ə-ˈrid-ət-ē, a-\ *n*

Ar·i·es \ˈar-ē-ˌēz, ˈer-\ *n* — see ZODIAC table

aright \ə-ˈrīt\ *adv* : RIGHTLY, CORRECTLY ⟨done *aright*⟩

arise \ə-ˈrīz\ *vb* **arose** \-ˈrōz\; **aris·en** \-ˈriz-ən\; **aris·ing** \-ˈrī-zing\ **1** : to move upward : ASCEND **2** : to get up from sleep or after lying down **3** : to come into existence : spring up : OCCUR ⟨a dispute *arose* between the leaders⟩

ar·is·toc·ra·cy \ˌar-ə-ˈstäk-rə-sē\ *n, pl* **-cies** **1** : government by the best individuals or by a small privileged class **2 a** : a government in which power is exercised by a small privileged class **b** : a state with such a government **3 a** : a governing body or upper class usu. made up of nobles **b** : a group felt to be superior (as in wealth, culture, or intelligence)

aris·to·crat \ə-ˈris-tə-ˌkrat\ *n* **1** : a member of an aristocracy; *esp* : NOBLE **2** : one who has habits and viewpoints that are typical of the aristocracy — **aris·to·crat·ic** \ə-ˌris-tə-ˈkrat-ik\ *adj* — **aris·to·crat·i·cal·ly** \-ˈkrat-i-k(ə-)lē\ *adv*

arith *abbr* arithmetic

ə abut	ər further	a back	ā bake
ä cot, cart	aù out	ch chin	e less	ē easy
g gift	i trip	ī life	j joke	ng sing	ō flow
ȯ flaw	ȯi coin	th thin	<u>th</u> this	ü loot
ù foot	y yet	yü few	yù furious	zh vision

arith·me·tic \ə-ˈrith-mə-ˌtik\ *n* **1** : a branch of mathematics that deals with real numbers and their addition, subtraction, multiplication, and division **2** : an act or method of computing : CALCULATION ⟨your *arithmetic* is faulty⟩ — **ar·ith·met·ic** \ˌar-ith-ˈmet-ik\ *or* **ar·ith·met·i·cal** \-ˈmet-i-kəl\ *adj* — **ar·ith·met·i·cal·ly** \-k(ə-)lē\ *adv* — **arith·me·ti·cian** \ə-ˌrith-mə-ˈtish-ən\ *n*

arithmetic mean \ˌar-ith-ˌmet-ik-\ *n* : a value that is computed by dividing the sum of a set of terms by the number of terms ⟨the *arithmetic mean* of 6, 4, and 5 is 5⟩

Ariz *abbr* Arizona

ark \ˈärk\ *n* **1 a** : the ship in which Noah and his family were saved from the Flood **b** : a clumsy boat or ship **2 a** : a sacred chest in which the ancient Hebrews kept the two tablets of the Law **b** : a repository in a synagogue for the scrolls of the Torah

Ark *abbr* Arkansas

[1]arm \ˈärm\ *n* **1 a** : a human upper limb; *esp* : the part between the shoulder and wrist **b** : a corresponding limb of a lower vertebrate **2 a** : something resembling an arm; *esp* : an inlet of water ⟨an *arm* of the sea⟩ **b** : a slender usu. functional projecting part (as of a machine) **3** : POWER, MIGHT ⟨the *arm* of the law⟩ **4** : a support (as on a chair) for the arm **5** : SLEEVE — **armed** \ˈärmd\ *adj* — **arm·less** \ˈärm-ləs\ *adj*

[2]arm *vb* **1** : to provide with weapons ⟨*arm* a regiment⟩ **2** : to provide with a means of defense ⟨*arm* oneself with facts⟩ **3** : to provide oneself with arms and armament ⟨the country *armed* for war⟩ **4** : to equip or ready for action or operation ⟨*arm* a bomb⟩

[3]arm *n* **1 a** : WEAPON; *esp* : FIREARM **b** : a branch of an army (as the infantry or artillery) that actually fights **c** : a branch of the military forces (as the navy) **2** *pl* : the heraldic devices of a family or a government **3 a** *pl* : active hostilities : WARFARE **b** *pl* : military service

ar·ma·da \är-ˈmäd-ə, -ˈmād-\ *n* **1** : a large fleet of warships **2** : a large force of moving objects (as airplanes)

ar·ma·dil·lo \ˌär-mə-ˈdil-ō\ *n, pl* **-los** : any of several small burrowing mammals of warm parts of the Americas having body and head encased in an armor of small bony plates

armadillo
(1 ft. high at shoulder)

ar·ma·ment \ˈär-mə-mənt\ *n* **1** : the military strength and equipment of a nation **2** : a supply of war materials **3** : means of protection : ARMOR **4** : the process of preparing for war

ar·ma·ture \ˈär-mə-chər, -ˌchù(ə)r\ *n* **1** : a protective or defensive mechanism or covering (as the spines of a cactus) **2** : the part of an electric generator that consists of coils of wire around an iron core and that induces an electric current when it is rotated in a magnetic field **3** : the part of an electric motor that consists of coils of wire around an iron core and that is caused to rotate in a magnetic field when an electric current is passed through the coils **4** : the movable part of an electromagnetic device (as an electric bell)

arm·chair \ˈärm-ˌche(ə)r, -ˌcha(ə)r, ˈärm-ˈ\ *n* : a chair with arms

A

armed forces *n pl* : the military, naval, and air forces of a nation

arm·ful \'ärm-ˌfu̇l\ *n, pl* **arm·fuls** \-ˌfu̇lz\ *or* **arms·ful** \'ärmz-ˌfu̇l\ : as much as a person's arm can hold ⟨an *armful* of books⟩

arm·hole \'ärm-ˌhōl\ *n* : an opening for the arm in a garment

ar·mi·stice \'är-mə-stəs\ *n* : a pause in fighting brought about by agreement between the two sides : TRUCE

Armistice Day *n* : VETERANS DAY

arm·let \'ärm-lət\ *n* : a bracelet or band for the upper arm

ar·mor \'är-mər\ *n* **1** : defensive covering for the body used esp. in combat **2** : a protective covering (as the steel plates of a battleship or a sheathing for wire) **3** : armored forces or vehicles (as tanks)

armor

ar·mored \-mərd\ *adj* **1** : protected by armor ⟨an *armored* car⟩ ⟨*armored* reptiles⟩ **2** : supplied with armored equipment ⟨an *armored* force⟩

armored scale *n* : any of numerous scale insects having a firm covering of wax

ar·mor·er \'är-mər-ər\ *n* **1** : one that makes armor or arms **2** : a person who repairs, assembles, and tests firearms or who services and loads aircraft armament

ar·mo·ri·al \är-'mōr-ē-əl, -'mȯr-\ *adj* : of, relating to, or bearing heraldic arms

ar·mo·ry \'ärm-(ə-)rē\ *n, pl* **-ries** **1** : a supply of arms **2** : ARSENAL 1 **3** : a place for training military reserve personnel

arm·pit \'ärm-ˌpit\ *n* : the hollow beneath the junction of the arm and shoulder

ar·my \'är-mē\ *n, pl* **ar·mies** **1 a** : a large body of men organized for land warfare **b** *often cap* : the complete military organization of a nation for land warfare **2** : a great multitude ⟨an *army* of insects⟩ **3** : a body of persons organized to advance a cause ⟨an *army* of dedicated doctors⟩

ar·my·worm \-ˌwərm\ *n* : any of numerous moths that in the larval stage travel in multitudes from field to field destroying crops (as grass or grain)

ar·ni·ca \'är-ni-kə\ *n* **1** : dried flower heads of a mountain herb related to the daisies and used esp. in solution as a liniment **2** : a medicinal solution prepared from arnica

aro·ma \ə-'rō-mə\ *n* : a distinctive pleasing often pungent or spicy odor (as of pine foliage or cloves)

ar·o·mat·ic \ˌar-ə-'mat-ik\ *adj* **1** : having aroma **2** : of, relating to, or characterized by the presence of at least one benzene ring — used of hydrocarbons and their derivatives ***syn*** see FRAGRANT ***ant*** acrid — **aromatic** *n*

arose *past of* ARISE

[1]**around** \ə-'rau̇nd\ *adv* **1** : in circumference ⟨a tree five feet *around*⟩ **2** : in or along a curving course **3** : on all sides ⟨papers lying *around*⟩ **4** : NEARBY ⟨stick *around*⟩ **5** : here and there : ABOUT ⟨travel *around*⟩ **6** : in rotation or succession ⟨pass the candy *around*⟩ **7** : in or to an opposite direction or position ⟨turn *around*⟩ **8** : APPROXIMATELY ⟨a price of *around* $20⟩

[2]**around** *prep* **1 a** : on all sides of ⟨fields *around* the village⟩ **b** : so as to encircle or enclose ⟨people seated *around* the table⟩ **c** : on or to another side of ⟨voyage *around* Cape Horn⟩ **2** : here and there in or throughout ⟨travel *around* the country⟩ **3** : near to ⟨selling at prices *around* $20⟩

arouse \ə-'rau̇z\ *vb* **1** : to awaken from sleep **2** : to rouse to action : EXCITE

ar·peg·gio \är-'pej-ō, -'pej-ē-ˌō\ *n, pl* **-gios** **1** : production of the tones of a chord in succession and not simultaneously **2** : a chord played in arpeggio

ar·que·bus \'är-\ *var of* HARQUEBUS

ar·raign \ə-'rān\ *vb* **1** : to call before a court to answer to an indictment : CHARGE **2** : ACCUSE, DENOUNCE — **ar·raign·ment** \-mənt\ *n*

ar·range \ə-'rānj\ *vb* **1** : to put in order; *esp* : to put in a particular order ⟨*arrange* books on shelves⟩ **2** : to make plans for : PREPARE ⟨*arrange* a meeting⟩ **3** : ADJUST, SETTLE ⟨*arrange* one's affairs to have the weekend free⟩ **4** : to make a musical arrangement of — **ar·rang·er** *n*

ar·range·ment \ə-'rānj-mənt\ *n* **1** : a putting in order : the order in which things are put ⟨the *arrangement* of furniture in a room⟩ **2** : PREPARATION, PLAN ⟨make *arrangements* for a trip⟩ **3** : something made by arranging ⟨a flower *arrangement*⟩ **4** : an adaptation of a piece of music to voices or instruments other than those orig. intended

ar·rant \'ar-ənt\ *adj* : THOROUGHGOING, CONFIRMED ⟨an *arrant* knave⟩ — **ar·rant·ly** *adv*

ar·ras \'ar-əs\ *n, pl* **arras** **1** : a tapestry of Flemish origin **2** : a wall hanging or screen of tapestry

[1]**ar·ray** \ə-'rā\ *vb* **1** : to set in order : draw up **2** : to dress esp. in splendid or impressive attire : ADORN — **ar·ray·er** *n*

[2]**array** *n* **1** : regular order or arrangement; *also* : persons (as troops) in array **2** : rich or beautiful apparel : FINERY **3** : an imposing group : large number **4** : a group of mathematical elements (as numbers or letters) arranged in rows and columns

ar·rears \ə-'ri(ə)rz\ *n pl* **1** : the state of being behind in the discharge of debts owed ⟨two months in *arrears* on his payments⟩ **2** : an unpaid and overdue debt

[1]**ar·rest** \ə-'rest\ *vb* **1** : to stop the progress or movement of : CHECK ⟨*arrest* a disease⟩ **2** : to take or keep in custody by authority of law ⟨*arrested* him on suspicion of robbery⟩ **3** : to attract and hold the attention of ⟨colors that *arrest* the eye⟩

[2]**arrest** *n* **1 a** : the act of stopping : CHECK **b** : the state of being stopped **2** : the act of taking or holding in custody by authority of law

ar·riv·al \ə-'rī-vəl\ *n* **1** : the act of arriving ⟨await the *arrival* of guests⟩ **2** : a person or thing that has arrived ⟨late *arrivals* at a concert⟩

ar·rive \ə-'rīv\ *vb* **1** : to reach a place and esp. one's destination ⟨*arrive* home at six o'clock⟩ **2** : to gain an end or object ⟨*arrive* at a decision⟩ **3** : COME ⟨the time *arrived* to begin⟩ **4** : to be successful

ar·ro·gance \'ar-ə-gən(t)s\ *n* : offensive pride : HAUGHTINESS

ar·ro·gant \-gənt\ *adj* **1** : exaggerating one's own worth or importance in an overbearing manner **2** : marked by arrogance ⟨*arrogant* remarks⟩ — **ar·ro·gant·ly** *adv*

ar·ro·gate \'ar-ə-ˌgāt\ *vb* **1** : to take or claim for one's own without right or in a haughty manner ⟨the dictator *arrogated* to himself the powers of parliament⟩ **2** : to ascribe to another esp. unduly or without right ⟨*arrogate* to a rival intentions he never had⟩ — **ar·ro·ga·tion** \ˌar-ə-'gā-shən\ *n*

ar·row \'ar-ō\ *n* **1** : a missile weapon shot from a bow and usu. having a slender shaft with a point at one end and feathers at the other **2 :** a mark (as on a map) to indicate direction

ar·row·head \-ˌhed\ *n* **:** the wedge-shaped striking end of an arrow

ar·row·root \-ˌrüt, -ˌru̇t\ *n* **1 :** any of several tropical American plants with starchy tuberous roots **2 :** an edible starch from arrowroot

arrow worm *n* **:** any of a small phylum of transparent tapering marine worms

ar·royo \ə-ˈrȯi-ō, -ˈrȯi-ə\ *n, pl* **-roy·os 1 :** a watercourse (as a creek) in a dry region **2 :** an often dry gully

ar·se·nal \ˈär-s(ə-)nəl\ *n* **1 a :** a place for the manufacture or storage of arms **b :** a collection of weapons **2 :** STORE, STOREHOUSE

ar·se·nate \ˈär-sə-nət, -ˌnāt\ *n* **:** a salt of arsenic acid

ar·se·nic \ˈär-s(ə-)nik\ *n* **1 :** a solid poisonous element commonly metallic steel-gray, crystalline, and brittle — see ELEMENT table **2 :** a white or transparent extremely poisonous oxide of arsenic used in making glass and insecticides

arsenic acid *n* **:** a white crystalline poisonous acid that consists of hydrogen, arsenic, and oxygen and is used in making chemicals

ar·sen·i·cal \är-ˈsen-i-kəl\ *adj* **:** of, relating to, or containing arsenic — **arsenical** *n*

ar·se·no·py·rite \ˌär-sə-nō-ˈpī-ˌrīt\ *n* **:** a hard bluish white mineral consisting of iron, arsenic, and sulfur

ar·sine \är-ˈsēn, ˈär-ˌ\ *n* **:** a colorless flammable extremely poisonous gas with an odor like garlic

ar·son \ˈär-sən\ *n* **:** the malicious burning of a building or property (as a dwelling house) — **ar·son·ist** \-s(ə-)nəst\ *n*

[1]**art** \(ˈ)ärt, ərt\ *archaic pres 2d sing of* BE

[2]**art** \ˈärt\ *n* **1 :** the power of doing something easily and skillfully **:** KNACK ⟨the *art* of making friends⟩ **2 :** an occupation that requires natural skill in addition to training and practice **3 :** the rules or ideas that a person must know in order to follow a profession or craft ⟨the *art* of medicine⟩ **4 :** a branch of learning; *esp* **:** one of the liberal arts — usu. used in pl. ⟨a bachelor's degree in *arts*⟩ **5 :** the study of drawing, painting, and sculpture **6 :** the works produced by artists (as painters, sculptors, or writers)

art *abbr* article

ar·te·ri·al \är-ˈtir-ē-əl\ *adj* **1 a :** of or relating to an artery **b :** being the bright red oxygen-rich blood present in most arteries **2 :** of, relating to, or being routes for through traffic ⟨*arterial* highways⟩ — **ar·te·ri·al·ly** \-ē-ə-lē\ *adv*

ar·te·ri·ole \är-ˈtir-ē-ˌōl\ *n* **:** a very small artery connecting a larger artery with capillaries — **ar·te·ri·o·lar** \är-ˌtir-ē-ˈō-ˌlär, -lər\ *adj*

ar·te·rio·scle·ro·sis \är-ˌtir-ē-ō-sklə-ˈrō-səs\ *n* **:** a chronic disease characterized by abnormal thickening and hardening of the arterial walls — **ar·te·rio·scle·rot·ic** \-ˈrät-ik\ *adj or n*

ar·tery \ˈärt-ə-rē\ *n, pl* **-ter·ies 1 :** one of the tubular branching muscular-walled and elastic-walled vessels that carry blood from the heart to all parts of the body **2 :** a channel (as a river or highway) of transportation or communication

ar·te·sian well \är-ˌtē-zhən-\ *n* **1 :** a bored well from which water flows up like a fountain **2 :** a deep-bored well

ə abut	ər further	a back	ā bake
ä cot, cart	au̇ out	ch chin	e less
ē easy	g gift	i trip	ī life
j joke	ng sing	ō flow	ȯ flaw
ȯi coin	th thin	th this	ü loot
u̇ foot	y yet	yü few	yu̇ furious
zh vision			

art·ful \ˈärt-fəl\ *adj* **1 :** performed with or showing art or skill **2 :** CRAFTY, WILY — **art·ful·ly** \-fə-lē\ *adv* — **art·ful·ness** *n*

ar·thri·tis \är-ˈthrīt-əs\ *n* **:** inflammation of the joints — **ar·thrit·ic** \-ˈthrit-ik\ *adj or n*

ar·thro·pod \ˈär-thrə-ˌpäd\ *n* **:** any of a phylum of invertebrate animals (as insects, arachnids, and crustaceans) with a segmented body, jointed limbs, and a chitinous shell that is shed periodically — **arthropod** *adj*

ar·ti·choke \ˈärt-ə-ˌchōk\ *n* **:** a tall thistlelike herb with coarse leaves that are sharply divided; *also* **:** the edible flower head of an artichoke which is cooked as a vegetable

ar·ti·cle \ˈärt-i-kəl\ *n* **1 :** a distinct part of a document (as a contract) dealing with a single subject **2 :** a nonfictional prose composition forming an independent part of a publication **3 :** a word (as *a, an,* or *the*) used with nouns to limit or give definiteness to their application **4 :** a member of a class of things ⟨*articles* of commerce⟩

ar·tic·u·lar \är-ˈtik-yə-lər\ *adj* **:** of or relating to a joint

[1]**ar·tic·u·late** \är-ˈtik-yə-lət\ *adj* **1 a :** divided clearly into words and syllables **:** INTELLIGIBLE **b :** able to speak; *esp* **:** able to express oneself effectively **2 :** consisting of segments united by joints **:** JOINTED ⟨*articulate* animals⟩ — **ar·tic·u·late·ly** *adv* — **ar·tic·u·late·ness** *n*

[2]**ar·tic·u·late** \-ˌlāt\ *vb* **1 a :** to speak in distinct syllables or words **b :** to express clearly and distinctly ⟨*articulate* every shade of meaning⟩ **2 :** to unite or become united or connected by or as if by a joint — **ar·tic·u·la·tor** \-ˌlāt-ər\ *n*

ar·tic·u·la·tion \(ˌ)är-ˌtik-yə-ˈlā-shən\ *n* **1 :** the making of articulate sounds (as in pronunciation) ⟨his *articulation* was distinct⟩ **2 :** a joint between rigid parts of an animal; *esp* **:** one between bones or cartilages

ar·ti·fact *or* **ar·te·fact** \ˈärt-ə-ˌfakt\ *n* **:** a usu. simple object (as a tool or ornament) showing human workmanship or modification

ar·ti·fice \ˈärt-ə-fəs\ *n* **1 :** SKILL, INGENUITY **2 a :** a clever or crafty device **:** TRICK **b :** GUILE, TRICKERY

ar·tif·i·cer \är-ˈtif-ə-sər, ˈärt-ə-fə-sər\ *n* **:** a skilled or artistic workman **:** CRAFTSMAN

ar·ti·fi·cial \ˌärt-ə-ˈfish-əl\ *adj* **1 :** not natural **:** MAN-MADE ⟨an *artificial* lake⟩ **2 :** made or changed to resemble something natural ⟨*artificial* flowers⟩ **3 :** not genuine or sincere **:** FORCED ⟨*artificial* gaiety⟩ — **ar·ti·fi·ci·al·i·ty** \-ˌfish-ē-ˈal-ət-ē\ *n* — **ar·ti·fi·cial·ly** \-ˈfish-(ə-)lē\ *adv*

artificial heart *n* **:** a device designed to maintain the flow of blood to the tissues of the body esp. during a surgical operation on the heart

artificial respiration *n* **:** the rhythmic forcing of air into and out of the lungs of a person whose breathing has stopped

artificial selection *n* **:** the process of modifying organisms (as domestic plants and animals) by selective breeding controlled by man

ar·til·lery \är-ˈtil-(ə-)rē\ *n* **1 :** large caliber crew-served mounted firearms (as guns, howitzers, rockets) **:** ORDNANCE **2 :** a branch of an army armed with artillery — **ar·til·lery·man** \-mən\ *n*

ar·ti·san \ˈärt-ə-zən\ *n* **:** a person (as a carpenter) who works at a trade requiring skill with the hands

art·ist \ˈärt-əst\ *n* **1 :** a person skilled in one of the arts (as painting, sculpture, music, or writing); *esp* **:** PAINTER **2 :** a person showing unusual ability in an occupation requiring skill

A

ar·tis·tic \är-'tis-tik\ *adj* **1** : relating to or characteristic of art or artists **2** : showing taste in arrangement or execution — **ar·tis·ti·cal·ly** \-'tis-ti-k(ə-)lē\ *adv*

art·ist·ry \'ärt-ə-strē\ *n* **1** : artistic quality of effect or workmanship **2** : artistic ability

art·less \'ärt-ləs\ *adj* **1** : lacking art, knowledge, or skill : UNCULTURED **2 a** : made without skill : RUDE **b** : being simple and sincere : NATURAL ⟨*artless* grace⟩ **3** : free from deceit — **art·less·ly** *adv* — **art·less·ness** *n*

art song *n* : a song whose melody and accompaniment are of artistic rather than popular or traditional origin and character

ar·um \'ar-əm, 'er-\ *n* : any of a family of plants (as the jack-in-the-pulpit or the skunk cabbage) having heart-shaped or sword-shaped leaves and flowers in a fleshy spike enclosed in a leafy sheath

ARV *abbr* American Revised Version

[1]**-ary** *n suffix*, *pl* **-aries** : thing or person belonging to or connected with ⟨function*ary*⟩

[2]**-ary** *adj suffix* : of, relating to, or connected with ⟨budget*ary*⟩

[1]**as** \əz, (,)az\ *adv* **1** : to the same degree or extent ⟨*as* deaf as a post⟩ ⟨a number twice *as* large⟩ **2** : for instance ⟨various trees, *as* oak or pine⟩

[2]**as** *conj* **1** : in or to the same degree that ⟨deaf *as* a post⟩ **2** : in the way or manner that ⟨do *as* I do⟩ **3** : WHILE, WHEN ⟨spilled the milk *as* she got up⟩ **4** : THOUGH ⟨improbable *as* it seems, it's true⟩ **5** : BECAUSE ⟨stayed home *as* she had no car⟩ **6** : that the result is — used after *so* or *such* ⟨so clearly guilty *as* to leave no doubt⟩

[3]**as** *pron* **1** : THAT, WHO, WHICH ⟨the same school *as* his father attended⟩ **2** : a fact that ⟨he is rich, *as* you know⟩

[4]**as** *prep* **1** : LIKE ⟨all rose *as* one man⟩ **2** : in the character or position of ⟨working *as* an editor⟩

as- — see AD-

as·a·fet·i·da *or* **as·a·foe·ti·da** \,as-ə-'fit-əd-ē, -'fet-əd-ə\ *n* : a hard gum that has an unpleasant smell and taste, comes from several oriental plants related to the carrot, and was once thought to ward off disease

as·bes·tos \as-'bes-təs, az-\ *n* : a noncombustible and heat-resistant grayish mineral that readily separates into long flexible fibers and is used in making various fireproof, nonconducting, and chemically resistant materials

as·ca·rid \'as-kə-rəd\ *n* : any of a family of roundworms that includes the common large roundworm parasitic in the human intestine

as·ca·ris \'as-kə-rəs\ *n*, *pl* **as·car·i·des** \a-'skar-ə-,dēz\ : ASCARID

as·cend \ə-'send\ *vb* : to go upward : CLIMB, RISE ⟨*ascend* a hill⟩ ⟨smoke *ascends*⟩ — **as·cend·a·ble** *or* **as·cend·i·ble** \-'sen-də-bəl\ *adj*

as·cend·an·cy \ə-'sen-dən-sē\ *or* **as·cend·ance** \-dən(t)s\ *n* : governing or controlling influence

[1]**as·cend·ant** \ə-'sen-dənt\ *n* : a state or position of dominant power ⟨his influence is in the *ascendant*⟩

[2]**ascendant** *adj* **1** : moving upward : RISING **2 a** : in a superior position **b** : inclined to dominate

as·cen·sion \ə-'sen-chən\ *n* : the act or process of ascending

Ascension Day *n* : the Thursday 40 days after Easter observed in commemoration of Christ's ascension into heaven

as·cent \ə-'sent\ *n* **1** : ASCENSION, CLIMB **2** : an upward slope : RISE

as·cer·tain \,as-ər-'tān\ *vb* : to learn with certainty : find out ⟨*ascertain* the date of the concert⟩ — **as·cer·tain·a·ble** \-'tā-nə-bəl\ *adj* — **as·cer·tain·ment** \-'tān-mənt\ *n*

as·cet·ic \ə-'set-ik\ *adj* **1** : practicing strict self-denial esp. as a means of religious discipline ⟨*ascetic* way of life⟩ **2** : AUSTERE ⟨*ascetic* surroundings⟩ — **ascetic** *n* — **as·cet·i·cism** \ə-'set-ə-,siz-əm\ *n*

as·co·my·cete \,as-kō-'mī-,sēt, -mī-'sēt\ *n* : any of a class of higher fungi (as yeasts and molds) with hyphae divided by septa and spores formed in asci — **as·co·my·ce·tous** \-mī-'sēt-əs\ *adj*

ascor·bic acid \ə-,skȯr-bik-\ *n* : VITAMIN C

as·cot \'as-kət, -,kät\ *n* : a broad neck scarf that is looped under the chin

as·cribe \ə-'skrīb\ *vb* : to refer to a supposed cause, source, or author : ATTRIBUTE — **as·crib·a·ble** \-'skrī-bə-bəl\ *adj*

as·crip·tion \ə-'skrip-shən\ *n* : the act of ascribing : ATTRIBUTION

as·cus \'as-kəs\ *n*, *pl* **as·ci** \'as-,(k)ī, -,kē\ : a membranous oval or tubular spore sac of an ascomycete usu. bearing eight spores

as·dic \'az-(,)dik\ *n* : SONAR

-ase \,ās\ *n suffix* : enzyme ⟨malt*ase*⟩

asep·sis \(')ā-'sep-səs, ə-\ *n* : the condition of being aseptic; *also* : the methods of making or keeping aseptic

asep·tic \-'sep-tik\ *adj* **1** : preventing infection; *also* : free or freed from disease-causing microorganisms **2 a** : lacking life, emotion, or warmth ⟨*aseptic* essays⟩ ⟨*aseptic* apartments⟩ **b** : DETACHED, OBJECTIVE ⟨an *aseptic* view of civilization⟩

asex·u·al \(')ā-'sek-sh(ə-w)əl\ *adj* **1** : lacking sex ⟨*asexual* organisms⟩ **2** : occurring or formed without the production and union of two kinds of reproductive cells ⟨*asexual* reproduction⟩ ⟨*asexual* spores⟩ — **asex·u·al·ly** \-ē\ *adv*

as for *prep* : with regard to : CONCERNING ⟨*as for* me⟩

[1]**ash** \'ash\ *n* **1** : any of a genus of trees related to the olive and having thin furrowed bark and winged seeds **2** : the tough elastic wood of an ash

[2]**ash** *n* **1 a** : the solid residue left when material is thoroughly burned or is oxidized by chemical means **b** : fine particles of mineral matter from a volcanic vent **2** *pl* **a** : a collection of ash left after something has been burned **b** : the remains of the dead human body esp. after cremation **c** : the last traces of something : RUINS

ashamed \ə-'shāmd\ *adj* **1** : feeling shame, guilt, or disgrace ⟨*ashamed* of his behavior⟩ **2** : kept back by pride ⟨*ashamed* to beg⟩ — **asham·ed·ly** \-'shā-məd-lē\ *adv*

[1]**ash·en** \'ash-ən\ *adj* : of, relating to, or made of ash

[2]**ashen** *adj* **1** : of the color of ashes **2** : deadly pale

ashore \ə-'shō(ə)r, -'shȯ(ə)r\ *adv or adj* : on or to the shore

Ash Wednesday *n* : the first day of Lent

ashy \'ash-ē\ *adj* **ash·i·er**; **-est** **1** : of, relating to, or resembling ashes **2** : deadly pale

Asian \'ā-zhən, 'ā-shən\ *adj* : of, relating to, or characteristic of Asia or its people — **Asian** *n*

Asi·at·ic \,ā-zhē-'at-ik\ *adj* : ASIAN — often taken to be offensive — **Asiatic** *n*

[1]**aside** \ə-'sīd\ *adv* **1** : to or toward the side ⟨stepped *aside*⟩ **2** : out of the way : AWAY ⟨took him *aside*⟩ **3** : away from one's thought : APART ⟨all kidding *aside*⟩

[2]**aside** *n* : words meant to be inaudible to someone; *esp* : an actor's words supposedly not heard by others on the stage

aside from *prep* **1** : in addition to : BESIDES **2** : except for

as if *conj* **1** : as it would be if ⟨it was *as if* he had lost his last friend⟩ **2** : as one would do if ⟨he ran *as if* ghosts were chasing him⟩ **3** : THAT ⟨it seemed *as if* the day would never end⟩

as·i·nine \'as-ə-ˌnīn\ *adj* **1** : OBSTINATE **2** : SILLY, FOOLISH ⟨an *asinine* remark⟩ — **as·i·nine·ly** *adv* — **as·i·nin·i·ty** \ˌas-ə-'nin-ət-ē\ *n*

ask \'ask\ *vb* **1** : to seek information : INQUIRE **2** : to make a request ⟨*ask* for help⟩ **3** : to set as a price : DEMAND ⟨*ask* $20 for a bicycle⟩ **4** : INVITE ⟨*asked* to a party⟩ **5** : LOOK ⟨*asking* for trouble⟩ — **ask·er** *n*

askance \ə-'skan(t)s\ *adv* **1** : with a side glance : OBLIQUELY **2** : with distrust, suspicion, or disapproval

askew \ə-'skyü\ *adv or adj* : out of line : AWRY

[1]**aslant** \ə-'slant\ *adv* : in a slanting direction

[2]**aslant** *prep* : over or across in a slanting direction

[1]**asleep** \ə-'slēp\ *adj* **1** : SLEEPING **2** : lacking sensation : NUMB

[2]**asleep** *adv* : into a state of sleep

asp \'asp\ *n* : a small venomous snake of Egypt

as·par·a·gus \ə-'spar-ə-gəs\ *n* : a tall branching perennial herb related to the lily and widely grown for its thick edible young shoots

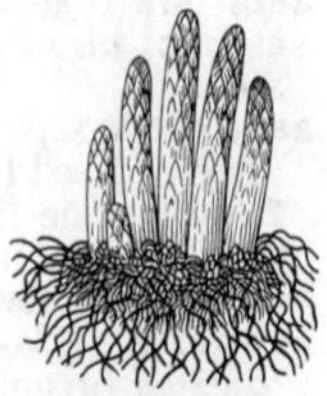
asparagus

as·par·tic acid \ə-ˌspärt-ik-\ *n* : a crystalline amino acid found esp. in plants

as·pect \'as-ˌpekt\ *n* **1 a** : the position of planets or stars with respect to one another held by astrologers to influence human affairs **b** : a position facing a particular direction : EXPOSURE **2** : a particular way in which something appears or may be regarded ⟨studied every *aspect* of the question⟩

as·pen \'as-pən\ *n* : any of several poplars with leaves that flutter in the lightest breeze

as·per·i·ty \a-'sper-ət-ē, ə-'sper-\ *n, pl* **-ties** **1** : RIGOR, SEVERITY **2** : harshness of temper, manner, or tone

as·perse \ə-'spərs, a-\ *vb* : to make aspersions against : SLANDER ⟨*asperse* a man's character⟩

as·per·sion \ə-'spər-zhən\ *n* : an injurious or offensive charge or implication ⟨cast *aspersions* on a person⟩

[1]**as·phalt** \'as-ˌfȯlt\ *or* **as·phal·tum** \as-'fȯl-təm\ *n* **1** : a brown to black substance that is found in natural beds or obtained as a residue in petroleum or coal-tar refining and that consists chiefly of hydrocarbons **2** : any of various compositions of asphalt having diverse uses (as for pavement or for waterproof cement or paint) — **as·phal·tic** \as-'fȯl-tik\ *adj*

[2]**asphalt** *vb* : to cover or impregnate with asphalt

as·pho·del \'as-fə-ˌdel\ *n* : any of several herbs related to the lilies and bearing white or yellow flowers in long erect spikes

as·phyx·ia \as-'fik-sē-ə\ *n* : a lack of oxygen or excess of carbon dioxide in the body usu. caused by interruption of breathing and resulting in unconsciousness

as·phyx·i·ate \as-'fik-sē-ˌāt\ *vb* : to cause asphyxia in; *also* : to kill or make unconscious by interference with the normal oxygen intake — **as·phyx·i·a·tion** \(ˌ)as-ˌfik-sē-'ā-shən\ *n*

as·pic \'as-pik\ *n* : a jelly of fish or meat stock used cold esp. to make a mold of meat, fish, or vegetables

as·pi·dis·tra \ˌas-pə-'dis-trə\ *n* : an Asiatic plant related to the lilies, having large basal leaves, and often grown as a houseplant

as·pi·rant \'as-p(ə-)rənt, ə-'spī-rənt\ *n* : one who aspires

[1]**as·pi·rate** \'as-pə-ˌrāt\ *vb* **1** : to pronounce with an initial *h*-sound ⟨we do not *aspirate* the word *hour*⟩ **2** : to draw or remove by suction

[2]**as·pi·rate** \'as-p(ə-)rət\ *n* : the sound \h\ or a character (as the letter *h*) representing it

as·pi·ra·tion \ˌas-pə-'rā-shən\ *n* **1** : pronunciation with or as an aspirate **2** : a drawing of something in, out, up, or through by suction **3 a** : a strong desire to achieve something high or great **b** : an object of such desire

as·pi·ra·tor \'as-pə-ˌrāt-ər\ *n* : an apparatus for producing suction or moving or collecting materials by suction

as·pire \ə-'spī(ə)r\ *vb* : to seek to attain something high or great — **as·pir·er** *n*

as·pi·rin \'as-p(ə-)rən\ *n* **1** : a white crystalline drug used as a remedy for pain and fever **2** : a tablet of aspirin

ass \'as\ *n* **1** : an animal resembling but smaller than the related horse and having a shorter mane, shorter hair on the tail, and longer ears : DONKEY **2** : a stupid or obstinate person

ass
(3 to 4 ft. at shoulder)

as·sa·fet·i·da *or* **as·sa·foe·ti·da** *var of* ASAFETIDA

as·sail \ə-'sāl\ *vb* : to attack violently with blows or words — **as·sail·a·ble** \-'sā-lə-bəl\ *adj* — **as·sail·ant** \-'sā-lənt\ *n*

as·sas·sin \ə-'sas-ən\ *n* [originally meaning a member of a secret order of Muslims sworn to commit murder of Christians and other enemies while under the influence of hashish, from Arabic *ḥashshāshīn*, plural of *ḥashshāsh*, "hashish addict", from *ḥashīsh* "hashish"] : a person who kills another by a surprise or secret attack; *esp* : a hired murderer of a prominent person

as·sas·si·nate \ə-'sas-ə-ˌnāt\ *vb* : to murder a usu. prominent person by a surprise or secret attack esp. for pay *syn* see KILL — **as·sas·si·na·tion** \ə-ˌsas-ə-'nā-shən\ *n*

as·sault \ə-'sȯlt\ *n* : a violent or sudden attack : ONSLAUGHT — **assault** *vb*

[1]**as·say** \'as-ˌā, a-'sā\ *n* : examination or analysis (as of an ore, metal, or drug) for the purpose of determining composition, measure, or quality

[2]**as·say** \a-'sā, 'as-ˌā\ *vb* **1** : TRY, ATTEMPT **2** : to analyze for one or more valuable components ⟨*assay* an ore⟩ — **as·say·er** *n*

ə abut ər further a back ā bake
ä cot, cart au̇ out ch chin e less ē easy
g gift i trip ī life j joke ng sing ō flow
ȯ flaw ȯi coin th thin t͟h this ü loot
u̇ foot y yet yü few yu̇ furious zh vision

as·sem·blage \ə-ˈsem-blij, *for 3 also* ˌa-ˌsäm-ˈbläzh\ *n* **1 :** a collection of persons or things : GATHERING **2 :** the act of assembling **3 :** something constructed out of parts; *esp* : an artistic composition made out of scraps or junk

as·sem·ble \ə-ˈsem-bəl\ *vb* **-bled; -bling** \-b(ə-)liŋ\ **1 :** to collect into one place or group ⟨*assembled* the crew⟩ **2 :** to fit together the parts of ⟨*assemble* a machine gun⟩ **3 :** to meet together : CONVENE ⟨the right to *assemble* peacefully⟩ ***syn*** see GATHER — **as·sem·bler** \-b(ə-)lər\ *n*

as·sem·bly \ə-ˈsem-blē\ *n, pl* **-blies 1 :** a body of persons gathered together (as for deliberation, worship, or entertainment) **2** *cap* **:** a legislative body; *esp* : the lower house of a legislature **3 :** ASSEMBLAGE **4 :** a signal for troops to assemble **5 :** a collection of parts that go to make up a complete unit ⟨the tail *assembly* of an airplane⟩

assembly line *n* **:** an arrangement of machines, equipment, and workers in which work passes from operation to operation in direct line until the product is assembled

as·sem·bly·man \ə-ˈsem-blē-mən\ *n* **:** a member of a legislative assembly

as·sent \ə-ˈsent\ *vb* **:** AGREE, CONCUR — **assent** *n*

as·sert \ə-ˈsərt\ *vb* **1 :** to state clearly and strongly : declare positively ⟨*assert* an opinion in a loud voice⟩ **2 :** MAINTAIN, DEFEND ⟨*assert* your rights⟩ — **assert oneself :** to demand that others recognize one's rights

as·ser·tion \ə-ˈsər-shən\ *n* **:** the act of asserting; *also* : something asserted : DECLARATION

as·sert·ive \ə-ˈsərt-iv\ *adj* **:** BOLD, CONFIDENT — **as·sert·ive·ly** *adv* — **as·sert·ive·ness** *n*

as·sess \ə-ˈses\ *vb* **1 :** to determine the rate or amount of ⟨the jury *assessed* damages of $5000⟩ **2 :** to set a value on (as property) for purposes of taxation ⟨a house *assessed* at $6300⟩ **3 :** to lay a tax or charge on ⟨the city *assessed* all car owners five dollars⟩ **4 :** to determine the importance, size, or value of — **as·sess·a·ble** \ə-ˈses-ə-bəl\ *adj*

as·sess·ment \ə-ˈses-mənt\ *n* **1 :** the act of assessing : APPRAISAL **2 :** the amount or value assessed

as·ses·sor \ə-ˈses-ər\ *n* **:** an official who assesses property for taxation

as·set \ˈas-ˌet\ *n* **1** *pl* **:** all the property of a person, corporation, or estate that may be used in payment of debts **2 :** ADVANTAGE, RESOURCE

as·sev·er·ate \ə-ˈsev-ə-ˌrāt\ *vb* **:** to declare positively : AVER — **as·sev·er·a·tion** \ə-ˌsev-ə-ˈrā-shən\ *n*

as·sid·u·ous \ə-ˈsij-(ə-)wəs\ *adj* **:** steadily attentive : DILIGENT — **as·si·du·i·ty** \ˌas-ə-ˈd(y)ü-ət-ē\ *n* — **as·sid·u·ous·ly** *adv* — **as·sid·u·ous·ness** *n*

as·sign \ə-ˈsīn\ *vb* **1 :** to transfer to another ⟨*assign* a patent to his son⟩ **2 a :** to appoint to a post or duty **b :** PRESCRIBE ⟨*assign* the lesson⟩ **3 :** to fix authoritatively : SPECIFY ⟨*assign* a limit⟩ — **as·sign·a·ble** \ə-ˈsī-nə-bəl\ *adj* — **as·sign·er** \ə-ˈsī-nər\ *or* **as·sign·or** \ə-ˈsī-nər; ə-ˌsī-ˈnȯ(ə)r, ˌas-ˌī-, ˌas-ə-\ *n* — **as·sign·ment** \ə-ˈsīn-mənt\ *n*

as·sign·ee \ə-ˌsī-ˈnē, ˌas-ˌī-, ˌas-ə-\ *n* **:** a person to whom something is assigned

as·sim·i·late \ə-ˈsim-ə-ˌlāt\ *vb* **:** to take something in and make it part of and like the thing it has joined ⟨the nation *assimilated* millions of immigrants⟩ — **as·sim·i·la·ble** \-ˈsim-ə-lə-bəl\ *adj* — **as·sim·i·la·tor** \-ˌlāt-ər\ *n*

as·sim·i·la·tion \ə-ˌsim-ə-ˈlā-shən\ *n* **:** the act or process of assimilating; *esp* : the conversion of nutrients (as digested food) into protoplasm — **as·sim·i·la·tive** \-ˈsim-ə-ˌlāt-iv\ *adj*

1**as·sist** \ə-ˈsist\ *vb* **:** to give support or aid : HELP

2**assist** *n* **1 :** an act of assistance : AID **2 :** the act of a player who enables a teammate to make a putout or score a goal

as·sist·ance \ə-ˈsis-tən(t)s\ *n* **:** the act of assisting or the aid supplied : SUPPORT

as·sist·ant \ə-ˈsis-tənt\ *n* **:** one who assists : HELPER; *also* : one who serves in a subordinate capacity — **assistant** *adj*

as·size \ə-ˈsīz\ *n* **:** a session of an English superior court held periodically in most counties by judges traveling on circuit — usu. used in pl.

assn *abbr* association

assoc *abbr* association

1**as·so·ci·ate** \ə-ˈsō-s(h)ē-ˌāt\ *vb* **1 :** to join or come together as partners, friends, or companions **2 :** to connect or bring together ⟨*associate* ideas⟩ **3 :** to combine or join with other parts : UNITE

2**as·so·ci·ate** \ə-ˈsō-s(h)ē-ət, -shət, -s(h)ē-ˌāt\ *n* **1 :** a fellow worker : COLLEAGUE **2 :** COMPANION **3** *often cap* **:** a degree conferred esp. by a junior college ⟨*associate* in arts⟩ — **associate** *adj*

as·so·ci·a·tion \ə-ˌsō-sē-ˈā-shən, -ˌsō-shē-\ *n* **1 :** the act of associating : the state of being associated **2 :** an organization of persons having a common interest : SOCIETY **3 :** a feeling, memory, or thought connected with a person, place, or thing ⟨pleasant *associations* with the beach⟩ **4 :** the formation of polymers by linkage through hydrogen bonds **5 :** a major ecological unit characterized by essential uniformity

association area *n* **:** an area of the brain that links and coordinates other areas of the brain

association neuron *n* **:** INTERNUNCIAL NEURON

as·so·ci·a·tive \ə-ˈsō-s(h)ē-ˌāt-iv, -shət-iv\ *adj* **1 :** of or relating to association **2 :** combining elements in such a way that the result is independent of the original order of the terms joined ⟨addition of real numbers is an *associative* operation⟩ — **as·so·ci·a·tive·ly** *adv* — **as·so·cia·tiv·i·ty** \ə-ˌsō-s(h)ē-ə-ˈtiv-ət-ē, -ˌsō-shə-ˈtiv-\ *n*

as soon as *conj* **:** immediately at or just after the time that ⟨left *as soon as* the meeting was over⟩

as·sort \ə-ˈsȯrt\ *vb* **1 :** to sort into groups : CLASSIFY **2 :** AGREE, HARMONIZE ⟨the dress *assorted* well with her complexion⟩

as·sort·a·tive \ə-ˈsȯrt-ət-iv\ *adj* **1 :** sorting into groups **2 :** of or relating to selection on the basis of likeness

assortative mating *n* **:** nonrandom mating; *esp* : selective mating between persons whose choice of marriage partners is controlled by similarity of social environment

as·sort·ed \ə-ˈsȯrt-əd\ *adj* **1 :** consisting of various kinds **2 :** MATCHED, SUITED ⟨an ill-*assorted* pair⟩

as·sort·ment \ə-ˈsȯrt-mənt\ *n* **1 a :** arrangement in classes **b :** VARIETY **2 :** a collection of assorted things ⟨an *assortment* of tools⟩

asst *abbr* assistant

as·suage \ə-ˈswāj\ *vb* **1 :** SOOTHE, EASE **2 :** SATISFY, QUENCH — **as·suage·ment** \-mənt\ *n*

as·sume \ə-ˈsüm\ *vb* **1 :** to take upon oneself : UNDERTAKE **2 :** SEIZE, USURP **3 :** to put on in appearance only : FEIGN ⟨*assume* the manner of a physician⟩ **4 :** to take for granted : SUPPOSE

as·sum·ing *adj* **:** PRESUMPTUOUS, ARROGANT

as·sump·tion \ə-ˈsəm(p)-shən\ *n* **1** *cap* **:** August 15 observed as a church festival in commemoration of the taking up of the Virgin Mary into heaven **2 :** the act of assuming; *esp* : the supposition that something is true **3 :** a fact or statement taken for granted

as·sur·ance \ə-ˈshu̇r-ən(t)s\ *n* **1** : the act of assuring : PLEDGE **2** : the state of being sure or certain : CONFIDENCE **3** *chiefly Brit* : INSURANCE **4** : SELF-CONFIDENCE

as·sure \ə-ˈshu̇(ə)r\ *vb* **1** : INSURE **2** : REASSURE ⟨tried to *assure* the worried children⟩ **3** : to make sure or certain ⟨*assure* himself that the door was locked⟩ **4** : to inform positively ⟨can *assure* you of his dependability⟩

[1]**as·sured** \ə-ˈshu̇(ə)rd\ *adj* : CONFIDENT, SELF-CONFIDENT — **as·sur·ed·ly** \-ˈshu̇r-əd-lē\ *adv* — **as·sur·ed·ness** \-əd-nəs\ *n*

[2]**assured** *n* : a person whose life or property is insured

As·syr·i·an \ə-ˈsir-ē-ən\ *adj* : of, relating to, or characteristic of Assyria or its people — **Assyrian** *n*

as·ta·tine \ˈas-tə-ˌtēn\ *n* : a radioactive element discovered by bombarding bismuth with helium nuclei — see ELEMENT table

as·ter \ˈas-tər\ *n* **1** : any of various mostly fall-blooming leafy-stemmed composite herbs usu. with showy white, pink, purple, or yellow flower heads **2** : a system of radiating fibers about a centrosome of a cell esp. during cell division

as·ter·isk \ˈas-tə-ˌrisk\ *n* [from Greek *asteriskos*, literally "little star", from *astēr* "star", the source of English *astronomy* and *astronaut*] : a character * used to refer a reader to a note or to show an omission

astern \ə-ˈstərn\ *adv* **1** : in, at, or toward the stern **2** : BACKWARD ⟨full speed *astern*⟩

as·ter·oid \ˈas-tə-ˌrȯid\ *n* : one of thousands of small planets between Mars and Jupiter with diameters from a fraction of a mile to nearly 500 miles

asth·ma \ˈaz-mə\ *n* : a condition that is marked by labored breathing with wheezing, a feeling of tightness in the chest, and coughing — **asth·mat·ic** \az-ˈmat-ik\ *adj or n* — **asth·mat·i·cal·ly** \-ˈmat-i-k(ə-)lē\ *adv*

as though *conj* : as if

astig·ma·tism \ə-ˈstig-mə-ˌtiz-əm\ *n* : a defect of an optical system (as of the eye) that prevents light from focusing accurately and results in a blurred image or indistinct vision — **as·tig·mat·ic** \ˌas-tig-ˈmat-ik\ *adj*

astir \ə-ˈstər\ *adj* **1** : being in a state of activity : STIRRING **2** : out of bed : UP

as·ton·ish \ə-ˈstän-ish\ *vb* : to strike with sudden wonder : surprise greatly : AMAZE — **as·ton·ish·ing·ly** \-ing-lē\ *adv* — **as·ton·ish·ment** \-mənt\ *n*

as·tound \ə-ˈstau̇nd\ *vb* : ASTONISH

astrad·dle \ə-ˈstrad-əl\ *adv or prep* : ASTRIDE

as·tra·khan *or* **as·tra·chan** \ˈas-trə-kən, -ˌkan\ *n*, *often cap* **1** : karakul of Russian origin **2** : a cloth with a curled and looped pile resembling karakul

as·tral \ˈas-trəl\ *adj* : of or relating to the stars

astray \ə-ˈstrā\ *adv or adj* **1** : off the right path or route **2** : into error : MISTAKEN

[1]**astride** \ə-ˈstrīd\ *adv* : with one leg on each side

[2]**astride** *prep* : with one leg on each side of ⟨*astride* a horse⟩

[1]**as·trin·gent** \ə-ˈstrin-jənt\ *adj* **1** : able or tending to shrink body tissues : CONTRACTING, PUCKERY ⟨*astringent* lotions⟩ ⟨an *astringent* fruit⟩ **2** : STERN, AUSTERE ⟨an *astringent* manner⟩ — **as·trin·gen·cy** \-jən-sē\ *n* — **as·trin·gent·ly** *adv*

[2]**astringent** *n* : an astringent agent or substance

astro– *comb form* : star : heavens : astronomical ⟨*astro*physics⟩

as·tro·bi·ol·o·gy \ˌas-trō-bī-ˈäl-ə-jē\ *n* : the science dealing with life originating or existing outside the earth or its atmosphere — **as·tro·bi·o·log·i·cal** \-ˌbī-ə-ˈläj-i-kəl\ *adj* — **as·tro·bi·ol·o·gist** \-bī-ˈäl-ə-jəst\ *n*

as·tro·gate \ˈas-trə-ˌgāt\ *vb* : to navigate in interplanetary space — **as·tro·ga·tion** \ˌas-trə-ˈgā-shən\ *n* — **as·tro·ga·tor** \ˈas-trə-ˌgāt-ər\ *n*

as·tro·labe \ˈas-trə-ˌlāb\ *n* : a compact instrument for observing the positions of celestial bodies that is superseded by the sextant

astrolabe

as·trol·o·gy \ə-ˈsträl-ə-jē\ *n* : the discovery of the supposed influences of the stars on human affairs by their positions and aspects — **as·trol·o·ger** \-jər\ *n* — **as·tro·log·i·cal** \ˌas-trə-ˈläj-i-kəl\ *adj*

as·tro·naut \ˈas-trə-ˌnȯt\ *n* : a traveler in a spacecraft — **as·tro·nau·ti·cal** \ˌas-trə-ˈnȯt-i-kəl\ *adj* — **as·tro·nau·ti·cal·ly** \-i-k(ə-)le\ *adv*

as·tro·nau·tics \ˌas-trə-ˈnȯt-iks\ *n* **1** : the science of the construction and operation of spacecraft **2** : ASTROGATION

as·tro·nom·i·cal \ˌas-trə-ˈnäm-i-kəl\ *or* **as·tro·nom·ic** \-ˈnäm-ik\ *adj* **1** : of or relating to astronomy **2** : extremely or unimaginably large ⟨an *astronomical* amount of money⟩ — **as·tro·nom·i·cal·ly** \-ˈnäm-i-k(ə-)lē\ *adv*

astronomical unit *n* : a unit of length used in astronomy equal to the mean distance of the earth from the sun or about 93 million miles

as·tron·o·my \ə-ˈsträn-ə-mē\ *n*, *pl* **-mies** **1** : the science of the celestial bodies and of their magnitudes, motions, and constitution **2** : a treatise on astronomy — **as·tron·o·mer** \-mər\ *n*

as·tro·phys·ics \ˌas-trə-ˈfiz-iks\ *n* : a branch of astronomy dealing with the physical and chemical constitution of the celestial bodies — **as·tro·phys·i·cal** \-ˈfiz-i-kəl\ *adj* — **as·tro·phys·i·cist** \-ˈfiz-ə-səst\ *n*

as·tute \ə-ˈst(y)üt, a-\ *adj* **1** : WISE, SHREWD ⟨an *astute* businessman⟩ **2** : WILY — **as·tute·ly** *adv* — **as·tute·ness** *n*

asun·der \ə-ˈsən-dər\ *adv or adj* **1** : into parts ⟨torn *asunder*⟩ **2** : APART

ASV *abbr* American Standard Version

as yet *adv* : up to the present time : YET

asy·lum \ə-ˈsī-ləm\ *n* **1** : a place of safety : SHELTER **2** : protection given esp. to political refugees **3** : an institution for the relief or care of those unable to care for themselves and esp. for the insane

asym·met·ric \ˌā-sə-ˈme-trik\ *adj* : not symmetrical — **asym·met·ri·cal** \-tri-kəl\ *adj* — **asym·met·ri·cal·ly** \-tri-k(ə-)lē\ *adv* — **asym·me·try** \(ˈ)ā-ˈsim-ə-trē\ *n*

at \ət, (ˈ)at\ *prep* — used to indicate (1) location in space or time ⟨staying *at* a hotel⟩ ⟨be here *at* six⟩ ⟨sick *at* heart⟩, (2) a goal ⟨aim *at* the target⟩ ⟨laugh *at* him⟩, (3) a condition ⟨*at* work⟩ ⟨*at* liberty⟩ ⟨*at* rest⟩, (4) how or why ⟨sold *at* auction⟩ ⟨angry *at* his answer⟩, or (5) rate, degree, or position in a scale or series ⟨the temperature *at* 90⟩ ⟨retire *at* 65⟩

A

at- — see AD-
at *abbr* atomic
at all \ət-'ȯl *also esp for 2* ə-'tȯl\ *adv* : with no qualifications or reservations : in any way or respect : under any circumstances ⟨will go anywhere *at all*⟩ ⟨doesn't smoke *at all*⟩ ⟨not *at all* likely⟩
atax·ia \ə-'tak-sē-ə\ *n* : inability to coordinate voluntary muscular movements — **atax·ic** \-sik\ *adj*
ate *past of* EAT
¹-ate \ət, ˌāt\ *n suffix* : office : function : rank : group of persons holding a specified office or rank ⟨professor*ate*⟩
²-ate *adj suffix* **1** : acted on (in a specified way) : brought into or being in a (specified) state ⟨temper*ate*⟩ **2** : marked by having ⟨chord*ate*⟩
³-ate \ˌāt\ *vb suffix* : cause to be modified or affected by ⟨camphor*ate*⟩ : cause to become ⟨activ*ate*⟩ : furnish with ⟨aer*ate*⟩
a tem·po \ä-'tem-pō\ *adv or adj* : in time — used as a direction in music to return to the original speed
athe·ism \'ā-thē-ˌiz-əm\ *n* : the belief that there is no God — **athe·ist** \-thē-əst\ *n* — **athe·is·tic** \ˌā-thē-'is-tik\ *adj*
Athe·ni·an \ə-'thē-nē-ən\ *adj* : of, relating to, or characteristic of Athens or its people — **Athenian** *n*
ath·ero·scle·ro·sis \ˌath-ə-rō-sklə-'rō-səs\ *n* : hardening and thickening of the walls of the arteries due to the deposit of fatty substances in the inner layer
athirst \ə-'thərst\ *adj* **1** : THIRSTY **2** : EAGER, LONGING
ath·lete \'ath-ˌlēt\ *n* : a person who is trained in or good at games and exercises that require physical skill, endurance, and strength
athlete's foot *n* : ringworm of the feet
ath·let·ic \ath-'let-ik\ *adj* **1** : of, relating to, or characteristic of athletes or athletics **2** : VIGOROUS, ACTIVE **3** : STRONG, MUSCULAR — **ath·let·i·cal·ly** \-'let-i-k(ə)lē\ *adv*
ath·let·ics \ath-'let-iks\ *n sing or pl* : games, sports, and exercises requiring strength and skill
¹athwart \ə-'thwȯrt, *naut often* -'thȯrt\ *adv* : ACROSS
²athwart *prep* **1** : ACROSS **2** : in opposition to
-a·tion \'ā-shən\ *n suffix* **1** : action or process ⟨flirt*ation*⟩ **2** : something connected with an action or process ⟨discolor*ation*⟩
-a·tive \ˌāt-iv, ət-\ *adj suffix* **1** : of, relating to, or connected with ⟨authorit*ative*⟩ **2** : tending to ⟨talk*ative*⟩
Atl *abbr* Atlantic
at·las \'at-ləs\ *n* **1** : a book of maps **2** : the first vertebra of the neck
atm *abbr* **1** atmosphere **2** atmospheric
at·mo·sphere \'at-mə-ˌsfi(ə)r\ *n* **1 a** : the whole mass of air surrounding the earth **b** : a gaseous mass surrounding a celestial body (as a planet) **2** : the air in a particular place ⟨the stuffy *atmosphere* of this room⟩ **3** : a surrounding influence or condition : ENVIRONMENT ⟨the home *atmosphere*⟩ **4** : a unit of pressure equal to the pressure of the air at sea level or approximately 14.7 pounds to the square inch
at·mo·spher·ic \ˌat-mə-'sfi(ə)r-ik, -'sfer-\ *adj* : of or relating to the atmosphere ⟨*atmospheric* pressure⟩ — **at·mo·spher·i·cal·ly** \-i-k(ə-)lē\ *adv*
at. no. *abbr* atomic number
atoll \'a-ˌtȯl, -ˌtäl, -ˌtōl, 'ā-\ *n* : a ring-shaped coral island or string of islands consisting of a coral reef surrounding a lagoon
at·om \'at-əm\ *n* [from Greek *atomos* "elementary particle", from *atomos* "indivisible", from *a-* "un-" and *tom-*, root of *temnein* "to cut"] **1** : a tiny particle : BIT **2 a** : the smallest particle of an element that has the properties of the element and can exist either alone or in combination ⟨an *atom* of hydrogen⟩ ⟨an *atom* of iron⟩ **b** : an atom that is a source of vast potential energy
atom bomb *n* **1** : a bomb whose violent explosive power is due to the sudden release of atomic energy resulting from the splitting of nuclei of a heavy chemical element (as plutonium or uranium) by neutrons in a very rapid chain reaction — called also *fission bomb* **2** : FUSION BOMB — **atom–bomb** *vb*
atom·ic \ə-'täm-ik\ *adj* **1** : of, relating to, or concerned with atoms, atomic energy, or atomic bombs **2** : extremely small : MINUTE **3** : existing in the state of separate atoms ⟨*atomic* hydrogen⟩
atomic age *n* : the period of history characterized by the use of atomic energy
atomic bomb *n* : ATOM BOMB
atomic clock *n* : a precision clock that depends for its operation on the natural vibrations of atoms or molecules (as of cesium)
atomic energy *n* : energy that can be liberated by changes (as by fission of a heavy nucleus or fusion of light nuclei into heavier ones with accompanying loss of mass) in the nucleus of an atom
atomic mass *n* : the mass of any species of atom usu. expressed in atomic mass units
atomic mass unit *n* : a unit of mass for expressing masses of atoms, molecules, or nuclear particles equal to $\frac{1}{12}$ of the atomic mass of the most abundant kind of carbon
atomic number *n* : a number that is characteristic of a chemical element and represents the number of protons in the nucleus
atomic pile *n* : REACTOR 2
atomic theory *n* **1** : a theory of the nature of matter: all material substances are composed of minute particles or atoms of a comparatively small number of kinds and all the atoms of the same kind are uniform in size, weight, and other properties **2** : any of several theories of the structure of the atom; *esp* : one holding that the atom is composed essentially of a small positively charged comparatively heavy nucleus surrounded by a comparatively large arrangement of electrons
atomic weight *n* : the relative weight of an atom of a chemical element in comparison with that of an oxygen atom assigned a relative weight of 16 or a carbon atom assigned a relative weight of 12 taken as a standard
at·om·ize \'at-ə-ˌmīz\ *vb* : to reduce to minute particles or to a fine spray
at·om·iz·er \'at-ə-ˌmī-zər\ *n* : a device for spraying a liquid (as a perfume or disinfectant)
atom smasher *n* : ACCELERATOR 3

atoll

aton·al \(ˈ)ā-'tōn-əl, (ˈ)a-\ *adj* : characterized by avoidance of traditional musical tonality — **ato·nal·i·ty** \ˌā-tō-'nal-ət-ē\ *n* — **aton·al·ly** \(ˈ)ā-'tōn-ə-lē, (ˈ)a-\ *adv*

atone \ə-'tōn\ *vb* : to do something to make up for a wrong done : make amends
atone·ment \-mənt\ *n* **1** : the reconciliation of God and man through the death of Jesus Christ **2** : reparation for an offense or injury
atop \ə-'täp\ *prep* : on top of
ATP \ˌā-ˌtē-'pē, ā-'tē-ˌpē\ *n* : a compound that occurs widely in living tissue and serves as a major source of energy
atri·um \'ā-trē-əm\ *n, pl* **atria** \-trē-ə\ *also* **atri·ums** : an anatomical cavity or passage; *esp* : the main chamber of an auricle of the heart or the entire auricle
atro·cious \ə-'trō-shəs\ *adj* **1** : savagely wicked, brutal, or cruel **2** : very bad : ABOMINABLE ⟨*atrocious* weather⟩ — **atro·cious·ly** *adv* — **atro·cious·ness** *n*
atroc·i·ty \ə-'träs-ət-ē\ *n, pl* **-ties** **1** : the quality or state of being atrocious **2** : an atrocious act, object, or situation
¹**at·ro·phy** \'a-trə-fē\ *n, pl* **-phies** : decrease in size or wasting away of a body part or tissue
²**atrophy** *vb* **-phied**; **-phy·ing** : to undergo atrophy
at·ro·pine \'a-trə-ˌpēn, -pən\ *n* : a poisonous white crystalline compound from belladonna and related plants used esp. to relieve spasms and to dilate the pupil of the eye
att *abbr* **1** attention **2** attorney
at·tach \ə-'tach\ *vb* **1** : to take money or property by legal authority esp. to secure payment of a debt ⟨*attach* a man's salary⟩ **2** : to fasten or join one thing to another : TIE ⟨*attach* a bell to a bicycle⟩ **3** : to tie or bind by feelings of affection ⟨the boy was *attached* to his dog⟩ **4** : to assign by authority : APPOINT ⟨*attach* an officer to a headquarters⟩ **5** : to think of as belonging to something : ATTRIBUTE ⟨*attach* no importance to a remark⟩ **6** : to be associated or connected ⟨the interest that *attaches* to his activities⟩ — **at·tach·a·ble** \-ə-bəl\ *adj*
at·ta·ché \ˌat-ə-'shā, ˌa-ˌta-, ə-ˌta-\ *n* : a technical expert on a diplomatic staff ⟨military *attaché*⟩
at·taché case \ə-'tash-ē-\ *n* : a small suitcase esp. for carrying papers and documents
at·tach·ment \ə-'tach-mənt\ *n* **1** : a seizure by legal process **2** : strong affection : FONDNESS **3** : a device attached to a machine or implement ⟨*attachments* for a vacuum cleaner⟩ **4** : the connection by which one thing is attached to another **5** : the process of physically attaching
¹**at·tack** \ə-'tak\ *vb* **1** : to set upon forcefully **2** : to use unfriendly or bitter words against **3** : to begin to affect or to act upon injuriously ⟨*attacked* by fever⟩ **4** : to set to work on ⟨*attack* a problem⟩ — **at·tack·er** *n*
²**attack** *n* **1** : the act or action of attacking : ASSAULT **2** : a setting to work : START **3** : a fit of sickness; *esp* : an active episode of a chronic or recurrent disease
at·tain \ə-'tān\ *vb* **1** : ACHIEVE, ACCOMPLISH **2** : OBTAIN **3** : to arrive at : REACH ⟨*attain* the top of the mountain⟩ — **at·tain·a·bil·i·ty** \ə-ˌtā-nə-'bil-ət-ē\ *n* — **at·tain·a·ble** \-'tā-nə-bəl\ *adj* — **at·tain·a·ble·ness** *n*
at·tain·der \ə-'tān-dər\ *n* : the taking away of a person's civil rights when he has been declared an outlaw or sentenced to death

ə abut	ər further	a back	ā bake	
ä cot, cart	aù out	ch chin	e less	ē easy
g gift	i trip	ī life	j joke	ng sing	ō flow
ȯ flaw	ȯi coin	th thin	th this	ü loot
ù foot	y yet	yü few	yù furious	zh vision

at·tain·ment \ə-'tān-mənt\ *n* **1** : the act of attaining : the state of being attained **2** : something attained : ACCOMPLISHMENT
at·tar \'at-ər, 'a-ˌtär\ *n* : a perfume obtained from flowers
attar of roses : a fragrant essential oil obtained from rose petals
¹**at·tempt** \ə-'tem(p)t\ *vb* **1** : to try to do or perform : make an effort to accomplish ⟨*attempt* an escape⟩ **2** : to try to take by force : ATTACK ⟨*attempt* a man's life⟩ **3** : ENDEAVOR ⟨*attempt* to solve the problem⟩
²**attempt** *n* : the act or an instance of attempting; *esp* : an unsuccessful effort
at·tend \ə-'tend\ *vb* **1** : to care for : look after **2** : to wait on : SERVE ⟨nurses *attend* the sick⟩ **3** : to go or stay with as a servant or companion ⟨a king *attended* by his court⟩ **4** : to be present at ⟨*attend* a party⟩ **5** : to be present with ⟨illness *attended* by fever⟩ **6** : to pay attention ⟨*attend* to his remarks⟩ *syn* see ACCOMPANY
at·tend·ance \ə-'ten-dən(t)s\ *n* **1** : the act of attending **2 a** : the number of persons attending **b** : the number of times a person attends
¹**at·tend·ant** \ə-'ten-dənt\ *adj* : accompanying or following as a consequence
²**attendant** *n* **1** : one who attends another to perform a service ⟨a bride and her *attendants*⟩ **2** : an employee who waits on customers ⟨gas station *attendant*⟩
at·ten·tion \ə-'ten-chən\ *n* **1** : the act or power of fixing one's mind upon something : careful listening or watching **2** : careful consideration of something with a view to taking action on it ⟨a matter requiring *attention*⟩ **3** : an act of kindness, care, or courtesy **4** : a military position of readiness to act on the next command
at·ten·tive \ə-'tent-iv\ *adj* **1** : paying attention : HEEDFUL, OBSERVANT **2** : heedful of the comfort of others : COURTEOUS — **at·ten·tive·ly** *adv* — **at·ten·tive·ness** *n*
at·ten·u·ate \ə-'ten-yə-ˌwāt\ *vb* **1** : to make thin or slender **2** : to make less in amount or force : WEAKEN **3** : to become thin, fine, or less — **at·ten·u·a·tion** \ə-ˌten-yə-'wā-shən\ *n*
at·test \ə-'test\ *vb* : to give proof of : testify to : CERTIFY ⟨his conduct *attests* his innocence⟩ ⟨*attest* the truth of a statement⟩ — **at·tes·ta·tion** \ˌa-ˌtes-'tā-shən\ *n* — **at·test·er** \ə-'tes-tər\ *n*
at·tic \'at-ik\ *n* : a room or a space immediately below the roof of a building
¹**at·tire** \ə-'tī(ə)r\ *vb* **1** : DRESS, ARRAY **2** : to clothe in rich garments
²**attire** *n* : DRESS, CLOTHES; *esp* : fine clothing
at·ti·tude \'at-ə-ˌt(y)üd\ *n* **1** : the arrangement of the body or figure : POSTURE **2** : a mental position or feeling regarding a fact or state **3** : the position of something in relation to something else
at·tor·ney \ə-'tər-nē\ *n, pl* **-neys** : one who is legally appointed by another to transact business and esp. legal business for him
attorney general *n, pl* **attorneys general** *or* **attorney generals** : the chief law officer of a nation or state who represents the government in legal matters
at·tract \ə-'trakt\ *vb* **1** : to draw to or toward itself ⟨a magnet *attracts* iron⟩ **2** : to draw by appealing to interest or feeling ⟨*attract* attention⟩
at·trac·tion \ə-'trak-shən\ *n* **1** : the act, process, or power of attracting; *esp* : personal charm or beauty **2** : an attractive quality, object, or feature **3** : a force acting mutually between particles of matter, tending to draw them together, and resisting their separation

at·trac·tive \ə-'trak-tiv\ *adj* : having the power or quality of attracting; *esp* : CHARMING, PLEASING ⟨an *attractive* smile⟩ — **at·trac·tive·ly** *adv* — **at·trac·tive·ness** *n*

1**at·tri·bute** \'a-trə-ˌbyüt\ *n* **1** : a quality belonging to a particular person or thing **2** : an object closely associated with a person, thing, or office ⟨crown and scepter are *attributes* of royalty⟩ **3** : a word ascribing a quality; *esp* : ADJECTIVE

2**at·trib·ute** \ə-'trib-yət\ *vb* **1** : to explain by way of cause ⟨*attributes* his success to hard work⟩ **2** : to regard as a characteristic of a person or thing ⟨*attributed* the worst motives to him⟩ — **at·trib·ut·a·ble** \-yət-ə-bəl\ *adj* — **at·trib·ut·er** *n* — **at·tri·bu·tion** \ˌa-trə-'byü-shən\ *n*

at·trib·u·tive \ə-'trib-yət-iv\ *adj* : relating to or being an attribute; *esp* : joined directly to a modified noun without a verb ⟨*red* in *red hair* is an *attributive* adjective⟩ — compare PREDICATE

at·tri·tion \ə-'trish-ən\ *n* : the act of weakening or exhausting by constant harassment

at·tune \ə-'t(y)ün\ *vb* : to bring into harmony : TUNE — **at·tune·ment** \-mənt\ *n*

atty *abbr* attorney

at.wt. *abbr* atomic weight

atyp·i·cal \(')ā-'tip-i-kəl\ *adj* : not typical : IRREGULAR — **atyp·i·cal·ly** \-k(ə-)lē\ *adv*

Å̊U *abbr* angstrom unit

au·burn \'ö-bərn\ *adj* : of a reddish brown color ⟨*auburn* hair⟩

1**auc·tion** \'ök-shən\ *n* [from Latin *auction-*, stem of *auctio*, meaning literally "increase", from *augēre* "to increase", the source of English *augment*] : a public sale in which persons bid on property to be sold and the property is sold to the highest bidder

2**auction** *vb* **auc·tioned**; **auc·tion·ing** \-sh(ə-)ning\ : to sell at auction

auc·tion·eer \ˌök-shə-'ni(ə)r\ *n* : an agent who sells goods at auction — **auctioneer** *vb*

au·da·cious \ö-'dā-shəs\ *adj* **1** : DARING, BOLD **2** : IMPUDENT — **au·da·cious·ly** *adv* — **au·da·cious·ness** *n*

au·dac·i·ty \ö-'das-ət-ē\ *n, pl* **-ties** **1** : BOLDNESS, DARING **2** : IMPUDENCE

audi- *or* **audio-** *comb form* **1** : hearing ⟨*audio*meter⟩ **2** : sound ⟨*audio*phile⟩ **3** : auditory and ⟨*audio*visual⟩

au·di·ble \'öd-ə-bəl\ *adj* : loud enough to be heard ⟨the sound was barely *audible*⟩ — **au·di·bil·i·ty** \ˌöd-ə-'bil-ət-ē\ *n* — **au·di·bly** \'öd-ə-blē\ *adv*

au·di·ence \'öd-ē-ən(t)s\ *n* **1** : an assembled group that listens or watches (as at a play, concert, or sports event) **2** : an opportunity of being heard; *esp* : a formal interview with a person of high rank **3** : those of the general public who give attention to something said, done, or written ⟨the radio *audience*⟩ ⟨the *audience* for poetry⟩

1**au·dio** \'öd-ē-ˌō\ *adj* **1** : of or relating to electrical or other vibrational frequencies corresponding to normally audible sound waves **2 a** : of or relating to sound or its reproduction and esp. high-fidelity reproduction **b** : relating to or used in the transmission or reception of sound — compare VIDEO

2**audio** *n* **1** : the transmission, reception, or reproduction of sound **2** : the section of television equipment that deals with sound

au·di·om·e·ter \ˌöd-ē-'äm-ət-ər\ *n* : an instrument used in measuring acuteness of hearing — **au·dio·met·ric** \ˌöd-ē-ə-'me-trik\ *adj* — **au·di·om·e·try** \ˌöd-ē-'äm-ə-trē\ *n*

au·dio·phile \'öd-ē-ə-ˌfīl\ *n* : one who is enthusiastic about high-fidelity sound reproduction

au·dio·vi·su·al \ˌöd-ē-ō-'vizh-(ə-w)əl\ *adj* : of, relating to, or making use of both hearing and sight ⟨*audiovisual* teaching aids⟩

1**au·dit** \'öd-ət\ *n* : an examination and verification of accounts esp. of a business or society; *also* : the report of such an audit

2**audit** *vb* : to make an audit of ⟨*audit* accounts⟩

1**au·di·tion** \ö-'dish-ən\ *n* **1** : the power or sense of hearing **2** : a critical hearing; *esp* : a trial performance to appraise an entertainer's merits

2**audition** *vb* **-di·tioned**; **-di·tion·ing** \-'dish-(ə-)ning\ **1** : to test in an audition ⟨*audition* a new trumpeter⟩ **2** : to give a trial performance ⟨the singers *auditioned* for the choirmaster⟩

au·di·tor \'öd-ət-ər\ *n* **1** : HEARER, LISTENER **2** : a person authorized to examine and verify accounts

au·di·to·ri·um \ˌöd-ə-'tōr-ē-əm, -'tör-\ *n* **1** : the part of a public building where an audience sits **2** : a room, hall, or building used for public gatherings

au·di·to·ry \'öd-ə-ˌtōr-ē, -ˌtör-\ *adj* : of or relating to hearing or to the sense or organs of hearing ⟨*auditory* sensation⟩

auditory area *n* : a sensory area in the brain associated with the organ of hearing

auditory canal *n* : the passage leading from the external-ear opening to the eardrum

auditory nerve *n* : a nerve connecting the inner ear with the brain and transmitting impulses concerned with hearing and balance

Aug *abbr* August

au·ger \'ö-gər\ *n* **1** : a tool for boring holes in wood **2** : any of various instruments used for boring (as in soil)

1**aught** \'öt, 'ät\ *pron* : ALL ⟨for *aught* I care, he can stay home⟩

2**aught** *n* : ZERO, CIPHER

au·gite \'ö-ˌjīt\ *n* : a black to dark green variety of pyroxene

aug·ment \ög-'ment\ *vb* : to increase esp. in size, amount, or degree — **aug·ment·a·ble** \-ə-bəl\ *adj* — **aug·men·ta·tion** \ˌög-mən-'tā-shən, -ˌmen-\ *n*

1**au·gur** \'ö-gər\ *n* : SOOTHSAYER, DIVINER

2**augur** *vb* **1** : to predict esp. from signs or omens **2** : to serve as a sign : INDICATE ⟨the report *augurs* well for success⟩

au·gu·ry \'ö-gyə-rē, -gə-\ *n, pl* **-ries** **1** : divination esp. from omens **2** : an indication of the future : OMEN

au·gust \ö-'gəst\ *adj* : marked by majestic dignity or grandeur — **au·gust·ly** *adv* — **au·gust·ness** *n*

Au·gust \'ö-gəst\ *n* [from Latin *Augustus* named after *Augustus* Caesar, first Roman emperor] : the 8th month of the year

auk \'ök\ *n* [from Old Norse *ālka*] : any of several thickset black-and-white short-necked diving seabirds that breed in colder parts of the northern hemisphere

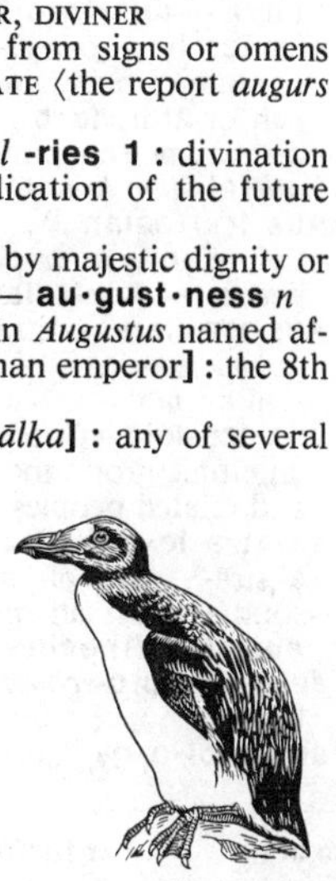

auk
(2 to 3 ft. high)

auld \'öl(d), 'äl(d)\ *adj, chiefly Scot* : OLD

auld lang syne \ˌōl-ˌ(d)ang-'zīn, ˌōl-ˌ(d)lang-, ˌöl-\ *n* [from Scottish, meaning "old long ago"] : the good old times

aunt \'ant, 'ånt\ *n* **1** : the sister of one's father or mother **2** : the wife of one's uncle

au·ra \'ör-ə\ *n* : a distinctive atmosphere or impression ⟨an *aura* of sanctity⟩

au·ral \'ȯr-əl\ *adj* : of or relating to the ear or sense of hearing — **au·ral·ly** \-ə-lē\ *adv*

au·re·ole \'ȯr-ē-ˌōl\ *or* **au·re·o·la** \ȯ-'rē-ə-lə\ *n* **1** : a radiant light around the head or body of a picture of a sacred person **2** : a bright area surrounding a bright light (as the sun) when seen through thin cloud or mist

au re·voir \ˌōr-əv-'wär, ˌȯr-\ *n* [from French, literally "till seeing again"] : GOOD-BYE

au·ri·cle \'ȯr-i-kəl\ *n* **1** : PINNA 2 **2** : the chamber or either of the chambers of the heart that receives blood from the veins

au·ric·u·lar \ȯ-'rik-yə-lər\ *adj* **1** : of or relating to the ear or the sense of hearing **2** : told privately ⟨*auricular* confession⟩ **3** : known by the sense of hearing **4** : of or relating to an auricle

au·ro·ra \ə-'rōr-ə, ȯ-'rōr-, -'rȯr-\ *n pl*, **-ras** *or* **-rae** **1** : the rising light of morning : DAWN **2** : AURORA BOREALIS **3** : AURORA AUSTRALIS — **au·ro·ral** \-əl\ *adj*

aurora aus·tra·lis \-ȯ-'strā-ləs, -ä-\ *n* : a display of light in the southern hemisphere corresponding to the aurora borealis

aurora bo·re·al·is \-ˌbōr-ē-'al-əs, -ˌbȯr-\ *n* : streamers or arches of light in the sky at night that are held to be of electrical origin and appear to best advantage in the arctic regions — called also *northern lights*

au·rum \'ȯr-əm\ *n* : GOLD

aus·pice \'ȯ-spəs\ *n, pl* **aus·pic·es** \-spə-səz, -ˌsēz\ [from Latin *auspicium*, from *avis* "bird" and *specere* "to look at", the source of English *spectacle*] **1** : augury esp. based upon the flight of birds **2** : OMEN; *esp* : a favorable sign **3** *pl* : SUPPORT, PROTECTION ⟨a concert given annually under the *auspices* of the school⟩

aus·pi·cious \ȯ-'spish-əs\ *adj* **1** : promising success : FAVORABLE ⟨an *auspicious* beginning⟩ **2** : PROSPEROUS, FORTUNATE ⟨an *auspicious* year⟩ — **aus·pi·cious·ly** *adv* — **aus·pi·cious·ness** *n*

aus·tere \ȯ-'sti(ə)r\ *adj* **1** : stern and forbidding in appearance and manner **2** : ASCETIC ⟨an *austere* old hermit⟩ **3** : UNADORNED, SIMPLE ⟨*austere* architecture⟩ — **aus·tere·ly** *adv*

aus·ter·i·ty \ȯ-'ster-ət-ē\ *n, pl* **-ties** **1** : the quality or state of being austere **2 a** : an austere act, manner, or attitude **b** : an ascetic practice **3** : enforced or extreme economy

Austral *abbr* Australian

Aus·tral·asian \ˌȯs-trə-'lā-zhən, ˌäs-, -shən\ *adj* : of, relating to, or characteristic of Australasia or its people — **Australasian** *n*

Aus·tra·lian \ȯ-'strāl-yən, ä-\ *adj* : of, relating to, or characteristic of Australia or its people — **Australian** *n*

Aus·tra·loid \'ȯs-trə-ˌlȯid, 'äs-\ *adj* : of or relating to an ethnic group including the Australian aborigines and related peoples — **Australoid** *n*

aus·tra·lo·pith·e·cine \ȯ-ˌstrā-lō-'pith-ə-ˌsīn, ä-ˌstrā-\ *adj* : of or relating to a group of extinct southern African apes with near-human dentition — **australopithecine** *n*

aut- *or* **auto-** *comb form* **1** : self : same one ⟨*auto*biography⟩ **2** : automatic : self-acting ⟨*auto*-rifle⟩

aut·ecol·o·gy \ˌȯt-i-'käl-ə-jē\ *n* : ecology dealing with individual organisms or individual kinds of organisms

au·then·tic \ȯ-'thent-ik, ə-\ *adj* **1** : being really what it seems to be : GENUINE ⟨an *authentic* signature of George Washington⟩ **2** : TRUE, CORRECT ⟨a report *authentic* in every detail⟩ — **au·then·ti·cal·ly** \-'thent-i-k(ə-)lē\ *adv* — **au·then·tic·i·ty** \ˌȯ-ˌthen-'tis-ət-ē, -thən-\ *n*

au·then·ti·cate \ȯ-'thent-i-ˌkāt, ə-\ *vb* : to prove, establish, or attest the authenticity of — **au·then·ti·ca·tion** \-ˌthent-i-'kā-shən\ *n*

au·thor \'ȯ-thər\ *n* **1** : one who writes or composes a literary work (as a book) **2** : one who originates or makes : CREATOR — **author** *vb* — **au·thor·ess** \'ȯ-th(ə-)rəs\ *n*

au·thor·i·tar·i·an \ə-ˌthȯr-ə-'ter-ē-ən, ȯ-, -ˌthär-\ *adj* : relating to or advocating submission to authority esp. as concentrated in a powerful leader or elite ⟨an *authoritarian* dictator⟩ — **authoritarian** *n* — **au·thor·i·tar·i·an·ism** \-ē-ə-ˌniz-əm\ *n*

au·thor·i·ta·tive \ə-'thȯr-ə-ˌtāt-iv, ȯ-, -'thär-\ *adj* **1** : having authority : coming from or based on authority ⟨*authoritative* teachings⟩ **2** : entitled to obedience or acceptance ⟨an *authoritative* order⟩ **3** : having an air of authority ⟨an *authoritative* manner⟩ — **au·thor·i·ta·tive·ly** *adv* — **au·thor·i·ta·tive·ness** *n*

au·thor·i·ty \ə-'thȯr-ət-ē, ȯ-, -'thär-\ *n, pl* **-ties** **1 a** : a person, text, or decision that is used to support a position **b** : a person appealed to as an expert **2** : the right to give commands or to carry out or enforce others' commands **3** : a person or persons having powers of government ⟨local *authorities*⟩

au·tho·rize \'ȯ-thə-ˌrīz\ *vb* **1** : to give authority to : EMPOWER ⟨*authorize* a son to act for his father⟩ **2** : to give legal or official approval to ⟨*authorize* a loan⟩ ⟨an *authorized* abridgment⟩ **3** : to establish by or as if by authority : SANCTION ⟨customs *authorized* by time⟩ — **au·tho·ri·za·tion** \ˌȯ-th(ə-)rə-'zā-shən\ *n* — **au·tho·riz·er** \'ȯ-thə-ˌrī-zər\ *n*

Authorized Version *n* : a revision of the English Bible carried out under James I, published in 1611, and widely used by Protestants — see BIBLE table

au·thor·ship \'ȯ-thər-ˌship\ *n* **1** : the profession of writing **2** : the origin esp. of a literary work ⟨a novel of unknown *authorship*⟩

au·to \'ȯt-ō, 'ät-\ *n* : AUTOMOBILE

au·to·bi·og·ra·phy \ˌȯt-ə-bī-'äg-rə-fē, -bē-\ *n* : the biography of a person narrated by himself — **au·to·bi·og·ra·pher** \-rə-fər\ *n* — **au·to·bio·graph·ic** \-ˌbī-ə-'graf-ik\ *or* **au·to·bio·graph·i·cal** \-'graf-i-kəl\ *adj* — **au·to·bio·graph·i·cal·ly** \-i-k(ə-)lē\ *adv*

au·toc·ra·cy \ȯ-'täk-rə-sē\ *n, pl* **-cies** **1** : government in which one person possesses unlimited power **2** : a state governed by autocracy

au·to·crat \'ȯt-ə-ˌkrat\ *n* : a person who has or acts as if he had unlimited authority

au·to·crat·ic \ˌȯt-ə-'krat-ik\ *adj* : of, relating to, or resembling autocracy or an autocrat : DESPOTIC ⟨*autocratic* rule⟩ — **au·to·crat·i·cal·ly** \-'krat-i-k(ə-)lē\ *adv*

[1]**au·to·graph** \'ȯt-ə-ˌgraf\ *n* : something written with one's own hand; *esp* : a person's handwritten signature

[2]**autograph** *vb* : to write one's signature in or on

au·to·mate \'ȯt-ə-ˌmāt\ *vb* **1** : to operate by automation **2** : to convert to automatic operation

[1]**au·to·mat·ic** \ˌȯt-ə-'mat-ik\ *adj* **1 a** : largely or wholly involuntary; *esp* : REFLEX 4 **b** : acting or done spontaneously or unconsciously ⟨an *automatic* reply⟩ **c** : resembling an automaton : MECHANICAL

ə abut	ər further	a back	ā bake	
ä cot, cart	au̇ out	ch chin	e less	ē easy
g gift	i trip	ī life	j joke	ng sing	ō flow
ȯ flaw	ȯi coin	th thin	t͟h this	ü loot
u̇ foot	y yet	yü few	yu̇ furious	zh vision

2 : having a self-acting or self-regulating mechanism ⟨*automatic* pistol⟩ ⟨*automatic* washer⟩ — **au·to·mat·i·cal·ly** \-'mat-i-k(ə-)lē\ *adv*

2**automatic** *n* : an automatic machine; *esp* : an automatic firearm

au·to·ma·tion \ˌȯt-ə-'mā-shən\ *n* **1** : the method of making an apparatus, a process, or a system operate automatically **2** : automatic operation of an apparatus, process, or system by mechanical or electronic devices that take the place of human operators

au·tom·a·tize \ȯ-'täm-ə-ˌtīz\ *vb* : to make automatic — **au·tom·a·ti·za·tion** \ȯ-ˌtäm-ət-ə-'zā-shən\ *n*

au·tom·a·ton \ȯ-'täm-ət-ən, -'täm-ə-ˌtän\ *n, pl* **-atons** *or* **-a·ta** \-ət-ə\ **1** : a machine that can move by itself; *esp* : one made to imitate the motions of a man or an animal **2** : a person who acts in a mechanical fashion

1**au·to·mo·bile** \ˌȯt-ə-mō-'bēl, -'mō-ˌbēl\ *adj* : AUTOMOTIVE

2**automobile** *n* : a usu. four-wheeled automotive vehicle designed for passenger transportation on streets and roadways and commonly propelled by an internal-combustion engine — **automobile** *vb* — **au·to·mo·bil·ist** \-mō-'bē-ləst\ *n*

au·to·mo·tive \ˌȯt-ə-'mōt-iv\ *adj* **1** : SELF-PROPELLED **2** : of, relating to, or concerned with automotive vehicles and esp. automobiles and motorcycles

au·to·nom·ic \ˌȯt-ə-'näm-ik\ *adj* : of, relating to, controlled by, or being part of the autonomic nervous system

autonomic nervous system *n* : the part of the vertebrate nervous system that sends nerves to smooth and heart muscle and to glands, that governs actions (as secretion or peristalsis) that are more or less automatic, and that consists of the sympathetic nervous system and the parasympathetic nervous system

au·ton·o·mous \ȯ-'tän-ə-məs\ *adj* : possessing autonomy : SELF-GOVERNING — **au·ton·o·mous·ly** *adv*

au·ton·o·my \-mē\ *n, pl* **-mies** : the power or right of self-government

au·top·sy \'ȯ-ˌtäp-sē, 'ȯt-əp-\ *n, pl* **-sies** : POSTMORTEM — **autopsy** *vb*

au·to·troph·ic \ˌȯt-ə-'träf-ik\ *adj* : able to live and grow on carbon from carbon dioxide or carbonates and nitrogen from a simple inorganic compound — **au·to·troph** \'ȯt-ə-ˌträf\ *n* — **au·tot·ro·phism** \ȯ-'tä-trə-ˌfiz-əm\ *or* **au·tot·ro·phy** \-'tä-trə-fē\ *n*

au·tumn \'ȯt-əm\ *n* **1** : the season between summer and winter — called also *fall* **2** : a time of full maturity beginning decline — **au·tum·nal** \ȯ-'təm-nəl\ *adj*

aux *abbr* auxiliary

1**aux·il·ia·ry** \ȯg-'zil-yə-rē\ *adj* : offering or providing help : SUPPLEMENTARY ⟨an *auxiliary* engine⟩

2**auxiliary** *n, pl* **-ries** **1** : an auxiliary person, group, or device **2** : AUXILIARY VERB

auxiliary verb *n* : a verb (as *have, be, may, do, shall, will, can, must*) that accompanies another and expresses such things as person, number, mood, or tense

aux·in \'ȯk-sən\ *n* : a plant hormone that stimulates shoot elongation and plays a role in water metabolism in the plant

av *abbr* **1** avenue **2** average **3** avoirdupois

AV *abbr* **1** audiovisual **2** Authorized Version

1**avail** \ə-'vāl\ *vb* : to be of use or advantage : HELP

2**avail** *n* : help or benefit toward attainment of a goal : USE ⟨effort was of little *avail*⟩

avail·a·ble \ə-'vā-lə-bəl\ *adj* **1** : USABLE; *esp* : present in a form that a plant or animal can use ⟨a food that contains *available* iron⟩ **2** : ACCESSIBLE, OBTAINABLE ⟨tried every *available* means⟩ — **avail·a·bil·i·ty** \ə-ˌvā-lə-'bil-ət-ē\ *n, pl* **-ties** — **avail·a·ble·ness** *n* — **avail·a·bly** \-blē\ *adv*

av·a·lanche \'av-ə-ˌlanch\ *n* **1** : a large mass of snow and ice or of earth and rock sliding down a mountainside or over a cliff **2** : a sudden overwhelming rush ⟨an *avalanche* of words⟩

av·a·rice \'av-(ə-)rəs\ *n* : excessive desire for wealth or gain : GREED

av·a·ri·cious \ˌav-ə-'rish-əs\ *adj* : greedy for gain : GRASPING — **av·a·ri·cious·ly** *adv* — **av·a·ri·cious·ness** *n*

avast \ə-'vast\ *imperative verb* — a nautical command to stop or cease

avaunt \ə-'vȯnt, -'vänt\ *adv, archaic* : AWAY

avdp *abbr* avoirdupois

ave *abbr* avenue

Ave Ma·ria \ˌäv-ˌā-mə-'rē-ə\ *n* : a salutation to the Virgin Mary combined with a prayer to her as mother of God

avenge \ə-'venj\ *vb* : to take vengeance for or on behalf of ⟨*avenge* an insult⟩ — **aveng·er** *n*

av·e·nue \'av-ə-ˌn(y)ü\ *n* **1** : a way or route to a place or goal : PATH **2** : a street esp. when broad and attractive

aver \ə-'vər\ *vb* **averred**; **aver·ring** : to declare positively : ASSERT

1**av·er·age** \'av-(ə-)rij\ *n* **1** : ARITHMETIC MEAN **2** : something typical of a group, class, or series **3** : a ratio of successful tries to total tries ⟨batting *average*⟩

2**average** *adj* **1** : equaling or approximating an arithmetic mean **2 a** : being about midway between extremes **b** : being not out of the ordinary : COMMON ⟨the *average* man⟩ — **av·er·age·ly** *adv* — **av·er·age·ness** *n*

3**average** *vb* **1** : to amount to on the average : be usually ⟨those children *average* four feet in height⟩ **2** : to find the average of

averse \ə-'vərs\ *adj* : having an active repugnance or distaste ⟨*averse* to strenuous exercise⟩ — **averse·ly** *adv* — **averse·ness** *n*

aver·sion \ə-'vər-zhən\ *n* **1** : a feeling of repugnance toward something with a desire to avoid or turn from it **2** : DISLIKE, ANTIPATHY

avert \ə-'vərt\ *vb* **1** : to turn away ⟨*avert* one's eyes⟩ **2** : to prevent from happening : ward off ⟨narrowly *averted* an accident⟩

avg *abbr* average

avi·an \'ā-vē-ən\ *adj* : of, relating to, or derived from birds

avi·ary \'ā-vē-ˌer-ē\ *n, pl* **-ar·ies** [from Latin *aviarium*, from *avis* "bird"] : a place (as a large cage or a building) where many live birds are kept usu. for exhibition

avi·a·tion \ˌā-vē-'ā-shən, ˌav-ē-\ *n* **1** : the operation of heavier-than-air aircraft **2** : military airplanes — **aviation** *adj*

avi·a·tor \'ā-vē-ˌāt-ər, 'av-ē-\ *n* : the pilot of a heavier-than-air aircraft — **avi·a·tress** \-ˌā-trəs\ *n* — **avi·a·trix** \ˌā-vē-'ā-triks, ˌav-ē-\ *n*

av·id \'av-əd\ *adj* **1** : craving eagerly : GREEDY **2** : ENTHUSIASTIC ⟨*avid* fans⟩ — **avid·i·ty** \ə-'vid-ət-ē, a-\ *n* — **av·id·ly** \'av-əd-lē\ *adv*

avi·ta·min·osis \ˌā-ˌvīt-ə-mə-'nō-səs\ *n, pl* **-min·oses** \-'nō-ˌsēz\ : disease resulting from a deficiency of one or more vitamins

av·o·ca·do \ˌav-ə-'käd-ō\ *n, pl* **-dos** : the usu. green pulpy pear-shaped edible fruit of a tropical American tree; *also* : the tree that bears this fruit

av·o·ca·tion \ˌav-ə-ˈkā-shən, ˈav-ə-ˌ\ *n* : a subordinate occupation pursued esp. for enjoyment : HOBBY — **av·o·ca·tion·al** \-sh(ə-)nəl\ *adj*

av·o·cet \ˈav-ə-ˌset\ *n* : any of several rather large long-legged shorebirds with webbed feet and slender upward-curving bill

Avo·ga·dro's law \ˌav-ə-ˌgäd-rōz-, ˌäv-\ *n* : a law in chemistry: equal volumes of all gases at the same temperature and pressure contain equal numbers of molecules

avoid \ə-ˈvȯid\ *vb* **1** : to make legally void : ANNUL ⟨*avoid* a contract⟩ **2** : to keep away from : SHUN ⟨*avoid* accidents⟩ — **avoid·a·ble** \-ə-bəl\ *adj* — **avoid·a·bly** \-blē\ *adv*

avoid·ance \ə-ˈvȯid-ən(t)s\ *n* **1** : the act of annulling **2** : the act of keeping away from or clear of

av·oir·du·pois \ˌav-ərd-ə-ˈpȯiz\ *n* [alteration of ME *avoir de pois* "goods sold by weight", from French, meaning literally "goods of weight"] **1** : AVOIRDUPOIS WEIGHT **2** : WEIGHT, HEAVINESS

avoirdupois weight *n* : the series of units of weight based on the pound of 16 ounces and the ounce of 16 drams — see MEASURE table

avouch \ə-ˈvau̇ch\ *vb* **1** : to declare positively : AFFIRM **2** : to vouch for : GUARANTEE — **avouch·ment** \-mənt\ *n*

avow \ə-ˈvau̇\ *vb* : to declare or acknowledge openly and frankly

avow·al \ə-ˈvau̇(-ə)l\ *n* : an open declaration or acknowledgment

avowed \ə-ˈvau̇d\ *adj* : openly acknowledged : ADMITTED — **avowed·ly** \-ˈvau̇(ə)d-lē\ *adv*

await \ə-ˈwāt\ *vb* **1** : to wait for : EXPECT ⟨*await* a train⟩ **2** : to be ready or waiting for ⟨a reward *awaits* him⟩

[1]**awake** \ə-ˈwāk\ *vb* **awoke** \-ˈwōk\ *or* **awaked** \-ˈwākt\; **awak·ing** **1** : to cease sleeping **2** : to become aware of something ⟨*awoke* to their danger⟩ **3** : to arouse from sleep **4** : to make or become active : STIR

[2]**awake** *adj* **1** : roused from sleep **2** : ALERT

awak·en \ə-ˈwā-kən\ *vb* **awak·ened**; **awak·en·ing** \-ˈwāk-(ə-)niŋ\ : AWAKE — **awak·en·er** \-(ə-)nər\ *n*

[1]**award** \ə-ˈwȯrd\ *vb* **1** : to give by judicial decision (as after a lawsuit) ⟨*award* damages⟩ **2** : to give or grant as a reward ⟨*award* a prize to the best speaker⟩

[2]**award** *n* : something that is conferred or bestowed : PRIZE

aware \ə-ˈwa(ə)r, -ˈwe(ə)r\ *adj* : having or showing realization, perception, or knowledge : CONSCIOUS — **aware·ness** *n*

awash \ə-ˈwȯsh, -ˈwäsh\ *adv or adj* **1** : washed by waves or tide **2** : washing about : AFLOAT **3** : overflowed by water

[1]**away** \ə-ˈwā\ *adv* **1** : on the way ⟨get *away* early⟩ **2** : from this or that place ⟨go *away*⟩ **3** : in another place or direction ⟨turn *away*⟩ **4** : out of existence ⟨echoes dying *away*⟩ **5** : from one's possession ⟨gave *away* a fortune⟩ **6** : without interruption or hesitation ⟨talk *away*⟩ **7** : FAR ⟨*away* back in 1910⟩

[2]**away** *adj* **1** : absent from a place : GONE ⟨be *away* from home⟩ **2** : DISTANT ⟨a lake 10 miles *away*⟩

ə abut	ər further	a back	ā bake
ä cot, cart	au̇ out	ch chin	e less	ē easy
g gift	i trip	ī life	j joke	ŋ sing	ō flow
ȯ flaw	ȯi coin	th thin	t͟h this	ü loot
u̇ foot	y yet	yü few	yu̇ furious	zh vision

[1]**awe** \ˈȯ\ *n* **1** : a profoundly humble and reverential attitude in the presence of deity or of something sacred or sublime **2** : abashed fear inspired by authority or power

[2]**awe** *vb* **1** : to inspire with awe **2** : to control or check by inspiring with awe ⟨*awed* him into submission⟩

awe·some \ˈȯ-səm\ *adj* **1** : expressive of awe **2** : inspiring awe — **awe·some·ly** *adv* — **awe·some·ness** *n*

awe·strick·en \ˈȯ-ˌstrik-ən\ *or* **awe·struck** \-ˌstrək\ *adj* : filled with awe

aw·ful \ˈȯ-fəl\ *adj* **1** : AWESOME **2** : extremely disagreeable or objectionable **3** : very great ⟨took an *awful* chance⟩ — **aw·ful·ness** *n*

aw·ful·ly *usu* ˈȯ-fə-lē *in sense 1*, ˈȯ-flē *in senses 2 & 3*\ *adv* **1** : in a manner to inspire awe **2** : in a disagreeable or objectionable manner **3** : EXTREMELY, VERY ⟨*awfully* nice of her⟩

awhile \ə-ˈhwīl\ *adv* : for a while : for a short time ⟨sit and rest *awhile*⟩

awhirl \ə-ˈhwərl\ *adv or adj* : in a whirl

awk·ward \ˈȯ-kwərd\ *adj* **1** : lacking dexterity in the use of the hands or of instruments **2** : not graceful : CLUMSY **3** : causing embarrassment ⟨an *awkward* situation⟩ **4** : difficult to use or handle — **awk·ward·ly** *adv* — **awk·ward·ness** *n*

awl \ˈȯl\ *n* : a pointed tool for making small holes (as in leather or wood)

aw·ning \ˈȯn-iŋ, ˈän-\ *n* : a cover esp. of canvas resembling a roof and extended over or in front of something to provide shade or shelter

AWOL \ˈā-ˌwȯl, ˌā-ˌdəb-əl-yü-ˌō-ˈel\ *n* [from a military abbreviation for "absent without leave"] : a person who is absent without permission — **AWOL** *adv or adj*

awry \ə-ˈrī\ *adv or adj* **1** : turned or twisted toward one side : ASKEW **2** : out of the right course : AMISS ⟨their plans went *awry*⟩

ax *or* **axe** \ˈaks\ *n* : a cutting tool that consists of a heavy edged head fixed to a handle and that is used for chopping and splitting wood

ax·i·al \ˈak-sē-əl\ *or* **ax·al** \-səl\ *adj* **1** : of, relating to, or functioning as an axis **2** : situated around, in the direction of, on, or along an axis ⟨*axial* flowers⟩ — **ax·i·al·ly** \-sē-ə-lē\ *adv*

axial skeleton *n* : the skeleton of the trunk and head

ax·il \ˈak-səl, -ˌsil\ *n* : the angle between a branch or leaf and the stem from which it arises

ax·il·la \ag-ˈzil-ə\ *n, pl* **ax·il·lae** \-ˈzil-(ˌ)ē, -ˈsil-, -ˌī\ *or* **axillas** : ARMPIT

ax·il·lary \ˈak-sə-ˌler-ē\ *adj* **1** : of, relating to, or located near the axilla **2** : situated in or growing from an axil ⟨an *axillary* bud⟩

ax·i·om \ˈak-sē-əm\ *n* : a truth or principle widely accepted as obvious

ax·i·om·at·ic \ˌak-sē-ə-ˈmat-ik\ *adj* **1** : of or relating to an axiom **2** : resembling an axiom : SELF-EVIDENT — **ax·i·om·at·i·cal·ly** \-ˈmat-i-k(ə-)lē\ *adv*

ax·is \ˈak-səs\ *n, pl* **ax·es** \ˈak-ˌsēz\ **1 a** : a straight line about which a body or a geometric figure rotates or may be supposed to rotate **b** : a straight line with respect to which a body or figure is symmetrical **c** : one of the reference lines of a coordinate system **2 a** : the second vertebra of the neck on which the head turns as on a pivot **b** : an anatomical structure around which parts of the body are arranged in a symmetrical way ⟨the cerebrospinal *axis*⟩; *esp* : the main stem of a plant from which leaves and branches arise **3** : PARTNERSHIP, ALLIANCE

ax·le \ˈak-səl\ *n* : a pin or shaft on or with which a wheel or pair of wheels revolves

A

ax·o·lotl \'ak-sə-ˌlät-əl\ *n* : any of several salamanders of mountain lakes of Mexico and the western U.S. that ordinarily live and breed while retaining the larval form

ax·on \'ak-ˌsän\ *also* **ax·one** \-ˌsōn\ *n* : a usu. long and single nerve-cell process that as a rule conducts impulses away from the cell body — **ax·o·nal** \'ak-sə-nəl\ *or* **ax·on·ic** \ak-'sän-ik\ *adj*

[1]**aye** *also* **ay** \'ā\ *adv* : FOREVER, ALWAYS

[2]**aye** *also* **ay** \'ī\ *adv* : YES

[3]**aye** *also* **ay** \'ī\ *n, pl* **ayes** : an affirmative vote or voter

aye–aye \'ī-ˌī\ *n* : a nocturnal lemur of Madagascar

Ayr·shire \'a(ə)r-ˌshi(ə)r, 'e(ə)r-, -shər\ *n* : any of a breed of hardy dairy cattle originated in Ayr that vary in color from white to red or brown

AZ *abbr* Arizona

aza·lea \ə-'zāl-yə\ *n* : any of numerous rhododendrons with funnel-shaped flowers and usu. deciduous leaves including many grown as ornamentals

az·i·muth \'az-(ə-)məth\ *n* : horizontal direction

azo \'az-ō\ *adj* : relating to or containing two nitrogen atoms united to each other and at both ends to carbon ⟨an *azo* dye⟩

azon·al \(')ā-'zōn-əl\ *adj* : of, relating to, or being a soil or a major soil group lacking well-developed horizons

Az·tec \'az-ˌtek\ *n* : a member of an Indian people that founded the Mexican empire and were conquered by Cortes in 1519

azure \'azh-ər\ *n* [from Old French *azur*, from Arabic *lāzuward* "lapis lazuli", from Persian *lāzhuward*] : the blue color of the clear sky — **azure** *adj*

azur·ite \'azh-ə-ˌrīt\ *n* : a blue mineral consisting of carbonate of copper, occurring in crystals, in mass, and in earthy form, and constituting an ore of copper

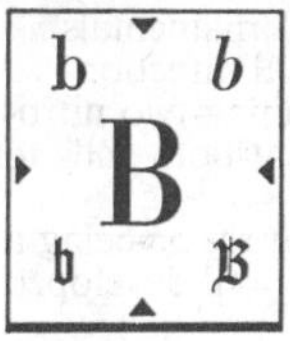

b \'bē\ *n, often cap* **1** : the 2d letter of the English alphabet **2** : the musical tone B **3** : a grade rating a student's work as good
b *abbr* **1** book **2** born
BA *abbr* **1** bachelor of arts **2** batting average
baa *or* **ba** \'ba, 'bä\ *n* : the bleat of a sheep — **baa** *vb*
bab·bitt metal \'bab-ət-\ *n* : an alloy used for lining bearings; *esp* : one containing tin, copper, and antimony
bab·ble \'bab-əl\ *vb* **bab·bled**; **bab·bling** \'bab-(ə-)ling\ **1 a** : to utter meaningless sounds **b** : to talk foolishly or excessively : PRATTLE **2** : to make sounds as though babbling ⟨a *babbling* brook⟩ **3** : to reveal by too free talk — **babble** *n* — **bab·bler** \'bab-(ə-)lər\ *n*
babe \'bāb\ *n* : INFANT, BABY
ba·bel \'bā-bəl, 'bab-əl\ *n, often cap* [from the Tower of *Babel* in Genesis 11:4–9, the building of which was interrupted by a confusion of tongues] **1** : a confusion of sounds or voices **2** : a scene of noise or confusion
ba·boon \ba-'bün\ *n* : any of several large African and Asiatic apes having doglike muzzles and usu. short tails — **ba·boon·ish** \-'bü-nish\ *adj*
ba·bush·ka \bə-'büsh-kə\ *n* [from the Russian word for "grandmother"; probably so called from the frequent wearing of such kerchiefs by elderly Russian peasant women] : a kerchief for the head usu. folded triangularly
[1]**ba·by** \'bā-bē\ *n, pl* **ba·bies** **1 a** : an extremely young child; *esp* : INFANT **b** : the youngest of a group **2** : a childish person — **ba·by·hood** \-bē-ˌhu̇d\ *n* — **ba·by·ish** \-ish\ *adj*
[2]**baby** *vb* **ba·bied**; **ba·by·ing** **1** : to treat as a baby : FONDLE, PET **2** : to operate or treat with care
Bab·y·lo·nian \ˌbab-ə-'lō-nyən, -nē-ən\ *adj* : of, relating to, or characteristic of ancient Babylonia or its people — **Babylonian** *n*
baby's breath *n* **1** : a tall much-branched herb related to the carnation and having clusters of small fragrant white or pink flowers **2** : a bedstraw with thin lance-shaped leaves and white flowers
ba·by–sit \'bā-bē-ˌsit\ *vb* **-sat** \-ˌsat\; **-sit·ting** : to care for children usu. during a short absence of the parents — **ba·by–sit·ter** *n*
baby's tears *n* : a creeping Corsican herb related to the nettle and often grown esp. as a houseplant for its mosslike small round short-stalked leaves
bac·ca·lau·re·ate \ˌbak-ə-'lȯr-ē-ət, -'lär-\ *n* **1** : the degree of bachelor conferred by universities and colleges **2** : a sermon to a graduating class or the service at which such a sermon is delivered
bach·e·lor \'bach-(ə-)lər\ *n* **1** : a person who has received the lowest degree conferred by a college, university, or professional school ⟨*bachelor* of arts⟩ **2 a** : an unmarried man **b** : an unmated male animal — **bach·e·lor·hood** \-ˌhu̇d\ *n*
bachelor's button *n* : any of numerous plants with flowers or flower heads that suggest buttons; *esp* : CORNFLOWER
bac·il·la·ry \'bas-ə-ˌler-ē, bə-'sil-ə-rē\ *or* **ba·cil·lar** \bə-'sil-ər, 'bas-ə-lər\ *adj* **1** : shaped like a rod; *also* : consisting of small rods **2** : of, relating to, or produced by bacilli
ba·cil·lus \bə-'sil-əs\ *n, pl* **-cil·li** \-'sil-ˌī, -'sil-ē\ : any of numerous straight rod-shaped bacteria that require oxygen for growth; *also* : a disease-producing bacterium
[1]**back** \'bak\ *n* **1 a** : the rear part of the human body esp. from the neck to the end of the spine **b** : the corresponding part of a four-footed or lower animal **2 a** : the hinder part : REAR **b** : the farther or reverse side **3** : something at or on the back for support ⟨*back* of a chair⟩ **4 a** : a position in some games behind the front line of players **b** : a player in this position — **backed** \'bakt\ *adj* — **back·less** \'bak-ləs\ *adj*
[2]**back** *adv* **1** : to, toward, or at the rear **2** : in or into a reclining position **3** : under control ⟨held *back*⟩ **4** : to, toward, or in a former place, state, or time ⟨go *back*⟩ **5** : in return or reply ⟨write *back*⟩
[3]**back** *adj* **1 a** : being at or in the back ⟨*back* door⟩ **b** : distant from a central or main area : REMOTE **2** : being in arrears : OVERDUE ⟨*back* rent⟩ **3** : not current ⟨*back* number of a magazine⟩
[4]**back** *vb* **1 a** : to give aid or support to : ASSIST ⟨*backed* the new enterprise by investing in it⟩ **b** : SUBSTANTIATE ⟨*backed* up his story with facts⟩ **2** : to move or cause to move back or backward **3** : to shift in a counterclockwise direction ⟨the wind *backed* around⟩ **4 a** : to furnish with a back **b** : to be or be at the back of — **back·er** *n*
back·ache \'bak-ˌāk\ *n* : pain in the back; *esp* : dull persistent pain in the lower back
back·bite \-ˌbīt\ *vb* **-bit** \-ˌbit\; **-bit·ten** \-ˌbit-ən\; **-bit·ing** \-ˌbīt-ing\ : to say mean or spiteful things about someone who is absent — **back·bit·er** *n*
back·board \-ˌbōrd, -ˌbȯrd\ *n* : a board placed at the back or serving as a back; *esp* : one rising vertically behind the basket on a basketball court
back·bone \-'bōn, -ˌbōn\ *n* **1** : SPINAL COLUMN **2** : the foundation or sturdiest part of something **3** : firm and resolute character — **back·boned** \-'bōnd, -ˌbōnd\ *adj*
back·cross \'bak-ˌkrȯs\ *vb* : to cross (a first-generation hybrid) with one parent or individual genetically identical with the parent — **backcross** *n*
back·drop \-ˌdräp\ *n* : a painted cloth hung across the rear of a stage
back·field \-ˌfēld\ *n* : the football players who line up behind the line of scrimmage
[1]**back·fire** \-ˌfī(ə)r\ *n* **1** : a fire started to check an advancing fire by clearing an area of combustible matter **2** : an improperly timed explosion of fuel mixture in the cylinder of an internal-combustion engine
[2]**backfire** *vb* **1** : to make or undergo a backfire **2** : to have an effect that is the reverse of the one desired or expected
back·gam·mon \'bak-ˌgam-ən\ *n* : a game played by two persons on a double board with 12 spaces on each side in which each player has 15 men whose movements are determined by throwing dice
back·ground \-ˌgrau̇nd\ *n* **1** : the scenery, ground, or surface behind an object seen or represented (as in a painting) **2** : an inconspicuous position ⟨keeps in the *background*⟩ **3 a** : the setting within which something takes place **b** : the events leading up to a situation **c** : information essential to understanding a problem or situation **d** : the total of a person's experience, knowledge, and education ⟨a strong *background* in mathematics⟩ **4 a** : undesired sound that is heard in a sound-reproducing system (as in radio or a tape recording) **b** : detectable radiation

ə abut	ər further	a back	ā bake	
ä cot, cart	au̇ out	ch chin	e less	ē easy
g gift	i trip	ī life	j joke	ng sing	ō flow
ȯ flaw	ȯi coin	th thin	t͟h this	ü loot
u̇ foot	y yet	yü few	yu̇ furious	zh vision

from sources other than those under consideration
¹**back·hand** \-ˌhand\ *n* **1** : a stroke made with the back of the hand turned in the direction of movement **2** : handwriting whose strokes slant downward from left to right

backhand 1

²**backhand** *adj* : using or made with a backhand
³**backhand** *vb* : to do, hit, or catch with a backhand
⁴**backhand** *or* **back·hand·ed** \-ˌhan-dəd\ *adv* : with a backhand
back·hand·ed \-ˌhan-dəd\ *adj* **1** : BACKHAND **2** : INDIRECT, DEVIOUS; *esp* : SARCASTIC ⟨a *backhanded* compliment⟩ **3** : written in backhand
back·ing \'bak-ing\ *n* **1** : something forming a back **2 a** : SUPPORT, AID **b** : ENDORSEMENT, APPROVAL **3** : those who support a person or enterprise ⟨a candidate with a wide *backing*⟩
back·lash \'bak-ˌlash\ *n* : a violent backward movement or reaction
back·log \-ˌlȯg, -ˌläg\ *n* **1** : a large log at the back of a hearth fire **2** : a reserve esp. of unfilled orders **3** : an accumulation of unperformed tasks
back of *prep* : BEHIND
back·rest \'bak-ˌrest\ *n* : a rest at or for the back
back·side \-'sīd\ *n* : BUTTOCKS
back·slide \-ˌslīd\ *vb* **-slid** \-ˌslid\; **-slid** *or* **-slid·den** \-ˌslid-ən\; **-slid·ing** \-ˌslīd-ing\ : to lapse morally or in the practice of religion — **back·slid·er** \-ˌslīd-ər\ *n*
back·spin \-ˌspin\ *n* : a backward rotary motion of a ball
¹**back·stage** \-'stāj\ *adv* **1** : in or to a backstage area **2** : SECRETLY, PRIVATELY
²**backstage** *adj* : of, relating to, or occurring in the area behind the proscenium and esp. in the dressing rooms
back·stop \-ˌstäp\ *n* **1** : a screen or fence used in some games to keep a ball from leaving the field of play **2** : a baseball catcher
back·stretch \-ˌstrech, -'strech\ *n* : the side opposite the homestretch on a racecourse
back·stroke \-ˌstrōk\ *n* : a swimming stroke executed by a swimmer lying on his back
back swimmer *n* : any of a family of aquatic bugs that are characterized by swimming on the back
back·track \'bak-ˌtrak\ *vb* **1** : to retrace one's course **2** : to reverse a position or stand
back·up \'bak-ˌəp\ *n* : a person or thing ready to take the place of another in an emergency — **backup** *adj*
¹**back·ward** \-wərd\ *or* **back·wards** \-wərdz\ *adv* **1** : toward the back ⟨look *backward*⟩ **2** : with the back foremost ⟨ride *backward*⟩ **3** : in a reverse or contrary direction or way ⟨count *backward*⟩ **4** : toward a worse state
²**backward** *adj* **1 a** : directed or turned backward ⟨a *backward* glance⟩ **b** : done backward **2** : SHY, BASHFUL **3** : retarded in development ⟨*backward* nations⟩ — **back·ward·ly** *adv* — **back·ward·ness** *n*
back·wash \'bak-ˌwȯsh, -ˌwäsh\ *n* **1** : backward movement (as of water or air) produced by motion of oars or other propelling force **2** : a later or secondary consequence : AFTERMATH
back·wa·ter \'bak-ˌwȯt-ər, -ˌwät-\ *n* **1** : water held, pushed, or turned back from its course **2** : a backward stagnant place or condition
back·woods \-'wu̇dz, -ˌwu̇dz\ *n pl* : wooded or partly cleared areas on the frontier — **back·woods·man** \-mən\ *n*
ba·con \'bā-kən\ *n* : salted and smoked meat from the sides and sometimes the back of a pig
bacteria *pl of* BACTERIUM
bac·te·ri·cid·al \bak-ˌtir-ə-'sīd-əl\ *adj* : destroying bacteria — **bac·te·ri·cide** \-'tir-ə-ˌsīd\ *n*
bac·te·ri·ol·o·gy \bak-ˌtir-ē-'äl-ə-jē\ *n* **1** : a science that deals with bacteria and their relations to medicine, industry, and agriculture **2** : bacterial life and phenomena — **bac·te·ri·o·log·ic** \-ē-ə-'läj-ik\ *or* **bac·te·ri·o·log·i·cal** \-'läj-i-kəl\ *adj* — **bac·te·ri·o·log·i·cal·ly** \-'läj-i-k(ə-)lē\ *adv* — **bac·te·ri·ol·o·gist** \-ē-'äl-ə-jəst\ *n*
bac·te·rio·phage \bak-'tir-ē-ə-ˌfāj\ *n* : any of various viruses that specifically attack bacteria
bac·te·ri·um \bak-'tir-ē-əm\ *n*, *pl* **-ria** \-ē-ə\ : any of a class of microscopic plants that live in soil, water, organic matter, or the bodies of plants and animals and are important to man because of their chemical effects and as a cause of disease — **bac·te·ri·al** \-ē-əl\ *adj*
Bac·tri·an camel \'bak-trē-ən-\ *n* : CAMEL b
¹**bad** \'bad\ *adj* **worse** \'wərs\; **worst** \'wərst\ **1 a** : below standard : POOR **b** : UNFAVORABLE ⟨*bad* impression⟩ **c** : DECAYED, SPOILED ⟨*bad* meat⟩ **2 a** : morally evil **b** : MISCHIEVOUS, DISOBEDIENT **3** : INADEQUATE ⟨*bad* lighting⟩ **4** : DISAGREEABLE, UNPLEASANT ⟨*bad* news⟩ **5 a** : HARMFUL ⟨too much candy is *bad* for you⟩ **b** : SEVERE ⟨*bad* cold⟩ **6** : INCORRECT, FAULTY ⟨*bad* spelling⟩ **7** : ILL, SICK ⟨feel *bad*⟩ **8** : SORROWFUL, SORRY ⟨don't feel *bad* about losing⟩ — **bad** *adv* — **bad·ly** *adv* — **bad·ness** *n*
²**bad** *n* **1** : something bad **2** : an evil or unhappy state ⟨went to the *bad*⟩
bade *past of* BID
badge \'baj\ *n* **1** : a mark or sign worn to show that a person belongs to a certain group, class, or rank ⟨a policeman's *badge*⟩ **2** : an outward sign
¹**badg·er** \'baj-ər\ *n* : any of several sturdy burrowing mammals widely distributed in the northern hemisphere; *also* : the pelt or fur of a badger

badger
(about 3½ ft. long)

²**badger** *vb* **badg·ered**; **badg·er·ing** \'baj-(ə-)ring\ : to harass or annoy persistently
bad·land \'bad-ˌland\ *n* : a region where erosion has formed the soft rocks into sharp and intricate shapes and where plant life is scarce ⟨*badlands* of So. Dakota⟩
bad·min·ton \'bad-ˌmint-ən\ *n* : a court game played with a light racket and a shuttlecock volleyed over a net
bad–mouth \-ˌmau̇th, -'mau̇th\ *vb* : to criticize severely
¹**baf·fle** \'baf-əl\ *vb* **baf·fled**; **baf·fling** \'baf-(ə-)ling\ **1** : to defeat or check by confusing : PERPLEX **2 a** : to check or turn the flow of by or as if by a baffle **b** : to prevent (sound waves) from interfering with each other (as by a baffle) ***syn*** see FRUSTRATE — **baf·fle·ment** \-əl-mənt\ *n* — **baf·fler** \-(ə-)lər\ *n*
²**baffle** *n* : a plate, screen, or other device to deflect, check, or regulate flow

1**bag** \'bag\ *n* **1 a** : a flexible container for holding, storing, or carrying something **b** : PURSE; *esp* : HANDBAG **c** : TRAVELING BAG **2 a** : a pouched or hanging bodily part or organ; *esp* : UDDER **b** : a puffed-out sag or bulge in cloth **c** : a square white canvas container to mark a base in baseball **3** : the amount contained in a bag **4** : a quantity of game taken or permitted to be taken **5** *slang* : a slovenly unattractive woman **6** *slang* : field of interest : SPECIALTY, INCLINATION ⟨rock is really his *bag*⟩ — **in the bag** : SURE, CERTAIN

2**bag** *vb* **bagged**; **bag·ging** **1** : to swell out : BULGE **2** : to put into a bag **3 a** : to take as game ⟨*bagged* a deer⟩ **b** : CAPTURE, SEIZE; *also* : to shoot down : DESTROY

ba·gel \'bā-gəl\ *n* : a hard glazed doughnut-shaped roll

bag·gage \'bag-ij\ *n* **1** : the traveling bags and personal belongings of a traveler : LUGGAGE **2** : the equipment carried with a military force

bag·gy \'bag-ē\ *adj* **bag·gi·er**; **-est** : loose, puffed out, or hanging like a bag ⟨*baggy* trousers⟩ — **bag·gi·ly** \'bag-ə-lē\ *adv* — **bag·gi·ness** \'bag-ē-nəs\ *n*

bag·pipe \'bag-,pīp\ *n* : a wind instrument consisting of a leather bag, a melody pipe, and three or four drone pipes — often used in pl. — **bag·pip·er** \-,pī-pər\ *n*

bagpipe

ba·guette \ba-'get\ *n* : a gem having the shape of a long narrow rectangle

bag·worm \'bag-,wərm\ *n* : a moth that as a larva lives in a silk case covered with plant debris and is destructive to foliage

1**bail** \'bāl\ *n* **1** : security given to guarantee the appearance of a prisoner at his trial in order to obtain his release from prison until that time **2** : one who provides bail

2**bail** *vb* **1** : to release under bail **2** : to gain the release of by giving bail

3**bail** *n* : a container used to remove water from a boat

4**bail** *vb* : to clear (water) from a boat by dipping and throwing over the side

5**bail** *n* **1** : a supporting half hoop **2** : the curved handle of a kettle or pail

bai·liff \'bā-ləf\ *n* **1** : any of various officials; *esp* : a minor officer of some U.S. courts usu. serving as a messenger or doorkeeper **2** *chiefly Brit* : one who manages an estate or farm

bail out *vb* **1** : to help from a predicament ⟨*bailed* him *out* with a loan⟩ **2** : to jump with a parachute from an airplane in flight

bairn \'ba(ə)rn, 'be(ə)rn\ *n, chiefly Scot* : CHILD

1**bait** \'bāt\ *vb* **1 a** : to exasperate by repeated attacks **b** : NAG, TEASE **2** : to harass with dogs usu. for sport **3 a** : to furnish with bait ⟨*bait* a hook⟩ **b** : ENTICE, LURE **4** : to give food and drink to esp. on the road ⟨*baited* his horses⟩ — **bait·er** *n*

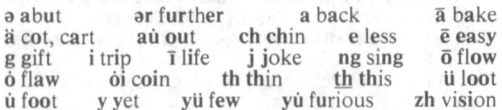

2**bait** *n* **1** : something used in luring esp. to a hook or trap **2** : a poisonous material distributed in food to kill pests **3** : LURE, TEMPTATION

baize \'bāz\ *n* : a coarse woolen or cotton fabric napped to imitate felt

1**bake** \'bāk\ *vb* **1** : to cook or become cooked in a dry heat esp. in an oven **2** : to dry or harden by heat ⟨*bake* bricks⟩ — **bak·er** *n*

2**bake** *n* **1** : the act or process of baking **2** : a social gathering at which a baked food is served

baker's dozen *n* : THIRTEEN

bakers' yeast *n* : a yeast used or suitable for use as leaven

bak·ery \'bā-k(ə-)rē\ *n, pl* **-er·ies** : a place where bread, cakes, and pastry are made or sold

bake·shop \'bāk-,shäp\ *n* : BAKERY

baking powder *n* : a powder that consists of a carbonate, an acid, and a starch and that makes the dough rise and become light in baking cakes and biscuits

baking soda *n* : SODIUM BICARBONATE

bal *abbr* balance

1**bal·ance** \'bal-ən(t)s\ *n* [from Old French, from Latin *bilanc-*, stem of *bilanx* "having two pans", from *bi-* and *lanx* "plate"] **1** : an instrument for weighing; *esp* : a beam that is supported freely in the center and has two pans of equal weight suspended from its ends **2** : a counterbalancing weight, force, or influence **3** : a vibrating wheel operating with a hairspring to regulate the movement of a timepiece **4** : a condition in which opposing forces offset each other ⟨a *balance* between right and need⟩ **5** : equality between the totals of the two sides of an account **6** : an aesthetically pleasing integration of elements : HARMONY **7** : something left over : REMAINDER; *esp* : the amount by which one side of an account is greater than the other ⟨a *balance* of $10 on the credit side⟩ **8** : mental and emotional steadiness **9** : the maintenance (as in a natural habitat) of a population in about the same condition and numbers

balance 1

2**balance** *vb* **1 a** : to compute the difference between the debits and credits of an account **b** : to pay the amount due on : SETTLE **2** : to make two parts exactly equal ⟨*balance* equations⟩ **3** : to complete (a chemical equation) so that the same number of atoms of each kind appears on each side **4 a** : COUNTERBALANCE, OFFSET **b** : to equal or equalize in weight, number, or proportion **5** : to compare the weight of in or as if in a balance **6 a** : to bring or come to a state or position of balance **b** : to poise in or as if in balance **c** : to bring into harmony or proportion; *also* : to so plan and prepare that all needed elements will be present ⟨*balance* a diet⟩ ⟨a *balanced* aquarium⟩ **7** : to move with a swaying or swinging motion — **bal·anc·er** *n*

balance of nature : the fine state of balance in a natural ecosystem due to interaction of the living and nonliving parts of the environment ⟨caused widespread destruction by upsetting the *balance of nature* of the western plains⟩

balance wheel *n* : a wheel that regulates or stabilizes the motion of a mechanism (as a timepiece or a sewing machine)

bal·co·ny \'bal-kə-nē\ *n, pl* **-nies** **1** : a platform enclosed by a low wall or railing and built out from the side of a building **2** : a gallery inside a building (as a theater or auditorium)

bald \'bȯld\ *adj* **1** : lacking a natural or usual covering (as of hair) **2** : UNADORNED, PLAIN ⟨a *bald* summary of the book⟩ — **bald·ly** *adv* — **bald·ness** \'bȯl(d)-nəs\ *n*

bald cypress *n* : either of two large swamp trees related to the pine and found in the southern U.S.

bald eagle *n* : the common eagle of No. America which is wholly dark when young but has white head and neck feathers when mature

bald eagle (up to 7½ ft. wingspread)

bal·dric \'bȯl-drik\ *n* : a belt worn over one shoulder to support a sword or bugle

bale *n* : a large bundle of goods tightly tied for storage or shipping and usu. wrapped ⟨a *bale* of cotton⟩ — **bale** *vb* — **bal·er** *n*

ba·leen \bə-'lēn\ *n* : WHALEBONE

baleen whale *n* : WHALEBONE WHALE

bale·ful \'bāl-fəl\ *adj* **1** : deadly or harmful in influence **2** : OMINOUS — **bale·ful·ly** \-fə-lē\ *adv* — **bale·ful·ness** *n*

Ba·li·nese \,bäl-i-'nēz, ,bal-, -'nēs\ *adj* : of, relating to, or characteristic of Bali or its people — **Balinese** *n*

1balk \'bȯk\ *n* **1** : HINDRANCE, CHECK **2** : failure of a player to complete a motion begun; *esp* : an illegal motion of a baseball pitcher while in position to pitch to a batter

2balk *vb* **1** : to check or stop by or as if by an obstacle : BLOCK **2** : to stop and refuse to go ⟨horse *balked* at the steep hill⟩ **3** : to commit a balk in sports — **balk·er** *n*

balky \'bȯ-kē\ *adj* **balk·i·er**; **-est** : likely to balk

1ball \'bȯl\ *n* **1 a** : a round or roundish body or mass **b** : a round or egg-shaped body used in a game or sport **c** : a usu. round solid shot for a firearm **d** : the rounded bulge at the base of the thumb or big toe **2** : a game in which a ball is thrown, kicked, or struck; *esp* : BASEBALL **3** : a pitched baseball not struck at by the batter that fails to pass through the strike zone

2ball *vb* : to form or gather into a ball

3ball *n* : a large formal gathering for social dancing

bal·lad \'bal-əd\ *n* **1** : a simple song : AIR **2** : a narrative poem usu. in stanzas of two or four lines and suitable for singing; *esp* : one of unknown authorship handed down orally from generation to generation **3** : a popular song; *esp* : a slow romantic or sentimental one

ball-and-socket joint *n* : a joint (as in the hip) in which a rounded part moves within a socket so as to allow movements in many directions

bal·last \'bal-əst\ *n* **1** : something heavy carried in a ship to steady it **2** : something heavy put into the car of a balloon to steady it or to control its ascent **3** : gravel, cinders, or crushed stone used in making a roadbed — **ballast** *vb*

ball bearing *n* **1** : a bearing in which the revolving part turns on steel balls that roll easily in a groove **2** : one of the balls in a ball bearing

ball·car·ri·er \'bȯl-,kar-ē-ər\ *n* : the football player carrying the ball in an offensive play

bal·le·ri·na \,bal-ə-'rē-nə\ *n* : a female ballet dancer

bal·let \'bal-,ā, ba-'lā\ *n* **1 a** : dancing combining conventional poses and steps with light flowing movements **b** : a theatrical art form using ballet to convey a story, theme, or atmosphere **2** : music for a ballet **3** : a group that performs ballets

bal·lis·tic \bə-'lis-tik\ *adj* : of or relating to ballistics or to a body in motion according to the laws of ballistics

ballistic missile *n* : a self-propelled missile that is guided during the ascent of a high-arch path and that falls freely in the descent

bal·lis·tics \bə-'lis-tiks\ *n sing or pl* **1 a** : the science that deals with the motion of projectiles (as bullets) **b** : the flight characteristics of a projectile **2** : the firing characteristics of a firearm or cartridge

1bal·loon \bə-'lün\ *n* **1** : an airtight bag filled with heated air or with a gas lighter than air so as to rise and float above the ground **2** : a toy consisting of an inflatable rubber bag — **bal·loon·ist** \-'lü-nəst\ *n*

2balloon *vb* **1** : to ascend or travel in a balloon **2** : to swell or puff out **3** : to increase rapidly

1bal·lot \'bal-ət\ *n* [from Italian *ballotta*, literally "little ball", from *balla* "ball"] **1** : a small ball used in secret voting or a sheet of paper used to cast a vote **2 a** : the action or system of voting **b** : the right to vote **3** : the number of votes cast

2ballot *vb* : to vote or decide by ballot

ball park *n* : a park or enclosed ground in which ball and esp. baseball is played

ball-point pen *n* : a pen having as the writing point a small rotating steel ball that inks itself by contact with an inner magazine

ball·room \'bȯl-,rüm, -,ru̇m\ *n* : a large room for dances

bal·ly·hoo \'bal-ē-,hü\ *n, pl* **-hoos** **1** : a noisy attention-getting demonstration or talk **2** : sensational advertising or propaganda — **ballyhoo** *vb*

balm \'bäm, 'bälm\ *n* **1** : a resin from small tropical evergreen trees **2** : a fragrant healing or soothing preparation (as an ointment) **3** : something that comforts or refreshes ⟨sleep is *balm* to a tired body⟩ **4** : LEMON BALM

balm of Gil·e·ad \-'gil-ē-əd\ **1 a** : a small African and Asiatic tree with aromatic evergreen leaves; *also* : a product from balm of Gilead consisting of its essential oil and resin **b** : any of several aromatic plant secretions **c** : either of two poplars often grown in cultivation **2** : an agency that soothes, relieves, or heals

balmy \'bäm-ē, 'bäl-mē\ *adj* **balm·i·er**; **-est** **1** : having the qualities of balm : SOOTHING, MILD **2** : FOOLISH, INSANE — **balm·i·ly** \'bäm-ə-lē, 'bäl-mə-\ *adv* — **balm·i·ness** \'bäm-ē-nəs, 'bäl-mē-\ *n*

bal·sa \'bȯl-sə\ *n* **1** : a tropical American tree with extremely light strong wood used esp. for floats; *also* : its wood **2** : a raft made of bundles of grass or reeds lashed together **3** : a life raft made of two cylinders of metal or wood joined by a framework

bal·sam \'bȯl-səm\ *n* **1 a** : a fragrant and usu. oily and resinous substance flowing from various plants **b** : a preparation containing or smelling like balsam **2 a** : a balsam-yielding tree (as balsam fir) **b** : IMPATIENS; *esp* : one grown as an ornamental **3** : BALM 2 — **bal·sam·ic** \bȯl-'sam-ik\ *adj*

balsam fir *n* : a resinous American evergreen tree related to the pines and widely used for pulpwood and as a Christmas tree

balsam poplar *n* : a No. American poplar that is often cultivated as a shade tree and has buds thickly coated with a resin

Bal·tic \'bȯl-tik\ *adj* **1** : of or relating to the Baltic

B

sea or to the states of Lithuania, Latvia, and Estonia **2 :** of or relating to a branch of the Indo-European languages containing Latvian, Lithuanian, and Old Prussian

Bal·ti·more oriole \\ˌbȯl-tə-ˌmōr-, -ˌmȯr-, -mər-\\ *n* **:** a common American oriole that builds a finely woven hanging nest of grass and fiber and in the male is black, white, and brilliant orange

bal·us·ter \\ˈbal-ə-stər\\ *n* **:** an upright support of a rail (as of a staircase)

bal·us·trade \\ˈbal-ə-ˌstrād\\ *n* **1 :** a row of balusters topped by a rail to serve as an open barrier (as along the edge of a terrace) **2 :** a stair railing

bam·boo \\bam-ˈbü\\ *n, pl* **bamboos :** any of various chiefly tropical tall woody grasses including some with strong hollow stems used for building, furniture, or utensils — **bamboo** *adj*

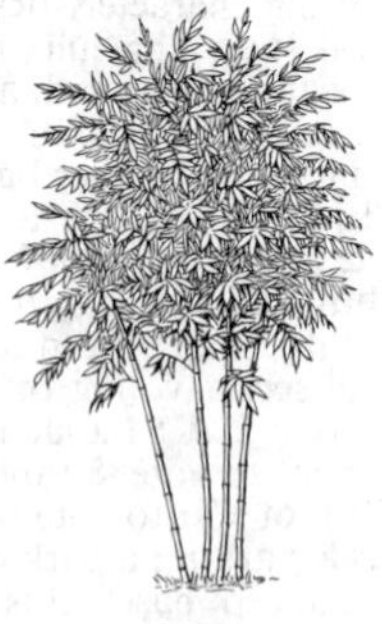
bamboo
(up to 120 ft. high)

1ban \\ˈban\\ *vb* **banned; ban·ning :** to prohibit esp. by legal means

2ban *n* **1 :** CURSE **2 :** an official prohibition

ba·nana \\bə-ˈnan-ə\\ *n* **:** a treelike tropical plant with large leaves and flower clusters that develop into a bunch of finger-shaped fruit which are yellow or red when ripe; *also* **:** its fruit

banana oil *n* **:** a colorless liquid acetate that has a fruity odor and is used as a solvent and in the manufacture of artificial fruit essences

1band \\ˈband\\ *n* **1 :** something that binds, ties, or goes around ⟨a rubber *band*⟩ **2 :** a strip distinguishable (as by color, texture, or composition) from adjacent matter ⟨a *band* of nerve fibers⟩ **3 :** a range of wavelengths or frequencies between two specified limits **4 :** a strip of grooves on a phonographic record containing a single piece or a section of a long piece — **band·ed** \\ˈban-dəd\\ *adj*

2band *vb* **1 :** to put a band on **2 :** to tie up with a band **3 :** to join in a group or for a common purpose ⟨*banded* together for warmth⟩ — **band·er** *n*

3band *n* **:** a group of persons, animals, or things; *esp* **:** a group of musicians usu. excluding players of stringed instruments organized for playing together

1ban·dage \\ˈban-dij\\ *n* **:** a strip of fabric used esp. to dress and bind up wounds

2bandage *vb* **:** to bind, dress, or cover with a bandage

ban·dan·na *or* **ban·dana** \\ban-ˈdan-ə\\ *n* **:** a large colored handkerchief

band·box \\ˈban(d)-ˌbäks\\ *n* **:** a usu. cylindrical box of pasteboard or thin wood (as for a hat)

ban·di·coot \\ˈban-di-ˌküt\\ *n* **:** any of various small insect-eating and plant-eating marsupial mammals esp. of Australia

ban·dit \\ˈban-dət\\ *n, pl* **bandits** *also* **ban·dit·ti** \\ban-ˈdit-ē\\ [from Italian *bandito*, meaning literally "one who is under a ban", from the past participle of *bandire* "to ban", "banish"] **:** OUTLAW, ROBBER — **ban·dit·ry** \\ˈban-də-trē\\ *n*

ə abut · ər further · a back · ā bake · ä cot, cart · aù out · ch chin · e less · ē easy · g gift · i trip · ī life · j joke · ng sing · ō flow · ȯ flaw · ȯi coin · th thin · th this · ü loot · u̇ foot · y yet · yü few · yu̇ furious · zh vision

band·mas·ter \\ˈban(d)-ˌmas-tər\\ *n* **:** a conductor of a musical band

ban·do·lier *or* **ban·do·leer** \\ˌban-də-ˈli(ə)r\\ *n* **:** a belt worn over the shoulder to carry something (as cartridges) or as part of a ceremonial dress

band saw *n* **:** a saw in the form of an endless steel belt running over pulleys

band·stand \\ˈban(d)-ˌstand\\ *n* **:** a usu. roofed outdoor platform on which a band or orchestra performs

1ban·dy \\ˈban-dē\\ *vb* **ban·died; ban·dy·ing 1 :** to toss or bat back and forth **2 :** EXCHANGE; *esp* **:** to exchange in argument ⟨*bandy* words⟩ **3 :** to discuss lightly or as a subject of gossip

2bandy *adj* **:** curved esp. outward **:** BOWED ⟨*bandy* legs⟩

ban·dy–legged \\ˌban-dē-ˈleg(-ə)d\\ *adj* **:** having bandy legs

bane \\ˈbān\\ *n* **1 :** something that destroys life; *esp* **:** deadly poison **2 :** a source of injury, harm, ruin, or woe — **bane·ful** \\ˈbān-fəl\\ *adj* — **bane·ful·ly** \\-fə-lē\\ *adv*

1bang \\ˈbang\\ *vb* **:** to beat, strike, shut, or explode with a loud noise

2bang *n* **1 :** a violent blow **2 :** a sudden loud noise **3 a :** a sudden striking effect **b :** a quick burst of energy ⟨start off with a *bang*⟩ **c :** THRILL

3bang *n* **:** hair cut short across the forehead

4bang *vb* **:** to cut (as front hair) short and squarely across

ban·gle \\ˈbang-gəl\\ *n* **1 :** a stiff bracelet or anklet **2 :** a small ornament hanging from a bracelet or necklace

bang–up \\ˈbang-ˌəp\\ *adj* **:** FIRST-RATE, EXCELLENT ⟨had a *bang-up* time⟩ ⟨a *bang-up* job⟩

ban·ian \\ˈban-yən\\ *var of* BANYAN

ban·ish \\ˈban-ish\\ *vb* **1 :** to compel to leave a country ⟨the king *banished* the traitors⟩ **2 :** to drive out from or as if from a home **:** EXPEL — **ban·ish·ment** \\-mənt\\ *n*

ban·is·ter \\ˈban-ə-stər\\ *n* **1 :** one of the slender posts used to support the handrail of a staircase **2 :** a stair rail and its supporting posts — usu. used in pl. **3 :** the handrail of a staircase

ban·jo \\ˈban-jō\\ *n, pl* **banjos** *also* **banjoes :** a musical instrument of the guitar class with a long neck and small round body — **ban·jo·ist** \\-ˌjō-əst\\ *n*

banjo

1bank \\ˈbangk\\ *n* **1 :** a mound or ridge of earth **2 :** a mass of cloud or fog **3 :** a rise in the sea bottom **:** SHOAL **4 :** the rising ground bordering a lake, river, or sea or forming the edge of a hollow **5 :** a steep slope (as of a hill) **6 :** the inward tilt of a surface along a curve or of a vehicle (as an airplane) when taking a curve ***syn*** see SHORE

2bank *vb* **1 :** to raise a bank about ⟨*bank* a cabin with dirt⟩ **2 :** to heap or pile in a bank **3 :** to rise in or form a bank **4 :** to cover with fresh fuel to reduce the speed of burning ⟨*bank* a fire⟩ **5 :** to build with the roadbed inclined upward from the inside edge ⟨*bank* a curve⟩ **6 :** to incline an airplane laterally when turning

3bank *n* **:** a group or series of objects arranged in a row or tier

4bank *n* [from Italian *banca*, literally "bench"; so called from the benches set up in the marketplace from which bankers formerly transacted their business] **1 :** a place of business that receives, lends, issues, exchanges, and takes care of money **2** : a small container in which coins or bills are saved **3** : a storage place for a reserve supply ⟨eye *bank*⟩

5**bank** *vb* **1** : to own or manage a bank **2** : to have an account in a bank **3** : to deposit in a bank ⟨*banks* $10 every week⟩ — **bank on** *or* **bank upon** : to depend upon

bank·book \'bangk-ˌbu̇k\ *n* : the depositor's book in which a bank enters his deposits and withdrawals

bank·er \'bang-kər\ *n* : one that engages in the business of banking

bank note *n* : a promissory note issued by a bank payable to bearer on demand without interest and acceptable as money

bank·roll \'bangk-ˌrōl\ *n* : supply of money : FUNDS

1**bank·rupt** \'bang-(ˌ)krəpt\ *n* : a person who becomes bankrupt; *esp* : one whose property by court order is turned over to be administered for the benefit of his creditors

2**bankrupt** *vb* : to reduce to bankruptcy

3**bankrupt** *adj* : unable to pay one's debts

bank·rupt·cy \'bang-(ˌ)krəp-(t)sē\ *n, pl* **-cies** : the condition of being bankrupt

1**ban·ner** \'ban-ər\ *n* **1** : 4FLAG **2** : a strip of cloth with a design, picture, or writing on it

2**banner** *adj* : OUTSTANDING, SUPERIOR ⟨a *banner* year for apples⟩

banns \'banz\ *n pl* : public announcement esp. in church of a proposed marriage

1**ban·quet** \'bang-kwət, 'ban-, -ˌkwet\ *n* : an elaborate meal for numerous people

2**banquet** *vb* : to treat or be treated with a banquet : FEAST — **ban·quet·er** *n*

ban·shee \'ban-(ˌ)shē\ *n* [from Scottish Gaelic *bean-sìth*, literally "woman of fairyland"] : a female spirit in Gaelic folklore whose wailing warns of approaching death

ban·tam \'bant-əm\ *n* **1** : any of numerous small domestic fowls that are often miniatures of members of the standard breeds **2** : a small often quarrelsome person — **bantam** *adj*

ban·tam·weight \-ˌwāt\ *n* : a boxer weighing more than 112 but not over 118 pounds

1**ban·ter** \'bant-ər\ *vb* **1** : to tease lightly **2** : to talk humorously — **ban·ter·er** \-ər-ər\ *n* — **ban·ter·ing·ly** \'bant-ə-ring-lē\ *adv*

2**banter** *n* : good-natured teasing or joking

ban·yan \'ban-yən\ *n* : a large East Indian tree from whose branches aerial roots grow downward into the ground and form new supporting trunks

bao·bab \'bau̇-ˌbab, 'bā-ə-ˌbab\ *n* : an Old World tropical tree with a broad trunk and an edible gourdlike acid fruit

bap·tism \'bap-ˌtiz-əm\ *n* **1** : a Christian sacrament signifying spiritual rebirth and admission to the Christian community through the use of water by immersion, pouring, or sprinkling **2** : an act or experience that purifies or initiates ⟨a soldier's *baptism* of fire⟩ — **bap·tis·mal** \bap-'tiz-məl\ *adj* — **bap·tis·mal·ly** \-mə-lē\ *adv*

bap·tis·tery *or* **bap·tis·try** \'bap-tə-strē\ *n, pl* **-ter·ies** *or* **-tries** : a place used for baptism

bap·tize \bap-'tīz, 'bap-ˌ\ *vb* **1** : to administer baptism to **2 a** : to purify spiritually by a cleansing experience or ordeal **b** : INITIATE **3** : to give a name to : CHRISTEN — **bap·tiz·er** *n*

1**bar** \'bär\ *n* **1 a** : a rigid piece (as of metal) longer than it is wide and used variously (as for a lever, barrier, or fastening) **b** : a bar-shaped piece or block of material ⟨a *bar* of soap⟩ **2** : something that obstructs or blocks : IMPEDIMENT **3** : a submerged or partly submerged bank along a shore or in a river **4 a** : the railing in a courtroom around the place where judicial business is transacted **b** : a court or system of courts **c** : an authority that renders judgment ⟨the *bar* of public opinion⟩ **d** : a body of lawyers ⟨the New York *bar*⟩ **e** : the profession of lawyer **5** : STRIPE **6 a** : a counter for serving food or esp. alcoholic beverages **b** : BARROOM **7 a** : a vertical line across the musical staff before the initial measure accent **b** : MEASURE

bar 7a

2**bar** *vb* **barred**; **bar·ring** **1** : to fasten with a bar **2** : to mark with bars : STRIPE **3** : to block off : OBSTRUCT ⟨*bar* the road with a chain⟩ **4 a** : to keep out : EXCLUDE ⟨*bar* reporters from a meeting⟩ **b** : PREVENT, FORBID ⟨*bar* the use of poison gas⟩

3**bar** *prep* : with the exception of ⟨*bar* none⟩

4**bar** *n* : a unit of pressure

barb \'bärb\ *n* : a sharp projection extending backward (as from the point of an arrow or fishhook) — **barb** *vb*

bar·bar·i·an \bär-'ber-ē-ən, bär-'bar-\ *adj* **1** : of, relating to, or being a land, culture, or people foreign to and usu. believed to be inferior to one's own **2** : lacking refinement, learning, or culture — **barbarian** *n*

bar·bar·ic \bär-'bar-ik\ *adj* **1** : BARBARIAN 1 **2** : PRIMITIVE, UNCIVILIZED **3** : SAVAGE, CRUEL

bar·ba·rism \'bär-bə-ˌriz-əm\ *n* **1** : a word or expression not accepted as belonging to the standard language **2 a** : a barbarian state of social or intellectual development **b** : barbarian acts, attitudes, or ideas

bar·bar·i·ty \bär-'bar-ət-ē\ *n, pl* **-ties** **1** : BARBARISM **2 a** : CRUELTY **b** : a cruel act

bar·ba·rous \'bär-b(ə-)rəs\ *adj* **1** : characterized by the use of barbarisms in speech or writing **2 a** : UNCIVILIZED **b** : BARBARIAN 2 **3** : SAVAGE, CRUEL — **bar·ba·rous·ly** *adv* — **bar·ba·rous·ness** *n*

Bar·ba·ry ape \ˌbär-b(ə-)rē-\ *n* : a tailless monkey of No. Africa and Gibraltar

1**bar·be·cue** \'bär-bi-ˌkyü\ *n* [from American Spanish *barbacoa* denoting at first an elevated platform or framework such as was used for barbecuing, a word of Caribbean Indian origin] **1** : a large animal (as a hog or steer) roasted or broiled over an open fire **2** : a social gathering esp. in the open air at which barbecued food is eaten

2**barbecue** *vb* **1** : to roast or broil on a rack over hot coals or on a revolving spit **2** : to cook in a highly seasoned sauce

barbed wire \'bä(r)b(d)-'wī(ə)r\ *n* : twisted wires armed with barbs or sharp points — called also *barbwire*

bar·bell \'bär-ˌbel\ *n* : a bar with adjustable weighted disks attached to each end used for exercise and in weight lifting

bar·ber \'bär-bər\ *n* [from medieval French *barbeor*, from *barbe* "beard", from Latin *barba*] : one whose business is cutting hair and shaving and trimming beards — **barber** *vb* — **bar·ber·shop** \-ˌshäp\ *n*

bar·ber·ry \'bär-ˌber-ē\ *n* : any of a genus of spiny yellow-flowered shrubs often grown for hedges or ornament

bar·bit·u·rate \bär-'bich-ə-rət, ˌbär-bə-'t(y)u̇r-ət\ *n* : any of various derivatives of barbituric acid used esp. as sedatives or hypnotics

bar·bi·tu·ric acid \ˌbär-bə-ˌt(y)u̇r-ik-\ *n* : a crystalline organic acid used in making plastics and drugs

bar·ca·role *or* **bar·ca·rolle** \'bär-kə-ˌrōl\ *n* **1 :** a Venetian gondoliers' song **2 :** a piece of music imitating a barcarole

bar chart *n* **:** a graphic means of comparing numbers by rectangles whose lengths are proportional to the numbers represented — called also *bar graph*

bard \'bärd\ *n* **1 :** a person in a primitive society who composes and sings verses about heroes and their deeds **2 :** POET — **bard·ic** \'bärd-ik\ *adj*

1**bare** \'ba(ə)r, 'be(ə)r\ *adj* **1 :** lacking a covering **:** NAKED ⟨trees *bare* of leaves⟩ **2 :** open to view **:** EXPOSED ⟨his guilt was laid *bare*⟩ **3 :** unfurnished or only scantily supplied ⟨*bare* of all safeguards⟩ **4 a :** just enough with nothing to spare **:** MERE ⟨a *bare* majority⟩ **b :** not adorned **:** PLAIN ⟨the *bare* facts⟩ — **bare·ly** *adv* — **bare·ness** *n*

2**bare** *vb* **:** to make or lay bare **:** UNCOVER, REVEAL

bare·back \-ˌbak\ *or* **bare·backed** \-'bakt\ *adv or adj* **:** on the bare back of a horse **:** without a saddle

bare·faced \-'fāst\ *adj* **:** SHAMELESS, BOLD ⟨a *barefaced* lie⟩

bare·foot \-ˌfu̇t\ *or* **bare·foot·ed** \-'fu̇t-əd\ *adv or adj* **:** with the feet bare **:** without shoes

bare·hand·ed \-'han-dəd\ *adv or adj* **1 :** with the hands bare **:** without gloves or mittens **2 :** without tools or weapons

bare·head·ed \-'hed-əd\ *adv or adj* **:** with the head bare **:** without a hat

1**bar·gain** \'bär-gən\ *n* **1 :** an agreement between parties settling what each is to give or receive in a transaction **2 :** something bought or offered for sale at a desirable price ⟨at 35 percent off, the suit was a real *bargain*⟩ ***syn*** see AGREEMENT

2**bargain** *vb* **1 :** to talk over the terms of a purchase or agreement; *esp* **:** to try to win advantageous terms in a bargain **2 :** to sell or dispose of by bargaining **:** BARTER — **bar·gain·er** *n* — **bargain for :** EXPECT ⟨more trouble than he *bargained for*⟩

1**barge** \'bärj\ *n* **:** a broad flat-bottomed boat used chiefly in harbors and on rivers and canals

2**barge** *vb* **1 :** to carry by barge **2 :** to move or thrust oneself clumsily or rudely ⟨*barged* right in without being invited⟩

bar graph *n* **:** BAR CHART

bar·ite \'ba(ə)r-ˌīt, 'be(ə)r-\ *n* **:** a white, yellow, or colorless mineral consisting of barium sulfate and occurring in crystals or as a mass

bar·i·tone \'bar-ə-ˌtōn\ *n* **1 a :** a male singing voice between bass and tenor **b :** a man having such a voice **2 :** the horn intermediate between althorn and tuba

bar·i·um \'bar-ē-əm, 'ber-\ *n* **:** a silver-white malleable toxic metallic element that occurs only in combination — see ELEMENT table

barium chloride *n* **:** a water-soluble toxic chloride of barium that is used esp. as a reagent

barium sulfate *n* **:** a colorless crystalline insoluble sulfate of barium used esp. as a pigment and filler

1**bark** \'bärk\ *vb* **1 :** to make the short loud cry of a dog or a similar noise **2 :** to speak or utter in a curt loud tone ⟨*bark* out an order⟩

2**bark** *n* **:** the sound made by a barking dog or a similar sound

3**bark** *n* **:** the tough largely corky covering of a woody root or stem

ə abut　ər further　a back　ā bake
ä cot, cart　au̇ out　ch chin　e less　ē easy
g gift　i trip　ī life　j joke　ng sing　ō flow
ȯ flaw　ȯi coin　th thin　th this　ü loot
u̇ foot　y yet　yü few　yu̇ furious　zh vision

4**bark** *vb* **1 :** to strip the bark from **2 :** to rub or scrape the skin of ⟨*barked* his knee⟩

5**bark** *or* **barque** \'bärk\ *n* **1 :** a small sailing craft **2 :** a 3-masted ship with foremast and mainmast square-rigged and mizzenmast fore-and-aft rigged

bark beetle *n* **:** any of a group of beetles that bore under bark of trees both as larvae and adults

bark·er \'bär-kər\ *n* **:** a person who stands at the entrance to a show or a store and tries to attract customers to it ⟨a sideshow *barker*⟩

bar·ley \'bär-lē\ *n* **:** a cereal grass with flowers in dense spikes with three spikelets at each joint; *also* **:** its seed used esp. in malt beverages and as food or stock feed

bar·ley·corn \-ˌkȯrn\ *n* **1 :** a grain of barley **2 :** an old unit of length equal to the average length of a grain of barley **:** a third of an inch

bar line *n* **:** BAR 7

bar magnet *n* **:** a magnet in the shape of a bar

bar mitz·vah \bär-'mits-və\ *n, often cap B&M* **1 :** a Jewish boy who reaches his 13th birthday and attains the age of religious duty and responsibility **2 :** the ceremony recognizing a boy as a bar mitzvah

barn \'bärn\ *n* **:** a building used chiefly for storing grain and hay and for housing farm animals

bar·na·cle \'bär-ni-kəl\ *n* **:** any of numerous marine crustaceans that are free-swimming as larvae but fixed (as to rocks or pilings) as adults — **bar·na·cled** \-kəld\ *adj*

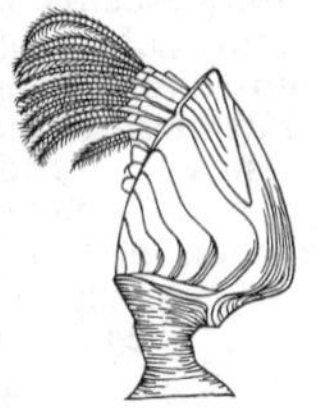

barnacle (about 6 in. long)

barn·storm \'bärn-ˌstȯrm\ *vb* **1 :** to tour through rural districts acting in plays **2 :** to travel from place to place making brief stops (as in a political campaign) **3 :** to pilot an airplane in sight-seeing flights or in exhibition stunts in an unscheduled course esp. in rural districts — **barn·storm·er** *n*

barn·yard \-ˌyärd\ *n* **:** the area around a barn

baro·graph \'bar-ə-ˌgraf\ *n* **:** a self-registering barometer

ba·rom·e·ter \bə-'räm-ət-ər\ *n* **1 :** an instrument that measures the pressure of the atmosphere to determine probable weather changes **2 :** something that registers changes (as in public opinion) — **bar·o·met·ric** \ˌbar-ə-'me-trik\ *adj*

barometric pressure *n* **:** the pressure of the atmosphere usu. expressed in terms of the height of a column of mercury

bar·on \'bar-ən\ *n* **1 a :** a tenant holding his rights and title directly from a feudal superior (as a king) **b :** NOBLEMAN, PEER **2 :** a member of the lowest grade of the British peerage **3 :** a man of great power or influence in some field ⟨cattle *baron*⟩ — **bar·on·ess** \-ə-nəs\ *n*

bar·on·age \-ə-nij\ *n* **:** the whole body of barons **:** NOBILITY

bar·on·et \-ə-nət\ *n* **:** a man holding a rank of honor below a baron but above a knight

ba·ro·ni·al \bə-'rō-nē-əl\ *adj* **:** of, relating to, or suitable for a baron ⟨*baronial* splendor⟩

bar·ony \'bar-ə-nē\ *n, pl* **bar·on·ies :** the domain, rank, or title of a baron

ba·roque \bə-'rōk, ba-, -'räk\ *adj* **:** of or relating to a style of artistic expression common in the 17th century: as **a :** using elaborate, exaggerated, and sometimes grotesquely ornamented figures in art and architecture **b :** marked by improvisation, tension, and the use of contrasting effects in music — **baroque** *n*

bar·racks \'bar-əks, -iks\ *n sing or pl* : a building or group of buildings in which soldiers are quartered

bar·ra·cu·da \ˌbar-ə-'küd-ə\ *n, pl* **-da** *or* **-das** : any of several large fierce marine fishes of warm seas with strong jaws, sharp teeth, and a cigar-shaped body

bar·rage \bə-'räzh, -'räj\ *n* **1** : a barrier formed by continuous artillery or machine-gun fire directed upon a narrow strip of ground **2** : a rapid or concentrated outpouring (as of speech or writing)

barred \'bärd\ *adj* : having alternate bands of different color

1**bar·rel** \'bar-əl\ *n* **1** : a round bulging container that is longer than it is wide and has flat ends **2 a** : the amount held by a barrel **b** : a great quantity **3** : a cylindrical or tubular part ⟨gun *barrel*⟩ ⟨the *barrel* of a pump⟩ — **bar·reled** \-əld\ *adj*

2**barrel** *vb* **-reled** *or* **-relled**; **-rel·ing** *or* **-rel·ling** **1** : to put or pack in a barrel **2** : to travel at a high speed

barrel organ *n* : a musical instrument consisting of a revolving cylinder studded with pegs that open a series of valves to admit air from a bellows to a set of pipes

1**bar·ren** \'bar-ən\ *adj* **1 a** : incapable of producing offspring ⟨a *barren* woman⟩ **b** : habitually failing to fruit **2 a** : producing inferior or scanty vegetation ⟨*barren* soils⟩ **b** : unproductive of results or gain : FRUITLESS ⟨a *barren* scheme⟩ **3** : lacking interest, information, or charm — **bar·ren·ly** *adv* — **bar·ren·ness** \-ən-nəs\ *n*

2**barren** *n* : a tract of barren land

bar·rette \bä-'ret, bə-\ *n* : a clip or bar for holding a woman's hair in place

bar·ri·cade \'bar-ə-ˌkād, ˌbar-ə-'\ *n* : a hastily made barrier for protection against attack or for blocking the way — **barricade** *vb*

bar·ri·er \'bar-ē-ər\ *n* **1** : something (as a fence, railing, or natural obstacle) that blocks the way ⟨a mountain *barrier*⟩ **2** : something immaterial that separates ⟨language *barriers* between peoples⟩ **3** : a factor that keeps organisms from interbreeding or spreading into new territory

barrier reef *n* : a coral reef roughly parallel to a shore and separated from it by a lagoon

bar·ring \'bär-ing\ *prep* **1** : with the exception of ⟨*barring* none⟩ **2** : apart from the possibility of ⟨will be there on time, *barring* accidents⟩

bar·room \'bär-ˌrüm, -ˌrum\ *n* : a room or establishment whose main feature is a bar for the sale of alcoholic beverages

1**bar·row** \'bar-ō\ *n* : a large burial mound of earth or stones

2**barrow** *n* **1** : a framework that has handles and sometimes a wheel and is used for carrying things **2** : a cart with a shallow box body, two wheels, and shafts for pushing it

bar·tend·er \'bär-ˌten-dər\ *n* : one that serves alcoholic beverages at a bar

1**bar·ter** \'bärt-ər\ *vb* : to trade one thing for another without the use of money ⟨*bartered* tobacco for furs⟩ — **bar·ter·er** \'bärt-ər-ər\ *n*

2**barter** *n* **1** : the exchange of goods without the use of money **2** : something given in barter

bar·yte \'ba(ə)r-ˌīt, 'be(ə)r-\ *or* **ba·ry·tes** \bə-'rīt-ēz\ *var of* BARITE

bar·y·tone \'bar-ə-ˌtōn\ *var of* BARITONE

bas·al \'bā-səl\ *adj* : relating to, situated at, or forming a base — **bas·al·ly** \-sə-lē\ *adv*

basal metabolic rate *n* : the rate at which heat is given off by an organism at complete rest

basal metabolism *n* : the energy turnover in a fasting and resting organism in which just enough energy is being used for cell activity, respiration, and circulation to maintain life

ba·salt \bə-'sölt, 'bā-ˌ\ *n* : a dark usu. fine-grained igneous rock — **ba·sal·tic** \bə-'söl-tik\ *adj*

1**base** \'bās\ *n, pl* **bas·es** \'bā-səz\ **1 a** : a supporting bottom : FOUNDATION ⟨the *base* of a lamp⟩ **b** : a part of a plant or animal organ by which it is attached to a more central structure ⟨leaf *base*⟩ **c** : one of the lines or surfaces of a geometric figure from which an altitude is or is thought to be constructed ⟨*base* of a triangle⟩ ⟨*bases* of a trapezoid⟩ **2** : a main ingredient **3** : a fundamental part : BASIS **4 a** : the point or line from which a start is made (as in a game or attack) **b** : a military installation ⟨naval *base*⟩ ⟨air *base*⟩ **c** : the number with reference to which a system of numbers is constructed; *esp* : the number of units in a given digit's place of a number system that is required to give one in the next higher place ⟨the decimal system uses a *base* of 10⟩ **d** : ROOT 5 **5 a** : the goal in various games **b** : any of the four stations a runner in baseball must touch in order to score **6** : a compound that reacts with an acid to form a salt, has a salty taste, and turns red litmus paper blue **7** : a sum of money in business which is multiplied by a rate (as of interest)

2**base** *vb* **1** : to make, form, or serve as a base for **2** : to use as a base or basis for : ESTABLISH

3**base** *adj* **1** *archaic* : BASEBORN **2 a** : of inferior quality; *esp* : alloyed with or made of inferior metal **b** : of comparatively little value; *esp* : of comparatively low value and relatively inferior in certain properties ⟨*base* metals⟩ **3** : morally low : CONTEMPTIBLE ⟨*base* conduct⟩ — **base·ly** *adv* — **base·ness** *n*

base·ball \'bās-ˌbol\ *n* : a game played with a bat and ball between two teams of nine players each on a field with four bases that mark the course a runner must take to score; *also* : the ball used in this game

base·board \-ˌbōrd, -ˌbord\ *n* : a line of boards or molding covering the joint of a wall and the adjoining floor

base·born \-'born\ *adj* **1** : of humble birth : LOWLY **2** : of illegitimate birth : BASTARD

based *adj* : having a base or having as a base ⟨a soundly *based* argument⟩ ⟨a 10-*based* number system⟩

base exchange *n* : a store at an air force base that sells to military personnel and authorized civilians

base hit *n* : a hit in baseball that enables the batter to reach base safely with no error made and no base runner forced out

base·less \'bās-ləs\ *adj* : having no basis or reason : GROUNDLESS ⟨a *baseless* accusation⟩

base line *n* **1** : a line used as a base **2** : the area within which a baseball player must keep when running between bases

base·man \'bās-mən\ *n* : a baseball player stationed at a base

base·ment \'bās-mənt\ *n* : the part of a building that is wholly or partly below ground level

ba·sen·ji \bə-'sen-jē\ *n* : any of an African breed of small compact curly-tailed chestnut-brown dogs that rarely bark

base path *n* : the marked area between the bases of a baseball field used by a base runner

base runner *n* : a baseball player of the team at bat who is on base or is attempting to reach a base

base word *n* : a word to which a prefix or a suffix can be added to form a new word

bash \'bash\ *vb* **1** : to strike violently : BEAT **2** : to smash by a blow **3** : CRASH

bash·ful \'bash-fəl\ *adj* : timid in the presence of others *syn* see SHY *ant* forward, brazen — **bash·ful·ly** \-fə-lē\ *adv* — **bash·ful·ness** *n*

[1]**ba·sic** \'bā-sik\ *adj* **1** : of, relating to, or forming the base or basis : FUNDAMENTAL ⟨*basic* research⟩ ⟨the *basic* facts⟩ **2** : of, relating to, containing, or having the character of a base ⟨*basic* salts⟩ — **ba·si·cal·ly** \-si-k(ə-)lē\ *adv*

[2]**basic** *n* : something basic : FUNDAMENTAL

ba·sic·i·ty \bā-'sis-ət-ē\ *n, pl* **-ties** : the quality or degree of being a base

basic sentence *n* : a sentence (as "she is a doctor" or "he borrowed the book") which is one of a set of simple sentence types from which all the sentences of a language can be derived by transformations

bas·il \'baz-əl, 'bās-, 'bas-, 'bāz-\ *n* : either of two mints with aromatic leaves used in cookery

ba·sil·i·ca \bə-'sil-i-kə, -'zil-\ *n* **1** : an oblong public building of ancient Rome ending in an apse **2** : an early Christian church building consisting of nave and aisles with clerestory and apse — **ba·sil·i·can** \-kən\ *adj*

bas·i·lisk \'bas-ə-,lisk, 'baz-\ *n* **1** : a legendary reptile with fatal breath and glance **2** : a crested tropical American lizard related to the iguanas

ba·sin \'bā-sən\ *n* **1 a** : a wide shallow bowl for holding liquid (as water) **b** : the amount that a basin holds **2** : a depression or enclosure containing water; *esp* : a partly enclosed water area for anchoring ships **3** : the land drained by a river and its branches

ba·sis \'bā-səs\ *n, pl* **ba·ses** \'bā-,sēz\ : the base, foundation, or chief supporting part

bask \'bask\ *vb* : to lie in or expose oneself to a pleasant warmth or atmosphere ⟨*bask* in the sun⟩

bas·ket \'bas-kət\ *n* **1 a** : a woven container (as of straw, cane, or strips of wood) **b** : the contents of a basket **2** : something that resembles a basket in shape or use **3 a** : a net open at the bottom and suspended from a metal ring that constitutes the goal in basketball **b** : a score made in basketball by tossing the ball through the basket while the ball is in play — **bas·ket·work** \-,wərk\ *n*

bas·ket·ball \-,bȯl\ *n* : a court game in which each of two teams tries to toss an inflated ball through a raised goal; *also* : the ball used in this game

bas·ket·ry \'bas-kə-trē\ *n* **1** : the art or craft of making baskets or objects woven like baskets **2** : objects produced by basketry

basking shark *n* **1** : a large shark that attains a length of 40 feet, feeds on plankton, and has a large liver that yields much oil **2** : WHALE SHARK

bas mitz·vah \bäs-'mits-və\ *n, often cap B&M* **1** : a Jewish girl who at about 13 years of age assumes religious responsibilities **2** : the ceremony recognizing a girl as a bas mitzvah

bas-relief

bas–re·lief \,bä-ri-'lēf\ *n* : a sculpture in relief in which the design is raised very slightly from the background

[1]**bass** \'bas\ *n, pl* **bass** *or* **bass·es 1** : any of several spiny-finned freshwater sport and food fishes of eastern No. America **2** : any of several saltwater fishes resembling the perch

[2]**bass** \'bās\ *n* **1** : a deep or low-pitched tone **2 a** : the lowest part in a musical composition **b** : the lowest male singing voice or a person having such a voice **c** : the lowest member of a family of instruments — **bass** *adj*

bass drum *n* : a large 2-headed drum producing a low booming sound

bas·set \'bas-ət\ *n* : any of an old French breed of short-legged slow-moving hunting dogs with very long ears and crooked front legs

bass horn *n* : TUBA

bas·si·net \,bas-ə-'net\ *n* : an infant's bed often with a hood over one end

bas·soon \ba-'sün, bə-\ *n* : a tenor or bass double reed woodwind instrument having a long doubled wooden body and a long curved mouthpiece — **bas·soon·ist** \-'sü-nəst\ *n*

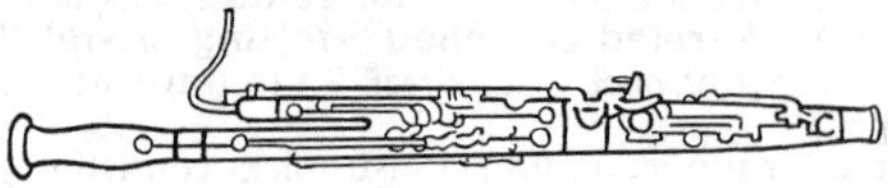
bassoon

bass viol *n* : DOUBLE BASS

bass·wood \'bas-,wu̇d\ *n* **1** : LINDEN **2** : TULIP TREE

bast \'bast\ *n* : a strong woody fiber obtained chiefly from the phloem of plants and used esp. in cordage and matting

bas·tard \'bas-tərd\ *n* : an illegitimate child — **bastard** *adj*

[1]**baste** \'bāst\ *vb* : to sew with long loose temporary stitches — **bast·er** *n*

[2]**baste** *vb* : to moisten (as roasting meat) with melted butter or fat — **bast·er** *n*

Bas·tille Day \ba-'stēl-\ *n* : July 14 observed in France as a national holiday in commemoration of the fall of the Bastille in 1789

bast·ing \'bā-sting\ *n* : the thread used in loose stitching or the stitching made by this thread

bas·tion \'bas-chən\ *n* : a projecting part of a fortification

[1]**bat** \'bat\ *n* **1** : a stout solid stick : CLUB ⟨a baseball *bat*⟩ **2** : a sharp blow **3** : a turn at batting

[2]**bat** *vb* **bat·ted; bat·ting 1** : to strike or hit with or as if with a bat **2** : to take one's turn at bat in baseball **3** : to have a batting average of ⟨is *batting* .300⟩

[3]**bat** *n* : any of an order of night-flying mammals with the forelimbs modified to form wings

[4]**bat** *vb* **bat·ted; bat·ting** : to wink esp. in surprise or emotion ⟨never *batted* an eye⟩

batch \'bach\ *n* **1** : a quantity used or made at one time ⟨a *batch* of cookies⟩ **2** : a group of persons or things : LOT ⟨a *batch* of letters⟩

bate \'bāt\ *vb* **1** : to reduce the force or intensity of ⟨listen with *bated* breath⟩ **2** : to take away : DEDUCT ⟨refuses to *bate* a jot of his claim⟩

bat (about 3½ in. long)

bath \'bath, 'bȧth\ *n, pl* **baths** \'bathz, 'baths, 'bȧthz, 'bȧths\ **1** : a washing or soaking (as in water or steam) of the body **2 a** : water used for bathing **b** : a liquid in which objects are placed so that it can act upon them; *also* : the container holding such a liquid **3 a** : BATHROOM **b** : a building containing rooms for bathing **c** : SPA — usu. used in pl.

ə abut	ər further	a back	ā bake
ä cot, cart	au̇ out	ch chin	e less
ē easy	g gift	i trip	ī life
j joke	ng sing	ō flow	ȯ flaw
ȯi coin	th thin	th this	ü loot
u̇ foot	y yet	yü few	yu̇ furious
zh vision			

bathe \'bāth\ *vb* **1 :** to take a bath **2 :** to go swimming **3 :** to wash in a liquid **4 :** to apply a liquid to ⟨*bathe* the eyes⟩ **5 :** to wash against : LAP ⟨waves *bathed* the shore⟩ **6 :** to surround or cover as a liquid does ⟨trees *bathed* in moonlight⟩ — **bath·er** \'bā-thər\ *n* — **bath·ing** \-thing\ *n*

bath·house \'bath-,haůs, 'báth-\ *n* **1 :** BATH 3b **2 :** a building containing dressing rooms for swimmers

bathing suit *n* **:** a garment worn esp. for swimming

batho·lith \'bath-ə-,lith\ *n* **:** a great mass of igneous rock that forced its way into or between other rocks and that stopped in its rise a considerable distance below the surface

bath·robe \'bath-,rōb, 'báth-\ *n* **:** a loose robe worn before or after bathing or as a dressing gown

bath·room \-,rüm, -,rům\ *n* **:** a room containing a bathtub or shower and usu. a washbowl and toilet

bath·tub \-,təb\ *n* **:** a usu. fixed tub for bathing

bathy·scaphe \'bath-i-,skaf, -,skāf\ *n* **:** a navigable submersible ship for deep-sea exploration having a spherical watertight cabin attached to its underside

bathy·sphere \'bath-i-,sfi(ə)r\ *n* **:** a strongly built steel diving sphere for deep-sea observation

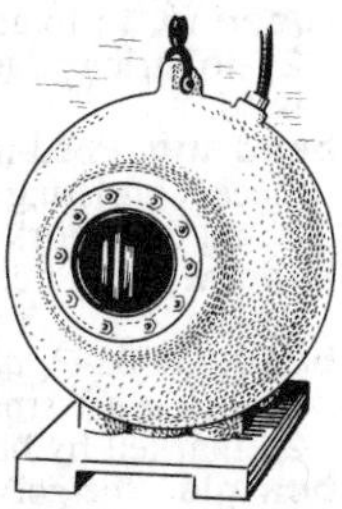

bathysphere

bathy·ther·mo·graph \,bath-i-'thər-mə-,graf\ *n* **:** an instrument that records the temperature of sea or fresh water in relation to depths

ba·tik \bə-'tēk, 'bat-ik\ *n* **1 a :** an Indonesian method of hand-printing textiles by coating with wax the parts not to be dyed **b :** a design so executed **2 :** a fabric printed by batik

ba·tiste \bə-'tēst, ba-\ *n* **:** a fine soft sheer fabric of plain weave

ba·ton \ba-'tän, bə-\ *n* **1 :** a staff borne as a symbol of office **2 :** a stick with which a leader directs a band or orchestra **3 :** a hollow cylinder passed from one member of a relay team to another **4 :** a staff with a ball at one end carried by a drum major or baton twirler

bat·tal·ion \bə-'tal-yən\ *n* **1 :** a large body of troops : ARMY **2 :** a military unit composed of two or more smaller units (as companies or batteries) **3 :** a large body of persons organized to act together

1**bat·ten** \'bat-ən\ *n* **1 :** a thin narrow strip of lumber **2 :** a strip, bar, or support like or used like a batten

2**batten** *vb* **:** to furnish or fasten with battens

1**bat·ter** \'bat-ər\ *vb* **1 :** to beat with heavy or shattering blows ⟨*batter* down the door⟩ **2 :** to wear or damage by blows or hard usage ⟨an old hat *battered* by long use⟩

2**batter** *n* **:** a thin mixture chiefly of flour and liquid ⟨pancake *batter*⟩

3**batter** *n* **:** one that bats; *esp* **:** the baseball player at bat

battering ram *n* **1 :** an ancient military siege engine consisting of a large iron-tipped wooden beam used to beat down the walls of a besieged place **2 :** a heavy metal bar with handles used to batter down doors and walls

battering ram

bat·tery \'bat-ə-rē, 'ba-trē\ *n, pl* **-ter·ies 1 a :** the act of beating **b :** the unlawful beating or use of force upon a person **2 a :** an artillery unit **b :** the guns of a warship **3 :** an electric cell or connected electric cells for furnishing electric current ⟨a flashlight *battery*⟩ **4 :** a number of machines or devices forming a unit ⟨a *battery* of lights or of cameras⟩ **5 :** the pitcher and catcher of a baseball team

battery jar *n* **:** a round, square, or rectangular glass container that has straight sides and is open at the top

bat·ting \'bat-ing\ *n* **1 a :** the act of one who bats **b :** use of or ability with a bat **2 :** layers of raw cotton or wool used for lining, stuffing, or packaging

batting average *n* **:** the average (as of a baseball batter) found by dividing the number of official times at bat into the number of base hits

1**bat·tle** \'bat-əl\ *n* **1 :** a general encounter between armies, warships, or airplanes **2 :** a combat between two persons ⟨trial by *battle*⟩ **3 :** an extended contest, struggle, or controversy ⟨a *battle* of wits⟩

2**battle** *vb* **bat·tled; bat·tling** \'bat-(ə-)ling\ **1 :** to engage in battle : FIGHT ⟨armies *battling* for a city⟩ **2 :** CONTEND, STRUGGLE ⟨*battle* for a cause⟩ **3 :** to fight against ⟨*battle* a storm⟩ ⟨*battling* a forest fire⟩

bat·tle–ax *or* **bat·tle–axe** \'bat-əl-,aks\ *n* **:** a broadax formerly used as a weapon of war

bat·tle·dore \'bat-əl-,dō(ə)r, -,dȯ(ə)r\ *n* **:** a badminton racket

bat·tle·field \-,fēld\ *n* **:** a place where a battle is fought

bat·tle·ground \-,graůnd\ *n* **:** BATTLEFIELD

bat·tle·ment \-mənt\ *n* **:** a low wall (as at the top of a tower) with open spaces to shoot through

bat·tle·ship \-,ship\ *n* **:** a warship of the largest and most heavily armed and armored class

bat·ty \'bat-ē\ *adj* **bat·ti·er; -est** *slang* **:** mentally unstable : CRAZY

bau·ble \'bȯ-bəl, 'bäb-əl\ *n* **:** TRINKET, TRIFLE

baux·ite \'bȯk-,sīt, 'bäk-\ *n* **:** a clayey substance that is the principal ore of aluminum

Ba·var·i·an \bə-'ver-ē-ən, -'var-\ *adj* **:** of, relating to, or characteristic of Bavaria or its people — **Bavarian** *n*

bawdy \'bȯd-ē\ *adj* **bawd·i·er; -est :** OBSCENE, LEWD — **bawd·i·ly** \'bȯd-ə-lē\ *adv* — **bawd·i·ness** \'bȯd-ē-nəs\ *n*

1**bawl** \'bȯl\ *vb* **1 :** to cry out loudly : YELL **2 :** to weep noisily — **bawl·er** *n*

2**bawl** *n* **:** a loud cry

bawl out *vb* **:** to scold severely

1**bay** \'bā\ *adj* **:** of the color bay

2**bay** *n* **1 :** a horse with a bay-colored body and black mane, tail, and points **2 :** a reddish brown

3**bay** *n* **1 a :** LAUREL 1 **b :** any of several shrubs or trees resembling the laurel **2 :** a laurel wreath given as a prize

4**bay** *n* **1 :** a section or compartment of a building or vehicle **2 :** BAY WINDOW

5**bay** *vb* **1 :** to bark with long deep tones **2 :** to bark at ⟨wolves *baying* the moon⟩

6**bay** *n* **1 :** the position of one unable to retreat and forced to face danger ⟨brought to *bay* in the blind alley⟩ **2 :** the position of one checked ⟨kept the hounds at *bay*⟩ **3 :** the baying of a dog : a deep bark

7**bay** *n* **:** an inlet of a body of water (as the sea) that is usu. smaller than a gulf

bay·ber·ry \'bā-ˌber-ē\ *n* **1 :** a West Indian tree that is related to the myrtle and yields a yellow aromatic oil **2 :** WAX MYRTLE; *also* **:** its fruit used esp. in making candles

[1]**bay·o·net** \'bā-ə-nət, ˌbā-ə-'net\ *n* **:** a steel blade made to be attached at the muzzle end of a rifle

[2]**bayonet** *vb* **-net·ed** *also* **-net·ted**; **-net·ing** *also* **-net·ting :** to stab with a bayonet

bay·ou \'bī-ō, 'bī-ü\ *n* **:** a marshy or sluggish body of water (as a branch of a river)

bay rum *n* **:** a fragrant cosmetic and medicinal liquid prepared from essential oils, alcohol, and water

bay window *n* **:** a window or set of windows in a compartment that projects outward from the wall of a building

ba·zaar \bə-'zär\ *n* **1 :** an Oriental market consisting of rows of shops or stalls **2 :** a place where many kinds of goods are sold **3 :** a fair for the sale of articles esp. for charitable purposes

ba·zoo·ka \bə-'zü-kə\ *n* **:** a light portable shoulder weapon that consists of an open tube and shoots an explosive rocket able to pierce armor

BB \'bē-ˌbē\ *n* **:** a small round shot pellet

BBC *abbr* British Broadcasting Corporation

bbl *abbr* barrel

B.C. *abbr* **1** before Christ **2** British Columbia

B complex *n* **:** VITAMIN B COMPLEX

bd *abbr* **1** board **2** bound

bdl *abbr* bundle

be \(')bē\ *vb, past 1st & 3d sing* **was** \(')wəz, 'wäz\; *2d sing* **were** \(')wər\; *pl* **were**; *past subjunctive* **were**; *past part* **been** \(')bin, *chiefly Brit* (')bēn\; *pres part* **be·ing** \'bē-ing\; *pres 1st sing* **am** \(ə)m, (')am\; *2d sing* **are** \ər, (')är\; *3d sing* **is** \(')iz, (ə)z\; *pl* **are**; *pres subjunctive* **be 1 a :** to have the same meaning as : serve as a sign for ⟨January *is* the first month⟩ ⟨let *x be* 10⟩ **b :** to have identity with ⟨the first person I met *was* my brother⟩ ⟨he *is* my father⟩ **c :** to have the quality or character of ⟨the leaves *are* green⟩ **d :** to belong to the class of ⟨the fish *is* a trout⟩ ⟨apes *are* mammals⟩ **2 a :** EXIST, LIVE ⟨I think, therefore I *am*⟩ **b :** to occupy a place, situation, or position ⟨the book *is* on the table⟩ ⟨*is* at ease⟩ **c :** OCCUR ⟨the concert *was* last night⟩ **3** — used with the past participle of transitive verbs to form the passive voice auxiliary ⟨the money *was* found⟩ ⟨the house is *being* built⟩ **4** — used as the auxiliary of the present participle to express continuous action ⟨he *is* reading⟩ ⟨I have *been* sleeping⟩ **5** — used with the infinitive with *to* to express futurity or obligation ⟨I *am* to go today⟩ ⟨he *was* to become famous⟩

be- *prefix* **1 :** on : around : over ⟨*be*smear⟩ **2 :** excessively ⟨*be*jewel⟩ ⟨*be*ribboned⟩ **3 :** about : to : upon ⟨*be*stride⟩ ⟨*be*speak⟩ **4 :** make : cause to be ⟨*be*little⟩ ⟨*be*fool⟩ **5 :** provide or cover with ⟨*be*whiskered⟩ ⟨*be*fog⟩

[1]**beach** \'bēch\ *n* **:** a shore of an ocean, sea, or lake or the bank of a river covered by sand or gravel ***syn*** see SHORE

[2]**beach** *vb* **:** to run or drive ashore ⟨*beach* a boat⟩

beach buggy *n* **:** a stripped-down soft-tired vehicle for travel on sand

beach bunny *n* **:** a girl who frequents beaches but does not swim

beach·comb·er \'bēch-ˌkō-mər\ *n* **:** one who searches along a shore for useful or salable flotsam and refuse

beach flea *n* **:** any of numerous small leaping crustaceans common on sea beaches

beach·head \'bēch-ˌhed\ *n* **:** an area on an enemy-held shore occupied by an advance attacking force to protect the later landing of troops or supplies

beach plum *n* **:** a shrubby plum with showy white flowers that grows along the Atlantic shores of the northern U.S. and Canada; *also* **:** its dark purple fruit often used in preserves

[1]**bea·con** \'bē-kən\ *n* **1 :** a signal fire commonly on a hill, tower, or pole **2 a :** a signal (as a lighthouse) for guidance **b :** a radio transmitter emitting signals for guidance of airplanes

[2]**beacon** *vb* **:** to shine or guide as a beacon

[1]**bead** \'bēd\ *n* [from Middle English *bede,* meaning first "prayer" and then denoting the bead of a rosary used in counting prayers] **1 :** a small piece of material pierced for threading on a string or wire **2 :** a small ball-shaped body ⟨*beads* of perspiration⟩ **3 :** a small metal knob on a firearm used as a front sight **4 :** a projecting rim or molding

[2]**bead** *vb* **1 :** to adorn or cover with beads or beading **2 :** to string together like beads **3 :** to form into a bead

bead·ing \'bēd-ing\ *n* **1 :** material or a part or a piece consisting of beads **2 :** a beaded molding **3 :** an openwork trimming **4 :** BEADWORK

bead·work \'bēd-ˌwərk\ *n* **:** ornamental work in beads

beady \'bēd-ē\ *adj* **bead·i·er**; **-est 1 :** resembling beads; *esp* **:** small, round, and shiny ⟨*beady* eyes⟩ **2 :** marked by beads

bea·gle \'bē-gəl\ *n* **:** a small short-legged smooth-coated hound

beak \'bēk\ *n* **1 a :** the bill of a bird; *esp* **:** the bill of a bird of prey adapted for striking and tearing **b :** any of various rigid projecting mouth structures (as of a turtle or octopus); *also* **:** the long sucking mouth of some insects **2 :** a pointed part or projection — **beaked** \'bēkt\ *adj*

bea·ker \'bē-kər\ *n* **:** a deep widemouthed cup or glass

[1]**beam** \'bēm\ *n* **1 :** a long heavy timber used esp. as a main horizontal support of a building or ship **2 :** the bar of a balance from which the scales hang **3 :** the width of a ship at its widest part **4 a :** a ray of light **b :** a collection of nearly parallel rays (as X rays) or a stream of particles (as electrons) **5 :** a constant directional radio signal sent out for the guidance of pilots along a particular course

[2]**beam** *vb* **1 :** to emit in beams or as a beam **2 :** to send out beams of light : SHINE **3 :** to smile with joy

bean \'bēn\ *n* **1 a :** BROAD BEAN **b :** the seed or pod that is characteristic of any of various erect or climbing plants related to the pea **c :** a plant bearing beans **2 :** a seed or fruit like a bean ⟨coffee *beans*⟩

[1]**bear** \'ba(ə)r, 'be(ə)r\ *n, pl* **bear** *or* **bears 1 :** any of a family of large heavy mammals having long shaggy hair and rudimentary tail, walking on the soles of its feet, and feeding largely on fruit and insects as well as on flesh **2 :** a gruff or sullen person **3 :** one that sells securities or commodities in expectation of a price decline — **bear·ish** \'ba(ə)r-ish, 'be(ə)r-\ *adj*

[2]**bear** *vb* **bore** \'bō(ə)r, 'bȯ(ə)r\; **borne** \'bōrn, 'bȯrn\ *also* **born** \'bȯrn\; **bear·ing 1 a :** CARRY ⟨arrived *bearing* gifts⟩ **b :** to have as a characteristic

B

⟨*bore* a resemblance to his uncle⟩ **c** : to hold in the mind : HARBOR ⟨*bear* a grudge⟩ **d** : to carry about and tell ⟨*bear* tales⟩ **e** : to relate as testimony ⟨*bears* false witness⟩ **f** : BEHAVE, CONDUCT ⟨*bore* himself like a gentleman⟩ ⟨*bears* up well in grief⟩ **2 a** : to give birth to ⟨has *borne* many children⟩ ⟨he was *born* last year⟩ **b** : PRODUCE, YIELD ⟨*bear* fruit⟩ **3 a** : to hold up : SUPPORT ⟨a colonnade *bore* the roof⟩ **b** : ENDURE ⟨can't *bear* walking all day⟩ **c** : ASSUME, ACCEPT ⟨*bore* the costs⟩ ⟨*bear* the blame⟩ **4** : THRUST, PRESS ⟨*borne* along by the crowd⟩ ⟨*bears* down on her pencil⟩ **5 a** : to move or lie in an indicated direction ⟨*bear* right at the next fork⟩ **b** : to become directed ⟨brought the gun to *bear* on the target⟩ **6 a** : APPLY, PERTAIN ⟨facts *bearing* on the question⟩ **b** : to exert influence or force ⟨bring pressure to *bear* to win votes⟩

bear·a·ble \'bar-ə-bəl, 'ber-\ *adj* : capable of being borne : TOLERABLE

bear·ber·ry \'ba(ə)r-ˌber-ē, 'be(ə)r-\ *n* : a trailing evergreen plant with glossy red berries that is related to the heath; *also* : any of several related plants (as a cranberry)

[1]**beard** \'bi(ə)rd\ *n* **1** : the hair that grows on a man's face often excluding the moustache **2** : a hairy or bristly growth or tuft (as on the chin of a goat or on a head of rye) — **beard·ed** \-əd\ *adj* — **beard·less** \-ləs\ *adj*

[2]**beard** *vb* : to confront and oppose daringly : DEFY

bear·er \'bar-ər, 'ber-\ *n* **1** : one that bears : PORTER **2** : a plant yielding fruit **3** : a person holding a check, draft, or order for payment

bear·ing \'ba(ə)r-ing, 'be(ə)r-\ *n* **1** : the manner in which one bears oneself : CARRIAGE, BEHAVIOR **2 a** : an object, surface, or point that supports something **b** : a machine part in which another turns **3 a** : the position or direction of one point with respect to another or to the compass **b** : a determination of position ⟨to take a *bearing*⟩ **c** *pl* : comprehension of one's location or situation ⟨lose one's *bearings*⟩ **4** : RELATION, CONNECTION ⟨the rain had no *bearing* on the decision to postpone the trip⟩

beast \'bēst\ *n* **1 a** : ANIMAL 1; *esp* : a lower mammal as distinguished from man and from lower vertebrate and invertebrate animals **b** : a domesticated mammal ⟨the care of a farmer for his *beasts*⟩; *esp* : a draft animal ⟨*beasts* of burden⟩ **2** : a vicious or brutal person

[1]**beast·ly** \'bēst-lē\ *adj* **beast·li·er**; **-est** **1** : of, relating to, or resembling a beast : BESTIAL **2** : ABOMINABLE, DISGUSTING — **beast·li·ness** *n*

[2]**beastly** *adv* : VERY ⟨a *beastly* cold day⟩

[1]**beat** \'bēt\ *vb* **beat**; **beat·en** \'bēt-ən\ *or* **beat**; **beat·ing** **1 a** : to strike repeatedly ⟨*beat* a child⟩ ⟨*beat* a drum⟩ ⟨rain *beating* on the roof⟩ **b** : to flap against ⟨wings *beating* the air⟩ **c** : to range over in or as if in quest of game **d** : to mix by stirring : WHIP **2 a** : to drive or force by blows ⟨*beat* off the intruder⟩ **b** : to make by treading ⟨*beat* a path⟩ **c** : to shape by blows ⟨*beat* swords into plowshares⟩ **d** : to express by drumbeat ⟨*beat* the alarm⟩ **3** : to cause to strike or flap repeatedly ⟨birds *beating* their wings⟩ **4 a** : OVERCOME, DEFEAT **b** : BEWILDER, BAFFLE ⟨it *beats* me where they are⟩ **5 a** : FORESTALL ⟨*beat* to the punch⟩ **b** : to report a news item in advance of **c** : to arrive before ⟨*beat* him home⟩ **6** : to indicate by beats ⟨*beat* the tempo⟩ **7** : to glare or strike harshly ⟨the sun *beat* down⟩ **8 a** : PULSATE, THROB **b** : TICK **c** : to sound upon being struck **9** : to progress with much tacking or with difficulty

[2]**beat** *n* **1 a** : a stroke or blow esp. in a series **b** : PULSATION, TICK **c** : a sound produced by or as if by beating ⟨the *beat* of waves against the rock⟩ **2** : each of the pulsations of amplitude produced by the union of sound or radio waves or electric currents having different frequencies **3 a** : a rhythmic stress in poetry or music or the effect of these stresses **b** : the tempo indicated to a musical performer **4** : a regular round ⟨a policeman's *beat*⟩ **5** : the reporting of a news story ahead of competitors

[3]**beat** *adj* **1** : EXHAUSTED **2** : sapped of resolution or morale **3** : of, relating to, or consisting of beatniks

beat·er \'bēt-ər\ *n* **1** : one that beats **2** : one that strikes bushes or other cover to rouse game

be·a·tif·ic \ˌbē-ə-'tif-ik\ *adj* : BLISSFUL

be·at·i·fy \bē-'at-ə-ˌfī\ *vb* **-fied**; **-fy·ing** : to declare to have attained the blessedness of heaven — **be·at·i·fi·ca·tion** \-ˌat-ə-fə-'kā-shən\ *n*

be·at·i·tude \bē-'at-ə-ˌt(y)üd\ *n* : any of the declarations made in the Sermon on the Mount (Matthew 5:3–12) beginning "Blessed are"

beat·nik \'bēt-nik\ *n* : a person who behaves and dresses unconventionally and is inclined to exotic philosophizing and extreme self-expression

beau \'bō\ *n, pl* **beaux** \'bōz\ *or* **beaus** \'bōz\ [from French, from the adjective *beau* "beautiful" (feminine *belle*), from Latin *bellus* "pretty"] **1** : a man who dresses carefully in the latest fashion : DANDY **2 a** : a man who is courting : LOVER **b** : ESCORT

Beau·fort scale \ˌbō-fərt-\ *n* : a scale in which the force of the wind is indicated by numbers from 0 to 17

beau·te·ous \'byüt-ē-əs\ *adj* : BEAUTIFUL — **beau·te·ous·ly** *adv* — **beau·te·ous·ness** *n*

beau·ti·cian \byü-'tish-ən\ *n* : COSMETOLOGIST

beau·ti·ful \'byüt-i-fəl\ *adj* : having beauty : LOVELY — **beau·ti·ful·ly** \-f(ə-)lē\ *adv* — **beau·ti·ful·ness** \-fəl-nəs\ *n*

beau·ti·fy \'byüt-ə-ˌfī\ *vb* **-fied**; **-fy·ing** : to make beautiful or more beautiful : ADORN — **beau·ti·fi·ca·tion** \ˌbyüt-ə-fə-'kā-shən\ *n*

beau·ty \'byüt-ē\ *n, pl* **beauties** **1** : the qualities of a person or a thing that give pleasure to the senses : LOVELINESS **2** : a lovely person or thing; *esp* : a lovely woman

beauty shop *n* : an establishment or department where hairdressing, facials, and manicures are done — called also *beauty parlor*

[1]**bea·ver** \'bē-vər\ *n, pl* **beaver** *or* **beavers** **1** : a large fur-bearing mammal that has webbed hind feet and a broad flat tail and builds dams and underwater houses of mud and branches **2 a** : the fur of a beaver **b** : a hat made of beaver or of a fabric imitating it

[2]**beaver** *n* : a piece of armor protecting the lower part of the face

be·calm \bi-'käm, -'kälm\ *vb* **1** : to bring to a stop by lack of wind **2** : to make calm : SOOTHE

be·cause \bi-'kȯz\ *conj* : for the reason that

because of *prep* : by reason of

beck \'bek\ *n* **1** : a beckoning gesture **2** : BIDDING, SUMMONS ⟨at his *beck* and call⟩

beck·et \'bek-ət\ *n* : a loop of rope with a knot at one end

beck·on \'bek-ən\ *vb* **beck·oned**; **beck·on·ing** \'bek-(ə-)ning\ **1** : to summon or signal to a person by a gesture (as a wave or nod) **2** : to appear inviting : ATTRACT

be·cloud \bi-'klau̇d\ *vb* : to obscure with or as if with a cloud

be·come \bi-'kəm\ *vb* **-came** \-'kām\; **-come**; **-com·ing** **1** : to move forward or reach the state of

⟨a tadpole *becomes* a frog⟩ ⟨the days *become* shorter as summer ends⟩ **2** : to look well on : SUIT ⟨her dress *becomes* her⟩ — **become of** : to happen to : be the state of ⟨whatever *became of* him⟩

be·com·ing \bi-'kəm-ing\ *adj* : SUITABLE; *esp* : attractively suitable ⟨a *becoming* dress⟩ — **be·com·ing·ly** \-ing-lē\ *adv*

1**bed** \'bed\ *n* **1 a** : a piece of furniture on which to lie or sleep **b** : a place or time for sleeping **2 a** : a plot of ground prepared for plants **b** : the bottom of a body of water **3** : a supporting surface or structure : FOUNDATION **4** : LAYER ⟨a *bed* of sandstone⟩

2**bed** *vb* **bed·ded**; **bed·ding** **1** : to put or go to bed **2** : to fix in or on a foundation ⟨*bedded* on rock⟩ **3** : to plant or arrange in beds

be·daub \bi-'dȯb, -'däb\ *vb* : to daub over : SMEAR

be·daz·zle \bi-'daz-əl\ *vb* : DAZZLE — **be·daz·zle·ment** \-mənt\ *n*

bed·bug \'bed-ˌbəg\ *n* : a wingless bloodsucking bug sometimes infesting houses and esp. beds

bed·clothes \'bed-ˌklō(th)z\ *n pl* : coverings (as sheets and blankets) for a bed

bed·ding \'bed-ing\ *n* **1** : BEDCLOTHES **2** : material for a bed

be·deck \bi-'dek\ *vb* : to deck out : ADORN

be·dew \bi-'d(y)ü\ *vb* : to wet with or as if with dew

bed·fast \'bed-ˌfast\ *adj* : BEDRIDDEN

bed·fel·low \'bed-ˌfel-ō\ *n* : one who shares a bed with another

be·dight \bi-'dīt\ *adj, archaic* : ADORNED

be·dim \bi-'dim\ *vb* : to make dim or obscure

be·di·zen \bi-'dī-zən, -'diz-ən\ *vb* : to dress or adorn esp. with gaudy finery

bed·lam \'bed-ləm\ *n* **[**from *Bedlam*, popular name for the Hospital of St. Mary of Bethlehem, a London insane asylum, from Middle English *Bedlem* "Bethlehem"**]** : a place or scene of uproar and confusion

Bed·ling·ton terrier \ˌbed-ling-tən-\ *n* : a swift rough-coated terrier of light build

bed·ou·in \'bed-ə-wən\ *n, pl* **bedouin** *or* **bedouins** *often cap* : a nomadic Arab of the Arabian, Syrian, or No. African deserts

bed·pan \'bed-ˌpan\ *n* : a shallow pan for use as a toilet by a person confined to bed

be·drag·gle \bi-'drag-əl\ *vb* : to wet and usu. soil thoroughly (as by rain or mud)

bed·rid·den \'bed-ˌrid-ən\ *adj* : confined to bed by illness or weakness

bed·rock \'bed-'räk, -ˌräk\ *n* **1** : the solid rock underlying surface materials (as soil) **2** : a solid foundation

bed·roll \'bed-ˌrōl\ *n* : bedding rolled up for carrying

bed·room \-ˌrüm, -ˌru̇m\ *n* : a room used for sleeping

bed·side \'bed-ˌsīd\ *n* : the place beside a bed esp. of a sick or dying person

bed·sore \-ˌsōr, -ˌsȯr\ *n* : a sore caused by constant pressure against a bed (as in a prolonged illness)

bed·spread \-ˌspred\ *n* : a decorative cover for a bed

bed·stead \-ˌsted\ *n* : the framework of a bed usu. including head, foot, and side rails

bed·straw \-ˌstrȯ\ *n* : an herb that is related to madder and has angled stems, leaves opposite or arranged in a circle around the stem, and small flowers

bed·time \'bed-ˌtīm\ *n* : time to go to bed

ə abut	ər further	a back	ā bake	
ä cot, cart	au̇ out	ch chin	e less	ē easy
g gift	i trip	ī life	j joke	ng sing	ō flow
ȯ flaw	ȯi coin	th thin	th this	ü loot
u̇ foot	y yet	yü few	yu̇ furious	zh vision

bee \'bē\ *n* **1** : a social colonial 4-winged insect often kept in hives for the honey that it produces; *also* : any of numerous related insects that differ from the wasps esp. in the heavier hairier body and in having sucking as well as chewing mouthparts **2** : a gathering of people for a specific purpose ⟨quilting *bee*⟩

bee balm *n* : any of several mints attractive to bees

bee·bread \'bē-ˌbred\ *n* : a bitter yellowish brown pollen mixture stored in honeycomb cells and used with honey by bees as food

beech \'bēch\ *n, pl* **beech·es** *or* **beech** : any of a genus of hardwood trees with smooth gray bark and small edible nuts; *also* : its wood — **beech·en** \'bē-chən\ *adj* — **beech·wood** \'bēch-ˌwu̇d\ *n*

beef \'bēf\ *n, pl* **beeves** \'bēvz\ *or* **beefs** **1** : the flesh of a steer, cow, or bull **2** : a steer, cow, or bull esp. when fattened for food

beef cattle *n pl* : cattle developed primarily for the efficient production of meat and marked by capacity for rapid growth, heavy well-fleshed body, and stocky build

beef·steak \'bēf-ˌstāk\ *n* : a slice of beef suitable for broiling or frying

beef up \'bēf-'əp\ *vb* : to add strength or power to ⟨*beef up* the army with new men⟩

beefy \'bē-fē\ *adj* **beef·i·er**; **-est** : BRAWNY, THICKSET

1**bee·hive** \'bē-ˌhīv\ *n* : a hive for bees

2**beehive** *adj* : resembling a dome-shaped beehive

bee·keep·er \-ˌkē-pər\ *n* : one that raises bees — **bee·keep·ing** *n*

bee·line \'bē-ˌlīn\ *n* : a straight direct course

been *past part of* BE

beer \'bi(ə)r\ *n* **1** : an alcoholic drink made from malt and flavored with hops **2** : a nonalcoholic drink made from roots or other parts of plants ⟨ginger *beer*⟩

bees·wax \'bēz-ˌwaks\ *n* : WAX 1

beet \'bēt\ *n* : a garden plant with thick long-stalked edible leaves and a swollen root used as a vegetable, as a source of sugar, or for forage; *also* : this root

1**bee·tle** \'bēt-əl\ *n* **1** : any of an order of insects having four wings of which the first pair are modified into stiff cases that fold over and protect the second pair when at rest **2** : any of various insects (as a cockroach) resembling a beetle

2**beetle** *n* : a heavy tool usu. with a wooden head for hammering

3**beetle** *adj* : being prominent and overhanging ⟨*beetle* brows⟩

4**beetle** *vb* **bee·tled**; **bee·tling** \'bēt-(ə-)ling\ : PROJECT, JUT

be·fall \bi-'fȯl\ *vb* **-fell** \-'fel\; **-fall·en** \-'fȯ-lən\; **-fall·ing** **1** : to come to pass : HAPPEN **2** : to happen to

be·fit \bi-'fit\ *vb* : to be suitable to or proper for ⟨clothes *befitting* the occasion⟩

be·fog \bi-'fȯg, -'fäg\ *vb* **1** : to make foggy : OBSCURE **2** : CONFUSE

be·fool \bi-'fül\ *vb* : DECEIVE

1**be·fore** \bi-'fō(ə)r, -'fȯ(ə)r\ *adv* **1** : in advance : AHEAD ⟨go on *before*⟩ **2** : EARLIER, PREVIOUSLY ⟨was here *before*⟩ ⟨tomorrow and not *before*⟩

2**before** *prep* **1 a** : in front of ⟨*before* one's eyes⟩ **b** : in the presence of ⟨stood *before* the judge⟩ **2** : under the consideration of ⟨the case *before* the court⟩ **3** : in advance of ⟨come *before* six o'clock⟩

3**before** *conj* **1** : earlier than the time when ⟨think *before* you speak⟩ **2** : more willingly than ⟨he will starve *before* he will steal⟩

be·fore·hand \-ˌhand\ *adv* : in advance : ahead of time

be·foul \bi-'fau̇l\ *vb* : to make dirty : SOIL
be·friend \bi-'frend\ *vb* : to act as a friend to
be·fud·dle \bi-'fəd-əl\ *vb* **1** : to dull the senses of : MUDDLE **2** : CONFUSE, PERPLEX — **be·fud·dle·ment** \-mənt\ *n*
beg \'beg\ *vb* **begged**; **beg·ging** **1** : to ask for money, food, or help as a charity ⟨*beg* in the streets⟩ **2** : to ask earnestly or politely ⟨*beg* a favor⟩ — **beg the question** : to assume as true or take for granted the thing that is the subject of the argument
be·gat \bi-'gat\ *archaic past of* BEGET
be·get \bi-'get\ *vb* **-got** \-'gät\; **-got·ten** \-'gät-ən\ *or* **-got**; **-get·ting** **1** : to become the father of : SIRE **2** : CAUSE — **be·get·ter** *n*
[1]**beg·gar** \'beg-ər\ *n* **1** : one that begs; *esp* : one that lives by begging **2** : PAUPER
[2]**beggar** *vb* **1** : to reduce to poverty **2** : to exceed the resources of ⟨*beggars* description⟩
beg·gar·ly \'beg-ər-lē\ *adj* : POOR, MEAN — **beg·gar·li·ness** *n*
beg·gar's–lice \'beg-ərz-ˌlīs\ *or* **beg·gar–lice** \-ər-ˌlīs\ *n sing or pl* : any of several plants with prickly or adhesive fruits; *also* : one of these fruits
beg·gar–ticks *or* **beg·gar's–ticks** \-ˌtiks\ *n sing or pl* **1** : BUR MARIGOLD; *also* : its prickly fruits **2** : BEGGAR'S-LICE
beg·gary \'beg-ə-rē\ *n* : extreme poverty or want
be·gin \bi-'gin\ *vb* **be·gan** \-'gan\; **be·gun** \-'gən\; **be·gin·ning** **1** : to do or be the first part of an action or course : START ⟨*begin* to type⟩ ⟨the road *begins* here⟩ **2** : to come or bring into existence : ORIGINATE ⟨*begin* a dynasty⟩ **3** : to do or succeed in the least degree ⟨does not *begin* to fill our needs⟩
be·gin·ner \bi-'gin-ər\ *n* : one that is beginning something or doing something for the first time : an inexperienced person
be·gin·ning \bi-'gin-ing\ *n* **1** : the point at which something begins **2** : the first part or stage ⟨the *beginnings* of American history⟩ **3** : ORIGIN, SOURCE
be·gone \bi-'gȯn, -'gän\ *vb* : to go away : DEPART — used esp. in the imperative mood
be·go·nia \bi-'gō-nyə\ *n* : any of a large genus of tropical herbs often grown for their shining leaves and bright waxy flowers
be·grime \bi-'grīm\ *vb* : to make dirty with grime
be·grudge \bi-'grəj\ *vb* **1** : to give, do, or concede reluctantly ⟨*begrudge* a person a favor⟩ **2** : to envy a person's possession or enjoyment of — **be·grudg·ing·ly** \-'grəj-ing-lē\ *adv*
be·guile \bi-'gīl\ *vb* **1** : to deceive by flattery or by a trick or lie **2** : to draw notice or interest by wiles or charm ⟨a *beguiling* manner⟩ **3** : to cause time to pass pleasantly : while away ⟨*beguile* the time by telling stories⟩ — **be·guile·ment** \-mənt\ *n* — **be·guil·er** *n*
be·half \bi-'haf, -'hȧf\ *n* : INTEREST, BENEFIT; *also* : SUPPORT, DEFENSE — used esp. in the phrase *in behalf of* or *on behalf of*
be·have \bi-'hāv\ *vb* **1** : to conduct oneself ⟨*behaved* badly at the party⟩ **2** : to conduct oneself properly ⟨if you don't *behave* you'll be punished⟩ **3** : to act, function, or react in a particular way ⟨the car *behaves* well on icy roads⟩
be·hav·ior \bi-'hā-vyər\ *n* **1** : the manner in which a person conducts himself **2** : the way in which something (as a machine or substance) behaves **3** : anything that an organism does that involves action and response to stimulation
be·head \bi-'hed\ *vb* : to cut off the head of
be·he·moth \bi-'hē-məth, 'bē-ə-ˌmȯth\ *n* **1** *often cap* : an animal described in the Bible that is prob. the hippopotamus **2** : something of monstrous size or power
be·hest \bi-'hest\ *n* : COMMAND, ORDER
[1]**be·hind** \bi-'hīnd\ *adv* **1 a** : in a place or time that is being or has been departed from ⟨stay *behind*⟩ ⟨leave your books *behind*⟩ **b** : at, to, or toward the back ⟨look *behind*⟩ ⟨fall *behind*⟩ **2** : not up to a general or expected level ⟨*behind* in school⟩ ⟨*behind* in his payments⟩
[2]**behind** *prep* **1** : at, to, or toward the back of ⟨look *behind* you⟩ ⟨a garden *behind* the house⟩ **2** : not up to the level of ⟨sales *behind* those of last year⟩ ⟨*behind* his class in school⟩
be·hind·hand \bi-'hīnd-ˌhand\ *adv or adj* : not keeping up : BEHIND ⟨*behindhand* with the rent⟩
be·hold \bi-'hōld\ *vb* : SEE, OBSERVE — **be·hold·er** *n*
be·hold·en \bi-'hōl-dən\ *adj* : being under obligation : INDEBTED
be·hoof \bi-'hüf\ *n* : ADVANTAGE, BENEFIT ⟨acted only for his own *behoof*⟩
be·hoove \bi-'hüv\ *or* **be·hove** \-'hōv\ *vb* : to be necessary, fitting, or proper for ⟨such behavior ill *behooves* you⟩ ⟨it *behooves* a soldier to obey orders⟩
beige \'bāzh\ *n* : a light grayish yellowish brown — **beige** *adj*
be·ing \'bē-ing\ *n* **1** : EXISTENCE, LIFE **2** : a living thing; *esp* : PERSON
be·la·bor \bi-'lā-bər\ *vb* **1** : to work on or at to absurd lengths ⟨*belabor* the obvious⟩ **2** : ASSAIL, ATTACK
be·lat·ed \bi-'lāt-əd\ *adj* : delayed beyond the usual time — **be·lat·ed·ly** *adv* — **be·lat·ed·ness** *n*
be·lay \bi-'lā\ *vb* **1** : to secure (as a rope) by turns around a cleat or pin **2** : STOP
belch \'belch\ *vb* **1** : to expel gas from the stomach through the mouth **2** : to eject, emit, or issue violently — **belch** *n*
bel·dam *or* **bel·dame** \'bel-dəm\ *n* : an old woman; *esp* : HAG
be·lea·guer \bi-'lē-gər\ *vb* **-guered**; **-guer·ing** \-g(ə-)ring\ : to surround with an army so as to prevent escape : BESIEGE
bel·fry \'bel-frē\ *n, pl* **belfries** : a tower or a room in a tower for a bell or set of bells
Belg *abbr* **1** Belgian **2** Belgium
Bel·gian \'bel-jən\ *n* **1** : a native or inhabitant of Belgium **2** : any of a Belgian breed of heavy usu. roan or chestnut draft horses — **Belgian** *adj*
Belgian hare *n* : any of a breed of slender dark red domestic rabbits
Belgian sheepdog *n* : any of a breed of hardy black or gray dogs developed in Belgium esp. for herding sheep
be·lie \bi-'lī\ *vb* **-lied**; **-ly·ing** **1** : MISREPRESENT ⟨his words *belie* his feelings⟩ **2** : to be false or unfaithful to ⟨*belied* his principles⟩ **3** : to show to be false ⟨his actions *belie* his promise⟩ — **be·li·er** *n*
be·lief \bə-'lēf\ *n* **1** : mental acceptance of something offered as true ⟨a *belief* in miracles⟩ **2** : religious faith; *esp* : CREED **3** : something believed : OPINION ⟨political *beliefs*⟩

syn BELIEF, CREDENCE, FAITH can mean acceptance of something or someone as true or reliable without asking proof. BELIEF, the most general term, may suggest nothing more than a going along uncritically; CREDENCE implies ready acceptance of rumors, reports, or opinions as a basis for belief; FAITH suggests trust and confidence in addition to uncritical acceptance ***ant*** unbelief, disbelief

be·lieve \bə-'lēv\ *vb* **1 :** to have a firm esp. religious belief **2 :** to take as true or honest ⟨*believe* the reports⟩ **3 :** to hold as an opinion : THINK ⟨*believe* it will rain⟩ — **be·liev·a·ble** \-'lē-və-bəl\ *adj* — **be·liev·a·bly** \-blē\ *adv* — **be·liev·er** *n*
be·like \bi-'līk\ *adv, archaic* : PROBABLY
be·lit·tle \bi-'lit-əl\ *vb* **-lit·tled; -lit·tling** \'lit-(ə-)ling\ **:** to make (a person or a thing) seem little or unimportant ⟨*belittle* the success of a rival⟩ — **be·lit·tle·ment** \-əl-mənt\ *n* — **be·lit·tler** \-'lit-(ə-)lər\ *n*
¹bell \'bel\ *n* **1 :** a hollow usu. cup-shaped metallic device that makes a ringing sound when struck **2 :** the stroke or sound of a bell that tells the hour esp. on shipboard **3 :** a half hour period of a watch on shipboard indicated by the strokes of a bell **4 :** something (as a flower or the flaring mouth of a trumpet) shaped like a bell **5** *pl* : BELL-BOTTOMS

No. of Bells	Hour (A.M. or P.M.)		
1	12:30	4:30	8:30
2	1:00	5:00	9:00
3	1:30	5:30	9:30
4	2:00	6:00	10:00
5	2:30	6:30	10:30
6	3:00	7:00	11:00
7	3:30	7:30	11:30
8	4:00	8:00	12:00

²bell *vb* **1 :** to provide with a bell **2 :** to take the form of a bell : FLARE
bel·la·don·na \,bel-ə-'dän-ə\ *n* [from Italian, from *bella donna* "beautiful lady"; so called from the use of its extract to enlarge the pupils of the eyes] **:** a European poisonous herb that is related to the nightshade and has reddish bell-shaped flowers, shining black berries, and root and leaves that yield atropine; *also* : a drug or extract from this plant
bell–bot·toms \'bel-'bät-əmz\ *n pl* **:** pants with legs that flare at the bottom — **bell–bottom** *or* **bell–bot·tomed** \-əmd\ *adj*
bell·boy \'bel-,bȯi\ *n* **:** a hotel or club employee who escorts guests to rooms, carries luggage, and runs errands
belle \'bel\ *n* **:** a popular attractive girl or woman
bell·flow·er \'bel-,flau̇(-ə)r\ *n* : CAMPANULA
bell·hop \-,häp\ *n* : BELLBOY
bel·li·cose \'bel-ə-,kōs\ *adj* **:** inclined to quarrel or fight : WARLIKE — **bel·li·cos·i·ty** \,bel-ə-'käs-ət-ē\ *n*
bel·lig·er·ence \bə-'lij-(ə-)rən(t)s\ *n* **:** belligerent attitude or disposition
bel·lig·er·en·cy \-(ə-)rən-sē\ *n* **1 :** the status of a nation that is at war **2 :** WARFARE
bel·lig·er·ent \bə-'lij-(ə-)rənt\ *adj* **1 :** waging war ⟨*belligerent* nations⟩ **2 :** inclined to or showing a readiness to fight — **belligerent** *n* — **bel·lig·er·ent·ly** *adv*
bell jar *n* **:** a bell-shaped usu. glass vessel designed to cover objects or to enclose gases or a vacuum
bell·man \'bel-mən\ *n* : BELLBOY

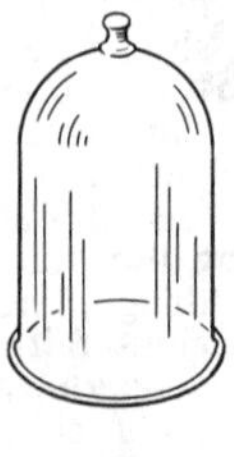
bell jar

ə abut	ər further	a back	ā bake	
ä cot, cart	au̇ out	ch chin	e less	ē easy
g gift	i trip	ī life	j joke	ng sing	ō flow
ȯ flaw	ȯi coin	th thin	t͟h this	ü loot
u̇ foot	y yet	yü few	yu̇ furious	zh vision

bel·low \'bel-ō\ *vb* **1 :** to make the loud deep hollow sound characteristic of a bull **2 :** to shout in a deep voice : BAWL — **bellow** *n*
bel·lows \'bel-ōz, -əz\ *n sing or pl* **1 :** a device that can be spread apart and then pressed together to force air through a tube at one end **2 :** the pleated expandable part of some cameras
bell·pull \'bel-,pu̇l\ *n* **:** a cord or wire or a handle or knob attached to it by which one rings a bell
bell·weth·er \'bel-'wet͟h-ər\ *n* **:** a belled sheep that identifies the location of a flock
¹bel·ly \'bel-ē\ *n, pl* **bellies 1 a :** ABDOMEN 1 **b :** the undersurface of an animal's body; *also* : hide from this part **c :** STOMACH 1a **2 :** the internal cavity : INTERIOR **3 :** a curved or rounded surface or object ⟨the *belly* of an airplane⟩
²belly *vb* **bel·lied; bel·ly·ing :** to swell or bulge out
¹bel·ly·ache \'bel-ē-,āk\ *n* **:** pain in the abdomen and esp. in the bowels : COLIC
²bellyache *vb* **:** to complain esp. in a whining or peevish way
belly button *n* : NAVEL 1
bel·ly–land \'bel-ē-,land\ *vb* **:** to land an airplane without use of landing gear — **belly landing** *n*
be·long \bə-'lȯng\ *vb* **1 a :** to be suitable, appropriate, or advantageous **b :** to be in a proper situation ⟨this book *belongs* on the top shelf⟩ **2 a :** to be the property of a person or thing ⟨this book *belongs* to me⟩ **b :** to become attached or bound ⟨feels that he *belongs*⟩ **3 :** to be a quality, part, or function of something ⟨parts *belonging* to a watch⟩ **4 :** to be classified ⟨whales *belong* among the mammals⟩
be·long·ings \bə-'lȯng-ingz\ *n pl* **:** the things that belong to a person : POSSESSIONS
Be·lo·rus·sian \,bel-ō-'rəsh-ən\ *adj* **:** of, relating to, or characteristic of Belorussia or its people — **Belorussian** *n*
be·loved \bi-'ləv(-ə)d\ *adj* **:** dearly loved — **beloved** *n*
¹be·low \bə-'lō\ *adv* **:** in or to a lower place
²below *prep* **:** lower than in place, rank, or value ⟨*below* average⟩
¹belt \'belt\ *n* **1 :** a strip of flexible material (as leather) worn around a person's body for holding in or supporting clothing or weapons or for ornament **2 :** something resembling a belt : BAND, CIRCLE ⟨a *belt* of trees⟩ **3 :** a flexible endless band running around wheels or pulleys and used for moving or carrying something ⟨a fan *belt* on a car⟩ **4 :** a region marked by some distinctive product or activity ⟨corn *belt*⟩ — **belt·ed** \'bel-təd\ *adj* — **below the belt :** UNFAIRLY
²belt *vb* **1 :** to put a belt on or around **2 :** to beat with or as if with a belt : STRIKE **3 :** to mark with a band
³belt *n* **:** a jarring blow
belt·ing \'bel-ting\ *n* **1 :** BELTS **2 :** material for making belts
be·lu·ga \bə-'lü-gə\ *n* **1 :** a white sturgeon esp. of the Black and Caspian seas **2 :** a mammal that is related to dolphins and becomes about 10 feet long and white when adult
be·moan \bi-'mōn\ *vb* **:** to express grief over
¹bench \'bench\ *n* **1 :** a long seat for two or more persons **2 :** a long table for holding work and tools (as of a carpenter) **3 a :** the seat where a judge sits in a court of law **b :** the position or rank of a judge **c :** a person or persons engaged in judging **4 :** a seat where the members of a team wait for an opportunity to play
²bench *vb* **1 :** to furnish with benches **2 :** to seat on a bench **3 :** to remove from or keep out of a game

bench mark *n* : a mark on a permanent object indicating elevation and serving as a reference in geological surveys

[1]**bend** \'bend\ *vb* **bent** \'bent\; **bend·ing** **1** : to pull tight ⟨*bend* a bow⟩ **2** : to curve or cause a change of shape ⟨*bend* a wire into a circle⟩ **3** : to turn in a certain direction : DIRECT ⟨*bent* his steps toward town⟩ **4** : to force to yield ⟨*bent* his family to his will⟩ **5** : to apply closely ⟨*bend* your energy to the task⟩ **6** : to curve out of line ⟨the road *bends* to the left⟩ **7** : to curve downward : STOOP **8** : YIELD, SUBMIT

[2]**bend** *n* **1** : the act or process of bending : the state of being bent **2** : something bent; *esp* : a curved part of a stream **3** *pl* : a severe disorder marked by pain (as in joints and limbs), distress in breathing, and often collapse and caused by release of gas bubbles in the tissues upon too rapid decrease in air pressure after a stay in a compressed atmosphere

[1]**be·neath** \bi-'nēth\ *adv* : in or to a lower position : BELOW

[2]**beneath** *prep* **1** : lower than : UNDER ⟨the ground *beneath* one's feet⟩ **2** : unworthy of ⟨*beneath* his dignity⟩

ben·e·dic·tion \ˌben-ə-'dik-shən\ *n* : BLESSING; *esp* : the short blessing at the end of a religious service

Benedict's solution \'ben-ə-ˌdik(t)s-\ *n* : a blue solution containing copper sulfate, sodium carbonate, and sodium citrate that is used esp. for detecting glucose

ben·e·fac·tion \'ben-ə-ˌfak-shən, ˌben-ə-'\ *n* **1** : the action of benefiting **2** : a benefit conferred; *esp* : a charitable donation

ben·e·fac·tor \'ben-ə-ˌfak-tər\ *n* : one that confers a benefit; *esp* : one that makes a gift or bequest — **ben·e·fac·tress** \-ˌfak-trəs\ *n*

ben·e·fice \'ben-ə-fəs\ *n* : a post held by a clergyman that gives him the right to use certain property and to receive income from stated sources — **benefice** *vb*

be·nef·i·cent \bə-'nef-ə-sənt\ *adj* : doing or producing good; *esp* : performing acts of charity — **be·nef·i·cence** \-sən(t)s\ *n* — **be·nef·i·cent·ly** *adv*

ben·e·fi·cial \ˌben-ə-'fish-əl\ *adj* : conferring benefits — **ben·e·fi·cial·ly** \-'fish-ə-lē\ *adv* — **ben·e·fi·cial·ness** *n*

syn BENEFICIAL, ADVANTAGEOUS, PROFITABLE can mean being favorable to one's interests. BENEFICIAL implies promotion of health or well-being; ADVANTAGEOUS suggests something leading to success or personal advancement; PROFITABLE implies the yielding of useful or enriching returns ***ant*** harmful, detrimental

ben·e·fi·ci·ary \-'fish-ē-ˌer-ē, -'fish-(ə-)rē\ *n, pl* **-ar·ies** : a person who benefits or is expected to benefit from something ⟨the *beneficiary* of a life insurance policy⟩

[1]**ben·e·fit** \'ben-ə-ˌfit\ *n* **1 a** : something that promotes well-being : ADVANTAGE **b** : useful aid : HELP **2** : money paid at death or when sick, retired, or unemployed (as by an insurance company or public agency) **3** : an entertainment or social event to raise funds for a person or cause

[2]**benefit** *vb* **-fit·ed** *or* **-fit·ted**; **-fit·ing** *or* **-fit·ting** **1** : to be useful or profitable to **2** : to receive benefit

be·nev·o·lence \bə-'nev(-ə)-lən(t)s\ *n* **1** : disposition to do good **2 a** : an act of kindness **b** : a generous gift

be·nev·o·lent \-lənt\ *adj* **1** : having or showing goodwill : KINDLY **2** : freely or generously giving to charity **3** : existing or operated to help others and not for profit ⟨*benevolent* institutions⟩ — **be·nev·o·lent·ly** *adv*

Ben·gal·ese \ˌben(g)-gə-'lēz, -'lēs\ *adj* : of, relating to, or characteristic of Bengal or its people — **Bengalese** *n*

be·night·ed \bi-'nīt-əd\ *adj* **1** : overtaken by night **2** : IGNORANT

be·nign \bi-'nīn\ *adj* **1** : of a gentle disposition : GRACIOUS **2** : FAVORABLE ⟨the weather remained *benign*⟩ **3** : of a mild character; *esp* : not malignant ⟨*benign* tumor⟩ — **be·nig·ni·ty** \-'nig-nət-ē\ *n* — **be·nign·ly** \-'nīn-lē\ *adv*

be·nig·nant \bi-'nig-nənt\ *adj* **1** : KINDLY, GENTLE **2** : FAVORABLE, BENEFICIAL — **be·nig·nant·ly** *adv*

ben·i·son \'ben-ə-sən, -zən\ *n* : BLESSING

[1]**bent** \'bent\ *n* : any of a genus of pasture and lawn grasses with fine velvety or wiry herbage

[2]**bent** *n* **1** : strong inclination or interest **2** : a natural capacity : TALENT

ben·thic \'ben(t)-thik\ *or* **ben·thon·ic** \ben-'thän-ik\ *adj* : of, relating to, or occurring in the depths of a body of water (as the ocean)

ben·thos \'ben-ˌthäs\ *n* : the benthic region or the organisms that live there

ben·ton·ite \'bent-ə-ˌnīt\ *n* : an absorptive and colloidal clay used esp. as a filler (as in paper)

be·numb \bi-'nəm\ *vb* : to make numb esp. by cold

ben·zene \'ben-ˌzēn, ben-'\ *n* : a colorless volatile flammable liquid that is obtained chiefly in the distillation of coal and that is used as a solvent and in making other chemicals (as dyes and drugs) — called also *benzol*

ben·zine \'ben-ˌzēn, ben-'\ *n* **1** : BENZENE **2** : any of various volatile flammable petroleum distillates used esp. as solvents for fatty substances or as motor fuels

ben·zo·ate of soda \ˌben-zə-ˌwāt-\ : SODIUM BENZOATE

ben·zo·ic acid \ben-ˌzō-ik-\ *n* : a white crystalline organic acid found naturally (as in cranberries) or made synthetically and used esp. as a preservative and as an antiseptic

ben·zol \'ben-ˌzȯl, -ˌzōl\ *n* : BENZENE

be·queath \bi-'kwēth, -'kwēt͟h\ *vb* **1** : to give or leave esp. personal property by will **2** : to hand down — **be·queath·al** \-əl\ *n*

be·quest \bi-'kwest\ *n* **1** : the action of bequeathing **2** : something bequeathed : LEGACY

be·rate \bi-'rāt\ *vb* : to scold violently

be·reave \bi-'rēv\ *vb* **be·reaved** \-'rēvd\ *or* **be·reft** \-'reft\; **be·reav·ing** : to deprive of something cherished esp. by death — **be·reave·ment** \-'rēv-mənt\ *n*

be·ret \bə-'rā\ *n* [from French *béret*, from Provençal *berret*, the source also, via Italian, of English *biretta*] : a soft flat wool cap without a visor

beret

berg \'bərg\ *n* : ICEBERG

ber·i·beri \ˌber-ē-'ber-ē\ *n* : a deficiency disease marked by weakness, wasting, and damage to nerves and caused by a dietary lack of or inability to assimilate thiamine

berke·li·um \'bər-

klē-əm, (ˌ)bər-'kē-lē-əm\ *n* : an artificially prepared radioactive chemical element — see ELEMENT table
Ber·mu·da grass \bər-'myüd-ə-\ *n* : a trailing grass that is native to Europe and is used for lawns and pasture esp. in the southern U.S.
Bermuda shorts *n pl* : knee-length walking shorts — called also *Bermudas*
¹ber·ry \'ber-ē\ *n, pl* **berries** **1** : a small pulpy and usu. edible fruit (as a strawberry or raspberry) **2** : a simple fruit (as a currant, grape, tomato, or banana) with the wall of the ripened ovary pulpy or fleshy **3** : the dry seed of some plants (as coffee) — **ber·ry·like** \-ē-ˌlīk\ *adj*
²berry *vb* **ber·ried**; **ber·ry·ing** **1** : to bear or produce berries **2** : to gather or seek berries ⟨go *berrying* every summer⟩
¹ber·serk \bə(r)-'sərk, -'zərk, 'bər-ˌ\ *or* **ber·serk·er** \-ər\ *n* : an ancient Scandinavian warrior frenzied in battle and held to be invulnerable
²berserk *adj* : FRENZIED, CRAZED — **berserk** *adv*
¹berth \'bərth\ *n* **1** : a place where a ship lies at anchor or at a wharf **2** : a place to sleep on a ship or vehicle **3** : a job esp. on a ship
²berth *vb* : to bring or come into a berth
ber·yl \'ber-əl\ *n* : a mineral consisting of a silicate of beryllium and aluminum of great hardness and occurring in green, bluish green, yellow, pink, or white prisms ⟨the emerald is a precious *beryl*⟩
be·ryl·li·um \bə-'ril-ē-əm\ *n* : a steel-gray light strong brittle metallic element — see ELEMENT table
be·seech \bi-'sēch\ *vb* **be·sought** \-'sȯt\ *or* **be·seeched**; **be·seech·ing** : to ask earnestly for : IMPLORE
be·seem \bi-'sēm\ *vb, archaic* : to be proper for : BEFIT
be·set \bi-'set\ *vb* **-set**; **-set·ting** **1** : to set upon : ASSAIL **2** : to hem in : SURROUND
be·set·ting *adj* : constantly present or attacking ⟨a *besetting* danger⟩
beside \bi-'sīd\ *prep* **1 a** : by the side of ⟨walk *beside* me⟩ **b** : in comparison with ⟨looks like a midget *beside* him⟩ **2** : BESIDES **3** : not relevant to ⟨*beside* the point⟩ — **beside oneself** : out of one's wits
¹be·sides \bi-'sīdz\ *adv* : in addition : ALSO
²besides *prep* : in addition to : other than
be·siege \bi-'sēj\ *vb* **1** : to surround with armed forces : lay siege to **2** : to crowd around : BESET — **be·sieg·er** *n*
be·smear \bi-'smi(ə)r\ *vb* : SMEAR
be·smirch \bi-'smərch\ *vb* : SULLY, SOIL
be·som \'bē-zəm\ *n* : a broom made of twigs
be·spat·ter \bi-'spat-ər\ *vb* : SPATTER
be·speak \bi-'spēk\ *vb* **-spoke** \-'spōk\; **-spo·ken** \-'spō-kən\; **-speak·ing** **1** : to ask or arrange for beforehand **2** : INDICATE, SIGNIFY ⟨her manners *bespeak* good training⟩
Bes·se·mer converter \ˌbes-ə-mər-\ *n* : the furnace used in the Bessemer process
Bessemer process *n* : a process of making steel from pig iron by burning out impurities (as carbon) by means of a blast of air forced through the molten metal
¹best \'best\ *adj, superlative of* GOOD **1** : good or useful in the highest degree : most excellent **2** : MOST, LARGEST ⟨the *best* part of a week⟩

ə abut	ər further	a back	ā bake
ä cot, cart	au̇ out	ch chin	e less
ē easy	g gift	i trip	ī life
j joke	ng sing	ō flow	ȯ flaw
ȯi coin	th thin	th this	ü loot
u̇ foot	y yet	yü few	yu̇ furious
zh vision			

²best *adv, superlative of* WELL **1** : in the best way **2** : to the highest degree : MOST ⟨*best* able to do the work⟩
³best *n* **1** : the best state or part **2** : one that is best ⟨the *best* falls short⟩ **3** : one's greatest effort ⟨do your *best*⟩ **4** : best clothes ⟨put on your Sunday *best*⟩
⁴best *vb* : to get the better of : OUTDO
be·stead \bi-'sted\ *adj, archaic* : BESET
bes·tial \'bes-chəl\ *adj* **1** : of or relating to beasts **2** : VICIOUS, BRUTAL — **bes·ti·al·i·ty** \ˌbes-chē-'al-ət-ē\ *n* — **bes·tial·ly** \'bes-chə-lē\ *adv*
be·stir \bi-'stər\ *vb* : to stir up : rouse to action
be·stow \bi-'stō\ *vb* : GIVE, GRANT — **be·stow·al** \-'stō-əl\ *n*
be·strew \bi-'strü\ *vb* **-strewed**; **-strewed** *or* **-strewn** \-'strün\; **-strew·ing** **1** : STREW **2** : to lie scattered over
be·stride \bi-'strīd\ *vb* **-strode** \-'strōd\; **-strid·den** \-'strid-ən\; **-strid·ing** \-'strīd-ing\ : to ride, sit, or stand astride : STRADDLE
¹bet \'bet\ *n* **1 a** : an agreement requiring the person whose guess about the result of a contest or the outcome of an event proves wrong to give something to a person whose guess proves right **b** : the making of such an agreement : WAGER **2** : the money or thing risked ⟨a *bet* of 10 cents⟩
²bet *vb* **bet** *or* **bet·ted**; **bet·ting** **1** : to risk in a bet **2** : to make a bet with **3** : to be certain enough to bet ⟨I *bet* it will rain⟩
bet *abbr* between
be·ta \'bāt-ə\ *n* : the 2d letter of the Greek alphabet — Β or β
be·take \bi-'tāk\ *vb* : to cause (oneself) to go
beta particle *n* : an electron or positron ejected from the nucleus of an atom during radioactive decay
beta ray *n* **1** : BETA PARTICLE **2** : a stream of beta particles
be·ta·tron \'bāt-ə-ˌträn\ *n* : a device that accelerates electrons by the action of a rapidly varying magnetic field
be·tel \'bēt-əl\ *n* : a climbing pepper whose dried leaves are chewed together with betel nut and lime as a stimulant esp. by southeastern Asians
betel nut *n* : the astringent seed of an Asiatic palm
beth·el \'beth-əl\ *n* [from Hebrew *bēth-Ēl* "house of God"] : a place of worship esp. for seamen
be·think \bi-'thingk\ *vb* **-thought** \-'thȯt\; **-think·ing** **1 a** : REMEMBER, RECALL **b** : to cause (oneself) to recall **2** : to cause (oneself) to consider
be·tide \bi-'tīd\ *vb* : to happen or happen to : BEFALL ⟨woe *betide* you if he finds out⟩
be·times \bi-'tīmz\ *adv* : in time : EARLY
be·to·ken \bi-'tō-kən\ *vb* : to be a sign of : INDICATE
be·tray \bi-'trā\ *vb* **1** : to give over to an enemy by treachery or fraud **2** : to be unfaithful to ⟨*betrayed* his trust⟩ **3** : to lead into error, sin, or danger : SEDUCE **4** : to reveal unintentionally ⟨*betray* his ignorance⟩ **5** : to tell in violation of a trust ⟨*betray* a secret⟩ — **be·tray·al** \-'trā(-ə)l\ *n* — **be·tray·er** \-'trā-ər\ *n*
be·troth \bi-'träth, -'trȯth, -'trōth, *or with* th\ *vb* : to promise to marry or give in marriage
be·troth·al \-'trōth-əl, -'trȯth-, -'trōth-\ *n* **1** : an engagement to be married **2** : the act or ceremony of becoming engaged
be·trothed \-'trätht, -'trȯtht, -'trōthd\ *n* : the person to whom one is betrothed
bet·ta \'bet-ə\ *n* : any of a genus of small brilliantly colored long-finned freshwater fishes of southeastern Asia
¹bet·ter \'bet-ər\ *adj, comparative of* GOOD **1** : more

than half ⟨the *better* part of a week⟩ **2** : improved in health **3** : of higher quality

2**better** *adv, comparative of* WELL **1** : in a more excellent manner **2 a** : to a higher or greater degree **b** : MORE

3**better** *n* **1 a** : a better thing or state ⟨a change for the *better*⟩ **b** : a superior esp. in merit or rank **2** : ADVANTAGE, VICTORY ⟨get the *better* of him⟩

4**better** *vb* **1** : to make better **2** : to surpass in excellence : EXCEL

bet·ter·ment \'bet-ər-mənt\ *n* : IMPROVEMENT

bet·tor *or* **bet·ter** \'bet-ər\ *n* : one that bets

1**be·tween** \bi-'twēn\ *prep* **1** : by the common action of ⟨ate six *between* them⟩ **2** : in the interval that separates ⟨*between* nine and ten o'clock⟩ ⟨*between* the desk and the wall⟩ **3** : DISTINGUISHING ⟨the difference *between* soccer and football⟩ **4** : by comparison of ⟨choose *between* the two coats⟩ **5** : CONNECTING ⟨the bond *between* friends⟩

2**between** *adv* : in an intermediate space or interval

be·twixt \bi-'twikst\ *adv or prep, archaic* : BETWEEN

1**bev·el** \'bev-əl\ *n* **1** : the angle that one surface or line makes with another **2** : the inclination of a bevel

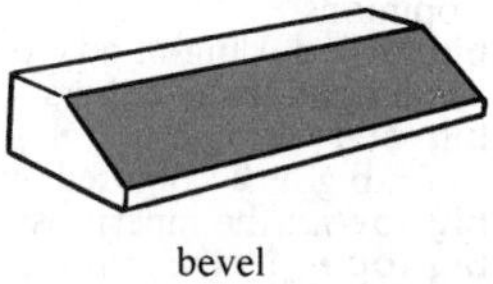
bevel

2**bevel** *vb* **bev·eled** *or* **bev·elled**; **bev·el·ing** *or* **bev·el·ling** \'bev-(ə-)liŋ\ **1** : to cut or shape (as an edge or surface) to a bevel **2** : INCLINE, SLANT — **bevel** *adj*

bev·er·age \'bev-(ə-)rij\ *n* : a liquid for drinking

bevy \'bev-ē\ *n, pl* **bev·ies** : GROUP, CLUSTER ⟨a *bevy* of girls⟩

be·wail \bi-'wāl\ *vb* **1** : to wail over **2** : to express deep regret for

be·ware \bi-'wa(ə)r, -'we(ə)r\ *vb* **1** : to be on one's guard ⟨*beware* of the dog⟩ **2** : to be wary of

be·wil·der \bi-'wil-dər\ *vb* **-dered**; **-der·ing** \-d(ə-)riŋ\ : to fill with uncertainty : CONFUSE — **be·wil·der·ment** \-dər-mənt\ *n*

be·witch \bi-'wich\ *vb* **1** : to gain an influence over by magic or witchcraft : put under a spell **2** : CHARM, FASCINATE — **be·witch·ment** \-mənt\ *n*

be·wray \bi-'rā\ *vb, archaic* : BETRAY, REVEAL

1**be·yond** \bē-'änd\ *adv* : on or to the farther side

2**beyond** *prep* **1** : on or to the farther side of ⟨*beyond* that tree⟩ **2** : out of the reach or sphere of ⟨*beyond* help⟩ ⟨beautiful *beyond* expression⟩

3**beyond** *n* : HEREAFTER

bg *abbr* bag

bhang \'baŋ\ *n* **1** : an intoxicating drug derived from the hemp plant **2** : the leaves and flowering tips of the hemp plant

B–ho·ri·zon \'bē-hə-ˌrī-zən\ *n* : the soil layer immediately below the A-horizon that contains materials transported down from the surface and often an accumulation of clay and compounds of iron and aluminum with oxygen

bi- *prefix* **1** : two ⟨*bi*racial⟩ **2** : coming or occurring every two ⟨*bi*monthly⟩ **3** : into two parts ⟨*bi*sect⟩ **4** : twice : doubly : on both sides ⟨*bi*convex⟩

bi·an·nu·al \(')bī-'an-yə(-wə)l\ *adj* : occurring twice a year — **bi·an·nu·al·ly** \-ē\ *adv*

1**bi·as** \'bī-əs\ *n* **1** : a line diagonal to the grain of a fabric **2** : an inclination of temperament or outlook; *esp* : strong prejudice **3** : the direct-current voltage in the grid circuit of an electron tube

2**bias** *vb* **bi·ased** *or* **bi·assed**; **bi·as·ing** *or* **bi·as·sing** : to give a bias to : PREJUDICE

bib \'bib\ *n* **1** : a cloth or plastic shield tied under a child's chin to protect the clothes **2** : the upper part of an apron or of overalls

bib *abbr* **1** Bible **2** biblical

Bi·ble \'bī-bəl\ *n* [from medieval Latin *biblia*, from Greek *ta biblia*, literally "the books"] **1** : the sacred writings of Christians comprising the Old Testament and the New Testament **2** : the sacred scriptures of Judaism or of some other religion — **bib·li·cal** \'bib-li-kəl\ *adj*

THE BOOKS OF THE OLD TESTAMENT

DOUAY VERSION	AUTHORIZED VERSION
Genesis	Genesis
Exodus	Exodus
Leviticus	Leviticus
Numbers	Numbers
Deuteronomy	Deuteronomy
Josue	Joshua
Judges	Judges
Ruth	Ruth
1 & 2 Kings	1 & 2 Samuel
3 & 4 Kings	1 & 2 Kings
1 & 2 Paralipomenon	1 & 2 Chronicles
1 Esdras	Ezra
2 Esdras	Nehemiah
Tobias	
Judith	
Esther	Esther
Wisdom	
Ecclesiasticus	
Isaias	Isaiah
Jeremias	Jeremiah
Lamentations	Lamentations
Baruch	
Ezechiel	Ezekiel
Daniel	Daniel
Osee	Hosea
Joel	Joel
Amos	Amos
Abdias	Obadiah
Jonas	Jonah
Micheas	Micah
Nahum	Nahum
Habacuc	Habakkuk
Sophonias	Zephaniah
Job	Job
Psalms	Psalms
Proverbs	Proverbs
Ecclesiastes	Ecclesiastes
Canticle of Canticles	Song of Solomon
Aggeus	Haggai
Zacharias	Zechariah
Malachias	Malachi
1 & 2 Machabees	

THE BOOKS OF THE NEW TESTAMENT
(*DV* and *AV* names the same)

Matthew
Mark
Luke
John
Acts of the Apostles
Romans
1 & 2 Corinthians
Galatians
Ephesians
Philippians
Colossians
1 & 2 Thessalonians
1 & 2 Timothy
Titus
Philemon
Hebrews
James
1 & 2 Peter
1, 2, 3 John
Jude
Revelation (*DV*: Apocalypse)

PROTESTANT APOCRYPHA

1 & 2 Esdras[1]
Tobit
Judith
part of Esther[2]
Wisdom of Solomon
Ecclesiasticus or the Wisdom of Jesus Son of Sirach
Baruch
Prayer of Azariah and the Song of the Three Holy Children[3]
Susanna[4]
Bel and the Dragon[5]
The Prayer of Manasses[6]
1 & 2 Maccabees

[1]not the same as 1 & 2 Esdras in *DV*
[2]ch. 11—16 in *DV*
[3]from ch. 3 of *DV* Daniel
[4]ch. 13 of *DV* Daniel
[5]ch. 14 of *DV* Daniel
[6]not in *DV*

bib·li·og·ra·phy \ˌbib-lē-'äg-rə-fē\ *n, pl* **-phies** **1** : the history, identification, or description of writings or publications **2** : a list of writings about a subject or author or by an author — **bib·li·og·ra·pher** \-fər\ *n* — **bib·li·o·graph·ic** \ˌbib-lē-ə-'graf-ik\ *or* **bib·li·o·graph·i·cal** \-'graf-i-kəl\ *adj*

bib·u·lous \'bib-yə-ləs\ *adj* **1** : ABSORBENT **2** : fond of alcoholic drinks — **bib·u·lous·ly** *adv* — **bib·u·lous·ness** *n*

bi·cam·er·al \(')bī-'kam-(ə-)rəl\ *adj* : consisting of two legislative chambers ⟨*bicameral* legislature⟩

bi·car·bon·ate \(')bī-'kär-bə-ˌnāt, -nət\ *n* : an acid carbonate

bicarbonate of soda : SODIUM BICARBONATE

bi·cen·ten·a·ry \ˌbī-sen-'ten-ə-rē, (')bī-'sent-

ə-ˌner-ē\ *adj* : BICENTENNIAL — **bicentenary** *n*
bi·cen·ten·ni·al \ˌbī-sen-ˈten-ē-əl\ *adj* : relating to a 200th anniversary — **bicentennial** *n*
bi·ceps \ˈbī-ˌseps\ *n* : a muscle having two heads; *esp* : a large muscle of the front of the upper arm
bi·chlo·ride \(ˈ)bī-ˈklōr-ˌīd, -ˈklȯr-\ *n* : DICHLORIDE
bick·er \ˈbik-ər\ *vb* **bick·ered**; **bick·er·ing** \ˈbik-(ə-)riŋ\ : to quarrel peevishly : WRANGLE — **bick·er** *n*
bi·col·or \ˈbī-ˌkəl-ər\ *adj* : two-colored — **bicolor** *n* — **bi·col·ored** \-ˈkəl-ərd\ *adj*
bi·con·cave \ˌbī-ˌkän-ˈkāv, (ˈ)bī-ˈkän-ˌ\ *adj* : concave on both sides ⟨red blood cells are *biconcave*⟩
bi·con·vex \ˌbī-ˌkän-ˈveks, (ˈ)bī-ˈkän-ˌ\ *adj* : convex on both sides
[1]**bi·cus·pid** \(ˈ)bī-ˈkəs-pəd\ *also* **bi·cus·pi·date** \-pə-ˌdāt\ *adj* : having or ending in two points
[2]**bicuspid** *n* : PREMOLAR
[1]**bi·cy·cle** \ˈbī-ˌsik-əl\ *n* : a light vehicle with two wheels behind one another, handlebars, and pedals by which it is propelled — **bi·cy·clist** \-ˌsik-(ə-)ləst\ *n*
[2]**bicycle** *vb* **bi·cy·cled**; **bi·cy·cling** \-ˌsik-(ə-)liŋ\ : to ride a bicycle — **bi·cy·cler** \-ˌsik-(ə-)lər\ *n*
[1]**bid** \ˈbid\ *vb* **bade** \ˈbad, ˈbād\ *or* **bid**; **bid·den** \ˈbid-ən\ *or* **bid**; **bid·ding** **1 a** : ORDER, COMMAND ⟨did as he was *bidden*⟩ **b** : INVITE **2** : to express to ⟨*bade* me farewell⟩ **3** *past* **bid** : to make an offer for something (as at an auction) ⟨*bid* $10 for a chair⟩ — **bid·der** *n* — **bid fair** : to seem likely — **bid up** : to raise the price of by bids at an auction
[2]**bid** *n* **1** : an offer to pay a certain sum for something or to perform certain work at a stated fee **2** : a turn to bid **3** : INVITATION **4 a** : an announcement of what a card player proposes to undertake **b** : the amount of such a bid **5** : an attempt to win, achieve, or attract ⟨made a strong *bid* for the job⟩
bide \ˈbīd\ *vb* **bode** \ˈbōd\ *or* **bid·ed**; **bided**; **bid·ing** **1** : WAIT **2** : to wait for ⟨*bided* his time before acting⟩
bi·en·ni·al \(ˈ)bī-ˈen-ē-əl\ *adj* **1** : occurring every two years **2 a** : lasting for two years **b** : growing vegetatively during the first year and fruiting and dying during the second — **biennial** *n* — **bi·en·ni·al·ly** \-ē-ə-lē\ *adv*
bier \ˈbi(ə)r\ *n* : a stand on which a coffin is placed
[1]**bi·fo·cal** \(ˈ)bī-ˈfō-kəl\ *adj* : having two focal lengths
[2]**bifocal** *n* **1** : a bifocal glass or lens **2** *pl* : eyeglasses with bifocal lenses that correct for near vision and for distant vision
big \ˈbig\ *adj* **big·ger**; **big·gest** **1** : of great force ⟨a *big* voice⟩ **2** : large in size, bulk, or extent ⟨a *big* house⟩ ⟨*big* business⟩ **3** : PREGNANT **4** : IMPORTANT — **big** *adv* — **big·ness** *n*
big·a·my \ˈbig-ə-mē\ *n* : the act of marrying one person while still legally married to another — **big·a·mist** \-məst\ *n* — **big·a·mous** \-məs\ *adj* — **big·a·mous·ly** *adv*
big bang theory *n* : a theory that the universe as it is today is a result of a giant explosion of compressed matter
Big Dipper *n* : the larger of the stellar dippers
big·eye \ˈbig-ˌī\ *n* : either of two small widely distributed marine reddish to silvery food fishes related to the perches

ə abut	ər further	a back	ā bake
ä cot, cart	aù out	ch chin	e less	ē easy
g gift	i trip	ī life	j joke	ŋ sing	ō flow
ȯ flaw	ȯi coin	th thin	t͟h this	ü loot
u̇ foot	y yet	yü few	yu̇ furious	zh vision

big·horn \ˈbig-ˌhȯrn\ *n, pl* **bighorn** *or* **bighorns** : a usu. grayish brown wild sheep of mountainous western No. America

bighorn
(about 3½ ft. at shoulder)

bight \ˈbīt\ *n* **1 a** : the slack middle part of a rope when it is fastened at both ends **b** : a loop or double part of a bent rope **2** : a bend or curve esp. in a river **3** : a bend in a coast or the bay it forms
big·it \ˈbij-ət\ *n* : [3]BIT 2
big·ot \ˈbig-ət\ *n* : a person obstinately or intolerantly devoted to his own group, beliefs, or opinions
big·ot·ed \ˈbig-ət-əd\ *adj* : intolerant of the ideas and opinions of others
big·ot·ry \ˈbig-ə-trē\ *n, pl* **-ries** **1** : the state of mind of a bigot **2** : bigoted acts or beliefs
big toe *n* : the innermost and largest toe of the foot
big top *n* **1** : the main tent of a circus **2** : CIRCUS 2
big tree \-ˌtrē\ *n* : GIANT SEQUOIA
big·wig \ˈbig-ˌwig\ *n* : an important person
bike \ˈbīk\ *n or vb* : BICYCLE — **bik·er** *n*
bi·ki·ni \bə-ˈkē-nē\ *n* : a woman's abbreviated two-piece bathing suit
bi·lat·er·al \(ˈ)bī-ˈlat-ə-rəl, -ˈla-trəl\ *adj* : having or involving two sides or parties ⟨a *bilateral* treaty⟩ — **bi·lat·er·al·ly** \-ē\ *adv*
bilateral symmetry *n* : animal symmetry in which similar parts are arranged so that one and only one plane can divide the individual into essentially identical halves — compare RADIAL SYMMETRY
bil·ber·ry \ˈbil-ˌber-ē\ *n* : any of several blueberries with flowers and fruit borne in leaf axils; *also* : the sweet edible bluish fruit
bile \ˈbīl\ *n* **1** : a thick bitter yellow or greenish fluid that is secreted by the liver and aids in the digestion and absorption of fats **2** : ill humor : ANGER
bile duct *n* : a canal by which bile passes from the liver or gall bladder to the duodenum
[1]**bilge** \ˈbilj\ *n* **1** : the bulging part of a cask or barrel **2** : the part of a ship's hull between the bottom and the point where the sides begin to rise nearly vertically
[2]**bilge** *vb* : to undergo damage in the bilge
bilge water *n* : water that collects in the bilge of a ship
bil·i·ary \ˈbil-ē-ˌer-ē, ˈbil-yə-rē\ *adj* : of, relating to, or conveying bile
bi·lin·gual \(ˈ)bī-ˈliŋ-g(yə-)wəl\ *adj* : of, expressed in, or using two languages ⟨a *bilingual* dictionary⟩
bil·ious \ˈbil-yəs\ *adj* **1 a** : of or relating to bile **b** : marked by or suffering from disordered liver function **2** : ILL-NATURED, IRRITABLE — **bil·ious·ly** *adv* — **bil·ious·ness** *n*

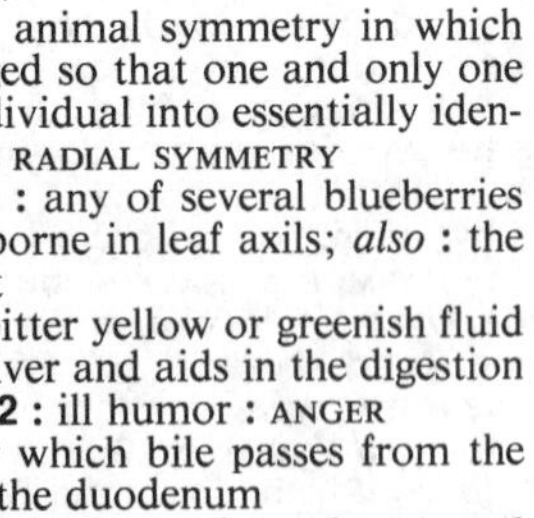
bill 1

[1]**bill** \ˈbil\ *n* **1** : the jaws of a bird together with their horny covering **2** : a mouth structure (as

the beak of a turtle) resembling a bird's bill **3** : the visor of a cap — **billed** \'bild\ *adj*

2**bill** *vb* **1** : to touch bills **2** : to caress affectionately ⟨lovers *billing* and cooing⟩

3**bill** *n* **1** : a draft of a law presented to a legislature for enactment **2** : a written declaration of a wrong one person has suffered from another or of a breach of law by some person **3** : an account of the cost of goods sold, services rendered, or work done : INVOICE **4 a** : an advertisement posted or distributed to announce an event (as a theatrical entertainment) **b** : an entertainment program or the entertainment presented on it **5** : NOTE 4a; *esp* : a piece of paper money

4**bill** *vb* **1 a** : to enter in a book of accounts : make a bill of ⟨*bill* the goods to my account⟩ **b** : to submit a bill to ⟨*bill* a customer for purchases⟩ **2** : to advertise esp. by posters — **bill·er** *n*

bill·board \'bil-ˌbōrd, -ˌbȯrd\ *n* : a flat surface on which bills are posted

1**bil·let** \'bil-ət\ *n* **1** : an official order directing that a soldier be lodged (as in a private home) **2** : quarters assigned by or as if by a billet **3** : BERTH, POSITION ⟨a soft *billet*⟩

2**billet** *vb* **1** : to assign lodging to : QUARTER **2** : to have quarters : LODGE

3**billet** *n* **1** : a chunky piece of wood (as for firewood) **2** : a bar of metal; *esp* : one of iron or steel

bil·let–doux \ˌbil-ā-'dü\ *n, pl* **bil·lets–doux** \-ā-'dü(z)\ : a love letter

bill·fold \'bil-ˌfōld\ *n* : a folding pocketbook for paper money

bil·liards \'bil-yərdz\ *n* : a game played on an oblong table by driving small balls against one another or into pockets with a cue — **billiard** *adj*

bil·lion \'bil-yən\ *n* **1** — see NUMBER table **2** : a very large number ⟨*billions* of dollars⟩ — **billion** *adj* — **bil·lionth** \-yən(t)th\ *adj or n*

bil·lion·aire \ˌbil-yə-'na(ə)r, -'ne(ə)r, 'bil-yə-ˌ\ *n* : one who is worth a billion dollars or more

bill of fare : MENU

bill of rights *often cap B&R* : a statement of fundamental rights and privileges guaranteed to a people; *esp* : the first 10 amendments to the U.S. Constitution

1**bil·low** \'bil-ō\ *n* **1** : WAVE; *esp* : a large wave **2** : a rolling mass like a high wave ⟨*billows* of smoke came pouring out of the burning building⟩

2**billow** *vb* **1** : to roll in waves ⟨the *billowing* ocean⟩ **2** : to bulge or swell out ⟨sails *billowing* in the breeze⟩ ⟨the wind *billowed* her skirt⟩

bil·lowy \'bil-ə-wē\ *adj* **bil·low·i·er**; **-est** : full of billows

bil·ly \'bil-ē\ *n, pl* **billies** : a heavy club; *esp* : a policeman's club

billy goat \'bil-ē-\ *n* : a male goat

bi·lobed \'bī-'lōbd\ *adj* : divided into two lobes

bi·met·al \'bī-ˌmet-əl\ *adj* : BIMETALLIC

bi·me·tal·lic \ˌbī-mə-'tal-ik\ *adj* : composed of two different metals — often used of devices having a part in which two metals that expand differently are bonded together

1**bi·month·ly** \(')bī-'mən(t)th-lē\ *adj* **1** : occurring every two months **2** : occurring twice a month : SEMIMONTHLY

2**bimonthly** *n* : a bimonthly publication

3**bimonthly** *adv* **1** : once every two months **2** : twice a month

bin \'bin\ *n* : a box or enclosed place for storage

bi·na·ry \'bī-nə-rē\ *adj* **1** : compounded or consisting of or characterized by two things or parts ⟨a *binary* mathematical operation⟩ **2** : relating to, being, or belonging to a system of numbers having two as its base ⟨*binary* digit⟩

binary fission *n* : reproduction of a cell by division into two approximately equal parts

binary star *n* : a system of two stars that revolve around each other under their mutual gravitation

bin·au·ral \(')bī-'nȯr-əl\ *adj* **1** : of, relating to, or used with two or both ears **2** : of, relating to, or characterized by the placement of sound sources (as in sound transmission and recording) to achieve in sound reproduction an effect of hearing the sound sources in their original positions — **bin·au·ral·ly** \-ə-lē\ *adv*

bind \'bīnd\ *vb* **bound** \'baủnd\; **bind·ing** **1 a** : to fasten by tying **b** : to confine, restrain, or restrict by force, obligation, or feeling ⟨*bound* by an oath⟩ ⟨*bound* by friendship⟩ **2** : BANDAGE **3** : to fasten together ⟨*bind* the stalks into sheaves⟩ **4 a** : to stick together **b** : to form a cohesive mass **c** : to take up and hold by chemical forces **5** : to make firm or sure ⟨a deposit *binds* the sale⟩ **6 a** : to protect or decorate by a band or binding **b** : to fasten the cover to ⟨*bind* a book⟩

bind·er \'bīn-dər\ *n* **1** : a person that binds something (as books) **2** : a cord or band used in binding **3** : a detachable cover for holding together sheets of paper **4** : a harvesting machine that cuts grain and ties it in bundles **5** : something (as tar or cement) that produces or promotes cohesion in loosely assembled substances

bind·ery \'bīn-d(ə-)rē\ *n, pl* **-er·ies** : a place where books are bound

bind·ing \'bīn-ding\ *n* **1** : the action of one that binds **2** : a material or device used to bind **3** : the cover and fastenings of a book **4** : a narrow fabric used to finish raw edges

binding energy *n* : the energy required to break up a molecule, atom, or atomic nucleus completely into its constituent particles

binding post *n* : a post attached to an electrical device for convenience in making connections

bind·weed \'bīnd-ˌwēd\ *n* : any of various twining plants related to the morning glory or to the buckwheat that mat or interlace with plants among which they grow

binge \'binj\ *n* : SPREE

bin·na·cle \'bin-i-kəl\ *n* : a box or stand containing a ship's compass and a lamp

1**bin·oc·u·lar** \bī-'näk-yə-lər, bə-\ *adj* : of, relating to, using, or adapted to the use of both eyes ⟨*binocular* microscope⟩ — **bin·oc·u·lar·ly** *adv*

2**bin·oc·u·lar** \bə-'näk-yə-lər, bī-\ *n* : a binocular optical instrument : FIELD GLASS — usu. used in pl. ⟨a pair of *binoculars*⟩

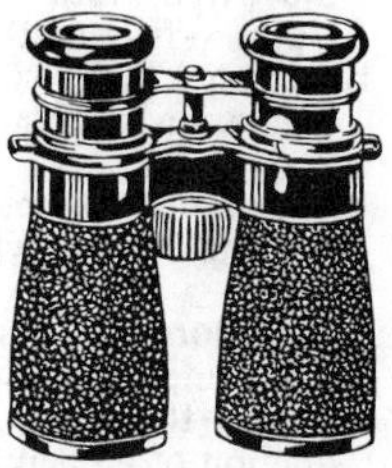
binoculars

bi·no·mi·al \bī-'nō-mē-əl\ *n* **1** : a mathematical expression consisting of two terms connected by a plus sign or minus sign **2** : a biological species name consisting of two terms — **binomial** *adj* — **bi·no·mi·al·ly** \-mē-ə-lē\ *adv*

binomial nomenclature *n* : a system of nomenclature in which each species of animal or plant receives a binomial name of which the first term identifies the genus to which it belongs and the second the species itself

bio- *comb form* **1** : life ⟨*bio*sphere⟩ **2** : living organisms or tissue ⟨*bio*luminescence⟩

B

biochem *abbr* biochemistry
bio·chem·is·try \ˌbī-ō-ˈkem-ə-strē\ *n* : chemistry that deals with the chemical compounds and processes occurring in organisms — **bio·chem·i·cal** \-ˈkem-i-kəl\ *adj* — **bio·chem·i·cal·ly** \-k(ə-)lē\ *adv* — **bio·chem·ist** \-ˈkem-əst\ *n*
bio·de·grad·a·ble \-di-ˈgrād-ə-bəl\ *adj* : capable of being broken down esp. into harmless products by the action of living things (as bacteria) ⟨*biodegradable* detergents⟩ — **bio·deg·ra·da·tion** \-ˌdeg-rə-ˈdā-shən\ *n* — **bio·de·grade** \-di-ˈgrād\ *vb*
bio·gen·e·sis \-ˈjen-ə-səs\ *n, pl* **-gen·e·ses** \-ˈjen-ə-ˌsēz\ **1** : the development of life from preexisting life **2** : a supposed tendency for stages in the evolutionary history of a kind of organism to briefly recur during the development from egg to adult of an individual — **bio·ge·net·ic** \-jə-ˈnet-ik\ *adj*
bio·ge·og·ra·phy \-jē-ˈäg-rə-fē\ *n* : a branch of biology that deals with the geographical distribution of animals and plants — **bio·ge·og·ra·pher** \-jē-ˈäg-rə-fər\ *n* — **bio·geo·graph·ic** \-ˌjē-ə-ˈgraf-ik\ *or* **bio·geo·graph·i·cal** \-ˈgraf-i-kəl\ *adj*
bi·og·ra·phy \bī-ˈäg-rə-fē, bē-\ *n, pl* **-phies** **1** : a history of a person's life **2** : biographical writings — **bi·og·ra·pher** \-fər\ *n* — **bio·graph·i·cal** \ˌbī-ə-ˈgraf-i-kəl\ *or* **bio·graph·ic** \-ik\ *adj* — **bio·graph·i·cal·ly** \-i-k(ə-)lē\ *adv*
biol *abbr* **1** biologic **2** biological **3** biology
¹**bi·o·log·i·cal** \ˌbī-ə-ˈläj-i-kəl\ *or* **bi·o·log·ic** \-ˈläj-ik\ *adj* : of or relating to biology or to life and living processes ⟨*biological* supplies⟩ — **bi·o·log·i·cal·ly** \-ˈläj-i-k(ə-)lē\ *adv*
²**biological** *or* **biologic** *n* : a medicinal product of biological origin
biological control *n* : attack upon pests (as vermin) by interference with their ecology without introducing artificial agents (as insecticides) into the environment
biological warfare *n* : warfare in which living organisms (as disease germs) are used to harm the enemy or his livestock and crops
bi·ol·o·gy \bī-ˈäl-ə-jē\ *n* [from German *biologie*, from Greek *bios* "life" and *-logia* "-logy"] **1** : a branch of knowledge that deals with living organisms and life processes **2 a** : the plant and animal life of a region or environment **b** : the laws and phenomena relating to an organism or group — **bi·ol·o·gist** \-jəst\ *n*
bi·ome \ˈbī-ˌōm\ *n* : a major ecological community type ⟨the grassland *biome*⟩
bio·phys·ics \ˈbī-ō-ˌfiz-iks\ *n* : a branch of knowledge concerned with the application of physical principles and methods to biological problems — **bio·phys·i·cal** \ˌbī-ō-ˈfiz-i-kəl\ *adj* — **bio·phys·i·cist** \-ˈfiz-ə-səst\ *n*
bi·op·sy \ˈbī-ˌäp-sē\ *n, pl* **-sies** : the removal and examination of tissue, cells, or fluids from the living body
bio·sat·el·lite \ˈbī-ō-ˌsat-ə-ˌlīt\ *n* : an artificial space satellite for carrying a living human, animal, or plant
bio·sphere \ˈbī-ə-ˌsfi(ə)r\ *n* : the part of the world in which life can exist
bio·syn·the·sis \ˌbī-ō-ˈsin(t)-thə-səs\ *n* : the production of a chemical compound by a living organism — **bio·syn·thet·ic** \-sin-ˈthet-ik\ *adj*
bi·o·ta \bī-ˈōt-ə\ *n* : the flora and fauna of a region
bi·ot·ic \bī-ˈät-ik\ *adj* : of or relating to life; *esp* : caused by living beings
bi·o·tin \ˈbī-ə-tən\ *n* : a colorless crystalline growth vitamin of the vitamin B complex found esp. in yeast, liver, and egg yolk
bi·o·tite \ˈbī-ə-ˌtīt\ *n* : a generally black or dark green mica containing iron, magnesium, potassium, and aluminum
bi·pa·ren·tal \ˌbī-pə-ˈrent-əl\ *adj* : involving or derived from two parents ⟨*biparental* reproduction⟩ ⟨*biparental* inheritance⟩
bi·par·ti·san \(ˈ)bī-ˈpärt-ə-zən\ *adj* : representing, composed of, or formulated by members of two parties ⟨a *bipartisan* foreign policy⟩ ⟨the bill received *bipartisan* support⟩
bi·par·tite \(ˈ)bī-ˈpär-ˌtīt\ *adj* **1** : being in two parts **2** : shared by two ⟨*bipartite* treaty⟩
bi·ped \ˈbī-ˌped\ *n* : a 2-footed animal — **biped** *or* **bi·ped·al** \(ˈ)bī-ˈped-əl\ *adj*
bi·plane \ˈbī-ˌplān\ *n* : an airplane with two wings usu. placed one above the other
bi·ra·di·al \(ˈ)bī-ˈrād-ē-əl\ *adj* : having both bilateral and radial symmetry — **bi·ra·di·al·ly** \-ē-ə-lē\ *adv*
bi·ra·mous \(ˈ)bī-ˈrā-məs\ *adj* : having two branches
¹**birch** \ˈbərch\ *n* **1** : any of a genus of deciduous usu. short-lived trees or shrubs with typically an outer bark that peels readily in thin layers; *also* : its hard pale close-grained wood **2** : a birch rod or bundle of twigs for flogging — **birch** *or* **birch·en** \ˈbər-chən\ *adj*
²**birch** *vb* : to whip with or as if with a birch
¹**bird** \ˈbərd\ *n* **1** : any of a class of warm-blooded egg-laying vertebrate animals with the body covered with feathers and the forelimbs modified as wings **2** *slang* : FELLOW; *esp* : a peculiar person **3** *slang* : GIRL
²**bird** *vb* : to observe or identify wild birds in their natural environment — **bird·er** *n*
bird·bath \ˈbərd-ˌbath, -ˌbȧth\ *n* : a basin set up for birds to bathe in
bird dog *n* : a dog that has been trained to hunt or retrieve birds
bird·house \ˈbərd-ˌhau̇s\ *n* : an artificial nesting place for birds; *also* : AVIARY
bird·lime \ˈbərd-ˌlīm\ *n* : a sticky substance smeared on twigs to catch and hold small birds
bird louse *n* : any of numerous wingless insects that are mostly parasitic on birds
bird·man \ˈbərd-mən\ *n* **1** : one who deals with birds **2** : AVIATOR
bird of paradise : any of numerous brilliantly colored plumed birds related to the crows and found in the New Guinea area
bird of passage : a migratory bird
bird of prey : a carnivorous bird that feeds wholly or chiefly on meat taken by hunting
bird·seed \ˈbərd-ˌsēd\ *n* : a mixture of small seeds (as of hemp or millet) used chiefly for feeding cage birds
bird's-eye \ˈbərd-ˌzī\ *adj* **1 a** : seen from above as if by a flying bird ⟨*bird's-eye* view⟩ **b** : CURSORY **2** : having spots resembling birds' eyes ⟨*bird's-eye* maple⟩; *also* : made of bird's-eye wood
bird's-foot trefoil \ˌbərdz-ˌfu̇t-\ *n* : a European legume with claw-shaped pods and yellow flowers that is widely used as a forage and fodder plant
bird watcher *n* : an observer of wild birds in their natural surroundings
bi·reme \ˈbī-ˌrēm\ *n* : a galley having two banks of oars

bi·ret·ta \bə-'ret-ə\ *n* : a square cap with three upright projecting pieces worn by Roman Catholic clergymen

biretta

birth \'bərth\ *n* **1 a** : the emergence of a new individual from the body of its parent **b** : the act or process of bringing forth young from the womb **2** : LINEAGE, DESCENT ⟨a man of noble *birth*⟩ **3** : BEGINNING, ORIGIN ⟨*birth* of an idea⟩

birth canal *n* : the channel formed by the cervix, vagina, and vulva through which the mammalian fetus is expelled

birth·day \'bərth-,dā\ *n* **1** : the day or anniversary of one's birth **2** : the day or anniversary of a beginning

birth·mark \-,märk\ *n* : an unusual mark or blemish on the skin at birth — **birthmark** *vb*

birth·place \-,plās\ *n* : place of birth or origin

birth·rate \-,rāt\ *n* : the number of births for every hundred or every thousand persons in a given area or group during a given time

birth·right \-,rīt\ *n* : a right or possession to which a person is entitled by birth

birth·stone \-,stōn\ *n* : a precious stone associated symbolically with the month of one's birth

bis·cuit \'bis-kət\ *n, pl* **biscuits** *also* **biscuit** [from medieval French *bescuit*, from an adjective meaning "twice cooked"] **1** : a crisp flat cake; *esp, Brit* : CRACKER 2 **2** : a small quick bread made from dough that has been rolled and cut or dropped from a spoon

bi·sect \'bī-,sekt, bī-'\ *vb* **1** : to divide into two usu. equal parts **2** : CROSS, INTERSECT **3** : FORK, DIVIDE

bi·sec·tor \'bī-,sek-tər, bī-'\ *n* : one that bisects; *esp* : a straight line that bisects an angle or a line segment

bi·sex·u·al \(')bī-'sek-sh(ə-w)əl\ *adj* **1** : possessing characters of or having sexual desire for both sexes **2** : of, relating to, or involving two sexes — **bisexual** *n* — **bi·sex·u·al·i·ty** \,bī-,sek-shə-'wal-ət-ē\ *n*

bish·op \'bish-əp\ *n* [from Old English *biscop*, from Greek *episkopos*, meaning literally "overseer", from *epi-* and *-skopos*, a combining form meaning "one that sees" found also in English *telescope* & *microscope*] **1** : a clergyman of high rank typically governing a diocese **2** : one of the pieces in chess

bish·op·ric \'bish-ə-(,)prik\ *n* **1** : DIOCESE **2** : the office of bishop

bis·muth \'biz-məth\ *n* : a heavy brittle grayish white metallic element that is chemically like arsenic and antimony and is used in alloys and medicine — see ELEMENT table

bi·son \'bī-sən, -zən\ *n, pl* **bison** : any of several large shaggy-maned mammals with a large head, short horns, and a large fleshy hump on the heavy forequarters; *esp* : BUFFALO b

bison
(about 6 ft. at shoulder)

bisque \'bisk\ *n* : a thick cream soup made of shellfish, meat, or vegetables

bi·sul·fide \(')bī-'səl-,fīd\ *n* : DISULFIDE

1**bit** \'bit\ *n* **1** : the part of a bridle inserted in the mouth of a horse **2** : the biting or cutting edge or part of a tool **3** : something that restrains

2**bit** *n* **1** : a small piece or amount **2** : a short time : WHILE ⟨rest a *bit*⟩ **3** : SOMEWHAT ⟨a *bit* of a fool⟩

3**bit** *n* **1** : a unit of information equivalent to the result of a choice between two alternatives (as *yes* or *no*, *on* or *off*) **2** : the physical representation of a bit (as a punched hole whose presence or absence in a card or tape indicates data)

bitch \'bich\ *n* : a female dog

1**bite** \'bīt\ *vb* **bit** \'bit\; **bit·ten** \'bit-ən\; **bit·ing** \'bīt-ing\ **1** : to seize, grip, or cut into with or as if with teeth ⟨*bite* an apple⟩ **2** : to wound or pierce with or as if with fangs ⟨*bitten* by a snake⟩ **3** : CUT, PIERCE ⟨the sword *bit* into his arm⟩ **4** : to cause to smart : STING ⟨pepper *bites* the mouth⟩ **5** : to eat into : CORRODE ⟨acid *bites* metal⟩ **6** : to respond to a lure : take a bait ⟨the fish are *biting*⟩ — **bite the dust** : to fall dead esp. in battle

2**bite** *n* **1 a** : a seizing of something by biting **b** : the grip taken in biting **2 a** : the amount of food taken at a bite **b** : a light informal meal : SNACK **3** : a wound made by biting **4** : a sharp penetrating quality or effect

bit·ing \'bīt-ing\ *adj* : SHARP, CUTTING

bit·ter \'bit-ər\ *adj* **1** : having or being a disagreeable acrid taste that is one of the four basic taste sensations ⟨*bitter* as quinine⟩ **2** : hard to bear : PAINFUL ⟨*bitter* disappointment⟩ **3** : sharp and resentful ⟨a *bitter* reply⟩ **4** : unpleasantly cold ⟨a *bitter* wind⟩ — **bit·ter·ly** \-ər-lē\ *adv* — **bit·ter·ness** *n*

bit·tern \'bit-ərn\ *n* : any of various small or medium-sized nocturnal herons with a characteristic booming cry

1**bit·ter·sweet** \'bit-ər-,swēt\ *n* **1** : a sprawling poisonous weedy nightshade with purple flowers and oval reddish orange berries **2** : a No. American woody climbing plant with yellow seedcases that open when ripe and show the scarlet seed covers

2**bittersweet** *adj* : being both bitter and sweet

bi·tu·men \bə-'t(y)ü-mən, bī-\ *n* : any of various mixtures of hydrocarbons (as asphalt, crude petroleum, or tar)

bi·tu·mi·nous \-mə-nəs\ *adj* **1** : resembling, containing, or impregnated with bitumen **2** : of or relating to bituminous coal

bituminous coal *n* : a coal that when heated yields considerable volatile matter — called also *soft coal*

1**bi·valve** \'bī-,valv\ *also* **bi·valved** \-,valvd\ *adj* **1** : having a shell composed of two movable valves **2** : having or consisting of two corresponding movable pieces

2**bivalve** *n* : an animal (as a clam) with a bivalve shell

biv·ouac \'biv-,wak, -ə-,wak\ *n* : a temporary encampment — **bivouac** *vb*

1**bi·week·ly** \(')bī-'wē-klē\ *adj* **1** : occurring, done, or produced every two weeks **2** : occurring, done, or produced twice a week — **biweekly** *adv*

2**biweekly** *n* : a biweekly publication

bi·year·ly \(')bī-'yi(ə)r-lē\ *adj* **1** : BIENNIAL **2** : BIANNUAL

bi·zarre \bə-'zär\ *adj* : strikingly unusual or odd esp. in fashion, design, or color ⟨*bizarre* costumes of gypsies⟩ — **bi·zarre·ly** *adv* — **bi·zarre·ness** *n*

bk *abbr* **1** bank **2** book

bkt *abbr* basket

BL *abbr* bats left

1**blab** \'blab\ *n* **1** : TATTLETALE **2** : CHATTER — **blabby** \'blab-ē\ *adj*

2**blab** *vb* **blabbed**; **blab·bing** **1** : to reveal by careless talk ⟨*blab* a secret⟩ **2** : PRATTLE — **blab·ber** *n*

blab·ber·mouth \'blab-ər-,maůth\ *n* : TATTLETALE

1**black** \'blak\ *adj* **1 a** : of the color black **b** : very dark **2 a** : having dark skin, hair, and eyes : SWARTHY **b** : NEGRO **3 a** : EVIL, WICKED ⟨a *black* deed⟩ **b** : GLOOMY, THREATENING ⟨the outlook was *black*⟩ **c** : SULLEN, HOSTILE — **black·ish** \-ish\ *adj* — **black·ly** *adv* — **black·ness** *n*

2**black** *n* **1** : a black pigment or dye; *esp* : one consisting largely of carbon **2** : the characteristic color of soot or coal **3** : black clothing ⟨dressed in *black*⟩ **4** : a person belonging to a dark-skinned race; *esp* : NEGRO **5** : absence of light : DARKNESS ⟨the *black* of night⟩ **6** : the condition of making a profit ⟨in the *black*⟩

3**black** *vb* : BLACKEN

black·a·moor \'blak-ə-ˌmu̇(ə)r\ *n* : a dark-skinned person; *esp* : NEGRO

black–and–blue \ˌblak-ən-'blü\ *adj* : darkly discolored (as from a bruise)

black art *n* : WITCHCRAFT

1**black·ball** \'blak-ˌbȯl\ *n* **1** : a small black ball used to cast a negative vote **2** : a negative vote

2**blackball** *vb* : to vote against; *esp* : to exclude from membership by casting a negative vote

black bass *n* : any of several highly prized freshwater sunfishes native to eastern and central No. America

black bear *n* : the usu. largely black-furred bear found in most of the less densely populated parts of No. America south of the tundra

black·ber·ry \'blak-ˌber-ē\ *n* **1** : the usu. black or dark purple juicy but seedy edible fruit of various brambles **2** : a plant that bears blackberries

black·bird \'blak-ˌbərd\ *n* : any of various birds of which the males are largely or entirely black: as **a** : a common and familiar British thrush **b** : any of several American birds (as a grackle or red-winged blackbird) related to the bobolink

black·board \'blak-ˌbōrd, -ˌbȯrd\ *n* : a hard smooth surface used for writing or drawing on with chalk or crayons

black·body \'blak-'bäd-ē\ *n* : a body or surface that completely absorbs all radiant energy falling upon it with no reflection

black book *n* : a book containing a blacklist

black·cap \'blak-ˌkap\ *n* **1** : any of several black-crowned birds (as the chickadee) **2** : a black-fruited raspberry of eastern No. America

black crappie *n* : a silvery black-mottled sunfish of the central and eastern U.S.

black death *n* : a form of epidemic plague present in Europe and Asia in the 14th century

black diamond *n* : CARBONADO

black·en \'blak-ən\ *vb* **black·ened**; **black·en·ing** \'blak-(ə-)ning\ **1** : to make or become black **2** : SOIL, DIRTY **3** : to injure the reputation of : DEFAME — **black·en·er** \-(ə-)nər\ *n*

black–eyed pea \ˌblak-ˌīd-\ *n* : COWPEA

black–eyed Su·san \-'sü-zən\ *n* : an American daisy with deep yellow or orange petals and a dark center

black-eyed Susan

black·fish \'blak-ˌfish\ *n* **1** : any of numerous dark-colored fishes; *esp* : a small food fish of Alaska and Siberia **2** : any of several small toothed whales related to the dolphins

black flag *n* : JOLLY ROGER

black·fly \'blak-ˌflī\ *n* : any of several small dark-colored insects; *esp* : a two-winged biting fly whose larvae live in flowing streams

Black·foot \-ˌfu̇t\ *n, pl* **Black·feet** \-ˌfēt\ *or* **Blackfoot** : a member of a people belonging to an Amerindian confederacy of Montana, Alberta, and Saskatchewan

1**black·guard** \'blag-ərd, -ˌärd; 'blak-ˌgärd\ *n* : a rude or unscrupulous person — **black·guard·ly** \-lē\ *adj or adv*

2**blackguard** *vb* : to abuse with bad language : REVILE, SCOLD

black gum *n* : an important timber tree of the southeastern U.S. with light and soft but tough wood

black·head \'blak-ˌhed\ *n* : a small oily plug blocking the duct of a fat-secreting gland in the skin

black·ing \'blak-ing\ *n* : a substance that makes things black; *esp* : a paste or liquid used in shining black shoes

black·jack \'blak-ˌjak\ *n* **1** : a small leather-covered club with a flexible handle **2** : a common often scrubby oak of the southern U.S. with black bark

black lead \-'led\ *n* : GRAPHITE

black light *n* : invisible ultraviolet or infrared light

black·list \'blak-ˌlist\ *n* : a list of persons who are disapproved of and are to be punished (as by refusal of jobs) — **blacklist** *vb*

black magic *n* : WITCHCRAFT

black·mail \'blak-ˌmāl\ *n* **1** : extortion of money from a person by a threat to reveal information that will disgrace him **2** : money got by blackmail — **blackmail** *vb* — **black·mail·er** *n*

black mark *n* : a mark placed beside a person's name to record a fault

black market *n* **1** : trade in violation of government controls (as price controls, rationing regulations, or official currency exchange rates) **2** : illegal trade in government property — **black mar·ket·er** \-'mär-kət-ər\ *or* **black mar·ke·teer** \-ˌmär-kə-'ti(ə)r\ *n*

black mica *n* : BIOTITE

Black Muslim *n* : a member of a black group that professes Islamic religious belief and advocates a separate black community

black oak *n* : a large timber tree of the central and eastern U.S. with a yellow inner bark used for tanning; *also* : any of several other American oaks

black·out \'blak-ˌau̇t\ *n* **1** : a period of darkness enforced as a precaution against air raids in wartime **2** : a temporary dulling or loss of vision or consciousness — **black out** \-'au̇t\ *vb*

black pepper *n* : a condiment prepared by grinding the fruit of the East Indian pepper with the black husk still on

black plague *n* : BUBONIC PLAGUE

black power *n* : the use of the political and economic power of American Negroes esp. to further racial equality

black·smith \'blak-ˌsmith\ *n* : a workman who shapes iron by heating it and then hammering it on an iron block — **black·smith·ing** *n*

black·snake \-ˌsnāk\ *n* **1** : any of several snakes largely black or dark in color; *esp* : either of two large harmless snakes of the U.S. **2** : a long braided whip of rawhide or leather

black·tail \-ˌtāl\ *n* : a deer of British Columbia, Oregon, and Washington — called also *black-tailed deer* \ˌblak-ˌtāld-\

black·thorn \'blak-ˌthȯrn\ *n* **1** : a European spiny plum with hard wood and small white flowers **2** : any of several American hawthorns

ə abut	ər further	a back	ā bake	
ä cot, cart	au̇ out	ch chin	e less	ē easy
g gift	i trip	ī life	j joke	ng sing	ō flow
ȯ flaw	ȯi coin	th thin	t͟h this	ü loot
u̇ foot	y yet	yü few	yu̇ furious	zh vision

black·top \-ˌtäp\ *n* : a bituminous material used esp. for surfacing roads — **blacktop** *vb*
black walnut *n* : a walnut of eastern No. America with hard strong heavy dark brown wood and oily edible nuts; *also* : its wood or nut
black widow *n* : a poisonous New World spider having the female black with an hourglass-shaped red mark on the underside of the abdomen
blad·der \'blad-ər\ *n* **1** : a membranous sac in an animal in which a liquid or gas is stored; *esp* : one in a vertebrate into which urine passes from the kidneys **2** : something resembling a bladder; *esp* : an inflatable bag or container — **blad·der·like** \-ˌlīk\ *adj*
blad·der·wort \-ˌwərt, -ˌwȯrt\ *n* : any of several slender plants growing in water or on wet shores and having insect-catching bladders on the stem, scalelike leaves, and irregular yellow or purple flowers
blade \'blād\ *n* **1 a** : a leaf of a plant and esp. of a grass **b** : the broad flat part of a leaf as distinguished from its stalk **2 a** : the broad flattened part of a paddle **b** : an arm of a propeller, electric fan, or steam turbine **3 a** : the cutting part of an implement **b** : SWORD **c** : the runner of an ice skate **4** : a jaunty dashing fellow ⟨a gay *blade*⟩ — **blad·ed** \'blād-əd\ *adj*
blain \'blān\ *n* : an inflammatory swelling or sore
¹**blame** \'blām\ *vb* **1** : to find fault with : CENSURE **2 a** : to hold responsible ⟨*blame* him for everything⟩ **b** : to place responsibility for ⟨*blames* it on me⟩ — **blam·a·ble** \'blā-mə-bəl\ *adj* — **blam·a·bly** \-ə-blē\ *adv* — **blam·er** *n*
²**blame** *n* **1** : expression of disapproval ⟨receive both *blame* and praise⟩ **2** : responsibility for something that fails : FAULT ⟨take the *blame* for the defeat⟩
blame·less \'blām-ləs\ *adj* : free from blame or fault — **blame·less·ly** *adv* — **blame·less·ness** *n*
blame·wor·thy \'blām-ˌwər-t͟hē\ *adj* : deserving blame — **blame·wor·thi·ness** *n*
blanch \'blanch\ *vb* **1 a** : to take the color out of : BLEACH **b** : to scald in order to remove the skin from or whiten ⟨*blanch* almonds⟩ **2** : to become white or pale — **blanch·er** *n*
bland \'bland\ *adj* **1** : smooth and soothing in manner : GENTLE ⟨a *bland* smile⟩ **2** : having soft and soothing qualities : not irritating ⟨*bland* diet⟩ — **bland·ly** *adv* — **bland·ness** \'blan(d)-nəs\ *n*
blan·dish \'blan-dish\ *vb* : to coax with flattery : CAJOLE — **blan·dish·ment** \-mənt\ *n*
¹**blank** \'blangk\ *adj* [from French *blanc* "white"] **1** : being without writing, printing, or marks ⟨*blank* sheet of paper⟩ **2** : having empty spaces to be filled in ⟨a *blank* form⟩ **3** : EXPRESSIONLESS ⟨a *blank* look⟩ **4** : lacking variety, change, or accomplishment : EMPTY ⟨a *blank* day⟩ **5** : ABSOLUTE, UNQUALIFIED ⟨*blank* refusal⟩ **6** : not shaped into finished form ⟨a *blank* key⟩ — **blank·ly** *adv* — **blank·ness** *n*
²**blank** *n* **1 a** : an empty space (as on a paper) or period **b** : a paper with spaces for the entry of data **2** : a piece of material prepared to be made into something (as a key) **3** : a cartridge loaded with powder but no bullet
³**blank** *vb* : to keep from scoring
¹**blan·ket** \'blang-kət\ *n* **1** : a heavy woven often woolen covering used for beds **2** : a covering of any kind ⟨a horse *blanket*⟩ ⟨a *blanket* of snow⟩
²**blanket** *vb* : to cover with or as if with a blanket
³**blanket** *adj* : covering all instances or members of a group or class ⟨*blanket* approval⟩
blank verse *n* : unrhymed verse; *esp* : unrhymed iambic pentameter verse
¹**blare** \'bla(ə)r, 'ble(ə)r\ *vb* **1** : to sound loud and harsh **2** : to utter or proclaim in a harsh noisy manner ⟨loudspeakers *blaring* advertisements⟩
²**blare** *n* : a loud strident noise ⟨the *blare* of trumpets⟩
blar·ney \'blär-nē\ *n* [from the *Blarney* stone, a stone in the wall of Blarney Castle, Ireland, believed to bestow skill in flattery on those who kiss it] : skillful flattery : BLANDISHMENT — **blarney** *vb*
blas·pheme \blas-'fēm, 'blas-ˌ\ *vb* **1** : to speak of or address with irreverence **2** : to utter blasphemy **3** : CURSE, SWEAR — **blas·phem·er** *n*
blas·phe·my \'blas-fə-mē\ *n, pl* **-mies** : great disrespect shown to God or to sacred persons or things — **blas·phe·mous** \-məs\ *adj* — **blas·phe·mous·ly** *adv* — **blas·phe·mous·ness** *n*
¹**blast** \'blast\ *n* **1** : a strong gust of wind **2** : a current of air or gas forced through an opening **3** : the blowing that a charge of ore or metal receives in a blast furnace **4** : the sound made by a wind instrument (as a horn) or by a whistle **5 a** : EXPLOSION **b** : an explosive charge for shattering rock **c** : the sudden air pressure produced in the vicinity of an explosion **6** : a sudden harmful effect from or as if from a hot wind; *esp* : a withering blight of plants
²**blast** *vb* **1** : to produce a strident sound **2** : to use an explosive **3** : to injure by or as if by the action of wind : BLIGHT **4** : to shatter by or as if by an explosive — **blast·er** *n*
blast furnace *n* : a furnace in which combustion is forced by a current of air under pressure; *esp* : one for the reduction of iron ore
blast off \'blas-'tȯf\ *vb* : to take off — used of rocket-propelled missiles and vehicles — **blast–off** \-ˌtȯf\ *n*
blas·tu·la \'blas-chə-lə\ *n, pl* **-las** \-ləz\ *or* **-lae** \-ˌlē, -ˌlī\ : an early embryo typically having the form of a hollow fluid-filled rounded cavity bounded by a single layer of cells — compare GASTRULA
bla·tant \'blāt-ənt\ *adj* **1** : NOISY, CLAMOROUS **2** : BRAZEN — **bla·tan·cy** \-ən-sē\ *n* — **bla·tant·ly** *adv*
¹**blaze** \'blāz\ *n* **1** : an intense burning fire **2** : intense direct light accompanied by heat **3** : a sudden outburst (as of flame) **4** : a dazzling display
²**blaze** *vb* **1 a** : to burn brightly **b** : to flare up : FLAME **2** : to be conspicuously brilliant **3** : to shoot rapidly and repeatedly ⟨*blaze* away⟩
³**blaze** *vb* : to make public : PROCLAIM ⟨*blaze* the news abroad⟩
⁴**blaze** *n* **1** : a white mark usu. running lengthwise on the face of an animal **2** : a mark made on a tree by chipping off a piece of the bark usu. to leave a trail
⁵**blaze** *vb* : to mark with blazes ⟨*blaze* a trail⟩
blaz·er \'blā-zər\ *n* : a sports jacket in bright stripes or solid color
bldg *abbr* building
¹**bleach** \'blēch\ *vb* **1** : to remove color or stains from **2** : to make whiter or lighter **3** : to grow white : lose color
²**bleach** *n* **1** : the act or process of bleaching **2** : a chemical used in bleaching
bleach·er \'blē-chər\ *n* : a usu. uncovered stand of tiered benches for spectators — usu. used in pl.
bleak \'blēk\ *adj* **1** : exposed to wind or weather ⟨a *bleak* coast⟩ **2** : DREARY, CHEERLESS **3** : COLD, RAW **4** : severely simple — **bleak·ly** *adv* — **bleak·ness** *n*
¹**blear** \'bli(ə)r\ *vb* **1** : to make (the eyes) sore or watery **2** : DIM, BLUR ⟨*bleared* sight⟩
²**blear** *adj* **1** : dim with water or tears **2** : DULL, DIM — **blear–eyed** \-'īd\ *adj* — **bleary** \'bli(ə)r-ē\ *adj*

B

bleat \'blēt\ *vb* **1** : to utter the natural cry of a sheep or goat **2** : to utter in a bleating manner — **bleat** *n*
bleed \'blēd\ *vb* **bled** \'bled\; **bleed·ing** **1** : to lose or shed blood ⟨a cut finger *bleeds*⟩ **2** : to be wounded ⟨*bleed* for one's country⟩ **3** : to feel pain or deep sympathy ⟨my heart *bleeds* for him⟩ **4** : to run out from a wounded surface **5 a** : to draw liquid from ⟨*bleed* a patient⟩ ⟨*bleed* a carburetor⟩ **b** : to diffuse or run when wetted ⟨dyes that *bleed*⟩ **6** : to extort money from
bleed·er \'blēd-ər\ *n* : one that bleeds; *esp* : HEMOPHILIAC
bleeding heart *n* : a garden plant related to the poppies and having drooping spikes of deep pink heart-shaped flowers
blem·ish \'blem-ish\ *n* : a mark that makes something imperfect — **blemish** *vb*
syn BLEMISH, DEFECT, FLAW can mean an imperfection that mars something. BLEMISH applies to something (as a spot or stain) that takes away from a thing's appearance; DEFECT implies an often hidden lack of something (as a functioning part) essential to completeness or wholeness ⟨a mechanical *defect*⟩; FLAW suggests a crack, nick, or break in smoothness or a weak spot that goes with these
¹**blench** \'blench\ *vb* : FLINCH
²**blench** *vb* : BLANCH
¹**blend** \'blend\ *vb* **1** : to mix thoroughly so that the things mixed cannot be distinguished **2** : to shade into each other : MERGE **3** : HARMONIZE ⟨furniture that *blends* with the draperies⟩ *syn* see MINGLE — **blend·er** *n*
²**blend** *n* **1** : a thorough mixture **2** : a product (as coffee) prepared by blending
blending inheritance *n* : inheritance of a character (as flower color in the four-o'clock) that in the hybrid genetic state is expressed as intermediate between the two pure strains
bless \'bles\ *vb* **blessed** \'blest\ *also* **blest** \'blest\; **bless·ing** [from Old English *blētsian*, derived from *blōd* "blood", and meaning originally "to sprinkle with the blood (of a sacrificial animal)"] **1** : to make holy : HALLOW **2** : to make the sign of the cross upon or over **3** : to invoke divine care or protection for **4** : PRAISE, GLORIFY **5** : to make prosperous or happy
blessed \'bles-əd, 'blest\ *or* **blest** \'blest\ *adj* **1** : HOLY ⟨the *blessed* Trinity⟩ **2** : enjoying happiness — **bless·ed·ly** \'bles-əd-lē\ *adv* — **bless·ed·ness** \'bles-əd-nəs\ *n*
bless·ing \'bles-ing\ *n* **1** : the act of one that blesses **2** : APPROVAL **3** : something that makes one happy or content **4** : grace said at a meal
blew *past of* BLOW
¹**blight** \'blīt\ *n* **1 a** : a disease of plants resulting in withering and death without rotting **b** : an organism that causes blight **2 a** : something that impairs or destroys **b** : an impaired or deteriorated condition
²**blight** *vb* **1** : to affect with blight **2** : to cause to deteriorate ⟨slums and *blighted* areas⟩ **3** : to suffer from or become affected with blight
blimp \'blimp\ *n* : a small cigar-shaped airship
¹**blind** \'blīnd\ *adj* **1 a** : SIGHTLESS **b** : having less than 1⁄10 normal vision in the best eye even with the aid of glasses **2** : lacking in judgment or understanding **3 a** : closed at one end ⟨a *blind* street⟩ **b** : having no opening ⟨a *blind* wall⟩ **4** : performed solely by the aid of instruments within an airplane ⟨a *blind* landing⟩ — **blind·ly** *adv* — **blind·ness** \'blīn(d)-nəs\ *n*
²**blind** *vb* **1** : to make blind **2** : to make temporarily blind : DAZZLE ⟨*blinded* by oncoming headlights⟩ **3** : to deprive of judgment or understanding ⟨love may *blind* parents to a child's faults⟩
³**blind** *n* **1** : a device (as a window shade) to hinder sight or keep out light **2** : a place of concealment esp. for hunters
⁴**blind** *adv* **1** : BLINDLY **2** : without seeing outside of an airplane ⟨fly *blind* with the aid of instruments⟩
blind·er \'blīn-dər\ *n* : either of two flaps on a horse's bridle to prevent sight of objects at his sides
¹**blind·fold** \'blīn(d)-ˌfōld\ *vb* : to cover the eyes of with or as if with a bandage — **blindfold** *adj*
²**blindfold** *n* : a bandage for covering the eyes
blind·man's buff \ˌblīn(d)-ˌmanz-'bəf\ *n* : a game in which a blindfolded player tries to catch and identify another
blind spot *n* **1 a** : a point in the retina through which the optic nerve enters and which is insensitive to light **b** : a portion of an area that cannot be seen with available equipment **2** : an area of weakness (as in judgment) **3** : a locality in which radio reception is poor
blind·worm \'blīnd-ˌwərm\ *n* : a small burrowing limbless lizard with minute eyes
¹**blink** \'blingk\ *vb* **1** : to look with half-shut winking eyes **2** : to wink quickly ⟨*blink* back tears⟩ **3** : to shine with a light that goes or seems to go on and off ⟨street lights *blinking* through rain⟩ **4** : to shut one's eyes to : IGNORE ⟨*blink* the facts⟩
²**blink** *n* **1** : GLIMMER, SPARKLE **2** : a shutting and opening of the eye : WINK — **on the blink** : not functioning properly : DISABLED
blink·er \'bling-kər\ *n* : one that blinks; *esp* : a blinking light used as a warning or for signaling
blip \'blip\ *n* : an image on a radar screen
bliss \'blis\ *n* : great happiness : JOY — **bliss·ful** \-fəl\ *adj* — **bliss·ful·ly** \-fə-lē\ *adv* — **bliss·ful·ness** *n*
¹**blis·ter** \'blis-tər\ *n* **1** : a raised area of the outer skin containing watery liquid **2** : a raised spot (as in paint) resembling a blister **3** : an agent that causes blistering **4** : any of various rounded bulging structures (as a gunner's compartment on an airplane) — **blis·tery** \-t(ə-)rē\ *adj*
²**blister** *vb* **blis·tered**; **blis·ter·ing** \-t(ə-)ring\ **1** : to develop a blister : rise in blisters **2** : to raise a blister on
blister beetle *n* : any of a family of soft-bodied beetles including some whose dried bodies are used medicinally to blister the skin
blister rust *n* : any of several diseases of pines caused by rust fungi and marked by external blisters
blithe \'blīth, 'blī<u>th</u>\ *adj* **1** : of a happy lighthearted character or disposition **2** : HEEDLESS — **blithe·ly** *adv*
blithe·some \'blīth-səm, 'blī<u>th</u>-\ *adj* : GAY, MERRY — **blithe·some·ly** *adv*
blitz \'blits\ *n* **1 a** : an intensive series of air raids **b** : AIR RAID **2** : a fast intensive campaign — **blitz** *vb*
blitz·krieg \'blits-ˌkrēg\ *n* [from German, meaning literally "lightning war"] : a violent swift surprise offensive
bliz·zard \'bliz-ərd\ *n* **1** : a long severe snowstorm **2** : an intensely strong cold wind filled with fine snow

ə abut	ər further	a back	ā bake
ä cot, cart	aù out	ch chin	e less	ē easy
g gift	i trip	ī life	j joke	ng sing	ō flow
ȯ flaw	ȯi coin	th thin	<u>th</u> this	ü loot
ù foot	y yet	yü few	yù furious	zh vision

blk *abbr* **1** black **2** block
[1]**bloat** \'blōt\ *vb* : to swell by filling with or as if with water or air : puff up
[2]**bloat** *n* : a disorder of cattle marked by abdominal bloating
blob \'bläb\ *n* : a small thick lump or drop of something (as paste or paint)
bloc \'bläk\ *n* : a combination of persons, groups, or nations united by treaty, agreement, or common interest ⟨the Soviet *bloc*⟩
[1]**block** \'bläk\ *n* **1 a** : a solid piece of material (as stone or wood) usu. with flat sides **b** : a hollow rectangular building unit (as of glass or concrete) **2 a** : a piece of wood on which condemned persons are beheaded **b** : a stand for something to be sold at auction **c** : a mold or form on which something is shaped ⟨a hat *block*⟩ **d** : the casting that contains the cylinders of an internal-combustion engine **3 a** : OBSTACLE **b** : an obstruction of an opponent's play in sports **c** : interruption of normal function ⟨a respiratory *block* due to carbon monoxide⟩ **4** : a wooden or metal case for one or more pulleys **5** : a number of things forming a group or unit ⟨a *block* of seats⟩ **6** : a large building divided into separate houses or shops ⟨an apartment *block*⟩ **7 a** : a space enclosed by streets **b** : the length of the side of such a block ⟨three *blocks* south⟩ **8** : a section of railroad track controlled by block signals **9** : a hand-carved piece of material from which impressions are to be printed
[2]**block** *vb* **1 a** : to stop up or close off : OBSTRUCT **b** : to hinder the progress or advance of; *esp* : to interfere with an opponent (as in football) **c** : to prevent normal functioning of; *esp* : to interrupt the passage of impulses along a nerve **2** : to mark the chief lines of ⟨*block* out a sketch⟩ **3** : to shape on, with, or as if with a block **4** : to make (lines of writing or type) flush at the left or at both left and right **5** : to secure, support, or provide with a block — **block·er** *n*
block·ade \blä-'kād\ *n* : the isolation of an area by means of troops or warships to prevent passage of persons or supplies in or out — **blockade** *vb* — **block·ad·er** *n*
block and tackle *n* : pulley blocks with associated rope or cable for hoisting or hauling
block·bust·er \'bläk-ˌbəs-tər\ *n* : a very large bomb
block·head \-ˌhed\ *n* : a stupid person
block·house \-ˌhaůs\ *n* **1** : a building of heavy timbers or of concrete built with holes in its sides through which persons inside may fire out at an enemy **2** : a building serving as an observation point for an operation likely to be accompanied by heat, blast, or radiation hazard

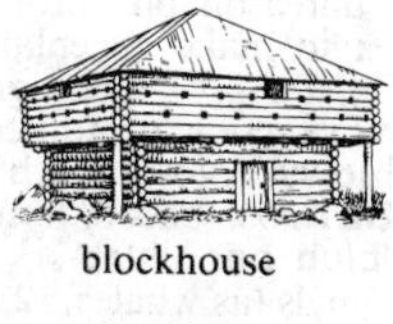
blockhouse

block letter *n* : a hand-printed usu. capital letter; *also* : a printed letter having all lines of equal thickness and no serifs
block mountain *n* : a mountain caused by faulting and uplifting
block signal *n* : a fixed signal at the entrance of a section of railroad track to govern trains entering and using it
bloke \'blōk\ *n, chiefly Brit* : MAN, FELLOW
[1]**blond** *also* **blonde** \'bländ\ *adj* **1** : of a pale yellowish brown color **2** : of a pale white or rosy white color — **blond·ness** \'blän(d)-nəs\ *n*
[2]**blond** *or* **blonde** *n* **1** : a blond person **2** : a light yellowish brown to dark grayish yellow
[1]**blood** \'bləd\ *n* **1 a** : the red fluid that circulates in the heart, arteries, capillaries, and veins of a vertebrate animal carrying nourishment and oxygen to and bringing away waste products from all parts of the body **b** : a fluid resembling blood **2 a** : LINEAGE, DESCENT; *esp* : royal lineage ⟨a prince of the *blood*⟩ **b** : relationship by descent from a common ancestor : KINSHIP **3** : ANGER
[2]**blood** *vb* : to give experience to ⟨troops already *blooded* in battle⟩
blood bank *n* : a reserve supply of blood or plasma or the place where it is stored
blood cell *n* : a cell normally present in blood
blood count *n* : the counting of the blood cells in a definite volume of blood; *also* : the number of cells so determined
blood·cur·dling \'bləd-ˌkərd-ling\ *adj* : seeming to have the effect of congealing the blood through fear or horror : TERRIFYING ⟨*bloodcurdling* screams⟩
blood·ed \'bləd-əd\ *adj* **1** : entirely or largely of pure blood or stock ⟨*blooded* horses⟩ **2** : having blood of a specified kind ⟨warm-*blooded*⟩

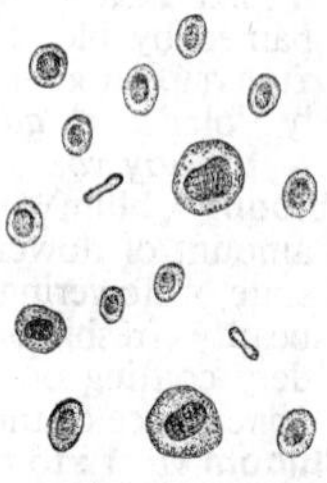
blood cells (magnified 150 times)

blood group *n* : one of the classes into which human beings can be separated on the basis of the presence or absence in their blood of specific antigens — **blood grouping** *n*
blood·hound \'bləd-ˌhaůnd\ *n* : a large powerful hound of a breed of European origin remarkable for keenness of smell
blood·less \-ləs\ *adj* **1** : deficient in blood **2** : done without bloodshed ⟨a *bloodless* revolution⟩ **3** : lacking in spirit or feeling — **blood·less·ly** *adv* — **blood·less·ness** *n*
blood·let·ting \-ˌlet-ing\ *n* : the act or practice of opening a vein for the purpose of drawing blood
blood·line \-ˌlīn\ *n* : a sequence of direct ancestors esp. in a pedigree; *also* : FAMILY, STRAIN
blood·mo·bile \-mō-ˌbēl\ *n* : an automobile staffed and equipped for collecting blood from donors
blood plasma *n* : the fluid portion of whole blood
blood platelet *n* : one of the minute disks of vertebrate blood that assist in blood clotting
blood poisoning *n* : a diseased condition of the blood caused by poisonous matter or organisms in it
blood pressure *n* : pressure of the blood on the walls of blood vessels and esp. arteries varying with physical condition and age
blood·root \'bləd-ˌrüt, -ˌrůt\ *n* : a plant related to the poppy, having a red root and sap and bearing a single lobed leaf and white flower in early spring
blood·shed \-ˌshed\ *n* **1** : the shedding of blood **2** : the taking of life : SLAUGHTER
blood·shot \-ˌshät\ *adj* : inflamed to redness ⟨*bloodshot* eyes⟩
blood·stain \-ˌstān\ *n* : a discoloration caused by blood — **blood·stained** \-ˌstānd\ *adj*
blood·stone \-ˌstōn\ *n* : a green quartz sprinkled with red spots
blood·stream \-ˌstrēm\ *n* : the flowing blood in a circulatory system
blood·suck·er \-ˌsək-ər\ *n* : an animal that sucks blood; *esp* : LEECH — **blood·suck·ing** \-ˌsək-ing\ *adj*
blood sugar *n* : the glucose in the blood; *esp* : the amount or proportion of such sugar normally from 0.08 to 0.11 percent

B

blood test *n* : a test of the blood; *esp* : a test for syphilis

blood·thirsty \'bləd-,thər-stē\ *adj* : eager to shed blood : CRUEL — **blood·thirst·i·ly** \-stə-lē\ *adv* — **blood·thirst·i·ness** \-stē-nəs\ *n*

blood transfusion *n* : the act or operation of transferring blood into a vein or artery of a man or animal

blood type *n* : BLOOD GROUP — **blood–type** *vb*

blood vessel *n* : a vessel in which blood circulates in an animal

bloody \'bləd-ē\ *adj* **blood·i·er**; **-est** **1 a** : smeared or stained with blood ⟨a *bloody* handkerchief⟩ **b** : BLEEDING ⟨a *bloody* nose⟩ **2** : causing or accompanied by bloodshed ⟨a *bloody* battle⟩ **3** : BLOODTHIRSTY, MURDEROUS ⟨a *bloody* deed ⟩ — **blood·i·ly** \'bləd-ə-lē\ *adv* — **blood·i·ness** \'bləd-ē-nəs\ *n* — **bloody** *vb*

1**bloom** \'blüm\ *n* **1 a** : FLOWER **b** : flowers or amount of flowers (as of a plant) **c** : the period or state of flowering **2** : a state, time, or appearance of beauty, freshness, and vigor **3 a** : a delicate powdery coating on some fruits and leaves **b** : a rosy appearance of the cheeks

2**bloom** *vb* **1** : to produce flowers : BLOSSOM **2** : to be in a state of youthful beauty or freshness : FLOURISH **3** : to glow with rosy color — **bloom·er** *n*

bloo·mers \'blü-mərz\ *n pl* : full loose trousers gathered at the knee formerly worn by women (as for athletics); *also* : underpants of similar design worn chiefly by girls

1**blos·som** \'bläs-əm\ *n* **1** : the flower of a seed plant ⟨apple *blossoms*⟩ **2** : the period or state of flowering — **blos·somy** \-ə-mē\ *adj*

2**blossom** *vb* **1** : BLOOM **2 a** : to flourish and prosper markedly **b** : DEVELOP, EXPAND

1**blot** \'blät\ *n* **1** : SPOT, STAIN **2** : DISGRACE, BLEMISH

2**blot** *vb* **blot·ted**; **blot·ting** **1** : SPOT, STAIN **2** : OBSCURE, DIM **3** : DISGRACE **4** : to dry with blotting paper or other absorbing agent **5** : to become marked with a blot

blotch \'bläch\ *n* **1** : IMPERFECTION, BLEMISH **2** : a spot or mark esp. when large or irregular — **blotch** *vb* — **blotched** \'blächt\ *adj* — **blotchy** \'bläch-ē\ *adj*

blot out *vb* **1** : to make obscure or invisible : HIDE **2** : DESTROY, KILL

blot·ter \'blät-ər\ *n* **1** : a piece of blotting paper **2** : a book in which entries are made temporarily ⟨a police *blotter*⟩

blotting paper *n* : a soft spongy paper used to absorb wet ink

blouse \'blaus, 'blauz\ *n* **1** : a loose outer garment like a shirt or smock varying from hip-length to calf-length **2** : the upper outer garment of a uniform **3** : a usu. loose-fitting garment covering the body from the neck to the waist

1**blow** \'blō\ *vb* **blew** \'blü\; **blown** \'blōn\; **blow·ing** **1** : to move or become moved esp. rapidly or with power ⟨wind *blowing* from the north⟩ **2** : to send forth a strong current of air (as from the mouth) ⟨*blow* on one's hands⟩ **3** : to drive or become driven by a current of air **4** : to make a sound or cause to sound by blowing ⟨*blow* a horn⟩ ⟨*blow* a whistle⟩ **5** : PANT, GASP **6 a** : to melt when overloaded ⟨the lights went out when a fuse *blew*⟩ **b** : to cause (a fuse) to blow **7** : to rupture by too much pressure ⟨*blew* a gasket⟩ ⟨the tire *blew* out⟩ **8** : to clear by forcing air through ⟨*blew* his nose⟩ **9** : to produce or shape by the action of blown or injected air ⟨*blow* bubbles⟩ ⟨*blow* glass⟩ **10** : to shatter or destroy by explosion **11** : to spend recklessly ⟨*blew* his money in one day⟩

2**blow** *n* **1** : a blowing of wind esp. when violent : GALE **2** : a forcing of air from the mouth or nose or through an instrument

3**blow** *vb* **blew** \'blü\; **blown** \'blōn\; **blow·ing** : FLOWER, BLOOM

4**blow** *n* **1** : a forcible stroke delivered with a part of the body or with an instrument **2** : a hostile act : COMBAT ⟨come to *blows*⟩ **3** : a sudden act or effort **4** : a sudden severe calamity ⟨a heavy *blow* to the nation⟩

syn BLOW, STROKE can mean the action of striking with impact. BLOW suggests violent impact and implies telling effect; STROKE suggests sweep or precision of movement

blow·er \'blō(-ə)r\ *n* **1** : one that blows **2** : a device for producing a current of air or gas

blow·fly \'blō-,flī\ *n* : any of various two-winged flies (as a bluebottle) that deposit their eggs or maggots on meat or in wounds

blow·gun \-,gən\ *n* : a tube from which an arrow or dart may be blown

blow·hole \-,hōl\ *n* **1** : a hole for the escape of air or gas **2** : a nostril in the top of the head of a whale or related animal **3** : a hole in the ice to which aquatic mammals (as seals) come to breathe

blown \'blōn\ *adj* **1** : SWOLLEN; *esp* : afflicted with bloat **2** : FLYBLOWN **3** : out of breath

blow·out \'blō-,aut\ *n* **1** *slang* : a big social affair **2** : a bursting of a container (as a tire) by pressure of the contents on a weak spot

blow·pipe \-,pīp\ *n* **1** : a small round tube for blowing a jet of gas (as air) into a flame so as to concentrate and increase the heat **2** : BLOWGUN

blow·torch \-,tȯrch\ *n* : a small portable burner that shoots out a very hot flame by means of a blast of air or oxygen

blowtorch

blow·up \'blō-,əp\ *n* **1** : EXPLOSION **2** : an outburst of temper **3** : a photographic enlargement

blow up \'blō-'əp\ *vb* **1** : to expand or become expanded to unreasonable proportions **2** : to make an enlargement of ⟨*blow up* a photograph⟩ **3 a** : EXPLODE **b** : to become violently angry

blowy \'blō-ē\ *adj* **blow·i·er**; **-est** : WINDY

BLT *abbr* bacon, lettuce, and tomato

1**blub·ber** \'bləb-ər\ *n* **1** : the fat of large sea mammals (as whales) **2** : the action of blubbering

2**blubber** *vb* **blub·bered**; **blub·ber·ing** \-(ə-)ring\ : to weep noisily and childishly or so as to swell or disfigure one's face

blud·geon \'bləj-ən\ *n* : a short club with one end thicker and heavier than the other — **bludgeon** *vb*

1**blue** \'blü\ *adj* **1** : of the color blue **2** : low in spirits : MELANCHOLY — **blue·ness** *n*

2**blue** *n* **1** : the color of the clear daytime sky or of the spectrum lying between green and violet **2** : blue clothing or cloth **3 a** : SKY **b** : SEA

3**blue** *vb* **blued**; **blue·ing** *or* **blu·ing** **1** : to make blue **2** : to add bluing to so as to make white ⟨*blue* the sheets⟩

blue baby *n* : an infant with a bluish tint usu. from a defect of the heart

blue·bell \'blü-ˌbel\ *n* : any of various plants (as a grape hyacinth) with blue bell-shaped flowers; *esp* : HAREBELL

blue·ber·ry \-ˌber-ē, -b(ə-)rē\ *n* : the edible blue or blackish small-seeded berry of any of several plants related to the cranberry; *also* : a low or tall shrub producing these berries — compare HUCKLEBERRY

blue·bird \-ˌbərd\ *n* : any of several small No. American songbirds related to the robin but more or less blue above

blue·bon·net \'blü-ˌbän-ət\ *n* **1** : CORNFLOWER **2** : a low-growing annual lupine of Texas with silky foliage and blue flowers

blue·bot·tle \-ˌbät-əl\ *n* : any of several blowflies with the abdomen or the whole body iridescent blue in color

blue·fish \-ˌfish\ *n* : an active saltwater food and sport fish that is related to the pompanos and is bluish above and silvery below

blue flag *n* : a blue-flowered iris; *esp* : a common iris of the eastern U.S. with a root formerly used medicinally

blue·gill \'blü-ˌgil\ *n* : a common food and sport sunfish of the eastern and central U.S.

blue·grass \-ˌgras\ *n* : a valuable pasture and lawn grass with bluish green stems

blue–green alga \ˌblü-ˌgrēn-\ *n* : any of a class of algae having the chlorophyll masked by bluish green pigments

blue heron *n* : any of several herons with bluish plumage

blue·jack·et \'blü-ˌjak-ət\ *n* : an enlisted man in the navy : SAILOR

blue jay \-ˌjā\ *n* : any of several crested and largely blue American jays

blue jeans *n pl* : pants or overalls made of blue denim

blue mold *n* : a fungus and esp. a penicillium that produces blue or blue-green surface growths

blue plate \-ˌplāt\ *n* : a main course (as of meat and vegetable) served as a single menu item

1**blue·print** \'blü-ˌprint\ *n* **1** : a photographic print in white on a blue ground used esp. for copying mechanical drawings and architects' plans **2** : a detailed plan or program of action

2**blueprint** *vb* : to make a blueprint of or for

blue racer *n* : a blacksnake of a bluish green variety occurring from Ohio to Texas

blue ribbon *n* : a blue ribbon awarded the first-place winner in a competition

blues \'blüz\ *n pl* **1** : low spirits : MELANCHOLY **2** : a song expressing melancholy and composed in a style originating among the American Negroes **3** : a blue uniform

blue·stem \'blü-ˌstem\ *n* : either of two important hay and forage grasses of the western U.S. with smooth bluish leaf sheaths

blu·et \'blü-ət\ *n* : a low American herb with small solitary bluish flowers

blue vitriol *n* : a hydrated copper sulfate

blue whale *n* : a whale held to reach a weight of 100 tons and a length of 100 feet and generally considered the largest living animal

1**bluff** \'bləf\ *adj* **1** : rising steeply with a broad front ⟨a *bluff* coastline⟩ **2** : frank and outspoken in a rough but good-natured manner — **bluff·ly** *adv* — **bluff·ness** *n*

syn BLUFF, BLUNT, CURT can mean speaking in a rough frank manner. BLUFF generally suggests hearty and good-natured roughness; BLUNT may suggest directness of speech not softened by tact; CURT usu. suggests briefness of speech that is disconcerting or rude ***ant*** suave

2**bluff** *n* : a high steep bank : CLIFF

3**bluff** *vb* : to deceive or frighten by pretending to have strength or confidence that one does not really have — **bluff·er** *n*

4**bluff** *n* **1 a** : an act or instance of bluffing **b** : the practice of bluffing **2** : one who bluffs

blu·ing *or* **blue·ing** \'blü-ing\ *n* : a preparation of blue or violet dyes used in laundering to counteract yellowing of white fabrics

blu·ish *or* **blue·ish** \'blü-ish\ *adj* : somewhat blue

1**blun·der** \'blən-dər\ *vb* **blun·dered**; **blun·der·ing** \-d(ə-)ring\ **1** : to move unsteadily or confusedly **2** : to make a blunder **3** : to say stupidly or thoughtlessly : BLURT **4** : BUNGLE — **blun·der·er** \-dər-ər\ *n*

2**blunder** *n* : a mistake resulting from stupidity, ignorance, confusion, or carelessness ***syn*** see ERROR

blun·der·buss \'blən-dər-ˌbəs\ *n* [a modification of

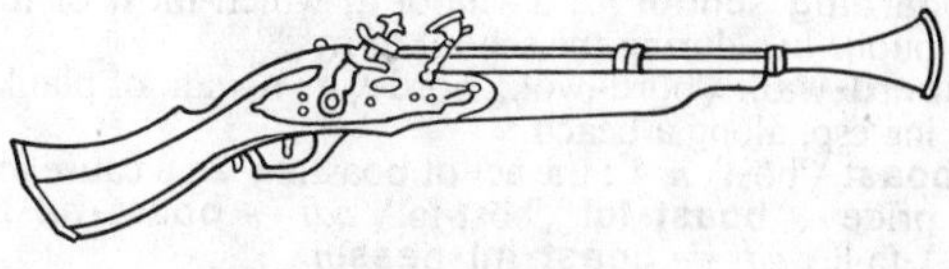

blunderbuss

obsolete Dutch *donderbus*, meaning literally "thunder gun"] **1** : an obsolete short firearm having a large bore and usu. a flaring muzzle for use at close range **2** : a blundering person

blunt \'blənt\ *adj* **1** : slow or deficient in feeling or understanding **2** : having an edge or point that is not sharp : DULL **3** : lacking refinement or tact : ABRUPT ***syn*** see BLUFF ***ant*** tactful — **blunt** *vb* — **blunt·ly** *adv* — **blunt·ness** *n*

1**blur** \'blər\ *n* **1** : a smear or stain that obscures but does not obliterate **2** : something vague or lacking definite outline — **blur·ry** \-ē\ *adj*

2**blur** *vb* **blurred**; **blur·ring 1** : to obscure or blemish by smearing **2** : to make or become vague, indistinct, or obscure

blurb \'blərb\ *n* : a brief notice esp. in advertising praising a product extravagantly

blurt \'blərt\ *vb* : to utter suddenly and without thinking ⟨*blurt* out a secret⟩

1**blush** \'bləsh\ *vb* **1** : to become red in the face esp. from shame, modesty, or confusion **2** : to feel shame or embarrassment **3** : to have a rosy or fresh color : BLOOM — **blush·er** *n*

2**blush** *n* **1** : APPEARANCE, VIEW ⟨at first *blush*⟩ **2** : a reddening of the face esp. from shame, modesty, or confusion **3** : a red or rosy tint

1**blus·ter** \'bləs-tər\ *vb* **blus·tered**; **blus·ter·ing** \-t(ə-)ring\ **1** : to blow violently and noisily **2** : to talk or act in a noisy boastful way — **blus·ter·er** \-tər-ər\ *n*

2**bluster** *n* **1** : a violent noise or commotion **2** : boastful empty speech — **blus·tery** \-t(ə-)rē\ *adj*

blvd *abbr* boulevard

BM *abbr* bowel movement

BMR *abbr* basal metabolic rate

BO *abbr* body odor

boa \'bō-ə\ *n* **1** : a large snake (as the boa constrictor, anaconda, or python) that crushes its prey **2** : a long fluffy scarf of fur, feathers, or fabric

boa con·stric·tor \-kən-'strik-tər\ *n* : a mottled brown tropical American boa

boar \'bō(ə)r, 'bȯ(ə)r\ *n* **1** : a male swine; *also* : the male of any of several mammals **2** : WILD BOAR

[1]**board** \'bōrd, 'bȯrd\ *n* **1** : the side of a ship ⟨star*board*⟩ ⟨over*board*⟩ **2 a** : a long thin flat piece of sawed lumber **b** *pl* : STAGE 2b ⟨trod the *boards* for 40 years⟩ **3 a** : a dining table **b** : daily meals esp. when furnished for pay ⟨room and *board*⟩ **4** : a group of persons who manage, direct, or investigate ⟨*board* of directors⟩ ⟨school *board*⟩ ⟨*board* of examiners⟩ **5 a** : a flat usu. rectangular piece of material (as of wood pulp or composition material) designed for a special purpose ⟨cutting *board*⟩ **b** : a surface, frame, or device for posting notices — **on board** : ABOARD

[2]**board** *vb* **1** : to go aboard : get on ⟨*board* a plane⟩ **2** : to cover with boards ⟨*board* up a window⟩ **3** : to provide or be provided with regular meals and often lodging

board·er \'bōrd-ər, 'bȯrd-\ *n* : one who pays for meals and sometimes lodging at another's house

board·ing·house \'bōrd-ing-ˌhau̇s, 'bȯrd-\ *n* : a house at which persons are boarded

boarding school *n* : a school at which most of the pupils live during the school term

board·walk \'bōrd-ˌwȯk, 'bȯrd-\ *n* : a walk of planking esp. along a beach

[1]**boast** \'bōst\ *n* **1** : the act of boasting **2** : a cause for pride — **boast·ful** \'bōst-fəl\ *adj* — **boast·ful·ly** \-fə-lē\ *adv* — **boast·ful·ness** *n*

[2]**boast** *vb* **1** : to praise one's own possessions, qualities, or accomplishments : BRAG ⟨*boasts* of his ability⟩ ⟨*boasting* about his money⟩ **2** : to have and display proudly ⟨a band *boasting* new uniforms⟩ — **boast·er** *n*

[1]**boat** \'bōt\ *n* **1** : a small vessel propelled by oars or paddles or by sail or power **2** : SHIP **3** : a boat-shaped utensil ⟨gravy *boat*⟩

[2]**boat** *vb* **1** : to put into or carry in a boat **2** : to travel by boat — **boat·er** *n*

boat·house \'bōt-ˌhau̇s\ *n* : a shelter for boats

boat·man \'bōt-mən\ *n* : a man who manages, works on, or deals in boats

boat·swain \'bō-sən\ *n* : a warrant officer on a warship or a petty officer on a merchant ship in charge of the hull and all related equipment

[1]**bob** \'bäb\ *vb* **bobbed**; **bob·bing 1 a** : to move or cause to move up and down in a short quick movement ⟨*bob* the head⟩ ⟨a cork *bobbing* in the water⟩ **b** : to emerge or appear suddenly or unexpectedly ⟨*bob* up again⟩ **2** : to grasp or make a grab with the teeth ⟨*bob* for apples⟩

[2]**bob** *n* : a short jerky motion ⟨a *bob* of the head⟩

[3]**bob** *n* **1** : a woman's or child's short haircut **2** : a weight hanging from a line **3** : a device for buoying up the baited end of a fishing line

[4]**bob** *vb* **bobbed**; **bob·bing 1** : to cut shorter : CROP **2** : to cut (hair) in the style of a bob

bob·ber \'bäb-ər\ *n* : one that bobs; *esp* : FLOAT 2a

bob·bin \'bäb-ən\ *n* : a spool or spindle on which yarn or thread is wound (as in a sewing machine)

bob·ble \'bäb-əl\ *vb* **bob·bled**; **bob·bling** \'bäb-(ə-)ling\ **1** : [1]BOB **2** : FUMBLE — **bobble** *n*

bob·by \'bäb-ē\ *n, pl* **bobbies** [from *Bobby*, nickname for Sir Robert Peel (1788–1850), who organized the London police force] *Brit* : POLICEMAN

ə abut ər further a back ā bake
ä cot, cart au̇ out ch chin e less ē easy
g gift i trip ī life j joke ng sing ō flow
ȯ flaw ȯi coin th thin t͟h this ü loot
u̇ foot y yet yü few yu̇ furious zh vision

bob·by pin \'bäb-ē-\ *n* : a flat wire hairpin with prongs that press close together

bobby socks *or* **bobby sox** *n pl* : girls' socks reaching above the ankle

bob·by-sox·er \'bäb-ē-ˌsäk-sər\ *or* **bob·by-sock·er** \-ˌsäk-ər\ *n* : an adolescent girl

bob·cat \'bäb-ˌkat\ *n* : a common usu. rusty-colored No. American lynx

bobcat (up to 3 ft. long)

bob·o·link \'bäb-ə-ˌlingk\ *n* : an American migratory songbird that has plumage which is streaky brown above and yellowish brown below except for the breeding plumage of the male which is chiefly black and white

bob·sled \'bäb-ˌsled\ *n* **1** : a short sled usu. used as one of a joined pair **2** : a sled formed of two coupled bobsleds — **bobsled** *vb* — **bob·sled·der** *n*

bob·tail \-ˌtāl\ *n* **1** : a short or bobbed tail **2** : an animal with a short or bobbed tail — **bobtail** *or* **bob·tailed** \-ˌtāld\ *adj*

bob·white \(')bäb-'hwīt\ *n* : any of several American quails; *esp* : a gray, white, and reddish game bird of the eastern and central U.S. — called also *partridge*

[1]**bode** \'bōd\ *vb* : to indicate beforehand : FORESHADOW

[2]**bode** *past of* BIDE

Bo·de's law \ˌbōd-əz-\ *n* : an empirical rule for calculating the distances of the planets from the sun

bod·ice \'bäd-əs\ *n* : the upper part of a woman's dress

bod·ied \'bäd-ēd\ *adj* : having a body or such a body ⟨long-*bodied*⟩

bodi·less \'bäd-i-ləs\ *adj* : having no body : INCORPOREAL

[1]**bodi·ly** \'bäd-ə-lē\ *adj* : of or relating to the body : PHYSICAL ⟨*bodily* comfort⟩ ⟨*bodily* organs⟩

[2]**bodily** *adv* **1** : in the flesh : by the body ⟨removed him *bodily*⟩ **2** : as a whole : ENTIRELY

bod·kin \'bäd-kən\ *n* **1 a** : DAGGER, STILETTO **b** : a sharp slender instrument for making holes in cloth **2** : a blunt needle with a large eye for drawing tape or ribbon through a loop or hem

body \'bäd-ē\ *n, pl* **bod·ies 1 a** : the physical whole of a living or dead organism **b** : the trunk or main part of an organism **c** : a human being : PERSON **2** : the main or central part ⟨the *body* of a truck⟩ ⟨the *body* of a letter⟩ **3** : the part of a garment covering the trunk **4** : a mass or portion of matter distinct from other masses ⟨a *body* of water⟩ ⟨a *body* of cold air⟩ **5** : a group of persons or things with a common aim or character ⟨a *body* of troops⟩ ⟨a *body* of laws⟩ **6** : richness of flavor or texture

body cavity *n* : a cavity within an animal body; *esp* : the space between the body wall and the digestive tract that in mammals is divided by the diaphragm into a cavity that contains the heart, lungs, and esophagus and a cavity that contains the rest of the digestive system, the internal parts of the reproductive system, and certain other organs

body-cen·tered \'bäd-ē-ˌsent-ərd\ *adj* : of or relating to a crystal structure in which the atoms are located at the corners and center of a unit cell

body·guard \'bäd-ē-ˌgärd\ *n* : a man or group of men whose duty it is to protect a person

body louse *n* : a sucking louse that lives in the clothing and feeds on the body of man

body shirt *n* : a tapered tight-fitting shirt

[1]**bog** \'bäg, 'bȯg\ *n* : wet spongy ground : MARSH — **bog·gy** \-ē\ *adj*

[2]**bog** *vb* **bogged**; **bog·ging** : to sink into or as if into a bog : MIRE

bo·gey *or* **bo·gy** *or* **bo·gie** *n, pl* **bogeys** *or* **bogies** **1** \'bu̇g-ē, 'bō-gē, 'bü-gē, 'bu̇g-ər\ : GHOST, GOBLIN **2** \'bō-gē *also* 'bu̇g-ē *or* 'bü-gē\ : something one is afraid of esp. without reason

bo·gey·man \'bu̇g-ē-ˌman, 'bō-gē-, 'bü-gē-, 'bu̇g-ər-\ *n* : an imaginary monster used in threatening children

bog rosemary *n* : any of several low evergreen shrubs with leathery leaves and drooping white or pinkish flowers

bo·gus \'bō-gəs\ *adj* : not genuine : SPURIOUS, SHAM

Bo·he·mi·an \bō-'hē-mē-ən\ *n* **1 a** : a native or inhabitant of Bohemia **b** : the Czech dialects used in Bohemia **2** *often not cap* **a** : VAGABOND, WANDERER; *esp* : GYPSY **b** : a writer or artist living an unconventional life — **bohemian** *adj, often cap* — **bo·he·mi·an·ism** \-mē-ə-ˌniz-əm\ *n, often cap*

[1]**boil** \'bȯil\ *n* : a painful swollen inflamed area in the skin resulting from infection — compare CARBUNCLE

[2]**boil** *vb* **1 a** : to produce bubbles of vapor when heated ⟨the water is *boiling*⟩ **b** : to come or bring to the boiling point ⟨the coffee *boiled*⟩ **2** : to become agitated like boiling water : SEETHE ⟨*boiling* flood waters⟩ **3** : to be excited or stirred up ⟨*boil* with anger⟩ **4** : to undergo or cause to undergo the action of a boiling liquid ⟨*boil* eggs⟩

[3]**boil** *n* : the act or state of boiling ⟨bring to a *boil*⟩

boil·er \'bȯi-lər\ *n* **1** : a container in which something is boiled **2** : a tank holding hot water **3** : a strong metal container used in making steam for heating buildings or for driving engines

boiling point *n* : the temperature at which a liquid boils

bois·ter·ous \'bȯi-st(ə-)rəs\ *adj* **1 a** : noisily turbulent : ROWDY ⟨a *boisterous* crowd⟩ **b** : marked by high spirits ⟨*boisterous* laughter⟩ **2** : STORMY, TUMULTUOUS ⟨*boisterous* winds⟩ — **bois·ter·ous·ly** *adv* — **bois·ter·ous·ness** *n*

bo·la \'bō-lə\ *or* **bo·las** \-ləs\ *n, pl* **bo·las** \-ləz\ : a weapon consisting of two or more stone or iron balls attached to the ends of a cord for hurling at and entangling an animal

bola

bold \'bōld\ *adj* **1 a** : willing to meet danger or take risks : DARING **b** : showing daring spirit ⟨a *bold* plan⟩ **2** : IMPUDENT, SAUCY **3** : SHEER, STEEP ⟨*bold* cliffs⟩ **4** : standing out prominently : CONSPICUOUS ⟨a dress with *bold* stripes⟩ — **bold·ly** *adv* — **bold·ness** \'bōl(d)-nəs\ *n*

bold·face \'bōl(d)-ˌfās\ *n* **1** : a type having thick dark lines — compare LIGHTFACE **2** : printing set in boldface

bold–faced \-'fāst\ *adj* **1** : BOLD, IMPUDENT **2** : set in boldface

bole \'bōl\ *n* : the trunk of a tree

bo·le·ro \bə-'le(ə)r-ō\ *n, pl* **-ros** **1** : a Spanish dance in ¾ time **2** : a loose waist-length jacket open at the front

bo·li·var \bə-'lē-ˌvär, 'bäl-ə-vər\ *n, pl* **bo·li·vars** *or* **bo·li·va·res** \ˌbäl-i-'vär-ˌās, ˌbō-li-\ **1** : the basic monetary unit of Venezuela **2** : a silver coin representing one bolivar

boll \'bōl\ *n* : a seedpod or capsule of a plant (as cotton)

boll weevil *n* : a small grayish weevil with a larva that lives in and feeds on the buds and bolls of the cotton plant

bo·lo \'bō-lō\ *n, pl* **bolos** : a long heavy single-edged knife used in the Philippines

bo·lo·gna \bə-'lō-nē *also* -n(y)ə\ *n* : a large smoked sausage of beef, veal, and pork

Bol·she·vik \'bōl-shə-ˌvik\ *n, pl* **Bolsheviks** *or* **Bol·she·vi·ki** \ˌbōl-shə-'vik-ē\ **1** : a member of the radical communist party that seized power in Russia by the revolution of November 1917 **2** : COMMUNIST — **Bolshevik** *adj* — **Bol·she·vism** \'bōl-shə-ˌviz-əm\ *n* — **Bol·she·vist** \-vəst\ *n or adj* — **Bol·she·vis·tic** \ˌbōl-shə-'vis-tik\ *adj*

[1]**bol·ster** \'bōl-stər\ *n* **1** : a long pillow or cushion extending the full width of a bed **2** : a structural part designed to eliminate friction or provide support

[2]**bolster** *vb* **bol·stered**; **bol·ster·ing** \-st(ə-)riŋ\ : to support with or as if with a bolster; *also* : REINFORCE — **bol·ster·er** \-stər-ər\ *n*

[1]**bolt** \'bōlt\ *n* **1** : a shaft or missile for a crossbow or catapult **2 a** : a lightning stroke : THUNDERBOLT **b** : a sudden surprise ⟨a *bolt* from the blue⟩ **3** : a sliding bar used to fasten a door **4** : the part of a lock worked by a key **5** : a metal pin or rod usu. with a head at one end and a screw thread at the other that is used to hold something in place **6** : a roll of cloth or wallpaper **7** : the device that closes the breech of a firearm

[2]**bolt** *vb* **1** : to move suddenly or nervously **2** : to move rapidly : DASH ⟨reporters *bolted* for the door⟩ **3** : to run away ⟨his horse shied and *bolted*⟩ **4** : to break away from or oppose one's political party **5** : to say impulsively : BLURT **6** : to fasten with a bolt **7** : to swallow hastily or without chewing ⟨*bolted* down his dinner and rushed out⟩ — **bolt·er** *n*

[3]**bolt** *n* : an act of bolting

bo·lus \'bō-ləs\ *n* : a rounded mass: as **a** : a large pill **b** : a soft mass of chewed food

[1]**bomb** \'bäm\ *n* **1** : a hollow case or shell containing explosives and dropped from an airplane, thrown by hand, or set off by a fuse **2** : a container in which a substance (as an insecticide) is stored under pressure and from which it is released in a fine spray

[2]**bomb** *vb* : to attack with bombs

bom·bard \bäm-'bärd, bəm-\ *vb* **1** : to attack with artillery : SHELL **2** : to assail vigorously or persistently ⟨*bombarded* him with questions⟩ **3** : to subject to the impact of rapidly moving particles (as electrons or alpha rays) — **bom·bard·ment** \-mənt\ *n*

bom·bar·dier \ˌbäm-bə(r)-'di(ə)r\ *n* : a bomber-crew member who releases the bombs

bombardier beetle *n* : any of numerous beetles that when disturbed discharge an irritating vapor

bom·bast \'bäm-ˌbast\ *n* [originally meaning "cotton batting", then "padding", from medieval French *bombace* "cotton"] : pompous speech or writing — **bom·bas·tic** \bäm-'bas-tik\ *adj* — **bom·bas·ti·cal·ly** \-ti-k(ə-)lē\ *adv*

bomb bay *n* : a bomb-carrying compartment in the underside of a combat airplane

bomb calorimeter *n* : a device with a chamber consisting of a strong steel shell that is used for measuring the heat evolved or absorbed in the complete burning of a substance

bomb·er \'bäm-ər\ *n* : one that bombs; *esp* : an airplane designed for dropping bombs

bomb·proof \'bäm-'prüf\ *adj* : safe against the explosive force of bombs

bomb·shell \-ˌshel\ *n* **1** : BOMB 1 **2** : a great surprise

bo·na fide \'bō-nə-ˌfīd, ˌbō-nə-'fīd-ē\ *adj* [from the Latin phrase *bona fide* "in good faith"] **1 a** : made or done in good faith ⟨*bona fide* offer⟩ **b** : acting in good faith ⟨*bona fide* purchaser⟩ **2** : GENUINE ⟨a *bona fide* cowboy⟩

bo·nan·za \bə-'nan-zə\ *n* **1** : a rich mass of ore in a mine **2** : something that brings a rich return

bon·bon \'bän-ˌbän\ *n* [from French, meaning literally "good good"] : a candy with chocolate or fondant coating and fondant center sometimes with fruits or nuts

[1]**bond** \'bänd\ *n* **1** : something that binds or confines **2 a** : a material or device for binding, joining, or cementing **b** : a means by which atoms, ions, or groups of atoms are held together in a molecule or crystal **3** : a tie of loyalty, sentiment, or friendship **4 a** : a pledge to do an act or pay a sum on or before a set date or forfeit a sum if the pledge is not fulfilled **b** : a certificate promising payment of a certain sum on or before a stated day and issued by a government or corporation as an evidence of debt **5** : a binding or connection made by overlapping parts of a structure (as in laying brick)

[2]**bond** *vb* **1** : to protect or secure by or operate under a bond ⟨*bonded* locksmiths⟩ **2** : to hold together or solidify by or as if by a bond — **bond·a·ble** \'bän-də-bəl\ *adj* — **bond·er** *n*

bond·age \'bän-dij\ *n* : SLAVERY

bond·hold·er \'bänd-ˌhōl-dər\ *n* : one that owns a government or corporation bond

bond·man \'bän(d)-mən\ *n* : SLAVE, SERF — **bond·wom·an** \'bänd-ˌwu̇m-ən\ *n*

[1]**bonds·man** \'bän(d)z-mən\ *n* : BONDMAN

[2]**bondsman** *n* : one who gives a bond or bail for another

[1]**bone** \'bōn\ *n* **1 a** : the hard largely calcareous material of which the skeleton of most vertebrate animals is formed; *also* : one of the hard pieces in which this tissue occurs ⟨break a *bone*⟩ **b** : a hard animal substance (as whalebone or ivory) similar to bone **2** : a cause of disagreement — used in the phrases *bone of contention* and *bone to pick* **3** *pl* : something usu. or orig. made from bone (as dice or clappers) **4** *pl* : an end man in a minstrel show — **bone·less** \-ləs\ *adj* — **bone·like** \-ˌlīk\ *adj*

[2]**bone** *vb* **1** : to remove the bones from ⟨*bone* a fish⟩ **2** : to study hard ⟨*bone* up on math⟩

bone black *n* : the black chiefly carbon residue of bones heated in a closed vessel that is used esp. as a pigment or a decolorizing material

bone meal *n* : fertilizer or feed made of crushed or ground bone

bon·er \'bō-nər\ *n* : a stupid or ridiculous mistake : BLUNDER

bon·fire \'bän-ˌfī(ə)r\ *n* [from Middle English *bonefire*, a large public fire in which bones were burned] : a large open-air fire

bon·go \'bäng-gō\ *n, pl* **bongos** *also* **bongoes** : one of a pair of small tuned drums played with the hands

bo·ni·to \bə-'nēt-ō\ *n, pl* **bonitos** *or* **bonito** : any of various medium-sized tunas

bon·net \'bän-ət\ *n* **1** : a head covering often tied under the chin and worn by women and small children **2** : a soft woolen cap worn by men in Scotland **3** : the headdress of an American Indian

bonnet monkey *n* : a monkey of the southern Indian peninsula that has a tuft of hair on the head suggesting a bonnet

bon·ny *also* **bon·nie** \'bän-ē\ *adj, chiefly Brit* : HANDSOME, ATTRACTIVE

bo·nus \'bō-nəs\ *n* : something given in addition to what is usual or what is strictly due; *esp* : money given in addition to an agreed salary or wages

bon voy·age \ˌbōn-ˌvwī-'äzh, -ˌvwä-'yäzh\ *n* : FAREWELL — often used interjectionally

bony \'bō-nē\ *adj* **bon·i·er**; **-est** **1** : of or relating to bone ⟨the *bony* structure of the body⟩ **2** : full of bones **3** : resembling bone esp. in hardness ⟨a *bony* substance⟩ **4** : having large or prominent bones ⟨a rugged *bony* face⟩ **5** : SKINNY, SCRAWNY ⟨*bony* underfed children⟩

bony fish *n* : any of a class comprising higher fishes with usu. well-developed bony skeletons

[1]**boo** \'bü\ *interj* — used to express contempt or disapproval or to startle or frighten

[2]**boo** *n* : a shout of disapproval or contempt — **boo** *vb*

boo·by \'bü-bē\ *n, pl* **boobies** **1** : a foolish person : DOPE **2** : any of several seabirds that resemble gulls but have longer necks and larger bills

booby 2
(up to 5 ft. wingspread)

booby trap *n* : a trap for a careless or unwary person; *esp* : a concealed explosive device set to go off when a harmless-looking object is touched — **boo·by-trap** \'bü-bē-ˌtrap\ *vb*

[1]**book** \'bu̇k\ *n* **1** : a set of sheets of paper bound together **2 a** : a long literary composition **b** : a major division of a literary work **3** : a volume of business records (as accounts) **4** *cap* : BIBLE **5** : a packet of items bound together ⟨a *book* of matches⟩ — **one for the book** : an act or occurrence worth noting

[2]**book** *vb* **1** : to engage transportation or reserve lodgings **2** : to schedule engagements for ⟨*book* an entertainer⟩ **3** : to enter charges against in a police register — **book·er** *n*

[3]**book** *adj* **1** : derived from books ⟨*book* learning⟩ **2** : shown by account books ⟨*book* value⟩

book·bind·ing \'bu̇k-ˌbīn-ding\ *n* **1** : the binding of a book **2** : the art or trade of binding books

book·case \'bu̇k-ˌkās\ *n* : a piece of furniture consisting of shelves to hold books

book·end \-ˌend\ *n* : a support placed at the end of a row of books to hold them up

book·ish \'bu̇k-ish\ *adj* **1** : fond of reading **2** : inclined to rely on knowledge from books rather than practical experience **3** : resembling the language of books : FORMAL — **book·ish·ly** *adv* — **book·ish·ness** *n*

book·keep·er \'bu̇k-ˌkē-pər\ *n* : a person who keeps

business accounts — **book·keep·ing** \-piŋ\ *n*
book·let \ˈbu̇k-lət\ *n* : a little book; *esp* : PAMPHLET
book louse *n* : any of several minute wingless insects injurious esp. to books
book lung *n* : a specialized breathing organ of spiders and related animals
book·mark \ˈbu̇k-ˌmärk\ *n* : a marker for finding a place in a book
book·mo·bile \ˈbu̇k-mō-ˌbēl\ *n* : a truck that serves as a traveling library
book·plate \ˈbu̇k-ˌplāt\ *n* : a label placed in a book showing who owns it
book·store \-ˌstō(ə)r, -ˌstȯ(ə)r\ *n* : a retail store where books are the main item for sale
book·worm \-ˌwərm\ *n* **1** : any of various insect larvae that feed on the binding and paste of books **2** : a person devoted to reading or study
Bool·ean algebra \ˌbü-lē-ən-\ *n* : any of several logical systems of combining abstract quantities; *esp* : an arithmetic of sets in which the intersection and union of sets are operations
1**boom** \ˈbüm\ *n* **1** : a long pole; *esp* : one for stretching the bottom of a sail **2 a** : a long beam projecting from the mast of a derrick to support or guide the thing that is being lifted **b** : a long movable arm used to manipulate a microphone **3** : a line of connected floating timbers to hold logs together in a river

boom 1

2**boom** *vb* **1** : to make a deep hollow sound **2** : to grow or develop rapidly ⟨business was *booming*⟩
3**boom** *n* **1** : a booming sound or cry **2** : a rapid expansion or increase; *esp* : a rapid widespread expansion of business
1**boo·mer·ang** \ˈbü-mə-ˌraŋ\ *n* [from its native name in Australia] **1** : a curved club that can be thrown so as to return to the thrower **2** : an act or utterance that reacts with harm to its maker or doer
2**boomerang** *vb* : to injure the originator instead of an intended target ⟨his backbiting *boomeranged* on him⟩
boom·town \ˈbüm-ˌtau̇n\ *n* : a town undergoing a sudden growth in business and population
1**boon** \ˈbün\ *n* **1** : BENEFIT, FAVOR **2** : a timely benefit : BLESSING
2**boon** *adj* : INTIMATE ⟨a *boon* companion⟩
boor \ˈbu̇(ə)r\ *n* **1 a** : PEASANT **b** : YOKEL **2** : a rude or insensitive person — **boor·ish** \-ish\ *adj* — **boor·ish·ly** *adv* — **boor·ish·ness** *n*
1**boost** \ˈbüst\ *vb* **1** : to push or shove up from below **2** : to increase in force, power, or amount ⟨*boost* production⟩ ⟨*boost* prices⟩ **3** : RAISE, PROMOTE **4** : to promote enthusiastically the cause or interests of
2**boost** *n* **1** : a push upward **2** : an increase in amount ⟨a *boost* in production⟩ **3** : an act giving needed help or encouragement

boost·er \ˈbü-stər\ *n* **1** : one that boosts **2** : an enthusiastic supporter **3** : an extra dose of an immunizing agent given to maintain or revive the effects of previously established immunity **4** : a device for strengthening radio or television signals in areas where reception is weak **5** : the first stage of a multistage rocket providing thrust for the launching and the initial part of the flight

1**boot** \ˈbüt\ *n* : something in addition — used in the phrase *to boot*
2**boot** *n* **1 a** : a covering (as of leather or rubber) for the foot and leg **b** : a high shoe **2** : KICK **3** : a navy or marine recruit undergoing basic training
3**boot** *vb* **1** : to put boots on **2** : KICK
boot·black \ˈbüt-ˌblak\ *n* : a person who shines boots and shoes
boot·ee *or* **boot·ie** \ˈbüt-ē\ *n* : an infant's knitted or crocheted sock
booth \ˈbüth\ *n, pl* **booths** \ˈbüt͟hz, ˈbüths\ **1** : a stall or stand for the sale or exhibition of goods (as at a fair) or for providing services ⟨information *booth*⟩ **2** : a small enclosure affording privacy for one person at a time ⟨voting *booth*⟩ ⟨telephone *booth*⟩ **3** : a table between two backed benches in a restaurant
boot·jack \ˈbüt-ˌjak\ *n* : a V-shaped device for use in pulling off one's boots
1**boot·leg** \-ˌleg\ *vb* **1** : to make or transport for sale alcoholic liquor contrary to law **2 a** : to produce or sell illicitly **b** : SMUGGLE — **boot·leg·ger** *n*
2**bootleg** *n* : something bootlegged; *esp* : MOONSHINE — **bootleg** *adj*
boot·less \ˈbüt-ləs\ *adj* : USELESS, UNPROFITABLE
boo·ty \ˈbüt-ē\ *n* **1** : SPOILS; *esp* : goods seized from the enemy in war **2** : a rich gain or prize
booze \ˈbüz\ *n* : alcoholic liquor
bor *abbr* borough
bo·rate \ˈbō(ə)r-ˌāt, ˈbȯ(ə)r-\ *n* : a salt of a boric acid
bo·rax \ˈbō(ə)r-ˌaks, ˈbȯ(ə)r-\ *n* : a borate of sodium that occurs as a mineral and is used in agricultural chemicals, as a cleansing agent, and as a water softener
bo·ra·zon \ˈbōr-ə-ˌzän, ˈbȯr-\ *n* : a crystalline compound of boron and nitrogen as hard as diamond but more resistant to high temperature
bor·deaux mixture \bȯr-ˈdō-, ˈbȯrd-ˌō-\ *n, often cap B* : a fungicide made by reaction of the sulfate of copper, lime, and water
1**bor·der** \ˈbȯrd-ər\ *n* **1** : an outer part or edge **2** : BOUNDARY, FRONTIER **3** : a narrow bed of plants along the edge of a garden or walk **4** : a design at the edge of a fabric or rug — **bor·dered** \-ərd\ *adj*
syn BORDER, MARGIN, EDGE can mean the outermost part of something. BORDER applies to an area on or just within a boundary line; MARGIN suggests a border of definite width; EDGE implies a sharp line marking an absolute limit
2**border** *vb* **bor·dered**; **bor·der·ing** \ˈbȯrd-(ə-)riŋ\ **1** : to put a border on **2** : to touch at or lie on the border ⟨the U.S. *borders* on Canada⟩ **3** : to come near to : VERGE ⟨that remark *borders* on the ridiculous⟩ — **bor·der·er** \-ər-ər\ *n*
bor·der·land \ˈbȯrd-ər-ˌland\ *n* **1** : territory at or near a border : FRONTIER **2** : an outlying or intermediate region often not clearly defined ⟨the *borderland* between sleeping and waking⟩
bor·der·line \-ˌlīn\ *adj* **1** : situated at or near a border or boundary **2** : having characteristics of a state or condition without clearly being in it : UNCERTAIN ⟨a *borderline* case of mental illness⟩ **3** : having characteristics of two states or conditions without clearly belonging to either : INTERMEDIATE

[1]**bore** \'bō(ə)r, 'bȯ(ə)r\ *vb* **1** : to make a hole in esp. with a drill : PIERCE **2** : to make by piercing or drilling ⟨*bore* a hole⟩ ⟨*bore* a well⟩

[2]**bore** *n* **1** : a hole made by or as if by boring **2** : the interior tube of a gun **3** : the diameter of a hole; *esp* : the interior diameter of a gun barrel

[3]**bore** *past of* BEAR

[4]**bore** *n* : a tidal flood with a high abrupt front usu. due to a rapidly narrowing inlet

[5]**bore** *n* : one that bores

[6]**bore** *vb* : to weary by being dull or monotonous

bore·dom \'bōrd-əm, 'bȯrd-\ *n* : the state of being bored

bor·er \'bōr-ər, 'bȯr-\ *n* **1** : one that bores; *esp* : a tool used for boring **2 a** : SHIPWORM **b** : an insect that as larva or adult bores in the woody parts of plants

bo·ric acid \ˌbōr-ik-, ˌbȯr-\ *n* : a white crystalline boron-containing weak acid that is used as a mild antiseptic

born \'bȯrn\ *adj* **1 a** : brought into life by birth **b** : NATIVE ⟨American-*born*⟩ **2** : having natural abilities or character ⟨a *born* leader⟩

borne *also* **born** *past part of* BEAR

born·ite \'bȯ(ə)r-ˌnīt\ *n* : a brittle metallic-looking mineral consisting of a sulfide of copper and iron and constituting a valuable ore of copper

bo·ron \'bō(ə)r-ˌän, 'bȯ(ə)r-\ *n* : a metalloid element found in nature only in combination (as in borax) — see ELEMENT table

bor·ough \'bər-ō\ *n* [from Old English *burg*, first meaning "fortress", and then "fortified town"] **1 a** : a town or urban area in Great Britain that sends one or more members to Parliament **b** : a self-governing urban area in Great Britain **2** : a self-governing town or village in some states **3** : one of the five political divisions of New York City

bor·row \'bär-ō\ *vb* **1** : to take or receive something with the promise or intention of returning it **2** : to take for one's own use : ADOPT ⟨*borrow* an idea⟩ **3** : to take 1 from a figure of the minuend in subtraction and add it as 10 to the next lower place — **bor·row·er** \'bär-ə-wər\ *n*

bor·zoi \'bȯr-ˌzȯi\ *n* : any of a breed of large long-haired dogs developed in Russia esp. for pursuing wolves

bo·s'n *or* **bo'·s'n** *or* **bo·sun** *or* **bo'·sun** \'bō-sən\ *var of* BOATSWAIN

[1]**bos·om** \'bu̇z-əm\ *n* **1** : the front of the human chest; *esp* : the female breasts **2 a** : the center of secret thoughts and feelings **b** : close relationship : EMBRACE ⟨in the *bosom* of her family⟩ **3** : the part of a garment covering the breast — **bos·omed** \-əmd\ *adj*

[2]**bosom** *adj* : CLOSE, INTIMATE ⟨*bosom* friends⟩

[1]**boss** \'bȯs, 'bäs\ *n* : a rounded projecting part; *esp* : an ornamental knob (as on a shield or a ceiling) : STUD

[2]**boss** *vb* : to ornament with bosses : EMBOSS

[3]**boss** \'bȯs\ *n* [from Dutch *baas* "master"] **1** : one who exercises control or authority; *esp* : one who directs or supervises workers **2** : a politician who controls votes or dictates appointments or legislative measures — **boss** *adj*

[4]**boss** \'bȯs\ *vb* : DIRECT, SUPERVISE

ə abut	ər further	a back	ā bake
ä cot, cart	au̇ out	ch chin	e less
ē easy	g gift	i trip	ī life
j joke	ng sing	ō flow	ȯ flaw
ȯi coin	th thin	th this	ü loot
u̇ foot	y yet	yü few	yu̇ furious
zh vision			

bossy \'bȯ-sē\ *adj* **boss·i·er**; **-est** : inclined to act like a boss : DICTATORIAL — **boss·i·ness** *n*

Bos·ton ivy \ˌbȯ-stən-\ *n* : a woody Asiatic vine that is related to the grape, has 3-lobed leaves, and often grows over walls

Boston terrier *n* : any of a breed of small smooth-coated brindle or black terriers with white markings — called also *Boston bull*

bot \'bät\ *n* : the larva of a botfly

[1]**bo·tan·i·cal** \bə-'tan-i-kəl\ *or* **bo·tan·ic** \-ik\ *adj* **1** : of or relating to plants or botany **2** : derived from plants ⟨*botanical* drugs⟩ — **bo·tan·i·cal·ly** \-i-k(ə-)lē\ *adv*

[2]**botanical** *n* : a vegetable drug esp. in the crude state

bot·a·nize \'bät-ə-ˌnīz\ *vb* : to collect and study plants

bot·a·ny \'bät-(ə-)nē\ *n* **1** : a branch of biology dealing with plant life **2 a** : plant life (as of a given region) **b** : the biology of a plant or plant group — **bot·a·nist** \'bät-(ə-)nəst\ *n*

[1]**botch** \'bäch\ *vb* **1** : REPAIR; *esp* : to patch clumsily **2** : BUNGLE

[2]**botch** *n* : a botched job : MESS — **botchy** \-ē\ *adj*

bot·fly \'bät-ˌflī\ *n* : any of various stout two-winged flies whose larvae are parasitic in various mammals

[1]**both** \'bōth\ *adj* : the two : the one and the other ⟨*both* feet⟩

[2]**both** *pron* : the one as well as the other ⟨*both* of us⟩ ⟨we are *both* well⟩

[3]**both** *conj* — used as a function word to indicate each of two things specified by coordinated words, phrases, or clauses ⟨*both* New York and London⟩

[1]**both·er** \'bäth-ər\ *vb* **both·ered**; **both·er·ing** \-(ə-)ring\ **1** : ANNOY, IRK **2 a** : to cause anxiety or concern to **b** : to feel concern or anxiety **3** : to take pains : make an effort ⟨don't *bother* to knock⟩

[2]**bother** *n* **1 a** : a state of petty annoyance **b** : something that causes petty annoyance **2** : FUSS, DISTURBANCE

both·er·some \'bäth-ər-səm\ *adj* : causing bother : VEXING

[1]**bot·tle** \'bät-əl\ *n* **1 a** : a container typically of glass or plastic with a narrow neck and mouth and no handle **b** : a bag made of skin **2** : the quantity held by a bottle — **bot·tle·ful** \-ˌfu̇l\ *n*

[2]**bottle** *vb* **bot·tled**; **bot·tling** \-(ə-)ling\ **1** : to put into a bottle **2** : to confine as if in a bottle — usu. used with *up* — **bot·tler** \-(ə-)lər\ *n*

bottled gas *n* : gas under pressure in portable cylinders; *esp* : LIQUEFIED PETROLEUM GAS

bot·tle·neck \'bät-əl-ˌnek\ *n* **1** : a narrow passageway **2** : a place, condition, or point where progress is held up ⟨a traffic *bottleneck*⟩

bot·tom \'bät-əm\ *n* **1 a** : the under surface of something **b** : a supporting surface or part : BASE **c** : BUTTOCKS, RUMP **2** : the bed of a body of water **3 a** : the part of a ship's hull lying below the water **b** : BOAT, SHIP **4** : the lowest part, place, or point **5** : low land along a river ⟨the Mississippi river *bottoms*⟩ **6** *pl* : the trousers of pajamas — **bot·tomed** \-əmd\ *adj* — **at bottom** : BASICALLY, REALLY

bot·tom·less \'bät-əm-ləs\ *adj* **1** : having no bottom **2** : very deep ⟨a *bottomless* pit⟩

bot·u·lism \'bäch-ə-ˌliz-əm\ *n* : an acute poisoning caused by eating food containing a toxin secreted by a spore-forming bacterium

bou·doir \'büd-ˌwär, 'bu̇d-, -ˌwȯr\ *n* [from French, meaning literally "a place to sulk in", from *bouder* "to pout", "sulk"] : a woman's dressing room, bedroom, or private sitting room

bough \'bau̇\ *n* : a branch of a tree; *esp* : a main branch ***syn*** see SHOOT — **boughed** \'bau̇d\ *adj*

bought *past of* BUY

bouil·lon \'bü-ˌyän; 'bu̇l-ˌyän, -yən\ *n* : a clear seasoned soup made usu. from beef

boul·der \'bōl-dər\ *n* : a large detached and rounded or much-worn mass of rock

bou·le·vard \'bu̇l-ə-ˌvärd, 'bül-\ *n* [from French, from medieval Dutch *bolwerc* "bulwark"; so called because the first boulevards followed the lines of abandoned city fortifications] : a broad often landscaped thoroughfare

1**bounce** \'bau̇n(t)s\ *vb* **1 a** : to cause to rebound ⟨*bounce* a ball⟩ **b** : to spring backward after striking **2** : to throw out violently from a place **3** : to leap suddenly : BOUND

2**bounce** *n* **1 a** : a sudden leap or bound **b** : a bouncing back : REBOUND **2** : LIVELINESS, VERVE

bounc·er \'bau̇n(t)-sər\ *n* : one that bounces; *esp* : a man employed in a public place to remove disorderly persons

bounc·ing \-siŋ\ *adj* : HEALTHY, ROBUST ⟨a *bouncing* baby⟩ — **bounc·ing·ly** \-siŋ-lē\ *adv*

bouncing bet \-'bet\ *n, often cap 2d B* : a narrow-leaved, smooth-stemmed plant about two feet tall and bearing pinkish white clusters of flowers with notched petals — called also *bouncing bess*

1**bound** \'bau̇nd\ *adj* : going or intending to go ⟨*bound* for home⟩

2**bound** *n* **1** : a boundary line **2** : a point or line beyond which one cannot go : LIMIT ⟨out of *bounds*⟩ **3** : the land within a boundary — usu. used in pl. — **bound·less** \-ləs\ *adj* — **bound·less·ly** *adv* — **bound·less·ness** *n*

3**bound** *vb* **1** : to set limits to : CONFINE **2** : to form the boundary of : ENCLOSE **3** : ADJOIN **4** : to name the boundaries of

4**bound** *past of* BIND

5**bound** *adj* **1 a** : FASTENED, TIED **b** : CONFINED **2** : CERTAIN, SURE ⟨*bound* to rain soon⟩ **3 a** : OBLIGED ⟨duty-*bound*⟩ **b** : RESOLVED, DETERMINED ⟨*bound* to have his own way⟩

6**bound** *n* **1** : LEAP, JUMP **2** : BOUNCE, REBOUND

7**bound** *vb* **1** : to move by leaping **2** : REBOUND, BOUNCE

bound·a·ry \'bau̇n-d(ə-)rē\ *n, pl* **-ries** : a line or strip that marks or shows a limit or end (as of a region or a piece of land)

bound·en \'bau̇n-dən\ *adj* : OBLIGATORY, BINDING

boun·te·ous \'bau̇nt-ē-əs\ *adj* **1** : GENEROUS **2** : given plentifully ⟨*bounteous* gifts⟩ — **boun·te·ous·ly** *adv* — **boun·te·ous·ness** *n*

boun·ti·ful \'bau̇nt-i-fəl\ *adj* **1** : GENEROUS **2** : PLENTIFUL, ABUNDANT ⟨a *bountiful* supply⟩ — **boun·ti·ful·ly** \-f(ə-)lē\ *adv* — **boun·ti·ful·ness** \-fəl-nəs\ *n*

boun·ty \'bau̇nt-ē\ *n, pl* **bounties** [from Old French *bonté* "goodness"] **1 a** : GENEROSITY **b** : something given generously **2** : money given as a reward or inducement (as for killing a destructive animal)

bou·quet \bō-'kā, bü-\ *n* **1** : a bunch of flowers **2** : FRAGRANCE, AROMA

1**bour·geois** \'bu̇(ə)rzh-ˌwä, bu̇rzh-'\ *n, pl* **bourgeois** \-ˌwä(z), -'wä(z)\ [from French, originally meaning "burgher", from *bourg* "town", from a prehistoric Germanic word meaning "fortress", "fortified town", the source of English *borough*] : a person of the middle class of society — **bourgeois** *adj*

bour·geoi·sie \ˌbu̇rzh-ˌwä-'zē\ *n, pl* **bourgeoisie** : the middle class of society

bourn *or* **bourne** \'bōrn, 'bȯrn, 'bu̇(ə)rn\ *n* **1** *archaic* : BOUNDARY, LIMIT **2** *archaic* : GOAL, DESTINATION

bour·rée \bu̇-'rā\ *n* : a lively 17th century French dance

bout \'bau̇t\ *n* **1** : a spell of activity **2** : an athletic match (as of boxing) **3** : OUTBREAK, ATTACK ⟨a *bout* of measles⟩

bou·tique \bü-'tēk\ *n* : a small retail store; *esp* : a fashionable specialty shop for women

bou·ton·niere \ˌbüt-ə-'ni(ə)r, ˌbü-tən-'ye(ə)r\ *n* : a flower or bouquet worn in a buttonhole

1**bo·vine** \'bō-ˌvīn, -ˌvēn\ *adj* **1** : of, relating to, or resembling the ox or cow **2** : sluggish or patient like an ox or cow

2**bovine** *n* : a bovine animal

1**bow** \'bau̇\ *vb* **1** : to bend the head, body, or knee in greeting, reverence, respect, or submission **2** : SUBMIT, YIELD ⟨*bow* to authority⟩ **3** : BEND ⟨*bowed* with age⟩ **4** : to express by bowing ⟨*bow* one's thanks⟩

2**bow** *n* : a bending of the head or body in respect, submission, assent, or greeting

3**bow** \'bō\ *n* **1** : RAINBOW **2** : a weapon for shooting arrows that is made of a strip of elastic material (as wood) bent by a cord connecting the two ends **3** : something that is curved like a bow **4** : a wooden rod with horsehairs stretched from end to end used for playing a violin or similar instrument **5** : a knot formed by doubling a ribbon or string into loops

bow 2

4**bow** \'bō\ *vb* **1** : to bend into a curve **2** : to play a stringed instrument with a bow

5**bow** \'bau̇\ *n* : the forward part of a ship

bow·el \'bau̇(-ə)l\ *n* **1 a** : INTESTINE, GUT — usu. used in pl. **b** : a division of the intestine **2** *pl* : the interior parts ⟨the *bowels* of the earth⟩

bow·er \'bau̇(-ə)r\ *n* **1** : a place for rest : RETREAT **2** : a shelter (as in a garden) made with tree boughs or vines twined together : ARBOR — **bow·ery** \-ē\ *adj*

bow·er·bird \'bau̇(-ə)r-ˌbərd\ *n* : any of various mostly Australian birds that build chambers or passages arched over with twigs and grasses

bow·ie knife \'bü-ē-, 'bō-ē-\ *n* : a stout straight single-edged hunting knife

1**bowl** \'bōl\ *n* **1** : a rounded hollow dish generally deeper than a basin and larger than a cup **2** : the contents of a bowl **3** : the bowl-shaped part of something (as a spoon or a tobacco pipe) **4** : a bowl-shaped amphitheater — **bowled** \'bōld\ *adj*

2**bowl** *n* **1 a** : a ball weighted or shaped to roll in a curved path **b** *pl* : a game played on a green in which bowls are rolled **2** : a cast of the ball in bowling or bowls

3**bowl** *vb* **1** : to roll a ball in bowling or bowls **2** : to travel smoothly and rapidly **3** : to strike with or as if with a swiftly moving object ⟨the news *bowled* him over⟩

bow·leg \'bō-ˌleg, -'leg\ *n* : a leg bowed outward at or below the knee — **bow·legged** \'bō-'leg(-ə)d\ *adj*

1**bowl·er** \'bō-lər\ *n* : one that bowls

2**bow·ler** \'bō-lər\ *n* : DERBY 3

bowl game *n* : a football game played after the regular season between specially invited teams

bow·line \'bō-lən, -ˌlīn\ *n* **1 :** a rope used to keep the weather edge of a square sail pulled forward **2 :** a knot used for making a loop that will not slip

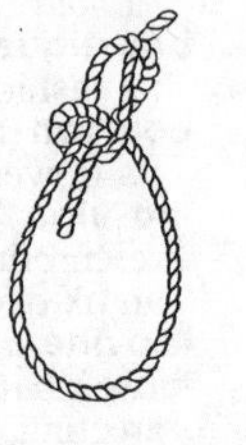

bowline 2

bowl·ing \'bō-ling\ *n* **1 :** a game played by rolling balls so as to knock down wooden pins set up at the far end of an alley **2 :** BOWL 1b

bow·man \'bō-mən\ *n* **:** ARCHER

bow·sprit \'bau̇-ˌsprit, 'bō-\ *n* **:** a large spar projecting forward from the bow of a ship

bow·string \'bō-ˌstring\ *n* **:** the cord connecting the two ends of a bow

bow window \'bō-\ *n* **:** a curved bay window

[1]**box** \'bäks\ *n, pl* **box** *or* **box·es :** an evergreen shrub or small tree used esp. for hedges

[2]**box** *n* **1 a :** a receptacle usu. having four sides, a bottom, and a cover **b :** the amount held by a box **2 :** a small compartment for a group of spectators in a theater **3 :** a stall for a horse **4 :** the driver's seat on a carriage **5 :** a shed that protects ⟨sentry *box*⟩ **6 :** a receptacle (as for a bearing) resembling a box **7 :** a space on a baseball diamond where a batter, coach, pitcher, or catcher stands

[3]**box** *vb* **:** to enclose in or as if in a box

[4]**box** *n* **:** a punch or slap esp. on the ear

[5]**box** *vb* **1 :** to strike with the hand **2 :** to engage in boxing **:** fight with the fists

box·car \'bäks-ˌkär\ *n* **:** a roofed freight car usu. with sliding doors in the sides

box elder *n* **:** a No. American maple with compound leaves

[1]**box·er** \'bäk-sər\ *n* **:** one that engages in the sport of boxing

[2]**boxer** *n* **:** a compact medium-sized short-haired usu. fawn or brindle dog of a breed originating in Germany

box·ing \'bäk-sing\ *n* **:** fighting with the fists practiced as a sport

Box·ing Day \'bäk-sing-\ *n* **:** the first weekday after Christmas observed as a legal holiday in parts of the British Commonwealth and marked by the giving of Christmas boxes (as to postmen)

boxing glove *n* **:** one of a pair of padded leather mittens worn in boxing

box office *n* **:** an office in a public place (as a theater or stadium) where admission tickets are sold

box score *n* **:** the complete score of a baseball game giving the names and positions of the players and a record of the play arranged in a table

box turtle *n* **:** any of several No. American land tortoises able to withdraw completely into the shell and to close it by hinged joints in the lower shell

box·wood \'bäks-ˌwu̇d\ *n* **:** the tough hard wood of the box; *also* **:** the box tree

boy \'bȯi\ *n* **1 :** a male child from birth to young manhood **2 :** SON **3 :** a male servant — **boy·hood** \-ˌhu̇d\ *n* — **boy·ish** \-ish\ *adj* — **boy·ish·ly** *adv* — **boy·ish·ness** *n*

[1]**boy·cott** \'bȯi-ˌkät\ *vb* [after Charles C. *Boycott* (1832-1897), an English land agent in Ireland who was ostracized for refusing to reduce rents] **:** to engage in a joint refusal to have dealings with a person, organization, or country usu. as an expression of disapproval or to force acceptance of terms

ə abut	ər further	a back	ā bake
ä cot, cart	au̇ out	ch chin	e less
ē easy	g gift	i trip	ī life
j joke	ng sing	ō flow	ȯ flaw
ȯi coin	th thin	t͟h this	ü loot
u̇ foot	y yet	yü few	yu̇ furious
zh vision			

[2]**boycott** *n* **:** the process or an instance of boycotting

boy·friend \'bȯi-ˌfrend\ *n* **:** a regular male companion of a girl or woman

Boyle's law \'bȯilz-\ *n* **:** a law that states that at constant temperature the volume of an enclosed gas will decrease as the pressure is increased and the volume of the gas will increase as the pressure is decreased

boy scout *n* **:** a member of the Boy Scouts of America

boy·sen·ber·ry \'bȯi-zən-ˌber-ē, -sən-\ *n* **1 :** a very large berry like a blackberry that resembles a raspberry in flavor and is valued for canning **2 :** the trailing hybrid bramble that produces boysenberries

bp *abbr* boiling point

bpl *abbr* birthplace

br *abbr* branch

Br *abbr* British

BR *abbr* bats right

bra \'brä\ *n* **:** BRASSIERE

[1]**brace** \'brās\ *n, pl* **brac·es** *or* **brace 1 :** two of a kind ⟨several *brace* of quail⟩ **2 :** something (as a clasp) that connects, fastens, or tightens **3 :** a crank-shaped handle for turning a wood-boring bit **4 a :** something that transmits, directs, resists, or supports weight or pressure; *esp* **:** an inclined timber used as a support **b** *pl* **:** SUSPENDERS **c :** a device for supporting a body part (as the shoulders) **d :** a usu. wire device worn on the teeth to correct irregularities of growth and position **5 a :** a mark { or } used to connect words or items or musical staffs that are to be taken together **b :** one of a pair of such marks enclosing words or symbols *syn* see COUPLE

[2]**brace** *vb* **1 a :** to make firm or taut **b :** to get ready ⟨*braced* himself for the test⟩ **2 :** to furnish or support with a brace **3 :** INVIGORATE, FRESHEN **4 :** to plant firmly ⟨*bracing* his feet in the stirrups⟩ **5 :** to take heart ⟨*brace* up, all is not lost⟩

brace·let \'brā-slət\ *n* [from medieval French, a derivative of *bras* "arm", from Latin *bracchium*] **:** an ornamental band or chain worn around the wrist

brach·i·al \'brāk-ē-əl\ *adj* **:** of or relating to the arm or a comparable process

brach·i·ate \'brak-ē-ˌāt, 'brā-kē-\ *vb* **:** to progress by swinging from one hold to another by the arms ⟨*brachiating* gibbons⟩ — **brach·i·a·tion** \ˌbrak-ē-'ā-shən, ˌbrā-kē-\ *n*

brach·io·pod \'brak-ē-ə-ˌpäd\ *n* **:** any of a phylum of marine invertebrate animals with bivalve shells and a pair of arms bearing tentacles — **brachiopod** *adj*

brack·en \'brak-ən\ *n* **:** a large coarse branching fern; *also* **:** a growth of such ferns

[1]**brack·et** \'brak-ət\ *n* **1 :** a support for a shelf or other weight usu. attached to a wall **2 :** a short wall shelf **3 a :** one of a pair of marks [ ] used to enclose words or usu. mathematical symbols to be taken together — called also *square bracket* **b :** one of a pair of marks ⟨ ⟩ used to enclose written or printed matter — called also *angle bracket* **4 :** CLASSIFICATION, GROUP; *esp* **:** one of a series of groups graded by income

[2]**bracket** *vb* **1 :** to place within or as if within brackets **2 :** to put into the same class **:** ASSOCIATE

bracket fungus *n* **:** a fungus that forms shelflike fruiting bodies

brack·ish \'brak-ish\ *adj* **:** somewhat salty

bract \'brakt\ *n* **1 :** a leaf from the axil of which a flower or inflorescence arises **2 :** a leaf that grows on a flower-bearing stem — **bract·ed** \'brak-təd\ *adj*

B

brad \'brad\ *n* : a thin wire nail

brae \'brā\ *n, chiefly Scot* : a hillside esp. along a river

[1]**brag** \'brag\ *n* **1** : a pompous or boastful statement **2** : arrogant talk or manner : COCKINESS **3** : BRAGGART

[2]**brag** *vb* **bragged**; **brag·ging** : to talk or assert boastfully — **brag·ger** \'brag-ər\ *n*

brag·ga·do·cio \ˌbrag-ə-'dō-s(h)ē-ˌō, -shō\ *n, pl* **-cios** **1** : BRAGGART **2** : BRAG

brag·gart \'brag-ərt\ *n* : a loud arrogant boaster — **braggart** *adj*

[1]**braid** \'brād\ *vb* **1** : to form strands into a braid ⟨*braided* her hair⟩ **2** : to ornament esp. with ribbon or braid — **braid·er** *n*

[2]**braid** *n* : a cord or ribbon or a length of hair formed of three or more intertwining strands

braille \'brāl\ *n, often cap* : a system of writing for the blind that uses characters made up of raised dots

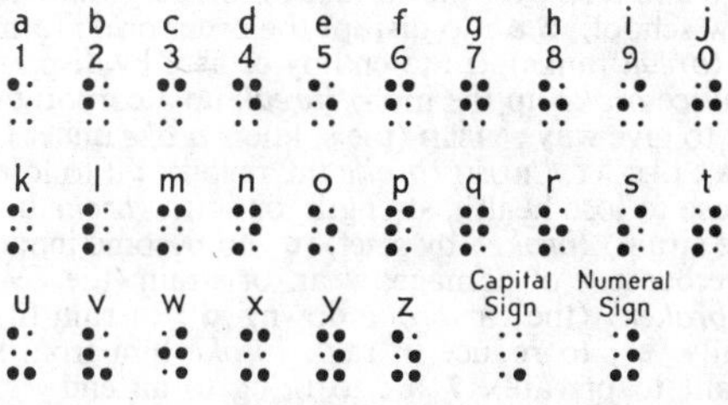

braille alphabet

[1]**brain** \'brān\ *n* **1 a** : the portion of the vertebrate central nervous system that is the organ of thought and nervous coordination, is enclosed within the skull, and is continuous with the spinal cord **b** : a major nervous center in an invertebrate animal **2 a** : UNDERSTANDING, INTELLIGENCE — often used in pl. **b** : a very intelligent or intellectual person

[2]**brain** *vb* **1** : to kill by smashing the skull **2** : to hit on the head

brain·case \'brān-ˌkās\ *n* : the cranium enclosing the brain

brain·less \-ləs\ *adj* : UNINTELLIGENT, SILLY — **brain·less·ly** *adv* — **brain·less·ness** *n*

brain stem *n* : the posterior and lower part of the brain including the midbrain and medulla oblongata

brain·storm \'brān-ˌstȯrm\ *n* **1** : a temporary violent mental disturbance **2** : a sudden burst of inspiration

brain·teas·er \-ˌtē-zər\ *n* : something demanding mental effort and sharpness for its solution : PUZZLE

brain·wash·ing \-ˌwȯsh-ing, -ˌwäsh-\ *n* : a forcible attempt to indoctrinate someone with political, social, or religious beliefs and attitudes he is opposed to

brain wave *n* : rhythmic fluctuations of voltage between parts of the brain

brainy \'brā-nē\ *adj* **brain·i·er**; **-est** : INTELLIGENT — **brain·i·ness** *n*

braise \'brāz\ *vb* : to cook slowly in fat and little moisture in a closed pot

[1]**brake** \'brāk\ *n* : a coarse fern often growing several feet high : BRACKEN

[2]**brake** *n* : a device for slowing up or stopping motion (as of a wheel, vehicle, or engine) esp. by friction

[3]**brake** *vb* : to retard or stop by or as if by a brake

[4]**brake** *n* : rough or marshy overgrown land : THICKET — **braky** \'brā-kē\ *adj*

brake·man \'brāk-mən\ *n* : a train crew member who inspects the train and assists the conductor

brake shoe *n* : SHOE 2c

bram·ble \'bram-bəl\ *n* : any of a large genus of usu. prickly shrubs (as a raspberry or blackberry) that are related to roses — **bram·bly** \-b(ə-)lē\ *adj*

bran \'bran\ *n* : the broken coat of the seed of cereal grain left after the grain has been ground and the flour or meal sifted out

[1]**branch** \'branch\ *n* **1** : a natural subdivision (as a bough arising from a trunk or a twig from a bough) of a plant stem **2** : something extending from a main line or body like a tree branch ⟨river *branch*⟩ ⟨a railroad *branch*⟩ **3** : DIVISION, SECTION ⟨executive *branch* of the government⟩ **4** : a subordinate office or part of a central system ⟨a *branch* of a bank⟩ *syn* see SHOOT — **branched** \'brancht\ *adj* — **branch·less** \'branch-ləs\ *adj*

[2]**branch** *vb* **1** : to put forth branches : spread or separate into branches ⟨a great elm *branches* over the yard⟩ **2** : to spring out from a main body or line : DIVERGE ⟨streets *branching* off the highway⟩ **3** : to extend activities ⟨the business is *branching* out all over the state⟩

bran·chi·al \'brang-kē-əl\ *adj* : of, relating to, or situated near the gills

[1]**brand** \'brand\ *n* **1** : a charred or burning piece of wood **2 a** : a mark made by burning (as on cattle) to show ownership or origin **b** : a mark made with a stamp or stencil for similar purposes **c** : TRADEMARK **3 a** : a mark put on criminals with a hot iron **b** : a mark of disgrace : STIGMA **4** : a class of goods identified as the product of a single maker : MAKE

[2]**brand** *vb* **1** : to mark with or as if with a brand **2** : to mark or expose as wicked : STIGMATIZE

bran·dish \'bran-dish\ *vb* : to shake or wave threateningly ⟨*brandish* a stick at a dog⟩

brand-new \'bran-'n(y)ü\ *adj* : conspicuously new and unused

[1]**bran·dy** \'bran-dē\ *n, pl* **-dies** [short for earlier *brandywine*, from Dutch *brandewijn*, meaning literally "burnt (i.e., distilled) wine"] : an alcoholic liquor distilled from wine or fermented fruit juice

[2]**brandy** *vb* **bran·died**; **bran·dy·ing** : to flavor, blend, or preserve with brandy ⟨*brandied* cherries⟩

brash \'brash\ *adj* **1** : IMPETUOUS, RASH ⟨a *brash* attack⟩ **2** : SAUCY, IMPUDENT ⟨a *brash* youth⟩ — **brash·ly** *adv* — **brash·ness** *n*

brass \'bras\ *n* **1** : an alloy consisting essentially of copper and zinc **2** : the reddish yellow color of brass **3** : brass musical instruments — often used in pl. **4** : bright metal fittings or utensils **5** : brazen self-assurance : GALL **6** : high-ranking esp. military officers — **brass** *adj*

bras·siere \brə-'zi(ə)r, ˌbras-ē-'e(ə)r\ *n* : a woman's close-fitting undergarment having cups for bust support

brassy \'bras-ē\ *adj* **brass·i·er**; **-est** **1** : BRAZEN, IMPUDENT **2** : resembling brass esp. in color **3** : resembling the sound of a brass instrument — **brass·i·ly** \'bras-ə-lē\ *adv* — **brass·i·ness** \'bras-ē-nəs\ *n*

brat \'brat\ *n* : CHILD; *esp* : an ill-mannered annoying child — **brat·tish** \'brat-ish\ *adj* — **brat·ty** \'brat-ē\ *adj*

bra·va·do \brə-'väd-ō\ *n, pl* **-does** *or* **-dos** : a show or pretense of bravery

[1]**brave** \'brāv\ *adj* **1** : resolute in facing odds : COURAGEOUS **2** : making a fine show : SPLENDID — **brave·ly** *adv*

[2]**brave** *vb* : to face or endure with courage ⟨*braved* the taunts of the mob⟩

[3]**brave** *n* : a No. American Indian warrior

brav·ery \'brāv-(ə-)rē\ *n, pl* **-er·ies** **1 a** : fine clothes **b** : showy display **2** : the quality or state of being brave : FEARLESSNESS ***syn*** see COURAGE

¹bra·vo \'bräv-ō\ *n, pl* **bravos** *or* **bravoes** : VILLAIN, DESPERADO; *esp* : a hired assassin

²bra·vo \'bräv-ō, brä-'vō\ *n, pl* **bravos** : a shout of approval — often used to applaud a performance

brawl \'bról\ *vb* **1** : to quarrel noisily : WRANGLE **2** : to make a loud confused noise — **brawl** *n* — **brawl·er** *n*

brawn \'brón\ *n* **1** : full strong muscles **2** : muscular strength — **brawn·i·ness** \'bró-nē-nəs\ *n* — **brawny** \'bró-nē\ *adj*

bray \'brā\ *vb* : to utter the characteristic loud harsh cry of a donkey — **bray** *n*

Braz *abbr* Brazilian

braze \'brāz\ *vb* : to solder with a relatively infusible alloy (as brass)

¹bra·zen \'brā-zən\ *adj* **1** : made of brass **2 a** : sounding harsh and loud like struck brass **b** : of the color of polished brass **3** : IMPUDENT, SHAMELESS — **bra·zen·ly** *adv* — **bra·zen·ness** \'brā-zən-(n)əs\ *n*

²brazen *vb* **bra·zened**; **bra·zen·ing** \'brāz-(ə-)ning\ : to face with defiance or impudence

bra·zier \'brā-zhər\ *n* **1** : a pan for holding burning coals **2** : a utensil on which food is exposed to heat through a wire grill

Bra·zil·ian \brə-'zil-yən\ *adj* : of, relating to, or characteristic of Brazil or its people — **Brazilian** *n*

Bra·zil nut \brə-,zil-\ *n* : one of the 3-sided oily edible nuts that occur packed inside the round fruit of a large Brazilian tree

Brazil nut

¹breach \'brēch\ *n* **1** : violation of a law, duty, or tie ⟨a *breach* of trust⟩ **2 a** : a broken, ruptured, or torn condition or area **b** : a gap (as in a wall) made by breaking through **3** : a break in friendly relations

²breach *vb* **1** : to make a breach in **2** : BREAK, VIOLATE

¹bread \'bred\ *n* **1** : a baked food made of flour or meal **2** : FOOD **3** *slang* : MONEY

²bread *vb* : to cover with bread crumbs ⟨*breaded* veal cutlet⟩

bread·bas·ket \'bred-,bas-kət\ *n* : a major cereal-producing region

bread·fruit \-,früt\ *n* : a round usu. seedless fruit that resembles bread in color and texture when baked; *also* : a tall tropical tree that is related to the mulberry and bears this fruit

breadfruit

bread·stuff \-,stəf\ *n* **1** : GRAIN, FLOUR **2** : BREAD

breadth \'bredth\ *n* **1** : distance from side to side : WIDTH **2 a** : something of full width **b** : a wide expanse **3** : COMPREHENSIVENESS, SCOPE

¹break \'brāk\ *vb* **broke** \'brōk\; **bro·ken** \'brō-kən\; **break·ing** **1 a** : to separate suddenly or violently into parts : SHATTER ⟨can't dry the dishes without *breaking* one⟩ ⟨the glass *broke* into a thousand pieces⟩ **b** (1) : FRACTURE ⟨*break* a bone⟩ (2) : to fracture the bone of (a bodily part) ⟨*broke* his arm⟩ **c** : to fracture the limbs of in torture : MAIM ⟨*broken* on the wheel⟩ **d** : to tear apart : CUT ⟨*break* the skin⟩ **e** : to curl over and fall apart ⟨waves *breaking* against the shore⟩ **2** : to fail to keep : VIOLATE ⟨*broke* the law⟩ ⟨*break* a promise⟩ **3 a** : to force a way into, out of, or through ⟨burglars *broke* into the house⟩ ⟨*break* jail⟩ **b** : to escape with sudden effort ⟨*broke* away from his captors⟩ **c** : to develop, appear, or burst forth suddenly ⟨day *breaks* in the east⟩ ⟨the storm *broke*⟩ ⟨*break* into tears⟩ **d** : to become fair ⟨wait for the weather to *break*⟩ **e** : to dash suddenly ⟨*break* for cover⟩ **f** : to make or effect by cutting, forcing, or pressing ⟨*break* open a package⟩ ⟨*break* a trail⟩ **g** : PENETRATE, PIERCE; *esp* : to penetrate the surface of ⟨fish *breaking* water⟩ **4** : to cut into and turn over the surface of ⟨*break* ground for a new school⟩ **5 a** : to disrupt the order or uniformity of ⟨*break* ranks⟩ **b** : to end by or as if by dispersing ⟨police *broke* up the mob⟩ ⟨*break* up a corporation⟩ **c** : to give way : YIELD ⟨the soldiers *broke* under fire⟩ **6 a** : DEFEAT, CRUSH ⟨*broke* the revolt⟩ **b** : to lose or cause to lose health, strength, or spirit ⟨*broke* under the strain⟩ ⟨*broken* by grief⟩ **c** : to become inoperative because of damage, wear, or strain ⟨the TV set is *broken*⟩ ⟨the car *broke* down⟩ **d** : to ruin financially **e** : to reduce in rank ⟨*broke* him from sergeant to private⟩ **7 a** : to bring to an end : STOP ⟨*break* a habit⟩ ⟨*broke* silence⟩ **b** : INTERRUPT ⟨*broke* in with a comment⟩ ⟨*broke* their tour for a rest⟩ **8 a** : to train an animal ⟨*break* a horse to the saddle⟩ **b** : to accustom to an activity ⟨*break* in a new worker⟩ **9** : to make known ⟨*break* the news to mother⟩ **10** : to turn aside or lessen the force of ⟨an awning *broke* his fall⟩ **11** : EXCEED, SURPASS ⟨*broke* all records⟩ **12** : OPEN ⟨*break* an electric circuit⟩ **13** : to cause to discontinue a habit ⟨*broke* the child of thumb-sucking⟩ **14** : SOLVE ⟨*broke* the code⟩ **15 a** : to curve, drop, or rise sharply ⟨the pitch *broke* over the plate for a strike⟩ **b** : to alter sharply in tone, pitch, or intensity ⟨his voice *broke*⟩ **c** : to shift abruptly from one register to another — **break·able** \'brā-kə-bəl\ *adj* — **break the ice** : to make a beginning esp. in friendly relations — **break wind** : to expel gas from the intestine

²break *n* **1** : an act, action, or result of breaking **2** : a gap in an electric circuit interrupting the flow of current **3 a** : a respite from work or duty **b** : a planned interruption in a radio or television program **c** : a noticeable change (as in a surface, course, movement, or direction) **d** : a notable variation in vocal pitch, intensity, or tone **e** : an abrupt run : DASH **4** : a place or situation at which a break occurs : GAP **5** : a stroke of luck ⟨a bad *break*⟩; *esp* : a stroke of good luck ⟨got all the *breaks*⟩

break·age \'brā-kij\ *n* **1 a** : the action of breaking **b** : a quantity broken **2** : an allowance for things broken

break·down \-,daůn\ *n* **1 a** : a failure to function properly **b** : a physical, mental, or nervous collapse **2** : DECOMPOSITION **3** : division into categories : CLASSIFICATION

break down \'brāk-'daůn\ *vb* **1** : to cease to work ⟨the engine *broke down*⟩ **2** : to collapse under stress ⟨*broke down* at the news⟩ **3 a** : to separate (as a protein) into simpler substances : DECOMPOSE **b** : to undergo decomposition **4 a** : ANALYZE, DIVIDE **b** : to become analyzed or divided

ə abut	ər further	a back	ā bake	
ä cot, cart	aů out	ch chin	e less	ē easy
g gift	i trip	ī life	j joke	ng sing	ō flow
ó flaw	ói coin	th thin	th this	ü loot
ů foot	y yet	yü few	yů furious	zh vision

break·er \'brā-kər\ *n* **1** : one that breaks **2** : a wave breaking into foam against the shore

break even *vb* : to emerge (as from a business transaction) with gains and losses balanced : reach a point where costs and profits balance

break·fast \'brek-fəst\ *n* : the first meal of the day — **breakfast** *vb*

breakfast food *n* : a breakfast cereal

break·neck \'brāk-ˌnek\ *adj* : extremely dangerous ⟨*breakneck* speed⟩

break out *vb* : to be affected with a skin eruption ⟨*broke out* with the measles⟩

break·through \'brāk-ˌthrü\ *n* : a sudden advance through resistance in knowledge or technique ⟨a *breakthrough* in medical science⟩

break·wa·ter \-ˌwȯt-ər, -ˌwät-\ *n* : a structure (as a wall) to protect a harbor or beach from the force of waves

bream \'brim\ *n, pl* **bream** *or* **breams** : any of various mostly freshwater spiny-finned fishes; *esp* : any of several sunfishes (as a bluegill)

[1]**breast** \'brest\ *n* **1** : either of two milk-producing organs situated on the front of the chest in the human female and some other mammals; *also* : any mammary gland **2** : the fore or ventral part of the body between the neck and the abdomen **3** : the seat of emotion and thought : BOSOM **4** : something resembling a breast — **breast·ed** \'bres-təd\ *adj*

[2]**breast** *vb* : FACE, CONFRONT ⟨*breasted* the waves⟩ ⟨*breast* a storm⟩

breast·bone \'bres(t)-'bōn, -ˌbōn\ *n* : STERNUM

breast–feed \'bres(t)-ˌfēd\ *vb* **-fed** \-ˌfed\; **-feed·ing** : to feed a baby milk from the breast

breast·plate \'bres(t)-ˌplāt\ *n* : metal armor for the breast

breast·stroke \'bres(t)-ˌstrōk\ *n* : a swimming stroke executed by extending the arms in front of the head while drawing the knees forward and outward and then sweeping the arms back with palms out while kicking backward and outward

breast·work \'brest-ˌwərk\ *n* : a hastily built fortification

breath \'breth\ *n* **1 a** : air filled with a fragrance or odor **b** : a slight indication : SUGGESTION **2 a** : the faculty of breathing **b** : an act of breathing **c** : RESPITE **3** : a slight breeze **4 a** : air inhaled and exhaled in breathing **b** : something (as moisture on a cold surface) produced by breathing **5** : a spoken sound : UTTERANCE — **out of breath** : breathing very rapidly (as from strenuous exercise)

breathe \'brēth\ *vb* **1** : to draw air into and expel it from the lungs **2** : LIVE **3** : to blow softly **4** : to send out by exhaling ⟨*breathe* a sigh of relief⟩ **5** : to instill by or as if by breathing ⟨*breathe* new life into the movement⟩ **6** : UTTER, EXPRESS ⟨never *breathed* a word of it⟩ **7** : to allow to rest after exertion ⟨*breathe* a horse⟩ **8** : to take in in breathing — **breath·a·ble** \'brē-thə-bəl\ *adj*

breath·er \'brē-thər\ *n* **1** : one that breathes **2** : a pause for rest

breath·less \'breth-ləs\ *adj* **1 a** : not breathing **b** : DEAD **2** : gasping for breath : PANTING — **breath·less·ly** *adv* — **breath·less·ness** *n*

breath·tak·ing \'breth-ˌtā-king\ *adj* **1** : making one out of breath ⟨*breathtaking* speed⟩ **2** : EXCITING, THRILLING ⟨*breathtaking* beauty⟩

brec·cia \'brech-(ē-)ə\ *n* : a rock consisting of sharp fragments embedded in a fine-grained material

breech \'brēch; "*breeches*" *(garment) is usu* 'brich-əz\ *n* **1** *pl* **a** : short trousers fitting snugly at or just below the knee **b** : PANTS **2** : BUTTOCKS **3** : the back part of a gun behind the bore

breech·es buoy \'brē-chəz-, 'brich-əz-\ *n* : a canvas sling in the form of a pair of short-legged breeches hung from a life buoy running along a rope that is used to take persons off a ship esp. in rescue operations

breeches buoy

[1]**breed** \'brēd\ *vb* **bred** \'bred\; **breed·ing** **1 a** : BEGET **1 b** : PRODUCE, ORIGINATE ⟨standing water *breeds* mosquitoes⟩ **2** : to propagate (plants or animals) sexually and usu. under controlled conditions (as for the development of improved forms) **3** : to bring up : NURTURE **4** : to mate with : MATE **5** : to produce offspring sexually ⟨*breed* like flies⟩ **6** : to produce (a fissionable element) by bombarding a nonfissionable element with neutrons from a radioactive element — **breed·er** *n*

[2]**breed** *n* **1** : a group of presumably related animals or plants visibly similar in most characters; *esp* : one originating in domestication **2** : CLASS, KIND

breed·ing *n* **1** : ANCESTRY **2** : training esp. in manners **3** : the sexual propagation of plants or animals

breeze \'brēz\ *n* : a gentle wind

breeze·way \'brēz-ˌwā\ *n* : a roofed open passage connecting two buildings or parts of a building

breezy \'brē-zē\ *adj* **breez·i·er**; **-est** **1** : swept by breezes **2** : BRISK, LIVELY — **breez·i·ly** \-zə-lē\ *adv* — **breez·i·ness** \-zē-nəs\ *n*

brethren *pl of* BROTHER — used chiefly in formal or solemn address

Bret·on \'bret-ən\ *n* : a native or inhabitant of Brittany

breve \'brēv, 'brev\ *n* [from Latin, the neuter of the adjective *brevis* "short" (the source of English *brief*)] : a mark ˘ placed over a vowel to show that the vowel is short

bre·via·ry \'brē-v(y)ə-rē, -vē-ˌer-ē\ *n, pl* **-ries** : a book containing prayers, hymns, and readings prescribed esp. for priests for each day of the year

brev·i·ty \'brev-ət-ē\ *n* **1** : shortness of duration **2** : expression in few words : CONCISENESS

[1]**brew** \'brü\ *vb* **1** : to prepare (as beer or ale) by steeping, boiling, and fermentation **2** : CONTRIVE, PLOT **3** : to prepare (as tea) by steeping in hot water **4** : to be forming ⟨a storm is *brewing*⟩ — **brew·er** \'brü-ər, 'bru̇(-ə)r\ *n*

[2]**brew** *n* : a brewed beverage

brewer's yeast *n* : a yeast used or suitable for use in brewing; *also* : the dried pulverized cells of such a yeast used as a source of B-complex vitamins

brew·ery \'brü-ə-rē, 'bru̇(-ə)r-ē\ *n, pl* **-er·ies** : a plant where malt liquors are brewed

bri·ar *var of* BRIER

[1]**bribe** \'brīb\ *n* : money or favor given or promised esp. to a person in a position of trust to influence dishonestly his judgment or conduct

[2]**bribe** *vb* : to influence by or as if by bribes — **brib·a·ble** \'brī-bə-bəl\ *adj* — **brib·er** *n*

brib·ery \'brī-b(ə-)rē\ *n, pl* **-er·ies** : the act or practice of bribing

bric–a–brac \'brik-ə-ˌbrak\ *n* : small ornamental articles : KNICKKNACKS

[1]**brick** \'brik\ *n* **1 a** : a building or paving material made from clay molded into blocks and hardened in the sun or baked **b** : a block made of brick **2** : a brick-shaped mass ⟨a *brick* of ice cream⟩

2**brick** *vb* : to close, face, or pave with bricks
brick·bat \'brik-ˌbat\ *n* : a piece of a broken brick; *esp* : one thrown as a missile
brick·lay·er \'brik-ˌlā-ər, -ˌle(-ə)r\ *n* : a person who builds with bricks — **brick·lay·ing** \-ˌlā-iŋ\ *n*
1**brid·al** \'brīd-əl\ *n* : WEDDING
2**bridal** *adj* : of or relating to a bride or a wedding
bride \'brīd\ *n* : a woman newly married or about to be married
bride·groom \-ˌgrüm, -ˌgru̇m\ *n* : a man just married or about to be married
brides·maid \'brīdz-ˌmād\ *n* : a woman who attends a bride at her wedding
1**bridge** \'brij\ *n* **1** : a structure built over a depression or an obstacle (as a river or a railroad) for use as a passageway **2** : a platform above and across the deck of a ship for the captain or officer in charge **3** : something resembling a bridge in form or function ⟨*bridge* of the nose⟩ **4** : an arch serving to raise the strings of a musical instrument **5** : a partial denture anchored to adjacent teeth
2**bridge** *vb* : to make a bridge over or across ⟨*bridge* a gap⟩ — **bridge·a·ble** \-ə-bəl\ *adj*
3**bridge** *n* : any of various card games for four players developed from whist
bridge·head \'brij-ˌhed\ *n* **1** : a fortified position protecting a bridge **2** : a position seized in enemy territory as a foothold for further advance
1**bri·dle** \'brīd-əl\ *n* **1** : the part of a horse's harness that fits over the head and is used to control the animal **2** : CURB, RESTRAINT
2**bridle** *vb* **bri·dled**; **bri·dling** \-(ə-)liŋ\ **1** : to put a bridle on **2** : to restrain with or as if with a bridle **3** : to show hostility or resentment esp. by drawing back the head and chin

bridle 1

bridle path *n* : a path for horseback riding
1**brief** \'brēf\ *adj* **1** : short in duration or extent **2** : CONCISE — **brief·ly** *adv* — **brief·ness** *n*
2**brief** *n* **1** : a concise statement of the case a lawyer will present in court **2** *pl* : short snug underpants
3**brief** *vb* **1** : to give final instructions to ⟨*brief* a bombing crew⟩ **2** : to give essential information to ⟨*brief* reporters⟩
brief·case \'brēf-ˌkās\ *n* : a flat flexible case usu. of leather for carrying papers
1**bri·er** \'brī(-ə)r\ *n* : a plant (as a blackberry or a wild rose) with a thorny or prickly woody stem — **bri·ery** \'brī(-ə)r-ē\ *adj*
2**brier** *n* : a heath of southern Europe the root of which is used for making tobacco pipes
1**brig** \'brig\ *n* : a 2-masted square-rigged ship
2**brig** *n* : a place (as on a ship) for temporary confinement of offenders in the U.S. Navy

brig

ə abut	ər further	a back	ā bake
ä cot, cart	au̇ out	ch chin	e less	ē easy
g gift	i trip	ī life	j joke	ŋ sing	ō flow
ȯ flaw	ȯi coin	th thin	t͟h this	ü loot
u̇ foot	y yet	yü few	yu̇ furious	zh vision

brig *abbr* **1** brigate **2** brigadier
bri·gade \brig-'ād\ *n* **1** : a military unit composed of one or more units of infantry or armor with supporting units **2** : a group of people organized for special activity ⟨fire *brigade*⟩ ⟨labor *brigade*⟩
brig·a·dier \ˌbrig-ə-'di(ə)r\ *n* : BRIGADIER GENERAL
brigadier general *n* : a commissioned officer (as in the army) ranking just below a major general
brig·and \'brig-ənd\ *n* : a person who lives by plunder usu. as a member of a band : BANDIT — **brig·and·age** \-ən-dij\ *n* — **brig·and·ism** \-ˌdiz-əm\ *n*
brig·an·tine \'brig-ən-ˌtēn\ *n* : a 2-masted square-rigged ship without a square mainsail
bright \'brīt\ *adj* **1** : shedding much light : GLOWING ⟨a *bright* fire⟩ ⟨a *bright* day⟩ ⟨a *bright* star⟩ **2** : very clear or vivid in color ⟨a *bright* red⟩ **3** : CLEVER, INTELLIGENT **4** : LIVELY, CHEERFUL **5** : PROMISING ⟨a *bright* future⟩ — **bright** *adv* — **bright·ly** *adv* — **bright·ness** *n*

syn BRIGHT, SHINING, BRILLIANT can mean emitting strong light. BRIGHT applies to a light that is strong by comparison with other lights from a similar source; SHINING suggests steady or constant brightness; BRILLIANT implies the shedding of a conspicuous, intense, or scintillating light ***ant*** dull, dim

bright·en \'brīt-ən\ *vb* **bright·ened**; **bright·en·ing** \-(ə-)niŋ\ : to make or become bright or brighter
brill \'bril\ *n, pl* **brill** : a European flatfish related to the turbot
1**bril·liant** \'bril-yənt\ *adj* **1 a** : very bright **b** : glittering brightly **2 a** : STRIKING, DISTINGUISHED **b** : unusually keen or alert in mind ***syn*** see BRIGHT ***ant*** subdued (*of light or color*) — **bril·liance** \-yən(t)s\ *or* **bril·lian·cy** \-yən-sē\ *n* — **bril·liant·ly** *adv*
2**brilliant** *n* : a gem (as a diamond) cut with many facets so as to sparkle
1**brim** \'brim\ *n* **1** : the rim esp. of a cup, bowl, or depression **2** : the projecting rim of a hat — **brim·ful** \-'fu̇l\ *adj* — **brim·less** \-ləs\ *adj*
2**brim** *vb* **brimmed**; **brim·ming** : to come to or overflow a brim
brim·stone \'brim-ˌstōn\ *n* : SULFUR
brin·dle \'brin-dəl\ *n* : a brindled color or animal
brin·dled \-dəld\ *or* **brin·dle** \-dəl\ *adj* : having faint dark streaks or spots on a gray or tawny ground
brine \'brīn\ *n* **1** : water containing a great deal of salt **2 a** : OCEAN **b** : the water of an ocean, sea, or salt lake
brine shrimp *n* : any of a genus of crustaceans found esp. in salt lakes
bring \'briŋ\ *vb* **brought** \'brȯt\; **bring·ing** \'briŋ-iŋ\ **1** : to cause to come with one by carrying or leading ⟨*bring* a lunch⟩ ⟨*bring* a friend⟩ **2** : PERSUADE, INDUCE ⟨*brought* him to agree⟩ **3** : to cause to come into a particular state or condition **4** : to cause to exist or occur ⟨winter will *bring* snow⟩ ⟨*bring* legal action⟩ **5** : to sell for ⟨apples will *bring* a good price⟩ — **bring forth** : to bear or give birth to : PRODUCE
bring about *vb* : to cause to take place : EFFECT
bring out *vb* : to present to the public ⟨*bring out* a new book⟩
bring to *vb* : to restore to consciousness
bring up *vb* **1** : REAR, EDUCATE **2** : to bring to attention : INTRODUCE **3** : VOMIT
brink \'briŋk\ *n* **1** : EDGE; *esp* : the edge at the top of a steep place **2** : the point of onset : VERGE ⟨*brink* of war⟩

briny \'brī-nē\ *adj* **brin·i·er; -est** : of or resembling brine : SALTY — **brin·i·ness** *n*
bri·quette *or* **bri·quet** \brik-'et\ *n* : a compacted mass of material ⟨charcoal *briquette*⟩
brisk \'brisk\ *adj* **1** : very active or alert : LIVELY **2** : INVIGORATING, REFRESHING ⟨*brisk* autumn weather⟩ **3** : ENERGETIC, QUICK ⟨a *brisk* pace⟩ — **brisk·ly** *adv* — **brisk·ness** *n*
bris·ket \'bris-kət\ *n* : the breast or lower chest of a four-footed animal
bris·ling *or* **bris·tling** \'briz-ling, 'bris-\ *n* : a small herring that resembles and is processed like a sardine
1**bris·tle** \'bris-əl\ *n* : a short stiff coarse hair or filament — **bris·tled** \-əld\ *adj* — **bris·tly** \-(ə-)lē\ *adj*
2**bristle** *vb* **bris·tled; bris·tling** \-(ə-)ling\ **1** : to stand stiffly erect ⟨quills *bristling* in all directions⟩ **2** : to show anger or defiance ⟨the boy *bristled* when he was criticized⟩ **3** : to appear as if covered with bristles — **bris·tly** \-(ə-)lē\ *adj*
bris·tle·cone pine \ˌbris-əl-ˌkōn-\ *n* : an extremely long-lived pine of the western U.S.
bris·tle·tail \'bris-əl-ˌtāl\ *n* : any of various wingless insects with two projecting tail bristles
bristle worm *n* : a segmented worm bearing setae
Brit *abbr* **1** Britain **2** British
bri·tan·nia metal \bri-ˌtan-yə-\ *n* : a silver-white alloy that is similar to pewter and is composed largely of tin, antimony, and copper
britch·es \'brich-əz\ *n pl* : BREECHES
1**Brit·ish** \'brit-ish\ *n* **1 British** *pl* : the people of Great Britain or their descendants **2** : ENGLISH
2**British** *adj* **1** : of or relating to the original inhabitants of Britain **2 a** : of or relating to Great Britain, the British Commonwealth, or the British **b** : ENGLISH
British system *n* : ENGLISH SYSTEM
British thermal unit *n* : the quantity of heat required to raise the temperature of one pound of water one degree Fahrenheit at or near 39.2° F — abbr. *Btu*
Brit·on \'brit-ən\ *n* **1** : a member of one of the peoples inhabiting Britain before the Anglo-Saxon invasions **2** : a native or subject of Great Britain; *esp* : ENGLISHMAN
Brit·ta·ny spaniel \ˌbrit-ə-nē-\ *n* : a large spaniel of a French breed developed by interbreeding pointers with spaniels of Brittany
brit·tle \'brit-əl\ *adj* : being hard but not tough : easily broken ⟨*brittle* glass⟩ — **brit·tle·ness** *n*
brittle star *n* : any of a group of sea animals similar to the related starfishes but having slender flexible arms
bro *abbr* brother
1**broach** \'brōch\ *n* : any of various pointed or tapered tools or parts; *esp* : one used for shaping a hole already bored
2**broach** *vb* **1** : to pierce (as a cask) in order to draw the contents : TAP **2** : to introduce for discussion ⟨*broach* a subject⟩
broad \'brȯd\ *adj* **1** : not narrow : WIDE ⟨a *broad* highway⟩ **2** : extending far and wide : SPACIOUS ⟨*broad* prairies⟩ **3** : CLEAR, FULL ⟨*broad* daylight⟩ **4** : PLAIN, OBVIOUS ⟨a *broad* hint⟩ **5** : COARSE, INDELICATE **6** : liberal in thought **7** : not limited : extended in range or amount ⟨a *broad* choice of subjects⟩ ⟨education in its *broadest* sense⟩ **8** : being main and essential ⟨*broad* outlines of a problem⟩ **9** : pronounced like the *a* in *father* — **broad·ly** *adv* — **broad·ness** *n*
broad·ax *or* **broad·axe** \'brȯd-ˌaks\ *n* : a broad-bladed ax
broad bean *n* **1** : an Old World upright vetch widely grown for its seeds and as fodder **2** : the large flat edible seed of a broad bean
1**broad·cast** \'brȯd-ˌkast\ *adj* **1** : scattered in all directions **2** : made public by means of radio or television — **broadcast** *adv*
2**broadcast** *n* **1** : the act of transmitting sound or images by radio or television **2** : a single radio or television program
3**broadcast** *vb* **broadcast** *also* **broad·cast·ed; broad·cast·ing 1** : to scatter or sow broadcast **2** : to send out by radio or television from a transmitting station — **broad·cast·er** *n*
broad·cloth \'brȯd-ˌklȯth\ *n* **1** : a fine woolen or worsted fabric made compact and glossy in finishing **2** : a fine cloth usu. of cotton, silk, or rayon made in plain and ribbed weaves
broad·en \'brȯd-ən\ *vb* **broad·ened; broad·en·ing** \-(ə-)ning\ : to make or become broad or broader
broad·leaf \'brȯd-ˌlēf\ *adj* : BROAD-LEAVED
broad–leaved \-'lēvd\ *or* **broad–leafed** \-'lēft\ *adj* : having broad leaves; *esp* : having leaves that are not needles
broad·loom \-ˌlüm\ *adj* : woven on a wide loom esp. in solid color ⟨*broadloom* rug⟩ — **broadloom** *n*
broad–mind·ed \-'mīn-dəd\ *adj* : tolerant of varied views or unorthodox behavior — **broad–mind·ed·ly** *adv* — **broad–mind·ed·ness** *n*
1**broad·side** \'brȯd-ˌsīd\ *n* **1** : the part of a ship's side above the waterline **2 a** : all the guns that can be fired from the same side of a ship **b** : a discharge of all these guns together **3** : a strongly worded attack ⟨a *broadside* of criticism⟩ **4** : a sheet of paper printed on one side (as for advertising)
2**broadside** *adv* : with the broadside toward a given object or point
broad·sword \'brȯd-ˌsōrd, -ˌsȯrd\ *n* : a broad-bladed sword
broad·tail \-ˌtāl\ *n* : the flat wavy fur of a young or premature karakul lamb
bro·cade \brō-'kād\ *n* : a rich fabric with raised patterns often in gold or silver thread — **bro·cad·ed** \-'kād-əd\ *adj*
broc·co·li \'bräk-(ə-)lē\ *n* : an open branching form of cauliflower whose young flowering shoots are used as a vegetable
bro·chure \brō-'shu̇(ə)r\ *n* : PAMPHLET
bro·gan \'brō-gən, brō-'gan\ *n* : a heavy shoe
1**brogue** \'brōg\ *n* **1** : BROGAN **2** : a shoe with decorative perforations along the seams
2**brogue** *n* : a marked dialect or regional pronunciation; *esp* : an Irish accent
1**broil** \'brȯil\ *vb* **1** : to cook or become cooked by direct exposure to fire or flame **2** : to make or become extremely hot ⟨a *broiling* sun⟩
2**broil** *vb* : BRAWL — **broil** *n*
broil·er \'brȯi-lər\ *n* **1** : a rack and pan or an oven equipped with a rack and pan for broiling meats **2** : a young chicken suitable for broiling
1**broke** \'brōk\ *past of* BREAK
2**broke** *adj* : having no money : PENNILESS
bro·ken \'brō-kən\ *adj* **1** : shattered into pieces ⟨*broken* glass⟩ **2 a** : ROUGH, UNEVEN ⟨*broken* country⟩ **b** : having gaps or breaks ⟨a *broken* line⟩ **3** : not kept ⟨a *broken* promise⟩ **4** : SUBDUED, CRUSHED ⟨a *broken* spirit⟩ **5** : imperfectly spoken ⟨*broken* English⟩ — **bro·ken·ly** *adv* — **bro·ken·ness** \-kən-(n)əs\ *n*
bro·ken–down \ˌbrō-kən-'dau̇n\ *adj* : infirm or worn to the point of breaking (as in strength, force, health, or structure)

bro·ken·heart·ed \ˌbrō-kən-ˈhärt-əd\ *adj* : crushed by grief or despair

broken line *n* **1** : a line made up of a series of dashes; *also* : a guideline painted in dashes on a highway to indicate where a driver may lawfully cross the midline of the road **2** : a line made up of segments of straight lines that join a number of given points

broken–line graph *n* : LINE GRAPH

bro·ker \ˈbrō-kər\ *n* : a person who acts as an agent in the purchase and sale of property

bro·ker·age \ˈbrō-k(ə-)rij\ *n* **1** : the business of a broker **2** : the fee or commission charged by a broker

bro·mide \ˈbrō-ˌmīd\ *n* : any of various compounds of bromine with another element or a radical including some (as potassium bromide) used as sedatives

bro·mid·ic \brō-ˈmid-ik\ *adj* : DULL, TIRESOME ⟨*bromidic* remarks⟩

bro·mine \ˈbrō-ˌmēn\ *n* [from French *brome*, from Greek *brōmos* meaning "a bad smell"] : an element that is normally a deep red corrosive liquid giving off an irritating reddish brown vapor of disagreeable odor — see ELEMENT table

bro·mo·thy·mol blue \ˌbrō-mə-ˌthī-ˌmȯl-, -ˌmōl-\ *n* : a chemical indicator

bronc \ˈbrängk\ *n* : BRONCO

bron·chi·al \ˈbräng-kē-əl\ *adj* : of, relating to, or involving the bronchi or their branches

bronchial pneumonia *n* : BRONCHOPNEUMONIA

bronchial tube *n* : a primary bronchus or any of its branches

bron·chi·ole \ˈbräng-kē-ˌōl\ *n* : a tiny thin-walled branch of a bronchial tube

bron·chi·tis \brän-ˈkīt-əs, bräng-\ *n* : acute or chronic inflammation of the bronchial tubes or a disease marked by this — **bron·chit·ic** \-ˈkit-ik\ *adj*

bron·cho·pneu·mo·nia \ˌbräng-kō-n(y)u̇-ˈmō-nyə, ˌbrän-\ *n* : pneumonia involving many relatively small areas of lung tissue

bron·cho·scope \ˈbräng-kə-ˌskōp\ *n* : a tubular instrument that may be passed through the trachea into the large bronchi and through which the bronchi can be inspected or worked on

bron·chus \ˈbräng-kəs\ *n, pl* **bron·chi** \ˈbrän-ˌkī, ˈbräng-, -ˌkē\ : either of the main divisions of the trachea each leading to a lung

bron·co \ˈbräng-kō, ˈbrän-\ *n, pl* **broncos** **1** : an unbroken or partly broken range horse of western No. America **2** : MUSTANG

bron·to·sau·rus \ˌbränt-ə-ˈsȯr-əs\ *also* **bron·to·saur** \ˈbränt-ə-ˌsȯr\ *n* : any of several very large four-footed and prob. herbivorous dinosaurs

[1]**bronze** \ˈbränz\ *vb* : to give the appearance of bronze to

[2]**bronze** *n* **1** : an alloy of copper and tin and sometimes other elements (as zinc) **2** : a work of art (as a statue, bust, or medallion) made of bronze **3** : a moderate yellowish brown — **bronzy** \ˈbrän-zē\ *adj*

Bronze Age *n* : a period of human culture characterized by the use of bronze tools and held to begin in Europe about 3500 B.C. and in western Asia and Egypt somewhat earlier

brooch \ˈbrōch, ˈbrüch\ *n* : an ornament held by a pin or clasp at or near the neck of a dress

[1]**brood** \ˈbrüd\ *n* : a family of young animals or children; *esp* : the young (as of a bird) hatched or cared for at one time

[2]**brood** *vb* **1** : to sit on eggs in order to hatch them **2** : to cover young with the wings **3** : to think anxiously or moodily ⟨*brooded* over his mistake⟩ — **brood·ing·ly** \-ing-lē\ *adv*

[3]**brood** *adj* : kept for breeding ⟨*brood* mare⟩ ⟨*brood* flock⟩

brood comb *n* : honeycomb made up of cells used for rearing bee larvae

brood·er \ˈbrüd-ər\ *n* **1** : a person or animal that broods **2** : a structure that can be heated and used for raising young fowl

broody \ˈbrüd-ē\ *adj* **1** : physiologically ready to brood **2** : inclined to brood : MOODY — **brood·i·ness** *n*

[1]**brook** \ˈbru̇k\ *vb* : to put up with : BEAR, TOLERATE ⟨*brooks* no interference⟩

[2]**brook** *n* : CREEK 2

brook·let \ˈbru̇k-lət\ *n* : a small brook

brook trout *n* : a common speckled cold-water char of eastern No. America

broom \ˈbrüm, ˈbru̇m\ *n* **1** : a plant that is related to the pea and has long slender branches along which grow many drooping yellow flowers **2** : a long-handled brush used for sweeping

broom·stick \-ˌstik\ *n* : the handle of a broom

bros *abbr* brothers

broth \ˈbrȯth\ *n, pl* **broths** \ˈbrȯths, ˈbrȯt͟hz\ : liquid in which meat, fish, or vegetables have been cooked

broth·er \ˈbrət͟h-ər\ *n, pl* **brothers** *or* **breth·ren** \ˈbret͟h-(ə-)rən, ˈbret͟h-ərn\ **1** : a male who has the same parents as another **2** : KINSMAN **3** : a fellow member **4** : one related to another by common ties or interests **5** *often cap* : a member of a male religious order who is not a priest ⟨a lay *brother*⟩

broth·er·hood \ˈbrət͟h-ər-ˌhu̇d\ *n* **1** : the state of being brothers or a brother **2** : an association of men for a particular purpose **3** : the persons engaged in a business or profession ⟨the legal *brotherhood*⟩

broth·er–in–law \ˈbrət͟h-(ə-)rən-ˌlȯ, ˈbrət͟h-ərn-ˌlȯ\ *n, pl* **broth·ers–in–law** \ˈbrət͟h-ər-zən-\ **1** : the brother of one's spouse **2** : the husband of one's sister

broth·er·ly \ˈbrət͟h-ər-lē\ *adj* **1** : of or relating to brothers **2** : natural or becoming to brothers : AFFECTIONATE ⟨*brotherly* love⟩ — **broth·er·li·ness** *n*

brougham \ˈbrü(-ə)m, ˈbrō-əm\ *n* **1** : a light closed carriage **2** : a 2-door sedan

brought *past of* BRING

brow \ˈbrau̇\ *n* **1 a** : EYEBROW **b** : the ridge on which the eyebrow grows **c** : FOREHEAD **2** : the upper edge of a steep slope

brow·beat \-ˌbēt\ *vb* **-beat**; **-beat·en** \-ˌbēt-ən\; **-beat·ing** : to frighten by a threatening manner or speech

[1]**brown** \ˈbrau̇n\ *adj* : of the color brown; *esp* : of dark or tanned complexion

[2]**brown** *n* : a color like that of coffee or chocolate that is a blend of red and yellow darkened by black — **brown·ish** \ˈbrau̇-nish\ *adj*

[3]**brown** *vb* : to make or become brown

brown alga *n* : any of a division of mostly marine algae with chlorophyll masked by brown pigment

brown coal *n* : LIGNITE

Brown·i·an movement \ˌbrau̇-nē-ən-\ *n* : a random movement of microscopic particles suspended in liquids or gases resulting from the impact of molecules of the fluid surrounding the particle

brown·ie \ˈbrau̇-nē\ *n* **1** : a good-natured goblin

ə abut	ər further	a back	ā bake	
ä cot, cart	au̇ out	ch chin	e less	ē easy
g gift	i trip	ī life	j joke	ng sing	ō flow
ȯ flaw	ȯi coin	th thin	t͟h this	ü loot
u̇ foot	y yet	yü few	yu̇ furious	zh vision

who performs helpful services at night **2 :** a member of a junior division of the Girl Scouts of the United States of America **3 :** a small square or rectangle of rich usu. chocolate cake containing nuts

brown rat *n* : the common domestic rat

brown·stone \'brau̇n-,stōn\ *n* **1 :** a reddish brown sandstone used for building **2 :** a dwelling faced with brownstone

brown sugar *n* : a somewhat moist cane sugar that is brown and contains some of the solids removed in refining white sugar

brown–tail moth \,brau̇n-,tāl-\ *n* : a tussock moth whose larvae feed on foliage and are irritating to the skin

brown trout *n* : a speckled European trout widely introduced as a game fish

brow·ridge \'brau̇-,rij\ *n* : a prominence on the bone above the eye caused by projection of air sinuses

1**browse** \'brau̇z\ *n* **1 :** tender shoots, twigs, and leaves fit for food for cattle **2 :** an act or instance of browsing

2**browse** *vb* **1 :** to nibble or feed on leaves and shoots **2 :** to read here and there in a book or library — **brows·er** *n*

bru·in \'brü-ən\ *n* [from *Bruin*, name of the bear in the medieval beast epic *Reynard the Fox*, from medieval Dutch *bruun* "brown"] : BEAR

1**bruise** \'brüz\ *vb* **1 :** to inflict a bruise on **2 :** to crush (as leaves or berries) by pounding **3 :** to hurt the feelings of **4 :** to become bruised or show the effects of bruises

2**bruise** *n* : an injury (as from a blow) in which the skin is not broken but is discolored from the breaking of small underlying blood vessels : CONTUSION

1**bruit** \'brüt\ *n, archaic* : REPORT, RUMOR

2**bruit** *vb* : to noise abroad : REPORT

brunch \'brənch\ *n* [from the first two letters of *breakfast* and the last four of *lunch*] : a late breakfast : an early lunch

bru·net *or* **bru·nette** \brü-'net\ *adj* : having brown or black hair and eyes — **brunet** *n*

brunt \'brənt\ *n* : the main force of a blow or an attack ⟨bore the *brunt* of the storm⟩

1**brush** \'brəsh\ *n* **1 :** BRUSHWOOD **2 a :** scrub vegetation **b :** land covered with scrub vegetation

2**brush** *n* **1 :** a device made of bristles set into a handle and used esp. for sweeping, scrubbing, or painting **2 :** a bushy tail (as of a fox or squirrel) **3 :** a conductor for an electric current between a moving and a nonmoving part of an electric motor or generator **4 a :** an act of brushing **b :** a quick light touch or momentary contact — **brush·like** \-,līk\ *adj*

3**brush** *vb* **1 a :** to clean, smooth, scrub, or paint with a brush **b :** to apply with a brush **2 :** to remove with or as if with a brush ⟨*brush* up dirt⟩ ⟨*brush* off criticism⟩ **3 :** to pass lightly across : GRAZE ⟨twigs *brushed* his cheek⟩ **4 :** to move so as to graze lightly ⟨*brushed* by the doorman⟩

4**brush** *n* : a brief encounter or skirmish

brush–off \'brəsh-,ȯf\ *n* : an abrupt or offhand dismissal

brush up *vb* : to refresh one's memory, skill, or knowledge ⟨*brush up* on arithmetic⟩ ⟨*brush up* your Shakespeare⟩

brush·wood \'brəsh-,wu̇d\ *n* **1 :** small branches cut from trees or shrubs **2 :** THICKET

1**brushy** \'brəsh-ē\ *adj* **brush·i·er; -est :** SHAGGY, ROUGH

2**brushy** *adj* **brush·i·er; -est :** covered with or abounding in brush or brushwood

brusque \'brəsk\ *adj* : abrupt in manner or speech — **brusque·ly** *adv* — **brusque·ness** *n*

brus·sels sprout \,brəs-əlz-\ *n, often cap B* : one of the edible small green heads borne on the stem of a plant related to the cabbage; *also* : this plant

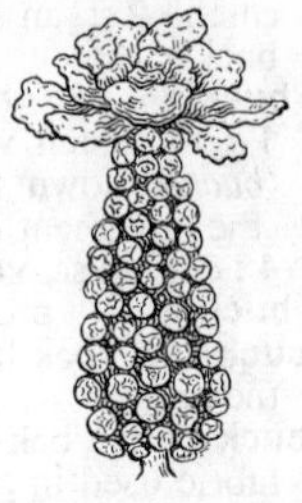

Brussels sprouts

bru·tal \'brüt-əl\ *adj* : ruthlessly violent : CRUEL, SAVAGE ⟨a *brutal* attack⟩ — **bru·tal·ly** \-ə-lē\ *adv*

bru·tal·i·ty \brü-'tal-ət-ē\ *n, pl* **-ties 1 :** the quality or state of being brutal **2 :** a brutal act or course of action

1**brute** \'brüt\ *adj* **1 :** of, relating to, or typical of beasts **2 :** CRUEL, SAVAGE **3 :** not guided by reason ⟨*brute* force⟩ **4 :** not softened or refined : CRUDE ⟨the *brute* facts⟩

2**brute** *n* **1 :** BEAST **2 :** a brutal or insensitive person — **brut·ish** \'brüt-ish\ *adj* — **brut·ish·ness** *n*

bry·ol·o·gy \brī-'äl-ə-jē\ *n* : a branch of botany that deals with mosses and liverworts

bry·o·phyl·lum \,brī-ə-'fil-əm\ *n* : a succulent Old World plant often grown as a foliage plant esp. from leaf cuttings — called also *air plant, life plant*

bry·o·phyte \'brī-ə-,fīt\ *n* : any of a division of nonflowering green plants comprising the mosses and liverworts — **bry·o·phyt·ic** \,brī-ə-'fit-ik\ *adj*

BS *abbr* bachelor of science

BSA *abbr* Boy Scouts of America

bskt *abbr* basket

Btu *abbr* British thermal unit

bu *abbr* bushel

1**bub·ble** \'bəb-əl\ *vb* **bub·bled; bub·bling** \-(ə-)ling\ **1 :** to form or produce bubbles **2 :** to flow with a gurgling sound **3 :** GURGLE

2**bubble** *n* **1 :** a small globule of gas within a liquid **2 :** a thin film of liquid filled with air or gas **3 :** a globule in a solid — **bub·bly** \'bəb-(ə-)lē\ *adj*

bubble chamber *n* : a chamber of heated liquid in which the path of an ionizing particle is made visible by a string of vapor bubbles

bu·bo \'b(y)ü-bō\ *n, pl* **buboes** : an inflammatory swelling of a lymph gland esp. in the groin — **bu·bon·ic** \b(y)ü-'bän-ik\ *adj*

bubonic plague *n* : a dangerous disease that is spread by rats and marked by chills and fever, weakness, and buboes

buc·ca·neer \,bək-ə-'ni(ə)r\ *n* : PIRATE

1**buck** \'bək\ *n, pl* **buck** *or* **bucks 1 :** a male animal; *esp* : a male deer or antelope **2 a :** MAN **b :** DANDY **3** *slang* : DOLLAR 3b

2**buck** *vb* **1 a :** to spring with a quick plunging leap ⟨*bucking* horse⟩ **b :** to throw (as a rider) by bucking **2 a :** to charge against something as if butting ⟨*buck* the line⟩ **b :** OPPOSE, RESIST ⟨*buck* change⟩ **3 :** to move or start jerkily — **buck·er** *n*

3**buck** *n* : an act or instance of bucking

buck·board \'bək-,bōrd, -,bȯrd\ *n* : a four-wheeled vehicle with a springy platform carrying the seat

1**buck·et** \'bək-ət\ *n* **1 :** a usu. round vessel for catching, holding, or carrying liquids or solids **2 :** an object for collecting, scooping, or carrying something **3 a :** BUCKETFUL **b :** a large quantity

bucket brigade *n* : a chain of persons passing buckets of water from hand to hand

buck·et·ful \'bək-ət-,fu̇l\ *n, pl* **buck·et·fuls** \-ət-,fu̇lz\ *or* **buck·ets·ful** \-əts-,fu̇l\ : the amount held by a bucket

bucket seat *n* : a low separate single seat used chiefly in automobiles and airplanes

buck·eye \'bək-,ī\ *n* : a shrub or tree related to the horse chestnut; *also* : its large nutlike seed

B

1**buck·le** \'bək-əl\ *n* **1** : a fastening for two loose ends that is attached to one and holds the other by a catch **2** : an ornamental device that suggests a buckle

2**buckle** *vb* **buck·led**; **buck·ling** \-(ə-)liŋ\ **1** : to fasten with a buckle **2** : to apply oneself ⟨*buckle* down to the job⟩ **3** : BEND, WARP, KINK ⟨the pavement *buckled* in the heat⟩ ⟨knees *buckled*⟩ **4** : COLLAPSE, YIELD

3**buckle** *n* : a product of buckling : BEND

buck·ler \'bək-lər\ *n* : a small round shield worn on the arm

buck·ram \'bək-rəm\ *n* : a stiff sized cotton or linen fabric used in garments, hats, and bookbindings — **buckram** *adj*

buck·saw \'bək-,sȯ\ *n* : a saw set in a usu. H-shaped frame that is used for sawing wood on a sawbuck

buck·shot \-,shät\ *n* : a coarse shot used in shotgun shells

buck·skin \-,skin\ *n* **1 a** : the skin of a buck **b** : a soft pliable leather **2** *pl* : buckskin breeches **3** : a horse of a light yellowish dun color usu. with dark mane and tail

buck·tooth \-'tüth\ *n* : a large projecting front tooth — **buck–toothed** \-'tütht\ *adj*

buck·wheat \'bək-,hwēt\ *n* : any of several herbs with pinkish white flowers and triangular seeds; *also* : the seeds used as feed or food

1**bu·col·ic** \byü-'käl-ik\ *adj* [from Greek *boukolikos*, from *boukolos* "cowherd", from *bous* "cow"] : PASTORAL, RURAL

2**bucolic** *n* : a pastoral poem

1**bud** \'bəd\ *n* **1** : a small growth at the tip or on the side of a plant stem that later develops into a flower, leaf, or new shoot **2** : a flower that has not fully opened **3** : a part that grows out from the body of an organism and develops into a new organism **4** : a stage in which something is not yet fully developed ⟨trees in *bud*⟩ ⟨a plan still in the *bud*⟩

2**bud** *vb* **bud·ded**; **bud·ding 1 a** : to set or put forth buds **b** : to reproduce asexually by forming and developing buds **2** : to be or develop like a bud (as in freshness and promise of growth) ⟨a *budding* diplomat⟩ **3** : to insert a bud from one plant into an opening cut in the bark of (another plant) in order to propagate a desired variety

budgerigar (about 7 in. long)

Bud·dhism \'bü-,diz-əm, 'bu̇d-,iz-\ *n* : a religion of eastern and central Asia growing out of the teaching of Gautama Buddha — **Bud·dhist** \'büd-əst, 'bu̇d-\ *n or adj* — **Bud·dhis·tic** \bü-'dis-tik, bu̇-\ *adj*

bud·dy \'bəd-ē\ *n, pl* **buddies** : COMPANION, PAL

budge \'bəj\ *vb* : MOVE, SHIFT; *esp* : YIELD

ə abut	ər further	a back	ā bake
ä cot, cart	au̇ out	ch chin	e less	ē easy
g gift	i trip	ī life	j joke	ŋ sing	ō flow
ȯ flaw	ȯi coin	th thin	t͟h this	ü loot
u̇ foot	y yet	yü few	yu̇ furious	zh vision

bud·ger·i·gar \'bəj-(ə-)ri-,gär, ,bəj-ə-'rē-,gär\ *n* : a small Australian parrot usu. light green with black and yellow markings in the wild but bred under domestication in many colors

1**bud·get** \'bəj-ət\ *n* [from medieval French *bougette*, meaning first "little bag", and then "the contents of a bag"] **1** : STOCK, SUPPLY **2 a** : a statement of estimated income and expenditures **b** : a plan for using money **c** : the amount of money available for some purpose

2**budget** *vb* **1** : to include in a budget ⟨*budget* $5 for entertainment⟩ **2** : to provide a budget for ⟨*budget* a trip abroad⟩ ⟨*budget* one's time⟩ **3** : to draw up and operate under a budget ⟨*budget* for a new car⟩ — **bud·get·ary** \'bəj-ə-,ter-ē\ *adj*

bud scale *n* : one of the leaves resembling scales that form the sheath of a plant bud

1**buff** \'bəf\ *n* **1** : a moderate orange yellow **2** : a device (as a stick or wheel) with a soft absorbent surface for applying polishing material **3** : FAN, ENTHUSIAST ⟨a tennis *buff*⟩

2**buff** *adj* : of the color buff

3**buff** *vb* : to polish with or as if with a buff

buf·fa·lo \'bəf-ə-,lō\ *n, pl* **-lo** *or* **-loes** : any of several wild oxen: as **a** : WATER BUFFALO **b** : a large shaggy-maned No. American wild ox with short horns and heavy forequarters bearing a large muscular hump

buffalo grass *n* : a low-growing native fodder grass of the American plains and prairies

1**buff·er** \'bəf-ər\ *n* : one that buffs

2**buf·fer** \'bəf-ər\ *n* **1** : a device or material for reducing shock due to contact **2** : a substance capable in solution of neutralizing both acids and bases

buffer state *n* : a small neutral state lying between two larger rival powers

1**buf·fet** \'bəf-ət\ *n* : a blow esp. with the hand

2**buffet** *vb* **1** : STRIKE, SLAP **2** : to pound repeatedly : BATTER ⟨*buffeted* by the crowd⟩ **3** : to struggle against ⟨*buffet* a storm⟩

3**buf·fet** \(,)bə-'fā, bü-\ *n* **1** : a cupboard or set of shelves for tableware : SIDEBOARD **2** : a counter for refreshments (as in a railway station) **3** : a meal set out on a buffet or table to be eaten without formal service

buf·fle·head \'bəf-əl-,hed\ *n* : a small No. American duck that obtains food by diving

buf·foon \(,)bə-'fün\ *n* : a person who amuses others by tricks, jokes, and antics : CLOWN

buf·foon·ery \-'fün-(ə-)rē\ *n, pl* **-er·ies** : the art or the conduct of a buffoon; *esp* : coarse clownish behavior

1**bug** \'bəg\ *n* **1 a** : an insect or other creeping or crawling invertebrate; *esp* : an obnoxious insect (as a bedbug or head louse) **b** : any of an order of insects with sucking mouthparts and incomplete metamorphosis that includes many destructive plant pests — called also *true bug* **2** : DEFECT, FLAW **3** : a disease-producing germ or a disease caused by it **4 a** : FAD, ENTHUSIASM **b** : ADDICT, FAN

2**bug** *vb* **bugged**; **bug·ging** : to plant a concealed microphone in

bug·a·boo \'bəg-ə-,bü\ *n, pl* **-boos** : BUGBEAR, BOGEY

bug·bear \'bəg-,ba(ə)r, -,be(ə)r\ *n* **1** : an imaginary goblin or specter used to excite fear **2** : an object or source of dread

1**bug·gy** \'bəg-ē\ *adj* **bug·gi·er**; **-est** **1** : infested with bugs ⟨it's too *buggy* out here — let's go inside⟩ **2** *slang* : CRAZY ⟨*buggy* about horses⟩

2**buggy** *n, pl* **buggies** : a light carriage having a single seat

bu·gle \'byü-gəl\ *n* [from Old French, meaning first "buffalo", then "instrument made of buffalo horn", coming from Latin *buculus* "wild ox", from *bos* "ox", "cow"] : a brass instrument like the trumpet but shorter and more conical — **bugle** *vb* — **bu·gler** \-glər\ *n*

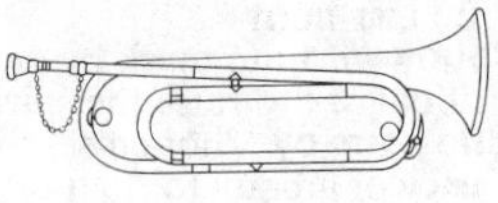

bugle

[1]**build** \'bild\ *vb* **built** \'bilt\; **build·ing 1** : to make by putting together parts or materials : CONSTRUCT ⟨*build* a house⟩ ⟨*build* a bridge⟩ **2** : to produce or create gradually ⟨*build* a winning team⟩ **3** : to progress toward a peak ⟨tension *building* up⟩

[2]**build** *n* : form or kind of structure; *esp* : PHYSIQUE

build·er \'bil-dər\ *n* : one that builds; *esp* : a person whose business is the building of houses and similar structures

build·ing \'bil-diŋ\ *n* **1** : a usu. roofed and walled structure (as for a dwelling) **2** : the art, work, or business of assembling materials into a structure

building block *n* **1** : BLOCK 1 **2** : a lightweight usu. solid wooden or plastic cubical toy that usu. is supplied in sets and is used in varied building and arranging activities **3** : one of many units comprising a whole ⟨*building blocks* of nucleic acid⟩

built-in \'bilt-'in\ *adj* : belonging to or fitted into the structure ⟨*built-in* bookcases⟩

bulb \'bəlb\ *n* **1 a** : a plant underground resting stage consisting of a short stem base bearing one or more buds enclosed in thickened storage leaves — compare CORM, TUBER **b** : a fleshy structure (as a tuber or corm) resembling a bulb in appearance or function **2** : a bulb-shaped object or part ⟨a lamp *bulb*⟩ — **bulb·like** \-ˌlīk\ *adj*

bul·bil \'bəl-bəl, -ˌbil\ *n* : a small or secondary plant bulb; *esp* : one produced in a leaf axil or replacing the flowers

bulb·ous \'bəl-bəs\ *adj* **1** : having a bulb : growing from or bearing bulbs **2** : resembling a bulb : ROUNDED, SWOLLEN — **bulb·ous·ly** *adv*

Bul·gar·i·an \ˌbəl-'gar-ē-ən, bu̇l-, -'ger-\ *n* **1** : a native or inhabitant of Bulgaria **2** : the Slavic language of the Bulgarians — **Bulgarian** *adj*

bulge \'bəlj\ *n* : a part that swells or bends outward — **bulge** *vb*

[1]**bulk** \'bəlk\ *n* **1** : greatness of size or mass : VOLUME **2** : a large body or mass **3** : the main or greater part — **in bulk** : in a mass : not divided into parts or packaged in separate units

[2]**bulk** *vb* **1** : SWELL, EXPAND **2** : to appear bulky

bulk·head \'bəlk-ˌhed\ *n* **1** : an upright partition separating compartments on a ship to resist pressure or to exclude water, fire, or gas **2** : a framework with a sloping door leading to a cellar stairway

bulky \'bəl-kē\ *adj* **bulk·i·er**; **-est 1** : large in size or mass **2** : being large and unwieldy — **bulk·i·ness** *n*

bull \'bu̇l\ *n* **1** : an adult male of a bovine animal or other large animals (as an elephant, moose, or whale) **2** : a person who buys securities in expectation of a price rise — **bull** *adj* — **bull·ish** \-ish\ *adj*

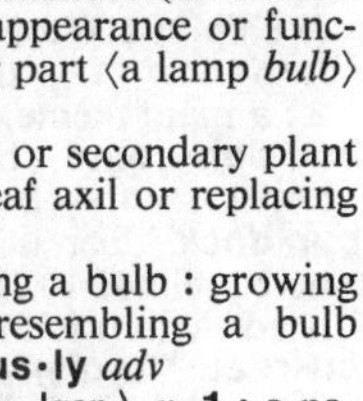

bulldog

[1]**bull·dog** \'bu̇l-ˌdȯg\ *n* : a compact muscular short-haired dog of English origin with forelegs set widely apart and an undershot lower jaw

[2]**bulldog** *adj* : resembling a bulldog : STUBBORN ⟨*bulldog* courage⟩

[3]**bulldog** *vb* : to throw a steer by seizing the horns and twisting the neck

bull·doze \'bu̇l-ˌdōz\ *vb* **1** : to move, clear, gouge out, or level with a bulldozer **2** : to force as if by using a bulldozer

bull·doz·er \-ˌdō-zər\ *n* : a tractor-driven machine having a broad blade for pushing (as in clearing land or building roads)

bul·let \'bu̇l-ət\ *n* [from medieval French *boulette*, diminutive of *boule* "ball", from Latin *bulla* "small round object"] : a shaped piece of metal made to be shot from a firearm

bul·le·tin \'bu̇l-ət-ən\ *n* **1** : a brief public notice usu. from an authoritative source ⟨weather *bulletin*⟩ ⟨special news *bulletin*⟩ **2** : a periodical publication esp. of a society

bulletin board *n* : a board for posting notices

bul·let·proof \ˌbu̇l-ət-'prüf\ *adj* : so made as to prevent the passing through of bullets

bull·fight \'bu̇l-ˌfīt\ *n* : an entertainment in which men excite and fight with bulls in an arena — **bull·fight·er** *n*

bull·finch \-ˌfinch\ *n* : a thick-billed red-breasted European songbird often kept as a cage bird

bull·frog \-ˌfrȯg, -ˌfräg\ *n* : a large heavy frog that makes a booming or bellowing sound

bull·head \-ˌhed\ *n* : any of various large-headed fishes; *esp* : any of several common freshwater catfishes of the U.S.

bull·head·ed \-'hed-əd\ *adj* : STUBBORN — **bull·head·ed·ness** *n*

bul·lion \'bu̇l-yən\ *n* : gold or silver esp. in bars or ingots

bull mastiff *n* : a large powerful dog of a breed developed by crossing bulldogs with mastiffs

bull·ock \'bu̇l-ək\ *n* **1** : a young bull **2** : a castrated bull : STEER

bull·pen \'bu̇l-ˌpen\ *n* : a place on a baseball field where relief pitchers warm up

bull's-eye \'bu̇l-ˌzī\ *n* **1** : the center of a target **2** : a shot that hits the bull's-eye **3** : a complete success

bull snake *n* : any of several large harmless No. American snakes feeding chiefly on rodents

bull·ter·ri·er \'bu̇l-'ter-ē-ər\ *n* : a short-haired terrier of a breed originated in England by crossing the bulldog with terriers

[1]**bul·ly** \'bu̇l-ē\ *n, pl* **bullies** : a person who is habitually cruel or abusive to others weaker than himself

[2]**bully** *vb* **bul·lied**; **bul·ly·ing** : to act like a bully : DOMINEER

bul·rush \'bu̇l-ˌrəsh\ *n* : any of several large sedges growing in wet land or water

bul·wark \'bu̇l-(ˌ)wərk, -ˌwȯrk\ *n* **1** : a solid wall built for defense : RAMPART **2** : a strong support or protection **3** : the side of a ship above the upper deck — usu. used in pl.

[1]**bum** \'bəm\ *vb* **bummed**; **bum·ming 1** : to wander like a tramp **2** : to obtain by begging ⟨*bum* a piece of candy⟩

[2]**bum** *n* **1** : a person who avoids work : LOAFER **2** : TRAMP, HOBO

[3]**bum** *adj* **1** : INFERIOR, WORTHLESS **2** : DISABLED ⟨a *bum* knee⟩

bum·ble·bee \'bəm-bəl-ˌbē\ *n* : any of numerous large robust hairy social bees

[1]**bump** \'bəmp\ *vb* **1** : to strike or knock against something with force or violence **2** : to proceed in a series of bumps : JOLT — **bump into** : to encounter esp. by chance

²**bump** *n* **1 :** a forceful blow, impact, or jolt **2 :** a rounded lump; *esp* **:** a swelling of tissue (as from a blow or sting)
¹**bum·per** \'bəm-pər\ *n* **:** a cup or glass filled to the brim
²**bumper** *adj* **:** unusually large or fine ⟨a *bumper* crop⟩
³**bump·er** \'bəm-pər\ *n* **:** a device for absorbing shock or preventing damage; *esp* **:** a metal bar at the end of an automobile
bump·kin \'bəm(p)-kən\ *n* **:** RUSTIC, YOKEL
bumpy \'bəm-pē\ *adj* **bump·i·er; -est :** marked by bumps or bumping ⟨a *bumpy* ride⟩ — **bump·i·ly** \-pə-lē\ *adv* — **bump·i·ness** \-pē-nəs\ *n*
bun \'bən\ *n* **1 :** a sweet or plain small bread **2 :** a knot of hair shaped like a bun
¹**bunch** \'bənch\ *n* **1 :** PROTUBERANCE, SWELLING **2 a :** a number of things of the same kind **:** CLUSTER ⟨a *bunch* of grapes⟩ **b :** GROUP, COLLECTION ⟨a *bunch* of his friends⟩ — **bunch·i·ly** \'bən-chə-lē\ *adv* — **bunchy** \-chē\ *adj*
²**bunch** *vb* **:** to form in or gather into a group or cluster
¹**bun·dle** \'bən-dəl\ *n* **1 a :** a group of things tied together **b :** PACKAGE, PARCEL **2 :** a small band of mostly parallel fibers (as of nerve)
²**bundle** *vb* **bun·dled; bun·dling** \-d(ə-)ling\ **1 :** to make into a bundle **:** WRAP **2 :** to hurry off **:** HUSTLE — **bun·dler** \-d(ə-)lər\ *n*
¹**bung** \'bəng\ *n* **1 :** the stopper in the bunghole of a cask **2 :** BUNGHOLE
²**bung** *vb* **1 :** to plug with a bung **2 :** BATTER, BRUISE ⟨badly *bunged* up⟩
bun·ga·low \'bəng-gə-ˌlō\ *n* [from Hindi *baṅglā* "(house) in the style of Bengal", from *Baṅgāl* "Bengal"] **:** a usu. one-storied house with low sweeping lines and a wide veranda
bung·hole \'bəng-ˌhōl\ *n* **:** a hole for filling or emptying a cask
bun·gle \'bəng-gəl\ *vb* **bun·gled; bun·gling** \-g(ə-)ling\ **:** to act, do, or make clumsily — **bungle** *n* — **bun·gler** \-g(ə-)ler\ *n*
bun·ion \'bən-yən\ *n* **:** an inflamed swelling on the first joint of the big toe
¹**bunk** \'bəngk\ *n* **1 :** a built-in bed (as on a ship) **2 :** a sleeping place — **bunk** *vb*
²**bunk** *n* **:** NONSENSE
bun·ker \'bəng-kər\ *n* **1 :** a large bin (as for coal or oil on a ship) **2 :** a fortified dugout **3 :** an obstacle on a golf course
bunk·house \'bəngk-ˌhau̇s\ *n* **:** a rough simple building providing sleeping quarters (as for construction workers)
bun·ny \'bən-ē\ *n, pl* **bunnies :** RABBIT
Bun·sen burner \ˌbən(t)-sən-\ *n* **:** a gas burner consisting typically of a tube with small holes at the bottom where air enters and mixes with the gas to produce a very hot blue flame
bunt *vb* **1 :** to strike or push with or as if with the head **:** BUTT **2 :** to push or tap a baseball lightly without swinging the bat — **bunt** *n* — **bunt·er** *n*
¹**bun·ting** \'bənt-ing\ *n* **:** any of various stout-billed finches of the size and habits of a sparrow
²**bunting** *n* **1 :** a thin fabric used chiefly for making flags and patriotic decorations **2 :** flags or decorations made of bunting

ə abut	ər further	a back	ā bake
ä cot, cart	au̇ out	ch chin	e less
ē easy	g gift	i trip	ī life
j joke	ng sing	ō flow	ȯ flaw
ȯi coin	th thin	t͟h this	ü loot
u̇ foot	y yet	yü few	yu̇ furious
zh vision			

¹**buoy** \'bü-ē, 'bȯi\ *n* **1 :** a floating object anchored in a body of water to mark a channel or warn of danger **2 :** LIFE BUOY
²**buoy** *vb* **1 :** to mark by or as if by a buoy **2 :** to keep afloat **3 :** to raise the spirits of ⟨*buoyed* up by hope⟩
buoy·an·cy \'bȯi-ən-sē, 'bü-yən-\ *n* **1 a :** the tendency of a body to float or to rise when submerged in a fluid ⟨the *buoyancy* of a cork in water⟩ **b :** the power of a fluid to exert an upward force on a body placed in it ⟨the *buoyancy* of seawater⟩ **2 :** lightness of spirit **:** LIGHTHEARTEDNESS
buoy·ant \'bȯi-ənt, 'bü-yənt\ *adj* **1 :** able to rise and float in the air or on the surface of a liquid **2 :** able to keep a body afloat ⟨gliding in *buoyant* currents of air⟩ **3 :** LIGHTHEARTED, CHEERFUL — **buoy·ant·ly** *adv*
bu·pres·tid \byü-'pres-təd\ *n* **:** any of a family of usu. small blue or bronze beetles with short heads and large eyes and long legless larvae some of which are destructive borers in the wood of fruit trees and other trees
bur *var of* BURR
bur *abbr* bureau
bur·ble \'bər-bəl\ *vb* **bur·bled; bur·bling** \'bər-b(ə-)ling\ **:** BABBLE, PRATTLE — **burble** *n* — **bur·bler** \-b(ə-)lər\ *n* — **bur·bly** \-b(ə-)lē\ *adv*
bur·bot \'bər-bət\ *n, pl* **burbot** *also* **burbots :** a northern freshwater fish related to the cod but somewhat resembling an eel
¹**bur·den** \'bərd-ən\ *n* **1 a :** something carried **:** LOAD **b :** something borne as a duty, obligation, or responsibility ⟨tax *burdens*⟩ **2 :** something hard to bear ⟨a *burden* of sorrow⟩ **3 a :** the carrying of loads ⟨beast of *burden*⟩ **b :** capacity for carrying cargo ⟨a ship of 100 tons *burden*⟩ — **burden** *vb*
²**burden** *n* **1 :** the refrain or chorus of a song **2 :** a main theme or central idea **:** GIST
bur·den·some \'bərd-ən-səm\ *adj* **:** difficult to bear **:** OPPRESSIVE — **bur·den·some·ness** *n*
bur·dock \'bər-ˌdäk\ *n* **:** any of a genus of coarse herbs related to the daisy that have globular flower heads with prickly bracts
bu·reau \'byu̇(ə)r-ō\ *n, pl* **bureaus** *also* **bu·reaux** \-ōz\ **1 :** a low chest of drawers with a mirror for a bedroom **2 a :** a subdivision of a governmental department ⟨Weather *Bureau*⟩ **b :** a commercial agency providing services for the public ⟨travel *bureau*⟩
bu·reau·cra·cy \byu̇-'räk-rə-sē\ *n, pl* **-cies 1 :** a body of officials; *esp* **:** appointed or hired government officials **2 :** administration by inflexible following of fixed rules and much delay
bu·reau·crat \'byu̇r-ə-ˌkrat\ *n* **:** a member of a bureaucracy; *esp* **:** one who carries out his duties in a narrow routine way — **bu·reau·crat·ic** \ˌbyu̇r-ə-'krat-ik\ *adj* — **bu·reau·crat·i·cal·ly** \-'krat-i-k(ə-)lē\ *adv*
bu·rette *or* **bu·ret** \byu̇-'ret\ *n* **:** a graduated glass tube usu. with a small aperture and stopcock for delivering measured quantities of liquid or for measuring the liquid or gas received or discharged
bur·geon \'bər-jən\ *vb* **1 a :** to put forth new growth (as buds) **b :** BLOSSOM, BLOOM **2 :** EXPAND, FLOURISH
bur·gess \'bər-jəs\ *n* **1 :** a citizen of a British borough **2 :** a member of the lower house of the legislature of colonial Virginia
burgh \'bər-ō, 'bə-rō\ *n* **:** BOROUGH; *esp* **:** a Scottish town with certain local lawmaking rights
burgh·er \'bər-gər\ *n* **:** an inhabitant of a borough or a town
bur·glar \'bər-glər\ *n* **:** one who commits burglary **:** THIEF

bur·glary \'bər-glə-rē\ *n, pl* **-glar·ies :** the act of breaking into a building (as a house) esp. at night to commit a crime (as stealing) — **bur·glar·ize** \-glə-ˌrīz\ *vb*
bur·go·mas·ter \'bər-gə-ˌmas-tər\ *n* **:** the mayor of a town in some European countries
Bur·gun·di·an \(ˌ)bər-'gən-dē-ən\ *adj* **:** of, relating to, or characteristic of Burgundy or its people — **Burgundian** *n*
bur·i·al \'ber-ē-əl\ *n* **:** the act of burying
bur·lap \'bər-ˌlap\ *n* **:** a coarse fabric made usu. from jute or hemp and used esp. for bags and wrappings
[1]**bur·lesque** \(ˌ)bər-'lesk\ *n* **1 :** a witty or derisive literary or dramatic imitation **2 :** theatrical entertainment consisting of low comedy and dance — **burlesque** *adj*
[2]**burlesque** *vb* **:** to mock or ridicule through burlesque
bur·ly \'bər-lē\ *adj* **bur·li·er; -est :** strongly and heavily built **:** HUSKY — **bur·li·ness** *n*
bur marigold *n* **:** any of a genus of coarse herbs related to the daisies having burs that adhere to clothing
Bur·mese \ˌbər-'mēz, -'mēs\ *n, pl* **Burmese 1 :** a native or inhabitant of Burma **2 :** the language of the Burmese people — **Burmese** *adj*
[1]**burn** *vb* **burned** \'bərnd\ *or* **burnt** \'bərnt\; **burning 1 :** to be or set on fire **2 a :** to feel hot or inflamed ⟨*burn* with anger⟩ **b :** SCORCH **c :** to appear as if on fire **:** GLOW **d :** to destroy by fire ⟨*burn* trash⟩ **e :** to use as fuel ⟨this furnace *burns* gas⟩ **f :** to consume fuel ⟨the rocket *burns*⟩ **3 :** to produce by the action of fire or heat ⟨*burn* a hole in the rug⟩ **4 :** to injure or alter by or as if by fire or heat ⟨*burn* out a bearing⟩ — **burn·a·ble** \'bər-nə-bəl\ *adj* — **burn·ing·ly** \-ning-lē\ *adv*
[2]**burn** *n* **1 :** injury, damage, or effect produced by or as if by burning **2 :** the process of burning ⟨energy gained during the rocket *burn*⟩
burn·er \'bər-nər\ *n* **:** one that burns; *esp* **:** the part of a device where a flame is produced
burning glass *n* **:** a convex lens for producing an intense heat by focusing the rays of the sun through it
bur·nish \'bər-nish\ *vb* **:** to make shiny or lustrous esp. by rubbing **:** POLISH — **burnish** *n* — **bur·nish·er** *n*
bur·noose *or* **bur·nous** \(ˌ)bər-'nüs\ *n* **:** a hooded cloak worn by Arabs and Moors

burnoose

burn·out \'bər-ˌnau̇t\ *n* **1 :** the process of burning out (as of a fuse or a building) **2 :** the cessation of operation of a jet or rocket engine as a result of the using up or shutting off of fuel **3 :** the point in a flight at which burnout occurs
burnt \'bərnt\ *adj* **:** consumed or altered by or as if by fire or heat
[1]**burp** \'bərp\ *n* **:** BELCH
[2]**burp** *vb* **1 :** BELCH **2 :** to help a baby expel gas from the stomach esp. by patting or rubbing the back
[1]**burr** \'bər\ *n* **1** *usu* **bur a :** a rough or prickly envelope of a fruit **b :** a plant that bears burs **2** *usu* **bur :** a bit used on a dental drill **3 :** roughness left in cutting or shaping metal **4 :** a rough trilled *r* as used esp. in northern England and in Scotland **5 :** a rough humming sound **:** WHIR — **burred** \'bərd\ *adj*
[2]**burr** *vb* **1 :** to speak or pronounce with a burr **2 :** to make a whirring sound **3 a :** to form into a rough edge **b :** to remove burrs from — **burr·er** \'bər-ər\ *n*
bur·ro \'bər-ō, 'bu̇r-; 'bə-rō\ *n, pl* **burros :** DONKEY; *esp* **:** a small one used as a pack animal
[1]**bur·row** \'bər-ō, 'bə-rō\ *n* **:** a hole in the ground made by an animal (as a rabbit) for shelter
[2]**burrow** *vb* **1 :** to construct by tunneling ⟨*burrow* a passage through the hill⟩ **2 :** to hide in or as if in a burrow **3 :** to move or enter by or as if by digging **4 :** to make a thorough search ⟨*burrowed* through his files⟩ — **bur·row·er** *n*
bur·sa \'bər-sə\ *n, pl* **bursas** *or* **bur·sae** \-ˌsē, -ˌsī\ **:** a bodily pouch or sac; *esp* **:** a small serous sac between a tendon and a bone — **bur·sal** \-səl\ *adj*
bur·sar \'bər-sər, -ˌsär\ *n* **:** a treasurer esp. of a college
bur·si·tis \(ˌ)bər-'sīt-əs\ *n* **:** inflammation of a bursa esp. of the shoulder or elbow
[1]**burst** \'bərst\ *vb* **burst; burst·ing 1 a :** to break open, apart, or into pieces from or as if from a blow or pressure from within ⟨buds ready to *burst* open⟩ ⟨bombs *bursting* in the air⟩ **b :** to cause to burst **2 a :** to give way from emotion ⟨his heart *burst* with grief⟩ **b :** to begin suddenly **:** BREAK ⟨*burst* into song⟩ ⟨*burst* into tears⟩ **3 :** to come or go suddenly ⟨*burst* out of a house⟩ **4 :** to be filled to the breaking point
[2]**burst** *n* **1 :** a sudden outbreak or effort ⟨a *burst* of laughter⟩ ⟨a *burst* of speed⟩ **2 :** a volley of shots **3 :** an act or result of bursting; *esp* **:** a visible puff accompanying the explosion of a shell
bur·then \'bər-t͟hən\ *archaic var of* BURDEN
bury \'ber-ē\ *vb* **bur·ied; bury·ing 1 :** to deposit a dead body in the earth, a tomb, or the sea **2 :** to place in the ground and cover over ⟨*buried* treasure⟩ **3 :** CONCEAL, HIDE ⟨*bury* her face in her hands⟩ **4 :** to remove from the world of action ⟨*bury* oneself in a book⟩ — **bur·i·er** *n*
bus \'bəs\ *n, pl* **bus·es** *or* **bus·ses** [short for *omnibus*, from a Latin word meaning "for everybody" (dative plural of *omnis* "all")] **:** a large passenger vehicle — **bus** *vb*
bus *abbr* business
bus·boy \'bəs-ˌbȯi\ *n* **:** a man or boy employed in a restaurant to remove soiled dishes and set tables
bush \'bu̇sh\ *n* **1 :** SHRUB; *esp* **:** a low densely branched shrub **2 :** a large uncleared or sparsely settled area (as in Australia) **3 :** a bushy tuft or mass
bush baby *n* **:** any of several small African lemurs
bush·el \'bu̇sh-əl\ *n* **1 :** any of various units of dry capacity — see MEASURE table **2 :** a container holding a bushel **3 :** a large quantity
bush·ing \'bu̇sh-ing\ *n* **1 :** a usu. removable cylindrical lining in an opening of a mechanical part to limit the size of the opening, resist wear (as in a bearing for an axle), or serve as a guide **2 :** an electrically insulating lining for a hole to protect a conductor
bush·man \'bu̇sh-mən\ *n* **1 :** a member of a nomadic hunting people of southern Africa **2 :** a person skilled at living in the bush or forest **:** WOODSMAN
bush·mas·ter \-ˌmas-tər\ *n* **:** a tropical American pit viper that is the largest New World venomous snake
bush pilot *n* **:** a pilot who flies a small plane over sparsely settled country
bushy \'bu̇sh-ē\ *adj* **bush·i·er; -est 1 :** full of or

overgrown with bushes **2 :** resembling a bush; *esp* **:** thickly spreading — **bush·i·ness** *n*

busi·ness \ˈbiz-nəs, -nəz\ *n* **1 :** an activity that takes a major part of the time, attention, or effort of a person or group; *esp* **:** OCCUPATION **2 :** an immediate task or goal ⟨state your *business*⟩ **3 a :** a commercial or industrial enterprise **b :** the making, buying, and selling of goods and services **4 :** AFFAIR, MATTER ⟨a strange *business*⟩ **5 :** a rightful interest **:** personal concern ⟨none of your *business*⟩

busi·ness·like \-ˌlīk\ *adj* **:** having or showing qualities desirable in business **:** EFFICIENT, PRACTICAL

busi·ness·man \-ˌman\ *n* **:** a business executive

[1]**bust** \ˈbəst\ *n* [from French *buste*, from Italian *busto*, from Latin *bustum* meaning "a tomb", on which a bust of the deceased was often placed] **1 :** a piece of sculpture representing the human head and neck **2 :** the upper portion of the human torso between neck and waist; *esp* **:** the breasts of a woman

[2]**bust** *vb* **bust·ed** *also* **bust**; **bust·ing** **1 :** HIT, PUNCH **2 :** BREAK, BURST **3 :** to ruin or become ruined financially **4 :** to demote esp. in military rank **5** *slang* **a :** ARREST **b :** RAID — **bust·er** *n*

[3]**bust** *n* **1** *slang* **:** [2]PUNCH 1 **2 :** a complete failure **3 :** SPREE **4** *slang* **:** a police raid

bus·tard \ˈbəs-tərd\ *n* **:** any of various Old World and Australian game birds

[1]**bus·tle** \ˈbəs-əl\ *vb* **bus·tled**; **bus·tling** \ˈbəs-(ə-)liŋ\ **:** to move about busily or noisily

[2]**bustle** *n* **:** noisy or energetic activity

[3]**bustle** *n* **:** a pad or light frame formerly worn by women just below the back waistline to give fullness to a skirt

[1]**busy** \ˈbiz-ē\ *adj* **bus·i·er**; **-est** **1 a :** engaged in action **:** OCCUPIED ⟨too *busy* to eat⟩ **b :** being in use ⟨a *busy* telephone⟩ **2 :** full of activity **:** BUSTLING ⟨a *busy* street⟩ — **bus·i·ly** \ˈbiz-ə-lē\ *adv*

syn BUSY, INDUSTRIOUS, DILIGENT can mean seriously occupied in accomplishing a purpose. BUSY suggests active occupation that demands one's time and attention; INDUSTRIOUS suggests constant or habitual devotion to work; DILIGENT may imply persevering application to a particular object or pursuit ***ant*** idle, unoccupied

[2]**busy** *vb* **bus·ied**; **busy·ing** **:** to make or keep busy

busy·body \ˈbiz-ē-ˌbäd-ē\ *n* **:** a person who meddles in the affairs of others

[1]**but** \(ˈ)bət\ *conj* **1 a :** except that **:** UNLESS ⟨it never rains *but* it pours⟩ **b :** that not ⟨not so stupid *but* he could learn⟩ **c :** THAT — used after a negative ⟨there is no doubt *but* he won⟩ **2 a :** on the contrary ⟨not peace *but* a sword⟩ **b :** despite that fact ⟨he tried *but* he failed⟩ **c :** with this exception, namely ⟨no one *but* he may enter⟩

[2]**but** *prep* **1 :** with the exception of ⟨no one there *but* me⟩ **2 :** other than ⟨this letter is nothing *but* an insult⟩

[3]**but** *adv* **:** ONLY, MERELY ⟨he is *but* a child⟩

bu·ta·di·ene \ˌbyüt-ə-ˈdī-ˌēn, -ˌdī-ˈ\ *n* **:** a flammable gaseous hydrocarbon used in making synthetic rubbers

bu·tane \ˈbyü-ˌtān\ *n* **:** either of two flammable gaseous hydrocarbons obtained usu. from petroleum or natural gas and used esp. as a fuel

ə abut	ər further	a back	ā bake
ä cot, cart	au̇ out	ch chin	e less
ē easy	g gift	i trip	ī life
j joke	ŋ sing	ō flow	ȯ flaw
ȯi coin	th thin	t͟h this	ü loot
u̇ foot	y yet	yü few	yu̇ furious
zh vision			

[1]**butch·er** \ˈbu̇ch-ər\ *n* [from Old French *bouchier*, from *bouc* "goat"] **1 a :** one who slaughters animals or dresses their flesh **b :** a dealer in meat **2 :** one that kills ruthlessly or brutally **3 :** a vendor esp. on trains or in theaters

[2]**butcher** *vb* **butch·ered**; **butch·er·ing** \-(ə-)riŋ\ **1 :** to slaughter and dress for meat **2 :** to kill in a barbarous manner **3 :** to make a mess of **:** BOTCH — **butch·er·er** \-ər-ər\ *n*

butch·er·bird \ˈbu̇ch-ər-ˌbərd\ *n* **:** any of various shrikes that impale their prey on thorns

butch·ery \ˈbu̇ch-(ə-)rē\ *n, pl* **-er·ies** **:** brutal murder **:** great slaughter

but·ler \ˈbət-lər\ *n* [from Old French *bouteillier* "servant in charge of wine", from *bouteille* "bottle"] **:** a chief male household servant

[1]**butt** \ˈbət\ *vb* **:** to strike with the head or horns

[2]**butt** *n* **:** a blow or thrust usu. with the head or horns

[3]**butt** *n* **1 a :** a mound for stopping missiles shot at a target **b :** TARGET **c** *pl* **:** RANGE 5b **2 :** a target of abuse or ridicule ⟨the *butt* of a joke⟩

[4]**butt** *n* **1 :** the thicker or handle end (as of a tool or weapon) **2 :** an unused remainder ⟨cigarette *butt*⟩

[5]**butt** *n* **:** a large cask esp. for wine or beer

butte \ˈbyüt\ *n* **:** an isolated hill with steep sides

[1]**but·ter** \ˈbət-ər\ *n* [from Latin *butyrum*, from Greek *boutyron*, from *bous* "cow" and *tyros* "cheese"] **1 :** a solid yellow fatty food made by churning milk or cream **2 :** a substance resembling butter in appearance, texture, or use ⟨apple *butter*⟩ ⟨cocoa *butter*⟩ — **but·tery** \-ə-rē\ *adj*

[2]**butter** *vb* **:** to spread with or as if with butter

but·ter–and–eggs \ˌbət-ər-ən-ˈegz\ *n sing or pl* **:** any of several plants related to the snapdragon having flowers of two shades of yellow

butter bean *n* **1 :** WAX BEAN **2 :** LIMA BEAN **3 :** a green shell bean esp. as opposed to a snap bean

but·ter·cup \ˈbət-ər-ˌkəp\ *n* **:** any of a genus of herbs having cuplike yellow flowers mostly with five petals and sepals and fruits that are achenes

but·ter·fat \-ˌfat\ *n* **:** the natural fat of milk and chief constituent of butter

but·ter·fish \-ˌfish\ *n* **:** any of numerous fishes with a slippery coating of mucus

but·ter·fly \-ˌflī\ *n* **1 :** any of numerous slender-bodied day-flying insects with scale-covered often brightly colored wings — compare MOTH **2 :** a frivolous or gaudily dressed person

butterfly

butterfly fish *n* **:** any of various fishes having variegated colors, broad expanded fins, or both

butterfly weed *n* **:** a showy orange-flowered milkweed of eastern No. America

but·ter·milk \ˈbət-ər-ˌmilk\ *n* **1 :** the liquid left after the butterfat has been churned from milk or cream **2 :** cultured milk made by the addition of certain organisms to sweet milk

but·ter·nut \-ˌnət\ *n* **:** the edible oily nut of an American tree related to the walnut; *also* **:** this tree

but·ter·scotch \-ˌskäch\ *n* **:** a candy or dessert topping made from sugar, corn syrup, and water — **butterscotch** *adj*

but·tery \'bət-ə-rē, 'bə-trē\ *n, pl* **-ter·ies** *chiefly dial* : PANTRY

but·tock \'bət-ək\ *n* **1** : the back of the hip which forms one of the fleshy parts on which a person sits **2** *pl* **a** : the seat of the body **b** : RUMP

[1]**but·ton** \'bət-ən\ *n* **1** : a small knob or disk used for holding parts of a garment together or or as an ornament **2** : something (as an immature mushroom) that resembles a button

[2]**button** *vb* **but·toned**; **but·ton·ing** \-(ə-)ning\ : to fasten with buttons — **but·ton·er** \-(ə-)nər\ *n*

[1]**but·ton·hole** \'bət-ən-ˌhōl\ *n* : a slit or loop for fastening a button

[2]**buttonhole** *vb* **1** : to furnish with buttonholes **2** : to detain in conversation by or as if by holding on to the clothes of — **but·ton·hol·er** *n*

but·ton·hook \'bət-ən-ˌhu̇k\ *n* : a hook for drawing small buttons through buttonholes

but·ton·wood \-ˌwu̇d\ *n* : SYCAMORE 3

but·tress \'bə-trəs\ *n* **1** : a projecting structure for supporting or giving stability to a wall or building **2** : something that supports, props, or strengthens — **buttress** *vb*

bu·tyr·ic acid \byü-ˌtir-ik-\ *n* : an organic acid of unpleasant odor found in rancid butter and sweat

bux·om \'bək-səm\ *adj* : vigorously or healthily plump — **bux·om·ness** *n*

[1]**buy** \'bī\ *vb* **bought** \'bȯt\; **buy·ing** : to get by giving money in exchange : PURCHASE — **buy·er** \'bī(-ə)r\ *n*

[2]**buy** *n* : BARGAIN

[1]**buzz** \'bəz\ *vb* **1** : to make a low continuous humming sound like that of a bee **2** : to be filled with a confused murmur ⟨the room *buzzed* with excitement⟩ **3** : to summon or signal with a buzzer **4** : to fly low and fast over ⟨planes *buzzed* the crowd⟩

[2]**buzz** *n* **1** : a persistent sound produced by or as if by fast pulsations (as of the wings of a bee) **2** : a confused murmur or flurry of activity **3** : a signal conveyed by buzzer

buz·zard \'bəz-ərd\ *n* : any of various usu. large slow-flying birds of prey (as a short-winged hawk) — compare TURKEY BUZZARD

buzz·er \'bəz-ər\ *n* : an electric signaling device that makes a buzzing sound

BV *abbr* Blessed Virgin

BWI *abbr* British West Indies

bx *abbr* box

BX \(')bē-'eks\ *n* : BASE EXCHANGE

[1]**by** \(')bī, *esp before consonants* bə\ *prep* **1** : close to : NEAR ⟨*by* the sea⟩ **2 a** : ALONG, THROUGH ⟨*by* a different route⟩ **b** : PAST ⟨went right *by* him⟩ **3 a** : AT, DURING ⟨studied *by* night⟩ **b** : not later than ⟨be there *by* 2 p.m.⟩ **4** : through the means or agency of ⟨*by* force⟩ **5 a** : in conformity with ⟨*by* the rules⟩ **b** : according to ⟨called *by* a different name⟩ ⟨sold *by* the pound⟩ **6** : with respect to ⟨a doctor *by* profession⟩ **7** : to the amount or extent of ⟨win *by* a nose⟩ **8** : in successive units of ⟨walk two *by* two⟩ **9** — used as a function word in multiplication and division and in measurements ⟨divide 6 *by* 2⟩ ⟨a room 15 feet *by* 20 feet⟩

[2]**by** \'bī\ *adv* **1 a** : close at hand : NEAR ⟨stand *by*⟩ **b** : at or to another's home ⟨stop *by* for a chat⟩ **2** : PAST ⟨the parade went *by*⟩ **3** : ASIDE, AWAY ⟨putting some money *by*⟩

[3]**by** *or* **bye** \'bī\ *adj* **1** : off the main route : SIDE **2** : INCIDENTAL

[4]**by** *or* **bye** \'bī\ *n, pl* **byes** \'bīz\ : something incidental — used esp. in the phrase *by the by*

by and by \ˌbī-ən-'bī\ *adv* : before long : SOON

by–and–by \ˌbī-ən-'bī\ *n* : a future time or occasion

by and large \ˌbī-ən-'lärj\ *adv* : on the whole : in general

by·gone \'bī-ˌgȯn, -ˌgän\ *adj* : gone by : PAST — **bygone** *n*

by·law \'bī-ˌlȯ\ *n* [from Middle English *bilage, bilawe*, from an Old Norse compound of *byr* "town" and *lög* "law"] : a rule adopted by an organization (as a club or municipality) for the regulation of its affairs

by–line \'bī-ˌlīn\ *n* : a line at the head of a newspaper or magazine article giving the writer's name

[1]**by·pass** \'bī-ˌpas\ *n* : a passage to one side or around a congested area

[2]**bypass** *vb* : to make a detour or circuit around ⟨*bypass* a city⟩

by·path \'bī-ˌpath, -ˌpȧth\ *n* : BYWAY

by–prod·uct \'bī-ˌpräd-(ˌ)əkt\ *n* : a secondary product or result

by·road \'bī-ˌrōd\ *n* : BYWAY

by·stand·er \'bī-ˌstan-dər\ *n* : a person standing near but taking no part

by·street \'bī-ˌstrēt\ *n* : a street off a main thoroughfare

by the way *adv* : INCIDENTALLY

by·way \'bī-ˌwā\ *n* : a little-traveled side road

by·word \'bī-ˌwərd\ *n* **1** : a proverbial saying **2** : a person or thing that is typical esp. of some bad class or quality

[1]**Byz·an·tine** \'biz-ən-ˌtēn, bə-'zan-, 'bīz-ən-; 'biz-ən-ˌtīn\ *n* : a native or inhabitant of Byzantium or of the Byzantine Empire

[2]**Byzantine** *adj* **1** : of, relating to, or characteristic of Byzantium or the Eastern Roman Empire **2** : of or relating to a style of architecture developed in the Byzantine Empire esp. in the 5th and 6th centuries characterized by a central dome over a square space and by much use of mosaics

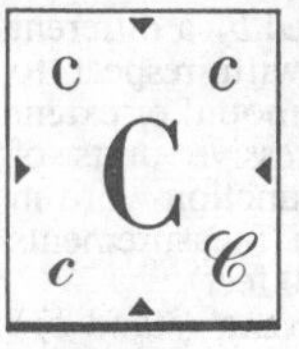

c \'sē\ *n, often cap* **1 :** the 3d letter of the English alphabet **2 :** the roman numeral 100 **3 :** the musical tone C **4 :** a grade rating a student's work as fair or mediocre
c *abbr* **1** cent **2** centimeter **3** century **4** chapter **5** cubic **6** cup
C *abbr* centigrade
CA *abbr* California
cab \'kab\ *n* **1 a :** a light closed carriage (as a hansom) **b :** a carriage for hire **2 :** TAXICAB **3 a :** the covered compartment for the engineer of a locomotive **b :** a similar compartment for the driver of a truck, tractor, or crane
ca·bal \kə-'bal\ *n* **:** a small group of persons working together to promote their own plans or interests esp. by secret schemes
ca·bana \kə-'ban-(y)ə\ *n* **:** a shelter resembling a tent at a beach or swimming pool
cab·a·ret \ˌkab-ə-'rā\ *n* **:** a restaurant serving liquor and providing entertainment
cab·bage \'kab-ij\ *n* **:** a vegetable with thick overlapping leaves in a round head
cab·by *or* **cab·bie** \'kab-ē\ *n, pl* **cabbies :** CABDRIVER
cab·driv·er \'kab-ˌdrī-vər\ *n* **:** a driver of a taxicab
cab·in \'kab-ən\ *n* **1 a :** a small room on a ship for officers or passengers **b :** a covered compartment on a boat for passengers or crew **c :** an airplane or airship compartment for cargo, crew, or passengers **2 :** a small simple dwelling
cabin boy *n* **:** a boy acting as a servant on a ship
cabin cruiser *n* **:** CRUISER 3
cab·i·net \'kab-(ə-)nət\ *n* **1 a :** a case or cupboard usu. having doors and shelves **b :** a case for a radio or television **2 :** a group of advisers to the political head of a government ⟨the British *cabinet*⟩ ⟨the president's *cabinet*⟩
cab·i·net·mak·er \-ˌmā-kər\ *n* **:** a skilled woodworker who makes fine furniture — **cab·i·net·mak·ing** \-king\ *n*
cab·i·net·work \-ˌwərk\ *n* **:** the finished work of a cabinetmaker
[1]**ca·ble** \'kā-bəl\ *n* **1 :** a very strong thick rope, wire, or chain **2 :** a wire or wire rope by which force is exerted to operate a mechanism ⟨brake *cable*⟩ **3 :** CABLE LENGTH **4 :** a bundle of electrical wires held together usu. around a central core **5 :** CABLEGRAM
[2]**cable** *vb* **ca·bled; ca·bling** \'kā-b(ə-)ling\ **1 :** to fasten or provide with a cable **2 :** to telegraph by cable
cable car *n* **:** a railway car moved by an endless cable or along an overhead cable
ca·ble·gram \'kā-bəl-ˌgram\ *n* **:** a message sent by submarine cable
cable length *n* **:** a maritime unit of length that is variously reckoned as 100 fathoms, 120 fathoms, or 608 feet
cable TV *n* **:** a system in which a television signal is received by means of a single antenna and then sent by cable to individual receivers of paying subscribers
ca·boose \kə-'büs\ *n* **:** a freight-train car attached usu. to the rear mainly for the use of the train crew and railroad workmen

ə abut	ər further	a back	ā bake	
ä cot, cart	au̇ out	ch chin	e less	ē easy
g gift	i trip	ī life	j joke	ng sing	ō flow
ȯ flaw	ȯi coin	th thin	th this	ü loot
u̇ foot	y yet	yü few	yu̇ furious	zh vision

ca·cao \kə-'kau̇, kə-'kā-ō\ *n, pl* **ca·caos :** a So. American tree with small yellowish flowers followed by fleshy yellow pods with many seeds; *also* **:** its dried partly fermented fatty seeds from which cocoa and chocolate are made

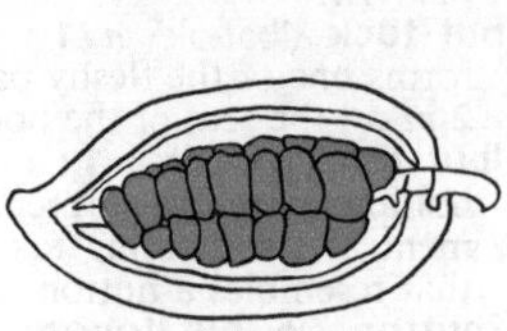
cacao

cache \'kash\ *n* **1 :** a place for hiding, storing, or safeguarding treasure, food, or supplies **2 :** the material hidden or stored in a cache — **cache** *vb*
cack·le \'kak-əl\ *vb* **cack·led; cack·ling** \-(ə-)ling\ **1 :** to make the sharp broken noise or cry characteristic of a hen esp. after laying **2 :** to laugh or chatter noisily — **cackle** *n* — **cack·ler** \-(ə-)lər\ *n*
cac·tus \'kak-təs\ *n, pl* **cac·ti** \-ˌtī, -(ˌ)tē\ *or* **cac·tus·es :** any of a large family of flowering plants able to live in dry regions and having fleshy stems and branches that bear scales or prickles instead of leaves
cad \'kad\ *n* **:** ungentlemanly person
ca·dav·er \kə-'dav-ər\ *n* **:** CORPSE — **ca·dav·er·ic** \-'dav-ə-rik\ *adj*
ca·dav·er·ous \kə-'dav-(ə-)rəs\ *adj* **:** resembling a corpse: as **a :** PALE, GHASTLY **b :** THIN, HAGGARD — **ca·dav·er·ous·ly** *adv*
cad·die *or* **cad·dy** \'kad-ē\ *n, pl* **caddies :** a person who carries a golfer's clubs — **caddie** *or* **caddy** *vb*
cad·dis fly \'kad-əs-\ *n* **:** any of an order of 4-winged insects with aquatic larvae — compare CADDISWORM
cad·dish \'kad-ish\ *adj* **:** resembling a cad or the behavior of a cad — **cad·dish·ly** *adv* — **cad·dish·ness** *n*
cad·dis·worm \'kad-əs-ˌwərm\ *n* **:** a larval caddis fly that lives in and carries around a silken case covered with bits of debris
cad·dy \'kad-ē\ *n, pl* **caddies :** a small box, can, or chest; *esp* **:** one to keep tea in
ca·dence \'kād-ən(t)s\ *n* **1 a :** rhythmic flow of sounds **b :** the beat or measure of rhythmical motion or activity **2 :** the close of a musical strain; *esp* **:** a musical chord sequence moving to a harmonic close or point of rest — **ca·denced** \-ən(t)st\ *adj*

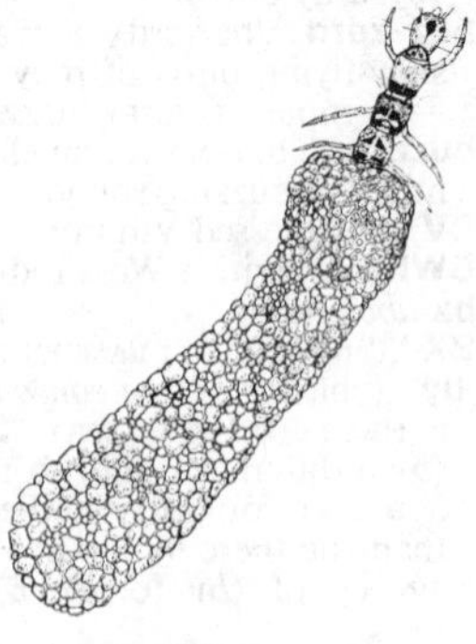
caddisworm
(less than ¼ in. long)

ca·den·za \kə-'den-zə\ *n* **:** a brilliant sometimes improvised solo passage usu. near the close of a musical composition
ca·det \kə-'det\ *n* [from French, from Gascon dialect *capdet* "captain" (younger sons of noble Gascon families frequently serving as captains in the 15th century French army), from Latin *capitellum*, diminutive of *caput* "head"] **1 :** a younger brother or son **2 :** a student military officer **3 :** a student at a military school **4 :** a boy or girl in any of various organizations — **ca·det·ship** \-ˌship\ *n*
cad·mi·um \'kad-mē-əm\ *n* **:** a grayish white malleable metallic element used esp. in protective coatings

(as to prevent rust) and in storage batteries — see ELEMENT table

ca·du·ce·us \kə-'d(y)ü-sē-əs\ *n, pl* **-cei** \-sē-ˌī\ **1** : a representation of a staff with two entwined snakes and two wings at the top **2** : an insignia bearing a caduceus and symbolizing a physician

cae·cal, cae·cum *var of* CECAL, CECUM

cae·sar·e·an *var of* CESAREAN

cae·su·ra \si-'z(h)u̇r-ə\ *n, pl* **-su·ras** *or* **-su·rae** \-'z(h)u̇(ə)r-(ˌ)ē\ : a break in the flow of sound usu. in the middle of a line of verse

ca·fé *also* **ca·fe** \ka-'fā, kə-\ *n* : RESTAURANT

caf·e·te·ria \ˌkaf-ə-'tir-ē-ə\ *n* [from American Spanish *cafetería* "coffee store", from Spanish *café* "coffee", from French] : a restaurant in which the customers serve themselves or are served at a counter but take the food to tables to eat

caf·feine \ka-'fēn, 'kaf-ē-ən\ *n* : a bitter stimulating compound found esp. in coffee, tea, and kola nuts

cage \'kāj\ *n* **1** : a largely openwork enclosure for an animal or bird **2** : an enclosure like a cage in form or purpose — **cage** *vb*

cage·ling \-ling\ *n* : a caged bird

ca·gey *also* **ca·gy** \'kā-jē\ *adj* **ca·gi·er**; **-est** : wary of being trapped or deceived : SHREWD — **ca·gi·ly** \-jə-lē\ *adv* — **ca·gi·ness** \-jē-nəs\ *n*

cai·man \kā-'man, kī-; 'kā-mən\ *n* : any of several Central and So. American reptiles closely related to alligators and crocodiles

cairn \'ka(ə)rn, 'ke(ə)rn\ *n* : a heap of stones piled up as a landmark or as a memorial

cairn·gorm \-ˌgȯrm\ *n* : a yellow or smoky brown crystalline quartz

cairn terrier *n* : a small compactly built hard-coated terrier of Scottish origin

cais·son \'kā-ˌsän, 'kā-sən\ *n* **1 a** : a chest for ammunition **b** : a 2-wheeled vehicle for artillery ammunition **2** : a watertight chamber used in construction work under water

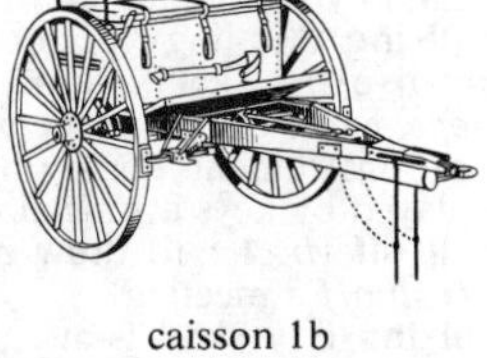
caisson 1b

caisson disease *n* : BENDS

cai·tiff \'kāt-əf\ *adj* : BASE, COWARDLY — **caitiff** *n*

ca·jole \kə-'jōl\ *vb* : to coax or persuade esp. by flattery : WHEEDLE — **ca·jol·ery** \-'jōl-(ə-)rē\ *n*

1**cake** \'kāk\ *n* **1** : a small mass of food (as dough or batter, meat, or fish) baked or fried **2** : a baked food made from a mixture of flour, sugar, eggs, and flavoring **3** : a substance hardened or molded into a solid mass ⟨a *cake* of soap⟩

2**cake** *vb* **1** : ENCRUST **2** : to form or harden into a mass

cal *abbr* calorie

Cal *abbr* **1** large calorie **2** California

cal·a·bash \'kal-ə-ˌbash\ *n* : GOURD; *esp* : one whose hard shell is used for a utensil (as a bottle)

ca·la·di·um \kə-'lād-ē-əm\ *n* : any of a genus of tropical American herbs that are often grown for their showy brightly colored leaves

cal·a·mine \'kal-ə-ˌmīn, -mən\ *n* : a mixture of zinc oxide and a small amount of ferric oxide used in lotions, liniments, and ointments in skin treatment

ca·lam·i·ty \kə-'lam-ət-ē\ *n, pl* **-ties** **1** : deep distress or misery **2** : an event marked by great loss and lasting distress — **ca·lam·i·tous** \-'lam-ət-əs\ *adj* — **ca·lam·i·tous·ly** *adv* — **ca·lam·i·tous·ness** *n*

cal·ca·ne·us \kal-'kā-nē-əs\ *n, pl* **-nei** \-nē-ˌī\ : a tarsal bone that in man is the great bone of the heel — **cal·ca·ne·al** \-nē-əl\ *adj*

cal·car·e·ous \kal-'kar-ē-əs, -'ker-\ *adj* **1** : resembling calcite or calcium carbonate esp. in hardness **2** : consisting of or containing calcium carbonate; *also* : containing calcium

cal·cif·er·ol \kal-'sif-ə-ˌrȯl, -ˌrōl\ *n* : a vitamin D that is used as a dietary supplement in human and animal nutrition and medicinally in the treatment esp. of various disorders of calcium metabolism

cal·cif·er·ous \kal-'sif-(ə-)rəs\ *adj* : producing or containing calcium carbonate and esp. calcite

cal·ci·fy \'kal-sə-ˌfī\ *vb* **-fied**; **-fy·ing** : to make or become stony by deposit of calcium salts — **cal·ci·fi·ca·tion** \ˌkal-sə-fə-'kā-shən\ *n*

cal·ci·mine \'kal-sə-ˌmīn\ *n* : a white or tinted thin paint used esp. on plastered surfaces (as ceilings) — **calcimine** *vb*

cal·cine \kal-'sīn\ *vb* : to heat to a high temperature to drive off volatile matter (as carbon dioxide from limestone) and often to reduce to powder — **cal·ci·na·tion** \ˌkal-sə-'nā-shən\ *n*

cal·cite \'kal-ˌsīt\ *n* : a crystalline mineral substance composed of calcium carbonate and found in numerous forms including limestone, chalk, and marble — **cal·cit·ic** \kal-'sit-ik\ *adj*

cal·ci·um \'kal-sē-əm\ *n* : a silver-white soft metallic element that is found only in combination with other elements (as in limestone) and is one of the essential constituents of the bodies of most plants and animals — see ELEMENT table

calcium carbonate *n* : a solid substance found in nature as limestone and marble and in plant ashes, bones, and shells and used esp. in making lime and portland cement

calcium chloride *n* : a salt that absorbs moisture from the air and that is used as a drying agent

calcium cyanamide *n* : CYANAMIDE

calcium phosphate *n* : any of various phosphates of calcium: as **a** : the phosphate used as a fertilizer **b** : a naturally occurring phosphate containing other elements (as fluorine) and occurring as the chief constituent of phosphate rock, bones, and teeth

calcium sulfate *n* : a compound of calcium; *esp* : GYPSUM

calcium tung·state \-'təng-ˌstāt\ *n* : a white crystalline salt found in nature as scheelite and used esp. for radiography, in luminous paints, and in fluorescent lamps

cal·cu·late \'kal-kyə-ˌlāt\ *vb* [from Latin *calculare*, from *calculus* "pebble", "stone used in reckoning", from *calc-*, stem of *calx* "lime", "stone", the source of English *chalk*, and more recently, of *calcium*] **1** : to determine mathematically : COMPUTE **2** : ESTIMATE **3** : to plan by careful thought ⟨a plan *calculated* to succeed⟩ **4** : RELY, DEPEND — **cal·cu·la·ble** \-kyə-lə-bəl\ *adj*

cal·cu·lat·ing \-ˌlāt-ing\ *adj* **1** : designed to make calculations ⟨*calculating* machine⟩ **2** : coldly and shrewdly analytical : SCHEMING — **cal·cu·lat·ing·ly** \-ing-lē\ *adv*

cal·cu·la·tion \ˌkal-kyə-'lā-shən\ *n* **1 a** : the process or an act of calculating **b** : the result of calculation **2** : care in planning : CAUTION — **cal·cu·la·tive** \'kal-kyə-ˌlāt-iv\ *adj*

cal·cu·la·tor \'kal-kyə-ˌlāt-ər\ *n* **1** : one that calculates **2** : a machine that solves mathematical problems

cal·cu·lus \'kal-kyə-ləs\ *n, pl* **-li** \-ˌlī, -ˌlē\ *also* **-lus·es** **1** : a mass usu. of mineral salts deposited in or around organic material in a hollow organ or bodily duct **2 :** a branch of higher mathematics concerned esp. with rates of change and irregular shapes

cal·de·ra \kal-'der-ə, kòl-, -'dir-\ *n* **:** a large crater formed by the collapse of the volcanic cone or by an explosion

cal·dron \'kòl-drən\ *n* **:** a large kettle or boiler

¹**cal·en·dar** \'kal-ən-dər\ *n* **[**from medieval Latin *kalendarium*, from Latin *kalendae*, name of the first day of each month**]** **1 a :** an arrangement of time into days, weeks, months, and years **b :** a record of such an arrangement for a certain period usu. a year **2 a :** an orderly list (as of cases to be tried in court) **b :** a schedule of coming events

²**calendar** *vb* **:** to enter in a calendar

calendar stone *n* **:** a stone with an inscription elucidating an ancient time-reckoning system

¹**cal·en·der** \'kal-ən-dər\ *vb* **:** to press (as cloth or paper) between rollers or plates in order to smooth and glaze or thin into sheets

²**calender** *n* **:** a machine for calendering cloth or paper

¹**calf** \'kaf, 'kȧf\ *n, pl* **calves** \'kavz, 'kȧvz\ **1 a :** the young of the domestic cow **b :** the young of various large animals (as the elephant or whale) **2** *pl* **calfs :** CALFSKIN **3 :** an awkward or silly boy or youth

²**calf** *n, pl* **calves :** the fleshy back part of the leg below the knee

calf·skin \'kaf-ˌskin, 'kȧf-\ *n* **:** a leather made of the skin of a calf

cal·i·ber *or* **cal·i·bre** \'kal-ə-bər\ *n* **1 :** the diameter of a projectile **2 :** the diameter of the bore of a gun **3 a :** mental ability or moral quality **b :** degree of excellence **:** QUALITY

cal·i·brate \'kal-ə-ˌbrāt\ *vb* **1 :** to measure the caliber of **2 a :** to determine, correct, or put the measuring marks on (as a thermometer tube) **b :** STANDARDIZE — **cal·i·bra·tion** \ˌkal-ə-'brā-shən\ *n*

cal·i·co \'kal-i-ˌkō\ *n, pl* **-coes** *or* **-cos** **1 :** cotton cloth; *esp* **:** cotton cloth with a colored pattern printed on one side **2 :** a blotched or spotted animal (as a piebald horse) — **calico** *adj*

Calif *abbr* California

Cal·i·for·nia condor \ˌkal-ə-ˌfòr-nyə-\ *n* **:** a very large nearly extinct No. American vulture that is related to the condor of So. America and is sometimes larger though of lighter build

California poppy *n* **:** any of a genus of poppies including one widely grown for its pale yellow to red flowers

cal·i·for·ni·um \ˌkal-ə-'fòr-nē-əm\ *n* **:** an artificially prepared radioactive element used as a neutron source in medicine and industry — see ELEMENT table

cal·i·per *or* **cal·li·per** \'kal-ə-pər\ *n* **:** a measuring instrument with two legs or jaws that can be adjusted to determine thickness, diameter, and distance between surfaces — usu. used in pl. ⟨a pair of *calipers*⟩

ca·liph *or* **ca·lif** \'kā-ləf, 'kal-əf\ *n* **[**from Arabic *khalīfah* "successor"**]** **:** a successor of Muhammad as temporal and spiritual head of Islam — used as a title — **ca·liph·ate** \-ˌāt\ *n*

cal·is·then·ics \ˌkal-əs-'then-iks\ *n sing or pl* **1 :** systematic bodily exercises without apparatus **2 :** the art or practice of calisthenics — **cal·is·then·ic** \-ik\ *adj*

¹**calk** \'kòk\ *var of* CAULK

²**calk** *n* **:** a tapered piece projecting downward from a shoe (as of a horse) to prevent slipping

³**calk** *vb* **1 :** to furnish with calks **2 :** to wound with a calk

¹**call** \'kòl\ *vb* **1 :** to speak so as to be heard at a distance **:** SHOUT **2 :** to utter in a loud clear voice ⟨*call* a roll⟩ ⟨*call* out a command⟩ **3 :** to announce with authority **:** PROCLAIM ⟨*call* a halt⟩ **4 :** SUMMON ⟨*call* him to dinner⟩ ⟨*call* a meeting⟩ **5 :** to bring into action or discussion ⟨*call* up reserves⟩ ⟨*call* a case in court⟩ **6 :** to make a request or demand ⟨*call* on a person's sense of decency⟩ **7 :** to make a telephone call to **8 :** to make a brief visit **9 a :** to give a name to **b :** to address by name **10 :** to regard as being of a certain kind **11 :** to estimate as being ⟨*call* the distance 10 miles⟩ **12 a :** to utter a characteristic note or cry ⟨crows *calling*⟩ **b :** to attract game by imitating its characteristic cry **13 :** HALT, SUSPEND ⟨*call* a game on account of bad weather⟩ ⟨*call* time⟩ — **call·er** *n*

²**call** *n* **1 a :** a loud shout or cry **b :** a speaking aloud esp. of a list of names **2 a :** a cry of an animal **b :** an imitation of an animal's cry or a device used to make such an imitation **3 a :** SUMMONS, INVITATION **b :** ATTRACTION, LURE ⟨the *call* of the wild⟩ **4 a :** DEMAND, CLAIM **b :** REQUEST ⟨many *calls* for Christmas stories⟩ **5 :** a short visit **6 :** the act of calling on the telephone **7 :** a ruling made by an official of a sports contest

cal·la \'kal-ə\ *n* **:** a plant often grown for its large white showy bract surrounding a fleshy spike of yellow florets

call·back \'kòl-ˌbak\ *n* **1 :** a return telephone call or visit **2 :** a calling back of defective merchandise (as cars) by a manufacturer for repairs

call·ing \'kò-ling\ *n* **:** OCCUPATION, PROFESSION

cal·li·o·pe \kə-'lī-ə-(ˌ)pē, 'kal-ē-ˌōp\ *n* **[**from *Calliope*, name of one of the nine Greek muses**]** **:** a musical instrument consisting of a series of whistles played by keys arranged as in an organ

call off *vb* **1 :** to draw away **:** DIVERT **2 :** CANCEL ⟨*call off* a meeting⟩

cal·los·i·ty \ka-'läs-ət-ē, kə-\ *n, pl* **-ties :** CALLUS 1

¹**cal·lous** \'kal-əs\ *adj* **1 :** so thickened and usu. hardened as to form callus or a callus **2 :** lacking sympathy or sensitivity **:** UNFEELING ⟨a *callous* disregard for human rights⟩ — **cal·lous·ly** *adv* — **cal·lous·ness** *n*

²**callous** *vb* **:** to make callous

cal·low \'kal-ō\ *adj* **:** lacking adult experience **:** IMMATURE — **cal·low·ness** *n*

call–up \'kòl-ˌəp\ *n* **:** an order to report for military service

¹**cal·lus** \'kal-əs\ *n* **1 :** a thickening of or a hard thickened area on skin or bark **2 :** a substance that surrounds a break in a bone and is converted into bone in the healing of the break

²**callus** *vb* **:** to form callus

¹**calm** \'käm, 'kälm\ *n* **1 a :** a period or state of freedom from storm, wind, or rough activity of water **b :** complete absence of wind or the presence of wind of no more than one mile per hour **2 :** a state of freedom from turmoil or agitation **:** PEACEFULNESS

²**calm** *adj* **1 :** marked by calm **:** STILL **2 :** free from agitation, excitement, or disturbance — **calm** *vb* — **calm·ly** *adv* — **calm·ness** *n*

cal·o·mel \'kal-ə-məl, -ˌmel\ *n* **:** a white tasteless chemical compound of mercury that occurs as a mineral or is made chemically and that is used as a strong laxative, fungicide, and insecticide

ca·lor·ic \kə-'lȯr-ik, -'lōr-, -'lär-\ *adj* **1** : of or relating to heat **2** : of or relating to calories — **ca·lor·i·cal·ly** \-i-k(ə-)lē\ *adv*

cal·o·rie *or* **cal·o·ry** \'kal-(ə-)rē\ *n, pl* **-ries** **1** : a unit of heat: **a** : the heat required to raise the temperature of one gram of water one degree centigrade — called also *small calorie;* abbr. *cal* **b** : 1000 small calories — used esp. to indicate the value of foods in the production of heat and energy; called also *large calorie;* abbr. *Cal* **2** : the amount of food producing one large calorie

cal·o·rif·ic \ˌkal-ə-'rif-ik\ *adj* : CALORIC

cal·o·rim·e·ter \ˌkal-ə-'rim-ət-ər\ *n* : an apparatus for measuring quantities of absorbed or evolved heat — **cal·o·ri·met·ric** \ˌkal-ə-rə-'me-trik\ *adj* — **cal·o·ri·met·ri·cal·ly** \-'me-tri-k(ə-)lē\ *adv*

calve \'kav, 'kȧv\ *vb* : to give birth to a calf

calves *pl of* CALF

ca·lyp·so \kə-'lip-sō\ *n, pl* **-sos** : an improvised rhythmic ballad originating in the West Indies that usu. satirizes current events

ca·lyx \'kā-liks, 'kal-iks\ *n, pl* **ca·lyx·es** *or* **ca·ly·ces** \'kā-lə-ˌsēz, 'kal-ə-\ : the external usu. green or leafy part of a flower consisting of sepals

cam \'kam\ *n* : a device by which circular motion may be transformed into intermittent or back-and-forth motion

ca·ma·ra·de·rie \ˌkam-(ə-)'rad-ə-rē, ˌkäm-(ə-)'räd-\ *n* : good feeling existing between comrades

cam·bi·um \'kam-bē-əm\ *n, pl* **-bi·ums** *or* **-bia** \-bē-ə\ : a thin cell layer between the xylem and phloem of most vascular plants from which new cells (as of wood and bark) develop — **cam·bi·al** \-bē-əl\ *adj*

Cam·bo·di·an \kam-'bōd-ē-ən\ *adj* : of, relating to, or characteristic of Cambodia or its people — **Cambodian** *n*

Cam·bri·an \'kam-brē-ən\ *n* : the earliest period of the Paleozoic era marked by fossils of every great animal type except the vertebrate and by scarcely recognizable plant fossils; *also* : the corresponding system of rocks — **Cambrian** *adj*

cam·bric \'kām-brik\ *n* : a fine white linen or cotton fabric

came *past of* COME

cam·el \'kam-əl\ *n* : either of two large cud-chewing

camels:
left, dromedary (about 90 in. at shoulder);
right, Bactrian camel (about 94 in. at shoulder)

mammals used as draft and saddle animals in desert regions esp. of Africa and Asia: **a** : DROMEDARY 2 **b** : a 2-humped camel of central Asian origin — called also *Bactrian camel*

ca·mel·lia *also* **ca·me·lia** \kə-'mēl-yə\ *n* : a greenhouse shrub that is related to the tea plant and has glossy evergreen leaves and showy roselike flowers

camel's hair *n* : a fabric made of the hair of camels or of this hair and wool

Cam·em·bert \'kam-əm-ˌbe(ə)r\ *n* : a soft cheese with a whitish rind ripened by the action of a mold on its surface

cam·eo \'kam-ē-ˌō\ *n, pl* **-e·os** : a carved gem in which the design is higher than its background

cam·era \'kam-(ə-)rə\ *n* **1** : a judge's private office ⟨hearings held in *camera*⟩ **2** [from scientific Latin *camera obscura,* literally "dark chamber"] : a lightproof box fitted with a lens through which the image of an object is recorded on a material sensitive to light **3** : the part of a television transmitting apparatus in which the image to be televised is formed for change into electrical impulses — **cam·era·man** \-ˌman, -mən\ *n*

camera 2

cam·i·sole \'kam-ə-ˌsōl\ *n* : a short sleeveless undergarment for women

camomile *var of* CHAMOMILE

cam·ou·flage \'kam-ə-ˌfläzh, -ˌfläj\ *n* **1 a** : the disguising of military equipment or installations with paint, nets, or foliage **b** : the disguise so applied **2** : concealment by means of disguise — **camouflage** *vb*

[1]**camp** \'kamp\ *n* **1 a** : ground on which temporary shelters are erected **b** : a group of tents, cabins, or huts **c** : TENT, CABIN, SHELTER **d** : an open-air location where persons camp **e** : a new lumbering or mining town **2** : a body of persons encamped

[2]**camp** *vb* **1** : to make or occupy a camp **2** : to live in a camp or outdoors

[3]**camp** *n* : something so outrageous, inappropriate, or in such bad taste as to be amusing — **camp** *adj* — **campy** \'kam-pē\ *adj*

cam·paign \kam-'pān\ *n* **1** : a series of military operations forming a distinct phase of a war **2** : a connected series of operations designed to bring about a particular result ⟨an election *campaign*⟩ — **campaign** *vb* — **cam·paign·er** *n*

cam·pa·ni·le \ˌkam-pə-'nē-lē\ *n* : a bell tower; *esp* : one built separate from another building

cam·pan·u·la \kam-'pan-yə-lə\ *n* : any of a large genus of herbs with regular bell-shaped flowers including several grown as ornamentals

camp·er \'kam-pər\ *n* **1** : one that camps **2** : a portable or self-propelled dwelling for use during casual travel and camping

camp fire girl *n* : a member of a national organization for girls from 7 to 18

cam·phor \'kam(p)-fər\ *n* : a tough gummy volatile fragrant crystalline compound obtained esp. from the wood and bark of the camphor tree and used as a stimulant and as an insect repellent

cam·phor·ate \-fə-ˌrāt\ *vb* : to impregnate with camphor ⟨*camphorated* oil⟩

camphor tree *n* : a large evergreen Asiatic tree related to the laurel

camp·o·ree \ˌkam-pə-'rē\ *n* : a gathering of boy or girl scouts from a given geographic area

camp·stool \'kamp-ˌstül\ *n* : a folding stool

cam·pus \'kam-pəs\ *n* [from Latin, "field", "plain"] : the grounds of a college or a school

cam·shaft \'kam-ˌshaft\ *n* : a shaft to which a cam is fastened

[1]**can** \kən, (ˈ)kan\ *auxiliary verb, past* **could** \kəd, (ˈ)ku̇d\; *pres sing & pl* **can** **1 a** : know how to

⟨he *can* read⟩ **b :** be able to ⟨he *can* lift 200 pounds⟩ **c :** be permitted by conscience or feeling ⟨you *can* hardly blame him⟩ **d :** have the power or right to **2 :** have permission to : MAY ⟨you *can* go now if you like⟩

2**can** \'kan\ *n* **1 :** a usu. cylindrical metal container or receptacle ⟨*can* of beans⟩ ⟨ash *can*⟩ **2 :** the contents of a can

3**can** \'kan\ *vb* **canned; can·ning :** to preserve by sealing in an airtight can or jar

Can *or* **Canad** *abbr* **1** Canada **2** Canadian

Can·a·da goose \,kan-əd-ə-\ *n* **:** the common wild goose of No. America that is mostly gray and brownish in color with black head and neck — called also *Canadian goose*

Canada goose

Canada lynx *n* : LYNX 1

Ca·na·di·an \kə-'nād-ē-ən\ *adj* **:** of, relating to, or characteristic of Canada or its people — **Canadian** *n*

ca·nal \kə-'nal\ *n* **1 :** a tubular anatomical passage or channel : DUCT **2 :** an artificial waterway for boats or for draining or irrigating land

ca·nary \kə-'ne(ə)r-ē\ *n, pl* **-nar·ies :** a small usu. yellow or greenish finch native to the Canary islands that is kept as a cage bird

ca·nas·ta \kə-'nas-tə\ *n* **[**from Spanish, literally "basket"**] :** rummy using two decks plus four jokers

canc *abbr* canceled

can·cel \'kan(t)-səl\ *vb* **-celed** *or* **-celled; -cel·ing** *or* **-cel·ling** \-s(ə-)ling\ **[**from Latin *cancellare*, literally "to make like a lattice", from *cancelli* "latticework", "grating"**] 1 :** to cross or strike out with a line : DELETE **2 a :** to destroy the force or validity of : ANNUL, WITHDRAW ⟨*cancel* an order⟩ ⟨*cancel* an appointment⟩ **b :** OFFSET **3 a :** to divide numerator and denominator by the same number **b :** to remove equivalents on opposite sides of an equation or account **4 :** to mark a postage stamp or check so that it cannot be reused — **can·cel·er** *or* **can·cel·ler** \-s(ə-)lər\ *n*

can·cel·la·tion \,kan(t)-sə-'lā-shən\ *n* **1 :** an act of canceling ⟨*cancellation* of a game because of bad weather⟩ **2 :** a mark made to cancel something ⟨a *cancellation* on a postage stamp⟩

can·cer \'kan(t)-sər\ *n* **1** *cap* — see ZODIAC table **2 :** a malignant tumor that tends to spread locally and to other parts of the body; *also* **:** an abnormal state marked by such tumors **3 :** a dangerous evil that eats away slowly but fatally — **can·cer·ous** \'kan(t)s-(ə-)rəs\ *adj*

can·de·la·bra \,kan-də-'läb-rə, -'lab-, -'lāb-\ *n* : CANDELABRUM

can·de·la·brum \-rəm\ *n, pl* **-bra** \-rə\ *or* **-brums :** a branching candlestick for several candles

can·did \'kan-dəd\ *adj* **1 :** free from prejudice : FAIR **2 :** marked by or showing sincere honesty : FRANK **3 :** relating to photography of subjects acting naturally without being posed ⟨*candid* picture⟩ — **can·did·ly** *adv* — **can·did·ness** *n*

can·di·da·cy \'kan-dəd-ə-sē\ *n, pl* **-cies :** the state of being a candidate ⟨announce one's *candidacy* for office⟩

can·di·date \'kan-də-,dāt, -dət\ *n* **[**from Latin *candidatus*, literally "one clothed in white", from *candidus* "white"; so called from the white toga worn by a candidate for office in ancient Rome**] :** one who offers himself or is proposed for an office or honor ⟨a *candidate* for mayor⟩

1**can·dle** \'kan-dəl\ *n* **1 :** a mass of tallow or wax containing a wick that is burned to give light **2 :** a unit of measurement for the intensity of light

2**candle** *vb* **can·dled; can·dling** \'kan-d(ə-)ling\ **:** to examine an egg by holding it between the eye and a light — **can·dler** \-d(ə-)lər\ *n*

can·dle·light \'kan-dəl-,(l)īt\ *n* **1 a :** the light of a candle **b :** soft artificial light **2 :** the time when candles are lit : TWILIGHT — **can·dle·lit** \-dəl-,(l)it\ *adj*

Can·dle·mas \'kan-dəl-məs\ *n* **:** February 2 observed as a church festival in commemoration of the presentation of Christ in the temple and the purification of the Virgin Mary

can·dle·pow·er \-,paů(-ə)r\ *n* **:** intensity of light expressed in candles

can·dle·stick \-,stik\ *n* **:** a holder with a socket for a candle

can·dor \'kan-dər\ *n* **1 :** freedom from prejudice **2 :** FRANKNESS

C & W *abbr* country and western

1**can·dy** \'kan-dē\ *n, pl* **-dies 1 :** crystallized sugar formed by boiling down sugar syrup **2 a :** a confection made of sugar often with flavoring and filling **b :** a piece of such confection

2**candy** *vb* **can·died; can·dy·ing 1 :** to coat or become coated with sugar **2 :** to bake in sugar syrup **3 :** to crystallize into sugar

can·dy·tuft \'kan-dē-,təft\ *n* **:** any of a genus of plants related to the mustards and grown for their white, pink, or purple flowers

1**cane** \'kān\ *n* **1 a :** a jointed plant stem that is usu. slender and more or less flexible **b :** any of various tall woody grasses or reeds; *esp* **:** SUGARCANE **2 a :** WALKING STICK **b :** a rod for flogging **c :** RATTAN; *esp* **:** split rattan for wickerwork or basketry

2**cane** *vb* **1 :** to beat with a cane **2 :** to make or repair with cane ⟨*cane* the seat of a chair⟩

cane·brake \'kān-,brāk\ *n* **:** a thicket of cane

1**ca·nine** \'kā-,nīn\ *adj* **:** of or relating to dogs or to the family that includes the dogs, wolves, jackals, and foxes

2**canine** *n* **1 :** a conical pointed tooth; *esp* **:** one situated between the outer incisor and the first premolar **2 :** DOG

can·is·ter \'kan-ə-stər\ *n* **1 :** a small box or can for holding a dry product (as coffee, flour, or sugar) **2 :** a shell for close-range artillery fire consisting of a number of bullets enclosed in a lightweight case that is burst by the firing charge **3 :** a perforated box that contains material to adsorb, filter, or make harmless a poisonous or irritating substance in the air and is used esp. with a gas mask

1**can·ker** \'kang-kər\ *n* **1 a :** an area of dead tissue in a plant part (as a stem) that is caused by various agents (as a fungus or a chemical) and may spread killing the affected part **b :** any of several animal disorders marked by chronic inflammatory changes **2 :** a source of corruption or destruction — **can·ker·ous** \'kang-k(ə-)rəs\ *adj*

2**canker** *vb* **can·kered; can·ker·ing** \'kang-

ə abut	ər further		a back	ā bake
ä cot, cart	aů out	ch chin	e less	ē easy
g gift	i trip	ī life	j joke	ng sing	ō flow
ȯ flaw	ȯi coin	th thin	th this	ü loot
ů foot	y yet	yü few	yů furious	zh vision

k(ə-)ring\ : to corrupt malignantly or undergo corruption
canker sore *n* : a small painful ulcer esp. of the mouth
can·ker·worm \'kang-kər-,wərm\ *n* : an insect larva (as a looper) that injures plants esp. by feeding on buds and foliage
can·na \'kan-ə\ *n* : a tall tropical herb with large leaves and an unbranched stem bearing bright-colored flowers at the end
can·na·bis \'kan-ə-bəs\ *n* : the dried flowering spikes of the hemp plant — compare HASHISH, MARIJUANA
can·ner \'kan-ər\ *n* : a person whose business or occupation is canning food
can·nery \'kan-(ə-)rē\ *n, pl* **-ner·ies** : a factory for the canning of food
can·ni·bal \'kan-ə-bəl\ *n* [from Spanish *Caníbal* "member of an Indian people of the Lesser Antilles", from a native word *Caniba* or *Carib*, the source of English *Caribbean*] **1** : a human being who eats human flesh **2** : an animal that eats its own kind — **cannibal** *adj* — **can·ni·bal·ism** \-bə-,liz-əm\ *n* — **can·ni·bal·is·tic** \,kan-ə-bə-'lis-tik\ *adj*
can·ni·bal·ize \'kan-ə-bə-,līz\ *vb* : to dismantle a machine for parts to be used as replacements in other machines
can·non \'kan-ən\ *n, pl* **cannons** *or* **cannon** [from Italian *cannone*, literally "large tube", from *canna* "reed", "tube", from Latin, "reed", "cane", the source of English *cane*] **1** : a heavy gun mounted on a carriage **2** : a heavy-caliber automatic gun on an airplane

cannon 1

can·non·ade \,kan-ə-'nād\ *n* : heavy firing of artillery — **cannonade** *vb*
can·non·ball \'kan-ən-,bȯl\ *n* : a round solid missile made for firing from a cannon
can·non·eer \,kan-ə-'ni(ə)r\ *n* : one who tends or fires cannon
can·not \'kan-(,)ät; kə-'nät, ka-'\ : can not — **cannot but** : to be bound to : MUST
can·ny \'kan-ē\ *adj* **can·ni·er**; **-est** : being cautious and shrewd : watchful of one's own interests ⟨a *canny* man with money⟩ — **can·ni·ly** \'kan-ə-lē\ *adv* — **can·ni·ness** \'kan-ē-nəs\ *n*
ca·noe \kə-'nü\ *n* : a long light narrow boat with sharp ends and curved sides that is usu. propelled by paddling — **canoe** *vb* — **ca·noe·ist** \-'nü-əst\ *n*
[1]**can·on** \'kan-ən\ *n* **1** : a church law or decree **2** : an official or authoritative list (as of the books of the Bible) **3** : an accepted principle or rule ⟨*canons* of good taste⟩ **4** : a musical composition in which one voice begins the melody and others imitate it exactly and completely
[2]**canon** *n* : a clergyman on the staff of a cathedral
ca·ñon \'kan-yən\ *var of* CANYON
ca·non·i·cal \kə-'nän-i-kəl\ *adj* **1** : complying with church law **2** : accepted as authoritative or genuine — **ca·non·i·cal·ly** \-i-k(ə-)lē\ *adv*
can·on·ize \'kan-ə-,nīz\ *vb* : to declare to be a saint and worthy of public veneration — **can·on·i·za·tion** \,kan-ə-nə-'zā-shən\ *n*
can·o·py \'kan-ə-pē\ *n, pl* **-pies** [from medieval Latin *canopeum* "mosquito net", from Greek *kōnōpion*, from *kōnōps* "mosquito"] **1 a** : a covering over a bed, throne, or shrine or carried on poles over a person of high rank or over some sacred object **b** : AWNING, MARQUEE **2** : an overhanging shade or shelter; *esp* : the uppermost spreading branchy layer of a forest **3** : the lifting or supporting surface of a parachute — **canopy** *vb*
canst \kən(t)st, (')kan(t)st\ *archaic pres 2d sing of* CAN
[1]**cant** \'kant\ *n* **1** : a slanting surface **2** : TILT, SLOPE, INCLINE — **cant** *vb*
[2]**cant** *n* **1 a** : ARGOT **b** : JARGON **2** : insincere speech; *esp* : pious words or statements
can't \'kant, 'kȧnt, *esp South* 'kānt\ : can not
can·ta·loupe \'kant-ə-,lōp\ *n* : MUSKMELON; *esp* : a muskmelon with a hard, thick skin and firm juicy reddish orange flesh which is eaten raw
can·tan·ker·ous \kan-'tang-k(ə-)rəs\ *adj* : ILL-NATURED, QUARRELSOME — **can·tan·ker·ous·ly** *adv* — **can·tan·ker·ous·ness** *n*
can·ta·ta \kən-'tät-ə\ *n* : a poem, story, or play set to music to be sung by a chorus and soloists
can·teen \kan-'tēn\ *n* **1** : a store (as in a camp or factory) in which food, drinks, and small supplies are sold **2** : a place of recreation and entertainment for servicemen **3** : a small container for carrying liquid (as drinking water)
can·ter \'kant-ər\ *n* : a 3-beat gait of a horse resembling but smoother and slower than the gallop — **canter** *vb*
Can·ter·bury bell \,kant-ə(r)-,ber-ē-\ *n* : a cultivated campanula
can·ti·cle \'kant-i-kəl\ *n* **1** : SONG **2** : a song taken from the Bible and used in church services
can·ti·le·ver \'kant-ə-,lē-vər, -,lev-ər\ *n* **1** : a projecting beam or similar structure fastened at one end **2** : either of two beams or structures that project from piers toward each other and when joined form a span in a bridge

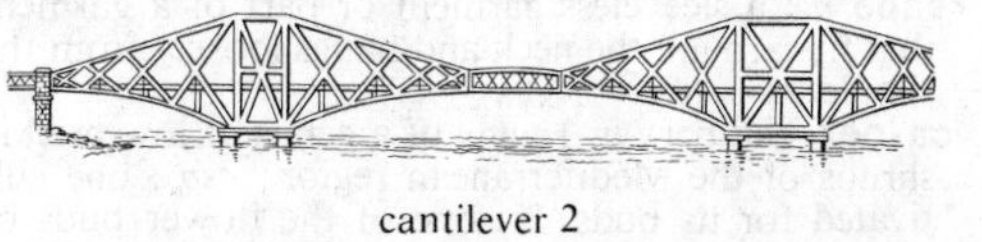
cantilever 2

can·tle \'kant-əl\ *n* : the rear part of a saddle
can·to \'kan-,tō\ *n, pl* **cantos** : a major division of a long poem
can·ton \'kant-ən, 'kan-,tän\ *n* **1** : a small division of a country; *esp* : one of the states of the Swiss confederation **2** : the top inner quarter of a flag
can·ton·ment \kan-'tōn-mənt, -'tän-\ *n* : a temporary camp for troops
can·tor \'kant-ər\ *n* **1** : a choir leader **2** : a synagogue official who sings or chants the liturgy and leads the congregation in prayer
can·vas \'kan-vəs\ *n* **1** : a strong cloth of hemp, flax, or cotton that is used for making tents and sails and as the material on which oil paintings are made **2** : something (as an oil painting) made of canvas or on canvas
can·vas·back \-,bak\ *n* : a No. American wild duck with reddish head and grayish back
can·vass \'kan-vəs\ *vb* **1 a** : to examine in detail; *esp* : to investigate officially ⟨*canvass* election returns⟩ **b** : DISCUSS, DEBATE ⟨*canvass* a question⟩ **2** : to go (as through an area or to persons) soliciting something (as information, contributions, or votes) — **canvass** *n* — **can·vass·er** *n*
can·yon \'kan-yən\ *n* : a deep valley with high steep slopes
caou·tchouc \kau̇-'chük\ *n* : RUBBER 2a

C

1**cap** \'kap\ *n* **1** : a head covering; *esp* : one for men and boys that has a visor and no brim **2** : something like a cap in appearance, position, or use ⟨bottle *cap*⟩ ⟨*cap* of a fountain pen⟩ **3** : a natural cover or top: as **a** : the umbrella-shaped part that bears the spores of a mushroom **b** : the top of a bird's head **4** : a paper or metal container holding an explosive charge (as for a toy pistol)

2**cap** *vb* **capped**; **cap·ping** **1** : to provide with a cap **2** : to match with something equal or better ⟨cap one story with another⟩

cap *abbr* capital

ca·pa·ble \'kā-pə-bəl\ *adj* **1** : having the ability, capacity, or power to do something ⟨a room *capable* of holding 50 people⟩ **2** : of such a nature as to permit : SUSCEPTIBLE ⟨a remark *capable* of being misunderstood⟩ **3** : EFFICIENT, COMPETENT ⟨a *capable* salesman⟩ — **ca·pa·bil·i·ty** \ˌkā-pə-'bil-ət-ē\ *n* — **ca·pa·bly** \'kā-pə-blē\ *adv*

ca·pa·cious \kə-'pā-shəs\ *adj* : able to contain much : ROOMY — **ca·pa·cious·ly** *adv* — **ca·pa·cious·ness** *n*

ca·pac·i·tor \kə-'pas-ət-ər\ *n* : a device for storing electric charge — called also *condenser*

ca·pac·i·ty \kə-'pas-ət-ē, -'pas-tē\ *n*, *pl* **-ties** **1** : the ability to hold or accommodate ⟨the seating *capacity* of a room⟩ **2** : a measure of content : VOLUME ⟨a jug with a *capacity* of one gallon⟩ **3** : ability to do or learn **4** : POSITION, FUNCTION ⟨in his *capacity* as a judge⟩

ca·par·i·son \kə-'par-ə-sən\ *n* **1** : an ornamental covering for a horse **2** : rich clothing or decoration : ADORNMENT — **caparison** *vb*

1**cape** \'kāp\ *n* : a point of land jutting out into water

2**cape** *n* : a sleeveless garment or part of a garment that fits around the neck and hangs loosely from the shoulders

1**ca·per** \'kā-pər\ *n* **1** : any of a genus of low prickly shrubs of the Mediterranean region; *esp* : one cultivated for its buds **2** : one of the flower buds or young berries of a caper pickled for use as a relish

2**caper** *vb* **ca·pered**; **ca·per·ing** \-p(ə-)ring\ : to leap about gaily : FROLIC

3**caper** *n* **1** : a gay bounding leap **2** : PRANK, TRICK

cap·il·lar·i·ty \ˌkap-ə-'lar-ət-ē\ *n* : the action by which the surface of a liquid where (as in a slender tube) it is in contact with a solid is raised or lowered depending upon the relative attraction of the molecules of the liquid for each other and for those of the solid

1**cap·il·lary** \'kap-ə-ˌler-ē\ *adj* **1** : resembling a hair in having a slender elongated form; *esp* : having a very small bore ⟨a *capillary* tube⟩ **2** : of or relating to capillaries or capillarity

2**capillary** *n*, *pl* **-lar·ies** : a capillary tube; *esp* : any of the tiny hairlike blood vessels connecting arteries and veins

1**cap·i·tal** \'kap-ət-əl\ *adj* **1 a** : punishable by death ⟨a *capital* crime⟩ **b** : resulting in death ⟨*capital* punishment⟩ **2** : belonging to the series A, B, C, etc. rather than a, b, c, etc. **3 a** : first in importance or influence : CHIEF **b** : being the seat of government ⟨*capital* city⟩ **4** : of or relating to capital ⟨*capital* investment⟩ **5** : EXCELLENT ⟨a *capital* performance⟩

2**capital** *n* **1 a** : accumulated goods and equipment and invested savings used in the process of production or to bring in income : ASSETS **b** : INVESTORS, CAPITALISTS **2** : ADVANTAGE, GAIN ⟨make *capital* out of his weakness⟩ **3** : a capital letter **4** : a capital city

3**capital** *n* : the top part or piece of an architectural column

cap·i·tal·ism \'kap-ət-ə-ˌliz-əm\ *n* : an economic system in which resources and means of production are privately owned and prices, production, and the distribution of goods are determined mainly by competition in a free market — **cap·i·tal·ist** \-ləst\ *or* **cap·i·tal·is·tic** \ˌkap-ət-ə-'lis-tik\ *adj* — **cap·i·tal·is·ti·cal·ly** \-ti-k(ə-)lē\ *adv*

cap·i·tal·ist \'kap-ət-ə-ləst\ *n* **1** : a person who has capital; *esp* : one who has or controls a great amount of business capital **2** : a person who favors capitalism

cap·i·tal·ize \'kap-ət-ə-ˌlīz\ *vb* **1** : to write or print with an initial capital or in capitals **2 a** : to supply capital for ⟨*capitalize* an enterprise at $50,000⟩ **b** : to use as capital ⟨*capitalize* reserve funds⟩ **3** : to take an advantage ⟨*capitalize* on an opponent's mistake⟩ — **cap·i·tal·i·za·tion** \ˌkap-ət-ə-lə-'zā-shən\ *n*

cap·i·tal·ly \'kap-ət-ə-lē\ *adv* : EXCELLENTLY ⟨got along *capitally* in school⟩

cap·i·tol \'kap-ət-əl\ *n* **1** : a building in which a state legislative body meets **2** *cap* : the building in which the U.S. Congress meets in Washington

ca·pit·u·late \kə-'pich-ə-ˌlāt\ *vb* : to surrender usu. on terms agreed upon in advance — **ca·pit·u·la·tion** \-ˌpich-ə-'lā-shən\ *n*

ca·pon \'kā-ˌpän, -pən\ *n* : a castrated male chicken

ca·price \kə-'prēs\ *n* **1** : a sudden unpredictable turn or change **2** : a disposition to change one's mind impulsively **3** : a musical composition in a free and lively form — **ca·pri·cious** \kə-'prish-əs, -'prē-shəs\ *adj* — **ca·pri·cious·ly** *adv* — **ca·pri·cious·ness** *n*

Cap·ri·corn \'kap-rə-ˌkȯrn\ *n* — see ZODIAC table

capri pants *n pl*, *often cap C* : close-fitting pants with a slit in the outer bottom of the leg worn esp. by women

caps *abbr* **1** capitals **2** capsule

cap·size \'kap-ˌsīz, kap-'\ *vb* : to turn over : UPSET ⟨canoes *capsize* easily⟩

cap·stan \'kap-stən\ *n* : an upright revolving drum to which a rope is fastened that is used on ships for moving or raising weights and for pulling

capstan

1**cap·sule** \'kap-səl, -sül\ *n* **1** : a surrounding cover ⟨the *capsule* of a joint⟩: as **a** : a case bearing spores or seeds **b** : an edible shell (as of gelatin) enclosing medicine **2** : a small pressurized compartment for an aviator or astronaut

2**capsule** *adj* **1** : extremely brief ⟨a *capsule* review of the news⟩ **2** : being small and compact

ə abut	ər further	a back	ā bake	
ä cot, cart	aủ out	ch chin	e less	ē easy
g gift	i trip	ī life	j joke	ng sing	ō flow
ȯ flaw	ȯi coin	th thin	th this	ü loot
ů foot	y yet	yü few	yů furious	zh vision

capt *abbr* captain

[1]**cap·tain** \'kap-tən\ *n* **1 :** a leader of a group ⟨the *captain* of a team⟩ **2 a :** a commissioned officer in the navy ranking just below a rear admiral **b :** a commissioned officer (as in the army) ranking just below a major **3 :** the commanding officer of a ship **4 :** a fire or police department officer usu. ranking between a chief and a lieutenant — **cap·tain·cy** \-sē\ *n*

[2]**captain** *vb* **:** to be captain of **:** LEAD

cap·tion \'kap-shən\ *n* **1 :** the heading esp. of an article or document **2 :** the explanation accompanying a pictorial illustration — **caption** *vb*

cap·tious \'kap-shəs\ *adj* **:** quick to find fault esp. over trifles — **cap·tious·ly** *adv* — **cap·tious·ness** *n*

cap·ti·vate \'kap-tə-ˌvāt\ *vb* **:** to attract with appeal and win over ⟨music that *captivated* everybody⟩ — **cap·ti·va·tion** \ˌkap-tə-'vā-shən\ *n* — **cap·ti·va·tor** \'kap-tə-ˌvāt-ər\ *n*

syn CAPTIVATE, CHARM, FASCINATE can mean to affect with personal appeal or magnetism. CAPTIVATE implies winning appeal that holds the attention strongly; CHARM may imply a seemingly magical personal influence; FASCINATE may imply alluring and holding with an irresistible charm ***ant*** repulse

[1]**cap·tive** \'kap-tiv\ *adj* **1 :** taken and held prisoner esp. in war **2 :** fastened so as to prevent escape ⟨*captive* balloon⟩ — **cap·tiv·i·ty** \kap-'tiv-ət-ē\ *n*

[2]**captive** *n* **:** one that is captive **:** PRISONER

cap·tor \'kap-tər\ *n* **:** one that has captured a person or thing

[1]**cap·ture** \'kap-chər\ *n* **1 :** the act of capturing **2 :** something or someone captured

[2]**capture** *vb* **cap·tured**; **cap·tur·ing** \'kap-chə-ring, 'kap-shring\ **1 :** to take captive **:** WIN, GAIN ⟨*capture* a city⟩ **2 :** PRESERVE ⟨*captured* her smile on film⟩

cap·u·chin \'kap-yə-shən, kə-'p(y)ü-\ *n* **:** a So. American monkey with the forehead bare and bordered by a fringe of dark hair

cap·y·bara \ˌkap-i-'bar-ə\ *n* **:** a tailless largely aquatic So. American rodent often exceeding four feet in length

capybara

car \'kär\ *n* **1 :** a vehicle (as a railroad coach or an automobile) moved on wheels **2 :** the cage of an elevator **3 :** the part of a balloon or an airship in which passengers or equipment are carried

car·a·bi·neer *or* **car·a·bi·nier** \ˌkar-ə-bə-'ni(ə)r\ *n* **:** a soldier armed with a carbine

car·a·cul \'kar-ə-kəl\ *n* **:** the pelt of a karakul lamb after the curl begins to loosen

ca·rafe \kə-'raf\ *n* **:** a bottle with a wide base and flaring lip used to hold water or beverages

car·a·mel \'kar-ə-məl, 'kär-məl\ *n* **1 :** a brittle brown substance obtained by heating sugar and used for coloring and flavoring **2 :** a firm chewy candy

car·a·pace \'kar-ə-ˌpās\ *n* **:** a bony or horny case or shield covering all or part of the back of an animal (as a turtle)

[1]**car·at** \'kar-ət\ *var of* KARAT

[2]**carat** *n* **:** a unit of weight for precious stones (as diamonds) equal to 200 milligrams

car·a·van \'kar-ə-ˌvan\ *n* **1 a :** a group of travelers through desert or hostile regions **b :** a train of pack animals or of vehicles traveling together **2 :** a covered vehicle; *esp* **:** one equipped as traveling living quarters

car·a·van·sa·ry \ˌkar-ə-'van(t)-sə-rē\ *n, pl* **-ries** **1 :** an inn in eastern countries where caravans rest at night **2 :** HOTEL, INN

car·a·vel \'kar-ə-ˌvel, -vəl\ *n* **:** a small 15th and 16th century ship with broad bows, high narrow poop, and lateen sails

car·a·way \'kar-ə-ˌwā\ *n* **:** a usu. white-flowered aromatic herb related to the carrot and having pungent fruits used in seasoning and medicine

car·bide \'kär-ˌbīd\ *n* **:** a compound of carbon with another element

car·bine \'kär-ˌbēn, -ˌbīn\ *n* **:** a short light rifle

car·bo·hy·drate \ˌkär-bō-'hī-ˌdrāt\ *n* **:** any of various compounds of carbon, hydrogen, and oxygen (as sugars, starches, or celluloses) some of which are formed by plants and are a major animal food

car·bol·ic acid \ˌkär-ˌbäl-ik-\ *n* **:** PHENOL 1

car·bon \'kär-bən\ *n* [from Latin *carbon-*, stem of *carbo* "ember", "charcoal"] **1 :** a nonmetallic element found native (as in the diamond and graphite) or as a constituent of coal, petroleum, and asphalt, of limestone and other carbonates, and of organic compounds or obtained artificially — see ELEMENT table **2 a :** a sheet of carbon paper **b :** a copy made with carbon paper **3 :** a carbon rod used in an arc lamp

car·bo·na·ceous \ˌkär-bə-'nā-shəs\ *adj* **:** relating to, containing, or composed of carbon

car·bo·na·do \ˌkär-bə-'nād-ō, -'näd-\ *n, pl* **-nados** **:** an impure opaque dark-colored fine-grained aggregate of diamond particles valuable for its superior toughness

carbon arc *n* **:** an arc lamp having carbon electrodes that gives off intense light

[1]**car·bon·ate** \'kär-bə-ˌnāt, -nət\ *n* **:** a salt or ester of carbonic acid

[2]**car·bon·ate** \-ˌnāt\ *vb* **1 :** to convert into a carbonate **2 :** to impregnate with carbon dioxide ⟨a *carbonated* beverage⟩ — **car·bon·a·tion** \ˌkär-bə-'nā-shən\ *n*

carbon black *n* **:** any of various colloidal black substances consisting wholly or principally of carbon obtained as soot and used esp. as pigments

carbon copy *n* **1 :** CARBON 2b **2 :** DUPLICATE

carbon cycle *n* **:** the cycle of carbon in living beings in which carbon dioxide fixed by photosynthesis to form food and growth substances is ultimately restored to the inorganic state by respiration and decay

carbon dioxide *n* **:** a heavy colorless gas that does not support combustion, dissolves in water to form carbonic acid, is formed esp. by the burning and breaking down of organic substances (as in animal respiration), is absorbed from the air by plants in photosynthesis, and has many industrial uses

carbon disulfide *n* **:** a colorless flammable poisonous liquid used esp. as a solvent for rubber and as an insecticide — called also *carbon bisulfide*

carbon 14 *n* **:** a heavy radioactive form of carbon that has mass number 14, is formed esp. by the action of cosmic rays on nitrogen in the atmosphere, and is used as a tracer or for determining the age of very old specimens of formerly living materials (as bones or charcoal)

car·bon·ic \kär-'bän-ik\ *adj* **:** of, relating to, or derived from carbon, carbonic acid, or carbon dioxide

carbonic acid *n* : an acid that decomposes readily into water and carbon dioxide
car·bon·if·er·ous \ˌkär-bə-ˈnif-(ə-)rəs\ *adj* **1** : producing or containing carbon or coal **2** *cap* : of, relating to, or being the Carboniferous
Carboniferous *n* : the period of the Paleozoic era between the Devonian and the Permian or the corresponding system of rocks that include coal beds
car·bon·ize \ˈkär-bə-ˌnīz\ *vb* : to convert or become converted into carbon : CHAR — **car·bon·i·za·tion** \ˌkär-bə-nə-ˈzā-shən\ *n*
carbon monoxide *n* : a colorless odorless very poisonous gas formed by the incomplete burning of carbon
carbon paper *n* : a thin paper faced with a pigmented coating and used for making copies of something written or typed
carbon tetrachloride *n* : a colorless nonflammable poisonous liquid that has an odor resembling that of chloroform and is used as a solvent esp. of grease and as a fire extinguisher
car·bun·cle \ˈkär-ˌbəŋ-kəl\ *n* **1** : a rounded and polished garnet **2** : a painful inflammation of the skin and deeper tissues that discharges pus from several openings — compare BOIL
car·bu·re·tor \ˈkär-b(y)ə-ˌrāt-ər\ *n* : an apparatus for supplying an internal-combustion engine with vaporized fuel mixed with air in an explosive mixture
car·cass \ˈkär-kəs\ *n* : a dead body; *esp* : the dressed body of a meat animal
car·cin·o·gen \kär-ˈsin-ə-jən, ˈkär-sə-nə-ˌjen\ *n* : a substance or agent producing or inciting cancer — **car·ci·no·gen·ic** \ˌkär-sə-nō-ˈjen-ik\ *adj*
car·ci·no·ma \ˌkär-sə-ˈnō-mə\ *n, pl* **-mas** *or* **-ma·ta** \-mət-ə\ : a malignant tumor consisting of epithelial cells
[1]**card** \ˈkärd\ *vb* : to cleanse and untangle fibers by combing with a card before spinning — **card·er** *n*
[2]**card** *n* : an instrument for combing fibers (as wool or cotton)
[3]**card** *n* **1** : PLAYING CARD **2** *pl* **a** : a game played with cards **b** : card playing **3** : an amusing person : WAG **4 a** : a flat stiff usu. rectangular piece of paper or paperboard **b** : a sports program
card·board \ˈkärd-ˌbōrd, -ˌbȯrd\ *n* : a stiff board made of paper pulp and used esp. for boxes and signs
car·di·ac \ˈkärd-ē-ˌak\ *adj* **1** : of, relating to, situated near, or acting on the heart **2** : of, relating to, or being the part of the stomach into which the esophagus opens
car·di·gan \ˈkärd-i-gən\ *n* : a usu. collarless sweater opening down the front
Cardigan *n* : a Welsh corgi with rounded ears, slightly bowed forelegs, and long tail
[1]**car·di·nal** \ˈkärd-(ə-)nəl\ *adj* [from Latin *cardinalis*, from *cardin-*, stem of *cardo* "hinge", "turning point"] **1** : MAIN, PRIMARY **2** : of or relating to a cardinal number — **car·di·nal·ly** \-ē\ *adv*
[2]**cardinal** *n* **1** : a high official of the Roman Catholic Church ranking next below the pope **2** : CARDINAL NUMBER **3** : any of several American finches of which the male is bright red with a black face and pointed crest

ə abut ər further a back ā bake ä cot, cart au̇ out ch chin e less ē easy g gift i trip ī life j joke ng sing ō flow ȯ flaw ȯi coin th thin t͟h this ü loot u̇ foot y yet yü few yu̇ furious zh vision

cardinal flower *n* : the brilliant red flower of a No. American lobelia; *also* : this plant
car·di·nal·i·ty \ˌkärd-ə-ˈnal-ət-ē\ *n, pl* **-ties** : the number of elements in a given mathematical set
cardinal number *n* : a number (as 1, 5, 15) that is used in simple counting and that answers the question how many? — see NUMBER table
cardinal point *n* : one of the four principal points of the compass: north, south, east, west
car·dio·gram \ˈkärd-ē-ə-ˌgram\ *n* : the curve or tracing made by a cardiograph
car·dio·graph \-ˌgraf\ *n* : an instrument that records graphically the duration and character of the heart movements — **car·dio·graph·ic** \ˌkärd-ē-ə-ˈgraf-ik\ *adj*
car·di·oid \ˈkärd-ē-ˌȯid\ *n* : a heart-shaped curve traced by a point on the circumference of a circle rolling completely around an equal fixed circle
car·dio·vas·cu·lar \ˌkärd-ē-ō-ˈvas-kyə-lər\ *adj* : of, relating to, or involving the heart and blood vessels
[1]**care** \ˈke(ə)r, ˈka(ə)r\ *n* **1** : a heavy sense of responsibility : CONCERN **2** : serious attention : HEED ⟨take *care* in crossing streets⟩ **3** : SUPERVISION ⟨under a doctor's *care*⟩ **4** : an object of one's care
[2]**care** *vb* **1 a** : to feel trouble or anxiety **b** : to feel interest or concern ⟨*care* about freedom⟩ **2** : to give care ⟨*care* for the sick⟩ **3 a** : to have a liking, fondness, or taste ⟨don't *care* for her cooking⟩ **b** : to have an inclination ⟨would you *care* for some pie?⟩ — **car·er** *n*
CARE \ˈke(ə)r, ˈka(ə)r\ *abbr* Co-operative for American Remittances to Everywhere
ca·reen \kə-ˈrēn\ *vb* **1** : to cause a boat to lean or tilt over on one side for cleaning, caulking, or repairing **2** : to sway from side to side : LURCH
[1]**ca·reer** \kə-ˈri(ə)r\ *n* **1 a** : COURSE, PROGRESS **b** : full speed or activity ⟨in full *career*⟩ **2** : a course of continued progress or activity **3** : a profession followed as a permanent calling
[2]**career** *vb* : to go at top speed
care·free \ˈke(ə)r-ˌfrē, ˈka(ə)r-\ *adj* : free from care : LIGHTHEARTED
care·ful \-fəl\ *adj* **1** : using care : taking care : WATCHFUL ⟨a *careful* driver⟩ **2** : made, done, or said with care ⟨*careful* examination⟩ — **care·ful·ly** \-f(ə-)lē\ *adv* — **care·ful·ness** \-fəl-nəs\ *n*
syn CAREFUL, CAUTIOUS, WARY can mean taking thought for security. CAREFUL suggests watchfulness and alertness to prevent mistakes or mishaps; CAUTIOUS suggests prudence in anticipating dangers; WARY often implies suspicion and fear of dangers or cunning in escaping them ***ant*** careless
care·less \ˈke(ə)r-ləs, ˈka(ə)r-\ *adj* **1** : CAREFREE **2** : not taking proper care : HEEDLESS ⟨*careless* of danger⟩ **3** : done, made, or said without due care ⟨a *careless* mistake⟩ — **care·less·ly** *adv* — **care·less·ness** *n*
ca·ress \kə-ˈres\ *n* : a tender or loving touch or embrace — **caress** *vb*
car·et \ˈkar-ət\ *n* [from Latin meaning "is missing", from *carēre* "to lack"] : a mark ∧ used to show where something is to be inserted
care·tak·er \ˈke(ə)r-ˌtā-kər, ˈka(ə)r-\ *n* : one that takes care of buildings or land often for an absent owner
care·worn \-ˌwōrn, -ˌwȯrn\ *adj* : showing the effect of grief or anxiety
car·fare \ˈkär-ˌfa(ə)r, -ˌfe(ə)r\ *n* : the fare charged for carrying a passenger (as on a bus or streetcar)
car·go \ˈkär-ˌgō\ *n, pl* **cargoes** *or* **cargos** : the

goods or merchandise conveyed in a ship, airplane, or vehicle : FREIGHT
car·hop \'kär-ˌhäp\ *n* : one who serves customers at a drive-in restaurant
Ca·rib·be·an \ˌkar-ə-'bē-ən, kə-'rib-ē-\ *adj* : of, relating to, or characteristic of the eastern and southern West Indies or the Caribbean sea
car·i·bou \'kar-ə-ˌbü\ *n, pl* **-bou** *or* **-bous** : any of several large deer of northern No. America closely related to the reindeer

caribou
(about 43 in. at shoulder)

car·i·ca·ture \'kar-i-kə-ˌchu̇(ə)r\ *n* **1** : exaggeration by means of comic distortion of parts or features **2** : a representation esp. in literature or art by means of caricature — **carica·ture** *vb* — **car·i·ca·tur·ist** \-ˌchu̇r-əst\ *n*
car·ies \'ka(ə)r-ēz, 'ke(ə)r-\ *n, pl* **caries** : a progressive destruction of bone or tooth; *esp* : tooth decay
car·il·lon \'kar-ə-ˌlän\ *n* : a set of bells sounded by hammers controlled by a keyboard
car·load \'kär-'lōd\ *n* : a load that fills a car
car·mine \'kär-mən, -ˌmīn\ *n* **1** : a rich crimson or scarlet coloring matter made from cochineal **2** : a vivid red
car·nage \'kär-nij\ *n* : great destruction of life (as in battle) : SLAUGHTER
car·nal \'kärn-əl\ *adj* **1** : of or relating to the body **2** : not spiritual : CORPOREAL **3** : SENSUAL — **car·nal·i·ty** \kär-'nal-ət-ē\ *n* — **car·nal·ly** \'kärn-ə-lē\ *adv*
car·na·tion \kär-'nā-shən\ *n* **1** : a moderate red **2** : any of the numerous cultivated usu. double-flowered pinks with reddish, pink, yellow, or white flowers
car·nau·ba wax \kär-ˌnȯ-bə-\ *n* : a brittle hard yellowish wax obtained from a Brazilian palm and used esp. in polishes
car·ne·lian \kär-'nēl-yən\ *n* : a hard tough reddish quartz used as a gem
car·ni·val \'kär-nə-vəl\ *n* **1** : a season or festival of merrymaking before Lent **2** : a merrymaking, feasting, or masquerading **3 a** : a traveling enterprise offering amusements **b** : an organized program of entertainment or exhibition
car·ni·vore \'kär-nə-ˌvō(ə)r, -ˌvȯ(ə)r\ *n* **1** : a flesh-eating animal; *esp* : any of an order of flesh-eating mammals **2** : an insect-eating plant
car·niv·o·rous \kär-'niv-(ə-)rəs\ *adj* **1** : subsisting or feeding on animal tissues **2** : of or relating to the carnivores — **car·niv·o·rous·ly** *adv* — **car·niv·o·rous·ness** *n*
[1]**car·ol** \'kar-əl\ *n* : a song of joy or mirth or praise ⟨Christmas *carol*⟩
[2]**carol** *vb* **-oled** *or* **-olled**; **-ol·ing** *or* **-ol·ling** **1** : to sing esp. in a joyful manner **2** : to sing carols — **car·ol·er** *or* **car·ol·ler** *n*
[1]**car·om** \'kar-əm\ *n* **1** : a shot in billiards in which the cue ball strikes each of two object balls **2** : a rebounding esp. at an angle
[2]**carom** *vb* **1** : to make a carom **2** : to strike and rebound at an angle : GLANCE
car·o·tene \'kar-ə-ˌtēn\ *or* **car·o·tin** \'kar-ət-ən\ *n* : any of several orange or red hydrocarbon pigments which occur in plants and in the fatty tissues of plant-eating animals and from which vitamin A is formed
ca·rot·id \kə-'rät-əd\ *n* : one of the pair of arteries that pass up each side of the neck and supply the head — called also *carotid artery* — **carotid** *adj*
ca·rous·al \kə-'rau̇-zəl\ *n* : CAROUSE
ca·rouse \kə-'rau̇z\ *n* : a drunken revel — **carouse** *vb* — **ca·rous·er** *n*
[1]**carp** \'kärp\ *vb* : to find fault : COMPLAIN — **carp·er** *n*
[2]**carp** *n, pl* **carp** *or* **carps** : a large variable Old World freshwater fish noted for its longevity and often raised for food; *also* : any of various related or similar fishes
[1]**car·pal** \'kär-pəl\ *adj* : relating to the wrist or carpus
[2]**carpal** *n* : a carpal bone or cartilage
car·pel \'kär-pəl\ *n* : one of the structures of a flower that together form the ovary of a seed plant
car·pen·ter \'kär-pən-tər\ *n* : a workman who builds or repairs wooden structures — **carpenter** *vb* — **car·pen·try** \-trē\ *n*
carpenter ant *n* : any of several ants that nest and gnaw passageways in dead or partially decayed wood
car·pet \'kär-pət\ *n* **1** : a heavy woven or felted fabric used as a floor covering **2** : a floor covering made of carpet — **carpet** *vb*
car·pet·bag \-ˌbag\ *n* : a traveling bag made of carpeting
car·pet·bag·ger \-ˌbag-ər\ *n* : a Northerner in the South during the reconstruction period seeking private gain by taking advantage of unsettled conditions and political corruption — **car·pet·bag** \-ˌbag\ *adj*
carpet beetle *n* : a small beetle whose larva damages woolen goods
car·pet·ing \'kär-pət-ing\ *n* : material for carpets; *also* : CARPETS
car·port \'kär-ˌpōrt, -ˌpȯrt\ *n* : an open-sided automobile shelter usu. formed by extension of a roof from the side of a building
car·pus \'kär-pəs\ *n, pl* **car·pi** \-ˌpī, -ˌpē\ : the wrist or its bones
car·riage \'kar-ij\ *n* **1 a** : the act of carrying **b** : manner of bearing the body : POSTURE **2** : the cost of carrying **3** : a horse-drawn wheeled vehicle designed for carrying persons **4** : a wheeled support carrying a load ⟨gun *carriage*⟩ **5** : a movable part of a machine for supporting or carrying some other movable object or part
car·ri·er \'kar-ē-ər\ *n* **1** : one that carries ⟨mail *carrier*⟩ **2** : a person or firm engaged in transporting passengers or goods **3** : a bearer and transmitter of disease germs; *esp* : one who carries in his system germs of a disease (as typhoid fever) to which he is immune **4** : a wave whose frequency or amplitude is varied in order to transmit a radio or television signal
car·ri·on \'kar-ē-ən\ *n* : dead and decaying flesh
car·rot \'kar-ət\ *n* : the long tapering edible root of a common garden plant that is eaten as a vegetable; *also* : a plant that produces a carrot
car·rou·sel *or* **car·ou·sel** \ˌkar-ə-'sel, -'zel\ *n* : MERRY-GO-ROUND
[1]**car·ry** \'kar-ē\ *vb* **car·ried**; **car·ry·ing** **1** : to support and take from one place to another : TRANSPORT ⟨*carry* a package⟩ **2** : to influence by mental or emotional appeal ⟨the speaker *carried* his audience⟩ **3** : WIN, CAPTURE ⟨*carry* an election⟩ **4** : to transfer from one place to another ⟨*carry* a number in addi-

tion⟩ **5 :** to contain and direct the course of : CONDUCT ⟨a pipe *carries* water⟩ **6 :** to wear or have on one's person or within one ⟨*carries* a gun⟩ ⟨*carries* a scar⟩ **7 :** IMPLY, INVOLVE ⟨the crime *carries* a penalty⟩ **8 :** to hold the body or a part of it ⟨*carries* his head high⟩ **9 :** to sing in correct pitch ⟨*carry* a tune⟩ **10 :** to stock for sale ⟨*carries* three brands of tires⟩ **11 :** to maintain on a list or record ⟨*carry* him on the payroll⟩ **12 :** SUPPORT, MAINTAIN ⟨pillars *carry* an arch⟩ **13 a :** to gain victory for ⟨*carry* your point⟩; *esp* **:** to secure the adoption or passage of ⟨*carry* a bill⟩ **b :** to win adoption ⟨the bill *carried*⟩ **14 :** to succeed in ⟨*carry* an election⟩ **15 :** PUBLISH ⟨the paper *carries* weather reports⟩ **16 :** to keep on one's books as a debtor **17 :** to reach or penetrate to a distance ⟨a voice that *carries* well⟩ : cover a distance ⟨the home run *carried* over 400 feet⟩

2**carry** *n, pl* **carries 1 :** the range of a gun or projectile or of a ball **2 a :** the act or method of carrying ⟨fireman's *carry*⟩ **b :** PORTAGE

car·ry·all \'kar-ē-ˌȯl\ *n* **1 :** a passenger automobile similar to a station wagon **2 :** a capacious bag or case

carry away *vb* **:** to arouse emotion or enthusiasm in

carrying charge *n* **:** a charge added to the price of merchandise sold on the installment plan

carry on *vb* **1 :** CONDUCT, MANAGE ⟨*carries on* a dry-cleaning business⟩ **2 :** to behave in a foolish, excited, or improper manner ⟨embarrassed at the way he *carried on*⟩ **3 :** to continue esp. in spite of hindrance or discouragement ⟨still *carrying on*⟩

carry out *vb* **:** to execute successfully ⟨*carry out* a plan⟩

car·sick \'kär-ˌsik\ *adj* **:** affected with motion sickness associated with riding in a car — **car sickness** *n*

1**cart** \'kärt\ *n* **1 :** a heavy usu. horse-drawn 2-wheeled wagon **2 :** a light usu. 2-wheeled vehicle ⟨pony *cart*⟩

2**cart** *vb* **:** to convey in or as if in a cart — **cart·er** *n*

cart·age \'kärt-ij\ *n* **:** the act of or rate charged for carting

car·tel \kär-'tel\ *n* **:** a combination of business firms to control world markets and fix prices

Car·te·sian product \kär-ˌtē-zhən-\ *n* **:** a set that is derived from two given sets and includes all pairs of the form (x, y) where x belongs to one set and y belongs to the other

Car·tha·gin·i·an \ˌkär-thə-'jin-ē-ən\ *adj* **:** of, relating to, or characteristic of Carthage or its people — **Carthaginian** *n*

car·ti·lage \'kärt-ə-lij\ *n* **1 :** an elastic tissue which composes most of the skeleton of the embryonic and very young vertebrates and much of which is converted to bone in the higher forms but remains throughout life the chief constituent of the skeleton in primitive forms **2 :** a part or structure composed of cartilage

car·ti·lag·i·nous \ˌkärt-ə-'laj-ə-nəs\ *adj* **:** of, relating to, or resembling cartilage

cartilaginous fish *n* **:** any of the fishes having the skeleton composed largely of cartilage

car·tog·ra·phy \kär-'täg-rə-fē\ *n* **:** the making of maps — **car·tog·ra·pher** \-fər\ *n* — **car·to·graph·ic** \ˌkärt-ə-'graf-ik\ *adj*

ə abut	ər further	a back	ā bake
ä cot, cart	aů out	ch chin	e less	ē easy
g gift	i trip	ī life	j joke	ng sing	ō flow
ȯ flaw	ȯi coin	th thin	t͟h this	ü loot
ů foot	y yet	yü few	yů furious	zh vision

car·ton \'kärt-ən\ *n* **:** a paperboard box or container ⟨an egg *carton*⟩

car·toon \kär-'tün\ *n* **1 :** a preparatory design, drawing, or painting **2 a :** a satirical drawing commenting on political matters **b :** COMIC STRIP **3 :** a series of drawings that when projected one after the other give the appearance of movement — **cartoon** *vb* — **car·toon·ist** \-'tü-nəst\ *n*

car·tridge \'kär-trij\ *n* **1 a :** a tube of metal or paper containing a charge for a firearm **b :** a case containing an explosive charge for blasting **2 :** a container of material (as film or recording tape) for insertion into a larger mechanism **3 :** a phonograph pickup that translates stylus motion into electrical voltage

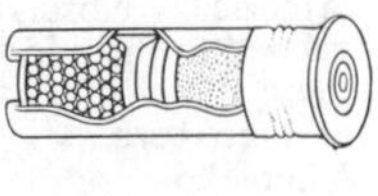

cartridge 1a

cart·wheel \'kärt-ˌhwēl\ *n* **1 :** a large coin (as a silver dollar) **2 :** a lateral handspring with arms and legs extended

carve \'kärv\ *vb* **1 :** to cut with care or precision esp. artistically ⟨*carve* friezes⟩ **2 :** to cut into pieces or slices **3 :** to cut up and serve meat

carv·en \'kär-vən\ *adj* **:** CARVED

carv·er \'kär-vər\ *n* **1 :** one that carves **2 :** a large knife for carving meat

carv·ing \'kär-ving\ *n* **1 :** the act or art of one who carves **2 :** a carved object, design, or figure

cary·at·id \ˌkar-ē-'at-əd\ *n, pl* **-at·ids** *or* **-at·i·des** \-'at-ə-ˌdēz\ **:** a sculptured figure of a woman in flowing robes used as an architectural column

ca·sa·ba \kə-'säb-ə\ *n* **:** any of several winter melons with yellow rind and sweet flesh

1**cas·cade** \kas-'kād\ *n* **:** a steep usu. small waterfall

2**cascade** *vb* **:** to fall in a cascade

Cas·ca·di·an \kas-'kād-ē-ən\ *adj* **:** of or relating to the mountain-making movements in the Cenozoic era

cas·cara \kas-'kar-ə\ *n* **:** the dried laxative bark of a tree that grows along the Pacific coast of the U.S.

1**case** \'kās\ *n* **1 :** a situation requiring investigation, action, or consideration ⟨a *case* for the police⟩ **2 a :** a form of a noun, pronoun, or adjective indicating its grammatical relation to other words ⟨the word *boy's* in "the boy's shirt" is in the possessive *case*⟩ **b :** such a relation whether indicated by inflection or not ⟨the subject of a verb is in the nominative *case*⟩ **3 :** what actually exists or happens **:** FACT **4 :** a legal suit or action **5 :** a supporting argument or evidence; *esp* **:** a convincing argument **6 a :** an instance of disease or injury **b :** PATIENT **7 :** INSTANCE, EXAMPLE ⟨a *case* of injustice⟩ — **in case 1 :** IF ⟨*in case* it rains, stay home⟩ **2 :** as a precaution ⟨carry an umbrella just *in case*⟩ **3 :** as a precaution against the event that ⟨has extra money *in case* he needs it⟩ — **in case of :** in the event of ⟨*in case of trouble*, yell⟩

2**case** *n* **1 a :** a box or receptacle to contain something **b :** a box with its contents **2 :** an outer covering or housing **3 :** CASING 2

case hard·en \'kās-ˌhärd-ən\ *vb* **:** to harden (an iron alloy) so that the surface layer is harder than the interior — **case–hard·ened** *adj*

ca·sein \kā-'sēn, 'kā-sē-ən\ *n* **1 :** a phosphorus-containing protein that is separated from milk by heating with an acid or by lactic acid in souring and that is used in making paints and adhesives **2 :** a phosphorus-containing protein that is produced when milk is curdled by rennet, that is one of the chief constituents of cheese, and that is used in making plastics

case knife *n* **1 :** SHEATH KNIFE **2 :** a table knife
case·ment \'kās-mənt\ *n* **1 :** a window sash opening on hinges like a door **2 :** a window with a casement
case·work \'kās-ˌwərk\ *n* **:** social work involving close contact with the problems and needs of a person or family — **case·work·er** \-ˌwər-kər\ *n*
[1]**cash** \'kash\ *n* [from French *casse* "money box", from Italian *cassa,* from Latin *capsa* "chest", "case"] **1 :** available money **2 :** money paid at the time of purchase
[2]**cash** *vb* **:** to pay or obtain cash for ⟨*cash* a check⟩
cash·ew \'kash-ü, kə-'shü\ *n* **:** a tropical American tree that is related to the sumacs and is grown chiefly for its enlarged edible flower stalk and kidney-shaped nut; *also* **:** its nut

cashew

[1]**cash·ier** \ka-'shi(ə)r\ *n* **1 :** a high officer of a bank responsible for all money received and paid out **2 :** an employee of a store or restaurant who receives and records payments made by customers
[2]**ca·shier** \ka-'shi(ə)r\ *vb* **:** DISCHARGE; *esp* **:** to discharge in disgrace from a position of responsibility or trust
cashier's check *n* **:** a check drawn by a bank upon its own funds and signed by its cashier
cash·mere \'kazh-ˌmi(ə)r, 'kash-\ *n* **1 :** fine wool from the undercoat of Kashmir goats **2 :** cashmere yarn **3 :** a soft twilled fabric made orig. from cashmere wool
cash register *n* **:** a business machine usu. with a money drawer that records the amount of money received and exhibits the amount of each sale
cash value *n* **:** the amount paid to the owner of a life insurance policy if it is surrendered to the insuring company before the beneficiary is eligible for the full benefits of the policy
cas·ing \'kā-sing\ *n* **1 a :** something that encases **b :** material for encasing **2 :** an enclosing frame around a door or window opening
ca·si·no \kə-'sē-nō\ *n, pl* **-nos :** a building or room used for social amusements; *esp* **:** a building or room used for gambling
cask \'kask\ *n* **1 :** a barrel-shaped container usu. for liquids **2 :** the quantity contained in a cask
cas·ket \'kas-kət\ *n* **1 :** a small chest or box (as for jewels) **2 :** COFFIN
casque \'kask\ *n* **:** HELMET
cas·sa·va \kə-'säv-ə\ *n* **:** any of several tropical plants with a fleshy rootstock that yields a nutritious starch; *also* **:** the rootstock or its starch — compare TAPIOCA
cas·se·role \'kas-ə-ˌrōl\ *n* **1 :** a dish in which food can be baked and served **2 :** the food cooked and served in a casserole
cas·sette \kə-'set, ka-\ *n* **:** a container for film, photographic plates, or recording tape
cas·sia \'kash-ə\ *n* **1 :** the coarse bark of any of several cinnamons **2 :** any of a genus of leguminous herbs, shrubs, and trees of warm regions some of which yield senna
cas·sit·er·ite \kə-'sit-ə-ˌrīt\ *n* **:** a brown or black mineral that consists of the dioxide of tin and is the chief source of tin
cas·sock \'kas-ək\ *n* **:** a close-fitting ankle-length gown worn by clergy esp. in the Roman Catholic and Anglican churches
cas·so·wary \'kas-ə-ˌwer-ē\ *n, pl* **-war·ies :** any of several tall swift-running birds of New Guinea and Australia closely related to the emu

cassowary
(about 5 ft. tall)

[1]**cast** \'kast\ *vb* **cast; cast·ing 1 a :** THROW, TOSS ⟨*cast* a stone⟩ **b :** to throw a fishing line **c :** DIRECT, PROJECT ⟨*cast* a glance⟩ ⟨*cast* doubt on his integrity⟩ **d** to deposit formally ⟨*cast* a ballot⟩ **e :** to throw off, out, or away ⟨the horse *cast* a shoe⟩ ⟨a snake *casts* its skin⟩ **2 a :** ADD, COMPUTE **b :** to calculate by astrology ⟨*cast* a horoscope⟩ **3 :** to assign parts to actors ⟨*cast* a play⟩ **4 :** to shape a substance by pouring it in liquid or plastic form into a mold and letting harden without pressure ⟨*cast* steel⟩ ⟨*cast* machine parts⟩ — **cast about :** to search here and there — **cast lots :** to draw lots to determine a matter by chance
[2]**cast** *n* **1 :** an act of casting **2 a :** the form in which a thing is constructed **b :** the actors in a play **3 :** the distance to which a thing can be thrown **4 a :** a glance of the eye **b :** EXPRESSION, APPEARANCE **5 a :** CASTING 2 **b :** a rigid dressing of plaster of paris for immobilizing a body part **6 :** FORECAST **7 :** a tinge of color **:** SHADE **8 :** something thrown out or off, shed, or ejected
cas·ta·net \ˌkas-tə-'net\ *n* [from Spanish *castañeta,* from *castaña* "chestnut", from Latin *castanea*] **:** a rhythm instrument that consists of two small ivory, wood, or plastic shells fastened to the thumb and clicked together by the fingers — usu. used in pl.
cast·away \'kas-tə-ˌwā\ *adj* **1 :** thrown away **2 :** cast adrift or ashore as a survivor of a shipwreck — **castaway** *n*

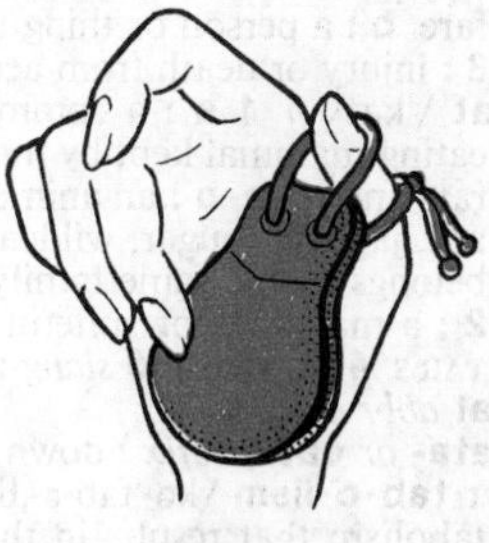
castanets

caste \'kast\ *n* **1 :** one of the hereditary classes formerly dividing Hindu society **2 a :** a division of society based upon differences of wealth, inherited rank, or occupation **b :** the position conferred by caste standing **:** PRESTIGE **3 :** a specialized form of a social insect (as the honeybee) that carries out a particular function in the colony ⟨the worker *caste*⟩
cas·tel·lat·ed \'kas-tə-ˌlāt-əd\ *adj* **:** having battlements
cast·er \'kas-tər\ *n* **1 :** one that casts **2 :** a small container (as for salt) with a perforated top **3 :** a small tray for cruets and other containers **4** *or* **cas·tor** \'kas-tər\ **:** a small wheel or set of wheels mounted in a swivel frame used for supporting furniture, trucks, and portable machines
cas·ti·gate \'kas-tə-ˌgāt\ *vb* **:** to punish, reprove, or criticize severely — **cas·ti·ga·tion** \ˌkas-tə-'gā-shən\ *n* — **cas·ti·ga·tor** \'kas-tə-ˌgāt-ər\ *n*
cas·tile soap \ˌkas-ˌtēl-\ *n, often cap C* **:** a fine hard bland soap made from olive oil and sodium hydroxide

cast·ing \'kas-tiŋ\ *n* **1** : the act of one that casts **2** : something cast in a mold ⟨a bronze *casting*⟩ **3** : CAST 8

casting vote *n* : a deciding vote cast by a presiding officer in case of a tied vote

cast iron *n* : a hard brittle alloy of iron, carbon, and silicon shaped by being poured into a mold while it is molten and being allowed to harden

1cas·tle \'kas-əl\ *n* **1 a** : a large fortified building or set of buildings **b** : a massive or imposing house **2** : 3ROOK

2castle *vb* **cas·tled**; **cas·tling** \'kas-(ə-)liŋ\ : to establish in a castle

cast–off \'kast-ˌȯf\ *adj* : thrown away : DISCARDED — **castoff** *n*

cas·tor bean \'kas-tər-\ *n* : the very poisonous seed of the castor-oil plant; *also* : CASTOR-OIL PLANT

castor oil *n* : a thick yellowish oil extracted from castor beans and used as a lubricant, in soap, and as a laxative

castor–oil plant *n* : a tropical Old World herb widely grown as an ornamental or for its oil-rich castor beans

cas·trate \'kas-ˌtrāt\ *vb* : to deprive of the sex glands and esp. the testes — **cas·tra·tion** \ka-'strā- shən\ *n*

ca·su·al \'kazh-(ə-)wəl, 'kazh-əl\ *adj* **1** : ACCIDENTAL, UNEXPECTED ⟨a *casual* meeting⟩ **2** : happening irregularly : OCCASIONAL **3 a** : feeling or showing little concern : NONCHALANT **b** : INFORMAL, NATURAL **c** : designed for ordinary or informal use ⟨a *casual* coat for town or country wear⟩ — **ca·su·al·ly** \-ē\ *adv* — **ca·su·al·ness** *n*

ca·su·al·ty \'kazh-əl-tē, 'kazh-(ə-)wəl-\ *n, pl* **-ties** **1** : serious or fatal accident : DISASTER **2 a** : a military person lost (as by death or capture) during warfare **b** : a person or thing injured, lost, or destroyed **3** : injury or death from accident

cat \'kat\ *n* **1 a** : a common small domestic flesh-eating mammal kept by man as a pet or for catching rats and mice **b** : an animal (as the lion, tiger, leopard, jaguar, cougar, wildcat, lynx, and cheetah) that belongs to the same family as the domesticated cat **2** : a malicious or spiteful woman **3** : CAT-O'-NINE-TAILS **4** : CATFISH **5** *slang* : GUY

cat *abbr* catalog

cata- *or* **cat-** *prefix* : down

ca·tab·o·lism \kə-'tab-ə-ˌliz-əm\ *n* : destructive metabolism that results in the breakdown of complex materials within the organisms and usu. involves the release of energy and formation of waste products — **cat·a·bol·ic** \ˌkat-ə-'bäl-ik\ *adj*

cat·a·clysm \'kat-ə-ˌkliz-əm\ *n* **1** : a great flood **2** : a violent and destructive natural event (as an earthquake) **3** : a violent social or political upheaval — **cat·a·clys·mic** \ˌkät-ə-'kliz-mik\ *adj*

cat·a·comb \'kat-ə-ˌkōm\ *n* : an underground place of burial; *esp* : one that has passages with hollowed places in the sides for tombs

cat·a·lep·sy \'kat-ə-ˌlep-sē\ *n* : a nervous condition in which the muscles become rigid and the body and limbs stay in any position in which they are placed — **cat·a·lep·tic** \ˌkat-ə-'lep-tik\ *adj or n*

1cat·a·log *or* **cat·a·logue** \'kat-ə-ˌlȯg\ *n* **1** : a list of names, titles, or articles arranged according to a system **2 a** : a book or file containing a catalog **b** : the items listed in such a book or file

2catalog *or* **catalogue** *vb* **1** : to make a catalog of **2** : to enter in a catalog ⟨*catalog* books⟩ — **cat·a·log·er** *or* **cat·a·logu·er** \-'lȯ-gər\ *n*

ca·tal·pa \kə-'tal-pə, -'tȯl-\ *n* : a small tree of America and Asia with broad oval leaves, flowers brightly striped inside and spotted outside, and long narrow pods

ca·tal·y·sis \kə-'tal-ə-səs\ *n* : the change and esp. increase in the rate of a chemical reaction brought about by a catalyst — **cat·a·lyt·ic** \ˌkat-ə-'lit-ik\ *adj*

cat·a·lyst \'kat-ə-ləst\ *n* : a substance that changes the rate of a chemical reaction but is itself unchanged at the end of the process; *esp* : such a substance that speeds up a reaction or enables it to proceed under milder conditions than otherwise possible

cat·a·lyze \'kat-ə-ˌlīz\ *vb* : to bring about or produce by chemical catalysis

cat·a·ma·ran \ˌkat-ə-mə-'ran\ *n* **1** : a raft of two joined logs **2** : a boat with twin hulls

cat·a·mount \'kat-ə-ˌmau̇nt\ *n* : any of various wild cats: as **a** : COUGAR **b** : LYNX

1cat·a·pult \'kat-ə-ˌpəlt, -ˌpu̇lt\ *n* **1** : an ancient military device for hurling missiles **2** : a device for launching an airplane (as from the deck of a ship)

2catapult *vb* : to throw or launch by or as if by a catapult

cat·a·ract \'kat-ə-ˌrakt\ *n* **1** : a clouding of the lens of the eye or of the saclike structure enclosing it obstructing the passage of light **2** : a large waterfall **3** : DOWNPOUR, FLOOD

ca·tarrh \kə-'tär\ *n* [from Greek *katarrhous,* from *katarrhein* "to flow down"] : inflammation of a mucous membrane; *esp* : one chronically affecting the human nose and air passages — **ca·tarrh·al** \-'tär-əl\ *adj*

ca·tas·tro·phe \kə-'tas-trə-(ˌ)fē\ *n* **1** : a sudden tragic event : DISASTER **2** : utter failure or ruin — **cat·a·stroph·ic** \ˌkat-ə-'sträf-ik\ *adj* — **cat·a·stroph·i·cal·ly** \-'sträf-i-k(ə-)lē\ *adv*

cat·bird \'kat-ˌbərd\ *n* : a dark gray American songbird with black cap and reddish under tail coverts

cat·boat \-ˌbōt\ *n* : a single-masted sailboat with the sail extended by a long boom

catboat

cat·call \-ˌkȯl\ *n* : a noise (as one like the cry of a cat) made to express disapproval — **catcall** *vb*

1catch \'kach, 'kech\ *vb* **caught** \'kȯt\; **catch·ing** **1 a** : to capture or seize in flight or motion ⟨*catch* butterflies⟩ **b** : TRAP **2 a** : to discover unexpectedly ⟨was *caught* in the act⟩ **b** : to check suddenly ⟨*caught* himself before he gave away the secret⟩ **3** : to take hold of : SNATCH **4 a** : to get entangled ⟨*catch* a sleeve on a nail⟩ **b** : to engage firmly ⟨this lock will not *catch*⟩ **c** : FASTEN **5** : to become affected by ⟨*catch* pneumonia⟩ **6** : to take or get momentarily or quickly ⟨*catch* a glimpse of a friend⟩ ⟨*catch* a little sleep⟩ **7 a** : OVERTAKE **b** : to get aboard in time ⟨*catch* the bus⟩ **8** : UNDERSTAND, APPREHEND ⟨didn't *catch* what he said⟩ **9** : to play ball as a catcher — **catch fire** **1** : to begin to burn **2** : to become excited or exciting — **catch one's**

ə abut	ər further	a back	ā bake
ä cot, cart	au̇ out	ch chin	e less	ē easy
g gift	i trip	ī life	j joke	ŋ sing	ō flow
ȯ flaw	ȯi coin	th thin	t͟h this	ü loot
u̇ foot	y yet	yü few	yu̇ furious	zh vision

breath : to pause or rest long enough to regain normal breathing

[2]**catch** *n* **1** : something caught; *esp* : the quantity caught at one time **2 a** : the act of catching **b** : a game in which a ball is thrown and caught **3** : something that checks or fastens; *esp* : LATCH **4** : one worth catching **5** : a round for three or more voices **6** : a concealed difficulty

catch·all \'kach-ˌȯl, 'kech-\ *n* : something to hold a variety of odds and ends

catch·er \'kach-ər, 'kech-\ *n* : one that catches; *esp* : a baseball player stationed behind home plate

catch·ing *adj* **1** : INFECTIOUS, CONTAGIOUS **2** : ALLURING

catch·ment \'kach-mənt, 'kech-\ *n* **1** : the action of catching water **2** : something that catches water

catch·up \'kech-əp, 'kach-; 'kat-səp\ *var of* CATSUP

catchy \'kach-ē, 'kech-ē\ *adj* **catch·i·er**; **-est** **1** : likely to attract attention **2** : easily remembered ⟨*catchy* music⟩ **3** : apt to entangle one : TRICKY ⟨a *catchy* question⟩

cat·e·chism \'kat-ə-ˌkiz-əm\ *n* **1** : a summary of religious doctrine in the form of questions and answers **2** : a set of formal questions

cat·e·chize \'kat-ə-ˌkīz\ *vb* : to instruct by means of a catechism — **cat·e·chist** \-ə-ˌkist, -i-ˌkəst\ *n* — **cat·e·chiz·er** *n*

cat·e·gor·i·cal \ˌkat-ə-'gȯr-i-kəl, -'gär-\ *also* **cat·e·gor·ic** \-ik\ *adj* **1** : UNQUALIFIED, ABSOLUTE ⟨a *categorical* denial⟩ **2** : of, relating to, or being a category — **cat·e·gor·i·cal·ly** \-i-k(ə-)lē\ *adv*

cat·e·go·rize \'kat-i-gə-ˌrīz\ *vb* : to put into a category : CLASSIFY — **cat·e·go·ri·za·tion** \ˌkat-i-gə-rə-'zā-shən\ *n*

cat·e·go·ry \'kat-ə-ˌgōr-ē, -ˌgȯr-\ *n, pl* **-ries** **1** : one of the divisions or groupings used in a system of classification ⟨"species" and "genus" are biological *categories*⟩ **2** : CLASS, KIND

ca·ter \'kāt-ər\ *vb* **1** : to provide a supply of food ⟨*cater* a banquet⟩ **2** : to supply the wants esp. of a special group ⟨*cater* to fishermen⟩ — **ca·ter·er** *n*

cat·er·cor·ner \ˌkat-ē-'kȯr-nər, ˌkat-ə-, ˌkit-ē-\ *or* **cat·er–cor·nered** \-nərd\ *adv or adj* : set crosswise : placed diagonally

cat·er·pil·lar \'kat-ə(r)-ˌpil-ər\ *n* [from Old French (northern dialect) *catepelose*, literally "hairy cat"] : the long wormlike larva of a butterfly or moth; *also* : any of various similar insect larvae (as of a sawfly)

caterpillar (about 1½ in. long)

cat·er·waul \'kat-ər-ˌwȯl\ *vb* : to make the characteristic harsh cry of a tomcat — **caterwaul** *n*

cat·fish \'kat-ˌfish\ *n* : any of numerous usu. stout-bodied large-headed fishes with long sensory barbels

cat·gut \-ˌgət\ *n* : a cord made usu. from sheep intestines and used for strings of musical instruments and rackets and for sewing in surgery

ca·thar·tic \kə-'thärt-ik\ *n* : a strong laxative — **cathartic** *adj*

ca·the·dral \kə-'thē-drəl\ *n* : the principal church of a diocese and the seat of its bishop

cath·ode \'kath-ˌōd\ *n* **1** : the negative electrode of an electrolytic cell — compare ANODE **2** : the positive terminal of a battery **3** : the electron-emitting electrode of an electron tube — **ca·thod·ic** \ka-'thäd-ik\ *adj*

cathode ray *n* **1** : one of the high-speed electrons projected in a stream from the heated cathode of a vacuum tube under the propulsion of a strong electric field **2** : a stream of cathode-ray electrons

cathode–ray tube *n* : a vacuum tube in which cathode rays usu. in the form of a slender beam are projected upon a fluorescent screen and produce a luminous spot

cath·o·lic \'kath-(ə-)lik\ *adj* **1** : broad in scope or interests **2** *cap* **a** : of or relating to the Christian church as a whole **b** : Roman Catholic — **Ca·thol·i·cism** \kə-'thäl-ə-ˌsiz-əm\ *n*

Catholic *n* **1** : CHRISTIAN **2** : ROMAN CATHOLIC

cat·ion \'kat-ˌī-ən\ *n* : the ion in an electrolyzed solution that migrates to the cathode; *also* : a positively charged ion

cat·kin \'kat-kən\ *n* : a flower cluster (as of the willow or birch) that is a usu. long ament densely crowded with bracts

cat·like \'kat-ˌlīk\ *adj* : resembling a cat; *esp* : STEALTHY

cat·nap \-ˌnap\ *n* : a short light nap — **catnap** *vb*

cat·nip \-ˌnip\ *n* : a common strong-scented mint that is esp. attractive to cats

cat–o'–nine–tails \ˌkat-ə-'nīn-ˌtālz\ *n, pl* **cat–o'–nine–tails** : a whip used in flogging and made of nine knotted cords fastened to a handle

cat's cradle *n* : a game played with a string looped on the fingers so as to resemble a small cradle

cat's–eye \'kats-ˌī\ *n* : any of various gems (as chalcedony) with a changeable luster suggestive of reflections from the eye of a cat

cat's–paw \'kats-ˌpȯ\ *n* **1** : a light breeze that ruffles the surface of the water **2** : a person used by another person for his own ends

cat·sup \'kech-əp, 'kach-; 'kat-səp\ *n* : a seasoned sauce of puree consistency usu. of tomatoes

cat·tail \'kat-ˌtāl\ *n* : a tall reedy marsh plant with brown furry spikes of very tiny flowers

cat·tle \'kat-əl\ *n, pl* **cattle** : domesticated four-footed animals held as property or raised for use; *esp* : bovine animals (as cows or oxen) kept on a farm or ranch — **cat·tle·man** \-mən, -ˌman\ *n*

cat·ty \'kat-ē\ *adj* **cat·ti·er**; **-est** **1** : resembling or held to resemble a cat **2** : slyly spiteful : MALICIOUS — **cat·ti·ly** \'kat-ə-lē\ *adv* — **cat·ti·ness** \'kat-ē-nəs\ *n*

cat·ty–cor·ner *or* **cat·ty–cor·nered** *var of* CATERCORNER

cat·walk \'kat-ˌwȯk\ *n* : a narrow raised walk (as along a bridge or over or around a large machine)

Cau·ca·sian \kȯ-'kā-zhən, -'kazh-ən\ *adj* **1** : of or relating to the Caucasus or its inhabitants **2** : of or relating to the white race of mankind — **Caucasian** *n*

cau·cus \'kȯ-kəs\ *n* : a closed meeting of members of a political party or faction usu. to select candidates or decide policy — **caucus** *vb*

cau·dal \'kȯd-əl\ *adj* **1** : of, relating to, or being a tail **2** : situated in or directed toward the hind part of the body — **cau·dal·ly** \-ə-lē\ *adv*

caudal fin *n* : the unpaired fin at the posterior end of the body of a fish

caught *past of* CATCH

cauldron *var of* CALDRON

cau·li·flow·er \'kȯ-li-ˌflau̇(-ə)r\ *n* [meaning literally "cabbage flower", from Latin *caulis* "cabbage"] : a garden plant closely related to the cabbage and grown for its compact edible head of usu. white undeveloped flowers

cauliflower ear *n* : an ear deformed from injury and excessive growth of scar tissue

[1]**caulk** \'kȯk\ *vb* : to make seams watertight by filling with waterproofing material ⟨*caulk* a boat⟩ ⟨*caulk* seams around a window⟩ — **caulk·er** *n*

[2]**caulk** *var of* CALK

1**cause** \ˈkȯz\ *n* **1** : something or someone that brings about a result : the occasion of an action or state **2** : a good or adequate reason ⟨a *cause* for anxiety⟩ **3 a** : a ground of legal action **b** : CASE 5a **c** : something supported or deserving support ⟨the *cause* of prison reform⟩ ⟨a worthy *cause*⟩ — **caus·al** \ˈkȯ-zəl\ *adj* — **cau·sal·i·ty** \kȯ-ˈzal-ət-ē\ *n* — **cau·sa·tion** \kȯ-ˈzā-shən\ *n* — **caus·a·tive** \ˈkȯz-ət-iv\ *adj* — **cause·less** \ˈkȯz-ləs\ *adj*

syn CAUSE, REASON, MOTIVE can mean a factor that explains an effect or result. CAUSE suggests an act that provokes a reaction ⟨never gave him *cause* for suspicion⟩; REASON implies thought that produces an explanation or justification; MOTIVE suggests actions accounted for by an emotion or desire

2**cause** *vb* : to be the cause of ⟨the fire *caused* considerable damage⟩ — **caus·er** *n*

cause·way \ˈkȯz-ˌwā\ *n* : a raised way esp. across wet ground or water

1**caus·tic** \ˈkȯ-stik\ *adj* **1** : capable of destroying or eating away by chemical action : CORROSIVE **2** : INCISIVE, BITING ⟨*caustic* wit⟩ — **caus·ti·cal·ly** \-sti-k(ə-)lē\ *adv*

2**caustic** *n* : a caustic substance (as caustic soda)

caustic soda *n* : SODIUM HYDROXIDE

cau·ter·ize \ˈkȯt-ə-ˌrīz\ *vb* : to burn with a hot iron or a caustic substance usu. to destroy infected tissue ⟨*cauterize* a wound⟩ — **cau·ter·i·za·tion** \ˌkȯt-ə-rə-ˈzā-shən\ *n*

1**cau·tion** \ˈkȯ-shən\ *n* **1** : WARNING **2** : prudent forethought to minimize risk

2**caution** *vb* **cau·tioned**; **cau·tion·ing** \ˈkȯ-sh(ə-)ning\ : to advise caution to : WARN

cau·tion·ary \ˈkȯ-shə-ˌner-ē\ *adj* : serving as or offering a warning ⟨a *cautionary* tale⟩

cau·tious \ˈkȯ-shəs\ *adj* : marked by or given to caution ⟨a *cautious* reply⟩ ⟨a *cautious* driver⟩ ***syn*** see CAREFUL ***ant*** adventurous — **cau·tious·ly** *adv* — **cau·tious·ness** *n*

cav·al·cade \ˌkav-əl-ˈkād, ˈkav-əl-ˌ\ *n* **1 a** : a procession of riders or carriages **b** : a procession of vehicles or ships **2** : a sequence of dramatic scenes : PAGEANT ⟨a *cavalcade* of American history⟩

1**cav·a·lier** \ˌkav-ə-ˈli(ə)r\ *n* **1** : a gentleman trained in arms and horsemanship **2** : a mounted soldier : KNIGHT **3** : a gallant gentleman

2**cavalier** *adj* **1** : DEBONAIR **2** : HAUGHTY, DISDAINFUL — **cav·a·lier·ly** *adv* — **cav·a·lier·ness** *n*

cav·al·ry \ˈkav-əl-rē\ *n, pl* **-ries** : highly mobile troops mounted on horseback or moving in motor vehicles or helicopters — **cav·al·ry·man** \-rē-mən, -ˌman\ *n*

1**cave** \ˈkāv\ *n* : a hollowed-out place in the earth or in the side of a hill or cliff; *esp* : CAVERN

2**cave** *vb* : to fall or cause to fall in or down : COLLAPSE ⟨the retaining wall *caved* in⟩

cave–in \ˈkāv-ˌin\ *n* **1** : the action of caving in **2** : a place where earth has caved in

cave·man \ˈkāv-ˌman\ *n* **1** : one who lives in a cave; *esp* : a man of the Stone Age **2** : a man who acts in a rough or violent way esp. toward women

cav·ern \ˈkav-ərn\ *n* : an underground cavity often of large or indefinite extent

ə abut	ər further	a back	ā bake	
ä cot, cart	aů out	ch chin	e less	ē easy
g gift	i trip	ī life	j joke	ng sing	ō flow
ȯ flaw	ȯi coin	th thin	t͟h this	ü loot
ů foot	y yet	yü few	yů furious	zh vision

cav·ern·ous \-ər-nəs\ *adj* **1** : having caverns or cavities **2** : resembling a cavern ⟨a large empty *cavernous* hall⟩ **3** : composed largely of spaces capable of filling with blood to bring about the enlargement of a body part — **cav·ern·ous·ly** *adv*

cav·i·ar *or* **cav·i·are** \ˈkav-ē-ˌär\ *n* [from obsolete Italian *caviaro*, from Turkish *havyar*] : processed salted roe of a large fish (as the sturgeon) prepared as an appetizer

cav·il \ˈkav-əl\ *vb* **-iled** *or* **-illed**; **-il·ing** *or* **-il·ling** \-(ə-)ling\ : to raise trivial and frivolous objections : QUIBBLE — **cavil** *n* — **cav·il·er** *or* **cav·il·ler** *n*

cav·i·ta·tion \ˌkav-ə-ˈtā-shən\ *n* : the formation and collapse of gas bubbles in a liquid esp. as a result of high-frequency sound waves passing through

cav·i·ty \ˈkav-ət-ē\ *n, pl* **-ties** : a hollow place: as **a** : an unfilled space within a man ⟨lung *cavity*⟩ **b** : a hole hollowed out often by decay ⟨*cavity* in a tooth⟩

ca·vort \kə-ˈvȯrt\ *vb* : CAPER, PRANCE

ca·vy \ˈkā-vē\ *n, pl* **cavies** : any of several short-tailed rough-haired So. American rodents; *esp* : GUINEA PIG

caw \ˈkȯ\ *vb* : to utter the harsh raucous natural call of the crow or a similar cry — **caw** *n*

cay \ˈkē, ˈkā\ *n* : 4KEY

cay·enne pepper \ˌkī-ˌen-, ˌkā-\ *n* : a very hot sharp-tasting powder consisting of the ground dried fruits or seeds of hot peppers; *also* : a plant bearing such fruits

cay·man *var of* CAIMAN

cay·use \ˈkī-ˌ(y)üs, kī-ˈ\ *n* : a native range horse of the western U.S.

CBC *abbr* Canadian Broadcasting Corporation

CBS *abbr* Columbia Broadcasting System

cc *abbr* cubic centimeter

Cc *abbr* cirrocumulus

CCTV *abbr* closed-circuit television

CCW *abbr* counterclockwise

cd *abbr* cord

CD *abbr* civil defense

cdr *abbr* commander

CE *abbr* civil engineer

cease \ˈsēs\ *vb* : to come or bring to an end : STOP

cease–fire \ˈsēs-ˈfī(ə)r\ *n* : a suspension of active hostilities

cease·less \ˈsēs-ləs\ *adj* : CONSTANT, CONTINUAL — **cease·less·ly** *adv* — **cease·less·ness** *n*

ce·cro·pia moth \si-ˌkrō-pē-ə-\ *n* : a large red and dark brown or black silkworm moth of the eastern U.S. that has a crescent-shaped spot on each wing

ce·cum \ˈsē-kəm\ *n, pl* **ce·ca** \-kə\ : a cavity open at one end; *esp* : the blind pouch in which the large intestine begins — **ce·cal** \-kəl\ *adj*

ce·dar \ˈsēd-ər\ *n* **1 a** : any of a genus of usu. tall trees related to the pine and noted for their fragrant durable wood **b** : any of numerous cone-bearing trees (as some junipers or arborvitaes) resembling the true cedars esp. in the fragrance and durability of their wood **2** : the wood of a cedar

sprig of cedar 1a

cede \ˈsēd\ *vb* : to yield or grant typically by treaty — **ced·er** *n*

ce·dil·la \si-ˈdil-ə\ *n* [from Spanish, originally the name of the obsolete letter ç (actually a medieval form of z), from a diminutive of *ceda, zeda*, name of the letter *z*, from Greek *zēta*] : a mark placed under the letter *c* (as ç) to show that it is to be pronounced like *s*

cei·ba \'sā-bə\ *n* : a massive tropical tree bearing large pods filled with seeds covered with a silky floss that yields kapok

ceil·ing \'sē-ling\ *n* **1** : the overhead inside lining of a room **2** : something that overhangs **3 a** : the greatest height at which an airplane can operate efficiently **b** : the height above the ground of the base of the lowest layer of clouds when over half of the sky is obscured **4** : an upper usu. prescribed limit ⟨price *ceiling*⟩

cel·an·dine \'sel-ən-ˌdīn, -ˌdēn\ *n* **1** : a yellow-flowered biennial herb related to the poppy **2** : a perennial tuber-forming buttercup

cel·e·brant \'sel-ə-brənt\ *n* : one who celebrates; *esp* : the priest who is celebrating a mass

cel·e·brate \'sel-ə-ˌbrāt\ *vb* **1** : to perform publicly and according to rule or form ⟨*celebrate* a mass⟩ ⟨*celebrate* a marriage⟩ **2** : to observe in some special way (as by merrymaking or by staying away from work) ⟨*celebrate* a birthday⟩ ⟨*celebrate* Christmas⟩ **3** : to praise or make known publicly — **cel·e·bra·tion** \ˌsel-ə-'brā-shən\ *n* — **cel·e·bra·tor** \'sel-ə-ˌbrāt-ər\ *n*

cel·e·brat·ed *adj* : widely known and often referred to : RENOWNED

ce·leb·ri·ty \sə-'leb-rət-ē\ *n, pl* **-ties** **1** : the state of being celebrated : FAME **2** : a celebrated person ⟨movie *celebrities*⟩

ce·ler·i·ty \sə-'ler-ət-ē\ *n, pl* **-ties** : SWIFTNESS, SPEED

cel·ery \'sel-(ə-)rē\ *n* : a European herb related to the carrot and widely grown for its thick edible leafstalks

ce·les·ta \sə-'les-tə\ *n* : a keyboard instrument with hammers that strike steel plates

ce·les·tial \sə-'les-chəl\ *adj* **1** : of or relating to heaven : HEAVENLY ⟨*celestial* beings⟩ **2** : of or relating to the sky ⟨a star is a *celestial* body⟩ — **ce·les·tial·ly** \-chə-lē\ *adv*

celestial equator *n* : the great circle on the celestial sphere midway between the celestial poles

celestial navigation *n* : navigation by observation of the positions of celestial bodies

celestial pole *n* : one of two points on the celestial sphere around which the diurnal rotation of the stars appears to take place

celestial sphere *n* : an imaginary sphere of infinite radius against which the celestial bodies appear to be projected

cel·i·ba·cy \'sel-ə-bə-sē\ *n* : the state of not being married; *esp* : the state of one bound by vow not to marry

cel·i·bate \'sel-ə-bət\ *n* : one who lives in celibacy — **celibate** *adj*

cell \'sel\ *n* **1 a** : a hermit's dwelling **b** : a single room (as in a convent or prison) usu. for one person **2** : a small compartment (as in a honeycomb), cavity (as in a plant ovary), or bounded space (as in an insect wing) **3** : one of the tiny units that are the basic structural elements of plant and animal tissues and that include a nucleus and are surrounded by a membrane **4 a** : a receptacle (as a jar) containing electrodes and an electrolyte either for generating electricity by chemical action or for use in electrolysis **b** : a single unit in a device for converting radiant energy into electrical energy ⟨solar *cell*⟩ — **celled** \'seld\ *adj*

cel·lar \'sel-ər\ *n* : BASEMENT

cell division *n* : a process by which cells multiply usu. involving division into similar parts of more or less equal size

cell membrane *n* **1** : a semipermeable limiting layer of cell protoplasm **2** : CELL WALL

cel·lo \'chel-ō\ *n, pl* **cellos** [short for *violoncello*, from Italian, diminutive of *violone* "bass viol", from *viola* "viol"] : the member of the violin family tuned an octave below the viola — **cel·list** \'chel-əst\ *n*

cel·lo·phane \'sel-ə-ˌfān\ *n* : a thin transparent usu. waterproof material made from cellulose and used esp. as a wrapping

cell sap *n* : a watery solution of nutrients and wastes that fills the vacuole of most plant cells

cell theory *n* : a generalization in biology that all living things consist of cells each of which has come from a previously existing cell

cel·lu·lar \'sel-yə-lər\ *adj* **1** : of, relating to, or consisting of cells **2** : containing cavities : having a porous texture

cel·lu·lose \'sel-yə-ˌlōs\ *n* : a complex carbohydrate that is the chief part of the cell walls of plants and is commonly obtained as a white stringy substance from vegetable matter (as wood or cotton) which is used in making various products (as rayon and cellophane)

cell wall *n* : the firm nonliving and usu. chiefly cellulose wall that encloses and supports most plant cells

Cel·si·us \'sel-sē-əs, 'sel-shəs\ *adj* : CENTIGRADE

Celt \'selt, 'kelt\ *n* **1** : a member of a division of the early Indo-European peoples distributed from the British Isles and Spain to Asia Minor **2** : a modern Gael, Highland Scot, Irishman, Welshman, Cornishman, or Breton

[1]**Celt·ic** \'sel-tik, 'kel-\ *adj* : of, relating to, or characteristic of the Celts or their languages

[2]**Celtic** *n* : a group of languages now confined to Brittany, Wales, western Ireland, and the Scottish Highlands

[1]**ce·ment** \si-'ment\ *n* **1** : a fine powder that is produced from a burned mixture chiefly of clay and limestone and used as an ingredient of mortar and concrete; *also* : CONCRETE, MORTAR **2 a** : a binding element or agency **b** : an adhesive substance **3 a** : CEMENTUM **b** : a material for filling cavities in teeth

[2]**cement** *vb* **1** : to unite by or as if by cement **2** : to overlay with concrete — **ce·ment·er** *n*

ce·men·tum \si-'ment-əm\ *n* : a specialized external bony layer that covers the root and neck and sometimes parts of the crown of the teeth of mammals

cem·e·tery \'sem-ə-ˌter-ē\ *n, pl* **-ter·ies** [from Greek *koimētērion*, literally "sleeping place", from *koiman* "to put to bed", from the same prehistoric root from which comes English *home*] : a burial ground

-cene \ˌsēn\ *adj comb form* : recent — in names of geologic periods ⟨Eocene⟩

cen·o·taph \'sen-ə-ˌtaf\ *n* : a tomb or a monument honoring a person whose body is elsewhere

Ce·no·zo·ic \ˌsē-nə-'zō-ik, ˌsen-ə-\ *n* : the most recent of the five eras of geologic history that extends to the present time and is marked by a rapid evolution of mammals and birds and of grasses, shrubs, and various flowering plants; *also* : the corresponding system of rocks — see GEOLOGIC TIME table — **Cenozoic** *adj*

cen·ser \'sen(t)-sər\ *n* : a container in which incense is burned

[1]**cen·sor** \'sen(t)-sər\ *n* **1** : one of two magistrates of ancient Rome acting as census takers, assessors, and inspectors of morals and conduct **2** : an official who examines publications or communications for objectionable matter

[2]**censor** *vb* **cen·sored**; **cen·sor·ing** \'sen(t)s-(ə-)ring\ : to examine in order to suppress or delete anything thought to be harmful or dangerous

C

cen·sor·ship \'sen(t)-sər-ˌship\ *n* : the system or practice of censoring

[1]**cen·sure** \'sen-chər\ *n* **1** : the act of blaming or condemning sternly **2** : an official reprimand

[2]**censure** *vb* **cen·sured**; **cen·sur·ing** \'sench-(ə-)ring\ : to find fault with — **cen·sur·a·ble** \'sench-(ə-)rə-bəl\ *adj* — **cen·sur·er** \'sen-chər-ər\ *n*

cen·sus \'sen(t)-səs\ *n* : a periodic governmental counting of population and usu. gathering of related statistics

cent \'sent\ *n* [from Latin *centum* "hundred"] **1** : a unit of value equal to 1/100 part of a basic monetary unit (as in the U.S. and Canada 1/100 dollar) **2** : a coin, token, or note representing one cent

cent *abbr* **1** centigrade **2** century

cent·are \'sen-ˌta(ə)r, -ˌte(ə)r, -ˌtär\ *or* **cen·ti·are** \'sent-ē-ˌa(ə)r, -ˌe(ə)r, -ˌär\ *n* — see METRIC SYSTEM table

cen·taur \'sen-ˌtȯr\ *n* : a creature in Greek mythology that is half man and half horse

[1]**cen·ta·vo** \sen-'täv-ō\ *n, pl* **-vos** **1** : a unit of value equal to 1/100 part of any of several basic monetary units (as the peso or rupee) **2** : a coin representing one centavo

[2]**cen·ta·vo** \-'täv-ü, -'täv-ō\ *n, pl* **-vos** **1** : a unit of value equal to 1/100 cruzeiro or Portuguese escudo **2** : a coin representing one centavo

cen·te·nar·i·an \ˌsent-ə-'ner-ē-ən\ *n* : one that is 100 years old or older — **centenarian** *adj*

cen·ten·a·ry \sen-'ten-ə-rē, 'sent-ə-ˌner-ē\ *adj or n* : CENTENNIAL

cen·ten·ni·al \sen-'ten-ē-əl\ *n* : a 100th anniversary or its celebration — **centennial** *adj* — **cen·ten·ni·al·ly** \-ē-ə-lē\ *adv*

[1]**cen·ter** \'sent-ər\ *n* **1 a** : the point at an equal distance from all points on the edge of a circle or sphere **b** : MIDDLE **2 a** : a place in or around which an activity concentrates or from which something originates ⟨*center* of government⟩ ⟨a railroad *center*⟩ **b** : a group of nerve cells having a common function ⟨respiratory *center*⟩ **c** : a region of concentrated population **3** : a middle part (as of an army or stage) **4** : a player occupying a middle position on a team ⟨a football *center*⟩

[2]**center** *vb* **cen·tered**; **cen·ter·ing** \'sent-ə-ring, 'sen-tring\ **1** : to place or fix at or around a center or central area **2** : to collect at or around a center

cen·ter·board \'sent-ər-ˌbōrd, -ˌbȯrd\ *n* : a retractable keel used esp. in sailboats

center of gravity : the point at which the entire weight of a body may be considered as concentrated

cen·ter·piece \'sent-ər-ˌpēs\ *n* : an object occupying a central position; *esp* : an adornment in the center of a table

[1]**cen·tes·i·mo** \chen-'tez-ə-ˌmō\ *n, pl* **-mi** \-(ˌ)mē\ **1** : a unit of value equal to 1/100 lira **2** : a coin representing one centesimo

[2]**cen·tes·i·mo** \sen-'tes-ə-ˌmō\ *n, pl* **-mi** \-(ˌ)mē\ **1** : a unit of value equal to 1/100 part of any of several basic monetary units (as the escudo) **2** : a coin representing one centesimo

centi- *comb form* [F, fr. L *centum* hundred] : hundredth part ⟨*centi*meter⟩ — used in terms of the metric system

ə abut	ər further	a back	ā bake
ä cot, cart	aù out	ch chin	e less	ē easy
g gift	i trip	ī life	j joke	ng sing	ō flow
ȯ flaw	ȯi coin	th thin	th this	ü loot
ù foot	y yet	yü few	yù furious	zh vision

cen·ti·grade \'sent-ə-ˌgrād, 'sänt-\ *adj* : relating to or having a thermometer scale on which the interval between the freezing point and the boiling point of water is divided into 100 degrees with 0° representing the freezing point and 100° the boiling point — abbr. *C*

cen·ti·gram \-ˌgram\ *n* — see METRIC SYSTEM table

cen·ti·li·ter \-ˌlēt-ər\ *n* — see METRIC SYSTEM table

cen·time \'sän-ˌtēm, 'sen-\ *n* **1** : a unit of value equal to 1/100 franc **2** : a coin representing one centime

cen·ti·me·ter \'sent-ə-ˌmēt-ər, 'sänt-\ *n* — see METRIC SYSTEM table

centimeter–gram–second *adj* : of, relating to, or being a system of units based upon the centimeter as the unit of length, the gram as the unit of mass, and the second as the unit of time — abbr. *cgs*

cen·ti·mo \'sent-ə-ˌmō\ *n, pl* **-mos** **1** : a unit of value equal to 1/100 part of any of several basic monetary units (as the peseta) **2** : a coin representing one centimo

cen·ti·pede \'sent-ə-ˌpēd\ *n* [from Latin *centipeda*, from *centum* "hundred" and *ped-*, stem of *pes* "foot"] : any of a class of long flattened many-segmented arthropods with each segment bearing one pair of legs of which the foremost pair is modified into poison fangs — compare MILLIPEDE

CENTO *abbr* Central Treaty Organization of the Middle East

[1]**cen·tral** \'sen-trəl\ *adj* **1** : containing or being a center **2** : CHIEF, PRINCIPAL ⟨the *central* figure in a story⟩ **3** : situated at, in, or near the center **4** : of, relating to, or comprising the brain and spinal cord; *also* : originating within the central nervous system — **cen·tral·i·ty** \sen-'tral-ət-ē\ *n* — **cen·tral·ly** \'sen-trə-lē\ *adv*

[2]**central** *n* : a telephone exchange or operator

central angle *n* : an angle with a vertex at the center of a circle and with sides that are radii of the circle

cen·tral·ize \'sen-trə-ˌlīz\ *vb* : to concentrate (as authority) in a center or central organization — **cen·tral·i·za·tion** \ˌsen-trə-lə-'zā-shən\ *n*

central nervous system *n* : the part of the nervous system that in vertebrates consists of the brain and spinal cord

central tendency *n* : a tendency of statistical data to pile up on or be distributed around some average value

cen·tre \'sent-ər\ *chiefly Brit var of* CENTER

cen·trif·u·gal \sen-'trif-yə-gəl, -'trif-i-gəl\ *adj* **1** : proceeding or acting in a direction away from a center or axis **2** : using or acting by centrifugal force

centrifugal force *n* : the force that tends to impel a thing or parts of a thing outward from a center of rotation

cen·tri·fuge \'sen-trə-ˌfyüj, 'sän-\ *n* : a machine using centrifugal force for separating substances of different densities, for removing moisture, or for simulating gravitational effects

cen·tri·ole \'sen-trē-ˌōl\ *n* **1** : a minute body forming the center of a centrosome **2** : CENTROSOME

cen·trip·e·tal \sen-'trip-ət-əl\ *adj* : proceeding or acting in a direction toward a center or axis — **cen·trip·e·tal·ly** \-ət-ə-lē\ *adv*

centripetal force *n* : the force that tends to impel a thing or parts of a thing inward toward a center of rotation

cen·tro·mere \'sen-trə-ˌmi(ə)r\ *n* : the point on a chromosome by which it appears to attach to the spindle in mitosis

cen·tro·some \'sen-trə-ˌsōm\ *n* : a minute body in the cell cytoplasm which divides at the beginning of mitosis and from which the spindle appears to rise

cen·trum \'sen-trəm\ *n, pl* **centrums** *or* **cen·tra** \-trə\ : the body of a vertebra
cen·tu·ry \'sench-(ə-)rē\ *n, pl* **-ries** **1** : a group of 100 things **2** : a period of 100 years
century plant *n* : a Mexican agave maturing and flowering only once in many years and then dying
ce·phal·ic \sə-'fal-ik\ *adj* **1** : of or relating to the head **2** : directed toward or situated on, in, or near the head
ceph·a·lo·pod \'sef-ə-lə-,päd\ *n* : any of a class of mollusks including the squids, cuttlefishes, and octopuses having a group of muscular sucker-bearing arms, highly developed eyes, and usu. a bag of inky fluid which they can eject — **cephalopod** *adj* — **ceph·a·lop·o·dan** \,sef-ə-'läp-əd-ən\ *adj or n*
ceph·a·lo·tho·rax \,sef-ə-lō-'thō(ə)r-,aks, -'thȯ(ə)r-\ *n* : a united head and thorax (as of a spider, scorpion, or crustacean) — **ceph·a·lo·tho·rac·ic** \-thə-'ras-ik\ *adj*
Ce·phe·id \'sē-fē-əd\ *n* : one of a class of pulsating stars whose light variations are very regular
[1]**ce·ram·ic** \sə-'ram-ik\ *adj* : of or relating to a product (as earthenware, porcelain, or brick) made from a nonmetallic mineral by firing at high temperatures
[2]**ceramic** *n* **1** *pl* : the art of making ceramic articles **2** : a product of ceramic manufacture
cer·cus \'sər-kəs\ *n, pl* **cer·ci** \'sər-,sī\ : a many-jointed posterior appendage of an insect
[1]**ce·re·al** \'sir-ē-əl\ *adj* [from Latin *cerealis*, literally "of Ceres", from *Ceres*, goddess of grain] : relating to grain or to the plants that produce it; *also* : made of grain
[2]**cereal** *n* **1** : a plant (as a grass) yielding starchy grain suitable for food; *also* : its grain **2** : a prepared foodstuff of grain
cer·e·bel·lum \,ser-ə-'bel-əm\ *n, pl* **-bellums** *or* **-bel·la** \-'bel-ə\ : a large projecting portion of the rear part of the brain that is concerned esp. with muscular coordination and bodily balance
ce·re·bral \sə-'rē-brəl, 'ser-ə-\ *adj* **1** : of or relating to the brain **2** : of, relating to, or being the cerebrum — **ce·re·bral·ly** \-brə-lē\ *adv*
cerebral hemisphere *n* : either of the two hollow many-ridged lateral halves of the cerebrum
cerebral palsy *n* : a disability resulting from damage to the brain usu. before or during birth and resulting in imperfect control of muscles, paralysis, and speech disturbances
ce·re·bro·spi·nal \sə-,rē-brō-'spīn-əl, ,ser-ə-brō-\ *adj* : of or relating to the brain and spinal cord
ce·re·brum \sə-'rē-brəm, 'ser-ə-brəm\ *n, pl* **-brums** *or* **-bra** \-brə\ **1** : BRAIN 1a **2** : the expanded front part of the brain that consists of cerebral hemispheres and connecting structures and is reported to be the seat of conscious mental processes
[1]**cer·e·mo·ni·al** \,ser-ə-'mō-nē-əl\ *adj* : of, relating to, or forming a ceremony — **cer·e·mo·ni·al·ism** \-nē-ə-,liz-əm\ *n* — **cer·e·mo·ni·al·ist** \-ləst\ *n* — **cer·e·mo·ni·al·ly** \-nē-ə-lē\ *adv* — **cer·e·mo·ni·al·ness** *n*
[2]**ceremonial** *n* : a ceremonial act, action, or system
cer·e·mo·ni·ous \,ser-ə-'mō-nē-əs\ *adj* **1** : CEREMONIAL **2** : careful to observe forms and ceremony : FORMAL **3** : according to formal usage — **cer·e·mo·ni·ous·ly** *adv* — **cer·e·mo·ni·ous·ness** *n*
cer·e·mo·ny \'ser-ə-,mō-nē\ *n, pl* **-nies** **1** : a formal act or series of acts prescribed by ritual or custom ⟨graduation *ceremonies*⟩ **2** : a conventional act of politeness or etiquette ⟨went through the *ceremony* of introductions⟩ **3** : the social behavior required by strict etiquette : FORMALITY
ce·rise \sə-'rēs, -'rēz\ *n* : a moderate red
ce·ri·um \'sir-ē-əm\ *n* : a malleable metallic element used esp. as a constituent in flints (as for lighters) — see ELEMENT table
cer·met \'sər-,met\ *n* : a strong alloy of a heat-resistant compound (as carbide of titanium) and a metal (as nickel) used esp. for turbine blades
[1]**cer·tain** \'sərt-ən\ *adj* **1** : FIXED, SETTLED ⟨receive a *certain* share of the profits⟩ **2** : not to be doubted : INDISPUTABLE ⟨it is *certain* that diamonds are hard⟩ **3** : implied as being specific but not named : PARTICULAR ⟨a *certain* town in Maine⟩ **4** : RELIABLE, SURE ⟨a *certain* cure⟩ **5 a** : INEVITABLE **b** : DESTINED ⟨*certain* to happen⟩ **6** : assured in mind or action ⟨feel *certain* he will come⟩ — **cer·tain·ly** *adv*
[2]**certain** *pron* : certain ones
cer·tain·ty \'sərt-ən-tē\ *n, pl* **-ties** **1** : something certain **2** : the quality or state of being or feeling certain
cer·tif·i·cate \(,)sər-'tif-i-kət\ *n* **1** : a document containing a certified statement; *esp* : one certifying that a person has fulfilled the requirements of a school or profession ⟨teaching *certificate*⟩ **2** : a document showing ownership or debt ⟨stock *certificate*⟩
certified milk *n* : milk of high quality produced under the rules and regulations of an authorized medical milk commission
cer·ti·fy \'sərt-ə-,fī\ *vb* **-fied**; **-fy·ing** **1** : to guarantee to be true or valid or as represented or meeting a standard **2** : LICENSE — **cer·ti·fi·a·ble** \-,fī-ə-bəl\ *adj* — **cer·ti·fi·ca·tion** \,sərt-ə-fə-'kā-shən\ *n* — **cer·ti·fi·er** \'sərt-ə-,fī(-ə)r\ *n*
cer·ti·tude \'sərt-ə-,t(y)üd\ *n* : CERTAINTY
ce·ru·le·an \sə-'rü-lē-ən\ *adj* : AZURE
cer·vi·cal \'sər-vi-kəl\ *adj* : of or relating to a neck or cervix
cer·vix \'sər-viks\ *n, pl* **cer·vi·ces** \'sər-və-,sēz\ *or* **cer·vix·es** : the narrow constricted outer end of the uterus
ce·sar·e·an *or* **ce·sar·i·an** \si-'zar-ē-ən, -'zer-\ *n* : a surgical operation opening the walls of the abdomen and uterus for delivery of offspring — **cesarean** *or* **cesarian** *adj*
ce·si·um \'sē-zē-əm\ *n* : a silver-white soft ductile element used in electron tubes — see ELEMENT table
ces·sa·tion \se-'sā-shən\ *n* : a ceasing of action : STOP
ces·sion \'sesh-ən\ *n* : a giving over (as of territory or rights) to another
cess·pool \'ses-,pül\ *n* : an underground pit or tank for liquid waste (as household sewage)
ces·tode \'ses-,tōd\ *n* : any of a group of internally parasitic flatworms comprising the tapeworms — **cestode** *adj*
ce·ta·cean \si-'tā-shən\ *n* : any of an order of aquatic mammals (as a whale, dolphin, or porpoise) — **cetacean** *adj* — **ce·ta·ceous** \-shəs\ *adj*
ce·tyl alcohol \,sēt-əl-\ *n* : a waxy crystalline organic alcohol used esp. in cosmetics and detergents
cg *abbr* centigram
CG *abbr* coast guard
cgs *abbr* centimeter-gram-second
ch *abbr* **1** chapter **2** church
chafe \'chāf\ *vb* **1 a** : IRRITATE, VEX **b** : to feel irritation or discontent : FRET **2** : to warm by rubbing **3 a** : to rub so as to wear away **b** : to make sore by or as if by rubbing ⟨the tight collar *chafed* his neck⟩
cha·fer \'chā-fər\ *n* : any of various large beetles
[1]**chaff** \'chaf\ *n* **1** : the debris (as seed coverings) separated from the seed in threshing grain **2** : something light and worthless — **chaffy** \-ē\ *adj*

2**chaff** *n* : light jesting talk : BANTER
3**chaff** *vb* : to tease good-naturedly
chaf·fer \'chaf-ər\ *vb* : to dispute about a price : BARGAIN
chaf·finch \'chaf-(,)inch\ *n* : a European finch that has a cheerful song and is often kept as a cage bird
chaf·ing dish \'chā-fing-\ *n* : a utensil for cooking or warming food at the table
1**cha·grin** \shə-'grin\ *n* : annoyance caused by failure or disappointment
2**chagrin** *vb* **cha·grined** \-'grind\; **cha·grin·ing** \-'grin-ing\ : to cause to feel chagrin
1**chain** \'chān\ *n* **1 a** : a series of connected links or rings **b** : a measuring instrument of 100 links used in surveying **c** : a unit of length equal to 66 feet **2** : something that confines or restrains **3 a** : a series of things linked, connected, or associated together ⟨a mountain *chain*⟩ **b** : a number of atoms united like links in a chain
2**chain** *vb* : to fasten, bind, or connect with or as if with a chain
chain reaction *n* **1** : a series of events so related to each other that each one initiates the succeeding one **2** : a chemical or nuclear reaction yielding energy or products that cause further reactions of the same kind and so becoming self-sustaining (as in the splitting of a uranium atom by a neutron whereby more neutrons are released that cause further splittings and so on)
chain saw *n* : a portable power saw that has teeth linked together to form an endless chain
chain store *n* : one of a number of stores under the same ownership and general management and selling the same lines of goods
chair \'che(ə)r, 'cha(ə)r\ *n* **1** : a seat with legs and a back for use by one person **2 a** : an official seat or a seat of authority or dignity **b** : an office or position of authority or dignity **c** : CHAIRMAN
chair·man \-mən\ *n* : the presiding officer of a meeting or an organization or committee — **chair·man·ship** \-,ship\ *n*
chaise \'shāz\ *n* **1** : a 2-wheeled carriage with a folding top **2** : a light carriage
chaise longue \'shāz-'lȯng\ *n, pl* **chaise longues** *also* **chaises longues** \'shāz-'lȯngz\ : a long chair for reclining — called also *chaise lounge* \-'laủnj\
chal·ced·o·ny \kal-'sed-ə-nē\ *n, pl* **-nies** : a translucent quartz commonly pale blue or gray with nearly waxy luster
chal·co·cite \'kal-kə-,sīt\ *n* : a black or gray mineral of metallic luster consisting of a sulfide of copper
chal·co·py·rite \,kal-kə-'pī(ə)r-,īt\ *n* : a yellow mineral consisting of a sulfide of copper and iron and constituting an important ore of copper
cha·let \sha-'lā\ *n* **1** : a remote herdsman's hut in the Alps **2 a** : a Swiss dwelling with a wide roof overhang **b** : a cottage in chalet style
chal·ice \'chal-əs\ *n* **1** : a drinking cup : GOBLET; *esp* : the cup used in the sacrament of Communion **2** : a flower cup
1**chalk** \'chȯk\ *n* **1** : a soft white, gray, or buff limestone chiefly composed of the shells of foraminifers **2** : chalk or a chalky material esp. when used in the form of a crayon — **chalky** \'chȯ-kē\ *adj*
2**chalk** *vb* **1** : to mark or draw with chalk **2** : to record or add up with or as if with chalk : CHARGE ⟨*chalk* it up to experience⟩
chalk·board \'chȯk-,bōrd, -,bȯrd\ *n* : BLACKBOARD
1**chal·lenge** \'chal-ənj\ *vb* **1** : to claim as due or deserved ⟨an act that *challenged* everyone's admiration⟩ **2** : to question and demand the countersign from **3 a** : to take exceptions to : DISPUTE ⟨*challenge* his right to speak⟩ **b** : to object to ⟨*challenge* a juror⟩ **4** : to issue an invitation to compete against one : DARE — **chal·leng·er** *n*
2**challenge** *n* **1** : an exception taken **2** : a sentry's command to halt and prove identity **3** : a summons or invitation to compete; *esp* : a summons to single combat
chal·lis \'shal-ē\ *n, pl* **chal·lises** \'shal-ēz\ : a lightweight soft clothing fabric esp. of cotton or wool
cha·lyb·e·ate \kə-'lib-ē-ət, -'lē-bē-\ *adj* : impregnated with salts of iron ⟨*chalybeate* springs⟩
1**cham·ber** \'chām-bər\ *n* **1** : ROOM; *esp* : BEDROOM **2** : an enclosed space or compartment ⟨the *chamber* of a pistol⟩ ⟨the *chambers* of the heart⟩ **3 a** : a meeting hall of a legislative or judicial body **b** : a room where a judge transacts business out of court **4 a** : a legislative body ⟨the lower *chamber* of Congress⟩ **b** : a voluntary board or council (as of businessmen) ⟨*chamber* of commerce⟩ — **cham·bered** \-bərd\ *adj*
2**chamber** *vb* : to place or hold in or as if in a chamber
cham·ber·lain \'chām-bər-lən\ *n* **1** : a chief officer in the household of a king or nobleman **2** : TREASURER
cham·ber·maid \-,mād\ *n* : a maid who takes care of bedrooms
chamber music *n* : music for performance by a few musicians for a small audience
cham·bray \'sham-,brā, -brē\ *n* : a lightweight clothing fabric with colored and white yarns
cha·me·leon \kə-'mēl-yən\ *n* **[**from Greek *chamaileōn*, from *chamai* "on the ground" and *leōn* "lion"**]** : a lizard that can vary the color of its skin
cham·ois \'sham-ē\ *n, pl* **cham·ois** \-ē(z)\ *also* **cham·oix** \-ē(z)\ **1** : a small goatlike mountain antelope of Europe and the Caucasus **2** *also* **cham·my** \'sham-ē\ : a soft pliant leather prepared from the skin of the chamois or from sheepskin

chamois 1
(about 29 in. at shoulder)

cham·o·mile \'kam-ə-,mīl, -,mēl\ *n* : any of a genus of strong-scented herbs related to the daisies with flower heads that contain a bitter medicinal principle
1**champ** \'champ\ *vb* **1** : to bite and chew noisily ⟨a horse *champing* his bit⟩ **2** : to show impatience
2**champ** *n* : CHAMPION
cham·pagne \sham-'pān\ *n* : a white sparkling wine made in Champagne, France; *also* : a similar wine made elsewhere
1**cham·pi·on** \'cham-pē-ən\ *n* **1** : one that fights for a cause (as another's rights or honor) **2** : a person formally acknowledged as better than all others in a sport or in a game of skill **3** : the winner of first place in a competition
2**champion** *vb* : to protect or fight for as a champion
cham·pi·on·ship \'cham-pē-ən-,ship\ *n* **1** : the act of defending as a champion ⟨his *championship* of

states' rights⟩ **2 :** the position or title of champion **3 :** a contest held to determine a champion

1**chance** \'chan(t)s\ *n* **1 :** the way in which things take place : FORTUNE ⟨occurred by *chance*⟩ **2 :** OPPORTUNITY ⟨had a *chance* to travel⟩ **3 :** RISK, GAMBLE ⟨take *chances*⟩ **4 a :** the possibility or likelihood of an indicated or a favorable outcome in an uncertain situation **b :** the degree of likelihood of such an outcome ⟨a good *chance* of success⟩ **5 :** a ticket in a raffle — **chance** *adj*

2**chance** *vb* **1 a :** to take place or come about by chance : HAPPEN **b :** to have the good or bad luck ⟨*chanced* to miss his train⟩ **2 :** to come casually and unexpectedly — used with *upon* **3 :** RISK ⟨*chance* an accident⟩

chan·cel \'chan(t)-səl\ *n* **:** the part of a church containing the altar and seats for the clergy and choir

chan·cel·lery *or* **chan·cel·lory** \'chan(t)-s(ə-)lə-rē\ *n, pl* **-ler·ies** *or* **-lor·ies 1 a :** the position or department of a chancellor **b :** the building or room where a chancellor has his office **2 :** the office or staff of an embassy or consulate

chan·cel·lor \'chan(t)-s(ə-)lər\ *n* **1 :** a high official of state (as in Great Britain or West Germany) **2 :** the head of a university — **chan·cel·lor·ship** \-,ship\ *n*

chan·cery \'chan(t)s-(ə-)rē\ *n, pl* **-cer·ies 1 :** a court of equity **2 :** a record office for public archives **3 :** CHANCELLERY

chan·cre \'shang-kər\ *n* **:** a sore or ulcer at the site of entry of an infective agent — **chan·crous** \-k(ə-)rəs\ *adj*

chan·de·lier \,shan-də-'li(ə)r\ *n* **:** a branched lighting fixture usu. suspended from a ceiling

1**change** \'chānj\ *vb* **1 :** to make or become different : ALTER **2 a :** to give a different position, course, or direction to **b :** REVERSE ⟨*change* one's vote⟩ **3 :** to replace with another : SWITCH, EXCHANGE ⟨*change* places⟩ **4 a :** to put fresh clothes or covering on ⟨*change* a bed⟩ **b :** to put on different clothes **5 :** to give or receive money as change for ⟨*change* a $10 bill⟩ — **chang·er** *n* — **change hands :** to pass from the possession of one person to that of another

2**change** *n* **1 :** the act, process, or result of changing ⟨a *change* of seasons⟩ ⟨a *change* for the better⟩ **2 :** a fresh set of clothes **3 a :** money in small denominations received in exchange for an equivalent sum in larger denominations **b :** money returned when a payment exceeds the amount due **c :** COINS — **change·ful** \'chānj-fəl\ *adj*

change·a·ble \'chān-jə-bəl\ *adj* **1 :** capable of or given to change : VARIABLE ⟨*changeable* weather⟩ **2 :** appearing different (as in color) from different points of view — **change·a·bil·i·ty** \,chān-jə-'bil-ət-ē\ *n* — **change·a·ble·ness** \'chān-jə-bəl-nəs\ *n* — **change·a·bly** \-blē\ *adv*

change·less \'chānj-ləs\ *adj* **:** UNCHANGING, CONSTANT — **change·less·ly** *adv* — **change·less·ness** *n*

change·ling \'chānj-ling\ *n* **:** a child secretly exchanged for another in infancy by fairies or elves

change of life : MENOPAUSE

1**chan·nel** \'chan-əl\ *n* **1 :** the bed of a stream **2 :** the deeper part of a river, harbor, or strait **3 :** a strait or a narrow sea between two landmasses ⟨the English *Channel*⟩ **4 :** a closed course through which something flows **5 :** a long gutter, groove, or furrow **6 :** a means of passage or transmission ⟨diplomatic *channels*⟩ **7 :** a range of frequencies of sufficient width for a single radio or television transmission

2**channel** *vb* **-neled** *or* **-nelled**; **-nel·ing** *or* **-nel·ling 1 :** to form a channel in : GROOVE **2 :** to direct into or through a channel

1**chant** \'chant\ *vb* **1 :** SING; *esp* **:** to sing a chant **2 :** to recite in a chant

2**chant** *n* **1 :** a melody in which several words or syllables are sung on one tone **2 :** SONG, SINGING **3 :** a rhythmic monotonous utterance

chan·tey *or* **chan·ty** \'shant-ē, 'chant-\ *n, pl* **chanteys** *or* **chanties :** a song sung by sailors in rhythm with their work

chan·ti·cleer \,chant-ə-'kli(ə)r, ,shant-\ *n* **:** 1COCK 1

cha·os \'kā-,äs\ *n* **:** complete confusion and disorder — **cha·ot·ic** \kā-'ät-ik\ *adj* — **cha·ot·i·cal·ly** \-i-k(ə-)lē\ *adv*

1**chap** \'chap\ *n* **:** FELLOW

2**chap** *vb* **chapped**; **chap·ping :** to open in slits **:** CRACK ⟨*chapped* lips⟩

3**chap** *n* **:** a crack or a sore roughening of the skin from exposure

chap *abbr* chapter

chap·ar·ral \,shap-ə-'ral, -'rel\ *n* **1 :** a thicket of dwarf evergreen oaks; *also* **:** a dense impenetrable thicket **2 :** an ecological community typical of parts of southern California that is composed of shrubby plants esp. adapted to dry sunny summers and moist winters

chap·el \'chap-əl\ *n* [from Old French *chapele*, from medieval Latin *cappella*, from Latin *cappa* "cloak", "cape"; so called from the preservation of the cloak of St. Martin of Tours in a chapel built for the purpose] **1 :** a small building or room or a recess for prayer or worship **2 :** a service of worship in a school or college

1**chap·er·on** *or* **chap·er·one** \'shap-ə-,rōn\ *n* **:** a person who accompanies and is responsible for a young woman or a group of young people (as at a dance)

2**chaperon** *or* **chaperone** *vb* **1 :** to act as a chaperon **2 :** ESCORT — **chap·er·on·age** \-,rō-nij\ *n*

chap·lain \'chap-lən\ *n* **1 :** a clergyman appointed to serve a dignitary, institution, or military force **2 :** a person chosen to conduct religious exercises for an organization — **chap·lain·cy** \-sē\ *n*

chap·let \'chap-lət\ *n* **1 :** a wreath worn on the head **2 a :** a string of beads **b :** a part of the rosary devoted to one group of sacred mysteries

chaps \'shaps\ *n pl* **:** leather leggings worn esp. by western ranch hands

chap·ter \'chap-tər\ *n* **1 :** a main division of a book or of a law code **2 :** a local branch of a society

1**char** \'chär\ *n, pl* **char** *or* **chars :** any of a genus of small-scaled trouts including the common brook trout

2**char** *vb* **charred**; **char·ring 1 :** to change to charcoal by burning **2 :** to burn partly with a blackened effect **3 :** to burn to a cinder ***syn*** see SINGE

char·ac·ter \'kar-ik-tər\ *n* [from Greek *charaktēr* "mark", "distinctive quality", from *charassein* "to scratch"] **1 :** a conventional marking; *esp* **:** a mark or symbol (as a letter or numeral) used in writing or printing **2 a :** a distinguishing feature : CHARACTERISTIC **b :** the sum total of the distinguishing qualities of a person, group, or thing : NATURE **c :** the bodily expression (as eye color or leaf shape) of the action of

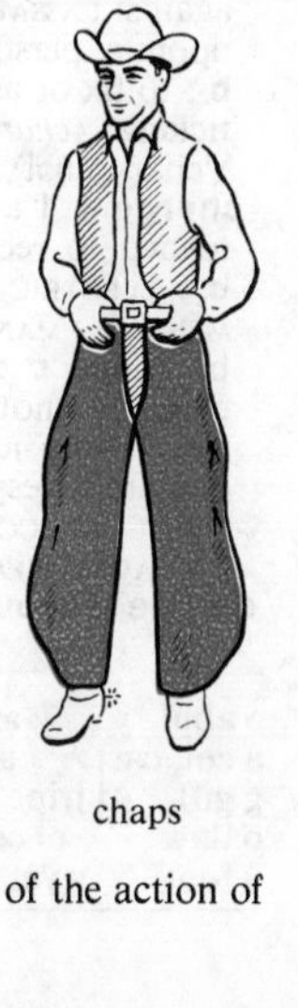

chaps

a gene or group of genes **3 :** POSITION, STATUS ⟨his *character* as a son⟩ **4 :** a person having notable traits or characteristics; *esp* : an odd or peculiar person **5 :** a person in a story, novel, or play **6 :** REPUTATION **7 :** moral excellence and strength — **char·ac·ter·less** \-ləs\ *adj*

¹**char·ac·ter·is·tic** \ˌkar-ik-tə-ˈris-tik\ *adj* : serving to mark the character of an individual or group : TYPICAL — **char·ac·ter·is·ti·cal·ly** \-ti-k(ə-)lē\ *adv*

²**characteristic** *n* : a distinguishing trait, quality, or property

syn CHARACTERISTIC, TRAIT, FEATURE can mean something that serves to identify or set off. CHARACTERISTIC suggests a mark or quality that distinguishes an individual or class from others of the same kind ⟨poison fangs, a *characteristic* of some snakes⟩; TRAIT applies to a highly distinctive usu. personal characteristic ⟨possessed the *trait* of physical courage⟩; FEATURE applies to a conspicuous identifying detail

char·ac·ter·i·za·tion \ˌkar-ik-tə-rə-ˈzā-shən\ *n* **1 :** the act of characterizing : description by a statement of characteristics **2 :** the creation of characters in fiction or drama

char·ac·ter·ize \ˈkar-ik-tə-ˌrīz\ *vb* **1 :** to indicate the character or characteristics of : DESCRIBE **2 :** to be characteristic of

character sketch *n* : a usu. short piece of writing dealing with a strongly marked character

cha·rades \shə-ˈrādz\ *n pl* : a game in which each syllable of a word to be guessed is acted out by some of the persons playing the game while the others try to guess the word

char·coal \ˈchär-ˌkōl\ *n* **1 :** a dark or black porous carbon prepared from vegetable or animal substances (as from wood by charring in a kiln from which air is excluded) **2 a :** a piece or pencil of fine charcoal used in drawing **b :** a charcoal drawing

chard \ˈchärd\ *n* : a beet that lacks a swollen root and forms large leaves and succulent stalks often cooked as a vegetable — called also *Swiss chard*

¹**charge** \ˈchärj\ *vb* **1 a :** LOAD, FILL **b :** to impart an electric charge to **c :** to restore the active materials in a storage battery by the passage of a direct current through in the opposite direction to that of discharge **2 a :** to impose a task or responsibility on **b :** to command, instruct, or exhort with right or authority ⟨*charge* a jury⟩ **3 :** ACCUSE, BLAME **4 :** to rush against : ASSAULT **5 a :** to impose a monetary charge upon a person ⟨*charged* him $50 for the goods⟩ **b :** to fix or ask as a fee or price ⟨*charge* $2.50 for a ticket⟩ ⟨*charges* too much⟩ — **charge·a·ble** \ˈchär-jə-bəl\ *adj*

²**charge** *n* **1 a :** the quantity that an apparatus is intended to receive ⟨a *charge* of powder for a gun⟩ **b :** ELECTRIC CHARGE **3 a :** OBLIGATION, REQUIREMENT **b :** MANAGEMENT, CUSTODY ⟨has *charge* of the building⟩ **c :** a person or thing committed to the care of another **4 :** INSTRUCTION, COMMAND ⟨a *charge* to a jury⟩ **5 a :** EXPENSE, COST **b :** the price demanded esp. for a service **c :** a debit to an account **6 :** ACCUSATION **7 :** a rush to attack an enemy : ASSAULT *syn* see PRICE

charge account *n* : a customer's account with a creditor (as a merchant) to which the purchase of goods is charged

¹**char·ger** \ˈchär-jər\ *n, archaic* : a large platter for carrying meat

²**charg·er** \ˈchär-jər\ *n* **1 :** a cavalry horse **2 :** a device for charging storage batteries

char·i·ot \ˈchar-ē-ət\ *n* : a 2-wheeled horse-drawn vehicle of ancient times used in battle and also in races and processions

chariot

char·i·ot·eer \ˌchar-ē-ə-ˈti(ə)r\ *n* : a driver of a chariot

char·i·ta·ble \ˈchar-ət-ə-bəl\ *adj* **1 :** liberal with money or help for poor and needy persons : GENEROUS **2 :** given for the needy : of service to the needy ⟨*charitable* funds⟩ ⟨a *charitable* institution⟩ **3 :** generous and kindly in judging other people : LENIENT — **char·i·ta·bly** \-blē\ *adv*

char·i·ty \ˈchar-ət-ē\ *n, pl* **-ties** **1 :** love for one's fellowmen **2 :** kindliness in judging others **3 a :** the giving of aid to the poor and suffering **b :** public aid for the poor **c :** an institution or fund for aiding the needy

char·la·tan \ˈshär-lə-tən\ *n* : a person who pretends to have knowledge or ability he does not have : QUACK — **char·la·tan·ry** \-rē\ *n*

Charles's law \ˌchärlz-əz-\ *n* : a law that states that the volume of a gas increases or decreases in direct proportion to the absolute temperature at constant pressure

char·ley horse \ˈchär-lē-ˌhȯrs\ *n* : pain and stiffness from muscular strain esp. in a leg

¹**charm** \ˈchärm\ *n* [from French *charme*, from Latin *carmen* "song", "incantation"] **1 :** a word, action, or thing believed to have magic powers **2 :** something worn or carried to keep away evil and bring good luck **3 :** a small decorative object worn on a chain or bracelet **4 a :** a quality that attracts and pleases **b :** physical grace or attractiveness

²**charm** *vb* **1 :** to affect or influence by or as if by magic ⟨*charm* a snake⟩ **2 :** to protect by or as if by a charm ⟨a *charmed* life⟩ **3 a :** DELIGHT **b :** to attract by grace or beauty *syn* see CAPTIVATE *ant* disgust — **charm·er** *n*

char·nel \ˈchärn-əl\ *n* : a building or chamber in which dead bodies or bones are deposited — **charnel** *adj*

¹**chart** \ˈchärt\ *n* **1 a :** MAP; *esp* : one showing features (as coasts, shoals, and currents) of importance to navigators **b :** an outline map exhibiting something (as climatic or magnetic differences) in its variations in different places at a given time **c :** a map for the use of navigators **2 :** a sheet giving information in the form of a table or of lists or by means of diagrams or graphs

²**chart** *vb* **1 :** to make a map or chart of **2 :** to lay out a plan for ⟨*charting* campaign strategy⟩

¹**char·ter** \ˈchärt-ər\ *n* : an official document granting, guaranteeing, or defining the rights and duties of the body to which it is issued

²**charter** *vb* **1 :** to grant a charter to **2 :** to hire (as a ship or a bus) for one's own use — **char·ter·er** \ˈchärt-ər-ər\ *n*

char·wom·an \'chär-ˌwu̇m-ən\ *n* : a cleaning woman usu. in a large building

chary \'cha(ə)r-ē, 'che(ə)r-\ *adj* **char·i·er**; **-est** **1** : cautiously sparing or frugal ⟨*chary* of giving praise⟩ **2** : cautiously watchful esp. in preserving something ⟨*chary* of his reputation⟩ — **char·i·ness** *n*

[1]**chase** \'chās\ *vb* **1** : to follow in order to capture or overtake **2** : HUNT **3** : to drive away or out ⟨*chase* a dog off the lawn⟩ — **chas·er** *n*

[2]**chase** *n* **1 a** : the act of chasing : PURSUIT **b** : HUNTING — used with *the* **2** : something pursued

[3]**chase** *vb* : to ornament metal by embossing or engraving ⟨*chased* bronze⟩

chasm \'kaz-əm\ *n* : a deep cleft in the earth : GORGE

chas·sis \'shas-ē, 'chas-ē\ *n, pl* **chas·sis** \-ēz\ : a supporting framework (as that bearing the body of an automobile or airplane or the parts of a radio or television receiving set)

chaste \'chāst\ *adj* **1** : CELIBATE **2** : pure in thought and act : MODEST **3** : pure or severe in design and expression — **chaste·ly** *adv* — **chaste·ness** \'chās(t)-nəs\ *n*

chas·ten \'chā-sən\ *vb* **chas·tened**; **chas·ten·ing** \'chā-s(ə-)niŋ\ **1** : to correct by punishment or suffering : DISCIPLINE **2** : to purify of excess, pretense, or falsity : REFINE

chas·tise \chas-'tīz\ *vb* **1** : to inflict punishment on (as by whipping) **2** : to censure severely : CASTIGATE — **chas·tise·ment** \chas-'tīz-mənt, 'chas-təz-\ *n* — **chas·tis·er** \chas-'tī-zər\ *n*

chas·ti·ty \'chas-tət-ē\ *n, pl* **-ties** : the quality or state of being chaste; *esp* : personal purity and modesty

cha·su·ble \'chaz(h)-ə-bəl, 'chas-ə-\ *n* : a sleeveless outer vestment worn by a priest at mass

[1]**chat** \'chat\ *vb* **chat·ted**; **chat·ting** : to talk in a light, informal, or familiar manner

[2]**chat** *n* **1 a** : light familiar talk **b** : an informal conversation **2** : any of several songbirds with a chattering call

châ·teau \sha-'tō\ *n, pl* **châ·teaus** \-'tōz\ *or* **châ·teaux** \-'tō(z)\ [from French, from Latin *castellum* "castle", from diminutive of *castra* "fortified camp"] : a castle or a large country house esp. in France

chat·tel \'chat-əl\ *n* **1** : SLAVE **2** : a piece of property (as animals, furniture, money, or goods) other than real estate

chat·ter \'chat-ər\ *vb* **1** : to utter rapid meaningless sounds suggesting speech ⟨squirrels *chattered* angrily⟩ **2** : to speak idly, incessantly, or rapidly : JABBER **3** : to click repeatedly or uncontrollably ⟨teeth *chattering* from the cold⟩ — **chatter** *n* — **chat·ter·er** \'chat-ər-ər\ *n*

chat·ter·box \'chat-ər-ˌbäks\ *n* : a person who talks unceasingly

chat·ty \'chat-ē\ *adj* **chat·ti·er**; **-est** **1** : fond of chatting : TALKATIVE **2** : having the style of light familiar conversation ⟨writes a *chatty* letter⟩ — **chat·ti·ly** \'chat-ə-lē\ *adv* — **chat·ti·ness** \'chat-ē-nəs\ *n*

[1]**chauf·feur** \'shō-fər, shō-'\ *n* : a person employed to drive an automobile

[2]**chauffeur** *vb* : to do the work of a chauffeur : DRIVE

cheap \'chēp\ *adj* **1** : of low cost or price ⟨a *cheap* watch⟩ **2** : of inferior quality ⟨*cheap* material wears out quickly⟩ **3 a** : gained with little effort **b** : not worth gaining **4** : lowered in one's own opinion : ABASHED ⟨feel *cheap*⟩ **5 a** : charging low prices **b** : dealing in inferior goods — **cheap** *adv* — **cheap·en** \'chēp-ən\ *vb* — **cheap·ly** *adv* — **cheap·ness** *n*

[1]**cheat** \'chēt\ *n* **1** : an act of cheating **2** : one that cheats : DECEIVER

[2]**cheat** *vb* **1** : to rob by deceit or fraud ⟨*cheated* him out of a large sum⟩ **2** : to influence or lead astray by deceit, trick, or artifice **3** : to violate rules dishonestly ⟨*cheat* at cards⟩

[1]**check** \'chek\ *n* **1** : exposure of a chess king to attack **2** : a stoppage of progress **3** : something that arrests, limits, or restrains : RESTRAINT ⟨constitutional *checks* and balances⟩ **4 a** : a standard for testing and evaluation **b** : EXAMINATION, INVESTIGATION, VERIFICATION **5** : a banked area of land that confines irrigation water admitted by flooding; *also* : a gate controlling the flow of irrigation water **6** : an order directing a bank to pay out money in accordance with instructions written on it **7 a** : a ticket or token that shows that the bearer has a claim to property or has made payment for a performance that did not take place ⟨baggage *check*⟩ ⟨rain *check*⟩ **b** : a slip indicating the amount due : BILL **8 a** : a pattern of squares **b** : a fabric with such a design **9** : a mark ✓ placed beside an item to show it has been noted **10** : CRACK, BREAK ⟨a *check* in wood⟩

[2]**check** *vb* **1** : to put a chess king in check **2 a** : to bring to a sudden pause : STOP **b** : to halt through caution, uncertainty, or fear : STOP **3** : RESTRAIN, CURB **4** : to make sure of the correctness or state of things **5** : to mark with a check **6** : to mark with squares ⟨a *checked* suit⟩ **7** : to leave or accept for safekeeping or for shipment as baggage **8** : to correspond point for point **9** : to develop small cracks

check·book \'chek-ˌbu̇k\ *n* : a book of blank bank checks

[1]**check·er** \'chek-ər\ *n* **1** : a square resembling the markings on a checkerboard **2** : a piece in the game of checkers

[2]**checker** *vb* **check·ered**; **check·er·ing** \-(ə-)riŋ\ **1** : to mark with squares of different colors ⟨a *checkered* tablecloth⟩ **2** : to subject to frequent changes (as of fortune) ⟨a *checkered* career⟩

[3]**checker** *n* : one that checks; *esp* : an employee who checks out purchases in a supermarket

check·er·ber·ry \'chek-ə(r)-ˌber-ē\ *n* : the spicy red fruit of an American wintergreen; *also* : this plant

check·er·board \-ə(r)-ˌbōrd, -ˌbȯrd\ *n* : a board used in games and marked with 64 squares in 2 alternating colors

check·ers \'chek-ərz\ *n* : a game played on a checkerboard by two persons each having 12 pieces

check·ing account \'chek-iŋ-\ *n* : an account in a bank from which the depositor can draw money by writing checks

check·list \'chek-ˌlist\ *n* : a list of items that may easily be referred to

[1]**check·mate** \'chek-ˌmāt\ *vb* **1** : to arrest or frustrate completely **2** : to check a chess opponent's king so that escape is impossible

[2]**checkmate** *n* **1 a** : the act of checkmating **b** : the situation of a checkmated king **2** : a complete check

check out *vb* : to total or have totaled the cost of purchases in a self-service store (as a supermarket) and make or receive payment for them

check·point \'chek-ˌpȯint\ *n* : a point at which traffic is halted for inspection or clearance

check·rein \-ˌrān\ *n* : a short rein that prevents a horse from lowering its head

check·room \-ˌrüm, -ˌru̇m\ *n* : a room at which baggage, parcels, or clothing is checked

check·up \'chek-ˌəp\ *n* : EXAMINATION; *esp* : a general physical examination

ched·dar \'ched-ər\ *n, often cap* : a hard pressed cheese of smooth texture

cheek \'chēk\ *n* **1** : the fleshy side of the face below the eye and above and to the side of the mouth **2** : something suggestive of the human cheek in position or form **3** : saucy speech or behavior : IMPUDENCE

cheek·bone \-'bōn, -ˌbōn\ *n* : the bone or the bony prominence below the eye

cheeky \'chē-kē\ *adj* **cheek·i·er; -est** : SAUCY, IMPUDENT — **cheek·i·ness** *n*

cheep \'chēp\ *vb* : PEEP, CHIRP — **cheep** *n*

1**cheer** \'chi(ə)r\ *n* **1** : state of mind or heart : SPIRIT ⟨be of good *cheer*⟩ **2** : ANIMATION, GAIETY **3** : food and drink for a feast : FARE **4** : something that gladdens ⟨words of *cheer*⟩ **5** : a shout of applause or encouragement

2**cheer** *vb* **1** : to give hope to or make happier : COMFORT ⟨*cheer* a sick person⟩ **2** : to urge on esp. with shouts or cheers ⟨*cheer* one's team to victory⟩ **3** : to shout with joy, approval, or enthusiasm ⟨the students *cheered* loudly at the end of the speech⟩ **4** : to grow or be cheerful : REJOICE — usu. used with *up*

cheer·ful \'chi(ə)r-fəl\ *adj* **1 a** : full of good spirits : GAY ⟨a *cheerful* outlook⟩ **b** : not grudging or reluctant : WILLING ⟨*cheerful* obedience⟩ **2** : pleasantly bright ⟨sunny *cheerful* room⟩ — **cheer·ful·ly** \-f(ə-)lē\ *adv* — **cheer·ful·ness** \-fəl-nəs\ *n*

cheer·lead·er \'chi(ə)r-ˌlēd-ər\ *n* : a person who directs organized cheering esp. at a sports event

cheer·less \'chi(ə)r-ləs\ *adj* : lacking in warmth or kindliness : DEPRESSING — **cheer·less·ly** *adv* — **cheer·less·ness** *n*

cheery \'chi(ə)r-ē\ *adj* **cheer·i·er; -est** : CHEERFUL — **cheer·i·ly** \'chir-ə-lē\ *adv* — **cheer·i·ness** \'chir-ē-nəs\ *n*

cheese \'chēz\ *n* : a food made from milk esp. by separating out the curd and molding or pressing and usu. ripening it

cheese·bur·ger \'chēz-ˌbər-gər\ *n* : a hamburger with a slice of melted cheese

cheese·cake \-ˌkāk\ *n* : a cake made from cream cheese or cottage cheese, eggs, and sugar in a pastry shell or a mold

cheese·cloth \-ˌklȯth\ *n* : a thin loose-woven cotton cloth

cheesy \'chē-zē\ *adj* **chees·i·er; -est** : resembling or suggestive of cheese

chee·tah \'chēt-ə\ *n* : a long-legged spotted African and formerly Asiatic cat that is the swiftest of all four-footed animals and is often trained to run down game

cheetah (about 31 in. at shoulder)

chef \'shef\ *n* : COOK; *esp* : a head cook

che·la \'kē-lə\ *n, pl* **che·lae** \-(ˌ)lē\ : a pincerlike organ or claw on a limb of a crustacean or arachnid

che·lic·era \ki-'lis-ə-rə\ *n, pl* **-er·as** *or* **-er·ae** \-ə-ˌrē\ : either of the front pair of appendages of an arachnid often specialized as fangs

che·li·ped \'kē-lə-ˌped\ *n* : either of the pair of appendages of a crustacean that bear chelae

chem- *or* **chemo-** *also* **chemi-** *comb form* : chemical : chemistry ⟨*chemo*taxis⟩

chem *abbr* **1** chemical **2** chemist **3** chemistry

1**chem·i·cal** \'kem-i-kəl\ *adj* **1** : of, relating to, used in, or produced by chemistry **2** : acting or operated or produced by chemicals — **chem·i·cal·ly** \-i-k(ə-)lē\ *adv*

2**chemical** *n* **1** : a substance formed when two or more other substances act upon one another to cause a permanent change ⟨sulfuric acid is a manufactured *chemical*⟩ **2 a** : a substance that is prepared for use in the manufacture of another substance ⟨a *chemical* used in making plastics⟩ **b** : a substance that acts upon something else to cause a permanent change ⟨a *chemical* that turns starch blue⟩

chemical engineering *n* : a branch of engineering dealing with the industrial application of chemistry and esp. with the design and operation of chemical plants and equipment — **chemical engineer** *n*

che·mise \shə-'mēz\ *n* **1** : a woman's one-piece undergarment **2** : a loose straight-hanging dress

chem·is·try \'kem-ə-strē\ *n* **1** : a science that deals with the composition, structure, and properties of elementary substances and compound substances and of the changes that they undergo **2** : chemical composition, properties, or processes ⟨the *chemistry* of gasoline⟩ ⟨the *chemistry* of iron⟩ ⟨the *chemistry* of blood⟩ — **chem·ist** \-əst\ *n*

che·mo·re·cep·tion \ˌkē-mō-ri-'sep-shən\ *n* : the physiological reception of chemical stimuli — **che·mo·re·cep·tor** \-'sep-tər\ *n*

che·mo·tax·is \-'tak-səs\ *n* : movement or positioning in relation to chemical agents — **che·mo·tac·tic** \-'tak-tik\ *adj*

che·mo·ther·a·py \-'ther-ə-pē\ *n* : the use of chemical agents in the treatment or control of disease — **che·mo·ther·a·peu·tic** \-ˌther-ə-'pyüt-ik\ *adj*

che·mot·ro·pism \kē-'mä-trə-ˌpiz-əm\ *n* : positioning of cells or organisms in relation to chemical stimuli — **che·mo·trop·ic** \ˌkē-mə-'träp-ik\ *adj*

che·nille \shə-'nēl\ *n* : a fabric with a deep fuzzy pile used for bedspreads and rugs

cheque \'chek\ *chiefly Brit var of* CHECK 6

cher·ish \'cher-ish\ *vb* **1** : to hold dear : feel or show affection for **2** : to keep with care and affection : NURTURE **3** : to harbor in the mind ⟨*cherish* a hope⟩

Cher·o·kee \'cher-ə-ˌkē\ *n* : a member of an Iroquoian Amerindian people orig. inhabiting the Appalachian mountains of Tennessee and No. Carolina

cher·ry \'cher-ē\ *n, pl* **cherries 1 a** : any of numerous trees and shrubs that are related to the roses and have rather small pale yellow to deep blackish red smooth-skinned fruits **b** : the fruit of a cherry **c** : the wood of a cherry **2** : a variable color averaging a moderate red — **cherry** *adj*

chert \'chərt\ *n* : a rock resembling flint and consisting essentially of fine crystalline quartz or fibrous chalcedony

cher·ub \'cher-əb\ *n* **1** *pl* **cher·u·bim** \'cher-(y)ə-ˌbim\ : an angel of high rank **2** *pl* **cher·ubs** \'cher-əbz\ **a** : a painting or drawing of a beautiful child usu. with wings **b** : a chubby rosy child — **che·ru·bic** \chə-'rü-bik\ *adj*

Ches·a·peake Bay retriever \ˌches-(ə-)ˌpēk-ˌbā-\ *n* : a large powerful sporting dog developed in Maryland by crossing Newfoundlands with native retrievers

ə abut	ər further	a back	ā bake	
ä cot, cart	aů out	ch chin	e less	ē easy
g gift	i trip	ī life	j joke	ng sing	ō flow
ȯ flaw	ȯi coin	th thin	th this	ü loot
ů foot	y yet	yü few	yů furious	zh vision

chess \'ches\ *n* : a game for 2 players played with 16 pieces on a checkerboard — **chess·board** \-ˌbōrd,-ˌbȯrd\ *n* — **chess·man** \-ˌman, -mən\ *n*

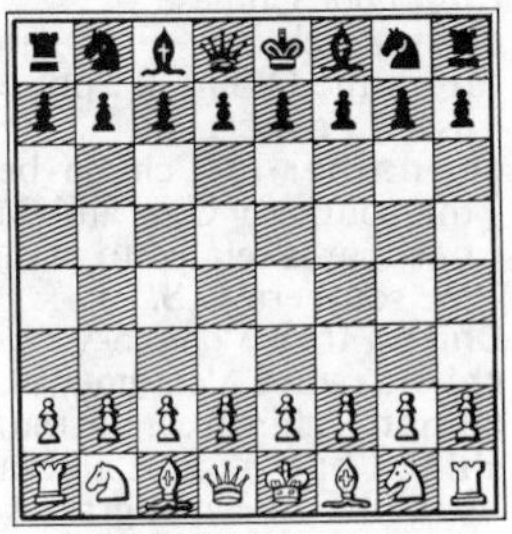

chess: diagram shows arrangement of pieces at beginning of game

chest \'chest\ *n* **1** : BOX, CASE; *esp* : a box with a lid esp. for safekeeping of belongings **2** : a public fund accumulated for some purpose ⟨campaign *chest*⟩ ⟨war *chest*⟩ **3** : the part of the body enclosed by the ribs and breastbone — **chest·ed** \'ches-təd\ *adj*

Ches·ter White \ˌches-tər-\ *n* : any of a breed of large white swine

[1]**chest·nut** \'ches-(ˌ)nət\ *n* **1 a** : an edible nut from several trees or shrubs related to the beech **b** : a plant bearing chestnuts **c** : the wood of a chestnut tree **2** : HORSE CHESTNUT **3** : a brown or reddish brown horse

[2]**chestnut** *adj* : of a grayish to reddish brown color

chestnut blight *n* : a destructive fungous disease of the American chestnut

chev·i·ot \'shev-ē-ət, 'chev-\ *n* **1** : any of a breed of hardy hornless British sheep **2 a** : a heavy napped woolen or worsted fabric **b** : a sturdy cotton shirting

chev·ron \'shev-rən\ *n* **1** : a figure resembling an upside-down V **2** : a sleeve badge usu. indicating the wearer's rank or service (as in the armed forces)

[1]**chew** \'chü\ *vb* : to crush or grind with the teeth — **chew·a·ble** \-ə-bəl\ *adj* — **chew·er** *n* — **chewy** \'chü-ē\ *adj*

[2]**chew** *n* **1** : the act of chewing **2** : something for chewing

chewing gum *n* : gum usu. of sweetened and flavored chicle prepared for chewing

che·wink \chi-'wiŋk\ *n* : a common towhee of eastern No. America

Chey·enne \shī-'an, -'en\ *n* : a member of an Amerindian people of the western plains

chg *abbr* **1** change **2** charge

chgd *abbr* charged

chi \'kī\ *n* : the 22d letter of the Greek alphabet — X or χ

[1]**chic** \'shēk\ *n* : STYLISHNESS

[2]**chic** *adj* : cleverly stylish : SMART ***syn*** see STYLISH

chi·ca·nery \shik-'ān-(ə-)rē\ *n, pl* **-ner·ies** : TRICKERY, DECEIT

Chi·ca·no \chi-'kän-(ˌ)ō\ *n* : an American of Mexican descent

chick \'chik\ *n* **1 a** : CHICKEN; *esp* : one newly hatched **b** : the young of any bird **2** : CHILD **3** *slang* : a young woman

chick·a·dee \'chik-əd-(ˌ)ē\ *n* : any of several crestless American titmice usu. with the crown of the head darker than the body

chick·en \'chik-ən\ *n* **1** : the common domestic fowl esp. when young; *also* : its flesh used as food **2** : any of various birds or their young

chicken cholera *n* : a highly destructive contagious bacterial disease of the blood in domestic poultry and most wild birds

chicken hawk *n* : a hawk that preys or is reputed to prey on chickens

chick·en·heart·ed \ˌchik-ən-'härt-əd\ *adj* : TIMID, COWARDLY

chicken pox *n* : a contagious virus disease esp. of children marked by low fever and a rash or small watery blisters

chick–pea \'chik-ˌpē\ *n* : an Asiatic herb related to the pea and cultivated for its short pods with one or two edible seeds; *also* : its seed

chick·weed \'chik-ˌwēd\ *n* : any of several low-growing small-leaved weedy plants related to the pinks

chi·cle \'chik-əl\ *n* : a gum from the latex of a tropical tree that is used as the chief ingredient of chewing gum

chic·o·ry \'chik-(ə-)rē\ *n, pl* **-ries** : a thick-rooted usu. blue-flowered European herb related to the daisies and grown for its roots and as a salad plant; *also* : its dried ground roasted root used to flavor or adulterate coffee

chide \'chīd\ *vb* **chid** \'chid\ *or* **chid·ed** \'chīd-əd\; **chid** *or* **chid·den** \'chid-ən\ *or* **chided**; **chid·ing** \'chīd-iŋ\ : SCOLD ***syn*** see REBUKE ***ant*** commend

[1]**chief** \'chēf\ *n* **[**from Old French, literally "head", from Latin *caput***]** : the head of a body or organization : LEADER ⟨an Indian *chief*⟩ ⟨*chief* of police⟩

[2]**chief** *adj* **1** : highest in rank, office, or authority ⟨*chief* executive⟩ **2** : of greatest importance, significance, or influence ⟨his *chief* claim to fame⟩

chief·ly \'chē-flē\ *adv* **1** : PRINCIPALLY, ESPECIALLY **2** : for the most part : MOSTLY, MAINLY

chief master sergeant *n* : a noncommissioned officer in the air force of the highest enlisted rank

chief of state : the formal head of a national state as distinguished from the head of the government

chief petty officer *n* : a petty officer in the navy ranking just below a senior chief petty officer

chief·tain \'chēf-tən\ *n* : a chief esp. of a band, tribe, or clan — **chief·tain·cy** \-sē\ *n* — **chief·tain·ship** \-ˌship\ *n*

chief warrant officer *n* : a warrant officer of senior rank

chif·fon \shif-'än, 'shif-ˌ\ *n* : a sheer silk fabric

chif·fo·nier \ˌshif-ə-'ni(ə)r\ *n* : a high narrow chest of drawers often with a mirror

chig·ger \'chig-ər, 'jig-\ *n* **1** : CHIGOE 1 **2** : a 6-legged mite larva that sucks the blood of vertebrates and causes intense itching

chi·gnon \'shēn-ˌyän\ *n* : a knot of hair worn at the back of the head

chig·oe \'chig-ō, 'chē-gō\ *n* **1** : a tropical flea of which the fertile female burrows under the skin causing great discomfort **2** : CHIGGER 2

Chi·hua·hua \chə-'wä-wä, shə-, -wə\ *n* : a very small round-headed large-eared short-coated dog

chil·blain \'chil-ˌblān\ *n* : redness and swelling sometimes with itching and burning esp. of the toes, fingers, nose, and ears caused by exposure to cold

child \'chīld\ *n, pl* **chil·dren** \'chil-drən, -dərn\ **1** : an unborn or recently born person **2 a** : a young person esp. between infancy and youth **b** : a childlike or childish person **3** : a son or daughter of human parents — **child·less** \'chīl(d)-ləs\ *adj* — **with child** : PREGNANT

child·bear·ing \'chīl(d)-ˌbar-iŋ, -ˌber-\ *n* : the act of giving birth to children : PARTURITION — **childbearing** *adj*

child·birth \'chīl(d)-ˌbərth\ *n* : the act or process of giving birth to children — called also *parturition*

child·hood \'chīld-ˌhu̇d\ *n* : the state or time of being a child

child·ish \'chīl-dish\ *adj* **1** : of, resembling, or suitable to a child ⟨*childish* games⟩ **2** : FOOLISH, SILLY ***syn*** see CHILDLIKE ***ant*** mature — **child·ish·ly** *adv* — **child·ish·ness** *n*

child·like \'chīl(d)-ˌlīk\ *adj* : of, relating to, or resembling a child or childhood; *esp* : marked by simplicity, innocence, and trust — **child·like·ness** *n*
syn CHILDLIKE, CHILDISH can mean befitting a child. CHILDLIKE usu. suggests such endearing qualities of childhood as innocence, simplicity, or trust; CHILDISH often suggests the more annoying characteristics such as silly immaturity or peevishness

chili *or* **chile** *or* **chil·li** \'chil-ē\ *n, pl* **chil·ies** *or* **chil·es** *or* **chil·lies** **1** : HOT PEPPER **2** : CHILI CON CARNE

chili con car·ne \ˌchil-ē-ˌkän-'kär-nē, -ē-kən-\ *n* : a stew of ground beef, chilies, and usu. beans

[1]**chill** \'chil\ *vb* **1** : to make or become cold or chilly **2** : to harden the surface of (metal) by sudden cooling — **chill·er** *n*

[2]**chill** *adj* **1 a** : fairly cold **b** : COLD, RAW **2** : not cordial : DISTANT ⟨a *chill* greeting⟩ — **chill·ness** *n*

[3]**chill** *n* **1** : a sensation of cold accompanied by shivering **2** : a moderate but disagreeable degree of cold

chilly \'chil-ē\ *adj* **chill·i·er**; **-est** **1** : noticeably cold : CHILLING **2** : unpleasantly affected by cold — **chill·i·ness** *n*

[1]**chime** \'chīm\ *n* **1** : a musically tuned set of bells **2** : the sound of a set of bells — usu. used in pl.

[2]**chime** *vb* **1 a** : to make a musical esp. harmonious sound **b** : to make the sounds of a chime **c** : to cause to chime **2** : to be or act in accord **3** : to call or indicate by chiming ⟨clock *chiming* midnight⟩

chime in *vb* : to break into or join in a conversation or discussion

chi·me·ra *or* **chi·mae·ra** \kī-'mir-ə, kə-\ *n* **1** *cap* : a she-monster in Greek mythology usu. with a lion's head vomiting flames, a goat's body, and a serpent's tail **2** : an often grotesque usu. fabricated combination of incongruous parts **3** : an illusion or fabrication of the mind or fancy — **chi·mer·i·cal** \-'mer-i-kəl, -'mir-\ *or* **chi·mer·ic** \-ik\ *adj*

chim·ney \'chim-nē\ *n, pl* **chimneys** **1** : a passage for smoke; *esp* : an upright structure of brick or stone extending above the roof of a building **2** : a glass tube around a lamp flame

chimney pot *n* : a usu. earthenware pipe at the top of a chimney to increase draft and carry off smoke

chimney sweep *n* : a person who cleans soot from chimneys

chimney swift *n* : a small sooty-gray bird with long narrow wings that often attaches its nest to the inside of an unused chimney

chimp \'chimp, 'shimp\ *n* : CHIMPANZEE

chim·pan·zee \ˌchim-ˌpan-'zē, ˌshim-; chim-'pan-zē, shim-\ *n* : an African manlike ape that is smaller and less fierce than the gorilla

chimpanzee (up to 5 ft. tall)

[1]**chin** \'chin\ *n* : the lower portion of the face lying below the lower lip and including the point of the lower jaw

[2]**chin** *vb* **chinned**; **chin·ning** **1** : to raise oneself with the hands until the chin is level with the support **2** *slang* : to talk idly : CHATTER

Chin *abbr* Chinese

chi·na \'chī-nə\ *n* **1** : vitreous porcelain ware orig. from the Orient **2** : pottery (as dishes) for domestic use **3** : PORCELAIN

chi·na·ber·ry \'chī-nə-ˌber-ē\ *n* **1** : a soapberry of the southern U.S. and Mexico **2** : a small Asiatic tree that is related to mahogany and is naturalized in the southern U.S.

Chi·na tree \'chī-nə-\ *n* : CHINABERRY 2

chi·na·ware \'chī-nə-ˌwa(ə)r, -ˌwe(ə)r\ *n* : CHINA 2

chinch \'chinch\ *n* : BEDBUG

chinch bug *n* : a small black-and-white bug very destructive to cereal grasses

chin·chil·la \chin-'chil-ə\ *n* **1** : a So. American rodent the size of a large squirrel widely bred in captivity for its very soft fur of a pearly gray color; *also* : its fur **2** : a heavy twilled woolen coating

chine \'chīn\ *n* **1** : BACKBONE, SPINE; *also* : a cut of meat or fish including the backbone or part of it and the surrounding flesh **2** : RIDGE, CREST

Chi·nese \chī-'nēz, -'nēs\ *n, pl* **Chinese** **1 a** : a native or inhabitant of China **b** : a person of Chinese descent **2** : a group of related languages used by the people of China — **Chinese** *adj*

Chinese evergreen *n* : an erect or climbing herb that is often kept as a houseplant for its green or variegated leaves

Chinese lantern *n* : a collapsible lantern of thin colored paper

Chinese puzzle *n* **1** : an intricate or ingenious puzzle **2** : something intricate and hard to solve

[1]**chink** \'chingk\ *n* : a narrow slit or crack (as in a wall)

[2]**chink** *vb* : to fill the chinks of (as by caulking) : stop up

[3]**chink** *n* : a short sharp sound

[4]**chink** *vb* : to make or cause to make a short sharp sound

chi·no \'chē-nō, 'shē-\ *n, pl* **-nos** **1** : a usu. khaki cotton twill fabric **2** : a garment made of chino — usu. used in pl.

Chi·nook \shə-'nu̇k, chə-\ *n* **1** : a member of an Amerindian people of the north shore of the Columbia river at its mouth **2** *not cap* **a** : a warm moist southwest wind of the coast from Oregon northward **b** : a warm dry wind that descends the eastern slopes of the Rocky mountains

chintz \'chin(t)s\ *n* : a usu. glazed printed cotton fabric

[1]**chip** \'chip\ *n* **1 a** : a small piece (as of wood, stone, or glass) broken off by a sharp blow : FLAKE **b** : a thin crisp slice of food ⟨potato *chip*⟩ **2 a** : a counter used in poker **b** *pl, slang* : MONEY **3** : a piece of dried dung ⟨cow *chip*⟩ **4** : a flaw left after a small piece has been broken off ⟨a cup with a *chip* in it⟩ — **chip off the old block** : a child that resembles his parent — **chip on one's shoulder** : a challenging or aggressive attitude

[2]**chip** *vb* **chipped**; **chip·ping** **1** : to cut or break a chip from something ⟨*chip* a cup⟩ **2** : to break off in small pieces

chipmunk (4 to 6 in. long)

chip in *vb* : CONTRIBUTE

chip·munk \'chip-ˌməŋk\ *n* : any of numerous small striped largely terrestrial American squirrels

chipped beef \'chip(t)-\ *n* : smoked dried beef sliced thin

chip·per \'chip-ər\ *adj* : GAY, SPRIGHTLY

Chip·pe·wa \'chip-ə-ˌwȯ, -ˌwä, -ˌwā\ *n* : OJIBWA

chip·ping sparrow \'chip-ing-\ *n* : a small eastern No. American sparrow whose song is a weak monotonous trill

chi·rop·o·dy \kə-'räp-əd-ē\ *n* : professional care and treatment of the human foot in health and disease — **chi·rop·o·dist** \-əd-əst\ *n*

chi·ro·prac·tic \'kī-rə-ˌprak-tik\ *n* : the treatment of bodily ailments according to a system of healing based on manipulation and adjustment by hand of body structures (as the spinal column) — **chi·ro·prac·tor** \-tər\ *n*

chirp \'chərp\ *n* : a short sharp sound characteristic of a small bird or cricket — **chirp** *vb*

chir·rup \'chər-əp, 'chir-; 'chə-rəp\ *n* : CHIRP — **chir·rup** *vb*

1**chis·el** \'chiz-əl\ *n* : a metal tool with a cutting edge at the end of a blade used to shape or chip away stone, wood, or metal

2**chisel** *vb* **-eled** *or* **-elled**; **-el·ing** *or* **-el·ling** \'chiz-(ə-)ling\ **1** : to cut or work with or as if with a chisel **2** : CHEAT — **chis·el·er** \'chiz-(ə-)lər\ *n*

chis·eled *or* **chis·elled** \'chiz-əld\ *adj* **1** : cut or shaped with a chisel **2** : appearing as if shaped with a chisel : finely cut ⟨sharply *chiseled* features⟩

chit·chat \'chit-ˌchat\ *n* : SMALL TALK, GOSSIP

chi·tin \'kīt-ən\ *n* : a horny substance that forms part of the hard outer body covering esp. of insects and crustaceans — **chi·tin·ous** \-əs\ *adj*

chi·ton \'kīt-ən, 'kī-ˌtän\ *n* : any of a class of bilaterally symmetrical marine mollusks with a shell of calcium-containing plates

chit·ter \'chit-ər\ *vb* **1** : TWITTER, CHIRP **2** : CHATTER

chit·ter·lings *or* **chit·lings** *or* **chit·lins** \'chit-lənz\ *n pl* : the intestines of hogs esp. prepared as food

chi·val·ric \shə-'val-rik\ *adj* : CHIVALROUS 2

chiv·al·rous \'shiv-əl-rəs\ *adj* **1** : VALIANT **2** : of or relating to chivalry **3 a** : having or displaying the qualities of an ideal knight **b** : courteously attentive to women — **chiv·al·rous·ly** *adv* — **chiv·al·rous·ness** *n*

chiv·al·ry \'shiv-əl-rē\ *n* [from Old French *chevalerie*, from *chevalier* "horseman", "knight", from Latin *caballarius*, from *caballus* "horse"] **1** : a body of knights **2** : the system, spirit, ways, or customs of medieval knighthood **3** : the qualities (as bravery, honor, protection of the weak, and generous treatment of foes) held to characterize an ideal knight

chive \'chīv\ *n* : a perennial herb related to the onion and used for flavoring

chlam·y·do·mo·nas \ˌklam-ə-də-'mō-nəs\ *n* : any of a genus of single-celled algae that have an eyespot and two flagella and are abundant in fresh water and damp soil

chlo·ral \'klōr-əl, 'klȯr-\ *n* : a bitter white crystalline drug used to bring sleep — called also *chloral hydrate*

chlor·am·phen·i·col \ˌklōr-ˌam-'fen-i-ˌkȯl, ˌklȯr-, -ˌkōl\ *n* : a colorless crystalline antibiotic that is effective against certain diseases caused by bacteria, rickettsiae, or viruses

chlor·dane \'klȯr-ˌdān\ *or* **chlor·dan** \-ˌdan\ *n* : an odorless liquid insecticide

chlo·rel·la \klə-'rel-ə\ *n* : any of a genus of single-celled green algae potentially a cheap source of protein and vitamins

chlo·ride \'klōr-ˌīd, 'klȯr-\ *n* : a chemical compound of chlorine with another element or radical; *esp* : a salt or ester of hydrochloric acid

chloride of lime : a white powder made by passing chlorine gas over slaked lime and used as a bleaching agent, disinfectant, and deodorant

chlo·rin·ate \'klōr-ə-ˌnāt, 'klȯr-\ *vb* : to treat or cause to combine with chlorine esp. for purifying — **chlo·rin·a·tion** \ˌklōr-ə-'nā-shən, ˌklȯr-\ *n* — **chlo·rin·a·tor** \'klōr-ə-ˌnāt-ər, 'klȯr-\ *n*

chlo·rine \'klōr-ˌēn, 'klȯr-, -ən\ *n* : an element that is a heavy greenish yellow irritating gas of pungent odor used esp. as a bleach, oxidizing agent, and disinfectant in water purification — see ELEMENT table

chlorine water *n* : a yellowish aqueous solution of chlorine in water used for bleaching

chlo·rite \'klōr-ˌīt, 'klȯr-\ *n* : a usu. green mineral associated with and resembling the micas

1**chlo·ro·form** \'klōr-ə-ˌfȯrm, 'klȯr-\ *n* : a colorless heavy poisonous liquid that smells like ether and is used esp. as a solvent or as an anesthetic

2**chloroform** *vb* : to treat with chloroform esp. so as to produce anesthesia or death

chlo·ro·phyll *also* **chlo·ro·phyl** \'klōr-ə-ˌfil, 'klȯr-\ *n* : the green coloring matter of plants that is found in chloroplasts and is necessary for the manufacture of plant food from carbon dioxide and water by photosynthesis

chlo·ro·plast \'klōr-ə-ˌplast, 'klȯr-\ *n* : a plastid that contains chlorophyll and is the seat of photosynthesis and starch formation in a plant cell

chlo·ro·sis \klə-'rō-səs\ *n, pl* **-ro·ses** \-'rō-ˌsēz\ : a disorder of green plants marked by yellowing or blanching — **chlo·rot·ic** \-'rät-ik\ *adj*

chm *or* **chmn** *abbr* chairman

1**chock** \'chäk\ *n* : a wedge or block for steadying or stopping a body or for filling in an unwanted space

2**chock** *vb* : to stop or make fast with or as if with chocks

chock–full \'chäk-'fu̇l\ *adj* : full to the limit

choc·o·late \'chäk-(ə-)lət, 'chȯk-\ *n* [from Spanish, from Nahuatl (the language of the Aztecs) *xocoatl*] **1** : a food prepared from ground roasted cacao beans **2** : a beverage of chocolate in water or milk **3** : a candy with a chocolate coating **4** : a brownish gray — **chocolate** *adj*

Choc·taw \'chäk-ˌtȯ\ *n* : a member of an Amerindian people of Mississippi, Alabama, and Louisiana

1**choice** \'chȯis\ *n* **1** : the act of choosing : SELECTION **2** : power of choosing : OPTION **3 a** : a person or thing chosen **b** : the best part : CREAM **4** : a sufficient number and variety for wide or free selection

2**choice** *adj* **1** : very fine ⟨*choice* fruits⟩ **2** : of a grade between prime and good ⟨*choice* meat⟩ — **choice·ly** *adv* — **choice·ness** *n*

1**choir** \'kwī(ə)r\ *n* **1** : an organized group of singers esp. in a church **2** : the part of a church between the sanctuary and the nave

choir·boy \-ˌbȯi\ *n* : a boy member of a church choir

choir·mas·ter \-ˌmas-tər\ *n* : the director of a choir

1**choke** \'chōk\ *vb* **1** : to hinder normal breathing by cutting off the supply of air ⟨thick smoke *choked* the firemen⟩ **2** : to have the windpipe stopped entirely or partly ⟨*choke* on a bone⟩ **3** : to check the growth or action of : SUPPRESS, SMOTHER ⟨*choke* a fire⟩ ⟨*choke* back tears⟩ **4** : to obstruct by clogging ⟨leaves *choked* the sewer⟩ **5** : to fill to the limit ⟨the store was *choked* with customers⟩ **6** : to decrease or shut off the air intake of a carburetor to make the fuel mixture richer — **chok·er** \'chō-kər\ *n*

2**choke** *n* **1** : a valve for choking a gasoline engine **2** : a narrowing toward the muzzle in the bore of a gun

choke·cher·ry \'chōk-ˌcher-ē, -'cher-\ *n* **:** any of several American wild cherries with pointed leaves, long clusters of white flowers, and fruit that is nearly black when ripe; *also* **:** this fruit

choke·damp \-ˌdamp\ *n* **:** a heavy nonexplosive mine gas that consists chiefly of carbon dioxide and will not support life

choky \'chō-kē\ *adj* **chok·i·er; -est 1 :** having the power to choke ⟨a *choky* gas⟩ **2 :** having a tendency to choke ⟨grow *choky* with fear⟩

chol·era \'käl-ə-rə\ *n* **:** any of several diseases usu. marked by severe vomiting and dysentery

chol·er·ic \'käl-ə-rik, kə-'ler-ik\ *adj* **:** easily moved to anger **:** hot-tempered

cho·les·ter·ol \kə-'les-tə-ˌrōl, -ˌrōl\ *n* **:** a physiologically important waxy substance that is present in animal cells and tissues and is sometimes a factor in the abnormal thickening and hardening of arteries

cho·line \'kō-ˌlēn, 'käl-ˌēn\ *n* **:** a substance that is widely distributed in animal and plant products and is a vitamin of the B complex essential to the liver function

chon·drus \'kän-drəs\ *n* **:** IRISH MOSS

choose \'chüz\ *vb* **chose** \'chōz\; **cho·sen** \'chō-zən\; **choos·ing** \'chü-zing\ **1 :** to select esp. freely and after consideration ⟨*choose* a leader⟩ **2 a :** DECIDE ⟨*chose* to go by train⟩ **b :** PREFER **3 :** to see fit **:** INCLINE ⟨take them if you *choose*⟩ — **choos·er** *n*

choosy *or* **choos·ey** \'chü-zē\ *adj* **choos·i·er; -est :** very careful in choosing **:** PARTICULAR

[1]**chop** \'chäp\ *vb* **chopped; chop·ping 1 :** to cut by striking esp. repeatedly with something sharp ⟨*chop* down a tree⟩ **2 :** to cut into small pieces **:** MINCE **3 :** to strike quickly or repeatedly

[2]**chop** *n* **1 a :** a forceful sudden stroke with a sharp instrument **b :** a sharp blow **2 :** a small cut of meat often including a part of a rib **3 :** a short quick motion (as of a wave)

[3]**chop** *vb* **chopped; chop·ping 1 :** to change direction **2 :** to veer with or as if with the wind

chop·per \'chäp-ər\ *n* **1 :** one that chops **2 :** HELICOPTER

[1]**chop·py** \'chäp-ē\ *adj* **chop·pi·er; -est :** CHANGEABLE, VARIABLE ⟨*choppy* wind⟩

[2]**choppy** *adj* **chop·pi·er; -est 1 :** rough with small waves **2 :** JERKY, DISCONNECTED

chops \'chäps\ *n pl* **:** the fleshy covering of the jaws

chop·stick \'chäp-ˌstik\ *n* **:** one of a pair of slender sticks used chiefly in oriental countries to lift food to the mouth

chopsticks

chop su·ey \chäp-'sü-ē\ *n* **:** a dish prepared chiefly from bean sprouts, bamboo shoots, onions, mushrooms, and meat or fish

ə abut	ər further	a back	ā bake
ä cot, cart	au̇ out	ch chin	e less	ē easy
g gift	i trip	ī life	j joke	ng sing	ō flow
ȯ flaw	ȯi coin	th thin	th this	ü loot
u̇ foot	y yet	yü few	yu̇ furious	zh vision

cho·ral \'kōr-əl, 'kȯr-\ *adj* **:** of, relating to, or performed by a chorus or choir — **cho·ral·ly** \-ə-lē\ *adv*

cho·rale \kə-'ral, -'räl\ *n* **1 :** a hymn or psalm sung to a traditional or composed melody **2 :** CHORUS, CHOIR

[1]**chord** \'kȯrd\ *n* **:** a combination of three or more tones sounded together — **chord·al** \-əl\ *adj*

[2]**chord** *vb* **1 :** ACCORD, HARMONIZE **2 :** to play chords

[3]**chord** *n* **1 :** a straight line joining two points on a curve **2 :** an individual emotion or disposition ⟨strike a familiar *chord*⟩

chor·date \'kȯrd-ət, 'kȯr-ˌdāt\ *n* **:** any of a major group of animals (as vertebrates and tunicates) having at least at some stage of development an elastic rod of cells forming a support along the back, a central nervous system situated in the back, and gill clefts — **chordate** *adj*

chore \'chō(ə)r, 'chȯ(ə)r\ *n* **1** *pl* **:** the regular light work of a household or farm **2 :** a routine task or job **3 :** a difficult or disagreeable task

cho·re·og·ra·phy \ˌkōr-ē-'äg-rə-fē, ˌkȯr-\ *n* **:** the art of dancing or of arranging dances and esp. ballets — **cho·re·og·ra·pher** \-fər\ *n* — **cho·re·o·graph·ic** \-ē-ə-'graf-ik\ *adj*

cho·ri·on \'kōr-ē-ˌän, 'kȯr-\ *n* **:** the outer embryonic membrane of higher vertebrates that in placental mammals joins in the formation of the placenta — **cho·ri·on·ic** \ˌkōr-ē-'än-ik, ˌkȯr-\ *adj*

cho·ris·ter \'kōr-ə-stər, 'kȯr-, 'kär-\ *n* **:** a singer in a choir

C-horizon *n* **:** the layer of soil below the B-horizon that consists mostly of the weathered rock that contributes the mineral part of the upper layers

cho·roid \'kōr-ˌȯid, 'kȯr-\ *also* **cho·ri·oid** \-ē-ˌȯid\ *adj* **:** of, relating to, or being the pigmented middle layer of the vertebrate eye lying between the sclera and the retina — **choroid** *n*

choroid coat *n* **:** the choroid layer of the eye

chor·tle \'chȯrt-əl\ *vb* **chor·tled; chor·tling** \'chȯrt-(ə-)ling\ **:** LAUGH, CHUCKLE — **chortle** *n* — **chor·tler** \'chȯrt-lər, -(ə-)lər\ *n*

[1]**cho·rus** \'kōr-əs, 'kȯr-\ *n* **1 a :** a group of singers and dancers in Greek drama participating in or commenting on the action **b :** an organized group of singers **:** CHOIR **c :** a group of supporting dancers and singers in a musical comedy or revue **2 a :** a recurring part of a song or hymn **b :** a composition to be sung by a chorus **c :** the main part of a popular song **3 :** something uttered simultaneously by a number of persons ⟨a *chorus* of boos⟩ — **in chorus :** in unison **:** as one voice

[2]**chorus** *vb* **:** to sing or utter in chorus

chose *past of* CHOOSE

chosen *past part of* CHOOSE

[1]**chow** \'chau̇\ *n* **:** a thick-coated straight-legged muscular dog with a blue-black tongue and a short tail curled close to the back — called also **chow chow** \'chau̇-ˌchau̇\

chow

[2]**chow** *n, slang* **:** FOOD, VICTUALS

chow·der \'chau̇d-ər\ *n* **:** a soup or stew made of fish, clams, or a vegetable usu. stewed in milk

chow mein \'chau̇-'mān\ *n* **1 :** fried noodles **2 :** a thick stew of shredded meat, mushrooms, and vegetables

chris·ten \'kris-ən\ *vb* **chris·tened; chris·ten-**

ing \-(ə-)niŋ\ **1 :** BAPTIZE **2 :** to name at baptism or with a ceremony ⟨*christen* a ship⟩

Chris·ten·dom \'kris-ən-dəm\ *n* **1 :** the entire body of Christians **2 :** countries or peoples that are predominantly Christian

[1]**Chris·tian** \'kris-chən\ *n* **1 :** a person who believes in Jesus Christ and follows his teachings **2 :** a member of a Christian church **3 :** a member of a group (as the Disciples of Christ or the Churches of Christ) seeking a return to New Testament Christianity

[2]**Christian** *adj* **1 :** of or relating to Jesus Christ or the religion deriving from him **2 :** of or relating to Christians ⟨a *Christian* nation⟩ **3 :** befitting a Christian **:** KIND

Chris·ti·an·i·ty \,kris-chē-'an-ət-ē\ *n* **1 :** the religion professed by Christians **2 :** Christian belief or practice

Chris·tian·ize \'kris-chə-,nīz\ *vb* **:** to make Christian — **Chris·tian·i·za·tion** \,kris-chə-nə-'zā-shən\ *n*

christian name *n, often cap C* **:** the name given to a person at birth or christening as distinct from the family name

Christ·mas \'kris-məs\ *n* **1 :** December 25 celebrated as a church festival in commemoration of the birth of Christ and observed as a legal holiday **2 :** CHRISTMASTIDE

Christmas fern *n* **:** a No. American evergreen fern often used for winter decorations

Christ·mas·tide \'kris-məs-,tīd\ *n* **:** the season of Christmas

Christmas tree *n* **:** a usu. evergreen tree decorated at Christmas

[1]**chro·mat·ic** \krō-'mat-ik\ *adj* **1 :** of or relating to color; *esp* **:** being a shade other than black, gray, or white **2 :** of, relating to, or giving all the tones of the chromatic scale — **chro·mat·i·cal·ly** \-'mat-i-k(ə-)lē\ *adv*

[2]**chromatic** *n* **:** ACCIDENTAL

chromatic aberration *n* **:** aberration caused by the differences in refraction of the colored rays of the spectrum

chromatic scale *n* **:** a musical scale that consists wholly of half steps

chro·ma·tin \'krō-mə-tən\ *n* **:** a material present in chromosomes that is a complex of DNA and protein and stains deeply with certain biological stains — **chro·ma·tin·ic** \,krō-mə-'tin-ik\ *adj*

chro·ma·tog·ra·phy \,krō-mə-'täg-rə-fē\ *n* **:** separation of chemical compounds by migration through an adsorbent medium (as paper) so that each compound becomes isolated in a separate layer or area — **chro·mato·graph·ic** \krō-,mat-ə-'graf-ik\ *adj*

chrome \'krōm\ *n* **1 a :** CHROMIUM **b :** a chromium pigment **2 :** something plated with an alloy of chromium

chro·mite \'krō-,mīt\ *n* **:** a mineral that consists of an oxide of iron and chromium and is an important ore of chromium

chro·mi·um \'krō-mē-əm\ *n* **:** a blue-white metallic element found in nature only in combination and used esp. in alloys, as a lustrous rust-resisting plating, and in its compounds in paints — see ELEMENT table

chro·mo·some \'krō-mə-,sōm\ *n* **:** one of the usu. elongated DNA-containing bodies of a cell nucleus that are usu. constant in number in any one kind of plant or animal, and can be seen esp. during mitosis or meiosis — **chro·mo·som·al** \,krō-mə-'sō-məl\ *adj*

chro·mo·sphere \'krō-mə-,sfi(ə)r\ *n* **:** the lower part of the atmosphere esp. of the sun composed chiefly of hydrogen

chron·ic \'krän-ik\ *adj* **1 :** marked by long duration or frequent recurrence **:** not acute **2 :** suffering from a chronic disease **3 :** HABITUAL, ACCUSTOMED ⟨a *chronic* complainer⟩ — **chron·i·cal·ly** \-i-k(ə-)lē\ *adv*

[1]**chron·i·cle** \'krän-i-kəl\ *n* **:** an historical account of events in order of time without analysis or interpretation

[2]**chronicle** *vb* **chron·i·cled; chron·i·cling** \-k(ə-)liŋ\ **:** to record in or as if in a chronicle **:** tell the story of — **chron·i·cler** \-k(ə-)lər\ *n*

Chron·i·cles \'krän-i-kəlz\ *n* — see BIBLE table

chrono·graph \'krän-ə-,graf, 'krō-nə-\ *n* **:** an instrument for measuring and recording time intervals with accuracy — **chrono·graph·ic** \,krän-ə-'graf-ik, ,krō-nə-\ *adj* — **chro·nog·ra·phy** \krə-'näg-rə-fē\ *n*

chron·o·log·i·cal \,krän-ə-'läj-i-kəl, ,krō-nə-\ *adj* **:** arranged in or according to the order of time ⟨*chronological* tables of American history⟩ — **chron·o·log·i·cal·ly** \-i-k(ə-)lē\ *adv*

chro·nol·o·gy \krə-'näl-ə-jē\ *n, pl* **-gies 1 :** the science that deals with measuring time and dating events **2 :** a chronological table or list **3 :** an arrangement (as of events) in order of occurrence — **chro·nol·o·gist** \-jəst\ *n*

chro·nom·e·ter \krə-'näm-ət-ər\ *n* **:** an instrument for measuring time; *esp* **:** one intended to keep time with great accuracy — **chrono·met·ric** \,krän-ə-'me-trik, ,krō-nə-\ *adj*

chrono·scope \'krän-ə-,skōp, 'krō-nə-\ *n* **:** an instrument for precise measurement of small time intervals

chrys·a·lid \'kris-ə-ləd\ *n* **:** CHRYSALIS — **chrysalid** *adj*

chrys·a·lis \'kris-ə-ləs\ *n, pl* **chry·sal·i·des** \kris-'al-ə-,dēz\ *or* **chrys·a·lis·es** \'kris-ə-lə-səz\ **:** the pupa of insects (as butterflies) that pass the pupal stage enclosed in a firm case without a cocoon

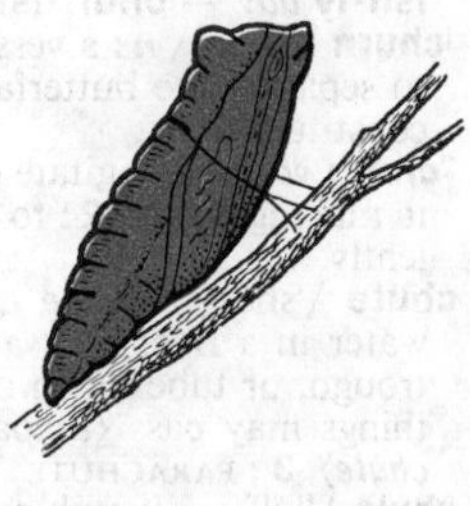
chrysalis

chry·san·the·mum \kris-'an(t)-thə-məm\ *n* **1 :** any of a genus of plants related to the daisies that include weeds, ornamentals grown for their brightly colored often double flower heads, and important sources of medicinals and insecticides **2 :** a flower head of an ornamental chrysanthemum

chryso·phyte \'kris-ə-,fīt\ *n* **:** any of a major group of algae (as diatoms) with yellowish green to golden brown pigments

chub·by \'chəb-ē\ *adj* **chub·bi·er; -est :** PLUMP ⟨a *chubby* boy⟩ — **chub·bi·ness** *n*

[1]**chuck** \'chək\ *vb* **1 :** to give a pat or a tap ⟨*chuck* her under the chin⟩ **2 :** to throw easily or carelessly **:** TOSS

[2]**chuck** *n* **1 :** a pat or nudge under the chin **2 :** TOSS, JERK

[3]**chuck** *n* **1 :** a portion of a side of dressed beef including most of the neck and the parts about the shoulder blade and the first three ribs **2 :** a device for holding work or a tool in a machine and esp. in a lathe

chuck–full \'chək-'fu̇l\ *var of* CHOCK-FULL

chuck·hole \'chək-,hōl, 'chəg-\ *n* **:** a hole or rut in a road

chuck·le \'chək-əl\ *vb* **chuck·led**; **chuck·ling** \'chək-(ə-)liŋ\ : to laugh inwardly or quietly — **chuckle** *n*

chuck wagon \'chək-\ *n* : a wagon carrying a stove and provisions for cooking (as on a ranch)

chuck·wal·la \'chək-,wäl-ə\ *n* : a large but harmless lizard of the desert regions of the southwestern U.S.

1**chug** \'chəg\ *n* : a dull explosive sound made by or as if by a laboring engine

2**chug** *vb* **chugged**; **chug·ging** : to move or go with chugs ⟨a locomotive *chugging* along⟩

chuk·ka \'chək-ə\ *n* : a usu. ankle-length leather boot with two pairs of eyelets

1**chum** \'chəm\ *n* [originally meaning "roommate", short for *chamber fellow*] : a steady companion : PAL

2**chum** *vb* **chummed**; **chum·ming** : to go about with a person regularly

chum·my \'chəm-ē\ *adj* **chum·mi·er**; **-est** : INTIMATE, SOCIABLE — **chum·mi·ly** \'chəm-ə-lē\ *adv* — **chum·mi·ness** \'chəm-ē-nəs\ *n*

chump \'chəmp\ *n* : FOOL, DUPE

chunk \'chəŋk\ *n* : a short thick piece or lump : HUNK

chunky \'chəŋ-kē\ *adj* **chunk·i·er**; **-est** : STOCKY

church \'chərch\ *n* [from Old English *cirice*, from Greek *kyriakon* "house of the Lord", from *kyrios* "lord"] **1** : a building for public worship esp. by a Christian parish or congregation **2** : a body or organization of religious believers **3** : public worship esp. in a church — **church·ly** \-lē\ *adj*

church·man \-mən\ *n* **1** : CLERGYMAN **2** : a church member

church·yard \-,yärd\ *n* : a yard that belongs to a church and is often used as a burial ground

churl \'chərl\ *n* **1** : an Anglo-Saxon freeman of the lowest rank **2** : a medieval peasant **3** : a rude or surly person — **churl·ish** \'chər-lish\ *adj* — **churl·ish·ly** *adv* — **churl·ish·ness** *n*

1**churn** \'chərn\ *n* : a vessel in which cream is agitated to separate the butterfat from the other constituents

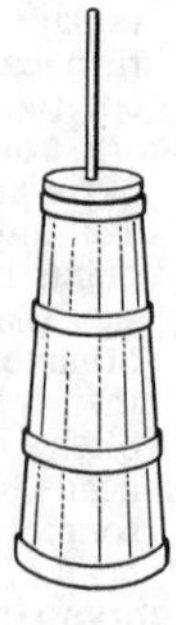
churn

2**churn** *vb* **1** : to agitate cream in a churn in making butter **2** : to stir or shake violently

chute \'shüt\ *n* **1** : a quick drop (as of water in a river) **2** : an inclined plane, trough, or tube down or through which things may pass ⟨a coal *chute*⟩ ⟨a mail *chute*⟩ **3** : PARACHUTE

chyle \'kīl\ *n* : lymph milky from bits of fat that is seen esp. in the lymph vessels surrounding the small intestine and carrying the digested fat to the blood

chyme \'kīm\ *n* : the semifluid mass of partly digested food that passes from the stomach into the duodenum

Ci *abbr* cirrus

CIA *abbr* Central Intelligence Agency

ci·ca·da \sə-'kād-ə, -'käd-\ *n* : any of a family of stout-bodied homopterous insects that have a wide blunt head and large transparent wings

cic·a·trix \'sik-ə-(,)triks, sə-'kā-triks\ *n, pl* **cic·a·tri·ces** \,sik-ə-'trī-(,)sēz, sə-'kā-trə-,sēz\ : a scar resulting from formation and contraction of tissue in a flesh wound

ə abut	ər further	a back	ā bake	
ä cot, cart	aù out	ch chin	e less	ē easy
g gift	i trip	ī life	j joke	ŋ sing
ō flow	ó flaw	ói coin	th thin	t͟h this
ü loot	ù foot	y yet	yü few	yù furious
zh vision				

-cide \,sīd\ *n comb form* **1** : killer ⟨pesti*cide*⟩ **2** : killing ⟨geno*cide*⟩

ci·der \'sīd-ər\ *n* : the expressed juice of fruit (as apples) used as a beverage or for making other products (as vinegar)

ci·gar \sig-'är\ *n* : a tight roll of tobacco for smoking

cig·a·rette *also* **cig·a·ret** \,sig-ə-'ret, 'sig-ə-,\ *n* : a small roll of cut tobacco wrapped in paper for smoking

cil·i·ary \'sil-ē-,er-ē\ *adj* **1** : of or relating to cilia **2** : of, relating to, or being the muscular body supporting the lens of the eye

1**cil·i·ate** \'sil-ē-ət, -,āt\ *or* **cil·i·at·ed** \-,āt-əd\ *adj* : provided with cilia

2**ciliate** *n* : any of a group of ciliate protozoans

cil·i·um \'sil-ē-əm\ *n, pl* **cil·ia** \-ē-ə\ **1** : EYELASH **2** : one of the tiny filaments of many cells that are capable of lashing movement

1**cinch** \'sinch\ *n* **1** : a strong girth for a pack or saddle **2** : a tight grip **3** : a thing done with ease **4** : a certainty to happen

2**cinch** *vb* **1** : to put a cinch on **2** : to make certain : ASSURE

cin·cho·na \siŋ-'kō-nə, sin-'chō-\ *n* : any of a genus of So. American trees and shrubs with bark containing substances (as quinine) that are used in treating malaria

cinc·ture \'siŋ(k)-chər\ *n* : GIRDLE, BELT

cin·der \'sin-dər\ *n* **1** : waste matter from the smelting of metal ores : SLAG **2 a** : a piece of partly burned coal or wood **b** : a hot coal without flame **3** *pl* : ASHES **4** : a fragment of lava from an erupting volcano — **cin·dery** \-d(ə-)rē\ *adj*

cinder block *n* : a building block made of concrete and coal cinders

cin·e·ma \'sin-ə-mə\ *n* **1** *chiefly Brit* **a** : MOTION PICTURE **b** : a motion-picture theater **2** : MOVIES — **cin·e·mat·ic** \,sin-ə-'mat-ik\ *adj* — **cin·e·mat·i·cal·ly** \-'mat-i-k(ə-)lē\ *adv*

cin·na·bar \'sin-ə-,bär\ *n* : a red mineral that consists of a sulfide of mercury and is the important ore of mercury

cin·na·mon \'sin-ə-mən\ *n* **1 a** : a spice consisting of the highly aromatic bark of any of several trees related to the laurel **b** : a tree that yields cinnamon **2** : a light yellowish brown — **cin·na·mon·ic** \,sin-ə-'män-ik\ *adj*

cinque·foil \'siŋk-,fóil, 'saŋk-\ *n* **1** : any of a group of plants that have 5-lobed leaves and are related to the roses **2** : a design enclosed by five joined foils

ci·on *var of* SCION

1**ci·pher** \'sī-fər\ *n* [from Arabic *ṣifr*, from *ṣifr* "empty"] **1 a** : the symbol 0 denoting the absence of all magnitude or quantity : ZERO — see NUMBER table **b** : an insignificant individual : NONENTITY **2 a** : a method of transforming a text in order to conceal its meaning **b** : a message in code **3** : the interwoven initials of a name : MONOGRAM

2**cipher** *vb* **ci·phered**; **ci·pher·ing** \-f(ə-)riŋ\ **1** : to use figures in a mathematical process **2** : ENCIPHER

cir *abbr* circle

1**cir·cle** \'sər-kəl\ *n* **1 a** : RING **b** : a closed plane curve every point of which is equally distant from a point within it **c** : the plane surface bounded by a circle **2** : something (as a traffic rotary) in the form of a circle **3** : CYCLE, ROUND **4** : a group bound by common ties or interests

2**circle** *vb* **cir·cled**; **cir·cling** \-k(ə-)liŋ\ **1** : to enclose in or as if in a circle **2** : to move or revolve around **3** : to move in or as if in a circle — **cir·cler** \-k(ə-)lər\ *n*

circle graph *n* : PIE CHART
cir·clet \'sər-klət\ *n* : a little circle; *esp* : an ornament in the form of a circle
cir·cuit \'sər-kət\ *n* **1 a** : a boundary around an enclosed space **b** : an enclosed space **2** : a moving or revolving around : CIRCLING ⟨the *circuit* of the earth around the sun⟩ **3 a** : a regular tour (as by a judge or preacher) around an assigned territory **b** : the route traveled **4 a** : LEAGUE **b** : a chain of theaters at which productions are successively presented **5** : the complete path of an electric current or any part of this path **6** : a radio or television hookup
circuit breaker *n* : a switch that automatically stops the flow of electric current under an abnormal condition (as overload)
cir·cu·i·tous \(ˌ)sər-'kyü-ət-əs\ *adj* **1** : marked by a circular or winding course ⟨a *circuitous* route⟩ **2** : marked by indirect procedure ⟨*circuitous* actions⟩ ⟨*circuitous* in speech⟩ — **cir·cu·i·tous·ly** *adv* — **cir·cu·i·tous·ness** *n*
cir·cuit·ry \'sər-kə-trē\ *n* : the plan or the components of an electric circuit
[1]**cir·cu·lar** \'sər-kyə-lər\ *adj* **1** : having the form of a circle : bounded by a circle : ROUND ⟨a *circular* driveway⟩ **2** : moving in or describing a circle or spiral **3** : CIRCUITOUS ⟨a *circular* explanation⟩ **4** : sent around to a number of persons ⟨a *circular* letter⟩ — **cir·cu·lar·i·ty** \ˌsər-kyə-'lar-ət-ē\ *n* — **cir·cu·lar·ly** \'sər-kyə-lər-lē\ *adv*
[2]**circular** *n* : a paper (as an advertising leaflet) intended for wide distribution
circular cylinder *n* : a cylinder with bases that are circles
cir·cu·lar·ize \'sər-kyə-lə-ˌrīz\ *vb* : to send circulars to
cir·cu·late \'sər-kyə-ˌlāt\ *vb* **1** : to move or cause to move in a circle or circuit; *esp* : to follow a course that returns to the starting point ⟨blood *circulates* through the body⟩ **2** : to pass from person to person or place to place ⟨*circulate* a rumor⟩ ⟨a magazine that *circulated* widely⟩ — **cir·cu·la·tor** \-ˌlāt-ər\ *n*
cir·cu·la·tion \ˌsər-kyə-'lā-shən\ *n* **1** : FLOW **2** : orderly movement through a circuit; *esp* : the movement of blood through the vessels of the body caused by the pumping action of the heart **3 a** : passage or transmission from person to person or place to place ⟨coins in *circulation*⟩ **b** : the number of copies of a publication sold over a given period — **cir·cu·la·tive** \'sər-kyə-ˌlāt-iv\ *adj*
cir·cu·la·to·ry \'sər-kyə-lə-ˌtōr-ē, -ˌtȯr-\ *adj* : of or relating to circulation (as of the blood)
circulatory system *n* : the system of blood, lymph, vessels, and heart concerned with circulation of body fluids
cir·cum·cise \'sər-kəm-ˌsīz\ *vb* : to cut off the foreskin of
cir·cum·ci·sion \ˌsər-kəm-'sizh-ən\ *n* **1** : the act of circumcising or being circumcised; *esp* : a Jewish rite performed on male infants as a sign of inclusion in the covenant between God and Abraham **2** *cap* : January 1 observed as a church festival in commemoration of the circumcision of Christ
cir·cum·fer·ence \sə(r)-'kəm(p)-fərn(t)s, -f(ə-)rən(t)s\ *n* **1** : a line that goes around or encloses a circle **2** : the outer boundary of a figure or area **3** : the distance around a figure or object
cir·cum·flex \'sər-kəm-ˌfleks\ *n* : a mark ˆ over a vowel used chiefly to indicate length, contraction, or a specific vowel quality — **circumflex** *adj*
cir·cum·lo·cu·tion \ˌsər-kəm-lō-'kyü-shən\ *n* : the use of many words to express an idea that could be expressed in few — **cir·cum·loc·u·to·ry** \-'läk-yə-ˌtōr-ē, -ˌtȯr-\ *adj*
cir·cum·lu·nar \ˌsər-kəm-'lü-nər\ *adj* : revolving about or surrounding the moon
cir·cum·nav·i·gate \-'nav-ə-ˌgāt\ *vb* : to go completely around esp. by water ⟨*circumnavigate* the earth⟩ — **cir·cum·nav·i·ga·tion** \-ˌnav-ə-'gā-shən\ *n*
cir·cum·po·lar \-'pō-lər\ *adj* **1** : continually visible above the horizon ⟨a *circumpolar* star⟩ **2** : occurring in both Old and New World arctic regions
cir·cum·scribe \'sər-kəm-ˌskrīb\ *vb* **1** : to draw a line around **2** : to limit esp. narrowly
cir·cum·spect \'sər-kəm-ˌspekt\ *adj* : careful to consider all circumstances and possible consequences : PRUDENT — **cir·cum·spect·ly** *adv*
cir·cum·spec·tion \ˌsər-kəm-'spek-shən\ *n* : circumspect action : CAUTION, PRUDENCE
cir·cum·stance \'sər-kəm-ˌstan(t)s\ *n* **1** : a fact or event that must be considered along with another fact or event **2** *pl* : surrounding conditions ⟨impossible under the *circumstances*⟩ **3** *pl* : financial condition ⟨in easy *circumstances*⟩ **4** : formality accompanying an event : CEREMONY ⟨with pomp and *circumstance*⟩ **5** : a happening or fact in a chain of events : DETAIL **6** : CHANCE, FATE ⟨a victim of *circumstance*⟩
cir·cum·stanced \-ˌstan(t)st\ *adj* : placed in particular circumstances esp. in regard to property or income
cir·cum·stan·tial \ˌsər-kəm-'stan-chəl\ *adj* **1** : consisting of, relating to, or dependent on circumstances ⟨*circumstantial* evidence⟩ **2** : INCIDENTAL **3** : containing full details ⟨a *circumstantial* account of what happened⟩ — **cir·cum·stan·tial·ly** \-'stanch-(ə-)lē\ *adv*
cir·cum·vent \ˌsər-kəm-'vent\ *vb* **1** : to go around **2** : to evade or defeat by ingenuity or stratagem ⟨*circumvent* the law⟩ — **cir·cum·ven·tion** \-'ven-chən\ *n*
cir·cus \'sər-kəs\ *n* [from Latin, literally "circle", "ring"] **1 a** : a large arena enclosed by tiers of seats and used for spectacles (as athletic contests or exhibitions of horsemanship) **b** : a public spectacle **2 a** : an arena often covered by a tent and used for variety shows usu. including feats of physical skill and daring, wild animal acts, and performances by jugglers and clowns **b** : a circus performance **c** : the equipment, livestock, and personnel of such a circus
cir·rho·sis \sə-'rō-səs\ *n* : an increase in fibrous tissue and hardening esp. of the liver — **cir·rhot·ic** \-'rät-ik\ *adj or n*
cir·ro·cu·mu·lus \ˌsir-ō-'kyü-myə-ləs\ *n* : a cloud form of small white rounded masses at a high altitude usu. in lines and regular groups
cir·ro·stra·tus \-'strāt-əs, -'strat-\ *n* : a fairly uniform layer of high stratus darker than cirrus
cir·rus \'sir-əs\ *n, pl* **cir·ri** \'sir-ˌī\ : a wispy white cloud usu. of minute ice crystals formed at altitudes of 20,000 to 40,000 feet
cis·lu·nar \(')sis-'lü-nər\ *adj* : lying between the earth and the moon or the moon's orbit
cis·tern \'sis-tərn\ *n* : an often underground artificial reservoir or tank for storing water
cit·a·del \'sit-əd-əl, -ə-ˌdel\ *n* **1** : a fortress that commands a city **2** : STRONGHOLD
ci·ta·tion \sī-'tā-shən\ *n* **1** : an official order to appear (as before a court) **2 a** : an act or instance of quoting **b** : a passage quoted **3** : MENTION; *esp* : reference in a military dispatch to meritorious performance of duty

cite \'sīt\ *vb* **1** : to summon to appear before a court **2** : to quote as an example, authority, or proof **3** : to refer to; *esp* : to mention formally in commendation

cit·i·fy \'sit-i-ˌfī\ *vb* **-fied**; **-fy·ing** : to accustom to urban ways

cit·i·zen \'sit-ə-zən\ *n* **1** : an inhabitant of a city or town **2 a** : a member of a state **b** : a person who by birth or naturalization owes allegiance to a government and is entitled to protection from it **3** : CIVILIAN

cit·i·zen·ry \-rē\ *n* : the whole body of citizens

cit·i·zen·ship \-ˌship\ *n* **1** : possession of the rights and privileges of a citizen **2** : the quality of an individual's response to membership in a community

cit·rate \'si-ˌtrāt\ *n* : a salt or ester of citric acid

cit·ric acid \ˌsi-trik-\ *n* : a pleasantly sour-tasting organic acid obtained esp. from lemon and lime juices or by fermentation of sugars and used as a flavoring

cit·ron \'si-trən\ *n* **1 a** : a fruit like the lemon in appearance and structure but larger; *also* : the citrus tree producing this fruit **b** : the preserved rind of the citron used esp. in fruitcake **2** : a small hard-fleshed watermelon used esp. in pickles and preserves

cit·ro·nel·la \ˌsi-trə-'nel-ə\ *n* : a fragrant grass of southern Asia that yields an oil used in perfumery and as an insect repellent

cit·rus \'si-trəs\ *n, pl* **citrus** *or* **cit·rus·es** : any of a genus of often thorny trees and shrubs grown in warm regions for their fruits (as orange, grapefruit, or lemon)

citrus canker *n* : a destructive disease of the leaves, twigs, and fruits of citrus trees that is caused by a bacterium

city \'sit-ē\ *n, pl* **cit·ies** **1** : an inhabited place of greater size or importance than a town **2** : a usu. large place in the U.S. governed under a charter granted by the state **3** : the people of a city

city manager *n* : an official employed by an elected council to direct the administration of a city government

city–state \'sit-ē-'stāt, -ˌstāt\ *n* : a self-governing state (as of ancient Greece) consisting of a city and surrounding territory

civ *abbr* **1** civil **2** civilian

civ·et \'siv-ət\ *n* : a thick yellowish musky-odored substance obtained from the civet cat and used in perfume

civet cat *n* **1** : a long-bodied short-legged African mammal that produces most of the civet of commerce **2** : any of the small spotted skunks of western No. America

civet cat 1
(about 16 in. at shoulder)

civ·ic \'siv-ik\ *adj* : of or relating to a citizen, a city, or citizenship ⟨*civic* pride⟩ ⟨*civic* duty⟩ — **civ·i·cal·ly** \'siv-i-k(ə-)lē\ *adv*

civ·ics \'siv-iks\ *n* : the study of the rights and duties of citizens

civ·il \'siv-əl\ *adj* **1** : of or relating to citizens **2** : of or relating to the state as an organized political body ⟨*civil* institutions⟩ **3** : of or relating to the general population as distinguished from military or church affairs **4** : marked by courtesy or politeness ⟨a *civil* answer⟩ **5** : relating to legal proceedings in connection with private rights and obligations distinct from criminal proceedings ⟨a *civil* suit⟩

civil defense *n* : protective measures and emergency relief activities carried on by civilians in case of enemy attack

civil engineering *n* : engineering that deals with the designing and construction of public works (as roads or harbors) — **civil engineer** *n*

ci·vil·ian \sə-'vil-yən\ *n* : one not on active duty in a military, police, or fire-fighting force — **civilian** *adj*

ci·vil·i·ty \sə-'vil-ət-ē\ *n, pl* **-ties** **1** : POLITENESS, COURTESY **2** : a polite act or expression

civ·i·li·za·tion \ˌsiv-ə-lə-'zā-shən\ *n* **1 a** : a high level of cultural and technological development **b** : the special culture of a people or a period ⟨Greek *civilization*⟩ ⟨18th century *civilization*⟩ **2** : the process of becoming civilized **3** : refinement of thought, manners, or taste

civ·i·lize \'siv-ə-ˌlīz\ *vb* **1** : to raise out of a savage state; *esp* : to bring to an advanced and ordered stage of cultural development **2** : REFINE — **civ·i·lized** *adj*

civ·il·ly \'siv-əl-(l)ē\ *adv* : in a civil manner : POLITELY

civil rights *n pl* : the nonpolitical rights of a citizen; *esp* : the rights of personal liberty guaranteed to U.S. citizens by the 13th and 14th amendments to the Constitution and by acts of Congress

civil service *n* : the administrative service of a government exclusive of the armed forces

civil war *n* : a war between opposing groups of citizens of the same country or nation

ck *abbr* check

cl *abbr* centiliter

clack \'klak\ *vb* **1** : CHATTER, PRATTLE **2** : CLATTER — **clack** *n* — **clack·er** *n*

clad \'klad\ *adj* : CLOTHED, COVERED

1**claim** \'klām\ *vb* **1 a** : to ask for as one's right or property ⟨*claim* the inheritance⟩ ⟨*claimed* his bags⟩ **b** : to call for : REQUIRE ⟨this matter *claims* our attention⟩ **2 a** : to state as a fact : MAINTAIN ⟨*claimed* that he'd been cheated⟩ **b** : PROFESS ⟨*claimed* to know nothing of the matter⟩ — **claim·a·ble** \'klā-mə-bəl\ *adj* — **claim·er** *n*

2**claim** *n* **1** : a demand for something due or believed to be due ⟨insurance *claim*⟩ **2 a** : a right or title to something **b** : an assertion open to challenge ⟨a *claim* of authenticity⟩ **3** : something claimed; *esp* : a tract of land marked out by a settler or prospector

claim·ant \'klā-mənt\ *n* : a person who asserts his right to something

clair·voy·ance \kla(ə)r-'vȯi-ən(t)s, kle(ə)r-\ *n* : the professed power of seeing or knowing about things that are not present to the senses — **clair·voy·ant** \-ənt\ *adj*

1**clam** \'klam\ *n* **1** : any of numerous edible marine mollusks that have two hinged shells and live in sand or mud **2** : a freshwater mussel

clam

ə abut	ər further	a back	ā bake	
ä cot, cart	au̇ out	ch chin	e less	ē easy
g gift	i trip	ī life	j joke	ng sing
ō flow	ȯ flaw	ȯi coin	th thin	t͟h this
ü loot	u̇ foot	y yet	yü few	yu̇ furious
zh vision				

2**clam** *vb* **clammed**; **clam·ming** : to gather clams esp. by digging

clam·bake \'klam-ˌbāk\ *n* : a party or gathering at which clams are cooked usu. on heated rocks covered by seaweed

clarinet

clam·ber \'klam-bər\ *vb* **clam·bered**; **clam·ber·ing** \-b(ə-)riŋ\ : to climb awkwardly ⟨*clamber* over steep rocks⟩ — **clam·ber·er** \-bər-ər\ *n*

clam·my \'klam-ē\ *adj* **clam·mi·er**; **-est** : being damp, soft, sticky, and usu. cool — **clam·mi·ness** *n*

clam·or \'klam-ər\ *n* **1 a** : noisy shouting **b** : a loud continuous noise **2** : vigorous and insistent protest or demand — **clamor** *vb* — **clam·or·ous** \-ə-rəs\ *adj* — **clam·or·ous·ly** *adv*

1**clamp** \'klamp\ *n* : a device that holds or presses parts together firmly

2**clamp** *vb* : to fasten or tighten with or as if with a clamp

clamp down *vb* : to impose harsh penalties and restrictions ⟨*clamp down* on speeders⟩

clam worm *n* : any of several large burrowing annelid worms often used as bait

clan \'klan\ *n* [from Scottish Gaelic *clann* "offspring", "clan", from Old Irish *cland* "plant", "offspring", borrowed from Latin *planta* "plant"] **1** : a group (as in the Scottish Highlands) made up of households whose heads claim descent from a common ancestor **2** : a group of persons united by a common interest

clan·des·tine \klan-'des-tən\ *adj* : managed with planned secrecy : UNDERHAND ⟨a *clandestine* meeting⟩ — **clan·des·tine·ly** *adv*

clang \'klaŋ\ *n* : a loud ringing sound like that made by pieces of metal striking each other ⟨the *clang* of a fire alarm⟩ — **clang** *vb*

clan·gor \'klaŋ-(g)ər\ *n* : CLANG, DIN — **clan·gor·ous** \-(g)ə-rəs\ *adj*

1**clank** \'klaŋk\ *vb* : to make or move with a clank or series of clanks

2**clank** *n* : a sharp brief metallic ringing sound

clan·nish \'klan-ish\ *adj* : tending to associate only with one's own group — **clan·nish·ness** *n*

clans·man \'klanz-mən\ *n* : a member of a clan

1**clap** \'klap\ *vb* **clapped**; **clap·ping** **1** : to strike noisily : BANG ⟨*clap* two boards together⟩ ⟨the door *clapped* shut⟩ **2** : to strike the hands together repeatedly in applause : APPLAUD **3** : to strike with the open hand ⟨*clapped* his friend on the shoulder⟩ **4** : to put hastily ⟨*clapped* him in jail⟩ ⟨*clapped* on his hat and left⟩

2**clap** *n* **1** : a sound made by or as if by clapping ⟨a *clap* of thunder⟩ **2** : a hard slap ⟨a *clap* on the shoulder⟩

clap·board \'klab-ərd; 'kla(p)-ˌbōrd, -ˌbȯrd\ *n* : a narrow board thicker at one edge than at the other used horizontally for covering the outside of wooden buildings — **clapboard** *vb*

clap·per \'klap-ər\ *n* **1** : the tongue of a bell **2** : one of a pair of flat sticks held between the fingers and used to produce musical rhythms **3** : a person who applauds by clapping

clar·et \'klar-ət\ *n* **1** : a dry red table wine **2** : a dark purplish red — **claret** *adj*

clar·i·fy \'klar-ə-ˌfī\ *vb* **-fied**; **-fy·ing** **1** : to make or become pure or clear ⟨*clarify* a liquid⟩ **2** : to make or become more readily understandable ⟨*clarify* your meaning⟩ — **clar·i·fi·ca·tion** \ˌklar-ə-fə-'kā-shən\ *n* — **clar·i·fi·er** \'klar-ə-ˌfī(-ə)r\ *n*

clar·i·net \ˌklar-ə-'net, 'klar-ə-nət\ *n* : a single-reed woodwind instrument in the form of a cylindrical tube with flaring end — **clar·i·net·ist** *or* **clar·i·net·tist** \ˌklar-ə-'net-əst\ *n*

1**clar·i·on** \'klar-ē-ən\ *n* : a trumpet having very clear and shrill tones

2**clarion** *adj* : brilliantly clear ⟨a *clarion* call to action⟩

clar·i·ty \'klar-ət-ē\ *n* : CLEARNESS

1**clash** \'klash\ *vb* **1** : to make a clash ⟨*clashing* cymbals⟩ **2 a** : to come into conflict ⟨rebels *clashed* with the police⟩ **b** : to be sharply out of harmony ⟨some colors *clash*⟩ **3** : to cause to clash ⟨the deer rushed together, *clashing* their horns⟩ — **clash·er** *n*

2**clash** *n* **1 a** : a noisy usu. metallic sound of collision ⟨the *clash* of swords⟩ **b** : a noisy collision **2 a** : a hostile encounter ⟨a *clash* between two armies⟩ **b** : a sharp conflict ⟨a *clash* of opinion⟩

1**clasp** \'klasp\ *n* **1** : a device for holding together two objects or parts ⟨the *clasp* of a necklace⟩ **2** : EMBRACE, GRASP ⟨the warm *clasp* of his hand⟩

2**clasp** *vb* **1** : to fasten with or as if with a clasp **2** : EMBRACE **3** : GRASP — **clasp·er** *n*

clasp knife *n* : POCKETKNIFE; *esp* : one having a clasp for holding the blade open

1**class** \'klas\ *n* **1 a** : a group of persons of the same general economic or social status ⟨the working *class*⟩ **b** *pl* : persons of high social or economic status ⟨the *classes* as opposed to the masses⟩ **c** : high quality ⟨the team was competent but lacked *class*⟩ **2 a** : a course of instruction ⟨a *class* in arithmetic⟩ **b** : the group of pupils meeting regularly in a course ⟨a big *class* this year⟩ **c** : the period during which a study group meets **d** : a group of students who graduate together ⟨*class* of 1975⟩ **3 a** : a group or set alike in some way; *esp* : a major category in biological taxonomy ranking above the order and below the phylum or division **b** : a grouping based on quality ⟨a *class* A movie⟩ — **class·less** \-ləs\ *adj*

2**class** *vb* : CLASSIFY

1**clas·sic** \'klas-ik\ *adj* **1 a** : serving as a standard of excellence **b** : TRADITIONAL, ENDURING ⟨a *classic* heritage⟩ **2** : CLASSICAL 2 **3** : notable as the best or most typical instance ⟨the *classic* example of a dictator⟩

2**classic** *n* **1** : a literary work of ancient Greece or Rome **2** : a work of enduring excellence; *also* : its author **3** : something regarded as perfect of its kind **4** : a traditional event ⟨a football *classic*⟩

clas·si·cal \'klas-i-kəl\ *adj* **1** : CLASSIC 1a **2** : of or relating to the classics of literature or art; *esp* : of or relating to the ancient Greek and Roman classics ⟨*classical* studies⟩ **3** : TRADITIONAL, AUTHENTIC **4** : concerned with a general study of the arts and sciences and not specializing in technical studies ⟨a *classical* high school⟩ **5** : composed in accordance with a long-established musical form : appealing to a highly developed musical taste ⟨*classical* music⟩

clas·si·cal·ly \'klas-i-k(ə-)lē\ *adv* : in a classic or classical manner

clas·si·cism \'klas-ə-ˌsiz-əm\ *n* **1** : the principles or style embodied in the literature, art, or architecture of ancient Greece and Rome **2** : adherence to traditional standards (as of formal correctness, order, proportion) in music and art

clas·si·fi·ca·tion \ˌklas-ə-fə-'kā-shən\ *n* **1** : the act or process of classifying **2 a** : systematic arrange-

C

ment in groups; *esp* : TAXONOMY **b** : CLASS, CATEGORY — **clas·si·fi·ca·to·ry** \'klas-(ə-)fə-kə-ˌtōr-ē, -ˌtȯr-\ *adj*

clas·si·fied \'klas-ə-ˌfīd\ *adj* **1** : divided into classes or placed in a class **2** : withheld from general circulation for reasons of national security ⟨*classified* information⟩

clas·si·fy \'klas-ə-ˌfī\ *vb* **-fied; -fy·ing** : to arrange in or assign to classes ⟨*classify* books by subjects⟩ — **clas·si·fi·a·ble** \-ˌfī-ə-bəl\ *adj* — **clas·si·fi·er** \-ˌfī(-ə)r\ *n*

class·mate \'klas-ˌmāt\ *n* : a member of the same class in a school or college

class·room \-ˌrüm, -ˌru̇m\ *n* : a room in a school or college in which classes meet

1**clat·ter** \'klat-ər\ *vb* **1** : to make or cause to make a rattling sound ⟨*clattering* the dishes⟩ **2** : to move with a clatter — **clat·ter·er** \-ər-ər\ *n* — **clat·ter·ing·ly** \'klat-ə-ring-lē\ *adv*

2**clatter** *n* **1** : a rattling sound (as of hard bodies striking together) **2** : COMMOTION **3** : noisy chatter — **clat·tery** \'klat-ə-rē\ *adj*

clause \'klȯz\ *n* **1** : a separate distinct part of an article or document ⟨a *clause* in a will⟩ **2** : a group of words having its own subject and predicate but forming only part of a compound or complex sentence (as "when it rained" or "they went inside" in the sentence "when it rained they went inside")

claus·tro·pho·bia \ˌklȯ-strə-'fō-bē-ə\ *n* : abnormal fear of being in closed or narrow spaces — **claus·tro·pho·bic** \-bik\ *adj*

clav·i·chord \'klav-ə-ˌkȯrd\ *n* : an early keyboard instrument in use before the piano

clav·i·cle \'klav-i-kəl\ *n* : a bone of the shoulder that joins the breastbone and the shoulder blade — called also *collarbone*

1**claw** \'klȯ\ *n* **1 a** : a sharp usu. slender and curved nail on the toe of an animal **b** : a sharp curved process esp. if at the end of a limb (as of an insect); *also* : one of the pincerlike organs on some limbs of arthropods (as a lobster or scorpion) **2** : something (as the forked end of a hammer) that resembles a claw in shape or use — **claw·like** \-ˌlīk\ *adj*

2**claw** *vb* : to rake, seize, or dig with or as if with claws

clawed \'klȯd\ *adj* : having claws

clay \'klā\ *n* **1 a** : an earthy material that is plastic when moist but hard when fired, is composed chiefly of compounds of silica, aluminum, and water, and is used for brick, tile, and earthenware **b** : soil composed chiefly of this material **2** : wet earth : MUD **3** : a plastic substance used for modeling — **clay·ish** \-ish\ *adj*

clay·ey \'klā-ē\ *adj* **clay·i·er; -est** : resembling clay or containing much clay ⟨a *clayey* soil⟩

1**clean** \'klēn\ *adj* **1** : free from dirt or foreign matter ⟨*clean* clothes⟩ ⟨a *clean* plate⟩ **2** : PURE, HONORABLE **3** : THOROUGH, COMPLETE ⟨made a *clean* sweep⟩ **4** : SKILLFUL ⟨a good *clean* job⟩ **5** : SHAPELY, TRIM ⟨a ship with *clean* lines⟩ **6** : EVEN, SMOOTH ⟨a sharp knife makes a *clean* cut⟩ **7** : habitually neat — **clean·ness** \'klēn-nəs\ *n*

2**clean** *adv* **1 a** : so as to clean ⟨a new broom sweeps *clean*⟩ **b** : in a clean manner ⟨fight *clean*⟩ **2** : COMPLETELY ⟨bullet went *clean* through his arm⟩

ə abut	ər further	a back	ā bake	
ä cot, cart	au̇ out	ch chin	e less	ē easy
g gift	i trip	ī life	j joke	ng sing
ō flow	ȯ flaw	ȯi coin	th thin	th this
ü loot	u̇ foot	y yet	yü few	yu̇ furious
zh vision				

3**clean** *vb* **1** : to make or become clean ⟨*clean* this room⟩ ⟨*cleaned* up for supper⟩ **2** : to exhaust the contents or resources of ⟨tourists *cleaned* out the shops⟩ — **clean·er** *n*

clean–cut \'klēn-'kət\ *adj* : wholesomely neat ⟨a *clean-cut* young man⟩

1**clean·ly** \'klen-lē\ *adj* **clean·li·er; -est** **1** : careful to keep clean ⟨a *cleanly* animal⟩ **2** : habitually kept clean ⟨*cleanly* surroundings⟩ — **clean·li·ness** *n*

2**clean·ly** \'klēn-lē\ *adv* : in a clean manner ⟨hit a ball *cleanly*⟩

cleanse \'klenz\ *vb* : to make clean

cleans·er \'klen-zər\ *n* : a preparation (as a scouring powder or cold cream) used for cleaning

1**clear** \'kli(ə)r\ *adj* **1 a** : BRIGHT, LUMINOUS ⟨*clear* sunlight⟩ **b** : free from clouds, haze, or mist ⟨a *clear* day⟩ **c** : UNTROUBLED, SERENE ⟨a *clear* gaze⟩ **2 a** : free of blemishes ⟨a *clear* complexion⟩ **b** : easily seen through : TRANSPARENT ⟨*clear* glass⟩ **3** : easily heard, seen, or understood ⟨a *clear* voice⟩ ⟨his meaning was *clear*⟩ **4** : free from doubt : SURE ⟨a *clear* understanding of the issue⟩ **5** : INNOCENT ⟨a *clear* conscience⟩ **6** : free from restriction, obstruction, or entanglement ⟨a *clear* profit⟩ ⟨the coast is *clear*⟩ — **clear·ly** *adv* — **clear·ness** *n*

2**clear** *adv* **1** : in a clear manner ⟨shout loud and *clear*⟩ **2** : all the way : COMPLETELY ⟨can see *clear* to the mountains⟩

3**clear** *vb* **1 a** : to make or become clear ⟨*clear* the water by filtering⟩ ⟨the sky is *clearing*⟩ **b** : to go away : DISPERSE ⟨clouds *cleared* away after the rain⟩ **2 a** : to free from accusation or blame ⟨*cleared* his name⟩ **b** : to certify as trustworthy ⟨*cleared* for defense work⟩ **3** : EXPLAIN ⟨*cleared* the matter up for me⟩ **4** : to free from obstruction, restriction, or entanglement ⟨*clear* land for crops⟩ ⟨*clear* a path⟩ **5 a** : AUTHORIZE **b** : to gain official approval ⟨all bills must be *cleared* with the committee⟩ **6** : SETTLE ⟨*clear* an account⟩ **7** : to go through customs **8** : NET ⟨*cleared* a profit⟩ **9** : to get rid of : REMOVE ⟨*clear* away that trash⟩ **10 a** : to jump or go by without touching ⟨*cleared* the fence⟩ **b** : PASS ⟨the bill *cleared* the legislature⟩

4**clear** *n* : a clear space or part — **in the clear** **1** : free of resistance or obstruction **2** : free of suspicion

clear·ance \'klir-ən(t)s\ *n* **1 a** : an act or process of clearing; *esp* : the passage of checks and claims among banks through a clearinghouse **b** : a document stating that a person or ship has cleared or been cleared **2** : an offering of goods for quick sale usu. at reduced prices **3** : the distance by which one object clears another or the clear space between them

clear–cut \'kli(ə)r-'kət\ *adj* : sharply outlined : DISTINCT, DEFINITE ⟨a *clear-cut* case of fraud⟩

clear·ing \'kli(ə)r-ing\ *n* **1** : the act or process of making or becoming clear **2** : a tract of land cleared of wood and brush

clear·ing·house \-ˌhau̇s\ *n* **1** : an institution established and maintained by banks for exchanging of checks and claims **2** : a central agency for collecting and distributing information

1**cleat** \'klēt\ *n* **1** : a wedge-shaped piece fastened to something and used as a support or check (as for a rope on the spar of a ship) **2** : a wooden or metal device around which a rope may be made fast **3** : a strip or projecting piece fastened on or across something to give strength, to provide a grip, or to prevent slipping ⟨*cleats* on a football shoe⟩

2**cleat** *vb* **1** : to fasten to or by a cleat **2** : to provide with a cleat

cleav·age \'klē-vij\ *n* **1** : the quality possessed by a crystallized substance or rock of splitting along definite planes **2** : the action of cleaving : the state of being cleaved **3** : cell division; *esp* : the series of mitotic divisions of the egg that changes the single cell into a multicellular embryo

[1]**cleave**\ 'klēv\ *vb* **cleaved** \'klēvd\ *or* **clove** \'klōv\; **cleav·ing** : ADHERE, CLING

[2]**cleave** *vb* **cleaved** \'klēvd\ *also* **cleft** \'kleft\ *or* **clove** \'klōv\; **cleaved** *also* **cleft** *or* **clo·ven** \'klō-vən\; **cleav·ing** : to split by or as if by a cutting blow ⟨*cleaved* the pole with one swing⟩

cleav·er \'klē-vər\ *n* : one that cleaves; *esp* : a heavy knife with a broad blade used by a butcher esp. for chopping through bone

clef \'klef\ *n* : a sign placed on the staff in music to show what pitch is represented by each line and space

[1]**cleft** \'kleft\ *n* **1** : a space or opening made by splitting : FISSURE **2** : a hollow resembling a cleft

[2]**cleft** *adj* : partially split or divided

clem·a·tis \'klem-ət-əs, kli-'mat-əs\ *n* : a vine or herb related to the buttercups that has leaves with three leaflets and is widely grown for its showy usu. white or purple flowers

clem·en·cy \'klem-ən-sē\ *n, pl* **-cies** **1 a** : disposition to be merciful **b** : an act or instance of leniency **2** : mildness of weather ***syn*** see MERCY ***ant*** harshness

clem·ent \'klem-ənt\ *adj* **1** : inclined to be merciful : LENIENT **2** : TEMPERATE, MILD ⟨*clement* weather⟩ — **clem·ent·ly** *adv*

clench \'klench\ *vb* **1** : CLINCH 1 **2** : to hold fast : CLUTCH **3** : to set or close tightly ⟨*clenched* his hands⟩ — **clench** *n*

clere·sto·ry \'kli(ə)r-,stōr-ē, -,stȯr-\ *n, pl* **-ries** : an outside wall of a room or building that rises above an adjoining roof and contains windows

cler·gy \'klər-jē\ *n, pl* **clergies** : the body of religious officials (as priests, ministers, and rabbis) authorized to conduct services

cler·gy·man \-ji-mən\ *n* : a member of the clergy

cler·ic \'kler-ik\ *n* : CLERGYMAN

cler·i·cal \'kler-i-kəl\ *adj* **1** : of, relating to, or characteristic of the clergy or a clergyman **2** : of or relating to a clerk or office worker — **cler·i·cal·ly** \'kler-i-k(ə-)lē\ *adv*

clerical collar *n* : a narrow stiffly upright white collar buttoned at the back of the neck and worn by clergymen

[1]**clerk** \'klərk\ *n* **1** : an official responsible for correspondence, records, and accounts ⟨town *clerk*⟩ **2** : one employed to keep records or accounts or to perform general office work **3** : a salesman in a store

[2]**clerk** *vb* : to act or work as a clerk

clev·er \'klev-ər\ *adj* **1** : showing skill or resourcefulness **2** : quick in learning **3** : marked by wit or ingenuity — **clev·er·ish** \-(ə-)rish\ *adj* — **clev·er·ly** \-ər-lē\ *adv* — **clev·er·ness** \-ər-nəs\ *n*

[1]**clew** *or* **clue** \'klü\ *n* **1** : a ball of thread, yarn, or cord **2** *usu clue* : something that guides a person in solving something difficult or perplexing; *esp* : a piece of evidence in a crime **3** : a metal loop attached to the lower corner of a sail

[2]**clew** *or* **clue** *vb* **clewed** *or* **clued**; **clew·ing** *or* **clue·ing** *or* **clu·ing** **1** : to roll into a ball **2** *usu clue* : to provide with a clue **3** : to haul a sail up or down by ropes through the clews

cli·ché \kli-'shā\ *n* : a trite phrase or expression or the idea expressed by it

[1]**click** \'klik\ *n* : a slight sharp noise

[2]**click** *vb* **1** : to make or cause to make a click **2** : to fit or work together smoothly **3** : SUCCEED ⟨his idea *clicked*⟩

click beetle *n* : any of a family of beetles that are able when turned over to flip into the air by a sudden thoracic movement that produces a distinct click

cli·ent \'klī-ənt\ *n* **1** : a person who engages the professional services of another ⟨a lawyer's *clients*⟩ **2** : PATRON, CUSTOMER

cli·en·tele \,klī-ən-'tel\ *n* : a body of clients and esp. of customers

cliff \'klif\ *n* : a high steep face of rock

cli·mac·tic \klī-'mak-tik\ *adj* : of, relating to, or constituting a climax

cli·mate \'klī-mət\ *n* **[**from Latin *climat-*, stem of *clima*, from Greek *klima* "angle of inclination", "latitude", "zone", from *klinein* "to lean"**]** **1 a** : a region with specified weather conditions **b** : the average weather conditions of a particular place or region over a period of years **2** : the prevailing mood or conditions ⟨a favorable financial *climate*⟩ ⟨a *climate* of fear⟩ — **cli·mat·ic** \klī-'mat-ik\ *adj*

cli·ma·tol·o·gy \,klī-mə-'täl-ə-jē\ *n* : the science that deals with climates — **cli·ma·tol·o·gist** \-jəst\ *n*

[1]**cli·max** \'klī-,maks\ *n* **1** : a series of ideas or statements so arranged that they increase in force and power from the first to the last **2** : the highest or most forceful in a series **3** : the highest point : CULMINATION ⟨the storm had reached its *climax*⟩ **4** : ORGASM **5** : a relatively stable ecological stage or community

[2]**climax** *vb* : to come or bring to a climax

[1]**climb** \'klīm\ *vb* **1 a** : to go up or down by grasping or clinging with hands and feet ⟨*climb* a flagpole⟩ ⟨*climb* down a ladder⟩ **b** : to ascend in growth (as by twining) ⟨a *climbing* vine⟩ **2** : to rise gradually to a higher point ⟨*climb* from poverty to wealth⟩ **3** : to slope upward ⟨the road *climbs* steeply to the summit⟩ — **climb·a·ble** \'klī-mə-bəl\ *adj* — **climb·er** \-mər\ *n*

[2]**climb** *n* **1** : a place where climbing is necessary **2** : the act of climbing

clime \'klīm\ *n* : CLIMATE

[1]**clinch** \'klinch\ *vb* **1 a** : to turn over or flatten the protruding end of ⟨*clinch* a nail⟩ **b** : to fasten by clinching **2** : CONFIRM, SETTLE ⟨the evidence *clinched* the case⟩ **3** : to seize or grasp one another : GRAPPLE

[2]**clinch** *n* **1 a** : a fastening by means of a clinched nail, rivet, or bolt **b** : the clinched part of a nail, bolt, or rivet **2** : an act or instance of clinching in boxing

clinch·er \'klin-chər\ *n* : one that clinches; *esp* : a decisive fact or argument

cling \'kling\ *vb* **clung** \'kləng\; **cling·ing** \'kling-ing\ **1** : to adhere as if glued : STICK ⟨the shirt *clung* to his back⟩ **2** : to hold or hold on tightly or tenaciously ⟨*clung* desperately to the ladder⟩ **3** : to have a strong emotional attachment or dependence ⟨*clings* to her family⟩

cling·stone \'kling-,stōn\ *n* : a fruit (as a peach) whose flesh adheres strongly to the pit

clin·ic \'klin-ik\ *n* **1 a** : a class of medical instruction in which patients are examined and discussed **b** : a facility (as of a hospital) for the treatment of outpatients **2** : a class meeting devoted to the analysis and treatment of cases in a special field ⟨a writing *clinic* for poor students⟩

clin·i·cal \'klin-i-kəl\ *adj* **1** : of, relating to, or conducted in or as if in a clinic ⟨*clinical* examination⟩ **2** : involving or based on direct observation of the

C

patient ⟨*clinical* studies⟩ — **clin·i·cal·ly** \ˈklin-i-k(ə-)lē\ *adv*

clinical thermometer *n* : a thermometer for measuring body temperature that has a constriction in the tube where the column of liquid breaks and continues to indicate the maximum temperature to which the thermometer was exposed until reset by shaking

clink \ˈkliŋk\ *vb* : to make or cause to make a slight sharp short metallic sound ⟨glasses *clinked*⟩ — **clink** *n*

clin·ker \ˈkliŋ-kər\ *n* : a mass of stony matter fused together by fire (as in a furnace from impurities in the coal) : SLAG

cli·nom·e·ter \klī-ˈnäm-ət-ər\ *n* : an instrument for measuring angles of elevation or inclination

1**clip** \ˈklip\ *vb* **clipped**; **clip·ping** : to fasten with a clip ⟨*clip* the papers together⟩

2**clip** *n* **1** : a device that grips, clasps, or hooks **2** : a device to hold cartridges for a firearm **3** : a piece of jewelry held by a clip

3**clip** *vb* **clipped**; **clip·ping** **1 a** : to cut or cut off with or as if with shears ⟨*clip* a dog's hair⟩ ⟨*clipping* out news items⟩ **b** : to cut off or trim the hair or wool of **2** : HIT, PUNCH ⟨*clipped* him on the chin⟩

4**clip** *n* **1** : a 2-bladed instrument for cutting esp. the nails **2 a** : something (as the wool of a sheep) that is clipped **b** : a crop of wool **3** : a section of filmed material **4** : an act of clipping **5** : a sharp blow **6** : a rapid pace ⟨move along at a good *clip*⟩

clip·board \ˈklip-ˌbōrd, -ˌbȯrd\ *n* : a small writing board with a clip at the top for holding papers

clip·per \ˈklip-ər\ *n* **1** : one that clips **2** *pl* : an implement for clipping ⟨hair *clippers*⟩ **3** : a fast sailing vessel with an overhanging bow, tall masts, and a large sail area

clip·ping \ˈklip-iŋ\ *n* **1** : a cutting or shearing of something **2** : a piece clipped or cut out or off ⟨a newspaper *clipping*⟩ ⟨hedge *clippings*⟩

clique \ˈklēk, ˈklik\ *n* : a small exclusive group or set of people

clit·o·ris \ˈklit-ə-rəs, ˈklīt-\ *n* : a small structure in the female mammal corresponding to the male penis — **clit·o·ral** \-rəl\ *adj*

clk *abbr* clerk

clo·a·ca \klō-ˈā-kə\ *n*, *pl* **clo·a·cae** \-ˌkē, -ˌsē\ : a chamber into which the intestinal, urinary, and reproductive canals discharge in birds, reptiles, amphibians, and many fishes; *also* : a comparable chamber of an invertebrate — **clo·a·cal** \-ˈā-kəl\ *adj*

1**cloak** \ˈklōk\ *n* **1** : a loose outer garment usu. longer than a cape **2** : something that conceals or covers ⟨under the *cloak* of darkness⟩

2**cloak** *vb* : to cover or hide with a cloak

clob·ber \ˈkläb-ər\ *vb* **1** *slang* : to pound mercilessly **2** *slang* : to defeat overwhelmingly

1**clock** \ˈkläk\ *n* **1** : a device for measuring or telling the time; *esp* : one not intended to be worn or carried about by a person **2** : a registering device (as a dial) attached to a machine to measure or record its performance

2**clock** *vb* **1** : to time with a stopwatch or by an electric device **2** : to register on a mechanical recording device

ə abut	ər further	a back	ā bake	
ä cot, cart	aů out	ch chin	e less	ē easy
g gift	i trip	ī life	j joke	ŋ sing	ō flow
ȯ flaw	ȯi coin	th thin	th this	ü loot
ů foot	y yet	yü few	yů furious	zh vision

3**clock** *n* : an ornamental figure on a stocking

clock arithmetic *n* : MODULAR ARITHMETIC

clock·face \ˈkläk-ˌfās\ *n* : the dial face of a clock

clock·wise \-ˌwīz\ *adv* : in the direction in which the hands of a clock rotate — **clockwise** *adj*

clock·work \-ˌwərk\ *n* : machinery (as in a mechanical toy) containing a train of small wheels

clod \ˈkläd\ *n* **1** : a lump or mass esp. of earth or clay **2** : a dull or insensitive person : OAF — **clod·dish** \ˈkläd-ish\ *adj*

clod·hop·per \ˈkläd-ˌhäp-ər\ *n* **1** : RUSTIC, HICK **2** : a large heavy shoe

1**clog** \ˈkläg\ *n* **1 a** : a weight attached to a man or an animal to hinder motion **b** : something that hinders or restrains **2** : a shoe having a thick typically wooden sole

2**clog** *vb* **clogged**; **clog·ging** **1** : HINDER **2** : to obstruct passage through **3** : to fill or become filled beyond capacity (as with leaves or debris) ⟨the gutters *clogged* quickly⟩ **4** : to dance a clog dance

clog dance *n* : a dance in which the performer wears clogs and beats out a clattering rhythm on the floor — **clog dancing** *n*

1**clois·ter** \ˈklȯi-stər\ *n* **1 a** : MONASTERY, CONVENT **b** : monastic life **2** : a covered passage on the side of or around a court usu. having one side walled and the other open

2**cloister** *vb* **1** : to shut away from the world in or as if in a cloister ⟨leads a *cloistered* life⟩ **2** : to surround with a cloister ⟨*cloistered* gardens⟩

clone \ˈklōn\ *n* : the whole asexual progeny of an individual (as a plant increased by grafting) — **clon·al** \ˈklōn-əl\ *adj*

clop \ˈkläp\ *n* : a sound made by or as if by a hoof or wooden shoe against pavement — **clop** *vb*

1**close** \ˈklōz\ *vb* **1 a** : to move so as to bar passage through something ⟨*close* the gate⟩ ⟨*close* the switch⟩ **b** : to fill or block up ⟨*close* a gap⟩ ⟨*close* a street⟩ **2** : to stop the operations of ⟨*close* school⟩ **3** : to bring or come to an end : TERMINATE ⟨*close* a meeting⟩ **4** : to bring or bind together the parts or edges of ⟨a *closed* fist⟩ **5 a** : to draw near **b** : to engage in a struggle at close quarters : GRAPPLE ⟨*close* with the enemy⟩ **6** : to complete an agreement ⟨*close* a bargain⟩

2**close** \ˈklōz\ *n* : CONCLUSION, END

3**close** \ˈklōs\ *n* : an enclosed area

4**close** \ˈklōs\ *adj* **1** : having no openings : CLOSED **2 a** : SECLUDED, SECRET **b** : SECRETIVE **3** : STRICT, RIGOROUS ⟨keep *close* watch⟩ **4** : SULTRY, STUFFY **5** : STINGY, TIGHTFISTED **6** : having little space between items or units ⟨flying in *close* formation⟩ **7** : fitting tightly or exactly **8** : SHORT ⟨*close* haircut⟩ **9** : being near in time, space, effect, or degree **10** : INTIMATE, FAMILIAR ⟨a *close* friend⟩ **11** : ACCURATE, PRECISE ⟨*close* measurements⟩ ⟨a *close* observer⟩ **12** : decided by a narrow margin ⟨a *close* election⟩ — **close·ly** *adv* — **close·ness** *n*

5**close** \ˈklōs\ *adv* : in a close position or manner : NEAR

closed \ˈklōzd\ *adj* **1** : not open : ENCLOSED **2** : formed by a line that returns to its starting point ⟨*closed* curve⟩ **3** : having elements that when subjected to an operation produce only elements of the same set ⟨the whole numbers are *closed* under addition⟩ **4** : not admitting or not readily admitting new members ⟨a *closed* meeting⟩ ⟨a *closed* society⟩

closed circuit \ˈklōz(d)-\ *n* **1** : a circuit whose path goes completely around a course **2** : a television installation in which the signal is transmitted by wire to a limited number of receivers

close·fist·ed \ˈklōs-ˈfis-təd\ *adj* : STINGY

close·mouthed \-'mau̇thd, -'mau̇tht\ *adj* : rarely speaking

1**clos·et** \'kläz-ət\ *n* **1** : a small private room **2** : a cabinet or recess for china, household utensils, or clothing **3** : WATER CLOSET

2**closet** *vb* **1** : to shut up in or as if in a closet **2** : to take into a private room for an interview ⟨he was *closeted* for an hour with the governor⟩

close–up \'klōs-,əp\ *n* **1** : a photograph or movie shot taken at close range **2** : an intimate view or examination

clos·ing \'klō-zing\ *n* : a concluding part (as of a speech)

clo·sure \'klō-zhər\ *n* **1 a** : an act of closing **b** : the condition of being closed **c** : the property of being closed under a mathematical operation — called also *closure property* **2** : something that closes

1**clot** \'klät\ *n* : a mass or lump made by a liquid substance thickening and sticking together

2**clot** *vb* **clot·ted**; **clot·ting** : to become or cause to become a clot : form clots

cloth \'klȯth\ *n*, *pl* **cloths** \'klȯthz, 'klȯths\ **1** : a pliable sheet of material made usu. by weaving, felting, or knitting natural or synthetic fibers and filaments **2** : a piece of cloth used for a particular purpose **3** : the distinctive dress of a profession or calling and esp. of the clergy

clothe \'klōth\ *vb* **clothed** *or* **clad** \'klad\; **cloth·ing 1 a** : to cover with or as if with clothing : DRESS **b** : to provide with clothes **2** : to express by suitable language ⟨*clothed* his thought effectively⟩

clothes \'klō(th)z\ *n pl* **1** : CLOTHING **2** : BEDCLOTHES

clothes·horse \-,hȯrs\ *n* : a frame on which to hang clothes

clothes moth *n* : any of several small yellowish moths whose larvae eat wool, fur, or feathers

clothes·pin \-,pin\ *n* : a forked piece of wood or plastic or a small clamp for fastening clothes on a line

clothes·press \-,pres\ *n* : a receptacle for clothes

clothes tree *n* : an upright stand with hooks or pegs at the top on which to hang clothes

cloth·ier \'klōth-yər, 'klō-thē-ər\ *n* : one who makes or sells cloth or clothing

cloth·ing \'klō-thing\ *n* **1** : CLOTHES **2** : COVERING

1**cloud** \'klau̇d\ *n* [from Old English *clūd* "rock", "hill"] **1** : a visible mass of particles of water or ice in the form of fog, mist, or haze suspended usu. at a considerable height in the air **2** : a visible mass of minute particles in the air or a mass of obscuring matter in interstellar space **3** : a great crowd massed together : SWARM ⟨a *cloud* of mosquitoes⟩ **4** : something that appears dark or threatening ⟨war *clouds*⟩ **5** : something that obscures or blemishes ⟨a *cloud* on his reputation⟩ **6** : a dark vein or spot (as in marble) — **cloud·less** \-ləs\ *adj*

2**cloud** *vb* **1** : to make or become cloudy **2** : to darken, envelop, or hide with or as if by a cloud

cloud·burst \'klau̇d-,bərst\ *n* : a sudden heavy rainfall

cloud chamber *n* : a vessel containing saturated water vapor whose sudden cooling reveals the path of an ionizing particle (as an electron) by a trail of visible droplets

cloud·let \'klau̇d-lət\ *n* : a small cloud

cloudy \'klau̇d-ē\ *adj* **cloud·i·er**; **-est 1** : darkened by gloom or anxiety **2** : overcast with clouds ⟨a *cloudy* sky⟩ **3** : dimmed or dulled as if by clouds : not clear : MURKY **4** : marked with veins or spots — **cloud·i·ly** \'klau̇d-ə-lē\ *adv* — **cloud·i·ness** \'klau̇d-ē-nəs\ *n*

clout \'klau̇t\ *n* : a blow esp. with the hand or a bat — **clout** *vb*

1**clove** \'klōv\ *past of* CLEAVE

2**clove** *n* : the dried flower bud of a tropical tree related to myrtle that is used as a spice and as the source of an oil used in perfumery and medicine; *also* : this tree

clo·ven \'klō-vən\ *past part of* CLEAVE

cloven foot *n* : a foot (as of a sheep) divided into two parts at its outer extremity — **clo·ven–foot·ed** \,klō-vən-'fu̇t-əd\ *adj*

cloven hoof *n* : CLOVEN FOOT — **clo·ven–hoofed** \,klō-vən-'hu̇ft, -'hüft, -'hu̇vd, -'hüvd\ *adj*

clo·ver \'klō-vər\ *n* : any of a genus of leguminous herbs having leaves with three leaflets and flowers in dense heads and including many plants valuable for forage and as a source of nectar for bees; *also* : any of various related plants

clover

clo·ver·leaf \-,lēf\ *n* : a road plan that in shape resembles a four-leaf clover and that is used for passing one highway over another and routing traffic for turns by turnoffs that lead around to enter the other highway from the right

1**clown** \'klau̇n\ *n* **1** : a rude ill-bred person : BOOR **2** : a fool or comedian in an entertainment; *esp* : a grotesquely dressed comedy performer in a circus — **clown·ish** \'klau̇-nish\ *adj* — **clown·ish·ly** *adv* — **clown·ish·ness** *n*

2**clown** *vb* : to act like a clown

clown fish *n* : a brilliantly colored fish of southeastern Asia and Borneo that is often kept in the tropical aquarium

cloy \'klȯi\ *vb* : to make something orig. pleasing distasteful through an excess of it — **cloy·ing·ly** \-ing-lē\ *adv*

1**club** \'kləb\ *n* **1 a** : a heavy usu. tapering staff esp. of wood used as a weapon **b** : a stick or bat used for hitting a ball in a game **2 a** : a black figure resembling a clover leaf used to distinguish a suit of playing cards **b** : a card of the suit bearing clubs **3 a** : an association of persons for some common object **b** : the meeting place of a club

2**club** *vb* **clubbed**; **club·bing 1** : to beat or strike with or as if with a club **2** : to unite or combine for a common cause ⟨*club* together to buy a boat⟩

club·foot \'kləb-'fu̇t\ *n* : a misshapen foot twisted out of position from birth; *also* : this deformity — **club·foot·ed** \-əd\ *adj*

club moss *n* : any of an order of low often trailing evergreen plants (as the ground pine) having branching stems covered with small mosslike leaves and reproducing by spores usu. borne in club-shaped cones

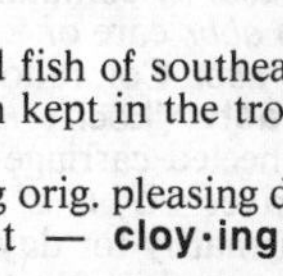
club moss

cluck \'klək\ *n* : the characteristic sound made by a hen esp. in calling her chicks — **cluck** *vb*

clue *var of* CLEW

clum·ber spaniel \,kləm-bər-\ *n*, *often cap* C & S : a large massive heavyset spaniel with a dense silky largely white coat

1**clump** \'kləmp\ *n* **1** : a group of things clustered together **2** : a compact mass : LUMP **3** : a heavy tramping sound — **clumpy** \'kləm-pē\ *adj*

2**clump** *vb* **1** : to tread clumsily and noisily **2** : to form or cause to form clumps

clum·sy \'kləm-zē\ *adj* **clum·si·er**; **-est** **1 a** : lacking dexterity, nimbleness, or grace ⟨*clumsy* fingers⟩ **b** : lacking tact or subtlety ⟨a *clumsy* joke⟩ **2** : awkwardly or poorly made : hard to use : UNWIELDY ⟨a *clumsy* tool⟩ — **clum·si·ly** \-zə-lē\ *adv* — **clum·si·ness** \-zē-nəs\ *n*

clung *past of* CLING

[1]**clus·ter** \'kləs-tər\ *n* : a number of similar things growing, collected, or grouped together : BUNCH

[2]**cluster** *vb* **clus·tered**; **clus·ter·ing** \-t(ə-)riŋ\ : to grow, collect, or gather in a cluster

[1]**clutch** \'kləch\ *vb* **1** : to grip with or as if with the hand or claws : GRASP **2** : to try to grasp and hold ⟨*clutch* at a swinging rope⟩

[2]**clutch** *n* **1 a** : the claws or a hand in the act of grasping **b** : CONTROL, POWER **2** : a device for gripping an object **3 a** : a coupling used to connect and disconnect a driving and a driven part of a mechanism **b** : a lever operating a clutch **4** : a tight or critical situation : PINCH

[3]**clutch** *n* : a nest or batch of eggs or a brood of chicks

[1]**clut·ter** \'klət-ər\ *vb* : to fill or cover with a disorderly scattering of things ⟨*clutter* up a room⟩

[2]**clutter** *n* : a crowded or confused collection

cm *abbr* centimeter

CNS *abbr* central nervous system

co- *prefix* **1** : with : together : joint : jointly ⟨*co*exist⟩ ⟨*co*heir⟩ **2** : in or to the same degree ⟨*co*extensive⟩ **3** : fellow : partner ⟨*co*author⟩ ⟨*co*-worker⟩

co *abbr* **1** company **2** county

c/o *abbr* care of

CO *abbr* Colorado

[1]**coach** \'kōch\ *n* **1 a** : a large usu. closed four-wheeled carriage with a raised seat in front for the driver **b** : a railroad passenger car intended primarily for day travel **c** : BUS **d** : a closed 2-door automobile for 4 or 5 passengers **2** : a class of passenger air transportation at a lower fare than first class **3 a** : a private tutor **b** : one who instructs or trains a performer or team

[2]**coach** *vb* : to instruct, direct, or prompt as a coach

coach dog *n* : DALMATIAN

coach·man \'kōch-mən\ *n* : a man whose business is driving a coach or carriage

co·ad·ju·tor \ˌkō-ə-'jüt-ər, kō-'aj-ət-ər\ *n* **1** : ASSISTANT **2** : a bishop who assists a diocesan bishop with the right to succeed him — **coadjutor** *adj*

co·ag·u·la·ble \kō-'ag-yə-lə-bəl\ *adj* : capable of being coagulated — **co·ag·u·la·bil·i·ty** \-ˌag-yə-lə-'bil-ət-ē\ *n*

co·ag·u·lant \-'ag-yə-lənt\ *n* : something that produces coagulation

co·ag·u·late \kō-'ag-yə-ˌlāt\ *vb* : to become or cause to become thickened into a compact mass : CLOT — **co·ag·u·la·tion** \-ˌag-yə-'lā-shən\ *n*

coagulation time *n* : the time required for shed blood to clot

[1]**coal** \'kōl\ *n* **1** : a piece of glowing or charred wood : EMBER **2** : a black solid mineral that is formed by the partial decay of vegetable matter under the influence of moisture and often increased pressure and temperature within the earth and that is mined for use as a fuel

ə abut	ər further	a back	ā bake	
ä cot, cart	aù out	ch chin	e less	ē easy
g gift	i trip	ī life	j joke	ŋ sing	ō flow
ȯ flaw	ȯi coin	th thin	th this	ü loot
ù foot	y yet	yü few	yù furious	zh vision

[2]**coal** *vb* **1** : to supply with coal **2** : to take in coal

Coal Age *n* : a geologic period (as the late Carboniferous) during which extensive coal deposits were formed

co·a·lesce \ˌkō-ə-'les\ *vb* **1** : to grow together ⟨the ends of the broken bones *coalesced*⟩ **2** : to unite into a whole : FUSE ***syn*** see MINGLE

coal gas *n* : gas from coal; *esp* : gas made by distilling bituminous coal and used for heating

co·a·li·tion \ˌkō-ə-'lish-ən\ *n* : UNION, COMBINATION; *esp* : a temporary union of persons, parties, or countries for a common purpose — **co·a·li·tion·ist** \-'lish-(ə-)nəst\ *n*

coal oil *n* **1** : a refined oil prepared from petroleum : PETROLEUM **2** : KEROSENE

coal tar *n* : tar obtained by distilling bituminous coal and used in making drugs, dyes, and explosives

coarse \'kōrs, 'kȯrs\ *adj* **1** : of ordinary or inferior quality or appearance : COMMON **2** : composed of large parts or particles ⟨*coarse* sand⟩ **3** : ROUGH, HARSH ⟨*coarse* skin⟩ **4** : not precise or detailed with respect to adjustment or discrimination **5** : crude in taste, manners, or language — **coarse·ly** *adv* — **coars·en** \-ən\ *vb* — **coarse·ness** *n*

[1]**coast** \'kōst\ *n* **1** : the land at or near esp. a long stretch of shoreline **2 a** : a slope suited to sliding (as on a sled) downhill **b** : a slide down such a slope

[2]**coast** *vb* **1** : to sail along a coast **2 a** : to slide or glide downhill by the force of gravity **b** : to move along (as on a bicycle when not pedaling) without applying power

coast·al \'kō-stəl\ *adj* **1** : relating to a coast **2** : located on, near, or along a coast ⟨*coastal* trade⟩

coastal plain *n* : a plain extending inland from a seashore

coast·er \'kō-stər\ *n* **1** : one that coasts; *esp* : a ship engaged in coastal trade **2 a** : a round tray often on wheels **b** : a shallow container or a plate or a mat to protect a surface **c** : a sled or wagon used in coasting

coast guard *n* **1** : a military force employed in guarding or patrolling a coast **2** : a member of a coast guard — **coast·guards·man** \'kōs(t)-ˌgärdz-mən\ *n*

coast·line \'kōst-ˌlīn\ *n* : the outline or shape of a coast

coast·wise \'kōst-ˌwīz\ *adv* : by way of or along the coast — **coastwise** *adj*

[1]**coat** \'kōt\ *n* **1** : an outer garment varying in length and style according to fashion and use **2** : the external growth (as of fur) on an animal **3** : a covering layer ⟨a *coat* of paint⟩ — **coat·ed** \-əd\ *adj*

[2]**coat** *vb* : to cover with a coat

co·a·ti \kə-'wät-ē, ˌkō-ə-'tē\ *n* : a tropical American mammal related to the raccoon but with a longer body and tail and a long flexible snout

coati
(about 11 in. at shoulder)

coat·ing \'kōt-iŋ\ *n* **1** : COAT, COVERING ⟨a *coating* of ice on the pond⟩ **2** : cloth for coats

coat of arms : heraldic arms (as of a person or family) displayed on a shield or surface

coat of mail : a garment of metal scales or rings worn as armor

co·au·thor \(ˈ)kō-ˈȯ-thər\ *n* : a joint author

coax \ˈkōks\ *vb* : to influence or gain by gentle urging, caressing, or flattering — **coax·er** *n*

co·ax·i·al cable \kō-ˌak-sē-əl-\ *n* : a cable that consists of a tube of electrically conducting material surrounding a central conductor and is used to transmit telegraph, telephone, and television signals

cob \ˈkäb\ *n* **1** : a male swan **2** : CORNCOB **3** : a short-legged stocky horse usu. with a high stylish step

co·bal·a·min \kō-ˈbal-ə-mən, -mēn\ *n* : a member of the vitamin B_{12} group; *also* : the vitamin B_{12} group

co·balt \ˈkō-ˌbȯlt\ *n* [from German *kobalt*, alteration of *kobold*, literally "goblin", "kobold"; so called from its appearance in silver ore where it was believed to have been placed by silver-stealing goblins] : a tough shiny silver-white magnetic metallic element that occurs with iron and nickel — see ELEMENT table

cobalt chloride *n* : a chloride of cobalt; *esp* : the dichloride which is dark red when hydrated, blue when dehydrated, and used in solution as a secret ink

cobalt 60 *n* : a heavy radioactive isotope of cobalt of the mass number 60 produced in nuclear reactors and used as a source of gamma rays

[1]**cob·ble** \ˈkäb-əl\ *vb* **cob·bled**; **cob·bling** \-(ə-)liŋ\ : to make roughly or hastily

[2]**cobble** *n* : a rounded stone larger than a pebble and smaller than a boulder

[3]**cobble** *vb* : to pave with cobbles

cob·bler \ˈkäb-lər\ *n* **1** : a mender or maker of shoes **2** : a deep-dish fruit pie with a thick top crust

cob·ble·stone \ˈkäb-əl-ˌstōn\ *n* : COBBLE

co·bra \ˈkō-brə\ *n* : any of several venomous Asiatic and African snakes that when excited expand the skin of the neck into a hood; *also* : any of several related African snakes

cob·web \ˈkäb-ˌweb\ *n* **1** : SPIDERWEB **2** : a single thread spun by a spider or insect larva — **cob·webbed** \-ˌwebd\ *adj* — **cob·web·by** \-ˌweb-ē\ *adj*

co·ca \ˈkō-kə\ *n* : a So. American shrub with leaves resembling tea that are chewed by the natives to impart endurance and are the source of cocaine; *also* : its dried leaves

co·caine \kō-ˈkān\ *n* : a bitter addictive narcotic drug obtained from coca leaves and used esp. to deaden pain

coc·cid \ˈkäk-səd\ *n* : SCALE INSECT, MEALYBUG

coc·cus \ˈkäk-əs\ *n, pl* **coc·ci** \ˈkäk-ˌ(s)ī, ˈkäk-(ˌ)(s)ē\ : a spherical bacterium — **coc·cal** \ˈkäk-əl\ *adj*

coc·cyx \ˈkäk-siks\ *n, pl* **coc·cy·ges** \ˈkäk-sə-ˌjēz\ *also* **coc·cyx·es** : the bone at the end of the spinal column that is composed of four fused vertebrae

coch·i·neal \ˈkäch-ə-ˌnēl, ˈkō-chə-\ *n* : a red dyestuff consisting of the dried bodies of female cochineal insects used esp. as a biological stain

cochineal insect *n* : a small bright red insect that is related to and resembles the mealybug, feeds on cactus, and yields cochineal

co·chlea \ˈkō-klē-ə, ˈkäk-lē-\ *n, pl* **-chle·ae** \-klē-ˌē, -lē-ˌē, -ˌī\ *or* **-le·as** : a part of the inner ear of higher vertebrates that is usu. coiled like a snail shell and is the seat of the hearing organ — **coch·le·ar** \-ər\ *adj*

[1]**cock** \ˈkäk\ *n* **1** : the adult male of a bird and esp. the domestic fowl **2** : a faucet or valve for regulating the flow of a liquid **3** : the cocked position of the hammer of a firearm

[2]**cock** *vb* **1** : to draw back the hammer of ⟨*cock* a pistol⟩ **2** : to turn, tip, or tilt upward or to one side

[3]**cock** *n* : TILT, SLANT

[4]**cock** *n* : a small pile (as of hay)

[5]**cock** *vb* : to put (as hay) into cocks

cock·ade \kä-ˈkād\ *n* : an ornament (as a rosette) worn on the hat as a badge

cock·a·too \ˈkäk-ə-ˌtü\ *n, pl* **-toos** : any of numerous large noisy usu. showy and crested chiefly Australasian parrots

cock·cha·fer \ˈkäk-ˌchā-fər\ *n* : a large European beetle destructive to vegetation; *also* : any of various related beetles

cock·crow \-ˌkrō\ *n* : the time of day at which cocks first crow : early morning

cock·er·el \ˈkäk-(ə-)rəl\ *n* : a young male domestic fowl

cock·er spaniel \ˌkäk-ər-\ *n* : a small spaniel with long ears, square muzzle, and silky coat

cock·eyed \ˈkäk-ˈīd\ *adj* **1** : having a squinting eye **2** *slang* **a** : ASKEW, AWRY **b** : slightly crazy

[1]**cock·le** \ˈkäk-əl\ *n* : any of several grainfield weeds; *esp* : CORN COCKLE

[2]**cockle** *n* **1** : an edible mollusk with a heart-shaped 2-valved shell **2** : COCKLESHELL

cock·le·bur \ˈkäk-əl-ˌbər, ˈkək-\ *n* : any of a genus of prickly-fruited plants related to the thistles; *also* : one of its fruits

cock·le·shell \ˈkäk-əl-ˌshel\ *n* **1 a** : a shell or shell valve of a cockle **b** : a shell (as a scallop) suggesting a cockleshell **2** : a light flimsy boat

cock·ney \ˈkäk-nē\ *n, pl* **cockneys** *often cap* **1** : a native of London and esp. of the East End of London **2** : the dialect spoken by the cockneys — **cockney** *adj*

cockleshell 1a

cock·pit \ˈkäk-ˌpit\ *n* **1** : an open space aft of a decked area of a small boat **2** : a space in the fuselage of an airplane for the pilot or the pilot and passengers or the pilot and crew

cock·roach \ˈkäk-ˌrōch\ *n* : any of an order of swift-running insect pests that have long antennae and a leathery body wall, are found in houses and ships, and are active chiefly at night

cocks·comb \ˈkäks-ˌkōm\ *n* : a garden plant related to the amaranth and grown for its showy flower clusters

cock·sure \ˈkäk-ˈshu̇(ə)r\ *adj* **1** : perfectly sure : CERTAIN **2** : OVERCONFIDENT, COCKY

cock·tail \-ˌtāl\ *n* **1** : an iced drink of distilled liquor mixed with flavoring ingredients **2** : an appetizer (as tomato juice) served as a first course at a meal

cocky \ˈkäk-ē\ *adj* **cock·i·er**; **-est** : PERT, CONCEITED — **cock·i·ly** \ˈkäk-ə-lē\ *adv* — **cock·i·ness** \ˈkäk-ē-nəs\ *n*

[1]**co·co** \ˈkō-kō\ *n, pl* **cocos** : the coconut palm or its fruit

[2]**coco** *adj* : made from the fibrous husk of the coconut

co·coa \ˈkō-kō\ *n* **1** : a cacao tree **2 a** : chocolate freed of some of its fat and ground **b** : a beverage prepared by cooking cocoa powder with water or milk

cocoa butter *n* : a pale fat obtained from cacao

co·co·nut *also* **co·coa·nut** \ˈkō-kə-(ˌ)nət\ *n* : the egg-shaped, husk-covered nutlike fruit of the coconut palm

coconut oil *n* : a nearly colorless oil or soft white fat extracted from coconuts or copra and used in soaps and foods

coconut palm *n* : a tall tropical palm with finely divided leaves that is prob. of American origin

co·coon \kə-'kün\ *n* **1** : a usu. silken envelope which an insect larva (as a caterpillar) forms about itself and in which it passes the pupa stage **2** : a covering suggesting a cocoon

coconut palm and section of fruit

cod \'käd\ *n, pl* **cod** *also* **cods** : a soft-finned fish of the colder parts of the No. Atlantic that is a major food fish; *also* : any of several related fishes

COD *abbr* **1** cash on delivery **2** collect on delivery

co·da \'kōd-ə\ *n* : a closing section in a musical composition

cod·dle \'käd-əl\ *vb* **cod·dled**; **cod·dling** \-(ə-)liŋ\ **1** : to cook slowly in water below the boiling point ⟨*coddle* eggs⟩ **2** : to treat as a little child or a pet : PAMPER

[1]**code** \'kōd\ *n* **1** : a systematic collection of laws **2** : a system of principles or rules ⟨moral *code*⟩ **3** : a system of signals for communicating **4** : a system of letters or symbols used (as in secret communications or in a computing machine) with special meanings

[2]**code** *vb* : to put into the form of a code — **cod·er** *n*

co·deine *or* **co·dein** \'kō-ˌdēn, 'kōd-ē-ən\ *n* : a drug that is obtained from opium, is weaker than morphine, and is used in cough remedies

cod·fish \'käd-ˌfish\ *n* : COD

cod·ger \'käj-ər\ *n* : an odd or cranky fellow

cod·i·fy \'käd-ə-ˌfī, 'kōd-\ *vb* **-fied**; **-fy·ing** : to arrange (as a collection of laws) in a systematic form — **cod·i·fi·ca·tion** \ˌkäd-ə-fə-'kā-shən, ˌkōd-\ *n*

cod·ling \'käd-liŋ\ *or* **cod·lin** \-lən\ *n* : a small immature apple; *also* : any of several elongated greenish English cooking apples

codling moth *n* : a small stout-bodied moth whose larva lives in apples, pears, quinces, and English walnuts

cod–liver oil *n* : an oil obtained from the liver of the cod and closely related fishes and used as a source of vitamins A and D

coed \'kō-ˌed\ *n* : a female student in a coeducational institution

co·ed·u·ca·tion \(ˌ)kō-ˌej-ə-'kā-shən\ *n* : education of male and female students at the same school or college — **co·ed·u·ca·tion·al** \-sh(ə-)nəl\ *adj*

co·ef·fi·cient \ˌkō-ə-'fish-ənt\ *n* **1** : a number or symbol (as *3* in *3x*) that is a multiplier of another **2** : a number that serves as a measure of some property or characteristic (as of a substance or device)

coe·la·canth \'sē-lə-ˌkan(t)th\ *n* : a fish or fossil of a family of mostly extinct fishes — **coelacanth** *adj*

coe·len·ter·ate \si-'lent-ə-ˌrāt, -rət\ *n* : any of a phylum of invertebrate animals that include the corals, sea anemones, jellyfishes, and hydroids and usu. have radial body symmetry — **coelenterate** *adj*

coe·lom \'sē-ləm\ *n, pl* **coe·loms** *or* **coe·lo·ma·ta** \si-'lō-mət-ə\ : the usu. epithelium-lined body cavity that occurs in animals above the lower worms — **coe·lo·mate** \'sē-lə-ˌmāt\ *adj or n* — **coe·lom·ic** \si-'läm-ik, -'lō-mik\ *adj*

co·en·zyme \(')kō-'en-ˌzīm\ *n* : a substance (as a vitamin) intimately associated with an enzyme and essential for its normal function

co·equal \(')kō-'ē-kwəl\ *adj* : equal esp. in rank or status — **co·equal·ly** \-kwə-lē\ *adv*

co·erce \kō-'ərs\ *vb* **1** : to restrain or dominate by threat or force **2** : to enforce by force : COMPEL ⟨*coerce* obedience⟩ — **co·er·cion** \-'ər-zhən, -shən\ *n* — **co·er·cive** \-'ər-siv\ *adj*

co·eval \kō-'ē-vəl\ *adj* : of the same age or duration

co·ex·ist \ˌkō-ig-'zist\ *vb* **1** : to exist together or at the same time **2** : to live in peace with each other — **co·ex·ist·ence** \-'zis-tən(t)s\ *n* — **co·ex·ist·ent** \-tənt\ *adj*

co·ex·ten·sive \ˌkō-ik-'sten(t)-siv\ *adj* : having the same scope or extent in space or time — **co·ex·ten·sive·ly** *adv*

cof·fee \'kȯ-fē, 'käf-ē\ *n* [from Turkish *kahve*, from Arabic *qahwah*] **1** : a drink made from the roasted and ground or pounded seeds of a tropical tree or shrub related to the madder **2** : coffee seeds or a plant producing them

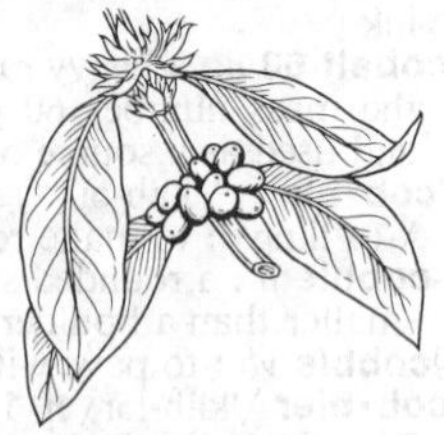

coffee 2

cof·fee·pot \-ˌpät\ *n* : a covered utensil for preparing or serving coffee

coffee table *n* : a low table placed in front of a sofa

cof·fer \'kȯ-fər, 'käf-ər\ *n* **1** : CHEST, BOX; *esp* : a strongbox for valuables **2** : TREASURY, FUNDS — usu. used in pl.

cof·fin \'kȯ-fən\ *n* : a box for a corpse to be buried in : CASKET

cog \'käg\ *n* : a tooth on the rim of a wheel adjusted to fit notches in another wheel or bar and to give or receive motion

co·gent \'kō-jənt\ *adj* : having power to compel; *esp* : appealing forcibly to the mind : CONVINCING — **co·gen·cy** \-jən-sē\ *n* — **co·gent·ly** *adv*

cog·i·tate \'käj-ə-ˌtāt\ *vb* : to think over : PONDER — **cog·i·ta·tion** \ˌkäj-ə-'tā-shən\ *n*

co·gnac \'kōn-ˌyak\ *n* : a French brandy

cog·ni·tion \käg-'nish-ən\ *n* **1** : the act or process of knowing **2** : something known by cognition — **cog·ni·tive** \'käg-nət-iv\ *adj*

cog·ni·zance \'käg-nə-zən(t)s\ *n* **1** : KNOWLEDGE **2** : NOTICE, HEED ⟨take *cognizance* of what is happening⟩ — **cog·ni·zant** \-zənt\ *adj*

cog·no·men \käg-'nō-mən, 'käg-nə-mən\ *n, pl* **-nomens** *or* **-no·mi·na** \-'näm-ə-nə, -'nō-mə-\ **1** : SURNAME **2** : NAME; *esp* : NICKNAME

cog·wheel \'käg-ˌhwēl\ *n* : a wheel with cogs on the rim

co·hab·it \kō-'hab-ət\ *vb* : to live together as husband and wife — **co·hab·i·ta·tion** \kō-ˌhab-ə-'tā-shən\ *n*

co·here \kō-'hi(ə)r\ *vb* **1 a** : to hold together firmly as parts of the same mass **b** : to consist of parts that cohere **2 a** : to become united in principles, relationships, or interests **b** : to be consistent — **co·her·ence** \-'hir-ən(t)s, -'her-\ *n* — **co·her·ent** \-ənt\ *adj* — **co·her·ent·ly** *adv*

co·he·sion \kō-'hē-zhən\ *n* **1** : the action of sticking together tightly **2** : molecular attraction by which the particles of a body are united throughout the

ə abut	ər further	a back	ā bake	
ä cot, cart	aů out	ch chin	e less	ē easy
g gift	i trip	ī life	j joke	ŋ sing	ō flow
ȯ flaw	ȯi coin	th thin	t͟h this	ü loot
ů foot	y yet	yü few	yů furious	zh vision

mass — **co·he·sive** \-'hē-siv, -ziv\ *adj* — **co·he·sive·ness** *n*

co·hort \'kō-ˌhȯrt\ *n* **1 a :** one of 10 divisions of an ancient Roman legion **b :** a group of warriors or followers **2 :** COMPANION, ACCOMPLICE

[1]**coif** \'kȯif, *in sense 2 usu* 'kwäf\ *n* **1 :** a close-fitting cap **2 :** COIFFURE

[2]**coif** \'kȯif, 'kwäf\ *or* **coiffe** \'kwäf\ *vb* **coiffed** *or* **coifed; coiff·ing** *or* **coif·ing :** to provide with a coif

coif·fure \kwä-'fyu̇(ə)r\ *n* **:** a manner of arranging the hair

[1]**coil** \'kȯil\ *vb* **1 :** to wind into or lie in a coil **2 :** to move in a circular, spiral, or winding course

[2]**coil** *n* **1 a :** a series of loops **:** SPIRAL **b :** a single loop of a coil **2 :** a number of turns of wire esp. in spiral form usu. for electromagnetic effect or for providing electrical resistance **3 :** a series of connected pipes (as in water-heating apparatus) in rows, layers, or windings

[1]**coin** \'kȯin\ *n* **1 :** a piece of metal **2 :** metal money

[2]**coin** *vb* **1 a :** to make (a coin) esp. by stamping **:** MINT **b :** to convert (metal) into coins **2 :** CREATE, INVENT ⟨*coin* a phrase⟩ — **coin·er** *n*

coin·age \'kȯi-nij\ *n* **1 :** the act or process of coining **2 :** COINS **3 :** something (as a word) made up or invented

co·in·cide \ˌkō-ən-'sīd\ *vb* **1 :** to occupy the same place in space or time ⟨his birthday *coincides* with Christmas⟩ **2 :** to be the same shape and size **3 :** to correspond or agree exactly

co·in·ci·dence \kō-'in(t)-səd-ən(t)s\ *n* **1 :** the act or condition of coinciding **2 a :** two things that happen at the same time by accident but seem to have some connection **b :** either one of these happenings

co·in·ci·dent \-səd-ənt\ *adj* **1 :** occupying the same space or time ⟨*coincident* events⟩ **2 :** of similar nature **:** HARMONIOUS ⟨a theory *coincident* with the facts⟩ — **co·in·ci·dent·ly** *adv*

co·in·ci·den·tal \(ˌ)kō-ˌin(t)-sə-'dent-əl\ *adj* **1 :** resulting from a coincidence **2 :** COINCIDENT 1 — **co·in·ci·den·tal·ly** \-'dent-(ə-)lē\ *adv*

co·i·tus \'kō-ət-əs\ *n* **:** sexual intercourse

coke \kōk\ *n* **:** gray porous lumps of fuel made by heating soft coal in a closed chamber until some of its gases have passed off

col- — see COM-

col *abbr* colonel

co·la \'kō-lə\ *n* **:** a carbonated soft drink usu. containing caffeine, sugar, and flavoring (as extract of kola nut, caramel, and acid and aromatic substances)

col·an·der \'kəl-ən-dər, 'käl-\ *n* **:** a perforated utensil for draining food

col·chi·cine \'käl-chə-ˌsēn, 'käl-kə-\ *n* **:** a poisonous substance from the corms or seeds of the meadow saffron used on cells to induce variation in chromosome numbers and produce new varieties of plants

[1]**cold** \'kōld\ *adj* **1 :** having a low temperature or one decidedly below normal ⟨a *cold* day⟩ ⟨a *cold* drink⟩ **2 :** lacking warmth of feeling **:** UNFRIENDLY ⟨a *cold* welcome⟩ **3 :** suffering or uncomfortable from lack of warmth ⟨feel *cold*⟩ — **cold·ly** *adv* — **cold·ness** \'kōl(d)-nəs\ *n* — **in cold blood :** with premeditation **:** DELIBERATELY

[2]**cold** *n* **1 a :** a condition of low temperature **b :** cold weather **2 :** bodily sensation produced by loss or lack of heat **:** CHILL **3 :** a bodily disorder popularly associated with chilling; *esp* **:** COMMON COLD

cold–blood·ed \'kōl(d)-'bləd-əd\ *adj* **1 :** lacking or showing a lack of natural human feelings ⟨a *cold-blooded* criminal⟩ **2 :** having cold blood; *esp* **:** having a body temperature close to that of the environment **3 :** sensitive to cold — **cold–blood·ed·ly** *adv*

cold chisel *n* **:** a strong steel chisel for chipping and cutting cold metal

cold cream *n* **:** a creamy preparation for cleansing, softening, and soothing the skin

cold cuts *n pl* **:** sliced assorted cold meats

cold frame *n* **:** a usu. glass-covered frame without artificial heat used to protect plants and seedlings

cold front *n* **:** the boundary between an advancing mass of cold or cool air and a mass of warmer air

cold shoulder *n* **:** intentionally cold or unsympathetic treatment — **cold–shoulder** *vb*

cold sore *n* **:** a group of blisters about or within the mouth caused by a common virus

cold sweat *n* **:** perspiration and chill occurring together and usu. associated with fear, pain, or shock

cold war *n* **:** a struggle or a state of strife between two nations or groups of nations carried on by means short of war (as propaganda, economic pressure, formation of political alliances, and threatening military maneuvers)

cold wave *n* **:** a period of unusually cold weather

cole \'kōl\ *n* **:** any of a large genus of herbs (as cabbage, cauliflower, turnip, and mustard) that produce a cylindrical pod with a cone-shaped beak and a single row of seeds

co·le·op·ter·on \ˌkō-lē-'äp-tə-ˌrän\ *n, pl* **co·le·op·tera** \-rə\ **:** [1]BEETLE 1 — **co·le·op·ter·ous** \-rəs\ *adj*

cole·slaw \'kōl-ˌslȯ\ *n* **:** a salad made of sliced or chopped raw cabbage

co·le·us \'kō-lē-əs\ *n* **:** any of a large genus of herbs related to the mints and often grown for their varicolored leaves

col·ic \'käl-ik\ *n* **:** sharp sudden pain in the abdomen — **col·icky** \-i-kē\ *adj*

co·li·form \'kō-lə-ˌfȯrm\ *adj* **:** relating to, resembling, or being the colon bacillus — **coliform** *n*

col·i·se·um \ˌkäl-ə-'sē-əm\ *n* [from medieval Latin *Colosseum, Coliseum,* name given in the Middle Ages to the great amphitheater built in Rome in the first century, from Latin *colosseus* "colossal"] **:** a large building, amphitheater, or stadium for athletic contests or public entertainments

col·lab·o·rate \kə-'lab-ə-ˌrāt\ *vb* **1 :** to work jointly with others (as in writing a book) **2 :** to cooperate with or assist an enemy force occupying one's country — **col·lab·o·ra·tion** \-ˌlab-ə-'rā-shən\ *n* — **col·lab·o·ra·tion·ist** \-sh(ə-)nəst\ *n* — **col·lab·o·ra·tor** \-'lab-ə-ˌrāt-ər\ *n*

col·la·gen \'käl-ə-jən\ *n* **:** an insoluble fibrous protein that occurs in connective tissue and yields gelatin and glue on prolonged heating with water — **col·lag·e·nous** \kə-'laj-ə-nəs\ *adj*

[1]**col·lapse** \kə-'laps\ *vb* **1 :** to break down completely **:** DISINTEGRATE ⟨the enemy's resistance *collapsed*⟩ **2 :** to shrink together abruptly ⟨a balloon *collapses*⟩ **3 :** to fall in **:** give way ⟨the tunnel *collapsed*⟩ **4 :** to suddenly lose value or effectiveness ⟨the country's currency *collapsed*⟩ **5 :** to break down physically or mentally through exhaustion or disease **6 :** to fold together ⟨*collapse* a card table⟩ — **col·laps·i·ble** \-'lap-sə-bəl\ *adj*

[2]**collapse** *n* **:** the act or an instance of collapsing **:** BREAKDOWN

[1]**col·lar** \'käl-ər\ *n* **1 a :** a band, strip, or chain worn around the neck or the neckline of a garment **b :** a part of the harness of draft animals fitted over

the shoulders **2** : something resembling a collar (as a ring to hold something in place) — **col·lar·less** \-ləs\ *adj*

2collar *vb* **1 a** : to seize by the collar **b** : CAPTURE, GRAB **2** : to put a collar on

col·lar·bone \ˌkäl-ər-ˈbōn, ˈkäl-ər-ˌ\ *n* : CLAVICLE

col·lard \ˈkäl-ərd\ *n* : a stalked smooth-leaved kale — usu. used in pl.

1col·lat·er·al \kə-ˈlat-ə-rəl, -ˈla-trəl\ *adj* **1** : associated but of secondary importance **2** : descended from the same ancestors but not in the same line ⟨cousins are *collateral* relatives⟩ — **col·lat·er·al·ly** \-ē\ *adv*

2collateral *n* : property (as stocks, bonds, or a mortgage) pledged as security for the repayment of a loan

col·league \ˈkäl-ˌēg\ *n* : an associate in a profession or office; *also* : a fellow worker

1col·lect \ˈkäl-ikt, -ˌekt\ *n* : an opening prayer in the communion service or the mass

2col·lect \kə-ˈlekt\ *vb* **1 a** : to bring together into one body or place **b** : to gather from a number of sources ⟨*collect* taxes⟩ **2** : to gain or regain control of ⟨*collect* his thoughts⟩ **3** : to take payment for ⟨*collect* a bill⟩ **4 a** : ASSEMBLE **b** : ACCUMULATE ***syn*** see GATHER — **col·lect·a·ble** *or* **col·lect·i·ble** \-ˈlek-tə-bəl\ *adj*

3col·lect \kə-ˈlekt\ *adv or adj* : to be paid for by the receiver ⟨he telephoned *collect*⟩

col·lect·ed \kə-ˈlek-təd\ *adj* : SELF-POSSESSED, CALM — **col·lect·ed·ly** *adv* — **col·lect·ed·ness** *n*

col·lec·tion \kə-ˈlek-shən\ *n* **1** : the act or process of collecting **2 a** : something collected; *esp* : an accumulation of objects gathered for study, comparison, or exhibition **b** : SET 7 **3** : a gathering of money (as for charitable purposes) ⟨take up a *collection* in church⟩

1col·lec·tive \kə-ˈlek-tiv\ *adj* **1** : denoting a number of persons or things considered as one group ⟨*flock* is a *collective* noun⟩ **2** : formed by collecting : AGGREGATED ⟨the *collective* experience of mankind⟩ **3** : of or relating to a group of individuals **4** : shared or assumed by all members of the group ⟨*collective* leadership⟩ — **col·lec·tive·ly** *adv*

2collective *n* **1** : a collective body : GROUP **2** : a cooperative unit or organization; *esp* : COLLECTIVE FARM

collective bargaining *n* : negotiation between an employer and union representatives over wages, hours, and working conditions

collective farm *n* : a farm jointly operated by a group under governmental supervision esp. in a communist country

col·lec·tor \kə-ˈlek-tər\ *n* **1** : an official or agent who collects funds or money due ⟨tax *collector*⟩ ⟨bill *collector*⟩ **2** : one that makes a collection ⟨stamp *collector*⟩ **3** : an object or device that collects

col·leen \kä-ˈlēn, ˈkäl-ˌēn\ *n* : an Irish girl

col·lege \ˈkäl-ij\ *n* **1** : a building used for an educational or religious purpose **2 a** : a subordinate school in a university **b** : a school higher than a high school; *esp* : a 4-year school offering courses in the sciences and humanities leading to a bachelor's degree **3** : an organized body of persons having common interests or duties ⟨*college* of cardinals⟩

col·le·gian \kə-ˈlē-j(ē-)ən\ *n* : a college student

col·le·giate \kə-ˈlē-j(ē-)ət\ *adj* **1** : of or relating to a college **2** : of, relating to, or characteristic of college students ⟨*collegiate* clothes⟩

col·lide \kə-ˈlīd\ *vb* **1** : to come together with solid impact **2** : CLASH

col·lie \ˈkäl-ē\ *n* : a large, usu. long-coated dog of a Scottish breed used in herding sheep

col·lier \ˈkäl-yər\ *n* **1** : a coal miner **2** : a ship for carrying coal

col·liery \ˈkäl-yə-rē\ *n, pl* **-lier·ies** : a coal mine and the buildings connected with it

col·li·mate \ˈkäl-ə-ˌmāt\ *vb* : to make (as rays of light) parallel

col·li·sion \kə-ˈlizh-ən\ *n* : an act or instance of colliding

col·lo·ca·tion \ˌkäl-ə-ˈkā-shən\ *n* : a placing together or side by side or the result of such placing

col·lo·di·on \kə-ˈlōd-ē-ən\ *n* : a viscous solution of pyroxylin used esp. as a coating for wounds or for photographic films

col·loid \ˈkäl-ˌȯid\ *n* : a substance in the form of very fine particles that are not visible in an ordinary microscope but when in suspension in a liquid or gas can be made visible by a beam of light and do not settle out; *also* : a system consisting of such a substance together with the gaseous, liquid, or solid substance in which it is dispersed — **col·loi·dal** \kə-ˈlȯid-əl, kä-\ *adj*

col·lo·qui·al \kə-ˈlō-kwē-əl\ *adj* **1** : used in or characteristic of familiar and informal conversation **2** : using conversational style — **col·lo·qui·al·ly** \-kwē-ə-lē\ *adv*

col·lo·qui·al·ism \-kwē-ə-ˌliz-əm\ *n* **1** : a colloquial expression **2** : colloquial style

col·lo·quy \ˈkäl-ə-kwē\ *n, pl* **-quies** : CONVERSATION; *esp* : a formal conversation or conference

col·lu·sion \kə-ˈlü-zhən\ *n* : secret agreement or cooperation for a fraudulent or deceitful purpose — **col·lu·sive** \-ˈlü-siv, -ziv\ *adj*

Colo *abbr* Colorado

co·logne \kə-ˈlōn\ *n* [from the city of *Cologne*, Germany, where it was first manufactured] : a perfumed toilet water composed of alcohol and aromatic oils

1co·lon \ˈkō-lən\ *n* : the part of the large intestine that extends from the cecum to the rectum — **co·lon·ic** \kō-ˈlän-ik\ *adj*

2colon *n* : a punctuation mark : used chiefly to direct attention to what follows (as a list, explanation, or quotation)

colon bacillus *n* : a bacillus regularly present in the intestine and used as an index of fecal contamination (as of water)

col·o·nel \ˈkərn-əl\ *n* [alteration of earlier *coronel*, from medieval French, from Italian *colonnelo*, from *colonna* "column", from Latin *columna*] : a commissioned officer (as in the army) ranking just below a brigadier general — **col·o·nel·cy** \-sē\ *n*

1co·lo·ni·al \kə-ˈlō-nē-əl, -nyəl\ *adj* **1** : of, relating to, or characteristic of a colony **2** *often cap* : of or relating to the original 13 colonies forming the United States **3** : possessing, forming, or composed of colonies ⟨a *colonial* nation and its *colonial* empire⟩

2colonial *n* : COLONIST 1

co·lo·ni·al·ism \kə-ˈlō-nē-ə-ˌliz-əm, -nyə-ˌliz-\ *n* : control by one nation over a dependent area or people or a policy advocating or based on such control — **co·lo·ni·al·ist** \-ləst\ *n or adj*

col·o·nist \ˈkäl-ə-nəst\ *n* **1** : an inhabitant or member of a colony **2** : a person who takes part in founding a colony

col·o·nize \-ˌnīz\ *vb* **1** : to establish a colony in or on ⟨England *colonized* Australia⟩ **2** : to establish in a colony **3** : to make or establish a colony : SETTLE — **col·o·ni·za·tion** \ˌkäl-ə-nə-ˈzā-shən\ *n* — **col·o·niz·er** \ˈkäl-ə-ˌnī-zər\ *n*

col·on·nade \ˌkäl-ə-ˈnād\ *n* : a row of columns set at regular intervals — **col·on·nad·ed** \-ˈnād-əd\ *adj*

col·o·ny \ˈkäl-ə-nē\ *n, pl* **-nies** **1 a** : a body of people sent out by a state to a new territory **b** : the territory inhabited by such colonists **c** : a distant territory belonging to a nation **2 a** : a distinguishable local population of organisms belonging to one species ⟨*colony* of termites⟩ **b** : a mass of microorganisms usu. growing in or on a solid medium **c** : an incompletely developed ecological community consisting of two or more species of organisms

[1]**col·or** \ˈkəl-ər\ *n* **1 a** : a quality of visible things distinct from form and from light and shade ⟨the *color* of blood is red⟩ ⟨the green *color* of grass⟩ **b** : the aspect of objects and light sources that may be described in terms of hue, lightness, and saturation for objects and hue, brightness, and saturation for light sources — used in this sense as the psychological basis for definitions of color in this dictionary **c** : a chromatic color **2** : an outward show : APPEARANCE ⟨his story has the *color* of truth⟩ **3 a** : COMPLEXION; *esp* : a healthy complexion **b** : BLUSH **4** : the use or combination of colors ⟨a painter who is a master of *color*⟩ **5** *pl* **a** : an identifying flag, ensign, or pennant **b** : service in the armed forces ⟨a call to the *colors*⟩ **c** : true nature ⟨showed his *colors* during the fight⟩ **6** : VITALITY, INTEREST **7** : something used to give color : PIGMENT **8** : skin pigmentation other than white that is characteristic of race

[2]**color** *vb* **1 a** : to give color to ⟨a blush *colored* the girl's cheeks⟩ **b** : to change the color of : PAINT **2** : MISREPRESENT, DISTORT ⟨his story is *colored* by his prejudices⟩ **3** : to take on or change color; *esp* : BLUSH ⟨she *colored* at his glance⟩

Col·o·ra·do potato beetle \ˌkäl-ə-ˈrad-ō-, -ˈräd-\ *n* : a black-and-yellow striped beetle that feeds on the leaves of the potato

col·or·a·tion \ˌkəl-ə-ˈrā-shən\ *n* : use or arrangement of colors or shades : COLORING ⟨study the *coloration* of a flower⟩

col·or–blind \ˈkəl-ər-ˌblīnd\ *adj* : affected with partial or total inability to distinguish one or more colors — **color blindness** *n*

col·or·cast \-ˌkast\ *n* : a television broadcast in color — **col·or·cast·ing** *n*

col·ored \ˈkəl-ərd\ *adj* **1** : having color ⟨*colored* pictures⟩ **2 a** : of a race other than the white; *esp* : NEGRO **b** : of or relating to colored persons

col·or·fast \ˈkəl-ər-ˌfast\ *adj* : having color that does not fade or run — **col·or·fast·ness** \-ˌfas(t)-nəs\ *n*

color filter *n* : a usu. glass device that absorbs light of certain colors and is used for modifying the light that reaches a sensitized photographic material

col·or·ful \ˈkəl-ər-fəl\ *adj* **1** : having striking colors **2** : full of variety or interest — **col·or·ful·ly** \-f(ə-)lē\ *adv* — **col·or·ful·ness** \-fəl-nəs\ *n*

col·or·im·e·ter \ˌkəl-ə-ˈrim-ət-ər\ *n* : a device for determining colors; *esp* : one used for chemical analysis by comparison of a liquid's color with standard colors

col·or·ing \ˈkəl-ə-ring\ *n* **1** : the act of applying colors **2** : something that produces color **3** : the effect produced by applying or combining colors **4** : COMPLEXION, COLORATION **5** : change of appearance (as by adding color)

col·or·less \ˈkəl-ər-ləs\ *adj* **1** : lacking color **2** : PALE, BLANCHED **3** : DULL, UNINTERESTING — **col·or·less·ly** *adv* — **col·or·less·ness** *n*

co·los·sal \kə-ˈläs-əl\ *adj* **1** : of, relating to, or resembling a colossus; *esp* : of very great size **2** : EXCEPTIONAL, ASTONISHING ⟨*colossal* growth⟩ ***syn*** see MONSTROUS — **co·los·sal·ly** \-ə-lē\ *adv*

Co·los·sians \kə-ˈläsh-ənz, -ˈläs-ē-ənz\ *n* — see BIBLE table

co·los·sus \kə-ˈläs-əs\ *n, pl* **-los·sus·es** *or* **-los·si** \-ˈläs-ˌī, -(ˌ)ē\ **1** : a huge statue **2** : a huge person or thing

co·los·trum \kə-ˈläs-trəm\ *n* : milk secreted for a few days after parturition and characterized by high protein and antibody content

colt \ˈkōlt\ *n* **1** : FOAL **2** : a young male horse

colt·ish \ˈkōl-tish\ *adj* : FRISKY, PLAYFUL

col·um·bine \ˈkäl-əm-ˌbīn\ *n* : any of a genus of plants that are related to the buttercups and have showy flowers with usu. five spurred petals

co·lum·bi·um \kə-ˈləm-bē-əm\ *n* : NIOBIUM

Co·lum·bus Day \kə-ˈləm-bəs-\ *n* **1** : October 12 formerly observed as a legal holiday in many states of the U.S. in commemoration of the landing of Columbus in the Bahamas in 1492 **2** : the second Monday in October observed as a legal holiday in many states of the U.S.

col·umn \ˈkäl-əm\ *n* **1 a** : a printed or written vertical arrangement of items ⟨add a *column* of figures⟩ ⟨a mistake in the dollars' *column*⟩ **b** : one of two or more vertical sections of a printed page separated by a rule or blank space **c** : a special department in a newspaper or periodical **2** : a supporting pillar; *esp* : one consisting of a usu. round shaft, a capital, and a base **3** : something resembling a column in form, position, or function ⟨a *column* of water⟩ **4** : a long row (as of soldiers) — **co·lum·nar** \kə-ˈləm-nər\ *adj*

col·um·nist \ˈkäl-əm-(n)əst\ *n* : a person who writes a newspaper column

com- *or* **col-** *or* **con-** *prefix* : with : together : jointly — usu. *com-* before *b*, *p*, or *m* ⟨*com*mingle⟩, *col-* before *l* ⟨*col*linear⟩, and *con-* before other sounds ⟨*con*centrate⟩

com *abbr* **1** commander **2** committee

[1]**co·ma** \ˈkō-mə\ *n* : a sleeplike state of unconsciousness caused by disease, injury, or poison — **co·ma·tose** \-ˌtōs\ *adj*

[2]**coma** *n, pl* **co·mae** \-ˌmē, -ˌmī\ : the head of a comet usu. containing a nucleus

Co·man·che \kə-ˈman-chē\ *n* : a member of an Amerindian people ranging from Wyoming and Nebraska south into New Mexico and northwestern Texas

Co·man·che·an \-chē-ən\ *n* : the period of the Mesozoic era between the Jurassic and the Upper Cretaceous; *also* : the corresponding system of rocks — **Comanchean** *adj*

[1]**comb** \ˈkōm\ *n* **1 a** : a toothed implement to smooth and arrange the hair or worn in the hair to hold it in place **b** : a toothed instrument for separating fibers (as of wool or flax) **2** : a fleshy crest on the head of the domestic fowl and some related birds **3** : HONEYCOMB — **combed** \ˈkōmd\ *adj*

[2]**comb** *vb* **1** : to smooth, arrange, or untangle with a comb ⟨*comb* one's hair⟩ ⟨*comb* wool⟩ **2** : to go over or through carefully in search of something

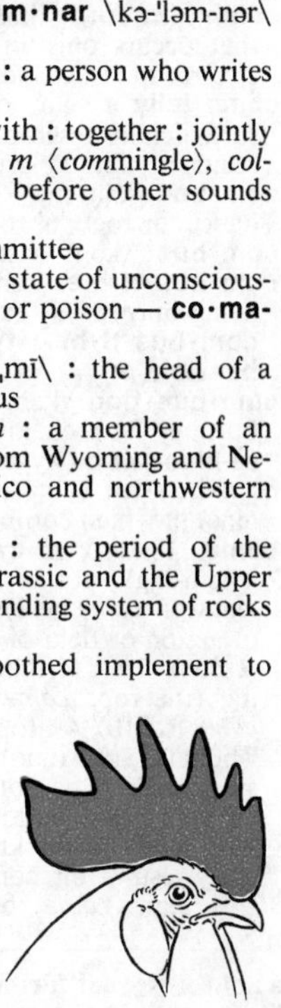

comb 2

[1]**com·bat** \kəm-ˈbat, ˈkäm-ˌ\ *vb* **-bat·ed** *or* **-bat·ted**; **-bat·ing** *or* **-bat·ting** **1** : to fight with : BATTLE **2** : to struggle against; *esp* : to strive to reduce or eliminate ⟨*combat* disease⟩

[2]**com·bat** \ˈkäm-ˌbat\ *n* **1** : FIGHT, STRUGGLE **2** : active fighting in a war : ACTION ⟨soldiers experienced in *combat*⟩

com·bat·ant \kəm-ˈbat-ənt, ˈkäm-bət-\ *adj* : engaging in or ready to engage in combat — **combatant** *n*

com·bat·ive \kəm-ˈbat-iv\ *adj* : eager to fight : PUGNACIOUS — **com·bat·ive·ness** *n*

comb·er \ˈkō-mər\ *n* **1** : one that combs fibers **2** : a long curling wave rolling in from the ocean

com·bi·na·tion \ˌkäm-bə-ˈnā-shən\ *n* **1** : a result or product of combining; *esp* : an alliance of persons or groups to achieve some end **2 a** : a sequence of letters or numbers chosen in setting a lock **b** : any of the possible subsets of a set without regard to order **3** : a one-piece undergarment for the upper and lower parts of the body **4** : the act or process of combining; *esp* : that of uniting to form a chemical compound

[1]**com·bine** \kəm-ˈbīn\ *vb* **1** : to bring into close relationship : UNIFY **2** : INTERMIX, BLEND **3 a** : to become one **b** : to unite to form a chemical compound ***syn*** see JOIN ***ant*** separate — **com·bin·a·ble** \-ˈbī-nə-bəl\ *adj*

[2]**com·bine** \ˈkäm-ˌbīn\ *n* **1** : a combination to gain an often illicit end **2** : a harvesting machine that harvests, threshes, and cleans grain while moving over a field

comb·ings \ˈkō-mingz\ *n pl* : loose hairs or fibers removed by a comb

combining form \kəm-ˌbī-ning-\ *n* : a linguistic form that occurs only in compounds or derivatives (as *electro-* in *electromagnetic* or *mal-* in *malodorous*)

comb jelly *n* : any of a phylum of marine animals superficially resembling jellyfishes but having eight bands of ciliated swimming plates

com·bo \ˈkäm-ˌbō\ *n, pl* **combos** : a small jazz, dance, or rock 'n' roll band

com·bust \kəm-ˈbəst\ *vb* : BURN

com·bus·ti·ble \kəm-ˈbəs-tə-bəl\ *adj* **1** : capable of being burned **2** : catching fire or burning easily — **com·bus·ti·bil·i·ty** \-ˌbəs-tə-ˈbil-ət-ē\ *n* — **combustible** *n*

com·bus·tion \kəm-ˈbəs-chən\ *n* **1** : the process of burning **2** : a chemical process in which substances combine with oxygen

com·bus·tor \-ˈbəs-tər\ *n* : a chamber (as in a jet engine) in which combustion occurs

come \(ˈ)kəm\ *vb* **came** \ˈkām\; **come**; **com·ing** \ˈkəm-ing\ **1** : to move toward something : APPROACH ⟨*come* here⟩ **2** : to arrive at or enter a scene of action or field of interest ⟨the police *came* to our rescue⟩ **3 a** : to reach the point of being or becoming ⟨the rope *came* untied⟩ **b** : AMOUNT ⟨the bill *came* to $10⟩ **4** : to take place ⟨the holiday *came* on Thursday⟩ **5** : ORIGINATE, ARISE ⟨*comes* from sturdy stock⟩ **6** : to be obtainable or attainable ⟨the dress *comes* in three colors⟩ **7** : EXTEND, REACH ⟨a coat that *comes* to the knees⟩ **8 a** : to arrive at a place, end, result, or conclusion ⟨*came* to his senses⟩ ⟨his plans *came* to naught⟩ **b** : HAPPEN, OCCUR ⟨no harm will *come* to you⟩ **9** : to fall within a scope ⟨*comes* under the terms of the treaty⟩ **10** : BECOME ⟨things will *come* clear if we are patient⟩ — **comer** \ˈkəm-ər\ *n* — **come across** : to meet or find by chance — **come by** : ACQUIRE — **come into one's own** : to reach one's appropriate level of importance, skill, or recognition — **come to be** : to arrive at or attain to being : BECOME — **come to pass** : HAPPEN — used with *it*

come about *vb* **1** : to come to pass : HAPPEN **2** : to change direction

come around *vb* : to come round

come·back \ˈkəm-ˌbak\ *n* : a return to a former position or condition (as of health, power, popularity, or prosperity) : RECOVERY

co·me·di·an \kə-ˈmēd-ē-ən\ *n* **1** : an actor who plays in comedy **2** : a comical individual; *esp* : a professional entertainer who tells jokes or who performs comical body movements

co·me·di·enne \kə-ˌmēd-ē-ˈen\ *n* : a female comedian

come down \(ˌ)kəm-ˈdau̇n\ *vb* : to fall sick ⟨*came down* with the measles⟩

come·down \ˈkəm-ˌdau̇n\ *n* : a descent in rank or dignity

com·e·dy \ˈkäm-əd-ē\ *n, pl* **-dies** **1** : a light amusing play with a happy ending **2** : a play or a medieval narrative that ends happily ⟨Dante's Divine *Comedy*⟩ **3** : comedies as a class

come·ly \ˈkəm-lē\ *adj* **come·li·er**; **-est** : PRETTY, ATTRACTIVE — **come·li·ness** *n*

come round *vb* **1** : to come to **2** : to change direction or opinion

com·et \ˈkäm-ət\ *n* **[**from Greek *komētēs*, literally "long-haired one", from *komē* "head of hair"**]** : a bright celestial body that develops a cloudy tail as it moves in an orbit around the sun

come to *vb* : to recover consciousness

com·fit \ˈkəm(p)-fət, ˈkäm(p)-\ *n* : a confection consisting of a piece of fruit, a root, or a seed coated and preserved with sugar

[1]**com·fort** \ˈkəm(p)-fərt\ *n* **1** : acts or words that comfort **2** : the feeling of the one that is comforted ⟨find *comfort* in a mother's love⟩ **3** : something that makes a person comfortable ⟨the *comforts* of home⟩ — **com·fort·less** \-ləs\ *adj*

[2]**comfort** *vb* **1** : to give strength and hope to : CHEER **2** : to ease the grief or trouble of : CONSOLE

com·fort·a·ble \ˈkəm(p)(f)-tə-bəl, ˈkəm(p)-fərt-ə-bəl\ *adj* **1** : giving comfort; *esp* : providing physical comfort **2** : more than adequate ⟨*comfortable* income⟩ **3** : enjoying comfort : at ease — **com·fort·a·ble·ness** *n* — **com·fort·a·bly** \-blē\ *adv*

com·fort·er \ˈkəm(p)-fə(r)t-ər\ *n* **1** : one that gives comfort **2** : a long narrow neck scarf **3** : QUILT

[1]**com·ic** \ˈkäm-ik\ *adj* **1** : of or relating to comedy **2** : causing laughter or amusement : FUNNY **3** : of or relating to comic strips

[2]**comic** *n* **1** : COMEDIAN **2** *pl* : the part of a newspaper devoted to comic strips

com·i·cal \ˈkäm-i-kəl\ *adj* : amusingly whimsical : LAUGHABLE — **com·i·cal·ly** \-i-k(ə-)lē\ *adv*

syn COMICAL, LUDICROUS, DROLL can mean arousing laughter. COMICAL applies to what calls forth lighthearted spontaneous laughter; LUDICROUS suggests obvious absurdity that excites laughter; DROLL may imply amusing oddity or quaintness ***ant*** pathetic

comic book *n* : a magazine made up of a series of comic strips

comic strip *n* : a sequence of cartoons that tell a story or part of a story

ə abut	ər further	a back	ā bake	
ä cot, cart	au̇ out	ch chin	e less	ē easy
g gift	i trip	ī life	j joke	ng sing	ō flow
ȯ flaw	ȯi coin	th thin	th this	ü loot
u̇ foot	y yet	yü few	yu̇ furious	zh vision

com·ing \'kəm-iŋ\ *adj* **1 :** APPROACHING, NEXT ⟨the *coming* year⟩ **2 :** gaining importance ⟨recognized as a *coming* young star⟩

com·i·ty \'käm-ət-ē, 'kō-mət-\ *n, pl* **-ties :** courteous behavior **:** CIVILITY

com·ma \'käm-ə\ *n* **:** a punctuation mark , used chiefly to show separation of words or word groups within a sentence

1**com·mand** \kə-'mand\ *vb* **1 a :** to direct authoritatively **:** ORDER **b :** to have authority and control over **:** be commander of **2 :** to have at one's disposal **3 :** to demand as one's due **:** EXACT ⟨*commands* a high fee⟩ **4 :** to overlook from a strategic position ⟨the hill *commands* the town⟩

2**command** *n* **1 :** the act of commanding ⟨march on *command*⟩ **2 :** an order given **3 a :** the ability to control **:** MASTERY ⟨has *command* of the subject⟩ ⟨a good *command* of French⟩ **b :** the authority, right, or power to command **4 :** the personnel, area, or unit under a commander **5 :** a position from which military operations are directed — called also *command post*

com·man·dant \'käm-ən-ˌdant, -ˌdänt\ *n* **:** an officer in command

com·man·deer \ˌkäm-ən-'di(ə)r\ *vb* **:** to take arbitrary or forcible possession of esp. for military purposes

com·mand·er \kə-'man-dər\ *n* **1 :** one in official command esp. of a military force or base **2 :** a commissioned officer in the navy ranking just below a captain — **com·mand·er·ship** \-ˌship\ *n*

commander in chief : one who holds the supreme command of an armed force

com·mand·ment \kə-'man(d)-mənt\ *n* **:** something commanded; *esp* **:** one of the biblical Ten Commandments said in the Bible to have been given by God to Moses on Mount Sinai

command module *n* **:** a space vehicle module designed to carry the crew, the chief communications equipment, and the equipment for reentry

com·man·do \kə-'man-dō\ *n, pl* **-dos** *or* **-does** **1 :** a military unit trained and organized for surprise raids into enemy territory **2 :** a member of a commando

com·mem·o·rate \kə-'mem-ə-ˌrāt\ *vb* **1 :** to call to remembrance **2 :** to mark by a ceremony **:** OBSERVE **3 :** to be a memorial of — **com·mem·o·ra·tor** \-ˌrāt-ər\ *n*

com·mem·o·ra·tion \kə-ˌmem-ə-'rā-shən\ *n* **1 :** the act of commemorating **2 :** a ceremony that commemorates

com·mem·o·ra·tive \kə-'mem-ə-ˌrāt-iv, -rət-\ *adj* **:** intended to commemorate an event ⟨a *commemorative* postage stamp⟩ — **commemorative** *n*

com·mence \kə-'men(t)s\ *vb* **:** BEGIN, START — **com·menc·er** *n*

com·mence·ment \-'men(t)s-mənt\ *n* **1 :** an act, instance, or time of commencing **2 :** the ceremonies or the day for conferring degrees or diplomas upon graduates of a school or college

com·mend \kə-'mend\ *vb* **1 :** to give into another's care **:** ENTRUST **2 :** to speak of someone or something with approval **:** PRAISE — **com·mend·a·ble** \-'men-də-bəl\ *adj* — **com·mend·a·bly** \-blē\ *adv*

com·men·da·tion \ˌkäm-ən-'dā-shən, -ˌen-\ *n* **1 :** an act of commending **2 :** something that commends — **com·men·da·to·ry** \kə-'men-də-ˌtōr-ē, -ˌtȯr-\ *adj*

com·men·sal \kə-'men(t)-səl\ *adj* **:** relating to or living in a state of commensalism — **commensal** *n* — **com·men·sal·ly** \-sə-lē\ *adv*

com·men·sal·ism \-sə-ˌliz-əm\ *n* **:** a relation between two kinds of organisms in which one obtains a benefit (as food) from the other without either damaging or benefiting it

com·men·su·rate \kə-'men(t)s-(ə-)rət, -'mench-(ə-)rət\ *adj* **1 :** equal in measure or extent **2 :** CORRESPONDING, PROPORTIONATE ⟨an income *commensurate* with one's needs⟩ — **com·men·su·rate·ly** *adv*

1**com·ment** \'käm-ˌent\ *n* **1 :** an expression of opinion or attitude in speech or writing **2 :** an explanatory, illustrative, or critical note or observation ***syn*** see REMARK

2**comment** *vb* **:** to make a comment **:** REMARK

com·men·tary \'käm-ən-ˌter-ē\ *n, pl* **-tar·ies** **1 :** an explanatory or narrative writing — often used in pl. ⟨Caesar's *Commentaries* on the Gallic Wars⟩ **2 :** a series of oral comments or written notes

com·men·ta·tor \'käm-ən-ˌtāt-ər\ *n* **:** one who gives a commentary; *esp* **:** one who reports and discusses news on radio or television

com·merce \'käm-(ˌ)ərs\ *n* **:** buying and selling of goods esp. on a large scale and between different places **:** TRADE

1**com·mer·cial** \kə-'mər-shəl\ *adj* **1 :** of or relating to commerce **2 :** designed mainly for profit; *esp* **:** designed for mass appeal ⟨the *commercial* theater⟩ **3 :** paid for by advertisers ⟨*commercial* TV⟩ — **com·mer·cial·ly** \-'mərsh-(ə-)lē\ *adv*

2**commercial** *n* **:** an advertisement broadcast on radio or television

com·mer·cial·ize \kə-'mər-shə-ˌlīz\ *vb* **1 :** to manage on a business basis for profit **2 :** to exploit for profit ⟨*commercialize* Christmas⟩ — **com·mer·cial·i·za·tion** \-ˌmər-shə-lə-'zā-shən\ *n*

com·min·gle \kə-'miŋ-gəl\ *vb* **:** MIX, INTERMIX

com·mis·er·ate \kə-'miz-ə-ˌrāt\ *vb* **:** to feel or express sorrow or compassion for — **com·mis·er·a·tion** \-ˌmiz-ə-'rā-shən\ *n*

com·mis·sar \'käm-ə-ˌsär\ *n* **:** the head of a government department in the U.S.S.R. before 1946

com·mis·sar·i·at \ˌkäm-ə-'ser-ē-ət\ *n* **1 :** a system for supplying an army with food **2 :** a government department headed by a commissar

com·mis·sary \'käm-ə-ˌser-ē\ *n, pl* **-sar·ies** **1 :** a person to whom a duty or office is entrusted by a superior **2 :** a store supplying provisions esp. to military personnel and dependents **3 :** a lunchroom in a motion-picture studio

1**com·mis·sion** \kə-'mish-ən\ *n* **1 a :** an order granting the power to perform various acts or duties **b :** a certificate conferring military rank and authority or the rank and authority so conferred **2 a :** authority to act as agent for another **b :** a matter entrusted to an agent **3 :** a group of persons directed to perform some duty ⟨park *commission*⟩ **4 :** an act of committing ⟨*commission* of a theft⟩ **5 :** a fee paid to an agent or employee for transacting a piece of business ⟨a 5% sales *commission*⟩ — **in commission :** in use or ready for use ⟨put a ship *in commission*⟩ — **out of commission 1 :** out of service or use **2 :** out of working order

2**commission** *vb* **-mis·sioned; -mis·sion·ing** \-'mish-(ə-)niŋ\ **1 :** to confer a commission on **2 :** to order to be made **3 :** to put (a ship) in commission

commissioned officer *n* **:** a military or naval officer holding by a commission a rank of second lieutenant or ensign or a higher rank

com·mis·sion·er \kə-'mish-(ə-)nər\ *n* **1 :** a member of a commission **2 :** an official in charge of a government department ⟨*Commissioner* of Public Safety⟩

C

com·mis·sure \'käm-ə-ˌshu̇(ə)r\ *n* : a connecting band of nerve tissue in the brain or spinal cord

com·mit \kə-'mit\ *vb* **com·mit·ted; com·mit·ting** **1 a** : to put into charge or trust : ENTRUST ⟨*commit* the poem to memory⟩ **b** : to place in a prison or mental institution **2** : to bring about : PERFORM ⟨*commit* a crime⟩ **3** : to pledge or assign to some particular course or use ⟨*committed* himself to come on Thursday⟩ — **com·mit·ta·ble** \-'mit-ə-bəl\ *adj*

com·mit·ment \kə-'mit-mənt\ *n* **1** : an act of committing to a charge or trust **2 a** : an agreement or pledge to do something in the future **b** : something pledged ⟨financial *commitments*⟩

com·mit·tee \kə-'mit-ē\ *n* : a body of persons appointed or elected to consider or take action on some matter ⟨a legislative *committee*⟩ — **com·mit·tee·man** \-mən, -ˌman\ *n* — **com·mit·tee·wom·an** \-ˌwu̇m-ən\ *n*

com·mode \kə-'mōd\ *n* **1** : a low chest of drawers **2** : a movable washstand with a cupboard underneath **3** : TOILET 2b

com·mo·di·ous \kə-'mōd-ē-əs\ *adj* : comfortably or conveniently spacious : ROOMY — **com·mo·di·ous·ness** *n*

com·mod·i·ty \kə-'mäd-ət-ē\ *n, pl* **-ties** **1** : a product of agriculture or mining **2** : an article exchanged in commerce

com·mo·dore \'käm-ə-ˌdō(ə)r, -ˌdo̊(ə)r\ *n* **1** : a commissioned officer in the navy ranking just below a rear admiral **2** : the chief officer of a yacht club **3** : the senior captain of a line of merchant ships

[1]**com·mon** \'käm-ən\ *adj* **1** : relating or belonging to or used by everybody : PUBLIC ⟨the *common* good⟩ **2** : belonging to or shared by two or more individuals or by the members of a group or set ⟨a *common* ancestor⟩ ⟨all points *common* to two intersecting circles⟩ **3** : widely or generally known, met, or seen ⟨facts of *common* knowledge⟩ **4** : FREQUENT, FAMILIAR ⟨a *common* sight⟩ **5** : not above the average in rank, merit, or social position ⟨a *common* soldier⟩ ⟨of the *common* people⟩ **6** : PLAIN, PRACTICAL ⟨advice full of good *common* sense⟩ **7 a** : falling below ordinary standards : SECOND-RATE **b** : lacking refinement : VULGAR — **com·mon·ly** *adv* — **com·mon·ness** \-ən-(n)əs\ *n*

[2]**common** *n* **1** *pl* : the common people **2** : a piece of land subject to common use esp. for pasture — often used in pl. — **in common** : shared together ⟨intersecting lines have one point *in common*⟩

common cold *n* : a virus disease of nose and structures associated in breathing that is marked by congestion and inflammation of mucous membranes and usu. by excessive secretion of mucus and coughing and sneezing

common denominator *n* : a common multiple of the denominators of a number of fractions

common divisor *n* : a number that divides two or more numbers without remainder — called also *common factor*

com·mon·er \'käm-ə-nər\ *n* : one of the common people : one who is not of noble rank

common multiple *n* : a multiple of each of two or more numbers

common noun *n* : a noun (as *chair* or *fear*) used with limiting modifiers (as *a*, *some*, *my*) that names a class of persons or things or any individual of a class

ə abut	ər further	a back	ā bake
ä cot, cart	au̇ out	ch chin	e less
ē easy	g gift	i trip	ī life
j joke	ng sing	ō flow	o̊ flaw
o̊i coin	th thin	th this	ü loot
u̇ foot	y yet	yü few	yu̇ furious
zh vision			

[1]**com·mon·place** \'käm-ən-ˌplās\ *n* : an obvious or trite remark or observation

[2]**commonplace** *adj* : very common or ordinary : UNINTERESTING

common salt *n* : SALT 1a

com·mon·weal \'käm-ən-ˌwēl\ *n* **1** : the general welfare **2** *archaic* : COMMONWEALTH

com·mon·wealth \-ˌwelth\ *n* **1** : STATE, NATION **2** : a state of the U.S. — used officially of Kentucky, Massachusetts, Pennsylvania, and Virginia

com·mo·tion \kə-'mō-shən\ *n* **1** : disturbed or violent motion : AGITATION **2** : noisy excitement and confusion : TUMULT

com·mu·nal \kə-'myün-əl, 'käm-yən-\ *adj* **1** : of or relating to a commune or community **2** : shared or used in common by members of a group or community

[1]**com·mune** \kə-'myün\ *vb* **1** : to receive Communion **2** : to communicate intimately ⟨*commune* with nature⟩

[2]**com·mune** \'käm-ˌyün, kə-'myün\ *n* **1** : the smallest administrative district of many countries esp. in Europe **2** : a large collectivized farm in the People's Republic of China **3** : a small group practicing joint ownership and sharing of duties and experiences

com·mu·ni·ca·ble \kə-'myü-ni-kə-bəl\ *adj* : capable of being communicated or carried from one person or thing to another ⟨*communicable* diseases⟩ — **com·mu·ni·ca·bil·i·ty** \-ˌmyü-ni-kə-'bil-ət-ē\ *n*

com·mu·ni·cant \kə-'myü-ni-kənt\ *n* **1** : a person who takes Communion : a church member **2** : a person who communicates

com·mu·ni·cate \kə-'myü-nə-ˌkāt\ *vb* **1 a** : to make known ⟨*communicate* the news⟩ **b** : TRANSFER, TRANSMIT ⟨*communicate* a disease⟩ **2** : to be in communication **3** : JOIN, CONNECT ⟨the rooms *communicate*⟩ — **com·mu·ni·ca·tor** \-ˌkāt-ər\ *n*

com·mu·ni·ca·tion \kə-ˌmyü-nə-'kā-shən\ *n* **1** : an act or instance of transmitting **2** : information communicated : MESSAGE **3** : an exchange of information **4** *pl* **a** : a system (as of telephones) for communicating **b** : a system of routes for moving troops, supplies, and vehicles

com·mu·ni·ca·tive \kə-'myü-nə-ˌkāt-iv, -ni-kət-\ *adj* **1** : tending to communicate : TALKATIVE **2** : of or relating to communication — **com·mu·ni·ca·tive·ness** *n*

com·mu·nion \kə-'myü-nyən\ *n* **1** *cap* **a** : a Christian sacrament in which bread and wine are partaken of as a commemoration of the death of Christ **b** : the part of the Mass in which the Eucharist is received **2** : COMMUNICATION, INTERCOURSE **3** : a Christian denomination

com·mu·ni·qué \kə-'myü-nə-ˌkā, -ˌmyü-nə-'\ *n* : an official communication : BULLETIN

com·mu·nism \'käm-yə-ˌniz-əm\ *n* **1** : a social system in which property and goods are owned in common or a theory advocating such a system **2** *cap* : a system of government in which a single party controls state-owned means of production with the aim of establishing a stateless society — **com·mu·nist** \-nəst\ *n or adj, often cap* — **com·mu·nis·tic** \ˌkäm-yə-'nis-tik\ *adj, often cap*

com·mu·ni·ty \kə-'myü-nət-ē\ *n, pl* **-ties** **1 a** : the people living in an area or the area itself **b** : a group of one or more ecologically interacting populations of organisms in a common location (as a bog) **c** : a group of people with common interests esp. when living together ⟨a *community* of monks⟩ **2 a** : joint ownership or participation ⟨*community* of goods⟩ **b** : LIKENESS ⟨a *community* of ideas⟩ **c** : FELLOWSHIP

community college *n* : a public junior college that fits its instruction to the community's needs

com·mu·ta·tion \ˌkäm-yə-ˈtā-shən\ *n* **1** : EXCHANGE, REPLACEMENT **2** : a reduction of a legal penalty **3** : an act of commuting **4** : the process of reversing the direction of an electric circuit

commutation ticket *n* : a transportation ticket sold at a reduced rate for a fixed number of trips over the same route during a limited period

com·mu·ta·tive \ˈkäm-yə-ˌtāt-iv, kə-ˈmyüt-ət-\ *adj* : combining elements to produce a result independent of the order in which the elements are taken ⟨addition of real numbers is *commutative*⟩ — **com·mu·ta·tiv·i·ty** \kə-ˌmyüt-ə-ˈtiv-ət-ē\ *n*

com·mu·ta·tor \ˈkäm-yə-ˌtāt-ər\ *n* : a device for reversing the direction of an electric current so that the alternating currents generated in the armature of a dynamo are converted to direct current

com·mute \kə-ˈmyüt\ *vb* **1** : EXCHANGE, INTERCHANGE; *esp* : to substitute a less severe penalty for a greater one ⟨*commute* a death sentence to life imprisonment⟩ **2** : to travel back and forth regularly — **com·mut·a·ble** \-ˈmyüt-ə-bəl\ *adj* — **com·mut·er** *n*

1**com·pact** \kəm-ˈpakt, ˈkäm-ˌ\ *adj* **1** : closely united or packed : SOLID, FIRM **2** : arranged so as to save space ⟨a *compact* house⟩ **3** : not wordy : BRIEF — **com·pact·ly** *adv* — **com·pact·ness** \-ˈpak(t)-nəs, -ˌpak(t)-\ *n*

2**compact** *vb* **1** : COMBINE, CONSOLIDATE **2** : COMPRESS **3** : to become compacted — **com·pac·tor** *or* **com·pact·er** \-ˈpak-tər, -ˌpak-\ *n*

3**com·pact** \ˈkäm-ˌpakt\ *n* **1** : a small cosmetic case **2** : a relatively small automobile

4**com·pact** \ˈkäm-ˌpakt\ *n* : AGREEMENT, CONTRACT

com·pan·ion \kəm-ˈpan-yən\ *n* [from medieval Latin *companion-*, stem of *companio*, literally "one who shares bread", from Latin *com-* and *panis* "bread"] **1** : one that often accompanies another : COMRADE **2 a** : one of a pair of matching things **b** : one employed to live with and serve another

com·pan·ion·a·ble \kəm-ˈpan-yə-nə-bəl\ *adj* : fitted to be a companion : SOCIABLE — **com·pan·ion·a·bly** \-blē\ *adv*

com·pan·ion·ship \kəm-ˈpan-yən-ˌship\ *n* : FELLOWSHIP

com·pan·ion·way \-ˌwā\ *n* : a ship's stairway from one deck to another

com·pa·ny \ˈkamp-(ə-)nē\ *n, pl* **-nies 1 a** : association with another : FELLOWSHIP **b** : COMPANIONS, ASSOCIATES **c** : VISITORS, GUESTS **2 a** : a group of persons or things **b** : a body of soldiers; *esp* : a unit consisting of two or more platoons **c** : an organization of musical or dramatic performers ⟨opera *company*⟩ **d** : the officers and men of a ship **e** : a fire-fighting unit **3 a** : an association of persons carrying on a business **b** : those members of a partnership whose names do not appear in the firm name ⟨John Doe and *Company*⟩

com·pa·ra·ble \ˈkäm-p(ə-)rə-bəl\ *adj* **1** : capable of being compared **2** : worthy of being compared ⟨cloth *comparable* to the best⟩ — **com·pa·ra·bly** \-blē\ *adv*

1**com·par·a·tive** \kəm-ˈpar-ət-iv\ *adj* **1** : of, relating to, or constituting the degree of grammatical comparison that denotes increase in the quality, quantity, or relation expressed by an adjective or adverb **2** : measured by comparison : RELATIVE ⟨*comparative* stranger⟩ **3** : involving systematic study of comparable elements ⟨*comparative* literature⟩ ⟨*comparative* anatomy⟩ — **com·par·a·tive·ly** *adv* — **com·par·a·tive·ness** *n*

2**comparative** *n* : the comparative degree or a word form expressing it ⟨*taller* is the *comparative* of *tall*⟩

1**com·pare** \kəm-ˈpa(ə)r, -ˈpe(ə)r\ *vb* **1** : to represent as similar : LIKEN ⟨*compare* an anthill to a town⟩ **2** : to examine in order to discover likenesses or differences ⟨*compare* two bicycles⟩ **3** : to be worthy of comparison : be like ⟨roller skating does not *compare* with ice skating⟩ **4** : to inflect or modify (an adjective or adverb) according to the degrees of comparison

2**compare** *n* : COMPARISON ⟨beauty beyond *compare*⟩

com·par·i·son \kəm-ˈpar-ə-sən\ *n* **1** : the act of comparing : the state of being compared **2** : change in the form of an adjective or an adverb (as by having *-er* or *-est* added or *more* or *most* prefixed) to show different levels of quality, quantity, or relation

com·part·ment \kəm-ˈpärt-mənt\ *n* **1** : one of the parts into which an enclosed space is divided **2** : a separate division or section

1**com·pass** \ˈkəm-pəs, ˈkäm-\ *vb* **1** : to travel entirely around **2** : ACHIEVE, ACCOMPLISH

2**compass** *n* **1 a** : BOUNDARY, CIRCUMFERENCE **b** : an enclosed space **c** (1) : RANGE, SCOPE (2) : the range of pitch lying within the capacity of a voice or instrument **2 a** : a device for determining directions by means of a magnetic needle pointing to the magnetic north **b** : any of various other devices that indicate direction **3** : an instrument for drawing circles or transferring measurements that consists of two pointed branches joined at the top — often used in pl.

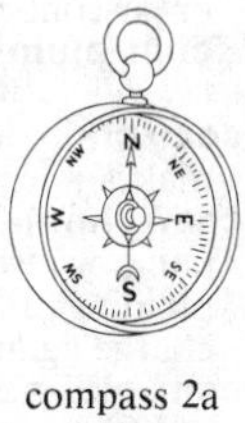

compass 2a

com·pas·sion \kəm-ˈpash-ən\ *n* : sorrow or pity aroused by the suffering or misfortune of another : SYMPATHY — **com·pas·sion·ate** \-ˈpash-(ə-)nət\ *adj* — **com·pas·sion·ate·ly** *adv*

com·pat·i·ble \kəm-ˈpat-ə-bəl\ *adj* **1** : capable of existing together in harmony ⟨*compatible* colors⟩ **2** : able to cross-fertilize freely ⟨*compatible* plants⟩ — **com·pat·i·bil·i·ty** \-ˌpat-ə-ˈbil-ət-ē\ *n* — **com·pat·i·bly** \-ˈpat-ə-blē\ *adv*

com·pa·tri·ot \kəm-ˈpā-trē-ət, -ˌät\ *n* : a fellow countryman

com·pel \kəm-ˈpel\ *vb* **com·pelled**; **com·pel·ling 1** : to drive or urge by physical force, pressure, threat, or necessity : CONSTRAIN **2** : EXACT, EXTORT ⟨*compel* obedience⟩ — **com·pel·ler** *n* — **com·pel·ling·ly** \-ˈpel-ing-lē\ *adv*

com·pen·di·ous \kəm-ˈpen-dē-əs\ *adj* : marked by a brief presentation of a comprehensive subject : CONCISE

com·pen·sate \ˈkäm-pən-ˌsāt\ *vb* **1** : to be equivalent to in value or effect : COUNTERBALANCE **2** : to make amends ⟨*compensate* for a rude act⟩ **3** : to make equal return to : PAY ⟨*compensate* a workman for his labor⟩ — **com·pen·sa·to·ry** \kəm-ˈpen(t)-sə-ˌtōr-ē, -ˌtȯr-\ *adj*

com·pen·sa·tion \ˌkäm-pən-ˈsā-shən\ *n* **1** : the act of compensating : the state of being compensated **2 a** : something that compensates; *esp* : payment to an unemployed or injured worker or his dependents **b** : SALARY, WAGES

com·pete \kəm-ˈpēt\ *vb* : to vie with another for or as if for a prize : CONTEST

com·pe·tence \ˈkäm-pət-ən(t)s\ *n* **1** : means sufficient for the necessities of life **2** : the quality or state of being competent

com·pe·ten·cy \-ən-sē\ *n* : COMPETENCE

com·pe·tent \'käm-pət-ənt\ *adj* : CAPABLE, QUALIFIED, FIT — **com·pe·tent·ly** *adv*

com·pe·ti·tion \ˌkäm-pə-'tish-ən\ *n* **1** : the act or process of competing **2 a** : a contest between rivals **b** : RIVALRY **c** : an individual or group one is competing against ⟨look over the *competition*⟩ **3** : the effort of persons or firms acting independently to secure business by offering the most favorable terms

com·pet·i·tive \kəm-'pet-ət-iv\ *adj* : relating to, characterized by, or based on competition ⟨*competitive* sports⟩ ⟨*competitive* bidding⟩ — **com·pet·i·tive·ly** *adv* — **com·pet·i·tive·ness** *n*

com·pet·i·tor \kəm-'pet-ət-ər\ *n* : one that competes esp. in the selling of goods or services : RIVAL

com·pi·la·tion \ˌkäm-pə-'lā-shən\ *n* **1** : the act or process of compiling **2** : something compiled; *esp* : a book of materials gathered from other books

com·pile \kəm-'pīl\ *vb* **1** : to collect into a volume **2** : to put together in a new form out of materials already existing ⟨*compile* a history of India⟩ — **com·pil·er** *n*

com·pla·cence \kəm-'plās-ən(t)s\ *n* : calm or secure satisfaction : SELF-SATISFACTION — **com·pla·cent** \kəm-'plās-ənt\ *adj* — **com·pla·cent·ly** *adv*

com·pla·cen·cy \-ən-sē\ *n* : COMPLACENCE

com·plain \kəm-'plān\ *vb* **1** : to express grief, pain, or discontent **2** : to make a formal accusation — **com·plain·er** *n* — **com·plain·ing·ly** \-'plā-ning-lē\ *adv*

com·plain·ant \kəm-'plā-nənt\ *n* : the party who makes a legal complaint

com·plaint \kəm-'plānt\ *n* **1** : expression of grief, pain, or resentment **2 a** : a cause or reason for complaining **b** : a bodily ailment or disease **3** : a formal charge against a person

com·plai·sance \kəm-'plās-ən(t)s, 'käm-plā-ˌzan(t)s\ *n* : disposition to please or oblige — **com·plai·sant** \-ənt, -ˌzant\ *adj*

¹**com·ple·ment** \'käm-plə-mənt\ *n* **1** : something that fills up, completes, or makes perfect **2** : full quantity, number, or amount ⟨a ship's *complement* of officers and men⟩ **3** : the angle that when added to a given angle equals 90 degrees **4** : an added word or group of words by which the predicate of a sentence is made complete ⟨*president* in "they elected him president" and *to work* in "he wants to work" are different kinds of *complements*⟩ **5** : a heat-sensitive substance in normal blood that in combination with antibodies destroys antigens (as bacteria and foreign blood corpuscles) **6** : the set of all elements not included in a given mathematical set

²**com·ple·ment** \-ˌment\ *vb* : to form or serve as a complement to ⟨a hat that *complements* a dress⟩

com·ple·men·ta·ry \ˌkäm-plə-'ment-ə-rē, -'men-trē\ *adj* : forming or serving as a complement

complementary angles *n pl* : two angles whose sum is 90 degrees

¹**com·plete** \kəm-'plēt\ *adj* **1** : possessing all necessary parts : ENTIRE **2** : brought to an end : CONCLUDED **3** : THOROUGH, ABSOLUTE ⟨*complete* freedom⟩ ⟨a *complete* failure⟩ — **com·plete·ly** *adv* — **com·plete·ness** *n*

²**complete** *vb* **1** : to bring to an end : accomplish or achieve fully **2** : to make whole or perfect; *esp* : to provide with all lacking parts

ə abut	ər further	a back	ā bake	
ä cot, cart	au̇ out	ch chin	e less	ē easy
g gift	i trip	ī life	j joke	ng sing	ō flow
ȯ flaw	ȯi coin	th thin	t͟h this	ü loot
u̇ foot	y yet	yü few	yu̇ furious	zh vision

complete metamorphosis *n* : insect metamorphosis (as of a butterfly) in which there is a pupal stage between the immature stage and the adult and in which the young insect is very different in form from the adult

com·ple·tion \kəm-'plē-shən\ *n* : the act or process of completing : the state of being complete ⟨a job near *completion*⟩

¹**com·plex** \käm-'pleks, kəm-', 'käm-ˌ\ *adj* **1 a** : composed of two or more and esp. many parts ⟨a *complex* mixture⟩ **b** : consisting of a main clause and one or more subordinate clauses ⟨*complex* sentence⟩ **c** : formed by union of simpler substances ⟨a *complex* protein⟩ **d** : characterized by many often intricately related parts, details, ideas, or functions ⟨*complex* behavior⟩ ⟨*complex* organisms like man⟩ **2** : having many interrelated parts, patterns, or elements esp. when hard to analyze or solve ⟨a *complex* problem⟩ — **com·plex·ly** *adv*

²**com·plex** \'käm-ˌpleks\ *n* **1** : a whole made up of complicated or interrelated parts **2** : a system of repressed desires and memories that exerts a dominating influence upon a person

complex fraction *n* : a fraction with a fraction or mixed number in the numerator or denominator or both

com·plex·ion \kəm-'plek-shən\ *n* **1** : the hue or appearance of the skin and esp. of the face **2** : general appearance : CHARACTER ⟨information that changes the whole *complexion* of a situation⟩ — **com·plex·ioned** \-shənd\ *adj*

com·plex·i·ty \kəm-'plek-sət-ē, käm-\ *n, pl* **-ties 1** : the quality or state of being complex **2** : something complex

com·pli·ance \kəm-'plī-ən(t)s\ *n* **1** : the act or process of complying **2** : a readiness or disposition to yield to others — **in compliance with** : in accordance with : in obedience to ⟨*in compliance with* your request for samples⟩

com·pli·an·cy \-ən-sē\ *n* : COMPLIANCE

com·pli·ant \-ənt\ *adj* : ready or disposed to comply : SUBMISSIVE — **com·pli·ant·ly** *adv*

com·pli·cate \'käm-plə-ˌkāt\ *vb* : to make or become complex, intricate, or difficult

com·pli·cat·ed *adj* **1** : consisting of parts intricately combined **2** : difficult to analyze, understand, or explain — **com·pli·cat·ed·ly** *adv* — **com·pli·cat·ed·ness** *n*

com·pli·ca·tion \ˌkäm-plə-'kā-shən\ *n* **1** : a making difficult, involved, or intricate **2** : a complex or intricate feature or element **3** : something that makes a situation more complicated or difficult **4** : a disease existing at the same time as and affecting the course or severity of another disease

com·plic·i·ty \kəm-'plis-ət-ē\ *n, pl* **-ties** : association or participation in a wrongful act

¹**com·pli·ment** \'käm-plə-mənt\ *n* **1** : an expression of esteem, respect, affection, or admiration; *esp* : a flattering remark **2** *pl* : best wishes : REGARDS *syn* COMPLIMENT, FLATTERY can mean praise directed to someone. COMPLIMENT implies sincerity in expressing esteem or giving credit; FLATTERY is more likely to imply insincerity and an appeal to vanity, often for selfish or insincere purposes *ant* taunt

²**com·pli·ment** \-ˌment\ *vb* : to pay a compliment to

com·pli·men·ta·ry \ˌkäm-plə-'ment-ə-rē, -'men-trē\ *adj* **1** : expressing or containing a compliment **2** : given free as a courtesy or favor ⟨*complimentary* ticket⟩

com·ply \kəm-'plī\ *vb* **com·plied**; **com·ply·ing** : to conform or adapt one's actions to another's wishes, to a rule, or to necessity ⟨*comply* with a request⟩ — **com·pli·er** \\-ˈplī(-ə)r\\ *n*

1**com·po·nent** \\kəm-ˈpō-nənt, ˈkäm-ˌ\\ *n* **:** a constituent part or element ⟨*components* of an electric circuit⟩ ⟨*components* of a stew⟩

2**component** *adj* **:** being or forming a part **:** CONSTITUENT

com·port \\kəm-ˈpōrt, -ˈpȯrt\\ *vb* **1 :** ACCORD, SUIT ⟨acts that *comport* with ideals⟩ **2 :** CONDUCT ⟨*comports* himself with dignity⟩

com·port·ment \\-mənt\\ *n* **:** BEHAVIOR, BEARING

com·pose \\kəm-ˈpōz\\ *vb* **1 a :** to form by putting together **:** FASHION **b :** to make up **:** CONSTITUTE ⟨a cake *composed* of many ingredients⟩ **c :** to arrange type in order for printing **:** SET **2 :** to create by mental or artistic labor ⟨*compose* a song⟩ **3 :** to arrange in proper form **4 :** QUIET, CALM ⟨try to *compose* your feelings⟩

com·posed \\-ˈpōzd\\ *adj* **:** free from agitation **:** CALM; *esp* **:** SELF-POSSESSED — **com·pos·ed·ly** \\-ˈpō-zəd-lē\\ *adv*

com·pos·er \\kəm-ˈpō-zər\\ *n* **:** one that composes; *esp* **:** a person who writes music

1**com·pos·ite** \\käm-ˈpäz-ət, kəm-\\ *adj* **1 :** made up of various distinct parts or elements ⟨a *composite* photograph⟩ **2 :** of or relating to a very large family of dicotyledonous plants (as a daisy or aster) that are characterized by florets arranged in dense heads that resemble single flowers

2**composite** *n* **1 :** something composite **:** COMPOUND **2 :** a composite plant

composite cone *n* **:** a volcanic cone composed of intermingled masses of alternate layers of lava and fragmentary material

composite number *n* **:** a product of two or more whole numbers each greater than 1

com·po·si·tion \\ˌkäm-pə-ˈzish-ən\\ *n* **1 :** the act or process of composing **2 :** the manner in which the parts of a thing are put together **:** MAKEUP ⟨the *composition* of a painting⟩ **3 :** the elements of a compound ⟨the *composition* of rubber⟩ **4 :** a product of combining ingredients **:** COMBINATION ⟨a *composition* made of several different metals⟩ **5 a :** a literary, musical, or artistic production **b :** the art of writing or of creating new pieces of music

com·pos·i·tor \\kəm-ˈpäz-ət-ər\\ *n* **:** one who sets type

com·post \\ˈkäm-ˌpōst\\ *n* **:** a mixing largely of decayed organic matter used for fertilizing and conditioning land

com·po·sure \\kəm-ˈpō-zhər\\ *n* **:** CALMNESS, SELF-POSSESSION

com·pote \\ˈkäm-ˌpōt\\ *n* **1 :** fruits cooked in syrup **2 :** a bowl usu. with a base and stem from which compotes, fruits, nuts, or sweets are served

1**com·pound** \\käm-ˈpau̇nd, kəm-ˈ, ˈkäm-ˌ\\ *vb* **1 :** to put together or be joined to form a whole **:** COMBINE **2 :** to form by combining parts ⟨*compound* a medicine⟩ **3 :** to settle peaceably **:** COMPROMISE **4 :** to increase by an increment that itself increases ⟨interest *compounded* quarterly⟩ — **com·pound·er** *n*

2**com·pound** \\ˈkäm-ˌpau̇nd, käm-ˈ, kəm-ˈ\\ *adj* **1 :** made of or by the union of separate elements or parts ⟨a *compound* substance⟩ **2 :** made up of two or more similar parts forming a common whole ⟨*compound* fruit⟩ **3 a :** being a word that is a compound ⟨the *compound* noun *steamboat*⟩ **b :** consisting of two or more main clauses ⟨"I told him to leave and he left" is a *compound* sentence⟩

3**com·pound** \\ˈkäm-ˌpau̇nd\\ *n* **1 :** a word consisting of parts that are words ⟨*rowboat*, *high school*, and *light-year* are *compounds*⟩ **2 :** something compound; *esp* **:** a distinct substance formed by the union of two or more chemical elements in definite proportion by weight

4**com·pound** \\ˈkäm-ˌpau̇nd\\ *n* **1 :** an enclosure of European residences and commercial buildings esp. in the Orient **2 :** a large fenced or walled-in area

compound bar *n* **:** a bimetallic bar

compound–complex *adj* **:** having two or more main clauses and one or more subordinate clauses ⟨*compound-complex* sentence⟩

compound event *n* **:** a subset containing more than one element and belonging to an event space

compound eye *n* **:** an eye (as of an insect) made up of many separate visual units

compound fracture *n* **:** a breaking of a bone in such a way as to produce an open wound through which bone fragments stick out

compound interest *n* **:** interest paid or to be paid both on the principal and on accumulated unpaid interest

compound leaf *n* **:** a leaf in which the blade is divided to the midrib forming two or more leaflets on a common axis

compound microscope *n* **:** a microscope consisting of an objective and an eyepiece mounted in a telescoping tube

compound transform *n* **:** a sentence that is the result of joining two sentences by means of a coordinating conjunction

com·pre·hend \\ˌkäm-pri-ˈhend\\ *vb* **1 :** to grasp the meaning of **:** UNDERSTAND **2 :** to take in **:** EMBRACE — **com·pre·hend·i·ble** \\-ˈhen-də-bəl\\ *adj* — **com·pre·hen·si·bil·i·ty** \\-ˌhen(t)-sə-ˈbil-ət-ē\\ *n* — **com·pre·hen·si·ble** \\-ˈhen(t)-sə-bəl\\ *adj* — **com·pre·hen·si·bly** \\-ˈhen(t)-sə-blē\\ *adv*

com·pre·hen·sion \\ˌkäm-pri-ˈhen-chən\\ *n* **1 :** the act of comprehending **2 :** knowledge gained by comprehending **3 :** the capacity for understanding

com·pre·hen·sive \\-ˈhen(t)-siv\\ *adj* **1 :** including much or all **:** FULL ⟨*comprehensive* insurance⟩ ⟨a *comprehensive* examination⟩ **2 :** having wide mental comprehension — **com·pre·hen·sive·ness** *n*

1**com·press** \\kəm-ˈpres\\ *vb* **1 :** to press or become pressed together **2 :** to reduce the volume of by pressure — **com·press·i·bil·i·ty** \\-ˌpres-ə-ˈbil-ət-ē\\ *n* — **com·press·i·ble** \\-ˈpres-ə-bəl\\ *adj*

2**com·press** \\ˈkäm-ˌpres\\ *n* **1 :** a folded cloth or pad applied so as to press upon a body part ⟨a cold *compress*⟩ **2 :** a machine for compressing cotton into bales

com·pressed air \\kəm-ˌprest-\\ *n* **:** air under pressure greater than that of the atmosphere

com·pres·sion \\kəm-ˈpresh-ən\\ *n* **1 :** the act or process of compressing **:** the state of being compressed **2 :** the process of compressing the fuel mixture in the cylinders of an internal-combustion engine — **com·pres·sion·al** \\-(ə-)nəl\\ *adj*

com·pres·sor \\kəm-ˈpres-ər\\ *n* **:** a person or machine that compresses ⟨air *compressor*⟩

com·prise \\kəm-ˈprīz\\ *vb* **1 :** to include within a scope **:** CONTAIN **2 :** to be made up of **3 :** to make up **:** CONSTITUTE

1**com·pro·mise** \\ˈkäm-prə-ˌmīz\\ *n* **1 :** a settlement of a dispute by each party giving up some demands **2 :** a giving up to something objectionable or dangerous **:** SURRENDER ⟨a *compromise* of one's principles⟩ **3 :** the thing agreed upon as a result of concessions

2**compromise** *vb* **1 :** to adjust or settle differences by means of a compromise **2 :** to expose to discredit, suspicion, or danger ⟨*compromised* his reputation⟩ — **com·pro·mis·er** *n*

comp·trol·ler \kən-ˈtrō-lər, ˈkäm(p)-ˌ\ *n* : a public official who examines and certifies accounts

com·pul·sion \kəm-ˈpəl-shən\ *n* **1** : an act of compelling : the state of being compelled **2** : a force or agency that compels **3** : an irresistible impulse

com·pul·sive \-ˈpəl-siv\ *adj* : caused by or subject to psychological compulsion ⟨*compulsive* behavior⟩ — **com·pul·sive·ly** *adv*

com·pul·so·ry \-ˈpəls-(ə-)rē\ *adj* **1** : ENFORCED, REQUIRED ⟨*compulsory* education⟩ **2** : having the power of compelling

com·punc·tion \kəm-ˈpəŋ(k)-shən\ *n* **1** : sharp uneasiness caused by a sense of guilt : REMORSE **2** : a passing feeling of regret for some slight wrong ***syn*** see QUALM

com·pu·ta·tion \ˌkäm-pyu̇-ˈtā-shən\ *n* **1** : the act or action of computing : CALCULATION **2** : a system of reckoning **3** : an amount computed

com·pute \kəm-ˈpyüt\ *vb* : to determine or calculate esp. by mathematical means : RECKON — **com·put·a·ble** \-ˈpyüt-ə-bəl\ *adj*

com·put·er \-ˈpyüt-ər\ *n* : one that computes; *esp* : an automatic electronic machine for performing calculations

com·rade \ˈkäm-ˌrad, -rəd\ *n* : an intimate friend or associate : COMPANION — **com·rade·ship** \-ˌship\ *n*

[1]**con** \ˈkän\ *vb* **conned**; **con·ning** **1** : to study carefully **2** : MEMORIZE

[2]**con** *adv* : on the negative side : in opposition

[3]**con** *n* : the negative side in a debate or one holding it

con- — see COM-

conc *abbr* concentrated

con·cave \kän-ˈkāv, ˈkän-ˌ\ *adj* : hollowed or rounded inward like the inside of a bowl ⟨*concave* lens⟩ — **con·cav·i·ty** \-ˈkav-ət-ē\ *n*

con·ceal \kən-ˈsēl\ *vb* **1** : to hide from sight ⟨carry a *concealed* weapon⟩ **2** : to keep secret ⟨*conceal* a fact⟩ — **con·ceal·a·ble** \-ə-bəl\ *adj*

con·ceal·ment \-mənt\ *n* **1** : the act of hiding : the state of being hidden **2** : a hiding place ⟨attack from *concealment*⟩

con·cede \kən-ˈsēd\ *vb* **1** : to grant as a right or privilege **2** : to acknowledge or admit grudgingly : YIELD — **con·ced·er** *n*

con·ceit \kən-ˈsēt\ *n* **1** : excessive pride in one's own worth or virtue **2 a** : a fanciful idea **b** : an elaborate way of expressing something ***syn*** see PRIDE ***ant*** humility

con·ceit·ed \-ˈsēt-əd\ *adj* : having an excessively high opinion of oneself — **con·ceit·ed·ly** *adv* — **con·ceit·ed·ness** *n*

con·ceive \kən-ˈsēv\ *vb* **1** : to become pregnant **2 a** : to take into the mind ⟨*conceived* a liking for the man⟩ **b** : to form an idea of : IMAGINE ⟨*conceive* a new system⟩ **3** : to have an opinion : THINK ⟨*conceived* of him as a genius⟩ — **con·ceiv·a·ble** \-ˈsē-və-bəl\ *adj* — **con·ceiv·a·bly** \-blē\ *n* — **con·ceiv·er** *n*

[1]**con·cen·trate** \ˈkän(t)-sən-ˌtrāt\ *vb* **1 a** : to bring, direct, or come toward or meet in a common center or objective **b** : to gather into one body, mass, or force **2** : to make stronger by removing the diluting or admixing material ⟨*concentrate* syrup⟩ ⟨*concentrate* ore⟩ **3** : to fix one's powers, efforts, or attention on one thing ⟨*concentrate* on a problem⟩ — **con·cen·tra·tor** \-ˌtrāt-ər\ *n*

[2]**concentrate** *n* : something concentrated ⟨frozen orange juice *concentrate*⟩

con·cen·tra·tion \ˌkän(t)-sən-ˈtrā-shən\ *n* **1** : the act or process of concentrating : the state of being concentrated; *esp* : direction of attention on a single object **2** : a concentrated mass **3** : the relative content of a component : STRENGTH ⟨the *concentration* of salt in a solution⟩

concentration camp *n* : a camp where persons (as prisoners of war, political prisoners, or refugees) are detained or confined

con·cen·tric \kən-ˈsen-trik, (ˈ)kän-\ *adj* : having a common center ⟨*concentric* circles⟩

con·cept \ˈkän-ˌsept\ *n* **1** : something conceived in the mind : THOUGHT, NOTION **2** : a general idea ⟨arrive at the *concept* of a flower by studying many different kinds of flowers⟩ — **con·cep·tu·al** \kən-ˈsep-chə(-wə)l\ *adj*

con·cep·tion \kən-ˈsep-shən\ *n* **1 a** : the act of becoming pregnant **b** : the state of being brought into being as an embryo **2** : BEGINNING **3 a** : the function or process of conceiving ideas **b** : CONCEPT **4** : the originating of an idea ⟨*conception* of a new device⟩

[1]**con·cern** \kən-ˈsərn\ *vb* **1** : to relate to : be about ⟨the novel *concerns* three soldiers⟩ **2** : to be the business or affair of ⟨the problem *concerns* us all⟩ **3** : to make anxious or worried ⟨his mother's illness *concerns* him⟩ **4** : ENGAGE, OCCUPY ⟨*concerned* himself in the matter⟩

syn CONCERN, AFFECT can mean to have a bearing on. CONCERN suggests a matter that bears indirectly ⟨urban problems that *concern* people in the suburbs⟩; AFFECT suggests a factor that bears more directly ⟨the amount of rainfall *affects* plant growth⟩

[2]**concern** *n* **1** : something that concerns one : AFFAIR ⟨the *concerns* of the day⟩ **2** : marked regard or care : ANXIETY ⟨deep *concern* for his friend's welfare⟩ ⟨public *concern* over the war danger⟩ **3** : a business or manufacturing establishment

con·cerned \-ˈsərnd\ *adj* : DISTURBED, ANXIOUS ⟨*concerned* for his health⟩

con·cern·ing \-ˈsər-niŋ\ *prep* : relating to ⟨news *concerning* friends⟩

[1]**con·cert** \kən-ˈsərt\ *vb* : to plan or arrange together : settle by agreement

[2]**con·cert** \ˈkän(t)-(ˌ)sərt\ *n* **1** : agreement in design or plan ⟨work in *concert*⟩ **2** : musical harmony : CONCORD **3** : a musical performance usu. by several voices or instruments or both

con·cert·ed \kən-ˈsərt-əd\ *adj* **1 a** : mutually contrived or agreed ⟨*concerted* effort⟩ **b** : performed in unison ⟨*concerted* artillery fire⟩ **2** : arranged in parts for several voices ⟨*concerted* music⟩

con·cer·ti·na \ˌkän(t)-sər-ˈtē-nə\ *n* : a musical instrument of the accordion family

concertina

ə abut | ər further | a back | ā bake | ä cot, cart | au̇ out | ch chin | e less | ē easy | g gift | i trip | ī life | j joke | ŋ sing | ō flow | ȯ flaw | ȯi coin | th thin | t͟h this | ü loot | u̇ foot | y yet | yü few | yu̇ furious | zh vision

con·cert·mas·ter \'kän(t)-sərt-ˌmas-tər\ *or* **con·cert·meis·ter** \-ˌmī-stər\ *n* : the leader of the first violins and assistant conductor
con·cer·to \kən-'chert-ō\ *n, pl* **-tos** *or* **-ti** \-(ˌ)ē\ : a piece for one or more soloists and orchestra usu. in three movements
concert overture *n* : an independent orchestral composition that is often descriptive in nature
con·ces·sion \kən-'sesh-ən\ *n* **1** : the act or an instance of conceding **2** : something conceded : ACKNOWLEDGMENT **3 a** : a grant of property or of a right by a government ⟨mining *concession*⟩ **b** : a lease of a part of premises for some purpose ⟨a soft-drink *concession*⟩
con·ces·sion·aire \kən-ˌsesh-ə-'na(ə)r, -'ne(ə)r\ *n* : the recipient or operator of a concession
conch \'käŋk, 'känch\ *n, pl* **conchs** \'käŋks\ *or* **conch·es** \'kän-chəz\ : a large spiral-shelled marine gastropod mollusk; *also* : its shell used esp. for cameos
con·chol·o·gy \käŋ-'käl-ə-jē\ *n* : a branch of zoology that deals with shells
con·cil·i·ate \kən-'sil-ē-ˌāt\ *vb* **1** : to make friendly : RECONCILE **2** : to gain the goodwill or favor of ⟨*conciliate* the opposition⟩ — **con·cil·i·a·tion** \-ˌsil-ē-'ā-shən\ *n* — **con·cil·i·a·tor** \-'sil-ē-ˌāt-ər\ *n* — **con·cil·ia·to·ry** \-'sil-yə-ˌtōr-ē, -'sil-ē-ə-, -ˌtȯr-\ *adj*
con·cise \kən-'sīs\ *adj* : marked by brevity of expression ⟨a *concise* review of the year's work⟩ — **con·cise·ly** *adv* — **con·cise·ness** *n*
con·clave \'kän-ˌklāv\ *n* : a private or secret meeting or assembly
con·clude \kən-'klüd\ *vb* **1** : to bring or come to an end : FINISH ⟨*conclude* a speech⟩ **2** : to form an opinion : decide by reasoning ⟨*conclude* that he is right⟩ **3** : to bring about as a result : ARRANGE ⟨*conclude* an agreement⟩ — **con·clud·er** *n*
con·clu·sion \kən-'klü-zhən\ *n* **1** : a final decision reached by reasoning **2** : END, RESULT **3** : a final summing up ⟨the *conclusion* of a speech⟩ **4** : an act or instance of concluding
con·clu·sive \kən-'klü-siv, -ziv\ *adj* : DECISIVE, CONVINCING ⟨*conclusive* proof⟩ — **con·clu·sive·ly** *adv* — **con·clu·sive·ness** *n*
con·coct \kən-'käkt, kän-\ *vb* **1** : to prepare by combining various ingredients ⟨*concoct* a stew⟩ **2** : to make up : INVENT ⟨*concoct* a likely story⟩ — **con·coc·tion** \-'käk-shən\ *n*
con·com·i·tant \kən-'käm-ət-ənt, kän-\ *adj* : accompanying esp. in a subordinate or incidental way — **concomitant** *n* — **con·com·i·tant·ly** *adv*
con·cord \'kän-ˌkȯrd, 'käŋ-\ *n* : HARMONY
con·cord·ance \kən-'kȯrd-ən(t)s\ *n* **1** : an alphabetical index of the principal words in a book or in the works of an author with their immediate contexts **2** : CONCORD
con·cord·ant \-ənt\ *adj* : AGREEING, CONSONANT — **con·cord·ant·ly** *adv*
con·course \'kän-ˌkōrs, -ˌkȯrs\ *n* **1** : a flocking together : GATHERING **2** : a place (as a boulevard, open area, or hall) where many people pass or congregate ⟨the *concourse* of the bus terminal⟩
[1]**con·crete** \kän-'krēt, 'kän-ˌ\ *adj* **1** : naming a real thing or class of things : not abstract ⟨*man* is a *concrete* noun but *goodness* is not⟩ **2 a** : belonging to or derived from actual experience ⟨*concrete* examples⟩ **b** : REAL, TANGIBLE ⟨*concrete* evidence⟩ **3** \'kän-ˌ, kän-'\ : relating to or made of concrete ⟨*concrete* mixer⟩ — **con·crete·ly** *adv* — **con·crete·ness** *n*
[2]**con·crete** \'kän-ˌkrēt, kän-'\ *n* : a hard strong material made by mixing cement, sand, and gravel or broken rock with water and used esp. for pavements and in building
[3]**con·crete** \'kän-ˌkrēt, kän-'\ *vb* **1** : SOLIDIFY **2** : to cover with, form of, or set in concrete
con·cre·tion \kän-'krē-shən\ *n* **1** : the act or process of concreting or solidifying **2** : something concreted; *esp* : a hard usu. inorganic mass formed in a living body
con·cu·bine \'käŋ-kyə-ˌbīn, 'kän-\ *n* : a woman who lives with a man and among some peoples has a legally recognized position in his household less than that of a wife
con·cur \kən-'kər\ *vb* **con·curred**; **con·cur·ring** **1** : to happen together : COINCIDE **2** : to act together : COMBINE ⟨several mishaps *concurred* to spoil the occasion⟩ **3** : to be in agreement : ACCORD ⟨four justices *concurred* in the decision⟩
con·cur·rence \kən-'kər-ən(t)s, -'kə-rən(t)s\ *n* **1** : agreement in action, opinion, or intent : COOPERATION **2** : CONSENT **3** : a coming together : CONJUNCTION
con·cur·rent \kən-'kər-ənt, -'kə-rənt\ *adj* **1** : coming together : CONVERGING **2** : operating at the same time ⟨*concurrent* expeditions to the Antarctic⟩ **3** : acting in conjunction — **con·cur·rent·ly** *adv*
con·cus·sion \kən-'kəsh-ən\ *n* **1** : SHAKING, AGITATION **2** : bodily injury esp. of the brain resulting from a sudden sharp jar (as from a blow) — **con·cus·sive** \-'kəs-iv\ *adj*
cond *abbr* conductivity
con·demn \kən-'dem\ *vb* **1** : to declare to be wrong : CENSURE ⟨*condemned* his behavior⟩ **2 a** : to pronounce guilty : CONVICT **b** : SENTENCE **3** : to declare to be unfit for use or consumption — **con·dem·na·tion** \ˌkän-ˌdem-'nā-shən, -dəm-\ *n* — **con·demn·er** *or* **con·demn·or** \kən-'dem-ər\ *n*
con·den·sate \'kän-dən-ˌsāt, kən-'den-\ *n* : a product of condensation
con·den·sa·tion \ˌkän-ˌden-'sā-shən, -dən-\ *n* **1** : the act or process of condensing **2** : the quality or state of being condensed **3** : a product of condensing; *esp* : an abridgment of a literary work
con·dense \kən-'den(t)s\ *vb* **1** : to make or become more close, compact, concise, or dense : CONCENTRATE ⟨*condense* a paragraph into a sentence⟩ **2** : to change from a less dense to a denser form ⟨steam *condenses* into water⟩
con·dens·er \kən-'den(t)-sər\ *n* **1** : one that condenses **2** : CAPACITOR
con·de·scend \ˌkän-di-'send\ *vb* **1** : to descend to a level considered less dignified or humbler than one's own **2** : to grant favors with a superior air — **con·de·scend·ing·ly** \-'sen-diŋ-lē\ *adv*
con·de·scen·sion \ˌkän-di-'sen-chən\ *n* : a patronizing attitude
con·di·ment \'kän-də-mənt\ *n* [from Latin *condimentum*, from *condire* "to pickle", "season"] : something used to give an appetizing taste to food; *esp* : a pungent seasoning
[1]**con·di·tion** \kən-'dish-ən\ *n* **1** : a provision upon which the carrying out of an agreement depends ⟨*conditions* of employment⟩ **2** : something essential to the appearance or occurrence of something else **3** : a restricting factor : QUALIFICATION **4 a** : a state of being **b** : social status : RANK **c** *pl* : attendant circumstances **5** : state of health or fitness
[2]**condition** *vb* **-di·tioned**; **-di·tion·ing** \-'dish-(ə-)niŋ\ **1** : to put into a proper or desired condition **2 a** : to adapt, modify, or mold to respond in a particular way **b** : to change the behavior of (an organism) in such a way that a response to a given stimulus becomes associated with a different and

C

formerly unrelated stimulus ⟨dogs can be *conditioned* to salivate at the sound of a bell⟩ — **con·di·tion·er** \-'dish-(ə-)nər\ *n*

con·di·tion·al \kən-'dish-(ə-)nəl\ *adj* **1 :** dependent upon a condition ⟨a *conditional* sale⟩ **2 :** expressing, containing, or implying a supposition ⟨*conditional* clause⟩ — **con·di·tion·al·ly** \-ē\ *adv*

con·di·tioned *adj* **:** determined or established by conditioning ⟨a *conditioned* response to a stimulus⟩

con·dole \kən-'dōl\ *vb* **:** to express sympathetic sorrow ⟨*condole* with a widow in her grief⟩ — **con·do·lence** \kən-'dō-lən(t)s, 'kän-də-\ *n*

con·done \kən-'dōn\ *vb* **:** to pardon or overlook voluntarily ⟨*condones* his friend's faults⟩ ***syn*** see EXCUSE ***ant*** condemn — **con·do·na·tion** \ˌkän-dō-'nā-shən, -də-\ *n* — **con·don·er** \kən-'dō-nər\ *n*

con·dor \'kän-dər, -ˌdȯr\ *n* **:** a very large American

condor
(wingspread over 9 ft.)

vulture having the head and neck bare and the plumage dull black with a downy white neck ruff

con·duce \kən-'d(y)üs\ *vb* **:** to lead or tend to a usu. desirable result — **con·du·cive** \-'d(y)ü-siv\ *adj* — **con·du·cive·ness** *n*

¹**con·duct** \'kän-(ˌ)dəkt\ *n* **1 :** the act, manner, or process of carrying on **:** MANAGEMENT ⟨the *conduct* of foreign affairs⟩ **2 :** personal behavior ⟨marked down for bad *conduct*⟩

²**con·duct** \kən-'dəkt\ *vb* **1 :** GUIDE, ESCORT **2 :** LEAD, DIRECT ⟨*conduct* a business⟩ **3 a :** to convey in a channel **b :** to act as a medium for conveying ⟨copper *conducts* electricity⟩ **4 :** BEHAVE ⟨*conducted* himself well at the party⟩ **5 :** to act as leader or director ⟨*conduct* an orchestra⟩ — **con·duct·i·bil·i·ty** \-ˌdək-tə-'bil-ət-ē\ *n* — **con·duct·i·ble** \-'dək-tə-bəl\ *adj*

con·duct·ance \kən-'dək-tən(t)s\ *n* **1 :** conducting power **2 :** the readiness with which a conductor transmits an electric current **:** the reciprocal of electrical resistance

con·duc·tion \kən-'dək-shən\ *n* **1 :** the act of conducting or conveying **2 a :** transmission through a conductor **b :** CONDUCTIVITY **3 :** the transmission of stimulus-produced irritability through living and esp. nervous tissue

con·duc·tive \kən-'dək-tiv\ *adj* **:** having conductivity

con·duc·tiv·i·ty \ˌkän-ˌdək-'tiv-ət-ē, kən-\ *n, pl* **-ties :** the quality or power of conducting or transmitting

con·duc·tom·e·ter \-'täm-ət-ər\ *n* **:** an instrument for measuring conductivity; *esp* **:** one for comparing the rates at which rods of different materials transmit heat

con·duc·tor \kən-'dək-tər\ *n* **1 :** a person in charge of a public conveyance (as a bus or railroad train) **2 :** the leader of a musical ensemble **3 :** a substance or body capable of transmitting electricity, heat, or sound — **con·duc·tress** \-trəs\ *n*

con·duit \'kän-ˌd(y)ü-ət, -dət\ *n* **1 :** a channel through which water or other fluid is conveyed **2 :** a pipe, tube, or tile for protecting electric wires or cables

cone \'kōn\ *n* **1 :** a mass of overlapping woody scales that esp. in the pine and related trees are arranged on an axis and bear seeds between them; *also* **:** any of several flower or fruit clusters resembling such cones **2 a :** a solid generated by rotating a right triangle about one of its legs — called also *right circular cone* **b :** a solid figure tapering evenly to a point from a usu. circular base **3 a :** a cone-shaped object **b :** a sense organ of the retina that functions in color vision **c :** the apex of a volcano

cone 1

cone·nose \'kōn-ˌnōz\ *n* **:** any of various large bloodsucking bugs

Con·es·to·ga \ˌkän-ə-'stō-gə\ *n* **:** a broad-wheeled covered wagon formerly used for transporting freight across the prairies — called also *Conestoga wagon*

co·ney \'kō-nē\ *n* **1 a :** RABBIT; *esp* **:** the common European rabbit **b :** rabbit fur **2 :** PIKA

con·fec·tion \kən-'fek-shən\ *n* **:** a fancy dish or sweet

con·fec·tion·er \-sh(ə-)nər\ *n* **:** a manufacturer of or dealer in confections

con·fec·tion·ery \-shə-ˌner-ē\ *n, pl* **-er·ies 1 :** CONFECTIONS; *esp* **:** CANDY **2 :** a confectioner's art or business **3 :** a confectioner's shop

confed *abbr* confederate

con·fed·er·a·cy \kən-'fed-(ə-)rə-sē\ *n, pl* **-cies 1 :** a loose league of persons, parties, or states **:** ALLIANCE **2** *cap* **:** the Confederate States of America composed of the 11 southern states that seceded from the U.S. in 1860 and 1861

¹**con·fed·er·ate** \kən-'fed-(ə-)rət\ *adj* **1 :** united in a league **:** ALLIED **2** *cap* **:** of or relating to the Confederate States of America

²**confederate** *n* **1 :** ALLY, ACCOMPLICE **2** *cap* **:** a soldier, citizen, or adherent of the Confederate States of America

³**con·fed·er·ate** \-'fed-ə-ˌrāt\ *vb* **:** to unite in a confederacy

Confederate Memorial Day *n* **:** any of several days appointed for the commemoration of servicemen of the Confederacy: **a :** April 26 in Alabama, Florida, Georgia, and Mississippi **b :** May 10 in No. and So. Carolina **c :** May 30 in Virginia **d :** June 3 in Kentucky, Louisiana, and Texas

con·fed·er·a·tion \kən-ˌfed-ə-'rā-shən\ *n* **1 :** an act

ə abut	ər further	a back	ā bake	
ä cot, cart	aù out	ch chin	e less	ē easy
g gift	i trip	ī life	j joke	ng sing	ō flow
ȯ flaw	ȯi coin	th thin	th this	ü loot
ù foot	y yet	yü few	yù furious	zh vision

of confederating : a state of being confederated **2** : LEAGUE, ALLIANCE

con·fer \kən-'fər\ *vb* **con·ferred**; **con·fer·ring** **1** : to give to grant publicly ⟨*confer* knighthood on him⟩ **2** : to compare views : CONSULT ⟨*confer* with the committee⟩ — **con·fer·ral** \-'fər-əl\ *n* — **con·fer·rer** \-'fər-ər\ *n*

con·fer·ee *or* **con·fer·ree** \ˌkän-fə-'rē\ *n* : one taking part in a conference

con·fer·ence \'kän-f(ə-)rən(t)s, -fərn(t)s\ *n* **1** : a meeting for formal discussion or exchange of opinions or the discussion itself **2** : a meeting of committees of two branches of a legislature to adjust differences esp. concerning laws in process of adoption **3** : an association of athletic teams representing educational institutions

con·fess \kən-'fes\ *vb* **1** : ACKNOWLEDGE, ADMIT ⟨*confess* one's guilt⟩ **2 a** : to admit one's sins to God or to a priest **b** : to act as confessor for ⟨the priest *confessed* the penitents⟩ ***syn*** see ACKNOWLEDGE ***ant*** renounce (*beliefs, principles*)

con·fessed·ly \-'fes-əd-lē, -'fest-lē\ *adv* : by confession : ADMITTEDLY

con·fes·sion \kən-'fesh-ən\ *n* **1** : an act of confessing; *esp* : a disclosure of one's sins to a priest **2** : a statement of something confessed ⟨the thief signed a *confession*⟩ **3** : a formal statement of religious beliefs : CREED **4** : a religious denomination

con·fes·sion·al \-'fesh-(ə-)nəl\ *n* **1** : the enclosed place in which a priest sits and hears confessions **2** : the practice of confessing to a priest

con·fes·sor \kən-'fes-ər\ *n* **1** : one that confesses **2** : a priest who hears confessions

con·fet·ti \kən-'fet-ē\ *n* [from Italian, literally "confections" denoting bonbons or plaster or paper imitations of these thrown at carnivals] : small bits of brightly colored paper made for throwing (as at weddings)

con·fi·dant \'kän-fə-ˌdant, -ˌdänt\ *n* : one to whom secrets are entrusted : a confidential friend

con·fi·dante \'kän-fə-ˌdant, -ˌdänt\ *n* : a female confidant

con·fide \kən-'fīd\ *vb* **1** : to have confidence : TRUST ⟨*confide* in a doctor's skill⟩ **2** : to show confidence by imparting secrets ⟨*confided* in her mother⟩ **3** : to tell confidentially ⟨*confide* a secret to a friend⟩ **4** : ENTRUST ⟨*confide* one's safety to the police⟩ — **con·fid·er** *n*

con·fi·dence \'kän-fəd-ən(t)s, -fə-ˌden(t)s\ *n* **1** : FAITH, TRUST ⟨had *confidence* in his coach⟩ **2** : consciousness of feeling sure : ASSURANCE ⟨spoke with great *confidence*⟩ **3 a** : reliance on another's secrecy or loyalty ⟨told a girl friend in *confidence*⟩ **b** : legislative support ⟨vote of *confidence*⟩ **4** : something told in confidence : SECRET

confidence game *n* : a swindle in which the swindler takes advantage of the trust he has persuaded the victim to place in him

confidence man *n* : a swindler in a confidence game

con·fi·dent \'kän-fəd-ənt, -fə-ˌdent\ *adj* : having or showing confidence : SURE, SELF-ASSURED ⟨*confident* of winning⟩ ⟨a *confident* manner⟩ — **con·fi·dent·ly** *adv*

con·fi·den·tial \ˌkän-fə-'den-chəl\ *adj* **1** : SECRET, PRIVATE ⟨*confidential* information⟩ **2** : INTIMATE, FAMILIAR ⟨a *confidential* tone of voice⟩ **3** : trusted with secret matters ⟨a *confidential* secretary⟩ — **con·fi·den·tial·ly** \-'dench-(ə-)lē\ *adv*

con·fid·ing \kən-'fīd-ing\ *adj* : tending to confide : TRUSTFUL — **con·fid·ing·ly** \-ing-lē\ *adv*

con·fig·u·ra·tion \kən-ˌfig-(y)ə-'rā-shən\ *n* : arrangement of parts or the pattern produced by such arrangement

1**con·fine** \'kän-ˌfīn\ *n* : BOUNDARY, LIMIT ⟨the *confines* of a city⟩

2**con·fine** \kən-'fīn\ *vb* **1** : to keep within limits : RESTRICT ⟨*confined* to quarters⟩ **2 a** : to shut up : IMPRISON ⟨*confined* for life⟩ **b** : to keep indoors ⟨*confined* with a cold⟩ — **con·fine·ment** \kən-'fīn-mənt\ *n* — **con·fin·er** *n*

con·firm \kən-'fərm\ *vb* **1** : to make firm or firmer (as in a habit, faith, or intention) : STRENGTHEN **2** : to make sure of the truth of : VERIFY ⟨*confirm* a suspicion by investigation⟩ **3** : APPROVE, RATIFY ⟨*confirm* a treaty⟩ **4** : to administer confirmation to — **con·firm·a·ble** \-'fər-mə-bəl\ *adj*

con·fir·ma·tion \ˌkän-fər-'mā-shən\ *n* **1** : an act or process of confirming **2** : a Christian rite admitting a baptized person to full church privileges **3** : something that confirms : PROOF — **con·firm·a·to·ry** \kən-'fər-mə-ˌtōr-ē, -ˌtȯr-\ *adj*

con·firmed \kən-'fərmd\ *adj* **1** : made firm : STRENGTHENED **2** : deeply established ⟨*confirmed* distrust of change⟩ **3** : HABITUAL, CHRONIC

con·fis·cate \'kän-fə-ˌskāt\ *vb* : to seize by authority for public use or as a penalty ⟨smuggled goods may be *confiscated*⟩ — **con·fis·ca·tion** \ˌkän-fə-'skā-shən\ *n* — **con·fis·ca·tor** \'kän-fə-ˌskāt-ər\ *n* — **con·fis·ca·to·ry** \kən-'fis-kə-ˌtōr-ē, -ˌtȯr-\ *adj*

con·fla·gra·tion \ˌkän-flə-'grā-shən\ *n* : a large disastrous fire

1**con·flict** \'kän-ˌflikt\ *n* **1** : FIGHT, BATTLE; *esp* : a prolonged struggle **2** : a clashing or sharp disagreement (as between ideas, interests, or purposes)

2**con·flict** \kən-'flikt, 'kän-ˌ\ *vb* : to be in opposition : CLASH ⟨duty and desire often *conflict*⟩

con·flu·ence \'kän-ˌflü-ən(t)s, kən-'\ *n* **1** : a flocking together to one place **2** : a flowing together or place of meeting esp. of streams

con·flu·ent \-ənt\ *adj* : flowing or coming together ⟨*confluent* rivers⟩

con·form \kən-'fȯrm\ *vb* **1** : to bring into harmony ⟨*conforms* his behavior to the circumstances⟩ **2** : to be similar or identical ⟨the data *conform* to the pattern⟩ **3** : to be obedient or compliant; *esp* : to adapt oneself to prevailing standards or customs — **con·form·er** *n* — **con·form·ist** \-'fȯr-məst\ *n*

con·form·a·ble \kən-'fȯr-mə-bəl\ *adj* **1** : corresponding in form or character ⟨*conformable* to established practice⟩ **2** : SUBMISSIVE, COMPLIANT — **con·form·a·bly** \-blē\ *adv*

con·for·mal \kən-'fȯr-məl, (')kän-\ *adj* : representing small areas in their true shape ⟨a *conformal* map⟩

con·for·ma·tion \ˌkän-(ˌ)fȯr-'mā-shən, -fər-\ *n* **1** : the act of conforming or producing conformity : ADAPTATION **2** : a shaping or putting into form **3 a** : STRUCTURE **b** : the form or outline esp. of an animal

con·for·mi·ty \kən-'fȯr-mət-ē\ *n, pl* **-ties** **1** : correspondence in form, manner, or character : AGREEMENT ⟨behaved in *conformity* with his beliefs⟩ **2** : action in accordance with a standard or authority : OBEDIENCE ⟨*conformity* to social custom⟩

con·found \kən-'fau̇nd, kän-\ *vb* **1** : DAMN **2** : to throw into disorder : mix up : CONFUSE — **con·found·ed·ly** *adv*

con·front \kən-'frənt\ *vb* **1** : to face esp. in challenge : OPPOSE ⟨*confront* an enemy⟩ **2** : to bring face-to-face : cause to meet ⟨*confront* him with his accuser⟩ ⟨*confronted* with difficulties⟩ — **con·fron·ta·tion** \ˌkän-(ˌ)frən-'tā-shən\ *n*

Con·fu·cian \kən-'fyü-shən\ *adj* : of or relating to the Chinese philosopher Confucius or his teachings or followers — **Con·fu·cian·ism** \-shə-ˌniz-əm\ *n* — **Con·fu·cian·ist** \-shə-nəst\ *n or adj*

con·fuse \kən-ˈfyüz\ *vb* **1 a :** to make mentally unclear or uncertain : PERPLEX ⟨a complicated problem *confuses* him⟩ **b :** DISCONCERT ⟨heckling *confused* the speaker⟩ **2 :** to make indistinct : BLUR ⟨stop *confusing* the issue⟩ **3 :** to mix up : JUMBLE ⟨his motives were hopelessly *confused*⟩ **4 :** to fail to distinguish between ⟨teachers always *confused* the twins⟩ — **con·fused·ly** \-ˈfyüz(-ə)d-lē\ *adv* — **con·fus·ing·ly** \-ˈfyü-zing-lē\ *adv* — **con·fu·sion** \-ˈfyü-zhən\ *n*

con·fute \kən-ˈfyüt\ *vb* : to overwhelm by argument : REFUTE — **con·fu·ta·tion** \ˌkän-fyu̇-ˈtā-shən\ *n*

cong *abbr* congress

con·ga \ˈkäng-gə\ *n* : a Cuban dance of African origin performed by a group usu. in single file

con game \ˈkän-\ *n* : CONFIDENCE GAME

con·geal \kən-ˈjēl\ *vb* **1 :** to change from a fluid to a solid state by or as if by cold **2 :** to make or become stiff, thick, or curdled : COAGULATE **3 :** to make or become rigid or inflexible — **con·geal·ment** \-mənt\ *n*

con·ge·nial \kən-ˈjē-nyəl\ *adj* **1 :** having the same disposition, interests, or tastes **2 :** suited to one's nature or tastes : AGREEABLE — **con·ge·ni·al·i·ty** \-ˌjē-nē-ˈal-ət-ē, -ˌjēn-ˈyal-\ *n* — **con·ge·nial·ly** \-nyə-lē\ *adv*

con·gen·i·tal \kən-ˈjen-ə-təl\ *adj* : existing at or dating from birth but usu. not hereditary ⟨*congenital* disease⟩ ***syn*** see INNATE

con·ger eel \ˌkäng-gər-\ *n* : a scaleless saltwater eel that sometimes grows to a length of eight feet and is an important food fish of Europe

con·gest \kən-ˈjest\ *vb* **1 :** to cause an excessive fullness of the blood vessels of (as an organ) **2 :** to block or obstruct by filling too full : CLOG, OVERCROWD ⟨*congested* streets⟩ — **con·ges·tion** \-ˈjes-chən\ *n* — **con·ges·tive** \-ˈjes-tiv\ *adj*

[1]**con·glom·er·ate** \kən-ˈgläm-(ə-)rət\ *adj* **1 :** made up of parts from various sources or of various kinds **2 :** densely clustered ⟨*conglomerate* flowers⟩

[2]**con·glom·er·ate** \-ˈgläm-ə-ˌrāt\ *vb* : to collect or form into a mass — **con·glom·er·a·tion** \-ˌgläm-ə-ˈrā-shən\ *n*

[3]**con·glom·er·ate** \kən-ˈgläm-(ə-)rət\ *n* **1 :** a composite mass or mixture; *esp* : rock composed of rounded fragments varying from small pebbles to large boulders in a cement (as of hardened clay) **2 :** a corporation engaging in many different kinds of business

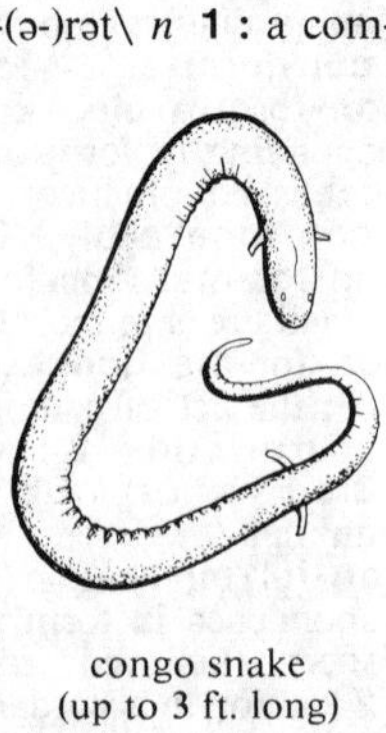
congo snake (up to 3 ft. long)

Con·go red \ˌkäng-ˌgō-\ *n* : a dye that is red in alkaline and blue in acid solution

con·go snake \ˈkäng-ˌgō-\ *n* : a long bluish black amphibian of the southeastern U.S. that has two pairs of very short limbs — called also *congo eel*

con·grat·u·late \kən-ˈgrach-ə-ˌlāt\ *vb* : to express sympathetic pleasure to on account of success or good fortune ⟨*congratulate* the winner⟩

ə abut ər further a back ā bake
ä cot, cart au̇ out ch chin e less ē easy
g gift i trip ī life j joke ng sing ō flow
ȯ flaw ȯi coin th thin t͟h this ü loot
u̇ foot y yet yü few yu̇ furious zh vision

con·grat·u·la·tion \-ˌgrach-ə-ˈlā-shən\ *n* **1 :** the act of congratulating **2 :** an expression of pleasure at another's success, happiness, or good fortune — usu. used in pl.

con·grat·u·la·to·ry \-ˈgrach-ə-lə-ˌtōr-ē, -ˌtȯr-\ *adj* : expressing congratulations ⟨a *congratulatory* smile⟩

con·gre·gate \ˈkäng-gri-ˌgāt\ *vb* : to collect into a group or crowd : ASSEMBLE — **con·gre·ga·tor** \-ˌgāt-ər\ *n*

con·gre·ga·tion \ˌkäng-gri-ˈgā-shən\ *n* **1 :** the action of congregating : the state of being congregated **2 :** a collection of things **3 :** an assembly of persons; *esp* : one for religious worship **4 :** the members of a church or synagogue

con·gre·ga·tion·al \-ˈgā-sh(ə-)nəl\ *adj* **1 :** of or relating to a congregation **2** *often cap* : of or relating to church government placing final authority in the local congregation — **con·gre·ga·tion·al·ism** \-ˌiz-əm\ *n, often cap* — **con·gre·ga·tion·al·ist** \-əst\ *n or adj, often cap*

con·gress \ˈkäng-grəs\ *n* **1 :** a formal meeting of delegates for discussion and action **2 :** the supreme legislative body of a nation and esp. of a republic **3 :** an association of constituent organizations **4 :** a single meeting or session of a congress — **con·gres·sion·al** \kən-ˈgresh-(ə-)nəl\ *adj* — **con·gres·sion·al·ly** \-ē\ *adv*

con·gress·man \ˈkäng-grəs-mən\ *n* : a member of a congress; *esp* : a member of the U.S. House of Representatives — **con·gress·wom·an** \-ˌwu̇m-ən\ *n*

con·gru·ence \kən-ˈgrü-ən(t)s, ˈkän-grə-wən(t)s\ *n* : the quality or state of having the same size and shape

con·gru·en·cy \-ən-sē, -wən-\ *n* : CONGRUENCE

con·gru·ent \kən-ˈgrü-ənt, ˈkäng-grə-wənt\ *adj* **1 :** SUITABLE, AGREEING ⟨the report proved to be *congruent* with the facts⟩ **2 :** capable of being placed over another figure so that all points of the one correspond to all points of the other : having the same size and shape ⟨*congruent* triangles⟩ — **con·gru·ent·ly** *adv*

con·gru·i·ty \kən-ˈgrü-ət-ē, kän-\ *n* **1 :** the quality or state of being congruent or congruous : AGREEMENT, HARMONY **2 :** a point of agreement

con·gru·ous \ˈkäng-grə-wəs\ *adj* **1 a :** being in agreement, harmony, or correspondence **b :** SUITABLE, APPROPRIATE **2 :** marked by harmony among parts — **con·gru·ous·ly** *adv*

con·ic \ˈkän-ik\ *adj* **1 :** CONICAL **2 :** of or relating to a cone

con·i·cal \ˈkän-i-kəl\ *adj* : resembling a cone esp. in shape — **con·i·cal·ly** \-i-k(ə-)lē\ *adv*

conic section *n* : a curve formed of the intersection of a plane and a cone

con·i·fer \ˈkän-ə-fər, ˈkō-nə-\ *n* : any of an order of mostly evergreen trees and shrubs including forms (as pines) with true cones — **co·nif·er·ous** \kō-ˈnif-(ə-)rəs, kə-\ *adj*

conj *abbr* conjunction

con·jec·tur·al \kən-ˈjek-chə-rəl\ *adj* **1 :** of the nature of, involving, or based on conjecture **2 :** given to conjectures — **con·jec·tur·al·ly** \-rə-lē\ *adv*

[1]**con·jec·ture** \kən-ˈjek-chər\ *n* **1 :** inference from inadequate evidence **2 :** a conclusion reached by surmise or guesswork

[2]**conjecture** *vb* **-jec·tured**; **-jec·tur·ing :** GUESS, SURMISE — **con·jec·tur·er** *n*

con·join \kən-ˈjȯin, kän-\ *vb* : to join together for a common purpose

con·joint \-ˈjȯint\ *adj* **1 :** UNITED, CONJOINED **2 :** made up of or carried on by two or more in combination : JOINT — **con·joint·ly** *adv*

con·ju·gal \'kän-ji-gəl, kən-'jü-\ *adj* : of or relating to marriage : MATRIMONIAL — **con·ju·gal·ly** \-gə-lē\ *adv*

con·ju·gant \'kän-ji-gənt\ *n* : either of a pair of conjugating gametes or organisms

[1]**con·ju·gate** \'kän-ji-gət, -jə-ˌgāt\ *adj* : joined together esp. in pairs : COUPLED — **con·ju·gate·ly** *adv*

[2]**con·ju·gate** \'kän-jə-ˌgāt\ *vb* **1** : to give the various forms of a verb in order **2** : to join together : COUPLE **3** : to unite chemically so that the product is easily broken down into the original compounds **4** : to pair and fuse in conjugation

con·ju·ga·tion \ˌkän-jə-'gā-shən\ *n* **1** : the act of conjugating : the state of being conjugated **2** : a class of verbs having the same type of inflectional forms **3** : fusion of usu. similar gametes that in some lower plants serves as a simple form of sexual reproduction

con·junc·tion \kən-'jəng(k)-shən\ *n* **1** : the act or instance of conjoining : the state of being conjoined **2** : a word or expression that joins together words or word groups

con·junc·ti·va \ˌkän-ˌjəngk-'tī-və, -'tē-\ *n, pl* **-tivas** *or* **-ti·vae** \-'tī-(ˌ)vē, -'tē-ˌvī\ : the mucous membrane that lines the inner surface of the eyelids and is continued over the front part of the eyeball — **con·junc·ti·val** \-vəl\ *adj*

con·junc·tive \kən-'jəng(k)-tiv\ *adj* **1** : CONNECTIVE **2** : done or existing in conjunction **3** : being or functioning like a conjunction ⟨*conjunctive* adverbs such as *however* and *therefore*⟩ — **conjunctive** *n* — **con·junc·tive·ly** *adv*

con·junc·ti·vi·tis \kən-ˌjəng(k)-ti-'vīt-əs\ *n* : inflammation of the conjunctiva

con·ju·ra·tion \ˌkän-jə-'rā-shən, ˌkən-\ *n* **1** : the act of conjuring : INCANTATION **2** : an expression or trick used in conjuring

con·jure \'kän-jər, 'kən-; *in sense 1* kən-'jů(ə)r\ *vb* **1** : to entreat earnestly : BESEECH **2 a** : to summon by invocation or incantation **b** : to affect or effect by or as if by magic ⟨*conjure* up a scheme⟩ **3** : to practice magic or magical tricks — **con·jur·er** *or* **con·ju·ror** \'kän-jər-ər, 'kən-\ *n*

conk \'kängk, 'kȯngk\ *vb* : to break down; *esp* : STALL ⟨the motor *conked* out⟩

con man \'kän-ˌman\ *n* : CONFIDENCE MAN

con mo·to \kän-'mō-tō, kōn-\ *adv* : with movement : SPIRITEDLY — used as a direction in music

Conn *abbr* Connecticut

con·nate \kä-'nāt, 'kän-ˌāt\ *adj* : entrapped in sediments at the time of deposition ⟨*connate* water⟩

con·nect \kə-'nekt\ *vb* **1** : to join or link together directly or by something coming between : UNITE ⟨towns *connected* by a railroad⟩ ⟨the two bones *connect* at the elbow⟩ **2** : to attach by personal relationship or association ⟨*connected* by marriage⟩ **3** : to associate in the mind ⟨*connect* two ideas⟩ **4** : to be related ⟨an event *connected* with his death⟩ **5** : to meet at a time and place suitable for transferring passengers or freight ⟨*connecting* trains⟩ ***syn*** see JOIN ***ant*** disconnect — **con·nec·tor** *or* **con·nect·er** \-'nek-tər\ *n*

con·nect·ed·ly *adv* : in a connected manner : COHERENTLY

con·nec·tion \kə-'nek-shən\ *n* **1** : the act of connecting **2** : the fact or condition of being connected : RELATIONSHIP ⟨the *connection* between dirt and disease⟩ **3** : a thing that connects : BOND, LINK ⟨a loose *connection* in a radio⟩ ⟨a telephone *connection*⟩ **4 a** : a person connected with others ⟨a *connection* by marriage⟩ **b** : a social, professional, or commercial relationship ⟨business *connections* in the city⟩ **5** : a means of continuing a journey by transferring to another conveyance ⟨make a *connection* for San Francisco at Chicago⟩

[1]**con·nec·tive** \kə-'nek-tiv\ *adj* : connecting or tending to connect — **con·nec·tive·ly** *adv* — **con·nec·tiv·i·ty** \ˌkä-ˌnek-'tiv-ət-ē\ *n*

[2]**connective** *n* : something that connects; *esp* : a word or expression (as a conjunction or a relative pronoun) that connects words or word groups

connective tissue *n* : a tissue with much intercellular substance or many interlacing processes that forms a supporting framework (as of bone, cartilage, and fibrous tissue) for the body and its parts

conn·ing tower \'kän-ing-\ *n* **1** : an armored pilothouse (as on a battleship) **2** : a raised structure on the deck of a submarine used as an observation post and as an entrance

conning tower 2

con·nive \kə-'nīv\ *vb* [from Latin *conivēre*, literally "to shut the eyes"] **1** : to pretend ignorance of something that one ought to oppose or stop **2** : to cooperate secretly or have a secret understanding — **con·niv·ance** \kə-'nī-vən(t)s\ *n* — **con·niv·er** *n*

con·nois·seur \ˌkän-ə-'sər, -'sů(ə)r\ *n* : a person competent to act as a judge in matters of taste and appreciation : EXPERT ⟨a *connoisseur* of rare books⟩

con·no·ta·tion \ˌkän-ə-'tā-shən\ *n* : a meaning or significance suggested by a word or an expression apart from and in addition to its denotation ⟨the word *home* with all its heart-warming *connotations*⟩

con·note \kə-'nōt\ *vb* : to suggest or mean along with or in addition to the exact meaning ⟨the word *cell* means a small compartment but it may *connote* imprisonment⟩

con·nu·bi·al \kə-'n(y)ü-bē-əl\ *adj* : CONJUGAL — **con·nu·bi·al·ly** \-bē-ə-lē\ *adv*

con·quer \'käng-kər\ *vb* **con·quered**; **con·quer·ing** \-k(ə-)riŋ\ **1** : to get or gain by force of arms ⟨*conquer* a country⟩ **2** : to overcome by force of arms : DEFEAT ⟨*conquered* all his enemies⟩ **3** : OVERCOME, SUBDUE ⟨*conquer* a habit⟩ **4** : to be victorious — **con·quer·or** \-kər-ər\ *n*

con·quest \'kän-ˌkwest, 'käng-\ *n* **1** : the act or process of conquering **2 a** : something conquered; *esp* : territory taken in war **b** : a person whose affections have been won

con·quis·ta·dor \kȯng-'kēs-tə-ˌdȯr, kän-'k(w)is-\ *n, pl* **con·quis·ta·do·res** \-ˌkēs-tə-'dȯr-ēz, -ˌk(w)is-, -'dōr-\ *or* **con·quis·ta·dors** : CONQUEROR; *esp* : a leader in the Spanish conquest of America in the 16th century

cons *abbr* consonant

con·san·guin·e·ous \ˌkän-ˌsan-'gwin-ē-əs, -ˌsang-\ *adj* : descended from the same ancestor — **con·san·guin·i·ty** \-'gwin-ət-ē\ *n*

con·science \'kän-chən(t)s\ *n* : the sense of the moral goodness or blameworthiness of one's own conduct, intentions, or character together with a feeling of obligation to do right

con·sci·en·tious \ˌkän-chē-'en-chəs\ *adj* **1** : governed by or in accordance with one's conscience

: SCRUPULOUS **2** : METICULOUS, CAREFUL ⟨a *conscientious* worker⟩ — **con·sci·en·tious·ly** *adv* — **con·sci·en·tious·ness** *n*

conscientious objector *n* : a person who refuses to serve in the armed forces or to bear arms as contrary to his moral or religious principles

con·scious \'kän-chəs\ *adj* **1** : perceiving or noticing facts or feelings : AWARE **2** : known or felt by one's inner self ⟨*conscious* guilt⟩ **3** : capable of or marked by thought, will, design, or perception ⟨a rock is not *conscious*⟩ **4** : mentally alert or active : AWAKE ⟨became *conscious* again⟩ **5** : KNOWING, INTENTIONAL ⟨a *conscious* smile⟩ — **con·scious·ly** *adv*

con·scious·ness \'kän-chəs-nəs\ *n* **1** : awareness of something ⟨*consciousness* of evil⟩ **2** : the condition of having ability to feel, think, and react : MIND **3** : the normal state of conscious life as distinguished from sleep or insensibility **4** : the part of mental life that is characterized by conscious thought and awareness

1**con·script** \'kän-ˌskript\ *adj* **1** : CONSCRIPTED **2** : made up of conscripted persons ⟨a *conscript* army⟩

2**conscript** *n* : a conscripted person

3**con·script** \kən-'skript\ *vb* : to enroll into service and esp. military service by compulsion — **con·scrip·tion** \kən-'skrip-shən\ *n*

con·se·crate \'kän(t)-sə-ˌkrāt\ *vb* **1** : to set apart to the service of God **2** : to devote to a purpose with deep solemnity or dedication **3** : to make inviolate ⟨rules *consecrated* by time⟩ — **con·se·cra·tor** \-ˌkrāt-ər\ *n*

con·se·cra·tion \ˌkän(t)-sə-'krā-shən\ *n* **1** : the act or ceremony of consecrating **2** : the state of being consecrated

con·sec·u·tive \kən-'sek-(y)ət-iv\ *adj* : following one after the other in order often with small intervals : SUCCESSIVE ⟨*consecutive* even numbers⟩ — **con·sec·u·tive·ly** *adv*

con·sen·sus \kən-'sen(t)-səs\ *n* **1** : general agreement (as in opinion or testimony) : ACCORD **2** : the trend of opinion

1**con·sent** \kən-'sent\ *vb* : to give assent or approval : AGREE — **con·sent·er** *n*

2**consent** *n* : approval of what is done or proposed

con·se·quence \'kän(t)-sə-ˌkwen(t)s, -si-kwən(t)s\ *n* **1** : RESULT, EFFECT **2** : a conclusion that results from reason or argument **3** : IMPORTANCE, SIGNIFICANCE ⟨a person of no *consequence*⟩

con·se·quent \-kwənt, -ˌkwent\ *adj* : following as a consequence ⟨a shipwreck with *consequent* loss of life⟩

con·se·quen·tial \ˌkän(t)-sə-'kwen-chəl\ *adj* **1** : CONSEQUENT **2** : having significant consequences : IMPORTANT **3** : SELF-IMPORTANT ⟨a *consequential* manner⟩

con·se·quent·ly \'kän(t)-sə-ˌkwent-lē, -si-kwənt-\ *adv* : as a result : ACCORDINGLY

con·ser·va·tion \ˌkän(t)-sər-'vā-shən\ *n* : a careful preservation and protection of something; *esp* : planned management of a natural resource to prevent exploitation, pollution, destruction, or neglect — **con·ser·va·tion·al** \-sh(ə-)nəl\ *adj* — **con·ser·va·tion·ist** \-sh(ə-)nəst\ *n*

ə abut   ər further   a back   ā bake
ä cot, cart   au̇ out   ch chin   e less   ē easy
g gift   i trip   ī life   j joke   ng sing   ō flow
ȯ flaw   ȯi coin   th thin   th this   ü loot
u̇ foot   y yet   yü few   yu̇ furious   zh vision

conservation of energy : a principle in physics that states that energy can neither be created nor destroyed and that the total energy of an isolated system remains constant

conservation of mass : a principle in physics that states that mass can neither be created nor destroyed and that the total mass of any material system is neither increased nor decreased by reactions between the parts — called also *conservation of matter*

con·ser·va·tism \kən-'sər-və-ˌtiz-əm\ *n* **1** : a political viewpoint supporting tradition and established institutions and preferring gradual development to abrupt change **2** : tendency to prefer an existing situation or ways and to be suspicious of change

1**con·ser·va·tive** \kən-'sər-vət-iv\ *adj* **1** : tending to conserve or preserve **2** : of or relating to conservatism **3** : tending or disposed to maintain existing views, conditions, or institutions : TRADITIONAL **4** : MODERATE, CAUTIOUS ⟨a *conservative* estimate⟩ **5** : marked by traditional standards of taste, elegance, or manners ⟨a *conservative* suit⟩ ⟨a *conservative* dresser⟩ — **con·ser·va·tive·ly** *adv* — **con·ser·va·tive·ness** *n*

2**conservative** *n* **1 a** : an adherent or advocate of conservatism **b** *cap* : a member or supporter of a conservative political party **2** : a cautious or discreet person

Conservative Judaism *n* : a movement in Judaism that holds sacred the Torah and the religious traditions but accepts some liturgical and ritual change

con·ser·va·to·ry \kən-'sər-və-ˌtōr-ē, -ˌtȯr-\ *n, pl* **-ries** **1** : a greenhouse for growing or displaying plants **2** : a school specializing in one of the fine arts

1**con·serve** \kən-'sərv\ *vb* **1** : to keep in a safe or sound state : PRESERVE **2** : to preserve with sugar — **con·serv·er** *n*

2**con·serve** \'kän-ˌsərv\ *n* **1** : CONFECTION; *esp* : a candied fruit **2** : PRESERVE; *esp* : one prepared from a mixture of fruits

con·sid·er \kən-'sid-ər\ *vb* **-sid·ered; -sid·er·ing** \-'sid-(ə-)ring\ **1** : to think over carefully : PONDER **2** : to regard highly : ESTEEM **3** : to think of in a certain way : regard as being ⟨*consider* the price too high⟩

con·sid·er·a·ble \kən-'sid-ər(-ə)-bəl, -'sid-rə-bəl\ *adj* **1** : deserving consideration : IMPORTANT **2** : large in extent, amount, or quantity ⟨a *considerable* area⟩ ⟨a *considerable* number⟩ — **con·sid·er·a·bly** \-blē\ *adv*

con·sid·er·ate \kən-'sid-(ə-)rət\ *adj* **1** : marked by or given to careful consideration **2** : thoughtful of the rights and feelings of others — **con·sid·er·ate·ly** *adv* — **con·sid·er·ate·ness** *n*

con·sid·er·a·tion \kən-ˌsid-ə-'rā-shən\ *n* **1** : careful thought : DELIBERATION **2** : thoughtfulness for other people **3** : MOTIVE, REASON **4** : RESPECT, REGARD ⟨a writer held in high *consideration*⟩ **5** : a payment made in return for something : COMPENSATION

con·sid·er·ing *prep* : in view of : taking into account

con·sign \kən-'sīn\ *vb* **1** : to give over to another's care : ENTRUST **2** : to give, transfer, or deliver formally ⟨*consign* a body to the grave⟩ **3** : to send or address to an agent to be cared for or sold — **con·sign·a·ble** \-'sī-nə-bəl\ *adj* — **con·sign·ee** \kən-ˌsī-'nē, ˌkän-ˌsī-, ˌkän(t)-sə-\ *n* — **con·sign·or** \kən-'sī-nər; kən-ˌsī-'nȯ(ə)r, ˌkän-ˌsī-, ˌkän(t)-sə-\ *n*

con·sign·ment \kən-'sīn-mənt\ *n* **1** : the act or process of consigning **2** : something consigned; *esp* : a single shipment of goods delivered to an agent for sale

con·sist \kən-'sist\ *vb* **1** : to be contained : LIE, RE-

SIDE ⟨honesty *consists* in telling the truth⟩ **2** : to be made up or composed ⟨breakfast *consisted* of cereal, milk, and fruit⟩

con·sis·tence \kən-'sis-tən(t)s\ *n* : CONSISTENCY

con·sis·ten·cy \kən-'sis-tən-sē\ *n, pl* **-cies** **1** : the degree of density, firmness, viscosity, or resistance to movement or separation of constituent particles ⟨mud with the *consistency* of glue⟩ **2** : AGREEMENT, HARMONY **3** : harmony with past performance or with stated aims

con·sis·tent \kən-'sis-tənt\ *adj* **1** : possessing firmness or coherence **2** : AGREEING, HARMONIOUS ⟨*consistent* statements⟩ **3** : uniform throughout — **con·sis·tent·ly** *adv*

con·so·la·tion \ˌkän(t)-sə-'lā-shən\ *n* **1** : the act or an instance of consoling : the state of being consoled **2** : something that consoles — **con·sol·a·to·ry** \kən-'säl-ə-ˌtōr-ē, -sō-lə-, -ˌtȯr-\ *adj*

¹**con·sole** \kən-'sōl\ *vb* : to comfort in times of grief, distress, or suffering ⟨try to *console* a child who has lost a pet⟩ — **con·sol·a·ble** \-'sō-lə-bəl\ *adj*

²**con·sole** \'kän-ˌsōl\ *n* **1** : an ornamental architectural bracket or support **2 a** : the desk from which an organ is played **b** : a panel or cabinet with dials and switches for controlling electrical or mechanical devices **3** : a cabinet (as for a radio or television set) designed to rest on the floor

con·sol·i·date \kən-'säl-ə-ˌdāt\ *vb* **1** : to join together into one whole : UNITE **2** : to make firm or secure : STRENGTHEN ⟨*consolidate* a beachhead⟩ — **con·sol·i·da·tion** \-ˌsäl-ə-'dā-shən\ *n*

consolidated school *n* : a public school usu. elementary and in a rural district that is formed by merging other schools

con·som·mé \ˌkän(t)-sə-'mā\ *n* : a clear soup chiefly of meat stock

con·so·nance \'kän(t)-s(ə-)nən(t)s\ *n* : harmony or agreement esp. of musical tones or speech sounds — **con·so·nant** \-s(ə-)nənt\ *adj* — **con·so·nant·ly** *adv*

con·so·nant \'kän(t)-s(ə-)nənt\ *n* **1** : a speech sound (as \p\, \n\, or \s\) characterized by narrowing or stoppage at one or more points in the breath channel **2** : a letter representing a consonant; *esp* : any letter of the English alphabet except *a, e, i, o,* and *u* — **con·so·nan·tal** \ˌkän(t)-sə-'nant-əl\ *adj*

¹**con·sort** \'kän-ˌsȯrt\ *n* **1** : a wife or husband : SPOUSE **2** : a ship sailing in company with another

²**con·sort** \kən-'sȯrt\ *vb* **1** : to keep company : ASSOCIATE **2** : ACCORD, HARMONIZE

con·spe·cif·ic \ˌkän(t)-spi-'sif-ik\ *adj* : of the same species

con·spic·u·ous \kən-'spik-yə-wəs\ *adj* **1** : obvious to the eye or mind **2** : attracting attention : STRIKING **3** : noticeably violating good taste ***syn*** see PROMINENT ***ant*** inconspicuous — **con·spic·u·ous·ly** *adv* — **con·spic·u·ous·ness** *n*

con·spir·a·cy \kən-'spir-ə-sē\ *n, pl* **-cies** **1** : the act of conspiring together **2 a** : an agreement among conspirators **b** : a group of conspirators

con·spir·a·tor \kən-'spir-ət-ər\ *n* : one that conspires : PLOTTER

con·spir·a·to·ri·al \kən-ˌspir-ə-'tōr-ē-əl, -'tȯr-\ *adj* : of, relating to, or characteristic of a conspiracy — **con·spir·a·to·ri·al·ly** \-ē-ə-lē\ *adv*

con·spire \kən-'spī(ə)r\ *vb* **1** : to agree secretly to do an unlawful act : PLOT ⟨*conspire* to overthrow the government⟩ **2** : to act in harmony

const *abbr* **1** constant **2** constitution **3** constitutional

con·sta·ble \'kän(t)-stə-bəl, 'kən(t)-\ *n* [from Old French *conestable,* from Latin *comes stabuli,* literally "officer of the stable"; see ³COUNT] **1** : a high officer of a medieval royal or noble household **2** : the warden of a royal castle or a fortified town **3** : a public officer responsible for keeping the peace

con·stab·u·lary \kən-'stab-yə-ˌler-ē\ *n, pl* **-lar·ies** **1** : an organized body of constables or of policemen **2** : an armed police force organized on military lines

con·stan·cy \'kän(t)-stən-sē\ *n* **1 a** : firmness in one's beliefs : STEADFASTNESS **b** : FIDELITY, LOYALTY **2** : freedom from change

¹**con·stant** \'kän(t)-stənt\ *adj* **1** : STEADFAST, FIRM **2** : FAITHFUL, LOYAL **3** : INVARIABLE, UNIFORM **4** : continually recurring : REGULAR — **con·stant·ly** *adv*

²**constant** *n* : something unchanging; *esp* : a number whose value does not change in a given mathematical discussion

con·stan·tan \'kän(t)-stən-ˌtan\ *n* : an alloy of copper and nickel used for electrical resistors and in thermocouples

con·stel·la·tion \ˌkän(t)-stə-'lā-shən\ *n* : any of 88 groups of stars forming patterns (as the Big Dipper) or an area of the heavens including one of these groups

con·ster·na·tion \ˌkän(t)-stər-'nā-shən\ *n* : amazement or dismay that hinders or throws into confusion

con·sti·pate \'kän(t)-stə-ˌpāt\ *vb* : to cause constipation in

con·sti·pa·tion \ˌkän(t)-stə-'pā-shən\ *n* : abnormally difficult or infrequent bowel movement

con·stit·u·en·cy \kən-'stich-(ə-)wən-sē\ *n, pl* **-cies** **1** : a body of citizens entitled to elect a representative to a legislative or other public body **2** : the residents in an electoral district **3** : an electoral district

¹**con·stit·u·ent** \kən-'stich-(ə-)wənt\ *n* **1** : one of the parts of which a thing is made up : ELEMENT ⟨flour is the chief *constituent* of bread⟩ **2** : a voter or resident in a constituency

²**constituent** *adj* **1** : forming a part of a whole : COMPONENT **2** : having the power to create a government or frame or amend a constitution ⟨a *constituent* assembly⟩

con·sti·tute \'kän(t)-stə-ˌt(y)üt\ *vb* **1** : to appoint to an office or duty ⟨a duly *constituted* representative⟩ **2** : to set up : ESTABLISH ⟨a fund was *constituted* to help needy students⟩ **3** : to make up : FORM ⟨twelve months *constitute* a year⟩

con·sti·tu·tion \ˌkän(t)-stə-'t(y)ü-shən\ *n* **1** : the act of establishing, making, or setting up **2 a** : the physical makeup of the individual : PHYSIQUE **b** : the structure, composition, or nature of something **3 a** : the basic principles and laws of a nation, state, or social group that determine the powers and duties of the government and guarantee certain rights to the people in it **b** : a document containing a constitution

¹**con·sti·tu·tion·al** \-sh(ə-)nəl\ *adj* **1** : of or relating to a person's physical or mental makeup **2** : of, relating to, or in accordance with the constitution of a nation or state ⟨a *constitutional* amendment⟩ ⟨*constitutional* rights⟩ — **con·sti·tu·tion·al·ly** \-ē\ *adv*

²**constitutional** *n* : a walk or other exercise taken for one's health

con·sti·tu·tion·al·i·ty \ˌkän(t)-stə-ˌt(y)ü-shə-'nal-ət-ē\ *n* : the quality or state of being in accordance with the provisions of a constitution

constr *abbr* construction

con·strain \kən-'strān\ *vb* **1** : COMPEL **2** : CONFINE **3** : RESTRAIN

con·straint \kən-'strānt\ *n* **1** : the act of con-

C

straining : the state of being constrained **2 :** a constraining agency or force : CHECK **3 :** a holding back of one's feelings, behavior, or actions : EMBARRASSMENT

con·strict \kən-'strikt\ *vb* : to make or become narrower or smaller : SQUEEZE, TIGHTEN — **con·stric·tive** \-'strik-tiv\ *adj*

con·stric·tion \kən-'strik-shən\ *n* **1 :** an act of constricting : the state of being constricted : TIGHTENING ⟨the *constriction* of a snake's coils⟩ **2 :** something that constricts : a part that is constricted

con·stric·tor \kən-'strik-tər\ *n* **1 :** one that constricts **2 :** a constricting snake that kills prey by compression in its coils

con·struct \kən-'strəkt\ *vb* **1 :** to make or form by combining parts : BUILD **2 :** to draw (a geometrical figure) with suitable instruments and under specified conditions — **con·struct·i·ble** \-'strək-tə-bəl\ *adj* — **con·struc·tor** \-'strək-tər\ *n*

con·struc·tion \kən-'strək-shən\ *n* **1 :** the arrangement and connection of words or groups of words in a sentence **2 :** the process, art, or manner of constructing **3 :** a thing constructed : STRUCTURE **4 :** an interpretation or explanation of a statement or a fact ⟨put the wrong *construction* on a remark⟩

construction paper *n* : colored paper used for making cutouts and for crayon, ink, or watercolor drawings

con·struc·tive \kən-'strək-tiv\ *adj* **1 :** fitted for or given to constructing ⟨Edison was a *constructive* genius⟩ **2 :** helping to develop, improve, or reinforce something ⟨*constructive* suggestions⟩ — **con·struc·tive·ly** *adv* — **con·struc·tive·ness** *n*

con·strue \kən-'strü\ *vb* **1 :** to explain the grammatical relationships of the words in a sentence, clause, or phrase **2 :** to understand or explain the meaning of : INTERPRET — **con·stru·a·ble** \-'strü-ə-bəl\ *adj*

con·sul \'kän(t)-səl\ *n* **1 :** either of two chief magistrates of the Roman republic **2 :** an official appointed by a government to reside in a foreign country to represent the commercial interests of citizens of the appointing country — **con·sul·ar** \-s(ə-)lər\ *adj* — **con·sul·ship** \-səl-,ship\ *n*

con·sul·ate \'kän(t)-s(ə-)lət\ *n* **1 :** government by consuls **2 :** the office or term of office of a consul **3 :** the residence or office of a consul

con·sult \kən-'səlt\ *vb* **1 :** to seek the opinion or advice of ⟨*consult* a doctor⟩ **2 :** to seek information from ⟨*consult* an encyclopedia⟩ **3 :** to have regard to : CONSIDER ⟨*consult* one's best interests⟩ **4 :** to engage in deliberation : CONFER — **con·sult·er** *n*

con·sult·ant \kən-'səlt-ənt\ *n* **1 :** one who consults another **2 :** one who gives professional advice or services

con·sul·ta·tion \,kän(t)-səl-'tā-shən\ *n* **1 :** COUNCIL, CONFERENCE; *esp* : a deliberation between physicians on a case or its treatment **2 :** the act of consulting or conferring

con·sume \kən-'süm\ *vb* **1 :** to destroy by or as if by fire **2 :** to use up : EXPEND **3 :** to eat or drink up **4 :** to engage one's interest or attention ***syn*** see EAT — **con·sum·a·ble** \-'sü-mə-bəl\ *adj*

con·sum·er \kən-'sü-mər\ *n* **1 :** one that consumes; *esp* : one that buys and uses economic goods **2 :** an organism that requires complex organic compounds for food which it obtains by preying on other organisms or eating particles of organic matter

consumer sentence *n* : a basic sentence into which an input sentence is incorporated by a transformation and which provides the underlying structure of the output sentence

[1]**con·sum·mate** \kən-'səm-ət, 'kän(t)-sə-mət\ *adj* : of the highest degree or quality : COMPLETE, PERFECT ⟨*consummate* skill⟩ — **con·sum·mate·ly** *adv*

[2]**con·sum·mate** \'kän(t)-sə-,māt\ *vb* **1 :** to make perfect : FINISH, COMPLETE **2 :** to make (marital union) complete by sexual intercourse — **con·sum·ma·tion** \,kän(t)-sə-'mā-shən\ *n*

con·sump·tion \kən-'səm(p)-shən\ *n* **1 a :** the act or process of consuming **b :** the amount consumed ⟨weekly food *consumption*⟩ **2 a :** a progressive wasting away of the body esp. from tuberculosis of the lungs **b :** TUBERCULOSIS

[1]**con·sump·tive** \kən-'səm(p)-tiv\ *adj* **1 :** DESTRUCTIVE, WASTEFUL **2 :** of, relating to, or affected with consumption — **con·sump·tive·ly** *adv*

[2]**consumptive** *n* : a person affected with consumption

cont *abbr* **1** contents **2** continent

[1]**con·tact** \'kän-,takt\ *n* **1 :** union or touching of surfaces **2 :** the connection of two electrical conductors through which a current passes or a part made for such a connection **3 a :** a social or business connection : RELATIONSHIP **b :** a person with whom one has contact ⟨has *contacts* in government⟩ **4 :** communication or an establishing of communication ⟨make *contact* by radio⟩

[2]**con·tact** \'kän-,takt, kən-'\ *vb* : to bring or come into contact

[3]**con·tact** \'kän-,takt\ *adj* : involving contact ⟨football is a *contact* sport⟩

con·tact lens \,kän-,takt-\ *n* : a thin lens designed to fit over the cornea

con·ta·gion \kən-'tā-jən\ *n* **1 :** the passing of a disease from one individual to another by direct or indirect contact **2 :** a contagious disease or its causative agent (as a virus) **3 :** transmission of an influence to the mind of others or the influence transmitted ⟨the *contagion* of enthusiasm⟩ — **con·ta·gious** \-jəs\ *adj*

contagious disease *n* : a disease that can be communicated by contact with a person suffering from it, his bodily discharges, or something that has touched the patient or his bodily discharges

con·tain \kən-'tān\ *vb* **1 :** to keep within limits : hold back : RESTRAIN ⟨try to *contain* your anger⟩ **2 :** to have within : HOLD, ENCLOSE **3 :** COMPRISE, INCLUDE ⟨a gallon *contains* four quarts⟩ **4 :** to be divisible by esp. without a remainder ⟨20 *contains* 5 four times⟩ — **con·tain·a·ble** \-'tā-nə-bəl\ *adj* — **con·tain·ment** \-'tān-mənt\ *n*

con·tain·er \kən-'tā-nər\ *n* : one that contains; *esp* : RECEPTACLE

con·tam·i·nant \kən-'tam-ə-nənt\ *n* : something that contaminates

con·tam·i·nate \kən-'tam-ə-,nāt\ *vb* **1 :** to soil, stain, or infect by contact **2 :** to make impure or unfit for use ⟨water *contaminated* by sewage⟩ — **con·tam·i·na·tion** \-,tam-ə-'nā-shən\ *n* — **con·tam·i·na·tor** \-'tam-ə-,nāt-ər\ *n*

con·temn \kən-'tem\ *vb* : to view or treat with contempt

con·tem·plate \'känt-əm-,plāt, 'kän-,tem-\ *vb* **1 :** to consider long and carefully : MEDITATE **2 :** to have in mind : INTEND — **con·tem·pla·tor** \-,plāt-ər\ *n*

con·tem·pla·tion \ˌkänt-əm-ˈplā-shən, ˌkän-ˌtem-\ *n* **1** : concentration on spiritual things : MEDITATION **2** : the act of looking at or thinking about something steadily **3** : INTENTION, EXPECTATION ⟨store food in *contemplation* of winter⟩

con·tem·pla·tive \kən-ˈtem-plət-iv; ˈkänt-əm-ˌplāt-, ˈkän-ˌtem-\ *adj* : marked by or given to contemplation : MEDITATIVE — **con·tem·pla·tive·ly** *adv* — **con·tem·pla·tive·ness** *n*

con·tem·po·ra·ne·ous \kən-ˌtem-pə-ˈrā-nē-əs\ *adj* [from Latin *contemporaneus*, from *com-* and *tempor-*, stem of *tempus* "time"] : existing, occurring, or originating during the same time — **con·tem·po·ra·ne·ous·ly** *adv* — **con·tem·po·ra·ne·ous·ness** *n*

1**con·tem·po·rary** \kən-ˈtem-pə-ˌrer-ē\ *adj* **1** : CONTEMPORANEOUS ⟨*contemporary* events in different countries⟩ **2** : of the same age **3** : of the present time : LIVING, MODERN ⟨our *contemporary* writers⟩

2**contemporary** *n, pl* **-rar·ies** **1** : one that is contemporary with another ⟨Washington and Jefferson were *contemporaries*⟩ **2** : one of about the same age as another ⟨your *contemporaries* in school⟩

con·tempt \kən-ˈtem(p)t\ *n* **1** : the state of mind of one who despises : SCORN **2** : the state of being despised **3** : disobedience or disrespect to a court, judge, or legislative body

con·tempt·i·ble \kən-ˈtem(p)-tə-bəl\ *adj* : deserving contempt ⟨a *contemptible* lie⟩ — **con·tempt·i·bly** \-blē\ *adv*

con·temp·tu·ous \kən-ˈtem(p)-chə-wəs\ *adj* : feeling or showing contempt ⟨a *contemptuous* sneer⟩ — **con·temp·tu·ous·ly** *adv*

syn CONTEMPTUOUS, SCORNFUL, DISDAINFUL can mean feeling or showing contempt. CONTEMPTUOUS suggests a lofty attitude toward a despised object; SCORNFUL may imply anger and disgust often expressed in mockery; DISDAINFUL suggests haughty or insolent disregard (as of something considered unworthy of notice) ***ant*** respectful

con·tend \kən-ˈtend\ *vb* **1** : to compete with another in opposition or in rivalry **2** : STRIVE, STRUGGLE ⟨*contend* against difficulties⟩ **3** : ARGUE, MAINTAIN ⟨*contends* that his opinion is right⟩ — **con·tend·er** *n*

1**con·tent** \kən-ˈtent\ *adj* : SATISFIED

2**content** *vb* : to appease the desires of : SATISFY

3**content** *n* : CONTENTMENT; *esp* : freedom from care or discomfort

4**con·tent** \ˈkän-ˌtent\ *n* **1** : something contained — usu. used in pl. ⟨the *contents* of a jar⟩ **2** : the subject matter or topics treated (as in a book) ⟨table of *contents*⟩ **3** : the essential meaning ⟨I enjoy the rhythm of the poem but I don't understand its *content*⟩ **4** : CAPACITY ⟨a jug with a *content* of one gallon⟩

con·tent·ed \kən-ˈtent-əd\ *adj* : satisfied with one's situation or lot — **con·tent·ed·ly** *adv* — **con·tent·ed·ness** *n*

con·ten·tion \kən-ˈten-chən\ *n* **1** : an act or instance of contending : STRIFE, DISPUTE **2** : a point advanced or maintained in a debate or argument

con·ten·tious \kən-ˈten-chəs\ *adj* : inclined to argue : QUARRELSOME — **con·ten·tious·ness** *n*

con·tent·ment \kən-ˈtent-mənt\ *n* : the state of being contented : peaceful satisfaction

1**con·test** \kən-ˈtest, ˈkän-ˌ\ *vb* **1** : DISPUTE, CHALLENGE ⟨*contest* a divorce⟩ **2** : to struggle over or for ⟨a *contested* territory⟩

2**con·test** \ˈkän-ˌtest\ *n* **1** : a struggle for victory or superiority : COMPETITION ⟨a boxing *contest*⟩ ⟨a spelling *contest*⟩ **2** : OPPOSITION, RIVALRY ⟨meet in friendly *contest*⟩

con·test·ant \kən-ˈtes-tənt, ˈkän-ˌtes-\ *n* : one who contests; *esp* : one who takes part in a contest

con·text \ˈkän-ˌtekst\ *n* : the parts of a written or spoken passage that are near a certain word or group of words and that help to explain its meaning — **con·tex·tu·al** \kän-ˈteks-chə(-wə)l\ *adj* — **con·tex·tu·al·ly** \-ē\ *adv*

con·ti·gu·i·ty \ˌkänt-ə-ˈgyü-ət-ē\ *n* : the state of being contiguous

con·tig·u·ous \kən-ˈtig-yə-wəs\ *adj* **1** : being in contact : TOUCHING **2** : very near though not in contact : NEIGHBORING — **con·tig·u·ous·ly** *adv*

con·ti·nence \ˈkänt-ə-nən(t)s\ *n* : self-restraint esp. in the face of bodily temptation — **con·ti·nent** \-ə-nənt\ *adj*

con·ti·nent \ˈkänt-(ə-)nənt\ *n* [from Latin *continent-*, stem of *continens*, from present participle of *continēre* "to hold together", "hold in", "contain", from *com-* + *tenēre* "to hold"] **1** : one of the great divisions of land (as North America, South America, Europe, Asia, Africa, Australia, or Antarctica) on the globe **2** *cap* : the continent of Europe ⟨visit the *Continent*⟩

1**con·ti·nen·tal** \ˌkänt-ə-ˈnent-əl\ *adj* **1** : of, relating to, or characteristic of a continent ⟨*continental* waters⟩; *esp* : of or relating to the continent of Europe **2** *often cap* : of or relating to the colonies later forming the U.S. ⟨*Continental* Congress⟩

2**continental** *n* **1 a** *often cap* : a soldier in the Continental army **b** : a piece of paper currency issued by the Continental Congress **2** : EUROPEAN

continental glacier *n* : an ice cap covering a considerable part of a continent

continental shelf *n* : a shallow submarine plain of varying width forming a border to a continent and typically ending in a steep slope to the depths of the ocean

continental slope *n* : a usu. steep slope from a continental shelf to the oceanic depths

con·tin·gen·cy \kən-ˈtin-jən-sē\ *n, pl* **-cies** **1** : the state of being contingent **2** : a chance happening or event **3** : a possible event or one foreseen as possible if another occurs ⟨prepared for every *contingency*⟩

1**con·tin·gent** \kən-ˈtin-jənt\ *adj* **1** : likely to happen : POSSIBLE **2** : happening by change or unforeseen causes **3** : dependent on or conditioned by something else ⟨plans *contingent* on the weather⟩ — **con·tin·gent·ly** *adv*

2**contingent** *n* : a number of persons representing or drawn from an area or group ⟨a *contingent* of troops from each regiment⟩

con·tin·u·al \kən-ˈtin-yə(-wə)l\ *adj* **1** : continuing indefinitely without interruption ⟨*continual* fear⟩ **2** : recurring in rapid succession ⟨*continual* interruptions⟩ — **con·tin·u·al·ly** \-ē\ *adv*

con·tin·u·ance \kən-ˈtin-yə-wən(t)s\ *n* **1** : the act of continuing ⟨during the *continuance* of the illness⟩ **2** : unbroken succession : CONTINUATION **3** : postponement of proceedings in a court of law to a specified day

con·tin·u·a·tion \kən-ˌtin-yə-ˈwā-shən\ *n* **1** : continuance in or prolongation of a state or activity **2** : resumption after an interruption **3** : something that continues, increases, or adds ⟨a *continuation* of last week's story⟩

con·tin·ue \kən-ˈtin-yü\ *vb* **1** : to remain in a place or condition : STAY ⟨*continue* in one's present job⟩ **2** : ENDURE, LAST ⟨cold weather *continued*⟩ **3** : to go on or carry forward in a course ⟨*continue* to study hard⟩ ⟨*continue* the study of French⟩ **4** : to go on or carry on after an interruption : RESUME ⟨the play *continued* after the intermission⟩ **5** : to postpone a legal proceeding to a later date **6** : to allow or cause to remain esp. in a position ⟨the town officials were *continued* in office⟩ — **con·tin·u·er** *n*

continued fraction *n* : an expression in the form of a fraction whose numerator is an integer and whose denominator is an integer plus a fraction whose numerator is an integer and whose denominator is an integer plus a fraction and so on; thus:

$$\cfrac{a}{a' + \cfrac{b}{b' + \cfrac{c}{c' + \ldots}}}$$

con·ti·nu·i·ty \\,känt-ə-'n(y)ü-ət-ē\\ *n, pl* **-ties** **1 a** : uninterrupted connection, succession, or union **b** : persistence without change **2 a** : a motion-picture, radio, or television script **b** : transitional spoken or musical matter for a radio or television program

con·tin·u·ous \\kən-'tin-yə-wəs\\ *adj* : being without break or interruption : CONTINUED ⟨*continuous* showing of a movie⟩ — **con·tin·u·ous·ly** *adv* — **con·tin·u·ous·ness** *n*

continuous miner *n* : a machine that cuts and loads coal in one continuous operation

con·tort \\kən-'tȯrt\\ *vb* : to twist into an unusual appearance or unnatural shape : DEFORM, DISTORT

con·tor·tion \\kən-'tȯr-shən\\ *n* **1** : a contorting or a being contorted **2** : a contorted shape or thing

con·tor·tion·ist \\-sh(ə-)nəst\\ *n* : an acrobat who puts himself into unusual postures

1con·tour \\'kän-,tu̇(ə)r\\ *n* **1** : the outline of a figure, body, or surface ⟨*contour* of the land⟩ **2** : a line or drawing representing a contour **3** : CONTOUR LINE

2contour *vb* **1** : to shape the contour of **2** : to shape to fit contours

3contour *adj* **1** : following contour lines; *esp* : forming furrows or ridges along them to retard erosion ⟨*contour* farming⟩ **2** : made to fit the contour of something

contour line *n* : a line (as on a map) connecting the points on a land surface that have the same elevation

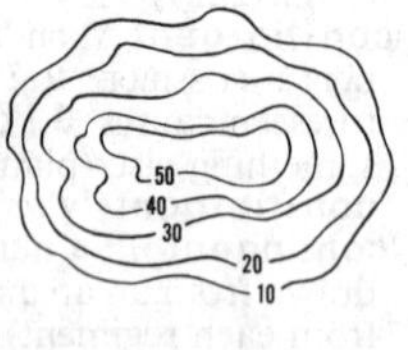

contour lines

contra- *prefix* **1** : against : contrary : contrasting ⟨*contra*distinction⟩ **2** : pitched below normal bass ⟨*contra*-octave⟩

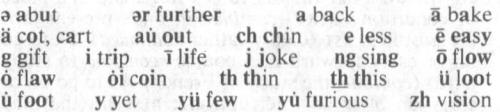

con·tra·band \\'kän-trə-,band\\ *n* [from Italian *contrabbando*, from medieval Latin *contrabannum*, from *contra-* and *bannum* "decree", "ban"] **1** : goods whose importation, exportation, or possession is forbidden **2** : smuggled goods — **contraband** *adj*

con·tra·cep·tion \\,kän-trə-'sep-shən\\ *n* : prevention of conception by abstinence or artificial means

1con·tra·cep·tive \\-'sep-tiv\\ *adj* : relating to or used for contraception

2contraceptive *n* : a contraceptive agent or device

1con·tract \\'kän-,trakt\\ *n* **1** : a legally binding agreement between persons or parties **2** : a document stating the terms of a contract ***syn*** see AGREEMENT

ə abut	ər further	a back	ā bake
ä cot, cart	au̇ out	ch chin	e less	ē easy
g gift	i trip	ī life	j joke	ng sing	ō flow
ȯ flaw	ȯi coin	th thin	th this	ü loot
u̇ foot	y yet	yü few	yu̇ furious	zh vision

2con·tract \\kən-'trakt, *oftenest for 2* 'kän-,\\ *vb* **1** : to enter into by contract ⟨*contract* a marriage⟩ **2** : to undertake by contract ⟨*contract* to build a bridge⟩ **3** : to draw together or up so as to make or become shorter and broader ⟨brows *contracting* in puzzlement⟩ ⟨*contract* a muscle⟩ **4 a** : SHORTEN, SHRINK ⟨metal *contracts* in cold weather⟩ **b** : to shorten by omitting one or more sounds or letters ⟨*contract he will* into *he'll*⟩ **5 a** : GET, CATCH ⟨*contract* a cold⟩ **b** : FORM ⟨it is easier to *contract* a habit than to break one⟩ — **con·tract·i·ble** \\kən-'trak-tə-bəl, 'kän-,\\ *adj*

con·trac·tile \\kən-'trak-təl\\ *adj* : having the power or property of contracting — **con·trac·til·i·ty** \\,kän-,trak-'til-ət-ē\\ *n*

contractile vacuole *n* : a vacuole in a single-celled organism that contracts regularly to discharge fluid from the cell

con·trac·tion \\kən-'trak-shən\\ *n* **1 a** : the act or process of contracting : the state of being contracted **b** : the shortening and thickening of a functioning muscle or muscle fiber **2 a** : a shortening of a word, syllable, or word group by omission of a sound or letter **b** : a form produced by such shortening ⟨*aren't* is a *contraction* of *are not*⟩ — **con·trac·tive** \\-'trak-tiv\\ *adj*

con·trac·tor \\'kän-,trak-tər, kən-'\\ *n* : one that enters into a contract; *esp* : one who agrees to perform work or provide supplies at a given price or within a given time ⟨building *contractor*⟩

con·trac·tu·al \\kən-'trak-chə(-wə)l, kän-\\ *adj* : of, relating to, or being a contract ⟨*contractual* agreements⟩ — **con·trac·tu·al·ly** \\-ē\\ *adv*

con·tra·dict \\,kän-trə-'dikt\\ *vb* **1** : to deny the truth of ⟨*contradict* a story⟩ **2** : to state the opposite of what another has said ⟨*contradicted* him⟩ **3** : to be contrary or opposed to ⟨his actions *contradict* his words⟩ — **con·tra·dic·tor** \\-'dik-tər\\ *n*

con·tra·dic·tion \\-'dik-shən\\ *n* **1 a** : a statement that contradicts another **b** : denial of the truth of something said **2** : opposition between things

con·tra·dic·to·ry \\,kän-trə-'dik-t(ə-)rē\\ *adj* **1** : tending to contradict **2** : involving contradiction : OPPOSED ⟨*contradictory* statements⟩ — **con·tra·dic·to·ri·ness** *n*

con·tra·dis·tinc·tion \\,kän-trə-dis-'ting(k)-shən\\ *n* : distinction by contrast ⟨painting in *contradistinction* to sculpture⟩

con·trail \\'kän-,trāl\\ *n* : streaks of condensed water vapor created in the air by an airplane or rocket at high altitudes

con·tral·to \\kən-'tral-tō\\ *n, pl* **-tos** **1 a** : the lowest female singing voice **b** : a singer with such a voice **2** : the part sung by a contralto

con·trap·tion \\kən-'trap-shən\\ *n* : DEVICE, GADGET

con·trari·wise \\'kän-,trer-ē-,wīz, kən-'\\ *adv* **1** : on the contrary **2** : vice versa : CONVERSELY **3** : PERVERSELY, CONTRARILY

1con·trary \\'kän-,trer-ē\\ *n, pl* **-trar·ies** **1** : a fact or statement incompatible with another : OPPOSITE **2** : one of a pair of opposites

2con·trary \\'kän-,trer-ē, *4 is often* kən-'tre(ə)r-ē\\ *adj* **1** : exactly opposite : wholly different ⟨*contrary* opinions⟩ **2** : OPPOSED ⟨an act *contrary* to law⟩ **3** : UNFAVORABLE ⟨a *contrary* wind⟩ **4** : inclined to oppose or resist : WAYWARD ⟨a *contrary* child⟩ — **con·trar·i·ly** \\-,trer-ə-lē, -'trer-\\ *adv* — **con·trar·i·ness** \\-,trer-ē-nəs, -'trer-\\ *n*

1con·trast \\'kän-,trast\\ *n* **1** : a person or thing that exhibits differences when contrasted **2** : difference esp. when sharp or striking between associated things ⟨the *contrast* between light and dark⟩

2**con·trast** \kən-'trast, 'kän-ˌ\ *vb* **1** : to show noticeable differences ⟨black and gold *contrast* sharply⟩ **2** : to compare two persons or things so as to show the differences between them ⟨*contrast* winter and summer⟩

con·trib·ute \kən-'trib-yət\ *vb* **1** : to give along with others ⟨*contribute* to charities⟩ **2** : to have a share in something ⟨everybody *contributed* to the success of the exhibit⟩ **3** : to supply for publication ⟨*contribute* a poem to an anthology⟩ — **con·trib·u·tive** \kən-'trib-yət-iv\ *adj* — **con·trib·u·tor** \-yət-ər\ *n*

con·tri·bu·tion \ˌkän-trə-'byü-shən\ *n* **1** : the act of contributing **2** : a sum or a thing contributed **3** : a writing for a publication

con·trib·u·to·ry \kən-'trib-yə-ˌtōr-ē, -ˌtȯr-ē\ *adj* : that contributes or serves to contribute; *esp* : helping to accomplish a result

con·trite \'kän-ˌtrīt, kən-'\ *adj* : sorrowful for a wrong that one has done : deeply repentant — **con·trite·ly** *adv* — **con·trite·ness** *n*

con·tri·tion \kən-'trish-ən\ *n* : the state of being contrite

con·triv·ance \kən-'trī-vən(t)s\ *n* **1** : the act or faculty of contriving **2** : a thing contrived; *esp* : a mechanical device

con·trive \kən-'trīv\ *vb* **1** : PLAN, PLOT ⟨*contrive* a means of escape⟩ **2** : to form or make in a skillful or ingenious way : INVENT **3** : to bring about : MANAGE ⟨a hard time *contriving* to make ends meet⟩ — **con·triv·er** *n*

1**con·trol** \kən-'trōl\ *vb* **con·trolled**; **con·trol·ling** **1** : to exercise restraining or directing influence over : REGULATE ⟨*control* your temper⟩ ⟨*control* a plane⟩ **2** : to have power over : RULE **3** : to kill (animals) when not wanted at a particular time and place ⟨*control* insects by spraying⟩ — **con·trol·la·ble** \-'trō-lə-bəl\ *adj*

2**control** *n* **1** : the power or authority to control ⟨a child under his parents' *control*⟩ **2** : ability to control ⟨a car out of *control*⟩ ⟨lose *control* of one's temper⟩ **3** : a means or a mechanism for controlling ⟨the *controls* of an airplane⟩ ⟨price *controls*⟩ **4** : something used in an experiment or a study to provide a basis for comparing results or for checking their accuracy **5** : reduction or regulation of an animal population of an area by killing ⟨insect *control*⟩

control experiment *n* : an experiment to check the results of other experiments

controlled experiment *n* : a complex experiment including one or more control experiments along with the actual experimental tests

con·trol·ler \kən-'trō-lər, 'kän-ˌ\ *n* **1 a** : COMPTROLLER **b** : the chief accounting officer of a business or institution **2** : one that controls ⟨air traffic *controller*⟩

con·tro·ver·sial \ˌkän-trə-'vər-shəl, -'vər-sē-əl\ *adj* **1** : of or relating to controversy **2** : open to or likely to cause controversy ⟨a *controversial* question⟩ **3** : fond of controversy : ARGUMENTATIVE — **con·tro·ver·sial·ly** \-ē\ *adv*

con·tro·ver·sy \'kän-trə-ˌvər-sē\ *n, pl* **-sies** **1** : a discussion marked esp. by expression of opposing views : DISPUTE **2** : QUARREL, STRIFE

con·tro·vert \'kän-trə-ˌvərt, 'kän-trə-'\ *vb* : DENY, CONTRADICT ⟨a theory *controverted* by facts⟩

con·tu·me·ly \kən-'t(y)ü-mə-lē; 'kän-t(y)ə-ˌmē-lē\ *n, pl* **-lies** : contemptuous language or treatment

con·tuse \kən-'t(y)üz\ *vb* : to injure (tissue) usu. without breaking the skin : BRUISE — **con·tu·sion** \-'t(y)ü-zhən\ *n*

co·nun·drum \kə-'nən-drəm\ *n* **1** : RIDDLE, PUZZLE **2** : an intricate problem

con·ur·ba·tion \ˌkän-(ˌ)ər-'bā-shən\ *n* : a continuous network of urban communities

con·va·lesce \ˌkän-və-'les\ *vb* : to recover health and strength gradually after illness or weakness

con·va·les·cence \ˌkän-və-'les-ən(t)s\ *n* : the process or period of convalescing — **con·va·les·cent** \-ənt\ *adj or n*

con·vec·tion \kən-'vek-shən\ *n* : the circulatory motion that occurs in a gas or liquid at a nonuniform temperature owing to currents caused by differences in density with the warmer portions rising and the colder denser portions sinking; *also* : the transfer of heat by this automatic circulation of a fluid — **con·vec·tion·al** \-sh(ə-)nəl\ *adj* — **con·vec·tive** \-'vek-tiv\ *adj*

con·vec·tor \-'vek-tər\ *n* : a heating unit in which air heated by contact with a heating device in a casing circulates by convection

con·vene \kən-'vēn\ *vb* **1** : to come together in a group or body : MEET ⟨the legislature *convened* Tuesday⟩ **2** : to cause to convene : call together ⟨the chairman *convened* the meeting⟩

con·ve·nience \kən-'vē-nyən(t)s\ *n* **1** : fitness or suitability for meeting a requirement ⟨the *convenience* of prepared foods⟩ **2** : personal comfort : freedom from trouble **3** : a suitable time : OPPORTUNITY ⟨come at your earliest *convenience*⟩ **4** : something that gives comfort or advantage ⟨a house with all modern *conveniences*⟩

con·ve·nient \kən-'vē-nyənt\ *adj* **1** : suited to personal comfort or to easy use ⟨*convenient* tools⟩ ⟨a *convenient* location⟩ **2** : near at hand : HANDY ⟨schools, churches, and stores are all *convenient*⟩ — **con·ve·nient·ly** *adv*

con·vent \'kän-vənt, -ˌvent\ *n* [from medieval Latin *conventus*, from Latin, "assembly," from *convenire* "to convene," from *com-* and *venire* "to come"] : a local branch of a religious order; *esp* : an establishment of nuns

con·ven·tion \kən-'ven-chən\ *n* **1** : AGREEMENT, COVENANT ⟨an international *convention* for treatment of prisoners of war⟩ **2 a** : generally accepted custom, practice, or belief **b** : something accepted by convention as true, useful, or convenient : RULE ⟨the *convention* of driving on the right⟩ **3** : an assembly of persons met for a common purpose ⟨a constitutional *convention*⟩ ⟨teachers' *convention*⟩

con·ven·tion·al \kən-'vench-(ə-)nəl\ *adj* **1** : behaving according to convention ⟨a very *conventional* man⟩ **2** : settled or prescribed by convention : CUSTOMARY ⟨*conventional* signs and symbols⟩ **3** : COMMONPLACE, ORDINARY ⟨offered a few *conventional* remarks⟩ **4** : according to established rules or traditions : not showing originality ⟨a *conventional* tale⟩ ⟨a *conventional* cowboy movie⟩ — **con·ven·tion·al·ly** \-ē\ *adv*

con·ven·tion·al·i·ty \kən-ˌven-chə-'nal-ət-ē\ *n, pl* **-ties** **1** : the quality or state of being conventional ⟨the *conventionality* of his remarks⟩ **2** : a conventional practice, custom, or rule : CONVENTION

con·verge \kən-'vərj\ *vb* **1** : to tend or move toward one point or one another : MEET **2** : to come together and unite in a common interest

con·ver·gence \kən-'vər-jən(t)s\ *n* : the act or condition of converging — **con·ver·gent** \-jənt\ *adj*

con·ver·sant \kən-'vərs-ənt\ *adj* : having knowledge or experience : FAMILIAR ⟨*conversant* with the facts of the case⟩

con·ver·sa·tion \ˌkän-vər-'sā-shən\ *n* **1** : oral exchange of sentiments, observations, opinions, or ideas **2** : an instance of such exchange : TALK

con·ver·sa·tion·al \ˌkän-vər-'sā-sh(ə-)nəl\ *adj*

1 : of, relating to, or suitable for informal friendly talk ⟨written in *conversational* style⟩ 2 : fond of or given to conversation — **con·ver·sa·tion·al·ly** \-ē\ *adv*

con·ver·sa·tion·al·ist \-sh(ə-)nə-ləst\ *n* : a person who is fond of or good at conversation

1**con·verse** \kən-'vərs\ *vb* : to engage in conversation : TALK — **con·vers·er** *n*

2**con·verse** \'kän-ˌvərs\ *n* : CONVERSATION

3**con·verse** \kən-'vərs, 'kän-ˌ\ *adj* : reversed in order, relation, or action — **con·verse·ly** *adv*

4**con·verse** \'kän-ˌvərs\ *n* : something that is the opposite of something else

con·ver·sion \kən-'vər-zhən\ *n* 1 : the act of converting : the state of being converted 2 : a change in nature or form ⟨*conversion* of water into steam by boiling⟩ 3 : a spiritual change in a person associated with a change of religious belief or with the definite adoption of religion

1**con·vert** \kən-'vərt\ *vb* 1 a : to bring over from one belief, view, or party to another b : to bring about a religious conversion in 2 a : to change from one form or function to another ⟨*convert* starch into sugar⟩ ⟨*convert* iron into steel⟩ b : to exchange for an equivalent ⟨*convert* diamonds into cash⟩ 3 : to undergo conversion 4 : to make good on a try for point after touchdown or on a free throw

2**con·vert** \'kän-ˌvərt\ *n* : one that is converted

con·vert·er *also* **con·ver·tor** \kən-'vərt-ər\ *n* 1 : one that converts 2 : a device employing mechanical rotation for changing alternating current to direct current 3 : a device for adapting a television receiver to receive channels for which it was not orig. designed

1**con·vert·i·ble** \kən-'vərt-ə-bəl\ *adj* 1 : capable of being converted ⟨a sofa *convertible* into a bed⟩ 2 : having a top that may be lowered or removed ⟨*convertible* coupe⟩ — **con·vert·i·bil·i·ty** \-ˌvərt-ə-'bil-ət-ē\ *n*

2**convertible** *n* : something convertible; *esp* : a convertible automobile

con·vex \kän-'veks, 'kän-ˌ, kən-'\ *adj* : curved or rounded like the outside of a sphere or circle ⟨*convex* lens⟩ — **con·vex·i·ty** \kən-'vek-sət-ē, kän-\ *n* — **con·vex·ly** *adv* — **con·vex·ness** *n*

con·vey \kən-'vā\ *vb* **con·veyed**; **con·vey·ing** 1 : to carry from one place to another : TRANSPORT 2 : to serve as a means of transferring or transmitting ⟨pipes *convey* water⟩ 3 : to communicate or serve as a means of communicating ⟨words that *conveyed* his meaning⟩ ⟨a flashing red light *conveys* a warning⟩ 4 : to transfer to another; *esp* : to transfer title to real estate by a legal document

con·vey·ance \kən-'vā-ən(t)s\ *n* 1 : the act of conveying 2 : a legal document by which title to property is conveyed 3 : a means of transport : VEHICLE

con·vey·er *or* **con·vey·or** \kən-'vā-ər\ *n* 1 : one that conveys 2 *usu conveyor* : a mechanical apparatus for carrying (as by an endless moving belt) packages or bulk material from place to place

1**con·vict** \kən-'vikt\ *vb* : to find or prove to be guilty

2**con·vict** \'kän-ˌvikt\ *n* 1 : a person convicted of a crime 2 : a person serving a prison sentence

con·vic·tion \kən-'vik-shən\ *n* 1 : the act of convicting : the state of being convicted; *esp* : a decision that a person is guilty of a crime or offense 2 : the state of being convinced : CERTITUDE ⟨speaks with *conviction*⟩ 3 : a strong belief or opinion ⟨a man with firm *convictions*⟩

con·vince \kən-'vin(t)s\ *vb* : to bring by argument or evidence to agreement or belief : overcome the disbelief or objections of ⟨was *convinced* of the man's innocence⟩ ⟨*convinced* me that he was qualified⟩ — **con·vinc·er** *n*

con·vinc·ing \-'vin(t)-sing\ *adj* : having the power or the effect of overcoming objection or disbelief ⟨a *convincing* argument⟩ ⟨a *convincing* speaker⟩ — **con·vinc·ing·ly** \-sing-lē\ *adv* — **con·vinc·ing·ness** *n*

con·viv·i·al \kən-'viv-ē-əl\ *adj* [from Latin *convivium* "feast," from *com-* and *vivere* "to live"] : fond of feasting, drinking, and good company — **con·viv·i·al·ly** \-ē-ə-lē\ *adv*

con·viv·i·al·i·ty \-ˌviv-ē-'al-ət-ē\ *n*, *pl* **-ties** : convivial spirit : FESTIVITY

con·vo·ca·tion \ˌkän-və-'kā-shən\ *n* 1 : a summons to a meeting 2 : ASSEMBLY, MEETING

con·voke \kən-'vōk\ *vb* : to call together to a meeting

1**con·vo·lute** \'kän-və-ˌlüt\ *vb* : TWIST, COIL

2**convolute** *adj* : rolled or wound together one part upon another : COILED ⟨a *convolute* shell⟩ — **con·vo·lute·ly** *adv*

con·vo·lu·tion \ˌkän-və-'lü-shən\ *n* 1 : one of the irregular ridges on the surface of the brain and esp. of the cerebrum of higher mammals 2 : a convoluted form or structure

con·vol·vu·lus \kən-'väl-vyə-ləs, -'vȯl-\ *n*, *pl* **-lus·es** *or* **-li** \-ˌlī, -ˌlē\ : any of a genus of erect, trailing, or twining herbs and shrubs that are related to the morning glory

1**con·voy** \'kän-ˌvȯi, kən-'\ *vb* : to accompany for protection : ESCORT ⟨a destroyer *convoying* merchant shipping⟩

2**con·voy** \'kän-ˌvȯi\ *n* 1 : a protective escort for ships, persons, or goods 2 : the act of convoying : the state of being convoyed ⟨ships traveling in *convoy*⟩ 3 : a group convoyed ⟨a *convoy* of freighters⟩

con·vulse \kən-'vəls\ *vb* : to shake or agitate violently; *esp* : to shake with or as if with irregular spasms ⟨was *convulsed* with laughter⟩ ⟨land *convulsed* by an earthquake⟩

con·vul·sion \kən-'vəl-shən\ *n* 1 : an abnormal violent and involuntary contraction or series of contractions of the muscles 2 : a violent disturbance

con·vul·sive \-'vəl-siv\ *adj* 1 : being or producing a convulsion 2 : attended or affected with convulsions — **con·vul·sive·ly** *adv* — **con·vul·sive·ness** *n*

co·ny *var of* CONEY

coo \'kü\ *vb* 1 : to make the low soft cry of a dove or pigeon or a similar sound 2 : to talk fondly or amorously — **coo** *n*

1**cook** \'ku̇k\ *n* : one who prepares food for eating

2**cook** *vb* 1 : to prepare food for eating by a heating process 2 : to undergo being cooked 3 : CONCOCT, INVENT ⟨*cook* up a scheme⟩ — **cook·er** *n*

cook·book \'ku̇k-ˌbu̇k\ *n* : a book of cooking directions and recipes

cook·ery \'ku̇k-(ə-)rē\ *n* : the art or practice of cooking

cook·ie *or* **cooky** \'ku̇k-ē\ *n*, *pl* **cook·ies** : a small sweet flat or slightly raised cake

cook·out \'ku̇k-ˌau̇t\ *n* 1 : an outing at which a meal is cooked and served in the open 2 : the meal cooked at a cookout

cook·stove \'ku̇k-ˌstōv\ *n* : a stove for cooking; *esp* : a cast-iron stove for wood or coal

1**cool** \'kül\ *adj* **1** : moderately cold : lacking in warmth **2** : not admitting or retaining heat ⟨*cool* clothes⟩ **3** : marked by steady calmness and self-control **4** : lacking ardor, excitement, or friendliness **5** : producing an impression of coolness ⟨blue is a *cool* color⟩ — **cool·ish** \'kü-lish\ *adj* — **cool·ly** \'kül-(l)ē\ *adv* — **cool·ness** \'kül-nəs\ *n*

2**cool** *vb* **1** : to make or become cool **2** : MODERATE, CALM ⟨allow tempers to *cool*⟩

3**cool** *n* : a cool time or place ⟨the *cool* of the night⟩

cool·ant \'kü-lənt\ *n* : a usu. fluid cooling agent

cool·er \'kü-lər\ *n* : one that cools; *esp* : a container for keeping foods cool

coo·lie \'kü-lē\ *n* : an unskilled laborer or porter usu. in or from the Far East

coon \'kün\ *n* : RACCOON

coon·skin \-ˌskin\ *n* : the fur or pelt of the raccoon

1**coop** \'küp, 'ku̇p\ *n* : a cage or small enclosure or building for housing poultry or small animals

2**coop** *vb* : to place or keep in or as if in a coop : PEN

co–op \'kō-ˌäp, kō-'äp, 'küp\ *n* : COOPERATIVE

coo·per \'kü-pər, 'ku̇p-ər\ *n* : one that makes or repairs wooden casks or tubs

coo·per·age \'kü-p(ə-)rij, 'ku̇p-(ə-)rij\ *n* **1** : a cooper's place of business **2** : a cooper's work or products

co·op·er·ate \kō-'äp-(ə-)ˌrāt\ *vb* : to act, work, or associate with others esp. for mutual benefit

co·op·er·a·tion \kō-ˌäp-ə-'rā-shən\ *n* **1** : the act or process of cooperating **2** : association of individuals or groups for the purpose of mutual benefit

1**co·op·er·a·tive** \kō-'äp-(ə-)rət-iv, -'äp-ə-ˌrāt-\ *adj* **1** : willing to cooperate ⟨*cooperative* neighbors⟩ **2** : of, relating to, or organized as a cooperative ⟨a *cooperative* store⟩ — **co·op·er·a·tive·ly** *adv* — **co·op·er·a·tive·ness** *n*

2**cooperative** *n* : an association formed to enable its members to buy or sell to better advantage

Coo·per's hawk \ˌkü-pərz-, ˌku̇p-ərz-\ *n* : a common American hawk that has a rounded tail and is slightly smaller than a crow

1**co·or·di·nate** \kō-'ȯrd-(ə-)nət\ *adj* **1** : equal in rank or order **2 a** : being of equal rank in a compound sentence ⟨*coordinate* clauses⟩ **b** : COORDINATING — **co·or·di·nate·ly** *adv*

2**coordinate** *n* **1** : one that is coordinate with another **2** : any of a set of numbers used in specifying the location of a point on a line or surface or in space

3**co·or·di·nate** \kō-'ȯrd-ə-ˌnāt\ *vb* **1** : to make or become coordinate **2** : to bring into a common action, movement, or condition : HARMONIZE ⟨*coordinated* the efforts of all the investigating agencies⟩ — **co·or·di·na·tion** \-ˌȯrd-ə-'nā-shən\ *n* — **co·or·di·na·tor** \-ˌnāt-ər\ *n*

co·or·di·nat·ing *adj* : joining words or word groups of the same grammatical rank ⟨*coordinating* conjunction⟩

coot \'küt\ *n* **1** : any of various sluggish slow-flying slaty-black birds that somewhat resemble ducks but are related to the rails **2** : a No. American scoter **3** : a harmless simple person

coo·tie \'küt-ē\ *n* : BODY LOUSE

cop \'käp\ *n* : POLICEMAN

1**cope** \'kōp\ *n* : a long garment like a cape worn by a priest or bishop

2**cope** *vb* : to struggle or contend esp. with success ⟨*cope* with a situation⟩

co·pe·pod \'kō-pə-ˌpäd\ *n* : any of a large group of usu. tiny freshwater and marine crustaceans — **copepod** *adj*

Co·per·ni·can \kō-'pər-ni-kən\ *adj* : of or relating to Copernicus or his theory that the earth rotates daily on its axis and the planets revolve in orbits round the sun

copi·er \'käp-ē-ər\ *n* : one that copies

co·pi·lot \'kō-ˌpī-lət\ *n* : an assistant aircraft pilot

cop·ing \'kō-piŋ\ *n* : the top or covering layer of a wall usu. with a sloping top

co·pi·ous \'kō-pē-əs\ *adj* : very plentiful : ABUNDANT — **co·pi·ous·ly** *adv* — **co·pi·ous·ness** *n*

co·pol·y·mer \(ˈ)kō-'päl-ə-mər\ *n* : a product of copolymerization

co·po·lym·er·ize \ˌkō-pə-'lim-ə-ˌrīz, (ˈ)kō-'päl-ə-mə-\ *vb* : to polymerize together — **co·po·lym·er·i·za·tion** \ˌkō-pə-ˌlim-ə-rə-'zā-shən, (ˌ)kō-ˌpäl-ə-mə-rə-\ *n*

cop·per \'käp-ər\ *n* **1** : a reddish metallic element that is ductile and malleable and one of the best conductors of heat and electricity — see ELEMENT table **2** : a copper or bronze coin **3** : any of various small butterflies with copper-colored wings — **cop·pery** \'käp-(ə-)rē\ *adj*

Copper Age *n* : the transitional period between the Neolithic and Bronze Ages in which some copper was used

cop·per·as \'käp-(ə-)rəs\ *n* : a green sulfate of iron used in making inks and in dyeing

cop·per·head \'käp-ər-ˌhed\ *n* **1** : a common largely coppery brown pit viper of the eastern U.S. **2** : a person in the northern states who sympathized with the South during the Civil War

copperhead
(about 3 ft. long)

copper oxide *n* : either of two compounds of copper and oxygen that occur in nature as minerals and are used chiefly as pigments, as fungicides, or as catalysts

copper sulfate *n* : a usu. blue crystalline compound that is used in solutions to destroy algae and fungi, in dyeing and printing, and in electric batteries

cop·pice \'käp-əs\ *n* : a thicket, grove, or growth of small trees

co·pra \'kō-prə\ *n* : dried coconut meat yielding coconut oil

copse \'käps\ *n* : COPPICE

cop·u·late \'käp-yə-ˌlāt\ *vb* : to engage in sexual intercourse — **cop·u·la·tion** \ˌkäp-yə-'lā-shən\ *n* — **cop·u·la·to·ry** \'käp-yə-lə-ˌtōr-ē, -ˌtȯr-\ *adj*

1**copy** \'käp-ē\ *n, pl* **cop·ies** **1** : an imitation or reproduction of an original **2** : one of the printed reproductions of an original text, engraving, or photograph **3** : matter to be set up for printing

2**copy** *vb* **cop·ied**; **copy·ing** **1** : to make a copy : DUPLICATE **2** : to model oneself on : IMITATE

copy·book \'käp-ē-ˌbu̇k\ *n* : a book containing copies esp. of penmanship for learners to imitate

copy·boy \-ˌbȯi\ *n* : one that carries copy and runs errands (as in a newspaper office)

copy·ist \'käp-ē-əst\ *n* **1** : one who makes copies **2** : IMITATOR

copy·read·er \'käp-ē-ˌrēd-ər\ *n* **1** : one who edits and writes headlines for newspaper copy **2** : an employee of a publishing house who corrects manuscript copy

1**copy·right** \-ˌrīt\ *n* : the sole legal right to re-

C

produce, publish, and sell the matter and form of a literary, musical, or artistic work — **copyright** *adj*

[2]**copyright** *vb* : to secure a copyright on

co·quet·ry \'kō-kə-trē, kō-'ke-trē\ *n, pl* **-ries** : the conduct or art of a coquette : FLIRTATION

co·quette \kō-'ket\ *n* : FLIRT — **co·quett·ish** \-'ket-ish\ *adj* — **co·quett·ish·ly** *adv*

co·qui·na \kō-'kē-nə\ *n* **1** : a small marine clam used for broth or chowder **2** : a soft whitish limestone formed of broken shells and corals cemented together and used for building

cor·a·cle \'kȯr-ə-kəl, 'kär-\ *n* : a boat made of hoops covered with horsehide or tarpaulin

cor·al \'kȯr-əl, 'kär-\ *n* **1 a** : the stony or horny skeletal deposit produced by various polyps; *esp* : a richly red material used in jewelry **b** : a polyp or polyp colony together with its membranes and skeleton **2** : a deep pink — **coral** *adj*

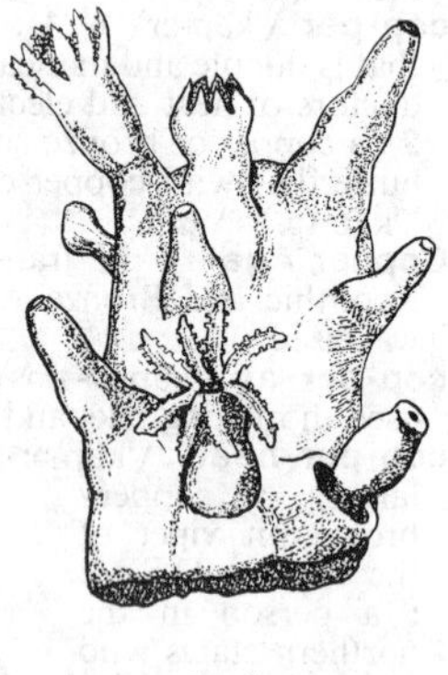

coral

coral reef *n* : a reef made up of corals, other organic deposits, and the solid limestone resulting from their fusion

coral snake *n* : any of several poisonous chiefly tropical New World snakes brilliantly banded in red, black, and yellow or white; *also* : any of several harmless snakes resembling the coral snakes

[1]**cord** \'kȯrd\ *n* **1** : a string or small rope **2** : an anatomical structure (as a tendon or nerve) resembling a cord **3** : a small flexible insulated electrical cable with fittings for connecting an appliance with a receptacle ⟨lamp *cord*⟩ **4** : a unit of wood cut for fuel equal to a stack 4 × 4 × 8 feet **5 a** : a rib like a cord on a textile **b** : a fabric with such ribs **c** *pl* : trousers made of cord — **cord·ed** \'kȯrd-əd\ *adj*

[2]**cord** *vb* **1** : to furnish, bind, or connect with a cord **2** : to pile up wood in cords

cord·age \'kȯrd-ij\ *n* **1** : CORDS; *esp* : the ropes in the rigging of a ship **2** : the number of cords of wood on a given area

cord·ed \'kȯrd-əd\ *adj* : having or drawn into ridges or cords ⟨*corded* muscles⟩ ⟨*corded* cloth⟩

[1]**cor·dial** \'kȯr-jəl\ *adj* [from Latin *cordialis*, "of the heart", "hearty", from *cord-*, stem of *cor* "heart", from the same prehistoric source as English *heart*] **1** : tending to revive or cheer **2** : HEARTFELT, HEARTY ⟨a *cordial* greeting⟩ — **cor·di·al·i·ty** \ˌkȯr-jē-'al-ət-ē\ *n* — **cor·dial·ly** \'kȯrj-(ə-)lē\ *adv*

[2]**cordial** *n* **1** : a stimulating medicine or drink **2** : LIQUEUR

cord·ite \'kȯr-ˌdīt\ *n* : a smokeless gunpowder composed of nitroglycerin, guncotton, and a stabilizing jelly

cord·less \'kȯrd-ləs\ *adj* : having no cord; *esp* : powered by a battery ⟨a *cordless* electric shaver⟩

ə abut	ər further	a back	ā bake	
ä cot, cart	au̇ out	ch chin	e less	ē easy
g gift	i trip	ī life	j joke	ng sing	ō flow
ȯ flaw	ȯi coin	th thin	<u>th</u> this	ü loot
u̇ foot	y yet	yü few	yu̇ furious	zh vision

cor·don \'kȯrd-ən, 'kȯr-ˌdän\ *n* **1** : an ornamental cord used esp. on costumes **2** : a line of persons or things around a person or place ⟨a *cordon* of police⟩ **3** : a cord or ribbon worn as a badge or decoration

cor·do·van \'kȯrd-ə-vən\ *n* : a fine-grained colored leather — **cordovan** *adj*

cor·du·roy \'kȯrd-ə-ˌrȯi\ *n* **1 a** : a durable ribbed usu. cotton fabric **b** *pl* : trousers of corduroy **2** : a road built of logs laid side by side — **corduroy** *adj*

cord·wood \'kȯrd-ˌwu̇d\ *n* : wood cut for fuel and sold by the cord

[1]**core** \'kō(ə)r, 'kȯ(ə)r\ *n* **1 a** : a central or essential part **b** : the central part of the earth displaying different properties from the surrounding mantle and crust **2** : the usu. inedible central part of some fruits (as a pineapple or apple) **3** : a bar of iron or a bundle of wires used to intensify an induced magnetic field (as in a transformer or an armature)

[2]**core** *vb* : to remove the core from — **cor·er** *n*

co·rin·thi·an \kə-'rin(t)-thē-ən\ *adj* : of or relating to a style of Greek architecture characterized by a bell-shaped capital enveloped with sculptured leaves

Co·rin·thi·ans \-ənz\ *n* — see BIBLE table

Co·ri·o·lis force \ˌkȯr-ē-ˌō-ləs-, ˌkȯr-, -ē-ə-ˌlēs-\ *n* : a deflecting force due to the earth's rotation that acts on a body in motion (as an airplane or projectile)

[1]**cork** \'kȯrk\ *n* [probably from Arabic *qurq*, from Latin *cortic-*, stem of *cortex* "bark", "cork"] **1 a** : the elastic tough outer tissue of a European oak used esp. for stoppers and insulation **b** : the tissue of a woody plant making up most of the bark and arising from an inner cambium **2** : a usu. cork stopper for a bottle or jug **3** : an angling float

[2]**cork** *vb* **1** : to furnish, fit, or seal with a cork **2** : to blacken with burnt cork

cork·er \'kȯr-kər\ *n* **1** : one that corks containers **2** *slang* : an outstanding person or thing

[1]**cork·screw** \'kȯrk-ˌskrü\ *n* : a pointed spiral tool for drawing corks from bottles

[2]**corkscrew** *adj* : resembling a corkscrew : SPIRAL

cork·wood \'kȯrk-ˌwu̇d\ *n* : any of several trees having light or corky wood

corky \'kȯr-kē\ *adj* **cork·i·er**; **-est** : resembling cork esp. in dry porous quality

corm \'kȯrm\ *n* : a solid bulblike underground stem (as of the crocus or gladiolus) bearing membranous or scaly leaves and buds

cor·mo·rant \'kȯrm-(ə-)rənt\ *n* [from medieval French, from Old French *cormareng*, from *corp* "raven" and *marenc* "of the sea", "marine"] : any of various dark-colored web-footed seabirds with a long neck, a wedge-shaped tail, a hooked bill, and a patch of bare often brightly colored skin under the mouth

[1]**corn** \'kȯrn\ *n* [from Old English, from an Indo-European noun from which is descended also Latin *granum*, the source of English *grain*] **1 a** : the seeds of a cereal plant and esp. of the important cereal crop of a particular region (as in Britain wheat, in Scotland and Ireland oats, and in the New World and Australia Indian corn) **b** : sweet corn served as a vegetable while the kernels are still soft and milky **2** : a plant that produces corn **3** : corny actions or speech

[2]**corn** *vb* : to preserve by packing with salt or by soaking in brine ⟨*corned* beef⟩

[3]**corn** *n* [from medieval French *corne* "horn", from Latin *cornu*, from the same prehistoric source as English *horn*] : a local hardening and thickening of skin (as on a toe)

corn belt *n* : an area (as the central portion of the

U.S.) in which more land is used for the cultivation of corn than any other single crop

corn borer *n* : any of several insects that bore in corn; *esp* : a moth whose larva is a major pest esp. in the stems and crowns of Indian corn, dahlias, and potatoes

corn bread *n* : bread made with cornmeal

corn·cob \'kȯrn-,käb\ *n* **1** : the woody core on which the kernels of Indian corn are arranged **2** : a tobacco pipe with a bowl made by hollowing out a piece of corncob

corn cockle *n* : an annual hairy weed with purplish red flowers found in grainfields

corn·crib \'kȯrn-,krib\ *n* : a crib for storing ears of Indian corn

cor·nea \'kȯr-nē-ə\ *n* : the transparent part of the coat of the eyeball that covers the iris and pupil and admits light to the interior — **cor·ne·al** \-nē-əl\ *adj*

corn ear·worm \-'i(ə)r-,wərm\ *n* : a large striped yellow-headed moth whose larva is esp. destructive to the ear of Indian corn

1**cor·ner** \'kȯr-nər\ *n* **1 a** : the point or place where edges or sides meet : ANGLE **b** : the place where two streets or roads meet **c** : a piece designed to form, mark, or protect a corner **2** : a place remote from ordinary affairs or life ⟨a quiet *corner* of the town⟩ **3** : a position from which escape or retreat is difficult or impossible **4** : control or ownership of enough of the available supply of something to control its price — **cor·nered** \-nərd\ *adj*

2**corner** *vb* **1** : to drive into a corner **2** : to get a corner on ⟨*corner* wheat⟩ **3** : to turn a corner ⟨a car that *corners* well⟩

3**corner** *adj* **1** : situated at a corner **2** : used or fitted for use in or on a corner

cor·ner·stone \-,stōn\ *n* **1** : a stone forming part of a corner in a wall **2** : something of basic importance

cor·net \kȯr-'net\ *n* **1** : a brass instrument like the trumpet but having less brilliant tone **2** : something conical (as a piece of paper twisted for use as a container) — **cor·net·ist** *or* **cor·net·tist** \-'net-əst\ *n*

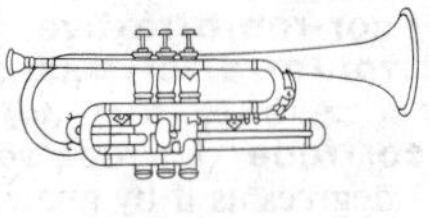
cornet

corn·flakes \'kȯrn-,flāks\ *n pl* : a breakfast cereal of dried and toasted flakes made from the coarse meal of hulled corn

corn·flow·er \-,flau̇(-ə)r\ *n* : a European plant related to the daisies and often grown for its showy blue, pink, or white flower heads — called also *bachelor's-button*

cor·nice \'kȯr-nəs\ *n* **1** : the ornamental projecting piece that forms the top edge of the front of a building or of a pillar **2** : an ornamental molding where the walls meet the ceiling of a room **3** : a decorative band of metal or wood to conceal curtain fixtures

Cor·nish \'kȯr-nish\ *n* : any of an English breed of domestic fowls much used in crossbreeding for meat production

Cor·nish·man \-mən\ *n* : a native or inhabitant of Cornwall, England

corn·meal \'kȯrn-'mēl\ *n* : meal ground from corn

corn oil *n* : a yellow fatty oil obtained from the germ of corn kernels and used chiefly in salad oil, in soft soap, and in margarine

corn pone *n, South & Midland* : corn bread often made without milk or eggs and baked or fried

corn·stalk \'kȯrn-,stȯk\ *n* : a stalk of Indian corn

corn·starch \-,stärch\ *n* : a fine starch made from corn and used in cooking

corn syrup *n* : a syrup obtained from cornstarch and used in baked goods and candy

cor·nu·co·pia \,kȯr-n(y)ə-'kō-pē-ə\ *n* **1** : a horn-shaped container overflowing with fruits and flowers used as a symbol of abundance **2** : a container shaped like a horn or a cone

corny \'kȯr-nē\ *adj* **corn·i·er**; **-est** : tastelessly old-fashioned or countrified : tiresomely simple or sentimental ⟨*corny* music⟩ ⟨*corny* jokes⟩

co·rol·la \kə-'räl-ə\ *n* : the inner floral envelope of a flower consisting of petals and enclosing the stamens and pistil

cor·ol·lary \'kȯr-ə-,ler-ē, 'kär-\ *n, pl* **-lar·ies** **1** : something that follows directly from something that has been proved **2** : something that naturally follows : RESULT

co·ro·na \kə-'rō-nə\ *n* **1** : a usu. colored circle often seen around and close to a luminous body (as the sun or moon) **2** : the outermost part of the atmosphere of the sun appearing as a gray halo around the moon's black disk during a total eclipse of the sun **3** : a crownlike part on the inner side of the corolla in some flowers (as the daffodil) **4** : a discharge of electricity seen as a faint glow adjacent to the surface of an electrical conductor at high voltage — **cor·o·nal** \'kȯr-ən-əl, 'kär-; kə-'rōn-\ *adj*

1**cor·o·nary** \'kȯr-ə-,ner-ē, 'kär-\ *adj* : of, relating to, or being the vessels that supply blood to the heart; *also* : of or relating to the heart

2**coronary** *n, pl* **-nar·ies** **1** : a coronary blood vessel **2** : CORONARY THROMBOSIS

coronary artery *n* : either of the two arteries, right and left, that arise from the aorta and supply the tissues of the heart

coronary sclerosis *n* : hardening of the coronary arteries of the heart

coronary thrombosis *n* : the blocking of an artery of the heart by a thrombus — called also *coronary occlusion*

cor·o·na·tion \,kȯr-ə-'nā-shən, ,kär-\ *n* : the act or ceremony of crowning a king or queen

cor·o·ner \'kȯr-ə-nər, 'kär-\ *n* : a public officer whose chief duty is to discover the causes of any death possibly not due to natural causes

cor·o·net \,kȯr-ə-'net, ,kär-\ *n* **1** : a small crown worn by a noble **2** : an ornamental wreath or band worn around the head ⟨a *coronet* of flowers⟩

corp *abbr* **1** corporal **2** corporation

1**cor·po·ral** \'kȯr-p(ə-)rəl\ *adj* : of or relating to the body ⟨whipping and other *corporal* punishments⟩ — **cor·po·ral·ly** \-ē\ *adv*

2**corporal** *n* : an enlisted man (as in the army) of the lowest noncommissioned rank

cor·po·rate \'kȯr-p(ə-)rət\ *adj* **1 a** : INCORPORATED **b** : of, relating to, or being a corporation **2** : of, relating to, or being a whole composed of individuals — **cor·po·rate·ly** *adv*

cor·po·ra·tion \,kȯr-pə-'rā-shən\ *n* : a group that is authorized by law to carry on an activity (as a business enterprise) with the rights and duties of a single person

cor·po·re·al \kȯr-'pōr-ē-əl, -'pȯr-\ *adj* **1** : not spiritual or immaterial : PHYSICAL, MATERIAL **2** : of or relating to a human body : BODILY — **cor·po·re·al·i·ty** \-,pōr-ē-'al-ət-ē, -,pȯr-\ *n* — **cor·po·re·al·ly** \-'pōr-ē-ə-lē, -'pȯr-\ *adv*

corps \'kō(ə)r, 'kȯ(ə)r\ *n, pl* **corps** \'kōrz, 'kȯrz\ **1 a** : an organized branch of the military establishment ⟨Marine *Corps*⟩ ⟨*Corps* of Engineers⟩ **b** : a military unit consisting of two or more divisions **2** : a group of persons acting under common direction ⟨diplomatic *corps*⟩

corpse \'kȯrps\ *n* : a dead body

corps·man \'kōr(z)-mən, 'kȯr(z)-\ *n* : a navy enlisted man trained to give first aid

cor·pu·lent \'kȯr-pyə-lənt\ *adj* : very fat : OBESE — **cor·pu·lence** \-lən(t)s\ *or* **cor·pu·lency** \-lən-sē\ *n* — **cor·pu·lent·ly** *adv*

Cor·pus Chris·ti \ˌkȯr-pəs-'kris-tē\ *n* : the Thursday after Trinity Sunday observed as a Roman Catholic festival in honor of the Eucharist

cor·pus·cle \'kȯr-(ˌ)pəs-əl\ *n* **1** : a minute particle **2** : a living cell; *esp* : one (as a blood or cartilage cell) not aggregated into continuous tissues — **cor·pus·cu·lar** \kȯr-'pəs-kyə-lər\ *adj*

cor·pus lu·te·um \ˌkȯr-pəs-'lüt-ē-əm\ *n, pl* **cor·po·ra lu·tea** \ˌkȯr-p(ə-)rə-'lüt-ē-ə\ : a yellowish mass of tissue formed in an ovarian follicle after the egg is released

1**cor·ral** \kə-'ral\ *n* [from Spanish, probably from an assumed Latin noun *currale* meaning "an enclosure for vehicles", from *currus* "chariot", from *currere* to run] **1** : a pen or enclosure for confining or capturing livestock **2** : an enclosure made with wagons for defense of an encampment

2**corral** *vb* **cor·ralled**; **cor·ral·ling** **1** : to confine in or as if in a corral **2** : SURROUND, CAPTURE **3** : to arrange wagons so as to form a corral

1**cor·rect** \kə-'rekt\ *vb* **1 a** : to make or set right **b** : COUNTERACT, NEUTRALIZE **c** : to alter or adjust so as to bring to some standard or required condition **2 a** : REBUKE, PUNISH **b** : to indicate the faults or errors of and show how they can be made right ⟨*correct* a student's composition⟩ — **cor·rect·a·ble** \-'rek-tə-bəl\ *adj*

syn CORRECT, RECTIFY, AMEND can mean to set right. CORRECT suggests action taken to point up or remove errors; RECTIFY suggests alteration to make accurate or to bring something under proper control or direction; AMEND implies improving or restoring by making changes

2**correct** *adj* **1** : conforming to an approved or conventional standard **2** : agreeing with fact, logic, or known truth — **cor·rect·ly** *adv* — **cor·rect·ness** \-'rek(t)-nəs\ *n*

syn CORRECT, ACCURATE, EXACT, PRECISE can mean brought to conformity with a standard. CORRECT suggests either freedom from error or compliance with convention; ACCURATE implies conformity to truth or fact through care to avoid error; EXACT suggests strict agreement with fact; PRECISE implies an even sharper definition or delimitation (as in making measurements) than EXACT *ant* incorrect

cor·rec·tion \kə-'rek-shən\ *n* **1** : the action or an instance of correcting **2** : a change that corrects something **3** : punishment or rebuke intended to correct faults of character or behavior — **cor·rec·tion·al** \-sh(ə-)nəl\ *adj*

cor·rec·tive \kə-'rek-tiv\ *adj* : serving to correct : having the power of making right, normal, or regular — **corrective** *n*

cor·re·late \'kȯr-ə-ˌlāt, 'kär-\ *vb* : to put into a systematic esp. part-for-part relation to each other ⟨*correlate* history and literature lessons⟩

cor·re·la·tion \ˌkȯr-ə-'lā-shən, ˌkär-\ *n* **1** : the act or process of correlating **2** : the state of being correlated; *esp* : a mutual relation discovered to exist between things ⟨the apparent *correlation* between the degree of poverty in a society and the crime rate⟩ — **cor·re·la·tion·al** \-sh(ə-)nəl\ *adj*

1**cor·rel·a·tive** \kə-'rel-ət-iv\ *adj* **1** : mutually related **2** : having a mutual grammatical relation and regularly used together ⟨*either* and *or* are *correlative* conjunctions⟩ — **cor·rel·a·tive·ly** *adv*

2**correlative** *n* : either of two correlative things

cor·re·spond \ˌkȯr-ə-'spänd, ˌkär-\ *vb* **1** : to be in conformity or agreement : SUIT **2 a** : to be like or equivalent : AGREE **b** : to be connected by means of a mathematical relationship ⟨point A *corresponds* to the number 1⟩ **3** : to communicate by means of letters — **cor·re·spond·ing·ly** \-'spän-ding-lē\ *adv*

cor·re·spond·ence \-'spän-dən(t)s\ *n* **1 a** : AGREEMENT, LIKENESS **b** : a point of similarity **c** : association of members of one set with each member of a second and of members of the second with each member of the first **2 a** : communication by letters **b** : the letters exchanged

1**cor·re·spond·ent** \-'spän-dənt\ *adj* **1** : SIMILAR **2** : CONFORMING, FITTING

2**correspondent** *n* **1** : something that corresponds to something else **2 a** : one who communicates with another by letter **b** : one who has regular commercial relations with another **c** : one who contributes news to a newspaper or newscast from a distant place

corresponding angle *n* : one of a pair of nonadjacent angles which are on the same side of a line intersected by two lines and of which one angle is inside and the other outside the two lines

cor·ri·dor \'kȯr-əd-ər, 'kär-, -ə-ˌdȯr\ *n* **1** : a passageway into which compartments or rooms open (as in a school) **2** : a narrow strip of land esp. through foreign-held territory

cor·rob·o·rate \kə-'räb-ə-ˌrāt\ *vb* : to support with evidence or authority ⟨*corroborated* his brother's story⟩ — **cor·rob·o·ra·tion** \-ˌräb-ə-'rā-shən\ *n* — **cor·rob·o·ra·tive** \-'räb-ə-ˌrāt-iv\ *adj* — **cor·rob·o·ra·tor** \-ˌrāt-ər\ *n* — **cor·rob·o·ra·to·ry** \-rə-ˌtōr-ē, -ˌtȯr-\ *adj*

cor·rode \kə-'rōd\ *vb* : to eat or be eaten away by degrees as if by gnawing ⟨a bridge *corroded* by rust⟩

cor·ro·sion \kə-'rō-zhən\ *n* : the action, process, or effect of corroding

1**cor·ro·sive** \kə-'rō-siv, -ziv\ *adj* : tending or having the power to corrode ⟨*corrosive* acids⟩ — **cor·ro·sive·ly** *adv* — **cor·ro·sive·ness** *n*

2**corrosive** *n* : something corrosive

corrosive sublimate *n* : a poisonous chloride of mercury used as a disinfectant and fungicide and in photography

cor·ru·gate \'kȯr-ə-ˌgāt, 'kär-\ *vb* : to form or shape into wrinkles or folds : FURROW ⟨*corrugated* paper⟩

cor·ru·ga·tion \ˌkȯr-ə-'gā-shən, ˌkär-\ *n* **1** : the act of corrugating : the state of being corrugated **2** : a ridge or groove of a corrugated surface

1**cor·rupt** \kə-'rəpt\ *vb* **1** : to change from good to bad in morals, manners, or actions; *esp* : to influence a public official improperly **2** : TAINT, ROT **3** : to alter from the original or correct form or version ⟨*corrupt* a text⟩ **4** : to become debased — **cor·rupt·er** *or* **cor·rup·tor** \-'rəp-tər\ *n*

2**corrupt** *adj* **1** : morally corrupted : DEPRAVED **2** : characterized by improper conduct ⟨a *corrupt* government⟩ — **cor·rupt·ly** *adv* — **cor·rupt·ness** \-'rəp(t)-nəs\ *n*

cor·rupt·i·ble \kə-'rəp-tə-bəl\ *adj* : capable of being corrupted — **cor·rupt·i·bil·i·ty** \-ˌrəp-tə-'bil-ət-ē\ *n*

cor·rup·tion \kə-'rəp-shən\ *n* **1** : physical decay or rotting **2** : moral impairment : DEPRAVITY **3** : inducement (as by bribery) to do wrong **4** : a departure from what is pure or correct

cor·sage \kȯr-'säzh, -'säj, 'kȯr-ˌ\ *n* [originally meaning "the waist of a woman's dress", from French, from Old French *cors* "body", from Latin *corpus*] : an arrangement of flowers to be worn by a woman

cor·sair \'kȯr-ˌsa(ə)r, -ˌse(ə)r\ *n* : PIRATE

corse \'kȯrs\ *n, archaic* : CORPSE

corse·let *n* **1** *or* **cors·let** \'kȯr-slət\ : the body armor worn by a knight esp. on the upper part of the body **2** \ˌkȯr-sə-'let\ : a woman's undergarment somewhat like a corset

cor·set \'kȯr-sət\ *n* : a tight-fitting stiffened undergarment worn by women to support or give shape to waist and hips — **corset** *vb*

cor·tege *also* **cor·tège** \'kȯr-ˌtezh, kȯr-'\ *n* **1** : a train of attendants : RETINUE **2** : PROCESSION; *esp* : a funeral procession

cor·tex \'kȯr-ˌteks\ *n, pl* **cor·ti·ces** \'kȯrt-ə-ˌsēz\ *or* **cor·tex·es** : an outer layer of an organism or one of its parts ⟨the *cortex* of the kidney⟩: as **a** : the outer layer of gray matter of the brain **b** : the layer of tissue outside the xylem and phloem and inside the corky or epidermal tissues of a vascular plant; *also* : all tissues external to the xylem — **cor·ti·cal** \'kȯrt-i-kəl\ *adj* — **cor·ti·cal·ly** \-i-k(ə-)lē\ *adv*

cor·ti·sone \'kȯrt-ə-ˌsōn, -ˌzōn\ *n* : a hormone of the adrenal cortex used esp. in the treatment of arthritis

co·run·dum \kə-'rən-dəm\ *n* : a very hard mineral of aluminum oxide used as an abrasive or in some crystalline forms as a gem (as ruby or sapphire)

cor·vette \kȯr-'vet\ *n* **1** : a naval sailing ship smaller than a frigate **2** : a highly maneuverable armed escort ship smaller than a destroyer

cos *abbr* cosine

cosily, cosiness *var of* COZILY, COZINESS

co·sine \'kō-ˌsīn\ *n* : the ratio between the side adjacent to the acute angle in a right triangle and the hypotenuse

1**cos·met·ic** \käz-'met-ik\ *n* : a cosmetic preparation

2**cosmetic** *adj* [from Greek *kosmein* "to adorn", from *kosmos* "order", "adornment", "cosmos"] : intended to beautify the hair or complexion

cos·me·tol·o·gist \ˌkäz-mə-'täl-ə-jəst\ *n* : one who gives beauty treatments (as to skin and hair) — **cos·me·tol·o·gy** \-jē\ *n*

cos·mic \'käz-mik\ *adj* **1** : of or relating to the cosmos ⟨*cosmic* theories⟩ **2** : extremely vast : GRAND ⟨*cosmic* dimensions⟩

cosmic dust *n* : very fine particles of solid matter in any part of the universe and esp. in interstellar space

cosmic radiation *n* : radiation consisting of cosmic rays

cosmic ray *n* : a stream of atomic nuclei of extremely penetrating character that enter the earth's atmosphere from outer space at speeds approaching that of light

cos·mol·o·gy \käz-'mäl-ə-jē\ *n, pl* **-gies** : a study that deals with the origin, structure, and space-time relationships of the universe — **cos·mol·o·gist** \-jəst\ *n*

cos·mo·naut \'käz-mə-ˌnȯt, -ˌnät\ *n* : ASTRONAUT; *specif* : a Soviet astronaut

cos·mo·pol·i·tan \ˌkäz-mə-'päl-ət-ən\ *adj* **1** : having a worldwide scope or outlook : not limited or parochial ⟨*cosmopolitan* world travelers⟩ **2** : composed of persons or elements from many parts of the world ⟨a *cosmopolitan* city⟩ **3** : found in most parts of the world and under varied ecological conditions ⟨a *cosmopolitan* herb⟩ — **cosmopolitan** *n*

cos·mos \'käz-məs, *1 & 2 also* -ˌmōs, -ˌmäs\ *n* **1** : the orderly systematic universe **2** : a complex harmonious system **3** : a tall garden plant that is related to the daisies and has showy white, pink, or rose-colored flower heads with usu. yellow centers

cos·sack \'käs-ˌak, -ək\ *n* [from Russian *kazak* and Ukrainian *kozak*, from Turkish *kazak* "independent person", "adventurer"] : a member of a group of frontiersmen of southern Russia formerly used as cavalry

1**cost** \'kȯst\ *n* **1** : the amount paid or charged for something : PRICE **2** : the outlay or effort made to achieve a goal ⟨won the battle at the *cost* of many lives⟩ **3** *pl* : expenses charged to a party before a court of law ⟨fined $50 and *costs*⟩

2**cost** *vb* **cost**; **cost·ing** **1** : to have a price of : require payment of ⟨each ticket *costs* one dollar⟩ **2** : to cause one to pay, spend, or lose ⟨selfishness *cost* him many friends⟩

cos·ta \'käs-tə\ *n, pl* **cos·tae** \-(ˌ)tē, -ˌtī\ : a rib or a body part (as the midrib of a leaf) resembling a rib — **cos·tal** \'käs-təl\ *adj* — **cos·tate** \-ˌtāt\ *adj*

cos·ter \'käs-tər\ *n, Brit* : COSTERMONGER

cos·ter·mon·ger \'käs-tər-ˌməng-gər, -ˌmäng-\ *n, Brit* : a person who sells fruit or vegetables in the street from a stand or cart

cos·tive \'käs-tiv\ *adj* **1** : CONSTIPATED **2** : causing constipation ⟨a *costive* diet⟩

cost·ly \'kȯst-lē\ *adj* **cost·li·er**; **-est** **1** : of great cost or value ⟨*costly* furs⟩ **2** : made at heavy expense or sacrifice ⟨*costly* victory⟩ — **cost·li·ness** *n*

cost·mary \'kȯst-ˌmer-ē\ *n, pl* **-mar·ies** : an aromatic herb related to the daisies and used as a potherb and in flavoring

1**cos·tume** \'käs-ˌt(y)üm\ *n* **1** : the prevailing dress of a period, country, or class **2** : a suit or dress characteristic of a period, country, class, or occupation esp. as worn on the stage or at a masquerade party **3** : a suit of clothes; *esp* : a woman's dress with coat or jacket — **costume** *adj*

2**costume** *vb* : to provide with a costume

cos·tum·er \'käs-ˌt(y)ü-mər\ *or* **cos·tu·mi·er** \käs-'t(y)ü-mē-ər\ *n* : one that makes, sells, or rents costumes

co·sy \'kō-zē\ *var of* COZY

1**cot** \'kät\ *n* : COTTAGE

2**cot** *n* : a small often collapsible bed usu. of fabric stretched on a frame

cote \'kōt, 'kät\ *n* : a shed or coop for small domestic animals (as sheep or pigeons)

co·te·rie \'kōt-ə-(ˌ)rē, ˌkōt-ə-'\ *n* : an intimate often exclusive group of persons with a common interest

co·til·lion \kō-'til-yən\ *n* **1** : an elaborate dance with frequent changing of partners led by one couple at formal balls **2** : a formal ball

cot·tage \'kät-ij\ *n* **1** : a small frame one-family house **2** : a small house for vacation use

cottage cheese *n* : a soft uncured cheese made from soured skim milk

cottage pudding *n* : plain cake covered with a hot sweet sauce

cot·tag·er \'kät-ij-ər\ *n* : one who lives in a cottage; *esp* : one occupying a private house at a vacation resort

1**cot·ter** *or* **cot·tar** \'kät-ər\ *n* : a peasant or rural laborer occupying a small holding

2**cot·ter** \'kät-ər\ *n* : a wedge-shaped piece used to fasten parts together

cotter pin *n* : a half-round metal strip bent into a pin whose ends can be flared after insertion through a slot or hole

C

1**cot·ton** \'kät-ən\ *n* **1 a :** a soft usu. white fibrous substance composed of the hairs surrounding the seeds of various plants **b :** any of several erect freely branching plants that produce cotton **2 a :** fabric made of cotton **b :** yarn spun from cotton — **cotton** *adj*

cotton 1b: leaves and flower

2**cotton** *vb* **cot·toned; cot·ton·ing** \'kät-(ə-)niŋ\ **:** to take a liking ⟨*cottoned* to him at their first meeting⟩

cotton gin *n* **:** a machine that separates the seeds, hulls, and foreign material from cotton

cotton grass *n* **:** any of a group of bog sedges characterized by a cottony fruiting spike

cot·ton·mouth \'kät-ən-ˌmau̇th\ *n* **:** WATER MOCCASIN

cot·ton·seed \-ˌsēd\ *n* **:** the seed of the cotton plant yielding a protein-rich meal and an oil

cottonseed oil *n* **:** a pale yellow fatty oil that is obtained from cottonseed and is used chiefly in salad and cooking oils and in shortening and margarine

cot·ton·tail \'kät-ən-ˌtāl\ *n* **:** any of several small brownish gray rabbits with white-tufted tail

cot·ton·wood \-ˌwu̇d\ *n* **1 :** a poplar with a tuft of cottony hairs on the seed; *esp* **:** one of the eastern and central U.S. noted for its rapid growth and luxuriant foliage **2 :** the wood of a cottonwood

cot·tony \'kät-(ə-)nē\ *adj* **1 :** covered with soft hairs **:** DOWNY **2 :** SOFT

cot·y·le·don \ˌkät-ə-'lēd-ən\ *n* **:** the first leaf or one of the first leaves developed by the embryo of a seed plant that is usually folded within the seed until germination and serves as a storehouse of food

1**couch** \'kau̇ch\ *vb* **1 :** to recline for rest or sleep **2 :** to bring down **:** LOWER ⟨a knight charging with *couched* lance⟩ **3 :** to phrase in a specified manner ⟨a letter *couched* in polite terms⟩

2**couch** *n* **:** BED; *esp* **:** SOFA

couch grass \'kau̇ch-, 'küch-\ *n* **:** a European creeping grass naturalized in No. America as a weed

cou·gar \'kü-gər, -ˌgär\ *n, pl* **cougars** *also* **cougar :** a large powerful tawny brown cat formerly widespread in the Americas but now extinct in many areas — called also *mountain lion, panther, puma*

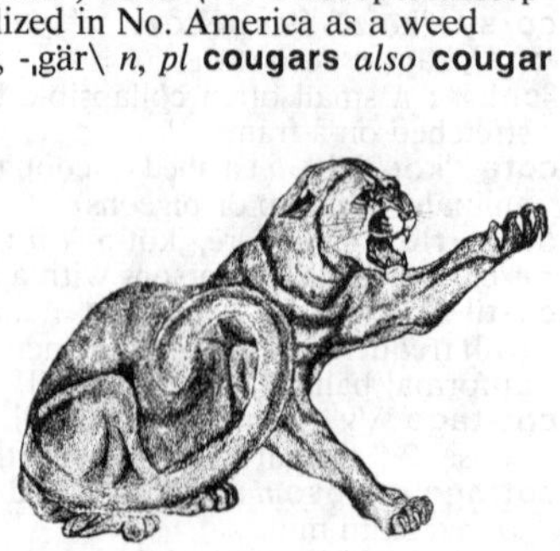
cougar (about 29 in. at shoulder)

1**cough** \'kȯf\ *vb* **1 :** to force air from the lungs with a sharp short noise or series of noises **2 :** to get rid of by coughing

ə abut	ər further	a back	ā bake
ä cot, cart	au̇ out	ch chin	e less	ē easy
g gift	i trip	ī life	j joke	ŋ sing	ō flow
ȯ flaw	ȯi coin	th thin	t͟h this	ü loot
u̇ foot	y yet	yü few	yu̇ furious	zh vision

2**cough** *n* **1 :** a condition marked by repeated or frequent coughing **2 :** an act or sound of coughing

could \kəd, (')ku̇d\ *past of* CAN — used as an auxiliary verb in the past ⟨he found he *could* go⟩ ⟨he said he would go if he *could*⟩ and as a polite or less forceful alternative to *can* ⟨*could* you do this for me⟩

couldn't \'ku̇d-ənt\ **:** could not

couldst \kədst, (')ku̇dst\ *archaic past 2d sing of* CAN

cou·lee \'kü-lē\ *n* **1** *chiefly West* **a :** a dry creek bed **b :** a steep-walled valley **2 :** a thick sheet or stream of lava

cou·lomb \'kü-ˌläm, -ˌlōm\ *n* **:** the practical mks unit of electric charge equal to the quantity of electricity transferred by a current of one ampere in one second

coun·cil \'kau̇n(t)-səl\ *n* **1 :** a meeting for consultation **2 :** an advisory or legislative body ⟨governor's *council*⟩ **3 :** an administrative body ⟨city *council*⟩

coun·cil·lor *or* **coun·cil·or** \'kau̇n(t)-s(ə-)lər\ *n* **:** a member of a council

coun·cil·man \'kau̇n(t)-səl-mən\ *n* **:** a member of a council esp. in a city government

1**coun·sel** \'kau̇n(t)-səl\ *n* **1 :** advice given **2 :** DELIBERATION, CONSULTATION **3** *pl* **counsel :** a lawyer engaged in the trial or management of a case in court

2**counsel** *vb* **-seled** *or* **-selled; -sel·ing** *or* **-sel·ling** \-s(ə-)liŋ\ **1 :** to give counsel **:** ADVISE ⟨*counsel* a student on a choice of studies⟩ **2 :** to seek counsel **:** CONSULT ⟨*counsel* with friends⟩

coun·sel·or *or* **coun·sel·lor** \'kau̇n(t)-s(ə-)lər\ *n* **1 :** ADVISER **2 :** LAWYER **3 :** a supervisor of campers or activities at a summer camp

1**count** \'kau̇nt\ *vb* [from French *compter*, from Latin *computare* "to compute"] **1 a :** to name one by one so as to find the total number ⟨*count* the apples in a box⟩ **b :** to name the consecutive numbers up to and including ⟨*count* ten⟩ **c :** to recite the numbers in order by units or groups ⟨*count* to one hundred by fives⟩ **d :** to include in a tally ⟨forty present, *counting* children⟩ **2 a :** CONSIDER ⟨*counts* himself lucky⟩ **b :** to include or exclude by or as if by counting ⟨*count* me out⟩ **3 a :** DEPEND, RELY ⟨a man you can *count* on⟩ **b :** RECKON, PLAN ⟨*counted* on going⟩ **4 :** to have value or importance ⟨every vote *counts*⟩ — **count·a·ble** \-ə-bəl\ *adj*

2**count** *n* **1 a :** the act or process of counting **b :** a total obtained by counting **:** TALLY **2 :** CHARGE; *esp* **:** a separate item in a legal accusation ⟨guilty on all *counts*⟩

3**count** *n* [from French *comte*, from medieval Latin *comit-*, stem of *comes*, from Latin, "companion", from *com-* and *ire* "to go"; so called because the count was subordinate to the duke; compare DUKE] **:** a European nobleman whose rank corresponds to that of a British earl

count·down \'kau̇nt-ˌdau̇n\ *n* **:** an audible backward counting off in fixed units (as seconds) from an arbitrary starting number of the time remaining before an event (as the launching of a rocket)

1**coun·te·nance** \'kau̇nt-(ə-)nən(t)s\ *n* **1 a :** calm expression **b :** facial expression **2 :** FACE **3 :** calmness of mind **4 :** APPROVAL, ENCOURAGEMENT ⟨gave no *countenance* to the plan⟩

2**countenance** *vb* **:** TOLERATE, ENCOURAGE ⟨refused to *countenance* his habitual lateness⟩

1**count·er** \'kau̇nt-ər\ *n* **1 :** a piece (as of metal or ivory) used in counting or in games **2 :** a level surface (as a table) over which business is transacted or food is served or on which goods are displayed

2**count·er** *n* **:** one that counts; *esp* **:** a device for indicating a number or amount

3**coun·ter** \'kau̇nt-ər\ *vb* **coun·tered; coun·ter-**

ing \'kaủnt-ə-ring, 'kaủn-tring\ **1 :** to act in opposition to : OPPOSE ⟨*countering* the claim for damages⟩ **2 :** to give a blow in return ⟨*counter* with a left hook⟩

4**coun·ter** *adv* **:** in a contrary manner or direction ⟨acting *counter* to his wishes⟩

5**coun·ter** *n* **1 a :** the act of giving a retaliatory blow **b :** the blow given **2 :** a stiffener for a shoe upper around the heel

6**coun·ter** *adj* **1 :** moving in an opposite direction ⟨ship slowed by *counter* tides⟩ **2 :** designed to oppose ⟨a *counter* offer⟩

counter- *prefix* **1 a :** contrary : opposite ⟨*counter*clockwise⟩ ⟨*counter*march⟩ **b :** opposing : retaliatory ⟨*counter*offensive⟩ **2 :** complementary : corresponding ⟨*counter*part⟩ **3 :** duplicate : substitute ⟨*counter*foil⟩

count·ter·act \,kaủnt-ər-'akt\ *vb* **:** to lessen the force of : OFFSET ⟨a drug that *counteracts* a poison⟩ — **coun·ter·ac·tion** \-'ak-shən\ *n* — **coun·ter·ac·tive** \-'ak-tiv\ *adj*

coun·ter·at·tack \'kaủnt-ər-ə-,tak\ *n* **:** an attack made to counter an enemy's attack — **counterattack** *vb*

1**coun·ter·bal·ance** \'kaủnt-ər-,bal-ən(t)s, ,kaủnt-ər-'\ *n* **1 :** a weight that balances another **2 :** a force or influence that offsets or checks an opposing force

2**counterbalance** *vb* **:** to oppose with an equal weight or force

counter check *n* **:** a blank check obtainable at a bank; *esp* **:** one to be cashed at the bank by the drawer

coun·ter·claim \'kaủnt-ər-,klām\ *n* **:** an opposing claim — **counterclaim** *vb* — **coun·ter·claim·ant** \-,klā-mənt\ *n*

coun·ter·clock·wise \,kaủnt-ər-'kläk-,wīz\ *adv* **:** in a direction opposite to that in which the hands of a clock rotate — **counterclockwise** *adj*

coun·ter·cur·rent \'kaủnt-ər-,kər-ənt, -,kə-rənt\ *n* **:** a current flowing in a direction opposite to that of another

1**coun·ter·feit** \'kaủnt-ər-,fit\ *vb* **1 :** to imitate or copy esp. with intent to deceive ⟨*counterfeiting* money⟩ **2 :** PRETEND, FEIGN ⟨*counterfeit* an air of indifference⟩ — **coun·ter·feit·er** *n*

2**counterfeit** *adj* **1 :** made in imitation of something else with intent to deceive : FORGED ⟨*counterfeit* money⟩ **2 :** FEIGNED, SHAM

3**counterfeit** *n* **:** something counterfeit : FORGERY

coun·ter·foil \'kaủnt-ər-,fỏil\ *n* **:** a stub usu. serving as a record or receipt (as on a check or ticket)

coun·ter·force \-,fōrs, -,fỏrs\ *n* **:** a force, power, or trend that opposes another

coun·ter·in·tel·li·gence \,kaủnt-ər-in-'tel-ə-jən(t)s\ *n* **:** activities designed to counter the activities of an enemy's intelligence service by blocking its sources of information and to deceive the enemy through ruses and misinformation

coun·ter·mand \'kaủnt-ər-,mand\ *vb* **1 :** to cancel a former command **2 :** to recall or order back by a contrary order

coun·ter·march \'kaủnt-ər-,märch\ *n* **:** a marching back; *esp* **:** a maneuver by which a marching unit reverses direction but keeps the same order — **countermarch** *vb*

coun·ter·mel·o·dy \-,mel-əd-ē\ *n* **:** a secondary melody sounded or to be sounded at the same time with the principal melody

coun·ter·of·fen·sive \'kaủnt-ər-ə-,fen(t)-siv\ *n* **:** a large-scale counterattack

coun·ter·pane \-,pān\ *n* **:** BEDSPREAD

coun·ter·part \'kaủnt-ər-,pärt\ *n* **1 :** a part or thing corresponding to another ⟨the left arm is the *counterpart* of the right⟩ **2 :** something that serves to complete another : COMPLEMENT **3 :** a person closely resembling another

coun·ter·point \'kaủnt-ər-,pỏint\ *n* **1 :** one or more independent melodies added above or below another **2 :** combination of two or more melodies into a single harmonic texture in which each retains its linear character

coun·ter·poise \-,pỏiz\ *vb* **:** COUNTERBALANCE — **counterpoise** *n*

coun·ter·rev·o·lu·tion \,kaủnt-ər-,rev-ə-'lü-shən\ *n* **:** a revolution intended to counteract an earlier one — **coun·ter·rev·o·lu·tion·ary** \-shə-,ner-ē\ *adj or n* — **coun·ter·rev·o·lu·tion·ist** \-sh(ə-)nəst\ *n*

C

1**coun·ter·sign** \'kaủnt-ər-,sīn\ *n* **:** a sign used in reply to another; *esp* **:** PASSWORD

2**countersign** *vb* **:** to add one's signature to a document after another's in order to confirm its genuineness — **coun·ter·sig·na·ture** \,kaủnt-ər-'sig-nə-,chủ(ə)r, -chər\ *n*

1**coun·ter·sink** \'kaủnt-ər-,singk\ *vb* **-sunk** \-,səngk\; **-sink·ing** **1 :** to form a hollowed-out place around the top of a hole into which a screw or bolt is to be placed **2 :** to sink the head of a screw, bolt, or nail even with or below the surface

2**countersink** *n* **1 :** a countersunk hole **2 :** a bit or drill for making a countersink

coun·ter·spy \'kaủnt-ər-,spī\ *n* **:** a spy employed in counterintelligence

coun·ter·ten·or \-,ten-ər\ *n* **:** a tenor with an unusually high range

coun·ter·weight \-,wāt\ *n* **:** COUNTERBALANCE

count·ess \'kaủnt-əs\ *n* **1 :** the wife or widow of a count or an earl **2 :** a woman who holds the rank of a count or an earl in her own right

count·ing·house \'kaủnt-ing-,haủs\ *n* **:** a building, room, or office used for keeping books and transacting business

counting number *n* **:** NATURAL NUMBER

count·less \'kaủnt-ləs\ *adj* **:** too numerous to be counted : INNUMERABLE

count noun *n* **:** a noun that forms a plural and that can be used with a numeral

coun·tri·fied *or* **coun·try·fied** \'kən-trē-,fīd\ *adj* **:** looking or acting like a person from the country : RUSTIC

1**coun·try** \'kən-trē\ *n, pl* **countries** **1 :** an indefinite usu. extended expanse of land : REGION ⟨hill *country*⟩ **2 a :** the land of a person's birth, residence, or citizenship **b :** a nation or its territory **3 :** the people of a state or district : POPULACE **4 :** rural as distinguished from urban areas ⟨lives out in the *country*⟩

2**country** *adj* **:** of, relating to, or characteristic of the country : RURAL, RUSTIC

country club *n* **:** a suburban club for social life and recreation

coun·try·man \'kən-trē-mən, *3 is often* -,man\ *n* **1 :** an inhabitant or native of a specified country **2 :** a native or inhabitant of the same country as another ⟨hated by his *countrymen*⟩ **3 :** one living in the country or marked by country ways : RUSTIC — **coun·try·wom·an** \-,wủm-ən\ *n*

country music *n* **:** music derived from or imitating the folk style of the southern U.S. or the western cowboy

coun·try·seat \,kən-trē-'sēt\ *n* **:** a dwelling or estate in the country

coun·try·side \'kən-trē-,sīd\ *n* **:** a rural area or its people

coun·ty \'kaủnt-ē\ *n, pl* **counties** **1 :** the domain of a count or earl **2 :** a division of a state or of a country for local government

county agent *n* : a government agent employed to promote agricultural improvement in a county

county seat *n* : a town that is the seat of county administration

coup \'kü\ *n, pl* **coups** \'küz\ **1** : a brilliant, sudden, and usu. highly successful stroke **2** : COUP D'ETAT

coup d'e·tat \ˌküd-ə-'tä, ˌküd-ā-\ *n, pl* **coups d'e·tat** \ˌküd-ə-'tä(z), ˌküd-ā-\ : a sudden overthrowing of a government by a small group

cou·pé *or* **coupe** \kü-'pā, *2 is often* 'küp\ *n* [from French *coupé*, literally "something cut", from past participle of *couper* "to cut"] **1** : a four-wheeled closed horse-drawn carriage for two persons with an outside seat for the driver **2** *usu coupe* **a** : an enclosed 2-door automobile for two persons **b** : a usu. enclosed 2-door automobile with a full-width rear seat

¹**cou·ple** \'kəp-əl\ *vb* **cou·pled**; **cou·pling** \'kəp-(ə-)liŋ\ **1** : to join together : CONNECT **2** : to join in pairs — **cou·pler** \-p(ə-)lər\ *n*

²**couple** *n* **1** : a man and woman paired or associated together (as by marriage or on a date) **2** : two persons or things paired together

syn COUPLE, PAIR, BRACE can mean a group of two considered together. COUPLE applies esp. to two closely associated things (as man and wife) of the same class; PAIR is more likely to apply to things of different classes that are associated ⟨the horse and rider made a fine *pair*⟩; BRACE applies esp. to a couple of certain animals ⟨a *brace* of quail⟩

cou·plet \'kəp-lət\ *n* : two successive lines of verse forming a unit; *esp* : two rhyming lines of the same length

cou·pling \'kəp-liŋ (*usual for 2*), -ə-liŋ\ *n* **1** : the act of bringing or coming together **2** : something that connects two parts or things ⟨a car *coupling*⟩ ⟨a pipe *coupling*⟩ **3** : means of electric connection of two electric circuits by having a part common to both

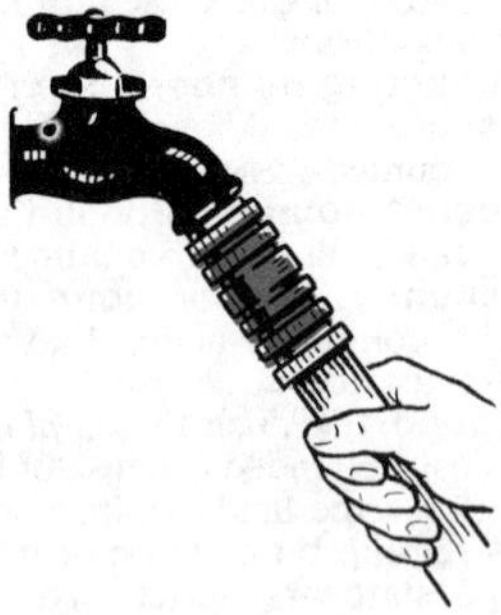

coupling 2

cou·pon \'k(y)ü-ˌpän\ *n* **1** : a statement of interest due to be cut from a bond and presented for payment on a stated date **2 a** : one of a series of tickets to be detached and presented as needed **b** : a ticket or form authorizing purchases of rationed commodities **c** : a certificate of a purchase redeemable in premiums **d** : a part of an advertisement to be cut off for use as an order blank or inquiry form

cour·age \'kər-ij, 'kə-rij\ *n* : strength of mind to venture, persevere, and withstand danger, fear, or difficulty

syn COURAGE, BRAVERY, VALOR, HEROISM can mean greatness of heart in carrying on in the face of danger or difficulty. COURAGE suggests fearlessness or the overcoming of fear; BRAVERY may imply bold and daring defiance of danger; VALOR applies esp. to bravery in combat; HEROISM implies high bravery in accepting risk or making a sacrifice for a noble or generous purpose *ant* cowardice

cou·ra·geous \kə-'rā-jəs\ *adj* : having or marked by courage : BRAVE — **cou·ra·geous·ly** *adv* — **cou·ra·geous·ness** *n*

cou·ri·er \'ku̇r-ē-ər, 'kər-ē-, 'kə-rē-\ *n* : a messenger esp. in the diplomatic service

¹**course** \'kōrs, 'kȯrs\ *n* **1** : motion or progress from point to point : PASSAGE ⟨met with difficulties in his *course*⟩ ⟨during the *course* of a year⟩ **2** : the direction or route of motion or progress ⟨the *course* of a river⟩ ⟨a ship's *course*⟩ **3** : land laid out for golf **4** : normal or accustomed procedure ⟨the disease ran its *course*⟩ **5** : manner of proceeding : CONDUCT ⟨a wise *course*⟩ **6** : an ordered process or series; *esp* : a series of classes in a subject or a series of such courses constituting a curriculum **7** : a part of a meal served at one time **8** : a layer of brick or masonry in a wall — **of course 1** : following the ordinary way or procedure ⟨did it as a matter *of course*⟩ **2** : NATURALLY, CERTAINLY

²**course** *vb* **1** : to run through or over ⟨buffalo *coursed* the plains⟩ **2** : to move rapidly : RACE ⟨blood *coursing* through the veins⟩

cours·er \'kōr-sər, 'kȯr-\ *n* : a swift or spirited horse

¹**court** \'kōrt, 'kȯrt\ *n* **1 a** : the residence of a king or similar dignitary **b** : a sovereign's formal assembly of his councillors and officers and his officials **c** : the family and retinue of a sovereign **2 a** : an open space wholly or partly surrounded by buildings **b** : a short street or lane **c** : a space for playing a ball game ⟨tennis *court*⟩ **3 a** : an assembly for carrying out judicial business **b** : a session of a judicial assembly ⟨*court* is now adjourned⟩ **c** : a building or room for administering justice **d** : a judge in session **4** : attention designed to win favor ⟨paying *court* to a woman⟩

²**court** *vb* **1 a** : to try to gain ⟨*court* favor⟩ **b** : to act so as to provoke ⟨*court* disaster⟩ **2** : to seek the affections or favor of ⟨*courted* the neighbor's daughter⟩ ⟨the candidate *courted* the voters⟩ **3 a** : to make love : WOO ⟨go *courting*⟩ **b** : to engage in activity leading to mating ⟨a pair of robins *courting*⟩

cour·te·ous \'kərt-ē-əs\ *adj* **1** : marked by polished manners suitable to a court **2** : marked by respect for and consideration of others — **cour·te·ous·ly** *adv* — **cour·te·ous·ness** *n*

cour·te·sy \'kərt-ə-sē\ *n, pl* **-sies 1** : courtly politeness ⟨old-world *courtesy*⟩ **2** : a favor courteously performed **3** : a favor as distinguished from a right ⟨a title by *courtesy* only⟩

court·house \'kōrt-ˌhau̇s, 'kȯrt-\ *n* : a building in which courts of law are held or county offices are housed

court·i·er \'kōrt-ē-ər, 'kȯrt-\ *n* **1** : a person in attendance at a royal court **2** : a person who practices flattery

court·ly \'kōrt-lē, 'kȯrt-\ *adj* : suitable to a royal court : ELEGANT ⟨*courtly* manners⟩ — **court·li·ness** *n*

¹**court–mar·tial** \'kōrt-ˌmär-shəl, 'kȯrt-\ *n, pl* **courts–martial** *also* **court–martials 1** : a military court **2** : a trial by court-martial

²**court–martial** *vb* **-mar·tialed** *also* **-mar·tialled**; **-mar·tial·ing** *also* **-mar·tial·ling** \-ˌmärsh-(ə-)liŋ\ : to try by court-martial

court plaster *n* : an adhesive plaster esp. of silk coated with isinglass and glycerin

court·room \'kōrt-ˌrüm, 'kȯrt-, -ˌru̇m\ *n* : a room in which a court of law is held
court·ship \-ˌship\ *n* : the act or process of courting
court·yard \'kōrt-ˌyärd, 'kȯrt-\ *n* : an enclosure attached to a building (as a palace)
cous·in \'kəz-ən\ *n* **1 a** : a child of one's uncle or aunt **b** : a relative descended from a common ancestor in a different line **2** : a person belonging to a related group ⟨our English *cousins*⟩ : COUSIN 1a
co·va·lent \(')kō-'vā-lənt\ *adj* : characterized by the sharing of electrons in pairs by two atoms in a chemical compound ⟨*covalent* bond⟩ — **co·va·lent·ly** *adv*
cove \'kōv\ *n* **1** : a small sheltered inlet or bay **2** : a level area sheltered by hills or mountains
cov·en \'kəv-ən\ *n* : an assembly or band of witches
[1]**cov·e·nant** \'kəv-(ə-)nənt\ *n* : a solemn agreement : CONTRACT
[2]**cov·e·nant** \'kəv-(ə-)nənt, -ə-ˌnant\ *vb* **1** : to promise by a covenant : PLEDGE **2** : to enter into a covenant : CONTRACT
[1]**cov·er** \'kəv-ər\ *vb* **cov·ered**; **cov·er·ing** \'kəv-(ə-)ring\ **1 a** : to guard from attack ⟨*cover* the landing with a naval bombardment⟩ **b** : to have within gunshot range **c** : to provide protection to or against : INSURE ⟨the policy *covered* water damage⟩ ⟨state police *covering* the highways⟩ **2 a** : to hide something from sight or knowledge ⟨*cover* up a scandal⟩ ⟨*covered* for his friend in the investigation⟩ **b** : to act as a substitute or replacement ⟨*covered* for me during my vacation⟩ **3 a** : to spread or lie over or on ⟨*covered* him with a blanket⟩ ⟨water *covered* the floor⟩ **b** : to put something protective or concealing over ⟨*cover* the mouth while coughing⟩ **4 a** : INCLUDE, EMBRACE ⟨an exam *covering* a semester's work⟩ **b** : to provide or plan for ⟨plans *covering* an enemy attack⟩ **5** : to have as one's territory or field of activity ⟨one salesman *covers* the state⟩ ⟨a reporter *covering* the courthouse⟩ **6** : to pass over or through ⟨*cover* 500 miles a day⟩— **cov·er·er** \-ər-ər\ *n*
[2]**cover** *n* **1** : something that protects, shelters, or conceals (as a natural shelter for an animal or natural features that shelter or conceal) **2 a** : something that is placed over or about another (as the lid of a box or a sheet or blanket on a bed) **b** : a binding or case for a book or the front or back of such a binding **c** : something (as vegetation or snow) that covers the ground **3** : an envelope or wrapper for mail
cov·er·age \'kəv-(ə-)rij\ *n* **1** : the act or fact of covering or something that covers ⟨insurance *coverage*⟩ ⟨news *coverage* at a political convention⟩ **2** : the number or amount covered : SCOPE
cov·er·all \'kəv-ər-ˌȯl\ *n* : a one-piece outer garment worn to protect clothes — usu. used in pl.
cover charge *n* : a charge made by a restaurant or nightclub in addition to the charge for food and drink
cover crop *n* : a crop planted to prevent soil erosion and to provide humus
covered wagon *n* : a wagon with an arched canvas top
cover glass *n* : a piece of very thin transparent material used to cover something mounted on a microscope slide
cov·er·ing \'kəv-(ə-)ring\ *n* : COVER
cov·er·let \'kəv-ər-lət\ *n* : BEDSPREAD
cov·er·slip \'kəv-ər-ˌslip\ *n* : COVER GLASS
[1]**cov·ert** \'kəv-ərt, 'kō-(ˌ)vərt\ *adj* **1** : partly hidden ⟨a *covert* smile⟩ **2** : covered over : SHELTERED ⟨a *covert* nook⟩ — **cov·ert·ly** *adv* — **cov·ert·ness** *n*
[2]**cov·ert** \'kəv-ərt, 'kō-vərt\ *n* **1 a** : hiding place : SHELTER **b** : a thicket affording cover for game **2** : a firm durable twilled cloth usu. of mixed-color yarns
cov·et \'kəv-ət\ *vb* : to wish enviously esp. for what belongs to another — **cov·et·er** \-ər\ *n* — **cov·et·ing·ly** \-ing-lē\ *adv*
cov·et·ous \'kəv-ət-əs\ *adj* : marked by a too eager desire esp. for another's possessions — **cov·et·ous·ly** *adv* — **cov·et·ous·ness** *n*
cov·ey \'kəv-ē\ *n, pl* **coveys** **1 a** : a mature bird or pair of birds with a brood of young **b** : a small flock **2** : COMPANY, GROUP
[1]**cow** \'kau̇\ *n* **1** : the mature female of cattle or of any animal (as the moose) the male of which is called *bull* **2** : a domestic bovine animal regardless of sex or age
[2]**cow** *vb* : to lessen the spirits or courage of : FRIGHTEN ⟨was *cowed* into submission⟩
cow·ard \'kau̇(-ə)rd\ *n* [from Old French *coart*, from *coue, coe* "tail", from Latin *cauda*] : one who shows ignoble fear or timidity — **coward** *adj*
cow·ard·ice \'kau̇(-ə)rd-əs\ *n* : lack of courage to face danger : shameful fear
cow·ard·ly \'kau̇(-ə)rd-lē\ *adj* **1** : lacking courage : disgracefully timid ⟨a *cowardly* rascal⟩ **2** : characteristic of a coward ⟨a *cowardly* attack from behind⟩ — **cowardly** *adv* — **cow·ard·li·ness** *n*
cow·bell \'kau̇-ˌbel\ *n* : a bell hung about the neck of a cow to indicate its whereabouts
cow·bird \-ˌbərd\ *n* : a small No. American blackbird that lays its eggs in the nests of other birds
cow·boy \-ˌbȯi\ *n* : one who tends or drives cattle; *esp* : a mounted cattle ranch hand — **cow·girl** \-ˌgərl\ *n*
cow·catch·er \-ˌkach-ər, -ˌkech-\ *n* : PILOT 3
cow·er \'kau̇(-ə)r\ *vb* : to crouch down (as from fear or cold)
cow·hand \'kau̇-ˌhand\ *n* : COWBOY
cow·herd \-ˌhərd\ *n* : one who tends cows
[1]**cow·hide** \-ˌhīd\ *n* **1** : the hide of a cow or leather made from it **2** : a coarse whip of rawhide or braided leather
[2]**cowhide** *vb* : to whip with a cowhide
cowl \'kau̇l\ *n* **1** : a monk's hood or long hooded cloak **2** : the top part of an automobile body forward of the two front doors to which are attached the windshield and instrument panel **3** : COWLING — **cowled** \'kau̇ld\ *adj*
cow·lick \'kau̇-ˌlik\ *n* : a lock or tuft of hair that grows in a different direction from the rest of the hair and cannot be made to lie flat
cowl·ing \'kau̇-ling\ *n* : a removable metal covering for the engine and sometimes a part of the fuselage of an airplane
cow·man \'kau̇-mən, -ˌman\ *n* **1** : COWBOY **2** : a cattle owner or rancher
co–work·er \'kō-ˌwər-kər\ *n* : a fellow worker
cow·pea \'kau̇-ˌpē\ *n* : a sprawling herb related to the bean and grown in the southern U.S. esp. for forage and green manure; *also* : its edible seed
Cow·per's gland \ˌkau̇-pərz-, ˌkü-pərz-, ˌku̇p-ərz-\ *n* : either of two small glands discharging into the male urethra
cow·poke \'kau̇-ˌpōk\ *n* : COWBOY
cow pony *n* : a light saddle horse trained for herding cattle
cow·pox \'kau̇-ˌpäks\ *n* : a mild disease of the cow that when communicated to man produces a temporary rash and protects against smallpox
cow·punch·er \-ˌpən-chər\ *n* : COWBOY
cow·rie *or* **cow·ry** \'kau̇(ə)r-ē\ *n, pl* **cowries** : any

of numerous small snails of warm seas with glossy often brightly colored shells

cow·slip \'kaů-,slip\ *n* **1** : a common Old World primrose with fragrant yellow or purplish flowers **2** : MARSH MARIGOLD

cox \'käks\ *n* : COXSWAIN — **cox** *vb*

cox·comb \'käks-,kōm\ *n* : a conceited foolish person : FOP

cox·swain \'käk-sən, -,swān\ *n* **1** : a sailor who has charge of a ship's boat and its crew **2** : the steerer of a racing shell

coy \'kȯi\ *adj* [from medieval French *coi* "quiet", from Latin *quietus*] **1** : BASHFUL, SHY **2** : affecting shyness — **coy·ly** *adv* — **coy·ness** *n*

coy·ote \'kī-,ōt, kī-'ōt-ē\ *n, pl* **coyotes** *or* **coyote** : a small wolf native to western No. America

coyote
(about 1½ ft. at shoulder)

coy·pu \'kȯi-pü\ *n* **1** : a So. American aquatic rodent with webbed feet and mammary glands on its back **2** : NUTRIA 2

coz·en \'kəz-ən\ *vb* : CHEAT — **coz·en·er** *n*

1**co·zy** \'kō-zē\ *adj* **co·zi·er**; **-est** : SNUG, COMFORTABLE — **co·zi·ly** \-zə-lē\ *adv* — **co·zi·ness** \-zē-nəs\ *n*

2**cozy** *n, pl* **cozies** : a padded cover for a teapot to keep the contents hot

CP *abbr* **1** candlepower **2** chemically pure **3** Communist party

cpd *abbr* compound

cpl *abbr* corporal

cr *abbr* **1** credit **2** creditor

1**crab** \'krab\ *n* **1** : a crustacean with a short broad usu. flattened chitinous shell, a small abdomen curled forward beneath the body, and a front pair of limbs with strong pincers; *also* : any of various other crustaceans resembling true crabs in having a reduced abdomen **2** : any of various machines for raising or hauling heavy weights

2**crab** *vb* **crabbed**; **crab·bing** : to fish for crabs — **crab·ber** *n*

3**crab** *vb* **crabbed**; **crab·bing** : to find fault : COMPLAIN

4**crab** *n* **1** : CRAB APPLE **2** : a sour ill-tempered person

crab apple *n* **1** : a small wild sour apple **2** : a cultivated apple with small usu. highly colored acid fruit

crab·bed \'krab-əd\ *adj* **1** : PEEVISH, CROSS **2** : difficult to read or understand — **crab·bed·ly** *adv* — **crab·bed·ness** *n*

crab·by \'krab-ē\ *adj* **crab·bi·er**; **-est** : CROSS, ILL-NATURED

crab·grass \'krab-,gras\ *n* : a weedy grass with creeping or sprawling stems that root freely at the nodes

ə abut	ər further	a back	ā bake
ä cot, cart	aů out	ch chin	e less	ē easy
g gift	i trip	ī life	j joke	ng sing	ō flow
ȯ flaw	ȯi coin	th thin	t͟h this	ü loot
ů foot	y yet	yü few	yů furious	zh vision

crab louse *n* : a louse infesting the human pubic region

1**crack** \'krak\ *vb* **1 a** : to break with a sudden sharp sound : SNAP **b** : to make or cause to make such a sound ⟨*crack* a whip⟩ **2** : to break wholly or partially ⟨the ice *cracked* in several places⟩ **3** : to tell esp. in a clever or witty way ⟨*crack* jokes⟩ **4** : PRAISE, EXTOL ⟨not all he is *cracked* up to be⟩ **5 a** : to lose control **b** : to fail in tone ⟨voice *cracked*⟩ **c** : to wreck a vehicle ⟨*cracked* up on a curve⟩ **d** : to give or receive a sharp blow ⟨*cracked* his head⟩ **6 a** : to puzzle out : SOLVE ⟨*crack* a code⟩ **b** : to break into or through ⟨*crack* a safe⟩ ⟨*crack* the sound barrier⟩ **7 a** : to subject hydrocarbons to cracking ⟨*crack* petroleum⟩ **b** : to produce by cracking ⟨*cracked* gasoline⟩

2**crack** *n* **1** : a sudden sharp noise **2** : a sharp witty remark : QUIP **3** : a narrow break or opening ⟨a *crack* in the glass⟩ ⟨open the window a *crack*⟩ **4 a** : WEAKNESS, FLAW **b** : a broken tone of the voice **5** : MOMENT, INSTANT ⟨the *crack* of dawn⟩ **6** : a sharp resounding blow **7** : TRY ⟨take a *crack* at it⟩

3**crack** *adj* : of superior quality ⟨*crack* troops⟩

crack·brain \'krak-,brān\ *n* : CRACKPOT — **crack-brained** \-'brānd\ *adj*

crack down \'krak-'daůn\ *vb* : to take strong action esp. to control or repress ⟨*crack down* on crime⟩ — **crack·down** \-,daůn\ *n*

crack·er \'krak-ər\ *n* **1** : something (as a firecracker) that makes a cracking noise **2** : a dry thin crisp bakery product made of flour and water **3** : the equipment in which cracking is carried out

crack·ing \'krak-ing\ *n* : a process in which relatively heavy hydrocarbons (as oils from petroleum) are broken up by heat into lighter products (as gasoline)

crack·le \'krak-əl\ *vb* **crack·led**; **crack·ling** \-(ə-)ling\ : to make small sharp sudden repeated noises — **crackle** *n*

crack·ling *n* **1** \'krak-(ə-)ling\ : a series of small sharp cracks or reports **2** \'krak-lən, 'krak-ling\ : the crisp residue left after the fat has been separated from the fibrous tissue (as in frying the skin of pork) — usu. used in pl.

crack·pot \'krak-,pät\ *n* : a crazy or eccentric person — **crack·pot** *adj*

crack–up \'krak-,əp\ *n* : CRASH, WRECK

1**cra·dle** \'krād-əl\ *n* **1** : a bed for a baby usu. on rockers **2** : a place of origin **3** : something serving as a framework or support (as the support for a telephone receiver or handset) **4** : an implement with rods like fingers attached to a scythe and used formerly for harvesting grain **5** : a rocking device used in panning for gold

2**cradle** *vb* **cra·dled**; **cra·dling** \'krād-(ə-)ling\ **1 a** : to place or keep in or as if in a cradle ⟨*cradled* a doll in her arms⟩ **b** : to protect and cherish lovingly **2** : to cut grain with a cradle **3** : to wash in a miner's cradle

craft \'kraft\ *n* **1** : DEXTERITY, SKILL **2** : an occupation requiring manual dexterity : TRADE **3** : skill in deceiving to gain an end **4** : the members of a trade **5** *pl usu* **craft a** : a boat esp. of small size **b** : AIRCRAFT **c** : SPACECRAFT ***syn*** see TRADE

crafts·man \'kraf(t)s-mən\ *n* **1** : a workman who practices a trade or handicraft : ARTISAN **2** : a highly skilled worker — **crafts·man·ship** \-,ship\ *n*

crafty \'kraf-tē\ *adj* **craft·i·er**; **-est** : skillful at deceiving others ***syn*** see CUNNING ***ant*** artless — **craft·i·ly** \-tə-lē\ *adv* — **craft·i·ness** \-tē-nəs\ *n*

crag \'krag\ *n* : a steep rugged rock or cliff — **crag·gy** \'krag-ē\ *adj*

cram \'kram\ *vb* **crammed**; **cram·ming** **1** : to stuff or crowd in ⟨*cram* clothes into a bag⟩ **2** : to fill full ⟨barns *crammed* with hay⟩ **3** : to study hastily in preparation for an examination **4** : to eat greedily : STUFF — **cram·mer** *n*

[1]**cramp** \'kramp\ *n* **1** : a sudden painful involuntary contraction of muscle **2** : sharp abdominal pain — usu. used in pl.

[2]**cramp** *n* : a usu. iron device bent at the ends and used to hold timbers or blocks of stone together

[3]**cramp** *vb* **1** : to affect with or as if with cramp **2 a** : CONFINE, RESTRAIN ⟨felt *cramped* in the tiny room⟩ **b** : HAMPER — used in the phrase *cramp one's style* **3** : to fasten or hold with a cramp

cram·pon \'kram-ˌpän\ *n* : a steel framework with spikes to be attached to boots for climbing — usu. used in pl.

crampon

cran·ber·ry \'kran-ˌber-ē, -b(ə-)rē\ *n* : the bright red sour berry of any of several trailing plants related to the blueberry; *also* : a plant producing these

[1]**crane** \'krān\ *n* **1** : any of a family of tall wading birds related to the rails **2** : any of several herons **3 a** : a machine for raising and carrying heavy weights by means of a swinging arm or a hoisting apparatus supported on an overhead track **b** : an iron arm in a fireplace for supporting kettles **c** : a long movable support for a motion-picture or television camera

[2]**crane** *vb* **1** : to raise or lift by a crane **2** : to stretch out one's neck to see better

crane fly *n* : any of numerous long-legged slender two-winged flies that resemble large mosquitoes but do not bite

cranes·bill \'krānz-ˌbil\ *n* : GERANIUM 1

cra·ni·al \'krā-nē-əl\ *adj* **1** : of or relating to the skull or cranium **2** : CEPHALIC

cranial nerve *n* : any of the paired nerves that arise from the lower surface of the brain and pass through openings in the skull

cra·ni·um \'krā-nē-əm\ *n, pl* **-ni·ums** *or* **-nia** \-nē-ə\ : SKULL; *esp* : the part that encloses the brain

[1]**crank** \'krangk\ *n* **1** : a bent part or arm at right angles to the end of a shaft by which circular motion is imparted to or received from it **2 a** : an eccentric person **b** : a bad-tempered person : GROUCH

[2]**crank** *vb* : to start or operate by turning a crank

crank·case \'krangk-ˌkās\ *n* : the housing of a crankshaft

crank·shaft \-ˌshaft\ *n* : a shaft turning or driven by a crank

cranky \'krang-kē\ *adj* **crank·i·er**; **-est** **1** : difficult to handle ⟨a *cranky* boat⟩ **2 a** : QUEER, ODD **b** : IRRITABLE — **crank·i·ness** *n*

cran·ny \'kran-ē\ *n, pl* **crannies** : a small break or slit : CREVICE

crape \'krāp\ *n* **1** : CREPE **2** : a band of crepe worn on a hat or sleeve as a sign of mourning

crap·pie \'kräp-ē\ *n* **1** : BLACK CRAPPIE **2** : WHITE CRAPPIE

craps \'kraps\ *n pl* : a gambling game played with two dice

crap·shoot·er \'krap-ˌshüt-ər\ *n* : a person who plays craps — **crap·shoot·ing** \-ˌshüt-ing\ *n*

[1]**crash** \'krash\ *vb* **1 a** : to break violently and noisily : SMASH **b** : to damage an airplane in landing **2 a** : to make or cause to make a loud noise **b** : to force through with loud crashing noises ⟨*crash* one's way through the underbrush⟩ **3** : to enter or attend without invitation or without paying ⟨*crash* a party⟩ **4** : to decline or fail suddenly — **crash·er** *n*

[2]**crash** *n* **1** : a loud sound (as of things smashing) **2** : a breaking to pieces by or as if by collision **3** : COLLISION, SMASHUP **4** : a sudden decline or failure (as of a business or prices) ⟨stock-market *crash*⟩

[3]**crash** *adj* : done hastily on an emergency basis with all available means ⟨a *crash* program⟩

[4]**crash** *n* : a coarse fabric used for draperies, toweling, and clothing

crash–land \'krash-'land\ *vb* : to land an airplane in an emergency usu. with damage to it — **crash landing** *n*

crass \'kras\ *adj* : GROSS, INSENSITIVE — **crass·ly** *adv* — **crass·ness** *n*

crate \'krāt\ *n* **1** : a box usu. made of wooden slats for packing fruit or vegetables **2** : an enclosing framework for protecting something in shipment — **crate** *vb*

cra·ter \'krāt-ər\ *n* **1** : a bowl-shaped depression around the opening of a volcano **2** : a crater formed by the impact of a meteorite **3** : a hole in the ground made by the explosion of a bomb or shell

cra·vat \krə-'vat\ *n* : NECKTIE

crave \'krāv\ *vb* **1** : to ask earnestly : BEG **2** : to have a strong desire for **3** : REQUIRE, NEED

[1]**cra·ven** \'krā-vən\ *adj* : COWARDLY — **cra·ven·ly** *adv* — **cra·ven·ness** \-vən-(n)əs\ *n*

[2]**craven** *n* : COWARD

crav·ing \'krā-ving\ *n* : a great desire or longing; *esp* : an abnormal desire (as for a habit-forming drug)

craw \'krȯ\ *n* **1** : the crop of a bird or insect **2** : the stomach esp. of a lower animal

craw·fish \'krȯ-ˌfish\ *n* **1** : CRAYFISH 1 **2** : SPINY LOBSTER

[1]**crawl** \'krȯl\ *vb* **1** : to move slowly with the body close to the ground : CREEP **2** : to move along slowly or feebly **3** : to be swarming with or have the sensation of swarming with creeping things ⟨the floor was *crawling* with ants⟩ — **crawl·er** *n*

[2]**crawl** *n* **1** : the act or motion of crawling **2** : a racing stroke in which a swimmer lying flat in the water propels himself by overarm strokes and a thrashing kick

cray·fish \'krā-ˌfish\ *n* **1** : any of numerous freshwater crustaceans resembling but usu. much smaller than the lobster **2** : SPINY LOBSTER

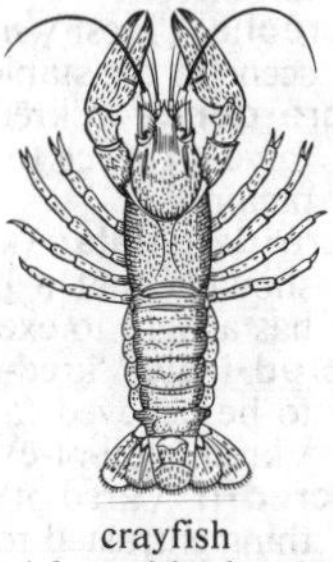

crayfish (about 4 in. long)

[1]**cray·on** \'krā-ˌän, -ən\ *n* **1** : a stick of white or colored chalk or of colored wax used for writing or drawing **2** : a crayon drawing

[2]**crayon** *vb* : to draw or color with a crayon

[1]**craze** \'krāz\ *vb* **1** : to make or become insane **2** : to develop a mesh of fine cracks

[2]**craze** *n* **1** : a strong but temporary interest in something or the object of such an interest : FAD ⟨the latest *craze* among schoolgirls⟩ **2** : a tiny crack in glaze or enamel

cra·zy \'krā-zē\ *adj* **cra·zi·er**; **-est** [originally meaning "cracked", from Middle English *crasen* "to break in pieces", of Scandinavian origin] **1** : mentally disordered : INSANE **2** : wildly impractical

C

3 : ERRATIC 4 : wildly excited or desirous — **cra·zi·ly** \-zə-lē\ *adv* — **cra·zi·ness** \-zē-nəs\ *n*

crazy bone *n* : FUNNY BONE

crazy quilt *n* : a patchwork quilt without a unified design

creak \'krēk\ *vb* : to make a prolonged grating or squeaking sound — **creak** *n* — **creak·i·ly** \'krē-kə-lē\ *adv* — **creaky** \'krē-kē\ *adj*

[1]**cream** \'krēm\ *n* **1** : the yellowish part of milk containing butterfat **2 a** : a food prepared with cream **b** : something having the consistency of cream (as a medicinal or cosmetic preparation) **3** : the choicest part **4** : a pale yellow — **creamy** \'krē-mē\ *adj*

[2]**cream** *vb* **1** : to form cream **2** : to skim the cream from **3** : to put cream into ⟨*cream* tea⟩ **4** : to work or blend to the consistency of cream

cream cheese *n* : an unripened soft white cheese made from whole milk enriched with cream

cream·er \'krē-mər\ *n* **1** : a device for separating cream from milk **2** : a small vessel for serving cream

cream·ery \'krēm-(ə-)rē\ *n, pl* **-er·ies** : a place where butter and cheese are made or where milk and cream are sold or prepared

cream of tartar : a white crystalline acid-tasting salt used esp. in baking powder

cream puff *n* : a round shell of light pastry filled with whipped cream or a cream filling

[1]**crease** \'krēs\ *n* **1** : a line or mark made by or as if by folding **2** : a specially marked area in a sport (as hockey)

[2]**crease** *vb* **1** : to make a crease in or on **2** : to wound slightly esp. by grazing **3** : to become creased

cre·ate \krē-'āt, 'krē-ˌ\ *vb* : to bring into existence : MAKE, PRODUCE

cre·at·i·nine \krē-'at-ə-ˌnēn\ *n* : a white crystalline compound that is found esp. in blood, muscle, and urine

cre·a·tion \krē-'ā-shən\ *n* **1** : the act of creating or fact of being created; *esp* : the bringing of the world into existence out of nothing **2** : something created **3** : all created things : WORLD

cre·a·tive \krē-'āt-iv\ *adj* : able to create; *esp* : having the power to produce original artistic work — **cre·a·tive·ly** *adv* — **cre·a·tive·ness** *n* — **cre·a·tiv·i·ty** \ˌkrē-ā-'tiv-ət-ē, ˌkrē-ə-\ *n*

cre·a·tor \krē-'āt-ər\ *n* **1** : one that creates or produces : MAKER **2** *cap* : [2]GOD

crea·ture \'krē-chər\ *n* **1** : ANIMAL **2** : a human being **3** : one who is the servile dependent or tool of another

crèche \'kresh\ *n* : a representation of the Nativity scene in the stable at Bethlehem

cre·dence \'krēd-ən(t)s\ *n* : mental acceptance ⟨give *credence* to a rumor⟩ ***syn*** see BELIEF ***ant*** suspicion

cre·den·tials \kri-'den-chəlz\ *n pl* : documents showing that a person is entitled to confidence or has a right to exercise official power

cred·i·ble \'kred-ə-bəl\ *adj* : capable of or deserving to be believed ⟨a *credible* story⟩ — **cred·i·bil·i·ty** \ˌkred-ə-'bil-ət-ē\ *n* — **cred·i·bly** \'kred-ə-blē\ *adv*

[1]**cred·it** \'kred-ət\ *n* [from Latin *creditum* "something entrusted to another", from neuter of past participle of *credere* "to believe", "trust"] **1** : a favorable balance in an account ⟨debits and *credits*⟩ **2** : an amount or sum put at the disposal of a person or firm by a bank **3 a** : the right or privilege of buying now and paying later ⟨extended him *credit*⟩ ⟨buy on *credit*⟩ **b** : reputation for fulfilling financial obligations ⟨his *credit* is good⟩ **4 a** : CREDENCE, BELIEF ⟨a story that deserves little *credit*⟩ **b** : reputation for honesty or integrity : good name **5 a** : something that adds to a person's reputation or honor ⟨give a person *credit* for a discovery⟩ **b** : a source of honor ⟨a *credit* to her school⟩ **6 a** : official certification of the completion of a course of study **b** : a unit of academic work for which such acknowledgment is made

[2]**credit** *vb* **1** : BELIEVE **2** : to enter a sum upon the credit side of ⟨*credit* his account with $10⟩ **3 a** : to give credit to **b** : to attribute to some person ⟨*credit* him with the victory⟩

cred·it·a·ble \'kred-ət-ə-bəl\ *adj* **1** : worthy of belief **2** : worthy of esteem or praise — **cred·it·a·bil·i·ty** \ˌkred-ət-ə-'bil-ət-ē\ *n* — **cred·it·a·bly** \'kred-ət-ə-blē\ *adv*

credit card *n* : a card authorizing purchases on credit

cred·i·tor \'kred-ət-ər\ *n* : a person to whom a debt is owed

cre·do \'krēd-ō, 'krād-\ *n, pl* **credos** : CREED

cre·du·li·ty \kri-'d(y)ü-lət-ē\ *n* : a willingness to believe statements esp. on little or no evidence

cred·u·lous \'krej-ə-ləs\ *adj* : ready to believe esp. on slight evidence — **cred·u·lous·ly** *adv* — **cred·u·lous·ness** *n*

Cree \'krē\ *n* : a member of an Amerindian people ranging from Ontario to Saskatchewan and south into Montana

creed \'krēd\ *n* [from Old English *crēda*, from Latin *crēdo* "I believe", the first word of several well-known creeds] **1** : a statement of the essential beliefs of a religious faith **2** : a set of guiding principles or beliefs

creek \'krēk, 'krik\ *n* **1** *chiefly Brit* : a small narrow inlet **2** : a stream of water usu. smaller than a river

Creek \'krēk\ *n* : a member of a confederacy of Amerindian peoples formerly occupying most of Alabama and Georgia and parts of Florida

creel \'krēl\ *n* : a basket for fish

[1]**creep** \'krēp\ *vb* **crept** \'krept\; **creep·ing** **1** : to move along with the body close to the ground or on hands and knees **2** : to advance slowly, timidly, or stealthily **3** : to spread or grow over a surface usu. rooting at intervals ⟨*creeping* vine⟩ **4** : to slip or gradually shift position ⟨soil *creeping* down a slope⟩ **5** : to feel as though insects were crawling on the body ⟨the shriek made my flesh *creep*⟩

[2]**creep** *n* **1** : a creeping movement **2 a** : a distressing sensation like that of insects creeping over one's flesh **b** : a feeling of horror — usu. used in pl.

creep·er \'krē-pər\ *n* **1 a** : one that creeps **b** : a creeping plant **c** : a bird that creeps about on trees or bushes searching for insects **2** : a spiked device worn on the shoe to prevent slipping **3** : an infant's garment like a romper

creepy \'krē-pē\ *adj* **creep·i·er**; **-est** : having or producing a sensation as of insects creeping on the skin; *esp* : EERIE — **creep·i·ness** *n*

cre·mate \'krē-ˌmāt, kri-'\ *vb* : to reduce a dead body to ashes by fire or heat — **cre·ma·tion** \kri-'mā-shən\ *n*

cre·ma·to·ri·um \ˌkrē-mə-'tōr-ē-əm, ˌkrem-ə-, -'tȯr-\ *n, pl* **-ri·ums** *or* **-ria** \-ē-ə\ : CREMATORY

[1]**cre·ma·to·ry** \'krē-mə-ˌtōr-ē, 'krem-ə-, -ˌtȯr-\ *n, pl* **-ries** : a furnace for cremating or a building containing such a furnace

2**crematory** *adj* : of, relating to, or used in cremation

Cre·ole \ˈkrē-ˌōl\ *n* **1** : a white person descended from early French or Spanish settlers in the U.S. Gulf states or Latin America **2** : a person of mixed French or Spanish and Negro descent — **Creole** *adj*

cre·o·sol \ˈkrē-ə-ˌsȯl, -ˌsōl\ *n* : a colorless organic liquid obtained from the tar made from beech and a resin

cre·o·sote \ˈkrē-ə-ˌsōt\ *n* **1** : a clear or yellowish oily liquid mixture of compounds obtained by the distillation of wood tar esp. from beechwood **2** : a brownish oily liquid obtained by distillation of coal tar and used esp. as a wood preservative

crepe *or* **crêpe** \ˈkrāp\ *n* : a thin crinkled fabric (as of silk, wool, or cotton) — **crepe** *adj*

crepe paper *n* : paper with a crinkled or puckered texture

cres *abbr* crescent

cresc *abbr* crescendo

cre·scen·do \kri-ˈshen-dō\ *n, pl* **-dos** *or* **-does** : a gradual increase in volume of sound in music or a passage so performed — **crescendo** *adv or adj*

1**cres·cent** \ˈkres-ənt\ *n* [from Latin *crescent-*, stem of *crescens* "growing", present participle of *crescere* "to increase"] **1 a** : the moon between new moon and first quarter or between last quarter and the next new moon **b** : the figure of the moon at these times **2** : something shaped like a crescent

2**crescent** *adj* **1** : INCREASING **2** : shaped like a crescent

cre·sol \ˈkrē-ˌsȯl, -ˌsōl\ *n* : any of three poisonous colorless crystalline or liquid organic substances obtained from coal tar and used as disinfectants or in making resins

cress \ˈkres\ *n* : any of numerous plants related to the mustard and having leaves that are used in salads

1**crest** \ˈkrest\ *n* **1 a** : a showy tuft or process on the head of an animal (as a bird) **b** : a plume worn on a knight's helmet **c** : a heraldic design placed above the escutcheon and also used (as to mark table silver) separately **2** : an upper part, edge, or limit ⟨the *crest* of a hill⟩ ⟨the *crest* of a wave⟩ — **crest·ed** \ˈkres-təd\ *adj* — **crest·less** \ˈkrest-ləs\ *adj*

2**crest** *vb* **1** : to furnish with a crest : CROWN **2** : to reach the crest of ⟨*crest* the hill⟩ **3** : to rise to a crest ⟨the river *crested* at eight feet⟩

crest·fall·en \ˈkres(t)-ˌfȯ-lən\ *adj* : having a drooping crest or hanging head : DEJECTED

cre·ta·ceous \kri-ˈtā-shəs\ *n* : the 3d and latest period of the Mesozoic era or the corresponding system of rocks with the deposits including chalk and most of the coal of the U.S. west of the Great Plains — **Cretaceous** *adj*

Cre·tan \ˈkrēt-ən\ *adj* : of, relating to, or characteristic of Crete or its people — **Cretan** *n*

cre·tin \ˈkrēt-ən\ *n* : one having cretinism; *also* : one having a marked mental deficiency

cre·tin·ism \-ˌiz-əm\ *n* : a usu. congenital abnormal condition marked by physical and mental stunting and caused by deficient functioning of the thyroid gland

cre·tonne \ˈkrē-ˌtän, kri-ˈ\ *n* : a strong printed cotton or linen cloth used esp. for furniture coverings and curtains

cre·vasse \kri-ˈvas\ *n* **1** : a deep crevice (as in a glacier) **2** : a break in a levee

crev·ice \ˈkrev-əs\ *n* : a narrow opening caused by a split or crack : FISSURE

crew \ˈkrü\ *n* **1** : a group or gathering of persons esp. when associated in joint work ⟨a train *crew*⟩ ⟨a gun *crew*⟩ **2** : the seamen who man a ship **3** : the oarsmen and steersman of a rowboat or racing shell **4** : the persons who man an airplane — **crew·man** \-mən\ *n*

crew cut *n* : a short haircut in which the hair resembles the surface of a brush

1**crib** \ˈkrib\ *n* **1** : a manger for feeding animals **2** : a small child's bedstead with high sides **3** : a bin or building for storing grain **4** : an open framework; *esp* : one used in building **5** : the cards discarded in cribbage **6** : PONY 3

2**crib** *vb* **cribbed**; **crib·bing** **1** : to copy (as an idea or passage) and use as one's own : PLAGIARIZE **2** : to make use of a translation or notes dishonestly — **crib·ber** *n*

crib·bage \ˈkrib-ij\ *n* : a card game in which the object is to form various counting combinations and in which each player is dealt six cards and discards one or two to make up the crib

crick \ˈkrik\ *n* : a painful spasm of muscles (as of the neck or back)

1**crick·et** \ˈkrik-ət\ *n* : a small leaping insect that has leathery fore wings and thin hind wings and is noted for the chirping notes of the males

cricket (about ⅝ in. long)

2**cricket** *n* : a game played with a ball and bat by two sides of usu. 11 players each on a large field centering upon two wickets — **crick·et·er** *n*

cri·er \ˈkrī(-ə)r\ *n* : one that cries; *esp* : one who proclaims orders or announcements

crime \ˈkrīm\ *n* **1** : the doing of an act forbidden by law or the failure to do an act required by law esp. when serious **2** : SIN **3** : criminal activity ⟨the war on *crime*⟩

1**crim·i·nal** \ˈkrim-ə-nəl\ *adj* **1** : involving or being a crime ⟨a *criminal* act⟩ **2** : relating to crime ⟨*criminal* court⟩ **3** : guilty of crime — **crim·i·nal·i·ty** \ˌkrim-ə-ˈnal-ət-ē\ *n* — **crim·i·nal·ly** \ˈkrim-ə-nə-lē\ *adv*

2**criminal** *n* : one that has committed a crime

crim·i·nol·o·gy \ˌkrim-ə-ˈnäl-ə-jē\ *n* : a scientific study of crime, of criminals, and of their punishment or correction — **crim·i·no·log·i·cal** \ˌkrim-ə-nə-ˈläj-i-kəl\ *adj* — **crim·i·nol·o·gist** \ˌkrim-ə-ˈnäl-ə-jəst\ *n*

1**crimp** \ˈkrimp\ *vb* : to make wavy, bent, or warped — **crimp·er** *n*

2**crimp** *n* **1** : something produced by or as if by crimping **2** : something that cramps or inhibits

crimpy \ˈkrim-pē\ *adj* **crimp·i·er**; **-est** : having a crimped appearance : FRIZZY

1**crim·son** \ˈkrim-zən\ *n* : deep purplish red — **crimson** *adj*

2**crimson** *vb* : to make or become crimson

cringe \ˈkrinj\ *vb* **cringed**; **cring·ing** \ˈkrin-jing\ **1** : to draw in or contract one's muscles involuntarily **2** : to shrink in fear : COWER **3** : to behave in a servile manner — **cring·er** \ˈkrin-jər\ *n*

1**crin·kle** \ˈkring-kəl\ *vb* **crin·kled**; **crin·kling** \-k(ə-)ling\ **1** : to form little waves on the surface : WRINKLE **2** : RUSTLE ⟨*crinkling* silk⟩

2**crinkle** *n* : WRINKLE, RIPPLE — **crin·kly** \-k(ə-)lē\ *adj*

cri·noid \ˈkrī-ˌnȯid\ *n* : any of a large class of echinoderms having usu. a cup-shaped body with five or more feathery arms — **crinoid** *or* **cri·noi·dal** \krī-ˈnȯid-əl\ *adj*

crin·o·line \ˈkrin-ə-lən\ *n* **1** : a cloth originally of horsehair and linen thread used for stiffening and lining **2 :** a full stiff skirt; *esp* **:** one lined with crinoline **3 :** HOOPSKIRT — **crinoline** *adj*

1crip·ple \'krip-əl\ *n* **:** a lame or disabled individual

2cripple *vb* **crip·pled**; **crip·pling** \'krip-(ə-)liŋ\ **1 :** to deprive of the use of a limb and esp. a leg **2 :** to deprive of strength, wholeness, or capability — **crip·pler** \-(ə-)lər\ *n*

cri·sis \'krī-səs\ *n, pl* **cri·ses** \'krī-ˌsēz\ **1 :** the turning point for better or worse in an acute disease or fever **2 :** a decisive moment or turning point **3 :** an unstable or crucial time or state of affairs ⟨a business *crisis*⟩

1crisp \'krisp\ *adj* **1 :** CURLY, WAVY ⟨*crisp* hair⟩ **2 :** easily crumbled **:** FLAKY ⟨*crisp* pastry⟩ **3 :** being firm and fresh ⟨*crisp* lettuce⟩ **4 :** being sharp and clear ⟨*crisp* outlines⟩ **5 :** FROSTY, SNAPPY ⟨*crisp* weather⟩ — **crisp·i·ness** \'kris-pē-nəs\ *n* — **crisp·ly** *adv* — **crisp·ness** *n* — **crispy** \'kris-pē\ *adj*

2crisp *vb* **:** to make or become crisp — **crisp·er** *n*

3crisp *n* **:** something crisp or brittle

1criss·cross \'kris-ˌkrȯs\ *n* **:** a pattern formed by crossed lines — **crisscross** *adj or adv*

2crisscross *vb* **1 :** to mark with intersecting lines **2 :** to go or pass back and forth

crit *abbr* **1** critical **2** criticism

cri·te·ri·on \krī-'tir-ē-ən\ *n, pl* **-ria** \-ē-ə\ *also* **-ri·ons :** a standard on which a judgment or decision may be based

crit·ic \'krit-ik\ *n* **1 :** a person who gives his judgment of the value, worth, beauty, or excellence of something; *esp* **:** one whose profession is to express trained judgment on work in art, music, drama, or literature **2 :** FAULTFINDER

crit·i·cal \'krit-i-kəl\ *adj* **1 a :** inclined to criticize unfavorably **b :** consisting of or involving criticism ⟨*critical* writings⟩ **c :** using or involving careful judgment **2 a :** of, relating to, or being a turning point ⟨*critical* phase⟩ **b :** CRUCIAL, DECISIVE ⟨*critical* test⟩ **3 :** NECESSARY, INDISPENSABLE **4 :** of sufficient size to sustain a chain reaction — used of a mass of fissionable material — **crit·i·cal·ly** \-i-k(ə-)lē\ *adv*

critical temperature *n* **:** the temperature above which a gas cannot be liquefied

crit·i·cism \'krit-ə-ˌsiz-əm\ *n* **1 :** the act of criticizing; *esp* **:** FAULTFINDING **2 :** a critical remark or observation **3 :** a careful judgment or review esp. by a critic **4 :** the art of a critic

crit·i·cize \'krit-ə-ˌsīz\ *vb* **1 :** to examine and judge as a critic **:** EVALUATE **2 :** to express criticism esp. of an unfavorable kind **3 :** to find fault with ⟨some people are quick to *criticize* others⟩

crit·ter \'krit-ər\ *n, dial* **:** CREATURE

croak \'krōk\ *vb* **1 a :** to make a deep harsh sound **b :** to speak in a hoarse throaty voice **2 :** GRUMBLE, COMPLAIN **3** *slang* **a :** DIE **b :** KILL — **croak** *n*

croak·er \'krō-kər\ *n* **1 :** one that croaks **2 :** any of various fishes that produce croaking or grunting noises

Croat \'krōt, 'krō-ˌat\ *n* **:** CROATIAN

Cro·atian \krō-'ā-shən\ *n* **1 :** a native or inhabitant of Croatia **2 :** a south Slavic language spoken by the Croatian people and distinct from Serbian chiefly in its use of the Latin alphabet — **Croatian** *adj*

cro·chet \krō-'shā\ *n* [from French, literally "little hook", from *croche* "hook"] **:** needlework consisting of interlocked looped stitches formed with a hooked needle — **crochet** *vb* — **cro·chet·er** \-'shā-ər\ *n*

crock \'kräk\ *n* **:** a thick earthenware pot or jar

crock·ery \'kräk-(ə-)rē\ *n* **:** EARTHENWARE

croc·o·dile \'kräk-ə-ˌdīl\ *n* **:** any of several large thick-skinned long-bodied aquatic reptiles of tropical and subtropical waters — compare ALLIGATOR

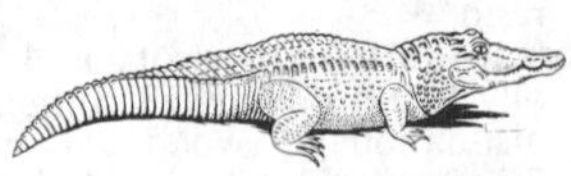

crocodile (usually 12 to 15 ft. long)

crocodile tears *n pl* **:** pretended tears or sorrow

cro·cus \'krō-kəs\ *n, pl* **cro·cus·es 1** *pl also* **cro·ci** \-ˌkē, -ˌkī, -ˌsī\ **:** any of a large genus of small herbs that are related to the iris and have showy solitary long-tubed flowers and slender linear leaves **2 :** SAFFRON 1b

croft \'krȯft\ *n* **1** *chiefly Brit* **:** a small enclosed field **2** *chiefly Brit* **:** a small farm worked by a tenant — **croft·er** *n*

Cro–Mag·non \krō-'mag-nən, -'man-yən\ *n* **:** any of a tall erect race of men known from skeletal remains chiefly from southern France and often placed in the same species as recent man — **Cro–Magnon** *adj*

crone \'krōn\ *n* **:** a withered old woman

cro·ny \'krō-nē\ *n, pl* **cronies :** an intimate companion

1crook \'krük\ *n* **1 a :** an implement having a bent or hooked form ⟨a shepherd's *crook*⟩ **b :** CROSIER **2 :** CRIMINAL **3 :** BEND, CURVE **4 :** a curved or hooked part

2crook *vb* **:** BEND, CURVE

crook·ed \'krük-əd\ *adj* **1 :** having a crook or curve **:** BENT **2 :** DISHONEST, CRIMINAL — **crook·ed·ly** *adv* — **crook·ed·ness** *n*

Crookes tube \'krüks-\ *n* **:** an electron tube evacuated to a high degree for demonstrating the properties of cathode rays

crook·neck \'krük-ˌnek\ *n* **:** a squash with a long curved neck

crook·necked \-'nekt\ *adj* **:** having a bent or curved neck ⟨a *crooknecked* flask⟩

croon \'krün\ *vb* [from medieval Dutch *cronen* "to bellow"] **1 :** to hum or sing in a low voice ⟨*croon* a lullaby⟩ **2 :** to sing popular songs in an exaggerated sentimental style — **croon·er** *n*

1crop \'kräp\ *n* **1 a :** the stock or handle of a whip **b :** a short riding whip with a loop **2 :** a pouched enlargement of the gullet of a bird or insect that receives food and prepares it for digestion **3 :** a close haircut **4 a :** a plant or animal or plant or animal product that can be grown and harvested **b :** the product or yield esp. of a harvested crop **c :** BATCH, LOT

2crop *vb* **cropped**; **crop·ping 1 a :** to remove the upper or outer parts of ⟨*crop* a hedge⟩ **b :** to cut off short **:** CLIP **2 a :** to cause land to bear produce **b :** to grow as a crop ⟨*crop* cotton⟩ **c :** HARVEST **3 :** to yield or make a crop ⟨the apple trees *cropped* well⟩ **4 :** to appear unexpectedly or casually ⟨problems *crop* up daily⟩

crop·land \'kräp-ˌland\ *n* **:** land devoted to the production of plant crops

1crop·per \'kräp-ər\ *n* **:** one that crops; *esp* **:** SHARECROPPER

2cropper *n* **1 :** a severe fall **2 :** a sudden or violent failure or collapse

crop rotation *n* **:** the practice of growing different crops in succession on the same land chiefly to preserve the capacity of the soil to yield crops

cro·quet \krō-ˈkā\ *n* [from French dialect, "hockey stick", from Old French, northern dialect form of *crochet* "little hook"] **:** a game in which the players use mallets to drive wooden balls through a series of hoops set in the ground

cro·quette \krō-ˈket\ *n* **:** a roll or ball of hashed meat, fish, or vegetables fried in deep fat

cro·sier \ˈkrō-zhər\ *n* **:** a staff carried by bishops and abbots as a symbol of office

1**cross** \ˈkrȯs\ *n* **1 a :** a structure consisting of an upright beam and a crossbar **b** *often cap* **:** the cross on which Jesus Christ was crucified **2 :** a trying affliction **3 a :** a cross-shaped mark or structure; *esp* **:** one used as a Christian emblem **b :** such a mark on paper; *esp* **:** one used as a signature **4 a :** an act of crossing unlike individuals **b :** a crossbred individual or kind **5 :** a hook crossed over an opponent's lead in boxing

crosses 3a

2**cross** *vb* **1 a :** to lie or be situated across **b :** INTERSECT ⟨where two roads *cross*⟩ **c :** to move, pass, or extend across ⟨*cross* the river⟩ **2 :** to make the sign of the cross on or over **3 :** to cancel by marking a cross on or drawing a line through ⟨*cross* names off a list⟩ **4 :** to place or fold crosswise one over the other ⟨*cross* the arms⟩ **5 :** OPPOSE, OBSTRUCT ⟨gets angry when he's *crossed*⟩ **6 :** to draw a line across ⟨*cross* a *t*⟩ **7 :** INTERBREED, HYBRIDIZE **8 :** to meet and pass on the way ⟨our letters *crossed* in the mail⟩

3**cross** *adj* **1 :** lying or moving across ⟨*cross* traffic⟩ **2 :** running counter **:** OPPOSING, OPPOSED ⟨a *cross* wind⟩ **3 :** marked by bad temper **:** GRUMPY ***syn*** see PEEVISH — **cross·ly** *adv* — **cross·ness** *n*

cross·arm \ˈkrȯs-ˌärm\ *n* **:** an arm fastened at right angles to an upright (as on a telephone pole)

cross·bar \-ˌbär\ *n* **:** a bar, piece, or stripe placed crosswise

cross·bill \-ˌbil\ *n* **:** any of a genus of finches with mandibles strongly curved and crossing each other

cross·bones \-ˌbōnz\ *n pl* **:** two leg or arm bones depicted crosswise

cross·bow \-ˌbō\ *n* **:** a short bow mounted crosswise near the end of a wooden stock that discharges stones and square-headed arrows — **cross·bow·man** \-mən\ *n*

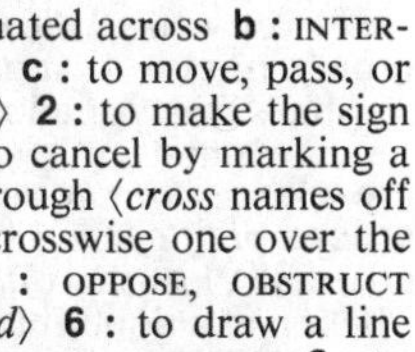

crossbow

cross·bred \ˈkrȯs-ˈbred\ *adj* **:** HYBRID; *esp* **:** produced by interbreeding two pure but different breeds, strains, or varieties — **cross·bred** \-ˌbred\ *n*

1**cross·breed** \-ˌbrēd, -ˈbrēd\ *vb* **:** HYBRIDIZE; *esp* **:** to interbreed two varieties or breeds of the same species

2**cross·breed** \-ˌbrēd\ *n* **:** HYBRID

cross–coun·try \-ˈkən-trē\ *adj* **1 :** extending or moving across a country ⟨a *cross-country* railroad⟩ ⟨a *cross-country* concert tour⟩ **2 :** proceeding over the countryside rather than by roads ⟨a *cross-country* race⟩ — **cross–country** *adv*

1**cross·cut** \-ˌkət, -ˈkət\ *vb* **-cut; -cut·ting :** to cut or saw crosswise esp. of the grain of wood

2**crosscut** *adj* **1 :** made or used for cutting transversely ⟨a *crosscut* saw⟩ **2 :** cut across or transversely

3**cross·cut** \-ˌkət\ *n* **:** something that cuts across or through

cross–ex·am·i·na·tion \ˌkrȯs-ig-ˌzam-ə-ˈnā-shən\ *n* **:** the questioning of a witness called by the opposing party to a legal action — **cross–ex·am·ine** \-ˈzam-ən\ *vb* — **cross–ex·am·in·er** *n*

cross–eyed \ˈkrȯs-ˈīd\ *adj* **:** affected with an abnormality in which one or both eyes turn inward toward the nose

cross–fer·til·i·za·tion \ˈkrȯs-ˌfərt-ə-lə-ˈzā-shən\ *n* **1 :** fertilization between gametes produced by separate individuals or sometimes by individuals of different kinds **2 :** CROSS-POLLINATION — **cross–fer·tile** \-ˈfərt-əl\ *adj* — **cross–fer·til·ize** \-ˈfərt-ə-ˌlīz\ *vb*

cross–grained \ˈkrȯs-ˈgrānd\ *adj* **1 :** having the grain running crosswise or irregularly **2 :** difficult to deal with **:** CONTRARY

cross hair *n* **:** one of the fine wires or threads in the eyepiece of an optical instrument used as a reference line

cross·hatch \ˈkrȯs-ˌhach\ *vb* **:** to mark with a series of parallel lines that cross esp. obliquely

cross·ing \ˈkrȯ-sing\ *n* **1 a :** the act of one that crosses **b :** a voyage across water **c :** the act or process of interbreeding or hybridizing **2 :** a point of intersection (as of a street and a railroad track) **3 :** a place where a street or stream is crossed

cross·ing–over \ˌkrȯ-sing-ˈō-vər\ *n* **:** an interchange of genes or segments between associated parts of homologous chromosomes during meiosis

cross–legged \ˈkrȯs-ˈleg(-ə)d\ *adv* **:** with the legs crossed and the knees spread wide

cross·over \ˈkrȯs-ˌō-vər\ *n* **:** an instance or product of genetic crossing-over

cross·piece \ˈkrȯs-ˌpēs\ *n* **:** a horizontal member (as of a figure or a structure)

cross–pol·li·nate \-ˈpäl-ə-ˌnāt\ *vb* **:** to subject to cross-pollination

cross–pol·li·na·tion \ˌkrȯs-ˌpäl-ə-ˈnā-shən\ *n* **:** the transfer of pollen from one flower to the stigma of another

cross–pur·pose \ˈkrȯs-ˈpər-pəs\ *n* **:** an opposing purpose — **at cross–pur·pos·es :** acting contrary to another without meaning to do so

cross–ques·tion \ˈkrȯs-ˈkwes-chən\ *vb* **:** CROSS-EXAMINE

cross–re·fer \ˌkrȯs-ri-ˈfər\ *vb* **:** to refer by a notation or direction from one place to another (as in a book) — **cross–ref·er·ence** \ˈkrȯs-ˈref-ərn(t)s, -ˈref-(ə-)rən(t)s\ *n*

cross·road \ˈkrȯs-ˌrōd, -ˈrōd\ *n* **1 :** a road that crosses a main road or runs cross-country between main roads **2 a :** a place where roads cross — usu. used in pl. **b :** a small community at a crossroads

cross section *n* **1 a :** a cutting made across something (as a log) **b :** a representation of a cutting made across something ⟨a *cross section* of a bridge⟩ **2 :** a number of persons or things selected to represent the general nature of a group ⟨a *cross section* of society⟩ — **cross–sec·tion·al** \ˈkrȯs-ˈsek-sh(ə-)nəl\ *adj*

cross·tie \ˈkrȯs-ˌtī\ *n* **:** a railroad tie

cross·town \'krȯs-ˌtau̇n, -'tau̇n\ *adj* **1** : situated at opposite points of a town ⟨*crosstown* neighbors⟩ **2** : running across a town ⟨a *crosstown* bus⟩ ⟨a *crosstown* route⟩ — **crosstown** *adv*

cross·tree \'krȯs-(ˌ)trē\ *n* : two horizontal crosspieces near the top of a ship's mast to spread apart the upper ropes that support the mast — usu. used in pl.

cross·walk \'krȯs-ˌwȯk\ *n* : a marked path for pedestrians crossing a street or road

cross·way \-ˌwā\ *n* : CROSSROAD — often used in pl.

cross·wise \-ˌwīz\ *also* **cross·ways** \-ˌwāz\ *adv* : so as to cross something : ACROSS — **crosswise** *adj*

cross·word puzzle \ˌkrȯs-ˌwərd-\ *n* : a puzzle in which words are filled into a pattern of numbered squares in answer to clues so that they read across and down

crotch \'kräch\ *n* : an angle formed by the parting of two legs, branches, or members

crotch·et \'kräch-ət\ *n* : a peculiar opinion or habit : WHIM — **crotch·et·i·ness** \-ət-ē-nəs\ *n* — **crotch·ety** \-ət-ē\ *adj*

cro·ton \'krōt-ən\ *n* : any of several herbs and shrubs related to the spurge; *esp* : an East Indian plant yielding an oil used as a strong purgative

Cro·ton bug \'krōt-ən-\ *n* : a small active winged cockroach common where food and moisture are found

crouch \'krau̇ch\ *vb* **1** : to stoop with the limbs close to the body **2** : to bend or bow servilely : CRINGE — **crouch** *n*

1**croup** \'krüp\ *n* : the rump of a four-footed animal

2**croup** *n* : a laryngitis esp. of infants marked by episodes of difficult breathing and a hoarse metallic cough — **croupy** \'krü-pē\ *adj*

crou·ton \'krü-ˌtän, krü-'\ *n* : a small cube of bread toasted or fried crisp

1**crow** \'krō\ *n* **1** : any of various large usu. entirely glossy black perching birds related to the jays **2** : CROWBAR **3** *cap* : a member of a Siouan Amerindian people living in the region between the Platte and Yellowstone rivers — **as the crow flies** : in a straight line

2**crow** *vb* **crowed** \'krōd\; **crow·ing** **1** : to make the loud shrill sound characteristic of a cock **2** : to utter a sound expressive of pleasure **3 a** : EXULT, GLOAT **b** : BRAG

3**crow** *n* **1** : the cry of the cock **2** : a sound of joy or triumph

crow·bar \'krō-ˌbär\ *n* : a metal bar usu. wedge-shaped at one end for use as a pry or lever

1**crowd** \'krau̇d\ *vb* **1** : to press forward or close ⟨*crowd* around the speaker⟩ **2** : to collect in numbers : THRONG ⟨people *crowded* the beach⟩ **3** : to press or squeeze tightly or fully ⟨*crowd* clothes into a trunk⟩

2**crowd** *n* **1** : a large number of persons or things crowded or crowding together **2** : the masses of the people : POPULACE ⟨his books appeal to the *crowd*⟩ **3** : a large number of things close together **4** : a group of people having a common interest ⟨our *crowd*⟩ ***syn*** see MULTITUDE

crow·foot \'krō-ˌfu̇t\ *n, pl* **crow·feet** \-ˌfēt\ **1** *pl usu* **crowfoots** : any of numerous plants with cleft lobes on the leaves; *esp* : BUTTERCUP **2** : CROW'S-FOOT 1 — usu. used in pl.

1**crown** \'krau̇n\ *n* **1 a** : a wreath or band for the head; *esp* : one worn as a mark of victory or honor **b** : REWARD **2** : a royal headdress **3 a** : the topmost part of the skull or head **b** : the summit of a mountain **c** : the head of foliage of a tree or shrub **d** : the part of a hat covering the crown **e** : the part of a tooth external to the gum or an artificial substitute for this **4** : something resembling a crown **5 a** : royal power : SOVEREIGNTY **b** *cap* : the executive part of the British government including the monarch and the ministers **c** : SOVEREIGN **6** : any of several coins; *esp* : an English silver coin worth five shillings — **crown** *adj, often cap* — **crowned** \'krau̇nd\ *adj* — **crown·like** \'krau̇n-ˌlīk\ *adj*

2**crown** *vb* **1 a** : to place a crown on; *esp* : to invest with regal dignity and power **b** : to recognize officially as ⟨was *crowned* champion⟩ **2 a** : SURMOUNT, TOP ⟨a statue *crowned* the dome⟩ **b** : to top a checker with a checker to make a king **3** : to bring to a successful conclusion : CLIMAX ⟨the victory *crowned* his career⟩ **4** : to put an artificial crown upon (a tooth)

crown glass *n* : a very clear glass that is used for optical instruments

crown prince *n* : the heir apparent to a crown or throne

crown princess *n* **1** : the wife of a crown prince **2** : a female heir apparent to a crown or throne

crow's-foot \'krōz-ˌfu̇t\ *n, pl* **crow's-feet** \-ˌfēt\ **1** : one of the wrinkles around the outer corners of the eyes — usu. used in pl. **2** : CROWFOOT 1

crow's nest *n* **1** : a partly enclosed platform high on a ship's mast for a lookout **2** : a lookout resembling a crow's nest

cro·zier *var of* CROSIER

cruces *pl of* CRUX

cru·cial \'krü-shəl\ *adj* **1** : marked by final determination of a doubtful issue : DECISIVE **2** : SEVERE, TRYING ⟨go through a *crucial* period⟩ — **cru·cial·ly** \'krüsh-(ə-)lē\ *adv*

cru·ci·ble \'krü-sə-bəl\ *n* **1** : a heat-resisting container in which material can be subjected to great heat **2** : a severe test

cru·ci·fer \'krü-sə-fər\ *n* : any of a family of plants (as the cabbage or mustard) that have flowers with four petals

cru·ci·fix \'krü-sə-ˌfiks\ *n* : a representation of Christ on the cross

cru·ci·fix·ion \ˌkrü-sə-'fik-shən\ *n* : an act of crucifying; *esp, cap* : the crucifying of Christ

cru·ci·form \'krü-sə-ˌfȯrm\ *adj* : forming or arranged in a cross

cru·ci·fy \'krü-sə-ˌfī\ *vb* **-fied**; **-fy·ing** **1** : to put to death by nailing or binding the hands and feet to a cross **2** : to treat cruelly : TORTURE

1**crude** \'krüd\ *adj* **1** : existing in a natural state and unaltered by processing : RAW ⟨*crude* oil⟩ **2** : lacking refinement, grace, or tact; *esp* : GROSS, VULGAR **3** : rough in plan or execution : RUDE **4** : not concealed or glossed over : BARE ⟨the *crude* facts⟩ — **crude·ly** *adv* — **crude·ness** *n* — **cru·di·ty** \'krüd-ət-ē\ *n*

2**crude** *n* : unrefined petroleum

cru·el \'krü-əl\ *adj* **cru·el·er** *or* **cru·el·ler**; **cru·el·est** *or* **cru·el·lest** **1** : disposed to inflict pain **2** : causing or helping to cause injury, grief, or pain — **cru·el·ly** \-ə-lē\ *adv* — **cru·el·ness** *n*

cru·el·ty \'krü-əl-tē\ *n, pl* **-ties** **1** : the quality or state of being cruel **2 a** : a cruel action **b** : inhuman treatment

ə abut	ər further	a back	ā bake	
ä cot, cart	au̇ out	ch chin	e less	ē easy
g gift	i trip	ī life	j joke	ng sing	ō flow
ȯ flaw	ȯi coin	th thin	th this	ü loot
u̇ foot	y yet	yü few	yu̇ furious	zh vision

cru·et \'krü-ət\ *n* : a small glass bottle for vinegar, oil, or sauce

cruise \'krüz\ *vb* [from Dutch *kruisen*, literally "to make a cross", from medieval Dutch *crūce* "cross", from Latin *crux*] **1** : to sail about touching at a series of ports **2** : to travel for enjoyment or at random **3** : to travel at the most efficient operating speed ⟨the *cruising* speed of an airplane⟩ — **cruise** *n*

cruis·er \'krü-zər\ *n* **1** : SQUAD CAR **2** : a large fast moderately armored and gunned warship **3** : a motorboat with arrangements for living aboard — called also *cabin cruiser*

crul·ler \'krəl-ər\ *n* [from Dutch *krulle*, from *krul* "curly"] : a small sweet cake in the form of a twisted strip fried in deep fat

[1]**crumb** \'krəm\ *n* **1** : a small fragment esp. of bread **2** : BIT

[2]**crumb** *vb* **1** : to break into crumbs : CRUMBLE **2** : to cover or thicken with crumbs **3** : to remove crumbs from ⟨*crumb* a table⟩

[1]**crum·ble** \'krəm-bəl\ *vb* **crum·bled**; **crum·bling** \-b(ə-)ling\ : to break into small pieces : DISINTEGRATE ⟨*crumble* bread in one's hand⟩ ⟨the wall *crumbled*⟩

[2]**crumble** *n* : crumbling substance : fine debris

crum·bly \-b(ə-)lē\ *adj* **crum·bli·er**; **-est** : easily crumbled

crum·pet \'krəm-pət\ *n* : a small round cake made of unsweetened batter cooked on a griddle

crum·ple \'krəm-pəl\ *vb* **crum·pled**; **crum·pling** \-p(ə-)ling\ **1** : WRINKLE, RUMPLE **2** : COLLAPSE

crunch \'krənch\ *vb* : to chew, grind, or press with a crushing noise — **crunch** *n* — **crunchy** \'krən-chē\ *adj*

crup·per \'krəp-ər, 'krůp-\ *n* **1** : a leather loop passing under a horse's tail and buckled to the saddle of the harness **2** : the rump of a horse : CROUP

[1]**cru·sade** \krü-'sād\ *n* **1** *cap* : any of the military expeditions undertaken by Christian countries in the 11th, 12th, and 13th centuries to recover the Holy Land from the Muslims **2** : a campaign undertaken with zeal and enthusiasm ⟨a *crusade* against gambling⟩

[2]**crusade** *vb* : to engage in a crusade — **cru·sad·er** *n*

cruse \'krüz, 'krüs\ *n* : a jar, pot, or cup for holding a liquid (as water or oil)

[1]**crush** \'krəsh\ *vb* **1** : to squeeze or force by pressure so as to break or bruise or to destroy the natural shape or condition ⟨*crush* grapes⟩ ⟨*crushed* his hat by sitting on it⟩ **2** : to break into fine pieces by pounding or grinding ⟨*crush* stone⟩ **3** : SUPPRESS, DEFEAT ⟨*crush* an attack⟩ **4** : to become crushed — **crush·er** *n*

[2]**crush** *n* **1** : an act of crushing **2** : a tightly packed crowd **3** : INFATUATION

crust \'krəst\ *n* **1 a** : the hardened exterior surface of bread **b** : a piece of dry hard bread **2** : the pastry portion of a pie **3 a** : a hard outer covering or surface layer ⟨a *crust* of snow⟩ **b** : the outer part of the earth — **crust** *vb*

crus·ta·cea \,krəs-'tā-sh(ē-)ə\ *n pl* : CRUSTACEANS

crus·ta·cean \,krəs-'tā-shən\ *n* : any of a large class of mostly aquatic arthropods (as lobsters, shrimps, crabs, wood lice, water fleas, and barnacles) having an exoskeleton of chitin or chitin and a compound of calcium — **crustacean** *adj*

crust·al \'krəs-təl\ *adj* : relating to a crust esp. of the earth or the moon

crusty \'krəs-tē\ *adj* **crust·i·er**; **-est** **1** : having or being a crust **2** : SURLY, IRASCIBLE — **crust·i·ness** *n*

crutch \'krəch\ *n* **1** : a support typically fitting under the armpit for use by the disabled in walking **2** : a usu. forked support or prop

crux \'krəks, 'krůks\ *n*, *pl* **crux·es** *also* **cru·ces** \'krü-,sēz\ **1** : a puzzling or difficult problem **2** : a crucial or critical point

cru·zei·ro \krü-'ze(ə)r-ō, -ü\ *n*, *pl* **-ros** **1** : the basic monetary unit of Brazil **2** : a coin representing one cruzeiro

[1]**cry** \'krī\ *vb* **cried**; **cry·ing** **1** : to call loudly : SHOUT **2** : WEEP, LAMENT **3** : to utter a characteristic sound or call **4** : BEG, BESEECH **5** : to proclaim publicly : call out — **cry havoc** : to sound an alarm — **cry wolf** : to give alarm without a reason

[2]**cry** *n*, *pl* **cries** **1** : a loud call or shout (as of pain, fear, or joy) **2** : APPEAL ⟨hear my *cry*⟩ **3** : a fit of weeping **4** : the characteristic sound of an animal (as a bird) **5** : SLOGAN — **a far cry** : a great distance or change — **in full cry** : in full pursuit

cry·ba·by \'krī-,bā-bē\ *n* : one who cries easily or often

cry down *vb* : DISPARAGE, BELITTLE

cry·ing \'krī-ing\ *adj* **1** : calling for attention and correction ⟨a *crying* need⟩ **2** : NOTORIOUS ⟨a *crying* evil⟩

cry·o·gen·ics \,krī-ə-'jen-iks\ *n* : a branch of physics that relates to the production and effects of very low temperatures

cry·o·lite \'krī-ə-,līt\ *n* : a mineral consisting of sodium, aluminum, and fluorine that is used esp. in producing aluminum

crypt \'kript\ *n* : an underground vault or room; *esp* : one under the floor of a church used as a burial place

cryp·tic \'krip-tik\ *adj* **1** : HIDDEN, SECRET **2** : having or seeming to have a hidden meaning ⟨a *cryptic* remark⟩ **3** : serving to conceal — **cryp·ti·cal·ly** \-ti-k(ə-)lē\ *adv*

cryp·to·gam \'krip-tə-,gam\ *n* : a plant (as a fern, moss, alga, or fungus) reproducing by spores and not producing flowers or seed — **cryp·to·gam·ic** \,krip-tə-'gam-ik\ *or* **cryp·tog·a·mous** \krip-'täg-ə-məs\ *adj*

cryp·to·gram \'krip-tə-,gram\ *n* : a writing in cipher or code

cryp·to·graph \-,graf\ *n* : CRYPTOGRAM — **cryp·to·graph·ic** \,krip-tə-'graf-ik\ *adj*

cryp·tog·ra·phy \krip-'täg-rə-fē\ *n* : the coding and deciphering of secret messages — **cryp·tog·ra·pher** \-fər\ *n*

cryst *abbr* crystalline

[1]**crys·tal** \'kris-təl\ *n* [from Greek *krystallos* "ice"] **1** : a quartz that is transparent or nearly so and that is either colorless or only slightly tinged **2** : something resembling crystal in transparency **3** : a body that is formed by the solidification of a substance or mixture and has a regularly repeating internal arrangement of its atoms and often external plane faces ⟨a *crystal* of quartz⟩ ⟨a snow *crystal*⟩ ⟨a salt *crystal*⟩ **4** : a clear high-quality glass **5** : the transparent cover over a watch or clock dial

[2]**crystal** *adj* **1** : consisting of or resembling crystal : CLEAR **2** : using a crystal ⟨a *crystal* radio⟩

crys·tal·line \'kris-tə-lən\ *adj* **1** : made of crystal or crystals **2** : resembling crystal : TRANSPARENT **3** : of or relating to a crystal

crystalline lens *n* : the lens of the vertebrate eye

crys·tal·lize \'kris-tə-,līz\ *vb* **1 a** : to cause to form crystals or assume crystalline form **b** : to become crystallized **2** : to give a definite form to ⟨tried to *crystallize* his thoughts⟩ — **crys·tal·li·za·tion** \,kris-tə-lə-'zā-shən\ *n*

crys·tal·log·ra·phy \ˌkris-tə-'läg-rə-fē\ *n* : a science that deals with the form and structure of crystals — **crys·tal·log·ra·pher** \-fər\ *n*
crys·tal·loid \'kris-tə-ˌlȯid\ *n* : a substance that forms a true solution and is capable of being crystallized
crystal set *n* : a radio receiver having a crystal for a detector and no vacuum tubes
c/s *abbr* cycles per second
Cs *abbr* cirrostratus
csc *abbr* cosecant
cswy *abbr* causeway
ct *abbr* **1** cent **2** court
CT *abbr* Connecticut
cten·o·phore \'ten-ə-ˌfōr, -ˌfȯr\ *n* : any of a phylum of marine animals superficially resembling jellyfishes and swimming by means of eight bands of ciliated plates — **cte·noph·o·ran** \ti-'näf-ə-rən\ *adj or n*
ctn *abbr* **1** carton **2** cotangent
ctr *abbr* center
cts *abbr* courts
cu *abbr* cubic
Cu *abbr* cumulus
cub \'kəb\ *n* **1 a** : a young flesh-eating mammal ⟨bear *cubs*⟩ ⟨lion *cubs*⟩ **b** : a young shark **2** : a young person **3** : APPRENTICE; *esp* : an inexperienced newspaper reporter — **cub** *adj*
Cu·ban \'kyü-bən\ *adj* : of, relating to, or characteristic of Cuba or its people — **Cuban** *n*
cub·by·hole \'kəb-ē-ˌhōl\ *n* : a snug or confined place (as for hiding or storing things)
¹**cube** \'kyüb\ *n* **1** : the solid body having six equal square sides **2** : the product obtained by taking a number three times as a factor ⟨the *cube* of 2 is 8⟩
²**cube** *vb* **1** : to raise to the third power **2** : to form or cut into cubes
cube root *n* : a number whose cube is a given number ⟨the *cube root* of 27 is 3⟩
cu·bic \'kyü-bik\ *adj* **1** : having the form of a cube **2** : being the volume of a cube whose edge is a specified unit **3 a** : having length, width, and height **b** : relating to volume — **cu·bi·cal** \-bi-kəl\ *adj* — **cu·bi·cal·ly** \-bi-k(ə-)lē\ *adv*
cubic centimeter *n* : a unit of volume equal to the volume of a cube one centimeter long on each side
cubic foot *n* : a unit of volume equal to the volume of a cube one foot long on each side
cubic inch *n* : a unit of volume equal to the volume of a cube one inch long on each side
cu·bi·cle \'kyü-bi-kəl\ *n* : a partitioned compartment esp. for sleeping
cubic measure *n* : a unit (as a cubic inch or cubic centimeter) for measuring volume — see MEASURE table, METRIC SYSTEM table
cubic meter *n* : a unit of volume equal to the volume of a cube one meter long on each side
cubic yard *n* : a unit of volume equal to the volume of a cube one yard long on each side
cu·bit \'kyü-bət\ *n* : a unit of length based on the length of the forearm from the elbow to the tip of the middle finger and usu. equal to about 18 inches
cub scout *n* : a member of the Boy Scouts of America program for boys of the age range 8–10
¹**cuck·oo** \'kük-ü, 'ku̇k-\ *n, pl* **cuckoos** **1** : a largely grayish brown European bird that lays its eggs in the nests of other birds for them to hatch; *also* : any of various related birds **2** : the call of a cuckoo
²**cuckoo** *adj* : SILLY, CRAZY
cuckoo spit *n* **1** : a frothy secretion exuded upon plants by the nymphs of spittlebugs **2** : SPITTLEBUG
cu·cum·ber \'kyü-(ˌ)kəm-bər\ *n* : the long fleshy many-seeded fruit of a vine related to the gourd and grown as a garden vegetable; *also* : this vine
cud \'kəd, 'ku̇d\ *n* : food brought up into the mouth by some animals (as a cow) from the rumen to be chewed again
cud·dle \'kəd-əl\ *vb* **cud·dled**; **cud·dling** \'kəd-(ə-)liŋ\ **1** : to hold close for warmth or comfort or in affection **2** : to lie close : SNUGGLE — **cuddle** *n* — **cud·dly** \'kəd-(ə-)lē\ *adj*
¹**cud·gel** \'kəj-əl\ *n* : a short heavy club
²**cudgel** *vb* **-geled** *or* **-gelled**; **-gel·ing** *or* **-gel·ling** : to beat with or as if with a cudgel — **cudgel one's brains** : to think hard (as for a solution to a problem)
¹**cue** \'kyü\ *n* **1** : a word, phrase, or action in a play serving as a signal for the next actor to speak or act **2** : something serving as a signal or suggestion : HINT — **cue** *vb*
²**cue** *n* **1** : QUEUE 2 **2** : a tapering rod for striking a ball in billiards or pool
cue ball *n* : the ball a player strikes with his cue in billiards or pool
¹**cuff** \'kəf\ *n* **1** : a part of a sleeve or glove encircling the wrist **2** : the turned-back hem of a trouser leg **3** : an inflatable band that is wrapped around a limb to control the flow of blood through the part when measuring blood pressure
²**cuff** *vb* : to strike with or as if with the palm of the hand : SLAP
³**cuff** *n* : a blow with the hand esp. when open : SLAP
cui·rass \kwi-'ras\ *n* : a piece of armor covering the body from neck to waist or the breastplate of such a piece
cuir·as·sier \ˌkwir-ə-'si(ə)r\ *n* : a mounted soldier wearing a cuirass
cui·sine \kwi-'zēn\ *n* : manner of preparing food
cu·lex \'kyü-ˌleks\ *n* : any of a large cosmopolitan genus of mosquitoes that includes the common house mosquito of Europe and No. America
cul·i·nary \'kəl-ə-ˌner-ē, 'kyü-lə-\ *adj* : of or relating to the kitchen or cookery
¹**cull** \'kəl\ *vb* **1** : to select from a group : CHOOSE **2** : to identify and remove the culls from — **cull·er** *n*
²**cull** *n* : something rejected as inferior or worthless
cul·mi·nate \'kəl-mə-ˌnāt\ *vb* : to reach the highest or climactic point — **cul·mi·na·tion** \ˌkəl-mə-'nā-shən\ *n*
cu·lotte \k(y)u̇-'lät\ *n* : a divided skirt or a garment with a divided skirt — often used in pl.
cul·pa·ble \'kəl-pə-bəl\ *adj* : BLAMEWORTHY, GUILTY — **cul·pa·bil·i·ty** \ˌkəl-pə-'bil-ət-ē\ *n* — **cul·pa·bly** \'kəl-pə-blē\ *adv*
cul·prit \'kəl-prət, -ˌprit\ *n* **1** : one accused of a crime **2** : one who has committed an offense
cult \'kəlt\ *n* **1** : formal worship **2** : a system of religious rites or those who practice it **3 a** : enthusiastic and usu. temporary devotion to a person, idea, or thing **b** : a group of persons showing such devotion — **cult·ist** \'kəl-təst\ *n*
cul·ti·gen \'kəl-tə-jən\ *n* : a cultivated organism (as Indian corn) of a variety or species for which a wild ancestor is unknown
cul·ti·vate \'kəl-tə-ˌvāt\ *vb* **1 a** : to prepare for the raising of crops : TILL **b** : to loosen or break up the

soil about (growing plants) **2 a :** to foster the growth of ⟨*cultivate* vegetables⟩ **b :** CULTURE 2 **c :** REFINE, IMPROVE ⟨*cultivate* the mind⟩ **3 :** FURTHER, ENCOURAGE ⟨*cultivate* the arts⟩ **4 :** to seek the society of — **cul·ti·va·bil·i·ty** \ˌkəl-tə-və-ˈbil-ət-ē\ *n* — **cul·ti·va·ble** \ˈkəl-tə-və-bəl\ *adj* — **cul·ti·vat·a·ble** \ˈkəl-tə-ˌvāt-ə-bəl\ *adj*

cul·ti·vat·ed *adj* **1 :** subjected to or produced under cultivation ⟨*cultivated* farms⟩ ⟨*cultivated* fruits⟩ **2 :** REFINED, EDUCATED ⟨*cultivated* speech⟩

cul·ti·va·tion \ˌkəl-tə-ˈvā-shən\ *n* **1 :** the act or art of cultivating; *esp* **:** TILLAGE **2 :** CULTURE, REFINEMENT

cul·ti·va·tor \ˈkəl-tə-ˌvāt-ər\ *n* **:** one that cultivates; *esp* **:** an implement to loosen the soil while crops are growing

cul·tur·al \ˈkəlch-(ə-)rəl\ *adj* **1 :** of or relating to culture **2 a :** produced by breeding **b :** of or relating to the culture of a plant — **cul·tur·al·ly** \-ē\ *adv*

cultural anthropology *n* **:** the division of anthropology that deals with the study of culture in all its aspects

1**cul·ture** \ˈkəl-chər\ *n* **1 :** CULTIVATION, TILLAGE **2 a :** the rearing or development of a particular product, stock, or crop ⟨bee *culture*⟩ ⟨the *culture* of grapes⟩ **b :** professional or expert care and training ⟨voice *culture*⟩ **3 :** improvement of the mind, tastes, and manners through careful training or the refinement so acquired **4 :** a particular form or stage of civilization ⟨ancient Greek *culture*⟩ **5 :** cultivation of living material in prepared nutrient media; *also* **:** a product of such cultivation

2**culture** *vb* **cul·tured**; **cul·tur·ing** \ˈkəlch-(ə-)ring\ **1 :** CULTIVATE **2 :** to grow in a prepared medium

cul·tured \ˈkəl-chərd\ *adj* **1 :** CULTIVATED **2 :** produced under artificial conditions ⟨*cultured* viruses⟩ ⟨*cultured* pearls⟩

cul·vert \ˈkəl-vərt\ *n* **1 :** a drain crossing under a road or railroad **2 :** a conduit for a culvert

cum·ber \ˈkəm-bər\ *vb* **cum·bered**; **cum·ber·ing** \-b(ə-)ring\ **1 :** to hinder or hamper by being in the way **2 :** to weigh down **:** BURDEN ⟨*cumbered* with cares and responsibilities⟩

cum·ber·some \ˈkəm-bər-səm\ *adj* **1 :** CLUMSY, UNWIELDY **2 :** slow-moving **:** LUMBERING — **cum·ber·some·ly** *adv* — **cum·ber·some·ness** *n*

cum·brous \ˈkəm-brəs\ *adj* **:** CUMBERSOME — **cum·brous·ly** *adv*

cum·mer·bund \ˈkəm-ər-ˌbənd\ *n* **:** a broad sash worn as a waistband

cu·mu·la·tive \ˈkyü-myə-lət-iv, -ˌlāt-\ *adj* **:** increasing (as in force, strength, or amount) by successive additions ⟨*cumulative* effects⟩ — **cu·mu·la·tive·ly** *adv* — **cu·mu·la·tive·ness** *n*

cu·mu·lo·nim·bus \ˌkyü-myə-lō-ˈnim-bəs\ *n* **:** a cumulus often spread out in the shape of an anvil extending to great heights

cu·mu·lo·stra·tus \-ˈstrāt-əs, -ˈstrat-\ *n* **:** a cumulus whose base extends horizontally as a stratus cloud

cu·mu·lus \ˈkyü-myə-ləs\ *n, pl* **cu·mu·li** \-ˌlī, -ˌlē\ **1 :** HEAP, ACCUMULATION **2 :** a massy cloud form having a flat base and rounded outlines often piled up like a mountain

cu·ne·ate \ˈkyü-nē-ˌāt, -nē-ət\ *adj* **:** narrowly triangular with the acute angle toward the base ⟨a *cuneate* leaf⟩ — **cu·ne·ate·ly** *adv*

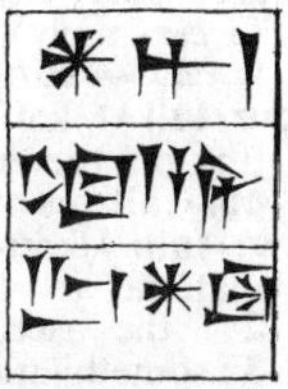
cuneiform

1**cu·ne·i·form** \kyu̇-ˈnē-ə-ˌfȯrm, ˈkyü-n(ē-)ə-\ *adj* **1 :** having the shape of a wedge **2 :** composed of or written in wedge-shaped characters ⟨*cuneiform* script⟩

2**cuneiform** *n* **:** cuneiform writing (as of ancient Assyria and Babylonia)

cun·ner \ˈkən-ər\ *n* **:** a small American food fish that is abundant on the rocky shores of New England

1**cun·ning** \ˈkən-ing\ *adj* **1 :** exhibiting skill **2 :** marked by esp. animal cleverness in gaining ends **:** ARTFUL **3 :** prettily appealing **:** CUTE — **cun·ning·ly** \-ing-lē\ *adv*

syn CUNNING, CRAFTY, SLY, WILY can mean skillful at trickery. CUNNING suggests animal cleverness or skill in coping with dangers or obstacles; CRAFTY suggests skill in deceiving with shrewd devices and schemes; SLY may imply secret or furtive deception; WILY implies a crafty attempt to catch or ensnare someone unprepared ***ant*** ingenuous

2**cunning** *n* **1 :** SKILL, DEXTERITY **2 :** SLYNESS, CRAFTINESS

1**cup** \ˈkəp\ *n* **1 :** an open bowl-shaped drinking vessel usu. with a handle **2 :** the contents of a cup **:** CUPFUL **3 :** a large ornamental cup offered as a prize **4 :** something (as the corolla of a flower) resembling a cup **5 :** a food served in a cup-shaped vessel ⟨fruit *cup*⟩ — **in one's cups :** DRUNK

2**cup** *vb* **cupped**; **cup·ping** **1 :** to curve into the shape of a cup ⟨*cupped* his hands⟩ **2 :** to place in or as if in a cup

cup·bearer \ˈkəp-ˌbar-ər, -ˌber-\ *n* **:** one who has the duty of filling and handing cups of wine

cup·board \ˈkəb-ərd\ *n* **1 :** a closet with shelves for cups, dishes, or food **2 :** a small closet

cup·cake \ˈkəp-ˌkāk\ *n* **:** a small cake baked in a cup-shaped mold

cup·ful \ˈkəp-ˌfu̇l\ *n, pl* **cup·fuls** \-ˌfu̇lz\ *or* **cups·ful** \ˈkəps-ˌfu̇l\ **1 :** the amount held by a cup **2 :** a half pint **:** eight ounces

cu·pid \ˈkyü-pəd\ *n* **:** a winged naked figure of an infant often with a bow and arrow that represents the Roman god of love Cupid

cu·pid·i·ty \kyu̇-ˈpid-ət-ē\ *n* **:** excessive desire esp. for wealth **:** GREED

cu·po·la \ˈkyü-pə-lə, -ˌlō\ *n* **1 :** a rounded roof or ceiling **2 :** a small structure built on top of a roof

cu·prite \ˈk(y)ü-ˌprīt\ *n* **:** a mineral that is an oxide of copper and an ore of copper

cur \ˈkər\ *n* **1 :** a mongrel or inferior dog **2 :** a low contemptible person

cur *abbr* **1** currency **2** current

cur·a·ble \ˈkyu̇r-ə-bəl\ *adj* **:** capable of being cured

cu·ra·re \k(y)u̇-ˈrär-ē\ *n* **:** a dried extract in water esp. of a tropical American vine used in native arrow poisons and in medicine to produce muscular relaxation

cu·rate \ˈkyu̇r-ət\ *n* **:** a clergyman serving as assistant to a rector

cu·ra·tive \ˈkyu̇r-ət-iv\ *adj* **:** relating to or used in the cure of diseases

cu·ra·tor \kyu̇-ˈrāt-ər, ˈkyu̇r-ˌāt-\ *n* **:** one that has the care and superintendence of something; *esp* **:** one in charge esp. of a museum or zoo — **cu·ra·tor·ship** *n*

1**curb** \ˈkərb\ *n* **1 :** a chain or strap on a bit used to restrain a horse **2 :** CHECK, RESTRAINT ⟨price *curbs*⟩ **3 :** a frame or a raised edge or margin to strengthen or confine ⟨the *curb* of a well⟩ **4 :** an edging built along a street

2**curb** *vb* **:** to control by or furnish with a curb ⟨legislation to *curb* price and wage increases⟩

curb·ing \ˈkər-bing\ *n* **1 :** the material for a curb **2 :** CURB

cur·cu·lio \(ˌ)kər-ˈkyü-lē-ˌō\ *n* : any of various weevils; *esp* : one that injures fruit
[1]**curd** \ˈkərd\ *n* : the thick casein-rich part of coagulated milk — **curdy** \-ē\ *adj*
[2]**curd** *vb* : COAGULATE, CURDLE
cur·dle \ˈkərd-əl\ *vb* **cur·dled**; **cur·dling** \ˈkərd-(ə-)liŋ\ **1** : to cause curds to form in **2** : to form curds : COAGULATE **3** : SPOIL, SOUR
[1]**cure** \ˈkyu̇(ə)r\ *n* **1** : pastoral charge of a parish **2 a** : recovery or relief from a disease **b** : REMEDY **c** : a course or period of treatment **3** : a process or method of curing — **cure·less** \-ləs\ *adj*
[2]**cure** *vb* **1 a** : to restore to health, soundness, or normality **b** : to bring about recovery from **2** : RECTIFY, REMEDY **3 a** : to process for keeping ⟨*cure* bacon⟩ **b** : to undergo a curing process ⟨hay *curing* in the sun⟩ — **cur·er** *n*
cure–all \ˈkyu̇(ə)r-ˌȯl\ *n* : a remedy for all ills
cur·few \ˈkər-ˌfyü\ *n* [from medieval French *covrefeu*, a signal given to bank the hearth fire, from *covrir* "to cover" and *feu* "fire"] **1** : an order or regulation requiring usu. specified persons to be off the streets at a stated time **2** : a signal to announce the beginning of a curfew **3** : the time when a curfew is sounded
cu·rie \ˈkyu̇(ə)r-(ˌ)ē, kyu̇-ˈrē\ *n* : a unit of radioactivity equal to 37 billion disintegrations per second
cu·rio \ˈkyu̇r-ē-ˌō\ *n, pl* **-ri·os** : a rare or unusual article
cu·ri·os·i·ty \ˌkyu̇r-ē-ˈäs-ət-ē\ *n, pl* **-ties** **1** : an eager desire to learn and often to learn what does not concern one : INQUISITIVENESS **2** : something strange or unusual; *esp* : CURIO
cu·ri·ous \ˈkyu̇r-ē-əs\ *adj* **1** : eager to learn ⟨a *curious* scholar⟩ **2** : INQUISITIVE, NOSY **3** : STRANGE, UNUSUAL ⟨a *curious* insect⟩ **4** : ODD, ECCENTRIC ⟨*curious* ideas⟩ — **cu·ri·ous·ly** *adv* — **cu·ri·ous·ness** *n*
cu·ri·um \ˈkyu̇r-ē-əm\ *n* : a metallic radioactive element artificially produced and used esp. as a source of neutrons — see ELEMENT table
[1]**curl** \ˈkərl\ *vb* **1** : to form into or grow in coils or ringlets **2** : CURVE, TWIST
[2]**curl** *n* **1** : a lock of hair that coils : RINGLET **2** : a spiral or winding form : COIL **3** : the state of being curled **4** : an abnormal rolling or curling of leaves
curl·er \ˈkər-lər\ *n* **1** : one that curls; *esp* : a device for putting a curl into hair **2** : a player in the game of curling
cur·lew \ˈkərl-(y)ü\ *n, pl* **curlews** *or* **curlew** : any of various largely brownish mostly migratory birds related to the woodcocks and distinguished by long legs and a long slender down-curved bill

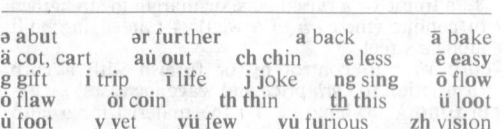

curlew (about 13 in. long)

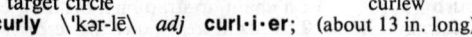

curl·i·cue *also* **curly·cue** \ˈkər-li-ˌkyü\ *n* : a fancy curve or spiral
curl·ing \ˈkər-liŋ\ *n* : a game in which two 4-man teams slide special stones over ice toward a target circle
curly \ˈkər-lē\ *adj* **curl·i·er**; **-est** **1** : tending to curl **2** : having curls — **curl·i·ness** *n*
cur·rant \ˈkər-ənt, ˈkə-rənt\ *n* [from Middle English *raison of Coraunte*, literally "raisin of Corinth", from *Corinth*, city in Greece from which it was exported] **1** : a small seedless raisin grown chiefly in the Levant **2** : the acid edible fruit of several shrubs related to the gooseberries; *also* : a plant bearing currants
cur·ren·cy \ˈkər-ən-sē, ˈkə-rən-\ *n, pl* **-cies** **1** : general use or acceptance ⟨a belief that has wide *currency*⟩ **2** : coins and paper money circulating as a medium of exchange
[1]**cur·rent** \ˈkər-ənt, ˈkə-rənt\ *adj* **1 a** : now passing ⟨the *current* month⟩ **b** : occurring in or belonging to the present time ⟨*current* events⟩ **2** : generally accepted, used, or practiced ⟨the *current* meaning of a word⟩ — **cur·rent·ly** *adv* — **cur·rent·ness** *n*
[2]**current** *n* **1 a** : the part of a fluid body moving continuously in a certain direction **b** : the swiftest part of a stream **c** : a strong or forceful flow **2** : general course or movement : TREND **3** : a movement of electricity analogous to the flow of a stream of water; *also* : the rate of such movement
cur·ric·u·lum \kə-ˈrik-yə-ləm\ *n, pl* **-la** \-lə\ *or* **-lums** : a course of study; *esp* : the body of courses offered in a school or college or in one of its departments — **cur·ric·u·lar** \-lər\ *adj*
[1]**cur·ry** \ˈkər-ē, ˈkə-rē\ *vb* **cur·ried**; **cur·ry·ing** **1** : to dress the coat of with a currycomb **2** : to treat (tanned leather) especially by incorporating oil or grease — **cur·ri·er** *n* — **curry fa·vor** \-ˈfā-vər\ : to seek to gain favor by flattery or attentions
[2]**cur·ry** *also* **cur·rie** \ˈkər-ē, ˈkə-rē\ *n, pl* **curries** **1** : CURRY POWDER **2** : a food seasoned with curry powder
[3]**curry** *vb* **cur·ried**; **cur·ry·ing** : to flavor or cook with curry powder
cur·ry·comb \ˈkər-ē-ˌkōm, ˈkə-rē-\ *n* : a comb with rows of metallic teeth or ridges used to curry horses — **curry·comb** *vb*
curry powder *n* : a pungent seasoning of ground spices
[1]**curse** \ˈkərs\ *n* **1** : a prayer that harm or injury may come upon someone **2** : a word or an expression used in cursing or swearing **3** : evil or misfortune that comes as if in answer to a curse ⟨floods are the *curse* of this region⟩
[2]**curse** *vb* **1** : to call upon divine or supernatural power to send injury upon **2** : to use profane language : SWEAR **3** : to bring great evil upon : AFFLICT
cursed \ˈkər-səd, ˈkərst\ *also* **curst** \ˈkərst\ *adj* : being under or deserving a curse — **cursed·ly** *adv* — **cursed·ness** *n*
cur·sive \ˈkər-siv\ *adj* : written or formed with the strokes of the letters joined together and the angles rounded ⟨*cursive* handwriting⟩ — **cur·sive·ly** *adv*
cur·so·ry \ˈkərs(-ə)-rē\ *adj* : rapidly and often superficially performed : HASTY — **cur·so·ri·ly** \-rə-lē\ *adv* — **cur·so·ri·ness** \-rē-nəs\ *n*
curt \ˈkərt\ *adj* : rudely abrupt or brief in language ⟨a *curt* reply⟩ ***syn*** see BLUFF ***ant*** voluble — **curt·ly** *adv* — **curt·ness** *n*
cur·tail \(ˌ)kər-ˈtāl\ *vb* : to shorten or reduce by cutting off the end or a part of — **cur·tail·er** *n* — **cur·tail·ment** \-ˈtāl-mənt\ *n*
cur·tain \ˈkərt-ən\ *n* **1** : a piece of cloth or other material to darken, conceal, divide, or decorate **2** : the ascent or descent of a theater curtain **3** : something that covers, conceals, or separates like a curtain — **curtain** *vb*
curt·sy *or* **curt·sey** \ˈkərt-sē\ *n, pl* **curtsies** *or*

ə abut	ər further	a back	ā bake	
ä cot, cart	au̇ out	ch chin	e less	ē easy
g gift	i trip	ī life	j joke	ŋ sing	ō flow
ȯ flaw	ȯi coin	th thin	t͟h this	ü loot
u̇ foot	y yet	yü few	yu̇ furious	zh vision

curtseys : a bow made esp. by women that consists of a slight lowering of the body and bending of the knees — **curtsy** *or* **curtsey** *vb*

cur·va·ture \'kər-və-ˌchu̇(ə)r, -chər\ *n* **1** : the state of being curved **2** : a measure or amount of curving **3** : an abnormal curving ⟨*curvature* of the spine⟩

1**curve** \'kərv\ *vb* **1** : to turn or deviate gradually from a straight line **2** : to cause to curve : BEND

2**curve** *n* **1** : a curving line or surface : BEND **2** : something curved **3** : a ball thrown so that it swerves from its normal course — called also *curve ball* — **curved** \'kərvd\ *adj*

1**cur·vet** \(ˌ)kər-'vet\ *n* : a leap of a horse in which first the forelegs and then the hind are raised so that for an instant all the legs are in the air

2**curvet** *vb* **cur·vet·ted** *or* **cur·vet·ed**; **cur·vet·ting** *or* **cur·vet·ing** **1** : to make a curvet **2** : CAPER, PRANCE

cur·vi·lin·e·ar \ˌkər-və-'lin-ē-ər\ *adj* : consisting of or bounded by curved lines

1**cush·ion** \'ku̇sh-ən\ *n* **1** : a soft pillow or pad to rest on or against **2** : something resembling a cushion in use, shape, or softness **3** : a rubber pad along the inner rim of a billiard table **4** : something serving to lessen the effects of disturbances or disorders

2**cushion** *vb* **cush·ioned**; **cush·ion·ing** \-(ə-)ning\ **1** : to place on a cushion **2** : to furnish with a cushion **3 a** : to lessen the effects of ⟨*cushion* the blow⟩ **b** : to protect from harm or injury ⟨*cushioned* the children from fear⟩

cusp \'kəsp\ *n* : POINT, APEX: as **a** : either of the pointed ends of a crescent moon **b** : a pointed projection formed by or arising from the intersection of two arcs **c** : a point on the grinding surface of a tooth

cus·pid \'kəs-pəd\ *n* : a canine tooth

cus·pi·dor \'kəs-pə-ˌdȯr\ *n* : SPITTOON

cus·tard \'kəs-tərd\ *n* : a sweetened mixture of milk and eggs baked, boiled, or frozen

custard apple *n* **1** : any of several chiefly tropical American soft-fleshed edible fruits; *also* : a tree or shrub bearing this fruit **2** : PAPAW 2

cus·to·di·an \ˌkəs-'tōd-ē-ən\ *n* : one that guards and protects or maintains; *esp* : JANITOR — **cus·to·di·al** \-ē-əl\ *adj* — **cus·to·di·an·ship** \-ˌship\ *n*

cus·to·dy \'kəs-təd-ē\ *n* **1** : CARE, CHARGE **2** : legal confinement; *esp* : IMPRISONMENT ⟨taken into *custody*⟩

1**cus·tom** \'kəs-təm\ *n* **1** : a practice common to many or habitual with an individual : the usual way of doing things **2** *pl* : duties or taxes imposed by law on imports or exports **3 a** : business patronage **b** : CUSTOMERS

2**custom** *adj* **1** : made or done to order ⟨*custom* clothes⟩ **2** : specializing in custom work ⟨a *custom* tailor⟩

cus·tom·ary \'kəs-tə-ˌmer-ē\ *adj* **1** : based on or established by custom ⟨*customary* rent⟩ **2** : commonly practiced or observed: HABITUAL ⟨*customary* courtesy⟩ ***syn*** see USUAL ***ant*** occasional — **cus·tom·ar·i·ly** \ˌkəs-tə-'mer-ə-lē\ *adv*

cus·tom·er \'kəs-tə-mər\ *n* **1** : one that buys; *esp* : one that regularly patronizes the same firm **2** : PERSON, FELLOW ⟨a queer *customer*⟩

cus·tom·house \'kəs-təm-ˌhau̇s\ *also* **cus·toms·house** \-təmz-\ *n* : a building where customs are paid or collected and where ships are entered and cleared at a port

cus·tom–made \ˌkəs-təm-'mād\ *adj* : made to individual order

1**cut** \'kət\ *vb* **cut**; **cut·ting** **1** : to penetrate with or as if with a knife : GASH ⟨*cut* his hand⟩ ⟨*cut* hay⟩ ⟨*cut* bread⟩ **2** : to experience the growth of through the gum ⟨*cut* a tooth⟩ **3** : to hurt emotionally **4** : to strike sharply or at an angle ⟨*cut* him across the legs with a whip⟩ **5** : to lessen in amount, length, or strength ⟨*cut* costs⟩ **6** : to remove with or as if with an edged tool ⟨*cut* a piece of cake⟩ ⟨*cut* two players from the squad⟩ **7 a** : to go straight rather than around ⟨*cut* across the campus⟩ **b** : INTERSECT, CROSS ⟨lines *cutting* other lines⟩ **8** : to divide a deck of cards **9** : STOP ⟨*cut* the nonsense⟩ ⟨*cut* the engine⟩ **10** : to refuse to recognize ⟨*cut* an old friend⟩ **11** : to fail to attend ⟨*cut* a class⟩ **12 a** : to make or shape with or as if with an edged tool ⟨*cut* a hole in the wall⟩ ⟨*cut* a diamond⟩ **b** : to record sounds on ⟨*cut* a record⟩ **13** : PERFORM, DO ⟨*cut* a caper⟩ **14** : to give the appearance of ⟨*cut* a fine figure⟩

2**cut** *n* **1 a** : something cut or cut off **b** : a part of a meat carcass ⟨a rib *cut*⟩ **c** : an allotted part : SHARE ⟨took his *cut* and left⟩ **2 a** : a wound made by something sharp : GASH **b** : a surface or outline made by cutting ⟨a smooth *cut* in a board⟩ **c** : a passage made by cutting ⟨a railroad *cut*⟩ **d** : a grade or step esp. in a social scale ⟨a *cut* above his neighbors⟩ **e** : a pictorial illustration **3 a** : a gesture or expression that wounds the feelings ⟨an unkind *cut*⟩ **b** : a straight path or course **c** : a cutting stroke or blow ⟨took a *cut* at the ball⟩ **d** : REDUCTION ⟨a *cut* in pay⟩ **4** : a voluntary absence from a class **5** : an abrupt transition from one sound or image to another in motion pictures, radio, or television **6** : the shape and style in which a thing is cut, formed, or made ⟨clothes of the latest *cut*⟩

cu·ta·ne·ous \kyu̇-'tā-nē-əs\ *adj* : of, relating to, or affecting the skin ⟨*cutaneous* infection⟩ — **cu·ta·ne·ous·ly** *adv*

cut·away \'kət-ə-ˌwā\ *n* **1** : a coat with skirts tapering from the front waistline to form tails at the back **2** : an illustration in which the surface or cover of an object is not fully shown and in which inner details are made apparent

cut back \'kət-'bak\ *vb* **1** : PRUNE **2** : REDUCE, DECREASE ⟨*cut back* production⟩ — **cut·back** \-ˌbak\ *n*

cute \'kyüt\ *adj* **1** : CLEVER, SHREWD **2** : attractive or pretty esp. by reason of daintiness — **cute·ly** *adv* — **cute·ness** *n*

cut glass *n* : glass ornamented by cutting and polishing

cu·ti·cle \'kyüt-i-kəl\ *n* **1** : SKIN, PELLICLE: as **a** : an external sheathing layer secreted usu. by epidermal cells **b** : the epidermis when it is the outermost layer **c** : a thin continuous fatty film on the outside surface of many higher plants **2** : dead or horny epidermis — **cu·tic·u·lar** \kyu̇-'tik-yə-lər\ *adj*

cu·tin \'kyüt-ən\ *n* : a substance containing waxes, fatty acids, soaps, and resinous matter that forms a continuous layer on the outer epidermal wall of a plant

cut in *vb* **1** : INTRUDE ⟨*cut in* on a conversation⟩ **2** : INCLUDE ⟨*cut* me *in* on the profits⟩ **3** : to swerve sharply in front of another vehicle

cut·lass \'kət-ləs\ *n* : a short curved sword formerly used by sailors

cut·ler \'kət-lər\ *n* : one who makes, deals in, or repairs cutlery

cut·lery \'kət-lə-rē\ *n, pl* **-ler·ies** **1** : cutting tools; *esp* : implements for cutting and eating food **2** : the business of a cutler

cut·let \'kət-lət\ *n* **1** : a small slice of meat broiled or fried **2** : a piece of food shaped like a cutlet

cut·off \'kət-ˌȯf\ *n* **1** : the action of cutting off **2** : SHORTCUT **3** : a device for cutting off

cut off \'kət-'ȯf\ *vb* **1** : to strike off : SEVER **2** : to kill suddenly or prematurely ⟨*cut off* in the prime of life⟩ **3** : to stop the passage of ⟨*cut off* our supplies⟩ **4** : SEPARATE, ISOLATE ⟨*cut off* by the sudden attack⟩ **5** : DISINHERIT ⟨was *cut off* without a cent⟩ **6** : to stop or interrupt while in communication ⟨the telephone operator *cut* me *off*⟩

cut·out \'kət-ˌau̇t\ *n* : something cut from or prepared for cutting from something else ⟨a page of animal *cutouts*⟩

1cut out \'kət-'au̇t\ *vb* **1** : to form by cutting ⟨*cut out* a pattern⟩ **2** : to determine through necessity ⟨his work is *cut out* for him⟩ **3** : DISCONNECT **4** : STOP ⟨*cut out* that noise⟩ **5** : ELIMINATE ⟨*cut out* waste⟩

2cut out *adj* : naturally fitted ⟨not *cut out* to be a lawyer⟩

cut·over \ˌkət-ˌō-vər\ *adj* : having most of its salable timber cut ⟨*cutover* land⟩

cut–rate \'kət-'rāt\ *adj* **1** : selling or offered at reduced prices ⟨a *cut-rate* store⟩ **2** : SECOND-RATE, CHEAP

cut·ter \'kət-ər\ *n* **1** : one that cuts ⟨a diamond *cutter*⟩ ⟨a cookie *cutter*⟩ **2 a** : a boat used by warships for carrying passengers and stores between a warship and the shore **b** : a small one-masted sailing boat **c** : a small armed coast guard boat **3** : a small sleigh

1cut·throat \'kət-ˌthrōt\ *n* : MURDERER

2cutthroat *adj* **1** : MURDEROUS, CRUEL ⟨a *cutthroat* rogue⟩ **2** : MERCILESS, RUTHLESS ⟨*cutthroat* competition⟩

1cut·ting \'kət-ing\ *n* **1** : something cut or cut off or out; *esp* : a section of a plant or animal capable of developing into a new organism **2** : RECORDING

2cutting *adj* **1** : designed for cutting : SHARP ⟨the *cutting* edge of a knife⟩ **2** : piercingly cold ⟨*cutting* wind⟩ **3** : SARCASTIC ⟨*cutting* remarks⟩ — **cutting·ly** \-ing-lē\ *adv*

cut·tle·bone \'kət-əl-ˌbōn\ *n* : the shell of cuttlefishes used for making polishing powder or for supplying caged birds with lime and salts

cut·tle·fish \-ˌfish\ *n* : a 10-armed marine mollusk differing from the related squid in having an internal shell composed of compounds of calcium

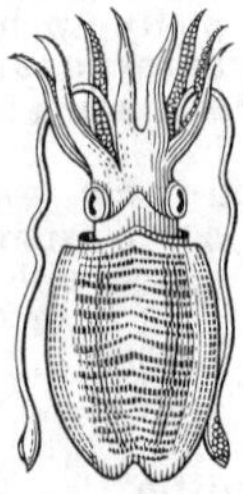

cuttlefish (about 2 ft. long)

cut up \'kət-'əp\ *vb* **1** : to cut into parts or pieces **2** : to act boisterously : CLOWN — **cut·up** \-ˌəp\ *n*

cut·worm \'kət-ˌwərm\ *n* : any of various smooth-bodied moth larvae that hide by day and feed on plants at night

CV *abbr* cardiovascular

cw *abbr* clockwise

cwt *abbr* hundredweight

-cy \sē\ *n suffix, pl* **-cies** **1** : action : practice ⟨piracy⟩ **2** : rank : office ⟨baronet*cy*⟩ ⟨chaplain*cy*⟩ **3** : body : class ⟨democra*cy*⟩ **4** : state : quality ⟨accura*cy*⟩ ⟨bankrupt*cy*⟩

cy·an·a·mide *also* **cy·an·a·mid** \sī-'an-ə-məd\ *n* : a grayish black lumpy or powdered compound of calcium, carbon, and nitrogen that is used as a fertilizer and weed killer — called also *calcium cyanamide*

ə abut	ər further	a back	ā bake
ä cot, cart	au̇ out	ch chin	e less	ē easy
g gift	i trip	ī life	j joke	ng sing	ō flow
ȯ flaw	ȯi coin	th thin	th this	ü loot
u̇ foot	y yet	yü few	yu̇ furious	zh vision

1cy·a·nide \'sī-ə-ˌnīd, -nəd\ *n* : a very poisonous compound consisting of a carbon and nitrogen radical with either sodium or potassium and used esp. in electroplating

2cy·a·nide \-ˌnīd\ *vb* : to treat with a cyanide

cy·an·o·gen \sī-'an-ə-jən\ *n* : a colorless flammable poisonous gas consisting of carbon and nitrogen and having an odor of crushed peach leaves

cy·ber·net·ics \ˌsī-bər-'net-iks\ *n* : comparative study of automatic control systems (as that of the nervous system and brain and mechanical-electrical communication systems) — **cy·ber·net·ic** *adj* — **cy·ber·net·i·cist** \-ə-səst\ *n*

cy·cad \'sī-kəd\ *n* : any of a family of tropical palmlike evergreen plants — **cy·ca·de·an** \ˌsī-kə-'dē-ən\ *adj* — **cy·cad·i·form** \sī-'kad-ə-ˌfȯrm\ *adj*

cy·cla·men \'sī-klə-mən, 'sik-lə-\ *n* : any of a genus of plants related to the primrose and grown as pot plants for their showy nodding flowers

1cy·cle \'sī-kəl, *4 also* 'sik-əl\ *n* **1** : a period of time taken up by a series of events or actions that repeat themselves regularly and in the same order ⟨the *cycle* of the seasons⟩ **2 a** : a course or series of events or operations that recur regularly and usu. lead back to the starting point ⟨the *cycle* of the blood from the heart, through the blood vessels, and back again⟩ **b** : one complete round of a cycle; *esp* : one complete series of changes of value of an alternating electric current **3** : a long period of time : AGE **4 a** : BICYCLE **b** : MOTORCYCLE — **cy·clic** \'sī-klik, 'sik-lik\ *or* **cy·cli·cal** \'sī-kli-kəl, 'sik-li-\ *adj* — **cy·cli·cal·ly** \-k(ə-)lē\ *adv*

2cy·cle \'sī-kəl, 'sik-əl\ *vb* **cy·cled**; **cy·cling** \'sī-k(ə-)ling, 'sik(-ə)-ling\ : to ride a cycle — **cy·cler** \'sī-k(ə-)lər, 'sik(-ə)-lər\ *n*

cy·clist \'sī-k(ə-)ləst, 'sik(-ə)-ləst\ *n* : one who cycles

cy·cloid \'sī-ˌklȯid\ *n* : a curve generated by a point on the circumference of a circle that is rolling along a straight line

cy·clone \'sī-ˌklōn\ *n* **1** : a storm or system of winds that rotates about a center of low atmospheric pressure counterclockwise in the northern hemisphere, advances at a speed of 20 to 30 miles an hour, and often brings abundant rain **2** : TORNADO — **cy·clon·ic** \sī-'klän-ik\ *adj*

cy·clo·pe·dia *or* **cy·clo·pae·dia** \ˌsī-klə-'pēd-ē-ə\ *n* : ENCYCLOPEDIA — **cy·clo·pe·dic** \-'pēd-ik\ *adj*

cy·clops \'sī-ˌkläps\ *n, pl* **cyclops** : WATER FLEA

cy·clo·stome \'sī-klə-ˌstōm\ *n* : any of a class of lower vertebrates with a large sucking mouth and no jaws — **cyclostome** *adj*

cy·clo·tron \'sī-klə-ˌträn\ *n* : a device for giving high speeds to charged particles by means of the combined action of a large magnetic force and a rapidly oscillating electric force

cyg·net \'sig-nət\ *n* : a young swan

cyl·in·der \'sil-ən-dər\ *n* **1** : a closed space figure or surface that has two congruent and parallel bases and can be formed by moving a line along the curve bounding one base so that it is always parallel to a certain fixed line **2** : a long round solid or hollow body (as the piston chamber of an engine, the barrel of a pump, or the part of a revolver which turns and holds the cartridges) — **cy·lin·dri·cal** \sə-'lin-dri-kəl\ *adj* — **cy·lin·dri·cal·ly** \-dri-k(ə-)lē\ *adv*

cym·bal \'sim-bəl\ *n* : a brass plate that is struck with a drumstick or used in pairs struck together to make a brilliant clashing tone — **cym·bal·ist** \-bə-ləst\ *n*

cyn·ic \'sin-ik\ *n* [originally denoting a member of

an ancient Greek philosophical sect preaching the virtue of independence and scorning ordinary social conventions, from Greek *kynikos*, from *kynixos* "like a dog" from *kyn-*, stem of *kyōn* "dog", from the same source as English *hound*] : one who distrusts people; *esp* : one who believes that human conduct is motivated wholly by self-interest — **cyn·i·cal** \'sin-i-kəl\ *adj* — **cyn·i·cal·ly** \-i-k(ə-)lē\ *adv*

cyn·i·cism \'sin-ə-ˌsiz-əm\ *n* **1** : cynical character or quality **2** : a cynical remark

cy·no·sure \'sī-nə-ˌshu̇r, 'sin-ə-\ *n* : a center of attraction or attention ⟨the *cynosure* of all eyes⟩

CYO *abbr* Catholic Youth Organization

cy·press \'sī-prəs\ *n* **1** : any of a genus of mostly evergreen trees that are related to the pines and have overlapping scalelike leaves **2** : either of two large swamp trees of the southern U.S. with hard red wood used for shingles **3** : the wood of a cypress tree

Cyp·ri·ot \'sip-rē-ət, -rē-ˌät\ *or* **Cyp·ri·ote** \-rē-ˌōt, -rē-ət\ *adj* : of, relating to, or characteristic of Cyprus or its people — **Cypriot** *or* **Cypriote** *n*

cyst \'sist\ *n* **1** : a closed pouch or sac of fluid that develops in the body in some diseased conditions **2** : a covering resembling a cyst or a body (as a spore) with such a covering — **cys·tic** \'sis-tik\ *adj*

cystic fibrosis *n* : an hereditary glandular disease that appears usu. in early childhood and is marked esp. by malnutrition, diarrhea, cough, and wheezing respiration

cy·to·chrome \'sīt-ə-ˌkrōm\ *n* : any of several iron-containing pigments that are important in oxidation reactions occurring in the living cell

cy·tol·o·gy \sī-'täl-ə-jē\ *n* : a branch of biology dealing with cells — **cy·to·log·i·cal** \ˌsīt-ə-'läj-i-kəl\ *or* **cy·to·log·ic** \-'läj-ik\ *adj* — **cy·tol·o·gist** \sī-'täl-ə-jəst\ *n*

cy·to·plasm \'sīt-ə-ˌplaz-əm\ *n* : the protoplasm of a plant or animal cell exclusive of the nucleus — **cy·to·plas·mic** \ˌsīt-ə-'plaz-mik\ *adj*

cy·to·sine \'sīt-ə-ˌsēn\ *n* : a base regularly present in DNA and RNA

CZ *abbr* Canal Zone

czar \'zär\ *n* **1** : the ruler of Russia until the 1917 revolution **2** : one having great power or authority ⟨baseball *czar*⟩ — **czar·dom** \'zärd-əm\ *n*

cza·ri·na \zä-'rē-nə\ *n* **1** : the wife of a czar **2** : a woman who has the rank of czar in her own right

Czech \'chek\ *n* **1** : CZECHOSLOVAK; *esp* : a native or inhabitant of Bohemia, Moravia, or Silesia **2** : the Slavic language of the Czechs — **Czech** *adj*

Czecho·slo·vak \ˌchek-ə-'slō-ˌväk, -ˌvak\ *or* **Czecho·slo·va·ki·an** \-slō-'väk-ē-ən, -'vak-\ *adj* : of, relating to, or characteristic of Czechoslovakia or its people — **Czechoslovak** *or* **Czechoslovakian** *n*

C

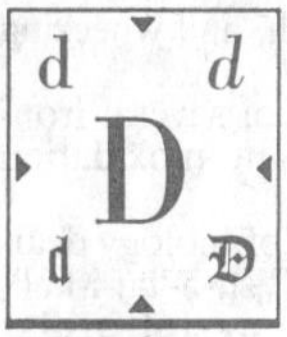

d \'dē\ *n, often cap* **1** : the 4th letter of the English alphabet **2** : the roman numeral 500 **3** : the musical tone D **4** : a grade rating a student's work as poor
d *abbr* **1** daughter **2** day **3** density **4** died **5** pence **6** penny
D *abbr* **1** Democrat **2** Democratic **3** diameter **4** doctor
DA *abbr* district attorney
1**dab** \'dab\ *n* **1** : a sudden blow or thrust : POKE **2** : a gentle touch or stroke : PAT
2**dab** *vb* **dabbed**; **dab·bing** **1** : to strike or touch lightly ⟨*dabs* at her eyes with a handkerchief⟩ **2** : to apply lightly or irregularly : DAUB — **dab·ber** *n*
3**dab** *n* **1** : DAUB **2** : a small amount ⟨just a *dab* more ice cream⟩
4**dab** *n* : FLATFISH; *esp* : any of several flounders
dab·ble \'dab-əl\ *vb* **dab·bled**; **dab·bling** \-(ə-)ling\ **1** : to wet by splashing : SPATTER **2 a** : to paddle or play in or as if in water **b** : to reach with the bill to the bottom of shallow water to obtain food **3** : to work or concern oneself lightly or superficially — **dab·bler** \-(ə-)lər\ *n*
da ca·po \dä-'käp-ō\ *adv or adj* : from the beginning — used as a direction in music to repeat
dace \'dās\ *n, pl* **dace** : any of various No. American freshwater fishes related to the carp
dachs·hund \'däks-ˌhu̇nt\ *n* [from German, meaning literally "badger dog"] : a small long-bodied short-legged droopy-eared dog of a breed of German origin

dachshund

dac·tyl \'dak-təl\ *n* [from Greek *daktylos* "finger", used in Greek also for a metrical foot of one long syllable followed by two shorts thus resembling the three joints of a finger] : a metrical foot consisting of one accented syllable followed by two unaccented syllables (as in *tenderly*) — **dac·tyl·ic** \dak-'til-ik\ *adj*
dad \'dad\ *n* : FATHER
dad·dy \'dad-ē\ *n, pl* **daddies** : FATHER
dad·dy long·legs \ˌdad-ē-'lo̊ng-ˌlegz\ *n* : any of various arachnids that resemble true spiders but have a small rounded body and very long slender legs
da·do \'dād-ō\ *n, pl* **dadoes** **1** : the part of a pedestal of a column between the base and the top moldings **2** : the lower part of an interior wall when specially decorated or faced
daemon *var of* DEMON
daf·fo·dil \'daf-ə-ˌdil\ *n* [originally applied to the asphodel, and probably borrowed from Dutch *de affodil* "the asphodel"] : any of a genus of bulbous herbs with long slender leaves and yellow, white, or pinkish flowers borne in spring; *esp* : one with petals whose inner parts are arranged to form a trumpet-shaped tube — compare JONQUIL

ə abut ər further a back ā bake
ä cot, cart au̇ out ch chin e less ē easy
g gift i trip ī life j joke ng sing ō flow
o̊ flaw o̊i coin th thin th this ü loot
u̇ foot y yet yü few yu̇ furious zh vision

daf·fy \'daf-ē\ *adj* **daf·fi·er**; **-est** : CRAZY, FOOLISH
daft \'daft\ *adj* **1** : SILLY, FOOLISH **2** : MAD, INSANE — **daft·ly** *adv* — **daft·ness** \'daf(t)-nəs\ *n*
dag *abbr* dekagram
dag·ger \'dag-ər\ *n* **1** : a short weapon for stabbing **2** : a character † used as a reference mark or to indicate a death date
da·guerre·o·type \də-'ger-(ē-)ə-ˌtīp\ *n* : an early photograph produced on a silver or a silver-covered copper plate; *also* : the process of producing such pictures
dahl·ia \'dal-yə, 'däl-\ *n* : any of a genus of American herbs related to the daisies and having opposite pinnate leaves, bright-rayed flower heads, and a tuberous root
1**dai·ly** \'dā-lē\ *adj* **1 a** : occurring, done, produced, or used every day or every weekday ⟨*daily* newspaper⟩ **b** : of or relating to every day ⟨*daily* visitor⟩ **2** : computed in terms of one day ⟨*daily* wages⟩ — **daily** *adv*
2**daily** *n, pl* **dailies** : a newspaper published every weekday
1**dain·ty** \'dānt-ē\ *n, pl* **dainties** : something delicious to the taste : DELICACY
2**dainty** *adj* **dain·ti·er**; **-est** **1** : TASTY, DELICIOUS **2** : delicately pretty ⟨a *dainty* flower⟩ **3 a** : having or showing delicate or finical taste **b** : FASTIDIOUS ⟨a *dainty* eater⟩ — **dain·ti·ly** \'dānt-ə-lē\ *adv* — **dain·ti·ness** \'dānt-ē-nəs\ *n*
dai·qui·ri \'dī-kə-rē\ *n* : a cocktail made of rum, lime juice, and sugar
dairy \'de(ə)r-ē\ *n, pl* **dair·ies** **1** : a place where milk is kept and butter or cheese is made **2** : a farm devoted to the production of milk — called also *dairy farm* **3** : an establishment for the sale or distribution of milk and milk products
dairy cattle *n* : cattle raised esp. to produce milk
dairy·ing \'der-ē-ing\ *n* : the business of operating a dairy
dairy·maid \-ē-ˌmād\ *n* : a woman employed in a dairy
dairy·man \-ē-mən, -ˌman\ *n* : a person who operates a dairy farm or works in a dairy
da·is \'dā-əs\ *n* : a raised platform in a hall or large room
dai·sy \'dā-zē\ *n, pl* **daisies** [from Old English *dægesēage*, meaning literally "day's eye"] **1** : any of numerous composite plants having flower heads with well-developed ray flowers usu. in one or a few whorls: as **a** : a low-growing European herb with white or pink ray flowers **b** : a tall leafy-stemmed American wild flower with yellow disk and long white ray flowers **2** : the flower head of a daisy
Da·ko·ta \də-'kōt-ə\ *n* : a member of a Siouan Amerindian people of the northern Mississippi valley
dal *abbr* dekaliter
dale \'dāl\ *n* : VALLEY
dal·li·ance \'dal-ē-ən(t)s\ *n* **1** : PLAY; *esp* : FLIRTATION **2** : frivolous action : TRIFLING
dal·ly \'dal-ē\ *vb* **dal·lied**; **dal·ly·ing** **1** : to act playfully : TRIFLE **2 a** : to waste time ⟨*dally* at one's work⟩ **b** : LINGER, DAWDLE ⟨*dally* on the way home⟩ — **dal·li·er** *n*
dal·ma·tian \dal-'mā-shən\ *n, often cap* : one of a breed of dogs that have a white short-haired coat with black or brown spots
dal se·gno \däl-'sān-yō\ *adv* — used as a direction in music to return to the sign that marks the beginning of a repeat
Dal·ton's atomic model \'do̊l-tənz-\ *n* : ATOMIC THEORY 1

[1]**dam** \'dam\ *n* : a female parent — used esp. of a domestic animal

[2]**dam** *n* **1** : a barrier preventing the flow of water **2** : a body of water confined by a dam

[3]**dam** *vb* **dammed**; **dam·ming** **1** : to provide or restrain with a dam ⟨*dam* a stream⟩ **2** : to stop up : BLOCK ⟨*dammed*-up feelings⟩

dam *abbr* dekameter

[1]**dam·age** \'dam-ij\ *n* **1** : a loss or harm resulting from injury to person, property, or reputation **2** *pl* : compensation in money imposed by law for loss or injury

[2]**damage** *vb* : to cause damage to

dam·ask \'dam-əsk\ *n* **1** : a firm lustrous reversible figured fabric used esp. for household linen **2** : a tough steel having decorative wavy lines — **damask** *adj*

dame \'dām\ *n* [from Old French, from Latin *domina* "mistress", feminine of *dominus* "master"; compare [1]DON] **1** : a woman of rank, station, or authority: as **a** *archaic* : the mistress of a household **b** : the wife or daughter of a lord **c** : a female member of an order of knighthood — used as a title prefixed to the given name **2** *slang* : WOMAN

[1]**damn** \'dam\ *vb* **1** : to condemn to a punishment or fate; *esp* : to condemn to hell **2** : to condemn as bad or as a failure **3** : to swear at : CURSE — **damn·ing·ly** \'dam-ing-lē\ *adv*

[2]**damn** *n* **1** : the utterance of the word *damn* as a curse **2** : something of little value ⟨not worth a *damn*⟩

dam·na·ble \'dam-nə-bəl\ *adj* **1** : liable to or deserving condemnation ⟨*damnable* conduct⟩ **2** : very bad : EXECRABLE ⟨*damnable* weather⟩ — **dam·na·bly** \-blē\ *adv*

dam·na·tion \dam-'nā-shən\ *n* **1** : the act of damning **2** : the state of being damned

[1]**damp** \'damp\ *n* **1** : a harmful gas esp. in a coal mine **2** : MOISTURE, HUMIDITY **3** : DISCOURAGEMENT, CHECK

[2]**damp** *vb* **1 a** : DEPRESS, DEJECT ⟨failure *damped* his spirits⟩ **b** : RESTRAIN, CHECK ⟨*damp* down a furnace⟩ ⟨*damp* his enthusiasm⟩ **c** : to check the vibration or oscillation of (as a piano string) **2** : DAMPEN

[3]**damp** *adj* : slightly wet ***syn*** see MOIST — **damp·ness** *n*

damp·en \'dam-pən\ *vb* **damp·ened**; **damp·en·ing** \'damp-(ə-)ning\ **1** : to check or diminish in activity or vigor : DEADEN **2** : to make or become damp — **damp·en·er** \'damp-(ə-)nər\ *n*

damp·er \'dam-pər\ *n* : one that damps ⟨put a *damper* on the celebration⟩: as **a** : a valve or plate (as in the flue of a furnace) for regulating the draft **b** : a device (as one of the felt-covered pieces of wood in a piano) used to deaden vibrations or oscillations

dam·sel \'dam-zəl\ *or* **dam·o·sel** *or* **dam·o·zel** \'dam-ə-zel\ *n* [from Old French *dameisele*, a diminutive of *dame* "lady"] : GIRL, MAIDEN

dam·sel·fly \'dam-zəl-ˌflī\ *n* : any of a group of insects that are closely related to the dragonflies, have laterally projecting eyes, and fold the wings above the body when at rest

Dan *abbr* Danish

[1]**dance** \'dan(t)s\ *vb* **1** : to engage in or perform a dance **2** : to move quickly up and down or about **3** : to perform or take part in as a dancer — **danc·er** *n*

[2]**dance** *n* **1** : an act or instance of dancing **2** : a series of rhythmic and patterned bodily movements usu. performed to music **3** : a social gathering for dancing **4** : a piece of music by which dancing may be guided **5** : the art of dancing

dan·de·li·on \'dan-də-ˌlī-ən\ *n* [from French *dent de lion*, meaning literally "lion's tooth"; so called from the shape of its leaves] **1** : any of a genus of yellow-flowered weedy plants related to chicory; *esp* : one with long deeply toothed stemless leaves sometimes grown as a potherb **2** : a flower of a dandelion

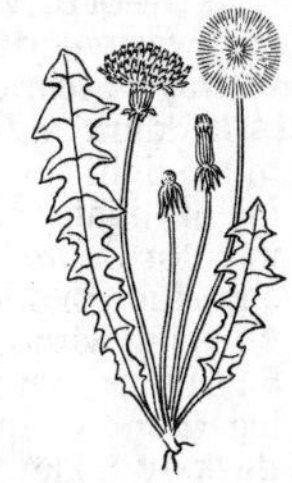

dandelion

dan·der \'dan-dər\ *n* : ANGER, TEMPER ⟨got his *dander* up⟩

dan·dle \'dan-dəl\ *vb* **dan·dled**; **dan·dling** \-d(ə-)ling\ **1** : to move up and down in one's arms or on one's knee in affectionate play **2** : PAMPER, PET

dan·druff \'dan-drəf\ *n* : a thin whitish flaky crust that forms on the scalp and is shed as scales — **dan·druffy** \-drə-fē\ *adj*

dan·dy \'dan-dē\ *n, pl* **dandies** **1** : a man markedly attentive to dress **2** : something excellent in its class — **dandy** *adj* — **dan·dy·ish** \-dē-ish\ *adj*

Dane \'dān\ *n* **1** : a native or inhabitant of Denmark **2** : a person of Danish descent

dan·ger \'dān-jər\ *n* **1** : exposure or liability to injury, harm, or evil **2** : something that may cause injury or harm ⟨the *dangers* of the jungle⟩

syn DANGER, PERIL, HAZARD, RISK mean a threat of loss, injury, or death. DANGER may suggest a threat constantly in prospect; PERIL is likely to suggest an immediate and fearful danger; HAZARD implies danger from a chance occurrence; RISK implies danger following on a chance voluntarily taken ***ant*** security

dan·ger·ous \'dānj-(ə-)rəs\ *adj* **1** : exposing to or involving danger ⟨a *dangerous* mission⟩ **2** : able or likely to inflict injury ⟨*dangerous* weapons⟩ — **dan·ger·ous·ly** *adv* — **dan·ger·ous·ness** *n*

dan·gle \'dang-gəl\ *vb* **dan·gled**; **dan·gling** \-g(ə-)ling\ **1** : to hang loosely esp. with a swinging motion **2** : to be a hanger-on or dependent **3** : to be left without proper grammatical connection in a sentence ⟨a *dangling* participle⟩ **4** : to cause to dangle : SWING — **dan·gler** \-g(ə-)lər\ *n*

Dan·iel \'dan-yəl\ *n* — see BIBLE table

[1]**Dan·ish** \'dā-nish\ *adj* : of, relating to, or characteristic of Denmark, the Danes, or Danish

[2]**Danish** *n* : the Germanic language of the Danes

dank \'dangk\ *adj* : unpleasantly moist or wet ***syn*** see MOIST — **dank·ly** *adv* — **dank·ness** *n*

dan·seuse \dän-'sə(r)z, -'süz\ *n* : a female ballet dancer

daph·nia \'daf-nē-ə\ *n* : any of a genus of tiny freshwater crustaceans : WATER FLEA

dap·per \'dap-ər\ *adj* **1** : being neat and trim in dress or appearance : SPRUCE **2** : being alert and lively in movement and manners

[1]**dap·ple** \'dap-əl\ *n* **1** : a dappled state **2** : a dappled animal

[2]**dapple** *vb* **dap·pled**; **dap·pling** \-(ə-)ling\ : to mark or become marked with numerous usu. cloudy and rounded spots of color or shade different from their background ⟨a *dappled* horse⟩

[1]**dare** \'da(ə)r, 'de(ə)r\ *vb* **1 a** : to have sufficient courage : be bold enough to ⟨try it if you *dare*⟩ **b** — used as an auxiliary verb ⟨no one *dared* say a word⟩ **2** : to challenge to perform an action esp. as a proof of courage ⟨I *dare* you⟩ **3** : to confront boldly ⟨*dared* the dangerous crossing⟩

[2]**dare** *n* : an act or instance of daring : CHALLENGE ⟨dived from the bridge on a *dare*⟩

D

dare·dev·il \'da(ə)r-ˌdev-əl, 'de(ə)r-\ *n* : a recklessly bold person — **daredevil** *adj*

1**dar·ing** \'da(ə)r-ing, 'de(ə)r-\ *adj* : ready to take risks : BOLD, VENTURESOME ***syn*** see ADVENTUROUS ***ant*** wary — **dar·ing·ly** \-ing-lē\ *adv*

2**daring** *n* : fearless boldness

1**dark** \'därk\ *adj* **1 a** : being without light or without much light ⟨in winter it gets *dark* early⟩ **b** : not giving off light ⟨the *dark* side of the moon⟩ **2** : not light in color ⟨a *dark* suit⟩ ⟨*dark* blue⟩ **3** : not bright and cheerful : GLOOMY ⟨look on the *dark* side of things⟩ **4** : being without knowledge and culture : IGNORANT **5** : SILENT, SECRETIVE **6** : not clear to the understanding ⟨*dark* sayings⟩ — **dark·ish** \'där-kish\ *adj* — **dark·ly** \-klē\ *adv* — **dark·ness** \'därk-nəs\ *n*

2**dark** *n* **1 a** : absence of light : DARKNESS **b** : a place or time of little or no light : NIGHT, NIGHTFALL ⟨get home before *dark*⟩ **2** : a dark or deep color

Dark Ages *n pl* : the period from about A.D. 476 to about 1000; *also* : MIDDLE AGES

dark·en \'där-kən\ *vb* **dark·ened**; **dark·en·ing** \'därk-(ə-)ning\ **1** : to make or grow dark or darker ⟨the sky *darkened*⟩ **2** : to make or become gloomy or forbidding ⟨his face *darkened* in anger⟩ — **dark·en·er** \'därk-(ə-)nər\ *n*

dark horse *n* : a contestant or a political figure whose abilities and chances as a contender are not known ⟨the convention nominated a *dark horse*⟩

dark lantern *n* : a lantern with an opening that can be closed to conceal the light

dark·ling \'där-kling\ *adj* **1** : DARK ⟨a *darkling* plain⟩ **2** : MYSTERIOUS ⟨*darkling* secrets⟩

dark·room \'därk-ˌrüm, -ˌru̇m\ *n* : a room protected from rays of light harmful in the process of developing sensitive photographic plates and film

dark·some \'därk-səm\ *adj* : gloomily somber : DARK

1**dar·ling** \'där-ling\ *n* **1** : a dearly loved person **2** : FAVORITE

2**darling** *adj* **1** : dearly loved : FAVORITE **2** : very pleasing : CHARMING

1**darn** \'därn\ *vb* : to mend with interlacing stitches ⟨*darn* socks⟩

2**darn** *n* : a place that has been darned

3**darn** *vb* : DAMN — **darn** \'därn\ *or* **darned** \'därn(d)\ *adj or adv*

4**darn** *n* : 2DAMN 2 ⟨not worth a *darn*⟩

dar·nel \'därn-əl\ *n* : any of several usu. weedy grasses with bristly flower clusters

darning needle *n* **1** : a long needle with a large eye for use in darning **2** : DRAGONFLY, DAMSELFLY

1**dart** \'därt\ *n* **1 a** : a small missile usu. pointed at one end and feathered on the other **b** *pl* : a game in which darts are thrown at a target **2** : something causing a sudden pain **3** : a stitched tapering fold in a garment **4** : a quick movement

2**dart** *vb* **1** : to throw with a sudden movement **2** : to thrust or move suddenly or rapidly ⟨the toad *darted* its tongue at a fly⟩ ⟨*darted* through the traffic⟩

Dar·win·ian \där-'win-ē-ən\ *adj* : of or relating to Charles Darwin, his theories, or his followers — **Darwinian** *n*

Dar·win·ism \'där-wə-ˌniz-əm\ *n* : a theory explaining the origin and perpetuation of new kinds of animals and plants by means of natural selection operating on chance variations — **Dar·win·ist** \-wə-nəst\ *n* — **darwinist** *or* **dar·win·is·tic** \ˌdär-wə-'nis-tik\ *adj, often cap* — **dar·win·is·ti·cal·ly** \-ti-k(ə-)lē\ *adv, often cap*

Dar·win's finches \ˌdär-wənz-\ *n pl* : finches (as the ground finches) of the Galapagos Islands that differ strikingly in size and shape of bill among the various species and were studied by Darwin prior to his discovery of the theory of evolution

DAS *abbr* dekastere

1**dash** \'dash\ *vb* **1** : to knock, hurl, or thrust violently ⟨the storm *dashed* the boat against a reef⟩ **2** : to break by striking or knocking ⟨*dashed* a plate against the wall⟩ **3** : SPLASH, SPATTER **4** : DESTROY, RUIN ⟨*dash* one's hopes⟩ **5** : to affect by mixing in something different ⟨*dashed* with vinegar⟩ **6** : to perform or finish hastily ⟨*dash* off a letter⟩ **7** : to move with sudden speed ⟨*dashed* upstairs⟩ — **dash·er** *n*

2**dash** *n* **1** : a sudden burst or splash ⟨a *dash* of cold water⟩ **2 a** : a stroke of a pen **b** : a punctuation mark — used chiefly to indicate a break in the thought or structure of a sentence **3** : a small usu. distinctive addition ⟨add a *dash* of salt⟩ **4** : animation in style and action ⟨a man of *dash* and vigor⟩ **5 a** : a sudden rush or attempt ⟨made a *dash* for the exit⟩ **b** : a short fast race **6** : a long click or buzz forming a letter or part of a letter (as in the Morse code) **7** : DASHBOARD 2

dash·board \'dash-ˌbōrd, -ˌbȯrd\ *n* **1** : a screen on the front of a vehicle (as a carriage) to keep out water, mud, or snow **2** : a panel extending across an automobile or airplane below the windshield and usu. containing dials and controls

dashed *adj* : made up of a series of dashes

da·shi·ki \də-'shē-kē\ *n* : a usu. brightly colored one-piece pullover garment worn esp. by men

dash·ing *adj* **1** : marked by vigorous action ⟨a *dashing* attack⟩ **2** : marked by smartness esp. in dress and manners ⟨made a *dashing* appearance⟩ — **dash·ing·ly** \-ing-lē\ *adv*

das·tard \'das-tərd\ *n* : COWARD; *esp* : one who sneakily commits malicious acts — **das·tard·li·ness** *n* — **das·tard·ly** \-lē\ *adj*

da·ta \'dāt-ə, 'dat-, 'dät-\ *n sing or pl* **1** : factual information (as measurements or statistics) **2** : DATUM

1**date** \'dāt\ *n* [from Old French, from Latin *dactylus*, from Greek *daktylos* meaning literally "finger"] : the oblong edible fruit of a tall Old World palm; *also* : this palm

2**date** *n* [from French, from Latin *data* "given", found in such phrases as *data Romae* "given at Rome" used in dating letters] **1 a** : the time at which an event occurs **b** : a statement giving the time of execution or making (as of a coin or check) **2** : DURATION **3** : the period of time to which something belongs **4 a** : APPOINTMENT; *esp* : a social engagement between two persons of opposite sex **b** : a person of the opposite sex with whom one has a social engagement — **to date** : up to the present moment ⟨have received no complaints *to date*⟩

3**date** *vb* **1** : to record the date of or on ⟨*date* a letter⟩ **2** : to mark or determine the date, age, or period of ⟨the architecture *dates* the house⟩ ⟨*dating* geological periods⟩ **3** : to make or have a date with ⟨*dated* only older men⟩ **4 a** : ORIGINATE ⟨*dates* from the sixth century⟩ **b** : EXTEND ⟨*dating* back to childhood⟩ **5** : to show qualities typical of a past period ⟨such formality is *dated*⟩ — **dat·a·ble** *or* **date·a·ble** \'dāt-ə-bəl\ *adj* — **dat·er** *n*

date·less \'dāt-ləs\ *adj* **1** : ENDLESS **2** : having no date **3** : too ancient to be dated **4** : TIMELESS

da·tive \'dāt-iv\ *adj* : of, relating to, or being the grammatical case that marks typically the indirect object of a verb or the object of some prepositions — **dative** *n*

da·tum \'dāt-əm, 'dat-, 'dät-\ *n, pl* **da·ta** \-ə\ *or* **datums** : a single piece of data : FACT

1**daub** \'dȯb, 'däb\ *vb* **1** : to cover with soft adhesive matter : PLASTER **2** : SMEAR, SMUDGE **3** : to apply coloring material crudely to — **daub·er** *n*

2**daub** *n* **1** : something daubed on : SMEAR **2** : a crude picture

1**daugh·ter** \'dȯt-ər\ *n* **1 a** : a female offspring esp. of human beings **b** : a human female having a specified ancestor or belonging to a group of common ancestry **2** : something derived from its origin as if feminine — **daugh·ter·ly** \-lē\ *adj*

2**daughter** *adj* **1** : having the characteristics or relationship of a daughter ⟨*daughter* cities⟩ **2** : being first generation offspring ⟨*daughter* cell⟩

daugh·ter–in–law \'dȯt-ə-rən-ˌlȯ, -ərn-ˌlȯ\ *n, pl* **daugh·ters–in–law** \-ər-zən-\ : the wife of one's son

daunt \'dȯnt, 'dänt\ *vb* : to lessen the courage of : make afraid

daunt·less \-ləs\ *adj* : FEARLESS, UNDAUNTED — **daunt·less·ly** *adv* — **daunt·less·ness** *n*

dau·phin \'dȯ-fən\ *n, often cap* : the eldest son of a king of France

dav·en·port \'dav-ən-ˌpōrt, -ˌpȯrt\ *n* : a large upholstered sofa

da·vit \'dā-vət, 'dav-ət\ *n* : one of a pair of posts with curved arms fitted with ropes and pulleys used esp. on ships for raising and lowering small boats

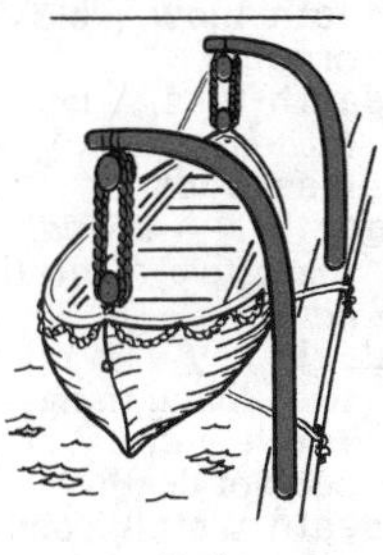

davit

Da·vy Jones's locker \ˌdā-vē-ˌjōnz(-əz)-\ *n* : the bottom of the sea

daw \'dȯ\ *n* : JACKDAW

daw·dle \'dȯd-əl\ *vb* **daw·dled**; **daw·dling** \-(ə-)liŋ\ **1** : to spend time wastefully or idly : LINGER ⟨*dawdled* over her homework⟩ **2** : LOITER ⟨*dawdles* on the way home⟩ **3** : IDLE ⟨*dawdle* the time away⟩ — **daw·dler** \-(ə-)lər\ *n*

1**dawn** \'dȯn, 'dän\ *vb* **1** : to begin to grow light as the sun rises ⟨waited for the day to *dawn*⟩ **2** : to begin to appear or develop ⟨the space age *dawned* with the first sputnik⟩ **3** : to begin to be perceived or understood ⟨the solution *dawned* on him⟩

2**dawn** *n* **1** : the first appearance of light in the morning **2** : a first appearance : BEGINNING ⟨the *dawn* of a new era⟩

day \'dā\ *n* **1 a** : the time of light between one night and the next **b** : DAYLIGHT **2** : the time the earth takes to make one turn on its axis **3** : a period of 24 hours beginning at midnight **4** : a specified day or date ⟨the *day* of the picnic⟩ ⟨their wedding *day*⟩ **5** : a specified time or period : AGE ⟨in grandfather's *day*⟩ **6** : the conflict or contention of the day ⟨played hard and carried the *day*⟩ **7** : the time set apart by usage or law for work ⟨the 8-hour *day*⟩

day·bed \'dā-ˌbed\ *n* : a couch with low head and foot pieces

day·break \-ˌbrāk\ *n* : DAWN

day coach *n* : COACH 1b

1**day·dream** \'dā-ˌdrēm\ *n* : a dreamy sequence of usu. happy or pleasant imaginings about oneself or one's future

2**daydream** *vb* : to have a daydream — **day·dream·er** *n*

day laborer *n* : one who works by the day or for daily wages esp. as an unskilled laborer

day·light \'dā-ˌlīt\ *n* **1** : the light of day **2** : DAWN **3** : completion of a problem or task ⟨began to see *daylight* on the problem⟩

daylight saving time *n* : time usu. one hour ahead of standard time — called also *daylight time*

day lily *n* : any of various Eurasian plants that have short-lived flowers resembling lilies and are widespread in cultivation and as escapes

Day of Atonement : YOM KIPPUR

day·star \'dā-ˌstär\ *n* : MORNING STAR

day·time \-ˌtīm\ *n* : the period of daylight

1**daze** \'dāz\ *vb* **1** : to stupefy esp. by a blow : STUN **2** : to dazzle with light

2**daze** *n* : the state of being dazed

daz·zle \'daz-əl\ *vb* **daz·zled**; **daz·zling** \-(ə-)liŋ\ **1** : to overpower with light ⟨the desert sunlight *dazzled* him⟩ **2** : to impress greatly or confound with brilliance ⟨*dazzled* the crowds with his oratory⟩ — **dazzle** *n* — **daz·zler** \-(ə-)lər\ *n* — **daz·zling·ly** \-(ə-)liŋ-lē\ *adv*

db *abbr* decibel

dbl *abbr* double

DC *abbr* **1** da capo **2** direct current **3** District of Columbia

DDS *abbr* **1** doctor of dental science **2** doctor of dental surgery

DDT \ˌdēd-(ˌ)ē-'tē\ *n* : a colorless odorless insecticide that is toxic to many higher animals

de- *prefix* **1 a** : do the opposite of ⟨*de*vitalize⟩ **b** : reverse of ⟨*de*-emphasis⟩ **2 a** : remove (a specified thing) from ⟨*de*louse⟩ **b** : remove from (a specified thing) ⟨*de*throne⟩ **3** : reduce ⟨*de*value⟩ **4** : get off of (a specified thing) ⟨*de*train⟩

DE *abbr* Delaware

dea·con \'dē-kən\ *n* [from Greek *diakonos*, meaning literally "a servant", "attendant"] **1** : a clergyman next below a priest **2** : a clergyman or layman in various Christian churches having specified functions — **dea·con·ess** \'dē-kə-nəs\ *n*

1**dead** \'ded\ *adj* **1** : deprived of life : having died : LIFELESS **2 a** : having the appearance of death : DEATHLY ⟨in a *dead* faint⟩ **b** : NUMB **c** : very tired **d** : UNRESPONSIVE ⟨*dead* to pity⟩ **e** : EXTINGUISHED ⟨*dead* coals⟩ **3 a** : INANIMATE, INERT ⟨*dead* matter⟩ **b** : no longer producing or functioning : EXHAUSTED ⟨*dead* battery⟩ **4 a** : no longer in use or effect : OBSOLETE ⟨*dead* language⟩ **b** : no longer active : EXTINCT ⟨*dead* volcano⟩ **c** : lacking in gaiety or animation ⟨*dead* party⟩ **d** : lacking in activity : QUIET **e** : lacking elasticity ⟨*dead* tennis ball⟩ **f** : being out of action or out of use ⟨a *dead* telephone line⟩ **g** : being out of play ⟨*dead* ball⟩ **5** : MUFFLED **6** : not running or circulating : STAGNANT ⟨*dead* air⟩ **7 a** : absolutely uniform ⟨*dead* level⟩ **b** : UNERRING, EXACT ⟨a *dead* shot⟩ ⟨*dead* center of the target⟩ **c** : being sudden and complete ⟨a *dead* stop⟩ **d** : COMPLETE, ABSOLUTE ⟨a *dead* loss⟩

2**dead** *n, pl* **dead** **1** : one that is dead — usu. used collectively ⟨the living and the *dead*⟩ **2** : the time of greatest quiet ⟨the *dead* of night⟩

3**dead** *adv* **1** : UTTERLY ⟨*dead* right⟩ **2** : suddenly and completely ⟨stopped *dead*⟩ **3** : DIRECTLY ⟨*dead* ahead⟩

dead–air space \ded-'a(ə)r-, -'e(ə)r-\ *n* : a sealed or unventilated air space

dead·beat \'ded-ˌbēt\ *n* : one who fails to pay his debts or his way

dead·en \'ded-ən\ *vb* **dead·ened**; **dead·en·ing**

D

\-(ə-)ning\ **1 :** to impair in vigor or sensation **:** BLUNT ⟨*deaden* pain with drugs⟩ **2 :** to make (as a wall) soundproof

dead end *n* **:** an end (as of a street) without an exit

dead–end \ˌded-ˌend\ *adj* **1 :** leading nowhere ⟨a *dead-end* job⟩ **2 :** TOUGH ⟨*dead-end* kids⟩

dead·eye \'ded-ˌī\ *n* **:** a rounded wood block pierced with holes to receive a lanyard that is used esp. to set up shrouds and stays

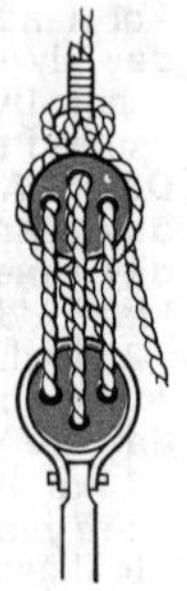

deadeye

dead heat *n* **:** a contest in which two or more contestants tie

dead letter *n* **1 :** something that has lost its force or authority without being formally abolished **2 :** a letter that is undeliverable and unreturnable by the post office

dead·line \'ded-ˌlīn\ *n* **:** a date or time before which something must be done

dead·lock \-ˌläk\ *n* **:** a stoppage of action because both sides in a struggle are equally powerful and neither will give in — **deadlock** *vb*

1**dead·ly** \'ded-lē\ *adj* **dead·li·er; -est** **1 :** likely to cause or capable of causing death ⟨a *deadly* weapon⟩ **2 a :** aiming to kill or destroy **:** IMPLACABLE ⟨a *deadly* enemy⟩ **b :** very accurate **:** UNERRING ⟨a *deadly* marksman⟩ **3 :** fatal to spiritual progress ⟨a *deadly* sin⟩ **4 :** very great **:** EXTREME ⟨a *deadly* bore⟩ — **dead·li·ness** *n*

2**deadly** *adv* **1 :** suggesting death ⟨*deadly* pale⟩ **2 :** EXTREMELY ⟨*deadly* dull⟩

deadly nightshade *n* **:** the belladonna plant

dead march *n* **:** a solemn march for a funeral

dead pan *n* **:** an expressionless immobile face — **dead·pan** \'ded-ˌpan\ *adj or adv*

dead reckoning *n* **:** the determination of the position of a ship or airplane by figuring the distances it has covered and the direction it has traveled without taking observations of celestial bodies

dead·weight \'ded-'wāt\ *n* **:** the full weight of an inert mass

dead·wood \-ˌwu̇d\ *n* **1 :** wood dead on the tree **2 :** useless personnel or material

deaf \'def\ *adj* **1 :** wholly or partly unable to hear **2 :** unwilling to hear or listen ⟨*deaf* to all suggestions⟩ — **deaf·ness** *n*

deaf·en \'def-ən\ *vb* **deaf·ened; deaf·en·ing** \-(ə-)ning\ **1 :** to make deaf **2 :** to stun with noise — **deaf·en·ing·ly** \-(ə-)ning-lē\ *adv*

deaf–mute \'def-ˌmyüt\ *n* **:** a deaf person who cannot speak or has not been taught to speak — **deaf–mute** *adj*

1**deal** \'dēl\ *n* **1 a :** an indefinite quantity or degree ⟨means a great *deal*⟩ **b :** a large quantity **2 a :** the act or right of distributing cards to players in a card game **b :** HAND 11b

2**deal** *vb* **dealt** \'delt\; **deal·ing** \'dē-ling\ **1 :** to give as one's portion **:** DISTRIBUTE ⟨*deal* out sandwiches⟩ ⟨*deal* the cards⟩ **2 :** ADMINISTER, BESTOW ⟨*dealt* him a blow⟩ **3 :** to have to do **:** TREAT ⟨the book *deals* with education⟩ **4 :** to take action ⟨*deal* with offenders⟩ **5 a :** to engage in bargaining **:** TRADE **b :** to sell or distribute something as a business ⟨*deals* in insurance⟩ — **deal·er** \'dē-lər\ *n*

3**deal** *n* **1 a :** an act of dealing **:** BARGAINING **b :** the result of bargaining **:** a mutual agreement ⟨make a *deal* for a used car⟩ **2 :** treatment received ⟨a dirty *deal*⟩ **3 :** a secret or underhand agreement **4 :** a purchase at a fair or very low price **:** BARGAIN ⟨a good *deal* in a new car⟩

4**deal** *n* **:** wood or a board of fir or pine — **deal** *adj*

deal·ing \'dē-ling\ *n* **1** *pl* **:** NEGOTIATIONS; *esp* **:** business transactions ⟨*dealings* with an automobile agency⟩ **2 :** a way of acting or of doing business ⟨fair in his *dealing*⟩

dean \'dēn\ *n* **1 :** the head of the chapter of a cathedral church **2 a :** the head of a division, faculty, college, or school of a university **b :** a college or secondary school administrator in charge of students or instruction **3 :** the senior member of a group ⟨the *dean* of the diplomatic corps⟩ — **dean·ship** \-ˌship\ *n*

1**dear** \'di(ə)r\ *adj* **1 :** highly valued **:** PRECIOUS **2 —** used as a form of address in letters and sometimes in speech ⟨*Dear* Sir⟩ **3 :** high-priced **:** EXPENSIVE **4 :** HEARTFELT ⟨my *dearest* wish⟩ — **dear** *adv* — **dear·ly** *adv* — **dear·ness** *n*

2**dear** *n* **:** a loved one **:** DARLING

dearth \'dərth\ *n* **:** SCARCITY, LACK

death \'deth\ *n* **1 :** a permanent cessation of all vital functions **:** the end of life **2 :** the cause of loss of life **3** *cap* **:** the destroyer of life represented usu. as a skeleton with a scythe **4 :** the state of being dead **5 :** DESTRUCTION, EXTINCTION — **death·like** \-ˌlīk\ *adj*

death·bed \-'bed\ *n* **1 :** the bed in which a person dies **2 :** the last hours of life

death·blow \-'blō\ *n* **:** a destructive or killing stroke or event

death·less \-ləs\ *adj* **:** IMMORTAL, IMPERISHABLE ⟨*deathless* fame⟩ — **death·less·ly** *adv* — **death·less·ness** *n*

death·ly \-lē\ *adj* **1 :** FATAL **2 :** of, relating to, or suggestive of death ⟨a *deathly* pallor⟩ — **deathly** *adv*

death ray *n* **:** a ray (as of radiant energy) able to destroy living things

death's–head \'deths-ˌhed\ *n* **:** a human skull symbolic of death

death·watch \'deth-ˌwäch\ *n* **:** a vigil kept with the dead or dying

deb \'deb\ *n* **:** DEBUTANTE

de·bar \di-'bär\ *vb* **:** to bar from having or doing something — **de·bar·ment** \-mənt\ *n*

de·bark \di-'bärk\ *vb* **:** DISEMBARK — **de·bar·ka·tion** \ˌdē-ˌbär-'kā-shən\ *n*

de·base \di-'bās\ *vb* **:** to lower in character, dignity, quality, or value — **de·base·ment** \-mənt\ *n* — **de·bas·er** *n*

de·bat·a·ble \di-'bāt-ə-bəl\ *adj* **:** open to question or dispute ⟨a *debatable* decision⟩

1**de·bate** \di-'bāt\ *n* **:** a verbal argument: as **a :** the formal discussion of a motion before a deliberative body **b :** a regulated discussion of a proposition between two matched sides

2**debate** *vb* **1 :** to discuss or examine a question often publicly by presenting and considering arguments on both sides **2 :** to take part in a debate **3 :** to present or consider the reasons for and against **:** CONSIDER *syn* see DISCUSS — **de·bat·er** *n*

1**de·bauch** \di-'bȯch, -'bäch\ *vb* **:** to lead away from virtue or morality **:** CORRUPT — **de·bauch·er** *n*

2**debauch** *n* **:** an act, occasion, or period of debauchery

de·bauch·ery \di-'bȯch-(ə-)rē, -'bäch-\ *n, pl* **-er·ies :** excessive indulgence in sensual pleasures

de·bil·i·tate \di-'bil-ə-ˌtāt\ *vb* **:** to impair the

strength of : WEAKEN — **de·bil·i·ta·tion** \-ˌbil-ə-ˈtā-shən\ *n*

de·bil·i·ty \di-ˈbil-ət-ē\ *n, pl* **-ties** : an infirm or weakened state

1**deb·it** \ˈdeb-ət\ *n* : an entry in an account representing an amount paid out or owed

2**debit** *vb* : to enter as a debit : charge with or as a debit

deb·o·nair \ˌdeb-ə-ˈna(ə)r, -ˈne(ə)r\ *adj* : gaily and gracefully charming ⟨a *debonair* manner⟩ — **deb·o·nair·ly** *adv* — **deb·o·nair·ness** *n*

de·brief \di-ˈbrēf, ˈdē-\ *vb* : to interrogate (as an astronaut back from a mission) in order to obtain useful information

de·bris \də-ˈbrē, ˈdā-ˌbrē\ *n, pl* **de·bris** \-ˈbrēz, -ˌbrēz\ **1** : the remains of something broken down or destroyed : RUINS **2** : an accumulation of fragments of rock

debt \ˈdet\ *n* [from Latin *debitum* "something owed", from the neuter of *debitus*, past participle of *debēre* "to owe"] **1** : SIN, TRESPASS **2** : something owed to another : a thing or amount due ⟨pay a *debt* of $10⟩ **3** : a condition of owing; *esp* : the state of owing money in amounts greater than one can pay ⟨hopelessly in *debt*⟩

debt·or \ˈdet-ər\ *n* **1** : SINNER **2** : one that owes a debt

de·bunk \(ˈ)dē-ˈbəngk\ *vb* : to expose the sham or falseness in — **de·bunk·er** *n*

de·but \ˈdā-ˌbyü, dā-ˈ\ *n* **1** : a first public appearance ⟨his *debut* as a pianist⟩ **2** : a formal entrance into society

deb·u·tante \ˈdeb-yu̇-ˌtänt\ *n* : a young woman making her debut

dec *abbr* decrease

Dec *abbr* December

deca- *or* **dec-** *or* **deka-** *or* **dek-** *comb form* : ten

dec·ade \ˈdek-ˌād, -əd; de-ˈkād\ *n* **1** : a group or set of 10 **2** : a period of 10 years **3** : a part of the rosary devoted to one sacred mystery and made up of ten Hail Marys preceded by the Lord's Prayer and followed by the Gloria Patri

dec·a·dence \ˈdek-əd-ən(t)s, di-ˈkād-ən(t)s\ *n* : the process of becoming or the quality or state of being in decline or decay — **dec·a·dent** \-ənt\ *adj* — **decadent** *n* — **dec·a·dent·ly** *adv*

dec·a·gon \ˈdek-ə-ˌgän\ *n* : a polygon of 10 angles and 10 sides

de·cal \ˈdē-ˌkal, di-ˈkal, ˈdek-əl\ *n* [short for earlier *decalcomania* which originally meant "the art of transferring pictures", taken from a French noun formed from *décalquer* "to copy by tracing" and *manie* "mania", "craze"] : a design made to be transferred (as to glass) from specially prepared paper

dec·a·logue \ˈdek-ə-ˌlȯg\ *n* **1** *cap* : TEN COMMANDMENTS **2** : a basic set of rules carrying binding authority

de·camp \di-ˈkamp\ *vb* **1** : to break up a camp **2** : to depart suddenly : ABSCOND ⟨*decamped* with the funds⟩ — **de·camp·ment** \-mənt\ *n*

de·cant \di-ˈkant\ *vb* **1** : to pour from one vessel into another **2** : to pour gently without disturbing any sediment ⟨*decant* wine⟩ — **de·can·ta·tion** \ˌdē-ˌkan-ˈtā-shən\ *n*

de·cant·er \di-ˈkant-ər\ *n* : an ornamental glass bottle used esp. for serving wine

de·cap·i·tate \di-ˈkap-ə-ˌtāt\ *vb* : to cut off the head of : BEHEAD — **de·cap·i·ta·tion** \-ˌkap-ə-ˈtā-shən\ *n*

de·cath·lon \di-ˈkath-lən\ *n* : an athletic contest in which each competitor participates in each of a series of 10 track-and-field events

1**de·cay** \di-ˈkā\ *vb* **1** : to decline in soundness, health, strength, or vigor **2** : to undergo or cause to undergo decomposition ⟨a radioactive element *decays*⟩ ⟨apples that *decayed* in storage⟩

2**decay** *n* **1** : gradual decline in strength, soundness, health, or vigor **2** : ROT **3** : spontaneous decrease in the number of radioactive atoms in radioactive material

de·cease \di-ˈsēs\ *n* : DEATH 1 — **decease** *vb*

de·ceased \-ˈsēst\ *n, pl* **deceased** : a dead person ⟨the will of the *deceased*⟩

de·ce·dent \di-ˈsēd-ənt\ *n* : a deceased person

de·ceit \di-ˈsēt\ *n* **1** : the act or practice of deceiving : DECEPTION **2** : an attempt or device to deceive : TRICK **3** : DECEITFULNESS

de·ceit·ful \-fəl\ *adj* **1** : practicing or tending to practice deceit **2** : showing or containing deceit or fraud : DECEPTIVE ⟨a *deceitful* answer⟩ — **de·ceit·ful·ly** \-fə-lē\ *adv* — **de·ceit·ful·ness** *n*

de·ceive \di-ˈsēv\ *vb* **1** : to cause to believe what is untrue : MISLEAD ⟨*deceived* his father about his real intentions⟩ **2** : to deal with dishonestly : CHEAT **3** : to use or practice deceit — **de·ceiv·er** *n* — **de·ceiv·ing·ly** \-ˈsē-ving-lē\ *adv*

de·cel·er·ate \(ˈ)dē-ˈsel-ə-ˌrāt\ *vb* : to move or cause to move at decreasing speed : slow down — **de·cel·er·a·tion** \(ˌ)dē-ˌsel-ə-ˈrā-shən\ *n* — **de·cel·er·a·tor** \(ˈ)dē-ˈsel-ə-ˌrāt-ər\ *n*

De·cem·ber \di-ˈsem-bər\ *n* [from Latin, originally the tenth month of the Roman year, from *decem* "ten"] : the 12th month of the year

de·cen·cy \ˈdē-sən-sē\ *n, pl* **-cies** **1 a** : the quality or state of being decent : PROPRIETY **b** : conformity to standards of taste, propriety, or quality **2** : standard of propriety — usu. used in pl.

de·cen·ni·al \di-ˈsen-ē-əl\ *adj* **1** : consisting of 10 years **2** : happening every 10 years ⟨*decennial* census⟩ — **decennial** *n* — **de·cen·ni·al·ly** \-ē-ə-lē\ *adv*

de·cent \ˈdē-sənt\ *adj* **1 a** : conforming to standards of propriety, good taste, or morality **b** : modestly clothed **2** : free from immodesty or obscenity **3** : fairly good : ADEQUATE ⟨*decent* housing⟩ — **de·cent·ly** *adv*

de·cen·tral·ize \(ˈ)dē-ˈsen-trə-ˌlīz\ *vb* **1** : to disperse or distribute among various regional or local authorities ⟨*decentralize* the administration of schools⟩ **2** : to cause to withdraw from urban centers to outlying areas ⟨*decentralize* industries⟩ — **de·cen·tral·i·za·tion** \(ˌ)dē-ˌsen-trə-lə-ˈzā-shən\ *n*

de·cep·tion \di-ˈsep-shən\ *n* **1 a** : the act of deceiving **b** : the fact or condition of being deceived **2** : something that deceives : TRICK

de·cep·tive \di-ˈsep-tiv\ *adj* : tending or having power to deceive — **de·cep·tive·ly** *adv* — **de·cep·tive·ness** *n*

deci- *comb form* : tenth part ⟨*decigram*⟩

dec·i·bel \ˈdes-ə-ˌbel, -bəl\ *n* : a unit for measuring the relative loudness of sounds — abbr. *db*

de·cide \di-ˈsīd\ *vb* **1** : to render a judgment on : SETTLE ⟨*decided* the case in favor of the defendant⟩ **2** : to bring to a definitive end ⟨one blow *decided* the fight⟩ **3** : to induce to come to a choice ⟨attractions that *decided* his mind⟩ **4** : to make a choice or judgment ⟨*decided* to go⟩ — **de·cid·a·ble** \-ˈsīd-ə-bəl\ *adj* — **de·cid·er** *n*

de·cid·ed \-ˈsīd-əd\ *adj* **1** : CLEAR, UNMISTAKABLE ⟨a *decided* smell of gas⟩ **2** : FIRM, DETERMINED ⟨a *decided* tone of voice⟩ — **de·cid·ed·ly** *adv* — **de·cid·ed·ness** *n*

de·cid·u·ous \di-ˈsij-ə-wəs\ *adj* **1** : falling off (as at the end of a growing period or stage of develop-

ment) ⟨antlers are *deciduous*⟩ **2** : having deciduous parts ⟨*deciduous* trees⟩
deciduous tooth *n* : MILK TOOTH
deci·gram \'des-ə-ˌgram\ *n* — see METRIC SYSTEM table
deci·li·ter \'des-ə-ˌlēt-ər\ *n* — see METRIC SYSTEM table
de·cil·lion \di-'sil-yən\ *n* — see NUMBER table
1dec·i·mal \'des-ə-məl\ *adj* **1** : numbered or proceeding by tens **2** : based on the number 10 ⟨a *decimal* system of currency⟩ **3** : expressed in a decimal fraction — **dec·i·mal·ly** \-mə-lē\ *adv*
2decimal *n* : a proper fraction in which the denominator is a power of 10 usu. not expressed but signified by a point placed at the left of the numerator (as .2 = $^2/_{10}$, .25 = $^{25}/_{100}$, .025 = $^{25}/_{1000}$)
decimal equivalent *n* : a number written as a decimal or as the combination of a whole number and a decimal ⟨3.25 is the *decimal equivalent* of 3¼⟩
decimal point *n* : the dot at the left of the decimal in a decimal fraction
dec·i·mate \'des-ə-ˌmāt\ *vb* **1** : to take or destroy the tenth part of **2** : to destroy a large part of ⟨a population *decimated* by an epidemic⟩ — **dec·i·ma·tion** \ˌdes-ə-'mā-shən\ *n*
deci·me·ter \'des-ə-ˌmēt-ər\ *n* — see METRIC SYSTEM table
de·ci·pher \(')dē-'sī-fər\ *vb* **1** : to convert into understandable form; *esp* : to translate from code **2** : to make out the meaning of despite indistinctness or obscurity ⟨*decipher* illegible handwriting⟩ — **de·ci·pher·a·ble** \-f(ə-)rə-bəl\ *adj* — **de·ci·pher·ment** \-fər-mənt\ *n*
de·ci·sion \di-'sizh-ən\ *n* **1** : the act or result of deciding ⟨the *decision* of the court⟩ **2** : promptness and firmness in deciding : DETERMINATION ⟨a man of courage and *decision*⟩
de·ci·sive \di-'sī-siv\ *adj* **1** : having the power to decide ⟨the *decisive* vote⟩ **2** : of such nature as to settle a question or dispute ⟨a *decisive* victory⟩ **3** : marked by or showing decision ⟨a *decisive* manner⟩ — **de·ci·sive·ly** *adv* — **de·ci·sive·ness** *n*
deci·stere \'des-ə-ˌsti(ə)r, -ˌste(ə)r\ *n* — see METRIC SYSTEM table
1deck \'dek\ *n* **1** : a platform extending from side to side in a ship forming a floor **2** : a flat structure resembling the deck of a ship **3** : a pack of playing cards — **on deck** : next in line
2deck *vb* **1 a** : to clothe elegantly : ARRAY ⟨*decked* out in a new suit⟩ **b** : DECORATE **2** : to furnish (as a ship) with a deck
deck·hand \'dek-ˌhand\ *n* : a seaman who performs manual duties
de·claim \di-'klām\ *vb* : to speak or deliver in the manner of a formal oration — **de·claim·er** *n* — **dec·la·ma·tion** \ˌdek-lə-'mā-shən\ *n* — **de·clam·a·to·ry** \di-'klam-ə-ˌtōr-ē, -ˌtȯr-\ *adj*
dec·la·ra·tion \ˌdek-lə-'rā-shən\ *n* **1** : the act of declaring : ANNOUNCEMENT **2** : something declared or a document containing such a declaration ⟨the *Declaration* of Independence⟩
de·clar·a·tive \di-'klar-ət-iv\ *adj* : making a declaration or statement ⟨*declarative* sentence⟩
de·clare \di-'kla(ə)r, -'kle(ə)r\ *vb* **1** : to make known formally or explicitly ⟨*declare* war⟩ **2** : to state emphatically : AFFIRM ⟨*declares* his innocence⟩ **3** : to make a full statement of (taxable or dutiable property) ⟨*declare* one's income⟩ — **de·clar·a·to·ry** \-'klar-ə-ˌtōr-ē, -ˌtȯr-\ *adj* — **declarer** *n*
de·clen·sion \di-'klen-chən\ *n* **1 a** : the giving of noun, adjective, or pronoun inflections esp. in prescribed order **b** : a class of nouns or adjectives having the same type of inflectional forms **2** : DECLINE, DETERIORATION **3** : DESCENT, SLOPE — **de·clen·sion·al** \-'klench-(ə-)nəl\ *adj*
dec·li·na·tion \ˌdek-lə-'nā-shən\ *n* **1** : angular distance north or south from the celestial equator measured along a great circle passing through the celestial poles ⟨the *declination* of a star⟩ **2** : a bending downward : INCLINATION **3** : a formal refusal **4** : the angle that the magnetic needle makes with a true north and south line
1de·cline \di-'klīn\ *vb* **1 a** : to slope downward : DESCEND **b** : to bend down ⟨*declined* his head⟩ **2** : to pass toward a lower level : RECEDE **3** : to draw to a close : WANE **4 a** : to refuse esp. politely to undertake, engage in, or comply with ⟨*declined* to run for a second term⟩ **b** : to refuse to accept ⟨*declined* the invitation⟩ **5** : to give the declension of a noun, pronoun, or adjective — **de·clin·a·ble** \-'klī-nə-bəl\ *adj*

syn DECLINE, REFUSE, REJECT mean to indicate unwillingness to go along with a demand or request. DECLINE suggests polite refusal; REFUSE suggests plainspoken emphatic denial; REJECT implies refusal even to consider a demand or request ***ant*** accept

2decline *n* **1** : the process of declining: **a** : a gradual sinking and wasting away **b** : a change to a lower state or level **2** : the time when something is approaching its end **3** : a downward slope
de·cliv·i·ty \di-'kliv-ət-ē\ *n, pl* **-ties** **1** : downward inclination **2** : a descending slope
de·code \(')dē-'kōd\ *vb* : to change (as a secret message) from code into ordinary language — **de·cod·er** *n*
de·col·or·ize \(')dē-'kəl-ə-ˌrīz\ *vb* : to remove color from
de·com·mis·sion \ˌdē-kə-'mish-ən\ *vb* : to take out of commission ⟨a *decommissioned* battleship⟩
de·com·pose \ˌdē-kəm-'pōz\ *vb* **1** : to separate a thing into its parts or into simpler compounds **2** : to break down through chemical change : ROT — **de·com·pos·a·ble** \-'pō-zə-bəl\ *adj* — **de·com·po·si·tion** \(ˌ)dē-ˌkäm-pə-'zish-ən\ *n*
de·com·pos·er \ˌdē-kəm-'pō-zər\ *n* : one that decomposes; *esp* : an organism (as a bacterium or a fungus) that lives on and decomposes dead organisms
de·com·press \ˌdē-kəm-'pres\ *vb* : to release (as a diver) from pressure or compression — **de·com·pres·sion** \-'presh-ən\ *n*
de·con·tam·i·nate \ˌdē-kən-'tam-ə-ˌnāt\ *vb* : to rid of contamination esp. that caused by chemical or biological warfare agents or radioactive material
dec·o·rate \'dek-ə-ˌrāt\ *vb* **1** : to make more attractive by adding something beautiful or becoming ⟨*decorate* a room⟩ **2** : to award a decoration of honor to ⟨*decorate* a soldier for bravery⟩
dec·o·ra·tion \ˌdek-ə-'rā-shən\ *n* **1** : the act or action of decorating **2** : something that adorns or beautifies : ORNAMENT ⟨Christmas tree *decorations*⟩ **3** : a badge of honor (as a medal, cross, or ribbon)
Decoration Day *n* : MEMORIAL DAY
dec·o·ra·tive \'dek-(ə-)rət-iv, 'dek-ə-ˌrāt-\ *adj* : serving to decorate : ORNAMENTAL — **dec·o·ra·tive·ly** *adv* — **dec·o·ra·tive·ness** *n*

dec·o·ra·tor \'dek-ə-ˌrāt-ər\ *n* : one that decorates; *esp* : a person who decorates the interiors of buildings

dec·o·rous \'dek-ə-rəs; di-'kōr-əs, -'kȯr-\ *adj* : marked by propriety and good taste : CORRECT ⟨*decorous* conduct⟩ — **dec·o·rous·ly** *adv* — **dec·o·rous·ness** *n*

de·co·rum \di-'kōr-əm, -'kȯr-\ *n* **1** : conformity to accepted standards of conduct : proper behavior ⟨social *decorum*⟩ **2** : ORDERLINESS ⟨disturb the *decorum* of the meeting⟩

1de·coy \di-'kȯi, 'dē-ˌ\ *n* [from Dutch *de kooi*, meaning literally "the cage"] **1** : something intended to lure into a trap; *esp* : an artificial bird used to attract live birds within shooting range **2** : a person used to lead another into a trap

2decoy *vb* : to lure by or as if by a decoy : ENTICE

1de·crease \di-'krēs, 'dē-ˌ\ *vb* : to grow or cause to grow less

2de·crease \'dē-ˌkrēs, di-'\ *n* **1** : a process of decreasing : DIMINISHING, LESSENING ⟨a *decrease* in accidents⟩ **2** : the amount by which a thing decreases ⟨a *decrease* of three dollars in wages⟩

1de·cree \di-'krē\ *n* : an order or decision given by one in authority

2decree *vb* **de·creed**; **de·cree·ing** : to command or order by decree

dec·re·ment \'dek-rə-mənt\ *n* : DECREASE

de·crep·it \di-'krep-ət\ *adj* : broken down with age : worn out

de·crep·i·tude \di-'krep-ə-ˌt(y)üd\ *n* : the quality or state of being decrepit : infirmity esp. from old age

decresc *abbr* decrescendo

1de·cre·scen·do \ˌdā-krə-'shen-dō\ *adv or adj* : with diminishing volume — used as a direction in music

2decrescendo *n, pl* **-dos** : a lessening in volume of sound

de·cry \di-'krī\ *vb* **1** : to speak slightingly of : BELITTLE ⟨*decry* a hero's deeds⟩ **2** : to find fault with : CONDEMN ⟨*decried* the waste of resources⟩ — **de·cri·er** \-'krī(-ə)r\ *n*

ded·i·cate \'ded-i-ˌkāt\ *vb* **1** : to set apart for some purpose and esp. a sacred or serious purpose : DEVOTE ⟨*dedicated* his life to helping others⟩ **2** : to address or inscribe as a compliment ⟨*dedicated* his book to his mother⟩ — **ded·i·ca·tor** \-ˌkāt-ər\ *n*

ded·i·ca·tion \ˌded-i-'kā-shən\ *n* **1 a** : an act or rite of dedicating to a divine being or to a sacred use **b** : a setting aside for a particular purpose **2** : the inscription dedicating a literary work **3** : self-sacrificing devotion — **ded·i·ca·tive** \'ded-i-ˌkāt-iv\ *adj* — **ded·i·ca·to·ry** \'ded-i-kə-ˌtōr-ē, -ˌtȯr-\ *adj*

de·duce \di-'d(y)üs\ *vb* **1** : to trace the course or derivation of **2 a** : to draw (a conclusion) necessarily from given premises **b** : to infer from a general principle — **de·duc·i·ble** \-'d(y)ü-sə-bəl\ *adj*

de·duct \di-'dəkt\ *vb* : to take away (an amount) from a total : SUBTRACT — **de·duct·i·ble** \-'dək-tə-bəl\ *adj*

de·duc·tion \di-'dək-shən\ *n* **1 a** : an act of taking away **b** : the deriving of a conclusion by reasoning; *esp* : inference in which the conclusion follows necessarily from the premises **2 a** : a conclusion reached by mental deduction **b** : something that is or may be subtracted ⟨*deductions* from taxable income⟩ — **de·duc·tive** \-'dək-tiv\ *adj* — **de·duc·tive·ly** *adv*

dee \'dē\ *n* : either of two hollow D-shaped metal electrodes in a cyclotron

1deed \'dēd\ *n* **1** : something that is done : ACT ⟨judge a person by his *deeds*⟩ **2** : a legal document by which one person transfers real property to another — **deed·less** \-ləs\ *adj*

2deed *vb* : to convey or transfer by deed

deem \'dēm\ *vb* : to have an opinion : BELIEVE, SUPPOSE ⟨*deemed* it wise to go slow⟩

1deep \'dēp\ *adj* **1 a** : extending far downward ⟨a *deep* well⟩ : having a great distance between the top and bottom surfaces ⟨*deep* water⟩ : not shallow **b** : extending well inward from an outer or front surface ⟨a *deep* gash⟩ **c** : extending far outward from a center ⟨*deep* space⟩ **d** : occurring or located near the outer limits ⟨*deep* right field⟩ **2** : having a specified extension downward or backward ⟨a shelf 20 inches *deep*⟩ **3 a** : difficult to understand ⟨a *deep* book⟩ **b** : MYSTERIOUS, OBSCURE ⟨a *deep* dark secret⟩ **c** : PROFOUND ⟨a *deep* thinker⟩ **d** : ENGROSSED, INVOLVED ⟨*deep* in thought⟩ **e** : INTENSE, HEAVY ⟨*deep* sleep⟩ **4 a** : dark and rich in color ⟨a *deep* red⟩ **b** : having a low musical pitch or range ⟨a *deep* voice⟩ **5 a** : coming from or situated well within ⟨a *deep* sigh⟩ ⟨a house *deep* in the forest⟩ **b** : covered, enclosed, or filled often to a specified degree ⟨knee-*deep* in water⟩ ⟨a road *deep* with snow⟩ — **deep·ly** *adv*

2deep *adv* **1** : to a great depth : DEEPLY **2** : far on : LATE ⟨*deep* in the night⟩

3deep *n* **1 a** : an extremely deep place or part (as of the ocean) **b** : OCEAN **2** : the middle or most intense part ⟨the *deep* of night⟩

deep-dish pie *n* : a pie baked in a deep dish and having no bottom crust

deep·en \'dē-pən\ *vb* **deep·ened**; **deep·en·ing** \'dēp-(ə-)ning\ : to make or become deep or deeper

deep-root·ed \'dēp-'rüt-əd, -'rut-\ *adj* : deeply implanted or established ⟨a *deep-rooted* loyalty⟩

deep-sea \ˌdēp-ˌsē\ *adj* : of, relating to, or occurring in the deeper parts of the sea

deep-seat·ed \'dēp-'sēt-əd\ *adj* **1** : situated far below the surface **2** : firmly established ⟨a *deep-seated* tradition⟩

deep-set \-'set\ *adj* : set far in ⟨*deep-set* eyes⟩

deep·wa·ter \ˌdēp-ˌwȯt-ər, -ˌwät-\ *adj* : of or relating to water of great depth; *esp* : DEEP-SEA ⟨*deepwater* sailors⟩

deer \'di(ə)r\ *n, pl* **deer** [from Old English *dēor*

deer: left, black-tailed deer; center, white-tailed deer; right, mule deer

meaning "wild animal", but later narrowed to denote the wild animal most familiar in England] : any of a family of cloven-hoofed cud-chewing mammals with antlers borne by the males of nearly all and by the females of a few forms

deer mouse *n* : any of numerous No. American field and woodland mice related to the hamsters

D

deer·skin \'di(ə)r-ˌskin\ *n* **1** : leather made from the skin of a deer **2** : a garment of deerskin

de–es·ca·late \(')dē-'es-kə-ˌlāt\ *vb* : to diminish in extent, volume, or scope : REDUCE ⟨*de-escalate* the war⟩ — **de–es·ca·la·tion** \(ˌ)dē-ˌes-kə-'lā-shən\ *n*

def *abbr* definition

de·face \di-'fās\ *vb* : to destroy or mar the face or surface of — **de·face·ment** \-'fās-mənt\ *n* — **de·fac·er** *n*

de·fal·cate \di-'fal-ˌkāt, -'fȯl-; 'def-əl-\ *vb* : to engage in embezzlement — **de·fal·ca·tion** \ˌdē-ˌfal-'kā-shən, -ˌfȯl-; ˌdef-əl-\ *n* — **de·fal·ca·tor** \-ˌkāt-ər\ *n*

de·fame \di-'fām\ *vb* : to injure or destroy the good name of : speak evil of : LIBEL — **def·a·ma·tion** \ˌdef-ə-'mā-shən\ *n* — **de·fam·a·to·ry** \di-'fam-ə-ˌtōr-ē, -ˌtȯr-\ *adj* — **de·fam·er** *n*

1**de·fault** \di-'fȯlt\ *n* : failure to do something required by law or duty

2**default** *vb* : to fail to carry out a contract, obligation, or duty — **de·fault·er** *n*

1**de·feat** \di-'fēt\ *vb* **1** : NULLIFY, FRUSTRATE **2** : to win a victory over : BEAT

2**defeat** *n* **1** : frustration by prevention of success ⟨*defeat* of one's hopes⟩ **2 a** : an overthrow of an army in battle **b** : loss of a contest (as by a team)

de·feat·ism \di-'fēt-ˌiz-əm\ *n* : an attitude of expecting the defeat of one's own cause or of accepting such defeat on the ground that further effort would be useless or unwise — **de·feat·ist** \-'fēt-əst\ *n or adj*

def·e·cate \'def-i-ˌkāt\ *vb* : to discharge feces from the bowels — **def·e·ca·tion** \ˌdef-i-'kā-shən\ *n*

1**de·fect** \'dē-ˌfekt, di-'\ *n* : a lack of something necessary for completeness or perfection : FAULT, IMPERFECTION ***syn*** see BLEMISH

2**de·fect** \di-'fekt\ *vb* : to desert a cause or party often in order to take up another — **de·fec·tion** \-'fek-shən\ *n* — **de·fec·tor** \-'fek-tər\ *n*

1**de·fec·tive** \di-'fek-tiv\ *adj* : lacking something essential : FAULTY ⟨*defective* brakes⟩ — **de·fec·tive·ly** *adv* — **de·fec·tive·ness** *n*

2**defective** *n* : a person who is subnormal physically or mentally

de·fend \di-'fend\ *vb* **1** : to repel danger or attack **2** : to act as attorney for **3** : to oppose the claim of another in a lawsuit : CONTEST **4** : to maintain against opposition — **de·fend·er** *n*

de·fend·ant \di-'fen-dənt\ *n* : a person required to make answer in a legal action or suit

de·fense *or* **de·fence** \di-'fen(t)s\ *n* **1** : the act of defending : resistance against attack **2** : capability of resisting attack **3 a** : means or method of defending **b** : an argument in support or justification **4 a** : a defending party or group **b** : a defensive team **5** : the answer made by the defendant in a legal action or suit — **de·fense·less** \-ləs\ *adj* — **de·fense·less·ly** *adv* — **de·fense·less·ness** *n* — **de·fen·si·bil·i·ty** \di-ˌfen(t)-sə-'bil-ət-ē\ *n* — **de·fen·si·ble** \-'fen(t)-sə-bəl\ *adj* — **de·fen·si·bly** \-'fen(t)-sə-blē\ *adv*

1**de·fen·sive** \di-'fen(t)-siv\ *adj* **1** : of or relating to defense : serving or intended to defend or protect ⟨a *defensive* alliance⟩ **2** : of or relating to the attempt to keep an opponent from scoring in a game or contest — **de·fen·sive·ly** *adv* — **de·fen·sive·ness** *n*

2**defensive** *n* : a defensive position ⟨put on the *defensive* by an attack⟩

1**de·fer** \di-'fər\ *vb* **de·ferred**; **de·fer·ring** : to put off : DELAY ⟨*defer* payment⟩ — **de·fer·ra·ble** \-'fər-ə-bəl\ *adj* — **de·fer·rer** *n*

2**defer** *vb* **de·ferred**; **de·fer·ring** : to submit or yield to another's wish or opinion

def·er·ence \'def-(ə-)rən(t)s\ *n* : courteous, respectful, or ingratiating regard for another's wishes

def·er·en·tial \ˌdef-ə-'ren-chəl\ *adj* : showing or expressing deference ⟨*deferential* attention⟩ — **def·er·en·tial·ly** \-'rench-(ə-)lē\ *adv*

de·fer·ment \di-'fər-mənt\ *n* : the act of delaying; *esp* : official postponement of military service

de·fi·ance \di-'fī-ən(t)s\ *n* **1** : the act or an instance of defying : CHALLENGE **2** : disposition to resist : contempt of opposition

de·fi·ant \-ənt\ *adj* : full of defiance : BOLD, INSOLENT — **de·fi·ant·ly** *adv*

de·fi·cien·cy \di-'fish-ən-sē\ *n, pl* **-cies** **1** : the quality or state of being deficient **2** : INADEQUACY; *esp* : a shortage of substances necessary to health

deficiency disease *n* : a disease (as scurvy or beriberi) caused by a lack of one or more essential substances (as a vitamin or mineral) in the diet

1**de·fi·cient** \di-'fish-ənt\ *adj* : lacking something necessary for completeness : not up to a given or normal standard ⟨a diet *deficient* in proteins⟩ ⟨*deficient* in arithmetic on his report card⟩ — **de·fi·cient·ly** *adv*

2**deficient** *n* : a person who is deficient

def·i·cit \'def-ə-sət\ *n* : a deficiency in amount; *esp* : an excess of expenditures over revenue

1**de·file** \di-'fīl\ *vb* **1** : to make filthy : DIRTY ⟨stored grain *defiled* by rats⟩ **2** : to corrupt the purity or perfection of ⟨*defile* the language⟩ **3** : DESECRATE ⟨a shrine *defiled* by the invaders⟩ **4** : DISHONOR ⟨*defiled* his good name⟩ — **de·file·ment** \-mənt\ *n* — **de·fil·er** *n*

2**de·file** \di-'fīl, 'dē-ˌ\ *n* : a narrow passage or gorge

de·fine \di-'fīn\ *vb* **1 a** : to fix or mark the limits of **b** : to make distinct in outline **2 a** : to determine the essential qualities of ⟨*define* the concept of loyalty⟩ ⟨*define* a circle⟩ **b** : to set forth the meaning of ⟨*define* a word⟩ — **de·fin·a·ble** \-'fī-nə-bəl\ *adj* — **de·fin·er** *n*

def·i·nite \'def-(ə-)nət\ *adj* **1** : having certain or distinct limits : FIXED ⟨a *definite* period of time⟩ **2** : clear in meaning : EXACT, EXPLICIT ⟨a *definite* answer⟩ **3** : typically designating an identified or immediately identifiable person or thing ⟨the *definite* article *the*⟩ — **def·i·nite·ly** *adv* — **def·i·nite·ness** *n*

def·i·ni·tion \ˌdef-ə-'nish-ən\ *n* **1** : an act of determining or settling the limits **2 a** : a statement of the meaning of a word or word group or a sign or symbol **b** : the action or process of stating such a meaning **3 a** : the action or the power of making definite and clear **b** : CLARITY, DISTINCTNESS — **def·i·ni·tion·al** \-'nish-(ə-)nəl\ *adj*

de·fin·i·tive \di-'fin-ət-iv\ *adj* **1** : serving to provide a final solution : CONCLUSIVE ⟨a *definitive* victory⟩ **2** : being authoritative and apparently exhaustive ⟨the *definitive* book on the subject⟩ **3** : serving to define or specify precisely — **de·fin·i·tive·ly** *adv* — **de·fin·i·tive·ness** *n*

definitive host *n* : a host in which the sexual reproduction of a parasite takes place

de·flate \di-'flāt, 'dē-\ *vb* **1** : to release air or gas from **2** : to cause to contract from a high level

: reduce from a state of inflation ⟨*deflate* the currency⟩ **3 :** to become deflated : COLLAPSE — **de·fla·tor** \-'flāt-ər\ *n*

de·fla·tion \-'flā-shən\ *n* **1 :** an act or instance of deflating : the state of being deflated **2 :** a contraction in the volume of available money or credit resulting in a decline of the general price level — **de·fla·tion·ary** \-shə-ˌner-ē\ *adj*

de·flect \di-'flekt\ *vb* : to turn or cause to turn aside (as from a course, direction, or position) ⟨a bullet *deflected* by striking a wall⟩ — **de·flec·tion** \-'flek-shən\ *n*

de·fo·li·ant \(')dē-'fō-lē-ənt\ *n* : a chemical applied to plants to cause the leaves to drop off prematurely

de·fo·li·ate \-lē-ˌāt\ *vb* : to deprive of leaves esp. prematurely — **de·fo·li·ate** \-lē-ət\ *adj* — **de·fo·li·a·tion** \(ˌ)dē-ˌfō-lē-'ā-shən\ *n* — **de·fo·li·a·tor** \(')dē-'fō-lē-ˌāt-ər\ *n*

de·for·est \(')dē-'fȯr-əst, -'fär-\ *vb* : to clear of forests — **de·for·es·ta·tion** \(ˌ)dē-ˌfȯr-ə-'stā-shən, -ˌfär-\ *n*

de·form \di-'fȯrm, 'dē-\ *vb* : to make or become misshapen or changed in shape — **de·for·ma·tion** \ˌdē-ˌfȯr-'mā-shən, ˌdef-ər-\ *n*

de·formed *adj* : distorted or unshapely in form : MISSHAPEN

de·for·mi·ty \di-'fȯr-mət-ē\ *n, pl* **-ties 1 :** the state of being deformed **2 :** a physical blemish or distortion : DISFIGUREMENT **3 :** a moral or aesthetic flaw

de·fraud \di-'frȯd\ *vb* : to deprive of something by trickery, deception, or fraud — **de·frau·da·tion** \ˌdē-ˌfrȯ-'dā-shən\ *n* — **de·fraud·er** \di-'frȯd-ər\ *n*

de·fray \di-'frā\ *vb* : to pay or provide for the payment of ⟨more money to *defray* expenses⟩ — **de·fray·a·ble** \-'frā-ə-bəl\ *adj* — **de·fray·al** \-'frā(-ə)l\ *n*

de·frost \di-'frȯst, 'dē-\ *vb* **1 :** to release from a frozen state : thaw out ⟨*defrost* meat⟩ **2 :** to free from ice ⟨*defrost* a refrigerator⟩ — **de·frost·er** *n*

deft \'deft\ *adj* : quick and neat in action : SKILLFUL ⟨knitting with *deft* fingers⟩ — **deft·ly** *adv* — **deft·ness** \'def(t)-nəs\ *n*

de·funct \di-'fəŋ(k)t\ *adj* : having finished the course of life or existence : DEAD, EXTINCT ⟨a *defunct* organization⟩

de·fy \di-'fī\ *vb* **de·fied; de·fy·ing 1 :** to challenge to do something considered impossible : DARE ⟨the magician *defied* his audience to explain the trick⟩ **2 :** to refuse boldly to obey or to yield to : DISREGARD ⟨*defy* public opinion⟩ **3 :** to resist attempts at : WITHSTAND, BAFFLE ⟨a scene that *defies* description⟩ — **de·fi·er** \-'fī(-ə)r\ *n*

deg *abbr* degree

de·gas \(')dē-'gas\ *vb* : to free from gas

de·gen·er·a·cy \di-'jen-(ə-)rə-sē\ *n, pl* **-cies 1 :** the state of being or process of becoming degenerate : DEGRADATION, DEBASEMENT **2 :** sexual perversion

¹de·gen·er·ate \di-'jen-(ə-)rət\ *adj* : having degenerated : DEBASED, DEGRADED — **de·gen·er·ate·ly** *adv* — **de·gen·er·ate·ness** *n*

²degenerate *n* : a degenerate person; *esp* : a sexual pervert

³de·gen·er·ate \di-'jen-ə-ˌrāt\ *vb* **1 :** to pass from a higher to a lower type or condition : DETERIORATE ⟨*degenerate* from the ancestral stock⟩ **2 :** to evolve toward an earlier or less highly organized biological form

de·gen·er·a·tion \di-ˌjen-ə-'rā-shən\ *n* **1 :** a lowering of power, vitality, or essential quality to a feebler and poorer kind or state **2 a :** a change in a tissue or an organ resulting in diminished activity or usefulness ⟨kidney *degeneration* in old age⟩ **b :** a condition marked by degeneration and esp. by loss of organs present in related forms ⟨tapeworms exhibit extreme *degeneration*⟩

de·gen·er·a·tive \di-'jen-əˌrāt-iv, -rət-\ *adj* : of, relating to, or tending to cause degeneration ⟨a *degenerative* disease⟩

deg·ra·da·tion \ˌdeg-rə-'dā-shən\ *n* **1 a :** a reduction in rank, dignity, or standing **b :** removal from office **2 :** DISGRACE, HUMILIATION **3 :** DETERIORATION, DEGENERATION

de·grade \di-'grād\ *vb* **1 :** to reduce from a higher to a lower rank or degree : deprive of an office or position **2 :** to lower the character of : DEBASE **3 :** to reduce the complexity of a chemical compound : DECOMPOSE — **de·grad·a·ble** \-'grād-ə-bəl\ *adj* — **de·grad·er** *n*

de·gree \di-'grē\ *n* **1 :** a step or stage in a process or series ⟨advance by *degrees*⟩ **2 a :** the intensity of something as measured by degrees ⟨murder in the first *degree*⟩ **b :** one of the forms used in the comparison of an adjective or adverb **3 a :** a rank or grade of official or social position ⟨persons of high *degree*⟩ **b :** the civil condition or status of a person **4 a :** a grade of membership attained in a ritualistic order or society **b :** the formal ceremonies observed in the conferral of a ritualistic distinction **c :** a title conferred upon students by a college, university, or professional school upon completion of a program of study ⟨a *degree* of doctor of medicine⟩ **d :** an academic title conferred honorarily **5 :** one of the divisions on an instrument (as a thermometer or barometer) that measures the amount of something (as heat) — symbol ° **6 :** a 360th part of the circumference of a circle **7 a :** a line or space of the musical staff **b :** a step, note, or tone of a musical scale — **to a degree 1 :** to a remarkable extent **2 :** in a small way

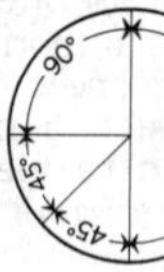

degrees 6

de·hu·mid·i·fy \ˌdē-hyü-'mid-ə-ˌfī, ˌdē-yü-\ *vb* : to remove moisture from (as the air) — **de·hu·mid·i·fi·er** \-ˌfī(-ə)r\ *n*

de·hy·drate \(')dē-'hī-ˌdrāt\ *vb* **1 :** to remove water from **2 :** to lose water or body fluids — **de·hy·dra·tion** \ˌdē-ˌhī-'drā-shən\ *n*

de·hy·drog·e·nase \ˌdē-ˌhī-'dräj-ə-ˌnās, (')dē-'hī-drə-jə-\ *n* : an enzyme that accelerates the removal and transfer of hydrogen

de·hy·drog·e·nate \ˌdē-ˌhī-'dräj-ə-ˌnāt, (')dē-'hī-drə-jə-\ *vb* : to remove hydrogen from

de·ice \(')dē-'īs\ *vb* : to keep free or rid of ice — **de·ic·er** *n*

de·i·fy \'dē-ə-ˌfī\ *vb* **-fied; -fy·ing 1 a :** to make a god of **b :** to take as an object of worship **2 :** to glorify as of supreme worth ⟨*deify* money⟩ — **de·i·fi·ca·tion** \ˌdē-ə-fə-'kā-shən\ *n*

deign \'dān\ *vb* : to think fit or in keeping with one's dignity : CONDESCEND ⟨did not *deign* to reply to the rude remark⟩

de·ion·ize \(')dē-'ī-ə-ˌnīz\ *vb* : to remove ions from

de·i·ty \'dē-ət-ē\ *n, pl* **-ties 1 a :** DIVINITY 1 **b** *cap* : ²GOD ⟨the *Deity*⟩ **2 a :** ¹GOD **b :** GODDESS

de·ject·ed \di-'jek-təd\ *adj* : cast down in spirits : LOW-SPIRITED, SAD, DEPRESSED — **de·ject·ed·ly** *adv* — **de·ject·ed·ness** *n*

de·jec·tion \di-'jek-shən\ *n* : lowness of spirits ***syn*** see MELANCHOLY

deka- *or* **dek-** — see DECA-

deka·gram *or* **deca·gram** \'dek-ə-ˌgram\ *n* — see METRIC SYSTEM table

deka·li·ter *or* **deca·li·ter** \-ˌlēt-ər\ *n* — see METRIC SYSTEM table

deka·me·ter *or* **deca·me·ter** \-ˌmēt-ər\ *n* — see METRIC SYSTEM table

deka·stere *or* **deca·stere** \-ˌsti(ə)r, -ˌste(ə)r\ *n* — see METRIC SYSTEM table

del *abbr* **1** delete **2** deletion

Del *abbr* Delaware

de·lam·i·na·tion \(ˌ)dē-ˌlam-ə-ˈnā-shən\ *n* : separation or splitting into distinct layers

[1]**de·lay** \di-ˈlā\ *n* **1** : the act of delaying : the state of being delayed **2** : the time during which something is delayed

[2]**delay** *vb* **1** : to put off : POSTPONE **2** : to stop, detain, or hinder for a time ⟨*delayed* by a storm⟩ **3** : to move or act slowly — **delay·er** *n*

syn DELAY, DETAIN, RETARD mean to check the progress of. DELAY usu. implies interference that slows completion or arrival beyond a set time; DETAIN often implies holding by force (as of police authority); RETARD is likely to suggest reducing speed of movement or development *ant* hasten, hurry

de·lec·ta·ble \di-ˈlek-tə-bəl\ *adj* **1** : highly pleasing : DELIGHTFUL **2** : DELICIOUS — **de·lec·ta·bly** \-blē\ *adv*

de·lec·ta·tion \ˌdē-ˌlek-ˈtā-shən\ *n* **1** : DELIGHT **2** : PLEASURE, ENJOYMENT, DIVERSION

[1]**del·e·gate** \ˈdel-i-gət, -ˌgāt\ *n* : a person sent with power to act for another : REPRESENTATIVE

[2]**del·e·gate** \-ˌgāt\ *vb* **1** : to entrust to another **2** : to appoint as one's delegate

del·e·ga·tion \ˌdel-i-ˈgā-shən\ *n* **1** : the act of delegating power or authority to another **2** : one or more persons chosen to represent others

de·lete \di-ˈlēt\ *vb* : to eliminate esp. by blotting out, cutting out, or erasing — **de·le·tion** \di-ˈlē-shən\ *n*

del·e·te·ri·ous \ˌdel-ə-ˈtir-ē-əs\ *adj* : HARMFUL, NOXIOUS — **del·e·te·ri·ous·ly** *adv* — **del·e·te·ri·ous·ness** *n*

delft \ˈdelft\ *or* **delft·ware** \-ˌwa(ə)r, -ˌwe(ə)r\ *n* : a Dutch pottery with a white glaze and blue decoration

[1]**de·lib·er·ate** \di-ˈlib-(ə-)rət\ *adj* **1** : decided upon as a result of careful thought : carefully considered ⟨a *deliberate* judgment⟩ **2** : characterized by awareness of the consequences ⟨a *deliberate* lie⟩ **3** : weighing facts and arguments : careful and slow in deciding ⟨a *deliberate* man⟩ **4** : slow in action : not hurried ⟨*deliberate* movements⟩ *syn* see VOLUNTARY *ant* accidental, impulsive — **de·lib·er·ate·ly** *adv* — **de·lib·er·ate·ness** *n*

[2]**de·lib·er·ate** \di-ˈlib-ə-ˌrāt\ *vb* : to think about deliberately : ponder issues and decisions carefully : CONSIDER ⟨*deliberate* before answering⟩

de·lib·er·a·tion \di-ˌlib-ə-ˈrā-shən\ *n* **1** : the act of deliberating **2** : a discussion and consideration of the reasons for and against a measure or question **3** : the quality of being deliberate : DELIBERATENESS

del·i·ca·cy \ˈdel-i-kə-sē\ *n, pl* **-cies** **1** : something pleasing to eat because it is rare or luxurious **2 a** : FINENESS, DAINTINESS ⟨lace of great *delicacy*⟩ **b** : FRAILTY **3** : nicety or subtle expressiveness of touch (as in painting or music) **4** : precise and refined perception and discrimination (as in feeling or conduct) **5** : extreme sensitivity : PRECISION **6** : SQUEAMISHNESS **7** : the quality or state of requiring delicate treatment ⟨the *delicacy* of a situation⟩

del·i·cate \ˈdel-i-kət\ *adj* **1** : satisfying or pleasing because of fineness or subtlety ⟨a *delicate* flavor⟩ ⟨*delicate* blossoms⟩ **2** : marked by keen sensitivity or fine discrimination : FASTIDIOUS **3** : exhibiting extreme sensitivity ⟨a *delicate* instrument⟩ **4** : precariously balanced **5** : marked by fineness of structure, workmanship, or texture ⟨*delicate* lace⟩ **6** : easily torn or hurt; *also* : WEAK, SICKLY ⟨a *delicate* child⟩ **7** : marked by tact; *also* : requiring tact ⟨*delicate* negotiations⟩ — **del·i·cate·ly** *adv* — **del·i·cate·ness** *n*

del·i·ca·tes·sen \ˌdel-i-kə-ˈtes-ən\ *n pl* [from German, plural of *delicatesse* (now spelled *delikatesse*) "delicacy", from French *délicatesse*, from *délicat* "delicate"] **1** : ready-to-eat food products (as cooked meats and prepared salads) **2** *sing, pl* **delicatessens** : a store where delicatessen are sold

de·li·cious \di-ˈlish-əs\ *adj* : affording great pleasure : DELIGHTFUL; *esp* : very pleasing to the taste — **de·li·cious·ly** *adv* — **de·li·cious·ness** *n*

[1]**de·light** \di-ˈlīt\ *n* **1** : extreme pleasure or satisfaction : JOY **2** : something that gives great pleasure

[2]**delight** *vb* **1** : to take great pleasure **2** : to give joy or satisfaction to : please greatly

de·light·ed *adj* : highly pleased : GRATIFIED, JOYOUS — **de·light·ed·ly** *adv* — **de·light·ed·ness** *n*

de·light·ful \di-ˈlīt-fəl\ *adj* : highly pleasing : giving delight — **de·light·ful·ly** \-fə-lē\ *adv* — **de·light·ful·ness** *n*

de·lim·it \di-ˈlim-ət\ *vb* : to fix the limits of : BOUND — **de·lim·i·ta·tion** \-ˌlim-ə-ˈtā-shən\ *n* — **de·lim·i·ta·tive** \-ˈlim-ə-ˌtāt-iv\ *adj*

de·lin·e·ate \di-ˈlin-ē-ˌāt\ *vb* **1** : to indicate by lines : SKETCH **2** : to describe in sharp or vivid detail ⟨*delineate* the characters in a story⟩ — **de·lin·e·a·tion** \-ˌlin-ē-ˈā-shən\ *n* — **de·lin·e·a·tor** \-ˈlin-ē-ˌāt-ər\ *n*

[1]**de·lin·quent** \di-ˈling-kwənt\ *n* : a delinquent person

[2]**delinquent** *adj* **1** : offending by neglect or violation of duty or of law **2** : being in arrears in payment — **de·lin·quen·cy** \-kwən-sē\ *n* — **de·lin·quent·ly** *adv*

del·i·quesce \ˌdel-ə-ˈkwes\ *vb* : to melt away; *esp* : to dissolve gradually by absorbing moisture from the air ⟨a *deliquescing* substance⟩ — **del·i·ques·cence** \-ˈkwes-ən(t)s\ *n*

del·i·ques·cent \-ˈkwes-ənt\ *adj* **1** : showing deliquescence **2** : having repeated division into branches ⟨elms are *deliquescent* trees⟩

de·lir·i·ous \di-ˈlir-ē-əs\ *adj* **1** : marked by delirium **2** : wildly excited — **de·lir·i·ous·ly** *adv* — **de·lir·i·ous·ness** *n*

de·lir·i·um \-ē-əm\ *n* **1** : a disordered mental condition characterized by confusion, disordered speech, and hallucinations **2** : frenzied excitement

de·liv·er \di-ˈliv-ər\ *vb* **de·liv·ered**; **de·liv·er·ing** \-(ə-)riŋ\ **1** : to set free : SAVE ⟨*deliver* us from evil⟩ **2** : to hand over : CONVEY, TRANSFER ⟨*deliver* a letter⟩ **3** : to assist in giving birth; *also* : to aid in the birth of **4** : UTTER, RELATE, COMMUNICATE ⟨*deliver* a speech⟩ **5** : to send to an intended target or destination ⟨*deliver* a pitch⟩ — **de·liv·er·a·ble** \-(ə-)rə-bəl\ *adj* — **de·liv·er·er** \-ər-ər\ *n*

de·liv·er·ance \di-ˈliv-(ə-)rən(t)s\ *n* **1** : a delivering or a being delivered : LIBERATION, RESCUE ⟨*deliverance* from the hands of the enemy⟩ **2** : something delivered or communicated; *esp* : a publicly expressed opinion

ə abut	ər further	a back	ā bake	
ä cot, cart	au̇ out	ch chin	e less	ē easy
g gift	i trip	ī life	j joke	ng sing	ō flow
ȯ flaw	ȯi coin	th thin	t͟h this	ü loot
u̇ foot	y yet	yü few	yu̇ furious	zh vision

de·liv·ery \di-'liv-(ə-)rē\ *n, pl* **-er·ies** **1** : a delivering from restraint ⟨jail *delivery*⟩ **2 a** : the act of handing over **b** : a legal conveyance of right or title **c** : something delivered at one time or in one unit **3** : the act of giving birth **4** : a delivering esp. of a speech **5** : manner or style of delivering

dell \'del\ *n* : a secluded small valley

de·louse \(')dē-'laůs, -'laůz\ *vb* : to remove lice from

del·phin·i·um \del-'fin-ē-əm\ *n* : any of a large genus of erect branching herbs related to the buttercups and having irregular flowers in showy spikes

del·ta \'del-tə\ *n* **1** : the 4th letter of the Greek alphabet — Δ or δ **2** : something shaped like a capital Δ; *esp* : the triangular or fan-shaped piece of land made by deposits of mud and sand at the mouth of a river — **del·ta·ic** \del-'tā-ik\ *adj*

de·lude \di-'lüd\ *vb* : to lead into error : mislead the judgment of : DECEIVE, TRICK ⟨*deluded* by false promises⟩ — **de·lud·er** *n*

1**del·uge** \'del-yüj\ *n* [from French, from Latin *diluvium*, from *diluere* "to wash away", from *dis-* "apart" and *lavere* "to wash"] **1 a** : an overflowing of the land by water : FLOOD **b** : a drenching rain **2** : an irresistible rush ⟨a *deluge* of Christmas mail⟩

2**deluge** *vb* **1** : to overflow with water : INUNDATE, FLOOD **2** : to overwhelm as if with a deluge ⟨*deluged* with inquiries⟩

de·lu·sion \di-'lü-zhən\ *n* **1** : the act of deluding : the state of being deluded **2 a** : something that is falsely or delusively believed **b** : a false belief that persists despite the facts and is common in some psychotic states — **de·lu·sion·al** \-'lüzh-(ə-)nəl\ *adj*

de·lu·sive \-'lü-siv, -ziv\ *adj* : deluding or apt to delude — **de·lu·sive·ly** *adv* — **de·lu·sive·ness** *n*

de·lu·so·ry \-sə-rē, -zə-\ *adj* : DECEPTIVE, DELUSIVE

de·luxe \di-'lůks, -'ləks, -'lüks\ *adj* : notably luxurious or elegant ⟨a *deluxe* edition⟩

delve \'delv\ *vb* **1** : to dig or labor with a spade **2** : to seek laboriously for information in written records — **delv·er** *n*

dem *abbr* demonstrative

Dem *abbr* **1** Democrat **2** Democratic

de·mag·ne·tize \(')dē-'mag-nə-ˌtīz\ *vb* : to deprive of magnetic properties — **de·mag·ne·ti·za·tion** \(ˌ)dē-ˌmag-nət-ə-'zā-shən\ *n*

dem·a·gogue *or* **dem·a·gog** \'dem-ə-ˌgäg\ *n* : a person who appeals to the emotions and prejudices of people in order to arouse discontent and advance his own political ends — **dem·a·gog·ic** \ˌdem-ə-'gäj-ik, -'gäg-\ *or* **dem·a·gog·i·cal** \-i-kəl\ *adj* — **dem·a·gogu·ery** \'dem-ə-ˌgäg-(ə-)rē\ *n* — **dem·a·gogy** \-ˌgäj-ē, -ˌgäg-\ *n*

1**de·mand** \di-'mand\ *n* **1 a** : an act of demanding **b** : something claimed as due **2 a** : an expressed desire **b** : the ability and desire to purchase goods or services at a specified time and price **c** : the quantity of an article or service that is wanted at a stated price **3** : a seeking or state of being sought after ⟨tickets are in great *demand*⟩ **4** : a pressing need or requirement ⟨*demands* that taxed his energy⟩ — **on demand** : upon request for payment

2**demand** *vb* **1** : to ask or call for with authority : claim as one's right ⟨*demand* payment of a debt⟩ ⟨*demand* an apology⟩ **2** : to ask earnestly or in the manner of a command ⟨the sentry *demanded* the password⟩ **3** : to call for : REQUIRE, NEED ⟨an illness that *demands* constant care⟩ — **de·mand·a·ble** \-'man-də-bəl\ *adj* — **de·mand·er** *n*

de·mand·ing *adj* : making difficult demands : EXACTING ⟨a *demanding* job⟩ — **de·mand·ing·ly** \-'man-ding-lē\ *adv*

de·mar·cate \di-'mär-ˌkāt, 'dē-ˌmär-\ *vb* **1** : to mark the limits or boundaries of **2** : to set apart : SEPARATE — **de·mar·ca·tion** \ˌdē-ˌmär-'kā-shən\ *n*

1**de·mean** \di-'mēn\ *vb* : to conduct or behave (oneself) usu. in a proper manner ⟨he *demeans* himself like a true American⟩

2**demean** *vb* : DEGRADE, DEBASE ⟨*demeaned* himself by dishonesty⟩

de·mean·or \di-'mē-nər\ *n* : outward manner or behavior : CONDUCT, BEARING

de·ment·ed \di-'ment-əd\ *adj* : MAD, INSANE — **de·ment·ed·ly** *adv* — **de·ment·ed·ness** *n*

de·men·tia \di-'men-chə\ *n* : INSANITY

de·mer·it \(')dē-'mer-ət\ *n* **1** : a quality that deserves blame : FAULT **2** : a mark placed against a person's record for some fault or offense

de·mesne \di-'mān, -'mēn\ *n* **1** : manorial land actually possessed by the lord and not held by free tenants **2 a** : the land attached to a mansion **b** : landed property : ESTATE **c** : REGION, TERRITORY **3** : REALM, DOMAIN

demi- *prefix* **1** : half **2** : one that partly belongs to (a specified type or class) ⟨*demi*god⟩

demi·god \'dem-ē-ˌgäd\ *n* : a mythological being with more power than a mortal but less than a god

demi·john \-ˌjän\ *n* : a large bottle of glass or stoneware enclosed in wickerwork

de·mil·i·ta·rize \(')dē-'mil-ə-tə-ˌrīz\ *vb* : to strip of military forces, weapons, or fortification ⟨a *demilitarized* zone⟩ — **de·mil·i·ta·ri·za·tion** \(ˌ)dē-ˌmil-ə-tə-rə-'zā-shən\ *n*

de·mise \di-'mīz\ *n* **1** : DEATH 1 **2** : a cessation of existence or activity ⟨the *demise* of a newspaper⟩

demi·tasse \'dem-ē-ˌtas\ *n* : a small cup of black coffee; *also* : the cup used to serve it

de·mo·bi·lize \di-'mō-bə-ˌlīz\ *vb* **1** : to dismiss from military service ⟨*demobilize* an army⟩ **2** : to change from a state of war to a state of peace — **de·mo·bi·li·za·tion** \-ˌmō-bə-lə-'zā-shən\ *n*

de·moc·ra·cy \di-'mäk-rə-sē\ *n, pl* **-cies** [from Greek *dēmokratia*, from *dēmos* "the people" and *kratein* "to rule", "govern", from *kratos* "power"] **1 a** : government by the people; *esp* : rule of the majority **b** : government in which the supreme power is vested in the people and exercised by them directly or indirectly through representation **2** : a political unit that has a democratic government **3 a** : the absence of hereditary or arbitrary class distinctions or privileges **b** : belief in or practice of social or economic equality

dem·o·crat \'dem-ə-ˌkrat\ *n* **1 a** : an adherent of democracy **b** : one who practices social equality **2** *cap* : a member of the Democratic party of the U.S.

dem·o·crat·ic \ˌdem-ə-'krat-ik\ *adj* **1** : of, relating to, or favoring political, social, or economic democracy **2** *cap* : of or relating to a major U.S. political party associated with policies of broad social reform and internationalism **3** : of, relating to, or appealing to the masses **4** : favoring social equality : not snobbish — **dem·o·crat·i·cal·ly** \-i-k(ə-)lē\ *adv*

Democratic–Republican *adj* : of or relating to an early 19th century American political party favoring strict interpretation of the constitution and emphasizing states' rights

de·moc·ra·tize \di-'mäk-rə-ˌtīz\ *vb* : to make democratic — **de·moc·ra·ti·za·tion** \-ˌmäk-rət-ə-'zā-shən\ *n*

de·mog·ra·phy \di-'mäg-rə-fē\ *n* : the statistical study of human populations — **de·mog·ra·pher** \-fər\ *n*

de·mol·ish \di-'mäl-ish\ *vb* **1 a** : to tear down : RAZE **b** : to break to pieces : SMASH **2** : to do away with : put an end to — **de·mol·ish·er** *n* — **de·mol·ish·ment** \-ish-mənt\ *n*

dem·o·li·tion \ˌdem-ə-'lish-ən, ˌdē-mə-\ *n* : the act of demolishing; *esp* : destruction by means of explosives

de·mon *or* **dae·mon** \'dē-mən\ *n* **1** *usu daemon* : an attendant power or spirit : GENIUS **2** : an evil spirit **3** *usu daemon* : DEMIGOD **4** : one that has unusual drive or effectiveness ⟨he is a *demon* for work⟩ — **de·mon·ic** \di-'män-ik\ *adj*

[1]**de·mo·ni·ac** \di-'mō-nē-ˌak\ *also* **de·mo·ni·a·cal** \ˌdē-mə-'nī-ə-kəl\ *adj* **1** : possessed or influenced by a demon **2** : of, relating to, or suggestive of a demon : DEVILISH, FIENDISH ⟨*demoniac* cruelty⟩ — **de·mo·ni·a·cal·ly** \ˌdē-mə-'nī-ə-k(ə-)lē\ *adv*

[2]**demoniac** *n* : one possessed by a demon

de·mon·stra·ble \di-'män(t)-strə-bəl, 'dem-ən-strə-\ *adj* : capable of being demonstrated or proved — **de·mon·stra·bil·i·ty** \di-ˌmän(t)-strə-'bil-ət-ē, ˌdem-ən-strə-\ *n* — **de·mon·stra·ble·ness** \di-'män(t)-strə-bəl-nəs, 'dem-ən-strə-\ *n* — **de·mon·stra·bly** \-blē\ *adv*

dem·on·strate \'dem-ən-ˌstrāt\ *vb* **1** : to show clearly **2 a** : to prove or make clear by reasoning or evidence **b** : to illustrate and explain esp. with examples **3** : to show publicly the good qualities of a product ⟨*demonstrate* a new car⟩ **4** : to make a public display (as of feeling or military force) ⟨citizens *demonstrated* in protest⟩

dem·on·stra·tion \ˌdem-ən-'strā-shən\ *n* **1** : an outward expression or display ⟨a *demonstration* of joy⟩ **2** : an act, process, or means of demonstrating the truth of something: **a** : conclusive evidence **b** : an explanation (as of a theory) by experiment **c** : a course of reasoning intended to prove that a conclusion must follow when certain conditions are accepted **d** : a showing to a prospective buyer of the merits of a product **3** : a show of armed force **4** : a public display of group feelings toward a person or cause — **dem·on·stra·tion·al** \-sh(ə-)nəl\ *adj*

[1]**de·mon·stra·tive** \di-'män(t)-strət-iv\ *adj* **1** : characterized or established by demonstration ⟨*demonstrative* reasoning⟩ **2** : pointing out the one referred to and distinguishing it from others of the same class ⟨the *demonstrative* pronoun *this* in "this is my hat"⟩ ⟨the *demonstrative* adjective *that* in "that boy"⟩ **3** : marked by display of feeling ⟨a *demonstrative* greeting⟩ — **de·mon·stra·tive·ly** *adv* — **de·mon·stra·tive·ness** *n*

[2]**demonstrative** *n* : a demonstrative word; *esp* : a demonstrative pronoun

dem·on·stra·tor \'dem-ən-ˌstrāt-ər\ *n* **1** : a person who makes or takes part in a demonstration **2** : a manufactured article (as an automobile) used for purposes of demonstration

de·mor·al·ize \di-'mȯr-ə-ˌlīz, -'mär-\ *vb* **1** : to corrupt in morals : make bad **2** : to destroy the morale of : weaken in discipline or spirit ⟨fear *demoralized* the army⟩ — **de·mor·al·i·za·tion** \-ˌmȯr-ə-lə-'zā-shən, -ˌmär-\ *n* — **de·mor·al·iz·er** \-'mȯr-ə-ˌlī-zər, -'mär-\ *n*

de·mote \di-'mōt, 'dē-\ *vb* : to reduce to a lower grade or rank — **de·mo·tion** \-'mō-shən\ *n*

ə abut	ər further	a back	ā bake
ä cot, cart	au̇ out	ch chin	e less
ē easy	g gift	i trip	ī life
j joke	ng sing	ō flow	ȯ flaw
ȯi coin	th thin	th this	ü loot
u̇ foot	y yet	yü few	yu̇ furious
zh vision			

de·mount \(ˈ)dē-'mau̇nt\ *vb* **1** : to remove from a mounted position **2** : DISASSEMBLE — **de·mount·a·ble** \-ə-bəl\ *adj*

[1]**de·mur** \di-'mər\ *vb* **de·murred**; **de·mur·ring** : to take exception : OBJECT

[2]**demur** *n* : the act of objecting : PROTEST ⟨accepted without *demur*⟩

de·mure \di-'myu̇(ə)r\ *adj* **1** : MODEST, RESERVED **2** : affectedly modest, reserved, or serious : COY — **de·mure·ly** *adv* — **de·mure·ness** *n*

den \'den\ *n* **1** : the shelter or resting place of a wild animal **2** : a hiding place (as for thieves) **3** : a dirty wretched place in which people live or gather ⟨*dens* of misery⟩ **4** : a quiet snug room; *esp* : one set apart for reading and relaxation

Den *abbr* Denmark

de·na·ture \(ˈ)dē-'nā-chər\ *vb* **de·na·tured**; **de·na·tur·ing** \-'nāch-(ə-)riŋ\ : to deprive of natural qualities: as **a** : to make (alcohol) unfit for drinking without impairing usefulness for other purposes **b** : to modify the structure of (as an enzyme) so that the original properties are removed or diminished — **de·na·tur·a·tion** \(ˌ)dē-ˌnā-chə-'rā-shən\ *n*

den·drite \'den-ˌdrīt\ *n* **1** : a branching figure (as in a mineral or stone) resembling a tree **2** : any of the usu. branching protoplasmic extensions of a nerve cell over which impulses travel toward the body of the cell — **den·drit·ic** \den-'drit-ik\ *adj*

den·drol·o·gy \den-'dräl-ə-jē\ *n* : the study of trees — **den·drol·o·gist** \-jist\ *n*

de·ni·al \di-'nī(-ə)l\ *n* **1** : a refusal to grant something asked for **2** : a refusal to admit the truth of a statement : CONTRADICTION ⟨a flat *denial* of the charges⟩ **3** : a refusal to acknowledge something; *esp* : a statement of disbelief or rejection ⟨make a public *denial* of political beliefs once held⟩ **4** : a cutting down or limiting : RESTRICTION ⟨*denial* of her appetite⟩

[1]**de·ni·er** \di-'nī(-ə)r\ *n* : one that denies

[2]**den·ier** \'den-yər\ *n* : a unit of fineness for silk, rayon, or nylon yarn

den·im \'den-əm\ *n* [from French *serge de Nîmes* "serge of Nîmes", from the French city of *Nîmes* where it was made] **1** : a firm durable twilled usu. cotton fabric **2** *pl* : overalls or trousers of denim

de·ni·tri·fi·ca·tion \(ˌ)dē-ˌnī-trə-fə-'kā-shən\ *n* : a process by which various nitrogen compounds are transformed or broken down and which is usu. brought about (as in the soil or in sewage) by denitrifying bacteria with formation of free nitrogen

de·ni·tri·fy \(ˈ)dē-'nī-trə-ˌfī\ *vb* : to convert a nitrogen compound to free nitrogen or to a different state esp. as a step in the nitrogen cycle

de·ni·tri·fy·ing bacteria \(ˈ)dē-'nī-trə-ˌfī-iŋ-\ *n pl* : bacteria that bring about denitrification esp. with the formation of nitrogen gas

den·i·zen \'den-ə-zən\ *n* : INHABITANT; *esp* : a person, animal, or plant found or naturalized in a particular region or environment

de·nom·i·nate \di-'näm-ə-ˌnāt\ *vb* : to give a name to : DESIGNATE

de·nom·i·nate number \di-ˌnäm-ə-nət-\ *n* : a number (as *7* in *7 feet*) that specifies a quantity in terms of a unit of measurement

de·nom·i·na·tion \di-ˌnäm-ə-'nā-shən\ *n* **1** : an act of denominating **2** : NAME, DESIGNATION; *esp* : a general name for a class of things **3** : a religious body comprising a number of congregations with similar beliefs **4** : one of a series of related values each having a special name ⟨a 1-dollar bill and a 10-dollar bill represent two *denominations* of U.S. money⟩ —

de·nom·i·na·tion·al \-sh(ə-)nəl\ *adj* — **de·nom·i·na·tion·al·ly** \-ē\ *adv*

de·nom·i·na·tor \di-ˈnäm-ə-ˌnāt-ər\ *n* : the part of a fraction that is below the line signifying division and that in fractions with 1 as the numerator indicates into how many parts the unit is divided : DIVISOR

de·no·ta·tion \ˌdē-nō-ˈtā-shən\ *n* **1** : an act or process of denoting **2** : MEANING; *esp* : a direct specific meaning as distinct from connotations **3** : a denoting term or label : NAME, SIGN — **de·no·ta·tive** \ˈdē-nō-ˌtāt-iv, di-ˈnōt-ət-iv\ *adj*

de·note \di-ˈnōt\ *vb* **1** : to mark out plainly : point out : INDICATE ⟨the hands of a clock *denote* the time⟩ **2** : to make known : SHOW ⟨smiled to *denote* pleasure⟩ **3** : to have the meaning of : MEAN, NAME ⟨in the U.S. the word *corn denotes* Indian corn⟩

de·noue·ment \ˌdā-ˌnü-ˈmäⁿ, dā-ˈnü-ˌ\ *n* [from French *dénouement* "the untying of a knot", from Old French *desnoer* "to untie", a derivative from Latin *nodus* "knot"] **1** : the final solution or untangling of the conflicts or difficulties that make up the plot of a literary work **2** : a solution or working out esp. of a complex or difficult situation

de·nounce \di-ˈnau̇n(t)s\ *vb* **1** : to point out as deserving blame or punishment **2** : to inform against : ACCUSE **3** : to announce formally the termination of (as a treaty) — **de·nounce·ment** \-mənt\ *n* — **de·nounc·er** *n*

dense \ˈden(t)s\ *adj* **1** : marked by compactness or crowding together of parts ⟨a *dense* forest⟩ **2** : mentally dull **3** : having high opacity ⟨*dense* fog⟩ **4** : having between any two mathematical elements at least one element ⟨the set of rational numbers is *dense*⟩ — **dense·ly** *adv* — **dense·ness** *n*

den·si·ty \ˈden(t)-sət-ē\ *n, pl* **-ties** **1** : the quality or state of being dense **2** : the quantity of something per unit volume, unit area, or unit length: as **a** : the mass of a substance per unit volume ⟨*density* expressed in grams per cubic centimeter⟩ **b** : the average number of individuals or units in a unit of area or volume **3** : STUPIDITY

[1]**dent** \ˈdent\ *n* **1** : a depression or hollow made by a blow or by pressure **2 a** : an impression or effect made usu. against resistance **b** : initial progress

[2]**dent** *vb* **1** : to make a dent in or on **2** : to become marked by a dent

dent *abbr* **1** dental **2** dentistry

den·tal \ˈdent-əl\ *adj* : of or relating to the teeth or dentistry

dental floss *n* : a usu. flattened waxed thread used to clean between the teeth

dental hygienist *n* : one who assists a dentist esp. in cleaning teeth

dent corn *n* : an Indian corn having kernels that contain both hard and soft starch and that become indented at maturity

den·ti·frice \ˈdent-ə-frəs\ *n* [from Latin *dentifricium*, from *denti-*, stem of *dens* "tooth" and *fricare* "to rub", the source of English *friction*] : a powder, paste, or liquid for cleaning the teeth

den·tin \ˈdent-ən\ *or* **den·tine** \ˈden-ˌtēn, den-ˈ\ *n* : a calcareous bonelike material that composes the principal mass of a tooth — **den·tin·al** \den-ˈtēn-əl, ˈdent-ə-nəl\ *adj*

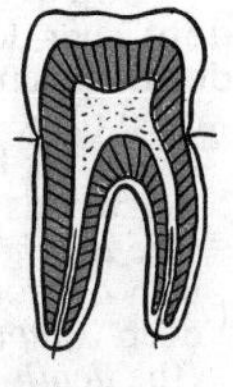

dentin

den·tist \ˈdent-əst\ *n* : one whose profession is the care, treatment, and repair of the teeth and the fitting of artificial teeth

den·tist·ry \ˈdent-ə-strē\ *n* : the profession or practice of a dentist

den·ti·tion \den-ˈtish-ən\ *n* **1** : the development and cutting of teeth **2** : the number, kind, and arrangement of teeth (as of a person or animal)

den·ture \ˈden-chər\ *n* : a set of teeth; *esp* : a partial or complete set of false teeth

de·nude \di-ˈn(y)üd\ *vb* : to strip of covering : lay bare ⟨erosion that *denudes* the rocks of soil⟩ — **de·nu·da·tion** \ˌdē-(ˌ)n(y)ü-ˈdā-shən, ˌden-yu̇-\ *n*

de·nun·ci·a·tion \di-ˌnən(t)-sē-ˈā-shən\ *n* : the act of denouncing; *esp* : a public accusation ⟨publish a *denunciation* of an official⟩ — **de·nun·ci·a·to·ry** \-ˈnən(t)-sē-ə-ˌtōr-ē, -ˌtȯr-\ *adj*

de·ny \di-ˈnī\ *vb* **de·nied**; **de·ny·ing** **1** : to declare not to be true : CONTRADICT ⟨*deny* a report⟩ **2** : to refuse to grant ⟨*deny* a request⟩ **3** : to refuse to acknowledge : DISOWN ⟨*denied* his faith⟩ **4** : to reject as false ⟨*deny* the theory of evolution⟩

de·odor·ant \dē-ˈōd-ə-rənt\ *n* : a preparation that destroys or masks unpleasant odors — **deodorant** *adj*

de·odor·ize \dē-ˈōd-ə-ˌrīz\ *vb* : to eliminate or prevent the offensive odor of — **de·odor·i·za·tion** \(ˌ)dē-ˌōd-ə-rə-ˈzā-shən\ *n* — **de·odor·iz·er** *n*

de·ox·i·dize \(ˈ)dē-ˈäk-sə-ˌdīz\ *vb* : to remove oxygen from

de·oxy·ri·bo·nu·cle·ic acid \(ˌ)dē-ˌäk-sē-ˈrī-bō-n(y)u̇-ˌklē-ik-, -ˌklā-\ *n* : DNA

de·oxy·ri·bose \dē-ˌäk-sē-ˈrī-ˌbōs\ *n* : a sugar that has five carbon atoms in the molecule and is a constituent of nucleic acids

dep *abbr* deposit

de·part \di-ˈpärt\ *vb* **1 a** : to go away or go away from : LEAVE **b** : DIE **2** : to turn aside : DEVIATE

de·part·ed *adj* **1** : BYGONE **2** : no longer living

de·part·ment \di-ˈpärt-mənt\ *n* **1** : a distinct sphere : PROVINCE **2 a** : a major administrative division of a government or business **b** : a major territorial administrative division **c** : a division of a college or school giving instruction in a particular subject **d** : a section of a department store — **de·part·men·tal** \di-ˌpärt-ˈment-əl, ˌdē-\ *adj* — **de·part·men·tal·ly** \-ē\ *adv*

department store *n* : a store having separate departments for a wide variety of goods

de·par·ture \di-ˈpär-chər\ *n* **1** : the act of going away **2** : a setting out (as on a new course) **3** : DIVERGENCE

de·pend \di-ˈpend\ *vb* **1** : to hang down ⟨a vine *depending* from a tree⟩ **2** : to rely for support ⟨children *depend* on their parents⟩ **3** : to be determined by or based on some action or condition ⟨success of the picnic will *depend* on the weather⟩ **4** : TRUST, RELY ⟨a man you can *depend* on⟩

de·pend·a·ble \di-ˈpen-də-bəl\ *adj* : capable of being depended on : TRUSTWORTHY, RELIABLE — **de·pend·a·bil·i·ty** \-ˌpen-də-ˈbil-ət-ē\ *n* — **de·pend·a·bly** \-ˈpen-də-blē\ *adv*

de·pend·ence \di-ˈpen-dən(t)s\ *n* **1** : the quality or state of being dependent; *esp* : the quality or state of being influenced by or subject to another **2** : RELIANCE, TRUST **3** : something on which one relies ⟨he was his mother's sole *dependence*⟩

de·pend·en·cy \-dən-sē\ *n, pl* **-cies** **1** : DEPENDENCE 1 **2** : a territory under the jurisdiction of a nation but not formally annexed by it

[1]**de·pend·ent** \di-ˈpen-dənt\ *adj* **1** : hanging down **2 a** : determined or conditioned by another **b** : relying on another for support ⟨*dependent* children⟩ **c** : subject to another's jurisdiction ⟨a *dependent* territory⟩ **3** : SUBORDINATE 3a — **de·pend·ent·ly** *adv*

2**dependent** *also* **de·pend·ant** \-dənt\ *n* : a person who relies on another for support

de·pict \di-'pikt\ *vb* **1** : to represent by a picture **2** : to describe in words — **de·pic·tion** \-'pik-shən\ *n*

de·plete \di-'plēt\ *vb* : to reduce in amount by using up : exhaust esp. of strength or resources ⟨soil *depleted* of minerals⟩ ⟨a *depleted* treasury⟩ — **de·ple·tion** \-'plē-shən\ *n*

de·plor·a·ble \di-'plōr-ə-bəl, -'plȯr-\ *adj* **1** : deserving to be deplored : LAMENTABLE ⟨a *deplorable* accident⟩ **2** : very bad : WRETCHED ⟨*deplorable* conditions⟩ — **de·plor·a·ble·ness** *n* — **de·plor·a·bly** \-blē\ *adv*

de·plore \di-'plō(ə)r, -'plȯ(ə)r\ *vb* **1 a** : to feel or express grief for **b** : to regret strongly **2** : to consider unfortunate or deserving of disapproval — **de·plor·er** *n* — **de·plor·ing·ly** \-ing-lē\ *adv*

de·ploy \di-'plȯi\ *vb* : to spread out or place in position for some purpose ⟨troops *deployed* for battle⟩ ⟨*deploy* police to prevent a riot⟩ — **de·ploy·ment** \-mənt\ *n*

de·po·nent \di-'pō-nənt\ *n* : a person who gives evidence

de·pop·u·late \(')dē-'päp-yə-ˌlāt\ *vb* : to reduce greatly the population of (as a city or region) by destroying or driving away the inhabitants ⟨*depopulated* by plague⟩ — **de·pop·u·la·tion** \(ˌ)dē-ˌpäp-yə-'lā-shən\ *n*

de·port \di-'pōrt, -'pȯrt\ *vb* **1** : CONDUCT, BEHAVE ⟨*deported* himself disgracefully⟩ **2** : to force (an alien whose presence is unlawful or harmful) to leave a country — **de·por·ta·tion** \ˌdē-ˌpōr-'tā-shən, -ˌpȯr-\ *n* — **de·por·tee** \ˌdē-ˌpōr-'tē, -ˌpȯr-\ *n*

de·port·ment \di-'pōrt-mənt, -'pȯrt-\ *n* : manner of conducting oneself : BEHAVIOR

de·pose \di-'pōz\ *vb* **1** : to remove from a high office ⟨*deposed* the king⟩ **2** : to testify under oath or by affidavit

1**de·pos·it** \di-'päz-ət\ *vb* **1** : to place for safekeeping; *esp* : to put money in a bank **2** : to give as a pledge that a purchase will be made or a service used ⟨*deposit* $10 on a new bicycle⟩ **3** : to lay down : PLACE, PUT ⟨*deposit* a parcel on a table⟩ **4** : to let fall or sink ⟨sand and silt *deposited* by a flood⟩ — **de·pos·i·tor** \-ət-ər\ *n*

2**deposit** *n* **1** : the state of being deposited ⟨money on *deposit*⟩ **2 a** : something placed for safekeeping; *esp* : money deposited in a bank **b** : money given as a pledge **3** : an act of depositing **4** : something laid or thrown down ⟨a *deposit* of silt left by the flood⟩ **5** : an accumulation of mineral matter (as ore, oil, or gas) in nature

dep·o·si·tion \ˌdep-ə-'zish-ən, ˌdē-pə-\ *n* **1** : the act of deposing a person from high office ⟨the *deposition* of the king⟩ **2** : a statement esp. in writing made under oath **3** : the action or process of depositing ⟨the *deposition* of silt by a stream⟩ **4** : something deposited : DEPOSIT — **dep·o·si·tion·al** \-'zish-(ə-)nəl\ *adj*

de·pos·i·to·ry \di-'päz-ə-ˌtōr-ē, -ˌtȯr-\ *n*, *pl* **-ries** : a place where something is deposited esp. for safekeeping

de·pot *1 & 3 are* 'dep-ˌō *also* 'dē-ˌpō, *2 is* 'dē-ˌpō *also* 'dep-ˌō\ *n* **1** : a place of deposit for goods : STOREHOUSE **2** : a building for railroad or bus passengers or freight : STATION **3** : a place where military supplies are kept or where troops are assembled and trained

de·prave \di-'prāv\ *vb* : to make evil : corrupt the morals of : PERVERT — **de·praved** \-'prāvd\ *adj* — **de·praved·ly** \-'prāv(-ə)d-lē\ *adv* — **de·praved·ness** \-'prāv(-ə)d-nəs\ *n*

de·prav·i·ty \di-'prav-ət-ē\ *n*, *pl* **-ties** **1** : the quality or state of being depraved **2** : a corrupt act or practice

dep·re·cate \'dep-ri-ˌkāt\ *vb* **1** : to express disapproval of **2** : to represent as of little value : DEPRECIATE — **dep·re·cat·ing·ly** \-ˌkāt-ing-lē\ *adv* — **dep·re·ca·tion** \ˌdep-ri-'kā-shən\ *n*

dep·re·ca·to·ry \'dep-ri-kə-ˌtōr-ē, -ˌtȯr-\ *adj* : seeking to avert disapproval : APOLOGETIC

de·pre·ci·ate \di-'prē-shē-ˌāt\ *vb* **1** : to lower the price or value of ⟨*depreciate* the currency⟩ **2** : to represent as of little value : DISPARAGE **3** : to fall in value ⟨new cars *depreciate* rapidly⟩ — **de·pre·cia·tive** \-shē-ˌāt-iv, -sh(ē-)ət-\ *adj* — **de·pre·cia·to·ry** \-sh(ē-)ə-ˌtōr-ē, -ˌtȯr-\ *adj*

de·pre·ci·a·tion \di-ˌprē-shē-'ā-shən\ *n* **1** : a decline in the purchasing power or exchange value of money **2** : the act of belittling : DISPARAGEMENT **3** : a decline (as from age or wear and tear) in the value of something

dep·re·da·tion \ˌdep-rə-'dā-shən\ *n* : the action or an act of plundering or laying waste : RAVAGING, PILLAGING

de·press \di-'pres\ *vb* **1 a** : to press down **b** : to cause to sink to a lower position **2** : to lessen the activity or strength of **3** : SADDEN, DISCOURAGE **4** : to lessen in price or value : DEPRECIATE — **de·press·i·ble** \-ə-bəl\ *adj* — **de·press·ing·ly** \-ing-lē\ *n*

de·pres·sant \di-'pres-ənt\ *n* : an agent (as a drug) that reduces bodily functional activity — **depressant** *adj*

de·pressed \di-'prest\ *adj* **1 a** : low in spirits : SAD **b** : suffering from mental depression **2** : suffering from economic depression

de·pres·sion \di-'presh-ən\ *n* **1** : an act of depressing : a state of being depressed: as **a** : a pressing down : LOWERING **b** : DEJECTION; *also* : a mental disorder marked by sadness, inactivity, and loss of a sense of one's own worth **c** (1) : a reduction in activity, amount, quality, or force (2) : a lowering of bodily functional activity **2** : a depressed place or part : HOLLOW **3** : a period of low general economic activity with widespread unemployment

de·pres·sor \-'pres-ər\ *n* : one that depresses: as **a** : a muscle that draws down a part **b** : a device for pressing a part (as the tongue) down or aside

de·pres·sur·ize \(')dē-'presh-ə-ˌrīz\ *vb* : to release (as a pressurized aircraft) from pressure

de·prive \di-'prīv\ *vb* **1** : to take something away from ⟨*deprive* a king of his power⟩ **2** : to stop from having something ⟨*deprived* of sleep by street noises⟩ — **dep·ri·va·tion** \ˌdep-rə-'vā-shən\ *n*

dept *abbr* department

depth \'depth\ *n* **1 a** : something that is deep : a deep place or part (as of a body of water) **b** : a part that is far from the outside or surface ⟨the *depths* of the woods⟩ **c** : ABYSS **d** : the middle of a time ⟨the *depth* of winter⟩ **2** : distance from top to bottom or from front to back **3** : the quality of being deep ⟨*depth* of insight⟩ **4** : degree of intensity ⟨the *depth* of a color⟩ — **depth·less** \-ləs\ *adj*

depth charge *n* : an explosive projectile for use under water esp. against submarines

dep·u·ta·tion \ˌdep-yə-'tā-shən\ *n* **1** : the act of ap-

ə abut	ər further	a back		ā bake
ä cot, cart	au̇ out	ch chin	e less	ē easy
g gift	i trip	ī life	j joke	ng sing	ō flow
ȯ flaw	ȯi coin	th thin	t͟h this	ü loot
u̇ foot	y yet	yü few	yu̇ furious	zh vision

pointing a deputy **2** : a group of people appointed to represent others
de·pute \di-'pyüt\ *vb* : DELEGATE
dep·u·tize \'dep-yə-ˌtīz\ *vb* **1** : to appoint as deputy **2** : to act as deputy
dep·u·ty \'dep-yət-ē\ *n, pl* **-ties** **1** : a person appointed to act for or in place of another **2** : an assistant empowered to act as a substitute in the absence of his superior — **deputy** *adj*
de·rail \di-'rāl\ *vb* : to cause to run off the rails ⟨a train *derailed* by heavy snow⟩ — **de·rail·ment** \-mənt\ *n*
de·rail·leur \di-'rā-lər\ *n* **1** : a multiple-speed gear mechanism on a bicycle that involves the moving of the chain from one sprocket to another **2** : a bicycle having a derailleur
de·range \di-'rānj\ *vb* **1** : to put out of order : DISARRANGE, UPSET **2** : to make insane — **de·range·ment** \-mənt\ *n*
der·by \'dər-bē, *esp Brit* 'där-\ *n, pl* **derbies** **1** : a horse race usu. for three-year-olds held annually **2** : a race or contest open to all comers **3** : a man's stiff felt hat with dome-shaped crown and narrow brim

derby

[1]**der·e·lict** \'der-ə-ˌlikt\ *adj* **1** : abandoned by the owner or occupant ⟨a *derelict* ship⟩ **2** : NEGLECTFUL, NEGLIGENT ⟨*derelict* in one's duty⟩
[2]**derelict** *n* **1** : something voluntarily abandoned; *esp* : a ship abandoned on the high seas **2** : a person no longer able to support himself : BUM
der·e·lic·tion \ˌder-ə-'lik-shən\ *n* **1** : the act of abandoning : the state of being abandoned ⟨the *dereliction* of a cause by its leaders⟩ **2** : a failure in duty : DELINQUENCY
de·ride \di-'rīd\ *vb* **de·rid·ed**; **de·rid·ing** : to laugh at scornfully : make fun of — **de·rid·er** *n* — **de·rid·ing·ly** \-'rīd-ing-lē\ *adv*
de·ri·sion \di-'rizh-ən\ *n* **1** : scornful or contemptuous ridicule **2** : an object of ridicule — **de·ri·sive** \-'rī-siv\ *adj* — **de·ri·sive·ly** *adv* — **de·ri·sive·ness** *n* — **de·ri·so·ry** \-'rī-sə-rē\ *adj*
deriv *abbr* **1** derivation **2** derivative
der·i·va·tion \ˌder-ə-'vā-shən\ *n* **1 a** : the formation (as by the addition of an affix) of a word from another word or root **b** : an act of ascertaining or stating the derivation of a word **c** : ETYMOLOGY 1 **2 a** : SOURCE, ORIGIN **b** : ORIGINATION, DESCENT **c** : an act or process of deriving — **der·i·va·tion·al** \-sh(ə-)nəl\ *adj*
[1]**de·riv·a·tive** \di-'riv-ət-iv\ *adj* : formed by derivation; *esp* : not original or fundamental ⟨*derivative* poetry⟩ — **de·riv·a·tive·ly** *adv*
[2]**derivative** *n* **1** : a word formed by derivation ⟨the word *kindness* is a *derivative* of *kind*⟩ **2** : something derived **3** : a substance that can be made from another substance in one or more steps ⟨a *derivative* of coal tar⟩
de·rive \di-'rīv\ *vb* **de·rived**; **de·riv·ing** **1** : to receive or obtain from a source **2** : to trace the origin, descent, or derivation of **3** : to come from a certain source or basis ⟨*derived* unit⟩ **4** : INFER, DEDUCE — **de·riv·a·ble** \-'rī-və-bəl\ *adj*
der·ma \'dər-mə\ *n* : DERMIS
der·mal \'dər-məl\ *adj* : of or relating to the dermis or epidermis : CUTANEOUS
der·map·ter·an \(ˌ)dər-'map-tə-rən\ *n* : any of an order of insects (as an earwig) that have biting mouthparts, short leathery fore wings without veins, and a pair of unjointed forcepslike structures on the end of the abdomen — **dermapteran** *adj* — **der·map·ter·ous** \-rəs\ *adj*
der·mis \'dər-məs\ *n* : the layer of skin directly under the epidermis
de·rog·a·to·ry \di-'räg-ə-ˌtōr-ē, -ˌtȯr-\ *adj* : intended to lower the reputation of a person or thing : DISPARAGING ⟨*derogatory* remarks⟩ — **de·rog·a·to·ri·ly** \-ˌräg-ə-'tōr-ə-lē, -'tȯr-\ *adv*
der·rick \'der-ik\ *n* [originally meaning "gallows", and so called after *Derick*, a 17th century hangman] **1** : any of various machines for moving or hoisting heavy weights by means of a long beam fitted with pulleys and cables **2** : a framework or tower built over an oil well for supporting machinery
der·ring–do \ˌder-ing-'dü\ *n* : daring action : DARING
der·vish \'dər-vish\ *n* : a member of a Muslim religious order noted for devotional exercises (as bodily movements leading to a trance)
de·sal·i·ni·za·tion \(ˌ)dē-ˌsal-ə-nə-'zā-shən\ *n* : removal of salt (as from seawater)
de·salt \(')dē-'sȯlt\ *vb* : to remove salt from (as seawater)
[1]**des·cant** \'des-ˌkant\ *n* **1** : a melody sung above a principal melody **2** : the art of composing or singing part music; *also* : a piece of music so composed **3** : a strain of melody : SONG **4** : a discourse or comment on a subject
[2]**des·cant** \'des-ˌkant, des-'\ *vb* **1 a** : to sing or play a descant **b** : SING, WARBLE **2** : to talk or write at length ⟨*descanted* on his favorite author⟩
de·scend \di-'send\ *vb* **1 a** : to pass from a higher to a lower place or level **b** : to pass, move, or climb down or down along **2 a** : to come down from a stock or source : DERIVE ⟨*descended* from an ancient family⟩ **b** : to pass by inheritance or transmission ⟨the manor *descended* to a son⟩ **3** : to incline, lead, or extend downward ⟨the road *descends* to the river⟩ **4** : to swoop down in a sudden attack **5** : to sink in status, dignity, or condition
[1]**de·scend·ant** *or* **de·scend·ent** \di-'sen-dənt\ *adj* **1** : DESCENDING **2** : proceeding from an ancestor or source
[2]**descendant** *or* **descendent** *n* **1** : one descended from another or from a common stock **2** : one deriving directly from a precursor or prototype
de·scent \di-'sent\ *n* **1** : the act or process of descending **2** : a downward step (as in station or value) : DECLINE **3** : derivation from an ancestor : BIRTH, LINEAGE **4 a** : an inclination downward : SLOPE **b** : a descending way (as a downgrade or stairway) **5** : a sudden hostile raid or assault
de·scribe \di-'skrīb\ *vb* **1** : to represent or give an account of in words **2** : to trace or traverse the outline of ⟨*describe* a circle⟩ — **de·scrib·a·ble** \-'skrī-bə-bəl\ *adj* — **de·scrib·er** *n*
de·scrip·tion \di-'skrip-shən\ *n* **1** : an account of something; *esp* : an account that presents a picture to a person who reads or hears it **2** : KIND, SORT ⟨people of every *description*⟩
de·scrip·tive \di-'skrip-tiv\ *adj* : serving to describe ⟨*descriptive* account⟩ ⟨*descriptive* adjective⟩ — **de·scrip·tive·ly** *adv* — **de·scrip·tive·ness** *n*
de·scry \di-'skrī\ *vb* **de·scried**; **de·scry·ing** **1** : to catch sight of : spy out or discover by the eye **2** : to discover or detect by observation or investigation
des·e·crate \'des-i-ˌkrāt\ *vb* : to violate the sanctity of : PROFANE — **des·e·crat·er** *or* **des·e·cra·tor** \-ˌkrāt-ər\ *n* — **des·e·cra·tion** \ˌdes-i-'krā-shən\ *n*

de·seg·re·gate \(ˈ)dē-ˈseg-ri-ˌgāt\ *vb* : to eliminate segregation in; *esp* : to end by law the isolation of members of a particular race in separate units ⟨*desegregate* the armed services⟩ — **de·seg·re·ga·tion** \(ˌ)dē-ˌseg-ri-ˈgā-shən\ *n*

1**des·ert** \ˈdez-ərt\ *n* : an arid barren tract with sparse vegetation and little rainfall

2**des·ert** \ˈdez-ərt\ *adj* : of, relating to, or resembling a desert; *esp* : being barren and without life ⟨a *desert* island⟩

3**de·sert** \di-ˈzərt\ *n* **1** : worthiness of reward or punishment ⟨rewarded according to his *deserts*⟩ **2** : a just reward or punishment

4**de·sert** \di-ˈzərt\ *vb* **1** : to withdraw from : LEAVE ⟨the town was *deserted*⟩ **2** : to leave or forsake someone or something one should stay with ⟨*deserted* his family⟩ **3** : to fail one in time of need ⟨his courage *deserted* him⟩ **4** : to quit one's post without permission esp. with the intent to remain away permanently ***syn*** see ABANDON ***ant*** stick (to), cleave (to) — **de·sert·er** *n* — **de·ser·tion** \di-ˈzər-shən\ *n*

de·serve \di-ˈzərv\ *vb* : to be worthy of : MERIT ⟨*deserves* another chance⟩ — **de·serv·ed·ly** \-ˈzər-vəd-lē\ *adv* — **de·serv·ed·ness** \-vəd-nəs\ *n* — **de·serv·er** *n*

de·serv·ing \-ˈzər-viŋ\ *adj* : MERITORIOUS, WORTHY — **de·serv·ing·ly** \-viŋ-lē\ *adv* — **de·serv·ing·ness** *n*

des·ic·ca·tor \ˈdes-i-ˌkāt-ər\ *n* : a container for drying substances and keeping them free of moisture

de·sid·er·a·tum \di-ˌsid-ə-ˈrät-əm, -ˌzid-, -ˈrāt-\ *n*, *pl* **-ta** \-ə\ : something desired as essential or needed

1**de·sign** \di-ˈzīn\ *vb* **1 a** : to conceive and plan out in the mind **b** : to have as a purpose : INTEND ⟨a plan *designed* to bring down the prime minister⟩ **c** : to devise for a specific function or end ⟨*design* a training program for auto mechanics⟩ **2 a** : to make a pattern or sketch of ⟨*design* new fashions⟩ **b** : to conceive and draw the plans for ⟨*design* an airplane⟩ — **de·sign·er** *n*

2**design** *n* **1** : a project or scheme in which means to an end are laid down **2** : deliberate purposive planning **3** : a secret project or scheme : PLOT — often used in pl. with *on* or *against* ⟨had *designs* on the money⟩ ⟨has no *designs* against friendly governments⟩ **4** : a sketch or plan showing the main features of something to be executed **5** : the arrangement of elements that make up a structure or a work of art **6** : a decorative pattern

des·ig·nate \ˈdez-ig-ˌnāt\ *vb* **1** : to mark or point out : INDICATE **2** : to appoint or choose by name for a special purpose ⟨*designate* someone as chairman⟩ **3** : to call by a name or title — **des·ig·na·tive** \-ˌnāt-iv\ *adj* — **des·ig·na·tor** \-ˌnāt-ər\ *n*

des·ig·na·tion \ˌdez-ig-ˈnā-shən\ *n* **1** : the act of indicating or identifying **2** : a distinguishing name, sign, or title **3** : appointment to or selection for an office, post, or service

de·sign·ed·ly \di-ˈzī-nəd-lē\ *adv* : PURPOSELY

de·sign·ing \-ˈzī-niŋ\ *adj* : CRAFTY, SCHEMING ⟨a *designing* woman⟩

de·sir·a·ble \di-ˈzī-rə-bəl\ *adj* **1** : having pleasing qualities or properties : ATTRACTIVE ⟨a *desirable* location⟩ **2** : worth seeking or doing as advantageous, beneficial, or wise : ADVISABLE ⟨*desirable* legislation⟩ — **de·sir·a·bil·i·ty** \-ˌzī-rə-ˈbil-ət-ē\ *n* — **de·sir·a·ble·ness** \-ˈzī-rə-bəl-nəs\ *n* — **de·sir·a·bly** \-blē\ *adv*

1**de·sire** \di-ˈzī(ə)r\ *vb* **1** : to long for : wish earnestly ⟨*desire* wealth⟩ ⟨*desire* peace⟩ **2** : to call for : express a wish for : REQUEST ⟨the librarian *desires* us to return all overdue books⟩

2**desire** *n* **1** : a strong wish : LONGING; *also* : the mental power or capacity to experience desires **2** : an expressed wish : REQUEST **3** : something desired

de·sir·ous \di-ˈzī(ə)r-əs\ *adj* : eagerly wishing : DESIRING ⟨*desirous* of an invitation⟩ — **de·sir·ous·ly** *adv* — **de·sir·ous·ness** *n*

de·sist \di-ˈzist, -ˈsist\ *vb* : to cease to proceed or act

desk \ˈdesk\ *n* **1 a** : a table, frame, or case with a flat or sloping surface esp. for writing and reading **b** : a counter at which a person performs his duties **c** : a music stand **2** : a specialized division of an organization (as a newspaper) ⟨city *desk*⟩

des·mid \ˈdez-məd\ *n* : any of numerous single-celled colonial green algae

1**des·o·late** \ˈdes-ə-lət, ˈdez-\ *adj* **1** : lacking inhabitants and visitors : DESERTED **2** : FORSAKEN, LONELY **3 a** : showing the effects of abandonment and neglect : DILAPIDATED **b** : BARREN, LIFELESS **c** : CHEERLESS, GLOOMY — **des·o·late·ly** *adv* — **des·o·late·ness** *n*

2**des·o·late** \-ˌlāt\ *vb* : to make desolate: **a** : to lay waste **b** : to make wretched

des·o·la·tion \ˌdes-ə-ˈlā-shən, ˌdez-\ *n* **1** : the action of desolating **2** : the condition of being desolated : DEVASTATION, RUIN **3** : a barren wasteland **4 a** : GRIEF, SADNESS **b** : LONELINESS

des·oxy·ri·bo·nu·cle·ic acid \de-ˌzäk-sē-ˈrī-bō-n(y)u̇-ˌklē-ik-, -ˌklā-\ *n* : DNA

1**de·spair** \di-ˈspa(ə)r, -ˈspe(ə)r\ *vb* : to lose all hope or confidence

2**despair** *n* **1** : utter loss of hope : feeling of complete hopelessness **2** : a cause of hopelessness — **despair·ing** *adj* — **de·spair·ing·ly** \-iŋ-lē\ *adv*

des·patch \dis-ˈpatch\ *var of* DISPATCH

des·per·a·do \ˌdes-pə-ˈräd-ō, -ˈrād-\ *n*, *pl* **-does** *or* **-dos** : a bold or reckless criminal

des·per·ate \ˈdes-p(ə-)rət\ *adj* **1** : being beyond or almost beyond hope : causing despair ⟨a *desperate* illness⟩ **2** : reckless because of despair : RASH ⟨a *desperate* attempt⟩ — **des·per·ate·ly** *adv* — **des·per·ate·ness** *n*

des·per·a·tion \ˌdes-pə-ˈrā-shən\ *n* **1** : a loss of hope and surrender to misery or dread **2** : a state of hopelessness leading to extreme recklessness

de·spic·a·ble \di-ˈspik-ə-bəl, ˈdes-(ˌ)pik-\ *adj* : deserving to be despised ⟨*despicable* traitor⟩ — **despic·a·ble·ness** *n* — **de·spic·a·bly** \-blē\ *adv*

de·spise \di-ˈspīz\ *vb* **1** : to look down on with contempt or aversion **2** : to regard as negligible, worthless, or distasteful — **de·spis·er** *n*

1**de·spite** \di-ˈspīt\ *n* **1** : CONTEMPT **2** : MALICE, SPITE **3 a** : an act of contempt or defiance **b** : HARM, INJURY — **in despite of** : in spite of

2**despite** *prep* : in spite of ⟨ran *despite* his injury⟩

de·spite·ful \di-ˈspīt-fəl\ *adj* : expressing malice or hate — **de·spite·ful·ly** \-fə-lē\ *adv* — **de·spite·ful·ness** *n*

de·spoil \di-ˈspȯil\ *vb* : to strip of belongings, possessions, or value : PLUNDER, PILLAGE — **despoil·er** *n* — **de·spoil·ment** \-ˈspȯil-mənt\ *n*

de·spo·li·a·tion \di-ˌspō-lē-ˈā-shən\ *n* : the act of despoiling : the state of being despoiled

de·spond \di-ˈspänd\ *vb* : to become discouraged or disheartened

de·spond·en·cy \di-'spän-dən-sē\ *n* : the state of being despondent : DEJECTION, DISCOURAGEMENT

de·spond·ent \-dənt\ *adj* : feeling extreme discouragement, dejection, or depression — **de·spond·ent·ly** *adv*

des·pot \'des-pət, -ˌpät\ *n* [from Greek *despotēs* "master", "lord", literally "master of the house"] **1** : a ruler with absolute power and authority **2** : a person exercising power abusively, oppressively, or tyrannously — **des·pot·ic** \des-'pät-ik\ *adj* — **des·pot·i·cal·ly** \-i-k(ə-)lē\ *adv*

des·po·tism \'des-pə-ˌtiz-əm\ *n* **1** : rule by a despot : TYRANNY **2** : a state or a system of government in which the ruler has unlimited power

des·sert \di-'zərt\ *n* : a course of sweet food, fruit, or cheese served at the close of a meal

des·ti·na·tion \ˌdes-tə-'nā-shən\ *n* **1** : an act of appointing, setting aside for a purpose, or predetermining **2** : purpose for which something is destined **3** : a place which is the goal of a journey or to which something is sent

des·tine \'des-tən\ *vb* **1** : to settle in advance ⟨a plan *destined* to fail⟩ **2** : to designate, assign, or dedicate in advance ⟨*destined* his son for the study of law⟩ **3** : to be bound or directed ⟨a ship *destined* for New York⟩

des·ti·ny \'des-tə-nē\ *n, pl* **-nies** **1** : something to which a person or thing is destined : FORTUNE **2** : a predetermined course of events often held to be a resistless power or agency

syn DESTINY, FATE, DOOM mean a predetermined lot or end. DESTINY suggests a preordained goal toward which sure progress is made; FATE suggests a course which must be accepted as inevitable; DOOM usu. suggests a grim judgment or end

des·ti·tute \'des-tə-ˌt(y)üt\ *adj* **1** : lacking something needed or desirable ⟨*destitute* of the necessities of life⟩ **2** : extremely poor : suffering great want — **des·ti·tu·tion** \ˌdes-tə-'t(y)ü-shən\ *n*

de·stroy \di-'strȯi\ *vb* **1** : to put an end to : do away with : RUIN **2** : SLAUGHTER, KILL

de·stroy·er \-'strȯi(-ə)r\ *n* **1** : a destroying agent or agency **2** : a small fast warship armed with guns, depth charges, torpedoes, and sometimes guided missiles

destroyer escort *n* : a warship similar to but smaller than a destroyer

de·struct \di-'strəkt\ *n* : the deliberate destruction of a rocket after launching

de·struc·ti·ble \di-'strək-tə-bəl\ *adj* : capable of being destroyed — **de·struc·ti·bil·i·ty** \-ˌstrək-tə-'bil-ət-ē\ *n*

de·struc·tion \di-'strək-shən\ *n* **1** : the action or process of destroying something **2** : the state or fact of being destroyed : RUIN

de·struc·tive \di-'strək-tiv\ *adj* **1** : causing destruction : RUINOUS ⟨*destructive* storm⟩ **2** : designed or tending to destroy or nullify ⟨*destructive* criticism⟩ ⟨*destructive* interference of light waves⟩ — **de·struc·tive·ly** *adv* — **de·struc·tive·ness** *n*

destructive distillation *n* : decomposition of a substance (as coal or oil) by heat in a closed container and collection of the volatile products produced

des·ul·to·ry \'des-əl-ˌtōr-ē, -ˌtȯr-\ *adj* : passing aimlessly from one thing or subject to another : DISCONNECTED ⟨*desultory* reading⟩ — **des·ul·to·ri·ly** \ˌdes-əl-'tōr-ə-lē, -'tȯr-\ *adv* — **des·ul·to·ri·ness** \'des-əl-ˌtōr-ē-nəs, -ˌtȯr-\ *n*

de·tach \di-'tach\ *vb* : to separate esp. from a larger mass and usu. without violence or damage — **de·tach·a·ble** \-ə-bəl\ *adj* — **de·tach·a·bly** \-blē\ *adv*

de·tached \-'tacht\ *adj* **1** : not joined or connected : SEPARATE ⟨a *detached* house⟩ **2** : ALOOF, UNCONCERNED, IMPARTIAL ⟨a *detached* attitude⟩ — **de·tached·ly** \-'tach-əd-lē, -'tach-tlē\ *adv* — **de·tached·ness** \-'tach-əd-nəs, -'tach(t)-nəs\ *n*

de·tach·ment \di-'tach-mənt\ *n* **1** : the action or process of detaching : SEPARATION **2 a** : the dispatching of a body of troops or part of a fleet from the main body **b** : a small military unit with a special task or function **3 a** : indifference to worldly concerns **b** : freedom from bias or prejudice : IMPARTIALITY

1de·tail \di-'tāl, 'dē-ˌ\ *n* **1 a** : a dealing with something item by item ⟨go into *detail* about an event⟩ **b** : a small part or feature : ITEM ⟨the *details* of a story⟩ **2 a** : selection (as of a group of soldiers) for some special service **b** : a soldier or group of soldiers appointed for special duty — **in detail** : item by item omitting nothing : THOROUGHLY ⟨explain *in detail*⟩

2detail *vb* **1** : to report in detail **2** : ENUMERATE, SPECIFY **3** : to assign to a task — **de·tail·er** *n*

de·tailed \di-'tāld, 'dē-ˌ\ *adj* **1** : including many details ⟨a *detailed* report⟩ **2** : furnished with finely finished details ⟨beautifully *detailed* hats⟩ — **de·tailed·ly** \di-'tāl(-ə)d-lē, 'dē-ˌ\ *adv* — **de·tailed·ness** \di-'tā-ləd-nəs, -'tāl(d)-nəs, 'dē-ˌ\ *n*

de·tain \di-'tān\ *vb* **1** : to hold or keep in or as if in custody **2** : to keep back (as something due) : WITHHOLD **3** : to restrain esp. from proceeding : STOP ***syn*** see DELAY — **de·tain·ment** \-mənt\ *n*

de·tect \di-'tekt\ *vb* : to discover the nature, existence, presence, or fact of ⟨*detect* the approach of an airplane⟩ — **de·tect·a·ble** \-'tek-tə-bəl\ *adj* — **de·tec·tion** \-'tek-shən\ *n*

1de·tec·tive \di-'tek-tiv\ *adj* **1** : fitted for or used in detecting something ⟨a *detective* device for coal gas⟩ **2** : of or relating to detectives or their work ⟨a *detective* story⟩

2detective *n* : an individual (as a policeman) whose business is solving crimes and catching criminals or gathering information that is not readily accessible

de·tec·tor \di-'tek-tər\ *n* **1** : one that detects or warns **2** : a device in a radio receiving set for converting the high-frequency current of radio waves into current that can vibrate a loudspeaker to reproduce the original sound

de·tent \'dē-ˌtent, di-'\ *n* : a mechanism that locks or unlocks a movement : PAWL

de·ten·tion \di-'ten-chən\ *n* : the act of detaining : the state of being detained; *esp* : temporary custody awaiting trial

de·ter \di-'tər\ *vb* **de·terred**; **de·ter·ring** [fr. Latin *deterrēre*, meaning literally "to frighten off", from *de-* "off" and *terrēre* "to terrify"] **1** : to turn aside, discourage, or prevent from acting (as by fear) **2** : INHIBIT — **de·ter·ment** \-'tər-mənt\ *n*

de·ter·gen·cy \di-'tər-jən-sē\ *n* : cleansing quality or power

1de·ter·gent \di-'tər-jənt\ *adj* [fr. Latin *detergent-*, stem of *detergens*, present participle of *detergēre* "to wipe off", from *de-* "off" and *tergēre* "to wipe"] : CLEANSING ⟨*detergent* oil for engines⟩

2detergent *n* : a cleansing agent; *esp* : a chemical preparation that is like soap in its ability to cleanse

de·te·ri·o·rate \di-'tir-ē-ə-ˌrāt\ *vb* : to make or become worse or of less value : DEGENERATE — **de·te·ri·o·ra·tion** \-ˌtir-ē-ə-'rā-shən\ *n* — **de·te·ri·o·ra·tive** \-'tir-ē-ə-ˌrāt-iv\ *adj*

de·ter·mi·nant \di-'tər-mə-nənt\ *n* : something that determines or conditions : FACTOR

de·ter·mi·nate \-nət\ *adj* **1** : having fixed limits

: DEFINITE **2** : definitely settled ⟨arranged in a *determinate* order⟩ — **de·ter·mi·nate·ly** *adv* — **de·ter·mi·nate·ness** *n*

de·ter·mi·na·tion \di-ˌtər-mə-ˈnā-shən\ *n* **1** : the act of coming to a decision; *also* : the decision or conclusion reached **2** : the act of fixing the extent, position, or character of something ⟨*determination* of the position of a ship⟩ **3** : accurate measurement (as of length or volume) **4** : firm or fixed purpose : FIRMNESS

de·ter·mine \di-ˈtər-mən\ *vb* **1 a** : to fix conclusively or authoritatively ⟨*determine* fiscal policy⟩ **b** : REGULATE **2** : to come to a decision : SETTLE, RESOLVE ⟨*determine* to learn to spell⟩ **3** : to find out the limits, nature, dimensions, or scope of : gain definite knowledge about ⟨*determine* the size of a room⟩ **4** : to be the cause of or reason for : DECIDE ⟨the quality of a pupil's work *determines* his mark⟩

de·ter·mined \-mənd\ *adj* **1** : DECIDED, RESOLVED **2** : FIRM, RESOLUTE — **de·ter·mined·ly** \-mən-dlē, -mə-nəd-lē\ *adv* — **de·ter·mined·ness** \-mən(d)-nəs\ *n*

de·ter·min·er \-mə-nər\ *n* : a word belonging to a group of noun modifiers that can occur before descriptive adjectives modifying the same noun ⟨*the* in "the red house" is a *determiner*⟩

de·ter·rence \di-ˈtər-ən(t)s, -ˈter-\ *n* : the act, process, or capacity of deterring

de·ter·rent \-ənt\ *adj* : serving to deter — **deterrent** *n*

de·test \di-ˈtest\ *vb* : to dislike intensely : LOATHE, ABHOR ***syn*** see HATE ***ant*** adore (sense 2) — **de·test·er** *n*

de·test·a·ble \di-ˈtes-tə-bəl\ *adj* : arousing or meriting intense dislike : ABOMINABLE — **de·test·a·ble·ness** *n* — **de·test·a·bly** \-blē\ *adv*

de·throne \di-ˈthrōn\ *vb* : to remove from a throne : DEPOSE — **de·throne·ment** \-mənt\ *n*

det·o·nate \ˈdet-ə-ˌnāt\ *vb* : to explode or cause to explode with sudden violence — **det·o·na·tion** \ˌdet-ə-ˈnā-shən\ *n*

det·o·na·tor \ˈdet-ə-ˌnāt-ər\ *n* : a device or small quantity of explosive used for detonating a high explosive

1**de·tour** \ˈdē-ˌtu̇(ə)r, di-ˈ\ *n* : a deviation from a direct course or the usual procedure; *esp* : a roundabout way temporarily replacing a regular route

2**detour** *vb* : to send or proceed by a detour

de·tract \di-ˈtrakt\ *vb* **1** : to make or represent as of less worth ⟨*detract* from a person's reputation⟩ **2** : DISTRACT ⟨*detract* attention⟩ — **de·trac·tion** \-ˈtrak-shən\ *n* — **de·trac·tive** \-ˈtrak-tiv\ *adj* — **de·trac·tive·ly** *adv* — **de·trac·tor** \-ˈtrak-tər\ *n*

det·ri·ment \ˈde-trə-mənt\ *n* : injury or damage or its cause : HURT — **det·ri·men·tal** \ˌde-trə-ˈment-əl\ *adj* — **det·ri·men·tal·ly** \-ə-lē\ *adv*

de·tri·tus \di-ˈtrīt-əs\ *n* **1** : loose material that results directly from the natural breaking up of rocks (as by the action of frost) **2** : a product of disintegration or wearing away

deuce \ˈd(y)üs\ *n* [from Middle French *deus* "two", from Latin *duos*, the accusative case of *duo* "two"] **1 a** (1) : the face of a dice that bears two spots (2) : a playing card bearing the number two **b** : a cast of dice yielding a point of two **2** : a tie in tennis with each side having a score of 40 **3** : DEVIL, DICKENS — used chiefly as a mild oath

deu·te·ri·um \d(y)ü-ˈtir-ē-əm\ *n* : the hydrogen isotope that is twice the mass of ordinary hydrogen — symbol *D*; called also *heavy hydrogen*

Deu·ter·on·o·my \ˌd(y)üt-ə-ˈrän-ə-mē\ *n* — see BIBLE table

dev·as·tate \ˈdev-ə-ˌstāt\ *vb* : to reduce to ruin : lay waste — **dev·as·tat·ing·ly** \-ˌstāt-ing-lē\ *adv* — **dev·as·ta·tion** \ˌdev-ə-ˈstā-shən\ *n*

de·vel·op \di-ˈvel-əp\ *vb* **1 a** : to unfold gradually or in detail ⟨as the story *developed*⟩ **b** : to apply chemicals to a photographic negative in order to bring out the picture **c** : to elaborate (a musical theme) by working out rhythmic and harmonic changes **2** : to bring to a more advanced or more nearly perfect state ⟨regular exercise *developed* his muscles⟩ ⟨study to *develop* the mind⟩ **3** : to make more available or usable ⟨*develop* resources⟩ **4** : to acquire gradually ⟨*developed* a taste for olives⟩ **5 a** : to go through a process of natural growth or evolution ⟨a blossom *develops* from a bud⟩ **b** : GROW — **de·vel·op·a·ble** \-ˈvel-ə-pə-bəl\ *adj*

de·vel·op·er \-ˈvel-ə-pər\ *n* : one that develops; *esp* : a chemical used to develop photographic film

de·vel·op·ment \di-ˈvel-əp-mənt\ *n* **1** : the act, process, or result of developing **2** : the state of being developed **3** : EVOLUTION **4** : the process of growth and specialization of cells and structure by which a fertilized egg, spore, or embryo is transformed into a mature organism — **de·vel·op·men·tal** \-ˌvel-əp-ˈment-əl\ *adj* — **de·vel·op·men·tal·ly** \-ə-lē\ *adv*

de·vi·ant \ˈdē-vē-ənt\ *adj* **1** : deviating esp. from some accepted standard **2** : characterized by deviation — **de·vi·ance** \-ən(t)s\ *n* — **deviant** *n*

de·vi·ate \ˈdē-vē-ˌāt\ *vb* : to turn aside esp. from an established way

de·vi·a·tion \ˌdē-vē-ˈā-shən\ *n* : an act or instance of deviating: as **a** : the difference found by subtracting some fixed number (as the arithmetic mean of a series of statistical data) from any item of the series **b** : noticeable departure from accepted standards (as of behavior)

de·vice \di-ˈvīs\ *n* **1 a** : a scheme to deceive : STRATAGEM **b** : a piece of equipment or a mechanism to serve a special purpose **2** : DESIRE, INCLINATION ⟨left to his own *devices*⟩ **3** : an emblematic design; *esp* : one used in heraldry

1**dev·il** \ˈdev-əl\ *n* [from Old English *dēofol*, borrowed from Latin *diabolus*, from Greek *diabolos*, meaning literally "the slanderer"] **1** *often cap* : the personal supreme spirit of evil often represented as the ruler of hell — often used with *the* as a mild oath or expression of surprise, vexation, or emphasis **2** : DEMON **3 a** : a wicked person **b** : a reckless or dashing person **c** : a pitiable person — usu. used with *poor*

2**devil** *vb* **dev·iled** *or* **dev·illed**; **dev·il·ing** *or* **dev·il·ling** \ˈdev-(ə-)ling\ **1** : TEASE, ANNOY **2** : to chop fine and season highly ⟨*deviled* eggs⟩

dev·il·fish \ˈdev-əl-ˌfish\ *n* **1** : any of several extremely large rays widely distributed in warm seas **2** : OCTOPUS

dev·il·ish \ˈdev-(ə-)lish\ *adj* **1** : characteristic of or resembling the devil ⟨*devilish* tricks⟩ **2** : EXTREME, EXCESSIVE ⟨in a *devilish* hurry⟩ — **devilish** *adv* — **dev·il·ish·ly** *adv* — **dev·il·ish·ness** *n*

dev·il·ment \ˈdev-əl-mənt, -ˌment\ *n* : DEVILRY

dev·il·ry \ˈdev-əl-rē\ *or* **dev·il·try** \-əl-trē\ *n*, *pl* **-ries** *or* **-tries** : reckless unrestrained conduct : MISCHIEF

devil's advocate *n* **1** : a Roman Catholic official whose duty is to point out defects in the evidence on which a demand for beatification or canonization rests **2** : a person who champions the worse cause for the sake of argument

devil's darning needle *n* **1** : DRAGONFLY **2** : DAMSELFLY

devil's paintbrush *n* : any of various hawkweeds found in the eastern U.S.

de·vi·ous \'dē-vē-əs\ *adj* **1** : deviating from a straight course : ROUNDABOUT **2** : not straightforward : TRICKY ⟨*devious* conduct⟩ — **de·vi·ous·ly** *adv* — **de·vi·ous·ness** *n*

de·vise \di-'vīz\ *vb* **1** : to form in the mind by new combinations or applications of ideas or principles : INVENT **2** : to give (real estate) by will — **de·vis·er** *n*

de·void \di-'vȯid\ *adj* : entirely lacking : DESTITUTE ⟨a book *devoid* of interest⟩

De·vo·ni·an \di-'vō-nē-ən\ *n* **1** : the period of the Paleozoic era between the Silurian and Mississippian — called also *Age of Fishes* **2** : the system of rocks formed during the Devonian and containing abundant fossils esp. of ferns and their allies, a few gymnosperms, primitive fish, and some air-breathing invertebrates — **Devonian** *adj*

de·vote \di-'vōt\ *vb* **1** : to set apart for a special purpose (as by a vow) : DEDICATE ⟨*devote* an hour to worship⟩ **2** : to give up to wholly ⟨*devoted* herself to her family⟩

de·vot·ed *adj* **1** : ZEALOUS, ARDENT, DEVOUT ⟨*devoted* admirers⟩ **2** : AFFECTIONATE, LOVING ⟨a *devoted* mother⟩ — **de·vot·ed·ly** *adv* — **de·vot·ed·ness** *n*

dev·o·tee \ˌdev-ə-'tē, -'tā\ *n* **1** : an ardent adherent of a religion or deity **2** : ENTHUSIAST, FAN

de·vo·tion \di-'vō-shən\ *n* **1 a** : religious fervor : PIETY **b** : a religious exercise or practice other than the regular worship of a church **2 a** (1) : the act of devoting (2) : the quality of being devoted **b** : ardent love, affection, or dedication — **de·vo·tion·al** \-sh(ə-)nəl\ *adj* — **de·vo·tion·al·ly** \-ē\ *adv*

de·vour \di-'vau̇(ə)r\ *vb* **1** : to eat up greedily **2 a** : to lay waste : CONSUME **b** : to use up wastefully **3** : to take in eagerly by the senses or mind ⟨*devour* a book⟩ ***syn*** see EAT

de·vout \di-'vau̇t\ *adj* **1** : devoted to religion or to religious duties or exercises **2** : expressing devotion or piety **3** : warmly devoted : SINCERE ⟨gave him *devout* thanks⟩ — **de·vout·ly** *adv* — **de·vout·ness** *n*

dew \'d(y)ü\ *n* **1** : moisture condensed upon the surfaces of cool bodies at night **2** : something resembling dew in purity, freshness, or power to refresh — **dewy** \'d(y)ü-ē\ *adj*

Dew·ar flask \ˌd(y)ü-ər-\ *n* : VACUUM BOTTLE

dew·ber·ry \'d(y)ü-ˌber-ē\ *n* **1** : any of several blackberries with trailing stems that root at the joints or tip **2** : the small purplish fruit of a dewberry

dew·drop \-ˌdräp\ *n* : a drop of dew

dew·lap \'d(y)ü-ˌlap\ *n* : a hanging fold of skin under the neck esp. of a cud-chewing animal — **dew·lapped** \-ˌlapt\ *adj*

dew point *n* : the temperature at which the moisture in the air begins to condense

dex·ter·i·ty \dek-'ster-ət-ē\ *n, pl* **-ties** **1** : readiness and grace in physical activity; *esp* : skill and ease in using the hands **2** : mental skill or quickness **3** : RIGHT-HANDEDNESS

dex·ter·ous *or* **dex·trous** \'dek-st(ə-)rəs\ *adj* **1** : skillful and competent with the hands **2** : mentally adroit and skillful : EXPERT **3** : done with skill — **dex·ter·ous·ly** *adv* — **dex·ter·ous·ness** *n*

dex·trose \'dek-ˌstrōs\ *n* : a naturally occurring form of glucose that is found in plants, fruits, and blood and is a source of energy for living things

dg *abbr* decigram

di- *comb form* **1** : twice : twofold : double ⟨*di*chromatic⟩ **2** : containing two atoms, radicals, or groups ⟨*di*chloride⟩

dia- *also* **di-** *prefix* : through : across

dia *or* **diam** *abbr* diameter

di·a·be·tes \ˌdī-ə-'bēt-ēz, -'bēt-əs\ *n* : a disease marked by discharge of excessive amounts of urine; *esp* : a disorder in which insulin is deficient and the urine and blood contain excess sugar — **di·a·bet·ic** \-'bet-ik\ *adj or n*

di·a·bol·ic \ˌdī-ə-'bäl-ik\ *adj* : of, relating to, or characteristic of the devil : FIENDISH — **di·a·bol·i·cal** \-'bäl-i-kəl\ *adj* — **di·a·bol·i·cal·ly** \-i-k(ə-)lē\ *adv* — **di·a·bol·i·cal·ness** \-i-kəl-nəs\ *n*

di·a·crit·ic \ˌdī-ə-'krit-ik\ *n* : a mark used with a letter or group of letters and indicating a sound value different from that given the unmarked or otherwise marked letter or combination of letters — called also *di·a·crit·i·cal mark* \-ˌkrit-i-kəl-\

di·a·dem \'dī-ə-ˌdem, -əd-əm\ *n* : CROWN; *esp* : a headband worn as a badge of royalty

di·aer·e·sis \dī-'er-ə-səs\ *n, pl* **di·aer·e·ses** \-'er-ə-ˌsēz\ : a mark ¨ placed over a vowel to show that it is pronounced in a separate syllable (as in *naïve* or *Brontë*)

diag *abbr* **1** diagonal **2** diagram

di·ag·nose \'dī-əg-ˌnōs, -ˌnōz\ *vb* : to recognize by signs and symptoms : make a diagnosis ⟨*diagnose* a disease⟩ ⟨*diagnose* a play in football⟩

di·ag·no·sis \ˌdī-əg-'nō-səs\ *n, pl* **-no·ses** \-'nō-ˌsēz\ **1** : the art or act of identifying a disease from its signs and symptoms **2 a** : a careful critical study of something esp. to determine its nature or importance **b** : the conclusion reached after a critical study — **di·ag·nos·tic** \-'näs-tik\ *adj* — **di·ag·nos·ti·cian** \-ˌnäs-'tish-ən\ *n*

[1]di·ag·o·nal \dī-'ag-ən-əl\ *adj* **1** : joining two opposite corners of a 4-sided figure **2** : running in a slanting direction — **di·ag·o·nal·ly** \-ē\ *adv*

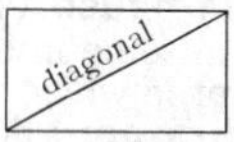

[2]diagonal *n* **1** : a diagonal line or direction **2** : a diagonal row, arrangement, or pattern

[1]di·a·gram \'dī-ə-ˌgram\ *n* : a drawing, sketch, plan, or chart that makes something clearer or easier to understand — **di·a·gram·mat·ic** \ˌdī-ə-grə-'mat-ik\ *or* **di·a·gram·mat·i·cal** \-'mat-i-kəl\ *adj* — **di·a·gram·mat·i·cal·ly** \-'mat-i-k(ə-)lē\ *adv*

[2]diagram *vb* **-gramed** *or* **-grammed** \-ˌgramd\; **-gram·ing** *or* **-gram·ming** \-ˌgram-ing\ : to represent by or put into the form of a diagram ⟨*diagram* a sentence⟩

[1]di·al \'dī(-ə)l\ *n* [from Latin *dialis* "of day", from *dies* "day"; so called because it showed the time of day] **1 a** : the face of a watch or clock **b** : SUNDIAL **2 a** : a face or scale upon which some measurement is registered usu. by means of numbers and a pointer **b** : a disk usu. with a knob or slots that may be turned to make electrical connections (as on a telephone) or to regulate the operation of a device (as a radio)

[2]dial *vb* **di·aled** *or* **di·alled**; **di·al·ing** *or* **di·al·ling** **1** : to manipulate a dial so as to operate, regulate, or select **2** : to make a call on a dial telephone

dial *abbr* **1** dialect **2** dialectal

di·a·lect \'dī-ə-ˌlekt\ *n* **1 :** a regional variety of a language differing from the standard language **2 :** a variety of a language used by the members of an occupational group or a social class ⟨peasant *dialect*⟩ — **dialect** *or* **di·a·lec·tal** \ˌdī-ə-'lek-təl\ *adj* — **di·a·lec·tal·ly** \ˌdī-ə-'lek-tə-lē\ *adv* — **di·a·lec·ti·cal** \-ti-kəl\ *adj*

di·a·logue *or* **di·a·log** \'dī-ə-ˌlȯg\ *n* **1 :** a conversation between two or more persons **2 :** the parts of a literary or dramatic composition that represent conversation

di·al·y·sis \dī-'al-ə-səs\ *n, pl* **-y·ses** \-ə-ˌsēz\ **:** the separation of substances in solution by means of their unequal diffusion through semipermeable membranes; *esp* **:** such a separation of colloids from soluble substances

di·am·e·ter \dī-'am-ət-ər\ *n* **[**from Greek *diametros*, from *dia-* "through" and *metron* "measure"**] 1 :** a straight line passing through the center of a figure or body **2 :** the length of a straight line through the center of an object

di·a·met·ric \ˌdī-ə-'me-trik\ *adj* **1 :** of or relating to a diameter **2 :** completely opposed or opposite — **di·a·met·ri·cal** \-'me-tri-kəl\ *adj* — **di·a·met·ri·cal·ly** \-tri-k(ə-)lē\ *adv*

di·a·mond \'dī-(ə-)mənd\ *n* **1 a :** a very hard stone of crystallized carbon that is used as a precious gem and industrially as an abrasive powder and in cutting tools **b :** a piece of this stone esp. when cut and polished **2 :** a figure formed by four equal straight lines enclosing two acute and two obtuse angles **3 :** a red lozenge used to distinguish a suit of playing cards; *also* **:** a card of the suit bearing diamonds **4 a :** INFIELD **b :** the entire playing field in baseball or softball

[1]**di·a·mond·back** \'dī-(ə-)mən(d)-ˌbak\ *also* **di·a·mond·backed** \ˌdī-(ə-)mən(d)-'bakt\ *adj* **:** having marks like diamonds on the back

[2]**diamondback** *n* **:** a large and deadly rattlesnake of the southern U.S.

diamondback terrapin *n* **:** any of several edible terrapins of coastal salt marshes of the southeastern U.S.

dia·pause \'dī-ə-ˌpȯz\ *n* **:** a period of dormancy (as in some insects) in which development slows down or in which activity is decreased

[1]**di·a·per** \'dī-(ə-)pər\ *n* **1 :** a usu. white linen or cotton fabric woven in a pattern formed by the repetition of a simple usu. geometric design; *also* **:** the design on such cloth **2 :** a garment for infants consisting of a piece of absorbent material drawn up between the legs and fastened about the waist

[2]**diaper** *vb* **1 :** to ornament with diaper designs **2 :** to put a diaper on ⟨*diaper* a baby⟩

di·a·phragm \'dī-ə-ˌfram\ *n* **1 :** a body partition of muscle and connective tissue; *esp* **:** the partition separating the chest and abdominal cavities in mammals **2 :** a device that regulates the size of an opening in order to control the amount of light passing through a lens (as of a camera or microscope) **3 :** a thin flexible disk that vibrates when struck by sound waves (as in a microphone) or that vibrates to produce sound waves (as in a loudspeaker) — **di·a·phrag·mat·ic** \ˌdī-ə-ˌfrag-'mat-ik\ *adj*

di·ar·rhea *or* **di·ar·rhoea** \ˌdī-ə-'rē-ə\ *n* **:** an abnormally frequent or abundant discharge of loose or fluid material from the bowels

di·a·ry \'dī-(ə-)rē\ *n, pl* **-ries :** a daily record esp. of personal experiences, observations, and thoughts; *also* **:** a book for keeping such private notes and records

di·a·stase \'dī-ə-ˌstās\ *n* **:** AMYLASE

di·as·to·le \dī-'as-tə-(ˌ)lē\ *n* **:** the stretching of the cavities of the heart during which they fill with blood — **di·a·stol·ic** \ˌdi-ə-'stäl-ik\ *adj*

di·as·tro·phism \dī-'as-trə-ˌfiz-əm\ *n* **:** the process of deformation that produces in the earth's crust its continents and ocean basins, plateaus and mountains, folds of strata, and faults — **di·a·stroph·ic** \ˌdī-ə-'sträf-ik\ *adj*

di·a·tom \'dī-ə-ˌtäm\ *n* **:** any of a class of minute floating single-celled or colonial algae that are abundant in fresh and salt water and in soil and have a cell wall of silica that persists as a skeleton after death — **di·a·to·ma·ceous** \ˌdī-ət-ə-'mā-shəs\ *adj*

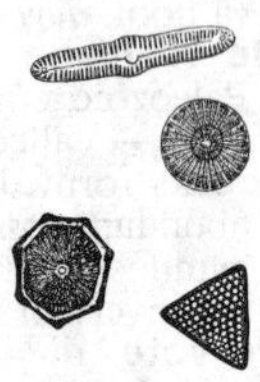

diatoms (magnified 150 times)

di·atom·ic \ˌdī-ə-'täm-ik\ *adj* **:** having two atoms in the molecule

di·at·o·mite \dī-'at-ə-ˌmīt\ *n* **:** a light crumbly silica-containing material derived chiefly from diatom remains and used esp. as a filter and for heat insulation

dia·ton·ic \ˌdī-ə-'tän-ik\ *adj* **:** relating to or being a standard major or minor scale of eight tones to the octave without chromatic deviation — **dia·ton·i·cal·ly** \-'tän-i-k(ə-)lē\ *adv*

di·a·tribe \'dī-ə-ˌtrīb\ *n* **:** a bitter or violent attack in speech or writing

dib·ble \'dib-əl\ *n* **:** a small hand tool for making holes in the ground for plants, seeds, or bulbs

[1]**dice** \'dīs\ *n, pl* **dice [** from Middle English *dees*, *dyce*, plural of *dee* "die", misunderstood as a singular**] 1 :** a small cube marked on each face with one to six spots and used usu. in pairs in various games **2 :** a gambling game played with dice

[2]**dice** *vb* **1 :** to cut into small cubes ⟨*diced* carrots⟩ **2 :** to play games with dice — **dic·er** *n*

di·chlo·ride \(')dī-'klō(ə)r-ˌīd, -'klȯ(ə)r-\ *n* **:** a compound containing two atoms of chlorine combined with an element or radical

di·chro·mat·ic \ˌdī-krō-'mat-ik\ *adj* **:** having or exhibiting two colors

dick·ens \'dik-ənz\ *n* **:** DEVIL, DEUCE — used chiefly as a mild oath

dick·er \'dik-ər\ *vb* **dick·ered**; **dick·er·ing** \'dik-(ə-)ring\ **:** BARGAIN, HAGGLE — **dicker** *n*

dick·ey *or* **dicky** \'dik-ē\ *n, pl* **dick·eys** *or* **dick·ies 1 :** any of various articles of clothing: as **a :** a separate or detachable front of a shirt **b :** a small cloth insert worn to fill in the neckline **2 :** a small bird

Dick test \'dik-\ *n* **:** a test to determine whether one can contract scarlet fever made by an injection of scarlet fever toxin

di·cot \'dī-ˌkät\ *also* **di·cot·yl** \-ˌkät-əl\ *n* **:** DICOTYLEDON — **dicot** *adj*

di·cot·y·le·don \ˌdī-ˌkät-ə-'lēd-ən\ *n* **:** any of a group of flowering plants (as an aster, an oak, or a cabbage) having an embryo with two cotyledons and usu. net-veined leaves and flower parts not in threes — **di·cot·y·le·don·ous** \-'lēd-ə-nəs\ *adj*

ə abut	ər further	a back	ā bake
ä cot, cart	au̇ out	ch chin	e less	ē easy
g gift	i trip	ī life	j joke	ng sing	ō flow
ȯ flaw	ȯi coin	th thin	th this	ü loot
u̇ foot	y yet	yü few	yu̇ furious	zh vision

dict *abbr* dictionary

¹dic·tate \'dik-ˌtāt\ *vb* **1 :** to speak or read for a person to transcribe or for a machine to record ⟨*dictate* a letter to a secretary⟩ **2 :** to say or state with authority or power : give orders ⟨*dictate* terms of surrender⟩ ⟨few people enjoy being *dictated* to⟩

²dictate *n* : an authoritative rule, prescription, or injunction : COMMAND ⟨the *dictates* of conscience⟩ ⟨the *dictates* of good taste⟩

dic·ta·tion \dik-'tā-shən\ *n* **1 :** the act or process of giving arbitrary commands **2 a :** the dictating of words ⟨write from *dictation*⟩ **b :** something that is dictated or is taken down from dictation

dic·ta·tor \'dik-ˌtāt-ər, dik-'\ *n* **1 :** a person ruling absolutely and often brutally and oppressively **2 :** one that dictates — **dic·ta·to·ri·al** \ˌdik-tə-'tōr-ē-əl, -'tȯr-\ *adj* — **dic·ta·to·ri·al·ly** \-ē-ə-lē\ *adv* — **dic·ta·to·ri·al·ness** *n*

dic·ta·tor·ship \dik-'tāt-ər-ˌship\ *n* **1 :** the office or term of office of a dictator **2 :** autocratic rule, control, or leadership **3 :** a government, form of government, or country in which absolute power is held by a dictator or a small clique

dic·tion \'dik-shən\ *n* **1 :** choice of words esp. with regard to correctness, clearness, or effectiveness : WORDING ⟨careless *diction* in his essay⟩ **2 :** quality of vocal expression : ENUNCIATION ⟨a good singer with excellent *diction*⟩

dic·tio·nary \'dik-shə-ˌner-ē\ *n, pl* **-nar·ies** **1 :** a reference book containing words usu. alphabetically arranged along with information about their forms, pronunciations, functions, etymologies, meanings, and syntactical and idiomatic uses **2 :** a reference book listing alphabetically terms or names important to a particular subject along with discussion of their meanings and applications ⟨a law *dictionary*⟩ **3 :** a reference book giving words of one language and their meanings in another ⟨an English-French *dictionary*⟩

dic·tum \'dik-təm\ *n, pl* **dic·ta** \-tə\ *also* **dic·tums** **1 :** an authoritative statement : PRONOUNCEMENT **2 :** a formal statement of an opinion

did *past of* DO

di·dac·tic \dī-'dak-tik\ *adj* **1 :** intended primarily to instruct rather than to entertain; *esp* : intended to teach a moral lesson ⟨*didactic* literature⟩ **2 :** having or showing a tendency to instruct or lecture others ⟨a *didactic* manner⟩ — **di·dac·ti·cal** \-ti-kəl\ *adj* — **di·dac·ti·cal·ly** \-ti-k(ə-)lē\ *adv* — **di·dac·ti·cism** \-tə-ˌsiz-əm\ *n*

didn't \'did-ənt\ : did not

didst \(')didst\ *archaic past 2d sing of* DO

¹die \'dī\ *vb* **died**; **dy·ing** \'dī-ing\ **1 :** to stop living : EXPIRE ⟨*died* of old age⟩ **2 a :** to pass out of existence ⟨a *dying* race⟩ **b :** to disappear or subside gradually ⟨the wind *died* down⟩ **3 :** to long keenly or desperately ⟨*dying* to go⟩ **4 :** STOP ⟨the motor sputtered and *died*⟩

²die \'dī\ *n* **1** *pl* **dice** \'dīs\ : DICE 1 **2** *pl* **dies** \'dīz\ : any of various devices used for cutting, shaping, or stamping a material or object

diel·drin \'dēl-drən\ *n* : a white crystalline chlorine-containing insecticide

di·er·e·sis *var of* DIAERESIS

die·sel \'dē-zəl, -səl\ *n* **1 :** DIESEL ENGINE **2 :** a vehicle (as a truck or train) driven by a diesel engine

diesel engine *n* : an internal-combustion engine in which air is compressed to generate sufficient heat to ignite the oil in the cylinder

¹di·et \'dī-ət\ *n* **1 :** the food and drink that a person, animal, or group usu. takes : customary nourishment **2 :** the kind and amount of food selected for a person or animal for a special reason (as ill health or overweight) ⟨a high-protein *diet*⟩

²diet *vb* : to eat or cause to eat less or according to prescribed rules — **di·et·er** *n*

³diet *n* : a formal deliberative assembly; *esp* : any of various national or provincial legislatures

di·e·tary \'dī-ə-ˌter-ē\ *adj* : of or relating to a diet or to the rules of diet

di·e·tet·ic \ˌdī-ə-'tet-ik\ *adj* : of or relating to diet or dietetics — **di·e·tet·i·cal·ly** \-'tet-i-k(ə-)lē\ *adv*

di·e·tet·ics \-'tet-iks\ *n* : the science of applying the principles of nutrition to feeding

di·e·ti·tian *or* **di·e·ti·cian** \ˌdī-ə-'tish-ən\ *n* : a specialist in dietetics

diff *abbr* difference

dif·fer \'dif-ər\ *vb* **dif·fered**; **dif·fer·ing** \'dif-(ə-)ring\ **1 :** to be not the same : be unlike ⟨brothers who *differ* in looks⟩ **2 :** DISAGREE

dif·fer·ence \'dif-ərn(t)s, 'dif-(ə-)rən(t)s\ *n* **1 :** unlikeness between persons or things ⟨the striking *difference* in the sisters' looks⟩ **2 :** the degree or amount by which things differ; *esp* : the number that is obtained by subtracting one number from another ⟨the *difference* between 4 and 6 is 2⟩ **3 :** a disagreement in opinion : DISPUTE ⟨persons unable to settle their *differences*⟩

dif·fer·ent \'dif-ərnt, 'dif-(ə-)rənt\ *adj* **1 :** not of the same kind : partly or totally unlike another ⟨this apple is *different* from the others in size and color⟩ **2 :** not the same : OTHER, SEPARATE ⟨see the same person at *different* times⟩ — **dif·fer·ent·ly** *adv*

¹dif·fer·en·tial \ˌdif-ə-'ren-chəl\ *adj* **1 a :** of, relating to, or constituting a distinction : DISTINGUISHING **b :** making a distinction between individuals or classes : DISCRIMINATORY **2 :** functioning or proceeding differently or at a different rate ⟨*differential* permeability of a membrane⟩ — **dif·fer·en·tial·ly** \-'rench-(ə-)lē\ *adv*

²differential *n* : DIFFERENTIAL GEAR

differential gear *n* : an arrangement of gears in an automobile that allows one wheel to turn faster than another (as in going around a curve)

dif·fer·en·ti·ate \ˌdif-ə-'ren-chē-ˌāt\ *vb* **1 :** to make or become different in some way ⟨the color of their eyes *differentiates* the twins⟩ **2 :** to undergo or cause to undergo differentiation in the course of development **3 :** to recognize or state the difference or differences ⟨*differentiate* between two plants⟩

dif·fer·en·ti·a·tion \-ˌren-chē-'ā-shən\ *n* **1 :** the act or process of differentiating **2 :** the sum of the processes whereby cells, tissues, and structures attain their specialized adult form and function; *also* : the result of these processes

dif·fi·cult \'dif-i-(ˌ)kəlt\ *adj* **1 :** hard to do, make, or carry out : ARDUOUS ⟨a *difficult* climb⟩ **2 a :** hard to deal with, manage, or overcome ⟨a *difficult* child⟩ **b :** hard to understand : PUZZLING ⟨*difficult* reading⟩ — **dif·fi·cult·ly** *adv*

dif·fi·cul·ty \-(ˌ)kəl-tē\ *n, pl* **-ties** **1 :** difficult nature ⟨slowed up by the *difficulty* of a task⟩ **2 :** great effort ⟨accomplish a task with *difficulty*⟩ **3 :** something that is hard to do : OBSTACLE ⟨overcome *difficulties*⟩ **4 :** a difficult or trying situation : TROUBLE ⟨in financial *difficulties*⟩ **5 :** DISAGREEMENT ⟨the partners ironed out their *difficulties*⟩

dif·fi·dent \'dif-əd-ənt, -ə-ˌdent\ *adj* **1 :** lacking confidence : TIMID **2 :** RESERVED, UNASSERTIVE ***syn*** see SHY ***ant*** brash, confident — **dif·fi·dence** \-əd-ən(t)s, -ə-ˌden(t)s\ *n* — **dif·fi·dent·ly** *adv*

dif·fract \dif-'rakt\ *vb* : to undergo or cause to undergo diffraction ⟨*diffract* light⟩

D

dif·frac·tion \dif-'rak-shən\ *n* **:** the bending or spreading of a beam of light esp. when passing through a narrow opening or when reflected from a ruled surface

diffraction grating *n* **:** a series of closely and equally spaced parallel lines or bars used for producing spectra by diffraction of light

1**dif·fuse** \dif-'yüs\ *adj* **1 :** poured or spread out **:** not concentrated ⟨*diffuse* daylight⟩ **2 :** marked by wordiness **:** VERBOSE ⟨a *diffuse* writer⟩ **3 :** spreading widely or loosely **:** SCATTERED ⟨*diffuse* branches⟩ — **dif·fuse·ly** *adv* — **dif·fuse·ness** *n*

2**dif·fuse** \dif-'yüz\ *vb* **1 :** to pour out and spread freely **2 :** to subject to or undergo diffusion ⟨gases *diffuse* at different rates⟩ **3 :** to break up (light) by reflection (as from a rough surface)

dif·fu·sion \dif-'yü-zhən\ *n* **1 :** a diffusing or a being diffused **2 :** the intermingling of the particles of liquids or gases **3 :** the reflection of light from a rough surface or the transmission of light through a translucent material (as frosted glass)

1**dig** \'dig\ *vb* **dug** \'dəg\; **dig·ging 1 a :** to turn up the soil (as with a spade or hoe) **b :** to hollow out or form by removing earth ⟨*dig* a hole⟩ ⟨*dig* a cellar⟩ **2 :** to uncover or seek by turning up earth ⟨*dig* potatoes⟩ ⟨*dig* for gold⟩ **3 :** to bring to light **:** DISCOVER ⟨*dig* up information⟩ **4 :** POKE, THRUST ⟨*dig* a person in the ribs⟩ **5** *slang* **a :** to pay attention to ⟨*dig* that crazy hat⟩ **b :** UNDERSTAND ⟨you *dig* me?⟩ **c :** LIKE ⟨really *digs* rock music⟩ — **dig·ger** *n*

2**dig** *n* **1 :** THRUST, POKE **2 :** a cutting remark **:** GIBE

1**di·gest** \'dī-ˌjest\ *n* **:** a summary or condensation of a body of information or of a literary work ⟨a *digest* of the laws⟩

2**di·gest** \dī-'jest, də-\ *vb* **1 :** to think over and arrange in the mind **:** assimilate mentally **2 :** to convert food into simpler forms that can be taken in and used by the body **3 :** to compress into a short summary **4 :** to become digested — **di·gest·i·ble** \dī-'jes-tə-bəl, də-\ *adj* — **di·gest·i·bil·i·ty** \(ˌ)dī-ˌjes-tə-'bil-ət-ē, də-\ *n*

di·ges·tion \dī-'jes-chən, də-\ *n* **:** the process or power of digesting something and esp. food

di·ges·tive \-'jes-tiv\ *adj* **1 :** of or relating to digestion **2 :** having the power to cause or promote digestion ⟨*digestive* enzymes⟩

dig·ger wasp \'dig-ər-\ *n* **:** a burrowing wasp; *esp* **:** one that digs nest burrows in the soil and provisions them with insects or spiders paralyzed by stinging

dig·gings \'dig-ingz\ *n pl* **1 :** a place where ore, metals, or precious stones are dug **2 :** LODGINGS

dig·it \'dij-ət\ *n* [from Latin *digitus* "finger" or "toe", descended from the same source as English *toe*; applied to the ten numerals because reckoning was done on the ten fingers] **1 a :** any of the arabic numerals 1 to 9 and usu. the symbol 0 **b :** one of the elements that combine to form numbers in a system other than the decimal system **2 :** FINGER, TOE — **dig·i·tal** \'dij-ət-əl\ *adj* — **dig·i·tal·ly** \-ə-lē\ *adv*

digital computer *n* **:** a computer that operates with numbers expressed as digits (as in the binary system) — compare ANALOG COMPUTER

dig·i·tal·is \ˌdij-ə-'tal-əs\ *n* **:** a powerful drug used as a heart stimulant and prepared from the dried leaves of the common foxglove

dig·ni·fied \'dig-nə-ˌfīd\ *adj* **:** showing or expressing dignity

dig·ni·fy \-ˌfī\ *vb* **-fied; -fy·ing :** to give dignity or distinction to **:** HONOR

dig·ni·tary \'dig-nə-ˌter-ē\ *n, pl* **-tar·ies :** a person of high position or honor ⟨*dignitaries* of the church⟩

dig·ni·ty \'dig-nət-ē\ *n, pl* **-ties 1 :** the quality or state of being worthy, honored, or esteemed **2 :** high rank, office, or position **3 :** formal reserve of manner or language

di·gress \dī-'gres, də-\ *vb* **:** to turn aside esp. from the main subject in writing or speaking — **di·gres·sion** \-'gresh-ən\ *n* — **di·gres·sive** \-'gres-iv\ *adj* — **di·gres·sive·ly** *adv* — **di·gres·sive·ness** *n*

di·he·dral angle \(ˌ)dī-ˌhē-drəl-\ *n* **:** the angle between two intersecting planes

1**dike** \'dīk\ *n* **1 :** an artificial watercourse **:** DITCH **2 :** a bank of earth constructed to control or confine water **:** LEVEE

2**dike** *vb* **:** to surround or protect with a dike; *also* **:** to drain by a dike — **dik·er** *n*

dil *abbr* dilute

di·lap·i·dat·ed \də-'lap-ə-ˌdāt-əd\ *adj* **:** partly ruined or decayed ⟨a *dilapidated* old house⟩

di·lap·i·da·tion \də-ˌlap-ə-'dā-shən\ *n* **:** a dilapidated condition **:** partial ruin (as from neglect)

di·late \dī-'lāt, 'dī-ˌ\ *vb* **:** to make or grow larger or wider **:** SWELL, DISTEND ⟨eyes *dilated* with fear⟩ ⟨lungs *dilated* with air⟩ — **di·lat·a·ble** \dī-'lāt-ə-bəl\ *adj* — **di·la·tor** \dī-'lāt-ər, 'dī-ˌ\ *n*

di·la·tion \dī-'lā-shən\ *n* **:** the act of dilating **:** the state of being dilated **:** EXPANSION

dil·a·to·ry \'dil-ə-ˌtōr-ē, -ˌtȯr-\ *adj* **1 :** tending or intended to cause delay ⟨*dilatory* tactics⟩ **2 :** characterized by procrastination **:** TARDY — **dil·a·to·ri·ly** \ˌdil-ə-'tōr-ə-lē, -'tȯr-\ *adv* — **dil·a·to·ri·ness** \'dil-ə-ˌtōr-ē-nəs, -ˌtȯr-\ *n*

di·lem·ma \də-'lem-ə\ *n* **:** a choice or a situation in which one has to choose between two or more things, ways, or plans that are equally unsatisfactory **:** a difficult choice

dil·et·tante \ˌdil-ə-'tänt(-ē), -'tant(-ē)\ *n, pl* **-tantes** *or* **-tan·ti** \-'tänt-ē, -'tant-ē\ **1 :** an admirer or lover of the arts **2 :** a person who engages usu. superficially in an art or branch of knowledge as a pastime — **dilettante** *adj* — **dil·et·tan·tism** \-'tän-ˌtiz-əm, -'tan-\ *n*

1**dil·i·gence** \'dil-ə-jən(t)s\ *n* **:** careful and continued work **:** conscientious effort **:** INDUSTRY

2**dil·i·gence** \'dil-ə-ˌzhäns, 'dil-ə-jən(t)s\ *n* **:** STAGECOACH

dil·i·gent \'dil-ə-jənt\ *adj* **:** characterized by steady, earnest, and energetic application and effort **:** PAINSTAKING ***syn*** see BUSY ***ant*** dilatory — **dil·i·gent·ly** *adv*

dill \'dil\ *n* **:** an herb with aromatic foliage and with seeds used in flavoring pickles

dil·ly·dal·ly \'dil-ē-ˌdal-ē\ *vb* **:** DELAY, DAWDLE

di·lute \dī-'lüt, də-\ *vb* **:** to make thinner or more liquid by admixture (as with water) — **dilute** *adj* — **di·lute·ness** *n* — **di·lut·er** *or* **di·lu·tor** \-'lüt-ər\ *n* — **di·lu·tion** \dī-'lü-shən, də-\ *n*

1**dim** \'dim\ *adj* **dim·mer; dim·mest 1 :** not bright or distinct **:** OBSCURE, FAINT ⟨a *dim* light⟩ **2 :** being without luster **:** DULL **3 a :** not seeing or understanding clearly **b :** not seen or understood clearly — **dim·ly** *adv* — **dim·ness** *n*

2**dim** *vb* **dimmed; dim·ming 1 :** to make or become dim **2 :** to reduce the light from headlights by switching to the low beam — **dim·mer** *n*

ə abut	ər further	a back	ā bake	
ä cot, cart	aù out	ch chin	e less	ē easy
g gift	i trip	ī life	j joke	ng sing	ō flow
ȯ flaw	ȯi coin	th thin	t͟h this	ü loot
ù foot	y yet	yü few	yù furious	zh vision

dim *or* **dimin** *abbr* diminuendo

dime \'dīm\ *n* [from medieval French *dime* "a tenth part", from Latin *decima*, from *decem* "ten"] **:** a U.S. coin worth 1⁄10 dollar

di·men·sion \də-'men-chən, dī-\ *n* **1 a :** extension in one direction **b :** magnitude of extension in one direction or in all directions **:** SIZE **2 :** the range over which something extends **:** SCOPE — **di·men·sion·al** \-'mench-(ə-)nəl\ *adj* — **di·men·sion·al·ly** \-ē\ *adv* — **di·men·sion·less** \-'men-chən-ləs\ *adj*

di·min·ish \də-'min-ish\ *vb* **1 a :** to make less or cause to appear less **b :** to reduce by subtracting ⟨8 *diminished* by 5⟩ **2 :** DWINDLE — **di·min·ish·a·ble** \-ish-ə-bəl\ *adj* — **di·min·ish·ment** \-ish-mənt\ *n*

di·min·u·en·do \də-ˌmin-(y)ə-'wen-dō\ *adv or adj* **:** DECRESCENDO — **diminuendo** *n*

dim·i·nu·tion \ˌdim-ə-'n(y)ü-shən\ *n* **:** the act, process, or an instance of diminishing **:** DECREASE

1**di·min·u·tive** \də-'min-yət-iv\ *n* **1 :** a diminutive word or affix **2 :** a diminutive object or individual

2**diminutive** *adj* **1 :** indicating small size and sometimes the state or quality of being lovable, pitiable, or contemptible ⟨the *diminutive* suffixes *-ette* and *-ling*⟩ ⟨the *diminutive* noun *duckling*⟩ **2 :** extremely small **:** TINY — **di·min·u·tive·ly** *adv* — **di·min·u·tive·ness** *n*

dim·i·ty \'dim-ət-ē\ *n, pl* **-ties :** a usu. corded cotton fabric in checks or stripes

1**dim·ple** \'dim-pəl\ *n* **1 :** a slight natural indentation in the surface of some part of the human body **2 :** a slight hollow

2**dimple** *vb* **dim·pled**; **dim·pling** \-p(ə-)ling\ **:** to mark with or form dimples

1**din** \'din\ *n* **:** a loud noise; *esp* **:** a welter of confused or discordant sounds

2**din** *vb* **dinned**; **din·ning 1 :** to make a din **2 :** to impress by insistent repetition ⟨*dinned* in our ears the consequences of failure⟩

dine \'dīn\ *vb* **1 :** to eat dinner **2 :** to give a dinner to **:** FEED

din·er \'dī-nər\ *n* **1 :** one that dines **2 a :** DINING CAR **b :** a restaurant in the shape of a railroad car

di·nette \dī-'net\ *n* **:** an alcove or small room used for dining

ding \'ding\ *vb* **:** to make a ringing sound **:** CLANG

1**ding·dong** \'ding-ˌdȯng, -ˌdäng\ *n* **:** the sound of repeated strokes on a bell or a similar sound

2**dingdong** *adj* **:** vigorously contested ⟨a *dingdong* battle⟩

din·ghy \'ding-(k)ē\ *n, pl* **dinghies 1 :** a ship's small boat **2 :** a rowboat used as a tender **3 :** a rubber life raft

din·gle \'ding-gəl\ *n* **:** a small and narrow wooded valley

din·go \'ding-gō\ *n, pl* **dingoes :** a reddish brown bushy-tailed wild dog of Australia

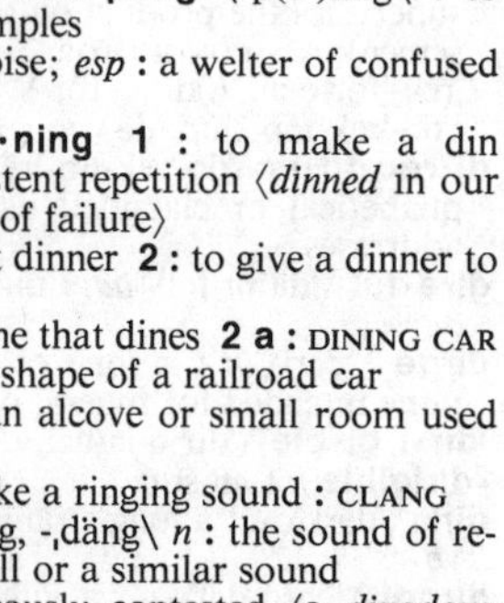

dingo
(21 in. at shoulder)

din·gy \'din-jē\ *adj* **din·gi·er**; **-est 1 :** DARK, DULL ⟨a *dingy* unlighted room⟩ **2 :** not fresh or clean **:** GRIMY ⟨*dingy* wallpaper⟩ — **din·gi·ly** \-jə-lē\ *adv* — **din·gi·ness** \-jē-nəs\ *n*

din·ich·thy·id \dī-'nik-thē-əd\ *n* **:** any of a genus of Devonian fishes or their fossils attaining a length as great as 30 feet and having the anterior bony armor reduced — **dinichthyid** *adj*

din·ing car \'dī-ning-\ *n* **:** a railroad car in which meals are served

din·key *or* **din·ky** \'ding-kē\ *n, pl* **dinkeys** *or* **dinkies :** a small locomotive used esp. for hauling freight, logging, and shunting

din·ky \'ding-kē\ *adj* **din·ki·er**; **-est :** SMALL, INSIGNIFICANT

din·ner \'din-ər\ *n* **1 :** the main meal of the day **2 :** a formal banquet

di·no·flag·el·late \ˌdī-nō-'flaj-ə-lət\ *n* **:** any of an order of chiefly marine floating organisms that resemble both algae and protozoa and are important in marine food chains

di·no·saur \'dī-nə-ˌsȯr\ *n* [from Greek *deinos* "terrible" and *sauros* "lizard"] **:** any of a group of extinct chiefly land-dwelling long-tailed reptiles with limbs adapted for walking — **di·no·sau·ri·an** \ˌdī-nə-'sȯr-ē-ən\ *adj or n*

1**dint** \'dint\ *n* **1** *archaic* **:** BLOW **2 :** FORCE, POWER — used chiefly in the phrase *by dint of* **3 :** DENT

2**dint** *vb* **:** DENT

1**di·oc·e·san** \dī-'äs-ə-sən\ *adj* **:** of or relating to a diocese

2**diocesan** *n* **:** a bishop having jurisdiction over a diocese

di·o·cese \'dī-ə-səs, -ˌsēz, -ˌsēs\ *n* **:** the district over which a bishop has authority

di·ode \'dī-ˌōd\ *n* **:** an electron tube consisting of a filament and a plate to which the electrons flow

di·o·rama \ˌdī-ə-'ram-ə, -'räm-\ *n* **:** a scenic representation in which lifelike sculptured figures and surrounding details are realistically illuminated against a painted background

di·ox·ide \(ˈ)dī-'äk-ˌsīd\ *n* **:** an oxide containing two atoms of oxygen in the molecule

1**dip** \'dip\ *vb* **dipped**; **dip·ping 1 a :** to plunge momentarily or partially under the surface (as of a liquid) so as to moisten, cool, or coat **b :** to thrust in a way to suggest immersion ⟨*dips* a hand into his pocket⟩ **2 :** to lift a portion of by reaching below the surface with something that holds liquid **:** LADLE ⟨*dip* water from a pail⟩ **3 :** to lower and then raise again ⟨*dip* a flag in salute⟩ **4 a :** to plunge into a liquid and quickly emerge ⟨oars *dipping* rhythmically⟩ **b :** to immerse something into a processing liquid or finishing material **5 a :** to drop down or out of sight ⟨the road *dipped* below the crest⟩ **b :** to decrease moderately and usu. temporarily ⟨prices *dipped*⟩ **6 :** to reach down inside or as if inside or below a surface esp. to withdraw a part of the contents ⟨*dipped* into their savings⟩ **7 :** to concern oneself casually or tentatively with something; *esp* **:** to read superficially ⟨*dip* into a book⟩

2**dip** *n* **1 :** an act of dipping; *esp* **:** a brief plunge into the water for sport or exercise **2 a :** inclination downward **b :** a sharp or slight downward course **:** DROP **3 :** the angle formed with the horizon by a magnetic needle free to rotate in a vertical plane **4 :** something obtained by or used in dipping **5 :** a sauce or soft mixture into which food (as potato chips) may be dipped **6 :** a liquid preparation into which something may be dipped (as for disinfecting or coating)

diph·the·ria \dif-'thir-ē-ə, dip-\ *n* **:** a contagious bacterial disease with fever in which the air passages become coated with a membranous layer that often obstructs breathing — **diph·the·ri·al** \-ē-əl\ *or* **diph·the·rit·ic** \ˌdif-thə-'rit-ik\ *adj*

diph·thong \'dif-ˌthȯng, 'dip-\ *n* **:** a 2-element speech sound that begins with the tongue position for one vowel and ends with the tongue position for another all within one syllable ⟨the sounds of *ou* in *out* and of *oy* in *boy* are *diphthongs*⟩

di·plo·ma \də-'plō-mə\ *n* **:** a document conferring a privilege, honor, or power; *esp* **:** an official paper showing graduation from or a degree conferred by an educational institution

di·plo·ma·cy \də-'plō-mə-sē\ *n* **1 :** the art and practice of conducting negotiations between nations **2 :** skill in handling affairs without arousing hostility **:** TACT

dip·lo·mat \'dip-lə-ˌmat\ *n* **:** a person employed or skilled in diplomacy

dip·lo·mat·ic \ˌdip-lə-'mat-ik\ *adj* **1 :** of, relating to, or concerned with diplomacy or diplomats ⟨*diplomatic* immunity⟩ **2 :** TACTFUL ⟨found a *diplomatic* way to say no⟩ — **dip·lo·mat·i·cal·ly** \-'mat-i-k(ə-)lē\ *adv*

di·plo·ma·tist \də-'plō-mət-əst\ *n* **:** DIPLOMAT

dip·lo·pod \'dip-lə-ˌpäd\ *n* **:** MILLIPEDE

dip needle *n* **:** a magnetized needle pivoted so that it moves vertically and points in the direction of the earth's greatest magnetic intensity at any place — called also *dipping needle*

dip net *n* **:** a small bag-shaped net with a long handle that is used to scoop small fishes and other aquatic life from the water

di·pole \'dī-ˌpōl\ *n* **:** a pair of equal and opposite electric charges or magnetic poles of opposite sign separated by a small distance

dip needle

dip·per \'dip-ər\ *n* **1 :** one that dips; *esp* **:** something (as a long-handled cup) used for dipping **2** *cap* **:** seven stars arranged in a form resembling a dipper: **a :** BIG DIPPER **b :** LITTLE DIPPER **3 :** any of several birds skilled in diving

dip·stick \'dip-ˌstik\ *n* **:** a graduated rod for indicating depth (as of the oil in an automobile)

dip·ter·an \'dip-tə-rən\ *adj* **:** of, relating to, or being a two-winged fly — **dipteran** *n*

dip·ter·ous \-tə-rəs\ *adj* **1 :** having two wings or appendages like wings **2 :** DIPTERAN

dire \'dī(ə)r\ *adj* **1 :** exciting horror **:** DREADFUL **2 :** warning of disaster ⟨a *dire* forecast⟩ **3 :** EXTREME ⟨*dire* need⟩ — **dire·ly** *adv* — **dire·ness** *n*

dir *abbr* director

[1]**di·rect** \də-'rekt, dī-\ *vb* **1 :** to mark with a name and address ⟨*direct* a letter⟩ **2 :** to cause to turn, move, or point or to follow a straight course **3 :** to point, extend, or project in a specified line, course, or direction **4 :** to show or point out the way for **5 :** to regulate the activities or course of ⟨*direct* the project⟩ ⟨*direct* a play⟩ **6 :** to request or instruct with authority ⟨the court *directed* the jury to acquit him⟩

[2]**direct** *adj* **1 :** proceeding from one point to another in time or space without deviation or interruption **:** STRAIGHT **2 a :** stemming immediately from a source, cause, or reason ⟨*direct* result⟩ **b :** operating without an intervening agency or step ⟨*direct* action⟩ ⟨census by *direct* count⟩ **c :** being or passing in a straight line of descent from parent to offspring **:** LINEAL ⟨*direct* ancestor⟩ **3 :** NATURAL, STRAIGHTFORWARD ⟨*direct* manner⟩ **4 :** consisting of or reproducing the exact words of a speaker ⟨*direct* discourse⟩ — **direct** *adv* — **di·rect·ness** \-'rek(t)-nəs\ *n*

direct current *n* **:** an electric current flowing in one direction only — abbr. *DC*

directed number *n* **:** a number preceded by a plus or minus sign

direct evidence *n* **:** evidence that if true immediately establishes the fact to be proved by it

di·rec·tion \də-'rek-shən, dī-\ *n* **1 :** guidance or supervision of action or conduct **:** MANAGEMENT **2** *archaic* **:** SUPERSCRIPTION **3 :** an authoritative instruction, indication, or order **4 :** the line or course along which something moves, lies, or points **5 :** TENDENCY, TREND — **di·rec·tion·less** \-ləs\ *adj*

di·rec·tion·al \-sh(ə-)nəl\ *adj* **1 :** relating to or indicating direction ⟨*directional* signal lights on an automobile⟩ **2 :** relating to direction or guidance esp. of thought or effort

di·rec·tive \də-'rek-tiv, dī-\ *n* **:** a general instruction as to procedure from a high-level body or official

di·rect·ly \də-'rek-(t)lē, dī-, *in sense 2 also* 'drek-lē\ *adv* **1 :** in a direct manner **2 :** without delay **:** IMMEDIATELY

direct object *n* **:** a grammatical object that is the primary goal or the result of the action of its verb ⟨*me* in "he hit me" and *house* in "we built a house" are *direct objects*⟩

di·rec·tor \də-'rek-tər, dī-\ *n* **:** one that directs: as **a :** one of a group of persons who direct the affairs of an organized body (as a corporation) **b :** one that supervises the production of a show (as for stage or screen) **c :** CONDUCTOR 2 — **di·rec·to·ri·al** \də-ˌrek-'tōr-ē-əl, (ˌ)dī-, -'tȯr-\ *adj* — **di·rec·tor·ship** \də-'rek-tər-ˌship, dī-\ *n*

di·rec·to·ry \də-'rek-t(ə-)rē, dī-\ *n, pl* **-ries :** an alphabetical or classified list containing names and addresses

dire·ful \'dī(ə)r-fəl\ *adj* **:** DIRE — **dire·ful·ly** \-fə-lē\ *adv*

dirge \'dərj\ *n* **:** a song or hymn of mourning; *esp* **:** one intended for funeral or memorial rites

[1]**dir·i·gi·ble** \'dir-ə-jə-bəl, də-'rij-ə-\ *adj* **:** STEERABLE

[2]**dirigible** *n* **:** AIRSHIP

dirk \'dərk\ *n* **:** a long straight-bladed dagger — **dirk** *vb*

dirndl \'dərn-dəl\ *n* **:** a full skirt with a tight waistband

dirt \'dərt\ *n* **1 :** a filthy or soiling substance (as mud, dust, or grime) **2 :** loose or packed earth **:** SOIL **3 :** moral uncleanness: as **a :** OBSCENITY **b :** CORRUPTION **4 :** scandalous gossip

[1]**dirty** \'dərt-ē\ *adj* **dirt·i·er; -est 1 :** not clean **:** FILTHY, SOILED ⟨*dirty* clothes⟩ **2 :** BASE, UNFAIR ⟨a *dirty* trick⟩ **3 :** INDECENT, SMUTTY ⟨*dirty* talk⟩ **4 :** FOGGY, STORMY ⟨*dirty* weather⟩ **5 :** not clear in color **:** DULL ⟨a *dirty* red⟩ — **dirt·i·ly** \'dərt-ə-lē\ *adv* — **dirt·i·ness** \'dərt-ē-nəs\ *n*

[2]**dirty** *vb* **dirt·ied; dirty·ing :** to make or become dirty

dis- *prefix* **1 a :** do the opposite of ⟨*dis*establish⟩ **b :** deprive of ⟨*dis*able⟩ ⟨*dis*frock⟩ **c :** exclude or expel from ⟨*dis*bar⟩ **2 :** opposite or absence of ⟨*dis*union⟩ ⟨*dis*affection⟩ **3 :** not ⟨*dis*agreeable⟩

dis·abil·i·ty \ˌdis-ə-'bil-ət-ē\ *n, pl* **-ties 1 :** the condition of being disabled **:** lack of ability, power, or fitness to do something **2 :** a source of disability (as a physical injury); *also* **:** a legal disqualification that prevents a person from serving or acting in a particular capacity

---

ə abut ər further a back ā bake
ä cot, cart au̇ out ch chin e less ē easy
g gift i trip ī life j joke ng sing ō flow
ȯ flaw ȯi coin th thin th this ü loot
u̇ foot y yet yü few yu̇ furious zh vision

dis·able \dis-'ā-bəl\ *vb* **dis·abled; dis·abling** \-b(ə-)ling\ **1** : to make unable or incapable : deprive of force, strength, or power of action : CRIPPLE ⟨a *disabling* illness⟩ **2** : to disqualify legally — **dis·able·ment** \-bəl-mənt\ *n*

dis·abuse \ˌdis-ə-'byüz\ *vb* : to free from mistakes or false beliefs ⟨*disabuse* him of his errors⟩

¹dis·ad·van·tage \ˌdis-əd-'vant-ij\ *n* **1** : loss or damage esp. to reputation or finances ⟨the deal worked to his *disadvantage*⟩ **2 a** : an unfavorable, inferior, or prejudicial condition ⟨at a *disadvantage* in educated company⟩ **b** : HANDICAP

²disadvantage *vb* : to place at a disadvantage : HARM

dis·ad·van·ta·geous \(ˌ)dis-ˌad-ˌvan-'tā-jəs, -vən-\ *adj* : constituting a disadvantage — **dis·ad·van·ta·geous·ly** *adv* — **dis·ad·van·ta·geous·ness** *n*

dis·af·fect \ˌdis-ə-'fekt\ *vb* : to alienate the affection or loyalty of : cause discontent in ⟨the troops were *disaffected*⟩ — **dis·af·fec·tion** \-'fek-shən\ *n*

dis·agree \ˌdis-ə-'grē\ *vb* **1** : to fail to agree ⟨the two stories *disagree*⟩ **2** : to differ in opinion ⟨*disagree* over the price⟩ **3** : to be unsuitable ⟨fried foods *disagree* with me⟩

dis·agree·a·ble \-'grē-ə-bəl\ *adj* **1** : causing discomfort : UNPLEASANT, OFFENSIVE ⟨a *disagreeable* taste⟩ **2** : marked by ill temper : PEEVISH ⟨a *disagreeable* man⟩ — **dis·agree·a·ble·ness** *n* — **dis·agree·a·bly** \-blē\ *adv*

dis·agree·ment \ˌdis-ə-'grē-mənt\ *n* **1** : the act of disagreeing **2 a** : the state of being different or at variance **b** : QUARREL

dis·al·low \ˌdis-ə-'lau̇\ *vb* : to refuse to admit or recognize : REJECT ⟨*disallow* a claim⟩ — **dis·al·low·ance** \-'lau̇-ən(t)s\ *n*

dis·ap·pear \ˌdis-ə-'pi(ə)r\ *vb* **1** : to cease to be visible : pass out of sight : VANISH **2** : to cease to be ⟨the dinosaur *disappeared* ages ago⟩ **3** : to become lost ⟨the book has *disappeared* from my desk⟩ — **dis·ap·pear·ance** \-'pir-ən(t)s\ *n*

dis·ap·point \ˌdis-ə-'pȯint\ *vb* : to fail to come up to the expectation or hope of

dis·ap·point·ed *adj* : defeated in expectation or hope : THWARTED

dis·ap·point·ment \ˌdis-ə-'pȯint-mənt\ *n* **1** : the act or an instance of disappointing : the state or emotion of being disappointed **2** : one that disappoints ⟨the play was a *disappointment*⟩

dis·ap·pro·ba·tion \(ˌ)dis-ˌap-rə-'bā-shən\ *n* : DISAPPROVAL

dis·ap·prov·al \ˌdis-ə-'prü-vəl\ *n* **1** : the act of disapproving : the state of being disapproved **2** : unfavorable opinion or judgment : CENSURE ⟨the plan met with *disapproval*⟩

dis·ap·prove \-'prüv\ *vb* **1** : to pass unfavorable judgment on : CONDEMN ⟨*disapproved* the boy's conduct⟩ **2** : to refuse approval to : REJECT ⟨*disapproved* the architect's plans⟩ **3** : to feel or express disapproval ⟨*disapproves* of smoking⟩ — **dis·ap·prov·ing·ly** \-'prü-ving-lē\ *adv*

dis·arm \(')dis-'ärm\ *vb* **1** : to deprive of arms : take arms or weapons from **2** : to disband or reduce the size and strength of the armed forces of a country **3** : to make harmless, peaceable, or friendly : remove dislike or suspicion ⟨a *disarming* smile⟩ — **dis·ar·ma·ment** \-'är-mə-mənt\ *n*

dis·ar·range \ˌdis-ə-'rānj\ *vb* : to disturb the arrangement or order of — **dis·ar·range·ment** \-mənt\ *n*

¹dis·ar·ray \ˌdis-ə-'rā\ *n* **1** : a lack of order or sequence : CONFUSION **2** : disorderly dress

²disarray *vb* : to throw into disorder

dis·as·sem·ble \ˌdis-ə-'sem-bəl\ *vb* : to take apart ⟨*disassemble* an engine⟩

di·sas·ter \diz-'as-tər, dis-\ *n* : a sudden great misfortune; *esp* : one bringing with it destruction of life or property or causing complete ruin — **di·sas·trous** \-'as-trəs\ *adj* — **di·sas·trous·ly** *adv*

dis·avow \ˌdis-ə-'vau̇\ *vb* : to refuse to acknowledge : deny responsibility for ⟨will *disavow* any knowledge of your activities⟩ — **dis·avow·al** \-'vau̇(-ə)l\ *n*

dis·band \dis-'band\ *vb* : to break up the organization of : DISPERSE ⟨*disband* an army⟩ — **dis·band·ment** \-'ban(d)-mənt\ *n*

dis·bar \dis-'bär\ *vb* **dis·barred; dis·bar·ring** : to deprive (a lawyer) of the rights and privileges of membership in the legal profession — **dis·bar·ment** \-'bär-mənt\ *n*

dis·be·lief \ˌdis-bə-'lēf\ *n* : the act or state of disbelieving : rejection of a statement as untrue

dis·be·lieve \-'lēv\ *vb* **1** : to hold not to be true or real ⟨*disbelieved* the man's testimony⟩ **2** : to withhold or reject belief ⟨came to *disbelieve* in his sincerity⟩ — **dis·be·liev·er** *n*

dis·bur·den \(')dis-'bərd-ən\ *vb* : UNBURDEN — **dis·bur·den·ment** \-mənt\ *n*

dis·burse \dis-'bərs\ *vb* : to pay out : EXPEND — **dis·burs·er** *n*

dis·burse·ment \-'bərs-mənt\ *n* : the act of disbursing; *also* : funds paid out

disc *var of* DISK

disc *abbr* discount

¹dis·card \dis-'kärd, 'dis-ˌ\ *vb* **1** : to let go a playing card from one's hand **2** : to get rid of as useless or unwanted

²dis·card \'dis-ˌkärd\ *n* **1** : the act of discarding **2** : a person or thing cast off or rejected

dis·cern \dis-'ərn, diz-\ *vb* **1** : to detect with the eyes : make out : DISTINGUISH ⟨*discern* an airplane in the clouds⟩ **2** : to come to know, recognize, or discriminate ⟨*discern* the basic issue⟩ ⟨*discern* right from wrong⟩ — **dis·cern·i·ble** \-'ər-nə-bəl\ *adj* — **dis·cern·i·bly** \-blē\ *adv*

dis·cern·ing *adj* : revealing insight and understanding : DISCRIMINATING ⟨a *discerning* critic⟩ — **dis·cern·ing·ly** \-'ər-ning-lē\ *adv*

dis·cern·ment \dis-'ərn-mənt, diz-\ *n* : skill in discerning or discriminating : keenness of insight

¹dis·charge \dis-'chärj, 'dis-ˌ\ *vb* **1** : to relieve of a charge, load, or burden : UNLOAD **2** : SHOOT ⟨*discharge* a gun⟩ **3** : to set free ⟨*discharge* a prisoner⟩ **4** : to dismiss from service or employment ⟨*discharge* a soldier⟩ **5** : to let go or let off ⟨*discharge* passengers⟩ **6** : to give forth fluid or other contents ⟨this river *discharges* into the ocean⟩ **7** : to get rid of by paying or doing ⟨*discharge* a debt⟩ ⟨*discharge* a function⟩ — **dis·charg·er** *n*

²dis·charge \'dis-ˌchärj, dis-'\ *n* **1 a** : the act of discharging **b** : something that discharges; *esp* : a certification of release or payment **2** : a firing off **3 a** : a flowing or issuing out; *also* : a rate of flow **b** : something that is emitted ⟨a *discharge* from a wound⟩ **4 a** : release or dismissal esp. from an office or employment **b** : complete separation from military service **5** : a flow of electricity (as in lightning or through a gas)

discharge tube *n* : an electron tube which contains gas or vapor at low pressure and through which electrical conduction takes place when a high voltage is applied

dis·ci·ple \dis-'ī-pəl\ *n* : a pupil or follower who accepts and helps to spread his master's teachings — **dis·ci·ple·ship** \-ˌship\ *n*

D

dis·ci·pli·nar·i·an \ˌdis-ə-plə-ˈner-ē-ən\ *n* : one who disciplines or enforces order — **disciplinarian** *adj*

dis·ci·plin·ary \ˈdis-ə-plə-ˌner-ē\ *adj* : of or relating to discipline : CORRECTIVE

1**dis·ci·pline** \ˈdis-ə-plən\ *n* **1** : a field of study : SUBJECT **2** : training that corrects, molds, or perfects **3** : PUNISHMENT **4** : control gained by obedience or training : orderly conduct **5** : a system of rules governing conduct or practice

2**discipline** *vb* **1** : to punish or penalize for the sake of discipline **2** : to train or develop by instruction and exercise esp. in self-control **3** : to bring under control ⟨*discipline* troops⟩ — **dis·ci·plin·er** *n*

disc jockey *n* : a person who conducts and announces a radio or television program of musical recordings

dis·claim \dis-ˈklām\ *vb* : to deny having a connection with or responsibility for : DISOWN ⟨the prisoner *disclaimed* any part in the crime⟩

dis·claim·er \-ˈklā-mər\ *n* : an act of disclaiming : a statement that disclaims : DENIAL

disc·like *var of* DISKLIKE

dis·close \dis-ˈklōz\ *vb* : to expose to view : make known : REVEAL ⟨*disclose* secrets⟩ — **dis·clos·er** *n*

dis·clo·sure \-ˈklō-zhər\ *n* **1** : the act or an instance of disclosing : EXPOSURE **2** : something that is disclosed : REVELATION

dis·col·or \(ˈ)dis-ˈkəl-ər\ *vb* : to alter or change in hue or color : STAIN, FADE — **dis·col·or·a·tion** \(ˌ)dis-ˌkəl-ə-ˈrā-shən\ *n*

dis·com·fit \dis-ˈkəm(p)-fət, *esp South* ˌdis-kəm-ˈfit\ *vb* : to throw into confusion : UPSET, FRUSTRATE ⟨the speaker was *discomfited* by hecklers⟩ — **dis·com·fi·ture** \dis-ˈkəm(p)-fə-ˌchu̇r, -fə-chər\ *n*

dis·com·fort \dis-ˈkəm(p)-fərt\ *vb* : to make uncomfortable or uneasy : DISTRESS — **discomfort** *n*

dis·com·mode \ˌdis-kə-ˈmōd\ *vb* : to cause inconvenience to

dis·com·pose \ˌdis-kəm-ˈpōz\ *vb* **1** : to disturb the calmness or peace of : AGITATE ⟨*discomposed* by the bad news⟩ **2** : DISARRANGE ⟨hair *discomposed* by the wind⟩ — **dis·com·po·sure** \-ˈpō-zhər\ *n*

dis·con·cert \ˌdis-kən-ˈsərt\ *vb* **1** : UPSET ⟨the unexpected event *disconcerted* their plans⟩ **2** : to disturb the composure of ⟨her frank stare *disconcerted* him⟩ ***syn*** see EMBARRASS — **dis·con·cert·ing·ly** \-iŋ-lē\ *adv*

dis·con·nect \ˌdis-kə-ˈnekt\ *vb* : to undo or break the connection of ⟨*disconnect* two pipes⟩ ⟨*disconnect* a telephone⟩ — **dis·con·nec·tion** \-ˈnek-shən\ *n*

dis·con·nect·ed *adj* : not connected : RAMBLING, INCOHERENT — **dis·con·nect·ed·ly** *adv* — **dis·con·nect·ed·ness** *n*

dis·con·so·late \dis-ˈkän(t)-sə-lət\ *adj* **1** : lacking consolation : hopelessly sad **2** : causing or suggestive of dejection : CHEERLESS — **dis·con·so·late·ly** *adv* — **dis·con·so·late·ness** *n*

1**dis·con·tent** \ˌdis-kən-ˈtent\ *adj* : DISCONTENTED

2**discontent** *vb* : to make discontented — **dis·con·tent·ment** \-mənt\ *n*

3**discontent** *n* **1** : lack of contentment : UNEASINESS **2** : a yearning for improvement or perfection

dis·con·tent·ed *adj* : DISSATISFIED, MALCONTENT — **dis·con·tent·ed·ly** *adv* — **dis·con·tent·ed·ness** *n*

ə abut	ər further	a back	ā bake
ä cot, cart	au̇ out	ch chin	e less
ē easy	g gift	i trip	ī life
j joke	ŋ sing	ō flow	ȯ flaw
ȯi coin	th thin	t͟h this	ü loot
u̇ foot	y yet	yü few	yu̇ furious
zh vision			

dis·con·tin·ue \ˌdis-kən-ˈtin-yü\ *vb* **1** : to break the continuity of : cease to operate, use, or take **2** : END; *esp* : to cease publication — **dis·con·tin·u·ance** \-ˈtin-yə-wən(t)s\ *n* — **dis·con·tin·u·a·tion** \-ˌtin-yə-ˈwā-shən\ *n*

dis·con·tin·u·ous \-ˈtin-yə-wəs\ *adj* : not continuous : having interruptions or gaps : BROKEN ⟨a *discontinuous* flight⟩ — **dis·con·ti·nu·i·ty** \(ˌ)dis-ˌkänt-ə-ˈn(y)ü-ət-ē\ *n* — **dis·con·tin·u·ous·ly** \ˌdis-kən-ˈtin-yə-wəs-lē\ *adv*

dis·cord \ˈdis-ˌkȯrd\ *n* **1** : lack of agreement or harmony : CONFLICT **2 a** : a harsh combination of musical sounds **b** : a harsh or unpleasant sound

dis·cord·ance \dis-ˈkȯrd-ən(t)s\ *n* **1** : the state or an instance of being discordant **2** : discordant sounds or noise

dis·cord·ant \-ənt\ *adj* **1 a** : being at variance : DISAGREEING **b** : QUARRELSOME **2** : relating to or producing a discord : JARRING — **dis·cord·ant·ly** *adv*

dis·co·theque \ˈdis-kə-ˌtek\ *n* : a small intimate nightclub for dancing esp. to recorded music

1**dis·count** \ˈdis-ˌkau̇nt\ *n* **1** : a reduction made from a regular or list price ⟨two percent *discount* for cash⟩ **2** : a deduction of interest in advance when lending money

2**dis·count** \ˈdis-ˌkau̇nt, dis-ˈ\ *vb* **1 a** : to reduce or deduct from the amount of a bill, debt, or charge **b** : to sell or offer for sale at a discount **2 a** : MINIMIZE **b** : to make allowance for exaggeration in **c** : to take into account in present calculations ⟨the stock market has already *discounted* the company's better prospects for next year⟩ — **dis·count·a·ble** \-ə-bəl\ *adj*

dis·coun·te·nance \dis-ˈkau̇nt-(ə-)nən(t)s\ *vb* **1** : EMBARRASS, DISCONCERT **2** : to look with disfavor on

dis·cour·age \dis-ˈkər-ij, -ˈkə-rij\ *vb* **1** : to lessen the courage or confidence of : DISHEARTEN **2 a** : to hinder by inspiring fear of consequences : DETER ⟨laws that *discourage* speeding⟩ **b** : to advise against a course of action : DISSUADE ⟨*discouraged* his son from becoming a musician⟩ — **dis·cour·ag·ing·ly** \-ˈkər-ij-iŋ-lē, -ˈkə-rij-\ *adv*

dis·cour·age·ment \-ˈkər-ij-mənt, -ˈkə-rij-\ *n* **1** : an act of discouraging : the state of being discouraged **2** : something that discourages

1**dis·course** \ˈdis-ˌkōrs, -ˌkȯrs, dis-ˈ\ *n* **1** : verbal interchange of ideas : CONVERSATION **2** : formal and orderly expression of thought on a subject **3** : an oral or written work embodying discourse

2**dis·course** \dis-ˈkōrs, -ˈkȯrs, ˈdis-ˌ\ *vb* : to express oneself in discourse : hold forth

dis·cour·te·ous \(ˈ)dis-ˈkərt-ē-əs\ *adj* : lacking courtesy : UNCIVIL, RUDE — **dis·cour·te·ous·ly** *adv* — **dis·cour·te·ous·ness** *n*

dis·cour·te·sy \-ˈkərt-ə-sē\ *n, pl* **-sies** : RUDENESS; *also* : a rude act

dis·cov·er \dis-ˈkəv-ər\ *vb* **dis·cov·ered; dis·cov·er·ing** \-ˈkəv-(ə-)riŋ\ **1** : to make known or visible **2 a** : to obtain sight or knowledge of for the first time ⟨*discovered* America⟩ ⟨*discovered* the law of gravity⟩ **b** : to detect the presence of : FIND ⟨*discovered* arsenic in the victim's coffee⟩ **c** : to find out ⟨was surprised to *discover* that he had lost his keys⟩ — **dis·cov·er·a·ble** \-ˈkəv-(ə-)rə-bəl\ *adj* — **dis·cov·er·er** \-ˈkəv-ər-ər\ *n*

dis·cov·ery \dis-ˈkəv-(ə-)rē\ *n, pl* **-er·ies** **1** : the act or process of discovering **2** : something discovered

1**dis·cred·it** \(ˈ)dis-ˈkred-ət\ *vb* **1** : to refuse to accept as true or accurate : DISBELIEVE ⟨*discredit* a rumor⟩ **2** : to cause disbelief in the accuracy or authority of ⟨*discredit* a witness⟩ **3** : to destroy the reputation of : DISGRACE ⟨involvement in graft *discredited* him⟩ — **dis·cred·it·a·ble** \-ə-bəl\ *adj* — **dis·cred·it·a·bly** \-blē\ *adv*

2discredit *n* **1** : loss of credit or reputation ⟨knew something to the man's *discredit*⟩ **2** : lack or loss of belief or confidence ⟨bring a story into *discredit*⟩

dis·creet \dis-'krēt\ *adj* : having or showing good judgment in conduct : PRUDENT; *esp* : capable of observing prudent silence — **dis·creet·ly** *adv* — **dis·creet·ness** *n*

dis·crep·an·cy \dis-'krep-ən-sē\ *n, pl* **-cies** **1** : the quality or state of being discrepant : DIFFERENCE **2** : an instance of discrepancy : something discrepant ⟨*discrepancies* in the firm's financial statements⟩

dis·crep·ant \-ənt\ *adj* : being at variance : DISAGREEING — **dis·crep·ant·ly** *adv*

dis·crete \dis-'krēt, 'dis-ˌ\ *adj* : individually distinct : SEPARATE — **dis·crete·ly** *adv* — **dis·crete·ness** *n*

dis·cre·tion \dis-'kresh-ən\ *n* **1** : the quality of being discreet : PRUDENCE **2 a** : individual choice or judgment ⟨left the decision to your *discretion*⟩ **b** : power of free decision or latitude of choice ⟨reached the age of *discretion*⟩ — **dis·cre·tion·ary** \-'kresh-ə-ˌner-ē\ *adj*

dis·crim·i·nate \dis-'krim-ə-ˌnāt\ *vb* **1 a** : to perceive the distinguishing features of **b** : DISTINGUISH, DIFFERENTIATE ⟨*discriminate* hundreds of colors⟩ **2** : to see and note the differences; *esp* : to distinguish one like object from another ⟨*discriminate* between a tree and a bush⟩ **3** : to make a distinction in favor of or against one person or thing as compared with others ⟨*discriminated* against because of his race⟩ — **dis·crim·i·na·ble** \-ə-nə-bəl\ *adj*

dis·crim·i·nat·ing \-ˌnāt-ing\ *adj* : marked by discrimination; *esp* : DISCERNING, JUDICIOUS ⟨a *discriminating* taste⟩ — **dis·crim·i·nat·ing·ly** \-ing-lē\ *adv*

dis·crim·i·na·tion \dis-ˌkrim-ə-'nā-shən\ *n* **1** : the act of discriminating : DIFFERENTIATION **2** : the quality or power of finely distinguishing **3** : distinction and esp. unjust distinction made against one person or group in favor of another ⟨laws to end racial *discrimination*⟩ — **dis·crim·i·na·tion·al** \-sh(ə-)nəl\ *adj*

dis·crim·i·na·tive \dis-'krim-ə-ˌnāt-iv\ *adj* **1** : making distinctions **2** : DISCRIMINATORY — **dis·crim·i·na·tive·ly** *adv*

dis·crim·i·na·to·ry \dis-'krim-(ə-)nə-ˌtōr-ē, -ˌtȯr-\ *adj* : marked by unjust discrimination ⟨*discriminatory* treatment⟩

dis·cur·sive \dis-'kər-siv\ *adj* : passing from one topic to another : RAMBLING — **dis·cur·sive·ly** *adv* — **dis·cur·sive·ness** *n*

dis·cus \'dis-kəs\ *n, pl* **dis·cus·es** : a heavy disk thicker in the center than at the perimeter that athletes throw for distance

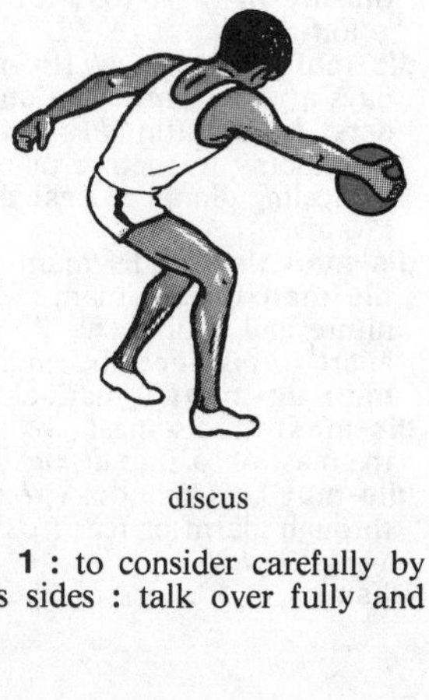

discus

dis·cuss \dis-'kəs\ *vb* **1** : to consider carefully by presenting the various sides : talk over fully and openly ⟨*discuss* a proposal⟩ **2** : to talk about ⟨*discuss* the weather⟩

syn DISCUSS, ARGUE, DEBATE mean to talk about with a view to reaching conclusions in common or to advancing different points of view. DISCUSS suggests a cooperative exchange of views to clarify an issue; ARGUE implies an exchange of fixed views between persons in disagreement; DEBATE implies an often public contest between persons taking opposite sides on a clear-cut issue

dis·cus·sion \dis-'kəsh-ən\ *n* : consideration of a question in open usu. informal debate

1dis·dain \dis-'dān\ *n* : a feeling of contempt for something regarded as beneath one : SCORN

2disdain *vb* **1** : to look with scorn on **2** : to reject or refrain from because of disdain

dis·dain·ful \-fəl\ *adj* : full of or expressing disdain : SCORNFUL ***syn*** see CONTEMPTUOUS ***ant*** deferential — **dis·dain·ful·ly** \-fə-lē\ *adv*

dis·ease \diz-'ēz\ *n* : a condition of the living plant or animal body in which the normal state is altered and the performance of the vital functions is impaired : ILLNESS — **dis·eased** \-'ēzd\ *adj*

dis·em·bark \ˌdis-əm-'bärk\ *vb* : to go or put ashore from a ship — **dis·em·bar·ka·tion** \(ˌ)dis-ˌem-ˌbär-'kā-shən, -bər-\ *n*

dis·em·body \ˌdis-əm-'bäd-ē\ *vb* : to deprive of bodily existence ⟨*disembodied* spirits⟩

dis·en·chant \ˌdis-ən-'chant\ *vb* : to free from enchantment : DISILLUSION — **dis·en·chant·ment** \-mənt\ *n*

dis·en·cum·ber \ˌdis-ən-'kəm-bər\ *vb* : to free from something that burdens or obstructs

dis·en·fran·chise \ˌdis-ən-'fran-ˌchīz\ *vb* : DISFRANCHISE — **dis·en·fran·chise·ment** \-ˌchīz-mənt, -chəz-\ *n*

dis·en·gage \ˌdis-ən-'gāj\ *vb* : to free or release from an engagement, entanglement, or encumbrance : EXTRICATE, DISENTANGLE ⟨*disengage* a clutch⟩; *esp* : to remove oneself from military commitments, alliances, or positions — **dis·en·gage·ment** \-mənt\ *n*

dis·en·tan·gle \ˌdis-ən-'tang-gəl\ *vb* : to free from entanglement : straighten out — **dis·en·tan·gle·ment** \-mənt\ *n*

1dis·fa·vor \(')dis-'fā-vər\ *n* **1** : DISAPPROVAL, DISLIKE **2** : the state or fact of being deprived of favor ⟨in *disfavor* at school⟩

2disfavor *vb* : to regard with disfavor

dis·fig·ure \dis-'fig-yər, *esp Brit* -'fig-ər\ *vb* : to spoil the appearance of ⟨*disfigured* by a scar⟩ — **dis·fig·ure·ment** \-mənt\ *n*

dis·fran·chise \(')dis-'fran-ˌchīz\ *vb* : to deprive of a franchise, a legal right, or a privilege or immunity; *esp* : to deprive of the right to vote — **dis·fran·chise·ment** \-ˌchīz-mənt, -chəz-\ *n*

dis·gorge \(')dis-'gȯrj\ *vb* **1** : VOMIT **2** : to discharge violently, confusedly, or as a result of force **3** : to discharge contents

1dis·grace \dis-'grās\ *vb* : to bring reproach or shame to — **dis·grac·er** *n*

2disgrace *n* **1** : the condition of being out of favor : loss of respect ⟨in *disgrace* with his schoolmates⟩ **2** : SHAME, DISHONOR ⟨the *disgrace* of being a coward⟩ **3** : a cause of shame ⟨that child's manners are a *disgrace*⟩ — **dis·grace·ful** \-'grās-fəl\ *adj* — **dis·grace·ful·ly** \-fə-lē\ *adv* — **dis·grace·ful·ness** *n*

dis·grun·tle \dis-'grənt-əl\ *vb* **dis·grun·tled; dis·grun·tling** \-'grənt-(ə-)ling\ : to put in bad humor — **dis·grun·tle·ment** \-əl-mənt\ *n*

1dis·guise \dis-'gīz\ *vb* **1** : to change the dress or looks of so as to conceal the identity or so as to resemble another ⟨special agents *disguised* as tourists⟩ **2 a** : HIDE, CONCEAL ⟨*disguised* their true feelings⟩ **b** : ALTER ⟨tried to *disguise* her voice⟩ — **dis·guised·ly** \-'gīz(-ə)d-lē\ *adv* — **dis·guis·er** \-'gī-zər\ *n*

2**disguise** *n* **1** : clothing put on to conceal one's identity or counterfeit another's **2** : an outward form hiding or misrepresenting a true nature or identity

1**dis·gust** \dis-'gəst\ *n* : marked aversion to something distasteful or loathsome : REPUGNANCE

2**disgust** *vb* : to provoke to loathing, repugnance, or aversion : be offensive to — **dis·gust·ed** *adj* — **dis·gust·ed·ly** *adv* — **dis·gust·ing** *adj* — **dis·gust·ing·ly** \-'gəs-ting-lē\ *adv*

1**dish** \'dish\ *n* [from Old English *disc*, borrowed from Latin *discus* "discus", "dish"; modern English *discus* and *disk* were much later borrowings from the same Latin word] **1** : a concave vessel from which food is served **2 a** : the food served in a dish ⟨a *dish* of strawberries⟩ **b** : food prepared in a particular way **3** : something resembling a dish esp. in being shallow and concave

2**dish** *vb* **1** : to put into a dish or dishes **2** : to make concave like a dish

dis·heart·en \(')dis-'härt-ən\ *vb* : to deprive of courage and hope : DISCOURAGE — **dis·heart·en·ing** \-'härt(-ə)-ning\ *adj* — **dis·heart·en·ing·ly** \-ning-lē\ *adv* — **dis·heart·en·ment** \-'härt-ən-mənt\ *n*

di·shev·el \dish-'ev-əl\ *vb* **di·shev·eled** *or* **di·shev·elled**; **di·shev·el·ing** *or* **di·shev·el·ling** \-'ev-(ə-)ling\ : to let hang or fall loosely in disorder

dis·hon·est \(')dis-'än-əst\ *adj* **1** : not honest : UNTRUSTWORTHY **2** : marked by fraud : CORRUPT ⟨*dishonest* dealings⟩ — **dis·hon·est·ly** *adv*

dis·hon·es·ty \-'än-ə-stē\ *n* : lack of honesty or integrity : disposition to defraud or deceive

1**dis·hon·or** \(')dis-'än-ər\ *n* **1** : loss of honor or reputation **2** : the state of one who has lost honor or prestige **3** : something dishonorable : a cause of disgrace — **dis·hon·or·a·ble** \(')dis-'än-(ə-)rə-bəl, -'än-ər-bəl\ *adj* — **dis·hon·or·a·bly** \-blē\ *adv*

2**dishonor** *vb* **1** : to bring shame on : DISGRACE **2** : to refuse to accept or pay (as a bill or check) — **dis·hon·or·er** *n*

dish·wash·er \'dish-,wȯsh-ər, -,wäsh-\ *n* : a person or a machine that washes dishes

dish·wa·ter \-,wȯt-ər, -,wät-\ *n* : water in which dishes have been or are to be washed

dis·il·lu·sion \,dis-ə-'lü-zhən\ *vb* **dis·il·lu·sioned**; **dis·il·lu·sion·ing** \-'lüzh-(ə-)ning\ : to free from or deprive of illusion — **dis·il·lu·sion·ment** \-'lü-zhən-mənt\ *n*

dis·in·cline \,dis-in-'klīn\ *vb* : to make or be unwilling — **dis·in·cli·na·tion** \(,)dis-,in-klə-'nā-shən\ *n*

dis·in·fect \,dis-in-'fekt\ *vb* : to cleanse of germs that might cause disease — **dis·in·fec·tion** \-'fek-shən\ *n*

dis·in·fect·ant \-'fek-tənt\ *n* : an agent that destroys harmful germs but not ordinarily spores of bacteria — **disinfectant** *adj*

dis·in·her·it \,dis-in-'her-ət\ *vb* : to prevent from inheriting property that would naturally be passed on

dis·in·te·grate \(')dis-'int-ə-,grāt\ *vb* **1** : to break or decompose into constituent elements, parts, or small particles **2** : to destroy the unity or integrity of **3** : to undergo a change in composition ⟨an atomic nucleus that *disintegrates* because of radioactivity⟩ — **dis·in·te·gra·tion** \(,)dis-,int-ə-'grā-shən\ *n* — **dis·in·te·gra·tor** \(')dis-'int-ə-,grāt-ər\ *n*

dis·in·ter \,dis-in-'tər\ *vb* **1** : to take out of the grave or tomb **2** : to bring to light : UNEARTH — **dis·in·ter·ment** \-mənt\ *n*

dis·in·ter·est·ed \(')dis-'in-trəs-təd, -'int-ə-rəs-\ *adj* **1** : not interested **2** : free from selfish motive or interest : UNBIASED ⟨a *disinterested* decision⟩ — **dis·in·ter·est·ed·ly** *adv* — **dis·in·ter·est·ed·ness** *n*

dis·join \(')dis-'jȯin\ *vb* : to end the union of or become separated

1**dis·joint** \(')dis-'jȯint\ *vb* **1** : to separate the parts of **2** : to take apart or become parted at the joints

2**disjoint** *adj* : completely separate; *esp* : having no members in common ⟨*disjoint* mathematical sets⟩

dis·joint·ed *adj* **1** : separated at or as if at the joint **2** : DISCONNECTED, DISORDERED; *esp* : INCOHERENT ⟨*disjointed* conversation⟩ — **dis·joint·ed·ly** *adv* — **dis·joint·ed·ness** *n*

1**disk** *or* **disc** \'disk\ *n* **1 a** : the central part of the flower head of a typical composite plant (as a daisy or aster) made up of closely packed tubular flowers **b** : any of various rounded and flattened animal anatomical structures **2 a** : a thin circular object : an object that appears to be thin and circular **b** *usu disc* : a phonograph record **3** *usu disc* : a tilling implement (as a harrow) with sharp-edged circular cutting blades; *also* : one of these blades — **disk·like** \-,līk\ *adj*

2**disk** *or* **disc** *vb* : to cultivate (land) with a disc

disk flower *n* : one of the tubular flowers in the disk of a composite plant

1**dis·like** \(')dis-'līk\ *vb* : to regard with dislike : DISAPPROVE

2**dislike** *n* : a feeling of distaste or disapproval

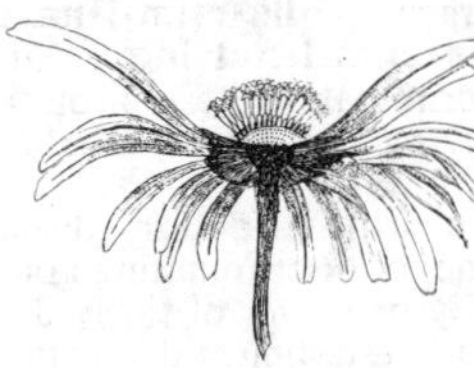
disk flower

dis·lo·cate \'dis-lō-,kāt, (')dis-'lō-\ *vb* **1** : to put out of place; *esp* : to displace (a bone) from normal connections with another bone **2** : DISRUPT — **dis·lo·ca·tion** \,dis-(,)lō-'kā-shən\ *n*

dis·lodge \(')dis-'läj\ *vb* : to force out of a place of rest, hiding, or defense

dis·loy·al \(')dis-'lȯi(-ə)l\ *adj* : lacking in loyalty — **dis·loy·al·ly** \-'lȯi-ə-lē\ *adv* — **dis·loy·al·ty** \-'lȯi(-ə)l-tē\ *n*

dis·mal \'diz-məl\ *adj* [from *dismal days*, a set of 24 days a year regarded as unlucky in medieval calendars, from Latin *dies mali*, literally "evil days"] **1** : gloomy to the eye or ear : DREARY, DEPRESSING **2** : feeling gloom : DEPRESSED — **dis·mal·ly** \-mə-lē\ *adv*

dis·man·tle \(')dis-'mant-əl\ *vb* **dis·man·tled**; **dis·man·tling** \-'mant-(ə-)ling\ **1** : to strip of furniture and equipment **2** : to take to pieces : take apart ⟨*dismantled* the engine to repair it⟩ — **dis·man·tle·ment** \-'mant-əl-mənt\ *n*

dis·mast \(')dis-'mast\ *vb* : to remove or break off the mast of ⟨a ship *dismasted* in a storm⟩

1**dis·may** \dis-'mā, diz-\ *vb* : to cause to lose courage through alarm or fear : DAUNT — **dis·may·ing·ly** \-ing-lē\ *adv*

2**dismay** *n* **1** : loss of courage from alarm or fear

ə abut	ər further	a back	ā bake	
ä cot, cart	au̇ out	ch chin	e less	ē easy
g gift	i trip	ī life	j joke	ng sing	ō flow
ȯ flaw	ȯi coin	th thin	th this	ü loot
u̇ foot	y yet	yü few	yu̇ furious	zh vision

2 : a feeling of alarm or disappointment

dis·mem·ber \(')dis-'mem-bər\ *vb* **dis·mem·bered; dis·mem·ber·ing** \-b(ə-)riŋ\ **1 :** to cut off or separate the limbs, members, or parts of **2 :** to break up or tear into pieces — **dis·mem·ber·ment** \-bər-mənt\ *n*

dis·miss \dis-'mis\ *vb* **1 :** to send away : cause or allow to go ⟨*dismiss* a messenger⟩ **2 :** to discharge from office, service, or employment **3 :** to put aside or out of mind ⟨*dismiss* the thought⟩ **4 :** to refuse further judicial hearing or consideration to ⟨the judge *dismissed* the charge⟩ — **dis·miss·al** \-'mis-əl\ *n*

dis·mount \(')dis-'maůnt\ *vb* **1 :** to get down from something (as a horse) **2 :** to throw down from a horse : UNHORSE **3 :** to take (as a cannon) from the carriage or mountings **4 :** to take apart (as a machine) : DISASSEMBLE

dis·obe·di·ence \ˌdis-ə-'bēd-ē-ən(t)s\ *n* : lack of obedience : neglect or refusal to obey — **dis·obe·di·ent** \-ənt\ *adj* — **dis·obe·di·ent·ly** *adv*

dis·obey \ˌdis-ə-'bā\ *vb* : to fail to obey : be disobedient

dis·oblige \ˌdis-ə-'blīj\ *vb* **1 :** to go counter to the wishes of **2 :** to cause inconvenience to

1**dis·or·der** \(')dis-'ȯrd-ər\ *vb* **1 :** to disturb the order of **2 :** to disturb the regular or normal functions of

2**disorder** *n* **1 a :** lack of order **b :** a disturbing, neglecting, or breaking away from a due order **2 :** an abnormal physical or mental condition : AILMENT — **dis·or·dered** \-'ȯrd-ərd\ *adj*

dis·or·der·ly \-ər-lē\ *adj* **1 a :** UNRULY, TURBULENT **b** (1) : offensive to public order or decency ⟨*disorderly* behavior⟩ (2) : guilty of disorderly conduct ⟨*disorderly* persons⟩ **2 :** not orderly : DISARRANGED ⟨a *disorderly* mass of papers⟩ — **dis·or·der·li·ness** *n*

dis·or·ga·nize \(')dis-'ȯr-gə-ˌnīz\ *vb* : to break up the regular arrangement of : throw into disorder : CONFUSE — **dis·or·ga·ni·za·tion** \(ˌ)dis-ˌȯrg-(ə-)nə-'zā-shən\ *n*

dis·own \(')dis-'ōn\ *vb* : to refuse to acknowledge as one's own : REPUDIATE, RENOUNCE, DISCLAIM

dis·par·age \dis-'par-ij\ *vb* **1 :** to lower in rank or reputation : DEGRADE **2 :** to speak slightingly of : BELITTLE ⟨*disparaged* his acts⟩ — **dis·par·age·ment** \-mənt\ *n* — **dis·par·ag·ing·ly** \-ij-iŋ-lē\ *adv*

dis·par·ate \dis-'par-ət, 'dis-p(ə-)rət\ *adj* : markedly or incongruously different : distinct in quality or character — **dis·par·ate·ly** *adv* — **dis·par·ate·ness** *n* — **dis·par·i·ty** \dis-'par-ət-ē\ *n*

dis·pas·sion·ate \(')dis-'pash-(ə-)nət\ *adj* : not influenced by strong feeling : CALM, IMPARTIAL — **dis·pas·sion·ate·ly** *adv*

1**dis·patch** \dis-'pach\ *vb* **1 :** to send away promptly or rapidly to a particular place or for a particular purpose ⟨*dispatch* a messenger⟩ ⟨*dispatch* a train⟩ **2 :** to attend to or dispose of speedily ⟨*dispatch* business⟩ **3 :** to put to death — **dis·patch·er** *n*

2**dispatch** *n* **1 a :** the sending of a message or messenger **b :** the shipment of goods **2 :** MESSAGE; *esp* : an important official message **3 :** the act of putting to death **4 :** a news item sent in by a correspondent **5 :** promptness and efficiency in performing a task

dis·pel \dis-'pel\ *vb* **dis·pelled; dis·pel·ling :** to drive away by scattering : DISSIPATE

dis·pens·a·ble \dis-'pen(t)-sə-bəl\ *adj* : capable of being dispensed with : NONESSENTIAL — **dis·pens·a·bil·i·ty** \-ˌpen(t)-sə-'bil-ət-ē\ *n*

dis·pen·sa·ry \dis-'pen(t)s-(ə-)rē\ *n, pl* **-ries :** a place where medical or dental aid is dispensed

dis·pen·sa·tion \ˌdis-pən-'sā-shən, -ˌpen-\ *n* **1 a :** a system of rules for ordering affairs **b :** a particular arrangement or provision esp. of nature **2 :** an exemption from a rule or from a vow or oath **3 a :** the act of dispensing **b :** something dispensed or distributed — **dis·pen·sa·tion·al** \-sh(ə-)nəl\ *adj*

dis·pense \dis-'pen(t)s\ *vb* **1 a :** to deal out in portions **b :** ADMINISTER ⟨*dispense* justice⟩ **2 :** to prepare and distribute (medicines) to the sick — **dispense with :** to do or get along without

dis·pens·er \dis-'pen(t)-sər\ *n* : one that dispenses; *esp* : a container (as a bottle or package) so made as to release part of its contents without being fully opened

dis·pers·al \dis-'pər-səl\ *n* : the act or result of dispersing

dis·perse \dis-'pərs\ *vb* **1 :** to cause to become spread widely : SCATTER **2 :** to subject (as light) to dispersion **3 :** to move in different directions — **dis·pers·i·ble** \-'pər-sə-bəl\ *adj*

dis·per·sion \dis-'pər-zhən\ *n* **1 :** the act or process of dispersing : the state of being dispersed **2 :** the separation of light (as by a prism) into colors with formation of a spectrum — **dis·per·sive** \-'pər-siv, -ziv\ *adj* — **dis·per·sive·ly** *adv* — **dis·per·sive·ness** *n*

dispir·it \(')dis-'pir-ət\ *vb* : to deprive of cheerful spirit : DISHEARTEN — **dispir·it·ed·ly** *adv* — **dispir·it·ed·ness** *n*

dis·place \(')dis-'plās\ *vb* **1 :** to remove from a usual or proper place; *esp* : to expel or force to flee from home or homeland ⟨*displaced* persons⟩ **2 :** to take the place of : REPLACE — **dis·place·a·ble** \-ə-bəl\ *adj*

dis·place·ment \-'plās-mənt\ *n* **1 :** the act of displacing : the state of being displaced **2 a :** the volume or weight of a fluid (as water) displaced by a floating body (as a ship) with the weight of the displaced fluid being equal to that of the displacing body ⟨a ship of 3000 tons *displacement*⟩ **b :** the difference between the initial position of an object and any later position

1**dis·play** \dis-'plā\ *vb* **1 :** to show outwardly ⟨*display* anger⟩ **2 a :** to spread before the view **b :** to set in display

2**display** *n* **1 :** a showing of something; *esp* : a device that gives information in visual form in communications ⟨a radar *display*⟩ **2 :** ostentatious show **3 :** an exhibition intended to draw attention by visual appeal

dis·please \(')dis-'plēz\ *vb* **1 :** to arouse the disapproval and dislike of **2 :** to be offensive to : give displeasure

dis·plea·sure \(')dis-'plezh-ər, -'plāzh-\ *n* : a feeling of annoyance and dislike accompanying disapproval : DISSATISFACTION

dis·port \dis-'pōrt, -'pȯrt\ *vb* **1 a :** DIVERT, AMUSE ⟨*disporting* themselves on the beach⟩ **b :** FROLIC **2 :** DISPLAY

dis·pos·a·ble \dis-'pō-zə-bəl\ *adj* : designed to be used once and then thrown away ⟨a *disposable* bottle⟩ ⟨*disposable* diapers⟩

dis·pos·al \dis-'pō-zəl\ *n* **1 :** an orderly distribution : ARRANGEMENT ⟨the *disposal* of troops for battle⟩ **2 :** a getting rid of or putting out of the way ⟨trash *disposal*⟩ **3 :** MANAGEMENT, ADMINISTRATION **4 :** the transfer of something into new hands ⟨a *disposal* of property⟩ **5 :** the power to dispose of something : CONTROL, COMMAND ⟨funds at his *disposal*⟩

dis·pose \dis-ˈpōz\ *vb* **1** : to distribute and put in place : ARRANGE **2 a** : to give a tendency to **b** : to be inclined ⟨*disposed* to refuse⟩ — **dispose of 1** : to settle or determine the fate, condition, or use of : deal with conclusively ⟨has the right to *dispose of* his personal property⟩ **2** : to get rid of : put out of the way : finish with : DISCARD ⟨*dispose of* rubbish⟩ ⟨*dispose of* the morning's mail⟩ **3** : to transfer to the control of another

dis·po·si·tion \ˌdis-pə-ˈzish-ən\ *n* **1** : the act or power of disposing : DISPOSAL **2** : the giving up or transferring of something ⟨*disposition* of real estate⟩ **3** : ARRANGEMENT ⟨the *disposition* of furniture in a room⟩ **4 a** : TENDENCY, INCLINATION ⟨a natural *disposition* to avoid pain⟩ **b** : natural attitude toward things ⟨a cheerful *disposition*⟩

dis·pos·sess \ˌdis-pə-ˈzes\ *vb* : to deprive of the occupancy of land or houses : put out : OUST ⟨the landlord *dispossessed* the tenants for not paying their rent⟩ — **dis·pos·ses·sion** \-ˈzesh-ən\ *n*

dis·proof \(ˈ)dis-ˈprüf\ *n* **1** : a proving that something is not as believed or stated **2** : evidence that disproves

¹**dis·pro·por·tion** \ˌdis-prə-ˈpōr-shən, -ˈpȯr-\ *n* : lack of proportion, symmetry, or proper relation : DISPARITY; *also* : an instance of such disparity — **dis·pro·por·tion·al** \-sh(ə-)nəl\ *adj* — **dis·pro·por·tion·ate** \-sh(ə-)nət\ *adj* — **dis·pro·por·tion·ate·ly** *adv*

²**disproportion** *vb* : to make out of proportion : MISMATCH

dis·prove \(ˈ)dis-ˈprüv\ *vb* : to prove to be false

dis·put·a·ble \dis-ˈpyüt-ə-bəl, ˈdis-pyət-\ *adj* : open to dispute, debate, or contest : DEBATABLE — **dis·put·a·bly** \-blē\ *adv*

dis·pu·tant \dis-ˈpyüt-ənt, ˈdis-pyət-\ *n* : a person who takes part in a dispute : DISPUTER

dis·pu·ta·tion \ˌdis-pyù-ˈtā-shən\ *n* : the act of disputing : DEBATE

dis·pu·ta·tious \-shəs\ *adj* : inclined to dispute : ARGUMENTATIVE — **dis·pu·ta·tious·ly** *adv* — **dis·pu·ta·tious·ness** *n*

¹**dis·pute** \dis-ˈpyüt\ *vb* **1** : to engage in argument : DEBATE **2** : WRANGLE **3** : to call into question : deny the truth or rightness of **4** : to struggle over : CONTEST — **dis·put·er** *n*

²**dispute** *n* : verbal controversy : DEBATE; *esp* : an angry one resulting in strained relations

syn DISPUTE, QUARREL mean an exchange of words in peevish or angry disagreement. DISPUTE lays emphasis on a bone of contention; QUARREL suggests feelings of anger or annoyance attending on and lingering after a dispute

dis·qual·i·fy \(ˈ)dis-ˈkwäl-ə-ˌfī\ *vb* **1** : to make or declare unfit or ineligible ⟨*disqualify* all voters who cannot write⟩ **2** : to deprive of necessary qualifications ⟨*disqualified* for military service by poor vision⟩ — **dis·qual·i·fi·ca·tion** \(ˌ)dis-ˌkwäl-ə-fə-ˈkā-shən\ *n*

¹**dis·qui·et** \(ˈ)dis-ˈkwī-ət\ *vb* : to make uneasy or restless : DISTURB — **dis·qui·et·ing·ly** \-ing-lē\ *adv*

²**disquiet** *n* : lack of peace or tranquillity : ANXIETY

dis·qui·etude \(ˈ)dis-ˈkwī-ə-ˌt(y)üd\ *n* : AGITATION, ANXIETY

ə abut	ər further	a back	ā bake	
ä cot, cart	aù out	ch chin	e less	ē easy
g gift	i trip	ī life	j joke	ng sing	ō flow
ȯ flaw	ȯi coin	th thin	t͟h this	ü loot
ù foot	y yet	yü few	yù furious	zh vision

dis·qui·si·tion \ˌdis-kwə-ˈzish-ən\ *n* : a formal inquiry or discussion : DISCOURSE

¹**dis·re·gard** \ˌdis-ri-ˈgärd\ *vb* : to pay no attention to : treat as unworthy of regard or notice

²**disregard** *n* : the act of disregarding : the state of being disregarded : intentional slight or neglect ⟨made the charge in utter *disregard* of the facts⟩ — **dis·re·gard·ful** \-fəl\ *adj*

dis·rel·ish \(ˈ)dis-ˈrel-ish\ *n* : lack of relish : DISTASTE, DISLIKE

dis·re·pair \ˌdis-ri-ˈpa(ə)r, -ˈpe(ə)r\ *n* : the state of being in need of repair

dis·rep·u·ta·ble \(ˈ)dis-ˈrep-yət-ə-bəl\ *adj* : not reputable : DISCREDITABLE, DISGRACEFUL; *esp* : having a bad reputation — **dis·rep·u·ta·ble·ness** *n* — **dis·rep·u·ta·bly** \-blē\ *adv*

dis·re·pute \ˌdis-ri-ˈpyüt\ *n* : loss or lack of reputation : low esteem : DISCREDIT

dis·re·spect \ˌdis-ri-ˈspekt\ *n* : lack of respect : DISCOURTESY — **dis·re·spect·ful** \-fəl\ *adj* — **dis·re·spect·ful·ly** \-fə-lē\ *adv*

dis·robe \(ˈ)dis-ˈrōb\ *vb* : UNDRESS

dis·rupt \dis-ˈrəpt\ *vb* **1** : to break apart : RUPTURE **2** : to throw into disorder : break up — **dis·rupt·er** *n* — **dis·rup·tion** \-ˈrəp-shən\ *n* — **dis·rup·tive** \-ˈrəp-tiv\ *adj* — **dis·rup·tive·ly** *adv* — **dis·rup·tive·ness** *n*

dis·sat·is·fac·tion \(ˌ)dis-ˌ(s)at-əs-ˈfak-shən\ *n* : the quality or state of being dissatisfied — **dis·sat·is·fac·to·ry** \-ˈfak-t(ə-)rē\ *adj*

dis·sat·is·fy \(ˈ)dis-ˈ(s)at-əs-ˌfī\ *vb* : to fail to satisfy : DISPLEASE

dis·sect \dis-ˈekt\ *vb* **1** : to cut up (as a plant or animal) into separate parts for examination and study **2** : to make a searching analysis : analyze minutely ⟨*dissect* a proposed plan⟩ — **dis·sec·tion** \-ˈek-shən\ *n*

dis·sem·ble \dis-ˈem-bəl\ *vb* **-bled; -bling** \-b(ə-)ling\ **1** : to hide under or put on a false appearance **2** : to put on the appearance of : SIMULATE — **dis·sem·bler** \-b(ə-)lər\ *n*

dis·sem·i·nate \dis-ˈem-ə-ˌnāt\ *vb* : to spread abroad as though sowing seed ⟨*disseminate* ideas⟩ — **dis·sem·i·na·tion** \-ˌem-ə-ˈnā-shən\ *n* — **dis·sem·i·na·tor** \-ˈem-ə-ˌnāt-ər\ *n*

dis·sen·sion \dis-ˈen-chən\ *n* : disagreement in opinion : DISCORD, QUARRELING

¹**dis·sent** \dis-ˈent\ *vb* **1** : to withhold assent **2** : to differ in opinion

²**dissent** *n* **1** : difference of opinion; *esp* : religious nonconformity **2** : a written statement in which a justice disagrees with the majority — called also *dissenting opinion*

dis·sent·er \dis-ˈent-ər\ *n* **1** : one that dissents **2** *cap* : an English Nonconformist

dis·sen·tient \dis-ˈen-chənt\ *adj* : expressing dissent — **dissentient** *n*

dis·ser·ta·tion \ˌdis-ər-ˈtā-shən\ *n* : an extended usu. written treatment of a subject

dis·ser·vice \(ˈ)dis-ˈ(s)ər-vəs\ *n* : HARM, INJURY; *also* : a harmful act

dis·sev·er \dis-ˈev-ər\ *vb* : to sever thoroughly : SEPARATE, DISUNITE — **dis·sev·er·ance** \-ˈev-(ə-)rən(t)s\ *n* — **dis·sev·er·ment** \-ˈev-ər-mənt\ *n*

dis·si·dence \ˈdis-əd-ən(t)s\ *n* : DISSENT, DISAGREEMENT

dis·si·dent \-əd-ənt\ *adj* : openly and often violently differing with an opinion or a group : DISAFFECTED — **dissident** *n*

dis·sim·i·lar \(ˈ)dis-ˈ(s)im-ə-lər\ *adj* : UNLIKE — **dis·sim·i·lar·i·ty** \(ˌ)dis-ˌ(s)im-ə-ˈlar-ət-ē\ *n* — **dis·sim·i·lar·ly** \(ˈ)dis-ˈ(s)im-ə-lər-lē\ *adv*

dis·sim·u·late \(ˈ)dis-ˈim-yə-ˌlāt\ *vb* : DISSEMBLE — **dis·sim·u·la·tion** \(ˌ)dis-ˌim-yə-ˈlā-shən\ *n* — **dis·sim·u·la·tor** \(ˈ)dis-ˈim-yə-ˌlāt-ər\ *n*

dis·si·pate \ˈdis-ə-ˌpāt\ *vb* **1** : to cause to spread out to the point of vanishing : DISSOLVE ⟨the breeze *dissipated* the fog⟩ **2** : to expend aimlessly or foolishly : SQUANDER ⟨*dissipated* his fortune⟩ **3** : to separate into parts and scatter or vanish **4** : to be extravagant or uncontrolled in the pursuit of pleasure; *esp* : to drink to excess

dis·si·pat·ed *adj* : given to or marked by dissipation : DISSOLUTE — **dis·si·pat·ed·ly** *adv* — **dis·si·pat·ed·ness** *n*

dis·si·pa·tion \ˌdis-ə-ˈpā-shən\ *n* : the act of dissipating : the state of being dissipated: **a** : DISPERSION, DIFFUSION **b** : wasteful expenditure **c** : intemperate living; *esp* : excessive drinking

dis·so·ci·ate \(ˈ)dis-ˈō-s(h)ē-ˌāt\ *vb* **1** : to separate from association or union with another : DISCONNECT **2** : DISUNITE — **dis·so·ci·a·tion** \(ˌ)dis-ˌō-sē-ˈā-shən, -ˌō-shē-\ *n* — **dis·so·cia·tive** \(ˈ)dis-ˈō-s(h)ē-ˌāt-iv, -shət-iv\ *adj*

dis·sol·u·ble \dis-ˈäl-yə-bəl\ *adj* : capable of being dissolved — **dis·sol·u·bil·i·ty** \dis-ˌäl-yə-ˈbil-ət-ē\ *n*

dis·so·lute \ˈdis-ə-ˌlüt\ *adj* : lacking restraint; *esp* : loose in morals or conduct — **dis·so·lute·ly** *adv* — **dis·so·lute·ness** *n*

dis·so·lu·tion \ˌdis-ə-ˈlü-shən\ *n* **1** : the action or process of dissolving **2** : the termination or breaking up of an assembly or a partnership or corporation

dis·solve \diz-ˈälv, -ˈȯlv\ *vb* **1** : to break up into component parts **2** : to pass or cause to pass into solution : MELT, LIQUEFY ⟨sugar *dissolves* in water⟩ **3** : to bring to an end : TERMINATE ⟨*dissolve* parliament⟩ **4** : to waste or fade away as if by breaking up or melting ⟨his courage *dissolved* in the face of danger⟩ **5** : to appear or fade out gradually so that one scene is replaced by another (as in moving pictures or television) **6** : to be overcome emotionally **7** : to resolve itself as if by dissolution — **dis·solv·a·ble** \-ˈäl-və-bəl, -ˈȯl-\ *adj* — **dis·solv·er** *n*

dis·so·nance \ˈdis-ə-nən(t)s\ *n* **1** : a mingling of discordant sounds **2** : lack of agreement : DISCORD **3** : an unresolved musical note or chord — **dis·so·nant** \-nənt\ *adj* — **dis·so·nant·ly** *adv*

dis·suade \dis-ˈwād\ *vb* : to advise against a course of action : persuade or try to persuade not to do something — **dis·sua·sion** \-ˈwā-zhən\ *n* — **dis·sua·sive** \-ˈwā-siv, -ziv\ *adj* — **dis·sua·sive·ly** *adv* — **dis·sua·sive·ness** *n*

dist *abbr* distance

dis·taff \ˈdis-ˌtaf\ *n, pl* **distaffs** **1 a** : a staff for holding the flax, tow, or wool in spinning **b** : woman's work **2** : the female branch or side of a family — **distaff** *adj*

[1]**dis·tance** \ˈdis-tən(t)s\ *n* **1 a** : separation in time **b** : the shortest space or amount of space between two points, lines, surfaces, or objects **c** : EXPANSE **d** : a full course ⟨go the *distance*⟩ **2** : the quality or state of being distant: as **a** : spatial remoteness **b** : COLDNESS, RESERVE **c** : DIFFERENCE, DISPARITY **3** : a distant point or region ⟨a light seen in the *distance*⟩

distaff

[2]**distance** *vb* : to leave far behind : OUTSTRIP

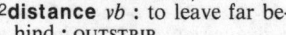

dis·tant \ˈdis-tənt\ *adj* **1 a** : separated in space : AWAY **b** : situated at a great distance : FAR-OFF **2** : not close in relationship ⟨*distant* cousin⟩ **3** : reserved or aloof in personal relationship : COLD — **dis·tant·ly** *adv* — **dis·tant·ness** *n*

dis·taste \(ˈ)dis-ˈtāst\ *n* **1** : dislike of food or drink **2** : DISINCLINATION, AVERSION ⟨a *distaste* for work⟩

dis·taste·ful \-fəl\ *adj* **1** : unpleasant to the taste : LOATHSOME **2** : OFFENSIVE, DISAGREEABLE ⟨a *distasteful* task⟩ — **dis·taste·ful·ly** \-fə-lē\ *adv* — **dis·taste·ful·ness** *n*

dis·tem·per \dis-ˈtem-pər\ *n* : a disordered or abnormal bodily state; *esp* : a highly contagious virus disease esp. of dogs marked by fever and by respiratory and sometimes nervous symptoms

dis·tend \dis-ˈtend\ *vb* : to stretch out or bulge out in all directions : SWELL — **dis·ten·sion** *or* **dis·ten·tion** \-ˈten-chən\ *n*

dis·till *also* **dis·til** \dis-ˈtil\ *vb* **dis·tilled**; **dis·till·ing** **1** : to fall or let fall in drops **2 a** : to purify by distillation ⟨*distill* water⟩ **b** : to obtain by distillation ⟨*distill* brandy from wine⟩

dis·til·late \ˈdis-tə-ˌlāt, dis-ˈtil-ət\ *n* : a liquid product condensed from vapor during distillation

dis·til·la·tion \ˌdis-tə-ˈlā-shən\ *n* **1** : a process that consists of expelling gas or vapor from liquids by heating and then condensing to liquid products **2** : something obtained by or as if by a process of distilling : ESSENCE

dis·till·er \dis-ˈtil-ər\ *n* : one that distills; *esp* : a person whose business is distilling alcoholic liquors

dis·till·ery \dis-ˈtil-(ə-)rē\ *n, pl* **-er·ies** : a place where distilling esp. of alcoholic liquors is carried on

dis·tinct \dis-ˈting(k)t\ *adj* **1** : distinguished from others : SEPARATE, DIFFERENT ⟨guilty of three *distinct* crimes⟩ **2** : clearly seen, heard, or understood : PLAIN, UNMISTAKABLE — **dis·tinct·ly** *adv* — **dis·tinct·ness** *n*

dis·tinc·tion \dis-ˈting(k)-shən\ *n* **1 a** : the act of distinguishing a difference **b** : something that makes a difference **2** : a distinguishing quality or mark **3 a** : a special recognition **b** : a mark or sign of such recognition **4** : HONOR ⟨served with *distinction*⟩

dis·tinc·tive \dis-ˈting(k)-tiv\ *adj* : clearly marking a person or a thing as different from others : CHARACTERISTIC ⟨a *distinctive* way of speaking⟩ — **dis·tinc·tive·ly** *adv* — **dis·tinc·tive·ness** *n*

dis·tin·guish \dis-ˈting-gwish\ *vb* **1** : to recognize one thing from others by some mark or characteristic ⟨*distinguish* the sound of a piano in an orchestra⟩ **2** : to hear or see clearly : make out : DISCERN ⟨*distinguish* a light in the distance⟩ **3** : to make distinctions ⟨*distinguish* between right and wrong⟩ **4** : to set apart : mark as different **5** : to separate from others by a mark of honor : make outstanding ⟨*distinguished* himself in athletics⟩ — **dis·tin·guish·a·ble** \-ə-bəl\ *adj* — **dis·tin·guish·a·bly** \-blē\ *adv*

dis·tin·guished *adj* : marked by eminence, distinction, or excellence

distn *abbr* distillation

dis·tort \dis-ˈtȯrt\ *vb* **1** : to twist out of the true meaning : MISREPRESENT **2** : to twist out of a natural, normal, or original shape or condition — **dis·tort·er** *n*

dis·tor·tion \dis-ˈtȯr-shən\ *n* **1** : the act of distorting **2** : the condition of being distorted or a product of distortion — **dis·tor·tion·al** \-sh(ə-)nəl\ *adj*

dis·tract \dis-ˈtrakt\ *vb* **1** : to turn aside : DIVERT; *esp* : to draw (the attention or mind) to a different object **2** : to stir up or confuse with conflicting emotions or motives : HARASS

dis·trac·tion \dis-'trak-shən\ *n* **1** : the act of distracting or the state of being distracted; *esp* : mental confusion **2** : something that distracts; *esp* : AMUSEMENT — **dis·trac·tive** \-'trak-tiv\ *adj*

dis·traught \dis-'tròt\ *adj* **1** : agitated with doubt or mental conflict **2** : CRAZED — **dis·traught·ly** *adv*

1**dis·tress** \dis-'tres\ *n* **1** : great suffering of body or mind : PAIN, ANGUISH **2** : MISFORTUNE, TROUBLE, SORROW **3** : a condition of danger or desperate need

2**distress** *vb* **1** : to subject to great strain or difficulties **2** : to cause to worry or be troubled : UPSET — **dis·tress·ing·ly** \-ing-lē\ *adv*

dis·tress·ful \-fəl\ *adj* : causing distress : full of distress — **dis·tress·ful·ly** \-fə-lē\ *adv* — **dis·tress·ful·ness** *n*

dis·trib·ute \dis-'trib-yət\ *vb* **1** : to divide among several or many : APPORTION **2** : to spread out so as to cover something : SCATTER **3** : to divide or separate esp. into kinds **4** : to market a line of goods in a particular area usu. as a wholesaler — **dis·trib·ut·a·ble** \-yət-ə-bəl\ *adj*

dis·tri·bu·tion \ˌdis-trə-'byü-shən\ *n* **1** : the act or process of distributing **2 a** : the position, arrangement, or frequency of occurrence (as of the members of a group) **b** : the natural geographic range of an organism **3 a** : something distributed **b** : FREQUENCY DISTRIBUTION ⟨population age *distribution*⟩ — **dis·tri·bu·tion·al** \-sh(ə-)nəl\ *adj*

dis·trib·u·tive \dis-'trib-yət-iv\ *adj* **1** : of or relating to distribution : serving to distribute **2** : producing the same element when operating on a whole as when operating on each part and collecting the results ⟨if multiplication is *distributive* over addition then a (b + c)=ab + ac⟩ — **dis·trib·u·tive·ly** *adv* — **dis·trib·u·tive·ness** *n*

dis·trib·u·tor \dis-'trib-yət-ər\ *n* **1** : one that distributes **2** : an agent or agency for marketing goods **3** : a device for distributing electric current to the spark plugs of an engine

1**dis·trict** \'dis-(ˌ)trikt\ *n* **1** : a territorial division marked off or defined (as for administrative or electoral purposes) ⟨school *district*⟩ ⟨judicial *district*⟩ **2** : a distinctive area or region

2**district** *vb* : to divide or organize into districts

district attorney *n* : a public official who prosecutes cases for a state or federal government

1**dis·trust** \(ˈ)dis-'trəst\ *vb* : to have no confidence in : SUSPECT

2**distrust** *n* : a lack of trust or confidence : SUSPICION, WARINESS ***syn*** see DOUBT ***ant*** trust — **dis·trust·ful** \-fəl\ *adj* — **dis·trust·ful·ly** \-fə-lē\ *adv* — **dis·trust·ful·ness** *n*

dis·turb \dis-'tərb\ *vb* **1 a** : to interfere with : INTERRUPT **b** : to alter the position or arrangement of **2 a** : to destroy the tranquillity or composure of : make uneasy **b** : to throw into disorder **c** : to put to inconvenience — **dis·turb·er** *n*

dis·turb·ance \dis-'tər-bən(t)s\ *n* **1** : the act of disturbing **2** : mental confusion : UPSET **3** : public turmoil : DISORDER

dis·turbed \-'tərbd\ *adj* : showing symptoms of mental or emotional illness

di·sul·fide \(ˈ)dī-'səl-ˌfīd\ *n* : a compound containing two atoms of sulfur combined with an element or radical

ə abut	ər further	a back	ā bake
ä cot, cart	aù out	ch chin	e less	ē easy
g gift	i trip	ī life	j joke	ng sing	ō flow
ȯ flaw	ȯi coin	th thin	th this	ü loot
u̇ foot	y yet	yü few	yu̇ furious	zh vision

dis·union \dish-'ü-nyən, (ˈ)dis-'yü-\ *n* : lack of union or agreement : SEPARATION

dis·unite \ˌdish-ü-'nīt, ˌdis-yu̇-\ *vb* : DIVIDE, SEPARATE

dis·uni·ty \dish-'ü-nət-ē, (ˈ)dis-'yü-\ *n* : lack of unity; *esp* : DISSENSION

1**dis·use** \dish-'üz, (ˈ)dis-'yüz\ *vb* : to discontinue the use or practice of

2**dis·use** \dish-'üs, (ˈ)dis-'yüs\ *n* : cessation of use or practice

1**ditch** \'dich\ *n* : a long narrow excavation dug in the earth (as for defense, drainage, or irrigation)

2**ditch** *vb* **1 a** : to enclose with a ditch **b** : to dig a ditch in **2** : to drive (a car) into a ditch **3** : to get rid of : DISCARD **4** : to make a forced landing of (an airplane) on water

dith·er \'dith-ər\ *n* : a highly nervous, excited, or agitated state — **dith·ery** \-ə-rē\ *adj*

dit·to \'dit-ō\ *n, pl* **dittos** **[**from Italian dialect, meaning "said" (i.e. "aforesaid"), from Latin *dictus*, past participle of *dicere* "to say"**]** **1** : SAME : more of the same : ANOTHER — used to avoid repeating a word ⟨lost : one shirt (white); *ditto* (blue)⟩ **2** : a mark composed of a pair of inverted commas or apostrophes used as a symbol for the word *ditto*

dit·ty \'dit-ē\ *n, pl* **ditties** : SONG; *esp* : a short simple song

di·ur·nal \dī-'ərn-əl\ *adj* **1** : recurring every day : DAILY ⟨*diurnal* task⟩ **2 a** : of, relating to, or occurring in the daytime ⟨the city's *diurnal* noises⟩ **b** : opening during the day and closing at night ⟨*diurnal* flowers⟩ — **di·ur·nal·ly** \-'ərn-ə-lē\ *adv*

div *abbr* **1** divided **2** dividend **3** division

di·van \'dī-ˌvan\ *n* : a large couch or sofa usu. without back or arms often designed for use as a bed

1**dive** \'dīv\ *vb* **dived** \'dīvd\ *or* **dove** \'dōv\; **diving** **1 a** : to plunge into water headfirst; *esp* : to execute a dive **b** : SUBMERGE **2 a** : to descend or fall precipitously **b** : to descend in a dive ⟨the airplane *dived*⟩ **3 a** : to plunge into some matter or activity **b** : DART, LUNGE ⟨*dived* for his legs⟩

2**dive** *n* **1** : the act or an instance of diving: as **a** (1) : a plunge into water executed in a prescribed manner (2) : a submerging of a submarine (3) : a steep descent of an airplane with or without power **b** : a sharp decline **2** : a disreputable bar

dive–bomb \'dīv-ˌbäm\ *vb* : to bomb from an airplane by making a steep dive toward the target before releasing the bomb — **dive–bomb·er** *n*

div·er \'dī-vər\ *n* **1** : one that dives **2 a** : a person who stays under water for long periods by having air supplied from the surface or by carrying a supply of compressed air **b** : any of various diving birds; *esp* : LOON

di·verge \də-'vərj, dī-\ *vb* **1 a** : to move or extend in different directions from a common point : draw apart ⟨*diverging* rays of light⟩ **b** : to differ in character, form, or opinion **2** : to turn aside from a path or course : DEVIATE

di·ver·gence \-'vər-jən(t)s\ *n* **1** : a drawing apart (as of lines extending from a common center) **2** : DIFFERENCE, DISAGREEMENT **3** : a deviation from a course or standard

di·ver·gent \-jənt\ *adj* **1** : diverging from each other : SPREADING **2** : differing from each other or from a standard : DEVIANT ⟨they frowned on his *divergent* behavior⟩ — **di·ver·gent·ly** *adv*

di·vers \'dī-vərz\ *adj* : VARIOUS

di·verse \dī-'vərs, də-, 'dī-ˌ\ *adj* : differing from one another : UNLIKE — **di·verse·ly** *adv* — **di·verse·ness** *n*

di·ver·si·fy \də-'vər-sə-ˌfī, dī-\ *vb* **-fied**; **-fy·ing** **1** : to make diverse : give variety to **2** : to increase the variety of a business's activities **3** : to engage in varied operations — **di·ver·si·fi·ca·tion** \də-ˌvər-sə-fə-ˈkā-shən, (ˌ)dī-\ *n*

di·ver·sion \də-ˈvər-zhən, dī-\ *n* **1** : the act or an instance of diverting from a course, activity, or use : DEVIATION **2** : something that diverts or amuses : PASTIME **3** : an attack made to draw the attention of an enemy from the scene of a principal operation — **di·ver·sion·ary** \-zhə-ˌner-ē\ *adj*

di·ver·si·ty \də-ˈvər-sət-ē, dī-\ *n, pl* **-ties** **1** : the condition of being different or having differences **2** : an instance or a point of difference

di·vert \də-ˈvərt, dī-\ *vb* **1 a** : to turn from one course or use to another : DEFLECT **b** : DISTRACT **2** : to give pleasure to : AMUSE

di·vest \dī-ˈvest, də-\ *vb* **1** : to strip esp. of clothing, ornament, or equipment **2** : to deprive esp. of a right

[1]**di·vide** \də-ˈvīd\ *vb* **1 a** : to separate into two or more parts, areas, or groups **b** : to separate into classes, categories, or divisions **c** : CLEAVE, PART **2 a** : to give out in shares : DISTRIBUTE **b** : to possess or make use of in common : SHARE **3** : to cause to be separate, distinct, or apart from one another **4 a** : to mark divisions on : GRADUATE ⟨*divide* a sextant⟩ **b** : to subject (a number) to the operation of finding how many times it contains another number ⟨*divide* 42 by 14⟩ **c** : to use as a divisor ⟨*divide* 14 into 42⟩ **5 a** : to undergo fission ⟨the cell *divides*⟩ **b** : BRANCH, FORK

[2]**divide** *n* : a dividing ridge between drainage areas : WATERSHED

di·vid·ed *adj* **1 a** : separated into parts or pieces ⟨finely *divided* particles of iron⟩ **b** : having the opposing streams of traffic separated ⟨a *divided* highway⟩ **2 a** : disagreeing with each other : DISUNITED **b** : directed or moved toward conflicting goals

div·i·dend \ˈdiv-ə-ˌdend, -əd-ənd\ *n* **1** : a sum to be distributed or a share of such a sum: as **a** : a share of profits distributed to stockholders or of surplus to an insurance policyholder **b** : interest paid on a bank account **2** : BONUS **3** : a number to be divided by another

di·vid·er \də-ˈvīd-ər\ *n* **1** : one that divides or separates ⟨a room *divider*⟩ **2** *pl* : an instrument for measuring or marking (as in dividing lines and transferring dimensions)

div·i·na·tion \ˌdiv-ə-ˈnā-shən\ *n* **1** : the art or practice that seeks to foresee future events or discover hidden knowledge usu. by means of augury or by the aid of supernatural powers **2** : unusual insight or intuitive perception

[1]**di·vine** \də-ˈvīn\ *adj* **1 a** : of, relating to, or proceeding directly from deity **b** : being deity ⟨the *divine* Savior⟩ **c** : directed to deity ⟨*divine* worship⟩ **2 a** : supremely good : SUPERB **b** : GODLIKE, HEAVENLY — **di·vine·ly** *adv*

[2]**divine** *n* : CLERGYMAN

[3]**divine** *vb* **1** : to discover or perceive intuitively : INFER **2** : to practice divination : PROPHESY — **di·vin·er** *n*

diving bell *n* : a diving apparatus consisting of a container open only at the bottom and supplied with compressed air by a hose

div·ing board \ˈdī-ving-\ *n* : SPRINGBOARD

di·vin·ing rod \də-ˈvī-ning-\ *n* : a forked rod believed to reveal the presence of water or minerals by dipping downward when held over a vein

di·vin·i·ty \də-ˈvin-ət-ē\ *n, pl* **-ties** **1** : the quality or state of being divine : GODHEAD **2 a** *often cap* : [2]GOD **b** (1) : [1]GOD (2) : GODDESS **c** : DEMIGOD **3** : THEOLOGY

di·vis·i·ble \də-ˈviz-ə-bəl\ *adj* : capable of being divided — **di·vis·i·bil·i·ty** \-ˌviz-ə-ˈbil-ət-ē\ *n*

di·vi·sion \də-ˈvizh-ən\ *n* **1 a** : the act or process of dividing : the state of being divided **b** : DISTRIBUTION **c** : CELL DIVISION **2** : one of the parts, sections, or groupings into which a whole is divided **3** : a large self-contained military or air unit **4** : an administrative or operating unit of a governmental, business, or educational organization **5** : something that divides, separates, or marks off **6** : difference in opinion or interest : DISAGREEMENT **7** : the mathematical operation of dividing — **di·vi·sion·al** \-ˈvizh-(ə-)nəl\ *adj*

di·vi·sor \də-ˈvī-zər\ *n* : the number by which a dividend is divided

[1]**di·vorce** \də-ˈvōrs, -ˈvȯrs\ *n* **1** : a complete legal dissolution of a marriage **2** : complete separation : SEVERANCE ⟨the *divorce* of religion and politics⟩

[2]**divorce** *vb* **1 a** : to get rid of one's spouse by divorce **b** : to dissolve the marriage between two spouses **2** : SEPARATE, DISUNITE — **di·vorce·ment** \-mənt\ *n*

di·vor·cée \də-ˌvōr-ˈsā\ *n* : a divorced woman

di·vulge \də-ˈvəlj, dī-\ *vb* : to make public : DISCLOSE, REVEAL ⟨*divulge* a secret⟩ — **di·vul·gence** \-ˈvəl-jən(t)s\ *n*

diz·zy \ˈdiz-ē\ *adj* **diz·zi·er**; **-est** **1 a** : having a whirling sensation in the head : GIDDY **b** : mentally confused **2 a** : causing or caused by giddiness ⟨a *dizzy* height⟩ **b** : extremely rapid — **diz·zi·ly** \ˈdiz-ə-lē\ *adv* — **diz·zi·ness** \ˈdiz-ē-nəs\ *n* — **dizzy** *vb*

DJ *abbr* disc jockey

dk *abbr* dark

dkg *abbr* dekagram

dkl *abbr* dekaliter

dkm *abbr* dekameter

dks *abbr* dekastere

dl *abbr* deciliter

D layer \ˈdē-\ *n* : the lowest of the ionized layers of the atmosphere that occurs between 25 and 40 miles above the earth's surface

D–line \ˈdē-\ *n* : a yellow line in the spectrum of sodium

dm *abbr* decimeter

DMD *abbr* doctor of dental medicine

DMT \ˌdē-ˌem-ˈtē\ *n* : a fast-acting hallucinogenic drug

dn *abbr* down

DNA \ˌdē-ˌen-ˈā\ *n* : any of various nucleic acids that are localized esp. in cell nuclei and are the molecular basis of heredity

[1]**do** \(ˈ)dü\ *vb* **did** \(ˈ)did\; **done** \ˈdən\; **do·ing** \ˈdü-ing\; **does** \(ˈ)dəz\ **1 a** : to engage in or carry out : PERFORM, ACCOMPLISH ⟨*do* some work⟩ ⟨crime *done* deliberately⟩ **b** : ACT, BEHAVE ⟨*do* as I say⟩ **2 a** : to work at **b** : to take appropriate action on ⟨*do* your homework⟩ ⟨*do* the dishes⟩ **c** : DECORATE ⟨*did* the bedroom in blue⟩ **3** : to get along ⟨*does* well in school⟩ **4** : to act so as to bring : RENDER ⟨sleep will *do* you good⟩ ⟨*do* honor to his memory⟩ **5** : FINISH ⟨turn out the light when you are *done* reading⟩ **6** : to put forth : EXERT ⟨*did* his best to win⟩ **7 a** : TRAVERSE ⟨*did* 500 miles that day⟩ **b** : to travel at a speed of ⟨*doing* 80 on the turnpike⟩ **8** : to serve in prison ⟨*did* five years for forgery⟩ **9 a** : to serve the purpose ⟨half of that will *do*⟩ **b** : to be fitting or proper ⟨it won't *do* to be late⟩ **10** — used with *so* or a pronoun object to stand for a preceding predicate ⟨he wants to make the varsity, but to *do* so he'll have to work hard⟩ ⟨if you must sing, *do* it somewhere else⟩ **11** — used as an auxiliary verb

(1) before the subject in an interrogative sentence ⟨*does* he work⟩ and after some adverbs ⟨never *did* he work so hard⟩, (2) in a negative statement ⟨he *doesn't* work⟩, (3) for emphasis ⟨he *does* work⟩, and (4) as a substitute for a preceding predicate ⟨he works harder than I *do*⟩ ⟨he doesn't work, *does* he⟩ ⟨he likes lobster and she *does* too⟩ — **do away with** **1** : to get rid of **2** : DESTROY, KILL — **do by** : to act toward in a specified manner ⟨*did* right *by* her⟩ — **do for** : to bring about the death or ruin of ⟨he's *done for* if we don't help him⟩

2**do** \'dō\ *n* : the 1st note of the diatonic scale

do *abbr* ditto

DO *abbr* doctor of osteopathy

DOA *abbr* dead on arrival

do·a·ble \'dü-ə-bəl\ *adj* : capable of being done

dob·bin \'däb-ən\ *n* **1** : a farm horse **2** : a quiet plodding horse

Do·ber·man pin·scher \ˌdō-bər-mən-'pin-chər\ *n* : a short-haired medium-sized working dog of a breed of German origin

Doberman pinscher

dob·son·fly \'däb-sən-ˌflī\ *n* : a large-eyed winged insect with a large carnivorous aquatic larva

doc *abbr* document

doc·ile \'däs-əl\ *adj* [from Latin *docilis* "teachable", from *docēre* "to teach"] : easily taught, led, or managed : TRACTABLE ⟨a *docile* child⟩ — **doc·ile·ly** \'däs-ə(l)-lē\ *adv* — **do·cil·i·ty** \dä-'sil-ət-ē, dō-\ *n*

1**dock** \'däk\ *n* : any of a genus of coarse weedy plants related to buckwheat that are used as potherbs and in folk medicine

2**dock** *n* : the solid part of an animal's tail as distinguished from the hair

3**dock** *vb* **1** : to cut off the end of : cut short **2** : to take away a part of : make a deduction from ⟨*dock* a man's wages⟩

4**dock** *n* **1** : an artificial basin to receive ships that has gates to keep the water in or out **2** : a slip or waterway usu. between two piers to receive ships **3** : a wharf or platform for the loading or unloading of materials

5**dock** *vb* **1** : to haul or guide into a dock **2** : to come or go into dock **3** : to maneuver and bring a spacecraft together with something (as another spacecraft)

6**dock** *n* : the place in a court where a prisoner stands or sits during trial

1**dock·et** \'däk-ət\ *n* **1 a** : a list of legal cases to be tried **b** : a list of matters to be acted on : AGENDA **2** : a label attached to a parcel containing directions (as for handling)

2**docket** *vb* **1** : to mark with an identifying statement : LABEL **2** : to place on the docket for legal action

dock·yard \'däk-ˌyärd\ *n* : a place where ships are built or repaired or where naval supplies or shipbuilding materials are stored

ə abut	ər further		a back	ā bake
ä cot, cart	au̇ out		ch chin	e less
g gift	i trip	ī life	j joke	ng sing
ȯ flaw	ȯi coin		th thin	t͟h this
u̇ foot	y yet		yü few	yu̇ furious

ē easy · ō flow · ü loot · zh vision

1**doc·tor** \'däk-tər\ *n* [from Latin *doctor* "teacher", from *docēre* "to teach"] **1** : a person holding one of the highest academic degrees (as a PhD) conferred by a university **2** : one skilled or specializing in healing; *esp* : a physician, surgeon, dentist, or veterinarian licensed to practice his profession — **doc·tor·al** \-t(ə-)rəl\ *adj*

2**doctor** *vb* **doc·tored**; **doc·tor·ing** \-t(ə-)ring\ **1 a** : to give medical treatment to **b** : to practice medicine **c** : to restore to good condition : REPAIR ⟨*doctor* an old clock⟩ **2 a** : to adapt or modify for a desired end ⟨*doctored* the play by abridging the last act⟩ **b** : to alter deceptively ⟨*doctored* the election returns⟩

doc·tor·ate \'däk-t(ə-)rət\ *n* : the degree, title, or rank of a doctor

doc·trine \'däk-trən\ *n* **1** : something that is taught **2** : a principle or the principles in a branch of knowledge or system of belief — **doc·tri·nal** \-trə-nəl\ *adj* — **doc·tri·nal·ly** \-nə-lē\ *adv*

1**doc·u·ment** \'däk-yə-mənt\ *n* : a written or printed paper furnishing information or used as proof of something else — **doc·u·men·tal** \ˌdäk-yə-'ment-əl\ *adj*

2**doc·u·ment** \'däk-yə-ˌment\ *vb* : to furnish documentary evidence of — **doc·u·ment·a·ble** \-ə-bəl\ *adj*

1**doc·u·men·ta·ry** \ˌdäk-yə-'ment-ə-rē, -'men-trē\ *adj* **1** : consisting of documents : of the nature of documents; *also* : contained or certified in writing ⟨*documentary* proof⟩ **2** : giving a factual presentation in artistic form ⟨a *documentary* film⟩ — **doc·u·men·tar·i·ly** \-mən-'ter-ə-lē, -ˌmen-\ *adv*

2**documentary** *n, pl* **-ries** : a documentary presentation (as a film)

doc·u·men·ta·tion \ˌdäk-yə-mən-'tā-shən, -ˌmen-\ *n* **1** : the providing of documents in proof of something **2** : evidence in the form of documents or references (as in footnotes) to documents

dod·der \'däd-ər\ *vb* **dod·dered**; **dod·der·ing** \-(ə-)ring\ **1** : to tremble or shake from weakness or age **2** : to progress feebly

doddering *adj* : FOOLISH, SENILE

1**dodge** \'däj\ *vb* **1 a** : to move suddenly aside **b** : to avoid by moving quickly aside **2** : to avoid by trickery or evasion

2**dodge** *n* **1** : an act of evading by sudden bodily movement **2 a** : an artful device to evade, deceive, or trick **b** : TECHNIQUE, METHOD — **dodg·er** *n*

do·do \'dōd-ō\ *n, pl* **dodoes** *or* **dodos** [from Portuguese *doudo*, from the adjective *doudo* meaning "crazy"] **1** : a large heavy flightless extinct bird related to the pigeons and formerly found on some of the islands of the Indian ocean **2 a** : a person who is hopelessly behind the times **b** : a stupid person

dodo (about 3 ft. long)

doe \'dō\ *n, pl* **does** *or* **doe** : the female esp. when adult of any mammal (as a deer, an antelope, or a hare) of which the male is called *buck*

do·er \'dü-ər\ *n* : one that does

does *pres 3d sing of* DO

doe·skin \'dō-ˌskin\ *n* **1** : the skin of does or leather made of it; *also* : soft leather from sheepskins or lambskins **2** : a soft firm woolen cloth

doesn't \'dəz-ənt\ : does not

doff \'däf, 'dȯf\ *vb* [from a contraction of *do off*] : to take off one's clothes; *esp* : to take off or lift up (one's hat)

[1]**dog** \'dȯg\ *n* **1 a :** a variable flesh-eating domesticated mammal related to the wolves and foxes **b :** an animal of the family to which the dog belongs **c :** a male dog **2 a :** any of various devices for holding, gripping, or fastening that consist of a spike, rod, or bar **b :** ANDIRON **3 :** affected stylishness or dignity ⟨put on the *dog*⟩ — **dog·like** \-ˌlīk\ *adj*

[2]**dog** *vb* **dogged; dog·ging 1 :** to hunt or track like a hound **2 :** to worry as if by dogs **:** HOUND ⟨*dogged* by bad luck⟩

dog·cart \'dȯg-ˌkärt\ *n* **1 :** a cart drawn by a dog **2 :** a light one-horse carriage with two seats back to back

dog days *n pl* **:** the hot sultry period of summer between early July and early September

doge \'dōj\ *n* **:** the chief magistrate in the republics of Venice and Genoa

dog–ear \'dȯg-ˌi(ə)r\ *n* **:** the turned-down corner of a leaf of a book — **dog–ear** *vb*

dog–eared \-ˌi(ə)rd\ *adj* **1 :** having dog-ears **2 :** SHABBY, WORN

dog·face \'dȯg-ˌfās\ *n, slang* **:** SOLDIER; *esp* **:** INFANTRYMAN

dog·fight \-ˌfīt\ *n* **:** a fight at close quarters between fighter planes

dog·fish \-ˌfish\ *n* **:** any of various small sharks that hunt in schools near shore

dog·ged \'dȯg-əd\ *adj* **:** stubbornly determined **:** TENACIOUS ⟨*dogged* persistence⟩ ***syn*** see OBSTINATE ***ant*** faltering — **dog·ged·ly** *adv* — **dog·ged·ness** *n*

[1]**dog·ger·el** \'dȯg-(ə-)rəl, 'däg-\ *adj* **:** loosely styled and irregular in measure

[2]**doggerel** *n* **:** doggerel verse

dog·gie bag \'dȯ-gē-\ *n* **:** a bag provided by a restaurant to a customer for taking home food (as for a dog)

dog·house \'dȯg-ˌhau̇s\ *n* **:** a shelter for a dog — **in the doghouse :** in a state of disfavor

do·gie \'dō-gē\ *n, chiefly West* **:** a motherless calf in a range herd

dog·ma \'dȯg-mə, 'däg-\ *n, pl* **dog·mas** *also* **dog·ma·ta** \-mət-ə\ **1 :** something held as an established opinion; *esp* **:** a tenet set forth as authoritative **2 :** a doctrine or body of doctrines concerning faith or morals laid down by a church

dog·mat·ic \dȯg-'mat-ik, däg-\ *adj* **1 :** characterized by or given to the use of dogmatism ⟨a *dogmatic* critic⟩ **2 :** of or relating to dogma — **dog·mat·i·cal·ly** \-'mat-i-k(ə-)lē\ *adv*

dog·ma·tism \'dȯg-mə-ˌtiz-əm, 'däg-\ *n* **:** positiveness in assertion of opinion esp. when unwarranted or arrogant — **dog·ma·tist** \-mət-əst\ *n*

dog·ma·tize \-mə-ˌtīz\ *vb* **:** to speak or write dogmatically — **dog·ma·tiz·er** *n*

dog·tooth violet \ˌdȯg-ˌtüth-\ *n* **:** any of a genus of small spring-flowering bulbous herbs related to the lily

dog·trot \'dȯg-ˌträt\ *n* **:** a gentle trot — **dogtrot** *vb*

dog watch *n* **:** a shipboard watch from 4 to 6 or from 6 to 8 p.m.

dog·wood \'dȯg-ˌwu̇d\ *n* **:** any of a group of trees and shrubs having small flowers often surrounded by four broad petallike leaves

dogwood

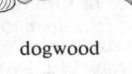

doi·ly \'dȯi-lē\ *n, pl* **doilies 1 :** a small napkin **2 :** a small often decorative mat

do in *vb* **1 :** RUIN **2 :** KILL ⟨*did* him *in* with a club⟩ **3 :** to wear out **:** EXHAUST ⟨*done in* at the end of the day⟩

do·ing \'dü-ing\ *n* **1 :** the act of performing or executing **:** ACTION ⟨takes some *doing* to beat him⟩ **2** *pl* **a :** things that are done or that occur ⟨everyday *doings*⟩ **b** *dial* **:** social activities ⟨big *doings* tonight⟩

do–it–your·self \ˌdü-ə-chər-'self\ *adj* **:** of, relating to, or designed for use by an amateur or hobbyist ⟨*do-it-yourself* tools⟩ ⟨*do-it-yourself* car model kit⟩

dol *abbr* dollar

dol·drums \'dōl-drəmz, 'däl-\ *n pl* **1 :** a spell of listlessness or despondency **2 :** a part of the ocean near the equator abounding in calms **3 :** a state of inactivity or slump

[1]**dole** \'dōl\ *n* **1 a** (1) **:** a giving out of food, money, or clothing to the needy (2) **:** money, food, or clothing so given **b :** a grant of government funds to the unemployed **2 :** something portioned out and distributed

D

[2]**dole** *vb* **1 :** to give or distribute as a charity **2 :** to give or deliver in small portions **:** PARCEL — usu. used with *out*

dole·ful \'dōl-fəl\ *adj* **:** full of grief **:** SAD — **dole·ful·ly** \-fə-lē\ *adv* — **dole·ful·ness** *n*

doll \'däl, 'dȯl\ *n* **1 :** a small-scale figure of a human being used esp. as a child's plaything **2 :** a pretty young woman

dol·lar \'däl-ər\ *n* [from Dutch *daler*, taken from German *taler*, short for *joachimstaler*, meaning a coin made in Sankt Joachimstal ("Saint Joachim's Valley") in Bohemia] **1 :** TALER **2 :** a coin (as a Spanish piece of eight) patterned after the taler **3 a :** a basic monetary unit (as of the U.S. and Canada) **b :** a coin, note, or token representing one dollar

dollar sign *n* **:** a mark **$** or $ placed before a number to indicate that it stands for dollars — called also *dollar mark*

doll up *vb* **:** to dress or adorn formally or elegantly

dolly \'däl-ē, 'dȯ-lē\ *n, pl* **doll·ies 1 :** DOLL **2 :** a platform on a roller or on wheels for transporting heavy objects; *esp* **:** a wheeled platform for a television or motion-picture camera

dol·man sleeve \ˌdōl-mən-, ˌdȯl-, ˌdäl-\ *n* **:** a sleeve that is very wide at the armhole and tight at the wrist

do·lo·mite \'dō-lə-ˌmīt, 'däl-ə-\ *n* **:** a mineral that includes much of the common white marble

do·lor \'dō-lər, 'däl-ər\ *n* **:** mental suffering or anguish **:** SORROW — **do·lor·ous** \'dō-lə-rəs, 'däl-ə-\ *adj* — **do·lor·ous·ly** *adv* — **do·lor·ous·ness** *n*

dol·phin \'däl-fən, 'dȯl-\ *n* **1 a :** any of various small long-nosed toothed whales **b :** PORPOISE 1 **2 :** either of two active spiny-finned marine food fishes noted for their brilliant coloring when dying out of water

dolphin 1a
(about 11 ft. long)

dolt \'dōlt\ *n* **:** a stupid person — **dolt·ish** \'dōl-tish\ *adj* — **dolt·ish·ly** *adv* — **dolt·ish·ness** *n*

-dom \dəm\ *n suffix* **1 a :** dignity **:** office ⟨duke*dom*⟩ **b :** realm **:** jurisdiction ⟨king*dom*⟩ **c :** geographical area ⟨Anglo-Saxon*dom*⟩ **2 :** state or fact of being ⟨free*dom*⟩ **3 :** those having a (specified) office, occupation, interest, or character ⟨official*dom*⟩

dom *abbr* domestic

do·main \dō-'mān, də-\ *n* **1** : a territory over which dominion is exercised **2** : a sphere of influence or activity **3** : a small region of a magnetic substance that contains a group of atoms all aligned in the same direction so that each group has the effect of a tiny magnet pointing in a certain direction

1dome \'dōm\ *n* **1** : a large hemispherical roof or ceiling **2** : a natural formation that resembles the dome of a building ⟨elevated rock *domes*⟩

2dome *vb* **1** : to cover with or as if with a dome **2** : to form into or swell upward or outward like a dome

1do·mes·tic \də-'mes-tik\ *adj* **1** : of or relating to the household or the family **2** : of, relating to, or produced or carried on within one country ⟨*domestic* politics⟩ **3 a** : living near or about the habitations of man ⟨*domestic* vermin⟩ **b** : DOMESTICATED, TAME **4** : devoted to home life ⟨a man *domestic* in his habits⟩ — **do·mes·ti·cal·ly** \-ti-k(ə-)lē\ *adv*

2domestic *n* : a household servant

domestic animal *n* : any of various animals (as the horse or sheep) domesticated by man so as to live and breed in a tame condition

do·mes·ti·cate \də-'mes-ti-ˌkāt\ *vb* **1** : to bring into domestic use : ADOPT ⟨European customs *domesticated* in America⟩ **2** : to fit for domestic life ⟨tried to *domesticate* her explorer husband⟩ **3** : to adapt to living with man and to serving his purposes ⟨man *domesticated* the dog⟩ — **do·mes·ti·ca·tion** \-ˌmes-ti-'kā-shən\ *n*

do·mes·tic·i·ty \ˌdō-ˌmes-'tis-ət-ē, də-\ *n, pl* **-ties** **1** : the quality or state of being domestic or domesticated **2** *pl* : domestic affairs

domestic science *n* : instruction and training in domestic management and the household arts (as cooking and sewing)

1dom·i·cile \'däm-ə-ˌsīl, 'dō-mə-; 'däm-ə-səl\ *n* : a dwelling place : place of residence : HOME

2domicile *vb* : to establish in or provide with a domicile

1dom·i·nant \'däm-ə-nənt\ *adj* **1** : commanding, controlling, or prevailing over all others ⟨a *dominant* political figure⟩ **2** : overlooking from a higher elevation **3** : PREDOMINANT, OUTSTANDING **4** : expressed in an observable trait of the organism when paired with a contrasting recessive factor **5** : of, relating to, or being an ecological dominant — **dom·i·nance** \-nən(t)s\ *n* — **dom·i·nant·ly** *adv*

2dominant *n* **1 a** : a dominant gene or a character determined by a dominant gene **b** : a kind of organism (as a species) that exerts a controlling influence on the environment of an ecological community **2** : the 5th note of the diatonic scale

dom·i·nate \'däm-ə-ˌnāt\ *vb* **1** : RULE, CONTROL ⟨refuse to be *dominated* by his friends⟩ **2** : to have a commanding position or controlling power over ⟨the rock of Gibraltar *dominates* the straits⟩ **3** : to rise high above ⟨the mountain range was *dominated* by a single snow-capped peak⟩ — **dom·i·na·tion** \ˌdäm-ə-'nā-shən\ *n* — **dom·i·na·tive** \-ˌnāt-iv\ *adj* — **dom·i·na·tor** \-ˌnāt-ər\ *n*

dom·i·neer \ˌdäm-ə-'ni(ə)r\ *vb* **1** : to rule in an arrogant manner **2** : to be overbearing

dom·i·neer·ing *adj* : inclined to domineer — **dom·i·neer·ing·ly** \-ing-lē\ *adv* — **dom·i·neer·ing·ness** *n*

Do·min·i·can \də-'min-i-kən\ *n* : a member of the Roman Catholic mendicant Order of Preachers founded in 1215 — **Dominican** *adj*

do·min·ion \də-'min-yən\ *n* **1** : supreme authority : SOVEREIGNTY **2** : DOMAIN **3** *often cap* : a self-governing nation of the British Commonwealth other than the United Kingdom that acknowledges the British monarch as chief of state

Dominion Day *n* : July 1 observed in Canada as a legal holiday in commemoration of the proclamation of dominion status in 1867

dom·i·no \'däm-ə-ˌnō\ *n, pl* **-noes** *or* **-nos** **1** : a long loose hooded cloak usu. worn with a half mask as a masquerade costume **2 a** : a flat rectangular block whose face is divided into two equal parts that are blank or bear dots **b** *pl* : any of several games played with dominoes

1don \'dän\ *n* [from Spanish, from Latin *dominus* "master", "lord"; compare DAME] **1** : a Spanish nobleman or gentleman — used as a title prefixed to the Christian name **2** : a head, tutor, or fellow in a college of Oxford or Cambridge University

2don *vb* **donned**; **don·ning** [from a contraction of *do on*] : to put on : dress oneself in

do·nate \'dō-ˌnāt, dō-'\ *vb* : to make a gift of : CONTRIBUTE ⟨*donate* blood⟩ *syn* see GIVE — **do·na·tor** \-ˌnāt-ər, -'nāt-\ *n*

do·na·tion \dō-'nā-shən\ *n* **1** : the action of making a gift esp. to a charity **2** : a free contribution : GIFT *syn* see PRESENT

done *past part of* DO

don·jon \'dän-jən, 'dən-\ *n* : a massive inner tower in a medieval castle

don·key \'däng-kē, 'dəng-, 'dȯng-\ *n, pl* **donkeys** **1** : the domestic ass **2** : a stupid or obstinate person

do·nor \'dō-nər, -ˌnȯr\ *n* **1** : one that donates **2** : one used as a source of bodily parts ⟨a blood *donor*⟩

donjon

don't \(')dōnt\ : do not

1doo·dle \'düd-əl\ *vb* **doo·dled**; **doo·dling** \'düd-(ə-)ling\ : to draw or scribble aimlessly while occupied with something else — **doo·dler** \-(ə-)lər\ *n*

2doodle *n* : something produced by doodling

doo·dle·bug \'düd-əl-ˌbəg\ *n* : the larva of an ant lion

1doom \'düm\ *n* **1 a** : JUDGMENT, DECISION **b** : a final determining of what is just **c** : JUDGMENT DAY **2 a** : DESTINY; *esp* : unfortunate destiny **b** : DEATH, RUIN *syn* see DESTINY

2doom *vb* **1** : CONDEMN **2** : to fix the fate of : DESTINE

dooms·day \'dümz-ˌdā\ *n* : JUDGMENT DAY

door \'dō(ə)r, 'dȯ(ə)r\ *n* **1** : a barrier by which an entry is closed and opened; *also* : a similar part of a piece of furniture **2** : DOORWAY **3** : a means of access ⟨the *door* to success⟩

door·bell \-ˌbel\ *n* : a bell, gong, or set of chimes to be rung usu. by a push button at an outside door

door·keep·er \-ˌkē-pər\ *n* : one that tends a door

door·knob \-ˌnäb\ *n* : a knob that when turned releases a door latch

ə abut	ər further	a back	ā bake
ä cot, cart	aů out	ch chin	e less	ē easy
g gift	i trip	ī life	j joke	ng sing	ō flow
ȯ flaw	ȯi coin	th thin	th this	ü loot
ů foot	y yet	yü few	yů furious	zh vision

door·man \-ˌman, -mən\ *n* **1** : DOORKEEPER **2** : one who tends a door (as of a hotel) and assists people by calling taxis and helping them in and out of cars
door·step \-ˌstep\ *n* : a step or steps before an outer door
door·way \-ˌwā\ *n* **1** : the opening that a door closes **2** : a means of gaining access
door·yard \-ˌyärd\ *n* : a yard right outside the door of a house
1**dope** \'dōp\ *n* **1** : a thick liquid or pasty preparation **2** : a drug preparation esp. when narcotic or addictive and used illicitly **3** : a stupid person **4** : information esp. from a reliable source
2**dope** *vb* **1** : to treat or affect with dope; *esp* : to give a narcotic to **2** *slang* : to guess the result of : predict esp. by means of special information or skill ⟨*dope* out which team will win⟩ — **dop·er** *n*
dop·ey \'dō-pē\ *adj* **dop·i·er**; **-est** **1** : dulled by or as if by alcohol or a narcotic **2** : DULL, STUPID — **dop·i·ness** *n*
Dopp·ler effect \'däp-lər-\ *n* : a change in the frequency with which waves (as of sound or light) from a given source reach an observer when the source and the observer are in rapid motion with respect to each other
Dor·ic \'dȯr-ik, 'där-\ *adj* : belonging to the oldest and simplest Greek architectural order
dor·mant \'dȯr-mənt\ *adj* **1** : not active but capable of resuming activity ⟨*dormant* volcano⟩ **2 a** : sleeping or appearing to be asleep : SLUGGISH **b** : having growth or other biological activity much reduced or suspended ⟨a *dormant* bud⟩ **3** : of, relating to, or used during dormancy ***syn*** see LATENT ***ant*** active — **dor·man·cy** \-mən-sē\ *n*
dor·mer \'dȯr-mər\ *n* [originally meaning "dormitory", and used to describe the sort of window frequently found in top-floor dormitories; from French *dormoir*, from Latin *dormitorium*, from *dormire* "to sleep"] : a window placed upright in a sloping roof; *also* : a roofed structure containing such a window
dor·mi·to·ry \'dȯr-mə-ˌtōr-ē, -ˌtȯr-\ *n, pl* **-ries** **1** : a room for sleeping; *esp* : a large room containing a number of beds **2** : a residence hall providing sleeping rooms
dor·mouse \'dȯ(ə)r-ˌmau̇s\ *n, pl* **dor·mice** \-ˌmīs\ : any of numerous Old World rodents that resemble small squirrels

dormouse
(about 3 in. long)

dor·sal \'dȯr-səl\ *adj* : relating to or situated near or on the back (as of an animal) — **dor·sal·ly** \-sə-lē\ *adv*
dorsal fin *n* : a fin on the median ridge of the back of a fish
do·ry \'dōr-ē, 'dȯr-\ *n, pl* **dories** : a flat-bottomed boat with a sharp bow and high sides that curve upward and outward
dos·age \'dō-sij\ *n* **1 a** : the giving of medicine in doses **b** : the amount of a single dose **2** : the addition of a substance or the application of an agent in a measured dose
1**dose** \'dōs\ *n* **1 a** : the measured amount of a medicine to be taken at one time **b** : the quantity of radiation administered or absorbed **2** : a portion of a substance added during a process **3** : an experience to which one is exposed ⟨a *dose* of defeat⟩
2**dose** *vb* **1** : to give medicine to **2** : to treat with an application or agent
do·sim·e·ter \dō-'sim-ət-ər\ *n* : an instrument for measuring doses of X rays or of radioactivity
dos·sier \'dȯs-ˌyā, 'däs-ē-ˌā\ *n* : a file of papers containing a detailed report
dost \(')dəst\ *archaic pres 2d sing of* DO
1**dot** \'dät\ *n* **1** : a small spot : SPECK **2** : a small mark made with or as if with a pen: as **a** : a point after a note or rest in music indicating increase of the time value by one half **b** : DECIMAL POINT **c** : a sign of multiplication **3** : a precise point in time or space ⟨arrived on the *dot*⟩ **4** : a short click or buzz forming a letter or part of a letter in the Morse code
2**dot** *vb* **dot·ted**; **dot·ting** **1** : to mark with a dot ⟨*dot* an *i*⟩ **2** : to cover with or as if with dots ⟨a lake *dotted* with boats⟩ — **dot·ter** *n*
dot·age \'dōt-ij\ *n* : SENILITY
dot·ard \'dōt-ərd\ *n* : a person in his dotage
dote \'dōt\ *vb* **1** : to be feebleminded esp. from old age **2** : to show excessive or foolish affection or fondness ⟨*doted* on her only nephew⟩ — **dot·ing·ly** \'dōt-ing-lē\ *adv*
doth \(')dəth\ *archaic pres 3d sing of* DO
dot·tle \'dät-əl\ *n* : unburned and partially burned tobacco caked in the bowl of a pipe
dot·ty \'dät-ē\ *adj* **dot·ti·er**; **-est** : mentally unbalanced : CRAZY
Dou·ay Version \dü-'ā-\ *n* : an English translation of the Vulgate used by Roman Catholics — see BIBLE table
1**dou·ble** \'dəb-əl\ *adj* **1** : TWOFOLD, DUAL ⟨a *double* function⟩ **2** : consisting of two members or parts **3** : being twice as great or as many **4** : folded in two **5** : having more than the usual number of floral parts and esp. petals ⟨*double* roses⟩ — **dou·ble·ness** *n*
2**double** *n* **1 a** : something twice another ⟨12 is the *double* of 6⟩ **b** : a hit that enables a batter to reach second base safely **2** : COUNTERPART, DUPLICATE; *esp* : a person who closely resembles another **3** : a sharp turn : REVERSAL **4** : FOLD **5** *pl* : a game between two pairs of players ⟨tennis *doubles*⟩
3**double** *adv* **1** : DOUBLY **2** : two together ⟨sleep *double*⟩
4**double** *vb* **dou·bled**; **dou·bling** \'dəb-(ə-)ling\ **1** : to make, be, or become twice as great or as many **2 a** : to make of two thicknesses : FOLD **b** : to close tightly the fingers of : CLENCH ⟨*doubled* his fist⟩ **c** : to cause to stoop at the waist **d** : to become bent or folded usu. in the middle **3** : to sail around (as a cape) by reversing direction **4** : to take the place of another **5** : to make a double **6** : to turn sharply and go back on one's course — **dou·bler** \'dəb-(ə-)lər\ *n*
double bass *n* : the largest instrument of the viol family
dou·ble-breast·ed \ˌdəb-əl-'bres-təd\ *adj* : having one half of the front lapped over the other and usu. two rows of buttons ⟨*double-breasted* jacket⟩
double cross *n* : an act of betraying or cheating esp. an associate — **dou·ble-cross** \ˌdəb-əl-'krȯs\ *vb* — **dou·ble-cross·er** *n*
dou·ble-deal·ing \ˌdəb-əl-'dē-ling\ *n* : DUPLICITY — **dou·ble-deal·er** *n* — **double-dealing** *adj*
dou·ble-deck·er \-'dek-ər\ *n* **1** : something (as a ship, bus, or bed) having two decks **2** : a sandwich having two layers
dou·ble·head·er \ˌdəb-əl-'hed-ər\ *n* **1** : a train pulled by two locomotives **2** : two games played consecutively on the same day
dou·ble-joint·ed \-'jȯint-əd\ *adj* : having one or more joints that permit the parts joined to be bent freely to unusual angles

double play *n* : a play in baseball or softball by which two base runners are put out

double pneumonia *n* : pneumonia involving both lungs

dou·ble–quick \'dəb-əl-ˌkwik\ *n* : DOUBLE TIME — **double–quick** *vb*

double star *n* : two stars very near to each other and generally seen as separate by means of a telescope

dou·blet \'dəb-lət\ *n* **1** : a close-fitting jacket worn by men of western Europe chiefly in the 16th century **2** : one of two similar or identical things **3** : one of two or more words in the same language derived by different routes from the same source ⟨*dish* and *disk* are *doublets*⟩

dou·ble–talk \'dəb-əl-ˌtȯk\ *n* : language that appears to be meaningful but in fact is a mixture of sense and nonsense

double time *n* **1** : a marching cadence of 180 36-inch steps per minute **2** : payment of a worker at twice his regular wage rate

dou·ble–time \'dəb-əl-ˌtīm\ *vb* : to move at double time

dou·bloon \ˌdə-'blün\ *n* : an old gold coin of Spain and Spanish America worth 16 pieces of eight

dou·bly \'dəb-lē\ *adv* **1** : to twice the degree **2** : in a twofold manner

1**doubt** \'dau̇t\ *vb* **1** : to be uncertain about **2** : to lack confidence in : DISTRUST, FEAR **3** : to consider unlikely ⟨I *doubt* that he will come⟩ — **doubt·a·ble** \-ə-bəl\ *adj* — **doubt·er** *n* — **doubt·ing·ly** \-iŋ-lē\ *adv*

2**doubt** *n* **1** : uncertainty of belief or opinion **2** : the condition of being objectively uncertain ⟨the outcome is in *doubt*⟩ **3 a** : a lack of confidence : DISTRUST **b** : an inclination not to believe or accept
syn DOUBT, DISTRUST, SUSPICION mean a feeling of unsureness about the truth or reality of something. DOUBT suggests a negative feeling that makes a decision or commitment difficult; DISTRUST implies wariness about a person's intentions; SUSPICION suggests an often unfounded feeling that good or innocent appearances about something or someone mask an underlying falseness or guilt ***ant*** certitude, faith

doubt·ful \'dau̇t-fəl\ *adj* **1** : not clear or certain as to fact ⟨a *doubtful* claim⟩ **2** : questionable in character ⟨*doubtful* intentions⟩ **3** : not settled in opinion : UNDECIDED ⟨*doubtful* about what to do⟩ **4** : not certain in outcome ⟨a *doubtful* battle⟩ — **doubt·ful·ly** \-fə-lē\ *adv* — **doubt·ful·ness** *n*

1**doubt·less** \'dau̇t-ləs\ *adv* **1** : without doubt : CERTAINLY **2** : PROBABLY

2**doubtless** *adj* : free from doubt : CERTAIN

douche \'düsh\ *n* **1 a** : a jet of fluid (as water) directed against a part or into a cavity of the body **b** : a cleansing with a douche **2** : a device for giving douches — **douche** *vb*

dough \'dō\ *n* **1 a** : a soft mass of moistened flour or meal thick enough to knead or roll **b** : any similar soft pasty mass **2** : MONEY — **doughy** \'dō-ē\ *adj*

dough·boy \'dō-ˌbȯi\ *n* : an American infantryman esp. in World War I

dough·nut \-(ˌ)nət\ *n* **1** : a small usu. ring-shaped cake fried in fat **2** : something resembling a doughnut esp. in shape

ə abut	ər further	a back	ā bake
ä cot, cart	au̇ out	ch chin	e less	ē easy
g gift	i trip	ī life	j joke	ŋ sing	ō flow
ȯ flaw	ȯi coin	th thin	t͟h this	ü loot
u̇ foot	y yet	yü few	yu̇ furious	zh vision

dough·ty \'dau̇t-ē\ *adj* **dough·ti·er**; **-est** : being strong and valiant : BOLD — **dough·ti·ly** \'dau̇t-ə-lē\ *adv* — **dough·ti·ness** \'dau̇t-ē-nəs\ *n*

Doug·las fir \ˌdəg-ləs-\ *n* : a tall evergreen cone-bearing timber tree of the western U.S.

dour \'dau̇(ə)r, 'du̇(ə)r\ *adj* **1** : STERN, HARSH **2** : GLOOMY, SULLEN — **dour·ly** *adv* — **dour·ness** *n*

douse \'dau̇s, 'dau̇z\ *vb* **1 a** : to plunge into water **b** : to throw a liquid on : DRENCH **2** : to put out : EXTINGUISH

1**dove** \'dəv\ *n* **1** : any of numerous pigeons; *esp* : a small wild pigeon **2** : a person who advocates negotiation and compromise in a dispute

2**dove** \'dōv\ *past of* DIVE

dove·cote \'dəv-ˌkōt, -ˌkät\ *or* **dove·cot** \-ˌkät\ *n* : a small raised house or box with compartments for domestic pigeons

1**dove·tail** \-ˌtāl\ *n* : something shaped like a dove's tail; *esp* : a ridge or groove cut in the end of a board

2**dovetail** *vb* **1 a** : to join by means of dovetails **b** : to cut to a dovetail **2** : to fit skillfully together to form a whole

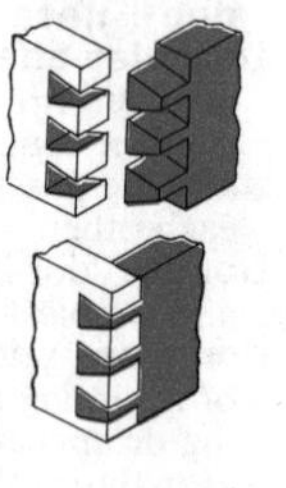
dovetail

dov·ish \'dəv-ish\ *adj* : advocating peace or peaceful policies

dow·a·ger \'dau̇-i-jər\ *n* **1** : a widow holding property or a title received from her deceased husband **2** : a dignified elderly woman

dowdy \'dau̇d-ē\ *adj* **dowd·i·er**; **-est** **1** : not neatly or becomingly dressed or cared for : SHABBY, UNTIDY **2** : lacking in style or smartness : out of date — **dowd·i·ly** \'dau̇d-ə-lē\ *adv* — **dowd·i·ness** \'dau̇d-ē-nəs\ *n*

1**dow·el** \'dau̇(-ə)l\ *n* : a pin or peg projecting from one of two parts or surfaces (as of wood) to be fastened together and fitting into a hole prepared in the other part

2**dowel** *vb* **-eled** *or* **-elled**; **-el·ing** *or* **-el·ling** : to fasten by or furnish with dowels

1**dow·er** \'dau̇(-ə)r\ *n* **1** : the part of or interest in the real estate of a deceased husband given by law to his widow during her life **2** : DOWRY

2**dower** *vb* : to supply with a dower or dowry : ENDOW

1**down** \'dau̇n\ *n* : an undulating usu. treeless upland with sparse soil — usu. used in pl.

2**down** *adv* **1 a** : toward or in a lower physical position **b** : to a lying or sitting position **c** : toward or to the ground, floor, or bottom **2** : in cash ⟨paid $10 *down*⟩ **3** : in a direction that is conventionally the opposite of up ⟨folded the bed covers *down*⟩ **4** : to or in a lower or worse condition, level, or status ⟨his pencil was worn *down*⟩ **5** : from a past time ⟨heirlooms that have been handed *down*⟩ **6** : to or in a state of less activity ⟨excitement died *down*⟩

3**down** *adj* **1 a** : occupying a low position; *esp* : lying on the ground **b** : directed or going downward ⟨a *down* car⟩ **c** : being at a lower level ⟨sales are *down*⟩ **2 a** : being in a state of reduced or low activity **b** (1) : DEPRESSED, DEJECTED (2) : SICK ⟨*down* with flu⟩ (3) : having a low opinion or dislike ⟨*down* on him⟩ **3** : FINISHED, DONE ⟨eight *down* and two to go⟩ **4** : made at the time of purchase or delivery ⟨a *down* payment⟩

4**down** *prep* : down along : down through : down toward : down in : down into : down on ⟨*down* the road⟩ ⟨*down* the well⟩

5**down** *n* **1** : a low or falling period ⟨the ups and *downs* of the business cycle⟩ **2** : the ending of an attempt to advance a football by the referee's signal; *also* : the attempt itself

6**down** *vb* : to go or cause to go or come down ⟨*downed* a duck with the first shot⟩

7**down** *n* **1** : a covering of soft fluffy feathers **2** : something soft and fluffy like down

down·beat \'dau̇n-ˌbēt\ *n* : the downward stroke of a conductor indicating the principally accented note of a measure of music

down·cast \-ˌkast\ *adj* **1** : DISCOURAGED, DEJECTED **2** : directed down ⟨a *downcast* glance⟩

down·draft \-ˌdraft, -ˌdråft\ *n* : a downward current of gas (as air in a chimney or during a thunderstorm)

down·fall \-ˌfȯl\ *n* **1** : FALL; *esp* : a sudden or heavy fall (as of rain) **2** : a sudden descent (as from a high position) : RUIN — **down·fall·en** \-ˌfȯ-lən\ *adj*

1**down·grade** \-ˌgrād\ *n* **1** : a downward grade or slope **2** : a decline toward a worse condition ⟨a neighborhood on the *downgrade*⟩ — **down·grade** \-'grād\ *adv*

2**down·grade** \-ˌgrād\ *vb* : to lower in grade, rank, position, or status

down·heart·ed \'dau̇n-'härt-əd\ *adj* : DEJECTED — **down·heart·ed·ly** *adv* — **down·heart·ed·ness** *n*

down·hill \-'hil\ *adv* : toward the bottom of a hill — **downhill** \-ˌhil\ *adj*

down·pour \-ˌpōr, -ˌpȯr\ *n* : a heavy rain

1**down·right** \-ˌrīt\ *adv* : THOROUGHLY ⟨*downright* mean⟩

2**downright** *adj* **1** : ABSOLUTE, THOROUGH ⟨a *downright* lie⟩ **2** : BLUNT, OUTSPOKEN ⟨a *downright* man⟩ — **down·right·ly** *adv* — **down·right·ness** *n*

1**down·stairs** \'dau̇n-'sta(ə)rz, -'ste(ə)rz\ *adv* : down the stairs : on or to a lower floor — **down·stairs** \-ˌsta(ə)rz, -ˌste(ə)rz\ *adj*

2**down·stairs** \'dau̇n-', 'dau̇n-ˌ\ *n* : the lower floor of a building

down·stream \'dau̇n-'strēm\ *adv or adj* : in the direction of flow of a stream

down·stroke \-ˌstrōk\ *n* : a stroke made in a downward direction

down–to–earth \ˌdau̇n-tə-'(w)ərth\ *adj* : PRACTICAL, REALISTIC

1**down·town** \-'tau̇n\ *adv* : to, toward, or in the lower part or business center of a town or city

2**downtown** \-ˌtau̇n\ *adj* **1** : situated downtown **2** : of or relating to the business center of a town or city

down·trod·den \'dau̇n-'träd-ən\ *adj* : crushed by superior power : OPPRESSED

1**down·ward** \-wərd\ *also* **down·wards** \-wərdz\ *adv* **1** : in a direction from higher to lower **2** : from a higher to a lower condition **3** : from an earlier time

2**downward** *adj* : moving or extending downward

down·wind \'dau̇n-'wind\ *adv or adj* : in the direction that the wind is blowing : LEEWARD

downy \'dau̇-nē\ *adj* **down·i·er**; **-est** **1 a** : resembling a bird's down **b** : covered with or made of down **2** : SOFT, SOOTHING

dow·ry \'dau̇(ə)r-ē\ *n, pl* **dowries** : the property that a woman brings to her husband in marriage

dox·ol·o·gy \däk-'säl-ə-jē\ *n, pl* **-gies** : an expression of praise to God; *esp, cap* : a hymn beginning "Praise God from whom all blessings flow"

doz *abbr* dozen

doze \'dōz\ *vb* : to sleep lightly — **doze** *n* — **doz·er** *n*

doz·en \'dəz-ən\ *n, pl* **dozens** *or* **dozen** **[**from Old French *dozaine*, from *doze* "twelve", from Latin *duodecim*, from *duo* "two" and *decem* "ten"**]** : a group of twelve — **dozen** *adj* — **doz·enth** \-ən(t)th\ *adj*

DP \(')dē-'pē\ *n* : a displaced person

DP *abbr* double play

dpt *abbr* department

dr *abbr* drive

Dr *abbr* doctor

1**drab** \'drab\ *n* : a light olive brown

2**drab** *adj* **drab·ber**; **drab·best** **1** : of the color drab **2** : being dull and monotonous : CHEERLESS — **drab·ly** *adv* — **drab·ness** *n*

dra·cae·na \drə-'sē-nə\ *n* : any of a genus of trees or shrubs that are related to the lilies, have branches terminated by clusters of sword-shaped leaves, and bear clusters of small greenish white flowers

drach·ma \'drak-mə\ *n, pl* **drach·mas** *or* **drach·mae** \-(ˌ)mē, -ˌmī\ *or* **drach·mai** \-ˌmī\ **1 a** : any of various ancient Greek units of weight **b** : any of various modern units of weight; *esp* : DRAM 1 **2 a** : an ancient Greek silver coin **b** : the basic monetary unit of modern Greece; *also* : a coin representing this unit

D

1**draft** \'draft, 'dråft\ *n* **1 a** : the act of drawing, hauling, or pulling **b** : a thing or amount that is drawn, hauled, or pulled **2** : the act or an instance of drinking or inhaling; *also* : the portion drunk or inhaled **3 a** : DELINEATION, REPRESENTATION; *esp* : a construction plan **b** : a preliminary sketch, outline, or version **4 a** : the act of drawing (as from a cask) **b** : a portion of liquid so drawn **5** : the depth of water a ship draws esp. when loaded **6 a** : the selection of a person esp. for compulsory military service **b** : a group of persons selected **7** : an order issued by one party to another to pay money to a third party **8** : a heavy demand : STRAIN ⟨a *draft* on national resources⟩ **9 a** : a current of air **b** : a device for regulating the flow of air (as in a fireplace) — **on draft** : ready to be drawn from a receptacle ⟨beer *on draft*⟩

2**draft** *adj* **1** : used for drawing loads ⟨*draft* animals⟩ **2** : constituting a preliminary or tentative version, sketch, or outline ⟨a *draft* treaty⟩ **3** : being on draft; *also* : DRAWN ⟨*draft* beer⟩

3**draft** *vb* **1** : to select usu. on a compulsory basis; *esp* : to conscript for military service **2 a** : to draw up a preliminary sketch, version, or plan of **b** : COMPOSE, PREPARE — **draft·er** *n*

draft·ee \draf-'tē, dråf-\ *n* : a person who is drafted esp. into the armed forces

drafts·man \'draf(t)s-mən, 'dråf(t)s-\ *n* : one who draws plans and sketches — **drafts·man·ship** \-ˌship\ *n*

drafty \'draf-tē, 'dråf-\ *adj* **draf·ti·er**; **-est** : exposed to a draft : subject to drafts ⟨a *drafty* hall⟩ — **draft·i·ly** \-tə-lē\ *adv* — **draft·i·ness** \-tē-nəs\ *n*

1**drag** \'drag\ *n* **1** : something that is dragged, pulled, or drawn along or over a surface: as **a** : HARROW **b** : a sledge for carrying heavy loads **2** : a device for dragging under water or along the bottom to detect or obtain objects **3 a** : something that retards motion **b** : the retarding force acting on a body (as an airplane) moving through a fluid (as air) **c** : something that hinders or obstructs progress **4 a** : the act or an instance of dragging or drawing **b** : a draw on a pipe, cigarette, or cigar : PUFF; *also* : a draft of liquid **5** : an event which passes painfully slowly ⟨the party was a *drag*⟩ **6** *slang* : influence securing special favor or partiality **7** *slang* : STREET, ROAD ⟨the main *drag*⟩ **8** : a contest between cars to see which can accelerate fastest — called also *drag race*

2**drag** *vb* **dragged**; **drag·ging** **1 a** : to draw slowly or heavily : HAUL **b** : to move, pass, or cause to move with painful slowness or difficulty ⟨he *drags* one leg⟩ ⟨the story *drags*⟩ **c** : PROTRACT ⟨*drag* out a story⟩ **2** : to hang or lag behind **3** : to trail along on the ground **4** : to explore, search, or fish with a drag **5** : DRAW, PUFF ⟨*drag* on a cigarette⟩ **6** : to engage in a drag race — **drag·ger** *n*

drag·gle \'drag-əl\ *vb* **drag·gled**; **drag·gling** \-(ə-)ling\ **1** : to make or become wet and dirty by dragging **2** : to follow slowly : STRAGGLE

drag·net \'drag-ˌnet\ *n* **1 a** : a net drawn along the bottom of a body of water : TRAWL **b** : a net used (as for capturing small game) on the ground **2** : a network of planned actions for pursuing and catching a criminal

drag·on \'drag-ən\ *n* [from Old French, from Latin *dracon-*, stem of *draco* "serpent", "dragon", from Greek *drakōn* "serpent", from a verb meaning "to look at", "gaze"] : a fabulous animal usu. represented as a monstrous winged and scaly serpent or lizard with a crested head and enormous claws

drag·on·fly \-ˌflī\ *n* : any of a group of large harmless insects that have four long wings held horizontal when at rest and feed esp. on flies, gnats, and mosquitoes — compare DAMSELFLY

1**dra·goon** \drə-'gün, dra-\ *n* : a cavalry soldier

2**dragoon** *vb* : to force or attempt to force into submission by violent measures

drag·ster \'drag-stər\ *n* : a hot rod specially designed for drag races

1**drain** \'drān\ *vb* **1 a** : to draw off or flow off gradually or completely ⟨*drain* water from a tank⟩ **b** : to cause the gradual disappearance of : DWINDLE **c** : to exhaust physically or emotionally **2 a** : to make or become gradually dry or empty ⟨let the dishes *drain*⟩ **b** : to carry away the surface water of : discharge surface or surplus water **c** : EMPTY, EXHAUST — **drain·er** *n*

2**drain** *n* **1** : a means by which liquid or other matter is drained **2 a** : the act of draining **b** : a gradual outflow or withdrawal : DEPLETION **3** : something that causes depletion : BURDEN ⟨a *drain* on one's resources⟩

drain·age \'drā-nij\ *n* **1** : the act, process, or mode of draining; *also* : something drained off ⟨*drainage* from a swamp⟩ **2** : a means for draining : DRAIN; *also* : a system of drains **3** : an area or district drained

drain·pipe \'drān-ˌpīp\ *n* : a pipe for drainage

drake \'drāk\ *n* : a male duck

dram \'dram\ *n* **1 a** — see MEASURE table **b** : FLUIDRAM **2** : a small portion of something to drink

dra·ma \'dräm-ə, 'dram-\ *n* [from Greek *drama*, meaning literally "action", from *dran* "to do", "act"] **1** : a composition telling a story through action and dialogue and designed for theatrical performance : PLAY **2** : dramatic art, literature, or affairs **3 a** : a series of events involving interesting or intense conflict of forces ⟨the *drama* of a hockey game⟩ **b** : dramatic effect

dra·mat·ic \drə-'mat-ik\ *adj* **1** : of or relating to the drama **2 a** : suitable to or characteristic of the drama **b** : striking in appearance or effect — **dra·mat·i·cal·ly** \-'mat-i-k(ə-)lē\ *adv*

dra·mat·ics \-'mat-iks\ *n sing or pl* **1 a** : performance of plays esp. as an extracurricular activity in school or college **b** : theatrical technique ⟨studying *dramatics*⟩ **2** : dramatic behavior or expression

dra·ma·tis per·so·nae \ˌdram-ət-əs-pər-'sō-(ˌ)nē, -ˌnī\ *n pl* : the characters or actors in a drama

dram·a·tist \'dram-ət-əst, 'dräm-\ *n* : PLAYWRIGHT

dram·a·tize \'dram-ə-ˌtīz, 'dräm-\ *vb* **1** : to adapt for theatrical presentation **2** : to present or represent in a dramatic manner — **dram·a·ti·za·tion** \ˌdram-ət-ə-'zā-shən, ˌdräm-\ *n*

drank *past of* DRINK

1**drape** \'drāp\ *vb* **1** : to cover or adorn with or as if with folds of cloth **2** : to cause to hang or stretch out loosely or carelessly ⟨he *draped* himself over the counter⟩ **3** : to arrange or become arranged in flowing lines or folds ⟨*drape* a gown⟩

2**drape** *n* **1** : a drapery esp. for a window : CURTAIN **2** : arrangement in or of folds **3** : the cut or hang of clothing ⟨the *drape* of his jacket⟩

drap·er \'drā-pər\ *n, Brit* : a dealer in cloth and sometimes also in clothing and dry goods

drap·ery \'drā-p(ə-)rē\ *n, pl* **-er·ies** **1 a** : a decorative fabric hung in loose folds **b** : hangings of heavy fabric for use as a curtain **2** : the draping or arranging of materials

dras·tic \'dras-tik\ *adj* **1** : acting rapidly or violently **2** : extreme in effect : SEVERE — **dras·ti·cal·ly** \-ti-k(ə-)lē\ *adv*

draught \'draft, 'dråft\ *chiefly Brit var of* DRAFT

1**draw** \'dro̊\ *vb* **drew** \'drü\; **drawn** \'dro̊n\; **drawing** **1** : to cause to move by pulling : HAUL, DRAG **2** : to move or go steadily or gradually ⟨night *draws* near⟩ **3 a** : ATTRACT, ENTICE ⟨honey *draws* flies⟩ **b** : PROVOKE ⟨*drew* enemy fire⟩ **4** : INHALE ⟨*drew* a deep breath⟩ **5 a** : to bring or pull out ⟨*draw* a sword⟩ **b** : to extract the contents or essence from : ELICIT **c** : EVISCERATE ⟨*drawn* and plucked chickens⟩ **6** : to require (a specified depth) to float in **7 a** : ACCUMULATE, GAIN ⟨*draw* interest⟩ **b** : to take money from a place of deposit : WITHDRAW **c** : to receive regularly from a source ⟨*draw* a salary⟩ **8 a** : to take (cards) from a stack or the dealer **b** : to receive or take at random ⟨*drew* a winning number⟩ **9** : to bend (a bow) by pulling back the string **10** : to change shape by or as if by pulling or stretching ⟨a face *drawn* with sorrow⟩ **11** : to leave (a contest) undecided : TIE **12 a** : to produce a likeness of by making lines on a surface : SKETCH **b** : to write out in due form : DRAFT ⟨*draw* up a will⟩ **c** : to describe in words **13** : DEDUCE ⟨*draw* a conclusion⟩ **14** : STRETCH, LENGTHEN **15** : to produce or make use of a draft or current of air ⟨the furnace *draws* well⟩

2**draw** *n* **1** : the act, process, or result of drawing **2** : a lot or chance drawn at random ⟨a win at the first *draw*⟩ **3** : the movable part of a drawbridge **4** : a contest or game in which there is no winner : TIE **5** : something that draws attention **6** : a gully shallower than a ravine

draw·back \'dro̊-ˌbak\ *n* : an objectionable feature

draw·bar \-ˌbär\ *n* **1** : a removable bar in a fence **2** : a beam across the rear of a tractor to which implements are hitched

draw·bridge \-ˌbrij\ *n* : a bridge made to be wholly or partly raised up, let down, or drawn aside so as to permit or hinder passage

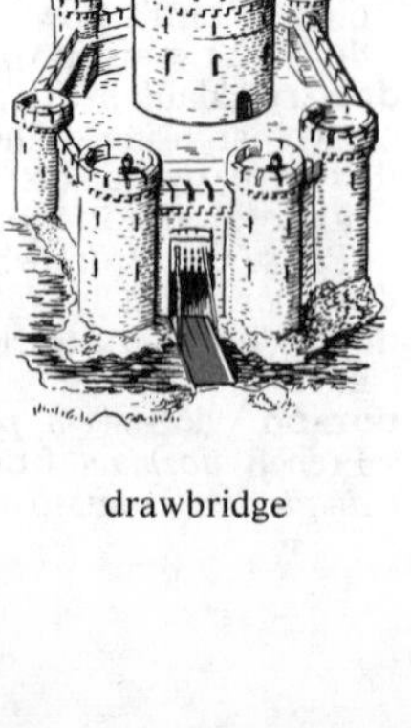
drawbridge

ə abut	ər further	a back	ā bake	
ä cot, cart	au̇ out	ch chin	e less	ē easy
g gift	i trip	ī life	j joke	ng sing	ō flow
o̊ flaw	o̊i coin	th thin	th this	ü loot
u̇ foot	y yet	yü few	yu̇ furious	zh vision

draw·er \'dró(-ə)r\ *n* **1 :** one that draws **2 :** a sliding box or receptacle (as in a desk) **3** *pl* **:** an undergarment for the lower part of the body

draw·ing \'dró-ing\ *n* **1 a :** an act or instance of drawing **b :** an occasion when something (as the winner of a raffle) is decided by drawing lots **2 :** the act, art, or technique of representing an object by means of lines **3 :** a representation formed by drawing **:** SKETCH

drawing board *n* **:** a board on which paper to be drawn on is fastened

drawing room *n* **:** a formal reception room

drawl \'dról\ *vb* **:** to speak slowly with vowels greatly prolonged — **drawl** *n* — **drawl·er** *n* — **drawl·ing·ly** \'dró-ling-lē\ *adv*

drawn butter \'drón-\ *n* **:** melted butter often with seasoning

draw·string \'dró-ˌstring\ *n* **:** a string, cord, or tape used in closing a bag or controlling fullness in garments or curtains

dray \'drā\ *n* **:** a strong low cart or wagon without sides used to haul goods

dray·man \-mən\ *n* **:** one who drives a dray

1**dread** \'dred\ *vb* **:** to fear greatly **:** be apprehensive or fearful

2**dread** *n* **1 a :** great fear esp. in the face of impending harm **b** *archaic* **:** AWE **2 :** one causing fear or awe *syn* see FEAR

3**dread** *adj* **1 :** causing great fear or anxiety **2 :** inspiring awe

dread·ful \'dred-fəl\ *adj* **1 :** inspiring dread or awe **:** FRIGHTENING **2 :** extremely distasteful, unpleasant, or shocking — **dread·ful·ly** \-f(ə-)lē\ *adv* — **dread·ful·ness** \-fəl-nəs\ *n*

dread·nought \'dred-ˌnót, -ˌnät\ *n* **:** a battleship armed with big guns of the same caliber

1**dream** \'drēm\ *n* **1 :** a series of thoughts, images, or emotions occurring during sleep **2 a :** a visionary creation of the imagination **:** DAYDREAM **b :** a state of mind in which a person is lost in fancies or reveries **c :** an object seen in a dream **:** VISION **3 :** something notable for its beauty, excellence, or enjoyable quality **4 :** a goal or purpose ardently desired **:** IDEAL — **dream·like** \-ˌlīk\ *adj*

2**dream** \'drēm\ *vb* **dreamed** \'drem(p)t, 'drēmd\ *or* **dreamt** \'drem(p)t\; **dream·ing** \'drē-ming\ **1 :** to have a dream **2 :** to indulge in daydreams **:** pass time in reverie **3 :** to conceive as possible, fitting, or proper **:** IMAGINE ⟨*dreamed* of success⟩

dream·er \'drē-mər\ *n* **1 :** one that dreams **2 a :** one who lives in a world of fancy and imagination **b :** one who constantly conceives of impractical projects

dream·land \'drēm-ˌland\ *n* **:** an unreal delightful country existing only in imagination

dreamy \'drē-mē\ *adj* **dream·i·er; -est 1 :** VAGUE, HAZY **2 :** given to dreaming or fantasy **3 a :** having the quality or characteristics of a dream **b :** quiet and soothing ⟨*dreamy* music⟩ **c :** DELIGHTFUL, PLEASING — **dream·i·ly** \-mə-lē\ *adv* — **dream·i·ness** \-mē-nəs\ *n*

drear \'dri(ə)r\ *adj* **:** DREARY

drea·ry \'dri(ə)r-ē\ *adj* **drea·ri·er** \'drir-ē-ər\; **-est 1 :** DOLEFUL, SAD **2 :** causing feelings of cheerlessness **:** GLOOMY — **drea·ri·ly** \'drir-ə-lē\ *adv* — **drea·ri·ness** \'drir-ē-nəs\ *n*

1**dredge** \'drej\ *n* **1 :** an iron frame with an attached bag net used esp. for gathering fish and shellfish **2 :** a machine for scooping up earth (as in deepening a river) usu. by buckets on an endless chain or a suction tube

2**dredge** *vb* **1 :** to dig, gather, or pull out with or as if with a dredge ⟨*dredge* a channel⟩ **2 :** to search with or as if with a dredge

dregs \'dregz\ *n pl* **1 :** sediment contained in a liquid or precipitated from it **:** LEES **2 :** the most undesirable part ⟨the *dregs* of humanity⟩

drench \'drench\ *vb* **:** to wet thoroughly **:** SATURATE *syn* see SOAK

1**dress** \'dres\ *vb* **1 :** to make or set straight (as troops in formation) **:** ALIGN **2 a :** to put clothes on **b :** to provide with clothing **c :** to put on or wear formal or fancy clothes **3 :** to add decorative details to **:** EMBELLISH ⟨*dress* a store window⟩ **4 :** to put in order **5 a :** to apply dressings or medicaments to ⟨*dress* a wound⟩ **b :** to arrange (the hair) by combing, brushing, or curling **c :** GROOM **d :** to kill and prepare for market ⟨*dress* a chicken⟩ **e :** CULTIVATE, TEND; *esp* **:** to apply manure or fertilizer to **6 :** SMOOTH, FINISH

2**dress** *n* **1 :** APPAREL, CLOTHING **2 :** an outer garment with a skirt for a woman or child **:** GOWN **3 :** clothing appropriate or peculiar to a particular time or occasion ⟨Roman *dress*⟩ ⟨evening *dress*⟩

3**dress** *adj* **1 :** relating to or used for a dress ⟨*dress* goods⟩ **2 :** suitable for a formal occasion ⟨*dress* clothes⟩

dress down *vb* **:** to reprove severely — **dressing down** *n*

1**dress·er** \'dres-ər\ *n* **1 :** a cupboard to hold dishes and cooking utensils **2 :** a chest of drawers or bureau with a mirror

2**dresser** *n* **:** one that dresses ⟨a window *dresser*⟩

dress·ing \'dres-ing\ *n* **1 a :** the act or process of one that dresses **b :** an instance of dressing **2 a :** a sauce for adding to a dish **b :** a seasoned mixture used as a stuffing (as for poultry) **3 a :** material used to cover an injury **b :** fertilizing material

dressing gown *n* **:** a loose robe worn esp. while dressing or resting

dressing room *n* **:** a room used chiefly for dressing; *esp* **:** a room in a theater for changing costumes and makeup

dressing table *n* **:** a low table with a mirror at which one sits while dressing

dress·mak·ing \'dres-ˌmā-king\ *n* **:** the process or occupation of making dresses — **dress·mak·er** \-kər\ *n*

dress rehearsal *n* **:** a full rehearsal of a play in costume and with stage properties shortly before the first performance

dressy \'dres-ē\ *adj* **dress·i·er; -est 1 :** showy in dress **2 :** suitable for formal occasions ⟨too *dressy* for daytime wear⟩

drew *past of* DRAW

1**drib·ble** \'drib-əl\ *vb* **drib·bled; drib·bling** \-(ə-)ling\ **1 :** to fall or flow or let fall in a series of drops **:** TRICKLE **2 :** DROOL **3 :** to propel by tapping, bouncing, or kicking ⟨*dribble* a basketball⟩ — **dribbler** \-(ə-)lər\ *n*

2**dribble** *n* **1 a :** a small trickling stream or flow **b :** a drizzling shower **2 :** an act or instance of dribbling a ball

drib·let \'drib-lət\ *n* **1 :** a small amount **2 :** a falling drop

dri·er *also* **dry·er** \'drī(-ə)r\ *n* **1 a :** something that dries **b** *usu dryer* **:** a device for drying something by heat or air **2 :** a substance used (as in paints or varnishes) to speed up drying

1**drift** \'drift\ *n* **1 a :** a drifting motion or course **b :** the flow of a river or ocean stream **2 a :** wind-driven snow, rain, or smoke usu. near the ground **b :** a mass of matter (as sand) deposited by or as if by wind or water **c :** a deposit of clay, sand, gravel, and boulders transported by a glacier or by running water from a glacier **3 a :** a general underlying tendency **b :** the meaning of what is spoken or written **4 :** a gradual shift in position or state

[2]**drift** *vb* **1 a :** to become or cause to be driven or carried along by a current of water, wind, or air **b :** to move or float smoothly and effortlessly **2 :** to move along without guidance or effort **3 :** to be piled up in heaps by wind or water — **drift·er** *n* — **drift·ing·ly** \'drif-ting-lē\ *adv*

drift·wood \'drift-ˌwu̇d\ *n* **:** wood drifted or floated by water

[1]**drill** \'dril\ *vb* **1 :** to pierce or bore with or as if with a drill ⟨*drill* a tooth⟩ ⟨*drill* a hole⟩ **2 :** to instruct or train by repetition ⟨*drill* a child in arithmetic⟩ ⟨*drill* troops⟩ — **drill·er** *n*

[2]**drill** *n* **1 :** a tool for making holes in hard substances **2 :** the training of soldiers in military skill and discipline **3 :** a physical or mental exercise regularly practiced **4 :** a marine snail that bores through oyster shells and feeds on the soft parts

[3]**drill** *n* **1 :** a shallow furrow or trench into which seed is sown **2 :** a planting machine that makes holes or furrows, drops in seed, and covers it with earth

[4]**drill** *vb* **:** to sow with or as if with a drill

[5]**drill** *n* **:** a durable cotton fabric in twill weave

dril·ling \'dril-ing\ *n* **:** [5]DRILL

drill·mas·ter \'dril-ˌmas-tər\ *n* **:** an instructor in military drill

drily *var of* DRYLY

[1]**drink** \'dringk\ *vb* **drank** \'drangk\; **drunk** \'drəngk\ *or* **drank**; **drink·ing** **1 a :** to swallow liquid **:** IMBIBE **b :** ABSORB **c :** to take in through the senses ⟨*drink* in the scenery⟩ **2 :** to give or join in a toast ⟨*drink* to the bride⟩ **3 :** to drink alcoholic beverages esp. to excess — **drink·a·ble** \'dring-kə-bəl\ *adj*

[2]**drink** *n* **1 a :** liquid suitable for swallowing **:** BEVERAGE **b :** alcoholic liquor **2 :** a draft or portion of liquid

drink·er \'dring-kər\ *n* **1 :** one that drinks **2 :** one that drinks alcoholic beverages esp. to excess

[1]**drip** \'drip\ *vb* **dripped**; **drip·ping** **1 :** to fall or let fall in drops **2 :** to let fall drops of moisture or liquid ⟨a *dripping* faucet⟩ — **drip·per** *n*

[2]**drip** *n* **1 a :** a falling in drops **b :** liquid that drips **2 :** the sound made by drops **3** *slang* **:** a tiresomely dull person

drip–dry \'drip-'drī\ *vb* **:** to dry with few or no wrinkles when hung dripping wet — **drip–dry** \-ˌdrī\ *adj*

drip·pings \'drip-ingz\ *n pl* **:** fat and juices drawn from meat during cooking

[1]**drive** \'drīv\ *vb* **drove** \'drōv\; **driv·en** \'driv-ən\; **driv·ing** \'drī-ving\ **1 a :** to urge, push, or force onward **b :** to cause to penetrate with force ⟨*drive* a nail⟩ **2 a :** to direct the movement or course of (as a vehicle or animals drawing a vehicle) **b :** to convey or transport in a vehicle **3 :** to set or keep in motion ⟨*drive* machinery by electricity⟩ **4 :** to carry through strongly ⟨*drive* a bargain⟩ **5 a :** to force to act ⟨*driven* by hunger to steal⟩ **b :** to project, inject, or impress forcefully ⟨*drove* the lesson home⟩ **6 :** to bring into a specified condition ⟨noise enough to *drive* a person crazy⟩ **7 :** to produce by opening a way (as by drilling) ⟨*drive* a well⟩ **8 :** to rush and press with violence ⟨the police *drove* into the mob⟩

[2]**drive** *n* **1 :** an act of driving: as **a :** a trip in a carriage or automobile **b :** a driving together of animals **c :** the guiding of logs downstream to a mill **d :** the act of driving a ball **e :** the flight of a ball **2 a :** DRIVEWAY **b :** a public road for driving **3 :** a sustained or intensive campaign ⟨an armored *drive* into the enemy stronghold⟩ ⟨a *drive* for charity⟩ **4 a :** an urgent or basic need or longing **b :** dynamic quality ⟨full of *drive*⟩ **5 a :** the means for giving motion to a machine or machine part ⟨a chain *drive*⟩ **b :** the means by which the movement of an automotive vehicle is controlled and directed

drive–in \'drīv-ˌin\ *adj* **:** arranged and equipped so as to accommodate patrons while they remain in their automobiles ⟨*drive-in* theater⟩ ⟨*drive-in* bank⟩ — **drive–in** *n*

[1]**driv·el** \'driv-əl\ *vb* **driv·eled** *or* **driv·elled**; **driv·el·ing** *or* **driv·el·ling** \-(ə-)ling\ **1 :** to let saliva dribble from the mouth **:** SLOBBER **2 :** to talk or utter stupidly, carelessly, or in an infantile way — **driv·el·er** *or* **driv·el·ler** \-(ə-)lər\ *n*

[2]**drivel** *n* **:** NONSENSE

driv·er \'drī-vər\ *n* **1 :** one that drives; *esp* **:** the operator of a motor vehicle **2 :** a golf club having a wooden head with a nearly straight face **3 :** a tool (as a hammer) for driving

drive·way \'drīv-ˌwā\ *n* **1 :** a road or way along which animals are driven **2 :** a short private road leading from the street to a house, garage, or parking lot

[1]**driz·zle** \'driz-əl\ *vb* **driz·zled**; **driz·zling** \-(ə-)ling\ **:** to rain in very small drops **:** SPRINKLE

[2]**drizzle** *n* **:** a fine misty rain — **driz·zly** \'driz-(ə-)lē\ *adj*

drogue \'drōg\ *n* **:** a small attached parachute for slowing down or stabilizing something (as an astronaut's capsule in landing)

droll \'drōl\ *adj* **:** having a humorous, whimsical, or odd quality ⟨a *droll* expression⟩ ***syn*** see COMICAL — **droll·ness** *n* — **drol·ly** \'drōl-lē\ *adv*

droll·ery \'drōl-(ə-)rē\ *n, pl* **-er·ies** **1 :** something droll **2 :** droll behavior **3 :** whimsical humor

-drome \ˌdrōm\ *n comb form* **1 :** racecourse ⟨motor*drome*⟩ **2 :** large specially prepared place ⟨aero*drome*⟩

drom·e·dary \'dräm-ə-ˌder-ē\ *n, pl* **-dar·ies** **1 :** a swift camel bred and trained esp. for riding **2 :** the one-humped camel of western Asia and northern Africa — called also *Arabian camel;* see CAMEL illustration

[1]**drone** \'drōn\ *n* **1 :** the stingless male bee (as of the honeybee) that gathers no honey **2 :** one that lives on the labors of others **:** PARASITE **3 :** a pilotless airplane or ship controlled by radio signals

[2]**drone** *vb* **:** to make or speak with a low dull monotonous humming sound

[3]**drone** *n* **1 :** one of the pipes on a bagpipe that sound fixed continuous tones **2 :** a deep monotonous sound **:** HUM

drool \'drül\ *vb* **1 a :** to water at the mouth **b :** to let saliva or some other substance flow from the mouth **:** SLAVER **2 :** to talk foolishly **:** DRIVEL

[1]**droop** \'drüp\ *vb* **1 :** to hang or incline downward **2 :** to sink gradually **3 :** to become depressed or weakened **:** LANGUISH — **droop·ing·ly** \'drü-ping-lē\ *adv* — **droopy** \'drü-pē\ *adj*

[2]**droop** *n* **:** the condition or appearance of drooping

[1]**drop** \'dräp\ *n* **1 a** (1) **:** the quantity of fluid that falls in one spherical mass (2) *pl* **:** a dose of medicine measured by drops **b :** a small quantity of drink **c :** the smallest practical unit of liquid measure

2 : something (as a hanging ornament on jewelry or a round candy) shaped like a drop **3 a** : the act or an instance of dropping : FALL **b** : a decline in quantity or quality ⟨a *drop* in water pressure⟩ ⟨a *drop* in prices⟩ **c** : a descent by parachute or helicopter **4** : the distance through which something drops **5** : a slot into which something is to be dropped **6** : an unframed piece of cloth scenery in a theater

[2]**drop** *vb* **dropped**; **drop·ping** **1** : to fall or let fall in drops **2 a** : to let fall ⟨*drop* a book⟩ **b** : to let fall gradually : LOWER ⟨*dropped* his voice⟩ **3** : SEND ⟨*drop* me a letter⟩ **4** : DISMISS ⟨*drop* the subject⟩ ⟨*drop* several workmen⟩ **5** : to knock or shoot down : cause to fall ⟨*drop* a deer with one shot⟩ **6** : to go lower ⟨prices *dropped*⟩ **7** : to come or go unexpectedly or informally ⟨*drop* in for a chat⟩ **8** : to pass into a less active state ⟨*drop* off to sleep⟩ **9** : to move downward or with a current **10** : to withdraw from participation or membership : QUIT ⟨*drop* out of school⟩ **11** : to leave (a letter) unsounded ⟨*drop* the *r* in *farm*⟩ **12** : to give birth to ⟨the cow *dropped* her calf⟩

drop·kick \'dräp-ˈkik\ *n* : a kick made by dropping a football to the ground and kicking it as it starts to rebound — **drop–kick** *vb* — **drop–kick·er** *n*

drop·let \'dräp-lət\ *n* : a very small drop

drop·out \'dräp-ˌau̇t\ *n* : one who drops out (as from school) esp. before achieving his goal

drop·per \'dräp-ər\ *n* **1** : one that drops **2** : a short glass or plastic tube with a rubber bulb used to measure out liquids by drops

drop·sy \'dräp-sē\ *n* : EDEMA — **drop·si·cal** \-si-kəl\ *adj*

dro·soph·i·la \drō-'säf-ə-lə\ *n* : any of a genus of small two-winged flies used esp. in genetics

dross \'dräs, 'drȯs\ *n* **1** : the scum formed on molten metal **2** : waste or foreign matter : IMPURITY

drought *or* **drouth** \'drau̇th, 'drau̇t\ *n* **1** : lack of rain or water **2** : a long period of dry weather — **droughty** \-ē\ *adj*

drove \'drōv\ *n* **1** : a group of animals driven or moving in a body **2** : a crowd of people moving or acting together

drov·er \'drō-vər\ *n* : one that drives cattle or sheep

drown \'drau̇n\ *vb* **1 a** : to suffocate by submersion esp. in water **b** : to become drowned **2** : to cover with water : INUNDATE **3** : OVERCOME, OVERPOWER

drowse \'drau̇z\ *vb* : DOZE — **drowse** *n*

drowsy \'drau̇-zē\ *adj* **drows·i·er**; **-est** **1** : ready to fall asleep **2** : making one sleepy ⟨a *drowsy* afternoon⟩ ***syn*** see SLEEPY — **drows·i·ly** \-zə-lē\ *adv* — **drows·i·ness** \-zē-nəs\ *n*

drub \'drəb\ *vb* **drubbed**; **drub·bing** **1** : to beat severely with or as if with a stick **2** : to defeat decisively

[1]**drudge** \'drəj\ *vb* : to do hard, menial, or monotonous work — **drudg·er** *n*

[2]**drudge** *n* : a person who drudges

drudg·ery \'drəj-(ə-)rē\ *n, pl* **-er·ies** : tiresome or menial work

[1]**drug** \'drəg\ *n* **1** : a substance used as a medicine or in making medicines **2** : something for which there is no demand ⟨a *drug* on the market⟩ **3** : a physiologically active and often harmful substance (as heroin, LSD, or marijuana) taken for other than medical reasons

[2]**drug** *vb* **drugged**; **drug·ging** **1** : to affect or treat with a drug; *esp* : to stupefy by a drug **2** : to lull or stupefy as if with a drug

drug·gist \'drəg-əst\ *n* : one who sells drugs and medicines; *also* : PHARMACIST

drug·store \'drəg-ˌstōr, -ˌstȯr\ *n* : a retail store where medicines and miscellaneous articles are sold : PHARMACY

dru·id \'drü-əd\ *n, often cap* : a member of an ancient Celtic priesthood of Gaul, Britain, and Ireland — **dru·id·ic** \drü-'id-ik\ *or* **dru·id·i·cal** \-'id-i-kəl\ *adj, often cap* — **dru·id·ism** \'drü-ə-ˌdiz-əm\ *n, often cap*

[1]**drum** \'drəm\ *n* **1** : a musical percussion instrument usu. consisting of a hollow cylinder with a skin head stretched over each end that is beaten with a stick or pair of sticks **2** : the sound of a drum; *also* : a similar sound **3** : a drum-shaped object: as **a** : a cylindrical mechanical device or part **b** : a cylindrical container; *esp* : a metal barrel with a capacity of 12 to 110 gallons **c** : a disk-shaped magazine for an automatic weapon

[2]**drum** *vb* **drummed**; **drum·ming** **1** : to beat or play on or as if on a drum **2** : to sound rhythmically : THROB, BEAT **3** : to summon or enlist by or as if by beating a drum ⟨*drum* up customers⟩ **4** : to dismiss ignominiously : EXPEL ⟨*drummed* out of the army⟩ **5** : to drive or force by steady effort or reiteration ⟨*drum* a lesson into his head⟩

drum·beat \'drəm-ˌbēt\ *n* : a stroke on a drum or its sound

drum·lin \'drəm-lən\ *n* : a long or oval hill of material left by a glacier

drum major *n* : the marching leader of a band or drum corps

drum ma·jor·ette \ˌdrəm-ˌmā-jə-'ret\ *n* : a female drum major

drum·mer \'drəm-ər\ *n* **1** : one that plays a drum **2** : TRAVELING SALESMAN

drum·stick \'drəm-ˌstik\ *n* **1** : a stick for beating a drum **2** : the lower segment of a fowl's leg

[1]**drunk** \'drəngk\ *adj* **1** : having the faculties impaired by alcohol **2** : controlled by some feeling as if under the influence of alcohol ⟨a dictator *drunk* with power⟩

[2]**drunk** *n* **1 a** : a person who is drunk **b** : DRUNKARD **2** : a period of excessive drinking : SPREE

drunk·ard \'drəng-kərd\ *n* : one who is habitually drunk

drunk·en \'drəng-kən\ *adj* **1 a** : DRUNK 1 **b** : given to habitual excessive use of alcohol **2** : of, relating to, or resulting from intoxication ⟨a *drunken* brawl⟩ **3** : unsteady or lurching as if from intoxication ⟨a *drunken* stagger⟩ — **drunk·en·ly** *adv* — **drunk·en·ness** \-kən-(n)əs\ *n*

drupe \'drüp\ *n* : a fleshy fruit (as the plum, cherry, or peach) having one seed enclosed in a hard bony stone

drupe·let \'drüp-lət\ *n* : a small drupe; *esp* : one of the individual parts of an aggregate fruit (as the raspberry)

[1]**dry** \'drī\ *adj* **dri·er** \'drī(-ə)r\; **dri·est** \'drī-əst\ **1** : free or freed from water or liquid ⟨*dry* weight⟩ ⟨*dry* steam⟩ **2** : characterized by loss or lack of water: as **a** : lacking precipitation and humidity ⟨a *dry* climate⟩ **b** : lacking freshness : STALE **c** : low in or deprived of natural juices or moisture ⟨*dry* hay⟩ **3** : not being in or under water ⟨*dry* land⟩ **4 a** : THIRSTY **b** : marked by the absence of alcoholic beverages ⟨a *dry* party⟩ **c** : no longer liquid or sticky ⟨the paint is *dry*⟩ **5** : containing or employing no liquid (as water) ⟨a *dry* creek⟩ ⟨*dry* heat⟩ **6** : not giving milk ⟨a *dry* cow⟩ **7** : not producing phlegm ⟨*dry* cough⟩ **8** : not productive : BARREN **9** : marked by a matter-of-fact, ironic, or terse manner of expression ⟨*dry* humor⟩ **10** : UNINTERESTING, WEARISOME ⟨*dry* passages of description⟩ **11** : not sweet ⟨*dry* wines⟩ **12** : relating to, favoring, or practicing

prohibition of alcoholic beverages ⟨a *dry* state⟩ — **dry·ly** *adv* — **dry·ness** *n*

2**dry** *vb* **dried**; **dry·ing** : to make or become dry

3**dry** *n, pl* **drys** \'drīz\ : PROHIBITIONIST

dry·ad \'drī-əd, -ˌad\ *n* : a nymph living in woods

dry–bulb thermometer *n* : a thermometer (as in a psychrometer) with unmoistened bulb

dry cell *n* : a small cell producing electricity by the reaction of chemicals that are not spillable ⟨a *dry cell* for a flashlight⟩

dry cleaning *n* : the cleansing of fabrics with organic solvents (as naphtha) — **dry–clean** *vb* — **dry cleaner** *n*

dry dock *n* : a dock that can be kept dry during the construction or repair of ships

dry·er *var of* DRIER

dry farm *n* : a farm on dry land operated without irrigation on the basis of moisture-conserving methods of cultivation and drought-resistant crops — **dry–farm** *vb* — **dry farmer** *n* — **dry farming** *n*

dry fly *n* : an artificial angling fly designed to float upon the surface of the water

dry fruit *n* : a fruit (as a capsule or achene) in which the walls of the ovary do not become succulent or pulpy

dry goods \'drī-ˌgu̇dz\ *n pl* : textiles, ready-to-wear clothing, and notions as distinguished from other goods

dry ice *n* : solidified carbon dioxide usu. in the form of blocks that at −78.5° C changes directly to a gas and that is used chiefly as a refrigerant

dry land *n* **1** : a region of low or inadequate rainfall **2** : TERRA FIRMA

dry measure *n* : a series of units of capacity for dry commodities — see MEASURE table, METRIC SYSTEM table

dry rot *n* : a fungous decay of seasoned timber in which the cellulose of wood is consumed leaving a soft skeleton readily reduced to powder

dry run *n* **1** : a practice firing without ammunition **2** : a practice exercise : TRIAL, REHEARSAL ⟨*dry run* of a television show⟩

dry–shod \'drī-'shäd\ *adj* : having dry shoes or feet

DS *abbr* dal segno

DST *abbr* daylight saving time

Du *abbr* Dutch

du·al \'d(y)ü-əl\ *adj* **1** : consisting of two parts or elements : having two like parts : DOUBLE **2** : having a double character or nature — **du·al·i·ty** \d(y)ü-'al-ət-ē\ *n* — **du·al·ly** \'d(y)ü-ə-lē\ *adv*

1**dub** \'dəb\ *vb* **dubbed**; **dub·bing** **1** : to confer knighthood upon **2** : NAME

2**dub** *vb* **dubbed**; **dub·bing** : to add sound effects to a film or broadcast

du·bi·ous \'d(y)ü-bē-əs\ *adj* **1** : occasioning doubt : UNCERTAIN **2** : feeling doubt : UNDECIDED ⟨was *dubious* about our chances in the race⟩ **3** : of uncertain outcome ⟨a *dubious* battle⟩ **4** : questionable in value, quality, or origin ⟨won by *dubious* means⟩ — **du·bi·ous·ly** *adv* — **du·bi·ous·ness** *n*

du·cal \'d(y)ü-kəl\ *adj* : of or relating to a duke or dukedom

duc·at \'dək-ət\ *n* : a former gold coin of various European countries

duch·ess \'dəch-əs\ *n* **1** : the wife or widow of a duke **2** : a woman who holds a ducal title in her own right

ə abut	ər further	a back	ā bake
ä cot, cart	au̇ out	ch chin	e less	ē easy
g gift	i trip	ī life	j joke	ng sing	ō flow
ȯ flaw	ȯi coin	th thin	th this	ü loot
u̇ foot	y yet	yü few	yu̇ furious	zh vision

duchy \'dəch-ē\ *n, pl* **duch·ies** : the territory of a duke or duchess

1**duck** \'dək\ *n, pl* **duck** *or* **ducks** : any of various swimming birds with the neck and legs short, the body heavy, the bill often broad and flat, and the sexes almost always different from each other in plumage

2**duck** *vb* **1** : to thrust or plunge under water **2** : to lower the head or body suddenly **3** : DODGE, EVADE ⟨*duck* a blow⟩ ⟨tried to *duck* the issue⟩ — **duck·er** *n*

3**duck** *n* **1** : a durable closely woven usu. cotton fabric **2** *pl* : clothes made of duck

4**duck** *n* : an amphibious truck

duck·bill \'dək-ˌbil\ *n* : PLATYPUS — called also *duck-billed platypus* \ˌdək-ˌbil(d)-\

duck·ling \-ling\ *n* : a young duck

duck·weed \-ˌwēd\ *n* : a tiny free-floating stemless plant found on a body of still water (as a pond)

duct \'dəkt\ *n* **1** : a tube or vessel carrying a bodily fluid (as the secretion of a gland) **2** : a pipe, tube, or channel that conveys a fluid (as air or water) — **duct·less** \'dək-tləs\ *adj*

duc·tile \'dək-təl\ *adj* **1** : capable of being drawn out (as into a wire) or hammered thin ⟨*ductile* metal⟩ **2** : easily led or influenced : DOCILE — **duc·til·i·ty** \ˌdək-'til-ət-ē\ *n*

ductless gland *n* : ENDOCRINE GLAND

dud \'dəd\ *n* **1** *pl* **a** : CLOTHES **b** : personal belongings **2** : one that fails completely **3** : a missile (as a bomb or shell) that fails to explode

dude \'d(y)üd\ *n* **1** : a man who pays excessive attention to his dress : DANDY **2 a** : a city man **b** : an Easterner in the West **3** *slang* : GUY, MAN — **dud·ish** \'d(y)üd-ish\ *adj* — **dud·ish·ly** *adv*

dude ranch *n* : a vacation resort offering horseback riding and other activities typical of western ranches

dud·geon \'dəj-ən\ *n* : ill humor : RESENTMENT ⟨stomped off in high *dudgeon*⟩

1**due** \'d(y)ü\ *adj* **1** : owed or owing as a debt or right ⟨respect *due* to the aged⟩ **2** : APPROPRIATE, FITTING **3 a** : SUFFICIENT, ADEQUATE ⟨arrived in *due* time⟩ **b** : REGULAR, LAWFUL ⟨*due* process of law⟩ **4** : ATTRIBUTABLE, ASCRIBABLE — used with *to* ⟨an accident *due* to negligence⟩ **5** : having reached the date at which payment is required : PAYABLE **6** : required or expected to happen : SCHEDULED ⟨*due* to arrive any time⟩

2**due** *n* **1** : something owed : DEBT ⟨pay a man his *due*⟩ **2** *pl* : a regular or legal charge or fee ⟨membership *dues*⟩

3**due** *adv* : DIRECTLY, EXACTLY ⟨*due* north⟩

1**du·el** \'d(y)ü-əl\ *n* [from medieval Latin *duellum*, from an archaic form of Latin *bellum* "war", revived in the Middle Ages to denote combat between two persons because the *du-* suggested Latin *duo* "two"] **1** : a combat between two persons; *esp* : one fought with weapons in the presence of witnesses **2** : a conflict between two persons or forces

2**duel** *vb* **du·eled** *or* **du·elled**; **du·el·ing** *or* **du·el·ling** : to fight in a duel — **du·el·er** *n* — **du·el·ist** \'d(y)ü-ə-ləst\ *n*

du·en·na \d(y)ü-'en-ə\ *n* **1** : an elderly woman in charge of the younger ladies in a Spanish or Portuguese family **2** : GOVERNESS, CHAPERON

du·et \d(y)ü-'et\ *n* : a composition for two performers

due to *prep* : because of

duf·fel \'dəf-əl\ *n* : an outfit of supplies (as for camping) : KIT

duffel bag *n* : a large fabric bag for belongings
dug *past of* DIG
du·gong \'dü-ˌgäng, -ˌgȯng\ *n* [from Malay *duyong*] : an aquatic plant-eating mammal related to the manatees but having a 2-lobed tail and tusks in the male

dugong
(about 9 ft. long)

dug·out \'dəg-ˌau̇t\ *n* **1** : a boat made by hollowing out a log **2** : a shelter dug in a hillside or in the ground **3** : a low shelter facing a baseball diamond for the players
duke \'d(y)ük\ *n* [from French *duc*, from Latin *duc-*, stem of *dux* "leader", from *ducere* "to lead", the source of English *induce*, *product*, *abduct*, and many others] **1** : a sovereign ruler of a duchy **2** : a nobleman of the highest rank esp. of the British peerage **3** *slang* : FIST, HAND — usu. used in pl. ⟨put up your *dukes*⟩ — **duke·dom** \-dəm\ *n*
dul·cet \'dəl-sət\ *adj* : sweet to the ear : MELODIOUS
dul·ci·mer \'dəl-sə-mər\ *n* : a wire-stringed instrument played with light hammers held in the hands
1**dull** \'dəl\ *adj* **1** : mentally slow : STUPID **2** : lacking zest or vivacity : LISTLESS **3** : slow in action : SLUGGISH ⟨a *dull* market⟩ **4** : lacking sharpness of edge or point **5** : lacking brilliance or luster **6** : not resonant or ringing **7** : CLOUDY, OVERCAST **8** : TEDIOUS, UNINTERESTING ⟨*dull* sermon⟩ **9** : not vivid in color ⟨*dull* blue⟩ — **dull·ness** *or* **dul·ness** \'dəl-nəs\ *n* — **dul·ly** \'dəl-(l)ē\ *adv*
2**dull** *vb* : to make or become dull
du·ly \'d(y)ü-lē\ *adv* : in a due manner, time, or degree ⟨*duly* authorized⟩ ⟨your request will be *duly* considered⟩
dumb \'dəm\ *adj* **1 a** : lacking the normal power of speech **b** : naturally incapable of speech ⟨*dumb* animals⟩ **2** : not willing to speak **3** : STUPID, FOOLISH — **dumb·ly** \'dəm-lē\ *adv* — **dumb·ness** *n*

syn DUMB, MUTE, SPEECHLESS mean unable to speak. Distinctively, DUMB can suggest an organic lack or defect ⟨*dumb* animals⟩ and MUTE a functional problem ⟨teaching *mute* children to speak⟩; SPEECHLESS usually implies a brief loss of ability to speak ⟨*speechless* with rage⟩ ***ant*** articulate (sense 1b)

dumb·bell \'dəm-ˌbel\ *n* **1** : a weight consisting of two spheres connected by a short bar and used usu. in pairs for exercise **2** : a stupid person
dumb·found *or* **dum·found** \ˌdəm-'fau̇nd\ *vb* : to strike dumb with astonishment
dumb·wait·er \'dəm-'wāt-ər\ *n* **1** : a portable serving table **2** : a small elevator for conveying food or goods from one story to another
dum·dum \'dəm-ˌdəm\ *n* : a soft-nosed bullet that expands upon hitting an object
1**dum·my** \'dəm-ē\ *n, pl* **dum·mies** **1** : a person who lacks or seems to lack the power of speech **2** : one who seems to be acting for himself but is really acting for another **3** : a stupid person **4** : an imitation of something to be used as a substitute or model or to confuse; *esp* : EFFIGY ⟨*dummies* in a store window⟩ **5 a** : an exposed hand in bridge played by one of the players in addition to his own **b** : a bridge player whose hand is a dummy
2**dummy** *adj* : having the appearance of being real but lacking ability to function ⟨a *dummy* corporation⟩ ⟨*dummy* wooden guns⟩
1**dump** \'dəmp\ *vb* **1** : to let fall in a heap or mass ⟨*dump* coal⟩ **2** : to get rid of quickly or unceremoniously **3** : to dump refuse ⟨no *dumping* allowed⟩ — **dump·er** *n*
2**dump** *n* **1** : a place where discarded materials (as refuse) are dumped **2** : a place where reserve military supplies are stored
dump·ling \'dəm-pling\ *n* **1** : a portion of dough cooked by boiling or steaming **2** : a dessert of fruit baked in biscuit dough
dumps \'dəm(p)s\ *n pl* : a dull gloomy state of mind : low spirits ⟨in the *dumps*⟩
dumpy \'dəm-pē\ *adj* **dump·i·er**; **-est** : short and thick in build : SQUAT — **dump·i·ness** *n*
1**dun** \'dən\ *n* **1** : a pale horse usu. with dark mane and tail and a dorsal stripe **2** : a nearly neutral slightly brownish dark gray — **dun** *adj*
2**dun** *vb* **dunned**; **dun·ning** : to make persistent demands upon for payment
3**dun** *n* **1** : a person who duns another **2** : an urgent demand for payment
dunce \'dən(t)s\ *n* [so called after John *Duns* Scotus, 13th century Scottish theologian, whose once accepted writings were ridiculed in the 16th century] : a mentally dull person
dune \'d(y)ün\ *n* : a hill or ridge of sand piled up by the wind
dune buggy *n* : a stripped automotive vehicle with over-sized tires for driving in sand
dung \'dəng\ *n* : waste matter of an animal : MANURE
dun·ga·ree \ˌdəng-gə-'rē\ *n* **1** : a heavy coarse cotton cloth **2** *pl* : trousers or work clothes made of dungaree
dung beetle *n* : a beetle (as a tumblebug) that rolls balls of dung in which to lay eggs and on which the larvae feed
dun·geon \'dən-jən\ *n* **1** : DONJON **2** : a close dark usu. underground prison
dung·hill \'dəng-ˌhil\ *n* : a manure pile
dunk \'dəngk\ *vb* **1** : to dip (as bread) into liquid while eating **2** : to dip or submerge temporarily in liquid **3** : to submerge oneself in water
dun·nage \'dən-ij\ *n* **1** : loose materials used around a cargo to prevent damage; *also* : padding in a shipping container **2** : baggage or personal effects esp. of a sailor
duo \'d(y)ü-ō\ *n, pl* **du·os** **1** : DUET; *esp* : a duet for two performers at two pianos **2** : PAIR
duo·dec·i·mal \ˌd(y)ü-ə-'des-ə-məl\ *adj* : of, relating to, or proceeding by twelve or the scale of twelves — **duodecimal** *n*
du·o·de·num \ˌd(y)ü-ə-'dē-nəm, d(y)u̇-'äd-ə-nəm\ *n, pl* **-de·na** \-'dē-nə, -ə-nə\ *or* **-denums** : the first part of the small intestine extending from the pylorus to the jejunum — **du·o·de·nal** \-'dēn-əl, -ə-nəl\ *adj*
dup *or* **dupl** *abbr* duplicate
dupe \'d(y)üp\ *vb* : DECEIVE, CHEAT — **dupe** *n* — **dup·er** *n*
du·ple \'d(y)ü-pəl\ *adj* **1** : taken by twos : TWOFOLD **2** : having two beats or a multiple of two beats to the measure ⟨*duple* time⟩
1**du·plex** \'d(y)ü-ˌpleks\ *adj* : DOUBLE, TWOFOLD
2**duplex** *n* : something duplex; *esp* : a 2-family house
duplex apartment *n* : an apartment having rooms on two floors
1**du·pli·cate** \'d(y)ü-pli-kət\ *adj* **1** : consisting of or existing in two corresponding or identical parts or examples **2** : being the same as another or others
2**duplicate** *n* : a thing that exactly resembles another : COPY
3**du·pli·cate** \'d(y)ü-pli-ˌkāt\ *vb* **1** : to make double

2 : to make a duplicate of — **du·pli·ca·tive** \'d(y)ü-pli-ˌkāt-iv\ *adj*

du·pli·ca·tion \ˌd(y)ü-pli-'kā-shən\ *n* **1 a** : an act or process of duplicating **b** : the state of being duplicated **2** : DUPLICATE, COUNTERPART

du·pli·ca·tor \'d(y)ü-pli-ˌkāt-ər\ *n* : one that duplicates; *esp* : a machine for making copies of typed, drawn, or printed matter

du·plic·i·ty \d(y)u̇-'plis-ət-ē\ *n, pl* **-ties** : deception by pretending to feel and act one way while acting another

du·ra·ble \'d(y)u̇r-ə-bəl\ *adj* : able to last a long time ⟨*durable* clothing⟩ — **du·ra·bil·i·ty** \ˌd(y)u̇r-ə-'bil-ət-ē\ *n* — **du·ra·ble·ness** \'d(y)u̇r-ə-bəl-nəs\ *n* — **du·ra·bly** \-blē\ *adv*

du·rance \'d(y)u̇r-ən(t)s\ *n* : IMPRISONMENT

du·ra·tion \d(y)u̇-'rā-shən\ *n* **1** : continuance in time ⟨a storm of short *duration*⟩ **2** : the time during which something lasts ⟨the *duration* of the war⟩

du·ress \d(y)u̇-'res\ *n* **1** : forcible restraint or restriction **2** : compulsion by threat ⟨a confession obtained under *duress*⟩

du·ri·an \'d(y)u̇r-ē-ən\ *n* : a large oval tasty but foul-smelling fruit with a prickly rind and soft pulp; *also* : the East Indian tree that bears it

dur·ing \ˌd(y)u̇r-ing\ *prep* **1** : throughout the duration of ⟨*during* his whole lifetime⟩ **2** : at some time or times in the course of ⟨occasional showers *during* the day⟩

du·rum wheat \ˌd(y)u̇r-əm-\ *n* : a hard red wheat that yields a flour used esp. in macaroni and spaghetti

dusk \'dəsk\ *n* **1** : the darker part of twilight esp. at night **2** : partial darkness : GLOOM

dusky \'dəs-kē\ *adj* **dusk·i·er**; **-est 1** : somewhat dark in color **2** : somewhat deficient in light : DIM — **dusk·i·ly** \-kə-lē\ *adv* — **dusk·i·ness** \-kē-nəs\ *n*

[1]**dust** \'dəst\ *n* **1 a** : fine particles (as of earth or in space) **b** : a fine powder **2** : the earthy remains of bodies once alive **3** : the surface of the ground **4** : something worthless

[2]**dust** *vb* **1** : to make free of dust : brush or wipe away dust **2** : to sprinkle with dust or as a dust ⟨*dust* a pan with flour⟩ ⟨*dust* insecticide on plants⟩

dust bowl *n* : a region that suffers from prolonged droughts and dust storms

dust·er \'dəs-tər\ *n* **1** : one that dusts **2** : a short housecoat

dust jacket *n* : a removable usu. decorative paper cover for a book

dust·pan \'dəs(t)-ˌpan\ *n* : a shovel-shaped pan for sweepings

dust storm *n* : a dust-laden whirlwind moving across a dry region

dusty \'dəs-tē\ *adj* **dust·i·er**; **-est 1** : filled or covered with dust **2** : consisting of or resembling dust : POWDERY — **dust·i·ly** \-tə-lē\ *adv* — **dust·i·ness** \-tē-nəs\ *n*

[1]**Dutch** \'dəch\ *adj* **1** *slang* : GERMAN **2** : of or relating to the Netherlands, its inhabitants, or their language

[2]**Dutch** *n* **1** : the Germanic language of the Netherlands **2 Dutch** *pl* : the people of the Netherlands **3** : DISFAVOR ⟨was in *Dutch* with the teacher⟩

Dutch door *n* : a door divided so that the lower part can be shut while the upper part remains open

Dutch elm disease *n* : a fungous disease of elms characterized by yellowing of the foliage, loss of leaves, and death

Dutch·man \'dəch-mən\ *n* **1 a** : a native or inhabitant of the Netherlands **b** : a person of Dutch descent **2** *slang* : GERMAN

Dutch·man's–breech·es \ˌdəch-mənz-'brich-əz\ *n pl* : a delicate spring-flowering herb of the eastern U.S. resembling the related bleeding heart but having cream-white double-spurred flowers

Dutchman's-breeches (up to 10 in. high)

Dutch oven *n* **1** : a brick oven for cooking **2 a** : a kettle with a tight cover used for baking in an open fire **b** : a heavy pot with a tight-fitting domed cover

Dutch treat *n* : a treat for which each person pays his own way

du·te·ous \'d(y)üt-ē-əs\ *adj* : DUTIFUL, OBEDIENT — **du·te·ous·ly** *adv* — **du·te·ous·ness** *n*

du·ti·a·ble \'d(y)üt-ē-ə-bəl\ *adj* : subject to a duty ⟨*dutiable* imports⟩

du·ti·ful \'d(y)üt-i-fəl\ *adj* **1** : motivated by a sense of duty ⟨a *dutiful* son⟩ **2** : proceeding from a sense of duty ⟨*dutiful* affection⟩ — **du·ti·ful·ly** \-fə-lē\ *adv* — **du·ti·ful·ness** *n*

du·ty \'d(y)üt-ē\ *n, pl* **duties 1** : conduct due to parents and superiors : RESPECT **2** : the action required by one's position or occupation **3 a** : a moral or legal obligation **b** : the force of moral obligation ⟨obey the call of *duty*⟩ **4** : TAX; *esp* : a tax on imports **5** : the service required (as of a machine) : USE ⟨a drill designed to withstand heavy *duty*⟩ ***syn*** see OBLIGATION

DV *abbr* Douay Version

DVM *abbr* doctor of veterinary medicine

[1]**dwarf** \'dwȯrf\ *n, pl* **dwarfs** \'dwȯrfs\ *also* **dwarves** \'dwȯrvz\ **1** : a person, animal, or plant much below normal size **2** : a small legendary man-like being usu. misshapen and ugly — **dwarf** *adj* — **dwarf·ish** \'dwȯr-fish\ *adj* — **dwarf·ness** *n*

[2]**dwarf** *vb* **1** : to restrict the growth or development of : STUNT **2** : to cause to appear smaller

dwell \'dwel\ *vb* **dwelt** \'dwelt\ *or* **dwelled** \'dweld, 'dwelt\; **dwell·ing 1** : to remain for a time **2** : to live as a resident : RESIDE **3** : to linger over something : keep the attention directed ⟨*dwelt* on the scene before him⟩ — **dwell·er** *n*

dwell·ing \'dwel-ing\ *n* : a shelter in which people live : HOUSE

dwin·dle \'dwin-dəl\ *vb* **dwin·dled**; **dwin·dling** \'dwin-d(ə-)ling\ : to make or become less : DIMINISH ⟨*dwindling* supply of coal⟩

dwt *abbr* pennyweight

[1]**dye** \'dī\ *n* **1** : color produced by dyeing **2** : a material used for dyeing or staining

[2]**dye** *vb* **dyed**; **dye·ing** : to stain or color usu. permanently : take up color in dyeing ⟨wool *dyes* beautifully⟩ — **dy·er** \'dī(-ə)r\ *n*

dye·ing \'dī-ing\ *n* : the process of fixing coloring matters in fibers (as of wool or cotton)

dy·ing \'dī-ing\ *adj* **1** : being about to die : being in the process of dying or dying out **2** : of or relating to dying or death ⟨his *dying* wish⟩

dyke *var of* DIKE

dy·nam·ic \dī-'nam-ik\ *adj* **1 a** : of or relating to

ə abut ər further a back ā bake
ä cot, cart au̇ out ch chin e less ē easy
g gift i trip ī life j joke ng sing ō flow
ȯ flaw ȯi coin th thin th this ü loot
u̇ foot y yet yü few yu̇ furious zh vision

physical force or energy **b** : of or relating to dynamics : ACTIVE **2 a** : marked by continuous activity or change **b** : marked by energy : FORCEFUL — **dy·nam·i·cal** \-'nam-i-kəl\ *adj* — **dy·nam·i·cal·ly** \-i-k(ə-)lē\ *adv*

dy·nam·ics \dī-'nam-iks\ *n sing or pl* **1** : the science of the motion of bodies and the action of forces in producing or changing their motion **2** : physical, moral, or intellectual forces or the laws relating to them **3** : the pattern of change or growth **4** : variation in force or intensity (as in music)

[1]**dy·na·mite** \'dī-nə-ˌmīt\ *n* [from Swedish *dynamit*, the name given to it by its inventor, Alfred Nobel, and derived from Greek *dynamis* "power"] : an explosive usu. used in blasting that is made chiefly of nitroglycerin absorbed in a porous material

[2]**dynamite** *vb* : to blow up with dynamite — **dy·na·mit·er** *n*

dy·na·mo \'dī-nə-ˌmō\ *n, pl* **-mos** : GENERATOR 3

dy·nas·ty \'dī-nə-stē, -ˌnas-tē\ *n, pl* **-ties** : a succession of rulers of the same line of descent — **dy·nas·tic** \dī-'nas-tik\ *adj* — **dy·nas·ti·cal·ly** \-ti-k(ə-)lē\ *adv*

dyne \'dīn\ *n* : the unit of force in the cgs system equal to the force that would give a free mass of one gram an acceleration of one centimeter per second per second

dys·en·tery \'dis-ən-ˌter-ē\ *n* **1** : a disease characterized by severe diarrhea with passage of mucus and blood from the bowels **2** : DIARRHEA — **dys·en·ter·ic** \ˌdis-ən-'ter-ik\ *adj*

dys·pep·sia \dis-'pep-shə, -sē-ə\ *n* : INDIGESTION

[1]**dys·pep·tic** \-'pep-tik\ *adj* **1** : relating to or having dyspepsia **2** : GLOOMY, CROSS — **dys·pep·ti·cal·ly** \-ti-k(ə-)lē\ *adv*

[2]**dyspeptic** *n* : a person having dyspepsia

dys·pro·si·um \dis-'prō-zē-əm, -zh(ē-)əm\ *n* : a chemical element that forms highly magnetic compounds — see ELEMENT table

dz *abbr* dozen

e \'ē\ *n, often cap* **1 :** the 5th letter of the English alphabet **2 :** the musical tone E **3 :** a grade rating a student's work as poor and usu. constituting a conditional pass
e- *prefix* **1 :** not ⟨*e*dentate⟩ **2 :** out : forth ⟨*e*radiate⟩
E *abbr* **1** east **2** eastern **3** English **4** error **5** excellent
ea *abbr* each
[1]**each** \'ēch\ *adj* **:** being one of two or more distinct individuals
[2]**each** *pron* **:** each one ⟨*each* of us took a turn⟩
[3]**each** *adv* **:** to or for each : APIECE ⟨50 cents *each*⟩
each other *pron* **:** each of two or more in mutual action or relation ⟨looked at *each other*⟩
ea·ger \'ē-gər\ *adj* **:** marked by keen, enthusiastic, or expectant desire or interest — **ea·ger·ly** *adv* — **ea·ger·ness** *n*
ea·gle \'ē-gəl\ *n* **1 :** any of various large day-flying, sharp-eyed, predatory birds with a powerful flight that are related to the hawks **2 :** a seal or standard bearing an eagle **3 :** a 10-dollar gold coin of the U.S. **4 :** a golf score of two strokes less than par on a hole
ea·glet \'ē-glət\ *n* **:** a young eagle
-ean — see -AN
[1]**ear** \'i(ə)r\ *n* **1 a :** the vertebrate organ of hearing and balance consisting in the typical mammal of a sound-collecting outer ear separated by a membranous drum from a sound-transmitting middle ear that in turn is separated from a sensory inner ear **b :** OUTER EAR **2 :** the sense of hearing ⟨a good *ear* for music⟩ **3 :** ATTENTION ⟨lend an *ear*⟩ **4 :** something resembling an ear in shape or position — **eared** \'i(ə)rd\ *adj* — **ear·less** \'i(ə)r-ləs\ *adj*
[2]**ear** *n* **:** the fruiting spike of a cereal (as Indian corn) including both the seeds and protective structures — **ear** *vb*
ear·ache \'i(ə)r-,āk\ *n* **:** an ache or pain in the ear
ear·drum \-,drəm\ *n* **:** the thin membrane that separates the outer and middle ear and transmits sound waves as vibrations to the chain of tiny bones in the middle ear
eared seal *n* **:** any of a family of seals including the sea lions and fur seals and having small well-developed external ears
earl \'ərl\ *n* **:** a member of the British peerage ranking below a marquess and above a viscount — **earl·dom** \-dəm\ *n*
ear·less seal \,i(ə)r-ləs-\ *n* **:** any of a family of seals with hairy coats and no external ears
ear·lobe \'i(ə)r-,lōb\ *n* **:** the pendent part of the ear of man or some fowls
[1]**ear·ly** \'ər-lē\ *adv* **ear·li·er; -est 1 :** near the beginning of a period of time or of a process or series **2 :** before the usual time
[2]**early** *adj* **ear·li·er; -est 1 :** of, relating to, or occurring near the beginning of a period or of a process or series **2 a :** occurring before the usual time ⟨peaches are *early* this year⟩ **b :** maturing or producing sooner than related forms ⟨an *early* peach⟩ — **ear·li·ness** *n*
[1]**ear·mark** \'i(ə)r-,märk\ *n* **1 :** a mark of identification on the ear of an animal **2 :** a distinguishing or identifying mark

ə abut	ər further	a back	ā bake
ä cot, cart	aù out	ch chin	e less
ē easy	g gift	i trip	ī life
j joke	ng sing	ō flow	ȯ flaw
ȯi coin	th thin	t͟h this	ü loot
ù foot	y yet	yü few	yù furious
zh vision			

[2]**earmark** *vb* **1 :** to mark with or as if with an earmark **2 :** to set aside for a specific purpose
ear·muff \'i(ə)r-,məf\ *n* **:** one of a pair of pads joined by a flexible band and worn to protect the ears against cold
earn \'ərn\ *vb* **1 :** to deserve as a result of labor or service ⟨*earned* every cent he was paid⟩ ⟨scored three *earned* runs in the sixth inning⟩ **2 :** to get for services given ⟨*earn* a good salary⟩ — **earn·er** *n*
[1]**ear·nest** \'ər-nəst\ *n* **:** an earnest mental state ⟨in *earnest*⟩
[2]**earnest** *adj* **1 :** characterized by or proceeding from an intense and serious state of mind : not light or playful **2 :** not trivial : IMPORTANT — **ear·nest·ly** *adv* — **ear·nest·ness** \-nəs(t)-nəs\ *n*
[3]**earnest** *n* **1 :** something of value given to bind a bargain **2 :** a token of what is to come : PLEDGE
earn·ings \'ər-ningz\ *n pl* **1 :** something earned; *esp* : WAGES **2 :** revenue after deduction of expenses
ear·phone \'i(ə)r-,fōn\ *n* **:** a device that converts electrical energy into sound waves and is worn over or inserted into the ear ⟨a radio *earphone*⟩

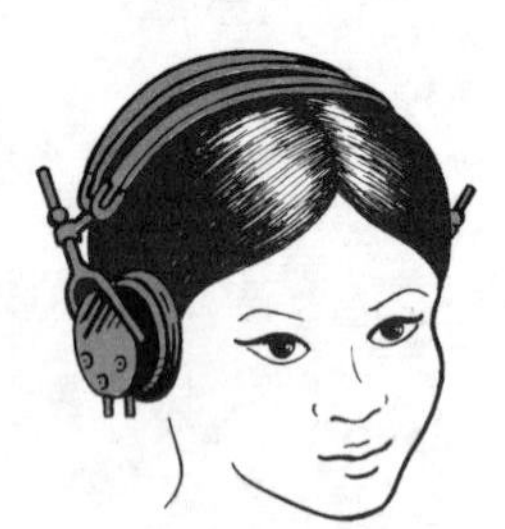
earphones

ear·ring \'i(ə)r-,ring\ *n* **:** an ornament for the earlobe
ear·shot \-,shät\ *n* **:** the range within which the unaided voice may be heard
ear·split·ting \-,split-ing\ *adj* **:** intolerably loud or shrill
earth \'ərth\ *n* **1 :** the soft or granular material composing part of the surface of the globe; *esp* : cultivable soil **2 :** the sphere of mortal life as distinguished from heaven and hell **3 :** land as distinguished from sea and air : GROUND **4** *often cap* **:** the planet on which we live — see PLANET table **5 :** the lair of a burrowing animal **6 :** any of several metallic oxides (as alumina)
earth·bound \-,baùnd\ *adj* **:** being on the way to or toward the earth
earth·en \'ər-thən, -t͟hən\ *adj* **:** made of earth or of baked clay ⟨an *earthen* floor⟩ ⟨*earthen* dishes⟩
earth·en·ware \-,wa(ə)r, -,we(ə)r\ *n* **:** articles (as utensils or ornaments) made of baked clay esp. of the coarser kinds
earth·light \'ərth-,līt\ *n* **:** EARTHSHINE
earth·ling \-ling\ *n* **:** an inhabitant of the earth
earth·ly \'ərth-lē\ *adj* **1 :** of, relating to, or characteristic of the earth : not heavenly or spiritual ⟨*earthly* joys⟩ **2 :** POSSIBLE, IMAGINABLE ⟨that tool is of no *earthly* use⟩ — **earth·li·ness** *n*
earth·quake \-,kwāk\ *n* **:** a shaking or trembling of a portion of the earth caused by movement of rock masses or by volcanic shocks
earth science *n* **:** any of the sciences (as geology or geography) that deal with the earth or one of its parts — **earth scientist** *n*
earth·shine \'ərth-,shīn\ *n* **:** sunlight reflected by the earth that illuminates the dark part of the moon
earth·work \-,wərk\ *n* **:** an embankment or construction of earth; *esp* : one made as a fortification
earth·worm \-,wərm\ *n* **:** a long slender worm with segmented body that lives in damp earth and moves with the aid of setae
earthy \'ər-thē, -t͟hē\ *adj* **earth·i·er; -est 1 :** consisting of or resembling earth ⟨an *earthy* flavor⟩

2 a : DOWN-TO-EARTH, PRACTICAL **b** : CRUDE, GROSS ⟨*earthy* humor⟩ — **earth·i·ness** *n*

ear·wax \ˈi(ə)r-ˌwaks\ *n* : a brownish yellow or orange waxlike substance produced by the glands of the external ear

ear·wig \-ˌwig\ *n* [from Old Engligh *ēarwicga*, from *ēare* "ear" and *wicga* "insect", literally "something that wiggles", so called from the belief that the insect crawled into the ear] : any of numerous insects with slender many-jointed antennae and a large forcepslike organ at the end of the body

1ease \ˈēz\ *n* **1** : freedom from pain or trouble : comfort of body or mind **2** : freedom from any feeling of difficulty or embarrassment ⟨speak with *ease*⟩

2ease *vb* **1** : to free from discomfort or worry : RELIEVE ⟨*ease* his pain⟩ **2** : to make less tight : LOOSEN

ea·sel \ˈē-zəl\ *n* [from Dutch *ezel* meaning literally "donkey"; compare the use of *horse* in *clotheshorse* and *sawhorse*] : a frame for supporting something (as an artist's canvas) esp. upright

easel

eas·i·ly \ˈēz-(ə-)lē\ *adv* **1** : in an easy manner ⟨won the game *easily*⟩ **2** : by far ⟨*easily* the best man⟩

1east \ˈēst\ *adv* [from Old English *ēast*, from an Indo-European root meaning "dawn"] : to or toward the east

2east *adj* **1** : situated toward or at the east **2** : coming from the east

3east *n* **1 a** : the general direction of sunrise **b** : the compass point directly opposite to west **2** *cap* : regions or countries east of a specified or implied point

east·bound \ˈēs(t)-ˌbau̇nd\ *adj* : going east

Eas·ter \ˈē-stər\ *n* : a feast observed on the first Sunday after the ecclesiastical full moon on or next after March 21 in commemoration of Christ's resurrection

Easter lily *n* : any of several white cultivated lilies that bloom in early spring

east·er·ly \ˈē-stər-lē\ *adv or adj* **1** : from the east **2** : toward the east

east·ern \ˈē-stərn\ *adj* **1** *often cap* : of, relating to, or characteristic of a region conventionally designated East **2** : lying toward or coming from the east — **east·ern·most** \-ˌmōst\ *adj*

East·ern·er \ˈē-stə(r)-nər\ *n* : a native or inhabitant of the East (as of the U.S.)

1east·ward \ˈēs-twərd\ *adv or adj* : toward the east — **east·ward·ly** \-lē\ *adv or adj* — **east·wards** \-twərdz\ *adv*

2eastward *n* : eastward direction or part

1easy \ˈē-zē\ *adj* **eas·i·er**; **-est** **1** : not hard to do or get : not difficult ⟨an *easy* lesson⟩ **2** : not severe : LENIENT ⟨an *easy* teacher⟩ **3** : COMFORTABLE ⟨an *easy* chair⟩ **4** : NATURAL UNAFFECTED ⟨an *easy* manner⟩ **5** : free from pain, trouble, or worry ⟨feels *easy* in his mind⟩ **6** : UNHURRIED, LEISURELY ⟨an *easy* pace⟩ **7** : not steep or abrupt ⟨*easy* slope⟩ *syn* see SIMPLE *ant* hard — **eas·iness** *n*

2easy *adv* **eas·i·er**; **-est** **1** : EASILY ⟨take life *easy*⟩ **2** : with slow care : CAUTIOUSLY ⟨go *easy*⟩

easy·go·ing \ˌē-zē-ˈgō-ing\ *adj* : taking life easily : CAREFREE — **easy·go·ing·ness** *n*

eat \ˈēt\ *vb* **ate** \ˈāt\; **eat·en** \ˈēt-ən\; **eat·ing** **1** : to take into the mouth and swallow food : chew and swallow in turn **2** : to take a meal **3** : to destroy, use up, or waste as if by eating : wear away ⟨rocks *eaten* away by waves⟩ **4** : to affect something by gradual destruction or consumption — used with *into* ⟨acid *ate* into the metal⟩ — **eat·er** *n*

syn EAT, CONSUME, DEVOUR mean to swallow usu. after chewing. EAT conveys the simple idea of chewing and swallowing; CONSUME implies eating up completely; DEVOUR suggests consuming with greedy abandon

1eat·a·ble \ˈēt-ə-bəl\ *adj* : fit to be eaten

2eatable *n* **1** : something to eat **2** *pl* : FOOD

eaves \ˈēvz\ *n sing or pl* : the overhanging lower edge of a roof projecting beyond the wall of a building

eaves·drop \ˈēvz-ˌdräp\ *vb* : to listen secretly to what is said in private — **eaves·drop·per** *n*

EB *abbr* eastbound

1ebb \ˈeb\ *n* **1** : the flowing back from the shore of water brought in by the tide **2** : a passing from a high to a low point : a time of decline

2ebb *vb* **1** : to recede from the flood state **2** : DECLINE, WEAKEN

ebb tide *n* **1** : the tide while ebbing **2** : a period or state of decline

eb·on \ˈeb-ən\ *adj* : EBONY

1eb·o·ny \ˈeb-ə-nē\ *n*, *pl* **-nies** **1** : a hard heavy wood yielded by various Old World tropical trees related to the persimmon **2** : a tree yielding ebony

2ebony *adj* **1** : made of or resembling ebony **2** : BLACK, DARK

eb·ul·lism \ˈeb-ə-ˌliz-əm\ *n* : the formation of bubbles (as of water vapor) in body fluids because of reduced environmental pressure

1ec·cen·tric \ik-ˈsen-trik, ek-\ *adj* **1** : not having the same center ⟨*eccentric* spheres⟩ **2** : deviating from some established pattern or from conventional or accepted usage or conduct **3** : deviating from a circular path ⟨an *eccentric* orbit⟩ — **ec·cen·tri·cal·ly** \-tri-k(ə-)lē\ *adv*

2eccentric *n* **1** : a disklike device that turns around a shaft not at its center and is used in machinery for changing circular motion into back-and-forth motion **2** : an eccentric person

ec·cen·tric·i·ty \ˌek-ˌsen-ˈtris-ət-ē\ *n*, *pl* **-ties** **1 a** : the quality or state of being eccentric **b** : deviation from an established pattern, rule, or norm; *esp* : odd or whimsical behavior **2** : the degree of deviation from a circular path ⟨a planet's *eccentricity*⟩

eccl *abbr* **1** ecclesiastic **2** ecclesiastical

Ec·cle·si·as·tes \ik-ˌlē-zē-ˈas-(ˌ)tēz\ *n* — see BIBLE table

ec·cle·si·as·tic \-ˈas-tik\ *n* : CLERGYMAN

ec·cle·si·as·ti·cal \-ti-kəl\ *or* **ec·cle·si·as·tic** \-tik\ *adj* : of or relating to the church or its organization or government ⟨*ecclesiastical* history⟩ — **ec·cle·si·as·ti·cal·ly** \-ti-k(ə-)lē\ *adv*

ec·dy·sis \ˈek-də-səs\ *n*, *pl* **-dy·ses** \-də-ˌsēz\ : the act of molting or of shedding (as by insects and crustaceans) an outer cuticular layer

ech·e·lon \ˈesh-ə-ˌlän\ *n* **1** : a formation of units (as airplanes) resembling a series of steps or a unit in such a formation **2** : one of a series of levels esp. of authority or those at such a level

echid·na \i-ˈkid-nə\ *n* : a spiny-coated toothless burrowing egg-laying mammal of Australia with a tapering snout and long tongue for eating ants

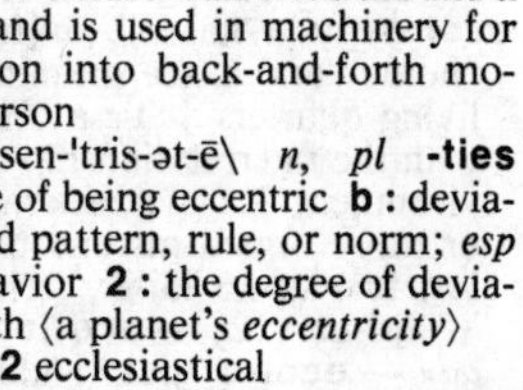

echidna (about 18 in. long)

echi·no·derm \i-ˈkī-nə-ˌdərm\ *n* : any of a phylum of marine animals (as starfishes and sea urchins) that have radially arranged body parts, a true coelom, often a calcium-containing outer skeleton, and a water-vascular system — **echi·no·der·ma·tous** \i-ˌkī-nə-'dər-mət-əs\ *adj*

1echo \'ek-ō\ *n, pl* **ech·oes 1 :** the repetition of a sound caused by reflection of sound waves **2 a :** a repetition or imitation of another **b :** REPERCUSSION, RESULT **3 :** one who closely imitates or repeats another — **echo·ic** \i-'kō-ik, e-\ *adj*

2echo *vb* **1 :** to resound with echoes **2 :** to produce an echo : send back or repeat a sound **3 :** REPEAT, IMITATE

echo·lo·ca·tion \ˌek-ō-lō-'kā-shən\ *n* **:** a process for locating distant or invisible objects by means of sound waves reflected back to the sender by the objects

echo sounder *n* **:** SONIC DEPTH FINDER

echo sounding *n* **:** the sounding of a body of water by means of a sonic depth finder or a radar device

éclair \ā-'kla(ə)r, -'kle(ə)r, 'ā-ˌ\ *n* **:** an oblong cream puff with whipped cream or custard filling

éclat \ā-'klä\ *n* **1 :** brilliance esp. in performance or achievement **2 :** demonstration of approval

1eclipse \i-'klips\ *n* **1 :** a complete or partial hiding or darkening of the sun or the moon caused when the sun is obscured by the moon's passing between the sun and the earth or when the moon is obscured by its entering the shadow of the earth **2 :** a falling into obscurity, decline, or disgrace

2eclipse *vb* **1 :** to cause an eclipse of **2 :** to dim the memory of ⟨the flight was *eclipsed* by later events⟩ **3 :** to surpass greatly : OUTSHINE

eclip·tic \i-'klip-tik\ *n* **:** the great circle of the celestial sphere that is the apparent path of the sun among the stars

ecol *abbr* **1** ecological **2** ecology

ecol·o·gy \i-'käl-ə-jē\ *n* [from Greek *oikos* "house", "home" and hence meaning literally "the science of living quarters"] **1 :** a branch of science concerned with the interrelationship of organisms and their environment **2 :** the pattern of relations between one or more organisms and their environment — **eco·log·ic** \ˌē-kə-'läj-ik, ˌek-ə-\ *or* **eco·log·i·cal** \-'läj-i-kəl\ *adj* — **eco·log·i·cal·ly** \-'läj-i-k(ə-)lē\ *adv* — **ecol·o·gist** \i-'käl-ə-jəst\ *n*

econ *abbr* **1** economics **2** economist **3** economy

ec·o·nom·ic \ˌek-ə-'näm-ik, ˌē-kə-\ *adj* **1 a :** of or relating to the science of economics **b :** of, relating to, or based on the production, distribution, and consumption of goods and services **2 :** having practical or industrial uses : affecting material resources ⟨*economic* pests⟩

ec·o·nom·i·cal \-'näm-i-kəl\ *adj* **1 :** given to thrift **2 :** operating with little waste or at a saving ⟨an *economical* car⟩ ***syn*** see FRUGAL ***ant*** extravagant — **ec·o·nom·i·cal·ly** \-i-k(ə-)lē\ *adv*

ec·o·nom·ics \ˌek-ə-'näm-iks, ˌē-kə-\ *n* **1 :** a social science concerned with discription and analysis of the production, distribution, and consumption of goods and services **2 :** economic aspect or significance — **econ·o·mist** \i-'kän-ə-məst\ *n*

econ·o·mize \i-'kän-ə-ˌmīz\ *vb* **1 :** to practice economy : be frugal ⟨*economize* on fuel⟩ **2 :** to use more economically : SAVE — **econ·o·miz·er** *n*

econ·o·my \i-'kän-ə-mē\ *n, pl* **-mies** [from Greek *oikonomia* meaning literally "household management", from *oikos* "house"] **1 a :** thrifty use of material resources or of available means **b :** an act of economizing **2 :** systematic arrangement : ORGANIZATION **3 :** the structure of economic life in a country, area, or period

eco·sys·tem \'ē-kō-ˌsis-təm, 'ekō-\ *n* **:** the whole complex formed in nature by an ecological community interacting with its environment

ec·ru \'ek-rü, 'ā-krü\ *adj* **:** BEIGE

ec·sta·sy \'ek-stə-sē\ *n, pl* **-sies 1 :** a state of being beyond reason and self-control **2 :** a state of overwhelming emotion; *esp* **:** rapturous delight — **ec·stat·ic** \ek-'stat-ik\ *adj* — **ec·stat·i·cal·ly** \-i-k(ə-)lē\ *adv*

ec·to·derm \'ek-tə-ˌdərm\ *n* **1 :** the outer cellular layer of a 2-layered animal (as a jellyfish) **2 :** the outermost of the three primary layers of an embryo from which skin, nerves, and certain other structures develop — **ec·to·der·mal** \ˌek-tə-'dər-məl\ *adj*

ec·to·plasm \'ek-tə-ˌplaz-əm\ *n* **1 :** an outer relatively rigid layer of the cytoplasm **2 :** a substance held to be the material form of a ghost — **ec·to·plas·mic** \ˌek-tə-'plaz-mik\ *adj*

Ecua *abbr* Ecuador

ec·u·men·i·cal \ˌek-yə-'men-i-kəl\ *adj* [originally meaning "of the whole world", from Greek *oikoumenē* (*gē*) "the inhabited (earth)", from the participle of a verb meaning "to inhabit", from *oikos* "house", the source of *ecology* and *economy*] **1 :** of, relating to, or representing the whole of a body of churches **2 :** promoting Christian unity or cooperation — **ec·u·men·i·cal·ly** \-i-k(ə-)lē\ *adv*

ec·ze·ma \ig-'zē-mə, 'ek-sə-mə, 'eg-zə-\ *n* **:** a skin disease marked by redness, itching, and scaly or crusted lesions

1-ed \d *after a vowel or* b, g, j, l, m, n, ng, r, th, v, z, zh; əd, id *after* d, t; t *after other sounds; exceptions are pronounced at their subentries or entries*\ *vb suffix or adj suffix* **1 —** used to form the past participle of regular weak verbs ⟨end*ed*⟩ ⟨fad*ed*⟩ ⟨tri*ed*⟩ ⟨patt*ed*⟩ **2 a :** having : characterized by ⟨cultur*ed*⟩ ⟨two-legg*ed*⟩ **b :** having the characteristics of ⟨bigot*ed*⟩

2-ed *vb suffix* **—** used to form the past tense of regular weak verbs ⟨judg*ed*⟩ ⟨deni*ed*⟩ ⟨dropp*ed*⟩

ed *abbr* **1** edited **2** edition **3** editor **4** education

edaph·ic \i-'daf-ik\ *adj* **:** of, relating to, or resulting from the soil — **edaph·i·cal·ly** \-'daf-i-k(ə-)lē\ *adv*

1ed·dy \'ed-ē\ *n, pl* **eddies :** a current of air or water running contrary to the main current; *esp* **:** a current moving in a circle like a whirlpool

2eddy *vb* **ed·died; ed·dy·ing :** to move in an eddy or so as to form an eddy

eddy current *n* **:** an electric current induced by an alternating magnetic field in a conductor (as the core of a transformer)

edel·weiss \'ād-əl-ˌwīs\ *n* **:** a small perennial woolly herb that is related to the thistles and grows high in the Alps

ede·ma \i-'dē-mə\ *n* **1 :** abnormal accumulation of watery fluid in a bodily tissue or cavity **2 :** an illness marked by edema — **edem·a·tous** \i-'dem-ət-əs, -'dē-mət-\ *adj*

eden·tate \(')ē-'den-ˌtāt\ *n* **:** any of a group of mammals having few or no teeth and including the sloths, armadillos, and New World anteaters — **edentate** *adj*

1edge \'ej\ *n* **1 a :** the cutting side of a blade **b :** the sharpness of a blade **c :** penetrating power : KEENNESS ⟨his voice had a sarcastic *edge*⟩ **2 a :** the

ə abut	ər further	a back	ā bake	
ä cot, cart	aù out	ch chin	e less	ē easy
g gift	i trip	ī life	j joke	ng sing	ō flow
ȯ flaw	ȯi coin	th thin	th this	ü loot
ù foot	y yet	yü few	yù furious	zh vision

line where an object or surface begins or ends; *also* : the narrow adjacent part **b** : the intersection of two plane faces of a solid ⟨*edge* of a prism⟩ **3** : a favorable margin : ADVANTAGE ***syn*** see BORDER — **edged** \'ejd\ *adj* — **on edge** : ANXIOUS, NERVOUS

²**edge** *vb* **1** : to give an edge to ⟨*edge* a sleeve with lace⟩ **2** : to move or advance slowly or by short moves ⟨*edged* his chair closer⟩

edge·ways \'ej-,wāz\ *or* **edge·wise** \-,wīz\ *adv* : with the edge foremost : SIDEWAYS

edg·ing \'ej-iŋ\ *n* : something that forms an edge or border ⟨a lace *edging*⟩

edgy \'ej-ē\ *adj* **edg·i·er**; **-est** **1** : having an edge : SHARP **2** : being on edge : IRRITABLE — **edg·i·ly** \'ej-ə-lē\ *adv* — **edg·i·ness** \'ej-ē-nəs\ *n*

ed·i·ble \'ed-ə-bəl\ *adj* : fit or safe to be eaten — **edible** *n* — **ed·i·ble·ness** *n*

edict \'ē-,dikt\ *n* : a law or order proclaimed by a sovereign — **edic·tal** \i-'dik-təl\ *adj*

ed·i·fice \'ed-ə-fəs\ *n* : BUILDING; *esp* : a large or impressive building (as a church)

ed·i·fy \'ed-ə-,fī\ *vb* **-fied**; **-fy·ing** : to instruct and improve morally or spiritually esp. by depicting good examples — **ed·i·fi·ca·tion** \,ed-ə-fə-'kā-shən\ *n*

ed·it \'ed-ət\ *vb* **1 a** : to correct, revise, and prepare for publication ⟨*edited* Poe's works⟩ **b** : to assemble (as a film or tape recording) for use or publication by cutting and rearranging **2** : to direct the publication of

edi·tion \i-'dish-ən\ *n* **1** : the form in which a text (as a printed book) is published **2** : the number of copies printed or published at one time ⟨a third *edition*⟩ **3** : one of the several issues of a newspaper for a single day

ed·i·tor \'ed-ət-ər\ *n* **1** : one that edits esp. as an occupation **2** : a person who writes editorials — **ed·i·tor·ship** \-,ship\ *n*

¹**ed·i·to·ri·al** \,ed-ə-'tōr-ē-əl, -'tȯr-\ *adj* **1** : of or relating to an editor ⟨an *editorial* staff⟩ **2** : being or resembling an editorial ⟨an *editorial* statement⟩ — **ed·i·to·ri·al·ly** \-ē-ə-lē\ *adv*

²**editorial** *n* : a newspaper or magazine article that gives the opinions of its editors or publishers

educ *abbr* **1** education **2** educational

ed·u·ca·ble \'ej-ə-kə-bəl\ *also* **ed·u·cat·a·ble** \-,kāt-ə-bəl\ *adj* : capable of being educated

ed·u·cate \'ej-ə-,kāt\ *vb* **1** : to provide schooling for **2 a** : to develop mentally and morally esp. by formal instruction **b** : TRAIN — **ed·u·ca·tor** \-,kāt-ər\ *n*

ed·u·cat·ed *adj* **1** : having an education; *esp* : having an education beyond the average **2** : giving evidence of education ⟨*educated* speech⟩ **3** : based on some knowledge of fact ⟨an *educated* guess⟩

ed·u·ca·tion \,ej-ə-'kā-shən\ *n* **1 a** : the action or process of educating or of being educated **b** : the knowledge and development resulting from an educational process ⟨a man of little *education*⟩ **2** : the field of study that deals mainly with methods and problems of teaching — **ed·u·ca·tion·al** \-sh(ə-)nəl\ *adj* — **ed·u·ca·tion·al·ly** \-ē\ *adv*

syn EDUCATION, TRAINING mean an action or process of learning. EDUCATION implies a usu. academic and general course of instruction for intellectual development; TRAINING usu. implies practical and specific exercise for developing skills (as in an art or trade)

ed·u·ca·tive \'ej-ə-,kāt-iv\ *adj* : tending to educate : INSTRUCTIVE

educe \i-'d(y)üs\ *vb* : to bring out : draw forth : ELICIT — **educ·i·ble** \-'d(y)ü-sə-bəl\ *adj*

¹**-ee** \'ē, (,)ē\ *n suffix* **1** : recipient or beneficiary of (a specified action or thing) ⟨appoint*ee*⟩ ⟨grant*ee*⟩ ⟨patent*ee*⟩ **2** : person that performs (a specified action) ⟨escap*ee*⟩

²**-ee** *n suffix* **1** : a particular esp. small kind of ⟨boot*ee*⟩ **2** : one resembling or suggestive of ⟨goat*ee*⟩

EEC *abbr* European Economic Community

EEG *abbr* electroencephalogram

eel \'ēl\ *n, pl* **eels** *or* **eel** **1** : any of numerous long snakelike fishes with smooth slimy skin and no pelvic fins **2** : EELWORM — **eel·like** \'ēl-,līk\ *adj*

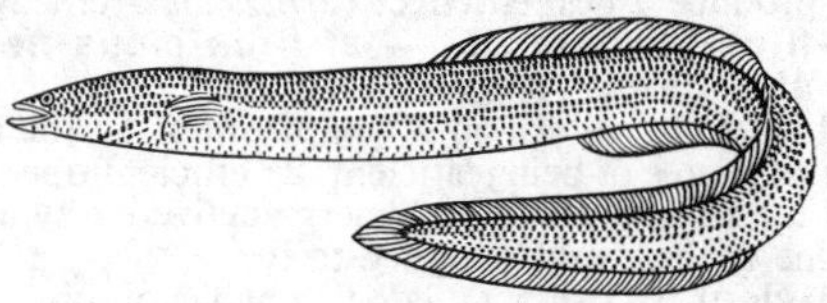

eel 1 (up to 6 ft. long)

eel·grass \'ēl-,gras\ *n* : a monocotyledonous plant that grows underwater and has long ribbonlike leaves

eel·worm \-,wərm\ *n* : a nematode worm; *esp* : one living in soil or parasitic on plants

e'en \(')ēn\ *adv* : EVEN

-eer \'i(ə)r\ *n suffix* : one that is concerned with or conducts or produces professionally ⟨auction*eer*⟩ ⟨pamphlet*eer*⟩

e'er \(')e(ə)r, (')a(ə)r\ *adv* : EVER

ee·rie *also* **ee·ry** \'i(ə)r-ē\ *adj* **ee·ri·er**; **-est** : arousing fear or uneasiness because of strangeness or gloominess : WEIRD — **ee·ri·ly** \'ir-ə-lē\ *adv* — **ee·ri·ness** \'ir-ē-nəs\ *n*

ef·face \i-'fās, e-\ *vb* **1** : to wipe out : OBLITERATE **2** : to make indistinct by or as if by rubbing out ***syn*** see ERASE — **ef·face·a·ble** \-'fā-sə-bəl\ *adj* — **ef·face·ment** \-'fās-mənt\ *n* — **ef·fac·er** *n*

¹**ef·fect** \i-'fekt\ *n* **1** : an event, condition, or state of affairs that is produced by a cause **2** : FULFILLMENT, EXECUTION, OPERATION ⟨the law went into *effect* today⟩ **3** : REALITY, FACT ⟨an excuse that was in *effect* a plain refusal⟩ **4** : the act of making a particular impression ⟨talked merely for *effect*⟩ **5** : INFLUENCE ⟨the *effect* of climate on growth⟩ **6** *pl* : GOODS, POSSESSIONS ⟨household *effects*⟩

²**effect** *vb* : to bring about ***syn*** see ACCOMPLISH — **ef·fect·er** *n*

¹**ef·fec·tive** \i-'fek-tiv\ *adj* **1 a** : producing or able to produce a desired effect **b** : IMPRESSIVE, STRIKING **2** : being in effect : OPERATIVE — **ef·fec·tive·ly** *adv* — **ef·fec·tive·ness** *n*

²**effective** *n* : a serviceman equipped and ready for duty

ef·fec·tor \i-'fek-tər\ *n* : a bodily organ (as a gland or muscle) that becomes active in response to stimulation

ef·fec·tu·al \i-'fek-chə(-wə)l\ *adj* : EFFECTIVE ⟨an *effectual* remedy⟩ — **ef·fec·tu·al·ly** \-ē\ *adv* — **ef·fec·tu·al·ness** *n*

ef·fec·tu·ate \i-'fek-chə-,wāt\ *vb* : to bring about : EFFECT

ef·fem·i·nate \ə-'fem-ə-nət\ *adj* : marked by qualities more suited to women than to men : UNMANLY — **ef·fem·i·na·cy** \-nə-sē\ *n* — **ef·fem·i·nate·ly** *adv* — **ef·fem·i·nate·ness** *n*

ef·fer·ent \'ef-ə-rənt, -,er-ənt, 'ē-,fer-\ *adj* : conducting outward from a part or organ; *esp* : conveying nervous impulses to an effector — **efferent** *n*

ef·fer·vesce \,ef-ər-'ves\ *vb* **1** : to bubble, hiss, and foam as gas escapes ⟨ginger ale *effervesces*⟩ **2** : to

E

show liveliness or exhilaration ⟨*effervesced* with excitement⟩ — **ef·fer·ves·cence** \-'ves-ən(t)s\ *n* — **ef·fer·ves·cent** \-ənt\ *adj* — **ef·fer·ves·cent·ly** *adv*

ef·fete \e-'fēt, i-\ *adj* **1** : no longer productive **2** : worn out : EXHAUSTED **3** : having lost character, courage, or vitality : OVERREFINED, DECADENT ⟨*effete* snobs⟩ — **ef·fete·ly** *adv* — **ef·fete·ness** *n*

ef·fi·ca·cious \ˌef-ə-'kā-shəs\ *adj* : having the power to produce a desired effect ⟨*efficacious* remedy⟩ — **ef·fi·ca·cious·ly** *adv* — **ef·fi·ca·cious·ness** *n* — **ef·fi·ca·cy** \'ef-i-kə-sē\ *n*

ef·fi·cien·cy \i-'fish-ən-sē\ *n, pl* **-cies** **1** : the quality or degree of being efficient **2** : efficient operation **3** : the ratio of the useful energy delivered by a machine to the energy supplied to it

ef·fi·cient \i-'fish-ənt\ *adj* : capable of producing desired effects; *esp* : productive without waste — **ef·fi·cient·ly** *adv*

ef·fi·gy \'ef-ə-jē\ *n, pl* **-gies** : an image or likeness esp. of a person: as **a** : a sculptured image on a tomb **b** : a crude figure representing a hated person ⟨hung him in *effigy*⟩

ef·flu·ent \'ef-ˌlü-ənt; e-'flü-, ə-\ *n* : liquid (as sewage or industrial by-products) discharged as waste — **effluent** *adj*

ef·fort \'ef-ərt, -ˌȯrt\ *n* **1** : conscious exertion of power **2** : a serious attempt : TRY **3** : something produced by exertion

ef·fort·less \'ef-ərt-ləs\ *adj* : showing or requiring little or no effort : EASY, SMOOTH — **ef·fort·less·ly** *adv* — **ef·fort·less·ness** *n*

ef·fron·tery \i-'frənt-ə-rē, e-\ *n, pl* **-ter·ies** : shameless boldness : INSOLENCE ⟨had the *effrontery* to deny his guilt⟩

ef·ful·gence \i-'fu̇l-jən(t)s, e-, -'fəl-\ *n* : radiant splendor : BRILLIANCE — **ef·ful·gent** \-jənt\ *adj*

ef·fu·sion \i-'fyü-zhən, e-\ *n* **1** : unrestrained expression of words or feelings **2 a** : escape of a fluid from containing vessels **b** : the fluid that escapes

ef·fu·sive \i-'fyü-siv, e-, -ziv\ *adj* : excessively demonstrative or emotional : GUSHING ⟨*effusive* thanks for his birthday present⟩ — **ef·fu·sive·ly** *adv* — **ef·fu·sive·ness** *n*

eft \'eft\ *n* : NEWT

eft·soons \eft-'sünz\ *or* **eft·soon** \-'sün\ *adv, archaic* : soon afterward; *also* : AGAIN, OFTEN

e.g. *abbr* [for Latin *exempli gratia*] for example

Eg *abbr* **1** Egypt **2** Egyptian

egad \i-'gad\ *interj* — used as a mild oath

egest \i-'jest\ *vb* : to rid the body of waste; *esp* : DEFECATE — **eges·tion** \-'jes-chən\ *n*

[1]**egg** \'eg\ *vb* [from Old English *eggen*, from Old Norse *eggja* meaning literally "to sharpen", from a noun related to English *edge*] : to incite to action : URGE, ENCOURAGE — usu. used with *on* ⟨*egged* him on to fight⟩

[2]**egg** *n* [from medieval English *egge*, from Old Norse *egg*] **1 a** : the hard-shelled reproductive body produced by a bird and esp. by domestic poultry **b** : an animal reproductive body consisting of an ovum with its nutritive and protective envelopes and being capable of development into a new individual **c** : a female germ cell — called also *ovum* **2** : something shaped like an egg ⟨darning *egg*⟩

ə abut	ər further	a back	ā bake
ä cot, cart	au̇ out	ch chin	e less
ē easy	g gift	i trip	ī life
j joke	ng sing	ō flow	ȯ flaw
ȯi coin	th thin	th this	ü loot
u̇ foot	y yet	yü few	yu̇ furious
zh vision			

egg·beat·er \'eg-ˌbēt-ər\ *n* : a rotary beater for beating eggs or liquids (as cream)

egg cell *n* : EGG

egg glass *n* : a timer similar to an hourglass for measuring short intervals (as that required for cooking an egg)

egg·head \'eg-ˌhed\ *n* : INTELLECTUAL, HIGHBROW

egg·nog \-ˌnäg\ *n* : a drink consisting of eggs beaten up with sugar, milk or cream, and often alcoholic liquor

egg·plant \-ˌplant\ *n* **1** : a widely cultivated perennial herb that is related to the potato and yields edible fruit **2** : the usu. glossy purple ovoid fruit of an eggplant

[1]**egg·shell** \-ˌshel\ *n* : the shell of an egg

[2]**eggshell** *adj* **1** : being thin and fragile ⟨*eggshell* china⟩ **2** : slightly glossy

egg white *n* : the clear semifluid mass of material surrounding the yolk of an egg

eg·lan·tine \'eg-lən-ˌtīn, -ˌtēn\ *n* : SWEETBRIER

ego \'ē-gō\ *n, pl* **egos** **1** : SELF; *esp* : the conscious self **2 a** : CONCEIT **b** : SELF-ESTEEM

ego·ism \'ē-gə-ˌwiz-əm\ *n* **1** : excessive interest in oneself : a self-centered attitude **2** : EGOTISM — **ego·ist** \-wəst\ *n* — **ego·is·tic** \ˌē-gə-'wis-tik\ *adj* — **ego·is·ti·cal·ly** \-'wis-ti-k(ə-)lē\ *adv*

ego·tism \'ē-gə-ˌtiz-əm\ *n* **1** : too frequent reference (as by use of the word *I*) to oneself **2** : an exaggerated sense of self-importance : CONCEIT **3** : EGOISM — **ego·tist** \-təst\ *n* — **ego·tis·tic** \ˌē-gə-'tis-tik\ *or* **ego·tis·ti·cal** \-'tis-ti-kəl\ *adj* — **ego·tis·ti·cal·ly** \-'tis-ti-k(ə-)lē\ *adv*

egre·gious \i-'grē-jəs\ *adj* [from Latin *egregius* "outstanding", "excellent", meaning literally "standing out from the herd"] : conspicuously bad : SHOCKING, FLAGRANT ⟨*egregious* errors⟩ — **egre·gious·ly** *adv* — **egre·gious·ness** *n*

egret
(about 2 ft. long)

egress \'ē-ˌgres\ *n* **1** : the act or right of going or coming out **2** : a way out : EXIT

egret \'ē-grət, i-'gret, 'ē-ˌgret, 'eg-rət\ *n* : any of various herons that bear long plumes during the breeding season

Egyp·tian \i-'jip-shən\ *n* **1** : a native or inhabitant of Egypt **2** : the language spoken by the ancient Egyptians — **Egyptian** *adj*

ei·der \'īd-ər\ *n* **1** : a large northern sea duck that is mostly white above and black below and has very soft down — called also *eider duck* **2** : EIDERDOWN 1

eider 1
(about 2 ft. long)

ei·der·down \-ˌdau̇n\ *n* **1** : the down of the eider **2** : a comforter filled with eiderdown

eight \'āt\ *n* **1** — see NUMBER table **2** : the eighth in a set or series **3** : something having eight units or members — **eight** *adj or pron*

eigh·teen \(')ā(t)-'tēn\ *n* — see NUMBER table — **eighteen** *adj or pron* — **eigh·teenth** \-'tēn(t)th\ *adj or n*

eighth \'ātth\ *n* — see NUMBER table — **eighth** *adj or adv*
eighth note *n* : a musical note equal in time to 1/8 of a whole note
eighty \'āt-ē\ *n, pl* **eight·ies** — see NUMBER table — **eight·i·eth** \-ē-əth\ *adj or n* — **eighty** *adj or pron*
ein·stei·ni·um \īn-'stī-nē-əm\ *n* : a radioactive element produced artificially — see ELEMENT table
1**ei·ther** \'ē-thər, 'ī-\ *adj* **1** : the one and the other of two : EACH ⟨flowers blooming on *either* side of the walk⟩ **2** : the one or the other of two ⟨take *either* road⟩
2**either** *pron* : the one or the other
3**either** *conj* — used before the first of two or more words or word groups of which the last is preceded by *or* to indicate that they represent alternatives ⟨a statement is *either* true or false⟩
4**either** *adv* **1** : LIKEWISE, MOREOVER — used after a negative ⟨not wise or handsome *either*⟩ **2** : so far as that is concerned — used after an alternative following a question or conditional clause esp. where negation is implied ⟨if his father had come or his mother *either* all would have gone well⟩
ejac·u·late \i-'jak-yə-,lāt\ *vb* **1** : to utter or eject suddenly and vigorously **2** : to eject a fluid and esp. semen — **ejac·u·la·to·ry** \-yə-lə-,tōr-ē, -,tȯr-\ *adj*
ejac·u·la·tion \i-,jak-yə-'lā-shən\ *n* **1** : an act of ejaculating; *esp* : a sudden discharging of a fluid from a duct **2** : something ejaculated; *esp* : a short sudden emotional utterance (as an exclamation)
eject \i-'jekt\ *vb* **1 a** : to drive out esp. by physical force **b** : to evict from property **2** : to throw out or off from within — **ejec·tion** \-'jek-shən\ *n* — **ejec·tor** \-'jek-tər\ *n*
eke out \'ēk-\ *vb* **1 a** : SUPPLEMENT ⟨she *eked out* her small income by sewing for neighbors⟩ **b** : to make (a supply) last by economy **2** : to gain by scanty or laborious means ⟨*eked out* a meager living from the poor soil of his farm⟩
el \'el\ *n* : ELEVATED RAILROAD
el *abbr* elevation
1**elab·o·rate** \i-'lab-(ə-)rət\ *adj* **1** : carried out with great care : DETAILED ⟨*elaborate* preparations⟩ **2** : marked by complexity, fullness of detail, or ornateness ⟨an *elaborate* design⟩ — **elab·o·rate·ly** *adv* — **elab·o·rate·ness** *n*
2**elab·o·rate** \i-'lab-ə-,rāt\ *vb* **1** : to work out in detail : DEVELOP ⟨*elaborate* an idea⟩ **2** : to give additional details ⟨*elaborate* on a story⟩ — **elab·o·ra·tion** \-,lab-ə-'rā-shən\ *n* — **elab·o·ra·tive** \-'lab-ə-,rāt-iv\ *adj* — **elab·o·ra·tor** \-,rāt-ər\ *n*
eland \'ē-lənd\ *n* : either of two large African antelopes resembling oxen and having short spirally twisted horns in both sexes

eland (about 6 ft. at shoulder)

elapse \i-'laps\ *vb* : to slip or glide away : PASS ⟨weeks *elapsed* before he wrote home⟩
elas·mo·branch \i-'laz-mə-,brangk\ *n, pl* **-branchs** : any of a class of fishes (as a shark or ray) with cartilaginous skeletons and platelike gills — **elasmobranch** *adj*
1**elas·tic** \i-'las-tik\ *adj* **1 a** : capable of recovering shape or size after being stretched, pressed, or squeezed : SPRINGY ⟨sponges are *elastic*⟩ **b** : capable of indefinite expansion ⟨gases are *elastic* substances⟩ **2** : able to recover quickly esp. from depression or fatigue ⟨youthful, *elastic* spirit⟩ **3** : FLEXIBLE, ADAPTABLE ⟨a plan *elastic* enough to be changed at any time⟩ — **elas·tic·i·ty** \i-,las-'tis-ət-ē, ,ē-,las-\ *n*
2**elastic** *n* **1 a** : an elastic fabric **b** : something made from elastic fabric **2** : a small oval rubber cord
elate \i-'lāt\ *vb* : to fill with joy or pride
elat·ed \i-'lāt-əd\ *adj* : marked by high spirits : EXULTANT — **elat·ed·ly** *adv* — **elat·ed·ness** *n*
el·a·ter \'el-ət-ər\ *n* : CLICK BEETLE
E layer *n* : a layer of the ionosphere that occurs at about 60 miles above the earth's surface and is capable of reflecting radio waves
1**el·bow** \'el-,bō\ *n* **1 a** : the joint of the arm; *also* : the outer curve of a bent arm **b** : a corresponding joint in the front limb of an animal **2** : something resembling an elbow; *esp* : an angular pipe fitting

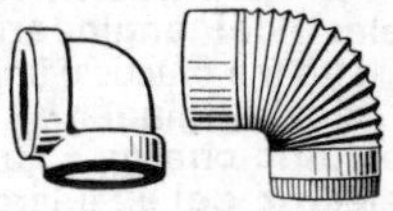

elbows 2

2**elbow** *vb* **1** : to push or shove with the elbow : JOSTLE **2** : to advance by or as if by pushing with the elbow ⟨*elbowed* their way through the crowd⟩
el·bow·room \'el-,bō-,rüm, -,ru̇m\ *n* **1** : room for moving the elbows freely **2** : enough space for work or operation
eld \'eld\ *n* **1** *archaic* : old age **2** *archaic* : ancient times : ANTIQUITY
1**el·der** \'el-dər\ *n* : any of a genus of shrubs or trees related to honeysuckle with flat clusters of small white or pink flowers and black or red drupes resembling berries
2**elder** *adj* : OLDER
3**elder** *n* **1** : one who is older : SENIOR **2** : a person having authority by virtue of age and experience ⟨the village *elders*⟩ **3** : any of various church officers — **el·der·ship** \-,ship\ *n*
el·der·ber·ry \'el-də(r)-,ber-ē\ *n* **1** : the edible fruit of an elder **2** : 1ELDER
el·der·ly \'el-dər-lē\ *adj* **1** : rather old; *esp* : past middle age **2** : of, relating to, or characteristic of later life ⟨*elderly* pursuits⟩ ***syn*** see OLD ***ant*** youthful — **el·der·li·ness** *n*
elder statesman *n* : a retired statesman who unofficially advises current leaders
el·dest \'el-dəst\ *adj* : OLDEST
elec *abbr* **1** electric **2** electrical **3** electricity
1**elect** \i-'lekt\ *adj* **1** : carefully selected : CHOSEN **2** : chosen for office or position but not yet installed ⟨president-*elect*⟩
2**elect** *n pl* : a carefully chosen group — used with *the*
3**elect** *vb* **1** : to select by vote for an office, position, or membership **2** : SELECT
elec·tion \i-'lek-shən\ *n* **1** : an act or process of electing; *esp* : the process of voting to choose a person for office **2** : the fact of being elected
elec·tion·eer \i-,lek-shə-'ni(ə)r\ *vb* : to work in the interest of a candidate or party in an election
1**elec·tive** \i-'lek-tiv\ *adj* **1** : chosen by election ⟨an *elective* official⟩ **2** : filled by a person who is elected ⟨the presidency is an *elective* office⟩ **3** : followed or taken by choice : not required ⟨an *elective* subject in school⟩ — **elec·tive·ly** *adv* — **elec·tive·ness** *n*
2**elective** *n* : an elective course or subject in school
elec·tor \i-'lek-tər\ *n* **1** : one qualified to vote in an election **2** : a member of the electoral college in the U.S.
elec·tor·al \i-'lek-t(ə-)rəl\ *adj* : of or relating to an election or electors

electoral college *n* : a body of electors; *esp* : one that elects the president and vice-president of the U.S.
elec·tor·ate \i-'lek-t(ə-)rət\ *n* : a body of people entitled to vote
electr- *or* **electro-** *comb form* : electricity : electric
1**elec·tric** \i-'lek-trik\ *or* **elec·tri·cal** \-tri-kəl\ *adj* [from Greek *ēlektron* "amber"; so called from the static electricity produced by rubbing a piece of amber] **1** : of, relating to, operated by, or produced by electricity ⟨*electric* motor⟩ ⟨*electric* shock⟩ **2** : ELECTRIFYING, THRILLING ⟨an *electric* performance⟩ — **elec·tri·cal·ly** \-tri-k(ə-)lē\ *adv* — **elec·tri·cal·ness** \-kəl-nəs\ *n*
2**electric** *n* : something operated by electricity; *esp* : an electric automobile
electrical engineering *n* : engineering that deals with the practical applications of electricity — **electrical engineer** *n*
electric charge *n* : a quantity of electricity
electric eel *n* : a large So. American eel-shaped fish able to give a severe electric shock
electric eye *n* : PHOTOELECTRIC CELL
elec·tri·cian \i-,lek-'trish-ən\ *n* : one who installs, operates, or repairs electrical equipment
elec·tric·i·ty \i-,lek-'tris-ət-ē, -'tris-tē\ *n* **1** : a source of energy found in nature that is observable in the attractions and repulsions of bodies electrically charged by friction and in natural phenomena (as lightning) **2** : electric current
electric ray *n* : any of various round-bodied short-tailed rays of warm seas able to give a severe electric shock
electric shock therapy *n* : the treatment of mental illness by the induction of coma through use of an electric current
elec·tri·fy \i-'lek-trə-,fī\ *vb* **-fied; -fy·ing 1 a** : to charge with electricity ⟨*electrify* a glass rod⟩ **b** : to equip for use of electric power or supply with electric power ⟨*electrify* a farm⟩ **2** : to excite intensely or suddenly : THRILL — **elec·tri·fi·ca·tion** \-,lek-trə-fə-'kā-shən\ *n*
elec·tro·cute \i-'lek-trə-,kyüt\ *vb* : to kill by electric shock; *esp* : to execute (a criminal) in this way — **elec·tro·cu·tion** \-,lek-trə-'kyü-shən\ *n*
elec·trode \i-'lek-,trōd\ *n* : either terminal of an electric source (as a battery); *esp* : either conductor by which the current enters or leaves an electrolyte
elec·tro·en·ceph·a·lo·gram \i-,lek-trō-en-'sef-ə-lō-,gram\ *n* : the tracing of brain waves that is made by an electroencephalograph
elec·tro·en·ceph·a·lo·graph \-,graf\ *n* : an apparatus for detecting and recording brain waves — **elec·tro·en·ceph·a·lo·graph·ic** \-en-,sef-ə-lō-'graf-ik\ *adj* — **elec·tro·en·ceph·a·log·ra·phy** \-,sef-ə-'läg-rə-fē\ *n*
elec·trol·y·sis \i-,lek-'träl-ə-səs\ *n* **1** : the producing of chemical changes by passage of an electric current through an electrolyte with the ions carrying the current by migrating to the electrodes where they may form new substances that are given off as gases or deposited as solids **2** : the destruction of hair roots with an electric current
elec·tro·lyte \i-'lek-trə-,līt\ *n* **1** : a liquid conductor containing ions through which an electric current can be passed with a resulting liberation of matter at the electrodes **2** : a substance that when dissolved in a suitable solvent or when fused becomes an ionic conductor
elec·tro·lyt·ic \i-,lek-trə-'lit-ik\ *adj* : of or relating to electrolysis or an electrolyte — **elec·tro·lyt·i·cal·ly** \-'lit-i-k(ə-)lē\ *adv*
elec·tro·mag·net \i-,lek-trō-'mag-nət\ *n* : a core of magnetic material (as soft iron) surrounded by a coil of wire through which an electric current is passed to magnetize the core
electromagnetic spectrum *n* : the entire range of wavelengths or frequencies of electromagnetic waves extending from gamma rays to the longest radio waves and including visible light
electromagnetic wave *n* : a wave (as a radio wave, wave of visible light, or X ray) that consists of an associated electric and magnetic effect and travels at the speed of light
elec·tro·mag·ne·tism \i-,lek-trō-'mag-nə-,tiz-əm\ *n* : magnetism developed by a current of electricity — **elec·tro·mag·net·ic** \-mag-'net-ik\ *adj*
elec·tro·mo·tive force \i-,lek-trə-,mōt-iv-\ *n* : a force that moves or tends to move electricity — abbr. *EMF* or *emf*
elec·tron \i-'lek-,trän\ *n* : a charge of negative electricity that forms the part of an atom outside the nucleus
electron cloud *n* : the system of electrons surrounding the nucleus of an atom
electron gun *n* : the part of a cathode-ray tube that produces, accelerates, and focuses a stream of electrons
elec·tron·ic \i-,lek-'trän-ik\ *adj* **1** : of or relating to electrons **2** : of, relating to, or utilizing devices constructed or working by principles of electronics — **elec·tron·i·cal·ly** \-'trän-i-k(ə-)lē\ *adv*
electronic brain *n* : a large computing machine that depends primarily on electronic devices for its operation
elec·tron·ics \-'trän-iks\ *n* : a branch of physics that deals with the emission, behavior, and effects of electrons in vacuums and gases and with the use of electronic devices (as electron tubes, radar, radio, and television)
electron microscope *n* : an instrument in which a beam of electrons is used to produce an enlarged image of a minute object on a fluorescent screen or a photographic plate in a way similar to that in which light is used to form the image in an ordinary microscope
electron tube *n* : a device in which conduction by electrons takes place through a vacuum or a gas within a sealed glass or metal container and which has various common uses (as in radio and television) based on the controlled flow of electrons — called also *electronic tube*
elec·tro·plate \i-'lek-trə-,plāt\ *vb* : to cover with a coating (as of metal or rubber) by means of electrolysis
elec·tro·scope \-,skōp\ *n* : any of various instruments for detecting the presence of an electric charge on a body, for determining whether the charge is positive or negative, or for indicating and measuring intensity of radiation
elec·tro·stat·ic \i-,lek-trə-'stat-ik\ *adj* : of or relating to static electricity or electrostatics
electrostatic generator *n* : an apparatus for the production of electrical discharges at high voltage commonly consisting of an insulated hollow conductor (as a sphere) that accumulates large quantities of electric charge

elec·tro·stat·ics \i-ˌlek-trə-ˈstat-iks\ *n* : physics that deals with phenomena due to attractions or repulsions of electric charges but not dependent upon their motion

elec·tro·type \i-ˈlek-trə-ˌtīp\ *n* **1** : a plate for use in printing made by making a mold of the matter to be printed, covering this mold with a thin shell of metal by electrolysis, and putting on a backing (as of heavy metal or plastic) **2** : a print made from an electrotype

el·e·gance \ˈel-i-gən(t)s\ *n* **1** : refined gracefulness **2** : tasteful richness of design or ornamentation

el·e·gan·cy \-gən-sē\ *n, pl* **-cies** : ELEGANCE

el·e·gant \ˈel-i-gənt\ *adj* **1** : marked by elegance **2** : EXCELLENT, SPLENDID — **el·e·gant·ly** *adv*

el·e·gy \ˈel-ə-jē\ *n, pl* **-gies** **1** : a poem expressing sorrow for one who is dead **2** : a poem that is mournful in spirit — **el·e·gi·ac** \ˌel-ə-ˈjī-ək\ *adj* — **el·e·gize** \ˈel-ə-ˌjīz\ *vb*

elem *abbr* elementary

el·e·ment \ˈel-ə-mənt\ *n* **1 a** : one of the four substances air, water, fire, or earth formerly believed to compose the physical universe **b** *pl* : forces of nature; *esp* : stormy or cold weather **c** : the state or sphere natural or suited to a person or an organism **2** : a basic or constituent part: as **a** *pl* : the simplest principles of a subject of study : RUDIMENTS **b** : a basic member of a mathematical class or set **c** : any of more than 100 fundamental substances that consist of atoms of only one kind and that cannot be separated by ordinary chemical means into simpler substances **3** *pl* : the bread and wine used in the sacrament of Communion

el·e·men·tal \ˌel-ə-ˈment-əl\ *adj* **1 a** : of, relating to, or being an element; *esp* : existing as an uncombined chemical element **b** : BASIC, ELEMENTARY **2** : of, relating to, or resembling a force of nature — **el·e·men·tal·ly** \-ˈment-ə-lē\ *adv*

el·e·men·ta·ry \ˌel-ə-ˈment-ə-rē, -ˈmen-trē\ *adj* **1** : of or relating to the simplest principles of a subject **2** : of, relating to, or teaching the basic subjects of education ⟨*elementary* school⟩

CHEMICAL ELEMENTS
with international atomic weights

ELEMENT & SYMBOL	ATOMIC NUMBER	ATOMIC WEIGHT
actinium (Ac)	89	
aluminum (Al)	13	26.98
americium (Am)	95	
antimony (Sb)	51	121.75
argon (Ar)	18	39.94
arsenic (As)	33	74.92
astatine (At)	85	
barium (Ba)	56	137.34
berkelium (Bk)	97	
beryllium (Be)	4	9.01
bismuth (Bi)	83	208.98
boron (B)	5	10.81
bromine (Br)	35	79.90
cadmium (Cd)	48	112.40
calcium (Ca)	20	40.08
californium (Cf)	98	
carbon (C)	6	12.01
cerium (Ce)	58	140.12
cesium (Cs)	55	132.90
chlorine (Cl)	17	35.45
chromium (Cr)	24	51.99
cobalt (Co)	27	58.93
columbium (Cb)	(see niobium)	
copper (Cu)	29	63.54
curium (Cm)	96	
dysprosium (Dy)	66	162.50
einsteinium (Es)	99	
erbium (Er)	68	167.26
europium (Eu)	63	151.96
fermium (Fm)	100	
fluorine (F)	9	18.99
francium (Fr)	87	
gadolinium (Gd)	64	157.25
gallium (Ga)	31	69.72
germanium (Ge)	32	72.59
gold (Au)	79	196.96
hafnium (Hf)	72	178.49
helium (He)	2	4.00
holmium (Ho)	67	164.93
hydrogen (H)	1	1.00
indium (In)	49	114.82
iodine (I)	53	126.90
iridium (Ir)	77	192.2
iron (Fe)	26	55.84
krypton (Kr)	36	83.80
lanthanum (La)	57	138.91
lawrencium (Lw)	103	
lead (Pb)	82	207.19
lithium (Li)	3	6.93
lutetium (Lu)	71	174.97
magnesium (Mg)	12	24.31
manganese (Mn)	25	54.93
mendelevium (Md)	101	

ELEMENT & SYMBOL	ATOMIC NUMBER	ATOMIC WEIGHT
mercury (Hg)	80	200.59
molybdenum (Mo)	42	95.94
neodymium (Nd)	60	144.24
neon (Ne)	10	20.18
neptunium (Np)	93	
nickel (Ni)	28	58.71
niobium (Nb)	41	92.90
nitrogen (N)	7	14.00
nobelium (No)	102	
osmium (Os)	76	190.2
oxygen (O)	8	15.99
palladium (Pd)	46	106.4
phosphorus (P)	15	30.97
platinum (Pt)	78	195.09
plutonium (Pu)	94	
polonium (Po)	84	
potassium (K)	19	39.10
praseodymium (Pr)	59	140.90
promethium (Pm)	61	
protactinium (Pa)	91	
radium (Ra)	88	
radon (Rn)	86	
rhenium (Re)	75	186.2
rhodium (Rh)	45	102.90
rubidium (Rb)	37	85.47
ruthenium (Ru)	44	101.07
samarium (Sm)	62	150.35
scandium (Sc)	21	44.95
selenium (Se)	34	78.96
silicon (Si)	14	28.08
silver (Ag)	47	107.87
sodium (Na)	11	22.98
strontium (Sr)	38	87.62
sulfur (S)	16	32.06
tantalum (Ta)	73	180.94
technetium (Tc)	43	
tellurium (Te)	52	127.60
terbium (Tb)	65	158.92
thallium (Tl)	81	204.37
thorium (Th)	90	232.03
thulium (Tm)	69	168.93
tin (Sn)	50	118.69
titanium (Ti)	22	47.90
tungsten (W)	74	183.85
uranium (U)	92	238.03
vanadium (V)	23	50.94
wolfram (W)	(see tungsten)	
xenon (Xe)	54	131.30
ytterbium (Yb)	70	173.04
yttrium (Y)	39	88.90
zinc (Zn)	30	65.37
zirconium (Zr)	40	91.22

elementary particle *n* : any of the submicroscopic constituents (as electrons or protons) of matter and energy whose existence has not been attributed to the combination of other more fundamental entities

el·e·phant \'el-ə-fənt\ *n* : a huge thickset nearly hairless mammal having the snout prolonged as a trunk and two incisors in the upper jaw developed into long outward-curving pointed tusks which furnish ivory

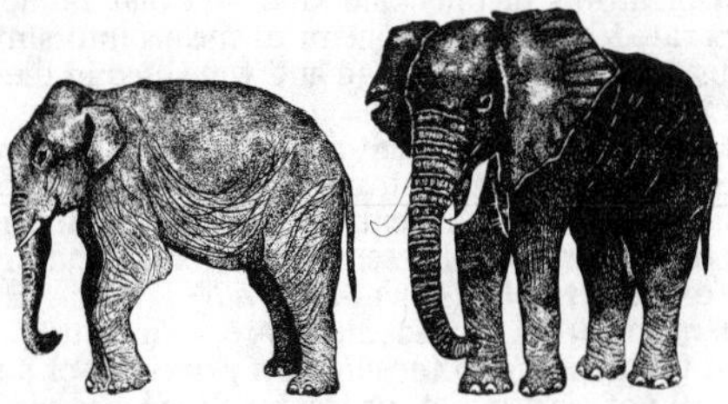

elephant: left, Indian (about 10 ft. at shoulder); right, African (about 11 ft. at shoulder)

el·e·phan·tine \ˌel-ə-'fan-ˌtēn, -ˌtīn\ *adj* **1 a** : very big : HUGE, MASSIVE **b** : PONDEROUS, UNGAINLY **2** : of or relating to an elephant

elev *abbr* elevation

el·e·vate \'el-ə-ˌvāt\ *vb* **1** : to lift up : RAISE **2** : to raise in rank or status **3** : to improve morally, intellectually, or culturally

1**el·e·vat·ed** \-ˌvāt-əd\ *adj* **1** : raised esp. above the ground ⟨*elevated* highway⟩ **2 a** : morally or intellectually on a high plane ⟨*elevated* mind⟩ **b** : FORMAL, DIGNIFIED ⟨*elevated* diction⟩

2**elevated** *n* : ELEVATED RAILROAD

elevated railroad *n* : a railroad supported by a structure of trestles and girders high enough to permit movement of traffic underneath — called also *elevated railway*

el·e·va·tion \ˌel-ə-'vā-shən\ *n* **1 a** : the height to which something is elevated **b** : the height above sea level : ALTITUDE **2** : an act or instance of elevating **3** : an elevated place : HILL **4** : the quality or state of being elevated **5** : a scale drawing showing a vertical section (as of a building) ***syn*** see HEIGHT

el·e·va·tor \'el-ə-ˌvāt-ər\ *n* **1 a** : an endless belt or chain conveyor for raising material **b** : a cage or platform for conveying persons or goods to different levels **c** : a building for storing grain **2** : a movable airfoil usu. attached to the tail plane of an airplane for producing motion up or down (as in climbing or diving)

elev·en \i-'lev-ən\ *n* **1** — see NUMBER table **2** : the eleventh in a set or series **3** : something having 11 units or members — **eleven** *adj or pron* — **elev·enth** \-ən(t)th\ *n* — **eleventh** *adj or adv*

elf \'elf\ *n, pl* **elves** \'elvz\ : a small and often mischievous fairy — **elf·ish** \'el-fish\ *adj* — **elf·ish·ly** *adv*

elf·in \'el-fən\ *adj* **1** : of or relating to elves **2** : resembling an elf; *esp* : having a strange beauty or charm

elf owl *n* : a very small insect-eating owl living in or about the giant cacti of desert areas of the southwestern U.S. and northern Mexico

elic·it \i-'lis-ət\ *vb* : to draw forth or bring out often by skillful questioning or discussion ⟨*elicit* the truth from an unwilling witness⟩

el·i·gi·ble \'el-ə-jə-bəl\ *adj* **1** : qualified to be chosen ⟨*eligible* to be president⟩ **2** : ENTITLED ⟨*eligible* to retire⟩ — **el·i·gi·bil·i·ty** \ˌel-i-jə-'bil-ət-ē\ *n* — **eligible** *n* — **el·i·gi·bly** \'el-i-jə-blē\ *adv*

elim·i·nate \i-'lim-ə-ˌnāt\ *vb* **1 a** : to get rid of : REMOVE ⟨*eliminate* the causes of an epidemic⟩ **b** : to remove by a process of selection ⟨the candidate was *eliminated* on the first ballot⟩ **2** : to expel from the living body — **elim·i·na·tion** \i-ˌlim-ə-'nā-shən\ *n* — **elim·i·na·tive** \i-'lim-ə-ˌnāt-iv\ *adj*

elite \ā-'lēt\ *n* **1** : the choice part; *esp* : a socially superior group **2** : a small group exercising power by virtue of real or claimed superiority — **elite** *adj*

elix·ir \i-'lik-sər\ *n* **1 a** : a substance held to be capable of changing metals into gold **b** : a substance held to be capable of prolonging life indefinitely **c** : CURE-ALL **2** : a sweetened usu. alcoholic liquid containing medicinal agents **3** : the essential principle

elk \'elk\ *n, pl* **elk** *or* **elks** **1** : the largest existing deer of Europe and Asia related to the American moose and having broad spreading antlers **2** : a large North American deer with curved antlers having many branches — called also *wapiti*

elk 2 (up to 5 ft. at shoulder)

1**ell** \'el\ *n* : a former English unit of length for cloth equal to 45 inches

2**ell** *n* : an extension at right angles to a building

el·lipse \i-'lips, e-\ *n* : a closed plane curve that is a conic section of oval shape

el·lip·sis \i-'lip-səs, e-\ *n, pl* **-lip·ses** \-'lip-ˌsēz\ : the omission of one or more words that can be obviously understood and supplied ⟨"fire when ready" for "fire when you are ready" is an example of *ellipsis*⟩

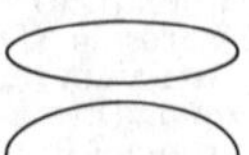

ellipses

el·lip·tic \i-'lip-tik, e-\ *or* **el·lip·ti·cal** \-ti-kəl\ *adj* **1** : OVAL **2** : of, relating to, or marked by ellipsis — **el·lip·ti·cal·ly** \-ti-k(ə-)lē\ *adv*

elm \'elm\ *n* **1** : any of a genus of large graceful trees that have alternate toothed leaves, small flowers without petals, and nearly circular one-seeded winged fruits and are often grown as shade trees; *esp* : AMERICAN ELM **2** : the wood of an elm

el·o·cu·tion \ˌel-ə-'kyü-shən\ *n* **1** : the art of effective public speaking **2** : a style of speaking esp. in public — **el·o·cu·tion·ary** \-shə-ˌner-ē\ *adj* — **el·o·cu·tion·ist** \-sh(ə-)nəst\ *n*

elo·dea \i-'lōd-ē-ə\ *n* : any of a small genus of American submerged aquatic herbs with leafy stems

elon·gate \i-'lȯng-ˌgāt\ *vb* **1** : to extend the length of **2** : to grow in length — **elon·ga·tion** \(ˌ)ē-ˌlȯng-'gā-shən\ *n*

elon·gat·ed \i-'lȯng-ˌgāt-əd\ *adj* : stretched out; *esp*

: being of relatively greater length than width

elope \i-'lōp\ *vb* : to run away secretly esp. with the intention of getting married without parental consent — **elope·ment** \-mənt\ *n* — **elop·er** *n*

el·o·quence \'el-ə-kwən(t)s\ *n* : discourse marked by force and persuasiveness; *also* : the art or power of using such discourse

el·o·quent \-kwənt\ *adj* **1** : marked by forceful and fluent expression **2** : vividly or movingly expressive or revealing — **el·o·quent·ly** *adv*

1else \'els\ *adv* **1** : in a different or additional manner or place or at a different time ⟨how *else* could it be done⟩ ⟨where *else* can we meet⟩ **2** : if the facts are or were different : if not : OTHERWISE

2else *adj* : OTHER: **a** : being different in identity ⟨somebody *else*⟩ **b** : being in addition ⟨what *else*⟩

else·where \'els-ˌhwe(ə)r, -ˌhwa(ə)r\ *adv* : in or to another place

elu·ci·date \i-'lü-sə-ˌdāt\ *vb* : to make clear or plain : EXPLAIN — **elu·ci·da·tion** \i-ˌlü-sə-'dā-shən\ *n* — **elu·ci·da·tive** \i-'lü-sə-ˌdāt-iv\ *adj* — **elu·ci·da·tor** \-ˌdāt-ər\ *n*

elude \ē-'lüd\ *vb* : to avoid or escape by being quick, skillful, or tricky

elu·sive \ē-'lü-siv, -ziv\ *adj* **1** : tending to elude : EVASIVE **2** : hard to comprehend or define ⟨an *elusive* idea⟩ — **elu·sive·ly** *adv* — **elu·sive·ness** *n*

elu·so·ry \i-'lüs-(ə-)rē, -'lüz-\ *adj* : ELUSIVE

el·ver \'el-vər\ *n* : a young eel

elves *pl of* ELF

elv·ish \'el-vish\ *adj* : ELFISH, MISCHIEVOUS

Ely·si·um \i-'liz(h)-ē-əm\ *n* : a place or condition of ideal happiness : PARADISE — **Ely·sian** \-'lizh-ən\ *adj*

el·y·tron \'el-ə-ˌträn\ *also* **el·y·trum** \-trəm\ *n, pl* **-tra** \-trə\ : one of the thick modified anterior wings in beetles and some other insects that protect the posterior pair of functional wings

em- — see EN-

ema·ci·ate \i-'mā-shē-ˌāt\ *vb* : to cause to lose flesh so as to become thin — **ema·ci·a·tion** \-ˌmā-s(h)ē-'ā-shən\ *n*

em·a·nate \'em-ə-ˌnāt\ *vb* **1** : to come out from a source **2** : to give out : EMIT — **em·a·na·tion** \ˌem-ə-'nā-shən\ *n* — **em·a·na·tion·al** \-sh(ə-)nəl\ *adj* — **em·a·na·tive** \'em-ə-ˌnāt-iv\ *adj*

eman·ci·pate \i-'man(t)-sə-ˌpāt\ *vb* : to free from restraint or control; *esp* : to free from slavery — **eman·ci·pa·tion** \-ˌman(t)-sə-'pā-shən\ *n* — **eman·ci·pa·tor** \-'man(t)-sə-ˌpāt-ər\ *n*

emas·cu·late \i-'mas-kyə-ˌlāt\ *vb* **1** : CASTRATE **2** : to deprive of masculine vigor or spirit : WEAKEN — **emas·cu·la·tion** \-ˌmas-kyə-'lā-shən\ *n* — **emas·cu·la·tor** \-'mas-kyə-ˌlāt-ər\ *n*

em·balm \im-'bäm, -'bälm\ *vb* **1** : to treat a dead body with special preparations to preserve it from decay **2** : to preserve as if by embalming ⟨*embalm* a poet in school anthologies⟩ — **em·balm·er** *n* — **em·balm·ment** \-'bäm-mənt, -'bälm-\ *n*

em·bank \im-'bangk\ *vb* : to enclose or confine by an embankment

em·bank·ment \-mənt\ *n* **1** : the action of embanking **2** : a raised bank or wall to carry a roadway, prevent floods, or hold back water

em·bar·go \im-'bär-gō\ *n, pl* **-goes** [from Spanish, a noun derived from the verb *embargar* to impede, literally "to put a barrier on", from Latin *barra* "bar"] **1** : an order of a government prohibiting the departure of commercial ships from its ports **2** : legal prohibition or restriction of commerce **3** : STOPPAGE, IMPEDIMENT; *esp* : PROHIBITION — **embargo** *vb*

em·bark \im-'bärk\ *vb* **1** : to go or put on board a ship or airplane **2** : to enter into an enterprise or undertaking ⟨*embark* on a career⟩ — **em·bar·ka·tion** \ˌem-ˌbär-'kā-shən\ *n* — **em·bark·ment** \im-'bärk-mənt\ *n*

em·bar·rass \im-'bar-əs\ *vb* **1** : to hamper the freedom of action of : IMPEDE **2** : to make confused or upset in mind : cause a feeling of uneasiness in ⟨unexpected laughter *embarrassed* the speaker⟩ **3** : to involve in financial difficulties — **em·bar·rass·ing·ly** \-'bar-ə-sing-lē\ *adv*

syn EMBARRASS, DISCONCERT, ABASH mean to make upset, uncomfortable, or confused emotionally. EMBARRASS suggests a feeling of uneasiness or discomfort; DISCONCERT suggests emotional upset or confusion from a source having strong and immediate impact; ABASH implies complete loss of composure (as from a feeling of guilt or inferiority)

em·bar·rass·ment \im-'bar-əs-mənt\ *n* **1** : the state of being embarrassed **2 a** : something that embarrasses : IMPEDIMENT **b** : an excessive quantity from which to select — used esp. in the phrase *embarrassment of riches*

E

em·bas·sy \'em-bə-sē\ *n, pl* **-sies** **1** : the function or position of an ambassador **2** : the business entrusted to an ambassador **3** : the person or group of persons sent as ambassadors **4** : the residence or office of an ambassador

em·bat·tle \im-'bat-əl\ *vb* **1** : to arrange in order of battle : prepare for battle **2** : FORTIFY

em·bed \im-'bed\ *vb* **1** : to enclose in or as if in a surrounding mass : set solidly in or as if in a bed ⟨*embed* a post in concrete⟩ **2** : to prepare (material for microscopic examination) for sectioning by infiltrating with and enclosing in a supporting substance (as paraffin)

em·bel·lish \im-'bel-ish\ *vb* **1** : to make beautiful with ornamentation : DECORATE **2** : to heighten the attractiveness of by adding ornamental details — **em·bel·lish·ment** \-mənt\ *n*

em·ber \'em-bər\ *n* **1** : a glowing piece of coal or wood from a fire; *esp* : such a piece smoldering in ashes **2** *pl* : smoldering remains of a fire

em·bez·zle \im-'bez-əl\ *vb* **-bez·zled; -bez·zling** \-(ə-)ling\ : to take (property entrusted to one's care) dishonestly for one's own use — **em·bez·zle·ment** \-əl-mənt\ *n* — **em·bez·zler** \-(ə-)lər\ *n*

em·bit·ter \im-'bit-ər\ *vb* : to make bitter or more bitter; *esp* : to arouse bitter feeling in — **em·bit·ter·ment** \-mənt\ *n*

em·bla·zon \im-'blā-zən\ *vb* **1** : to inscribe or ornament with markings or emblems used in heraldry **2 a** : to deck in bright colors **b** : GLORIFY, EXTOL ⟨a name *emblazoned* in history⟩

em·blem \'em-bləm\ *n* **1** : an object or likeness used to suggest a thing that cannot be pictured ⟨the flag is the *emblem* of one's country⟩ **2** : a device, symbol, design, or figure used as an identifying mark

syn EMBLEM, TOKEN, SYMBOL all mean a sign for something else. EMBLEM applies to an often pictorial object that is commonly understood to stand for an idea ⟨the spread eagle, an *emblem* of the United States⟩; TOKEN applies to an act, gesture, or object that is taken as a sign of sentiment ⟨take this check as a *token* of my appreciation⟩; SYMBOL applies broadly to anything that is understood as a sign of something else ⟨letters, the written *symbols* of spoken sounds⟩

em·blem·at·ic \ˌem-blə-'mat-ik\ *also* **em·blem·at·i·cal** \-'mat-i-kəl\ *adj* : of, relating to, or constituting an emblem : SYMBOLIC

em·bod·i·ment \im-'bäd-i-mənt\ *n* **1 :** the act of embodying : the state of being embodied **2 :** a thing that embodies something
em·body \im-'bäd-ē\ *vb* **-bod·ied; -body·ing 1 :** to bring together so as to form a body or system ⟨the Constitution *embodies* the fundamental laws of the United States⟩ **2 :** to make a part of a body or system **3 :** to express in a concrete or definite form ⟨*embodied* his ideas in suitable words⟩ **4 :** to represent in visible form ⟨a man who *embodies* courage⟩ — **em·bodi·er** *n*
em·bold·en \im-'bōl-dən\ *vb* **:** to make bold
em·bo·lism \'em-bə-ˌliz-əm\ *n* **1 :** the sudden obstruction of a blood vessel by an embolus **2 :** EMBOLUS
em·bo·lus \'em-bə-ləs\ *n, pl* **-li** \-ˌlī, -ˌlē\ **:** an abnormal particle (as an air bubble) circulating in the blood — compare THROMBUS
em·bo·som \im-'bu̇z-əm\ *vb* **1 :** to take to one's heart : EMBRACE **2 :** ENCLOSE, SHELTER
em·boss \im-'bäs, -'bȯs\ *vb* **:** to ornament with a raised pattern or design — **em·boss·er** *n* — **em·boss·ment** \-mənt\ *n*
em·bow·er \im-'bau̇(-ə)r\ *vb* **:** to shelter or enclose in or as if in a bower
[1]**em·brace** \im-'brās\ *vb* [from Old French *embracier*, from *en-* "in" + *brace* "pair of arms", from Latin *bracchium* arm] **1 a :** to clasp in the arms : HUG **b :** CHERISH, LOVE **2 :** ENCIRCLE, ENCLOSE **3 a :** to take up readily or gladly ⟨*embrace* a cause⟩ **b :** to avail oneself of : WELCOME **4 :** to take in : INCLUDE — **em·brace·a·ble** \-'brā-sə-bəl\ *adj* — **em·brac·er** *n*
[2]**embrace** *n* **:** a close encircling with the arms : HUG
em·bra·sure \im-'brā-zhər\ *n* **1 :** a recess of a door or window **2 :** an opening with sides flaring outward in a wall or parapet for the firing of cannon
em·bro·cate \'em-brə-ˌkāt\ *vb* **:** to moisten and rub (a part of the body) with a medicinal lotion or liniment — **em·bro·ca·tion** \ˌem-brə-'kā-shən\ *n*
em·broi·der \im-'brȯid-ər\ *vb* **em·broi·dered; em·broi·der·ing** \-(ə-)riŋ\ **1 :** to make or fill in a design with needlework **2 :** to ornament with needlework **3 :** to elaborate on : EXAGGERATE — **em·broi·der·er** \-ər-ər\ *n*
em·broi·dery \im-'brȯid-(ə-)rē\ *n, pl* **-der·ies 1 a :** the process or art of embroidering **b :** decorative needlework **2 :** elaboration in details esp. to add interest
em·broil \im-'brȯil\ *vb* **1 :** to throw into disorder or confusion **2 :** to involve in conflict or difficulties — **em·broil·ment** \-mənt\ *n*
em·bryo \'em-brē-ˌō\ *n, pl* **-bry·os 1 :** an animal in the early stages of development that are characterized by cleavage, the laying down of fundamental tissues, and the formation of primitive organs and organ systems — compare FETUS **2 :** the young sporophyte within a seed usu. having the form of a rudimentary plant **3 :** a beginning or undeveloped stage — used esp. in the phrase *in embryo*

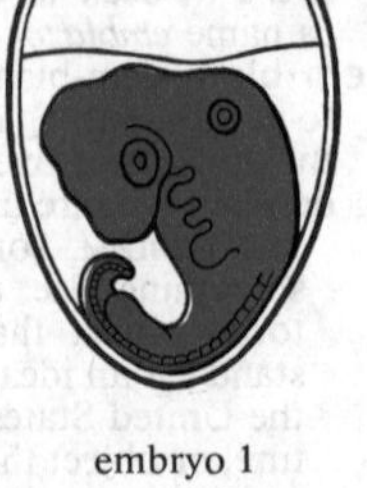
embryo 1

embryol *abbr* embryology
em·bry·ol·o·gy \ˌem-brē-'äl-ə-jē\ *n* **1 :** a branch of biology dealing with embryos and their development **2 :** the facts and events characteristic of the development of an embryo — **em·bry·o·log·ic** \ˌem-brē-ə-'läj-ik\ *or* **em·bry·o·log·i·cal** \-'läj-i-kəl\ *adj* — **em·bry·o·log·i·cal·ly** \-i-k(ə-)lē\ *adv* — **em·bry·ol·o·gist** \ˌem-brē-'äl-ə-jəst\ *n*
em·bry·on·ic \ˌem-brē-'än-ik\ *adj* **1 :** of or relating to an embryo **2 :** being in an early or undeveloped stage : being in embryo ⟨an *embryonic* idea⟩ — **em·bry·on·i·cal·ly** \-i-k(ə-)lē\ *adv*
em·cee \'em-'sē\ *n* **:** MASTER OF CEREMONIES — **emcee** *vb*
emend \ē-'mend\ *vb* **:** to correct usu. by textual alterations — **emen·da·tion** \(ˌ)ē-ˌmen-'dā-shən, ˌem-ən-\ *n*
[1]**em·er·ald** \'em-(ə-)rəld\ *n* **:** a rich green precious stone
[2]**emerald** *adj* **:** brightly or richly green
emerge \i-'mərj\ *vb* **1 :** to rise from or as if from an enveloping fluid : come out into view **2 :** to become known or apparent **3 :** to rise from an obscure or inferior condition
emer·gence \i-'mər-jən(t)s\ *n* **:** the act or an instance of emerging
emer·gen·cy \i-'mər-jən-sē\ *n, pl* **-cies 1 :** an unforeseen combination of circumstances or the resulting state that calls for immediate action **2 :** a pressing need : EXIGENCY
emer·i·tus \i-'mer-ət-əs\ *adj* **:** holding after retirement an honorary title corresponding to that held last during active service ⟨professor *emeritus*⟩ — **emeritus** *n*
em·ery \'em-(ə-)rē\ *n* **:** a dark granular corundum used esp. in the form of powder or grains for grinding and polishing
emet·ic \i-'met-ik\ *n* **:** an agent that induces vomiting — **emetic** *adj* — **emet·i·cal·ly** \-'met-i-k(ə-)lē\ *adv*
EMF *abbr* electromotive force
em·i·grant \'em-i-grənt\ *n* **1 :** one that emigrates **2 :** a migrant plant or animal — **emigrant** *adj*
em·i·grate \'em-ə-ˌgrāt\ *vb* **:** to leave a country or region to live or reside elsewhere — **em·i·gra·tion** \ˌem-ə-'grā-shən\ *n*
em·i·nence \'em-ə-nən(t)s\ *n* **1 :** a condition or station of prominence or superiority **2 —** used as a title for a cardinal **3 a :** a person of high rank or attainments **b :** a natural elevation : HEIGHT — **em·i·nent** \-nənt\ *adj* — **em·i·nent·ly** *adv*
eminent domain *n* **:** a right of a government to take private property for public use
emir \i-'mi(ə)r, ā-\ *n* **:** a Muslim prince — **emir·ate** \-'mi(ə)r-ət, -ˌāt\ *n*
em·is·sary \'em-ə-ˌser-ē\ *n, pl* **-sar·ies :** one sent as the agent of another to negotiate or gather information
emis·sion \ē-'mish-ən\ *n* **1 :** an act or instance of emitting **2 :** something emitted : DISCHARGE — **emis·sive** \ē-'mis-iv\ *adj*
emit \ē-'mit\ *vb* **emit·ted; emit·ting 1 a :** to throw or give off or out ⟨*emit* light⟩ **b :** EJECT **2 :** to give utterance to : EXPRESS — **emit·ter** *n*
em·mer \'em-ər\ *n* **:** a hard red wheat having spikelets with two kernels
em·met \'em-ət\ *n, chiefly dial* **:** ANT
emol·lient \i-'mäl-yənt\ *adj* **:** making soft or supple; *also* **:** soothing esp. to the skin or mucous membrane — **emollient** *n*

emol·u·ment \i-ˈmäl-yə-mənt\ *n* **:** profit from one's employment or from an office held **:** SALARY, WAGES
emote \i-ˈmōt\ *vb* **:** to give expression to emotion in or as if in a play
emo·tion \i-ˈmō-shən\ *n* **1 :** strong feeling **:** EXCITEMENT ⟨speak with *emotion*⟩ **2 :** a mental and bodily reaction (as anger, joy, hate, or fear) marked by strong feeling
emo·tion·al \i-ˈmō-sh(ə-)nəl\ *adj* **1 :** of or relating to the emotions ⟨an *emotional* upset⟩ **2 :** inclined to show or express emotion **:** easily moved ⟨an *emotional* person⟩ **3 :** appealing to or arousing emotion ⟨an *emotional* speech⟩ — **emo·tion·al·ly** \-ē\ *adv*
em·per·or \ˈem-pər-ər\ *n* **:** the sovereign ruler of an empire
emph *abbr* emphatic
em·pha·sis \ˈem(p)-fə-səs\ *n, pl* **-pha·ses** \-fə-ˌsēz\ **1 a :** forcefulness of expression ⟨spoke with *emphasis*⟩ **b :** prominence given in speaking to a word or syllable **2 :** special stress or insistence upon something
em·pha·size \ˈem(p)-fə-ˌsīz\ *vb* **:** to place emphasis on **:** STRESS
em·phat·ic \im-ˈfat-ik, em-\ *adj* **1 :** uttered with or marked by emphasis **2 :** tending to express oneself in forceful speech or action **3 :** attracting special attention ⟨an *emphatic* contrast⟩ — **em·phat·i·cal·ly** \-ˈfat-i-k(ə-)lē\ *adv*
em·phy·se·ma \ˌem(p)-fə-ˈzē-mə, -ˈsē-\ *n* **:** a disorder marked by air-filled expansions of tissues esp. of the lung — **em·phy·se·ma·tous** \-ˈzē-mət-əs, -ˈsē-\ *adj*
em·pire \ˈem-ˌpī(ə)r\ *n* **1 a** (1) **:** a major political unit with a large territory or a number of territories or peoples under one sovereign authority; *esp* **:** one having an emperor as chief of state (2) **:** the territory of such a unit **b :** something held to resemble an empire; *esp* **:** an extensive enterprise under one control **2 :** imperial sovereignty, rule, or dominion
em·pir·ic \im-ˈpir-ik, em-\ *n* **:** a physician or other person who relies on experience alone
em·pir·i·cal \-ˈpir-i-kəl\ *or* **em·pir·ic** \-ˈpir-ik\ *adj* **1 :** relying on experience or observation usu. without due regard for system and theory ⟨*empirical* medicine⟩ **2 :** originating in or based on observation or experience ⟨*empirical* data⟩ **3 :** capable of being verified or disproved by observation or experiment ⟨*empirical* laws⟩ — **em·pir·i·cal·ly** \-ˈpir-i-k(ə-)lē\ *adv*
empirical formula *n* **:** a chemical formula showing the simplest ratio of elements in a compound
em·pir·i·cism \im-ˈpir-ə-ˌsiz-əm, em-\ *n* **1 :** QUACKERY, CHARLATANRY **2 :** reliance on observation and experiment in the natural sciences **3 :** a theory that knowledge originates in experience — **em·pir·i·cist** \-səst\ *adj or n*
em·place \im-ˈplās\ *vb* **:** to put into place
em·place·ment \-mənt\ *n* **1 :** a prepared position for weapons **2 :** a putting into position **:** PLACEMENT
1**em·ploy** \im-ˈplȯi\ *vb* **1 :** to make use of **:** USE **2 a :** to use or engage the services of ⟨*employ* a lawyer⟩ **b :** to provide with a job that pays wages or a salary **3 :** to devote to or direct toward a particular activity or person — **em·ploy·a·ble** \-ə-bəl\ *adj*
2**employ** *n* **:** employment esp. for wages or a salary ⟨generous to men in his *employ*⟩
em·ploy·ee *or* **em·ploye** \im-ˌplȯi-ˈē, (ˌ)em-; im-ˈplȯi-ˌē\ *n* **:** one employed by another for wages or a salary
em·ploy·er \im-ˈplȯi(-ə)r\ *n* **:** one that employs others
em·ploy·ment \im-ˈplȯi-mənt\ *n* **1 :** USE, PURPOSE; *also* **:** the act of using **2 a :** the act of engaging a person for work **:** HIRING **b :** the work at which one is employed **:** OCCUPATION **c :** the state of being employed ⟨*employment* in the machine trade⟩ **d :** the extent or degree to which a labor force is employed ⟨*employment* is high⟩
em·po·ri·um \im-ˈpōr-ē-əm, em-, -ˈpȯr-\ *n, pl* **-riums** *or* **-ria** \-ē-ə\ **1 a :** MARKETPLACE **b :** a commercial center **2 :** a store carrying a wide variety of merchandise
em·pow·er \im-ˈpau̇(-ə)r\ *vb* **:** to give official authority or legal power to
em·press \ˈem-prəs\ *n* **1 :** the wife or widow of an emperor **2 :** a woman who holds an imperial title in her own right
1**emp·ty** \ˈem(p)-tē\ *adj* **emp·ti·er; -est 1 :** containing nothing ⟨*empty* box⟩ **2 :** UNOCCUPIED, VACANT ⟨*empty* house⟩ **3 :** being without reality or substance ⟨*empty* dreams⟩ **4 :** lacking in value, sense, effect, or sincerity ⟨*empty* pleasures⟩ ⟨*empty* threats⟩ **5 :** HUNGRY ⟨feel *empty* before dinner⟩ **6 :** NULL 3 — **emp·ti·ly** \-tə-lē\ *adv* — **emp·ti·ness** \-tē-nəs\ *n*
2**empty** *vb* **1 :** to make empty **:** remove the contents of ⟨*empty* a barrel⟩ **2 :** to transfer by emptying ⟨*empty* flour from a bag⟩ **3 :** to become empty **4 :** to give forth contents (as fluid) **:** DISCHARGE ⟨the river *empties* into the ocean⟩
3**empty** *n, pl* **empties :** an empty container
em·pur·ple \im-ˈpər-pəl\ *vb* **em·pur·pled; em·pur·pling** \-ˈpər-p(ə-)liŋ\ **:** to tinge or color purple
em·py·re·an \ˌem-ˌpī-ˈrē-ən, -pə-\ *n* **1 :** the highest heaven or heavenly sphere **2 :** FIRMAMENT, HEAVENS — **em·py·re·al** \-ˈrē-əl\ *adj* — **empyrean** *adj*
emu \ˈē-myü\ *n* **:** a swift-running Australian bird with undeveloped wings that is related to but smaller than the ostrich

emu (about 5 ft. high)

em·u·late \ˈem-yə-ˌlāt\ *vb* **:** to strive to equal or excel — **em·u·la·tor** \-ˌlāt-ər\ *n*
em·u·la·tion \ˌem-yə-ˈlā-shən\ *n* **:** ambition or endeavor to equal or excel — **em·u·la·tive** \ˈem-yə-ˌlāt-iv\ *adj*
em·u·lous \ˈem-yə-ləs\ *adj* **:** eager or ambitious to equal or excel — **em·u·lous·ly** *adv* — **em·u·lous·ness** *n*
emul·si·fy \i-ˈməl-sə-ˌfī\ *vb* **-fied; -fy·ing :** to convert (as an oil) into an emulsion — **emul·si·fi·a·ble** \-ˌfī-ə-bəl\ *adj* — **emul·si·fi·ca·tion** \i-ˌməl-sə-fə-ˈkā-shən\ *n*
emul·sion \i-ˈməl-shən\ *n* **:** a material consisting of a mixture of liquids that do not dissolve in each other and having droplets of one liquid dispersed throughout the other ⟨an *emulsion* of oil in water⟩
en- *also* **em-** \e *also occurs in these prefixes although only* i *may be shown as in "engage"*\ *prefix* **1 :** put into or on to ⟨*en*cradle⟩ ⟨*en*throne⟩ **:** go into or on to ⟨*em*bus⟩ **2 :** cause to be ⟨*en*slave⟩ **3 :** provide with ⟨*em*power⟩ **4 :** so as to cover ⟨*en*wrap⟩ **:** thoroughly ⟨*en*tangle⟩ — in all senses usu. *em-* before *b, m,* or *p*
1**-en** \ən\ *also* **-n** \n\ *adj suffix* **:** made of **:** consisting of ⟨earth*en*⟩ ⟨wool*en*⟩
2**-en** *vb suffix* **1 :** become or cause to be ⟨sharp*en*⟩ **2 :** cause or come to have ⟨length*en*⟩
en·able \in-ˈā-bəl\ *vb* **en·abled; en·abling** \-b(ə-)liŋ\ **1 a :** to make able ⟨glasses *enable* him to read⟩ **b :** to make possible, practical, or easy **2 :** to give legal power, capacity, or sanction to

en·act \in-'akt\ *vb* **1** : to make (as a bill) into law ⟨*enact* legislation⟩ **2** : to act out : REPRESENT — **en·ac·tor** \-'ak-tər\ *n*

en·act·ment \-'ak(t)-mənt\ *n* **1** : the act of enacting : the state of being enacted **2** : LAW, STATUTE

1**enam·el** \in-'am-əl\ *vb* **-eled** *or* **-elled**; **-el·ing** *or* **-el·ling** \-'am-(ə-)ling\ : to cover or inlay with enamel

2**enamel** *n* **1** : a usu. opaque vitreous composition applied by fusion to the surface of metal, glass, or pottery **2** : a surface that resembles enamel **3** : a paint that flows out to a smooth hard coat when applied and usu. dries with a glossy appearance **4** : a very hard outer layer covering the crown of a tooth

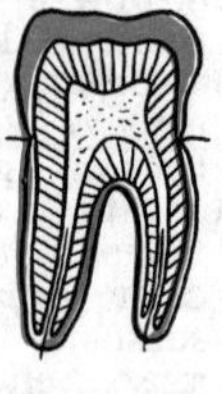
enamel 4

enam·el·ware \-əl-ˌwa(ə)r, -ˌwe(ə)r\ *n* : metal utensils (as pots and pans) coated with enamel

en·am·or \in-'am-ər\ *vb* : to inflame with love

en·camp \in-'kamp\ *vb* **1** : to set up and occupy a camp : CAMP **2** : to place or establish in a camp ⟨*encamp* troops⟩

en·camp·ment \-mənt\ *n* **1** : the act of encamping : the state of being encamped **2** : CAMP

en·cap·su·late \in-'kap-sə-ˌlāt\ *vb* : to encase or become encased in a capsule — **en·cap·su·la·tion** \-ˌkap-sə-'lā-shən\ *n*

en·case \in-'kās\ *vb* : to enclose in or as if in a case — **en·case·ment** \-mənt\ *n*

-ence \ən(t)s\ *n suffix* **1** : action or process ⟨emerg*ence*⟩ : instance of an action or process ⟨refer*ence*⟩ **2** : quality or state ⟨despond*ence*⟩

encephal- *or* **encephalo-** *comb form* : brain ⟨*encephal*itis⟩ ⟨*encephalo*gram⟩

en·ceph·a·li·tis \in-ˌsef-ə-'līt-əs, (ˌ)en-\ *n* : any of several infectious or contagious diseases (as sleeping sickness) characterized by inflammation of the brain — **en·ceph·a·lit·ic** \-'lit-ik\ *adj*

en·chain \in-'chān\ *vb* : to bind with or as if with chains — **en·chain·ment** \-mənt\ *n*

en·chant \in-'chant\ *vb* **1** : to influence by charms and incantation : BEWITCH **2** : THRILL, ENRAPTURE

en·chant·er \-ər\ *n* : one that enchants; *esp* : SORCERER

en·chant·ing *adj* : CHARMING, ATTRACTIVE — **en·chant·ing·ly** \-ing-lē\ *adv*

en·chant·ment \in-'chant-mənt\ *n* **1** : the act or art of enchanting : the state of being enchanted **2** : something that enchants : SPELL, CHARM

en·chant·ress \in-'chan-trəs\ *n* **1** : a woman who practices magic : SORCERESS **2** : a fascinating woman

en·ci·pher \in-'sī-fər, en-\ *vb* : to convert (a message) into cipher

en·cir·cle \in-'sər-kəl\ *vb* **1** : to form a circle around : SURROUND **2** : to pass completely around — **en·cir·cle·ment** \-kəl-mənt\ *n*

en·close \in-'klōz\ *vb* **1 a** : to close in : SURROUND ⟨*enclose* a porch with glass⟩; *esp* : to mark off (land) by or as if by a fence **b** : to hold in : CONFINE **2** : to place in a parcel or envelope

en·clo·sure \in-'klō-zhər\ *n* **1** : the act of enclosing : the state of being enclosed **2** : an enclosed space **3** : something (as a fence) that encloses **4** : something enclosed ⟨a letter with two *enclosures*⟩

en·code \in-'kōd\ *vb* : to convert (a message) into code

en·co·mi·um \en-'kō-mē-əm\ *n, pl* **-mi·ums** *or* **-mia** \-mē-ə\ : warm or high praise esp. when formally expressed : EULOGY

en·com·pass \in-'kəm-pəs, -'käm-\ *vb* **1** : to form a circle about : ENCLOSE **2 a** : ENVELOP **b** : INCLUDE — **en·com·pass·ment** \-mənt\ *n*

1**en·core** \'än-ˌkō(ə)r, -ˌkȯ(ə)r\ *n* : a demand for repetition or reappearance made by an audience; *also* : a further performance in response to such a demand

2**encore** *vb* : to call for a further performance or appearance of or by

1**en·coun·ter** \in-'kau̇nt-ər\ *vb* **en·coun·tered**; **en·coun·ter·ing** \-'kau̇nt-ə-ring, -'kau̇n-tring\ **1** : to meet as an adversary : FIGHT **2** : to come upon face to face : MEET **3** : to come upon unexpectedly

2**encounter** *n* **1** : a hostile meeting : COMBAT **2 a** : a chance meeting **b** : a meeting face to face

en·cour·age \in-'kər-ij, -'kə-rij\ *vb* **1** : to inspire with courage, spirit, or hope : HEARTEN **2** : to spur on : STIMULATE **3** : to give help to : FOSTER — **en·cour·age·ment** \-mənt\ *n* — **en·cour·ag·ing·ly** \-ij-ing-lē, -rij-\ *adv*

en·croach \in-'krōch\ *vb* **1** : to enter or force oneself gradually upon another's property or rights : TRESPASS, INTRUDE ⟨*encroach* on a neighbor's land⟩ **2** : to advance beyond the usual or proper limits ⟨the gradually *encroaching* sea⟩ — **en·croach·ment** \-mənt\ *n*

en·crust \in-'krəst\ *vb* **1** : to cover with a crust **2** : to form a crust

en·crus·ta·tion \(ˌ)in-ˌkrəs-'tā-shən, ˌen-\ *var of* INCRUSTATION

en·cum·ber \in-'kəm-bər\ *vb* **en·cum·bered**; **en·cum·ber·ing** \-b(ə-)ring\ **1** : to place an excessive burden on : HAMPER **2** : to impede the function or activity of

en·cum·brance \in-'kəm-brən(t)s\ *n* **1** : something that encumbers : LOAD, BURDEN **2** : a legal claim (as a mortgage) against property

-en·cy \ən-sē\ *n suffix, pl* **-encies** : quality or state ⟨despond*ency*⟩

ency *or* **encyc** *abbr* encyclopedia

1**en·cyc·li·cal** \in-'sik-li-kəl, en-\ *adj* : addressed to all the individuals of a group : GENERAL

2**encyclical** *n* : an encyclical letter; *esp* : a papal letter to the bishops of the church as a whole or to those in one country

en·cy·clo·pe·dia *also* **en·cy·clo·pae·dia** \in-ˌsī-klə-'pēd-ē-ə\ *n* [from Greek *enkyklopaideia*, "general education", from *enkyklios* "all-round" (from *kyklos* "circle", the source of English *cycle*) and *paideia* "education"] : a work that contains information on all branches of knowledge or treats comprehensively a particular branch of knowledge usu. in articles arranged alphabetically by subject

en·cy·clo·pe·dic *also* **en·cy·clo·pae·dic** \-'pēd-ik\ *adj* **1** : of or relating to an encyclopedia **2** : covering a wide range of subjects ⟨*encyclopedic* knowledge⟩ — **en·cy·clo·pe·di·cal·ly** \-'pēd-i-k(ə-)lē\ *adv*

en·cyst \in-'sist, en-\ *vb* : to form or become enclosed in a cyst — **en·cyst·ment** \-'sis(t)-mənt\ *n*

1**end** \'end\ *n* **1 a** : the part at the boundary of an area **b** : a point that marks the extent, limit, or cessation of something ⟨the *end* of the month⟩ **c** : the last part lengthwise : TIP **2 a** : cessation of a process, pursuit, or activity **b** : DEATH, DESTRUCTION

3 : something left over : REMNANT **4** : the goal toward which an agent acts or should act **5** : a football lineman whose position is at the end of the line **6** : a phase of an undertaking ⟨the advertising *end* of the business⟩ — **end·ed** \'en-dəd\ *adj*

²**end** *vb* : to bring or come to an end : STOP

end- *or* **endo-** *comb form* **1** : within : inside ⟨*endo*skeleton⟩ — compare EXO- **2** : taking in ⟨*endo*thermal⟩

en·dan·ger \in-'dān-jər\ *vb* **en·dan·gered**; **en·dan·ger·ing** \-'dānj-(ə-)riŋ\ : to bring into danger or peril

en·dan·gered *adj* : threatened with extinction ⟨an *endangered* species⟩

en·dear \in-'di(ə)r\ *vb* : to cause to become dear or beloved

en·dear·ment \-mənt\ *n* : a word or an act (as a caress) showing love or affection

en·deav·or \in-'dev-ər\ *vb* **en·deav·ored**; **en·deav·or·ing** \-(ə-)riŋ\ : to make an effort : work for a particular end : TRY — **endeavor** *n*

¹**en·dem·ic** \en-'dem-ik\ *adj* : restricted or peculiar to a locality or region ⟨*endemic* diseases⟩ ⟨an *endemic* plant⟩

²**endemic** *n* : NATIVE 3

end·ing \'en-diŋ\ *n* : the final part : CONCLUSION, END ⟨a novel with a happy *ending*⟩

en·dive \'en-,dīv\ *n* **1** : an annual or biennial herb closely related to chicory and widely grown as a salad plant — called also *escarole* **2** : the developing shoot of chicory when blanched for use as salad

end·less \'en-dləs\ *adj* **1** : being or seeming to be without end **2** : joined at the ends : CONTINUOUS ⟨an *endless* belt⟩ — **end·less·ly** *adv* — **end·less·ness** *n*

end line *n* : a line marking an end or boundary ⟨*end line* of a half plane⟩

end man *n* : a comedian at either end of the line of performers in a minstrel show

end·most \'en(d)-,mōst\ *adj* : situated at the very end

¹**en·do·crine** \'en-də-krən, -,krīn, -,krēn\ *adj* **1** : producing secretions that are distributed in the body by way of the bloodstream **2** : of, relating to, or resembling that of an endocrine gland **3** : HORMONAL

²**endocrine** *n* **1** : HORMONE **2** : ENDOCRINE GLAND

endocrine gland *n* : any of various glands that have no duct and pour their secretions directly into the lymph or blood circulating through them

en·do·derm \'en-də-,dərm\ *n* : the innermost of the three primary layers of an embryo giving rise to the epithelium of the digestive tract and its derivatives — **en·do·der·mal** \,en-də-'dər-məl\ *or* **en·do·der·mic** \-mik\ *adj*

en·do·plasm \'en-də-,plaz-əm\ *n* : the inner relatively fluid part of the cytoplasm — **en·do·plas·mic** \,en-də-'plaz-mik\ *adj*

endoplasmic reticulum *n* : a system of cavities and minute connecting canals that occupy much of the cytoplasm of the cell

en·dorse \in-'dȯrs\ *vb* **1** : to sign the back of (a commercial document) for some special purpose ⟨*endorse* a check⟩ **2** : to give one's support to ⟨*endorse* a candidate⟩ — **en·dors·er** *n*

en·dorse·ment \in-'dȯrs-mənt\ *n* **1** : the act or process of endorsing **2** : a signature often with additional writing endorsing a check or note **3** : SANCTION, APPROVAL

en·do·skel·e·ton \,en-dō-'skel-ət-ən\ *n* : an internal skeleton or supporting framework in an animal — **en·do·skel·e·tal** \-ət-əl\ *adj*

en·do·sperm \'en-də-,spərm\ *n* : a nutritive tissue formed within the seed in seed plants — **en·do·sper·mic** \,en-də-'spər-mik\ *adj* — **en·do·sper·mous** \-məs\ *adj*

en·do·ther·mic \,en-də-'thər-mik\ *or* **en·do·ther·mal** \-məl\ *adj* : characterized by or formed with absorption of heat ⟨*endothermic* chemical reactions⟩

en·dow \in-'dau̇\ *vb* **1** : to furnish with money for support or maintenance ⟨*endow* a hospital⟩ **2** : to furnish with something freely or naturally ⟨man is *endowed* with reason⟩

en·dow·ment \-mənt\ *n* **1** : the providing of a permanent fund for support or the fund provided ⟨a college with a large *endowment*⟩ **2** : a person's natural ability or talent

end·point \'en(d)-,pȯint\ *n* : either of two points that mark the ends of a line segment or a point that marks the end of a ray

end run *n* : a football play in which the ballcarrier attempts to run wide around the end

end table *n* : a small table used beside a larger piece of furniture

en·due \in-'d(y)ü\ *vb* : to provide with a quality or power ⟨*endued* with grace⟩

en·dur·ance \in-'d(y)u̇r-ən(t)s\ *n* **1** : PERMANENCE, DURATION **2** : the ability to withstand hardship, adversity, or stress **3** : SUFFERING, TRIAL

en·dure \in-'d(y)u̇(ə)r\ *vb* **1** : to continue in the same state : LAST **2** : to bear patiently : SUFFER **3** : TOLERATE, PERMIT — **en·dur·a·ble** \-'d(y)u̇r-ə-bəl\ *adj* — **en·dur·ing** *adj* — **en·dur·ing·ly** \-'d(y)u̇r-iŋ-lē\ *adv* — **en·dur·ing·ness** *n*

end·ways \'en-,dwāz\ *or* **end·wise** \-,dwīz\ *adv or adj* **1** : with the end forward **2** : LENGTHWISE

end zone *n* : the area at each end of a football field bounded by the end line, the goal line, and the sidelines

-ene \,ēn\ *n suffix* : unsaturated carbon compound ⟨benz*ene*⟩; *esp* : carbon compound with one double bond ⟨ethyl*ene*⟩

en·e·ma \'en-ə-mə\ *n* : the injection of liquid into the rectum by way of the anus usu. to clear the bowels; *also* : the material injected

en·e·my \'en-ə-mē\ *n, pl* **-mies** [from French *enemi*, from Latin *inimicus*, from *in-* "un-" and *amicus* "friend"] **1** : one that hates another : one that attacks or tries to harm another **2** : something that harms **3 a** : a nation with which a country is at war **b** : a military force, a ship, or a person belonging to such a nation

en·er·get·ic \,en-ər-'jet-ik\ *adj* : having or showing energy : ACTIVE, FORCEFUL ⟨an *energetic* salesman⟩ — **en·er·get·i·cal·ly** \-'jet-i-k(ə-)lē\ *adv*

en·er·gize \'en-ər-,jīz\ *vb* **1** : to put forth energy : ACT **2** : to impart energy to **3** : to apply voltage to — **en·er·giz·er** *n*

en·er·gy \'en-ər-jē\ *n, pl* **-gies** **1** : power or capacity to be active : strength of body or mind to do things or to work ⟨a man of great intellectual *energy*⟩ **2** : natural power vigorously exerted : vigorous action ⟨work with *energy*⟩ **3** : the capacity (as of heat, light, or running water) for performing work — compare KINETIC ENERGY, POTENTIAL ENERGY *syn* see POWER

energy level *n* : one of the stable states of constant energy that may be assumed by a physical system — used esp. of the states in which electrons occur in atoms

en·er·vate \'en-ər-,vāt\ *vb* : to cause to decline in strength or vigor : WEAKEN — **en·er·va·tion** \,en-ər-'vā-shən\ *n*

en·fee·ble \in-'fē-bəl\ *vb* **en·fee·bled**; **en·fee-**

E

bling \-b(ə-)ling\ : to make feeble — **en·fee·ble·ment** \-bəl-mənt\ *n*
en·fold \in-ˈfōld\ *vb* **1** : to cover with folds : ENVELOP **2** : to clasp within the arms : EMBRACE
en·force \in-ˈfōrs, -ˈfȯrs\ *vb* **1** : FORCE, COMPEL ⟨*enforce* obedience⟩ **2** : to carry out effectively ⟨*enforce* the law⟩ — **en·force·a·ble** \-ə-bəl\ *adj* — **en·force·ment** \-mənt\ *n* — **en·forc·er** *n*
en·fran·chise \in-ˈfran-ˌchīz\ *vb* **1** : to set free (as from slavery) **2** : to admit to the privileges of a citizen; *esp* : to admit to the right of suffrage — **en·fran·chise·ment** \-ˌchīz-mənt, -chəz-\ *n*
eng *abbr* **1** engine **2** engineer
Eng *abbr* **1** England **2** English
en·gage \in-ˈgāj\ *vb* **1** : to interlock with : MESH; *also* : to cause to mesh **2** : to bind oneself to do something; *esp* : to bind by a pledge to marry **3 a** : to arrange for the use or services of : HIRE **b** : ENGROSS, OCCUPY ⟨the task *engaged* his attention⟩ **4** : to enter into contest with ⟨*engage* the enemy⟩ **5** : to take part in : carry on ⟨*engage* in sports⟩
en·gaged \in-ˈgājd\ *adj* **1** : OCCUPIED, EMPLOYED, BUSY ⟨*engaged* in conversation⟩ **2** : pledged to be married : BETROTHED ⟨an *engaged* couple⟩
en·gage·ment \in-ˈgāj-mənt\ *n* **1 a** : the act of engaging : the state of being engaged **b** : BETROTHAL **2** : PLEDGE, OBLIGATION ⟨financial *engagements* to fulfill⟩ **3 a** : a promise to be present at a specified time and place **b** : employment esp. for a stated time **4** : a military battle
en·gag·ing \in-ˈgā-jing\ *adj* : ATTRACTIVE, PLEASING — **en·gag·ing·ly** \-jing-lē\ *adv*
en·gen·der \in-ˈjen-dər\ *vb* **en·gen·dered**; **en·gen·der·ing** \-d(ə-)ring\ **1** : BEGET, PROCREATE **2** : PRODUCE, CREATE
en·gine \ˈen-jən\ *n* **1 a** : a mechanical device; *esp* : a machine used in war **b** : a mechanical appliance **2** : a machine that converts energy into mechanical motion **3** : a railroad locomotive
[1]**en·gi·neer** \ˌen-jə-ˈni(ə)r\ *n* **1** : a member of a military group devoted to engineering work **2 a** : a designer or builder of engines **b** : a person who is trained in or follows as a profession a branch of engineering **3** : a person who runs or supervises an engine or an apparatus
[2]**engineer** *vb* **1** : to plan, build, or manage as an engineer **2** : to guide the course of ⟨*engineer* a fund-raising campaign⟩
en·gi·neer·ing \ˌen-jə-ˈni(ə)r-ing\ *n* : the science or profession of developing and using nature's power and resources in ways that are useful to man (as in designing and building roads, structures, or machines and in creating new products)
[1]**En·glish** \ˈing-glish\ *adj* [from Old English *englisc*, derived from *Engle* "the Angles", one of the Germanic peoples that settled in England in the 5th century A.D.] : of, relating to, or characteristic of England, the English people, or the English language
[2]**English** *n* **1 a** : the language of the people of England and the U.S. and many areas now or formerly under British control **b** : English language, literature, or composition that is a subject of study **2 English** *pl* : the people of England **3** : a sideways spin given to a ball (as in pool or bowling)

ə abut	ər further	a back	ā bake	
ä cot, cart	au̇ out	ch chin	e less	ē easy
g gift	i trip	ī life	j joke	ng sing	ō flow
ȯ flaw	ȯi coin	th thin	t͟h this	ü loot
u̇ foot	y yet	yü few	yu̇ furious	zh vision

English daisy *n* : DAISY 1a
English horn *n* : a double-reed woodwind instrument

English horn

similar to the oboe but lower in pitch
English ivy *n* : IVY 1
En·glish·man \ˈing-glish-mən\ *n* : a native or inhabitant of England — **En·glish·wom·an** \-ˌwu̇m-ən\ *n*
English setter *n* : any of a breed of bird dogs with a flat silky coat of white or white with color
English shepherd *n* : any of a breed of medium-sized dogs with a long and glossy black coat and usu. tan to brown markings
English sparrow *n* : an Old World sparrow widely naturalized in the New World — called also *house sparrow*
English springer spaniel *n* : any of a breed of springer spaniels characterized by muscular build and a moderately long straight or slightly wavy silky coat of usu. black and white hair
English system *n* : a system of weights and measures in which the foot is the unit of length and the pound is the unit of weight
en·gorge \in-ˈgȯrj\ *vb* **1** : GORGE, GLUT **2** : to fill with blood : CONGEST — **en·gorge·ment** \-mənt\ *n*
en·grave \in-ˈgrāv\ *vb* **1** : to impress deeply ⟨the incident was *engraved* in his memory⟩ **2 a** : to cut (as figures or letters) upon a surface (as wood or metal) esp. for printing **b** : to print from an engraved plate — **en·grav·er** *n*
en·grav·ing \in-ˈgrā-ving\ *n* **1** : the art of cutting letters, pictures, or patterns in wood, stone, or metal **2** : a print made from an engraved surface
en·gross \in-ˈgrōs\ *vb* **1 a** : to copy or write in a large hand **b** : to prepare the final text of (an official document) **2** : to take up the whole interest of : ABSORB — **en·gross·er** *n* — **en·gross·ment** \-ˈgrōs-mənt\ *n*
en·gulf \in-ˈgəlf\ *vb* : to flow over and enclose : SWALLOW — **en·gulf·ment** \-mənt\ *n*
en·hance \in-ˈhan(t)s\ *vb* : to make greater in value, desirability, or attractiveness : HEIGHTEN — **en·hance·ment** \-mənt\ *n*
enig·ma \i-ˈnig-mə\ *n* : something hard to understand or explain : PUZZLE ⟨his behavior was an *enigma* to his family⟩ — **en·ig·mat·ic** \ˌen-ig-ˈmat-ik, ˌē-nig-\ *or* **en·ig·mat·i·cal** \-ˈmat-i-kəl\ *adj* — **en·ig·mat·i·cal·ly** \-i-k(ə-)lē\ *adv*
en·join \in-ˈjȯin\ *vb* **1** : to direct or impose by authoritative order **2** : FORBID, PROHIBIT
en·joy \in-ˈjȯi\ *vb* **1** : to take pleasure or satisfaction in **2** : to have for one's use or benefit — **en·joy·a·ble** \-ə-bəl\ *adj* — **en·joy·a·ble·ness** *n* — **en·joy·a·bly** \-blē\ *adv*
en·joy·ment \in-ˈjȯi-mənt\ *n* **1** : the condition of enjoying something : possession and use of something with satisfaction ⟨the *enjoyment* of good health⟩ **2** : PLEASURE, SATISFACTION ⟨find *enjoyment* in skating⟩ **3** : something that gives pleasure
en·kin·dle \in-ˈkin-dəl\ *vb* : KINDLE
en·large \in-ˈlärj\ *vb* **1** : to make or grow larger : INCREASE, EXPAND **2** : ELABORATE ⟨*enlarge* on a story⟩ — **en·larg·er** *n*
en·large·ment \in-ˈlärj-mənt\ *n* **1** : an act or in-

stance of enlarging : the state of being enlarged **2** : a photographic print made larger than the negative

en·light·en \in-'līt-ən\ *vb* **en·light·ened; en·light·en·ing** \-(ə-)ning\ : to furnish knowledge or insight to : INSTRUCT — **en·light·en·ment** \-ən-mənt\ *n*

en·list \in-'list\ *vb* **1** : to enroll for military or naval service; *esp* : to join one of the armed services voluntarily **2** : to obtain the help or support of ⟨*enlisted* her friends in the campaign⟩; *also* : to participate heartily (as in a cause or drive) — **en·list·ment** \-'lis(t)-mənt\ *n*

en·list·ed *adj* : of, relating to, or constituting the part of a military or naval force below commissioned or warrant officers

en·liv·en \in-'lī-vən\ *vb* : to give life, action, or spirit to : ANIMATE

en masse \än-'mas\ *adv* : in a body : as a whole

en·mesh \in-'mesh\ *vb* : to entangle in or as if in meshes

en·mi·ty \'en-mət-ē\ *n, pl* **-ties** : ILL WILL, HATRED; *esp* : mutual hatred or ill will

en·no·ble \in-'ō-bəl\ *vb* **-bled; -bling** \-b(ə-)ling\ **1** : to make noble : ELEVATE **2** : to raise to the rank of nobility — **en·no·ble·ment** \-bəl-mənt\ *n*

en·nui \'än-'wē\ *n* : a feeling of weariness and dissatisfaction : BOREDOM

enor·mi·ty \i-'nȯr-mət-ē\ *n, pl* **-ties 1** : great wickedness : OUTRAGEOUSNESS ⟨the *enormity* of the offense⟩ **2** : an outrageous act or offense

enor·mous \i-'nȯr-məs\ *adj* [from L *enormis* meaning literally "out of the ordinary" from *e-* "out" and *norma* "norm"] : extraordinarily great in size, number, or degree — **enor·mous·ly** *adv* — **enor·mous·ness** *n*

[1]**enough** \i-'nəf\ *adj* : equal to the demands or needs : SUFFICIENT

[2]**enough** *adv* **1** : in sufficient amount or degree : SUFFICIENTLY ⟨ran fast *enough*⟩ **2** : FULLY, QUITE ⟨ready *enough* to admit the truth⟩ **3** : TOLERABLY ⟨sang well *enough*⟩

[3]**enough** *n* : a sufficient quantity ⟨*enough* to meet our needs⟩

enow \i-'nau̇\ *adv or adj, archaic* : ENOUGH

en·plane \in-'plān\ *vb* : to board an airplane

en·quire \in-'kwī(ə)r\, **en·qui·ry** \'in-ˌkwī(ə)r-ē, in-'; 'in-kwə-rē, 'ing-\ *var of* INQUIRE, INQUIRY

en·rage \in-'rāj\ *vb* : to fill with rage : MADDEN

en·rap·ture \in-'rap-chər\ *vb* : to fill with delight

en·rich \in-'rich\ *vb* **1** : to make rich or richer ⟨*enrich* the mind⟩ **2** : ADORN, ORNAMENT **3 a** : to make (soil) more fertile **b** : to improve (a food) in nutritive value by adding vitamins and minerals in processing **c** : to increase the proportion of valuable metal or mineral in ⟨*enrich* uranium⟩ — **en·rich·ment** \-mənt\ *n*

en·roll *or* **en·rol** \in-'rōl\ *vb* **en·rolled; en·roll·ing 1** : to enter in a list or roll : REGISTER **2 a** : to take into membership **b** : JOIN, ENTER ⟨*enroll* in the army⟩ ⟨*enroll* in school⟩ — **en·roll·ment** \-'rōl-mənt\ *n*

en route \än-'rüt, en-, in-\ *adv* : on or along the way

ens *abbr* ensign

en·sconce \in-'skän(t)s\ *vb* **1** : to place or hide securely : CONCEAL ⟨*ensconced* himself behind a tree⟩ **2** : to establish comfortably : settle snugly

en·sem·ble \än-'säm-bəl\ *n* [from French, from *ensemble* "together", from L *insimul*, *simul* "at the same time", related to English *same*] : a group constituting a whole or producing a single effect: as **a** : music of two or more parts or the musicians that perform it **b** : a complete set of harmonizing clothes

en·shrine \in-'shrīn\ *vb* **1** : to enclose in or as if in a shrine **2** : to preserve or cherish as sacred

en·shroud \in-'shrau̇d\ *vb* : SHROUD

en·sign \'en(t)-sən, *in senses 1 & 2 also* 'en-ˌsīn\ *n* **1** : a flag flown as the symbol of nationality **2** : a badge of office, rank, or power **3** : a commissioned officer of the lowest rank in the navy

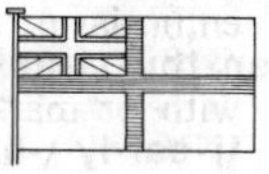

ensign 1

en·si·lage \'en(t)-sə-lij\ *n* : SILAGE

en·sile \en-'sīl\ *vb* : to prepare and store (fodder) for silage

en·slave \in-'slāv\ *vb* : to make a slave of — **en·slave·ment** \-mənt\ *n* — **en·slav·er** *n*

en·snare \in-'sna(ə)r, -'sne(ə)r\ *vb* : SNARE, ENTRAP

en·sue \in-'sü\ *vb* : to come after in time or as a result : FOLLOW ⟨*ensuing* effects⟩

en·sure \in-'shu̇(ə)r\ *vb* : to make sure, certain, or safe : GUARANTEE

[1]**en·tail** \in-'tāl\ *vb* **1** : to limit the inheritance of (property) to the owner's direct descendants or to a class thereof **2** : to involve as a necessary result — **en·tail·ment** \-mənt\ *n*

[2]**entail** *n* **1 a** : an entailing esp. of lands **b** : an entailed estate **2** : the rule fixing descent by entailment

en·tan·gle \in-'tang-gəl\ *vb* **1** : TANGLE, CONFUSE **2** : to involve in or as if in a tangle — **en·tan·gle·ment** \-gəl-mənt\ *n*

en·ter \'ent-ər\ *vb* **en·tered; en·ter·ing** \'ent-ə-ring, 'en-tring\ **1** : to go or come in or into ⟨*enter* a room⟩ ⟨*enter* and leave by the same door⟩ **2** : PENETRATE, PIERCE **3** : to cause to be admitted to ⟨*enter* a child in kindergarten⟩ **4** : to become a member of : JOIN **5** : to make a beginning ⟨*enter* into business⟩ **6** : to take part or play a part ⟨*enter* into a discussion⟩ **7** : to take possession ⟨*entered* upon their inheritance⟩ **8** : to set down in a book or list ⟨*entered* his name on the roster⟩ **9** : to place formally before a legal authority (as a court) ⟨*enter* a complaint⟩ — **en·ter·a·ble** \'ent-ə-rə-bəl\ *adj*

en·ter·ic \en-'ter-ik\ *adj* : of or relating to the alimentary canal : INTESTINAL

en·ter·i·tis \ˌent-ə-'rīt-əs\ *n* : inflammation of the intestines or a disease marked by this

en·ter·prise \'ent-ər-ˌprīz\ *n* **1** : a difficult, complicated, or risky project or undertaking : VENTURE **2** : a business organization **3** : readiness to engage in daring or difficult action : INITIATIVE — **en·ter·pris·er** \-ˌprī-zər\ *n*

en·ter·pris·ing \-ˌprī-zing\ *adj* : bold, active, and energetic in undertaking or experimenting

en·ter·tain \ˌent-ər-'tān\ *vb* **1** : to receive and provide for as host : have as a guest ⟨*entertain* friends over the weekend⟩ **2** : to provide entertainment esp. for guests **3** : to have in mind : CONSIDER ⟨*entertained* thoughts of quitting⟩ **4** : AMUSE, DIVERT ⟨*entertained* us with stories⟩

en·ter·tain·er \-'tā-nər\ *n* : one that entertains; *esp* : one who gives or takes part in public entertainments

en·ter·tain·ment \-'tān-mənt\ *n* **1** : provision for guests esp. in public places (as hotels and inns) **2** : AMUSEMENT, RECREATION **3** : a means of amusement or recreation; *esp* : a public performance

en·thrall *or* **en·thral** \in-'thrȯl\ *vb* **en·thralled; en·thrall·ing 1** : ENSLAVE **2** : to hold spellbound : CHARM — **en·thrall·ment** \-'thrȯl-mənt\ *n*

en·throne \in-'thrōn\ *vb* **1 a** : to seat ceremonially on a throne **b** : to install in office by enthroning **2** : to place on high : EXALT — **en·throne·ment** \-mənt\ *n*

en·thuse \in-'th(y)üz\ *vb* **1** : to make enthusiastic **2** : to show enthusiasm

en·thu·si·asm \in-'th(y)ü-zē-ˌaz-əm\ *n* **1** : strong excitement of feeling : FERVOR **2** : something inspiring zeal or fervor

en·thu·si·ast \-zē-ˌast, -əst\ *n* : a person filled with enthusiasm

en·thu·si·as·tic \in-ˌth(y)ü-zē-'as-tik\ *adj* : filled with or marked by enthusiasm — **en·thu·si·as·ti·cal·ly** \-ti-k(ə-)lē\ *adv*

en·tice \in-'tīs\ *vb* : to attract by arousing hope or desire : TEMPT — **en·tice·ment** \-mənt\ *n*

en·tire \in-'tī(ə)r, 'en-ˌ\ *adj* **1** : having no element or part left out : COMPLETE **2** : TOTAL, FULL **3** : INTACT **4** : having the margin continuous and free from indentations ⟨an *entire* leaf⟩ — **entire** *adv* — **en·tire·ly** *adv* — **en·tire·ness** *n*

en·tire·ty \in-'tī-rət-ē, -'tī(ə)rt-ē\ *n* **1** : the state of being entire or complete **2** : SUM TOTAL, WHOLE

en·ti·tle \in-'tīt-əl\ *vb* **en·ti·tled**; **en·ti·tling** \-(ə-)ling\ **1** : to give a title to : DESIGNATE **2** : to give a right to : QUALIFY ⟨the card *entitles* him to a discount⟩ — **en·ti·tle·ment** \-əl-mənt\ *n*

en·ti·ty \'ent-ət-ē\ *n, pl* **-ties** : something existing or thought of as existing : THING, BEING

entom *or* **entomol** *abbr* entomology

en·tomb \in-'tüm\ *vb* : to place in a tomb : BURY — **en·tomb·ment** \-'tüm-mənt\ *n*

en·to·mol·o·gy \ˌent-ə-'mäl-ə-jē\ *n* : a branch of zoology that deals with insects — **en·to·mo·log·ic** \ˌent-ə-mə-'läj-ik\ *or* **en·to·mo·log·i·cal** \-'läj-i-kəl\ *adj* — **en·to·mo·log·i·cal·ly** \-i-k(ə-)lē\ *adv* — **en·to·mol·o·gist** \ˌent-ə-'mäl-ə-jəst\ *n*

en·to·mos·tra·can \ˌent-ə-'mäs-tri-kən\ *n* : any of a large group of small simple crustaceans (as copepods or barnacles)

en·trails \'en-trəlz, -ˌtrālz\ *n pl* : internal parts : VISCERA; *esp* : INTESTINES

en·train \in-'trān\ *vb* : to put or go aboard a train

1**en·trance** \'en-trən(t)s\ *n* **1** : the act of entering **2** : the means or place of entry **3** : the right to enter : ADMISSION

2**en·trance** \in-'tran(t)s\ *vb* **1** : to put into a trance **2** : to fill with delight, wonder, or rapture — **entrance·ment** \-mənt\ *n*

en·trant \'en-trənt\ *n* : one that enters; *esp* : one that enters a contest

en·trap \in-'trap\ *vb* : to catch in or as if in a trap — **en·trap·ment** \-mənt\ *n*

en·treat \in-'trēt\ *vb* : to ask earnestly or urgently : PLEAD, BEG ⟨*entreated* the king to pardon her son⟩ — **en·treat·ing·ly** \-ing-lē\ *adv*

en·treaty \in-'trēt-ē\ *n, pl* **-treat·ies** : earnest request : APPEAL, PLEA

en·trée *or* **en·tree** \'än-ˌtrā\ *n* **1 a** : ENTRANCE **b** : freedom of entry or access **2 a** : a dish served between the main courses **b** : the principal dish of the meal

en·trench \in-'trench\ *vb* **1 a** : to dig, place within, surround with, or occupy a trench esp. for defense **b** : to establish solidly **2** : to cut into : FURROW; *esp* : to erode downward so as to form a trench **3** : ENCROACH — used with *on* or *upon*

en·trench·ment \in-'trench-mənt\ *n* **1** : the act of entrenching : the state of being entrenched **2** : DEFENSE; *esp* : a defensive work consisting of a trench and a wall of earth

en·trust \in-'trəst\ *vb* **1** : to give into the care of another ⟨*entrust* your savings to a bank⟩ **2** : to give custody, care, or charge of something to ⟨*entrusted* a bank with his savings⟩ — **en·trust·ment** \-'trəs(t)-mənt\ *n*

en·try \'en-trē\ *n, pl* **entries** **1** : the act of entering : ENTRANCE **2** : a place through which entrance is made : HALL, VESTIBULE **3 a** : the act of making (as in a book or list) a written record of something **b** : the thing thus recorded ⟨dictionary *entries*⟩

en·try·way \-trē-ˌwā\ *n* : ENTRY 2

en·twine \in-'twīn\ *vb* : to twine together or around

enu·mer·ate \i-'n(y)ü-mə-ˌrāt\ *vb* **1** : to ascertain the number of : COUNT **2** : to specify one after another : LIST — **enu·mer·a·ble** \-'n(y)üm-(ə-)rə-bəl\ *adj* — **enu·mer·a·tion** \-ˌn(y)ü-mə-'rā-shən\ *n* — **enu·mer·a·tive** \-'n(y)ü-mə-ˌrāt-iv, -'n(y)üm-(ə-)rət-\ *adj* — **enu·mer·a·tor** \-'n(y)ü-mə-ˌrāt-ər\ *n*

enun·ci·ate \ē-'nən(t)-sē-ˌāt\ *vb* **1** : ANNOUNCE, PROCLAIM **2** : ARTICULATE, PRONOUNCE — **enun·ci·a·tion** \-ˌnən(t)-sē-'ā-shən\ *n* — **enun·ci·a·tor** \-'nən(t)-sē-ˌāt-ər\ *n*

env *abbr* envelope

en·vel·op \in-'vel-əp\ *vb* : to enfold completely with or as if with a covering — **en·vel·op·ment** \-mənt\ *n*

en·ve·lope \'en-və-ˌlōp, 'än-\ *n* **1** : something that envelops **2** : a flat usu. paper container (as for a letter) **3** : the bag containing the gas in a balloon or airship **4** : a natural enclosing covering (as a membrane)

en·ven·om \in-'ven-əm\ *vb* **1** : to taint or fill with poison **2** : EMBITTER

en·vi·a·ble \'en-vē-ə-bəl\ *adj* : worthy of envy : highly desirable — **en·vi·a·ble·ness** *n* — **en·vi·a·bly** \-blē\ *adv*

en·vi·ous \'en-vē-əs\ *adj* : feeling or showing envy : caused by or proceeding from envy ⟨*envious* of a neighbor's wealth⟩ — **en·vi·ous·ly** *adv* — **en·vi·ous·ness** *n*

syn ENVIOUS, JEALOUS can mean intolerant of another's success or possessions. ENVIOUS suggests a brooding desire to have what another has; JEALOUS suggests resentment or hostility toward someone more successful

en·vi·ron \in-'vī-rən\ *vb* : ENCIRCLE, SURROUND

en·vi·ron·ment \in-'vī-rən-mənt\ *n* **1** : something that environs : SURROUNDINGS **2** : the surrounding conditions or forces that influence or modify: as **a** : the whole complex of factors (as soil, climate, and living things) that determine the form and survival of an organism or ecological community **b** : the social and cultural conditions that influence the life of a person or human community — **en·vi·ron·men·tal** \-ˌvī-rən-'ment-əl\ *adj* — **en·vi·ron·men·tal·ly** \-ə-lē\ *adv*

en·vi·rons \in-'vī-rənz, 'en-və-\ *n pl* **1** : the districts around a city **2** : SURROUNDINGS

en·vis·age \in-'viz-ij\ *vb* : to have a mental picture of : VISUALIZE

en·voy \'en-ˌvȯi, 'än-\ *n* **1 a** : a diplomatic representative who ranks between an ambassador and a minister **b** : a representative sent by one government to another **2** : MESSENGER, REPRESENTATIVE

1**en·vy** \'en-vē\ *n, pl* **envies** **[**via Old French *envie* from Latin *invidia*, from *invidēre* "to envy", meaning literally "to look at" (from *in-* "in", "on" and *vidēre* "to see") with the implication of casting an evil eye upon**]** **1** : painful or resentful awareness of an advantage enjoyed by another joined with a desire to possess the same advantage **2 :** an object of envy

2**envy** *vb* **en·vied**; **en·vy·ing :** to feel envy toward or on account of — **en·vi·er** *n* — **en·vy·ing·ly** \-iŋ-lē\ *adv*

en·wrap \in-'rap\ *vb* **:** ENFOLD, ENVELOP

en·zyme \'en-ˌzīm\ *n* **:** any of various complex proteins produced by living cells that bring about or accelerate reaction (as in the digestion of food) at body temperatures without being permanently altered — **en·zy·mat·ic** \ˌen-zə-'mat-ik\ *adj* — **en·zy·mat·i·cal·ly** \-'mat-i-k(ə-)lē\ *adv*

Eo·cene \'ē-ə-ˌsēn\ *n* **:** the epoch of the Tertiary between the Paleocene and the Oligocene when mammals became the dominant form of animal life; *also* **:** the corresponding system of rocks — **Eocene** *adj*

eo·hip·pus \ˌē-ō-'hip-əs\ *n* **:** any of a genus of small primitive 4-toed horses from the Eocene of the western U.S.

eo·li·an \ē-'ō-lē-ən\ *adj* **:** borne, deposited, produced, or eroded by the wind ⟨*eolian* sand⟩

eo·lith \'ē-ə-ˌlith\ *n* **:** a very crudely chipped flint from the earliest phase of human culture

Eo·lith·ic \ˌē-ə-'lith-ik\ *adj* **:** of or relating to the earliest period of the Stone Age and the earliest stage of human culture characterized by the use of eoliths

eon \'ē-ən, 'ē-ˌän\ *var of* AEON

-eous *adj suffix* **:** like **:** resembling ⟨aque*ous*⟩

ep·au·let *also* **ep·au·lette** \ˌep-ə-'let\ *n* **:** a shoulder ornament on a uniform esp. of a military or naval officer

epaulets

ephed·rine \i-'fed-rən\ *n* **:** a crystalline basic substance extracted from Chinese woody plants or synthesized and used as a salt in relieving hay fever, asthma, and nasal congestion

ephem·er·al \i-'fem-(ə-)rəl\ *adj* **1 :** lasting one day only **2 :** lasting a very short time — **ephem·er·al·ly** \-ē\ *adv*

ephem·er·id \i-'fem-ə-rəd\ *n* **:** MAYFLY — **ephemerid** *adj*

Ephe·sians \i-'fē-zhənz\ *n* — see BIBLE table

epi- *or* **ep-** *prefix* **:** upon ⟨*epi*phyte⟩ **:** over ⟨*epi*center⟩

ep·ic \'ep-ik\ *n* **:** a long poem in elevated style relating the deeds of a hero — **epic** *adj*

epi·cen·ter \'ep-ə-ˌsent-er\ *n* **:** the part of the earth's surface directly above the focus of an earthquake

ep·i·cure \'ep-i-ˌkyu̇r\ *n* [named for *Epicurus*, a Greek philosopher of the 4th–3d century B.C., who believed pleasure to be the chief aim of life] **:** a person with refined tastes in food or wine — **ep·i·cu·re·an** \ˌep-i-kyu̇-'rē-ən, -'kyu̇r-ē-\ *adj or n*

epi·cy·cle \'ep-ə-ˌsī-kəl\ *n* **:** a circle according to an early astronomy theory in which a planet moves and which has a center that is itself carried around at the same time on the circumference of a larger circle

1**ep·i·dem·ic** \ˌep-ə-'dem-ik\ *adj* **:** affecting many individuals at one time — **ep·i·dem·i·cal·ly** \-'dem-i-k(ə-)lē\ *adv* — **ep·i·de·mic·i·ty** \-de-'mis-ət-ē\ *n*

2**epidemic** *n* **1 :** an outbreak of epidemic disease **2 :** a sudden rapidly spreading outbreak

ep·i·de·mi·ol·o·gy \ˌep-ə-ˌdē-mē-'äl-ə-jē\ *n* **1 :** a branch of medical science that deals with the incidence, distribution, and control of disease in a population **2 :** the sum of the factors controlling the presence or absence of a particular disease — **ep·i·de·mi·o·log·ic** \-mē-ə-'läj-ik\ *or* **ep·i·de·mi·o·log·i·cal** \-'läj-i-kəl\ *adj* — **ep·i·de·mi·o·log·i·cal·ly** \-i-k(ə-)lē\ *adv* — **ep·i·de·mi·ol·o·gist** \-mē-'äl-ə-jəst\ *n*

epi·der·mis \ˌep-ə-'dər-məs\ *n* **1 :** the thin outer layer of the animal body that in vertebrates forms an insensitive covering over the dermis **2 :** a thin surface layer of protecting cells in seed plants and ferns **3 :** any of various covering layers resembling the epidermis of the skin — **epi·der·mal** \-məl\ *adj*

ep·i·did·y·mis \ˌep-ə-'did-ə-məs\ *n, pl* **-did·y·mi·des** \-'did-ə-mə-ˌdēz\ **:** a mass at the back of the testis composed of coiled tubes in which sperms are stored — **epi·did·y·mal** \-'did-ə-məl\ *adj*

epi·glot·tis \ˌep-ə-'glät-əs\ *n* **:** a thin plate of flexible cartilage in front of the glottis that folds back over and protects the glottis during swallowing — see LARYNX illustration — **epi·glot·tal** \-'glät-əl\ *adj*

ep·i·gram \'ep-ə-ˌgram\ *n* **1 :** a short poem ending with a clever turn of thought **2 :** a brief witty saying — **ep·i·gram·ma·tist** \ˌep-ə-'gram-ət-əst\ *n*

ep·i·gram·mat·ic \ˌep-i-grə-'mat-ik\ *adj* **1 :** of, relating to, or resembling an epigram **2 :** given to the use of epigrams — **ep·i·gram·mat·i·cal** \-'mat-i-kəl\ *adj* — **ep·i·gram·mat·i·cal·ly** \-i-k(ə-)lē\ *adv*

ep·i·lep·sy \'ep-ə-ˌlep-sē\ *n* **:** a disorder marked by disturbed electrical rhythms of the central nervous system and characterized by convulsive fits and loss of consciousness — **ep·i·lep·tic** \ˌep-ə-'lep-tik\ *adj or n*

ep·i·logue \'ep-ə-ˌlȯg\ *n* **1 :** a final section that rounds out the design of a literary work **2 :** a speech often in verse addressed to the audience by an actor at the end of a play

ep·i·neph·rine \ˌep-ə-'nef-ˌrēn, -rən\ *n* **:** a hormone of the adrenal gland acting esp. on smooth muscle, causing narrowing of blood vessels, and raising blood pressure

Epiph·a·ny \i-'pif-ə-nē\ *n* **:** January 6 observed as a church festival celebrating the coming of the three wise men to Jesus at Bethlehem

ep·i·phyte \'ep-ə-ˌfīt\ *n* **:** a plant that derives its moisture and nutrients from the air and rain and grows usu. on another plant

ep·i·phyt·ic \ˌep-ə-'fit-ik\ *adj* **1 :** of, relating to, or being an epiphyte **2 :** living on the surface of plants

epis·co·pa·cy \i-'pis-kə-pə-sē\ *n, pl* **-cies 1 :** government of a church by bishops **2 :** EPISCOPATE

epis·co·pal \i-'pis-kə-pəl\ *adj* [from Greek *episkopos* "bishop" (the source, via Old English *biscop*, also of English *bishop*); literally it means "overseer"] **1 :** of or relating to a bishop or episcopacy **2** *cap* **:** of or relating to the Protestant Episcopal Church — **epis·co·pal·ly** \-pə-lē\ *adv*

Epis·co·pa·lian \i-ˌpis-kə-'pāl-yən\ *n* **1 :** an adherent of episcopacy **2 :** a member of the Protestant Episcopal Church — **Episcopalian** *adj* — **Epis·co·pa·lian·ism** \-yə-ˌniz-əm\ *n*

epis·co·pate \i-'pis-kə-pət\ *n* **1 :** the rank, office, or term of office of a bishop **2 :** the whole body of bishops

ep·i·sode \'ep-ə-ˌsōd\ *n* **1 :** a distinct and complete event that is part of a longer story **2 :** a distinct and separate event in history or in a life — **ep·i·sod·ic** \ˌep-ə-'säd-ik\ *adj*

epis·tle \i-'pis-əl\ *n* **:** LETTER; *esp* **:** a formal or elegant letter

epis·to·lary \i-'pis-tə-ˌler-ē\ *adj* **:** of, relating to, or suitable to a letter

ep·i·taph \'ep-ə-ˌtaf\ *n* **:** an inscription (as on a tombstone) in memory of a dead person

ep·i·the·li·um \\,ep-ə-'thē-lē-əm\\ *n, pl* **-lia** \\-lē-ə\\ **1 :** a membranous cellular tissue that covers a free surface or lines a tube or cavity of an animal body **2 :** a usu. thin layer of parenchyma that lines a cavity or tube of a plant — **ep·i·the·li·al** \\-lē-əl\\ *adj*

ep·i·thet \\'ep-ə-,thet\\ *n* **1 :** a word or phrase (as *Lion-Hearted* in "Richard the Lion-Hearted") that expresses a quality held to be characteristic of a person or thing **2 :** the part of a taxonomic name identifying a subordinate unit within a genus — **ep·i·thet·ic** \\,ep-ə-'thet-ik\\ *or* **ep·i·thet·i·cal** \\-'thet-i-kəl\\ *adj*

epit·o·me \\i-'pit-ə-mē\\ *n* **1 :** SUMMARY, ABSTRACT **2 :** a part considered as typical of a whole ⟨his response was the *epitome* of good sense⟩

epit·o·mize \\-,mīz\\ *vb* **:** to make or serve as an epitome of **:** SUMMARIZE

ep·och \\'ep-ək, -,äk\\ *n* **1 :** an event or a time that begins a new period of development **2 :** a memorable event, date, or period **3 :** a division of geologic time less than a period and greater than an age — **ep·och·al** \\-əl\\ *adj* — **ep·och·al·ly** \\-ə-lē\\ *adv*

ep·oxy \\'ep-,äk-sē, ep-'\\ *n* **:** EPOXY RESIN

epoxy resin *n* **:** a synthetic resin used chiefly in coatings and adhesives

ep·si·lon \\'ep-sə-,län, -lən\\ *n* **:** the 5th letter of the Greek alphabet — Ε or ϵ

Ep·som salt *n* \\,ep-səm-\\ **:** a bitter colorless or white crystalline salt used esp. as a cathartic — usu. used in pl.

eq *abbr* equation

eq·ua·ble \\'ek-wə-bəl, 'ē-kwə-\\ *adj* **:** EVEN, UNIFORM; *esp* **:** free from extremes or sudden or harsh changes ⟨an *equable* temper⟩ ⟨an *equable* climate⟩ — **eq·ua·bly** \\-blē\\ *adv*

[1]**equal** \\'ē-kwəl\\ *adj* **1 a :** exactly the same in number, amount, degree, rank, or quality ⟨an *equal* number of apples and oranges⟩ ⟨officers of *equal* rank⟩ **b :** identical in mathematical value **:** EQUIVALENT **2 :** not varying **:** UNIFORM **3 a :** evenly balanced **b :** IMPARTIAL **4 :** EQUABLE **5 :** capable of meeting requirements **:** SUFFICIENT ⟨*equal* to the task⟩ ***syn*** see IDENTICAL ***ant*** unequal — **equally** *adv*

[2]**equal** *n* **1 :** one that is equal ⟨has no *equal* at chess⟩ **2 :** an equal quantity

[3]**equal** *vb* **equaled** *or* **equalled; equal·ing** *or* **equal·ling 1 :** to be equal to **2 :** to produce something equal to **:** MATCH

equal·i·ty \\i-'kwäl-ət-ē\\ *n, pl* **-ties :** the quality or state of being equal

equal·ize \\'ē-kwə-,līz\\ *vb* **1 :** to make equal **2 :** to make uniform; *esp* **:** to distribute evenly **:** BALANCE — **equal·i·za·tion** \\,ē-kwə-lə-'zā-shən\\ *n* — **equal·iz·er** \\'ē-kwə-,lī-zər\\ *n*

equal sign *n* **:** a sign = indicating mathematical or logical equivalence — called also *equality sign, equals sign*

equa·nim·i·ty \\,ē-kwə-'nim-ət-ē, ,ek-wə-\\ *n* **:** evenness of mind **:** calm temper **:** COMPOSURE ⟨accept misfortunes with *equanimity*⟩

equate \\i-'kwāt\\ *vb* **:** to make or treat as equal **:** represent or express as equal or equivalent

equa·tion \\i-'kwā-zhən, -shən\\ *n* **1 :** the act or process of equating **:** the state of being equated **2 a :** a statement of the equality of two mathematical expressions **b :** an expression representing a chemical reaction by means of chemical symbols

equa·tor \\i-'kwāt-ər, 'ē-,\\ *n* **:** the great circle midway between the poles of rotation of a planet, star, or other celestial body; *esp* **:** a great circle of the earth that is everywhere equally distant from the north pole and the south pole and divides the earth's surface into the northern and southern hemispheres

equa·to·ri·al \\,ē-kwə-'tōr-ē-əl, ,ek-wə-, -'tȯr-\\ *adj* **1 :** of, relating to, or located at the equator **2 :** suggesting the region around the equator ⟨*equatorial* heat⟩

eq·uer·ry \\'ek-wə-rē, i-'kwer-ē\\ *n, pl* **-ries 1 :** an officer in charge of the horses of a prince or nobleman **2 :** a personal attendant of a member of the British royal family

[1]**eques·tri·an** \\i-'kwes-trē-ən\\ *adj* **1 :** of or relating to horses, horsemen, or horsemanship **2 :** mounted on horseback ⟨*equestrian* troops⟩

[2]**equestrian** *n* **:** one who rides on horseback

eques·tri·enne \\i-,kwes-trē-'en\\ *n* **:** a female equestrian

equi- *comb form* **:** equal ⟨*equi*poise⟩ **:** equally ⟨*equi*probable⟩

equi·an·gu·lar \\,ē-kwi-'ang-gyə-lər\\ *adj* **:** having all or corresponding angles equal

equi·dis·tant \\,ē-kwə-'dis-tənt\\ *adj* **:** equally distant

equi·lat·er·al \\,ē-kwə-'lat-ə-rəl, -'la-trəl\\ *adj* **:** having all sides or faces equal

equi·lib·ri·um \\,ē-kwə-'lib-rē-əm, ,ek-wə-\\ *n, pl* **-riums** *or* **-ria** \\-rē-ə\\ **1 :** a state of balance between opposing forces, actions, or influences **2 :** the normal oriented state of the animal body in respect to its environment that in higher vertebrates is controlled by sense organs in the inner ear

equine \\'ē-,kwīn\\ *adj* **:** of, relating to, or resembling a horse or its close relatives — **equine** *n* — **equinely** *adv*

[1]**equi·noc·tial** \\,ē-kwə-'näk-shəl, ,ek-wə-\\ *adj* **1 :** of, relating to, or occurring at or near an equinox **2 :** EQUATORIAL

[2]**equinoctial** *n* **:** an equinoctial storm

equi·nox \\'ē-kwə-,näks, 'ek-wə-\\ *n* **:** either of the two times each year when the sun crosses the equator and day and night are everywhere of equal length that occur about March 21 and September 23 — called also respectively *vernal equinox, autumnal equinox*

equip \\i-'kwip\\ *vb* **equipped; equip·ping :** to furnish for service or action **:** PREPARE

equip *abbr* equipment

eq·ui·page \\'ek-wə-pij\\ *n* **1 :** material or articles used in equipment **:** OUTFIT **2 :** a horse-drawn carriage with its attendants or such a carriage alone

equip·ment \\i-'kwip-mənt\\ *n* **1 a :** the equipping of a person or thing **b :** the state of being equipped **2 :** the articles serving to equip a person or thing

eq·ui·poise \\'ek-wə-,pȯiz, 'ē-kwə-\\ *n* **1 :** a state of balance **:** EQUILIBRIUM **2 :** a weight used to balance another weight

equi·po·tent \\,ē-kwə-'pōt-ənt\\ *adj* **:** having equal effects or capacities ⟨*equipotent* genes⟩

eq·ui·se·tum \\,ek-wə-'sēt-əm\\ *n* **:** any of a genus of primitive perennial vascular plants with creeping rhizomes and leaves reduced to sheaths at the nodes of the hollow jointed grooved shoots — called also *horsetail, scouring rush*

eq·ui·ta·ble \\'ek-wət-ə-bəl\\ *adj* **:** having or exhibiting equity **:** JUST — **eq·ui·ta·ble·ness** *n* — **eq·ui·ta·bly** \\-blē\\ *adv*

eq·ui·ty \\'ek-wət-ē\\ *n, pl* **-ties 1 :** fairness or justice

ə abut		ər further	a back	ā bake
ä cot, cart		au̇ out	ch chin	e less	ē easy
g gift	i trip	ī life	j joke	ng sing	ō flow
ȯ flaw		ȯi coin	th thin	t͟h this	ü loot
u̇ foot	y yet	yü few	yu̇ furious	zh vision

in dealings between persons **2 :** a system of law that is a more flexible supplement to common and statute law and is designed to protect rights and enforce duties fixed by substantive law **3 :** the value of an owner's interest in a property in excess of claims against it

equiv·a·lent \i-'kwiv(-ə)-lənt\ *adj* **1 a :** alike or equal in number, value, or meaning **b :** having the same numerical value ⟨*equivalent* fractions⟩ ⟨*equivalent* numerals⟩ **c :** having the same solution ⟨y = z and zy = 4 are *equivalent* equations⟩ **2 :** corresponding in effect or function **3 :** capable of being placed in a one-to-one correspondence ⟨*equivalent* sets⟩ ***syn*** see IDENTICAL ***ant*** different — **equiv·a·lence** \-lən(t)s\ *n* — **equivalent** *n* — **equiv·a·lent·ly** *adv*

equiv·o·cal \i-'kwiv-ə-kəl\ *adj* **1 :** having two or more possible meanings **:** AMBIGUOUS ⟨an *equivocal* answer⟩ **2 :** UNCERTAIN, DOUBTFUL ⟨an *equivocal* result⟩ **3 :** SUSPICIOUS, QUESTIONABLE ⟨*equivocal* behavior⟩ — **equiv·o·cal·ly** \-k(ə-)lē\ *adv* — **equiv·o·cal·ness** \-kəl-nəs\ *n*

equiv·o·cate \i-'kwiv-ə-ˌkāt\ *vb* **:** to use equivocal language esp. with intent to deceive **:** LIE — **equiv·o·ca·tion** \-ˌkwiv-ə-'kā-shən\ *n* — **equiv·o·ca·tor** \-'kwiv-ə-ˌkāt-ər\ *n*

[1]**-er** \ər; *after some vowels, often* r; *after* ng, *usu* gər\ *adj suffix or adv suffix* — used to form the comparative degree of adjectives and adverbs of one syllable ⟨hott*er*⟩ ⟨dri*er*⟩ and of some adjectives and adverbs of two or more syllables ⟨complet*er*⟩

[2]**-er** \ər; *after some vowels, often* r\ *also* **-ier** \ē-ər, yər\ *or* **-yer** \yər\ *n suffix* **1 a :** person occupationally connected with ⟨hatt*er*⟩ ⟨furr*ier*⟩ ⟨law*yer*⟩ **b :** person or thing belonging to or associated with ⟨old-tim*er*⟩ **c :** native of **:** resident of ⟨New York*er*⟩ ⟨cottag*er*⟩ **d :** one that has ⟨three-deck*er*⟩ **e :** one that produces or yields ⟨pork*er*⟩ **2 a :** one that does or performs (a specified action) ⟨report*er*⟩ — sometimes added to both elements of a compound ⟨build*er*-upp*er*⟩ **b :** one that is a suitable object of (a specified action) ⟨broil*er*⟩ **3 :** one that is ⟨foreign*er*⟩

ER *abbr* earned runs

era \'ir-ə, 'er-ə, 'ē-rə\ *n* **1 :** a period of time reckoned from some special date or event ⟨the Christian *era*⟩ **2 :** an important or distinctive period of history ⟨the Revolutionary *era*⟩ **3 :** one of the major divisions of geologic time

erad·i·cate \i-'rad-ə-ˌkāt\ *vb* **[**from L *eradicare*, from *e-* "out" and *radic-*, stem of *radix* "root"**] :** to remove by or as if by uprooting **:** ELIMINATE, DESTROY ⟨*eradicate* weeds⟩ ⟨*eradicating* an endemic disease⟩ — **erad·i·ca·ble** \-'rad-i-kə-bəl\ *adj* — **erad·i·ca·tion** \-ˌrad-ə-'kā-shən\ *n* — **erad·i·ca·tor** \-'rad-ə-ˌkāt-ər\ *n*

erase \i-'rās\ *vb* **1 :** to rub out (as something written) **2 :** to remove as if by erasing ⟨*erased* the event from his memory⟩ — **eras·a·ble** \-'rā-sə-bəl\ *adj*

syn ERASE, EFFACE mean to remove (as by rubbing away) from a surface. ERASE may imply removing something (as pencil writing) by quick deliberate action; EFFACE may suggest removing something slowly but effectively so as to make indistinct or cause to vanish without trace

eras·er \i-'rā-sər\ *n* **:** one that erases; *esp* **:** a piece of rubber or cloth used to erase marks

era·sure \i-'rā-shər, -zhər\ *n* **:** an act or instance of erasing

er·bi·um \'ər-bē-əm\ *n* **:** a metallic element that occurs with yttrium — see ELEMENT table

[1]**ere** \(ˌ)e(ə)r, (ˌ)a(ə)r\ *prep* **:** [2]BEFORE 3

[2]**ere** *conj* **:** [3]BEFORE

[1]**erect** \i-'rekt\ *adj* **1 :** straight up and down **:** UPRIGHT ⟨an *erect* pole⟩ ⟨*erect* poplars⟩ **2 :** straight in posture ⟨a man of *erect* bearing⟩ **3 :** directed upward **:** RAISED ⟨a tree with *erect* branches⟩ — **erect·ly** *adv* — **erect·ness** \-'rek(t)-nəs\ *n*

[2]**erect** *vb* **1 :** to put up or together by fitting together materials **:** BUILD, ASSEMBLE ⟨*erect* a building⟩ ⟨*erect* a machine⟩ **2 :** to set upright ⟨*erect* a flagpole⟩ **3 :** to construct (as a perpendicular) on a given base — **erec·tor** \-'rek-tər\ *n*

erec·tile \i-'rek-təl, -ˌtīl\ *adj* **:** capable of being raised to an erect position

erec·tion \i-'rek-shən\ *n* **1 :** the process of erecting **:** the state of being erected **2 a :** the state marked by firm turgid form and erect position of a previously limp or flabby bodily part whose tissue becomes dilated with blood **b :** an occurrence of such a state in the penis or clitoris **3 :** something erected

ere·long \e(ə)r-'lȯŋ, a(ə)r-\ *adv* **:** before long **:** SOON

er·e·mite \'er-ə-ˌmīt\ *n* **:** HERMIT

erep·sin \i-'rep-sən\ *n* **:** a mixture of peptidases from the intestinal juice

erg \'ərg\ *n* **:** a unit of work equal to the work done by a force of one dyne acting through a distance of one centimeter

er·go \'e(ə)r-gō, 'ər-\ *adv* **:** THEREFORE, HENCE

er·i·ca·ceous \ˌer-ə-'kā-shəs\ *adj* **:** of, relating to, or being heath plants

Er·len·mey·er flask \ˌər-lən-ˌmī(-ə)r-, ˌer-lən-\ *n* **:** a flat-bottomed laboratory flask

er·mine \'ər-mən\ *n, pl* **ermine** *or* **ermines** **1 a :** any of several weasels that assume a white winter coat usu. with more or less black on the tail **b :** the white fur of an ermine **2 :** a rank or office whose robe is ornamented with ermine — **er·mined** \-mənd\ *adj*

Erlenmeyer flask

erne *or* **ern** \'ərn, 'e(ə)rn\ *n* **:** EAGLE; *esp* **:** a white-tailed sea eagle

erode \i-'rōd\ *vb* **1 a :** to eat into **:** CORRODE **b :** to wear away by or as if by the action of water, wind, or glacial ice **2 :** to undergo erosion

ero·sion \i-'rō-zhən\ *n* **:** the process of eroding **:** the state of being eroded — **ero·sion·al** \-'rōzh-(ə-)nəl\ *adj*

ero·sive \i-'rō-siv, -ziv\ *adj* **:** eating or wearing away ⟨the *erosive* effect of water⟩ — **ero·sive·ness** *n*

erot·ic \i-'rät-ik\ *adj* **:** of, relating to, or marked by sexual love or desire — **erot·i·cal·ly** \-'rät-i-k(ə-)lē\ *adv* — **erot·i·cism** \-'rät-ə-ˌsiz-əm\ *n*

err \'e(ə)r, 'ər\ *vb* **1 :** to make a mistake ⟨*erred* in his calculations⟩ **2 :** to do wrong **:** SIN

er·rand \'er-ənd\ *n* **:** a short trip taken to attend to some business esp. for another; *also* **:** the object or purpose of such a trip

er·rant \'er-ənt\ *adj* **1 :** wandering esp. in search of adventure ⟨an *errant* knight⟩ **2 a :** straying outside proper bounds ⟨an *errant* calf⟩ **b :** ERRING — **er·rant·ry** \-ən-trē\ *n*

er·rat·ic \ir-'at-ik\ *adj* **1 :** having no fixed course **:** WANDERING ⟨an *erratic* comet⟩ **2 :** marked by lack of consistency or regularity **:** ECCENTRIC ⟨*erratic* behavior⟩ — **er·rat·i·cal·ly** \-'at-i-k(ə-)lē\ *adv*

er·ro·ne·ous \ir-'ō-nē-əs, e-'rō-\ *adj* **:** MISTAKEN, INCORRECT — **er·ro·ne·ous·ly** *adv* — **er·ro·ne·ous·ness** *n*

er·ror \'er-ər\ *n* **1 a :** deviation from a code of behavior ⟨the *error* of his ways⟩ **b :** an unintentional deviation from truth, accuracy, or a goal **c :** a defensive misplay made by a baseball player when normal play would have resulted in an out or prevented an advance by a base runner **2** : the quality or state of erring **3** : a false belief or a set of false beliefs **4** : something produced by mistake **5** : the difference between an observed or calculated value and a true value; *esp* : variation in measurements, calculations, or observations of a quantity due to mistakes or to uncontrollable factors **6** : degree or amount of error — **er·ror·less** \-ləs\ *adj*

syn ERROR, MISTAKE, BLUNDER mean a failure to speak or act in accordance with truth, accuracy, or good judgment. ERROR may imply a deviation from logic, belief, or procedure; MISTAKE suggests a lapse of judgment or understanding; BLUNDER suggests a gross mistake or error

erst·while \'ərst-ˌhwīl\ *adv* : in the past : FORMERLY — **erstwhile** *adj*

eruct \i-'rəkt\ *vb* : BELCH — **eruc·ta·tion** \i-ˌrək-'tā-shən, ˌē-ˌrək-\ *n*

er·u·dite \'er-(y)ə-ˌdīt\ *adj* : possessing or displaying erudition — **er·u·dite·ly** *adv*

er·u·di·tion \ˌer-(y)ə-'dish-ən\ *n* : extensive knowledge gained chiefly from books : LEARNING

erupt \i-'rəpt\ *vb* **1** : to burst forth or cause to burst forth : EXPLODE **2** : to break through a surface ⟨teeth *erupting* from the gum⟩ **3** : to break out (as with a skin eruption) — **erupt·i·ble** \-'rəp-tə-bəl\ *adj*

erup·tion \i-'rəp-shən\ *n* **1** : an act, process, or instance of erupting **2** : a product (as a skin rash) of erupting — **erup·tive** \-'rəp-tiv\ *adj*

-ery \(ə-)rē\ *n suffix, pl* **-er·ies** **1** : qualities collectively : character : -NESS ⟨snobb*ery*⟩ **2** : art : practice ⟨cook*ery*⟩ **3** : place of doing, keeping, producing, or selling (the thing specified) ⟨fish*ery*⟩ ⟨bak*ery*⟩ **4** : collection : aggregate ⟨fin*ery*⟩ **5** : state or condition ⟨slav*ery*⟩

eryth·ro·cyte \i-'rith-rə-ˌsīt\ *n* : RED BLOOD CELL — **eryth·ro·cyt·ic** \-ˌrith-rə-'sit-ik\ *adj*

1**-es** \əz, iz *after* s, z, sh, ch; z *after* v *or a vowel*\ *n pl suffix* **1** — used to form the plural of most nouns that end in *s* ⟨glass*es*⟩, *z* ⟨fuzz*es*⟩, *sh* ⟨bush*es*⟩, *ch* ⟨peach*es*⟩, or a final *y* that changes to *i* ⟨ladi*es*⟩ and of some nouns ending in *f* that changes to *v* ⟨loav*es*⟩ **2** : 1-s 2

2**-es** *vb suffix* — used to form the third person singular present of most verbs that end in *s* ⟨bless*es*⟩, *z* ⟨fizz*es*⟩, *sh* ⟨hush*es*⟩, *ch* ⟨catch*es*⟩, or a final *y* that changes to *i* ⟨defi*es*⟩

es·ca·late \'es-kə-ˌlāt\ *vb* : to increase in extent, volume, or scope : EXPAND ⟨*escalate* the war⟩ — **es·ca·la·tion** \ˌes-kə-'lā-shən\ *n*

es·ca·la·tor \'es-kə-ˌlāt-ər\ *n* : a moving set of stairs arranged like an endless belt

es·cal·lop \is-'käl-əp, -'kal-\ *var of* SCALLOP

es·ca·pade \'es-kə-ˌpād\ *n* : a mischievous adventure : PRANK

1**es·cape** \is-'kāp\ *vb* **1 a** : to get away (as by flight) ⟨*escape* from a burning building⟩ **b** : to leak out from confinement ⟨gas is *escaping*⟩ **c** : to run wild from cultivation **2** : to get out of the way of : AVOID **3** : to fail to be noticed or recallable by ⟨*escape* attention⟩ ⟨his name *escapes* me⟩ **4** : to come out from or be uttered by involuntarily ⟨a sigh *escaped* him⟩ — **es·cap·er** *n*

2**escape** *n* **1** : an act or instance of escaping **2** : a means of escaping **3** : a cultivated plant run wild

es·cape·ment \is-'kāp-mənt\ *n* **1** : a device in a timepiece which controls the wheel movement and through which the energy of the weight or spring is transmitted to the pendulum or balance by means of impulses that permit one tooth on a wheel to escape from a projecting part at regular intervals **2** : the mechanism in a typewriter that controls movement of the carriage

escape velocity *n* : the minimum velocity that a moving body (as a rocket) must have to escape from the gravitational field of the earth or of a celestial body and move outward into space

es·cap·ism \is-'kā-ˌpiz-əm\ *n* : habitual thinking on purely imaginary things in order to escape from reality or routine — **es·cap·ist** \-pəst\ *adj or n*

es·ca·role \'es-kə-ˌrōl\ *n* : ENDIVE 1

es·carp·ment \is-'kärp-mənt\ *n* **1** : a steep slope in front of a fortification **2** : a long cliff

es·chew \is-'chü\ *vb* : SHUN, AVOID

1**es·cort** \'es-ˌkȯrt\ *n* **1** : a person or group of persons accompanying another to give protection or show courtesy **2** : the man who goes on a date with a woman **3** : a protective screen of vehicles, warships, or planes ⟨motorcycle *escort*⟩ ⟨fighter *escort*⟩

2**es·cort** \is-'kȯrt, es-', 'es-ˌ\ *vb* : to accompany as an escort *syn* see ACCOMPANY

escort carrier *n* : a small aircraft carrier

es·cu·do \is-'küd-ō\ *n, pl* **-dos** **1** : the basic monetary unit of Portugal and Chile **2** : a coin representing one escudo

es·cu·lent \'es-kyə-lənt\ *adj* : EDIBLE — **esculent** *n*

es·cutch·eon \is-'kəch-ən\ *n* : the usu. shield-shaped surface on which a coat of arms is shown

1**-ese** \'ēz, 'ēs\ *adj suffix* : of, relating to, or originating in (a specified place or country) ⟨Japan*ese*⟩

2**-ese** *n suffix, pl* **-ese** **1** : native or resident of (a specified place or country) ⟨Chin*ese*⟩ **2 a** : language of (a specified place, country, or nationality) ⟨Vietnam*ese*⟩ **b** : speech or literary style peculiar to (a specified place, person, or group) ⟨journal*ese*⟩

Esk *abbr* Eskimo

es·ker \'es-kər\ *n* : a long narrow mound of material (as sand or gravel) deposited by a stream flowing on, within, or beneath a stagnant glacier

Es·ki·mo \'es-kə-ˌmō\ *n* **1** : a member of a group of peoples of northern North America and eastern Siberia **2** : the language of the Eskimo people — **Es·ki·mo·an** \ˌes-kə-'mō-ən\ *adj*

Eskimo dog *n* **1** : a broad-chested powerful dog native to Greenland and Labrador that has a heavy double coat **2** : any sled dog of American origin

esoph·a·gus \i-'säf-ə-gəs\ *n, pl* **-gi** \-ˌgī, -ˌjī, -ˌgē\ : a muscular tube that leads from the pharynx to the stomach — see LARYNX illustration — **esoph·a·ge·al** \-ˌsäf-ə-'jē-əl\ *adj*

es·o·ter·ic \ˌes-ə-'ter-ik\ *adj* **1** : taught to or understood by the initiated alone ⟨an *esoteric* ritual⟩ **2** : of or relating to knowledge that is restricted to a small group ⟨*esoteric* writings⟩ — **es·o·ter·i·cal·ly** \-'ter-i-k(ə-)lē\ *adv*

esp *abbr* **1** especial **2** especially

ESP *abbr* extrasensory perception

es·pal·ier \is-'pal-yər\ *n* : a plant (as a fruit tree) trained to grow flat against a support (as a wall or trellis) — **espalier** *vb*

es·pe·cial \is-'pesh-əl\ *adj* : SPECIAL, PARTICULAR — **es·pe·cial·ly** \-'pesh-(ə-)lē\ *adv*

es·pi·o·nage \'es-pē-ə-ˌnäzh, -nij, -ˌnäj\ *n* : the practice of spying : the use of spies

es·pla·nade \'es-plə-ˌnäd, -ˌnād\ *n* : a level open stretch or area; *esp* : one for walking or driving along a shore

es·pous·al \is-'paů-zəl, -səl\ *n* **1 a** : BETROTHAL **b** : WEDDING **c** : MARRIAGE **2** : a taking up of a cause or belief as a supporter

es·pouse \is-'paůz, -'paůs\ *vb* **1** : MARRY **2** : to take up the cause of : SUPPORT — **es·pous·er** *n*

espres·so \e-'spres-ō\ *n* : coffee brewed by forcing steam through finely ground darkly roasted coffee beans

es·prit \is-'prē\ *n* [from French, meaning literally "spirit", from L *spiritus*] : vivacious cleverness or wit

es·prit de corps \is-ˌprēd-ə-'kō(ə)r, -'kȯ(ə)r\ *n* : enthusiastic devotion of members to a group and strong regard for the honor of the group

es·py \is-'pī\ *vb* **es·pied**; **es·py·ing** : to catch sight of

esq *abbr* esquire

es·quire \'es-ˌkwī(ə)r, is-'\ *n* [from medieval French *esquier* "squire"] **1** : a member of the English gentry ranking immediately below a knight **2** : a candidate for knighthood serving as attendant to a knight **3** — used as a title of courtesy usu. placed in its abbreviated form after the surname ⟨John Smith, *Esq.*⟩

-ess \əs, is *also* ˌes\ *n suffix* : female ⟨author*ess*⟩

1**es·say** \'es-ˌā, *in sense 1 also* e-'sā\ *n* **1** : ATTEMPT, TRY; *esp* : a tentative effort **2** : a nonfictional usu. short literary composition dealing with its subject from a personal point of view

2**es·say** \e-'sā, 'es-ˌā\ *vb* : ATTEMPT, TRY

es·say·ist \'es-ˌā-əst\ *n* : a writer of essays

es·sence \'es-ən(t)s\ *n* **1** : the basic nature of a thing : the quality or qualities that make a thing what it is ⟨the *essence* of love is unselfishness⟩ **2** : a substance extracted from another substance (as a plant or drug) and having the special qualities of the original substance ⟨*essence* of peppermint⟩ **3** : PERFUME, SCENT

1**es·sen·tial** \i-'sen-chəl\ *adj* **1** : forming or belonging to the essence ⟨free speech is an *essential* right of citizenship⟩ **2** : containing or having the character of a volatile essence ⟨*essential* oils⟩ **3** : important in the highest degree : NECESSARY ⟨food is *essential* to life⟩ — **es·sen·ti·al·i·ty** \-ˌsen-chē-'al-ət-ē\ *n* — **es·sen·tial·ly** \-'sench-(ə-)lē\ *adv* — **es·sen·tial·ness** \-'sen-chəl-nəs\ *n*

2**essential** *n* : something basic, necessary, or indispensable ⟨the *essentials* for success⟩

essential amino acid *n* : an amino acid that is necessary for proper growth of the animal body and that cannot be manufactured by the body unassisted but must be obtained from protein food

1**-est** \əst, ist\ *adj suffix or adv suffix* — used to form the superlative degree of adjectives and adverbs of one syllable ⟨fatt*est*⟩ ⟨lat*est*⟩ and of some adjectives and adverbs of two or more syllables ⟨lucki*est*⟩ ⟨often*est*⟩

2**-est** \əst, ist\ *or* **-st** \st\ *suffix* — used to form the archaic second person singular of verbs (with *thou*) ⟨gett*est*⟩ ⟨did*st*⟩

est *abbr* **1** established **2** estimate

es·tab·lish \is-'tab-lish\ *vb* **1** : to make firm or stable ⟨*establish* a gun on its base⟩ **2** : to enact permanently ⟨*establ'sh* a constitution⟩ **3 a** : to bring into existence : FOUND ⟨*establish* a republic⟩ **b** : to bring about : EFFECT ⟨*establish* a good relationship⟩ **4 a** : to set on a firm basis ⟨*establish* his son in business⟩ **b** : to put into a favorable position ⟨the *established* order⟩ **5** : to gain full recognition or acceptance of : PROVE ⟨*establish* a claim⟩ ⟨*established* his innocence⟩ — **es·tab·lish·er** *n*

established church *n* : a church recognized by law as the official church of a state

es·tab·lish·ment \is-'tab-lish-mənt\ *n* **1 a** : the act of establishing : the state or fact of being established **b** : the granting of a privileged position ⟨*establishment* of a church⟩ **2** : a permanent civil or military organization **3** : a place for residence or business ⟨a dry-cleaning *establishment*⟩ **4** : an established order of society; *also* : the social, economic, and political leaders of such an order ⟨hostile to the *establishment*⟩

es·tate \is-'tāt\ *n* **1** : STATE, CONDITION **2 a** : social standing or rank **b** : a social or political class **3 a** : POSSESSIONS, PROPERTY; *esp* : a person's property in land **b** : the assets and liabilities left by a person at death **c** : a large country house with extensive land

1**es·teem** \is-'tēm\ *n* : high regard

2**esteem** *vb* **1** : REGARD, CONSIDER ⟨*esteem* it a privilege⟩ **2** : to regard highly

es·ter \'es-tər\ *n* : an organic compound formed by the reaction between an acid and an alcohol

Es·ther \'es-tər\ *n* — see BIBLE table

esthetic, esthetics *var of* AESTHETIC, AESTHETICS

1**es·ti·mate** \'es-tə-ˌmāt\ *vb* **1** : to judge tentatively or approximately the value, size, or cost of ⟨*estimate* a distance⟩ ⟨*estimate* a painting job⟩ **2** : to form an opinion of : JUDGE, CONCLUDE — **es·ti·ma·tor** \-ˌmāt-ər\ *n*

2**es·ti·mate** \-mət\ *n* **1** : the act of estimating : CALCULATION **2** : an opinion or judgment of the nature, character, or quality of a thing **3** : a rough or approximate calculation **4** : a statement by a contractor of what he would charge for a job

es·ti·ma·tion \ˌes-tə-'mā-shən\ *n* **1** : JUDGMENT, OPINION **2** : ESTIMATE **3** : ESTEEM, HONOR

Es·to·nian \e-'stō-nē-ən, -nyən\ *n* **1** : a member of a Caucasian people chiefly of Estonia **2** : the language of the Estonians — **Estonian** *adj*

es·tra·di·ol \ˌes-trə-'dī-ˌȯl, -ˌōl\ *n* : a powerful estrogenic hormone usu. made synthetically for medicinal use

es·trange \is-'trānj\ *vb* : to destroy the affection of : ALIENATE ⟨*estranged* from his wife⟩ — **es·trange·ment** \-mənt\ *n*

es·trin \'es-trən\ *n* : an estrogenic hormone

es·tri·ol \'es-ˌtrī-ˌȯl, e-'strī-, -ˌōl\ *n* : a crystalline estrogenic hormone usu. obtained from the urine of pregnant women

es·tro·gen \'es-trə-jən\ *n* : a substance (as a sex hormone) tending to promote estrus and stimulate the development of secondary sex characteristics in the female — **es·tro·gen·ic** \ˌes-trə-'jen-ik\ *adj*

es·trone \'es-ˌtrōn\ *n* : an estrogenic hormone from the urine of pregnant females

estrous cycle *n* : the correlated cycle of physiological changes of the endocrine and reproductive systems of a female mammal from the beginning of one period of estrus to the beginning of the next

es·trus \'es-trəs\ *n* **1** : a regularly recurring state of sexual excitability during which the female of most mammals will accept the male and is capable of conceiving : HEAT **2** : ESTROUS CYCLE — **es·trous** \-trəs\ *adj*

es·tu·ary \'es-chə-ˌwer-ē\ *n, pl* **-ar·ies** : a passage where the tide meets a river current; *esp* : an arm of the sea at the lower end of a river — **es·tu·a·rine** \'es-chə-wə-ˌrīn\ *adj*

-et \'et, ˌet, ət, it\ *n suffix* **1** : small one : lesser one ⟨isl*et*⟩ **2** : group ⟨oct*et*⟩

eta \'āt-ə\ *n* : the 7th letter of the Greek alphabet — H or *η*

etc *abbr* et cetera

et cet·era \et-'set-ə-rə, -'se-trə\ : and others esp. of the same kind : and so forth

etch \'ech\ *vb* [from Dutch *etsen*, from German *ätzen* meaning literally "to cause to eat", a derivative of the verb which is the source of English *eat*] **1** : to produce esp. on metal or glass by lines eaten into the substance by acid **2** : to impress sharply — **etch·er** *n*

etch·ing *n* **1** : the art of producing pictures or designs by printing from an etched plate **2** : an impression from an etched plate

eter·nal \i-'tərn-əl\ *adj* **1** : having no beginning and no end : lasting forever **2** : continuing without interruption : UNCEASING ⟨that dog's *eternal* barking⟩ — **eter·nal·ly** \-ə-lē\ *adv* — **eter·nal·ness** *n*

eter·ni·ty \i-'tər-nət-ē\ *n, pl* **-ties** **1** : the quality or state of being eternal **2** : infinite time **3** : the state after death : IMMORTALITY **4** : a seemingly endless time

[1]**-eth** \əth, ith\ *or* **-th** \th\ *vb suffix* — used to form the archaic third person singular present of verbs ⟨go*eth*⟩ ⟨do*th*⟩

[2]**-eth** — see -TH

eth·ane \'eth-,ān\ *n* : a colorless odorless gas that consists of carbon and hydrogen, is found in natural gas, and is used esp. as a fuel

ether \'ē-thər\ *n* **1** : the upper regions of space : HEAVENS **2** : the invisible substance formerly held to permeate all space and transmit waves (as light) **3** : a strong-smelling flammable liquid that evaporates easily, is obtained by the distillation of alcohol with sulfuric acid, and is used chiefly as a solvent esp. of fats and as an anesthetic

ethe·re·al \i-'thir-ē-əl\ *adj* **1** : HEAVENLY ⟨*ethereal* spirits⟩ **2** : being light and airy : DELICATE ⟨*ethereal* music⟩ — **ethe·re·al·ly** \-ē-ə-lē\ *adv* — **ethe·re·al·ness** *n*

ether·ize \'ē-thə-,rīz\ *vb* : to treat or anesthetize with ether — **ether·i·za·tion** \,ē-thə-rə-'zā-shən\ *n*

eth·i·cal \'eth-i-kəl\ *or* **eth·ic** \-ik\ *adj* **1** : of or relating to ethics **2 a** : conforming to an accepted or a correct moral code **b** : conforming to professional standards of conduct **3** : sold only on a doctor's prescription ⟨*ethical* drugs⟩ — **eth·i·cal·ly** \'eth-i-k(ə-)lē\ *adv*

eth·ics \'eth-iks\ *n sing or pl* **1** : a branch of philosophy dealing with what is morally good or bad and with moral duty and obligation **2** : the principles of moral conduct governing an individual or a group

Ethi·o·pi·an \,ē-thē-'ō-pē-ən\ *n* : a native or inhabitant of Ethiopia — **Ethiopian** *adj*

Ethi·op·ic \-'äp-ik, -'ō-pik\ *n* : a Semitic language formerly spoken in Ethiopia and still used in church services there

eth·nic \'eth-nik\ *adj* : of or relating to races or large groups of people classed according to common traits and customs ⟨*ethnic* minorities⟩ — **eth·ni·cal·ly** \-ni-k(ə-)lē\ *adv*

eth·no·cen·tric \,eth-nō-'sen-trik\ *adj* : favoring one's own ethnic group ⟨*ethnocentric* views⟩

ethnol *abbr* ethnology

eth·nol·o·gy \eth-'näl-ə-jē\ *n* **1** : a science that deals with the origin, distribution, relations, and characteristics of human races **2** : the comparative study of cultures : CULTURAL ANTHROPOLOGY — **eth·no·log·ic** \,eth-nə-'läj-ik\ *or* **eth·no·log·i·cal** \-'läj-i-kəl\ *adj* — **eth·no·log·i·cal·ly** \-i-k(ə-)lē\ *adv* — **eth·nol·o·gist** \eth-'näl-ə-jəst\ *n*

ethol·o·gy \ē-'thäl-ə-jē\ *n* : the scientific study of animal behavior — **etho·log·i·cal** \,ē-thə-'läj-i-kəl\ *adj* — **ethol·o·gist** \ē-'thäl-ə-jəst\ *n*

ethyl alcohol *n* : ALCOHOL 1a

eth·yl·ene \'eth-ə-,lēn\ *n* : a colorless flammable gas found in coal gas or obtained from petroleum and used to ripen fruits or as an anesthetic

ethylene gly·col \-'glī-,kȯl, -,kōl\ *n* : a thick liquid alcohol used as an antifreeze and in making resins

eti·ol·o·gy \,ēt-ē-'äl-ə-jē\ *n* : the cause or origin esp. of a disease — **eti·o·log·ic** \,ēt-ē-ə-'läj-ik\ *or* **eti·o·log·i·cal** \-'läj-i-kəl\ *adj* — **eti·o·log·i·cal·ly** \-i-k(ə-)lē\ *adv*

et·i·quette \'et-i-kət, -,ket\ *n* : the body of rules governing the way in which people behave socially, ceremonially, or in office

-ette \'et, ,et, ət, it\ *n suffix* **1** : little one ⟨kitchen*ette*⟩ **2** : female ⟨farmer*ette*⟩ **3** : imitation

étude \'ā-,t(y)üd\ *n* **1** : a piece of music for practice to develop technical skill **2** : a composition built on a technical motive but played for its artistic value

et·y·mol·o·gy \,et-ə-'mäl-ə-jē\ *n, pl* **-gies** **1** : the history of a word or part of a word (as an affix or a base) as shown by identifying its related forms in other languages and tracing these to their origin in a common form in an earlier parent language or by tracing the transmission of a word from one language to another **2** : a branch of language study concerned with etymologies — **et·y·mo·log·i·cal** \-mə-'läj-i-kəl\ *adj* — **et·y·mo·log·i·cal·ly** \-'läj-i-k(ə-)lē\ *adv* — **et·y·mol·o·gist** \-'mäl-ə-jəst\ *n*

eu·ca·lypt \'yü-kə-,lipt\ *n* : EUCALYPTUS

eu·ca·lyp·tus \,yü-kə-'lip-təs\ *n, pl* **-ti** \-,tī, -(,)tē\ *or* **-tus·es** : any of a genus of mostly Australian evergreen trees that are related to the myrtle and include many that are widely cultivated for their gums, resins, oils, and useful woods

Eu·cha·rist \'yü-kə-rəst\ *n* : COMMUNION 1a; *esp* : a Roman Catholic sacrament renewing Christ's sacrifice of his body and blood — **eu·cha·ris·tic** \,yü-kə-'ris-tik\ *adj, often cap*

eu·gen·ic \yu̇-'jen-ik\ *adj* **1** : relating to or fitted for the production of good offspring **2** : of or relating to eugenics — **eu·gen·i·cal·ly** \-'jen-i-k(ə-)lē\ *adv*

eu·gen·ics \yu̇-'jen-iks\ *n* : a science that deals with the improvement of hereditary qualities of a race or breed and esp. of human beings

eu·gle·na \yu̇-'glē-nə\ *n* : any of a large genus of green freshwater flagellates often classed as algae — **eu·gle·noid** \-,nȯid\ *adj or n*

euglenoid movement *n* : writhing protoplasmic movement typical of some euglenoid flagellates

eu·lo·gize \'yü-lə-,jīz\ *vb* : to speak or write in high praise of : EXTOL — **eu·lo·gist** \-jəst\ *n* — **eu·lo·gis·tic** \,yü-lə-'jis-tik\ *adj* — **eu·lo·gis·ti·cal·ly** \-ti-k(ə-)lē\ *adv*

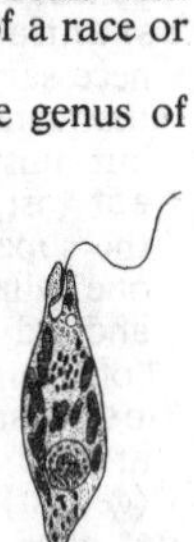

euglena (magnified 150 times)

eu·lo·gy \'yü-lə-jē\ *n, pl* **-gies** **1** : discourse in praise of a person or thing; *esp* : a formal speech in praise of a dead person **2** : high praise

eu·nuch \'yü-nək\ *n* : a castrated man; *esp* : one placed in charge of a harem or employed as a chamberlain in a palace

eu·phe·mism \'yü-fə-ˌmiz-əm\ *n* : the substitution of an agreeable or inoffensive expression for one that may offend or suggest something unpleasant or the expression so substituted ⟨*pass away* is a widely used *euphemism* for *die*⟩ — **eu·phe·mis·tic** \ˌyü-fə-'mis-tik\ *adj* — **eu·phe·mis·ti·cal·ly** \-ti-k(ə-)lē\ *adv*

eu·pho·ni·um \yu̇-'fō-nē-əm\ *n* : a tenor tuba like a baritone but mellower in tone

eu·pho·ny \'yü-fə-nē\ *n, pl* **-nies** [from Greek *euphōnia,* from *eu-* "good" and *phōnē* "sound", the source of English *phonograph*] : pleasing or sweet sound; *esp* : the effect of words so combined as to please the ear — **eu·pho·ni·ous** \yu̇-'fō-nē-əs\ *adj*

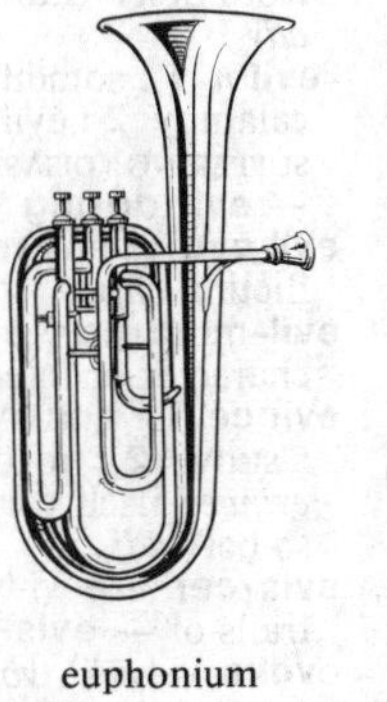

euphonium

eu·pho·ria \yu̇-'fōr-ē-ə, -'fȯr-\ *n* : a strong feeling of well-being or elation — **eu·phor·ic** \-'fȯr-ik, -'fär-\ *adj*

Eur *abbr* **1** Europe **2** European

Eur·asian \yu̇-'rā-zhən, -shən\ *adj* **1** : of or relating to Eurasia **2** : of mixed European and Asiatic origin — **Eurasian** *n*

Eu·ro·pe·an \ˌyu̇r-ə-'pē-ən\ *n* **1** : a native or inhabitant of Europe **2** : a person of European descent — **European** *adj*

European plan *n* : a hotel rate whereby guests are charged a fixed sum for room without meals

eu·ro·pi·um \yu̇-'rō-pē-əm\ *n* : a metallic chemical element found in a sand — see ELEMENT table

eu·sta·chian tube \yu̇-ˌstā-shən-, -ˌstā-kē-ən-\ *n, often cap E* : a tube connecting the middle ear with the throat and equalizing air pressure on both sides of the eardrum

eu·tha·na·sia \ˌyü-thə-'nā-zh(ē-)ə\ *n* : MERCY KILLING

eu·then·ics \yu̇-'then-iks\ *n* : a science that deals with human improvement by control and improvement of environment

evac·u·ate \i-'vak-yə-ˌwāt\ *vb* **1** : to make empty **2** : to discharge waste matter from the body **3** : to remove something (as a gas) from esp. by pumping **4** : to remove or withdraw from a military or occupation zone or from a dangerous place — **evac·u·a·tion** \-ˌvak-yə-'wā-shən\ *n* — **evac·u·a·tive** \-'vak-yə-ˌwāt-iv\ *adj*

evac·u·ee \i-ˌvak-yə-'wē\ *n* : a person who has been evacuated from a place

evade \i-'vād\ *vb* **1** : to get away from or avoid by skill or trickery ⟨*evade* a question⟩ ⟨*evade* punishment⟩ **2** : BAFFLE, FOIL ⟨the problem *evades* solution⟩ — **evad·a·ble** \-'vād-ə-bəl\ *adj* — **evad·er** *n*

evag·i·nate \i-'vaj-ə-ˌnāt\ *vb* : to turn inside out — **evag·i·na·tion** \-ˌvaj-ə-'nā-shən\ *n*

eval·u·ate \i-'val-yə-ˌwāt\ *vb* : to determine or fix the value, quality, or degree of — **eval·u·a·tion** \-ˌval-yə-'wā-shən\ *n* — **eval·u·a·tive** \-'val-yə-ˌwāt-iv\ *adj*

ev·a·nes·cent \ˌev-ə-'nes-ənt\ *adj* : tending to vanish like vapor : not lasting : quickly passing ⟨*evanescent* pleasures⟩

evan·gel·i·cal \ˌē-ˌvan-'jel-i-kəl, ˌev-ən-\ *also* **evan·gel·ic** \-'jel-ik\ *adj* **1** : of, relating to, or being in agreement with the Christian gospel esp. as presented in the four Gospels **2** : emphasizing salvation by faith in Jesus Christ through conversion, the authority of Scripture, and the importance of preaching — **Evan·gel·i·cal·ism** \-i-kə-ˌliz-əm\ *n* — **evan·gel·i·cal·ly** \-i-k(ə-)lē\ *adv*

evan·ge·lism \i-'van-jə-ˌliz-əm\ *n* : the winning or revival of personal commitments to Christ — **evan·ge·lis·tic** \-ˌvan-jə-'lis-tik\ *adj*

evan·ge·list \i-'van-jə-ləst\ *n* [from Greek *euangelistēs,* from *euangelion* gospel, literally "good news", from *eu-* "good" and *angelos* "messenger"] **1** *often cap* : a writer of any of the four Gospels **2** : one who evangelizes; *esp* : a preacher at services of evangelism

evan·ge·lize \i-'van-jə-ˌlīz\ *vb* **1** : to preach the gospel **2** : to convert to Christianity — **evan·ge·li·za·tion** \-ˌvan-jə-lə-'zā-shən\ *n* — **evan·ge·liz·er** \-'van-jə-ˌlī-zər\ *n*

evap *abbr* evaporation

evap·o·rate \i-'vap-ə-ˌrāt\ *vb* [from Latin *evaporare,* from *e-* "out" and *vapor* "steam", "vapor"] **1** : to pass off or cause to pass off into vapor **2 a** : to pass off or away : DISAPPEAR **b** : to diminish quickly **3** : to expel moisture from (as by heat) ⟨*evaporate* apples⟩

evap·o·ra·tion \i-ˌvap-ə-'rā-shən\ *n* : the process of evaporating; *esp* : the conversion of liquid into vapor — **evap·o·ra·tor** \-ˌrāt-ər\ *n*

eva·sion \i-'vā-zhən\ *n* **1** : the act or an instance of evading : ESCAPE ⟨tax *evasion*⟩ **2** : a means of evading

eva·sive \i-'vā-siv, -ziv\ *adj* : marked by a tendency or purpose to evade ⟨gave an *evasive* answer⟩ — **eva·sive·ly** *adv* — **eva·sive·ness** *n*

eve \'ēv\ *n* **1** : EVENING **2** : the evening or the day before a special day ⟨Christmas *Eve*⟩ **3** : the period just before an event

¹even \'ē-vən\ *n, archaic* : EVENING

²even *adj* **1 a** : having a horizontal surface : FLAT **b** : being without break or irregularity : SMOOTH **c** : being in the same plane or line **2 a** : equal in size, number, or amount ⟨*even* distances apart⟩ **b** : being without variation : UNIFORM ⟨*even* breathing⟩ **3 a** : without advantage on either side : FAIR ⟨start out *even*⟩ ⟨an *even* trade⟩ **b** : leaving nothing due : paid up ⟨*even* with his creditors⟩ **c** : BALANCED; *esp* : showing neither profit nor loss **4** : being exactly divisible by two ⟨an *even* number⟩ **5** : EXACT, PRECISE ⟨an *even* dozen⟩ — **even·ly** *adv* — **even·ness** \-vən-(n)əs\ *n*

³even *adv* **1 a** : PRECISELY, EXACTLY ⟨*even* as you and I⟩ **b** : at the very same time ⟨*even* as the clock struck⟩ **2 a** — used as an intensive to indicate something unexpected ⟨honored *even* by his enemies⟩ **b** — used as an intensive to stress the comparative degree ⟨are *even* more at home⟩

⁴even *vb* **evened; even·ing** \'ēv-(ə-)ning\ : to make or become even — **even·er** \'ēv-(ə-)nər\ *n*

even·hand·ed \ˌē-vən-'han-dəd\ *adj* : FAIR, IMPARTIAL

eve·ning \'ēv-ning\ *n* **1** : the latter part of the day and early part of the night **2** : the latter part ⟨the *evening* of life⟩

evening primrose *n* **1** : a coarse biennial herb with yellow flowers that open in the evening **2** : any of several plants related to the evening primrose

evening star *n* : a bright planet (as Venus) seen in the western sky at or after sunset

even·song \'ē-vən-ˌsȯng\ *n, often cap* : VESPERS

event \i-'vent\ *n* [from Latin *eventus* "outcome", from the past participle of *evenire* "to turn out", from *e-* "out" and *venire* "to come"] **1 a** : something that happens : OCCURRENCE **b** : a noteworthy happening **c** : a social occasion or activity **2 a** : OUT-

COME, RESULT **b** : EVENTUALITY ⟨in the *event* of rain the ceremony will be held indoors⟩ **3** : any of the contests in a program of sports ⟨track-and-field *events*⟩

event·ful \i-ˈvent-fəl\ *adj* **1** : full of events ⟨an *eventful* day⟩ **2** : MOMENTOUS — **event·ful·ly** \-fə-lē\ *adv* — **event·ful·ness** *n*

even·tide \ˈē-vən-ˌtīd\ *n* : EVENING

event space *n* : the set of all possible outcomes of an experiment (as tossing a pair of dice)

even·tu·al \i-ˈvench-(ə-)wəl, -ˈven-chəl\ *adj* : taking place at an unspecified later time : ULTIMATE ⟨*eventual* success⟩ — **even·tu·al·ly** \-ē\ *adv*

even·tu·al·i·ty \i-ˌven-chə-ˈwal-ət-ē\ *n, pl* **-ties** : a possible outcome : POSSIBILITY

ev·er \ˈev-ər\ *adv* **1** : ALWAYS ⟨*ever* faithful⟩ **2 a** : at any time ⟨seldom if *ever* home⟩ **b** : in any way : at all ⟨how can I *ever* thank you⟩ **3** — used as an intensive esp. with *so* ⟨thank you *ever* so much⟩

ev·er·bloom·ing \ˌev-ər-ˈblü-ming\ *adj* : blooming more or less continuously throughout the growing season

ev·er·glade \ˈev-ər-ˌglād\ *n* : a low-lying tract of swampy or marshy land

[1]**ev·er·green** \ˈev-ər-ˌgrēn\ *adj* : having foliage that remains green and functional through more than one growing season ⟨most conifers are *evergreen* trees⟩ — compare DECIDUOUS

[2]**evergreen** *n* **1** : an evergreen plant; *also* : CONIFER **2** *pl* : twigs and branches of evergreen plants used for decoration

[1]**ev·er·last·ing** \ˌev-ər-ˈlas-ting\ *adj* **1** : lasting through all time : ETERNAL **2 a** : continuing long or too long ⟨*everlasting* complaints⟩ **b** : retaining form or color when dried ⟨*everlasting* flowers⟩ **3** : DURABLE — **ev·er·last·ing·ly** \-ting-lē\ *adv* — **ev·er·last·ing·ness** *n*

[2]**everlasting** *n* **1** : ETERNITY **2** : a plant (as a composite) with everlasting flowers **3** : an everlasting flower

ev·er·more \ˌev-ər-ˈmō(ə)r, -ˈmȯ(ə)r\ *adv* : ALWAYS, FOREVER

evert \i-ˈvərt\ *vb* : to turn outward or inside out — **ever·si·ble** \-ˈvər-sə-bəl\ *adj* — **ever·sion** \-ˈvər-zhən\ *n*

ev·ery \ˈev-rē\ *adj* **1** : being each individual or part of a group without exception **2** : COMPLETE, ENTIRE ⟨have *every* confidence in him⟩

ev·ery·body \ˈev-ri-ˌbäd-ē\ *pron* : every person

ev·ery·day \ˈev-rē-ˌdā\ *adj* : encountered or used routinely or typically : ORDINARY ⟨*everyday* clothes⟩

ev·ery·one \-(ˌ)wən\ *pron* : EVERYBODY

ev·ery·thing \-ˌthing\ *pron* **1 a** : all that exists **b** : all that relates to the subject ⟨tell *everything*⟩ **2** : the most important thing ⟨to some people money is *everything*⟩

ev·ery·where \-ˌhwe(ə)r, -ˌhwa(ə)r\ *adv* : in or to every place

evict \i-ˈvikt\ *vb* : to put (a person) out from property by legal process — **evic·tion** \-ˈvik-shən\ *n* — **evic·tor** \-ˈvik-tər\ *n*

[1]**ev·i·dence** \ˈev-əd-ən(t)s, -ə-ˌden(t)s\ *n* **1** : an outward sign : INDICATION **2** : something that furnishes proof; *esp* : material legally submitted to a tribunal to ascertain the truth — **ev·i·den·tial** \ˌev-ə-ˈden-chəl\ *adj* — **in evidence** : to be easily seen : CONSPICUOUS

[2]**evidence** *vb* : to serve as or offer evidence of

ev·i·dent \ˈev-əd-ənt, -ə-ˌdent\ *adj* : clear to the sight or mind : PLAIN ⟨*evident* that they were twins⟩ — **ev·i·dent·ly** *adv*

[1]**evil** \ˈē-vəl\ *adj* **evil·er** *or* **evil·ler**; **evil·est** *or* **evil·lest** **1** : not good morally : WICKED **2 a** : HARMFUL, INJURIOUS **b** : marked by misfortune : UNLUCKY ⟨fall on *evil* days⟩ — **evil·ly** \-vəl-(l)ē\ *adv*

[2]**evil** *n* **1** : something that brings sorrow, distress, or calamity **2** : evil conduct or nature **3** : MISFORTUNE, SUFFERING, DISASTER — **evil·do·er** \ˌē-vəl-ˈdü-ər\ *n* — **evil·do·ing** \-ˈdü-ing\ *n*

evil eye *n* : an eye or glance held to be capable of inflicting harm

evil–mind·ed \ˌē-vəl-ˈmīn-dəd\ *adj* : having an evil character or intentions

evince \i-ˈvin(t)s\ *vb* **1** : to constitute evidence of : SHOW **2** : to display clearly : REVEAL ⟨his talent *evinced* itself early in life⟩ — **evinc·i·ble** \-ˈvin(t)-sə-bəl\ *adj*

evis·cer·ate \i-ˈvis-ə-ˌrāt\ *vb* : to take out the entrails of — **evis·cer·a·tion** \-ˌvis-ə-ˈrā-shən\ *n*

evoke \i-ˈvōk\ *vb* : to call forth : SUMMON, ELICIT — **evo·ca·tion** \ˌē-vō-ˈkā-shən, ˌev-ə-\ *n* — **evoc·a·tive** \-ˈväk-ət-iv\ *adj*

ev·o·lu·tion \ˌev-ə-ˈlü-shən, ˌē-və-\ *n* **1 a** : a process of change esp. from a lower or simple to a higher or complex state : GROWTH **b** : something evolved **2** : one of a set of prescribed movements **3** : the process of working out or developing **4 a** : PHYLOGENY **b** : the process by which through a series of changes or steps a living organism acquired its distinguishing characters **c** : a theory that the various types of animals and plants have their origin in other preexisting types and that the distinguishable differences are due to inherited changes occurring in successive generations — **ev·o·lu·tion·ary** \-shə-ˌner-ē\ *adj* — **ev·o·lu·tion·ism** \-shə-ˌniz-əm\ *n* — **ev·o·lu·tion·ist** \-sh(ə-)nəst\ *n or adj*

evolve \i-ˈvälv, -ˈvȯlv\ *vb* **1** : to derive or produce from something else : DEVELOP **2** : to produce by a process of evolution **3** : to undergo evolutionary change — **evolve·ment** \-mənt\ *n*

ewe \ˈyü\ *n* : the female of the sheep or a related animal esp. when mature

ew·er \ˈyü-ər, ˈyu̇(-ə)r\ *n* : a vase-shaped pitcher or jug

[1]**ex-** \(ˌ)eks, ˈeks\ *prefix* : former ⟨*ex*-president⟩ ⟨*ex*-child actor⟩

[2]**ex-** — see EXO-

ex *abbr* **1** example **2** extra

[1]**ex·act** \ig-ˈzakt\ *vb* **1** : to demand and get by force or threat ⟨*exact* a ransom⟩ ⟨*exact* vengeance⟩ **2** : to call for as necessary, appropriate, or desirable : REQUIRE ⟨the situation *exacts* caution⟩ — **ex·act·a·ble** \-ˈzak-tə-bəl\ *adj* — **ex·ac·tion** \-ˈzak-shən\ *n*

[2]**exact** *adj* **1** : fully and completely in accordance with fact ⟨the *exact* time⟩ **2** : marked by thorough attention to facts ⟨the *exact* sciences⟩ ⟨an *exact* replica⟩ **3** : providing great accuracy ⟨*exact* instruments⟩ *syn* see CORRECT ***ant*** inexact — **exact·ness** \-ˈzak(t)-nəs\ *n*

ex·act·ing \ig-ˈzak-ting\ *adj* : making many or difficult demands : TRYING ⟨an *exacting* task⟩ ⟨an *exacting* teacher⟩ — **ex·act·ing·ly** \-ting-lē\ *adv* — **ex·act·ing·ness** *n*

ex·ac·ti·tude \ig-ˈzak-tə-ˌt(y)üd\ *n* : EXACTNESS

ex·act·ly \ig-ˈzak-(t)lē\ *adv* **1** : in an exact manner

: PRECISELY ⟨copy *exactly*⟩ ⟨at *exactly* three⟩ **2** : quite so : just as you say — used to express agreement

ex·ag·ger·ate \ig-'zaj-ə-ˌrāt\ *vb* [from Latin *exaggerare* "to heap up", from *ex-* "out" and *agger* "mound of earth", "heap"] : to enlarge a fact or statement beyond what is actual or true — **ex·ag·ger·at·ed·ly** \-ˌrāt-əd-lē\ *adv* — **ex·ag·ger·a·tion** \-ˌzaj-ə-'rā-shən\ *n* — **ex·ag·ger·a·tor** \-'zaj-ə-ˌrāt-ər\ *n*

ex·alt \ig-'zȯlt\ *vb* **1** : to raise high : ELEVATE **2** : to raise in rank, power, or character **3** : to elevate by praise or in estimation : GLORIFY — **ex·alt·er** *n*

ex·al·ta·tion \ˌeg-ˌzȯl-'tā-shən\ *n* **1** : the act of exalting : the state of being exalted **2** : a greatly heightened sense of personal well-being, power, or importance

ex·am \ig-'zam\ *n* : EXAMINATION

ex·am·i·na·tion \ig-ˌzam-ə-'nā-shən\ *n* **1** : the act or process of examining : the state of being examined **2** : an exercise to determine progress, qualifications, or knowledge

syn EXAMINATION, INSPECTION mean close observation of something in the course of investigating. EXAMINATION generally suggests an intent to determine the true nature or quality of something; INSPECTION more often implies looking for errors, flaws, or defects

ex·am·ine \ig-'zam-ən\ *vb* **1 a** : to look at or inspect closely ⟨*examine* rock specimens⟩ **b** : to inquire into carefully : INVESTIGATE **2** : to test the condition of ⟨had his eyes *examined*⟩ **3** : to question closely in order to determine progress, fitness, or knowledge ⟨*examine* a class in arithmetic⟩ — **ex·am·in·er** *n*

ex·am·ple \ig-'zam-pəl\ *n* **1** : a sample of something taken to show what the whole is like ⟨a striking *example* of scientific method⟩ **2** : a problem to be solved in order to show how a rule works ⟨an *example* in arithmetic⟩ **3** : something to be imitated : MODEL ⟨set a good *example*⟩ **4** : punishment inflicted as a warning to others — **for example** : as an example

ex·as·per·ate \ig-'zas-pə-ˌrāt\ *vb* **1** : to make angry : ENRAGE **2** : ANNOY, IRRITATE

ex·as·per·a·tion \ig-ˌzas-pə-'rā-shən\ *n* **1** : the act of exasperating : PROVOCATION **2** : the state of being exasperated : extreme irritation or annoyance : ANGER **3** : a source of exasperation

exc *abbr* excellent

ex·ca·vate \'ek-skə-ˌvāt\ *vb* **1** : to hollow out : form a hole in **2** : to make by hollowing out ⟨*excavate* a tunnel⟩ **3** : to dig out and remove ⟨*excavate* sand⟩ **4** : to uncover by digging away covering earth — **ex·ca·va·tor** \-ˌvāt-ər\ *n*

ex·ca·va·tion \ˌek-skə-'vā-shən\ *n* **1** : the act or process of excavating **2** : a hollowed-out place formed by excavating

ex·ceed \ik-'sēd\ *vb* **1** : to be greater than or superior to : SURPASS ⟨*exceeds* his earlier performance⟩ **2** : to go or be beyond a limit or bound ⟨*exceeded* his authority⟩ ⟨*exceed* the speed limit⟩

ex·ceed·ing \ik-'sēd-ing\ *adj* : exceptional in amount, quality, or degree : EXTRAORDINARY

ex·ceed·ing·ly \-ing-lē\ *or* **exceeding** *adv* : EXTREMELY

ex·cel \ik-'sel\ *vb* **ex·celled**; **ex·cel·ling** : to outdo others (as in good qualities or ability) : be better than others : SURPASS ⟨a pupil who *excels* in arithmetic⟩ ⟨*excels* his brother at tennis⟩

ex·cel·lence \'ek-s(ə-)lən(t)s\ *n* **1** : the quality of being excellent : MERIT **2** : an excellent quality : VIRTUE

ex·cel·len·cy \'ek-s(ə-)lən-sē\ *n, pl* **-cies** **1** : EXCELLENCE **2** — used as a title for high dignitaries of state (as an ambassador) and church (as a Roman Catholic bishop)

ex·cel·lent \'ek-s(ə-)lənt\ *adj* : extremely good of its kind : very good — **ex·cel·lent·ly** *adv*

ex·cel·si·or \ik-'sel-sē-ər\ *n* : curled wood shavings used esp. for packing fragile items

[1]**ex·cept** \ik-'sept\ *vb* : to leave out from a number or a whole : OMIT

[2]**except** *also* **ex·cept·ing** *prep* **1** : not including ⟨everybody *except* him⟩ **2** : other than ⟨take no orders *except* from me⟩

[3]**except** *also* **excepting** *conj* : UNLESS ⟨*except* you repent⟩

ex·cep·tion \ik-'sep-shən\ *n* **1** : the act of excepting : EXCLUSION **2** : one that is excepted ⟨an *exception* to the rule⟩ **3** : an objection or a ground for objection

ex·cep·tion·a·ble \ik-'sep-sh(ə-)nə-bəl\ *adj* : OBJECTIONABLE — **ex·cep·tion·a·bly** \-blē\ *adv*

ex·cep·tion·al \ik-'sep-sh(ə-)nəl\ *adj* **1** : constituting an exception : RARE **2** : better than average : SUPERIOR — **ex·cep·tion·al·ly** \-ē\ *adv* — **ex·cep·tion·al·ness** *n*

[1]**ex·cerpt** \ek-'sərpt, 'ek-ˌ; eg-'zərpt, 'eg-ˌ\ *vb* : to select for quoting : EXTRACT

[2]**ex·cerpt** \'ek-ˌsərpt, 'eg-ˌzərpt\ *n* : a passage selected or copied : EXTRACT

[1]**ex·cess** \ik-'ses, 'ek-ˌ\ *n* **1 a** : a state of being more than enough : SUPERFLUITY **b** : an amount in excess of what is usual, proper, or specified **c** : the amount by which one thing or quantity exceeds another **2** : INTEMPERANCE

[2]**excess** *adj* : more than the usual, proper, or specified amount ⟨*excess* baggage⟩

ex·ces·sive \ik-'ses-iv\ *adj* : exceeding the usual, proper, or specified ⟨*excessive* bail⟩; *esp* : too much ⟨*excessive* rain⟩ — **ex·ces·sive·ly** *adv* — **ex·ces·sive·ness** *n*

[1]**ex·change** \iks-'chānj, 'eks-ˌ\ *n* **1** : a giving or taking of one thing in return for another : TRADE **2** : the act of substituting one thing for another **3** : interchange of money of different countries with allowance for difference in value **4** : a place where things or services are exchanged: as **a** : a center for trading in securities or commodities **b** : a central office in which telephone lines are connected to permit communication

[2]**exchange** *vb* **1** : to give in exchange : TRADE, SWAP **2** : to part with for a substitute ⟨unwilling to *exchange* his home for a palace⟩ — **ex·change·a·ble** \-ə-bəl\ *adj* — **ex·chang·er** *n*

exchange student *n* : a student from a foreign country received into a school in exchange for one sent to that country

ex·che·quer \'eks-ˌchek-ər, iks-'\ *n* **1** : the department of the British Government concerned with the national revenue **2** : TREASURY; *esp* : a national or royal treasury **3** : money available : FUNDS

[1]**ex·cise** \'ek-ˌsīz, -ˌsīs\ *n* : a tax on the manufacture, sale, or use of a commodity within a country

[2]**ex·cise** \ek-'sīz\ *vb* : to remove by cutting out — **ex·ci·sion** \-'sizh-ən\ *n*

ex·cit·a·ble \ik-'sīt-ə-bəl\ *adj* **1** : easily excited **2** : capable of activation by and reaction to stimuli : exhibiting irritability — **ex·cit·a·bil·i·ty** \-ˌsīt-ə-'bil-ət-ē\ *n*

ex·ci·ta·tion \ˌek-sī-'tā-shən, ˌek-sə-\ *n* : EXCITEMENT; *esp* : the irritability induced in protoplasm by a stimulus

E

ex·cit·a·to·ry \ik-'sīt-ə-,tōr-ē, -,tȯr-\ *adj* : exhibiting or marked by excitement or excitation
ex·cite \ik-'sīt\ *vb* **1** : to stir the activity or passion of : ROUSE ⟨*excited* to anger by injustice⟩ **2** : to cause to be felt or done ⟨*excite* admiration⟩ **3 a** : ENERGIZE **b** : to produce a magnetic field in **4** : to increase the activity of (as nervous tissue) : STIMULATE **5** : to raise (as an atom) to a higher energy level
ex·cit·ed \-'sīt-əd\ *adj* : having or showing strong feeling : worked up : STIRRED — **ex·cit·ed·ly** *adv*
excited state *n* : any of the states of a physical system (as an atom) that is higher in energy than the ground state
ex·cite·ment \ik-'sīt-mənt\ *n* **1** : the act of exciting : the state of being excited : AGITATION **2** : something that excites
ex·cit·er \-'sīt-ər\ *n* : one that excites
ex·cit·ing \-'sīt-ing\ *adj* : causing excitement : STIRRING — **ex·cit·ing·ly** \-ing-lē\ *adv*
ex·claim \iks-'klām\ *vb* : to cry out or speak in strong or sudden emotion
ex·cla·ma·tion \,eks-klə-'mā-shən\ *n* **1** : a sharp or sudden utterance : OUTCRY **2** : forceful expression of protest or complaint **3** : a word, phrase, clause, or sentence used to exclaim
exclamation point *n* : a punctuation mark ! used chiefly after an exclamation to show forceful utterance or strong feeling
ex·clam·a·to·ry \iks-'klam-ə-,tōr-ē, -,tȯr-\ *adj* : expressing, using, or relating to exclamation ⟨an *exclamatory* phrase⟩
ex·clude \iks-'klüd\ *vb* **1 a** : to shut out **b** : to bar from participation, consideration, or inclusion **2** : to put out : EXPEL — **ex·clud·a·ble** \-'klüd-ə-bəl\ *adj* — **ex·clud·er** *n* — **ex·clu·sion** \-'klü-zhən\ *n*
exclusion principle *n* : a principle that states that no two electrons in an atom can have the same four quantum numbers
ex·clu·sive \iks-'klü-siv, -ziv\ *adj* **1** : excluding or inclined to exclude certain persons or classes (as from ownership, membership, or privileges): as **a** : catering to a special esp. fashionable class ⟨an *exclusive* neighborhood⟩ **b** : DISCRIMINATORY **2** : SOLE, SINGLE ⟨*exclusive* use of a beach⟩ **3** : COMPLETE, UNDIVIDED ⟨gave their *exclusive* attention⟩ **4** : not including ⟨for five days *exclusive* of today⟩ — **ex·clu·sive·ly** *adv* — **ex·clu·sive·ness** *n*
ex·com·mu·ni·cate \,eks-kə-'myü-nə-,kāt\ *vb* : to bar officially from the rights of church membership — **ex·com·mu·ni·ca·tion** \-,myü-nə-'kā-shən\ *n* — **ex·com·mu·ni·ca·tor** \-'myü-nə-,kāt-ər\ *n*
ex·co·ri·ate \ek-'skōr-ē-āt, -'skȯr-\ *vb* : to censure scathingly — **ex·co·ri·a·tion** \(,)ek-,skōr-ē-'ā-shən, -,skȯr-\ *n*
ex·cre·ment \'ek-skrə-mənt\ *n* : waste matter discharged from the body and esp. from the alimentary canal — **ex·cre·men·tal** \,ek-skrə-'ment-əl\ *adj*
ex·cres·cence \ek-'skres-ən(t)s\ *n* : OUTGROWTH; *esp* : an abnormal outgrowth (as a wart) on the body
ex·cres·cent \-ənt\ *adj* : being or forming an excrescence
ex·cre·ta \ek-'skrēt-ə\ *n pl* : waste matter eliminated or separated from an organism

ə abut	ər further	a back	ā bake
ä cot, cart	aù out	ch chin	e less	ē easy
g gift	i trip	ī life	j joke	ng sing	ō flow
ȯ flaw	ȯi coin	th thin	th this	ü loot
ù foot	y yet	yü few	yù furious	zh vision

ex·crete \ek-'skrēt\ *vb* : to separate and eliminate (waste) from the blood or tissues or from the active protoplasm usu. in the form of sweat or urine
ex·cre·tion \ek-'skrē-shən\ *n* **1** : the act or process of excreting **2** : excreted matter
ex·cre·to·ry \'ek-skrə-,tōr-ē, -,tȯr-\ *adj* : of, relating to, or functioning in excretion
ex·cru·ci·at·ing \ik-'skrü-shē-,āt-ing\ *adj* : causing great pain or anguish : AGONIZING — **ex·cru·ci·at·ing·ly** \-ing-lē\ *adv*
ex·cul·pate \'ek-(,)skəl-,pāt, ek-'\ *vb* : to clear from a charge of fault or guilt — **ex·cul·pa·tion** \,ek-(,)skəl-'pā-shən\ *n* — **ex·cul·pa·to·ry** \ek-'skəl-pə-,tōr-ē, -,tȯr-\ *adj*
ex·cur·rent \ek-'skər-ənt, -'skə-rənt\ *adj* : characterized by a current that flows outward ⟨*excurrent* canals of a sponge⟩
ex·cur·sion \ik-'skər-zhən\ *n* [from Latin *excursio*, from *excurrere* "to run out", from *ex-* "out" and *currere* "to run"] **1** : a brief pleasure trip; *esp* : such a trip at special reduced rates **2** : deviation from a direct or proper course; *esp* : DIGRESSION
ex·cur·sion·ist \ik-'skərzh-(ə-)nəst\ *n* : a person who goes on an excursion
¹**ex·cuse** \ik-'skyüz\ *vb* **1** : to make apology for : try to remove blame from ⟨*excused* himself for being late⟩ **2** : to accept an excuse for **3** : to free or let off from doing something ⟨*excuse* a person from a debt⟩ **4** : to serve as an acceptable reason or explanation for something said or done : JUSTIFY ⟨nothing can *excuse* dishonesty⟩ — **ex·cus·a·ble** \-'skyü-zə-bəl\ *adj* — **ex·cus·a·bly** \-blē\ *adv* — **ex·cus·er** *n*

syn EXCUSE, CONDONE, PARDON, FORGIVE mean in common not to exact retribution for (an offense) or hold a grudge or claim against (a person). EXCUSE usu. implies passing over a fault or error; CONDONE suggests accepting without protest a blameworthy act or condition; PARDON implies freeing from due penalty; FORGIVE implies giving up all resentment and desire for retaliation ***ant*** punish

²**ex·cuse** \ik-'skyüs\ *n* **1** : grounds for being excused : JUSTIFICATION **2** : an expression of a person's grounds for being excused
ex·e·cra·ble \'ek-si-krə-bəl\ *adj* : DETESTABLE, ABOMINABLE — **ex·e·cra·ble·ness** *n* — **ex·e·cra·bly** \-blē\ *adv*
ex·e·crate \'ek-sə-,krāt\ *vb* **1** : to declare to be evil or detestable : DENOUNCE **2** : to detest utterly : ABHOR — **ex·e·cra·tion** \,ek-sə-'krā-shən\ *n* — **ex·e·cra·tor** \'ek-sə-,krāt-ər\ *n*
ex·e·cute \'ek-sə-,kyüt\ *vb* **1** : to put into effect : carry out : PERFORM **2** : to do what is provided or required by ⟨*execute* a decree⟩ **3** : to put to death in compliance with a legal sentence **4** : to make or produce esp. by carrying out a design
ex·e·cu·tion \,ek-sə-'kyü-shən\ *n* **1** : the act or process of executing : PERFORMANCE ⟨put a plan into *execution*⟩ **2** : a putting to death as a legal penalty **3** : a judicial writ empowering an officer to carry out a judgment **4** : manner of performance
ex·e·cu·tion·er \-'kyü-sh(ə-)nər\ *n* : one who puts into effect a sentence of death
¹**ex·ec·u·tive** \ig-'zek-(y)ət-iv\ *adj* **1** : designed for or relating to the execution of affairs ⟨*executive* ability⟩ **2** : of or relating to the execution of the laws and the conduct of public affairs **3** : of or relating to an executive
²**executive** *n* **1** : the executive branch of a government **2** : one who holds a position of administrative or managerial responsibility

ex·ec·u·tor \ig-'zek-(y)ət-ər, *in sense 1 also* 'ek-sə-ˌkyüt-\ *n* **1** : one who executes something **2** : the person designated in a will to carry out its provisions

ex·ec·u·trix \ig-'zek-(y)ə-(ˌ)triks\ *n, pl* **ex·ec·u·trix·es** *or* **ex·ec·u·tri·ces** \-ˌzek-(y)ə-'trī-ˌsēz\ : a female executor

ex·em·plar \ig-'zem-ˌplär, -plər\ *n* **1** : one that serves as a model or pattern; *esp* : an ideal model **2** : a typical instance : EXAMPLE; *esp* : a typical or standard specimen

ex·em·pla·ry \ig-'zem-plə-rē\ *adj* **1 a** : serving as an example or pattern **b** : deserving imitation : COMMENDABLE **2** : serving as a warning — **ex·em·plar·i·ly** \ˌeg-zəm-'pler-ə-lē\ *adv*

ex·em·pli·fy \ig-'zem-plə-ˌfī\ *vb* **-fied**; **-fy·ing** **1** : to show or illustrate by example **2** : to serve as an example of — **ex·em·pli·fi·ca·tion** \-ˌzem-plə-fə-'kā-shən\ *n*

[1]**ex·empt** \ig-'zem(p)t\ *adj* : free or released from an obligation or requirement to which others are subject

[2]**exempt** *vb* : to make exempt

ex·emp·tion \ig-'zem(p)-shən\ *n* **1** : the act of exempting : the state of being exempt : IMMUNITY **2** : something exempted; *esp* : a part of property or income that is exempt from taxation

[1]**ex·er·cise** \'ek-sər-ˌsīz\ *n* **1** : the act of bringing into play or realizing in action : USE ⟨by the *exercise* of his authority as governor⟩ **2** : bodily exertion for the sake of physical fitness **3** : something performed or practiced to develop, improve, or display a specific power or skill **4** *pl* : a program including speeches, announcements of awards and honors, and various traditional practices ⟨graduation *exercises*⟩

[2]**exercise** *vb* **1** : to bring to bear : EXERT ⟨*exercise* patience⟩ **2 a** : to use repeatedly in order to strengthen or develop ⟨*exercise* a muscle⟩ **b** : to put through exercises : give exercise to ⟨*exercise* a dog⟩ **3** : to cause anxiety, alarm, or indignation in ⟨found his family greatly *exercised* about his absence⟩ **4** : to take exercise — **ex·er·cis·a·ble** \-ˌsī-zə-bəl\ *adj* — **ex·er·cis·er** *n*

ex·ert \ig-'zərt\ *vb* **1** : to put forth (as strength, force, power, or influence) : bring into play **2** : to put (oneself) into action or to tiring effort

ex·er·tion \ig-'zər-shən\ *n* : the act or an instance of exerting; *esp* : laborious or perceptible effort

ex·e·unt \'ek-sē-(ˌ)ənt\ [Latin, meaning "(they) go out", from *exire* "to go out"] — used as a stage direction that all or some characters leave the stage

ex·fo·li·ate \(')eks-'fō-lē-ˌāt\ *vb* : to shed or remove (as rock or skin) in thin layers or scales — **ex·fo·li·a·tion** \(ˌ)eks-ˌfō-lē-'ā-shən\ *n*

ex·ha·la·tion \ˌeks-(h)ə-'lā-shən\ *n* : an act or product of exhaling ⟨*exhalation* of breath⟩ ⟨*exhalations* of steam from a geyser⟩

ex·hale \eks-'hāl\ *vb* **1** : to breathe out **2** : to send forth (as gas or odor) : EMIT ⟨the fragrance that flowers *exhale*⟩

[1]**ex·haust** \ig-'zȯst\ *vb* **1 a** : to draw off or let out completely ⟨*exhaust* the air from the jar⟩ **b** : to empty by drawing something from; *esp* : to create a vacuum in **2 a** : to use up all of ⟨*exhaust* his patience⟩ **b** : to tire out : FATIGUE **3 a** : to develop (a subject) completely **b** : to try out all of ⟨they *exhausted* all possibilities⟩ **4** : to destroy the fertility of (soil) **5** : to pass or flow out : DISCHARGE, EMPTY ***syn*** see TIRE — **ex·haust·er** *n* — **ex·haust·i·bil·i·ty** \-ˌzȯ-stə-'bil-ət-ē\ *n* — **ex·haust·i·ble** \-'zȯ-stə-bəl\ *adj*

[2]**exhaust** *n* **1 a** : the escape of used steam or gas from an engine **b** : the gas thus escaping **2 a** : a conduit through which used gases escape **b** : an arrangement (as of fans) for withdrawing fumes, dusts, or odors from an enclosure (as a kitchen or factory room)

ex·haus·tion \ig-'zȯs-chən\ *n* **1** : the act or process of exhausting **2** : the state of being exhausted; *esp* : extreme weariness or fatigue

ex·haus·tive \ig-'zȯ-stiv\ *adj* **1** : serving or tending to exhaust **2** : THOROUGH, COMPLETE — **ex·haus·tive·ly** *adv* — **ex·haus·tive·ness** *n*

[1]**ex·hib·it** \ig-'zib-ət\ *vb* **1** : to show outwardly : REVEAL ⟨*exhibit* an interest in music⟩ **2** : to put on display ⟨*exhibit* a collection of paintings⟩ **3** : to present in legal form (as to a court) — **ex·hib·i·tor** \-ət-ər\ *n*

[2]**exhibit** *n* **1** : an act or instance of exhibiting **2** : something exhibited; *esp* : a document or object produced in court as evidence

ex·hi·bi·tion \ˌek-sə-'bish-ən\ *n* **1** : an act or instance of exhibiting **2** : a public showing (as of works of art, manufactured goods, or athletic skill)

ex·hil·a·rate \ig-'zil-ə-ˌrāt\ *vb* **1** : to make cheerful : GLADDEN **2** : to fill with a lively sense of well-being : INVIGORATE ⟨an *exhilarating* autumn day⟩ — **ex·hil·a·ra·tive** \-ˌrāt-iv\ *adj*

ex·hil·a·ra·tion \ig-ˌzil-ə-'rā-shən\ *n* **1** : the action of exhilarating **2** : the state or the feeling of being exhilarated : high spirits

ex·hort \ig-'zȯrt\ *vb* : to arouse by words (as of advice, encouragement, or warning) : urge or appeal strongly — **ex·hort·er** *n*

ex·hor·ta·tion \ˌeks-ȯr-'tā-shən, ˌegz-\ *n* **1** : an act or instance of exhorting **2** : a speech intended to exhort

ex·hume \igz-'(y)üm, iks-'(h)yüm\ *vb* : to dig out of the ground; *esp* : to remove from a place of burial — **ex·hu·ma·tion** \ˌeks-(h)yü-'mā-shən, ˌegz-(y)ü-\ *n*

ex·i·gence \'ek-sə-jən(t)s\ *n* : EXIGENCY

ex·i·gen·cy \'ek-sə-jən-sē, ig-'zij-ən-\ *n, pl* **-cies** : a case or a state of affairs demanding immediate action or remedy : an urgent need

[1]**ex·ile** \'eg-ˌzīl, 'ek-ˌsīl\ *n* **1** : forced removal or voluntary absence from one's native country; *also* : the state of one so absent **2** : a person expelled from his country by authority

[2]**exile** *vb* : to banish or expel from one's own country or home

ex·ist \ig-'zist\ *vb* **1** : to have actual being : be real : BE ⟨do unicorns *exist*⟩ **2** : to continue to be : LIVE ⟨earn hardly enough to *exist* on⟩ **3** : to be found : OCCUR ⟨a disease that no longer *exists*⟩

ex·ist·ence \ig-'zis-tən(t)s\ *n* **1** : the fact or the state of having being or of being real ⟨believed in the *existence* of dragons⟩ ⟨the largest animal in *existence*⟩ **2** : continuance in living or way of living : LIFE ⟨owed his *existence* to a doctor's skill⟩ **3** : actual occurrence ⟨recognized the *existence* of a state of war⟩ **4** : the sum total of existing things

ex·ist·ent \-tənt\ *adj* **1** : having being : EXISTING **2** : existing now : EXTANT

[1]**ex·it** \'eg-zət, 'ek-sət\ [Latin, meaning "(he or she) goes out", from *exire* "to go out"] — used as a stage direction to specify who goes off stage

[2]**exit** *n* **1** : a departure from a stage **2** : the act of going out or going away **3** : a way out of an enclosed place or space — **exit** *vb*

exo- *or* **ex-** *comb form* : outside : outer ⟨*exo*skeleton⟩ — compare END-

exo·crine \'ek-sə-krən, -ˌkrīn, -ˌkrēn\ *adj* : secreting or secreted externally

E

exocrine gland *n* : a gland (as a salivary gland or a sweat gland) that produces an exocrine secretion

ex·o·dus \'ek-səd-əs\ *n* [from Greek *exodos* "a journey out", from *ex-* "out" and *hodos* "road"; the Bible book is so called from its containing the story of the Israelites' departure from Egypt] **1** *cap* — see BIBLE table **2** : a mass departure

ex of·fi·cio \ˌeks-ə-'fish-ē-ˌō\ *adv or adj* : by virtue or because of an office ⟨*ex officio* chairman⟩

ex·on·er·ate \ig-'zän-ə-ˌrāt\ *vb* : to clear from an accusation or from blame : declare innocent — **ex·on·er·a·tion** \ig-ˌzän-ə-'rā-shən\ *n*

ex·or·bi·tant \ig-'zȯr-bət-ənt\ *adj* : going beyond the limits of what is fair, reasonable, or expected : EXCESSIVE ⟨*exorbitant* prices⟩ — **ex·or·bi·tance** \-bət-ən(t)s\ *n* — **ex·or·bi·tant·ly** *adv*

ex·or·cise \'ek-ˌsȯr-ˌsīz, -sər-\ *vb* **1** : to drive (as an evil spirit) off by calling upon some holy name or by spells **2** : to free (as a person or place) from an evil spirit — **ex·or·cis·er** *n*

ex·or·cism \-ˌsiz-əm\ *n* **1** : the act or practice of exorcising **2** : a spell or formula used in exorcising — **ex·or·cist** \-ˌsist, -səst\ *n*

exo·skel·e·ton \ˌek-sō-'skel-ət-ən\ *n* : a hard supporting or protective structure (as of an insect, spider, or crustacean) developed on the outside of the body — **exo·skel·e·tal** \-ət-əl\ *adj*

exo·sphere \'ek-sō-ˌsfi(ə)r\ *n* : the outermost region of the atmosphere

exo·ther·mic \ˌek-sō-'thər-mik\ *or* **exo·ther·mal** \-məl\ *adj* : characterized by or formed by the giving off of heat ⟨an *exothermic* chemical reaction⟩

[1]**ex·ot·ic** \ig-'zät-ik\ *adj* **1** : introduced from another country ⟨*exotic* plants⟩ **2** : strikingly or excitingly different or unusual (as in color or design) — **ex·ot·i·cal·ly** \-'zät-i-k(ə-)lē\ *adv* — **ex·ot·ic·ness** \-ik-nəs\ *n*

[2]**exotic** *n* : something (as a plant) that is exotic

exp *abbr* **1** expanse **2** export **3** express

ex·pand \ik-'spand\ *vb* **1** : to open wide : UNFOLD ⟨a bird with wings *expanded*⟩ **2** : to take up or cause to take up more space : ENLARGE, SWELL ⟨metals *expand* under heat⟩ **3** : to develop more fully : work out in greater detail ⟨*expand* an argument⟩ **4** : to state in enlarged form or in a series : write out in full ⟨*expand* an equation⟩ — **ex·pand·a·ble** \-'span-də-bəl\ *adj* — **ex·pand·er** *n*

ex·panse \ik-'span(t)s\ *n* : a wide space, area, or stretch ⟨the vast *expanse* of the ocean⟩

ex·pan·sion \ik-'span-chən\ *n* **1** : the act or process of expanding **2** : the quality or state of being expanded **3** : something expanded or a result of expansion **4** : the result of an indicated operation ⟨the *expansion* of $(a + b)^2$ is $a^2 + 2ab + b^2$⟩

expansion valve *n* : a valve through which liquid or gas under pressure is allowed to expand to a lower pressure and greater volume

ex·pan·sive \ik-'span(t)-siv\ *adj* **1** : having a capacity or a tendency to expand ⟨gases are *expansive*⟩ **2** : causing or tending to cause expansion ⟨an *expansive* force⟩ **3** : characterized by high spirits or benevolent inclinations ⟨in an *expansive* mood⟩ **4** : having considerable extent : BROAD — **ex·pan·sive·ly** *adv* — **ex·pan·sive·ness** *n*

ex·pa·ti·ate \ek-'spā-shē-ˌāt\ *vb* : to speak or write at length or in detail — **ex·pa·ti·a·tion** \(ˌ)ek-ˌspā-shē-'ā-shən\ *n*

[1]**ex·pa·tri·ate** \ek-'spā-trē-ˌāt\ *vb* **1** : to drive into exile : BANISH **2** : to leave one's native country; *esp* : to renounce allegiance to one's native country — **ex·pa·tri·ate** \-trē-ˌāt, -trē-ət\ *adj or n* — **ex·pa·tri·a·tion** \(ˌ)ek-ˌspā-trē-'ā-shən\ *n*

ex·pect \ik-'spekt\ *vb* [from Latin *exspectare*, from *ex-* "out" and *spectare* "to look"] **1** : to believe that something will occur and await its happening ⟨*expect* rain⟩ ⟨*expect* him home soon⟩ **2** : to be pregnant ⟨she is *expecting*⟩ **3** : SUPPOSE, THINK **4 a** : to consider reasonable, due, or necessary ⟨*expect* an honest day's work⟩ **b** : to consider obligated ⟨*expect* him to pay his dues⟩ — **ex·pect·a·ble** \-'spek-tə-bəl\ *adj*

ex·pect·an·cy \ik-'spek-tən-sē\ *n, pl* **-cies** **1** : EXPECTATION **2** : the expected amount (as of years of life) based on statistical probability

ex·pect·ant \-tənt\ *adj* **1** : characterized by or being in a state of expectation **2** : expecting the birth of a child ⟨*expectant* fathers⟩; *esp* : PREGNANT — **expectant** *n* — **ex·pect·ant·ly** *adv*

ex·pec·ta·tion \ˌek-ˌspek-'tā-shən, ik-\ *n* **1** : the act or state of expecting : a looking forward to or waiting for something **2** : prospects of good or bad fortune — usu. used in pl. **3** : something expected

ex·pec·to·rant \ik-'spek-tə-rənt\ *adj* : tending to promote discharge of mucus from the respiratory tract — **expectorant** *n*

ex·pec·to·rate \ik-'spek-tə-ˌrāt\ *vb* : to discharge (as phlegm) from the throat or lungs by coughing and spitting; *also* : SPIT — **ex·pec·to·ra·tion** \-ˌspek-tə-'rā-shən\ *n*

ex·pe·di·ence \ik-'spēd-ē-ən(t)s\ *n* : EXPEDIENCY

ex·pe·di·en·cy \ik-'spēd-ē-ən-sē\ *n, pl* **-cies** **1** : suitability to the end in view or in a particular situation **2** : the use of means and methods advantageous to oneself without regard to principles of fairness and rightness

[1]**ex·pe·di·ent** \ik-'spēd-ē-ənt\ *adj* : suitable for bringing about a desired result often without regard to fairness or rightness — **ex·pe·di·ent·ly** *adv*

[2]**expedient** *n* : a means to accomplish an end; *esp* : one used in place of a better means that is not available

ex·pe·dite \'ek-spə-ˌdīt\ *vb* **1** : to carry out rapidly : execute promptly **2** : to hasten the process or progress of : FACILITATE **3** : to send out : DISPATCH

ex·pe·dit·er *also* **ex·pe·di·tor** \-ˌdīt-ər\ *n* : one that expedites; *esp* : one employed to ensure adequate supplies of raw materials and equipment or to coordinate the flow of materials, tools, parts, and processed goods within a plant

ex·pe·di·tion \ˌek-spə-'dish-ən\ *n* **1** : efficient promptness **2 a** : a sending or setting forth for some object or purpose **b** : a journey or trip undertaken for a specific purpose (as war or exploring) **c** : a group making such a journey

ex·pe·di·tion·ary \-'dish-ə-ˌner-ē\ *adj* : sent on military service abroad ⟨an *expeditionary* force⟩

ex·pe·di·tious \ˌek-spə-'dish-əs\ *adj* : characterized by or acting with promptness and efficiency : SPEEDY — **ex·pe·di·tious·ly** *adv* — **ex·pe·di·tious·ness** *n*

ex·pel \ik-'spel\ *vb* **ex·pelled**; **ex·pel·ling** **1** : to drive or force out ⟨*expel* air from the lungs⟩ **2** : to drive away; *esp* : DEPORT **3** : to cut off from membership ⟨*expelled* from college⟩ — **ex·pel·la·ble** \-'spel-ə-bəl\ *adj*

ex·pend \ik-'spend\ *vb* **1** : to pay out : SPEND **2** : to consume by use : use up

ex·pend·a·ble \ik-'spen-də-bəl\ *adj* : that may be used up in an ordinary way or sacrificed to accomplish a mission ⟨*expendable* ammunition⟩ ⟨*expendable* troops⟩ — **ex·pend·a·bil·i·ty** \-ˌspen-də-'bil-ət-ē\ *n* — **expendable** *n* — **ex·pend·a·bly** \-'spen-də-blē\ *adv*

ex·pen·di·ture \ik-'spen-di-chər, -də-ˌchu̇r\ *n* **1** : the act or process of expending **2** : an amount (as of money or time) expended

ex·pense \ik-'spen(t)s\ *n* **1 a** : something expended to secure a benefit or bring about a result **b** : financial burden or outlay : COST **2** : a cause of expenditure ⟨a car is a great *expense*⟩ **3** : SACRIFICE — usu. used in the phrase *at the expense of*

ex·pen·sive \ik-'spen(t)-siv\ *adj* **1** : occasioning great expense : COSTLY ⟨an *expensive* mistake⟩ **2** : high-priced : DEAR — **ex·pen·sive·ly** *adv* — **ex·pen·sive·ness** *n*

1**ex·pe·ri·ence** \ik-'spir-ē-ən(t)s\ *n* **1** : the living through an event or series of events esp. with awareness ⟨learn by *experience*⟩ **2** : something that one has done or lived through ⟨a soldier's *experiences* in war⟩ **3** : skill or knowledge gained by actually doing or feeling a thing ⟨a job that requires men with *experience*⟩ **4** : the amount or kind of work done or the time during which work has been done ⟨a man with five years' *experience*⟩ — **ex·pe·ri·en·tial** \-ˌspir-ē-'en-chəl\ *adj*

2**experience** *vb* **1** : to have experience of : UNDERGO **2** : to learn by experience ⟨*experience* what war is like⟩

ex·pe·ri·enced \ik-'spir-ē-ən(t)st\ *adj* : made skillful or wise through experience ⟨an *experienced* pilot⟩

1**ex·per·i·ment** \ik-'sper-ə-mənt\ *n* : TEST, TRIAL; *esp* : an operation carried out under controlled conditions in order to discover something, to test a hypothesis, or to serve as an example

2**ex·per·i·ment** \-ˌment\ *vb* : to make experiments — **ex·per·i·men·ta·tion** \ik-ˌsper-ə-mən-'tā-shən, -ˌmen-\ *n* — **ex·per·i·ment·er** \-'sper-ə-ˌment-ər\ *n*

1**ex·per·i·men·tal** \ik-ˌsper-ə-'ment-əl\ *adj* **1** : of, relating to, or based on experience or experiment **2** : having the characteristics of experiment : TENTATIVE — **ex·per·i·men·tal·ly** \-ə-lē\ *adv*

2**experimental** *n* : a plant or animal actually subjected to an experiment as contrasted to one kept for a control

experiment station *n* : an establishment for scientific research (as in agriculture) esp. of practical importance and for the dissemination of information

1**ex·pert** \'ek-ˌspərt, ik-'\ *adj* : having, involving, or displaying special skill or knowledge derived from training or experience ***syn*** see SKILLFUL ***ant*** amateurish — **ex·pert·ly** *adv* — **ex·pert·ness** *n*

2**ex·pert** \'ek-ˌspərt\ *n* : one who has acquired special skill in or knowledge of a subject

ex·pi·ate \'ek-spē-ˌāt\ *vb* **1** : to atone for : pay the penalty for **2** : to make amends for — **ex·pi·a·ble** \-spē-ə-bəl\ *adj* — **ex·pi·a·tion** \ˌek-spē-'ā-shən\ *n* — **ex·pi·a·tor** \'ek-spē-ˌāt-ər\ *n* — **ex·pi·a·to·ry** \'ek-spē-ə-ˌtōr-ē, -ˌtȯr-\ *adj*

ex·pi·ra·tion \ˌek-spə-'rā-shən\ *n* **1 a** : the expelling of air from the lungs in breathing **b** : air or vapor expelled from the lungs **2** : the fact of coming to an end : TERMINATION

ex·pi·ra·to·ry \ik-'spī-rə-ˌtōr-ē, ek-, -ˌtȯr-; 'ek-sp(ə-)rə-\ *adj* : of, relating to, or used in respiratory expiration

ex·pire \ik-'spī(ə)r, *oftenest for 3* ek-\ *vb* **1** : DIE **2** : to come to an end : STOP **3 a** : to emit the breath **b** : to breathe out from or as if from the lungs

ex·plain \ik-'splān\ *vb* **1** : to make plain or understandable **2** : to give the reason for or cause of — **ex·plain·a·ble** \-'splā-nə-bəl\ *adj* — **ex·plain·er** *n* — **ex·plan·a·to·ry** \ik-'splan-ə-ˌtōr-ē, -ˌtȯr-\ *adj* — **ex·plan·a·to·ri·ly** \-ˌsplan-ə-'tōr-ə-lē, -'tȯr-\ *adv*

ex·pla·na·tion \ˌek-splə-'nā-shən\ *n* **1** : the act or process of explaining **2** : something that explains : a statement that makes clear

ex·ple·tive \'ek-splət-iv\ *n* **1** : a word that anticipates a subsequent word or phrase which supplies the meaning ⟨*it* in "it is easy to say so" and in "make it clear which you prefer" is an *expletive*⟩ **2** : an exclamatory word or phrase; *esp* : one that is obscene or profane — **expletive** *adj*

ex·pli·cate \'ek-splə-ˌkāt\ *vb* : to give a detailed explanation of — **ex·plic·a·ble** \ek-'splik-ə-bəl, 'ek-(ˌ)splik-\ *adj* — **ex·pli·ca·tion** \ˌek-splə-'kā-shən\ *n* — **ex·plic·a·tive** \ek-'splik-ət-iv, 'ek-splə-ˌkāt-\ *adj* — **ex·pli·ca·tor** \'ek-splə-ˌkāt-ər\ *n* — **ex·plic·a·to·ry** \ek-'splik-ə-ˌtōr-ē, 'ek-(ˌ)splik-, -ˌtȯr-\ *adj*

ex·plic·it \ik-'splis-ət\ *adj* : so clear in statement that there is no doubt about the meaning : fully stated ⟨*explicit* instructions⟩ — **ex·plic·it·ly** *adv* — **ex·plic·it·ness** *n*

ex·plode \ik-'splōd\ *vb* **1** : to cause to be given up or rejected : DISCREDIT ⟨science has *exploded* many old ideas⟩ **2 a** : to burst or cause to burst violently and noisily **b** : to burn suddenly so that there is a violent expansion of hot gases with great disruptive force and a loud noise; *also* : to undergo an atomic nuclear reaction with similar but more violent effects **3** : to burst forth (as with anger or laughter)

ex·plod·ed \-'splōd-əd\ *adj* : showing the parts separated but in correct relationship to each other ⟨an *exploded* view of a carburetor⟩

1**ex·ploit** \'ek-ˌsplȯit, ik-'\ *n* : DEED, ACT; *esp* : a notable or heroic act

2**ex·ploit** \ik-'splȯit, 'ek-ˌ\ *vb* **1** : to extract value or use from : UTILIZE ⟨*exploit* a mine⟩ **2** : to make use of unfairly for one's own advantage — **ex·ploit·a·ble** \-ə-bəl\ *adj* — **ex·ploi·ta·tion** \ˌek-ˌsplȯi-'tā-shən\ *n* — **ex·ploit·er** \ik-'splȯit-ər, 'ek-ˌ\ *n*

ex·plo·ra·tion \ˌek-splə-'rā-shən\ *n* : the act or an instance of exploring — **ex·plor·a·tive** \ik-'splōr-ət-iv, -'splȯr-\ *adj* — **ex·plor·a·to·ry** \-ə-ˌtōr-ē, -ˌtȯr-\ *adj*

ex·plore \ik-'splō(ə)r, -'splȯ(ə)r\ *vb* **1 a** : to search through : look into **b** : to examine carefully and in detail esp. for diagnostic purposes ⟨*explore* a wound⟩ **c** : to penetrate into or range over for purposes of discovery ⟨*explore* the moon⟩ **2** : to make or conduct a systematic search ⟨*explore* for oil⟩

ex·plor·er \ik-'splōr-ər, -'splȯr-\ *n* : one that explores; *esp* : a person who travels in search of geographical or scientific information

ex·plo·sion \ik-'splō-zhən\ *n* **1** : the act or an instance of exploding **2** : a large-scale, rapid, and spectacular expansion, outbreak, or upheaval **3** : a violent outburst of feeling

1**ex·plo·sive** \ik-'splō-siv, -ziv\ *adj* **1** : relating to, characterized by, or operated by explosion **2** : tending to explode — **ex·plo·sive·ly** *adv* — **ex·plo·sive·ness** *n*

2**explosive** *n* : an explosive substance

ex·po·nent \ik-'spō-nənt, 'ek-ˌ\ *n* **1** : a symbol written above and to the right of a mathematical expression to indicate how many times the expression is to be repeated as a factor ⟨in the expression a^3, the *exponent 3* indicates that a is to be taken as a factor three times⟩ **2 a** : one that expounds or interprets

b : one that champions or advocates — **ex·po·nen·tial** \ˌek-spə-ˈnən-chəl\ *adj* — **ex·po·nen·tial·ly** \-ˈnench-(ə-)lē\ *adv*

1**ex·port** \ek-ˈspōrt, -ˈspȯrt, ˈek-ˌ\ *vb* : to carry or send to another country or place esp. for sale — **ex·port·a·ble** \-ə-bəl\ *adj* — **ex·por·ta·tion** \ˌek-ˌspōr-ˈtā-shən, -ˌspȯr-, -spər-\ *n* — **ex·port·er** \ek-ˈspōrt-ər, -ˈspȯrt-, ˈek-ˌ\ *n*

2**ex·port** \ˈek-ˌspōrt, -ˌspȯrt\ *n* **1** : something exported; *esp* : a commodity conveyed from one country or region to another for purposes of trade **2** : an act of exporting : EXPORTATION — **export** *adj*

ex·pose \ik-ˈspōz\ *vb* **1 a** : to deprive of shelter, protection, or care ⟨*expose* troops needlessly⟩ **b** : to submit or subject to an action or influence; *esp* : to subject (as a sensitive photographic film) to the action of light **c** : to abandon (an infant) in the open **2** : to lay open to view : DISPLAY **3** : to bring to light : UNMASK ⟨*expose* a murderer⟩ — **ex·pos·er** *n*

ex·po·sé \ˌek-spō-ˈzā\ *n* : an exposure of something discreditable

ex·po·si·tion \ˌek-spə-ˈzish-ən\ *n* **1** : an explaining of the meaning or purpose of something **2** : a composition that explains **3** : a public exhibition or show **4** : the first part of a musical composition in which the theme is presented — **ex·pos·i·tor** \ik-ˈspäz-ət-ər\ *n* — **ex·pos·i·to·ry** \ik-ˈspäz-ə-ˌtōr-ē, -ˌtȯr-\ *adj*

ex·pos·tu·late \ik-ˈspäs-chə-ˌlāt\ *vb* : to reason earnestly with a person against something he has done or intends to do : REMONSTRATE — **ex·pos·tu·la·tion** \-ˌspäs-chə-ˈlā-shən\ *n* — **ex·pos·tu·la·to·ry** \-ˈspäs-chə-lə-ˌtōr-ē, -ˌtȯr-\ *adj*

ex·po·sure \ik-ˈspō-zhər\ *n* **1** : the act or an instance of exposing: as **a** : disclosure to view **b** : UNMASKING **c** : abandonment of an infant in the open **2 a** : a condition of being exposed esp. to danger ⟨*exposure* to hostile fire⟩ ⟨*exposure* to the storm⟩ **b** : a position with respect to direction or to general weather conditions ⟨a southern *exposure*⟩ **3 a** : a section of a film for a single picture **b** : the time during which a photographic film is exposed

ex·pound \ik-ˈspau̇nd\ *vb* **1** : to set forth : STATE **2** : to state clearly and in detail the meaning of : INTERPRET — **ex·pound·er** *n*

1**ex·press** \ik-ˈspres\ *adj* **1 a** : directly and distinctly stated : EXPLICIT **b** : EXACT, PRECISE **2** : SPECIAL **3 a** : traveling at high speed; *esp* : traveling with few or no stops ⟨*express* train⟩ **b** : adapted or suitable for travel at high speed ⟨an *express* route⟩

2**express** *adv* : by express ⟨send a package *express*⟩

3**express** *n* **1 a** : a system for special transportation of goods at premium rates **b** : a company operating such a service or the goods or shipments so transported **2** : an express vehicle

4**express** *vb* **1 a** : to represent esp. in words : STATE **b** : to give expression to one's opinions, feelings, or abilities **c** : SYMBOLIZE **2** : to press or squeeze out **3** : to send by express — **ex·press·er** *n* — **ex·press·i·ble** \-ə-bəl\ *adj*

ex·pres·sion \ik-ˈspresh-ən\ *n* **1** : the act or process of expressing esp. in words **2 a** : a word, phrase, or sign that represents a thought, feeling, or quality; *esp* : a significant word or phrase **b** : a mathematical symbol or a combination of symbols and signs representing a quantity or operation **3** : a way of speaking or singing or of playing an instrument so as to show mood or feeling ⟨sing with *expression*⟩ **4** : LOOK, APPEARANCE ⟨a pleased *expression*⟩ **5** : the detectable effect of a gene **6** : an act or product of pressing out — **ex·pres·sion·less** \-ləs\ *adj*

ex·pres·sive \ik-ˈspres-iv\ *adj* **1** : of or relating to expression **2** : serving to express **3** : full of expression : MEANINGFUL — **ex·pres·sive·ly** *adv* — **ex·pres·sive·ness** *n*

ex·press·ly \ik-ˈspres-lē\ *adv* **1** : PLAINLY, EXPLICITLY **2** : for the express purpose : ESPECIALLY ⟨came *expressly* to congratulate him⟩

ex·press·man \ik-ˈspres-ˌman, -mən\ *n* : a person employed in the express business

ex·press·way \-ˌwā\ *n* : a divided superhighway that is for through traffic and that may be entered and left only at special places

expt *abbr* experiment

exptl *abbr* experimental

ex·pul·sion \ik-ˈspəl-shən\ *n* : the act of expelling : the state of being expelled — **ex·pul·sive** \-ˈpəl-siv\ *adj*

ex·punge \ik-ˈspənj\ *vb* **1** : to blot out : rub out : ERASE **2** : CANCEL — **ex·pung·er** *n*

ex·pur·gate \ˈek-spər-ˌgāt\ *vb* : to clear of something wrong or objectionable; *esp* : to clear (as a book) of objectionable words or passages — **ex·pur·ga·tion** \ˌek-spər-ˈgā-shən\ *n* — **ex·pur·ga·tor** \ˈek-spər-ˌgāt-ər\ *n*

ex·quis·ite \ek-ˈskwiz-ət, ˈek-(ˌ)skwiz-\ *adj* [from Latin *exquisitus* meaning literally "sought out", "searched for"] **1** : marked by flawless craftsmanship or delicate execution **2** : keenly appreciative **3** : pleasing through beauty, fitness, or perfection **4** : ACUTE, INTENSE ⟨*exquisite* pain⟩ — **ex·quis·ite·ly** *adv* — **ex·quis·ite·ness** *n*

ext *abbr* extension

ex·tant \ˈek-stənt, ek-ˈstant\ *adj* : currently existing : not destroyed or lost

ex·tem·po·ra·ne·ous \(ˌ)ek-ˌstem-pə-ˈrā-nē-əs\ *adj* : composed, performed, or uttered on the spur of the moment : IMPROMPTU — **ex·tem·po·ra·ne·ous·ly** *adv* — **ex·tem·po·ra·ne·ous·ness** *n*

ex·tem·po·re \ik-ˈstem-pə-(ˌ)rē\ *adv* : EXTEMPORANEOUSLY — **extempore** *adj*

ex·tem·po·rize \ik-ˈstem-pə-ˌrīz\ *vb* : to do, make, or utter extempore : IMPROVISE — **ex·tem·po·ri·za·tion** \-ˌstem-pə-rə-ˈzā-shən\ *n* — **ex·tem·po·riz·er** \-ˈstem-pə-ˌrī-zər\ *n*

ex·tend \ik-ˈstend\ *vb* **1** : to straighten out or stretch forth ⟨*extended* his arm⟩ **2** : EXERT **3 a** : to offer to someone ⟨*extend* an apology⟩ **b** : to make available ⟨*extend* credit⟩ **4 a** : to stretch out : LENGTHEN **b** : ENLARGE **c** : BROADEN **5 a** : to span a distance, space, or time : REACH, RANGE ⟨the woods *extend* over a wide area⟩ ⟨the road *extends* to the town⟩ **b** : to span an interval of distance, space, or time ⟨the bridge *extends* across the river⟩ — **ex·tend·i·ble** \-ˈsten-də-bəl\ *or* **ex·ten·si·ble** \-ˈsten(t)-sə-bəl\ *adj* — **ex·ten·si·bil·i·ty** \-ˌsten(t)-sə-ˈbil-ət-ē\ *n*

ex·ten·sion \ik-ˈsten-chən\ *n* **1 a** : the act of extending : the state of being extended **b** : something extended **2** : EXTENT, RANGE **3** : the property of occupying space **4** : a granting of extra time to fulfill an obligation **5** : education by special programs (as correspondence courses) at a distance from a school **6 a** : a part forming an addition or increase **b** : an extra telephone connected to the principal line — **ex·ten·sion·al** \-ˈstench-(ə-)nəl\ *adj* — **ex·ten·sion·al·ly** \-ē\ *adv*

ex·ten·sive \ik-'sten(t)-siv\ *adj* : having wide or considerable extent — **ex·ten·sive·ly** *adv* — **ex·ten·sive·ness** *n*
ex·ten·sor \ik-'sten(t)-sər\ *n* : a muscle serving to extend a bodily part (as a limb)
ex·tent \ik-'stent\ *n* **1 a** : the range, distance, or space over or through which something extends **b** : the point, degree, or limit to which something extends **2** : an extended tract or region
ex·ten·u·ate \ik-'sten-yə-,wāt\ *vb* **1** : to make excuses for **2** : to serve as a partial excuse for ⟨his extreme youth *extenuated* his behavior⟩ — **ex·ten·u·a·tion** \-,sten-yə-'wā-shən\ *n* — **ex·ten·u·a·tor** \-'sten-yə-,wāt-ər\ *n* — **ex·ten·u·a·to·ry** \-wə-,tōr-ē, -,tȯr-\ *adj*
[1]**ex·te·ri·or** \ek-'stir-ē-ər\ *adj* : EXTERNAL, OUTER ⟨an *exterior* surface⟩ ⟨*exterior* paint⟩ — **ex·te·ri·or·ly** *adv*
[2]**exterior** *n* **1** : OUTSIDE **2** : outward manner or appearance ⟨a calm *exterior*⟩
exterior angle *n* : an angle formed by a transversal cutting two lines and lying outside the latter
ex·ter·mi·nate \ik-'stər-mə-,nāt\ *vb* : to get rid of completely : ANNIHILATE — **ex·ter·mi·na·tion** \-,stər-mə-'nā-shən\ *n* — **ex·ter·mi·na·tor** \-'stər-mə-,nāt-ər\ *n*
[1]**ex·ter·nal** \ek-'stərn-əl\ *adj* **1** : outwardly visible ⟨*external* signs⟩ **2 a** : of, relating to, or connected with the outside or an outer part **b** : applied or applicable to the outside **3 a** : situated outside, apart, or beyond **b** : arising or acting from outside ⟨*external* force⟩ **4** : of or relating to relationships with foreign countries — **ex·ter·nal·ly** \-ə-lē\ *adv*
[2]**external** *n* : an external feature or aspect — usu. used in pl.
external–combustion engine *n* : a heat engine (as a steam engine) that derives its heat from fuel consumed outside the engine cylinder
external ear *n* : the outer part of the ear consisting of the sound-collecting pinna and the canal leading from this to the eardrum
ex·tinct \ik-'sting(k)t, 'ek-,\ *adj* **1** : no longer active ⟨an *extinct* volcano⟩ **2** : no longer existing in the living state ⟨an *extinct* species of animal⟩ — **ex·tinc·tion** \ik-'sting(k)-shən\ *n*
ex·tin·guish \ik-'sting-gwish\ *vb* **1** : to cause to cease burning or glowing **2** : DESTROY, CRUSH — **ex·tin·guish·a·ble** \-ə-bəl\ *adj*
ex·tin·guish·er \-ər\ *n* : one that extinguishes; *esp* : FIRE EXTINGUISHER
ex·tir·pate \'ek-stər-,pāt, ek-'\ *vb* **1** : to pull up by the roots **2** : to eradicate or destroy wholly — **ex·tir·pa·tion** \,ek-(,)stər-'pā-shən\ *n* — **ex·tir·pa·tive** \'ek-stər-,pāt-iv, ek-'stər-pət-\ *adj* — **ex·tir·pa·tor** \-,pāt-ər, -pət-\ *n*
ex·tol *also* **ex·toll** \ik-'stōl\ *vb* **ex·tolled**; **ex·tol·ling** : to praise highly : GLORIFY — **ex·tol·ler** *n* — **ex·tol·ment** \-'stōl-mənt\ *n*
ex·tort \ik-'stȯrt\ *vb* : to get (as money or a confession) from a person by the use of force or threats — **ex·tort·er** *n* — **ex·tor·tion** \ik-'stȯr-shən\ *n* — **ex·tor·tion·er** \-sh(ə-)nər\ *n* — **ex·tor·tion·ist** \-sh(ə-)nəst\ *n* — **ex·tor·tive** \-'stȯrt-iv\ *adj*
ex·tor·tion·ate \ik-'stȯr-sh(ə-)nət\ *adj* **1** : characterized by extortion **2** : EXCESSIVE, EXORBITANT ⟨*extortionate* prices⟩ ⟨*extortionate* fees⟩ — **ex·tor·tion·ate·ly** *adv*
[1]**ex·tra** \'ek-strə\ *adj* **1 a** : more than is due, usual, or necessary : ADDITIONAL ⟨*extra* work⟩ **b** : subject to an additional charge **2** : SUPERIOR ⟨*extra* quality⟩
[2]**extra** *n* : something extra: as **a** : a special edition of a newspaper **b** : an additional actor hired to act in a group scene (as in a motion picture, television show, or stage production)
[3]**extra** *adv* : beyond the usual size, extent, or degree ⟨*extra* long⟩
extra- *prefix* : outside : beyond ⟨*extra*judicial⟩
ex·tra·cel·lu·lar \,ek-strə-'sel-yə-lər\ *adj* : situated or occurring outside a cell or the cells of the body — **ex·tra·cel·lu·lar·ly** *adv*
[1]**ex·tract** \ik-'strakt, *oftenest in sense 5* 'ek-,\ *vb* **1** : to draw forth : pull out **2** : to separate or otherwise obtain (as a juice or a constituent element) by physical or chemical process **3** : to separate (a metal) from an ore **4** : to calculate a mathematical root **5** : to select (excerpts) and copy out — **ex·tract·a·ble** *or* **ex·tract·i·ble** \ik-'strak-tə-bəl, 'ek-,\ *adj* — **ex·trac·tor** \-tər\ *n*
[2]**ex·tract** \'ek-,strakt\ *n* **1** : a selection from a writing or discourse : EXCERPT **2** : a product (as an essence or concentrate) prepared by extracting; *esp* : a solution of essential components of a complex material ⟨vanilla *extract*⟩
ex·trac·tion \ik-'strak-shən\ *n* **1** : the act or process of extracting ⟨*extraction* of a tooth⟩ **2** : the origin of a person : DESCENT ⟨a man of French *extraction*⟩ **3** : something extracted
ex·tra·cur·ric·u·lar \,ek-strə-kə-'rik-yə-lər\ *adj* : not falling within the curriculum; *esp* : of or relating to those activities (as debating and athletics) that form part of the life of students but are not part of the courses of study
ex·tra·dite \'ek-strə-,dīt\ *vb* : to cause to be delivered or given up to a different legal authority as an alleged criminal for trial ⟨the prisoner was *extradited* from New York to New Jersey⟩ — **ex·tra·dit·a·ble** \-,dīt-ə-bəl\ *adj* — **ex·tra·di·tion** \,ek-strə-'dish-ən\ *n*
ex·tra·ne·ous \ek-'strā-nē-əs\ *adj* **1** : not forming an essential or vital part : ACCIDENTAL **2** : IRRELEVANT — **ex·tra·ne·ous·ly** *adv* — **ex·tra·ne·ous·ness** *n*
ex·traor·di·nary \ik-'strȯrd-ə-,ner-ē, ,ek-strə-'ȯrd-\ *adj* **1 a** : going beyond what is usual, regular, or customary ⟨*extraordinary* powers⟩ **b** : very exceptional : REMARKABLE ⟨a girl of *extraordinary* beauty⟩ **2** : employed on a special service ⟨an ambassador *extraordinary*⟩ — **ex·traor·di·nar·i·ly** \ik-,strȯrd-ə-'ner-ə-lē, ,ek-strə-,ȯrd-\ *adv* — **ex·traor·di·nar·i·ness** \ik-'strȯrd-ə-,ner-ē-nəs, ,ek-strə-'ȯrd-\ *n*
extra point *n* **1** : a point scored in football after a touchdown by drop-kicking or place-kicking **2** *pl* : two points scored after a touchdown by advancing the ball across the goal line in one play
ex·trap·o·late \ik-'strap-ə-,lāt\ *vb* : to infer unknown facts from known facts — **ex·trap·o·la·tion** \-,strap-ə-'lā-shən\ *n* — **ex·trap·o·la·tor** \-'strap-ə-,lāt-ər\ *n*
ex·tra·sen·so·ry \,ek-strə-'sen(t)s-(ə-)rē\ *adj* : extending or occurring beyond the known senses
extrasensory perception *n* : an awareness of events or facts that cannot be explained by communication using any of the known senses
ex·tra·ter·res·tri·al \-tə-'res-trē-əl\ *adj* : originating or existing outside the earth or its atmosphere ⟨*extraterrestrial* life⟩
ex·tra·ter·ri·to·ri·al \-,ter-ə-'tōr-ē-əl, -'tȯr-\ *adj* **1** : located outside a jurisdiction **2** : of or relating to extraterritoriality ⟨*extraterritorial* rights⟩ — **ex·tra·ter·ri·to·ri·al·ly** \-ē-ə-lē\ *adv*
ex·tra·ter·ri·to·ri·al·i·ty \-,tōr-ē-'al-ət-ē, -,tȯr-\ *n* : exemption from local law ⟨diplomats enjoy *extraterritoriality*⟩
extratropical cyclone *n* : a cyclone outside the trop-

E

ics that is often 1500 miles in diameter and may exhibit great variation in wind strength

ex·trav·a·gance \ik-'strav-i-gən(t)s\ *n* **1 a** : an extravagant act; *esp* : an excessive outlay of money **b** : something extravagant **2** : the quality or fact of being extravagant

ex·trav·a·gant \-gənt\ *adj* **1** : going beyond what is reasonable or suitable ⟨*extravagant* praise⟩ **2** : wasteful esp. of money **3** : too high : EXCESSIVE ⟨an *extravagant* price⟩ — **ex·trav·a·gant·ly** *adv*

ex·trav·a·gan·za \ik-ˌstrav-ə-'gan-zə\ *n* **1** : a literary or musical work marked by extreme freedom of style and structure **2** : a spectacular show

ex·tra·ve·hic·u·lar \ˌek-strə-vē-'hik-yə-lər\ *adj* : taking place outside a vehicle (as a spacecraft)

1ex·treme \ik-'strēm\ *adj* **1** : existing in the greatest possible degree ⟨*extreme* poverty⟩ **2** : FARTHEST **3** : UTMOST — **ex·treme·ly** *adv* — **ex·treme·ness** *n*

2extreme *n* **1** : an extreme state, condition, or degree **2** : something situated as far away as possible from another ⟨*extremes* of heat and cold⟩ **3** : the first term or the last term of a mathematical proportion **4** : an extreme measure or expedient

ex·trem·ism \ik-'strē-ˌmiz-əm\ *n* : advocacy or practice of extreme measures esp. in politics — **ex·trem·ist** \-məst\ *n or adj*

ex·trem·i·ty \ik-'strem-ət-ē\ *n, pl* **-ties 1** : the farthest or most remote part, section, or point **2** : a limb of the body; *esp* : a human hand or foot **3** : extreme danger or critical need **4** : the utmost degree (as of emotion or pain) **5** : a drastic or desperate act or measure

ex·tri·cate \'ek-strə-ˌkāt\ *vb* : to free or remove from an entanglement or difficulty — **ex·tri·ca·ble** \ek-'strik-ə-bəl, 'ek-(ˌ)strik-\ *adj* — **ex·tri·ca·tion** \ˌek-strə-'kā-shən\ *n*

ex·trin·sic \ek-'strin-zik, -'strin(t)-sik\ *adj* : not forming part of or belonging to a thing : EXTRANEOUS — **ex·trin·si·cal·ly** \-zi-k(ə-)lē, -si-\ *adv*

ex·tro·vert \'ek-strə-ˌvərt\ *n* : a person more interested in what he does and what goes on about him than in what he thinks or imagines — **ex·tro·ver·sion** \ˌek-strə-'vər-zhən\ *n* — **ex·tro·vert·ed** \'ek-strə-ˌvərt-əd\ *or* **extrovert** *adj*

ex·trude \ik-'strüd\ *vb* **1** : to force, press, or push out **2** : to shape (as metal) by forcing through a die **3** : to become extruded — **ex·tru·sion** \-'strü-zhən\ *n*

ex·tru·sive \ik-'strü-siv, -ziv\ *adj* : formed by crystallization of lava poured out at the earth's surface ⟨*extrusive* rock⟩

ex·u·ber·ant \ig-'zü-b(ə-)rənt\ *adj* **1** : ABUNDANT **2** : filled with life, vigor, and high spirits **3** : carried to or experienced in an extreme degree — **ex·u·ber·ance** \-b(ə-)rən(t)s\ *n* — **ex·u·ber·ant·ly** *adv*

ex·u·date \'eks-ə-ˌdāt, 'egz-\ *n* : exuded matter

ex·ude \ig-'züd\ *vb* [from Latin *exsudare*, from *ex-* "out" and *sudor* "sweat", from the same source as English *sweat*] **1** : to discharge slowly through pores or cuts : OOZE ⟨*exude* sweat⟩ ⟨sap *exuding* from a cut stem⟩ **2** : to give forth : EMIT ⟨*exuded* charm⟩ — **ex·u·da·tion** \ˌeks-ə-'dā-shən, ˌegz-\ *n*

ex·ult \ig-'zəlt\ *vb* : to be extremely joyful : REJOICE — **ex·ult·ing·ly** \-'zəl-ting-lē\ *adv*

ə abut	ər further	a back	ā bake
ä cot, cart	aù out	ch chin	e less	ē easy
g gift	i trip	ī life	j joke	ng sing	ō flow
ȯ flaw	ȯi coin	th thin	th this	ü loot
ů foot	y yet	yü few	yů furious	zh vision

ex·ult·ant \ig-'zəlt-ənt\ *adj* : EXULTING, JUBILANT — **ex·ult·ant·ly** *adv*

ex·ul·ta·tion \ˌeks-(ˌ)əl-'tā-shən, ˌegz-\ *n* : the act of exulting : the state of being exultant

ex·urb \'ek-ˌsərb, 'eg-ˌzərb\ *n* : a region or district outside a city and its suburbs inhabited chiefly by well-to-do families — **ex·ur·ban·ite** \ek-'sər-bə-ˌnīt, eg-'zər-\ *n* — **ex·ur·bia** \ek-'sər-bē-ə, eg-'zər-\ *n*

-ey — see -Y

1eye \'ī\ *n* **1** : an organ of sight; *esp* : a rounded hollow organ lined with a sensitive retina and lodged in a bony orbit in the vertebrate skull **2 a** : ability to see or appreciate ⟨a good *eye* for painting⟩ **b** : LOOK, GLANCE ⟨gave her the *eye*⟩ **c** : close attention ⟨keep an *eye* on the store while I'm gone⟩ **d** : POINT OF VIEW, JUDGMENT ⟨guilty in the *eyes* of the law⟩ **3** : something suggestive of an eye: as **a** : the hole through the head of a needle **b** : a loop to receive a hook **c** : an undeveloped bud (as on a potato) **d** : a device (as a photoelectric cell) that functions in a manner analogous to human vision **4** : something central : CENTER ⟨the *eye* of a hurricane⟩ — **eyed** \'īd\ *adj* — **eye·less** \'ī-ləs\ *adj* — **eye·like** \-ˌlīk\ *adj*

eye 3b

2eye *vb* **eyed**; **eye·ing** *or* **ey·ing** : to watch closely

eye·ball \'ī-ˌbȯl\ *n* : the vertebrate eye

eye·brow \-ˌbraů\ *n* : the ridge over the eye or hair growing on it

eye·cup \-ˌkəp\ *n* : a small oval cup with a rim curved to fit the orbit of the eye used for applying liquid remedies to the eyes

eye·drop·per \-ˌdräp-ər\ *n* : DROPPER 2

eye·drop·per·ful \-ˌfůl\ *n* : the amount held by an eyedropper

eye·ful \'ī-ˌfůl\ *n* **1** : a full or satisfying view **2** : one that is visually attractive

eye·glass \-ˌglas\ *n* **1 a** : a glass lens used to improve faulty eyesight **b** *pl* : GLASSES **2** : EYEPIECE

eye·hole \-ˌhōl\ *n* **1** : EYE SOCKET **2** : PEEPHOLE

eye·lash \-ˌlash\ *n* **1** : the fringe of hair edging the eyelid **2** : a single hair of the eyelash

eye·let \'ī-lət\ *n* **1** : a small hole designed to receive a cord or used for decoration **2** : a small ring to reinforce an eyelet : GROMMET

eye·lid \-ˌlid\ *n* : one of the movable lids of skin and muscle that can be closed over the eyeball

eye·piece \-ˌpēs\ *n* : the lens or combination of lenses at the eye end of an optical instrument

eye·sight \-ˌsīt\ *n* : SIGHT, VISION ⟨keen *eyesight*⟩

eye socket *n* : one of the bone-lined cavities for the eyes in the vertebrate skull

eye·sore \'ī-ˌsōr, -ˌsȯr\ *n* : something displeasing to the sight

eye·spot \-ˌspät\ *n* : a simple or primitive visual organ

eye·stalk \-ˌstȯk\ *n* : a movable stalk bearing an eye at the tip in a crustacean

eye·strain \'ī-ˌstrān\ *n* : weariness or a strained state of the eye

eye·tooth \-'tüth\ *n* : a canine tooth of the upper jaw

eye·wash \-ˌwȯsh, -ˌwäsh\ *n* : an eye lotion

eye·wit·ness \-'wit-nəs\ *n* : a person who sees an occurrence and is able to give a firsthand account of it

ey·rie \'ī(ə)r-ē, *or like* AERIE\ *var of* AERIE

Eze·kiel \i-'zē-kyəl, -kē-əl\ *n* — see BIBLE table

Ez·ra \'ez-rə\ *n* — see BIBLE table

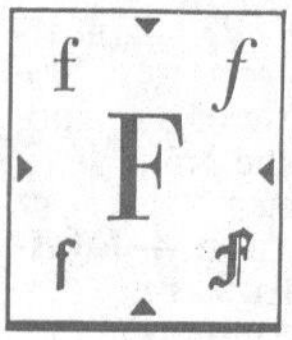

f \'ef\ *n, often cap* **1 :** the 6th letter of the English alphabet **2 :** the musical tone F **3 :** a grade rating a student's work as failing
f *abbr* **1** female **2** feminine **3** focal length **4** folio **5** following **6** forte **7** frequency
F *abbr* **1** Fahrenheit **2** fair **3** French
fa \'fä\ *n* **:** the 4th note of the diatonic scale
fa·ble \'fā-bəl\ *n* **:** a fictitious story; *esp* **:** one intended to teach a lesson and in which animals speak and act like human beings — **fab·u·list** \'fab-yə-ləst\ *n*
fa·bled \'fā-bəld\ *adj* **1 :** FICTITIOUS **2 :** told or celebrated in fable ⟨*fabled* mountain of glass⟩
fab·ric \'fab-rik\ *n* **1 :** STRUCTURE, FRAMEWORK ⟨the *fabric* of society⟩ **2 :** CLOTH
fab·ri·cate \'fab-ri-ˌkāt\ *vb* **1 :** CONSTRUCT, MANUFACTURE **2 :** INVENT, CREATE **3 :** to make up in order to deceive — **fab·ri·ca·tion** \ˌfab-ri-'kā-shən\ *n* — **fab·ri·ca·tor** \'fab-ri-ˌkāt-ər\ *n*
fab·u·lous \'fab-yə-ləs\ *adj* **1 :** told in or based on fable ⟨*fabulous* animals⟩ **2 :** resembling a fable esp. in exaggeration **:** EXTRAORDINARY, WONDERFUL ⟨*fabulous* adventures of an explorer⟩ — **fab·u·lous·ly** *adv* — **fab·u·lous·ness** *n*
fa·cade *also* **fa·çade** \fə-'säd\ *n* **1 :** the front of a building **2 :** a false, superficial, or artificial appearance ⟨a *facade* of wealth⟩
¹face \'fās\ *n* **1 :** the front part of the head **2 :** PRESENCE ⟨brave in the *face* of danger⟩ **3 a :** facial expression ⟨put a sad *face* on⟩ **b :** GRIMACE ⟨make a *face*⟩ **4 a :** outward appearance ⟨suspicious on the *face* of it⟩ **b :** DIGNITY, PRESTIGE ⟨afraid to lose *face*⟩ **5 a :** a front, upper, or outer surface ⟨the *face* of a cliff⟩ **b :** any of the plane surfaces that bound a geometric solid ⟨*faces* of a crystal⟩ ⟨*faces* of a pyramid⟩ **c :** a surface or side that is marked or specially prepared ⟨the *face* of a clock⟩ **6 :** the end (as of a mine tunnel) at which work is progressing — **faced** \'fāst\ *adj*
²face *vb* **1 a :** to line near the edge esp. with a different material ⟨*face* a hem⟩ **b :** to cover the front or surface of ⟨*faced* the building with marble⟩ **2 :** to bring face to face ⟨*faced* him with the evidence⟩ **3 a :** to stand or sit with the face toward ⟨*face* the class⟩ **b :** to front on ⟨a house *facing* the park⟩ **4 :** to oppose firmly ⟨*faces* danger bravely⟩ ⟨*faced* up to his foe⟩ **5 :** to turn toward ⟨*face* the east⟩
face card *n* **:** a king, queen, or jack in a deck of cards
face–lift·ing \'fās-ˌlif-ting\ *n* **1 :** plastic surgery for removal of facial defects (as wrinkles or sagging) **2 :** MODERNIZATION
fac·et \'fas-ət\ *n* [from French *facette*, meaning "a little face"] **1 :** a small plane surface (as on a cut gem) **2 :** ASPECT, PHASE **3 :** the surface of a functional unit of vision of a compound eye — **fac·et·ed** \'fas-ət-əd\ *adj*

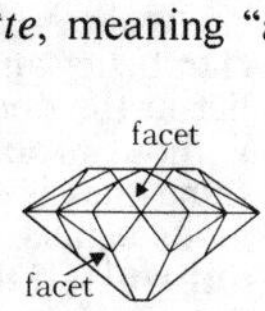

facet 1

fa·ce·tious \fə-'sē-shəs\ *adj* **1 :** JOCULAR **2 :** marked by unseemly jesting or ironic levity **:** FLIPPANT ⟨welcomes serious and relevant but not *facetious* questions⟩ — **fa·ce·tious·ly** *adv* — **fa·ce·tious·ness** *n*
face–to–face \ˌfās-tə-'fās\ *adv or adj* **1 :** within each other's close presence ⟨we met *face-to-face* for the first time⟩ **2 :** having to make a decision or to take action ⟨*face-to-face* with an emergency case⟩
face value *n* **1 :** the value indicated on the face of a bill or note **2 :** the apparent value or significance ⟨can't take a braggart's statement at *face value*⟩
¹fa·cial \'fā-shəl\ *adj* **:** of or relating to the face — **fa·cial·ly** \-shə-lē\ *adv*
²facial *n* **:** a facial treatment or massage
fac·ile \'fas-əl\ *adj* **1 :** easily done, handled, or attained **2 :** mild or yielding in disposition **:** PLIANT **3 :** READY, FLUENT ⟨a *facile* writer⟩ — **fac·ile·ly** \-ə(l)-lē\ *adv*
fa·cil·i·tate \fə-'sil-ə-ˌtāt\ *vb* **:** to make easier — **fa·cil·i·ta·tion** \-ˌsil-ə-'tā-shən\ *n*
fa·cil·i·ty \fə-'sil-ət-ē\ *n, pl* **-ties 1 :** freedom from difficulty **:** EASE ⟨can be handled with *facility*⟩ **2 :** APTITUDE, SKILL **3 a :** something that facilitates an action, operation, or course of conduct — usu. used in pl. ⟨library *facilities*⟩ **b :** something (as a hospital) that is built, installed, or established to serve a particular purpose
fac·ing \'fā-sing\ *n* **1 a :** a lining at the edge esp. of a garment **b** *pl* **:** the collar, cuffs, and trimmings of a uniform coat **2 :** an ornamental or protective layer ⟨a frame house with brick *facing*⟩ **3 :** material for facing
fac·sim·i·le \fak-'sim-ə-lē\ *n* **1 :** an exact copy **2 :** the process of transmitting printed matter or still pictures by wire or radio for reproduction
fact \'fakt\ *n* **1 :** a thing done **:** DEED; *esp* **:** CRIME ⟨accessory after the *fact*⟩ **2 :** the quality of being actual **3 a :** something that exists or occurs **:** EVENT, ACTUALITY **b :** an occurrence, quality, or relation that can be experienced or inferred ⟨a number *fact*⟩ **c :** a piece of information about a fact ⟨a book filled with *facts*⟩
fac·tion \'fak-shən\ *n* **1 :** a group acting together within a larger body **:** CLIQUE **2 :** DISSENSION *syn* see PARTY — **fac·tion·al** \-sh(ə-)nəl\ *adj* — **fac·tion·al·ism** \-ˌiz-əm\ *n*
fac·tious \'fak-shəs\ *adj* **1 :** of, relating to, or caused by faction **2 :** inclined to faction or the formation of factions ⟨*factious* politicians⟩ — **fac·tious·ly** *adv* — **fac·tious·ness** *n*
fac·ti·tious \fak-'tish-əs\ *adj* **:** not natural or genuine **:** ARTIFICIAL ⟨a *factitious* display of grief⟩ — **fac·ti·tious·ly** *adv* — **fac·ti·tious·ness** *n*
¹fac·tor \'fak-tər\ *n* **1 :** one that buys or sells property for another **:** AGENT **2 :** something that contributes to the production of a result **:** INGREDIENT **3 :** GENE **4 :** any of the numbers or symbols in mathematics that when multiplied together form a product — **fac·to·ri·al** \fak-'tōr-ē-əl, -'tȯr-\ *adj*
²factor *vb* **fac·tored; fac·tor·ing** \-t(ə-)ring\ **:** to resolve into mathematical factors — **fac·tor·a·ble** \-t(ə-)rə-bəl\ *adj*
fac·tor·iza·tion \ˌfak-tə-rə-'zā-shən\ *n* **:** the act or process or an instance of factoring
fac·to·ry \'fak-t(ə-)rē\ *n, pl* **-ries 1 :** a trading station where resident factors trade **2 :** a building or set of buildings with facilities for manufacturing
fac·to·tum \fak-'tōt-əm\ *n* **:** an employee with many varied duties
fac·tu·al \'fak-chə(-wə)l\ *adj* **1 :** of or relating to facts **2 :** restricted to or based on fact — **fac·tu·al·i·ty** \ˌfak-chə-'wal-ət-ē\ *n* — **fac·tu·al·ly** \'fak-chə(-wə)-lē\ *adv* — **fac·tu·al·ness** \-chə(-wə)l-nəs\ *n*
fac·ul·ty \'fak-əl-tē\ *n, pl* **-ties 1 :** ability to do something **:** TALENT ⟨a *faculty* for making friends⟩ **2 :** one of the powers of the mind or body ⟨the *faculty* of hearing⟩ **3 a :** the teachers in a school or college **b :** a department of instruction in a university ⟨the *faculty* of law⟩
fad \'fad\ *n* **:** a practice or interest followed for a

time with exaggerated zeal : CRAZE — **fad·dist** \'fad-əst\ *n*
[1]**fade** \'fād\ *vb* **1** : to lose freshness or vitality : WITHER **2** : to lose or cause to lose brilliance of color **3** : to grow dim or faint : disappear gradually **4** : to change gradually in loudness or visibility — used of a motion-picture image or of an electronics signal and usu. with *in* or *out*
[2]**fade** *n* : a gradual changing of one picture to another in a motion-picture or television sequence
fa·er·ie *also* **fa·ery** \'fā-(ə-)rē, 'fa(ə)r-ē, 'fe(ə)r-ē\ *n, pl* **fa·er·ies** **1** : FAIRYLAND **2** : FAIRY — **faery** *adj*
[1]**fag** \'fag\ *vb* **fagged**; **fag·ging** **1** : DRUDGE **2** : to act as a fag **3** : to tire by strenuous activity : EXHAUST
[2]**fag** *n* **1** : an English public-school boy who acts as servant to another **2** : MENIAL, DRUDGE
[3]**fag** *n* : CIGARETTE
fag end *n* **1 a** : the last part or coarser end of a web of cloth **b** : the untwisted end of a rope **2 a** : a poor or worn-out end : REMNANT **b** : the extreme end
fag·ot *or* **fag·got** \'fag-ət\ *n* : a bundle of sticks or twigs
fag·ot·ing *or* **fag·got·ing** \'fag-ət-ing\ *n* : embroidery produced by tying threads in hourglass-shaped clusters
Fahr *abbr* Fahrenheit
Fahr·en·heit \'far-ən-,hīt\ *adj* [named for Gabriel *Fahrenheit* (1686–1736), a German physicist who invented the scale] : relating or conforming to or having a thermometer scale on which under standard atmospheric pressure the boiling point of water is at 212 degrees above the zero of the scale and the freezing point is at 32 degrees above zero — abbr. *F*
[1]**fail** \'fāl\ *vb* **1 a** : to lose strength : WEAKEN **b** : to stop functioning ⟨the engine *failed*⟩ **2 a** : to fall short ⟨*failed* in his duty⟩ ⟨*failed* of reelection⟩ **b** : to become absent or inadequate ⟨the water supply *failed*⟩ **c** : to be unsuccessful (as in passing an examination) **d** : to grade as not passing ⟨*fail* a student⟩ **e** : to become bankrupt **3** : DISAPPOINT, DESERT ⟨*fail* a friend in his need⟩ **4 a** : to be deficient or inadequate esp. in operating or working ⟨the light *failed* to go on⟩ ⟨his legs *failed* to support him⟩ **b** : NEGLECT ⟨*fail* to answer the telephone⟩
[2]**fail** *n* : FAILURE — usu. used in the phrase *without fail*
[1]**fail·ing** \'fā-ling\ *n* : WEAKNESS, SHORTCOMING
[2]**failing** *prep* : in the absence or lack of ⟨*failing* a purchaser, he rented the house⟩
faille \'fīl\ *n* : a somewhat shiny ribbed silk, rayon, or cotton fabric
fail·ure \'fāl-yər\ *n* **1 a** : a failing to do or perform **b** : neglect of an assigned, expected, or appropriate action **c** : inability to perform a normal function adequately ⟨heart *failure*⟩ **2 a** : a lack of success **b** : BANKRUPTCY **3 a** : a falling short : DEFICIENCY ⟨crop *failure*⟩ **b** : DETERIORATION, BREAKDOWN ⟨a *failure* of memory⟩ **4** : one that has failed
[1]**fain** \'fān\ *adj* **1** *archaic* : GLAD **2** *archaic* : INCLINED **3** *archaic* : OBLIGED
[2]**fain** *adv* **1** *archaic* : WILLINGLY **2** *archaic* : RATHER
[1]**faint** \'fānt\ *adj* **1** : TIMID, COWARDLY ⟨*faint* heart⟩ **2** : being weak, dizzy, and likely to faint ⟨feels *faint* at the sight of blood⟩ **3** : lacking strength : FEEBLE ⟨*faint* praise⟩ **4** : lacking distinctness : barely perceptible ⟨a *faint* sound⟩ — **faint·ly** *adv* — **faint·ness** *n*
[2]**faint** *vb* : to lose consciousness because of a temporary decrease in the blood supply to the brain
[3]**faint** *n* : an act or condition of fainting
faint·heart·ed \'fānt-'härt-əd\ *adj* : TIMID — **faint·heart·ed·ly** *adv* — **faint·heart·ed·ness** *n*
[1]**fair** \'fa(ə)r, 'fe(ə)r\ *adj* **1** : attractive in appearance : BEAUTIFUL ⟨*fair* lady⟩ ⟨our *fair* city⟩ **2 a** : CLEAN, PURE ⟨sullied her *fair* name⟩ **b** : CLEAR, LEGIBLE ⟨make a *fair* copy⟩ **3** : not stormy or cloudy ⟨*fair* weather⟩ **4 a** : marked by impartiality and honesty : JUST **b** : conforming with the rules : ALLOWED ⟨*fair* play⟩ **c** : open to legitimate pursuit or attack ⟨*fair* game⟩ **5 a** : PROMISING, LIKELY ⟨a *fair* chance of winning⟩ **b** : favorable to a ship's course ⟨a *fair* wind⟩ **6** : not dark : BLOND **7** : ADEQUATE ⟨made a *fair* grade⟩ — **fair·ness** *n*
[2]**fair** *adv* **1** : FAIRLY **2** : so as to be a fair ball
[3]**fair** *n* **1** : a gathering of buyers and sellers for trade **2** : a competitive exhibition (as of farm products) usu. with accompanying entertainment and amusements **3** : a sale of articles usu. for a charitable purpose
fair ball *n* : a batted baseball that settles within the foul lines in the infield, that first touches the ground within the foul lines in the outfield, or that is within the foul lines when bounding to the outfield past first or third base or when going beyond the outfield for a home run
fair·ground \'fa(ə)r-,graůnd, 'fe(ə)r-\ *n* : an area set aside for fairs and similar gatherings
fair·ly \'fa(ə)r-lē, 'fe(ə)r-\ *adv* **1** : FAVORABLY ⟨*fairly* situated⟩ **2** : QUITE, COMPLETELY ⟨*fairly* bursting with pride⟩ **3** : in a fair manner : JUSTLY ⟨treat each person *fairly*⟩ **4** : MODERATELY ⟨a *fairly* easy job⟩
fair·way \-,wā\ *n* : the mowed part of a golf course between a tee and a green
fairy \'fa(ə)r-ē, 'fe(ə)r-\ *n, pl* **fair·ies** : a mythical being of folklore and romance usu. having diminutive human form and magic powers — **fairy** *adj* — **fairy·like** \-ē-,līk\ *adj*
fairy·land \-ē-,land\ *n* **1** : the land of fairies **2** : a place of delicate beauty or magical charm
fairy ring *n* : a ring of mushrooms in a lawn or meadow that is produced at the edge of a body of mycelium which is growing outward from a central point
fairy shrimp *n* : any of several delicate transparent freshwater crustaceans
fairy tale *n* **1** : a simple children's story about supernatural beings — called also *fairy story* **2** : a made-up story usu. designed to mislead
faith \'fāth\ *n* **1 a** : allegiance to duty or a person : LOYALTY **b** : fidelity to one's promises **2 a** (1) : belief and trust in and loyalty to God (2) : belief in the doctrines of a religion **b** (1) : firm belief without proof (2) : complete confidence **3** : something that is firmly believed; *esp* : a system of religious beliefs *syn* see BELIEF *ant* doubt
[1]**faith·ful** \'fāth-fəl\ *adj* **1** : full of faith esp. in God **2** : steadfast in keeping promises or in fulfilling duties ⟨a *faithful* worker⟩ **3** : LOYAL ⟨a *faithful* friend⟩ **4** : true to the facts : ACCURATE ⟨*faithful* copy⟩ — **faith·ful·ly** \-fə-lē\ *adv* — **faith·ful·ness** *n*
[2]**faithful** *n, pl* **faith·ful** *or* **faith·fuls** : one that is faithful
faith·less \'fāth-ləs\ *adj* **1** : not having faith **2** : not worthy of trust : DISLOYAL — **faith·less·ly** *adv* — **faith·less·ness** *n*
[1]**fake** \'fāk\ *vb* **1** : to treat so as to falsify : DOCTOR

ə abut	ər further	a back	ā bake
ä cot, cart	aů out	ch chin	e less	ē easy
g gift	i trip	ī life	j joke	ng sing	ō flow
ȯ flaw	ȯi coin	th thin	th this	ü loot
ů foot	y yet	yü few	yů furious	zh vision

⟨*faked* statistics to make them support an argument⟩ **2** : COUNTERFEIT ⟨*fake* a rare first edition⟩ **3** : PRETEND, SIMULATE ⟨*fake* surprise⟩ — **fak·er** \'fā-kər\ *n* — **fak·ery** \-k(ə-)rē\ *n*

2**fake** *n* **1** : an imitation or fabrication that is passed off as genuine : FRAUD, COUNTERFEIT **2** : IMPOSTOR, CHARLATAN — **fake** *adj*

fa·kir \fə-'ki(ə)r\ *n* [from Arabic *faqīr*, meaning literally "poor man"] **1** : DERVISH **2** : a wandering Hindu ascetic or wonder-worker

fal·con \'fal-kən, 'fȯl-; 'fȯ-kən\ *n* **1** : a hawk trained for use in falconry; *esp* : a female peregrine falcon **2** : any of various long-winged hawks having a notch and tooth on the upper jaw

falcon 2 (up to 4½ ft. wingspread)

fal·con·er \-kə-nər\ *n* : one that hunts with hawks or breeds or trains hawks for hunting

fal·con·ry \-kən-rē\ *n* **1** : the art of training falcons to pursue game **2** : the sport of hunting with falcons

1**fall** \'fȯl\ *vb* **fell** \'fel\; **fall·en** \'fȯ-lən\; **fall·ing 1 a** : to descend freely by the force of gravity **b** : to hang freely **c** : to drop oneself to a lower position ⟨*fell* to his knees⟩ **d** : to come as if by descending ⟨night *fell*⟩ **2 a** : to become of lower degree or level ⟨the temperature *fell* 10°⟩ **b** : to become lowered ⟨her eyes *fell*⟩ **3 a** : to leave an erect position suddenly and involuntarily **b** : to enter blindly : STRAY ⟨*fell* into a trap⟩ **c** : to drop down wounded or dead **d** : to undergo capture or defeat ⟨the fortress *fell*⟩ **e** : to suffer ruin or failure **4** : to fail to live up to a standard of conduct **5 a** : to move or extend downward ⟨the ground *falls* away to the east⟩ **b** : SUBSIDE, ABATE ⟨the tide is *falling*⟩ **c** : to decline in quality, activity, quantity, or value **d** : to assume a look of shame or dejection ⟨his face *fell* when he lost⟩ **6 a** : to occur at a certain time ⟨his birthday *falls* on the 5th⟩ **b** : DEVOLVE ⟨it *fell* to him to break the news⟩ **c** : to have the proper place or station ⟨the accent *falls* on the second syllable⟩ **7** : to come within the scope of something **8** : to pass from one condition of body or mind to another ⟨*fall* ill⟩ ⟨*fall* asleep⟩ **9** : to set about heartily or actively ⟨*fell* to work⟩ — **fall flat** : to produce no response or result — **fall for 1** : to fall in love with **2** : to become a victim of — **fall from grace** : to lapse morally : SIN, BACKSLIDE — **fall on** *or* **fall upon 1** : ATTACK, ASSAULT **2** : to meet or discover by chance : come across — **fall short 1** : to be deficient **2** : to fail to attain something

2**fall** *n* **1** : the act of falling by the force of gravity ⟨a *fall* from a horse⟩ **2 a** : a falling out, off, or away : DROPPING ⟨the *fall* of the leaves⟩ **b** : AUTUMN **c** : a thing or quantity that falls ⟨a heavy *fall* of snow⟩ **3 a** : loss of greatness : COLLAPSE **b** : the surrender or capture of a besieged place **c** : departure from innocence or goodness **4 a** : SLOPE **b** : WATERFALL — usu. used in pl. **5** : a decrease in size, quantity, degree, activity, or value **6** : the distance which something falls **7 a** : an act of forcing a wrestler's shoulders to the mat **b** : a bout of wrestling

fal·la·cious \fə-'lā-shəs\ *adj* **1** : embodying a fallacy ⟨a *fallacious* argument⟩ **2** : MISLEADING, DELUSIVE ⟨cherish a *fallacious* hope⟩ — **fal·la·cious·ly** *adv* — **fal·la·cious·ness** *n*

fal·la·cy \'fal-ə-sē\ *n, pl* **-cies 1** : a false or mistaken idea **2** : illogical reasoning or an instance of such reasoning

fall back *vb* : RETREAT, RECEDE

fal·li·ble \'fal-ə-bəl\ *adj* : liable to err or be erroneous — **fal·li·bil·i·ty** \ˌfal-ə-'bil-ət-ē\ *n* — **fal·li·bly** \'fal-ə-blē\ *adv*

fall in *vb* : to take one's proper place in a military formation

fall·ing–out \ˌfȯ-ling-'au̇t\ *n, pl* **fallings–out** *or* **falling–outs** : QUARREL

falling star *n* : METEOR

fal·lo·pi·an tube \fə-ˌlō-pē-ən-\ *n, often cap F* : either of the pair of tubes conducting the egg from the ovary to the uterus

fall·out \'fȯl-ˌau̇t\ *n* : the often radioactive particles stirred up by or resulting from a nuclear explosion and descending through the atmosphere

fall out \-'au̇t\ *vb* **1** : HAPPEN **2** : to have a quarrel **3 a** : to leave one's place in the ranks **b** : to leave a building to join a military formation

1**fal·low** \'fal-ō\ *n* **1** : land for crops allowed to lie idle during the growing season **2** : the tilling of land without sowing it for a season

2**fallow** *vb* : to till (land) without seeding

3**fallow** *adj* **1** : left untilled or unsown **2** : DORMANT, INACTIVE

fallow deer *n* : a small European deer with broad antlers and a pale yellow coat spotted white in the summer

fallow deer (up to 3 ft. high at shoulder)

1**false** \'fȯls\ *adj* **1** : not genuine ⟨*false* documents⟩ ⟨*false* teeth⟩ **2 a** : intentionally untrue ⟨*false* testimony⟩ **b** : intended or tending to mislead ⟨*false* promise⟩ **3** : not true : INCORRECT **4** : not faithful or loyal : TREACHEROUS **5** : not essential to structure ⟨*false* ceiling⟩ ⟨*false* front⟩ **6** : inaccurate in pitch ⟨a *false* note⟩ **7** : based on mistaken ideas ⟨*false* pride⟩ — **false·ly** *adv* — **false·ness** *n*

2**false** *adv* : FAITHLESSLY, TREACHEROUSLY ⟨she played him *false*⟩

false·hood \'fȯls-ˌhu̇d\ *n* **1** : an untrue statement : LIE **2** : absence of truth or accuracy **3** : the practice of lying

fal·set·to \fȯl-'set-ō\ *n, pl* **-tos 1** : an artificially high voice; *esp* : an artificial singing voice that extends above the range of the full voice esp. of a tenor **2** : a singer who uses falsetto — **falsetto** *adv*

fal·si·fy \'fȯl-sə-ˌfī\ *vb* **-fied**; **-fy·ing 1** : to make false : change so as to deceive ⟨*falsify* financial accounts⟩ **2 a** : to tell lies : LIE **b** : MISREPRESENT **3** : to prove to be false ⟨promises *falsified* by events⟩ — **fal·si·fi·ca·tion** \ˌfȯl-sə-fə-'kā-shən\ *n* — **fal·si·fi·er** \'fȯl-sə-ˌfī(-ə)r\ *n*

fal·si·ty \'fȯl-sət-ē\ *n, pl* **-ties 1** : something false : LIE **2** : the quality or state of being false

fal·ter \'fȯl-tər\ *vb* **fal·tered**; **fal·ter·ing** \'fȯl-t(ə-)ring\ **1** : to move unsteadily : WAVER **2** : STAMMER **3** : to hesitate in purpose or action ⟨courage that never *falters*⟩ — **falter** *n* — **fal·ter·er** \-tər-ər\ *n* — **fal·ter·ing·ly** \-t(ə-)ring-lē\ *adv*

fame \'fām\ *n* : the fact or condition of being known to the public : RENOWN — **famed** \'fāmd\ *adj*

1**fa·mil·iar** \fə-'mil-yər\ *n* **1** : an intimate associate : COMPANION **2** : a spirit held to serve or guard a person — called also *familiar spirit* **3** : one that frequents a place

[2]**familiar** *adj* **1** : closely acquainted : INTIMATE **2 a** : INFORMAL ⟨*familiar* essay⟩ **b** : overly intimate : FORWARD, PRESUMPTUOUS **3 a** : frequently seen or experienced **b** : of everyday occurrence **4** : having a good knowledge ⟨*familiar* with the rules of soccer⟩ — **fa·mil·iar·ly** *adv*

fa·mil·iar·i·ty \fə-ˌmil-ˈyar-ət-ē, -ˌmil-ē-ˈar-\ *n, pl* **-ties 1** : close friendship : INTIMACY **2** : close acquaintance with or knowledge of something ⟨acquire a *familiarity* with French⟩ **3** : lack of formality : freedom and ease in personal relations **4** : an unduly bold or forward act or expression

fa·mil·iar·ize \fə-ˈmil-yə-ˌrīz\ *vb* **1** : to make thoroughly acquainted : ACCUSTOM ⟨*familiarized* himself with his new job⟩ **2** : to make well known ⟨advertising *familiarizes* the name of a product⟩ — **fa·mil·iar·i·za·tion** \-ˌmil-yə-rə-ˈzā-shən\ *n*

fam·i·ly \ˈfam-(ə-)lē\ *n, pl* **-lies 1** : a group of persons of common ancestry : CLAN **2** : a group of individuals living under one roof and under one head : HOUSEHOLD **3** : a group of things having common characteristics or properties **4** : a social group composed of one or two parents and their children **5** : a group of related plants or animals ranking in biological classification above a genus and below an order — **fa·mil·ial** \fə-ˈmil-yəl\ *adj*

family name *n* : SURNAME 2

family tree *n* **1** : GENEALOGY **2** : a diagram showing genealogical relationships

fam·ine \ˈfam-ən\ *n* **1** : an extreme general scarcity of food **2** : a great shortage

fam·ish \ˈfam-ish\ *vb* **1** : STARVE **2** : to suffer or cause to suffer from extreme hunger — **fam·ish·ment** \-mənt\ *n*

fa·mous \ˈfā-məs\ *adj* **1** : much talked about : very well known ⟨*famous* explorer⟩ **2** : deserving to be remembered : EXCELLENT

fa·mous·ly \ˈfā-məs-lē\ *adv* : SPLENDIDLY, EXCELLENTLY ⟨got along *famously* together⟩

[1]**fan** \ˈfan\ *n* **1** : any of various devices for winnowing grain **2** : an instrument for producing a current of air: as **a** : a device that is often in the shape of a segment of a circle and is waved to and fro by hand **b** : a device that consists of a series of vanes rotated by a motor **3** : something shaped like a hand fan

[2]**fan** *vb* **fanned**; **fan·ning 1** : WINNOWING **2** : to move or impel air with a fan **3 a** : to direct a current of air upon with a fan **b** : to stir up to activity as if by fanning : STIMULATE **4** : to spread out or move like a fan **5** : to strike out in baseball — **fan·ner** *n*

[3]**fan** *n* : an enthusiastic follower or admirer ⟨sports *fans*⟩

fa·nat·ic \fə-ˈnat-ik\ *adj* : marked or moved by excessive enthusiasm and intense uncritical devotion — **fanatic** *n* — **fa·nat·i·cal** \-i-kəl\ *adj* — **fa·nat·i·cal·ly** \-i-k(ə-)lē\ *adv* — **fa·nat·i·cism** \-ˈnat-ə-ˌsiz-əm\ *n*

fan·ci·er \ˈfan(t)-sē-ər\ *n* : one with a special liking or interest; *esp* : a person who breeds or grows a particular animal or plant for points of excellence

fan·ci·ful \ˈfan(t)-si-fəl\ *adj* **1 a** : full of fancy ⟨a *fanciful* tale of an imaginary kingdom⟩ **b** : guided by fancy ⟨a *fanciful* impractical person⟩ **2** : coming from the fancy rather than from reason ⟨a *fanciful* scheme for getting rich⟩ **3** : curiously made or shaped ⟨*fanciful* forms of ice on a windowpane⟩ — **fan·ci·ful·ly** \-f(ə-)lē\ *adv* — **fan·ci·ful·ness** \-fəl-nəs\ *n*

[1]**fan·cy** \ˈfan(t)-sē\ *n, pl* **fancies 1** : the power of the mind to think of things not present : IMAGINATION **2** : LIKING ⟨take a *fancy* to a person⟩ **3** : THOUGHT, IDEA, WHIM ⟨a passing *fancy*⟩ **4** : taste or judgment esp. in art, literature, or decoration

[2]**fancy** *vb* **fan·cied**; **fan·cy·ing 1** : to have a fancy for : LIKE **2** : to form a conception of : IMAGINE **3** : to believe without evidence

[3]**fancy** *adj* **fan·ci·er**; **-est 1** : based on fancy : WHIMSICAL **2 a** : not plain : ORNAMENTAL **b** : of particular excellence **c** : bred primarily for showiness **3** : executed with technical skill and superior grace ⟨*fancy* diving⟩ — **fan·ci·ly** \ˈfan(t)-sə-lē\ *adv* — **fan·ci·ness** \-sē-nəs\ *n*

fancy dress *n* : a costume (as for a masquerade) chosen to suit the wearer's fancy — **fancy–dress** *adj*

fan·cy–free \ˈfan(t)-sē-ˌfrē\ *adj* : not centering the attention on any one person or thing; *esp* : not in love

fan·cy·work \-ˌwərk\ *n* : ornamental needlework (as embroidery)

fan·dan·go \fan-ˈdang-gō\ *n, pl* **-gos** : a lively Spanish or Spanish-American dance

fan·fare \ˈfan-ˌfa(ə)r, -ˌfe(ə)r\ *n* **1** : a flourish of trumpets **2** : a showy outward display

fang \ˈfang\ *n* **1 a** : one of the long sharp teeth by which an animal's prey is seized and held or torn **b** : one of the long hollow or grooved teeth of a venomous snake **2** : the root of a tooth — **fanged** \ˈfangd\ *adj*

fan·light \ˈfan-ˌlīt\ *n* : a semicircular window with radiating bars placed over a door or window

fan·tail \ˈfan-ˌtāl\ *n* **1** : a fan-shaped tail or end **2 a** : a domestic pigeon having a broad rounded tail **b** : a fancy goldfish with the tail fins double **3** : an overhang at the stern of a ship

fan·ta·sia \fan-ˈtā-zhə, ˌfant-ə-ˈzē-ə\ *also* **fan·ta·sie** \ˌfant-ə-ˈzē\ *n* : a musical composition in free form

fan·tas·tic \fan-ˈtas-tik, fən-\ *also* **fan·tas·ti·cal** \-ti-kəl\ *adj* **1** : produced by the fancy or resembling something produced by the fancy : IMAGINARY, UNREAL ⟨*fantastic* dreams⟩ ⟨a *fantastic* scheme⟩ **2** : going beyond belief : incredible or hardly credible ⟨airplanes now travel at *fantastic* speeds⟩ **3** : extremely individual or eccentric ⟨*fantastic* behavior⟩ — **fan·tas·ti·cal·ly** \-ti-k(ə-)lē\ *adv* — **fan·tas·ti·cal·ness** \-kəl-nəs\ *n*

fan·ta·sy \ˈfant-ə-sē, -ə-zē\ *n, pl* **-sies 1** : IMAGINATION, FANCY **2** : something imagined; *esp* : ILLUSION **3** : FANTASIA

[1]**far** \ˈfär\ *adv* **far·ther** \-thər\ *or* **fur·ther** \ˈfər-\; **far·thest** *or* **fur·thest** \-thəst\ **1** : at or to a considerable distance in space or time ⟨*far* from home⟩ **2** : by a broad interval : WIDELY, MUCH ⟨*far* better⟩ **3** : to or at a definite distance, point, or degree ⟨as *far* as I know⟩ **4** : to an advanced point or extent : a long way ⟨go *far* in his field⟩ — **by far** : GREATLY — **far and away** : DECIDEDLY

[2]**far** *adj* **farther** *or* **further**; **farthest** *or* **furthest 1** : very distant in space or time **2** : LONG ⟨a *far* journey⟩ **3** : the more distant of two ⟨the *far* side of the lake⟩

far·away \ˌfär-ə-ˌwā\ *adj* **1** : DISTANT ⟨*faraway* lands⟩ **2** : DREAMY, ABSTRACTED ⟨a *faraway* look⟩

farce \ˈfärs\ *n* **1** : a play about ridiculous situations and happenings that is intended to make people laugh **2** : humor characteristic of a farce **3** : a ridiculous action, display, or pretense — **far·ci·cal** \'fär-si-kəl\ *adj*

[1]**fare** \'fa(ə)r, 'fe(ə)r\ *vb* **1** : GO, TRAVEL **2** : to get along : SUCCEED **3** : EAT, DINE

[2]**fare** *n* **1** : the money a person pays to travel on a public conveyance **2** : a person paying a fare : PASSENGER **3** : FOOD

[1]**fare·well** \fa(ə)r-'wel, fe(ə)r-\ *imperative verb* : get along well — used interjectionally to or by one departing

[2]**farewell** *n* **1** : a wish of welfare at parting : GOOD-BYE **2** : an act of departure : LEAVE-TAKING

[3]**fare·well** \ˌfa(ə)r-ˌwel, ˌfe(ə)r-\ *adj* : PARTING, FINAL ⟨a *farewell* concert⟩

far·fetched \'fär-'fecht\ *adj* : not easily or naturally deduced or introduced : IMPROBABLE

far–flung \'fär-'fləŋ\ *adj* : covering great areas : having wide range ⟨a *far-flung* empire⟩

fa·ri·na \fə-'rē-nə\ *n* : a fine meal made chiefly from cereal grains and used esp. for puddings or as a breakfast cereal

[1]**farm** \'färm\ *n* **1 a** : a tract of land used for growing crops or raising livestock **b** : a tract of water used for the cultivation of aquatic animals **2** : a minor-league subsidiary of a major-league baseball club to which recruits are assigned for training

[2]**farm** *vb* **1** : to turn over for performance or use usu. on contract or for an agreed payment — usu. used with *out* ⟨*farm* out the electrical work to a subcontractor⟩ **2 a** : to devote to agriculture : CULTIVATE ⟨*farm* 60 acres⟩ **b** : to engage in raising crops or livestock — **farm·er** *n*

farm·hand \'färm-ˌhand\ *n* : a farm laborer

farm·house \-ˌhau̇s\ *n* : a dwelling on a farm

farm·ing \'fär-miŋ\ *n* : the occupation or business of a person who farms : AGRICULTURE

farm·land \'färm-ˌland\ *n* : land used or suitable for farming

farm·stead \-ˌsted\ *n* : FARM

farm·yard \-ˌyärd\ *n* : space around or enclosed by farm buildings

far–off \'fär-'ȯf\ *adj* : remote in time or space

far–out \-'au̇t\ *adj* **1** : exceedingly strange or unusual; *esp* : being or practicing the newest and most bizarre modes of conduct **2** : HIGH 9b

far–reach·ing \'fär-'rē-chiŋ\ *adj* : having a wide range, influence, or effect ⟨a *far-reaching* decision⟩

[1]**far·row** \'far-ō\ *vb* : to give birth to pigs

[2]**farrow** *n* : a litter of pigs

far·see·ing \'fär-'sē-iŋ\ *adj* : FARSIGHTED

far·sight·ed \-'sīt-əd\ *adj* **1** : able to see distant things more clearly than near ones **2** : having foresight — **far·sight·ed·ly** *adv*

far·sight·ed·ness *n* **1** : the condition of having foresight **2** : a visual condition in which the image focuses behind the retina

[1]**far·ther** \'fär-t͟hər\ *adv* **1** : at or to a greater distance or more advanced point **2** : more completely

[2]**farther** *adj* **1** : more distant : REMOTER **2** : [2]FURTHER 2

far·ther·most \-ˌmōst\ *adj* : FARTHEST

[1]**far·thest** \'fär-t͟həst\ *adj* : most distant in space or time

[2]**farthest** *adv* **1** : to or at the greatest distance in space or time : REMOTEST **2** : to the most advanced point **3** : by the greatest degree or extent : MOST

far·thing \'fär-t͟hiŋ\ *n* : a former British monetary unit equal to ¼ of a penny; *also* : a coin representing this unit

fas·ci·cle \'fas-i-kəl\ *n* **1** : a small bundle or cluster (as of flowers or roots) **2** : one of the divisions of a book published in parts — **fas·ci·cled** \-kəld\ *adj* — **fas·cic·u·lar** \fə-'sik-yə-lər, fa-\ *adj* — **fas·cic·u·late** \-lət\ *adj*

fas·ci·nate \'fas-ə-ˌnāt\ *vb* **1** : to grip the attention of esp. so as to take away the power to move, act, or think for oneself **2** : to allure and hold by charming qualities ***syn*** see CAPTIVATE — **fas·ci·na·tion** \ˌfas-ə-'nā-shən\ *n* — **fas·ci·na·tor** \'fas-ə-ˌnāt-ər\ *n*

fas·ci·nat·ing \'fas-ə-ˌnāt-iŋ\ *adj* : extremely interesting or charming — **fas·ci·nat·ing·ly** \-iŋ-lē\ *adv*

fas·cism \'fash-ˌiz-əm\ *n, often cap* : a political philosophy, movement, or regime (as that of Italy 1922–1943) that advocates nationalism and racial superiority, a centralized dictatorial regime, economic and social regimentation, and forcible suppression of opposition — **fas·cist** \'fash-əst\ *n or adj, often cap* — **fas·cis·tic** \fa-'shis-tik\ *adj, often cap* — **fas·cis·ti·cal·ly** \-'shis-ti-k(ə-)lē\ *adv, often cap*

[1]**fash·ion** \'fash-ən\ *n* **1** : the make or form of something **2** : MANNER, WAY ⟨behave in a strange *fashion*⟩ **3** : a prevailing style esp. of dress during a particular time or among a certain esp. innovative group ⟨*fashions* in women's hats⟩ ⟨an idea that is out of *fashion*⟩

[2]**fashion** *vb* **fash·ioned**; **fash·ion·ing** \'fash-(ə-)niŋ\ : to give shape or form to : MOLD, CONSTRUCT — **fash·ion·er** \-(ə-)nər\ *n*

fash·ion·a·ble \'fash-(ə-)nə-bəl\ *adj* **1 a** : following the fashion : STYLISH ⟨*fashionable* clothes⟩ **b** : dressing according to fashion ⟨*fashionable* people⟩ **2** : of or relating to the world of fashion : popular among those who set fashions ⟨*fashionable* stores⟩ ***syn*** see STYLISH ***ant*** unfashionable — **fash·ion·a·ble·ness** *n* — **fash·ion·a·bly** \-blē\ *adv*

[1]**fast** \'fast\ *adj* **1 a** : firmly fixed or bound **b** : tightly shut **c** : adhering firmly **d** : UNCHANGEABLE **2** : firmly loyal : STAUNCH **3 a** : moving or able to move rapidly : SWIFT **b** : taking a short time ⟨a *fast* trip⟩ **c** : imparting quickness of motion or action ⟨a *fast* bowler⟩ **d** : conducive to speed ⟨the *faster* route⟩ **4** : indicating ahead of the correct time **5** : not fading readily **6** : loose in morals or conduct ⟨a *fast* crowd⟩

[2]**fast** *adv* **1** : in a fixed manner ⟨stuck *fast* in the mud⟩ **2** : SOUNDLY, DEEPLY ⟨*fast* asleep⟩ **3** : SWIFTLY **4** : in a dissipated manner : RECKLESSLY

[3]**fast** *vb* **1** : to abstain from food **2** : to eat sparingly or abstain from some foods

[4]**fast** *n* **1** : the act of fasting **2** : a time of fasting

fast·back \'fas(t)-ˌbak\ *n* **1** : a back roof on a car sloping in a long unbroken line to the rear bumper **2** : an automobile having a fastback

fas·ten \'fas-ən\ *vb* **fas·tened**; **fas·ten·ing** \-(ə-)niŋ\ **1** : to attach or join by or as if by pinning, tying, or nailing ⟨*fasten* clothes on a line⟩ ⟨*fasten* blame on someone⟩ **2** : to make fast : fix securely ⟨*fasten* a door⟩ **3** : to fix or set steadily ⟨*fastened* his eyes on the distant ship⟩ **4** : to become fixed or joined ⟨a shoe that *fastens* with a buckle⟩ — **fas·ten·er** \-(ə-)nər\ *n*

fas·ten·ing \'fas-(ə-)niŋ\ *n* : something that fastens : FASTENER

fas·tid·i·ous \fa-'stid-ē-əs\ *adj* : overly difficult to please esp. in matters of taste or cleanliness — **fas·tid·i·ous·ly** *adv* — **fas·tid·i·ous·ness** *n*

fast·ness \'fas(t)-nəs\ *n* **1** : the quality or state of being fast **2** : a fortified or secure place : STRONGHOLD

[1]**fat** \'fat\ *adj* **fat·ter**; **fat·test** **1 a** : PLUMP, FLESHY

F

b : OILY, GREASY **2** : well stocked : ABUNDANT ⟨a *fat* purse⟩ **3** : PROFITABLE — **fat·ness** *n*

2fat *n* **1** : animal tissue consisting chiefly of cells containing much greasy or oily matter **2 a** : any of numerous compounds of carbon, hydrogen, and oxygen that are the chief constituents of plant and animal fat, are a major class of energy-rich food, and are soluble in ether but not in water **b** : a solid or semisolid fat (as lard) as distinguished from an oil **3** : the best or richest part ⟨lived on the *fat* of the land⟩ **4** : excess matter

3fat *vb* **fat·ted**; **fat·ting** : to make fat : FATTEN

fa·tal \ˈfāt-əl\ *adj* **1** : causing death or ruin : MORTAL, DISASTROUS ⟨a *fatal* accident⟩ **2** : determining one's fate : FATEFUL ⟨a *fatal* day in his life⟩ — **fa·tal·ly** \-ə-lē\ *adv*

fa·tal·ism \ˈfāt-ə-ˌliz-əm\ *n* : the belief or attitude that events are determined in advance by powers beyond man's control — **fa·tal·ist** \-ləst\ *n* — **fa·tal·is·tic** \ˌfāt-ə-ˈlis-tik\ *adj* — **fa·tal·is·ti·cal·ly** \-ti-k(ə-)lē\ *adv*

fa·tal·i·ty \fā-ˈtal-ət-ē, fə-\ *n, pl* **-ties 1 a** : the quality or state of causing death : DEADLINESS **b** : the quality or condition of being destined for disaster **2** : FATE 1 **3** : a death resulting from a disaster or accident

1fate \ˈfāt\ *n* [from Latin *fatum*, meaning literally "what has been spoken", from the past participle of *fari* "to speak"; compare INFANT] **1** : a power beyond men's control that is held to determine what happens : DESTINY ⟨blamed his failure on *fate*⟩ **2** : something that happens as though determined by fate : FORTUNE ⟨it was his *fate* to outlive his children⟩ **3** : END, OUTCOME ⟨awaited news of the *fate* of the polar expedition⟩ **4** : DISASTER; *esp* : DEATH ***syn*** see DESTINY

2fate *vb* **1** : DESTINE **2** : DOOM

fate·ful \ˈfāt-fəl\ *adj* **1** : having or marked by serious consequences : IMPORTANT ⟨a *fateful* decision⟩ **2** : OMINOUS, PROPHETIC ⟨the *fateful* circling of vultures overhead⟩ **3** : DEADLY, DESTRUCTIVE — **fate·ful·ly** \-fə-lē\ *adv* — **fate·ful·ness** *n*

1fa·ther \ˈfäth-ər\ *n* **1 a** : a male parent **b** *cap* (1) : 2GOD (2) : the first person of the Trinity **2** : FOREFATHER **3 a** : one who cares for as a father might **b** : one deserving the respect and love given to a father ⟨the *father* of his country⟩ **4** : ORIGINATOR, AUTHOR **5** : PRIEST — used esp. as a title **6** : one of the leading men ⟨city *fathers*⟩ — **fa·ther·hood** \ˈfäth-ər-ˌhu̇d\ *n* — **fa·ther·less** \-ləs\ *adj*

2father *vb* **fa·thered**; **fa·ther·ing** \ˈfäth-(ə-)riŋ\ **1 a** : BEGET **b** : to be the founder, producer, or author of **2** : to treat or care for as a father

fa·ther–in–law \ˈfäth-(ə-)rən-ˌlȯ, -ərn-ˌlȯ\ *n, pl* **fathers–in–law** \ˈfäth-ər-zən-\ : the father of one's spouse

fa·ther·land \ˈfäth-ər-ˌland\ *n* **1** : one's native land **2** : the native land of one's ancestors

fa·ther·ly \-lē\ *adj* **1** : of or resembling a father **2** : showing the affection or concern of a father ⟨*fatherly* advice⟩ — **fa·ther·li·ness** *n*

Father's Day *n* : the 3d Sunday in June appointed for the honoring of fathers

1fath·om \ˈfath-əm\ *n* : a unit of length equal to 6 feet used esp. for measuring the depth of water

ə abut	ər further	a back	ā bake	
ä cot, cart	au̇ out	ch chin	e less	ē easy
g gift	i trip	ī life	j joke	ŋ sing
ō flow	ȯ flaw	ȯi coin	th thin	th this
ü loot	u̇ foot	y yet	yü few	yu̇ furious
zh vision				

2fathom *vb* **1** : to measure by a sounding line **2** : to penetrate and come to understand ⟨couldn't *fathom* the reasons for her decision⟩ — **fath·om·a·ble** \ˈfath-ə-mə-bəl\ *adj*

fath·om·less \ˈfath-əm-ləs\ *adj* : incapable of being fathomed

1fa·tigue \fə-ˈtēg\ *n* **1 a** : weariness from labor or exertion **b** : the condition of a part of the body (as a sense organ or gland) that suffers temporary loss of power to respond after prolonged stimulation **2 a** : manual or menial work performed by military personnel **b** *pl* : the uniform worn on fatigue and in the field **3** : the tendency of a material (as metal) to break under repeated stress (as bending)

2fatigue *vb* **1** : to weary or become weary with exertion **2** : to induce a condition of fatigue in ***syn*** see TIRE

fat·ten \ˈfat-ən\ *vb* **fat·tened**; **fat·ten·ing** \-(ə-)niŋ\ **1** : to make or become fat ⟨*fatten* pigs for market⟩ ⟨cattle *fattening* on the range⟩ **2** : to make fertile : ENRICH — **fat·ten·er** \-(ə-)nər\ *n*

fat·ty \ˈfat-ē\ *adj* **fat·ti·er**; **-est 1** : containing fat esp. in unusual amounts **2** : overly stout **3** : GREASY — **fat·ti·ly** \ˈfat-ə-lē\ *adv* — **fat·ti·ness** \ˈfat-ē-nəs\ *n*

fatty acid *n* : any of numerous saturated or unsaturated acids that contain only carbon, hydrogen, and oxygen and that occur naturally in fats and various oils

fau·cet \ˈfȯ-sət, ˈfäs-ət\ *n* : a fixture for drawing a liquid from a pipe or tank

1fault \ˈfȯlt\ *n* **1 a** : a weakness in character : FAILING; *esp* : a minor moral weakness **b** : IMPERFECTION, FLAW ⟨a *fault* in the weave of the cloth⟩ **2 a** : a wrongful act **b** : MISTAKE ⟨a *fault* in the text⟩ **3** : responsibility for wrongdoing or failure ⟨it's all my *fault*⟩ **4** : a break in the earth's crust accompanied by a displacement of rock masses parallel to the fracture — **fault·less** \-ləs\ *adj* — **fault·less·ly** *adv* — **fault·less·ness** *n* — **at fault** : open to blame : RESPONSIBLE — **to a fault** : EXCESSIVELY ⟨generous *to a fault*⟩

2fault *vb* **1** : to fracture so as to produce a geologic fault **2** : to find a fault in ⟨could not *fault* his argument⟩

fault·find·er \ˈfȯlt-ˌfīn-dər\ *n* : a person who is inclined to find fault — **fault·find·ing** \-diŋ\ *n or adj*

fault line *n* : the geologic line determined by the intersection of a fault with the earth's surface

fault mountain *n* : BLOCK MOUNTAIN

faulty \ˈfȯl-tē\ *adj* : marked by fault, blemish, or defect : IMPERFECT — **fault·i·ly** \-tə-lē\ *adv* — **fault·i·ness** \-tē-nəs\ *n*

faun \ˈfȯn, ˈfän\ *n* : an ancient Italian deity of fields and herds represented as part goat and part man

fau·na \ˈfȯn-ə, ˈfän-\ *n, pl* **faunas** *also* **fau·nae** \-ˌē, -ˌī\ : animals or animal life esp. of a region, period, or environment — **fau·nal** \ˈfȯ-nəl\ *adj*

faun

1fa·vor \ˈfā-vər\ *n* **1 a** : friendly regard shown toward another ⟨enjoyed the *favor* of the king⟩ **b** : APPROVAL, APPROBATION ⟨look with *favor* on a project⟩ **c** : PARTIALITY ⟨the judge showed *favor* to the defendant⟩ **d** : POPULARITY ⟨a fad loses *favor* quickly⟩ **2** : an act of kindness ⟨do a friend a *favor*⟩ **3 a** : a token of love (as a ribbon) usu. worn conspicuously **b** : a small gift given out at a party **4** : a special privilege or right granted or conceded ⟨granted the reporter an interview as a *favor*⟩ — **in favor of 1** : in accord or sympathy with **2** : in support of ⟨voted *in favor of* the bill⟩

2favor *vb* **fa·vored**; **fa·vor·ing** \'fāv-(ə-)ring\ **1 a** : to regard or treat with favor **b** : to do a kindness for : OBLIGE **c** : ENDOW ⟨*favored* by nature⟩ **d** : to treat gently or carefully : SPARE ⟨*favor* a lame leg⟩ **2** : PREFER **3** : to make possible or easy : help to succeed ⟨darkness *favored* the attack⟩ **4** : to look like : RESEMBLE ⟨*favors* his father⟩ — **fa·vor·er** \'fā-vər-ər\ *n*

fa·vor·a·ble \'fāv-(ə-)rə-bəl, 'fā-vər-bəl\ *adj* **1** : showing favor : APPROVING ⟨a *favorable* opinion⟩ **2** : PROMISING, ADVANTAGEOUS ⟨*favorable* weather⟩ — **fa·vor·a·ble·ness** *n* — **fa·vor·a·bly** \-blē\ *adv*

1fa·vor·ite \'fāv-(ə-)rət\ *n* **1** : a person or a thing that is favored **2** : the contestant regarded as having the best chance to win

2favorite *adj* : constituting a favorite : best-liked ⟨playing his *favorite* tune⟩

fa·vor·it·ism \'fāv-(ə-)rət-,iz-əm\ *n* : unfairly favorable treatment of some to the neglect of others

1fawn \'fȯn, 'fän\ *vb* **1** : to show affection — used esp. of a dog **2** : to try to win favor by behavior that shows lack of self-respect — **fawn·er** *n* — **fawn·ing·ly** \-ing-lē\ *adv*

2fawn *n* **1** : a young deer; *esp* : one in its first year **2** : a variable color averaging a light grayish brown

fay \'fā\ *n* [from French *fée*, from Latin *Fata* "goddess of fate", from *fatum* "fate"] : FAIRY, ELF — **fay** *adj*

faze \'fāz\ *vb* : to disturb the composure or courage of : DAUNT

FBI *abbr* Federal Bureau of Investigation

FD *abbr* fire department

FDA *abbr* Food and Drug Administration

fe·al·ty \'fē(-ə)l-tē\ *n* **1** : the loyalty of a feudal vassal to his lord **2** : LOYALTY, ALLEGIANCE

1fear \'fi(ə)r\ *n* **1 a** : an unpleasant often strong emotion caused by expectation or awareness of danger **b** : an instance of fear or a state marked by fear ⟨live in *fear* of assassination⟩ **2** : anxious concern : WORRY **3** : reverential awe esp. toward God

syn FEAR, DREAD, ALARM, FRIGHT can mean an unpleasant emotion in the presence or expectation of danger. FEAR suggests a usu. persistent anxiety that may cause timid reactions; DREAD implies intense reluctance to face something; ALARM may imply intense emotional upset brought on by unexpected and often imminent danger; FRIGHT suggests the shock of sudden startling and often only brief fear ***ant*** fearlessness

2fear *vb* **1** : to have a reverential awe of ⟨*fear* God⟩ **2** : to be afraid of : have fear **3** : to be apprehensive ⟨*feared* he would miss the train⟩ — **fear·er** *n*

fear·ful \'fi(ə)r-fəl\ *adj* **1** : causing fear ⟨the *fearful* roar of a lion⟩ **2** : filled with fear ⟨*fearful* of danger⟩ **3** : showing or caused by fear ⟨a *fearful* glance⟩ **4** : extremely bad, large, or intense ⟨*fearful* cold⟩ — **fear·ful·ly** \-fə-lē\ *adv* — **fear·ful·ness** *n*

fear·less \-ləs\ *adj* : free from fear : BRAVE — **fear·less·ly** *adv* — **fear·less·ness** *n*

fear·some \-səm\ *adj* **1** : causing fear **2** : TIMID — **fear·some·ly** *adv* — **fear·some·ness** *n*

fea·si·ble \'fē-zə-bəl\ *adj* **1** : capable of being done or carried out ⟨a *feasible* plan⟩ **2** : capable of being used : SUITABLE **3** : REASONABLE, LIKELY — **fea·si·bil·i·ty** \,fē-zə-'bil-ət-ē\ *n* — **fea·si·ble·ness** \'fē-zə-bəl-nəs\ *n* — **fea·si·bly** \-blē\ *adv*

1feast \'fēst\ *n* **1** : an elaborate meal : BANQUET **2** : a day on which a religious festival falls

2feast *vb* **1** : to eat plentifully : participate in a feast **2** : to entertain with rich and plentiful food **3** : DELIGHT ⟨*feasted* his eyes on a beautiful scene⟩ — **feast·er** *n*

feat \'fēt\ *n* **1** : ACT, DEED **2 a** : a deed notable esp. for courage **b** : an act or product of skill, endurance, or ingenuity

1feath·er \'feth-ər\ *n* **1 a** : one of the light horny outgrowths that form the external covering of the body of a bird **b** : the vane of an arrow **2 a** : KIND, NATURE ⟨birds of a *feather*⟩ **b** : ATTIRE, DRESS ⟨in full *feather*⟩ **c** : CONDITION, MOOD ⟨in fine *feather*⟩ **3** : a feathery tuft or fringe of hair **4** : a projecting strip — **feath·ered** \-ərd\ *adj* — **feath·er·less** \-ər-ləs\ *adj* — **feath·ery** \-(ə-)rē\ *adj* — **a feather in one's cap** : a mark of distinction : HONOR

feather 1a

2feather *vb* **feath·ered**; **feath·er·ing** \'feth-(ə-)ring\ **1 a** : to furnish (as an arrow) with a feather **b** : to cover, clothe, or adorn with feathers **2 a** : to turn (an oar blade) horizontal when lifting from the water at the end of a stroke **b** : to change the angle of (airplane propeller blades) toward the line of flight **3** : to grow feathers — **feather one's nest** : to provide for one's own comfort

feather bed *n* : a mattress filled with feathers; *also* : a bed with such a mattress

feath·er·bed·ding \'feth-ər-,bed-ing\ *n* : the requiring of an employer to employ more workers than are needed or to limit production

feath·er·brain \-,brān\ *n* : a foolish scatterbrained person — **feath·er·brained** \,feth-ər-'brānd\ *adj*

feath·er·edge \'feth-ər-,ej\ *n* : a very thin sharp edge; *esp* : one that is easily broken or bent — **featheredge** *vb*

feath·er·weight \-,wāt\ *n* **1** : a very light weight **2** : one that weighs little; *esp* : a boxer weighing more than 118 but not over 126 pounds

1fea·ture \'fē-chər\ *n* **1 a** : the shape or appearance of the face ⟨a man stern of *feature*⟩ **b** : a single part of the face (as the nose or the mouth) **2** : a prominent part or detail **3** : a main or outstanding attraction: as **a** : the principal motion picture on a program **b** : a special column or section in a newspaper or magazine ***syn*** see CHARACTERISTIC — **fea·ture·less** \-ləs\ *adj*

2feature *vb* **fea·tured**; **fea·tur·ing** \'fēch-(ə-)ring\ **1** : to be a feature of something **2** : to have as a feature; *esp* : to give special prominence to ⟨*feature* a story in a newspaper⟩

Feb *abbr* February

Feb·ru·ary \'feb-(y)ə-,wer-ē, 'feb-rə-\ *n* [from Latin *Februarius*, derived from *Februa*, a feast of purification held on the 15th of the month] : the 2d month of the year

fe·ces \'fē-(,)sēz\ *n pl* : bodily waste discharged through the anus : EXCREMENT — **fe·cal** \'fē-kəl\ *adj*

fe·cund \'fek-ənd, 'fē-kənd\ *adj* **1** : FRUITFUL, PROLIFIC **2** : intellectually productive or inventive — **fe·cun·di·ty** \fi-'kən-dət-ē\ *n*

fec·un·date \'fē-kən-,dāt, 'fek-ən-\ *vb* : FERTILIZE — **fec·un·da·tion** \,fē-kən-'dā-shən, ,fek-ən-\ *n*

fed *abbr* federal

fed·er·al \'fed-(ə-)rəl\ *adj* [from Latin *foeder-*, stem of *foedus* "compact", "treaty", related to *fides* "faith", the source of English *fidelity*] **1 a :** formed by a compact between political units that surrender sovereignty to a central authority but retain certain powers **b :** of or constituting a form of government in which power is distributed between a central authority and constituent units **c :** of or relating to the central government of a federation **2** *often cap* **:** of, relating to, or loyal to the federal government of the U.S. esp. in the Civil War — **fed·er·al·ly** \-ē\ *adv*

Federal *n* **1 :** a supporter of the government of the U.S. in the Civil War; *esp* **:** a soldier in the federal armies **2 :** a federal agent or officer

fed·er·al·ist \'fed-(ə-)rə-ləst\ *n* **1 :** an advocate of federal government; *esp, often cap* **:** an advocate of the adoption of the U.S. Constitution **2** *cap* **:** a member of a major political party in the early years of the U.S. favoring a strong centralized national government — **fed·er·al·ism** \-ˌliz-əm\ *n, often cap* — **federalist** *adj, often cap*

fed·er·al·ize \'fed-(ə-)rə-ˌlīz\ *vb* **1 :** to unite in or under a federal system **2 :** to bring under the jurisdiction of a federal government ⟨*federalize* the National Guard⟩ — **fed·er·al·i·za·tion** \ˌfed-(ə-)rə-lə-'zā-shən\ *n*

fed·er·ate \'fed-ə-ˌrāt\ *vb* **:** to join in a federation

fed·er·a·tion \ˌfed-ə-'rā-shən\ *n* **1 :** the act of federating; *esp* **:** the formation of a federal union **2 :** something formed by federation: as **a :** a federal government **b :** a union of organizations

fe·do·ra \fi-'dōr-ə, -'dȯr-\ *n* **:** a low soft felt hat with the crown creased lengthwise

fed up *adj* **:** exhausted of patience

fee \'fē\ *n* **1 a :** an estate in land held from a feudal lord in return for homage and service **b :** an inherited or heritable estate in land **2 a :** a fixed charge ⟨admission *fee*⟩ ⟨license *fee*⟩ **b :** a charge for a professional service ⟨a doctor's *fees*⟩ ***syn*** see PRICE — **in fee :** as a fee ⟨land held *in fee*⟩

fee·ble \'fē-bəl\ *adj* **fee·bler** \-b(ə-)lər\; **-blest** \-b(ə-)ləst\ [from Old French *feble*, from Latin *flebilis* "lamentable", from *flēre* "to weep"] **1 :** lacking in strength or endurance **2 :** not vigorous or loud **:** INEFFECTIVE, INADEQUATE ⟨a *feeble* cry⟩ ⟨a *feeble* protest⟩ ***syn*** see WEAK ***ant*** robust, sturdy — **fee·ble·ness** \-bəl-nəs\ *n* — **fee·bly** \-blē\ *adv*

fee·ble·mind·ed \ˌfē-bəl-'mīn-dəd\ *adj* **:** lacking normal intelligence **:** mentally deficient — **fee·ble·mind·ed·ness** *n*

1**feed** \'fēd\ *vb* **fed** \'fed\; **feed·ing 1 a :** to give food to **b :** to give as food **c :** to consume food **:** EAT **d :** PREY — used with *on, upon,* or *off* **2 a :** to furnish with something essential ⟨*feed* a furnace with coal⟩ **b :** to nourish or become nourished as if by food ⟨*feed* on praise⟩ **3 :** to supply (as material) for use or consumption

2**feed** *n* **1 :** MEAL; *esp* **:** a large meal **2 :** food for livestock **3 :** a mechanism by which material is fed

feed·back \'fēd-ˌbak\ *n* **:** the return to the input of a part of the output of a machine, system, or process

feed·er \'fēd-ər\ *n* **1 a :** a device for supplying food ⟨bird *feeder*⟩ **b :** FEED 3 **c :** a branch (as of a river or a transportation system) that supplies another

ə abut	ər further	a back	ā bake
ä cot, cart	aů out	ch chin	e less	ē easy
g gift	i trip	ī life	j joke	ng sing	ō flow
ȯ flaw	ȯi coin	th thin	t͟h this	ü loot
ů foot	y yet	yü few	yů furious	zh vision

2 a : one that eats **b :** an animal being fattened or suitable for fattening — **feeder** *adj*

feed·stuff \'fēd-ˌstəf\ *n* **:** FEED 2

1**feel** \'fēl\ *vb* **felt** \'felt\; **feel·ing 1 a :** to perceive through direct contact ⟨*feel* a blow⟩; *esp* **:** TOUCH **b :** to examine or test by touching **:** HANDLE ⟨*felt* the silk between her fingers⟩ **2 a :** EXPERIENCE ⟨*felt* his scorn⟩ **b :** to suffer from ⟨*feels* the cold⟩ **3 :** to discover by cautious trial — often used with *out* **4 a :** to be aware of ⟨*feel* the joy of victory⟩ ⟨*feel* trouble brewing⟩ **b :** to be conscious of a physical or emotional state ⟨*feel* happy⟩ ⟨*feel* sick⟩ **c :** BELIEVE, THINK ⟨I *feel* he's wrong about that⟩ **5 :** to search for something with the fingers **6 :** to seem esp. to the touch ⟨*feels* like wool⟩ **7 :** to have sympathy or pity ⟨I *feel* for you⟩

2**feel** *n* **1 :** the sense of touch ⟨soft to the *feel*⟩ **2 :** SENSATION, FEELING **3 :** the quality of a thing as imparted through touch ⟨the *feel* of sandpaper⟩

feel·er \'fē-lər\ *n* **1 :** one that feels; *esp* **:** a movable organ (as an antenna) of an animal that usually functions for touch **2 :** a proposal or remark made to find out the views of other people

feeler gauge *n* **:** a thin metal strip of known thickness used as a gauge

1**feel·ing** \'fē-ling\ *n* **1 a :** a sense by which the hardness or softness, hotness or coldness, or heaviness or lightness of things is determined; *esp* **:** TOUCH 3 **b :** a sensation experienced through this sense **2 a :** a state of mind; *esp* **:** EMOTION ⟨a *feeling* of loneliness⟩ **b :** such a state with regard to something ⟨a *feeling* of dislike⟩ **c** *pl* **:** general emotional condition **:** SENSIBILITIES ⟨hurt their *feelings*⟩ **3 :** the quality of one's awareness **:** SENSITIVITY ⟨a man of deep *feeling*⟩ **4 :** an opinion or belief esp. when ungrounded ⟨a *feeling* that it will rain⟩ **5 :** SYMPATHY

2**feeling** *adj* **:** easily moved emotionally — **feel·ing·ly** \'fē-ling-lē\ *adv* — **feel·ing·ness** *n*

feet *pl of* FOOT

feet·first \'fēt-'fərst\ *adv* **:** with both feet or all four feet foremost ⟨jumped into the water *feetfirst*⟩

Feh·ling's solution \'fā-lingz-\ *n* **:** a blue solution prepared by mixing solutions of Rochelle salt and copper sulfate and used esp. in testing for the presence of sugars

feign \'fān\ *vb* **1 :** to represent by a false appearance of **:** SHAM ⟨*feign* illness⟩ **2 :** to assert as if true ⟨*feign* an excuse⟩ — **feign·er** *n*

feint \'fānt\ *n* **:** something feigned; *esp* **:** a mock blow or attack at one point in order to distract attention from the point one really intends to attack — **feint** *vb*

feist \'fīst\ *n, chiefly dial* **:** a small dog

feld·spar \'fel(d)-ˌspär\ *n* **:** any of a group of crystalline minerals that consist of silicates of aluminum with either potassium, sodium, calcium, or barium and that are an essential constituent of nearly all crystalline rocks

fe·lic·i·tate \fi-'lis-ə-ˌtāt\ *vb* **:** CONGRATULATE — **fe·lic·i·ta·tion** \-ˌlis-ə-'tā-shən\ *n* — **fe·lic·i·ta·tor** \-'lis-ə-ˌtāt-ər\ *n*

fe·lic·i·tous \fi-'lis-ət-əs\ *adj* **1 :** suitably expressed **:** APT ⟨*felicitous* wording⟩ **2 :** possessing a talent for apt expression ⟨a *felicitous* speaker⟩ — **fe·lic·i·tous·ly** *adv* — **fe·lic·i·tous·ness** *n*

fe·lic·i·ty \fi-'lis-ət-ē\ *n, pl* **-ties 1 :** great happiness **:** BLISS **2 :** something that causes happiness **3 :** a talent for apt expression **4 :** an apt expression

fe·line \'fē-ˌlīn\ *adj* [from Latin *felinus*, from *felis* "cat"] **1 a :** belonging to the family of lithe-bodied, soft-furred, flesh-eating mammals that includes the cats, lions, tigers, leopards, pumas, and lynxes

b : of or resembling a cat : characteristic of cats **2** : SLY, STEALTHY — **feline** *n* — **fe·line·ly** *adv* — **fe·lin·i·ty** \fē-'lin-ət-ē\ *n*

1**fell** \'fel\ *n* : SKIN, HIDE, PELT

2**fell** *vb* **1 a** : to cut, beat, or knock down ⟨*fell* trees for lumber⟩ **b** : KILL **2** : to sew (a seam) by folding one edge under the other — **fell·a·ble** \-ə-bəl\ *adj*

3**fell** *past of* FALL

4**fell** *adj* : FIERCE, CRUEL; *also* : DEADLY

fel·lah \'fel-ə, fə-'lä\ *n, pl* **fel·la·hin** \ˌfel-ə-'hēn, fə-ˌlä-'hēn\ : a peasant or agricultural laborer in Arab countries (as Egypt or Syria)

1**fel·low** \'fel-ō\ *n* **1** : COMRADE, ASSOCIATE **2 a** : an equal in rank, power, or character : PEER **b** : one of a pair : MATE **3 a** : a member of an incorporated literary or scientific society **b** : a person holding any of various positions at a university **4 a** : MAN, BOY **b** : BOYFRIEND **5** : a person granted funds for advanced study

2**fellow** *adj* : being a companion, mate, or associate ⟨a *fellow* lodge member⟩

fel·low·man \ˌfel-ō-'man\ *n* : a kindred human being

fel·low·ship \'fel-ō-ˌship\ *n* **1** : the condition of friendly relationship existing among persons **2** : a community of interest or feeling **3** : a group with similar interests **4 a** : the position of a fellow (as of a university) **b** : the funds granted a fellow

fel·ly \'fel-ē\ *or* **fel·loe** \-ō\ *n, pl* **fellies** *or* **felloes** : the outside rim or a part of the rim of a wheel

1**fel·on** \'fel-ən\ *n* : CRIMINAL; *esp* : one who has committed a felony

2**felon** *n* : a deep inflammation of the finger or toe esp. near the end or around the nail and usu. with pus

fel·o·ny \'fel-ə-nē\ *n, pl* **-nies** : a serious crime punishable by a heavy sentence — **fe·lo·ni·ous** \fə-'lō-nē-əs\ *adj* — **fe·lo·ni·ous·ly** *adv* — **fe·lo·ni·ous·ness** *n*

1**felt** \'felt\ *n* **1** : a cloth made of wool and fur often mixed with natural or synthetic fibers and pressed **2** : an article (as a hat) made of felt **3** : a material resembling felt

2**felt** *vb* **1** : to make into felt **2** : to mat together **3** : to cover with felt

3**felt** *past of* FEEL

fem *abbr* feminine

1**fe·male** \'fē-ˌmāl\ *n* : a female plant or animal

2**female** *adj* **1 a** : of, relating to, or being the sex that bears young **b** : having only seed-producing flowers ⟨a *female* holly⟩ **2 a** : of, relating to, or characteristic of the female sex ⟨a high *female* voice⟩ **b** : made up of females ⟨a large *female* population⟩ — **female·ness** *n*

1**fem·i·nine** \'fem-ə-nən\ *adj* **1** : FEMALE **2** : characteristic of or belonging to women : WOMANLY ⟨a *feminine* concern with clothes⟩ **3** : of, relating to, or constituting the class of words that ordinarily includes most of those referring to females ⟨a *feminine* noun⟩ ⟨*feminine* gender⟩ — **fem·i·nin·i·ty** \ˌfem-ə-'nin-ət-ē\ *n*

2**feminine** *n* **1** : a word or form of the feminine gender **2** : the feminine gender

fem·i·nism \'fem-ə-ˌniz-əm\ *n* **1** : the theory of the political, economic, and social equality of the sexes **2** : organized activity on behalf of women's rights and interests — **fem·i·nist** \-nəst\ *n or adj* — **fem·i·nis·tic** \ˌfem-ə-'nis-tik\ *adj*

fe·mur \'fē-mər\ *n, pl* **fe·murs** *or* **fem·o·ra** \'fem-(ə-)rə\ **1** : the long bone of the hind or lower limb extending from the hip to the knee and supporting the thigh **2** : the segment of an insect's leg that is third from the body — **fem·o·ral** \'fem-(ə-)rəl\ *adj*

fen \'fen\ *n* : low land covered wholly or partly by water

1**fence** \'fen(t)s\ *n* **1** : a barrier intended to prevent escape or intrusion or to mark a boundary; *esp* : such a barrier made of posts and wire or boards **2** : a person who receives stolen goods or a shop where stolen goods are disposed of — **fence·less** \-ləs\ *adj* — **on the fence** : not having one's mind made up : UNDECIDED

2**fence** *vb* **1 a** : to enclose with a fence **b** : to keep in or out with a fence **2** : to engage in fencing **3** : to sell (stolen property) to a fence — **fenc·er** *n*

fenc·ing *n* **1 a** : the art or practice of attack and defense with a sword **b** : debating tactics resembling fencing **2 a** : the fences of a property or region **b** : material for fences

fend \'fend\ *vb* **1** : to keep or ward off : REPEL **2** : to try to get along without help : SHIFT ⟨*fend* for himself⟩

fend·er \'fen-dər\ *n* : a device that protects: as **a** : a guard over the wheel of a motor vehicle **b** : a low metal frame placed on the hearth before an open fireplace

fen·nec \'fen-ik\ *n* : a small large-eared African fox

fen·nel \'fen-əl\ *n* : a garden plant related to the carrot and grown for its aromatic seeds

fennec
(about 8 in. at shoulder)

fe·ral \'fir-əl, 'fer-\ *adj* : having escaped from domestication and become wild

fer-de-lance \ˌferd-ə-'lan(t)s, -'län(t)s\ *n, pl* **fer-de-lance** : a large extremely poisonous pit viper of Central and So. America

1**fer·ment** \(ˌ)fər-'ment\ *vb* **1** : to undergo or cause to undergo fermentation **2** : to be or cause to be in a state of agitation or intense activity : EXCITE — **fer·ment·a·ble** \-ə-bəl\ *adj* — **fer·ment·er** *n*

2**fer·ment** \'fər-ˌment\ *n* **1** : an agent that is capable of causing fermentation **2** : a state of unrest : AGITATION

fer·men·ta·tion \ˌfər-mən-'tā-shən, -ˌmen-\ *n* **1** : chemical breaking down of an organic substance (as in the souring of milk or the formation of alcohol from sugar) produced by an enzyme and often accompanied by the formation of a gas **2** : FERMENT 2 — **fer·men·ta·tive** \(ˌ)fər-'ment-ət-iv\ *adj*

fer·mi·um \'fer-mē-əm, 'fər-\ *n* : a radioactive metallic element artificially produced (as by bombardment of plutonium with neutrons) — see ELEMENT table

fern \'fərn\ *n* : any of an order of flowerless seedless vascular plants resembling seed plants in having root, stem, and leaflike fronds but reproducing by spores instead of seeds — **fern·like** \-ˌlīk\ *adj* — **ferny** \'fər-nē\ *adj*

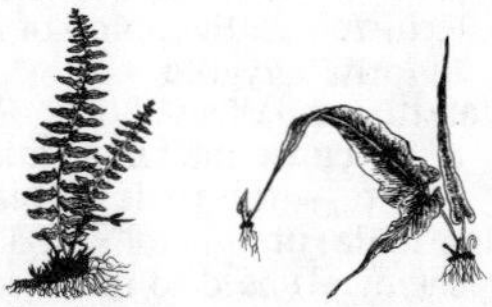
ferns

fe·ro·cious \fə-'rō-shəs\ *adj* **1** : CRUEL, SAVAGE **2** : unbearably intense ⟨*ferocious* heat⟩ — **fe·ro·cious·ly** *adv* — **fe·ro·cious·ness** *n* — **fe·roc·i·ty** \fə-'räs-ət-ē\ *n*

-f·er·ous \f-(ə-)rəs\ *adj comb form* : bearing : producing ⟨carboni*ferous*⟩

[1]**fer·ret** \'fer-ət\ *n* : a partially domesticated usu. albino European mammal related to the weasel and used esp. for hunting rodents

ferret
(about 19 in. long)

[2]**ferret** *vb* **1** : to drive out of a hiding place **2** : to find and bring to light by searching — usu. used with *out* — **fer·ret·er** *n*

fer·ric \'fer-ik\ *adj* : of, relating to, or containing iron

ferric oxide *n* : the red or black oxide of iron found in nature as hematite and as rust and also manufactured and used as a pigment and for polishing

Fer·ris wheel \'fer-əs-\ *n* : an amusement device consisting of a large upright power-driven wheel carrying seats around its rim

fer·ro·mag·net·ic \ˌfer-ō-mag-'net-ik\ *adj* : of or relating to substances (as iron and nickel) that are easily magnetized

fer·rous \'fer-əs\ *adj* : of, relating to, or containing iron

ferrous sulfate *n* : a salt that consists of iron, sulfur, and oxygen and is used in making pigments and ink, in treating industrial wastes, and in medicine

fer·ru·gi·nous \fə-'rü-jə-nəs, fe-\ *or* **fer·ru·gin·e·ous** \ˌfer-(y)u̇-'jin-ē-əs\ *adj* : resembling iron rust in color

fer·rule \'fer-əl\ *n* : a metal ring or cap placed around the end of a wooden shaft or handle to prevent splitting or to provide a strong joint

[1]**fer·ry** \'fer-ē\ *vb* **fer·ried**; **fer·ry·ing 1 a** : to carry by boat over a body of water **b** : to cross by a ferry **2 a** : to fly (an airplane) to a delivery point **b** : to transport in an airplane

[2]**ferry** *n, pl* **ferries 1** : a place where persons or things are carried across a body of water in a boat **2** : FERRYBOAT — **fer·ry·man** \'fer-ē-mən\ *n*

fer·ry·boat \'fer-ē-ˌbōt\ *n* : a boat used to ferry passengers, vehicles, or goods

fer·tile \'fərt-əl\ *adj* **1** : producing vegetation or crops plentifully : RICH ⟨*fertile* farmland⟩ **2** : producing abundantly in any way ⟨a *fertile* mind⟩ **3 a** : capable of growing and developing ⟨a *fertile* seed⟩ **b** : capable of reproducing or of producing reproductive cells ⟨a *fertile* bull⟩ ⟨*fertile* fungous hyphae⟩ — **fer·tile·ly** \-əl-(l)ē\ *adv* — **fer·tile·ness** \-əl-nəs\ *n* — **fer·til·i·ty** \(ˌ)fər-'til-ət-ē\ *n*

syn FERTILE, FRUITFUL, PROLIFIC can mean having productivity. FERTILE suggests inherent power to produce; FRUITFUL suggests actual production in abundance; PROLIFIC suggests rapid production or multiplying ***ant*** infertile, sterile

fer·til·i·za·tion \ˌfərt-ə-lə-'zā-shən\ *n* **1** : an act or process of making fertile; *esp* : the application of fertilizer **2** : the union of male and female germ cells to form a zygote

fer·til·ize \'fərt-ə-ˌlīz\ *vb* : to make fertile: as **a** : to cause the fertilization of **b** : to apply a fertilizer to — **fer·til·iz·a·ble** \-ˌlī-zə-bəl\ *adj*

fer·til·iz·er \-ˌlī-zər\ *n* : a substance (as manure or a chemical) used to make soil produce more plant life

fer·ule \'fer-əl\ *n* : a rod or ruler used in punishing children

fer·vent \'fər-vənt\ *adj* : marked by great warmth of feeling : ARDENT — **fer·ven·cy** \-vən-sē\ *n* — **fer·vent·ly** *adv*

fer·vid \'fər-vəd\ *adj* : ARDENT, ZEALOUS — **fer·vid·ly** *adv* — **fer·vid·ness** *n*

fer·vor \'fər-vər\ *n* : intensity of feeling : ardent zeal

fes·cue \'fes-kyü\ *n* : a tufted perennial grass

fes·tal \'fes-təl\ *adj* : FESTIVE — **fes·tal·ly** \-tə-lē\ *adv*

[1]**fes·ter** \'fes-tər\ *n* : a pus-filled sore

[2]**fester** *vb* **fes·tered**; **fes·ter·ing** \-t(ə-)riŋ\ **1 a** : to form pus **b** : to become painful and inflamed **2** : ROT **3** : to grow or cause to grow more acute and harder to bear : RANKLE ⟨resentment *festered* in his mind⟩

fes·ti·val \'fes-tə-vəl\ *n* **1** : a time of celebration marked by special observances **2** : a periodic season or program of cultural events or entertainment ⟨a music *festival*⟩ — **festival** *adj*

fes·tive \'fes-tiv\ *adj* **1** : of, relating to, or suitable for a feast or festival **2** : JOYOUS, GAY — **fes·tive·ly** *adv* — **fes·tive·ness** *n*

fes·tiv·i·ty \fe-'stiv-ət-ē\ *n, pl* **-ties 1** : FESTIVAL 1 **2** : GAIETY **3** : festive activity

[1]**fes·toon** \fe-'stün\ *n* **1** : a decorative chain or strip hanging between two points **2** : a carved, molded, or painted ornament representing a festoon

[2]**festoon** *vb* **1** : to hang or form festoons on **2** : to shape into festoons

fetch \'fech\ *vb* **1** : to go after and bring back ⟨teach a dog to *fetch* a stick⟩ **2** : to cause to come : bring out ⟨*fetched* tears from the eyes⟩ **3** : to bring as a price : sell for — **fetch·er** *n*

fetch·ing *adj* : ATTRACTIVE, PLEASING — **fetch·ing·ly** \-iŋ-lē\ *adv*

[1]**fete** *or* **fête** \'fāt\ *n* **1** : FESTIVAL **2** : a lavish entertainment or party

[2]**fete** *or* **fête** *vb* **1** : to honor or commemorate with a fete **2** : to pay high honor to

fet·er·i·ta \ˌfet-ə-'rēt-ə\ *n* : a grain sorghum with compact heads of soft white seeds

fet·id \'fet-əd\ *adj* : STINKING — **fet·id·ly** *adv* — **fet·id·ness** *n*

fet·ish *or* **fet·ich** \'fet-ish, 'fēt-\ *n* **1** : an object (as an idol or image) believed to have supernatural or magical powers **2** : an object of unreasoning devotion or concern — **fet·ish·ism** \-ˌiz-əm\ *n*

fet·lock \'fet-ˌläk\ *n* **1** : a projection with a tuft of hair on the back of a horse's leg above the hoof **2** : the tuft of hair growing out of the fetlock

fet·ter \'fet-ər\ *n* **1** : a chain or shackle for the feet **2** : something that confines : RESTRAINT — **fetter** *vb*

fet·tle \'fet-əl\ *n* : a state of fitness or order : CONDITION ⟨in fine *fettle*⟩

fe·tus \'fēt-əs\ *n* : a young animal while in the body of its mother or in the egg esp. in the later stages of development — **fe·tal** \'fēt-əl\ *adj*

feud \'fyüd\ *n* : a prolonged quarrel; *esp* : a lasting conflict between families or clans marked by violent attacks undertaken for revenge — **feud** *vb*

feu·dal·ism \-əl-ˌiz-əm\ *n* : a system of political organization (as in medieval Europe) in which a vassal rendered service to a lord and received protection and land in return — **feu·dal** \'fyüd-əl\ *adj* — **feu·dal·is·tic** \ˌfyüd-ə-'lis-tik\ *adj* — **feu·dal·ly** \'fyüd-ə-lē\ *adv*

[1]**feu·da·to·ry** \'fyüd-ə-ˌtōr-ē, -ˌtȯr-\ *adj* : owing feudal allegiance

[2]**feudatory** *n, pl* **-ries 1** : a person who holds lands by feudal law or usage **2** : FIEF

ə abut	ər further	a back	ā bake	
ä cot, cart	au̇ out	ch chin	e less	ē easy
g gift	i trip	ī life	j joke	ŋ sing	ō flow
ȯ flaw	ȯi coin	th thin	t͟h this	ü loot
u̇ foot	y yet	yü few	yu̇ furious	zh vision

fe·ver \'fē-vər\ *n* **1 a :** a rise of body temperature above the normal **b :** a disease of which fever is a prominent symptom **2 a :** a state of heightened or intense emotion or activity **b :** CRAZE, RAGE

fever blister *n* : COLD SORE

fe·ver·ish \'fēv-(ə-)rish\ *adj* **1 a :** marked by fever **b :** of, relating to, or being fever **c :** tending to cause fever **2 :** marked by intense emotion, activity, or instability — **fe·ver·ish·ly** *adv* — **fe·ver·ish·ness** *n*

fever thermometer *n* : CLINICAL THERMOMETER

1**few** \'fyü\ *pron* : not many persons or things

2**few** *adj* **1 :** amounting to only a small number ⟨one of his *few* pleasures⟩ **2 :** not many but some ⟨caught a *few* fish⟩ — **few·ness** *n*

3**few** *n* **1 :** a small number of units or individuals ⟨a *few* of them⟩ **2 :** a special limited number ⟨the discriminating *few*⟩

1**few·er** \'fyü-ər\ *adj* : not so many : a smaller number of

2**fewer** *pron* : a smaller number of persons or things ⟨*fewer* came than were expected⟩

fez \'fez\ *n, pl* **fez·zes :** a round flat-crowned hat made of red felt and worn by men in eastern Mediterranean countries

fez

ff *abbr* fortissimo

fi·an·cé \ˌfē-ˌän-'sā, fē-'än-ˌsā\ *n* [from French, from past participle of *fiancer* "to pledge", "betroth", from *fiance* "trust", "promise", ultimately derived from Latin *fides* "faith"] : a man engaged to be married

fi·an·cée \ˌfē-ˌän-'sā, fē-'än-ˌsā\ *n* : a woman engaged to be married

fi·as·co \fē-'as-kō\ *n, pl* **-coes** : a complete or ridiculous failure

fi·at \'fī-ˌat, 'fē-ˌät\ *n* [from the Latin verb form *fiat* meaning "let it be done"] : an authoritative decree

fib \'fib\ *n* : a lie about some trivial matter — **fib** *vb* — **fib·ber** *n*

fi·ber *or* **fi·bre** \'fī-bər\ *n* **1 :** a thread or a structure or object resembling a thread: as **a :** a slender root (as of a grass) **b :** a long tapering thick-walled plant cell esp. of vascular tissue **c :** a muscle cell **d** : AXON, DENDRITE **e :** a slender and greatly elongated natural or synthetic unit of material (as wool, cotton, asbestos, gold, glass, or rayon) typically capable of being spun into yarn **2 :** material made of fibers; *esp* : a tough hard or flexible material made from cellulose fibers and used for luggage **3 :** basic toughness : STRENGTH ⟨moral *fiber*⟩

fi·ber·board \'fī-bər-ˌbōrd, -ˌbȯrd\ *n* : a material made by compressing fibers (as of wood) into stiff sheets

fiber glass *n* : glass in fibrous form used in making various products (as yarn and insulation)

fi·brin \'fī-brən\ *n* : a white insoluble fibrous substance formed in clotting of the blood

fi·brous \'fī-brəs\ *adj* **1 :** containing, consisting of, or resembling fibers **2 :** TOUGH, STRINGY

fibrous root *n* : a root that is one of many similar slender roots branching directly from the base of the stem of a plant — compare TAPROOT

fib·u·la \'fib-yə-lə\ *n, pl* **-lae** \-ˌlē, -ˌlī\ *or* **-las** : the outer and usu. the smaller of the two bones of the hind limb below the knee — **fib·u·lar** \-lər\ *adj*

fick·le \'fik-əl\ *adj* : not firm or steadfast in disposition or character : INCONSTANT ⟨*fickle* friends⟩ — **fick·le·ness** *n*

fic·tion \'fik-shən\ *n* **1 :** something told or written that is not fact : something made up ⟨both fact and *fiction* in that story⟩ **2 :** a made-up story about real or imaginary persons or events; *also* : such stories as a class ⟨a writer of *fiction*⟩ — **fic·tion·al** \-sh(ə-)nəl\ *adj* — **fic·tion·al·ly** \-ē\ *adv*

fic·tion·al·ize \'fik-sh(ə-)nəl-ˌīz\ *or* **fic·tion·ize** \-shə-ˌnīz\ *vb* : to make into fiction ⟨the novel is a *fictionalized* version of the author's youth⟩ — **fic·tion·al·i·za·tion** \ˌfik-sh(ə-)nəl-ə-'zā-shən\ *or* **fic·tion·i·za·tion** \-shə-nə-'zā-shən\ *n*

fic·ti·tious \fik-'tish-əs\ *adj* : not real : MADE-UP, IMAGINARY ⟨a *fictitious* alibi⟩ — **fic·ti·tious·ly** *adv* — **fic·ti·tious·ness** *n*

1**fid·dle** \'fid-əl\ *n* : VIOLIN

2**fiddle** *vb* **fid·dled; fid·dling** \-(ə-)liŋ\ **1 :** to play on a fiddle **2 a :** to move the hands or fingers restlessly **b :** PUTTER **c :** MEDDLE, TAMPER — **fid·dler** \-(ə-)lər\ *n*

fid·dle–leaf fig \ˌfid-əl-ˌ(l)ēf-\ *n* : an African fig tree with violin-shaped leaves that is often cultivated as a pot plant

fiddler crab *n* : a burrowing crab with one claw much enlarged in the male

fid·dle·stick \-ˌstik\ *n* **1 :** a violin bow **2** *pl* : NONSENSE — used as an interjection

fi·del·i·ty \fə-'del-ət-ē, fī-\ *n, pl* **-ties 1 a :** the quality or state of being faithful **b :** accuracy in details : EXACTNESS **2 :** the degree to which an electronic device (as a radio or phonograph) accurately reproduces its effect (as sound) ***syn*** see LOYALTY ***ant*** faithlessness, perfidy

1**fid·get** \'fij-ət\ *n* **1** *pl* : uneasiness or restlessness as shown by nervous movements **2 :** one that fidgets — **fid·gety** \-ət-ē\ *adj*

2**fidget** *vb* : to move or cause to move or act nervously or restlessly

fie \'fī\ *interj* — used to express slight shock or disapproval

fief \'fēf\ *n* : a feudal estate : FEE

1**field** \'fēld\ *n* **1 a :** open country — usu. used in pl. **b :** a piece of open land **c :** a piece of land put to some special use or yielding some special product ⟨athletic *field*⟩ ⟨gas *field*⟩ **d :** a place where a battle is fought : the region in which military operations are carried on **e :** an open space or expanse ⟨a *field* of ice⟩ **2 :** a sphere of activity or influence ⟨the *field* of science⟩ **3 :** a background on which something is drawn, painted, or mounted ⟨the American flag has white stars on a blue *field*⟩ **4 :** the individuals that make up all or part of a sports activity **5 :** a region or space in which a given effect (as gravity, electricity, or magnetism) exists **6 :** the area visible through the lens of an optical instrument

2**field** *vb* **1 :** to put into the field ⟨*field* an army⟩ **2 :** to catch, stop, or throw a ball as a fielder ⟨*fielded* a ground ball⟩

3**field** *adj* : of or relating to a field: as **a :** growing in or inhabiting open country ⟨*field* flowers⟩ **b :** made, conducted, used, or operating in the field ⟨*field* artillery⟩

field corn *n* : an Indian corn with starchy kernels grown for feeding livestock or for market grain

field day *n* **1 :** a day devoted to outdoor sports and athletic competition **2 :** a time of unusual pleasure or unexpected success

field·er \'fēl-dər\ *n* : a baseball player stationed in the outfield

field event *n* : an event in a track meet other than a race

field glass *n* : a hand-held optical instrument for use

F

outdoors usu. consisting of two telescopes on a single frame — usu. used in pl.
field goal *n* **1** : a score in football made by drop-kicking or place-kicking the ball over the crossbar from ordinary play **2** : a basket in basketball made while the ball is in play
field lens *n* : the one of the two lenses at the eye end of a telescope or microscope that is nearer the object under study
field magnet *n* : a magnet for producing and maintaining a magnetic field esp. in a generator or electric motor
field marshal *n* : an officer (as in the British army) of the highest rank
field mouse *n* : any of various mice that inhabit open fields
field trip *n* : a visit (as to a factory, farm, or museum) made by students and usu. a teacher for purposes of firsthand observation
fiend \'fēnd\ *n* [from Old English *fēond*, *fīend* meaning originally "an enemy", then "the devil" regarded as the enemy of mankind] **1** : DEMON, DEVIL **2** : an extremely wicked or cruel person **3 a** : FANATIC ⟨golf *fiend*⟩ **b** : ADDICT ⟨dope *fiend*⟩ — **fiend·ish** \'fēn-dish\ *adj* — **fiend·ish·ly** *adv* — **fiend·ish·ness** *n*
fierce \'fi(ə)rs\ *adj* **1 a** : violently hostile or aggressive in temperament **b** : given to fighting or killing : PUGNACIOUS **2** : marked by unrestrained zeal or vehemence : INTENSE **3** : furiously active or determined **4** : wild or menacing in aspect — **fierce·ly** *adv* — **fierce·ness** *n*
fi·ery \'fī-(ə-)rē\ *adj* **fi·eri·er**; **-est** **1** : being on fire : BLAZING **2** : hot or glowing like a fire **3 a** : full of emotion or spirit ⟨a *fiery* speech⟩ **b** : easily provoked ⟨a *fiery* temper⟩ — **fi·eri·ness** *n*
fi·es·ta \fē-'es-tə\ *n* : FESTIVAL; *esp* : a saint's day celebrated in Spain and Latin America with processions and dances
fife \'fīf\ *n* : a small shrill musical instrument resembling a flute
fif·teen \(')fif-'tēn\ *n* — see NUMBER table — **fifteen** *adj or pron* — **fif·teenth** \-'tēn(t)th\ *adj or n*
fifth \'fif(t)th\ *n* **1** — see NUMBER table **2** : a musical interval embracing five diatonic degrees **3** : a unit of measure for liquor equal to one fifth of a U.S. gallon — **fifth** *adj or adv* — **fifth·ly** *adv*
fif·ty \'fif-tē\ *n, pl* **fifties** — see NUMBER table — **fif·ti·eth** \-tē-əth\ *adj or n* — **fifty** *adj or pron*
fif·ty–fif·ty \,fif-tē-'fif-tē\ *adj* **1** : shared equally **2** : half favorable and half unfavorable ⟨a *fifty-fifty* chance to live⟩ — **fifty–fifty** *adv*
fig \'fig\ *n* : the usu. edible oblong or pear-shaped fruit of a tree related to the mulberry; *also* : a tree bearing figs
fig *abbr* figure
¹fight \'fīt\ *vb* **fought** \'fȯt\; **fight·ing** **1 a** : to contend against another in battle or physical combat **b** : to engage in prizefighting : BOX **2** : to try hard **3 a** : to act in opposition : STRUGGLE, CONTEND ⟨*fight* for the right⟩ ⟨*fight* a fire⟩ ⟨*fight* discrimination⟩ **b** : to attempt to prevent the success or effectiveness of **4** : to carry on : WAGE ⟨*fight* a war⟩ **5** : to gain by struggle ⟨*fights* his way through⟩
²fight *n* **1 a** : a hostile encounter : COMBAT, BATTLE

ə abut	ər further	a back	ā bake
ä cot, cart	au̇ out	ch chin	e less	ē easy
g gift	i trip	ī life	j joke	ng sing	ō flow
ȯ flaw	ȯi coin	th thin	t͟h this	ü loot
u̇ foot	y yet	yü few	yu̇ furious	zh vision

b : a boxing match **c** : a verbal disagreement **2** : a struggle for a goal or an objective **3** : strength or disposition for fighting ⟨full of *fight*⟩
fight·er \'fīt-ər\ *n* : one that fights: **a** : WARRIOR, SOLDIER **b** : BOXER **c** : a fast maneuverable airplane with armament for destroying enemy aircraft
fig·ment \'fig-mənt\ *n* : something imagined or made up
fig·u·ra·tive \'fig-(y)ə-rət-iv\ *adj* **1** : representing by a figure : EMBLEMATIC **2 a** : expressing one thing in terms normally denoting another : METAPHORICAL **b** : marked by figures of speech — **fig·u·ra·tive·ly** *adv* — **fig·u·ra·tive·ness** *n*
¹fig·ure \'fig-yər, *esp Brit* 'fig-ər\ *n* **1 a** : NUMERAL **b** *pl* : arithmetical calculations **c** : a written or printed character **d** : PRICE **2 a** : the shape or outline of something **b** : bodily shape or form esp. of a person **c** : an object noticeable only as a shape or form **3 a** : a representation of a form esp. of a person **b** : a diagram or pictorial illustration of a text **c** : a combination of points, lines, or surfaces in geometry ⟨a circle is a closed plane *figure*⟩ **4** : FIGURE OF SPEECH **5** : PATTERN, DESIGN **6** : impression produced ⟨the couple cut quite a *figure*⟩ **7** : a series of movements in a dance **8** : a prominent personality : PERSONAGE — **fig·ured** \-(y)ərd\ *adj*
²figure *vb* **1** : to represent by or as if by a figure or outline : PORTRAY **2** : to decorate with a pattern **3 a** : BELIEVE, DECIDE ⟨*figured* he might win⟩ **b** : CONSIDER ⟨*figure* yourself lucky⟩ **4** : to be or appear important or conspicuous ⟨*figure* in the news⟩ **5** : COMPUTE, CALCULATE — **fig·ur·er** \-(y)ər-ər\ *n* — **figure on** **1** : to take into consideration **2** : to rely on **3** : PLAN
fig·ure·head \'fig-(y)ər-,hed\ *n* **1** : a figure, statue, or bust on the bow of a ship **2** : a person who has the title but not the powers of the head of something

figurehead 1

figure of speech : a form of expression (as a simile or metaphor) used to convey meaning or heighten effect often by comparing or identifying one thing with another that has a meaning or connotation familiar to the reader or listener
fig·u·rine \,fig-(y)ə-'rēn\ *n* : a small carved or molded figure
fig·wort \'fig-,wərt, -,wȯrt\ *n* : any of a genus of chiefly coarse erect herbs with toothed leaves and clustered flowers
fil·a·ment \'fil-ə-mənt\ *n* : a single thread or a thin flexible threadlike object, process, or appendage: as **a** : a wire in an electric lamp made incandescent by the passage of an electric current; *esp* : a cathode in the form of a metal wire in an electron tube **b** : the anther-bearing stalk of a stamen — **fil·a·men·tous** \,fil-ə-'ment-əs\ *adj*
fil·bert \'fil-bərt\ *n* **1** : either of two European hazels; *also* : the sweet thick-shelled nut of a filbert **2** : HAZELNUT
filch \'filch\ *vb* : to steal furtively : PILFER
¹file \'fīl\ *n* : a usu. steel tool with sharp ridges or teeth on its surface for smoothing or rubbing down a hard substance
²file *vb* : to rub, smooth, or cut away with a file
³file *vb* [from medieval French *filer* "to string documents on a string or wire", from *fil* "thread", "string", from Latin *filum*] **1** : to arrange in order for preservation or reference **2** : to enter or record as

prescribed by law ⟨*file* a mortgage⟩ ⟨*file* for elective office⟩

4**file** *n* **1 :** a device (as a folder, case, or cabinet) for keeping papers or records in order **2 :** a collection of papers or records kept in a file

5**file** *n* **:** a row of persons, animals, or things arranged one behind the other

6**file** *vb* **:** to march or proceed in file

fi·let \fi-ˈlā\ *n* **:** a lace with a square mesh and geometric designs

fil·i·al \ˈfil-ē-əl,ˈfil-yəl\ *adj* **1 :** of, relating to, or befitting a son or daughter **2 :** having or assuming the relation of a child or offspring — **fil·i·al·ly** \-ē\ *adv*

1**fil·i·bus·ter** \ˈfil-ə-ˌbəs-tər\ *n* [from Spanish *filibustero*, itself borrowed, probably via French *flibustier*, from English *freebooter*, which in turn came from Dutch *vrijbuiter*, a word related to the sources of English *free* and *booty*] **1 :** an irregular military adventurer; *esp* **:** an American engaged in stirring up rebellions in Latin America in the mid-19th century **2 a :** the use of delaying tactics (as long speeches) to delay or prevent action esp. in a legislative assembly **b :** an instance of this practice

2**filibuster** *vb* **fil·i·bus·tered**; **fil·i·bus·ter·ing** \-t(ə-)ring\ **1 :** to carry out revolutionary activities in a foreign country **2 :** to engage in a legislative filibuster — **fil·i·bus·ter·er** \-tər-ər\ *n*

fil·i·gree \ˈfil-ə-ˌgrē\ *n* **1 :** ornamental work esp. of fine wire applied chiefly to gold and silver surfaces **2 a :** ornamental openwork of delicate or intricate design **b :** a pattern or design resembling this openwork

fil·ing \ˈfī-ling\ *n* **1 :** the act of one that files **2 :** a small piece scraped off in filing ⟨iron *filings*⟩

Fil·i·pi·no \ˌfil-ə-ˈpē-nō\ *n, pl* **-nos 1 :** a native or inhabitant of the Philippines **2 :** a person of Filipino descent — **Filipino** *adj*

1**fill** \ˈfil\ *vb* **1 :** to put into as much as can be held or conveniently contained ⟨*fill* one's plate⟩ **2 :** to become full **3 :** SATISFY ⟨*fill* all requirements⟩ **4 :** to occupy fully **:** take up whatever space there is ⟨clothes *filled* the closet⟩ **5 :** to spread through ⟨laughter *filled* the room⟩ **6 :** to stop up (as crevices or holes) **:** PLUG ⟨*fill* a crack with putty⟩ ⟨*fill* a tooth⟩ **7 a :** to perform the duties of **:** OCCUPY ⟨*fill* the office of president⟩ **b :** to put a person in ⟨*filled* several vacancies⟩ **8 :** to supply according to directions ⟨*fill* a prescription⟩ — **fill one's shoes :** to take one's place or position

2**fill** *n* **1 :** a full supply; *esp* **:** a quantity that satisfies or satiates ⟨eat one's *fill*⟩ **2 :** material used esp. for filling a ditch or hollow in the ground

fill·er \ˈfil-ər\ *n* **:** one that fills: as **a :** a substance added to another substance to increase bulk or weight **b :** a material used for filling cracks and pores in wood before painting **c :** a pack of paper for insertion in a binder

1**fil·let** \ˈfil-ət\ *also* **fi·let** \fi-ˈlā, ˈfil-(ˌ)ā\ *n* **1 :** a narrow headband **2 :** a thin narrow strip of material; *esp* **:** a piece or slice of boneless meat or fish

2**fillet** *vb* **1 :** to bind or adorn with a fillet **2 :** to cut into fillets

fill in *vb* **1 :** to furnish with specified information ⟨*fill in* an application⟩ ⟨*filled* him *in* on the latest news⟩ **2 :** to fill a vacancy usu. temporarily **:** SUBSTITUTE ⟨*filled in* during the emergency⟩

fill·ing \ˈfil-ing\ *n* **1 :** material that is used to fill something ⟨a *filling* for a tooth⟩ **2 :** something that completes: as **a :** the yarn interlacing the warp in a fabric **b :** a food mixture used to fill pastry or sandwiches

filling station *n* **:** a retail establishment for servicing motor vehicles esp. with gasoline and oil

1**fil·lip** \ˈfil-əp\ *n* **1 :** a blow or gesture made by the sudden forcible straightening of a finger curled against the thumb **2 :** a feature added to attract interest

2**fillip** *vb* **1 :** to tap with the finger by flicking the fingernail outward across the end of the thumb **2 :** STIMULATE

fill out *vb* **1 :** to put on flesh **2 :** to complete by filling in blanks ⟨*fill out* an application⟩

fil·ly \ˈfil-ē\ *n, pl* **fillies :** a young female horse usu. of less than four years

1**film** \ˈfilm\ *n* **1 :** a thin skin or membrane **2 :** a thin coating or layer ⟨a *film* of ice on a windshield⟩ **3 :** a roll or strip of thin flexible transparent material coated with a chemical substance sensitive to light and used in taking pictures **4 :** MOTION PICTURE

2**film** *vb* **1 :** to cover or become covered with film ⟨eyes *filmed* with tears⟩ **2 :** to photograph on a film; *esp* **:** to make a motion picture

film·strip \ˈfilm-ˌstrip\ *n* **:** a strip of film bearing photographs, diagrams, or graphic matter for projecting still pictures on a screen

filmy \ˈfil-mē\ *adj* **film·i·er**; **-est 1 :** of, resembling, or composed of film **2 :** covered with a haze or film — **film·i·ness** *n*

1**fil·ter** \ˈfil-tər\ *n* **1 :** a porous substance through which a gas or liquid is passed to separate out matter in suspension **2 :** an apparatus containing a filter **3 :** COLOR FILTER

F

2**filter** *vb* **fil·tered**; **fil·ter·ing** \-t(ə-)ring\ **1 :** to subject to the action of a filter **2 :** to remove by means of a filter **3 :** to pass through or as if through a filter

fil·ter·a·ble *also* **fil·tra·ble** \ˈfil-t(ə-)rə-bəl\ *adj* **:** capable of being separated by or of passing through a filter ⟨*filterable* microorganisms⟩ ⟨a *filterable* liquid⟩ — **fil·ter·a·bil·i·ty** \ˌfil-t(ə-)rə-ˈbil-ət-ē\ *n*

filter bed *n* **:** a bed of sand or gravel through which liquid (as from sewage) is passed to purify it

filter paper *n* **:** porous paper used for filtering

filth \ˈfilth\ *n* **1 :** foul or putrid matter; *esp* **:** loathsome dirt or refuse **2 a :** moral corruption or defilement **b :** something that tends to corrupt or defile

filthy \ˈfil-thē\ *adj* **filth·i·er**; **-est 1 :** covered with or containing filth **:** disgustingly dirty **2 a :** UNDERHANDED, VILE **b :** OBSCENE — **filth·i·ly** \-thə-lē\ *adv* — **filth·i·ness** \-thē-nəs\ *n*

fil·trate \ˈfil-ˌtrāt\ *n* **:** the fluid that has passed through a filter

fil·tra·tion \fil-ˈtrā-shən\ *n* **:** the act or process of filtering

fin \ˈfin\ *n* **1 :** a thin external process of an aquatic animal (as a fish or whale) used in propelling or guiding the body **2 a :** a fin-shaped part (as on an airplane, boat, or automobile) **b :** FLIPPER 2 **c :** a projecting rib on a radiator or an engine cylinder — **fin·like** \-ˌlīk\ *adj* — **finned** \ˈfind\ *adj*

fin *abbr* finish

fi·na·gle \fə-ˈnā-gəl\ *vb* **fi·na·gled**; **fi·na·gling** \-g(ə-)ling\ **:** to use trickery to gain one's ends — **fi·na·gler** \-g(ə-)lər\ *n*

1**fi·nal** \ˈfīn-əl\ *adj* **1 :** not to be altered or undone **:** CONCLUSIVE ⟨my *final* offer⟩ **2 :** relating to or occurring at the end or conclusion **:** ULTIMATE — **fi·nal·ly** \ˈfīn-(ə-)lē\ *adv*

2**final** *n* **:** something final: as **a :** a deciding match, game, or trial **b :** the last examination in a course

fi·na·le \fə-ˈnal-ē, fi-ˈnäl-\ *n* **:** the close or termination of something; *esp* **:** the last section of a musical composition

fi·nal·ist \'fīn-ə-ləst\ *n* : a contestant in the finals of a competition

fi·nal·i·ty \fī-'nal-ət-ē, fə-\ *n, pl* **-ties** **1** : the character or state of being final, settled, or complete **2** : something final

fi·nal·ize \'fīn-ə-,līz\ *vb* : to put in final or finished form

1**fi·nance** \fə-'nan(t)s, 'fī-,, fī-'\ *n* [from Middle English, meaning "the settlement of debts", from French, from *finer* "to pay up", literally "to bring to an end", from *fin* "end", from Latin *finis*] **1** *pl* : resources (as money) available esp. to a government or business **2** : the obtaining or provision of funds or capital : FINANCING — **fi·nan·cial** \fə-'nan-chəl, fī-\ *adj* — **fi·nan·cial·ly** \-'nanch-(ə-)lē\ *adv*

2**finance** *vb* : to raise or provide funds or capital for ⟨*finance* a new car⟩

fin·an·cier \,fin-ən-'si(ə)r, fə-,nan-, ,fī-,nan-\ *n* : a person who supplies large sums of money as investments

finch \'finch\ *n* : any of numerous songbirds (as the sparrows, grosbeaks, crossbills, goldfinches, linnets, and buntings) having a short stout conical bill adapted for crushing seeds

1**find** \'fīnd\ *vb* **found** \'fau̇nd\; **find·ing** **1** : to meet with someone or something by chance ⟨*find* a kitten on the porch⟩ **2** : to come upon by searching or study : DISCOVER **3** : to obtain by effort or management ⟨*find* time to do it⟩ **4** : to arrive at : REACH ⟨*find* his place in the world⟩ **5** : to make a decision and declare it ⟨*find* a verdict⟩ ⟨*find* for the defendant⟩ **6** : to know by experience ⟨people *found* the boy honest⟩ **7** : to gain or regain the use of ⟨*found* her voice again⟩ **8** : PROVIDE, SUPPLY ⟨*find* room for a guest⟩ — **find fault** : to discover real or imaginary faults : CRITICIZE, COMPLAIN

2**find** *n* **1** : an instance of finding **2** : something found; *esp* : a valuable item found

find·er \'fīn-dər\ *n* : one that finds: as **a** : a small telescope attached to a larger one for finding an object **b** : a lens on a camera that shows the view being photographed by the camera

find·ing \'fīn-ding\ *n* **1** : FIND **2** : the result of a judicial proceeding or inquiry

find out *vb* **1** : to learn by study or observation : DISCOVER ⟨didn't know the way and *found out* for himself⟩ ⟨*find out* a secret⟩ **2** : UNMASK ⟨*found* the impostor *out*⟩

1**fine** \'fīn\ *n* : a sum of money imposed as punishment

2**fine** *vb* : to punish by a fine

3**fine** *adj* **1** : free from impurity **2 a** : not thick, coarse, or dull ⟨*fine* thread⟩ ⟨*fine* sand⟩ ⟨knife with a *fine* edge⟩ **b** : SMALL ⟨*fine* print⟩ **c** : DELICATE ⟨*fine* china⟩ ⟨*fine* adjustment⟩ **3** : SUBTLE ⟨a *fine* distinction⟩ **4** : superior in quality, conception, or appearance **5** : to one's liking : AGREEABLE ⟨that's *fine* with me⟩ — **finely** *adv* — **fine·ness** \'fīn-nəs\ *n*

4**fine** *adv* **1** : FINELY **2** : very well ⟨did *fine* on the test⟩ ⟨I liked it *fine*⟩

5**fi·ne** \'fē-(,)nā\ *n* : END — used as a direction in music to mark the closing point after a repeat

fine art *n* : art or an art (as painting, sculpture, or music) concerned primarily with the creation of beautiful objects

ə abut	ər further	a back	ā bake
ä cot, cart	au̇ out	ch chin	e less	ē easy
g gift	i trip ī life	j joke	ng sing	ō flow
ȯ flaw	ȯi coin	th thin	t͟h this	ü loot
u̇ foot	y yet	yü few	yu̇ furious	zh vision

fin·ery \'fīn-(ə-)rē\ *n, pl* **-er·ies** : ORNAMENTS; *esp* : showy clothing and jewels

1**fi·nesse** \fə-'nes\ *n* **1** : refinement or delicacy of workmanship, structure, or texture ⟨a painting executed with *finesse*⟩ **2** : skillful handling of a situation : CUNNING, SUBTLETY ⟨did by *finesse* what could not be done by force⟩

2**finesse** *vb* : to bring about a result by finesse

1**fin·ger** \'fing-gər\ *n* **1** : one of the five divisions of the end of the hand; *esp* : one other than the thumb **2 a** : something that resembles or does the work of a finger **b** : a part of a glove into which a finger is inserted **3** : the breadth of a finger — **fin·gered** \-gərd\ *adj* — **fin·ger·like** \-gər-,līk\ *adj*

2**finger** *vb* **fin·gered**; **fin·ger·ing** \-g(ə-)ring\ **1** : to touch with the fingers : HANDLE **2** : to perform with the fingers or with a certain fingering **3** : to point out : IDENTIFY

fin·ger·board \'fing-gər-,bōrd, -,bȯrd\ *n* : the part of a stringed instrument against which the fingers press the strings to vary the pitch

finger hole *n* : a hole in a wind instrument by means of which the pitch of the tone is changed when it is left open or closed by the finger

fin·ger·ing \'fing-g(ə-)ring\ *n* **1** : the act or process of handling or touching with the fingers **2 a** : the method of using the fingers in playing an instrument **b** : the marking on a piece of music that shows what fingers are to be used

fin·ger·nail \'fing-gər-,nāl, ,fing-gər-'\ *n* : the nail of a finger

finger painting *n* **1** : a method of spreading pigment on wet paper chiefly with the fingers **2** : a picture produced by finger painting

fin·ger·print \'fing-gər-,print\ *n* : the pattern of marks made by pressing the tip of a finger on a surface; *esp* : an ink impression of the lines on the tip of a finger taken for the purpose of identification — **finger·print** *vb*

fin·i·cal \'fin-i-kəl\ *adj* : FINICKY — **fin·i·cal·ly** \-k(ə-)lē\ *adv* — **fin·i·cal·ness** \-kəl-nəs\ *n*

fin·ick·ing \'fin-i-king, -kən\ *adj* : FINICKY

fin·icky \'fin-i-kē\ *adj* : too nice, exacting, or demanding in taste or standards : FUSSY — **fin·ick·i·ness** *n*

fin·is \'fin-əs, 'fī-nəs\ *n* : END, CONCLUSION

1**fin·ish** \'fin-ish\ *vb* **1** : to bring or come to an end : TERMINATE **2** : to bring to completion or issue : PERFECT **3** : to put a final coat or surface on **4** : to come to the end of a course, task, or undertaking ⟨the pianist *finished* with a flourish⟩ ⟨*finished* second in the race⟩ — **fin·ish·er** *n*

2**finish** *n* **1** : END, CONCLUSION ⟨a close *finish* in a race⟩ **2** : the treatment given a surface or the appearance given by finishing ⟨shiny *finish* on a new car⟩ **3** : cultivation in manners and speech : social polish

finishing nail *n* : a small-headed wire nail used esp. where a large head would be undesirably conspicuous

fi·nite \'fī-,nīt\ *adj* **1** : having definite or definable limits : limited in scope or nature : not infinite **2** : showing distinction of grammatical person and number ⟨a *finite* verb⟩ — **fi·nite·ly** *adv* — **fi·nite·ness** *n*

finite arithmetic *n* : MODULAR ARITHMETIC

Finn \'fin\ *n* **1** : a member of a people speaking Finnish **2 a** : a native or inhabitant of Finland **b** : a person of Finnish descent

Finn *abbr* Finnish

fin·nan had·die \,fin-ən-'had-ē\ *n* : smoked haddock — called also *finnan haddock*

[1]**Finn·ish** \'fin-ish\ *adj* : of, relating to, or characteristic of Finland, the Finns, or Finnish
[2]**Finnish** *n* : a language spoken in Finland, Karelia, and small areas of Sweden and Norway
fin·ny \'fin-ē\ *adj* **1** : resembling or having fins **2** : of, relating to, or full of fish
fiord *var of* FJORD
fir \'fər\ *n* **1** : any of various usu. large symmetrical evergreen trees related to the pines some of which yield useful lumber or resins **2** : the wood of a fir
[1]**fire** \'fī(ə)r\ *n* **1** : the light and heat and esp. the flame produced by burning **2** : fuel that is burning (as in a fireplace or stove) **3** : the destructive burning of something (as a building or a forest) **4** : ardent liveliness : ENTHUSIASM **5** : the discharge of firearms : SHOOTING — **on fire 1** : BURNING **2** : ARDENT, EAGER — **under fire 1** : exposed to the firing of an enemy's guns **2** : under attack
[2]**fire** *vb* **1 a** : to set on fire : KINDLE, IGNITE **b** : STIR, ENLIVEN ⟨*fires* the imagination⟩ ⟨all *fired* up⟩ **2** : to dismiss from employment **3** : to cause to explode ⟨*fire* dynamite⟩ **4 a** : to propel from or as if from a gun : LAUNCH ⟨*fire* an arrow⟩ ⟨*fire* a rocket⟩ **b** : to throw with speed : HURL ⟨*fired* the ball to first base⟩ **c** : to shoot off a firearm : DISCHARGE **5 a** : to subject to intense heat ⟨*fire* pottery⟩ **b** : to feed the fire of ⟨*fire* a furnace⟩ **6 a** : to begin to burn : catch fire **b** : to become ignited at the proper time ⟨cylinder that does not *fire* right⟩ — **fir·er** *n*
fire alarm *n* : an alarm sounded to signal the outbreak of a fire; *also* : an apparatus for sounding such an alarm
fire·arm \'fī(ə)r-,ärm\ *n* : a weapon from which a shot is discharged by gunpowder — usu. used only of a small arm (as a rifle or pistol)
fire·ball \-,bȯl\ *n* **1** : a ball of fire **2** : a brilliant meteor **3** : the luminous cloud of vapor and dust created by a nuclear explosion (as of an atom bomb)
fire·boat \-,bōt\ *n* : a ship equipped with apparatus (as pumps) for fighting fire
fire·box \-,bäks\ *n* **1** : a chamber (as of a furnace or steam boiler) that contains a fire **2** : a box containing a fire alarm
fire·brand \-,brand\ *n* **1** : a piece of burning wood **2** : a person who creates unrest or strife : AGITATOR
fire·break \-,brāk\ *n* : a barrier of cleared or plowed land intended to check a forest or grass fire
fire·brick \-,brik\ *n* : a brick capable of withstanding great heat and used for lining furnaces or fireplaces
fire·bug \-,bəg\ *n* : a person who deliberately sets destructive fires : ARSONIST
fire·crack·er \-,krak-ər\ *n* : a paper tube containing an explosive and usu. discharged for amusement
fire·damp \-,damp\ *n* : a combustible mine gas that consists chiefly of methane; *also* : the explosive mixture of this gas with air
fire·dog \-,dȯg\ *n* : ANDIRON
fire engine *n* : an apparatus for directing water or an extinguishing chemical on fires; *esp* : a motortruck equipped with such an apparatus
fire escape *n* : a stairway or ladder that provides a means of escape from a building in case of fire
fire extinguisher *n* : something used to put out a fire; *esp* : a portable hand-operated metal contrivance for ejecting a stream or spray of fire-extinguishing chemicals
fire·fly \'fī(ə)r-,flī\ *n* : a winged nocturnal insect producing a bright soft intermittent light; *esp* : the male of various long flat beetles
fire·house \-,hau̇s\ *n* : FIRE STATION
fire irons *n pl* : implements for tending a fire in a fireplace
fire·light \'fī(ə)r-,līt\ *n* : the light of a fire and esp. of one in a fireplace
fire·man \-mən\ *n* **1** : a member of a company organized to fight fires **2** : one who tends fires : STOKER
fire·place \-,plās\ *n* **1** : a framed rectangular opening in a chimney to hold an open fire **2** : an outdoor structure of brick or stone made for an open fire
fire·plug \-,pləg\ *n* : a hydrant to which a large hose can be attached for drawing water to extinguish fires
fire·pow·er \-,pau̇(-ə)r\ *n* : the ability to deliver gunfire or warheads on a target
[1]**fire·proof** \-'prüf\ *adj* : proof against or resistant to fire
[2]**fireproof** *vb* : to make fireproof
fire·side \'fī(ə)r-,sīd\ *n* **1** : a place near the hearth **2** : HOME
fire station *n* : a building housing fire apparatus and usu. firemen
fire tower *n* **1** : a tower from which a watch for fires is kept (as in a forest) **2** : a fireproof compartment containing a stairway in a building
fire·trap \'fī(ə)r-,trap\ *n* : a building or place apt to catch on fire or difficult to escape from in case of fire
fire wall *n* : a wall for preventing the spread of fire
fire·wa·ter \'fī(ə)r-,wȯt-ər, -,wät-\ *n* : intoxicating liquor
fire·weed \-,wēd\ *n* : a plant with pinkish purple flowers that springs up in clearings or burned areas
fire·wood \-,wu̇d\ *n* : wood cut for fuel
fire·work \-,wərk\ *n* **1** : an explosive or flammable device for producing a striking display (as of light, noise, or smoke) **2** *pl* : a display of fireworks **3** *pl* : a display of temper
fir·kin \'fər-kən\ *n* **1** : a small wooden vessel or cask **2** : any of various British units of capacity usu. equal to 1/4 barrel
[1]**firm** \'fərm\ *adj* **1 a** : securely or solidly fixed in place **b** : SOLID, VIGOROUS **c** : having a solid or compact texture **2 a** : not subject to change or fluctuation : STEADY ⟨a *firm* offer⟩ ⟨*firm* prices⟩ **b** : not easily moved or disturbed : STEADFAST **c** : WELL-FOUNDED ⟨*firm* evidence⟩ **3** : indicating firmness or resolution — **firm** *vb* — **firm·ly** *adv* — **firm·ness** *n*
[2]**firm** *n* [from German *firma*, originally "the name under which a company does business", from Italian, "signature", from *firmare* "to sign", from Latin *firmare* "to make firm", "confirm"] : a business enterprise or organization ⟨law *firm*⟩
fir·ma·ment \'fər-mə-mənt\ *n* : the arch of the sky : HEAVENS
[1]**first** \'fərst\ *adj* **1** — see NUMBER table **2** : preceding all others in time, order, or importance: as **a** : EARLIEST **b** : being the lowest forward gear or speed in an automotive shift **c** : highest or most prominent in carrying the melody ⟨*first* violin⟩
[2]**first** *adv* **1 a** : before any other in time, space, or importance **b** : for the first time **2** : in preference to something else ⟨surrender? We will die *first*⟩
[3]**first** *n* **1** — see NUMBER table **2 a** : the first gear or speed in an automotive vehicle **b** : the winning place in a competition or contest
first aid *n* : emergency treatment given to an ill or injured person
first base *n* : the base that must be touched first by a base runner in baseball or the position of the player defending that — **first base·man** \-'bās-mən\ *n*
first·born \'fərs(t)-'bȯrn\ *adj* : born first : ELDEST — **firstborn** *n*
first class *n* : the best or highest group in a classification — **first-class** *adj*
first cousin *n* : COUSIN 1 a

first–degree burn *n* : a mild burn characterized by heat, pain, and reddening of the burned surface but not exhibiting blistering or charring of tissues
first·hand \'fərst-'hand\ *adj* : coming directly from the original source — **firsthand** *adv*
first lady *n, often cap F&L* : the wife or hostess of the chief executive of a state or nation
first lieutenant *n* : a military officer ranking below a captain
first·ling \'fərst-ling\ *n* **1** : the first of a class **2** : the first product or result of something
first·ly \-lē\ *adv* : in the first place
first–rate \'fərst-'rāt\ *adj* : of the first order of size, importance, or quality — **first–rate** *adv*
firth \'fərth\ *n* : a narrow arm of the sea
fis·cal \'fis-kəl\ *adj* **1** : of or relating to public finances **2** : FINANCIAL — **fis·cal·ly** \-kə-lē\ *adv*
¹**fish** \'fish\ *n, pl* **fish** *or* **fish·es** **1 a** : an aquatic animal — usu. used in combination ⟨star*fish*⟩ ⟨cuttle*fish*⟩ **b** : a cold-blooded water-inhabiting water-breathing vertebrate animal with a typically long scaly tapering body, limbs developed as fins, and a vertical tail fin **2** : the flesh of fish used as food **3** : FELLOW, CHAP ⟨a queer *fish*⟩ — **fish·like** \'fish-ˌlīk\ *adj*
²**fish** *vb* **1** : to catch or try to catch fish **2** : to catch or try to catch fish in ⟨*fish* the stream⟩ **3** : to seek something by or as if by groping or feeling
fish·er \'fish-ər\ *n* **1** : one that fishes **2** : a large dark brown No. American aboreal carnivorous mammal related to the weasels; *also* : its valuable fur or pelt

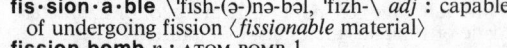

fisher 2 (about 36 in. long)

fish·er·man \-mən\ *n* **1** : one who fishes **2** : a ship used in commercial fishing
fish·ery \'fish-(ə-)rē\ *n, pl* **-er·ies** **1** : the activity or business of fishing **2** : a place or establishment for catching fish
fish–eye \'fish-ˌī\ *adj* : being, having, or produced by a lens covering an angle of about 180° ⟨*fish-eye* view⟩
fish hawk *n* : OSPREY
fish·hook \'fish-ˌhu̇k\ *n* : a usu. barbed hook for catching fish
fish ladder *n* : an arrangement of pools by which fish can pass around a dam
fish·wife \'fish-ˌwīf\ *n* **1** : a woman who sells fish **2** : a loudly abusive woman
fishy \'fish-ē\ *adj* **fish·i·er**; **-est** **1** : of, relating to, or resembling fish ⟨a *fishy* odor⟩ **2** : inspiring doubt or suspicion : QUESTIONABLE ⟨that story sounds *fishy* to me⟩
¹**fis·sion** \'fish-ən, 'fizh-\ *n* [from Latin *fiss-*, past participle stem of *findere* "to split", coming from the same source as English *bite*] **1** : a splitting or breaking up into parts **2** : reproduction by spontaneous division of a body or a cell into two or more parts each of which grows into a complete individual **3** : the splitting of an atomic nucleus resulting in the release of large amounts of energy
²**fission** *vb* : to undergo or cause to undergo fission

ə abut	ər further	a back	ā bake		
ä cot, cart	au̇ out	ch chin	e less	ē easy	
g gift	i trip	ī life	j joke	ng sing	ō flow
ȯ flaw	ȯi coin	th thin	<u>th</u> this	ü loot	
u̇ foot	y yet	yü few	yu̇ furious	zh vision	

fis·sion·a·ble \'fish-(ə-)nə-bəl, 'fizh-\ *adj* : capable of undergoing fission ⟨*fissionable* material⟩
fission bomb *n* : ATOM BOMB 1
fis·sure \'fish-ər\ *n* : a narrow opening or crack ⟨a *fissure* in rock⟩ — **fissure** *vb*
fist \'fist\ *n* **1** : the hand clenched with fingers doubled into the palm **2** : INDEX 5
fist·i·cuffs \'fis-ti-ˌkəfs\ *n pl* : a fight with fists
fis·tu·la \'fis-chə-lə\ *n, pl* **-las** *or* **-lae** \-ˌlē, -ˌlī\ : an abnormal passage leading from an abscess or hollow organ — **fis·tu·lous** \-ləs\ *adj*
¹**fit** \'fit\ *n* **1** : a sudden violent attack of a disorder (as epilepsy) esp. when marked by convulsions or loss of consciousness **2** : a sudden outburst (as of laughter)
²**fit** *adj* **fit·ter**; **fit·test** **1** : adapted to an end or design ⟨water *fit* for drinking⟩; *esp* : so adapted to the environment as to be capable of surviving — often used in the phrase *survival of the fittest* **2** : BECOMING, PROPER **3** : READY, PREPARED **4** : QUALIFIED, COMPETENT **5** : sound physically and mentally : HEALTHY — **fit·ly** *adv* — **fit·ness** *n*

syn FIT, APT, SUITABLE, APPROPRIATE can mean right with respect to the nature, condition, or use of the thing referred to. FIT may imply adaptability or qualification for an end in view; APT often applies to words and suggests a discriminating choice for a particular need or occasion; SUITABLE implies a fulfillment of requirements of a situation; APPROPRIATE suggests a marked or distinctive suitability ***ant*** unfit

³**fit** *vb* **fit·ted**; **fit·ting** **1** : to be suitable for or to : BEFIT **2 a** : to be of the right size and shape ⟨the suit *fits*⟩ **b** : to insert or adjust until correctly in place **c** : to make a place or room for **3** : to be in accord with ⟨*fit* the facts⟩ **4 a** : to make ready : PREPARE **b** : to bring to a required form and size : ADJUST **c** : to cause to conform to or suit something else ⟨*fit* words to a song⟩ **5** : SUPPLY, EQUIP ⟨*fit* out an expedition⟩ **6** : to be in harmony or accord : BELONG
⁴**fit** *n* **1** : the state or manner of fitting ⟨a tight *fit*⟩ **2** : a piece of clothing that fits
fitch \'fich\ *or* **fitch·ew** \'fich-ü\ *n* : POLECAT 1; *also* : its fur or pelt
fitch·et \'fich-ət\ *n* : POLECAT 1
fit·ful \'fit-fəl\ *adj* : not regular : RESTLESS ⟨*fitful* sleep⟩ — **fit·ful·ly** \-fə-lē\ *adv* — **fit·ful·ness** *n*
fit·ter \'fit-ər\ *n* : one that fits: as **a** : a person who tries on and adjusts articles of dress **b** : a person who fits, adjusts, or assembles parts (as of machinery)
¹**fit·ting** *adj* : APPROPRIATE, SUITABLE — **fit·ting·ly** \-ing-lē\ *adv* — **fit·ting·ness** *n*
²**fitting** *n* **1** : the action of one that fits; *esp* : a trying on of clothes being made or altered **2** : a small often standardized accessory part ⟨a pipe *fitting*⟩
five \'fīv\ *n* **1** — see NUMBER table **2** : the fifth in a set or series **3** : something having five units or members; *esp* : a male basketball team — **five** *adj or pron*
five–and–ten \ˌfī-vən-'ten\ *also* **five–and–dime** \-vən-'dīm\ *n* : a store selling inexpensive articles
¹**fix** \'fiks\ *vb* **1 a** : to make firm, stable, or fast **b** : to give a permanent or final form to **c** : to change into a stable or available form ⟨bacteria that *fix* nitrogen⟩ **d** : to kill, harden, and preserve for microscopic study **e** : to make the image of (a photographic film or print) permanent by chemical treatment **f** : AFFIX, ATTACH **2** : to hold or direct steadily ⟨*fixes* his eyes on the horizon⟩ **3 a** : to set or place definitely : ESTABLISH ⟨*fix* the date of a

meeting⟩ **b** : ASSIGN ⟨*fix* blame⟩ **4** : to get ready : PREPARE ⟨*fix* dinner⟩ **5** : REPAIR **6** : to influence the outcome of by improper or illegal methods ⟨*fix* a horse race⟩ — **fix·a·ble** \'fik-sə-bəl\ *adj* — **fix·er** *n*

[2]**fix** *n* **1** : a position of difficulty or embarrassment : PREDICAMENT **2** : the position (as of a ship) determined by taking bearings; *also* : a taking of bearings **3** : a shot of a narcotic

fix·ate \'fik-ˌsāt\ *vb* **1** : to make fixed or unchanging **2 a** : to focus one's eyes upon **b** : to concentrate one's attention — **fix·a·tion** \fik-'sā-shən\ *n*

fix·a·tive \'fik-sət-iv\ *n* : something that stabilizes or sets: as **a** : a substance added to a perfume esp. to prevent too rapid evaporation **b** : a varnish used esp. for the protection of crayon drawings

fixed \'fikst\ *adj* **1 a** : securely placed or fastened ⟨a *fixed* gaze⟩ **b** : not subject to change or fluctuation : SETTLED, FINAL ⟨a *fixed* income⟩ **2** : supplied with a definite amount of something needed ⟨well *fixed* for troops⟩ — **fix·ed·ly** \'fik-səd-lē\ *adv* — **fix·ed·ness** \'fik-səd-nəs\ *n*

fixed star *n* : a star so distant that it seems not to move

fix·ing \'fik-sing, *2 is often* -sənz\ *n* **1** : a putting in permanent form **2** *pl* : TRIMMINGS, EXTRAS ⟨turkey with all the *fixings*⟩

fix·ture \'fiks-chər\ *n* **1** : the act of fixing : the state of being fixed **2** : one firmly established in a place **3** : something attached to another as a permanent part ⟨bathroom *fixtures*⟩

[1]**fizz** \'fiz\ *vb* : to make a hissing or sputtering sound

[2]**fizz** *n* **1** : a hissing sound **2** : a bubbling drink — **fizzy** \'fiz-ē\ *adj*

fiz·zle \'fiz-əl\ *vb* **fiz·zled**; **fiz·zling** \-(ə-)ling\ **1** : FIZZ **2** : to fail after a promising start — **fizzle** *n*

fjord \fē-'ȯrd, 'fyȯrd\ *n* : a narrow inlet of the sea between cliffs or steep slopes

fl *abbr* fluid

Fla *or* **FL** *abbr* Florida

flab·ber·gast \'flab-ər-ˌgast\ *vb* : ASTONISH, DUMBFOUND

flab·by \'flab-ē\ *adj* **flab·bi·er**; **-est** : not firm and elastic : SOFT ⟨*flabby* muscles⟩ — **flab·bi·ly** \'flab-ə-lē\ *adv* — **flab·bi·ness** \'flab-ē-nəs\ *n*

[1]**flag** \'flag\ *n* : any of various irises; *esp* : a wild iris

[2]**flag** *n* **1** : a hard stone that easily splits into flat pieces **2** : a piece of flag used for paving

[3]**flag** *vb* **flagged**; **flag·ging** : to pave (as a walk) with flags

[4]**flag** *n* **1** : a piece of cloth with a distinctive design that is used as a symbol (as of nationality) or for signaling **2** : a small mark or marker

[5]**flag** *vb* **flagged**; **flag·ging** **1** : to put a flag on ⟨*flag* important letters⟩ **2** : to signal with or as if with a flag; *esp* : to signal to stop ⟨*flag* a taxi⟩

[6]**flag** *vb* **flagged**; **flag·ging** **1** : to be limp : DROOP **2** : to become weak ⟨his interest *flagged*⟩

Flag Day *n* : June 14 observed in some states in commemoration of the adoption in 1777 of the U.S. flag

[1]**flag·el·late** \'flaj-ə-ˌlāt\ *vb* : WHIP — **flag·el·la·tion** \ˌflaj-ə-'lā-shən\ *n*

[2]**flag·el·late** \'flaj-ə-lət, flə-'jel-ət\ *adj* **1 a** *or* **flag·el·lat·ed** \'flaj-ə-ˌlāt-əd\ : having flagella **b** : resembling a flagellum **2** : of, relating to, or caused by flagellates

[3]**flagellate** *like* [2]\ *n* : a flagellate protozoan or alga

fla·gel·lum \flə-'jel-əm\ *n, pl* **-gel·la** \-'jel-ə\ *also* **-gellums** : a tapering process that projects singly or in groups from a cell and is the primary organ of motion of many microorganisms — **fla·gel·lar** \-'jel-ər\ *adj*

fla·geo·let \ˌflaj-ə-'let\ *n* : a small woodwind instrument belonging to the flute class

flag·ging \'flag-ing\ *n* : a pavement of flagstones

flag·man \'flag-mən\ *n* : one who signals with or as if with a flag

flag·on \'flag-ən\ *n* : a container for liquids usu. having a handle, spout, and lid

flag·pole \'flag-ˌpōl\ *n* : a pole from which a flag flies

flag rank *n* : any of the ranks in the navy above a captain

fla·grant \'flā-grənt\ *adj* : conspicuously bad : OUTRAGEOUS, NOTORIOUS ⟨*flagrant* disobedience⟩ ⟨a *flagrant* criminal⟩ — **fla·gran·cy** \-grən-sē\ *n* — **fla·grant·ly** *adv*

flag·ship \'flag-ˌship\ *n* : the ship that carries the commander of a fleet or squadron

flag·staff \-ˌstaf\ *n* : FLAGPOLE

flag·stone \-ˌstōn\ *n* : [2]FLAG 2

[1]**flail** \'flāl\ *n* : a hand threshing tool consisting of a wooden handle with a free-swinging stout short stick at the end

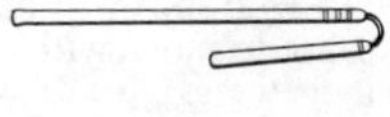
flail

[2]**flail** *vb* : to strike with or as if with a flail ⟨*flailed* out with his arms⟩

flair \'fla(ə)r, 'fle(ə)r\ *n* : natural aptitude : BENT ⟨a *flair* for acting⟩

flak \'flak\ *n* : antiaircraft guns or the bursting shells fired from them

[1]**flake** \'flāk\ *n* : a thin flat usu. loose piece : CHIP ⟨a *flake* of snow⟩ ⟨a *flake* of dandruff⟩ ⟨soap *flakes*⟩

[2]**flake** *vb* : to form or separate into flakes : make or become flaky ⟨this paint *flakes* off⟩

flaky \'flā-kē\ *adj* **flak·i·er**; **-est** **1** : consisting of flakes **2** : tending to flake ⟨pie with a crisp *flaky* crust⟩ — **flak·i·ness** *n*

flam·beau \'flam-ˌbō\ *n, pl* **flam·beaux** \-ˌbōz\ *or* **flambeaus** : a flaming torch

flam·boy·ant \flam-'bȯi-ənt\ *adj* **1** *often cap* : marked by waving curves suggesting flames **2** : FLORID, ORNATE; *also* : RESPLENDENT ⟨*flamboyant* fall colors⟩ **3** : given to dashing display : SHOWY — **flam·boy·ance** \-ən(t)s\ *n* — **flam·boy·ant·ly** *adv*

[1]**flame** \'flām\ *n* **1** : the glowing gaseous part of a fire **2** : a state of blazing combustion ⟨burst into *flame*⟩ ⟨a building in *flames*⟩ **3** : a condition or appearance suggesting a flame **4** : SWEETHEART ⟨an old *flame* of his⟩

[2]**flame** *vb* **1** : to burn with a flame : BLAZE **2** : to burst or break out violently or passionately

fla·min·go \flə-'ming-gō\ *n, pl* **-gos** *also* **-goes** [from obsolete Spanish *flamengo*, where it meant originally "a Fleming", from Dutch *Vlaminc*; it was applied to the bird whose color reminded the Spaniards of the ruddy complexions of the Flemings] : any of several aquatic long-legged and long-necked birds with a broad bill bent downward at the end and usu. rosy-white plumage with scarlet wings

flamingo
(about 5 ft. tall)

flam·ma·ble \'flam-ə-bəl\ *adj* : capable of being easily ignited and of burning rapidly ⟨a *flammable* liquid⟩ — **flam·ma·bil·i·ty** \ˌflam-ə-'bil-ət-ē\ *n* — **flammable** *n*

flange \'flanj\ *n* : a rib or rim used for strength, for guiding, or for attachment to another object ⟨the *flange* on a locomotive wheel⟩ — **flanged** \'flanjd\ *adj*

1**flank** \'flangk\ *n* **1 a** : the fleshy part of the side between the ribs and the hip **b** : a cut of meat from this part of an animal **2 a** : SIDE **b** : the right or left of a military formation

2**flank** *vb* **1 a** : to attack or threaten the flank of **b** : to pass around the flank of **2** : to be situated at the side of : BORDER

flank·er \'flang-kər\ *n* **1** : one that flanks **2** : a football halfback who lines up on the flank as a pass receiver — called also *flanker back*

flan·nel \'flan-əl\ *n* **1** : a soft napped wool or cotton fabric **2** *pl* : flannel underwear or trousers

flan·nel·ette \ˌflan-ə-'let\ *n* : a cotton flannel napped on one or both sides

1**flap** \'flap\ *n* **1** : SLAP **2** : a broad and limber or flat and thin piece that hangs loose (as on a pocket or envelope) **3** : the motion or sound of a flap **4** : a movable airfoil attached to the trailing edge of an airplane wing for a steeper gliding angle in landing

2**flap** *vb* **flapped**; **flap·ping** **1** : SLAP **2** : to move or cause to move with a beating motion ⟨birds *flapping* their wings⟩ **3** : to sway loosely usu. with a noise of striking ⟨the tent *flapped* in the rising breeze⟩

flap·jack \'flap-ˌjak\ *n* : GRIDDLE CAKE

flap·per \'flap-ər\ *n* **1** : one that flaps **2** : a bold and unconventional young woman of the 1920s

1**flare** \'fla(ə)r, 'fle(ə)r\ *vb* **1** : to burn with an unsteady flame **2 a** : to shine or blaze suddenly **b** : to become suddenly excited or angry ⟨*flare* up⟩ **3** : to open or spread outward

2**flare** *n* **1** : an unsteady glaring light **2** : a fire or blaze of light used to signal, illuminate, or attract attention; *also* : a device or material that produces such a flare **3** : FLARE-UP **4** : a spreading outward; *also* : a place or part that spreads ⟨the *flare* of a vase⟩ ⟨the *flare* of a trumpet⟩ **5** *pl* : bell-bottomed trousers

flare–up \-ˌəp\ *n* : a sudden burst (as of flame or anger)

1**flash** \'flash\ *vb* **1** : to shine in or like a sudden flame ⟨lightning *flashed*⟩ ⟨her eyes *flashed* with excitement⟩ **2** : to send out in or as if in flashes ⟨*flash* a message⟩ **3** : to appear or pass very suddenly ⟨a car *flashed* by⟩ **4** : to gleam or glow intermittently **5** : to expose to view briefly ⟨*flash* a badge⟩

2**flash** *n* **1 a** : a sudden burst of light, flame, or heat **b** : a movement of a flag or light in signaling **2** : a sudden and brilliant burst ⟨a *flash* of wit⟩ **3** : a brief time **4** : one that attracts notice; *esp* : an outstanding athlete **5** : FLASHLIGHT 2

3**flash** *adj* : of sudden origin and short duration ⟨a *flash* fire⟩

flash·bulb \-ˌbəlb\ *n* : an electric flash lamp in which metal foil or wire is burned

flash card *n* : a card bearing words, numbers, or pictures held up briefly by a teacher to a class during drills (as in spelling or arithmetic)

flash·cube \'flash-ˌkyüb\ *n* : a cubical device incorporating four flashbulbs for taking four photographs in succession

flash·er \'flash-ər\ *n* : BLINKER

ə abut	ər further	a back	ā bake
ä cot, cart	aů out	ch chin	e less	ē easy
g gift	i trip	ī life	j joke	ng sing	ō flow
ȯ flaw	ȯi coin	th thin	th this	ü loot
ů foot	y yet	yü few	yů furious	zh vision

flash·gun \'flash-ˌgən\ *n* : a device for holding and operating a flashbulb

flash lamp *n* : a lamp for producing a brief intense flash of light for taking photographs

flash·light \'flash-ˌlīt\ *n* **1 a** : a sudden bright artificial light used in taking photographs **b** : a photograph taken by such a light **2** : a small portable electric light

flashy \'flash-ē\ *adj* **flash·i·er**; **-est** : GAUDY, SHOWY — **flash·i·ly** \'flash-ə-lē\ *adv* — **flash·i·ness** \'flash-ē-nəs\ *n*

flask \'flask\ *n* : a bottle-shaped container often narrowed toward the outlet

1**flat** \'flat\ *adj* **flat·ter**; **flat·test** **1** : having a smooth level horizontal surface ⟨*flat* ground⟩ **2** : having a smooth even surface ⟨a *flat* wall⟩ **3** : spread out on or along a surface ⟨was *flat* on the ground⟩ **4** : having a broad smooth surface and little thickness ⟨a phonograph record is *flat*⟩ **5** : DOWNRIGHT, POSITIVE ⟨a *flat* refusal⟩ **6** : FIXED, UNCHANGING ⟨charge a *flat* rate⟩ **7** : EXACT **8** : DULL, INSIPID ⟨a *flat* story⟩ ⟨water that tastes *flat*⟩ **9** : DEFLATED — used of tires **10 a** : lower than the true pitch **b** : lower by a half step ⟨tone of A *flat*⟩ **11** : free from gloss ⟨*flat* paint⟩ — **flat·ly** *adv* — **flat·ness** *n*

2**flat** *n* **1** : a level surface of land : PLAIN **2** : a flat part or surface ⟨the *flat* of his hand⟩ **3 a** : a musical tone one half step lower than a specified tone **b** : a character ♭ indicating such a note **4** : a shoe or slipper having a flat heel or no heel **5** : a deflated tire

3**flat** *adv* **1** : on or against a flat surface ⟨lie *flat*⟩ **2** : EXACTLY ⟨four minutes *flat*⟩ **3** : below the true musical pitch

4**flat** *vb* **flat·ted**; **flat·ting** : to lower in pitch esp. by a half step

5**flat** *n* : an apartment on one floor

flat·boat \'flat-ˌbōt\ *n* : a large flat-bottomed riverboat for carrying freight

flat·car \-ˌkär\ *n* : a railroad freight car without sides or roof

flat·fish \-ˌfish\ *n* : any of a group of marine fishes (as halibuts, flounders, or soles) that as adults swim on one side of the flattened body and have both eyes on the upper side

flatboat

flat·foot \-ˌfu̇t, -'fu̇t\ *n*, *pl* **flat·feet** \-ˌfēt, -'fēt\ **1** : a condition in which the main arch of the foot is so flattened that the entire sole rests upon the ground **2** : a foot affected with flatfoot

flat·iron \-ˌī(-ə)rn\ *n* : an iron for pressing clothes

flat·ten \'flat-ən\ *vb* **flat·tened**; **flat·ten·ing** \-(ə-)ning\ : to make or become flat

flat·ter \'flat-ər\ *vb* **1** : to praise too much and without sincerity **2** : to represent too favorably ⟨a picture that *flatters* her⟩ **3** : to judge oneself as better than another ⟨*flattered* himself on his skill as a swimmer⟩ — **flat·ter·er** \-ər-ər\ *n* — **flat·ter·ing·ly** \'flat-ə-ring-lē\ *adv*

flat·tery \'flat-ə-rē\ *n*, *pl* **-ter·ies** **1** : the act of flattering **2** : flattering speech or attentions : insincere or excessive praise ***syn*** see COMPLIMENT

flat·top \'flat-ˌtäp\ *n* : AIRCRAFT CARRIER

flat·worm \-ˌwərm\ *n* : any of a phylum of flat bilaterally symmetrical unsegmented worms (as trematodes and tapeworms) that lack a body cavity and are mostly parasites

flaunt \'flȯnt, 'flänt\ *vb* **1 :** to wave or flutter showily **2 :** to display ostentatiously or impudently : PARADE

flau·tist \'flȯt-əst, 'flau̇t-\ *n* : FLUTIST

fla·vor \'flā-vər\ *n* **1 a :** the quality of something that affects the sense of taste : SAVOR **b :** the blend of taste and smell sensations evoked by a substance in the mouth **2 :** a substance that flavors **3 :** characteristic or predominant quality — **flavor** *vb* — **fla·vored** \-vərd\ *adj* — **fla·vor·ful** \-vər-fəl\ *adj* — **fla·vor·less** \-ləs\ *adj*

fla·vor·ing *n* : FLAVOR 2

flaw \'flȯ\ *n* : an imperfect part : CRACK, FAULT ⟨a *flaw* in a plan⟩ ⟨a *flaw* in a diamond⟩ ***syn*** see BLEMISH — **flaw** *vb* — **flaw·less** \-ləs\ *adj* — **flaw·less·ly** *adv* — **flaw·less·ness** *n*

flax \'flaks\ *n* : a slender erect blue-flowered plant grown for its fiber and seeds; *also* : its fiber esp. prepared for spinning — compare LINEN

flax·en \'flak-sən\ *adj* **1 :** made of flax **2 :** of a pale straw color

flax·seed \'flak-ˌsēd\ *n* : the seed of flax used as a source of linseed oil and medicinally

flay \'flā\ *vb* **1 :** to strip off the skin or surface of : SKIN **2 :** to criticize harshly : SCOLD

F layer *n* : the highest and most densely ionized layer of the ionosphere occurring at night and dividing into an inner F_1 layer and an outer F_2 layer during the day

flea \'flē\ *n* : any of an order of wingless bloodsucking insects with a hard laterally compressed body and legs adapted to leaping

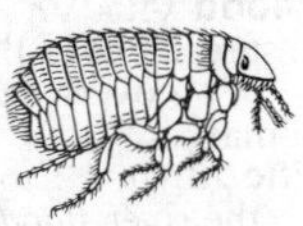

flea (up to ⅜ in. long)

flea·bane \'flē-ˌbān\ *n* : any of various plants related to the daisies

1**fleck** \'flek\ *vb* : STREAK, SPOT

2**fleck** *n* **1 :** SPOT, MARK **2 :** FLAKE, PARTICLE

flec·tion \'flek-shən\ *n* : FLEXION

fledge \'flej\ *vb* **1 :** to develop the feathers necessary for flying **2 :** to furnish with feathers ⟨*fledge* an arrow⟩

fledg·ling \'flej-ling\ *n* **1 :** a young bird just fledged **2 :** an immature or inexperienced person

flee \'flē\ *vb* **fled** \'fled\; **flee·ing 1 a :** to run away from danger or evil : FLY **b :** to run away from : SHUN **2 :** to pass away swiftly : VANISH

1**fleece** \'flēs\ *n* : the coat of wool covering an animal (as a sheep) — **fleecy** \'flē-sē\ *adj*

2**fleece** *vb* **1 :** to remove the fleece from : SHEAR **2 :** to rob by fraud or extortion

1**fleet** \'flēt\ *n* **1 a :** a group of warships under one command **b :** a country's navy **2 :** a group of ships or vehicles that move together or are operated under one management ⟨a *fleet* of trucks⟩

2**fleet** *adj* : swift in motion : NIMBLE — **fleet·ly** *adv* — **fleet·ness** *n*

fleet admiral *n* : an admiral of the highest rank

fleet–foot·ed \'flēt-'fu̇t-əd\ *adj* : swift of foot

fleet·ing \'flēt-ing\ *adj* : not lasting : passing swiftly

Flem *abbr* Flemish

Flem·ing \'flem-ing\ *n* : a member of the Germanic people inhabiting northern Belgium

Flem·ing valve \ˌflem-ing-\ *n* : DIODE

Flem·ish \'flem-ish\ *n* **1 :** the Germanic language of the Flemings **2 Flemish** *pl* : FLEMINGS — **Flemish** *adj*

1**flesh** \'flesh\ *n* **1 a :** the soft parts of the body of an animal and esp. the muscular parts **b :** sleek well-fatted condition of body **2 :** parts of an animal used as food **3 :** the physical being of man as distinguished from the soul **4 a :** human beings **b :** living beings **c :** STOCK, KINDRED **5 :** a fleshy plant part used as food; *esp* : the fleshy part of a fruit — **fleshed** \'flesht\ *adj*

2**flesh** *vb* **1 :** to give substance to ⟨*flesh* out a story with details⟩ **2 :** to remove flesh from **3 :** to become fleshy — often used with *up* or *out*

flesh·ly \'flesh-lē\ *adj* **1 :** CORPOREAL, BODILY **2 :** SENSUAL, WORLDLY

flesh·pot \'flesh-ˌpät\ *n* : a place of luxurious entertainment

fleshy \'flesh-ē\ *adj* **flesh·i·er; -est 1 a :** resembling or consisting of flesh **b :** PLUMP, FAT **2 :** SUCCULENT, PULPY — **flesh·i·ness** *n*

fleshy fruit *n* : a fruit (as a berry, drupe, or pome) consisting largely of soft succulent flesh

fleur–de–lis *or* **fleur–de–lys** \ˌflərd-ə-'lē, ˌflu̇rd-\ *n*, *pl* **fleurs–de–lis** *or* **fleur–de–lis** *or* **fleurs–de–lys** *or* **fleur–de–lys** \ˌflərd-ə-'lē(z), ˌflu̇rd-\ [from French, meaning literally "flower of the lily"] **1 :** IRIS 2 **2 :** a conventionalized iris in art and heraldry

fleur-de-lis 2

flew *past of* FLY

flex \'fleks\ *vb* : BEND

flex·i·ble \'flek-sə-bəl\ *adj* **1 :** capable of being bent : PLIANT **2 :** readily changed or changing : ADAPTABLE ⟨a *flexible* mind⟩ — **flex·i·bil·i·ty** \ˌflek-sə-'bil-ət-ē\ *n* — **flex·i·bly** \'flek-sə-blē\ *adv*

flex·ion \'flek-shən\ *n* : muscular movement that lessens the angle between bones or parts; *also* : the resulting state or relation of parts

flex·or \'flek-sər\ *n* : a muscle that produces flexion — **flexor** *adj*

flex·ure \'flek-shər\ *n* **1 :** the quality or state of being flexed **2 :** TURN, FOLD, BEND — **flex·ur·al** \-shə-rəl\ *adj*

1**flick** \'flik\ *n* **1 :** a light sharp jerky stroke or movement **2 :** a sound produced by a flick **3 :** STREAK, DAUB

2**flick** *vb* **1 :** to strike lightly with a quick sharp motion ⟨*flicked* a speck off her coat⟩ **2 :** FLICKER

1**flick·er** \'flik-ər\ *vb* **flick·ered; flick·er·ing** \-(ə-)ring\ **1 a :** to waver unsteadily : FLUTTER **b :** FLIT, DART **2 :** to burn fitfully or with a fluctuating light ⟨a *flickering* candle⟩

2**flicker** *n* **1 :** a brief interval of brightness **2 :** a flickering light **3 :** a brief stirring ⟨a *flicker* of interest⟩ — **flick·ery** \'flik-(ə-)rē\ *adj*

3**flicker** *n* : a large insect-eating North American woodpecker with a black crescent on the breast, red on the back of the neck, and yellow shafts on tail feathers and wing feathers

flied *past of* FLY

fli·er \'flī(-ə)r\ *n* **1 :** one that flies; *esp* : AVIATOR **2 :** something that travels very fast **3 :** a speculative undertaking; *esp* : an attempt to gain large profits in a business venture by one who is inexperienced or uninformed **4 :** a brief printed notice or message distributed in large numbers

1**flight** \'flīt\ *n* **1 :** an act or instance of passing through the air by the use of wings ⟨a *flight* in a plane⟩ ⟨the *flight* of birds⟩ **2 a :** a passing through the air or through space outside the earth's atmosphere ⟨a balloon *flight*⟩ ⟨the *flight* of a bullet⟩ ⟨a *flight* to the moon⟩ **b :** the distance covered in a flight **3 :** an airplane making a scheduled flight **4 :** a group of similar things flying through the air together ⟨a *flight* of ducks⟩ ⟨a *flight* of bombers⟩ **5 :** a brilliant, imaginative, or unrestrained exercise or display ⟨a *flight* of fancy⟩ **6 :** a continuous series of stairs from one landing or floor to another

2**flight** *n* : an act or instance of running away

flight control *n* : the control from a ground station of an airplane esp. by radio

flight engineer *n* : a flight crewman of an airplane responsible for mechanical operation

flight·less \ˈflīt-ləs\ *adj* : unable to fly ⟨*flightless* birds⟩

flight path *n* : the path of the center of gravity of an airplane in flight

flighty \ˈflīt-ē\ *adj* **flight·i·er**; **-est** **1** : easily excited : SKITTISH ⟨*flighty* horses⟩ **2** : SILLY, FRIVOLOUS ⟨a *flighty* young girl⟩ — **flight·i·ly** \ˈflīt-ə-lē\ *adv* — **flight·i·ness** \ˈflīt-ē-nəs\ *n*

flim·sy \ˈflim-zē\ *adj* **flim·si·er**; **-est** **1** : lacking strength or substance ⟨a *flimsy* cardboard suitcase⟩ **2** : having little worth or plausibility ⟨a *flimsy* excuse⟩ — **flim·si·ly** \-zə-lē\ *adv* — **flim·si·ness** \-zē-nəs\ *n*

flinch \ˈflinch\ *vb* : to shrink from or as if from physical pain : WINCE — **flinch** *n* — **flinch·er** *n*

flin·ders \ˈflin-dərz\ *n pl* : SPLINTERS, FRAGMENTS

1**fling** \ˈfling\ *vb* **flung** \ˈfləng\; **fling·ing** \ˈfling-ing\ **1** : to move in a brusque or headlong manner ⟨*flung* himself onto the chair⟩ **2** : to kick or plunge vigorously **3 a** : to throw or swing with force ⟨*flung* back his head⟩ **b** : to cast aside : DISCARD **4** : to put suddenly and unexpectedly into a state or condition ⟨*flung* the enemy into confusion⟩ ***syn*** see THROW — **fling·er** \ˈfling-ər\ *n*

2**fling** *n* **1** : an act or instance of flinging **2** : a casual try **3** : a period of self-indulgence

flint \ˈflint\ *n* **1** : a grayish or dark hard quartz that strikes fire with steel **2** : an alloy (as of iron and cerium) used for striking fire in cigarette lighters **3** : something very hard ⟨a heart of *flint*⟩ — **flint·i·ly** \-ə-lē\ *adv* — **flint·i·ness** \-ē-nəs\ *n* — **flinty** \-ē\ *adj*

flint glass *n* : heavy glass that contains an oxide of lead and is used for optical structures (as lenses)

flint lock \ˈflint-ˌläk\ *n* **1** : a lock for a 17th and 18th century firearm using a flint to ignite the charge **2** : a firearm fitted with a flintlock

1**flip** \ˈflip\ *vb* **flipped**; **flip·ping** **1** : to turn by tossing ⟨*flip* a coin⟩ **2** : to turn quickly ⟨*flip* the pages of a book⟩ **3** : FLICK, JERK ⟨*flip* a switch⟩ **4** : to lose self-control ⟨he really *flipped* over her⟩ — **flip** *n*

2**flip** *adj* : FLIPPANT

flip·pant \ˈflip-ənt\ *adj* : treating lightly something serious or worthy of respect : SAUCY — **flip·pan·cy** \-ən-sē\ *n* — **flip·pant·ly** *adv*

flip·per \ˈflip-ər\ *n* **1** : a broad flat limb (as of a seal) adapted for swimming **2** : a flat rubber shoe with the front end widened and flattened into a paddle for use in skin diving

1**flirt** \ˈflərt\ *vb* **1** : FLIT **2 a** : to play at making love **b** : TOY — **flir·ta·tion** \ˌflər-ˈtā-shən\ *n* — **flir·ta·tious** \-shəs\ *adj* — **flir·ta·tious·ness** *n* — **flirt·er** \ˈflərt-ər\ *n*

2**flirt** *n* **1** : an act or instance of flirting **2** : a person who flirts

flit \ˈflit\ *vb* **flit·ted**; **flit·ting** : to move or progress in quick erratic darts — **flit** *n*

fliv·ver \ˈfliv-ər\ *n* : a small cheap usu. old automobile

1**float** \ˈflōt\ *n* **1** : an act or instance of floating **2** : something that floats: as **a** : a cork or bob buoying up the baited end of a fishing line **b** : a floating platform anchored near a shoreline for use by swimmers or boats **c** : a hollow ball that controls the flow or level of the liquid it floats on (as in a tank or cistern); *also* : a similar usu. horseshoe-shaped device in a carburetor of a gasoline engine **d** : a watertight structure giving an airplane buoyancy on water **3 a** : a vehicle with a platform used to carry a display in a parade **b** : the vehicle and display together **4** : a drink consisting of ice cream floating in a beverage

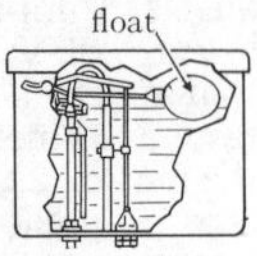

float 2c

2**float** *vb* **1** : to rest in or on the surface of a fluid **2** : to drift on or through or as if on or through a fluid ⟨dust *floating* through the air⟩ **3** : to cause to float ⟨*float* logs down a river⟩ — **float·er** *n*

floating rib *n* : a rib (as one of the last two pairs in man) that has no attachment to the sternum

1**flock** \ˈfläk\ *n* **1** : a group of birds or mammals assembled or herded together **2** : a group under the guidance of a leader **3** : a large number

2**flock** *vb* : to gather or move in a crowd ⟨they *flocked* to the beach⟩

floe \ˈflō\ *n* : a sheet or mass of floating ice

flog \ˈfläg\ *vb* **flogged**; **flog·ging** : to beat severely with a rod or whip — **flog·ger** *n*

1**flood** \ˈfləd\ *n* **1** : a great flow of water that rises and spreads over the land **2** : the flowing in of the tide **3** : an overwhelming quantity or volume ⟨a *flood* of mail⟩

2**flood** *vb* **1** : to cover or become filled with a flood ⟨the river *flooded* the lowlands⟩ ⟨the cellar *floods* after a rain⟩ **2** : to fill abundantly or excessively ⟨a room *flooded* with light⟩ ⟨*flood* a carburetor⟩ **3** : to pour forth in a flood

flood·gate \ˈfləd-ˌgāt\ *n* : a gate (as in a canal) for controlling a body of water : SLUICE

flood·light \-ˌlīt\ *n* **1** : artificial light in a broad beam **2** : a light that projects a broad beam — **floodlight** *vb*

flood·plain \-ˌplān\ *n* **1** : low flat land along a stream that may flood **2** : a plain built up by deposits of earth from floodwaters

flood tide *n* **1** : the tide while rising or at its greatest height **2 a** : an overwhelming quantity **b** : a high point : PEAK ⟨his success was at *flood tide*⟩

flood·wa·ter \ˈfləd-ˌwȯt-ər, -ˌwät-\ *n* : the water of a flood

1**floor** \ˈflō(ə)r, ˈflȯ(ə)r\ *n* **1** : the part of a room on which one stands **2 a** : the lower inside surface of a hollow structure ⟨the *floor* of a car⟩ **b** : a ground surface ⟨the ocean *floor*⟩ ⟨the *floor* of a forest⟩ **3** : a story of a building ⟨lives on the first *floor*⟩ **4** : the surface of a structure on which one travels ⟨the *floor* of a bridge⟩ **5 a** : a main floor (as in a legislative chamber) as distinguished from a platform or gallery **b** : the right to speak from the floor ⟨the senator has the *floor*⟩ **6** : a lower limit (as of prices)

2**floor** *vb* **1** : to cover with a floor or flooring **2 a** : to knock to the floor **b** : SHOCK, OVERWHELM ⟨the news *floored* us⟩

floor·ing \ˈflōr-ing, ˈflȯr-\ *n* **1** : FLOOR **2** : material for floors

floor show *n* : entertainment presented in a nightclub and usu. consisting of singing, dancing, or comedy routines

floor·walk·er \ˈflō(ə)r-ˌwȯ-kər, ˈflȯ(ə)r-\ *n* : an em-

ə abut	ər further	a back	ā bake	
ä cot, cart	au̇ out	ch chin	e less	ē easy
g gift	i trip	ī life	j joke	ng sing	ō flow
ȯ flaw	ȯi coin	th thin	t͟h this	ü loot
u̇ foot	y yet	yü few	yu̇ furious	zh vision

ployee of a retail store who oversees the sales force and aids customers

[1]**flop** \'fläp\ *vb* **flopped**; **flop·ping** **1** : to swing or bounce loosely : flap about ⟨a hat brim *flopping* in the wind⟩ **2 a** : to throw oneself down heavily or clumsily ⟨*flopped* into the chair with a sigh⟩ **b** : to throw or drop suddenly and heavily or noisily ⟨she *flopped* her bundles on the table⟩ **3** : to fail completely ⟨in spite of good reviews the play *flopped*⟩

[2]**flop** *n* **1** : an act or sound of flopping **2** : a complete failure : DUD ⟨he was a *flop* as a teacher⟩

flop·py \'fläp-ē\ *adj* **flop·pi·er**; **-est** : being soft and flexible

flo·ra \'flōr-ə, 'flȯr-\ *n, pl* **floras** *also* **flo·rae** \'flō(ə)r-,ē, 'flȯ(ə)r-, -,ī\ : plants or plant life esp. of a region, period, or environment

flo·ral \'flōr-əl, 'flȯr-\ *adj* : of or relating to flowers or a flora ⟨a *floral* pattern in wallpaper⟩ — **flo·ral·ly** \-ə-lē\ *adv*

Flor·ence flask \,flȯr-ən(t)s, ,flär-\ *n* : a round usu. flat-bottomed glass laboratory vessel with a long neck

Flor·en·tine \'flȯr-ən-,tēn, 'flär-\ *adj* : of, relating to, or characteristic of Florence or its people — **Florentine** *n*

flo·ret \'flōr-ət, 'flȯr-\ *n* : a small flower; *esp* : one of the small flowers forming the head of a composite plant (as a daisy)

flor·id \'flȯr-əd, 'flär-\ *adj* **1** : FLOWERY, ORNATE ⟨*florid* writing⟩ **2** : tinged with red : RUDDY ⟨a *florid* complexion⟩ — **flor·id·ly** *adv*

flor·in \'flȯr-ən, 'flär-, 'flōr-\ *n* **1** : an old gold coin first struck at Florence in 1252 **2** : any of various coins patterned after the florin

flo·rist \'flōr-əst, 'flȯr-, 'flär-\ *n* : one who sells flowers and ornamental plants

floss \'fläs, 'flȯs\ *n* **1** : soft silk or cotton thread used for embroidery **2** : fluffy fibrous material; *esp* : SILK COTTON — **flossy** \-ē\ *adj*

flo·ta·tion \flō-'tā-shən\ *n* **1** : the act, process or state of floating **2** : the separation of the particles of a mass of pulverized ore according to their relative capacity for floating on a given liquid

flo·til·la \flō-'til-ə\ *n* : FLEET; *esp* : a fleet of small ships

flot·sam \'flät-səm\ *n* : floating wreckage of a ship or its cargo

[1]**flounce** \'flaun(t)s\ *vb* **1** : to move with exaggerated jerky motions **2** : to go with sudden determination ⟨she *flounced* out of the room in anger⟩

[2]**flounce** *n* : an act or instance of flouncing

[3]**flounce** *n* : a strip of fabric attached by the upper edge ⟨a wide *flounce* at the bottom of her skirt⟩

[4]**flounce** *vb* : to trim with flounces

[1]**floun·der** \'flaun-dər\ *n, pl* **flounder** *or* **flounders** : FLATFISH; *esp* : any of various important marine food fishes

[2]**flounder** *vb* **floun·dered**; **floun·der·ing** \-d(ə-)riŋ\ : to struggle or proceed clumsily ⟨*flounder* in deep mud⟩

flounder
(about 1½ ft. long)

[1]**flour** \'flau̇(ə)r\ *n* [from Middle English, just an older spelling of *flower*, and used for "the flower (or best part) of the grain"] **1** : finely ground powdery meal of wheat or of any cereal grain or edible seed **2** : a fine soft powder

[2]**flour** *vb* : to coat with flour

flour beetle *n* : any of several usu. elongated flattened brown beetles that are economic pests esp. in flour or meal

[1]**flour·ish** \'flər-ish, 'flə-rish\ *vb* **1** : to grow luxuriantly : THRIVE **2 a** : PROSPER, SUCCEED **b** : to be active ⟨*flourished* around 1850⟩ **3** : to make bold and sweeping gestures **4** : BRANDISH ⟨*flourish* a sword⟩

[2]**flourish** *n* **1** : a flowery embellishment or passage ⟨handwriting with *flourishes*⟩ ⟨a *flourish* of drums⟩ **2 a** : an act or instance of brandishing : WAVE ⟨a *flourish* of his cane⟩ **b** : a dramatic gesture

floury \'flau̇(ə)r-ē\ *adj* **1** : of, relating to, or resembling flour **2** : covered with flour

flout \'flau̇t\ *vb* : to treat with contemptuous disregard : jeer at : SCORN ⟨*flouting* her mother's advice⟩ — **flout·er** *n*

[1]**flow** \'flō\ *vb* **1** : to issue or move in a stream ⟨molasses *flows* slowly⟩ **2** : RISE ⟨the tide ebbs and *flows*⟩ **3** : to glide or pass smoothly and readily ⟨words *flowed* from his mouth⟩ ⟨traffic *flowing* over a bridge⟩ **4** : to hang loose and billowing ⟨a flag *flowing* in the breeze⟩ — **flow·ing·ly** \-iŋ-lē\ *adv*

[2]**flow** *n* **1** : an act of flowing **2** : FLOOD 1, 2 **3 a** : a smooth uninterrupted movement **b** : STREAM, CURRENT ⟨a *flow* of electricity⟩ **c** : a mass of matter that has flowed ⟨a lava *flow*⟩ **4** : the quantity that flows in a certain time ⟨the *flow* of water over a dam⟩

[1]**flow·er** \'flau̇(-ə)r\ *n* **1 a** : BLOSSOM, INFLORESCENCE **b** : a shoot of the sporophyte of a higher plant that is specialized for reproduction and bears modified leaves (as petals or sporophylls) **c** : a plant cultivated or esteemed for its blossoms **2 a** : the best part or example ⟨the *flower* of the family⟩ **b** : a state or time of flourishing ⟨when knighthood was in *flower*⟩ — **flow·er·less** \-ləs\ *adj* — **flow·er·like** \-,līk\ *adj*

[2]**flower** *vb* **1** : to produce flowers : BLOOM **2** : DEVELOP ⟨*flowered* into young womanhood⟩ **3** : FLOURISH

flow·ered \'flau̇(-ə)rd\ *adj* **1** : having or bearing flowers **2** : decorated with flowers or flowerlike figures ⟨*flowered* silk⟩

flow·er·et \'flau̇(-ə)r-ət\ *n* : FLORET

flower head *n* : a tight cluster of small sessile flowers so arranged that the whole looks like a single flower

flowering plant *n* : any of a major group of higher plants that produce flowers, fruits, and seeds — compare SEED PLANT

flow·er·pot \'flau̇(-ə)r-,pät\ *n* : a pot in which to grow plants

flow·ery \'flau̇(-ə)r-ē\ *adj* **flow·er·i·er**; **-est** **1** : full of or covered with flowers **2** : full of fine words or phrases ⟨*flowery* language⟩ — **flow·er·i·ness** *n*

flown *past part of* FLY

fl oz *abbr* fluidounce

flu \'flü\ *n* **1** : INFLUENZA **2** : any of several virus diseases marked esp. by respiratory symptoms

flub \'fləb\ *vb* **flubbed**; **flub·bing** : BOTCH, BLUNDER — **flub** *n*

fluc·tu·ate \'flək-chə-,wāt\ *vb* **1** : to move up and down or back and forth like a wave **2** : to be constantly changing esp. up and down : WAVER ⟨*fluctuating* temperatures⟩ ⟨*fluctuated* in his mind between hope and fear⟩ — **fluc·tu·a·tion** \,flək-chə-'wā-shən\ *n*

flue \'flü\ *n* : an enclosed passageway for directing a current: as **a** : a channel in a chimney for conveying

F

flame and smoke to the outer air **b :** an air channel to the lip of a wind instrument

flu·ent \'flü-ənt\ *adj* **1 :** FLUID **2 a :** ready or facile in speech ⟨*fluent* in Spanish⟩ **b :** effortlessly smooth and rapid : POLISHED ⟨*fluent* speech⟩ — **flu·en·cy** \-ən-sē\ *n* — **flu·ent·ly** *adv*

[1]**fluff** \'fləf\ *n* **1 :** NAP, DOWN ⟨soft *fluff* from a pillow⟩ **2 :** something fluffy

[2]**fluff** *vb* : to make or become fluffy ⟨*fluff* up a pillow⟩

fluffy \'fləf-ē\ *adj* **fluff·i·er; -est 1 :** having, covered with, or resembling down ⟨the *fluffy* fur of a kitten⟩ **2 :** being light and soft or airy ⟨a *fluffy* omelet⟩ — **fluff·i·ness** *n*

[1]**flu·id** \'flü-əd\ *adj* **1 a :** capable of flowing like a liquid or gas : being liquid or gaseous **b :** likely or tending to change or move **2 :** smoothly flowing ⟨a *fluid* style⟩ **3 :** readily available ⟨*fluid* assets⟩ — **flu·id·i·ty** \flü-'id-ət-ē\ *n* — **flu·id·ly** \'flü-əd-lē\ *adv* — **flu·id·ness** *n*

[2]**fluid** *n* : a substance tending to flow or conform to the outline of its container ⟨liquids and gases are *fluids*⟩

fluid mechanics *n* : a branch of mechanics that deals with the special properties of liquids and gases

flu·id·ounce \,flü-əd-'au̇n(t)s\ *n* : a unit of liquid capacity equal to 1/16 pint — see MEASURE table

flu·i·dram \,flü-ə(d)-'dram\ *n* : a unit of liquid capacity equal to 1/8 fluidounce — see MEASURE table

[1]**fluke** \'flük\ *n* **1 :** FLATFISH **2 :** TREMATODE

[2]**fluke** *n* **1 :** the part of an anchor that fastens in the ground **2 :** a barbed head (as of a harpoon) **3 :** one of the lobes of a whale's tail

[3]**fluke** *n* : a stroke of good luck ⟨won by a *fluke*⟩ — **fluky** \'flü-kē\ *adj*

flume \'flüm\ *n* **1 :** a ravine or gorge with a stream running through it **2 :** an inclined channel for conveying water (as for power)

flung *past of* FLING

flunk \'fləngk\ *vb* **1 :** to fail an examination or course ⟨*flunked* English⟩ **2 :** to give a failing grade to — **flunk** *n*

flunk out *vb* : to dismiss or be dismissed from a school for failure

flun·ky *or* **flun·key** \'fləng-kē\ *n, pl* **flunkies** *or* **flunkeys 1 :** a servant in livery; *esp* : FOOTMAN **2 :** a person who fawns upon or does menial duties for another : TOADY

flu·o·resce \(,)flu̇(-ə)r-'es\ *vb* : to produce, undergo, or exhibit fluorescence

flu·o·res·cence \(,)flu̇(-ə)r-'es-ən(t)s\ *n* : the property of a substance of emitting radiation usu. as visible light when exposed to radiation from another source (as ultraviolet light); *also* : the radiation emitted — **flu·o·res·cent** \-ənt\ *adj*

fluorescent lamp *n* : a tubular electric lamp in which light is produced on the inside fluorescent coating by the action of ultraviolet light

flu·o·ri·date \'flu̇r-ə-,dāt\ *vb* : to add a fluoride to ⟨the water was *fluoridated*⟩ — **flu·o·ri·da·tion** \,flu̇r-ə-'dā-shən\ *n*

flu·o·ride \'flu̇(-ə)r-,īd\ *n* : a compound of fluorine with another element or a radical

flu·o·rin·ate \'flu̇r-ə-,nāt\ *vb* : to treat or cause to combine with fluorine or a compound of fluorine — **flu·o·rin·a·tion** \,flu̇r-ə-'nā-shən\ *n*

ə abut	ər further	a back	ā bake
ä cot, cart	au̇ out	ch chin	e less
ē easy	g gift	i trip	ī life
j joke	ng sing	ō flow	ȯ flaw
ȯi coin	th thin	th this	ü loot
u̇ foot	y yet	yü few	yu̇ furious
zh vision			

flu·o·rine \'flu̇(-ə)r-,ēn, -ən\ *n* : a nonmetallic element that is normally a pale yellowish flammable irritating toxic gas — see ELEMENT table

flu·o·rite \'flu̇(-ə)r-,īt\ *n* : a transparent or translucent mineral of different colors that consists of a fluoride of calcium and is used as a flux and in making glass

flu·o·ro·car·bon \,flu̇(-ə)r-ō-'kär-bən\ *n* : any of various compounds of carbon and fluorine used chiefly as lubricants and in making resins and plastics

[1]**flu·o·ro·scope** \'flu̇r-ə-,skōp\ *n* : an instrument that is useful in examining inner parts of the body (as the lungs) by observing light and shadows produced on a screen by the action of X rays — **flu·o·ro·scop·ic** \,flu̇r-ə-'skäp-ik\ *adj* — **flu·o·ros·co·py** \(,)flu̇(-ə)r-'äs-kə-pē\ *n*

[2]**fluoroscope** *vb* : to examine by fluoroscopy

flu·or·spar \'flu̇(-ə)r-,spär\ *n* : FLUORITE

flur·ry \'flər-ē, 'flə-rē\ *n, pl* **flurries 1 a :** a gust of wind **b :** a brief light snowfall **2 :** nervous commotion : BUSTLE ⟨the news caused a *flurry*⟩ **3 :** a brief outburst of activity ⟨a *flurry* of trading in the stock exchange⟩ — **flurry** *vb*

[1]**flush** \'fləsh\ *vb* : to fly up or cause to fly up suddenly ⟨*flushed* a covey of quail⟩

[2]**flush** *n* **1 :** a sudden flow **2 :** a sudden increase; *esp* : a surge of emotion ⟨a *flush* of triumph⟩ **3 a :** BLUSH **b :** a fresh and vigorous state ⟨the *flush* of youth⟩ **4 :** a brief sensation of heat

[3]**flush** *vb* **1 :** to flow and spread suddenly and freely **2 a :** to glow brightly **b :** BLUSH **3 :** to pour liquid over or through; *esp* : to wash out with a rush of liquid **4 :** INFLAME, EXCITE ⟨troops *flushed* with victory⟩ **5 :** to make red or hot ⟨face *flushed* with fever⟩

[4]**flush** *adj* **1 a :** filled to overflowing **b :** fully supplied esp. with money **2 a :** full of life and vigor : LUSTY **b :** of a ruddy healthy color **3 a :** having an unbroken surface ⟨*flush* paneling⟩ **b :** even with an adjacent surface ⟨a river *flush* with the top of its bank⟩ — **flush·ness** *n*

[5]**flush** *adv* **1 :** so as to be flush **2 :** SQUARELY ⟨a blow *flush* on the chin⟩

flushing bar *n* : a device attached in front of a mowing machine to flush ground-nesting game birds

flus·ter \'fləs-tər\ *vb* **flus·tered; flus·ter·ing** \-t(ə-)ring\ : to make nervous and unsure : UPSET ⟨*flustered* by his stares⟩ — **fluster** *n*

[1]**flute** \'flüt\ *n* **1 :** a woodwind instrument played by

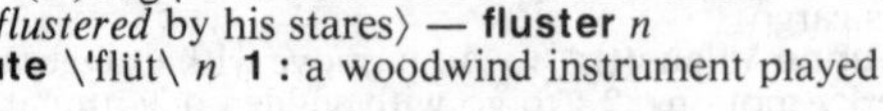

flute 1

blowing across a hole near the closed end **2 :** a rounded groove; *esp* : one on a classical architectural column — **flute·like** \-,līk\ *adj*

[2]**flute** *vb* **1 :** to play a flute **2 :** to make a sound like that of a flute **3 :** to form flutes in ⟨*fluted* columns⟩

flut·ing \'flüt-ing\ *n* : fluted decoration

flut·ist \'flüt-əst\ *n* : a flute player

[1]**flut·ter** \'flət-ər\ *vb* **1 :** to move or cause the wings to move rapidly without flying or in short flights ⟨butterflies *flutter*⟩ **2 :** to move with quick wavering or flapping motions ⟨flags *fluttered* in the breeze⟩ **3 :** to move about or behave in an agitated aimless manner — **flut·tery** \'flət-ə-rē\ *adj*

[2]**flutter** *n* **1 :** an act of fluttering **2 :** FLURRY, COMMOTION

[1]**flux** \'fləks\ *n* **1 :** an excessive fluid discharge from

the body and esp. the bowels **2 a** : a flowing in ⟨*flux* of the tide⟩ **b** : a series of changes : a state of continuous change **3** : a substance used to promote fusion (as by removing impurities) esp. of metals or minerals

[2]**flux** *vb* **1** : to become or cause to become fluid : FUSE **2** : to treat with a flux

[1]**fly** \ˈflī\ *vb* **flew** \ˈflü\; **flown** \ˈflōn\; **fly·ing** **1 a** : to move in or pass through the air with wings **b** : to move through the air or before the wind **c** : to float or cause to float, wave, or soar in the air ⟨flags *flying*⟩ ⟨*fly* a kite⟩ **2** : to take flight : FLEE, SHUN **3** : to move or pass swiftly ⟨*fly* to the rescue⟩ ⟨time *flies*⟩ **4** *past or past part* **flied** \ˈflīd\ : to hit a fly in baseball **5 a** : to operate or travel in an aircraft **b** : to journey over by flying ⟨to *fly* the Atlantic⟩ **c** : to transport by aircraft ⟨to *fly* passengers⟩

[2]**fly** *n, pl* **flies** **1 a** : a garment closing concealed by a fold of cloth **b** : the outer canvas of a tent with double top **c** : the length of an extended flag; *also* : the loose end of a flag **2** : a baseball hit high into the air — **on the fly** : in motion esp. while still in the air

[3]**fly** *n, pl* **flies** **1** : a winged insect **2** : any of a group of mostly two-winged insects (as horseflies, houseflies, or mosquitoes); *esp* : HOUSEFLY **3** : a fishhook dressed to suggest an insect — **fly in the ointment** : a detracting factor or element

fly·blown \ˈflī-ˌblōn\ *adj* : TAINTED, SPOILED

fly·by \-ˌbī\ *n* : a usu. low-altitude flight past an appointed place by an aircraft or spacecraft

fly·catch·er \-ˌkach-ər, -ˌkech-\ *n* : a small bird that feeds on insects that it captures in the air

fly·er *var of* FLIER

fly·ing \ˈflī-iŋ\ *adj* **1 a** : rapidly moving **b** : HASTY **2** : ready to move or act quickly ⟨a *flying* squad⟩

flying boat *n* : a seaplane with a hull adapted for floating

flying buttress *n* : a projecting arched structure to support a wall or building

flying fish *n* : any of numerous sea fishes that have long fins suggesting wings and are able to glide some distance through the air

flying machine *n* : AIRCRAFT

flying saucer *n* : any of various unidentified moving objects repeatedly reported as seen in the air and usu. alleged to be saucer-shaped or disk-shaped

flying squirrel *n* : a squirrel with folds of skin connecting the forelegs and hind legs and enabling it to make long gliding leaps

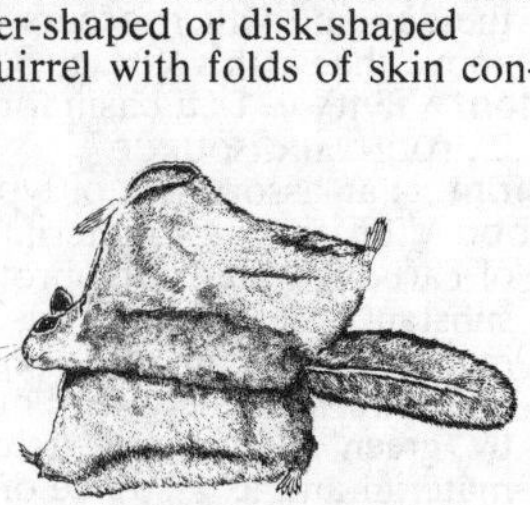

flying squirrel (about 9 in. long)

fly·leaf \ˈflī-ˌlēf\ *n* : a blank leaf at the beginning or end of a book

fly·pa·per \-ˌpā-pər\ *n* : paper poisoned or coated with a sticky substance for killing or catching flies

fly·speck \-ˌspek\ *n* **1** : a speck of fly dung **2** : something small and insignificant — **flyspeck** *vb*

fly·way \-ˌwā\ *n* : an established air route of migratory birds

fly·weight \-ˌwāt\ *n* : a boxer weighing 112 pounds or less

fly·wheel \-ˌhwēl\ *n* : a heavy wheel for regulating the speed of machinery

FM *abbr* frequency modulation

[1]**foal** \ˈfōl\ *n* : the young of an animal of the horse family; *esp* : one under one year

[2]**foal** *vb* : to give birth to a foal

[1]**foam** \ˈfōm\ *n* **1** : a light frothy mass of fine bubbles formed in or on a liquid **2** : a froth formed (as by a horse) in salivating or sweating **3** : a stabilized froth produced chemically and used esp. in fighting oil fires **4** : a material (as rubber) in a light-weight cellular form resulting from introduction of gas bubbles during manufacture — **foamy** \-mē\ *adj* — **foam·i·ly** \ˈfō-mə-lē\ *adv* — **foam·i·ness** \-mē-nəs\ *n*

[2]**foam** *vb* **1** : to produce or form foam : FROTH **2** : to be angry

foam rubber *n* : rubber prepared in the form of a spongy foam

fob \ˈfäb\ *n* **1** : a watch chain or ribbon; *esp* : one hanging from a small watch pocket near the waistband in trousers **2** : a small ornament worn on a watch chain

FOB *abbr* free on board

fo·cal \ˈfō-kəl\ *adj* : of, relating to, or having a focus — **fo·cal·ly** \-kə-lē\ *adv*

focal length *n* : the distance from the surface of a lens or mirror to the point where the rays from it come together

fo'·c'sle *var of* FORECASTLE

[1]**fo·cus** \ˈfō-kəs\ *n, pl* **fo·cus·es** *or* **fo·ci** \-ˌsī\ [from Latin, meaning "fireplace", "hearth", a word which has come to mean "fire" in the Romance languages (e.g. Italian *fuoco*, Spanish *fuego*, French *feu*)] **1** : a point at which rays (as of light, heat, or sound) converge or from which they diverge or appear to diverge; *esp* : the point at which an image is formed by a mirror, lens, or optical system **2 a** : FOCAL LENGTH **b** : adjustment (as of the eye or field glasses) for distinct vision ⟨bring into *focus*⟩ **3** : a center of activity or interest **4** : one of the two points within an ellipse the sum of whose distances from any point on the ellipse is a constant

[2]**focus** *vb* **fo·cused** *also* **fo·cussed**; **fo·cus·ing** *also* **fo·cus·sing** **1** : to bring to a focus ⟨*focus* rays of light⟩ **2** : to cause to be concentrated ⟨*focus* public attention on a problem⟩ **3** : to adjust the focus of ⟨*focus* the eyes⟩ ⟨*focus* a telescope⟩ **4** : to come to a focus **5** : to adjust one's eye or a camera to a particular range ⟨*focus* at 8 feet⟩

fod·der \ˈfäd-ər\ *n* : coarse dry food (as cornstalks) for livestock — **fodder** *vb*

foe \ˈfō\ *n* **1** : one who hates another : ENEMY **2** : an enemy in war : ADVERSARY

foehn \ˈfə(r)n, ˈfān\ *n* : a warm dry wind blowing down the side of a mountain

foe·tal \ˈfēt-əl\, **foe·tus** *var of* FETAL, FETUS

[1]**fog** \ˈfȯg, ˈfäg\ *n* **1 a** : fine particles of water suspended in the atmosphere near the ground **b** : a fine spray or a foam for fire fighting **2** : a murky condition of the atmosphere or a substance causing it **3** : a state of mental confusion

[2]**fog** *vb* **fogged**; **fog·ging** **1** : to cover or become covered with or as if with fog **2** : to make confused

fog·gy \ˈfȯg-ē, ˈfäg-\ *adj* **fog·gi·er**; **-est** **1** : filled with fog **2** : MUDDLED — **fog·gi·ly** \-ə-lē\ *adv* — **fog·gi·ness** \-ē-nəs\ *n*

fog·horn \ˈfȯg-ˌhȯrn, ˈfäg-\ *n* : a horn sounded in foggy weather to warn ships

fo·gy *also* **fo·gey** \ˈfō-gē\ *n, pl* **fogies** *also* **fogeys** : a person with old-fashioned ideas — usu. used with *old* — **fo·gy·ish** \-gē-ish\ *adj* — **fo·gy·ism** \-gē-ˌiz-əm\ *n*

foi·ble \ˈfȯi-bəl\ *n* : a minor shortcoming in personal character or behavior : WEAKNESS

[1]**foil** \ˈfȯil\ *vb* **1** : to prevent from attaining an end **2** : to cause to fail ⟨*foil* a plot⟩

[2]**foil** *n* : a fencing sword with a light flexible blade tapering to a blunt point

[3]**foil** *n* [from medieval French, meaning "leaf", from Latin *folium*] **1** : a very thin sheet of metal ⟨tin or aluminum *foil*⟩ **2** : a thin leaf of polished and colored metal used in jewelry to give color and brilliance to paste and inferior stones **3** : one that serves as a contrast to another

foist \'fȯist\ *vb* : to pass off (something false) as genuine

[1]**fold** \'fōld\ *n* **1** : a pen for sheep **2** : a group of people with a common faith or interest

[2]**fold** *vb* : to confine in a fold

[3]**fold** *vb* **1** : to double or become doubled over itself ⟨*fold* a blanket⟩ **2** : CLASP, EMBRACE ⟨*folded* his hands⟩ **3** : to lay one part over or against another part ⟨birds *folding* their wings⟩ ⟨*fold* the leaves of the table⟩ **4** : to enclose in or as if in a fold ⟨a letter with a circular *folded* in it⟩ **5** : to bend (a surface or stratum) into folds **6** : FAIL, COLLAPSE ⟨the new enterprise *folded* rapidly⟩

[4]**fold** *n* **1** : a folding over **2** : a part doubled or laid over another part **3** : a bend produced in rock

-fold \ˌfōld, 'fōld\ *suffix* **1** : multiplied by (a specified number) : times — in adjectives ⟨a twelve*fold* increase⟩ and adverbs ⟨repay you ten*fold*⟩ **2** : having (so many) parts ⟨a three*fold* problem⟩

fold·er \'fōl-dər\ *n* **1** : one that folds **2** : a printed circular of folded sheets **3** : a folded cover or large envelope for holding loose papers

fo·li·age \'fō-l(ē-)ij, 'fōl-yij\ *n* : the mass of leaves of a plant : LEAFAGE — **fo·li·aged** \-l(ē-)ijd, -yijd\ *adj*

fo·li·ate *vb* \'fo-lē-ˌāt\ : to divide into layers or leaves — **fo·li·at·ed** \-ˌāt-əd\ *adj*

fo·lic acid \ˌfō-lik-\ *n* : a crystalline vitamin of the B complex used esp. in the treatment of nutritional anemias

fo·lio \'fō-lē-ˌō\ *n, pl* **fo·li·os** **1** : a leaf of a manuscript or book **2 a** : a book printed on sheets of paper folded once **b** : a very large book

[1]**folk** \'fōk\ *n, pl* **folk** *or* **folks** **1** : a group of people forming a tribe or nation **2** : people in general : persons as a group ⟨country *folk*⟩ ⟨old *folks*⟩ **3** : the persons of one's own family ⟨visit her *folks* during the holidays⟩

[2]**folk** *adj* : of, relating to, or originating among the common people ⟨*folk* music⟩

folk·lore \'fōk-ˌlō(ə)r, -ˌlȯ(ə)r\ *n* : customs, beliefs, stories, and sayings of a people handed down from generation to generation — **folk·lor·ist** \-ˌlōr-əst, -ˌlȯr-\ *n*

folk song *n* : a song originated or traditional among the common people of a country or region — **folk singer** *n*

folk·tale \'fōk-ˌtāl\ *n* : an anonymous tale circulated orally among a people

fol·li·cle \'fäl-i-kəl\ *n* **1** : a small cavity in the body or a deep narrow-mouthed depression (as from which a hair grows) **2** : a dry one-celled fruit (as in the peony, larkspur, or milkweed) that develops from a single ovary and splits open by one seam only when ripe — **fol·lic·u·lar** \fə-'lik-yə-lər, fä-\ *adj* — **fol·lic·u·late** \-lət\ *also* **fol·lic·u·lat·ed** \-ˌlāt-əd\ *adj*

[1]**follow** \'fäl-ō\ *vb* **1** : to go or come after or behind **2** : be guided by : OBEY ⟨*followed* her conscience⟩ ⟨*follow* instructions⟩ **3** : PURSUE ⟨*follow* a clue⟩ **4** : to proceed along ⟨*follow* a path⟩ **5** : engage in as a business or way of life steadily ⟨*follow* the sea⟩ **6** : to come after in order of rank or natural sequence ⟨two *follows* one⟩ **7** : to keep one's eyes or attention fixed on ⟨*follow* a speech⟩ **8** : to result from something ⟨disaster *followed* the captain's blunder⟩ ⟨it *follows* that the accused is guilty⟩

syn FOLLOW, SUCCEED can mean to come after or later. FOLLOW may apply to a coming after in time, position or sequence; SUCCEED may imply a replacement of what went before

fol·low·er \'fäl-ə-wər\ *n* **1** : ATTENDANT **2** : SUPPORTER, ADHERENT **3** : DISCIPLE **4** : IMITATOR

[1]**fol·low·ing** \'fäl-ə-wing\ *adj* **1** : next after ⟨the *following* day⟩ **2** : that immediately follows ⟨trains will leave at the *following* times⟩

[2]**following** *n* : a group of followers

[3]**following** *prep* : subsequent to ⟨*following* the lecture tea was served⟩

follow up *vb* : to pursue closely : show continued interest in ⟨*follow up* a news story⟩

fol·ly \'fäl-ē\ *n, pl* **follies** **1** : lack of good sense or normal prudence and foresight **2 a** : a foolish act or idea **b** : foolish actions or conduct **3** : a costly or unprofitable undertaking

fo·ment \fō-'ment\ *vb* **1** : to treat (as for easing pain) with warm water or a medicinal liquid **2** : to stir up : ROUSE, INSTIGATE ⟨*foment* rebellion⟩ — **fo·men·ta·tion** \ˌfō-mən-'tā-shən, -ˌmen-\ *n* — **fo·ment·er** \fō-'ment-ər\ *n*

fond \'fänd\ *adj* **1 a** : prizing highly : DESIROUS ⟨*fond* of praise⟩ **b** : strongly attracted or predisposed ⟨*fond* of music⟩ **2** : TENDER, AFFECTIONATE **3** : doted on : CHERISHED ⟨his *fondest* hopes⟩ — **fond·ly** *adv* — **fond·ness** \'fän(d)-nəs\ *n*

fon·dant \'fän-dənt\ *n* **1** : a creamy preparation of sugar used as a basis for candies **2** : a candy consisting chiefly of fondant

fon·dle \'fän-dəl\ *vb* **fon·dled**; **fon·dling** \-d(ə-)ling\ : to touch or handle in a tender or loving manner : CARESS, PET — **fon·dler** \-d(ə-)lər\ *n*

F_1 layer \'ef-'wən-\ *n* : the inner of the two layers into which the F layer of the ionosphere divides during the day and which occurs between 90 to 150 miles above the earth's surface

[1]**font** \'fänt\ *n* **1** : a basin for baptismal or holy water **2** : FOUNTAIN, SOURCE

[2]**font** *n* : an assortment of type all of one size and style

food \'füd\ *n* **1 a** : material containing or consisting of carbohydrates, fats, proteins, and supplementary substances (as minerals) used in the body of an animal to sustain growth, repair, and vital processes and to furnish energy **b** : organic material produced by green plants and used by them as building material and as a source of energy **2** : nourishment in solid form **3** : something that nourishes, sustains, or supplies

food chain *n* : a sequence of organisms in which each uses the next usu. lower member of the sequence as a food source

food color *n* : a dye or pigment permitted for use in foods

food poisoning *n* : an acute digestive disorder caused by bacteria or by chemicals in food

food·stuff \'füd-ˌstəf\ *n* : a substance with food value; *esp* : a specific nutrient (as protein or fat)

food vacuole *n* : a vacuole (as in an amoeba) in which ingested food is digested

food web *n* : the totality of interacting food chains in an ecological community

¹**fool** \'fül\ *n* **1** : a person who lacks sense or judgment **2** : a person formerly kept in a noble or royal household to amuse with jests and pranks — called also *jester*
²**fool** *vb* **1 a** : to spend time idly or aimlessly **b** : to meddle or tamper thoughtlessly or ignorantly ⟨don't *fool* with that gun⟩ **2** : to speak or act in jest : JOKE ⟨I was only *fooling*⟩ **3** : to make a fool of : DECEIVE
fool·ery \'fül-(ə-)rē\ *n, pl* **-er·ies** **1** : foolish behavior **2** : a foolish act : HORSEPLAY
fool·har·dy \'fül-ˌhärd-ē\ *adj* : foolishly adventurous and bold : RASH — **fool·har·di·ly** \-ˌhärd-ə-lē\ *adv* — **fool·har·di·ness** \-ˌhärd-ē-nəs\ *n*
fool·ish \'fü-lish\ *adj* : showing or arising from folly : SENSELESS, SILLY — **fool·ish·ly** *adv* — **fool·ish·ness** *n*
fool·proof \'fül-'prüf\ *adj* : so simple, plain, or reliable as to leave no opportunity for error, misuse, or failure ⟨*foolproof* directions⟩ ⟨a *foolproof* plan⟩
fools·cap \'fül-ˌskap\ *n* [named after the watermark of a jester's cap formerly applied to such paper] : a size of paper typically 16 × 13 inches
fool's gold *n* : PYRITE
¹**foot** \'fu̇t\ *n, pl* **feet** \'fēt\ *also* **foot** **1 a** : the terminal part of the vertebrate leg below the ankle **b** : an organ upon which an invertebrate stands or moves; *esp* : a ventral muscular part of a mollusk **2** : a unit of length equal to ⅓ yard and comprising 12 inches ⟨a 10-*foot* pole⟩ ⟨6 *feet* tall⟩ — see MEASURE table **3** : the basic unit of verse meter consisting of a group of accented and unaccented syllables **4** : something resembling an animal's foot in position or use or in being opposite the head ⟨the *foot* of a mountain⟩ ⟨the *foot* of a bed⟩ **5** *foot pl, chiefly Brit* : INFANTRY — **on foot** **1** : by walking ⟨toured the campus *on foot*⟩ **2** : under way : in progress ⟨plans for a new building are *on foot*⟩
²**foot** *vb* **1 a** : DANCE **b** : WALK **c** : RUN **2 a** : to add up **b** : to pay or provide for paying ⟨*foot* the bill⟩
foot·ball \'fu̇t-ˌbȯl\ *n* **1** : any of several games that are played on a rectangular field by two teams whose object is to get an inflated ball over a goal line or between goalposts: as **a** *Brit* : SOCCER **b** *Brit* : RUGBY **c** : a game played between two teams of 11 players each in which the ball is advanced by running or passing **2** : the ball used in football
foot·board \-ˌbōrd, -ˌbȯrd\ *n* **1** : a narrow platform on which to stand or brace the feet **2** : a board forming the foot of a bed
foot·bridge \-ˌbrij\ *n* : a bridge for pedestrians
foot·can·dle \-'kan-dəl\ *n* : a unit for measuring illumination equal to the illumination on a suface all parts of which are one foot from a light of one candle
foot·ed \'fu̇t-əd\ *adj* **1** : having a foot or feet **2** : having such or so many feet ⟨flat-*footed*⟩ ⟨four-*footed*⟩
foot·fall \'fu̇t-ˌfȯl\ *n* : FOOTSTEP
foot·hill \-ˌhil\ *n* : a hill at the foot of higher hills
foot·hold \-ˌhōld\ *n* **1** : a hold for the feet : FOOTING **2** : a position usable as a base for further advance
foot·ing \'fu̇t-ing\ *n* **1 a** : the placing of one's feet in a position to secure a firm or safe stand **b** : a place for the foot to rest securely **2 a** : position with respect to one another : STATUS ⟨nations on a friendly *footing*⟩ **b** : BASIS **3 a** : the action of adding up a column of figures **b** : the total amount of such a column
foot·lights \'fu̇t-ˌlīts\ *n pl* **1** : a row of lights set across the front of a stage floor **2** : the stage as a profession
foot·loose \-ˌlüs\ *adj* : having no ties : FREE, UNBOUND
foot·man \-mən\ *n* : a male servant who attends a carriage, waits on table, admits visitors, and runs errands
foot·note \-ˌnōt\ *n* : a note of reference, explanation, or comment placed below the text on a printed page — **foot·note** *vb*
¹**foot·pad** \-ˌpad\ *n* : a highwayman or robber on foot
²**footpad** *n* : a round somewhat flat foot on the leg of a spacecraft for distributing weight to minimize sinking into a surface (as on the moon)
foot·path \-ˌpath, -ˌpȧth\ *n* : a narrow path for pedestrians
foot–pound \-'pau̇nd\ *n, pl* **foot–pounds** : a unit of work equal to the work done by a force of one pound acting through a distance of one foot
foot–pound–second *adj* : being or relating to a system of units based upon the foot as the unit of length, the pound as the unit of weight or mass, and the second as the unit of time — abbr. *fps*
foot·print \'fu̇t-ˌprint\ *n* : an impression left by the foot
foot·race \-ˌrās\ *n* : a race run on foot
foot·rest \-ˌrest\ *n* : a support for the feet
foot soldier *n* : INFANTRYMAN
foot·sore \'fu̇t-ˌsō(ə)r, -ˌsȯ(ə)r\ *adj* : having sore or tender feet (as from much walking)
foot·step \-ˌstep\ *n* **1 a** : a step or tread of the foot **b** : distance covered by a step : PACE **2 a** : FOOTPRINT **b** : the sound of a footstep **3** : a step on which to ascend or descend
foot·stool \-ˌstül\ *n* : a low stool to support the feet
foot·wear \-ˌwa(ə)r, -ˌwe(ə)r\ *n* : covering (as shoes) for the feet
foot·work \-ˌwərk\ *n* : the management of the feet (as in boxing)
foo·zle \'fü-zəl\ *vb* **foo·zled**; **foo·zling** \'füz-(ə-)ling\ : BUNGLE — **foozle** *n*
fop \'fäp\ *n* : a man who is vain about his dress or appearance : DANDY — **fop·pish** \'fäp-ish\ *adj* — **fop·pish·ly** *adv* — **fop·pish·ness** *n*
fop·pery \'fäp-(ə-)rē\ *n, pl* **fop·per·ies** : the distinguishing marks (as behavior or dress) of a fop
¹**for** \fər, (')fȯ(ə)r\ *prep* **1** — used as a function word to indicate a purpose or object toward which a desire or activity is directed or intended ⟨money *for* lunch⟩ ⟨left *for* home⟩ ⟨now *for* a good rest⟩ **2** : as being ⟨take him *for* a fool⟩ **3** : because of ⟨cried *for* joy⟩ **4 a** : in support of ⟨fighting *for* their country⟩ **b** : directed at ⟨medicine *for* a cold⟩ **c** : so as to bring about a certain state ⟨shouted the news *for* all to hear⟩ **5 a** : in place of ⟨Doe batting *for* Roe⟩ **b** : in exchange ⟨paid $10 *for* a hat⟩ **6** : in spite of ⟨unconvinced *for* all his clever arguments⟩ **7** : CONCERNING ⟨a stickler *for* detail⟩ **8** — used as a function word to indicate equality or proportion ⟨point *for* point⟩ ⟨tall *for* his age⟩ **9** — used as a function word to indicate duration of time or extent of space ⟨waited *for* several hours⟩ **10** : ²AFTER 3b ⟨named *for* his grandfather⟩
²**for** *conj* : for this reason or on this ground : SINCE ⟨he was certainly there, *for* I heard him⟩
for *abbr* **1** foreign **2** forestry
¹**for·age** \'fȯr-ij, 'fär-\ *n* **1** : food for animals esp. when taken by browsing or grazing **2** : a search for food or provisions
²**forage** *vb* **1** : BROWSE, GRAZE **2** : to make a search esp. for food or provisions ⟨*forage* for grain⟩ ⟨*forage* for firewood⟩ **3** : to get by foraging — **for·ag·er** *n*
for·a·min·i·fer \ˌfȯr-ə-'min-ə-fər, ˌfär-\ *n* : any of an

F

order of large chiefly marine ameboid protozoans usu. having perforated shells that are important sources of chalk and limestone — **fo·ram·i·nif·er·al** \fə-ˌram-ə-ˈnif-(ə-)rəl; ˌfȯr-ə-mə-ˈnif-, ˌfär-\ *or* **fo·ram·i·nif·er·ous** \-(ə-)rəs\ *adj* — **fo·ram·i·nif·er·an** \-(ə-)rən\ *adj or n*

for·as·much as \ˌfȯr-əz-ˌməch-əz\ *conj* : in view of the fact that : SINCE

for·ay \ˈfȯr-ˌā\ *vb* : to raid esp. in search of plunder : PILLAGE — **foray** *n*

1**for·bear** \fȯr-ˈba(ə)r, fər-, -ˈbe(ə)r\ *vb* **-bore** \-ˈbō(ə)r, -ˈbȯ(ə)r\; **-borne** \-ˈbōrn, -ˈbȯrn\; **-bear·ing 1** : to refrain or desist from : ABSTAIN **2** : to control oneself when provoked : be patient — **for·bear·er** *n*

2**for·bear** \ˈfȯr-ˌba(ə)r, -ˌbe(ə)r\ *var of* FOREBEAR

for·bear·ance \fȯr-ˈbar-ən(t)s, fər-, -ˈber-\ *n* **1** : the act of forbearing **2** : the quality of being forbearing : PATIENCE

for·bid \fər-ˈbid, fȯr-\ *vb* **-bade** \-ˈbad, -ˈbād\ *or* **-bad** \-ˈbad\; **-bid·den** \-ˈbid-ən\; **-bid·ding 1** : to command not to do or to be done or used ⟨I *forbid* you to go⟩ ⟨cameras are *forbidden*⟩ **2** : to hinder or prevent as if by command ⟨space *forbids* quoting in full⟩ — **for·bid·der** *n*

for·bid·ding *adj* : frightening away : REPELLENT — **for·bid·ding·ly** \-ing-lē\ *adv* — **for·bid·ding·ness** *n*

1**force** \ˈfōrs, ˈfȯrs\ *n* **1 a** : strength or energy exerted : active power ⟨*forces* of nature⟩ **b** : moral or mental strength **c** : capacity to persuade or convince ⟨the *force* of his arguments⟩ **d** : legal effectiveness ⟨that law is still in *force*⟩ **2** : a body of persons or things available for a particular end ⟨labor *force*⟩ ⟨air *force*⟩ ⟨a *force* of ships⟩ **3** : violence or compulsion exerted upon a person or thing ⟨open a door by *force*⟩ **4** : an influence (as a push or pull) that if applied to a material free body results chiefly in an acceleration of the body and sometimes in other effects (as deformation) — **force·less** \-ləs\ *adj*

2**force** *vb* **1** : to compel by force : COERCE ⟨*forced* him to quit⟩ **2** : to attain or effect against resistance ⟨*force* your way through⟩ **3 a** : to gain by struggle or violence ⟨*forced* his way in⟩ **b** : to break open or through ⟨*force* a lock⟩ **4** : to produce with unnatural effort ⟨*forced* laughter⟩ **5** : to hasten the progress or growth of ⟨*forcing* lilies for Easter⟩ **6** : to urge upon someone unwilling ⟨*forced* his attentions on her⟩ — **forc·er** *n*

forced \ˈfōrst, ˈfȯrst\ *adj* **1** : compelled by force or circumstances : INVOLUNTARY ⟨*forced* labor⟩ **2** : done or produced with effort, exertion, or pressure ⟨a *forced* march⟩ — **forc·ed·ly** \ˈfōr-səd-lē, ˈfȯr-\ *adv*

force·ful \ˈfōrs-fəl, ˈfȯrs-\ *adj* : possessing much force : VIGOROUS ⟨a *forceful* speech⟩ — **force·ful·ly** \-fə-lē\ *adv* — **force·ful·ness** *n*

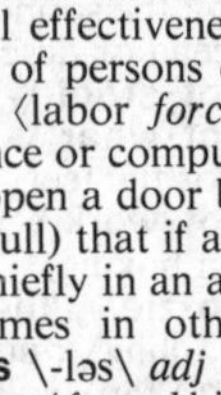
forceps

for·ceps \ˈfȯr-səps\ *n, pl* **forceps** [from Latin, literally "something for holding hot objects", from *formus* "hot" (from the same prehistoric source as English *warm*) and *capere* "to take" (from which English *capture* is derived)] : an instrument for grasping or holding objects esp. in delicate operations (as by jewelers or surgeons) — **for·ceps·like** \-ˌlīk\ *adj*

forc·i·ble \ˈfōr-sə-bəl, ˈfȯr-\ *adj* **1** : got, made, or done by force or violence ⟨a *forcible* entrance⟩ **2** : FORCEFUL — **forc·i·bly** \-blē\ *adv*

1**ford** \ˈfōrd, ˈfȯrd\ *n* : a shallow part of a body of water that may be crossed by wading

2**ford** *vb* : to cross (a body of water) by wading — **ford·a·ble** \-ə-bəl\ *adj*

1**fore** \ˈfō(ə)r, ˈfȯ(ə)r\ *adv* : in, toward, or near the front : FORWARD

2**fore** *adj* : being or coming before in time, order, or space

3**fore** *n* : a prominent place or position : FRONT

4**fore** *interj* — used by a golfer to warn anyone within range of the probable line of flight of his ball

fore- *comb form* **1 a** : earlier : beforehand ⟨*fore*see⟩ **b** : occurring earlier : occurring beforehand ⟨*fore*payment⟩ **2 a** : situated at the front : in front ⟨*fore*leg⟩ **b** : front part of (something specified) ⟨*fore*arm⟩

fore–and–aft \ˌfōr-ən-ˈaft, ˌfȯr-\ *adj* **1** : lying, running, or acting along the length of a ship ⟨*fore-and-aft* sails⟩ **2** : having no square sails

fore–and–aft rig *n* : a sailing ship rig in which most or all of the sails are not attached to yards but are bent to gaffs or set on the masts or on stays in a fore-and-aft line — **fore–and–aft rigged** *adj*

1**fore·arm** \(ˈ)fōr-ˈärm, (ˈ)fȯr-\ *vb* : to arm in advance : PREPARE

2**fore·arm** \ˈfōr-ˌärm, ˈfȯr-\ *n* : the part of the arm between the elbow and the wrist

fore·bear *or* **for·bear** \ˈfōr-ˌba(ə)r, ˈfȯr-, -ˌbe(ə)r\ *n* : ANCESTOR, FOREFATHER

for·bode \fōr-ˈbōd, fȯr-\ *vb* **1** : FORETELL, PORTEND ⟨such heavy air *forebodes* storm⟩ **2** : to have a feeling that something esp. unfortunate is going to happen — **fore·bod·er** *n* — **fore·bod·ing** \-ˈbōd-ing\ *n* — **fore·bod·ing·ly** \-ing-lē\ *adv* — **fore·bod·ing·ness** *n*

fore·brain \ˈfōr-brān, ˈfȯr-\ *n* : the anterior division of the embryonic vertebrate brain or the parts developed from it

1**fore·cast** \ˈfōr-ˌkast, ˈfȯr-\ *vb* **forecast** *or* **fore·cast·ed**; **fore·cast·ing** : to calculate or predict (a future event or state) usu. by study and analysis of data ⟨*forecast* the weather⟩ ***syn*** see FORETELL — **fore·cast·er** *n*

2**forecast** *n* : a prophecy, estimate, or prediction of a future happening or condition ⟨weather *forecasts*⟩

fore·cas·tle \ˈfōk-səl; ˈfōr-ˌkas-əl, ˈfȯr-\ *n* **1** : the part of the upper deck of a ship forward of the foremast **2** : the forward part of a merchantman containing the crew quarters

fore·close \fōr-ˈklōz, fȯr-\ *vb* **1** : to shut out : EXCLUDE ⟨didn't *foreclose* the possibility of a second term⟩ **2** : to take legal measures to terminate a mortgage and take possession of the mortgaged property because the conditions of the mortgage have not been met — **fore·clo·sure** \-ˈklō-zhər\ *n*

fore·deck \ˈfōr-ˌdek, ˈfȯr-\ *n* : the forepart of a ship's main deck

fore·doom \fōr-ˈdüm, fȯr-\ *vb* : to doom beforehand ⟨efforts *foredoomed* to failure⟩

fore·fa·ther \ˈfōr-ˌfäth-ər, ˈfȯr-\ *n* **1** : ANCESTOR 1 **2** : a person of an earlier period to whom one owes much (as political independence, culture, or beliefs)

fore·fin·ger \-ˌfing-gər\ *n* : the finger next to the thumb

fore·foot \-ˌfu̇t\ *n* : one of the front feet of a four-footed animal

ə abut	ər further	a back	ā bake	
ä cot, cart	au̇ out	ch chin	e less	ē easy
g gift	i trip	ī life	j joke	ng sing	ō flow
ȯ flaw	ȯi coin	th thin	th this	ü loot
u̇ foot	y yet	yü few	yu̇ furious	zh vision

fore·front \-ˌfrənt\ *n* : the foremost part or place : FOCUS ⟨an event in the *forefront* of the news⟩
foregather *var of* FORGATHER
[1]**fore·go** \fōr-ˈgō, fȯr-\ *vb* **-went** \-ˈwent\; **-gone** \-ˈgȯn, -ˈgän\; **-go·ing** \-ˈgō-ing\ : to go before : PRECEDE — **fore·go·er** \-ˈgō(-ə)r\ *n*
[2]**forego** *var of* FORGO
fore·go·ing \fōr-ˈgō-ing, fȯr-\ *adj* : PRECEDING ⟨the *foregoing* paragraphs⟩
fore·gone \ˌfōr-ˌgȯn, ˌfȯr-, -ˌgän\ *adj* : settled in advance ⟨his success was a *foregone* conclusion⟩
fore·ground \ˈfōr-ˌgraund, ˈfȯr-\ *n* : the part of a scene or representation that is nearest to and in front of the spectator
fore·hand \-ˌhand\ *n* : a stroke made with the palm of the hand turned in the direction of movement — **forehand** *adv or adj*
fore·hand·ed \-ˈhan-dəd\ *adj* : mindful of the future : THRIFTY — **fore·hand·ed·ly** *adv* — **fore·hand·ed·ness** *n*
fore·head \ˈfȯr-əd, ˈfär-; ˈfōr-ˌhed, ˈfȯr-\ *n* : the part of the face above the eyes
for·eign \ˈfȯr-ən, ˈfär-\ *adj* [from Old French *forein*, from the Latin adjective *foranus* "outside", from the adverb *foris* "outside", literally "at the doors"; from the same source as English *door*] **1** : situated outside a place or country; *esp* : situated outside one's own country ⟨*foreign* nations⟩ **2** : born in, belonging to, or characteristic of another place or country ⟨*foreign* language⟩ ⟨*foreign* customs⟩ **3** : not connected or pertinent ⟨material *foreign* to the topic at hand⟩ **4** : related to or dealing with other nations ⟨*foreign* affairs⟩ ⟨*foreign* office⟩ **5** : not normally found in an area or part ⟨a *foreign* body in the eye⟩ ⟨*foreign* matter in milk⟩ — **for·eign·ness** \-ən-nəs\ *n*
for·eign·er \ˈfȯr-ə-nər, ˈfär-\ *n* : a person belonging to or owing allegiance to a foreign country : ALIEN
foreign minister *n* : a governmental minister for foreign affairs
fore·know \(ˈ)fōr-ˈnō, (ˈ)fȯr-\ *vb* **-knew** \-ˈn(y)ü\; **-known** \-ˈnōn\; **-know·ing** : to have prior knowledge of : know beforehand — **fore·knowl·edge** \-ˈnäl-ij\ *n*
fore·land \ˈfōr-lənd, ˈfȯr-\ *n* : PROMONTORY, HEADLAND
fore·leg \-ˌleg\ *n* : a front leg
fore·limb \-ˌlim\ *n* : an arm, fin, wing, or leg that is a foreleg or homologous to it
fore·lock \-ˌläk\ *n* : a lock of hair growing from the front of the head
fore·man \ˈfōr-mən, ˈfȯr-\ *n* **1** : a member of a jury who acts as chairman and spokesman **2** : a workman in charge of a group of workers — **fore·la·dy** \-ˌlād-ē\ *n*
fore·mast \-ˌmast, -məst\ *n* : the mast nearest the bow of a ship
fore·most \ˈfōr-ˌmōst, ˈfȯr-\ *adj* : first in time, place, or order : most important — **foremost** *adv*
fore·name \-ˌnām\ *n* : the first of the names that a person bears (as "John" in "John Smith")
fore·noon \ˈfōr-ˌnün, ˈfȯr-\ *n* : the part of the day ending with noon : MORNING
fo·ren·sic \fə-ˈren(t)-sik, -ˈren-zik\ *adj* [from Latin *forensis* "belonging to the forum"; from the location of the law courts in the forum of ancient Rome] : belonging to, used in, or suitable to courts of law or to public discussion and debate — **fo·ren·si·cal·ly** \-si-k(ə-)lē-, -zi-\ *adv*
fore·or·dain \ˌfōr-ȯr-ˈdān\ *vb* : to ordain in advance : PREDESTINE ⟨a *foreordained* course of events⟩ — **fore·or·di·na·tion** \-ˌȯrd-ə-ˈnā-shən\ *n*
fore·part \ˈfōr-ˌpärt, ˈfȯr-\ *n* : the part most advanced or first in place or in time
fore·paw \-ˌpȯ\ *n* : the paw of a foreleg
fore·quar·ter \-ˌkwȯrt-ər\ *n* : the left or right half of a front half of the body or carcass of a four-footed animal
fore·run·ner \ˈfōr-ˌrən-ər, ˈfȯr-\ *n* **1** : one going or sent before to give notice of the approach of others : HARBINGER ⟨the dark clouds were *forerunners* of a storm⟩ **2** : PREDECESSOR, ANCESTOR
fore·sail \ˈfōr-ˌsāl, ˈfȯr-, -səl\ *n* **1** : the lowest sail on the foremast of a square-rigged ship **2** : the lower sail set toward the stern on the foremast of a schooner
fore·see \fōr-ˈsē, fȯr-\ *vb* **-saw** \-ˈsȯ\; **-seen** \-ˈsēn\; **-see·ing** : to see or realize beforehand : EXPECT — **fore·see·a·ble** \-ˈsē-ə-bəl\ *adj* — **fore·se·er** \-ˈsē-ər\ *n*
fore·shad·ow \-ˈshad-ō\ *vb* : to give a hint or suggestion of beforehand : represent beforehand ⟨events *foreshadowed* a victory⟩ — **fore·shad·ow·er** *n*
fore·short·en \-ˈshȯrt-ən\ *vb* : to shorten (a detail) in a drawing or painting so that the composition appears to have depth
fore·sight \ˈfōr-ˌsīt, ˈfȯr-\ *n* **1** : the act or power of foreseeing : FOREKNOWLEDGE **2** : care or provision for the future : PRUDENCE — **fore·sight·ed** \-ˌsīt-əd\ *adj* — **fore·sight·ed·ly** *adv* — **fore·sight·ed·ness** *n*
fore·skin \-ˌskin\ *n* : a fold of skin that covers the end of the penis — called also *prepuce*
for·est \ˈfȯr-əst, ˈfär-\ *n* : a dense growth of trees and underbrush covering a large area
fore·stall \fōr-ˈstȯl, fȯr-\ *vb* : to keep out, hinder, or prevent by measures taken in advance ⟨*forestall* unnecessary questions by careful directions⟩ — **fore·stall·er** *n* — **fore·stall·ment** \-ˈstȯl-mənt\ *n*
for·es·ta·tion \ˌfȯr-ə-ˈstā-shən, ˌfär-\ *n* : the planting and care of a forest
for·est·ed \ˈfȯr-ə-stəd, ˈfär-\ *adj* : covered with trees or forests : WOODED
for·est·er \ˈfȯr-ə-stər, ˈfär-\ *n* **1** : a person trained in forestry **2** : a dweller in a forest
forest fire *n* : an uncontrolled fire in a wooded area
forest floor *n* : the upper layer of mixed soil and organic debris typical of forested land
forest ranger *n* : a person in charge of the management and protection of a forest
for·est·ry \ˈfȯr-ə-strē, ˈfär-\ *n* : the science and practice of caring for forests
foreswear *var of* FORSWEAR
fore·taste \ˈfōr-ˌtāst, ˈfȯr-\ *n* : a preliminary experience of something that will not be fully experienced until later ⟨through maneuvers a soldier gets a *foretaste* of war⟩
fore·tell \fōr-ˈtel, fȯr-\ *vb* **-told** \-ˈtōld\; **-tell·ing** : to tell of or describe beforehand : PROPHESY — **fore·tell·er** *n*

syn FORETELL, PREDICT, FORECAST can mean to tell of in advance. FORETELL may imply unexplained powers by which the future is revealed; PREDICT is likely to suggest experience or knowledge of natural laws as a basis of accurate foreseeing; FORECAST implies dealing with probabilities rather than certainties

fore·thought \ˈfōr-ˌthȯt, ˈfȯr-\ *n* : thought or care taken in advance — **fore·thought·ful** \-fəl\ *adj* — **fore·thought·ful·ly** \-fə-lē\ *adv* — **fore·thought·ful·ness** *n*
fore·top \ˈfōr-ˌtäp, ˈfȯr-; ˈfōrt-əp, ˈfȯrt-\ *n* : the platform at the head of a ship's foremast

F

for·ev·er \fə-'rev-ər\ *adv* **1** : for a limitless time : EVERLASTINGLY **2** : ALWAYS, CONSTANTLY ⟨a dog that was *forever* chasing cars⟩

for·ev·er·more \-ˌrev-ə(r)-'mō(ə)r, -'mȯ(ə)r\ *adv* : FOREVER

fore·warn \fōr-'wȯrn, fȯr-\ *vb* : to warn in advance ⟨*forewarned* of danger⟩

fore wing *n* : either of the front wings of a 4-winged insect

fore·word \'fōr-(ˌ)wərd, 'fȯr-\ *n* : PREFACE

¹**for·feit** \'fȯr-fət\ *n* **1** : something forfeited : PENALTY, FINE **2** *pl* : a game in which the players redeem personal articles by paying amusing or embarrassing penalties

²**forfeit** *vb* : to lose or lose the right to as a punishment for an error, offense, or crime — **for·feit·er** *n*

³**forfeit** *adj* : forfeited or subject to forfeiture ⟨if they caught the spy his life would be *forfeit*⟩

for·fei·ture \'fȯr-fə-ˌchu̇r, -chər\ *n* **1** : the act of forfeiting **2** : something forfeited : PENALTY

for·gath·er *or* **fore·gath·er** \fȯr-'gat͟h-ər, fōr-\ *vb* : to come together : ASSEMBLE, MEET

¹**forge** \'fōrj, 'fȯrj\ *n* [from Old French, from Latin *fabrica* "workshop"] **1** : a furnace or a shop with its furnace where metal is heated and wrought **2** : a workshop where wrought iron is produced or where iron is made malleable

²**forge** *vb* **1 a** : to form (as metal) by heating and hammering **b** : to form (metal) by a press **2** : to form or shape out : FASHION ⟨*forged* an agreement⟩ **3** : to make or imitate falsely esp. with intent to defraud : COUNTERFEIT ⟨*forge* a check⟩ ⟨*forge* a signature⟩ — **forg·er** *n*

³**forge** *vb* : to move forward steadily but gradually ⟨*forge* ahead in the voting for class president⟩

forg·ery \'fōrj-(ə-)rē, 'fȯrj-\ *n, pl* **-er·ies** **1** : the crime of falsely making or changing a written paper or signing someone else's name **2** : something (as a signature) that has been forged

for·get \fər-'get, fȯr-\ *vb* **-got** \-'gät\; **-got·ten** \-'gät-ən\ *or* **-got**; **-get·ting** **1** : to be unable to think of or recall ⟨*forgot* his address⟩ ⟨he *forgets* easily⟩ **2 a** : to fail to recall at the proper time ⟨*forgot* about paying the bill⟩ **b** : NEGLECT ⟨*forgot* his old friends⟩ — **for·get·ter** *n* — **forget oneself** : to lose one's dignity, temper, or self-control

for·get·ful \-'get-fəl\ *adj* **1** : having a poor memory **2** : CARELESS, NEGLECTFUL ⟨*forgetful* of responsibilities⟩ — **for·get·ful·ly** \-fə-lē\ *adv* — **for·get·ful·ness** *n*

for·get–me–not \fər-'get-mē-ˌnät, fȯr-\ *n* : any of a genus of small herbs with bright blue or white flowers

forg·ing \'fōr-jing, 'fȯr-\ *n* : a piece of forged work ⟨aluminum *forgings*⟩

for·give \fər-'giv, fȯr-\ *vb* **-gave** \-'gāv\; **-giv·en** \-'giv-ən\; **-giv·ing** **1** : to cease to feel resentment against (an offender) : PARDON ⟨*forgive* your enemies⟩ **2 a** : to give up resentment of or claim to requital for ⟨*forgive* an insult⟩ **b** : to grant relief from payment of ⟨*forgive* a debt⟩ ***syn*** see EXCUSE — **for·giv·a·ble** \-'giv-ə-bəl\ *adj* — **for·giv·er** *n*

for·give·ness \-'giv-nəs\ *n* : the act of forgiving : PARDON

ə abut	ər further	a back	ā bake
ä cot, cart	au̇ out	ch chin	e less	ē easy
g gift	i trip	ī life	j joke	ng sing	ō flow
ȯ flaw	ȯi coin	th thin	t͟h this	ü loot
u̇ foot	y yet	yü few	yu̇ furious	zh vision

for·giv·ing \-'giv-ing\ *adj* : showing forgiveness : inclined or ready to forgive ⟨a person with a *forgiving* nature⟩ — **for·giv·ing·ly** \-ing-lē\ *adv* — **for·giv·ing·ness** *n*

for·go *or* **fore·go** \fȯr-'gō, fōr-\ *vb* **-went** \-'went\; **-gone** \-'gȯn, -'gän\; **-go·ing** \-'gō-ing\ : to give up : let pass : go without ⟨*forgo* lunch⟩ ⟨*forgo* an opportunity⟩

¹**fork** \'fȯrk\ *n* **1** : a pronged implement used esp. for taking up (as in eating), pitching, or digging **2** : a forked part, tool, or piece of equipment **3 a** : a dividing into branches or the place where something divides into branches ⟨a *fork* in the road⟩ **b** : a branch of a fork ⟨take the left *fork* at the crossroads⟩

²**fork** *vb* **1** : to divide into two or more branches ⟨the road *forks*⟩ **2** : to give the form of a fork to ⟨*forking* her fingers⟩ **3** : to raise or pitch with a fork ⟨*fork* hay⟩ — **fork·er** *n*

forked \'fȯrkt, 'fȯr-kəd\ *adj* : having a fork : shaped like a fork ⟨*forked* lightning⟩ ⟨a *forked* tongue⟩

fork·lift \'fȯrk-ˌlift\ *n* : a machine for hoisting heavy objects by means of steel fingers inserted under the load

for·lorn \fər-'lȯrn\ *adj* **1** : DESERTED, FORSAKEN **2** : feeling deserted or neglected : WRETCHED **3** : nearly hopeless ⟨a *forlorn* cause⟩ — **for·lorn·ly** *adv* — **for·lorn·ness** \-'lȯrn-nəs\ *n*

¹**form** \'fȯrm\ *n* **1 a** : the shape and structure of something as distinguished from its material **b** : a body (as of a person) esp. in its external appearance or as distinguished from the face **2** : an established manner of doing or saying something ⟨a *form* of worship⟩ **3** : a printed or typed document with blank spaces for inserting information ⟨tax *form*⟩ **4 a** : conduct regulated by custom or etiquette : CEREMONY, CONVENTION; *also* : show without substance ⟨outward *forms* of mourning⟩ **b** : manner of performing according to recognized standards ⟨such behavior is bad *form*⟩ **5** : a long seat : BENCH **6 a** : a model of the human figure used for displaying clothes **b** : a mold in which concrete is placed to set **7** : printing type or matter arranged and secured for printing **8** : one of the different manifestations of a particular thing or substance ⟨coal is a *form* of carbon⟩ **9 a** : orderly method of arrangement (as in the presentation of ideas or of artistic elements); *also* : a kind or instance of such arrangement ⟨painting is an art *form*⟩ **b** : the structural element, plan, or design of a work of art **10** : a bounded surface or volume **11** : a grade in a British secondary school or in some American private schools **12 a** : ability as shown by past performance **b** : condition for performing (as in athletic competition) ⟨in top *form*⟩ **13** : any of the different pronunciations or spellings a word may take in inflection or compounding **14** : a particular way of stating a mathematical expression ⟨the number 2.5 can be written in fractional *form* as 5/2⟩

²**form** *vb* **1** : to give form or shape to : FASHION, MAKE ⟨*form* the letter A⟩ **2** : TRAIN, INSTRUCT ⟨education *forms* the mind⟩ **3** : DEVELOP, GET, CONTRACT ⟨*form* a habit⟩ **4** : to make up : CONSTITUTE ⟨bonds *formed* the bulk of the estate⟩ **5** : to arrange in order ⟨*form* a battle line⟩ **6** : to take form : ARISE ⟨fog *forms* in the valleys⟩ **7** : to take a definite form, shape, or arrangement ⟨the infantry *formed* in line⟩ — **form·er** *n*

¹**for·mal** \'fȯr-məl\ *adj* **1** : of, relating to, or being the outward form of something **2 a** : following or according with established form, custom, or rule : CONVENTIONAL **b** : relating to, suitable for, or be-

ing an event requiring conventionally elaborate dress and behavior ⟨a *formal* ball⟩ ⟨*formal* dress⟩ **3 :** done in due or lawful form ⟨a *formal* contract⟩ **4 :** ALOOF, RESERVED ⟨a *formal* manner⟩ **5 :** NOMINAL ⟨a purely *formal* requirement⟩ — **for·mal·ly** \-mə-lē\ *adv*

²**formal** *n* **:** something (as a social event) formal in character

form·al·de·hyde \fȯr-ˈmal-də-ˌhīd, fər-\ *n* **:** a colorless gas that consists of carbon, hydrogen, and oxygen, has a sharp irritating odor, and in solution is used as a disinfectant and preservative

for·ma·lin \ˈfȯr-mə-lən\ *n* **:** a clear water solution of formaldehyde

for·mal·ism \ˈfȯr-mə-ˌliz-əm\ *n* **:** the strict observance of forms or conventions (as in religion or art) — **for·mal·ist** \-ləst\ *n* — **for·mal·is·tic** \ˌfȯr-mə-ˈlis-tik\ *adj* — **for·mal·is·ti·cal·ly** \-ti-k(ə-)lē\ *adv*

for·mal·i·ty \fȯr-ˈmal-ət-ē\ *n, pl* **-ties 1 :** the quality or state of being formal **2 :** compliance with formal or conventional rules **:** CEREMONY **3 :** required or conventional form

for·mal·ize \ˈfȯr-mə-ˌlīz\ *vb* **1 :** FORM, SHAPE **2 a :** to make formal **b :** to give formal status or approval to — **for·mal·iz·er** *n*

¹**for·mat** \ˈfȯr-ˌmat\ *n* **:** the general organization or arrangement of something

²**format** *vb* **for·mat·ted; for·mat·ting :** to arrange in a particular format

for·ma·tion \fȯr-ˈmā-shən\ *n* **1 :** a forming of something ⟨the *formation* of good habits during childhood⟩ **2 :** something formed **3 :** the manner in which a thing is formed **:** STRUCTURE, SHAPE ⟨an abnormal *formation* of the jaw⟩ **4 :** an arrangement or grouping of persons, ships, or airplanes ⟨battle *formation*⟩ ⟨planes flying in *formation*⟩ **5 :** a bed of rocks or series of beds recognizable as a unit — **for·ma·tion·al** \-sh(ə-)nəl, shə-nəl\ *adj*

for·ma·tive \ˈfȯr-mət-iv\ *adj* **1 :** giving or capable of giving form **:** CONSTRUCTIVE ⟨a *formative* influence⟩ **2 :** of, relating to, or characterized by important growth or formation ⟨*formative* years⟩ — **for·ma·tive·ly** *adv* — **for·ma·tive·ness** *n*

for·mer \ˈfȯr-mər\ *adj* **1 :** coming before in time; *esp* **:** of, relating to, or occurring in the past ⟨*former* correspondence⟩ **2 :** FOREGOING ⟨*former* part of the chapter⟩ **3 :** first mentioned or in order of two things mentioned or understood ⟨of these two evils the *former* is the lesser⟩

for·mer·ly \-mər-lē\ *adv* **:** at an earlier time **:** PREVIOUSLY

for·mic acid \ˌfȯr-mik-\ *n* **:** a colorless strong-smelling organic acid that irritates the skin, is found in insects (as ants) and in many plants, and is used chiefly in dyeing and finishing textiles

for·mi·da·ble \ˈfȯr-məd-ə-bəl, fȯr-ˈmid-\ *adj* **1 :** arousing fear ⟨a *formidable* foe⟩ **2 :** imposing serious difficulties or hardships ⟨the mountains were a *formidable* barrier⟩ **3 :** tending to inspire awe or wonder ⟨*formidable* feats of daring⟩ — **for·mi·da·bil·i·ty** \ˌfȯr-məd-ə-ˈbil-ət-ē, fȯr-ˌmid-\ *n* — **for·mi·da·ble·ness** \ˈfȯr-məd-ə-bəl-nəs, fȯr-ˈmid-\ *n* — **for·mi·da·bly** \-blē\ *adv*

form·less \ˈfȯrm-ləs\ *adj* **:** having no regular form or shape — **form·less·ly** *adv* — **form·less·ness** *n*

for·mu·la \ˈfȯr-myə-lə\ *n, pl* **-las** *also* **-lae** \-ˌlē, -ˌlī\ **1 :** a set form of words for use in a ceremony or ritual **2 a :** RECIPE, PRESCRIPTION **b :** a milk mixture or substitute for a baby **3 a :** a general fact, rule, or principle expressed in symbols **b :** a symbolic expression of the composition or constitution of a substance ⟨the *formula* for water is H_2O⟩ **4 :** a prescribed or set form or method — **for·mu·la·ic** \ˌfȯr-myə-ˈlā-ik\ *adj* — **for·mu·la·ical·ly** \-ˈlā-ə-k(ə-)lē\ *adv*

for·mu·late \ˈfȯr-myə-ˌlāt\ *vb* **1 :** to express in a formula **2 :** to put in systematic form **:** state definitely and clearly ⟨*formulate* a plan⟩ — **for·mu·la·tion** \ˌfȯr-myə-ˈlā-shen\ *n* — **for·mu·la·tor** \ˈfȯr-myə-ˌlāt-ər\ *n*

formula weight *n* **:** the weight of the smallest chemically identifiable unit of a substance that is equal to the sum of the weights of all the atoms contained in it **:** MOLECULAR WEIGHT

for·ni·ca·tion \ˌfȯr-nə-ˈkā-shən\ *n* **:** sexual intercourse between unmarried people — **for·ni·cate** \ˈfȯr-nə-ˌkāt\ *vb* — **for·ni·ca·tor** \-ˌkāt-ər\ *n*

for·sake \fər-ˈsāk, fȯr-\ *vb* **for·sook** \-ˈsu̇k\; **for·sak·en** \-ˈsā-kən\; **for·sak·ing 1 :** to give up **:** RENOUNCE **2 :** to quit or leave entirely ⟨*forsook* the theater for other work⟩; *also* **:** DESERT ⟨*forsaken* by false friends⟩ ***syn*** see ABANDON ***ant*** return (to), revert (to)

for·sooth \fər-ˈsüth\ *adv* **:** in truth **:** INDEED

for·swear *or* **fore·swear** \fȯr-ˈswa(ə)r, fōr-, -ˈswe(ə)r\ *vb* **-swore** \-ˈswō(ə)r, -ˈswȯ(ə)r\; **-sworn** \-ˈswōrn, -ˈswȯrn\; **-swear·ing 1 :** to swear falsely **:** commit perjury **2 :** to promise to give up ⟨*forswear* gambling⟩

for·syth·ia \fər-ˈsith-ē-ə\ *n* **:** any of a genus of shrubs related to the olive and having yellow bell-shaped flowers appearing before the leaves in early spring

fort \ˈfōrt, ˈfȯrt\ *n* [from medieval French, from the adjective *fort* "strong", from Latin *fortis*] **1 :** a strong or fortified place; *esp* **:** a place surrounded with defenses and occupied by soldiers **2 :** a permanent army post

¹**forte** \ˈfōrt, ˈfȯrt, ˈfȯr-ˌtā\ *n* [from medieval French *fort*, from the adjective *fort* "strong"] **:** something in which a person shows special ability **:** a strong point ⟨baseball was that boy's *forte*⟩

²**for·te** \ˈfȯr-ˌtā, ˈfȯrt-ē\ *adv or adj* **:** LOUDLY — used as a direction in music

forth \ˈfōrth, ˈfȯrth\ *adv* **1 :** FORWARD, ONWARD ⟨from that time *forth*⟩ ⟨and so *forth*⟩ ⟨back and *forth*⟩ **2 :** out into view ⟨plants putting *forth* leaves⟩

¹**forth·com·ing** \(ˈ)fōrth-ˈkəm-ing, (ˈ)fȯrth-\ *adj* **1 :** being about to appear **:** APPROACHING ⟨the *forthcoming* holidays⟩ **2 :** readily available or approachable ⟨supplies will be *forthcoming*⟩

²**forthcoming** *n* **:** a coming forth **:** APPROACH

forth·right \ˈfōrth-ˌrīt, ˈfȯrth-\ *adj* **:** STRAIGHTFORWARD, DIRECT ⟨a *forthright* answer⟩ — **forth·right·ly** *adv* — **forth·right·ness** *n*

forth·with \(ˈ)fōrth-ˈwith, (ˈ)fȯrth-, -ˈwith\ *adv* **:** IMMEDIATELY ⟨expect an answer *forthwith*⟩

for·ti·fi·ca·tion \ˌfȯrt-ə-fə-ˈkā-shən\ *n* **1 :** the act of fortifying **2 a :** a construction built for the defense of a place **:** FORT **b** *pl* **:** defensive works

for·ti·fy \ˈfȯrt-ə-ˌfī\ *vb* **-fied; -fy·ing :** to make strong: as **a :** to strengthen and secure by military defenses ⟨*fortify* a town⟩ **b :** to give strength, courage, or endurance to ⟨*fortify* the body against illness⟩ **c :** to add material to for strengthening or improving **:** ENRICH ⟨*fortify* a soil with fertilizer⟩ — **for·ti·fi·er** \-ˌfī(-ə)r\ *n*

for·tis·si·mo \fȯr-ˈtis-ə-ˌmō\ *adv or adj* **:** very loudly — used as a direction in music

for·ti·tude \ˈfȯrt-ə-ˌt(y)üd\ *n* **:** strength of mind that enables a person to meet danger or bear pain or adversity with courage

fort·night \ˈfōrt-ˌnīt, ˈfȯrt-\ *n* [from Middle English *fourtene night* "fourteen nights"] **:** the space of 14 days **:** two weeks — **fort·night·ly** \-lē\ *adv or adj*

FOR·TRAN \'fȯr-ˌtran\ *n* : a language for programming a computer
for·tress \'fȯr-trəs\ *n* : a fortified place; *esp* : a large permanent fortification
for·tu·i·tous \fȯr-'t(y)ü-ət-əs, fər-\ *adj* : occurring by chance — **for·tu·i·tous·ly** *adv* — **for·tu·i·tous·ness** *n*
for·tu·nate \'fȯrch-(ə-)nət\ *adj* **1** : coming or happening by good luck : bringing a benefit or good that was not expected **2** : receiving some unexpected or unearned good : LUCKY ⟨a *fortunate* man⟩ — **for·tu·nate·ly** *adv* — **for·tu·nate·ness** *n*
for·tune \'fȯr-chən\ *n* **1** : an apparent cause of something that happens to one suddenly and unexpectedly : CHANCE, LUCK **2** : what happens to a person : good or bad luck ⟨the *fortunes* of war⟩ **3** : a person's destiny ⟨offered to tell his *fortune* with cards⟩ **4 a** : WEALTH ⟨a man of *fortune*⟩ **b** : a store of material possessions : RICHES ⟨was left a *fortune* by his father⟩
for·tune–tell·er \-ˌtel-ər\ *n* : a person who professes to foretell future events — **for·tune–tell·ing** \-ˌtel-iŋ\ *n or adj*
for·ty \'fȯrt-ē\ *n, pl* **forties** — see NUMBER table — **for·ti·eth** \-ē-əth\ *adj or n* — **forty** *adj or pron*
for·ty–five \ˌfȯrt-ē-'fīv\ *n* **1** : a 45 caliber pistol — usu. written .45 **2** : a phonograph record for play at 45 revolutions per minute
for·ty–nin·er \ˌfȯrt-ē-'nī-nər\ *n* : a person who went to California in the gold rush of 1849
fo·rum \'fōr-əm, 'fȯr-\ *n, pl* **forums** *also* **fo·ra** \-ə\ **1** : the marketplace or public place of an ancient Roman city **2** : a medium of open discussion **3** : a judicial body : COURT **4** : a meeting, program, or lecture involving discussion
1**for·ward** \'fȯr-wərd\ *adj* **1** : near, being at, or belonging to the front ⟨a ship's *forward* gun⟩ **2 a** : EAGER **b** : BRASH **3** : notably advanced or developed : PRECOCIOUS **4** : moving, tending, or leading toward the front — **forward** *adv* — **for·ward·ly** *adv* — **for·ward·ness** *n*
2**forward** *n* : a player in any of several games (as basketball) stationed at or near the front of his team
3**forward** *vb* **1** : to help onward : ADVANCE ⟨*forwarded* his friend's career⟩ **2** : to send on or forward : TRANSMIT ⟨*forward* a letter⟩
for·ward·er \'fȯr-wərd-ər\ *n* : one that forwards; *esp* : an agent who forwards goods ⟨a freight *forwarder*⟩
forward pass *n* : a pass in football thrown in the direction of the opponents' goal
for·wards \'fȯr-wərdz\ *adv* : FORWARD
1**fos·sil** \'fäs-əl\ *n* **1** : a trace or impression or the remains of a plant or animal of a past age preserved in the earth's crust **2 a** : a person whose ideas are out-of-date **b** : something that has become rigidly fixed
2**fossil** *adj* : being or resembling a fossil
fossil fuel *n* : a fuel (as coal, oil, or natural gas) that is formed in the earth from plant or animal remains
fos·sil·ize \'fäs-ə-ˌlīz\ *vb* **1** : to convert or become converted into a fossil **2** : to make outmoded, rigid, or fixed — **fos·sil·i·za·tion** \ˌfäs-ə-lə-'zā-shən\ *n*
1**fos·ter** \'fȯs-tər, 'fäs-\ *adj* : affording, receiving, or sharing parental care though not related by blood or legal ties ⟨*foster* parent⟩ ⟨*foster* child⟩ ⟨his *foster* brother⟩

ə abut · ər further · a back · ā bake
ä cot, cart · au̇ out · ch chin · e less · ē easy
g gift · i trip · ī life · j joke · ŋ sing · ō flow
ȯ flaw · ȯi coin · th thin · t͟h this · ü loot
u̇ foot · y yet · yü few · yu̇ furious · zh vision

2**foster** *vb* **fos·tered**; **fos·ter·ing** \-t(ə-)riŋ\ **1** : to give parental care to : NURTURE **2** : to promote the growth or development of : ENCOURAGE ⟨*foster* the spread of higher education⟩ — **fos·ter·er** \-tər-ər\ *n*
Fou·cault pendulum \ˌfü-ˌkō-\ *n* : a device consisting of a weight suspended by a wire that swings in one direction although the direction seems to change giving proof of the rotation of the earth
fought *past of* FIGHT
1**foul** \'fau̇l\ *adj* **1 a** : offensive to the senses : LOATHSOME ⟨a *foul* sewer⟩ **b** : clogged or covered with dirt **2** : morally or spiritually odious : DETESTABLE ⟨*foul* crimes⟩ **3** : OBSCENE, ABUSIVE ⟨*foul* language⟩ **4** : being wet and stormy ⟨*foul* weather⟩ **5 a** : TREACHEROUS, DISHONORABLE ⟨fair means or *foul*⟩ **b** : violating a rule in a game or sport ⟨a *foul* blow in boxing⟩ **6** : ENTANGLED **7** : being outside the foul lines in baseball ⟨*foul* grounder⟩ — **foul** *adv* — **foul·ly** \'fau̇l-(l)ē\ *adv* — **foul·ness** \'fau̇l-nəs\ *n*
2**foul** *n* **1** : an entanglement or collision esp. in angling or sailing **2 a** : an infringement of the rules in a game or sport **b** : FREE THROW **3** : FOUL BALL
3**foul** *vb* **1** : to make or become foul ⟨*foul* the air⟩ ⟨*foul* a stream⟩ **2** : DISGRACE, DISHONOR ⟨*fouled* his good name⟩ **3 a** : to commit a violation of the rules in a sport or game **b** : to hit a foul ball **4** : to entangle or become entangled ⟨*foul* a rope⟩ ⟨the anchor *fouled*⟩ **5** : to collide with ⟨*foul* a launch in moving away from the dock⟩
fou·lard \fü-'lärd\ *n* **1** : a lightweight silk usu. decorated with a printed pattern **2** : an article of clothing (as a scarf) made of foulard
foul ball *n* : a baseball batted into foul territory
foul line *n* **1** : either of two straight lines extending from home plate through first and third base on to the boundary of a baseball field **2** : a line across a bowling alley that a bowler must not step over when delivering the ball
foul play *n* : unfair dealing : dishonest conduct; *esp* : VIOLENCE ⟨a victim of *foul play*⟩
1**found** \'fau̇nd\ *past of* FIND
2**found** *vb* [from Old French *fonder*, from Latin *fundare*, from *fundus* "bottom"] **1** : to take the first steps in building : ESTABLISH ⟨*found* a colony⟩ **2** : to set on something solid : BASE ⟨a house *founded* on rock⟩ — **found·er** *n*
3**found** *vb* [from medieval French *fondre* "to pour", "melt", from Latin *fundere*, the source of English *funnel*] : to melt (metal) and pour into a mold — **found·er** *n*
foun·da·tion \fau̇n-'dā-shən\ *n* **1** : the act of founding **2** : the base or basis upon which something stands or is supported ⟨a house with a cinder-block *foundation*⟩ ⟨suspicions with no *foundation* in fact⟩ **3** : funds given for the permanent support of an institution : ENDOWMENT; *also* : an organization or institution so endowed — **foun·da·tion·al** \-sh(ə-)nəl\ *adj*
foun·der \'fau̇n-dər\ *vb* **foun·dered**; **foun·der·ing** \-d(ə-)riŋ\ **1** : to become or make disabled; *esp* : to go lame ⟨his horse *foundered*⟩ **2** : to sink below the surface of the water ⟨a *foundering* ship⟩ **3** : FAIL ⟨their efforts all *foundered*⟩
found·ling \'fau̇n-dliŋ\ *n* : an infant found after its unknown parents have abandoned it
found·ry \'fau̇n-drē\ *n, pl* **foundries** **1** : the act, process, or art of casting metals; *also* : CASTINGS **2** : an establishment where founding is carried on
fount \'fau̇nt\ *n* : FOUNTAIN, SOURCE
foun·tain \'fau̇nt-ən\ *n* **1** : a spring of water issuing from the earth **2** : SOURCE **3** : an artificially pro-

duced jet of water; *also* : the structure from which it rises **4** : a reservoir containing a liquid that can be drawn off as needed

foun·tain·head \-ˌhed\ *n* **1** : a spring that is the source of a stream **2** : a primary source : ORIGIN ⟨the *fountainhead* of our liberties⟩ ⟨a *fountainhead* of wisdom⟩

fountain pen *n* : a pen with a reservoir that automatically feeds the writing point with ink

four \ˈfō(ə)r, ˈfȯ(ə)r\ *n* **1** — see NUMBER table **2** : the fourth in a set or series **3** : something having four units or members — **four** *adj or pron*

four–foot·ed \-ˈfu̇t-əd\ *adj* : having four feet : QUADRUPED

4–H \-ˈāch\ *adj* : of or relating to a program set up by the U.S. Department of Agriculture to instruct rural young people in modern farm practices and in good citizenship ⟨*4-H* club⟩

four–o'clock \-ə-ˌkläk\ *n* : an American herb with fragrant solitary yellow, red, or white flowers opening late in the afternoon

four–post·er \-ˈpō-stər\ *n* : a bed with tall corner posts orig. designed to support curtains or a canopy

four·score \ˈfōr-ˈskōr, ˈfȯr-ˈskȯr\ *adj* : being four times twenty : EIGHTY

four·some \ˈfōr-səm, ˈfȯr-\ *n* **1** : a group of four persons or things **2** : a golf match between two pairs of partners

four·square \-ˈskwa(ə)r, -ˈskwe(ə)r\ *adj* **1** : SQUARE **2** : marked by boldness and conviction : FORTHRIGHT — **foursquare** *adv*

four·teen \(ˈ)fōr(t)-ˈtēn, (ˈ)fȯr(t)-\ *n* — see NUMBER table — **fourteen** *adj or pron* — **four·teenth** \-ˈtēn(t)th\ *adj or n*

fourth \ˈfōrth, ˈfȯrth\ *n* **1** — see NUMBER table **2** : the musical interval embracing four diatonic degrees — **fourth** *adj or adv* — **fourth·ly** *adv*

fourth estate *n, often cap F & E* : the public press

Fourth of July : INDEPENDENCE DAY

four–wheel \ˌfōr-ˌhwēl, ˌfȯr-\ *or* **four–wheeled** \-ˈfōr-ˈhwēld, ˈfȯr-\ *adj* **1** : having four wheels **2** : acting on or by means of four wheels of an automotive vehicle ⟨*four-wheel* drive⟩

[1]**fowl** \ˈfau̇l\ *n, pl* **fowl** *or* **fowls** **1** : BIRD 1: as **a** : a domestic cock or hen; *esp* : a full-grown hen **b** : any of several domesticated or wild birds related to the common domestic fowl **2** : the meat of fowl used as food

[2]**fowl** *vb* : to seek, catch, or kill wildfowl — **fowl·er** *n*

fowling piece *n* : a light gun for shooting birds or small quadrupeds

[1]**fox** \ˈfäks\ *n, pl* **fox·es** *or* **fox** **1 a** : any of various alert flesh-eating mammals related to the wolves but smaller and with shorter legs and more pointed muzzle **b** : the fur of a fox **2** : a clever crafty person

fox 1a
(about 11 in. at shoulder)

[2]**fox** *vb* : to trick by ingenuity or cunning : OUTWIT

fox·glove \ˈfäks-ˌgləv\ *n* : any of a genus of erect herbs related to the snapdragon; *esp* : a tall herb with showy dotted white or purple tubular flowers that is a source of digitalis

fox·hole \-ˌhōl\ *n* : a pit dug hastily during combat for individual cover against enemy fire

fox·hound \-ˌhau̇nd\ *n* : a large swift powerful hound of any of several breeds often trained to hunt foxes

fox·tail \-ˌtāl\ *n* **1** : the tail of a fox **2** : a meadow grass with brushlike leaves

fox terrier *n* : a small lively terrier formerly used to dig out foxes and known in smooth-haired and wire-haired varieties

fox–trot \ˈfäks-ˌträt\ *n* **1** : a short broken slow trotting gait of the horse **2** : a ballroom dance in duple time — **fox–trot** *vb*

foxy \ˈfäk-sē\ *adj* **fox·i·er**; **-est** **1** : resembling a fox in appearance ⟨a *foxy* face⟩ **2** : being alert and knowing : WILY, CLEVER — **fox·i·ly** \-sə-lē\ *adv* — **fox·i·ness** \-sē-nəs\ *n*

foy·er \ˈfȯi(-ə)r, ˈfȯi-ˌ(y)ā\ *n* : an entrance hallway : VESTIBULE, LOBBY

fp *abbr* freezing point

fpm *abbr* feet per minute

fps *abbr* **1** feet per second **2** foot-pound-second

fr *abbr* **1** father **2** from

Fr *abbr* French

fra·cas \ˈfrā-kəs, ˈfrak-əs\ *n* : a noisy quarrel : BRAWL

frac·tion \ˈfrak-shən\ *n* **1** : a number (as $\frac{1}{2}$ or $\frac{3}{4}$) that designates one or more equal parts or the division of one number by another; *also* : a number (as 3.323) consisting of a whole number and a decimal **2** : PORTION, SECTION

frac·tion·al \-sh(ə-)nəl\ *adj* **1** : of, relating to, or being a fraction **2** : quite small : INCONSIDERABLE **3** : of, relating to, or involving a separating of components from a mixture through differences in physical or chemical properties ⟨*fractional* distillation⟩ — **frac·tion·al·ly** \-ē\ *adv*

frac·tion·ate \ˈfrak-shə-ˌnāt\ *vb* : to separate into different portions; *esp* : to subject to fractional distillation — **frac·tion·ation** \ˌfrak-shə-ˈnā-shən\ *n*

frac·ture \ˈfrak-chər\ *n* **1** : the act or process of breaking or the state of being broken; *esp* : the breaking of a bone **2** : the result of fracturing; *esp* : an injury resulting from fracture of a bone — **fracture** *vb*

frag·ile \ˈfraj-əl, -ˌīl\ *adj* : easily broken or destroyed : DELICATE — **fra·gil·i·ty** \frə-ˈjil-ət-ē\ *n*

frag·ment \ˈfrag-mənt\ *n* **1** : a part broken off, detached, or incomplete **2** : SENTENCE FRAGMENT — **frag·ment** \-ˌment\ *vb*

frag·men·tal \frag-ˈment-əl\ *adj* : FRAGMENTARY

frag·men·tary \ˈfrag-mən-ˌter-ē\ *adj* : consisting of fragments : INCOMPLETE ⟨*fragmentary* evidence⟩

fra·grance \ˈfrā-grən(t)s\ *n* : a sweet, pleasing, and often flowery or fruity odor

fra·grant \-grənt\ *adj* : sweet or agreeable in smell — **fra·grant·ly** *adv*

syn FRAGRANT, AROMATIC can mean having a pleasant smell often associated with plants or plant products. FRAGRANT usu. implies a sweet often flowery or fruity odor; AROMATIC may imply an odor (as of coffee or cloves) that is spicy or pungent and often penetrating ***ant*** fetid

frail \ˈfrāl\ *adj* **1** : morally or physically weak ⟨*frail* humanity⟩ **2** : FRAGILE — **frail·ly** \ˈfrāl-lē\ *adv* — **frail·ness** *n*

frail·ty \ˈfrā(-ə)l-tē\ *n, pl* **frailties** **1** : the quality or state of being frail **2** : a fault due to weakness esp. of character

[1]**frame** \ˈfrām\ *vb* **1 a** : PLAN, CONTRIVE **b** : FORMULATE **c** : SHAPE, CONSTRUCT **d** : COMPOSE ⟨*frame* a constitution⟩ **2** : to enclose in a frame ⟨*frame* a picture⟩ **3** : to make (an innocent person) appear guilty — **fram·er** *n*

[2]**frame** *n* **1 a** : something composed of parts fitted

together and united **b** : the physical makeup of a body : PHYSIQUE **2 a** : an arrangement of structural parts that gives form or support ⟨the *frame* of a house⟩ **b** : a skeletal structure on or in which something rests ⟨the *frame* of an auto⟩; *also* : a machine built on or in a frame ⟨a spinning *frame*⟩ **c** : a supporting or enclosing border or casing (as for a window or a picture) **d** : matter or an area enclosed by a border; *esp* : one picture of the series on a length of film or in a television transmission **3** : a particular state of mind : MOOD

[3]**frame** *adj* : having a wood frame ⟨*frame* houses⟩

frame of reference : a set or system (as of facts or ideas) serving to orient or give particular meaning

frame–up \'frām-ˌəp\ *n* : a scheme to cause an innocent person to be accused of a crime; *also* : the result of such a scheme

frame·work \-ˌwərk\ *n* **1** : a skeletal, openwork, or structural frame **2** : a basic structure ⟨build a speech around a *framework* of ideas⟩

franc \'frangk\ *n* **1** : the basic monetary unit of any of several countries (as France, Belgium, or Switzerland) **2** : a coin representing one franc

fran·chise \'fran-ˌchīz\ *n* **1** : a special privilege granted to an individual or group; *esp* : the right to market a company's goods or services in a particular territory; *also* : the territory covered by such a grant **2** : the right to vote

fran·ci·um \'fran(t)-sē-əm\ *n* : a radioactive element obtained artificially by the bombardment of thorium with protons and used esp. in making phosphors — see ELEMENT table

Franco- *comb form* : French and ⟨*Franco*-German⟩ : French ⟨*Franco*phile⟩

frank \'frangk\ *adj* : free in expressing one's feelings and opinions : OUTSPOKEN — **frank·ly** *adv* — **frank·ness** *n*

frank·furt·er *or* **frank·fort·er** \'frangk-fə(r)t-ər\ *or* **frank·furt** *or* **frank·fort** \-fərt\ *n* [from German *Frankfurter* "coming from Frankfurt", from *Frankfurt*, a city in Germany] : a seasoned beef or beef and pork sausage

frank·in·cense \'frang-kən-ˌsen(t)s\ *n* : a fragrant gum resin from African or Arabian trees that is burned as incense

fran·tic \'frant-ik\ *adj* : wildly or uncontrollably excited : FRENZIED ⟨*frantic* with pain⟩ ⟨*frantic* cries for help⟩ — **fran·ti·cal·ly** \-i-k(ə-)lē\ *adv* — **fran·tic·ly** \-i-klē\ *adv*

frap·pé \fra-'pā\ *or* **frappe** \'frap, fra-'pā\ *n* **1** : an iced or frozen mixture or drink **2** : a thick milk shake — **frappé** *adj*

Frasch process \'frash-\ *n* : a method of mining sulfur by forcing into the deposit very hot water and pumping out the melted sulfur

fra·ter·nal \frə-'tərn-əl\ *adj* **1 a** : of, relating to, or involving brothers **b** : of, relating to, or being a fraternity **2** : FRIENDLY, BROTHERLY — **fra·ter·nal·ism** \-ˌiz-əm\ *n* — **fra·ter·nal·ly** \-ē\ *adv*

fraternal twins *n pl* : twins developed from different fertilized egg cells and not necessarily of the same sex, appearance, or disposition

fra·ter·ni·ty \frə-'tər-nət-ē\ *n, pl* **-ties** **1** : a social, honorary, or professional organization; *esp* : a social club of male college students **2** : BROTHERLINESS, BROTHERHOOD **3 a** : the entire progeny of a single mating **b** : a group of siblings

frat·er·nize \'frat-ər-ˌnīz\ *vb* **1** : to associate or mingle as friends **2** : to associate on intimate terms with citizens or troops of a hostile nation — **frat·er·ni·za·tion** \ˌfrat-ər-nə-'zā-shən\ *n* — **frat·er·niz·er** \'frat-ər-ˌnī-zər\ *n*

fraud \'frȯd\ *n* **1 a** : DECEIT; *esp* : misrepresentation in order to induce another to part with something of value or to surrender a legal right **b** : an act of deceiving : TRICK **2 a** : IMPOSTOR **b** : one who defrauds : CHEAT

fraud·u·lent \'frȯ-jə-lənt\ *adj* : characterized by, based on, or done by fraud : DECEITFUL — **fraud·u·lence** \-lən(t)s\ *n* — **fraud·u·lent·ly** *adv* — **fraud·u·lent·ness** *n*

fraught \'frȯt\ *adj* : FULL, LOADED ⟨words *fraught* with meaning⟩; *esp* : full of promise or menace ⟨*fraught* with danger⟩

Fraun·ho·fer lines \ˌfrau̇n-ˌhō-fər-\ *n pl* : the dark lines in the spectrum of the sun

[1]**fray** \'frā\ *n* : BRAWL, FIGHT

[2]**fray** *vb* **1** : to wear into shreds or so that the threads show ⟨a coat *frayed* at the elbows⟩ **2** : STRAIN, IRRITATE

fraz·zle \'fraz-əl\ *vb* **fraz·zled**; **fraz·zling** \-(ə-)ling\ **1** : FRAY **2** : to tire physically or mentally — **frazzle** *n*

[1]**freak** \'frēk\ *n* **1 a** : WHIM **b** : a seemingly capricious action or event **2** : something markedly unusual or abnormal ⟨sideshow *freaks*⟩ **3** *slang* : ENTHUSIAST ⟨a car *freak*⟩ **4** *slang* : a person who uses drugs — **freak·ish** \'frē-kish\ *adj* — **freak·ish·ly** *adv* — **freak·ish·ness** *n*

[2]**freak** *adj* : having the character of a freak : UNLIKELY ⟨involved in a *freak* accident⟩

freck·le \'frek-əl\ *n* : a small brownish spot in the skin usu. caused by formation of pigment upon exposure to sunlight — **freckle** *vb* — **freck·ly** \-(ə-)lē\ *adv*

[1]**free** \'frē\ *adj* **fre·er** \'frē-ər\; **fre·est** \'frē-əst\ **1 a** : having liberty : not being a slave **b** : not controlled or influenced by others : INDEPENDENT ⟨a *free* country⟩ ⟨a *free* press⟩ **c** : not allowing slavery ⟨*free* territory⟩ ⟨*free* state⟩ **2** : not subject to a duty, tax, or other charge **3** : released or not suffering from something unpleasant or painful ⟨*free* from worry⟩ ⟨*free* from disease⟩ **4** : given without charge ⟨*free* ticket⟩ ⟨*free* lunch⟩ **5** : made or done voluntarily ⟨a *free* offer⟩ **6** : LAVISH ⟨a *free* spender⟩ **7** : PLENTIFUL, COPIOUS ⟨a *free* supply⟩ **8** : OPEN, FRANK ⟨*free* expression of opinion⟩ **9** : not restricted by conventional forms ⟨*free* verse⟩ **10** : not literal or exact ⟨a *free* translation⟩ **11 a** : not obstructed : CLEAR ⟨a road *free* of ice⟩ **b** : not being used or occupied ⟨*free* time⟩ ⟨waved with his *free* hand⟩ **c** : not fastened or bound : able to act, move, or turn ⟨*free* electrons⟩ **12** : performed under the rules without interference from the opponents ⟨a *free* kick⟩ **13** : UNCOMBINED ⟨*free* oxygen⟩ **14** : capable of being used meaningfully apart from another linguistic form ⟨the word *hats* is a *free* form⟩ — compare BOUND — **free·ly** *adv*

[2]**free** *adv* **1** : FREELY **2** : without charge ⟨children admitted *free*⟩

[3]**free** *vb* **freed**; **free·ing** **1** : to cause to be free : set free ⟨*free* a prisoner⟩ **2** : RELIEVE, RID ⟨*free* a patient from pain⟩ **3** : DISENTANGLE, CLEAR ⟨*free* a road of ice⟩

free·board \'frē-ˌbōrd, -ˌbȯrd\ *n* : the distance between the waterline and the deck of a ship

free·boo·ter \'frē-ˌbüt-ər\ *n* : PLUNDERER, PIRATE

free·born \'frē-'bȯrn\ *adj* **1 :** not born in vassalage or slavery **2 :** relating to or befitting one that is freeborn
free city *n* **:** a self-governing city having many sovereign powers
freed·man \'frēd-mən\ *n* **:** a man freed from slavery
free·dom \'frēd-əm\ *n* **1 a :** the state of being free **:** LIBERTY, INDEPENDENCE **b :** EXEMPTION, RELEASE ⟨*freedom* from care⟩ **c :** EASE, FACILITY ⟨*freedom* of movement⟩ **d :** FRANKNESS, OUTSPOKENNESS **e :** unrestricted use ⟨grant a visitor the *freedom* of one's house⟩ **2 a :** a political right **b :** RIGHT, PRIVILEGE
free–for–all \'frē-fər-ˌȯl\ *n* **:** a fight open to all comers and usu. with no rules **:** BRAWL
free·hand \'frē-ˌhand\ *adj* **:** done without mechanical aids or devices ⟨*freehand* drawing⟩ — **freehand** *adv*
free·hand·ed \-'han-dəd\ *adj* **:** GENEROUS
free lance *n* **1 :** a knight whose services could be bought by any ruler or state **2 :** one who pursues a profession (as writing, art, or acting) on his own without being committed to work for one employer for a long period — **free–lance** *adj* — **free–lance** *vb* — **free–lanc·er** *n*
free·man \'frē-mən\ *n* **1 :** a person enjoying civil or political liberty **2 :** CITIZEN
free·mar·tin \-ˌmärt-ən\ *n* **:** a usu. sterile female calf born as a twin with a male
free on board *adv or adj* **:** delivered without charge onto a means of transportation
free–spo·ken \'frē-'spō-kən\ *adj* **:** speaking freely **:** OUTSPOKEN
free·stone \-ˌstōn\ *n* **1 :** a stone that may be cut freely without splitting **2 a :** a fruit stone to which the flesh does not cling **b :** a fruit (as a peach or cherry) having such a stone
free–swim·ming \-ˌswim-ing\ *adj* **:** able to swim about **:** not attached
free·think·er \-'thing-kər\ *n* **:** one who forms opinions independently; *esp* **:** one who doubts or denies religious dogma — **free·think·ing** \-king\ *n or adj*
free throw *n* **:** an unhindered shot in basketball made from behind a set line and usu. awarded because of a foul by an opponent
free trade *n* **:** the unrestricted international exchange of goods without high tariffs
free verse *n* **:** verse whose meter is irregular or whose rhythm is not metrical
free·way \'frē-ˌwā\ *n* **1 :** an expressway with fully controlled access **2 :** a toll-free highway
free·will \ˌfrē-ˌwil\ *adj* **:** by one's own free choice **:** VOLUNTARY ⟨a *freewill* offering⟩
1freeze \'frēz\ *vb* **froze** \'frōz\; **fro·zen** \'frō-zən\; **freez·ing 1 :** to harden into ice or a like solid by loss of heat ⟨the river *froze* over⟩ ⟨*freeze* cream⟩ **2 a :** to chill or become chilled with cold ⟨almost *froze* to death⟩ **b :** to become coldly formal in manner ⟨*froze* when introduced to him⟩ **3 a :** to act on usu. destructively by frost ⟨*froze* the tomato plants⟩ **b :** to anesthetize by cold **4 :** to cling or stick by or as if by freezing ⟨the clothes *froze* to the line⟩ ⟨fear *froze* the driver to the wheel⟩ **5 :** to clog or become clogged with ice ⟨the water pipes *froze*⟩ **6 :** to make or become fixed or motionless ⟨the engine *froze*⟩ ⟨*froze* in his tracks⟩ **7 :** to fix at a certain stage or level ⟨*freeze* rents to avoid inflation⟩
2freeze *n* **1 :** a state of weather marked by low temperature **2 a :** an act or instance of freezing ⟨a price *freeze*⟩ **b :** the state of being frozen
freeze–dry \'frēz-'drī\ *vb* **:** to dry in a frozen state under high vacuum esp. for preservation ⟨*freeze-dry* coffee⟩
freez·er \'frē-zər\ *n* **:** one that freezes or keeps cool; *esp* **:** an insulated compartment, box, or room for keeping food at a temperature below freezing or for freezing perishable food
freezing point *n* **:** the temperature at which a liquid solidifies ⟨the *freezing point* of water is 0° C or 32° F⟩
1freight \'frāt\ *n* **1 :** the amount paid (as to a railroad) for carrying goods **2 :** goods or cargo carried by a vehicle; *also* **:** the carrying of goods from one place to another by vehicle ⟨ship the order by *freight*⟩ **3 :** a train that carries freight
2freight *vb* **1 :** to load with goods for transportation **2 :** to transport or ship by freight
freight·er \'frāt-ər\ *n* **1 :** SHIPPER **2 :** a ship or airplane used chiefly to carry freight
1French \'french\ *adj* **:** of, relating to, or characteristic of France, its people, or their language — **French·man** \-mən\ *n* — **French·wom·an** \-ˌwu̇m-ən\ *n*
2French *n* **1 :** the Romance language of the French **2 French** *pl* **:** the French people
French door *n* **:** a door with glazed panels extending the full length
1french fry *vb, often cap 1st F* **:** to fry in deep fat until brown
2french fry *n, often cap 1st F* **:** a strip of potato fried in deep fat
French horn *n* **:** a curved conical brass instrument with a funnel-shaped mouthpiece and a flaring bell

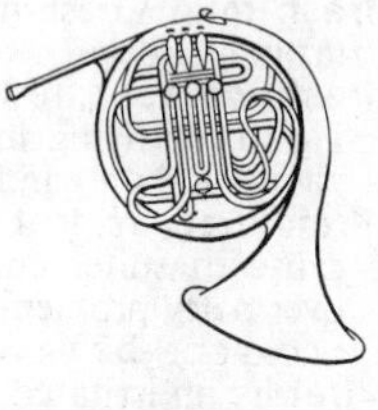
French horn

fre·net·ic \fri-'net-ik\ *adj* **:** FRENZIED, FRANTIC — **fre·net·i·cal·ly** \-'net-i-k(ə-)lē\ *adv*
fren·zy \'fren-zē\ *n, pl* **fren·zies 1 :** a temporary madness or violent agitation **2 :** intense and usu. wild and often disorderly activity — **fren·zied** \-zēd\ *adj* — **frenzy** *vb*
freq *abbr* **1** frequent **2** frequently
fre·quence \'frē-kwən(t)s\ *n* **:** FREQUENCY
fre·quen·cy \'frē-kwən-sē\ *n, pl* **-cies 1 :** the fact or condition of occurring frequently **2 :** rate of occurrence **3 :** the number of repetitions of a periodic process in a unit of time: as **a :** the number of complete alternations per second of an alternating current ⟨a current having a *frequency* of 60 cycles per second⟩ **b :** the number of sound waves per second produced by a sounding body ⟨a sound having a *frequency* of 1500 cycles per second⟩ **c :** the number of complete oscillations per second of an electromagnetic wave ⟨the *frequency* of a radio wave⟩ ⟨the *frequency* of yellow light⟩
frequency distribution *n* **:** an arrangement of statistical data that exhibits the frequency of the occurrence of the values of a variable
frequency modulation *n* **:** variation of the frequency of the carrier wave in accordance with the strength of the audio or video signal; *esp* **:** the system of broadcasting using this method of modulation — abbr. *FM*
1fre·quent \'frē-kwənt\ *adj* **1 :** happening often or at short intervals ⟨made *frequent* trips to town⟩ **2 :** HABITUAL, CONSTANT ⟨a *frequent* visitor⟩ — **fre·quent·ly** *adv* — **fre·quent·ness** *n*
2fre·quent \frē-'kwent, 'frē-kwənt\ *vb* **:** to visit often **:** associate with or go to habitually ⟨*frequent* a café⟩ — **fre·quent·er** *n*
fres·co \'fres-kō\ *n, pl* **frescoes** *or* **frescos**

1 : the art of painting on freshly spread moist plaster **2** : a painting executed in fresco — **fresco** *vb*

fresh \ˈfresh\ *adj* **1 a** : not salt ⟨*fresh* water⟩ **b** : PURE, INVIGORATING ⟨*fresh* air⟩ **c** : fairly strong : BRISK ⟨*fresh* breeze⟩ **2 a** : not altered by processing (as freezing, canning, or pickling) ⟨*fresh* vegetables⟩ **b** : having its original qualities unimpaired: as (1) : full of or renewed in vigor : REFRESHED (2) : not stale, sour, or decayed ⟨*fresh* bread⟩ (3) : not faded (4) : not worn or rumpled **3 a** (1) : experienced, made, or received newly or anew ⟨*fresh* reinforcements⟩ (2) : ADDITIONAL, ANOTHER ⟨make a *fresh* start⟩ **b** : ORIGINAL, VIVID ⟨*fresh* in his mind⟩ **c** : INEXPERIENCED, RAW ⟨*fresh* recruits⟩ **d** : newly arrived ⟨*fresh* from school⟩ **4** : disposed to take liberties : IMPUDENT ***syn*** see NEW ***ant*** stale — **fresh·ly** *adv* — **fresh·ness** *n*

fresh breeze *n* : wind having a speed of 19 to 24 miles per hour

fresh·en \ˈfresh-ən\ *vb* **fresh·ened**; **fresh·en·ing** \-(ə-)ning\ **1** : to make or become fresh : REFRESH ⟨*freshen* up with a shower⟩ **2** : to become brisk or strong ⟨the wind *freshened*⟩ **3** : to brighten in appearance ⟨*freshen* up a room with a spot of color⟩ **4** : to come into milk ⟨when the cow *freshens*⟩ — **fresh·en·er** \-(ə-)nər\ *n*

fresh·et \ˈfresh-ət\ *n* : a rise or overflowing of a stream caused by heavy rains or melted snow

fresh gale *n* : wind having a speed of 39 to 46 miles per hour

fresh·man \ˈfresh-mən\ *n* : a student in his first year (as in a college)

fresh·wa·ter \ˌfresh-ˌwȯt-ər, -ˌwät-\ *adj* **1** : of, relating to, or living in fresh water **2** : accustomed to navigating only in fresh waters

[1]**fret** \ˈfret\ *vb* **fret·ted**; **fret·ting** **1** : to suffer or cause to suffer emotional strain : WORRY ⟨*fretted* over petty problems⟩ **2 a** : to eat into or wear away : CORRODE **b** : FRAY

[2]**fret** *n* : an irritated or worried state ⟨be in a *fret*⟩

[3]**fret** *vb* **fret·ted**; **fret·ting** : to decorate with interlaced designs

[4]**fret** *n* : ornamental work consisting of small intersecting bars

[5]**fret** *n* : one of a series of ridges across the fingerboard of a stringed instrument — **fret·ted** \ˈfret-əd\ *adj*

fret·ful \ˈfret-fəl\ *adj* : disposed to fret : IRRITABLE ***syn*** see PEEVISH — **fret·ful·ly** \-fə-lē\ *adv* — **fret·ful·ness** *n*

fret·work \ˈfret-ˌwərk\ *n* : decoration consisting of frets

frets

Fri *abbr* Friday

fri·a·ble \ˈfrī-ə-bəl\ *adj* : easily crumbled or pulverized — **fri·a·bil·i·ty** \ˌfrī-ə-ˈbil-ət-ē\ *n* — **fri·a·ble·ness** \ˈfrī-ə-bəl-nəs\ *n*

fri·ar \ˈfrī(-ə)r\ *n* [from Middle English *frere*, from Old French, meaning literally "brother", from Latin *frater*, the source of English *fraternity*, and coming from the same earlier source as English *brother*] : a member of one of several Roman Catholic religious orders for men in which monastic life is combined with preaching and other priestly duties

ə abut	ər further	a back	ā bake	
ä cot, cart	au̇ out	ch chin	e less	ē easy
g gift	i trip	ī life	j joke	ng sing	ō flow
ȯ flaw	ȯi coin	th thin	th this	ü loot
u̇ foot	y yet	yü few	yu̇ furious	zh vision

fri·ary \ˈfrī-(ə-)rē\ *n*, *pl* **-ar·ies** : a monastery of friars

[1]**fric·as·see** \ˈfrik-ə-ˌsē\ *n* : a dish of meat (as chicken or veal) cut into pieces and stewed in a gravy

[2]**fricassee** *vb* **-seed**; **-see·ing** : to cook as a fricassee

fric·tion \ˈfrik-shən\ *n* **1 a** : the rubbing of one body against another **b** : resistance to motion between two bodies in contact ⟨the *friction* of a box sliding along the floor⟩ ⟨lubrication reduces *friction*⟩ **2** : discord between two persons or parties — **fric·tion·al** \-sh(ə-)nəl\ *adj* — **fric·tion·al·ly** \-ē\ *adv* — **fric·tion·less** \-ləs\ *adj*

Fri·day \ˈfrīd-ē\ *n* [from Old English *frīgedæg* "day of Frigga", named after the goddess *Frigga*] : the 6th day of the week

fried·cake \ˈfrīd-ˌkāk\ *n* : DOUGHNUT, CRULLER

friend \ˈfrend\ *n* **1 a** : one attached to another by affection or esteem **b** : ACQUAINTANCE **2** : one who is not hostile ⟨are you *friend* or foe⟩ **3** : one who supports or favors something ⟨a *friend* of liberal education⟩ **4** *cap* : a member of a Christian group that stresses Inner Light, rejects ostentation, outward rites, and an ordained ministry, and opposes war — called also *Quaker* — **friend·less** *adj* — **friend·less·ness** *n*

friend·ly \ˈfren-dlē\ *adj* **friend·li·er**; **-est** : of, relating to, or befitting a friend: as **a** : showing kindly interest and goodwill ⟨a *friendly* gesture⟩ **b** : not hostile ⟨*friendly* Indians⟩ **c** : BENEFICIAL, HELPFUL, FAVORABLE ⟨a *friendly* breeze⟩ **d** : COMFORTING, CHEERFUL ⟨the *friendly* glow of the fire⟩ — **friend·li·ness** *n*

friend·ship \ˈfren(d)-ˌship\ *n* **1** : the state of being friends **2** : FRIENDLINESS

fri·er *var of* FRYER

[1]**frieze** \ˈfrēz, frē-ˈzā\ *n* : a woolen cloth with a shaggy surface

[2]**frieze** \ˈfrēz\ *n* : a sculptured or ornamented band (as around a building)

frig·ate \ˈfrig-ət\ *n* **1** : a medium-sized square-rigged warship **2** : a British or Canadian escort ship smaller than a destroyer and larger than a corvette **3** : a U.S. warship smaller than a cruiser and larger than a destroyer

frigate bird *n* : any of several seabirds noted for their power of flight and the habit of robbing other birds of fish

frieze

fright \ˈfrīt\ *n* **1** : fear caused by sudden danger : sudden terror : ALARM ⟨cry out in *fright*⟩ **2** : something that frightens **3** : something that is ugly or shocking ⟨his beard was a *fright*⟩ ***syn*** see FEAR

fright·en \ˈfrīt-ən\ *vb* **fright·ened**; **fright·en·ing** \-(ə-)ning\ **1** : to make afraid : TERRIFY **2** : to drive away or out by frightening **3** : to become frightened — **fright·en·ing·ly** \-(ə-)ning-lē\ *adv*

fright·ful \ˈfrīt-fəl\ *adj* **1** : causing fear or alarm : TERRIFYING **2** : causing shock or horror : STARTLING **3** : EXTREME ⟨*frightful* thirst⟩ — **fright·ful·ly** \-fə-lē\ *adv* — **fright·ful·ness** *n*

frig·id \ˈfrij-əd\ *adj* **1** : intensely cold **2** : lacking warmth or ardor : INDIFFERENT — **fri·gid·i·ty** \frij-ˈid-ət-ē\ *n* — **frig·id·ly** \ˈfrij-əd-lē\ *adv* — **frig·id·ness** *n*

frigid zone *n* : the area or region between the arctic

circle and the north pole or between the antarctic circle and the south pole

frill \'fril\ *n* **1** : a gathered, pleated, or ruffled edging (as of lace) **2** : a merely ornamental addition : something unessential **3** : a ruff of hair or feathers about the neck of an animal — **frill** *vb* — **frilly** \'fril-ē\ *adj*

[1]**fringe** \'frinj\ *n* **1** : an ornamental border consisting of hanging threads or strips **2** : EDGE, BORDER ⟨the *fringe* of the forest⟩

[2]**fringe** *vb* **1** : to furnish or adorn with a fringe **2** : to serve as a fringe for : BORDER

frip·pery \'frip-(ə-)rē\ *n, pl* **-per·ies** **1** : cheap showy finery **2** : affected elegance : pretentious display — **frippery** *adj*

frisk \'frisk\ *vb* **1** : to leap, skip, or dance in a lively or playful way : GAMBOL **2** : to search (a person) rapidly esp. for concealed weapons — **frisk·er** *n*

frisky \'fris-kē\ *adj* **frisk·i·er**; **-est** : inclined to frisk : FROLICSOME — **frisk·i·ly** \-kə-lē\ *adv* — **frisk·i·ness** \-kē-nəs\ *n*

frit·il·lary \'frit-ə-ˌler-ē\ *n, pl* **-laries** : any of numerous spotted butterflies

[1]**frit·ter** \'frit-ər\ *n* : a small quantity of fried or sautéed batter often containing fruit or meat

[2]**fritter** *vb* : to reduce or waste piecemeal ⟨*frittering* away his time on trifles⟩ — **frit·ter·er** \-ər-ər\ *n*

friv·o·lous \'friv-(ə-)ləs\ *adj* **1** : of little importance : TRIVIAL **2** : lacking in seriousness : PLAYFUL — **fri·vol·i·ty** \friv-'äl-ət-ē\ *n* — **friv·o·lous·ly** \'friv-(ə-)ləs-lē\ *adv* — **friv·o·lous·ness** *n*

[1]**frizz** \'friz\ *vb* : to curl in small tight curls

[2]**frizz** *n* : a tight curl or hair that is tightly curled — **frizzy** \'friz-ē\ *adj*

[1]**friz·zle** \'friz-əl\ *vb* **friz·zled**; **friz·zling** \-(ə-)ling\ : FRIZZ — **frizzle** *n* — **friz·zly** \-(ə-)lē\ *adj*

[2]**frizzle** *vb* **1** : to fry until crisp and curled **2** : SIZZLE

fro \'frō\ *adv* : BACK, AWAY — used in the phrase *to and fro*

frock \'fräk\ *n* **1** : a friar's habit **2** : a woman's or child's dress

frog \'frȯg, 'fräg\ *n* **1 a** : any of various smooth-skinned web-footed largely aquatic tailless leaping amphibians — compare TOAD **b** : hoarseness in the throat ⟨had a *frog* in his throat⟩ **2** : an ornamental braid or loop for buttoning the front of a garment

frog 2

frog·man \-ˌman, -mən\ *n* : a swimmer equipped to stay under water for some time; *esp* : a member of a military unit so equipped

frog spit *n* : CUCKOO SPIT 1 — called also *frog spittle*

[1]**frol·ic** \'fräl-ik\ *vb* **frol·icked**; **frol·ick·ing** **1** : to make merry **2** : to play about happily : ROMP

[2]**frolic** *n* **1** : a playful mischievous action **2** : FUN, MERRIMENT

frol·ic·some \'fräl-ik-səm\ *adj* : full of gaiety : SPORTIVE

from \(')frəm, 'främ\ *prep* **1** — used as a function word to indicate a starting point ⟨came here *from* the city⟩ ⟨cost *from* $5 to $10⟩ ⟨an avid reader *from* childhood⟩ **2** — used as a function word to indicate separation or exclusion ⟨a child taken *from* its mother⟩ ⟨refrain *from* interrupting⟩ ⟨far *from* safe⟩ **3** — used as a function word to indicate the source, cause, agent, or basis ⟨reading aloud *from* a book⟩ ⟨suffering *from* a cold⟩

frond \'fränd\ *n* : a leaf or leaflike part: as **a** : a palm leaf **b** : a fern leaf **c** : a leaflike shoot or plant body (as of a lichen)

[1]**front** \'frənt\ *n* **1** : external often feigned appearance ⟨put up a good *front*⟩ **2 a** : a region in which active warfare or struggle is taking place **b** : the lateral space occupied by a military unit ⟨advanced on a 4-mile *front*⟩ **3** : the forward part or surface ⟨the *front* of a shirt⟩ ⟨the *front* of the house⟩ **4** : the boundary between two dissimilar air masses **5** : a position directly before or ahead of something else ⟨stood in *front* of them⟩ **6** : a person, group, or thing used to mask the identity or true character of the actual controlling agent **7** : a coalition of political groups

[2]**front** *vb* **1** : FACE ⟨the cottage *fronts* on the lake⟩ ⟨the house *fronts* the street⟩ **2** : to serve as a front **3** : CONFRONT

[3]**front** *adj* : of, relating to, or situated at the front

front·age \'frənt-ij\ *n* **1 a** : the front face (as of a building) **b** : the direction in which something faces **2** : the front boundary line of a lot or its length

front·al \'frənt-əl\ *adj* **1** : of, relating to, or adjacent to the forehead **2 a** : of, relating to, or situated at the front **b** : directed against the front or at the main issue : DIRECT ⟨*frontal* assault⟩ — **fron·tal·ly** \-ə-lē\ *adv*

fron·tier \ˌfrən-'ti(ə)r, frän-\ *n* **1** : a border between two countries **2 a** : a region that forms the margin of settled territory **b** : the outer limits of knowledge or achievement ⟨the *frontiers* of science⟩ — **frontier** *adj*

fron·tiers·man \-'ti(ə)rz-mən\ *n* : a man living on the frontier

fron·tis·piece \'frənt-ə-ˌspēs\ *n* : an illustration facing the title page of a book

front·let \'frənt-lət\ *n* **1** : a band worn on the forehead **2** : the forehead esp. of a bird when distinctively marked

[1]**frost** \'frȯst\ *n* **1** : the temperature that causes freezing **2** : a covering of minute ice crystals on a cold surface

[2]**frost** *vb* **1 a** : to cover with or as if with frost; *esp* : to put icing on (as cake) **b** : to produce a fine-grained slightly rough surface on (as glass) **2** : to injure or kill by frost : FREEZE

frost·bite \'frȯs(t)-ˌbīt\ *n* : the freezing or the local effect of a partial freezing of some part of the body — **frostbite** *vb*

frost·ed \'frȯ-stəd\ *adj* **1** : covered with frost or with something resembling frost ⟨*frosted* glass⟩ **2** : ornamented with frosting ⟨a *frosted* cake⟩ **3** : QUICK-FROZEN ⟨*frosted* foods⟩

frost·ing \'frȯ-sting\ *n* **1** : ICING **2** : a dull finish on metal or glass

frosty \'frȯ-stē\ *adj* **frost·i·er**; **-est** **1** : attended with or producing frost : FREEZING **2** : covered or appearing as if covered with frost : HOARY **3** : cool or reserved in manner — **frost·i·ly** \-stə-lē\ *adv* — **frost·i·ness** \-stē-nəs\ *n*

froth \'frȯth\ *n* **1 a** : bubbles formed in or on a liquid by fermentation or agitation **b** : the foam produced by saliva in certain diseases or nervous excitement **2** : something light or frivolous and of little value — **froth** \'frȯth\ *vb* — **froth·i·ly** \'frȯ-thə-lē\ *adv* — **froth·i·ness** \-thē-nəs\ *n* — **frothy** \-thē\ *adj*

fro·ward \'frō-(w)ərd\ *adj* : disposed to disobey and oppose : WILLFUL — **fro·ward·ly** *adv* — **fro·ward·ness** *n*

frown \'fraùn\ *vb* **1** : to wrinkle the forehead (as in anger, displeasure, or thought) : put on a stern look **2** : to look with disapproval ⟨*frowns* on rudeness⟩ **3** : to express with a frown ⟨*frowned* her disapproval⟩ — **frown** *n* — **frown·er** *n* — **frown·ing·ly** \'fraù-ning-lē\ *adv*

frow·zy *or* **frow·sy** \'frau̇-zē\ *adj* **frow·zi·er** *or* **frow·si·er; -est** : having a slovenly or uncared-for appearance
froze *past of* FREEZE
fro·zen \'frō-zən\ *adj* **1 a** : affected or crusted over by freezing **b** : subject to long and severe cold ⟨the *frozen* north⟩ **c** : CHILLED, REFRIGERATED **2 a** : expressing or characterized by cold unfriendliness ⟨a *frozen* stare⟩ **b** : incapable of being changed, moved, or undone : FIXED ⟨wages were *frozen*⟩ — **fro·zen·ly** *adv* — **fro·zen·ness** \-zən-(n)əs\ *n*
frozen food *n* : food that has been subjected to rapid freezing and is kept frozen until used
FRS *abbr* Federal Reserve System
frt *abbr* freight
fruc·tose \'frək-,tōs\ *n* : a very sweet soluble sugar that occurs esp. in fruit juices and honey
fru·gal \'frü-gəl\ *adj* : characterized by or reflecting economy in the expenditure of resources — **fru·gal·i·ty** \frü-'gal-ət-ē\ *n* — **fru·gal·ly** \'frü-gə-lē\ *adv*
syn FRUGAL, THRIFTY, ECONOMICAL mean in common careful with money and other resources. FRUGAL suggests a husbanding of resources by living simply and cutting expenses; THRIFTY suggests habitual saving and avoidance of waste; ECONOMICAL implies wise management of resources ***ant*** wasteful
[1]**fruit** \'früt\ *n* [from French, from Latin *fructus*, meaning literally "enjoyment"] **1 a** : a usu. useful product of plant growth ⟨*fruits* of the earth⟩ **b** : the usu. edible reproductive body of a seed plant; *esp* : one (as a strawberry or apple) having a sweet pulp **c** : a product of fertilization in a plant with its envelopes or appendages; *esp* : the ripened ovary of a plant (as the pod of a pea, a nut, a grain, or a berry) with or without the attached parts **2** : CONSEQUENCE, RESULT — **fruit·ed** \-əd\ *adj* — **fruity** \-ē\ *adj*
[2]**fruit** *vb* : to bear or cause to bear fruit
fruit·age \'früt-ij\ *n* **1** : the condition or process of bearing fruit **2** : FRUIT
fruit·cake \'früt-,kāk\ *n* : a rich cake containing nuts, dried or candied fruits, and spices
fruit fly *n* : any of various small two-winged flies whose larvae feed on fruit or decaying vegetable matter
fruit·ful \'früt-fəl\ *adj* **1** : yielding or producing fruit **2** : abundantly productive : bringing results ⟨*fruitful* idea⟩ ***syn*** see FERTILE ***ant*** unfruitful — **fruit·ful·ly** \-fə-lē\ *adv* — **fruit·ful·ness** *n*
fruiting body *n* : a plant organ specialized for producing spores
fru·i·tion \frü-'ish-ən\ *n* **1** : the state of bearing fruit **2** : REALIZATION, ACCOMPLISHMENT ⟨bring his dreams to *fruition*⟩
fruit·less \'früt-ləs\ *adj* **1** : not bearing fruit **2** : productive of no good effect : UNSUCCESSFUL ⟨a *fruitless* attempt⟩ — **fruit·less·ly** *adv* — **fruit·less·ness** *n*
frus·trate \'frəs-,trāt\ *vb* **1** : to prevent from carrying out a purpose : DEFEAT, BLOCK **2** : to bring to nothing : NULLIFY — **frus·tra·tion** \(,)frəs-'trā-shən\ *n*
syn FRUSTRATE, THWART, BAFFLE can mean to balk in an endeavor or purpose. FRUSTRATE implies bringing someone's best and most persistent efforts to nothing; THWART implies a deliberate crossing or opposing; BAFFLE implies frustrating by outwitting or confusing ***ant*** fulfill
frwy *abbr* freeway
[1]**fry** \'frī\ *vb* **fried; fry·ing** : to cook or be cooked in a pan or on a griddle esp. with the use of fat
[2]**fry** *n, pl* **fries** **1** : a dish of something fried **2** : a social gathering where fried food is eaten
[3]**fry** *n, pl* **fry** **1 a** : recently hatched fish **b** : the young of animals other than fish **2** : very small adult fish **3** : PERSONS, INDIVIDUALS ⟨small *fry*⟩
fry·er \'frī(-ə)r\ *n* **1** : a young chicken suitable for frying **2** : a deep utensil for frying foods
frying pan *n* : a shallow metal pan for frying foods
ft *abbr* **1** feet **2** foot **3** fort
FTC *abbr* Federal Trade Commission
ft lb *abbr* foot-pound
F_2 layer \'ef-'tü-\ *n* : the outer of the two layers into which the F layer of the ionosphere divides during the day and which occurs between 150 to 250 miles above the earth's surface
fuch·sia \'fyü-shə\ *n* [from its scientific Latin name derived from the name of Leonhard *Fuchs* (1501–1566), a German botanist] **1** : any of a genus of shrubs related to the evening primrose and having showy nodding flowers usu. in deep pinks, reds, and purples **2** : a vivid reddish purple
fuch·sine *or* **fuch·sin** \'fyük-sən, -,sēn\ *n* : a synthetic dye that yields a brilliant bluish red
fu·cus \'fyü-kəs\ *n* : any of various brown algae common along rocky shores
fud·dle \'fəd-əl\ *vb* **fud·dled; fud·dling** \'fəd-(ə-)liŋ\ : BEFUDDLE
fud·dy–dud·dy \'fəd-ē-,dəd-ē\ *n, pl* **-dies** : one who is old-fashioned, pompous, unimaginative, or concerned about trifles
[1]**fudge** \'fəj\ *vb* **1** : to avoid commitment : HEDGE **2** : FAKE, FALSIFY
[2]**fudge** *n* **1** : foolish nonsense **2** : a soft creamy candy of sugar, milk, butter, and flavoring
[1]**fu·el** \'fyü-əl\ *n* **1 a** : a material used to produce heat or power by burning **b** : a material from which atomic energy can be liberated esp. in a reactor **2** : a source of energy : INCENTIVE
[2]**fuel** *vb* **-eled** *or* **-elled; -el·ing** *or* **-el·ling** **1** : to provide with or take in fuel **2** : SUPPORT, STIMULATE
fuel cell *n* : a device that converts the chemical energy of a fuel (as hydrogen) directly into electrical energy
fuel oil *n* : an oil that is used for fuel and that usu. ignites at a higher temperature than kerosene
[1]**fu·gi·tive** \'fyü-jət-iv\ *adj* **1** : running away or trying to escape ⟨a *fugitive* slave⟩ **2** : likely to vanish suddenly : not fixed or lasting ⟨*fugitive* thoughts⟩ — **fu·gi·tive·ly** *adv* — **fu·gi·tive·ness** *n*
[2]**fugitive** *n* : one who flees or tries to escape
fugue \'fyüg\ *n* : a musical composition in which one or two themes are stated and then taken up and developed — **fu·gal** \'fyü-gəl\ *adj*
[1]**-ful** \fəl\ *adj suffix, sometimes* **-ful·ler**; *sometimes* **-ful·lest** **1** : full of ⟨event*ful*⟩ **2** : characterized by ⟨peace*ful*⟩ **3** : having the qualities of ⟨master*ful*⟩ **4** : -ABLE ⟨mourn*ful*⟩
[2]**-ful** \,fu̇l\ *n suffix* : number or quantity that fills or would fill ⟨room*ful*⟩
ful·crum \'fu̇l-krəm, 'fəl-\ *n, pl* **fulcrums** *or* **ful·cra** \-krə\ : the support about which a lever turns
ful·fill *or* **ful·fil** \fu̇l-'fil\ *vb* **ful·filled; ful·fill·ing** **1** : to put into effect : ACCOMPLISH ⟨*fulfill* a promise⟩ **2** : to measure up to : SATISFY ⟨*fulfill* requirements⟩ — **ful·fill·er** *n* — **ful·fill·ment** \-mənt\ *n*

[1]**full** \ˈfu̇l\ *adj* **1 :** containing as much or as many as is possible or normal ⟨a bin *full* of corn⟩ **2 a :** complete in number, amount, or duration ⟨a *full* set of silver⟩ **b :** having all the characteristics ⟨a *full* member⟩ **c :** being at the highest degree : MAXIMUM ⟨*full* strength⟩ **3 a :** plump and rounded in outline ⟨a *full* figure⟩ **b :** having an abundance of material ⟨a *full* skirt⟩ **4 a :** possessing or containing an abundance ⟨a *full* life⟩ **b :** DETAILED ⟨a *full* report⟩ **5 :** satisfied esp. with food or drink **6 :** having both parents in common ⟨*full* sisters⟩ **7 :** having volume or depth of sound ⟨*full* tones⟩ **8 :** completely occupied esp. with a thought or plan ⟨*full* of his own concerns⟩ — **full·ness** *also* **ful·ness** *n*

[2]**full** *adv* **1 a :** VERY, EXTREMELY **b :** ENTIRELY ⟨fill a glass *full*⟩ **2 :** EXACTLY, SQUARELY ⟨the blow hit him *full* in the face⟩

[3]**full** *n* **1 :** the highest state, extent, or degree **2 :** the complete amount ⟨paid in *full*⟩

[4]**full** *vb* **:** to shrink and thicken (woolen cloth) by moistening, heating, and pressing — **full·er** *n*

full·back \ˈfu̇l-ˌbak\ *n* **:** an offensive football back who usu. lines up between the halfbacks

full–blown \-ˈblōn\ *adj* **1 :** being at the height of bloom **2 :** fully mature or developed

full dress *n* **:** formal or ceremonial dress — **full–dress** *adj*

fuller's earth *n* **:** a clayish earthy substance used in fulling cloth, as a filter medium, and as a catalyst

full–fledged \ˈfu̇l-ˈflejd\ *adj* **1 :** fully developed **:** MATURE **2 :** having full plumage

full moon *n* **:** the moon with its whole apparent disk illuminated

ful·ly \ˈfu̇l-(l)ē\ *adv* **1 :** COMPLETELY **2 :** at least ⟨*fully* nine tenths of us⟩

ful·mi·nate \ˈfu̇l-mə-ˌnāt, ˈfəl-\ *vb* [from Latin *fulminere* "to strike with lightning", from *fulmen* "lightning", from *fulgēre* "to flash"] **1 :** to utter loud or forceful complaints, censure, or invective **2 :** to make a sudden loud noise : EXPLODE — **ful·mi·na·tion** \ˌfu̇l-mə-ˈnā-shən, ˌfəl-\ *n* — **ful·mi·na·tor** \ˈfu̇l-mə-ˌnāt-ər, ˈfəl-\ *n*

ful·some \ˈfu̇l-səm\ *adj* **:** offensive esp. from insincerity or baseness of motive ⟨*fulsome* praise⟩ — **fulsome·ly** *adv* — **ful·some·ness** *n*

fu·ma·role \ˈfyü-mə-ˌrōl\ *n* **:** a hole in a volcanic region from which hot gases and vapors issue

fum·ble \ˈfəm-bəl\ *vb* **fum·bled**; **fum·bling** \-b(ə-)ling\ **1 :** to feel or grope about clumsily ⟨*fumbled* in his pocket for a key⟩ **2 :** to handle or manage something clumsily; *esp* **:** to fail to hold, catch, or handle the ball properly in a game — **fumble** *n* — **fum·bler** \-b(ə-)lər\ *n*

[1]**fume** \ˈfyüm\ *n* **1 :** a usu. irritating or offensive smoke, vapor, or gas — usu. used in pl. ⟨automobile *fumes*⟩ ⟨acid *fumes*⟩ **2 :** a state of excited irritation or anger — **fumy** \ˈfyü-mē\ *adj*

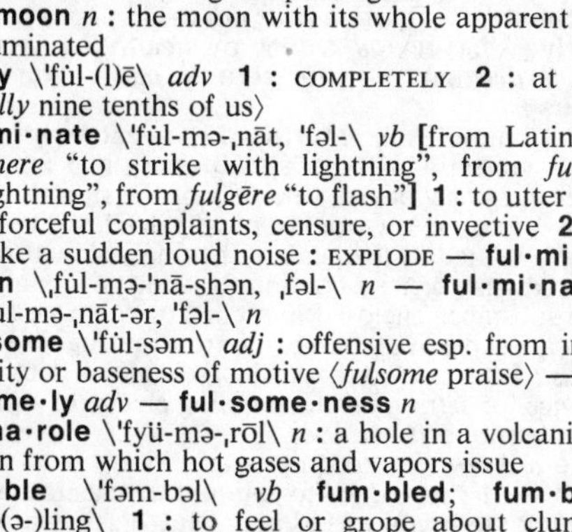

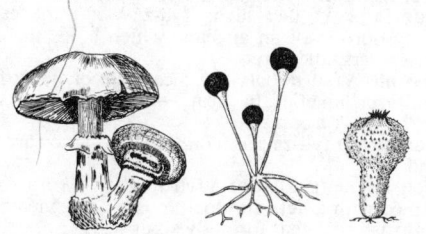

fungi 1:
left, mushrooms; center, mold; right, puffball

[2]**fume** *vb* **1 :** to expose to or treat with fumes **2 :** to give off fumes **3 :** to show bad temper : express annoyance or irritation

fu·mi·gant \ˈfyü-mi-gənt\ *n* **:** a substance used in fumigating

fu·mi·gate \ˈfyü-mə-ˌgāt\ *vb* **:** to apply smoke, vapor, or gas to esp. for the purpose of disinfecting or of destroying pests — **fu·mi·ga·tion** \ˌfyü-mə-ˈgā-shən\ *n* — **fu·mi·ga·tor** \ˈfyü-mə-ˌgāt-ər\ *n*

[1]**fun** \ˈfən\ *n* **1 :** something that provides amusement or enjoyment; *esp* **:** playful boisterous action or speech **2 :** AMUSEMENT, ENJOYMENT

[2]**fun** *vb* **funned**; **fun·ning** **:** to indulge in banter or play : JOKE

[1]**func·tion** \ˈfəng(k)-shən\ *n* **1 :** professional position or duties : OCCUPATION **2 a :** the particular purpose for which a person or thing is specially fitted or used or for which a thing exists ⟨the *function* of a knife is cutting⟩ **b :** the natural or proper action of a bodily part in a living organism ⟨the *function* of the heart⟩ **3 :** an impressive, elaborate, or formal ceremony or social gathering **4 a :** a mathematical entity that assigns to each element of one set at least one element of the same or another set **b :** a quality dependent on another — **func·tion·less** \-ləs\ *adj*

[2]**function** *vb* **func·tioned**; **func·tion·ing** \-sh(ə-)ning\ **1 :** to have a function : SERVE **2 :** to be in action : OPERATE

func·tion·al \ˈfəng(k)-sh(ə-)nəl\ *adj* **1 a :** of, connected with, or being a function **b :** affecting functions but not structure ⟨*functional* heart disease⟩ **2 :** serving in a larger whole; *also* **:** designed or developed chiefly from the point of view of use ⟨*functional* architecture⟩ **3 :** performing or able to perform a regular function **4 :** organized by functions — **func·tion·al·ly** \-ē\ *adv*

func·tion·ary \ˈfəng(k)-shə-ˌner-ē\ *n, pl* **-ar·ies** **:** a person charged with performing a given function; *esp* **:** OFFICIAL

function word *n* **:** a word expressing primarily grammatical relationship

fund \ˈfənd\ *n* **1 :** an available quantity of material or intangible resources **:** SUPPLY **2 a :** a sum of money or other resources set apart for a specific objective **b :** available money — usu. used in pl. **3 :** an organization administering a special fund

[1]**fun·da·men·tal** \ˌfən-də-ˈment-əl\ *adj* **1 a :** serving as an origin or source **:** PRIMARY **b :** serving as a basic support or essential structure or function **:** BASIC **2 :** of or relating to essential structure or function : RADICAL ⟨*fundamental* change⟩ **3 :** of central importance : PRINCIPAL ⟨*fundamental* purpose⟩ — **fun·da·men·tal·ly** \-ə-lē\ *adv*

[2]**fundamental** *n* **1 :** something fundamental; *esp* **:** one of the basic constituents essential to a thing or system ⟨*fundamentals* of arithmetic⟩ **2 :** the harmonic component of a wave that has the lowest frequency and commonly the greatest amplitude

fu·ner·al \ˈfyün-(ə-)rəl\ *n* **:** the ceremonies held for a dead person usu. before burial or cremation — **funeral** *adj*

fu·ne·re·al \fyu̇-ˈnir-ē-əl\ *adj* **1 :** of or relating to a funeral **2 :** suggesting a funeral ⟨*funereal* gloom⟩ — **fu·ne·re·al·ly** \-ē-ə-lē\ *adv*

fun·gi·cide \ˈfən-jə-ˌsīd, ˈfəng-gə-\ *n* **:** a substance that destroys fungi — **fun·gi·cid·al** \ˌfən-jə-ˈsīd-əl, ˌfəng-gə-\ *adj* — **fun·gi·cid·al·ly** \-ə-lē\ *adv*

fun·gous \ˈfəng-gəs\ *or* **fun·gal** \-gəl\ *adj* **1 :** of, relating to, or resembling fungi **2 :** caused by a fungus

fun·gus \ˈfəng-gəs\ *n, pl* **fun·gi** \ˈfən-ˌjī, ˈfəng-ˌgī\

also **fun·gus·es** **1** : any of a major group of flowerless plants (as molds, rusts, mildews, smuts, and mushrooms) that lack chlorophyll and are saprophytic or parasitic **2** : infection with a fungus — **fungus** *adj*
fu·nic·u·lar \fyů-ˈnik-yə-lər, fə-\ *n* : a cable railway ascending a mountain
funk \ˈfəngk\ *n* : a state of paralyzed fear : PANIC — **funk** *vb*
funky \ˈfəng-kē\ *adj* : relating to or in the style of the blues
[1]**fun·nel** \ˈfən-əl\ *n* **1** : a utensil usu. shaped like a hollow cone with a tube extending from the point and designed to catch and direct a downward flow (as of liquid) **2** : something shaped like a funnel **3** : a stack or flue for the escape of smoke or for ventilation
[2]**funnel** *vb* **-neled** *also* **-nelled**; **-nel·ing** *also* **-nel·ling** **1** : to pass through or as if through a funnel **2** : to move or cause to move to a focal point or into a central channel
fun·ny \ˈfən-ē\ *adj* **fun·ni·er**; **-est** **1 a** : affording light mirth and laughter : AMUSING **b** : seeking or intended to amuse : FACETIOUS **2** : differing from the ordinary in a suspicious way : QUEER **3** : involving trickery or deception ⟨*funny* business⟩ — **fun·ni·ly** \ˈfən-ə-lē\ *adv* — **fun·ni·ness** \ˈfən-ē-nəs\ *n*
funny bone *n* : a place at the back of the elbow where a blow causes a painful tingling sensation
fur \ˈfər\ *n* **1** : a piece of the dressed pelt of an animal used to make, trim, or line wearing apparel **2** : an article of clothing made of or with fur **3** : the hairy coat of a mammal esp. when fine, soft, and thick **4** : a coating (as on the tongue) resembling fur — **fur** *vb* — **fur·less** \-ləs\ *adj* — **furred** \ˈfərd\ *adj*
fur·bear·er \ˈfər-ˌbar-ər, -ˌber-\ *n* : an animal that bears fur
fur·be·low \ˈfər-bə-ˌlō\ *n* **1** : FLOUNCE, RUFFLE **2** : showy trimming
fur·bish \ˈfər-bish\ *vb* **1** : to make lustrous : POLISH **2** : RENOVATE, REVIVE
fu·ri·ous \ˈfyůr-ē-əs\ *adj* **1** : being in a fury : FIERCE, ANGRY **2** : RUSHING, VIOLENT ⟨a *furious* assault⟩ — **fu·ri·ous·ly** *adv*
[1]**furl** \ˈfərl\ *vb* : to wrap or roll (as a sail or a flag) close to or around something
[2]**furl** *n* **1** : the act of furling **2** : a furled coil
fur·long \ˈfər-ˌlȯng\ *n* : a unit of distance equal to 220 yards
[1]**fur·lough** \ˈfər-lō\ *n* : a leave of absence from duty granted esp. to a soldier
[2]**furlough** *vb* **1** : to grant a furlough to **2** : to lay off from work
fur·nace \ˈfər-nəs\ *n* : an enclosed structure in which heat is produced (as for heating a house or melting metals)
fur·nish \ˈfər-nish\ *vb* **1** : to provide with what is needed; *esp* : to equip with furniture **2** : SUPPLY, GIVE — **fur·nish·er** *n*
fur·nish·ings \-nish-ingz\ *n pl* **1** : articles or accessories of dress **2** : FURNITURE
fur·ni·ture \ˈfər-ni-chər\ *n* : EQUIPMENT; *esp* : movable articles (as chairs, tables, or beds) used in making a room ready for occupancy or use
fu·ror \ˈfyůr-ˌȯr, -ˌōr\ *n* **1** : ANGER, RAGE **2** : a fashionable craze : VOGUE **3** : an outburst of public excitement or indignation : UPROAR
fu·rore \-ˌōr, -ˌȯr\ *n* **1** : FUROR 2 **2** : FUROR 3
fur·ri·er \ˈfər-ē-ər\ *n* : a person who prepares or deals in furs — **fur·ri·ery** \-ē-ə-rē\ *n*
fur·ring \ˈfər-ing\ *n* **1** : a fur trimming or lining **2** : the application of thin wood, brick, or metal to joists, studs, or walls to form a level surface or an air space; *also* : the material used in this process
fur·row \ˈfər-ō, ˈfə-rō\ *n* **1** : a trench in the earth made by or as if by a plow **2** : something (as a groove or wrinkle) that resembles a furrow — **furrow** *vb*
furrow irrigation *n* : irrigation of farmland by water run in furrows between the crop rows
fur·ry \ˈfər-ē\ *adj* **fur·ri·er**; **-est** **1** : consisting of or resembling fur **2** : covered with fur
fur seal *n* : any of various seals with a valuable dense soft undercoat
[1]**fur·ther** \ˈfər-t͟hər\ *adv* **1** : [1]FARTHER 1 **2** : in addition : MOREOVER **3** : to a greater degree or extent
[2]**further** *adj* **1** : [2]FARTHER 1 **2** : going or extending beyond : ADDITIONAL ⟨*further* education⟩
[3]**further** *vb* **fur·thered**; **fur·ther·ing** \ˈfərt͟h-(ə-)ring\ : to help forward : PROMOTE — **fur·ther·er** \ˈfər-t͟hər-ər\ *n*
fur·ther·ance \ˈfərt͟h-(ə-)rən(t)s\ *n* : the act of furthering : ADVANCEMENT
fur·ther·more \ˈfər-t͟hə(r)-ˌmōr, -ˌmȯr\ *adv* : in addition to what precedes : BESIDES
fur·ther·most \-ˌmōst\ *adj* : most distant : FARTHEST
fur·thest \ˈfər-t͟həst\ *adv or adj* : FAPTHEST
fur·tive \ˈfərt-iv\ *adj* : done by stealth : SLY, SECRET ⟨a *furtive* look⟩ — **fur·tive·ly** *adv* — **fur·tive·ness** *n*
fu·ry \ˈfyů(ə)r-ē\ *n, pl* **furies** **1** : violent anger : RAGE **2** : a violently angry or spiteful person **3** : extreme fierceness or violence ⟨the *fury* of the storm⟩
furze \ˈfərz\ *n* : a prickly mostly leafless evergreen shrub related to the pea and having yellow flowers
[1]**fuse** \ˈfyüz\ *n* **1** : a continuous train of a combustible substance enclosed in a cord or cable for setting off an explosive charge by transmitting fire to it **2** *usu* **fuze** : a mechanical or electrical detonating device for setting off the bursting charge of a projectile, bomb, or torpedo
[2]**fuse** *or* **fuze** *vb* : to equip with a fuse
[3]**fuse** *vb* **1** : to reduce to a liquid or plastic state by heat **2** : to become fluid with heat **3** : to unite by or as if by melting together : BLEND, INTEGRATE
[4]**fuse** *n* : an electrical safety device consisting of or including a wire or strip of fusible metal that melts and interrupts the circuit when the current becomes too strong
fu·see \fyü-ˈzē\ *n* **1** : a friction match with a bulbous head not easily blown out **2** : a red signal flare used esp. for protecting stalled trains and trucks
fu·se·lage \ˈfyü-sə-ˌläzh, ˈfyü-zə-\ *n* : the central body portion of an airplane which holds the crew, passengers, and cargo
fus·i·ble \ˈfyü-zə-bəl\ *adj* : capable of being fused and esp. liquefied by heat — **fus·i·bil·i·ty** \ˌfyü-zə-ˈbil-ət-ē\ *n*
fu·si·form \ˈfyü-zə-ˌfȯrm\ *adj* : tapering toward each end
fu·sil·ier *or* **fu·sil·eer** \ˌfyü-zə-ˈli(ə)r\ *n* : a soldier armed with a light flintlock musket or a member of a British regiment formerly so armed
fu·sil·lade \ˈfyü-sə-ˌlād, ˈfyü-zə-, -ˌläd\ *n* **1** : a number of shots fired simultaneously or in rapid succession **2** : a spirited outburst
fu·sion \ˈfyü-zhən\ *n* **1** : the process of melting or

making fluid by heat **2 :** union by or as if by melting; *esp* : a merging of diverse elements into a unified whole **3 :** the union of atomic nuclei to form heavier nuclei resulting in the release of enormous quantities of energy when certain light elements unite

fusion bomb *n* **:** a bomb in which nuclei of a light chemical element unite to form nuclei of heavier elements with a release of energy; *esp* **:** HYDROGEN BOMB

[1]**fuss** \\'fəs\\ *n* **:** needless bustle or excitement esp. over a trivial matter

[2]**fuss** *vb* **1 :** to create or be in a state of restless activity; *esp* **:** to shower flattering attentions **2 :** to pay undue attention to small details **3 :** WORRY — **fusser** *n*

fussy \\'fəs-ē\\ *adj* **fuss·i·er; -est 1 :** easily upset **:** IRRITABLE **2 a :** requiring or giving close attention to details **b :** too particular **:** FASTIDIOUS — **fuss·i·ly** \\'fəs-ə-lē\\ *adv* — **fuss·i·ness** \\'fəs-ē-nəs\\ *n*

fus·tian \\'fəs-chən\\ *n* **1 :** a strong cotton and linen fabric **2 :** pretentious writing or speech — **fustian** *adj*

fus·ty \\'fəs-tē\\ *adj* **fus·ti·er; -est 1 :** MOLDY, MUSTY **2 :** rigidly conservative **:** OLD-FASHIONED — **fus·ti·ly** \\-tə-lē\\ *adv* — **fus·ti·ness** \\-tē-nəs\\ *n*

fu·tile \\'fyüt-əl, 'fyü-ˌtīl\\ *adj* **1 :** having no result or effect **:** USELESS ⟨a *futile* struggle against overwhelming forces⟩ ⟨waste time in *futile* talk⟩ **2 :** UNIMPORTANT, TRIVIAL — **fu·tile·ly** \\-əl-(l)ē, -ˌtīl-lē\\ *adv* — **fu·til·i·ty** \\fyü-'til-ət-ē\\ *n*

[1]**fu·ture** \\'fyü-chər\\ *adj* [from Latin *futurus* "going to be", used as the future participle of *esse* "to be"; it is from the same prehistoric source as English *be*] **1 a :** that is to be **b :** existing after death **2 :** of, relating to, or constituting a verb tense expressive of time yet to come

[2]**future** *n* **1 a :** time that is to come **b :** what is going to happen **2 :** expectation of advancement or development ⟨a promising *future*⟩ **3 :** a stock or commodity sold for delivery at a future time — usu. used in pl. **4 a :** the future tense **b :** a verb form in the future tense

fu·ture·less \\-ləs\\ *adj* **:** having no prospect of future success

future perfect *adj* **:** of, relating to, or constituting a verb tense formed in English with *will have* and *shall have* and expressing completion of an action by a specified time that is yet to come — **future perfect** *n*

fu·tur·is·tic \\ˌfyü-chə-'ris-tik\\ *adj* **:** being or resembling the style or type predicted for the future ⟨*futuristic* automobiles⟩ — **fu·tur·is·ti·cal·ly** \\-ti-k(ə-)lē\\ *adv*

fu·tu·ri·ty \\fyu̇-'t(y)u̇r-ət-ē, -'chu̇r-\\ *n, pl* **-ties 1 :** FUTURE **2 :** the quality or state of being future **3** *pl* **:** future events or prospects

fuze, fuzee *var of* FUSE, FUSEE

fuzz \\'fəz\\ *n* **1 :** fine light particles or fibers (as of down or fluff) **2** *slang* **:** the police **:** COPS

fuzzy \\'fəz-ē\\ *adj* **fuzz·i·er; -est 1 :** covered with or resembling fuzz **2 :** not clear **:** INDISTINCT — **fuzz·i·ly** \\'fəz-ə-lē\\ *adv* — **fuzz·i·ness** \\'fəz-ē-nəs\\ *n*

FW *abbr* fresh water

fwd *abbr* forward

fwy *abbr* freeway

-fy \\ˌfī\\ *vb suffix* **-fied; -fy·ing** [from French *-fier*, from Latin *-ficare*, a verb suffix from the same root as *facere* "to make"] **1 :** make **:** form into ⟨dandi*fy*⟩ **2 :** invest with the attributes of **:** make similar to ⟨citi*fy*⟩

fy *abbr* ferry

FYI *abbr* for your information

g \'jē\ *n, often cap* **1** : the 7th letter of the English alphabet **2** : the musical tone G **3** : a unit of force equal to a person's weight and used to express forces he experiences (as when he is in an airplane that is pulling out of a dive) ⟨a force of three *G's*⟩

g *abbr* **1** acceleration of gravity **2** gram **3** gravity

G *abbr* **1** games **2** German **3** goal **4** good

Ga *or* **GA** *abbr* Georgia

gab \'gab\ *vb* **gabbed**; **gab·bing** : to talk idly : CHATTER — **gab** *n*

gab·ar·dine \'gab-ər-ˌdēn\ *n* **1** : GABERDINE **2 a** : a firm durable twilled fabric having diagonal ribs **b** : a garment of gabardine

gab·ble \'gab-əl\ *vb* **gab·bled**; **gab·bling** \'gab-(ə-)ling\ : JABBER, BABBLE — **gabble** *n* — **gab·bler** \'gab-(ə-)lər\ *n*

gab·bro \'gab-rō\ *n, pl* **gabbros** : a granular igneous rock rich in magnesium and low in quartz — **gab·bro·ic** \ga-'brō-ik\ *adj*

gab·by \'gab-ē\ *adj* **gab·bi·er**; **-est** : TALKATIVE, GARRULOUS

gab·er·dine \'gab-ər-ˌdēn\ *n* **1 a** : a long smock worn by Jews in medieval times **b** : an English laborer's smock **2** : GABARDINE

gab·fest \'gab-ˌfest\ *n* **1** : an informal gathering for general talk **2** : an extended conversation

ga·ble \'gā-bəl\ *n* **1** : the triangular part of a wall of a building that is formed by the sides of the roof sloping down from the ridgepole to the eaves **2** : a triangular structure (as over a door or window) — **ga·bled** \-bəld\ *adj*

gable 1

gable roof *n* : a double-sloping roof that forms a gable at each end

[1]gad \'gad\ *vb* **gad·ded**; **gad·ding** : to roam about without purpose — **gad·der** *n*

[2]gad *interj* — used as a mild oath

gad·about \'gad-ə-ˌbau̇t\ *n* : a person who moves about in social activity — **gadabout** *adj*

gad·fly \'gad-ˌflī\ *n* **1** : any of various flies (as a horsefly or botfly) that are pests esp. of livestock **2** : a person who intentionally criticizes a lot and thus provokes or stimulates people

gad·get \'gaj-ət\ *n* : CONTRIVANCE, DEVICE ⟨a *gadget* for peeling potatoes⟩ — **gad·get·eer** \ˌgaj-ə-'ti(ə)r\ *n* — **gad·get·ry** \'gaj-ə-trē\ *n*

gad·o·lin·i·um \ˌgad-ə-'lin-ē-əm\ *n* : a magnetic metallic chemical element occurring in several minerals — see ELEMENT table

Gael \'gāl\ *n* **1** : a Scottish Highlander **2** : a Celtic esp. Gaelic-speaking inhabitant of Ireland, Scotland, or the Isle of Man

Gael·ic \'gāl-ik, 'gal-, 'gäl-\ *adj* **1** : of or relating to the Gaels and esp. the Celtic Highlanders of Scotland **2** : of, relating to, or constituting the Celtic speech of the inhabitants of Ireland, the Isle of Man, and the Scottish Highlands — **Gaelic** *n*

gaff \'gaf\ *n* **1** : a spear or hook for lifting heavy fish **2** : the spar upon which the head of a fore-and-aft sail is extended **3** : rough treatment : ABUSE ⟨couldn't stand the *gaff*⟩ — **gaff** *vb*

[1]gag \'gag\ *vb* **gagged**; **gag·ging** **1** : to prevent from speaking or crying out by or as if by stopping up the mouth **2 a** : to retch or cause to retch **b** : OBSTRUCT, CHOKE **3** : BALK **4** : to make quips

[2]gag *n* **1 a** : something thrust into the mouth esp. to prevent speech or outcry **b** : a check to free speech **2** : a laugh-provoking remark or act **3** : HOAX, TRICK

[1]gage \'gāj\ *n* **1** : a token of defiance; *esp* : a glove or cap cast on the ground as a pledge of combat **2** : something deposited as a pledge : SECURITY

[2]gage *var of* GAUGE

gai·e·ty \'gā-ət-ē\ *n, pl* **gai·e·ties** **1** : MERRYMAKING **2** : gay spirits or manner **3** : FINERY

gai·ly \'gā-lē\ *adv* : in a gay manner

[1]gain \'gān\ *n* **1** : an increase in or addition to what is of profit **2** : the obtaining of profit or possessions **3** : an increase in amount, magnitude, or degree

[2]gain *vb* **1 a** : to get possession of : EARN **b** : to win in competition or conflict ⟨*gain* a victory⟩ **c** : to get by a natural development or process : ACHIEVE ⟨*gain* strength⟩ **d** : to arrive at ⟨*gained* the river that night⟩ **2** : to win to one's side : PERSUADE **3** : to increase in ⟨*gain* momentum⟩ **4** : to run fast ⟨my watch *gains* a minute a day⟩ **5** : to get advantage : PROFIT **6 a** : INCREASE **b** : to improve in health — **gain ground** : to make progress

gain·er \'gā-nər\ *n* **1** : one that gains **2** : a fancy dive in which the diver rotates backward and enters the water feetfirst and facing away from the board

gain·ful \'gān-fəl\ *adj* : producing gain : PROFITABLE, PAID ⟨*gainful* employment⟩ — **gain·ful·ly** \-fə-lē\ *adv* — **gain·ful·ness** *n*

gain·say \gān-'sā\ *vb* **gain·said** \-'sād, -'sed\; **gain·say·ing** \-'sā-ing\ **1** : DENY, DISPUTE **2** : CONTRADICT — **gain·say·er** *n*

gait \'gāt\ *n* : manner of moving on foot ⟨his *gait* was deliberate⟩; *also* : a particular style of such movement ⟨the walk, trot, and canter are *gaits* of the horse⟩ — **gait·ed** \-əd\ *adj*

gai·ter \'gāt-ər\ *n* **1** : a leg covering reaching from the instep to ankle, mid calf, or knee **2 a** : an ankle-high shoe with elastic gores **b** : an overshoe with fabric upper

gal \'gal\ *n* : GIRL

gal *abbr* gallon

ga·la \'gā-lə, 'gal-ə\ *n* : a gay celebration : FESTIVITY — **gala** *adj*

ga·lac·tic \gə-'lak-tik\ *adj* : of or relating to a galaxy

ga·lac·tose \gə-'lak-ˌtōs\ *n* : a sugar less soluble and less sweet than glucose

Ga·la·tians \gə-'lā-shənz\ *n* — see BIBLE table

gal·axy \'gal-ək-sē\ *n, pl* **gal·ax·ies** [from Greek *galaxias*, from *galakt-*, stem of *gala* "milk"] **1** : MILKY WAY GALAXY **2** : one of billions of systems each including stars, nebulae, clusters of stars, gas, and dust that make up the universe

gale \'gāl\ *n* **1** : a strong current of air; *esp* : a wind of from 32 to 63 miles per hour **2** : an emotional outburst

ga·le·na \gə-'lē-nə\ *n* : a bluish gray mineral with metallic luster consisting of sulfide of lead and constituting the principal ore of lead

Gal·i·le·an \ˌgal-ə-'lē-ən\ *adj* : of or relating to Galileo Galilei, founder of experimental physics and astronomy

[1]gall \'gȯl\ *n* **1 a** : BILE **b** : something bitter to endure **c** : bitterness of spirit **2** : EFFRONTERY, IMPUDENCE

[2]gall *n* : a skin sore (as on a horse's back) caused by chronic irritation

ə abut	ər further	a back	ā bake	
ä cot, cart	au̇ out	ch chin	e less	ē easy
g gift	i trip	ī life	j joke	ng sing
ō flow	ȯ flaw	ȯi coin	th thin	t͟h this
ü loot	u̇ foot	y yet	yü few	yu̇ furious
zh vision				

[3]**gall** *vb* **1 a :** CHAFE **b :** to become sore or worn by rubbing **2 :** IRRITATE, VEX **3 :** HARASS

[4]**gall** *n* : a swelling or growth of plant tissue usu. due to fungi or insect parasites

gall (on oak leaf)

[1]**gal·lant** \gə-'lant, gə-'länt, 'gal-ənt\ *n* **1 :** a young man of fashion **2 a :** a man who is fond of the company of women and is attentive to them **b :** SUITOR

[2]**gal·lant** \'gal-ənt (*usu in sense 2b*); gə-'lant, gə-'länt (*usu in sense 3*)\ *adj* **1 :** showy in dress or bearing **2 a :** SPLENDID, STATELY ⟨a *gallant* ship⟩ **b :** SPIRITED, BRAVE ⟨made a *gallant* stand⟩ **c :** CHIVALROUS, NOBLE ⟨a *gallant* knight⟩ **3 :** polite and attentive to women — **gal·lant·ly** *adv*

gal·lant·ry \'gal-ən-trē\ *n, pl* **-ries 1 a :** an act of marked courtesy **b :** courteous attention to a woman **2 :** conspicuous bravery

gall·blad·der \'gȯl-,blad-ər\ *n* : a membranous muscular sac in which bile from the liver is stored

gal·le·on \'gal-ē-ən\ *n* : a heavy square-rigged sailing ship of the 15th to 18th centuries used esp. by the Spanish

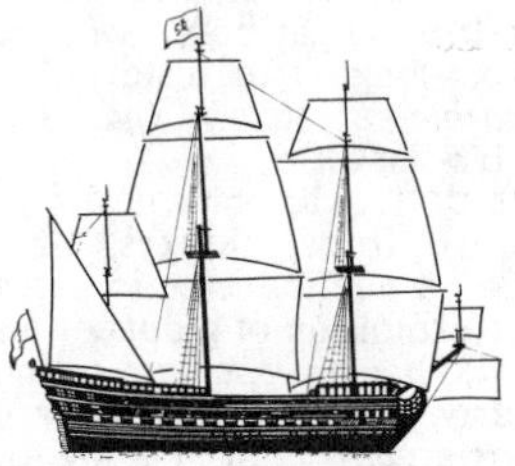

galleon

gal·lery \'gal(-ə)-rē\ *n, pl* **gal·ler·ies 1 a :** an outdoor balcony **b :** a balcony in a theater, auditorium, or church; *esp* **:** the highest balcony in a theater or the people who sit there ⟨play to the *gallery*⟩ **2 :** a body of spectators at a tennis or golf match **3 a :** a long narrow room, hall, or passage; *esp* **:** one having windows along one side **b :** an underground passageway (as in a mine) **c :** a passage (as in earth or wood) made by an animal and esp. an insect **4 a :** a room or building devoted to the exhibition of works of art **b :** an institution or business exhibiting or dealing in works of art **5 :** a photographer's studio

gal·ley \'gal-ē\ *n, pl* **galleys 1 :** a large low ship propelled by oars and sails and used in ancient times and in the Middle Ages chiefly in the Mediterranean sea **2 :** the kitchen of a ship

gall·fly \'gȯl-,flī\ *n* : an insect that deposits its eggs in plants and causes galls in which the larvae feed

Gal·lic \'gal-ik\ *adj* : of or relating to Gaul or France

gall·ing \'gȯ-ling\ *adj* : CHAFING, VEXING

gal·li·nule \'gal-ə-,n(y)ül\ *n* : any of several aquatic birds related to the rails

gal·li·um \'gal-ē-əm\ *n* : a bluish white metallic element that is hard and brittle at low temperatures but melts just above room temperature — see ELEMENT table

gal·li·vant \'gal-ə-,vant\ *vb* : to travel or roam about for pleasure

gal·lon \'gal-ən\ *n* — see MEASURE table

gal·lop \'gal-əp\ *n* **1 :** a springing gait of a quadruped with all four feet off the ground at the same time once in each stride; *esp* **:** a fast natural 3-beat gait of the horse — compare CANTER **2 :** a ride or run at a gallop — **gallop** *vb* — **gal·lop·er** *n*

gal·lows \'gal-ōz\ *n, pl* **gallows** *or* **gal·lows·es** : a structure consisting of an upright frame with a crosspiece from which criminals are hanged

gall·stone \'gȯl-,stōn\ *n* : a hard pebblelike mass formed in the gallbladder or bile passages

gall wasp *n* : a wasp that is a gallfly

ga·lore \gə-'lō(ə)r, -'lȯ(ə)r\ *adj* [from Irish Gaelic *go leor* "in plenty"] **:** ABUNDANT, PLENTIFUL — used after the word it modifies ⟨presents *galore*⟩

ga·losh \gə-'läsh\ *n* : a high overshoe worn esp. in snow and slush — **ga·loshed** \-'läsht\ *adj*

gal·van·ic \gal-'van-ik\ *adj* **1 :** of, relating to, or producing a direct current of electricity by chemical action ⟨a *galvanic* cell⟩ **2 :** having an electric effect : STIMULATING ⟨a *galvanic* personality⟩ — **gal·van·i·cal·ly** \-i-k(ə-)lē\ *adv*

gal·va·nism \'gal-və-,niz-əm\ *n* : a direct current of electricity produced by chemical action

gal·va·nize \'gal-və-,nīz\ *vb* **1 a :** to subject to the action of an electric current **b :** to stimulate or excite by or as if by an electric shock ⟨*galvanize* a muscle⟩ **2 :** to coat (as iron) with zinc for protection esp. from rust — **gal·va·ni·za·tion** \,gal-və-nə-'zā-shən\ *n*

gal·va·nom·e·ter \,gal-və-'näm-ət-ər\ *n* : an instrument for detecting or measuring a small electric current

gal·vano·scope \gal-'van-ə-,skōp\ *n* : an instrument for detecting the presence and direction of an electric current by the deflection of a magnetic needle

[1]**gam·ble** \'gam-bəl\ *vb* **gam·bled**; **gam·bling** \-b(ə-)ling\ **1 a :** to play a game for money or other stakes **b :** to bet on an uncertain outcome **2 :** to stake something on a doubtful event : BET, WAGER **3 :** RISK, HAZARD — **gam·bler** \-blər\ *n*

[2]**gamble** *n* : a risky undertaking

gam·boge \gam-'bōj, -'büzh\ *n* : an orange to brown gum resin from southeast Asian trees that is used as a yellow pigment and cathartic

gam·bol \'gam-bəl\ *vb* **gam·boled** *or* **gam·bolled**; **gam·bol·ing** *or* **gam·bol·ling** \-b(ə-)ling\ **:** to skip about in play : FRISK — **gambol** *n*

gam·brel roof \,gam-brəl-\ *n* : a roof with a lower steeper slope and an upper flatter one on each side — see ROOF illustration

[1]**game** \'gām\ *n* **1 a :** AMUSEMENT, DIVERSION **b :** FUN, SPORT **2 a :** PLAN, STRATAGEM **b :** a line of work : PROFESSION **3 a :** a physical or mental contest or a division of one **b :** the number of points necessary to win **c :** the manner of playing in a contest **4 a** (1) **:** animals pursued or taken by hunting (2) **:** the flesh of game animals **b :** an object of ridicule or attack — often used in the phrase *fair game*

[2]**game** *vb* : GAMBLE

[3]**game** *adj* **:** having a resolute unyielding spirit ⟨*game* to the end⟩ — **game·ly** *adv* — **game·ness** *n*

[4]**game** *adj* : LAME ⟨a *game* leg⟩

game bird *n* : a bird that may be hunted legally

game·cock \'gām-,käk\ *n* : a male game fowl

game fish *n* : a fish regularly fished for sport

game fowl *n* : a domestic fowl developed for the production of fighting cocks

game·keep·er \'gām-,kē-pər\ *n* **:** one that has charge of the breeding and protection of game animals or birds on a private preserve

ga·mete \gə-'mēt, 'gam-,ēt\ *n* : a matured sex cell capable of uniting with another such cell to form a new plant or animal individual — **ga·met·ic** \gə-

G

'met-ik\ *adj* — **ga·met·i·cal·ly** \-'met-i-k(ə-)lē\ *adv*

ga·me·to·phyte \gə-'mēt-ə-ˌfīt\ *n* : the individual or generation of plants with alternating sexual and asexual generations that produces the gametes from which the asexual sporophyte develops — **ga·me·to·phyt·ic** \-ˌmēt-ə-'fit-ik\ *adj*

game warden *n* : an official whose duties are to enforce the laws regulating the taking of game

gam·in \'gam-ən\ *n* : URCHIN

ga·mine \ga-'mēn\ *n* : a female urchin

gam·ma \'gam-ə\ *n* : the 3d letter of the Greek alphabet — Γ or γ

gamma globulin *n* : a blood plasma protein rich in antibodies

gamma rays *n pl* : very penetrating radiation of the same nature as X rays but of shorter wavelength emitted by various radioactive atomic nuclei — called also *gamma radiation*

gam·ut \'gam-ət\ *n* [from medieval Latin *gamma*, name of the lowest note of the whole scale, and *ut*, name of the lowest note of an octave] : an entire range or series

gamy \'gā-mē\ *adj* **gam·i·er**; **-est** **1** : GAME, PLUCKY **2** : having the flavor of game esp. when slightly tainted ⟨*gamy* meat⟩ — **gam·i·ly** \'gā-mə-lē\ *adv* — **gam·i·ness** \'gā-mē-nəs\ *n*

1**gan·der** \'gan-dər\ *n* : a male goose

2**gander** *n, slang* : LOOK, GLANCE

1**gang** \'gang\ *n* **1** : a group of persons working or going about together ⟨a *gang* of laborers⟩ ⟨a *gang* of boys in swimming⟩ **2** : a group of persons associated together for unlawful or antisocial purposes ⟨a *gang* of thieves⟩ **3** : two or more similar implements or devices arranged to work together ⟨a *gang* of saws⟩

2**gang** *vb* **1** : to attack in a gang — usu. used with *up* ⟨the crowd *ganged* up on the referee⟩ **2** : to form into or move or act as a gang

gang·land \'gang-ˌland\ *n* : the world of organized crime

gan·gling \'gang-gling, -glən\ *adj* : LANKY, SPINDLING

gan·gli·on \'gang-glē-ən\ *n, pl* **-glia** \-glē-ə\ *also* **-gli·ons** : a mass of neural tissue lying external to the brain or spinal cord and containing nerve cells; *also* : NUCLEUS c — **gan·gli·on·ic** \ˌgang-glē-'än-ik\ *adj*

gang·plank \'gang-ˌplangk\ *n* : a movable bridge used in boarding or leaving a ship at a pier

gang·plow \-ˌplau̇\ *n* : a plow designed to turn two or more furrows at one time

1**gan·grene** \'gang-ˌgrēn, gang-'\ *n* : local death of soft tissues due to loss of blood supply — **gan·gre·nous** \'gang-grə-nəs\ *adj*

2**gangrene** *vb* : to make or become gangrenous

gang·ster \'gang-stər\ *n* : a member of a gang of criminals : RACKETEER — **gang·ster·ism** \-stə-ˌriz-əm\ *n*

gangue \'gang\ *n* : the worthless rock or vein matter in which valuable metals or minerals occur

gang·way \'gang-ˌwā\ *n* **1** : a passage into, through, or out of an enclosed place **2** : GANGPLANK **3** : a clear passage through a crowd — often used as an interjection

ə abut	ər further	a back	ā bake
ä cot, cart	au̇ out	ch chin	e less	ē easy
g gift	i trip	ī life	j joke	ng sing	ō flow
ȯ flaw	ȯi coin	th thin	th this	ü loot
u̇ foot	y yet	yü few	yu̇ furious	zh vision

gan·net \'gan-ət\ *n, pl* **gannets** *also* **gannet** : any of several large fish-eating seabirds that breed chiefly on offshore islands

gan·try \'gan-trē\ *n, pl* **gantries** **1** : a platform made to carry a traveling crane and supported by towers running on parallel tracks **2** : a movable structure with platforms at different levels used for erecting and servicing rockets before launching **3** : a structure spanning several railroad tracks and displaying signals

gaol \'jāl\, **gaol·er** *chiefly Brit var of* JAIL, JAILER

gap \'gap\ *n* **1** : an opening made by a break or a parting : BREACH, CLEFT **2** : a mountain pass **3** : a break or separation in continuity : a blank space **4** : the distance between two electrodes (as in a spark plug)

1**gape** \'gāp\ *vb* **1 a** : to open the mouth wide **b** : to open or part widely **2** : to stare openmouthed **3** : YAWN — **gap·er** *n* — **gap·ing·ly** *adv*

2**gape** *n* : an act or instance of gaping: **a** : YAWN **b** : an openmouthed stare

gar \'gär\ *n* : any of various fishes with a long body like that of a pike and long narrow jaws

gar *abbr* garage

1**ga·rage** \gə-'räzh, -'räj\ *n* **1** : a building where automobiles are housed **2** : a repair shop for automobiles — **ga·rage·man** \-ˌman\ *n*

2**garage** *vb* : to keep or put in a garage

garb \'gärb\ *n* **1** : style of dress **2** : CLOTHING, DRESS — **garb** *vb*

gar·bage \'gär-bij\ *n* : food waste : REFUSE

gar·ble \'gär-bəl\ *vb* **gar·bled**; **gar·bling** \-b(ə-)ling\ : to distort the meaning or sound of ⟨*garble* a story⟩ ⟨*garble* words⟩ — **gar·bler** \-b(ə-)lər\ *n*

1**gar·den** \'gärd-ən\ *n* **1** : a plot of ground where herbs, fruits, flowers, or vegetables are grown **2 a** : a public recreation area or park; *esp* : one for the exhibition of plants or animals ⟨a botanical *garden*⟩ **b** : an open-air eating or drinking place — **garden** *vb* — **gar·den·er** \'gärd-(ə-)nər\ *n*

2**garden** *adj* **1** : of, relating to, or frequenting gardens **2** : of a kind grown under cultivation esp. in the open **3** : ORDINARY, COMMONPLACE

gar·de·nia \gär-'dē-nyə\ *n* [from scientific Latin, named after Alexander *Garden* (1730–1791), a Scottish-American naturalist] : any of various Old World tropical trees and shrubs with leathery leaves and fragrant white or yellow flowers; *also* : one of the flowers

1**gar·gle** \'gär-gəl\ *vb* **gar·gled**; **gar·gling** \-g(ə-)ling\ : to rinse the throat with a liquid kept in motion by air forced through it from the lungs

2**gargle** *n* : a liquid used in gargling

gar·goyle \'gär-ˌgȯil\ *n* [from French *gargouille*, from Old French *gargoule*, a name imitating the sound of water gurgling] : a waterspout in the form of a grotesque human or animal figure

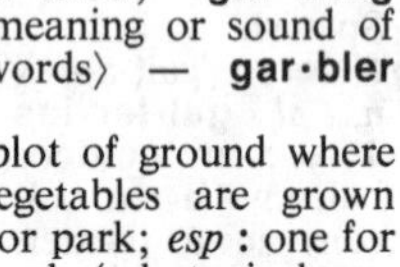

gargoyle

gar·ish \'ga(ə)r-ish, 'ge(ə)r-\ *adj* : tastelessly bright or showy : FLASHY, GAUDY — **gar·ish·ly** *adv* — **gar·ish·ness** *n*

gar·land \'gär-lənd\ *n* : a wreath or rope of leaves or flowers — **garland** *vb*

gar·lic \'gär-lik\ *n* : a European herb related to the lilies and having pungent compound bulbs much used in cookery; *also* : one of the bulbs — **gar·licky** \-li-kē\ *adj*

gar·ment \'gär-mənt\ *n* : an article of clothing — **garment** *vb*

gar·ner \'gär-nər\ *vb* **1** : to acquire by effort : EARN **2** : ACCUMULATE, COLLECT

gar·net \'gär-nət\ *n* **1** : a transparent usu. deep red silicate mineral that is used as a semiprecious stone and as an abrasive **2** : a deep red color

gar·net·if·er·ous \ˌgär-nət-'if-(ə-)rəs\ *adj* : containing garnets

garnet paper *n* : an abrasive paper with crushed garnet as the abrasive

gar·nish \'gär-nish\ *vb* **1** : DECORATE, EMBELLISH **2** : to add decorative or savory touches to (food) — **garnish** *n* — **gar·nish·ment** \-mənt\ *n*

gar·ni·ture \'gär-ni-chər, -nə-ˌchu̇r\ *n* : EMBELLISHMENT, TRIMMING

gar·ret \'gar-ət\ *n* : a room or unfinished part of a house just under the roof

[1]**gar·ri·son** \'gar-ə-sən\ *n* **1** : a military post; *esp* : a permanent military installation **2** : the troops stationed at a garrison

[2]**garrison** *vb* **1** : to furnish (as a fort or a town) with troops for defense **2** : to protect with forts and soldiers ⟨*garrison* a frontier⟩

garrison house *n* **1** : a house fortified against Indian attack **2** : a house having the second story overhanging the first in the front

[1]**gar·rote** *or* **ga·rotte** \gə-'rät, -'rōt\ *n* **1 a** : a method of execution by strangling with an iron collar **b** : the iron collar used **2 a** : strangulation esp. for the purpose of robbery **b** : an implement for this purpose

[2]**garrote** *or* **garotte** *vb* : to strangle with or as if with a garrote — **gar·rot·er** *n*

gar·ru·lous \'gar-ə-ləs\ *adj* : very talkative esp. about trifles : WORDY ***syn*** see TALKATIVE ***ant*** taciturn — **gar·ru·li·ty** \gə-'rü-lət-ē, ga-\ *n* — **gar·ru·lous·ly** \'gar-ə-ləs-lē\ *adv* — **gar·ru·lous·ness** *n*

gar·ter \'gärt-ər\ *n* : a band or strap worn to hold up a stocking

garter snake *n* : any of numerous harmless viviparous American snakes with stripes along the back

[1]**gas** \'gas\ *n*, *pl* **gas·es** *also* **gas·ses** [from modern Latin, an alteration of Latin *chaos* "empty space", from Greek *chaōs* "chaos"] **1** : a fluid (as hydrogen or air) that has no fixed shape and tends to expand indefinitely **2 a** : a gas or gaseous mixture used as a fuel or as an anesthetic **b** : a gaseous, liquid, or solid substance (as tear gas or mustard gas) that can be used to produce a poisonous, asphyxiating, or irritant atmosphere **3** *slang* : empty talk : BOMBAST **4** : GASOLINE **5** *slang* : something exciting or very funny ⟨the movie is a *gas*⟩

[2]**gas** *vb* **gassed**; **gas·sing 1 a** : to treat chemically with gas **b** : to poison with gas **2** : to supply with gas or esp. gasoline ⟨*gas* up the automobile⟩ **3** *slang* : to talk idly

Gas·con \'gas-kən\ *n* : a native of Gascony — **Gascon** *adj*

gas·e·ous \'gas-ē-əs, 'gash-əs\ *adj* **1** : having the form of or being gas **2** : of or relating to gas ⟨*gaseous* explosions⟩

gash \'gash\ *vb* : to make a long deep cut in — **gash** *n*

gas·ket \'gas-kət\ *n* **1** : a line or band used to lash a furled sail **2** : material (as abestos, rubber, or metal) used as packing (as for pistons or pipe joints)

gas·light \'gas-ˌlīt\ *n* **1** : light made by burning illuminating gas **2 a** : a gas flame **b** : a gas lighting fixture — **gas·light·ing** \-ing\ *n* — **gas·lit** \-ˌlit\ *adj*

gas mask *n* : a mask connected to a chemical air filter and used to protect the face and lungs against poison gases

gas mask

gas·o·line \'gas-ə-ˌlēn, ˌgas-ə-'\ *n* : a flammable liquid produced usu. by blending products from natural gas and petroleum and used esp. as a motor fuel and cleaning fluid

gasoline engine *n* : an internal-combustion engine using gasoline as fuel

gasoline pump *n* : a device that measures and supplies gasoline to motor vehicles

gas·om·e·ter \ga-'säm-ət-ər\ *n* : a laboratory apparatus for holding and measuring gases

gasp \'gasp\ *vb* **1** : to catch the breath with shock or other emotion **2** : to breathe laboriously : PANT **3** : to utter in a gasping manner — **gasp** *n*

gas·ser \'gas-ər\ *n* : an oil well that yields gas

gas station *n* : FILLING STATION

gas·sy \'gas-ē\ *adj* **gas·si·er**; **-est 1** : full of or containing gas **2** : having the characteristics of gas **3** : having or being likely to cause gases in the alimentary tract — **gas·si·ness** *n*

gas·tric \'gas-trik\ *adj* : of, relating to, or located near the stomach

gastric juice *n* : a watery acid digestive fluid secreted by glands in the walls of the stomach

gas·tri·tis \ga-'strīt-əs\ *n* : inflammation of the stomach and esp. of its mucous membrane

gas·tron·o·my \ga-'strän-ə-mē\ *n* : the art of good eating — **gas·tro·nom·ic** \ˌgas-trə-'näm-ik\ *adj* — **gas·tro·nom·i·cal** \-'näm-i-kəl\ *adj*

gas·tro·pod \'gas-trə-ˌpäd\ *n* : any of a large class of mollusks (as snails) having a muscular ventral foot and usu. a distinct head bearing sensory organs and a spiral shell into which the body can be withdrawn — **gastropod** *also* **gas·trop·o·dan** \ga-'sträp-əd-ən\ *or* **gas·trop·o·dous** \-əd-əs\ *adj*

gas·tro·trich \'gas-trə-ˌtrik\ *n* : any of a small group of minute freshwater multicellular animals superficially resembling infusorians — **gas·trot·ri·chan** \ga-'strä-tri-kən\ *adj or n*

gas·tru·la \'gas-trə-lə\ *n*, *pl* **-las** *or* **-lae** \-ˌlē, -ˌlī\ : an early embryo typically consisting of a double cup-shaped layer of cells produced by a folding in of the wall of the blastula — **gas·tru·lar** \-lər\ *adj*

gas·tru·late \-ˌlāt\ *vb* : to become or form a gastrula — **gas·tru·la·tion** \ˌgas-trə-'lā-shən\ *n*

gas turbine *n* : an engine in which turbine blades are driven by hot compressed gases produced during combustion

gas·works \'gas-ˌwərks\ *n pl* : a plant for manufacturing gas

gate \'gāt\ *n* **1** : an opening in a wall or fence **2** : a city or castle entrance often with defensive structures **3** : the frame or door that closes a gate **4** : a means of entrance or exit **5** : a door, valve, or other device for controlling the passage of fluid **6** : the total admission receipts or the number of spectators at a sports event

gate·keep·er \-ˌkē-pər\ *n* : a person who tends or guards a gate

gate·way \'gāt-ˌwā\ *n* **1** : an opening for a gate in a wall or fence **2** : a passage into or out of a place or state ⟨knowledge is the *gateway* to wisdom⟩

[1]**gath·er** \'gat͟h-ər\ *vb* **gath·ered**; **gath·er·ing** \'gat͟h-(ə-)ring\ **1** : to bring together ⟨*gathered* up

his tools⟩ **2** : PICK, HARVEST **3** : to gain by gradual increase ⟨*gather* speed⟩ **4** : to prepare (as oneself) by mustering strength ⟨*gather* courage to dive⟩ **5** : to draw together, about, or close ⟨*gathering* his cloak about him⟩ **6** : GUESS, DEDUCE ⟨I *gathered* he did not want to come⟩ **7** : to come together in a body or around a focus of attraction ⟨a crowd *gathered* round⟩ — **gath·er·er** \'gath-ər-ər\ *n*

syn GATHER, COLLECT, ASSEMBLE can mean to come or bring together. GATHER applies broadly to the coming or bringing together of units often not of one class; COLLECT may imply careful, orderly, or crowded gathering of units often of one kind; ASSEMBLE suggests a gathering of units into an ordered whole

[2]**gather** *n* : a puckering in cloth made by gathering

gath·er·ing *n* **1 a** : ASSEMBLY, MEETING **b** : a pus-filled swelling (as an abscess) **2** : the collecting of food and raw materials from the wild **3** : COLLECTION **4** : a gather in cloth

gauche \'gōsh\ *adj* **[**from French, meaning "left-hand", and then "awkward" because in most people the left hand is more awkward than the right**]** : lacking social experience or grace — **gauche·ness** *n*

gau·cho \'gau̇-chō\ *n, pl* **gauchos** : a cowboy of the So. American pampas

gaud \'gȯd, 'gäd\ *n* : ORNAMENT, TRINKET

gaudy \-ē\ *adj* **gaud·i·er**; **-est** : showily or tastelessly ornamented — **gaud·i·ly** \-ə-lē\ *adv* — **gaud·i·ness** \-ē-nəs\ *n*

[1]**gauge** \'gāj\ *n* **1** : measurement according to some standard or system **2** : an instrument for measuring, testing, or registering ⟨steam *gauge*⟩ **3** : the distance between the rails of a railroad **4** : the size of a shotgun expressed as the number of lead balls each just fitting the interior diameter of the barrel required to make a pound ⟨a 12-*gauge* shotgun⟩ **5** : the thickness of sheet metal or the diameter of wire or a screw **6** : the fineness of a knitted fabric in loops per 1½ inch

[2]**gauge** *vb* **1 a** : to measure exactly the size, dimensions, or other measurable quantity of **b** : to determine the capacity or contents of **2** : ESTIMATE, JUDGE — **gauge·a·ble** \'gā-jə-bəl\ *adj* — **gaug·er** *n*

gaunt \'gȯnt, 'gänt\ *adj* **1** : being thin and bony (as from hunger, suffering, or weariness) **2** : BARREN, DESOLATE *syn* see THIN — **gaunt·ly** *adv* — **gaunt·ness** *n*

[1]**gaunt·let** \'gȯnt-lət, 'gänt-\ *n* **1** : a protective glove worn with medieval armor **2** : a protective glove used in industry **3** : a dress glove extending above the wrist — **gaunt·let·ed** \-lət-əd\ *adj*

[2]**gauntlet** *n* : a double file of men armed with weapons (as clubs) with which to strike at a person who is made to run between them

gauze \'gȯz\ *n* **1** : a thin often transparent fabric **2** : a loosely woven cotton surgical dressing — **gauzy** \'gȯ-zē\ *adj*

gave *past of* GIVE

gav·el \'gav-əl\ *n* : the mallet of a presiding officer or auctioneer

ga·votte \gə-'vät\ *n* : a French peasant dance in moderately quick 4/4 time — **gavotte** *vb*

[1]**gawk** \'gȯk\ *vb* : to gape or stare stupidly

[2]**gawk** *n* : a clumsy stupid person : LOUT

gawky \'gȯ-kē\ *adj* **gawk·i·er**; **-est** : AWKWARD, CLUMSY ⟨a tall *gawky* youth⟩ — **gawk·i·ly** \-kə-lē\ *adv* — **gawk·i·ness** \-kē-nəs\ *n*

gay \'gā\ *adj* **1** : happily excited : MERRY **2 a** : BRIGHT, LIVELY **b** : brilliant in color **3** : SOCIABLE **4** : HOMOSEXUAL — **gay** *adv* — **gay·ness** *n*

gay·e·ty *var of* GAIETY

gay·ly *var of* GAILY

gaze \'gāz\ *vb* : to fix the eyes in a steady intent look — **gaze** *n* — **gaz·er** *n*

syn GAZE, STARE, PEER can mean to look at with concentration. GAZE suggests a long and intent look; STARE suggests a wide-eyed often curious, rude, or vacant gaze; PEER suggests a curious or furtive look esp. at something hard to make out

ga·zelle \gə-'zel\ *n, pl* **gazelles** *also* **gazelle** : any of numerous small graceful swift antelopes with soft bright eyes

ga·zette \gə-'zet\ *n* **1** : NEWSPAPER **2** : an official journal

gaz·et·teer \ˌgaz-ə-'ti(ə)r\ *n* : a geographical dictionary

GB *abbr* Great Britain

gds *abbr* goods

ge- *or* **geo-** *comb form* : earth : ground : soil ⟨*ge*anticline⟩ ⟨*geo*logy⟩

ge·an·ti·cline \jē-'ant-i-ˌklīn\ *n* : a great upward flexure of the earth's crust

[1]**gear** \'gi(ə)r\ *n* **1** : EQUIPMENT, PARAPHERNALIA ⟨fishing *gear*⟩ ⟨camping *gear*⟩ ⟨electronic *gear*⟩ **2 a** : a mechanism that performs a specific function in a machine ⟨steering *gear*⟩ **b** : a toothed wheel : COGWHEEL **3 a** : working relation or adjustment ⟨in *gear*⟩ **b** : one of the adjustments of a motor-vehicle transmission that determine the direction of travel and the relative speed of the engine and the vehicle — **gear·less** \-ləs\ *adj*

[2]**gear** *vb* **1 a** : to provide or connect with gearing **b** : to put into gear **2** : to prepare for operation ⟨*gear* up for full-scale production⟩ **3** : to be in or come into gear

gear·ing \'gi(ə)r-ing\ *n* **1** : the act or process of providing or fitting with gears **2** : the parts by which motion is transmitted from one portion of machinery to another

gear·shift \'gi(ə)r-ˌshift\ *n* : a mechanism by which transmission gears are engaged and disengaged

gear train *n* : a system of gears

gear wheel *n* : COGWHEEL

gecko \'gek-ō\ *n, pl* **geck·os** *or* **geck·oes** : any of numerous small harmless chiefly tropical and nocturnal insect-eating lizards

gee \'jē\ *imperative verb* — used as a direction to a draft animal to turn to the right or move ahead

geese *pl of* GOOSE

ge·gen·schein \'gā-gən-ˌshīn\ *n, often cap* : a faint light on the celestial sphere opposite the sun

Gei·ger counter \ˌgī-gər-\ *or* **Geiger–Mül·ler counter** \-'myül-ər-, -'mil-, -'məl-\ *n* : an electronic instrument for indicating (as by clicks) the presence of cosmic rays or radioactive substances

gei·sha \'gā-shə, 'gē-\ *n, pl* **geisha** *or* **geishas** : a Japanese girl who is trained to provide entertaining company for men

Geiss·ler tube \ˌgīs-lər-\ *n* : a glass tube provided with electrodes and filled with gas which becomes luminous when an electrical discharge is passed through it

[1]**gel** \'jel\ *n* : a colloid in a more solid form than a sol ⟨fruit jelly and gelatin dessert are *gels*⟩

[2]**gel** *vb* **gelled**; **gel·ling** : to change into or take on the form of a gel — **gel·a·ble** \'jel-ə-bəl\ *adj*

ə abut	ər further	a back	ā bake
ä cot, cart	au̇ out	ch chin	e less	ē easy
g gift	i trip	ī life	j joke	ng sing	ō flow
ȯ flaw	ȯi coin	th thin	th this	ü loot
u̇ foot	y yet	yü few	yu̇ furious	zh vision

gel·a·tin *also* **gel·a·tine** \'jel-ət-ən\ *n* **1** : gummy or sticky protein obtained from animal tissues by boiling and used as food, in photography, and in medicine **2 a** : an edible jelly formed with gelatin **b** : a thin colored transparent sheet used to color a stage light
ge·lat·i·nous \jə-'lat-(ə-)nəs\ *adj* **1** : resembling gelatin or jelly ⟨a *gelatinous* precipitate⟩ **2** : of, relating to, or containing gelatin — **ge·lat·i·nous·ly** *adv* — **ge·lat·i·nous·ness** *n*
geld \'geld\ *vb* : CASTRATE; *also* : SPAY
geld·ing \'gel-ding\ *n* : a castrated animal; *esp* : a castrated male horse
gem \'jem\ *n* **1 a** : JEWEL **b** : a precious or semiprecious stone cut and polished for ornament **2** : something small or brief and beautiful or perfect — **gem** *vb*
Gem·i·ni \'jem-ə-(,)nē, -,nī\ *n* — see ZODIAC table
gem·stone \'jem-,stōn\ *n* : a mineral or petrified material that when cut and polished can be used in jewelry
gen *abbr* **1** general **2** genitive
gen·darme \'zhän-,därm, 'jän-\ *n* [from French, intended as a singular of *gensdarmes* "police force", literally "people of arms"] : a member of an armed national police force esp. in France
gen·dar·mer·ie *or* **gen·dar·mery** \jän-'därm-ə-rē, zhän-\ *n, pl* **-mer·ies** : a body of gendarmes
gen·der \'jen-dər\ *n* **1** : SEX **2** : any of two or more classes of words (as nouns or pronouns) or of forms of words (as adjectives) that are partly based on sex and that determine agreement with other words or grammatical forms
gene \'jēn\ *n* : a specific part of DNA or sometimes RNA that transmits a hereditary character and is usually located in a chromosome in the cell nucleus
ge·ne·al·o·gy \,jē-nē-'äl-ə-jē, ,jen-ē-, -'al-\ *n, pl* **-gies** **1** : the descent of a person or family from an ancestor or a history of such descent **2** : the study of family pedigrees — **ge·ne·a·log·i·cal** \,jē-nē-ə-'läj-i-kəl, ,jen-ē-\ *adj* — **ge·ne·al·o·gist** \-'äl-ə-jəst, -'al-\ *n*
gene mutation *n* : mutation due to fundamental change in a gene
genera *pl of* GENUS
[1]**gen·er·al** \'jen-(ə-)rəl\ *adj* **1** : of or relating to the whole : not local or partial ⟨a *general* election⟩ **2** : taken as a whole ⟨the *general* body of citizens⟩ **3** : relating to or covering all instances or all members of a class ⟨a *general* conclusion⟩ **4** : not specific or in detail ⟨a *general* outline⟩ **5** : common to many ⟨a *general* custom⟩ **6** : not special : not specialized ⟨a *general* store⟩ **7** : superior in rank : concerned with administration or counseling ⟨*general* manager⟩ ⟨inspector *general*⟩
[2]**general** *n* : a military officer ranking above a colonel; *esp* : one ranking above a lieutenant general — **gen·er·al·ship** \-,ship\ *n* — **in general** : for the most part : GENERALLY
gen·er·a·lis·si·mo \,jen-(ə-)rə-'lis-ə-,mō\ *n, pl* **-mos** : the commander in chief of an army or of all armed forces
gen·er·al·ist \-əst\ *n* : one that is proficient in several fields or skills or is adaptable to a variety of environments
gen·er·al·i·ty \,jen-ə-'ral-ət-ē\ *n, pl* **-ties** **1** : the quality or state of being general **2 a** : GENERALIZATION 2 **b** : a vague or inadequate statement **3** : the greatest part : BULK
gen·er·al·i·za·tion \,jen-(ə-)rə-lə-'zā-shən\ *n* **1** : the act or process of generalizing **2** : a general statement, law, principle, or proposition
gen·er·al·ize \'jen-(ə-)rə-,līz\ *vb* **1** : to make general **2** : to draw general conclusions from ⟨*generalized* their experiences⟩ **3** : to reach a general conclusion esp. on the basis of instances — **gen·er·al·iz·er** *n*
gen·er·al·ly \'jen-(ə-)rə-lē, 'jen-ər-lē\ *adv* **1** : in disregard of specific instances : for the most part ⟨*generally* speaking⟩ **2** : as a rule : USUALLY
general of the air force : a general of the highest rank in the air force
general of the army : a general of the highest rank in the army
general practitioner *n* : a physician or veterinarian who does not limit his practice to a specialty
gen·er·ate \'jen-ə-,rāt\ *vb* : to bring into existence : PRODUCE; *esp* : to originate by a vital or chemical process ⟨*generate* an electric current⟩ ⟨heat *generated* by friction⟩ — **gen·er·a·tive** \-ə-,rāt-iv, -rət-\ *adj*
gen·er·a·tion \,jen-ə-'rā-shən\ *n* **1 a** : a body of living beings constituting a single step in the line of descent from an ancestor **b** : a group of individuals born and living at the same time **c** : a type or class of objects developed from an earlier type **2** : the average span of time between the birth of parents and that of their offspring **3** : the action or process of generating ⟨*generation* of an electric current⟩
generation gap *n* : a difference in culture and outlook that makes understanding between one generation and the next difficult
gen·er·a·tor \'jen-ə-,rāt-ər\ *n* **1** : one that generates **2** : an apparatus in which vapor or gas is formed **3** : a machine by which mechanical energy is changed into electrical energy
ge·ner·ic \jə-'ner-ik\ *adj* **1** : of, relating to, or characteristic of a whole group or class : GENERAL **2** : of, relating to, or ranking as a biological genus — **ge·ner·i·cal·ly** \-'ner-i-k(ə-)lē\ *adv*
gen·er·os·i·ty \,jen-ə-'räs-ət-ē\ *n, pl* **-ties** **1** : freedom in spirit or act; *esp* : readiness in giving **2** : a generous act
gen·er·ous \'jen-(ə-)rəs\ *adj* [from Latin *generosus*, literally "highborn", "noble", from *gener-*, stem of *genus* "birth", "family", a word from the same prehistoric source as English *kin*] **1** : free in giving or sharing : UNSELFISH ⟨a *generous* giver⟩ **2** : HIGH-MINDED, NOBLE ⟨*generous* in dealing with a defeated enemy⟩ **3** : ABUNDANT, PLENTIFUL, AMPLE ⟨a *generous* supply⟩ — **gen·er·ous·ly** *adv* — **gen·er·ous·ness** *n*
gen·e·sis \'jen-ə-səs\ *n, pl* **-e·ses** \-ə-,sēz\ : the origin or coming into being of something
Genesis — see BIBLE table
ge·net·ic \jə-'net-ik\ *adj* **1** : of or relating to the origin, development, or causes of something **2** : of, relating to, or involving genetics — **ge·net·i·cal** \-i-kəl\ *adj* — **ge·net·i·cal·ly** \-i-k(ə-)lē\ *adv*
genetic code *n* : the arrangement of chemical groups within the molecular structure of the genes by which genetic information is conveyed
ge·net·ics \jə-'net-iks\ *n* : a branch of biology that deals with the heredity and variation of organisms — **ge·net·i·cist** \-'net-ə-səst\ *n*
ge·nial \'jē-nyəl\ *adj* **1** : favorable to growth or comfort ⟨a *genial* climate⟩ **2** : being cheerful and cheering : KINDLY ⟨a *genial* host⟩ ⟨a *genial* disposition⟩ — **ge·ni·al·i·ty** \,jē-nē-'al-ət-ē, jēn-'yal-\ *n* — **ge·nial·ly** \'jē-nyə-lē, -nē-ə-lē\ *adv* — **ge·nial·ness** *n*
ge·nie \'jē-nē\ *n, pl* **ge·nies** \-nēz\ : JINN
gen·i·tal \'jen-ə-təl\ *adj* : of or relating to reproduction or the sexual organs
[2]**genital** *n* : one of the genitalia

G

gen·i·ta·lia \ˌjen-ə-ˈtā-lē-ə, -ˈtāl-yə\ *n pl* **:** reproductive organs; *esp* **:** the external genital organs — **gen·i·tal·ic** \-ˈtal-ik\ *adj*

gen·i·tive \ˈjen-ət-iv\ *adj* **:** of, relating to, or constituting a grammatical case marking typically possession or source — compare POSSESSIVE — **gen·i·ti·val** \ˌjen-ə-ˈtī-vəl\ *adj* — **genitive** *n*

gen·i·to·uri·nary \ˌjen-ə-tō-ˈyůr-ə-ˌner-ē\ *adj* **:** of or relating to the genital and urinary organs or functions

ge·nius \ˈjē-nyəs\ *n, pl* **ge·nius·es** *or* **ge·nii** \-nē-ˌī\ **1** *pl genii* **:** an attendant spirit **2 :** a strong leaning or inclination **:** PENCHANT ⟨a *genius* for getting into trouble⟩ **3 :** a peculiar, distinctive, or identifying character ⟨the *genius* of a nation⟩ **4 a** *pl genii* **:** JINN **b :** a person who influences another for good or bad ⟨his evil *genius*⟩ **5** *pl geniuses* **a :** a marked aptitude **b :** extraordinary intellectual power esp. as manifested in creative activity **c :** a person with such power

gen·o·cide \ˈjen-ə-ˌsīd\ *n* **:** the deliberate and systematic destruction of a racial, political, or cultural group — **gen·o·cid·al** \ˌjen-ə-ˈsīd-əl\ *adj*

ge·no·type \ˈjē-nə-ˌtīp, ˈjen-ə-\ *n* **:** the genetic constitution of an individual or group — **ge·no·typ·ic** \ˌjē-nə-ˈtip-ik, ˌjen-ə-\ *also* **ge·no·typ·i·cal** \-ˈtip-i-kəl\ *adj* — **ge·no·typ·i·cal·ly** \-i-k(ə-)lē\ *adv*

genre \ˈzhän-rə\ *n* **:** a distinctive type or category of literary or artistic composition

gent \ˈjent\ *n* **:** MAN, FELLOW

gent *abbr* gentleman

gen·teel \jen-ˈtēl\ *adj* **1 :** ARISTOCRATIC **2 :** ELEGANT, GRACEFUL **3 :** POLITE, REFINED — **gen·teel·ly** \-ˈtēl-lē\ *adv* — **gen·teel·ness** *n* — **gen·til·i·ty** \jen-ˈtil-ət-ē\ *n*

gen·tian \ˈjen-chən\ *n* **:** any of various fall-flowering herbs with opposite smooth leaves and showy bell-shaped or funnel-shaped usu. blue flowers

gen·tile \ˈjen-ˌtīl\ *n* [from Latin *gentilis* "belonging to a people", from *gent-*, stem of *gens* "people"; since the plural of the latter word, *gentes*, was used by the early Christians as a translation of the Hebrew word for non-Jews *gōyīm*, literally "the nations", the derivative *gentilis* came to mean "heathen" for the Christians] **1 :** a person who is not Jewish **2 :** HEATHEN, PAGAN **3 :** a person who is not a Mormon — **gentile** *adj*

gen·tle \ˈjen-təl\ *adj* **1 :** belonging or suitable to a family of high social station **2 a :** easily handled **:** DOCILE **b :** not harsh or stern **:** MILD **3 :** SOFT, SOOTHING ⟨a *gentle* murmur⟩ **4 :** MODERATE ⟨*gentle* slopes⟩ — **gentle** *vb* — **gen·tle·ness** *n* — **gen·tly** \ˈjent-lē\ *adv*

gen·tle·folk \ˈjen-təl-ˌfōk\ *also* **gen·tle·folks** \-ˌfōks\ *n pl* **:** GENTRY

gen·tle·man \ˈjen-təl-mən\ *n* **1 :** a man of good family **2 :** a well-bred man of good education and social position **3 :** MAN — used in the plural as a form of address in speaking to a group of men — **gen·tle·man·li·ness** *n* — **gen·tle·man·ly** \-lē\ *adj*

gen·tle·wom·an \ˈjen-təl-ˌwům-ən\ *n* **1 :** a woman of good family **2 :** a woman attending a lady of rank

gen·try \ˈjen-trē\ *n* **1 :** people of good birth, breeding, and education **:** ARISTOCRACY **2 :** the class of English people between the nobility and the yeomanry **3 :** PEOPLE; *esp* **:** persons of a designated class

gen·u·flect \ˈjen-yə-ˌflekt\ *vb* **:** to kneel on one knee and then rise again as an act of reverence

gen·u·ine \ˈjen-yə-wən\ *adj* **1 :** being actually what it seems to be **:** REAL ⟨*genuine* gold⟩ ⟨a *genuine* antique⟩ **2 :** SINCERE, HONEST ⟨a *genuine* interest in classical music⟩ — **gen·u·ine·ly** *adv* — **gen·u·ine·ness** *n*

ge·nus \ˈjē-nəs\ *n, pl* **gen·era** \ˈjen-ə-rə\ [scientific Latin, from Latin, where it meant first "birth", then "family", and then "kind", "sort"; compare GENEROUS] **:** a category of biological classification ranking between the family and the species, comprising structurally or genetically related species and called by a capitalized noun formed in Latin

geo- — see GE-

geo·cen·tric \ˌjē-ō-ˈsen-trik\ *adj* **1 :** relating to or measured from the earth's center **2 :** having or relating to the earth as a center

geo·chem·is·try \-ˈkem-ə-strē\ *n* **:** a science that deals with the chemical composition of and chemical changes in the crust of the earth — **geo·chem·i·cal** \-ˈkem-i-kəl\ *adj* — **geo·chem·ist** \-ˈkem-əst\ *n*

ge·ode \ˈje-ˌōd\ *n* **:** a nodule of stone having a cavity lined with crystals or mineral matter

ge·od·e·sy \jē-ˈäd-ə-sē\ *n* **:** a branch of mathematics that determines the exact positions of points and the figures and areas of large portions of the earth's surface, the shape and size of the earth, and the variations of terrestrial gravity and magnetism — **ge·o·det·ic** \ˌjē-ə-ˈdet-ik\ *adj*

geodetic surveying *n* **:** surveying in which account is taken of and corrections made for the curvature of the earth

geog *abbr* **1** geographic **2** geography

geographical mile *n* **:** MILE 2

ge·og·ra·phy \jē-ˈäg-rə-fē\ *n, pl* **-phies** **1 :** a science that deals with the natural features of the earth and its climate, products, and inhabitants **2 :** the natural features of an area — **ge·og·ra·pher** \-fər\ *n* — **ge·o·graph·ic** \ˌjē-ə-ˈgraf-ik\ *or* **ge·o·graph·i·cal** \-i-kəl\ *adj* — **ge·o·graph·i·cal·ly** \-i-k(ə-)lē\ *adv*

geol *abbr* **1** geologic **2** geological **3** geology

geologic time *n* **:** the long period of time that deals with the sequence of events in the earth's geological history

ge·ol·o·gy \jē-ˈäl-ə-jē\ *n, pl* **-gies** **1 a :** a science that deals with the history of the earth and its life esp. as recorded in rocks **b :** a study of the features of a celestial body (as the moon) **2 :** the geologic features of an area — **ge·o·log·ic** \ˌjē-ə-ˈläj-ik\ *or* **ge·o·log·i·cal** \-i-kəl\ *adj* — **ge·o·log·i·cal·ly** \-i-k(ə-)lē\ *adv* — **ge·ol·o·gist** \jē-ˈäl-ə-jəst\ *n*

geom *abbr* **1** geometrical **2** geometry

geo·mag·net·ic \ˌjē-ō-mag-ˈnet-ik\ *adj* **:** of or relating to the magnetism of the earth — **geo·mag·ne·tism** \-ˈmag-nə-ˌtiz-əm\ *n*

ge·o·met·rid \ˌjē-ə-ˈme-trəd, jē-ˈäm-ə-\ *n* **:** any of a family of medium-sized moths with large wings and larvae that are loopers — **geometrid** *adj*

ge·om·e·try \jē-ˈäm-ə-trē\ *n* **1 :** a branch of mathematics that deals with points, lines, angles, surfaces, and solids **2 :** ARRANGEMENT, SHAPE ⟨the *geometry* of a crystal⟩ — **ge·om·e·ter** \-ət-ər\ *n* — **ge·o·met·ric** \ˌjē-ə-ˈme-trik\ *or* **ge·o·met·ri·cal** \-tri-kəl\ *adj* — **ge·o·met·ri·cal·ly** \-tri-k(ə-)lē\ *adv* — **ge·om·e·tri·cian** \jē-ˌäm-ə-ˈtrish-ən\ *n*

geo·phys·ics \ˌjē-ə-ˈfiz-iks\ *n* **:** the physics of the earth including the fields of meteorology, hydrology,

ə abut	ər further	a back		ā bake
ä cot, cart	aů out	ch chin	e less	ē easy
g gift	i trip	ī life	j joke	ng sing / ō flow
ȯ flaw	ȯi coin	th thin	th this	ü loot
ů foot	y yet	yü few	yů furious	zh vision

GEOLOGIC TIME AND FORMATIONS

ERAS	PERIODS AND SYSTEMS	EPOCHS AND SERIES	APPROXIMATE NO. OF YEARS AGO	EARLIEST RECORD OF ANIMALS	EARLIEST RECORD OF PLANTS
	Quaternary	Holocene (Recent) Pleistocene (Glacial)			
Cenozoic				mankind	
	Tertiary	Pliocene Miocene Oligocene Eocene Paleocene	70,000,000		
				placental mammals	
	Cretaceous (Upper Cretaceous)				
Mesozoic	Comanchean (Lower Cretaceous)				grasses and cereals
	Jurassic		160,000,000	birds mammals	flowering plants
	Triassic				
					ginkgos
	Permian		230,000,000		cycads and conifers
	Pennsylvanian				
				insects	primitive gymnosperms
	Mississippian			reptiles	
Paleozoic	Devonian		390,000,000	amphibians	vascular plants: lycopodiums, equisetums, ferns, etc.
	Silurian				
				fishes	
	Ordovician				
	Cambrian		500,000,000		mosses
			620,000,000		
Proterozoic				invertebrates	spores of uncertain relationship marine algae
	not divided into periods		1,420,000,000		
Archeozoic			2,300,000,000		

oceanography, seismology, volcanology, magnetism, radioactivity, and geodesy — **geo·phys·i·cal** \-'fiz-i-kəl\ *adj* — **geo·phys·i·cist** \-'fiz-ə-səst\ *n*

Geor·gian \'jȯr-jən\ *adj* : of, relating to, or characteristic of the reign of the first four British kings named George ⟨*Georgian* architecture⟩

geo·sci·ence \ˌjē-ō-'sī-ən(t)s\ *n* : any of the sciences dealing with the earth — **geo·sci·en·tist** \-ən-təst\ *n*

geo·syn·cline \ˌjē-ō-'sin-ˌklīn\ *n* : a great downward flexure of the earth's crust

ge·ot·ro·pism \jē-'ä-trə-ˌpiz-əm\ *n* : a tropism involving turning or movement toward the earth — **ge·o·trop·ic** \ˌjē-ə-'träp-ik\ *adj*

ger *abbr* gerund

Ger *abbr* **1** German **2** Germany

ge·ra·ni·um \jə-'rā-nē-əm\ *n* [from Greek *geranion*, derived from *geranos* "a crane", and applied to the plant because of the long projections of the carpels resembling cranes' bills] **1** : any of a genus of herbs with usu. deeply cut leaves, flowers in which glands alternate with the petals, and long slender dry fruits **2** : any of a genus of herbs that are distinguished by clusters of scarlet, pink, or white flowers having the sepals joined at the base into a hollow spur and are popular as window plants

ger·i·at·ric \ˌjer-ē-'a-trik\ *adj* : of or relating to geriatrics, the aged, or the process of aging

ger·i·a·trics \ˌjer-ē-'a-triks\ *n* : a branch of medicine that deals with the problems and diseases of old age and aging people

germ \'jərm\ *n* **1** : a small mass of living substance capable of developing into an organism or one of its parts **2** : a small source or origin ⟨the *germ* of an idea⟩ **3** : MICROBE

Ger·man \'jər-mən\ *n* **1 a** : a native or inhabitant of Germany **b** : a person of German descent **2** : the Germanic language of Germany, Austria, and parts of Switzerland — **German** *adj*

ger·mane \(ˌ)jər-'mān\ *adj* : having a significant connection : PERTINENT — **ger·mane·ly** *adv*

[1]**Ger·man·ic** \(ˌ)jər-'man-ik\ *adj* **1** : GERMAN **2** : of, relating to, or characteristic of the Germanic-speaking peoples **3** : of, relating to, or constituting Germanic

[2]**Germanic** *n* : a branch of the Indo-European language family containing English, German, Dutch, and the Scandinavian languages

ger·ma·ni·um \(ˌ)jər-'mā-nē-əm\ *n* : a grayish white hard brittle element that resembles silicon and is used as a semiconductor — see ELEMENT table

German measles *n sing or pl* : a contagious virus disease like but usu. milder than typical measles

German shepherd *n* : a large erect-eared intelligent dog of a breed originating in northern Europe that is often used in police work and as a guide dog for the blind

German silver *n* : NICKEL SILVER

germ cell *n* : an egg or sperm or one of the cells reserved by the body for forming eggs and sperms

ger·mi·cid·al \ˌjər-mə-'sīd-əl\ *adj* : of or relating to a germicide; *also* : destroying germs

ger·mi·cide \'jər-mə-ˌsīd\ *n* : an agent that destroys germs

ger·mi·nate \'jər-mə-ˌnāt\ *vb* **1** : to cause to sprout or develop **2** : to begin to grow : SPROUT **3** : to come into being : EVOLVE — **ger·mi·na·tion** \ˌjər-mə-'nā-shən\ *n*

germ theory *n* **1** : the theory that living organisms can be produced only by development from living parts (as a fertilized egg produced by combination of egg and sperm) from other living organisms **2** : the theory that infectious and contagious disease results from the action of living organisms

ger·on·tol·o·gy \ˌjer-ən-'täl-ə-jē\ *n* : a branch of knowledge dealing with aging and the problems of the aged

[1]**ger·ry·man·der** \ˌjer-ē-'man-dər, ˌger-\ *n* : the act or result of gerrymandering

[2]**gerrymander** *vb* **ger·ry·man·dered**; **ger·ry·man·der·ing** \-d(ə-)riŋ\ : to divide (as a state or county) into election districts so as to give one political party an advantage over its opponents

ger·und \'jer-ənd\ *n* : an English noun formed from a verb by the addition of *-ing* that is capable of taking adverbial modifiers and having an object ⟨*eating* in "Doctors recommend eating slowly" is a *gerund*⟩

ges·ta·tion \je-'stā-shən\ *n* : the carrying of young in the uterus : PREGNANCY

ges·tic·u·late \je-'stik-yə-ˌlāt\ *vb* : to make gestures esp. when speaking — **ges·tic·u·la·tion** \-ˌstik-yə-'lā-shən\ *n*

ges·ture \'jes-chər\ *n* **1** : a movement of the body or limbs that expresses or emphasizes an idea, sentiment, or attitude **2** : the use of gestures as a means of expression **3** : something said or done merely for effect or as a formality ⟨providing a meal for the flood victims was a mere *gesture*⟩ — **gesture** *vb*

get \(ˈ)get, *esp when unemphatic also* git\ *vb* **got** \(ˈ)gät\; **got** *or* **got·ten** \'gät-ən\; **get·ting** **1 a** : to gain possession of (as by receiving, acquiring, earning, buying, or winning) ⟨*get* a present⟩ ⟨*got* first prize⟩ ⟨*get* a dog⟩ **b** : FETCH ⟨*get* his slippers⟩ **2 a** : to succeed in coming or going ⟨*got* to the city on time⟩ ⟨*got* home early⟩ **b** : to cause to come or go ⟨*got* the dog out in a hurry⟩ **c** : GO ⟨*get* away from here⟩ ⟨*get* on a bus⟩ **3** : BEGET **4 a** : to cause to be in a certain condition ⟨*got* his hair cut⟩ ⟨*got* his feet wet⟩ **b** : BECOME ⟨*get* sick⟩ ⟨*get* better⟩ ⟨it's *getting* warmer⟩ **c** : PREPARE ⟨started *getting* dinner⟩ **5 a** : SEIZE ⟨*got* the thief by the leg⟩ **b** : to move emotionally ⟨a song that always *got* him⟩ **c** : BAFFLE, PUZZLE ⟨the third question *got* everybody⟩ **d** : IRRITATE ⟨don't let it *get* you⟩ **e** : HIT ⟨*got* him in the leg⟩ **f** : KILL ⟨swore to *get* him⟩ **6 a** : to be subjected to ⟨*got* the measles⟩ **b** : to receive as punishment ⟨*got* six months for larceny⟩ **7 a** : to find out by calculation ⟨*got* the right answer⟩ **b** : to hear correctly ⟨I didn't *get* your name⟩ **c** : UNDERSTAND ⟨now I've *got* it⟩ ⟨I *get* you⟩ **8** : PERSUADE, INDUCE ⟨couldn't *get* him to agree⟩ **9 a** : HAVE — used in the present perfect form with present meaning ⟨I've *got* no money⟩ **b** : to have to : MUST — used in the present perfect form with present meaning ⟨he has *got* to come⟩ **10** : to establish communication with ⟨*got* him on the telephone⟩ **11** : to leave at once ⟨told him to *get*⟩ ⟨*get* out or else⟩ **12** : to put out in baseball

syn GET, OBTAIN, PROCURE, SECURE can mean to bring into one's possession. GET implies merely the fact of gaining possession; OBTAIN may imply getting by planning or effort; PROCURE often applies specifically to obtaining by official action; SECURE implies bringing into safe and sure possession

— **get ahead** : to achieve success — **get around**

1 : to get the better of **2** : EVADE — **get at 1** : to reach effectively **2** : to try to prove or make clear ⟨what is he *getting at?*⟩ — **get away with** : to perform without suffering unpleasant consequences — **get back at** : to get even with — **get even** : to get revenge — **get even with** : to repay in kind — **get it** : to receive a scolding or punishment — **get one's goat** : to make one angry or annoyed — **get over** : to recover from — **get to 1** : BEGIN **2** : to have an effect on : INFLUENCE — **get together 1** : to bring or come together : ASSEMBLE **2** : to reach agreement — **get wind of** : to become aware of

get along *vb* **1 a** : PROGRESS ⟨*getting along* well in history⟩ **b** : to approach old age ⟨*getting along* in years⟩ **2** : MANAGE ⟨*get along* on a small pension⟩ **3** : to be or remain on congenial terms ⟨easy to *get along* with⟩

get·away \'get-ə-ˌwā\ *n* **1** : ESCAPE **2** : the action of starting or getting under way (as by horses in a race or an automobile starting from a dead stop)

get away *vb* : ESCAPE ⟨you should have seen the one that *got away*⟩

get by *vb* : to avoid failure or catastrophe : barely succeed

get off *vb* **1** : UTTER ⟨*get off* a joke⟩ **2** : START **3** : to escape or help to escape punishment or harm ⟨his lawyer *got* him *off* with a suspended sentence⟩

get on *vb* : to get along

get out *vb* **1** : PUBLISH **2** : to escape or help to escape **3** : to become known : leak out ⟨their secret *got out*⟩

get–to·geth·er \'get-tə-ˌgeth-ər\ *n* : MEETING; *esp* : an informal social gathering

get·up \'get-ˌəp\ *n* : OUTFIT, COSTUME

get up \get-'əp, git-\ *vb* **1 a** : to arise from bed **b** : to rise to one's feet **2** : PREPARE, ORGANIZE ⟨*get up* a petition⟩ **3** : DRESS ⟨was *got up* as a pirate⟩

gew·gaw \'g(y)ü-ˌgȯ\ *n* : TRINKET, BAUBLE

gey·ser \'gī-zər\ *n* [from *Geysir*, name of a geyser in Haukadal, Iceland, meaning in Icelandic "gusher"] : a spring that throws forth intermittent jets of hot water and steam

ghast·ly \'gast-lē\ *adj* **ghast·li·er**; **-est 1** : HORRIBLE, SHOCKING ⟨a *ghastly* crime⟩ **2** : resembling a ghost : DEATHLIKE, PALE ⟨a *ghastly* face⟩ — **ghast·li·ness** *n* — **ghastly** *adv*

gher·kin \'gər-kən\ *n* **1** : the small prickly fruit of a trailing West Indian cucumber vine that is used for pickling; *also* : the vine that bears it **2** : the immature fruit of the common cultivated cucumber

ghet·to \'get-ō\ *n, pl* **ghettos** *or* **ghettoes** : a quarter of a city in which Jews are required to live; *also* : a quarter of a city in which members of a minority group live because of social, legal, or economic pressure

[1]**ghost** \'gōst\ *n* **1** : the seat of life : SOUL ⟨give up the *ghost*⟩ **2** : a disembodied soul; *esp* : the soul of a dead person believed to be an inhabitant of the unseen world or to appear to the living in bodily likeness **3** : SPIRIT, DEMON **4** : a faint shadowy trace or suggestion ⟨a *ghost* of a smile⟩ **5** : a false image in a photographic negative or on a television screen caused esp. by reflection **6** : one who ghostwrites

[2]**ghost** *vb* : GHOSTWRITE

ghost·ly \'gōst-lē\ *adj* **ghost·li·er**; **-est 1** : SPIRITUAL **2** : of, relating to, or having the characteristics of a ghost : SPECTRAL — **ghost·li·ness** *n*

ghost town *n* : a once flourishing town deserted or nearly so often after exhaustion of some natural resource (as gold)

ghost·write \'gōst-ˌrīt\ *vb* **-wrote** \-ˌrōt\; **-writ·ten** \-ˌrit-ən\; **-writ·ing** \-ˌrīt-iŋ\ : to write for and in the name of another — **ghost–writ·er** *n*

ghoul \'gül\ *n* **1** : a legendary evil being that robs graves and feeds on corpses **2** : a person (as a grave robber) whose activities suggest those of a ghoul — **ghoul·ish** \'gü-lish\ *adj* — **ghoul·ish·ly** *adv* — **ghoul·ish·ness** *n*

gi *abbr* gill

[1]**GI** \(')jē-'ī\ *adj* [from the abbreviation for *galvanized iron* used in listing such articles as garbage cans, but taken as standing for *government issue*] **1** : provided by a U.S. military supply department ⟨*GI* shoes⟩ **2** : of, relating to, or characteristic of U.S. military personnel **3** : conforming to military regulations or customs ⟨a *GI* haircut⟩

[2]**GI** *n, pl* **GI's** *or* **GIs** : a member or former member of the U.S. armed forces; *esp* : an enlisted man in the army

gi·ant \'jī-ənt\ *n* **1** : a legendary being of great size and strength **2** : a living being or a thing of great size or unusual power — **giant** *adj* — **gi·ant·ess** \'jī-ənt-əs\ *n*

giant cactus *n* : SAGUARO

giant sequoia *n* : a California evergreen that often exceeds 300 feet in height and 30 feet in girth — called also *big tree*

giant squid *n* : any of a group of gigantic squids that include the largest mollusks known with some being 40 feet long inclusive of the long arms

giant star *n* : a star of great luminosity and of large mass

Gib *abbr* Gibraltar

gib·ber \'jib-ər\ *vb* **gib·bered**; **gib·ber·ing** \-(ə-)riŋ\ : to speak gibberish : CHATTER — **gib·ber** *n*

gib·ber·el·lin \ˌjib-ə-'rel-ən\ *n* : any of several plant growth regulators produced by a fungus that in low concentrations promote shoot growth

gib·ber·ish \'jib-(ə-)rish, 'gib-\ *n* : rapid meaningless speech or language

gib·bet \'jib-ət\ *n* : GALLOWS; *esp* : an upright post with a projecting arm for hanging the bodies of executed criminals as a warning — **gibbet** *vb*

gib·bon \'gib-ən\ *n* : any of several tailless apes of southeastern Asia and the East Indies that are the smallest and most arboreal manlike apes

gibbon (about 3 ft. tall)

gib·bous \'jib-əs, 'gib-\ *adj* **1** : convexly rounded : HUMPED **2** : seen with more than half but not all of the apparent disk illuminated ⟨*gibbous* moon⟩ — **gib·bous·ly** *adv* — **gib·bous·ness** *n*

gibe \'jīb\ *vb* : to reproach with taunting or sarcastic words : JEER — **gibe** *n* — **gib·er** *n*

gib·let \'jib-lət\ *n* : an edible inner organ (as the heart or liver) of a fowl ⟨*giblet* gravy⟩ — usu. used in pl.

gid·dap \gid-'ap\ *imperative verb* — used as a command to a horse to go ahead or go faster

gid·dy \'gid-ē\ *adj* **gid·di·er**; **-est 1** : having a feeling of whirling or reeling about : DIZZY **2** : causing dizziness ⟨a *giddy* height⟩ **3** : lightheartedly silly : FRIVOLOUS — **gid·di·ly** \'gid-ə-lē\ *adv* — **gid·di·ness** \'gid-ē-nəs\ *n*

gift \'gift\ *n* **1** : the act or power of giving ⟨the appointment was not in his *gift*⟩ **2** : something given : PRESENT **3** : a special ability : TALENT ⟨a *gift* for music⟩ ***syn*** see PRESENT — **gift·ed** \'gif-təd\ *adj*

G

gig \'gig\ *n* **1 :** a long light ship's boat **2 :** a light two-wheeled one-horse carriage

gi·gan·tic \jī-'gant-ik\ *adj* **:** extremely large or great **:** HUGE — **gi·gan·ti·cal·ly** \-'gant-i-k(ə-)lē\ *adv*

gig·gle \'gig-əl\ *vb* **gig·gled**; **gig·gling** \-(ə-)ling\ **:** to laugh in a light silly manner — **giggle** *n* — **gig·gler** \-(ə-)lər\ *n* — **gig·gly** \'gig-(ə-)lē\ *adj*

Gi·la monster \,hē-lə-\ *n* **:** a large orange and black venomous lizard of the southwestern U.S.; *also* **:** a related Mexican lizard

Gila monster
(up to 21 in. long)

1gild \'gild\ *vb* **gild·ed** *or* **gilt** \'gilt\; **gild·ing 1 :** to cover with or as if with a thin coating of gold **2 :** to give a falsely attractive appearance to — **gild·er** *n*

2gild *var of* GUILD

1gill \'jil\ *n* — see MEASURE table

2gill \'gil\ *n* **1 :** an organ (as of a fish) of thin plates or threadlike processes for obtaining oxygen from water **2 :** the flesh under or about the chin or jaws — usu. used in pl. **3 :** one of the radiating plates forming the undersurface of the cap of a mushroom

gill filament *n* **:** one of the threadlike processes making up a gill

gill slit *n* **1 :** any of the openings or clefts in vertebrates with gills through which water taken in at the mouth moves to the outside bathing the gills **2 :** a rudiment of a gill slit that occurs at some stage of development in all vertebrate embryos

1gilt \'gilt\ *adj* **:** of the color of gold

2gilt *n* **:** gold or something that resembles gold laid on a surface

gim·crack \'jim-,krak\ *n* **:** a showy object of little use or value **:** GEWGAW — **gimcrack** *adj* — **gim·crack·ery** \-,krak-(ə-)rē\ *n*

gim·let \'gim-lət\ *n* **:** a small tool with a screw point and cross handle for boring holes

gim·mick \'gim-ik\ *n* **1 :** an ingenious scheme or device **2 :** a hidden feature **:** CATCH — **gim·micky** \-i-kē\ *adj*

gimlet

1gin \'jin\ *n* [from Old French *engin* "device", "engine", the source of English *engine*] **1 :** a snare or trap for game **2 :** COTTON GIN

2gin *vb* **ginned**; **gin·ning 1 :** SNARE **2 :** to separate (cotton fiber) from seeds and waste material — **gin·ner** *n*

3gin *n* [a shortened form of older *geneva*, from obsolete Dutch *genever*, literally "juniper", coming via Old French *genevre* from Latin *juniperus*] **:** a clear strong alcoholic beverage made from grain alcohol usu. flavored with juniper berries

gin·ger \'jin-jər\ *n* **1 :** any of a genus of tropical Old World herbs with pungent aromatic rhizomes used for flavoring and in medicine; *also* **:** this rhizome **2 :** high spirit **:** PEP — **gin·gery** \'jinj-(ə-)rē\ *adj*

ginger ale *n* **:** a nonalcoholic drink flavored with ginger extract

gin·ger·bread \'jin-jər-,bred\ *n* **1 :** a cake made with molasses and flavored with ginger **2 :** lavish or superfluous ornament esp. in architecture — **gingerbread** *adj*

gin·ger·ly \'jin-jər-lē\ *adj* **:** very cautious or careful — **gingerly** *adv*

gin·ger·snap \-,snap\ *n* **:** a thin brittle cookie flavored with ginger

ging·ham \'ging-əm\ *n* **:** a cotton clothing fabric in plain weave

gin·gi·vi·tis \,jin-jə-'vīt-əs\ *n* **:** inflammation of the gums

gink·go *also* **ging·ko** \'ging-kō\ *n, pl* **ginkgoes :** a large Chinese tree with fan-shaped leaves and foul-smelling fruit that is often grown as a shade tree

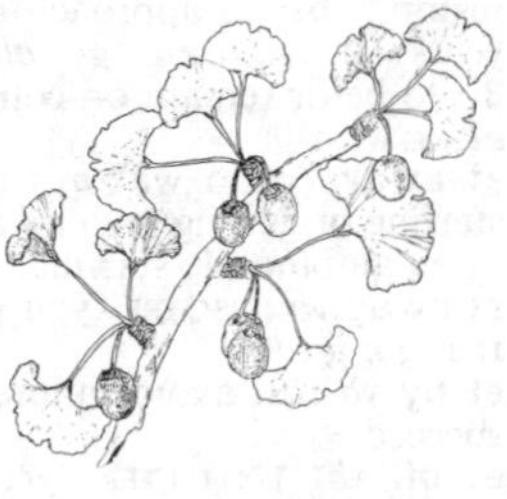

ginkgo

gin rummy *n* **:** a rummy game for two players in which a player may win a hand by matching all his cards

gin·seng \'jin-,sang, -,seng\ *n* **1 :** a perennial Chinese herb with small greenish flowers in a rounded cluster and scarlet berries; *also* **:** a closely related No. American herb **2 :** the forked aromatic root of the ginseng used in oriental medicine

Gipsy *var of* GYPSY

gi·raffe \jə-'raf\ *n, pl* **giraffe** *or* **giraffes** [from Italian *giraffa*, from Arabic *zarāfah*] **:** a large fleet cud-chewing long-necked spotted African mammal that is the tallest of living four-footed animals

giraffe
(up to 18 ft. tall)

gird \'gərd\ *vb* **gird·ed** *or* **girt** \'gərt\; **gird·ing 1 :** to encircle or fasten with or as if with a belt or cord **:** GIRDLE ⟨*gird* on a sword⟩ **2 :** to invest esp. with power or authority **3 :** to make ready **:** BRACE ⟨*girded* themselves for a struggle⟩

gird·er \'gərd-ər\ *n* **:** a horizontal main supporting beam

1gir·dle \'gərd-əl\ *n* **1 :** a belt or sash encircling the waist **2 :** a woman's supporting undergarment that extends from the waist to below the hips **3 :** a bony arch for the support of a limb **4 :** a ring made by the removal of the bark and cambium around a plant stem

2girdle *vb* **gir·dled**; **gir·dling** \'gərd-(ə-)ling\ **1 :** to bind or encircle with or as if with a girdle **:** CIRCLE **2 :** to cut a girdle around (a plant)

girl \'gərl\ *n* **1 a :** a female child **b :** a young woman **2 :** a female servant **3 :** GIRL FRIEND 2 — **girl·hood** \-,hu̇d\ *n* — **girl·ish** \'gər-lish\ *adj* — **girl·ish·ness** *n*

girl friend *n* **1 :** a female friend **2 :** a girl who is a regular companion of a male and the object of his affections

ə abut	ər further	a back	ā bake
ä cot, cart	au̇ out	ch chin	e less	ē easy
g gift	i trip	ī life	j joke	ng sing	ō flow
ȯ flaw	ȯi coin	th thin	th this	ü loot
u̇ foot	y yet	yü few	yu̇ furious	zh vision

girl scout *n* : a member of the Girl Scouts of the United States of America
girt \'gərt\ *vb* **1** : GIRD **2** : to fasten by means of a girth
girth \'gərth\ *n* **1** : a band around the body of an animal to fasten something (as a saddle) upon its back **2** : a measure around a body ⟨a man of large *girth*⟩ ⟨the *girth* of a tree trunk⟩ — **girth** *vb*
gist \'jist\ *n* : the main point of a subject : DRIFT
[1]**give** \'giv\ *vb* **gave** \'gāv\; **giv·en** \'giv-ən\; **giv·ing 1** : to make a present of or to ⟨*gave* him a book⟩ **2 a** : GRANT, BESTOW **b** : to make a donation ⟨*give* blood⟩ ⟨we already *gave* at the office⟩ **c** : to accord or yield to another ⟨*gave* her confidence to him⟩ **3 a** : to put into the possession or keeping of another : HAND **b** : to offer to another : PROFFER ⟨*gave* his hand to the visitor⟩ **c** : DELIVER; *esp* : to deliver in exchange **d** : PAY ⟨*give* a fair price⟩ **4 a** : to present in public performance ⟨*give* a concert⟩ **b** : to present to view ⟨*gave* the signal to start⟩ **5** : to provide by way of entertainment ⟨*give* a party⟩ **6** : to designate as a share or portion : ALLOT **7** : ATTRIBUTE, ASCRIBE ⟨*gave* all the glory to God⟩ **8** : PRODUCE ⟨cows *give* milk⟩ ⟨84 divided by 12 *gives* 7⟩ **9 a** : to deliver by some bodily action ⟨*gave* him a push⟩ **b** : to carry out a movement : EXECUTE ⟨*gave* a sudden leap⟩ **c** : UTTER, PRONOUNCE ⟨*give* judgment⟩ **10** : to offer for consideration or acceptance ⟨*gives* no reason for his absence⟩ **11** : to apply fully : DEVOTE ⟨*gave* himself to the cause⟩ **12** : to cause to have ⟨*gave* pleasure to the reader⟩ **13** : to yield or collapse under force or pressure ⟨the bank *gave* under his foot⟩ — **giv·er** *n*
syn GIVE, PRESENT, DONATE can mean to pass over freely to another. GIVE applies to delivering in any manner; PRESENT suggests more ceremony or formality; DONATE implies a free contribution (as to a charity)
— **give it to** : to attack vigorously ⟨*gave it to* him right between the eyes⟩ — **give way 1** : RETREAT **2** : to lose control of oneself **3** : COLLAPSE
[2]**give** *n* : tendency to yield to force or strain; *esp* : SPRINGINESS
give·away \'giv-ə-ˌwā\ *n* **1** : an unintentional revelation or betrayal **2** : a radio or television program on which prizes are given away
give away \ˌgiv-ə-'wā\ *vb* **1** : to deliver (a bride) to the bridegroom at a wedding **2 a** : BETRAY **b** : DISCLOSE, REVEAL
give in *vb* : to yield to insistence or entreaty : SURRENDER
giv·en \'giv-ən\ *adj* **1** : INCLINED, DISPOSED ⟨*given* to swearing⟩ **2** : SPECIFIED, FIXED ⟨at a *given* time⟩ **3** : granted as true : ASSUMED
given name *n* : FORENAME
give off *vb* : EMIT
give out *vb* **1** : EMIT **2** : to become exhausted : COLLAPSE **3** : to break down
give up *vb* **1** : SURRENDER **2** : to abandon (oneself) to a feeling, influence, or activity **3** : STOP
giz·zard \'giz-ərd\ *n* : a muscular enlargement of the digestive canal (as of a bird) that follows the crop and has usu. a horny lining for grinding the food
Gk *abbr* Greek
gla·cial \'glā-shəl\ *adj* **1 a** : extremely cold : FRIGID **b** : lacking warmth and cordiality **2 a** : of, relating to, or produced by glaciers **b** : of, relating to, or being any of those parts of geologic time when a large portion of the earth was covered by glaciers **c** *cap* : PLEISTOCENE
gla·ci·a·tion \ˌglā-s(h)ē-'ā-shən\ *n* : the condition of being covered by ice caps or glaciers
gla·cier \'glā-shər\ *n* : a large body of ice moving slowly down a slope or valley or spreading outward on a land surface
gla·ci·ol·o·gy \ˌglā-s(h)ē-'äl-ə-jē\ *n* : a branch of geology dealing with snow or ice accumulation, glaciation, or glacial epochs — **gla·ci·ol·o·gist** \-jəst\ *n*
glad \'glad\ *adj* **glad·der**; **glad·dest 1 a** : experiencing pleasure, joy, or delight : made happy **b** : GRATIFIED, PLEASED **c** : very willing ⟨*glad* to do it⟩ **2** : causing happiness and joy : PLEASANT ⟨*glad* tidings⟩ **3** : BRIGHT, GAY — **glad·den** \'glad-ən\ *vb* — **glad·ly** *adv* — **glad·ness** *n*
glade \'glād\ *n* : a grassy open space in a forest
glad·i·a·tor \'glad-ē-ˌāt-ər\ *n* [from Latin, meaning literally "swordsman", from *gladius* "sword"] **1** : a person engaged in a fight to the death for public entertainment in ancient Rome **2** : a person engaging in a fierce fight or controversy — **glad·i·a·to·ri·al** \ˌglad-ē-ə-'tōr-ē-əl, -'tȯr-\ *adj*
glad·i·o·lus \ˌglad-ē-'ō-ləs\ *n, pl* **-o·li** \-'ō-(ˌ)lē, -'ō-ˌlī; -ə-ˌlī\ *or* **-o·lus** *or* **-o·lus·es** [from Latin, diminutive of *gladius* "sword"] **1** : any of a genus of chiefly African plants related to the irises and having erect sword-shaped leaves and spikes of brilliantly colored irregular flowers **2** : the flower of a gladiolus plant
glad·some \'glad-səm\ *adj* : giving or showing joy : CHEERFUL — **glad·some·ly** *adv* — **glad·some·ness** *n*
glam·our *or* **glam·or** \'glam-ər\ *n* : romantic, exciting, and often illusory attractiveness — **glam·or·ize** \'glam-ə-ˌrīz\ *vb* — **glam·or·ous** \-rəs\ *adj* — **glam·or·ous·ly** *adv* — **glam·or·ous·ness** *n*
[1]**glance** \'glan(t)s\ *vb* **1** : to strike and fly off at an angle ⟨the arrow *glanced* off the shield⟩ **2** : to give a quick or hasty look ⟨*glanced* at his watch⟩ ⟨*glanced* up from a book⟩ **3** : GLINT — **glanc·ing·ly** \'glan(t)-sing-lē\ *adv*
[2]**glance** *n* **1** : a quick intermittent flash or gleam **2** : a deflected impact or blow **3 a** : a swift movement of the eyes **b** : a quick or hasty look
gland \'gland\ *n* : a cell or group of cells that prepares and secretes a product (as saliva, sweat, bile, or shell) for further use in the body or for elimination from the body
glan·ders \'glan-dərz\ *n sing or pl* : a destructive bacterial disease esp. of horses
glan·du·lar \'glan-jə-lər\ *adj* **1** : of, relating to, or involving glands, gland cells, or their products **2** : having the characteristics or function of a gland — **glan·du·lar·ly** *adv*
glans \'glanz\ *n, pl* **glan·des** \'glan-ˌdēz\ : a conical vascular body forming the extremity of the penis or clitoris
[1]**glare** \'gla(ə)r, 'gle(ə)r\ *vb* **1 a** : to shine with a harsh uncomfortably brilliant light **b** : to stand out offensively : OBTRUDE **2** : to stare angrily or fiercely — **glare** *n* — **glary** \'gla(ə)r-ē, 'gle(ə)r-\ *adj*
[2]**glare** *n* : a smooth slippery surface or sheet of ice
glar·ing *adj* : painfully obvious ⟨a *glaring* mistake⟩ — **glar·ing·ly** \-ing-lē\ *adv* — **glar·ing·ness** *n*
[1]**glass** \'glas\ *n* **1** : a hard brittle usu. transparent substance commonly formed by melting a mixture (as of silica sand and metallic oxides) and cooling to a rigid condition **2 a** : something (as a water tumbler, lens, mirror, barometer, or telescope) that is made of glass or has a glass lens **b** *pl* : a pair of glass lenses used to correct defects of vision **3** : the quantity held by a glass — **glass·ful** \-ˌfu̇l\ *n* — **glass·ware** \-ˌwa(ə)r, -ˌwe(ə)r\ *n*
[2]**glass** *vb* : to fit or protect with glass

G

glass·blow·ing \-ˌblō-ing\ *n* : the art of shaping a mass of hot glass by blowing air into it through a tube — **glass·blow·er** \-ˌblō(-ə)r\ *n*

glass snake *n* : a limbless lizard of the southern U.S. resembling a snake and having a fragile tail that readily breaks into pieces

glass wool *n* : glass fibers in a mass resembling wool and being used esp. for thermal insulation and air filters

glassy \'glas-ē\ *adj* **glass·i·er**; **-est 1** : resembling glass **2** : DULL, LIFELESS ⟨*glassy* eyes⟩ — **glass·i·ly** \'glas-ə-lē\ *adv* — **glass·i·ness** \'glas-ē-nəs\ *n*

1glaze \'glāz\ *vb* **1** : to furnish or fit with glass **2** : to coat with or as if with glass **3** : to become glazed — **glaz·er** *n*

2glaze *n* **1** : a smooth slippery coating of thin ice **2 a** : a transparent or translucent substance used as a coating (as on food or pottery) to produce a gloss **b** : a smooth glossy finish

gla·zier \'glā-zhər\ *n* : a person who sets glass in window frames

gleam \'glēm\ *n* **1** : a small briefly visible light : GLINT **2** : a brief or faint appearance : TRACE ⟨*gleam* of hope⟩ — **gleam** *vb*

glean \'glēn\ *vb* **1** : to gather from a field or vineyard what has been left (as by reapers) **2** : to gather little by little ⟨*glean* knowledge from books⟩ — **glean·er** *n*

glean·ings \'glē-ningz\ *n pl* : things acquired by gleaning

glee \'glē\ *n* **1** : exultant high-spirited joy **2** : an unaccompanied song for three or more voices — **glee·ful** \'glē-fəl\ *adj* — **glee·ful·ly** \-fə-lē\ *adv* — **glee·ful·ness** *n*

glee club *n* : a chorus organized for singing usu. short choral pieces

glen \'glen\ *n* : a small secluded narrow valley

glib \'glib\ *adj* **glib·ber**; **glib·best** : speaking or spoken with careless ease and often with little regard for truth ⟨a *glib* excuse⟩ — **glib·ly** *adv* — **glib·ness** *n*

glide \'glīd\ *vb* **1** : to move smoothly, continuously, and effortlessly **2** : to descend at a normal angle without engine power sufficient for level flight ⟨*glide* in an airplane⟩ — **glide** *n*

glid·er \'glīd-ər\ *n* **1** : an aircraft without an engine that glides on air currents **2** : a porch seat suspended from a frame by short chains or straps

gliding joint *n* : a movable joint of the body in which one surface glides over the other without any angular or rotatory motion

glim·mer \'glim-ər\ *n* **1 a** : a feeble or intermittent light **b** : a soft shimmer **2 a** : a faint idea : INKLING **b** : a small amount : BIT — **glimmer** *vb*

1glimpse \'glim(p)s\ *vb* : to take a brief look : see momentarily or incompletely — **glimps·er** *n*

2glimpse *n* **1** : a short hurried view ⟨catch a *glimpse* of something rushing by⟩ **2** : a faint idea : GLIMMER

glint \'glint\ *vb* : to shine by reflection: **a** : to shine with small bright flashes **b** : GLITTER **c** : GLEAM — **glint** *n*

gliss *abbr* glissando

glis·san·do \gli-'sän-dō\ *n, pl* **-di** \-(ˌ)dē\ *or* **-dos** : a rapid sliding up or down the musical scale

glis·ten \'glis-ən\ *vb* **glis·tened**; **glis·ten·ing** \-(ə-)ning\ : to shine by reflection with a soft luster or sparkle — **glisten** *n*

glis·ter \'glis-tər\ *vb* **glis·tered**; **glis·ter·ing** \-t(ə-)ring\ : GLISTEN — **glister** *n*

1glit·ter \'glit-ər\ *vb* **1** : to shine with brilliant or metallic luster ⟨*glittering* sequins⟩ **2** : SPARKLE **3** : to shine with a cold glassy brilliance ⟨eyes *glittered* cruelly⟩

2glitter *n* **1** : sparkling brilliancy **2** : small glittering objects used for ornamentation — **glit·tery** \'glit-ə-rē\ *adj*

gloam·ing \'glō-ming\ *n* : TWILIGHT, DUSK

gloat \'glōt\ *vb* : to gaze at or think about something with great satisfaction or joy ⟨*gloating* over his enemy's loss⟩ — **gloat·er** *n*

glob \'gläb\ *n* : a small drop : BLOB

glob·al \'glō-bəl\ *adj* **1** : SPHERICAL **2** : WORLDWIDE ⟨*global* war⟩ — **glob·al·ly** \-bə-lē\ *adv*

globe \'glōb\ *n* : something spherical or rounded: as **a** : a spherical model of the earth or heavens **b** : EARTH — usu. used with *the* — **glob·u·lar** \'gläb-yə-lər\ *adj*

glob·ule \'gläb-yül\ *n* : a tiny globe or ball ⟨*globules* of fat⟩

glob·u·lin \'gläb-yə-lən\ *n* : any of a class of simple proteins insoluble in pure water but soluble in dilute salt solutions that occur widely in plant and animal tissues

glock·en·spiel \'gläk-ən-ˌs(h)pēl\ *n* [from German, meaning literally "bell play"] : a percussion instrument consisting of a series of metal bars played with two hammers

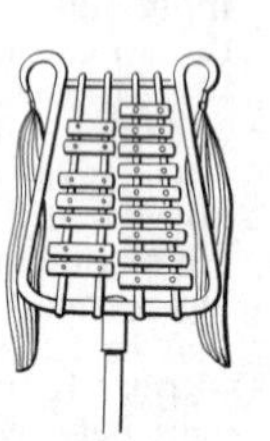
glockenspiel

1gloom \'glüm\ *vb* **1** : to look sullen or despondent **2** : to be or become overcast

2gloom *n* **1** : partial or total darkness **2 a** : pervasive lowness of spirits : DESPONDENCY **b** : an atmosphere of despair *syn* see MELANCHOLY *ant* glee — **gloom·i·ly** \-mə-lē\ *adv* — **gloom·i·ness** \-mē-nəs\ *n* — **gloomy** \'glü-mē\ *adj*

Glo·ria Pa·tri \ˌglōr-ē-ə-'pä-(ˌ)trē, ˌglȯr-\ *n* : a Christian doxology beginning "Glory be to the Father"

glo·ri·fy \'glōr-ə-ˌfī, 'glȯr-\ *vb* **-fied**; **-fy·ing 1** : WORSHIP, ADORE **2** : to praise highly or to the utmost **3** : to present in a highly often overly favorable light ⟨*glorify* war⟩ — **glo·ri·fi·ca·tion** \ˌglōr-ə-fə-'kā-shən, ˌglȯr-\ *n* — **glo·ri·fi·er** \'glōr-ə-ˌfī(-ə)r, 'glȯr-\ *n*

glo·ri·ous \'glōr-ē-əs, 'glȯr-\ *adj* **1 a** : possessing or deserving glory : ILLUSTRIOUS **b** : conferring glory ⟨*glorious* victory⟩ **2** : RESPLENDENT, MAGNIFICENT ⟨a *glorious* sunset⟩ **3** : DELIGHTFUL — **glo·ri·ous·ly** *adv* — **glo·ri·ous·ness** *n*

1glo·ry \'glōr-ē, 'glȯr-\ *n, pl* **glories 1 a** : praise, honor, or distinction extended by common consent : RENOWN **b** : worshipful praise, honor, and thanksgiving **2 a** : something that brings praise or renown **b** : a brilliant asset **3 a** : RESPLENDENCE, MAGNIFICENCE **b** : the splendor and bliss of heaven **4** : a height of prosperity or achievement

2glory *vb* : to rejoice proudly : EXULT

1gloss \'gläs, 'glȯs\ *n* **1** : brightness from a smooth surface : LUSTER, SHEEN **2** : a deceptively attractive appearance ⟨a thin *gloss* of good manners⟩

2gloss *vb* **1** : to give a deceptive appearance to **2** : to pass over quickly in an attempt to ignore ⟨*gloss* over one's mistakes⟩

gloss *abbr* glossary

ə abut	ər further	a back	ā bake	
ä cot, cart	aù out	ch chin	e less	ē easy
g gift	i trip	ī life	j joke	ng sing
ō flow	ȯ flaw	ȯi coin	th thin	th this
ü loot	ù foot	y yet	yü few	yù furious
zh vision				

glos·sa·ry \'gläs-(ə-)rē, 'glòs-\ *n, pl* **-ries** **1 :** a list of the hard or unusual words found in a book **2 :** a dictionary of the special terms in a particular field
glossy \'gläs-ē, 'glòs-\ *adj* **gloss·i·er**; **-est :** having a superficial luster or brightness — **gloss·i·ness** *n*
glot·tis \'glät-əs\ *n, pl* **glot·tis·es** *or* **glot·ti·des** \'glät-ə-ˌdēz\ **:** the elongated opening between the vocal cords in the larynx — **glot·tal** \'glät-əl\ *adj*
glove \'gləv\ *n* **1 :** a covering for the hand having separate sections for each finger **2 a :** a padded leather covering for the hand used in baseball **b :** BOXING GLOVE — **gloved** \'gləvd\ *adj*
[1]**glow** \'glō\ *vb* **1 :** to shine with or as if with an intense heat **:** give off light without flame ⟨*glowing* coals⟩ **2 :** to have a rich warm usu. ruddy color **3 :** to be or look warm and flushed (as from exercise, feeling, or excitement) ⟨*glow* with pride⟩
[2]**glow** *n* **1 :** brightness or warmth of color ⟨a rosy *glow* of health⟩ **2 a :** warmth of emotion **b :** a sensation of warmth **3 :** light such as is emitted by something that is intensely hot but not flaming
glow·er \'glau̇(-ə)r\ *vb* **:** GLARE, SCOWL — **glower** *n*
glow·worm \'glō-ˌwərm\ *n* **:** an insect or insect larva that gives off light
gloze \'glōz\ *vb* **:** to make appear right or acceptable **:** GLOSS ⟨*gloze* over a person's faults⟩
glu·cose \'glü-ˌkōs\ *n* **1 :** a sugar known in three different forms and found esp. in blood, plant sap, and fruits; *esp* **:** DEXTROSE **2 :** CORN SYRUP
[1]**glue** \'glü\ *n* **1 :** any of various strong adhesive substances; *esp* **:** a hard protein substance that absorbs water to form a viscous solution with strong adhesive properties and is obtained by cooking down animal materials (as hides or bones) **2 :** a solution of glue used to stick things together — **glu·ey** \'glü-ē\ *adj*
[2]**glue** *vb* **glued**; **glu·ing** *also* **glue·ing :** to make fast with or as if with glue
glum \'gləm\ *adj* **glum·mer**; **glum·mest** **1 :** MOROSE, SULLEN **2 :** GLOOMY — **glum·ly** *adv* — **glum·ness** *n*
[1]**glut** \'glət\ *vb* **glut·ted**; **glut·ting** **1 :** to fill with food to the point of discomfort **:** STUFF **2 :** to flood with an excess supply ⟨the market was *glutted* with fruit⟩
[2]**glut** *n* **:** an excessive quantity **:** OVERSUPPLY
glu·tam·ic acid \glü-ˌtam-ik-\ *n* **:** an amino acid widely distributed in plant and animal proteins and used in the form of a sodium salt as a seasoning
glu·ten \'glüt-ən\ *n* **:** a tough elastic protein substance in flour esp. from wheat that holds together dough and makes it sticky
glu·ti·nous \'glüt-(ə-)nəs\ *adj* **:** resembling glue **:** STICKY — **glu·ti·nous·ly** *adv*
glut·ton \'glət-ən\ *n* **1 :** one that eats too much **2 a :** a shaggy thickset carnivorous mammal of northern Europe and Asia related to the marten and the sable **b :** WOLVERINE — **glut·ton·ous** \'glət-(ə-)nəs\ *adj* — **glut·ton·ous·ly** *adv*
glut·tony \'glət-(ə-)nē\ *n, pl* **-ton·ies :** excess in eating or drinking
glyc·er·in *or* **glyc·er·ine** \'glis-(ə-)rən\ *n* **:** GLYCEROL
glyc·er·ol \'glis-ə-ˌrȯl, -ˌrōl\ *n* **:** a sweet colorless syrupy alcohol usu. obtained from fats and oils and used esp. as a solvent and in making explosives
glyc·er·yl stearate \ˌglis-ə-rəl-\ *n* **:** STEARIN 1
gly·co·gen \'glī-kə-jən\ *n* **:** a white tasteless substance that is the chief storage carbohydrate of animals
gm *abbr* gram
GM *abbr* general manager
G–man \'jē-ˌman\ *n* [probably short for *Government man*] **:** a special agent of the Federal Bureau of Investigation
gnarl \'närl\ *n* **:** a large or hard knot in wood or on a tree — **gnarled** \'närld\ *adj* — **gnarly** \'när-lē\ *adj*
gnash \'nash\ *vb* **:** to strike or grind the teeth together
gnat \'nat\ *n* **:** any of various small usu. biting two-winged flies
gnaw \'nȯ\ *vb* **1 a :** to bite or chew with the teeth; *esp* **:** to wear away by persistent biting or nibbling ⟨dog *gnawing* a bone⟩ **b :** to make by gnawing ⟨rats *gnawed* a hole⟩ **2 a :** VEX, IRRITATE **b :** to affect like gnawing ⟨*gnawing* hunger⟩ — **gnaw·er** \'nȯ(-ə)r\ *n*

gnat (about 1/4 in. long)

gneiss \'nīs\ *n* **:** a rock in layers that is similar in composition to granite or feldspar
gnome \'nōm\ *n* **:** a dwarf of folklore living inside the earth and guarding precious ore or treasure — **gnom·ish** \'nō-mish\ *adj*
gno·mon \'nō-ˌmän, -mən\ *n* **:** an object that by the position or length of its shadow serves as an indicator of the hour of the day; *esp* **:** the style of an ordinary sundial
GNP *abbr* gross national product
gnu \'n(y)ü\ *n, pl* **gnu** *or* **gnus :** any of several large African antelopes with a head like that of an ox, short mane, long tail, and horns in both sexes that curve downward and outward

gnu (less than 4 ft. at shoulder)

[1]**go** \'gō\ *vb* **went** \'went\; **gone** \'gȯn, 'gän\; **go·ing** \'gō-iŋ\; **goes** \'gōz\ **1 :** to move on a course **:** PROCEED ⟨*go* slow⟩ ⟨*go* by way of Dubuque⟩ **2 a :** to move away from one point to or toward another **:** LEAVE, DEPART **b :** FOLLOW, TRAVERSE ⟨*go* the whole route⟩ ⟨*go* my way⟩ **c :** to leave one's home ⟨*gone* for the day⟩ ⟨just *going* out⟩ **3 a :** to pass by a process like journeying ⟨the message *went* by wire⟩ ⟨the prize *went* to the winner⟩ **b** (1) **:** EXTEND, RUN ⟨his land *goes* to the river⟩ (2) **:** to give access **:** LEAD ⟨that door *goes* to the cellar⟩ **4 :** to be habitually in a certain state ⟨*goes* bareheaded⟩ ⟨*goes* armed after dark⟩ **5 a :** to become lost, consumed, or spent ⟨funds *going* for research⟩ **b :** ELAPSE, PASS ⟨where did the time *go*⟩ **c :** to pass by sale ⟨*went* for a good price⟩ **d :** to become impaired or weakened ⟨his hearing started to *go*⟩ **e :** to give way under force or pressure **:** BREAK **6 a :** to take place **:** HAPPEN ⟨what's *going* on⟩ **b :** to be in general or on an average ⟨cheap, as yachts *go*⟩ **c :** to become esp. as the result of a contest ⟨decision *went* against him⟩ **7 :** to put or subject oneself ⟨*go* to great expense⟩ **8 :** to have recourse **:** RESORT ⟨*go* to court to recover damages⟩ **9 a :** to begin or maintain an action or motion ⟨*go* when the light turns⟩ ⟨drums *going* strong⟩ **b :** to function properly ⟨get the motor to *go*⟩ **10 :** to have currency **:** CIRCULATE ⟨the report *goes*⟩ **11 :** to be or act in accordance ⟨a good rule to *go* by⟩ **12 :** to contribute to a result ⟨qualities that *go* to make a hero⟩ **13 a :** to be about, intending, or expecting ⟨is *going* to leave town⟩ **b :** to come or arrive at a certain state

or condition ⟨*go* to sleep⟩ **c** : to come to be ⟨the tire *went* flat⟩ **14 a** : FIT ⟨these clothes will *go* in your suitcase⟩ **b** : to have a usual or proper place : BELONG ⟨these books *go* on the top shelf⟩ **c** : to be capable of being contained in another quantity ⟨5 *goes* into 60 12 times⟩ **15** : TEND, CONDUCE ⟨*goes* to show he can be trusted⟩ **16** : to be acceptable : DO ⟨any kind of dress *goes*⟩ **17** : BET, BID ⟨willing to *go* $50⟩ — **go at 1** : ATTACK **2** : UNDERTAKE — **go back on** : BETRAY — **go for 1** : to pass for or serve as **2** : to have an interest in or liking for : FAVOR — **go in for** : to take part in out of interest or liking ⟨*go in for* stamp collecting⟩ — **go one better** : OUTDO, SURPASS — **go over 1** : STUDY, REVIEW **2** : REVISE — **go places** : to be on the way to success — **go steady** : to date one person exclusively and frequently — **go through 1** : EXAMINE, STUDY **2** : EXPERIENCE, UNDERGO **3** : to carry out : PERFORM ⟨*went through* his act perfectly⟩ — **to go 1** : REMAINING, LEFT ⟨five minutes *to go*⟩ **2** : to be taken from a restaurant ⟨ham sandwich *to go*⟩

2**go** *n, pl* **goes 1** : the height of fashion ⟨that dress is all the *go*⟩ **2** : ENERGY, VIGOR ⟨full of *go*⟩ **3 a** : ATTEMPT, TRY ⟨have a *go* at it⟩ **b** : a spell of activity ⟨did it in one *go*⟩ **c** : SUCCESS ⟨make a *go* of a business⟩ — **no go** : to no avail : USELESS — **on the go** : constantly or restlessly active

3**go** *adj* : ready to go : fully prepared ⟨everything is *go* for launch⟩

goad \'gōd\ *n* **1** : a pointed rod used to urge an animal on **2** : something that urges : SPUR — **goad** *vb*

goal \'gōl\ *n* **1** : the terminal point of a race **2** : the end toward which effort is directed : AIM **3 a** : an area or object toward which players in various games attempt to advance a ball or puck to score points **b** : the score resulting from such an act

goal·keep·er \-,kē-pər\ *n* : a player who defends the goal in various games — called also *goal·ie* \'gō-lē\, *goal·tend·er* \'gōl-,ten-dər\

goal·post \'gōl-,pōst\ *n* : one of two vertical posts that with a crossbar constitute the goal in various games

goat \'gōt\ *n, pl* **goat** *or* **goats 1** : any of various hollow-horned cud-chewing mammals related to the sheep but of lighter build and with backwardly arching horns, a short tail, and usu. straight hair **2** : SCAPEGOAT — **goat·like** \'gōt-,līk\ *adj*

goa·tee \gō-'tē\ *n* : a small trim pointed or tufted beard on a man's chin

goat·herd \'gōt-,hərd\ *n* : a person who tends goats

goat·skin \-,skin\ *n* : the skin of a goat or a leather made from it

goat·suck·er \-,sək-ər\ *n* : any of various medium-sized long-winged insect-eating nocturnal birds (as the whippoorwills and nighthawks) having a short wide bill, short legs, and soft mottled plumage

1**gob** \'gäb\ *n* **1** : LUMP, MASS **2** : a large amount — usu. used in pl. ⟨*gobs* of money⟩

2**gob** *n* : SAILOR

gob·bet \'gäb-ət\ *n* : LUMP, MASS

1**gob·ble** \'gäb-əl\ *vb* **gob·bled**; **gob·bling** \-(ə-)liŋ\ **1** : to swallow or eat greedily **2** : to take eagerly : GRAB — usu. used with *up*

2**gobble** *vb* : to make the natural guttural noise of a male turkey — **gobble** *n*

ə abut	ər further	a back		ā bake
ä cot, cart	aü out	ch chin	e less	ē easy
g gift	i trip	ī life	j joke	ŋ sing	ō flow
ȯ flaw	ȯi coin	th thin	th this	ü loot
u̇ foot	y yet	yü few	yu̇ furious	zh vision

gob·ble·dy·gook *or* **gob·ble·de·gook** \,gäb-əl-dē-'gu̇k\ *n* : GIBBERISH

gob·bler \'gäb-lər\ *n* : a male turkey

go–be·tween \'gō-bə-,twēn\ *n* : a person who acts as a messenger or an intermediary between two parties

gob·let \'gäb-lət\ *n* : a drinking glass with a foot and stem

gob·lin \'gäb-lən\ *n* : a grotesque, evil, or mischievous sprite

go–cart \'gō-,kärt\ *n* **1** : STROLLER **2** : a light open carriage

1**god** \'gäd, 'gȯd\ *n* **1** : a being possessing more than human powers ⟨ancient peoples worshiped many *gods*⟩ **2** : a physical object (as an image or idol) worshiped as divine **3** : something held to be the most important thing in existence ⟨make a *god* of money⟩ — **god·hood** \-,hu̇d\ *n* — **god·like** \-,līk\ *adj*

2**God** *n* : the supreme or ultimate reality; *esp* : the Being perfect in power, wisdom, and goodness whom men worship as creator and ruler of the universe

god·child \-,chīld\ *n* : a person for whom another person stands as sponsor at baptism

god·daugh·ter \-,dȯt-ər\ *n* : a female godchild

god·dess \'gäd-əs\ *n* **1** : a female god **2** : a woman whose great charm or beauty arouses adoration

god·fa·ther \'gäd-,fäth-ər, 'gȯd-\ *n* : a male godparent

god·for·sak·en \-fər-,sā-kən\ *adj* : REMOTE, DESOLATE ⟨the most *godforsaken* hole in the world⟩

god·head \-,hed\ *n* **1** : divine nature : DIVINITY **2** *cap* : 2GOD

god·less \'gäd-ləs, 'gȯd-\ *adj* : not acknowledging a deity or divine law — **god·less·ness** *n*

god·ly \-lē\ *adj* **god·li·er**; **-est** : PIOUS, DEVOUT ⟨a *godly* man⟩ — **god·li·ness** *n*

god·moth·er \-,məth-ər\ *n* : a female godparent

god·par·ent \-,par-ənt, -,per-\ *n* : a sponsor at baptism

god·send \-,send\ *n* : a desirable or needed thing or event that comes unexpectedly

god·son \-,sən\ *n* : a male godchild

God·speed \-'spēd\ *n* : a wish for success given to a person on parting

go·er \'gō(-ə)r\ *n* : one that goes

goes *pres 3d sing of* GO, *pl of* GO

go–get·ter \'gō-,get-ər\ *n* : an aggressively enterprising person : HUSTLER — **go–get·ting** \-,get-iŋ\ *adj or n*

1**gog·gle** \'gäg-əl\ *vb* **gog·gled**; **gog·gling** \-(ə-)liŋ\ : to stare with goggle eyes — **gog·gler** \-(ə-)lər\ *n*

2**goggle** *adj* : PROTUBERANT, STARING ⟨*goggle* eyes⟩ — **gog·gly** \'gäg-(ə-)lē\ *adj* — **gog·gle–eyed** \,gäg-əl-'īd\ *adj*

gog·gles \'gäg-əlz\ *n pl* : protective eyeglasses typically with shields at the side

go–go \'gō-,gō\ *adj* : of, relating to, featuring, or being dances or dancers typical of a discotheque ⟨*go-go* girl⟩ ⟨*go-go* club⟩

1**go·ing** \'gō-iŋ\ *n* **1** : DEPARTURE **2** : the condition of the ground esp. for walking or driving **3** : advance toward an objective : PROGRESS

2**going** *adj* **1** : EXISTING, LIVING ⟨best novelist *going*⟩ **2** : CURRENT, PREVAILING ⟨*going* price⟩ **3** : being successful and likely to continue successful ⟨a *going* concern⟩

go·ings–on \,gō-iŋz-'ȯn, -'än\ *n pl* : ACTIONS, EVENTS

goi·ter *also* **goi·tre** \'gȯit-ər\ *n* **1** : an enlargement of the thyroid gland visible as a swelling of the front of the neck **2** : a diseased condition characterized by enlargement of the thyroid gland

gold \'gōld\ *n* **1** : a malleable ductile yellow metallic element that occurs chiefly free but also in a few minerals and is used esp. in coins and jewelry — see ELEMENT table **2 a** : gold coins **b** : MONEY **3** : a variable color averaging deep yellow — **gold** *adj*
gold·brick \'gōl(d)-ˌbrik\ *n* : a person (as a soldier) who shirks assigned work — **goldbrick** *vb*
gold·en \'gōl-dən\ *adj* **1** : consisting of, relating to, or containing gold **2** : having the color of gold ⟨*golden* hair⟩ **3** : FLOURISHING, PROSPEROUS ⟨a *golden* age⟩ **4** : of precious rarity ⟨a *golden* opportunity⟩ **5** : MELLOW, RESONANT ⟨smooth *golden* tenor⟩
gold·en–ag·er \-ˌā-jər\ *n* : an elderly person; *esp* : one leading an active contented life
golden eagle *n* : a large and powerful eagle of the northern hemisphere that has brownish yellow tips on head and neck feathers
golden glow *n* : a tall branching herb related to the daisies that has showy yellow many-petaled flowers
golden mean *n* : the medium between extremes : MODERATION
golden plover *n* : any of a group of migratory plovers that in adult summer plumage are speckled golden-yellow and white above with the lower parts being black
gold·en·rod \'gōl-dən-ˌräd\ *n* : any of numerous chiefly No. American plants related to the asters that have stems resembling wands and heads of small yellow or sometimes white flowers most often in one-sided clusters
golden rule *n* : a rule that one should treat others as he would like others to treat him
gold–filled \'gōl(d)-'fild\ *adj* : covered with a layer of gold ⟨a *gold-filled* bracelet⟩
gold·finch \-ˌfinch\ *n* **1** : a small largely red, black, and yellow European finch often kept as a cage bird **2** : any of several small American finches usu. having the male in summer plumage yellow with black wings, tail, and crown
gold·fish \-ˌfish\ *n* : a small usu. golden yellow or orange carp much used as an aquarium and pond fish
gold leaf *n* : a very thin sheet of gold used esp. for gilding
gold·smith \'gōl(d)-ˌsmith\ *n* : one who makes articles of gold
golf \'gälf, 'gȯlf\ *n* : a game whose object is to sink a ball into each of 9 or 18 holes with as few strokes of a club as possible — **golf** *vb* — **golf·er** *n*
-gon \ˌgän\ *n comb form* : figure having (so many) angles ⟨deca*gon*⟩
go·nad \'gō-ˌnad\ *n* : a sperm or egg-producing gland : TESTIS, OVARY
gon·do·la \'gän-də-lə (*usual for sense 1*), gän-'dō-\ *n* **1** : a long narrow boat with a high prow and stern used on the canals of Venice **2** : a railroad car with low sides and no top used for hauling bulk commodities **3 a** : an enclosure suspended from the underside of an airship or a balloon for carrying passengers or instruments **b** : an enclosure suspended from a cable and used esp. as a lift for skiers

gondola 1

gon·do·lier \ˌgän-də-'li(ə)r\ *n* : one who propels a gondola
gone \'gȯn, 'gän\ *adj* **1 a** : ADVANCED, ABSORBED ⟨far *gone* in hysteria⟩ **b** : INFATUATED ⟨she's *gone* on him⟩ **2 a** : DEAD **b** : WEAK, SINKING ⟨a *gone* feeling from hunger⟩
gon·er \'gȯn-ər, 'gän-\ *n* : one whose case is hopeless
gong \'gäng, 'gȯng\ *n* **1** : a metallic disk that resounds when struck **2** : a flat saucer-shaped bell
gono·coc·cus \ˌgän-ə-'käk-əs\ *n, pl* **-coc·ci** \-'käk-ˌ(s)ī, -'käk-(ˌ)(s)ē\ : a pus-producing bacterium that causes gonorrhea
go–no–go \'gō-'nō-ˌgō\ *adj* **1** : being or relating to a required decision to continue or stop a course of action **2** : being or relating to a time such a decision must be made
gon·or·rhea \ˌgän-ə-'rē-ə\ *n* : a contagious inflammatory disease of the genitourinary tract caused by the gonococcus — **gon·or·rhe·al** \-'rē-əl\ *adj*
goo \'gü\ *n* : a viscid or sticky substance — **goo·ey** \'gü-ē\ *adj*
goo·ber \'gü-bər, 'gu̇b-ər\ *n, dial* : PEANUT
1**good** \'gu̇d\ *adj* **bet·ter** \'bet-ər\; **best** \'best\ **1 a** : of a favorable character or tendency ⟨*good* news⟩ **b** : BOUNTIFUL, FERTILE ⟨*good* land⟩ **c** : COMELY, ATTRACTIVE ⟨*good* looks⟩ **d** : AGREEABLE, PLEASANT ⟨a *good* place to live⟩ **e** : SUITABLE, FIT ⟨*good* to eat⟩ ⟨medicine *good* for a cold⟩ **f** : RELIABLE ⟨a *good* man in a pinch⟩ **g** : SOUND, WHOLE ⟨one *good* arm⟩ **2 a** : certain to last or live ⟨*good* for another year⟩ **b** : certain to provide or produce ⟨always *good* for a laugh⟩ **3 a** : CONSIDERABLE, AMPLE ⟨present in *good* numbers⟩ **b** : FULL ⟨*good* measure⟩ **4 a** : WELL-FOUNDED, COGENT ⟨*good* reasons⟩ **b** : TRUE ⟨holds *good* for society at large⟩ **c** : recognized or valid esp. in law ⟨member in *good* standing⟩ ⟨has a *good* title⟩ **5 a** : ADEQUATE, SATISFACTORY ⟨*good* care⟩ **b** : conforming to a standard ⟨*good* English⟩ **c** : DISCRIMINATING, CHOICE ⟨*good* taste⟩ **6 a** : VIRTUOUS, JUST ⟨a *good* man⟩ **b** : RIGHT ⟨*good* conduct⟩ **c** : KIND, BENEVOLENT ⟨*good* intentions⟩ **d** : UPPER-CLASS ⟨*good* family⟩ **e** : COMPETENT, SKILLFUL ⟨a *good* doctor⟩ **f** : LOYAL ⟨a *good* Catholic⟩ — **good·ness** *n* — **as good as** : in effect : VIRTUALLY ⟨*as good as* dead⟩ — **good and** : VERY, ENTIRELY ⟨was *good and* mad⟩

G

2**good** *n* **1** : something good, useful, or desirable ⟨health and prosperity are *goods*⟩ **2** : PROSPERITY, BENEFIT, WELFARE ⟨*good* of the community⟩ **3** *pl* : CLOTH **4** *pl* : WARES, COMMODITIES **5** : good persons — used with *the* **6** *pl* : proof of wrongdoing ⟨got the *goods* on him⟩
3**good** *adv* : WELL
good–bye *or* **good–by** \gu̇d-'bī\ *n* [a shortened and altered form of *God be with you*] : a concluding remark at parting — often used interjectionally
Good Friday *n* : the Friday before Easter observed as the anniversary of the crucifixion of Christ
good–heart·ed \'gu̇d-'härt-əd\ *adj* : having a kindly generous disposition — **good–heart·ed·ly** *adv* — **good–heart·ed·ness** *n*
good–hu·mored \-'hyü-mərd, -'yü-\ *adj* : GOOD-NATURED, CHEERFUL — **good–hu·mored·ly** *adv* — **good–hu·mored·ness** *n*
good·ish \'gu̇d-ish\ *adj* : fairly good
good·ly \'gu̇d-lē\ *adj* **good·li·er**; **-est** **1** : of pleasing appearance **2** : LARGE, CONSIDERABLE ⟨a *goodly* number⟩
good·man \'gu̇d-mən\ *n* **1** *archaic* : the head of a household : HUSBAND **2** *archaic* : MISTER
good–na·tured \'gu̇d-'nā-chərd\ *adj* : of a pleasant cheerful disposition — **good–na·tured·ly** *adv* — **good–na·tured·ness** *n*
good–sized \-'sīzd\ *adj* : fairly large
good–tem·pered \-'tem-pərd\ *adj* : having an even temper — **good–tem·pered·ly** *adv* — **good–tem·pered·ness** *n*
good·wife \'gu̇d-ˌwīf\ *n* **1** *archaic* : the mistress of a

household **2** *archaic* — used as a title equivalent to *Mrs.*

good·will \-'wil\ *n* **1** : kindly feeling : BENEVOLENCE **2** : the value of the trade a business has built up **3 a** : cheerful consent **b** : willing effort

goody \'gu̇d-ē\ *n, pl* **good·ies** : something that is particularly good to eat or otherwise attractive

goody–goody \ˌgu̇d-ē-'gu̇d-ē\ *adj* : affectedly good — **goody–goody** *n*

goof \'güf\ *vb* : BLUNDER — **goof** *n*

go off *vb* **1** : EXPLODE **2** : to take place : PROCEED ⟨the dance *went off* as planned⟩

goofy \'gü-fē\ *adj* **goof·i·er**; **-est** : CRAZY, SILLY — **goof·i·ly** \-fə-lē\ *adv* — **goof·i·ness** \-fē-nəs\ *n*

goose \'güs\ *n, pl* **geese** \'gēs\ **1 a** : any of numerous long-necked birds intermediate in size between the related swans and ducks **b** : a female goose as distinguished from a gander **2** : SIMPLETON, DOLT **3** *pl* **goos·es** : an iron with a goose-neck handle used by tailors for smoothing clothes

goose·ber·ry \'güs-ˌber-ē, 'güz-\ *n* : the acid usu. prickly fruit of any of several shrubs related to the currant

goose egg *n* : ZERO, NOTHING

goose·flesh \'güs-ˌflesh\ *n* : a roughening of the skin caused usu. by cold or fear

goose·foot *n, pl* **goosefoots** : any of numerous mostly woody smooth herbs with branched clusters of small greenish or whitish flowers without petals

goose·neck \-ˌnek\ *n* : something (as a flexible jointed metal pipe) curved like the neck of a goose or U-shaped — **goose·necked** \-ˌnekt\ *adj*

goose pimples *n pl* : GOOSEFLESH

goose step *n* : a straight-legged stiff-kneed step used by troops of some armies on parade — **goose–step** \'güs-ˌstep\ *vb*

go out *vb* : to become a candidate ⟨*went out* for the football team⟩

go over *vb* : to be favorably received : SUCCEED ⟨the joke *went over* with a bang⟩

GOP *abbr* Grand Old Party (Republican)

go·pher \'gō-fər\ *n* **1** : a burrowing American land tortoise **2 a** : any of several burrowing American rodents with large cheek pouches **b** : a small striped ground squirrel of the prairie region of the U.S.

gopher 2a
(about 14 in. long)

gopher snake *n* : BULL SNAKE

¹gore \'gō(ə)r, 'gȯ(ə)r\ *n* : BLOOD; *esp* : clotted blood

²gore *n* : a tapering or triangular piece of cloth (as in a skirt)

³gore *vb* **1** : to cut into a tapering triangular form **2** : to provide with a gore

⁴gore *vb* : to pierce or wound with or as if with a tusk

¹gorge \'gȯrj\ *n* **1** : THROAT **2** : a narrow passage (as between two mountains) **3** : a mass of matter that chokes up a passage ⟨an ice *gorge* in the river⟩

²gorge *vb* : to eat greedily : stuff oneself — **gorg·er** *n*

gor·geous \'gȯr-jəs\ *adj* : resplendently beautiful ⟨*gorgeous* sunset⟩ — **gor·geous·ly** *adv* — **gor·geous·ness** *n*

Gor·gon·zo·la \ˌgȯr-gən-'zō-lə\ *n* : a cheese of Italian origin ripened by veins of greenish blue mold

go·ril·la \gə-'ril-ə\ *n* [from Greek *Gorillai*, represent-

gorilla
(up to 6 ft. tall)

ing a name reported by 6th century B.C. Carthaginian explorers for West African creatures believed to be a race of hairy women] : the largest of the manlike apes that is closest to man in structure and is found in west equatorial Africa

gor·man·dize \'gȯr-mən-ˌdīz\ *vb* : to eat greedily or ravenously — **gor·man·diz·er** *n*

gorse \'gȯrs\ *n* : FURZE

gory \'gō(ə)r-ē, 'gȯ(ə)r-\ *adj* **gor·i·er**; **-est** **1** : covered with gore : BLOODSTAINED **2** : BLOODCURDLING

gos·hawk \'gäs-ˌhȯk\ *n* : any of several long-tailed short-winged hawks noted for their powerful flight, activity, and vigor

gos·ling \'gäz-liŋ, 'gȯz-, -lən\ *n* : a young goose

¹gos·pel \'gäs-pəl\ *n* [from Old English *gōdspel*, from *gōd* "good" and *spell* "tale", "tidings"; a translation of Greek *euangelion*; see EVANGELIST] **1 a** *often cap* : the Christian message concerning Christ, the kingdom of God, and salvation **b** *cap* : one of the first four New Testament books telling of the life, death, and resurrection of Jesus Christ **2** : something accepted as infallible truth or as a guiding principle

²gospel *adj* **1** : relating to or in accordance with the gospel : EVANGELICAL **2** : EVANGELISTIC ⟨a *gospel* team⟩ **3** : of or relating to religious songs associated with evangelism ⟨a *gospel* singer⟩

gos·sa·mer \'gäs-ə-mər, 'gäz-\ *n* **1** : a film of cobwebs floating in air **2** : something light, delicate, or tenuous — **gossamer** *adj* — **gos·sa·mery** \-mə-rē\ *adj*

¹gos·sip \'gäs-əp\ *n* **1** : a person who habitually reveals personal or sensational facts **2 a** : rumor or report of an intimate nature **b** : chatty talk — **gossip** *vb* — **gos·sip·er** *n* — **gos·sipy** \-ə-pē\ *adj*

got *past and past part of* GET

gotten *past part of* GET

¹gouge \'gau̇j\ *n* **1** : a chisel with a curved blade for scooping or cutting holes **2** : a hole or groove made with or as if with a gouge

²gouge *vb* **1** : to cut holes or grooves in with or as if with a gouge **2** : to force out (an eye) with the thumb **3** : to charge an excessive price : CHEAT — **goug·er** *n*

gou·lash \'gü-ˌläsh, -ˌlash\ *n* [from Hungarian *gulyás*, meaning first "a cowherd" (from *gulya* "herd of cattle"), and then "a stew popular with herdsmen"] : a beef stew with onion, paprika, and caraway

gourd \'gōrd, 'gȯrd, 'gu̇rd\ *n* **1** : any of a family of chiefly herbaceous tendril-bearing vines (as the cucumber, melon, squash, and pumpkin) **2** : the hard-shelled many-seeded fruit of a gourd **3** : the cleaned dried shell of the fruit of a gourd used for decoration or as a bottle, bowl, or dipper — **gourd-like** \-ˌlīk\ *adj*

gour·mand \'gu̇(ə)r-ˌmänd\ *n* **1** : GLUTTON 1 **2** : GOURMET — **gour·mand·ism** \'gu̇(ə)r-ˌmän-ˌdiz-əm, -mən-\ *n*

gour·met \-ˌmā\ *n* : a connoisseur in eating and drinking

gout \'gau̇t\ *n* **1** : a disease marked by a painful inflammation and swelling of the joints **2** : a drop or clot usu. of blood — **gouty** \-ē\ *adj*

gov *abbr* governor

gov·ern \'gəv-ərn\ *vb* [from Old French *governer*, from Latin *gubernare*, literally "to pilot", "steer", from Greek *kybernan*] **1** : to exercise authority over : RULE **2** : to control the speed of by automatic means **3 a** : to control, direct, or strongly influence the actions and conduct of **b** : to hold in check : RESTRAIN **4** : to require a word to be in a certain case or mood ⟨in English a transitive verb *governs* a pronoun in the objective case⟩ **5** : to constitute a rule or law for — **gov·ern·a·ble** \-ər-nə-bəl\ *adj*

syn GOVERN, RULE mean to exercise power over others. GOVERN implies the aim of keeping in a straight course or smooth operation for the common good; RULE more often suggests the exercise of arbitrary or despotic power

gov·ern·ance \'gəv-ər-nən(t)s\ *n* : the exercise of control : GOVERNMENT

gov·ern·ess \'gəv-ər-nəs\ *n* : a woman who teaches and trains a child esp. in a private home

gov·ern·ment \'gəv-ər(n)-mənt\ *n* **1 a** : the act or process of governing; *esp* : authoritative direction of a political unit **b** : the making of policy as distinguished from the administration of policy decisions **2 a** : the agency through which a political unit exercises authority **b** : manner of governing : the institutions, laws, and customs through which a political unit is governed ⟨republican *government*⟩ **3 a** : the officials comprising the governing body of a political unit **b** *cap* : the executive branch of the U.S. federal government **4** : POLITICAL SCIENCE — **government** *adj* — **gov·ern·men·tal** \ˌgəv-ər(n)-'ment-əl\ *adj* — **gov·ern·men·tal·ly** \-ə-lē\ *adv*

gov·er·nor \'gəv-ə(r)-nər\ *n* **1** : one that governs; *esp* : an official elected or appointed to act as ruler, chief executive, or nominal head of a political unit (as a colony, state, or province) **2** : an attachment to a machine for automatic control of speed — **gov·er·nor·ship** \-ˌship\ *n*

govt *abbr* government

gown \'gau̇n\ *n* **1** : an official robe worn esp. by a judge, clergyman, or teacher **2** : a woman's dress; *esp* : one suitable for afternoon or evening wear **3** : a loose robe (as a dressing gown or a nightgown) — **gown** *vb*

gp *abbr* group

GP *abbr* **1** games played **2** general practitioner

GPO *abbr* general post office

gr *abbr* **1** grade **2** grain **3** gram **4** gravity **5** gross

Graaf·ian follicle \ˌgräf-ē-ən-, ˌgraf-\ *n* : a vesicle in a mammal ovary enclosing a developing egg

[1]**grab** \'grab\ *vb* **grabbed**; **grab·bing** : to take hastily : CLUTCH, SNATCH — **grab·ber** *n*

[2]**grab** *n* **1 a** : a sudden snatch **b** : an unlawful or unethical seizure ⟨land *grab*⟩ **c** : something grabbed **2** : a device for clutching an object

[1]**grace** \'grās\ *n* **1 a** : help given man by God in overcoming temptation **b** : a state of freedom from sin enjoyed through divine grace **2** : a short prayer at a meal **3 a** : KINDNESS, FAVOR **b** : a temporary respite granted from the performance of an obligation (as the payment of a debt) **c** : APPROVAL, ACCEPTANCE ⟨stayed in his good *graces*⟩ **4 a** : a charming trait or quality **b** : ease of movement : charm of bearing ⟨walks with *grace*⟩ **5** — used as a title for a duke, a duchess, or an archbishop — **grace·ful** \-fəl\ *adj* — **grace·ful·ly** \-fə-lē\ *adv* — **grace·ful·ness** *n*

[2]**grace** *vb* **1** : HONOR **2** : ADORN, EMBELLISH

grace·less \'grās-ləs\ *adj* : having no grace, charm, or elegance; *esp* : showing lack of feeling for what is fitting ⟨*graceless* behavior⟩ — **grace·less·ly** *adv* — **grace·less·ness** *n*

grace note *n* : a short musical note added before another as an ornament

gra·cious \'grā-shəs\ *adj* **1** : marked by kindness and courtesy **2** : GRACEFUL **3** : characterized by charm, good taste, and urbanity ⟨*gracious* living⟩ — **gra·cious·ly** *adv* — **gra·cious·ness** *n*

grack·le \'grak-əl\ *n* : any of several rather large American blackbirds with glossy black plumage showing changeable green, purple, and bronze colors

grad *abbr* graduate

gra·da·tion \grā-'dā-shən, grə-\ *n* **1 a** : a series of grades **b** : GRADE 1 **2** : the act or process of grading — **gra·da·tion·al** \-sh(ə-)nəl\ *adj* — **gra·da·tion·al·ly** \-ē\ *adv*

[1]**grade** \'grād\ *n* **1** : a stage, step, or degree in a series, order, or ranking **2** : position in a scale of rank, quality, or order ⟨the *grade* of sergeant⟩ ⟨leather of the highest *grade*⟩ **3** : a class of things that are of the same rank, quality, or order **4 a** : a division of the school course representing a year's work ⟨finish the fourth *grade*⟩ **b** : the pupils in a school division **c** *pl* : the elementary school system ⟨teach in the *grades*⟩ **5** : a mark or rating esp. of accomplishment in school ⟨a *grade* of 90 in a test⟩ **6** : a standard of quality ⟨government *grades* for meat⟩ **7** : the rate at which something (as a road, railroad track, or embankment) slopes downward or upward

[2]**grade** *vb* **1** : to arrange in grades : SORT ⟨*grade* apples⟩ **2** : to make level or evenly sloping ⟨*grade* a highway⟩ **3** : to give a grade to ⟨*grade* a pupil in arithmetic⟩ **4** : to assign to a grade **5** : to form a series having only slight differences ⟨colors that *grade* into one another⟩

grade crossing *n* : a crossing of highways, railroad tracks, or pedestrian walks or combinations of these on the same level

grad·er \'grād-ər\ *n* **1** : one that grades **2** : a machine for leveling earth **3** : a pupil in a school grade ⟨a 5th *grader*⟩

grade school *n* : a public school including the first six or the first eight grades

gra·di·ent \'grād-ē-ənt\ *n* **1** : SLOPE, GRADE **2** : a continuous graded change in measure, activity, or substance ⟨vertical temperature *gradient* in a lake⟩ ⟨a *gradient* in developmental activity in a seedling⟩

grad·u·al \'graj-(ə-w)əl\ *adj* **1** : proceeding by steps or degrees **2** : moving or changing by slight

degrees — **grad·u·al·ly** \'graj-ə-(wə-)lē\ *adv* — **grad·u·al·ness** \'graj-(ə-w)əl-nəs\ *n*
grad·u·al·ism \'graj-ə(-wə)-ˌliz-əm\ *n* : the policy of approaching a desired end by gradual stages — **grad·u·al·ist** \-ləst\ *n or adj*
1**grad·u·ate** \'graj-ə-wət, -ˌwāt\ *n* **1** : a holder of an academic degree or diploma **2** : a graduated cup, cylinder, or flask for measuring contents
2**graduate** *adj* **1** : holding an academic degree or diploma **2** : of or relating to studies beyond the bachelor's degree
3**grad·u·ate** \'graj-ə-ˌwāt\ *vb* **1** : to grant or receive an academic degree or diploma **2** : to divide into grades, classes, or intervals ⟨*graduated* income tax⟩ ⟨*graduated* thermometer⟩ — **grad·u·a·tor** \-ˌwāt-ər\ *n*
graduate school *n* : a school or division of a university or college devoted entirely to studies beyond the bachelor's degree and having authority to grant advanced degrees
grad·u·a·tion \ˌgraj-ə-'wā-shən\ *n* **1** : a mark or the marks on an instrument or vessel indicating degrees or quantity **2 a** : an act or process of graduating **b** : the ceremony marking the completion by a student of a course of study at a school or college : COMMENCEMENT **3** : arrangement in degrees or ranks
graf·fi·to \gra-'fēt-ō\ *n, pl* **-ti** \-(ˌ)ē\ : a writing or drawing on a rock or wall
1**graft** \'graft\ *vb* **1 a** : to insert a shoot from one plant into another plant so that they are joined and grow together **b** : to join one thing to another as if by grafting ⟨*graft* skin over a scar⟩ **2** : to gain money or advantage by graft — **graft·er** *n*
2**graft** *n* **1 a** : a grafted plant **b** : the point of insertion of a scion in a plant **2 a** : the act of grafting **b** : something used in grafting: as (1) : SCION (2) : living tissue used in surgical grafting **3 a** : the getting of money or advantage by dishonest means through misuse of an official position ⟨exposed *graft* in the city government⟩ **b** : the money or advantage gained ⟨accused of taking *graft*⟩
gra·ham cracker \ˌgrā-əm-\ *n* : a slightly sweet cracker made chiefly of whole wheat flour
1**grain** \'grān\ *n* **1 a** : the seed or fruit of a cereal grass (as wheat, Indian corn, or oats) **b** : the threshed seed or fruits of various food plants (as cereal grasses, flax, peas, or sugarcane) **c** : plants producing grain **2** : a small hard particle ⟨*grain* of sand⟩ **3 a** : a granulated surface or appearance **b** : the outer or hair side of a skin or hide **4** : a unit of weight based on the weight of a grain of wheat — see MEASURE table **5 a** : the arrangement of fibers in wood **b** : appearance or texture due to constituent particles or fibers ⟨the *grain* of a rock⟩ **6** : natural disposition : TEMPER ⟨lying went against his *grain*⟩ — **grainy** \'grā-nē\ *adj* — **with a grain of salt** : with reservations : SKEPTICALLY ⟨take his predictions *with a grain of salt*⟩
2**grain** *vb* : to paint in imitation of the grain of wood or stone — **grain·er** *n*
grain alcohol *n* : ALCOHOL 1
grained \'grānd\ *adj* **1** : having, consisting of, or producing grains ⟨small-*grained* wheat⟩ **2** : having grain ⟨fine-*grained* wood⟩

ə abut	ər further	a back	ā bake	
ä cot, cart	aù out	ch chin	e less	ē easy
g gift	i trip	ī life	j joke	ng sing	ō flow
ȯ flaw	ȯi coin	th thin	th this	ü loot
ù foot	y yet	yü few	yù furious	zh vision

grain·field \'grān-ˌfēld\ *n* : a field where grain is grown
grain sorghum *n* : any of several sorghums cultivated primarily for grain — compare SORGO
gram \'gram\ *n* : a metric unit of mass and weight equal to 1/1000 kilogram and nearly equal to one cubic centimeter of water at its maximum density — see METRIC SYSTEM table
-gram \ˌgram\ *n comb form* : drawing : writing : record ⟨tele*gram*⟩
grama \'gram-ə\ *n* : a pasture grass of the western U.S.
gra·mer·cy \grə-'mər-sē\ *interj, archaic* — used to express gratitude or astonishment
gram·mar \'gram-ər\ *n* **1** : the study of the classes of words, their inflections, and their functions and relations in a language **2** : the facts of language with which grammar deals **3 a** : a grammar textbook **b** : speech or writing evaluated according to its conformity to grammatical rules ⟨"Him and I went" is bad *grammar*⟩
gram·mar·i·an \grə-'mer-ē-ən\ *n* : a specialist in or a teacher of grammar
grammar school *n* : an elementary school
gram·mat·i·cal \grə-'mat-i-kəl\ *adj* **1** : of or relating to grammar **2** : conforming to the rules of grammar — **gram·mat·i·cal·i·ty** \-ˌmat-ə-'kal-ət-ē\ *n* — **gram·mat·i·cal·ly** \-k(ə-)lē\ *adv* — **gram·mat·i·cal·ness** \-'mat-i-kəl-nəs\ *n*
gram·pus \'gram-pəs\ *n* **1** : a sea mammal related to the whales and having teeth in the lower jaw only **2 a** : KILLER WHALE **b** : BLACKFISH 1
gra·na·ry \'grān-(ə-)rē, 'gran-\ *n, pl* **-ries** **1** : a storehouse for grain **2** : a region producing grain in abundance
1**grand** \'grand\ *adj* **1** : higher in rank than others of the same class : FOREMOST, PRINCIPAL ⟨*grand* champion⟩ ⟨*grand* prize⟩ **2** : great in size **3** : INCLUSIVE, COMPLETE ⟨a *grand* total⟩ **4 a** : marked by magnificence : SPLENDID ⟨a *grand* coronation ceremony⟩ **b** : showing wealth or high social standing ⟨the airs of a *grand* lady⟩ **5** : IMPRESSIVE, STATELY, ADMIRABLE ⟨a *grand* old man⟩ **6** : very good : FINE ⟨*grand* weather⟩ ⟨have a *grand* time⟩ — **grand·ly** *adv* — **grand·ness** \'gran(d)-nəs\ *n*
syn GRAND, MAGNIFICENT, MAJESTIC can mean impressive for beauty and size or range. GRAND suggests dignity that is seen in huge and handsome proportions ⟨a *grand* arch⟩; MAGNIFICENT suggests overwhelming splendor and vast extent ⟨a *magnificent* marble palace⟩; MAJESTIC may suggest severe beauty and a tremendous scope that inspires awe ⟨the *majestic* vault of heaven⟩
2**grand** *n* **1** : GRAND PIANO **2** *slang* : a thousand dollars
gran·dam \'gran-ˌdam, -dəm\ *or* **gran·dame** \-ˌdām, -dəm\ *n* **1** : GRANDMOTHER **2** : an old woman
grand·aunt \'gran-'dant, -'dȧnt\ *n* : an aunt of one's father or mother
grand·child \'gran(d)-ˌchīld\ *n* : a child of one's son or daughter
grand·daugh·ter \'gran-ˌdȯt-ər\ *n* : a daughter of one's son or daughter
gran·dee \gran-'dē\ *n* : a man of elevated rank or station; *esp* : a high-ranking Spanish or Portuguese nobleman
gran·deur \'gran-jər\ *n* **1** : the quality or state of being grand : awe-inspiring magnificence **2** : something that is grand
grand·fa·ther \'gran(d)-ˌfäth-ər\ *n* : the father of one's father or mother; *also* : ANCESTOR 1

grandfather clock *n* **:** a tall pendulum clock standing directly on the floor — called also *grandfather's clock*
gran·dil·o·quence \gran-ˈdil-ə-kwən(t)s\ *n* **:** lofty or pompous eloquence — **gran·dil·o·quent** \-kwənt\ *adj* — **gran·dil·o·quent·ly** *adv*
gran·di·ose \ˈgran-dē-ˌōs\ *adj* **1 :** impressive because of uncommon largeness, scope, effect, or grandeur **2 :** characterized by deliberately assumed grandeur or splendor or by absurd exaggeration ⟨*grandiose* schemes⟩ — **gran·di·ose·ly** *adv* — **gran·di·os·i·ty** \ˌgran-dē-ˈäs-ət-ē\ *n*

grandfather clock

grand jury *n* **:** a jury that chiefly examines accusations of crime made against persons and if the evidence warrants makes formal charges on which the accused persons are later tried
grand·moth·er \ˈgran(d)-ˌməth-ər\ *n* **:** the mother of one's father or mother; *also* **:** a female ancestor
grand·neph·ew \-ˈnef-yü\ *n* **:** a grandson of one's brother or sister
grand·niece \-ˈnēs\ *n* **:** a granddaughter of one's brother or sister
grand opera *n* **:** opera in which the plot is elaborated as in serious drama and the entire text set to music
grand·par·ent \ˈgran(d)-ˌpar-ənt, -ˌper-\ *n* **:** a parent of one's father or mother
grand piano *n* **:** a piano with horizontal frame and strings
grand·sire \ˈgran(d)-ˌsī(ə)r\ *or* **grand·sir** \ˈgran(t)-sər\ *n* **1** *dial* **:** GRANDFATHER **2** *archaic* **:** an aged man
grand·son \ˈgran(d)-ˌsən\ *n* **:** a son of one's son or daughter
grand·stand \ˈgran(d)-ˌstand\ *n* **:** a usu. roofed stand for spectators at a racecourse or stadium
grand·un·cle \ˈgran-ˈdəng-kəl\ *n* **:** an uncle of one's father or mother
grange \ˈgrānj\ *n* **1 :** FARM; *esp* **:** a farmhouse with its various buildings **2** *cap* **:** one of the lodges of a national fraternal association of farmers; *also* **:** the association itself
grang·er \ˈgrān-jər\ *n* **:** a member of a Grange
gran·ite \ˈgran-ət\ *n* **:** a very hard rock that takes a high polish and is used for building and for monuments
gran·ny *or* **gran·nie** \ˈgran-ē\ *n, pl* **grannies 1 :** GRANDMOTHER **2 :** a fussy person **3 :** an ankle-length dress usu. with long sleeves and a high waist
granny glasses *n pl* **:** metal-rimmed eyeglasses with small lenses
granny knot *n* **:** an insecure knot often made instead of a square knot
¹grant \ˈgrant\ *vb* **1 a :** to consent to **:** ALLOW **b :** to permit as a right, privilege, or favor **2 :** to give the possession or benefit of formally or legally **3 :** to concede something not yet proved to be true — **grant·er** \-ər\ *n* — **grant·or** \ˈgrant-ər, grant-ˈȯr\ *n*
²grant *n* **1 :** the act of granting ⟨land ceded by *grant*⟩ **2 :** something granted: as **a :** a gift for a particular purpose ⟨a *grant* for a summer's study in Europe⟩ **b :** a tract of land granted by a government
grant·ee \grant-ˈē\ *n* **:** one to whom a grant is made
gran·u·lar \ˈgran-yə-lər\ *adj* **1 :** consisting of grains **2 :** having a grainy texture or appearance — **gran·u·lar·i·ty** \ˌgran-yə-ˈlar-ət-ē\ *n*
gran·u·late \ˈgran-yə-ˌlāt\ *vb* **:** to form or crystallize into grains or granules — **gran·u·lat·ed** *adj*
gran·u·la·tion \ˌgran-yə-ˈlā-shən\ *n* **1 :** the act or process of granulating or the condition of being granulated **2 :** one of the small raised places of a granulated surface
gran·ule \ˈgran-yül\ *n* **1 :** a small grain or particle ⟨*granules* of sugar⟩ **2 :** one of the short-lived brilliant spots on the sun
grape \ˈgrāp\ *n* **1 :** a smooth-skinned juicy greenish white to deep red or purple berry eaten dried or fresh as a fruit or fermented to produce wine **2 :** a woody vine widely grown for its clustered grapes **3 :** GRAPESHOT — **grapy** \ˈgrā-pē\ *adj*
grape·fruit \ˈgrāp-ˌfrüt\ *n* **1 :** a large citrus fruit with a bitter yellow rind and a highly flavored somewhat acid juicy pulp **2 :** a tree that bears grapefruit
grape hyacinth *n* **:** any of several small spring-flowering herbs related to the lilies and having usu. blue flowers
grape ivy *n* **:** an evergreen climbing vine with tendrils and leaves having three leaflets and reddish hairy lower surfaces that is used widely as a houseplant
grape·shot \ˈgrāp-ˌshät\ *n* **:** a cluster of small iron balls used as a cannon charge
grape sugar *n* **:** DEXTROSE
grape·vine \ˈgrāp-ˌvīn\ *n* **1 :** GRAPE 2 **2 :** an informal means of spreading information or gossip
graph \ˈgraf\ *n* **1 :** a diagram that represents change in one variable factor in comparison with that of one or more other factors **2 :** a pictorial representation of a set of points (as a line or curve) symbolizing a mathematical equation or set

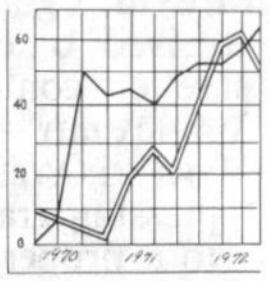

graph 1

-graph \ˌgraf\ *n comb form* **1 :** something written ⟨auto*graph*⟩ **2 :** instrument for making or transmitting records ⟨chrono*graph*⟩
graph·ic \ˈgraf-ik\ *or* **graph·i·cal** \-i-kəl\ *adj* **1 :** clearly and vividly told or described **2 :** of, relating to, or being arts such as painting, engraving, printing, or photography **3 :** of, relating to, or represented by a graph — **graph·i·cal·ly** \-i-k(ə-)lē\ *adv* — **graph·ic·ness** *n*
graph·ite \ˈgraf-ˌīt\ *n* [from German, from Greek *graphein* "to write"] **:** a soft black carbon with a metallic luster that conducts electricity and is used in making lead pencils, as a dry lubricant, and for electrodes
graph paper *n* **:** paper ruled (as into small squares) for drawing graphs or making diagrams
-g·ra·phy \g-rə-fē\ *n comb form, pl* **-graphies :** writing or representation in a (specified) manner or by a (specified) means or of a (specified) object ⟨photo*graphy*⟩ ⟨steno*graphy*⟩
grap·nel \ˈgrap-nəl\ *n* **:** a small anchor with claws used in dragging or grappling
¹grap·ple \ˈgrap-əl\ *n* **1 :** the act of grappling **:** GRIP, HOLD **2 :** an implement for grappling
²grapple *vb* **grap·pled; grap·pling** \ˈgrap-(ə-)ling\ **1 :** to seize or hold with or as if with a hooked implement **2 :** to seize and struggle with one another **3 :** to attempt to deal **:** COPE — **grap·pler** \-(ə-)lər\ *n*
¹grasp \ˈgrasp\ *vb* **1 :** to make the motion of seizing **:** CLUTCH ⟨*grasp* at straws⟩ **2 :** to clasp or embrace with or as if with the fingers or arms **3 :** to lay hold of with the mind **:** COMPREHEND — **grasp·a·ble** \ˈgras-pə-bəl\ *adj* — **grasp·er** *n*

[2]**grasp** *n* **1** : EMBRACE **2** : HOLD, CONTROL ⟨money in his *grasp*⟩ **3 a** : the reach of the arms ⟨the limb was beyond his *grasp*⟩ **b** : the power of seizing and holding **4** : COMPREHENSION

grasp·ing *adj* : AVARICIOUS — **grasp·ing·ly** \'gras-ping-lē\ *adv* — **grasp·ing·ness** *n*

[1]**grass** \'gras\ *n* **1** : herbage suitable or used for grazing animals **2** : any of a large family of mostly herbaceous monocotyledonous plants (as wheat, Indian corn, bamboo, or sugarcane) with jointed usually hollow stems, slender sheathing leaves, and fruit consisting of a seedlike grain **3** : grass-covered land; *esp* : LAWN **4** *slang* : MARIJUANA — **grass·like** \-,līk\ *adj* — **grassy** \'gras-ē\ *adj*

[2]**grass** *vb* **1** : to seed to grass **2** : to furnish with pasture or with grass for food

grass·hop·per \'gras-,häp-ər\ *n* : any of numerous plant-eating insects having the hind legs adapted for leaping

grass·land \-,land\ *n* : land covered naturally or under cultivation with grasses and other low-growing herbs

grass roots *n pl* : society at the local and popular level as distinguished from political or cultural centers

[1]**grate** \'grāt\ *n* **1** : GRATING **2** : a frame or basket of iron bars for holding burning fuel (as in a furnace or a fireplace)

[2]**grate** *vb* **1** : to make into small particles by rubbing against something rough ⟨*grate* cheese⟩ **2** : to grind or rub against something with a rasping noise **3** : to have a harsh or rasping effect — **grat·er** *n*

grate·ful \'grāt-fəl\ *adj* **1 a** : appreciative of benefits received **b** : expressing gratitude **2** : affording pleasure or contentment : PLEASING — **grate·ful·ly** \-fə-lē\ *adv* — **grate·ful·ness** *n*

syn GRATEFUL, THANKFUL mean feeling or expressing gratitude. GRATEFUL commonly applies to a proper sense of favors received from one's fellowmen; THANKFUL may apply to a more generalized acknowledgment of what is vaguely felt to be providential ***ant*** obnoxious

grat·i·fy \'grat-ə-,fī\ *vb* **-fied**; **-fy·ing** **1** : to give or be a source of pleasure or satisfaction to **2** : to confer a favor on : INDULGE — **grat·i·fi·ca·tion** \,grat-ə-fə-'kā-shən\ *n*

grat·ing \'grāt-ing\ *n* **1** : a frame of parallel bars or crossbars **2** : a ruled surface used in the diffraction of light to produce spectra

gra·tis \'grāt-əs, 'grat-\ *adv or adj* : without charge : FREE

grat·i·tude \'grat-ə-,t(y)üd\ *n* : the state of being grateful

gra·tu·i·tous \grə-'t(y)ü-ət-əs\ *adj* **1** : done or provided freely without regard to claim or merit **2** : not called for by the circumstances : UNWARRANTED ⟨a *gratuitous* insult⟩ — **gra·tu·i·tous·ly** *adv* — **gra·tu·i·tous·ness** *n*

gra·tu·i·ty \grə-'t(y)ü-ət-ē\ *n, pl* **-ties** : something given freely; *esp* : TIP

[1]**grave** \'grāv\ *vb* **graved**; **grav·en** \'grā-vən\ *or* **graved**; **grav·ing** **1** : CARVE, SCULPTURE **2** : ENGRAVE

[2]**grave** *n* : an excavation for burial of a body; *also* : TOMB

ə abut	ər further	a back		ā bake
ä cot, cart	aủ out	ch chin	e less	ē easy
g gift	i trip	ī life	j joke	ng sing	ō flow
ȯ flaw	ȯi coin	th thin	<u>th</u> this	ü loot
ủ foot	y yet	yü few	yủ furious	zh vision

[3]**grave** \'grāv, *in sense 3 also* 'gräv\ *adj* **1 a** : meriting serious consideration : IMPORTANT ⟨a *grave* matter⟩ **b** : threatening great harm or danger ⟨received a *grave* injury⟩ **2** : dignified in appearance or demeanor : SOLEMN, SERIOUS **3** : of, marked by, or being an accent mark having the form ˋ — **grave·ly** *adv* — **grave·ness** *n*

[4]**gra·ve** \'gräv-(,)ā\ *adv or adj* : in a slow and solemn manner — used as a direction in music

[1]**grav·el** \'grav-əl\ *n* **1** : loose rounded fragments of rock coarser than sand **2** : a deposit of small pebblelike bodies in the kidneys and urinary bladder

[2]**gravel** *adj* : GRAVELLY 2

[3]**gravel** *vb* **grav·eled** *or* **grav·elled**; **grav·el·ing** *or* **grav·el·ling** \'grav-(ə-)ling\ : to cover or spread with gravel

grav·el·ly \'grav-(ə-)lē\ *adj* **1** : of, containing, or covered with gravel **2** : having a harsh grating sound ⟨a *gravelly* voice⟩

grav·er \'grā-vər\ *n* **1** : ENGRAVER, SCULPTOR **2** : any of various cutting or shaving tools

grave·stone \'grāv-,stōn\ *n* : a burial monument

grave·yard \-,yärd\ *n* : CEMETERY

gra·vim·e·ter \grə-'vim-ət-ər, 'grav-ə-,mēt-\ *n* **1** : a device similar to a hydrometer for determining specific gravity **2** : an instrument for measuring differences in the force of gravity at different places

grav·i·tate \'grav-ə-,tāt\ *vb* **1** : to move or tend to move under the influence of gravitation **2** : to move toward something

grav·i·ta·tion \,grav-ə-'tā-shən\ *n* **1** : the force that attracts objects or material bodies toward each other **2** : the action or process of gravitating — **grav·i·ta·tion·al** \-sh(ə-)nəl\ *adj* — **grav·i·ta·tion·al·ly** \-ē\ *adv* — **grav·i·ta·tive** \'grav-ə-,tāt-iv\ *adj*

grav·i·ty \'grav-ət-ē\ *n, pl* **-ties** **1 a** : dignity or sobriety of bearing **b** : IMPORTANCE, SIGNIFICANCE; *esp* : SERIOUSNESS **2** : WEIGHT — used chiefly in the phrase *center of gravity* **3 a** : the gravitational attraction of the earth's mass for bodies at or near its surface toward the center of the earth **b** : GRAVITATION **c** : ACCELERATION OF GRAVITY

gra·vy \'grā-vē\ *n, pl* **gravies** **1** : a sauce made from the thickened and seasoned juices of cooked meat **2** : unearned, extra, or illicit gain; *esp* : GRAFT

[1]**gray** \'grā\ *adj* **1** : of the color gray; *also* : dull in color **2** : having gray hair **3** : dull in mood or outlook : DISMAL ⟨a *gray* day⟩ — **gray·ness** *n*

[2]**gray** *n* **1** : one of the series of neutral colors ranging between black and white **2** : something gray **3** *slang* : a white man — **gray** *vb* — **gray·ish** \'grā-ish\ *adj*

gray·beard \'grā-,bi(ə)rd\ *n* : an old man

gray·ling \'grā-ling\ *n, pl* **grayling** *also* **graylings** **1** : any of several freshwater fishes related to the trouts and valued for food and sport **2** : any of various gray and brown butterflies

gray matter *n* **1** : nerve tissue esp. of the brain and spinal cord that contains nerve-cell bodies as well as nerve fibers and has a brownish gray color **2** : BRAINS, INTELLECT

gray moss *n* : SPANISH MOSS

[1]**graze** \'grāz\ *vb* **1** : to feed on growing herbage **2** : to feed or put cattle to feed on herbage

[2]**graze** *vb* **1** : to rub or touch lightly in passing : touch against and glance off ⟨the car's wheel *grazed* the curb⟩ **2** : to scratch or scrape by rubbing against something ⟨*grazed* his elbow⟩

[3]**graze** *n* : an act or result of grazing; *esp* : a superficial skin injury

[1]**grease** \'grēs\ *n* **1** : rendered animal fat **2** : oily matter **3** : a thick lubricant

2**grease** \'grēs, 'grēz\ *vb* **1 :** to smear or daub with grease **2 :** to lubricate with grease — **greas·er** *n*
grease·paint \'grēs-ˌpānt\ *n* **:** theatrical makeup
grease pencil *n* **:** a pencil in which the marking substance is pigment and grease
greasy \'grē-sē, -zē\ *adj* **greas·i·er; -est** **1 :** smeared with grease **2 :** containing grease ⟨*greasy* food⟩ **3 :** resembling grease or oil **:** SMOOTH, SLIPPERY — **greas·i·ly** \-sə-lē, -zə-\ *adv* — **greas·i·ness** \-sē-nəs, -zē-\ *n*
great \'grāt, *in South also* 'gre(ə)t\ *adj* **1 :** large in size **:** not small or little **2 :** large in number **:** NUMEROUS ⟨a *great* crowd⟩ **3 :** long continued ⟨a *great* while⟩ **4 :** beyond the average or ordinary **:** MIGHTY, HEAVY, INTENSE ⟨a *great* weight⟩ ⟨in *great* pain⟩ **5 :** EMINENT, DISTINGUISHED ⟨a *great* artist⟩ ⟨*great* men⟩ **6 :** remarkable in knowledge of or skill in something ⟨the boy is *great* at dividing⟩ **7 :** FAVORITE ⟨a *great* joke of my father's⟩ **8 :** EXCELLENT, FINE ⟨a *great* time at the beach⟩ **9 :** more distant in relationship by one generation ⟨*great*-grandchildren⟩ — **great·ly** *adv* — **great·ness** *n*
great ape *n* **:** any of the anthropoid apes existing at the present time and including the gibbon, chimpanzee, gorilla, and orangutan
great auk *n* **:** an extinct large flightless auk formerly abundant along No. Atlantic coasts
great–aunt *n* **:** GRANDAUNT
great blue heron *n* **:** a large slaty-blue American heron with a crested head
great circle *n* **:** a circle formed on the surface of a sphere by the intersection of a plane that passes through the center of the sphere; *esp* **:** one on the surface of the earth an arc of which constitutes the shortest distance between two terrestrial points
great·coat \'grāt-ˌkōt\ *n* **:** a heavy overcoat
Great Dane *n* **:** any of a breed of tall massive powerful smooth-coated dogs
great divide *n* **:** a watershed between major drainage systems
great·heart·ed \'grāt-'härt-əd\ *adj* **1 :** COURAGEOUS **2 :** nobly generous — **great·heart·ed·ly** *adv* — **great·heart·ed·ness** *n*
great–nephew *n* **:** GRANDNEPHEW
great–niece *n* **:** GRANDNIECE
great power *n* **:** one of the nations that figure most decisively in international affairs
great–uncle *n* **:** GRANDUNCLE
great white shark *n* **:** a large man-eating shark that is bluish when young but becomes whitish when older and is widespread in warm and tropical seas
greave \'grēv\ *n* **:** armor for the leg below the knee — usu. used in pl.
grebe \'grēb\ *n* **:** any of a family of swimming and diving birds closely related to the loons

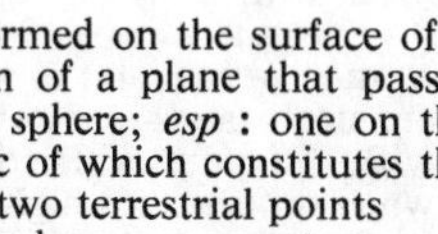

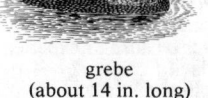

grebe
(about 14 in. long)

Gre·cian \'grē-shən\ *adj* **:** GREEK — **Gre·cian** *n*
greed \'grēd\ *n* **:** excessive or blameworthy desire for food, money, or possessions
greedy \'grēd-ē\ *adj* **greed·i·er; -est** **1 :** having a keen appetite **2 :** having an eager and often selfish desire or longing ⟨*greedy* for praise⟩ **3 :** wanting more than one needs or more than one's fair share (as of food or wealth) — **greed·i·ly** \'grēd-ə-lē\ *adv* — **greed·i·ness** \'grēd-ē-nəs\ *n*
Greek \'grēk\ *n* **1 a :** a native or inhabitant of Greece **b :** a person of Greek descent **2 :** the Indo-European language of the Greeks — **Greek** *adj*
1**green** \'grēn\ *adj* **1 :** of the color green **2 a :** covered by green foliage or herbage ⟨*green* hills⟩ **b :** consisting of green plants or of the leafy part of a plant ⟨a *green* salad⟩ **3 :** not fully grown or ripe ⟨*green* apples⟩ **4 :** marked by a sickly appearance ⟨*green* with envy⟩ **5 :** lacking training, knowledge, or experience ⟨*green* troops⟩ — **green·ly** *adv* — **green·ness** \'grēn-nəs\ *n*
2**green** *n* **1 :** a color (as that of growing fresh grass or of the emerald) lying between blue and yellow in the spectrum **2 a :** green vegetation **b** *pl* **:** leafy parts of plants used for some purpose (as ornament or food) **3 :** a grassy plain or plot; *esp* **:** a smooth grassy area around the hole into which the ball must be played in golf — **green·ish** \'grē-nish\ *adj*
green alga *n* **:** an alga in which the chlorophyll is not masked by other pigments
green·back \'grēn-ˌbak\ *n* **:** a piece of U.S. paper money
green bean *n* **:** a kidney bean with the pods green when ready for harvest
green·belt \'grēn-ˌbelt\ *n* **:** a belt of parkways or farmlands that encircles a community
green·ery \'grēn-(ə-)rē\ *n, pl* **-er·ies** **:** green foliage or plants **:** VERDURE
green·gro·cer \'grēn-ˌgrō-sər\ *n, chiefly Brit* **:** a retailer of fresh vegetables and fruit — **green·gro·cery** \-ˌgrōs-(ə-)rē\ *n*
green·horn \'grēn-ˌhȯrn\ *n* **:** an inexperienced person; *esp* **:** one easily tricked or cheated
green·house \-ˌhau̇s\ *n* **:** a glassed enclosure for cultivation of plants
greenhouse effect *n* **:** the warming effect produced by the trapping of the sun's radiation after it is absorbed by the earth and reemitted as longer wavelengths that can be absorbed by carbon dioxide and water vapor in the atmosphere
green manure *n* **1 :** an herbaceous crop (as clover) plowed under while green to enrich the soil **2 :** fresh or undecayed barn manure
green mold *n* **:** a green or green-spored mold (as a penicillium)
green snake *n* **:** either of two bright green harmless largely insect-eating No. American snakes
green·sward \'grēn-ˌswȯrd\ *n* **:** turf green with growing grass
green thumb *n* **:** an unusual ability to make plants grow — **green–thumbed** \'grēn-'thəmd\ *adj*
green turtle *n* **:** a large edible sea turtle with a smooth greenish shell
green vegetable *n* **:** a vegetable that has the edible parts rich in chlorophyll and is an important source of vitamins
Green·wich time \'grin-ij-, 'gren-, -ich-\ *n* **:** the time of the meridian of Greenwich used as the basis of standard time throughout the world
green·wood \'grēn-ˌwu̇d\ *n* **:** a forest green with foliage
greet \'grēt\ *vb* **1 :** to address upon arrival or meeting with expressions of kind wishes **2 :** to meet or react to in a specified manner ⟨candidate was *greeted* with cheers and catcalls⟩ **3 :** to be perceived by ⟨a sight *greeted* her eyes⟩ — **greet·er** *n*
greet·ing *n* **1 :** SALUTATION **2 :** an expression of good wishes **:** REGARDS — usu. used in pl.
gre·gar·i·ous \gri-'gar-ē-əs, -'ger-\ *adj* **1 :** tending to associate with others of one's kind **:** SOCIABLE **2 :** habitually living or moving with others of one's own kind **:** tending to flock together — **gre·gar·i·ous·ly** *adv* — **gre·gar·i·ous·ness** *n*
Gre·go·ri·an calendar \gri-ˌgōr-ē-ən-, -ˌgȯr-\ *n*

G

: a calendar introduced by Pope Gregory XIII in 1582 and adopted in Great Britain and the American colonies in 1752 — compare JULIAN CALENDAR

Gregorian chant *n* : a rhythmically free unaccompanied melody sung in unison in services of the Roman Catholic Church

grem·lin \'grem-lən\ *n* : a small gnome held to be responsible for equipment failure esp. in an airplane

gre·nade \grə-'nād\ *n* [from French, meaning first "pomegranate", from Latin *granatum*, from the neuter of *granatus* "grainy"; the fruit was so called from its numerous seeds, the bomb from the pellets with which it was filled] : a small bomb to be hurled by hand or from a small launcher

gren·a·dier \ˌgren-ə-'di(ə)r\ *n* : a member of a European regiment formerly armed with grenades

grew *past of* GROW

grey *var of* GRAY

grey·hound \'grā-ˌhau̇nd\ *n* : a tall slender graceful smooth-coated dog noted for swiftness and keen sight and used for chasing game and racing

greyhound

grid \'grid\ *n* **1** : GRATING **2** : a perforated or ridged metal plate used as a conductor in a storage battery **3** : an electrode consisting of a mesh or a spiral of fine wire placed between two other elements of an electron tube so as to control the amount of current that flows between them **4** : a network of horizontal and perpendicular lines (as for locating points on a map by means of coordinates or for counting a sample of particles or organisms on a microscope slide)

grid·dle \'grid-əl\ *n* : a flat surface or pan on which food is cooked

griddle cake *n* : a flat cake made of thin batter and cooked on both sides on a griddle

grid·iron \'grid-ˌī(-ə)rn\ *n* **1** : a grate for broiling food **2** : something consisting of or covered with a grid; *esp* : a football field

grief \'grēf\ *n* **1** : deep sorrow : SADNESS, DISTRESS **2** : a cause of sorrow **3** : MISHAP, DISASTER ⟨the boat came to *grief* on the rocks⟩

griev·ance \'grē-vən(t)s\ *n* **1** : a cause of distress affording reason for complaint **2** : the formal expression of a grievance : COMPLAINT

grieve \'grēv\ *vb* **1** : to cause grief or suffering to : DISTRESS **2** : to feel or express grief — **griev·er** *n*

griev·ous \'grē-vəs\ *adj* **1** : HEAVY, SEVERE ⟨the *grievous* cost of war⟩ **2** : causing or characterized by pain, suffering, or sorrow ⟨a *grievous* wound⟩ **3** : SERIOUS, GRAVE ⟨*grievous* fault⟩ — **griev·ous·ly** *adv* — **griev·ous·ness** *n*

griffin

grif·fin *or* **grif·fon** \'grif-ən\ *n* : a fabulous animal typically half eagle and half lion

1**grill** \'gril\ *vb* **1** : to broil on a grill **2 a** : to torment as if by broiling **b** : to question intensely

2**grill** *n* **1** : a grate on which food is broiled **2** : broiled food **3** : a restaurant featuring broiled foods

grille *also* **grill** \'gril\ *n* **1** : a grating forming a barrier or screen **2** : an opening covered with a grille

grill·work \'gril-ˌwərk\ *n* : work constituting or resembling a grille

grim \'grim\ *adj* **grim·mer**; **grim·mest** **1** : SAVAGE, FIERCE **2 a** : harsh and forbidding in appearance **b** : ghastly, repellent, or sinister in character **3** : UNFLINCHING, UNYIELDING ⟨*grim* determination⟩ — **grim·ly** *adv* — **grim·ness** *n*

grim·ace \'grim-əs, grim-'ās\ *n* : a twisting or distortion of the face or features expressive usu. of disgust or disapproval — **grimace** *vb*

grime \'grīm\ *n* : soot, smut, or dirt adhering to or embedded in a surface; *also* : accumulated dirtiness and disorder — **grime** *vb* — **grim·i·ness** \'grī-mē-nəs\ *n* — **grimy** \'grī-mē\ *adj*

grin \'grin\ *vb* **grinned**; **grin·ning** : to draw back the lips so as to show the teeth esp. in amusement or laughter — **grin** *n*

1**grind** \'grīnd\ *vb* **ground** \'grau̇nd\; **grind·ing** **1** : to reduce to powder or fragments by friction (as in a mill or with the teeth) **2** : to wear down, polish, or sharpen by friction : WHET ⟨*grind* lenses⟩ **3** : to press with a grating noise : GRIT ⟨*grind* the teeth⟩ **4** : OPPRESS, HARASS **5 a** : to operate or produce by turning a crank **b** : to produce in a laborious or mechanical way ⟨*grind* out a composition⟩ **6** : to move with difficulty or friction so as to grate the gears when shifting into high

2**grind** *n* **1** : an act of grinding **2 a** : monotonous labor or routine; *esp* : intensive study **b** : a student who studies excessively **3** : the result of grinding; *esp* : the size of particle obtained by grinding

grind·er \'grīn-dər\ *n* **1** *pl* : TEETH **2** : one that grinds **3** : SUBMARINE 2

grind·stone \'grīn-ˌstōn\ *n* : a sandstone disk that revolves on an axle and is used for grinding, shaping, or smoothing

grindstone

1**grip** \'grip\ *vb* **gripped**; **grip·ping** **1** : to seize firmly **2** : to hold strongly the interest of ⟨the story *grips* the reader⟩

2**grip** *n* **1 a** : a firm grasp **b** : strength in gripping **c** : a way of clasping the hand by which members of a secret order recognize or greet one another **2 a** : CONTROL, MASTERY **b** : mental grasp : UNDERSTANDING **3** : a part or device for gripping or by which something is grasped; *esp* : HANDLE **4** : SUITCASE

1**gripe** \'grīp\ *vb* **1** : SEIZE, GRIP **2 a** : AFFLICT, DISTRESS **b** : IRRITATE, VEX ⟨his ingratitude *gripes* me⟩ **3** : to cause or experience spasms of pain in the bowels **4** : COMPLAIN — **grip·er** *n*

2**gripe** *n* **1** : GRIP **2 a** : AFFLICTION **b** : COMPLAINT **3** : a spasm of intestinal pain

grippe \'grip\ *n* : an acute virus disease identical with or resembling influenza — **grippy** \'grip-ē\ *adj*

gris·ly \'griz-lē\ *adj* **gris·li·er**; **-est** : HORRIBLE, GRUESOME — **gris·li·ness** *n*

grist \'grist\ *n* : grain to be ground or already ground

gris·tle \'gris-əl\ *n* : CARTILAGE — **gris·tli·ness** \'gris-(ə-)lē-nəs\ *n* — **gris·tly** \'gris-(ə-)lē\ *adj*

ə abut	ər further	a back	ā bake	
ä cot, cart	au̇ out	ch chin	e less	ē easy
g gift	i trip	ī life	j joke	ng sing	ō flow
ȯ flaw	ȯi coin	th thin	th this	ü loot
u̇ foot	y yet	yü few	yu̇ furious	zh vision

grist·mill \'grist-ˌmil\ *n* : a mill for grinding grain
[1]**grit** \'grit\ *n* **1 a** : a hard sharp granule (as of sand) **b** : material (as an abrasive) composed of grits **2** : firmness of mind or spirit : unyielding courage — **grit·ty** \'grit-ē\ *adj*
[2]**grit** *vb* **grit·ted**; **grit·ting** : to grind or cause to grind : GRATE ⟨*grit* one's teeth⟩
grits \'grits\ *n pl* : coarsely ground hulled grain
griz·zled \'griz-əld\ *adj* : sprinkled, streaked, or mixed with gray
[1]**griz·zly** \'griz-lē\ *adj* **griz·zli·er**; **-est** : GRIZZLED
[2]**grizzly** *n, pl* **grizzlies** : GRIZZLY BEAR
grizzly bear *n* : a large powerful usu. brownish yellow bear of western No. America
gro *abbr* gross
groan \'grōn\ *vb* **1** : to utter a deep moan of pain, grief, or annoyance **2** : to make a harsh sound under strain ⟨the chair *groaned* under his weight⟩ — **groan** *n* — **groan·er** *n*

grizzly bear (up to 3½ ft. at shoulder)

gro·cer \'grō-sər\ *n* [from medieval French *grossier* "wholesale dealer", from *gros* "gross", "wholesale"] : a dealer in staple foodstuffs and household supplies
gro·cery \'grōs-(ə-)rē\ *n, pl* **-cer·ies** **1** *pl* : foodstuffs sold by a grocer ⟨went out to buy the *groceries*⟩ **2** : a grocer's store
grog \'gräg\ *n* [named after Old *Grog*, nickname of British Admiral Edward Vernon (1684–1757) who issued orders to cut the sailors' rum with water] : alcoholic liquor; *esp* : liquor (as rum) cut with water — **grog·gery** \'gräg-ə-rē\ *n* — **grog·shop** \'gräg-ˌshäp\ *n*
grog·gy \'gräg-ē\ *adj* **grog·gi·er**; **-est** : being weak and dazed and unsteady on the feet or in action — **grog·gi·ly** \'gräg-ə-lē\ *adv* — **grog·gi·ness** \'gräg-ē-nəs\ *n*
[1]**groin** \'gròin\ *n* **1** : the junction of the lower abdomen and thigh or the part of the body about this junction **2** : the projecting curved line along which two intersecting structural vaults meet
[2]**groin** *vb* : to build or equip with groins
grom·met \'gräm-ət, 'grəm-\ *n* **1** : a ring of rope **2** : a small usu. metal ring to reinforce an eyelet
[1]**groom** \'grüm, 'grủm\ *n* **1** : a male servant; *esp* : one in charge of horses **2** : BRIDEGROOM
[2]**groom** *vb* **1** : to clean and care for (an animal) **2** : to make neat, attractive, or acceptable : POLISH
grooms·man \'grümz-mən, 'grủmz-\ *n* : a male friend who attends a bridegroom at his wedding
[1]**groove** \'grüv\ *n* **1** : a long narrow channel, depression, or indentation **2** : a fixed routine : RUT — **in the groove** : in top form
[2]**groove** *vb* **1 a** : to form a groove in **b** : to become grooved **2** : to enjoy fully an experience or event : DIG
groovy \'grü-vē\ *adj* **groov·i·er**; **-est** : very good : EXCELLENT
grope \'grōp\ *vb* **1** : to feel about or cast about blindly or uncertainly in search ⟨*groped* for his arm⟩ ⟨*grope* for the right word⟩ **2** : to feel one's way by groping ⟨*grope* along a wall⟩
gros·beak \'grōs-ˌbēk\ *n* : any of several finches (as the pine grosbeak or rose-breasted grosbeak) of Europe or America having large stout conical bills
[1]**gross** \'grōs\ *adj* **1 a** : glaringly noticeable ⟨*gross* error⟩ **b** : SHAMEFUL ⟨*gross* injustice⟩ **2 a** : BIG, BULKY; *esp* : excessively fat **b** : excessively luxuriant : RANK **3** : consisting of a whole before any deductions ⟨*gross* earnings⟩ **4** : COARSE, VULGAR ⟨*gross* epithets⟩ — **gross·ly** *adv* — **gross·ness** *n*
[2]**gross** *n* : a whole before any deductions (as for taxes or expenses)
[3]**gross** *vb* : to earn before deductions ⟨*grossed* $50,000 before taxes⟩
[4]**gross** *n, pl* **gross** : 12 dozen ⟨a *gross* of pencils⟩
gross national product *n* : the total value of the goods and services produced in a nation during a year
grot \'grät\ *n* : GROTTO
gro·tesque \grō-'tesk\ *adj* **1** : combining (as in a painting or poem) details never found together in nature : using distortion for artistic effect **2** : absurdly awkward or incongruous — **gro·tesque·ly** *adv* — **gro·tesque·ness** *n*
grot·to \'grät-ō\ *n, pl* **grottoes** *also* **grottos** **1** : CAVE **2** : an artificial recess or structure made to resemble a natural cave
grouch \'graủch\ *n* **1** : a fit of bad temper **2** : an habitually irritable or complaining person — **grouch** *vb* — **grouch·i·ly** \'graủ-chə-lē\ *adv* — **grouch·i·ness** \-chē-nəs\ *n* — **grouchy** \-chē\ *adj*
[1]**ground** \'graủnd\ *n* **1 a** : the bottom of a body of water ⟨the boat struck *ground*⟩ **b** *pl* : sediment at the bottom of a liquid : LEES **2** : BASIS, FOUNDATION ⟨*grounds* for divorce⟩ **3** : a surrounding area : BACKGROUND ⟨a picture on a gray *ground*⟩ **4 a** : the surface of the earth **b** : an area used for a particular purpose ⟨parade *ground*⟩ **c** *pl* : the area around and belonging to a building ⟨the capitol *grounds*⟩ **5** : SOIL, EARTH **6** : distance ahead or behind ⟨gain *ground* on the other racers⟩ **7 a** : an object that makes an electrical connection with the earth **b** : a large conducting body (as the earth) used as a common return for an electric circuit — **ground** *adj*
[2]**ground** *vb* **1** : to bring to or place on the ground ⟨*ground* a rifle⟩ **2 a** : to provide a reason or justification for **b** : to instruct in fundamentals ⟨well *grounded* in mathematics⟩ **3** : to connect electrically with a ground **4** : to restrict to the ground ⟨*ground* a pilot⟩ **5** : to run aground ⟨the ship *grounded* on a reef⟩ **6** : to hit a grounder ⟨*grounded* to the shortstop⟩
[3]**ground** *past of* GRIND
ground crew *n* : the mechanics and technicians who maintain and service an aircraft
ground·er \'graủn-dər\ *n* : a batted ball that strikes the ground almost immediately — called also *ground ball*
ground finch *n* : any of several dull-colored large-billed finches that occur in the Galapagos islands
ground·hog \'graủnd-ˌhòg, -ˌhäg\ *n* : WOODCHUCK
Groundhog Day *n* [from the legend that the groundhog comes out of hibernation on this date, but is frightened back for six more weeks if the day is sunny and he sees his shadow, thus betokening six more weeks of winter] : February 2
ground·less \'graủn-dləs\ *adj* : being without basis or reason ⟨*groundless* fears⟩ — **ground·less·ly** *adv* — **ground·less·ness** *n*
ground·ling \'graủn-dling\ *n* **1 a** : a spectator in the cheaper part of a theater **b** : a person of inferior taste **2** : one that lives or works on or near the ground
ground·mass \'graủn(d)-ˌmas\ *n* : the fine-grained base of a rock in which larger crystals are embedded
ground pine *n* : any of several club mosses with long creeping stems and erect branches

ground plan *n* **1 :** a plan of a floor of a building **2 :** a first or basic plan
ground squirrel *n* **:** any of numerous burrowing rodents (as the gophers and chipmunks) differing from true squirrels in having cheek pouches and shorter fur
ground state *n* **:** the energy level of a physical system (as an atom) having the least energy of all its possible states
ground swell *n* **:** a broad deep ocean swell caused by a distant storm or earthquake
ground·wa·ter \'grau̇nd-ˌwȯt-ər, -ˌwät-\ *n* **:** water within the earth that supplies wells and springs
ground·work \'grau̇nd-ˌwərk\ *n* **:** FOUNDATION, BASIS
¹**group** \'grüp\ *n* **1 :** a number of objects or persons regarded as a unit **2 a :** a number of plants or animals having some natural relationship **b :** an assemblage of atoms forming part of a molecule ⟨a methyl *group*⟩ **3 :** a small band **:** COMBO ⟨a rock *group*⟩
²**group** *vb* **:** to arrange or combine in a group ⟨*group* children by ages⟩
grou·per \'grü-pər\ *n, pl* **groupers** *also* **grouper :** any of numerous mostly large solitary bottom fishes of warm seas related to the sea basses
group·ie \'grü-pē\ *n, slang* **:** a girl who admires a rock group and follows it on tour
¹**grouse** \'grau̇s\ *n, pl* **grouse :** any of numerous plump-bodied game birds usu. protectively colored and less brilliant in plumage than the related pheasants
²**grouse** *vb* **:** COMPLAIN, GRUMBLE — **grous·er** *n*
grove \'grōv\ *n* **:** a small wood; *esp* **:** a group of trees without underbrush ⟨an orange *grove*⟩
grov·el \'gräv-əl, 'grəv-\ *vb* **-eled** *or* **-elled; -el·ing** *or* **-el·ling** \-(ə-)liŋ\ **1 :** to lie or creep with the body prostrate esp. as a sign of subservience **2 :** to abase oneself **:** CRINGE — **grov·el·er** *or* **grov·el·ler** \-(ə-)lər\ *n*
grow \'grō\ *vb* **grew** \'grü\; **grown** \'grōn\; **growing 1 a :** to spring up and develop to maturity **b :** to be able to grow in some place or situation ⟨rice *grows* in water⟩ **c :** to assume some relation through or as if through growth ⟨a tree with limbs *grown* together⟩ **2 :** INCREASE, EXPAND ⟨the city is *growing* rapidly⟩ ⟨*grows* in wisdom⟩ **3 :** ORIGINATE ⟨the project *grew* out of a mere suggestion⟩ **4 a :** to pass into a condition **:** BECOME ⟨*grew* pale⟩ **b :** to obtain influence ⟨habit *grows* on a man⟩ **5 :** to cause to grow **:** CULTIVATE, RAISE ⟨*grow* wheat⟩ — **grow·er** \'grō(-ə)r\ *n*
growing point *n* **:** the tip of a plant shoot from which additional shoot tissues differentiate
growing season *n* **:** the period of the year warm enough for growth esp. of cultivated plants; *esp* **:** the period between the last spring and the first fall killing frost
growl \'grau̇l\ *vb* **1 a :** RUMBLE **b :** to utter a deep guttural threatening sound ⟨the dog *growled* at the stranger⟩ **2 :** COMPLAIN — **growl** *n* — **growl·er** *n*
grown \'grōn\ *adj* **:** fully grown **:** MATURE ⟨*grown* man⟩
grown–up \'grōn-ˌəp\ *adj* **:** ADULT ⟨*grown-up* books⟩ — **grown–up** *n*
growth \'grōth\ *n* **1 a :** stage or condition attained in growing **:** SIZE ⟨hasn't reached his full *growth*⟩ **b :** a process of growing esp. through orderly increase in amount of protoplasm or inorganic substance ⟨*growth* of a crystal⟩ **c :** progressive development ⟨the *growth* of civilization⟩; *also* **:** INCREASE ⟨*growth* of wealth⟩ **2 :** a result or product of growing ⟨covered with a *growth* of mold⟩ ⟨a thick *growth* of underbrush⟩ **3 :** an abnormal mass of tissue (as a tumor)

ə abut	ər further	a back	ā bake
ä cot, cart	au̇ out	ch chin	e less	ē easy
g gift	i trip	ī life	j joke	ŋ sing	ō flow
ȯ flaw	ȯi coin	th thin	t͟h this	ü loot
u̇ foot	y yet	yü few	yu̇ furious	zh vision

growth hormone *n* **:** a hormone in plants or animals that regulates growth; *esp* **:** one produced by the pituitary gland
¹**grub** \'grəb\ *vb* **grubbed; grub·bing 1 :** to clear or root out by digging ⟨*grub* up roots⟩ ⟨*grub* for potatoes⟩ **2 :** to work hard **:** DRUDGE — **grub·ber** *n*
²**grub** *n* **1 :** a soft thick wormlike larva of an insect **2 :** DRUDGE **3 :** FOOD
grub·by \'grəb-ē\ *adj* **grub·bi·er; -est :** DIRTY, SLOVENLY — **grub·bi·ly** \'grəb-ə-lē\ *adv* — **grub·bi·ness** \'grəb-ē-nəs\ *n*
grub·stake \'grəb-ˌstāk\ *n* **:** supplies or funds furnished a mining prospector in return for a promise of a share in his finds — **grubstake** *vb* — **grub·stak·er** *n*
¹**grudge** \'grəj\ *vb* **:** BEGRUDGE — **grudg·er** *n* — **grudg·ing·ly** \'grəj-iŋ-lē\ *adv*
²**grudge** *n* **:** a feeling of deep-seated resentment or ill will
gru·el \'grü-əl\ *n* **:** a thin food made by boiling cereal (as oatmeal or cornmeal) in water or milk
gru·el·ing *or* **gru·el·ling** \'grü-ə-liŋ\ *adj* **:** requiring extreme effort **:** EXHAUSTING ⟨a *grueling* race⟩
grue·some \'grü-səm\ *adj* **:** inspiring horror or repulsion **:** GRISLY — **grue·some·ly** *adv* — **grue·some·ness** *n*
gruff \'grəf\ *adj* **1 :** rough or stern in manner, speech, or look ⟨a *gruff* reply⟩ **2 :** being deep and harsh **:** HOARSE ⟨a *gruff* voice⟩ — **gruff·ly** *adv* — **gruff·ness** *n*
grum·ble \'grəm-bəl\ *vb* **grum·bled; grum·bling** \-b(ə-)liŋ\ **1 :** to mutter in discontent **2 :** RUMBLE — **grumble** *n* — **grum·bler** \-b(ə-)lər\ *n*
grump \'grəmp\ *n* **1** *pl* **:** a fit of ill humor **2 :** a person given to complaining — **grump·i·ly** \'grəm-pə-lē\ *adv* — **grump·i·ness** \-pē-nəs\ *n* — **grumpy** \-pē\ *adj*
grunt \'grənt\ *n* **1 a :** the deep short sound characteristic of a hog **b :** a similar sound **2 :** any of numerous marine fishes related to the snappers — **grunt** *vb* — **grunt·er** *n*
grv *abbr* grove
gryph·on *var of* GRIFFIN
GSA *abbr* Girl Scouts of America
G suit *n* **:** an aviator's or astronaut's suit designed to counteract the physiological effects of acceleration
gt *abbr* great
Gt Brit *abbr* Great Britain
GU *abbr* Guam
gua·nine \'gwän-ˌēn\ *n* **:** a base regularly present in DNA and RNA
gua·no \'gwän-ō\ *n, pl* **guanos :** a substance composed chiefly of the excrement of seabirds and used as a fertilizer
¹**guar·an·tee** \ˌgar-ən-'tē\ *n* **1 :** GUARANTOR **2 :** an agreement by which a person or firm guarantees something or someone **3 :** something given as security **:** PLEDGE
²**guarantee** *vb* **-teed; -tee·ing 1 :** to undertake to answer for the debt, failure to perform, or faulty performance of another **2 :** to promise that some condition holds or will be fulfilled ⟨*guarantee* a car against defects for one year⟩ ⟨*guaranteed* annual wage⟩ **3 :** to give security **:** SECURE

guar·an·tor \ˌgar-ən-'tȯ(ə)r, 'gar-ən-tər\ *n* : a person who gives a guarantee

guar·an·ty \'gar-ən-tē\ *n, pl* **-ties** : GUARANTEE — **guaranty** *vb*

[1]**guard** \'gärd\ *n* **1** : a posture of defense ⟨on *guard*⟩ **2 a** : the act or duty of protecting or defending **b** : PROTECTION **3 a** : a man or body of men that guard **b** *pl* : a body of troops whose duties include guarding a head of state or one patterned on such a body **4 a** : a football player who lines up inside the tackle and next to the center **b** : either of two primarily defensive players stationed to the rear of the court in basketball **5** : a protective or safety device (as on a machine)

[2]**guard** *vb* **1** : to protect from danger : DEFEND **2** : to watch over so as to restrain, control, or check ⟨*guard* a prisoner⟩ ⟨a closely *guarded* secret⟩ ⟨*guard* his tongue⟩ **3** : to attempt to prevent an opponent from scoring **4** : to be on guard : take precautions ⟨*guard* against infection⟩

guard cell *n* : one of the two crescent-shaped epidermal cells that border and open and close a plant stoma

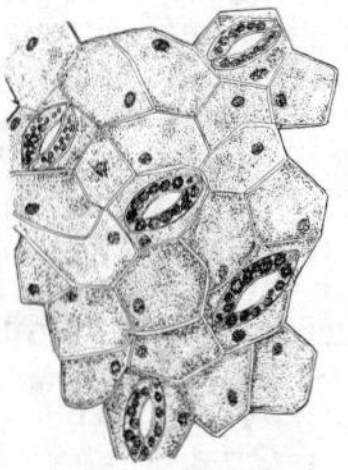

guard cells in leaf epidermis (magnified 150 times)

guard·ed \'gärd-əd\ *adj* : CAUTIOUS, NONCOMMITTAL ⟨a *guarded* answer⟩ — **guard·ed·ly** *adv*

guard·house \'gärd-ˌhau̇s\ *n* **1** : a building occupied by a guard or used as a headquarters by soldiers on guard duty **2** : a military jail

guard·i·an \'gärd-ē-ən\ *n* **1** : one that guards : CUSTODIAN **2** : one who has the care of the person or property of another — **guard·i·an·ship** \-ˌship\ *n*

guard·room \'gärd-ˌrüm, -ˌru̇m\ *n* **1** : a room used by a military guard while on duty **2** : a room where military prisoners are confined

guards·man \'gärdz-mən\ *n* : a member of a military body called *guard* or *guards*

gua·va \'gwäv-ə\ *n* **1** : any of several tropical American shrubs or small trees related to the myrtle; *esp* : one widely grown for its sweet-to-acid yellow fruit **2** : the fruit of a guava used esp. for making jelly and jam

gu·ber·na·to·ri·al \ˌgü-bə(r)-nə-'tōr-ē-əl, ˌgyü-, -'tȯr-\ *adj* : of or relating to a governor

gud·geon \'gəj-ən\ *n* **1** : a small European freshwater fish related to the carps **2** : any of various minnows

guern·sey \'gərn-zē\ *n, pl* **guernseys** : any of a breed of fawn and white dairy cattle that are larger than jerseys and produce rich yellowish milk

guer·ril·la *or* **gue·ril·la** \gə-'ril-ə\ *n* [from Spanish *guerrilla* "band of skirmishers", diminutive of *guerra* "war"] : a person who engages in irregular warfare esp. as a member of an independent unit carrying out harassment and sabotage — **guerrilla** *adj*

guess \'ges\ *vb* **1** : to form an opinion from little or no evidence **2** : to conjecture correctly about : DISCOVER **3** : BELIEVE, SUPPOSE ⟨I *guess* you're right⟩ — **guess** *n* — **guess·er** *n* — **guess·work** \'ges-ˌwərk\ *n*

guest \'gest\ *n* **1** : a person entertained in one's house **2** : a person to whom hospitality is extended ⟨*guests* at a school banquet⟩ ⟨*guests* on a TV show⟩ **3** : a patron of a hotel, motel, inn, or restaurant

guf·faw \(ˌ)gə-'fȯ\ *n* : a loud burst of laughter — **guf·faw** *vb*

guid·ance \'gīd-ən(t)s\ *n* **1** : the act or process of guiding **2** : advice on vocational or educational problems given to students **3** : the process of controlling the course of a projectile (as a missile) by a built-in mechanism ⟨*guidance* system⟩

[1]**guide** \'gīd\ *n* **1 a** : one who leads or directs another on his course **b** : one who exhibits and explains points of interest **c** : something that provides guiding information ⟨a street *guide*⟩ **d** : a principle of conduct ⟨let your conscience be your *guide*⟩ **2** : a device or organ for steadying or directing the motion of something

[2]**guide** *vb* **1** : to act as a guide : CONDUCT ⟨*guide* a group on a tour⟩ **2 a** : MANAGE, DIRECT ⟨*guide* a boat through the rapids⟩ **b** : to superintend the training or conduct of : INSTRUCT, COUNSEL — **guid·a·ble** \'gīd-ə-bəl\ *adj*

guide·book \'gīd-ˌbu̇k\ *n* : a book of information for travelers

guid·ed missile \ˌgīd-əd-\ *n* : a missile whose course toward a target may be changed (as by radio signals or a built-in target-seeking device) during flight

guide·line \'gīd-ˌlīn\ *n* **1** : a means of identification (as a number) or orientation (as a line) by which one is guided **2** : an outline of criteria for future policy or action

guide·post \-ˌpōst\ *n* **1** : a post (as at the fork of a road) with directions for travelers **2** : INDICATION, SIGN

guide word *n* : either of the terms at the left and right of the head of a page of an alphabetical reference work (as a dictionary) indicating the first and last entries on the page

guild \'gild\ *n* : an association of men with common interests or aims; *esp* : a medieval association of merchants or craftsmen — **guild·ship** \-ˌship\ *n*

guild·hall \'gild-ˌhȯl\ *n* : a hall where a guild or corporation assembles : TOWN HALL

guile \'gīl\ *n* : deceitful cunning : DUPLICITY — **guile·ful** \-fəl\ *adj* — **guile·ful·ly** \-fə-lē\ *adv* — **guile·ful·ness** *n*

guile·less \'gīl-ləs\ *adj* : free from deceit or cunning : INNOCENT, NAÏVE ⟨a *guileless* person⟩ ⟨a *guileless* smile⟩ — **guile·less·ly** *adv* — **guile·less·ness** *n*

guil·lo·tine \'gil-ə-ˌtēn, 'gē-(y)ə-\ *n* : a machine for cutting off a person's head by means of a heavy blade sliding in two upright grooved posts — **guillotine** *vb*

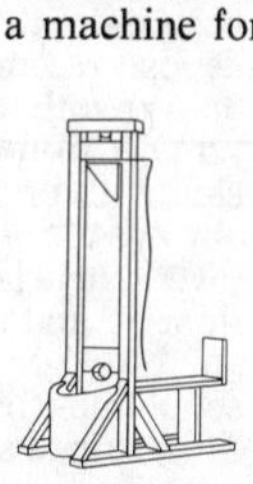

guillotine

guilt \'gilt\ *n* **1** : the fact of having committed an offense and esp. one that is punishable by law **2** : BLAMEWORTHINESS **3** : a feeling of responsibility for offenses — **guilt·less** \-ləs\ *adj*

guilty \'gil-tē\ *adj* **guilt·i·er**; **-est 1** : having committed a breach of conduct **2 a** : suggesting or involving guilt ⟨a *guilty* manner⟩ **b** : aware of or suffering from guilt — **guilt·i·ly** \-tə-lē\ *adv* — **guilt·i·ness** \-tē-nəs\ *n*

guin·ea \'gin-ē\ *n* **1** : a British gold coin no longer issued worth 21 shillings **2** : a former unit of value equal to 21 shillings

guin·ea fowl \'gin-ē-\ *n* : a gray and white spotted game and farm bird related to the pheasants, widely raised for food, and marked by a bare neck and head

guinea hen *n* : GUINEA FOWL; *esp* : a female guinea fowl

guinea pig *n* **1** : a small stout-bodied short-eared

nearly tailless rodent often kept as a pet and widely used in biological research **2 :** a person or thing experimented on

guise \'gīz\ *n* **1 :** a form or style of dress : COSTUME ⟨in the *guise* of a shepherd⟩ **2 :** external appearance : SEMBLANCE ⟨swindled people under the *guise* of friendship⟩

gui·tar \gə-'tär\ *n* **:** a flat-bodied stringed instrument with a long fretted neck and usu. six strings plucked with a plectrum or with the fingers

gulch \'gəlch\ *n* **:** RAVINE, COULEE

gulf \'gəlf\ *n* **1 :** a part of an ocean or sea extending into the land **2 :** a deep hollow in the earth : CHASM, ABYSS **3 :** a wide separation : an unbridgeable gap

Gulf Stream *n* **:** a warm ocean current in the north Atlantic flowing from the Gulf of Mexico along the eastern coast of the U.S. to Nantucket Island and thence eastward

1**gull** \'gəl\ *n* **:** any of numerous mostly white or gray long-winged web-footed hook-billed aquatic birds

2**gull** *vb* **:** to make a dupe of : DECEIVE

3**gull** *n* **:** a person easily deceived or cheated : DUPE

gul·let \'gəl-ət\ *n* **1 :** the tube that leads from the back of the mouth to the stomach : ESOPHAGUS **2 :** THROAT

gull·i·ble \'gəl-ə-bəl\ *adj* **:** easily deceived, cheated, or duped — **gull·i·bil·i·ty** \ˌgəl-ə-'bil-ət-ē\ *n* — **gull·i·bly** \'gəl-ə-blē\ *adv*

gul·ly \'gəl-ē\ *n, pl* **gullies :** a trench worn in the earth by running water after rains — **gully** *vb*

gully erosion *n* **:** soil erosion produced by running water

gulp \'gəlp\ *vb* **1 :** to swallow hurriedly or greedily or in one swallow **2 :** to keep back as if by swallowing ⟨*gulp* down a sob⟩ **3 :** to catch the breath as if in taking a long drink — **gulp** *n* — **gulp·er** *n*

1**gum** \'gəm\ *n* **:** the tissue along the jaws of animals that surrounds the necks of the teeth

2**gum** *n* **1 :** any of numerous complex colloidal substances (as gum arabic) that are exuded by plants or are extracted from them by solvents, that are thick or sticky when moist but harden on drying and are either soluble in water or swell up in contact with water, and that are used in pharmacy, for adhesives, as food thickeners, and in inks; *also* **:** any of various gummy plant exudates including natural resins, rubber, and rubberlike substances **2 :** a substance or deposit resembling a plant gum (as in sticky quality) **3 :** a tree that yields a gum **4 :** CHEWING GUM

3**gum** *vb* **gummed; gum·ming :** to smear, seal, or clog with or as if with gum ⟨*gum* up the works⟩

gum arabic *n* **:** a water-soluble gum obtained from several acacias and used esp. in adhesives, in confectionery, and in pharmacy

gum·bo \'gəm-bō\ *n, pl* **gumbos 1 :** OKRA **2 :** a soup thickened with okra pods **3 :** any of various fine-grained silty soils that become very sticky when wet

gum·boil \'gəm-ˌbȯil\ *n* **:** an abscess in the gums

gum·drop \-ˌdräp\ *n* **:** a candy made usu. from corn syrup with gelatin or gum arabic and coated with sugar crystals

gum·my \'gəm-ē\ *adj* **gum·mi·er; -est 1 :** consisting of, containing, or covered with gum **2 :** VISCOUS, STICKY — **gum·mi·ness** *n*

ə abut	ər further	a back	ā bake
ä cot, cart	aů out	ch chin	e less
ē easy	g gift	i trip	ī life
j joke	ng sing	ō flow	ȯ flaw
ȯi coin	th thin	th this	ü loot
ů foot	y yet	yü few	yů furious
zh vision			

gump·tion \'gəm(p)-shən\ *n* **1 :** shrewd common sense **2 :** courageous or vigorous initiative : SPUNK

1**gun** \'gən\ *n* **1 a :** a piece of artillery usu. with a relatively long barrel and comparatively flat trajectory : CANNON **b :** a portable firearm (as a rifle or pistol) **2 a :** a discharge of a gun ⟨a 21-*gun* salute⟩ **b :** a signal marking a beginning or ending ⟨the opening *gun* of his campaign⟩ **3 :** something suggesting a gun in shape or function ⟨grease *gun*⟩ **4 :** THROTTLE — **gunned** \'gənd\ *adj*

2**gun** *vb* **gunned; gun·ning 1 :** to hunt or shoot with a gun ⟨*gunning* for rabbits⟩ **2 :** to open up the throttle of so as to increase speed ⟨*gun* the engine⟩

gun·boat \'gən-ˌbōt\ *n* **:** a small lightly armed ship for use in shallow waters

gun·cot·ton \-ˌkät-ən\ *n* **:** an explosive usu. made by soaking cotton with nitric and sulfuric acids

gun·fight \-ˌfīt\ *n* **:** a duel with guns — **gun·fight·er** *n*

gun·fire \-ˌfī(ə)r\ *n* **:** the firing of guns

gun·lock \-ˌläk\ *n* **:** a device on a firearm by which the charge is ignited

gun·man \-mən\ *n* **:** a man armed with a gun; *esp* **:** an armed criminal

gun·met·al \-ˌmet-əl\ *n* **1 a :** a bronze formerly much used for making cannon **b :** a metal treated to look like gunmetal **2 :** a slightly purplish dark gray

gun·ner \'gən-ər\ *n* **1 :** a soldier or airman who operates or aims a gun **2 :** one that hunts with a gun

gun·nery \'gən-(ə-)rē\ *n* **1 :** the use of guns **2 :** the science of the flight of projectiles and of the effective use of guns

gun·ny \'gən-ē\ *n, pl* **gunnies 1 :** coarse jute sacking **2 :** BURLAP

gun·ny·sack \-ˌsak\ *n* **:** a sack made of gunny

gun·point \'gən-ˌpȯint\ *n* **:** the point of a gun — **at gunpoint :** under a threat of death by being shot

gun·pow·der \-ˌpaůd-ər\ *n* **:** an explosive mixture used in guns and blasting

gun·ship \-ˌship\ *n* **:** an aircraft armed with rockets and machine guns for protection of ground troops or aircraft carrying them

gun·shot \-ˌshät\ *n* **1 :** shot or a projectile fired from a gun **2 :** the range of a gun ⟨within *gunshot*⟩

gun·smith \-ˌsmith\ *n* **:** one whose business is the making and repair of firearms

gun·wale *or* **gun·nel** \'gən-əl\ *n* **:** the upper edge of a ship's side

gup·py \'gəp-ē\ *n, pl* **guppies :** a small tropical minnow often kept as an aquarium fish

gur·gle \'gər-gəl\ *vb* **gur·gled; gur·gling** \'gər-g(ə-)liŋ\ **1 :** to flow in a broken irregular current **2 :** to make a sound like that of a gurgling liquid — **gurgle** *n*

gu·ru \gə-'rü, 'gů(ə)r-ü\ *n* **:** a personal religious teacher and spiritual guide in Hinduism

gush \'gəsh\ *vb* **1 :** to issue or pour forth copiously or violently : SPOUT ⟨oil *gushed* from the new well⟩ **2 :** to make an exaggerated display of affection or enthusiasm ⟨*gushed* over the latest movie star⟩ — **gush** *n*

gush·er \'gəsh-ər\ *n* **:** one that gushes; *esp* **:** an oil well with a copious natural flow

gus·set \'gəs-ət\ *n* **:** a usu. triangular or diamond-shaped insert (as in a glove) to give width or strength

gust \'gəst\ *n* **1 :** a sudden brief rush of wind **2 :** a sudden outburst : SURGE ⟨a *gust* of anger⟩ — **gusty** \'gəs-tē\ *adj*

gus·to \'gəs-tō\ *n* **:** keen enjoyment or appreciation ⟨eat with *gusto*⟩

1**gut** \'gət\ *n* **1 a :** VISCERA, ENTRAILS — usu. used in pl. **b :** the alimentary canal or part of it; *esp* **:** the intestine of an animal prepared for some special use (as stringing tennis rackets) **c** : BELLY, ABDOMEN **2** *pl* : the inner essential parts **3** *pl* : COURAGE

²**gut** *vb* **gut·ted**; **gut·ting** **1** : to remove the entrails from ⟨scale and *gut* a fish⟩ **2** : to destroy the inside of ⟨fire *gutted* the building⟩

gut·ta–per·cha \ˌgət-ə-ˈpər-chə\ *n* : a tough plastic substance that resembles rubber, is used esp. as insulation and in dentistry, and is derived from several Malaysian trees

¹**gut·ter** \ˈgət-ər\ *n* **1 a** : a trough along the eaves to catch and carry off water from a roof **b** : a low area (as at a roadside) to carry off surface water **2** : a narrow channel or groove

²**gutter** *vb* **1** : to form gutters in **2 a** : to flow in small streams **b** : to melt away by becoming channeled ⟨a *guttering* candle⟩ **3** : to flicker in a draft

gut·tur·al \ˈgət-ə-rəl\ *adj* **1** : of or relating to the throat **2 a** : formed or pronounced in the throat ⟨*guttural* sounds⟩ **b** : formed with the back of the tongue touching or near the palate — **guttural** *n* — **gut·tur·al·ly** \-rə-lē\ *adv*

¹**guy** \ˈgī\ *n* : a rope, chain, or rod attached to something as a brace or guide

²**guy** *vb* **guyed**; **guy·ing** : to steady or reinforce with a guy

³**guy** *n* : MAN, FELLOW

⁴**guy** *vb* **guyed**; **guy·ing** : to make fun of : RIDICULE

guz·zle \ˈgəz-əl\ *vb* **guz·zled**; **guz·zling** \-(ə-)liŋ\ : to drink greedily — **guz·zler** \-(ə-)lər\ *n*

gybe \ˈjīb\ *var of* JIBE

gym \ˈjim\ *n* : GYMNASIUM

gym·na·si·um \jim-ˈnā-zē-əm\ *n, pl* **-si·ums** *or* **-sia** \-zē-ə\ : a room or building for sports activities

gym·nast \ˈjim-ˌnast\ *n* : an expert in gymnastics

gym·nas·tics \jim-ˈnas-tiks\ *n sing or pl* : physical exercises developing or exhibiting skill, strength, and control in the use of the body — **gym·nas·tic** \-tik\ *adj*

gym·no·sperm \ˈjim-nə-ˌspərm\ *n* : any of a group of woody vascular seed plants that produce naked seeds not enclosed in a true fruit — **gym·no·sper·mous** \ˌjim-nə-ˈspər-məs\ *adj*

gyn·an·dro·morph \jin-ˈan-drə-ˌmȯrf, gīn-\ *n* : an abnormal individual having characters of both sexes in various parts of the body — **gyn·an·dro·mor·phic** \-ˌan-drə-ˈmȯr-fik\ *adj* — **gyn·an·dro·mor·phism** \-ˌfiz-əm\ *n* — **gyn·an·dro·mor·phous** \-fəs\ *adj*

gy·ne·col·o·gy \ˌgīn-i-ˈkäl-ə-jē, ˌjin-\ *n* : a branch of medicine that deals with women, their diseases, and their hygiene — **gy·ne·co·log·ic** \-kə-ˈläj-ik\ *or* **gy·ne·co·log·i·cal** \-ˈläj-i-kəl\ *adj* — **gy·ne·col·o·gist** \-ˈkäl-ə-jəst\ *n*

¹**gyp** \ˈjip\ *n* **1** : CHEAT, SWINDLER **2** : FRAUD, SWINDLE

²**gyp** *vb* **gypped**; **gyp·ping** : CHEAT, SWINDLE

gyp·sum \ˈjip-səm\ *n* : a colorless mineral that consists of calcium sulfate occurring in crystals or masses and that is used esp. as a soil improver and in making plaster of paris

Gyp·sy \ˈjip-sē\ *n, pl* **Gypsies** [a shortened and altered form of *Egyptian*, so called because Gypsies were once believed to have come from Egypt] **1** : one of a dark Caucasian people coming orig. from India to Europe in the 14th or 15th century and living and maintaining a migratory way of life **2** : ROMANY 2

gypsy moth *n* : an Old World moth introduced about 1869 into the U.S. that has a grayish mottled hairy caterpillar which is a destructive defoliator of many trees

gy·rate \ˈjī-ˌrāt\ *vb* **1** : to revolve around a point or axis **2** : SPIN, WHIRL — **gy·ra·tion** \jī-ˈrā-shən\ *n* — **gy·ra·tion·al** \-sh(ə-)nəl *adj*

gyr·fal·con \ˈjər-ˌfal-kən, -ˌfȯl-; -ˌfȯ-kən\ *n* : a large arctic falcon that is more powerful though less active than the peregrine falcon and may be blackish, white, or grayish

gy·ro \ˈjī-rō\ *n, pl* **gyros** **1** : GYROSCOPE **2** : GYROCOMPASS

gy·ro·com·pass \ˈjī-rō-ˌkəm-pəs, -ˌkäm-\ *n* : a compass in which the horizontal axis of a constantly spinning gyroscope points to the north and which is often used instead of a magnetic compass where metal in the vicinity (as on a ship) would interfere with the working of a magnetic compass

gy·ro·scope \ˈjī-rə-ˌskōp\ *n* : a wheel or disk mounted to spin rapidly about an axis that is free to turn in various directions

gyve \ˈjīv\ *n* : FETTER — usu. used in pl. — **gyve** *vb*

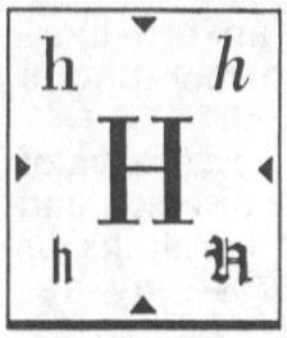

h \'āch\ *n, often cap* **1** : the 8th letter of the English alphabet **2** *slang* : HEROIN

h *abbr* **1** hard **2** hardness **3** hour **4** husband

H *abbr* hit

ha \'hä\ *interj* — used to express surprise, joy, grief, or doubt

Hab·ak·kuk \'hab-ə-ˌkək, hə-'bak-ək\ *n* — see BIBLE table

ha·be·as cor·pus \ˌhā-bē-əs-'kȯr-pəs\ *n* [from the formula used in such writs in medieval Latin, meaning "that you should have the body", addressed to jailers ordering them to produce a prisoner] **1** : a writ ordering an inquiry to determine whether a person has been lawfully imprisoned **2** : the right of a citizen to obtain a writ of habeas corpus as a protection against illegal imprisonment

hab·er·dash·er \'hab-ə(r)-ˌdash-ər\ *n* : a dealer in men's clothing and accessories

hab·er·dash·ery \-ˌdash-(ə-)rē\ *n, pl* **-er·ies** **1** : goods sold by a haberdasher **2** : a haberdasher's shop

ha·bil·i·ment \hə-'bil-ə-mənt\ *n* : CLOTHES — usu. used in pl.

hab·it \'hab-ət\ *n* **1** : a costume characteristic of a calling, rank, or function ⟨riding *habit*⟩ **2** : a usual manner of behavior or thinking : CUSTOM **3** : a behavior pattern acquired and fixed by frequent repetition; *esp* : one that has become nearly or completely involuntary **4** : characteristic mode of growth or occurrence ⟨elms have a spreading *habit*⟩

hab·it·a·ble \'hab-ət-ə-bəl\ *adj* : suitable or fit to live in ⟨the *habitable* parts of the earth⟩ — **hab·it·a·bil·i·ty** \ˌhab-ət-ə-'bil-ət-ē\ *n* — **hab·it·a·ble·ness** \'hab-ət-ə-bəl-nəs\ *n* — **hab·it·a·bly** \-blē\ *adv*

hab·i·tant \'hab-ət-ənt\ *n* : INHABITANT, RESIDENT

hab·i·tat \'hab-ə-ˌtat\ *n* [from the Latin verb form meaning "it dwells"] : the place or type of place where a plant or animal naturally or normally lives or grows

hab·i·ta·tion \ˌhab-ə-'tā-shən\ *n* **1** : the act of inhabiting : OCCUPANCY **2** : a dwelling place : RESIDENCE

hab·it–form·ing *adj* : inducing the formation of an addiction

ha·bit·u·al \hə-'bich-(ə-w)əl\ *adj* **1** : according to or constituting a habit ⟨*habitual* tardiness⟩ **2** : doing or acting by force of habit ⟨*habitual* smoker⟩ **3** : REGULAR ⟨*habitual* evening walk⟩ ***syn*** see USUAL ***ant*** occasional — **ha·bit·u·al·ly** \-ē\ *adv* — **ha·bit·u·al·ness** *n*

ha·bit·u·ate \hə-'bich-ə-ˌwāt\ *vb* : to make used to : ACCUSTOM — **ha·bit·u·a·tion** \-ˌbich-ə-'wā-shən\ *n*

ha·chure \ha-'shu̇(ə)r\ *n* : a short line used in drawing and engraving for shading or esp. to show different levels or slopes on a map

ha·ci·en·da \ˌ(h)äs-ē-'en-də\ *n* : a large estate in Spanish-speaking countries

1**hack** \'hak\ *vb* **1** : to cut or sever with repeated irregular or unskillful blows : CHOP **2** : to cough in a short dry manner — **hack·er** *n*

2**hack** *n* **1** : NICK, NOTCH **2** : a short dry cough

ə abut	ər further	a back	ā bake
ä cot, cart	au̇ out	ch chin	e less	ē easy
g gift	i trip	ī life	j joke	ng sing	ō flow
ȯ flaw	ȯi coin	th thin	th this	ü loot
u̇ foot	y yet	yü few	yu̇ furious	zh vision

3**hack** *n* **1 a** (1) : a horse let out for common hire (2) : a horse used in all kinds of work **b** : a worn-out horse **c** : a light easy saddle horse; *esp* : a three-gaited saddle horse **2 a** : HACKNEY **b** (1) : TAXICAB (2) : a driver of a cab **3 a** : a writer who works mainly for hire **b** : one who serves a cause merely for reward ⟨party *hacks* in a political campaign⟩

4**hack** *adj* **1** : working for hire **2** : done by or characteristic of a hack ⟨*hack* writing⟩

5**hack** *vb* **1** : to ride or drive at an ordinary pace or over the roads rather than across country **2** : to operate a taxicab

hack·ber·ry \'hak-ˌber-ē\ *n* **1** : any of a genus of trees and shrubs that are related to the elm and have small often edible berries **2** : the wood of a hackberry

hack·le \'hak-əl\ *n* **1** : a comb for dressing fibers (as flax or hemp) **2** : one of the long narrow feathers on the neck or lower back of a bird **3** : erectile hairs along the neck and back esp. of a dog

hack·ma·tack \'hak-mə-ˌtak\ *n* **1** : TAMARACK **2** : BALSAM POPLAR

1**hack·ney** \'hak-nē\ *n, pl* **hackneys** **1** : any of a breed of compact English horses with a high knee and hock flexion **2** : a carriage or automobile kept for hire

hackney 1

2**hackney** *adj* **1** : kept for public hire **2** : HACKNEYED

hack·neyed \'hak-nēd\ *adj* : worn out from too long or too much use : COMMONPLACE ⟨a *hackneyed* expression⟩

hack·saw \'hak-ˌsȯ\ *n* : a fine-tooth saw with blade clamped in a bow-shaped frame for cutting hard materials (as metal)

had *past of* HAVE

had·dock \'had-ək\ *n, pl* **haddock** *also* **haddocks** : an important Atlantic food fish usu. smaller than the related common cod

ha·des \'hād-(ˌ)ēz\ *n* **1** *cap* : the abode of the dead in Greek mythology **2** : HELL

hadn't \'had-ənt\ : had not

hadst \(')hadst, (h)ədst\ *archaic past 2d sing of* HAVE

hae \(')hā\ *chiefly Scot var of* HAVE

haf·ni·um \'haf-nē-əm\ *n* : a metallic element that resembles zirconium chemically and is useful because of its ready emission of electrons — see ELEMENT table

haft \'haft\ *n* : the handle of a weapon or tool

hag \'hag\ *n* **1** : WITCH **2** : an ugly, dirty, or evil-looking old woman

Hag·gai \'hag-ē-ˌī, 'hag-ˌī\ *n* — see BIBLE table

hag·gard \'hag-ərd\ *adj* : gaunt esp. from great hunger, worry, or pain

hag·gle \'hag-əl\ *vb* **hag·gled**; **hag·gling** \-(ə-)liŋ\ : to dispute or argue esp. in bargaining — **haggle** *n* — **hag·gler** \-(ə-)lər\ *n*

Hag·i·og·ra·pha \ˌhag-ē-'äg-rə-fə, ˌhā-jē-\ *n sing or pl* : the third part of the Jewish scriptures — compare LAW, PROPHETS

1**hail** \'hāl\ *n* **1** : small lumps of ice that fall from clouds esp. during thunderstorms **2** : something that gives the effect of falling hail ⟨a *hail* of bullets⟩

2**hail** *vb* **1** : to precipitate hail **2** : to pour down like hail

3**hail** *interj* **1** — used to express enthusiastic approval **2** *archaic* — used as a greeting

4**hail** *vb* **1 a :** GREET **b :** to greet with enthusiastic approval : ACCLAIM ⟨*hailed* him as a hero⟩ **2 :** to summon by calling ⟨*hail* a taxi⟩ **3 :** to call out to ⟨*hail* a passing ship⟩ — **hail from :** to come from ⟨he *hails from* New York⟩

5**hail** *n* **1 :** an act or instance of hailing **2 :** hailing distance ⟨within *hail*⟩

Hail Mary *n* **:** AVE MARIA

hail·stone \ˈhāl-ˌstōn\ *n* **:** a pellet of hail **:** a frozen drop of rain

hail·storm \-ˌstȯrm\ *n* **:** a storm accompanied by hail

hair \ˈha(ə)r, ˈhe(ə)r\ *n* **1 a :** a slender threadlike outgrowth from the skin of an animal; *esp* **:** one of the usu. pigmented filaments that form the characteristic coat of a mammal **b :** the hairy covering of an animal or a body part **2 a :** a tiny distance or amount ⟨won by a *hair*⟩ **b :** a precise degree ⟨aligned to a *hair*⟩ **3 :** a threadlike structure that resembles hair ⟨leaf *hair*⟩ — **haired** \ˈha(ə)rd, ˈhe(ə)rd\ *adj* — **hair·less** \ˈha(ə)r-ləs, ˈhe(ə)r-\ *adj* — **hair·like** \-ˌlīk\ *adj*

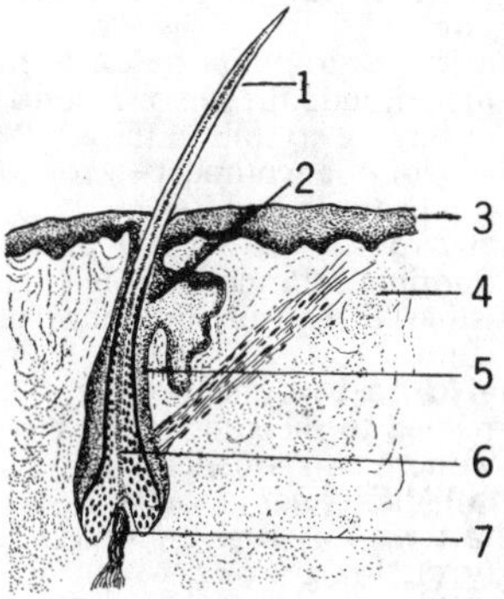

hair 1a:
1, shaft; 2, sebaceous gland; 3, epidermis; 4, dermis; 5, hair follicle; 6, bulb; 7, papilla

hair·breadth \ˈha(ə)r-ˌbredth, ˈhe(ə)r-\ *or* **hairs·breadth** \ˈha(ə)rz-, ˈhe(ə)rz-\ *n* **:** a very small distance or margin — **hairbreadth** *adj*

hair·brush \ˈha(ə)r-ˌbrəsh, ˈhe(ə)r-\ *n* **:** a brush for the hair

hair cell *n* **:** a sensory cell (as of the organ of hearing) bearing hairlike processes

hair·cloth \ˈha(ə)r-ˌklȯth, ˈhe(ə)r-\ *n* **:** any of various stiff wiry fabrics esp. of horsehair or camel's hair used for upholstery or stiffening in garments

hair·cut \-ˌkət\ *n* **:** the act, process, or style of cutting and shaping the hair — **hair·cut·ter** \-ˌkət-ər\ *n* — **hair·cut·ting** \-ˌkət-ing\ *n*

hair·do \-ˌdü\ *n, pl* **hairdos :** a way of dressing a woman's hair **:** COIFFURE ⟨the very latest in *hairdos*⟩

hair·dress·er \-ˌdres-ər\ *n* **:** one who dresses or cuts women's hair — **hair·dress·ing** \-ˌdres-ing\ *n*

hair follicle *n* **:** the tubular sheath surrounding the lower part of a hair shaft

hair hygrometer *n* **:** a hygrometer that employs one or more strands of human hair that expand with increasing humidity and contract with decreasing humidity and are connected to a pointer on a scale

hair·line \ˈha(ə)r-ˌlīn, ˈhe(ə)r-\ *n* **1 :** a very slender line **2 :** the outline of the hair on the head — **hairline** *adj*

hair·pin \-ˌpin\ *n* **1 :** a 2-pronged U-shaped pin to hold the hair in place **2 :** something shaped like a hairpin; *esp* **:** an extremely sharp turn in a road — **hairpin** *adj*

hair–rais·ing \-ˌrā-zing\ *adj* **:** causing terror, excitement, or astonishment ⟨a *hair-raising* climax⟩ — **hair–rais·ing·ly** \-zing-lē\ *adv*

hair seal *n* **:** any of a family of seals with a coarse hairy coat and no external ears — compare FUR SEAL

hair·snake \ˈha(ə)r-ˌsnāk, ˈhe(ə)r-\ *n* **:** HORSEHAIR WORM

hair·split·ter \-ˌsplit-ər\ *n* **:** a person who makes unnecessarily fine distinctions in reasoning — **hair·split·ting** \-ˌsplit-ing\ *adj or n*

hair·spring \-ˌspring\ *n* **:** a slender spiraled spring that regulates the motion of the balance wheel of a timepiece

hair·streak \-ˌstrēk\ *n* **:** any of various small usu. dark butterflies with hairlike projections from the hind wings

hair trigger *n* **:** a trigger so adjusted as to permit a firearm to be fired by a very slight pressure

hair·worm \ˈha(ə)r-ˌwərm, ˈhe(ə)r-\ *n* **:** any of various slender elongated worms (as a horsehair worm)

hairy \ˈha(ə)r-ē, ˈhe(ə)r-\ *adj* **hair·i·er; -est 1 :** bearing or covered with or as if with hair **2 :** made of or resembling hair — **hair·i·ness** *n*

hake \ˈhāk\ *n* **:** any of several marine food fishes related to the cod

hal·berd \ˈhal-bərd, ˈhȯl-\ *or* **hal·bert** \-bərt\ *n* **:** a long-handled weapon used both as a spear and as a battle-ax esp. in the 15th and 16th centuries — **hal·berd·ier** \ˌhal-bər-ˈdi(ə)r, ˌhȯl-\ *n*

1**hal·cy·on** \ˈhal-sē-ən\ *n* **1 :** a bird identified with the kingfisher and held in ancient legend to nest at sea in December and calm the waves **2 :** KINGFISHER

2**halcyon** *adj* **:** CALM, PEACEFUL ⟨*halcyon* days⟩

1**hale** \ˈhāl\ *adj* **:** SOUND, HEALTHY ⟨grandfather was still *hale* and hearty at eighty⟩

2**hale** *vb* **1 :** HAUL, PULL **2 :** to compel to go ⟨*haled* him into court⟩

1**half** \ˈhaf, ˈhȧf\ *n, pl* **halves** \ˈhavz, ˈhȧvz\ **1 :** one of two equal or nearly equal parts into which a thing is divisible **2 :** one of a pair: as **a :** one of the two periods that make up the playing time of various games **b :** the turn of one team to bat in baseball — **in half :** into two halves

H

2**half** *adj* **1 :** being one of two halves **2 :** of half the usual size or extent — **half·ness** *n*

3**half** *adv* **1 a :** to the extent of half ⟨*half* full⟩ **b :** PARTIALLY ⟨*half* persuaded⟩ **2 :** at all **:** by any means ⟨the song wasn't *half* bad⟩

half·back \ˈhaf-ˌbak, ˈhȧf-\ *n* **:** a football back who lines up on or near either flank; *also* **:** one of the players stationed behind the forward line in other games

half–breed \-ˌbrēd\ *n* **:** the offspring of parents of different races; *esp* **:** the offspring of an American Indian and a white person — **half–breed** *adj*

half brother *n* **:** a brother by one parent only

half–caste \ˈhaf-ˌkast, ˈhȧf-\ *n* **:** HALF-BREED — **half–caste** *adj*

half–dol·lar \-ˈdäl-ər\ *n* **1 :** a coin representing one half of a dollar **2 :** the sum of fifty cents

half·heart·ed \-ˈhärt-əd\ *adj* **:** lacking spirit or interest — **half·heart·ed·ly** *adv* — **half·heart·ed·ness** *n*

half hitch *n* **:** a simple knot so made as to be easily unfastened

half hour *n* **1 :** thirty minutes **2 :** the middle point of an hour — **half–hour·ly** \ˈhaf-ˈau̇(ə)r-lē, ˈhȧf-\ *adv or adj*

half–knot \ˈhaf-ˌnät, ˈhȧf-\ *n* **:** a knot joining the ends of two cords and used in tying other knots

half–life \-ˌlīf\ *n* **:** the time required for half of the atoms of a radioactive substance to become disintegrated

half line *n* : a straight line extending from a point in one direction only
half–mast \'haf-'mast, 'håf-\ *n* : a point about halfway down below the top of a mast or staff ⟨flags hanging at *half-mast*⟩
half–moon \-ˌmün\ *n* : the moon when half its disk appears illuminated
half note *n* : a musical note equal in time to ½ of a whole note
half·pen·ny \'hāp-(ə-)nē, *US also* 'haf-ˌpen-ē, 'håf-\ *n, pl* **half·pence** \'hā-pən(t)s, *US also* 'haf-ˌpen(t)s, 'håf-\ *or* **halfpennies** : a former British coin representing one half of a penny
half plane *n* : the part of a plane on one side of an indefinitely extended straight line drawn in it
half sister *n* : a sister by one parent only
half sole *n* : a shoe sole extending from the shank forward — **half–sole** \'haf-'sōl, 'håf-\ *vb*
half step *n* : the pitch interval between any two adjacent tones on a keyboard instrument — called also *semitone*
half·tone \'haf-ˌtōn, 'håf-\ *n* : a medium tint or tone in a painting, engraving, or photograph
half–track \-ˌtrak\ *n* **1** : an endless-chain track used in place of a rear wheel on a heavy-duty vehicle **2** : a motor vehicle propelled by half-tracks
half–truth \-ˌtrüth\ *n* : a statement that is only partially true; *esp* : one that deliberately mingles truth and falsehood
half·way \-'wā\ *adj* **1** : midway between two points ⟨stop at the *halfway* mark⟩ **2** : PARTIAL ⟨*halfway* measures⟩ — **halfway** *adv*
half–wit \-ˌwit\ *n* : a foolish or imbecilic person — **half–wit·ted** \-'wit-əd\ *adj*
hal·i·but \'hal-ə-bət, 'häl-\ *n, pl* **halibut** *also* **halibuts** [from Middle English *halybutte*, from *haly* "holy" and *butte* "flatfish"; so called because it was eaten on holy days] : a marine food fish that is the largest flatfish of both the Atlantic and Pacific oceans
hal·ide \'hal-ˌīd, 'hā-ˌlīd\ *n* : a compound of a halogen with another element or a radical
hal·ite \'hal-ˌīt, 'hā-ˌlīt\ *n* : native sodium chloride
hall \hȯl\ *n* **1 a** : a large or imposing residence or public building ⟨city *hall*⟩ **b** : one of the buildings of a college or university ⟨Science *Hall*⟩ ⟨residence *halls*⟩ **2 a** : the entrance room of a building : LOBBY **b** : a corridor or passage in a building **3** : a large room for assembly : AUDITORIUM **4** : a place used for public entertainment
¹**hal·le·lu·jah** \ˌhal-ə-'lü-yə\ *interj* [from Hebrew *halălū-yāh* "praise ye Jehovah"] — used to express praise, joy, or thanks
²**hallelujah** *n* : a shout or song of praise or thanksgiving
hall·mark \'hȯl-ˌmärk\ *n* **1** : an official mark stamped on gold and silver articles in England to attest their purity **2** : a mark of excellence, quality, or purity ⟨bears the *hallmarks* of genius⟩ — **hallmark** *vb*
hal·low \'hal-ō\ *vb* **1** : to make holy or set apart for holy use : CONSECRATE **2** : to respect greatly : VENERATE — **hal·lowed** \'hal-ōd, *in the Lord's Prayer also* 'hal-ə-wəd\ *adj*
Hal·low·een \ˌhal-ə-'wēn, ˌhäl-\ *n* : October 31 observed with merrymaking and pranks by children during the evening
Hal·low·mas \'hal-ō-ˌmas, -məs\ *n* : ALL SAINTS' DAY
Hall process \'hȯl-\ *n* : an electrolytic process by which aluminum is produced from aluminum oxide
hal·lu·ci·na·tion \hə-ˌlüs-ə-'nā-shən\ *n* : the perceiving of objects or the experiencing of feelings that have no cause outside one's mind esp. as the result of a mental disorder or as the effect of a drug; *also* : something so perceived or experienced — **hal·lu·ci·nate** \-'lüs-ə-ˌnāt\ *vb* — **hal·lu·ci·na·tion·al** \-ˌlüs-ə-'nā-sh(ə-)nəl\ *adj* — **hal·lu·ci·na·to·ry** \-'lü-sə-nə-ˌtōr-ē, -ˌtȯr-\ *adj*
hal·lu·ci·no·gen·ic \hə-ˌlü-sə-nə-'jen-ik\ *adj* : tending to produce hallucinations esp. when taken by mouth — **hal·lu·ci·no·gen** \-'lü-sə-nə-jən\ *n*
hall·way \'hȯl-ˌwā\ *n* **1** : an entrance hall **2** : CORRIDOR
ha·lo \'hā-lō\ *n, pl* **halos** *or* **haloes** **1** : a circle of light around the sun or moon caused by the presence of tiny ice crystals in the air **2** : NIMBUS **3** : the aura of glory or sentiment surrounding an idealized person or thing
hal·o·gen \'hal-ə-jən\ *n* : any of the five elements fluorine, chlorine, bromine, iodine, and astatine existing in the free state normally as diatomic molecules
hal·o·ge·ton \ˌhal-ə-'jēt-ən\ *n* : a coarse annual herb related to the goosefoots that is a noxious weed in western No. America
¹**halt** \'hȯlt\ *adj* : LAME
²**halt** *vb* **1** : LIMP **2** : WAVER, FALTER — **halt·ingly** \'hȯl-ting-lē\ *adv*
³**halt** *n* : STOP ⟨call a *halt*⟩
⁴**halt** *vb* **1** : to cease marching or journeying **2** : to bring to a stop : END
¹**hal·ter** \'hȯl-tər\ *n* **1** : a rope or strap for leading or tying an animal **2** : a rope for hanging criminals : NOOSE **3** : a woman's article of clothing that covers the upper body, that is held in place by straps, and that leaves the back, arms, and midriff bare — **halter** *vb*
²**hal·ter** \'hȯl-tər\ *or* **hal·tere** \-ˌti(ə)r\ *n, pl* **halteres** \hȯl-'ti(ə)r-(ˌ)ēz, 'hȯl-ˌti(ə)rz\ : one of a pair of club-shaped organs that are the modified second pair of wings of a two-winged fly and serve to maintain balance in flight
halve \'hav, 'håv\ *vb* **1** : to divide into two halves **2** : to reduce to one half ⟨*halving* the cost⟩
halves *pl of* HALF
hal·yard *or* **hal·liard** \'hal-yərd\ *n* : a rope or tackle for hoisting and lowering
¹**ham** \'ham\ *n* **1** : a buttock with its associated thigh — usu. used in pl. **2** : a cut of meat consisting of a thigh; *esp* : one from a hog **3 a** : an unskillful but showy performer **b** : an operator of an amateur radio station — **ham** *adj*
²**ham** *vb* **hammed**; **ham·ming** : to act with exaggerated speech or gestures
ham·burg·er \'ham-ˌbər-gər\ *or* **ham·burg** \-ˌbərg\ *n* **1 a** : ground beef **b** : a cooked patty of ground beef **2** : a sandwich consisting of a patty of hamburger in a split round bun
ham·let \'ham-lət\ *n* : a small village
¹**ham·mer** \'ham-ər\ *n* **1 a** : a hand tool that consists of a solid head set crosswise on a handle and is used for pounding (as in driving nails) **b** : a power tool for pounding **2** : something that resembles a hammer in shape or action (as the part of a gun whose striking action causes explosion of the charge) **3** : MALLEUS **4** : a heavy metal sphere that is hurled in an athletic event

[2]**hammer** *vb* **ham·mered; ham·mer·ing** \ˈham-(ə-)riŋ\ **1 :** to strike blows with or as if with a hammer : POUND **2 :** to make repeated efforts ⟨*hammer* away at one's lessons⟩ **3 :** to fasten, build, or shape with or as if with a hammer ⟨*hammer* out a policy⟩ — **ham·mer·er** \ˈham-ər-ər\ *n*

ham·mer·head \ˈham-ər-ˌhed\ *n* **:** any of various active voracious medium-sized sharks that have the eyes at the ends of lateral extensions of the flattened head

ham·mock \ˈham-ək\ *n* [from Spanish *hamaca*, from Taino, a West Indian language] **:** a swinging couch or bed usu. made of netting or canvas and slung by cords from supports at each end

[1]**ham·per** \ˈham-pər\ *vb* **ham·pered; ham·per·ing** \-p(ə-)riŋ\ **:** to restrict or interfere with the movement or operation of : IMPEDE, DISRUPT

[2]**hamper** *n* **:** a large basket usu. with a cover ⟨a clothes *hamper*⟩

ham·ster \ˈham(p)-stər\ *n* **:** any of various stocky short-tailed Old World rodents with large cheek pouches

hamster (about 7 in. long)

[1]**ham·string** \ˈham-ˌstriŋ\ *n* **1 :** either of two groups of tendons at the back of the human knee **2 :** a large tendon above and behind the hock of a four-footed animal

[2]**hamstring** *vb* **-strung** \-ˌstrəŋ\; **-string·ing** \-ˌstriŋ-iŋ\ **1 :** to cripple by cutting the leg tendons **2 :** to make ineffective or powerless : CRIPPLE

[1]**hand** \ˈhand\ *n* **1 a :** the free end part of the forelimb when modified (as in man) for handling, grasping, and holding **b :** any of various anatomical parts (as the hind foot of an ape or the pincers of a crab) that are similar to the hand in structure or function **2 :** something resembling a hand: as **a :** an indicator or pointer on a dial; *esp* **:** one of the pointers on a timepiece indicating the hour, minute, or second **b :** a figure of a hand with forefinger extended to point something out **c :** a cluster of bananas **3 :** personal possession : CONTROL, DIRECTION ⟨in the *hands* of the enemy⟩ **4 a :** SIDE, DIRECTION ⟨fighting on either *hand*⟩ **b :** a side or aspect of an issue or argument ⟨on the one *hand* . . . on the other *hand*⟩ **5 :** a pledge esp. of marriage ⟨gave him her *hand*⟩ **6 :** HANDWRITING **7 a :** SKILL, ABILITY ⟨try one's *hand* at chess⟩ **b :** a part or share in doing something ⟨take a *hand* in the work⟩ **8 :** SOURCE ⟨learn at first *hand*⟩ **9 :** a unit of measure equal to 4 inches used esp. for the height of horses **10 :** a round of applause ⟨give him a *hand*⟩ **11 a :** the cards or pieces held by a player in a game **b :** a single round in a game **12 a :** one who performs or executes a work ⟨two portraits by the same *hand*⟩ **b :** a hired worker : LABORER **c :** a member of a ship's crew ⟨all *hands* on deck⟩ **d :** one skilled in a particular activity or field **13 :** WORKMANSHIP ⟨the *hand* of a master⟩ — **at hand :** NEAR — **by hand :** with the hands — **in hand 1 :** in one's possession or control **2 :** in preparation — **on hand 1 :** in present possession ⟨goods *on hand*⟩ **2 :** in attendance : PRESENT — **out of hand :** out of control — **out of one's hands :** out of one's control

[2]**hand** *vb* **1 :** to guide or assist with the hand : CONDUCT ⟨*hand* a lady into a bus⟩ **2 :** to give or pass with the hand ⟨*hand* a person a letter⟩

hand·bag \ˈhan(d)-ˌbag\ *n* **1 :** TRAVELING BAG **2 :** a woman's bag for carrying small personal articles and money

hand·ball \-ˌbȯl\ *n* **1 :** a game played in a walled court or against a single wall or board by two or four players who use their hands to strike a ball **2 :** the ball used in handball

hand·bill \-ˌbil\ *n* **:** a printed sheet to be distributed by hand

hand·book \-ˌbu̇k\ *n* **:** a small book of facts or useful information usu. about a particular subject : MANUAL

hand·car \ˈhan(d)-ˌkär\ *n* **:** a small railroad car propelled by hand or by a small motor

[1]**hand·craft** \-ˌkraft\ *n* : HANDICRAFT

[2]**handcraft** *vb* **:** to fashion by handicraft

hand·cuff \ˈhan(d)-ˌkəf\ *n* **:** a metal fastening locking around a wrist and usu. connected by a chain or bar with another such fastening — usu. used in pl. — **handcuff** *vb*

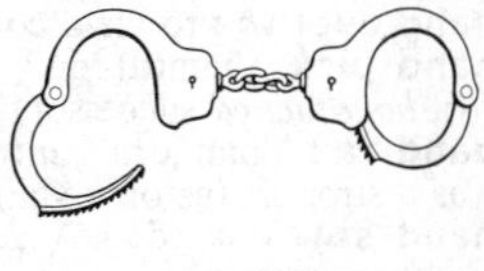

handcuffs

hand down *vb* **1 :** to transmit in succession ⟨*handed down* from generation to generation⟩ **2 :** to make formulation of and express a judicial decision

hand·ed \ˈhan-dəd\ *adj* **:** having or using such or so many hands ⟨a right-*handed* person⟩ — **hand·ed·ness** *n*

hand·ful \ˈhan(d)-ˌfu̇l\ *n, pl* **handfuls** \-ˌfu̇lz\ *or* **hands·ful** \ˈhan(d)z-ˌfu̇l\ **1 :** as much or as many as the hand will grasp **2 :** a small quantity or number **3 :** as much as one can control or manage

hand·gun \ˈhan(d)-ˌgən\ *n* **:** a firearm held and fired with one hand

[1]**hand·i·cap** \ˈhan-di-ˌkap\ *n* **1 :** a race or contest in which an artificial disadvantage is imposed on a contestant to equalize chances of winning; *also* **:** the disadvantage imposed **2 :** a disadvantage that makes progress or success difficult ⟨his overweight was a *handicap*⟩

[2]**handicap** *vb* **-capped; -cap·ping 1 :** to give a handicap to **2 :** to put at a disadvantage ⟨*handicapped* by poor health⟩

hand·i·craft \ˈhan-di-ˌkraft\ *n* **1 :** an occupation (as weaving or pottery making) requiring skill with the hands **2 :** articles fashioned by handicraft — **hand·i·craft·er** \-ˌkraf-tər\ *n* — **hand·i·crafts·man** \-ˌkraf(t)s-mən\ *n*

hand·i·ly \ˈhan-də-lē\ *adv* **1 :** CONVENIENTLY **2 :** EASILY ⟨won *handily*⟩

hand·i·ness \-dē-nəs\ *n* **:** the quality or state of being handy

hand·i·work \ˈhan-di-ˌwərk\ *n* **:** work done by the hands or by oneself ⟨proud of his *handiwork*⟩

hand·ker·chief \ˈhaŋ-kər-chəf, -(ˌ)chif, -ˌchēf\ *n, pl* **-chiefs** *also* **-chieves** \-chəfs, -(ˌ)chifs, -ˌchēvz, -ˌchēfs\ **1 :** a small piece of cloth used for wiping the face, nose, or eyes **2 :** KERCHIEF 1

[1]**han·dle** \ˈhan-dəl\ *n* **1 :** a part that is designed to be grasped by the hand **2** *slang* **:** NAME — **han·dled** \-dəld\ *adj* — **off the handle :** into a state of sudden and violent anger ⟨flew *off the handle* and punched him in the nose⟩

[2]**handle** *vb* **han·dled; han·dling** \-d(ə-)liŋ\ **1 a :** to touch, feel, hold, or move with the hand **b :** to manage with the hands ⟨*handle* a horse⟩ **2 a :** to deal with **b :** CONTROL, DIRECT **3 :** to deal or trade in ⟨a store that *handles* rugs⟩ **4 :** to act, behave, or feel in a certain way when managed or directed ⟨a car that *handles* well⟩ — **han·dler** \-d(ə-)lər\ *n*

H

han·dle·bar \'han-dəl-ˌbär\ *n* : a bar with a handle (as for steering a bicycle) at each end

hand lens *n* : a magnifying glass to be held in the hand

hand·made \'han(d)-'mād\ *adj* : made by hand and not by machine

hand·maid \-ˌmād\ *or* **hand·maid·en** \-ˌmād-ən\ *n* : a female servant or attendant

hand–me–down \'han(d)-mē-ˌdau̇n\ *adj* : USED, SECONDHAND — **hand–me–down** *n*

hand organ *n* : a barrel organ operated by a hand crank

hand·out \'han-ˌdau̇t\ *n* **1** : food, clothing, or money given to a beggar **2** : an information sheet for free distribution **3** : a prepared statement released to the press

hand over *vb* : to yield control of

hand·pick \'han(d)-'pik\ *vb* : to select personally ⟨a *handpicked* successor⟩

hand·rail \'han-ˌdrāl\ *n* : a narrow rail for grasping as a support (as on a staircase)

hand·saw \'han(d)-ˌsȯ\ *n* : a saw designed to be used with one hand

hand·set \'han(d)-ˌset\ *n* : a combined telephone transmitter and receiver mounted on a handle

hand·shake \-ˌshāk\ *n* : a clasping of hands by two people esp. in greeting or farewell

hand·some \'han(t)-səm\ *adj* **1** : moderately large : SIZABLE ⟨a *handsome* fortune⟩ **2** : GENEROUS, LIBERAL ⟨a *handsome* tribute⟩ ⟨a *handsome* tip⟩ **3** : having a pleasing and usu. impressive or dignified appearance — **hand·some·ly** *adv* — **hand·some·ness** *n*

hand·spring \'han(d)-ˌspring\ *n* : a feat of tumbling in which the body turns forward or backward in a full circle from a standing position and lands first on the hands and then on the feet

hand–to–hand \ˌhan-tə-'hand\ *adj* : being at very close quarters ⟨*hand-to-hand* combat⟩

hand–to–mouth \-tə-'mau̇th\ *adj* : having or providing nothing to spare : PRECARIOUS ⟨a *hand-to-mouth* existence⟩

hand·work \'hand-ˌwərk\ *n* : work done with the hands and not by machine

hand·writ·ing \'han-ˌdrīt-ing\ *n* **1** : writing done by hand **2** : the form of writing peculiar to a particular person **3** : MANUSCRIPT — **hand·writ·ten** \-ˌdrit-ən\ *adj*

handy \'han-dē\ *adj* **hand·i·er; -est 1 a** : conveniently near **b** : easily handled or used ⟨a *handy* sloop⟩ ⟨a *handy* reference book⟩ **2** : clever in using the hands : DEXTEROUS ⟨*handy* with a needle⟩

handy·man \-dē-ˌman\ *n* : a man who does odd jobs

1**hang** \'hang\ *vb* **hung** \'həng\ *also* **hanged** \'hangd\; **hang·ing** \'hang-ing\ **1 a** : to fasten or be fastened to an elevated point without support from below : SUSPEND, DANGLE **b** : to kill or be killed by hanging from a rope tied round the neck ⟨sentenced to be *hanged*⟩ **c** : to fasten so as to allow free motion upon a point of suspension ⟨*hang* a door⟩ **2** : to cover, decorate, or furnish by hanging pictures, trophies, or drapery **3** : DROOP ⟨*hung* his head in shame⟩ **4** : to fasten to a wall ⟨*hang* wallpaper⟩ **5** : to display pictures in a gallery **6** : HOVER ⟨clouds *hanging* low overhead⟩ **7** : to stay with persistence **8** : DEPEND ⟨election *hangs* on one vote⟩ **9 a** : to take hold for support : CLING ⟨she *hung* on his arm⟩ **b** : to be burdensome or oppressive ⟨time *hangs* on his hands⟩ **10** : to leave unsettled ⟨the decision is still *hanging*⟩ **11** : to be in a state of rapt attention ⟨*hung* on his every word⟩ **12** : LINGER, LOITER — **hang·able** \'hang-ə-bəl\ *adj*

2**hang** *n* **1** : the manner in which a thing hangs ⟨the *hang* of a skirt⟩ **2 a** : MEANING, SENSE ⟨the *hang* of an argument⟩ **b** : a special method : KNACK ⟨get the *hang* of driving⟩ — **give a hang** *or* **care a hang** : to be concerned or worried

hang·ar \'hang-ər, 'hang-gər\ *n* : a shelter for housing and repairing aircraft

hang around *vb* **1** : LOITER **2** : to spend time in company ⟨*hangs around* with older kids⟩

hang back *vb* **1** : to linger behind others **2** : to be reluctant : HESITATE

hang·dog \'hang-ˌdȯg\ *adj* **1** : ASHAMED, GUILTY ⟨a *hangdog* look⟩ **2** : ABJECT, COWED

hang in *vb* : to refuse to be discouraged or intimidated : show pluck : PERSIST ⟨*hang in* there, kid! Don't quit⟩

hang·er \'hang-ər\ *n* **1** : one that hangs **2** : a device by which something hangs; *esp* : a device for hanging a garment from a hook or rod

hang·er–on \'hang-ər-ˌȯn, -ˌän\ *n, pl* **hangers–on** : one that hangs around a person, place, or institution in hope of personal gain

1**hang·ing** \'hang-ing\ *n* **1** : an execution by strangling or breaking the neck by a suspended noose **2** : something hung (as a curtain or tapestry) — usu. used in pl.

2**hanging** *adj* **1** : situated on steeply sloping ground ⟨*hanging* gardens⟩ **2 a** : OVERHANGING **b** : supported only by the wall on one side ⟨a *hanging* staircase⟩ **3** : adapted for sustaining a hanging object **4** : punishable by hanging ⟨a *hanging* offense⟩

hang·man \'hang-mən\ *n* : a person who hangs condemned criminals

hang·nail \-ˌnāl\ *n* : a bit of skin hanging loose at the side or base of a fingernail

hang on *vb* **1** : to keep hold or possession esp. tightly ⟨*hang on* or you'll fall⟩ ⟨*hang on* to your money⟩ **2** : to persist tenaciously ⟨a cold that *hung on* all spring⟩ **3** : to depend upon ⟨his going *hangs on* the weather⟩

hang·out \'hang-ˌau̇t\ *n* : a place in which a person hangs out

hang out \-'au̇t\ *vb* : to habitually spend one's time idly ⟨*hangs out* at the corner store⟩

hang·over \'hang-ˌō-vər\ *n* **1** : something (as a surviving custom) that remains from what is past **2** : disagreeable aftereffects from drinking too much alcohol

hang–up \'hang-ˌəp\ *n, slang* : a mental quirk or obsession ⟨what's his *hang-up?*⟩

hang up \-'əp\ *vb* **1 a** : to place on a hook or hanger ⟨told the child to *hang up* his coat⟩ **b** : to replace a telephone receiver on the cradle so that the connection is broken; *also* : to end a telephone conversation ⟨I've got to *hang up* now⟩ **2** : to snag or cause to snag so as to be immovable ⟨the ship *hung up* on a sandbar⟩

hank \'hangk\ *n* : COIL, SKEIN; *esp* : a coil of yarn

han·ker \'hang-kər\ *vb* **han·kered; han·ker·ing** \-k(ə-)ring\ : to have an eager or persistent desire ⟨*hanker* after fame and fortune⟩ — **han·ker·er** \-kər-ər\ *n*

han·ky–pan·ky \ˌhang-kē-'pang-kē\ *n* : questionable or underhand activity : TRICKERY

Han·sen's disease \'han(t)-sənz-\ *n* : LEPROSY

han·som \'han(t)-səm\ *n* : a light 2-wheeled covered carriage with the driver's seat elevated behind

hansom

Ha·nuk·kah \'k̲än-ə-kə, 'hän-\ *n* [from Hebrew *ḥănukkāh* meaning "dedication"] : an 8-day Jewish festival celebrated in November or December in commemoration of the rededication of the Temple of Jerusalem after its defilement by Antiochus of Syria

hap \'hap\ *n* **1** : HAPPENING **2** : CHANCE, FORTUNE — **hap** *vb* — **hap·ly** \-lē\ *adv*

hap·haz·ard \hap-'haz-ərd\ *adj* : marked by lack of plan, order, or direction — **haphazard** *adv or n* — **hap·haz·ard·ly** *adv* — **hap·haz·ard·ness** *n*

hapl- *or* **haplo-** *comb form* : single : simple

hap·less \'hap-ləs\ *adj* : having no luck : UNFORTUNATE — **hap·less·ly** *adv* — **hap·less·ness** *n*

hap·pen \'hap-ən\ *vb* **hap·pened**; **hap·pen·ing** \-(ə-)ning\ **1** : to occur or come about by chance **2** : to take place : OCCUR **3** : to have occasion or opportunity : CHANCE ⟨*happened* to overhear⟩ **4 a** : to meet or find something by chance ⟨*happened* on the right answer⟩ **b** : to appear casually or by chance **5** : to come by way of injury or harm ⟨I promise nothing will *happen* to you⟩

hap·pen·ing \'hap-(ə-)ning\ *n* **1** : EVENT, OCCURRENCE **2** : an apparently aimless stage performance intended to create startling chance effects

hap·pi·ly \'hap-ə-lē\ *adv* **1** : FORTUNATELY, LUCKILY ⟨*happily*, no one was injured⟩ **2** : in a happy manner or state ⟨lived *happily* ever after⟩ **3** : APTLY, SUCCESSFULLY ⟨his remarks were *happily* worded⟩

hap·pi·ness \'hap-i-nəs\ *n* **1** : a state of well-being and contentment : JOY **2** : APTNESS

hap·py \'hap-ē\ *adj* **hap·pi·er**; **-est** [from *hap*, and like *lucky* and *fortunate* specialized to refer to good luck rather than bad] **1** : FORTUNATE, LUCKY **2** : FITTING, SUITABLE ⟨a *happy* choice for governor⟩ **3 a** : enjoying well-being and contentment : JOYOUS ⟨*happy* in his work⟩ **b** : expressing or suggestive of happiness : PLEASANT ⟨*happy* laughter⟩ **c** : PLEASED, GRATIFIED ⟨*happy* to accept an invitation⟩

hap·py–go–lucky \ˌhap-ē-ˌgō-'lək-ē\ *adj* : blithely unconcerned : CAREFREE

ha·rangue \hə-'rang\ *n* **1** : a speech addressed to a public assembly **2** : a ranting or scolding speech or writing — **harangue** *vb* — **ha·rangu·er** \-'rang-ər\ *n*

ha·rass \hə-'ras, 'har-əs\ *vb* **1** : to tire out by persistent efforts : worry or annoy with repeated attacks **2** : to lay waste : HARRY — **ha·rass·ment** \-mənt\ *n*

har·bin·ger \'här-bən-jər\ *n* : one that announces or shows what is coming : FORERUNNER ⟨warm rains that come as *harbingers* of spring⟩ — **harbinger** *vb*

[1]**har·bor** \'här-bər\ *n* **1** : a place of safety and comfort : REFUGE **2** : a part of a body of water protected and deep enough to furnish anchorage; *esp* : one with port facilities — **har·bor·less** \-ləs\ *adj*

[2]**harbor** *vb* **har·bored**; **har·bor·ing** \-b(ə-)ring\ **1** : to give shelter or refuge to ⟨*harbor* an escaped convict⟩ **2** : to hold a thought or feeling of ⟨*harbor* a grudge⟩ **3** : to take shelter in or as if in a harbor — **har·bor·er** *n*

har·bor·age \'här-bə-rij\ *n* : SHELTER, HARBOR

harbor porpoise *n* : a common porpoise of the north Atlantic and Pacific

[1]**hard** \'härd\ *adj* **1** : not easily penetrated, cut, or divided into parts : not soft **2 a** : high in alcoholic content ⟨*hard* distilled liquors⟩ **b** : containing substances that prevent lathering with soap ⟨*hard* water⟩ **3** : stable and substantial in value and often convertible into gold ⟨*hard* currency⟩ **4 a** : physically fit **b** : HARDY **5 a** (1) : FIRM, DEFINITE ⟨*hard* agreement⟩ (2) : based on clear fact ⟨*hard* evidence⟩ **b** : CLOSE, SEARCHING ⟨*hard* look⟩ **c** : lacking sympathy or sentiment **6 a** : difficult to endure : HARSH, SEVERE ⟨*hard* words⟩ ⟨a *hard* winter⟩ ⟨*hard* times⟩ **b** : RESENTFUL ⟨*hard* feelings⟩ **c** : STRICT, UNRELENTING ⟨drives a *hard* bargain⟩ **d** : physically or mentally difficult ⟨a *hard* problem⟩ ⟨*hard* work⟩ **7** : DILIGENT, ENERGETIC ⟨a *hard* worker⟩ **8 a** : sharply or harshly defined : STARK ⟨*hard* shadows⟩ **b** : sounding as in *arcing* and *geese* respectively — used of *c* and *g* — **hard up 1** : short of money : POOR **2** : poorly provided ⟨*hard up* for friends⟩

[2]**hard** *adv* **1 a** : with great effort or energy : STRENUOUSLY ⟨work *hard*⟩ ⟨try *hard*⟩ **b** : COMPLETELY ⟨turn the wheel *hard* left⟩ **2 a** : HARSHLY, SEVERELY **b** : with rancor, bitterness, or grief ⟨took his defeat *hard*⟩ **3** : TIGHTLY, FIRMLY ⟨hold *hard* to something⟩ **4** : to the point of hardness ⟨dry *hard*⟩ **5** : CLOSE ⟨the school stood *hard* by a church⟩

hard–and–fast \ˌhärd-ən-'fast\ *adj* : rigidly binding : STRICT ⟨a *hard-and-fast* rule⟩

hard·back \'härd-ˌbak\ *n* : a book bound in hard covers

hard·ball \-ˌbȯl\ *n* : BASEBALL

hard–bit·ten \-'bit-ən\ *adj* : TOUGH, DOGGED ⟨*hard-bitten* campaigners⟩

hard·board \-ˌbōrd, -ˌbȯrd\ *n* : a board made by compressing shredded wood chips often with a binder at high temperatures

hard–boiled \-'bȯild\ *adj* **1** : boiled until both white and yolk have solidified ⟨*hard-boiled* eggs⟩ **2** : lacking sentiment : CALLOUS ⟨a *hard-boiled* drill sergeant⟩

hard coal *n* : ANTHRACITE

hard core *n* : a resistant and enduring central part; *esp* : a militant nucleus of a group — **hard–core** *adj*

hard·en \'härd-ən\ *vb* **hard·ened**; **hard·en·ing** \-(ə-)ning\ **1** : to make or become hard or harder **2** : to make or become hardy or strong ⟨muscles *hardened* by exercise⟩ **3 a** : to make or become stubborn, unfeeling, or unsympathetic ⟨*harden* his heart⟩ **b** : to become confirmed ⟨a *hardened* criminal⟩ **4** : to protect from blast or heat by a thick concrete or earth barrier or by placing underground ⟨*hardened* missile sites⟩ — **hard·en·er** \-(ə-)nər\ *n*

hard·hack \'härd-ˌhak\ *n* : a shrubby American spirea with rusty hairy leaves and dense clusters of pink or occas. white flowers

hard hat *n* **1** : a protective helmet worn esp. by construction workers **2** : a construction worker

hard·head·ed \-'hed-əd\ *adj* **1** : STUBBORN **2** : marked by sound judgment : REALISTIC ⟨a *hard-headed* reappraisal⟩ — **hard·head·ed·ly** *adv* — **hard·head·ed·ness** *n*

hard·heart·ed \-'härt-əd\ *adj* : UNFEELING, PITILESS — **hard·heart·ed·ly** *adv* — **hard·heart·ed·ness** *n*

har·di·hood \'härd-ē-ˌhu̇d\ *n* **1** : BRAVERY **2** : VIGOR, ROBUSTNESS

hard·ly \'härd-lē\ *adv* **1** : SEVERELY, HARSHLY ⟨dealt *hardly* with him⟩ **2** : with difficulty : PAIN-

FULLY **3 :** only just : BARELY, SCARCELY ⟨it *hardly* ever rains there⟩ **4 :** very probably not ⟨a wish that will *hardly* come true⟩

hard·ness *n* **1 :** the quality or state of being hard **2 :** the comparative capacity of a substance (as a mineral) to scratch another substance or be itself scratched

hard–of–hearing \ˌhärd-ə(v)-ˈhi(ə)r-ing\ *adj* **1 :** partially deaf **2 :** of or relating to partial deafness

hard·pan \ˈhärd-ˌpan\ *n* **1 :** a very hard and often clayey layer in soil that roots cannot readily penetrate **2 :** a fundamental part : BASIS

hard put *adj* : barely able ⟨*hard put* to find an explanation⟩

hard rubber *n* : a firm rubber or rubber product that is relatively incapable of being stretched

hard–shell crab \ˌhärd-ˌshel-\ *n* : a crab that has not recently shed its shell — called also *hard-shelled crab* \-ˌshel(d)-\

hard–shelled \ˈhärd-ˈsheld\ *adj* : having a hard shell

hard·ship \ˈhärd-ˌship\ *n* **1 :** SUFFERING, PRIVATION **2 :** something that causes suffering or privation

hard·tack \-ˌtak\ *n* : a hard biscuit or bread made of flour and water without salt

hard·top \-ˌtäp\ *n* : an automobile styled to resemble a convertible but having a rigid top

hard·ware \-ˌwa(ə)r, -ˌwe(ə)r\ *n* : articles (as fittings, cutlery, tools, utensils, or parts of machines) made of metal

hard wheat *n* : a wheat with hard flinty kernels that yield a flour esp. suitable for bread and macaroni

1**hard·wood** \ˈhärd-ˌwu̇d\ *n* **1 :** the wood of a tree (as an oak or maple) producing enclosed seeds as distinguished from that of a tree bearing cones **2 :** a tree that yields hardwood

2**hardwood** *adj* **1 :** having or made of hardwood ⟨*hardwood* floors⟩ **2 :** consisting of mature woody tissue ⟨a *hardwood* cutting⟩

har·dy \ˈhärd-ē\ *adj* **har·di·er**; **-est** **1 :** BOLD, BRAVE **2 :** inured to fatigue or hardships : ROBUST **3 :** able to withstand adverse conditions (as of weather) ⟨a *hardy* rose⟩ — **har·di·ly** \ˈhärd-ə-lē\ *adv* — **har·di·ness** \ˈhärd-ē-nəs\ *n*

hare \ˈha(ə)r, ˈhe(ə)r\ *n, pl* **hare** *or* **hares :** any of various swift timid long-eared mammals with a divided upper lip, long hind legs, a short cocked tail, and the young open-eyed and furred at birth

hare·bell \-ˌbel\ *n* : a slender herb with bright blue bell-shaped flowers

hare·brained \-ˈbrānd\ *adj* : FLIGHTY, GIDDY

hare·lip \-ˈlip\ *n* : a deformity in which the upper lip is split like that of a hare — **hare·lipped** \-ˈlipt\ *adj*

har·em \ˈhar-əm, ˈher-\ *n* **1 a :** the rooms assigned to the women in a Muslim household **b :** the women of a Muslim household **2 :** a group of females controlled by and usu. mating with one male — used of polygamous animals

hark \ˈhärk\ *vb* : LISTEN

hark back *vb* : to recall or cause to recall something earlier ⟨*hark back* to the good old days⟩

har·le·quin \ˈhär-li-k(w)ən\ *n* **1 :** CLOWN **2 :** a variegated pattern of usu. diamond-shaped figures — **harlequin** *adj*

har·lot \ˈhär-lət\ *n* : PROSTITUTE

ə abut	ər further	a back	ā bake	
ä cot, cart	au̇ out	ch chin	e less	ē easy
g gift	i trip	ī life	j joke	ng sing	ō flow
ȯ flaw	ȯi coin	th thin	t͟h this	ü loot
u̇ foot	y yet	yü few	yu̇ furious	zh vision

har·lot·ry \-lə-trē\ *n* : PROSTITUTION

harm \ˈhärm\ *n* **1 :** physical or mental damage : INJURY **2 :** MISCHIEF, HURT — **harm** *vb*

harm·ful \ˈhärm-fəl\ *adj* : DAMAGING, INJURIOUS — **harm·ful·ly** \-fə-lē\ *adv* — **harm·ful·ness** *n*

harm·less \ˈhärm-ləs\ *adj* **1 :** free from harm **2 :** unable to harm ⟨a *harmless* joke⟩ — **harm·less·ly** *adv* — **harm·less·ness** *n*

1**har·mon·ic** \här-ˈmän-ik\ *adj* : of or relating to musical harmony as opposed to melody or rhythm — **har·mon·i·cal·ly** \-ˈmän-i-k(ə-)lē\ *adv*

2**harmonic** *n* : OVERTONE; *esp* : a flutelike tone produced (as on a violin) by lightly touching a vibrating string with a finger

har·mon·i·ca \här-ˈmän-i-kə\ *n* : a small rectangular wind instrument with free metallic reeds sounded by exhaling and inhaling

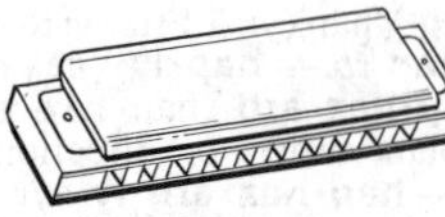

harmonica

har·mo·ni·ous \här-ˈmō-nē-əs\ *adj* **1 :** musically concordant ⟨a *harmonious* song⟩ ⟨*harmonious* voices⟩ **2 :** having the parts agreeably related : CONGRUOUS ⟨decorated in *harmonious* colors⟩ **3 :** marked by accord in sentiment or action ⟨a *harmonious* family⟩ — **har·mo·ni·ous·ly** *adv* — **har·mo·ni·ous·ness** *n*

har·mo·nize \ˈhär-mə-ˌnīz\ *vb* **1 :** to play or sing in harmony **2 :** to be in harmony **3 :** to bring into harmony **4 :** to provide or accompany with harmony — **har·mo·ni·za·tion** \ˌhär-mə-nə-ˈzā-shən\ *n* — **har·mo·niz·er** \ˈhär-mə-ˌnī-zər\ *n*

har·mo·ny \ˈhär-mə-nē\ *n, pl* **-nies** **1 a :** the combination of simultaneous musical notes in a chord **b :** the structure of music with respect to the composition and progression of chords **c :** the science of harmony **2 a :** pleasing or congruent arrangement of parts **b :** CORRESPONDENCE, ACCORD ⟨lives in *harmony* with her neighbors⟩

1**har·ness** \ˈhär-nəs\ *n* **1 :** the straps and fastenings by which a draft animal pulls a load **2 :** an arrangement that resembles a harness

2**harness** *vb* **1 :** to put a harness on **2 :** to tie together : YOKE **3 :** to put to work : UTILIZE ⟨*harness* a waterfall⟩

harness racing *n* : the sport of racing standardbred horses harnessed to 2-wheeled sulkies

1**harp** \ˈhärp\ *n* : an instrument having strings stretched across an open triangular frame and plucked with the fingers — **harp·ist** \ˈhär-pəst\ *n*

2**harp** *vb* **1 :** to play on a harp **2 :** to dwell on or recur to a subject tiresomely ⟨always *harping* on his shortcomings⟩ — **harp·er** *n*

har·poon \här-ˈpün\ *n* : a barbed spear used esp. in hunting large fish or whales — **harpoon** *vb* — **har·poon·er** *n*

harp·si·chord \ˈhärp-si-ˌkȯrd\ *n* : a keyboard instrument that sounds by the plucking of wire strings with quills or leather points

har·py \ˈhär-pē\ *n, pl* **harpies** **1** *cap* : a foul creature of classical mythology that is part woman and part bird **2 a :** a greedy or grasping person **b :** a shrewish woman

har·que·bus \ˈhär-kwi-(ˌ)bəs\ *n* : a portable firearm of the 15th and 16th centuries later replaced by the musket

1**har·ri·er** \ˈhar-ē-ər\ *n* : a hunting dog like a small foxhound used esp. for hunting rabbits

2**harrier** *n* **1 :** one that harries **2 :** any of various slender long-legged hawks (as the marsh hawk)

[1]har·row \'har-ō\ *n* : a cultivating implement set with spikes, teeth, or disks and used for pulverizing and smoothing the soil

[2]harrow *vb* **1** : to cultivate with a harrow **2** : TORMENT, VEX — **har·row·er** *n*

har·ry \'har-ē\ *vb* **har·ried**; **har·ry·ing 1** : RAID, PILLAGE **2** : TORMENT, WORRY

harsh \'härsh\ *adj* **1** : disagreeable to the touch **2** : causing discomfort or pain **3** : unduly exacting : SEVERE ⟨*harsh* discipline⟩ **4** : aesthetically jarring ⟨*harsh* combination of colors⟩ — **harsh·ly** *adv* — **harsh·ness** *n*

hart \'härt\ *n*, *chiefly Brit* : a male red deer esp. over five years old : STAG

harte·beest \'härt-(ə-)ˌbēst\ *n* : a large nearly extinct African antelope with ringed horns

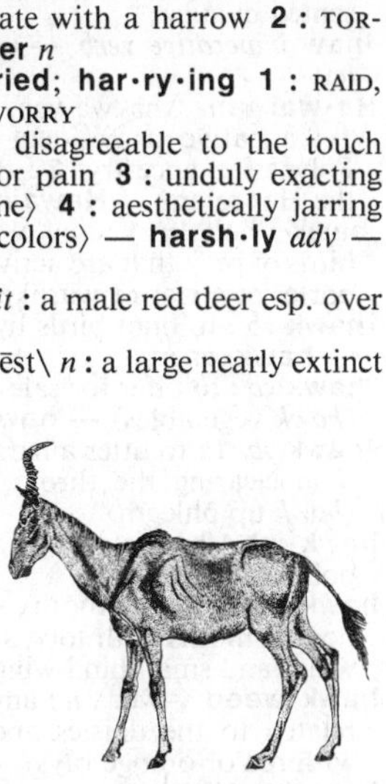

hartebeest
(about 4 ft. at shoulder)

harts·horn \'härts-ˌhȯrn\ *n* : a preparation of ammonia used as smelling salts

har·um–scar·um \ˌhar-əm-'skar-əm, ˌher-əm-'sker-\ *adj* : RECKLESS, IRRESPONSIBLE — **harum–scarum** *n* — **harum–scarum** *adv*

har·vest \'här-vəst\ *n* **1** : the season when crops are gathered **2** : the gathering of a crop **3** : a ripe crop (as of grain or fruit); *also* : the quantity of a crop gathered in a single season — **harvest** *vb* — **har·vest·er** *n*

har·vest·man \'här-vəs(t)-mən\ *n* : DADDY LONGLEGS

harvest moon *n* : the full moon nearest the time of the September equinox

has *pres 3d sing of* HAVE

has–been \'haz-ˌbin\ *n* : one that has passed the peak of ability, power, or popularity

[1]hash \'hash\ *vb* [from French *hacher*, from *hache* ax] **1 a** : to chop into small pieces **b** : CONFUSE, MUDDLE **2** : to talk about : CONSIDER ⟨*hash* over a question⟩

[2]hash *n* **1** : chopped meat mixed with potatoes and browned **2** : HODGEPODGE, JUMBLE

hash·ish \'hash-ˌēsh, -(ˌ)ish\ *n* : a drug prepared from hemp that is smoked, chewed, or drunk for its intoxicating effect

hasn't \'haz-ənt\ : has not

hasp \'hasp\ *n* : a device for fastening; *esp* : a fastener esp. for a door or lid consisting of a hinged metal strap that fits over a staple and is secured by a pin or padlock

has·sle \'has-əl\ *n* : ARGUMENT, FIGHT — **hassle** *vb*

has·sock \'has-ək\ *n* **1** : TUSSOCK **2 a** : a cushion to kneel on in prayer **b** : a cushion that serves as a seat or as a leg rest

hast \(')hast, (h)əst\ *archaic pres 2d sing of* HAVE

has·tate \'has-ˌtāt\ *adj* : shaped like an arrowhead with flaring barbs ⟨*hastate* leaf⟩

[1]haste \'hāst\ *n* **1** : rapidity of motion or action : SWIFTNESS **2** : rash or headlong action **3** : undue eagerness to act : HURRY

[2]haste *vb* : HASTEN

has·ten \'hā-sən\ *vb* **has·tened**; **has·ten·ing** \'-s(ə-)ning\ **1** : to urge on **2** : to speed up : ACCELERATE ⟨*hastened* his steps⟩ **3** : to move or act quickly : HURRY ⟨*hasten* home⟩ — **has·ten·er** \-s(ə-)nər\ *n*

hasty \'hā-stē\ *adj* **hast·i·er**; **-est 1 a** : done or made in a hurry ⟨made a *hasty* sketch of the scene⟩ **b** : fast and often superficial ⟨made a *hasty* survey of the problem⟩ **2** : acting or done without forethought : RASH **3** : quick to anger : IRRITABLE ⟨a *hasty* temper⟩ — **hast·i·ly** \-stə-lē\ *adv* — **hast·i·ness** \-stē-nəs\ *n*

hasty pudding *n* **1** *Brit* : a porridge of oatmeal or flour boiled in water **2** *New Eng* : cornmeal mush

hat \'hat\ *n* : a covering for the head usu. having a shaped crown and brim

hat·box \'hat-ˌbäks\ *n* : a round piece of luggage for carrying hats

[1]hatch \'hach\ *n* **1** : an opening in a deck, floor, or roof **2** : a small door or opening (as in an airplane) **3** : the covering for a hatch

[2]hatch *vb* **1** : to produce young by incubation : INCUBATE **2** : to bring into being : ORIGINATE; *esp* : to concoct in secret ⟨*hatch* a plot⟩ **3** : to emerge from an egg or chrysalis — **hatch·a·bil·i·ty** \ˌhach-ə-'bil-ət-ē\ *n* — **hatch·a·ble** \'hach-ə-bəl\ *adj*

[3]hatch *n* **1** : an act or instance of hatching **2** : a brood of hatched young

[4]hatch *vb* : to mark (as the shading in a picture) with hatching

hatch·ery \'hach-(ə-)rē\ *n*, *pl* **-er·ies** : a place for hatching eggs

hatch·et \'hach-ət\ *n* [from French *hachette*, diminutive of *hache* "ax"] : a short-handled ax for use with one hand

hatch·ing \'hach-ing\ *n* : the engraving or drawing of fine lines close together chiefly to give an effect of shading; *also* : the pattern so created

hatch·way \'hach-ˌwā\ *n* : a hatch usu. with a ladder or stairs

[1]hate \'hāt\ *n* **1** : intense hostility : HATRED **2** : an object of hatred

[2]hate *vb* **1** : to feel extreme enmity toward ⟨*hates* his country's enemies⟩ **2 a** : to have a strong aversion to ⟨*hate* hypocrisy⟩ **b** : to find distasteful : DISLIKE ⟨*hates* cold weather⟩ — **hat·er** *n*

syn HATE, DETEST, ABHOR, LOATHE mean to have strong feelings against (someone or something). HATE implies feelings of hostility or malice; DETEST implies strong dislike but usu. without active hostility; ABHOR conveys a suggestion of deep repugnance; LOATHE suggests utter disgust or intolerance ***ant*** love

hate·ful \'hāt-fəl\ *adj* **1** : full of hate : MALICIOUS ⟨*hateful* enemies⟩ **2** : exciting or deserving hate ⟨a *hateful* crime⟩ — **hate·ful·ly** \-fə-lē\ *adv* — **hate·ful·ness** *n*

hath \(')hath, (h)əth\ *archaic pres 3d sing of* HAVE

ha·tred \'hā-trəd\ *n* : strong dislike and ill will : HATE

hat·ter \'hat-ər\ *n* : one that makes, sells, or cleans and repairs hats

hau·berk \'hȯ-(ˌ)bərk\ *n* : a tunic of chain mail worn as defensive armor from the 12th to the 14th century

haugh·ty \'hȯt-ē, 'hät-\ *adj* **haugh·ti·er**; **-est** [from Middle English *haute*, from medieval French *haut* meaning literally "high", from Latin *altus*, the source of English *altitude*] : disdainfully proud or overbearing : ARROGANT ⟨a *haughty* old woman⟩ — **haugh·ti·ly** \'hȯt-ə-lē, 'hät-\ *adv* — **haugh·ti·ness** \'hȯt-ē-nəs, 'hät-\ *n*

[1]haul \'hȯl\ *vb* **1** : to change the course of a ship esp. so as to sail closer to the wind **2 a** : to exert traction : DRAW, PULL ⟨the horse *hauled* a cart⟩ **b** : to obtain or move by hauling **c** : to transport in a vehicle — **haul·er** *n*

[2]haul *n* **1** : the act or process of hauling : PULL

2 a : an amount collected : TAKE ⟨a burglar's *haul*⟩ **b** : the fish taken in a single drawing of a net **3** : the distance over which a load is hauled ⟨a long *haul*⟩

haul off *vb* **1** : to draw back : WITHDRAW **2** : to draw back the arm to gain force ⟨*hauled off* and hit him⟩

haunch \'hȯnch, 'hänch\ *n* **1 a** : HIP **b** : HINDQUARTER 2 — usu. used in pl. **2** : HINDQUARTER 1

[1]**haunt** \'hȯnt, 'hänt\ *vb* **1** : to visit often : FREQUENT ⟨she *haunted* the antique shops⟩ **2** : to recur constantly and against the will to ⟨the tune *haunted* her all day⟩ **3** : to visit or inhabit as a ghost ⟨the murdered man *haunted* the house⟩ — **haunt·ing·ly** \-ing-lē\ *adv*

[2]**haunt** \'hȯnt, 'hänt, *2 is usu* 'hant\ *n* **1** : a place habitually frequented or repeatedly visited ⟨favorite *haunts* of birds⟩ **2** : GHOST

haut·bois *or* **haut·boy** \'(h)ō-ˌbȯi\ *n*, *pl* **hautbois** \-ˌbȯiz\ *or* **hautboys** : OBOE

hau·teur \hō-'tər\ *n* : HAUGHTINESS, ARROGANCE

have \(')hav, (h)əv, v; *before "to" usu* 'haf\ *vb*, *past & past part* **had** \(')had, (h)əd, d\; *pres part* **hav·ing** \'hav-ing\; *pres 3d sing* **has** \(')haz, (h)əz, z, s; *before "to" usu* 'has\ **1 a** : POSSESS, OWN ⟨*have* a car⟩ ⟨*have* the right to vote⟩ **b** : to consist of : CONTAIN ⟨April *has* 30 days⟩ **2** : to be obliged in regard to : MUST ⟨*have* to go⟩ ⟨*have* a letter to write⟩ **3** : to stand in relationship to ⟨*have* enemies⟩ **4 a** : OBTAIN, GET ⟨best to be *had*⟩ **b** : RECEIVE **c** : ACCEPT; *esp* : to accept in marriage ⟨she wouldn't *have* him⟩ **5 a** : to be marked or characterized by ⟨*have* red hair⟩ **b** : SHOW ⟨*had* the gall to refuse⟩ **c** : USE, EXERCISE ⟨*have* mercy⟩ **6 a** : EXPERIENCE, UNDERGO ⟨*have* a good time⟩ ⟨*have* a cold⟩ **b** : to carry on : PERFORM ⟨*have* a look at that cut⟩ ⟨*have* a fight⟩ **c** : to entertain in the mind ⟨*have* an opinion⟩ ⟨*have* doubts⟩ **7 a** : to cause to do or be done ⟨*had* his hair cut⟩ ⟨please *have* the children stay⟩ **b** : to cause to be ⟨*has* everyone confused⟩ **8** : ALLOW ⟨we'll *have* no more of that⟩ **9 a** : to hold an advantage over ⟨we *have* him now⟩ **b** : TRICK, FOOL ⟨been *had* by a partner⟩ **10** : BEGET, BEAR ⟨*have* a baby⟩ **11** : to partake of ⟨*have* dinner⟩ **12** : BRIBE ⟨can be *had* for a price⟩ **13** — used as an auxiliary verb with the past participle of another verb ⟨*has* gone home⟩ ⟨*had* already eaten⟩ ⟨will *have* finished dinner by then⟩ — **have at** \ha-'vat\ : to go at or deal with : ATTACK — **have done** : FINISH, STOP — **have to do with 1** : to deal with ⟨the book *has to do with* fish⟩ **2** : to be connected or related to

ha·ven \'hā-vən\ *n* **1** : HARBOR, PORT **2** : a place of safety : SHELTER

haven't \'hav-ənt\ : have not

hav·er·sack \'hav-ər-ˌsak\ *n* : a bag similar to a knapsack but worn over one shoulder

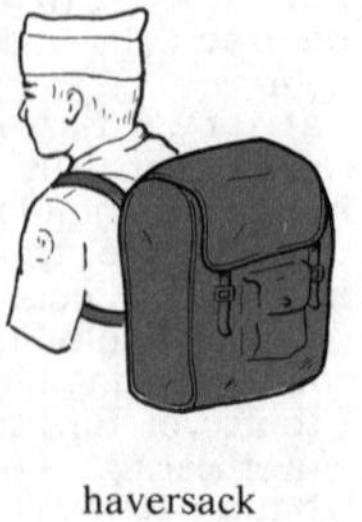
haversack

hav·oc \'hav-ək\ *n* **1** : wide and general destruction : DEVASTATION ⟨*havoc* caused by a tornado⟩ **2** : great confusion and disorder

[1]**haw** \'hȯ\ *n* **1** : a hawthorn berry **2** : HAWTHORN

[2]**haw** *vb* **1** : to utter the sound represented by *haw* ⟨hemmed and *hawed* before answering⟩ **2** : to hesitate in speaking

[3]**haw** *n* : a pause in speaking filled by the sound represented by *haw*

[4]**haw** *imperative verb* — used as a direction to turn left

Ha·wai·ian \hə-'wä-yən, -'wī-(y)ən, -'wȯ-yən\ *n* **1** : a native or resident of Hawaii; *esp* : one of Polynesian ancestry **2** : the Polynesian language of the Hawaiians — **Hawaiian** *adj*

[1]**hawk** \'hȯk\ *n* **1** : any of numerous relatively small birds of prey that are active mostly by day **2** : a supporter of a war or warlike policy

[2]**hawk** *vb* : to hunt birds by means of a trained hawk — **hawk·er** *n*

[3]**hawk** *vb* : to offer for sale by calling out in the street ⟨*hawk* vegetables⟩ — **hawk·er** *n*

[4]**hawk** *vb* **1** : to utter a harsh coughing sound in or as if in clearing the throat **2** : to raise by hawking ⟨*hawk* up phlegm⟩

hawk·ish \'hȯ-kish\ *adj* : advocating war or warlike policies

hawk·moth \'hȯk-ˌmȯth\ *n* : any of numerous stout-bodied moths with long strong narrow pointed fore wings and small hind wings

hawk·weed \-ˌwēd\ *n* : any of several plants that are related to the daisies and usu. have flower heads with red or orange rays

haw·ser \'hȯ-zər\ *n* : a large rope for towing or mooring a ship

haw·thorn \'hȯ-ˌthȯrn\ *n* : any of a genus of spring-flowering spiny shrubs or small trees that are related to the rose and have glossy and often lobed leaves, white or pink fragrant flowers, and small red fruits

[1]**hay** \'hā\ *n* : herbage (as grass) mowed and cured for fodder

[2]**hay** *vb* **1** : to cut, cure, and store herbage for hay **2** : to feed with hay — **hay·er** *n*

hay·cock \'hā-ˌkäk\ *n* : a conical pile of hay

hay fever *n* : an acute allergic catarrh of the mucous membranes of the eyes, nose, and throat

hay·field \'hā-ˌfēld\ *n* : a field where grass is grown for hay

hay·fork \-ˌfȯrk\ *n* **1** : PITCHFORK **2** : a mechanically operated fork for loading or unloading hay

hay·loft \-ˌlȯft\ *n* : a loft for hay

hay·mow \-ˌmau̇\ *n* : a mow of or for hay

hay·rack \-ˌrak\ *n* : a frame mounted on a wagon and used esp. in hauling hay or straw; *also* : the wagon and frame

hay·rick \-ˌrik\ *n* : a large outdoor stack of hay

hay·stack \-ˌstak\ *n* : a stack of hay

hay·wire \-ˌwī(ə)r\ *adj* **1** : being out of order : not working ⟨the radio went *haywire*⟩ **2** : emotionally or mentally upset : CRAZY

[1]**haz·ard** \'haz-ərd\ *n* [from medieval French *hasard*, from Arabic *az-zahr* "the die"] **1** : a game of chance played with dice **2** : CHANCE, ACCIDENT **3** : RISK, PERIL ⟨the *hazards* of war⟩ **4** : a source of danger ⟨a fire *hazard*⟩ **5** : an obstruction on a golf course ***syn*** see DANGER

[2]**hazard** *vb* : VENTURE, RISK ⟨*hazard* a guess⟩

haz·ard·ous \'haz-ərd-əs\ *adj* : DANGEROUS, RISKY ⟨a *hazardous* voyage⟩ — **haz·ard·ous·ly** *adv* — **haz·ard·ous·ness** *n*

[1]**haze** \'hāz\ *vb* : to make or become hazy or cloudy

[2]**haze** \'hāz\ *n* **1** : fine dust, smoke, or light vapor causing lack of transparency in the air **2** : vagueness of mind or perception : DAZE

[3]**haze** *vb* : to play abusive and humiliating tricks on or force to perform humiliating tasks or stunts by way of initiation — **haz·er** *n*

ha·zel \'hā-zəl\ *n* **1** : any of a genus of shrubs or small trees related to birches and bearing edible nuts enclosed in a leafy case **2** : a light brown to a strong yellowish brown — **hazel** *adj* — **ha·zel·ly** \'hāz-(ə-)lē\ *adj*

ha·zel·nut \'hā-zəl-ˌnət\ *n* : the nut of a hazel

hazy \'hā-zē\ *adj* **haz·i·er**; **-est** **1** : obscured or darkened by or as if by haze ⟨*hazy* weather⟩ **2** : VAGUE, INDEFINITE ⟨a *hazy* idea⟩ — **haz·i·ly** \-zə-lē\ *adv* — **haz·i·ness** \-zē-nəs\ *n*

H–bomb \'āch-ˌbäm\ *n* : HYDROGEN BOMB

hd *abbr* head

HD *abbr* heavy-duty

hdbk *abbr* handbook

hdkf *abbr* handkerchief

hdqrs *abbr* headquarters

he \(')hē, ē\ *pron* **1** : that male one ⟨*he* is my father⟩ **2** : that person or animal ⟨everyone should do the best *he* can⟩

1head \'hed\ *n* **1** : the upper or front division of the body (as of a man or an insect) that contains the brain, the chief sense organs, and the mouth **2 a** : MIND, UNDERSTANDING ⟨a good *head* for figures⟩ **b** : emotional control : POISE ⟨a level *head*⟩ **3** : the side of a coin bearing a head or the major design **4 a** : each one among a number : INDIVIDUAL **b** *pl* **head** : a unit of number (as of livestock) ⟨100 *head* of cattle⟩ **5 a** : the end that is upper or higher or opposite the foot ⟨the *head* of the bed⟩ **b** : the front part ⟨*head* of the column⟩ **c** : the uppermost part : TOP **d** : an end of a drum over which a skin or membrane is stretched **6** : HEADMASTER **7** : a compact mass of plant parts (as leaves or flowers) ⟨a *head* of cabbage⟩ **8 a** : the source of a stream **b** : a body of water kept in reserve at a height **c** : the difference in elevation between two points in a body of fluid **d** : the resulting pressure at the lower point; *also* : pressure of a fluid ⟨a *head* of steam⟩ **9 a** : the place of leadership or command ⟨the man at the *head* of the group⟩ **b** : a person in this place : CHIEF, LEADER **10** : the foam that rises on an effervescing liquid **11 a** : the part of a boil, pimple, or abscess at which it is likely to break **b** : CRISIS ⟨events came to a *head*⟩ **12** : a part of a machine, tool, weapon, or apparatus that performs the main function ⟨*head* of a lance⟩ ⟨a machine with a grinding *head*⟩ ⟨a shower *head*⟩ **13** : a user of drugs — often used in combination ⟨acid*head*⟩ **14** : a device used in recording, reproducing, or erasing sound — **head·ed** \-əd\ *adj* — **head·ship** \'hed-ˌship\ *n* — **out of one's head** : DELIRIOUS — **over one's head** **1** : beyond one's comprehension **2** : bypassing or ignoring one with a higher position

2head *adj* **1** : PRINCIPAL, CHIEF ⟨*head* cook⟩ **2** : situated at the head ⟨sat at the *head* table at the banquet⟩ **3** : coming from in front ⟨*head* sea⟩

3head *vb* **1** : to form a head ⟨this cabbage *heads* early⟩ **2** : to be or put oneself at the head of : LEAD ⟨*head* a revolt⟩ ⟨*head* the list of heroes⟩ **3 a** : to get in front of so as to hinder, stop, or turn back ⟨*head* him off at the pass⟩ **b** : to take a lead over (as in a race) **4** : to go or point in a specified course ⟨*head* for home⟩ ⟨*head* the ship north⟩

head·ache \'hed-ˌāk\ *n* **1** : pain in the head **2** : an annoying or baffling situation or problem — **head·achy** \-ˌā-kē\ *adj*

head·band \-ˌband\ *n* : a band worn on or around the head

head·board \-ˌbōrd, -ˌbȯrd\ *n* : a board forming the head (as of a bed)

head cold *n* : a common cold centered in the nasal passages and adjacent mucous tissues

head·dress \'hed-ˌ(d)res\ *n* : a covering or ornament for the head

headdresses

head·ed \'hed-əd\ *adj* : having such a head or so many heads ⟨curly-*headed*⟩

head·er \'hed-ər\ *n* **1** : a grain-harvesting machine that cuts off the grain heads and lifts them into a wagon **2** : a fall or dive head foremost ⟨took a *header* downstairs⟩

head·first \'hed-'fərst\ *also* **head·fore·most** \-'fōr-ˌmōst, -'fȯr-\ *adv* : with the head foremost — **headfirst** *adj*

head·gear \-ˌgi(ə)r\ *n* **1** : a covering (as a hat or helmet) for the head **2** : harness for a horse's head

head·hunt·ing \-ˌhənt-ing\ *n* : the practice of cutting off and preserving the heads of enemies — **head·hunt·er** *n*

head·ing \'hed-ing\ *n* **1** : the direction in which a ship or aircraft points **2** : an inscription, headline, or title standing at the top or beginning (as of a letter or chapter)

head·land \'hed-lənd, -ˌland\ *n* : a point of land jutting out into the sea : PROMONTORY

head·less \-ləs\ *adj* **1** : having no head **2** : having no chief **3** : lacking good sense or prudence : FOOLISH — **head·less·ness** *n*

head·light \-ˌlīt\ *n* : a light on the front of a vehicle

1head·line \-ˌlīn\ *n* **1** : a line at the top of a page (as in a book) giving a heading **2** : the title over an item or article in a newspaper

2headline *vb* **1** : to provide with a headline **2** : to publicize highly

1head·long \'hed-'lȯng\ *adv* **1** : HEADFIRST **2** : without deliberation : RECKLESSLY ⟨dash *headlong* into traffic⟩

2headlong *adj* **1** : PRECIPITATE, RASH ⟨*headlong* flight⟩ **2** : plunging headfirst ⟨a *headlong* dive⟩

head louse *n* : a louse that lives on the scalp of man

head·man \'hed-'man, -ˌman\ *n* : one who is a leader (as of a tribe, clan, or village) : CHIEF

head·mas·ter \-ˌmas-tər\ *n* : a male head of a private school — **head·mis·tress** \-ˌmis-trəs\ *n*

head–on \-'ȯn, -'än\ *adj* : having the head or front facing forward : front to front ⟨a *head-on* collision⟩

head over heels *adv* **1** : in or as if in a somersault ⟨fell *head over heels* down the hill⟩ **2** : HOPELESSLY, DEEPLY ⟨*head over heels* in love⟩

head·phone \'hed-ˌfōn\ *n* : an earphone held over the ear by a band worn on the head

head·piece \-ˌpēs\ *n* **1** : a protective covering for the head **2** : BRAINS, INTELLIGENCE **3** : an ornament at the beginning of a chapter

head·pin \-ˌpin\ *n* : a pin that stands at the apex in a triangular arrangement of bowling pins

head·quar·ters \-ˌkwȯrt-ərz\ *n sing or pl* **1** : a place from which a commander exercises command **2** : the administrative center of an enterprise

head·rest \-ˌrest\ *n* : a support for the head

head·set \-ˌset\ *n* : a pair of headphones

heads·man \'hedz-mən\ *n* : one that beheads : EXECUTIONER

head·stand \'hed-ˌstand\ *n* : the gymnastic feat of standing on one's head

head·stone \-ˌstōn\ *n* : a memorial stone placed at the head of a grave

head·strong \-ˌstrȯng\ *adj* **1** : not easily restrained : WILLFUL ⟨a *headstrong* child⟩ **2** : directed by ungovernable will ⟨violent *headstrong* actions⟩

head·wait·er \-ˈwāt-ər\ *n* : the head of the dining-room staff of a restaurant or hotel

head·wa·ters \-ˌwȯt-ərz, -ˌwät-\ *n pl* : the source and upper part of a stream

head·way \-ˌwā\ *n* **1 a** : motion forward **b** : PROGRESS **2** : clear space (as under an arch)

head wind *n* : a wind blowing in a direction opposite to a course esp. of a ship or aircraft

head·work \ˈhed-ˌwərk\ *n* : mental work : THINKING

heady \ˈhed-ē\ *adj* **head·i·er**; **-est** **1** : WILLFUL, RASH **2** : likely to make one dizzy ⟨*heady* wine⟩ ⟨a *heady* height⟩ — **head·i·ly** \ˈhed-ə-lē\ *adv* — **head·i·ness** \ˈhed-ē-nəs\ *n*

heal \ˈhēl\ *vb* : to make or become healthy or whole ⟨*heal* the sick⟩ ⟨a cut that *heals* slowly⟩

heal·er \ˈhē-lər\ *n* : one that heals

health \ˈhelth\ *n* **1 a** : the condition of being sound in body, mind, or spirit; *esp* : freedom from disease **b** : general condition ⟨in poor *health*⟩ **2** : flourishing condition **3** : a toast to someone's health or prosperity ⟨drink a *health*⟩

health·ful \-fəl\ *adj* **1** : beneficial to health of body or mind ⟨*healthful* exercise⟩ **2** : HEALTHY — **health·ful·ly** \-fə-lē\ *adv* — **health·ful·ness** *n*

syn HEALTHFUL, WHOLESOME, SALUBRIOUS can mean favorable to good health. HEALTHFUL implies a positive contribution to a healthy condition; WHOLESOME may only imply doing the body no harm; SALUBRIOUS suggests the refreshing effect of healthful climate or air

healthy \ˈhel-thē\ *adj* **health·i·er**; **-est** **1 a** : enjoying good health : WELL **b** : typical of good health ⟨*healthy* complexion⟩ **2** : HEALTHFUL 1 **3 a** : PROSPEROUS, FLOURISHING **b** : not small or feeble : CONSIDERABLE — **health·i·ly** \-thə-lē\ *adv* — **health·i·ness** \-thē-nəs\ *n*

[1]**heap** \ˈhēp\ *n* **1** : a collection of things thrown one on another : PILE ⟨a rubbish *heap*⟩ **2** : a great number or large quantity : LOT ⟨*heaps* of people⟩ ⟨a *heap* of fun⟩

[2]**heap** *vb* **1** : to throw or lay in a heap : AMASS, PILE ⟨*heap* up leaves⟩ **2** : to cast or bestow in large quantities ⟨*heaped* scorn upon him⟩ **3** : to fill a measure or container more than even full

hear \ˈhi(ə)r\ *vb* **heard** \ˈhərd\; **hear·ing** \ˈhi(ə)r-ing\ **1** : to take in by the ear ⟨*hear* music⟩; *also* : to have the power of taking in sound ⟨doesn't *hear* well⟩ **2** : to gain knowledge of by hearing : LEARN ⟨*heard* you're leaving⟩ **3** : to listen to : HEED ⟨*hear* me out⟩ **4 a** : to give a legal hearing to ⟨*hear* a case⟩ **b** : to take testimony from ⟨*hear* witnesses⟩ **5 a** : to get news ⟨*heard* from him yesterday⟩ **b** : to have knowledge ⟨never *heard* of such a thing⟩ **6** : to entertain the idea ⟨wouldn't *hear* of it⟩ — **hear·er** \ˈhir-ər\ *n*

hear·ing *n* **1 a** : the process or power of taking in sound **b** : EARSHOT ⟨stay within *hearing*⟩ **2 a** : a chance to present one's case ⟨demanded a *hearing*⟩ **b** : a listening to arguments or testimony **c** : a session in which testimony is heard ⟨held public *hearings* on the bill⟩

hearing aid *n* : an electronic device usu. worn by a person for amplifying sound

hearing canal *n* : the passage leading from the external opening of the ear to the eardrum

ə abut · ər further · a back · ā bake
ä cot, cart · aů out · ch chin · e less · ē easy
g gift · i trip · ī life · j joke · ng sing · ō flow
ȯ flaw · ȯi coin · th thin · th this · ü loot
ů foot · y yet · yü few · yů furious · zh vision

hear·ken \ˈhär-kən\ *vb* **hear·kened**; **hear·ken·ing** \ˈhärk-(ə-)ning\ : LISTEN, ATTEND

hear·say \ˈhi(ə)r-ˌsā\ *n* **1** : something heard from another : RUMOR **2** : evidence based not on a witness's personal knowledge but on matters told him by another

hearse \ˈhərs\ *n* : a vehicle for conveying the dead to the grave

heart \ˈhärt\ *n* **1 a** : a hollow muscular organ of vertebrate animals that by its rhythmic contraction acts as a pump maintaining the circulation of the blood **b** : a structure in an invertebrate animal with function like that of the vertebrate heart **2** : the central or most important part ⟨the *heart* of a forest⟩ ⟨the *heart* of the argument⟩ **3 a** : something resembling a heart in shape **b** : a playing card marked with red stylized hearts **c** *pl* : a card game whose object is to avoid taking tricks with hearts **4 a** : human feelings : AFFECTION, KINDNESS ⟨a man without *heart*⟩ **b** : COURAGE, SPIRIT ⟨take *heart*⟩ **c** : MOOD ⟨a light *heart*⟩ **5** : MEMORY ⟨learn by *heart*⟩ **6** : PERSON ⟨dear *heart*⟩ ⟨a crew of stout *hearts*⟩ — **heart·ed** \-əd\ *adj* — **to heart** : with deep concern

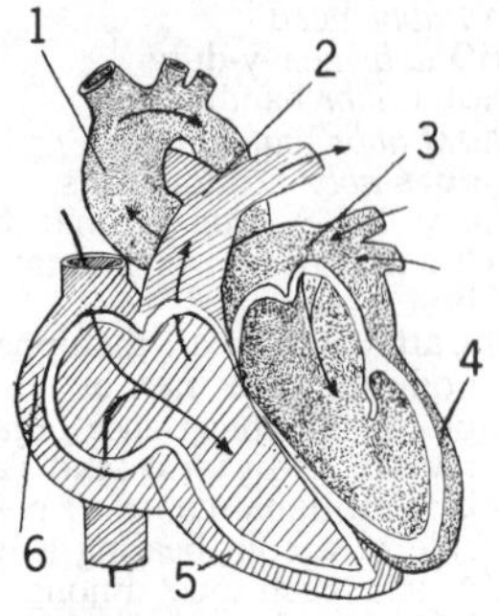

heart 1a: 1, aorta; 2, pulmonary artery; 3, left auricle; 4, left ventricle; 5, right ventricle; 6, right auricle

heart·ache \ˈhärt-ˌāk\ *n* : SORROW, ANGUISH

heart attack *n* : an acute episode of heart disease or disorder; *esp* : CORONARY THROMBOSIS

heart·beat \ˈhärt-ˌbēt\ *n* : one complete pulsation of the heart

heart·break \-ˌbrāk\ *n* : crushing grief, anguish, or distress — **heart·break·ing** \-ˌbrā-king\ *adj* — **heart·break·ing·ly** \-king-lē\ *adv* — **heart·bro·ken** \-ˌbrō-kən\ *adj*

heart·burn \-ˌbərn\ *n* : a burning discomfort seeming to be localized about the heart and usu. related to spasm of the lower esophagus or the upper stomach

heart·burn·ing \-ˌbər-ning\ *n* : intense or rancorous jealousy or resentment

heart disease *n* : an abnormal condition of the heart or of the heart and circulation

heart·en \ˈhärt-ən\ *vb* **heart·ened**; **heart·en·ing** \-(ə-)ning\ : to cheer up : ENCOURAGE

heart·felt \ˈhärt-ˌfelt\ *adj* : deeply felt : EARNEST ⟨*heartfelt* thanks⟩

hearth \ˈhärth\ *n* **1 a** : the area in front of a fireplace **b** : the floor of a fireplace **c** : the lowest section of a blast furnace in which the molten metal and slag are collected **2** : HOME

hearth·side \-ˌsīd\ *n* : FIRESIDE

hearth·stone \-ˌstōn\ *n* **1** : stone forming a hearth **2** : FIRESIDE

heart·i·ly \ˈhärt-ə-lē\ *adv* **1** : with sincerity, goodwill, or enthusiasm ⟨set to work *heartily*⟩ ⟨eat *heartily*⟩ **2** : CORDIALLY ⟨make a guest *heartily* welcome⟩ **3** : COMPLETELY, THOROUGHLY ⟨*heartily* sick of his complaints⟩

heart·land \'härt-ˌland\ *n* : a central land area; *esp* : one thought of as economically and militarily self-sufficient
heart·less \-ləs\ *adj* : PITILESS, CRUEL — **heart·less·ly** *adv* — **heart·less·ness** *n*
heart murmur *n* : MURMUR 3
heart·rend·ing \-ˌren-ding\ *adj* : causing heartbreak ⟨a *heartrending* experience⟩
hearts·ease \'härts-ˌēz\ *n* **1** : peace of mind : TRANQUILLITY **2** : any of various small-flowered violas
heart·sick \'härt-ˌsik\ *adj* : very despondent : DEPRESSED — **heart·sick·ness** *n*
heart·sore \-ˌsōr, -ˌsȯr\ *adj* : HEARTSICK
heart·string \-ˌstring\ *n* : the deepest emotions or affections ⟨pulled at his *heartstrings*⟩
heart–to–heart \ˌhärt-tə-ˌhärt\ *adj* : SINCERE, FRANK ⟨a *heart-to-heart* talk⟩
heart·wood \'härt-ˌwu̇d\ *n* : the older harder nonliving and usu. darker wood of the central part of a tree trunk
[1]**hearty** \'härt-ē\ *adj* **heart·i·er**; **-est** **1 a** : WHOLEHEARTED, SINCERE ⟨*hearty* agreement⟩ **b** : enthusiastically cordial ⟨a *hearty* welcome⟩ **c** : UNRESTRAINED ⟨*hearty* laughter⟩ **2 a** : exhibiting vigorous good health ⟨a hale and *hearty* old man⟩ **b** (1) : having a good appetite ⟨a *hearty* eater⟩ (2) : being abundant and satisfying ⟨a *hearty* meal⟩ **c** : NOURISHING ⟨*hearty* beef stock⟩ **3** : ENERGETIC, VIGOROUS ⟨gave a *hearty* pull⟩ — **heart·i·ness** *n*
[2]**hearty** *n*, *pl* **heart·ies** : COMRADE; *also* : SAILOR
[1]**heat** \'hēt\ *vb* **1** : to make or become warm or hot **2** : to make or become excited or angry
[2]**heat** *n* **1 a** : a condition of being hot : WARMTH **b** : a high degree of hotness **c** : a hot place or period ⟨the *heat* of the day⟩ **d** : a form of energy that causes substances to rise in temperature or to undergo associated changes (as fusion, evaporation, or expansion) **2 a** : intensity of feeling; *esp* : ANGER ⟨answered with some *heat*⟩ **b** : the height of an action or condition ⟨the *heat* of battle⟩ **c** : sexual excitement esp. in a female mammal; *esp* : ESTRUS **3** : pungency of flavor **4 a** : a single course in a race **b** : one of the preliminary races held to eliminate less competent contenders **5** : PRESSURE, COERCION — **heat·less** \-ləs\ *adj*
heat·ed \'hēt-əd\ *adj* **1** : HOT ⟨a *heated* engine⟩ **2** : marked by emotional heat : ANGRY ⟨a *heated* debate⟩ — **heat·ed·ly** *adv*
heat engine *n* : a mechanism for converting heat energy into mechanical energy
heat·er \'hēt-ər\ *n* : a device that heats or holds something to be heated
heat exchange *n* : the transfer of heat energy between substances at different temperatures
heat exchanger *n* : a device (as an automobile radiator) for transferring heat from one fluid to another without allowing them to mix
heat exhaustion *n* : a condition marked by weakness, nausea, dizziness, and profuse sweating that results from physical exertion in a hot environment — called also *heat prostration*
heath \'hēth\ *n* **1** : any of a family of shrubby often evergreen plants that thrive on open barren usu. acid and ill-drained soil; *esp* : a low evergreen shrub with whorls of needlelike leaves and clusters of small flowers **2** : a usu. level tract of land overgrown with low shrubs — **heath·like** \-ˌlīk\ *adj* — **heathy** \'hē-thē\ *adj*
hea·then \'hē-t͟hən\ *n*, *pl* **heathens** *or* **heathen** **1** : a person who does not acknowledge the God of the Bible : PAGAN **2** : an uncivilized or irreligious person — **heathen** *adj* — **hea·then·dom** \-dəm\ *n* — **hea·then·ish** \-t͟hə-nish\ *adj* — **hea·then·ism** \-ˌniz-əm\ *n*
heath·er \'het͟h-ər\ *n* : HEATH 1; *esp* : a common evergreen heath of northern and alpine regions with small crowded stemless leaves and tiny usu. purplish pink flowers — **heath·ery** \-(ə-)rē\ *adj*
heath hen *n* : an extinct grouse of the northeastern U.S. related to the prairie chicken
heating element *n* : the part of an electrical heating appliance that changes electrical energy into heat by offering great resistance to the passage of an electrical current
heat lightning *n* : flashes of light without thunder seen near the horizon and ascribed to far-off lightning reflected by high clouds
heat of condensation : heat given up by one gram of vapor (as steam) as it condenses into liquid
heat of crystallization : heat lost by a gram of a substance when it freezes
heat of fusion : the amount of heat required to melt a gram of a substance
heat of vaporization : heat gained by a gram of a substance as it vaporizes
heat rash *n* : PRICKLY HEAT
heat seal *n* : a seal made by uniting two surfaces by heat and pressure to make a seam, closure, or attachment
heat shield *n* : an insulated barrier to protect a space capsule from heat on its reentry into the atmosphere
heat·stroke \'hēt-ˌstrōk\ *n* : a condition marked esp. by cessation of sweating, high body temperature, and collapse that results from prolonged exposure to high temperature
heat wave *n* **1** : a wave of thermal radiation **2** : a period of unusually hot weather

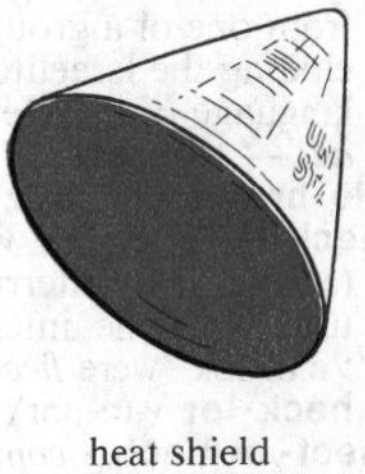
heat shield

[1]**heave** \'hēv\ *vb* **heaved** *or* **hove** \'hōv\; **heav·ing** **1** : to raise with effort : LIFT ⟨*heave* a trunk onto a truck⟩ **2** : THROW, CAST, HURL ⟨*heave* a rock⟩ **3** : to utter with effort ⟨*heave* a sigh⟩ **4** : to rise and fall repeatedly ⟨the runner's chest was *heaving*⟩ **5** : to be thrown up or raised ⟨the ground *heaved* during the earthquake⟩ — **heav·er** *n* — **heave in sight** : to seem to rise above the horizon and come into view — **heave to** : to bring a ship to a stop
[2]**heave** *n* **1 a** : an effort to heave or raise **b** : a forceful throw : CAST **2** : a rhythmical rising (as of the chest in breathing)
heav·en \'hev-ən\ *n* **1** : SKY 1 — usu. used in pl. **2 a** *often cap* : the dwelling place of God **b** : a spiritual state of everlasting communion with God **3** : a place or condition of utmost happiness
heav·en·ly \-lē\ *adj* **1** : of or relating to heaven or the heavens ⟨*heavenly* bodies such as the stars⟩ **2** : DIVINE, SACRED, BLESSED ⟨*heavenly* grace⟩ **3** : supremely delightful ⟨a *heavenly* day⟩ — **heav·en·li·ness** *n*
heav·en·ward \-wərd\ *adv or adj* : toward heaven
[1]**heavy** \'hev-ē\ *adj* **heavi·er**; **-est** **1 a** : having great weight or greater than usual weight **b** : weighty in proportion to bulk : having a high specific gravity ⟨gold is a *heavy* metal⟩ **c** : having or being atoms of greater than normal mass ⟨*heavy* isotopes⟩ **2** : hard to bear; *esp* : GRIEVOUS ⟨a *heavy* sorrow⟩ **3 a** : of weighty import : SERIOUS, DEEP ⟨words *heavy* with meaning⟩ **b** *slang* : KNOWLEDGE-

H

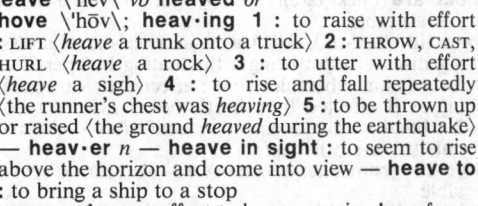

ABLE, AWARE ⟨a *heavy* talker⟩ **c** *slang* : ROUGH, UNPLEASANT ⟨the scene got *heavy* when the cops arrived⟩ **4** : lacking life, gaiety, or charm : DULL **5** : DROWSY **6** : greater in volume or force than the average ⟨*heavy* traffic⟩ ⟨*heavy* seas⟩ **7** : OVERCAST **8** : THICK ⟨a *heavy* growth of timber⟩ **9** : LABORIOUS, LABORED ⟨*heavy* breathing⟩ **10** : of large capacity or output ⟨a *heavy* drinker⟩ **11** : not easily digested **12** : producing goods (as coal or steel) used in the production of other goods ⟨*heavy* industry⟩ **13** : heavily armed or armored ⟨*heavy* tank⟩ — **heavi·ly** \'hev-ə-lē\ *adv* — **heavi·ness** \'hev-ē-nəs\ *n*

2**heavy** *adv* : in a heavy manner : HEAVILY ⟨time hung *heavy* on their hands⟩

3**heavy** *n, pl* **heav·ies** **1** : HEAVYWEIGHT 2 **2 a** : a theatrical role or an actor representing a dignified or imposing person **b** : VILLAIN **3** *slang* : a person who is very knowledgeable or aware ⟨a lot of *heavies* on campus⟩

heavy hydrogen *n* : DEUTERIUM

heavy·set \ˌhev-ē-'set\ *adj* : STOCKY; *also* : STOUT

heavy water *n* : water containing more than the usual proportion of heavy isotopes; *esp* : water enriched in deuterium

heavy·weight \'hev-ē-ˌwāt\ *n* **1** : one above average in weight **2** : one in the heaviest class of contestants; *esp* : a boxer weighing over 175 pounds

Heb *abbr* Hebrew

He·brew \'hē-brü\ *n* **1** : a member of or descendant from one of a group of northern Semitic peoples including the Israelites; *esp* : ISRAELITE **2** : the Semitic language of the Hebrews — **He·bra·ic** \hi-'brā-ik\ *adj* — **Hebrew** *adj*

He·brews \'hē-brüz\ *n* — see BIBLE table

heck·le \'hek-əl\ *vb* **heck·led**; **heck·ling** \'hek-(ə-)liŋ\ : to interrupt with questions or comments usu. with the intention of annoying or hindering : BADGER ⟨were *heckling* the speaker at the rally⟩ — **heck·ler** \-(ə-)lər\ *n*

hect- *or* **hecto-** *comb form* : hundred

hect·are \'hek-ˌta(ə)r, -ˌte(ə)r, -ˌtär\ *n* — see METRIC SYSTEM table

hec·tic \'hek-tik\ *adj* **1 a** : characteristic of a wasting disease; *esp* : being a fluctuating but persistent fever (as in tuberculosis) **b** : affected by or appearing as if affected by a hectic fever; *esp* : FLUSHED **2** : filled with excitement or confusion — **hec·ti·cal·ly** \-ti-k(ə-)lē\ *adv*

hec·to·gram \'hek-tə-ˌgram\ *n* — see METRIC SYSTEM table

hec·to·li·ter \-ˌlēt-ər\ *n* — see METRIC SYSTEM table

hec·to·me·ter \-ˌmēt-ər\ *n* — see METRIC SYSTEM table

hec·tor \'hek-tər\ *vb* **hec·tored**; **hec·tor·ing** \-t(ə-)riŋ\ **1** : SWAGGER **2** : to intimidate by bluster or personal pressure

he'd \(ˌ)hēd, ēd\ : he had : he would

1**hedge** \'hej\ *n* **1** : a boundary formed by a dense row of shrubs or low trees **2** : BARRIER, LIMIT

2**hedge** *vb* **1** : to enclose or protect with or as if with a hedge **2** : to obstruct with or as if with a barrier : HINDER ⟨*hedged* in by restrictions⟩ **3** : to avoid giving a direct or definite answer or promise ⟨*hedged* when asked for his support⟩ — **hedg·er** *n*

ə abut   ər further   a back   ā bake
ä cot, cart   au̇ out   ch chin   e less   ē easy
g gift   i trip   ī life   j joke   ŋ sing   ō flow
ȯ flaw   ȯi coin   th thin   t͟h this   ü loot
u̇ foot   y yet   yü few   yu̇ furious   zh vision

hedge·hog \'hej-ˌhȯg, -ˌhäg\ *n* **1** : an Old World insect-eating mammal having sharp spines mixed with the hair on its back and able to roll itself up into a spiny ball **2** : PORCUPINE

hedgehog 1
(about 10 in. long)

hedge·hop \-ˌhäp\ *vb* : to fly an airplane so low that it is necessary to climb to avoid obstacles (as trees) — **hedge·hop·per** *n*

hedge·row \-ˌrō\ *n* : a row of shrubs or trees bounding or separating fields

1**heed** \'hēd\ *vb* **1** : to pay attention **2** : to take notice of : MIND

2**heed** *n* : ATTENTION, NOTICE

heed·ful \'hēd-fəl\ *adj* : taking heed : CAREFUL ⟨*heedful* of the rights of others⟩ — **heed·ful·ly** \-fə-lē\ *adv* — **heed·ful·ness** *n*

heed·less \'hēd-ləs\ *adj* : not taking heed : CARELESS ⟨*heedless* of danger⟩ — **heed·less·ly** *adv* — **heed·less·ness** *n*

1**heel** \'hēl\ *n* **1** : the back part of the human foot behind the arch and below the ankle; *also* : the corresponding part of a lower vertebrate **2** : a part (as of a shoe) that covers or supports the human heel **3** : a lower, back, or end part; *esp* : one of the crusty ends of a loaf of bread **4** : a contemptible person — **heel·less** \'hēl-ləs\ *adj*

2**heel** *vb* : to furnish with a heel — **heel·er** *n*

3**heel** *vb* : to tilt to one side : LIST

4**heel** *n* : a tilt to one side

heel bone *n* : CALCANEUS

1**heft** \'heft\ *n* : WEIGHT, HEAVINESS

2**heft** *vb* **1** : to heave up : LIFT **2** : to test the weight of by lifting

hefty \'hef-tē\ *adj* **heft·i·er**; **-est** : HEAVY, BULKY — **heft·i·ly** \-tə-lē\ *adv* — **heft·i·ness** \-tē-nəs\ *n*

heif·er \'hef-ər\ *n* : a young cow; *esp* : one that has not had a calf

height \'hīt\ *n* **1** : the highest part or point : SUMMIT, CLIMAX ⟨the *height* of stupidity⟩ **2 a** : the distance from bottom to top **b** : the extent of elevation above a level **3** : the condition of being tall or high **4 a** : a landmass rising above the surrounding country **b** : a high point or position

syn HEIGHT, ALTITUDE, ELEVATION can mean distance upward. HEIGHT may imply measurement from bottom to top; ALTITUDE usu. implies height above a given level; ELEVATION may imply the height to which something is raised

height·en \'hīt-ən\ *vb* **height·ened**; **height·en·ing** \-(ə-)niŋ\ **1** : to make or become brighter or more intense : DEEPEN ⟨excitement *heightened* the pinkness of her cheeks⟩ ⟨*heightened* the citizens' awareness⟩ **2** : to raise high or higher : ELEVATE

hei·nous \'hā-nəs\ *adj* : shockingly evil : ABOMINABLE — **hei·nous·ly** *adv* — **hei·nous·ness** *n*

heir \'a(ə)r, 'e(ə)r\ *n* **1** : a person who inherits or is entitled to inherit property **2** : a person who has legal claim to a title or a throne when the person holding it dies — **heir·ess** \-əs\ *n* — **heir·ship** \-ˌship\ *n*

heir apparent *n, pl* **heirs apparent** : an heir who cannot legally be deprived of his right to succeed (as to a throne) if he survives the present holder

heir·loom \'a(ə)r-ˌlüm, 'e(ə)r-\ *n* : a piece of personal property handed down by inheritance esp. for several generations

heir presumptive *n, pl* **heirs presumptive** : an heir whose right to inherit could be lost through the birth of a nearer relative

held *past of* HOLD

hel·i·cop·ter \'hel-ə-ˌkäp-tər, 'hē-lə-\ *n* : an aircraft that is supported in the air by propellers revolving on a vertical axis

he·lio·cen·tric \ˌhē-lē-ō-'sen-trik\ *adj* **1** : referred to or measured from the sun's center or appearing as if seen from it **2** : having or relating to the sun as a center

he·lio·graph \'hē-lē-ə-ˌgraf\ *n* : an apparatus for telegraphing by means of the sun's rays reflected from a mirror — **heliograph** *vb*

he·lio·trope \'hēl-yə-ˌtrōp, 'hē-lē-ə-\ *n* : any of a genus of herbs or shrubs having small white or purple flowers

he·li·ot·ro·pism \ˌhē-lē-'ä-trə-ˌpiz-əm\ *n* : a turning or curving (as of a sunflower head) toward the sunlight — **he·lio·tro·pic** \ˌhē-lē-ə-'trōp-ik, -'träp-\ *adj* — **he·lio·tro·pi·cal·ly** \-i-k(ə-)lē\ *adv*

heli·port \'hel-ə-ˌpōrt, 'hē-lə-, -ˌpȯrt\ *n* : a landing and takeoff place for a helicopter

heliograph

he·li·um \'hē-lē-əm\ *n* [from Greek *hēlios* "sun"; so called because it was first observed in the sun's atmosphere] : a light colorless nonflammable gaseous element in various natural gases used esp. to inflate balloons — see ELEMENT table

he·lix \'hē-liks\ *n, pl* **he·li·ces** \'hel-ə-ˌsēz, 'hē-lə-\ *also* **he·lix·es** \'hē-lik-səz\ : a curve in space traced by a point rotating around an axis and moving forward in a direction parallel to the axis

hell \'hel\ *n* **1** : the abode of souls after death **2** : the place or state of punishment for the wicked after death : the home of evil spirits **3** : a place or condition of misery or wickedness **4** : something that causes torment; *esp* : a severe scolding

he'll \(ˌ)hēl, hil, ēl, il\ : he shall : he will

hell·ben·der \'hel-ˌben-dər\ *n* : a large aquatic salamander of the Ohio valley

hel·le·bore \'hel-ə-ˌbōr, -ˌbȯr\ *n* **1** : any of a genus of herbs related to the buttercup and having white, greenish, or purplish flowers; *also* : its dried root formerly used in medicine **2** : a poisonous herb related to the lily; *also* : its dried root or a product of this containing alkaloids used in medicine and insecticides

Hel·lene \'hel-ˌēn\ *n* : GREEK — **Hel·len·ic** \he-'len-ik, hə-\ *adj*

hell·gram·mite \'hel-grə-ˌmīt\ *n* : the carnivorous aquatic larva of a dobsonfly that is much used as a fish bait

hell·ish \'hel-ish\ *adj* : of, resembling, or befitting hell : DEVILISH — **hell·ish·ly** *adv* — **hell·ish·ness** *n*

hel·lo \hə-'lō, he-\ *n, pl* **hellos** : an expression or gesture of greeting — used interjectionally in greeting, in answering the telephone, or to express surprise

1helm \'helm\ *n* : HELMET 1

2helm *n* **1** : a lever or wheel controlling the rudder of a ship; *also* : the steering apparatus of a ship **2** : a position of control : HEAD

hel·met \'hel-mət\ *n* **1** : a covering or enclosing headpiece of armor **2** : any of various protective head coverings usu. made of a hard material to resist impact — **hel·met·like** \-ˌlīk\ *adj*

hel·minth \'hel-ˌmin(t)th\ *n* : WORM; *esp* : an intestinal worm (as a tapeworm) — **hel·min·thic** \hel-'min(t)-thik\ *adj*

hel·min·thol·o·gy \ˌhel-ˌmin-'thäl-ə-jē\ *n* : a branch of zoology concerned with helminths; *esp* : the study of parasitic worms

helms·man \'helmz-mən\ *n* : the man at the helm : STEERSMAN

hel·ot \'hel-ət\ *n* : SERF, SLAVE — **hel·ot·ry** \-ə-trē\ *n*

hel·ot·ism \'hel-ət-ˌiz-əm\ *n* : SERFDOM

1help \'help\ *vb* **1** : to provide with what is useful in achieving an end : AID, ASSIST ⟨*helped* me get a job⟩ ⟨*helped* him home⟩ **2** : REMEDY, RELIEVE ⟨rest *helps* a cold⟩ **3 a** : to refrain from ⟨couldn't *help* laughing⟩ **b** : PREVENT ⟨a mistake that could not be *helped*⟩ **4** : to serve with food or drink ⟨*help* yourself⟩

2help *n* **1** : an act or instance of helping : AID, ASSISTANCE ⟨give *help*⟩ ⟨thanked him for his *help*⟩ **2** : the state of being helped : RELIEF ⟨a situation beyond *help*⟩ **3** : a person or a thing that helps ⟨a *help* in time of trouble⟩ **4** : a hired helper or a body of hired helpers ⟨hire additional *help* in a business⟩

help·er \'hel-pər\ *n* : one that helps; *esp* : a person who helps with manual labor ⟨an electrician's *helper*⟩

help·ful \'help-fəl\ *adj* : furnishing help : ASSISTING, USEFUL ⟨a *helpful* neighbor⟩ ⟨a *helpful* reference book⟩ — **help·ful·ly** \-fə-lē\ *adv* — **help·ful·ness** *n*

help·ing \'hel-ping\ *n* : a portion of food : SERVING

helping verb *n* : AUXILIARY VERB

help·less \'help-ləs\ *adj* **1** : DEFENSELESS **2** : POWERLESS — **help·less·ly** *adv* — **help·less·ness** *n*

help·mate \'help-ˌmāt\ *n* : COMPANION, HELPER; *esp* : WIFE

help·meet \-ˌmēt\ *n* : HELPMATE

hel·ter–skel·ter \ˌhel-tər-'skel-tər\ *adv* **1** : in headlong disorder : PELL-MELL ⟨ran *helter-skelter* down the hill⟩ **2** : in random order : HAPHAZARDLY ⟨clothes strewn *helter-skelter* about the room⟩ — **helter–skelter** *adj*

helve \'helv\ *n* : HAFT

1hem \'hem\ *n* : a border of a garment or cloth; *esp* : one made by folding back an edge and sewing it down

2hem *vb* **hemmed**; **hem·ming** **1** : to finish with or make a hem in sewing **2** : to surround in a restrictive manner : CONFINE ⟨a town *hemmed* in by mountains⟩ — **hem·mer** *n*

3hem *a throat-clearing sound; often read as* 'hem\ *n* : a pause in speaking filled by the sound represented by *hem* — often used interjectionally to call attention or to express hesitation or doubt

4hem \'hem\ *vb* **hemmed**; **hem·ming** **1** : to utter the sound represented by *hem* **2** : to hesitate in speaking

hem- *or* **hemo-** *comb form* : blood ⟨*hem*al⟩

he·mal \'hē-məl\ *adj* : of or relating to the blood or blood vessels

he–man \'hē-'man\ *n* : a strong virile man

hemat- *or* **hemato-** *comb form* : HEM- ⟨*hemato*logy⟩

hem·a·tite \'hem-ə-ˌtīt, 'hē-mə-\ *n* : a mineral that consists of an oxide of iron and is a chief ore of iron

he·ma·tol·o·gy \ˌhē-mə-'täl-ə-jē\ *n* : a branch of biology that deals with the blood and blood-forming organs — **he·ma·to·log·ic** \ˌhē-mət-ə-'läj-ik\ *or* **he·ma·to·log·i·cal** \-'läj-i-kəl\ *adj* — **he·ma·tol·o·gist** \ˌhē-mə-'täl-ə-jəst\ *n*

he·ma·tox·y·lin \ˌhē-mə-'täk-sə-lən\ *n* : a crystalline compound found in logwood and used chiefly as a biological stain

H

heme \'hēm\ *n* : a deep red iron-containing pigment obtained from hemoglobin

hemi- *prefix* : half

he·mip·ter·an \hi-'mip-tə-rən\ *n* : any of a large order of insects comprising the true bugs (as the bedbug and chinch bug) and related forms (as plant lice) and having flattened bodies, two pairs of wings, and heads with piercing and sucking organs — **he·mip·ter·on** \-tə-ˌrän\ *n* — **he·mip·ter·ous** \-tə-rəs\ *adj*

hemi·sphere \'hem-ə-ˌsfi(ə)r\ *n* **1** : one of the halves of the earth as divided by the equator or by a meridian **2** : one of two halves of a sphere **3** : CEREBRAL HEMISPHERE — **hemi·spher·ic** \ˌhem-ə-'sfi(ə)r-ik, -'sfer-\ *or* **hemi·spher·i·cal** \-'sfir-i-kəl, -'sfer-\ *adj*

hem·line \'hem-ˌlīn\ *n* : the line formed by the hem of a dress, skirt, or coat

hem·lock \'hem-ˌläk\ *n* **1** : any of several poisonous herbs related to the carrot and having finely cut leaves and small white flowers **2** : any of a genus of evergreen trees related to the pine; *also* : the soft light splintery wood of a hemlock

hemlock looper *n* : a plain buff or gray geometrid moth whose larva is sometimes a serious defoliator of hemlock and other conifers and oak

hemo- — see HEM-

he·mo·glo·bin \'hē-mə-ˌglō-bən\ *n* : an iron-containing protein that is the chief means of oxygen transport in the vertebrate body where it occurs in the red blood cells and is able to combine loosely with oxygen in regions (as the lungs) of high concentration and release it in regions (as the visceral tissues) of low concentration

he·mo·phil·ia \ˌhē-mə-'fil-ē-ə\ *n* : a hereditary tendency to uncontrollable bleeding even from slight wounds — **he·mo·phil·i·ac** \-ē-ˌak\ *adj or n*

hem·or·rhage \'hem-(ə-)rij\ *n* : a copious discharge of blood from the blood vessels esp. when caused by injury — **hemorrhage** *vb* — **hem·or·rhag·ic** \ˌhem-ə-'raj-ik\ *adj*

hem·or·rhoid \'hem-(ə-)ˌrȯid\ *n* **1** : a swollen mass of dilated veins situated at or just within the anus **2** *pl* : the condition of one affected with hemorrhoids — called also *piles*

hemp \'hemp\ *n* : a tall Asiatic herb related to the mulberry and widely grown for its tough woody fiber that is used to make rope and for its flowers and leaves from which various intoxicating drugs (as hashish and marijuana) are derived — **hemp·en** \'hem-pən\ *adj*

hemp (up to 16 ft. high)

1hem·stitch \'hem-ˌstich\ *vb* : to embroider fabric by drawing out parallel threads and stitching the exposed threads in groups to form designs — **hem·stitch·er** *n*

2hemstitch *n* **1** : decorative needlework **2** : a stitch used in hemstitching

hen \'hen\ *n* **1** : a female domestic fowl esp. over a year old **2** : a female of any bird

hence \'hen(t)s\ *adv* **1** : from this place or time ⟨a week *hence*⟩ **2** : CONSEQUENTLY, THEREFORE ⟨was a newcomer and *hence* had no close friends in the city⟩

hence·forth \-ˌfōrth, -ˌfȯrth\ *adv* : from this point on

hence·for·ward \hen(t)s-'fȯr-wərd\ *adv* : HENCEFORTH

hench·man \'hench-mən\ *n* : a trusted follower or supporter

1hen·na \'hen-ə\ *n* **1** : an Old World tropical shrub with panicles of fragrant white flowers **2** : a reddish brown dye obtained from leaves of the henna and used esp. on hair

2henna *vb* **hen·naed** \'hen-əd\; **hen·na·ing** : to dye or tint with henna

hen·nery \'hen-ə-rē\ *n, pl* **-ner·ies** : a poultry farm; *also* : an enclosure for poultry

hen party *n* : a party for women only

hen·peck \'hen-ˌpek\ *vb* : to subject one's husband to persistent nagging and domination

1he·pat·ic \hi-'pat-ik\ *adj* [from Greek *hēpat-*, stem of *hēpar* "liver"] : of, relating to, or resembling the liver

2hepatic *n* : LIVERWORT

he·pat·i·ca \hi-'pat-i-kə\ *n* : any of a genus of herbs related to the buttercup and having lobed leaves and delicate white, pink, or bluish flowers; *also* : this flower

hep·a·ti·tis \ˌhep-ə-'tīt-əs\ *n* : inflammation of the liver; *also* : an acute virus disease marked by hepatitis, jaundice, and fever

hep·ta·gon \'hep-tə-ˌgän\ *n* : a polygon of seven angles and seven sides — **hep·tag·o·nal** \hep-'tag-ən-əl\ *adj*

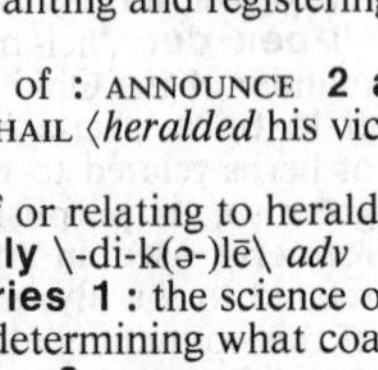

heptagons

1her \(h)ər, ˌhər\ *adj* : of, relating to, or belonging to her or herself ⟨*her* house⟩ ⟨*her* success⟩

2her \ər, (')hər\ *pron, objective case of* SHE

1her·ald \'her-əld\ *n* **1** : an official crier or messenger **2** : an officer responsible for granting and registering coats of arms **3** : HARBINGER

2herald *vb* **1** : to give notice of : ANNOUNCE **2 a** : to greet with enthusiasm **b** : HAIL ⟨*heralded* his victory⟩

he·ral·dic \he-'ral-dik\ *adj* : of or relating to heralds or heraldry — **he·ral·di·cal·ly** \-di-k(ə-)lē\ *adv*

her·ald·ry \'her-əl-drē\ *n, pl* **-ries** **1** : the science of tracing a person's family and determining what coat of arms he is entitled to have **2** : COAT OF ARMS **3** : heraldic pomp or ceremony

herb \'(h)ərb\ *n* **1** : a seed plant that does not develop persistent woody tissue but dies down at the end of a growing season **2** : a plant or plant part used for making medicine and seasonings — **her·ba·ceous** \ˌ(h)ər-'bā-shəs\ *adj* — **herb·like** \'(h)ərb-ˌlīk\ *adj*

herb·age \'(h)ər-bij\ *n* **1** : herbaceous vegetation (as grass) esp. when used for grazing **2** : the succulent parts of herbaceous plants

1herb·al \'(h)ər-bəl\ *n* : a book about plants esp. with reference to their medical properties

2herbal *adj* : of, relating to, or made of herbs

herb·al·ist \'(h)ər-bə-ləst\ *n* : one that collects, grows, or deals in herbs

her·bar·i·um \ˌ(h)ər-'bar-ē-əm, -'ber-\ *n, pl* **-ia** \-ē-ə\ **1** : a collection of dried plant specimens **2** : a place that houses an herbarium

her·bi·cide \'(h)ər-bə-ˌsīd\ *n* : an agent used to destroy or inhibit plant growth — **her·bi·cid·al** \ˌ(h)ər-bə-ˈsīd-əl\ *adj*

her·bi·vore \ˈ(h)ər-bə-ˌvōr, -ˌvȯr\ *n* : a plant-eating animal; *esp* : UNGULATE — **her·biv·o·rous** \ˌ(h)ər-ˈbiv-ə-rəs\ *adj*

her·cu·le·an \ˌhər-kyə-ˈlē-ən, ˌhər-ˈkyü-lē-\ *adj* **1** *cap* : of, relating to, or characteristic of Hercules **2** : of unusual power, size, or difficulty ⟨a *herculean* task⟩

1**herd** \ˈhərd\ *n* **1** : a number of animals of one kind kept or living together **2** : the common people

2**herd** *vb* **1** : to assemble or come together into a herd or group **2** : to gather, lead, or drive a herd ⟨*herd* cattle⟩ — **herd·er** *n*

herds·man \ˈhərdz-mən\ *n* : a manager, breeder, or tender of livestock

1**here** \ˈhi(ə)r\ *adv* **1** : in or at this place ⟨turn *here*⟩ **2** : at this point ⟨*here* we agree⟩ **3** : to or into this place ⟨come *here*⟩

2**here** *n* : this place ⟨get away from *here*⟩

here·abouts \ˈhi(ə)r-ə-ˌbau̇ts\ *or* **here·about** \-ˌbau̇t\ *adv* : near or around this place : in this vicinity

1**here·af·ter** \hi(ə)r-ˈaf-tər\ *adv* **1** : after this **2** : in some future time or state

2**hereafter** *n* **1** : FUTURE **2** : life after death ⟨belief in the *hereafter*⟩

here·by \hi(ə)r-ˈbī\ *adv* : by means of this

he·red·i·tary \hə-ˈred-ə-ˌter-ē\ *adj* **1** : genetically transmitted or capable of being transmitted from parent to offspring ⟨*hereditary* traits⟩ **2 a** : received or passing by inheritance ⟨*hereditary* rank⟩ **b** : having title or possession through inheritance ⟨*hereditary* ruler⟩ **3** : of or relating to inheritance or heredity ***syn*** see INNATE

he·red·i·ty \hə-ˈred-ət-ē\ *n, pl* **-ties** **1** : the genetic traits including both genes and their expressed characters derived from one's ancestors **2** : the transmission of characteristics from ancestor to descendant through genes

Her·e·ford \ˈhər-fərd, ˈher-ə-\ *n* : any of an English breed of hardy red white-faced beef cattle widely raised in the western U.S.

here·in \hi(ə)r-ˈin\ *adv* : in this

here·of \-ˈəv, -ˈäv\ *adv* : of this

here·on \-ˈȯn, -ˈän\ *adv* : on this

her·e·sy \ˈher-ə-sē\ *n, pl* **-sies** [from Greek *hairesis* "sect", literally "choice", from *haireisthai* "to take for oneself", "choose"] **1** : religious opinion contrary to the doctrines of a church **2** : opinion or doctrine contrary to a dominant or generally accepted belief

her·e·tic \ˈher-ə-ˌtik\ *n* : a person who believes or teaches heretical doctrines

he·ret·i·cal \hə-ˈret-i-kəl\ *adj* : of, relating to, or characterized by heresy : UNORTHODOX — **he·ret·i·cal·ly** \hə-ˈret-i-k(ə-)lē\ *adv* — **he·ret·i·cal·ness** \-kəl-nəs\ *n*

here·to·fore \ˈhi(ə)rt-ə-ˌfōr, -ˌfȯr\ *adv* : up to this time

here·un·to \hi(ə)r-ˈən-tü\ *adv* : to this; *esp* : to this document

here·up·on \ˈhi(ə)r-ə-ˌpȯn, -ˌpän\ *adv* : on this : immediately after this

here·with \hi(ə)r-ˈwith, -ˈwith\ *adv* : with this : enclosed in this

her·i·ta·ble \ˈher-ət-ə-bəl\ *adj* : capable of being inherited **2** : HEREDITARY — **her·i·ta·bil·i·ty** \ˌher-ət-ə-ˈbil-ət-ē\ *n*

her·i·tage \ˈher-ət-ij\ *n* **1** : property that descends to an heir **2** : something transmitted by or acquired from a predecessor

her·maph·ro·dite \(ˌ)hər-ˈmaf-rə-ˌdīt\ *n* : an animal or plant having both male and female reproductive organs — **hermaphrodite** *adj* — **her·maph·ro·dit·ic** \(ˌ)hər-ˌmaf-rə-ˈdit-ik\ *adj* — **her·maph·ro·dit·i·cal·ly** \-ˈdit-i-k(ə-)lē\ *adv* — **her·maph·ro·dit·ism** \(ˌ)hər-ˈmaf-rə-ˌdīt-ˌiz-əm\ *n*

her·met·ic \(ˌ)hər-ˈmet-ik\ *adj* : AIRTIGHT — **her·met·i·cal·ly** \-i-k(ə-)lē\ *adv*

her·mit \ˈhər-mət\ *n* [from Greek *erēmitēs*, from *erēmia* "solitude", "desert"] **1** : one that lives apart from others esp. for religious reasons : RECLUSE **2** : a spiced molasses cookie

her·mit·age \ˈhər-mət-ij\ *n* : a hermit's home; *also* : a secluded residence : RETREAT

hermit crab *n* : any of various crabs having soft asymmetrical abdomens and occupying empty mollusk shells

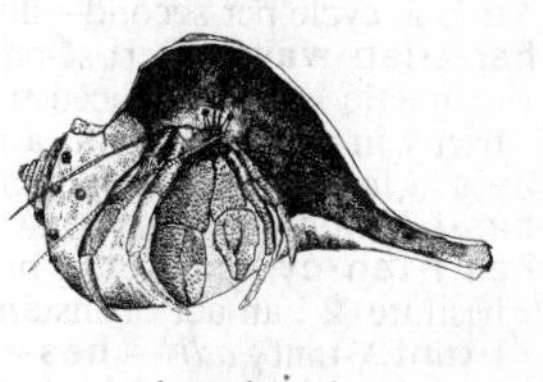

hermit crab (about 3 in. long)

her·nia \ˈhər-nē-ə\ *n, pl* **her·ni·as** *or* **her·ni·ae** \-nē-ˌē, -nē-ˌī\ : a protrusion of an organ or part through connective tissue or through a wall of the cavity in which it is normally enclosed — called also *rupture* — **her·ni·al** \-nē-əl\ *adj*

he·ro \ˈhē-rō, ˈhi(ə)r-ō\ *n, pl* **heroes** **1 a** : a mythological or legendary man of great strength or ability **b** : an illustrious warrior or soldier **c** : a man admired for his achievements and qualities **d** : one that shows great courage ⟨the *hero* of a rescue⟩ **2** : the chief male figure in a literary work or in an event or period **3** *pl* **heros** *chiefly New York* : SUBMARINE 2

he·ro·ic \hi-ˈrō-ik\ *adj* **1** : of or relating to heroes esp. of antiquity ⟨the *heroic* age⟩ ⟨*heroic* legends⟩ **2** : exhibiting or marked by courage, daring, or desperate enterprise ⟨a *heroic* rescue⟩ **3 a** : GRAND, NOBLE ⟨a *heroic* plan for civic improvement⟩ **b** : larger than life-size ⟨a *heroic* statue⟩ — **he·ro·i·cal** \-ˈrō-i-kəl\ *adj* — **he·ro·i·cal·ly** \-i-k(ə-)lē\ *adv*

he·ro·ics \-iks\ *n pl* : extravagant display of heroic attitudes in action or expression

her·o·in \ˈher-ə-wən\ *n* : a strongly addictive drug derived from the opium poppy and more potent than morphine — **her·o·in·ism** \-wə-ˌniz-əm\ *n*

her·o·ine \ˈher-ə-wən\ *n* **1** : a woman of courage and daring **2** : a woman admired for her achievements and qualities **3** : the chief female figure in a literary work or in an event or period

her·o·ism \ˈher-ə-ˌwiz-əm\ *n* : heroic conduct or qualities ***syn*** see COURAGE

her·on \ˈher-ən\ *n, pl* **herons** *also* **heron** : any of various long-necked wading birds with a long tapering bill, large wings, and soft plumage

her·pes \ˈhər-(ˌ)pēz\ *n* : any of several virus diseases characterized by the formation of blisters on the skin or mucous membranes

her·pe·tol·o·gy \ˌhər-pə-ˈtäl-ə-jē\ *n* : a branch of zoology dealing with reptiles and amphibians — **her·pe·to·log·ic** \ˌhər-pət-ə-ˈläj-ik\ *or* **her·pe·to·log·i·cal** \-ˈläj-i-kəl\ *adj* — **her·pe·to·log·i·cal·ly** \-i-k(ə-)lē\ *adv* — **her·pe·tol·o·gist** \ˌhər-pə-ˈtäl-ə-jəst\ *n*

her·ring \ˈher-ing\ *n, pl* **herring** *or* **herrings** : a valuable soft-rayed food fish abundant in the north Atlantic ocean; *also* : any of various similar and related fishes

1**her·ring·bone** \'her-ing-ˌbōn\ *n* **1** : a pattern of rows of parallel lines with every other row slanting in the opposite direction **2** : a fabric with a herringbone pattern

2**herringbone** *vb* **1** : to produce a herringbone pattern on a surface **2** : to arrange in a herringbone pattern

hers \'hərz\ *pron* : her one : her ones ⟨the book is *hers*⟩

her·self \(h)ər-'self\ *pron* **1** : that identical female one — used for emphasis or to show that the subject and object of the verb are the same ⟨she considers *herself* lucky⟩ ⟨she *herself* did it⟩ **2** : her normal, healthy, or sane self ⟨was *herself* again after a good night's sleep⟩

hertz \'he(ə)rts, 'hərts\ *n* : a unit of frequency equal to one cycle per second—abbr. *Hz*

hertz·ian wave \ˌhert-sē-ən-, ˌhərt-\ *n* : an electromagnetic wave produced by the oscillation of electricity in a conductor (as a radio antenna)

he's \(ˌ)hēz, ēz\ : he is : he has

hes·i·tance \'hez-ə-tən(t)s\ *n* : HESITANCY

hes·i·tan·cy \-tən-sē\ *n, pl* **-cies** **1** : a tendency to hesitate **2** : an act or instance of hesitating — **hes·i·tant** \-tənt\ *adj* — **hes·i·tant·ly** *adv*

hes·i·tate \'hez-ə-ˌtāt\ *vb* **1** : to stop or pause because of forgetfulness, uncertainty, or indecision ⟨*hesitate* before answering⟩ **2** : to be reluctant ⟨*hesitate* to ask a favor⟩ **3** : STAMMER — **hes·i·tat·er** *n* — **hes·i·tat·ing·ly** \-ˌtāt-ing-lē\ *adv* — **hes·i·ta·tion** \ˌhez-ə-'tā-shən\ *n*

Hes·sian fly \ˌhesh-ən-\ *n* : a small two-winged fly destructive to wheat in America

heter- *or* **hetero-** *comb form* : other than usual : other : different ⟨*hetero*sexual⟩

het·ero·chro·mat·ic \ˌhet-ə-rō-krə-'mat-ik\ *adj* : of, relating to, or having different colors esp. in a complex pattern — **het·ero·chro·ma·tism** \-'krō-mə-ˌtiz-əm\ *n*

het·er·o·dox \'het-ə-rə-ˌdäks\ *adj* **1** : contrary to prevailing opinions, beliefs, or standards; *esp* : not orthodox in religion **2** : holding or expressing unorthodox beliefs or opinions

het·er·o·doxy \-ˌdäk-sē\ *n, pl* **-dox·ies** **1** : the quality or state of being heterodox **2** : a heterodox opinion or doctrine

het·er·o·ge·ne·ous \ˌhet-ə-rə-'jē-nē-əs\ *adj* : differing in kind : consisting of dissimilar ingredients : MIXED ⟨a *heterogeneous* population⟩ — **het·er·o·ge·ne·ous·ly** *adv* — **het·er·o·ge·ne·ous·ness** *n*

het·er·op·ter·ous \ˌhet-ə-'räp-tə-rəs\ *adj* : of or relating to a group of insects comprising the true bugs — **het·er·op·ter·an** \-tə-rən\ *adj or n*

het·ero·sex·u·al \ˌhet-ə-rō-'sek-sh(ə-w)əl\ *adj* : of, relating to, or marked by sexual interest in members of the opposite sex — **heterosexual** *n* — **het·ero·sex·u·al·i·ty** \-ˌsek-shə-'wal-ət-ē\ *n*

het·ero·troph·ic \ˌhet-ə-rə-'träf-ik, -'trō-fik\ *adj* : unable to live and grow without complex organic compounds of nitrogen and carbon — **het·ero·troph** \'het-ə-rə-ˌträf\ *n* — **het·er·ot·ro·phism** \ˌhet-ə-'rä-trə-ˌfiz-əm\ *n* — **het·er·ot·ro·phy** \-trə-fē\ *n*

het·ero·zy·gote \-'zī-ˌgōt\ *n* : a heterozygous individual — **het·ero·zy·gos·i·ty** \-zī-'gäs-ət-ē\ *n*

ə abut	ər further	a back	ā bake
ä cot, cart	au̇ out	ch chin	e less
ē easy	g gift	i trip	ī life
j joke	ng sing	ō flow	ȯ flaw
ȯi coin	th thin	t͟h this	ü loot
u̇ foot	y yet	yü few	yu̇ furious
zh vision			

het·ero·zy·gous \-'zī-gəs\ *adj* : containing both members of at least one pair of alleles ⟨a plant *heterozygous* for yellow seed⟩

hew \'hyü\ *vb* **hewed**; **hewed** *or* **hewn** \'hyün\; **hew·ing** **1** : to chop down : CHOP ⟨*hew* logs⟩ ⟨*hew* trees⟩ **2** : to make or shape by cutting with an ax ⟨a cabin built of rough-*hewn* logs⟩ **3** : to conform strictly : ADHERE ⟨*hew* to the line⟩ — **hew·er** *n*

1**hex** \'heks\ *vb* **1** : to put a hex on **2** : to affect as if by an evil spell : JINX — **hex·er** *n*

2**hex** *n* **1** : SPELL, JINX **2** : WITCH

hexa- *or* **hex-** *comb form* : six

hexa·flu·o·ride \ˌhek-sə-'flu̇(-ə)r-ˌīd\ *n* : a fluoride containing six atoms of fluorine in a molecule ⟨uranium *hexafluoride*⟩

hex·a·gon \'hek-sə-ˌgän\ *n* : a polygon of six angles and six sides — **hex·ag·o·nal** \hek-'sag-ən-əl\ *adj*

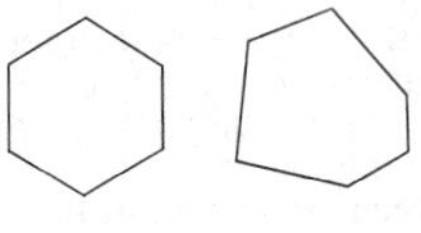

hexagons

hex·am·e·ter \hek-'sam-ət-ər\ *n* : a line of verse consisting of six metrical feet

hexa·meth·y·lene·di·a·mine \ˌhek-sə-ˌmeth-ə-ˌlēn-'dī-ə-ˌmēn, -dī-'am-ən\ *n* : a compound used in the manufacture of nylon

hex·ane \'hek-ˌsān\ *n* : a volatile liquid hydrocarbon found in petroleum

1**hex·a·pod** \'hek-sə-ˌpäd\ *n* : INSECT 2

2**hexapod** *adj* **1** : six-footed **2** : of or relating to insects

hex·ose \'hek-ˌsōs\ *n* : a sugar containing six carbon atoms in the molecule

hey \'hā\ *interj* — used esp. to call attention or to express interrogation, surprise, or exultation

hey·day \'hā-ˌdā\ *n* : the time of greatest strength or vigor ⟨a nation in the *heyday* of its power⟩

hf *abbr* **1** half **2** high frequency

hg *abbr* hectogram

hgt *abbr* height

hi \'hī(-ē)\ *interj* — used esp. as a greeting

HI *abbr* Hawaii

hi·a·tus \hī-'āt-əs\ *n* **1** : a gap in space or time; *esp* : a break where a part is missing **2** : the occurrence of two vowel sounds without pause or an intervening consonant sound

hi·ba·chi \hē-'bäch-ē\ *n* : a charcoal brazier

hi·ber·nate \'hī-bər-ˌnāt\ *vb* : to pass the winter in a torpid or resting state — **hi·ber·na·tion** \ˌhī-bər-'nā-shən\ *n* — **hi·ber·na·tor** \'hī-bər-ˌnāt-ər\ *n*

hi·bis·cus \hī-'bis-kəs, hə-\ *n* : any of a large genus of herbs, shrubs, or small trees related to the mallow and having toothed leaves and large showy flowers

1**hic·cup** *also* **hic·cough** \'hik-(ˌ)əp\ *n* : a spasmodic drawing in of breath that is stopped by sudden closure of the glottis and accompanied by a peculiar sound

2**hiccup** *also* **hiccough** *vb* **hic·cuped** *also* **hic·cupped**; **hic·cup·ing** *also* **hic·cup·ping** : to make a hiccup or be affected with hiccups

hick·o·ry \'hik-(ə-)rē\ *n, pl* **-ries** **1** : any of a genus of No. American hardwood trees related to the walnut and having a hard-shelled edible nut **2** : the usu. tough pale wood of a hickory

hi·dal·go \hid-'al-gō, ē-'t͟häl-\ *n, pl* **-gos** **[**from Spanish, a contraction of *hijo d'algo*, literally "son of something", and hence used of one with inherited wealth**]** : a member of the lower nobility of Spain

hidden hunger *n* : a bodily disorder caused by a badly balanced diet

[1]**hide** *vb* **hid** \'hīd\; **hid·den** \'hid-ən\ *or* **hid**; **hid·ing** \'hīd-ing\ **1** : to put or get out of sight : CONCEAL ⟨*hide* a treasure⟩ ⟨*hid* in a closet⟩ **2** : to keep secret ⟨*hid* her grief⟩ **3** : to screen from view ⟨a house *hidden* by trees⟩ ⟨clouds *hid* the sun⟩ **4** : to seek protection or evade responsibility ⟨*hides* behind dark glasses⟩ — **hid·er** \'hīd-ər\ *n*

[2]**hide** *n* : the skin of an animal whether raw or dressed

[3]**hide** *vb* **hid·ed**; **hid·ing** : to give a beating to : FLOG

hide-and-seek \ˌhīd-ən-'sēk\ *n* : a children's game in which all but one player hide and he tries to find and catch them — called also *hide-and-go-seek* \-ən-gō-'sēk\

hide·away \'hīd-ə-ˌwā\ *n* : RETREAT, HIDEOUT

hide·bound \'hīd-ˌbaund\ *adj* **1** : having a dry skin adhering closely to the underlying flesh ⟨a *hidebound* horse⟩ **2** : obstinately conservative

hid·e·ous \'hid-ē-əs\ *adj* : horribly ugly or disgusting : FRIGHTFUL — **hid·e·ous·ly** *adv* — **hid·e·ous·ness** *n*

hide·out \'hīd-ˌaut\ *n* : a place of refuge or concealment

[1]**hid·ing** \'hīd-ing\ *n* : a state or place of concealment

[2]**hiding** *n* : FLOGGING, WHIPPING ⟨got a severe *hiding*⟩

hie \'hī\ *vb* **hied**; **hy·ing** *or* **hie·ing** : HURRY, HASTEN

hi·er·ar·chy \'hī(-ə)-ˌrär-kē\ *n, pl* **-chies** **1** : a ruling body esp. of clergy organized into ranks each subordinate to the one above it **2 a** : an arrangement into a graded series **b** : persons or things arranged in ranks or classes — **hi·er·ar·chi·cal** \ˌhī(-ə)-'rär-ki-kəl\ *or* **hi·er·ar·chic** \-'rär-kik\ *adj* — **hi·er·ar·chi·cal·ly** \-'rär-ki-k(ə-)lē\ *adv*

hi·er·o·glyph \'hī(-ə)-rə-ˌglif\ *n* : a character used in hieroglyphic writing

hi·er·o·glyph·ic \ˌhī(-ə)-rə-'glif-ik\ *n* [from Greek *hieroglyphikos* "hieroglyphic" (adj.), from *hieros* "holy" and *glyphein* "to carve"] **1** : HIEROGLYPH **2** : a system of writing mainly in pictorial characters; *esp* : the picture script of the ancient Egyptian priesthood **3** : obscure or illegible signs or writing — **hieroglyphic** *adj*

hi-fi \'hī-'fī\ *n* **1** : HIGH FIDELITY **2** : equipment for reproduction of sound with high fidelity

hig·gle·dy-pig·gle·dy \ˌhig-əl-dē-'pig-əl-dē\ *adv* : in confusion : TOPSY-TURVY — **higgledy-piggledy** *adj*

[1]**high** \'hī\ *adj* **1 a** : extending or raised up : ELEVATED ⟨a *high* building⟩ **b** : having a specified elevation ⟨six feet *high*⟩ **2** : advanced toward fullness ⟨*high* summer⟩ **3** : SHRILL, SHARP ⟨*high* note⟩ **4** : relatively far from the equator ⟨*high* latitude⟩ **5** : exalted in character : NOBLE ⟨a man of *high* purpose⟩ **6** : of greater degree, size, amount, or content than average or ordinary ⟨*high* pressure⟩ ⟨*high* power of a microscope⟩ **7** : of relatively great importance: as **a** : foremost in rank, dignity, or standing ⟨*high* society⟩ **b** : SERIOUS, GRAVE ⟨*high* crimes⟩ **8** : FORCIBLE, STRONG ⟨*high* winds⟩ **9 a** : showing elation or excitement ⟨*high* spirits⟩ **b** : INTOXICATED; *also* : excited or stupefied by a narcotic substance (as heroin) **10** : COSTLY, DEAR ⟨everything's *high* nowadays⟩ **11** : advanced in complexity or development ⟨*higher* mathematics⟩ ⟨*higher* animals including man⟩

syn HIGH, TALL, LOFTY can mean extending upward to a marked degree. HIGH may imply extending upward from a base ⟨a *high* hill⟩; TALL applies to something that rises higher than others of its kind; LOFTY implies extent upward to an impressive height ***ant*** low

[2]**high** *adv* **1** : at or to a high place, altitude, or degree ⟨knocked the ball *high* into the bleachers⟩ **2** : RICHLY, LUXURIOUSLY ⟨lived *high* after getting his inheritance⟩

[3]**high** *n* **1 a** : HILL, KNOLL **b** : SKY, HEAVEN ⟨birds wheeling on *high*⟩ **2** : a region of high barometric pressure : ANTICYCLONE **3 a** : a high point or level : HEIGHT ⟨prices reached a new *high* this year⟩ **b** : the arrangement of gears (as in an automobile) that gives the highest speed and consequently the highest speed of travel **4** : a state of elation or excitement; *esp* : one induced by drugs

high·ball \'hī-ˌbȯl\ *n* : a drink of alcoholic liquor with water or a carbonated beverage served in a tall glass

high blood pressure *n* **1** : abnormally high blood pressure esp. in the arteries **2** : the condition resulting from high blood pressure that is characterized by nervousness, dizziness, and headache

high·born \'hī-'bȯrn\ *adj* : of noble birth

high·boy \'hī-ˌbȯi\ *n* : a high chest of drawers mounted on a base with long legs

high·brow \-ˌbrau\ *n* : a person of superior learning or culture : INTELLECTUAL — **highbrow** *adj*

high chair *n* : a child's chair with long legs, a feeding tray, and a footrest

high·fa·lu·tin \ˌhī-fə-'lüt-ən\ *adj* : PRETENTIOUS, POMPOUS ⟨*highfalutin* talk⟩ ⟨*highfalutin* people⟩

high fidelity *n* : the reproduction of sound with a high degree of faithfulness to the original

high-flown \'hī-'flōn\ *adj* **1** : ELEVATED, PROUD **2** : not plain or simple : EXTRAVAGANT ⟨*high-flown* language⟩

high frequency *n* : a radio frequency in the range between 3 and 30 megacycles — abbr. *hf*

high-grade \'hī-'grād\ *adj* : of a grade rated as superior

high-hand·ed \-'han-dəd\ *adj* : OVERBEARING, ARBITRARY ⟨*high-handed* actions⟩ — **high-hand·ed·ly** *adv* — **high-hand·ed·ness** *n*

[1]**high-hat** \-'hat\ *adj* : supercilious or snobbish in attitude or manner

[2]**high-hat** *vb* : to treat in a high-hat manner

high horse *n* : an arrogant mood or attitude

high jinks \-'jing(k)s\ *n pl* : wild or boisterous behavior

[1]**high·land** \'hī-lənd\ *n* : elevated or mountainous land

[2]**highland** *adj* **1** : of or relating to a highland **2** *cap* : of or relating to the Highlands of Scotland

high·land·er \-lən-dər\ *n* **1** : an inhabitant of a highland **2** *cap* : an inhabitant of the Highlands of Scotland

Highland fling *n* : a lively Scottish folk dance

[1]**high·light** \'hī-ˌlīt\ *n* **1 a** : one of the spots or areas on an object that reflect the most light **b** : the brightest spot (as in a painting or drawing) **2** : an event or scene of major interest ⟨the *highlights* of a trip⟩

[2]**highlight** *vb* **1** : to throw a strong light on **2 a** : to center attention on : EMPHASIZE **b** : to be a highlight of

high·ly \'hī-lē\ *adv* **1** : to a high degree : EXTREMELY ⟨*highly* pleased⟩ **2** : with approval ⟨speak *highly* of a person⟩

high-mind·ed \'hī-'mīn-dəd\ *adj* : having or marked by elevated principles and feelings — **high-mind·ed·ly** *adv* — **high-mind·ed·ness** *n*

high·ness \'hī-nəs\ *n* **1** : the quality or state of being high **2** — used as a title for persons (as a king or prince) of high rank ⟨His Royal *Highness*⟩

high-octane *adj* : having a high octane number and

H

hence good antiknock properties ⟨*high-octane* gasoline⟩

[1]**high-pressure** *adj* **1 a :** having or involving a high pressure esp. greatly exceeding that of the atmosphere **b :** having a high atmospheric pressure **2 :** using or involving aggressive and insistent sales techniques

[2]**high-pressure** *vb* **:** to sell or influence by high-pressure tactics

high-rise *adj* **:** having several stories and being equipped with elevators ⟨*high-rise* apartments⟩

high·road \'hī-ˌrōd\ *n, chiefly Brit* **:** HIGHWAY

high school *n* **:** a secondary school usu. comprising the 9th to 12th or 10th to 12th years of study

high seas *n pl* **:** the open part of a sea or ocean esp. outside territorial waters

high-sound·ing \'hī-'saủn-diŋ\ *adj* **:** POMPOUS, IMPOSING

high-spir·it·ed \'hī-'spir-ət-əd\ *adj* **:** characterized by a bold or lively spirit — **high-spir·it·ed·ly** *adv* — **high-spir·it·ed·ness** *n*

high-strung \-'strəŋ\ *adj* **:** highly nervous or sensitive

high-tension *adj* **1 :** having a high voltage **2 :** relating to or being apparatus to be used at high voltage

high-test *adj* **1 :** passing a difficult test **2 :** having a high volatility; *esp* **:** HIGH-OCTANE ⟨*high-test* gasoline⟩

high tide *n* **:** the tide when the water is at its greatest height

high treason *n* **:** TREASON 2

high·way \'hī-ˌwā\ *n* **:** a public road; *esp* **:** a main direct road

high·way·man \-mən\ *n* **:** a person who robs travelers on a highway

hi·jack *or* **high-jack** \'hī-ˌjak\ *vb* **1 :** to stop and steal from a moving vehicle ⟨*hijack* a truck⟩ ⟨*hijack* a load of furs⟩ **2 :** to force a pilot to fly an aircraft where one wants ⟨*hijack* an airliner to Cuba⟩ — **hi·jack·er** *n*

[1]**hike** \'hīk\ *vb* **1 :** to move or raise up ⟨*hike* rents⟩ **2 :** to go on a long walk — **hik·er** *n*

[2]**hike** *n* **1 :** a long walk esp. for pleasure or exercise **2 :** an upward movement **:** RISE ⟨a price *hike*⟩

hi·lar·i·ous \hil-'ar-ē-əs, -'er-; hī-'lar-, -'ler-\ *adj* **:** marked by or affording hilarity — **hi·lar·i·ous·ly** *adv* — **hi·lar·i·ous·ness** *n*

hi·lar·i·ty \-ət-ē\ *n* **:** boisterous merriment

[1]**hill** \'hil\ *n* **1 :** a usu. rounded height of land lower than a mountain **2 :** an artificial heap or mound (as of earth) **3 :** several seeds or plants planted in a group rather than a row ⟨a *hill* of beans⟩

[2]**hill** *vb* **1 :** to form into a heap **2 :** to draw earth around the roots or base of — **hill·er** *n*

hill·bil·ly \'hil-ˌbil-ē\ *n, pl* **-lies :** a person from a mountainous backwoods area

hillbilly music *n* **:** COUNTRY MUSIC

hill·ock \'hil-ək\ *n* **:** a small hill — **hill·ocky** \-ə-kē\ *adj*

hill·side \'hil-ˌsīd\ *n* **:** the side of a hill

hill·top \'hil-ˌtäp\ *n* **:** the highest part of a hill

hilly \'hil-ē\ *adj* **hill·i·er; -est 1 :** abounding in hills ⟨a *hilly* city⟩ **2 :** STEEP

hilt \'hilt\ *n* **:** a handle esp. of a sword or dagger — **to the hilt :** COMPLETELY

ə abut	ər further	a back	ā bake
ä cot, cart	aủ out	ch chin	e less	ē easy
g gift	i trip	ī life	j joke	ŋ sing	ō flow
ȯ flaw	ȯi coin	th thin	th this	ü loot
ủ foot	y yet	yü few	yủ furious	zh vision

hi·lum \'hī-ləm\ *n, pl* **hi·la** \-lə\ **:** a scar on a seed at the point of attachment of the ovule — **hi·lar** \-lər\ *adj*

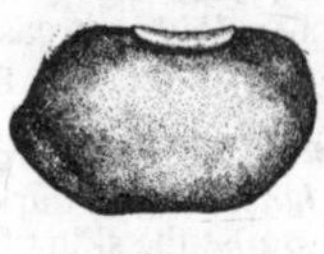
hilum (on bean seed)

him \im, (ˈ)him\ *pron, objective case of* HE

Him·a·lay·an \ˌhim-ə-'lā-ən, hə-'mäl-(ə-)yən\ *adj* **:** of, relating to, or characteristic of the Himalaya mountains or the people living there — **Himalayan** *n*

him·self \(h)im-'self\ *pron* **1 :** that identical male one **:** that identical one whose sex is unknown or immaterial — used for emphasis or to show that the subject and object of the verb are the same ⟨everyone must look out for *himself*⟩ ⟨he *himself* did it⟩ **2 :** his normal, healthy, or sane self ⟨he's *himself* again⟩

[1]**hind** \'hīnd\ *n, pl* **hinds** *also* **hind 1 :** a female red deer **2 :** any of various usu. spotted groupers

[2]**hind** *n, archaic* **:** RUSTIC

[3]**hind** *adj* **:** located behind **:** REAR ⟨*hind* legs⟩

hind·brain \'hīn(d)-ˌbrān\ *n* **:** the posterior division of the embryonic vertebrate brain or the parts developed from it

hin·der \'hin-dər\ *vb* **hin·dered; hin·der·ing** \-d(ə-)riŋ\ **1 :** to make slow or difficult **:** HAMPER ⟨progress was *hindered* by bad weather⟩ **2 :** to hold back **:** CHECK ⟨*hindered* by lack of money⟩ — **hin·der·er** \-dər-ər\ *n*

Hin·di \'hin-(ˌ)dē\ *n* **1 :** a literary and official language of northern India **2 :** a complex of Indic dialects of northern India for which Hindi is the usual literary language — **Hindi** *adj*

hind·most \'hīn(d)-ˌmōst\ *adj* **:** farthest to the rear

hind·quar·ter \-ˌkwȯrt-ər\ *n* **1 :** the back half of a lateral half of the body or carcass of a four-footed animal ⟨a *hindquarter* of beef⟩ **2** *pl* **:** the part of a four-footed animal behind the attachment of the hind legs to the trunk

hin·drance \'hin-drən(t)s\ *n* **1 :** the state of being hindered **2 :** the action of hindering **3 :** something that hinders **:** IMPEDIMENT

hind·sight \'hīn(d)-ˌsīt\ *n* **1 :** a rear sight of a firearm **2 :** perception of the significance of an event only after it has happened ⟨*hindsight* is easier than foresight⟩

Hin·du \'hin-dü\ *n* **1 :** an adherent of Hinduism **2 :** a native or inhabitant of India — **Hindu** *adj*

Hin·du·ism \-ˌiz-əm\ *n* **:** a body of social, cultural, and religious beliefs and practices native to the Indian subcontinent

hind wing *n* **:** a posterior wing of an insect

[1]**hinge** \'hinj\ *n* **1 :** a jointed piece on which one surface (as a door, gate, or lid) turns or swings on another **2 :** the joint between valves of a bivalve's shell

[2]**hinge** *vb* **1 :** to attach by or furnish with hinges **2 :** to hang or turn as if on a hinge **:** DEPEND ⟨success *hinges* on the decision⟩

hinge joint *n* **:** a joint between bones (as at the elbow) that permits motion in but one plane

hin·ny \'hin-ē\ *n, pl* **hinnies :** a hybrid between a stallion and a she ass

[1]**hint** \'hint\ *n* **1 :** a slight mention **:** an indirect suggestion or reminder ⟨a *hint* of winter in the air⟩ **2 :** a very small amount **:** TRACE ⟨a *hint* of garlic⟩

[2]**hint** *vb* **:** to bring to mind by or give a hint ⟨*hinting* at what she wanted for Christmas⟩ ⟨*hinted* that something was up⟩ — **hint·er** *n*

hin·ter·land \'hint-ər-ˌland\ *n* **1 :** a region behind a coast **2 :** a region remote from cities and towns

[1]**hip** \'hip\ *n* : the fruit of a rose

[2]**hip** *n* : the part of the body that curves outward below the waist on either side formed by the side part of the pelvis and the upper part of the thigh — **hipped** \'hipt\ *adj*

[3]**hip** *adj* **1** : keenly aware of or interested in the newest developments **2** : WISE, ALERT **3** : of, relating to, or being a hippie

hip·bone \'hip-'bōn, -ˌbōn\ *n* : either of two large flaring compound bones that make lateral halves of the pelvis in mammals, provide points of attachment for the skeleton of the leg, and fuse together in front and with the backbone in the rear to form a closed bony ring which supports the lower part of the trunk and the abdominal organs

hip girdle *n* : PELVIC GIRDLE

hip·pie *or* **hip·py** \'hip-ē\ *n, pl* **hippies** : a young person who rejects established ways of dressing and behaving, believes in the rejection of violence, and often claims that drugs are a way to religious experiences

hip·po \'hip-ō\ *n, pl* **hippos** : HIPPOPOTAMUS

hip·po·drome \'hip-ə-ˌdrōm\ *n* **1** : an oval stadium for horse and chariot races in ancient Greece **2** : an arena for performances featuring horses and riding

hip·po·pot·a·mus \ˌhip-ə-'pät-ə-məs\ *n, pl* **-muses** *or* **-mi** \-ˌmī, -(ˌ)mē\ [from Greek, from *hippos* "horse" and *potamos* "river"] : any of several large plant-eating 4-toed chiefly aquatic African mammals related to the swine and characterized by an extremely large head and mouth, very thick hairless skin, and short legs

hippopotamus
(about 5 ft. at shoulder)

hip·py \'hip-ē\ *adj* **hip·pi·er**; **-est** : having large hips

[1]**hire** \'hī(ə)r\ *n* **1 a** : payment for temporary use **b** : payment for services : WAGES ⟨not worth his *hire*⟩ **2 a** : the act of hiring **b** : the state of being hired : EMPLOYMENT

[2]**hire** *vb* **1** : to engage or grant the services of for a set sum ⟨*hire* a new crew⟩ ⟨*hired* out as a cook⟩ **2** : to engage the temporary use of for a set sum ⟨*hire* a hall⟩ — **hir·er** *n*

hire·ling \'hī(ə)r-ling\ *n* : a person who works for wages; *esp* : one whose only interest in his work is the money he receives

hir·sute \'hər-ˌsüt, 'hi(ə)r-\ *adj* : roughly hairy

[1]**his** \(h)iz, ˌhiz\ *adj* : of, relating to, or belonging to him or himself ⟨*his* house⟩ ⟨*his* writings⟩

[2]**his** \'hiz\ *pron* : his one : his ones ⟨the book is *his*⟩

His·pan·ic \his-'pan-ik\ *adj* : of or relating to Spain or Latin America or their people

hiss \'his\ *vb* : to make a prolonged sharp sound like that of the speech sound \s\ or that emitted by an alarmed snake usu. as a sign of disapproval ⟨*hissed* him off the stage⟩ — **hiss** *n* — **hiss·er** *n*

hist \s *often prolonged and usu with* p *preceding and* t *following*; *often read as* 'hist\ *interj* — used to attract attention

hist *abbr* **1** historical **2** history

his·ta·mine \'his-tə-ˌmēn, -mən\ *n* : a compound occurring in many animal tissues that is believed to play an important part in allergic reactions (as hives, asthma, and hay fever)

his·to·gram \'his-tə-ˌgram\ *n* : an arrangement of statistical data in classes usu. represented by vertical rectangles on a graph such that each rectangle is wide enough to include the values of one class and its height is proportional to the frequency or the relative frequency of the members of the class

his·tol·o·gy \his-'täl-ə-jē\ *n, pl* **-gies** **1** : a branch of anatomy that deals with the structure of animal and plant tissues as revealed by the microscope **2** : tissue structure or organization — **his·to·log·i·cal** \ˌhis-tə-'läj-i-kəl\ *or* **his·to·log·ic** \-'läj-ik\ *adj* — **his·to·log·i·cal·ly** \-i-k(ə-)lē\ *adv* — **his·tol·o·gist** \his-'täl-ə-jəst\ *n*

his·to·ri·an \his-'tōr-ē-ən, -'tȯr-\ *n* : a student or writer of history

his·tor·ic \his-'tȯr-ik, -'tär-\ *adj* **1** : HISTORICAL 1 **2** : famous in history ⟨*historic* events⟩

his·tor·i·cal \-i-kəl\ *adj* **1 a** : of, relating to, or having the character of history; *esp* : known to be true ⟨*historical* fact⟩ **b** : based on history ⟨*historical* novels⟩ **2** : HISTORIC 2 — **his·tor·i·cal·ly** \-i-k(ə-)lē\ *adv* — **his·tor·i·cal·ness** \-kəl-nəs\ *n*

his·to·ry \'his-t(ə-)rē\ *n, pl* **-ries** [from Greek *historia*, "investigation", "research"] **1** : TALE, STORY **2 a** : a written account of important events and their causes **b** : a branch of knowledge that records and explains past events **c** : events that form the subject matter of a history

his·tri·on·ic \ˌhis-trē-'än-ik\ *adj* **1** : of or relating to actors, acting, or the theater **2** : deliberately affected : EXAGGERATED, THEATRICAL — **his·tri·on·i·cal·ly** \-'än-i-k(ə-)lē\ *adv*

his·tri·on·ics \-'än-iks\ *n pl* **1** : theatrical performances **2** : exaggerated display of emotion

[1]**hit** \'hit\ *vb* **hit**; **hit·ting** **1 a** : to strike usu. with force ⟨*hit* a ball⟩ ⟨the ball *hit* the house⟩ ⟨the stone *hit* against the window⟩ **b** : to make or bring into contact with something ⟨tipped over and *hit* hard⟩ ⟨fell and *hit* his head against the wall⟩ **c** : to strike something aimed at ⟨*hit* the bull's-eye with the first shot⟩ **2 a** : ATTACK ⟨tried to guess where the enemy would *hit*⟩ **b** : to affect as if by a blow ⟨her death *hit* him pretty hard⟩ **3** : OCCUR, HAPPEN ⟨the storm *hit* just at sundown⟩ **4 a** : to come upon : DISCOVER ⟨*hit* upon the answer accidentally⟩ ⟨finally *hit* pay dirt⟩ **b** : to get to : REACH ⟨*hit* town that night⟩ ⟨prices *hit* a new high⟩ **c** : to reflect accurately ⟨*hits* the right note⟩ **5** : to fire the charge in the cylinders ⟨an automobile engine not *hitting*⟩ — **hit·ter** *n*

[2]**hit** *n* **1 a** : a blow striking an object aimed at ⟨made three *hits* out of five tries⟩ **b** : BLOW, COLLISION **2 a** : a stroke of luck **b** : a great success ⟨the show was a *hit*⟩ **3** : BASE HIT

hit–and–miss \ˌhit-ən-'mis\ *adj* : sometimes successful and sometimes not : HAPHAZARD

hit–and–run \-'rən\ *adj* : being or involving a motor-vehicle driver who does not stop after being involved in an accident

[1]**hitch** \'hich\ *vb* **1** : to move by jerks ⟨*hitched* his pants up⟩ **2** : to catch, fasten, or connect by or as if by a hook or knot ⟨*hitch* a horse to a rail⟩ **3** : HITCHHIKE — **hitch·er** *n*

[2]**hitch** *n* **1** : a jerky movement or pull ⟨gave his trousers a *hitch*⟩ **2** : an unexpected stop or obstacle ⟨the plan went off without a *hitch*⟩ **3** : the connection between something towed (as a plow or

H

trailer) and its mover (as a tractor, automobile, or animal) **4 :** a knot used for a temporary fastening ⟨barrel *hitch*⟩ **5** *slang* **:** a period of time ⟨do a *hitch* in the army⟩

hitches 4

hitch·hike \'hich-ˌhīk\ *vb* **:** to travel by or secure free rides — **hitch·hik·er** *n*

1**hith·er** \'hit͟h-ər\ *adv* **:** to this place ⟨come *hither*⟩

2**hither** *adj* **:** NEAR, NEARER ⟨the *hither* side of the hill⟩

hith·er·to \'hit͟h-ər-ˌtü\ *adv* **:** up to this time ⟨*hitherto* unknown facts⟩

hit off *vb* **1 :** to imitate usu. in order to ridicule **2 :** to be congenial **:** HARMONIZE ⟨they *hit* it *off* together on first meeting⟩

hit or miss *adv* **:** HAPHAZARDLY — **hit–or–miss** \ˌhit-ər-'mis\ *adj*

1**hive** \'hīv\ *n* **1 a :** a container for housing honeybees **b :** a colony of bees **2 :** a place swarming with busy occupants

2**hive** *vb* **1 a :** to collect as bees into a hive **b :** to enter and take over a hive or nesting place **2 :** to store up in or as if in a hive ⟨*hive* honey⟩ **3 :** to reside in close association

hives \'hīvz\ *n sing or pl* **:** an allergic disorder in which the skin or mucous membrane is affected by an itching rash

hl *abbr* hectoliter

H line *n* **:** a line in the spectrum of calcium that is found in the spectra of most stars

hm *abbr* hectometer

HMS *abbr* **1** Her Majesty's Ship **2** His Majesty's Ship

ho \'hō\ *interj* — used esp. to attract attention

hoa·gie \'hō-gē, 'hȯ-\ *n* **:** SUBMARINE 2

1**hoar** \'hō(ə)r, 'hȯ(ə)r\ *adj, archaic* **:** HOARY

2**hoar** *n* **:** FROST 2

hoard \'hōrd, 'hȯrd\ *n* **:** a hidden supply or fund stored up — **hoard** *vb* — **hoard·er** *n*

hoar·frost \'hō(ə)r-ˌfrȯst, 'hȯ(ə)r-\ *n* **:** FROST 2

hoarse \'hōrs, 'hȯrs\ *adj* **1 :** harsh in sound **2 :** having a rough grating voice ⟨a cold made him *hoarse*⟩ — **hoarse·ly** *adv* — **hoarse·ness** *n*

hoary \'hōr-ē, 'hȯr-\ *adj* **hoar·i·er; -est 1 :** grayish or whitish esp. from age ⟨bowed his *hoary* head⟩ **2 :** very old **:** ANCIENT ⟨*hoary* legends⟩ — **hoar·i·ness** *n*

hoax \'hōks\ *n* **1 :** an act intended to trick or dupe **2 :** something false passed off or accepted as genuine — **hoax** *vb* — **hoax·er** *n*

1**hob** \'häb\ *n* **1** *dial Eng* **:** HOBGOBLIN **2 :** MISCHIEF, TROUBLE ⟨raise *hob*⟩

2**hob** *n* **1 :** a projection at the back or side of a fireplace on which something may be kept warm **2 :** a tool for cutting the teeth of worm or gear wheels

1**hob·ble** \'häb-əl\ *vb* **hob·bled; hob·bling** \-(ə-)liŋ\ **1 a :** to walk with difficulty **:** LIMP ⟨*hobble* along on crutches⟩ **b :** to make lame **:** CRIPPLE ⟨*hobbled* by an ankle injury⟩ **2 a :** to keep from straying by tying two legs together ⟨*hobble* a horse⟩ **b :** HAMPER, IMPEDE — **hob·bler** \-(ə-)lər\ *n*

2**hobble** *n* **1 :** a hobbling walk **2 :** something used to hobble an animal

hob·ble·de·hoy \'häb-əl-di-ˌhȯi\ *n* **:** an awkward gawky youth

hob·by \'häb-ē\ *n, pl* **hobbies :** an interest or activity to which a person devotes much time for pleasure — **hob·by·ist** \-ē-əst\ *n*

hob·by·horse \-ē-ˌhȯrs\ *n* **1 :** a stick with a horse's head on which children pretend to ride **2 :** ROCKING HORSE **3 :** a toy horse suspended by springs from a frame

hob·gob·lin \'häb-ˌgäb-lən\ *n* **1 :** a mischievous elf or goblin **2 :** BOGEY 2

hob·nail \'häb-ˌnāl\ *n* **:** a large-headed nail used to stud the soles of heavy shoes as a protection against wear — **hob·nailed** \-ˌnāld\ *adj*

hob·nob \-ˌnäb\ *vb* **hob·nobbed; hob·nob·bing :** to associate familiarly ⟨*hobnobbing* with royalty⟩ — **hob·nob·ber** *n*

ho·bo \'hō-bō\ *n, pl* **hoboes** *also* **hobos :** TRAMP — **hobo** *vb*

1**hock** \'häk\ *n* **:** the tarsal joint or region in the hind limb of a four-footed animal (as the horse) corresponding to the ankle of man

2**hock** *n* **:** 1PAWN 2 ⟨got his watch out of *hock*⟩

3**hock** *vb* **:** PAWN

hock·ey \'häk-ē\ *n* **:** a game played on a field or on ice in which two sides try to drive a ball or puck through opposite goals by hitting it with a stick

ho·cus–po·cus \ˌhō-kəs-'pō-kəs\ *n* **1 :** a set form of words used by magicians **2 :** nonsense used to deceive

hod \'häd\ *n* **1 :** a long-handled tray used to carry mortar or bricks on the shoulder **2 :** a bucket for coal

hod 1

hodge·podge \'häj-ˌpäj\ *n* **:** MIXTURE, JUMBLE

hoe \'hō\ *n* **:** a farm or garden tool with a thin flat blade at nearly a right angle to a long handle that is used for weeding, loosening the earth, and hilling — **hoe** *vb* — **ho·er** \'hō(-ə)r\ *n*

hoe·cake \'hō-ˌkāk\ *n* **:** a cornmeal cake often baked on a griddle

1**hog** \'hȯg, 'häg\ *n, pl* **hogs** *also* **hog 1 a :** a domestic swine esp. when weighing more than 120 pounds **b :** any of various animals related to the domestic swine **2 :** a selfish, greedy, or filthy person — **hog·gish** \'hȯg-ish, 'häg-\ *adj* — **hog·gish·ly** *adv* — **hog·gish·ness** *n*

2**hog** *vb* **hogged; hog·ging :** to take more than one's share ⟨*hogged* all the cookies⟩

ho·gan \'hō-ˌgän\ *n* **:** an earth-covered dwelling of the Navaho Indians

hog cholera *n* **:** a highly infectious often fatal virus disease of swine

hogan

hog·nose snake \ˌhȯg-ˌnōz-, ˌhäg-\ *n* **:** any of several rather small harmless stout-bodied No. American snakes that hiss belligerently when disturbed — called also *hog-nosed snake* \-ˌnōz(d)-\

ə abut　ər further　a back　ā bake
ä cot, cart　au̇ out　ch chin　e less　ē easy
g gift　i trip　ī life　j joke　ŋ sing　ō flow
ȯ flaw　ȯi coin　th thin　t͟h this　ü loot
u̇ foot　y yet　yü few　yu̇ furious　zh vision

hogs·head \'hȯgz-ˌhed, 'hägz-\ *n* **1** : a large cask or barrel; *esp* : one containing from 63 to 140 gallons **2** : a U.S. measure for liquids equal to 63 gallons

[1]**hoist** \'hȯist, *chiefly dial* 'hīst\ *vb* : to raise or become raised into position esp. by means of tackle ***syn*** see RAISE — **hoist·er** *n*

[2]**hoist** *n* **1** : an act of hoisting : LIFT **2** : an apparatus for hoisting heavy loads

hol- *or* **holo-** *comb form* : complete : total

[1]**hold** \'hōld\ *vb* **held** \'held\; **hold·ing 1 a** : to keep in one's possession : POSSESS, HAVE ⟨*hold* this for me⟩ **b** : to have a right to : OWN ⟨*hold* property⟩ ⟨*hold* a bachelor's degree⟩ **2 a** : to retain or restrain by force ⟨the troops *held* the bridge⟩ ⟨*held* him from jumping⟩ **b** : DELAY ⟨*held* the plane⟩ **c** : to keep from advancing or succeeding ⟨his temper *held* him back⟩ **d** : to bind legally or morally : CONSTRAIN ⟨*held* him to his word⟩ **3 a** : to have or keep in the grasp ⟨*hold* the pen upright⟩ **b** : to fix or keep in a place, position, or situation ⟨*hold* the ladder steady⟩ **c** : to remain fastened ⟨the anchor *held* in the rough sea⟩ **d** : SUPPORT, SUSTAIN ⟨the floor will *hold* 10 tons⟩ **e** : to keep in custody ⟨*hold* a suspect for questioning⟩ **4** : BEAR, COMPORT ⟨*held* himself well⟩; *also* : to bear oneself ⟨*hold* still⟩ **5 a** : to keep in being or action ⟨*hold* silence⟩ **b** : to keep the interest or devotion of ⟨the play *held* the audience⟩ **6** : to receive and retain ⟨the can *holds* 20 gallons⟩ **7 a** : HARBOR, ENTERTAIN ⟨*hold* a theory⟩ **b** : CONSIDER, JUDGE ⟨truths *held* to be self-evident⟩ **8** : to carry on as a group ⟨*hold* a meeting⟩ **9** : to be or stand in ⟨each digit *holds* a place⟩ **10 a** : to maintain position : not retreat ⟨the line *held* under attack⟩ **b** : REMAIN, CONTINUE, LAST ⟨his interest *held* up⟩ ⟨hope the weather *holds*⟩ **11** : to be true : APPLY ⟨the rule *holds* in most cases⟩ **12** : to refrain from an act : HALT, PAUSE — **hold forth** : to preach or harangue at length — **hold good** : to remain true ⟨the rule *holds good* in this case⟩ — **hold one's own** : to maintain one's place or condition esp. against opposition — **hold the bag 1** : to be left empty-handed **2** : to bear the blame that should be shared by others — **hold water** : to stand up under criticism or examination ⟨your story doesn't *hold water*⟩ — **hold with** : to agree with : approve of

[2]**hold** \'hōld\ *n* **1** : STRONGHOLD **2** : something that holds, secures, or fastens **3** : the act or manner of holding : SEIZURE, GRASP ⟨lost his *hold* on the rope⟩ **4** : a manner of grasping the opponent in wrestling **5** : authority to take or keep : POWER ⟨the law has no *hold* over this man⟩ **6** : something that may be grasped or held **7** : a prolonged note or rest in music **8** : an order or indication that something is to be reserved or delayed **9** : STOPPAGE, HALT ⟨a *hold* in a rocket countdown⟩

[3]**hold** *n* **1** : the interior of a ship below decks; *esp* : the cargo deck of a ship **2** : the cargo compartment of an airplane

hold·back \'hōl(d)-ˌbak\ *n* **1** : a device that retains or restrains **2 a** : the act of holding back **b** : something held back

hold·er \'hōl-dər\ *n* **1** : a person that holds; *esp* : a legal owner **2** : a device that holds ⟨cigarette *holder*⟩

hold·fast \'hōl(d)-ˌfast\ *n* : a part by which a plant or animal clings (as to a flat surface or the body of a host)

hold in *vb* : RESTRAIN, CHECK

hold·ing \'hōl-ding\ *n* **1** : land or property (as bonds or stocks) owned **2** : a ruling of a court

hold off *vb* **1** : to keep away : WITHSTAND ⟨*held off* the attack⟩ **2 a** : DELAY, POSTPONE ⟨decided to *hold off* on the decision⟩ **b** : REFRAIN ⟨*held off* from smoking⟩

hold on *vb* **1** : to keep a hold **2** : to go on : CONTINUE **3** : STOP, WAIT

hold out \'hōl-'daủt\ *vb* **1** : to remain in being : LAST ⟨hope the food *holds out*⟩ **2** : to remain unyielding : refuse to surrender or compromise ⟨*held out* until help arrived⟩ — **hold·out** \-ˌdaủt\ *n* — **hold out on** : to keep a fair share from

hold over \'hōl-'dō-vər\ *vb* : to continue beyond a normal or planned time ⟨the movie was *held over* for three weeks⟩ — **hold·over** \-ˌdō-vər\ *n*

hold·up \'hōl-ˌdəp\ *n* **1** : a robbery at gunpoint **2** : DELAY

hold up \-'dəp\ *vb* **1** : DELAY, IMPEDE ⟨only *holding* things *up*⟩ **2** : to rob at gunpoint

hole \'hōl\ *n* **1** : an opening into or through a thing ⟨a *hole* in a wall⟩ **2 a** : a hollow place; *esp* : PIT, CAVE **b** : a deep place in a body of water ⟨trout *holes*⟩ **3** : a defect in a crystal (as of a semiconductor) that is due to an electron having left its normal position and is equivalent to a positive charge **4** : an underground habitation : BURROW ⟨a fox in its *hole*⟩ **5** : FLAW, FAULT ⟨a big *hole* in his argument⟩ **6** : the unit of play in golf **7** : a mean or dingy place ⟨lives in a real *hole*⟩ **8** : an awkward position : FIX — **hole** *vb* — **hol·ey** \'hō-lē\ *adj* — **in the hole** : in debt ⟨40 dollars *in the hole*⟩

holed \'hōld\ *adj* : having one or more holes — often used in combination ⟨two-*holed* stopper⟩

hol·i·day \'häl-ə-ˌdā\ *n* [from Old English *hāligdæg*, literally "holy day"] **1** : HOLY DAY **2** : a day of freedom from work; *esp* : a day of celebration or commemoration fixed by law **3** : a period of relaxation : VACATION — **holiday** *vb* — **hol·i·day·er** *n*

ho·li·ness \'hō-lē-nəs\ *n* **1** : the quality or state of being holy **2** — used as a title for various high religious dignitaries ⟨His *Holiness* Pope Paul VI⟩

hol·ler \'häl-ər\ *vb* **hol·lered**; **hol·ler·ing** \-(ə-)ring\ **1** : to cry or call out : SHOUT **2** : GRIPE, COMPLAIN — **holler** *n*

[1]**hol·low** \'häl-ō\ *adj* **1** : curved inward : SUNKEN ⟨*hollow* cheeks⟩ **2** : having a hole inside : not solid throughout ⟨*hollow* tree⟩ **3** : lacking value or meaning ⟨*hollow* victory⟩ **4** : being like a sound made in or by beating on a large empty enclosure : MUFFLED ⟨a *hollow* roar⟩ **5** : INSINCERE ⟨*hollow* promises⟩ — **hollow** *vb* — **hol·low·ly** *adv* — **hol·low·ness** *n*

[2]**hollow** *n* **1** : a low spot in a surface; *esp* : VALLEY **2** : an empty space within something : HOLE

hol·ly \'häl-ē\ *n, pl* **hollies 1** : any of a genus of trees and shrubs with thick glossy spiny-margined leaves and usu. bright red berries **2** : the foliage or branches of a holly

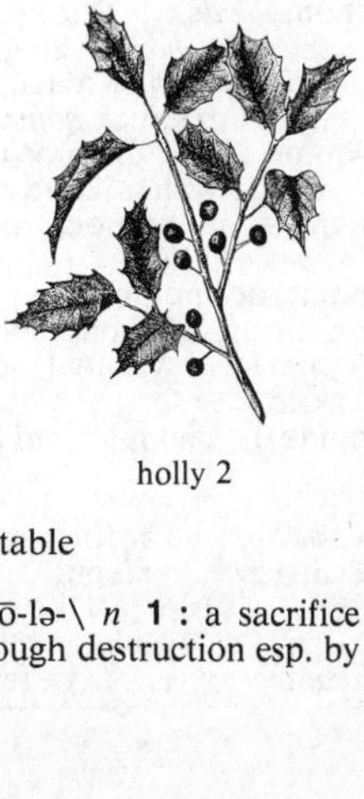
holly 2

hol·ly·hock \'häl-ē-ˌhäk, -ˌhȯk\ *n* : a tall widely grown perennial Chinese herb related to the mallow and having large coarse rounded leaves and tall spikes of showy flowers

hol·mi·um \'hō(l)-mē-əm\ *n* : a metallic element that occurs with yttrium and forms highly magnetic compounds — see ELEMENT table

holo- — see HOL-

hol·o·caust \'häl-ə-ˌkȯst, 'hō-lə-\ *n* **1** : a sacrifice consumed by fire **2** : a thorough destruction esp. by fire

Ho·lo·cene \'hō-lə-ˌsēn, 'häl-ə-\ *adj* : RECENT 2 — **Holocene** *n*

hol·o·gram \'häl-ə-ˌgram, 'hō-lə-\ *n* : a three-dimensional picture made by laser light reflected from an object onto photographic film without camera or lenses

hol·o·graph \-ˌgraf\ *n* : a document wholly in the handwriting of the author — **holograph** *or* **hol·o·graph·ic** \ˌhäl-ə-'graf-ik, ˌhō-lə-\ *adj*

hol·o·thu·ri·an \ˌhäl-ō-'th(y)u̇r-ē-ən, ˌhō-lō-\ *n* : any of a class of echinoderms having a long flexible tough muscular body — **holothurian** *adj*

hol·stein \'hōl-ˌstēn, -ˌstīn\ *n* : any of a breed of large black-and-white dairy cattle that produce large quantities of comparatively low-fat milk — called also *holstein-frie·sian* \-'frē-zhən\

hol·ster \'hōl(t)-stər\ *n* : a usu. leather case for carrying a pistol

ho·ly \'hō-lē\ *adj* **ho·li·er**; **-est** **1** : set apart to the service of God or a god : SACRED **2** : commanding absolute adoration and reverence **3** : spiritually pure : SAINTLY **4** : evoking or meriting veneration or awe ⟨*holy* places⟩

holy day *n* : a day observed as a religious feast or fast

Holy Ghost *n* : HOLY SPIRIT

Holy Saturday *n* : the Saturday before Easter

Holy Spirit *n* : the third person of the Trinity

ho·ly·stone \'hō-lē-ˌstōn\ *n* : a soft sandstone used to scrub a ship's decks — **holystone** *vb*

Holy Thursday *n* : MAUNDY THURSDAY

holy water *n* : water blessed by a priest and used to purify

Holy Week *n* : the week before Easter

Holy Writ *n* : BIBLE 1, 2

hom- *or* **homo-** *comb form* : one and the same : similar : alike ⟨*homo*graph⟩

hom·age \'(h)äm-ij\ *n* **1** : a ceremony in which a person pledged allegiance to a lord and became his vassal **2** : something done or given as an acknowledgment of a vassal's duty to his lord **3** : RESPECT, HONOR

[1]**home** \'hōm\ *n* **1** : the house in which a person or his family lives **2** : the country or place where one lives or where one's ancestors lived **3** : the place where something is usu. or naturally found : HABITAT ⟨the *home* of the elephant⟩ **4** : a place for the care of persons unable to care for themselves ⟨old people's *home*⟩ **5** : a family living together in one dwelling ⟨a city of 20,000 *homes*⟩ **6** : a dwelling house **7** : the goal or point to be reached in some games — **home·less** \-ləs\ *adj* — **home·like** \-ˌlīk\ *adj*

[2]**home** *adv* **1** : to or at home ⟨he went *home*⟩ ⟨she's not *home*⟩ **2** : to a final, closed, or standard position ⟨drive a nail *home*⟩ **3** : to a vital core ⟨the truth struck *home*⟩

[3]**home** *vb* **1** : to go or return home **2** : to send to or provide with a home

home- *or* **homeo-** *comb form* : like : similar ⟨*homeo*stasis⟩

home economics *n* : the study of the care and management of a household — **home economist** *n*

home·land \'hōm-ˌland\ *n* : native land : FATHERLAND

home·ly \'hōm-lē\ *adj* **home·li·er**; **-est** **1** : characteristic of home life : PLAIN, SIMPLE ⟨*homely* meals⟩ **2** : lacking polish or refinement : RUDE ⟨*homely* manners⟩ **3** : not handsome ⟨a *homely* person⟩ — **home·li·ness** *n*

home·made \'hōm-'(m)ād\ *adj* : made in the home or on the premises ⟨*homemade* bread⟩

home·mak·er \'hōm-ˌmā-kər\ *n* : one who manages a household esp. as a wife and mother — **home·mak·ing** \-king\ *n or adj*

ho·meo·sta·sis \ˌhō-mē-ō-'stā-səs\ *n* : a tendency toward keeping a relatively stable internal environment in the bodies of higher animals by means of complex physiological interactions — **ho·meo·stat·ic** \-'stat-ik\ *adj*

home plate *n* : a rubber slab at the apex of a baseball diamond that a base runner must touch in order to score

hom·er \'hō-mər\ *n* **1** : HOMING PIGEON **2** : HOME RUN

home·room \'hōm-ˌrüm, -ˌru̇m\ *n* : a schoolroom where pupils report at the opening of school

home rule *n* : self-government in local affairs by the citizens of a subordinate political unit

home run *n* : a hit in baseball that enables the batter to make a complete circuit of the bases and score a run

home·sick \'hōm-ˌsik\ *adj* : longing for home and family while absent from them — **home·sick·ness** *n*

home·spun \-ˌspən\ *n* : a loosely woven usu. woolen or linen fabric orig. made from yarn spun at home — **homespun** *adj*

[1]**home·stead** \-ˌsted\ *n* **1** : a home and surrounding land **2** : a tract of land acquired from U.S. public lands by living on and cultivating it

[2]**homestead** *vb* : to acquire or settle on public land for use as a homestead ⟨*homesteaded* in Alaska⟩ — **home·stead·er** *n*

home·stretch \-'strech\ *n* **1** : the part of a racecourse between the last curve and the winning post **2** : a final stage

home tone *n* : TONIC 2

home·ward \-wərd\ *or* **home·wards** \-wərdz\ *adv* : toward or in the direction of home — **homeward** *adj*

home·work \-ˌwərk\ *n* : work and esp. school lessons to be done at home

hom·ey \'hō-mē\ *adj* **hom·i·er**; **-est** : HOMELIKE, COZY — **hom·ey·ness** *or* **hom·i·ness** *n*

hom·i·cid·al \ˌhäm-ə-'sīd-əl, ˌhō-mə-\ *adj* : having or showing tendencies toward homicide : MURDEROUS — **hom·i·cid·al·ly** \-'sīd-ə-lē\ *adv*

hom·i·cide \'häm-ə-ˌsīd, 'hō-mə-\ *n* [from Latin *homicida* "killer of a man" and *homicidium* "killing of a man", from *homo* "man" and *caedere* "to cut", "slay"] **1** : a person who kills another **2** : a killing of one human being by another

hom·i·ly \'häm-ə-lē\ *n*, *pl* **-lies** **1** : SERMON **2** : a moral lecture

[1]**hom·ing** \'hō-ming\ *n* : an accurate return of an animal (as a pigeon or salmon) to a known place

[2]**homing** *adj* **1** : habitually returning to a known place **2** : guiding or being guided to an objective ⟨a *homing* torpedo⟩

homing pigeon *n* : a racing pigeon trained to return home

hom·i·nid \'häm-ə-nəd\ *n* : any of a family of 2-footed primate mammals comprising recent man, his immediate ancestors, and related extinct forms — **hominid** *adj*

hom·i·noid \'häm-ə-ˌnȯid\ *adj* : resembling or related to man — **hominoid** *n*

hom·i·ny \'häm-ə-nē\ *n* : hulled corn with the germ removed

ho·mo \'hō-mō\ *n* : any of a genus of primate mammals that consists of mankind and is usu. held to include a single recent species comprising all surviving and various extinct men

homo- — see HOM-

ho·mog·e·nate \hō-'mäj-ə-ˌnāt\ *n* : a product of homogenizing

ho·mo·ge·ne·ous \ˌhō-mə-'jē-nē-əs\ *adj* **1** : of the same or a similar kind or nature **2** : uniform throughout — **ho·mo·ge·ne·i·ty** \-jə-'nē-ət-ē\ *n* — **ho·mo·ge·ne·ous·ly** *adv*

ho·mog·e·nize \hō-'mäj-ə-ˌnīz\ *vb* **1** : to make homogeneous **2 a** : to reduce to small particles of uniform size and distribute evenly ⟨*homogenize* peanut butter⟩ ⟨*homogenize* paint⟩ **b** : to break up the fat globules of (milk) into very fine particles esp. by forcing through minute openings — **ho·mog·e·ni·za·tion** \-ˌmäj-ə-nə-'zā-shən\ *n* — **ho·mog·e·niz·er** \-'mäj-ə-ˌnī-zər\ *n*

ho·mog·e·nous \hō-'mäj-ə-nəs\ *adj* : HOMOGENEOUS

homo·graph \'häm-ə-ˌgraf, 'hō-mə-\ *n* : one of two or more words alike in spelling but different in origin or meaning ⟨*row* of seats and *row* (a fight) are *homographs*, as are *fair* (market) and *fair* (beautiful)⟩

ho·mol·o·gize \hō-'mäl-ə-ˌjīz\ *vb* **1** : to make homologous **2** : to demonstrate the homology of

ho·mol·o·gous \hō-'mäl-ə-gəs\ *adj* **1 a** : having the same relative position, value, or structure **b** : corresponding in structure or origin ⟨arms and wings are *homologous* structures⟩ **c** : belonging to or consisting of a chemical series whose members exhibit homology **2** : derived from or developed in response to organisms of the same species ⟨*homologous* tissue graft⟩

ho·mo·logue *or* **ho·mo·log** \'hō-mə-ˌlȯg, 'häm-ə-\ *n* : something that exhibits homology

ho·mol·o·gy \hō-'mäl-ə-jē\ *n, pl* **-gies** **1** : a similarity often due to common origin **2 a** : structural likeness between corresponding parts of different organisms due to evolution from a remote common ancestor **b** : structural likeness between different parts of the same individual **3** : the relation existing between chemical compounds in a series whose successive members have in composition a regular difference

hom·o·nym \'häm-ə-ˌnim, 'hō-mə-\ *n* **1** : HOMOPHONE **2** : HOMOGRAPH **3** : one of two or more words spelled and pronounced alike but different in meaning ⟨*pool* of water and *pool* (the game) are *homonyms*⟩ — **hom·o·nym·ic** \ˌhäm-ə-'nim-ik, ˌhō-mə-\ *adj*

hom·o·phone \'häm-ə-ˌfōn, 'hō-mə-\ *n* : one of two or more words pronounced alike but different in meaning, derivation, or spelling ⟨*to*, *too*, and *two* are *homophones*⟩ — **ho·moph·o·nous** \hō-'mäf-ə-nəs\ *adj*

ho·moph·o·ny \hō-'mäf-ə-nē\ *n* : music having a single accompanied melodic line — **hom·o·phon·ic** \ˌhäm-ə-'fän-ik, ˌhō-mə-\ *adj*

ho·mop·ter·ous \hō-'mäp-tə-rəs\ *adj* : of or relating to a group of insects (as the cicadas, aphids, or scale insects) having sucking mouthparts — **ho·mop·ter·an** \-rən\ *adj or n*

ho·mo sa·pi·ens \ˌhō-mō-'sap-ē-ənz, -sā-pē-\ *n* : MANKIND 1

ho·mo·sex·u·al \ˌhō-mə-'sek-sh(ə-w)əl\ *adj* : of, relating to, or exhibiting sexual desire toward a member of one's own sex — **homosexual** *n* — **ho·mo·sex·u·al·i·ty** \-ˌsek-shə-'wal-ət-ē\ *n*

ho·mo·zy·gote \-'zī-ˌgōt\ *n* : a homozygous individual — **ho·mo·zy·gos·i·ty** \-zī-'gäs-ət-ē\ *n*

ho·mo·zy·gous \-'zī-gəs\ *adj* : containing either but not both members of at least one pair of alleles ⟨a plant *homozygous* for yellow seed⟩

hone \'hōn\ *n* **1** : a fine whetstone; *esp* : one for sharpening razors **2** : a tool for enlarging holes to precise measurements — **hone** *vb*

hon·est \'än-əst\ *adj* **1** : free from fraud or deception : TRUTHFUL ⟨an *honest* plea⟩ **2** : GENUINE, REAL ⟨made an *honest* mistake⟩ **3** : REPUTABLE, RESPECTABLE ⟨poor but *honest* people⟩ **4** : TRUSTWORTHY **5** : FRANK, OPEN — **hon·est·ly** *adv*

syn HONEST, UPRIGHT, SINCERE can mean right-minded or straightforward in dealing with others. HONEST implies fairness or truthfulness in one's transactions; UPRIGHT implies holding without compromise to high moral principles in all areas of life; SINCERE implies honesty in expressing one's true feelings ***ant*** dishonest

hon·es·ty \'än-ə-stē\ *n* **1** : fairness and straightforwardness of conduct : INTEGRITY **2** : TRUTHFULNESS, SINCERITY ⟨*honesty* is the best policy⟩

hon·ey \'hən-ē\ *n, pl* **honeys** **1** : a thick sugary material prepared by bees from floral nectar and stored by them in a honeycomb for food **2 a** : SWEETHEART, DEAR — often used as a term of affection **b** : something very good ⟨a *honey* of a play⟩ **3** : SWEETNESS ⟨*honey* in her voice⟩ — **honey** *adj*

hon·ey·bee \-ˌbē\ *n* : a social honey-producing bee; *esp* : a European bee widely kept for its honey and wax

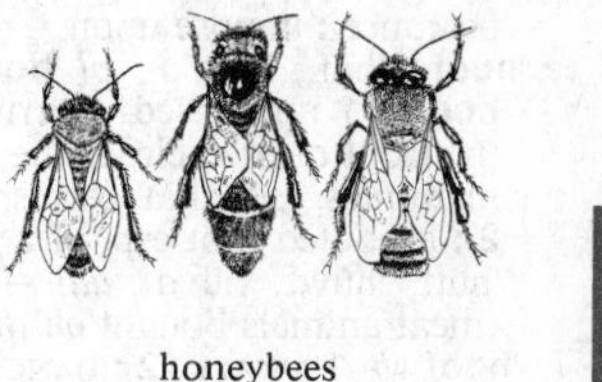

honeybees (left, worker; center, queen; right, drone)

1hon·ey·comb \'hən-ē-ˌkōm\ *n* **1** : a mass of 6-sided wax cells built by honeybees in their nest for rearing larvae and storing honey **2** : something that resembles a honeycomb in structure or appearance

2honeycomb *vb* : to make or become full of holes like a honeycomb

hon·ey·dew \'hən-ē-ˌd(y)ü\ *n* : a sugary deposit secreted on the leaves of plants usu. by aphids or scale insects but sometimes by a fungus

honeydew melon *n* : a pale smooth-skinned muskmelon with greenish sweet flesh

hon·ey·moon \'hən-ē-ˌmün\ *n* **1** : the time immediately after marriage **2** : the holiday spent by a couple after marriage — **honeymoon** *vb* — **hon·ey·moon·er** *n*

hon·ey·suck·le \-ˌsək-əl\ *n* : any of a genus of shrubs with opposite leaves and often showy flowers rich in nectar

honk \'häŋk, 'hȯŋk\ *n* : the cry of a goose; *also* : a similar sound (as of a horn) — **honk** *vb*

1hon·or \'än-ər\ *n* **1 a** : a good name : public esteem : REPUTATION **b** : outward respect : RECOGNITION ⟨a dinner in *honor* of a new coach⟩ **2** : PRIVILEGE **3 a** : a person of superior standing ⟨if your *Honor* please⟩ — used esp. as a title for a holder of high office **b** : one whose worth brings respect or fame : CREDIT ⟨an *honor* to his profession⟩ **4 a** : a mark of distinction (as a title or medal) **b** *pl* : superior marks in school **5 a** : CHASTITY, PURITY **b** : a keen sense of ethical conduct : INTEGRITY ⟨known to be a man of *honor*⟩ **6** *pl* : social courtesies ⟨did the *honors* at the table⟩

2honor *vb* **hon·ored**; **hon·or·ing** \ˈän-(ə-)riŋ\ **1 a** : to regard or treat with honor : RESPECT ⟨*honor* your parents⟩ **b** : to confer honor on **2** : to fulfill the terms of ⟨*honored* his contract⟩

hon·or·a·ble \ˈän-(ə-)rə-bəl, ˈän-ər-bəl\ *adj* **1** : deserving of honor **2** : performed or accompanied with marks of honor ⟨an *honorable* burial⟩ **3** — used as a title esp. for various government officials **4** : doing credit to the possessor **5** : characterized by integrity : ETHICAL — **hon·or·a·bly** \-blē\ *adv*

hon·or·ary \ˈän-ə-ˌrer-ē\ *adj* **1** : given or done as a sign of honor ⟨an *honorary* degree⟩ **2** : UNPAID, VOLUNTARY ⟨*honorary* chairman⟩ — **hon·or·ar·i·ly** \ˌän-ə-ˈrer-ə-lē\ *adv*

1hood \ˈhu̇d\ *n* **1** : a soft covering for the head and neck and sometimes the shoulders **2** : a marking, crest, or fold on the head of an animal **3 a** : something resembling a hood in form or use **b** : a cover for parts of mechanisms; *esp* : the movable metal covering over the engine of an automobile — **hood·ed** \-əd\ *adj* — **hood·like** \-ˌlīk\ *adj*

2hood \ˈhu̇d, ˈhüd\ *n, slang* : HOODLUM

-hood \ˌhu̇d\ *n suffix* **1** : state : condition : quality ⟨boy*hood*⟩ ⟨hardi*hood*⟩ **2** : instance of a state or quality ⟨false*hood*⟩ **3** : individuals sharing a state or character ⟨brother*hood*⟩

hood·lum \ˈhüd-ləm\ *n* **1** : THUG, MOBSTER **2** : a young ruffian

hoo·doo \ˈhüd-ü\ *n, pl* **hoodoos** **1** : VOODOO **2** : something that brings bad luck — **hoodoo** *vb* — **hoo·doo·ism** \-ˌiz-əm\ *n*

hood·wink \ˈhu̇d-ˌwiŋk\ *vb* : to deceive by false appearance : impose upon

1hoof \ˈhu̇f, ˈhüf\ *n, pl* **hooves** \ˈhu̇vz, ˈhüvz\ *or* **hoofs** **1** : a curved covering of horn that protects the front of or encloses the ends of the toes of some mammals and that corresponds to a nail or claw **2** : a hoofed foot esp. of a horse — **hoofed** \ˈhu̇ft, ˈhüft, ˈhu̇vd, ˈhüvd\ *adj* — **on the hoof** : LIVING ⟨meat animals bought *on the hoof*⟩

2hoof *vb* **1** : WALK **2** : DANCE — **hoof·er** *n*

1hook \ˈhu̇k\ *n* **1** : a curved or bent implement for catching, holding, or pulling **2** : something curved or bent **3** : a flight of a ball that veers in a direction opposite to the dominant hand of the player propelling it **4** : a short blow delivered with a circular motion by a boxer while the elbow remains bent and rigid — **by hook or by crook** : by any means — **off the hook** : out of trouble — **on one's own hook** : by oneself : INDEPENDENTLY

2hook *vb* **1** : to form into a hook : CROOK, CURVE **2 a** : to seize, make fast, or connect by or as if by a hook **b** : to become secured or connected by or as if by a hook **3** : STEAL, PILFER **4** : to strike or pierce as if with a hook **5** : to make by drawing loops of thread, yarn, or cloth through a coarse fabric with a hook ⟨*hook* a rug⟩ **6** : to hit or throw a ball so that a hook results

hooked \ˈhu̇kt\ *adj* **1** : shaped like or furnished with a hook **2** : made by hooking ⟨a *hooked* rug⟩

hook·up \ˈhu̇k-ˌəp\ *n* **1 a** : an assemblage (as of circuits) used for a specific purpose (as in radio) **b** : the diagram of such an assemblage **2** : an arrangement of mechanical parts **3** : CONNECTION, ALLIANCE ⟨a *hookup* between two countries⟩

ə abut	ər further	a back	ā bake	
ä cot, cart	au̇ out	ch chin	e less	ē easy
g gift	i trip	ī life	j joke	ŋ sing	ō flow
ȯ flaw	ȯi coin	th thin	t͟h this	ü loot
u̇ foot	y yet	yü few	yu̇ furious	zh vision

hook·worm \ˈhu̇k-ˌwərm\ *n* **1** : a parasitic nematode worm having strong hooks or plates about the mouth **2** : a disordered state marked by blood loss, paleness, and weakness due to hookworms in the intestine — called also *hookworm disease*

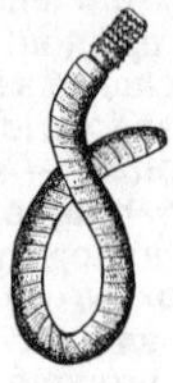

hookworm 1 (magnified 4 times)

hoop \ˈhu̇p, ˈhüp\ *n* **1** : a circular strip used for holding together the staves of a barrel; *also* : a similar strip used as a plaything **2** : a circular figure or object : RING **3** : a circle or series of circles of flexible material used to expand a woman's skirt — **hoop** *vb*

hoop·skirt \-ˈskərt\ *n* : a skirt stiffened with or as if with hoops

hoo·ray \hu̇-ˈrā\ *var of* HURRAH

hoose·gow \ˈhüs-ˌgau̇\ *n* [from Spanish *juzgado* "panel of judges", "court", from *juzgar* "to judge", from Latin *judicare*] *slang* : JAIL

1hoot \ˈhüt\ *vb* **1** : to utter a loud shout usu. in contempt **2** : to make the natural throat noise of an owl or a similar cry **3** : to drive out by hooting — **hoot·er** *n*

2hoot *n* **1** : a sound of hooting; *esp* : the cry of an owl **2** : a very small amount ⟨don't care a *hoot*⟩

hoo·te·nan·ny \ˈhüt-ə-ˌnan-ē\ *n, pl* **-nies** : a gathering at which folk singers entertain

1hop \ˈhäp\ *vb* **hopped**; **hop·ping** **1** : to move by a quick springy leap or series of leaps; *esp* : to jump on one foot **2** : to jump over ⟨*hop* a puddle⟩ **3** : to get aboard by or as if by hopping ⟨*hop* a train⟩ **4** : to make a quick trip esp. by air

2hop *n* **1 a** : a short brisk leap esp. on one leg **b** : BOUNCE **2** : DANCE, BALL ⟨the junior *hop*⟩ **3 a** : a flight in an airplane **b** : a short trip

3hop *n* **1** : a twining vine related to the mulberry and having lobed leaves and pistillate flowers in cone-shaped catkins **2** *pl* : the ripe dried pistillate catkins of a hop used esp. to impart a bitter flavor to malt liquors

4hop *vb* **hopped**; **hop·ping** **1** : to flavor with hops **2** : to increase the power of ⟨*hop* up an engine⟩

1hope \ˈhōp\ *vb* : to desire something and expect that it will happen or be obtained ⟨*hope* to succeed⟩ ⟨*hope* he'll accept the invitation⟩ ⟨*hope* for a bicycle⟩

2hope *n* **1** : TRUST, RELIANCE ⟨our *hope* is in the Lord⟩ **2 a** : desire accompanied by expectation of fulfillment ⟨in *hope* of an early recovery⟩ **b** : someone or something on which hopes are centered ⟨a home run was the only *hope* for victory⟩ **c** : something hoped for

1hope·ful \ˈhōp-fəl\ *adj* **1** : full of or inclined to hope **2** : having qualities which inspire hope — **hope·ful·ly** \-fə-lē\ *adv* — **hope·ful·ness** *n*

2hopeful *n* : a person who has hopes or is considered promising

hope·less \ˈhōp-ləs\ *adj* **1 a** : having no expectation of good or success : DESPAIRING **b** : INCURABLE **2 a** : giving no ground for hope : DESPERATE ⟨a *hopeless* situation⟩ **b** : incapable of solution or accomplishment : IMPOSSIBLE ⟨a *hopeless* task⟩ — **hope·less·ly** *adv* — **hope·less·ness** *n*

Ho·pi \ˈhō-pē\ *n* : a member of a Pueblo Amerindian people of northeastern Arizona

hop·per \ˈhäp-ər\ *n* **1 a** : one that hops **b** : a leaping insect; *esp* : an immature hopping form of an insect **2 a** : a usu. funnel-shaped receptacle for delivering material (as grain) **b** : a tank with a device for releasing its liquid through a pipe

hop·scotch \ˈhäp-ˌskäch\ *n* : a child's game in which a player hops through a figure drawn on the ground

hor *abbr* horizontal
horde \'hōrd, 'hȯrd\ *n* **1** : a nomadic people or tribe **2** : a great multitude : THRONG, SWARM ⟨*hordes* of tourists⟩
hore·hound \'hō(ə)r-ˌhau̇nd, 'hȯ(ə)r-\ *n* **1** : an aromatic bitter mint with hoary downy leaves **2** : an extract or confection made from horehound
ho·ri·zon \hə-'rī-zən\ *n* [from Greek *horizōn* (stem *horizont-*), present participle of *horizein* "to bound", from *horos* "limit", "boundary"] **1** : the apparent junction of earth and sky **2** : the limit or range of a person's outlook or experience ⟨reading broadens our *horizons*⟩ **3 a** : the geological deposit of a particular time **b** : a distinct layer of soil or its underlying material in a vertical section of land — **ho·ri·zon·al** \-'rīz-(ə-)nəl\ *adj*
[1]**hor·i·zon·tal** \ˌhȯr-ə-'zänt-əl, ˌhär-\ *adj* **1** : of or relating to the horizon **2** : parallel to the horizon : LEVEL **3** : being on the same level — **hor·i·zon·tal·ly** \-ə-lē\ *adv*
[2]**horizontal** *n* : a horizontal line or plane
hor·mone \'hȯr-ˌmōn\ *n* [from Greek *hormōn*, present participle of *horman* "to stir up", "set in motion"] : a product of living cells that circulates in body fluids or sap and produces a specific and usu. stimulatory effect on cells at a distance from its point of origin — **hor·mon·al** \hȯr-'mōn-əl\ *adj*
horn \'hȯrn\ *n* **1** : one of the hard bony growths that arise from the head of many hoofed animals and are found in some extinct mammals and reptiles: **a** : one of the permanent paired hollow sheaths of keratin usually present in both sexes of cattle and their relatives that function chiefly for defense and arise from a bony core anchored to the skull **b** : ANTLER **c** : a permanent solid horn of keratin occurring on a bone in the snout of a rhinoceros **d** : one of a pair of permanent bone outgrowths from the skull of a giraffe or okapi that are covered with hairy skin **2** : a part like an animal's horn **3 a** : a tough fibrous material that consists chiefly of keratin and forms the sheath of a true horn and horny parts (as hooves or nails) **b** : a manufactured product (as a plastic) resembling horn **4** : a hollow horn used to hold something ⟨powder *horn*⟩ **5** : something resembling a horn ⟨saddle *horn*⟩ ⟨*horns* of the moon's crescent⟩ **6 a** : a brass wind instrument; *esp* : FRENCH HORN **b** : a device that makes a noise like that of a horn ⟨an automobile *horn*⟩ — **horned** \'hȯrnd\ *adj* — **horn·less** \'hȯrn-ləs\ *adj*
horn·beam \'hȯrn-ˌbēm\ *n* : any of a genus of trees related to the birch having smooth gray bark and hard white wood
horn·bill \-ˌbil\ *n* : any of a family of large Old World birds having enormous bills
horn·blende \-ˌblend\ *n* : a mineral that is a black, dark green, or brown variety of amphibole
horn·book \-ˌbu̇k\ *n* : a child's primer consisting of a sheet of parchment or paper protected by a sheet of transparent horn

hornbill
(about 52 in. long)

horned owl *n* : any of several owls with conspicuous tufts of feathers on the head
horned pout *n* : a common bullhead of the eastern U.S.
horned toad *n* : any of several small harmless insect-eating lizards of the western U.S. and Mexico having hornlike spines
hor·net \'hȯr-nət\ *n* : any of the larger social wasps
horn·fels \'hȯrn-ˌfelz\ *n* : a fine-grained silicate rock formed by metamorphism
horn of plenty : CORNUCOPIA
horn·pipe \'hȯrn-ˌpīp\ *n* **1** : a wind instrument consisting of a wooden or bone pipe and a bell usu. of horn **2** : a lively folk dance originally accompanied by hornpipe playing
horn·tail \-ˌtāl\ *n* : any of various hymenopterous insects related to the sawflies
horn·wort \-ˌwərt, -ˌwȯrt\ *n* : any of an order of mostly aquatic plants related to the liverworts
horny \'hȯr-nē\ *adj* **horn·i·er**; **-est** **1** : made of or as if of horn **2 a** : resembling horn **b** : HARD, CALLOUS ⟨*horny*-handed⟩ **3** : having horns
ho·rol·o·gy \hə-'räl-ə-jē\ *n* **1** : the science of measuring time **2** : the art of constructing instruments for indicating time — **ho·rol·o·ger** \-jər\ *n* — **hor·o·log·ic** \ˌhȯr-ə-'läj-ik, ˌhär-, -'lōj-\ *adj* — **hor·o·log·i·cal** \-i-kəl\ *adj* — **ho·rol·o·gist** \hə-'räl-ə-jəst\ *n*
hor·o·scope \'hȯr-ə-ˌskōp, 'här-\ *n* : a diagram of the positions of planets and signs of the zodiac used by astrologers to foretell events of a person's life
hor·ren·dous \hȯ-'ren-dəs, hä-, hə-\ *adj* : DREADFUL, HORRIBLE — **hor·ren·dous·ly** *adv*
hor·ri·ble \'hȯr-ə-bəl, 'här-\ *adj* **1** : marked by or arousing horror **2** : extremely unpleasant or disagreeable — **hor·ri·bly** \-blē\ *adv*
hor·rid \'hȯr-əd, 'här-\ *adj* **1** : HIDEOUS, SHOCKING **2** : REPULSIVE, OFFENSIVE — **hor·rid·ly** *adv* — **hor·rid·ness** *n*
hor·ri·fy \'hȯr-ə-ˌfī, 'här-\ *vb* **-fied**; **-fy·ing** : to cause to feel horror
hor·ror \'hȯr-ər, 'här-\ *n* **1** : intense fear, dread, or dislike **2** : the quality of inspiring horror **3** : something horrible
hors d'oeuvre \ȯr-'dərv\ *n*, *pl* **hors d'oeuvres** *also* **hors d'oeuvre** \-'dərv(z)\ : any of various savory foods usu. served as appetizers
[1]**horse** \'hȯrs\ *n*, *pl* **hors·es** *also* **horse** **1 a** : a large

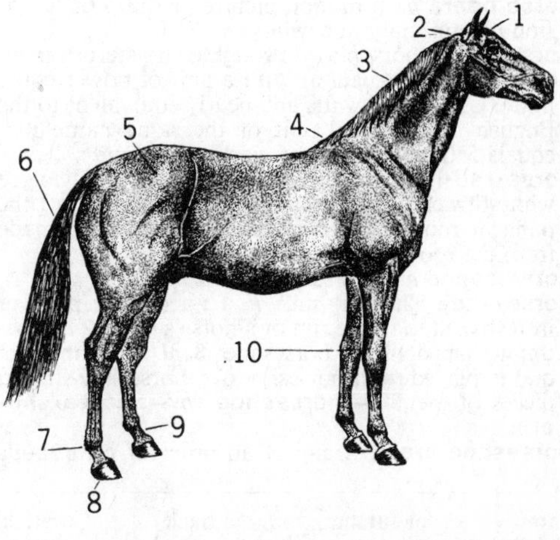

horse 1a: 1, forelock; 2, poll; 3, mane; 4, withers; 5, flank; 6, tail; 7, fetlock; 8, hoof; 9, pastern; 10, knee

H

solid-hoofed grazing mammal domesticated by man since a prehistoric period and used as a beast of burden, a draft animal, or for riding **b** : a male horse : STALLION **2 a** : a frame that supports something (as wood while being cut) **b** : a piece of gymnasium equipment used for vaulting exercises **3** *horse pl* : CAVALRY **4** *slang* : HEROIN — **horse** *adj*

2**horse** *vb* **1** : to provide with a horse **2** : to engage in horseplay : FOOL ⟨was *horsing* around instead of studying⟩

1**horse·back** \'hȯrs-ˌbak\ *n* : the back of a horse

2**horseback** *adv* : on horseback

horse·car \'hȯrs-ˌkär\ *n* **1** : a streetcar drawn by horses **2** : a car for transporting horses

horse chestnut *n* [so called from the former use of the nut in treating respiratory ailments in horses] **1** : a large Asiatic tree with palmate leaves and clusters of showy flowers widely grown as an ornamental and shade tree **2** : the large glossy brown seed of a horse chestnut

horse·fly \'hȯrs-ˌflī\ *n* : any of a family of swift usu. large two-winged flies with bloodsucking females

horse·hair \-ˌha(ə)r, -ˌhe(ə)r\ *n* **1** : hair of a horse esp. from the mane or tail **2** : cloth made from horsehair — **horsehair** *adj*

horsehair worm *n* : any of various long slender worms that are related to nematodes but have a true body cavity and a reduced digestive tract in the adult and are parasitic on arthropods as larvae — called also *horsehair snake*

horse·hide \'hȯrs-ˌhīd\ *n* : a horse's hide or leather made from it

horse latitudes *n pl* : either of two belts or regions in the neighborhood of 30° N. and 30° S. latitude characterized by high pressure, calms, and light changeable winds

horse·laugh \'hȯrs-ˌlaf, -ˌlȧf\ *n* : a loud boisterous laugh : GUFFAW

horse mackerel *n* : any of several large fishes (as a tuna)

horse·man \'hȯrs-mən\ *n* **1 a** : a rider on horseback **b** : one skilled in managing horses **2** : a breeder or raiser of horses — **horse·man·ship** \-ˌship\ *n* — **horse·wom·an** \'hȯrs-ˌwu̇m-ən\ *n*

horse nettle *n* : a coarse prickly yellow-flowered weed related to the nightshades

horse opera *n* : a motion picture or radio or television play usu. about cowboys

horse·play \'hȯrs-ˌplā\ *n* : rough or boisterous play

horse·pow·er \-ˌpau̇(-ə)r\ *n* : a unit of power equal in the U.S. to 746 watts and nearly equivalent to the English gravitational unit of the same name that equals 550 foot-pounds of work per second

horse·rad·ish \-ˌrad-ish, -ˌred-\ *n* **1 a** : a tall coarse white-flowered herb related to the mustard **b** : the pungent root of the horseradish **2** : a relish made from the root of the horseradish

horse sense *n* : COMMON SENSE

horse·shoe \'hȯrs(h)-ˌshü\ *n* **1** : a narrow plate of iron shaped to fit the rim of a horse's hoof **2** : something shaped like a horseshoe **3** *pl* : a game like quoits played with horseshoes or horseshoe-shaped pieces of metal — **horseshoe** *vb* — **horse·sho·er** *n*

horseshoe crab *n* : any of an order of arthropods that have a broad crescent-shaped united head and thorax with a pair of compound and a pair of simple eyes, a small abdomen, and a movable stiff tail spine

ə abut	ər further	a back	ā bake
ä cot, cart	au̇ out	ch chin	e less	ē easy
g gift	i trip	ī life	j joke	ng sing	ō flow
ȯ flaw	ȯi coin	th thin	th this	ü loot
u̇ foot	y yet	yü few	yu̇ furious	zh vision

horse·tail \'hȯrs-ˌtāl\ *n* : EQUISETUM

horse trade *n* : a shrewd bargain — **horse–trade** *vb* — **horse trader** *n*

horse·whip \'hȯrs-ˌhwip\ *vb* : to flog with or as if with a whip made to be used on a horse

hors·ey *or* **horsy** \'hȯr-sē\ *adj* **hors·i·er**; **-est** **1** : of, relating to, or suggesting a horse, horses, or horse racing **2** : characteristic of horsemen — **hors·i·ness** *n*

hort *abbr* **1** horticultural **2** horticulture

hor·ti·cul·ture \'hȯrt-ə-ˌkəl-chər\ *n* : the science of growing fruits, vegetables, flowers, or ornamental plants — **hor·ti·cul·tur·al** \ˌhȯrt-ə-'kəlch(-ə)-rəl\ *adj* — **hor·ti·cul·tur·ist** \-rəst\ *n*

ho·san·na \hō-'zan-ə\ *interj* — used as a cry of praise and adoration

1**hose** \'hōz\ *n* **1** *pl* **hose a** : STOCKINGS, SOCKS **b** : a close-fitting garment covering the legs and waist worn by men about 1600 **c** : short breeches reaching to the knee **2** *pl* **hose** *or* **hoses** : a flexible tube for conveying a fluid (as air or water)

2**hose** *vb* : to spray, water, or wash with a hose

Ho·sea \hō-'zē-ə, -'zā-\ *n* — see BIBLE table

ho·siery \'hōzh(-ə)-rē, 'hōz(-ə)-\ *n* : HOSE 1a

hosp *abbr* hospital

hos·pice \'häs-pəs\ *n* : an inn for travelers; *esp* : one kept by a religious order

hos·pit·a·ble \hä-'spit-ə-bəl, 'häs-(ˌ)pit-\ *adj* **1** : generous and cordial in receiving guests **2 a** : PLEASANT, INVITING **b** : beneficial to life ⟨a *hospitable* climate⟩ **3** : readily receptive : OPEN ⟨*hospitable* to new ideas⟩ — **hos·pit·a·bly** \-blē\ *adv*

hos·pi·tal \'häs-ˌpit-əl\ *n* [from medieval Latin *hospitale*, meaning originally "a hospice", from Latin *hospit-*, stem of *hospes* "host"] : an institution where the sick or injured are given medical or surgical care

hos·pi·tal·i·ty \ˌhäs-pə-'tal-ət-ē\ *n*, *pl* **-ties** : hospitable treatment of visitors and guests

hos·pi·tal·ize \'häs-ˌpit-ə-ˌlīz\ *vb* : to place in a hospital for care and treatment — **hos·pi·tal·i·za·tion** \ˌhäs-ˌpit-ə-lə-'zā-shən\ *n*

1**host** \'hōst\ *n* **1** : ARMY **2** : a great number ***syn*** see MULTITUDE

2**host** *n* **1** : one who receives or entertains guests socially or as a business **2** : a living animal or plant affording food or lodgment to a parasite — **host** *vb* — **host·ess** \'hō-stəs\ *n*

3**host** *n*, *often cap* : the bread or wafer consecrated in the Mass

hos·tage \'häs-tij\ *n* : a person held captive as a pledge that promises will be kept or terms met by another

hos·tel \'häs-təl\ *n* **1** : INN **2** : a lodging for use by youth esp. on bicycling trips — called also *youth hostel*

hos·tel·er \'häs-tə-lər\ *n* **1** : INNKEEPER **2** : a young traveler who stops at hostels

hos·tel·ry \'häs-təl-rē\ *n*, *pl* **-ries** : INN, HOTEL

hos·tile \'häs-təl, 'häs-ˌtīl\ *adj* [from Latin *hostilis*, from *hostis* "enemy"] **1** : of or relating to an enemy ⟨*hostile* troops⟩ **2** : showing ill will : UNFRIENDLY **3** : not hospitable : FORBIDDING ⟨a *hostile* environment⟩ — **hos·tile·ly** \-təl-(l)ē, -ˌtīl-lē\ *adv*

hos·til·i·ty \hä-'stil-ət-ē\ *n*, *pl* **-ties** **1** : a hostile state, attitude, or action **2** *pl* : acts of warfare

hos·tler \'(h)äs-lər\ *n* : one who takes care of horses or mules

hot \'hät\ *adj* **hot·ter**; **hot·test** **1** : having a relatively high temperature **2 a** : ARDENT, FIERY

⟨*hot* temper⟩ **b** : VIOLENT, RAGING **c** : EAGER ⟨*hot* for reform⟩ **d** : exciting in rhythm and mood ⟨*hot* jazz⟩ **3** : having or causing an uncomfortable degree of body heat ⟨his forehead is *hot*⟩ **4** : newly made : FRESH ⟨*hot* scent⟩; *also* : close to something sought **5** : suggestive of heat or of burning or glowing objects ⟨*hot* spicy foods⟩ **6 a** : temporarily capable of unusual performance **b** : currently popular ⟨*hot* items in ladies' wear⟩ **7 a** : electrically energized **b** : RADIOACTIVE **c** : dealing with radioactive material **8 a** : illegally obtained ⟨*hot* jewels⟩ **b** : sought by the police — **hot** *adv* — **hot·ly** *adv* — **hot·ness** *n*

hot air *n* : empty talk

hot·bed \'hät-ˌbed\ *n* **1** : a heated bed of soil enclosed in glass and used for forcing seedlings **2** : an environment that favors rapid growth or development ⟨a *hotbed* of dissent⟩

hot–blood·ed \-'bləd-əd\ *adj* : easily roused or excited : ARDENT — **hot–blood·ed·ness** *n*

hot·box \-ˌbäks\ *n* : a journal bearing (as of a railroad car) overheated by friction

hotch·potch \'häch-ˌpäch\ *n* : HODGEPODGE

hot dog \'hät-ˌdȯg\ *n* : FRANKFURTER; *esp* : a cooked frankfurter served in a long split roll

ho·tel \hō-'tel\ *n* [from French *hôtel*, from Old French *hostel* (from which came English *hostel*), from Latin *hospitale* "hospice"; compare HOSPITAL] : a building that provides lodging and usu. meals, entertainment, and personal services esp. for transients : INN

hot·head \'hät-ˌhed\ *n* : a hotheaded person

hot·head·ed \-'hed-əd\ *adj* : HASTY, RASH, FIERY — **hot·head·ed·ly** *adv* — **hot·head·ed·ness** *n*

hot·house \-ˌhau̇s\ *n* : a heated glass-enclosed house for raising plants — **hothouse** *adj*

hot pepper *n* **1** : a pungent often thin-walled and small pepper **2** : a pepper plant related to the potato that bears hot peppers

hot plate *n* : a portable appliance for heating or cooking

hot rod *n* : an automobile rebuilt or modified for high speed and fast acceleration — **hot–rod·der** \'hät-'räd-ər\ *n*

hot·shot \'hät-ˌshät\ *n* : a showily skillful person

hot war *n* : a conflict involving actual fighting

hot water *n* : a distressing predicament : DIFFICULTY ⟨in *hot water* for not doing his homework⟩

[1]**hound** \'hau̇nd\ *n* **1** : DOG **2** : a dog of any of various hunting breeds typically having large drooping ears and a deep voice and following their prey by scent

[2]**hound** *vb* : to pursue with or as if with hounds

hour \'au̇(ə)r\ *n* **1** : a time for daily devotion **2** : one of the 24 divisions of a day : 60 minutes **3** : the time of day **4** : a fixed or particular time ⟨lunch *hour*⟩ ⟨an *hour* of need⟩ **5** : the distance traveled in an hour ⟨lives two *hours* away⟩ **6** : a class session ⟨a 50-minute *hour*⟩ — **after hours** : after the regular hours of work or operation

hour·glass \-ˌglas\ *n* : an instrument for measuring time in which sand, water, or mercury runs from the upper to the lower part of a glass container in an hour — **hourglass** *adj*

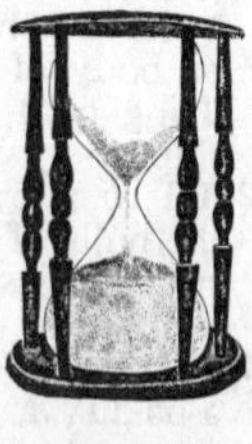
hourglass

hour·ly \'au̇(ə)r-lē\ *adj* **1 a** : occurring every hour ⟨*hourly* bus service⟩ **b** : FREQUENT, CONTINUAL **2** : computed in terms of one hour ⟨*hourly* wages⟩ — **hourly** *adv*

[1]**house** \'hau̇s\ *n, pl* **hous·es** \'hau̇-zəz\ **1** : a building in which one or more families dwell **2 a** : an animal's shelter or habitation **b** : a building in which something is housed ⟨carriage *house*⟩ **3 a** : one of the 12 equal sectors in which the celestial sphere is divided in astrology **b** : a zodiacal sign that is the seat of a planet's greatest influence **4 a** : HOUSEHOLD **b** : FAMILY 1; *esp* : a royal or noble family **5** : a residence for a religious community or for students **6** : a body of persons assembled to make and discuss laws; *esp* : the lower house when there are two houses **7 a** : a place of business or entertainment **b** : a business firm **c** : the audience in a theater or concert hall

[2]**house** \'hau̇z\ *vb* **1 a** : to provide with living quarters or shelter **b** : to store in a house **2** : to encase or enclose for protection **3** : to take shelter : LODGE

house·boat \'hau̇s-ˌbōt\ *n* : a barge fitted for use as a dwelling or for leisurely cruising

house·boy \-ˌbȯi\ *n* : a boy or man hired to act as a general household servant

house·break·ing \-ˌbrā-king\ *n* : the act of breaking into a person's house with the intent of committing a crime — **house·break·er** \-kər\ *n*

house·bro·ken \-ˌbrō-kən\ *adj* : trained to excretory habits acceptable in indoor living — **house·break** \-ˌbrāk\ *vb*

house cat *n* : CAT 1a

house·coat \'hau̇s-ˌkōt\ *n* : a woman's informal garment for wear around the house

house·fly \-ˌflī\ *n* : a two-winged fly that is common about human habitations and acts as a vector of diseases (as typhoid fever)

[1]**house·hold** \-ˌhōld\ *n* : those who dwell under the same roof and compose a family

[2]**household** *adj* **1** : of or relating to a household : DOMESTIC **2** : FAMILIAR, COMMON ⟨his name has become a *household* word⟩

house·hold·er \'hau̇s-ˌhōl-dər\ *n* : one who occupies a dwelling alone or as the head of a household

house·keep·er \-ˌkē-pər\ *n* : a woman employed to keep house

house·keep·ing *n* : the care and management of a house and home affairs

house·maid \-ˌmād\ *n* : a female servant who does housework

housemaid's knee *n* : a swelling over the knee due to an enlargement of the bursa in the front of the kneecap

House of Commons : the lower house of the British and Canadian parliaments

House of Lords : the upper house of the British Parliament

house of representatives : the lower house of a legislative body (as the U.S. Congress or a state legislature)

house·plant \'hau̇s-ˌplant\ *n* : a plant grown or kept indoors

house sparrow *n* : ENGLISH SPARROW

house·top \'hau̇s-ˌtäp\ *n* : ROOF

house·warm·ing \-ˌwȯr-ming\ *n* : a party to celebrate moving into a new home

house·wife \'hau̇s-ˌwīf, *2 is often* 'həz-əf, 'həs-əf\ *n* **1** : a married woman who keeps house in her own home **2** : a small container for small articles (as thread) — **house·wife·li·ness** \'hau̇s-ˌwīf-lē-nəs\ *n* — **house·wife·ly** \-lē\ *adj* — **house·wif·ery** \-ˌwīf-(ə-)rē\ *n*

house·work \'hau̇s-ˌwərk\ *n* : the work of keeping house

[1]**hous·ing** \'hau̇-zing\ *n* **1 a** : SHELTER, LODGING **b** : DWELLINGS **2 a** : something that covers or protects **b** : a support for mechanical parts

2**housing** *n* **1** : a usu. ornamental covering for the back and sides of a horse **2** *pl* : TRAPPINGS
hove *past of* HEAVE
hov·el \'həv-əl, 'häv-\ *n* **1** : an open shed or shelter **2** : a small mean house : HUT
hov·er \'həv-ər, 'häv-\ *vb* **hov·ered**; **hov·er·ing** \-(ə-)riŋ\ **1 a** : to hang fluttering in the air or on the wing ⟨hawks *hovering* over their prey⟩ **b** : to remain suspended over a place or object **2 a** : to move to and fro near a place ⟨waiters *hovered* about⟩ **b** : to be in a state of uncertainty, irresolution, or suspense ⟨*hovering* between life and death⟩ — **hover** *n* — **hov·er·er** \-ər-ər\ *n*
1**how** \(')hau̇\ *adv* **1**: in what manner or way ⟨study *how* plants grow⟩ ⟨*how* was it done⟩ **2** : for what reason : WHY ⟨*how* could you say that⟩ **3** : to what degree or extent ⟨*how* far is Denver⟩ **4** : in what state or condition ⟨*how* are you⟩ — **how about** : what do you say to or think of ⟨*how about* another game⟩
2**how** *conj* : in what manner or condition ⟨remember *how* they fought⟩ ⟨asked him *how* he was⟩
1**how·be·it** \hau̇-'bē-ət\ *adv* : NEVERTHELESS
2**howbeit** *conj* : ALTHOUGH
how·dah \'hau̇d-ə\ *n* : a seat or covered pavilion on the back of an elephant or camel
1**how·ev·er** \hau̇-'ev-ər\ *conj* : in whatever way or manner ⟨do it *however* you like⟩
2**however** *adv* **1 a** : to whatever degree or extent **b** : in whatever manner or way **2** : in spite of that : on the other hand : BUT ⟨I'd like to go; *however*, I'd better not⟩ **3** : HOW ⟨*however* did you manage to do it⟩
how·it·zer \'hau̇-ət-sər\ *n* [from Dutch *houwitser*, from German *haubitze*, from Czech *houfnice* catapult] : a short cannon used to fire projectiles in a high trajectory
howl \'hau̇l\ *vb* **1** : to emit a loud sustained mournful sound ⟨*howling* dogs⟩ **2** : to cry out or exclaim under strong impulse (as pain, grief, or rage) **3** : to utter or bring about with outcry — **howl** *n*

howdah

howl·er \'hau̇-lər\ *n* **1** : one that howls **2** : a stupid and ridiculous blunder
how·so·ev·er \ˌhau̇-sə-'wev-ər\ *adv* **1** : in whatever manner **2** : to whatever degree or extent
hoy·den \'hȯid-ən\ *n* : a saucy, boisterous girl : TOMBOY — **hoy·den·ish** \-ish\ *adj*
hp *abbr* horsepower
HP *abbr* high pressure
HQ *abbr* headquarters
hr *abbr* hour
HR *abbr* **1** home run **2** House of Representatives
HS *abbr* high school
ht *abbr* height
HT *abbr* high-tension
hts *abbr* heights
hua·ra·che \wə-'räch-ē\ *n* : a sandal held by leather thongs
hub \'həb\ *n* **1** : the central part of a wheel, propeller, or fan **2** : a center of activity
hub·bub \'həb-ˌəb\ *n* : UPROAR, TURMOIL
huck·le·ber·ry \'hək-əl-ˌber-ē\ *n* **1 a** : an American shrub related to the blueberry **b** : the edible dark blue to black usu. acid berry of a huckleberry **2** : BLUEBERRY
huck·ster \'hək-stər\ *n* **1** : HAWKER, PEDDLER **2** : a writer of advertising
1**hud·dle** \'həd-əl\ *vb* **hud·dled**; **hud·dling** \-(ə-)liŋ\ **1** : to crowd, push, or pile together ⟨people *huddled* in a doorway⟩ **2** : to gather together to receive signals from the quarterback in a football game **3** : to curl up : CROUCH ⟨a child *huddled* in its crib⟩ — **hud·dler** \-(ə-)lər\ *n*
2**huddle** *n* **1** : a close-packed group : BUNCH **2 a** : CONFERENCE **b** : a strategy conference of football players behind the line of scrimmage
Hud·son seal \ˌhəd-sən-\ *n* : the fur of the muskrat dressed to simulate seal
hue \'hyü\ *n* **1** : COLOR; *esp* : gradation of color **2** : a color other than white, gray, and black
hue and cry \ˌhyü-\ *n* **1** : a loud outcry formerly used in the pursuit of felons **2** : a clamor of alarm or protest
1**huff** \'həf\ *vb* : PUFF
2**huff** *n* : a fit of anger or pique
huffy \'həf-ē\ *adj* **huff·i·er**; **-est** **1** : easily offended : TOUCHY **2** : SULKY — **huff·i·ly** \'həf-ə-lē\ *adv* — **huff·i·ness** \'həf-ē-nəs\ *n*
hug \'həg\ *vb* **hugged**; **hug·ging** **1** : to press tightly esp. in the arms : EMBRACE **2** : to hold fast : CHERISH ⟨*hugged* her fancied grievances⟩ **3** : to stay close to ⟨drives along *hugging* the curb⟩ — **hug** *n*
huge \'hyüj, 'yüj\ *adj* **1** : of great size or area **2** : of great scale or degree **3** : of limitless scope or character — **huge·ly** *adv* — **huge·ness** *n*
hug·ger–mug·ger \'həg-ər-ˌməg-ər\ *n* **1** : SECRECY **2** : CONFUSION, MUDDLE — **hugger–mugger** *adj*
hu·la \'hü-lə\ *or* **hu·la–hu·la** \ˌhü-lə-'hü-lə\ *n* : a Polynesian dance composed of slow rhythmic body movements usu. accompanied by chants and drumming
1**hulk** \'həlk\ *n* **1** : a heavy clumsy ship **2** : a bulky or clumsy person or thing **3 a** : the body of an old ship unfit for service or of an abandoned wreck **b** : a ship used as a prison — usu. used in pl.
2**hulk** *vb* **1** : to appear impressively large : BULK **2** : to move heavily — **hulk·ing** \'həl-kiŋ\ *adj*
1**hull** \'həl\ *n* **1 a** : the outer covering of a fruit or seed **b** : the persistent calyx or involucre that clings to the base of some fruits **2** : the frame or body of a ship, flying boat, or airship
2**hull** *vb* : to remove the hulls of ⟨*hulling* strawberries⟩ — **hull·er** *n*
hul·la·ba·loo \'həl-ə-bə-ˌlü\ *n, pl* **-loos** : UPROAR, DIN

hull 2

hum \ˈhəm\ *vb* **hummed**; **hum·ming** **1 a** : to utter a sound like that of the speech sound \m\ prolonged **b** : to make the natural buzzing noise of an insect in motion : DRONE **c** : to give forth a low continuous blend of sound **2** : to sing with closed lips **3** : to be busily active ⟨the place was *humming*⟩ — **hum** *n* — **hum·mer** *n*

1**hu·man** \ˈhyü-mən, ˈyü-\ *adj* **1** : relating to or characteristic of man; *specif* : showing qualities typical of man ⟨a *human* failing⟩ **2 a** : being a man ⟨a *human* being⟩ **b** : consisting of men ⟨the *human* race⟩ **3** : having human form or attributes ⟨the dog's expression was almost *human*⟩ — **hu·man·ness** \-mən-nəs\ *n*

syn HUMAN, HUMANE can mean having a sympathetic character. HUMAN applies to any feeling or quality shared by mankind in general; HUMANE suggests the gentler side of human nature and implies compassion for people or animals in difficulty or need

2**human** *n* : a human being

hu·mane \hyü-ˈmān, yü-\ *adj* : marked by compassion, sympathy, or consideration for other human beings or for animals ***syn*** see HUMAN ***ant*** inhumane — **hu·mane·ly** *adv* — **hu·mane·ness** \-ˈmān-nəs\ *n*

hu·man·i·tar·i·an \(ˌ)hyü-ˌman-ə-ˈter-ē-ən, (ˌ)yü-\ *n* : a person promoting human welfare and social reform : PHILANTHROPIST — **humanitarian** *adj* — **hu·man·i·tar·i·an·ism** \-ē-ə-ˌniz-əm\ *n*

hu·man·i·ty \hyü-ˈman-ət-ē, yü-\ *n, pl* **-ties** **1** : the quality or state of being human or of being humane **2** *pl* : the branches of learning having primarily a cultural character **3** : MANKIND 1

hu·man·ize \ˈhyü-mə-ˌnīz, ˈyü-\ *vb* **1** : to adapt to human nature or use **2** : to make humane : CIVILIZE, REFINE — **hu·man·i·za·tion** \ˌhyü-mə-nə-ˈzā-shən, ˌyü-\ *n*

hu·man·kind \ˈhyü-mən-ˌkīnd, ˈyü-\ *n* : MANKIND 1

hu·man·ly \ˈhyü-mən-lē, ˈyü-\ *adv* **1** : within the range of human capacity ⟨a task not *humanly* possible⟩ **2** : in a human manner

1**hum·ble** \ˈhəm-bəl, ˈəm-\ *adj* **hum·bler** \-b(ə-)lər\; **hum·blest** \-b(ə-)ləst\ [from Old French, from Latin *humilis* "low", "lowly", from *humus* "ground", "earth"] **1** : modest or meek in spirit or manner : not proud or assertive ⟨a great man is often *humble*⟩ ⟨*humble* apology⟩ **2** : low in rank or status ⟨*humble* birth⟩ ⟨a *humble* position⟩ — **hum·bly** \-blē\ *adv*

2**humble** *vb* **hum·bled**; **hum·bling** \-b(ə-)ling\ **1** : to make humble in spirit or manner ⟨*humbled* himself before the king⟩ **2** : to destroy the power or prestige of ⟨*humbled* the enemy with a crushing attack⟩ — **hum·bler** \-b(ə-)lər\ *n*

hum·bug \ˈhəm-ˌbəg\ *n* **1** : a false or deceiving person or thing : FRAUD **2** : DRIVEL, NONSENSE — **humbug** *vb* — **hum·bug·gery** \-ˌbəg-(ə-)rē\ *n*

hum·drum \ˈhəm-ˌdrəm\ *adj* : MONOTONOUS, DULL

hu·mer·al \ˈhyüm-(ə-)rəl\ *adj* : of, relating to, or used or located in the region of the humerus or shoulder — **humeral** *n*

hu·mer·us \ˈhyüm-(ə-)rəs\ *n, pl* **hu·meri** \ˈhyü-mə-ˌrī, -ˌrē\ : the long bone of the upper arm or forelimb extending from the shoulder to the elbow

hu·mid \ˈhyü-məd, ˈyü-\ *adj* : DAMP, MOIST ⟨a *humid* climate⟩ — **hu·mid·ly** *adv*

hu·mid·i·fy \hyü-ˈmid-ə-ˌfī, yü-\ *vb* **-fied**; **-fy·ing** : to make (as the air of a room) humid : MOISTEN — **hu·mid·i·fi·ca·tion** \-ˌmid-ə-fə-ˈkā-shən\ *n* — **hu·mid·i·fi·er** \-ˈmid-ə-ˌfī(-ə)r\ *n*

hu·mid·i·ty \-ˈmid-ət-ē\ *n, pl* **-ties** : DAMPNESS, MOISTURE; *esp* : the amount of moisture in the air

hu·mi·dor \ˈhyü-mə-ˌdȯr, ˈyü-\ *n* : a case in which the air is kept properly humidified for storing cigars or tobacco

hu·mil·i·ate \hyü-ˈmil-ē-ˌāt, yü-\ *vb* : to reduce to a lower position in one's own eyes or others' eyes : HUMBLE ⟨the public reprimand *humiliated* him⟩ — **hu·mil·i·a·tion** \-ˌmil-ē-ˈā-shən\ *n*

hu·mil·i·ty \hyü-ˈmil-ət-ē, yü-\ *n* : the quality or state of being humble

hum·ming·bird \ˈhəm-ing-ˌbərd\ *n* : any of numerous tiny brightly colored American birds related to the swifts and having narrow swiftly beating wings, a slender bill, and a long tongue for sipping nectar

hummingbirds (about 3½ in. long)

hum·mock \ˈhəm-ək\ *n* **1** : a rounded mound of earth : KNOLL **2** : a ridge or pile of ice — **hum·mocky** \-ə-kē\ *adj*

1**hu·mor** \ˈhyü-mər, ˈyü-\ *n* [from Latin, meaning "moisture", "fluid", and related to the source of English *humidity*; in medieval Latin applied to human dispositions from the belief that these were influenced by the proportions of certain fluids (such as blood, phlegm, bile) in the body] **1** : an often whimsical or changeable state of mind or disposition ⟨he is in a good *humor*⟩ **2** : the amusing quality of things ⟨the *humor* of a situation⟩ **3** : the power to see or tell about the amusing or comic side of things **4** : humorous writings or entertainment ***syn*** see MOOD — **hu·mor·less** \-ləs\ *adj* — **hu·mor·less·ness** *n*

2**humor** *vb* **hu·mored**; **hu·mor·ing** \ˈhyüm-(ə-)ring, ˈyüm-\ : to comply with the wishes or mood of ⟨*humor* an invalid⟩

hu·mor·ist \ˈhyüm-(ə-)rəst, ˈyüm-\ *n* : a writer or performer of humor

hu·mor·ous \ˈhyüm-(ə-)rəs, ˈyüm-\ *adj* : full of, characterized by, or expressive of humor : AMUSING, DROLL ⟨a *humorous* story⟩ — **hu·mor·ous·ly** *adv* — **hu·mor·ous·ness** *n*

1**hump** \ˈhəmp\ *n* **1** : a rounded bulge or lump (as on the back of a camel) **2** : MOUND, HUMMOCK — **humped** \ˈhəm(p)t\ *adj*

2**hump** *vb* **1** : to exert oneself vigorously : HUSTLE **2** : to make hump-shaped : HUNCH

hump·back \ˈhəmp-ˌbak\ *n* **1** : a humped or crooked back **2** : HUNCHBACK 2 **3** : a large whalebone whale with very long flippers — **hump·backed** \-ˈbakt\ *or* **hump·back** \-ˌbak\ *adj*

hu·mus \ˈhyü-məs, ˈyü-\ *n* : a brown or black product of partial decay of plant or animal matter that forms the organic portion of soil

1**hunch** \ˈhənch\ *vb* **1** : to push oneself forward by jerks ⟨*hunch* nearer the fire⟩ **2** : to assume a bent or crooked posture ⟨sat *hunched* over the table⟩ **3** : to thrust into a hump ⟨*hunches* his shoulders⟩

2**hunch** *n* **1** : HUMP **2** : a strong feeling about what will happen : INTUITION

hunch·back \ˈhənch-ˌbak\ *n* **1** : HUMPBACK 1 **2** : a person with a humpback — **hunch·backed** \-ˈbakt\ *adj*

hun·dred \'hən-drəd, -dərd\ *n, pl* **hundreds** *or* **hundred 1** — see NUMBER table **2 :** the number in the third decimal place to the left of the decimal point in arabic numerals **3 :** a very large number ⟨*hundreds* of times⟩ — **hundred** *adj*
hun·dred–legged worm \,hən-drəd-,leg(-ə)d-, -dərd-\ *n* **:** CENTIPEDE — called also *hundred leg·ger* \-'leg-ər\
hun·dredth \-drədth\ *n* **1 :** one of 100 equal parts of something **2** — see NUMBER table — **hundredth** *adj*
hun·dred·weight \'hən-drəd-,wāt, -dərd-\ *n, pl* **-weight** *or* **-weights 1 :** a unit of weight equal to 100 pounds — called also *short hundredweight;* see MEASURE table **2** *Brit* **:** a unit of weight equal to 112 pounds — called also *long hundredweight*
hung *past of* HANG
Hung *abbr* **1** Hungarian **2** Hungary
Hun·gar·i·an \,həng-'ger-ē-ən, -'gar-\ *n* **1 a :** a native or inhabitant of Hungary **:** MAGYAR **b :** a person of Hungarian descent **2 :** MAGYAR 2 — **Hungarian** *adj*
1**hun·ger** \'həng-gər\ *n* **1 a :** a desire or a need for food **b :** an uneasy feeling or weakened condition resulting from lack of food **2 :** a strong desire **:** CRAVING ⟨a *hunger* for praise⟩ — **hunger** *adj*
2**hunger** *vb* **hun·gered**; **hun·ger·ing** \-g(ə-)ring\ **1 :** to feel or suffer hunger **2 :** to have an eager desire ⟨*hungered* for affection⟩
hunger strike *n* **:** refusal esp. by a prisoner to eat enough to sustain life
hung jury *n* **:** a jury that is unable to reach a unanimous verdict
hun·gry \'həng-grē\ *adj* **hun·gri·er**; **-est 1 :** feeling or showing hunger **2 :** EAGER, AVID **3 :** not rich or fertile **:** BARREN — **hun·gri·ly** \-grə-lē\ *adv* — **hun·gri·ness** \-grē-nəs\ *n*
hunk \'həngk\ *n* **:** a large lump or piece ⟨*hunks* of iron⟩ ⟨a *hunk* of bread⟩
1**hunt** \'hənt\ *vb* **1 a :** to pursue for food or in sport ⟨*hunt* squirrel⟩ **b :** to use in hunting game ⟨*hunts* a pack of dogs⟩ **2 a :** to pursue with intent to capture **b :** to search out **:** look for **:** SEEK ⟨*hunting* for his gloves⟩ ⟨*hunting* a new job⟩; *also* **:** to find by hunting ⟨enjoyed *hunting* down bargains⟩ **3 :** to drive or chase esp. by harrying ⟨*hunt* a tramp out of town⟩ **4 :** to search through in quest of prey ⟨*hunts* the woods⟩
2**hunt** *n* **1 :** the action, the practice, or an instance of hunting **2 :** a group of hunters; *esp* **:** persons with horses and dogs engaged in hunting
hunt·er \'hənt-ər\ *n* **1 :** a person who hunts; *esp* **:** one who hunts game **2 :** a dog or horse used or trained for hunting
hunt·ing *n* **:** the action of one that hunts; *esp* **:** the pursuit of game
hunt·ress \'hən-trəs\ *n* **:** a female hunter
hunts·man \'hən(t)s-mən\ *n* **1 :** a person who hunts game **2 :** a person who manages a hunt and looks after the hounds
1**hur·dle** \'hərd-əl\ *n* **1 :** a movable frame (as of woven twigs) used as a fence **2 :** a barrier to be jumped in a race **3 :** OBSTACLE
2**hurdle** *vb* **hur·dled**; **hur·dling** \'hərd-(ə-)ling\ **1 :** to leap over while running **2 :** OVERCOME, SURMOUNT — **hur·dler** \-(ə-)lər\ *n*

ə abut	ər further	a back	ā bake	
ä cot, cart	aü out	ch chin	e less	ē easy
g gift	i trip	ī life	j joke	ng sing	ō flow
ȯ flaw	ȯi coin	th thin	th this	ü loot
ü foot	y yet	yü few	yü furious	zh vision

hur·dy–gur·dy \,hərd-ē-'gərd-ē\ *n, pl* **-dies :** a musical instrument in which the sound is produced by turning a crank; *esp* **:** BARREL ORGAN

hurdy-gurdy

hurl \'hərl\ *vb* **1 :** to throw violently or powerfully ⟨*hurl* a spear⟩ **2 :** PITCH 6 *syn* see THROW — **hurl·er** *n*
hur·ly–bur·ly \,hər-lē-'bər-lē\ *n, pl* **-lies :** UPROAR, TUMULT
hur·rah \hü-'rȯ, -'rä\ *or* **hur·ray** \-'rā\ *interj* — used to express joy, approval, or encouragement
hur·ri·cane \'hər-ə-,kān, -i-kən, 'hə-rə-, 'hə-ri-\ *n* **[**from Spanish *huracán,* borrowed from an American Indian language of the West Indies**] :** a tropical cyclone with winds of 73 miles per hour or greater usu. accompanied by rain, thunder, and lightning
hur·ried \'hər-ēd, 'hə-rēd\ *adj* **1 :** going or working at speed ⟨the *hurried* life of the city⟩ **2 :** done in a hurry **:** HASTY ⟨a *hurried* meal⟩ — **hur·ried·ly** *adv*
1**hur·ry** \'hər-ē, 'hə-rē\ *vb* **hur·ried**; **hur·ry·ing 1 a :** to carry or cause to go with haste ⟨*hurry* him to the hospital⟩ **b :** to move or act with haste ⟨had to *hurry* to arrive in time⟩ **2 a :** to urge on to greater speed **:** PROD **b :** to hasten the doing of ⟨*hurry* a repair job⟩ — **hur·ri·er** *n*
2**hurry** *n, pl* **hurries 1 :** great speed; *esp* **:** unnecessary haste **2 :** a state of eagerness or urgency **:** RUSH ⟨in a *hurry* to get there⟩
1**hurt** \'hərt\ *vb* **hurt**; **hurt·ing 1 a :** to inflict with physical pain **b :** to do harm to **:** DAMAGE **2 a :** to cause anguish to **:** OFFEND **b :** HAMPER **3 :** to feel or cause pain ⟨my tooth *hurts*⟩ — **hurt·er** *n*
2**hurt** *n* **1 :** a cause of injury or damage **2 :** a bodily injury or wound **3 a :** bodily pain **b :** mental distress **:** SUFFERING **4 a :** WRONG, HARM **b :** DAMAGE
hurt·ful \'hərt-fəl\ *adj* **:** causing injury or suffering **:** DAMAGING — **hurt·ful·ly** \-fə-lē\ *adv* — **hurt·ful·ness** *n*
hur·tle \'hərt-əl\ *vb* **hur·tled**; **hur·tling** \-(ə-)ling\ **1 :** to move suddenly or violently ⟨boulders *hurtled* down the hill⟩ **2 :** HURL, FLING
1**hus·band** \'həz-bənd\ *n* **[**from Old English *hūsbonda* "master of a house", from Old Norse *hūsbōndi,* from *hūs* "house" and *bōndi* "householder"**] :** a married man
2**husband** *vb* **:** to manage prudently and economically **:** CONSERVE ⟨*husbanded* their resources⟩ — **hus·band·er** *n*
hus·band·man \'həz-bən(d)-mən\ *n* **:** FARMER
hus·band·ry \-bən-drē\ *n* **1 :** wise management of resources **:** ECONOMY **2 :** FARMING, AGRICULTURE
1**hush** \'həsh\ *vb* **1 :** to make quiet, calm, or still **:** SOOTHE ⟨*hush* a baby⟩ **2 :** to become quiet **3 :** to keep from public knowledge **:** SUPPRESS ⟨*hush* up a scandal⟩
2**hush** *n* **:** a silence or calm esp. following noise **:** QUIET
1**husk** \'həsk\ *n* **1 :** a usu. thin dry outer covering of a seed or fruit **2 :** an outer layer **:** SHELL
2**husk** *vb* **:** to strip the husk from — **husk·er** *n*
1**husky** \'həs-kē\ *adj* **husk·i·er**; **-est :** resembling, containing, or full of husks
2**hus·ky** \'həs-kē\ *adj* **hus·ki·er**; **-est :** HOARSE — **hus·ki·ly** \'həs-kə-lē\ *adv* — **hus·ki·ness** \-kē-nəs\ *n*

[3]**hus·ky** *adj* **hus·ki·er**; **-est** : BURLY, ROBUST
[4]**hus·ky** *n, pl* **huskies** : a heavy-coated working dog of the New World arctic region
hus·sar \(,)hə-'zär\ *n* : a member of any of various European originally cavalry military units
hus·sy \'həz-ē, 'həs-\ *n, pl* **hussies** **1** : a lewd or brazen woman **2** : a pert or mischievous girl
hus·tings \'həs-tingz\ *n pl* : a place where political campaign speeches are made
hus·tle \'həs-əl\ *vb* **hus·tled**; **hus·tling** \-(ə-)ling\ **1** : to push, crowd, or force forward roughly ⟨*hustled* the prisoner to jail⟩ **2** : to move or work rapidly and tirelessly; *also* : to obtain by such work ⟨*hustled* new customers⟩ — **hustle** *n* — **hus·tler** \-(ə-)lər\ *n*
hut \'hət\ *n* : a small and often temporary dwelling or shelter : SHACK — **hut** *vb*
hutch \'həch\ *n* **1 a** : a chest or compartment for storage **b** : a low cupboard topped by open shelves **2** : a pen or coop for an animal **3** : SHACK, SHANTY
huz·zah *or* **huz·za** \(,)hə-'zä\ *interj* — used to express joy or approval
hwy *abbr* highway
hy·a·cinth \'hī-ə-(,)sin(t)th\ *n* **1** : a red or brownish gem **2** : any of a genus of bulbous herbs related to the lily; *esp* : a common garden plant widely grown for the beauty and fragrance of its bell-shaped 6-lobed flowers in a thick spike
hy·a·lite \'hī-ə-,līt\ *n* : a colorless opal that is clear as glass, translucent, or whitish
hy·brid \'hī-brəd\ *n* **1** : an offspring of parents of different genetic constitution esp. when of different races, breeds, species, or genera **2** : something of mixed origin or composition — **hybrid** *adj* — **hy·brid·ism** \-,iz-əm\ *n*
hybrid corn *n* **1** : the grain of Indian corn developed by hybridizing two or more inbred strains **2** : the plant grown from hybrid corn esp. when conforming to standards of increased size, yield, or disease resistance
hy·brid·ize \'hī-brəd-,īz\ *vb* : to produce or cause to produce hybrids : INTERBREED — **hy·brid·i·za·tion** \,hī-brəd-ə-'zā-shən\ *n* — **hy·brid·iz·er** \'hī-brəd-,ī-zer\ *n*
hybrid vigor *n* : exceptional vigor or capacity for growth on the part of a hybrid
hydr- *or* **hydro-** *comb form* **1** : water ⟨*hydr*ous⟩ ⟨*hydro*electricity⟩ **2** : hydrogen : containing or combined with hydrogen ⟨*hydro*carbon⟩
hy·dra \'hī-drə\ *n* : any of numerous small tubular freshwater animals related to the jellyfishes and having a mouth surrounded by tentacles at one end

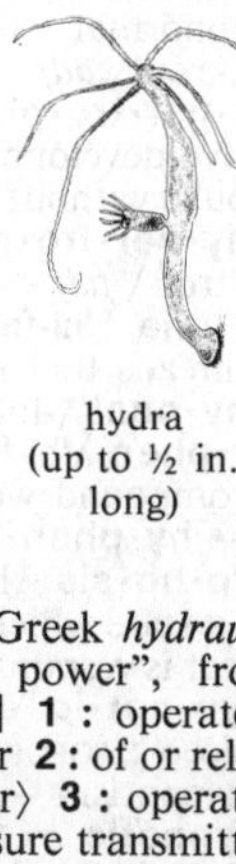

hydra (up to ½ in. long)

hy·dran·gea \hī-'drān-jə\ *n* : any of a genus of shrubby or woody plants with showy clusters of usu. sterile white, pink, or blue flowers
hy·drant \'hī-drənt\ *n* : a pipe with a valve and spout at which water may be drawn from a main
hy·drate \'hī-,drāt\ *vb* : to cause to take up or combine with water or the elements of water — **hy·dra·tion** \hī-'drā-shən\ *n*
hy·drau·lic \hī-'drȯ-lik\ *adj* [from Greek *hydraulis* "pipe organ operated by water power", from *hydr-* and *aulos* "reed instrument"] **1** : operated, moved, or effected by means of water **2** : of or relating to hydraulics ⟨*hydraulic* engineer⟩ **3** : operated by the resistance offered or the pressure transmitted when a quantity of liquid is forced through a comparatively small orifice or through a tube ⟨*hydraulic* brakes⟩ **4** : hardening or setting under water ⟨*hydraulic* cement⟩ — **hy·drau·li·cal·ly** \-li-k(ə-)lē\ *adv*
hy·drau·lics \-liks\ *n* : a science that deals with practical applications of liquid (as water) in motion
hy·dra·zine \'hī-drə-,zēn\ *n* : a colorless fuming corrosive liquid used esp. in fuels for rocket engines
hy·dro \'hī-drō\ *adj* : HYDROELECTRIC ⟨*hydro* power⟩
hy·dro·car·bon \,hī-drə-'kär-bən\ *n* : an organic compound (as acetylene or benzene) containing only carbon and hydrogen
hy·dro·chlo·ric acid \,hī-drə-,klōr-ik-, -,klȯr-\ *n* : an aqueous solution of hydrogen chloride that is a strong corrosive liquid acid, is normally present in dilute form in gastric juice, and is widely used in industry and in the laboratory
hy·dro·dy·nam·ics \,hī-drō-dī-'nam-iks\ *n* : a science that deals with the motion of fluids and the forces acting on solid bodies immersed in fluids and in motion relative to them — **hy·dro·dy·nam·ic** \-ik\ *adj*
hy·dro·elec·tric \,hī-drō-i-'lek-trik\ *adj* : of or relating to production of electricity by waterpower ⟨a *hydroelectric* power plant⟩ — **hy·dro·elec·tric·i·ty** \-,lek-'tris-ət-ē, -'tris-tē\ *n*
hy·dro·flu·or·ic acid \,hī-drō-flu̇-,ȯr-ik-, -,är-\ *n* : a weak poisonous acid that consists of a solution of hydrogen fluoride in water and is used esp. in finishing or etching glass
hy·dro·foil \'hī-drə-,fȯil\ *n* : a flat or curved plane surface similar to an airfoil but designed for action in or on the water
hy·dro·gen \'hī-drə-jən\ *n* [from French *hydrogène*, from *hydr-* and *-gène* "-gen"; so called because water is generated by its combustion] : an element that is the simplest and lightest of the elements and is normally a colorless odorless highly flammable diatomic gas — see ELEMENT table — **hy·drog·e·nous** \hī-'dräj-ə-nəs\ *adj*
hy·dro·gen·ate \'hī-drə-jə-,nāt, hī-'dräj-ə-\ *vb* : to combine or treat with hydrogen; *esp* : to add hydrogen to the molecule of ⟨*hydrogenate* a vegetable oil to form a fat⟩ — **hy·dro·gen·a·tion** \,hī-drə-jə-'nā-shən, (,)hī-,dräj-ə-\ *n*
hydrogen bomb *n* : a bomb whose violent explosive power is due to the sudden release of atomic energy resulting from the union of light nuclei (as of hydrogen atoms)
hydrogen chloride *n* : a colorless pungent poisonous gas that fumes in moist air and yields hydrochloric acid when dissolved in water
hydrogen fluoride *n* : a colorless corrosive fuming poisonous liquid or gas that yields hydrofluoric acid when dissolved in water
hydrogen peroxide *n* : an unstable liquid compound used esp. as an oxidizing and bleaching agent, an antiseptic, and a propellant
hydrogen sulfide *n* : a flammable poisonous gas with a disagreeable odor suggestive of rotten eggs that is found esp. in many mineral waters and in putrefying matter
hy·drog·ra·phy \hī-'dräg-rə-fē\ *n* **1** : the study of seas, lakes, rivers, and other waters esp. with reference to their use by man **2** : the mapping of bodies of water **3** : bodies of water — **hy·drog·ra·pher** \-fər\ *n* — **hy·dro·graph·ic** \,hī-drə-'graf-ik\ *adj*
[1]**hy·droid** \'hī-,drȯid\ *adj* : of or relating to the hydrozoans; *esp* : resembling a typical hydra
[2]**hydroid** *n* : HYDROZOAN; *esp* : a hydrozoan polyp as distinguished from a hydrozoan jellyfish
hy·dro·logic cycle \,hī-drə-,läj-ik-\ *n* : the sequence

of conditions through which water naturally passes from water vapor in the atmosphere through precipitation upon land or water surfaces and finally back into the atmosphere as a result of evaporation and transpiration

hy·drol·o·gy \hī-'dräl-ə-jē\ *n* : a science dealing with the properties, distribution, and circulation of water on and below the surface of the land and in the atmosphere — **hy·dro·log·ic** \ˌhī-drə-'läj-ik\ *adj* — **hy·drol·o·gist** \hī-'dräl-ə-jəst\ *n*

hy·drom·e·ter \hī-'dräm-ət-ər\ *n* : a floating instrument for determining specific gravities of liquids and the strength (as of alcoholic liquors, saline solutions)

hy·dro·pho·bia \ˌhī-drə-'fō-bē-ə\ *n* : RABIES — **hy·dro·pho·bic** \-'fō-bik, -'fäb-ik\ *adj*

hy·dro·phyte \'hī-drə-ˌfīt\ *n* : a plant growing in water or in waterlogged soil — **hy·dro·phyt·ic** \ˌhī-drə-'fit-ik\ *adj*

hy·dro·plane \'hī-drə-ˌplān\ *n* **1** : a speedboat with fins or a bottom so designed that the hull is raised wholly or partly out of the water **2** : SEAPLANE

hydroplane 1

hy·dro·pon·ics \ˌhī-drə-'pän-iks\ *n* : the growing of plants in nutrient solutions — **hy·dro·pon·ic** \-ik\ *adj*

hy·dro·sphere \'hī-drə-ˌsfi(ə)r\ *n* **1** : the water vapor that surrounds the earth as part of the atmosphere **2** : the surface waters of the earth and the water vapor in the atmosphere

hy·drot·ro·pism \hī-'drä-trə-ˌpiz-əm\ *n* : a tropism (as in plant roots) in which water or water vapor is the orienting factor — **hy·dro·trop·ic** \ˌhī-drə-'träp-ik\ *adj*

hy·drous \'hī-drəs\ *adj* : containing water usu. chemically combined

hy·drox·ide \hī-'dräk-ˌsīd\ *n* : a compound of hydroxyl with an element or radical

hy·drox·yl \hī-'dräk-səl\ *n* : a radical consisting of one atom of hydrogen and one of oxygen

hy·dro·zo·an \ˌhī-drə-'zō-ən\ *n* : any of a class of coelenterates including the hydras and various polyps and jellyfishes — **hydrozoan** *adj* — **hy·dro·zo·on** \-'zō-ˌän, -'zō-ən\ *n*

hy·e·na \hī-'ē-nə\ *n* : any of several large strong nocturnal flesh-eating Old World mammals

hy·giene \'hī-ˌjēn\ *n* **1** : a science dealing with the preservation of health **2** : conditions or practices (as of cleanliness) conducive to health — **hy·gi·en·ic** \ˌhī-jē-'en-ik, hī-'jen-, hī-'jēn-\ *adj* — **hy·gi·en·i·cal·ly** \-i-k(ə-)lē\ *adv*

hyena (about 31 in. at shoulder)

hy·gien·ist \hī-'jēn-əst, -'jen-, 'hī-ˌ\ *n* : a person skilled in hygiene; *esp* : DENTAL HYGIENIST

hy·gro·graph \'hī-grə-ˌgraf\ *n* : an instrument for automatic recording of variations in the amount of moisture in the air

hy·grom·e·ter \hī-'gräm-ət-ər\ *n* : an instrument for measuring the amount of moisture in the air

hy·gro·scop·ic \ˌhī-grə-'skäp-ik\ *adj* : readily taking up and retaining moisture ⟨salt is somewhat *hygroscopic*⟩

hying *pres part of* HIE

hy·men \'hī-mən\ *n* : a fold of mucous membrane partly closing the opening of the vagina — **hy·men·al** \-əl\ *adj*

hy·me·ne·al \ˌhī-mə-'nē-əl\ *adj* : of or relating to marriage : NUPTIAL

hy·me·nop·ter·on \ˌhī-mə-'näp-tə-ˌrän, -rən\ *n, pl* **-tera** \-rə\ : any of an order of highly specialized and often colonial insects (as bees, wasps, and ants) that have usu. four membranous wings and the abdomen on a slender stalk — **hy·me·nop·ter·an** \-rən\ *adj or n* — **hy·me·nop·ter·ous** \-rəs\ *adj*

hymn \'him\ *n* **1** : a song of praise esp. to God : PAEAN **2** : a religious song

hym·nal \'him-nəl\ *n* : a book of hymns

hymn·book \'him-ˌbu̇k\ *n* : HYMNAL

hyp- — see HYPO-

hyper- *prefix* **1** : above : beyond : SUPER- **2 a** : excessively ⟨*hyper*sensitive⟩ **b** : excessive

hy·per·ac·id \ˌhī-pər-'as-əd\ *adj* : containing more than the normal amount of acid — **hy·per·acid·i·ty** \-ə-'sid-ət-ē\ *n*

hy·per·bo·le \hī-'pər-bə-(ˌ)lē\ *n* : extravagant exaggeration used as a figure of speech — **hy·per·bol·ic** \ˌhī-pər-'bäl-ik\ *adj* — **hy·per·bol·i·cal** \-i-kəl\ *adj* — **hy·per·bol·i·cal·ly** \-i-k(ə-)lē\ *adv*

hy·per·crit·i·cal \ˌhī-pər-'krit-i-kəl\ *adj* : too critical — **hy·per·crit·i·cal·ly** \-k(ə-)lē\ *adv*

hy·per·opia \ˌhī-pə-'rō-pē-ə\ *n* : FARSIGHTEDNESS — **hy·per·ope** \'hī-pə-ˌrōp\ *n* — **hy·per·opic** \ˌhī-pə-'rōp-ik, -'räp-\ *adj*

hy·per·sen·si·tive \ˌhī-pər-'sen(t)-sət-iv, -'sen(t)-stiv\ *adj* : excessively or abnormally sensitive — **hy·per·sen·si·tive·ness** *n*

hy·per·sen·si·tiv·i·ty \-ˌsen(t)-sə-'tiv-ət-ē\ *n* : the condition or state of being hypersensitive; *esp* : an abnormal bodily state in which exposure to certain substances (as a particular pollen or food) causes a reaction and physical distress (as sneezing, hives, or asthma)

hy·per·ten·sion \ˌhī-pər-'ten-chən\ *n* : HIGH BLOOD PRESSURE

hy·per·thy·roid·ism \-'thī-ˌrȯi-ˌdiz-əm\ *n* : excessive activity of the thyroid gland; *also* : the resulting abnormal state of health — **hy·per·thy·roid** \-ˌrȯid\ *adj*

hy·per·tro·phy \hī-'pər-trə-fē\ *n, pl* **-phies** : excessive development of a bodily part; *esp* : increase in bulk without multiplication of constituent units — **hy·per·tro·phic** \hī-'pər-trə-fik; ˌhī-pər-'träf-ik, -'trōf-\ *adj* — **hypertrophy** *vb*

hy·pha \'hī-fə\ *n, pl* **hy·phae** \-(ˌ)fē\ : one of the threads that make up the mycelium of a fungus — **hy·phal** \-fəl\ *adj*

hy·phen \'hī-fən\ *n* : a mark - used to divide or to compound words or word elements — **hyphen** *vb* — **hy·phen·ate** \-fə-ˌnāt\ *vb*

hyp·no·sis \hip-'nō-səs\ *n, pl* **-no·ses** \-'nō-ˌsēz\ : a state which resembles sleep but in which the subject is responsive to suggestions of the hypnotizer

¹hyp·not·ic \hip-'nät-ik\ *adj* **1** : tending to cause sleep : SOPORIFIC **2** : of or relating to hypnosis or hypnotism — **hyp·not·i·cal·ly** \-i-k(ə-)lē\ *adv*

²hypnotic *n* **1** : a sleep-inducing agent : SOPORIFIC **2** : one that is or can be hypnotized

hyp·no·tism \'hip-nə-ˌtiz-əm\ *n* **1** : the study of or act of causing hypnosis **2** : HYPNOSIS — **hyp·no·tist** \-təst\ *n*

hyp·no·tize \-ˌtīz\ *vb* **1** : to cause hypnosis in **2** : to deaden judgment or resistance by or as if by hypnotic suggestion — **hyp·no·tiz·a·ble** \-ˌtī-zə-bəl\ *adj* — **hyp·no·ti·za·tion** \ˌhip-nət-ə-'zā-shən\ *n* — **hyp·no·tiz·er** \'hip-nə-ˌtī-zər\ *n*

[1]**hy·po** \'hī-pō\ *n* : sodium thiosulfate used in photography as a fixing agent

[2]**hypo** *n, pl* **hypos** : a hypodermic syringe or injection

hypo- *or* **hyp-** *prefix* **1** : under : beneath : down ⟨*hypo*dermic⟩ **2** : less than normal or normally ⟨*hypo*tension⟩ **3** : in a lower state of oxidation : in a low and usu. the lowest position in a series of compounds ⟨*hypo*nitrous acid⟩

hy·po·chon·dria \ˌhī-pə-'kän-drē-ə\ *n* : severe depression of mind often centered on imaginary physical ailments — **hy·po·chon·dri·ac** \-drē-ˌak\ *adj or n*

hy·po·cot·yl \'hī-pə-ˌkät-əl\ *n* : the part of the axis of a plant embryo or seedling below the cotyledons

hy·poc·ri·sy \hip-'äk-rə-sē\ *n, pl* **-sies** : a pretending to be what one is not or to believe what one does not; *esp* : a pretending to be more virtuous or religious than one really is

hyp·o·crite \'hip-ə-ˌkrit\ *n* [from Greek *hypokritēs*, originally meaning "actor", literally "one that answers"] : a person who practices hypocrisy — **hyp·o·crit·i·cal** \ˌhip-ə-'krit-i-kəl\ *adj* — **hyp·o·crit·i·cal·ly** \-i-k(ə-)lē\ *adv*

[1]**hy·po·der·mic** \ˌhī-pə-'dər-mik\ *adj* : of, relating to, or injected into the parts beneath the skin — **hy·po·der·mi·cal·ly** \-mi-k(ə-)lē\ *adv*

[2]**hypodermic** *n* **1** : HYPODERMIC INJECTION **2** : HYPODERMIC SYRINGE

hypodermic injection *n* : an injection made into the subcutaneous tissues

hypodermic needle *n* **1** : NEEDLE 1c **2** : a hypodermic syringe complete with needle

hypodermic syringe *n* : a small syringe used with a hollow needle for injection of material into or beneath the skin

hy·po·der·mis \ˌhī-pə-'dər-məs\ *n* : a layer of tissue just beneath the epidermis of a plant and often modified to serve as a supporting and protecting layer

hy·poph·y·sis \hī-'päf-ə-səs\ *n, pl* **-y·ses** \-ə-ˌsēz\ : PITUITARY BODY — **hy·poph·y·se·al** \(ˌ)hī-ˌpäf-ə-'sē-əl\ *adj*

hy·po·sen·si·tize \ˌhī-pō-'sen(t)-sə-ˌtīz\ *vb* : to reduce the sensitivity of esp. to an allergen : DESENSITIZE — **hy·po·sen·si·ti·za·tion** \-ˌsen-sət-ə-'zā-shən\ *n*

hy·po·ten·sion \ˌhī-pō-'ten-chən\ *n* : LOW BLOOD PRESSURE

hy·pot·e·nuse \hī-'pät-ə-ˌn(y)üs, -ˌn(y)üz\ *n* : the side opposite the right angle of a right-angled triangle

hy·poth·e·sis \hī-'päth-ə-səs\ *n, pl* **-e·ses** \-ə-ˌsēz\ : something not proved but assumed to be true for purposes of argument or further study or investigation

hy·poth·e·size \hī-'päth-ə-ˌsīz\ *vb* **1** : to make a hypothesis **2** : to adopt as a hypothesis

hy·po·thet·i·cal \ˌhi-pə-'thet-i-kəl\ *adj* **1** : involving hypothesis : ASSUMED **2** : imagined for purposes of example ⟨a *hypothetical* case⟩ — **hy·po·thet·i·cal·ly** \-i-k(ə-)lē\ *adv*

hy·po·thy·roid·ism \ˌhī-pō-'thī-ˌrȯi-ˌdiz-əm\ *n* : deficient activity of the thyroid gland; *also* : the resultant condition marked esp. by lowered metabolic rate and loss of vigor — **hy·po·thy·roid** \-ˌrȯid\ *adj*

hy·rax \'hī-ˌraks\ *n, pl* **hy·rax·es** *also* **hy·ra·ces** \'hī-rə-ˌsēz\ : any of several small thickset Old World hoofed mammals — called also *coney*

hyrax
(up to 18 in. long)

hys·sop \'his-əp\ *n* **1** : a plant used in purificatory sprinkling rites by the ancient Hebrews **2** : a woody European mint with pungent aromatic leaves sometimes used in folk medicine for bruises

hys·te·ria \his-'ter-ē-ə, -'tir-\ *n* **1** : a nervous disorder marked by emotional excitability **2** : unmanageable fear or emotional excess — **hys·ter·ic** \-'ter-ik\ *n* — **hysteric** *or* **hys·ter·i·cal** \-'ter-i-kəl\ *adj* — **hys·ter·i·cal·ly** \-i-k(ə-)lē\ *adv*

hys·ter·ics \his-'ter-iks\ *n sing or pl* : a fit of uncontrollable laughter or crying

Hz *abbr* hertz

H

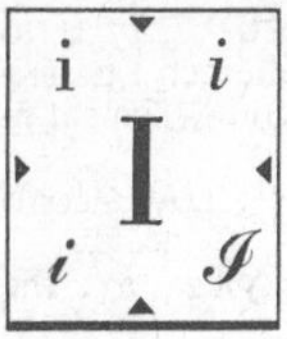

i \ˈī\ *n, often cap* **1 :** the 9th letter of the English alphabet **2 :** the roman numeral 1 **3 :** a grade rating a student's work as incomplete
I \(ˈ)ī, ə\ *pron* **:** the one who is speaking or writing ⟨*I* feel fine⟩
I *abbr* island
-ia *n suffix* **:** pathological condition ⟨hyster*ia*⟩
Ia *or* **IA** *abbr* Iowa
-ial *adj suffix* **:** [1]-AL ⟨proverb*ial*⟩
iamb \ˈī-ˌam\ *n* **:** a metrical foot consisting of one unaccented syllable followed by one accented syllable (as in *away*) — **iam·bic** \ī-ˈam-bik\ *adj*
iam·bus \ī-ˈam-bəs\ *n, pl* **-bus·es :** IAMB
-ian — see -AN
-i·a·sis \ˈī-ə-səs\ *n suffix, pl* **-i·a·ses** \ˈī-ə-ˌsēz\ **:** disease produced by (something specified) ⟨ameb*iasis*⟩
-i·a·try \ˈī-ə-trē, *in a few words* ē-ˌa-trē\ *n comb form* **:** medical treatment **:** healing ⟨psych*iatry*⟩
ibex \ˈī-ˌbeks\ *n, pl* **ibex** *or* **ibex·es :** any of several wild goats living chiefly in high mountain areas of the Old World and having large recurved ridged horns

ibex
(about 3 ft. at shoulder)

-ibility — see -ABILITY
ibis \ˈī-bəs\ *n, pl* **ibis** *or* **ibis·es :** any of several wading birds related to the herons but distinguished by a long slender bill that curves downward
-ible — see -ABLE
-ic \ik\ *adj suffix* **1 :** having the character or form of **:** being ⟨angel*ic*⟩ **:** consisting of ⟨run*ic*⟩ **2 :** derived from or containing ⟨alcohol*ic*⟩ **3 :** in the manner of **:** characteristic of ⟨puritan*ic*⟩ **4 :** associated or dealing with ⟨drama*tic*⟩ **:** utilizing ⟨electron*ic*⟩ **5 :** characterized by **:** exhibiting ⟨nostalg*ic*⟩ **:** affected with ⟨allerg*ic*⟩ **6 :** caused by ⟨ameb*ic*⟩
-i·cal \i-kəl\ *adj suffix* **:** -IC ⟨symmetr*ical*⟩ ⟨geolog*ical*⟩ — adjectives formed with *-ical* sometimes have a wider range of meaning than corresponding adjectives in *-ic*
ICBM *abbr* intercontinental ballistic missile
[1]**ice** \ˈīs\ *n* **1 a :** frozen water **b :** an expanse of frozen water ⟨skating on the *ice*⟩ **2 :** a state of coldness (as from formality or reserve) **3 :** a substance resembling ice **4 :** a frozen dessert; *esp* **:** one containing no milk or cream — **on ice :** in reserve — **on thin ice :** in a dangerous situation
[2]**ice** *vb* **1 a :** to coat or become coated with ice **b :** to change into ice **c :** to chill with ice **d :** to supply with ice **2 :** to cover with icing
Ice Age *n* **:** the Pleistocene glacial epoch
ice·berg \ˈīs-ˌbərg\ *n* [probably from Norwegian *isberg*, from *is* "ice" and *berg* "mountain"] **:** a large floating mass of ice detached from a glacier
ice·boat \-ˌbōt\ *n* **:** a boat or frame on runners propelled on ice usu. by sails
ice·bound \-ˌbau̇nd\ *adj* **:** surrounded or obstructed by ice
ice·box \-ˌbäks\ *n* **:** REFRIGERATOR
ice·break·er \-ˌbrā-kər\ *n* **:** a ship equipped to make and maintain a channel through ice
ice cap *n* **:** an extensive glacier forming on level land and flowing outward from its center
ice cream \(ˈ)īs-ˈkrēm, ˈīs-ˌ\ *n* **:** a frozen food containing cream or butterfat, flavoring, sweetening, and usu. eggs
Ice·land·er \ˈīs-ˌlan-dər, -lən-\ *n* **:** a native or inhabitant of Iceland
[1]**Ice·lan·dic** \īs-ˈlan-dik\ *adj* **:** of, relating to, or characteristic of Iceland, the Icelanders, or Icelandic
[2]**Icelandic** *n* **:** the Germanic language of the Icelandic people
ice·man \ˈīs-ˌman\ *n* **:** one who sells or delivers ice
ice pack *n* **:** a mass of floating chunks of ice
ice pick *n* **:** a hand tool ending in a spike for chipping ice
ice·quake \ˈīs-ˌkwāk\ *n* **:** the shaking and trembling caused by the breaking up of masses of ice
ice sheet *n* **:** ICE CAP
ice–skate \ˈī(s)-ˌskāt\ *vb* **:** to skate on ice — **ice skater** *n*
ice water *n* **:** chilled or iced water esp. for drinking
ich·neu·mon fly \ik-ˌn(y)ü-mən-\ *n* **:** any of numerous small insects which are related to wasps and whose larvae are usu. internal parasites of other insect larvae
ich·thy·ol·o·gy \ˌik-thē-ˈäl-ə-jē\ *n* **:** a branch of zoology that deals with fishes — **ich·thy·o·log·i·cal** \ˌik-thē-ə-ˈläj-i-kəl\ *adj* — **ich·thy·ol·o·gist** \ˌik-thē-ˈäl-ə-jəst\ *n*
ich·thy·o·saur \ˈik-thē-ə-ˌsȯr\ *n* **:** any of an order of extinct marine reptiles with fish-shaped body and elongated snout

ichthyosaur
(about 30 ft. long)

-i·cian \ˈish-ən\ *n suffix* **:** specialist **:** practitioner ⟨beaut*ician*⟩
ici·cle \ˈī-ˌsik-əl\ *n* **:** a hanging mass of ice formed by the freezing of dripping water
ic·ing \ˈī-sing\ *n* **:** a sweet coating for baked goods (as cakes)
icon \ˈī-ˌkän\ *n* **1 :** IMAGE **2 :** a conventional religious image typically painted on a small wooden panel — **icon·ic** \ī-ˈkän-ik\ *adj* — **icon·i·cal·ly** \-ˈkän-i-k(ə-)lē\ *adv*
icon·o·clast \ī-ˈkän-ə-ˌklast\ *n* [from medieval Greek *eikonoklastēs*, from Greek *eikōn* "image", "icon" and *klan* "to break"] **1 :** one who destroys religious images or opposes their veneration **2 :** one who attacks established beliefs or institutions — **icon·o·clasm** \-ˌklaz-əm\ *n* — **icon·o·clas·tic** \ī-ˌkän-ə-ˈklas-tik\ *adj* — **icon·o·clas·ti·cal·ly** \-ti-k(ə-)lē\ *adv*
icon·o·scope \ī-ˈkän-ə-ˌskōp\ *n* **:** a camera tube that transforms pictures into electrical signals for television
ic·tus \ˈik-təs\ *n* **:** the recurring stress or beat in a rhythmic or metrical series of sounds
icy \ˈī-sē\ *adj* **ic·i·er; -est 1 a :** covered with, full of, or consisting of ice ⟨*icy* roads⟩ **b :** intensely cold ⟨*icy* weather⟩ **2 :** COLD, UNFRIENDLY ⟨an *icy* stare⟩ — **ic·i·ly** \-sə-lē\ *adv* — **ic·i·ness** \-sē-nəs\ *n*

ID *abbr* **1** Idaho **2** identification

I'd \(,)īd\ : I had : I should : I would

-ide \,īd\ *also* **-id** \əd, (,)id\ *n suffix* : chemical compound consisting of two elements ⟨hydrogen sulf*ide*⟩

idea \ī-'dē-ə, *esp South* 'īd-ē\ *n* **1** : a plan of action : INTENTION ⟨his *idea* is to study law⟩ **2** : something imagined or pictured in the mind : NOTION ⟨form an *idea* of a foreign country from reading⟩ **3** : a central meaning or purpose ⟨the *idea* of the game is to keep from getting caught⟩ — **idea·less** \ī-'dē-ə-ləs\ *adj*

1**ide·al** \ī-'dē(-ə)l\ *adj* **1** : existing only in the mind : not real ⟨a purely *ideal* conception of society⟩ **2** : embodying or symbolizing an ideal : PERFECT ⟨an *ideal* place for a picnic⟩

2**ideal** *n* **1** : a standard of perfection, beauty, or excellence ⟨our nation's *ideals*⟩ **2** : a perfect type : a model for imitation ⟨considered the old man his *ideal*⟩ ***syn*** see PATTERN

ide·al·ism \ī-'dē-(ə-),liz-əm\ *n* **1** : the practice of forming ideals or living under their influence **2** : the tendency to idealize — **ide·al·ist** \-(ə-)ləst\ *n* — **ide·al·is·tic** \-,dē-(ə-)'lis-tik\ *adj* — **ide·al·is·ti·cal·ly** \-ti-k(ə-)lē\ *adv*

ide·al·ize \ī-'dē-(ə-),līz\ *vb* : to think of or represent things as one believes they should be rather than as they are ⟨*idealize* farm life⟩ — **ide·al·i·za·tion** \-,dē-(ə-)lə-'zā-shən\ *n* — **ide·al·iz·er** \-'dē-(ə-),lī-zər\ *n*

ide·al·ly \ī-'dē-(ə-)lē\ *adv* **1** : in idea : MENTALLY ⟨realizable only *ideally*, not in fact⟩ **2** : in agreement with an ideal : PERFECTLY ⟨*ideally* suited to the job⟩

iden·ti·cal \ī-'dent-i-kəl, ə-'dent-\ *adj* **1** : being one and the same ⟨the *identical* place we stopped before⟩ **2** : exactly alike ⟨*identical* hats⟩ — **iden·ti·cal·ly** \-i-k(ə-)lē\ *adv* — **iden·ti·cal·ness** \-kəl-nəs\ *n*

syn IDENTICAL, EQUIVALENT, EQUAL can mean comparable in essential matter. IDENTICAL implies complete agreement in all details; EQUIVALENT may imply comparable qualities (as of strength, importance, or value); EQUAL implies sameness in some essential property (as number or size) ***ant*** diverse

identical twin *n* : either member of a pair of twins that are produced from a single fertilized egg and that are usu. genetically identical

iden·ti·fi·ca·tion \ī-,dent-ə-fə-'kā-shən, ə-,dent-\ *n* **1** : an act of identifying : the state of being identified **2** : evidence of identity ⟨carry *identification* at all times⟩

iden·ti·fy \ī-'dent-ə-,fī, ə-'dent-\ *vb* **-fied**; **-fy·ing** **1** : to make identical **2** : to think of as identical ⟨*identifies* democracy with capitalism⟩ **3** : ASSOCIATE ⟨*identified* himself with the movement⟩ **4** : to establish the identity of ⟨*identified* the dog as her lost pet⟩ — **iden·ti·fi·a·ble** \-,fī-ə-bəl\ *adj* — **iden·ti·fi·a·bly** \-blē\ *adv* — **iden·ti·fi·er** \-,fī(-ə)r\ *n*

iden·ti·ty \ī-'dent-ət-ē, ə-'dent-\ *n, pl* **-ties** **1** : the condition of being exactly alike : SAMENESS ⟨an *identity* of interests⟩ **2** : distinctness of character : INDIVIDUALITY ⟨members of a mob often lose their *identity*⟩ **3** : the fact of being the same person or thing as one described or known to exist ⟨proved his *identity* with the wanted man⟩ **4** : an element of a mathematical set that leaves any element of the set unchanged under a specific operation (as addition or multiplication)

id·e·o·gram \'id-ē-ə-,gram, 'īd-\ *n* **1** : a picture or symbol used in a system of writing to represent a thing or an idea but not a particular word or phrase **2** : a character or symbol (as *3*) used in a system of writing to represent an entire word but not its individual sounds

id·e·o·graph \-,graf\ *n* : IDEOGRAM — **id·e·o·graph·ic** \,id-ē-ə-'graf-ik, ,īd-\ *adj* — **id·e·o·graph·i·cal·ly** \-'graf-i-k(ə-)lē\ *adv*

ide·ol·o·gy \,īd-ē-'äl-ə-jē, ,id-\ *n, pl* **-gies** : ideas characteristic of an individual, group, or political party — **ide·o·log·i·cal** \-ē-ə-'läj-i-kəl\ *adj* — **ide·o·log·i·cal·ly** \-i-k(ə-)lē\ *adv* — **ide·ol·o·gist** \-ē-'äl-ə-jəst\ *n*

ides \'īdz\ *n pl* : the 15th day of March, May, July, or October or the 13th day of any other month in the ancient Roman calendar

id·i·o·cy \'id-ē-ə-sē\ *n, pl* **-cies** **1** : extreme mental deficiency commonly due to incomplete or abnormal development of the brain **2** : something stupid or foolish

id·i·om \'id-ē-əm\ *n* [from Greek *idiōma* (stem *idiōmat-*) "individual peculiarity of language", from *idios* "one's own"] **1** : the language peculiar to a group ⟨doctors' professional *idiom*⟩ **2** : the characteristic form or structure of a language ⟨know the vocabulary of a foreign language but not its *idiom*⟩ **3** : an expression that cannot be understood from the meanings of its separate words but must be learned as a whole ⟨the expression *give way*, meaning "retreat", is an *idiom*⟩ — **id·i·om·at·ic** \,id-ē-ə-'mat-ik\ *adj* — **id·i·om·at·i·cal·ly** \-'mat-i-k(ə-)lē\ *adv*

id·i·o·syn·cra·sy \,id-ē-ə-'sing-krə-sē\ *n, pl* **-sies** : a way of behaving or thinking characteristic of a person : MANNERISM — **id·i·o·syn·crat·ic** \,id-ē-ō-sin-'krat-ik\ *adj* — **id·i·o·syn·crat·i·cal·ly** \-'krat-i-k(ə-)lē\ *adv*

id·i·ot \'id-ē-ət\ *n* [from Greek *idiōtēs* "person in private station", "layman", and then "ignorant person"; it is from the same source as *idiom*, from the adjective *idios* "one's own", "private"] **1** : a person afflicted with idiocy; *esp* : one requiring complete care **2** : a silly or foolish person — **idiot** *adj* — **id·i·ot·ic** \,id-ē-'ät-ik\ *adj* — **id·i·ot·i·cal·ly** \-'ät-i-k(ə-)lē\ *adv*

1**idle** \'īd-əl\ *adj* **idler** \'īd-(ə-)lər\; **idlest** \'īd-(ə-)ləst\ **1** : not based on facts ⟨*idle* rumor⟩ **2** : USELESS ⟨it is *idle* to want what you cannot have⟩ **3** : not employed : doing nothing ⟨*idle* workmen⟩ ⟨*idle* machines⟩ **4** : not willing to work ⟨*idle* boys hanging around the corner⟩ — **idle·ness** \'īd-əl-nəs\ *n* — **idly** \'īd-lē\ *adv*

syn IDLE, LAZY, INDOLENT can mean inclined to avoid activity or work. IDLE implies avoidance of work by habit of character; LAZY implies a strong dislike of work; INDOLENT implies a dislike of even moving or exerting oneself at all ***ant*** busy

2**idle** *vb* **idled**; **idling** \'īd-(ə-)ling\ **1 a** : to spend time in idleness **b** : to move slowly or aimlessly **2** : to run disconnected so that power is not used for useful work ⟨the engine is *idling*⟩ **3** : to pass in idleness : WASTE ⟨*idle* away one's time⟩ — **idler** \'īd-(ə-)lər\ *n*

idol \'īd-əl\ *n* **1** : an image of a god made or used as an object of worship **2** : one that is greatly loved and admired

idol·a·ter \ī-'däl-ət-ər\ *n* **1** : a worshiper of idols **2** : a person who admires or loves intensely — **idol·a·tress** \-'däl-ə-trəs\ *n*

idol·a·trous \ī-'däl-ə-trəs\ *adj* **1** : of, relating to, or having the character of idolatry **2** : given to idolatry — **idol·a·trous·ly** *adv*

idol·a·try \-trē\ *n, pl* **-tries** **1** : the worship of a physical object as a god **2** : excessive attachment or devotion to something

idol·ize \'īd-ə-,līz\ *vb* **1** : to worship idolatrously

I

2 : to love or admire to excess — **idol·i·za·tion** \\ˌīd-ə-lə-ˈzā-shən\\ *n* — **idol·iz·er** \\ˈīd-ə-ˌlī-zər\\ *n*

idyll *or* **idyl** \\ˈīd-əl\\ *n* **1** : a simple poetic or prose work that describes peaceful rustic life **2** : a suitable subject for an idyll — **idyl·lic** \\ī-ˈdil-ik\\ *adj* — **idyl·li·cal·ly** \\-ˈdil-i-k(ə-)lē\\ *adv*

-ie *also* **-y** \\ē\\ *n suffix, pl* **-ies** **1** : little one ⟨bird*ie*⟩ ⟨sonn*y*⟩ ⟨pant*ie*⟩ **2** : one belonging to : one having to do with ⟨town*y*⟩ **3** : one of such a kind or quality ⟨cut*ie*⟩ ⟨tough*ie*⟩

i.e. *abbr* [for Latin *id est*] that is

-ier — see -ER

if \\(ˌ)if, əf\\ *conj* **1** : with the provision that ⟨come *if* you can⟩ **2** : WHETHER ⟨asked *if* the mail had come⟩ **3** — used as a function word to introduce an exclamation expressing a wish ⟨*if* it would only rain⟩ **4** : even though : BUT ⟨an interesting *if* untenable argument⟩

if·fy \\ˈif-ē\\ *adj* : abounding in uncertain or unknown qualities or conditions ⟨an *iffy* venture⟩

-i·fy \\ə-ˌfī\\ *vb suffix* **-i·fied**; **-i·fy·ing** : -FY

ig·loo \\ˈig-lü\\ *n, pl* **igloos** : an Eskimo house often made of snow blocks and in the shape of a dome

igloo

ig·ne·ous \\ˈig-nē-əs\\ *adj* **1** : of, relating to, or resembling fire : FIERY **2** : formed by solidification of molten magma ⟨*igneous* rock⟩

ig·nite \\ig-ˈnīt\\ *vb* **1 a** : to set afire ⟨*ignite* a piece of paper⟩; *also* : KINDLE ⟨*ignite* a fire⟩ **b** : to cause a fuel mixture to burn **2** : to catch fire ⟨dry wood *ignites* quickly⟩ — **ig·nit·a·ble** \\-ˈnīt-ə-bəl\\ *adj* — **ig·nit·er** *or* **ig·ni·tor** \\-ˈnīt-ər\\ *n*

ig·ni·tion \\ig-ˈnish-ən\\ *n* **1** : the act of igniting : KINDLING **2** : the process or means (as an electric spark) of igniting a fuel mixture

ig·no·ble \\ig-ˈnō-bəl\\ *adj* **1** : of low birth **2** : not honorable : BASE, MEAN ⟨*ignoble* conduct⟩ — **ig·no·bly** \\-blē\\ *adv*

ig·no·min·i·ous \\ˌig-nə-ˈmin-ē-əs\\ *adj* : marked by or causing disgrace or shame : DISHONORABLE ⟨an *ignominious* defeat⟩ — **ig·no·min·i·ous·ly** *adv* — **ig·no·min·i·ous·ness** *n*

ig·no·mi·ny \\ˈig-nə-ˌmin-ē, ig-ˈnäm-ə-nē\\ *n, pl* **-nies** **1** : deep humiliation and disgrace : DISHONOR **2** : disgraceful conduct or qualities

ig·no·ra·mus \\ˌig-nə-ˈrā-məs\\ *n, pl* **-mus·es** [from *Ignoramus*, name of an ignorant lawyer in a 17th century play; the name in Latin means "we do not know", a phrase used in legal Latin] : an ignorant person : DUNCE

ig·no·rant \\ˈig-nə-rənt\\ *adj* **1** : having no knowledge or very little knowledge : not educated **2** : not knowing : UNAWARE ⟨*ignorant* of the true facts⟩ **3** : resulting from or showing lack of knowledge ⟨an *ignorant* mistake⟩ — **ig·no·rance** \\-rən(t)s\\ *n* — **ig·no·rant·ly** *adv* — **ig·no·rant·ness** *n*

syn IGNORANT, UNEDUCATED, UNLETTERED, ILLITERATE can mean not having knowledge instilled by education. IGNORANT implies a lack of knowledge either in general or in some particular field; UNEDUCATED implies such a lack resulting from deficient formal education; UNLETTERED implies a lack of the knowledge that wide reading offers; ILLITERATE implies a failure to meet minimum standards of education ***ant*** cognizant, conversant, informed

ig·nore \\ig-ˈnō(ə)r, -ˈnȯ(ə)r\\ *vb* : to refuse to take notice of ⟨*ignore* an interruption⟩ — **ig·nor·er** *n*

igua·na \\i-ˈgwän-ə\\ *n* : any of various large plant-eating tropical American lizards that have a crest of erect scales along the back and that are locally important as human food

iguana
(about 6 ft. long)

il- — see IN-

il·e·um \\ˈil-ē-əm\\ *n, pl* **il·ea** \\-ē-ə\\ : the part of the small intestine between the jejunum and the large intestine — **il·e·al** \\-ē-əl\\ *adj*

il·i·um \\ˈil-ē-əm\\ *n, pl* **il·ia** \\-ē-ə\\ : the dorsal and upper one of the three bones composing either lateral half of the pelvis — **il·i·ac** \\-ē-ˌak\\ *adj*

ilk \\ˈilk\\ *n* : SORT, FAMILY — used chiefly in the phrase *of that ilk*

[1]**ill** \\ˈil\\ *adj* **worse** \\ˈwərs\\; **worst** \\ˈwərst\\ **1** : showing evil intent ⟨*ill* deeds⟩ **2 a** : causing suffering or distress : DISAGREEABLE ⟨*ill* weather⟩ **b** : not normal or sound : FAILING ⟨*ill* health⟩ **c** : not in good health **d** : NAUSEATED ⟨felt *ill*⟩ **3** : UNFORTUNATE, UNLUCKY ⟨*ill* omen⟩ **4** : UNKIND, UNFRIENDLY ⟨*ill* feeling⟩ **5** : not right or proper

[2]**ill** *adv* **worse**; **worst** **1 a** : with displeasure ⟨the remark was *ill* received⟩ **b** : HARSHLY ⟨*ill* treated⟩ **2** : in a blameworthy manner ⟨an *ill*-spent youth⟩ ⟨*ill*-gotten gains⟩ **3** : SCARCELY ⟨can *ill* afford it⟩ **4** : BADLY, POORLY ⟨*ill* equipped⟩

[3]**ill** *n* **1** : EVIL, MISFORTUNE ⟨for good or *ill*⟩ **2 a** : SICKNESS, AILMENT ⟨childhood *ills*⟩ **b** : TROUBLE, AFFLICTION ⟨the *ills* of society⟩ **3** : unfavorable remarks ⟨speak no *ill* of the dead⟩

Ill *or* **IL** *abbr* Illinois

I'll \\(ˌ)īl\\ : I shall : I will

ill-ad·vised \\ˌil-əd-ˈvīzd\\ *adj* : UNWISE ⟨an *ill-advised* act⟩ — **ill-ad·vis·ed·ly** \\-ˈvī-zəd-lē\\ *adv*

ill-bred \\ˈil-ˈbred\\ *adj* : badly brought up : IMPOLITE

il·le·gal \\il-ˈ(l)ē-gəl\\ *adj* : not lawful — **il·le·gal·i·ty** \\ˌil-ē-ˈgal-ət-ē\\ *n* — **il·le·gal·ly** \\il-ˈ(l)ē-gə-lē\\ *adv*

il·leg·i·ble \\il-ˈ(l)ej-ə-bəl\\ *adj* : not legible : impossible or very hard to read ⟨*illegible* handwriting⟩ — **il·leg·i·bly** \\il-ˈ(l)ej-ə-blē\\ *adv*

il·le·git·i·mate \\ˌil-i-ˈjit-ə-mət\\ *adj* **1** : born of a father and mother who are not married **2** : not correctly deduced or reasoned ⟨an *illegitimate* conclusion⟩ **3** : not lawful or proper — **il·le·git·i·ma·cy** \\-ˈjit-ə-mə-sē\\ *n* — **il·le·git·i·mate·ly** *adv*

ill-fat·ed \\ˈil-ˈfāt-əd\\ *adj* : doomed to disaster : UNFORTUNATE ⟨an *ill-fated* expedition⟩

ill-fa·vored \\-ˈfā-vərd\\ *adj* **1** : unattractive esp. in facial features **2** : OFFENSIVE

ill-hu·mored \\ˈil-ˈhyü-mərd, ˈil-ˈyü-\\ *adj* : SURLY, IRRITABLE — **ill-hu·mored·ly** *adv*

il·lib·er·al \\il-ˈ(l)ib-(ə-)rəl\\ *adj* : not liberal or broad-minded : BIGOTED — **il·lib·er·al·i·ty** \\il-ˌib-ə-ˈral-ət-ē\\ *n* — **il·lib·er·al·ly** \\-ˈ(l)ib-(ə-)rə-lē\\ *adv*

il·lic·it \\il-ˈ(l)is-ət\\ *adj* : not permitted : UNLAWFUL ⟨*illicit* drug traffic⟩ — **il·lic·it·ly** *adv*

il·lim·it·a·ble \\il-ˈ(l)im-ət-ə-bəl\\ *adj* : incapable of being limited — **il·lim·it·a·bly** \\-blē\\ *adv*

il·lit·er·a·cy \il-'(l)it-ə-rə-sē, -'(l)i-trə-sē\ *n, pl* **-cies** **1 :** the quality or state of being illiterate; *esp* **:** inability to read or write **2 :** a mistake made by one who is illiterate

il·lit·er·ate \-'(l)it-ə-rət, -'(l)i-trət\ *adj* **1 :** having little or no education; *esp* **:** unable to read or write **2 :** showing illiteracy ***syn*** see IGNORANT ***ant*** literate — **illiterate** *n* — **il·lit·er·ate·ly** *adv* — **il·lit·er·ate·ness** *n*

ill–man·nered \'il-'man-ərd\ *adj* **:** marked by bad manners **:** RUDE

ill–na·tured \-'nā-chərd\ *adj* **:** having a bad disposition **:** CROSS, SURLY — **ill–na·tured·ly** *adv*

ill·ness \'il-nəs\ *n* **:** an unhealthy condition of body or mind **:** SICKNESS

il·log·i·cal \il-'(l)äj-i-kəl\ *adj* **:** not observing principles of good reasoning — **il·log·i·cal·ly** \-i-k(ə-)lē\ *adv* — **il·log·i·cal·ness** \-kəl-nəs\ *n*

ill–starred \'il-'stärd\ *adj* **:** ILL-FATED, UNLUCKY ⟨*ill-starred* lovers⟩

ill–tem·pered \-'tem-pərd\ *adj* **:** ILL-NATURED, QUARRELSOME — **ill–tem·pered·ly** *adv*

ill–treat \-'trēt\ *vb* **:** to treat cruelly or improperly **:** MALTREAT — **ill–treat·ment** \-mənt\ *n*

il·lu·mi·nate \il-'ü-mə-ˌnāt\ *vb* **1 :** to supply with light **:** light up ⟨*illuminate* a building⟩ **2 :** to make clear **:** EXPLAIN ⟨*illuminated* the subject with lengthy comments⟩ **3 :** to decorate with designs or pictures in gold or colors ⟨*illuminate* a manuscript⟩ — **il·lu·mi·na·tive** \-ˌnāt-iv\ *adj* — **il·lu·mi·na·tor** \-ˌnāt-ər\ *n*

il·lu·mi·na·tion \il-ˌü-mə-'nā-shən\ *n* **1 a :** the action of illuminating or state of being illuminated **b :** amount of light **2 :** spiritual or intellectual enlightenment **3 :** decorative lighting or lighting effects **4 :** gold or colored decoration (as in a manuscript)

il·lu·mine \il-'ü-mən\ *vb* **:** ILLUMINATE

ill–use \'il-'yüz\ *vb* **:** MALTREAT, ABUSE — **ill–us·age** \-'yü-sij, -'yü-zij\ *n*

il·lu·sion \il-'ü-zhən\ *n* **1 :** a misleading image presented to the eye **2 :** the state or fact of being led to accept as true something unreal or imagined **3 :** a mistaken idea ⟨*illusions* of childhood about the world of grown-ups⟩

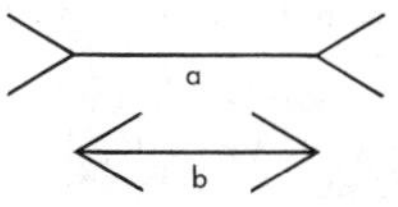

illusion 1: a equals b

il·lu·sive \il-'ü-siv, -'ü-ziv\ *adj* **:** ILLUSORY — **il·lu·sive·ly** *adv* — **il·lu·sive·ness** *n*

il·lu·so·ry \il-'üs(-ə)-rē, -'üz(-ə)-\ *adj* **:** based on or producing illusion **:** DECEPTIVE

illust *abbr* **1** illustrated **2** illustration

il·lus·trate \'il-ə-ˌstrāt\ *vb* **1 :** to make clear by an example or instance ⟨*illustrated* his point with cases from his own experience⟩ **2 a :** to provide with pictures or figures intended to explain or decorate ⟨*illustrate* a book with color plates⟩ **b :** to serve to explain or decorate ⟨the diagram *illustrates* the operation of a computer⟩ — **il·lus·tra·tor** \-ˌstrāt-ər\ *n*

il·lus·tra·tion \ˌil-ə-'strā-shən\ *n* **1 :** the action of illustrating **:** the condition of being illustrated **2 :** an example or instance or a picture or diagram intended to illustrate

il·lus·tra·tive \il-'əs-trət-iv\ *adj* **:** serving, tending, or designed to illustrate ⟨*illustrative* examples⟩ — **il·lus·tra·tive·ly** *adv*

il·lus·tri·ous \il-'əs-trē-əs\ *adj* **:** notably outstanding because of rank or achievement **:** EMINENT — **il·lus·tri·ous·ly** *adv* — **il·lus·tri·ous·ness** *n*

ill will *n* **:** unfriendly feeling

ill–wish·er \'il-'wish-ər\ *n* **:** one that wishes ill to another

il·ly \'il-(l)ē\ *adv* **:** BADLY, ILL ⟨*illy* chosen⟩

il·men·ite \'il-mə-ˌnīt\ *n* **:** an iron-black mineral composed of iron, titanium, and oxygen that is an ore of titanium

im- — see IN-

I'm \(ˌ)īm\ **:** I am

[1]**im·age** \'im-ij\ *n* **1 :** a reproduction or imitation of the form of a person or thing; *esp* **:** STATUE **2 :** a picture of an object produced by a lens, a mirror, an electronic system, or photography **3 :** a mental picture of something not actually present **:** IMPRESSION **4 :** a person strikingly like another person ⟨the very *image* of his father⟩

[2]**image** *vb* **1 :** to describe or portray in words or pictures **2 :** to call up a mental picture of **:** IMAGINE **3 :** REFLECT, MIRROR

im·ag·ery \'im-ij-(ə-)rē\ *n, pl* **-er·ies** **1 a :** IMAGES, STATUES **b :** the art of making images **2 :** figurative language ⟨*imagery* of a poem⟩ **3 :** mental images; *esp* **:** the products of imagination

imag·in·a·ble \im-'aj-(ə-)nə-bəl\ *adj* **:** capable of being imagined **:** CONCEIVABLE — **imag·in·a·bly** \-blē\ *adv*

imag·i·nary \im-'aj-ə-ˌner-ē\ *adj* **:** existing only in imagination **:** FANCIED

imaginary number *n* **1 :** an even root of a negative number — called also *imaginary* **2 :** a complex number in which the part (as $3\sqrt{-1}$ in $2 + 3\sqrt{-1}$) containing the positive square root of minus 1 is not equal to zero

imag·i·na·tion \im-ˌaj-ə-'nā-shən\ *n* **1 :** the power of forming a mental image or conception of something not present to the senses and esp. of something never before perceived in reality **2 :** creative ability **3 :** a creation of the mind; *esp* **:** an idealized or poetic creation

imag·i·na·tive \im-'aj-(ə-)nət-iv, -'aj-ə-ˌnāt-\ *adj* **1 :** of, relating to, or characterized by imagination ⟨*imaginative* writing⟩ **2 :** having a lively imagination — **imag·i·na·tive·ly** *adv* — **imag·i·na·tive·ness** *n*

imag·ine \im-'aj-ən\ *vb* **imag·ined**; **imag·in·ing** \-'aj-(ə-)ning\ **1 :** to form a mental image of something not present **:** use the imagination **2 :** THINK, SUPPOSE, GUESS ⟨I *imagine* it will rain⟩

ima·go \im-'ā-gō, -'äg-ō\ *n, pl* **imagoes** *or* **ima·gi·nes** \-'ā-gə-ˌnēz, -'äg-ə-\ **:** an insect in its final adult, sexually mature, and usu. winged state — **ima·gi·nal** \-'ā-gə-nəl, -'äg-ə-\ *adj*

im·bal·ance \(')im-'bal-ən(t)s\ *n* **:** lack of balance **:** the state of being out of equilibrium or out of proportion

im·be·cile \'im-bə-səl, -ˌsil\ *n* **:** a mentally deficient person; *esp* **:** a feebleminded person requiring supervision in the performance of routine daily tasks of caring for himself — **imbecile** *or* **im·be·cil·ic** \ˌim-bə-'sil-ik\ *adj*

im·be·cil·i·ty \ˌim-bə-'sil-ət-ē\ *n, pl* **-ties** **1 :** the quality or state of being imbecile or an imbecile **2 a :** utter foolishness **b :** FUTILITY **c :** something foolish

imbed *var of* EMBED

im·bibe \im-'bīb\ *vb* **1 :** to receive into the mind and retain ⟨*imbibe* knowledge⟩ **2 a :** DRINK **b :** ABSORB ⟨sponges *imbibe* moisture⟩ — **im·bib·er** *n*

im·bi·bi·tion \ˌim-bə-'bish-ən\ *n* **:** the act or action of imbibing; *esp* **:** the taking up of fluid by a colloidal system (as protoplasm in a cell) resulting in swelling — **im·bi·bi·tion·al** \-'bish-(ə-)nəl\ *adj*

I

im·bro·glio \im-ˈbrōl-yō\ *n, pl* **-glios** [from Italian, from *imbrogliare* "to throw into confusion", from French *embrouiller*, the source of English *embroil*] **1 :** a difficult or complicated situation **2 :** a painful or embarrassing misunderstanding

im·bue \im-ˈbyü\ *vb* **1 :** to tinge or dye deeply **2 :** to cause to become penetrated **:** PERMEATE ⟨*imbued* with a deep sense of loyalty⟩

im·i·ta·ble \ˈim-ət-ə-bəl\ *adj* **:** capable or worthy of being imitated or copied

im·i·tate \ˈim-ə-ˌtāt\ *vb* **1 :** to follow as a pattern, model, or example ⟨drama that *imitates* life⟩ **2 :** to be or appear similar to **:** RESEMBLE ⟨plastic finished to *imitate* leather⟩ **3 :** to copy exactly ⟨*imitate* the barking of a dog⟩ — **im·i·ta·tor** \-ˌtāt-ər\ *n*

syn IMITATE, APE, MIMIC, MOCK can mean to follow the example of another. IMITATE implies use of another's admired example as a model or pattern; APE suggests a close and often inept imitation of an admired example; MIMIC may suggest imitation of another's personal manner often for humorous effect; MOCK suggests mimicry of another in his presence intended to ridicule him

[1]**im·i·ta·tion** \ˌim-ə-ˈtā-shən\ *n* **1 :** an act of imitating **2 :** something produced as a copy **3 :** the repetition in a voice part of the melodic theme, phrase, or motive previously found in another part

[2]**imitation** *adj* **:** resembling something else esp. of better quality **:** not real ⟨*imitation* leather⟩

im·i·ta·tive \ˈim-ə-ˌtāt-iv\ *adj* **1 :** marked by imitation ⟨*buzz* is an *imitative* word⟩ **2 :** inclined to imitate **3 :** imitating something superior — **im·i·ta·tive·ly** *adv* — **im·i·ta·tive·ness** *n*

im·mac·u·late \im-ˈak-yə-lət\ *adj* **1 :** having no stain or blemish **:** PURE ⟨an *immaculate* record of service⟩ **2 :** spotlessly clean ⟨*immaculate* linen⟩ — **im·mac·u·late·ly** *adv* — **im·mac·u·late·ness** *n*

Immaculate Conception *n* **:** December 8 observed as a Roman Catholic festival in commemoration of the conception of the Virgin Mary as free from original sin

im·ma·te·ri·al \ˌim-ə-ˈtir-ē-əl\ *adj* **1 :** not consisting of matter **2 :** UNIMPORTANT

im·ma·ture \ˌim-ə-ˈt(y)u̇(ə)r\ *adj* **:** not mature or fully developed **:** YOUNG, UNRIPE — **im·ma·ture·ly** *adv* — **im·ma·tu·ri·ty** \-ˈt(y)u̇r-ət-ē\ *n*

im·mea·sur·a·ble \(ˈ)im-ˈezh-(ə-)rə-bəl, -ˈezh-ər-bəl, -ˈāzh-\ *adj* **:** incapable of being measured **:** indefinitely large — **im·mea·sur·a·bly** \-blē\ *adv*

im·me·di·a·cy \im-ˈēd-ē-ə-sē\ *n, pl* **-cies 1 a :** the quality or state of being immediate **b :** URGENCY **2 :** something that is of immediate importance ⟨*immediacies* of daily life⟩

im·me·di·ate \im-ˈēd-ē-ət\ *adj* **1 :** next in line or relationship ⟨the king's *immediate* heir⟩ **2 :** closest in importance ⟨his *immediate* interest⟩ **3 :** acting directly and alone without anything intervening ⟨an *immediate* cause of disease⟩ **4 :** not distant or separated **:** NEXT ⟨their *immediate* neighbors⟩ **5 :** close in time ⟨the *immediate* past⟩ **6 :** made or done at once ⟨ask for an *immediate* reply⟩ — **im·me·di·ate·ness** *n*

im·me·di·ate·ly *adv* **1 :** with nothing between **:** DIRECTLY ⟨the house *immediately* beyond this one⟩ **2 :** without delay **:** at once ⟨do it *immediately*⟩

im·me·mo·ri·al \ˌim-ə-ˈmōr-ē-əl, -ˈmȯr-\ *adj* **:** extending beyond the reach of memory or record — **im·me·mo·ri·al·ly** \-ē-ə-lē\ *adv*

im·mense \im-ˈen(t)s\ *adj* [from Latin *immensus* meaning literally "unmeasured", from *mensus* "measured", the source of English *measure*] **1 :** very great in size or degree **:** HUGE **2 :** EXCELLENT — **im·mense·ly** *adv* — **im·mense·ness** *n* — **im·men·si·ty** \-ˈen(t)-sət-ē\ *n*

im·merse \im-ˈərs\ *vb* **1 :** to plunge or dip into a fluid **2 :** to baptize by submerging in water **3 :** ENGROSS, ABSORB ⟨*immersed* himself in his studies⟩ — **im·mer·sion** \-ˈər-zhən, -shən\ *n*

im·mi·grant \ˈim-i-grənt\ *n* **1 :** a person who comes to a country to become a permanent resident **2 :** a plant or animal that becomes established in an area where it did not occur previously — **immigrant** *adj*

im·mi·grate \ˈim-ə-ˌgrāt\ *vb* **:** to come into a foreign country to become a permanent resident — **im·mi·gra·tion** \ˌim-ə-ˈgrā-shən\ *n*

im·mi·nent \ˈim-ə-nənt\ *adj* **:** ready to take place; *esp* **:** threatening to occur immediately ⟨in *imminent* danger⟩ — **im·mi·nence** \-nən(t)s\ *n* — **im·mi·nent·ly** *adv*

im·mo·bile \(ˈ)im-ˈō-bəl, -ˌbēl, -ˌbīl\ *adj* **1 :** incapable of being moved **:** FIXED **2 :** not moving — **im·mo·bil·i·ty** \ˌim-(ˌ)ō-ˈbil-ət-ē\ *n*

im·mo·bi·lize \im-ˈō-bə-ˌlīz\ *vb* **:** to make immobile ⟨*immobilize* a broken arm with a cast⟩ — **im·mo·bi·li·za·tion** \im-ˌō-bə-lə-ˈzā-shən\ *n* — **im·mo·bi·liz·er** \im-ˈō-bə-ˌlī-zər\ *n*

im·mod·er·ate \(ˈ)im-ˈäd-(ə-)rət\ *adj* **:** not moderate **:** EXCESSIVE — **im·mod·er·a·cy** \-(ə-)rə-sē\ *n* — **im·mod·er·ate·ly** *adv*

im·mod·est \(ˈ)im-ˈäd-əst\ *adj* **:** not modest; *esp* **:** INDECENT ⟨*immodest* clothing⟩ — **im·mod·est·ly** *adv* — **im·mod·es·ty** \-ə-stē\ *n*

im·mo·late \ˈim-ə-ˌlāt\ *vb* **:** to offer in sacrifice; *esp* **:** to kill as a sacrifice — **im·mo·la·tion** \ˌim-ə-ˈlā-shən\ *n* — **im·mo·la·tor** \ˈim-ə-ˌlāt-ər\ *n*

im·mor·al \(ˈ)im-ˈȯr-əl, -ˈär-\ *adj* **:** not moral **:** WICKED, LEWD — **im·mo·ral·i·ty** \ˌim-ˌȯ-ˈral-ət-ē, ˌim-ə-ˈral-\ *n* — **im·mor·al·ly** \(ˈ)im-ˈȯr-ə-lē, -ˈär-\ *adv*

[1]**im·mor·tal** \(ˈ)im-ˈȯrt-əl\ *adj* **:** not subject to death **:** living or lasting forever ⟨*immortal* gods⟩ ⟨*immortal* fame⟩ — **im·mor·tal·i·ty** \ˌim-ˌȯr-ˈtal-ət-ē\ *n* — **im·mor·tal·ly** \-ə-lē\ *adv*

[2]**immortal** *n* **1 :** an immortal being (as a god) **2 :** a person whose fame is lasting ⟨baseball *immortals*⟩

im·mor·tal·ize \im-ˈȯrt-ə-ˌlīz\ *vb* **:** to make immortal ⟨a man *immortalized* by his writings⟩ — **im·mor·tal·i·za·tion** \-ˌȯrt-ə-lə-ˈzā-shən\ *n*

im·mov·a·ble \(ˈ)im-ˈü-və-bəl\ *adj* **1 a :** incapable of being moved **b :** STATIONARY **2 :** STEADFAST ⟨an *immovable* purpose⟩ — **im·mov·a·bil·i·ty** \(ˌ)im-ˌü-və-ˈbil-ət-ē\ *n* — **im·mov·a·bly** \(ˈ)im-ˈü-və-blē\ *adv*

im·mune \im-ˈyün\ *adj* **1 :** FREE, EXEMPT ⟨*immune* from punishment⟩ **2 a :** not susceptible or responsive ⟨*immune* to persuasion⟩ **b :** having a high degree of natural or acquired resistance ⟨*immune* to diphtheria⟩ **3 :** containing or producing antibodies — **immune** *n*

immune serum *n* **:** ANTISERUM

im·mu·ni·ty \im-ˈyü-nət-ē\ *n, pl* **-ties :** the quality or state of being immune; *esp* **:** bodily power to resist an infectious disease usu. resulting from vaccination or inoculation, a previous attack of the disease, or a natural resistance

im·mu·nize \'im-yə-ˌnīz\ *vb* : to make immune — **im·mu·ni·za·tion** \ˌim-yə-nə-'zā-shən\ *n*

im·mu·no·gen·ic \ˌim-yə-nō-'jen-ik\ *adj* : producing immunity — **im·mu·no·ge·nic·i·ty** \-jə-'nis-ət-ē\ *n*

im·mu·nol·o·gy \ˌim-yə-'näl-ə-jē\ *n* : a science that deals with immunity to disease — **im·mu·no·log·ic** \ˌim-yə-nə-'läj-ik\ *or* **im·mu·no·log·i·cal** \-'läj-i-kəl\ *adj* — **im·mu·no·log·i·cal·ly** \-i-k(ə-)lē\ *adv* — **im·mu·nol·o·gist** \ˌim-yə-'näl-ə-jəst\ *n*

im·mure \im-'yu̇(ə)r\ *vb* : to enclose within or as if within walls : IMPRISON — **im·mure·ment** \-mənt\ *n*

im·mu·ta·ble \(')im-'yüt-ə-bəl\ *adj* : UNCHANGEABLE — **im·mu·ta·bil·i·ty** \(ˌ)im-ˌyüt-ə-'bil-ət-ē\ *n* — **im·mu·ta·bly** \(')im-'yüt-ə-blē\ *adv*

imp \'imp\ *n* **1** : a small demon : FIEND **2** : a mischievous child

imp *abbr* **1** imperative **2** imperfect

im·pact \'im-ˌpakt\ *n* **1** : a striking together of two bodies : COLLISION **2** : a forceful effect ⟨the full *impact* of war⟩

im·pact·ed \im-'pak-təd\ *adj* **1** : wedged into a bodily passage **2** : wedged between the jawbone and another tooth

im·pac·tion \im-'pak-shən\ *n* : the act of becoming or the state of being impacted; *also* : lodgment of something (as feces) in a body passage or cavity

im·pair \im-'pa(ə)r, -'pe(ə)r\ *vb* : to diminish in quantity, value, or strength : DAMAGE ⟨overwork *impaired* his health⟩ — **im·pair·er** *n* — **im·pair·ment** \-mənt\ *n*

im·pale \im-'pāl\ *vb* **1** : to pierce with or as if with something pointed **2** : to torture or kill by impaling — **im·pale·ment** \-mənt\ *n*

im·pal·pa·ble \(')im-'pal-pə-bəl\ *adj* **1** : incapable of being felt by the touch **2** : not readily perceived or understood ⟨an *impalpable* difference between two shades of green⟩ — **im·pal·pa·bil·i·ty** \(ˌ)im-ˌpal-pə-'bil-ət-ē\ *n* — **im·pal·pa·bly** \(')im-'pal-pə-blē\ *adv*

im·pan·el \im-'pan-əl\ *vb* **-eled** *or* **-elled**; **-el·ing** *or* **-el·ling** : to enter in or on a panel or list : ENROLL ⟨*impanel* a jury⟩

im·part \im-'pärt\ *vb* **1** : to give or grant from a supply : TRANSMIT ⟨the sun *imparts* warmth⟩ **2** : to make known : DISCLOSE ⟨*imparted* her plans⟩

im·par·tial \(')im-'pär-shəl\ *adj* : not partial : UNBIASED — **im·par·ti·al·i·ty** \(ˌ)im-ˌpär-shē-'al-ət-ē, -ˌpär-'shal-\ *n* — **im·par·tial·ly** \(')im-'pärsh-(ə-)lē\ *adv*

im·pass·a·ble \(')im-'pas-ə-bəl\ *adj* : incapable of being passed, traversed, or crossed ⟨roads made *impassable* by the hurricane⟩ — **im·pass·a·bil·i·ty** \(ˌ)im-ˌpas-ə-'bil-ət-ē\ *n* — **im·pass·a·bly** \(')im-'pas-ə-blē\ *adv*

im·passe \'im-ˌpas, im-'\ *n* **1** : an impassable road or way **2 a** : a predicament from which there is no escape **b** : DEADLOCK ⟨negotiations reached an *impasse*⟩

im·pas·si·ble \(')im-'pas-ə-bəl\ *adj* : incapable of feeling emotion — **im·pas·si·bil·i·ty** \(ˌ)im-ˌpas-ə-'bil-ət-ē\ *n* — **im·pas·si·bly** \(')im-'pas-ə-blē\ *adv*

im·pas·sioned \im-'pash-ənd\ *adj* : filled with passion or zeal : showing strong feeling ⟨*impassioned* plea for justice⟩

im·pas·sive \(')im-'pas-iv\ *adj* : not feeling or not showing emotion : CALM, UNMOVED ⟨an *impassive* expression⟩ — **im·pas·sive·ly** *adv* — **im·pas·sive·ness** *n* — **im·pas·siv·i·ty** \ˌim-ˌpas-'iv-ət-ē\ *n*

im·pa·tiens \im-'pā-shənz, -shən(t)s, -shē-ˌenz\ *n* : JEWELWEED

im·pa·tient \(')im-'pā-shənt\ *adj* **1** : not patient : restless or irritable esp. at delay or opposition ⟨an *impatient* disposition⟩ **2** : showing or arising from an impatient temper ⟨an *impatient* answer⟩ **3** : restlessly eager ⟨*impatient* to be on his way⟩ — **im·pa·tience** \-shən(t)s\ *n* — **im·pa·tient·ly** *adv*

im·peach \im-'pēch\ *vb* **1** : to charge a public official formally with misconduct in office **2** : to cast doubt on; *esp* : to challenge the credibility of ⟨*impeach* his honesty⟩ — **im·peach·a·ble** \-'pē-chə-bəl\ *adj* — **im·peach·ment** \-'pēch-mənt\ *n*

im·pec·ca·ble \(')im-'pek-ə-bəl\ *adj* : free from fault or blame : FLAWLESS — **im·pec·ca·bil·i·ty** \(ˌ)im-ˌpek-ə-'bil-ət-ē\ *n* — **im·pec·ca·bly** \(')im-'pek-ə-blē\ *adv*

im·pe·cu·ni·ous \ˌim-pi-'kyü-nē-əs, -nyəs\ *adj* : having little or no money : POOR — **im·pe·cu·ni·ous·ness** *n*

im·pede \im-'pēd\ *vb* [from Latin *impedire* meaning literally "to entangle or shackle the feet", from *in-* "in" and *ped-*, the stem of *pes* "foot", from the same source as English *foot*] : to interfere with the progress of : BLOCK, HINDER ⟨traffic *impeded* by heavy rain⟩ — **im·ped·er** *n*

im·ped·i·ment \im-'ped-ə-mənt\ *n* **1** : something that impedes, hinders, or obstructs **2** : a defect in speech

im·pel \im-'pel\ *vb* **im·pelled**; **im·pel·ling** **1** : to urge or drive forward or into action ⟨felt *impelled* to speak up⟩ **2** : PROPEL — **im·pel·ler** \-'pel-ər\ *n*

im·pend \im-'pend\ *vb* : to threaten to occur immediately ⟨*impending* danger⟩

im·pen·e·tra·ble \(')im-'pen-ə-trə-bəl\ *adj* **1** : incapable of being penetrated ⟨*impenetrable* jungle⟩ **2** : incapable of being understood ⟨*impenetrable* mystery⟩ — **im·pen·e·tra·bil·i·ty** \(ˌ)im-ˌpen-ə-trə-'bil-ət-ē\ *n* — **im·pen·e·tra·ble·ness** *n* — **im·pen·e·tra·bly** \-blē\ *adv*

im·pen·i·tent \(')im-'pen-ə-tənt\ *adj* : not penitent : not sorry for having done wrong — **im·pen·i·tence** \-tən(t)s\ *n* — **im·pen·i·tent·ly** *adv*

[1]**im·per·a·tive** \im-'per-ət-iv\ *adj* **1 a** : of, relating to, or constituting the grammatical mood that expresses a command, request, or encouragement **b** : being or expressing a command ⟨an *imperative* tone of voice⟩ **2** : not to be avoided or evaded : URGENT ⟨*imperative* business⟩ — **im·per·a·tive·ly** *adv* — **im·per·a·tive·ness** *n*

[2]**imperative** *n* **1** : the imperative mood of a verb or a verb in this mood **2 a** : COMMAND, ORDER **b** : an obligatory act or duty

im·per·cep·ti·ble \ˌim-pər-'sep-tə-bəl\ *adj* : not perceptible; *esp* : too slight to be perceived ⟨an *imperceptible* difference⟩ — **im·per·cep·ti·bil·i·ty** \-ˌsep-tə-'bil-ət-ē\ *n* — **im·per·cep·ti·bly** \-'sep-tə-blē\ *adv*

[1]**im·per·fect** \(')im-'pər-fikt\ *adj* **1** : not perfect : DEFECTIVE **2** : of, relating to, or constituting a verb tense used to designate a continuing state or an incomplete action esp. in the past — **im·per·fect·ly** \-fik-(t)lē\ *adv* — **im·per·fect·ness** \-fik(t)-nəs\ *n*

[2]**imperfect** *n* : the imperfect tense of a verb or a verb in this tense

imperfect flower *n* : a flower with stamens or pistils but not both

im·per·fec·tion \ˌim-pər-'fek-shən\ *n* **1** : the quality or state of being imperfect **2** : FAULT, BLEMISH

[1]**im·pe·ri·al** \im-'pir-ē-əl\ *adj* **1** : of, relating to, or befitting an empire or an emperor ⟨by *imperial* decree⟩ ⟨*imperial* splendor⟩ **2** : of unusual size or excellence — **im·pe·ri·al·ly** \-ē-ə-lē\ *adv*

2imperial *n* : a pointed beard growing below the lower lip

im·pe·ri·al·ism \im-'pir-ē-ə-ˌliz-əm\ *n* **1** : imperial government or authority **2** : the policy of extending the power or dominion of one nation over the political or economic life of other areas — **im·pe·ri·al·ist** \-ləst\ *n* — **imperialist** *or* **im·pe·ri·al·is·tic** \im-ˌpir-ē-ə-'lis-tik\ *adj* — **im·pe·ri·al·is·ti·cal·ly** \-ti-k(ə-)lē\ *adv*

im·per·il \im-'per-əl\ *vb* **-iled** *or* **-illed**; **-il·ing** *or* **-il·ling** : ENDANGER — **im·per·il·ment** \-əl-mənt\ *n*

im·pe·ri·ous \im-'pir-ē-əs\ *adj* **1** : COMMANDING, LORDLY **2** : ARROGANT, DOMINEERING **3** : IMPERATIVE, URGENT ⟨an *imperious* need⟩ — **im·pe·ri·ous·ly** *adv* — **im·pe·ri·ous·ness** *n*

im·per·ish·a·ble \(')im-'per-ish-ə-bəl\ *adj* : not perishable or subject to decay : INDESTRUCTIBLE — **im·per·ish·a·bil·i·ty** \(ˌ)im-ˌper-ish-ə-'bil-ət-ē\ *n* — **im·per·ish·a·bly** \(')im-'per-ish-ə-blē\ *adv*

im·per·ma·nent \(')im-'pər-mə-nənt\ *adj* : not permanent : TRANSIENT — **im·per·ma·nence** \-nən(t)s\ *n* — **im·per·ma·nent·ly** *adv*

im·per·me·a·ble \(')im-'pər-mē-ə-bəl\ *adj* : not permitting passage (as of a fluid) through its substance — **im·per·me·a·bil·i·ty** \(ˌ)im-ˌpər-mē-ə-'bil-ət-ē\ *n* — **im·per·me·a·bly** \(')im-'pər-mē-ə-blē\ *adv*

im·per·mis·si·ble \ˌim-pər-'mis-ə-bəl\ *adj* : not permissible

im·per·son·al \(')im-'pər-s(ə-)nəl\ *adj* **1** : having no expressed subject or no subject other than "it" ⟨*rained* in "it rained" is an *impersonal* verb⟩ **2** : not referring to a particular person ⟨*impersonal* criticism⟩ **3** : not involving personal feelings ⟨an *impersonal* professional attitude⟩ **4** : not existing as a person ⟨an *impersonal* deity⟩ — **im·per·son·al·i·ty** \(ˌ)im-ˌpər-sə-'nal-ət-ē\ *n* — **im·per·son·al·ize** \(')im-'pər-s(ə-)nə-ˌlīz\ *vb* — **im·per·son·al·ly** \-s(ə-)nə-lē\ *adv*

im·per·son·ate \im-'pər-sə-ˌnāt\ *vb* **1** : to pretend to be some other person ⟨*impersonate* a policeman⟩ **2** : PERSONIFY — **im·per·son·a·tion** \-ˌpər-sə-'nā-shən\ *n* — **im·per·son·a·tor** \-'pər-sə-ˌnāt-ər\ *n*

im·per·ti·nence \(')im-'pərt-ə-nən(t)s\ *also* **im·per·ti·nen·cy** \-nən-sē\ *n, pl* **-nences** *also* **-nencies** **1** : IRRELEVANCE **2 a** : INCIVILITY, INSOLENCE **b** : a rude or impudent act or remark

im·per·ti·nent \-nənt\ *adj* **1** : not pertinent : IRRELEVANT **2 a** : RUDE, INSOLENT **b** : SAUCY, IMPUDENT — **im·per·ti·nent·ly** *adv*

im·per·turb·a·ble \ˌim-pər-'tər-bə-bəl\ *adj* : not easily disturbed or excited : CALM — **im·per·turb·a·bil·i·ty** \-ˌtər-bə-'bil-ət-ē\ *n* — **im·per·turb·a·bly** \-'tər-bə-blē\ *adv*

im·per·vi·ous \(')im-'pər-vē-əs\ *adj* **1** : not allowing entrance or passage : IMPENETRABLE ⟨*impervious* soils⟩ **2** : not capable of being affected or disturbed ⟨*impervious* to criticism⟩ — **im·per·vi·ous·ly** *adv* — **im·per·vi·ous·ness** *n*

im·pe·ti·go \ˌim-pə-'tē-gō, -'tī-\ *n* : a contagious skin disease characterized by vesicles, pustules, and yellowish crusts

im·pet·u·ous \im-'pech-(ə-)wəs\ *adj* **1** : marked by force and violence **2** : IMPULSIVE, RASH — **im·pet·u·os·i·ty** \im-ˌpech-ə-'wäs-ət-ē\ *n* — **im·pet·u·ous·ly** *adv* — **im·pet·u·ous·ness** *n*

im·pe·tus \'im-pət-əs\ *n* **1 a** : a driving force : IMPULSE **b** : INCENTIVE, STIMULUS **2** : MOMENTUM

im·pi·e·ty \(')im-'pī-ət-ē\ *n, pl* **-ties** **1** : lack of piety **2** : an impious act

im·pinge \im-'pinj\ *vb* **1** : to strike or dash esp. with a sharp collision ⟨sound waves *impinge* on the eardrums⟩ **2** : ENCROACH, INFRINGE ⟨*impinge* on another's rights⟩ — **im·pinge·ment** \-mənt\ *n*

im·pi·ous \'im-pē-əs, (')im-'pī-\ *adj* **1** : not pious : IRREVERENT, PROFANE **2** : DISRESPECTFUL — **im·pi·ous·ly** *adv*

imp·ish \'im-pish\ *adj* : of or relating to an imp; *esp* : MISCHIEVOUS — **imp·ish·ly** *adv* — **imp·ish·ness** *n*

im·plac·a·ble \(')im-'plak-ə-bəl, -'plā-kə-\ *adj* : not capable of being pacified ⟨an *implacable* enemy⟩ — **im·plac·a·bly** \-blē\ *adv*

im·plant \im-'plant\ *vb* **1** : to fix or set securely or deeply ⟨*implant* a habit of study in a child⟩ **2** : to insert in a living site for growth or absorption — **im·plan·ta·tion** \ˌim-ˌplan-'tā-shən\ *n* — **im·plant·er** \im-'plant-ər\ *n*

im·plau·si·ble \(')im-'plȯ-zə-bəl\ *adj* : UNLIKELY — **im·plau·si·bil·i·ty** \(ˌ)im-ˌplȯ-zə-'bil-ət-ē\ *n* — **im·plau·si·bly** \(')im-'plȯ-zə-blē\ *adv*

1im·ple·ment \'im-plə-mənt\ *n* : an article intended for use in work : TOOL, INSTRUMENT ⟨*implements* of war⟩

2im·ple·ment \-ˌment\ *vb* : to carry out : put into effect : FULFILL ⟨*implement* the provisions of a treaty⟩ — **im·ple·men·ta·tion** \ˌim-plə-mən-'tā-shən, -ˌmen-\ *n*

im·pli·cate \'im-plə-ˌkāt\ *vb* : to bring into connection : INVOLVE ⟨his confession *implicated* others in the crime⟩

im·pli·ca·tion \ˌim-plə-'kā-shən\ *n* **1** : the act of implicating : the state of being implicated **2 a** : the act of implying : the state of being implied **b** : something implied

im·plic·it \im-'plis-ət\ *adj* **1** : understood though not directly stated ⟨an *implicit* agreement⟩ **2** : COMPLETE, UNQUESTIONING ⟨has *implicit* confidence in him⟩ — **im·plic·it·ly** *adv* — **im·plic·it·ness** *n*

im·plode \im-'plōd\ *vb* : to burst inward — **im·plo·sion** \-'plō-zhən\ *n* — **im·plo·sive** \-'plō-siv, -ziv\ *adj*

im·plore \im-'plō(ə)r, -'plȯ(ə)r\ *vb* **1** : to call on : BESEECH ⟨*implored* him to make peace⟩ **2** : to call or pray for : ENTREAT ⟨*implored* her help⟩

im·ply \im-'plī\ *vb* **im·plied**; **im·ply·ing** **1** : to include or involve as a natural or necessary though not expressly stated part or effect ⟨military maneuvers *implying* threats of war⟩ ⟨rights *imply* obligations⟩ **2** : to express indirectly : suggest rather than say plainly ⟨remarks that *implied* consent⟩ — **im·plied·ly** \-'plī(-ə)d-lē\ *adv*

im·po·lite \ˌim-pə-'līt\ *adj* : not polite : RUDE — **im·po·lite·ly** *adv* — **im·po·lite·ness** *n*

im·pon·der·a·ble \(')im-'pän-d(ə-)rə-bəl\ *adj* : incapable of being evaluated — **imponderable** *n*

1im·port \im-'pōrt, -'pȯrt, 'im-ˌ\ *vb* **1** : MEAN, SIGNIFY **2** : to be important : MATTER **3** : to bring in or introduce from a foreign country; *esp* : to bring in goods to be resold ⟨*imports* coffee⟩ ⟨*imported* sports cars⟩ — **im·port·er** *n*

2im·port \'im-ˌpōrt, -ˌpȯrt\ *n* **1** : MEANING **2** : IMPORTANCE **3** : something imported

im·por·tant \im-'pȯrt-ənt\ *adj* **1** : having great meaning or influence : SIGNIFICANT ⟨*important* remarks⟩ ⟨an *important* change⟩ **2** : having considerable power or authority ⟨an *important* official⟩ **3 :** POMPOUS — **im·por·tance** \-ən(t)s\ *n* — **im·por·tant·ly** *adv*

im·por·ta·tion \ˌim-ˌpōr-'tā-shən, -ˌpȯr-, -pər-\ *n* **1 :** the act or practice of importing **2 :** IMPORT 3

im·por·tu·nate \im-'pȯrch-(ə-)nət\ *adj* **:** overly persistent in requests or demands — **im·por·tu·nate·ly** *adv* — **im·por·tu·nate·ness** *n*

im·por·tune \ˌim-pər-'t(y)ün, im-'pȯr-chən\ *vb* **:** to press, beg, or urge with troublesome persistence — **im·por·tun·er** *n*

im·por·tu·ni·ty \ˌim-pər-'t(y)ü-nət-ē\ *n, pl* **-ties** **:** the quality or state of being importunate **:** persistence in requests or demands

im·pose \im-'pōz\ *vb* **1 a :** to establish or apply as a charge or penalty **:** LEVY ⟨*impose* a fine⟩ ⟨*impose* a tax⟩ **b :** to establish by force ⟨*imposed* his will on them⟩ **2 :** to use trickery or deception to get what one wants ⟨*impose* on an ignorant person⟩ **3 :** to take unwarranted advantage ⟨*impose* on a friend's good nature⟩ — **im·pos·er** *n*

im·pos·ing \im-'pō-zing\ *adj* **:** impressive in size, dignity, or grandeur ⟨an *imposing* building⟩ — **im·pos·ing·ly** \-zing-lē\ *adv*

im·po·si·tion \ˌim-pə-'zish-ən\ *n* **1 :** the act of imposing **2 a :** something imposed; *esp* **:** LEVY, TAX **b :** an overly burdensome requirement or demand **3 :** DECEPTION, TRICK

im·pos·si·bil·i·ty \(ˌ)im-ˌpäs-ə-'bil-ət-ē\ *n, pl* **-ties** **1 :** the quality or state of being impossible **2 :** something impossible

im·pos·si·ble \(')im-'päs-ə-bəl\ *adj* **1 a :** incapable of being or of occurring **b :** enormously difficult **:** HOPELESS ⟨an *impossible* situation⟩ **2 a :** extremely undesirable ⟨a treaty with *impossible* conditions⟩ **b :** difficult to deal with ⟨an *impossible* person⟩ — **im·pos·si·bly** \-blē\ *adv*

im·post \'im-ˌpōst\ *n* **:** TAX; *esp* **:** a customs duty

im·pos·tor \im-'päs-tər\ *n* **:** a person who deceptively represents himself as being someone else

im·pos·ture \im-'päs-chər\ *n* **:** fraudulent impersonation

im·po·tent \'im-pət-ənt\ *adj* **1 :** not potent **:** lacking in power, strength, or vigor **:** HELPLESS **2 :** unable to copulate; *also* **:** STERILE — usu. used of males — **im·po·tence** \-pət-ən(t)s\ *n* — **im·po·tent·ly** *adv*

im·pound \im-'paủnd\ *vb* **1 :** to shut up in a pound **:** CONFINE **2 :** to seize and hold in legal custody ⟨*impound* funds pending decision of a case⟩ **3 :** to collect in a reservoir ⟨*impound* water⟩ — **im·pound·ment** \-'paủn(d)-mənt\ *n*

im·pov·er·ish \im-'päv-(ə-)rish\ *vb* **1 :** to make poor **2 :** to deprive of strength, richness, or fertility ⟨*impoverished* soil⟩ — **im·pov·er·ish·ment** \-mənt\ *n*

im·prac·ti·ca·ble \(')im-'prak-ti-kə-bəl\ *adj* **:** not practicable **:** difficult to put into practice or use ⟨an *impracticable* plan⟩ — **im·prac·ti·ca·bil·i·ty** \(ˌ)im-ˌprak-ti-kə-'bil-ət-ē\ *n* — **im·prac·ti·ca·bly** \(')im-'prak-ti-kə-blē\ *adv*

im·prac·ti·cal \(')im-'prak-ti-kəl\ *adj* **1 :** not practical; *esp* **:** incapable of dealing sensibly or prudently with practical matters **2 :** IMPRACTICABLE — **im·prac·ti·cal·i·ty** \(ˌ)im-ˌprak-ti-'kal-ət-ē\ *n* — **im·prac·ti·cal·ness** \(')im-'prak-ti-kəl-nəs\ *n*

im·pre·cate \'im-pri-ˌkāt\ *vb* **:** to invoke evil on **:** CURSE — **im·pre·ca·tion** \ˌim-pri-'kā-shən\ *n* — **im·pre·ca·to·ry** \'im-pri-kə-ˌtōr-ē, im-'prek-ə-, -ˌtȯr-\ *adj*

im·pre·cise \ˌim-pri-'sīs\ *adj* **:** not precise — **im·pre·cise·ly** *adv* — **im·pre·cise·ness** *n* — **im·pre·ci·sion** \-'sizh-ən\ *n*

im·preg·na·ble \im-'preg-nə-bəl\ *adj* **:** incapable of being taken by assault **:** UNCONQUERABLE — **im·preg·na·bly** \-blē\ *adv*

im·preg·nate \im-'preg-ˌnāt\ *vb* **1 a** (1) **:** to make pregnant (2) **:** to introduce sperm cells into **b :** to make fertile or fruitful **2 :** to cause a substance to be filled, permeated, or saturated ⟨*impregnate* wood with preservative⟩ — **im·preg·na·tion** \ˌim-ˌpreg-'nā-shən\ *n* — **im·preg·na·tor** \im-'preg-ˌnāt-ər\ *n*

im·pre·sa·rio \ˌim-prə-'sär-ē-ˌō, -'sar-, -'ser-\ *n, pl* **-ri·os** **:** the manager of an opera or concert company

[1]**im·press** \im-'pres\ *vb* **1 :** STAMP, PRESS **2 :** to produce a vivid impression **:** affect forcibly or deeply — **im·press·i·bil·i·ty** \-ˌpres-ə-'bil-ət-ē\ *n* — **im·press·i·ble** \im-'pres-ə-bəl\ *adj* — **im·press·i·bly** \-'pres-ə-blē\ *adv*

[2]**im·press** \'im-ˌpres\ *n* **1 :** the act of impressing **2 :** a mark made by pressure **:** IMPRINT **3 :** a characteristic or special mark **:** STAMP **4 :** IMPRESSION, EFFECT

[3]**im·press** \im-'pres\ *vb* **1 :** to seize for public service; *esp* **:** to force into naval service **2 :** to enlist the aid or services of ⟨*impress* helpers into a fund-raising campaign⟩

im·pres·sion \im-'presh-ən\ *n* **1 :** the act or process of impressing **2 a :** a stamp, form, or figure impressed **b :** an influence or effect on feeling, sense, or mind ⟨the boy made a good *impression* on us⟩ **3 :** a characteristic trait or feature resulting from influence **4 a :** a single copy made by pressing material being printed onto a surface **b :** all the copies (as of a book) printed at one time **5 :** a vague recollection, belief, or opinion — **im·pres·sion·al** \-'presh-(ə-)nəl\ *adj*

im·pres·sion·a·ble \im-'presh-(ə-)nə-bəl\ *adj* **:** easily impressed **:** easily molded or influenced — **im·pres·sion·a·bil·i·ty** \-ˌpresh-(ə-)nə-'bil-ət-ē\ *n* — **im·pres·sion·a·ble·ness** \-'presh-(ə-)nə-bəl-nəs\ *n* — **im·pres·sion·a·bly** \-blē\ *adv*

im·pres·sion·ism \im-'presh-ə-ˌniz-əm\ *n* **1** *often cap* **:** a theory or practice in modern painting of depicting objects by means of dabs or strokes of primary colors to simulate actual reflected light **2 :** a style of musical composition designed to create moods through rich and varied harmonies — **im·pres·sion·ist** \-'presh-(ə-)nəst\ *n or adj* — **im·pres·sion·is·tic** \-ˌpresh-ə-'nis-tik\ *adj* — **impres·sion·is·ti·cal·ly** \-ti-k(ə-)lē\ *adv*

im·pres·sive \im-'pres-iv\ *adj* **:** making or tending to make a deep impression ⟨an *impressive* speech⟩ — **im·pres·sive·ly** *adv* — **im·pres·sive·ness** *n*

im·press·ment \im-'pres-mənt\ *n* **:** the act of seizing for public use or of impressing into public service

im·pri·ma·tur \ˌim-prə-'mät-ər\ *n* **1 a :** a license to print or publish **b :** official approval of a publication by a censor **2 :** SANCTION, APPROVAL

[1]**im·print** \im-'print, 'im-ˌ\ *vb* **1 :** to mark by or as if by pressure **:** STAMP, IMPRESS **2 :** to fix firmly ⟨her smile was *imprinted* on his memory⟩

[2]**im·print** \'im-ˌprint\ *n* **1 :** something imprinted or printed **:** IMPRESSION **2 :** a publisher's name often with address and date of publication printed on a title page

im·pris·on \im-'priz-ən\ *vb* **-pris·oned**; **-pris·on·ing** \-'priz-(ə-)ning\ **:** to put in or as if in prison **:** CONFINE — **im·pris·on·ment** \-'priz-ən-mənt\ *n*

im·prob·a·ble \(')im-'präb-ə-bəl\ *adj* **:** unlikely to be true or to occur — **im·prob·a·bil·i·ty** \(ˌ)im-ˌpräb-ə-'bil-ət-ē\ *n* — **im·prob·a·ble·ness** \(')im-'präb-ə-bəl-nəs\ *n* — **im·prob·a·bly** \-blē\ *adv*

im·promp·tu \im-'präm(p)-t(y)ü\ *adj* [from French,

I

from th atin phrase *in promptu* meaning "in readiness"] : not prepared or rehearsed : IMPROVISED, EXTEMPORANEOUS ⟨an *impromptu* speech⟩ — **impromptu** *adv or n*

im·prop·er \(')im-'präp-ər\ *adj* **1** : not fit or suitable ⟨*improper* dress for the occasion⟩ **2** : INCORRECT, INACCURATE ⟨*improper* deduction⟩ ⟨*improper* address on a letter⟩ **3** : not in accordance with good taste or good manners ⟨*improper* language⟩ — **im·prop·er·ly** *adv* — **im·prop·er·ness** *n*

improper fraction *n* : a fraction whose numerator is equal to or larger than the denominator

im·pro·pri·e·ty \,im-prə-'prī-ət-ē\ *n, pl* **-ties** **1** : the quality or state of being improper **2** : an improper or indecorous act or remark

im·prove \im-'prüv\ *vb* **1** : to make greater in amount or degree : INCREASE **2** : to increase in value or quality : make or grow better ⟨*improved* his health⟩ **3** : to make good use of ⟨*improved* their time by studying⟩ **4** : to make improvements ⟨*improve* on the carburetor⟩ — **im·prov·a·ble** \-'prü-və-bəl\ *adj* — **im·prov·er** *n*

im·prove·ment \im-'prüv-mənt\ *n* **1** : the act or process of improving **2 a** : the state of being improved; *esp* : increased value or excellence **b** : a result of improvement **c** : something that increases value ⟨make *improvements* in an old house⟩

im·prov·i·dent \(')im-'präv-əd-ənt, -ə-,dent\ *adj* : not providing for the future : THRIFTLESS — **im·prov·i·dence** \-əd-ən(t)s, -ə-,den(t)s\ *n* — **im·prov·i·dent·ly** *adv*

im·pro·vise \,im-prə-'vīz\ *vb* **1** : to compose, recite, or sing without preparation **2** : to make, invent, or arrange offhand — **im·prov·i·sa·tion** \im-,präv-ə-'zā-shən, ,im-prə-və-\ *n* — **im·pro·vis·er** \,im-prə-'vī-zər\ *n*

im·pru·dent \(')im-'prüd-ənt\ *adj* : not prudent : RASH, UNWISE — **im·pru·dence** \-ən(t)s\ *n* — **im·pru·dent·ly** *adv*

im·pu·dent \'im-pyəd-ənt\ *adj* : showing contempt for or disregard of others : INSOLENT, DISRESPECTFUL — **im·pu·dence** \-ən(t)s\ *n* — **im·pu·dent·ly** *adv*

im·pugn \im-'pyün\ *vb* : to attack as false : cast doubt on ⟨*impugn* the motives of an opponent⟩ — **im·pugn·er** \-'pyü-nər\ *n*

im·pulse \'im-,pəls\ *n* **1 a** : a force that starts a body into motion **b** : the motion produced by an impulse **2** : a sudden spontaneous notion to do something ⟨an *impulse* to run away⟩ ⟨acts on *impulse*⟩ **3** : a signal transmitted through nerves and muscles that conveys information and that results in altered activity of a bodily part

im·pul·sion \im-'pəl-shən\ *n* **1 a** : the action of impelling : the state of being impelled **b** : an impelling force **2** : IMPULSE 2

im·pul·sive \im-'pəl-siv\ *adj* **1** : having the power of driving or impelling **2** : acting or liable to act on impulse : moved or caused by an impulse : IMPETUOUS — **im·pul·sive·ly** *adv* — **im·pul·sive·ness** *n*

im·pu·ni·ty \im-'pyü-nət-ē\ *n* : freedom from punishment, harm, or loss

im·pure \(')im-'pyu̇(ə)r\ *adj* **1** : not pure : UNCLEAN, DIRTY **2** : UNCHASTE, OBSCENE **3** : mixed with some other usu. inferior substance ⟨an *impure* chemical⟩ — **im·pure·ly** *adv* — **im·pure·ness** *n*

ə abut	ər further	a back	ā bake	
ä cot, cart	au̇ out	ch chin	e less	ē easy
g gift	i trip	ī life	j joke	ng sing	ō flow
ȯ flaw	ȯi coin	th thin	th this	ü loot
u̇ foot	y yet	yü few	yu̇ furious	zh vision

im·pu·ri·ty \(')im-'pyu̇r-ət-ē\ *n, pl* **-ties** **1** : the quality or state of being impure **2** : something that is impure or that makes impure ⟨remove *impurities* from water⟩

im·pute \im-'pyüt\ *vb* **1** : to place the responsibility or blame for : CHARGE ⟨*imputed* the ruin of their plans to him⟩ **2** : to credit to : ATTRIBUTE ⟨*impute* the mistake to ignorance⟩ — **im·put·a·ble** \-'pyüt-ə-bəl\ *adj* — **im·pu·ta·tion** \,im-pyə-'tā-shən\ *n*

¹in \(')in, ən\ *prep* **1 a** : enclosed or surrounded by : WITHIN ⟨*in* a box⟩ **b** : INTO 1a ⟨went *in* the house⟩ **c** : DURING ⟨*in* summer⟩ **2** : by means of : WITH ⟨written *in* pencil⟩ **3 a** — used as a function word to indicate manner, state, or situation ⟨alike *in* some respects⟩ ⟨left *in* a hurry⟩ **b** : INTO 2a ⟨broke *in* pieces⟩ **4** — used as a function word to indicate purpose ⟨said *in* reply⟩

²in \'in\ *adv* **1 a** : to or toward the inside ⟨went *in* and closed the door⟩ **b** : to or toward a place ⟨flew *in* on the first plane⟩ **c** : NEAR ⟨play close *in*⟩ **d** : into the midst of something ⟨mix *in* the flour⟩ **e** : to or at its proper place ⟨fit a piece *in*⟩ **f** : into line ⟨fell *in* with our plans⟩ **2 a** : WITHIN **b** : on good terms ⟨he's *in* with the teacher⟩ **c** : in fashion **d** : at hand : on hand ⟨the evidence was all *in*⟩ ⟨harvests are *in*⟩

³in \'in\ *adj* **1 a** : being inside or within ⟨the *in* part⟩ **b** : being in power ⟨the *in* party⟩ **2** : directed or bound inward : INCOMING ⟨the *in* train⟩ **3 a** : keenly aware of and responsive to what is new and smart ⟨the *in* crowd⟩ **b** : highly fashionable ⟨the *in* thing to do⟩ ⟨the *in* place to go⟩

⁴in \'in\ *n* **1** : one who is in office or power **2** : INFLUENCE, PULL ⟨have an *in* with important people⟩

¹in- *or* **il-** *or* **im-** *or* **ir-** *prefix* : not : NON-, UN- — usu. *il-* before *l* ⟨*il*logical⟩ and *im-* before *b, m,* or *p* ⟨*im*balance⟩ ⟨*im*moral⟩ ⟨*im*practical⟩ and *ir-* before *r* ⟨*ir*reducible⟩ and *in-* before other sounds ⟨*in*conclusive⟩

²in- *or* **il-** *or* **im-** *or* **ir-** *prefix* **1** : in : within : into : toward : on ⟨*im*mingle⟩ ⟨*ir*radiance⟩ — usu. *il-* before *l*, *im-* before *b, m,* or *p*, *ir-* before *r*, and *in-* before other sounds **2** : ¹EN- ⟨*im*peril⟩ ⟨*in*spirit⟩

-in \ən\ *n suffix* : chemical compound ⟨stear*in*⟩ ⟨insul*in*⟩ ⟨niac*in*⟩

in *abbr* inch

IN *abbr* Indiana

in·abil·i·ty \,in-ə-'bil-ət-ē\ *n* : the condition of being unable : lack of ability, power, or means

in·ac·ces·si·ble \,in-ik-'ses-ə-bəl, ,in-ak-\ *adj* : not accessible — **in·ac·ces·si·bil·i·ty** \-,ses-ə-'bil-ət-ē\ *n* — **in·ac·ces·si·bly** \-'ses-ə-blē\ *adv*

in·ac·cu·ra·cy \(')in-'ak-yə-rə-sē\ *n, pl* **-cies** **1** : the quality or state of being inaccurate **2** : MISTAKE, ERROR

in·ac·cu·rate \-rət\ *adj* : not accurate : not exact : FAULTY — **in·ac·cu·rate·ly** *adv*

in·ac·tion \(')in-'ak-shən\ *n* : lack of action or activity : IDLENESS

in·ac·ti·vate \(')in-'ak-tə-,vāt\ *vb* : to make inactive — **in·ac·ti·va·tion** \(,)in-,ak-tə-'vā-shən\ *n*

in·ac·tive \(')in-'ak-tiv\ *adj* **1** : INDOLENT, SLUGGISH **2 a** : being out of use or activity **b** : relating to members of the armed forces who are not performing or available for military duties — **in·ac·tive·ly** *adv* — **in·ac·tiv·i·ty** \,in-,ak-'tiv-ət-ē\ *n*

in·ad·e·quate \(')in-'ad-i-kwət\ *adj* : not adequate : INSUFFICIENT — **in·ad·e·qua·cy** \-kwə-sē\ *n* — **in·ad·e·quate·ly** *adv* — **in·ad·e·quate·ness** *n*

in·ad·mis·si·ble \,in-əd-'mis-ə-bəl\ *adj* : not admissible — **in·ad·mis·si·bil·i·ty** \-,mis-ə-'bil-ət-ē\ *n* — **in·ad·mis·si·bly** \-'mis-ə-blē\ *adv*

in·ad·ver·tence \ˌin-əd-'vərt-ən(t)s\ *n* **1** : INATTENTION **2** : a result of inattention : OVERSIGHT

in·ad·ver·ten·cy \-'vərt-ən-sē\ *n, pl* **-cies** : INADVERTENCE

in·ad·ver·tent \-'vərt-ənt\ *adj* **1** : HEEDLESS, INATTENTIVE **2** : UNINTENTIONAL — **in·ad·ver·tent·ly** *adv*

in·ad·vis·a·ble \ˌin-əd-'vī-zə-bəl\ *adj* : not advisable : UNWISE — **in·ad·vis·a·bil·i·ty** \-ˌvī-zə-'bil-ət-ē\ *n*

in·alien·a·ble \(')in-'āl-yə-nə-bəl, -'ā-lē-ə-nə-\ *adj* : not capable of being taken away, given up, or transferred ⟨*inalienable* rights⟩ — **in·alien·a·bly** \(')in-'āl-yə-nə-blē, -'ā-lē-ə-nə-\ *adv*

inane \in-'ān\ *adj* **1** : EMPTY, INSUBSTANTIAL **2** : lacking meaning or point : SILLY — **inane·ly** *adv* — **inane·ness** \-'ān-nəs\ *n* — **inan·i·ty** \-'an-ət-ē\ *n*

in·an·i·mate \(')in-'an-ə-mət\ *adj* **1 a** : not endowed with life ⟨stones are *inanimate*⟩ **b** : lacking consciousness or power of motion ⟨*inanimate* organisms⟩ **2** : not animated or lively : DULL — **in·an·i·mate·ly** *adv* — **in·an·i·mate·ness** *n*

in·a·ni·tion \ˌin-ə-'nish-ən\ *n* : exhaustion from lack of food and water

in·ap·pli·ca·ble \(')in-'ap-li-kə-bəl, ˌin-ə-'plik-ə-\ *adj* : not applicable : IRRELEVANT — **in·ap·pli·ca·bil·i·ty** \(ˌ)in-ˌap-li-kə-'bil-ət-ē, ˌin-ə-ˌplik-ə-\ *n* — **in·ap·pli·ca·bly** \(')in-'ap-li-kə-blē, ˌin-ə-'plik-ə-\ *adv*

in·ap·pre·cia·ble \ˌin-ə-'prē-shə-bəl\ *adj* : very slight : IMPERCEPTIBLE — **in·ap·pre·cia·bly** \-blē\ *adv*

in·ap·pro·pri·ate \ˌin-ə-'prō-prē-ət\ *adj* : not appropriate : UNSUITABLE — **in·ap·pro·pri·ate·ly** *adv* — **in·ap·pro·pri·ate·ness** *n*

in·apt \(')in-'apt\ *adj* **1** : not suitable **2** : INEPT — **in·apt·ly** *adv* — **in·apt·ness** \-'ap(t)-nəs\ *n*

in·ap·ti·tude \-'ap-tə-ˌt(y)üd\ *n* : lack of aptitude

in·ar·tic·u·late \ˌin-är-'tik-yə-lət\ *adj* **1 a** : not understandable as spoken words ⟨*inarticulate* cries⟩ **b** : incapable of speech : MUTE **c** : incapable of being expressed ⟨*inarticulate* longings⟩ **2** : incapable of giving clear expression to ideas or feelings **3** : not jointed or segmented — **in·ar·tic·u·late·ly** *adv* — **in·ar·tic·u·late·ness** *n*

in·ar·tis·tic \ˌin-är-'tis-tik\ *adj* : not artistic — **in·ar·tis·ti·cal·ly** \-ti-k(ə-)lē\ *adv*

in·as·much as \ˌin-əz-ˌməch-əz\ *conj* **1** : to the extent that **2** : in view of the fact that : SINCE

in·at·ten·tion \ˌin-ə-'ten-chən\ *n* : failure to pay attention — **in·at·ten·tive** \-'tent-iv\ *adj* — **in·at·ten·tive·ly** *adv* — **in·at·ten·tive·ness** *n*

in·au·di·ble \(')in-'ȯd-ə-bəl\ *adj* : not audible — **in·au·di·bil·i·ty** \(ˌ)in-ˌȯd-ə-'bil-ət-ē\ *n* — **in·au·di·bly** \(')in-'ȯd-ə-blē\ *adv*

1in·au·gu·ral \in-'ȯ-gyə-rəl, -g(ə-)rəl\ *adj* **1** : of or relating to an inauguration ⟨*inaugural* address⟩ ⟨*inaugural* ball⟩ **2** : marking a beginning

2inaugural *n* **1** : an inaugural address **2** : INAUGURATION

in·au·gu·rate \in-'ȯ-g(y)ə-ˌrāt\ *vb* **1** : to introduce into office with ceremonies : INSTALL ⟨*inaugurate* a president⟩ **2** : to celebrate the opening of ⟨*inaugurate* a new gym⟩ **3** : BEGIN, INTRODUCE ⟨*inaugurate* reform⟩ — **in·au·gu·ra·tor** \-ˌrāt-ər\ *n*

in·au·gu·ra·tion \in-ˌȯ-g(y)ə-'rā-shən\ *n* : an act of inaugurating; *esp* : a ceremonial introduction into office

in·aus·pi·cious \ˌin-ȯ-'spish-əs\ *adj* : not auspicious — **in·aus·pi·cious·ly** *adv* — **in·aus·pi·cious·ness** *n*

in·board \'in-ˌbōrd, -ˌbȯrd\ *adv* **1** : inside a ship's hull : toward the center line of a ship **2** : toward the inside **3** : in a position closer or closest to the center line of an aircraft — **inboard** *adj*

in·born \'in-'bȯrn\ *adj* **1** : born in one : not acquired by training or experience : NATURAL **2** : genetically determined : INHERITED, HEREDITARY ⟨an *inborn* tendency toward mental instability⟩ ***syn*** see INNATE ***ant*** acquired

in·bound \'in-'baủnd\ *adj* : inward bound ⟨*inbound* traffic⟩

in·bred \'in-'bred\ *adj* **1 a** : present from birth **b** : established by early teaching or training **2** : subjected to or produced by inbreeding

in·breed·ing \'in-ˌbrēd-ing\ *n* : the interbreeding of closely related individuals esp. to preserve desirable and eliminate unfavorable characters — **in·breed** \'in-'brēd\ *vb*

inc *abbr* **1** incorporated **2** increase

In·ca \'ing-kə\ *n* **1** : a noble or a member of the ruling family of an Indian empire of Peru before the Spanish conquest **2** : an Indian of the leading people of the empire of the Incas — **In·can** \-kən\ *adj*

in·cal·cu·la·ble \(')in-'kal-kyə-lə-bəl\ *adj* **1** : not capable of being calculated; *esp* : too large or numerous to be calculated **2** : not capable of being known in advance : UNCERTAIN — **in·cal·cu·la·bil·i·ty** \(ˌ)in-ˌkal-kyə-lə-'bil-ət-ē\ *n* — **in·cal·cu·la·bly** \-blē\ *adv*

in·can·des·cence \ˌin-kən-'des-ən(t)s\ *n* : the glowing of a substance due to its high temperature

in·can·des·cent \-ənt\ *adj* **1 a** : white or glowing with intense heat **b** : SHINING, BRILLIANT **2 a** : of, relating to, or being light produced by incandescence **b** : producing light by incandescence — **in·can·des·cent·ly** *adv*

incandescent lamp *n* : a lamp whose light is produced by the glow of a filament heated by an electric current

in·can·ta·tion \ˌin-ˌkan-'tā-shən\ *n* : ritual use of spoken or sung magic spells or charms; *also* : a formula of words so used — **in·can·ta·tion·al** \-sh(ə-)nəl\ *adj* — **in·can·ta·to·ry** \in-'kant-ə-ˌtōr-ē, -ˌtȯr-\ *adj*

in·ca·pa·ble \(')in-'kā-pə-bəl\ *adj* : not capable; *esp* : not able or fit : UNQUALIFIED — **in·ca·pa·bil·i·ty** \(ˌ)in-ˌkā-pə-'bil-ət-ē\ *n* — **in·ca·pa·ble·ness** \(')in-'kā-pə-bəl-nəs\ *n* — **in·ca·pa·bly** \-blē\ *adv*

in·ca·pac·i·tate \ˌin-kə-'pas-ə-ˌtāt\ *vb* : to make incapable : DISABLE — **in·ca·pac·i·ta·tion** \-ˌpas-ə-'tā-shən\ *n*

in·ca·pac·i·ty \ˌin-kə-'pas-ət-ē, -'pas-tē\ *n, pl* **-ties** : lack of ability or power

in·car·cer·ate \in-'kär-sə-ˌrāt\ *vb* : IMPRISON, CONFINE — **in·car·cer·a·tion** \(ˌ)in-ˌkär-sə-'rā-shən\ *n*

1in·car·nate \in-'kär-nət, -ˌnāt\ *adj* **1** : provided with bodily and esp. human nature and form **2** : EMBODIED, PERSONIFIED ⟨a fiend *incarnate*⟩

2in·car·nate \-ˌnāt\ *vb* : to make incarnate ⟨believed that demons were *incarnated* as men⟩

in·car·na·tion \ˌin-ˌkär-'nā-shən\ *n* **1** : the act of incarnating : the state of being incarnate **2 a** : the embodiment of a deity or spirit in an earthly form; *esp, cap* : the union of divinity with humanity in Jesus Christ **b** : a concrete instance of a quality or concept : EMBODIMENT

in·cau·tious \(')in-'kȯ-shəs\ *adj* : not cautious : RASH — **in·cau·tious·ly** *adv* — **in·cau·tious·ness** *n*

1in·cen·di·ary \in-'sen-dē-ˌer-ē\ *n, pl* **-ar·ies** **1** : a person who maliciously sets fire to property **2** : a person who excites quarrels : AGITATOR

2**incendiary** *adj* **1 :** of, relating to, or involving malicious burning of property **2 :** tending to excite or inflame quarrels : INFLAMMATORY **3 :** relating to or being a missile containing chemicals that ignite on bursting or on contact

1**in·cense** \'in-ˌsen(t)s\ *n* **1 a :** material (as gums or spices) used to produce a fragrant odor when burned **b :** the odor so produced **2 :** a pleasing scent

2**in·cense** \in-'sen(t)s\ *vb* **:** to inflame with anger or indignation ⟨*incensed* by his bad behavior⟩

in·cen·tive \in-'sent-iv\ *n* **:** something that rouses or spurs one on to action or effort : STIMULUS — **incentive** *adj*

in·cep·tion \in-'sep-shən\ *n* **:** an act, process, or instance of beginning : COMMENCEMENT ⟨a success since its *inception*⟩

in·cer·ti·tude \(')in-'sərt-ə-ˌt(y)üd\ *n* **:** UNCERTAINTY

in·ces·sant \(')in-'ses-ənt\ *adj* **:** UNCEASING ⟨*incessant* rains⟩ — **in·ces·sant·ly** *adv*

in·cest \'in-ˌsest\ *n* **:** sexual intercourse between persons so closely related that they are forbidden by law to marry

in·ces·tu·ous \in-'ses-chə-wəs\ *adj* **1 :** constituting or involving incest **2 :** guilty of incest — **in·ces·tu·ous·ly** *adv* — **in·ces·tu·ous·ness** *n*

1**inch** \'inch\ *n* [from Old English *ynce,* from Latin *uncia* "twelfth part", "inch", "ounce"] **1 :** a unit of length equal to 1/12 foot — see MEASURE table **2 :** a small amount, distance, or degree ⟨won't move an *inch*⟩

2**inch** *vb* **:** to move by small degrees

inch·worm \'inch-ˌwərm\ *n* **:** LOOPER 1

in·ci·dence \'in(t)-səd-ən(t)s, -sə-ˌden(t)s\ *n* **1 :** rate of occurrence ⟨the *incidence* of skin cancer⟩ **2 :** ANGLE OF INCIDENCE

1**in·ci·dent** \'in(t)-səd-ənt, -sə-ˌdent\ *n* **1 a :** OCCURRENCE, EVENT **b :** an accompanying minor occurrence **2 :** an action likely to lead to grave diplomatic consequences

2**incident** *adj* **1 :** INCIDENTAL **2 :** falling or striking on something ⟨*incident* light rays⟩

1**in·ci·den·tal** \ˌin(t)-sə-'dent-əl\ *adj* **1 :** occurring merely by chance or without intention **2 :** happening or likely to happen as a chance or minor consequence ⟨*incidental* expenses of a trip⟩ — **in·ci·den·tal·ly** \-'dent-(ə-)lē\ *adv*

2**incidental** *n* **1 :** something that is incidental **2** *pl* **:** minor items (as of expense) that are not individually listed

in·cin·er·ate \in-'sin-ə-ˌrāt\ *vb* **:** to burn to ashes — **in·cin·er·a·tion** \(ˌ)in-ˌsin-ə-'rā-shən\ *n*

in·cin·er·a·tor \in-'sin-ə-ˌrāt-ər\ *n* **:** one that incinerates; *esp* **:** a furnace or a container for incinerating waste materials

in·cip·i·ent \in-'sip-ē-ənt\ *adj* **:** beginning to be or to become apparent — **in·cip·i·en·cy** \-ən-sē\ *also* **in·cip·i·ence** \-ən(t)s\ *n* — **in·cip·i·ent·ly** *adv*

in·cise \in-'sīz\ *vb* **1 a :** to cut into **b :** NOTCH, GROOVE **2 :** ENGRAVE

in·ci·sion \in-'sizh-ən\ *n* **1 a :** NOTCH **b :** CUT, GASH; *esp* **:** a surgical cut made into the body ⟨removed the diseased appendix through a neat small *incision*⟩ **2 :** an act of incising ⟨watched the flawless technique of the surgeon's skillful *incision*⟩ **3 :** incisive quality

ə abut	ər further	a back	ā bake
ä cot, cart	au̇ out	ch chin	e less	ē easy
g gift	i trip	ī life	j joke	ng sing	ō flow
ȯ flaw	ȯi coin	th thin	t͟h this	ü loot
u̇ foot	y yet	yü few	yu̇ furious	zh vision

in·ci·sive \in-'sī-siv\ *adj* **1 :** CUTTING, PENETRATING **2 :** able to see clearly or make hard decisions : ACUTE — **in·ci·sive·ly** *adv* — **in·ci·sive·ness** *n*

in·ci·sor \in-'sī-zər\ *n* **:** a tooth adapted for cutting; *esp* **:** one of the cutting teeth in front of the canines of a mammal

in·cite \in-'sīt\ *vb* **:** to move to action : stir up — **in·cit·er** *n*

in·cite·ment \in-'sīt-mənt\ *n* **1 :** the act of inciting : the state of being incited **2 :** something that incites : INCENTIVE

in·ci·vil·i·ty \ˌin(t)-sə-'vil-ət-ē\ *n, pl* **-ties 1 :** the quality or state of being uncivil : DISCOURTESY, RUDENESS **2 :** a rude or discourteous act

in·clem·ent \(')in-'klem-ənt\ *adj* **:** STORMY, ROUGH ⟨*inclement* weather⟩ — **in·clem·en·cy** \-ən-sē\ *n* — **in·clem·ent·ly** *adv*

in·cli·na·tion \ˌin-klə-'nā-shən, ˌing-\ *n* **1 a :** BOW, NOD **b :** an act of tilting **2 :** PROPENSITY, BENT; *esp* **:** LIKING **3 a :** a departure from the true vertical or horizontal : SLANT ⟨the *inclination* of the earth's axis⟩ **b :** the degree of such departure **c :** an inclined surface : SLOPE **4 :** a tendency to a particular state, character, or action **5 :** DIP 3 — **in·cli·na·tion·al** \-sh(ə-)nəl\ *adj*

1**in·cline** \in-'klīn\ *vb* **1 :** to bend the head or body forward : BOW **2 :** to lean in one's mind : be disposed : TEND ⟨*inclined* toward going swimming⟩ **3 :** to deviate from a line, direction, or course : LEAN, SLOPE, SLANT **4 :** to cause to bend, bow, slope, or slant **5 :** to have influence on ⟨the teacher's example *inclined* him to become a teacher too⟩ — **in·clin·a·ble** \in-'klī-nə-bəl\ *adj*

2**in·cline** \'in-ˌklīn\ *n* **:** GRADE, SLOPE

inclined plane *n* **:** a plane surface that makes an oblique angle with the plane of the horizon

in·cli·nom·e·ter \ˌin-klə-'näm-ət-ər, ˌing-\ *n* **1 :** an apparatus for determining the direction of the earth's magnetic field with reference to the plane of the horizon **2 :** an instrument for indicating the inclination to the horizontal of the lateral or longitudinal axis of an airplane

inclose, inclosure *var of* ENCLOSE, ENCLOSURE

in·clude \in-'klüd\ *vb* **:** to take in or comprise as a part of a whole — **in·clud·a·ble** *or* **in·clud·i·ble** \-'klüd-ə-bəl\ *adj* — **in·clu·sion** \-'klü-zhən\ *n*

in·clu·sive \in-'klü-siv, -ziv\ *adj* **1 :** INCLUDING ⟨the cost *inclusive* of materials⟩; *esp* **:** including one or more limits ⟨pages 10 to 20 *inclusive*⟩ **2 :** broad in scope ⟨an *inclusive* insurance policy⟩ — **in·clu·sive·ly** *adv* — **in·clu·sive·ness** *n*

1**in·cog·ni·to** \ˌin-ˌkäg-'nēt-ō, in-'käg-nə-ˌtō\ *adv or adj* [from Italian, from Latin *incognitus* "unknown"] **:** with one's identity concealed (as by a false name or title)

2**incognito** *n, pl* **-tos :** the state or disguise of a person traveling incognito

in·co·her·ent \ˌin-kō-'hir-ənt, -'her-\ *adj* **1 :** not sticking closely or compactly together : LOOSE **2 :** not clearly or logically connected : RAMBLING ⟨told an *incoherent* story⟩ — **in·co·her·ence** \-ən(t)s\ *n* — **in·co·her·ent·ly** *adv*

in·com·bus·ti·ble \ˌin-kəm-'bəs-tə-bəl\ *adj* **:** incapable of being burned

in·come \'in-ˌkəm\ *n* **:** a gain usu. measured in money that derives from capital or labor; *esp* **:** the amount of such gain received in a given period

income tax \'in-(ˌ)kəm-\ *n* **:** a tax on the net income of an individual or business concern

in·com·ing \'in-ˌkəm-ing\ *n* **:** the act of coming in — **incoming** *adj*

in·com·men·su·rate \ˌin-kə-'men(t)s-(ə-)rət,

-'mench-(ə-)rət\ *adj* : not commensurate; *esp* : not adequate : not enough to satisfy ⟨funds *incommensurate* with need⟩
in·com·mode \ˌin-kə-'mōd\ *vb* : INCONVENIENCE
in·com·mu·ni·ca·ble \ˌin-kə-'myü-ni-kə-bəl\ *adj* : not capable of being communicated — **in·com·mu·ni·ca·bil·i·ty** \-ˌmyü-ni-kə-'bil-ət-ē\ *n* — **in·com·mu·ni·ca·bly** \-'myü-ni-kə-blē\ *adv*
in·com·mu·ni·ca·do \ˌin-kə-ˌmyü-nə-'käd-ō\ *adv or adj* : without means of communication with others ⟨a prisoner held *incommunicado*⟩
in·com·mu·ni·ca·tive \ˌin-kə-'myü-nə-ˌkāt-iv, -ni-kət-\ *adj* : UNCOMMUNICATIVE
in·com·pa·ra·ble \(')in-'käm-p(ə-)rə-bəl\ *adj* **1** : eminent beyond comparison : MATCHLESS **2** : not able to be compared — **in·com·pa·ra·bil·i·ty** \(ˌ)in-ˌkäm-p(ə-)rə-'bil-ət-ē\ *n* — **in·com·pa·ra·bly** \(')in-'käm-p(ə-)rə-blē\ *adv*
in·com·pat·i·ble \ˌin-kəm-'pat-ə-bəl\ *adj* **1** : incapable of being brought together in a harmonious relationship ⟨temperamentally *incompatible*⟩ ⟨*incompatible* colors⟩ **2** : unsuitable for use in blood transfusion because of a tendency to react unfavorably when mixed with the recipient's blood ⟨*incompatible* blood types⟩ — **in·com·pat·i·bil·i·ty** \-ˌpat-ə-'bil-ət-ē\ *n* — **in·com·pat·i·bly** \-'pat-ə-blē\ *adv*
[1]**in·com·pe·tent** \(')in-'käm-pət-ənt\ *adj* **1** : lacking qualities (as knowledge, skill, or ability) necessary for effective action **2** : not legally qualified — **in·com·pe·tence** \(')in-'käm-pət-ən(t)s\ *also* **in·com·pe·ten·cy** \-ən-sē\ *n* — **in·com·pe·tent·ly** *adv*
[2]**incompetent** *n* : an incompetent person
in·com·plete \ˌin-kəm-'plēt\ *adj* **1** : not complete : UNFINISHED, IMPERFECT ⟨handed in an *incomplete* paper⟩ **2** : not caught ⟨an *incomplete* pass⟩ — **in·com·plete·ly** *adv* — **in·com·plete·ness** *n*
incomplete metamorphosis *n* : insect metamorphosis (as of a grasshopper) in which there is no pupal stage between the immature stage and the adult and in which the young insect usu. resembles the adult

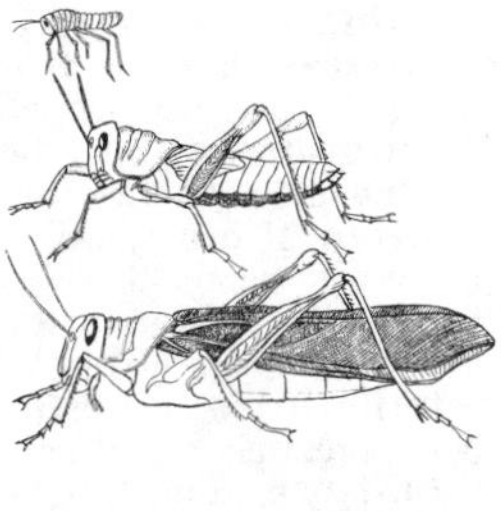
incomplete metamorphosis of a locust

in·com·pre·hen·si·ble \(ˌ)in-ˌkäm-pri-'hen(t)-sə-bəl\ *adj* : impossible to understand — **in·com·pre·hen·si·bil·i·ty** \-ˌhen(t)-sə-'bil-ət-ē\ *n* — **in·com·pre·hen·si·bly** \-'hen(t)-sə-blē\ *adv*
in·com·pre·hen·sion \(ˌ)in-ˌkäm-pri-'hen-chən\ *n* : lack of understanding
in·com·press·i·ble \ˌin-kəm-'pres-ə-bəl\ *adj* : incapable of or resistant to compression — **in·com·press·i·bil·i·ty** \-ˌpres-ə-'bil-ət-ē\ *n*
in·con·ceiv·a·ble \ˌin-kən-'sē-və-bəl\ *adj* : impossible to conceive : INCREDIBLE — **in·con·ceiv·a·bil·i·ty** \-ˌsē-və-'bil-ət-ē\ *n* — **in·con·ceiv·a·ble·ness** \-'sē-və-bəl-nəs\ *n* — **in·con·ceiv·a·bly** \-blē\ *adv*
in·con·clu·sive \ˌin-kən-'klü-siv, -ziv\ *adj* : leading to no conclusion or definite result — **in·con·clu·sive·ly** *adv* — **in·con·clu·sive·ness** *n*
in·con·gru·ous \(')in-'käng-grə-wəs\ *adj* : not harmonious, appropriate, or proper — **in·con·gru·i·ty** \ˌin-kən-'grü-ət-ē, -ˌkän-\ *n* — **in·con·gru·ous·ly** \(')in-'kang-grə-wəs-lē\ *adv* — **in·con·gru·ous·ness** *n*
in·con·se·quen·tial \(ˌ)in-ˌkän(t)-sə-'kwen-chəl\ *adj* : of no significance : UNIMPORTANT — **in·con·se·quen·tial·ly** \-'kwench-(ə-)lē\ *adv*
in·con·sid·er·a·ble \ˌin-kən-'sid-ər-(ə-)bəl, -'sid-rə-bəl\ *adj* : not worth considering : SLIGHT, TRIVIAL — **in·con·sid·er·a·ble·ness** *n* — **in·con·sid·er·a·bly** \-blē\ *adv*
in·con·sid·er·ate \ˌin-kən-'sid-(ə-)rət\ *adj* : careless of the rights or feelings of others — **in·con·sid·er·ate·ly** *adv* — **in·con·sid·er·ate·ness** *n*
in·con·sis·ten·cy \ˌin-kən-'sis-tən-sē\ *n, pl* **-cies** **1** : the quality or state of being inconsistent **2** : an instance of being inconsistent
in·con·sis·tent \ˌin-kən-'sis-tənt\ *adj* **1** : not being in agreement or harmony : INCOMPATIBLE ⟨an explanation *inconsistent* with the facts⟩ **2** : not constant or regular in purpose or behavior : CHANGEABLE ⟨a very *inconsistent* man⟩ — **in·con·sis·tent·ly** *adv*
in·con·sol·a·ble \ˌin-kən-'sō-lə-bəl\ *adj* : incapable of being consoled : DISCONSOLATE — **in·con·sol·a·ble·ness** *n* — **in·con·sol·a·bly** \-blē\ *adv*
in·con·spic·u·ous \ˌin-kən-'spik-yə-wəs\ *adj* : not readily noticeable — **in·con·spic·u·ous·ly** *adv* — **in·con·spic·u·ous·ness** *n*
in·con·stant \(')in-'kän(t)-stənt\ *adj* : likely to change frequently without apparent reason : CHANGEABLE — **in·con·stan·cy** \-stən-sē\ *n* — **in·con·stant·ly** *adv*
in·con·test·a·ble \ˌin-kən-'tes-tə-bəl\ *adj* : not open to doubt : UNQUESTIONABLE — **in·con·test·a·bil·i·ty** \-ˌtes-tə-'bil-ət-ē\ *n* — **in·con·test·a·bly** \-'tes-tə-blē\ *adv*
in·con·ti·nent \(')in-'känt-ə-nənt\ *adj* : lacking self-restraint esp. in the gratification of sensuous desires — **in·con·ti·nence** \-nən(t)s\ *n* — **in·con·ti·nent·ly** *adv*
in·con·tro·vert·i·ble \(ˌ)in-ˌkän-trə-'vərt-ə-bəl\ *adj* : INDISPUTABLE ⟨*incontrovertible* evidence⟩ — **in·con·tro·vert·i·bly** \-blē\ *adv*
[1]**in·con·ve·nience** \ˌin-kən-'vē-nyən(t)s\ *n* **1** : the quality or state of being inconvenient **2** : something inconvenient
[2]**inconvenience** *vb* : to cause discomfort to : put to trouble
in·con·ve·nient \-nyənt\ *adj* : not convenient : causing difficulty, discomfort, or annoyance — **in·con·ve·nient·ly** *adv*
in·cor·po·rate \in-'kȯr-pə-ˌrāt\ *vb* **1** : to unite or combine to form a single whole : BLEND **2** : EMBODY **3** : to form, form into, or become a corporation ⟨*incorporate* a firm⟩ ⟨an *incorporated* town⟩ — **in·cor·po·ra·tion** \(ˌ)in-ˌkȯr-pə-'rā-shən\ *n* — **in·cor·po·ra·tor** \in-'kȯr-pə-ˌrāt-ər\ *n*
in·cor·po·rat·ed \in-'kȯr-pə-ˌrāt-əd\ *adj* : united in one body; *esp* : formed into a corporation
in·cor·po·re·al \ˌin-kȯr-'pōr-ē-əl, -'pȯr-\ *adj* : having no material body or form : IMMATERIAL — **in·cor·po·re·al·ly** \-ə-lē\ *adv*
in·cor·rect \ˌin-kə-'rekt\ *adj* **1 a** : INACCURATE, FAULTY ⟨an *incorrect* job of copying⟩ **b** : not true : WRONG ⟨an *incorrect* answer⟩ **2** : UNBECOMING, IMPROPER — **in·cor·rect·ly** *adv* — **in·cor·rect·ness** \-'rek(t)-nəs\ *n*
[1]**in·cor·ri·gi·ble** \(')in-'kȯr-ə-jə-bəl, -'kär-\ *adj* **1** : incapable of being reformed ⟨an *incorrigible* gambler⟩ **2** : UNRULY, UNMANAGEABLE
[2]**incorrigible** *n* : an incorrigible person
in·cor·rupt·i·ble \ˌin-kə-'rəp-tə-bəl\ *adj* **1** : not

I

subject to decay **2** : incapable of being corrupted : HONEST — **in·cor·rupt·i·bil·i·ty** \-ˌrəp-tə-'bil-ət-ē\ *n* — **in·cor·rupt·i·bly** \-'rəp-tə-blē\ *adv*

1**in·crease** \in-'krēs, 'in-ˌ\ *vb* **1** : to make or become greater ⟨*increase* speed⟩ ⟨skill *increases* with practice⟩ **2** : to multiply by the production of young — **in·creas·a·ble** \-'krē-sə-bəl, -ˌkrē-\ *adj* — **in·creas·er** *n*

2**in·crease** \'in-ˌkrēs, in-'\ *n* **1** : the act of increasing **2** : something (as offspring, produce, or profit) added to an original stock by enlargement or growth

in·creas·ing·ly \in-'krē-sing-lē, 'in-ˌ\ *adv* : to an increasing degree : more and more

in·cred·i·ble \(')in-'kred-ə-bəl\ *adj* : UNBELIEVABLE — **in·cred·i·bil·i·ty** \(ˌ)in-ˌkred-ə-'bil-ət-ē\ *n* — **in·cred·i·bly** \(')in-'kred-ə-blē\ *adv*

in·cre·du·li·ty \ˌin-kri-'d(y)ü-lət-ē\ *n* : the quality or state of not believing or of doubting

in·cred·u·lous \(')in-'krej-ə-ləs\ *adj* **1** : not credulous : tending to disbelieve **2** : expressing incredulity ⟨listened with an *incredulous* smile⟩ — **in·cred·u·lous·ly** *adv*

in·cre·ment \'ing-krə-mənt, 'in-\ *n* **1** : a growth esp. in quantity or value : INCREASE **2 a** : something gained or added **b** : one of a series of regular consecutive additions — **in·cre·men·tal** \ˌing-krə-'ment-əl, ˌin-\ *adj*

in·crim·i·nate \in-'krim-ə-ˌnāt\ *vb* : to charge with or involve in a crime or fault : ACCUSE — **in·crim·i·na·tion** \(ˌ)in-ˌkrim-ə-'nā-shən\ *n* — **in·crim·i·na·to·ry** \in-'krim-(ə-)nə-ˌtōr-ē, -ˌtòr-\ *adj*

incrust *var of* ENCRUST

in·crus·ta·tion \ˌin-ˌkrəs-'tā-shən\ *n* **1** : the act of encrusting : the state of being encrusted **2** : a hard coating : CRUST **3 a** : OVERLAY **b** : INLAY

in·cu·bate \'ing-kyə-ˌbāt, 'in-kyə-\ *vb* **1** : to sit on eggs to hatch them by warmth **2** : to maintain (as bacteria or a chemically active system) under conditions favorable for development or reaction — **in·cu·ba·tion** \ˌing-kyə-'bā-shən, ˌin-kyə-\ *n*

incubation period *n* **1** : the period of brooding or incubating required to bring an egg to hatching **2** : the period between infection and the manifestation of a disease

in·cu·ba·tor \'ing-kyə-ˌbāt-ər, 'in-kyə-\ *n* : one that incubates; *esp* : an apparatus providing suitable conditions (as of warmth and moisture) for incubating something ⟨an *incubator* for premature babies⟩

in·cu·bus \'ing-kyə-bəs, 'in-kyə-\ *n, pl* **-bi** \-ˌbī, -ˌbē\ *also* **-bus·es** **1** : an evil spirit held to lie upon persons in their sleep **2** : NIGHTMARE 2 **3** : an oppressive burden

in·cul·cate \in-'kəl-ˌkāt, 'in-(ˌ)kəl-\ *vb* : to impress on the mind by frequent repetition ⟨childhood training *inculcated* a deep sense of responsibility⟩ — **in·cul·ca·tion** \ˌin-(ˌ)kəl-'kā-shən\ *n*

in·cum·ben·cy \in-'kəm-bən-sē\ *n, pl* **-cies** : the period of office of an incumbent

1**in·cum·bent** \-bənt\ *n* : the holder of an office or position

2**incumbent** *adj* **1** : lying or resting on something else **2** : imposed as a duty : OBLIGATORY **3** : being an incumbent

in·cur \in-'kər\ *vb* **in·curred**; **in·cur·ring** **1** : to meet with (as an inconvenience) ⟨*incur* expenses⟩ **2** : to become liable or subject to ⟨*incur* punishment⟩ — **in·cur·rence** \-'kər-ən(t)s, -'kə-rən(t)s\ *n*

1**in·cur·a·ble** \(')in-'kyu̇r-ə-bəl\ *adj* : not capable of being cured — **in·cur·a·bil·i·ty** \(ˌ)in-ˌkyu̇r-ə-'bil-ət-ē\ *n* — **in·cur·a·ble·ness** \(')in-'kyu̇r-ə-bəl-nəs\ *n* — **in·cur·a·bly** \-blē\ *adv*

2**incurable** *n* : a person suffering from a disease that is beyond cure

in·cur·sion \in-'kər-zhən\ *n* : a sudden usu. temporary invasion : RAID

in·cus \'ing-kəs\ *n, pl* **in·cu·des** \ing-'kyüd-(ˌ)ēz\ : ANVIL 2

ind *abbr* **1** index **2** industry

Ind *abbr* Indiana

in·debt·ed \in-'det-əd\ *adj* : being in debt : owing something (as money, gratitude, or services)

in·debt·ed·ness *n* **1** : the condition of being indebted **2** : an amount owed

in·de·cen·cy \(')in-'dēs-ən-sē\ *n, pl* **-cies** **1** : lack of decency **2** : an indecent act or word

in·de·cent \-ənt\ *adj* **1** : UNBECOMING, UNSEEMLY ⟨remarried in *indecent* haste⟩ **2** : morally offensive — **in·de·cent·ly** *adv*

in·de·ci·sion \ˌin-di-'sizh-ən\ *n* : slowness in deciding : hesitation in making up one's mind

in·de·ci·sive \-'sī-siv\ *adj* **1** : not decisive or final ⟨an *indecisive* battle⟩ **2** : characterized by indecision : UNCERTAIN ⟨an *indecisive* person⟩ — **in·de·ci·sive·ly** *adv* — **in·de·ci·sive·ness** *n*

in·de·clin·a·ble \ˌin-di-'klī-nə-bəl\ *adj* : having no grammatical inflections

in·dec·o·rous \(')in-'dek-ə-rəs; ˌin-di-'kōr-əs, -'kòr-\ *adj* : not decorous : UNBECOMING — **in·dec·o·rous·ly** *adv* — **in·dec·o·rous·ness** *n*

in·deed \in-'dēd\ *adv* **1** : in fact : in reality : TRULY — often used interjectionally to express disbelief or surprise **2** : ADMITTEDLY, UNDENIABLY

indef *abbr* indefinite

in·de·fat·i·ga·ble \ˌin-di-'fat-i-gə-bəl\ *adj* : capable of working a long time without tiring : TIRELESS — **in·de·fat·i·ga·bil·i·ty** \-ˌfat-i-gə-'bil-ət-ē\ *n* — **in·de·fat·i·ga·ble·ness** \-'fat-i-gə-bəl-nəs\ *n* — **in·de·fat·i·ga·bly** \-blē\ *adv*

in·de·fea·si·ble \ˌin-di-'fē-zə-bəl\ *adj* : not capable of being abolished or annulled ⟨*indefeasible* rights⟩ — **in·de·fea·si·bil·i·ty** \-ˌfē-zə-'bil-ət-ē\ *n* — **in·de·fea·si·bly** \-'fē-zə-blē\ *adv*

in·de·fen·si·ble \ˌin-di-'fen(t)-sə-bəl\ *adj* : not capable of being defended ⟨an *indefensible* position⟩ — **in·de·fen·si·bil·i·ty** \-ˌfen(t)-sə-'bil-ət-ē\ *n* — **in·de·fen·si·bly** \-'fen(t)-sə-blē\ *adv*

in·de·fin·a·ble \ˌin-di-'fī-nə-bəl\ *adj* : incapable of being precisely described or analyzed — **in·de·fin·a·bil·i·ty** \-ˌfī-nə-'bil-ət-ē\ *n* — **in·de·fin·a·ble·ness** \-'fī-nə-bəl-nəs\ *n* — **in·de·fin·a·bly** \-blē\ *adv*

in·def·i·nite \(')in-'def-(ə-)nət\ *adj* **1** : not clear or fixed in meaning or details : VAGUE ⟨an *indefinite* answer⟩ **2** : not fixed or limited (as in amount or length) ⟨an *indefinite* period⟩ **3** : being a pronoun or grammatical modifier that typically designates an unidentified or not immediately identifiable person or thing ⟨*some* is an *indefinite* determiner⟩ — **indefinite** *n* — **in·def·i·nite·ly** *adv* — **in·def·i·nite·ness** *n*

in·del·i·ble \in-'del-ə-bəl\ *adj* **1** : not capable of being erased, removed, or blotted out ⟨*indelible* impression⟩ **2** : making marks not easily erased ⟨an *indelible* pencil⟩ — **in·del·i·bly** \-blē\ *adv*

in·del·i·ca·cy \(')in-'del-i-kə-sē\ *n, pl* **-cies** **1** : the quality or state of being indelicate : COARSENESS **2** : an indelicate act or utterance

in·del·i·cate \-kət\ *adj* : offensive to good manners or taste : IMMODEST, COARSE — **in·del·i·cate·ly** *adv* — **in·del·i·cate·ness** *n*

in·dem·ni·fy \in-'dem-nə-ˌfī\ *vb* **-fied**; **-fy·ing** **1** : to insure or protect against loss, damage, or injury **2** : to make compensation to for loss, damage, or injury ⟨*indemnify* victims of a disaster⟩ **3** : to make compensation for : make good ⟨have their losses *indemnified*⟩ — **in·dem·ni·fi·ca·tion** \-ˌdem-nə-fə-'kā-shən\ *n* — **in·dem·ni·fi·er** \-'dem-nə-ˌfī(-ə)r\ *n*

in·dem·ni·ty \in-'dem-nət-ē\ *n, pl* **-ties** **1** : protection from loss, damage, or injury : INSURANCE **2** : freedom from penalty for past offenses **3** : compensation for loss, damage, or injury

1**in·dent** \in-'dent\ *vb* **1** : to notch the edge of : make jagged ⟨*indented* leaves⟩ **2** : to set in from the margin ⟨*indent* the first line of a paragraph⟩ — **in·dent·er** *n*

2**indent** *vb* **1** : to force inward so as to form a depression **2** : to form a dent in — **in·dent·er** *n*

in·den·ta·tion \ˌin-ˌden-'tā-shən\ *n* **1 a** : an angular cut in an edge : NOTCH **b** : a deep recess (as in a coastline) **2 a** : the action of indenting : the state of being indented **b** : a blank or empty space produced by indenting **3** : DENT

in·den·tion \in-'den-chən\ *n* : INDENTATION

1**in·den·ture** \in-'den-chər\ *n* **1** : a written agreement : CONTRACT **2** : a contract that binds a person to serve another for a specified period — usu. used in pl.

2**indenture** *vb* : to bind by indentures ⟨*indenture* an apprentice⟩

in·de·pend·ence \ˌin-də-'pen-dən(t)s\ *n* : the quality or state of being independent : freedom from outside control or support

Independence Day *n* : July 4 observed as a legal holiday in commemoration of the adoption of the Declaration of Independence in 1776

in·de·pend·en·cy \ˌin-də-'pen-dən-sē\ *n* : INDEPENDENCE

1**in·de·pend·ent** \ˌin-də-'pen-dənt\ *adj* **1** : not subject to control or rule by another : SELF-GOVERNING, FREE ⟨an *independent* nation⟩ **2** : not having connections with another : SEPARATE ⟨the same story told by *independent* witnesses⟩ **3** : not supported by or willing to accept support from another : having or providing enough money to live on ⟨a person of *independent* means⟩ **4** : not easily influenced ⟨an *independent* mind⟩ **5** : having full meaning in itself and capable of standing alone as a simple sentence : MAIN ⟨*independent* clause⟩ **6** : not committed to a political party **7** : having probabilities such that the occurrence or nonoccurrence of one event does not influence the outcome of another ⟨the outcomes of the tossing of two dice are *independent*⟩ — **in·de·pend·ent·ly** *adv*

2**independent** *n* : one that is independent; *esp* : one not committed to a political party

in·de·scrib·a·ble \ˌin-di-'skrī-bə-bəl\ *adj* : incapable of being described : beyond description ⟨*indescribable* beauty⟩ — **in·de·scrib·a·bly** \-bə-blē\ *adv*

in·de·struc·ti·ble \ˌin-di-'strək-tə-bəl\ *adj* : incapable of being destroyed — **in·de·struc·ti·bil·i·ty** \-ˌstrək-tə-'bil-ət-ē\ *n* — **in·de·struc·ti·ble·ness** \-'strək-tə-bəl-nəs\ *n* — **in·de·struc·ti·bly** \-blē\ *adv*

in·de·ter·min·a·ble \ˌin-di-'tər-mə-nə-bəl\ *adj* : incapable of being definitely decided or ascertained — **in·de·ter·min·a·bly** \-blē\ *adv*

in·de·ter·mi·nate \ˌin-di-'tər-mə-nət\ *adj* **1** : not definitely or precisely determined : VAGUE ⟨*indeterminate* plans⟩ **2** : not leading to a definite end or result — **in·de·ter·mi·na·cy** \-mə-nə-sē\ *n* — **in·de·ter·mi·nate·ly** *adv* — **in·de·ter·mi·nate·ness** *n*

1**in·dex** \'in-ˌdeks\ *n, pl* **in·dex·es** \-ˌdek-səz\ *or* **in·di·ces** \-də-ˌsēz\ **1** : an alphabetical list in a printed work that gives with each item listed the page number where it may be found **2** : POINTER, INDICATOR ⟨the *index* on a scale⟩ **3** : SIGN, INDICATION ⟨an *index* of his mood⟩ **4** *pl usu indices* : a mathematical figure, letter, or expression (as the figure *3* in a^3) showing a power or root of another : EXPONENT **5** : a character ☞ used to direct attention

2**index** *vb* **1** : to provide with or list in an index **2** : to serve as an index of — **in·dex·er** *n*

index finger *n* : the finger next to the thumb

index fossil *n* : a fossil that is found over a relatively short span of geological time and can be used in dating formations in which it is found

in·dia ink \ˌin-dē-ə-\ *n, often cap 1st I* **1** : a black pigment (as lampblack) used in drawing and lettering **2** : a fluid made from india ink

In·di·an \'in-dē-ən\ *n* **1** : a native or inhabitant of the Republic of India, the subcontinent of India, or the East Indies **2 a** [so called from Columbus' belief that the lands he discovered were part of the East Indies] : a member of any of the native peoples of No. and So. America except the Eskimos **b** : an American Indian language — **Indian** *adj*

Indian club *n* : a wooden club that is swung for gymnastic exercise

Indian corn *n* **1** : a tall widely cultivated American cereal grass bearing seeds on elongated ears **2** : the ears of Indian corn; *also* : its edible seeds

Indian meal *n* : CORNMEAL

Indian paintbrush *n* **1** : any of a large genus of American and northeast Asiatic herbs that have dense spikes of hooded flowers with brightly colored bracts **2** : ORANGE HAWKWEED

Indian pipe *n* : a waxy white leafless saprophytic herb with a solitary nodding bell-shaped flower

Indian pipe (up to 10 in. high)

Indian pudding *n* : a pudding made chiefly of cornmeal, milk, and molasses

Indian summer *n* : a period of mild weather in late autumn or early winter

India paper *n* : a thin tough printing paper

india rubber *n, often cap I* **1** : RUBBER **2** : something made of rubber

indic *abbr* indicative

In·dic \'in-dik\ *adj* : of, relating to, or constituting the Indian branch of the Indo-European languages

in·di·cate \'in-də-ˌkāt\ *vb* **1 a** : to point out : point to **b** : to be a sign, symptom, or index of ⟨perform the *indicated* operations⟩ **2** : to state or express briefly : SUGGEST

in·di·ca·tion \ˌin-də-'kā-shən\ *n* **1** : the action of indicating **2** : something that indicates : SIGN, SUGGESTION

1**in·dic·a·tive** \in-'dik-ət-iv\ *adj* **1** : of, relating to, or constituting the grammatical mood that represents the denoted act or state as an objective fact **2** : indicating something not visible or obvious : SUGGESTIVE ⟨remarks *indicative* of resentment⟩ — **in·dic·a·tive·ly** *adv*

2**indicative** *n* : the indicative mood of a verb or a verb in this mood

in·di·ca·tor \'in-də-ˌkāt-ər\ *n* **1** : one that indicates (as an index hand, dial, or gauge) **2** : a substance used to show visually (as by change of color) the condition of a solution esp. with respect to the presence of free acid or alkali — **in·dic·a·to·ry** \in-'dik-ə-ˌtōr-ē, -ˌtȯr-\ *adj*

indices *pl of* INDEX

in·dict \in-'dīt\ *vb* : ACCUSE; *esp* : to charge with a crime by the finding of a grand jury — **in·dict·a·ble** \-ə-bəl\ *adj* — **in·dict·er** *or* **in·dict·or** \-'dīt-ər\ *n*

in·dict·ment \in-'dīt-mənt\ *n* **1** : the act or process of indicting **2** : a formal statement charging a person with an offense drawn up by a prosecuting attorney and reported by a grand jury after an inquiry

in·dif·fer·ence \in-'dif-ərn(t)s, -'dif-(ə-)rən(t)s\ *n* **1** : lack of feeling for or against something **2** : lack of importance ⟨a matter of *indifference* to him⟩

in·dif·fer·ent \in-'dif-ərnt, -'dif-(ə-)rənt\ *adj* **1** : having no preference : not interested or concerned ⟨*indifferent* to the troubles of others⟩ **2** : showing neither interest nor dislike ⟨the audience was *indifferent*⟩ **3** : neither good nor bad : MEDIOCRE ⟨*indifferent* health⟩ **4** : of no special influence or value : not important — **in·dif·fer·ent·ly** *adv*

in·dig·e·nous \in-'dij-ə-nəs\ *adj* : produced, growing, or living naturally in a particular region or environment ***syn*** see NATIVE ***ant*** exotic, naturalized — **in·dig·e·nous·ly** *adv* — **in·dig·e·nous·ness** *n*

in·di·gent \'in-di-jənt\ *adj* : POOR, NEEDY — **in·di·gence** \-jən(t)s\ *n*

in·di·gest·i·ble \ˌin-dī-'jes-tə-bəl, -də-\ *adj* : not digestible or easily digested — **in·di·gest·i·bil·i·ty** \-ˌjes-tə-'bil-ət-ē\ *n*

in·di·ges·tion \-'jes-chən\ *n* **1** : inability to digest or difficulty in digesting something **2** : a case or attack of indigestion — **in·di·ges·tive** \-'jes-tiv\ *adj*

in·dig·nant \in-'dig-nənt\ *adj* : filled with or marked by indignation — **in·dig·nant·ly** *adv*

in·dig·na·tion \ˌin-dig-'nā-shən\ *n* : anger aroused by something unjust, unworthy, or mean

in·dig·ni·ty \in-'dig-nət-ē\ *n* **1** : an act that offends a person's dignity or self-respect : INSULT **2** : humiliating treatment

in·di·go \'in-di-ˌgō\ *n, pl* **-gos** *or* **-goes** [from Italian dialect, from Latin *indicum*, literally "Indian substance"] **1** : a blue dye made artificially and formerly obtained from plants and esp. indigo plants **2** : a variable color averaging a dark grayish blue

indigo plant *n* : any of various mostly leguminous plants that yield indigo

indigo snake *n* : a large harmless blue-black snake of the southern U.S.

in·di·rect \ˌin-də-'rekt, -dī-\ *adj* **1** : not straight : not the shortest ⟨an *indirect* route⟩ **2** : not straightforward : ROUNDABOUT ⟨*indirect* methods⟩ **3** : not having a plainly seen connection ⟨an *indirect* cause⟩ **4** : not straight to the point ⟨an *indirect* answer⟩ **5** : stating what an original speaker said with changes in wording that conform the statement grammatically to the sentence in which it is included ⟨"that he would come" in "He said that he would come" is in *indirect* discourse⟩ — **in·di·rect·ly** *adv* — **in·di·rect·ness** \-'rek(t)-nəs\ *n*

indirect evidence *n* : evidence that establishes immediately facts from which the most important fact has to be obtained by reasoning

indirect lighting *n* : lighting in which the light emitted by a source is diffusely reflected (as by the ceiling)

indirect object *n* : a grammatical object representing the secondary goal of the action of its verb ⟨*me* in "gave me the book" is an *indirect object*⟩

in·dis·creet \ˌin-dis-'krēt\ *adj* : not discreet : IMPRUDENT — **in·dis·creet·ly** *adv* — **in·dis·creet·ness** *n*

in·dis·cre·tion \-'kresh-ən\ *n* **1** : lack of discretion : IMPRUDENCE **2** : an indiscreet act or remark

in·dis·crim·i·nate \ˌin-dis-'krim-ə-nət\ *adj* : showing lack of discrimination : not making careful distinctions ⟨an *indiscriminate* reader⟩ ⟨*indiscriminate* enthusiasm⟩ — **in·dis·crim·i·nate·ly** *adv* — **in·dis·crim·i·nate·ness** *n*

in·dis·pens·a·ble \ˌin-dis-'pen(t)-sə-bəl\ *adj* : absolutely necessary ⟨an *indispensable* employee⟩ — **in·dis·pens·a·bil·i·ty** \-ˌpen(t)-sə-'bil-ət-ē\ *n* — **in·dis·pens·a·bly** \-'pen(t)-sə-blē\ *adv*

in·dis·posed \ˌin-dis-'pōzd\ *adj* **1** : slightly ill **2** : UNWILLING, AVERSE

in·dis·po·si·tion \(ˌ)in-ˌdis-pə-'zish-ən\ *n* **1** : a slight illness **2** : DISINCLINATION, UNWILLINGNESS

in·dis·put·a·ble \ˌin-dis-'pyüt-ə-bəl, (')in-'dis-pyət-\ *adj* : not disputable ⟨*indisputable* proof⟩ — **in·dis·put·a·ble·ness** *n* — **in·dis·put·a·bly** \-blē\ *adv*

in·dis·sol·u·ble \ˌin-dis-'äl-yə-bəl\ *adj* : not capable of being dissolved, undone, broken up, or decomposed ⟨an *indissoluble* contract⟩ — **in·dis·sol·u·bil·i·ty** \-dis-ˌäl-yə-'bil-ət-ē\ *n* — **in·dis·sol·u·ble·ness** \-dis-'äl-yə-bəl-nəs\ *n* — **in·dis·sol·u·bly** \-blē\ *adv*

in·dis·tinct \ˌin-dis-'ting(k)t\ *adj* **1** : not distinct : CONFUSED, BLURRED ⟨*indistinct* in the fog⟩ **2** : FAINT, DIM ⟨a far-off *indistinct* light⟩ — **in·dis·tinct·ly** *adv* — **in·dis·tinct·ness** *n*

in·dis·tin·guish·a·ble \ˌin-dis-'ting-gwish-ə-bəl\ *adj* : not capable of being clearly distinguished — **in·dis·tin·guish·a·ble·ness** *n* — **in·dis·tin·guish·a·bly** \-blē\ *adv*

in·dite \in-'dīt\ *vb* **1** : to make up : COMPOSE ⟨*indite* an epistle⟩ **2** : to compose and put down in writing — **in·dit·er** *n*

in·di·um \'in-dē-əm\ *n* : a malleable fusible silvery metallic element — see ELEMENT table

1**in·di·vid·u·al** \ˌin-də-'vij-(ə-w)əl\ *adj* **1** : of or relating to an individual ⟨*individual* traits⟩ **2** : intended for one person ⟨*individual* servings⟩ **3** : PARTICULAR, SEPARATE ⟨*individual* copies⟩ **4** : having marked individuality ⟨an *individual* style⟩ — **in·di·vid·u·al·ly** \-ē\ *adv*

2**individual** *n* : a particular person, animal, or thing in contrast to its class or species

in·di·vid·u·al·ism \-'vij-ə(-wə)-ˌliz-əm\ *n* **1** : a doctrine that the interests of the individual are primary **2** : a doctrine holding that the individual has certain political or economic rights with which the state must not interfere

in·di·vid·u·al·ist \-ləst\ *n* **1** : a person who shows marked individuality or independence in thought or behavior **2** : a supporter of individualism — **in·di·vid·u·al·is·tic** \-ˌvij-ə(-wə)-'lis-tik\ *adj* — **in·di·vid·u·al·is·ti·cal·ly** \-ti-k(ə-)lē\ *adv*

in·di·vid·u·al·i·ty \ˌin-də-ˌvij-ə-'wal-ət-ē\ *n, pl* **-ties** **1** : the qualities that distinguish one person or thing from all others **2** : the condition of having separate existence

ə abut	ər further	a back	ā bake
ä cot, cart	aü out	ch chin	e less	ē easy
g gift	i trip	ī life	j joke	ng sing	ō flow
ȯ flaw	ȯi coin	th thin	th this	ü loot
u̇ foot	y yet	yü few	yu̇ furious	zh vision

in·di·vid·u·al·ize \-'vij-(ə-w)əl-ˌīz\ *vb* **1** : to make individual in character **2** : to treat or notice individually — **in·di·vid·u·al·i·za·tion** \-ˌvij-(ə-w)əl-ə-'zā-shən\ *n*

in·di·vis·i·ble \ˌin-də-'viz-ə-bəl\ *adj* : not capable of being divided or separated — **in·di·vis·i·bil·i·ty** \-ˌviz-ə-'bil-ət-ē\ *n* — **in·di·vis·i·ble·ness** \-'viz-ə-bəl-nəs\ *n* — **in·di·vis·i·bly** \-blē\ *adv*

in·doc·tri·nate \in-'däk-trə-ˌnāt\ *vb* **1** : to instruct esp. in fundamentals **2** : to teach the principles or doctrines of a particular group — **in·doc·tri·na·tion** \(ˌ)in-ˌdäk-trə-'nā-shən\ *n* — **in·doc·tri·na·tor** \in-'däk-trə-ˌnāt-ər\ *n*

[1]**In·do–Eu·ro·pe·an** \ˌin-dō-ˌyůr-ə-'pē-ən\ *adj* : of, relating to, or constituting a family of languages comprising those spoken in most of Europe, in the parts of the world colonized by Europeans, and in parts of Asia

[2]**Indo–European** *n* **1** : the Indo-European languages **2** : a member of a people who originally spoke an Indo-European language

in·dole·ace·tic acid \ˌin-ˌdōl-ə-ˌsēt-ik-\ *n* : a crystalline plant hormone that promotes growth and rooting of plants

in·dole·bu·tyr·ic acid \-byü-ˌtir-ik-\ *n* : a crystalline acid similar to indoleacetic acid in its effects on plants

in·do·lent \'in-də-lənt\ *adj* : LAZY ⟨felt *indolent* every spring⟩ ***syn*** see IDLE ***ant*** industrious — **in·do·lence** \-lən(t)s\ *n* — **in·do·lent·ly** *adv*

in·dom·i·ta·ble \in-'däm-ət-ə-bəl\ *adj* : UNCONQUERABLE ⟨*indomitable* courage⟩ — **in·dom·i·ta·bil·i·ty** \-ˌdäm-ət-ə-'bil-ət-ē\ *n* — **in·dom·i·ta·ble·ness** \-'däm-ət-ə-bəl-nəs\ *n* — **in·dom·i·ta·bly** \-blē\ *adv*

In·do·ne·sian \ˌin-də-'nē-zhən, -shən\ *n* **1** : a native or inhabitant of the Republic of Indonesia **2** : the language based on Malay that is the national language of Indonesia — **Indonesian** *adj*

in·door \ˌin-ˌdōr, -ˌdȯr\ *adj* **1** : of or relating to the interior of a building **2** : done, living, or belonging within doors

in·doors \(')in-'dō(ə)rz, -'dȯ(ə)rz\ *adv* : in or into a building ⟨games to be played *indoors*⟩

in·du·bi·ta·ble \(')in-'d(y)ü-bət-ə-bəl\ *adj* : too evident to be doubted : UNQUESTIONABLE — **in·du·bi·ta·ble·ness** *n* — **in·du·bi·ta·bly** \-blē\ *adv*

in·duce \in-'d(y)üs\ *vb* **1** : to lead on to do something : PERSUADE **2** : to bring about : CAUSE ⟨an illness *induced* by overwork⟩ **3** : to conclude or infer by reasoning from particular instances **4** : to produce (as an electric current) by induction — **in·duc·er** *n* — **in·duc·i·ble** \-'d(y)ü-sə-bəl\ *adj*

in·duce·ment \in-'d(y)üs-mənt\ *n* **1** : the act of inducing **2** : something that induces ⟨a money-back guarantee is an *inducement* to buy⟩

in·duct \in-'dəkt\ *vb* **1** : to place formally in office : INSTALL **2** : to draft into military service — **in·duct·ee** \(ˌ)in-ˌdək-'tē\ *n*

in·duc·tion \in-'dək-shən\ *n* **1 a** : the act or process of inducting (as into office) **b** : an initial experience : INITIATION **c** : the procedure by which a civilian is inducted into military service **2** : reasoning from particular instances to a general conclusion or to an unobserved case : probable reasoning **3 a** : the act of causing or bringing on or about **b** : the process by which an electrical conductor becomes electrified when near a charged body, by which a body becomes magnetized when in a magnetic field or in the flux set up by a magnetizing force, or by which an electromotive force is produced in a circuit by varying the magnetic field linked with the circuit

induction coil *n* : an apparatus for transforming a direct current of electricity by induction into an alternating current of high potential

in·duc·tive \in-'dək-tiv\ *adj* : relating to, employing, or based on induction — **in·duc·tive·ly** *adv*

in·duc·tor \in-'dək-tər\ *n* **1** : one that inducts **2** : a part of an electrical apparatus that acts upon another or is itself acted upon by induction

in·dulge \in-'dəlj\ *vb* **1** : to be tolerant toward : HUMOR, GRATIFY ⟨*indulges* his wife's whims⟩ **2** : to allow oneself to take pleasure ⟨*indulge* himself in eating and drinking⟩ — **in·dulg·er** *n*

in·dul·gence \in-'dəl-jən(t)s\ *n* **1** : a release from punishment in this world or in purgatory gained by performing pious acts authorized by the Roman Catholic Church **2 a** : the act of indulging : the state of being indulgent **b** : an indulgent act **c** : something indulged in

in·dul·gent \-jənt\ *adj* : indulging or characterized by indulgence : LENIENT — **in·dul·gent·ly** *adv*

[1]**in·du·rate** \'in-d(y)ə-rət, in-'d(y)ůr-ət\ *adj* : physically hardened

[2]**in·du·rate** \'in-d(y)ə-ˌrāt\ *vb* **1** : to make fibrous or hard ⟨great heat *indurates* clay⟩ ⟨*indurated* tissue⟩ **2** : to grow hard : HARDEN — **in·du·ra·tion** \ˌin-d(y)ə-'rā-shən\ *n* — **in·du·ra·tive** \'in-d(y)ə-ˌrāt-iv, in-'d(y)ůr-ət-\ *adj*

in·dus·tri·al \in-'dəs-trē-əl\ *adj* **1** : of, relating to, or engaged in industry **2** : characterized by highly developed industries ⟨an *industrial* nation⟩ **3** : derived from or used in industry ⟨*industrial* diamonds⟩ — **in·dus·tri·al·ly** \-trē-ə-lē\ *adv*

industrial arts *n sing or pl* : a subject taught in elementary and secondary schools that aims at developing manual skill and familiarity with tools and machines

industrial engineering *n* : engineering that deals with the design or improvement of manufacturing systems and that utilizes the techniques of scientific management in order to maintain a high level of productivity at a desired cost — **industrial engineer** *n*

in·dus·tri·al·ist \in-'dəs-trē-ə-ləst\ *n* : an owner or manager of an industry : MANUFACTURER

in·dus·tri·al·ize \-ˌlīz\ *vb* : to make or become industrial : convert to an industrial economy ⟨*industrialize* an agricultural region⟩ — **in·dus·tri·al·i·za·tion** \-ˌdəs-trē-ə-lə-'zā-shən\ *n*

industrial revolution *n* : a rapid major change in an economy (as in England in the late 18th century) marked by the general introduction of power-driven machinery

in·dus·tri·ous \in-'dəs-trē-əs\ *adj* : constantly, regularly, or habitually occupied : DILIGENT ***syn*** see BUSY ***ant*** indolent, slothful — **in·dus·tri·ous·ly** *adv* — **in·dus·tri·ous·ness** *n*

in·dus·try \'in-(ˌ)dəs-trē\ *n, pl* **-tries** **1** : the habit of working hard and steadily : DILIGENCE **2** : systematic labor ⟨lived by his own *industry*⟩ **3 a** : a usu. large manufacturing firm **b** : the businesses engaged in providing a particular kind of goods or services ⟨the steel *industry*⟩ ⟨the tourist *industry*⟩ **c** : manufacturing activity as a whole ⟨commerce and *industry*⟩

ine·bri·ate \in-'ē-brē-ˌāt\ *vb* : to make drunk : INTOXICATE — **ine·bri·ate** \-brē-ət\ *adj or n* — **ine·bri·a·tion** \in-ˌē-brē-'ā-shən\ *n*

in·ed·i·ble \(')in-'ed-ə-bəl\ *adj* : not fit or safe for eating ⟨*inedible* mushrooms⟩

in·ef·fa·ble \(')in-'ef-ə-bəl\ *adj* : INEXPRESSIBLE — **in·ef·fa·bil·i·ty** \(ˌ)in-ˌef-ə-'bil-ət-ē\ *n* — **in·ef·fa·bly** \(')in-'ef-ə-blē\ *adv*

I

in·ef·fec·tive \ˌin-ə-'fek-tiv\ *adj* **1** : INEFFECTUAL ⟨an *ineffective* law⟩ **2** : not efficient : INCAPABLE ⟨an *ineffective* leader⟩ — **in·ef·fec·tive·ly** *adv* — **in·ef·fec·tive·ness** *n*

in·ef·fec·tu·al \ˌin-ə-'fek-chə(-wə)l\ *adj* : not producing the proper or usual effect — **in·ef·fec·tu·al·ly** \-ē\ *adv* — **in·ef·fec·tu·al·ness** *n*

in·ef·fi·cient \ˌin-ə-'fish-ənt\ *adj* **1** : INEFFECTUAL **2** : INCAPABLE, INCOMPETENT — **in·ef·fi·cien·cy** \-'fish-ən-sē\ *n* — **in·ef·fi·cient·ly** *adv*

in·elas·tic \ˌin-ə-'las-tik\ *adj* **1** : not elastic **2** : slow to react or respond to changing conditions — **in·elas·tic·i·ty** \ˌin-i-ˌlas-'tis-ət-ē\ *n*

in·el·e·gant \(')in-'el-i-gənt\ *adj* : lacking in refinement, grace, or good taste — **in·el·e·gant·ly** *adv*

in·el·i·gi·ble \(')in-'el-ə-jə-bəl\ *adj* : not qualified to be chosen or used — **in·el·i·gi·bil·i·ty** \(ˌ)in-ˌel-ə-jə-'bil-ət-ē\ *n* — **ineligible** *n*

in·ept \in-'ept\ *adj* **1** : lacking in fitness or aptitude : UNFIT **2** : not apt for the occasion : INAPPROPRIATE **3** : generally incompetent : BUNGLING — **in·ep·ti·tude** \-'ep-tə-ˌt(y)üd\ *n* — **in·ept·ly** *adv* — **in·ept·ness** \-'ep(t)-nəs\ *n*

in·equal·i·ty \ˌin-i-'kwäl-ət-ē\ *n* **1** : the quality of being unequal **2** : an instance of being unequal (as an irregularity in a surface) **3** : a formal logical or mathematical statement that two quantities are unequal

in·eq·ui·ta·ble \(')in-'ek-wət-ə-bəl\ *adj* : not equitable : UNFAIR — **in·eq·ui·ta·bly** \-blē\ *adv*

in·eq·ui·ty \-wət-ē\ *n, pl* **-ties 1** : INJUSTICE, UNFAIRNESS **2** : an instance of injustice or unfairness

in·erad·i·ca·ble \ˌin-i-'rad-i-kə-bəl\ *adj* : incapable of being eradicated — **in·erad·i·ca·bly** \-blē\ *adv*

in·ert \in-'ərt\ *adj* [from Latin *inert-*, stem of *iners* "idle", "sluggish", literally "lacking in skill", from *in-* "un-" and *art-*, stem of *ars* "art"] **1** : not having the power to move itself **2** : deficient in active properties; *esp* : lacking a usual or anticipated chemical or biological action ⟨*inert* ingredients in cough medicine⟩ ⟨*inert* gas⟩ **3** : very slow to move or act : SLUGGISH — **in·ert·ly** *adv* — **in·ert·ness** *n*

in·er·tia \in-'ər-shə, -shē-ə\ *n* **1** : a property of matter by which it remains at rest or in uniform motion in the same straight line unless acted on by some external force **2** : a disposition not to move, change, or exert oneself — **in·er·tial** \-shəl\ *adj*

inertial guidance *n* : guidance (as of an aircraft) by means of self-contained automatically controlling devices that respond to changes in velocity or direction

in·es·cap·a·ble \ˌin-ə-'skā-pə-bəl\ *adj* : incapable of being escaped — **in·es·cap·a·bly** \-blē\ *adv*

in·es·ti·ma·ble \(')in-'es-tə-mə-bəl\ *adj* : too valuable or excellent to be measured or appreciated — **in·es·ti·ma·bly** \-blē\ *adv*

in·ev·i·ta·ble \in-'ev-ət-ə-bəl\ *adj* : incapable of being avoided or evaded : bound to happen : CERTAIN — **in·ev·i·ta·bil·i·ty** \(ˌ)in-ˌev-ət-ə-'bil-ət-ē\ *n* — **in·ev·i·ta·ble·ness** \(')in-'ev-ət-ə-bəl-nəs\ *n* — **in·ev·i·ta·bly** \-blē\ *adv*

in·ex·act \ˌin-ig-'zakt\ *adj* : not precisely correct or true : INACCURATE — **in·ex·ac·ti·tude** \-'zak-tə-ˌt(y)üd\ *n* — **in·ex·act·ly** \-'zak-(t)lē\ *adv* — **in·ex·act·ness** \-'zak(t)-nəs\ *n*

ə abut	ər further	a back	ā bake
ä cot, cart	aù out	ch chin	e less / ē easy
g gift / i trip	ī life	j joke	ng sing / ō flow
ȯ flaw	ȯi coin	th thin	t͟h this / ü loot
ù foot / y yet	yü few	yù furious	zh vision

in·ex·cus·a·ble \ˌin-ik-'skyüz-ə-bəl\ *adj* : not to be excused : not justifiable ⟨*inexcusable* rudeness⟩ — **in·ex·cus·a·ble·ness** *n* — **in·ex·cus·a·bly** \-blē\ *adv*

in·ex·haust·i·ble \ˌin-ig-'zȯ-stə-bəl\ *adj* **1** : plentiful enough not to give out : UNFAILING ⟨an *inexhaustible* supply⟩ **2** : UNTIRING — **in·ex·haust·i·bil·i·ty** \-ˌzȯ-stə-'bil-ət-ē\ *n* — **in·ex·haust·i·bly** \-'zȯ-stə-blē\ *adv*

in·ex·o·ra·ble \(')in-'eks-(ə-)rə-bəl\ *adj* : not to be persuaded or moved by earnest requests : RELENTLESS — **in·ex·o·ra·bil·i·ty** \(ˌ)in-ˌeks-(ə-)rə-'bil-ət-ē\ *n* — **in·ex·o·ra·ble·ness** \(')in-'eks-(ə-)rə-bəl-nəs\ *n* — **in·ex·o·ra·bly** \-blē\ *adv*

in·ex·pe·di·ent \ˌin-ik-'spēd-ē-ənt\ *adj* : not suited to bring about a desired result : UNWISE — **in·ex·pe·di·en·cy** \-ən-sē\ *n* — **in·ex·pe·di·ent·ly** *adv*

in·ex·pen·sive \ˌin-ik-'spen(t)-siv\ *adj* : reasonable in price : CHEAP — **in·ex·pen·sive·ly** *adv* — **in·ex·pen·sive·ness** *n*

in·ex·pe·ri·ence \ˌin-ik-'spir-ē-ən(t)s\ *n* : lack of experience or of knowledge or skill gained by experience — **in·ex·pe·ri·enced** \-ən(t)st\ *adj*

in·ex·pert \(')in-'ek-ˌspərt, ˌin-ik-'\ *adj* : not expert : UNSKILLED — **in·ex·pert·ly** *adv* — **in·ex·pert·ness** *n*

in·ex·pi·a·ble \(')in-'ek-spē-ə-bəl\ *adj* : incapable of being atoned for ⟨an *inexpiable* crime⟩ — **in·ex·pi·a·bly** \-blē\ *adv*

in·ex·plic·a·ble \ˌin-ik-'splik-ə-bəl, (')in-'ek-(ˌ)splik-\ *adj* : incapable of being explained — **in·ex·plic·a·bil·i·ty** \ˌin-ik-ˌsplik-ə-'bil-ət-ē, (ˌ)in-ˌek-(ˌ)splik-ə-ˌbil-\ *n* — **in·ex·plic·a·ble·ness** \ˌin-ik-'splik-ə-bəl-nəs, (')in-'ek-(ˌ)splik-\ *n* — **in·ex·plic·a·bly** \-blē\ *adv*

in·ex·press·i·ble \ˌin-ik-'spres-ə-bəl\ *adj* : being beyond one's power to express : INDESCRIBABLE ⟨*inexpressible* joy⟩ — **in·ex·press·i·bil·i·ty** \-ˌspres-ə-'bil-ət-ē\ *n* — **in·ex·press·i·ble·ness** \-'spres-ə-bəl-nəs\ *n* — **in·ex·press·i·bly** \-blē\ *adv*

in·ex·pres·sive \-'spres-iv\ *adj* : not expressive ⟨an *inexpressive* face⟩ — **in·ex·pres·sive·ly** *adv* — **in·ex·pres·sive·ness** *n*

in·ex·tin·guish·a·ble \ˌin-ik-'sting-gwish-ə-bəl\ *adj* : not extinguishable : UNQUENCHABLE — **in·ex·tin·guish·a·bly** \-blē\ *adv*

in·ex·tric·a·ble \ˌin-ik-'strik-ə-bəl, (')in-'ek-(ˌ)strik- \ *adj* **1** : forming a tangle from which one cannot free oneself **2** : not capable of being disentangled — **in·ex·tric·a·bly** \-blē\ *adv*

inf *abbr* infinitive

in·fal·li·ble \(')in-'fal-ə-bəl\ *adj* **1** : not capable of being wrong : UNERRING **2** : not liable to fail : SURE ⟨an *infallible* remedy⟩ — **in·fal·li·bil·i·ty** \(ˌ)in-ˌfal-ə-'bil-ət-ē\ *n* — **in·fal·li·bly** \(')in-'fal-ə-blē\ *adv*

in·fa·mous \'in-fə-məs\ *adj* **1** : having an evil reputation ⟨an *infamous* person⟩ **2** : causing or bringing infamy : DETESTABLE, ABOMINABLE ⟨an *infamous* crime⟩ — **in·fa·mous·ly** *adv*

in·fa·my \-mē\ *n, pl* **-mies 1** : an evil reputation **2 a** : an infamous act **b** : the state of being infamous

in·fan·cy \'in-fən-sē\ *n, pl* **-cies 1** : early childhood **2** : a beginning or early period of existence

in·fant \'in-fənt\ *n* [from Latin *infant-*, stem of *infans*, meaning literally "not speaking", from *in-* "un-" and *fans*, present participle of *fari* "to speak"] : a child in the first period of life — **infant** *adj*

in·fan·ti·cide \in-'fant-ə-ˌsīd\ *n* **1** : the killing of an infant **2** : a person who kills an infant

in·fan·tile \'in-fən-,tīl, -təl, -,tēl\ *adj* : of, relating to, or resembling infants or infancy : CHILDISH — **in·fan·til·i·ty** \,in-fən-'til-ət-ē\ *n*

infantile paralysis *n* : POLIOMYELITIS

in·fan·til·ism \'in-fən-,tīl-,iz-əm, -təl-, -,tēl-\ *n* : retention of childish qualities in adult life

in·fan·try \'in-fən-trē\ *n, pl* **-tries** : soldiers trained, armed, and equipped to fight — **in·fan·try·man** \-mən\ *n*

in·fat·u·ate \in-'fach-ə-,wāt\ *vb* : to fill with a foolish or extravagant love or admiration — **in·fat·u·at·ed** *adj* — **in·fat·u·a·tion** \in-,fach-ə-'wā-shən\ *n*

in·fect \in-'fekt\ *vb* **1** : to contaminate with a disease-producing substance or organism ⟨*infected* bedding⟩ **2 a** : to communicate a germ or disease to ⟨coughing people who *infect* others⟩ **b** : to enter and cause disease in ⟨bacteria that *infect* wounds⟩ **3** : to cause to share one's feelings ⟨*infected* everyone with his enthusiasm⟩ — **in·fec·tious** \-'fek-shəs\ *adj* — **in·fec·tious·ly** *adv* — **in·fec·tious·ness** *n* — **in·fec·tor** \-'fek-tər\ *n*

in·fec·tion \in-'fek-shən\ *n* **1** : an act or process of infecting **2 a** : the state produced by an infective agent (as a germ or parasite) living in or on a suitable host **b** : CONTAGIOUS DISEASE, INFECTIOUS DISEASE **3 a** : an infective agent **b** : material contaminated with an infective agent **4** : the communication of emotions

infectious disease *n* : a disease caused by the presence, growth, and multiplication of microorganisms in the body

infectious jaundice *n* : a disease caused by a spirochete and characterized by chills, fever, muscle pain, inflammation of the liver, and more or less severe jaundice

in·fec·tive \in-'fek-tiv\ *adj* : producing or able to produce infection — **in·fec·tiv·i·ty** \(,)in-,fek-'tiv-ət-ē\ *n*

in·fe·lic·i·tous \,in-fi-'lis-ət-əs\ *adj* **1** : UNHAPPY, UNFORTUNATE ⟨an *infelicitous* time⟩ **2** : not well chosen : UNSUITABLE ⟨an *infelicitous* word⟩ — **in·fe·lic·i·tous·ly** *adv*

in·fe·lic·i·ty \-ət-ē\ *n, pl* **-ties** **1** : UNHAPPINESS, WRETCHEDNESS **2** : a lack of suitability **3** : an inappropriate act or expression

in·fer \in-'fər\ *vb* **in·ferred**; **in·fer·ring** **1** : to derive as a conclusion from facts or premises **2** : GUESS, SURMISE **3** : IMPLY — **in·fer·a·ble** *or* **in·fer·ri·ble** \-'fər-ə-bəl\ *adj* — **in·fer·rer** \-'fər-ər\ *n*

in·fer·ence \'in-f(ə-)rən(t)s\ *n* **1** : the act or process of inferring **2** : something inferred

in·fe·ri·or \in-'fir-ē-ər\ *adj* [from Latin, comparative of *inferus* "underneath"; from the same source as English *under*] **1** : situated lower down **2** : of low or lower degree or rank **3** : of little or less importance, value, or merit — **inferior** *n* — **in·fe·ri·or·i·ty** \(,)in-,fir-ē-'ór-ət-ē, -'är-\ *n*

inferior court *n* : a court (as of a justice of the peace) having limited rather than general jurisdiction

inferior vena cava *n* : a large vein returning blood to the right atrium of the heart from the viscera and the posterior parts of the body

in·fer·nal \in-'fər-nəl\ *adj* **1** : of or relating to hell **2** : suitable to hell : FIENDISH ⟨*infernal* cruelty⟩ —**in·fer·nal·ly** \-nə-lē\ *adv*

in·fer·no \in-'fər-nō\ *n, pl* **-nos** [from Italian, from Latin *infernus*, originally an adjective meaning "situated underneath"] **1** : HELL **2 a** : a very hot place **b** : a raging fire

in·fer·tile \(')in-'fərt-əl\ *adj* : not fertile : STERILE, BARREN — **in·fer·til·i·ty** \,in-(,)fər-'til-ət-ē\ *n*

in·fest \in-'fest\ *vb* **1** : to spread or swarm in or over in a troublesome manner **2** : to live in or on as a parasite — **in·fes·ta·tion** \,in-,fes-'tā-shən\ *n* — **in·fest·er** \in-'fes-tər\ *n*

in·fi·del \'in-fəd-əl, -fə-,del\ *n* : a person who does not believe in a particular religion — **infidel** *adj*

in·fi·del·i·ty \,in-fə-'del-ət-ē, -fī-\ *n, pl* **-ties** **1** : lack of faith in a religion **2** : unfaithfulness esp. to one's husband or wife

in·field \'in-,fēld\ *n* **1 a** : the part of a baseball field enclosed by the three bases and home plate and including the base paths **b** : the defensive positions comprising first base, second base, shortstop, and third base **2** : the area enclosed by a racetrack or running track — **in·field·er** \-,fēl-dər\ *n*

in·fil·trate \in-'fil-,trāt, 'in-(,)fil-\ *vb* **1** : to pass into or through by filtering or permeating **2** : to enter or become established gradually or unobtrusively — **in·fil·tra·tion** \,in-(,)fil-'trā-shən\ *n* — **in·fil·tra·tor** \'in-(,)fil-,trāt-ər, in-'fil-\ *n*

in·fi·nite \'in-fə-nət\ *adj* **1 a** : being without limits of any kind : ENDLESS ⟨*infinite* space⟩ **b** : having cardinality that cannot be indicated by a whole number **2** : seeming to be without limits : VAST ⟨*infinite* patience⟩ ⟨*infinite* wealth⟩ — **infinite** *n* — **in·fi·nite·ly** *adv* — **in·fi·nite·ness** *n*

in·fin·i·tes·i·mal \(,)in-,fin-ə-'tes-ə-məl\ *adj* : immeasurably small — **in·fin·i·tes·i·mal·ly** \-mə-lē\ *adv*

in·fin·i·tive \in-'fin-ət-iv\ *n* : a verb form serving as a noun or as a modifier and at the same time taking objects and adverbial modifiers ⟨*have* in "let him have it" and *to do* in "he has nothing to do" are *infinitives*⟩ — **infinitive** *adj*

in·fin·i·ty \in-'fin-ət-ē\ *n, pl* **-ties** **1** : the quality of being infinite **2 a** : an unlimited extent of time, space, or quantity **b** : a point infinitely far away **3** : an indefinitely great number or amount

in·firm \in-'fərm\ *adj* **1** : weakened in vitality; *esp* : feeble from age **2** : not solid or stable : INSECURE ***syn*** see WEAK ***ant*** hale — **in·firm·ly** *adv*

in·fir·ma·ry \in-'fərm-(ə-)rē\ *n, pl* **-ries** : a place where the infirm or sick are lodged for care and treatment

in·fir·mi·ty \in-'fər-mət-ē\ *n, pl* **-ties** **1** : the quality or state of being infirm : FEEBLENESS **2** : a cause of infirmity (as an ailment, handicap, or weakness of character)

in·flame \in-'flām\ *vb* **1** : to set on fire : KINDLE **2** : to excite to excessive action or feeling **3** : to cause to redden or grow hot from anger or excitement **4** : to cause inflammation in (bodily tissue) **5** : to become affected with inflammation — **in·flam·er** *n*

in·flam·ma·ble \in-'flam-ə-bəl\ *adj* **1** : FLAMMABLE **2** : easily inflamed : EXCITABLE — **in·flam·ma·bil·i·ty** \-,flam-ə-'bil-ət-ē\ *n* — **in·flam·ma·ble·ness** \-'flam-ə-bəl-nəs\ *n* — **in·flam·ma·bly** \-blē\ *adv*

in·flam·ma·tion \,in-flə-'mā-shən\ *n* **1** : the act of inflaming : the state of being inflamed **2** : a local bodily response to injury in which an affected area becomes red, hot, painful, and filled with blood

in·flam·ma·to·ry \in-'flam-ə-,tōr-ē, -,tór-\ *adj* **1** : tending to excite anger, disorder, or rebellion ⟨*inflammatory* speeches⟩ **2** : causing or accompanied by inflammation ⟨*inflammatory* diseases⟩

in·flate \in-'flāt\ *vb* **1** : to swell with a fluid (as gas) ⟨*inflate* a balloon⟩ **2** : to puff up : ELATE ⟨*inflated* with a sense of his own importance⟩ **3** : to increase abnormally ⟨*inflated* prices⟩ ⟨*inflated* currency⟩ — **in·flat·a·ble** \in-'flāt-ə-bəl\ *adj*

I

in·flat·ed \-'flāt-əd\ *adj* : hollow and stretched or swelled ⟨*inflated* pods of a plant⟩

in·fla·tion \in-'flā-shən\ *n* **1** : an act of inflating : the state of being inflated **2** : a substantial and continuing rise in prices

in·fla·tion·ary \-shə-,ner-ē\ *adj* : of, relating to, or tending to cause inflation

in·flect \in-'flekt\ *vb* **1** : to vary a word by inflection **2** : to vary the pitch of the voice

in·flec·tion \in-'flek-shən\ *n* **1** : a change in the pitch or tone of a person's voice **2** : the change in the form of a word showing its case, gender, number, person, tense, mood, voice, or comparison — **in·flec·tion·al** \-sh(ə-)nəl\ *adj*

in·flex·i·ble \(')in-'flek-sə-bəl\ *adj* **1** : not easily bent or twisted : RIGID, STIFF **2** : not easily influenced or persuaded : FIRM ⟨an *inflexible* judge⟩ **3** : incapable of change : UNALTERABLE ⟨*inflexible* laws⟩ — **in·flex·i·bil·i·ty** \(,)in-,flek-sə-'bil-ət-ē\ *n* — **in·flex·i·bly** \(')in-'flek-sə-blē\ *adv*

in·flict \in-'flikt\ *vb* **1** : to give esp. by striking ⟨*inflict* a wound⟩ **2** : to cause something damaging or painful to be endured : IMPOSE ⟨*inflict* punishment⟩ — **in·flic·tion** \-'flik-shən\ *n*

in·flo·res·cence \,in-flə-'res-ən(t)s\ *n* **1 a** : the

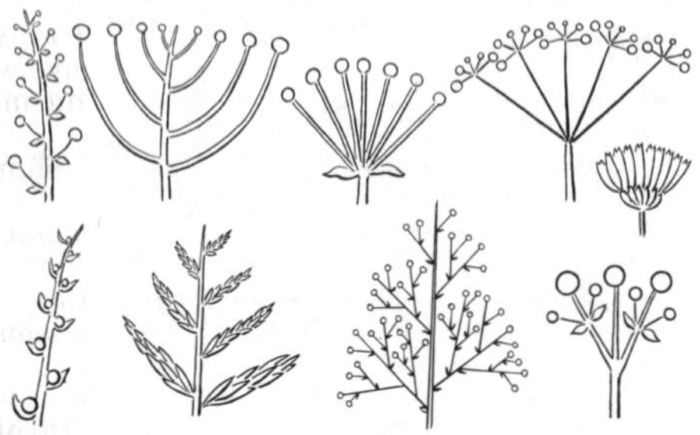

inflorescence 1a (types) top row: raceme, corymb, umbel, compound umbel, capitulum; bottom row: spike, compound spike, panicle, cyme

mode of development and arrangement of flowers on a stem **b** : a flowering stem with all its parts; *also* : a flower cluster or sometimes a solitary flower **2** : BLOSSOMING, FLOWERING — **in·flo·res·cent** \-ənt\ *adj*

in·flow \'in-,flō\ *n* **1** : the act of flowing in **2** : something that flows in

¹in·flu·ence \'in-,flü-ən(t)s\ *n* **1** : the act or power of producing an effect indirectly or without apparent use of force or exercise of command **2** : corrupt interference with authority **3** : a person or thing that exerts influence

²influence *vb* : to have an influence on : affect by influence — **in·flu·enc·er** *n*

in·flu·en·tial \,in-flü-'en-chəl\ *adj* : having or exerting influence — **in·flu·en·tial·ly** \-'ench-(ə-)lē\ *adv*

ə abut	ər further	a back	ā bake	
ä cot, cart	au̇ out	ch chin	e less	ē easy
g gift	i trip	ī life	j joke	ng sing	ō flow
ȯ flaw	ȯi coin	th thin	t͟h this	ü loot
u̇ foot	y yet	yü few	yu̇ furious	zh vision

in·flu·en·za \,in-flü-'en-zə\ *n* **1** : an acute and very contagious virus disease with sudden onset, fever, exhaustion, severe aches and pains, and inflammation of the respiratory tract **2** : any of various feverish usu. virus diseases of man or domestic animals typically with respiratory symptoms and inflammation and often affecting the body as a whole

in·flux \'in-,fləks\ *n* : a flowing in : INFLOW

in·fold *vb* **1** \in-'fōld\ : ENFOLD **2** \'in-,fōld\ : to fold inward

in·form \in-'fȯrm\ *vb* **1** : to let a person know something : TELL **2** : to give information so as to accuse or make suspect ⟨*inform* against him to the police⟩

in·for·mal \(')in-'fȯr-məl\ *adj* **1** : carried out without formality **2** : CASUAL ⟨*informal* clothes⟩ — **in·for·mal·i·ty** \,in-fȯr-'mal-ət-ē, -fər-\ *n* — **in·for·mal·ly** \(')in-'fȯr-mə-lē\ *adv*

in·form·ant \in-'fȯr-mənt\ *n* : INFORMER

in·for·ma·tion \,in-fər-'mā-shən\ *n* **1** : the communication of knowledge or intelligence **2 a** : knowledge obtained from investigation, study, or instruction : FACTS **b** : NEWS — **in·for·ma·tion·al** \-sh(ə-)nəl\ *adj*

in·form·a·tive \in-'fȯr-mət-iv\ *adj* : providing knowledge : INSTRUCTIVE — **in·form·a·tive·ly** *adv* — **in·form·a·tive·ness** *n*

in·form·er \in-'fȯr-mər\ *n* : someone who informs; *esp* : a person who informs against someone else

infra- *prefix* **1** : below ⟨*infra*human⟩ ⟨*infra*sonic⟩ **2** : below in a scale or series ⟨*infra*red⟩

in·fract \in-'frakt\ *vb* : VIOLATE — **in·frac·tion** \-'frak-shən\ *n* — **in·frac·tor** \-'frak-tər\ *n*

in·fra·red \,in-frə-'red, -(,)frä-\ *adj* **1** : lying outside the visible spectrum at its red end — used of heat radiation of wavelengths longer than those of visible light **2** : relating to, producing, or employing infrared radiation ⟨*infrared* photography⟩ **3** : sensitive to infrared radiation and capable of photographing in darkness ⟨*infrared* film⟩ — **infrared** *n*

in·fre·quent \(')in-'frē-kwənt\ *adj* **1** : seldom happening or occurring : RARE **2** : placed or occurring at considerable distances or intervals — **in·fre·quen·cy** \-kwən-sē\ *n* — **in·fre·quent·ly** *adv*

in·fringe \in-'frinj\ *vb* **1** : VIOLATE, TRANSGRESS ⟨*infringe* a treaty⟩ ⟨*infringe* a patent⟩ **2** : ENCROACH ⟨*infringe* on a person's rights⟩ — **in·fringe·ment** *n* — **in·fring·er** *n*

in·fu·ri·ate \in-'fyu̇r-ē-,āt\ *vb* : to make furious : ENRAGE — **in·fu·ri·at·ing·ly** \-,āt-ing-lē\ *adv* — **in·fu·ri·a·tion** \-,fyu̇r-ē-'ā-shən\ *n*

in·fuse \in-'fyüz\ *vb* **1** : to put in as if by pouring ⟨*infused* courage into his followers⟩ **2** : to steep without boiling ⟨*infuse* tea⟩ — **in·fus·er** *n*

in·fus·i·ble \(')in-'fyü-zə-bəl\ *adj* : incapable or very difficult of fusion

in·fu·sion \in-'fyü-zhən\ *n* **1** : the act or process of infusing **2** : a substance extracted esp. from a plant material by steeping or soaking in water ⟨a strong *infusion* of tea⟩ **3** : a watery suspension of decaying organic matter ⟨culturing protozoans in a hay *infusion*⟩

in·fu·so·ri·an \,in-fyü-'zōr-ē-ən, -'zȯr-\ *n* : any of a varied group of minute organisms found esp. in decomposing infusions of organic matter; *esp* : a ciliated protozoan — **in·fu·so·ri·al** \-ē-əl\ *or* **infusorian** *adj*

¹-ing \ing; *in some dialects usu, in other dialects informally,* ən *or* in\ *vb suffix or adj suffix* — used to form the present participle ⟨sail*ing*⟩ and sometimes to form an adjective not derived from a verb ⟨hulk*ing*⟩

²-ing *n suffix* **1** : action or process ⟨runn*ing*⟩

⟨sleep*ing*⟩ ⟨meet*ing*⟩ **2 :** product or result of an action or process ⟨an engrav*ing*⟩ ⟨earn*ings*⟩ **3 :** something used in or connected with making or doing ⟨bedd*ing*⟩ ⟨roof*ing*⟩

in·ge·nious \in-'jē-nyəs\ *adj* **:** marked by ingenuity ⟨an *ingenious* plan⟩ — **in·ge·nious·ly** *adv* — **in·ge·nious·ness** *n*

in·ge·nue *or* **in·gé·nue** \'an-jə-,nü, 'an-zhə-\ *n* **:** a naïve girl or young woman or an actress representing such a person

in·ge·nu·i·ty \,in-jə-'n(y)ü-ət-ē\ *n, pl* **-ties 1 :** skill or cleverness in discovering, inventing, or contriving **2 :** an ingenious device or contrivance

in·gen·u·ous \in-'jen-yə-wəs\ *adj* **1 :** STRAIGHTFORWARD, FRANK **2 :** showing innocent or childlike simplicity **:** NAÏVE — **in·gen·u·ous·ly** *adv* — **in·gen·u·ous·ness** *n*

in·gest \in-'jest\ *vb* **:** to take in for digestion — **in·gest·i·ble** \-'jes-tə-bəl\ *adj* — **in·ges·tion** \-'jes-chən\ *n* — **in·ges·tive** \-'jes-tiv\ *adj*

in·gle·nook \'ing-gəl-,nu̇k\ *n* **:** a corner by the fire or chimney

in·glo·ri·ous \(')in-'glōr-ē-əs, -'glȯr-\ *adj* **1 :** lacking fame or honor **2 :** bringing disgrace **:** SHAMEFUL ⟨*inglorious* defeat⟩ — **in·glo·ri·ous·ly** *adv* — **in·glo·ri·ous·ness** *n*

in·got \'ing-gət\ *n* **:** a mass of metal cast into a convenient shape for storage or transportation

[1]**in·grain** \(')in-'grān\ *vb* **1 :** to incorporate in the natural texture **2 :** to instill deeply **:** fix firmly ⟨an *ingrained* habit⟩

[2]**in·grain** \'in-,grān\ *adj* **1 :** made of fiber that is dyed before being spun into yarn **2 :** made of yarn that is dyed before being woven or knitted ⟨*ingrain* carpet⟩ — **ingrain** *n*

in·grate \'in-,grāt\ *n* **:** an ungrateful person

in·gra·ti·ate \in-'grā-shē-,āt\ *vb* **:** to gain favor or acceptance for by deliberate effort ⟨quickly *ingratiated* herself with her new pupils⟩ — **in·gra·ti·at·ing·ly** \-'grā-shē-,āt-ing-lē\ *adv* — **in·gra·ti·a·tion** \-,grā-shē-'ā-shən\ *n*

in·grat·i·tude \(')in-'grat-ə-,t(y)üd\ *n* **:** lack of gratitude

in·gre·di·ent \in-'grēd-ē-ənt\ *n* **:** one of the substances that make up a mixture ⟨*ingredients* of a cake⟩ — **ingredient** *adj*

in·gress \'in-,gres\ *n* **1 :** the act of entering **2 :** the power or liberty of entering **3 :** a means of entrance

in·grow·ing \'in-,grō-ing\ *adj* **:** growing or tending inward — **in·grown** \-,grōn\ *adj*

in·hab·it \in-'hab-ət\ *vb* **:** to live or dwell in — **in·hab·it·a·ble** \-ət-ə-bəl\ *adj* — **in·hab·it·er** \-'hab-ət-ər\ *n*

in·hab·it·ant \in-'hab-ət-ənt\ *n* **:** one who lives permanently in a place

in·hal·ant \in-'hā-lənt\ *n* **:** something (as an allergen or medicated spray) that is inhaled — **inhalant** *adj*

in·ha·la·tor \'in-(h)ə-,lāt-ər\ *n* **:** an apparatus used in inhaling something (as a mixture of oxygen and carbon dioxide)

in·hale \in-'hāl\ *vb* **1 :** to draw in by breathing **2 :** to breathe in — **in·ha·la·tion** \,in-(h)ə-'lā-shən\ *n*

in·hal·er \in-'hā-lər\ *n* **1 :** one that inhales **2 :** INHALATOR

in·har·mo·ni·ous \,in-(,)här-'mō-nē-əs\ *adj* **:** not harmonious **:** DISCORDANT — **in·har·mo·ni·ous·ly** *adv*

in·here \in-'hi(ə)r\ *vb* **:** to be inherent **:** BELONG

in·her·ent \in-'hir-ənt, -'her-\ *adj* **:** belonging to or being a part of the nature of a person or thing ⟨an *inherent* sense of fair play⟩ ⟨fluidity is an *inherent* quality of gas⟩ — **in·her·ence** \-ən(t)s\ *n* — **in·her·ent·ly** *adv*

in·her·it \in-'her-ət\ *vb* **1 :** to receive by legal right from a person at his death **2 :** to receive by genetic transmission ⟨*inherit* a strong constitution⟩ **3 :** to have handed on to one by a predecessor ⟨*inherit* a job⟩ — **in·her·it·a·ble** \-ət-ə-bəl\ *adj* — **in·her·i·tor** \-ət-ər\ *n* — **in·her·i·tress** \-ə-trəs\ *or* **in·her·i·trix** \-ə-(,)triks\ *n*

in·her·it·ance \in-'her-ət-ən(t)s\ *n* **1 :** the act of inheriting **2 :** something that is or may be inherited

in·hib·it \in-'hib-ət\ *vb* **1 :** to prohibit from doing something **2 :** to hold in check **:** RESTRAIN, REPRESS — **in·hib·i·tive** \-ət-iv\ *adj* — **in·hib·i·tor** \-ət-ər\ *n* — **in·hib·i·to·ry** \-ə-,tōr-ē, -,tȯr-\ *adj*

in·hib·it·ed \in-'hib-ət-əd\ *adj* **:** disposed to repress desires, feelings, and thoughts

in·hi·bi·tion \,in-(h)ə-'bish-ən\ *n* **1 a :** the act of inhibiting **:** the state of being inhibited **b :** something that inhibits **2 :** an inner force that prevents or impedes the free expression of thoughts, emotions, or desires

in·hos·pit·a·ble \,in-,häs-'pit-ə-bəl, (')in-'häs-(,)pit-\ *adj* **1 :** not showing hospitality **2 :** providing no shelter or food **:** BARREN ⟨an *inhospitable* desert⟩ — **in·hos·pit·a·ble·ness** \,in-,häs-'pit-ə-bəl-nəs, (')in-'häs-(,)pit-\ *n* — **in·hos·pit·a·bly** \-blē\ *adv* — **in·hos·pi·tal·i·ty** \(,)in-,häs-pə-'tal-ət-ē\ *n*

in·hu·man \(')in-'hyü-mən, (')in-'yü-\ *adj* **1 a :** SAVAGE, BRUTAL **b :** COLD, IMPERSONAL **2 :** unlike what is typically human ⟨an *inhuman* cry⟩ — **in·hu·man·ly** *adv*

in·hu·mane \,in-hyü-'mān, ,in-yü-\ *adj* **:** not humane **:** INHUMAN 1 — **in·hu·mane·ly** *adv*

in·hu·man·i·ty \-'man-ət-ē\ *n, pl* **-ties :** a cruel or barbarous act or attitude

in·im·i·cal \in-'im-i-kəl\ *adj* **1 :** HOSTILE, UNFRIENDLY **2 :** HARMFUL, DAMAGING ⟨habits *inimical* to health⟩ — **in·im·i·cal·ly** \-k(ə-)lē\ *adv*

in·im·i·ta·ble \(')in-'im-ət-ə-bəl\ *adj* **:** not capable of being imitated **:** MATCHLESS — **in·im·i·ta·bil·i·ty** \(,)in-,im-ət-ə-'bil-ət-ē\ *n* — **in·im·i·ta·ble·ness** \(')in-'im-ət-ə-bəl-nəs\ *n* — **in·im·i·ta·bly** \-blē\ *adv*

in·iq·ui·ty \in-'ik-wət-ē\ *n, pl* **-ties [**from Latin *iniquitas* "unfairness", from *iniquus* "unequal", from *in-* "un-" and *aequus* "equal"**] 1 :** complete injustice **:** WICKEDNESS **2 :** something that is unjust or wicked **:** SIN — **in·iq·ui·tous** \-wət-əs\ *adj* — **in·iq·ui·tous·ly** *adv* — **in·iq·ui·tous·ness** *n*

[1]**ini·tial** \in-'ish-əl\ *adj* **1 :** of, relating to, or existing at the beginning **:** EARLIEST ⟨*initial* stages of a disease⟩ **2 :** placed or standing at the beginning **:** FIRST ⟨*initial* letter of a word⟩ — **ini·tial·ly** \-'ish-(ə-)lē\ *adv* — **ini·tial·ness** \-'ish-əl-nəs\ *n*

[2]**initial** *n* **:** a first letter esp. of a name

[3]**initial** *vb* **ini·tialed** *or* **ini·tialled**; **ini·tial·ing** *or* **ini·tial·ling** \-'ish-(ə-)ling\ **:** to mark with initials or an initial ⟨*initial* a handkerchief⟩

[1]**ini·ti·ate** \in-'ish-ē-,āt\ *vb* **1 :** ORIGINATE, BEGIN ⟨*initiate* a new policy⟩ **2 :** to instruct in the basics of something **:** INTRODUCE ⟨*initiate* pupils into the mysteries of algebra⟩ **3 :** to induct into membership by special rites — **ini·ti·a·tor** \-,āt-ər\ *n* — **ini·tia·to·ry** \-'ish-(ē-)ə-,tōr-ē, -,tȯr-\ *adj*

[2]**ini·tiate** \in-'ish-(ē-)ət\ *n* **1 :** a person who is undergoing or has passed an initiation **2 :** an expert in a special field

ini·ti·a·tion \in-,ish-ē-'ā-shən\ *n* **1 :** the act of initiating **:** the process of being initiated **:** INTRODUCTION **2 :** the ceremonies with which a person is made a member of a society

ini·tia·tive \in-'ish-ət-iv\ *n* **1 :** a first step or movement ⟨take the *initiative* in becoming acquainted⟩ **2 :** energy in initiation of action : ENTERPRISE ⟨has ability but lacks *initiative*⟩ **3 :** a procedure enabling voters to propose or enact a law directly
in·ject \in-'jekt\ *vb* **1 a :** to throw, drive, or force into something ⟨*inject* fuel into an engine⟩ **b :** to force a fluid into esp. for medical purposes **2 :** to introduce as a subordinate element ⟨*injected* humor into his speech⟩ — **in·ject·a·ble** \-'jek-tə-bəl\ *adj* — **in·jec·tor** \-'jek-tər\ *n*
in·jec·tion \in-'jek-shən\ *n* **1 :** an act or instance of injecting **2 :** something (as a medication) that is injected
in·ju·di·cious \,in-jü-'dish-əs\ *adj* : not judicious : UNWISE — **in·ju·di·cious·ly** *adv* — **in·ju·di·cious·ness** *n*
in·junc·tion \in-'jəng(k)-shən\ *n* : a court order requiring a party to do or refrain from doing a specified act ⟨an *injunction* against the strike⟩
in·jure \'in-jər\ *vb* **in·jured**; **in·jur·ing** \'inj-(ə-)ring\ **1 :** to do an injustice to : WRONG **2 :** to inflict bodily hurt on **3 :** to impair the soundness of ⟨*injured* his arm⟩ ⟨*injured* his pride⟩ **4 :** to inflict material damage or loss on ⟨a tax that *injured* business⟩
in·ju·ri·ous \in-'jür-ē-əs\ *adj* : causing injury : HARMFUL — **in·ju·ri·ous·ly** *adv* — **in·ju·ri·ous·ness** *n*
in·ju·ry \'inj-(ə-)rē\ *n, pl* **-ries** **1 :** an act that damages or hurts : WRONG **2 :** hurt, damage, or loss sustained
in·jus·tice \(')in-'jəs-təs\ *n* **1 :** violation of the rights of another : UNFAIRNESS **2 :** an unjust act
[1]**ink** \'ingk\ *n* **1 :** a usu. liquid material for writing or printing **2 :** the black protective secretion of a cephalopod
[2]**ink** *vb* **1 :** to put ink on **2 :** to write or draw in ink — **ink·er** *n*
ink·ber·ry \'ingk-,ber-ē\ *n* **1 :** POKEWEED **2 :** the fruit of an inkberry
ink·horn \-,hórn\ *n* : a portable container for ink
in·kling \'ing-kling\ *n* : a vague notion : HINT ⟨didn't have an *inkling* of what it all meant⟩
ink·stand \'ingk-,stand\ *n* : INKWELL
ink·well \-,wel\ *n* : a container for ink
inky \'ing-kē\ *adj* **ink·i·er**; **-est** **1 :** consisting of or resembling ink ⟨*inky* blackness of the sea⟩ **2 :** soiled with ink **3 :** of the color of ink : BLACK — **ink·i·ness** *n*
inky cap *n* : a small mushroom whose cap dissolves into an inky fluid after the spores mature

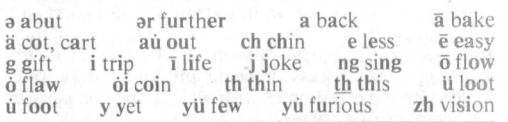

inky caps (about 3 in. high)

in·laid \'in-'lād\ *adj* **1 :** set into a surface in a decorative design; *also* : decorated with an inlaid design **2 :** having a design that goes all the way through ⟨*inlaid* linoleum⟩
in·land \'in-,land, -lənd\ *n* : the part of a country away from the coast or boundaries : INTERIOR — **inland** *adj or adv* — **in·land·er** \-,lan-dər, -lən-\ *n*

ə abut ər further a back ā bake
ä cot, cart aù out ch chin e less ē easy
g gift i trip ī life j joke ng sing ō flow
ȯ flaw ȯi coin th thin th this ü loot
ù foot y yet yü few yù furious zh vision

in–law \'in-,lȯ\ *n* : a relative by marriage
[1]**in·lay** \(')in-'lā\ *vb* **in·laid** \-'lād\; **in·lay·ing** : to set into a surface for decoration or reinforcement — **in·lay·er** *n*
[2]**in·lay** \'in-,lā\ *n* **1 :** inlaid work or material used in inlaying **2 :** a tooth filling shaped to fit a cavity and then cemented into place
in·let \'in-,let, -lət\ *n* **1 :** a small or narrow bay **2 :** an opening for intake esp. of fluids
in·mate \'in-,māt\ *n* : a member of a group occupying a single residence; *esp* : a person confined in an institution (as an asylum or prison)
in·most \'in-,mōst\ *adj* : INNERMOST
inn \'in\ *n* **1 :** a public house that provides lodging and food : HOTEL **2 :** TAVERN 1
in·nards \'in-ərdz\ *n pl* **1 :** the internal organs of a man or animal; *esp* : VISCERA **2 :** the internal parts of a structure or mechanism
in·nate \in-'āt, 'in-,\ *adj* **1 :** existing in or belonging to an individual from birth : NATIVE **2 :** NATURAL, INHERENT ⟨*innate* defects in the plan⟩ — **in·nate·ly** *adv* — **in·nate·ness** *n*
syn INNATE, INBORN, CONGENITAL, HEREDITARY can mean determined or seemingly determined in an individual at birth. INNATE applies to qualities or characteristics that are part of a person's or thing's essential nature ⟨man's *innate* sense of justice⟩; INBORN applies to qualities that form part of an individual's distinctive makeup seemingly from birth ⟨*inborn* aptitudes⟩; CONGENITAL applies chiefly to something that dates from the birth or beginning of the individual involved ⟨*congenital* blindness⟩; HEREDITARY applies specifically to natural traits received from parents ***ant*** acquired
in·ner \'in-ər\ *adj* **1 a :** situated farther in ⟨*inner* room⟩ **b :** near a center esp. of influence ⟨an *inner* circle of advisors⟩ **2 :** of or relating to the mind or spirit ⟨the *inner* life of man⟩ — **in·ner·ly** *adv*
inner ear *n* : a cavity in the temporal bone that contains a complex membranous labyrinth containing sense organs of hearing and of awareness of position in space
inner light *n, often cap I & L* : a divine presence held (as in Quaker doctrine) to enlighten and guide the soul
in·ner·most \'in-ər-,mōst\ *adj* : farthest inward
inner tube *n* : a tube of rubber inside a tire to hold air
in·ning \'in-ing\ *n* **1 :** a baseball team's turn at bat; *also* : a division of a baseball game consisting of a turn at bat for each team **2 :** a chance for action or accomplishment
inn·keep·er \'in-,kē-pər\ *n* : the landlord of an inn
in·no·cent \'in-ə-sənt\ *adj* **1 :** knowing nothing of evil : PURE **2 :** free from guilt or blame : GUILTLESS ⟨*innocent* of the crime⟩ **3 :** free from evil influence or effect : HARMLESS ⟨*innocent* fun⟩ **4 :** SIMPLE, UNSOPHISTICATED, NAÏVE ⟨an *innocent* country boy⟩ — **in·no·cence** \-sən(t)s\ *n* — **innocent** *n* — **in·no·cent·ly** *adv*
in·noc·u·ous \in-'äk-yə-wəs\ *adj* **1 :** producing no injury : HARMLESS ⟨treatment to make sewage *innocuous*⟩ **2 :** not likely to give offense : INOFFENSIVE ⟨the *innocuous* follies of his youth⟩ — **in·noc·u·ous·ly** *adv* — **in·noc·u·ous·ness** *n*
in·nom·i·nate bone \in-,äm-ə-nət-\ *n* : HIPBONE
in·no·vate \'in-ə-,vāt\ *vb* : to introduce novelties : make changes — **in·no·va·tion** \,in-ə-'vā-shən\ *n* — **in·no·va·tive** \-,vāt-iv\ *adj* — **in·no·va·tor** \-,vāt-ər\ *n*

in·nu·en·do \ˌin-yə-'wen-dō\ *n, pl* **-dos** *or* **-does** : a slight or veiled reference; *esp* : a disparaging insinuation

in·nu·mer·a·ble \in-'(y)üm-(ə-)rə-bəl\ *adj* : COUNTLESS — **in·nu·mer·a·bly** \-blē\ *adv*

in·oc·u·late \in-'äk-yə-ˌlāt\ *vb* [from Latin *inoculare* "to insert a bud or graft in a plant", from *oculus* "bud", literally, "eye"] **1** : to introduce a microorganism into ⟨beans *inoculated* with nitrogen-fixing bacteria⟩ **2** : to introduce a serum or agent into in order to treat or prevent a disease ⟨*inoculate* children against diphtheria⟩ — **in·oc·u·la·tion** \in-ˌäk-yə-'lā-shən\ *n* — **in·oc·u·la·tor** \-ˌlāt-ər\ *n*

in·of·fen·sive \ˌin-ə-'fen(t)-siv\ *adj* : not offensive : HARMLESS — **in·of·fen·sive·ly** *adv* — **in·of·fen·sive·ness** *n*

in·op·er·a·ble \(')in-'äp-(ə-)rə-bəl\ *adj* **1** : not suitable for surgery **2** : not in working order

in·op·er·a·tive \-'äp-(ə-)rət-iv, -'äp-ə-ˌrāt-\ *adj* : not functioning : producing no effect ⟨an *inoperative* law⟩ — **in·op·er·a·tive·ness** *n*

in·op·por·tune \(ˌ)in-ˌäp-ər-'t(y)ün\ *adj* : INCONVENIENT ⟨an *inopportune* time⟩ — **in·op·por·tune·ly** *adv* — **in·op·por·tune·ness** \-'t(y)ün-nəs\ *n*

in order that *conj* : THAT

in·or·di·nate \in-'ȯrd-(ə-)nət\ *adj* : not kept within bounds : IMMODERATE ⟨an *inordinate* curiosity⟩ — **in·or·di·nate·ly** *adv* — **in·or·di·nate·ness** *n*

in·or·gan·ic \ˌin-ȯr-'gan-ik\ *adj* **1** : being or composed of matter of other than plant or animal origin : MINERAL **2** : of or relating to a branch of chemistry concerned with substances not usu. classed as organic — **in·or·gan·i·cal·ly** \-'gan-i-k(ə-)lē\ *adv*

INP *abbr* International News Photo

in·put \'in-ˌpu̇t\ *n* **1** : power, energy, a signal, or data put into a machine or system **2** : a point at which an input is put in **3** : the act or process of putting in

input sentence *n* : a basic sentence which is incorporated into the structure of a consumer sentence

in·quest \'in-ˌkwest\ *n* : a judicial or official inquiry or investigation

in·quire \in-'kwī(ə)r\ *vb* **1** : to ask about ⟨*inquired* the way to the station⟩ **2** : to make investigation or inquiry : search into : INVESTIGATE **3** : to put a question : ASK ⟨*inquired* about the weather⟩ — **in·quirer** *n* — **in·quir·ing·ly** \-ing-lē\ *adv*

in·qui·ry \'in-ˌkwī(ə)r-ē, in-'; 'in-kwə-rē, 'ing-\ *n, pl* **-ries** **1 a** : the act of inquiring ⟨learn by *inquiry*⟩ **b** : a request for information ⟨make *inquiries* at the station⟩ **2** : a search for truth or knowledge **3** : a systematic examination : INVESTIGATION

in·qui·si·tion \ˌin-kwə-'zish-ən\ *n* **1** : the act of inquiring **2** : INQUEST **3 a** *cap* : a former Roman Catholic tribunal for the discovery and punishment of heresy **b** : an investigation conducted with little regard for individual rights **c** : a severe questioning — **in·qui·si·tion·al** \-'zish-(ə-)nəl\ *adj*

in·quis·i·tive \in-'kwiz-ət-iv\ *adj* : given to making inquiry : CURIOUS, QUESTIONING; *esp* : too curious about other people's affairs : PRYING — **in·quis·i·tive·ly** *adv* — **in·quis·i·tive·ness** *n*

in·quis·i·tor \in-'kwiz-ət-ər\ *n* : one who conducts an inquisition — **in·quis·i·to·ri·al** \-ˌkwiz-ə-'tōr-ē-əl, -'tȯr-\ *adj* — **in·quis·i·to·ri·al·ly** \-ē-ə-lē\ *adv*

INRI *abbr* [for Latin *Iesus Nazarenus Rex Iudaeorum*] Jesus of Nazareth, King of the Jews

in·road \'in-ˌrōd\ *n* **1** : a sudden hostile invasion : RAID **2** : a serious encroachment : an advance at the expense of another ⟨making *inroads* against the competition⟩

in·rush \'in-ˌrəsh\ *n* : a flooding in : INFLUX

in·sane \(')in-'sān\ *adj* **1** : not sane : unsound in mind : MAD, CRAZY **2** : showing evidence of an unsound mind ⟨an *insane* look⟩ **3** : used by or for the insane ⟨an *insane* asylum⟩ **4** : FOOLISH, WILD ⟨an *insane* attempt⟩ — **in·sane·ly** *adv*

in·san·i·tary \(')in-'san-ə-ˌter-ē\ *adj* : not sanitary : UNHEALTHY

in·san·i·ty \in-'san-ət-ē\ *n, pl* **-ties** **1** : extreme unsoundness or derangement of the mind esp. when sufficient to relieve one of civil or criminal responsibility **2** : a mental illness or disorder **3 a** : extreme folly or unreasonableness **b** : senseless conduct

in·sa·tia·ble \(')in-'sā-shə-bəl\ *adj* : incapable of being satisfied ⟨*insatiable* thirst⟩ ⟨an *insatiable* desire for knowledge⟩ — **in·sa·tia·bly** \-blē\ *adv*

in·scribe \in-'skrīb\ *vb* **1** : to write, engrave, or print characters on something as a lasting record **2** : to enter on a list : ENROLL **3** : to stamp deeply : IMPRESS ⟨a scene *inscribed* on her memory⟩ **4** : to dedicate to someone ⟨*inscribe* a poem⟩ **5** : to draw within a figure so as to touch in as many places as possible — **in·scrib·er** *n*

in·scrip·tion \in-'skrip-shən\ *n* : inscribed words or characters

in·scru·ta·ble \in-'skrüt-ə-bəl\ *adj* : not readily understood : INCOMPREHENSIBLE ⟨an *inscrutable* mystery⟩ — **in·scru·ta·bly** \-blē\ *adv*

in·sect \'in-ˌsekt\ *n* [from Latin *insectum*, from the past participle of *insecare* "to cut into", from *secare* "to cut", the source also of Latin *segmentum* "segment"] **1** : any of numerous small animals that are usu. more or less obviously segmented **2** : any of a class of arthropods (as bugs or bees) with well-defined head, thorax, and abdomen, three pairs of jointed legs, and typically one or two pairs of wings

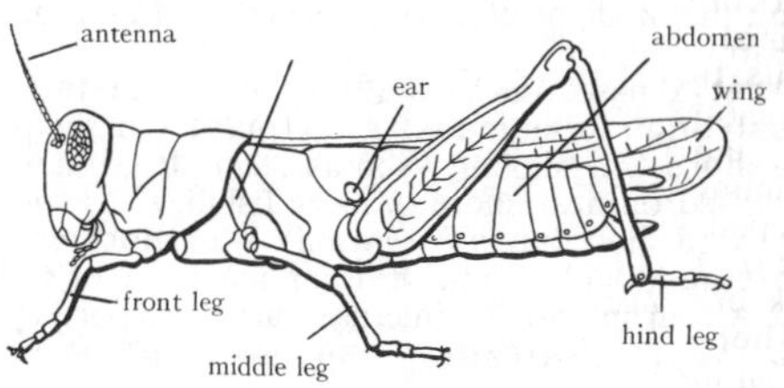

insect

in·sec·ta·ry \'in-ˌsek-tə-rē\ *or* **in·sec·tar·i·um** \-ˌin-ˌsek-'ter-ē-əm\ *n, pl* **-ta·ries** \-tə-rēz\ *or* **-tar·ia** \-'ter-ē-ə\ : a place for rearing or keeping live insects

in·sec·ti·cide \in-'sek-tə-ˌsīd\ *n* : an agent that destroys insects — **in·sec·ti·cid·al** \-ˌsek-tə-'sīd-əl\ *adj*

in·sec·ti·vore \in-'sek-tə-ˌvōr, -ˌvȯr\ *n* **1** : any of an order of mammals (as the moles, shrews, and hedgehogs) that are mostly small, insect-eating, and nocturnal **2** : an insect-eating plant or animal

in·sec·tiv·o·rous \ˌin-ˌsek-'tiv-(ə-)rəs\ *adj* : depending on insects as food

in·se·cure \ˌin(t)-si-'kyu̇(ə)r\ *adj* **1** : not confident or sure : UNCERTAIN ⟨felt *insecure* of his answers⟩ **2** : UNPROTECTED, UNSAFE ⟨*insecure* property⟩ **3** : LOOSE, SHAKY ⟨an *insecure* hinge⟩ **4** : not stable or well-adjusted ⟨*insecure* people⟩ — **in·se·cure·ly** *adv* — **in·se·cu·ri·ty** \-'kyu̇r-ət-ē\ *n*

in·sem·i·nate \in-'sem-ə-ˌnāt\ *vb* : to introduce semen into the genital tract of (a female) — **in·sem·i·na·tion** \-ˌsem-ə-'nā-shən\ *n*

in·sen·sate \(ˈ)in-ˈsen-ˌsāt\ *adj* **1** : INANIMATE **2** : lacking sense : FOOLISH **3** : UNFEELING, BRUTAL — **in·sen·sate·ly** *adv*

in·sen·si·ble \(ˈ)in-ˈsen(t)-sə-bəl\ *adj* **1 a** : INANIMATE **b** : UNCONSCIOUS **c** : lacking or deprived of sensory perception ⟨*insensible* to pain⟩ **2** : so slight as to be imperceptible ⟨*insensible* motion⟩ **3** : APATHETIC, INDIFFERENT ⟨*insensible* to fear⟩; *also* : UNAWARE ⟨*insensible* of their danger⟩ — **in·sen·si·bil·i·ty** \(ˌ)in-ˌsen(t)-sə-ˈbil-ət-ē\ *n* — **in·sen·si·bly** \(ˈ)in-ˈsen(t)-sə-blē\ *adv*

in·sen·si·tive \(ˈ)in-ˈsen(t)-sət-iv, -ˈsen(t)-stiv\ *adj* : not sensitive; *esp* : lacking feeling — **in·sen·si·tive·ly** *adv* — **in·sen·si·tive·ness** *n* — **in·sen·si·tiv·i·ty** \(ˌ)in-ˌsen(t)-sə-ˈtiv-ət-ē\ *n*

in·sep·a·ra·ble \(ˈ)in-ˈsep-(ə-)rə-bəl\ *adj* : incapable of being separated ⟨*inseparable* friends⟩ — **in·sep·a·ra·bil·i·ty** \(ˌ)in-ˌsep-(ə-)rə-ˈbil-ət-ē\ *n* — **inseparable** *n* — **in·sep·a·ra·bly** \(ˈ)in-ˈsep-(ə-)rə-blē\ *adv*

[1]**in·sert** \in-ˈsərt\ *vb* **1** : to put in ⟨*inserted* the key in the lock⟩ ⟨*insert* a word in a sentence⟩ **2** : to set in and make fast — **in·sert·er** *n*

[2]**in·sert** \ˈin-ˌsərt\ *n* : something inserted; *esp* : printed material inserted (as between the leaves of a book)

in·ser·tion \in-ˈsər-shən\ *n* **1** : the act or process of inserting **2 a** : something inserted; *esp* : the part of a muscle that is attached to a part to be moved **b** : the mode or place of attachment of an organ or part

in·set \ˈin-ˌset, in-ˈ\ *vb* **inset** *or* **in·set·ted**; **in·set·ting** : to set in : INSERT — **inset** \ˈin-ˌset\ *n*

in·shore \ˈin-ˈshō(ə)r, -ˈshȯ(ə)r\ *adj* **1** : situated or carried on near shore ⟨*inshore* fishing⟩ **2** : moving toward shore ⟨an *inshore* wind⟩ — **inshore** *adv*

[1]**in·side** \(ˈ)in-ˈsīd, ˈin-ˌ\ *n* **1** : an inner side or surface **2 a** : an interior or internal part : the part within **b** : VISCERA, ENTRAILS — usu. used in pl. — **inside** *adj*

[2]**inside** *prep* **1 a** : in or into the interior of ⟨went *inside* the house⟩ **b** : on the inner side of ⟨put the dot *inside* the curve⟩ **2** : before the end of : WITHIN ⟨*inside* an hour⟩

[3]**inside** *adv* **1** : on the inner side ⟨cleaned his car *inside* and out⟩ **2** : in or into the interior ⟨went *inside*⟩

inside of *prep* : INSIDE

in·sid·er \(ˈ)in-ˈsīd-ər\ *n* : a person who has access to secret information

in·sid·i·ous \in-ˈsid-ē-əs\ *adj* [from Latin *insidiae* "ambush", from *insidēre* "to sit in"; so called from a military force's lying in wait to surprise an enemy] **1** : awaiting a chance to trap : TREACHEROUS **2** : having a more harmful effect than is apparent ⟨an *insidious* disease⟩ — **in·sid·i·ous·ly** *adv* — **in·sid·i·ous·ness** *n*

insignia of the U.S. Army Medical Corps

in·sight \ˈin-ˌsīt\ *n* : the power or act of seeing into a situation

in·sig·nia \in-ˈsig-nē-ə\ *n, pl* **-nia** *or* **-ni·as** : a distinguishing mark esp. of authority, office, or honor : BADGE, EMBLEM

in·sig·nif·i·cant \ˌin(t)-sig-ˈnif-i-kənt\ *adj* : not significant : UNIMPORTANT — **in·sig·nif·i·cance** \-kən(t)s\ *n* — **in·sig·nif·i·cant·ly** *adv*

in·sin·cere \ˌin(t)-sin-ˈsi(ə)r\ *adj* : not sincere : HYPOCRITICAL — **in·sin·cere·ly** *adv* — **in·sin·cer·i·ty** \-ˈser-ət-ē, -ˈsir-\ *n*

in·sin·u·ate \in-ˈsin-yə-ˌwāt\ *vb* **1** : to introduce gradually or in a subtle, indirect, or disguised way ⟨*insinuated* herself into his confidence⟩ **2** : HINT, IMPLY — **in·sin·u·a·tion** \-ˌsin-yə-ˈwā-shən\ *n* — **in·sin·u·a·tor** \-ˌwāt-ər\ *n*

in·sip·id \in-ˈsip-əd\ *adj* **1** : lacking taste or flavor : TASTELESS **2** : lacking in interest, stimulation, or challenge : DULL, FLAT ⟨*insipid* fiction⟩ — **in·si·pid·i·ty** \ˌin(t)-sə-ˈpid-ət-ē\ *n* — **in·sip·id·ly** \in-ˈsip-əd-lē\ *adv*

in·sist \in-ˈsist\ *vb* **1** : to place special emphasis or great importance ⟨*insists* on punctuality⟩ **2** : to make a demand : request urgently ⟨*insisted* that I come⟩

in·sist·ent \in-ˈsis-tənt\ *adj* : compelling attention : DEMANDING, PERSISTENT — **in·sist·ence** \-tən(t)s\ *n* — **in·sist·ent·ly** *adv*

in·so·far as \ˌin(t)-sə-ˌfär-əz\ *conj* : to the extent or degree that

in·so·la·tion \ˌin-ˌsō-ˈlā-shən\ *n* : solar radiation that has been received (as by the earth)

in·sole \ˈin-ˌsōl\ *n* **1** : an inside sole of a shoe **2** : a loose thin strip placed inside a shoe for warmth or comfort

in·so·lent \ˈin(t)-sə-lənt\ *adj* **1** : arrogant in speech or conduct ⟨an *insolent* child⟩ **2** : exhibiting boldness or rudeness ⟨an *insolent* act⟩ — **in·so·lence** \-lən(t)s\ *n* — **in·so·lent·ly** *adv*

in·sol·u·ble \(ˈ)in-ˈsäl-yə-bəl\ *adj* **1** : having no solution ⟨an *insoluble* problem⟩ **2** : impossible or difficult to dissolve ⟨a substance *insoluble* in water⟩ — **in·sol·u·bil·i·ty** \(ˌ)in-ˌsäl-yə-ˈbil-ət-ē\ *n*

in·sol·vent \(ˈ)in-ˈsäl-vənt\ *adj* **1** : unable to pay debts **2** : insufficient to pay all debts ⟨an *insolvent* estate⟩ — **in·sol·ven·cy** \-vən-sē\ *n* — **insolvent** *n*

in·som·nia \in-ˈsäm-nē-ə\ *n* : prolonged inability to sleep : SLEEPLESSNESS — **in·som·ni·ac** \-nē-ˌak\ *adj or n*

in·spect \in-ˈspekt\ *vb* **1** : to examine closely (as for judging quality or condition) ⟨*inspect* foodstuffs⟩ **2** : to view and examine officially ⟨*inspect* the troops⟩

in·spec·tion \in-ˈspek-shən\ *n* **1** : the act of inspecting **2** : a checking or testing of an individual against established standards ***syn*** see EXAMINATION

in·spec·tor \in-ˈspek-tər\ *n* **1** : a person employed to make inspections ⟨meat *inspector*⟩ **2** : a police officer ranking just below a superintendent or deputy superintendent — **in·spec·tor·ship** \-ˌship\ *n*

in·spi·ra·tion \ˌin(t)-spə-ˈrā-shən\ *n* **1** : the drawing of air into the lungs in breathing : INHALATION **2 a** : the act or power of moving the intellect or emotions ⟨the *inspiration* of music⟩ **b** : the quality or state of being inspired ⟨the artist's *inspiration* came from many sources⟩ **c** : something that is inspired ⟨a scheme that was an *inspiration*⟩ **d** : someone or something that inspires ⟨his wife was his greatest *inspiration*⟩ — **in·spi·ra·tion·al** \-sh(ə-)nəl\ *adj* — **in·spi·ra·tion·al·ly** \-ē\ *adv*

in·spire \in-ˈspī(ə)r\ *vb* **1** : to move, guide, or communicate by divine or supernatural influence ⟨prophets *inspired* by God⟩ ⟨thoughts *inspired* by God⟩ **2 a** : to exert an animating, enlivening, or exalting influence on ⟨*inspired* by his mother⟩ **b** : AFFECT ⟨a childhood that *inspired* him with a desire for education⟩ **c** : to infuse or introduce into the mind : AROUSE ⟨*inspires* confidence in his followers⟩ **3** : INHALE **4** : to bring about ⟨studies that *inspired* several inventions⟩ — **in·spir·er** *n*

inst *abbr* instant

in·sta·bil·i·ty \ˌin(t)-stə-'bil-ət-ē\ *n* : the quality or state of being unstable

in·stall *or* **in·stal** \in-'stȯl\ *vb* **in·stalled; in·stall·ing** **1** : to place formally in office : induct into an office or rank **2** : to put in an indicated place, condition, or status ⟨*installed* himself in the best chair⟩ **3** : to set up for use or service ⟨*install* a TV set⟩ — **in·stall·er** *n*

in·stal·la·tion \ˌin(t)-stə-'lā-shən\ *n* **1** : the act of installing : the state of being installed **2** : something installed for use **3** : a military base

¹**in·stall·ment** *or* **in·stal·ment** \in-'stȯl-mənt\ *n* : INSTALLATION 1

²**installment** *or* **instalment** *n* **1** : one of the parts into which a debt is divided when payment is made at intervals **2** : one of several parts (as of a publication) presented at intervals — **installment** *adj*

installment plan *n* : a system of paying for goods or services in installments

¹**in·stance** \'in(t)-stən(t)s\ *n* **1** : SUGGESTION, REQUEST ⟨entered at the *instance* of his teacher⟩ **2** : EXAMPLE ⟨an *instance* of rare courage⟩ **3** : OCCASION, CASE ⟨in the first *instance*⟩ — **for instance** : as an example

²**instance** *vb* : to mention as an example : CITE

¹**in·stant** \'in(t)-stənt\ *n* : a very small space of time : MOMENT

²**instant** *adj* **1** : PRESSING, URGENT ⟨in *instant* need⟩ **2** : IMMEDIATE, DIRECT ⟨an *instant* reponse⟩ **3** : partially prepared by the manufacturer to make final preparation easy ⟨*instant* cake mix⟩; *esp* : immediately soluble in water ⟨*instant* coffee⟩

in·stan·ta·ne·ous \ˌin(t)-stən-'tā-nē-əs\ *adj* **1** : done or happening in an instant **2** : done without delay — **in·stan·ta·ne·ous·ly** *adv* — **in·stan·ta·ne·ous·ness** *n*

in·stan·ter \in-'stant-ər\ *adv* : IMMEDIATELY

in·stant·ly \'in(t)-stənt-lē\ *adv* : without delay : IMMEDIATELY

in·star \'in-ˌstär\ *n* : a stage in the life of an insect between two successive molts

in·state \in-'stāt\ *vb* : to install in a rank or office

in·stead \in-'sted\ *adv* : as a substitute or equivalent ⟨was going to write but called *instead*⟩

instead of \in-ˌsted-ə(v), -ˌstid-\ *prep* : as a substitute for or alternative to ⟨called *instead of* writing⟩

in·step \'in-ˌstep\ *n* **1** : the arched middle part of the human foot **2** : the part of a shoe or stocking over the instep

in·sti·gate \'in(t)-stə-ˌgāt\ *vb* : PROVOKE, INCITE — **in·sti·ga·tion** \ˌin(t)-stə-'gā-shən\ *n* — **in·sti·ga·tor** \'in(t)-stə-ˌgāt-ər\ *n*

in·still *also* **in·stil** \in-'stil\ *vb* **in·stilled; in·still·ing** **1** : to cause to enter drop by drop **2** : to impart gradually ⟨*instill* a love of music⟩ — **in·stil·la·tion** \ˌin(t)-stə-'lā-shən\ *n* — **in·still·er** \in-'stil-ər\ *n*

in·stinct \'in-ˌsting(k)t\ *n* **1** : a natural aptitude, impulse, or capacity **2** : a complex and usu. genetically determined response by an organism to environmental stimuli — **in·stinc·tive** \in-'sting(k)-tiv\ *adj* — **in·stinc·tive·ly** *adv* — **in·stinc·tu·al** \in-'sting(k)-chə(-wə)l\ *adj*

¹**in·sti·tute** \'in(t)-stə-ˌt(y)üt\ *vb* **1** : to set up : ESTABLISH, FOUND ⟨*institute* a society⟩ **2** : INAUGURATE, BEGIN ⟨*institute* an inquiry⟩ — **in·sti·tut·er** *or* **in·sti·tu·tor** \-ˌt(y)üt-ər\ *n*

²**institute** *n* **1** : something that is instituted **2 a** : an organization for the promotion of a cause : ASSOCIATION ⟨an *institute* for mental health⟩ **b** : an educational institution **3** : a meeting or a brief course of meetings for instruction ⟨teachers' *institute*⟩

in·sti·tu·tion \ˌin(t)-stə-'t(y)ü-shən\ *n* **1** : the act of instituting : ESTABLISHMENT **2** : an established custom, practice, or law ⟨turkey dinner is a Thanksgiving *institution*⟩ **3 a** : an established society or corporation; *esp* : a public one ⟨educational *institutions*⟩ ⟨a financial *institution*⟩ **b** : the building used by such an organization — **in·sti·tu·tion·al** \-sh(ə-)nəl\ *adj* — **in·sti·tu·tion·al·ly** \-ē\ *adv*

in·sti·tu·tion·al·ize \-sh(ə-)nə-ˌlīz\ *vb* **1** : to make into or treat like an institution ⟨*institutionalized* housing⟩ **2** : to put into an institution

in·struct \in-'strəkt\ *vb* **1** : to impart knowledge to : TEACH **2** : to give information to : INFORM **3** : to give directions or commands to

in·struc·tion \in-'strək-shən\ *n* **1 a** : LESSON **b** : COMMAND, ORDER **c** *pl* : an outline or manual of procedures to be followed : DIRECTIONS **2** : the action or practice of an instructor or teacher — **in·struc·tion·al** \-sh(ə-)nəl\ *adj*

in·struc·tive \in-'strək-tiv\ *adj* : giving knowledge : serving to instruct or inform ⟨an *instructive* experience⟩ — **in·struc·tive·ly** *adv* — **in·struc·tive·ness** *n*

in·struc·tor \-tər\ *n* : one that instructs : TEACHER — **in·struc·tor·ship** \-ˌship\ *n* — **in·struc·tress** \-'strək-trəs\ *n*

¹**in·stru·ment** \'in(t)-strə-mənt\ *n* **1** : a means whereby something is done **2 a** : IMPLEMENT, TOOL ⟨a surgical *instrument*⟩ **b** : a device used to produce music **3** : a formal legal document (as a deed, bond, or agreement) **4 a** : a measuring device for determining the present value of a quantity under observation **b** : an electrical or mechanical device used in navigating an airplane; *esp* : such a device used as the sole means of navigating

²**in·stru·ment** \-ˌment\ *vb* : to equip with instruments

in·stru·men·tal \ˌin(t)-strə-'ment-əl\ *adj* **1** : acting as an instrument or means ⟨*instrumental* in sending a thief to jail⟩ **2** : designed for or performed with or on a musical instrument **3** : of, relating to, or done with an instrument ⟨*instrumental* error⟩ — **in·stru·men·tal·ly** \-ē\ *adv*

in·stru·men·tal·ist \-'ment-ə-ləst\ *n* : a player on a musical instrument

in·stru·men·tal·i·ty \ˌin(t)-strə-mən-'tal-ət-ē, -ˌmen-\ *n*, *pl* **-ties** **1** : the quality or state of being instrumental **2** : MEANS, AGENCY

in·stru·men·ta·tion \ˌin(t)-strə-mən-'tā-shən, -ˌmen-\ *n* **1** : the arrangement or composition of music for instruments **2** : instruments for a particular purpose ⟨the *instrumentation* of an aircraft⟩

in·sub·or·di·nate \ˌin(t)-sə-'bȯrd-(ə-)nət\ *adj* : unwilling to submit to authority : DISOBEDIENT — **in·sub·or·di·nate·ly** *adv* — **in·sub·or·di·na·tion** \-ˌbȯrd-ə-'nā-shən\ *n*

in·sub·stan·tial \ˌin(t)-səb-'stan-chəl\ *adj* **1** : lacking substance or reality : IMAGINARY **2** : lacking firmness or solidity — **in·sub·stan·ti·al·i·ty** \-ˌstan-chē-'al-ət-ē\ *n*

in·suf·fer·a·ble \(ˈ)in-'səf-(ə-)rə-bəl\ *adj* : incapable of being endured : INTOLERABLE ⟨*insufferable* boredom⟩ — **in·suf·fer·a·ble·ness** *n* — **in·suf·fer·a·bly** \-blē\ *adv*

in·suf·fi·cien·cy \ˌin(t)-sə-'fish-ən-sē\ *n*, *pl* **-cies** **1** : the quality or state of being insufficient **2** : a lack of something : DEFICIENCY

I

in·suf·fi·cient \-'fish-ənt\ *adj* : not sufficient : INADEQUATE — **in·suf·fi·cient·ly** *adv*
in·su·lar \'in(t)s-(y)ə-lər, 'in-shə-lər\ *adj* [from Latin *insula* "island", the source of English *peninsula* and (through French) of *isle*] **1** : of, relating to, or forming an island **2** : ISOLATED, DETACHED **3** : of or relating to the inhabitants of islands **4** : not liberal : NARROW — **in·su·lar·i·ty** \,in(t)s-(y)ə-'lar-ət-ē, ,in-shə-'lar-\ *n* — **in·su·lar·ly** *adv*
in·su·late \'in(t)-sə-,lāt\ *vb* : to place in a detached situation : ISOLATE; *esp* : to separate from conducting bodies by means of nonconductors so as to prevent transfer of electricity, heat, or sound
in·su·la·tion \,in(t)-sə-'lā-shən\ *n* **1** : the act of insulating : the state of being insulated **2** : material used in insulating
in·su·la·tor \'in(t)-sə-,lāt-ər\ *n* : one that insulates; *esp* : a material that is a poor conductor of electricity or a device made of such material
in·su·lin \'in(t)-s(ə-)lən\ *n* : a pancreatic hormone necessary for the normal utilization of sugar by the body
insulin shock *n* : a condition of deficient blood sugar associated with excessive insulin in the system and marked by coma
1in·sult \in-'səlt\ *vb* : to treat or speak to with insolence, rudeness, or contempt — **in·sult·er** *n*
2in·sult \'in-,səlt\ *n* : an insulting act or speech
in·su·per·a·ble \(')in-'sü-p(ə-)rə-bəl\ *adj* : incapable of being overcome or passed over ⟨*insuperable* difficulties⟩ — **in·su·per·a·bly** \-blē\ *adv*
in·sup·port·a·ble \,in(t)-sə-'pōrt-ə-bəl, -'pȯrt-\ *adj* : not supportable : UNENDURABLE — **in·sup·port·a·bly** \-blē\ *adv*
in·sur·a·ble \in-'shu̇r-ə-bəl\ *adj* : capable of being insured against loss, damage, or death — **in·sur·a·bil·i·ty** \-,shu̇r-ə-'bil-ət-ē\ *n*
in·sur·ance \in-'shu̇r-ən(t)s\ *n* **1** : the act of insuring : the state of being insured **2 a** : the business of insuring persons or property **b** : coverage by contract whereby one party undertakes to guarantee another against loss (as from fire, theft, or death) **c** : the sum for which something is insured
in·sure \in-'shu̇(ə)r\ *vb* **1** : to give or procure insurance on or for **2** : to make certain : ENSURE — **in·sur·er** \in-'shu̇r-ər\ *n*
1in·sur·gent \in-'sər-jənt\ *n* : a person who revolts : REBEL
2insurgent *adj* : rising in opposition to authority : REBELLING — **in·sur·gen·cy** \-jən-sē\ *n* — **in·sur·gent·ly** *adv*
in·sur·mount·a·ble \,in(t)-sər-'mau̇nt-ə-bəl\ *adj* : INSUPERABLE
in·sur·rec·tion \,in(t)-sə-'rek-shən\ *n* : REBELLION — **in·sur·rec·tion·ary** \-shə-,ner-ē\ *adj or n* — **in·sur·rec·tion·ist** \-sh(ə-)nəst\ *n*
int *abbr* **1** interest **2** international
in·tact \in-'takt\ *adj* : untouched esp. by anything that harms or diminishes : ENTIRE, UNINJURED
in·ta·glio \in-'tal-yō, -'tag-lē-,ō\ *n, pl* **-glios** : an engraving or incised figure in a hard material (as stone) depressed below the surface of the material
in·take \'in-,tāk\ *n* **1** : a place where liquid or air is taken into something (as a pump) **2** : the act of taking in **3** : something taken in ⟨food *intake*⟩

ə abut ər further a back ā bake ä cot, cart au̇ out ch chin e less ē easy g gift i trip ī life j joke ng sing ō flow ȯ flaw ȯi coin th thin th this ü loot u̇ foot y yet yü few yu̇ furious zh vision

in·tan·gi·ble \(')in-'tan-jə-bəl\ *adj* **1** : incapable of being touched ⟨light is *intangible*⟩ **2** : incapable of being thought of as matter or substance : ABSTRACT ⟨goodwill is an *intangible* asset⟩ — **in·tan·gi·bil·i·ty** \(,)in-,tan-jə-'bil-ət-ē\ *n* — **intangible** *n* — **in·tan·gi·ble·ness** \(')in-'tan-jə-bəl-nəs\ *n* — **in·tan·gi·bly** \-blē\ *adv*
in·te·ger \'int-i-jər\ *n* : a number that is a natural number (as 1, 2, or 3), the negative of a natural number, or 0 — called also *whole number*
in·te·gral \'int-i-grəl (*usu so in mathematics*); in-'teg-rəl, -'tēg-\ *adj* **1** : needed for completeness ⟨an *integral* part of his plan⟩ **2** : of or relating to an integer **3** : composed of integral parts **4** : ENTIRE, COMPLETE, WHOLE — **in·te·gral·i·ty** \,int-ə-'gral-ət-ē\ *n* — **in·te·gral·ly** \'int-i-grə-lē; in-'teg-rə-; -'tēg-\ *adv*
in·te·grate \'int-ə-,grāt\ *vb* **1** : to form or unite into a whole ⟨*integrate* the countries' economies⟩ **2** : to incorporate into a larger unit; *esp* : to end the segregation of and bring into common and equal membership in society **3** : DESEGREGATE ⟨*integrate* school districts⟩ **4** : to become integrated
in·te·gra·tion \,int-ə-'grā-shən\ *n* : the act, the process, or an instance of integrating; *esp* : incorporation as equals into society of persons from different races
in·te·gra·tion·ist \-sh(ə-)nəst\ *n* : a person who favors integration
in·teg·ri·ty \in-'teg-rət-ē\ *n* **1** : an unimpaired condition : SOUNDNESS **2** : moral soundness : HONESTY, VIRTUE **3** : the quality or state of being complete or undivided
in·teg·u·ment \in-'teg-yə-mənt\ *n* : something that covers or encloses; *esp* : an outer enclosing layer (as a skin, membrane, or husk) of an organism or one of its parts — **in·teg·u·men·tal** \(,)in-,teg-yə-'ment-əl\ *adj* — **in·teg·u·men·ta·ry** \-'ment-ə-rē, -'men-trē\ *adj*
in·tel·lect \'int-ə-,lekt\ *n* **1 a** : the power of knowing **b** : the capacity for thought esp. when highly developed **2** : a person of notable intellect
1in·tel·lec·tu·al \,int-ə-'lek-ch(ə-w)əl\ *adj* **1 a** : relating to the intellect or understanding **b** : performed by the intellect ⟨*intellectual* processes⟩ **2** : having intellect to a high degree : engaged in or given to learning and thinking ⟨*intellectual* person⟩ **3** : requiring study and thought ⟨*intellectual* work⟩ — **in·tel·lec·tu·al·i·ty** \-,lek-chə-'wal-ət-ē\ *n* — **in·tel·lec·tu·al·ly** \-'lek-ch(ə-w)ə-lē\ *adv*
2intellectual *n* : an intellectual person
in·tel·li·gence \in-'tel-ə-jən(t)s\ *n* **1** : the ability to learn and understand or to deal with problems : REASON **2 a** : INFORMATION, NEWS **b** : information concerning an enemy or possible enemy; *also* : an agency engaged in obtaining such information
intelligence quotient *n* : a number held to express the intelligence of a person and determined by dividing his mental age by his chronological age and multiplying by 100
intelligence test *n* : a test designed to measure the mental capacity of a person
in·tel·li·gent \in-'tel-ə-jənt\ *adj* : having or showing intelligence or intellect ⟨an *intelligent* person⟩ ⟨an *intelligent* answer⟩ — **in·tel·li·gent·ly** *adv*
in·tel·li·gen·tsia \in-,tel-ə-'jen(t)-sē-ə, -'gen(t)-\ *n* : intellectuals as a group : the educated class
in·tel·li·gi·ble \in-'tel-ə-jə-bəl\ *adj* : capable of being understood — **in·tel·li·gi·bil·i·ty** \-,tel-ə-jə-'bil-ət-ē\ *n* — **in·tel·li·gi·ble·ness** \-'tel-ə-jə-bəl-nəs\ *n* — **in·tel·li·gi·bly** \-blē\ *adv*
in·tem·per·ance \(')in-'tem-p(ə-)rən(t)s\ *n* : lack of

moderation or self-restraint; *esp* : excessive use of alcoholic beverages

in·tem·per·ate \-p(ə-)rət\ *adj* **1** : not moderate or mild : SEVERE ⟨*intemperate* weather⟩ **2** : lacking or showing lack of restraint ⟨*intemperate* language⟩ **3** : given to excessive use of alcoholic beverages — **in·tem·per·ate·ly** *adv* — **in·tem·per·ate·ness** *n*

in·tend \in-'tend\ *vb* : to have in mind as a purpose or aim : PLAN ⟨*intend* to do better work⟩ ⟨*intend* no harm⟩

[1]**in·tend·ed** \in-'ten-dəd\ *adj* **1** : INTENTIONAL ⟨an *intended* insult⟩ **2** : BETROTHED ⟨the woman's *intended* husband⟩

[2]**intended** *n* : an intended person : BETROTHED

in·tense \in-'ten(t)s\ *adj* **1** : existing in an extreme degree ⟨an *intense* light⟩ **2** : very earnest or intent ⟨*intense* study⟩ **3** : feeling deeply ⟨an *intense* person⟩ — **in·tense·ly** *adv* — **in·tense·ness** *n*

in·ten·si·fy \in-'ten(t)-sə-ˌfī\ *vb* **-fied; -fy·ing** : to make or become intense or more intensive : HEIGHTEN — **in·ten·si·fi·ca·tion** \-ˌten(t)-sə-fə-'kā-shən\ *n* — **in·ten·si·fi·er** \-'ten(t)-sə-ˌfī(-ə)r\ *n*

in·ten·si·ty \in-'ten(t)-sət-ē\ *n, pl* **-ties** **1** : the quality or state of being intense; *esp* : extreme strength or force **2** : the degree or amount of a quality or condition ⟨the *intensity* of an electric field⟩

[1]**in·ten·sive** \in-'ten(t)-siv\ *adj* **1** : marked by special effort : THOROUGH ⟨an *intensive* campaign⟩ **2** : serving to give emphasis ⟨the *intensive* pronoun *himself* in the sentence "he himself was present"⟩ — **in·ten·sive·ly** *adv* — **in·ten·sive·ness** *n*

[2]**intensive** *n* : an intensive word

[1]**in·tent** \in-'tent\ *n* **1** : PURPOSE, INTENTION ⟨with *intent* to kill⟩ **2** : MEANING ⟨the *intent* of the letter⟩

[2]**intent** *adj* **1** : highly attentive ⟨an *intent* gaze⟩ **2 a** : closely occupied : ENGROSSED ⟨*intent* on his own thoughts⟩ **b** : set on some end or purpose ⟨*intent* on going⟩ — **in·tent·ly** *adv* — **in·tent·ness** *n*

in·ten·tion \in-'ten-chən\ *n* **1** : a determination to act in a certain way ⟨done without *intention*⟩ **2** : an intended goal : AIM ⟨complete victory was his *intention*⟩ **3** : a person or purpose that is especially prayed for ⟨universal peace was the special *intention* of the congregation⟩ **4** : MEANING, SIGNIFICANCE

in·ten·tion·al \in-'tench-(ə-)nəl\ *adj* : done by intention or design : not accidental : INTENDED ***syn*** see VOLUNTARY ***ant*** instinctive, unintentional — **in·ten·tion·al·ly** \-'tench-(ə-)nə-lē\ *adv*

in·ter \in-'tər\ *vb* **in·terred; in·ter·ring** [from the Latin phrase *in terra* "in the earth"] : BURY

inter- *prefix* **1** : between : among : in the midst ⟨*inter*mix⟩ ⟨*inter*stellar⟩ **2** : reciprocal ⟨*inter*relation⟩ : reciprocally ⟨*inter*marry⟩ **3** : located or occurring between ⟨*inter*lining⟩ ⟨*inter*glacial⟩ **4** : carried on between ⟨*inter*national⟩ **5** : shared by or derived from two or more

in·ter·act \ˌint-ər-'akt\ *vb* : to act on one another — **in·ter·ac·tion** \ˌint-ər-'ak-shən\ *n* — **in·ter·ac·tion·al** \-sh(ə-)nəl\ *n*

in·ter·atom·ic \ˌint-ər-ə-'täm-ik\ *adj* : situated or acting between atoms

in·ter·breed \ˌint-ər-'brēd\ *vb* **-bred** \-'bred\; **-breed·ing** : to breed or cause to breed together: as **a** : CROSSBREED **b** : to breed within a population

in·ter·cede \ˌint-ər-'sēd\ *vb* **1** : to act as a go-between between hostile parties **2** : to plead in behalf of another

in·ter·cel·lu·lar \ˌint-ər-'sel-yə-lər\ *adj* : lying between cells ⟨*intercellular* spaces⟩

in·ter·cept \ˌint-ər-'sept\ *vb* **1** : to take or seize on the way to or before arrival ⟨*intercept* a letter⟩ ⟨*intercept* an enemy bomber⟩ **2** : to cut through : INTERSECT ⟨a line *intercepted* between points A and B⟩ — **in·ter·cep·tion** \-'sep-shən\ *n*

in·ter·cep·tor \-'sep-tər\ *n* : one that intercepts; *esp* : a fast fighter plane designed for defense against bombers

in·ter·ces·sion \ˌint-ər-'sesh-ən\ *n* : the act of interceding : MEDIATION — **in·ter·ces·sor** \-'ses-ər\ *n*

[1]**in·ter·change** \ˌint-ər-'chānj\ *vb* **1** : to put each in the place of the other ⟨*interchange* the front tires⟩ **2** : EXCHANGE ⟨*interchange* ideas⟩ **3** : to change places mutually — **in·ter·change·a·bil·i·ty** \-ˌchān-jə-'bil-ət-ē\ *n* — **in·ter·change·a·ble** \-'chān-jə-bəl\ *adj* — **in·ter·change·a·bly** \-'chān-jə-blē\ *adv* — **in·ter·chang·er** *n*

[2]**in·ter·change** \'int-ər-ˌchānj\ *n* **1** : the act or process or an instance of interchanging : EXCHANGE **2** : a joining of two or more highways by a system of separate levels that permit traffic to pass from one to another without the crossing of traffic streams

in·ter·col·le·giate \ˌint-ər-kə-'lē-j(ē-)ət\ *adj* : existing or carried on between colleges

in·ter·com \'int-ər-ˌkäm\ *n* : INTERCOMMUNICATION SYSTEM

in·ter·com·mu·ni·cate \ˌint-ər-kə-'myü-nə-ˌkāt\ *vb* : to exchange communication with one another — **in·ter·com·mu·ni·ca·tion** \-ˌmyü-nə-'kā-shən\ *n*

intercommunication system *n* : a two-way communication system with microphone and loudspeaker at each end

in·ter·con·ti·nen·tal \ˌint-ər-ˌkänt-ə-'nent-əl\ *adj* **1** : extending among or carried on between continents ⟨*intercontinental* trade⟩ **2** : capable of traveling between continents ⟨*intercontinental* missile⟩

in·ter·con·vert·i·ble \ˌint-ər-kən-'vərt-ə-bəl\ *adj* : capable of being interchanged

in·ter·course \'int-ər-ˌkōrs, -ˌkȯrs\ *n* **1** : dealings between persons or groups : RELATIONS **2** : sexual intercourse

in·ter·crop \ˌint-ər-'kräp\ *vb* : to grow two or more crops at one time on the same piece of land ⟨*intercrop* corn and pumpkins⟩

in·ter·de·pend \ˌint-ər-di-'pend\ *vb* : to depend on one another — **in·ter·de·pend·ence** \-'pen-dən(t)s\ *n* — **in·ter·de·pend·en·cy** \-dən-sē\ *n* — **in·ter·de·pend·ent** \-dənt\ *adj* — **in·ter·de·pend·ent·ly** *adv*

[1]**in·ter·dict** \'int-ər-ˌdikt\ *n* **1** : a Roman Catholic ecclesiastical withdrawal of sacraments and Christian burial from a person or district **2** : PROHIBITION

[2]**in·ter·dict** \ˌint-ər-'dikt\ *vb* : to prohibit or forbid esp. by an interdict — **in·ter·dic·tion** \-'dik-shən\ *n*

[1]**in·ter·est** \'in-trəst, 'int-ə-rəst\ *n* **1** : a right, title, or legal share in something **2** : WELFARE, BENEFIT; *esp* : SELF-INTEREST **3 a** : a charge for borrowed money that is generally a percentage of the amount borrowed **b** : the return received by capital on its investments **4** *pl* : a group interested in an industry or enterprise ⟨mining *interests*⟩ **5 a** : readiness to be concerned with or moved by something ⟨show an *interest* in sports⟩ **b** : a quality that arouses interest ⟨her plans are of great *interest* to me⟩

[2]**interest** *vb* **1** : to involve the interest of : AFFECT, CONCERN ⟨had *interested* herself in his behalf⟩ **2** : to persuade to participate or take part **3** : to arouse or hold the interest of ⟨puzzles *interest* him⟩

in·ter·est·ing *adj* : holding the attention : arousing interest — **in·ter·est·ing·ly** \-iŋ-lē\ *adv*

I

in·ter·face \'int-ər-ˌfās\ *n* **:** a surface forming a common boundary of two bodies, spaces, or phases ⟨an *interface* between oil and water⟩ — **in·ter·fa·cial** \ˌint-ər-'fā-shəl\ *adj*

in·ter·fere \ˌint-ə(r)-'fi(ə)r\ *vb* **1 :** to come in collision or be in opposition **:** CLASH ⟨illness *interfered* with his plans⟩ **2 :** to take part in the concerns of others ⟨she *interferes* continually⟩ **3 :** to act on one another ⟨*interfering* light waves⟩ **4 :** to hinder illegally an attempt of a football player to receive a pass ***syn*** see MEDDLE — **in·ter·fer·er** *n*

in·ter·fer·ence \ˌint-ə(r)-'fir-ən(t)s\ *n* **1 a :** the act or process of interfering **b :** something that interferes **2 :** the mutual effect on meeting of two waves (as of light or sound) whereby the resulting neutralization at some points and reinforcement at others produces in the case of light waves alternate light and dark bands or colored bands **3 a :** the act of blocking an opponent in football **b :** the act of interfering illegally with a football pass reception **4 a :** confusion of received radio signals due to undesired signals or electrical effects **b :** an electrical effect that produces such confusion

in·ter·fer·om·e·ter \ˌint-ə(r)-ˌfir-'äm-ət-ər\ *n* **:** an instrument that utilizes light interference phenomena for precise determinations (as of wavelength)

in·ter·fuse \ˌint-ər-'fyüz\ *vb* **1 :** to combine by or as if by fusing **:** INTERMINGLE **2 :** PERVADE, PERMEATE — **in·ter·fu·sion** \-'fyü-zhən\ *n*

in·ter·ga·lac·tic \ˌint-ər-gə-'lak-tik\ *adj* **:** situated or occurring in the spaces between galaxies

in·ter·gla·cial \ˌint-ər-'glā-shəl\ *adj* **:** occurring or relating to the time between successive glaciations

in·ter·im \'in-tə-rəm, -ˌrim\ *n* **[**from the Latin adverb *interim* "meanwhile", from the preposition *inter* "between"**]** **:** a time intervening **:** INTERVAL — **interim** *adj*

[1]**in·te·ri·or** \in-'tir-ē-ər\ *adj* **1 :** existing or occurring within the limits **:** INNER **2 :** remote from the border or shore **:** INLAND — **in·te·ri·or·ly** *adv*

[2]**interior** *n* **1 :** the internal or inner part ⟨*interior* of a house⟩ **2 :** the inland part **3 :** the internal affairs of a state or nation ⟨secretary of the *Interior*⟩ — **in·te·ri·or·i·ty** \(ˌ)in-ˌtir-ē-'ȯr-ət-ē, -'är-\ *n*

interior angle *n* **:** any of the four angles formed in the area between a pair of lines when a third line cuts them

interior decoration *n* **:** the art of decorating and furnishing the interior of a building

interj *abbr* interjection

in·ter·ject \ˌint-ər-'jekt\ *vb* **:** to throw in between or among other things **:** INSERT ⟨*interject* a remark⟩ — **in·ter·jec·tor** \-'jek-tər\ *n* — **in·ter·jec·to·ry** \-t(ə-)rē\ *adj*

in·ter·jec·tion \-'jek-shən\ *n* **1 :** an interjecting of something **2 :** something interjected ⟨interrupted by *interjections* from the audience⟩ **3 :** a word or cry expressing sudden or strong feeling — **in·ter·jec·tion·al** \-sh(ə-)nəl\ *adj* — **in·ter·jec·tion·al·ly** \-ē\ *adv*

in·ter·lace \ˌint-ər-'lās\ *vb* **:** to unite or cross by or as if by lacing together **:** INTERWEAVE ⟨*interlaced* fibers⟩ ⟨*interlacing* boughs⟩ — **in·ter·lace·ment** \-mənt\ *n*

ə abut	ər further	a back	ā bake
ä cot, cart	aü out	ch chin	e less	ē easy
g gift	i trip	ī life	j joke	ng sing	ō flow
ȯ flaw	ȯi coin	th thin	t͟h this	ü loot
u̇ foot	y yet	yü few	yu̇ furious	zh vision

in·ter·lard \ˌint-ər-'lärd\ *vb* **:** to insert or introduce at intervals ⟨a speech *interlarded* with quotations⟩

[1]**in·ter·line** \ˌint-ər-'līn\ *vb* **:** to write between lines already written

[2]**interline** *vb* **:** to provide a garment with an interlining

in·ter·lin·e·ar \ˌint-ər-'lin-ē-ər\ *adj* **1 :** written between lines already written or printed **2 :** printed in different languages in alternate lines ⟨an *interlinear* translation⟩ — **in·ter·lin·e·ar·ly** *adv*

in·ter·lin·ing \'int-ər-ˌlī-ning\ *n* **:** a lining between the ordinary lining and the outside fabric

in·ter·lock \ˌint-ər-'läk\ *vb* **:** to lock together **:** interlace firmly **:** UNITE ⟨*interlocked* fingers⟩

in·ter·lop·er \ˌint-ər-'lō-pər, 'int-ər-ˌ\ *n* **:** a person who interferes wrongly or officiously **:** INTRUDER

in·ter·lude \'int-ər-ˌlüd\ *n* **1 :** a performance between the acts of a play **2 :** an intervening period, space, or event **:** INTERVAL ⟨an *interlude* of peace between wars⟩ **3 :** a musical composition inserted between the parts of a longer one, a drama, or a religious service

in·ter·mar·riage \ˌint-ər-'mar-ij\ *n* **:** marriage between members of different racial, social, or religious groups

in·ter·mar·ry \-'mar-ē\ *vb* **1 :** to marry each other **2 :** to become connected by intermarriage

in·ter·med·dle \ˌint-ər-'med-əl\ *vb* **:** MEDDLE

in·ter·me·di·ary \ˌint-ər-'mēd-ē-ˌer-ē\ *adj* **1 :** INTERMEDIATE ⟨an *intermediary* stage⟩ **2 :** acting as a mediator ⟨*intermediary* agent⟩ — **intermediary** *n*

in·ter·me·di·ate \ˌint-ər-'mēd-ē-ət\ *adj* **:** being or occurring in the middle or between — **intermediate** *n* — **in·ter·me·di·ate·ly** *adv*

intermediate host *n* **:** a host that is normally used by a parasite in the course of its life cycle and that may actively transmit it from one organism to another

in·ter·ment \in-'tər-mənt\ *n* **:** BURIAL

in·ter·mesh \ˌint-ər-'mesh\ *vb* **:** to mesh with one another

in·ter·mez·zo \ˌint-ər-'met-sō, -'med-zō\ *n, pl* **-zi** \-(ˌ)sē, -(ˌ)zē\ *or* **-zos** **1 :** a short light piece between the acts of a drama or opera **2 a :** a short movement connecting parts of a longer musical work **b :** a short independent instrumental composition

in·ter·mi·na·ble \(')in-'tərm-(ə-)nə-bəl\ *adj* **:** ENDLESS; *esp* **:** tiresomely long ⟨an *interminable* speech⟩ — **in·ter·mi·na·ble·ness** *n* — **in·ter·mi·na·bly** \-blē\ *adv*

in·ter·min·gle \ˌint-ər-'ming-gəl\ *vb* **:** INTERMIX

in·ter·mis·sion \ˌint-ər-'mish-ən\ *n* **1 :** INTERRUPTION ⟨continuing without *intermission*⟩ **2 :** a pause or interval esp. between the acts of a play

in·ter·mit \-'mit\ *vb* **-mit·ted; -mit·ting :** to stop for a time and then continue

in·ter·mit·tent \-'mit-ənt\ *adj* **:** starting, stopping, and starting again ⟨an *intermittent* fever⟩— **in·ter·mit·tence** \-'mit-ən(t)s\ *n* — **in·ter·mit·tent·ly** *adv*

in·ter·mix \ˌint-ər-'miks\ *vb* **:** to mix together — **in·ter·mix·ture** \-'miks-chər\ *n*

in·ter·mo·lec·u·lar \ˌint-ər-mə-'lek-yə-lər\ *adj* **:** existing or acting between molecules

[1]**in·tern** \'in-ˌtərn, in-'\ *vb* **:** to confine esp. during a war ⟨*interned* enemy aliens⟩

[2]**in·tern** *or* **in·terne** \'in-ˌtərn\ *n* **:** an advanced student or graduate esp. in medicine who is gaining supervised practical experience (as in a hospital) — **in·tern·ship** \-ˌship\ *n*

[3]**in·tern** \'in-ˌtərn\ *vb* **:** to act as an intern

in·ter·nal \in-'tər-nəl\ *adj* **1 :** existing or lying within : INNER ⟨*internal* structure⟩ **2 :** relating to, occurring, or situated in the interior of the body ⟨*internal* medicine⟩ ⟨*internal* fertilization⟩ **3 :** of or relating to the domestic affairs of a state ⟨*internal* revenue⟩ — **in·ter·nal·ly** \-ē\ *adv*

internal–combustion engine *n* : an engine run by a fuel mixture ignited within the engine cylinder

internal secretion *n* : HORMONE

1in·ter·na·tion·al \,int-ər-'nash-(ə-)nəl\ *adj* : of, relating to, affecting, or involving two or more nations ⟨*international* trade⟩ — **in·ter·na·tion·al·i·za·tion** \-,nash-(ə-)nəl-ə-'zā-shən\ *n* — **in·ter·na·tion·al·ize** \-,īz\ *vb* — **in·ter·na·tion·al·ly** \-'nash-(ə-)nəl-ē\ *adv*

2in·ter·na·tion·al \-'nash-(ə-)nəl *with reference to political organization, often* -,nash-ə-'nal, -'näl\ *n* : an organization having branches in more than one country

in·ter·na·tion·al·ism \,int-ər-'nash-(ə-)nəl-,iz-əm\ *n* : a policy of cooperation among nations or an attitude favoring such a policy — **in·ter·na·tion·al·ist** \-əst\ *n or adj*

in·ter·nec·ine \,int-ər-'nes-,ēn, -'nē-,sīn; in-'tər-nə-,sēn\ *adj* **1 :** marked by slaughter : DEADLY **2 :** of, relating to, or involving conflict within a group ⟨*internecine* feuds⟩

in·tern·ee \,in-,tər-'nē\ *n* : an interned person

in·ter·neu·ron \,int-ər-'n(y)ü-,rän, -'n(y)u̇(ə)r-,än\ *n* : a nerve cell that carries an impulse from one nerve cell to another

in·ter·nist \in-'tər-nəst\ *n* : a specialist in internal medicine

in·tern·ment \in-'tərn-mənt\ *n* : the act of interning : the state of being interned

in·ter·node \'int-ər-,nōd\ *n* : an interval or part between two nodes (as of a stem) : SEGMENT

in·ter·nun·ci·al neuron \,int-ər-'nən(t)-sē-əl-, -'nu̇n(t)-\ *n* : a nerve cell in the central nervous system that is an intermediary between a sensory and motor nerve — called also *association neuron*

in·ter·pen·e·trate \,int-ər-'pen-ə-,trāt\ *vb* **1 :** to penetrate between, within, or throughout **2 :** to penetrate mutually — **in·ter·pen·e·tra·tion** \-,pen-ə-'trā-shən\ *n*

in·ter·phase \'int-ər-,fāz\ *n* : the period between the end of one mitotic division and the beginning of the next

in·ter·phone \'int-ər-,fōn\ *n* : a telephone system for intercommunication between points (as in an office building) within a short distance of each other

in·ter·plan·e·tary \,int-ər-'plan-ə-,ter-ē\ *adj* : existing, carried on, or operating between planets ⟨*interplanetary* travel⟩

in·ter·plant \,int-ər-'plant\ *vb* : to plant (a crop) between plants of another kind

in·ter·play \'int-ər-,plā\ *n* : mutual action or influence : INTERACTION ⟨an *interplay* of thought and feeling⟩ — **interplay** \,int-ər-'plā\ *vb*

in·ter·po·late \in-'tər-pə-,lāt\ *vb* **1 :** to alter by inserting new matter ⟨*interpolate* a text⟩ **2 :** to insert between other things or parts — **in·ter·po·la·tion** \-,tər-pə-'lā-shən\ *n* — **in·ter·po·la·tive** \-'tər-pə-,lāt-iv\ *adj* — **in·ter·po·la·tor** \-,lāt-ər\ *n*

in·ter·pose \,int-ər-'pōz\ *vb* **1 a :** to place in an intervening position **b :** INTRUDE, INTERRUPT **2 :** to introduce in between the parts of a conversation or argument **3 :** to be or come between; *esp* : to step in between opposing parties — **in·ter·pos·er** *n* — **in·ter·po·si·tion** \-pə-'zish-ən\ *n*

in·ter·pret \in-'tər-prət\ *vb* **1 :** to explain the meaning of ⟨*interpret* a dream⟩ **2 :** to understand according to one's own belief, judgment, or interest ⟨*interpret* an action as unfriendly⟩ **3 :** to bring out the meaning or significance of by performing ⟨an actor *interprets* a role⟩ **4 :** to translate orally for others — **in·ter·pret·a·ble** \-prət-ə-bəl\ *adj* — **in·ter·pret·er** *n* — **in·ter·pre·tive** \-prət-iv\ *adj* — **in·ter·pre·tive·ly** *adv*

in·ter·pre·ta·tion \in-,tər-prə-'tā-shən\ *n* **1 :** the act or the result of interpreting : EXPLANATION **2 :** an instance of artistic interpretation in performance or adaptation — **in·ter·pre·ta·tive** \-'tər-prə-,tāt-iv\ *adj*

in·ter·ra·cial \,int-ə(r)-'rā-shəl\ *adj* : of, involving, or designed for members of different races

in·ter·reg·num \,int-ə-'reg-nəm\ *n, pl* **-nums** *or* **-na** \-nə\ **1 :** a period between two reigns or regimes **2 :** a pause in a continuous series

in·ter·re·late \,int-ə(r)-ri-'lāt\ *vb* : to bring into or have a mutual relationship — **in·ter·re·la·tion** \-'lā-shən\ *n* — **in·ter·re·la·tion·ship** \-shən-,ship\ *n*

interrog *abbr* interrogative

in·ter·ro·gate \in-'ter-ə-,gāt\ *vb* : to question formally and systematically ⟨*interrogate* a prisoner of war⟩ — **in·ter·ro·ga·tion** \-,ter-ə-'gā-shən\ *n* — **in·ter·ro·ga·tion·al** \-sh(ə-)nəl\ *adj* — **in·ter·ro·ga·tor** \-'ter-ə-,gāt-ər\ *n*

interrogation point *n* : QUESTION MARK

1in·ter·rog·a·tive \,int-ə-'räg-ət-iv\ *adj* **1 :** having the form or force of a question ⟨an *interrogative* phrase⟩ **2 :** used in a question ⟨an *interrogative* pronoun⟩ — **in·ter·rog·a·tive·ly** *adv*

2interrogative *n* : a word used in asking questions ⟨*who, what*, and *which* are *interrogatives*⟩

in·ter·rog·a·to·ry \,int-ə-'räg-ə-,tōr-ē, -,tȯr-\ *adj* : containing, expressing, or implying a question ⟨an *interrogatory* tone of voice⟩

in·ter·rupt \,int-ə-'rəpt\ *vb* **1 :** to stop or hinder by breaking in ⟨*interrupt* a conversation⟩ **2 :** to break the uniformity or continuity of ⟨*interrupt* a sequence⟩ — **in·ter·rup·tion** \-'rəp-shən\ *n* — **in·ter·rup·tive** \-'rəp-tiv\ *adj*

in·ter·scho·las·tic \,int-ər-skə-'las-tik\ *adj* : existing or carried on between schools ⟨*interscholastic* athletics⟩

1in·ter·sect \,int-ər-'sekt\ *vb* **1 :** to divide by passing through or across : CROSS ⟨one line *intersecting* another⟩ **2 :** to meet and cross at a point ⟨lines *intersecting* at right angles⟩

2intersect *n* : INTERSECTION 3a

in·ter·sec·tion \,int-ər-'sek-shən\ *n* **1 :** the act or process of intersecting **2 :** the place or point where two or more things and esp. streets intersect ⟨a busy *intersection*⟩ **3 a :** the set of mathematical elements common to two or more sets **b :** the set of points common to two geometric figures

in·ter·sex \'int-ər-,seks\ *n* : an intersexual individual

in·ter·sex·u·al \,int-ər-'sek-sh(ə-w)əl\ *adj* **1 :** existing between sexes ⟨*intersexual* hostility⟩ **2 :** intermediate in sexual character between a typical male and a typical female

1in·ter·space \'int-ər-,spās\ *n* : an intervening space : INTERVAL

2in·ter·space \,int-ər-'spās\ *vb* : to separate by spaces

in·ter·spe·cif·ic \,int-ər-spi-'sif-ik\ *or* **in·ter·spe·cies** \-'spē-(,)shēz, -(,)sēz\ *adj* : existing or arising between species ⟨*interspecific* hybrid⟩

in·ter·sperse \,int-ər-'spərs\ *vb* **1 :** to set here and there among other things ⟨*intersperse* pictures in a book⟩ **2 :** to vary with things inserted here and there ⟨a serious talk *interspersed* with jokes⟩ — **in·ter·sper·sion** \-'spər-zhən\ *n*

I

in·ter·state \ˌint-ər-ˈstāt\ *adj* : of, connecting, or existing between states esp. of the U.S. ⟨*interstate* commerce⟩

in·ter·stel·lar \-ˈstel-ər\ *adj* : located or taking place among the stars ⟨*interstellar* space⟩

in·ter·ster·ile \-ˈster-əl\ *adj* : unable to pollinate one another — **in·ter·ste·ril·i·ty** \-stə-ˈril-ət-ē\ *n*

in·ter·stice \in-ˈtər-stəs\ *n, pl* **in·ter·stic·es** \-stə-ˌsēz, -stə-səz\ : a little space between two things : CHINK, CREVICE

in·ter·sti·tial \ˌint-ər-ˈstish-əl\ *adj* : relating to or situated in the interstices — **in·ter·sti·tial·ly** \-ē\ *adv*

in·ter·tid·al \-ˈtīd-əl\ *adj* : of, relating to, or being the area that is above low-tide mark but exposed to tidal flooding

in·ter·twine \-ˈtwīn\ *vb* : to twine or cause to twine about one another : INTERLACE

in·ter·twist \-ˈtwist\ *vb* : INTERTWINE

in·ter·ur·ban \ˌint-ər-ˈər-bən\ *adj* : connecting cities or towns ⟨an *interurban* bus line⟩

in·ter·val \ˈint-ər-vəl\ *n* **1** : a space of time between events or states : PAUSE ⟨a 3-month *interval*⟩ **2** : a space between things ⟨the *interval* between two desks⟩ **3** : difference in pitch between tones

in·ter·vene \ˌint-ər-ˈvēn\ *vb* **1** : to happen as an unrelated event ⟨rain *intervened* and we postponed the match⟩ **2** : to come between points of time or between events ⟨a second *intervened* between the flash and the report⟩ **3** : to come between in order to stop, settle, or change ⟨*intervene* in a quarrel⟩ **4** : to be or lie between ⟨*intervening* mountains⟩ — **in·ter·ven·tion** \-ˈven-chən\ *n*

in·ter·view \ˈint-ər-ˌvyü\ *n* **1** : a meeting face to face esp. for the purpose of talking or consulting **2** : a meeting between a journalist and another person in order to get news or an article; *also* : the account of such a meeting — **interview** *vb* — **in·ter·view·er** *n*

in·ter·weave \ˌint-ər-ˈwēv\ *vb* **1** : to weave together **2** : to blend or cause to blend together : INTERMINGLE — **in·ter·wo·ven** \-ˈwō-vən\ *adj*

in·tes·tate \in-ˈtes-ˌtāt, -ˈtes-tət\ *adj* **1** : not having made a will ⟨he died *intestate*⟩ **2** : not disposed of by will — **in·tes·ta·cy** \-ˈtes-tə-sē\ *n*

in·tes·ti·nal \in-ˈtes-tə-nəl\ *adj* **1** : of or relating to the intestine **2** : affecting or occurring in the intestine — **in·tes·ti·nal·ly** \-ē\ *adv*

1in·tes·tine \in-ˈtes-tən\ *adj* : being or involving conflict within a country or group

2intestine *n* : the tubular part of the alimentary canal that extends from the stomach to the anus, that helps to digest food and absorb nutrients, and that carries waste matter to be discharged

in·ti·ma·cy \ˈint-ə-mə-sē\ *n, pl* **-cies** **1** : the state of being intimate : FAMILIARITY **2** : an instance of being intimate

1in·ti·mate \ˈint-ə-ˌmāt\ *vb* **1** : ANNOUNCE **2** : to communicate indirectly : HINT — **in·ti·mat·er** *n* — **in·ti·ma·tion** \ˌint-ə-ˈmā-shən\ *n*

2in·ti·mate \ˈint-ə-mət\ *adj* **1** : belonging to or characterizing one's deepest nature ⟨*intimate* reflections⟩ **2** : marked by very close association or contact **3 a** : marked by a warm friendship developing through long association ⟨on *intimate* terms with a neighbor⟩ **b** : suggesting informal warmth or privacy ⟨*intimate* clubs⟩ **4** : of a very personal or private nature ⟨*intimate* family affairs⟩ — **in·ti·mate·ly** *adv* — **in·ti·mate·ness** *n*

3in·ti·mate \ˈint-ə-mət\ *n* : an intimate friend : CONFIDANT

in·tim·i·date \in-ˈtim-ə-ˌdāt\ *vb* : to frighten esp. by threats — **in·tim·i·da·tion** \-ˌtim-ə-ˈdā-shən\ *n* — **in·tim·i·da·tor** \-ˈtim-ə-ˌdāt-ər\ *n*

in·to \ˈin-tə, -tü\ *prep* **1 a** : to the inside of ⟨came *into* the room⟩ **b** — used as a function word to indicate entry, introduction, or inclusion ⟨enter *into* an alliance⟩ **2 a** : to the state, condition, or form of ⟨got *into* trouble⟩ ⟨divide *into* four parts⟩ **b** : to the occupation, action, or possession of ⟨go *into* farming⟩ **3** : AGAINST ⟨ran *into* a wall⟩ **4** : engaged in or involved with ⟨wasn't *into* drugs anymore⟩

in·tol·er·a·ble \(ˈ)in-ˈtäl-(ə-)rə-bəl, -ˈtäl-ər-bəl\ *adj* : not tolerable : UNBEARABLE — **in·tol·er·a·bil·i·ty** \(ˌ)in-ˈtäl-(ə-)rə-ˈbil-ət-ē\ *n* — **in·tol·er·a·bly** \(ˈ)in-ˈtäl-(ə-)rə-blē, -ˈtäl-ər-blē\ *adv*

in·tol·er·ance \(ˈ)in-ˈtäl-ə-rən(t)s\ *n* **1** : the quality or state of being intolerant **2** : exceptional sensitivity (as to a drug or food)

in·tol·er·ant \-rənt\ *adj* **1** : unable or unwilling to endure **2** : unwilling to grant equality, freedom, or other social rights : BIGOTED — **in·tol·er·ant·ly** *adv*

in·to·na·tion \ˌin-tə-ˈnā-shən\ *n* **1** : the act of intoning; *also* : something intoned **2** : the act of producing tones on a musical instrument **3** : the rise and fall in pitch of the voice in speech — **in·to·na·tion·al** \-sh(ə-)nəl\ *adj*

in·tone \in-ˈtōn\ *vb* : to utter in musical or prolonged tones : CHANT — **in·ton·er** *n*

in·tox·i·cant \in-ˈtäk-si-kənt\ *n* : something that intoxicates; *esp* : an alcoholic drink — **intoxicant** *adj*

in·tox·i·cate \in-ˈtäk-sə-ˌkāt\ *vb* [from medieval Latin *intoxicare* "to poison", from Latin *toxicum* "poison", from Greek *toxikon*] **1** : to affect (as by alcohol or marijuana) esp. to the point where physical and mental control is markedly diminished **2** : to excite to enthusiasm or frenzy : ELATE ⟨*intoxicated* with joy⟩

in·tox·i·ca·tion \in-ˌtäk-sə-ˈkā-shən\ *n* **1 a** : an abnormal state that is essentially a poisoning ⟨intestinal *intoxication*⟩ **b** : the condition of being drunk : INEBRIATION **2** : a strong excitement or elation

in·tra- \ˌin-trə *also but not shown at individual entries* ˌin-ˌträ\ *prefix* **1** : within ⟨*intra*mural⟩ **2** : INTRO- ⟨an *intra*venous injection⟩

in·tra·cel·lu·lar \ˌin-trə-ˈsel-yə-lər\ *adj* : being or occuring within a cell — **in·tra·cel·lu·lar·ly** *adv*

in·trac·ta·ble \(ˈ)in-ˈtrak-tə-bəl\ *adj* **1** : not easily managed or controlled ⟨an *intractable* child⟩ **2** : not easily relieved or cured ⟨*intractable* pain⟩ — **in·trac·ta·bil·i·ty** \(ˌ)in-ˌtrak-tə-ˈbil-ət-ē\ *n*

in·tra·der·mal \ˌin-trə-ˈdər-məl\ *adj* : situated or done within or between the layers of the skin — **in·tra·der·mal·ly** \-mə-lē\ *adv*

in·tra·mo·lec·u·lar \ˌin-trə-mə-ˈlek-yə-lər\ *adj* : situated, acting, or occurring within the molecule

in·tra·mu·ral \-ˈmyu̇r-əl\ *adj* : being, occurring, or undertaken within the limits usu. of a school ⟨*intramural* sports⟩

intrans *abbr* intransitive

in·tran·si·tive \(ˈ)in-ˈtran(t)s-ət-iv, -ˈtranz-\ *adj* : not transitive; *esp* : not having or containing a direct object ⟨an *intransitive* verb⟩

in·tra·spe·cif·ic \ˌin-trə-spi-ˈsif-ik\ *also* **in·tra-**

ə abut	ər further	a back	ā bake	
ä cot, cart	au̇ out	ch chin	e less	ē easy
g gift	i trip	ī life	j joke	ng sing	ō flow
ȯ flaw	ȯi coin	th thin	<u>th</u> this	ü loot
u̇ foot	y yet	yü few	yu̇ furious	zh vision

spe·cies \-ˈspē-(ˌ)shēz, -(ˌ)sēz\ *adj* : occurring within a species or involving members of one species ⟨*intraspecific* variation⟩

in·tra·state \ˌin-trə-ˈstāt\ *adj* : existing or occurring within a state

in·tra·uter·ine \-ˈyüt-ə-rən, -ˌrīn\ *adj* : being or occurring within the uterus ⟨*intrauterine* growth⟩

intrauterine device : a device (as a spiral of plastic or a ring of stainless steel) inserted in the uterus and left there to prevent pregnancy

in·tra·ve·nous \ˌin-trə-ˈvē-nəs\ *adj* : being within or entering by way of the veins ⟨*intravenous* feeding⟩ — **in·tra·ve·nous·ly** *adv*

in·trep·id \in-ˈtrep-əd\ *adj* : resolutely fearless — **in·tre·pid·i·ty** \ˌin-trə-ˈpid-ət-ē\ *n* — **in·trep·id·ly** \in-ˈtrep-əd-lē\ *adv* — **in·trep·id·ness** *n*

in·tri·ca·cy \ˈin-tri-kə-sē\ *n, pl* **-cies 1** : the quality or state of being intricate **2** : something intricate ⟨the *intricacies* of a plot⟩

in·tri·cate \ˈin-tri-kət\ *adj* : difficult to follow, understand, or analyze : COMPLICATED ⟨an *intricate* machine⟩ ⟨an *intricate* problem⟩ — **in·tri·cate·ly** *adv* — **in·tri·cate·ness** *n*

¹in·trigue \in-ˈtrēg\ *vb* **1** : to make or accomplish by secret plotting ⟨*intrigued* his way into power⟩ **2** : PLOT, SCHEME **3** : to arouse the interest or curiosity of ⟨*intrigued* by the tale⟩ — **in·trigu·er** *n*

²in·trigue \ˈin-ˌtrēg, in-ˈ\ *n* **1** : a secret and involved scheme : PLOT **2** : a secret love affair

in·trin·sic \in-ˈtrin-zik, -ˈtrin(t)-sik\ *adj* : INHERENT, REAL ⟨has sentimental but no *intrinsic* value⟩ ⟨*intrinsic* brightness of light⟩ — **in·trin·si·cal** \-zi-kəl, -si-\ *adj* — **in·trin·si·cal·ly** \-k(ə-)lē\ *adv* — **in·trin·si·cal·ness** \-kəl-nəs\ *n*

intro- *prefix* **1** : in, into **2** : inward ⟨*intro*vert⟩

in·tro·duce \ˌin-trə-ˈd(y)üs\ *vb* **1** : to bring into practice or use ⟨*introduce* a new fashion⟩ **2** : to lead or bring in ⟨*introduce* birds from other countries⟩; *esp* : to present formally ⟨*introduce* a person into society⟩ ⟨*introduce* a legislative bill⟩ **3** : to cause to become acquainted : make known ⟨*introduce* the speaker⟩ **4** : to present or bring forward for discussion ⟨*introduce* a subject⟩ **5** : to put in : INSERT — **in·tro·duc·er** *n*

in·tro·duc·tion \ˌin-trə-ˈdək-shən\ *n* **1 a** : the action of introducing **b** : something introduced **2** : the part of a book that leads up to and explains what will be found in the main part : PREFACE **3** : a book for beginners in a subject ⟨an *introduction* to chemistry⟩ **4** : the action of making persons known to each other

in·tro·duc·to·ry \ˌin-trə-ˈdək-t(ə-)rē\ *adj* : serving to introduce : PRELIMINARY — **in·tro·duc·to·ri·ly** \-t(ə-)rə-lē\ *adv*

in·tro·mis·sion \ˌin-trə-ˈmish-ən\ *n* : the act or process of intromitting; *esp* : COPULATION

in·tro·mit \-ˈmit\ *vb* **in·tro·mit·ted**; **in·tro·mit·ting** : to send or put in : INSERT — **in·tro·mit·tent** \-ˈmit-ənt\ *adj* — **in·tro·mit·ter** \-ˈmit-ər\ *n*

in·tro·spec·tion \ˌin-trə-ˈspek-shən\ *n* : a reflective looking inward : an examination of one's own thoughts or feelings — **in·tro·spect** \-ˈspekt\ *vb* — **in·tro·spec·tive** \-ˈspek-tiv\ *adj* — **in·tro·spec·tive·ly** *adv*

in·tro·vert \ˈin-trə-ˌvərt\ *n* **1** : one that is or can be turned in or inward on itself **2** : a person who tends to be preoccupied with his own thoughts — **in·tro·ver·sion** \ˌin-trə-ˈvər-zhən\ *n* — **introvert** *adj* — **in·tro·vert·ed** \ˈin-trə-ˌvərt-əd\ *adj*

in·trude \in-ˈtrüd\ *vb* **1** : to bring or force in unasked ⟨*intruded* his views into the discussion⟩ **2** : to come or go in without invitation : TRESPASS ⟨*intrude* on another's property⟩ — **in·trud·er** *n*

in·tru·sion \in-ˈtrü-zhən\ *n* : the act of intruding : the state of being intruded

in·tru·sive \in-ˈtrü-siv, -ziv\ *adj* **1** : characterized by intrusion; *esp* : intruding where one is not welcome or invited **2** : having been forced while in a plastic state into cavities or between layers ⟨*intrusive* rocks⟩ —**in·tru·sive·ly** *adv* — **in·tru·sive·ness** *n*

in·tu·i·tion \ˌin-t(y)u̇-ˈish-ən\ *n* **1** : the power of knowing immediately and without conscious reasoning **2** : something known or understood at once and without an effort of the mind — **in·tu·i·tion·al** \-ˈish-(ə-)nəl\ *adj*

in·tu·i·tive \in-ˈt(y)ü-ət-iv\ *adj* **1** : knowing or understanding by intuition ⟨an *intuitive* person⟩ **2** : having or characterized by intuition ⟨an *intuitive* mind⟩ **3** : known or understood by intuition ⟨*intuitive* knowledge⟩ — **in·tu·i·tive·ly** *adj* — **in·tu·i·tive·ness** *n*

in·un·date \ˈin-ən-ˌdāt\ *vb* : to cover with a flood : OVERFLOW — **in·un·da·tion** \ˌin-ən-ˈdā-shən\ *n*

in·ure \in-ˈ(y)u̇(ə)r\ *vb* **1** : to make less sensitive : HARDEN ⟨*inured* to cold⟩ **2** : to become advantageous ⟨benefits that *inure* to our descendants⟩

in·vade \in-ˈvād\ *vb* **1** : to enter for conquest or plunder ⟨*invade* a country⟩ **2** : to encroach upon : INFRINGE ⟨*invaded* his privacy⟩ **3** : to spread progressively over or into usu. injuriously ⟨bacteria *invading* tissue⟩ — **in·vad·er** *n*

in·vag·i·nate \in-ˈvaj-ə-ˌnāt\ *vb* : to fold or cause to fold in so that an outer becomes an inner surface — **in·vag·i·na·tion** \-ˌvaj-ə-ˈnā-shən\ *n*

¹in·val·id \(ˈ)in-ˈval-əd\ *adj* : having no force or effect : not valid ⟨an *invalid* license⟩ — **in·va·lid·i·ty** \ˌin-və-ˈlid-ət-ē\ *n* — **in·val·id·ly** \(ˈ)in-ˈval-əd-lē\ *adv*

²in·va·lid \ˈin-və-ləd\ *adj* **1** : suffering from disease or disability : SICKLY **2** : of, relating to, or suited to an invalid

³invalid *like*²\ *n* : one that is sickly or disabled

⁴in·va·lid \ˈin-və-ləd, -ˌlid\ *vb* **1** : to make sickly or disabled **2** : to remove from active duty by reason of sickness or disability ⟨*invalided* home after the battle⟩

in·val·i·date \(ˈ)in-ˈval-ə-ˌdāt\ *vb* : to weaken or destroy the effect of ⟨*invalidate* a ballot because of fraud⟩ — **in·val·i·da·tion** \(ˌ)in-ˌval-ə-ˈdā-shən\ *n*

in·val·u·a·ble \(ˈ)in-ˈval-yə-(wə-)bəl\ *adj* : having value too great to be estimated : PRICELESS — **in·val·u·a·bly** \-blē\ *adv*

in·var·i·a·ble \(ˈ)in-ˈver-ē-ə-bəl, -ˈvar-\ *adj* : not changing or capable of change : CONSTANT ⟨an *invariable* routine⟩ — **in·var·i·a·bil·i·ty** \(ˌ)in-ˌver-ē-ə-ˈbil-ət-ē, -ˌvar-\ *n* — **invariable** *n* — **in·var·i·a·ble·ness** \(ˈ)in-ˈver-ē-ə-bəl-nəs, -ˈvar-\ *n* — **in·var·i·a·bly** \-blē\ *adv*

in·var·i·ant \(ˈ)in-ˈver-ē-ənt, -ˈvar-\ *adj* : CONSTANT, UNCHANGING — **invariant** *n*

in·va·sion \in-ˈvā-zhən\ *n* : an act of invading; *esp* : entrance of an army into a country for conquest

in·vec·tive \in-ˈvek-tiv\ *n* : harsh or bitter condemnation ⟨attacked his opponent with *invective*⟩

in·veigh \in-ˈvā\ *vb* : to protest or complain bitterly : RAIL ⟨*inveigh* against the tax laws⟩

in·vei·gle \in-ˈvā-gəl, -ˈvē-\ *vb* **in·vei·gled**; **in·vei·gling** \-g(ə-)liŋ\ **1** : to bring or lead by flattery : ENTICE ⟨*inveigled* him into marriage⟩ **2** : to acquire by ingenuity or flattery ⟨*inveigled* a loan⟩

in·vent \in-ˈvent\ *vb* **1** : to think up : make up ⟨*invent* an excuse⟩ **2** : to create or produce for the first time — **in·ven·tor** \-ˈvent-ər\ *n*

in·ven·tion \in-ˈven-chən\ *n* **1** : something in-

I

vented; *esp* : an original device or process **2** : an imaginary story : FALSEHOOD **3** : the act, process, or power of inventing

in·ven·tive \in-'vent-iv\ *adj* : gifted with the skill and imagination to invent — **in·ven·tive·ly** *adv* — **in·ven·tive·ness** *n*

[1]**in·ven·to·ry** \'in-vən-ˌtōr-ē, -ˌtȯr-\ *n, pl* **-ries** **1** : an itemized list of assets or of goods on hand **2** : the stock of goods on hand **3** : the act or process of making an inventory

[2]**inventory** *vb* **-ried**; **-ry·ing** : to make an inventory of

[1]**in·verse** \(ˈ)in-'vərs, 'in-ˌ\ *adj* : opposite in order, nature, or effect; *esp* : being a mathematical operation opposite in effect to another ⟨addition and subtraction are *inverse* operations⟩ — **in·verse·ly** *adv*

[2]**in·verse** \'in-ˌvərs, (ˈ)in-'\ *n* : something inverse or resulting in or from inversion

inversely proportional *adj* : having their product constant — used of two variable quantities one of which varies directly as the reciprocal of the other

inverse square law *n* : a statement in physics: a physical quantity (as illumination) varies with the distance from the source inversely as the square of the distance

in·ver·sion \in-'vər-zhən\ *n* **1** : the act or process of inverting **2** : a reversal of position, order, or relationship **3** : increase of temperature of the air with increasing altitude

in·vert \in-'vərt\ *vb* **1 a** : to turn inside out or upside down **b** : to turn inward **2** : to reverse the position, order, or relationship of

in·ver·te·brate \(ˈ)in-'vərt-ə-brət, -ˌbrāt\ *adj* : lacking a spinal column; *also* : of or relating to invertebrate animals — **invertebrate** *n*

[1]**in·vest** \in-'vest\ *vb* **1 a** : INSTALL 1 **b** : to furnish with power or authority **2** : to cover completely : ENVELOP **3** : CLOTHE, ADORN **4** : to surround with troops or ships : BESIEGE **5** : to infuse with a quality or characteristic ⟨*invest* an incident with mystery⟩

[2]**invest** *vb* **1** : to commit money so as to return a profit **2** : to expend for future benefits or advantages ⟨*invest* in a project⟩ — **in·ves·tor** \-'ves-tər\ *n*

in·ves·ti·gate \in-'ves-tə-ˌgāt\ *vb* : to study by close examination and systematic inquiry — **in·ves·ti·ga·tion** \-ˌves-tə-'gā-shən\ *n* — **in·ves·ti·ga·tive** \-'ves-tə-ˌgāt-iv\ *adj* — **in·ves·ti·ga·tor** \-ˌgāt-ər\ *n* — **in·ves·ti·ga·to·ry** \-'ves-ti-gə-ˌtōr-ē, -ˌtȯr-\ *adj*

in·ves·ti·ture \in-'ves-tə-ˌchu̇r, -chər\ *n* **1** : the action of investing a person esp. with the robes of office **2** : CLOTHING, APPAREL

[1]**in·vest·ment** \in-'ves(t)-mənt\ *n* **1** : INVESTITURE 1 **2** : BLOCKADE, SIEGE

[2]**investment** *n* **1** : the outlay of money for income or profit **2** : a sum of money invested or a property purchased

in·vet·er·ate \in-'vet-ə-rət, -'ve-trət\ *adj* **1** : firmly established by age or by long continuation **2** : HABITUAL — **in·vet·er·ate·ly** *adv*

in·vid·i·ous \in-'vid-ē-əs\ *adj* : tending to arouse dislike, ill will, or envy; *esp* : discriminating unfairly between two things ⟨an *invidious* comparison⟩ — **in·vid·i·ous·ly** *adv* — **in·vid·i·ous·ness** *n*

ə abut	ər further	a back	ā bake	
ä cot, cart	au̇ out	ch chin	e less	ē easy
g gift	i trip	ī life	j joke	ng sing	ō flow
ȯ flaw	ȯi coin	th thin	th this	ü loot
u̇ foot	y yet	yü few	yu̇ furious	zh vision

in·vig·o·rate \in-'vig-ə-ˌrāt\ *vb* : to give life and energy to : ANIMATE — **in·vig·o·ra·tion** \-ˌvig-ə-'rā-shən\ *n* — **in·vig·o·ra·tor** \-'vig-ə-ˌrāt-ər\ *n*

in·vin·ci·ble \(ˈ)in-'vin(t)-sə-bəl\ *adj* : incapable of being defeated, overcome, or subdued ⟨an *invincible* army⟩ — **in·vin·ci·bil·i·ty** \(ˌ)in-ˌvin(t)-sə-'bil-ət-ē\ *n* — **in·vin·ci·bly** \(ˈ)in-'vin(t)-sə-blē\ *adv*

in·vi·o·la·ble \(ˈ)in-'vī-ə-lə-bəl\ *adj* **1** : too sacred to be violated ⟨an *inviolable* oath⟩ **2** : incapable of being harmed or destroyed by violence — **in·vi·o·la·bil·i·ty** \(ˌ)in-ˌvī-ə-lə-'bil-ət-ē\ *n* — **in·vi·o·la·bly** \(ˈ)in-'vī-ə-lə-blē\ *adv*

in·vi·o·late \(ˈ)in-'vī-ə-lət\ *adj* : not violated; *esp* : PURE — **in·vi·o·late·ly** *adv* — **in·vi·o·late·ness** *n*

in·vis·i·ble \(ˈ)in-'viz-ə-bəl\ *adj* **1** : incapable of being seen ⟨sound is *invisible*⟩ **2** : inaccessible to view : HIDDEN ⟨the sun is *invisible* at night⟩ **3** : IMPERCEPTIBLE, INCONSPICUOUS ⟨an *invisible* plaid⟩ — **in·vis·i·bil·i·ty** \(ˌ)in-ˌviz-ə-'bil-ət-ē\ *n* — **in·vis·i·bly** \(ˈ)in-'viz-ə-blē\ *adv*

in·vi·ta·tion \ˌin-və-'tā-shən\ *n* **1** : the act of inviting **2** : the written, printed, or spoken expression by which a person is invited — **in·vi·ta·tion·al** \-sh(ə-)nəl\ *adj*

[1]**in·vite** \in-'vīt\ *vb* **1** : INDUCE, ATTRACT ⟨behavior that *invites* criticism⟩ ⟨*invite* disaster by speeding⟩ **2 a** : to request the presence or participation of **b** : to request formally or politely : ENCOURAGE ⟨*invite* suggestions⟩ — **in·vit·er** *n*

[2]**in·vite** \'in-ˌvīt\ *n, chiefly dial* : INVITATION

in·vit·ing \in-'vīt-ing\ *adj* : ATTRACTIVE, TEMPTING ⟨an *inviting* prospect⟩ — **in·vit·ing·ly** \-ing-lē\ *adv*

in vi·tro \in-'vē-trō\ *adv or adj* : outside the living body and in an artificial environment

in vi·vo \in-'vē-vō\ *adv or adj* : in the living body of a plant or animal

in·vo·ca·tion \ˌin-və-'kā-shən\ *n* **1** : the act or process of invoking **2** : a prayer for blessing or guidance at the beginning of a religious service **3** : a formula for conjuring : INCANTATION — **in·vo·ca·tion·al** \-sh(ə-)nəl\ *adj*

[1]**in·voice** \'in-ˌvȯis\ *n* : an itemized statement of goods or services with their prices and the terms of sale; *also* : a shipment of goods sent with an invoice

[2]**invoice** *vb* : to submit an invoice for : BILL

in·voke \in-'vōk\ *vb* **1** : to call on for aid or protection (as in prayer) ⟨*invoke* God's blessing⟩ **2** : to call forth by magic : CONJURE ⟨*invoke* spirits⟩ **3** : to appeal to as an authority or for support

in·vo·lu·cre \'in-və-ˌlü-kər\ *n* : one or more whorls of bracts immediately below a flower, flower cluster, or fruit — **in·vo·lu·cral** \ˌin-və-'lü-krəl\ *adj*

in·vol·un·tary \(ˈ)in-'väl-ən-ˌter-ē\ *adj* **1** : not made or done willingly or from choice : UNWILLING **2** : COMPULSORY **3** : not normally under the control of the will — **in·vol·un·tar·i·ly** \(ˌ)in-ˌväl-ən-'ter-ə-lē\ *adv* — **in·vol·un·tar·i·ness** \(ˈ)in-'väl-ən-ˌter-ē-nəs\ *n*

involuntary muscle *n* : SMOOTH MUSCLE

in·vo·lu·tion \ˌin-və-'lü-shən\ *n* : INTRICACY, COMPLEXITY

in·volve \in-'välv, -'vȯlv\ *vb* **1** : to draw in as a participant : ENGAGE ⟨*involved* in a lawsuit⟩ **2** : to occupy absorbingly ⟨*involved* in the hero's fate⟩ **3** : COMPLICATE ⟨an *involved* explanation⟩ **4** : to have within or as a part : INCLUDE ⟨one problem *involves* others⟩ **5** : DEMAND, REQUIRE ⟨the road job *involved* building 10 bridges⟩ **6** : AFFECT — **in·volve·ment** \-mənt\ *n* — **in·volv·er** *n*

in·vul·ner·a·ble \(ˈ)in-'vəl-nə-rə-bəl\ *adj* **1** : incapable of being wounded, injured, or damaged

2 : immune to or proof against attack : IMPREGNABLE — **in·vul·ner·a·bil·i·ty** \(ˌ)in-ˌvəl-nə-rə-ˈbil-ət-ē\ *n* — **in·vul·ner·a·bly** \(ˈ)in-ˈvəl-nə-rə-blē\ *adv*

¹in·ward \ˈin-wərd\ *adj* **1** : situated on the inside : INNER **2 a** : MENTAL **b** : SPIRITUAL **3** : directed toward the interior ⟨an *inward* flow⟩

²inward *or* **in·wards** \-wərdz\ *adv* **1** : toward the inside, center, or interior ⟨slope *inwards*⟩ **2** : toward the mind or spirit ⟨turned his thoughts *inward*⟩

in·ward·ly \ˈin-wərd-lē\ *adv* **1** : MENTALLY, SPIRITUALLY **2 a** : INTERNALLY ⟨bled *inwardly*⟩ **b** : to oneself : PRIVATELY ⟨cursed *inwardly*⟩ **3** : towards the inside ⟨curving *inwardly*⟩

in·weave \(ˈ)in-ˈwēv\ *vb* : to weave in or together : INTERLACE — **in·wo·ven** \ˈin-ˈwō-vən\ *adj*

in·wrought \(ˈ)in-ˈrȯt\ *adj* **1** : worked in among other things : inwoven in a fabric ⟨an *inwrought* design⟩ **2** : ADORNED, DECORATED

io·dide \ˈī-ə-ˌdīd\ *n* : a compound of iodine with another element or radical

io·dine \ˈī-ə-ˌdīn, -əd-ən, -ə-ˌdēn\ *also* **io·din** \ˈī-əd-ən\ *n* [from French *iode*, from Greek *ioeidēs* "violet-colored"; so called from the color of its vapor] **1** : a nonmetallic element that occurs in seawater, seaweeds, and underground brines, is obtained usu. as heavy shining blackish gray crystals, and is used esp. in medicine, photography, and analysis — see ELEMENT table **2** : a solution of iodine in alcohol used as an antiseptic

io·dize \ˈī-ə-ˌdīz\ *vb* : to treat with iodine or an iodide ⟨*iodized* salt⟩

io·do·form \ī-ˈōd-ə-ˌfȯrm, -ˈäd-\ *n* : a yellow crystalline volatile iodine compound that is used as an antiseptic dressing

io·dop·sin \ˌī-ə-ˈdäp-sən\ *n* : a violet light-sensitive pigment in the retinal cones of the eye that is important in daylight vision

io moth \ˌī-(ˌ)ō-\ *n* : a large yellowish American moth with a large spot on each hind wing

io moth
(about 3 in. across)

ion \ˈī-ən, ˈī-ˌän\ *n* [from Greek, present participle of the verb *ienai* "to go"; so called because in electrolysis it goes to one of the two poles] : an atom or group of atoms that carries a positive or negative electric charge as a result of having lost or gained one or more electrons

-ion *n suffix* **1 a** : act or process ⟨validat*ion*⟩ **b** : result of an act or process ⟨regulat*ion*⟩ **2** : state or condition ⟨hydrat*ion*⟩

ion·ic \ī-ˈän-ik\ *adj* : of, relating to, or existing in the form of ions — **ion·i·cal·ly** \-ˈän-i-k(ə-)lē\ *adv*

Ion·ic \ī-ˈän-ik\ *adj* : belonging to or resembling a style of Greek architecture characterized esp. by the scroll-like decoration of the capital of a column

ionic bond *n* : a chemical bond formed between ions of opposite charge

ion·ize \ˈī-ə-ˌnīz\ *vb* **1** : to convert wholly or partly into ions **2** : to become ionized — **ion·iz·a·ble** \-ˌnī-zə-bəl\ *adj* — **ion·i·za·tion** \ˌī-ə-nə-ˈzā-shən\ *n* — **ion·iz·er** \ˈī-ə-ˌnī-zər\ *n*

iono·sphere \ī-ˈän-ə-ˌsfi(ə)r\ *n* : the part of the earth's atmosphere beginning at an altitude of about 25 miles, extending outward 250 miles or more, and containing free electrically charged particles by means of which radio waves are transmitted to great distances around the earth — **iono·spher·ic** \(ˌ)ī-ˌän-ə-ˈsfi(ə)r-ik, -ˈsfer-\ *adj*

ion rocket *n* : a rocket deriving thrust from a stream of ionized particles

io·ta \ī-ˈōt-ə\ *n* **1** : the 9th letter of the Greek alphabet — Ι or ι **2** [from the fact that iota is the smallest letter of the Greek alphabet] : a tiny amount : JOT ⟨the story contained not one *iota* of truth⟩

IOU \ˌī-(ˌ)ō-ˈyü\ *n* : a paper that has on it the letters IOU, a stated sum, and a signature and that is given to acknowledge a debt

-ious *adj suffix* : -OUS ⟨capac*ious*⟩

IP *abbr* innings pitched

IQ *n* : INTELLIGENCE QUOTIENT

ir- — see IN-

Ir *abbr* Irish

Ira·ni·an \ir-ˈā-nē-ən\ *n* **1** : a native or inhabitant of Iran **2** : a branch of the Indo-European family of languages that includes Persian — **Iranian** *adj*

iras·ci·ble \ir-ˈas-ə-bəl, ī-ˈras-\ *adj* : easily provoked to anger : hot-tempered — **iras·ci·bil·i·ty** \ir-ˌas-ə-ˈbil-ət-ē, ī-ˌras-\ *n* — **iras·ci·bly** \ir-ˈas-ə-blē, ī-ˈras-\ *adv*

irate \ī-ˈrāt\ *adj* : ANGRY — **irate·ly** *adv* — **irate·ness** *n*

ire \ˈī(ə)r\ *n* : ANGER — **ire** *vb* — **ire·ful** \-fəl\ *adj* — **ire·ful·ly** \-fə-lē\ *adv*

Ire *abbr* **Ireland**

ir·i·des·cence \ˌir-ə-ˈdes-ən(t)s\ *n* : a play of colors producing rainbow effects (as in mother-of-pearl) — **ir·i·des·cent** \-ənt\ *adj* — **ir·i·des·cent·ly** *adv*

irid·i·um \ir-ˈid-ē-əm\ *n* : a silver-white hard brittle very heavy metallic element — see ELEMENT table

iris \ˈī-rəs\ *n, pl* **iris·es** \-rə-səz\ *or* **iri·des** \ˈī-rə-ˌdēz, ˈir-ə-\ **1** : the colored part of the eye that varies in size to control the amount of light entering the pupil **2** : any of a large genus of perennial plants with basal swordlike leaves and large showy flowers **3** : IRIS DIAPHRAGM

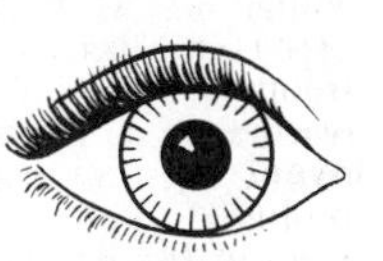
iris 1

iris diaphragm *n* : an adjustable diaphragm of thin opaque plates used for changing the diameter of a central opening to control the amount of light passing (as into a microscope or camera)

Irish \ˈī(ə)r-ish\ *n* **1 Irish** *pl* : the natives or inhabitants of Ireland or their descendants **2** : the Celtic language of Ireland — **Irish** *adj*

Irish·man \ˈī-rish-mən\ *n* **1** : a native or inhabitant of Ireland **2** : a man of Irish descent — **Irish·wom·an** \-ˌwu̇m-ən\ *n*

Irish moss *n* **1** : either of two red algae **2** : the dried and bleached plants of Irish moss used esp. in cooking and pharmacy

Irish potato *n* : POTATO 2b

Irish setter *n* : any of a breed of bird dogs similar to English setters but with a chestnut-brown or mahogany-red coat

irk \ˈərk\ *vb* : to make weary, irritated, or bored : ANNOY

irk·some \ˈərk-səm\ *adj* : TIRESOME, TEDIOUS, ANNOYING ⟨an *irksome* task⟩ — **irk·some·ly** *adv* — **irk·some·ness** *n*

Irish moss 1
(up to 10 in. long)

I

[1]**iron** \ˈī(-ə)rn\ *n* **1 :** a malleable magnetic silver-white metallic element that readily rusts in moist air, occurs in meteorites and combined in rocks, and is vital to biological processes — see ELEMENT table **2 a :** something made of iron **b** *pl* **:** handcuffs or chains used to bind or restrain **c :** a heated metal implement used for branding **d :** FLATIRON **e :** one of a set of golf clubs numbered 1 through 9 and having metal heads **3 :** STRENGTH, HARDNESS ⟨muscles of *iron*⟩

[2]**iron** *adj* **1 :** of, relating to, or made of iron **2 :** resembling iron (as in hardness or strength) **3 :** being strong and healthy **:** ROBUST ⟨an *iron* constitution⟩ **4 :** INFLEXIBLE, UNRELENTING ⟨*iron* determination⟩

[3]**iron** *vb* **:** to smooth or press clothes with a heated flatiron ⟨*iron* a shirt⟩ — **iron·er** *n*

Iron Age *n* **:** the period of human culture characterized by the smelting and use of iron and beginning somewhat before 1000 B.C. in western Asia and Egypt

[1]**iron·clad** \ˈī(-ə)rn-ˈklad\ *adj* **1 :** sheathed in iron armor **2 :** RIGOROUS, EXACTING ⟨*ironclad* laws⟩

[2]**iron·clad** \-ˌklad\ *n* **:** an armored naval vessel

iron curtain *n* **:** a barrier created by censorship and the banning of free travel that isolates an area from outside contact

iron·ic \ī-ˈrän-ik\ *or* **iron·i·cal** \-i-kəl\ *adj* **1 :** relating to, containing, or constituting irony ⟨an *ironic* turn of events⟩ ⟨an *ironic* laugh⟩ **2 :** given to irony — **iron·i·cal·ly** \-i-k(ə-)lē\ *adv*

iron lung *n* **:** a device for artificial respiration in which the air pressure in a chamber surrounding a patient's chest varies in a rhythm and forces air into and out of the lungs

iron out 1 : to remove by or as if by ironing ⟨*iron out* wrinkles⟩ **2 :** to bring into agreement **:** MODERATE ⟨*iron out* differences by negotiation⟩

iron oxide *n* **1 :** FERRIC OXIDE **2 :** a black magnetic oxide of iron used as a pigment and polishing material

iron pyrites *n* **:** PYRITE — called also *iron pyrite*

iron·stone \ˈī(-ə)rn-ˌstōn\ *n* **1 :** a hard rock rich in iron **2 :** a hard white pottery first made in England during the 18th century — called also *ironstone china*

iron sulfide *n* **:** a compound (as a pyrite or marcasite) of iron and sulfur

iron·ware \-ˌwa(ə)r, -ˌwe(ə)r\ *n* **:** articles made of iron

iron·wood \-ˌwu̇d\ *n* **1 :** any of numerous trees and shrubs with very tough hard wood **2 :** the wood of an ironwood

iron·work \-ˌwərk\ *n* **1 :** work in iron **2** *pl* **:** a mill or building where iron or steel is smelted or heavy iron or steel products are made — **iron·work·er** \-ˌwər-kər\ *n*

iro·ny \ˈī-rə-nē\ *n, pl* **-nies 1 a :** the humorous or sarcastic use of words that mean the opposite of what one really intends (as when words of praise are given but blame is intended) **b :** an ironic expression or utterance **2 a :** incongruity between an actual and an expected result **b :** a result marked by this incongruity

ə abut ər further a back ā bake ä cot, cart au̇ out ch chin e less ē easy g gift i trip ī life j joke ng sing ō flow ȯ flaw ȯi coin th thin th this ü loot u̇ foot y yet yü few yu̇ furious zh vision

syn IRONY, SARCASM can mean the use of words to convey somehow the opposite from what is actually said. IRONY applies esp. to a manner of expression intended to imply often by way of criticism the opposite of the literal meaning of the words used; SARCASM often applies to harsh malicious irony intended to ridicule or hurt

Ir·o·quois \ˈir-ə-ˌkwȯi\ *n, pl* **Iroquois** \-ˌkwȯi(z)\ **:** a member of any of the peoples of an Amerindian confederacy that existed originally in central New York state

ir·ra·di·ate \ir-ˈād-ē-ˌāt\ *vb* **1 a :** to cast rays of light on **:** ILLUMINATE **b :** to affect or treat by exposure to radiations (as of ultra-violet light, X rays, or gamma rays) **2 :** to emit like rays of light **:** RADIATE — **ir·ra·di·a·tion** \-ˌād-ē-ˈā-shən\ *n* — **ir·ra·di·a·tive** \-ˈād-ē-ˌāt-iv\ *adj*

ir·ra·tio·nal \(ˈ)ir-ˈash-(ə-)nəl\ *adj* **1 :** incapable of reasoning ⟨*irrational* beasts⟩ ⟨*irrational* from fever⟩ **2 :** not based on reason ⟨*irrational* fear⟩ — **ir·ra·tio·nal·i·ty** \(ˌ)ir-ˌash-ə-ˈnal-ət-ē\ *n* — **ir·ra·tio·nal·ly** \(ˈ)ir-ˈash-(ə-)nə-lē\ *adv*

irrational number *n* **:** a number that can be expressed as an infinite decimal with no set of consecutive digits repeating itself indefinitely but cannot be expressed as the quotient of two integers

ir·re·claim·a·ble \ˌir-i-ˈklā-mə-bəl\ *adj* **:** incapable of being reclaimed — **ir·re·claim·a·bly** \-blē\ *adv*

ir·rec·on·cil·a·ble \(ˌ)ir-ˌek-ən-ˈsī-lə-bəl, (ˈ)ir-ˈek-ən-ˌ\ *adj* **:** impossible to reconcile, adjust, or harmonize — **ir·rec·on·cil·ably** \-blē\ *adv*

ir·re·cov·er·a·ble \ˌir-i-ˈkəv-(ə-)rə-bəl\ *adj* **:** not capable of being recovered or rectified — **ir·re·cov·er·a·bly** \-blē\ *adv*

ir·re·deem·a·ble \ˌir-i-ˈdē-mə-bəl\ *adj* **1 :** not redeemable; *esp* **:** not convertible into gold or silver at the will of the holder **2 :** being beyond remedy **:** HOPELESS ⟨*irredeemable* mistakes⟩ — **ir·re·deem·a·bly** \-blē\ *adv*

ir·re·duc·i·ble \ˌir-i-ˈd(y)ü-sə-bəl\ *adj* **:** not reducible — **ir·re·duc·i·bil·i·ty** \-ˌd(y)ü-sə-ˈbil-ət-ē\ *n* — **ir·re·duc·i·bly** \-ˈd(y)ü-sə-blē\ *adv*

ir·re·fut·a·ble \ˌir-i-ˈfyüt-ə-bəl, (ˈ)ir-ˈef-yət-\ *adj* **:** not capable of being proved wrong **:** INDISPUTABLE — **ir·re·fut·a·bly** \-blē\ *adv*

irreg *abbr* irregular

[1]**ir·reg·u·lar** \(ˈ)ir-ˈeg-yə-lər\ *adj* **1 a :** not conforming to custom or rule **b :** not belonging to a recognized or organized body ⟨*irregular* troops⟩ **2 a :** not conforming to the normal or usual manner of inflection ⟨the *irregular* verb *sell*⟩ **b :** STRONG ⟨the *irregular* verb *write*⟩ **3 a :** having one or more similar parts unequal in size, form, or union ⟨*irregular* flowers⟩ **b :** UNEVEN ⟨*irregular* surface⟩ **4 :** lacking continuity or regularity of occurrence ⟨*irregular* intervals⟩ — **ir·reg·u·lar·ly** *adv*

[2]**irregular** *n* **:** an irregular soldier

ir·reg·u·lar·i·ty \(ˌ)ir-ˌeg-yə-ˈlar-ət-ē\ *n, pl* **-ties 1 :** the quality or state of being irregular **2 :** something (as dishonest conduct) that is irregular

ir·rel·e·vant \(ˈ)ir-ˈel-ə-vənt\ *adj* **:** not relevant **:** not applicable or pertinent — **ir·rel·e·vance** \-vən(t)s\ *or* **ir·rel·e·van·cy** \-vən-sē\ *n* — **ir·rel·e·vant·ly** *adv*

ir·re·li·gious \ˌir-i-ˈlij-əs\ *adj* **:** lacking religious emotions — **ir·re·li·gious·ly** *adv*

ir·re·me·di·a·ble \ˌir-i-ˈmēd-ē-ə-bəl\ *adj* **:** not remediable; *esp* **:** INCURABLE — **ir·re·me·di·a·bly** \-blē\ *adv*

ir·re·mov·a·ble \ˌir-i-ˈmü-və-bəl\ *adj* **:** not removable — **ir·re·mov·a·bil·i·ty** \-ˌmü-və-ˈbil-ət-ē\ *n* — **ir·re·mov·a·bly** \-ˈmü-və-blē\ *adv*

ir·rep·a·ra·ble \(')ir-'ep-(ə-)rə-bəl\ *adj* : not capable of being repaired or regained ⟨an *irreparable* loss⟩ — **ir·rep·a·ra·bly** \-blē\ *adv*

ir·re·place·a·ble \,ir-i-'plā-sə-bəl\ *adj* : not replaceable

ir·re·press·i·ble \,ir-i-'pres-ə-bəl\ *adj* : not capable of being repressed ⟨*irrepressible* laughter⟩ — **ir·re·press·i·bil·i·ty** \-,pres-ə-'bil-ət-ē\ *n* — **ir·re·press·i·bly** \-'pres-ə-blē\ *adv*

ir·re·proach·a·ble \-'prō-chə-bəl\ *adj* : not reproachable : BLAMELESS — **ir·re·proach·a·bly** \-blē\ *adv*

ir·re·sist·i·ble \,ir-i-'zis-tə-bəl\ *adj* : impossible to successfully resist or oppose ⟨an *irresistible* attraction⟩ — **ir·re·sist·i·bil·i·ty** \-,zis-tə-'bil-ət-ē\ *adj* — **ir·re·sist·i·bly** \-'zis-tə-blē\ *adv*

ir·res·o·lute \(')ir-'ez-ə-,lüt, -lət\ *adj* : not resolute : HESITANT — **ir·res·o·lute·ly** *adv* — **ir·res·o·lute·ness** *n* — **ir·res·o·lu·tion** \(,)ir-,ez-ə-'lü-shən\ *n*

ir·re·spec·tive of \,ir-i-'spek-tiv-əv\ *prep* : without regard to

ir·re·spon·si·ble \,ir-i-'spän(t)-sə-bəl\ *adj* **1** : not legally responsible ⟨a child is *irresponsible* for his debts⟩ **2** : having or showing no sense of responsibility ⟨*irresponsible* charges⟩ **3** : unable to bear responsibility — **ir·re·spon·si·bil·i·ty** \-,spän(t)-sə-'bil-ət-ē\ *n* — **ir·re·spon·si·bly** \-'spän(t)-sə-blē\ *adv*

ir·re·triev·a·ble \,ir-i-'trē-və-bəl\ *adj* : not capable of being recovered, regained, or remedied ⟨an *irretrievable* mistake⟩ — **ir·re·triev·a·bly** \-blē\ *adv*

ir·rev·er·ent \(')ir-'ev-(ə-)rənt, -'ev-ərnt\ *adj* : showing lack of reverence : DISRESPECTFUL — **ir·rev·er·ence** \-'ev-(ə-)rən(t)s, -'ev-ərn(t)s\ *n* — **ir·rev·er·ent·ly** *adv*

ir·re·vers·i·ble \,ir-i-'vər-sə-bəl\ *adj* : incapable of being reversed ⟨an *irreversible* chemical reaction⟩ — **ir·re·vers·i·bil·i·ty** \-,vər-sə-'bil-ət-ē\ *n* — **ir·re·vers·i·bly** \-'vər-sə-blē\ *adv*

ir·rev·o·ca·ble \(')ir-'ev-ə-kə-bəl\ *adj* : not capable of being revoked ⟨an *irrevocable* decision⟩ — **ir·rev·o·ca·bil·i·ty** \(,)ir-,ev-ə-kə-'bil-ət-ē\ *n* — **ir·rev·o·ca·bly** \(')ir-'ev-ə-kə-blē\ *adv*

ir·ri·gate \'ir-ə-,gāt\ *vb* **1** : to supply with water by artificial means ⟨*irrigate* a field⟩ ⟨*irrigate* crops⟩ **2** : to flush with a liquid ⟨*irrigate* a wound⟩ — **ir·ri·ga·tion** \,ir-ə-'gā-shən\ *n*

ir·ri·ta·bil·i·ty \,ir-ət-ə-'bil-ət-ē\ *n, pl* **-ties** **1** : the quality or state of being irritable; *esp* : readiness to become annoyed or angry : IMPATIENCE **2** : the property of protoplasm and of living organisms that permits them to react to stimuli

ir·ri·ta·ble \'ir-ət-ə-bəl\ *adj* : capable of being irritated; *esp* : easily irritated — **ir·ri·ta·ble·ness** *n* — **ir·ri·ta·bly** \-blē\ *adv*

ir·ri·tant \'ir-ə-tənt\ *adj* : IRRITATING; *esp* : tending to produce physical irritation — **irritant** *n*

ir·ri·tate \'ir-ə-,tāt\ *vb* **1** : to excite impatience, anger, or displeasure in : ANNOY **2** : to make sore or inflamed : act as an irritant toward — **ir·ri·ta·tion** \,ir-ə-'tā-shən\ *n*

ir·rupt \(')ir-'əpt\ *vb* **1** : to rush in forcibly or violently **2** : to increase suddenly in numbers ⟨rabbits *irrupt* in cycles⟩ — **ir·rup·tion** \(')ir-'əp-shən\ *n* — **ir·rup·tive** \-'əp-tiv\ *adj* — **ir·rup·tive·ly** *adv*

IRS *abbr* Internal Revenue Service

is *pres 3d sing of* BE

is- *or* **iso-** *comb form* : equal : uniform ⟨*iso*bar⟩

is *abbr* island

Isa·iah \ī-'zā-ə\ *or* **Isa·ias** \-'zā-əs\ *n* — see BIBLE table

is·chi·um \'is-kē-əm\ *n, pl* **-chia** \-kē-ə\ : the dorsal and posterior of the three principal bones composing either half of the pelvis — **is·chi·al** \-kē-əl\ *adj*

-ish \ish\ *adj suffix* **1** : of, relating to, or being ⟨Finn*ish*⟩ **2 a** : characteristic of ⟨boy*ish*⟩ ⟨mul*ish*⟩ **b** : somewhat ⟨purpl*ish*⟩ **c** : having the approximate age of ⟨forty*ish*⟩ **d** : being or occurring at the approximate time of ⟨arrive about eight*ish*⟩

isin·glass \'ī-zən-,glas, -zing-,glas\ *n* [from a modification (*-blas* being misunderstood as *glass*) of obsolete Dutch *huizenblas*, meaning literally "sturgeon's bladder"] **1** : a pure gelatin prepared from the air bladders of fish (as sturgeons) **2** : mica in thin sheets

Is·lam \is-'läm, iz-, -'lam, 'is-,, 'iz-,\ *n* **1** : a religion marked by belief in Allah as the sole deity, in Muhammad as his prophet, and in the Koran **2 a** : the civilization erected upon Islamic faith **b** : the believers in the Islamic religion **c** : the nations in which Islam is the dominant religion — **Is·lam·ic** \is-'läm-ik, iz-, -'lam-\ *adj*

is·land \'ī-lənd\ *n* [an alteration of earlier *iland*, from Old English *igland*, literally "island land"; the *s* comes from its synonym *isle*, with which it is otherwise quite unrelated; compare INSULAR] **1** : an area of land surrounded by water and smaller than a continent **2** : something (as a safety island in a street) suggestive of an island

is·land·er \'ī-lən-dər\ *n* : a native or inhabitant of an island

island of Langerhans : ISLET OF LANGERHANS

island universe *n* : a galaxy other than the Milky Way

isle \'īl\ *n* : ISLAND; *esp* : ISLET

is·let \'ī-lət\ *n* : a little island

islet of Lang·er·hans \-'läng-ər-,hän(t)s, -,hänz\ : any of the groups of small granular endocrine cells that form interlacing strands in the pancreas and secrete insulin

ism \'iz-əm\ *n* : a distinctive doctrine, cause, or theory

-ism \,iz-əm\ *n suffix* **1 a** : act : practice : process ⟨critic*ism*⟩ ⟨plagiar*ism*⟩ **b** : manner of action or behavior ⟨hero*ism*⟩ **2 a** : state : condition : property ⟨barbarian*ism*⟩ **b** : abnormal state or condition ⟨alcohol*ism*⟩ ⟨mongol*ism*⟩ **3** : doctrine : theory : cult ⟨Buddh*ism*⟩ ⟨social*ism*⟩ **4** : characteristic or peculiar feature ⟨colloquial*ism*⟩

isn't \'iz-ənt\ : is not

iso·bar \'ī-sə-,bär\ *n* : a line drawn on a map to indicate areas having the same atmospheric pressure at a given time or for a given period — **iso·bar·ic** \,ī-sə-'bär-ik, -'bar-\ *adj*

isobars

iso·late \'ī-sə-,lāt, 'is-ə-\ *vb* [derived from Italian *isolato* "isolated", literally "put on an island", from *isola* "island", from Latin *insula*; compare INSULATE] : to set or keep apart from others

iso·la·tion \,ī-sə-'lā-shən, ,is-ə-\ *n* **1** : the act of isolating : the condition of being isolated **2** : separation of a population of organisms from related forms in such a manner as to prevent crossbreeding

iso·la·tion·ism \-shə-,niz-əm\ *n* : a national policy of avoiding international political and economic relations (as alliances) — **iso·la·tion·ist** \-sh(ə-)nəst\ *n or adj*

iso·mer \'ī-sə-mər\ *n* : a compound, radical, or ion exhibiting isomerism with one or more others

isom·er·ism \ī-'säm-ə-,riz-əm\ *n* : the relation of

two or more chemical compounds, radicals, or ions that contain the same numbers of atoms of the same elements but differ in structural arrangement and properties — **iso·mer·ic** \ˌī-sə-ˈmer-ik\ *adj*

iso·met·ric drawing \ˌī-sə-ˌme-trik-\ *n* : the representation of an object on a single plane (as a piece of paper) with the three spatial axes of the object forming equal angles with the drawing surface and with the lines and edges parallel to the axes drawn to the same proportion of their true lengths

iso·met·rics \ˌī-sə-ˈme-triks\ *n sing or pl* : exercise or a system of exercises involving contraction of muscles against resistance but without much shortening of muscle fibers

iso·pod \ˈī-sə-ˌpäd\ *n* : any of a large order of small crustaceans having seven free thoracic segments each bearing a pair of similar legs — **isopod** *adj* — **isop·o·dan** \ī-ˈsäp-əd-ən\ *adj or n*

iso·prene \ˈī-sə-ˌprēn\ *n* : a compound used esp. in making synthetic rubber

iso·pro·pyl alcohol \ˌī-sə-ˌprō-pəl-\ *n* **1** : a volatile flammable liquid used esp. as a solvent and as rubbing alcohol **2** : ALCOHOL 1b

isop·ter·ous \ī-ˈsäp-tə-rəs\ *adj* : of or relating to the order of social insects comprising the termites

isos·ce·les trapezoid \ī-ˌsäs-ə-ˌlēz-\ *n* : a trapezoid whose two nonparallel sides are equal

isosceles triangle *n* : a triangle having two equal sides

isos·ta·sy \ī-ˈsäs-tə-sē\ *n* : general equilibrium in the earth's crust maintained by a yielding flow of rock material beneath the surface under the force of gravity — **iso·stat·ic** \ˌī-sə-ˈstat-ik\ *adj*

iso·therm \ˈī-sə-ˌthərm\ *n* : a line on a map connecting points having the same average temperature

iso·ther·mal \ˌī-sə-ˈthər-məl\ *adj* : of, relating to, or marked by equality of temperature

iso·tope \ˈī-sə-ˌtōp\ *n* [from *is-*, *iso-* and Greek *topos* "place"; so called because two or more isotopes of an element occupy the same place in the periodic table] : any of two or more species of atoms of a chemical element with the same atomic number and position in the periodic table and nearly identical chemical behavior but with differing atomic mass or mass number and different physical properties — **iso·top·ic** \ˌī-sə-ˈtäp-ik, -ˈtō-pik\ *adj* — **iso·top·i·cal·ly** \-ˈtäp-i-k(ə-)lē, -ˈtō-pi-\ *adv*

Isr *abbr* **1** Israel **2** Israeli

Is·rae·li \iz-ˈrā-lē\ *adj* : of, relating to, or characteristic of the republic of Israel or its people — **Israeli** *n*

Is·ra·el·ite \ˈiz-rē-ə-ˌlīt\ *n* : a descendant of the Hebrew patriarch Jacob; *esp* : a native or inhabitant of the ancient kingdom of Israel — **Israelite** *adj*

is·su·ance \ˈish-ü-ən(t)s\ *n* : the act of issuing esp. officially

[1]**is·sue** \ˈish-(ˌ)ü\ *n* **1** : the action of going, coming, or flowing out **2** : a means or place of going out : EXIT, OUTLET **3** : OFFSPRING, PROGENY **4** : final outcome : RESULT **5** : a point of debate or controversy **6** : a discharge (as of blood) from the body **7** : something issued or issuing; *esp* : the copies of a publication published at one time

[2]**issue** *vb* **1** : to go, come, or flow out : EMERGE, DISCHARGE ⟨water *issuing* from a pipe⟩ **2 a** : to cause to come forth : EMIT **b** : to distribute officially ⟨*issue* a new stamp⟩ **c** : to send out for sale or circulation : PUBLISH **3** : to come as an effect : RESULT — **is·su·er** *n*

[1]**-ist** \əst\ *n suffix* **1 a** : one that performs a (specified) action ⟨cycl*ist*⟩ : one that makes or produces ⟨novel*ist*⟩ **b** : one that plays a (specified) musical instrument ⟨harp*ist*⟩ **c** : one that operates a (specified) mechanical contrivance ⟨automobil*ist*⟩ **2** : one that specializes in a (specified) art or science or skill ⟨geolog*ist*⟩ **3** : one that adheres to or advocates a (specified) doctrine or system or code of behavior ⟨social*ist*⟩ or that of a (specified) individual ⟨Marx*ist*⟩

[2]**-ist** *adj suffix* : of, relating to, or characteristic of ⟨dilettant*ist*⟩

isth·mus \ˈis-məs\ *n* : a narrow strip of land connecting two larger land areas

-is·tic \ˈis-tik\ *or* **-is·ti·cal** \-is-ti-kəl\ *adj suffix* : of, relating to, or characteristic of

[1]**it** \(ˈ)it, ət\ *pron* **1** : that one — used usu. in reference to a lifeless thing ⟨caught the ball and threw *it* back⟩, an organism whose sex is unknown or disregarded ⟨don't know who *it* is⟩, a group, or an abstract entity **2** — used as subject of a verb that expresses a condition or action without reference to an agent ⟨*it* is raining⟩ **3 a** — used in the usual place of a noun, phrase, or clause not in its ordinary place ⟨*it* is necessary to repeat the whole thing⟩ ⟨*it* was here that I lost my way⟩ **b** — used as a direct object with little or no meaning ⟨footed *it* back to camp⟩ **4** : the general state of affairs ⟨how is *it* going⟩

[2]**it** \ˈit\ *n* : the player in a game (as tag) who has to catch the others

It *or* **Ital** *abbr* Italian

Ital·ian \ə-ˈtal-yən, i-\ *n* **1 a** : a native or inhabitant of Italy **b** : a person of Italian descent **2** : the Romance language of the Italians — **Italian** *adj*

Italian sandwich *n* : SUBMARINE 2

[1]**ital·ic** \ə-ˈtal-ik, i-, ī-\ *adj* **1** *cap* : of or relating to ancient Italy, its peoples, or their Indo-European languages **2** : of, relating to, or being a type style with characters that slant upward to the right (as in "*these words are italic*")

[2]**italic** *n* : an italic character or type

ital·i·cize \ə-ˈtal-ə-ˌsīz, i-, ī-\ *vb* **1** : to print in italics **2** : to underline with a single line

[1]**itch** \ˈich\ *vb* **1** : to have or produce an itch **2** : to cause to itch **3** : to have a strong persistent desire ⟨*itching* to get a new car⟩

[2]**itch** *n* **1 a** : an uneasy irritating sensation in the skin usu. held to result from mild stimulation of pain receptors **b** : a skin disorder accompanied by an itch; *esp* : SCABIES **2** : a constant irritating desire — **itch·i·ness** \ˈich-ē-nəs\ *n* — **itchy** \-ē\ *adj*

it'd \ˌit-əd\ : it had : it would

-ite \ˌīt\ *n suffix* **1 a** : native : resident ⟨Brooklyn*ite*⟩ **b** : descendant ⟨Israel*ite*⟩ **c** : adherent : follower ⟨Wagner*ite*⟩ **2** : product ⟨vulcan*ite*⟩ **3** : fossil ⟨ammon*ite*⟩ **4** : mineral ⟨hal*ite*⟩ : rock ⟨quartz*ite*⟩

item \ˈīt-əm\ *n* [from the Latin adverb *item* meaning "likewise"] **1** : a separate part in a list, account, or series ⟨one *item* in a bill⟩ **2** : a brief piece of news or an article reporting it

item·ize \ˈīt-ə-ˌmīz\ *vb* : to set down one by one : LIST ⟨*itemize* expenditures⟩ — **item·i·za·tion** \ˌīt-ə-mə-ˈzā-shən\ *n*

it·er·ate \ˈit-ə-ˌrāt\ *vb* : REITERATE — **it·er·a·tion** \ˌit-ə-ˈrā-shən\ *n* — **it·er·a·tive** \ˈit-ə-ˌrāt-iv, -rət-\ *adj*

itin·er·ant \ī-ˈtin-ə-rənt, ə-ˈtin-\ *adj* : traveling from place to place ⟨an *itinerant* preacher⟩

itin·er·ary \ī-ˈtin-ə-ˌrer-ē, ə-\ *n, pl* **-ar·ies** **1** : the route of a journey **2 :** a travel diary **3 :** a traveler's guidebook — **itinerary** *adj*

-i·tis \'īt-əs *also but not shown at individual entries* 'ēt-\ *n suffix, pl* **-i·tis·es** \'īt-ə-səz, 'ēt-\ *also* **-it·i·des** \'it-ə-ˌdēz\ *sometimes* **-i·tes** \'īt-(ˌ)ēz, 'ēt-\ **:** inflamed state or inflammatory disorder of ⟨bronch*itis*⟩

ivory-billed woodpecker (about 20 in. long)

it'll \ˌit-əl\ **:** it shall **:** it will

its \(ˌ)its, əts\ *adj* **:** of or relating to it or itself esp. as possessor ⟨*its* kennel⟩, agent ⟨a child proud of *its* first drawings⟩, or object of an action ⟨*its* enactment into law⟩

it's \(ˌ)its, əts\ **1 :** it is **2 :** it has

it·self \it-'self, ət-\ *pron* **1 :** that identical one — used to show that the subject and object of the verb are the same ⟨the cat gave *itself* a bath⟩ or for emphasis ⟨the letter *itself* was missing⟩ **2 :** its normal, healthy, or sane self

-ity \ət-ē\ *n suffix, pl* **-ities :** quality **:** state **:** degree ⟨alkalin*ity*⟩

-ive \iv\ *adj suffix* **:** that performs or tends toward an indicated action ⟨correct*ive*⟩

I've \(ˌ)īv\ **:** I have

ivied \'ī-vēd\ *adj* **:** overgrown with ivy

ivo·ry \'īv-(ə-)rē\ *n, pl* **-ries [**via Old French *ivoire* from Latin *eboreus* "of ivory", from *ebur* "ivory", from Egyptian *ꜣb* "elephant", "ivory"**] 1 :** the hard creamy-white modified dentine that composes the tusks of a tusked mammal (as an elephant) **2 :** a pale whitish yellow

ivo·ry–billed woodpecker \ˌīv-(ə-)rē-ˌbild-\ *n* **:** a nearly extinct large woodpecker with glossy black plumage, a large ivory-white bill, and in the male a large scarlet crest

ivy \'ī-vē\ *n, pl* **ivies 1 :** a climbing woody vine with glossy evergreen leaves, small yellowish flowers, and black berries — called also *English ivy* **2 :** any of several plants (as Virginia creeper) resembling ivy

ivy 1

IWW *abbr* Industrial Workers of the World

-ize \ˌīz\ *vb suffix* **1 :** cause to be or conform to or resemble ⟨american*ize*⟩ **:** form or cause to be formed into ⟨crystall*ize*⟩ ⟨union*ize*⟩ **2 a :** subject to a specified action ⟨satir*ize*⟩ **b :** saturate, treat, or combine with ⟨oxid*ize*⟩ ⟨macadam*ize*⟩ **3 :** treat like ⟨idol*ize*⟩ **4 :** engage in a (specified) activity ⟨philosoph*ize*⟩

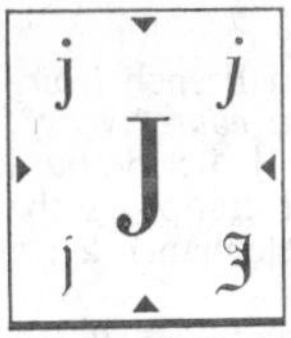

j \'jā\ *n, often cap* : the 10th letter of the English alphabet

jab \'jab\ *vb* **jabbed; jab·bing** : to thrust quickly or abruptly with or as if with something sharp : POKE — **jab** *n*

¹**jab·ber** \'jab-ər\ *vb* **jab·bered; jab·ber·ing** \-(ə-)riŋ\ : to talk or speak rapidly, indistinctly, or unintelligibly — **jab·ber·er** \-ər-ər\ *n*

²**jabber** *n* : GIBBERISH, CHATTER

jab·ber·wocky \'jab-ər-ˌwäk-ē\ *n* : meaningless speech or writing

ja·bot \zha-'bō, ja-\ *n* : a ruffle of cloth or lace that falls from the collar down the front of a dress or shirt

¹**jack** \'jak\ *n* **1** *often cap* : MAN; *esp* : SAILOR **2 a** : a device for turning a spit (as in roasting meat) **b** : any of various portable mechanisms for exerting pressure or lifting a heavy body (as an automobile or a building) a short distance **3** : any of various animals: as **a** : a male ass **b** : JACKRABBIT **4 a** : something small of its kind ⟨*jack* rafter⟩ **b** : a small national flag flown by a ship **c** : a small 6-pointed metal object used in a game **d** *pl* : a game played with jacks **5** : a playing card bearing the figure of a man **6** *slang* : MONEY **7** : a socket in an electric circuit used with a plug to make a connection with another circuit

²**jack** *vb* **1** : to move or lift by or as if by a jack **2** : INCREASE, RAISE ⟨*jack* up prices⟩ — **jack·er** *n*

jack·al \'jak-əl, -ˌöl\ *n* **1** : any of several Old World wild dogs smaller than the related wolves **2** : a person who performs menial tasks for another : LACKEY

jackal 1
(about 16 in. at shoulder)

jack·a·napes \'jak-ə-ˌnāps\ *n* : an impudent or conceited person

jack·ass \'jak-ˌas\ *n* **1** : a male ass; *also* : DONKEY **2** : a stupid person : FOOL

jack·boot \-ˌbüt\ *n* : a heavy military boot; *esp* : one reaching above the knee

jack·daw \-ˌdȯ\ *n* : a common black and gray Eurasian bird related to but smaller than the common crow

jack·et \'jak-ət\ *n* **1** : a garment for the upper body usu. having a front opening, collar, and sleeves **2** : an outer covering or casing: as **a** : a tough metal covering on a bullet or projectile **b** : a coating or covering of a nonconducting material used to prevent heat radiation **c** : a detachable outer paper wrapper on a bound book — **jack·et·ed** \-ət-əd\ *adj*

jack–in–the–box \'jak-ən-thə-ˌbäks\ *n, pl* **jack–in–the–boxes** *or* **jacks–in–the–box** : a small box out of which a figure (as of a clown's head) springs when the lid is raised

jack–in–the–pul·pit \ˌjak-ən-thə-'pu̇l-ˌpit\ *n, pl* **jack–in–the–pulpits** *or* **jacks–in–the–pulpit** : an American spring-flowering woodland herb with an upright club-shaped flower cluster arched over by a green and purple hoodlike bract

¹**jack·knife** \'jak-ˌnīf\ *n* **1** : a large strong clasp knife for the pocket **2** : a dive in which the diver bends from the waist and touches his ankles before straightening out

²**jackknife** *vb* : to double up like a jackknife ⟨the trailer truck *jackknifed*⟩

jack–of–all–trades \ˌjak-ə-'vȯl-ˌtrādz\ *n, pl* **jacks–of–all–trades** : a person who can work at various trades : HANDYMAN

jack–o'–lan·tern \'jak-ə-ˌlant-ərn\ *n* : a lantern made of a pumpkin cut to look like a human face

jack pine \'jak-\ *n* : a No. American pine with paired twisted needles that is used for pulp and box lumber

jack·pot \'jak-ˌpät\ *n* **1** : a large poker pot formed by the accumulation of stakes from previous play **2 a** : a combination on a slot machine that wins a top prize or all the coins in the machine **b** : the sum so won **3** : an impressive often unexpected success or reward

jack·rab·bit \-ˌrab-ət\ *n* : any of several large hares of western No. America with long ears and long hind legs

jack·screw \-ˌskrü\ *n* : a screw-operated jack for lifting or for exerting pressure

jack·stone \-ˌstōn\ *n* **1** : JACK 4c **2** *pl* : JACK 4d

jack·straw \-ˌstrȯ\ *n* **1** : one of the pieces used in the game jackstraws **2** *pl* : a game in which straws or thin strips are let fall in a heap with each player trying to remove them one at a time without disturbing the rest

jack–tar \-'tär\ *n, often cap* : SAILOR

jackrabbit
(about 24 in. long)

¹**jade** \'jād\ *n* **1** : a broken-down, vicious, or worthless horse **2** : a disreputable woman

²**jade** *vb* **1 a** : to wear out : TIRE **b** : to become weary **2** : to make dull or uninterested by too much : SATIATE ⟨an appetite *jaded* by too many sweets⟩

³**jade** *n* : a tough usu. green gemstone that takes a high polish

jade green *n* : a light bluish green

¹**jag** \'jag\ *n* : a sharp projecting part : BARB

²**jag** *n* **1** : a small load (as of hay) **2** : a period of excessive or uncontrolled indulgence (as in liquor or emotion) : SPREE ⟨a crying *jag*⟩ ⟨a marijuana *jag*⟩

jag·ged \'jag-əd\ *adj* : sharply notched : ROUGH ⟨a *jagged* edge⟩ — **jag·ged·ly** *adv* — **jag·ged·ness** *n*

jag·uar \'jag-(yə-)ˌwär\ *n* [from Spanish & Portuguese, from American Indian languages of Brazil and Paraguay] : a large cat of tropical America that is larger and stockier than the leopard and is brownish yellow or buff with black spots

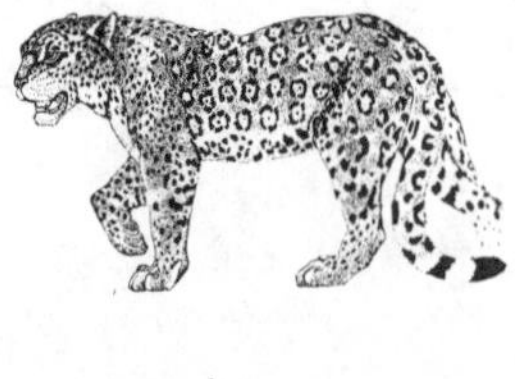

jaguar
(about 33 in. at shoulder)

jai alai \'hī-ˌlī, ˌhī-ə-'lī\ *n* : a court game for two or four

ə abut	ər further	a back	ā bake	
ä cot, cart	au̇ out	ch chin	e less	ē easy
g gift	i trip	ī life	j joke	ng sing
ō flow	ȯ flaw	ȯi coin	th thin	th this
ü loot	u̇ foot	y yet	yü few	yu̇ furious
zh vision				

players using a ball and a long wicker basket strapped to the wrist

jail \ˈjāl\ *n* [from Old French *jaiole*, from assumed Latin *caveola*, diminutive of Latin *cavea* "cage"] : PRISON; *esp* : a building for temporary custody of prisoners — **jail** *vb*

jail·bird \-ˌbərd\ *n* : a person who is or is often confined in jail

jail·break \-ˌbrāk\ *n* : a forcible escape from jail

jail·er *or* **jail·or** \ˈjā-lər\ *n* : a keeper of a jail

ja·lopy \jə-ˈläp-ē\ *n, pl* **-lop·ies** : a dilapidated old vehicle

jal·ou·sie \ˈjal-ə-sē\ *n* **1** : a blind with adjustable horizontal slats to admit light and air and exclude sun and rain **2** : a window made of adjustable glass louvers

1**jam** \ˈjam\ *vb* **jammed**; **jam·ming** **1 a** : to press into a close or tight position ⟨*jam* his hat on⟩ **b** : to be or cause to be wedged so as to be unworkable ⟨*jam* the typewriter keys⟩ ⟨the gun *jammed*⟩ **c** : to crowd into esp. so as to obstruct or to fill or overfill : PACK ⟨2000 people *jammed* the hall⟩ ⟨*jam* clothes into a suitcase⟩ **2** : to push suddenly and forcibly ⟨*jam* on the brakes⟩ **3** : to squeeze or crush painfully ⟨*jammed* his finger in the door⟩ **4** : to make unintelligible by sending out interfering signals or messages ⟨*jam* a radio program⟩ — **jammer** *n*

2**jam** *n* **1 a** : an act or instance of jamming **b** : a crowded mass that obstructs ⟨traffic *jam*⟩ **2** : a difficult state of affairs

3**jam** *n* : a food made of fruit and sugar thickened by boiling

Jam *abbr* Jamaica

jamb \ˈjam\ *n* : an upright piece forming the side of an opening (as of a door)

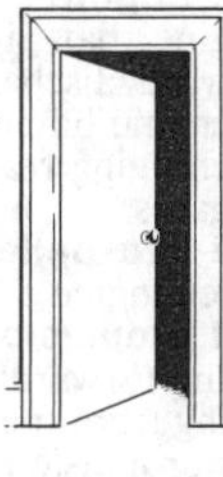

jamb

jam·bo·ree \ˌjam-bə-ˈrē\ *n* **1** : a large festive gathering **2** : a national or international camping assembly of boy scouts

James \ˈjāmz\ *n* — see BIBLE table

jam session *n* : a performance by a group of jazz musicians improvising together

Jan *abbr* January

jan·gle \ˈjang-gəl\ *vb* **jan·gled**; **jan·gling** \-g(ə-)ling\ : to make or cause to make a harsh or discordant ringing sound — **jangle** *n*

jan·i·tor \ˈjan-ət-ər\ *n* **1** : DOORKEEPER **2** : a person who has the care of a building — **jan·i·to·ri·al** \ˌjan-ə-ˈtōr-ē-əl, -ˈtȯr-\ *adj* — **jan·i·tress** \ˈjan-ə-trəs\ *n*

Jan·u·ary \ˈjan-yə-ˌwer-ē\ *n* [from Latin *Januarius*, from *Janus*, Roman god of gates and doors and of beginnings and endings] : the 1st month of the year

Jap *abbr* **1** Japan **2** Japanese

ja·pan \jə-ˈpan\ *n* **1** : a varnish giving a hard brilliant surface coating **2** : work varnished and figured in the Japanese manner — **japan** *vb*

Jap·a·nese \ˌjap-ə-ˈnēz, -ˈnēs\ *n, pl* **Japanese** **1 a** : a native or inhabitant of Japan **b** : a person of Japanese descent **2** : the language of the Japanese — **Japanese** *adj*

Japanese beetle *n* : a small lustrous green and brown beetle introduced into America from Japan that as a grub feeds on the roots of grasses and decaying vegetation and as an adult eats foliage and fruits

adult Japanese beetle and larva (up to ⅝ in. long)

1**jar** \ˈjär\ *vb* **jarred**; **jar·ring** **1 a** : to make a harsh or discordant sound **b** : to have a harsh or disagreeable effect ⟨noise that *jars* the nerves⟩ **2** : to cause to vibrate : SHAKE **3** : CLASH, CONFLICT ⟨*jarring* opinions⟩

2**jar** *n* **1** : a harsh sound **2** : JOLT **3** : QUARREL, DISPUTE **4** : a painful effect : SHOCK

3**jar** *n* **1** : a widemouthed container usu. of earthenware or glass **2** : JARFUL

jar·di·niere \ˌjärd-ə-ˈni(ə)r\ *n* : an ornamental stand or pot for plants or flowers

jar·ful \ˈjär-ˌfu̇l\ *n, pl* **jarfuls** \-ˌfu̇lz\ *or* **jars·ful** \ˈjärz-ˌfu̇l\ : the quantity held by a jar

jar·gon \ˈjär-gən, -ˌgän\ *n* **1** : a mixed language used for communication between peoples of different speech **2** : the special language of a particular activity or group **3** : obscure and often pretentious language

jas·mine \ˈjaz-mən\ *n* : any of numerous often climbing shrubs that are related to the olive and have extremely fragrant flowers; *also* : any of various plants noted for sweet-scented flowers

jas·per \ˈjas-pər\ *n* : an opaque fine-grained usu. red, yellow, or brown quartz; *esp* : green chalcedony — **jas·pery** \-pə-rē\ *adj*

ja·to unit \ˈjāt-ō-\ *n* : a special rocket engine to help an airplane take off

1**jaun·dice** \ˈjȯn-dəs, ˈjän-\ *n* **1** : yellowish discoloration of the skin, tissues, and body fluids caused by the presence of coloring matter from the bile; *also* : a disease or abnormal condition marked by jaundice **2** : a state or attitude marked by satiety, distaste, or hostility

2**jaundice** *vb* **1** : to affect with jaundice **2** : to affect by envy, distaste, or hostility

jaunt \ˈjȯnt, ˈjänt\ *n* : a short trip for pleasure — **jaunt** *vb*

jaun·ty \ˈjȯnt-ē, ˈjänt-\ *adj* **jaun·ti·er**; **-est** : sprightly in manner or appearance : LIVELY — **jaun·ti·ly** \ˈjȯnt-ə-lē, ˈjänt-\ *adv* — **jaun·ti·ness** \ˈjȯnt-ē-nəs, ˈjänt-\ *n*

Ja·va man \ˌjäv-ə-, ˌjav-\ *n* : either of two primitive small-brained prehistoric men known chiefly from skulls found in Java : PITHECANTHROPUS

jav·e·lin \ˈjav-(ə-)lən\ *n* **1** : a light spear **2** : a slender metal-tipped shaft of wood thrown for distance in an athletic field event

1**jaw** \ˈjȯ\ *n* **1 a** : either of two structures of bone or cartilage that support the soft parts enclosing the mouth and usu. bear teeth **b** : the parts constituting the walls of the mouth and serving to open and close it — usu. used in pl. **c** : any of various organs of invertebrates that perform the function of the vertebrate jaws **2** : something resembling the jaw of an animal in form or action; *esp* : one of a set of opposing parts that open and close for holding or crushing something between them — **jawed** \ˈjȯd\ *adj*

2**jaw** *vb* **1** : to talk at length **2** : SCOLD

jaw·bone \ˈjȯ-ˈbōn, -ˌbōn\ *n* : JAW 1a

jaw·break·er \-ˌbrā-kər\ *n* : a round hard candy

jay \ˈjā\ *n* : any of several noisy birds that are related to the crow but are smaller and more graceful and usu. more brightly colored

jay·walk \ˈjā-ˌwȯk\ *vb* : to cross a street carelessly without paying attention to traffic regulations — **jay·walk·er** *n*

1**jazz** \ˈjaz\ *vb* **1** : ENLIVEN — usu. used with *up* **2** : to play in the manner of jazz

2**jazz** *n* **1** : American music marked by lively rhythms in which the accents often fall on beats not usually accented **2** : empty talk ⟨don't give me any of that *jazz*⟩

jazzy \'jaz-ē\ *adj* **jazz·i·er; -est 1 :** having the characteristics of jazz **2 :** LIVELY, FLASHY — **jazz·i·ness** \'jaz-ē-nəs\ *n*
JCC *abbr* Junior Chamber of Commerce
jct *abbr* junction
Je *abbr* June
jeal·ous \'jel-əs\ *adj* **1 :** demanding complete devotion **2 :** fearful or spitefully envious of a rival or competitor **3 :** fearful of the loss of a loved one's devotion : emotionally possessive **4 :** WATCHFUL, CAREFUL ⟨*jealous* of her rights⟩ ***syn*** see ENVIOUS — **jeal·ous·ly** *adv*
jeal·ou·sy \'jel-ə-sē\ *n, pl* **-sies 1 :** a jealous disposition, attitude, or feeling **2 :** zealous vigilance ⟨cherished their liberty with determined *jealousy*⟩
jean \'jēn\ *n* [short for *jean fustian,* from Middle English *Gene, Jene* "Genoa"] **1 :** a durable twilled cotton cloth used esp. for sportswear and work clothes **2** *pl* **:** pants made of jean or denim
jeep \'jēp\ *n* **:** a small general-purpose motor vehicle with ¼-ton capacity and four-wheel drive used by the U.S. Army in World War II
jeer \'ji(ə)r\ *vb* **:** to scoff at : MOCK — **jeer** *n*
Je·ho·vah \ji-'hō-və\ *n* **:** [2]GOD
je·june \ji-'jün\ *adj* **1 :** lacking interest or significance : DULL **2 :** CHILDISH ⟨*jejune* remarks⟩ — **je·june·ly** *adv* — **je·june·ness** \-'jün-nəs\ *n*
je·ju·num \ji-'jü-nəm\ *n* **:** the section of the small intestine between the duodenum and the ileum
jell \'jel\ *vb* **1 :** to make or become jelly **2 :** to take shape : FORM ⟨an idea *jelled* ⟩
[1]**jel·ly** \'jel-ē\ *n, pl* **jellies 1 :** a food with a soft elastic consistency due usu. to gelatin or pectin; *esp* **:** a fruit product made by boiling sugar and the juice of fruit **2 :** a substance resembling jelly in consistency — **jel·ly·like** \-ē-,līk\ *adj*
[2]**jelly** *vb* **jel·lied; jel·ly·ing 1 :** JELL 1 **2 :** to set in jelly ⟨*jellied* tongue⟩
jel·ly·fish \'jel-ē-,fish\ *n* **:** a free-swimming sexually-reproducing coelenterate animal with a jellylike, disk-shaped, and usu. nearly transparent body; *also* **:** any of various similar sea animals (as a ctenophore)

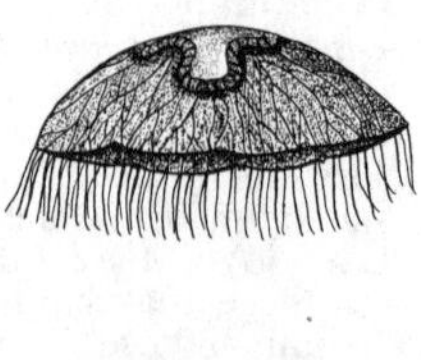
jellyfish
(up to 6 in. across)

jen·net \'jen-ət\ *n* **:** a small Spanish horse
jen·ny \'jen-ē\ *n, pl* **jennies 1 a :** a female bird ⟨*jenny* wren⟩ **b :** a female donkey **2 :** SPINNING JENNY
jeop·ar·dize \'jep-ər-,dīz\ *vb* **:** to expose to danger : IMPERIL; *also* **:** RISK
jeop·ar·dy \'jep-ərd-ē\ *n* **:** DANGER
jer·boa \jər-'bō-ə\ *n* **:** any of several social nocturnal Old World jumping rodents with long hind legs and long tail
Jer·e·mi·ah \,jer-ə-'mī-ə\ *n* — see BIBLE table
[1]**jerk** \'jərk\ *vb* **1 :** to give a sharp quick push, pull, or twist to **2 :** to make in jerks or with a jerk **3 :** to mix and dispense (as sodas)
[2]**jerk** *n* **1 :** a short quick pull or twist : TWITCH **2 :** an involuntary muscular movement or spasm **3 :** a stupid, foolish, or eccentric person — **jerk·i·ly** \'jər-kə-lē\ *adv* — **jerk·i·ness** \-kē-nəs\ *n* — **jerky** \-kē\ *adj*
[3]**jerk** *vb* **:** to cut into long strips and dry in the sun ⟨*jerked* beef⟩
jer·kin \'jər-kən\ *n* **:** a close-fitting hip-length sleeveless jacket
jer·sey \'jər-zē\ *n, pl* **jerseys** [from *Jersey,* one of the Channel islands] **1 :** a plain knitted fabric of various fibers **2 :** a close-fitting knitted garment (as a shirt) **3 :** any of a breed of small usu. fawn-colored dairy cattle noted for their rich milk
jes·sa·mine \'jes-(ə-)mən\ *var of* JASMINE
jest \'jest\ *n* **1 :** a comic act or remark : JOKE **2 :** a frivolous mood or manner ⟨spoken in *jest*⟩ **3 :** LAUGHINGSTOCK — **jest** *vb*
jest·er \'jes-tər\ *n* **1 :** FOOL 2 ⟨court *jester*⟩ **2 :** a person given to jests
[1]**jet** \'jet\ *n* **1 :** a compact black mineral that takes a good polish and is often used for jewelry **2 :** a very dark black
[2]**jet** *vb* **jet·ted; jet·ting :** to spout or emit in a stream : SPURT
[3]**jet** *n* **1 a :** a forceful rush of liquid, gas, or vapor through a narrow opening or a nozzle **b :** a nozzle for a jet of fluid (as gas or water) **2 a :** JET ENGINE **b :** JET AIRPLANE
[4]**jet** *vb* **jet·ted; jet·ting :** to travel by jet airplane
jet airplane *n* **:** an airplane having no propeller and powered by a jet engine — called also *jet plane*

jet airplane

jet assist *n* **:** the additional thrust given to a craft (as an airplane) usu. by auxiliary units
jet engine *n* **:** an engine that produces motion as a result of the rearward discharge of a jet of fluid; *esp* **:** an airplane engine having one or more exhaust nozzles for discharging rearwardly a jet of heated air and exhaust gases
jet–pro·pelled \,jet-prə-'peld\ *adj* **:** propelled by a jet engine
jet propulsion *n* **:** propulsion of a body produced by the forwardly directed forces of the reaction resulting from the rearward discharge of a jet of fluid; *esp* **:** propulsion of an airplane by jet engines
jet·sam \'jet-səm\ *n* **:** goods thrown overboard to lighten a ship in distress; *esp* **:** such goods when washed ashore
jet set *n* **:** an international social group of wealthy people who frequent fashionable resorts
jet stream *n* **:** a long narrow meandering current of high-speed winds blowing from a generally westerly direction several miles above the earth's surface
jet·ti·son \'jet-ə-sən\ *vb* **1 :** to throw goods overboard from a ship or airplane esp. to lighten it in distress **2 :** DISCARD — **jettison** *n*
jet·ty \'jet-ē\ *n, pl* **jetties 1 :** a pier built out into the water to influence the current or protect a harbor **2 :** a landing wharf
Jew \'jü\ *n* **1 :** one of the ancient Hebrews or a descendant of the ancient Hebrews **2 :** one whose religion is Judaism — **Jew·ish** \'jü-ish\ *adj*
[1]**jew·el** \'jü-əl\ *n* **1 :** an ornament of precious metal often set with stones and worn as an accessory of dress **2 :** one that is highly esteemed **3 :** a precious stone : GEM **4 :** a bearing in a watch made of a crystal or a precious stone
[2]**jewel** *vb* **-eled** *or* **-elled; -el·ing** *or* **-el·ling :** to adorn or equip with jewels

jew·el·er *or* **jew·el·ler** \'jü-ə-lər\ *n* **:** a person who makes or deals in jewelry and related articles

jew·el·ry \'jü-əl-rē\ *n* **:** JEWELS

jew·el·weed \'jü-əl-ˌwēd\ *n* **:** any of a large genus of watery-juiced annual herbs with often showy irregular flowers

jew·fish \'jü-ˌfish\ *n* **:** any of various large rough-scaled dusky green or blackish groupers with a broad head somewhat flattened on top

Jew·ry \'jü(ə)r-ē, 'jü-rē\ *n, pl* **Jewries 1 :** a district inhabited by Jews **:** GHETTO **2 :** the Jewish people

Jew's harp *or* **Jews' harp** \'jüz-ˌhärp\ *n* **:** a small lyre-shaped instrument that when placed between the teeth gives tones from a metal tongue struck by the finger

Jew's harp

jib \'jib\ *n* **:** a triangular sail set on a stay running from the bow to the head of the foremast

[1]**jibe** \'jīb\ *vb* **1 :** to shift or swing from one side to the other **2 :** to cause a sail to jibe

[2]**jibe** *var of* GIBE

[3]**jibe** *vb* **:** to be in accord **:** AGREE ⟨the two reports *jibed*⟩

jif·fy \'jif-ē\ *n, pl* **jiffies :** MOMENT, INSTANT ⟨in a *jiffy*⟩

[1]**jig** \'jig\ *n* **1 :** a lively springy dance in triple rhythm **2 :** TRICK, GAME — used chiefly in the phrase *the jig is up* **3 :** a fishing device that is jerked up and down or drawn through the water **4 :** a device used to guide a tool or to hold parts together during assembly

[2]**jig** *vb* **jigged; jig·ging 1 :** to dance a jig **2 :** to jerk up and down or to and fro

[1]**jig·ger** \'jig-ər\ *n* **1 :** one that jigs or operates a jig **2 :** JIG 3 **3 :** DEVICE, GADGET **4 :** a measure used in mixing drinks that usu. holds 1½ ounces

[2]**jigger** *n* **:** CHIGGER

jig·gle \'jig-əl\ *vb* **jig·gled; jig·gling** \-(ə-)liŋ\ **:** to move or cause to move with quick little jerks — **jiggle** *n*

jig·saw \'jig-ˌsȯ\ *n* **:** a machine saw with a narrow blade for cutting curved and irregular lines or openwork patterns

jigsaw puzzle *n* **:** a puzzle consisting of small irregular pieces fitted together to form a picture

[1]**jilt** \'jilt\ *n* **:** a woman who jilts a man

[2]**jilt** *vb* **:** to cast a lover aside unfeelingly

jim crow \'jim-'krō\ *n, often cap J & C* **:** discrimination against Negroes

jim–dan·dy \'jim-'dan-dē\ *n* **:** something very good — **jim–dandy** *adj*

[1]**jim·my** \'jim-ē\ *n, pl* **jimmies :** a short crowbar used by burglars

[2]**jimmy** *vb* **jim·mied; jim·my·ing :** to force open with or as if with a jimmy

jim·son·weed \'jim(p)-sən-ˌwēd\ *n, often cap* **:** a poisonous coarse annual weed that is related to the potato and has rank-smelling foliage and large white or violet trumpet-shaped flowers

[1]**jin·gle** \'jiŋ-gəl\ *vb* **jin·gled; jin·gling** \-g(ə-)liŋ\ **:** to make or cause to make a light clinking sound — **jin·gler** \-g(ə-)lər\ *n*

[2]**jingle** *n* **1 :** a light clinking sound **2 :** a catchy repetition of sounds in a poem **3 :** a verse or song marked by catchy repetition — **jin·gly** \-g(ə-)lē\ *adj*

jin·go \'jiŋ-gō\ *n, pl* **jingoes :** a person who favors a warlike policy toward other countries **:** HAWK — **jin·go·ism** \-ˌiz-əm\ *n* — **jin·go·is·tic** \ˌjiŋ-gō-'is-tik\ *adj*

jinn \'jin\ *or* **jin·ni** \jə-'nē, 'jin-ē\ *n, pl* **jinns** *or* **jinn :** a powerful spirit held by the Muslims to be able to take on various forms

jin·rik·i·sha \jin-'rik-shȯ\ *n* **:** a small 2-wheeled vehicle pulled by a man and used orig. in Japan

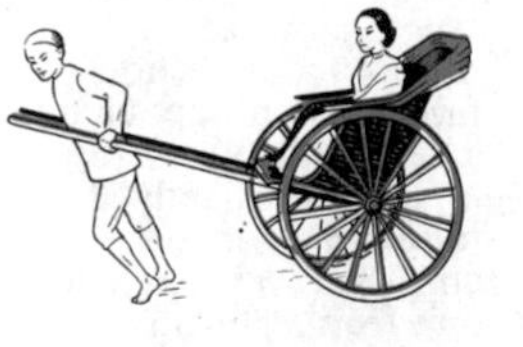

jinrikisha

jinx \'jiŋ(k)s\ *n* **:** someone or something that brings bad luck

jit·ney \'jit-nē\ *n, pl* **jitneys 1** *slang* **:** NICKEL 2a **2 :** a small bus that carries passengers over a regular route

jit·ter·bug \'jit-ər-ˌbəg\ *n* **1 :** a dance in which couples two-step, balance, and twirl with vigorous acrobatics **2 :** a person who dances the jitterbug — **jitterbug** *vb*

jit·ters \'jit-ərz\ *n pl* **:** extreme nervousness — **jit·tery** \-ə-rē\ *adj*

jiu·jit·su *or* **jiu·jut·su** *var of* JUJITSU

jive \'jīv\ *n* **1 :** swing music or dancing performed to it **2 a** *slang* **:** glib, deceptive, or foolish talk **b :** the jargon of swing musicians **c :** a special jargon of difficult or slang terms — **jive** *vb*

jo \'jō\ *n, pl* **joes** *chiefly Scot* **:** SWEETHEART, DEAR

job \'jäb\ *n* **1 a :** a piece of work; *esp* **:** one undertaken at a stated rate **b :** something produced by or as if by work ⟨that painting is a good *job*⟩ **2 :** DUTY, TASK ⟨your *job* is to mow the lawn⟩ **3 :** a position at which one regularly works for pay ⟨looked for a *job* as an accountant⟩ ⟨lost his *job*⟩ — **job·less** \-ləs\ *adj* — **job·less·ness** *n*

Job \'jōb\ *n* — see BIBLE table

job·ber \'jäb-ər\ *n* **1 :** a person who buys goods and then sells them to other dealers **2 :** a person who does work by the job

job·hold·er \'jäb-ˌhōl-dər\ *n* **:** one having a regular job; *esp* **:** a government employee

jo block \'jō-\ *n* **:** one of a set of gauge blocks ground to an accuracy of around one hundred-thousandth of an inch

job lot *n* **1 :** miscellaneous goods for sale as a lot usu. to a retailer **2 :** a miscellaneous and usu. inferior collection or group

job work *n* **:** commercial printing of miscellaneous orders

[1]**jock·ey** \'jäk-ē\ *n, pl* **jockeys 1 :** one who rides a horse esp. as a professional in a race **2 :** OPERATOR ⟨bus *jockey*⟩ ⟨elevator *jockey*⟩

[2]**jockey** *vb* **jock·eyed; jock·ey·ing 1 :** to ride a horse as a jockey **2 :** to move or manage with skill or so as to gain advantage ⟨*jockey* a truck into position⟩ ⟨*jockeying* for position⟩ **3 :** TRICK, CHEAT ⟨was *jockeyed* out of a political job⟩

jo·cose \jō-'kōs\ *adj* **:** MERRY, JOKING — **jo·cose·ly** *adv* — **jo·cose·ness** *n*

joc·u·lar \'jäk-yə-lər\ *adj* **1 :** given to jesting **2 :** said or done in jest **:** PLAYFUL — **joc·u·lar·i·ty** \ˌjäk-yə-'lar-ət-ē\ *n* — **joc·u·lar·ly** \'jäk-yə-lər-lē\ *adv*

joc·und \'jäk-ənd, 'jō-kənd\ *adj* **:** CHEERFUL, GAY — **joc·und·ly** *adv*

jodh·pur \'jäd-pər\ *n* **1** *pl* **:** riding breeches loose

J

above the knee and tight-fitting below **2 :** an ankle-high boot fastened with a strap that is buckled at the side
Jo·el \'jō-əl\ *n* — see BIBLE table
1jog \'jäg\ *vb* **jogged; jog·ging 1 :** to give a slight shake or push to **:** NUDGE **2 :** ROUSE, STIR ⟨*jogged* his memory⟩ **3 :** to move up and down or about with a short heavy motion **4 a :** to go or cause to go at a jog **b :** to run at a slow pace esp. for exercise ⟨*jogs* two miles every morning⟩ — **jog·ger** *n*
2jog *n* **1 :** a slight shake **:** PUSH **2 :** a slow jolting gait esp. of a horse
3jog *n* **1 :** a projection or indentation in a line or surface **2 :** an abrupt change in direction
jog·gle \'jäg-əl\ *vb* **jog·gled; jog·gling** \-(ə-)liŋ\ **1 :** to shake slightly **2 :** to move shakily or jerkily — **joggle** *n*
John \'jän\ *n* — see BIBLE table
John Doe \'jän-'dō\ *n* **:** a person whose true name is unknown or not mentioned
john·ny·cake \'jän-ē-ˌkāk\ *n* **:** a bread made with cornmeal, flour, eggs, and milk
John·ny–jump–up \ˌjän-ē-'jəmp-ˌəp\ *n* **:** any of various small-flowered pansies or violets
join \'jȯin\ *vb* **1 a :** to bring or fasten together in close contact ⟨*join* hands⟩ ⟨*join* two points by a line⟩ **b :** to become joined ⟨place where two roads *join*⟩ **c :** to combine the elements of ⟨*join* two sets⟩ **2 :** to come or bring into close association ⟨*join* a club⟩ ⟨*join* in marriage⟩ **3 :** to come into the company of ⟨*join* friends for lunch⟩ **4 :** ADJOIN **5 :** to take part with others in an activity ⟨*join* in singing⟩ — **join·a·ble** \-ə-bəl\ *adj*
syn JOIN, CONNECT, COMBINE, UNITE can mean to bring or come together in some degree of union. JOIN suggests a physical contact or conjunction between two or more things ⟨*join* the ends with glue⟩; CONNECT suggests in addition a loose or external attachment ⟨the bones that *connect* at the elbow⟩; COMBINE implies some degree of merger or mingling, with some loss of identity, of things that meet ⟨*combining* the ingredients for a cake⟩; UNITE implies a more complete merger, with greater loss of separate identity, that turns two or more things into one unit ⟨metal pieces *united* by welding⟩ ***ant*** disjoin
join·er \'jȯi-nər\ *n* **1 :** a woodworker who constructs articles by joining pieces of wood **2 :** a person who joins many organizations
1joint \'jȯint\ *n* **1 a :** the point of contact of two bones in the animal body often with the surrounding and supporting parts **b :** NODE 2 **c :** a part of space included between two joints, knots, or nodes ⟨the upper *joint* of the arm⟩ **2 :** a large piece of meat for roasting **3 a :** a place where two things or parts are joined ⟨a *joint* in a pipe⟩ **b :** a fracture or crack in rock **4 a :** a cheap or shabby place of entertainment **b :** PLACE, ESTABLISHMENT **5** *slang* **:** a marijuana cigarette — **joint·ed** \-əd\ *adj* — **out of joint :** DISLOCATED
2joint *adj* **1 :** UNITED, COMBINED ⟨a *joint* effort⟩ **2 :** done by or shared by two or more persons ⟨a *joint* account⟩ **3 :** sharing with another ⟨*joint* owner⟩ — **joint·ly** *adv*
3joint *vb* **1 a :** to fit together **b :** to provide with a joint **2 :** to separate the joints of — **joint·er** *n*
joist \'jȯist\ *n* **:** a small beam laid crosswise to support a floor or ceiling

joists

1joke \'jōk\ *n* **1 a :** something said or done to provoke laughter; *esp* **:** a brief story with a humorous climax **b :** the humorous element in something **c :** KIDDING ⟨can't take a *joke*⟩ **d :** LAUGHINGSTOCK **2 :** something trivial
2joke *vb* **:** to make jokes **:** JEST — **jok·ing·ly** \'jō-kiŋ-lē\ *adv*
jok·er \'jō-kər\ *n* **1 :** a person who jokes **2 :** an extra card used in some card games **3 :** a hidden or misleading part of an agreement that works to one party's disadvantage **:** CATCH
jol·li·fi·ca·tion \ˌjäl-i-fə-'kā-shən\ *n* **:** MERRYMAKING
jol·li·ty \'jäl-ət-ē\ *n, pl* **-ties :** GAIETY, MERRIMENT
1jol·ly \'jäl-ē\ *adj* **jol·li·er; -est 1 a :** MERRY, CHEERFUL **b :** JOVIAL **2 :** very pleasant or agreeable **:** SPLENDID
2jolly *adv* **:** VERY ⟨a *jolly* good time⟩
Jol·ly Rog·er \ˌjäl-ē-'räj-ər\ *n* **:** a black flag with a white skull and crossbones
1jolt \'jōlt\ *vb* **1 :** to give a quick hard blow to **:** JAR **2 :** to move jerkily — **jolt·er** *n*
2jolt *n* **1 :** a sudden jarring blow or movement **2 :** a sudden shock or surprise
Jo·nah \'jō-nə\ *n* — see BIBLE table
jon·quil \'jän(g)-kwəl, 'jäŋ-\ *n* **:** a Mediterranean perennial bulbous herb with long linear leaves that is widely grown for its yellow or white fragrant short-tubed clustered flowers — compare DAFFODIL
Jor·da·ni·an \jȯr-'dā-nē-ən\ *adj* **:** of, relating to, or characteristic of Jordan or its people — **Jordanian** *n*
Josh·ua \'jäsh-ə-wə\ *n* — see BIBLE table
Joshua tree *n* **:** a tall branched yucca of the southwestern U.S. with short leaves and clustered greenish white flowers

Joshua tree
(up to 35 ft. high)

1jos·tle \'jäs-əl\ *vb* **jos·tled; jos·tling** \-(ə-)liŋ\ **1 :** to run or knock against so as to jar **:** push roughly ⟨*jostled* by a crowd⟩ **2 :** to make one's way by jostling **:** ELBOW
2jostle *n* **:** a jostling blow **:** SHOVE, JAR
1jot \'jät\ *n* **:** the least bit
2jot *vb* **jot·ted; jot·ting :** to make a brief note of ⟨*jot* this down⟩
joule \'jül, 'jaủl\ *n* **:** a unit of work or energy equal to 10^7 ergs or approximately 0.7375 foot-pounds
jounce \'jaủn(t)s\ *vb* **:** JOLT — **jounce** *n*
jour·nal \'jərn-əl\ *n* [from medieval French, denoting a service book containing the day hours, from the adjective *journal* "daily", from Latin *diurnalis*, from *dies* "day"] **1 a :** a brief account of daily events

ə abut	ər further	a back	ā bake	
ä cot, cart	aủ out	ch chin	e less	ē easy
g gift	i trip	ī life	j joke	ŋ sing	ō flow
ȯ flaw	ȯi coin	th thin	th this	ü loot
ủ foot	y yet	yü few	yủ furious	zh vision

: DIARY **b** : a record of the proceedings of a conference or a legislative body **2 a** : a daily newspaper **b** : a news magazine **3** : the part of a rotating shaft, axle, roll, or spindle that turns in a bearing

jour·nal·ism \ˈjərn-ə-ˌliz-əm\ *n* **1** : the business of writing for, editing, or publishing periodicals (as newspapers) **2** : writing designed for or characteristic of newspapers or popular magazines — **journal·is·tic** \ˌjərn-ə-ˈlis-tik\ *adj*

jour·nal·ist \ˈjərn-ə-ləst\ *n* : an editor of or writer for a periodical

jour·ney \ˈjər-nē\ *n, pl* **journeys** : travel from one place to another : TRIP — **journey** *vb* — **jour·ney·er** *n*

jour·ney·man \ˈjər-nē-mən\ *n* **1** : a worker who has learned a trade and works for another person usu. by the day **2** : an experienced reliable workman

joust \ˈjau̇st, ˈjəst\ *n* : a combat on horseback between two knights with lances esp. as part of a tournament — **joust** *vb* — **joust·er** *n*

jo·vi·al \ˈjō-vē-əl\ *adj* : GOOD-HUMORED, CHEERFUL — **jo·vi·al·i·ty** \ˌjō-vē-ˈal-ət-ē\ *n* — **jo·vi·al·ly** \ˈjō-vē-ə-lē\ *adv*

[1]**jowl** \ˈjau̇l, ˈjōl\ *n* **1** : JAW; *esp* : the lower jaw **2** : CHEEK 1

[2]**jowl** *n* : loose flesh hanging from the lower jaw or throat — **jowly** \-ē\ *adj*

[1]**joy** \ˈjȯi\ *n* [from Old French *joie*, from Latin *gaudium*] **1** : a feeling of great pleasure or happiness that comes from success, good fortune, or a sense of well-being : GLADNESS **2** : something that gives joy ⟨a *joy* to behold⟩ — **joy·ful** \-fəl\ *adj* — **joy·ful·ly** \-fə-lē\ *adv* — **joy·ful·ness** *n* — **joy·less** \ˈjȯi-ləs\ *adj* — **joy·less·ness** *n*

[2]**joy** *vb* : to experience joy : REJOICE

joy·ous \ˈjȯi-əs\ *adj* : feeling, causing, or showing joy ⟨a *joyous* occasion⟩ — **joy·ous·ly** *adv* — **joy·ous·ness** *n*

JP *abbr* **1** jet propulsion **2** justice of the peace

jr *abbr* junior

JRC *abbr* Junior Red Cross

ju·bi·lant \ˈjü-bə-lənt\ *adj* : feeling or expressing great joy : EXULTANT — **ju·bi·lant·ly** *adv*

ju·bi·la·tion \ˌjü-bə-ˈlā-shən\ *n* : an act of rejoicing : the state of being jubilant

ju·bi·lee \ˈjü-bə-ˌlē\ *n* **1 a** : a special anniversary; *esp* : a 50th anniversary **b** : a celebration esp. of an anniversary **2** : a Negro folk song about a future happy time

Ju·da·ism \ˈjüd-ə-ˌiz-əm, ˈjüd-ē-\ *n* **1** : a religion developed among the ancient Hebrews that emphasizes belief in one God and adherence to the moral and ceremonial laws of the Old Testament **2** : the cultural practices of the Jews — **Ju·da·ic** \jü-ˈdā-ik\ *adj*

Jude \ˈjüd\ *n* — see BIBLE table

[1]**judge** \ˈjəj\ *vb* **1** : to form an authoritative opinion **2** : to decide as a judge : TRY **3** : to reach a conclusion esp. after inquiry and deliberation : CONSIDER

[2]**judge** *n* **1** : a public official authorized to decide questions brought before a court **2** : a person appointed to decide in a contest or competition : UMPIRE **3** : one who gives an authoritative opinion : CRITIC — **judge·ship** \-ˌship\ *n*

Judg·es \ˈjəj-əz\ *n* — see BIBLE table

judg·ment *or* **judge·ment** \ˈjəj-mənt\ *n* **1** : the act of judging **2** : a formal decision given by a court **3 a** : the process of forming an opinion by discerning and comparing **b** : an opinion so formed **4** : the capacity for judging : DISCERNMENT

Judgment Day *n* : the day of the final judging of mankind by God

ju·di·cial \jü-ˈdish-əl\ *adj* **1** : of or relating to courts or judges **2** : pronounced by a court ⟨a *judicial* decision⟩ **3** : JUDICIOUS — **ju·di·cial·ly** \-(ə-)lē\ *adv*

ju·di·ci·ary \jü-ˈdish-ē-ˌer-ē, -ˈdish-ə-rē\ *n, pl* **-aries** **1 a** : a system of courts of law **b** : the judges of these courts **2** : a branch of government in which judicial power is vested — **judiciary** *adj*

ju·di·cious \jü-ˈdish-əs\ *adj* : having, exercising, or characterized by sound judgment : DISCREET — **ju·di·cious·ly** *adv*

ju·do \ˈjüd-ō\ *n, pl* **judos** : a modern form of jujitsu that uses special applications of the principles of movement, balance, and leverage

[1]**jug** \ˈjəg\ *n* **1 a** : a large deep usu. earthenware or glass container with a narrow mouth and a handle **b** : JUGFUL **2** : JAIL

[2]**jug** *vb* **jugged**; **jug·ging** : IMPRISON

jug·ful \ˈjəg-ˌfu̇l\ *n, pl* **jugfuls** \-ˌfu̇lz\ *or* **jugs·ful** \ˈjəgz-ˌfu̇l\ : the quantity held by a jug

jug·gle \ˈjəg-əl\ *vb* **jug·gled**; **jug·gling** \-(ə-)ling\ **1** : to keep several objects in motion in the air at the same time **2** : to mix things up so as to deceive ⟨*juggle* an account to hide a loss⟩ **3** : to hold or balance insecurely — **jug·gler** \-(ə-)lər\ *n*

jug·glery \ˈjəg-lə-rē\ *n, pl* **-gler·ies** **1** : the art or practice of a juggler **2** : TRICKERY

jug·u·lar \ˈjəg-yə-lər\ *adj* **1** : of, relating to, or situated in or on the throat or neck **2** : of or relating to the jugular vein

jugular vein *n* : any of several veins of each side of the neck that return blood from the head — called also *jugular*

juice \ˈjüs\ *n* **1 a** : the liquid part that can be squeezed out of vegetables and fruits **b** : the fluid part of meat **2 a** : the natural fluids (as blood, lymph, and secretions) of an animal body **b** : the liquid or moisture contained in something **3** : a medium (as electricity or gasoline) that supplies power — **juiced** \ˈjüst\ *adj*

juicy \ˈjü-sē\ *adj* **juic·i·er**; **-est** **1** : having much juice : SUCCULENT **2 a** : rich in interest : COLORFUL **b** : RACY — **juic·i·ly** \-sə-lē\ *adv* — **juic·i·ness** \-sē-nəs\ *n*

ju·jit·su *or* **ju·jut·su** \jü-ˈjit-sü\ *n* : the Japanese art of defending oneself by grasping or striking an opponent so that his own strength and weight are used against him

juke·box \ˈjük-ˌbäks\ *n* : a coin-operated phonograph

Jul *abbr* July

ju·lep \ˈjü-ləp\ *n* : a drink of bourbon, sugar, and mint served with crushed ice

Ju·lian calendar \ˌjül-yən-\ *n* : a calendar introduced in Rome in 46 B.C. establishing the 12-month year of 365 days with each 4th year having 366 days and the months each having 31 or 30 days except for February which has 28 or in leap years 29 days — compare GREGORIAN CALENDAR

Ju·ly \jü-ˈlī\ *n* [from Latin *Julius*, after *Julius* Caesar, Roman dictator] : the 7th month of the year

jum·ble \ˈjəm-bəl\ *vb* **jum·bled**; **jum·bling** \-b(ə-)ling\ : to mix in a confused mass — **jumble** *n*

jum·bo \ˈjəm-bō\ *n, pl* **jumbos** [after *Jumbo*, a huge elephant exhibited by P. T. Barnum] : something very large of its kind — **jumbo** *adj*

[1]**jump** \ˈjəmp\ *vb* **1 a** : to spring into the air : LEAP **b** : to give a sudden movement : START **c** : to begin to move — usu. used with *off* **2** : to rise or raise suddenly in rank, status, or condition ⟨*jumped* him over the other candidates⟩ ⟨prices *jumped*⟩ **3** : to make a sudden attack ⟨*jumped* on him for being late⟩ **4** : to bustle with activity ⟨the joint is *jumping*⟩

5 a : to pass over or cause to pass over by a leap ⟨*jump* a hurdle⟩ **b** : BYPASS ⟨*jump* electrical connections⟩ **c** : ANTICIPATE ⟨*jump* the gun in starting the race⟩ **d** : to leap aboard ⟨*jump* a freight⟩ **6** : to abscond while at liberty under (bail) **7** : to depart from a normal course ⟨*jump* the track⟩ **8** : to occupy illegally ⟨*jump* a mining claim⟩

[2]**jump** *n* **1 a** (1) : an act of jumping : LEAP (2) : a sports competition featuring a leap, spring, or bound (3) : a space covered by a leap **b** : a sudden involuntary movement : START **c** : a move made in a board game by jumping **2 a** : a sharp sudden increase **b** : one in a series of moves ⟨keep one *jump* ahead⟩ **3** : an advantage at the start

[1]**jump·er** \'jəm-pər\ *n* : one that jumps

[2]**jumper** *n* **1** : a loose blouse or jacket worn by workmen **2** : a sleeveless dress worn usu. with a blouse

jumping bean *n* : a seed of any of several Mexican shrubs that tumbles about because of the movements of the larva of a small moth inside it

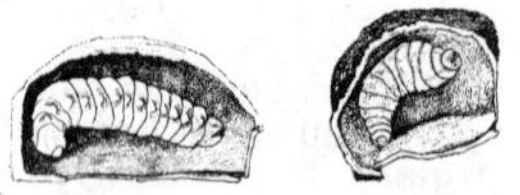

jumping beans

jumping jack *n* : a toy figure of a man jointed and made to jump or dance by means of strings or a sliding stick

jumping mouse *n* : any of several small hibernating No. American rodents with long hind legs and tail and no cheek pouches

jumping spider *n* : any of a family of small spiders that stalk and leap upon their prey

jumpy \'jəm-pē\ *adj* **jump·i·er; -est** : NERVOUS, JITTERY — **jump·i·ness** *n*

jun *abbr* junior

Jun *abbr* June

junc *abbr* junction

jun·co \'jəng-kō\ *n, pl* **juncos** *or* **juncoes** : any of a genus of small American finches usu. with a pink bill, ashy gray head and back, and conspicuous white tail feathers

junc·tion \'jəng(k)-shən\ *n* **1** : an act of joining : the state of being joined **2** : a place or point of meeting ⟨a railroad *junction*⟩

junc·ture \'jəng(k)-chər\ *n* **1** : an instance of joining : UNION **2** : JOINT, CONNECTION **3** : a critical point of time — **junc·tur·al** \-chə-rəl\ *adj*

June \'jün\ *n* [from Latin *Junius*] : the 6th month of the year

june beetle *n, often cap J* : any of various large leaf-eating beetles that fly chiefly in late spring and have as larvae white grubs that live in soil and feed on roots — called also *june bug*

jun·gle \'jəng-gəl\ *n* **1** : a thick tangled mass of tropical vegetation **2** : a tract overgrown with jungle or other rank vegetation

[1]**ju·nior** \'jü-nyər\ *n* **1** : a person who is younger or of lower rank than another **2** : a student in his next-to-last year in a high school, college, or university

[2]**junior** *adj* **1** : YOUNGER — used chiefly to distinguish a son with the same given name as his father **2** : lower in standing or rank ⟨*junior* partner⟩ **3** : of or relating to juniors in a school

junior college *n* : a school that offers two years of studies similar to those in the first two years of a four-year college

junior high school *n* : a school usu. including the 7th, 8th, and 9th grades

junior varsity *n* : a team representing a university, college, school, or club and composed of members lacking the experience or qualifications for the varsity

ju·ni·per \'jü-nə-pər\ *n* **1** : any of a genus of evergreen shrubs and trees that are related to the pine; *esp* : one of low spreading or shrubby habit **2** : any of various coniferous trees resembling true junipers

[1]**junk** \'jəngk\ *n* **1** : hard salted beef for use on shipboard **2 a** : old iron, glass, paper, or waste : discarded articles **b** : a shoddy product : TRASH — **junk·man** \-ˌman\ *n* — **junky** \'jəng-kē\ *adj*

[2]**junk** *vb* : to get rid of as worthless : SCRAP

[3]**junk** *n* : a ship of eastern Asia with a high poop and overhanging stem

junk

[1]**jun·ket** \'jəng-kət\ *n* **1** : a dessert of sweetened flavored milk set in a jelly **2** : TRIP; *esp* : a trip made by an official at public expense

[2]**junket** *vb* **1** : FEAST, BANQUET **2** : to go on a junket

jun·ta \'hu̇n-tə, 'jənt-ə\ *n* **1** : a group of persons controlling a government esp. after a revolution **2** : JUNTO

jun·to \'jənt-ō\ *n, pl* **juntos** : a group of persons joined for a common purpose

Ju·pi·ter \'jü-pət-ər\ *n* : the largest of the planets — see PLANET table

Ju·ras·sic \ju̇-'ras-ik\ *n* : the period of the Mesozoic era between the Triassic and Comanchean marked by the presence of dinosaurs and the first appearance of birds; *also* : the corresponding system of rocks — **Jurassic** *adj*

ju·ris·dic·tion \ˌju̇r-əs-'dik-shən\ *n* **1** : the power, right, or authority to interpret and apply the law **2** : the authority of a sovereign power to govern or legislate **3** : the limits or territory within which authority may be exercised

ju·ris·pru·dence \ˌju̇r-ə-'sprüd-ən(t)s\ *n* **1** : a system of laws **2** : the science of law **3** : a department of law ⟨medical *jurisprudence*⟩ — **ju·ris·pru·den·tial** \-sprü-'den-chəl\ *adj* — **ju·ris·pru·den·tial·ly** \-'dench-(ə-)lē\ *adv*

ju·rist \'ju̇r-əst\ *n* : one having a thorough knowledge of law

ju·ris·tic \ju̇-'ris-tik\ *adj* **1** : of or relating to a jurist or jurisprudence **2** : relating to or recognized in law

ju·ror \'ju̇r-ər\ *n* : a member of a jury

ju·ry \'ju̇(ə)r-ē\ *n, pl* **juries** **1** : a body of persons sworn to inquire into a matter of fact and give their verdict **2** : a committee that judges and awards prizes at an exhibition or contest — **ju·ry·man** \-mən\ *n*

[1]**just** \'jəst\ *adj* **1 a** : WELL-FOUNDED, REASONABLE ⟨a *just* comment⟩ **b** : conforming to a standard of correctness : PROPER ⟨*just* proportions⟩ **2 a** : morally right or good : RIGHTEOUS ⟨a *just* war⟩ **b** : MERITED, DESERVED ⟨*just* punishment⟩ **3** : legally right ⟨a *just* title⟩ — **just·ly** *adv*

[2]**just** \(ˌ)jəst, (ˌ)jist\ *adv* **1 a** : EXACTLY, PRECISELY ⟨*just* right⟩ **b** : very recently ⟨the bell *just* rang⟩

2 a : by a small margin : BARELY ⟨*just* over the line⟩ **b :** IMMEDIATELY, DIRECTLY ⟨*just* west of here⟩ **3 a :** ONLY, MERELY ⟨*just* a note⟩ **b :** QUITE, VERY ⟨*just* wonderful⟩

jus·tice \'jəs-təs\ *n* **1 :** just conduct, management, or treatment ⟨do *justice* to a book⟩ **2 a :** JUDGE **b :** the administration of law esp. when just ⟨the plaintiff received *justice*⟩ **3 a :** FAIRNESS, HONESTY **b :** basis in morality, the right, or the law : RIGHTFULNESS ⟨the *justice* of a complaint⟩

justice of the peace : a local magistrate empowered to try minor cases, to administer oaths, and to perform marriages

jus·ti·fi·ca·tion \,jəs-tə-fə-'kā-shən\ *n* **1 :** the act or an instance of justifying or of being justified **2 :** something that justifies : DEFENSE

jus·ti·fy \'jəs-tə-,fī\ *vb* **-fied; -fy·ing 1 :** to prove or show to be just, right, legal, or reasonable **2 :** to release from the guilt of sin — **jus·ti·fi·a·ble** \'jəs-tə-,fī-ə-bəl\ *adj* — **jus·ti·fi·a·bly** \-blē\ *adv* — **jus·ti·fi·er** \-,fī(-ə)r\ *n*

jut \'jət\ *vb* **jut·ted; jut·ting :** to stick out, up, or forward : PROJECT — **jut** *n*

jute \'jüt\ *n* **:** a glossy fiber from either of two East Indian plants that is used chiefly for sacking and twine

juv *abbr* juvenile

ju·ve·nal \'jü-vən-əl\ *adj* **:** JUVENILE

[1]**ju·ve·nile** \'jü-və-,nīl, -vən-əl\ *adj* **1 :** showing incomplete development : IMMATURE, CHILDISH **2 :** of, relating to, or characteristic of children or young people **3 :** MAGMATIC ⟨*juvenile* water⟩ — **ju·ve·nil·i·ty** \,jü-və-'nil-ət-ē\ *n*

[2]**juvenile** *n* **1 :** a young person, animal, or plant **2 :** a book for young people **3 :** an actor or actress who plays youthful parts

juvenile delinquency *n* **:** violation of the law or antisocial behavior by a juvenile — **juvenile delinquent** *n*

jux·ta·pose \'jək-stə-,pōz\ *vb* **:** to place side by side — **jux·ta·po·si·tion** \,jək-stə-pə-'zish-ən\ *n*

JV *abbr* junior varsity

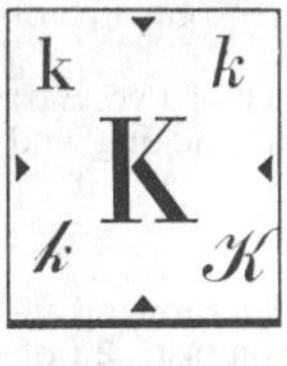

k \'kā\ *n, often cap* : the 11th letter of the English alphabet
k *abbr* knit
K *abbr* **1** Kelvin **2** kindergarten
kai·ser '\kī-zər\ *n* : EMPEROR; *esp* : the ruler of Germany from 1871 to 1918
kale \'kāl\ *n* : a hardy cabbage with curled often finely cut leaves that do not form a dense head
ka·lei·do·scope \kə-'līd-ə-ˌskōp\ *n* **1** : a device containing loose bits of colored glass between two flat plates and two plane mirrors so placed that changes of position of the bits of glass are reflected in an endless variety of patterns **2** : a changing pattern or scene — **ka·lei·do·scop·ic** \-ˌlīd-ə-'skäp-ik\ *adj* — **ka·lei·do·scop·i·cal·ly** \-'skäp-i-k(ə-)lē\ *adv*

kale

kame \'kām\ *n* : a short ridge or mound of material deposited by water from a melting glacier
kan·ga·roo \ˌkang-gə-'rü\ *n, pl* **-roos** : any of various plant-eating leaping marsupial mammals of Australia, New Guinea, and adjacent islands with small head, long powerful hind legs, and long thick tail used as a support and in balancing

kangaroo (about 6 ft. tall)

kangaroo rat *n* : a pouched burrowing rodent of dry regions of the western U.S.
Kans *abbr* Kansas
ka·o·lin *also* **ka·o·line** \'kā-ə-lən\ *n* : a fine usu. white clay used in ceramics
ka·o·lin·ite \-lə-ˌnīt\ *n* : a mineral that consists of the silicate of aluminum and is the principal mineral in kaolin
ka·pok \'kā-ˌpäk\ *n* : a mass of silky fibers that clothe the seeds of the ceiba tree and are used as a filling for mattresses, life preservers, and sleeping bags
kap·pa \'kap-ə\ *n* : the 10th letter of the Greek alphabet — Κ or κ
kar·a·kul \'kar-ə-kəl\ *n* **1** : any of a breed of hardy fat-tailed Asiatic sheep with coarse wiry brown fur **2** : the tightly curled glossy black coat of the newborn lamb of a karakul valued as fur
kar·at \'kar-ət\ *n* : a unit of fineness for gold equal to 1/24 part of pure gold in an alloy
ka·ra·te \kə-'rät-ē\ *n* [from Japanese, meaning literally "empty hand"] : a Japanese system of self-defense without a weapon
Kash·mir goat \ˌkash-ˌmi(ə)r-, ˌkazh-\ *n* : an Indian goat whose soft woolly undercoat forms cashmere wool
ka·ty·did \'kāt-ē-ˌdid\ *n* : any of several large green American long-horned grasshoppers having sound-producing organs on the fore wings of the males

katydid (about 2 in. long)

kay·ak \'kī-ˌak\ *n* **1** : an Eskimo canoe made of a frame entirely covered with skins except for a small opening in the center where one or two paddlers may sit **2** : a canvas-covered small canoe resembling a kayak

kayak 1

[1]**kayo** \(')kā-'ō, 'kā-ō\ *n, pl* **kay·os** : KNOCKOUT
[2]**kayo** *vb* **kay·oed**; **kayo·ing** : KO
ka·zoo \kə-'zü\ *n, pl* **kazoos** : a toy musical instrument consisting of a tube with a membrane sealing one end and a side hole into which one sings or hums
kc *abbr* kilocycle
kcal *abbr* kilocalorie
kc/s *abbr* kilocycles per second
[1]**keel** \'kēl\ *n* **1** : a timber or plate running lengthwise along the center of the bottom of a ship and usu. projecting from the bottom **2 a** : something (as the breastbone of a bird) like a ship's keel in form or use; *esp* : a ridged part **b** : the lower two petals of a pea flower
[2]**keel** *vb* **1 a** : to turn over **b** : to fall in or as if in a faint — usu. used with *over* **2** : to provide with a keel
keel·haul \'kēl-ˌhȯl\ *vb* **1** : to haul under the keel of a ship as punishment or torture **2** : to rebuke severely
keel·son \'kel-sən, 'kēl-\ *n* : a structure running above and fastened to the keel of a ship in order to stiffen and strengthen the keel
[1]**keen** \'kēn\ *adj* **1** : having a fine edge or point : SHARP ⟨a *keen* knife⟩ **2** : CUTTING, STINGING, SEVERE ⟨a *keen* wind⟩ **3** : ACUTE ⟨a *keen* sense of smell⟩ **4** : EAGER, ENTHUSIASTIC ⟨*keen* about baseball⟩ **5** : having or showing mental sharpness ⟨a *keen* mind⟩ ***syn*** see SHARP ***ant*** dull — **keen·ly** *adv* — **keen·ness** \'kēn-nəs\ *n*
[2]**keen** *vb* : to lament in a loud wailing voice — **keen** *n*
[1]**keep** \'kēp\ *vb* **kept** \'kept\; **keep·ing** **1** : to perform as a duty : FULFILL, OBSERVE ⟨*keep* a promise⟩ ⟨*keep* a holiday⟩ **2 a** : GUARD ⟨*keep* us from harm⟩ **b** : to take care of ⟨*keep* a garden⟩ **c** : to maintain in a good condition ⟨*keep* house⟩ **3** : to continue doing something : MAINTAIN ⟨*keep* silence⟩ ⟨*keep* on working⟩ **4** : to have in one's service or at one's disposal ⟨*keep* a car⟩ **5** : to preserve a record in ⟨*keep* a diary⟩ **6** : to have on hand for sale ⟨*keep* neckties⟩ **7** : to possess permanently ⟨*kept* what he earned⟩ **8** : HOLD, DETAIN ⟨*keep* a person in jail⟩ **9** : to hold back : WITHHOLD ⟨*keep* a secret⟩ **10 a** : to remain or cause to remain in a place, situation, or condition ⟨*keep* off the grass⟩ ⟨*keep* him waiting⟩ **b** : to continue in an unspoiled condition ⟨milk does not *keep* well in warm weather⟩ **11** : REFRAIN ⟨*keep* from talking⟩
[2]**keep** *n* **1** : the strongest part of a medieval castle **2** : the means by which one is kept; *esp* : one's food

ə abut	ər further	a back	ā bake	
ä cot, cart	au̇ out	ch chin	e less	ē easy
g gift	i trip	ī life	j joke	ng sing	ō flow
ȯ flaw	ȯi coin	th thin	th this	ü loot
u̇ foot	y yet	yü few	yu̇ furious	zh vision

and lodging ⟨a worker scarcely worth his *keep*⟩ — **for keeps 1 :** with the provision that one keep what he has won ⟨play marbles *for keeps*⟩ **2 :** PERMANENTLY

keep·er \'kē-pər\ *n* : a person who watches, guards, or takes care of something : WARDEN, CUSTODIAN

keep·ing \'kē-ping\ *n* **1 :** OBSERVANCE ⟨the *keeping* of a holiday⟩ **2 :** CARE, CUSTODY **3 :** AGREEMENT, HARMONY ⟨in *keeping* with good taste⟩

keep·sake \'kēp-ˌsāk\ *n* : something kept or given to be kept as a memento

keep up *vb* **1 :** MAINTAIN, SUSTAIN ⟨*keep* standards *up*⟩ **2 :** to keep informed ⟨*keep up* on the war⟩ **3 :** to continue without interruption ⟨rain *kept up* all night⟩ **4 :** to stay even with others (as in a race, thoughts, or studies)

keg \'keg, 'kag\ *n* **1 :** a small cask or barrel holding 30 gallons or less **2 :** the contents of a keg

kelp \'kelp\ *n* **1 :** any of various large brown seaweeds; *also* : a mass of these **2 :** the ashes of seaweed used esp. as a source of iodine

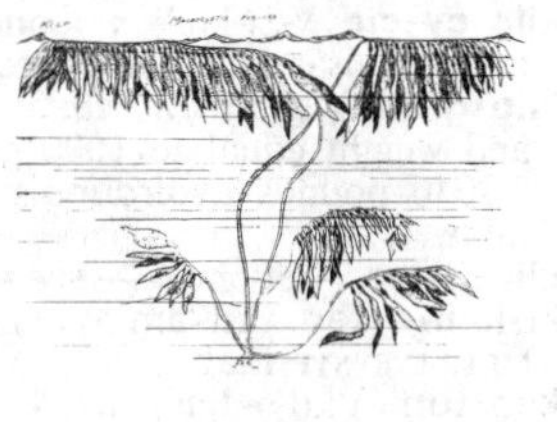

kelp 1
(up to 150 ft. long)

Kel·vin \'kel-vən\ *adj* : relating to, conforming to, or having a thermometer scale according to which absolute zero or −273.16°C is 0° — abbr. *K*

¹ken \'ken\ *vb* **kenned; ken·ning** *chiefly Scot* : KNOW

²ken *n* **1 a :** a range of vision **b :** SIGHT, VIEW **2 :** range of understanding

¹ken·nel \'ken-əl\ *n* **1 :** a shelter for a dog **2 :** a place where dogs are bred or boarded

²kennel *vb* **-neled** *or* **-nelled**; **-nel·ing** *or* **-nel·ling :** to put or keep in a kennel

Ken·nel·ly–Heav·i·side layer \ˌken-ə-lē-ˌhev-ē-ˌsīd-\ *n* : IONOSPHERE

Ken·tucky bluegrass \kən-ˌtək-ē-\ *n* : a valuable pasture, lawn, and meadow grass that has tall stalks and slender bright green leaves and is found in both Europe and America

Kentucky
bluegrass

Kentucky coffee tree *n* : a tall No. American leguminous tree with large woody pods whose seeds have been used as a substitute for coffee

Kep·ler's laws \ˌkep-lərz-\ *n pl* : laws in astronomy dealing with planetary motion

ker·a·tin \'ker-ət-ən\ *n* : a sulfur-containing fibrous protein that forms the chemical basis of hair and horny tissues

ker·chief \'kər-chəf, -ˌchēf\ *n, pl* **kerchiefs** \-chəfs, -ˌchēfs\ *also* **ker·chieves** \-ˌchēvz\ [from Middle English *courchef*, from Old French *couvrechef*, from *covrir* "to cover" and *chef* "head"] **1 :** a square of cloth worn as a head covering or around the neck **2 :** HANDKERCHIEF 1

ker·nel \'kərn-əl\ *n* **1 a :** the inner softer part of a seed, fruit stone, or nut **b :** a whole seed of a cereal (as wheat or corn) **2 :** a central or essential part

kern·ite \'kər-ˌnīt\ *n* : a mineral that consists of sodium, borate, and water and is an important source of borax

ker·o·sene *or* **ker·o·sine** \'ker-ə-ˌsēn\ *n* : a thin oil consisting of a mixture of hydrocarbons usu. obtained by distillation of petroleum and used for a fuel and as a solvent and thinner (as for paints)

Ker·ry blue terrier \ˌker-ē-\ *n* : any of an Irish breed of medium sized terriers with a long head, deep chest, and silky bluish coat

ketch \'kech\ *n* : a two-masted fore-and-aft-rigged ship similar to a yawl

ketch·up *var of* CATSUP

ket·tle \'ket-əl\ *n* : a metal vessel for boiling liquids; *esp* : TEAKETTLE

ket·tle·drum \-ˌdrəm\ *n* : a brass or copper kettle-shaped drum with parchment stretched across the top and capable of being tuned

ketch

¹key \'kē\ *n, pl* **keys 1 a :** an instrument by which the bolt of a lock is turned **b :** a device having the form or function of a key ⟨a *key* for opening a coffee can⟩ **2 :** a means of gaining or preventing entrance, possession, or control **3 a :** something that provides an explanation, solution, or means of identifying; *esp* : a map legend **b :** a numbered or lettered arrangement usu. of pairs of alternative characters of a group of plants or animals used for identification **4 :** one of the levers with a flat surface that is pressed by a finger in operating or playing an instrument (as a typewriter, piano, or clarinet) **5 :** a system of seven tones based on their relationship to a tonic; *esp* : the tonality of a scale ⟨the *key* of C⟩ **6 a :** characteristic style or tone ⟨sung in a sad *key*⟩ **b :** the tone or pitch of a voice **7 :** a small switch for opening or closing an electric circuit

²key *vb* **keyed; key·ing 1 :** to lock or secure by a key **2 :** to regulate the musical pitch of **3 :** to make nervous or tense — usu. used with *up* ⟨all *keyed* up about the test⟩

³key *adj* : of basic importance ⟨*key* men⟩ ⟨a *key* concept⟩

⁴key *n* : a low island or reef ⟨the Florida *keys*⟩

key·board \'kē-ˌbōrd, -ˌbȯrd\ *n* : a row or arrangement of keys (as on a piano or typewriter)

Key deer \'kē-\ *n* : a nearly extinct race of very small white-tailed deer native to the Florida keys

key·hole \'kē-ˌhōl\ *n* : a hole for receiving a key

key·note \-ˌnōt\ *n* **1 :** the first and fundamental tone of a scale **2 :** the fundamental or central fact, idea, or mood

key signature *n* : the sharps or flats placed after a clef in music to indicate the key

key·stone \-ˌstōn\ *n* **1 :** the wedge-shaped piece at the top of an arch that locks the other pieces in place **2 :** something on which other things depend

kg *abbr* kilogram

khaki \'kak-ē, 'käk-\ *n* **1 :** a light yellowish brown **2 a :** khaki-colored cloth **b** *pl* : a uniform of this cloth

¹khan \'kän, 'kan\ *n* **1 :** a Mongol leader **2 :** a local chieftain or man of rank in some countries of central Asia

²khan *n* : CARAVANSARY

khe·dive \kə-'dēv\ *n* : a governor of Egypt from 1867 to 1914

Khmer \kə-'me(ə)r\ *n* : a member of an aboriginal people of Cambodia

kib·butz \kib-'ůts, -'üts\ *n, pl* **kib·but·zim** \-ˌůt-'sēm, -ˌüt-\ : a collective farm or settlement in Israel
kib·itz·er \'kib-ət-sər\ *n* : one who looks on and often offers unwanted advice or comment esp. at a card game — **kib·itz** \-əts\ *vb*
1**kick** \'kik\ *vb* **1** : to strike out with the foot or feet **2** : to strike, thrust, or hit with the foot **3** : to object strongly : PROTEST ⟨*kick* because prices were raised⟩ **4** : to recoil when fired **5** : to score by kicking a ball ⟨*kick* the point after touchdown⟩ — **kick·er** *n*
2**kick** *n* **1 a** : a blow with the foot; *esp* : a propelling of a ball with the foot **b** : the power to kick **c** : a motion of the legs in swimming **2** : a forceful jolt or thrust; *esp* : the recoil of a gun **3 a** : a strong objection : PROTEST **b** : the grounds for objection **4** : a stimulating effect esp. of pleasure : THRILL
kick·ball \'kik-ˌbȯl\ *n* : a game resembling baseball but played with an inflated ball that is kicked instead of batted
kick off \'kik-'ȯf\ *vb* **1** : to start or resume play in football by a place-kick **2** : to begin proceedings — **kick·off** \-ˌȯf\ *n*
1**kid** \'kid\ *n* **1** : the young of a goat or of a related animal **2 a** : the flesh, fur, or skin of a kid **b** : something (as leather) made of kid **3** : CHILD, YOUNGSTER — **kid·dish** \'kid-ish\ *adj*
2**kid** *vb* **kid·ded**; **kid·ding** **1** : to deceive as a joke : FOOL **2** : TEASE — **kid·der** *n*
kid·nap \'kid-ˌnap\ *vb* **kid·napped** *or* **kid·naped** \-ˌnapt\; **kid·nap·ping** *or* **kid·nap·ing** \-ˌnap-iŋ\ : to carry away a person by unlawful force or by fraud and against his will — **kid·nap·per** *or* **kid·nap·er** \-ˌnap-ər\ *n*
kid·ney \'kid-nē\ *n, pl* **kidneys** **1** : either of a pair of oval to bean-shaped organs located in the back part of the abdomen near the spine that excrete waste products in the form of urine **2** : an excretory organ of an invertebrate animal
kidney bean *n* : a common garden bean grown esp. for its nutritious seeds; *also* : a rather large dark red bean seed
kid·skin \'kid-ˌskin\ *n* : the skin of a kid or leather made from or resembling it
kie·sel·guhr *or* **kie·sel·gur** \'kē-zəl-ˌgůr\ *n* : loose or porous diatomite
1**kill** \'kil\ *vb* **1** : to deprive of life : put to death **2** : DESTROY, RUIN ⟨*kill* all chance of success⟩ **3** : to use up ⟨*kill* time⟩ **4** : DEFEAT ⟨*kill* a proposed law⟩ **5** : STOP ⟨*kill* the engine⟩ — **kill·er** *n*

syn KILL, SLAY, MURDER, ASSASSINATE can mean to take the life of. KILL implies nothing about the manner of death and applies generally to the death of anything that dies ⟨plants *killed* by an early frost⟩ ⟨sheep-*killing* dogs⟩ ⟨a man *killed* in an accident⟩; SLAY implies deliberate and violent action in taking a person's or animal's life; MURDER applies to deliberate and unlawful killing of a person; ASSASSINATE implies an impersonal and often political motive for killing

2**kill** *n* **1** : an act of killing **2 a** : an animal killed in a hunt, season, or particular period of time **b** : an enemy aircraft, submarine, or ship destroyed
kill·deer \'kil-ˌdi(ə)r\ *n, pl* **killdeers** *or* **killdeer** : a No. American plover with a mournful and penetrating cry

ə abut ər further a back ā bake
ä cot, cart aů out ch chin e less ē easy
g gift i trip ī life j joke ŋ sing ō flow
ȯ flaw ȯi coin th thin t͟h this ü loot
ů foot y yet yü few yů furious zh vision

kill·er whale \'kil-ər-\ *n* : a fierce flesh-eating largely black whale 20 to 30 feet long that travels in groups — called also *killer*

killer whale (up to 30 ft. long)

kill·ing \'kil-iŋ\ *n* : a sudden large profit
kill·joy \'kil-ˌjȯi\ *n* : one who spoils the pleasure of others
kiln \'kil(n)\ *n* : an oven or furnace for hardening, burning, or drying something ⟨brick *kilns*⟩ ⟨a *kiln* for rapid drying of lumber⟩ — **kiln** *vb*
ki·lo \'kē-lō, 'kil-ō\ *n, pl* **kilos** **1** : KILOGRAM **2** : KILOMETER
kilo- *comb form* : thousand ⟨*kilo*ton⟩
kilo·cal·o·rie \'kil-ə-ˌkal-(ə-)rē\ *n* : CALORIE 1b
kilo·cy·cle \-ˌsī-kəl\ *n* : one thousand cycles; *esp* : one thousand cycles per second
kilo·gram \-ˌgram\ *n* : the basic metric unit of mass and weight equal to 1000 grams or approximately 2.2046 pounds avoirdupois — see METRIC SYSTEM table
kilo·li·ter \-ˌlēt-ər\ *n* — see METRIC SYSTEM table
ki·lom·e·ter \kil-'äm-ət-ər, 'kil-ə-ˌmēt-\ *n* — see METRIC SYSTEM table
kilo·ton \'kil-ə-ˌtən\ *n* **1** : one thousand tons **2** : an explosive force equivalent to that of 1000 tons of TNT
kilo·volt \-ˌvōlt\ *n* : a unit of electromotive force equal to 1000 volts
kilo·watt \'kil-ə-ˌwät\ *n* : a unit of power equal to 1000 watts
kilowatt–hour *n* : a unit of work or energy equal to that expended by one kilowatt in one hour
kilt \'kilt\ *n* **1** : a knee-length pleated skirt usu. of tartan worn by men in Scotland and by Scottish regiments in the British army **2** : a garment that resembles a kilt — **kilt·ed** \'kil-təd\ *adj*
kil·ter \'kil-tər\ *n* : proper condition : ORDER ⟨out of *kilter*⟩
ki·mo·no \kə-'mō-nə\ *n, pl* **-nos** **1** : a loose robe with wide sleeves and a broad sash traditionally worn as an outer garment by the Japanese **2** : a loose dressing gown worn by women

kimono 1

1**kin** \'kin\ *n* **1** : KINDRED 2 **2** : KINSMAN
2**kin** *adj* : KINDRED, RELATED
-kin \kən\ *also* **-kins** \kənz\ *n suffix* : little ⟨cat*kin*⟩ ⟨baby*kins*⟩
1**kind** \'kīnd\ *n* **1 a** : a natural group : SPECIES **b** : a group united by common traits or interests : CATEGORY **c** : VARIETY ⟨all *kinds* of people⟩ **d** : a doubtful or marginal member of a category ⟨a *kind* of gray⟩ **2** : essential quality or character ⟨differences in *kind*⟩ **3 a** : goods or commodities as distinguished from money ⟨pay in *kind*⟩ **b** : the equivalent of what has been offered or received ⟨returned the favor in *kind*⟩
2**kind** *adj* **1** : inclined to do good and to bring happiness to others **2** : showing or growing out of kindness ⟨a *kind* act⟩
kin·der·gar·ten \'kin-dər-ˌgärt-ən, -ˌgärd-\ *n* : a school or class for very young children in which teaching is done largely through activities based on the normal aptitudes and desire of the pupils for exercise and play

kin·der·gart·ner \-ˌgärt-nər, -ˌgärd-\ *n* **1 :** a kindergarten pupil **2 :** a kindergarten teacher

kind·heart·ed \'kīnd-'härt-əd\ *adj* **:** having or showing a kind and sympathetic nature — **kind·heart·ed·ly** *adv* — **kind·heart·ed·ness** *n*

kin·dle \'kin-dəl\ *vb* **kin·dled; kin·dling** \-d(ə-)ling\ **1 :** to set on fire or take fire **:** LIGHT **2 :** AROUSE, EXCITE ⟨*kindle* a person's anger⟩ **3 :** to begin to be excited **4 :** to light up as if with flame ⟨with eyes *kindling*⟩

kin·dling \'kin-dling\ *n* **:** material that burns easily for starting a fire

kin·dling temperature \'kin-d(ə-)ling-\ *n* **:** the lowest temperature at which burning occurs — called also *kindling point*

[1]**kind·ly** \'kīn-dlē\ *adj* **kind·li·er; -est** **1 :** AGREEABLE, PLEASANT ⟨a *kindly* climate⟩ **2 :** of a sympathetic or generous nature **:** FRIENDLY ⟨*kindly* men⟩ — **kind·li·ness** *n*

[2]**kindly** *adv* **1 :** READILY ⟨does not take *kindly* to criticism⟩ **2 a :** SYMPATHETICALLY **b :** as a gesture of goodwill **c :** COURTEOUSLY, OBLIGINGLY ⟨was *kindly* invited in⟩ ⟨*kindly* pass the salt⟩

kind·ness \'kīn(d)-nəs\ *n* **1 :** a kind deed **:** FAVOR **2 :** the quality or state of being kind

[1]**kin·dred** \'kin-drəd\ *n* **1 :** a group of related individuals **2 :** one's relatives

[2]**kindred** *adj* **:** of like nature or character

kine \'kīn\ *archaic pl of* cow

kin·e·mat·ics \ˌkin-ə-'mat-iks, ˌkī-nə-\ *n* **:** a science that deals with aspects of motion apart from considerations of mass and force — **kin·e·mat·ic** \-'mat-ik\ *adj*

kin·e·scope \'kin-ə-ˌskōp\ *n* **1 :** an electron tube on which the picture in a television set appears **2 :** a moving picture made from the image on a kinescope

ki·net·ic \kə-'net-ik, kī-\ *adj* **:** of or relating to the motion of material bodies and the forces and energy associated therewith

kinetic energy *n* **:** energy associated with motion

ki·net·ics \kə-'net-iks, kī-\ *n sing or pl* **:** a science that deals with the effects of forces upon the motions of material bodies or with changes in a physical or chemical system

kinetic theory *n* **:** a theory that states that all matter is composed of particles in motion and that the rate of motion varies directly with the temperature

kin·folk \'kin-ˌfōk\ *n* **:** RELATIVES

king \'king\ *n* **1 :** a male ruler of a country; *esp* **:** one who inherits his position and rules for life **2 :** a chief among competitors ⟨an oil *king*⟩ **3 :** the chief piece in the game of chess **4 :** a playing card bearing the figure of a king **5 :** a checker that has been crowned

king·bird \-ˌbərd\ *n* **:** an American tyrant flycatcher

king crab *n* **1 :** HORSESHOE CRAB **2 :** any of several very large crabs

king·dom \'king-dəm\ *n* **1 :** a country whose ruler is a king or queen **2 :** a realm or region in which something or someone is dominant ⟨the cotton *kingdom*⟩ **3 :** one of the three primary divisions of lifeless material, plants, and animals into which natural objects are grouped

king·fish \'king-ˌfish\ *n* **:** a large sport and food fish of the warm western Atlantic

king·fish·er \-ˌfish-ər\ *n* **:** any of a family of usu. crested and bright-colored birds with a short tail and a long stout sharp bill

King James Version \king-'jāmz-\ *n* **:** AUTHORIZED VERSION

king·let \'king-lət\ *n* **1 :** a weak or petty king **2 :** any of several small birds that resemble warblers but have some of the habits of titmice

king·ly \'king-lē\ *adj* **1 :** having the status of king or royal rank **2 :** of, relating to, or befitting a king — **king·li·ness** *n* — **kingly** *adv*

king·pin \'king-ˌpin\ *n* **1 :** any of several bowling pins: as **a :** HEADPIN **b :** the number 5 pin **2 :** the chief person in a group or undertaking **3 :** a vertical bolt by which the forward axle and wheels of a vehicle are connected with other parts

Kings \'kingz\ *n* — see BIBLE table

king·ship \'king-ˌship\ *n* **1 :** the position, office, or dignity of a king **2 :** the personality of a king **:** MAJESTY **3 :** government by a king

king–size \'king-ˌsīz\ *or* **king–sized** \-ˌsīzd\ *adj* **1 :** longer than the regular or standard size **2 :** unusually large

king snake *n* **:** any of numerous harmless brightly marked snakes of the southern and central U.S. that feed on rodents

[1]**kink** \'kingk\ *n* **1 :** a short tight twist or curl **2 :** QUIRK, WHIM **3 :** CRAMP **4 :** a flaw that causes difficulties in operation ⟨iron out the *kinks* in a new engine⟩ — **kinky** \'king-kē\ *adj*

[2]**kink** *vb* **:** to form a kink **:** make a kink in

kin·ka·jou \'king-kə-ˌjü\ *n* **:** a slender long-tailed mammal of Central and So. America related to the raccoon

kinkajou
(about 3 ft. long)

-kins — see -KIN

kins·folk \'kinz-ˌfōk\ *n* **:** RELATIVES

kin·ship \'kin-ˌship\ *n* **:** the quality or state of being kin **:** RELATIONSHIP

kins·man \'kinz-mən\ *n* **:** RELATIVE; *esp* **:** a male relative — **kins·wom·an** \-ˌwu̇m-ən\ *n*

ki·osk \'kē-ˌäsk, kē-'\ *n* **1 :** PAVILION 2 **2 :** a small light structure with one or more open sides used esp. as a newsstand or a telephone booth

[1]**kip·per** \'kip-ər\ *n* **:** a kippered herring or salmon

[2]**kipper** *vb* **kip·pered; kip·per·ing** \-(ə-)ring\ **:** to cure by splitting, cleaning, salting, and smoking

kirk \'ki(ə)rk, 'kərk\ *n, chiefly Scot* **:** CHURCH

kir·tle \'kərt-əl\ *n* **:** a medieval woman's dress, skirt, or petticoat

[1]**kiss** \'kis\ *vb* **1 :** to touch with the lips as a mark of affection or greeting **2 :** to touch gently or lightly ⟨wind gently *kissing* the trees⟩ — **kiss·a·ble** \-ə-bəl\ *adj*

[2]**kiss** *n* **1 :** a caress with the lips **2 :** a gentle touch or contact **3 :** a bite-size candy often wrapped in paper or foil

kiss·er \'kis-ər\ *n* **1 :** one that kisses **2** *slang* **:** MOUTH; *also* **:** FACE

kit \'kit\ *n* **1 a :** a collection of articles for personal use ⟨a shaving *kit*⟩ **b :** a set of tools or implements ⟨a carpenter's *kit*⟩ **c :** a set of parts to be assembled ⟨model-airplane *kit*⟩ **d :** a packaged collection of related material ⟨convention *kit*⟩ **2 :** a container (as a bag or case) for a kit

kitch·en \'kich-ən\ *n* **:** a place (as a room) with cooking facilities

kitch·en·ette \ˌkich-ə-'net\ *n* **:** a small kitchen or an alcove containing cooking facilities

kitchen police *n* **1 :** enlisted men detailed to assist the cooks in a military mess **2 :** the work done by kitchen police

kitch·en·ware \'kich-ən-ˌwa(ə)r, -ˌwe(ə)r\ *n* : hardware for use in a kitchen

kite \'kīt\ *n* **1** : any of various hawks with long narrow wings, a deeply forked tail, and feet adapted for taking insects and small reptiles as prey **2** : a light frame covered with paper or cloth flown in the air at the end of a long string

kite 1
(about 24 in. long)

kith \'kith\ *n* : familiar friends, neighbors, or relatives ⟨*kith* and kin⟩

kit·ten \'kit-ən\ *n* : the young of a small mammal and esp. of a cat

kit·ten·ish \'kit-(ə-)nish\ *adj* : resembling a kitten; *esp* : PLAYFUL — **kit·ten·ish·ly** *adv* — **kit·ten·ish·ness** *n*

kit·ti·wake \'kit-ē-ˌwāk\ *n* : any of various gulls having the hind toe short and the wing tips black

kit·ty \'kit-ē\ *n, pl* **kitties** : CAT 1a; *esp* : KITTEN

kit·ty–cor·ner *or* **kit·ty–cor·nered** *var of* CATER-CORNER

ki·wi \'kē-(ˌ)wē\ *n* : a flightless New Zealand bird with weak and undeveloped wings, stout legs, a long bill, and grayish brown hairlike plumage

kiwi
(up to 28 in. long)

KKK *abbr* Ku Klux Klan

kl *abbr* kiloliter

klep·to·ma·nia \ˌklep-tə-'mā-nē-ə, -nyə\ *n* : a persistent abnormal impulse to steal — **klep·to·ma·ni·ac** \-nē-ˌak\ *adj or n*

K–level \'kā-\ *n* : the lowest available energy level for electrons in an atom

klieg light *or* **kleig light** \'klēg-\ *n* : an arc lamp used in taking motion pictures

km *abbr* kilometer

knack \'nak\ *n* **1** : a clever way of doing something : TRICK **2** : a natural ability : TALENT ⟨has a *knack* for using tools⟩

knap·sack \'nap-ˌsak\ *n* : a canvas or leather case strapped on the back to carry supplies while on a march or hike

knave \'nāv\ *n* [from Middle English, meaning "a male servant", "a man of humble position", from Old English *cnafa* "boy"] **1** : a tricky deceitful fellow : ROGUE **2** : JACK 5 — **knav·ish** \'nā-vish\ *adj* — **knav·ish·ly** *adv*

knav·ery \'nāv-(ə-)rē\ *n, pl* **-er·ies** **1** : the practices of a knave : RASCALITY **2** : a roguish or mischievous act

knead \'nēd\ *vb* **1** : to work and press into a mass with or as if with the hands **2 a** : to form or shape as if by kneading **b** : to treat as if by kneading : MASSAGE — **knead·er** *n*

knee \'nē\ *n* **1** : the joint in the middle part of the human leg in which the femur, tibia, and kneecap come together; *also* : a corresponding part of a four-footed mammal **2** : something resembling the knee; *esp* : a cone-shaped process growing upward from the roots of a few swamp-growing trees and projecting above the surrounding water **3** : the part of a garment covering the knee — **kneed** \'nēd\ *adj*

knee·cap \'nē-ˌkap\ *n* : a thick flat movable bone forming the front part of the knee — called also *patella*

knee·hole \-ˌhōl\ *n* : a space (as under a desk) for the knees

knee jerk *n* : an involuntary forward kick produced by a light blow on the tendon below the kneecap

kneel \'nēl\ *vb* **knelt** \'nelt\ *or* **kneeled** \'nēld\; **kneel·ing** : to bend the knee : fall or rest on the knees — **kneel·er** *n*

[1]**knell** \'nel\ *vb* **1** : to ring esp. for a death, funeral, or disaster : TOLL **2** : to sound in an ominous manner or with an ominous effect **3** : to summon or announce by tolling

[2]**knell** *n* **1** : a stroke or sound of a bell esp. when rung slowly for a death, funeral, or disaster **2** : a sound or other indication of a death, ending, or failure

knew *past of* KNOW

knick·er·bock·ers \'nik-ə(r)-ˌbäk-ərz\ *n pl* : KNICKERS

knick·ers \'nik-ərz\ *n pl* : loose-fitting short pants gathered at the knee

knickers

knick·knack \'nik-ˌnak\ *n* : a small trivial article intended for ornament

[1]**knife** \'nīf\ *n, pl* **knives** \'nīvz\ **1 a** : a cutting instrument consisting of a sharp blade fastened to a handle **b** : a weapon resembling a knife **2** : a sharp cutting blade or tool in a machine

[2]**knife** *vb* **1** : to stab, slash, or wound with a knife **2** : to move like a knife : CUT ⟨ships *knifing* through the sea⟩

knife–edge \'nīf-ˌej\ *n* : a sharp wedge usu. of steel used as a fulcrum for a lever beam in a precision instrument (as a balance)

knife switch *n* : an electric switch in which contact is made by pushing one or more flat blades between the jaws of clips

[1]**knight** \'nīt\ *n* [from Old English *cniht* "boy", "youth", "military follower"] **1 a** : a mounted warrior of feudal times serving a superior; *esp* : one who after a period of early service has been awarded a special rank and has sworn to obey certain rules **b** : a man honored by a sovereign for merit and in Great Britain ranking below a baronet **c** : a member of any of various orders or societies **2** : one of the pieces in a game of chess — **knight·ly** \-lē\ *adj or adv*

[2]**knight** *vb* : to make a knight of : confer the rank of knight on

knight–er·rant \'nīt-'er-ənt\ *n, pl* **knights–errant** : a knight traveling in search of adventures in which to show his military skill and generosity — **knight–er·rant·ry** \'nīt-'er-ən-trē\ *n*

knight·hood \'nīt-ˌhu̇d\ *n* **1** : the rank, dignity, or profession of a knight **2** : the qualities befitting a knight : CHIVALRY **3** : knights as a class or body

knit \'nit\ *vb* **knit** *or* **knit·ted**; **knit·ting** **1 :** to form a fabric by interlacing yarn or thread in connected loops with needles ⟨*knit* a sweater⟩ **2 :** to draw or come together closely as if knitted ⟨*knit* by common interests⟩ ⟨wait for a broken bone to *knit*⟩ **3 :** WRINKLE ⟨*knit* her brow⟩ — **knit·ter** *n*

knit·ting *n* **1 :** the action or method of one that knits **2 :** work done or being done by one that knits

knit·wear \'nit-ˌwa(ə)r, -ˌwe(ə)r\ *n* **:** knitted clothing

knob \'näb\ *n* **1 a :** a rounded projection **:** LUMP **b :** a small rounded ornament or handle **2 :** a rounded usu. isolated hill or mountain — **knobbed** \'näbd\ *adj* — **knob·by** \'näb-ē\ *adj*

[1]**knock** \'näk\ *vb* **1 a :** to strike something with a sharp blow **b :** to drive, force, or make by so striking **2 :** to collide with something **3 :** MOVE, WANDER ⟨*knocked* about the woods all day⟩ **4 :** to make a pounding noise ⟨the engine *knocks*⟩ **5 :** to find fault with

[2]**knock** *n* **1 :** a sharp blow **2 :** a severe misfortune or hardship **3 :** a pounding noise

knock down **1 :** to sell to the highest bidder at an auction **2 :** to take or come apart **:** DISASSEMBLE

knock·er \'näk-ər\ *n* **:** one that knocks; *esp* **:** a device hinged to a door for use in knocking

knock–knee \'näk-'nē, -ˌnē\ *n* **:** a condition in which the legs curve inward at the knees — **knock–kneed** \-'nēd\ *adj*

knock off *vb* **:** STOP; *esp* **:** to quit working

knock·out \'näk-ˌau̇t\ *n* **1 a :** the act of knocking out **:** the condition of being knocked out **b :** a blow that knocks out an opponent in boxing **2 :** something sensationally striking or attractive — **knockout** *adj*

knock out \-'au̇t\ *vb* **:** to make unconscious

knoll \'nōl\ *n* **:** a small round hill **:** MOUND

[1]**knot** \'nät\ *n* **1 :** an interlacing (as of string or ribbon) that forms a lump or knob **2 :** something hard to solve **:** PROBLEM **3 :** a bond of union; *esp* **:** the marriage bond **4 a :** a lump or swelling in bodily tissue **b :** the base of a woody branch enclosed in the stem from which it arises; *also* **:** a section of a knot in lumber **5 :** a cluster of persons or things **:** GROUP **6 a :** one nautical mile per hour **b :** one nautical mile

[2]**knot** *vb* **knot·ted**; **knot·ting** **1 :** to tie in or with a knot **:** form knots in **2 :** to unite closely or intricately **:** ENTANGLE

knot·hole \'nät-ˌhōl\ *n* **:** a hole in a board or tree trunk where a knot has come out

knot·ted \'nät-əd\ *adj* **:** KNOTTY

knot·ty \'nät-ē\ *adj* **knot·ti·er**; **-est** **1 :** full of knots ⟨*knotty* wood⟩ **2 :** DIFFICULT ⟨a *knotty* problem⟩

knotty pine *n* **:** pine wood with decorative distribution of knots used esp. for interior finish

knout \'nau̇t, 'nüt\ *n* **:** a whip for flogging criminals

know \'nō\ *vb* **knew** \'n(y)ü\; **known** \'nōn\; **know·ing** **1 a :** to perceive directly **:** have direct awareness of **b :** to have understanding of ⟨*know* yourself⟩ **c :** to recognize the nature of ⟨*knew* him to be honest⟩ **2 a :** to recognize as being the same as something previously known ⟨*knew* him by his walk⟩ **b :** to be acquainted or familiar with ⟨*knows* the city very well⟩ **3 a :** to be aware of the truth or actuality of ⟨*know* that the earth is round⟩ **b :** to have a practical understanding of ⟨*knows* how to write⟩ **4 :** to have knowledge **5 :** to be or become aware ⟨*knew* about her⟩ — **know·a·ble** \'nō-ə-bəl\ *adj* — **know·er** \'nō(-ə)r\ *n*

know–how \'nō-ˌhau̇\ *n* **:** knowledge of how to do something smoothly and efficiently

know·ing \'nō-ing\ *adj* **1 :** having or showing knowledge, information, or intelligence ⟨a *knowing* glance⟩ **2 :** shrewdly and keenly alert **:** ASTUTE **3 :** DELIBERATE, INTENTIONAL — **know·ing·ly** \-ing-lē\ *adv*

knowl·edge \'näl-ij\ *n* **1 :** understanding or skill gained by experience ⟨a *knowledge* of carpentry⟩ **2 a :** the state of being aware of something or of having information **b :** range of information ⟨within my *knowledge*⟩ **3 :** the act of understanding **:** clear perception of truth **4 :** something learned and kept in the mind **:** LEARNING ⟨a man of vast *knowledge* of history⟩

knowl·edge·a·ble \'näl-i-jə-bəl\ *adj* **:** having or exhibiting knowledge or intelligence **:** WISE

know–noth·ing \'nō-ˌnəth-ing\ *n* **:** IGNORAMUS

[1]**knuck·le** \'nək-əl\ *n* **1 :** the rounded lump formed by the ends of two bones where they come together in a joint; *esp* **:** such a lump at a finger joint **2 :** any of several parts (as the hock or shank or a tarsal joint) of the leg of a four-footed animal as used for food

[2]**knuckle** *vb* **knuck·led**; **knuck·ling** \-(ə-)ling\ **1 :** to place the knuckles on the ground in shooting a marble **2 :** to give in **:** SUBMIT — usu. used with *under* **3 :** to apply oneself earnestly — usu. used with *down*

knurl \'nərl\ *n* **1 :** KNOB **2 :** a twisted knot of wood **3 :** one of a series of small ridges or beads on a metal surface (as of a thumbscrew) to aid in gripping — **knurled** \'nərld\ *adj*

KO \(')kā-'ō, 'kā-ō\ *vb* **KO'd**; **KO'·ing** **:** to knock out in boxing — **KO** *n*

ko·a·la \kō-'äl-ə\ *n* **:** an Australian tree-dwelling marsupial that has large hairy ears, gray fur, and no tail and feeds on eucalyptus leaves

koala
(about 2 ft. long)

Koch's postulates \'ko̊ks-\ *n pl* **:** a statement of the steps required to identify a germ as the cause of a disease: (1) it must be found in all cases of the disease; (2) it must be isolated from the one with the disease and grown in pure culture; (3) it must produce the disease when introduced into a healthy but susceptible host; (4) it must be found in the host that is experimentally infected

kohl \'kōl\ *n* **:** a preparation used by women esp. in Arabia and Egypt to darken the edges of the eyelids

kohl·rabi \kōl-'rab-ē, -'räb-\ *n, pl* **-rab·ies** **:** a cabbage that forms no head but has a swollen fleshy edible stem

ko·la nut \'kō-lə-\ *n* **:** the bitter seed of an African tree containing much caffeine and used in beverages and medicine for its stimulant effect

koo·doo *or* **ku·du** \'küd-ü\ *n* **:** a large grayish brown African antelope with large ringed spirally twisted horns

koodoo
(about 5 ft. at shoulder)

kook \'kük\ *n* **:** an eccentric or insane person **:** NUT — **kooky** \'kü-kē\ *adj*

kook·a·bur·ra \'ku̇k-ə-ˌbər-ə, -ˌbə-

K

rə\ *n* : an Australian kingfisher that is about the size of a crow and has a call resembling loud laughter — called also *laughing jackass*

ko·peck *also* **ko·pek** \ˈkō-ˌpek\ *n* **1** : a unit of value equal to 1/100 ruble **2** : a coin representing one kopeck

Ko·ran \kə-ˈran\ *n* : the book composed of writings accepted by Muslims as revelations made to Muhammad by Allah

Ko·re·an \kə-ˈrē-ən\ *n* **1** : a native or inhabitant of Korea **2** : the language of the Korean people — **Korean** *adj*

ko·sher \ˈkō-shər\ *adj* **1** : sanctioned by Jewish law; *esp* : ritually fit for use **2** : selling or serving food ritually fit according to Jewish law

kow·tow \kau-ˈtau̇, ˈkau̇-ˌ\ *vb* [from Chinese *k'o*[1] *t'ou*[2], from *k'o*[1] "to bump" and *t'ou*[2] "head"] **1** : to kneel and touch the forehead to the ground to show worship or respect **2** : to show slavish respect — **kowtow** *n*

KP \ˈkā-ˈpē\ *n* : KITCHEN POLICE

kraal \ˈkrȯl, ˈkräl\ *n* **1** : a village of southern African natives **2** : an enclosure for domestic animals in southern Africa

kraft \ˈkraft\ *n* : a strong paper or board made from wood pulp

krill \ˈkril\ *n* : small planktonic organisms (as crustaceans and larvae) that form a major food of whales

Kriss Kringle \ˈkris-ˈkring-gəl\ *n* : SANTA CLAUS

[1]**kro·na** \ˈkrō-nə\ *n, pl* **kro·nur** \-nər\ **1** : the basic monetary unit of Iceland **2** : a coin representing one krona

[2]**kro·na** \ˈkrō-nə, ˈkrü-\ *n, pl* **kro·nor** \-ˌnȯr\ **1** : the basic monetary unit of Sweden **2** : a coin representing one krona

[1]**kro·ne** \ˈkrō-nə\ *n, pl* **kro·nen** \-nən\ **1** : the basic monetary unit of Austria from 1892 to 1925 **2** : a coin representing one krone

[2]**kro·ne** \ˈkrō-nə, ˈkrü-\ *n, pl* **kro·ner** \-nər\ **1** : the basic monetary unit of Denmark and Norway **2** : a coin representing one krone

kryp·ton \ˈkrip-ˌtän\ *n* : a colorless gaseous element found in air and used esp. in electric lamps — see ELEMENT table

KS *abbr* Kansas

kud·zu \ˈku̇d-zü\ *n* : a trailing Asiatic vine that is related to the pea and is used widely for hay and forage and for erosion control

kum·quat \ˈkəm-ˌkwät\ *n* [from Cantonese Chinese *kam kwat*, from *kam* "gold" and *kwat* "orange"] **1** : a small citrus fruit with sweet spongy rind and somewhat acid pulp used esp. for preserves **2** : a tree or shrub that bears kumquats

kv *abbr* kilovolt

kw *abbr* kilowatt

kwa·shi·or·kor \ˌkwäsh-ē-ˈȯr-kər\ *n* : a disease of young children resulting from deficient intake of protein

kwh *or* **kwhr** *abbr* kilowatt-hour

Ky *or* **KY** *abbr* Kentucky

ə abut	ər further	a back	ā bake	
ä cot, cart	au̇ out	ch chin	e less	ē easy
g gift	i trip	ī life	j joke	ng sing	ō flow
ȯ flaw	ȯi coin	th thin	t͟h this	ü loot
u̇ foot	y yet	yü few	yu̇ furious	zh vision

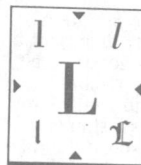

l \'el\ *n, often cap* **1** : the 12th letter of the English alphabet **2** : the roman numeral 50

l *abbr* **1** left **2** line **3** liter

L *abbr* **1** large **2** Latin **3** losses

la \'lä\ *n* : the 6th note of the diatonic scale

La *abbr* Louisiana

LA *abbr* **1** Los Angeles **2** Louisiana

lab \'lab\ *n* : LABORATORY

Lab *abbr* Labrador

[1]**la·bel** \'lā-bəl\ *n* **1** : a slip (as of paper or cloth) that is attached to something to identify or describe it **2** : a descriptive or identifying word or phrase

[2]**label** *vb* **la·beled** *or* **la·belled**; **la·bel·ing** *or* **la·bel·ling** \-b(ə-)liŋ\ **1** : to attach a label to **2** : to name or describe with a label ⟨*labeled* his opponent a visionary⟩ **3** : to make (a chemical element) traceable (as through the steps of a biochemical process) by incorporating a radioactive or special isotope into its structure

la·bi·al \'lā-bē-əl\ *adj* : of or relating to the lips or labia — **la·bi·al·ly** \-ə-lē\ *adv*

la·bi·ate \'lā-bē-ət, -bē-,āt\ *adj* **1** : LIPPED; *esp* : having a tubular corolla or calyx divided into two unequal parts projecting one over the other like lips **2** : of or relating to the mint

la·bi·um \'lā-bē-əm\ *n, pl* **-bia** \-bē-ə\ **1** : any of the folds at the margin of the vulva **2** : the lower lip of a labiate corolla **3** : the lower lip of an insect

[1]**la·bor** \'lā-bər\ *n* **1** : physical or mental effort esp. when hard or required : TOIL, WORK **2 a** : work with hands or machines (as in a factory) as opposed to clerical or brain work or sometimes farming **b** : those who do labor for wages **3** : the physical efforts and pain of childbirth; *also* : the period of such labor **4** : something that requires toil : TASK

[2]**labor** *vb* **la·bored**; **la·bor·ing** \-b(ə-)riŋ\ **1 a** : to exert one's body or mind strenuously : work hard **b** : to work for wages in production of goods or services **2** : to move with great effort **3** : to pitch or roll heavily ⟨the ship *labored* in a rough sea⟩ *syn* see WORK

lab·o·ra·to·ry \'lab-(ə-)rə-,tōr-ē, -,tȯr-\ *n, pl* **-ries** : a place equipped for scientific experiments for testing and analysis

Labor Day *n* : the 1st Monday in September observed as a legal holiday in recognition of the workingman

la·bored \'lā-bərd\ *adj* : produced or done with labor ⟨*labored* breathing⟩

la·bor·er \'lā-bər-ər\ *n* : one that works; *esp* : a worker on jobs requiring strength rather than skill

la·bo·ri·ous \lə-'bōr-ē-əs, -'bȯr-\ *adj* **1** : INDUSTRIOUS **2** : requiring hard effort — **la·bo·ri·ous·ly** *adv* — **la·bo·ri·ous·ness** *n*

la·bor·sav·ing \'lā-bər-,sā-viŋ\ *adj* : adapted to replace or decrease human labor and esp. manual labor

labor union *n* : an organization of workers formed to protect the rights and advance the interests of its members

Labrador duck \,lab-rə-,dȯr-\ *n* : an extinct black-and-white duck related to the eiders

lab·ra·dor·ite \'lab-rə-,dȯr-,īt\ *n* : a feldspar with changeable colors (as gray, blue, and green)

Labrador retriever *n* : a retriever characterized by a short dense usu. black coat and broad head and chest

la·brum \'lā-brəm\ *n* : the upper lip of an arthropod in front of or above the mandibles

la·bur·num \lə-'bər-nəm\ *n* : any of several poisonous Eurasian shrubs and trees related to the pea and having hanging clusters of bright yellow flowers

lab·y·rinth \'lab-ə-,rin(t)th\ *n* **1** : a place full of passageways and blind alleys so arranged as to make it difficult to find one's way around : MAZE **2** : something extremely complex or twisting **3** : the internal ear or its bony or membranous part — **lab·y·rin·thine** \,lab-ə-'rin(t)-thən\ *adj*

lac \'lak\ *n* : a resinous substance secreted by a scale insect and used in the manufacture of shellac, lacquers, and sealing wax

lac·co·lith \'lak-ə-,lith\ *n* : a mass of igneous rock that intrudes between sedimentary beds and produces a dome-shaped bulge

[1]**lace** \'lās\ *n* [from Old French *laz*, from Latin *laqueus* "noose"] **1** : a cord or string for drawing together two edges (as of a shoe) **2** : an ornamental braid for trimming **3** : a fine openwork fabric of thread or cord used chiefly for ornament of dress — **laced** \'lāst\ *adj* — **lace·like** \'lās-,līk\ *adj*

[2]**lace** *vb* **1** : to fasten or join with or as if with a lace **2** : to adorn with lace **3** : INTERTWINE **4** : BEAT, LASH

lac·er·ate \'las-ə-,rāt\ *vb* **1** : to tear roughly : injure by tearing ⟨flesh *lacerated* by a dog's teeth⟩ **2** : to afflict mentally : DISTRESS

lac·er·a·tion \,las-ə-'rā-shən\ *n* **1** : an act or instance of lacerating **2** : a torn and ragged wound

lace·wing \'lās-,wiŋ\ *n* : any of various neuropterous insects with delicate lacy wings, long antennae, and brilliant eyes

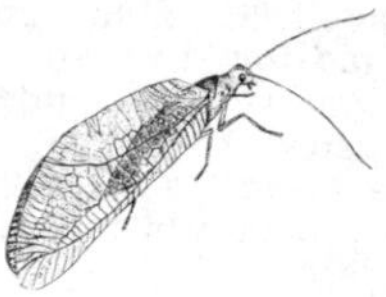
lacewing
(less than one inch long)

lach·ry·mose \'lak-rə-,mōs\ *adj* **1** : given to weeping : TEARFUL **2** : tending to cause tears : MOURNFUL ⟨*lachrymose* ballads⟩ — **lach·ry·mose·ly** *adv*

lac·ing \'lā-siŋ\ *n* **1** : the action of one that laces **2** : LACE

[1]**lack** \'lak\ *vb* **1** : to be wanting or missing ⟨the will to win is *lacking*⟩ **2** : to need, want, or be deficient in ⟨*lacks* money⟩

[2]**lack** *n* **1** : the fact or state of being wanting or deficient ⟨a *lack* of good manners⟩ **2** : something that is lacking or is needed ⟨money is our biggest *lack*⟩

lack·a·dai·si·cal \,lak-ə-'dā-zi-kəl\ *adj* : LANGUID, LISTLESS — **lack·a·dai·si·cal·ly** \-k(ə-)lē\ *adv*

lack·ey \'lak-ē\ *n, pl* **lackeys** **1** : a liveried retainer : FOOTMAN **2** : a servile follower : TOADY

lack·lus·ter \'lak-,ləs-tər\ *adj* : lacking in sheen, radiance, or vitality : DULL

la·con·ic \lə-'kän-ik\ *adj* : sparing of words : TERSE — **la·con·i·cal·ly** \-'kän-i-k(ə-)lē\ *adv*

lac·quer \'lak-ər\ *n* **1** : any of numerous preparations that consist of a substance in solution (as shellac in alcohol), dry rapidly usu. by evaporation of the solvent to form a glossy film, and are used to coat objects (as wood or metal) **2** : any of various durable natural varnishes; *esp* : one from an Asiatic sumac — **lacquer** *vb*

lac·ri·mal *also* **lach·ry·mal** \'lak-rə-məl\ *adj* : of, relating to, or being the glands that produce tears

lac·ri·ma·tion \,lak-rə-'mā-shən\ *n* : the secretion of tears esp. when abnormal or excessive

lac·ri·ma·tor *or* **lach·ry·ma·tor** \'lak-rə-,māt-ər\ *n* : TEAR GAS

la·crosse \lə-'krȯs\ *n* [from Canadian French *la crosse*, meaning literally "the crosier"; so called from the shape of the racket] : a field game in which the players use a long-handled racket to catch, carry, or throw the ball toward or into the opponents' goal

lac·tase \'lak-ˌtās\ *n* : an enzyme that breaks down lactose and related compounds and occurs esp. in the intestines of young mammals and in yeasts
lac·tate \'lak-ˌtāt\ *vb* : to secrete milk — **lac·ta·tion** \lak-'tā-shən\ *n*
1**lac·te·al** \'lak-tē-əl\ *adj* **1** : consisting of, producing, or resembling milk **2 a** : conveying or containing a milky fluid **b** : of or relating to the lacteals
2**lacteal** *n* : one of the lymphatic vessels arising from the villi of the small intestine and carrying chyle
lac·tic \'lak-tik\ *adj* **1** : of or relating to milk **2** : obtained from sour milk or whey **3** : involving the production of lactic acid
lactic acid *n* : an organic acid present in cells and esp. muscle, manufactured from carbohydrate usu. by bacterial fermentation, and used esp. in food and medicine
lac·tose \'lak-ˌtōs\ *n* : a sugar present in milk that breaks down to yield glucose and galactose and on fermentation yields esp. lactic acid
lacy \'lā-sē\ *adj* **lac·i·er**; **-est** : resembling or consisting of lace
lad \'lad\ *n* **1** : BOY, YOUTH **2** : FELLOW, CHAP
lad·der \'lad-ər\ *n* **1** : a structure for climbing that consists of two long parallel sidepieces joined at intervals by crosspieces on which one may step **2** : something that suggests a ladder in form or use **3** : a series of steps or stages : SCALE
lad·die \'lad-ē\ *n* : a young lad
lade \'lād\ *vb* **lad·ed**; **lad·ed** *or* **lad·en** \'lād-ən\; **lad·ing** **1** : LOAD ⟨*lade* a ship⟩ ⟨a truck *laden* with gravel⟩ **2** : to burden heavily : OPPRESS ⟨*laden* with cares⟩ **3** : LADLE
la·di·no \lə-'dī-nō, -nə\ *n*, *pl* **-nos** : a large rapidly growing white clover widely planted for hay or silage
la·dle \'lād-əl\ *n* : a deep-bowled long-handled spoon or dipper used in dipping — **ladle** *vb*
la·dy \'lād-ē\ *n*, *pl* **ladies** [from Old English *hlǣfdīge* "female head of a household", literally "one who kneads bread", from *hlāf* "loaf" and a root meaning "to knead" which appears in modern English *dough*] **1** : a woman of property, rank, or authority; *esp* : one having a standing equivalent to that of a lord — used as a title **2** *cap* : VIRGIN MARY — usu. used with *Our* **3** : a woman of superior social position or of refinement and gentle manners **4** : WOMAN **5** : WIFE
lady beetle *n* : LADYBUG
la·dy·bird \'lād-ē-ˌbərd\ *n* : LADYBUG
la·dy·bug \-ˌbəg\ *n* : any of numerous small roundish-backed often brightly colored beetles that usu. feed both as larvae and adults on other insects

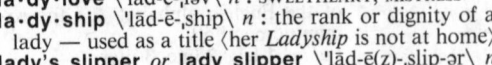

ladybug (less than one inch long)

la·dy–in–wait·ing \ˌlād-ē-in-'wāt-ing\ *n*, *pl* **ladies–in–waiting** : a lady appointed to attend or wait on a queen or princess
la·dy·like \'lād-ē-ˌlīk\ *adj* **1** : resembling a lady in appearance or manners **2** : suitable to a lady ⟨*ladylike* behavior⟩

ə abut	ər further	a back	ā bake	
ä cot, cart	aù out	ch chin	e less	ē easy
g gift	i trip	ī life	j joke	ng sing	ō flow
ȯ flaw	ȯi coin	th thin	th this	ü loot
u̇ foot	y yet	yü few	yu̇ furious	zh vision

la·dy·love \'lād-ē-ˌləv\ *n* : SWEETHEART, MISTRESS
la·dy·ship \'lād-ē-ˌship\ *n* : the rank or dignity of a lady — used as a title ⟨her *Ladyship* is not at home⟩
lady's slipper *or* **lady slipper** \'lād-ē(z)-ˌslip-ər\ *n* : any of several temperate-zone orchids with large drooping flowers whose shape suggests a slipper
1**lag** \'lag\ *vb* **lagged**; **lag·ging** **1** : to stay or fall behind ⟨was tired and *lagged* behind the other hikers⟩ **2** : to hang back : LINGER, LOITER **3** : to move, function, or develop comparatively slowly ⟨production *lagged* behind schedule⟩ **4** : to slacken little by little : FLAG ⟨his interest *lagged*⟩ ***syn*** see LINGER — **lag·ger** *n*
2**lag** *n* **1** : the action or condition of lagging : comparative slowness **2 a** : amount of lagging **b** : a time during which lagging continues
lag·gard \'lag-ərd\ *adj* : lagging or tending to lag : SLOW — **laggard** *n* — **lag·gard·ly** *adv or adj*
lago·morph \'lag-ə-ˌmȯrf\ *n* : any of an order of gnawing mammals having two pairs of upper incisors one behind the other and comprising the rabbits, hares, and pikas — compare RODENT — **lago·mor·phic** \ˌlag-ə-'mȯr-fik\ *adj*
la·goon \lə-'gün\ *n* : a shallow sound, channel, or pond near or connected with a larger body of water
laid *past of* LAY
lain *past part of* LIE
lair \'la(ə)r, 'le(ə)r\ *n* : the den or resting place of a wild animal; *also* : REFUGE, HIDEAWAY
laird \'la(ə)rd, 'le(ə)rd\ *n* : a Scottish landowner
lais·sez–faire \ˌles-ˌā-'fa(ə)r, -'fe(ə)r\ *n* [from French *laissez faire* meaning "let do"] : a doctrine opposing governmental interference in economic affairs — **laissez–faire** *adj*
la·i·ty \'lā-ət-ē\ *n*, *pl* **-ties** **1** : the people of a religious faith as distinguished from its clergy **2** : persons not of a particular profession or skill
1**lake** \'lāk\ *n* : a large inland body of standing water; *also* : a pool of liquid (as oil or pitch)
2**lake** *n* **1** : any of numerous bright pigments composed of a soluble dye adsorbed on or combined with another substance **2** : a vivid red
lake trout *n* : any of several lake fishes: as **a** : BROWN TROUT **b** : a large dark American char that is an important sport and commercial fish in northern lakes
la·ma \'läm-ə\ *n* : a Lamaist monk
La·ma·ism \'läm-ə-ˌiz-əm\ *n* : the Buddhism of Tibet and Mongolia marked by a dominant hierarchy of monks — **La·ma·ist** \'läm-ə-əst\ *n or adj* — **La·ma·is·tic** \ˌläm-ə-'is-tik\ *adj*
La·marck·ism \lə-'mär-ˌkiz-əm\ *n* : a theory of organic evolution asserting that environmental changes cause structural changes in animals and plants that are transmitted to offspring — **La·marck·i·an** \-'mär-kē-ən\ *adj or n*
la·ma·sery \'läm-ə-ˌser-ē\ *n*, *pl* **-ser·ies** : a monastery of lamas
1**lamb** \'lam\ *n* **1 a** : a young sheep esp. less than one year old or without permanent teeth **b** : the flesh of a lamb used as food **2** : an innocent, weak, or gentle person
2**lamb** *vb* : to give birth to a lamb
lam·baste *or* **lam·bast** \lam-'bāst, -'bast\ *vb* **1** : STRIKE, BEAT **2** : to scold roughly
lamb·da \'lam-də\ *n* : the 11th letter of the Greek alphabet — Λ or λ
lam·bent \'lam-bənt\ *adj* **1** : playing lightly over a surface : FLICKERING **2** : softly radiant ⟨*lambent* eyes⟩ **3** : BRILLIANT, WITTY — **lam·ben·cy** \-bən-sē\ *n*
lamb·skin \'lam-ˌskin\ *n* : a lamb's skin or a fine sheepskin or leather made from either

lamb's–quar·ters \'lamz-,kwȯrt-ərz\ *n* : a goosefoot with glaucous foliage that is sometimes used as a potherb

1**lame** \'lām\ *adj* **1 a** : physically disabled; *also* : having a part and esp. a limb so disabled as to impair freedom of movement **b** : halting in movement : LIMPING ⟨a *lame* gait⟩ **2** : lacking substance : WEAK ⟨made a pretty *lame* excuse⟩ — **lame·ly** *adv* — **lame·ness** *n*

2**lame** *vb* : to make lame : CRIPPLE ⟨*lamed* for life by a boyhood attack of polio⟩

la·mel·la \lə-'mel-ə\ *n, pl* **-mel·lae** \-'mel-(,)ē, -,ī\ *also* **-mellas** : a thin flat scale or part — **la·mel·lar** \-'mel-ər\ *adj*

la·mel·li·branch \lə-'mel-ə-,brangk\ *n, pl* **-branchs** \-,brang(k)s\ : any of a class of mollusks (as clams, oysters, or mussels) with a shell made up of right and left parts joined by a hinge — **lamellibranch** *adj*

la·ment \lə-'ment\ *vb* **1** : to mourn aloud : WAIL **2** : to express sorrow for : BEWAIL — **lament** *n* — **lam·en·ta·tion** \,lam-ən-'tā-shən\ *n*

lam·en·ta·ble \'lam-ən-tə-bəl, lə-'ment-ə-\ *adj* **1** : that is to be regretted or lamented : DEPLORABLE ⟨a *lamentable* error⟩ **2** : SORROWFUL — **lam·en·ta·ble·ness** *n* — **lam·en·ta·bly** \-blē\ *adv*

Lam·en·ta·tions \,lam-ən-'tā-shənz\ *n* — see BIBLE table

lam·i·na \'lam-ə-nə\ *n, pl* **-nae** \-,nē, -,nī\ *or* **-nas** : a thin plate or scale — **lam·i·nar** \-nər\ *adj*

lam·i·nar·ia \,lam-ə-'ner-ē-ə, -'nar-\ *n* : any of various large kelps with an unbranched cylindrical or flattened stalk and a smooth or wavy blade — **lam·i·nar·i·an** \-ē-ən\ *adj*

laminaria (about 10 ft. long)

lam·i·nate \'lam-ə-,nāt\ *vb* **1** : to roll or compress into a thin plate **2** : to make by uniting layers of one or more materials; *esp* : to bond or impregnate layers of paper, wood, or fabric with resin and compress under heat — **lam·i·na·tion** \,lam-ə-'nā-shən\ *n* — **lam·i·na·tor** \'lam-ə-,nāt-ər\ *n*

Lam·mas \'lam-əs\ *n* : August 1

lamp \'lamp\ *n* **1** : a vessel with a wick for burning a liquid (as oil) to produce light **2** : a device for producing light or heat ⟨an electric *lamp*⟩

lamp·black \-,blak\ *n* : a fine black soot made by incomplete burning of carbon-containing material and used esp. as a pigment in paints and ink

lamp·light·er \-,līt-ər\ *n* : one that lights a lamp; *esp* : a person employed to light gas street lights

1**lam·poon** \lam-'pün\ *n* : a satirical writing or drawing usu. aimed at a person

2**lampoon** *vb* : to satirize by a lampoon : RIDICULE — **lam·poon·er** *n*

lam·prey \'lam-prē\ *n, pl* **lampreys** : any of an order of aquatic vertebrates that resemble eels but have a large sucking mouth with no jaws

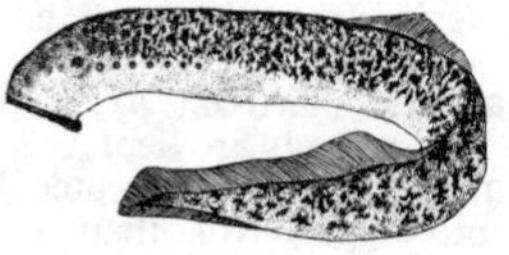

lamprey (up to 3 ft. long)

lamp·shell \'lamp-,shel\ *n* : BRACHIOPOD

1**lance** \'lan(t)s\ *n* **1** : a weapon consisting of a long shaft with a sharp steel head and carried by knights or light cavalry **2** : a sharp implement suggestive of a lance; *esp* : LANCET

2**lance** *vb* : to pierce or cut with a lance or lancet ⟨*lance* a boil⟩

lance·let \'lan(t)s-lət\ *n* : any of various small translucent marine animals related to the vertebrates — called also *amphioxus*

lanc·er \'lan(t)-sər\ *n* : one who carries a lance; *esp* : a light cavalryman armed with a lance

lan·cet \'lan(t)-sət\ *n* : a sharp-pointed and usu. 2-edged surgical instrument

1**land** \'land\ *n* **1** : the solid part of the surface of the earth **2** : a distinguishable portion of the earth's surface ⟨fenced *land*⟩ ⟨marshy *land*⟩ **3** : COUNTRY, NATION **4** : REAL ESTATE ⟨owns *land* in Alaska⟩ — **land·less** \'lan-dləs\ *adj*

2**land** *vb* **1 a** : to set or go ashore from a ship : DISEMBARK ⟨*land* troops⟩ ⟨he *landed* today⟩ **b** : to stop at or near a place on shore ⟨the ship *landed* at the dock⟩ **2** : to alight or cause to alight on a surface ⟨*land* a plane⟩ **3** : to bring to or arrive at a destination or a position or condition ⟨*land* in jail⟩ ⟨*landed* him in trouble⟩ **4 a** : to catch and bring in ⟨*land* a fish⟩ **b** : GAIN, SECURE ⟨*land* a job⟩ — **land·er** *n*

land breeze *n* : a breeze blowing toward the sea

land bridge *n* : a strip of land connecting two landmasses

land·ed \'lan-dəd\ *adj* **1** : owning land ⟨*landed* proprietors⟩ **2** : consisting of real estate ⟨*landed* property⟩

land·form \'lan(d)-,fȯrm\ *n* : a feature of the earth's surface attributable to natural causes

land·hold·er \'land-,hōl-dər\ *n* : an owner or possessor of land — **land·hold·ing** \-ding\ *n*

land·ing \'lan-ding\ *n* **1** : the action of one that lands **2** : a place (as a wharf) for discharging or taking on passengers and cargo **3** : the level part of a staircase at the end of a flight of stairs or connecting one flight with another

landing craft *n* : any of numerous naval craft designed for putting ashore troops and equipment

landing field *n* : a field where aircraft may land and take off

landing strip *n* : AIRSTRIP

land·locked \'lan(d)-,läkt\ *adj* **1** : enclosed or nearly enclosed by land ⟨a *landlocked* harbor⟩ **2** : confined to fresh water by a barrier ⟨*landlocked* salmon⟩

land·lord \-,lȯrd\ *n* **1** : the owner of property which he leases or rents to another **2** : a man who runs an inn or rooming house — **land·la·dy** \-,lād-ē\ *n*

land·lub·ber \-,ləb-ər\ *n* : LANDSMAN

land·mark \-,märk\ *n* **1** : an object that marks the boundary of land **2 a** : a conspicuous object on land that serves as a guide **b** : an important building or monument ⟨historical *landmarks*⟩ **3** : an event that marks a turning point

land·mass \-,mas\ *n* : a large area of land

land·own·er \'land-,ō-nər\ *n* : an owner of land — **land·own·ing** \-ning\ *adj*

1**land·scape** \'lan(d)-,skāp\ *n* **1** : a picture of natural scenery **2** : the land that can be seen in one glance

2**landscape** *vb* : to improve the natural beauties of a tract of land by grading, clearing, or gardening

land·slide \'lan(d)-,slīd\ *n* **1** : the slipping down of a mass of rocks or earth on a steep slope; *also* : the mass of material that slides **2** : an overwhelming victory esp. in a political contest

lands·man \'lan(d)z-mən\ *n* : a person who lives or works on land; *esp* : one who knows little or nothing of the sea and ships

land·ward \'land-wərd\ *adj* : lying or being toward

the land or on the side toward the land — **land·ward** *also* **land·wards** \-wərdz\ *adv*

lane \'lān\ *n* **1** : a narrow way or road usu. between fences, hedges, or buildings **2** : a relatively narrow way or track: as **a** : an ocean route for ships; *also* : AIR LANE **b** : a strip of roadway for a single line of vehicles **c** : a bowling alley

lang *abbr* language

lan·guage \'lang-gwij\ *n* **1 a** : the words, their pronunciation, and the methods of combining them used and understood by a large group of people **b** : a systematic means of communicating ideas ⟨sign *language*⟩ **2** : form or manner of verbal expression; *esp* : STYLE ⟨forceful *language*⟩ **3** : the words and expressions of a particular group or field ⟨the *language* of medicine⟩ **4** : the study of language **5** : the means by which animals communicate or are thought to communicate with each other ⟨*language* of the bees⟩

lan·guid \'lang-gwəd\ *adj* **1** : drooping or flagging from or as if from exhaustion **2** : sluggish in nature : LISTLESS **3** : lacking force or quickness of movement : SLOW ⟨*languid* life in the tropics⟩ — **lan·guid·ly** *adv*

lan·guish \'lang-gwish\ *vb* **1** : to become weak or languid : waste away ⟨*languish* in prison⟩ **2** : to become weak with longing : PINE **3** : to appeal for sympathy by putting on a weary or sorrowful look — **lan·guish·ing·ly** \-ing-lē\ *adv* — **lan·guish·ment** \-gwish-mənt\ *n*

lan·guor \'lang-(g)ər\ *n* **1** : weakness or weariness of body or mind **2** : a state of dreamy inactivity — **lan·guor·ous** \-(g)ə-rəs\ *adj* — **lan·guor·ous·ly** *adv*

lank \'langk\ *adj* **1** : not well filled out : THIN ⟨*lank* cattle⟩ **2** : hanging straight and limp without spring or curl ⟨*lank* hair⟩ — **lank·ly** *adv* — **lank·ness** *n*

lanky \'lang-kē\ *adj* **lank·i·er**; **-est** : being tall, thin, and usu. loose-jointed ⟨a *lanky* boy⟩ — **lank·i·ly** \-kə-lē\ *adv* — **lank·i·ness** \-kē-nəs\ *n*

lan·o·lin \'lan-ə-lən\ *n* : the fatty coating of sheep's wool esp. when refined for use in ointments and cosmetics

lan·ta·na \lan-'tän-ə\ *n* : any of a genus of tropical shrubs that have showy heads of small bright flowers

lan·tern \'lant-ərn\ *n* **1** : a usu. portable light with a protective covering **2** : PROJECTOR 2

lan·tha·num \'lan(t)-thə-nəm\ *n* : a white soft malleable metallic element — see ELEMENT table

lan·yard \'lan-yərd\ *n* **1** : a rope or line for fastening something in ships **2** : a cord worn around the neck or shoulder to hold a knife, whistle, or pistol or as a military decoration **3** : a strong cord used in firing cannon

Lao \'lau̇\ *or* **Lao·tian** \lā-'ō-shən, 'lau̇-shən\ *n* **1** : a member of a Buddhist people living in Laos and northeastern Thailand **2** : the Thai language of the Lao people — **Lao** *or* **Laotian** *adj*

1**lap** \'lap\ *n* **1** : a loose panel in a garment : FLAP **2 a** : the clothing that lies on the knees and thighs when one sits **b** : the front part of the lower trunk and thighs of a seated person **3** : a congenial environment ⟨the *lap* of luxury⟩

ə abut	ər further	a back	ā bake	
ä cot, cart	au̇ out	ch chin	e less	ē easy
g gift	i trip	ī life	j joke	ng sing	ō flow
ȯ flaw	ȯi coin	th thin	th this	ü loot
u̇ foot	y yet	yü few	yu̇ furious	zh vision

2**lap** *vb* **lapped**; **lap·ping** **1** : FOLD **2** : WRAP **3** : to lay or lie over or near something else so as to partly cover it ⟨*lap* one shingle over another⟩

3**lap** *n* **1 a** : the amount by which one object overlaps or projects beyond another ⟨shingles with a 2-inch *lap*⟩ **b** : the part of an object that overlaps another **2 a** : one circuit around a racecourse **b** : one part of a journey

4**lap** *vb* **lapped**; **lap·ping** **1** : to scoop up food or drink with the tongue or a tonguelike part ⟨the *lapping* mouthparts of a fly⟩ **2** : to wash or splash gently ⟨waves *lapping* against the dock⟩

5**lap** *n* : an act or sound of lapping

lap·dog \'lap-,dȯg\ *n* : a small dog that may be held in the lap

la·pel \lə-'pel\ *n* : the fold of the front of a coat that is usu. a part of the collar

lap·ful \'lap-,fu̇l\ *n*, *pl* **lapfuls** \-,fu̇lz\ *or* **laps·ful** \'laps-,fu̇l\ : as much as the lap can hold or support

lap·i·dary \'lap-ə-,der-ē\ *n*, *pl* **-dar·ies** : a person who cuts, polishes, and engraves precious stones — **lapidary** *adj*

la·pis la·zu·li \,lap-əs-'laz(h)-ə-lē\ *n* : a deep blue semiprecious stone

Lapp \'lap\ *n* : a member of a people of northern Scandinavia, Finland, and the Kola peninsula of Russia

lap·pet \'lap-ət\ *n* **1** : a fold or flap on a garment or headdress **2** : a flat overlapping or hanging piece (as the wattle of a bird)

1**lapse** \'laps\ *n* **1 a** : a slight error or slip ⟨*lapse* of memory⟩ **b** : a temporary deviation or fall ⟨*lapse* into sin⟩ **2** : the ending of a right or privilege through failure to meet requirements **3** : a passage of time; *also* : INTERVAL

2**lapse** *vb* **1** : to slip, pass, or fall gradually ⟨*lapse* into silence⟩ **2** : to fall into disuse ⟨a custom that had *lapsed*⟩ **3** : to come to an end : CEASE **4** : to pass to another because of failure to meet requirements ⟨his insurance *lapsed* for nonpayment⟩

lapse rate *n* : the rate of decrease of temperature with increase of height

lap·wing \'lap-,wing\ *n* : a crested Old World plover noted for its slow irregular flapping flight and its shrill wailing cry

lar·board \'lär-bərd\ *n* : 4PORT — **larboard** *adj*

lar·ce·ny \'lär-s(ə-)nē\ *n*, *pl* **-nies** : the unlawful taking of personal property with intent to keep it : THEFT — **lar·ce·nous** \-s(ə-)nəs\ *adj*

larch \'lärch\ *n* **1** : any of a genus of trees with short deciduous needles that are related to pines **2** : the wood of a larch

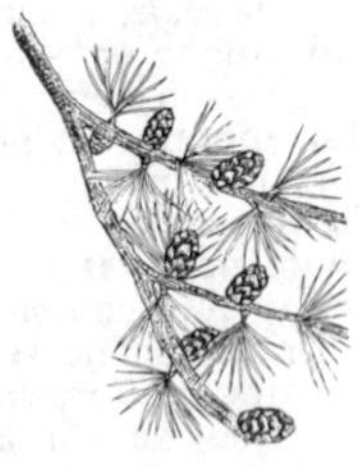

larch 1

1**lard** \'lärd\ *vb* **1** : to insert strips of usu. pork fat into meat before cooking **2** : to smear with lard, fat, or grease **3** : to add to; *esp* : ENRICH ⟨a book *larded* with illustrations⟩

2**lard** *n* : a soft white solid or semisolid fat obtained by rendering fatty tissue of the hog — **lardy** \'lärd-ē\ *adj*

lar·der \'lärd-ər\ *n* : a place where foods are kept

large \'lärj\ *adj* : greater, bigger, more extended, or more powerful than usual ⟨*large* expenditures⟩ ⟨a *large* house⟩ — **large·ness** *n* — **at large** **1** : at liberty : FREE ⟨the escapee is still *at large*⟩ **2** : as a whole : in general ⟨the public *at large*⟩ **3** : representing a whole state or area rather than one

of its divisions — used in combination ⟨congress-man-*at-large* from Ohio⟩ ⟨delegate-*at-large*⟩
large calorie *n* : CALORIE 1b
large intestine *n* : the posterior division of the vertebrate intestine consisting of the cecum, colon, and rectum and functioning esp. in the dehydration of digestive residues into feces
large·ly \'lärj-lē\ *adv* : for the most part : GENERALLY ⟨the statement is *largely* true⟩
large·mouth bass \ˌlärj-ˌmau̇th-\ *n* : a large bass of warm sluggish waters that is blackish green above and lighter or whitish below — called also *large-mouth black bass*
lar·gess *or* **lar·gesse** \lär-'jes, 'lär-ˌ\ *n* **1** : liberal giving **2** : a generous gift
larg·ish \'lär-jish\ *adj* : rather large
[1]**lar·go** \'lär-gō\ *adv or adj* : in a very slow and broad manner — used as a direction in music
[2]**largo** *n, pl* **largos** : a largo movement
lar·i·at \'lar-ē-ət\ *n* [from American Spanish *la reata*, meaning literally "the lasso"] : a rope to catch livestock or to picket grazing animals : LASSO
[1]**lark** \'lärk\ *n* **1** : any of numerous Old World singing birds; *esp* : SKYLARK **2** : any of various usu. dull-colored ground-living birds (as the meadowlark or titlark)
[2]**lark** *n* : FROLIC, ROMP; *also* : PRANK — **lark** *vb*
lark·spur \'lärk-ˌspər\ *n* : DELPHINIUM; *esp* : a cultivated annual delphinium grown for its flowers
lar·va \'lär-və\ *n, pl* **lar·vae** \-(ˌ)vē, -ˌvī\ *also* **larvas** [modern Latin, from Latin meaning "ghost" or "mask"; so called because the mature form was considered to be disguised in the larval stage] **1** : the immature, wingless, and often wormlike form that hatches from the egg of many insects **2** : the early form of any animal that at birth or hatching is fundamentally unlike its parent ⟨the tadpole is the *larva* of the frog⟩ — **lar·val** \-vəl\ *adj*
lar·vi·cide \'lär-və-ˌsīd\ *n* : an agent for killing larval pests — **lar·vi·cid·al** \ˌlär-və-'sīd-əl\ *adj*
lar·yn·gi·tis \ˌlar-ən-'jīt-əs\ *n* : inflammation of the larynx
lar·ynx \'lar-ing(k)s\ *n, pl* **la·ryn·ges** \lə-'rin-(ˌ)jēz\ *or* **lar·ynx·es** : the modified upper part of the windpipe that in man and most mammals contains the vocal cords

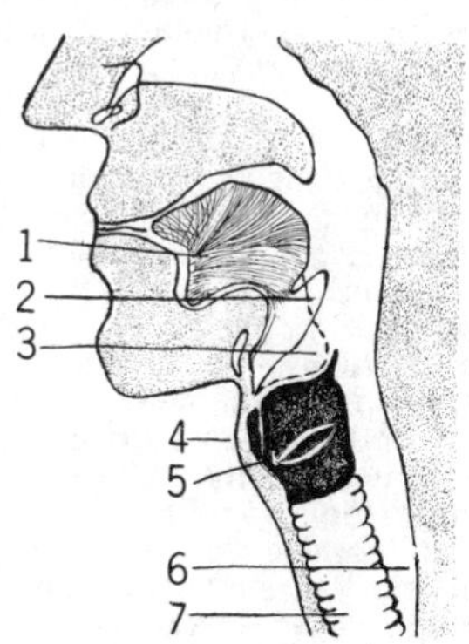

larynx: 1, tongue; 2, epiglottis opening larynx; 3, epiglottis closing larynx; 4, Adam's apple; 5, vocal cords; 6, esophagus; 7, trachea

las·civ·i·ous \lə-'siv-ē-əs\ *adj* : LEWD, LUSTFUL — **las·civ·i·ous·ly** *adv* — **las·civ·i·ous·ness** *n*
la·ser \'lā-zər\ *n* [from the initials of the descriptive phrase *l*ight *a*mplification by *s*timulated *e*mission of *r*adiation] : a device that utilizes the natural oscillations of atoms for amplifying or generating light waves
[1]**lash** \'lash\ *vb* **1** : to move violently or suddenly ⟨a lion *lashing* his tail⟩ **2** : to strike with or as if with a whip ⟨rain *lashing* the window⟩ **3** : to attack verbally
[2]**lash** *n* **1 a** : a stroke with a whip or switch **b** : the flexible part of a whip; *also* : WHIP **2** : a sudden swinging blow **3** : EYELASH
[3]**lash** *vb* : to bind with a rope, cord, or chain — **lash·er** *n*
lash·ing \'lash-ing\ *n* : something used for binding, wrapping, or fastening
lass \'las\ *n* : young woman : GIRL
lass·ie \'las-ē\ *n* : LASS, GIRL
las·si·tude \'las-ə-ˌt(y)üd\ *n* **1** : WEARINESS, FATIGUE **2** : LISTLESSNESS
las·so \'las-ō, la-'sü\ *n, pl* **lassos** *or* **lassoes** [from Spanish *lazo*, from Latin *laqueus* "noose"; compare English LACE] : a rope or long leather thong with a noose used esp. for catching livestock — **lasso** *vb*
[1]**last** \'last\ *vb* **1** : to continue in being or operation : go on ⟨the meeting *lasted* three hours⟩ **2** : to be enough for the needs of ⟨supplies to *last* you for a week⟩
[2]**last** *adj* **1 a** : following all the rest in time, place, or rank ⟨*last* one out⟩ ⟨*last* in his class⟩ **b** : being the only remaining ⟨his *last* dollar⟩ **2** : belonging to the final stage ⟨the four *last* things⟩ **3** : next before the present : LATEST ⟨*last* week⟩ **4** : least likely ⟨the *last* thing he'd want⟩
[3]**last** *adv* **1** : at the end ⟨ran *last* in the race⟩ **2** : most lately ⟨saw him *last* in New York⟩ **3** : in conclusion ⟨and *last*, I'd like to talk about money⟩
[4]**last** *n* : something that is last ⟨was the *last* to come⟩
[5]**last** *n* : a form which is shaped like the human foot and on which a shoe is shaped or repaired
[6]**last** *vb* : to shape with a last
last·ing *adj* : existing or continuing a long while : ENDURING — **last·ing·ly** \'las-ting-lē\ *adv* — **last·ing·ness** *n*
syn LASTING, PERMANENT mean remaining so long as to seem fixed or established. LASTING implies an often surprising capacity to continue indefinitely ⟨*lasting* friendships formed in youth⟩; PERMANENT applies to things that are designed, expected, or likely to endure without being removed or replaced ⟨our *permanent* editorial staff⟩ *ant* fleeting
last·ly \'last-lē\ *adv* : in conclusion : in the last place
last word *n* **1** : the final remark in a verbal exchange **2** : the power of final decision **3** : the most modern or fashionable one of its kind ⟨the *last word* in hats⟩
lat *abbr* latitude
Lat *abbr* Latin
[1]**latch** \'lach\ *vb* **1** : to get hold ⟨*latch* onto a pass⟩ **2** : to attach oneself
[2]**latch** *n* : a catch (as a spring bolt) that holds a door or gate closed
[3]**latch** *vb* : CATCH, FASTEN
latch·key \'lach-ˌkē\ *n* : a key for opening a door latch
latch·string \-ˌstring\ *n* : a string for raising a latch so as to release it
[1]**late** \'lāt\ *adj* **1 a** : coming or remaining after the due, usual, or proper time ⟨*late* spring⟩ **b** : far advanced toward the close esp. of the day or night ⟨*late* hours⟩ **2 a** : having died or held an office ⟨the *late* Mr. Smith⟩ ⟨the *late* president⟩ **b** : RECENT ⟨a *late* discovery⟩ — **late·ness** *n*
[2]**late** *adv* **1 a** : after the usual or proper time ⟨came in *late*⟩ **b** : at or to an advanced point in time ⟨saw her *later* in the day⟩ **2** : not long ago : RECENTLY ⟨a man *late* of Chicago⟩ — **of late** : LATELY, RECENTLY
late·com·er \'lāt-ˌkəm-ər\ *n* : one who arrives late; *also* : a recent arrival

la·teen \lə-ˈtēn\ *adj* : of, relating to, or being a sailing rig of the Mediterranean characterized by a triangular sail extended by a long spar slung to a low mast

late·ly \ˈlāt-lē\ *adv* : RECENTLY

la·tent \ˈlāt-ənt\ *adj* : present but not visible or active ⟨*latent* abilities⟩ ⟨*latent* infection⟩ — **la·ten·cy** \-ən-sē\ *n* — **la·tent·ly** *adv*

syn LATENT, DORMANT, QUIESCENT, POTENTIAL can mean present but not active at a given moment. LATENT applies to qualities or powers that lie hidden in an undeveloped state; DORMANT applies to something that has sunk from activity to inactivity but can become active again ⟨a *dormant* volcano⟩; QUIESCENT suggests present inactivity without regard to an active past or future; POTENTIAL implies never yet having been activated or brought into being as such ⟨*potential* markets for a new product⟩ *ant* patent

[1]**lat·er·al** \ˈlat-ə-rəl, ˈla-trəl\ *adj* **1** : of or relating to the side : situated on, directed toward, or coming from the side **2** : of, relating to, or being part of a geometric solid that is not part of the base ⟨*lateral* face of a prism⟩ ⟨*lateral* area of a cylinder⟩ — **lat·er·al·ly** \-ē\ *adv*

[2]**lateral** *n* **1** : a lateral part or branch **2** : a lateral pass in football

lateral moraine *n* : a moraine deposited at the side of a glacier

lateral pass *n* : a pass in football thrown parallel to the line of scrimmage or away from the opponent's goal

lat·er·ite \ˈlat-ə-ˌrīt\ *n* : a residual product of rock decay that is red in color and has a high content in the oxides of iron and hydroxide of aluminum

la·tex \ˈlā-ˌteks\ *n, pl* **lat·i·ces** \ˈlat-ə-ˌsēz, ˈlāt-\ *or* **la·tex·es** **1** : a milky juice produced by the cells of various plants (as milkweeds, poppies, and the rubber tree) **2** : a water emulsion of a synthetic rubber or plastic used esp. in paints and adhesives — **lat·i·cif·er·ous** \ˌlat-ə-ˈsif-(ə-)rəs\ *adj*

lath \ˈlath\ *n, pl* **laths** \ˈlat͟hz, ˈlaths\ **1** : a thin narrow strip of wood used esp. as a base for plaster **2** : material (as wire cloth) used in sheets as a substitute for wooden laths **3** : a quantity of laths together — **lath** *vb*

lathe \ˈlāt͟h\ *n* : a machine in which a piece of material is held and turned while being shaped by a tool

[1]**lath·er** \ˈlat͟h-ər\ *n* **1 a** : foam formed when a detergent is agitated in water **b** : foam from sweating (as on a horse) **2** : an agitated state : DITHER — **lath·ery** \-(ə-)rē\ *adj*

[2]**lather** *vb* **lath·ered**; **lath·er·ing** \ˈlat͟h-(ə-)ring\ **1** : to spread lather over ⟨*lathered* his face⟩ **2** : to form lather or a froth like lather ⟨this soap *lathers* well⟩

[3]**lath·er** \ˈlath-ər, ˈlat͟h-\ *n* : a workman who makes or applies laths

lath·ing \ˈlath-ing, ˈlat͟h-\ *n* **1** : the action or process of placing laths **2** : a quantity or an installation of laths

lat·i·me·ria \ˌlat-ə-ˈmir-ē-ə\ *n* : any of a genus of living coelacanth fishes of deep seas off southern Africa — compare LOBE-FIN

ə abut	ər further	a back	ā bake	
ä cot, cart	au̇ out	ch chin	e less	ē easy
g gift	i trip	ī life	j joke	ng sing	ō flow
ȯ flaw	ȯi coin	th thin	t͟h this	ü loot
u̇ foot	y yet	yü few	yu̇ furious	zh vision

[1]**Lat·in** \ˈlat-ən\ *adj* **1** : of, relating to, or composed in Latin ⟨*Latin* grammar⟩ **2** : of or relating to that part of the Catholic Church that formerly used a Latin rite ⟨*Latin* liturgy⟩ **3** : of, relating to, or characteristic of the countries or peoples of Latin America

[2]**Latin** *n* **1** : the Italic language of ancient Rome **2** : an ancient Roman **3** : a member of one of the peoples speaking Romance languages; *esp* : a native or inhabitant of Latin America

lat·ish \ˈlāt-ish\ *adj or adv* : somewhat late

lat·i·tude \ˈlat-ə-ˌt(y)üd\ *n* **1 a** : distance north or south from the equator measured in degrees **b** : a region or locality as marked by its latitude **2** : freedom from narrow restrictions ⟨allowed great *latitude* in his editorials⟩ — **lat·i·tu·di·nal** \ˌlat-ə-ˈt(y)üd-(ə-)nəl\ *adj* — **lat·i·tu·di·nal·ly** \-ē\ *adv*

latitude 1a : hemisphere marked with parallels of latitude

la·trine \lə-ˈtrēn\ *n* **1** : a receptacle (as a pit in the earth) for use as a toilet **2** : TOILET

lat·ter \ˈlat-ər\ *adj* **1 a** : more recent : LATER **b** : of or relating to the end : FINAL **2** : of, relating to, or being the second of two things referred to

lat·ter·ly \-lē\ *adv* : RECENTLY

lat·tice \ˈlat-əs\ *n* **1 a** : a framework or structure of crossed wood or metal strips **b** : a window, door, or gate having a lattice **2** : a regular geometrical arrangement of points or objects over an area or in space ⟨the *lattice* of atoms in a crystal⟩ — **lat·ticed** \-əst\ *adj* — **lat·tice·work** \ˈlat-əs-ˌwərk\ *n*

[1]**Lat·vi·an** \ˈlat-vē-ən\ *adj* : of, relating to, or characteristic of Latvia, the Latvians, or Latvian

[2]**Latvian** *n* **1** : a native or inhabitant of Latvia **2** : the Baltic language of the Latvian people

laud \ˈlȯd\ *n* : PRAISE — **laud** *vb* — **lau·da·tion** \lȯ-ˈdā-shən\ *n*

laud·a·ble \ˈlȯd-ə-bəl\ *adj* : PRAISEWORTHY — **laud·a·bil·i·ty** \ˌlȯd-ə-ˈbil-ət-ē\ *n* — **laud·a·bly** \-blē\ *adv*

lau·da·num \ˈlȯd-(ə-)nəm\ *n* **1** : a formerly used preparation of opium **2** : a tincture of opium

lau·da·to·ry \ˈlȯd-ə-ˌtōr-ē, -ˌtȯr-\ *adj* : expressing praise

[1]**laugh** \ˈlaf, ˈlȧf\ *vb* **1 a** : to show mirth, joy, or scorn with a smile and chuckle or explosive sound **b** : to become amused or derisive ⟨*laughed* at his early efforts⟩ **2** : to utter with a laugh ⟨*laughs* her consent⟩ — **laugh·er** *n*

[2]**laugh** *n* **1** : the act or sound of laughing **2** : something funny

laugh·a·ble \ˈlaf-ə-bəl, ˈlȧf-\ *adj* : provoking laughter or derision : RIDICULOUS — **laugh·a·ble·ness** *n* — **laugh·a·bly** \-blē\ *adv*

laugh·ing *adj* : fit to be laughed at : LAUGHABLE ⟨no *laughing* matter⟩

laughing gas *n* : NITROUS OXIDE

laughing jackass *n* : KOOKABURRA

laugh·ing·ly \ˈlaf-ing-lē, ˈlȧf-\ *adv* : with laughter

laugh·ing·stock \-ing-ˌstäk\ *n* : an object of ridicule

laugh·ter \ˈlaf-tər, ˈlȧf-\ *n* : the action or sound of laughing

[1]**launch** \ˈlȯnch, ˈlänch\ *vb* [from Old French (northern dialect) *lancher*, from Latin *lanceare* "to wield a lance", from *lancea* "lance"] **1 a** : to throw or spring forward : HURL ⟨*launch* a spear⟩ **b** : to send off a self-propelled object ⟨*launch* a rocket⟩ **c** : to set a ship afloat **2 a** : to put in operation : BEGIN

⟨*launch* an attack⟩ **b** : to give a person a start ⟨*launched* his son in business⟩ **c** : to make a start esp. energetically ⟨*launched* on a difficult course⟩

2**launch** *n* : an act of launching

3**launch** *n* : a small motorboat used for pleasure or short-distance transportation

launch·er \'lȯn-chər, 'län-\ *n* **1** : a device for firing a grenade from a rifle **2** : a device for launching a rocket

launcher 2

launching pad *n* : a nonflammable platform from which a rocket can be launched

laun·der \'lȯn-dər, 'län-\ *vb* **laun·dered**; **laun·der·ing** \-d(ə-)riŋ\ [from Middle English *launder* meaning "a laundryman", from French *lavandier*, from medieval Latin *lavandarius*, from Latin *lavanda* "things to be washed", from *lavare* "to wash"] **1** : to wash or wash and iron clothing or household linens **2** : to undergo washing and ironing ⟨fabrics guaranteed to *launder* well⟩ — **laun·der·er** \-dər-ər\ *n* — **laun·dress** \-drəs\ *n*

laun·dry \'lȯn-drē, 'län-\ *n, pl* **-dries** **1** : clothes or linens that have been or are to be laundered **2** : a place where laundering is done

laun·dry·man \-mən\ *n* : a male laundry worker — **laun·dry·wom·an** \-ˌwu̇m-ən\ *n*

lau·re·ate \'lȯr-ē-ət, 'lär-\ *n* : a person honored for his achievements in an art or science; *esp* : POET LAUREATE — **laureate** *adj*

lau·rel \'lȯr-əl, 'lär-\ *n* **1** : any of a genus of trees or shrubs related to the sassafras and cinnamon; *esp* : a small evergreen tree of southern Europe with foliage used by the ancient Greeks to crown victors in various contests **2** : a tree or shrub (as a mountain laurel) that resembles the true laurel **3 a** : a crown of laurel **b** : HONOR, FAME

lav *abbr* lavatory

la·va \'läv-ə, 'lav-\ *n* : melted rock coming from a volcano; *also* : such rock that has cooled and hardened

lav·a·to·ry \'lav-ə-ˌtōr-ē, -ˌtȯr-\ *n, pl* **-ries** **1** : a vessel for washing; *esp* : a fixed basin with running water and drainpipe **2** : a room with lavatories and usu. with toilets **3** : WATER CLOSET

lave \'lāv\ *vb* **1 a** : WASH **b** *archaic* : BATHE **2** : to flow along or against ⟨water *laving* the shore⟩

lav·en·der \'lav-ən-dər\ *n* **1 a** : a Mediterranean mint widely cultivated for its narrow aromatic leaves and spikes of lilac-purple flowers **b** : the dried leaves and flowers of lavender used to perfume clothes and bed linen **2** : a pale purple

1**lav·ish** \'lav-ish\ *adj* **1** : spending or giving more than is necessary : EXTRAVAGANT ⟨*lavish* with money⟩ ⟨*lavish* of praise⟩ **2** : spent, produced, or given freely ⟨*lavish* gifts⟩ ⟨*lavish* hospitality⟩ — **lav·ish·ly** *adv* — **lav·ish·ness** *n*

2**lavish** *vb* : to spend or give freely : SQUANDER ⟨*lavish* affection on a person⟩

law \'lȯ\ *n* **1 a** : a rule of conduct or action laid down and enforced by the supreme governing authority (as the legislature) of a community or established by custom **b** : the whole collection of such rules ⟨the *law* of the land⟩ **c** : the control brought about by enforcing rules ⟨forces of *law* and order⟩ **2** : a basic rule or principle ⟨the *laws* of poetry⟩ **3** : a rule or principle stating something that always works in the same way under the same conditions ⟨the *law* of gravity⟩ **4** *cap* : the first part of the Jewish scriptures — compare HAGIOGRAPHA, PROPHETS **5** : trial in a court to determine what is just and right according to the laws ⟨go to *law*⟩ **6** : the department of knowledge that deals with laws and their interpretation and application ⟨study *law*⟩ **7 a** : the profession of a lawyer **b** : lawyers as a group

law–abid·ing \'lȯ-ə-ˌbīd-iŋ\ *adj* : obedient to the law

law·break·er \'lȯ-ˌbrā-kər\ *n* : a person who breaks the law — **law·break·ing** \-kiŋ\ *adj or n*

law·ful \'lȯ-fəl\ *adj* **1** : permitted by law ⟨*lawful* conduct⟩ **2** : recognized by law : RIGHTFUL ⟨the *lawful* owner⟩ — **law·ful·ly** \-f(ə-)lē\ *adv* — **law·ful·ness** \-fəl-nəs\ *n*

law·giv·er \'lȯ-ˌgiv-ər\ *n* **1** : one who gives a code of laws to a people **2** : LEGISLATOR

law·less \'lȯ-ləs\ *adj* **1** : having no laws : not based on or regulated by law ⟨the *lawless* society of the frontier⟩ **2** : not controlled by law : UNRULY, DISORDERLY ⟨*lawless* mob⟩ — **law·less·ly** *adv* — **law·less·ness** *n*

law·mak·er \'lȯ-ˌmā-kər\ *n* : LEGISLATOR — **law·mak·ing** \-kiŋ\ *adj or n*

1**lawn** \'lȯn, 'län\ *n* : a fine sheer linen or cotton fabric

2**lawn** *n* : ground (as around a house or in a park) covered with grass that is kept mowed

lawn mower *n* : a machine for cutting grass on lawns

law of conservation of energy : CONSERVATION OF ENERGY

law of conservation of mass : CONSERVATION OF MASS

law of definite proportions : a law in chemistry that states that every specific compound always contains the same elements in the same proportions by weight

law of dominance : MENDEL'S LAW 3

law of independent assortment : MENDEL'S LAW 2

law of multiple proportions : a law in chemistry that states that when two elements combine in more than one proportion to form two or more compounds the weights of one element that combine with a given weight of the other element are in the ratios of small whole numbers

law of segregation : MENDEL'S LAW 1

law of unit characters : MENDEL'S LAW 2

law·ren·ci·um \lȯ-'ren(t)-sē-əm\ *n* : a short-lived radioactive element produced from californium — see ELEMENT table

law·suit \'lȯ-ˌsüt\ *n* : a suit in law : a case before a court

law·yer \'lȯ-yər\ *n* : one whose profession is to conduct lawsuits for clients or to advise as to legal rights and obligations

lax \'laks\ *adj* **1** : not firm or tight : LOOSE **2** : not strict or stringent ⟨*lax* discipline⟩ — **lax·ly** *adv* — **lax·ness** *n*

1**lax·a·tive** \'lak-sət-iv\ *adj* : having a tendency to loosen or relax; *esp* : relieving constipation

2**laxative** *n* : a usu. mild laxative drug — compare PURGATIVE

lax·i·ty \'lak-sət-ē\ *n* : the quality or state of being lax ⟨*laxity* in discipline⟩

1**lay** \'lā\ *vb* **laid** \'lād\; **lay·ing** **1** : to beat or strike down ⟨*laid* him in the dust⟩ **2 a** : to put or set on or against a surface or in order ⟨*lay* the book on the table⟩ ⟨*lay* bricks⟩ **b** : to place for rest or sleep; *also* : BURY **3** : to produce and deposit eggs **4** : to cause to settle ⟨a shower *laid* the dust⟩; *also* : CALM, ALLAY ⟨*laid* his fears⟩ **5** : to spread over a surface ⟨*lay* plaster⟩ **6** : PREPARE, ARRANGE ⟨*lay* plans⟩ ⟨*lay* a table⟩ **7** : to deposit as a wager : BET ⟨I'll *lay* you $10 on that⟩ **8** : IMPOSE ⟨*lay* a tax on li-

L

quor⟩ ⟨*laid* the blame on him⟩ **9 :** to place or assign in one's scheme of things ⟨*lays* great stress on manners⟩ **10 :** to bring to a specified condition ⟨*lay* waste the land⟩ **11 :** to put forward : SUBMIT ⟨*lay* claim to an estate⟩ ⟨*laid* his case before the committee⟩ — **lay hold of :** GRASP, SEIZE

²**lay** *n* **:** the way in which a thing lies in relation to something else ⟨*lay* of the land⟩

³**lay** *past of* LIE

⁴**lay** *n* **:** BALLAD, SONG

⁵**lay** *adj* [from Old French *lai*, from Latin *laicus*, from Greek *laikos* meaning "of the people", from *laos* "people"] **:** of or relating to laymen or the laity ⟨*lay* public⟩

lay away *vb* **:** to put aside for future use or delivery

lay down *vb* **1 :** ESTABLISH, PRESCRIBE ⟨*lay down* standards⟩ **2 :** to assert or command dogmatically ⟨*lay down* the law⟩

¹**lay·er** \'lā-ər, 'le(-ə)r\ *n* **1 :** one that lays ⟨his hens were poor *layers*⟩ **2 :** one thickness or fold over or under another ⟨a *layer* of rock⟩ **3 a :** a shoot or branch of a plant that is treated to induce rooting (as by bending to the ground and covering with soil) while still attached to the parent plant **b :** a plant so produced — **lay·ered** \'lā-ərd, 'le(-ə)rd\ *adj*

²**layer** *vb* **:** to propagate a plant by layers

lay·ette \lā-'et\ *n* **:** an outfit of clothing and equipment for a newborn infant

lay·man \'lā-mən\ *n* **:** a person who is not a clergyman or a member of a particular profession — **lay-wom·an** \-,wu̇m-ən\ *n*

lay·off \'lā-,ȯf\ *n* **1 :** the act of laying off an employee or a work force **2 :** a period of inactivity or idleness

lay off \-'ȯf\ *vb* **1 :** to mark or measure off **2 :** to cease to employ usu. temporarily ⟨*lay off* workers⟩ **3 a :** to leave undisturbed ⟨*lay off* him — he's had enough⟩ **b :** AVOID, QUIT ⟨*lay off* smoking⟩

lay on *vb* **:** ATTACK, BEAT ⟨*laid on* to him with a stick⟩

lay·out \'lā-,au̇t\ *n* **1 :** ARRANGEMENT, PLAN ⟨the *layout* of a house⟩ **2 :** something laid out ⟨a model train *layout*⟩ **3 :** a set or outfit esp. of tools

lay out \-'au̇t\ *vb* **1 :** PLAN, ARRANGE ⟨*lay out* a campaign⟩ **2 :** to arrange for display or for working upon ⟨*lay out* an exhibit⟩ ⟨*lay out* materials for a dress⟩ **3 :** SPEND

lay·over \'lā-,ō-vər\ *n* **:** STOPOVER

lay over \-'ō-vər\ *vb* **:** to make a temporary halt or stop

lay–up \'lā-,əp\ *n* **:** a jumping one-hand shot in basketball made off the backboard from close under the basket

lay up \-'əp\ *vb* **1 :** to store up **2 :** to disable or confine with illness or injury

la·zy \'lā-zē\ *adj* **la·zi·er**; **-est** **1 :** not willing to act or work : INDOLENT **2 :** SLOW, SLUGGISH ⟨a *lazy* stream⟩ ***syn*** see IDLE — **la·zi·ly** \-zə-lē\ *adv* — **la-zi·ness** \-zē-nəs\ *n*

la·zy·bones \'lā-zē-,bōnz\ *n* **:** a lazy person

la·zy·ish \'lā-zē-ish\ *adj* **:** somewhat lazy

lb *abbr* [for Latin *libra*] pound

LCD *abbr* least common denominator

LCM *abbr* lowest common multiple

LD *abbr* lethal dose

lea \'lē, 'lā\ *n* **:** MEADOW, PASTURE

ə abut	ər further	a back	ā bake
ä cot, cart	au̇ out	ch chin	e less	ē easy
g gift	i trip	ī life	j joke	ng sing	ō flow
ȯ flaw	ȯi coin	th thin	t͟h this	ü loot
u̇ foot	y yet	yü few	yu̇ furious	zh vision

leach \'lēch\ *vb* **:** to pass a liquid through to carry off the soluble components; *also* **:** to dissolve out by such means ⟨*leach* minerals from rocks⟩

¹**lead** \'lēd\ *vb* **led** \'led\; **lead·ing** \'lēd-ing\ **1 a :** to guide esp. by going in advance : CONDUCT **b :** to direct on a course or in a direction **c :** to serve as a channel for ⟨pipes *lead* water into canals⟩ **d :** to lie, go, or open in a specified direction ⟨path *leads* uphill⟩ ⟨study *leading* to a degree⟩ **2 :** to go through : LIVE ⟨*lead* a quiet life⟩ **3 a :** to direct the activity of : MANAGE, DIRECT ⟨*lead* an orchestra⟩ ⟨*lead* a campaign⟩ **b :** to be first or foremost in ⟨*lead* the league⟩; *also* **:** BEGIN, OPEN ⟨*lead* off for the home team⟩ **c :** to have a margin over ⟨*led* his opponent⟩

²**lead** *n* **1 a :** position at the front : LEADERSHIP **b :** EXAMPLE, PRECEDENT **c :** a margin or distance ahead ⟨a 10-yard *lead*⟩ **2 :** INDICATION, CLUE **3 :** a principal role in a play; *also* **:** one who plays such a role **4 :** an introductory section of a news story; *also* **:** a news story of chief importance **5 :** the first in a series; *also* **:** the right to be first **6 :** an insulated electrical conductor **7 :** a position taken by a base runner off a base toward the next — **lead** *adj*

³**lead** \'led\ *n* **1 :** a heavy soft malleable bluish white metallic element that is found mostly in combination and is used esp. in pipes, cable sheaths, solder, and for type in printing — see ELEMENT table **2 a :** a mass of lead used on a line for finding the depth of water (as in the ocean) **b** *pl* **:** lead framing for glass (as in windows) **c :** a thin strip of metal used to separate lines of type in printing **3 :** a thin stick of marking substance (as graphite) in or for a pencil **4 :** BULLETS, PROJECTILES **5 :** TETRAETHYL LEAD

⁴**lead** \'led\ *vb* **lead·ed**; **lead·ing** **1 :** to cover, line, or weight with lead **2 :** to fix (window glass) in position with lead **3 :** to place lead or other spacing material between the lines of (type matter) **4 :** to treat or mix with lead or a lead compound ⟨*leaded* gasoline⟩

lead acetate *n* **:** a poisonous soluble salt used in dyeing and printing

lead arsenate *n* **:** a poisonous salt used as an insecticide

lead dioxide *n* **:** a poisonous compound that occurs as a mineral and is produced artificially and that is used as an oxidizing agent and in chemical storage cells — called also *lead peroxide*

lead·en \'led-ən\ *adj* **1 a :** made of lead **b :** of the color of lead : dull gray **2 :** low in quality : POOR **3 a :** oppressively heavy **b :** SLUGGISH, DULL

lead·er \'lēd-ər\ *n* **1 :** something that leads: as **a :** a main shoot of a plant **b :** TENDON, SINEW **c :** a short line for attaching the end of a fishing line to a lure or hook **d :** a pipe for conducting fluid **e :** an article offered at an attractive special low price to stimulate business **2 :** a person that leads: as **a :** GUIDE **b :** COMMANDER **c :** CONDUCTOR 2 **d :** a person in charge or in control : BOSS, CHIEF **3 :** a horse placed in front of the other horses of a team — **lead·er·less** \-ləs\ *adj* — **lead·er·ship** \-,ship\ *n*

lead–in \'lēd-,in\ *n* **:** something that leads in; *esp* **:** the part of a radio antenna that runs to the transmitting or receiving set — **lead–in** *adj*

lead·ing \'lēd-ing\ *adj* **1 :** coming or ranking first or among the first : FOREMOST **2 :** exercising leadership **3 :** GUIDING, DIRECTING ⟨*leading* question⟩

leading lady *n* **:** an actress who plays the leading feminine role in a play or movie

leading man *n* : an actor who plays the leading male role in a play or movie
leading tone *n* : the seventh musical degree of a major or minor scale — called also *subtonic*
lead monoxide *n* : a yellow to brownish red poisonous compound used in rubber and glass manufacture
lead nitrate *n* : a poisonous soluble salt used esp. in making fireworks
lead·off \'lēd-ˌȯf\ *n* **1** : a beginning action **2** : the player who heads the batting order or bats first in an inning in baseball — **lead–off** *adj*
lead on *vb* : to entice or induce to proceed in a course esp. when unwise or mistaken ⟨*led* her *on* to believe him⟩
lead pencil \'led-\ *n* : a pencil using graphite as the marking material
lead peroxide *n* : LEAD DIOXIDE
lead sulfide *n* : GALENA
lead up \'lēd-\ *vb* : to make a gradual or indirect approach to a topic
[1]**leaf** \'lēf\ *n, pl* **leaves** \'lēvz\ **1 a** : a usu. flat lateral

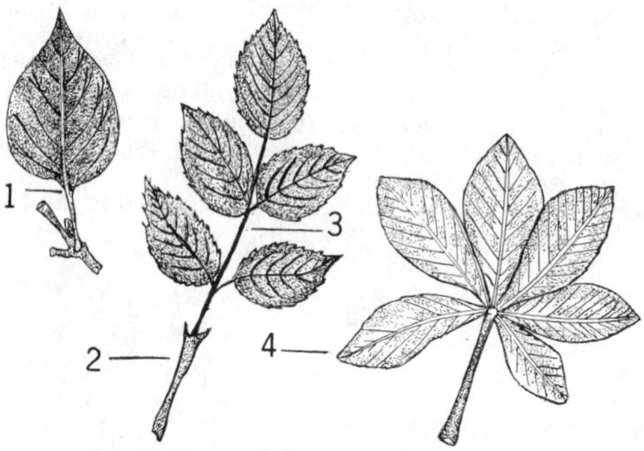

leaf 1a: 1, petiole; 2, stipule; 3, rachis; 4, leaflet

outgrowth from a plant stem that functions primarily in food manufacture by photosynthesis **b** : FOLIAGE **2 a** : a part of a book or folded sheet containing a page on each side **b** : a part (as of window shutters) that slides or is hinged **c** : the movable part of a table top **d** : a thin sheet (as of metal) **e** : one of the plates of a leaf spring — **leaf·less** \'lēf-ləs\ *adj* — **leaf·like** \-ˌlīk\ *adj*
[2]**leaf** *vb* **1** : to produce leaves **2** : to turn the pages of a book
leaf·age \'lē-fij\ *n* : FOLIAGE
leaf bud *n* : a bud that develops into a leafy shoot and does not produce flowers
leaf cutting *n* : a leaf or part of a leaf that is used to propagate a plant (as a begonia or African violet)
leaf·hop·per \'lēf-ˌhäp-ər\ *n* : any of numerous small leaping insects related to the cicadas that suck the juices of plants
leaf·let \'lēf-lət\ *n* **1 a** : one of the divisions of a compound leaf — see LEAF illustration **b** : a small or young foliage leaf **2** : PAMPHLET
leaf miner *n* : any of various small insects that as larvae burrow in and eat the tissue of leaves
leaf mold *n* : a compost or layer composed chiefly of decayed vegetable matter
leaf spring *n* : a spring made of overlying strips or leaves
leaf·stalk \'lēf-ˌstȯk\ *n* : PETIOLE
leafy \'lē-fē\ *adj* **leaf·i·er**; **-est** **1 a** : having or abounding in leaves ⟨*leafy* woodlands⟩ **b** : consisting mostly of leaves ⟨*leafy* vegetables⟩ **2** : resembling a leaf
[1]**league** \'lēg\ *n* : any of various units of distance from about 2.4 to 4.6 statute miles
[2]**league** *n* **1** : an association or alliance of nations **2** : an association of persons or groups united for common interests or goals ⟨baseball *leagues*⟩ — **league** *vb*
leagu·er \'lē-gər\ *n* : a member of a league
[1]**leak** \'lēk\ *vb* **1** : to enter or escape or permit to enter or escape accidentally or by mistake ⟨fumes *leak* in⟩ ⟨the secret *leaked* out⟩ **2** : to give out information surreptitiously ⟨*leaked* the story to the press before the official announcement⟩
[2]**leak** *n* **1** : something and esp. a crack or hole that admits or lets escape usu. accidentally **2** : LEAKAGE
leak·age \'lē-kij\ *n* **1 a** : the act, process, or an instance of leaking **b** : loss of electricity due esp. to faulty insulation **2** : something or the amount that is lost in a leak
leaky \'lē-kē\ *adj* **leak·i·er**; **-est** : permitting fluid to leak in or out ⟨a *leaky* boat⟩ ⟨a *leaky* fountain pen⟩ — **leak·i·ness** *n*
leal \'lēl\ *adj, chiefly Scot* : LOYAL, TRUE
[1]**lean** \'lēn\ *vb* **leaned** \'lēnd, *chiefly Brit* 'lent\; **lean·ing** \'lē-ning\ **1 a** : to incline or cause to incline or bend from an upright position ⟨the tree *leans* to one side⟩ ⟨*lean* a ladder against a wall⟩ **b** : to cast one's weight to one side for support ⟨*lean* on me⟩ **2** : to depend on **3** : to incline in opinion, taste, or desire ⟨*lean* toward simplicity⟩ ***syn*** see SLANT
[2]**lean** *n* : the act or an instance of leaning : INCLINATION
[3]**lean** *adj* **1 a** : lacking or deficient in flesh ⟨*lean* cattle⟩ **b** : containing little or no fat ⟨*lean* meat⟩ **2** : lacking richness or fullness ***syn*** see THIN ***ant*** fleshy — **lean·ness** \'lēn-nəs\ *n*
[4]**lean** *n* : the part of meat that consists principally of fat-free muscle
lean·ing \'lē-ning\ *n* : TENDENCY, INCLINATION
[1]**lean–to** \'lēn-ˌtü\ *n, pl* **lean–tos** : a wing of a building or a rough shed or shelter with a lean-to roof
[2]**lean–to** *adj* : having only one slope or pitch ⟨*lean-to* roof⟩
[1]**leap** \'lēp\ *vb* **leaped** *or* **leapt** \'lēpt, 'lept\; **leap·ing** \'lē-ping\ **1** : to spring or cause to spring free from or as if from the ground : JUMP ⟨*leap* over a fence⟩ **2 a** : to pass abruptly from one state or topic to another **b** : to act hastily ⟨*leaped* at the chance⟩ — **leap·er** \'lē-pər\ *n*
[2]**leap** *n* **1 a** : an act of leaping : SPRING, BOUND **b** : a place leaped over or from **c** : the distance covered by a leap **2** : a sudden change of state — **by leaps and bounds** : very rapidly ⟨improved *by leaps and bounds*⟩
leap·frog \'lēp-ˌfrȯg, -ˌfräg\ *n* : a game in which one player bends down and another leaps over him
leap year *n* : a year in the Gregorian calendar containing 366 days with February 29 as the extra day
learn \'lərn\ *vb* **learned** \'lərnd, 'lərnt\ *also* **learnt** \'lərnt\; **learn·ing** **1** : to gain knowledge or understanding of or skill in by study, instruction, or experience **2** : MEMORIZE ⟨*learn* the lines of a play⟩ **3 a** : to come to be able to ⟨*learn* to swim⟩ **b** : to come to realize **4** *substand* : TEACH **5** : to find out : ASCERTAIN **6** : to acquire knowledge ⟨never too late to *learn*⟩ — **learn·a·ble** \'lər-nə-bəl\ *adj* — **learn·er** *n*

L

learn·ed \'lər-nəd\ *adj* : possessing or displaying learning : SCHOLARLY — **learn·ed·ly** *adv* — **learn·ed·ness** *n*

learn·ing \'lər-niŋ\ *n* **1** : the act or experience of one that learns **2** : knowledge or skill acquired by instruction or study

[1]**lease** \'lēs\ *n* **1** : an agreement to hand over real estate for a period of time usu. for a specified rent; *also* : the act of leasing real estate **2** : the period for which something is leased ⟨a one-year *lease*⟩ **3** : property that is leased

[2]**lease** *vb* **1** : to grant by lease : LET **2** : to hold under a lease

leash \'lēsh\ *n* : a line for leading or restraining an animal — **leash** *vb*

[1]**least** \'lēst\ *adj* **1** : lowest in importance or position **2** : smallest in size or degree

[2]**least** *n* : one that is least : something of the lowest possible value, importance, or scope ⟨not to care in the *least*⟩ ⟨the *least* that can be said⟩ — **at least 1** : at the minimum **2** : in any case

[3]**least** *adv* : in the smallest or lowest degree

least common denominator *n* : the lowest common multiple of the denominators of two or more fractions

least common multiple *n* : LOWEST COMMON MULTIPLE

least·wise \'lēst-ˌwīz\ *adv* : at least

leath·er \'leth-ər\ *n* **1** : animal skin dressed for use **2** : something wholly or partly made of leather — **leather** *adj* — **leather** *vb*

leath·ern \'leth-ərn\ *adj* : made of or resembling leather

leath·er·neck \'leth-ər-ˌnek\ *n* : MARINE

leath·ery \'leth-(ə-)rē\ *adj* : resembling leather in appearance or texture : TOUGH

[1]**leave** \'lēv\ *vb* **left** \'left\; **leav·ing 1** : to allow or cause to remain behind ⟨*leave* your books at home⟩ **2** : DELIVER ⟨*leave* a book at the library⟩ ⟨the postman *left* three letters⟩ **3** : to have remaining ⟨*leave* a widow and two children⟩ ⟨taking 7 from 10 *leaves* 3⟩ **4** : to give by will : BEQUEATH **5** : to let stay without interference ⟨*leave* a kettle to boil⟩ ⟨*leave* someone alone⟩ **6** : to go away from a place ⟨*leave* at 10 o'clock⟩ ⟨*leave* the house⟩

[2]**leave** *n* **1 a** : PERMISSION **b** : authorized absence from duty or employment **2** : an act of leaving : DEPARTURE

[3]**leave** *vb* **leaved**; **leav·ing** : LEAF

leaved \'lēvd\ *adj* : having leaves ⟨broad-*leaved*⟩

[1]**leav·en** \'lev-ən\ *n* **1 a** : a substance (as yeast) used to produce a gaseous fermentation (as in dough) **b** : a material (as baking powder) used to produce a gas that makes dough or batter rise and become light **2** : something that modifies or lightens a mass ⟨a *leaven* of common sense⟩

[2]**leaven** *vb* **leav·ened**; **leav·en·ing** \'lev-(ə-)niŋ\ **1** : to raise (dough) with a leaven **2** : to mix or permeate with leaven

leave off *vb* : STOP, CEASE

leaves *pl of* LEAF

leave–tak·ing \'lēv-ˌtā-kiŋ\ *n* : an act of going away : FAREWELL

leav·ings \'lē-viŋz\ *n pl* : LEFTOVERS

Leb·a·nese \ˌleb-ə-'nēz, -'nēs\ *adj* : of, relating to, or characteristic of Lebanon or its people — **Lebanese** *n*

lec·tern \'lek-tərn\ *n* : a desk to read from while standing; *esp* : one from which scripture lessons are read in a church service

[1]**lec·ture** \'lek-chər\ *n* **1** : a discourse given before an audience or class esp. for instruction **2** : REPRIMAND, SCOLDING

[2]**lecture** *vb* **lec·tured**; **lec·tur·ing 1** : to give a lecture or a course of lectures **2** : to instruct by lectures **3** : REPRIMAND, SCOLD — **lec·tur·er** *n*

led *past of* LEAD

ledge \'lej\ *n* **1** : a projecting ridge or raised edge along a surface : SHELF **2** : an underwater ridge or reef esp. near the shore **3** : a narrow flat surface or shelf; *esp* : one that projects (as from a wall of rock)

led·ger \'lej-ər\ *n* : a book in which accounts are kept in final form

ledger line *n* : a short line added above or below a musical staff for notes that are too high or too low to be placed on the staff

[1]**lee** \'lē\ *n* **1** : protecting shelter **2** : the side (as of a ship) that is sheltered from the wind

[2]**lee** *adj* : of or relating to the lee

leech \'lēch\ *n* [formerly meaning "physician", from Old English *lǣce*; then applied to the worm which was frequently used by physicians for bleeding patients] **1** : any of numerous carnivorous or bloodsucking segmented usu. flattened worms having a sucker at each end **2** : a hanger-on who seeks advantage or gain : PARASITE

leek \'lēk\ *n* : a garden herb closely related to the onion and grown for its mildly pungent leaves and thick stalk

leek

leer \'li(ə)r\ *vb* : to cast a sly or sneering sidelong glance — **leer** *n*

leery \'li(ə)r-ē\ *adj* : SUSPICIOUS, WARY

lees \'lēz\ *n pl* : the settlings of liquor during fermentation and aging : DREGS

[1]**lee·ward** \'lē-wərd, 'lü-ərd\ *adj* : situated away from the wind : DOWNWIND — **leeward** *adv*

[2]**leeward** *n* : the lee side

lee·way \'lē-ˌwā\ *n* **1** : sideways movement of a ship when under way **2** : an allowable margin of freedom or variation : TOLERANCE ⟨allow enough *leeway* to arrive on time⟩

[1]**left** \'left\ *adj* **1** : of, relating to, or being the side of the body in which the heart is mostly located ⟨the *left* leg⟩ **2** : located nearer to the left side of the body than to the right ⟨the *left* arm of his chair⟩ — **left** *adv*

[2]**left** *n* **1** : the left side or the part on the left side **2** : the members of a European legislative body sitting to the left of the presiding officer and holding more radical views than other members **3** *cap* : political liberals or radicals; *also* : their beliefs

[3]**left** *past of* LEAVE

left–hand \ˌleft-ˌhand\ *adj* **1** : situated on the left **2** : LEFT-HANDED

left–hand·ed \'left-'han-dəd\ *adj* **1** : using the left hand more easily than the right **2** : relating to, designed for, or done with the left hand **3 a** : CLUMSY, AWKWARD **b** : INSINCERE, DUBIOUS ⟨*left-handed* compliment⟩ **4 a** : COUNTERCLOCKWISE **b** : having a structure involving a counterclockwise direction ⟨*left-handed* screw⟩ — **left–handed** *adv* — **left–**

ə abut	ər further	a back	ā bake	
ä cot, cart	au̇ out	ch chin	e less	ē easy
g gift	i trip	ī life	j joke	ŋ sing	ō flow
ȯ flaw	ȯi coin	th thin	th this	ü loot
u̇ foot	y yet	yü few	yu̇ furious	zh vision

hand·ed·ly *adv* — **left–hand·ed·ness** *n* — **left-hand·er** \-ˈhan-dər\ *n*
left·ist \ˈlef-təst\ *n* : a liberal or radical in politics — **leftist** *adj*
left·over \ˈleft-ˌō-vər\ *n* : something remaining; *esp* : food left over from one meal and served at another — **leftover** *adj*
left·ward \ˈleft-wərd\ *also* **left·wards** \-wərdz\ *adv* : toward or on the left — **leftward** *adj*
1leg \ˈleg\ *n* **1** : a limb of an animal used esp. for supporting the body and for walking; *esp* : the part of the vertebrate limb between the knee and foot **2** : something resembling an animal leg in shape or use ⟨*legs* of a table⟩ **3** : the part of an article of clothing that covers the leg **4** : either side of a triangle as distinguished from the base or hypotenuse **5 a** : a portion of a trip : STAGE **b** : one section of a relay race
2leg *vb* **legged**; **leg·ging 1** : WALK **2** : RUN
leg *abbr* legato
leg·a·cy \ˈleg-ə-sē\ *n, pl* **-cies** : something left to a person by or as if by will
le·gal \ˈlē-gəl\ *adj* **1** : of or relating to law or lawyers **2** : based on law ⟨a *legal* right⟩ **3** : permitted by law or established rules — **le·gal·ly** \-gə-lē\ *adv*
le·gal·i·ty \li-ˈgal-ət-ē\ *n, pl* **-ties** : the quality or state of being legal : LAWFULNESS
le·gal·ize \ˈlē-gə-ˌlīz\ *vb* : to make legal; *esp* : to give legal validity to — **le·gal·i·za·tion** \ˌlē-gə-lə-ˈzā-shən\ *n*
legal tender *n* : currency that the law authorizes a debtor to pay with and requires a creditor to accept
leg·ate \ˈleg-ət\ *n* : an official representative (as an ambassador or envoy)
leg·a·tee \ˌleg-ə-ˈtē\ *n* : a person to whom a legacy is bequeathed
le·ga·tion \li-ˈgā-shən\ *n* **1** : a diplomatic mission; *esp* : one headed by a minister **2** : the official residence and office of a diplomatic minister
le·ga·to \li-ˈgät-ō\ *adv or adj* : in a manner that is smooth and connected — used as a direction in music
leg bone *n* : any bone of a vertebrate leg; *esp* : TIBIA
leg·end \ˈlej-ənd\ *n* [from medieval Latin *legenda*, meaning "something to be read", from Latin *legere* "to read"] **1** : a story coming down from the past whose truth is popularly accepted but cannot be checked **2 a** : an inscription or title on an object **b** : CAPTION 2 **c** : an explanatory list of the symbols on a map or chart
leg·end·ary \ˈlej-ən-ˌder-ē\ *adj* **1** : of or resembling a legend ⟨*legendary* heroes⟩ **2** : consisting of legends ⟨*legendary* writings⟩
leg·er·de·main \ˌlej-ərd-ə-ˈmān\ *n* **1** : SLEIGHT OF HAND **2** : an artful deception
legged \ˈleg(-ə)d\ *adj* : having legs ⟨four-*legged*⟩
leg·ging \ˈleg-ən, ˈleg-ing\ *n* : a covering for the leg — usu. used in pl.
leg·horn \ˈleg-ˌ(h)ȯrn, ˈleg-ərn\ *n* [from *Leghorn*, city in Tuscany, Italy] **1 a** : a fine plaited straw made from an Italian wheat **b** : a hat of this straw **2** : any of a Mediterranean breed of small hardy fowls noted for their large production of white eggs
leg·i·ble \ˈlej-ə-bəl\ *adj* : capable of being read : PLAIN — **leg·i·bil·i·ty** \ˌlej-ə-ˈbil-ət-ē\ *n* — **leg·i·bly** \ˈlej-ə-blē\ *adv*
le·gion \ˈlē-jən\ *n* **1** : the principal unit of the Roman army comprising 3000 to 6000 foot soldiers with cavalry **2** : ARMY 1a **3** : a very large number : MULTITUDE
1le·gion·ary \ˈlē-jə-ˌner-ē\ *adj* : of, relating to, or constituting a legion
2legionary *n, pl* **-ar·ies** : LEGIONNAIRE
le·gion·naire \ˌlē-jə-ˈna(ə)r, -ˈne(ə)r\ *n* : a member of a legion
leg·is·late \ˈlej-ə-ˌslāt\ *vb* **1** : to make or enact laws **2** : to cause, create, or bring about by legislation
leg·is·la·tion \ˌlej-ə-ˈslā-shən\ *n* **1** : the action of making laws **2** : the laws made by a legislator or legislative body
leg·is·la·tive \ˈlej-ə-ˌslāt-iv\ *adj* **1** : having the power of legislating ⟨the *legislative* branch⟩ **2** : of or relating to a legislature or legislation — **leg·is·la·tive·ly** *adv*
leg·is·la·tor \ˈlej-ə-ˌslāt-ər\ *n* : a person who makes laws; *esp* : a member of a legislature
leg·is·la·ture \ˈlej-ə-ˌslā-chər\ *n* : an organized body of persons having the authority to make laws for a political unit
1le·git·i·mate \li-ˈjit-ə-mət\ *adj* **1** : born of parents who are married ⟨*legitimate* children⟩ **2** : LAWFUL ⟨a *legitimate* claim⟩ **3** : being in keeping with what is right or with standards ⟨a *legitimate* excuse for absence⟩ — **le·git·i·ma·cy** \-mə-sē\ *n* — **le·git·i·mate·ly** *adv*
2le·git·i·mate \-ˌmāt\ *vb* : to make lawful or legal — **le·git·i·ma·tion** \li-ˌjit-ə-ˈmā-shən\ *n*
le·git·i·mize \li-ˈjit-ə-ˌmīz\ *vb* : LEGITIMATE
leg·less \ˈleg-ləs\ *adj* : having no legs ⟨*legless* insect⟩
leg·man \ˈleg-ˌman\ *n* **1** : a newspaperman assigned usu. to gather information **2** : an assistant who gathers information and runs errands
leg·ume \ˈleg-ˌyüm, li-ˈgyüm\ *n* **1 a** : any of a large family of dicotyledonous herbs, shrubs, and trees having fruits that are dry single-celled pods and split into two valves when ripe, bearing nodules on the roots that contain nitrogen-fixing bacteria, and including important food and forage plants (as peas, beans, or clovers) **b** : the part (as seeds or pods) of a legume used as food **2** : the pod characteristic of a legume — **le·gu·mi·nous** \li-ˈgyü-mə-nəs, le-\ *adj*
leg·work \ˈleg-ˌwərk\ *n* : the work of a legman
lei \ˈlā, ˈlā-ˌē\ *n* [from Hawaiian] : a wreath or necklace usu. of flowers
lei·sure \ˈlēzh-ər, ˈlezh-, ˈlāzh-\ *n* **1** : freedom from work or duties **2** : EASE **3** : time at one's command : CONVENIENCE ⟨do the report at your *leisure*⟩ — **leisure** *adj*
lei·sure·ly \-ər-lē\ *adj* : characterized by leisure : UNHURRIED ⟨a *leisurely* pace⟩ — **lei·sure·li·ness** *n* — **leisurely** *adv*
LEM *abbr* lunar excursion module
lem·ming \ˈlem-ing\ *n* : any of several small short-tailed northern rodents with furry feet and small ears; *esp* : a European rodent that participates in recurring mass migrations which often continue into the sea where vast numbers are drowned

lemming (up to 7 in. long)

lem·on \ˈlem-ən\ *n* **1 a** : a yellow oblong citrus fruit with an acid juicy center and a rind that yields a fragrant oil **b** : the stout thorny citrus tree that bears lemons **2** : the color of ripe lemons **3** : DUD, FAILURE ⟨the new car is a *lemon*⟩ — **lemon** *adj*
lem·on·ade \ˌlem-ə-ˈnād\ *n* : a drink made of lemon juice, sugar, and water
lemon balm *n* : a perennial Old World mint often grown for its fragrant lemon-flavored leaves

le·mur \'lē-mər\ *n* : any of numerous tree-dwelling mostly nocturnal mammals that are related to the monkeys and usu. have a muzzle like a fox, large eyes, very soft woolly fur, and a long furry tail

lemur
(about 4 ft. long)

lend \'lend\ *vb* **lent** \'lent\; **lend·ing** **1** : to allow the use of something on the condition that it or its equivalent be returned ⟨*lend* a book⟩ ⟨*lend* money⟩ **2** : to give for the time being ⟨*lend* assistance⟩ **3** : to have the quality or nature that makes suitable ⟨a voice that *lends* itself to singing in opera⟩ — **lend·er** *n*

length \'leng(k)th\ *n* **1 a** : the longer or longest dimension of an object **b** : a measured distance or dimension ⟨10-inch *length*⟩ **c** : the quality or state of being long ⟨criticized the *length* of the story⟩ **2 a** : duration or extent in time ⟨the *length* of an interview⟩ **b** : relative duration or stress of a sound **3** : the length of something taken as a unit of measure ⟨horse led by a *length*⟩ **4** : a single piece constituting one of a series of pieces that may be joined together : SECTION ⟨a *length* of pipe⟩ — **at length** **1** : COMPREHENSIVELY, FULLY **2** : at last : FINALLY

length·en \'leng(k)-thən\ *vb* **length·ened**; **length·en·ing** \'leng(k)th-(ə-)ning\ : to make or become longer — **length·en·er** \-(ə-)nər\ *n*

length·ways \'leng(k)th-,wāz\ *adv* : LENGTHWISE

length·wise \-,wīz\ *adv* : in the direction of the length ⟨fold the paper *lengthwise*⟩ — **lengthwise** *adj*

lengthy \'leng(k)-thē\ *adj* **length·i·er**; **-est** : very long; *esp* : OVERLONG ⟨a *lengthy* speech⟩ — **length·i·ly** \-thə-lē\ *adv* — **length·i·ness** \-thē-nəs\ *n*

le·ni·en·cy \'lē-nē-ən-sē\ *or* **le·ni·ence** \-ən(t)s\ *n* : the quality or state of being lenient ***syn*** see MERCY

le·ni·ent \'lē-nē-ənt\ *adj* : of mild and tolerant disposition or effect : MERCIFUL — **le·ni·ent·ly** *adv*

len·i·ty \'len-ət-ē\ *n* : MILDNESS, LENIENCY

lens \'lenz\ *n* [from Latin (stem *lent-*) meaning "lentil"; so called from its shape; English *lentil* is from a Latin diminutive of this same word] **1** : a piece of transparent substance (as glass) that has two opposite regular surfaces either both curved or one curved and the other plane and that is used either singly or combined in an optical instrument for forming an image by focusing rays of light **2** : a device for directing or focusing radiation (as sound waves or electrons) other than light **3** : something shaped like a double-convex optical lens ⟨a mineral occurring in the form of *lenses*⟩ **4** : a transparent nearly spherical body in the eye that focuses light rays (as upon the retina)

Lent \'lent\ *n* [from Old English *lengten* "springtime", coming from a prehistoric Germanic compound meaning "long day"] : a period of penitence and fasting observed on the 40 weekdays from Ash Wednesday to Easter by many churches — **Lent·en** \'lent-ən\ *adj*

len·ti·cel \'lent-ə-,sel\ *n* : a pore in a stem of a woody plant through which gases are exchanged between the atmosphere and the stem tissues

len·til \'lent-əl\ *n* : a Eurasian annual legume widely grown for its flattened edible seeds and leafy stalks used as fodder; *also* : its seed

len·to \'len-,tō\ *adv or adj* : in a slow manner — used as a direction in music

Leo \'lē-ō\ *n* — see ZODIAC table

le·o·nine \'lē-ə-,nīn\ *adj* : of, relating to, or resembling a lion

leop·ard \'lep-ərd\ *n* : a large strong cat of southern Asia and Africa that is usu. tawny or buff with black spots arranged in broken rings or rosettes — called also *panther* — **leop·ard·ess** \-əs\ *n*

leopard
(about 2½ ft. at shoulder)

leopard frog *n* : the common spotted frog of the eastern U.S.

le·o·tard \'lē-ə-,tärd\ *n* **1** : a close-fitting garment usu. with long sleeves, a high neck, and ankle-length legs worn by dancers, acrobats, and aerialists **2** *pl* : TIGHTS

lep·er \'lep-ər\ *n* **1** : a person affected with leprosy **2** : OUTCAST

lep·i·dop·ter·an \,lep-ə-'däp-tə-rən\ *n* [from the scientific Latin name of the order *Lepidoptera*, from Greek *lepid-*, stem of *lepis* "scale" and *pteron* "wing"] : any of a large order of insects that comprise the butterflies, moths, and skippers and that as adults have four wings usu. covered with minute overlapping often brightly colored scales, and as larvae are caterpillars — **lepidopteran** *adj* — **lep·i·dop·ter·ous** \-tə-rəs\ *adj*

lep·i·dop·ter·on \-tə-rən, -,rän\ *n, pl* **-tera** \-rə\ : LEPIDOPTERAN

lep·re·chaun \'lep-rə-,kän, -,kȯn\ *n* : a mischievous elf of Irish folklore usu. believed to reveal the hiding place of treasure if caught

lep·ro·sy \'lep-rə-sē\ *n* : a chronic bacterial disease marked by slow-growing spreading swellings accompanied by loss of sensation, wasting, and deformities

lep·rous \'lep-rəs\ *adj* : infected with, relating to, or resembling leprosy — **lep·rous·ness** *n*

les·bi·an \'lez-bē-ən\ *adj, often cap* : of or relating to homosexuality between females — **lesbian** *n, often cap* — **les·bi·an·ism** \-bē-ə-,niz-əm\ *n*

lese maj·es·ty *or* **lèse ma·jes·té** \'lēz-'maj-ə-stē\ *n* **1 a** : a crime committed against a sovereign power **b** : an offense violating the dignity of a ruler **2** : AFFRONT

le·sion \'lē-zhən\ *n* **1** : INJURY, HARM **2** : a structural change in an organ or part due to injury or disease; *esp* : one that is clearly distinguishable from nearby healthy tissue

les·pe·de·za \,les-pə-'dē-zə\ *n* : any of a genus of herbaceous or shrubby leguminous plants including some widely used for forage, soil improvement, and esp. hay

[1]**less** \'les\ *adj* **1** : of a smaller number : FEWER ⟨*less* than three⟩ **2** : of lower rank, degree, or importance ⟨no *less* a person than the principal⟩ **3 a** : SMALLER, SLIGHTER **b** : more limited in quantity ⟨in *less* time⟩

[2]**less** *adv* : to a lesser extent or degree ⟨*less* difficult⟩

[3]**less** *prep* : diminished by ⟨full price *less* the discount⟩

ə abut ər further a back ā bake
ä cot, cart aủ out ch chin e less ē easy
g gift i trip ī life j joke ŋ sing ō flow
ȯ flaw ȯi coin th thin th this ü loot
ů foot y yet yü few yů furious zh vision

[4]**less** *n, pl* **less** **1** : a smaller portion or quantity ⟨spent *less* than usual⟩ **2** : something of less importance ⟨could have killed him for *less*⟩

-less \ləs\ *adj suffix* **1** : destitute of : not having ⟨wit*less*⟩ ⟨child*less*⟩ **2** : unable to be acted on or to act (in a specified way) ⟨daunt*less*⟩ ⟨fade*less*⟩

les·see \le-'sē\ *n* : a tenant under a lease

less·en \'les-ən\ *vb* **less·ened**; **less·en·ing** \-(ə-)niŋ\ : to make or become less : DECREASE ⟨the possibility of recovery *lessened*⟩

[1]**less·er** \'les-ər\ *adj* **1** : LESS, SMALLER ⟨the *lesser* evil⟩ **2** : INFERIOR ⟨the *lesser* nobility⟩

[2]**lesser** *adv* : LESS ⟨*lesser*-known⟩

lesser celandine *n* : CELANDINE 2

les·son \'les-ən\ *n* **1** : a passage from sacred writings read in a service of worship **2 a** : a piece or a short period of instruction : TEACHING; *esp* : a reading or exercise to be studied by a pupil **b** : something learned by study or experience ⟨the *lessons* of history⟩ **3** : an instructive example

les·sor \'les-,ȯr, le-'sȯ(ə)r\ *n* : one that leases property to another

lest \(,)lest\ *conj* **1** : for fear that ⟨bound him *lest* he should escape⟩ **2** : THAT — used after expressions of fear ⟨worried *lest* he should be late⟩

[1]**let** \'let\ *n* : HINDRANCE, OBSTACLE ⟨talk without *let* or hindrance⟩

[2]**let** *vb* **let**; **let·ting** **1** : to cause to : MAKE ⟨*let* it be known⟩ **2 a** : RENT, LEASE ⟨*let* rooms⟩ **b** : to assign esp. after bids ⟨*let* a contract⟩ **3 a** : to allow to ⟨live and *let* live⟩ **b** — used in the imperative to introduce a request or proposal ⟨*let* us pray⟩ **4** : to allow to go or pass ⟨*let* them through⟩

-let \lət\ *n suffix* **1** : small one ⟨book*let*⟩ **2** : article worn on ⟨wrist*let*⟩

let·down \'let-,dau̇n\ *n* **1** : DISAPPOINTMENT **2** : a slackening of effort : RELAXATION

let down \-'dau̇n\ *vb* **1** : to fail to support : DESERT ⟨*let down* a friend in a crisis⟩ **2** : DISAPPOINT ⟨the end of the story *lets* the reader *down*⟩

[1]**le·thal** \'lē-thəl\ *adj* : causing or capable of causing death — **le·thal·ly** \'lē-thə-lē\ *adv*

[2]**lethal** *n* : an abnormality of genetic origin causing the death of the organism possessing it

lethal gene *n* : a gene capable of preventing development or causing the death of an organism or its germ cells — called also *lethal factor*

leth·ar·gy \'leth-ər-jē\ *n* **1** : abnormal drowsiness **2** : the quality or state of being lazy or indifferent — **le·thar·gic** \lə-'thär-jik, le-\ *adj* — **le·thar·gi·cal·ly** \-ji-k(ə-)lē\ *adv*

let on *vb* **1** : ADMIT, REVEAL ⟨didn't *let on* he was the author⟩ ⟨don't *let on* that I told you⟩ **2** : PRETEND ⟨not so surprised as he *let on*⟩

let's \(,)lets, (,)les\ : let us

Lett \'let\ *n* : a member of a people closely related to the Lithuanians and mainly inhabiting Latvia : LATVIAN

[1]**let·ter** \'let-ər\ *n* **1** : a symbol in writing or print that stands for a speech sound and constitutes a unit of an alphabet **2** : a written or printed message addressed to a person or organization **3** *pl* **a** : LITERATURE **b** : LEARNING **4** : the strict meaning ⟨the *letter* of the law⟩ **5** : a single piece of type

[2]**letter** *vb* : to mark with letters — **let·ter·er** \-ər-ər\ *n*

let·tered \'let-ərd\ *adj* **1 a** : LEARNED, EDUCATED **b** : of or relating to learning **2** : inscribed with letters ⟨a *lettered* sign⟩

let·ter·head \'let-ər-,hed\ *n* : stationery having a printed or engraved heading; *also* : the heading itself

let·ter·ing *n* : letters used in an inscription

let·ter–per·fect \,let-ər-'pər-fikt\ *adj* : correct to the smallest detail; *esp* : VERBATIM

let·ter·press \'let-ər-,pres\ *n* **1** : printing done directly by impressing the paper on an inked raised surface **2** : printed reading matter

Lett·ish \'let-ish\ *adj* : of or relating to the Latvians or their language — **Lettish** *n*

let·tuce \'let-əs\ *n* : a common garden vegetable related to the daisies that has crisp succulent leaves used esp. in salads

let up \'let-'əp\ *vb* **1** : to slow down **2** : CEASE, STOP ⟨the rain *let up*⟩ **3** : to ease off ⟨*let up* on the gas⟩ — **let·up** \-,əp\ *n*

leu·cine \'lü-,sēn\ *n* : an amino acid that is essential in the nutrition of man

leu·co·plast \'lü-kə-,plast\ *n* : a colorless plastid of a plant cell usu. concerned with starch formation and storage

leu·ke·mia \lü-'kē-mē-ə\ *n* : a cancerous disease of warm-blooded animals (as man) in which leukocytes increase abnormally in the tissues and often in the blood — **leu·ke·mic** \-mik\ *adj*

leu·ko·cyte *also* **leu·co·cyte** \'lü-kə-,sīt\ *n* : a white or colorless blood cell having a nucleus — **leu·ko·cyt·ic** \,lü-kə-'sit-ik\ *adj*

lev- *or* **levo-** *comb form* : turning light to the left ⟨*lev*ulose⟩

le·va·tor \li-'vāt-ər\ *n, pl* **lev·a·to·res** \,lev-ə-'tōr-(,)ēz\ *or* **le·va·tors** \li-'vāt-ərz\ : a muscle that serves to raise a body part

[1]**lev·ee** \'lev-ē; lə-'vē, -'vā\ *n* : RECEPTION; *esp* : one held by a person of distinction orig. on rising from bed

[2]**lev·ee** \'lev-ē\ *n* **1** : an embankment to prevent flooding **2** : a river landing place

[1]**lev·el** \'lev-əl\ *n* **1** : a device for establishing a horizontal line or plane ⟨a carpenter's *level*⟩ **2** : horizontal position **3** : a condition of liquids marked by a horizontal surface ⟨water seeks its own *level*⟩ **4** : a horizontal line or surface taken as an index of altitude ⟨placed at eye *level*⟩ **5 a** : a flat surface **b** : FLOOR **6** : a step or stage in height, position, or rank ⟨students at the same *level* of learning⟩ — **on the level** : bona fide : HONEST ⟨find out if his offer is *on the level*⟩

[2]**level** *vb* **lev·eled** *or* **lev·elled**; **lev·el·ing** *or* **lev·el·ling** \'lev-(ə-)liŋ\ **1 a** : to make horizontal **b** : to make flat or level **2** : AIM, DIRECT **3** : to bring to a common level or plane : EQUALIZE **4** : to lay level with the ground : RAZE **5** : to attain or come to a level ⟨the plane *leveled* off at 10,000 feet⟩ — **lev·el·er** *or* **lev·el·ler** \-(ə-)lər\ *n*

[3]**level** *adj* **1** : having a flat even surface ⟨a *level* lawn⟩ **2** : being on a line with the floor or even ground : HORIZONTAL ⟨in a *level* position⟩ **3** : of the same height or rank : being on a line : EVEN ⟨water *level* with his shoulders⟩ **4** : steady and cool in judgment ⟨a *level* head⟩ — **level best** : very best

lev·el·head·ed \,lev-əl-'hed-əd\ *adj* : having sound judgment : SENSIBLE — **lev·el·head·ed·ness** *n*

[1]**lev·er** \'lev-ər, 'lē-vər\ *n* **1** : a bar used for prying or dislodging something **2** : a rigid bar used to exert a pressure or sustain a weight at one point of its length by the application of a force at a second and turning at a third on a fulcrum **3** : a projecting piece by which a mechanism is operated or adjusted

[2]**lever** *vb* **lev·ered**; **lev·er·ing** \'lev-(ə-)riŋ, 'lēv-\ : to pry, raise, or move with a lever

lev·er·age \'lev-(ə-)rij, 'lēv-\ *n* : the action of a lever or the mechanical advantage gained by it

le·vi·a·than \li-'vī-ə-thən\ *n* **1** *often cap* : a sea monster often symbolizing evil in the Old Testament and Christian literature **2** : something very large or powerful of its kind

Le·vi's \'lē-ˌvīz\ *trademark* — used for close-fitting heavy blue denim pants reinforced at strain points with copper rivets

Le·vit·i·cus \li-'vit-i-kəs\ *n* — see BIBLE table

lev·i·ty \'lev-ət-ē\ *n, pl* **-ties** : lack of earnestness in conduct or character : FRIVOLITY

lev·u·lose \'lev-yə-ˌlōs\ *n* : FRUCTOSE

1**levy** \'lev-ē\ *n, pl* **lev·ies** **1 a** : the imposition of an assessment **b** : an amount levied **2 a** : the raising of men for military service **b** : troops raised by levy

2**levy** *vb* **lev·ied**; **levy·ing** **1** : to impose or collect by legal authority ⟨*levy* a tax⟩ ⟨*levy* a fine⟩ **2** : to enlist or conscript for military service **3** : to carry on : WAGE ⟨*levy* war⟩ — **lev·i·er** *n*

lewd \'lüd\ *adj* **1** : sexually unchaste : LUSTFUL **2** : OBSCENE — **lewd·ly** *adv* — **lewd·ness** *n*

lex·i·cog·ra·phy \ˌlek-sə-'käg-rə-fē\ *n* **1** : the editing or making of a dictionary **2** : the principles and practices of dictionary making — **lex·i·cog·ra·pher** \-fər\ *n* — **lex·i·co·graph·ic** \-kō-'graf-ik\ *or* **lex·i·co·graph·i·cal** \-'graf-i-kəl\ *adj*

lex·i·con \'lek-sə-ˌkän, -si-kən\ *n* : DICTIONARY

Ley·den jar \ˌlīd-ən-\ *n* : a device for storing electric charge consisting of a glass jar coated inside and outside with metal foil and having the inner coating connected to a conducting rod passed through the insulating stopper

Leyden jar

lf *abbr* low frequency

lg *abbr* large

LH *abbr* left hand

LI *abbr* Long Island

li·a·bil·i·ty \ˌlī-ə-'bil-ət-ē\ *n, pl* **-ties** **1** : the state of being liable ⟨*liability* for his debts⟩ ⟨*liability* to disease⟩ **2** *pl* : that for which a person is liable : DEBTS **3** : DRAWBACK, DISADVANTAGE ⟨his short height is a *liability*⟩

li·a·ble \'lī-ə-bəl\ *adj* **1** : bound by law : OBLIGATED, RESPONSIBLE ⟨*liable* for damage done to a neighbor's property⟩ ⟨men *liable* for military service⟩ **2** : exposed to or likely to experience something undesirable ⟨*liable* to slip⟩ ⟨*liable* to be hurt⟩ **3** : SUSCEPTIBLE ⟨*liable* to disease⟩

li·ai·son \'lē-ə-ˌzän, lē-'ā-\ *n* **1** : a connecting link; *esp* : a linking or coordinating of activities **2** : communication esp. between parts of an armed force

li·a·na \lē-'än-ə, -'an-ə\ *or* **li·ane** \-'än, -'an\ *n* : a climbing plant; *esp* : one with a woody stem in a tropical rain forest

li·ar \'lī(-ə)r\ *n* : one that tells lies

lib \'lib\ *n* **1** *slang* : LIBERAL **2** *slang* : LIBERATION

lib *abbr* **1** librarian **2** library

li·ba·tion \lī-'bā-shən\ *n* : the act of pouring a liquid (as wine) in honor of a god; *also* : the liquid poured out — **li·ba·tion·ary** \-shə-ˌner-ē\ *adj*

1**li·bel** \'lī-bəl\ *n* **1** : the action or the crime of injuring a person's reputation in print or writing or by a visible representation (as a picture) — compare SLANDER **2** : a spoken or written statement or a representation that gives an unjustly unfavorable impression of a person or thing — **li·bel·ous** *or* **li·bel·lous** \-bə-ləs\ *adj*

ə abut	ər further	a back		ā bake
ä cot, cart	aú out	ch chin	e less	ē easy
g gift	i trip	ī life	j joke	ng sing
ō flow	ȯ flaw	ȯi coin	th thin	t͟h this
ü loot	u̇ foot	y yet	yü few	yu̇ furious
zh vision				

2**libel** *vb* **li·beled** *or* **li·belled**; **li·bel·ing** *or* **li·bel·ling** : to make or publish a libel against — **li·bel·er** *or* **li·bel·ler** \-bə-lər\ *n*

1**lib·er·al** \'lib(-ə)-rəl\ *adj* **1** : of, relating to, or based on the liberal arts ⟨a *liberal* education⟩ **2 a** : GENEROUS ⟨a *liberal* giver⟩ **b** : AMPLE, BOUNTIFUL ⟨a *liberal* portion of ham⟩ **3** : BROAD-MINDED, TOLERANT; *esp* : not bound by orthodox or traditional forms or beliefs **4** : of, favoring, or based on the principles of liberalism : not conservative — **lib·er·al·i·za·tion** \ˌlib(-ə)-rə-lə-'zā-shən\ *n* — **lib·er·al·ize** \-rə-ˌlīz\ *vb* — **lib·er·al·ly** \-rə-lē\ *adv*

2**liberal** *n* : one who is liberal esp. in politics

liberal arts *n pl* : the studies (as literature, philosophy, mathematics, history, or pure science) in a college or university intended to provide chiefly general knowledge and to develop general intellectual capacities

lib·er·al·ism \'lib(-ə)-rə-ˌliz-əm\ *n* : a political philosophy based on belief in progress, the essential goodness of man, and individual freedom and standing for the protection of political and civil liberties

lib·er·al·i·ty \ˌlib-ə-'ral-ət-ē\ *n, pl* **-ties** **1** : GENEROSITY **2** : BROAD-MINDEDNESS

lib·er·ate \'lib-ə-ˌrāt\ *vb* **1** : to free from bondage or restraint : set at liberty ⟨*liberate* a prisoner⟩ ⟨*liberate* the mind from worry⟩ **2** : to free (as a gas) from chemical combination — **lib·er·a·tion** \ˌlib-ə-'rā-shən\ *n* — **lib·er·a·tor** \'lib-ə-ˌrāt-ər\ *n*

lib·er·tar·i·an \ˌlib-ər-'ter-ē-ən\ *n* : one who upholds liberty of thought and action — **libertarian** *adj* — **lib·er·tar·i·an·ism** \-ē-ə-ˌniz-əm\ *n*

lib·er·tine \'lib-ər-ˌtēn\ *n* : a person who is unrestrained by convention or morality; *specif* : one leading a dissolute life — **libertine** *adj*

lib·er·ty \'lib-ərt-ē\ *n, pl* **-ties** **1** : the condition of those who are free and independent : FREEDOM **2** : power to do what one pleases : freedom from restraint ⟨give a child some *liberty*⟩ **3** : permission for a sailor to go ashore off duty **4** : the act of a person who is too free or bold or familiar ⟨take *liberties* with a stranger⟩ — **at liberty** **1** : not confined **2** : at leisure : not busy **3** : having the right : FREE ⟨*at liberty* to go or stay⟩

Li·bra \'lī-brə, 'lē-\ *n* — see ZODIAC table

li·brar·i·an \lī-'brer-ē-ən\ *n* : a specialist in the care or management of a library — **li·brar·i·an·ship** \-ˌship\ *n*

li·brary \'lī-ˌbrer-ē\ *n, pl* **-brar·ies** [from medieval Latin *librarium*, from Latin *liber* "book"] **1** : a place in which literary and artistic materials and esp. books are kept for use but not for sale **2** : a collection of literary or artistic materials (as books or prints)

li·bret·to \lə-'bret-ō\ *n, pl* **-tos** *or* **-ti** \-(ˌ)ē\ [from Italian, diminutive of *libro* "book", from Latin *liber*] : the text of an opera or musical; *also* : a book containing such a text

Lib·y·an \'lib-ē-ən\ *adj* : of, relating to, or characteristic of Libya or its people — **Libyan** *n*

lice *pl of* LOUSE

1**li·cense** *or* **li·cence** \'lī-sən(t)s\ *n* **1** : freedom of action esp. when carried too far **2 a** : permission granted by competent authority to do something **b** : a document, plate, or tag showing that license has been granted **3** : deviation from fact or rule by an artist or writer for the sake of effect

2**license** *also* **licence** *vb* : to permit or authorize by license — **li·cens·a·ble** \-sən-sə-bəl\ *adj*

li·cen·tious \lī-'sen-chəs\ *adj* : loose and lawless in behavior; *esp* : LUSTFUL — **li·cen·tious·ly** *adv* — **li·cen·tious·ness** *n*

li·chen \'lī-kən\ *n* : any of numerous complex plants

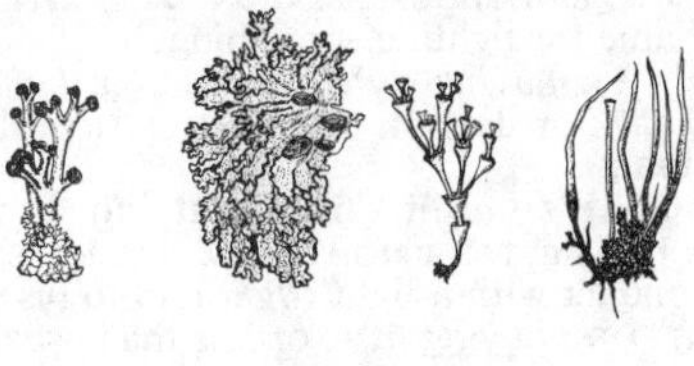

lichens

made up of an alga and a fungus growing in symbiotic association

1**lick** \'lik\ *vb* **1 a** : to draw the tongue over **b** : to flicker over like a tongue ⟨flames *licked* the ceiling⟩ **2** : to lap up **3 a** : to strike repeatedly : THRASH **b** : DEFEAT — **lick·ing** *n*

2**lick** *n* **1 a** : an act or instance of licking **b** : a small amount : BIT ⟨hasn't done a *lick* of work⟩ **c** : a hasty careless effort **2 a** : a sharp hit : BLOW ⟨got in some *licks* for his side⟩ **b** : OPPORTUNITY, TURN **3** : a place (as a spring) having a deposit of salt that animals regularly lick

lic·o·rice \'lik(-ə)-rish, -rəs\ *n* [from Old French, from Latin *liquiritia*, from Greek *glykyrrhiza*, from *glykys* "sweet" (seen in English *glycerine*) and *rhiza* "root"] **1** : a European leguminous plant **2** : the dried root of licorice; *also* : an extract from it used esp. in medicine, brewing, and confectionery

lid \'lid\ *n* **1** : a movable cover ⟨the *lid* of a box⟩ **2** : EYELID — **lid·ded** \'lid-əd\ *adj*

1**lie** \'lī\ *vb* **lay** \'lā\; **lain** \'lān\; **ly·ing** \'lī-ing\ **1 a** : to be in, stay in, or take up a horizontal position : RECLINE ⟨*lay* fast asleep⟩ ⟨*lie* down⟩ **b** : to stay in hiding or in ambush ⟨*lie* low⟩ ⟨*lie* in wait⟩ **2** : to be spread flat so as to cover ⟨snow *lying* on the ground⟩ **3** : to have direction : EXTEND ⟨the route *lay* to the west⟩ **4** : to be located ⟨Ohio *lies* east of Indiana⟩

2**lie** *vb* **lied**; **ly·ing** \'lī-ing\ **1** : to make an untrue statement with intent to deceive **2** : to create a false impression ⟨statistics sometimes *lie*⟩ — **lie** *n*

lief \'lēv, 'lēf\ *adv* : GLADLY, WILLINGLY ⟨I had as *lief* go as not⟩

1**liege** \'lēj\ *adj* **1** : having the right to receive service and allegiance ⟨*liege* lord⟩ **2** : owing or giving service to a lord

2**liege** *n* **1** : VASSAL **2** : a feudal superior

liege man *n* **1** : VASSAL **2** : a devoted follower

lien \'lēn, 'lē-ən\ *n* : a legal claim on the property of another person until he has met a certain obligation (as a debt)

lieu \'lü\ *n*, *archaic* : PLACE, STEAD — **in lieu of** : in the place of : instead of

lieut *abbr* lieutenant

lieu·ten·an·cy \lü-'ten-ən-sē\ *n*, *pl* **-cies** : the office, rank, or commission of a lieutenant

lieu·ten·ant \lü-'ten-ənt\ *n* [from French, from *lieu* "place" and *tenant* "holding"] **1** : an officer empowered to act for a higher official **2 a** (1) : FIRST LIEUTENANT (2) : SECOND LIEUTENANT **b** : a commissioned officer in the navy ranking next below a lieutenant commander **c** : a fire or police department officer ranking below a captain

lieutenant colonel *n* : a commissioned officer (as in the army) ranking next below a colonel

lieutenant commander *n* : a commissioned officer in the navy ranking next below a commander

lieutenant general *n* : a commissioned officer (as in the army) ranking next below a general

lieutenant governor *n* **1** : an elected official serving as deputy to the governor of an American state **2** : the formal head of the government of a Canadian province appointed to represent the crown

lieutenant junior grade *n* : a commissioned officer in the navy ranking next below a lieutenant

1**life** \'līf\ *n*, *pl* **lives** \'līvz\ **1 a** : the quality that distinguishes a vital and functional being from a dead body or inanimate matter **b** : a state of an organism characterized esp. by capacity for metabolism, growth, reaction to stimuli, and reproduction **2 a** : the sequence of experiences that make up the existence of an individual **b** : BIOGRAPHY 1 **3 a** : the period during which an organism lives **b** : a specific phase or aspect of such a life ⟨adult *life*⟩ ⟨sex *life*⟩ **4** : a way or manner of living ⟨the *life* of a scholar⟩ **5** : a living being; *esp* : PERSON ⟨saving *lives*⟩ **6** : ANIMATION, SPIRIT ⟨eyes full of *life*⟩ **7** : the period of utility, continuance, or existence of something ⟨*life* of a car⟩ ⟨*life* of an insurance policy⟩ **8** : living beings (as of a kind or place) ⟨forest *life*⟩ **9** : animate activity and movement ⟨stirrings of *life*⟩ ⟨streets humming with *life*⟩ **10** : one providing interest and vigor ⟨the *life* of the party⟩

2**life** *adj* **1** : of or relating to animate being ⟨the *life* force⟩ ⟨*life* situation⟩ **2** : LIFELONG ⟨*life* tenure⟩

life belt *n* : a life preserver in the form of a belt

life·blood \'līf-'bləd\ *n* : something that gives strength and energy : the vital force or essence ⟨free speech is the *lifeblood* of liberty⟩

life·boat \-ˌbōt\ *n* : a strong buoyant boat designed for use in saving lives at sea

life buoy *n* : a float consisting of a ring of buoyant material to support a person who has fallen into the water

life cycle *n* **1** : the series of stages through which an organism passes from a particular beginning stage of one individual to the corresponding stage of its offspring **2** : LIFE HISTORY 1a

life expectancy *n* : an expected number of years of life based on tables drawn from past experience

life·guard \'līf-ˌgärd\ *n* : a usu. expert swimmer employed to safeguard bathers

life history *n* **1** : a history of the changes through which an organism passes in its development from the initial stage to its natural death **2** : LIFE CYCLE 1

life insurance *n* : insurance providing for payment of a stipulated sum upon death of the insured

life jacket *n* : LIFE VEST

life·less \'līf-ləs\ *adj* **1 a** : DEAD **b** : INANIMATE ⟨*lifeless* as marble⟩ **2** : lacking animation and sparkle : DULL ⟨*lifeless* voice⟩ **3** : destitute of living beings ⟨a *lifeless* desert⟩ — **life·less·ly** *adv* — **life·less·ness** *n*

life·like \-ˌlīk\ *adj* : accurately representing or imitating real life — **life·like·ness** *n*

life·line \-ˌlīn\ *n* **1** : a line to which persons may cling to save or protect their lives **2** : a line attached to a diver's helmet by which he is lowered and raised **3** : a rope line for lowering a person to safety

life·long \-ˌlȯng\ *adj* : continuing through life ⟨a *lifelong* friendship⟩

life plant *n* : BRYOPHYLLUM

life preserver *n* : a device designed to save a person from drowning by buoying up the body while in the water

life raft *n* : a raft designed for use by people forced into the water

life·sav·ing \'līf-ˌsā-ving\ *n* : the art or practice of saving lives esp. of drowning persons — **life·sav·er** \-vər\ *n* — **lifesaving** *adj*

life–size \ˈlīf-ˈsīz\ *or* **life–sized** \-ˈsīzd\ *adj* : of natural size : of the size of the original ⟨a *life-size* statue⟩
life–span \-ˌspan\ *n* : the average length of life of an organism or of the persistence of a material object under specified circumstances or in a particular environment
life·time \-ˌtīm\ *n* : the duration of an individual's existence
life vest *n* : a life preserver in the form of a vest
life·work \ˈlīf-ˈwərk\ *n* : the entire or chief work of one's lifetime; *also* : a work extending over a lifetime
1lift \ˈlift\ *vb* **1** : to raise or rise to a higher position, rate, or amount **2** : STEAL **3** : to move from one place to another : TRANSPORT **4** : to disperse upward ⟨until the fog *lifts*⟩ **5** : to stop or remove often temporarily ⟨*lift* a blockade⟩ ⟨*lift* a ban⟩ ***syn*** see RAISE ***ant*** lower — **lift·er** *n*

life vest

2lift *n* **1** : the amount that may be lifted at one time : LOAD **2 a** : the action or an instance of lifting **b** : an upward tilt ⟨the proud *lift* of her head⟩ **3 a** : ASSISTANCE, HELP **b** : a ride along one's way **4** : the extent to which something rises ⟨the *lift* of a canal lock⟩ **5 a** *Brit* : ELEVATOR 1 **b** : a conveyor for carrying people up or down a mountain **6 a** : an elevating influence **b** : an elevation of the spirits ⟨his visits give me a *lift*⟩ **7** : the upward force acting on an airplane or airfoil
lift–off \ˈlift-ˌȯf\ *n* : a vertical takeoff (as by an aircraft or rocket vehicle)
lig·a·ment \ˈlig-ə-mənt\ *n* : a tough band of tissue that holds bones together or keeps an organ in place in the body — **lig·a·men·tous** \ˌlig-ə-ˈment-əs\ *adj*
li·gate \ˈlī-ˌgāt, lī-ˈ\ *vb* : to tie with a ligature — **li·ga·tion** \lī-ˈgā-shən\ *n*
lig·a·ture \ˈlig-ə-ˌchu̇r, -chər\ *n* **1** : a binding or tying of something **2** : something that binds or connects : BAND, BOND **3** : a thread or filament used in surgery esp. for tying blood vessels
1light \ˈlīt\ *n* **1 a** : something that makes vision possible **b** : the sensation aroused by stimulation of the visual receptors **c** : an electromagnetic radiation in the wavelength range including infrared, visible, ultraviolet, and X rays and traveling in a vacuum with a speed of about 186,281 miles per second; *esp* : the part of this range that is visible to the human eye **2 a** : DAYLIGHT **b** : DAWN **3** : a source of light; *esp* : LAMP **4 a** : mental or spiritual insight **b** : TRUTH ⟨see the *light*⟩ **c** : public knowledge ⟨facts brought to *light*⟩ **d** : a particular aspect presented to view ⟨saw the matter in a false *light*⟩ **5** : a particular illumination ⟨by the *light* of the moon⟩ **6 a** : WINDOW **b** : SKYLIGHT **7** *pl* : way of thinking : BELIEFS ⟨she was a good girl according to her *lights*⟩ **8** : a noteworthy person ⟨one of the leading *lights* of the stage⟩ **9 a** : LIGHTHOUSE, BEACON **b** : TRAFFIC SIGNAL **10** : a flame for lighting something
2light *adj* **1** : having light : BRIGHT ⟨a *light* room⟩ **2** : not dark or deep in color : PALE ⟨*light* blue⟩ — **light·ness** *n*
3light *vb* **light·ed** *or* **lit** \ˈlit\; **light·ing** **1** : to make or become light : BRIGHTEN **2** : KINDLE, IGNITE **3** : to conduct with a light ⟨*light* him to his room⟩
4light *adj* **1 a** : having little or less than usual weight : not heavy **b** : designed to carry a small load ⟨*light* truck⟩ **2 a** : not important or serious : TRIVIAL **b** : not abundant : SCANTY ⟨*light* rain⟩ **c** : SLIGHT, MODERATE ⟨a *light* case of measles⟩ **3 a** : easily disturbed ⟨*light* sleeper⟩ **b** : exerting or resulting from little force or pressure : GENTLE ⟨a *light* touch⟩ **4** : not hard to bear, do, pay, or digest ⟨*light* punishment⟩ ⟨*light* exercise⟩ ⟨*light* food⟩ **5** : capable of moving swiftly or nimbly **6 a** : FRIVOLOUS ⟨*light* conduct⟩ **b** : CHEERFUL **c** : intended chiefly to entertain ⟨*light* reading⟩ **7** : lightly armed or equipped ⟨*light* cavalry⟩ **8** : DIZZY, GIDDY **9** : producing goods for direct use by the consumer ⟨*light* industry⟩ **10** : having a clear soft quality ⟨a *light* voice⟩ — **light·ly** *adj* — **light·ness** *n*
5light *adv* **1** : in a light manner **2** : with little baggage ⟨travels *light*⟩
6light *vb* **light·ed** *or* **lit** \ˈlit\; **light·ing** **1** : SETTLE, ALIGHT ⟨birds *lit* on the lawn⟩ **2** : to come by chance ⟨the blow *lighted* on his arm⟩ ⟨*lit* upon a solution⟩
light air *n* : wind having a speed of 1 to 3 miles per hour
light breeze *n* : wind having a speed of 4 to 7 miles per hour
light bulb *n* : INCANDESCENT LAMP
1light·en \ˈlīt-ən\ *vb* **light·ened**; **light·en·ing** \-(ə-)niŋ\ **1** : to make or become light, lighter, or clear : BRIGHTEN **2** : to give out flashes of lightning — **light·en·er** \-(ə-)nər\ *n*
2lighten *vb* **light·ened**; **light·en·ing** \ˈlīt-(ə-)niŋ\ **1** : to relieve of a burden ⟨*lighten* the plane⟩ ⟨*lighten* his duties⟩ **2** : CHEER, GLADDEN **3** : to become less heavy — **light·en·er** \ˈlīt-(ə-)nər\ *n*
1ligh·ter \ˈlīt-ər\ *n* : a large barge used esp. in unloading or loading ships
2lighter *vb* : to convey by a lighter
3light·er \ˈlīt-ər\ *n* : one that lights; *esp* : a device for lighting ⟨cigarette *lighter*⟩
light·face \ˈlīt-ˌfās\ *n* : a type having light thin lines — compare BOLDFACE — **light·faced** \-ˈfāst\ *adj*
light–fin·gered \-ˈfiŋ-gərd\ *adj* : adroit in stealing esp. by picking pockets
light–foot·ed \-ˈfu̇t-əd\ *adj* : having a light and springy step or movement
light–head·ed \-ˈhed-əd\ *adj* **1** : DIZZY **2** : FRIVOLOUS — **light–head·ed·ness** *n*
light·heart·ed \-ˈhärt-əd\ *adj* : free from care or anxiety : GAY — **light·heart·ed·ly** *adv* — **light·heart·ed·ness** *n*
light·house \ˈlīt-ˌhau̇s\ *n* : a tower with a powerful light for guiding navigators at night
light·ing \ˈlīt-iŋ\ *n* **1 a** : ILLUMINATION **b** : IGNITION **2** : an artificial supply of light or the apparatus providing it
light meter *n* **1** : a small portable device for measuring illumination **2** : a device for

lighthouse

ə abut	ər further	a back	ā bake	
ä cot, cart	au̇ out	ch chin	e less	ē easy
g gift	i trip	ī life	j joke	ŋ sing	ō flow
ȯ flaw	ȯi coin	th thin	t͟h this	ü loot
u̇ foot	y yet	yü few	yu̇ furious	zh vision

indicating correct photographic exposure under varying conditions of illumination

light microscope *n* : MICROSCOPE 1

light–mind·ed \'līt-'mīn-dəd\ *adj* : lacking in seriousness : FRIVOLOUS — **light–mind·ed·ly** *adv* — **light–mind·ed·ness** *n*

light·ning \'līt-ning\ *n* : the flashing of light produced by a discharge of atmospheric electricity from one cloud to another or between a cloud and the earth; *also* : the discharge itself

lightning arrester *n* : a device for protecting electrical apparatus and radio and television sets from injury from lightning by carrying the discharges to the ground

lightning bug *n* : FIREFLY

lightning rod *n* : a metal rod set up on a building or a ship and connected with the earth or water below to decrease the chances of damage from lightning

light opera *n* : OPERETTA

light out *vb* : to leave in a hurry ⟨*lit out* for home⟩

light·proof \'līt-'prüf\ *adj* : impenetrable by light

lights \'līts\ *n pl* : the lungs esp. of a slaughtered animal

light·ship \'līt-ˌship\ *n* : a ship equipped with a brilliant light and moored at a place dangerous to navigation

light show *n* : a display of quickly changing colored lights, slides, and film loops designed to imitate the effects of psychedelic drugs

light·some \'līt-səm\ *adj* **1** : AIRY, NIMBLE **2** : free from care : CHEERFUL **3** : FRIVOLOUS — **light·some·ly** *adv* — **light·some·ness** *n*

light trap *n* : a device for collecting or destroying insects by attracting them to a light and trapping or killing them

light·weight \'līt-ˌwāt\ *n* **1** : one of less than average weight; *esp* : a boxer weighing more than 126 but not over 135 pounds **2** : a person of little ability or success — **lightweight** *adj*

light–year \'līt-ˌyi(ə)r\ *n* : a unit of length in astronomy equal to the distance that light travels in one year or 5,878,000,000,000 miles

lig·ne·ous \'lig-nē-əs\ *adj* : of or resembling wood : WOODY

lig·nin \'lig-nən\ *n* : a substance related to cellulose that occurs in the woody cell walls of plants and in the cementing material between them

lig·nite \'lig-ˌnīt\ *n* : a usu. brownish black coal intermediate between peat and bituminous coal; *esp* : one in which the texture of the original wood is distinct

lik·a·ble *or* **like·a·ble** \'lī-kə-bəl\ *adj* : easily liked : PLEASANT, AGREEABLE ⟨a *likable* fellow⟩ — **lik·a·ble·ness** *n*

1**like** \'līk\ *vb* **1** : to feel attraction toward or take pleasure in : ENJOY ⟨*likes* baseball⟩ **2** : to feel toward : REGARD ⟨how would you *like* a change⟩ **3** : to wish to have : WANT ⟨would *like* a drink⟩ **4** : to feel inclined : CHOOSE ⟨does as he *likes*⟩

2**like** *n* : LIKING, PREFERENCE ⟨knows his *likes* and dislikes⟩

3**like** *adj* **1 a** : ALIKE, SIMILAR ⟨suits of *like* design⟩ **b** : resembling or characteristic of — used after the word modified ⟨dog*like*⟩ ⟨bell-*like*⟩ **2 a** : LIKELY **b** : being about or as if about — used with an infinitive ⟨*like* to die⟩

4**like** *prep* **1** : similar or similarly to ⟨his house is *like* a barn⟩ ⟨acts *like* a fool⟩ **2** : typical of ⟨was *like* him to do that⟩ **3** : likely to ⟨looks *like* rain⟩ **4** : such as ⟨a subject *like* physics⟩

5**like** *n* : COUNTERPART, EQUAL ⟨may never see his *like* again⟩

6**like** *conj* **1** : in the same way that : AS **2** : as if ⟨looked *like* he was scared⟩

like·li·hood \'lī-klē-ˌhu̇d\ *n* : PROBABILITY

1**like·ly** \'lī-klē\ *adj* **like·li·er**; **-est** **1** : making a happening or result probable ⟨that bomb is *likely* to explode any time⟩ **2** : seeming like the truth : BELIEVABLE ⟨a *likely* story⟩ **3** : PROMISING ⟨a *likely* place to fish⟩

2**likely** *adv* : in all probability : PROBABLY ⟨most *likely* you are right⟩

lik·en \'lī-kən\ *vb* **lik·ened**; **lik·en·ing** \'līk-(ə-)ning\ : to represent as like something : COMPARE

like·ness \'līk-nəs\ *n* **1** : RESEMBLANCE **2** : APPEARANCE ⟨in the *likeness* of a clown⟩ **3** : COPY, PORTRAIT

like·wise \'līk-ˌwīz\ *adv* **1** : in like manner : SIMILARLY **2** : in addition : ALSO

lik·ing \'lī-king\ *n* : favorable regard : FONDNESS, TASTE

li·lac \'lī-lək, -ˌlak, -ˌläk\ *n* [from Arabic *līlak*, from Persian *nīlak* "bluish", from *nīl* "blue", from Sanskrit *nīla*] **1** : any of a genus of shrubs and trees related to the olive; *esp* : a European shrub widely grown for its showy clusters of fragrant pink, purple, or white flowers **2** : a variable color averaging a moderate purple

lilac 1

lil·i·a·ceous \ˌlil-ē-'ā-shəs\ *adj* : of or relating to lilies

1**lilt** \'lilt\ *vb* : to sing or play in a lively cheerful manner — **lilt·ing·ly** \'lil-ting-lē\ *adv*

2**lilt** *n* **1** : a lively and usu. gay song or tune **2** : a rhythmic swinging movement

1**lily** \'lil-ē\ *n, pl* **lil·ies** : any of a genus of erect perennial leafy-stemmed bulbous herbs widely grown for their showy funnel-shaped flowers; *also* : any of various related plants

2**lily** *adj* : of, relating to, or resembling a lily

lily of the valley : a low perennial herb that is related to the lilies and has usu. two large oblong leaves and a stalk of fragrant nodding bell-shaped flowers

lily pad *n* : a floating leaf of a water lily

lily–white \ˌlil-ē-'hwīt\ *adj* **1** : white as a lily **2** : characterized by or favoring the exclusion of Negroes **3** : FAULTLESS, PURE

li·ma bean \ˌlī-mə-\ *n* : any of various bush or tall-growing beans widely grown for their flat edible usu. pale green or whitish seeds; *also* : this seed

lily of the valley

1**limb** \'lim\ *n* **1** : one of the projecting paired appendages (as wings) of an animal body used esp. for movement and grasping; *esp* : a leg or arm of a human being **2** : a large primary branch of a tree ***syn*** see SHOOT — **limb·less** \'lim-ləs\ *adj*

2**limb** *vb* : to cut off the limbs of (a felled tree)

3**limb** *n* : the outer edge of the apparent disk of a celestial body ⟨the eastern *limb* of the sun⟩

1**lim·ber** \'lim-bər\ *adj* : bending easily : FLEXIBLE, SUPPLE ⟨a *limber* willow twig⟩ — **lim·ber·ly** *adv* — **lim·ber·ness** *n*

2**limber** *vb* **lim·bered**; **lim·ber·ing** \-b(ə-)ring\ : to make or become limber ⟨*limbered* up with calisthenics⟩

lim·bo \'lim-bō\ *n, pl* **limbos** **1** *often cap* : an abode of souls (as of unbaptized infants) barred from heaven through no fault of their own **2 a** : a place or state of confinement or oblivion **b** : an intermediate place or state

[1]**lime** \'līm\ *n* **1** : a caustic solid that consists primarily of an oxide of calcium, is obtained esp. by heating limestone or shells, and is used in mortar and plaster and in agriculture **2** : a dry white powder that is made by treating lime with water — called also *slaked lime* — **lime** *vb*

[2]**lime** *adj* : of, relating to, or containing lime or limestone

[3]**lime** *n* : a European linden tree

[4]**lime** *n* : a fruit like the lemon but smaller and with greenish yellow rind; *also* : the citrus tree that bears it

lime·ade \lī-'mād\ *n* : a drink made of lime juice, sugar, and water

lime·light \'līm-ˌlīt\ *n* **1** : a device formerly used for lighting a stage by means of a flame directed on a cylinder of lime; *also* : the light produced by this device **2** : the center of public attention

lim·er·ick \'lim-(ə-)rik\ *n* : a light or humorous verse form of 5 lines of which the 1st, 2d, and 5th follow one rhyme and the 3d and 4th another

lime·stone \'līm-ˌstōn\ *n* : a rock that is formed chiefly by accumulation of organic remains (as shells or coral), consists mainly of calcium carbonate, is extensively used in building, and yields lime when burned

lime·wa·ter \-ˌwȯt-ər, -ˌwät-\ *n* : an alkaline water solution of the hydroxide of calcium often used as an antacid

[1]**lim·it** \'lim-ət\ *n* **1** : BOUNDARY ⟨the city *limits*⟩ **2** : the highest or lowest possible amount, quantity, or number ⟨reach the *limit* of one's powers⟩ — **lim·it·less** \-ləs\ *adj*

[2]**limit** *vb* **1** : to set limits to : CONFINE **2** : to curtail or reduce in quantity or extent — **lim·it·a·ble** \-ə-bəl\ *adj* — **lim·i·ta·tion** \ˌlim-ə-'tā-shən\ *n* — **lim·it·er** *n*

lim·it·ed *adj* **1 a** : confined within limits : RESTRICTED **b** : taking a limited number of passengers **2** : relating to or being a government in which constitutional limitations are placed upon the powers of one or more of its branches ⟨a *limited* monarchy⟩ — **lim·it·ed·ly** *adv* — **lim·it·ed·ness** *n*

limited war *n* : a war with an objective less than the total defeat of the enemy

limiting factor *n* : an environmental factor that is important in restricting the size of a population

limn \'lim\ *vb* **limned**; **limn·ing** \'lim-(n)iŋ\ **1** : DRAW **2** : PAINT **3** : DESCRIBE, PORTRAY — **limn·er** \'lim-(n)ər\ *n*

lim·nol·o·gy \lim-'näl-ə-jē\ *n* : the scientific study of fresh waters — **lim·no·log·i·cal** \ˌlim-nə-'läj-i-kəl\ *adj* — **lim·nol·o·gist** \lim-'näl-ə-jəst\ *n*

li·mo·nite \'lī-mə-ˌnīt\ *n* : an ore of iron consisting of oxides of iron — **li·mo·nit·ic** \ˌlī-mə-'nit-ik\ *adj*

lim·ou·sine \'lim-ə-ˌzēn, ˌlim-ə-'\ *n* **1** : a small bus ⟨an airport *limousine*⟩ **2** : a large luxurious sedan

[1]**limp** \'limp\ *vb* **1** : to walk lamely **2** : to proceed slowly or with difficulty ⟨the ship *limped* into port⟩ — **limp·er** *n*

ə abut | ər further | a back | ā bake
ä cot, cart | au̇ out | ch chin | e less | ē easy
g gift | i trip | ī life | j joke | ŋ sing | ō flow
ȯ flaw | ȯi coin | th thin | th this | ü loot
u̇ foot | y yet | yü few | yu̇ furious | zh vision

[2]**limp** *n* : a limping movement or gait

[3]**limp** *adj* **1** : not stiff or rigid **2 a** : EXHAUSTED **b** : lacking in strength or firmness : SPIRITLESS — **limp·ly** *adv* — **limp·ness** *n*

lim·pet \'lim-pət\ *n* : a marine mollusk that has a low conical shell, browses over rocks or timbers, and clings very tightly when disturbed

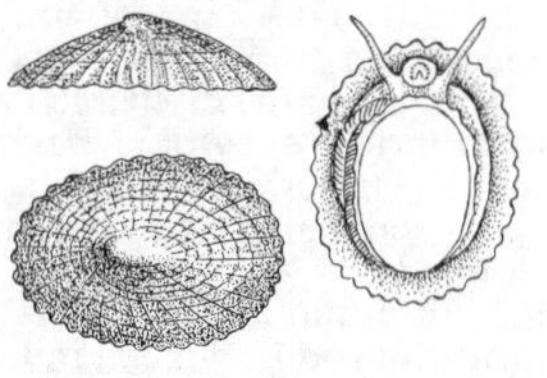

limpet

lim·pid \'lim-pəd\ *adj* : TRANSPARENT, CLEAR ⟨a *limpid* pool⟩ — **lim·pid·i·ty** \lim-'pid-ət-ē\ *n* — **lim·pid·ly** \'lim-pəd-lē\ *adv* — **lim·pid·ness** *n*

lim·u·lus \'lim-yə-ləs\ *n, pl* **-li** \-ˌlī, -ˌlē\ : HORSESHOE CRAB

limy \'lī-mē\ *adj* **lim·i·er**; **-est** : containing lime or limestone

linch·pin \'linch-ˌpin\ *n* : a locking pin inserted crosswise (as through the end of an axle or shaft)

Lin·coln's Birthday \ˌliŋ-kənz-\ *n* : February 12 observed as a legal holiday in many of the states of the U.S.

lin·dane \'lin-ˌdān\ *n* : an insecticide consisting of not less than 99 percent of a chloride of benzene

lin·den \'lin-dən\ *n* **1** : any of a genus of trees with large heart-shaped leaves and clustered yellowish flowers rich in nectar **2** : the light fine-grained white wood of a linden

[1]**line** \'līn\ *vb* **1** : to cover the inner surface of ⟨*line* a box with paper⟩ **2** : to serve as the lining of ⟨tapestries *lined* the walls⟩

[2]**line** *n* **1 a** : THREAD **b** : CORD, ROPE ⟨a fishing *line*⟩ **2** : a cord, wire, or tape used in measuring and leveling **3 a** : piping for conveying a fluid ⟨gas *line*⟩ ⟨water *line*⟩ ⟨steam *line*⟩ **b** : wire connecting one telegraph or telephone station with another or a system of such wires **c** : the principal circuits of an electric power system **4 a** : a horizontal row of written or printed characters **b** : a unit of verse formed by the grouping of metrical feet **c** : a short letter : NOTE ⟨drop me a *line*⟩ **d** *pl* : the words making up a part in a drama ⟨forgot her *lines*⟩ **5 a** : something (as a ridge, seam, or wrinkle) that is long and narrow **b** : the course of something in motion : ROUTE ⟨the *line* of flight of a bullet⟩ **c** : BOUNDS, LIMITS ⟨town *line*⟩ **d** : the track and roadbed of a railway **6** : a state of agreement ⟨bring ideas into *line*⟩ **7 a** : a course of conduct; *esp* : a publicly proclaimed policy ⟨a political *line*⟩ **b** : a field of activity or interest ⟨out of my *line*⟩ **c** : a glib persuasive way of talking **8** : FAMILY, RACE, STOCK ⟨descended from a noble *line*⟩ **9 a** : the position of military forces in actual combat with the enemy at the front **b** : a military or naval formation with the elements abreast **c** : fighting or sea forces or officers as opposed to staff or supply forces **10** : goods for sale of one general kind ⟨a *line* of clothing⟩ **11 a** : a system of public transportation or the firm operating it ⟨bus *line*⟩ **b** : a route over which such a firm operates ⟨the Broadway *line*⟩ **12** : an arrangement of manufacturing processes in sequence **13 a** : a long narrow mark **b** : a circle of latitude or longitude on a map **c** : EQUATOR **d** : any of the horizontal parallel strokes on a music staff **e** : LINE OF SCRIMMAGE; *also* : the football players who line up on or within a foot of it **14** : a geometric element that is generated

by a moving point and that has length but no width or thickness; *esp* : a straight line **15 a** : a defining outline : CONTOUR ⟨a ship's *lines*⟩ **b** : a general plan ⟨a play along the same *lines* as a novel⟩ — **in line for** : due to receive — **on the line 1** : in full view and at stake ⟨put his future *on the line*⟩ **2** : on the border between two classes **3** : IMMEDIATELY ⟨pay cash *on the line*⟩

³**line** *vb* **1** : to mark or cover with a line **2** : to depict by lines : DRAW **3** : to place or form a line along ⟨pedestrians *line* the walks⟩ **4** : to form a line : form into lines **5** : to hit a line drive

lin·e·age \'lin-ē-ij\ *n* **1** : lineal descent from a common progenitor **2** : a group of persons tracing descent from a common ancestor

lin·e·al \'lin-ē-əl\ *adj* **1** : LINEAR ⟨*lineal* measure⟩ **2 a** : consisting of or being in a direct line of ancestry or descent ⟨*lineal* descendants⟩ **b** : HEREDITARY — **lin·e·al·ly** \-ē-ə-lē\ *adv*

lin·e·a·ment \'lin-ē-ə-mənt\ *n* : a feature or contour of a body or figure and esp. of the face

lin·e·ar \'lin-ē-ər\ *adj* **1 a** : relating to, consisting of, or resembling a line : STRAIGHT **b** : involving a single dimension **c** : containing variables of the first degree only ⟨*linear* equation⟩ **2** : long and uniformly narrow ⟨*linear* leaf of the hyacinth⟩ — **lin·e·ar·i·ty** \,lin-ē-'ar-ət-ē\ *n* — **lin·e·ar·ly** \'lin-ē-ər-lē\ *adv*

linear accelerator *n* : a device in which charged particles are accelerated in a straight line by successive impulses from a series of electric fields

linear measure *n* **1** : a measure of length **2** : a system of measures of length

line·back·er \'līn-,bak-ər\ *n* : a defensive football player who acts either as a lineman or as a pass defender

line drive *n* : a batted baseball hit not far above the ground in a nearly straight line

line graph *n* : a graph in which the points representing specific values are connected by a broken line

line·man \'līn-mən\ *n* **1** : one who sets up or repairs electric wire communication or power lines **2** : a player in the line in football

lin·en \'lin-ən\ *n* **1** : cloth, thread, or yarn made from flax **2** : clothing or household articles made of linen or a similar fabric — **linen** *adj*

line of force : an imaginary line serving as a convenience in indicating the direction in space in which an electric or magnetic force acts

line of scrimmage : an imaginary line in football touching and at right angles to the nose of the ball as it lies on the ground before a scrimmage

¹**lin·er** \'lī-nər\ *n* **1** : one that draws lines **2** : something with which lines are made **3 a** : a ship belonging to a regular line of ships **b** : an airplane belonging to an airline

²**liner** *n* : one that lines or is used to line or back something

line segment *n* : SEGMENT 2b

lines·man \'līnz-mən\ *n* : an official who assists a referee in an athletic game (as football)

line·up \'līn-,əp\ *n* **1** : a line of persons arranged esp. for identification by police **2** : a list of players taking part in a game (as of baseball); *also* : the players on such a list

line up \-'əp\ *vb* **1** : to come together or arrange in a line or rows ⟨*line up* for inspection⟩ **2** : to put into alignment **3 a** : COLLECT, RAISE ⟨*line up* support for the party⟩ **b** : to take sides ⟨*lined up* behind the candidate⟩

-ling \ling\ *n suffix* **1** : one connected with or having the quality of ⟨hire*ling*⟩ **2** : young, small, or inferior one ⟨duck*ling*⟩

lin·ger \'ling-gər\ *vb* **lin·gered**; **lin·ger·ing** \-g(ə-)ring\ **1** : to be slow in quitting a place or activity ⟨*lingered* at the dinner table⟩ **2** : to be slow to act — **lin·ger·er** \-gər-ər\ *n* — **lin·ger·ing·ly** \-g(ə-)ring-lē\ *adv*

syn LINGER, LOITER, LAG can mean to pause without valid reason or explanation. LINGER suggests evident reluctance to leave a scene of pleasure immediately; LOITER suggests aimless sauntering or lagging behind; LAG implies inability or unwillingness to maintain a pace

lin·ge·rie \,län-jə-'rā, ,lan-zhə-, ,lan-jə-, -'rē\ *n* [from French, from *linge* "linen", from Latin *lineus* "made of linen", from *linum* "flax"] : women's nightclothes or underwear

lin·go \'ling-gō\ *n, pl* **lingoes** [probably from Provençal, meaning "tongue", "language", from Latin *lingua*] **1** : strange or incomprehensible language or speech; *esp* : a foreign language **2** : JARGON

lin·gual \'ling-gwəl\ *adj* **1** : of, relating to, or resembling a tongue **2** : produced by the tongue ⟨*lingual* sounds such as \t\ or \l\⟩ — **lin·gual·ly** \-gwə-lē\ *adv*

lin·guist \'ling-gwəst\ *n* **1** : a person skilled in languages **2** : one who specializes in linguistics

lin·guis·tic \ling-'gwis-tik\ *adj* : of or relating to language or linguistics — **lin·guis·ti·cal·ly** \-ti-k(ə-)lē\ *adv*

lin·guis·tics \-tiks\ *n* : the study of human speech including the units, nature, structure, and development of language, languages, or a language

lin·i·ment \'lin-ə-mənt\ *n* : a liquid preparation rubbed on the skin esp. to relieve pain

lin·ing \'lī-ning\ *n* : material used to line something (as a garment)

¹**link** \'lingk\ *n* **1 a** : a single ring or division of a chain **b** : a division of a surveyor's chain that is 7.92 inches long and is used as a measure of length **c** : a usu. ornamental device for fastening a cuff **d** : BOND 2b **e** : an intermediate rod or piece for transmitting force or motion **2 a** : a segment of sausage in a chain **b** : a connecting element : BOND ⟨a *link* with the past⟩

²**link** *vb* : to join by a link — **link·er** *n*

link·age \'ling-kij\ *n* **1** : the manner or style of being united: as **a** : the manner in which atoms or radicals are linked in a molecule **b** : BOND 2b **2** : the quality or state of being linked; *esp* : the occurring together of genes on the same chromosome with the result that the traits they control are not inherited independently of each other but tend to be found together **3** : a system of links; *esp* : a system of links or bars jointed together by means of which lines or curves may be traced

linked \'lingkt\ *adj* : exhibiting genetic linkage : tending to be inherited together

linking verb *n* : an intransitive verb (as *be* or *seem*) that links a subject with a word or words in the predicate ⟨*looks* in "he looks sick" and *were* in "they were at home" are *linking verbs*⟩

links \'ling(k)s\ *n pl* : COURSE 3

link·up \'lingk-,əp\ *n* **1** : MEETING **2** : something that serves as a link

Lin·nae·an *or* **Lin·ne·an** \lə-'nē-ən, 'lin-ē-\ *adj* : of, relating to, or following the method of the Swedish botanist Linné who established the system of binomial nomenclature

lin·net \'lin-ət\ *n* : a common small Old World finch with variable plumage

li·no·le·um \lə-'nō-lē-əm, -'nōl-yəm\ *n* : a floor covering with a canvas back and a surface of hardened linseed oil and a filler (as cork dust)

L

lin·seed \'lin-ˌsēd\ *n* : FLAXSEED
linseed oil *n* : a yellowish oil obtained from flaxseed and used esp. in paint, varnish, printing ink, and linoleum
lin·sey–wool·sey \ˌlin-zē-'wu̇l-zē\ *n* : a coarse fabric of wool and linen or cotton
lint \'lint\ *n* **1** : linen made into a soft fleecy substance for use in surgical dressings **2** : fine ravelings, fluff, or loose short fibers from yarn or fabrics **3** : fibers forming a close thick coating about cotton seeds and constituting the staple of cotton — **linty** \-ē\ *adj*
lin·tel \'lint-əl\ *n* : a horizontal piece or part across the top of an opening (as of a door) that carries the weight of the structure above it
li·on \'lī-ən\ *n, pl* **lion** *or* **lions** **1** : a large tawny

lions 1
(about 3 ft. at shoulder)

flesh-eating chiefly nocturnal cat of open or rocky areas of Africa and esp. formerly southern Asia with a tufted tail and a shaggy mane in the male **2 a** : a person resembling a lion (as in courage or ferocity) **b** : a person of outstanding interest or importance ⟨a literary *lion*⟩ — **li·on·ess** \'lī-ə-nəs\ *n* — **li·on·like** \'lī-ən-ˌlīk\ *adj*
¹**lip** \'lip\ *n* **1** : either of the two fleshy folds that surround the mouth **2 a** : a fleshy edge or margin ⟨*lips* of a wound⟩ **b** : the protruding part of an irregular corolla (as of a snapdragon or orchid) **3** : the edge of a hollow vessel esp. where it flares slightly ⟨the *lip* of a pitcher⟩ — **lipped** \'lipt\ *adj*
²**lip** *adj* : spoken with the lips only without intent to carry out : INSINCERE ⟨*lip* service⟩
li·pase \'lī-ˌpās, 'lip-ˌās\ *n* : an enzyme that accelerates the hydrolysis or synthesis of fats or the breakdown of fatty proteins
lip·id \'lip-əd\ *n* : any of various substances (as fats and waxes) that with proteins and carbohydrates constitute the principal structural components of living cells
lip·read·ing \'lip-ˌrēd-ing\ *n* : interpreting a speaker's words without hearing his voice by watching his lip and facial movements — **lip–read** \-ˌrēd\ *vb* — **lip–read·er** *n*
lip·stick \-ˌstik\ *n* : a waxy solid usu. colored cosmetic in stick form for the lips; *also* : a stick of such cosmetic with its case
liq *abbr* liquid
liq·ue·fac·tion \ˌlik-wə-'fak-shən\ *n* **1** : the process of liquefying **2** : the state of being liquid
liquefied petroleum gas *n* : a compressed gas consisting of flammable light hydrocarbons and used esp. as fuel or as raw material for chemical synthesis
liq·ue·fy \'lik-wə-ˌfī\ *vb* **-fied**; **-fy·ing** : to make or become liquid — **liq·ue·fi·a·ble** \-ˌfī-ə-bəl\ *adj*
li·queur \li-'kər, -'k(y)u̇(ə)r\ *n* : a flavored usu. sweetened alcoholic beverage
¹**liq·uid** \'lik-wəd\ *adj* **1** : flowing freely like water **2** : neither solid nor gaseous : characterized by free movement of the constituent molecules among themselves but without the tendency to separate ⟨*liquid* mercury⟩ **3** : resembling liquid in clarity or smoothness ⟨large *liquid* eyes⟩ ⟨*liquid* notes of a bird⟩ **4** : that is without friction and like a vowel ⟨the *liquid* consonant \l\⟩ **5** : consisting of cash or capable of ready conversion into cash ⟨*liquid* assets⟩ — **li·quid·i·ty** \lik-'wid-ət-ē\ *n* — **liq·uid·ly** \'lik-wəd-lē\ *adv*
²**liquid** *n* **1** : a liquid substance **2** : a liquid consonant
liquid air *n* : air in the liquid state prepared by subjecting it to great pressure and then cooling it by its own expansion and used chiefly as a refrigerant
liq·ui·date \'lik-wə-ˌdāt\ *vb* **1** : to pay off ⟨*liquidate* a debt⟩ **2** : to settle the accounts of and use the assets toward paying off the debts ⟨*liquidate* a business⟩ **3** : to kill ruthlessly and in secret ⟨*liquidate* a political opponent⟩ — **liq·ui·da·tion** \ˌlik-wə-'dā-shən\ *n* — **liq·ui·da·tor** \'lik-wə-ˌdāt-ər\ *n*
liquid measure *n* : a unit or series of units for measuring liquid capacity — see MEASURE table, METRIC SYSTEM table
li·quor \'lik-ər\ *n* : a liquid substance or solution ⟨dye *liquor*⟩; *esp* : a distilled alcoholic beverage
li·ra \'lir-ə\ *n* **1** *pl* **li·re** \'lē-ˌrā\ *or* **liras** **a** : the basic monetary unit of Italy **b** : a coin or note representing one lira **2** *pl* **liras** *also* **lire** : a Turkish or Syrian pound **3** *pl* **li·roth** *or* **li·rot** \'lē-ˌrōt(h)\ : the Israeli pound
lisle \'līl\ *n* : a smooth tightly twisted thread usu. made of long-staple cotton
¹**lisp** \'lisp\ *vb* **1** : to pronounce *s* and *z* by giving them the sound of *th* **2** : to speak falteringly, childishly, or with a lisp — **lisp·er** *n*
²**lisp** *n* **1** : the habit or act of lisping **2** : a sound resembling a lisp
lis·some *also* **lis·som** \'lis-əm\ *adj* **1** : easily flexed : LITHE **2** : NIMBLE — **lis·some·ly** *adv* — **lis·some·ness** *n*
¹**list** \'list\ *vb, archaic* : WISH, CHOOSE
²**list** *vb, archaic* : LISTEN, HEAR
³**list** *n* **1** : SELVAGE **2** *pl* **a** : an arena for jousting **b** : a field of competition or controversy
⁴**list** *n* : a roll, record, or catalog of names or objects ⟨guest *list*⟩ ⟨grocery *list*⟩
⁵**list** *vb* **1** : to make a list of : ENUMERATE **2** : to include on a list : REGISTER ⟨securities *listed* on the exchange⟩ ⟨*lists* himself as a plumber⟩ **3** : to become entered in a catalog with a selling price ⟨the coat *lists* at $25⟩
⁶**list** *vb* : to lean or cause to lean to one side : TILT
⁷**list** *n* : a deviation from the vertical : TILT
lis·ten \'lis-ən\ *vb* **lis·tened**; **lis·ten·ing** \-(ə-)ning\ **1** : to pay attention in order to hear ⟨*listen* for a signal⟩ ⟨*listen* to a new record⟩ **2** : to give heed : follow advice ⟨*listen* to a warning⟩ — **lis·ten·er** \-(ə-)nər\ *n*

listen in *vb* **1** : to listen to a broadcast **2** : EAVESDROP
list·ing \'lis-tiŋ\ *n* **1** : [4]LIST **2** : something listed
list·less \'list-ləs\ *adj* : LANGUID, SPIRITLESS — **list·less·ly** *adv* — **list·less·ness** *n*
list price *n* : the retail price of an item as published in a catalog, price list, or advertisement
lit *past of* LIGHT
lit·a·ny \'lit-ə-nē\ *n, pl* **-nies** : a prayer consisting of a series of supplications and responses said alternately by a leader and a group
li·tchi \'lī-(,)chē, 'lē-\ *n* : the oval fruit of an Asiatic tree having a hard outer covering and a seed surrounded by sweetish edible flesh that when dried is firm and black; *also* : the tree bearing this fruit
li·ter \'lēt-ər\ *n* : a metric unit of capacity equal to the volume of one kilogram of water at 4°C and at standard atmospheric pressure of 760 millimeters of mercury — see METRIC SYSTEM table
lit·er·a·cy \'lit-ə-rə-sē, 'li-trə-sē\ *n* : ability to read and write
lit·er·al \'lit-ə-rəl, 'li-trəl\ *adj* **1 a** : following the ordinary or usual meaning of the words **b** : true to fact : ACCURATE ⟨a *literal* account⟩ **c** : PLAIN, UNADORNED **d** : concerned mainly with facts : PROSAIC **2** : of, relating to, or expressed in letters ⟨*literal* equations⟩ **3** : reproduced word for word : EXACT, VERBATIM ⟨a *literal* translation⟩ — **lit·er·al·ly** \'lit-ər-(ə-)lē, 'li-trə-lē\ *adv* — **lit·er·al·ness** \'lit-ə-rəl-nəs, 'li-trəl-\ *n*
lit·er·ary \'lit-ə-,rer-ē\ *adj* : of, relating to, or having the characteristics of literature or of writers, critics, or readers of literature — **lit·er·ar·i·ly** \,lit-ə-'rer-ə-lē\ *adv* — **lit·er·ar·i·ness** \'lit-ə-,rer-ē-nəs\ *n*
lit·er·ate \'lit-ə-rət, 'li-trət\ *adj* **1** : EDUCATED, CULTURED **2** : able to read and write — **literate** *n* — **lit·er·ate·ly** *adv*
lit·er·a·ture \'lit-ə-rə-,chu̇r, 'li-trə-, -chər\ *n* **1** : the writing of literary work esp. as an occupation **2 a** : writings in prose or verse; *esp* : writings having permanent interest or value **b** : the body of writings on a particular subject or of a particular group, nation, or language ⟨medical *literature*⟩ ⟨classical *literature*⟩ ⟨French *literature*⟩ **c** : printed matter (as leaflets or circulars)
lith- *or* **litho-** *comb form* : stone ⟨*litho*logy⟩
-lith \,lith\ *n comb form* : structure or implement of stone ⟨mega*lith*⟩
li·tharge \'lith-,ärj, lith-'\ *n* : LEAD MONOXIDE
lithe \'līth, 'līth\ *adj* **1** : easily bent : FLEXIBLE ⟨long *lithe* stems⟩ **2** : gracefully limber ⟨*lithe* dancers⟩ — **lithe·ly** *adv* — **lithe·ness** *n*
lithe·some \'līth-səm, 'līth-\ *adj* : LISSOME
lith·i·um \'lith-ē-əm\ *n* : a soft silver-white element that is the lightest metal known and is used esp. in nuclear reactions and metallurgy — see ELEMENT table
lithium chloride *n* : a deliquescent salt used in hygrometers
[1]litho·graph \'lith-ə-,graf\ *vb* : to produce, copy, or portray by lithography — **li·thog·ra·pher** \-lith-'äg-rə-fər, 'lith-ə-,graf-ər\ *n*
[2]lithograph *n* : a print made by lithography — **litho·graph·ic** \,lith-ə-'graf-ik\ *adj* — **litho·graph·i·cal·ly** \-'graf-i-k(ə-)lē\ *adv*
li·thog·ra·phy \lith-'äg-rə-fē\ *n* : the process of printing from a plane surface (as a smooth stone or metal plate) on which the image to be printed is ink-receptive and the blank area ink-repellent
li·thol·o·gy \lith-'äl-ə-jē\ *n* : the study of rocks
litho·sphere \'lith-ə-,sfi(ə)r\ *n* : the outer part of the solid earth
Lith·u·a·ni·an \,lith-(y)ə-'wā-nē-ən, -nyən\ *n* **1** : a native or inhabitant of Lithuania **2** : the Baltic language of the Lithuanian people — **Lithuanian** *adj*
lit·i·gant \'lit-i-gənt\ *n* : a party to a lawsuit
lit·i·gate \'lit-ə-,gāt\ *vb* : to take legal measures to establish one's rights — **lit·i·ga·tion** \,lit-ə-'gā-shən\ *n*
lit·mus \'lit-məs\ *n* : a coloring matter from lichens that turns red in acid solutions and blue in alkaline solutions and is used as an acid-base indicator
litmus paper *n* : paper impregnated with litmus
li·tre \'lēt-ər\ *var of* LITER
[1]lit·ter \'lit-ər\ *n* **1 a** : a covered and curtained couch provided with shafts and used for carrying a passenger **b** : a device (as a stretcher) for carrying a sick or injured person **2** : material used as bedding for animals **3** : the offspring of an animal born at one time **4** : an untidy accumulation of objects lying about : RUBBISH
[2]litter *vb* **1** : to give birth to young **2 a** : to strew with litter **b** : to scatter about in disorder
lit·ter·bug \'lit-ər-,bəg\ *n* : one that litters a public area
littermate *n* : one of a litter of offspring considered in relation to the other members of the litter
[1]lit·tle \'lit-əl\ *adj* **lit·tler** \'lit-(ə-)lər\ *or* **less** \'les\ *or* **less·er** \'les-ər\; **lit·tlest** \'lit-(ə-)ləst\ *or* **least** \'lēst\ **1 a** : small in size or extent : TINY **b** : small in comparison with related forms ⟨*little* blue heron⟩ ⟨*little* celandine⟩ **c** : small in number **d** : small in condition, distinction, or scope **e** : NARROW, MEAN ⟨men of *little* natures⟩ **2 a** : small in quantity or degree : not much ⟨*little* food⟩ **b** : short in duration : BRIEF ⟨*little* time left⟩ **3** : small in importance or interest : TRIVIAL — **lit·tle·ness** \'lit-əl-nəs\ *n*
[2]little *adv* **less** \'les\; **least** \'lēst\ **1** : in only a small quantity or degree : SLIGHTLY ⟨had *little* more than he needed⟩ **2** : INFREQUENTLY, RARELY
[3]little *n* **1** : a small amount or quantity **2** : a short time or distance
Little Dipper *n* : the smaller of the stellar dippers
little finger *n* : the fourth finger of the hand counting the finger next to the thumb as one
[1]lit·to·ral \'lit-ə-rəl; ,lit-ə-'ral, -'räl\ *adj* : of, relating to, or situated or growing on or near a shore esp. of the sea
[2]littoral *n* : a coastal region; *esp* : the area between high and low watermarks
lit·ur·gy \'lit-ər-jē\ *n, pl* **-gies** : a rite or body of rites prescribed for public worship — **li·tur·gi·cal** \lə-'tər-ji-kəl\ *adj*
liv·a·ble *also* **live·a·ble** \'liv-ə-bəl\ *adj* **1** : suitable for living in or with **2** : ENDURABLE — **liv·a·bil·i·ty** \,liv-ə-'bil-ət-ē\ *n* — **liv·a·ble·ness** \'liv-ə-bəl-nəs\ *n*
[1]live \'liv\ *vb* **1** : to be or continue alive : have life **2** : to maintain oneself : SUBSIST ⟨*live* on fruits⟩ **3** : to conduct or pass one's life ⟨*lived* up to his principles⟩ **4** : DWELL, RESIDE **5** : to remain in human memory or record **6** : to pass through or spend the duration of ⟨*lives* a life of misery⟩ **7** : ENACT, PRACTICE ⟨*lives* what he preaches⟩
[2]live \'līv\ *adj* **1** : having life : LIVING **2** : LIVELY, VIVID **3 a** : AFIRE, GLOWING ⟨*live* cigar⟩ **b** : carrying an electric current ⟨a *live* wire⟩ **c** : charged with explosives and containing shot or a bullet ⟨*live* ammunition⟩; *also* : UNEXPLODED ⟨*live* bomb⟩ **4** : of continuing or current interest ⟨a *live* issue⟩ **5** : being in play ⟨a *live* ball⟩ **6 a** : of or involving the actual presence of people ⟨*live* audience⟩ **b** : broadcast directly at the time of production instead of from recorded or filmed material ⟨a *live* radio program⟩

lived \ˈlīvd, ˈlivd\ *adj* : having a life of a specified kind or length ⟨long-*lived*⟩

live down *vb* : to live so as to wipe out the memory or effects of ⟨*lived down* his evil reputation⟩

live·li·hood \ˈlīv-lē-ˌhu̇d\ *n* : means of support or subsistence

live·long \ˌliv-ˌlȯng\ *adj* : WHOLE, ENTIRE ⟨all the *livelong* day⟩

live·ly \ˈlīv-lē\ *adj* **live·li·er**; **-est** **1** : full of life : ACTIVE ⟨a *lively* puppy⟩ **2** : KEEN, VIVID ⟨a *lively* interest⟩ **3** : full of spirit or feeling : ANIMATED ⟨a *lively* debate⟩ **4** : showing activity or vigor ⟨a *lively* manner⟩ **5** : rebounding quickly ⟨a *lively* tennis ball⟩ — **live·li·ly** \ˈlīv-lə-lē\ *adv* — **live·li·ness** \ˈlīv-lē-nəs\ *n* — **lively** *adv*

liv·en \ˈlī-vən\ *vb* **liv·ened**; **liv·en·ing** \ˈlīv-(ə-)ning\ : ENLIVEN

live oak \ˈlīv-ˌōk\ *n* : any of several American evergreen oaks with hard durable wood; *esp* : one found in the southeastern states cultivated for its shelter and shade and formerly much used in building ships

[1]**liv·er** \ˈliv-ər\ *n* **1 a** : a large glandular organ of vertebrates that secretes bile and causes changes in the blood (as by converting sugars into glycogen) **b** : any of various large prob. digestive glands of invertebrate animals **2** : the tissue of the liver (as of a calf or pig) eaten as food — **liv·ered** \-ərd\ *adj*

[2]**liv·er** \ˈliv-ər\ : one that lives esp. in a specified way

liver fluke *n* : any of various trematode worms that invade the liver of mammals

liv·er·ied \ˈliv-(ə-)rēd\ *adj* : wearing a livery

liv·er·wort \ˈliv-ər-ˌwərt, -ˌwȯrt\ *n* : any of a class of flowerless plants related to and resembling the mosses but differing esp. in reproduction and development

liverworts: female and male plants (about life-size)

liv·er·wurst \ˈliv-ə(r)-ˌwərst, -ˌwu̇rst\ *n* : a sausage consisting chiefly of liver

liv·ery \ˈliv-(ə-)rē\ *n, pl* **-er·ies** **1** : a special uniform worn by the servants of a wealthy household ⟨a footman in *livery*⟩ **2** : distinctive dress ⟨the *livery* of a school⟩ **3 a** : the feeding, care, and stabling of horses for pay; *also* : the keeping of horses and vehicles for hire **b** : LIVERY STABLE

livery stable *n* : a stable where horses and vehicles are kept for hire and where stabling is provided

lives *pl of* LIFE

live steam *n* : steam direct from a boiler and under pressure so that it can do work

live·stock \ˈlīv-ˌstäk\ *n* : animals kept or raised; *esp* : farm animals kept for use and profit

live wire *n* : an alert active aggressive person

liv·id \ˈliv-əd\ *adj* **1** : discolored by bruising **2** : ASHEN, PALE ⟨*livid* with rage⟩ — **liv·id·ly** *adv* — **liv·id·ness** *n*

[1]**liv·ing** \ˈliv-ing\ *adj* **1 a** : not dead or inanimate : ALIVE ⟨*living* authors⟩ **b** : ACTIVE, FUNCTIONING ⟨a *living* faith⟩ **2** : naturally giving life : INVIGORATING ⟨*living* waters⟩ **3 a** : full of life or vigor ⟨made mathematics a *living* subject⟩ **b** : true to life ⟨the *living* image of his father⟩ **4** : suited or adequate for living ⟨the *living* area⟩

[2]**living** *n* **1** : the condition of being alive **2** : conduct or manner of life ⟨right *living*⟩ **3** : means of subsistence : LIVELIHOOD

living fossil *n* : an animal or plant (as the horseshoe crab or the ginkgo tree) that has remained almost unchanged from earlier geologic times and whose near relatives are nearly all extinct

living room *n* : a room in a residence used for common social activities

liz·ard \ˈliz-ərd\ *n* : any of a group of reptiles distinguished from the related snakes by a fused inseparable lower jaw, external ears, eyes with movable lids, and usu. two pairs of well-formed functional limbs

ll *abbr* lines

lla·ma \ˈläm-ə\ *n* : any of several wild and domesticated So. American cud-chewing hoofed mammals related to the camels but smaller and without a hump

llama (about 50 in. at shoulder)

lla·no \ˈlän-ō\ *n, pl* **llanos** : an open grassy plain esp. of tropical Spanish America

LLD *abbr* doctor of laws

L level \ˈel-ˌlev-əl\ *n* : the second available energy level for electrons in an atom

ln *abbr* lane

lo \ˈlō\ *interj* — used to call attention

[1]**load** \ˈlōd\ *n* **1 a** : whatever is put on a man or pack animal to be carried **b** : whatever is put in a ship or vehicle or aircraft for conveyance : CARGO **c** : the quantity that can be carried at one time ⟨10 *loads* of sand⟩ — often used in combination ⟨a boat*load* of tourists⟩ **2** : a mass or weight supported by something ⟨the *load* on a column⟩ **3 a** : something that oppresses the mind or spirits ⟨a *load* of care⟩ **b** : a burdensome responsibility **4** : a large quantity : LOT — usu. used in pl. **5** : a charge for a firearm **6 a** : amount of work performed or expected to be performed **b** : the demand upon the operating resources of a system (as a telephone exchange or a refrigerating apparatus)

[2]**load** *vb* **1 a** : to put a load in or on; *also* : to receive a load **b** : to place in or on a means of conveyance ⟨*load* coal⟩ **2 a** : to place or be a weight or stress upon ⟨vines *loaded* down with grapes⟩ **b** : to encumber or oppress with something laborious or disheartening : BURDEN ⟨a mind *loaded* with cares⟩ **c** : to place as a burden or obligation ⟨*load* more work on him⟩ **3 a** : to increase in weight by adding a heavy substance ⟨*loaded* dice⟩ **b** : to influence by factors supporting one side : BIAS ⟨*loaded* questions⟩ **4** : to supply in abundance or excess : HEAP ⟨*loaded* food on his plate⟩ ⟨*load* him with honors⟩ **5** : to place or insert a load or as a load ⟨*load* film in a camera⟩ ⟨*load* a gun⟩ — **load·er** *n*

load·ed \ˈlōd-əd\ *adj* **1** *slang* : DRUNK **2** : WEALTHY, RICH

load·star *var of* LODESTAR

load·stone *var of* LODESTONE

[1]**loaf** \ˈlōf\ *n, pl* **loaves** \ˈlōvz\ **1** : a shaped or

ə abut	ər further	a back	ā bake
ä cot, cart	au̇ out	ch chin	e less	ē easy
g gift	i trip	ī life	j joke	ng sing	ō flow
ȯ flaw	ȯi coin	th thin	t͟h this	ü loot
u̇ foot	y yet	yü few	yu̇ furious	zh vision

molded mass of bread **2 :** a regularly molded often rectangular mass **3 :** a dish (as of meat or fish) baked in the form of a loaf

2**loaf** *vb* **1 :** to spend time in idleness : LOUNGE **2 :** to pass idly ⟨*loaf* the time away⟩ — **loaf·er** *n*

loam \'lōm, 'lüm\ *n* : SOIL; *esp* : a soil consisting of a loose easily crumbled mixture of varying proportions of clay, silt, and sand — **loamy** \'lō-mē, 'lü-\ *adj*

1**loan** \'lōn\ *n* **1 :** something loaned; *esp* : money let out at interest **2 :** permission to use something temporarily

2**loan** *vb* : to give for temporary possession or use

loan shark *n* : a person who lends money at excessive rates of interest

loath \'lōth, 'lō*th*\ *adj* : unwilling to do something : RELUCTANT ⟨*loath* to go against his principles⟩

loathe \'lō*th*\ *vb* : to feel extreme disgust for or at : DETEST ⟨*loathe* the smell of burning rubber⟩ ***syn*** see HATE ***ant*** dote (on)

loath·ing \'lō-*th*ing\ *n* : extreme disgust : DETESTATION

loath·some \'lōth-səm, 'lō*th*-\ *adj* : exciting loathing : DISGUSTING — **loath·some·ness** *n*

1**lob** \'läb\ *vb* **lobbed; lob·bing 1 :** to throw, hit, or propel slowly in a high curve **2 :** to move slowly and heavily

2**lob** *n* : a tennis ball hit slowly in a high arc

lobar pneumonia *n* : acute pneumonia involving one or more lobes of the lung

lo·bate \'lō-ˌbāt\ *or* **lo·bat·ed** \-ˌbāt-əd\ *adj* : having lobes or rounded divisions ⟨a *lobate* leaf⟩

1**lob·by** \'läb-ē\ *n, pl* **lobbies 1 :** a hall (as of a hotel or theater) used as a passageway or waiting room **2 :** a group of persons engaged in lobbying for a single interest ⟨the oil *lobby*⟩

2**lobby** *vb* **lob·bied; lob·by·ing 1 :** to try to influence public officials and esp. members of a legislative body **2 :** to promote or secure the passage of by influencing public officials — **lob·by·ist** \-ē-əst\ *n*

lobe \'lōb\ *n* : a curved or rounded projection or division; *esp* : such a subdivision of a bodily organ or part — **lobed** \'lōbd\ *adj*

lobe–fin \'lōb-ˌfin\ *n* : any of a large group of mostly extinct fishes that have paired fins suggesting limbs and may be ancestral to the terrestrial vertebrates — compare LATIMERIA — **lobe–finned** \-'find\ *adj*

lo·be·lia \lō-'bēl-yə\ *n* : any of a genus of widely distributed herbs (as the cardinal flower) often grown for their terminal clusters of showy lipped flowers

lob·lol·ly pine \ˌläb-ˌläl-ē-\ *n* : a pine of the southern U.S. with thick flaky bark, long needles in threes, and spiny-tipped cones; *also* : its coarse-grained wood — called also *lob·lol·ly* \'läb-\

lob·ster \'läb-stər\ *n* : any of several large edible marine crustaceans with stalked eyes, a pair of large claws, and a long abdomen; *also* : SPINY LOBSTER — **lobster** *adj*

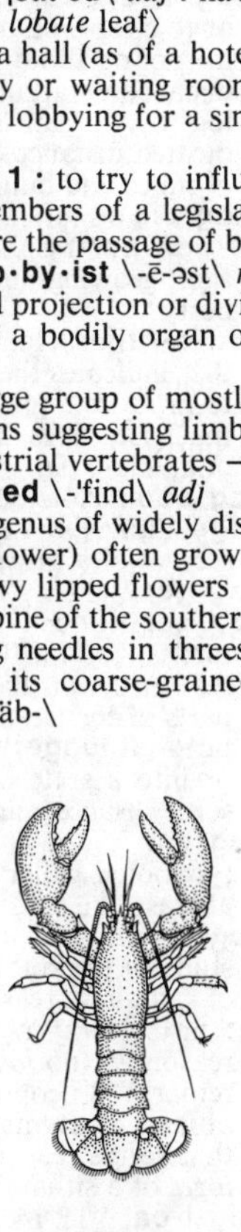

lobster
(about 9 in. long)

lobster pot *n* : a trap for catching lobsters

1**lo·cal** \'lō-kəl\ *adj* **1 :** characterized by or relating to position in space **2 :** characterized by, relating to, or occupying a particular place ⟨*local* news⟩ ⟨a *local* custom⟩ **3 :** involving or affecting only a small part of the body ⟨a *local* infection⟩ **4 :** primarily serving the needs of a particular limited district ⟨*local* government⟩ **5 :** making all the stops on a run ⟨a *local* train⟩ — **lo·cal·ly** \-kə-lē\ *adv*

2**local** *n* **1 :** a local train or other public conveyance **2 :** a local branch (as of a labor union)

local color *n* : features and peculiarities used in a story or play that suggest a particular locality and its inhabitants

lo·cale \lō-'kal\ *n* : PLACE, SCENE, LOCALITY ⟨the *locale* of the accident⟩ ⟨the *locale* of a play⟩

lo·cal·ism \'lō-kə-ˌliz-əm\ *n* **1 :** the inclination to be strongly interested in the affairs of one's own locality **2 :** a local manner of speech

lo·cal·i·ty \lō-'kal-ət-ē\ *n, pl* **-ties** : a particular spot, situation, or location

lo·cal·ize \'lō-kə-ˌlīz\ *vb* : to make or become local : fix in or assign or confine to a definite place or locality ⟨pain *localized* in a joint⟩ — **lo·cal·i·za·tion** \ˌlō-kə-lə-'zā-shən\ *n*

lo·cate \'lō-ˌkāt, lō-'\ *vb* **1 :** to establish oneself or one's business : set or establish in a particular spot : SETTLE **2 :** to determine or indicate the place, site, or limits of ⟨*locate* a lost ring⟩ **3 :** to find or fix the place of in a sequence ⟨*locate* an event in history⟩ — **lo·cat·er** *n*

lo·ca·tion \lō-'kā-shən\ *n* **1 :** the process of locating **2 :** SITUATION, PLACE; *esp* : a locality of or for a building **3 :** a tract of land (as a mining claim) whose boundaries and purpose have been designated **4 :** a place outside a studio where a motion picture is filmed ⟨on *location* in the desert⟩

loch \'läk, 'lä*k*\ *n* **1** *Scot* : LAKE **2** *Scot* : an arm of the sea esp. when nearly landlocked

loci *pl of* LOCUS

1**lock** \'läk\ *n* **1 :** a strand or ringlet of hair **2 :** a cohering bunch (as of wool, cotton, or flax)

2**lock** *n* **1 a :** a fastening (as for a door) in which a bolt is operated **b :** the mechanism for exploding the charge or cartridge of a firearm **2 :** an enclosure (as in a canal) with gates at each end used in raising or lowering boats as they pass from level to level **3 :** a hold in wrestling secured on one part of the body ⟨a leg *lock*⟩

3**lock** *vb* **1 :** to make or become fast with or as if with a lock ⟨*lock* up the house⟩ ⟨the door *locks* from the inside⟩ **2 a :** to enclose or confine by means of locks ⟨*locked* up her jewels⟩ ⟨*locked* in jail⟩ **b :** to make or become fast or inactive : FIX ⟨the wheels *locked*⟩ **3 a :** to make fast by the linking of parts ⟨*lock* arms⟩ **b :** to hold tight; *also* : to grapple in combat

lock·er \'läk-ər\ *n* **1 :** a drawer, cabinet, compartment, or chest for personal use usu. with a lock **2 :** an insulated compartment for storing food at a low temperature

lock·et \'läk-ət\ *n* : a small ornamental case usu. worn on a chain

lock·jaw \'läk-ˌjȯ\ *n* : a symptom of tetanus characterized by spasm of the jaw muscles and inability to open the jaws; *also* : TETANUS

lock·out \-ˌau̇t\ *n* : the suspension of work or closing of a plant by an employer during a labor dispute in order to make his employees accept his terms

lock·smith \-ˌsmith\ *n* : one who makes or repairs locks

lock·step \-ˌstep\ *n* : a mode of marching in step in a very close single file

lock·up \-ˌəp\ *n* : JAIL; *esp* : one where persons are detained prior to court hearing

lo·co \'lō-kō\ *adj, slang* : out of one's mind : CRAZY, MAD

lo·co·ism \'lō-kō-ˌiz-əm\ *n* : a nervous disease of horses, cattle, and sheep caused by chronic poisoning with locoweeds

L

lo·co·mo·tion \ˌlō-kə-ˈmō-shən\ *n* : the act or power of moving from place to place

1**lo·co·mo·tive** \ˌlō-kə-ˈmōt-iv\ *adj* **1** : of or relating to locomotion **2** : of, relating to, or being a locomotive

2**locomotive** *n* : an engine that moves under its own power; *esp* : one that hauls cars on a railroad

lo·co·mo·tor \ˌlō-kə-ˈmōt-ər\ *adj* : affecting or involving the locomotive organs

lo·co·weed \ˈlō-kō-ˌwēd\ *n* : any of several leguminous plants of western No. America that cause locoism in livestock

locoweed

lo·cus \ˈlō-kəs\ *n, pl* **lo·ci** \ˈlō-ˌsī\ **1** : PLACE, LOCALITY **2** : the set of all points whose location is determined by stated conditions

lo·cust \ˈlō-kəst\ *n* **1 a** : SHORT-HORNED GRASSHOPPER; *esp* : a migratory grasshopper often traveling in vast swarms and stripping the areas passed of vegetation **b** : CICADA **2 a** : any of various hard-wooded leguminous trees **b** : the wood of a locust

lo·cu·tion \lō-ˈkyü-shən\ *n* **1** : a particular form of expression ⟨involved *locutions*⟩ **2** : style of expression or speaking

lode \ˈlōd\ *n* **1** : a mass or strip of a mineral (as gold or copper ore) that fills a crack in rock **2** : a mass of ore in the earth or among rocks

lode·star \-ˌstär\ *n* : a star that leads or guides; *esp* : NORTH STAR

lode·stone \-ˌstōn\ *n* **1** : a rock having magnetic properties **2** : something that strongly attracts

1**lodge** \ˈläj\ *vb* **1 a** : to provide or serve as esp. temporary quarters for ⟨*lodged* his guests overnight⟩ **b** : to establish or settle oneself in a place **c** : DWELL **d** : to rent lodgings to **2** : to serve as a receptacle for : CONTAIN **3** : to bring or come to a rest and remain ⟨the bone *lodged* in his throat⟩ ⟨the bullet *lodged* in a tree⟩ **4** : to lay before a proper authority : FILE ⟨*lodge* a complaint⟩

2**lodge** *n* **1 a** : a house set apart for residence in a special season ⟨hunting *lodge*⟩ **b** : a resort hotel **c** : a house for an employee on an estate ⟨gamekeeper's *lodge*⟩ **2** : a den or lair of wild animals **3** : the meeting place of a branch (as of a fraternal organization); *also* : the members of such a branch **4 a** : WIGWAM **b** : a family of No. American Indians

lodge·pole pine \ˌläj-ˌpōl-\ *n* : either of two western No. American pines with needles in pairs and short irregular cones

lodg·er \ˈläj-ər\ *n* : one that lodges; *esp* : one that occupies a rented room in another's house

lodg·ing \ˈläj-ing\ *n* **1** : DWELLING; *esp* : a temporary dwelling or sleeping place **2** : a room or suite of rooms in another's house rented as a dwelling — usu. used in pl.

lodging house *n* : ROOMING HOUSE

lodg·ment *or* **lodge·ment** \ˈläj-mənt\ *n* **1 a** : a lodging place : SHELTER **b** : LODGINGS **2** : the act, fact, or manner of lodging; *esp* : a placing, depositing, or coming to rest **3** : an accumulation of something deposited in a place ⟨a *lodgment* of leaves in a gutter⟩

loess \ˈles, ˈlə(r)s, ˈlō-əs\ *n* : a usu. yellowish brown loamy deposit found in No. America, Europe, and Asia and believed to be chiefly deposited by the wind

1**loft** \ˈlȯft\ *n* **1** : ATTIC **2 a** : a gallery in a church or hall ⟨organ *loft*⟩ **b** : an upper floor of a warehouse or business building when not partitioned **c** : HAYLOFT **3 a** : the backward slant of the face of a golf club head **b** : HEIGHT ⟨the ball had too much *loft*⟩

2**loft** *vb* **1** : to place, house, or store in a loft **2** : to strike or throw a ball so that it rises high in the air ⟨*lofted* a high fly to center field⟩

lofty \ˈlȯf-tē\ *adj* **loft·i·er**; **-est** **1** : PROUD, HAUGHTY ⟨a *lofty* air⟩ **2 a** : NOBLE ⟨*lofty* ideals⟩ **b** : of high rank : SUPERIOR **3** : rising high : TOWERING ⟨a *lofty* oak⟩ ***syn*** see HIGH — **loft·i·ly** \-tə-lē\ *adv* — **loft·i·ness** \-tē-nəs\ *n*

1**log** \ˈlȯg, ˈläg\ *n* **1** : a bulky piece of unshaped timber; *esp* : a long piece of a tree trunk trimmed and ready for sawing **2** : an apparatus for measuring the rate of a ship's motion through the water that consists of a block fastened to a line and run out from a reel **3 a** : the daily record of a ship's speed and progress **b** : the full record of a ship's voyage or of an aircraft's flight **4** : a record of performance (as the operating history of an aircraft or the flying time of a pilot)

2**log** *vb* **logged**; **log·ging** **1** : to cut trees for lumber or to clear land of trees in lumbering **2** : to enter details of or about in a log **3 a** : to move an indicated distance or attain an indicated speed as noted in a log **b** : to sail a ship or fly an aircraft for an indicated distance or time ⟨the pilot *logged* thousands of miles and hundreds of hours⟩

3**log** *n* : LOGARITHM

lo·gan·ber·ry \ˈlō-gən-ˌber-ē\ *n* : a red-fruited upright-growing and prob. hybrid dewberry; *also* : its berry

log·a·rithm \ˈlȯg-ə-ˌrith-əm, ˈläg-\ *n* : the exponent that indicates the power to which a number is raised to produce a given number ⟨the *logarithm* of 100 to the base 10 is 2⟩ — **log·a·rith·mic** \ˌlȯg-ə-ˈrith-mik, ˌläg-\ *adj*

log·book \ˈlȯg-ˌbu̇k, ˈläg-\ *n* : LOG 3, 4

loge \ˈlōzh\ *n* **1** : a box in a theater **2** : the forward section of a theater mezzanine

log·ger \ˈlȯg-ər, ˈläg-\ *n* : one engaged in logging

log·ger·head \-ˌhed\ *n* : any of various very large turtles; *esp* : a flesh-eating sea turtle of the warmer parts of the western Atlantic — **at loggerheads** : in or into a state of quarrelsome disagreement

loggerhead (about 3 ft. long)

log·gia \ˈlō-jē-ə, ˈlȯ-jä\ *n* : a roofed gallery open on at least one side

log·ic \ˈläj-ik\ *n* **1** : the study of the rules and tests of sound reasoning **2** : REASONING; *esp* : sound reasoning ⟨no *logic* in that remark⟩ **3** : connection (as of facts or events) in a way that seems reasonable ⟨the *logic* of a situation⟩ — **lo·gi·cian** \lō-ˈjish-ən\ *n*

log·i·cal \ˈläj-i-kəl\ *adj* **1** : of or relating to logic : used in logic **2** : conforming to the rules of logic ⟨a *logical* argument⟩ **3** : skilled in logic ⟨a *logical* thinker⟩ **4 :** reasonably to be expected ⟨a *logical* result of an action⟩ — **log·i·cal·ly** \-k(ə-)lē\ *adv* — **log·i·cal·ness** \-kəl-nəs\ *n*

lo·gis·tics \lō-ˈjis-tiks\ *n sing or pl* **:** a branch of military science that deals with the transportation, quartering, and supplying of troops in military operations — **lo·gis·tic** \-tik\ *or* **lo·gis·ti·cal** \-ti-kəl\ *adj*

log·roll·ing \ˈlȯg-ˌrō-ling, ˈläg-\ *n* **1 :** the rolling of logs in water by treading **2 :** the trading of votes by two legislators to secure favorable action on projects of interest to each

log·wood \ˈlȯg-ˌwu̇d, ˈläg-\ *n* **:** a Central American and West Indian leguminous tree; *also* **:** its hard brown or brownish red heartwood used in dyeing or an extract of this

lo·gy \ˈlō-gē\ *adj* **lo·gi·er; -est :** SLUGGISH, TIRED — **lo·gi·ness** \-gē-nəs\ *n*

-l·o·gy \l-ə-jē\ *n comb form* **:** doctrine **:** theory **:** science ⟨bio*logy*⟩

loin \ˈlȯin\ *n* **1 a :** the part of the body on each side of the spinal column and between the hip and the lower ribs **b :** a cut of meat comprising the loin of one or both sides of a carcass with the adjoining half of the vertebrae included but without the flank **2** *pl* **a :** the pubic region **b :** the organs of reproduction

loin·cloth \-ˌklȯth\ *n* **:** a cloth worn as a garment about the loins

loi·ter \ˈlȯit-ər\ *vb* **1 :** to interrupt or delay an errand or a journey with aimless stops **2 a :** to hang around idly **b :** to lag behind ***syn*** see LINGER — **loi·ter·er** *n*

loll \ˈläl\ *vb* **1 :** to hang or let hang loosely **:** DROOP **2 :** to recline, lean, or move in a lax or indolent manner **:** LOUNGE ⟨*loll* around in the sun⟩

lol·li·pop *or* **lol·ly·pop** \ˈläl-ē-ˌpäp\ *n* **:** a lump of hard candy on the end of a stick

Lond *abbr* London

lone \ˈlōn\ *adj* **1 :** having no company **:** SOLITARY ⟨a *lone* traveler⟩ **2 :** situated by itself **:** ISOLATED ⟨*lone* outpost⟩

lone·ly \ˈlōn-lē\ *adj* **lone·li·er; -est 1 :** LONE **2 :** UNFREQUENTED, DESOLATE ⟨a *lonely* spot⟩ **3 :** LONESOME ⟨feeling *lonely*⟩ — **lone·li·ness** *n*

lone·some \ˈlōn(t)-səm\ *adj* **1 :** sad from lack of companionship or separation from others **2 :** REMOTE, UNFREQUENTED — **lone·some·ness** *n*

[1]**long** \ˈlȯng\ *adj* **long·er** \ˈlȯng-gər\; **long·est** \ˈlȯng-gəst\ **1 :** of great extent from end to end **:** not short **2 a :** having a specified length ⟨a yard *long*⟩ **b :** forming the chief linear dimension ⟨the *long* side⟩ **3 :** lasting for a considerable or specified time **4 :** unduly long **5 :** containing many or a specified number of units ⟨a *long* series of wins⟩ **6 :** being a syllable or speech sound of relatively great duration **7 :** extending far into the future ⟨take a *long* view of things⟩ **8 :** strong in or well furnished with something ⟨*long* on golf⟩ — **at long last :** after a long wait **:** FINALLY

[2]**long** *adv* **1 :** for or during a long time **2 :** for the duration of a specified period ⟨all summer *long*⟩ **3 :** at a distant point of time ⟨*long* before we came⟩ — **as long as** *or* **so long as 1 :** in view of the fact that **:** SINCE **2 :** PROVIDED, IF — **so long :** GOOD-BYE

[3]**long** *vb* **longed; long·ing** \ˈlȯng-ing\ **:** to feel a strong desire or wish **:** YEARN

long *abbr* longitude

long·boat \ˈlȯng-ˌbōt\ *n* **:** a large boat carried on a ship

long bone *n* **:** one of the bones supporting a vertebrate limb and consisting of a long nearly cylindrical shaft that contains marrow and ends in enlarged heads

long·bow \ˈlȯng-bō\ *n* **:** a wooden bow drawn by hand and usu. 5½ to 6 feet long

[1]**long-dis·tance** \-ˈdis-tən(t)s\ *adj* **:** of or relating to telephone communication with a distant point

[2]**long-distance** *adv* **:** by long-distance telephone

long distance *n* **1 :** communication by long-distance telephone **2 :** a telephone operator or exchange that gives long-distance connections

long division *n* **:** arithmetical division in which the several steps corresponding to the division of parts of the dividend by the divisor are indicated in detail

lon·gev·i·ty \län-ˈjev-ət-ē, lȯn-\ *n* **1 :** long life **2 :** length of life

long·hand \ˈlȯng-ˌhand\ *n* **:** the characters used in ordinary writing **:** HANDWRITING

long·horn \-ˌhȯrn\ *n* **:** any of the long-horned cattle of Spanish derivation formerly common in the southwestern U.S.

long-horned \-ˈhȯrnd\ *adj* **:** having long horns or antennae

long·ing \ˈlȯng-ing\ *n* **:** an eager desire **:** CRAVING — **long·ing·ly** \-ing-lē\ *adv*

long·ish \ˈlȯng-ish\ *adj* **:** somewhat long

lon·gi·tude \ˈlän-jə-ˌt(y)üd\ *n* **:** distance measured by degrees or time east or west from the prime meridian ⟨the *longitude* of New York is 74 degrees or about five hours west of Greenwich⟩

longitude : hemisphere marked with meridians of longitude

lon·gi·tu·di·nal \ˌlän-jə-ˈt(y)üd-(ə-)nəl\ *adj* **1 :** of or relating to length **2 :** placed or running lengthwise — **lon·gi·tu·di·nal·ly** \-ē\ *adv*

long johns \ˈlȯng-ˌjänz\ *n pl* **:** long underwear

long·leaf pine \ˌlȯng-ˌlēf-\ *also* **long-leaved pine** \-ˌlēv(d)-\ *n* **:** a large pine of the southern U.S. that has long slim clustered needles and long cones and is a major timber tree; *also* **:** its tough coarse-grained durable wood

long-lived \ˈlȯng-ˈlīvd, -ˈlivd\ *adj* **:** living or lasting long — **long-lived·ness** \-ˈlīv(d)-nəs, -ˈliv(d)-\ *n*

long-play·ing \ˈlȯng-ˈplā-ing\ *adj* **:** of, relating to, or being a record ordinarily having a diameter of 10 or 12 inches and turning at 33 1/3 revolutions per minute

long-range \-ˈrānj\ *adj* **1 :** capable of traveling or shooting over great distances ⟨a *long-range* gun⟩ **2 :** LONG-TERM ⟨*long-range* planning⟩

long·shore·man \ˈlȯng-ˈshōr-mən, -ˈshȯr-\ *n* **:** a laborer at a wharf who loads and unloads cargo

long shot \ˈlȯng-ˌshät\ *n* **:** an entry (as in a horse race) given little chance of winning

long-suf·fer·ing \-ˈsəf-(ə-)ring\ *or* **long-suf·fer·ance** \-(ə-)rən(t)s\ *n* **:** long and patient endurance — **long-suffering** *adj* — **long-suf·fer·ing·ly** \-(ə-)ring-lē\ *adv*

long-term \-ˈtərm\ *adj* **:** extending over or involving a long period of time

long-wind·ed \-ˈwin-dəd\ *adj* **:** tediously long in speaking or writing — **long-wind·ed·ly** *adv* — **long-wind·ed·ness** *n*

[1]**look** \ˈlu̇k\ *vb* **1 :** to exercise the power of vision **:** SEE **2 :** to express by the eyes or facial expression **3 a :** to have an appearance that befits or accords with ⟨*looks* her age⟩ **b :** APPEAR, SEEM ⟨it *looks* dangerous⟩ **4 :** to direct one's attention or eyes ⟨*look* in the mirror⟩ **5 :** POINT, FACE ⟨the house *looks*

east⟩ — **look after** : to take care of : attend to — **look daggers** : to look threateningly — **look down on** : to treat as an inferior : DESPISE — **look for 1** : EXPECT **2** : to search for : SEEK — **look forward to** : to expect with pleasure : ANTICIPATE — **look on** *or* **look upon** : CONSIDER, REGARD ⟨*looked upon* him as a friend⟩ — **look out for 1** : to be on guard against ⟨*look out for* the trains⟩ **2** : to care for : PROTECT ⟨*look out for* his interests⟩ — **look up** : to seek for or out ⟨*look up* a word in the dictionary⟩ ⟨*look up* a friend⟩

2**look** *n* **1 a** : the action of looking **b** : GLANCE **2 a** : the expression of the countenance **b** : physical appearance; *esp* : attractive physical appearance — usu. used in pl. **3** : the state or form in which something appears : ASPECT

look·er–on \ˌlu̇k-ər-ˈȯn, -ˈän\ *n, pl* **lookers–on** : ONLOOKER, SPECTATOR

looking glass *n* : MIRROR

look·out \ˈlu̇k-ˌau̇t\ *n* **1** : a person engaged in watching; *esp* : one assigned to watch a ship **2** : an elevated place or structure affording a wide view for observation **3** : a careful looking or watching **4** : VIEW, OUTLOOK **5** : a matter of care or concern

1**loom** \ˈlüm\ *n* : a frame or machine for weaving threads or yarns into cloth

2**loom** *vb* **1** : to appear in a large, indistinct, or distorted form ⟨*loomed* out of the fog⟩ **2** : to be about to happen : IMPEND

loon \ˈlün\ *n* : any of several fish-eating diving birds with webbed feet, black head, and white-spotted black back

loon (about 35 in. long)

loo·ny *or* **loo·ney** \ˈlü-nē\ *adj* **loo·ni·er; -est** : CRAZY, FOOLISH — **loony** *n*

1**loop** \ˈlüp\ *n* **1** : a fold or doubling of a line through which another line can be passed or into which a hook may be hooked **2** : a loop-shaped ornament, figure, bend, or course ⟨a *loop* in a river⟩ **3** : a circular airplane maneuver involving flying upside down **4** : a complete electric circuit **5** : a piece of film whose ends are spliced together to project the same things continuously — **for a loop** : into a state of amazement, confusion, or distress ⟨the news knocked her *for a loop*⟩

2**loop** *vb* **1** : to make or form a loop **2 a** : to make a loop in, on, or about **b** : to fasten with a loop **3** : to execute a loop in an airplane

loop·er \ˈlü-pər\ *n* **1** : any of numerous small caterpillars that are mostly larvae of moths, move with a looping movement, and have little or no hair **2** : one that loops

looper 1 (about 1½ in. long

loop·hole \ˈlüp-ˌhōl\ *n* **1** : a small opening; *esp* : one in a wall through which firearms may be discharged **2** : a means of escape; *esp* : a way of evading a law or regulation

1**loose** \ˈlüs\ *adj* **1 a** : not rigidly fastened or securely attached **b** : not attached : DISCONNECTED ⟨a boat *loose* from its moorings⟩ **c** : not tight-fitting **2 a** : free from confinement, restraint, or obligation **b** : not brought together in a bundle, container, or binding ⟨*loose* sheets of pages⟩ **3** : not dense or compact ⟨*loose* dirt⟩ ⟨cloth of *loose* weave⟩ **4** : lacking in restraint : IMMORAL ⟨*loose* conduct⟩ **5** : not tightly drawn or stretched : SLACK **6** : lacking in precision, exactness, or care ⟨a *loose* guess⟩ — **loose** *adv* — **loose·ly** *adv* — **loose·ness** *n*

2**loose** *vb* **1** : LOOSEN **2** : DISCHARGE, FIRE ⟨*loose* a volley⟩

loose–joint·ed \ˈlüs-ˈjȯint-əd\ *adj* : having a flexibility or lack of rigidity suggesting the absence of rigid joints; *esp* : moving with unusual freedom or ease — **loose–joint·ed·ness** *n*

loos·en \ˈlüs-ən\ *vb* **loos·ened; loos·en·ing** \-(ə-)niŋ\ **1** : to release from restraint **2** : to make or become loose or looser **3** : to cause or permit to become less strict

loose·strife \ˈlü(s)-ˌstrīf\ *n* **1** : any of a genus of plants that are related to the primrose and have leafy stems and yellow or white flowers **2** : any of a genus of herbs including some with showy spikes of purple flowers **3** : SWAMP LOOSESTRIFE

1**loot** \ˈlüt\ *n* [from Hindi *lūṭ*] : something stolen or taken by force : SPOILS, PLUNDER

2**loot** *vb* : PLUNDER, STEAL — **loot·er** *n*

lop \ˈläp\ *vb* **lopped; lop·ping 1** : to cut branches or twigs from a tree ⟨*lop* a tree⟩ **2** : to remove unnecessary or undesirable parts from something — usu. used with *off* — **lop·per** *n*

lope \ˈlōp\ *n* : an easy bounding gait (as of a wolf) — **lope** *vb* — **lop·er** *n*

lop–eared \ˈläp-ˈi(ə)rd\ *adj* : having ears that droop

lop·sid·ed \ˈläp-ˈsīd-əd\ *adj* : leaning to one side : UNBALANCED — **lop·sid·ed·ness** *n*

lo·qua·cious \lō-ˈkwā-shəs\ *adj* : overly talkative — **lo·qua·cious·ly** *adv* — **lo·qua·cious·ness** *n* — **lo·quac·i·ty** \-ˈkwas-ət-ē\ *n*

lo·quat \ˈlō-ˌkwät\ *n* : a small Asiatic evergreen tree bearing a yellow plumlike fruit; *also* : its fruit used esp. in preserves

1**lord** \ˈlȯrd\ *n* [from Old English *hlāford*, originally meaning "head of a household", from *hlāf* "loaf of bread" and *weard* "keeper", "ward"] **1 a** : a person who has power and authority; *esp* : a ruler to whom service and obedience are due **b** : a person from whom a feudal fee or estate is held **2** *cap* **a** : 2GOD **b** : JESUS CHRIST **3** : a man of rank or high position: as **a** : a feudal tenant holding directly of the king **b** : a British nobleman or a bishop entitled to sit in the House of Lords — used as a title **c** *pl, cap* : HOUSE OF LORDS

2**lord** *vb* : to act or command arrogantly : DOMINEER — used with *it*

lord·ly \ˈlȯrd-lē\ *adj* **lord·li·er; -est 1** : of, relating to, or having the characteristics of a lord : NOBLE **2** : PROUD, HAUGHTY — **lord·li·ness** *n* — **lordly** *adv*

lor·do·sis \lȯr-ˈdō-səs\ *n* : abnormal curvature of the spine forward

lord·ship \ˈlȯrd-ˌship\ *n* **1** : the rank or dignity of a lord — used as a title ⟨his *Lordship* is not at home⟩ **2** : the authority, power, or territory of a lord

Lord's Prayer *n* : the prayer in Matthew 6:9–13 that Christ taught his disciples

Lord's Supper *n* : COMMUNION 1a

lore \'lō(ə)r, 'lȯ(ə)r\ *n* : KNOWLEDGE; *esp* : a particular body of knowledge or tradition ⟨forest *lore*⟩

lor·gnette \lȯrn-'yet\ *n* : a pair of eyeglasses or opera glasses with a handle

lo·ris \'lōr-əs, 'lȯr-\ *n* : either of two small nocturnal slow-moving lemurs

loris
(up to 15 in. long)

lorn \'lȯrn\ *adj* : FORSAKEN, DESOLATE

lor·ry \'lȯr-ē, 'lär-\ *n, pl* **lorries** *Brit* : a large open truck

lose \'lüz\ *vb* **lost** \'lȯst\; **los·ing** \'lü-ziŋ\ **1** : RUIN, DESTROY ⟨ship was *lost* on the reef⟩ **2** : to be unable to find or have at hand : MISLAY ⟨*lose* a billfold⟩ **3** : to become deprived of esp. accidentally or by death ⟨*lose* his eyesight⟩ ⟨*lost* his son by drowning⟩ **4 a** : to fail to use to advantage : WASTE ⟨*lose* a day in sightseeing⟩ **b** : to fail to win, gain, or obtain ⟨*lose* a prize⟩ ⟨*lose* a contest⟩ ⟨*lose* with good grace⟩ **c** : to fail to catch with the senses or the mind ⟨*lost* part of what he said⟩ **5** : to cause the loss of ⟨one careless statement *lost* him the election⟩ **6** : to fail to keep, sustain, or maintain ⟨*lost* his balance⟩ **7 a** : to miss or cause to miss one's way or bearings ⟨*lost* himself in the maze of streets⟩ **b** : to make unconscious ⟨*lost* himself in daydreams⟩ **8** : OUTSTRIP ⟨*lost* his pursuers⟩ **9** : to free oneself from : get rid of ⟨dieting to *lose* some weight⟩ — **los·er** *n* — **lose ground** : to fail to advance or improve — **lose one's heart** : to fall in love

loss \'lȯs\ *n* **1 a** : the act or an instance of losing ⟨the *loss* of a ship⟩ **b** : the harm or privation resulting from losing ⟨her death was a *loss* to the community⟩ **2 a** : a person, thing, or amount lost **b** *pl* : killed, wounded, or captured soldiers **3** : failure to gain, win, obtain or utilize; *esp* : an amount by which the cost of an article exceeds the selling price **4** : decrease in amount, magnitude, or degree — **at a loss** : PUZZLED, UNCERTAIN ⟨was *at a loss* to explain his sudden interest in schoolwork⟩

lost \'lȯst\ *adj* **1** : not used, won, or claimed ⟨*lost* opportunities⟩ **2** : unable to find the way ⟨a *lost* puppy⟩ **3** : ruined or destroyed physically or morally **4** : no longer possessed or known ⟨a long *lost* uncle⟩ **5** : ABSORBED, RAPT ⟨*lost* in revery⟩

lot \'lät\ *n* **1** : an object used as a counter in determining a question by chance **2 a** : the use of lots as a means of deciding something ⟨choose by *lot*⟩ **b** : the choice resulting from deciding by lot **3 a** : something that comes to one by or as if by lot ⟨it fell my *lot* to do the dishes⟩ **b** : FATE, FORTUNE **4 a** : a piece or plot of land ⟨owns the corner *lot*⟩ ⟨a building *lot*⟩ **b** : a motion-picture studio and its adjoining property **5** : a number of articles offered for sale as one item **6** : a number (as at an auction) of associated persons : SET **7** : a considerable quantity or number ⟨a *lot* of books⟩ ⟨*lots* of food⟩ ⟨had been there *lots* of times⟩ — often used adverbially ⟨a *lot* worse⟩ ⟨feels *lots* better⟩

loth \'lōth, 'lō*th*\ *var of* LOATH

lo·tion \'lō-shən\ *n* : a liquid preparation for cosmetic or external medicinal use

lot·tery \'lät-ə-rē, 'lä-trē\ *n, pl* **-ter·ies** : a drawing of lots in which prizes are given to the winning names or numbers

lo·tus \'lōt-əs\ *n* **1** : a fruit held in Greek legend to cause forgetfulness; *also* : a tree bearing this fruit **2** : any of various water lilies including several represented in ancient Egyptian and Hindu art

lotus 2

loud \'lau̇d\ *adj* **1 a** : marked by intensity or volume of sound **b** : producing a loud sound **2** : CLAMOROUS, NOISY **3** : obtrusive or offensive in color or pattern ⟨a *loud* suit⟩ — **loud** *adv* — **loud·ly** *adv* — **loud·ness** *n*

loud·mouthed \'lau̇d-'mau̇*th*d, -'mau̇tht\ *adj* : having an offensively loud voice or blustering manner

loud·speak·er \-'spē-kər\ *n* : a device similar to a telephone receiver in operation but amplifying sound

^{1}**lounge** \'lau̇nj\ *vb* **1** : to move or act in a lazy, slow, or listless way : LOAF ⟨*lounge* away the afternoon⟩ **2** : to stand, sit, or lie in a slack manner — **loung·er** *n*

^{2}**lounge** *n* **1 a** : a room with comfortable lounging furniture **b** : a room in a public building or vehicle often combining lounging, smoking, and toilet facilities **2** : a long couch

lour \'lau̇(-ə)r\, **lour·ing** *var of* LOWER, LOWERING

louse \'lau̇s\ *n* **1** *pl* **lice** \'līs\ **a** : any of various small wingless usu. flat insects parasitic on warm-blooded animals **b** : any of several small arthropods **2** *pl* **lous·es** \'lau̇-səz\ : a contemptible person

louse 1a
(about $^{1}/_{6}$ in. long)

louse up *vb* : BOTCH, BUNGLE

lousy \'lau̇-zē\ *adj* **lous·i·er**; **-est** **1** : infested with lice **2 a** : MEAN, CONTEMPTIBLE **b** : miserably poor or inferior **c** : amply supplied ⟨*lousy* with money⟩ — **lous·i·ly** \-zə-lē\ *adv* — **lous·i·ness** \-zē-nəs\ *n*

lout \'lau̇t\ *n* : a stupid, clownish, or awkward fellow — **lout·ish** \-ish\ *adj* — **lout·ish·ly** *adv* — **lout·ish·ness** *n*

lou·ver *or* **lou·vre** \'lü-vər\ *n* **1** : an opening provided with one or more slanted strips to allow flow of air or light but to exclude rain or sun or to provide privacy **2** : one of the slanted strips of a louver — **lou·vered** \-vərd\ *adj*

lov·a·ble \'ləv-ə-bəl\ *adj* : having qualities that tend to make one loved — **lov·a·ble·ness** *n* — **lov·a·bly** \-blē\ *adv*

^{1}**love** \'ləv\ *n* **1** : strong affection based on admiration or benevolence ⟨motherly *love*⟩ **2 a** : warm attachment, enthusiasm, or devotion ⟨*love* of the sea⟩ **b** : the object of attachment or devotion **3 a** : attraction based on sexual desire : the ardent affection and tenderness felt by lovers **b** : a beloved person : DARLING **4** : a score of zero in tennis — **in love** : feeling love for and devotion toward someone

^{2}**love** *vb* **1** : to hold dear : CHERISH **2 a** : to feel a lover's passion, devotion, or tenderness for **b** : CARESS **3** : to like or desire actively : take pleasure in ⟨*loved* to play the violin⟩ **4** : to thrive in ⟨the rose *loves* sunlight⟩

love·bird \'ləv-ˌbərd\ *n* : any of various small usu. gray or green parrots that are noted for their attachment to their mates

love knot *n* : a stylized knot sometimes used as an emblem of love

L

love·lorn \'ləv-ˌlȯrn\ *adj* : deserted by one's lover

love·ly \'ləv-lē\ *adj* **love·li·er**; **-est** **1** : delicately beautiful ⟨a *lovely* dress⟩ **2** : beautiful in character **3** : highly pleasing : FINE ⟨a *lovely* view⟩ — **love·li·ness** *n*

lov·er \'ləv-ər\ *n* **1 a** : one that loves ⟨a *lover* of music⟩; *esp* : a man in love **b** *pl* : two persons in love with each other **2** : the male partner in a sexual relationship other than that of husband and wife

love seat *n* : a sofa or settee for two persons

love–sick \'ləv-ˌsik\ *adj* **1** : languishing with love : YEARNING **2** : expressing a lover's longing — **love·sick·ness** *n*

lov·ing \'ləv-ing\ *adj* : feeling or showing love : AFFECTIONATE ⟨*loving* care⟩ ⟨a *loving* glance⟩ — **lov·ing·ly** \-ing-lē\ *adv*

[1]**low** \'lō\ *n* : the deep sustained sound of a cow : MOO — **low** *vb*

[2]**low** \'lō\ *adj* **low·er** \'lō(-ə)r\; **low·est** \'lō-əst\ **1 a** : not high or tall ⟨*low* wall⟩ ⟨*low* bridge⟩ **b** : cut far down at the neck **2 a** : situated or passing below the normal level ⟨*low* ground⟩ **b** : marking a bottom ⟨*low* point of his career⟩ **3** : STRICKEN, PROSTRATE ⟨laid *low*⟩ **4 a** : not loud : SOFT ⟨a *low* whisper⟩ **b** : deep in pitch ⟨a *low* note⟩ **5 a** : being near the equator ⟨*low* northern latitudes⟩ **b** : being near the horizon ⟨the sun is *low*⟩ **6** : humble in status ⟨*low* birth⟩ **7 a** : FEEBLE, WEAK ⟨*low* with fever⟩ **b** : GLOOMY, DEPRESSED ⟨in *low* spirits⟩ **8** : less than usual (as in number, amount, or degree) ⟨*low* price⟩ ⟨*low* pressure⟩ **9 a** : lacking dignity or elevation ⟨*low* style of writing⟩ **b** : morally reprehensible : BASE ⟨*low* trick⟩ **c** : COARSE, VULGAR ⟨*low* language⟩ **10** : not advanced in complexity or development ⟨*low* organisms⟩ **11** : UNFAVORABLE, DISPARAGING ⟨*low* opinion of him⟩ — **low** *adv* — **low·ness** *n*

[3]**low** *n* **1** : something low; *esp* : a region of low barometric pressure **2** : the arrangement of gears (as of an automobile) that transmits the greatest power from the engine to the propeller shaft

low blood pressure *n* : abnormally low blood pressure esp. in the arteries

low·boy \'lō-ˌbȯi\ *n* : a chest of drawers about three feet high with long legs

low·bred \-'bred\ *adj* : RUDE, VULGAR

low·brow \-ˌbrau̇\ *n* : a person without intellectual interests or culture — **lowbrow** *adj*

Low Church *adj* : tending to minimize the priesthood, sacraments, and formal rites — **Low Churchman** *n*

low·down \-ˌdau̇n\ *n* : reliable information

[1]**low·er** \'lau̇(-ə)r\ *vb* **1** : to look sullen : FROWN **2** : to become dark, gloomy, and threatening

[2]**lower** *n* : FROWN

[3]**low·er** \'lō(-ə)r\ *adj* **1** : relatively low in position, rank, or order ⟨*lower* court⟩ ⟨the *lower* house of Congress⟩ **2** : less advanced in the scale of development through evolution ⟨*lower* animals⟩ **3** *usu cap* : being an earlier epoch or species of the geologic period or system named ⟨*Lower* Cretaceous⟩

[4]**low·er** \'lō(-ə)r\ *vb* **1** : DROP, DIMINISH ⟨*lowered* her voice⟩ **2 a** : to let fall ⟨*lower* a flag⟩ **b** : to make the aim or objective lower ⟨*lowered* the sights⟩ **c** : to reduce the height of ⟨*lower* a wall⟩ **3 a** : to reduce in value or amount ⟨*lower* the price⟩ **b** : to bring down : DEGRADE ⟨*lowered* himself by lying⟩ **c** : ABASE, HUMBLE — **lower the boom** : to crack down

low·er·case \ˌlō(-ə)r-'kās\ *adj* : being a letter that belongs to or conforms to the series a, b, c, etc. rather than A, B, C, etc. — **lowercase** *n*

low·er·ing \'lau̇-(ə-)ring\ *adj* **1** : FROWNING, SCOWLING **2** : OVERCAST, GLOOMY ⟨a *lowering* sky⟩

low·er·most \'lō(-ə)r-ˌmōst\ *adj* : LOWEST

low·er world \'lō(-ə)r-\ *n* : HADES

lowest common denominator *n* : LEAST COMMON DENOMINATOR

lowest common multiple *n* : the smallest multiple common to two or more numbers

lowest terms *n pl* : the form of a fraction in which the numerator and denominator have no common divisor

low frequency *n* : a radio frequency in the range between 30 and 300 kilocycles — abbr. *lf*

Low German *n* : the German dialects of northern Germany esp. since the end of the medieval period

low·land \'lō-lənd, -ˌland\ *n* : low and usu. level country — **lowland** *adj*

low·land·er \-lən-dər, -ˌlan-\ *n* : a native or inhabitant of a lowland region

[1]**low·ly** \'lō-lē\ *adv* : HUMBLY, MEEKLY

[2]**lowly** *adj* **low·li·er**; **-est** **1** : HUMBLE, MEEK ⟨a *lowly* hut⟩ **2** : of low rank or station — **low·liness** *n*

low–pres·sure \'lō-'presh-ər\ *adj* **1 a** : having, exerting, or operating under a relatively small pressure **b** : having or resulting from a low atmospheric pressure **2** : EASYGOING

low–spir·it·ed \'lō-'spir-ət-əd\ *adj* : DEJECTED, DEPRESSED

low–ten·sion \'lō-'ten-chən\ *adj* **1** : having a low potential or voltage **2** : constructed to be used at low voltage

low–test \-'test\ *adj* : having a low volatility ⟨*low-test* gasoline⟩

low tide *n* : the tide when the water is at its farthest ebb

[1]**lox** \'läks\ *n* : liquid oxygen

[2]**lox** *n, pl* **lox** *or* **lox·es** : smoked salmon

loy·al \'lȯi(-ə)l\ *adj* [from Old French *leial, loial*, from Latin *legalis* "legal", "law-observing", from *leg-*, stem of *lex* "law"] **1 a** : faithful to one's lawful government **b** : faithful to a person to whom fidelity is held to be due **2** : faithful to a cause or ideal — **loy·al·ly** \'lȯi-ə-lē\ *adv*

loy·al·ist \'lȯi-ə-ləst\ *n* : one who is or remains loyal to a political cause, government, or sovereign esp. in times of revolt

loy·al·ty \'lȯi(-ə)l-tē\ *n, pl* **-ties** : the quality or state of being loyal

syn LOYALTY, FIDELITY, ALLEGIANCE can mean constant devotion in upholding the interests of something or someone. LOYALTY implies personal steadfast adherence in the face of any pressure to desert or betray; FIDELITY implies strict unbroken faithfulness to an obligation, trust, or duty (as to a marriage partner); ALLEGIANCE implies adherence to a formal obligation (as to one's country) ***ant*** disloyalty

loz·enge \'läz-ənj\ *n* **1** : a diamond-shaped figure **2 a** : something shaped like a lozenge **b** : a small usu. medicated disk or tablet

LR *abbr* living room

LS *abbr* left side

LSD \ˌel-es-'dē\ *n* : a hallucinogenic drug that is capable of inducing psychotic symptoms similar to those of severe mental illness

lt *abbr* lieutenant

ə abut	ər further	a back	ā bake	
ä cot, cart	au̇ out	ch chin	e less	ē easy
g gift	i trip	ī life	j joke	ng sing	ō flow
ȯ flaw	ȯi coin	th thin	th this	ü loot
u̇ foot	y yet	yü few	yu̇ furious	zh vision

ltd *abbr* limited

ltr *abbr* letter

lu·au \'lü-ˌaů\ *n* : a Hawaiian feast

lub *abbr* **1** lubricant **2** lubricating

lub·ber \'ləb-ər\ *n* **1** : a big clumsy fellow **2** : an unskilled seaman — **lub·ber·ly** \-lē\ *adj or adv*

lube \'lüb\ *n* : LUBRICANT

lu·bri·cant \'lü-bri-kənt\ *n* : something (as a grease or oil) capable of reducing friction when applied between moving parts — **lubricant** *adj*

lu·bri·cate \'lü-brə-ˌkāt\ *vb* [from Latin *lubricare*, from *lubricus* "slippery"] **1** : to make smooth or slippery **2** : to apply a lubricant to ⟨*lubricate* a car⟩ **3** : to act as a lubricant — **lu·bri·ca·tion** \ˌlü-brə-'kā-shən\ *n* — **lu·bri·ca·tor** \'lü-brə-ˌkāt-ər\ *n*

lu·cent \'lü-sənt\ *adj* **1** : LUMINOUS, BRIGHT **2** : CLEAR, LUCID

lu·cid \'lü-səd\ *adj* **1 a** : suffused with light : LUMINOUS **b** : TRANSLUCENT **2** : having full use of one's faculties : clear-minded **3** : clear to the understanding : PLAIN — **lu·cid·i·ty** \lü-'sid-ət-ē\ *n* — **lu·cid·ly** \'lü-səd-lē\ *adv* — **lu·cid·ness** *n*

Lu·ci·fer \'lü-sə-fər\ *n* [from Latin, name of the Morning Star, literally "light bringer", from *luc-* (stem of *lux* "light") and *ferre* "to bear", "bring"] : DEVIL, SATAN

luck \'lək\ *n* **1** : whatever happens to a person apparently by chance : FORTUNE, CHANCE ⟨have good *luck* fishing⟩ **2** : the accidental way events occur ⟨happening by pure *luck*⟩ **3** : good fortune : SUCCESS ⟨have *luck*⟩ ⟨be out of *luck*⟩ — **luck·less** \'lək-ləs\ *adj*

luck·i·ly \'lək-ə-lē\ *adv* : by good luck : FORTUNATELY ⟨*luckily* no one was hurt⟩

lucky \'lək-ē\ *adj* **luck·i·er**; **-est** **1** : favored by luck : FORTUNATE **2** : producing a good result apparently by chance ⟨a *lucky* hit⟩ **3** : seeming to bring good luck ⟨a *lucky* coin⟩ — **luck·i·ness** *n*

lu·cra·tive \'lü-krət-iv\ *adj* : producing wealth : PROFITABLE — **lu·cra·tive·ly** *adv* — **lu·cra·tive·ness** *n*

lu·cre \'lü-kər\ *n* : monetary gain : PROFIT; *also* : MONEY

lu·di·crous \'lüd-ə-krəs\ *adj* **1** : laughable through obvious absurdity **2** : meriting scornful laughter as absurdly inept, false, or foolish ***syn*** see COMICAL — **lu·di·crous·ly** *adv* — **lu·di·crous·ness** *n*

luff \'ləf\ *vb* : to sail toward the wind — **luff** *n*

[1]**lug** \'ləg\ *vb* **lugged**; **lug·ging** : to pull or carry esp. laboriously

[2]**lug** *n* **1** : a part (as a handle) that projects like an ear **2** : BLOCKHEAD, LOUT

lug·gage \'ləg-ij\ *n* **1** : a traveler's belongings : BAGGAGE **2** : containers (as suitcases) for carrying personal belongings

lug·ger \'ləg-ər\ *n* : a boat that carries one or more lugsails

Lugol's solution \'lü-ˌgȯlz-\ *n* : any of several deep brown solutions of iodine in water or alcohol that are used in medicine or as microscopic stains — called also *Lugol's iodine solution*

lug·sail \'ləg-ˌsāl, -səl\ *n* : a 4-sided sail fastened at the top to a yard that hangs obliquely and is raised and lowered with the sail

lu·gu·bri·ous \lů-'g(y)ü-brē-əs\ *adj* : MOURNFUL; *esp* : exaggeratedly or affectedly mournful — **lu·gu·bri·ous·ly** *adv* — **lu·gu·bri·ous·ness** *n*

lug·worm \'ləg-wərm\ *n* : any of a genus of marine annelid worms that have a row of tufted gills along each side of the back and are used for bait

Luke \'lük\ *n* — see BIBLE table

luke·warm \'lük-'wȯrm\ *adj* **1** : neither hot nor cold : moderately warm : TEPID ⟨*lukewarm* bath⟩ **2** : not enthusiastic : INDIFFERENT ⟨his plan got a *lukewarm* reception⟩ — **luke·warm·ly** *adv* — **luke·warm·ness** *n*

[1]**lull** \'ləl\ *vb* **1** : to cause to sleep or rest : SOOTHE **2** : to cause to relax vigilance

[2]**lull** *n* **1** : a temporary calm before or during a storm **2** : a temporary drop in activity

lul·la·by \'ləl-ə-ˌbī\ *n, pl* **-bies** : a song to quiet children or lull them to sleep

lum·ba·go \ˌləm-'bā-gō\ *n* : usu. painful muscular rheumatism involving the lumbar region

lum·bar \'ləm-bər, -ˌbär\ *adj* : of, relating to, or adjacent to the loins or the bony regions of the lower spinal column ⟨*lumbar* region⟩

[1]**lum·ber** \'ləm-bər\ *vb* **lum·bered**; **lum·ber·ing** \-b(ə-)riŋ\ : to move heavily or clumsily; *also* : RUMBLE — **lum·ber·ing·ly** \-b(ə-)riŋ-lē\ *adv*

[2]**lumber** *n* **1** : surplus or disused household articles that are stored **2** : timber or logs esp. when sawed up for use

[3]**lumber** *vb* **lum·bered**; **lum·ber·ing** \-b(ə-)riŋ\ **1** : CLUTTER, ENCUMBER **2 a** : to cut logs **b** : to saw logs into lumber — **lum·ber·er** \-bər-ər\ *n*

lum·ber·jack \'ləm-bər-ˌjak\ *n* : LOGGER

lum·ber·man \-mən\ *n* : a person engaged in lumbering

lum·ber·yard \-ˌyärd\ *n* : a place where lumber is kept for sale

lumin- *or* **lumini-** *or* **lumino-** *comb form* : light ⟨*lumini*ferous⟩

lu·mi·naire \ˌlü-mə-'na(ə)r, -'ne(ə)r\ *n* : a complete lighting unit

lu·mi·nary \'lü-mə-ˌner-ē\ *n, pl* **-nar·ies** **1** : a very famous person **2** : a source of light; *esp* : one of the heavenly bodies — **luminary** *adj*

lu·mi·nes·cence \ˌlü-mə-'nes-ən(t)s\ *n* : emission of light at low temperatures esp. as a by-product of chemical (as physiological) processes; *also* : such light — **lu·mi·nesce** \-'nes\ *vb*

lu·mi·nes·cent \-'nes-ənt\ *adj* : relating to, exhibiting, or adapted for the production of luminescence ⟨*luminescent* paint⟩

lu·mi·nos·i·ty \ˌlü-mə-'näs-ət-ē\ *n, pl* **-ties** **1** : the quality or state of being luminous : BRIGHTNESS **2** : something luminous

lu·mi·nous \'lü-mə-nəs\ *adj* **1** : emitting light : SHINING **2** : LIGHTED ⟨a public square *luminous* with sunlight⟩ **3** : CLEAR, INTELLIGIBLE — **lu·mi·nous·ly** *adv* — **lu·mi·nous·ness** *n*

[1]**lump** \'ləmp\ *n* **1** : a small irregular mass **2** : AGGREGATE, TOTALITY ⟨taken in the *lump*⟩ **3** : an abnormal swelling or growth

[2]**lump** *adj* : not divided into parts : WHOLE ⟨*lump* sum⟩

[3]**lump** *vb* **1** : to group together **2** : to move noisily and clumsily **3** : to form into a lump

lump·ish \'ləm-pish\ *adj* **1** : DULL, STUPID **2** : HEAVY, AWKWARD — **lump·ish·ly** *adv* — **lump·ish·ness** *n*

lumpy \'ləm-pē\ *adj* **lump·i·er**; **-est** : having or full of lumps — **lump·i·ness** *n*

lu·na·cy \'lü-nə-sē\ *n, pl* **-cies** **1** : unsoundness of mind : INSANITY **2** : great foolishness : extreme folly

lu·na moth \ˌlü-nə-\ *n* : a large mostly pale green American moth with long tails on the hind wings

lu·nar \'lü-nər\ *adj* **1** : of or relating to the moon **2** : measured by the moon's revolution ⟨*lunar* month⟩

lunar eclipse *n* : an eclipse in which the moon passes partially or wholly through the umbra of the earth's shadow

lunar module *n* : a space vehicle module designed to carry astronauts from the command module to the surface of the moon and back — called also *lunar excursion module*

lunar module

lu·na·tic \'lü-nə-ˌtik\ *adj* [from Latin *lunaticus*, from *luna* "moon", so called from the former belief that lunacy fluctuated with the phases of the moon] **1 a :** INSANE **b :** designed for insane persons ⟨*lunatic* asylum⟩ **2 :** wildly foolish — **lunatic** *n*

lunch \'lənch\ *n* **1 :** a light meal; *esp* : one eaten in the middle of the day **2 :** the food prepared for a lunch — **lunch** *vb*

lun·cheon \'lən-chən\ *n* [alteration of dialect *nuncheon*, from Middle English *nonechench*, meaning literally "noon drink"] : a light meal at midday; *esp* : a formal lunch

lun·cheon·ette \ˌlən-chə-'net\ *n* : a place where light lunches are sold

lunch·room \'lənch-ˌrüm, -ˌrům\ *n* **1 :** LUNCHEONETTE **2 :** a room (as in a school) where lunches may be eaten

lung \'ləng\ *n* **1 a :** one of the usu. paired organs that form the special breathing apparatus of air-breathing vertebrates **b :** any of various respiratory organs of invertebrates **2 :** a device (as an iron lung) to promote and facilitate breathing

lunge \'lənj\ *n* **1 :** a sudden stretching thrust or pass (as with a sword) **2 :** the act of striding or leaping suddenly forward — **lunge** *vb*

lung·fish \'ləng-ˌfish\ *n* : any of various fishes that breathe by sacs resembling lungs as well as by gills

lu·nule \'lü-nyül\ *n* : a crescent-shaped body part or marking; *esp* : the whitish mark at the base of a fingernail

lu·pine \'lü-pən\ *n* : any of a genus of herbs that are related to the pea and have white, yellow, blue, or pink flowers in long upright clusters and flat pods with kidney-shaped seeds

1**lurch** \'lərch\ *n* : a lack of help or support ⟨left in the *lurch*⟩ — **in the lurch** : in a helpless or unsupported position

2**lurch** *n* **1 :** a sudden roll of a ship to one side **2 :** a sudden swaying or tipping movement ⟨the car gave a *lurch*⟩; *also* : a staggering gait — **lurch** *vb*

lure \'lů(ə)r\ *n* **1 a :** an inducement to pleasure or gain : ENTICEMENT **b :** APPEAL, ATTRACTION **2 :** a decoy for attracting animals to capture; *esp* : an artificial bait used for catching fish — **lure** *vb*

lu·rid \'lůr-əd\ *adj* **1 :** ghastly pale : WAN **2 :** shining with the red glow of fire seen through smoke **3 a :** causing horror or revulsion : GRUESOME ⟨*lurid* tales of murder⟩ **b :** highly colored : SENSATIONAL — **lu·rid·ly** *adv* — **lu·rid·ness** *n*

lurk \'lərk\ *vb* **1 a :** to stay in or about a place secretly **b :** to move furtively **2 :** to lie concealed; *esp* : to constitute a hidden threat — **lurk·er** *n*

syn LURK, SKULK, SNEAK can mean to go or act so as to escape attention. LURK usu. suggests lying in wait (as in ambush); SKULK strongly suggests moving about stealthily with an evil intention or sometimes from fear; SNEAK suggests moving into or out of a place in such a way as to avoid detection

lus·cious \'ləsh-əs\ *adj* **1 :** having a delicious taste or smell : SWEET ⟨*luscious* berries⟩ **2 :** appealing to the senses : DELIGHTFUL — **lus·cious·ly** *adv* — **lus·cious·ness** *n*

lush \'ləsh\ *adj* **1 :** being juicy and fresh ⟨*lush* grass⟩ **2 :** covered with luxuriant growth ⟨*lush* pastures⟩ — **lush·ly** *adv* — **lush·ness** *n*

1**lust** \'ləst\ *n* **1 :** sexual desire esp. if intense or unrestrained **2 :** an intense longing : CRAVING

2**lust** *vb* : to have an intense desire : CRAVE; *esp* : to have a strong sexual desire

lus·ter *or* **lus·tre** \'ləs-tər\ *n* **1 :** a shine or sheen esp. from reflected light : GLOSS **2 :** BRIGHTNESS, GLITTER **3 :** GLORY, SPLENDOR ⟨the *luster* of a famous name⟩ **4 :** a surface on pottery sometimes iridescent and always metallic in appearance — **lus·ter·less** \-tər-ləs\ *adj* — **lus·trous** \-trəs\ *adj*

lust·ful \'ləst-fəl\ *adj* : excited by lust — **lust·ful·ly** \-fə-lē\ *adv* — **lust·ful·ness** *n*

lusty \'ləs-tē\ *adj* **lust·i·er; -est** : full of vitality : VIGOROUS, ROBUST — **lust·i·ly** \-tə-lē\ *adv* — **lust·i·ness** \-tē-nəs\ *n*

lute \'lüt\ *n* : a stringed instrument with a pear-shaped body and a fretted fingerboard played by plucking the strings with the fingers

lute

lu·te·al \'lüt-ē-əl\ *adj* : of, relating to, or involving the corpus luteum

lu·te·fisk \'lüt-ə-ˌfisk\ *or* **lut·fisk** \'lüt-ˌfisk\ *n* : fish (as cod) that has been dried and soaked in lye water, skinned, boned and boiled

lu·te·tium *or* **lu·te·cium** \lü-'tē-sh(ē-)əm\ *n* : a metallic element — see ELEMENT table

lux·u·ri·ant \(ˌ)ləg-'zhůr-ē-ənt, (ˌ)lək-'shůr-\ *adj* **1 a :** yielding abundantly : PRODUCTIVE **b :** characterized by abundant growth : LUSH **2 :** LAVISH, PROFUSE — **lux·u·ri·ance** \-ən(t)s\ *n* — **lux·u·ri·ant·ly** *adv*

lux·u·ri·ate \-ē-ˌāt\ *vb* **1 :** to grow profusely : PROLIFERATE **2 :** to indulge oneself luxuriously: REVEL

lux·u·ri·ous \(ˌ)ləg-'zhůr-ē-əs, (ˌ)lək-'shůr-\ *adj* **1 :** of or relating to luxury **2 a :** fond of luxury or self-indulgence **b :** characterized by rich abundance; *esp* : excessively ornate — **lux·u·ri·ous·ly** *adv* — **lux·u·ri·ous·ness** *n*

lux·u·ry \'ləksh-(ə-)rē, 'ləgzh-\ *n, pl* **-ries** **1 a :** liberal use or possession of costly food, dress, or anything that pleases a person's appetite or desire **b :** great ease or comfort : rich surroundings ⟨live in *luxury*⟩ **2 a :** something desirable but costly or hard to get ⟨a *luxury* few can afford⟩ **b :** something adding to pleasure or comfort but not absolutely necessary — **luxury** *adj*

lv *abbr* **1** leave **2** leaves

1**-ly** \lē\ *adj suffix* [from Old English *-lic*, from *lic* "body"] **1 :** like in appearance, manner, or nature : having the characteristics of ⟨queen*ly*⟩ ⟨father*ly*⟩ **2 :** characterized by regular recurrence in (specified) units of time : every ⟨hour*ly*⟩

2**-ly** *adv suffix* **1 :** in a (specified) manner ⟨slow*ly*⟩ **2 :** from a (specified) point of view ⟨grammatical*ly*⟩

ə abut	ər further	a back	ā bake	
ä cot, cart	aů out	ch chin	e less	ē easy
g gift	i trip	ī life	j joke	ng sing
ō flow	ȯ flaw	ȯi coin	th thin	th this
ü loot	ů foot	y yet	yü few	yů furious
zh vision				

ly·ce·um \lī-'sē-əm, 'lī-sē-\ *n* **1** : a hall for public lectures or discussions **2** : an association providing public lectures, concerts, and entertainments
ly·co·po·di·um \ˌlī-kə-'pōd-ē-əm\ *n* : any of a large genus of erect or creeping club mosses with evergreen leaves in four to many ranks
lye \'lī\ *n* **1** : a strong alkaline solution obtained from wood ashes and used esp. in making soap and in washing **2** : any of various strong alkaline solutions **3** : a solid caustic (as caustic soda)
[1]**ly·ing** \'lī-ing\ *pres part of* LIE
[2]**lying** *adj* : UNTRUTHFUL, FALSE
lymph \'lim(p)f\ *n* : a pale colorless fluid that circulates in lymphatic vessels, bathes the cells of the body, and consists of white blood cells and a liquid portion resembling blood plasma — **lymph** *adj*
[1]**lym·phat·ic** \lim-'fat-ik\ *adj* **1** : of, relating to, or carrying lymph **2** : lacking physical or mental energy — **lym·phat·i·cal·ly** \-'fat-i-k(ə-)lē\ *adv*
[2]**lymphatic** *n* : a vessel that contains or transports lymph
lymph node *n* : one of the rounded masses of tissue occurring in association with the lymphatic vessels and giving rise to the colorless cells — called also *lymph gland*
lynch \'linch\ *vb* : to put to death by mob action without legal sanction or due process of law — **lyncher** *n*
lynx \'ling(k)s\ *n, pl* **lynx** *or* **lynx·es** **1** : a large No. American cat with relatively long legs, short stubby tail, mottled coat, soft fur, tufted ears, and large padded feet — called also *Canada lynx* **2** : any of several wildcats resembling the lynx

lynx 1
(about 3 ft. long)

lynx–eyed \'ling(k)s-'īd\ *adj* : having sharp sight
lyre \'lī(ə)r\ *n* : a stringed instrument of the harp class used by the ancient Greeks
lyre·bird \-ˌbərd\ *n* : either of two Australian birds of which the males have very long tail feathers displayed during courtship in the shape of a lyre

lyre

[1]**lyr·ic** \'lir-ik\ *adj* [from Greek *lyrikos*, from *lyra* "lyre"; applied to personal poetry because the lyre was the favorite instrument used to accompany this type of poetry] **1** : of or relating to a lyre **2 a** : resembling a song in form, feeling, or literary quality **b** : expressing a poet's own feeling : not narrative or dramatic ⟨*lyric* poetry⟩ **3** : having a light flexible quality ⟨a *lyric* tenor⟩
[2]**lyric** *n* **1** : a lyric poem or song **2** *pl* : the words of a song
lyr·i·cal \'lir-i-kəl\ *adj* **1** : resembling a song in mood or expression **2** : unrestrained in expressing enthusiasm, delight, or praise — **lyr·i·cal·ly** \-k(ə-)lē\ *adv*
ly·sin \'lī-sən\ *n* : any of a group of substances capable of causing lysis
ly·sine \'lī-ˌsēn\ *n* : a crystalline basic amino acid that is essential to animal nutrition
ly·sis \'lī-səs\ *n, pl* **ly·ses** \'lī-ˌsēz\ : a process of disintegration or dissolution (as of cells)

L

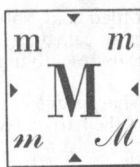

m \ˈem\ *n, often cap* **1 :** the 13th letter of the English alphabet **2 :** the roman numeral 1000
m *abbr* **1** male **2** masculine **3** [for Latin *meridies*] noon **4** meter **5** mile **6** minute
M *abbr* **1** medium **2** [for Latin *mille*] thousand
ma \ˈmä, ˈmȯ\ *n, pl* **mas :** MOTHER
ma *abbr* milliampere
MA *abbr* **1** Massachusetts **2** master of arts
ma'am \ˈmam, *after "yes" often* əm\ *n* **:** MADAM
ma·ca·bre \mə-ˈkäb(-rə)\ *adj* **1 :** having death as a subject **2 :** GRISLY, GRUESOME
mac·ad·am \mə-ˈkad-əm\ *n* [named after John L. *McAdam* (1756–1836), Scottish engineer who invented the macadamizing process] **1 :** a roadway or pavement of small closely packed broken stone **2 :** the broken stone used in macadamizing
mac·ad·am·ize \-ˌīz\ *vb* **:** to construct or surface (as a road) by packing a layer of small broken stone on an earth roadbed
ma·caque \mə-ˈkak, -ˈkäk\ *n* **:** any of several short-tailed monkeys of Asia and the East Indies; *esp* **:** RHESUS MONKEY
mac·a·ro·ni \ˌmak-ə-ˈrō-nē\ *n, pl* **-nis** *or* **-nies** **1 :** a food made chiefly of wheat flour paste dried in the form of slender tubes **2 :** DANDY, FOP
mac·a·roon \ˌmak-ə-ˈrün\ *n* **:** a cookie or small cake made of egg whites, sugar, and ground almonds or coconut
ma·caw \mə-ˈkȯ\ *n* **:** any of numerous parrots of South and Central America including some of the largest and showiest

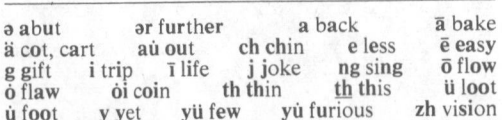

macaw
(about 30 in. long)

¹mace \ˈmās\ *n* **1 :** a heavy spiked club used as a weapon in the Middle Ages **2 :** an ornamental staff borne as a symbol of authority
²mace *n* **:** a spice consisting of the dried outer fibrous covering of the nutmeg
mac·er·ate \ˈmas-ə-ˌrāt\ *vb* **1 :** to waste away or cause to waste away **2 :** to cause to become soft or separated into constituent elements by or as if by steeping in fluid — **mac·er·a·tion** \ˌmas-ə-ˈrā-shən\ *n*
mach *abbr* **1** machine **2** machinery
Mach \ˈmäk\ *n* **:** MACH NUMBER
ma·chete \mə-ˈshet-ē, -ˈchet-ē\ *n* **:** a large heavy knife used esp. for cutting sugarcane and underbrush
Ma·chi·a·vel·li·an \ˌmak-ē-ə-ˈvel-ē-ən\ *adj* **1 :** of or relating to the doctrine that a ruler is justified in using any means to stay in power **2 :** characterized by cunning, deceitfulness, or bad faith — **Machiavellian** *n* — **Ma·chi·a·vel·li·an·ism** \-ˌiz-əm\ *n*
mach·i·nate \ˈmak-ə-ˌnāt, ˈmash-ə-\ *vb* **:** CONTRIVE, PLOT; *esp* **:** to scheme to do harm — **mach·i·na·tion** \ˌmak-ə-ˈnā-shən, ˌmash-\ *n* — **mach·i·na·tor** \ˈmak-ə-ˌnāt-ər, ˈmash-\ *n*
¹ma·chine \mə-ˈshēn\ *n* **1 a :** VEHICLE, CONVEYANCE; *esp* **:** AUTOMOBILE **b :** a combination of parts that transmit forces, motion, and energy to do some desired work ⟨a sewing *machine*⟩ ⟨a hoisting *machine*⟩ **c :** an instrument (as a lever or pulley) designed to transmit or modify the application of power, force, or motion **2 :** an organized group that controls a political party — **ma·chine·like** \-ˌlīk\ *adj*
²machine *adj* **1 :** characterized by widespread use of machinery ⟨the *machine* age⟩ **2 :** produced by or as if by machinery ⟨*machine* products⟩
³machine *vb* **:** to shape or finish by machine-operated tools — **ma·chin·a·ble** \-ˈshē-nə-bəl\ *adj*
machine gun *n* **:** an automatic gun capable of continuous firing — **machine–gun** *vb* — **machine gunner** *n*
ma·chin·ery \mə-ˈshēn-(ə-)rē\ *n* **1 :** MACHINES ⟨the *machinery* in a factory⟩ **2 :** the working parts of a machine or instrument having moving parts ⟨the *machinery* of a watch⟩ **3 :** the organization or system by which something is done or carried on ⟨the *machinery* of government⟩
machine shop *n* **:** a workshop in which metal articles are machined and assembled
machine tool *n* **:** a machine (as a lathe or drill) that is operated by power and is partly or wholly automatic
ma·chin·ist \mə-ˈshē-nəst\ *n* **:** a person who makes or works on machines and engines
Mach number \ˈmäk-\ *n* **:** a number representing the ratio of the speed of a body to the speed of sound in the surrounding atmosphere ⟨a *Mach number* of 2 indicates a speed that is twice the speed of sound⟩
mack·er·el \ˈmak-(ə-)rəl\ *n, pl* **-el** *or* **-els :** a No. Atlantic food fish that is green with blue bars above and silvery below; *also* **:** any of various usu. small or medium-sized related fishes
mackerel sky *n* **:** a sky covered with rows of clouds resembling the patterns on a mackerel's back
mack·i·naw \ˈmak-ə-ˌnȯ\ *n* **1 :** a flat-bottomed boat with pointed prow and square stern formerly much used on the upper Great Lakes **2 :** a short heavy woolen plaid coat reaching to about mid-thigh
mack·in·tosh *or* **mac·in·tosh** \ˈmak-ən-ˌtäsh\ *n* [named after Charles *Macintosh* (1766–1843), Scottish chemist who invented the material from which it was originally made] *chiefly Brit* **:** RAINCOAT
mac·ro·cosm \ˈmak-rə-ˌkäz-əm\ *n* **:** the world as a whole **:** UNIVERSE
ma·cron \ˈmāk-ˌrän, ˈmak-, -rən\ *n* **:** a mark ¯ placed over a vowel (as in \māk\) to show that the vowel is long
mac·ro·scop·ic \ˌmak-rə-ˈskäp-ik\ *adj* **1 :** large enough to be observed by the naked eye **2 :** considered in terms of large units or elements
mac·u·la·tion \ˌmak-yə-ˈlā-shən\ *n* **:** the arrangement of spots and markings on an animal or plant
mad \ˈmad\ *adj* **mad·der; mad·dest** **1 :** disordered in mind **:** INSANE **2 :** RASH, FOOLISH ⟨a *mad* promise⟩ **3 :** FURIOUS, ENRAGED ⟨make a bull *mad*⟩ **4 :** FRANTIC ⟨*mad* with pain⟩ **5 :** ENTHUSIASTIC ⟨*mad* about dancing⟩ **6 :** wildly gay ⟨a *mad* party⟩ **7 :** RABID ⟨a *mad* dog⟩ **8 :** ANGRY, DISPLEASED — **mad·ly** *adv* — **mad·ness** *n*
mad·am \ˈmad-əm\ *n, pl* **mes·dames** \mā-ˈdäm, -ˈdam\ [from French *madame*, from *ma dame* "my lady"; compare DAME] — used as a form of polite address to a woman
ma·dame \mə-ˈdam, *before a surname also* ˌmad-əm\ *n, pl* **mes·dames** \mā-ˈdäm, -ˈdam\ — used

ə abut	ər further	a back	ā bake	
ä cot, cart	au̇ out	ch chin	e less	ē easy
g gift	i trip	ī life	j joke	ng sing	ō flow
ȯ flaw	ȯi coin	th thin	t͟h this	ü loot
u̇ foot	y yet	yü few	yu̇ furious	zh vision

as a title equivalent to *Mrs.* for a married woman not of English-speaking nationality

mad·cap \'mad-ˌkap\ *adj* : WILD, RECKLESS — **mad-cap** *n*

mad·den \'mad-ən\ *vb* : to make mad : ENRAGE

mad·den·ing \'mad(-ə)-ning\ *adj* : INFURIATING, IRRITATING ⟨a *maddening* habit⟩ — **mad·den·ing·ly** \-ning-lē\ *adv*

mad·der \'mad-ər\ *n* **1** : a Eurasian herb with spear-shaped leaves and small yellowish flowers followed by berries; *also* : any of several related plants **2** : the red fleshy root of a madder that is used to make a dye; *also* : a dye made from madder root

made *past of* MAKE

ma·de·moi·selle \ˌmad(-ə)-mə-'zel, -mwə-'zel; mam-'zel\ *n, pl* **ma·de·moi·selles** \-'zelz\ *or* **mes·de·moi·selles** \ˌmād(-ə)-mə-'zel, -mwə-'zel\ — used as a title equivalent to *Miss* for an unmarried woman not of English-speaking and esp. of French nationality

made–up \'mād-'əp\ *adj* **1** : marked by the use of makeup ⟨*made-up* eyelids⟩ **2** : fancifully or falsely invented ⟨a *made-up* story⟩

mad·house \'mad-ˌhau̇s\ *n* **1** : an asylum for insane persons **2** : a place of uproar or confusion

mad·man \'mad-ˌman, -mən\ *n* : a man who is insane : LUNATIC — **mad·wom·an** \'mad-ˌwu̇m-ən\ *n*

ma·dras \mə-'dras, -'dräs; 'mad-rəs\ *n* : a fine usu. corded or striped cotton fabric

mad·ri·gal \'mad-ri-gəl\ *n* **1 a** : a short love poem that can be set to music **b** : music for a madrigal **2** : a 16th century part-song — **mad·ri·gal·ist** \-gə-ləst\ *n*

mael·strom \'māl-strəm\ *n* [from obsolete Dutch, from *malen* "to grind" and *strom* "stream"] **1** : a strong violent whirlpool dangerous to ships **2** : a great turmoil ⟨a *maelstrom* of emotions⟩

mae·sto·so \mī-'stō-sō\ *adv or adj* : so as to be majestic and stately — used as a direction in music

mae·stro \'mī-strō\ *n, pl* **maestros** *or* **mae·stri** \-ˌstrē\ : a master of an art and esp. of music

Ma·fia \'mäf-ē-ə, 'maf-\ *n* **1** : a Sicilian secret terrorist society **2** : a secret criminal organization held to control illicit activities (as racketeering) throughout the world

ma·fi·o·so \ˌmäf-ē-'ō-sō, ˌmaf-\ *n, pl* **ma·fi·o·si** \-sē\ : a member of the Mafia

mag *abbr* **1** magazine **2** magnetism

mag·a·zine \'mag-ə-ˌzēn, ˌmag-ə-'\ *n* **1** : a storehouse esp. for military supplies **2** : a place for keeping gunpowder in a fort or ship **3** : a publication usu. containing stories, articles, or poems and issued periodically (as weekly or monthly) **4** : a supply chamber: as **a** : a chamber in a gun for holding cartridges **b** : a chamber for film on a camera or motion-picture projector

ma·gen·ta \mə-'jent-ə\ *n* **1** : a deep red dye **2** : a deep purplish red

mag·got \'mag-ət\ *n* : a soft-bodied legless larva of a two-winged fly (as the housefly)

mag·goty \-ət-ē\ *adj* : infested with maggots

mag·ic \'maj-ik\ *n* **1** : the art of persons who claim to be able to do things by the help of supernatural creatures or by their own knowledge of nature's secrets **2 a** : something that charms ⟨the *magic* of his voice⟩ **b** : seemingly hidden or secret power ⟨the *magic* of a great name⟩ **3** : SLEIGHT OF HAND — **magic** *adj* — **mag·i·cal** \-i-kəl\ *adj* — **mag·i·cal·ly** \-ik(ə-)lē\ *adv*

ma·gi·cian \mə-'jish-ən\ *n* **1** : a person skilled in magic; *esp* : SORCERER **2** : a performer of sleight of hand

magic lantern *n* : an early type of slide projector

magic square *n* : a square containing a number of integers so arranged that the sum of the numbers in each row, column, and diagonal is always the same

4	9	2
3	5	7
8	1	6

6	3	10	15
9	16	5	4
7	2	11	14
12	13	8	1

magic square

mag·is·te·ri·al \ˌmaj-ə-'stir-ē-əl\ *adj* **1** : AUTHORITATIVE, COMMANDING ⟨a *magisterial* personality⟩ **2** : of or relating to a magistrate or his office or duties — **mag·is·te·ri·al·ly** \-ē-ə-lē\ *adv*

mag·is·tra·cy \'maj-ə-strə-sē\ *n, pl* **-cies** **1** : the state of being a magistrate **2** : the office, power, or dignity of a magistrate **3** : a body of magistrates

mag·is·trate \'maj-ə-ˌstrāt, -strət\ *n* **1** : an official exercising executive powers (as over a nation) ⟨the president is the chief *magistrate*⟩ **2** : an official having judicial powers

mag·ma \'mag-mə\ *n* : molten rock material within the earth from which an igneous rock results by cooling — **mag·mat·ic** \mag-'mat-ik\ *adj*

mag·na·nim·i·ty \ˌmag-nə-'nim-ət-ē\ *n, pl* **-ties** **1 a** : nobility of character : HIGH-MINDEDNESS **b** : GENEROSITY **2** : a magnanimous act

mag·nan·i·mous \mag-'nan-ə-məs\ *adj* **1** : showing or suggesting a lofty courageous spirit : NOBLE **2** : GENEROUS, FORGIVING — **mag·nan·i·mous·ly** \mag-'nan-ə-məs-lē\ *adv*

mag·nate \'mag-ˌnāt, -nət\ *n* : a person of rank, power, or influence (as in an industry)

mag·ne·sia \mag-'nē-shə, -'nē-zhə\ *n* : a white earthy solid that consists of magnesium and oxygen and is used in refractory materials, fertilizers, and rubber and as an antacid and mild laxative

mag·ne·si·um \mag-'nē-zē-əm, -zhəm\ *n* : a silver-white metallic element that is lighter than aluminum, is easily worked, burns with a dazzling light, and is used in making lightweight alloys — see ELEMENT table

magnesium chloride *n* : a bitter deliquescent salt that occurs dissolved in seawaters and underground brines and is used in producing magnesium metal

magnesium sulfate *n* : any of several sulfates of magnesium; *esp* : EPSOM SALT

mag·net \'mag-nət\ *n* **1** : a piece of some material (as the mineral iron oxide) that is able to attract iron; *esp* : a mass of iron or steel so treated that it has this property **2** : something that attracts ⟨the *magnet* of fame⟩

mag·net·ic \mag-'net-ik\ *adj* **1 a** : of or relating to a magnet or magnetism **b** : having the properties of a magnet **2** : of or relating to the earth's magnetism ⟨the *magnetic* meridian⟩ **3** : capable of being magnetized **4** : working by magnetic attraction **5** : having great power to attract ⟨a *magnetic* personality⟩ — **mag·net·i·cal·ly** \-i-k(ə-)lē\ *adv*

magnetic field *n* : the portion of space near a magnetic body or a body carrying an electric current within which forces due to the body or current can be detected

magnetic needle *n* : a narrow strip of magnetized steel that is free to swing horizontally or vertically to show the direction of the earth's magnetism and that is the essential part of a compass

magnetic north *n* : the northerly direction in the earth's magnetic field indicated by the north-seeking pole of the horizontal magnetic needle

magnetic pole *n* **1** : either of the poles of a magnet

2 : either of two small regions which are located respectively in the polar areas of the northern and southern hemispheres and toward which the compass needle points from any direction throughout adjacent regions

magnetic recording *n* **:** the process of recording sound, data, or a television program by producing varying local magnetization of a moving tape, wire, or disc

magnetic tape *n* **:** a ribbon of thin paper or plastic that is coated for use in magnetic recording

mag·ne·tism \'mag-nə-,tiz-əm\ *n* **1 a :** the property of attracting certain metals or producing a magnetic field as shown by a magnet, a magnetized material, or a conductor carrying an electric current **b :** the science that deals with magnetic occurrences or conditions **2 :** the power to attract or charm others

mag·ne·tite \'mag-nə-,tīt\ *n* **:** an iron ore that is an oxide of iron, is strongly attracted by a magnet, and sometimes acts like a magnet

mag·ne·tize \'mag-nə-,tīz\ *vb* **1 :** to cause to be magnetic : make into a magnet **2 :** CHARM, CAPTIVATE — **mag·ne·tiz·a·ble** \-,tī-zə-bəl\ *adj* — **mag·ne·ti·za·tion** \,mag-nət-ə-'zā-shən\ *n*

mag·ne·to \mag-'nēt-ō\ *n, pl* **-tos :** a small electric generator using permanent magnets; *esp* **:** one used to produce sparks in an internal-combustion engine

mag·ne·tom·e·ter \,mag-nə-'täm-ət-ər\ *n* **:** an instrument for measuring magnetic intensity esp. of the earth's magnetic field

mag·neto·sphere \mag-'nēt-ə-,sfi(ə)r\ *n* **:** a region of the upper atmosphere that extends out for thousands of miles and is dominated by the earth's magnetic field so that charged particles are trapped in it

mag·ni·fi·ca·tion \,mag-nə-fə-'kā-shən\ *n* **1 :** the act of magnifying : the state of being magnified **2 :** an apparent enlarging or reducing of an object by an optical instrument that equals the ratio of a dimension of the image formed to a corresponding dimension of the object

mag·nif·i·cent \mag-'nif-ə-sənt\ *adj* **1 :** having grandeur and beauty : SPLENDID ⟨*magnificent* palaces⟩ ⟨a *magnificent* view⟩ **2 :** EXALTED, NOBLE ⟨a *magnificent* character⟩ ***syn*** see GRAND — **mag·nif·i·cence** \-sən(t)s\ *n* — **mag·nif·i·cent·ly** *adv*

mag·ni·fy \'mag-nə-,fī\ *vb* **-fied; -fy·ing 1 :** PRAISE, EXTOL **2 a :** ENLARGE **b :** to make appear larger ⟨a microscope *magnifies* an object seen through it⟩ **3 :** to exaggerate in importance ⟨*magnify* a fault⟩ — **mag·ni·fi·er** \-,fī(-ə)r\ *n*

mag·ni·fy·ing glass *n* **:** a lens that magnifies an object seen through it

magnifying power *n* **:** magnification esp. as applied to visual instruments

mag·nil·o·quent \mag-'nil-ə-kwənt\ *adj* **:** speaking in a high-flown or bombastic manner : GRANDILOQUENT — **mag·nil·o·quence** \-kwən(t)s\ *n* — **mag·nil·o·quent·ly** *adv*

mag·ni·tude \'mag-nə-,t(y)üd\ *n* **1 a :** greatness esp. in size or extent : BIGNESS **b :** spatial quality : SIZE **2 :** greatness in influence or effect **3 :** degree of brightness; *esp* **:** a number representing the relative brightness of a star

mag·no·lia \mag-'nōl-yə\ *n* **:** any of a genus of No. American and Asiatic shrubs and trees with usu. showy white, yellow, rose, or purple flowers appearing in early spring

ə abut	ər further	a back		ā bake
ä cot, cart	aù out	ch chin	e less	ē easy
g gift	i trip ī life	j joke	ng sing	ō flow
ȯ flaw	ȯi coin	th thin	t͟h this	ü loot
u̇ foot	y yet	yü few	yu̇ furious	zh vision

mag·num opus \,mag-nəm-'ō-pəs\ *n* **:** a literary or artistic masterpiece

mag·pie \'mag-,pī\ *n* **1 :** any of numerous noisy birds related to the jays but having a long tapered tail and black-and-white plumage **2 :** a person who chatters constantly

ma·guey \mə-'gā\ *n, pl* **magueys 1 :** any of various fleshy-leaved agaves or closely related fiber-yielding plants **2 :** any of several hard fibers derived from magueys

Mag·yar \'mag-,yär, 'mäg-; 'mäj-,är\ *n* **1 :** a member of the dominant people of Hungary **2 :** the language of the Magyars — **Magyar** *adj*

ma·ha·ra·ja *or* **ma·ha·ra·jah** \,mä-hə-'räj-ə, -'räzh-ə\ *n* [from Sanskrit *mahārāja*, from *mahā-* "great" and *rāja* "king", "raja"] **:** a Hindu prince ranking above a raja

ma·ha·ra·ni *or* **ma·ha·ra·nee** \-'rän-ē\ *n* **1 :** the wife of a maharaja **2 :** a Hindu princess ranking above a rani

ma·hat·ma \mə-'hät-mə, -'hat-\ *n* [from Sanskrit *mahātman* "great-souled", from *mahā-* "great" and *atman* "self", "soul"] **:** a person revered for high-mindedness, wisdom, and selflessness — used as a title of honor esp. by Hindus

ma·hog·a·ny \mə-'häg-ə-nē\ *n, pl* **-nies 1 :** the wood of any of various chiefly tropical trees: as **a :** the durable usu. reddish brown and moderately hard and heavy wood of a West Indian tree that is widely used for cabinetwork **b :** any of several African woods that vary in color from pinkish to deep reddish brown **2 :** any of various woods resembling or substituted for true mahogany **3 :** a tree that yields mahogany **4 :** a moderate reddish brown

ma·hout \mə-'hau̇t\ *n* **:** a keeper and driver of an elephant

maid \'mād\ *n* **1 :** an unmarried girl or woman; *esp* **:** MAIDEN **2 :** a female servant

[1]**maid·en** \'mād-ən\ *n* **1 :** a young unmarried girl or woman **2 :** VIRGIN — **maid·en·hood** \-,hu̇d\ *n* — **maid·en·li·ness** \-lē-nəs\ *n* — **maid·en·ly** \-lē\ *adj*

[2]**maiden** *adj* **1 a :** UNMARRIED ⟨*maiden* aunt⟩ **b :** VIRGIN **2 :** of, relating to, or befitting a maiden **3 :** FIRST, EARLIEST ⟨*maiden* voyage⟩ **4 :** INTACT, FRESH

maid·en·hair \'mād-ən-,ha(ə)r, -,he(ə)r\ *n* **:** a fern with slender stems and delicate much-divided often feathery leaves

maidenhair (about 20 in. high)

maiden name *n* **:** the surname of a woman before she is married

maid of honor 1 : an unmarried woman usu. of noble birth who attends a queen or princess **2 :** an unmarried woman serving as the principal female attendant of a bride at her wedding

maid·ser·vant \'mād-,sər-vənt\ *n* **:** a female servant

[1]**mail** \'māl\ *n* **1 :** matter (as letters or parcels) sent under public authority from one person to another through the post office **2 :** the system used in the public sending and delivery of letters and parcels ⟨do business by *mail*⟩ **3 :** something that comes in the mail and esp. in a single delivery **4 :** a vehicle (as a train, truck, or boat) that carries mail

2**mail** *vb* : to send by mail : POST — **mail·a·ble** \'mā-lə-bəl\ *adj* — **mail·er** *n*

3**mail** *n* : a flexible network of small metal rings linked together for use as armor ⟨a coat of *mail*⟩ — **mailed** \'māld\ *adj*

a coat of mail

mail·box \'māl-ˌbäks\ *n* **1** : a public box for the collection of mail **2** : a private box for the delivery of mail

mailing tube *n* : a paperboard tube often with a screw cap in which small objects or rolled items (as calendars) are mailed

mail·man \-ˌman\ *n* : a man who delivers mail or who collects mail from public mailboxes

mail order *n* : an order for goods that is received and filled by mail — **mail–order** *adj*

maim \'mām\ *vb* : to mutilate, disfigure, or wound seriously : CRIPPLE — **maim·er** *n*

1**main** \'mān\ *n* **1** : physical strength : FORCE — used in the phrase *with might and main* **2 a** : MAINLAND **b** : HIGH SEAS **3** : a principal pipe, duct, or circuit of a utility system ⟨gas *main*⟩ ⟨water *main*⟩ — **in the main** : for the most part

2**main** *adj* **1** : OUTSTANDING, CHIEF, PRINCIPAL **2** : fully exerted : SHEER ⟨by *main* force⟩ **3** : being a clause that is capable of standing alone as a simple sentence but is part of a larger sentence that includes a subordinate clause or another main clause

main·land \'mān-ˌland, -lənd\ *n* : a continent or the main part of a continent as distinguished from an offshore island, cape, or peninsula — **main·land·er** \-ˌlan-dər, -lən-\ *n*

main·line \-'līn\ *vb, slang* : to inject a drug directly into a principal vein

main·ly \'mān-lē\ *adv* : for the most part : CHIEFLY

main·mast \'mān-ˌmast, -məst\ *n* : the principal mast of a sailing ship

main·sail \'mān-ˌsāl, 'mān(t)-səl\ *n* : the principal sail on the mainmast

main·spring \'mān-ˌspring\ *n* **1** : the principal spring in a mechanism esp. of a watch or clock **2** : the chief motive, cause, or force underlying or responsible for an action

main·stay \-ˌstā\ *n* **1** : a rope running from the maintop of a ship usu. to the foot of the foremast **2** : a chief support ⟨the *mainstay* of the family⟩

main·stream \-ˌstrēm\ *n* : a prevailing current of activity or influence

main·tain \mān-'tān, mən-\ *vb* **1** : to keep in an existing state; *esp* : to keep in good condition ⟨*maintain* one's health⟩ ⟨*maintain* machinery⟩ **2** : to defend by argument **3** : to continue in : carry on : keep up ⟨*maintain* his balance⟩ ⟨*maintain* a correspondence⟩ **4** : to provide for : SUPPORT ⟨*maintains* his family by working⟩ **5** : ASSERT, CLAIM ⟨*maintained* that all men are equal⟩ — **main·tain·a·ble** \-'tā-nə-bəl\ *adj* — **main·tain·er** *n*

main·te·nance \'mānt-(ə-)nən(t)s\ *n* **1** : the act of maintaining : the state of being maintained **2** : something that maintains or supports; *esp* : a supply of necessities and conveniences **3** : the upkeep of property or machinery

main·top \'mān-ˌtäp\ *n* : a platform about the head of the mainmast of a square-rigged ship

maize \'māz\ *n* : INDIAN CORN

maj *abbr* major

ma·jes·tic \mə-'jes-tik\ *adj* : being stately and dignified : NOBLE ***syn*** see GRAND — **ma·jes·ti·cal·ly** \-ti-k(ə-)lē\ *adv*

maj·es·ty \'maj-ə-stē\ *n, pl* **-ties** **1** : sovereign power, authority, or dignity **2** : the person of a sovereign — used as a title for a king, queen, emperor, or empress ⟨if your *Majesty* please⟩ **3 a** : royal bearing or quality : GRANDEUR **b** : greatness of quality or character

1**ma·jor** \'mā-jər\ *adj* **1 a** : greater in dignity, rank, or importance ⟨a *major* poet⟩ **b** : greater in number, quantity, or extent ⟨received the *major* part of the blame⟩ **2 a** : having half steps between the 3d and 4th and the 7th and 8th degrees ⟨*major* scale⟩ **b** : based on a major scale ⟨*major* key⟩ ⟨*major* chord⟩ **3** : of or relating to an academic major

2**major** *n* **1** : a commissioned officer (as in the army) ranking just below a lieutenant colonel **2 a** : the chief subject studied by a student **b** : a student specializing in a field ⟨a French *major*⟩

3**major** *vb* **ma·jored**; **ma·jor·ing** \'māj-(ə-)ring\ : to study an academic major ⟨*major* in English⟩

ma·jor·do·mo \ˌmā-jər-'dō-mō\ *n, pl* **-mos** : a man in charge of a great and esp. of a royal household

majorette *n* : DRUM MAJORETTE

major general *n* : a commissioned officer (as in the army) ranking just below a lieutenant general

ma·jor·i·ty \mə-'jȯr-ət-ē, -'jär-\ *n, pl* **-ties** **1 a** : the age at which one is given full civil rights **b** : the status of one who has attained this age **2 a** : a number greater than half of a total **b** : the amount by which such a number exceeds the smaller number ⟨won by a *majority* of seven⟩ **3** : the group or party that makes up the greater part of a whole body of persons ⟨the *majority* in the senate⟩ **4** : the military office or rank of a major

major league *n* : a league in the highest class of U.S. professional sports

1**make** \'māk\ *vb* **made** \'mād\; **mak·ing** **1 a** : to seem to begin an action ⟨he *made* as if to go⟩ **b** : to act so as to appear ⟨*make* merry⟩ **2** : to cause to exist or occur : CREATE ⟨*make* a noise⟩ ⟨*make* trouble⟩ ⟨he was *made* to be an actor⟩ **3 a** : to form or shape out of material or parts : FASHION, CONSTRUCT ⟨*make* a dress⟩ ⟨*make* a chair⟩ **b** : to comprise a whole : CONSTITUTE ⟨a house *made* of stone⟩ ⟨2 and 2 *make* 4⟩ **4** : to frame in the mind ⟨*make* plans⟩ **5 a** : COMPUTE, ESTIMATE ⟨I *make* it an even $5⟩ **b** : to regard as being : CONSIDER ⟨he is not the fool you *make* him⟩ **c** : UNDERSTAND ⟨unable to *make* anything of the story⟩ **6** : to set in order : PREPARE ⟨*make* a bed⟩ **7** : to cut and spread for drying ⟨*make* hay⟩ **8** : to cause to be or become ⟨*made* himself useful⟩ **9 a** : ENACT, ESTABLISH ⟨*make* laws⟩ **b** : EXECUTE ⟨*make* a will⟩ **10** : UNDERTAKE, PERFORM ⟨*make* war⟩ ⟨*make* a curtsy⟩ **11** : to produce or acquire by or as if by action or effort ⟨*made* a mess of the job⟩ ⟨*make* good money⟩ ⟨*make* friends⟩ **12** : to compel to act in some manner ⟨*made* him return home⟩ **13** : to cause or assure the success of ⟨the first case *made* the new lawyer⟩ **14 a** : REACH, ATTAIN ⟨the ship *makes* port tonight⟩ ⟨he *made* corporal in 10 months⟩ **b** : CATCH ⟨*make* the train⟩ **c** : to set out in pursuit ⟨*made* after the fox⟩ — **make away with 1** : to carry off **2** : KILL, DESTROY **3** : CONSUME, EAT — **make believe** : FEIGN, PRETEND — **make good 1** : FULFILL ⟨*made good* his promise⟩ **2** : to make up for a deficiency ⟨*make good* the loss⟩ **3** : SUCCEED ⟨*make good* as a salesman⟩ — **make love** : WOO, COURT — **make sail 1** : to raise or spread sail **2** : to set out on a voyage — **make time** : to travel fast ⟨can really *make time* on the new highway⟩ — **make way** : to open a path or passage ⟨the crowd *made way* for the injured man⟩

2**make** *n* **1** : the way in which a thing is made

M

: STRUCTURE **2** : KIND, BRAND ⟨looked at several *makes* of car before deciding⟩

[1]**make-be·lieve** \'māk-bə-,lēv\ *n* : a pretending to believe or be (as in the play of children) : PRETENSE

[2]**make-believe** *adj* **1** : IMAGINARY, PRETENDED ⟨was only a *make-believe* lion⟩ **2** : INSINCERE

make out *vb* **1** : to draw up in writing ⟨*make out* a shopping list⟩ **2** : UNDERSTAND ⟨how do you *make* that *out*⟩ **3** : to represent as being ⟨*made* him *out* a hero⟩ **4** : DISCERN, SEE ⟨*make out* a form in the fog⟩ **5** : SUCCEED ⟨*make out* well in business⟩ **6** : to engage in kissing and petting

make over *vb* **1** : to transfer the title of : CONVEY **2** : REMAKE, REMODEL

mak·er \'mā-kər\ *n* : one that makes: as **a** *cap* : [2]GOD **b** : a person who signs a promissory note

make·shift \'māk-,shift\ *n* : a temporary replacement : SUBSTITUTE — **makeshift** *adj*

make·up \'māk-,əp\ *n* **1** : the way the parts or elements of something are put together : COMPOSITION ⟨the *makeup* of a newspaper⟩ **2** : materials (as wigs or cosmetics) used in making up ⟨put on *makeup* for a play⟩ ⟨too young to wear *makeup*⟩

make up \-'əp\ *vb* **1 a** : CONSTRUCT, COMPOSE ⟨*make up* a poem⟩ **b** : COMPRISE ⟨nine players *make up* a team⟩ **2** : INVENT, CONCOCT ⟨*make up* an excuse⟩ **3** : to form by fitting together or assembling ⟨*make up* a suit⟩ ⟨*make up* a train⟩ **4** : to compensate for a lack **5** : to become reconciled ⟨they quarreled and *made up*⟩ **6** : SETTLE, DECIDE ⟨*made up* his mind to sell the house⟩ **7 a** : to put on costumes or makeup (as for a play) ⟨*made up* as a clown⟩ **b** : to apply cosmetics

mak·ing \'mā-king\ *n* **1** : the action of one that makes **2** : a process or means of advancement or success ⟨misfortune may be the *making* of a man⟩ **3** : material from which something can be developed : POTENTIALITY ⟨there is the *making* of a racehorse in this colt⟩ — often used in pl. ⟨has the *makings* of a great quarterback⟩ **4** \ *for cigarette materials usu* 'mā-kənz\ *pl* : the materials from which something can be made ⟨roll a cigarette from the *makings*⟩

mal- *comb form* **1 a** : bad ⟨*mal*practice⟩ **b** : badly ⟨*mal*odorous⟩ **2 a** : abnormal ⟨*mal*formation⟩ **b** : abnormally ⟨*mal*formed⟩

Mal·a·chi \'mal-ə-,kī\ *n* — see BIBLE table

mal·a·chite \'mal-ə-,kīt\ *n* : a green mineral that consists of copper, carbon, oxygen, and hydrogen and is used as an ore of copper and for ornamental objects

mal·a·col·o·gy \,mal-ə-'käl-ə-jē\ *n* : a branch of zoology dealing with mollusks — **mal·a·col·o·gist** \-jəst\ *n*

mal·adapt·ed \,mal-ə-'dap-təd\ *adj* : poorly suited to a particular use, purpose, or situation

mal·ad·just·ed \,mal-ə-'jəs-təd\ *adj* : poorly or inadequately adjusted esp. to one's environment — **mal·ad·just·ment** \-'jəs(t)-mənt\ *n*

mal·adroit \,mal-ə-'drȯit\ *adj* : AWKWARD, CLUMSY — **mal·adroit·ly** *adv* — **mal·adroit·ness** *n*

mal·a·dy \'mal-əd-ē\ *n, pl* **-dies** : a disease or disorder of the body or mind : AILMENT

Mal·a·gasy \,mal-ə-'gas-ē\ *n* **1** : a native or inhabitant of Madagascar or the Malagasy Republic **2** : the language of the Malagasy people — **Malagasy** *adj*

mal·aise \ma-'lāz\ *n* : an indefinite feeling of bodily or mental disorder

mal·a·mute *or* **mal·e·mute** \'mal-ə-,myüt\ *n* : a sled dog of northern No. America; *esp* : ALASKAN MALAMUTE

ma·lar·ia \mə-'ler-ē-ə\ *n* : a disease caused by parasites in the red blood cells, transmitted by the bite of mosquitoes, and characterized by periodic attacks of chills and fever — **ma·lar·i·al** \-ē-əl\ *adj*

mal·a·thi·on \,mal-ə-'thī-ən, -,än\ *n* : a pesticide that is less harmful to mammals then parathion and is used against insects and mites

Ma·lay \mə-'lā, 'mā-,lā\ *n* **1** : a member of a people of the Malay peninsula and adjacent islands **2** : the language of the Malay people — **Malay** *adj* — **Ma·lay·an** \mə-'lā-ən, 'mā-,lā-\ *adj or n*

Ma·lay·sian \mə-'lā-zhən\ *adj* : of, relating to, or characteristic of Malaysia or its people — **Malaysian** *n*

mal·con·tent \,mal-kən-'tent\ *adj* : not satisfied with the existing state of affairs : DISCONTENTED — **malcontent** *n*

male \'māl\ *adj* **1 a** : of, relating to, being, or characteristic of the sex that fathers young **b** : bearing only stamens; *esp* : having only stamens and not producing fruit or seeds ⟨a *male* holly⟩ **2** : made up or consisting of males ⟨a *male* choir⟩ — **male** *n* — **male·ness** *n*

mal·e·dic·tion \,mal-ə-'dik-shən\ *n* : a prayer for harm to befall someone : CURSE — **mal·e·dic·to·ry** \-'dik-t(ə-)rē\ *adj*

mal·e·fac·tion \-'fak-shən\ *n* : an evil deed : CRIME — **mal·e·fac·tor** \'mal-ə-,fak-tər\ *n*

ma·lev·o·lent \mə-'lev-ə-lənt\ *adj* : having or showing ill will : SPITEFUL — **ma·lev·o·lence** \-lən(t)s\ *n* — **ma·lev·o·lent·ly** *adv*

mal·fea·sance \(')mal-'fē-zən(t)s\ *n* : wrongful conduct esp. by a public official

mal·for·ma·tion \,mal-fȯr-'mā-shən, -fər-\ *n* : an irregular, abnormal, or faulty formation or structure ⟨physical and psychological *malformations*⟩ — **malformed** \(')mal-'fȯrmd\ *adj*

mal·func·tion \(')mal-'fəng(k)-shən\ *vb* : to fail to operate properly — **malfunction** *n*

mal·ice \'mal-əs\ *n* : ILL WILL; *esp* : the intention of doing harm for the satisfaction of doing it

ma·li·cious \mə-'lish-əs\ *adj* **1** : feeling malice **2** : done or carried on with malice or caused by malice ⟨*malicious* gossip⟩ — **ma·li·cious·ly** *adv* — **ma·li·cious·ness** *n*

[1]**ma·lign** \mə-'līn\ *adj* **1** : MALEVOLENT **2** : operating so as to injure or hurt ⟨hindered by *malign* influences⟩

[2]**malign** *vb* : to utter injurious or false reports about : DEFAME

ma·lig·nan·cy \mə-'lig-nən-sē\ *n, pl* **-cies** **1** : the quality or state of being malignant **2** : a malignant tumor

ma·lig·nant \-nənt\ *adj* **1** : evil in influence or effect : INJURIOUS **2** : MALICIOUS **3** : tending or likely to produce death ⟨*malignant* tumor⟩ — **ma·lig·nant·ly** *adv* — **ma·lig·ni·ty** \-nət-ē\ *n*

ma·lin·ger \mə-'ling-gər\ *vb* **ma·lin·gered**; **ma·lin·ger·ing** \-g(ə-)ring\ : to pretend to be sick or injured so as to avoid duty or work — **ma·lin·ger·er** \-gər-ər\ *n*

mall \'mȯl, 'mal\ *n* **1** : a shaded walk : PROMENADE **2** : a grassy strip between two roadways **3** : a group of stores arranged about an often covered way for pedestrians

ə abut	ər further	a back	ā bake	
ä cot, cart	au̇ out	ch chin	e less	ē easy
g gift	i trip	ī life	j joke	ng sing	ō flow
ȯ flaw	ȯi coin	th thin	th this	ü loot
u̇ foot	y yet	yü few	yu̇ furious	zh vision

mal·lard \'mal-ərd\ *n, pl* **mallard** *or* **mallards** : a common and widely distributed wild duck that is ancestral to the domestic ducks

mallard
(about 23 in. long)

mal·le·a·ble \'mal-ē-ə-bəl, 'mal-(y)ə-bəl\ *adj* **1** : capable of being beaten out, extended, or shaped by hammer blows or by the pressure of rollers ⟨a *malleable* metal⟩ **2** : ADAPTABLE, PLIABLE — **mal·le·a·bil·i·ty** \,mal-ē-ə-'bil-ət-ē, ,mal-(y)ə-'bil-\ *n*

mal·let \'mal-ət\ *n* **1** : a hammer usu. with a barrel-shaped head of soft material (as wood); *esp* : one with a short handle used for driving a tool (as a chisel) or for striking a surface without marring it **2** : a long-handled club with a cylindrical head used in playing croquet **3** : a polo stick

mal·le·us \'mal-ē-əs\ *n, pl* **mal·lei** \-ē-,ī, -ē-,ē\ : the outermost of the three small bones of the mammalian ear

mal·low \'mal-ō\ *n* : any of a group of herbs with lobed leaves, usu. showy flowers, and a disk-shaped fruit

mal·nour·ished \(')mal-'nər-isht, -'nə-risht\ *adj* : poorly nourished

mal·nu·tri·tion \,mal-n(y)ů-'trish-ən\ *n* : faulty and esp. inadequate nutrition — **mal·nu·tri·tion·al** \-'trish-(ə-)nəl\ *adj*

mal·odor·ous \(')mal-'ōd-ə-rəs\ *adj* : bad-smelling — **mal·odor·ous·ly** *adv* — **mal·odor·ous·ness** *n*

Mal·pigh·i·an tubule \mal-,pig-ē-ən-, -,pē-gē-\ *n* : any of a group of long vessels opening into the intestine in various arthropods and functioning in excretion

mal·prac·tice \(')mal-'prak-təs\ *n* : violation of professional standards esp. by negligence or improper conduct

1**malt** \'mȯlt\ *n* **1** : grain and esp. barley steeped in water and used chiefly in brewing and distilling **2** : MALTED MILK — **malt** *adj*

2**malt** *vb* **1** : to convert into malt **2** : to make or treat with malt or malt extract

malt·ase \'mȯl-,tās\ *n* : an enzyme that accelerates the breakdown of maltose to glucose

malted milk *n* **1** : a soluble powder prepared from dried milk and malted cereals **2** : a beverage made by dissolving malted milk in a liquid (as milk)

Mal·tese \mȯl-'tēz\ *n, pl* **Maltese** **1** : a native or inhabitant of Malta **2** : the Semitic language of the Maltese people — **Maltese** *adj*

Maltese cat *n* : a bluish gray domestic short-haired cat

Maltese cross *n* : a cross with four arms of equal size that increase in width toward the ends

malt·ose \'mȯl-,tōs\ *n* : a sugar formed esp. from starch by the action of enzymes and used in brewing and distilling

mal·treat \(')mal-'trēt\ *vb* : to treat unkindly or roughly : ABUSE — **mal·treat·ment** \-mənt\ *n*

mam·ba \'mäm-bə, 'mam-\ *n* : any of several African venomous snakes related to the cobras but lacking a hood

mam·bo \'mäm-bō\ *n, pl* **mambos** : a dance of Haitian origin related to the rumba — **mambo** *vb*

1**mam·ma** *or* **ma·ma** \'mäm-ə\ *n* : MOTHER

2**mam·ma** \'mam-ə\ *n, pl* **mam·mae** \'mam-,ē, -,ī\ : a mammary gland and its accessory parts

mam·mal \'mam-əl\ *n* : any of a class of higher vertebrates comprising man and all other animals that nourish their young with milk secreted by mammary glands and have the skin usu. more or less covered with hair — **mam·ma·li·an** \mə-'mā-lē-ən, ma-'mā-\ *adj or n*

mam·mal·o·gy \mə-'mal-ə-jē, ma-'mal-\ *n* : a branch of zoology dealing with mammals — **mam·mal·o·gist** \-jəst\ *n*

mam·ma·ry \'mam-ə-rē\ *adj* : of, relating to, lying near, or affecting the mammae

mammary gland *n* : one of the large glands that in female mammals are modified to secrete milk and in males are usu. relatively underdeveloped, are situated in pairs on the abdominal side of the organism, and usu. end in a nipple

1**mam·moth** \'mam-əth\ *n* : any of numerous large hairy extinct elephants with very long upward-curving tusks

mammoth
(about 14 ft. at shoulder)

2**mammoth** *adj* : very large : HUGE

mam·my \'mam-ē\ *n, pl* **mammies** **1** : MAMMA **2** : a Negro woman serving as a nurse to white children

1**man** \'man\ *n, pl* **men** \'men\ **1 a** : a human being; *esp* : an adult male human **b** : the human race : MANKIND **c** : HUSBAND, LOVER **d** : any member of the natural family that includes both human beings and extinct related forms known only from fossils **2 a** : VASSAL **b** : an adult male servant **c** *pl* : WORKERS **3** : an indefinite person : ANYONE ⟨a *man* could be killed there⟩ **4** : one of the pieces in a game (as chess) **5** *cap* **a** : POLICE **b** : the white establishment ⟨standing up to the *Man*⟩

2**man** *vb* **manned**; **man·ning** **1** : to supply with men ⟨*man* a ship⟩ **2** : to station members of a ship's crew at ⟨*man* the ropes⟩

man *abbr* manual

Man *abbr* Manitoba

man·a·cle \'man-i-kəl\ *n* **1** : HANDCUFF — usu. used in pl. **2** : something that restrains or restricts — **manacle** *vb*

man·age \'man-ij\ *vb* **1** : to oversee and make decisions about : DIRECT ⟨*manage* a factory⟩ **2** : to make responsive or submissive : HANDLE ⟨*manages* his skis well⟩ ⟨skill in *managing* horses⟩ **3** : to use to best advantage : HUSBAND ⟨there's enough food if it's *managed* well⟩ **4** : to succeed in one's purpose : get along ⟨*manages* despite a handicap⟩ ⟨always *manages* to win somehow⟩ — **man·age·a·bil·i·ty** \,man-ij-ə-'bil-ət-ē\ *n* — **man·age·a·ble** \'man-ij-ə-bəl\ *adj*

man·age·ment \'man-ij-mənt\ *n* **1** : the act or art of managing : CONTROL, DIRECTION **2** : skill in managing **3** : the persons who manage an enterprise

man·ag·er \'man-ij-ər\ *n* **1** : one that manages a business **2** : a person who directs a team or an athlete — **man·a·ge·ri·al** \,man-ə-'jir-ē-əl\ *adj*

man–at–arms \,man-ət-'ärmz\ *n, pl* **men–at–arms** : SOLDIER; *esp* : a heavily armed mounted soldier

M

man·a·tee \'man-ə-ˌtē\ *n* : any of several chiefly tropical plant-eating aquatic mammals that differ from the related dugong esp. in having the tail broad and rounded

manatee
(up to 15 ft. long)

Man·chu·ri·an \ˌman-'chu̇r-ē-ən\ *adj* : of, relating to, or characteristic of Manchuria or its people — **Manchurian** *n*

man·da·rin \'man-d(ə-)rən\ *n* **1** : a public official under the Chinese Empire **2** *cap* : the chief dialect of China centering about Peking **3** : a small spiny Chinese orange tree with yellow to reddish orange loose-skinned fruits; *also* : its fruit

1**man·date** \'man-ˌdāt\ *n* **1** : an authoritative command or instruction **2** : authorization or approval given to a representative esp. by voters **3 a** : a commission granted by the League of Nations to a member nation to administer a territory on its behalf **b** : a mandated territory

2**mandate** *vb* : to administer or assign under a mandate

man·da·to·ry \'man-də-ˌtōr-ē, -ˌtȯr-\ *adj* **1** : containing or constituting a command : OBLIGATORY **2** : of, relating to, or holding a mandate

man·di·ble \'man-də-bəl\ *n* **1 a** : JAW 1a; *esp* : a lower jaw consisting of a single bone or completely fused bones **b** : the lower jaw with its surrounding soft parts **c** : either the upper or lower segment of the bill of a bird **2** : an invertebrate mouthpart that holds or bites food; *esp* : either of the front pair of mouth appendages of an arthropod often forming strong biting jaws — **man·dib·u·lar** \man-'dib-yə-lər\ *adj*

man·do·lin \ˌman-də-'lin, 'man-də-lən\ *also* **man·do·line** \ˌman-də-'lēn, 'man-də-lən\ *n* : a stringed instrument with a pear-shaped body and fretted neck and four to six pairs of strings

man·drake \'man-ˌdrāk\ *n* : MAYAPPLE

man·drel \'man-drəl\ *n* **1** : an axle or spindle inserted into a hole in a piece of work to support it during machining **2** : a metal bar used as a core around which material may be cast, shaped, or molded

man·drill \'man-drəl\ *n* : a large fierce baboon of western Africa that usu. lives in groups

mane \'mān\ *n* **1** : long heavy hair growing about the neck of some mammals (as a horse) **2** : long heavy hair on a person's head — **maned** \'mānd\ *adj*

man–eat·er \'man-ˌēt-ər\ *n* : one (as a cannibal, shark, or tiger) that has or is thought to have an appetite for human flesh — **man–eat·ing** \-ˌēt-ing\ *adj*

1**ma·neu·ver** \mə-'n(y)ü-vər\ *n* **1 a** : a planned movement of troops or ships **b** : a military or naval training exercise **2** : a clever often evasive move or action

2**maneuver** *vb* **ma·neu·vered**; **ma·neu·ver·ing** \-'n(y)üv-(ə-)ring\ **1** : to move (as troops or ships) in a maneuver **2** : to perform a maneuver **3** : to manage skillfully **4** : to use stratagems — **ma·neu·ver·a·bil·i·ty** \-ˌn(y)üv-(ə-)rə-'bil-ət-ē\ *n* — **ma·neu·ver·a·ble** \-'n(y)üv-(ə-)rə-bəl\ *adj*

ə abut	ər further	a back	ā bake
ä cot, cart	au̇ out	ch chin	e less	ē easy
g gift	i trip	ī life	j joke	ng sing	ō flow
ȯ flaw	ȯi coin	th thin	t͟h this	ü loot
u̇ foot	y yet	yü few	yu̇ furious	zh vision

man·ful \'man-fəl\ *adj* : BRAVE, RESOLUTE — **man·ful·ly** \-fə-lē\ *adv* — **man·ful·ness** *n*

man·ga·nese \'mang-gə-ˌnēz, -ˌnēs\ *n* : a grayish white usu. hard and brittle metallic element that resembles iron but is not magnetic — see ELEMENT table

manganese dioxide *n* : a brown or gray-black insoluble compound of manganese and oxygen that is used as an oxidizing agent, in making glass, and in ceramics

mange \'mānj\ *n* : any of several contagious skin diseases of domestic animals and sometimes man that is marked esp. by itching and loss of hair; *esp* : one caused by a minute mite

man·ger \'mān-jər\ *n* : a trough or open box for livestock feed or fodder

1**man·gle** \'mang-gəl\ *vb* **man·gled**; **man·gling** \-g(ə-)ling\ **1** : to cut, bruise, or hack with repeated blows or strokes **2** : to spoil or injure in making or performing : BOTCH — **man·gler** \-g(ə-)lər\ *n*

2**mangle** *n* : a machine for ironing laundry by passing it between heated rollers

3**mangle** *vb* **man·gled**; **man·gling** \-g(ə-)ling\ : to press or smooth with a mangle — **man·gler** \-g(ə-)lər\ *n*

man·go \'mang-gō\ *n, pl* **mangoes** *or* **mangos** [from Portuguese *manga*, from a native name in southern India, *mān-kāy*] : a yellowish red tropical fruit with a firm skin, hard central stone, and juicy aromatic mildly acid pulp; *also* : the evergreen tree related to the sumacs that bears this fruit

man·go·steen \'mang-gə-ˌstēn\ *n* : a dark reddish brown fruit with thick rind and juicy flesh having a flavor suggestive of both peach and pineapple; *also* : an East Indian tree that bears this fruit

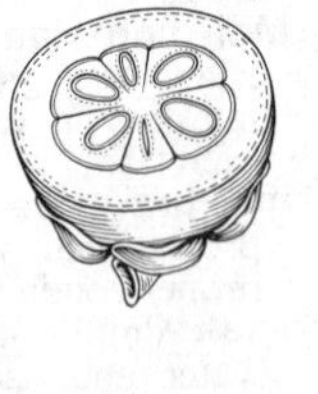

mangosteen

man·grove \'man-ˌgrōv, 'mang-\ *n* : any of various tropical trees or shrubs that throw out many prop roots and form dense masses in brackish marshes or shallow salt water

mangy \'mān-jē\ *adj* **mang·i·er**; **-est** **1** : affected with or resulting from mange **2** : SHABBY, SEEDY — **mang·i·ness** \'mān-jē-nəs\ *n*

man·han·dle \'man-ˌhan-dəl\ *vb* **1** : to move or manage by human force **2** : to handle roughly

man·hat·tan \man-'hat-ən, mən-\ *n, often cap* : a cocktail consisting of vermouth and whiskey

man·hole \'man-ˌhōl\ *n* : a hole (as in a pavement, tank, or boiler) through which a man may go

man·hood \'man-ˌhu̇d\ *n* **1** : COURAGE, MANLINESS **2** : the condition of being an adult male **3** : MEN

man–hour *n* : a unit of one hour's work by one man used esp. as a basis for wages and in accounting

man·hunt \'man-ˌhənt\ *n* : an organized hunt for a person and esp. for one charged with a crime

ma·nia \'mā-nē-ə, -nyə\ *n* **1** : MADNESS; *esp* : insanity characterized by uncontrollable emotion or excitement **2** : excessive enthusiasm : CRAZE

1**ma·ni·ac** \'mā-nē-ˌak\ *adj* : affected with or suggestive of madness — **ma·ni·a·cal** \mə-'nī-ə-kəl\ *adj* — **ma·ni·a·cal·ly** \-k(ə-)lē\ *adv*

2**maniac** *n* **1** : LUNATIC, MADMAN **2** : a person wildly enthusiastic about something : BUG

1**man·i·cure** \'man-ə-ˌkyu̇(ə)r\ *n* [from French, from Latin *manus* "hand" and *cura* "care"] **1** : MANI-

CURIST **2** : a beauty treatment for the hands and nails
2**manicure** *vb* **1** : to give a manicure to **2** : to trim closely and evenly ⟨*manicured* his lawn⟩
man·i·cur·ist \\-ˌkyu̇r-əst\\ *n* : a person who gives manicures
1**man·i·fest** \\'man-ə-ˌfest\\ *adj* : clear to the senses or mind : OBVIOUS — **man·i·fest·ly** *adv*
2**manifest** *vb* : to show plainly : DISPLAY
3**manifest** *n* : a list of cargo or passengers esp. for a ship or plane
man·i·fes·ta·tion \\ˌman-ə-fə-'stā-shən, -ˌfes-'tā-\\ *n* **1 a** : the act or an instance of manifesting : EXPRESSION **b** : something that manifests : EVIDENCE **2** : a public demonstration of power and purpose
man·i·fes·to \\ˌman-ə-'fes-tō\\ *n, pl* **-tos** *or* **-toes** : a public declaration of policy, purpose, or views
1**man·i·fold** \\'man-ə-ˌfōld\\ *adj* **1** : of many and various kinds ⟨*manifold* excuses⟩ **2** : including or uniting various features ⟨a *manifold* personality⟩ **3** : consisting of or operating many of one kind joined together ⟨a *manifold* pipe⟩ — **man·i·fold·ly** *adv*
2**manifold** *n* : something manifold; *esp* : a pipe fitting having several outlets for connecting one pipe with others
3**manifold** *vb* : to make several copies ⟨*manifold* a manuscript⟩
man·i·kin *or* **man·ni·kin** \\'man-i-kən\\ *n* **1** : MANNEQUIN **2** : a little man : DWARF
ma·nila \\mə-'nil-ə\\ *adj, often cap* : made of manila paper or from Manila hemp ⟨*manila* folder⟩ ⟨*manila* rope⟩
Manila hemp *n* : a strong fiber obtained from the leafstalk of a Philippine banana
manila paper *n, often cap M* : a tough brownish paper made orig. from Manila hemp and used esp. as a wrapping paper
man·i·oc \\'man-ē-ˌäk\\ *or* **man·i·o·ca** \\ˌman-ē-'ō-kə\\ *n* : CASSAVA
ma·nip·u·late \\mə-'nip-yə-ˌlāt\\ *vb* **1** : to treat or operate with the hands or by mechanical means esp. with skill ⟨*manipulate* the TV dials⟩ **2** : to manage or utilize skillfully ⟨*manipulate* masses of statistics⟩ **3** : to manage artfully or fraudulently ⟨*manipulate* accounts⟩ ⟨*manipulate* public opinion⟩ — **ma·nip·u·la·tion** \\-ˌnip-yə-'lā-shən\\ *n* — **ma·nip·u·la·tor** \\-'nip-yə-ˌlāt-ər\\ *n*
man·kind *n* **1** \\'man-'kīnd, -ˌkīnd\\ : the human race : all human beings **2** \\-ˌkīnd\\ : men as distinguished from women
man·like \\'man-ˌlīk\\ *adj* : resembling or characteristic of a man : MANNISH
man·ly \\'man-lē\\ *adj* **man·li·er**; **-est** **1** : having qualities appropriate to a man : BRAVE **2** : befitting a man ⟨*manly* sports⟩ — **man·li·ness** *n*
man–made \\'man-'mād\\ *adj* : made by man rather than nature ⟨*man-made* satellites⟩; *esp* : SYNTHETIC ⟨*man-made* fibers⟩
man·na \\'man-ə\\ *n* **1** : food miraculously supplied to the Israelites in the wilderness **2** : something much needed and joyfully received
manned \\'mand\\ *adj* : carrying or performed by a man ⟨*manned* spaceflight⟩
man·ne·quin \\'man-i-kən\\ *n* **1** : an artist's, tailor's, or dressmaker's jointed figure of the human body **2** : a figure of the human body used to display clothes **3** : a woman who models clothing : MODEL
man·ner \\'man-ər\\ *n* **1 a** : KIND ⟨what *manner* of man is he⟩ **b** : SORTS ⟨all *manner* of information⟩ **2 a** : a way of acting or proceeding ⟨worked in a brisk *manner*⟩ **b** : HABIT, CUSTOM ⟨spoke bluntly as was his *manner*⟩ **c** : STYLE ⟨painted in the artist's early *manner*⟩ **3** *pl* **a** : CUSTOMS ⟨the *manners* of a primitive people⟩ **b** : characteristic or habitual deportment : BEHAVIOR ⟨taught the child good *manners*⟩; *esp* : polite behavior — **man·nered** \\'man-ərd\\ *adj*
man·ner·ism \\'man-ə-ˌriz-əm\\ *n* : an esp. artificial peculiarity of action, bearing, or treatment ⟨the *mannerism* of constantly smoothing her hair⟩
man·ner·ly \\'man-ər-lē\\ *adj* : showing good manners : POLITE — **man·ner·li·ness** *n* — **mannerly** *adv*
man·nish \\'man-ish\\ *adj* : resembling, suggesting, suitable to, or characteristic of a man rather than a woman ⟨a *mannish* voice⟩ ⟨her *mannish* clothes⟩ — **man·nish·ly** *adv* — **man·nish·ness** *n*
ma·noeu·vre \\mə-'n(y)ü-vər\\ *var of* MANEUVER
man–of–war \\ˌman-ə(v)-'wȯ(ə)r\\ *n, pl* **men–of–war** : WARSHIP
ma·nom·e·ter \\mə-'näm-ət-ər\\ *n* : an instrument for measuring pressure (as of gases and vapors)
man·or \\'man-ər\\ *n* : a usu. large landed estate; *esp* : one granted to a feudal lord — **ma·no·ri·al** \\mə-'nōr-ē-əl, -'nȯr-\\ *adj*
manor house *n* : the house of the lord of a manor
man–o'–war bird \\ˌman-ə-'wȯr-\\ *n* : any of several long-winged web-footed seabirds noted for their powers of flight and the habit of robbing other birds of fish
man power *n* **1** : power available from or supplied by the physical effort of man **2** *usu* **man·pow·er** : the total supply of persons available and fitted for service ⟨military *manpower*⟩
man·sard \\'man-ˌsärd\\ *n* : a roof having two slopes on all sides with the lower slope steeper than the upper one

mansard

manse \\'man(t)s\\ *n* : the residence of a clergyman : PARSONAGE
man·ser·vant \\'man-ˌsər-vənt\\ *n, pl* **men·ser·vants** \\'men-ˌsər-vən(t)s\\ : a male servant
man·sion \\'man-chən\\ *n* : a large imposing residence
man–size \\'man-ˌsīz\\ *or* **man–sized** \\-ˌsīzd\\ *adj* : suitable for or requiring a man ⟨a *man-sized* job⟩
man·slaugh·ter \\'man-ˌslȯt-ər\\ *n* : the unlawful killing of a person without intent to do so
man·ta \\'mant-ə\\ *n* : DEVILFISH 1 — called also *manta ray*
man·tel \\'mant-əl\\ *n* : the beam, stone, arch, or shelf above a fireplace
man·tel·piece \\-ˌpēs\\ *n* **1** : a mantel with its side elements **2** : the shelf of a mantel
man·til·la \\man-'tē-(y)ə, -'til-ə\\ *n* **1** : a light scarf worn over the head and shoulders esp. by Spanish and Latin American women **2** : a short light cape or cloak
man·tis \\'mant-əs\\ *n, pl* **man·tis·es** *or* **man·tes** \\'man-ˌtēz\\ : any of various insects related to the grasshoppers and roaches that feed upon other insects and clasp the prey in stout forelegs held up as if in prayer

mantis
(about 2 in. long)

[1]**man·tle** \'mant-əl\ *n* **1 :** a loose sleeveless outer garment : CLOAK **2 a :** something that covers or envelops **b :** a fold or lobe or pair of lobes of the body wall of a mollusk or brachiopod lining and secreting the shell **3 :** the back, scapulars, and wings of a bird **4 :** a mesh sheath that gives a glowing light when placed over a flame **5 :** the portion of the earth lying between the crust and the core

[2]**mantle** *vb* **man·tled; man·tling** \'mant-(ə-)liŋ\ **:** to cover or envelop with or as if with a mantle

[1]**man·u·al** \'man-yə(-wə)l\ *adj* **1 :** of, relating to, or involving the hands ⟨*manual* dexterity⟩ **2 :** worked by hand ⟨*manual* choke⟩ **3 :** requiring or using physical skill and energy ⟨*manual* labor⟩ ⟨*manual* workers⟩ — **man·u·al·ly** \-ē\ *adv*

[2]**manual** *n* **1 :** a small book; *esp* : HANDBOOK **2 :** the set movements in the handling of a weapon during a military drill

manual training *n* **:** training to develop skill in using the hands (as in woodworking)

manuf *abbr* **1** manufacture **2** manufacturing

man·u·fac·to·ry \,man-(y)ə-'fak-t(ə-)rē\ *n, pl* **-ries :** FACTORY

[1]**man·u·fac·ture** \,man-(y)ə-'fak-chər\ *n* [from French, from Latin *manu factus* "made by hand"; opposed to "grown naturally"] **1 :** something made from raw materials **2 :** the making of products by hand or machinery **3 :** PRODUCTION ⟨the *manufacture* of blood in the body⟩

[2]**manufacture** *vb* **1 :** to make into a product suitable for use ⟨*manufacture* wool⟩ **2 :** to make from raw materials by hand or by machinery **3 :** INVENT, FABRICATE — **man·u·fac·tur·ing** *n*

man·u·fac·tur·er \-chər-ər\ *n* **:** one that manufactures; *esp* : an employer of workers in manufacturing

man·u·mis·sion \,man-yə-'mish-ən\ *n* **:** emancipation from slavery

man·u·mit \,man-yə-'mit\ *vb* **-mit·ted; -mit·ting :** to set free; *esp* : to release from slavery

[1]**ma·nure** \mə-'n(y)u̇(ə)r\ *vb* **:** to enrich by the application of manure ⟨*manure* a field⟩

[2]**manure** *n* **:** material that fertilizes land; *esp* : refuse of stables and barnyards consisting of bodily waste of birds and animals with or without litter

[1]**man·u·script** \'man-yə-,skript\ *adj* **:** written by hand or typed

[2]**manuscript** *n* **1 :** a written or typewritten composition or document **2 :** writing as opposed to print

Manx cat \'maŋ(k)s-\ *n* **:** a short-haired domestic cat having no external tail

[1]**many** \'men-ē\ *adj* **more** \'mō(ə)r, 'mȯ(ə)r\; **most** \'mōst\ **1 :** amounting to a large number ⟨worked for *many* years⟩ **2 :** being one of a large but indefinite number ⟨*many* a man⟩ — **as many :** the same in number ⟨saw three plays in *as many* days⟩

[2]**many** *pron* **:** a large number ⟨*many* came⟩

[3]**many** *n* **:** a large but indefinite number ⟨a good *many* of them⟩

[1]**map** \'map\ *n* **1 :** a drawing or picture showing selected features of an area (as the surface of the earth or the moon or a section of the brain) and usu. drawn to a given scale **2 :** a drawing or picture of the sky showing the position of stars and planets

[2]**map** *vb* **mapped; map·ping 1 :** to study and make a map of ⟨*map* the heavens⟩ **2 :** to chart the course of : plan in detail ⟨*map* out a campaign⟩ — **mapper** *n*

ma·ple \'mā-pəl\ *n* **:** any of a genus of trees or shrubs with opposite leaves and a 2-winged dry fruit; *also* **:** the hard light-colored close-grained wood of a maple

maple sugar *n* **:** a brown sugar made by boiling maple syrup

maple syrup *n* **:** syrup made by concentrating the sap of maples and esp. the sugar maple

mar \'mär\ *vb* **marred; mar·ring :** to make a blemish on : DAMAGE

Mar *abbr* March

mar·a·bou *or* **mar·a·bout** \'mar-ə-,bü\ *n* **1 a :** a large Old World stork **b :** the long soft feathers from under the tail and wings of this bird formerly used as trimming (as on hats) **2 :** a raw silk or a fabric made of it

ma·ra·ca \mə-'räk-ə, -'rak-\ *n* **:** a dried gourd or a rattle like a gourd that contains dried seeds or pebbles and is used as a percussion instrument

mar·a·schi·no \,mar-ə-'skē-nō, -'shē-\ *n, often cap* **1 :** a sweet liqueur distilled from the juice of a bitter wild cherry **2 :** a cherry preserved in true or imitation maraschino

mar·a·thon \'mar-ə-,thän\ *n* [from *Marathon*, Greece, site of a victory of Greeks over Persians in 490 B.C., the news of which was carried to Athens by a long-distance runner] **1 :** a long-distance footrace **2 :** an endurance contest — **marathon** *adj*

ma·raud \mə-'rȯd\ *vb* **:** to roam about and raid in search of plunder — **ma·raud·er** *n*

[1]**mar·ble** \'mär-bəl\ *n* **1 a :** a partly crystallized limestone that takes a high polish and is used in architecture and sculpture **b :** something made from marble; *esp* : a piece of sculpture **2 a :** a little ball (as of glass) used in various games **b** *pl* **:** a children's game played with these little balls — **marble** *adj*

[2]**marble** *vb* **mar·bled; mar·bling** \-b(ə-)liŋ\ **:** to give a veined or mottled appearance to (as by staining) ⟨*marble* the edges of a book⟩

mar·ca·site \'mär-kə-,sīt, ,mär-kə-'zēt\ *n* **:** a mineral consisting of iron and sulfur and having a metallic luster

[1]**march** \'märch\ *n* **1 :** a border region : FRONTIER **2** *pl* **:** the borderlands between England and Scotland and between England and Wales

[2]**march** *vb* **1 :** to move along with a steady regular stride esp. in step with others **2 :** to move in a direct purposeful manner : PROGRESS — **march·er** *n*

[3]**march** *n* **1 a :** the action of marching **b :** the distance covered within a period of time by marching **c :** a regular even step used in marching **2 :** forward movement : PROGRESS ⟨the *march* of time⟩ **3 :** a musical composition usu. in 4/4 time suitable to accompany marching

March \'märch\ *n* [from Old French, from Latin *Martius*, after *Mars* (stem *Mart-*), Roman god of war] **:** the 3d month of the year

mar·chio·ness \'mär-shə-nəs\ *n* **1 :** the wife or widow of a marquess **2 :** a woman who holds the rank of a marquess in her own right

Mar·di Gras \,märd-ē-'grä\ *n* **:** Shrove Tuesday often observed with parades and merrymaking

[1]**mare** \'ma(ə)r, 'me(ə)r\ *n* **:** a female horse; *also* **:** a female animal of the family to which the horse belongs

[2]**ma·re** \'mär-ā\ *n, pl* **ma·ria** \'mär-ē-ə\ **:** SEA 5

mar·ga·rine \'märj-(ə-)rən, 'märj-ə-,rēn\ *n* **:** a food product made from usu. vegetable oils and skim milk and used as a spread and a cooking fat

mar·gay \'mär-gā\ *n* : a small American spotted wildcat

[1]**mar·gin** \'mär-jən\ *n* **1** : the part of a page outside the main body of printed or written matter **2** : boundary area : VERGE **3** : an extra amount (as of time or money) allowed for use if needed **4 a** : the difference between net selling price and cost **b** : cash or collateral deposited with a broker to protect him from loss **c** : an allowance above or below a certain figure within which a sale is to be made ***syn*** see BORDER — **mar·gined** \-jənd\ *adj*

margay (about 2 ft. long)

[2]**margin** *vb* **1** : to provide with a margin **2** : BORDER

mar·gin·al \'märj(-ə)-nəl\ *adj* **1** : written or printed in the margin ⟨*marginal* notes⟩ **2** : of, relating to, or situated at a margin or border **3** : close to the lower limit of quality ⟨*marginal* ability⟩ ⟨*marginal* land⟩ — **mar·gin·al·ly** \-nə-lē\ *adv*

mar·gue·rite \ˌmär-g(y)ə-'rēt\ *n* **1** : DAISY 1a **2** : any of various single-flowered chrysanthemums

mari·gold \'mar-ə-ˌgōld, 'mer-\ *n* **1** : POT MARIGOLD **2** : any of a genus of tropical American herbs related to the daisies and grown for their showy yellow or red and yellow flower heads

mar·i·jua·na *or* **mar·i·hua·na** \ˌmar-ə-'(h)wän-ə\ *n* : any of various nonmedicinal drug preparations from the female hemp plant that contain THC as an active ingredient

ma·rim·ba \mə-'rim-bə\ *n* : a xylophone with resonators beneath each bar

ma·ri·na \mə-'rē-nə\ *n* : a dock or basin providing moorings for motorboats and yachts and often offering other facilities

[1]**mar·i·nade** \ˌmar-ə-'nād\ *vb* : MARINATE

[2]**marinade** *n* : a liquid preparation in which meat or fish is soaked to enrich its flavor

mar·i·nate \'mar-ə-ˌnāt\ *vb* : to soak in a marinade

[1]**ma·rine** \mə-'rēn\ *adj* **1 a** : of or relating to the sea ⟨*marine* life⟩ **b** : of the sea : NAUTICAL, MARITIME ⟨a *marine* chart⟩ ⟨*marine* insurance⟩ **2** : of or relating to marines ⟨*marine* barracks⟩

[2]**marine** *n* **1** : the commercial and naval shipping of a country **2** : one of a class of soldiers serving on shipboard or in association with a naval force; *esp* : a member of the U.S. Marine Corps

mar·i·ner \'mar-ə-nər\ *n* : SAILOR

mar·i·o·nette \ˌmar-ē-ə-'net, ˌmer-\ *n* : a puppet moved by strings or by hand

mar·i·tal \'mar-ət-əl\ *adj* : of or relating to marriage : CONJUGAL — **mar·i·tal·ly** \-ət-ə-lē\ *adv*

mar·i·time \'mar-ə-ˌtīm\ *adj* **1** : of or relating to navigation or commerce on the sea ⟨*maritime* law⟩ **2** : bordering on or living or situated near the ocean ⟨*maritime* nations⟩ **3** : being or having characteristics controlled primarily by oceanic winds and air masses ⟨a *maritime* climate⟩

mar·jo·ram \'märj-(ə-)rəm\ *n* : any of various usu. fragrant mints sometimes used in cookery

[1]**mark** \'märk\ *n* **1 a** : something (as a line, notch, or fixed object) designed to record position ⟨high-water *mark*⟩ **b** : a conspicuous object serving as a guide for travelers **c** : something aimed at : TARGET **d** : an object of ridicule **e** : the starting line or position in a track event **f** : a standard of performance, quality, or condition ⟨not up to the *mark*⟩ **2 a** : SIGN, INDICATION **b** : a characteristic or distinguishing trait or quality **c** : a cross made in place of a signature **d** : a written or printed symbol **e** : a symbol (as a brand or label) used for identification (as of ownership or quality) **f** : a symbol (as a number or letter) representing the quality of work or conduct : GRADE **3** : an impression (as a scar, scratch, or stain) made on a surface **4** : a lasting or strong impression **5** : IMPORTANCE, DISTINCTION

[2]**mark** *vb* **1 a** : to fix or trace out the bounds of by or as if by a mark **b** : to set apart by a boundary ⟨*mark* off a tennis court⟩ **2 a** : to designate as if by a mark ⟨*marked* for greatness⟩ **b** : to make a mark or notation on **c** : to furnish with natural marks **d** : to label so as to indicate price or quality **3 a** : to make note of in writing : JOT **b** : to indicate by a mark or symbol **c** : to determine the value of by means of marks : GRADE **4** : CHARACTERIZE, DISTINGUISH ⟨a disease *marked* by fever⟩ **5** : to take notice of : OBSERVE — **mark time 1** : to keep the time of a marching step by moving the feet alternately without advancing **2** : to function or operate without making progress

[3]**mark** *n* **1** : the basic monetary unit of Germany **2** : a coin representing one mark

Mark \'märk\ *n* — see BIBLE table

mark·down \'märk-ˌdau̇n\ *n* **1** : a lowering of price **2** : the amount by which a price is reduced

mark down \-'dau̇n\ *vb* : to put a lower price on

marked \'märkt\ *adj* **1** : having marks **2** : NOTICEABLE, CONSPICUOUS — **mark·ed·ly** \'mär-kəd-lē\ *adv*

mark·er \'mär-kər\ *n* **1** : one that marks **2** : something used for marking

[1]**mar·ket** \'mär-kət\ *n* [from Old French (northern dialect), from Latin *mercatus* "trade", "marketplace", from *mercari* "to trade", the source also of English *merchant* and *merchandise*] **1 a** : a meeting together of people to buy and sell **b** : the people at such a meeting **c** : a public place where a market is held; *esp* : a place where provisions are sold at wholesale **2** : a food store ⟨meat *market*⟩ **3** : a region in which things may be sold ⟨foreign *markets*⟩ **4** : an opportunity for selling ⟨a good *market* for used cars⟩

[2]**market** *vb* **1** : to deal in a market **2** : to offer for sale in a market : SELL — **mar·ket·ing** \-ing\ *n*

mar·ket·a·ble \'mär-kət-ə-bəl\ *adj* **1** : fit to be offered for sale **2** : wanted by purchasers : SALABLE — **mar·ket·a·bil·i·ty** \ˌmär-kət-ə-'bil-ət-ē\ *n*

market garden *n* : a plot in which vegetables are raised for market — **market gardener** *n* — **market gardening** *n*

mar·ket·place \'mär-kət-ˌplās\ *n* : an open square or place where markets are held

market value *n* : the value of a commodity determined by current prices

mark·ing \'mär-king\ *n* **1** : a mark made **2** : an arrangement or pattern of marks (as on the coat of an animal)

marks·man \'märks-mən\ *n* : one that shoots at a mark; *esp* : a person skilled at target shooting — **marks·man·ship** \-ˌship\ *n*

mark·up \'märk-ˌəp\ *n* **1** : a raising of price **2** : an amount added to the cost price of an article to determine the selling price

mark up \-'əp\ *vb* : to put a higher price on

marl \'märl\ *n* : a crumbling earthy deposit that consists of clay and calcium carbonate and is used to improve soils lacking lime

mar·lin \'mär-lən\ *n* : any of several large oceanic sport fishes related to sailfishes

mar·line·spike *also* **mar·lin·spike** \'mär-lən-ˌspīk\ *n* : a pointed iron tool used to separate strands of rope or wire

mar·ma·lade \'mär-mə-ˌlād\ *n* : a clear jelly containing pieces of fruit and fruit rind

mar·mo·re·al \mär-'mōr-ē-əl, mär-'mȯr-\ *adj* : of, relating to, or resembling marble

mar·mo·set \'mär-mə-ˌset, -mə-ˌzet\ *n* : any of numerous soft-furred bushy-tailed So. and Central American monkeys with claws instead of nails except on the big toe

marmoset
(about 30 in. long)

mar·mot \'mär-mət\ *n* : a stout-bodied short-legged burrowing rodent with coarse fur, a short bushy tail, and very small ears

[1]**ma·roon** \mə-'rün\ *vb* **1** : to put ashore and abandon on a desolate island or coast **2** : to leave isolated and helpless

[2]**maroon** *n* : a dark red

mar·quee \mär-'kē\ *n* **1** : a large tent for an outdoor party, reception, or exhibition **2** : a canopy projecting over an entrance ⟨a theater *marquee*⟩

mar·quess \'mär-kwəs\ *n* **1** : a nobleman of hereditary rank in Europe **2** : a member of the British peerage ranking below a duke — **mar·quess·ate** \-kwə-sət\ *n*

mar·quis \'mär-kwəs, mär-'kē\ *n, pl* **mar·quises** \-kwə-səz, -'kēz\ : MARQUESS

mar·quise \mär-'kēz\ *n, pl* **mar·quises** \-'kēz(-əz)\ : MARCHIONESS

mar·qui·sette \ˌmär-k(w)ə-'zet\ *n* : a sheer meshed fabric used for clothing, curtains, and mosquito nets

mar·riage \'mar-ij\ *n* **1 a** : the state of being married **b** : the mutual relation of husband and wife : WEDLOCK **c** : the institution whereby a man and a woman are joined in a special social and legal relationship for the purpose of making a home and raising a family **2** : an act of marrying; *esp* : a wedding ceremony **3** : an intimate or close union — **mar·riage·a·ble** \-ə-bəl\ *adj*

mar·ried \'mar-ēd\ *adj* **1** : united in marriage : WEDDED ⟨a *married* couple⟩ **2** : of or relating to marriage

mar·row \'mar-ō\ *n* **1 a** : a soft vascular tissue that fills the cavities of most bones **b** : the substance of the spinal cord **2** : the inmost, best, or essential part

mar·row·bone \'mar-ə-ˌbōn\ *n* : a bone (as a shinbone) rich in marrow

[1]**mar·ry** \'mar-ē\ *vb* **mar·ried**; **mar·ry·ing** **1** : to join as husband and wife according to law or custom ⟨they were *married* by a priest⟩ **2** : to give in marriage ⟨*married* his daughter to a lawyer⟩ **3** : to take as husband or wife ⟨*married* his secretary⟩ **4** : to take a spouse : WED ⟨decided to *marry*⟩

[2]**marry** *interj, archaic* — used to express agreement or surprise

Mars \'märz\ *n* — see PLANET table

ə abut	ər further	a back	ā bake
ä cot, cart	aù out	ch chin	e less
ē easy	g gift	i trip	ī life
j joke	ng sing	ō flow	ȯ flaw
ȯi coin	th thin	th this	ü loot
ù foot	y yet	yü few	yù furious
zh vision			

marsh \'märsh\ *n* : an area of soft wet land usu. overgrown by grasses and sedges — **marshy** \'mär-shē\ *adj*

[1]**mar·shal** \'mär-shəl\ *n* **1 a** : a high official in a medieval royal household **b** : a person who arranges and directs ceremonies **2** : an officer of the highest rank in some military forces **3 a** : a federal official having duties similar to those of a sheriff **b** : a municipal official having similar duties

[2]**marshal** *vb* **-shaled** *or* **-shalled**; **-shal·ing** *or* **-shal·ling** \'märsh-(ə-)liŋ\ **1** : to arrange in order **2** : to lead with ceremony : USHER

marsh gas *n* : METHANE

marsh hawk *n* : a common American hawk that feeds mostly on frogs and snakes

marsh·mal·low \'märsh-ˌmel-ō, -ˌmal-\ *n* **1** : a pink-flowered perennial herb related to the mallow that has a gluey root sometimes used in foods and in medicine **2** : a confection made from the root of the marshmallow or from corn syrup, sugar, albumen, and gelatin

marsh marigold *n* : a swamp herb having bright yellow flowers resembling those of the related buttercups — called also *cowslip*

marsh wren *n* : any of several American wrens that frequent marshes

[1]**mar·su·pi·al** \mär-'sü-pē-əl\ *adj* : of, relating to, or being a marsupial

[2]**marsupial** *n* : any of an order of lower mammals (as kangaroos and opossums) that have a pouch on the abdomen of the female containing the teats and serving to carry the young

mart \'märt\ *n* : a trading place : MARKET

mar·ten \'märt-ən\ *n, pl* **marten** *or* **martens** : a slim flesh-eating mammal larger than the related weasels; *also* : its soft gray or brown fur

marten
(about 25 in. long)

mar·tial \'mär-shəl\ *adj* **1** : of, relating to, or suited for war or a warrior ⟨a *martial* tune⟩ **2** : of or relating to an army or to military life ⟨a *martial* stride⟩ — **mar·tial·ly** \-shə-lē\ *adv*

syn MARTIAL, WARLIKE, MILITARY can mean associated with war. MARTIAL may suggest the pomp and ceremony of war ⟨*martial* music⟩; WARLIKE implies the aggressive feelings of those who are quick to resort to war ⟨*warlike* tribes⟩; MILITARY applies to anything concerned in the conduct of organized warfare

martial law *n* : the law applied by military forces in occupied territory or in an emergency

Mar·tian \'mär-shən\ *adj* : of or relating to the planet Mars or its hypothetical inhabitants — **Martian** *n*

mar·tin \'märt-ən\ *n* : a small European swallow with a forked tail, bluish black head and back, and white rump and underparts; *also* : any of various swallows and flycatchers

mar·ti·net \ˌmärt-ə-'net\ *n* : a strict disciplinarian

mar·tin·gale \'märt-ən-ˌgāl\ *n* : a strap connecting a horse's girth to the bit or reins so as to hold down its head

mar·ti·ni \mär-'tē-nē\ *n* : a cocktail consisting of gin and dry vermouth

Mar·tin·mas \'märt-ən-məs, -ˌmas\ *n* : November 11

1**mar·tyr** \'märt-ər\ *n* **1** : a person who suffers death rather than give up his religion **2** : one who sacrifices his life or something of great value for a principle or cause **3** : a great or constant sufferer

2**martyr** *vb* **1** : to put to death for adhering to a belief **2** : TORTURE

mar·tyr·dom \'märt-ər-dəm\ *n* **1** : the sufferings and death of a martyr **2** : TORTURE

1**mar·vel** \'mär-vəl\ *n* : something that causes wonder or astonishment

2**marvel** *vb* **mar·veled** *or* **mar·velled**; **mar·vel·ing** *or* **mar·vel·ling** \'märv-(ə-)liŋ\ : to become filled with surprise or astonishment ⟨*marveled* at the magician's skill⟩

mar·vel·ous *or* **mar·vel·lous** \'märv-(ə-)ləs\ *adj* **1** : causing wonder : ASTONISHING **2** : having the characteristics of a miracle **3** : of the highest kind or quality : SPLENDID — **mar·vel·ous·ly** *adv* — **mar·vel·ous·ness** *n*

mar·zi·pan \'märt-sə-ˌpän, 'mär-zə-ˌpan\ *n* : a confection of almond paste, sugar, and whites of eggs

masc *abbr* masculine

mas·cara \ma-'skar-ə\ *n* : a cosmetic for coloring the eyelashes and eyebrows

mas·cot \'mas-ˌkät, -kət\ *n* : a person, animal, or object supposed to bring good luck

1**mas·cu·line** \'mas-kyə-lən\ *adj* **1** : of the male sex **2** : characteristic of or belonging to men : MANLY ⟨a *masculine* voice⟩ **3** : of, relating to, or constituting the class of words that ordinarily includes most of those referring to males ⟨a *masculine* noun⟩ ⟨*masculine* gender⟩ — **mas·cu·lin·i·ty** \ˌmas-kyə-'lin-ət-ē\ *n*

2**masculine** *n* **1** : a word or form of the masculine gender **2** : the masculine gender

ma·ser \'mā-zər\ *n* : a device that utilizes the natural oscillations of atoms or molecules for amplifying or generating electromagnetic waves

1**mash** \'mash\ *n* **1** : crushed malt or grain meal steeped and stirred in hot water **2** : a mixture of ground feeds for livestock **3** : a soft pulpy mass

2**mash** *vb* **1** : to reduce to a soft pulpy state by beating or pressure **2** : to subject crushed malt to the action of water with heating and stirring — **mash·er** *n*

1**mask** \'mask\ *n* **1** : a cover for the face used for disguise or protection ⟨a Halloween *mask*⟩ ⟨a baseball catcher's *mask*⟩ **2** : a device usu. covering the mouth and nose either to aid in or prevent the inhaling of something (as a gas or spray) **3** : a covering (as of gauze) for the mouth and nose to prevent infective droplets from being blown into the air **4** : something that disguises or conceals : CLOAK **5** : MASKER **6** : a sculptured face made by a mold in plaster or wax ⟨a death *mask*⟩ **7** : the face of a mammal (as a fox or dog) **8** : MASQUE

2**mask** *vb* **1** : CONCEAL, DISGUISE ⟨*masked* his real purpose⟩ **2** : to cover for protection

masked \'maskt\ *adj* **1** : wearing or using a mask ⟨*masked* dancers⟩ ⟨*masked* bandit⟩ **2** : marked by or requiring the wearing of masks ⟨a *masked* ball⟩

mask·er \'mas-kər\ *n* : a person who wears a mask; *esp* : a participant in a masquerade

ma·son \'mā-sən\ *n* : a person who builds or works with stone, brick, or cement

ma·son·ry \'mā-sən-rē\ *n, pl* **-ries** **1** : the art, trade, or occupation of a mason **2** : the work done by a mason **3** : something built of stone, brick, or concrete

masque \'mask\ *n* **1** : MASQUERADE **2** : an old play performed by masked actors

masqu·er \'mas-kər\ *n* : MASKER

1**mas·quer·ade** \ˌmas-kə-'rād\ *n* **1** : a social gathering of persons wearing masks and often fantastic costumes **2** : an appearance that is mere disguise or outward show : POSE

2**masquerade** *vb* **1** : to take part in a masquerade **2** : to assume the appearance of something one is not : POSE — **mas·quer·ad·er** *n*

1**mass** \'mas\ *n* **1** *cap* : a sequence of prayers and ceremonies forming the eucharistic rite esp. of the Roman Catholic Church **2** *often cap* : a celebration of the Eucharist **3** : a musical setting for parts of the Mass

2**mass** *n* **1 a** : a quantity of matter or the form of matter that holds or clings together in one body ⟨a *mass* of metal⟩ **b** : SIZE, BULK **c** : the main body **2** : the quantity of matter in a body as measured by its inertia ⟨*mass* is responsible for weight but is independent of gravity⟩ **3** : a large amount or number **4** *pl* : the common people

3**mass** *vb* : to form or collect into a mass

4**mass** *adj* **1** : of, relating to, or designed for the masses ⟨*mass* market⟩ ⟨*mass* education⟩ **2** : participated in by or affecting a large number of individuals ⟨*mass* demonstrations⟩

Mass *abbr* Massachusetts

1**mas·sa·cre** \'mas-i-kər\ *vb* **-cred**; **-cring** \-k(ə-)riŋ\ : to kill in a massacre : SLAUGHTER — **mas·sa·crer** \-i-kər-ər, -i-krər\ *n*

2**massacre** *n* : the violent cruel indiscriminate killing of a number of persons

mas·sage \mə-'säzh, -'säj\ *n* : treatment (as of the body) by rubbing, stroking, kneading, or tapping — **massage** *vb*

mas·sa·sau·ga \ˌmas-ə-'sȯ-gə\ *n* : any of several small rattlesnakes

mas·seur \ma-'sər\ *n* : a man who practices massage

mas·seuse \-'sə(r)z, -'süz\ *n* : a woman who practices massage

mas·sive \'mas-iv\ *adj* **1 a** : WEIGHTY, HEAVY ⟨*massive* walls⟩ **b** : impressively large or ponderous **2 a** : large, solid, or heavy in structure ⟨a *massive* jaw⟩ **b** : large in scope or degree — **mas·sive·ly** *adv* — **mas·sive·ness** *n*

mass meeting *n* : a large or general assembly of people

mass noun *n* : a noun (as *sand*, *butter*, or *accuracy*) that denotes a homogeneous substance or idea and that is used in English only in the singular and is usu. preceded by *some* rather than *a* or *an*

mass number *n* : an integer that expresses the mass of an isotope and designates the number of nucleons in the nucleus

mass–pro·duce \ˌmas-prə-'d(y)üs\ *vb* : to produce in quantity usu. by machinery — **mass production** *n*

mass spectrometer *n* : an apparatus used to measure relative abundance of isotopes or to analyze mixtures of compounds by separating a stream of charged particles according to their mass and recording the resulting spectrum

massy \'mas-ē\ *adj* **mass·i·er**; **-est** : MASSIVE

mast \'mast\ *n* **1** : a long pole that rises from the keel or deck of a ship and supports the yards, booms, sails, and rigging **2** : an upright tall pole (as on a crane) — **mast·ed** \'mas-təd\ *adj* — **before the mast** : as a common sailor

1**mas·ter** \'mas-tər\ *n* **1 a** : a male teacher **b** : a person holding an academic degree between a bachelor's and a doctor's **2 a** : an independent skilled workman; *esp* : one employing journeymen and apprentices **b** : an artist or performer of consummate skill **3 a :** one having authority **b :** VICTOR **c :** the captain of a merchant ship **d :** an owner of a slave or animal **e :** EMPLOYER **4** — used as a title for a boy too young to be called *mister* — **mas·ter·ship** \-ˌship\ *n*

2**master** *vb* **mas·tered; mas·ter·ing** \-t(ə-)riŋ\ **1 :** OVERCOME, SUBDUE ⟨*master* an enemy⟩ ⟨*master* a desire⟩ **2 :** to become skilled at ⟨*master* arithmetic⟩

3**master** *adj* **1 :** being a master ⟨a *master* carpenter⟩ **2 :** GOVERNING, MAIN ⟨a *master* plan⟩ **3 :** controlling the operation of other mechanisms ⟨a *master* clock⟩

master chief petty officer *n* **:** a petty officer of the highest rank

mas·ter·ful \ˈmas-tər-fəl\ *adj* **1 :** inclined to take control or dominate **2 :** having or showing the technical or artistic skill of a master — **mas·ter·ful·ly** \-fə-lē\ *adv* — **mas·ter·ful·ness** *n*

mas·ter·ly \ˈmas-tər-lē\ *adj* **:** MASTERFUL — **masterly** *adv*

mas·ter·mind \-ˌmīnd\ *n* **:** a person who invents or directs an ingenious joint project — **mastermind** *vb*

master of ceremonies : a person who acts as host at a formal event or on an entertainment program (as on television)

mas·ter·piece \ˈmas-tər-ˌpēs\ *n* **:** a work done with great skill; *esp* **:** a supreme intellectual or artistic achievement

master sergeant *n* **:** a noncommissioned officer ranking in the army just below a sergeant major and in the air force just below a senior master sergeant

mas·tery \ˈmas-t(ə-)rē\ *n, pl* **-ter·ies 1 :** the position or authority of a master **2 :** VICTORY **3 :** skill or knowledge that makes one master of something **:** COMMAND ⟨a *mastery* of French⟩

mast·head \ˈmast-ˌhed\ *n* **1 :** the top of a mast **2 :** the name of a newspaper displayed on the top of the first page

mas·tic \ˈmas-tik\ *n* **1 :** a yellowish to greenish resin of a small southern European tree used in varnish **2 :** a pasty material (as a preparation of asphalt) used as protective coating or cement

mas·ti·cate \ˈmas-tə-ˌkāt\ *vb* **1 :** to grind or crush with the teeth before swallowing **:** CHEW **2 :** to soften or reduce to pulp by crushing or kneading — **mas·ti·ca·tion** \mas-tə-ˈkā-shən\ *n*

mas·tiff \ˈmas-təf\ *n* **:** a large powerful deep-chested smooth-coated dog used chiefly as a watchdog and guard dog

mas·to·don \ˈmas-tə-ˌdän, -dən\ *n* **:** any of numerous huge extinct mammals related to the mammoths and existing elephants — **mas·to·dont** \-ˌdänt\ *adj or n*

1**mas·toid** \ˈmas-ˌtȯid\ *adj* **:** of, relating to, or occurring in the region of a somewhat cone-shaped process of a bone of the skull behind the ear

2**mastoid** *n* **:** a mastoid bone or process

1**mat** \ˈmat\ *n* **1 a :** a piece of coarse fabric of rush, straw, or wool **b :** a piece of material in front of a door to wipe the shoes on **c :** a piece of material (as straw or cloth) used under a dish or vase or as an ornament **d :** a pad or cushion for gymnastics or wrestling **2 :** something made up of many intertwined or tangled strands ⟨a thick *mat* of vegetation⟩

2**mat** *vb* **mat·ted; mat·ting 1 :** to provide with a mat or matting **2 :** to form into a tangled mass

3**mat** *adj* **:** lacking luster or gloss

4**mat** *vb* **mat·ted; mat·ting 1 :** to give a dull effect to **2 :** to border (a picture) with a mat

5**mat** *n* **1 :** a border around a picture between picture and frame or serving as the frame **2 :** a dull finish

MAT *abbr* master of arts in teaching

mat·a·dor \ˈmat-ə-ˌdȯr\ *n* [from Spanish, meaning literally "killer"] **:** the bullfighter who kills the bull with a sword

1**match** \ˈmach\ *n* **1 a :** a person or thing that is equal or similar to or exactly like another **b :** one that is able to cope with another ⟨a *match* for the enemy⟩ **2 :** two persons or things that go well together ⟨curtains and carpet are a good *match*⟩ **3 a :** MARRIAGE ⟨both daughters made good *matches*⟩ **b :** a person to be considered as a marriage partner **4 :** a contest between parties ⟨a tennis *match*⟩

2**match** *vb* **1 :** to meet usu. successfully as a competitor **2 a :** to place in competition with **b :** to provide with a worthy competitor **3 :** to join or give in marriage **4 a :** to make or find the equal or the like of **b :** to make correspond **c :** to be the same or suitable to one another ⟨do these colors *match*?⟩ **5 :** to flip or toss coins and compare exposed faces — **match·er** *n*

3**match** *n* **1 :** a wick or cord that burns evenly and is used to ignite a charge of powder **2 :** a short slender piece of material tipped with a mixture that ignites when subjected to friction

match·book \ˈmach-ˌbu̇k\ *n* **:** a small folder containing rows of paper matches

match·less \-ləs\ *adj* **:** having no equal **:** better than any other — **match·less·ly** *adv*

match·lock \-ˌläk\ *n* **:** an old gun in which the charge was lighted by a cord match

match·mak·er \-ˌmā-kər\ *n* **:** one that arranges marriages — **match·mak·ing** \-kiŋ\ *n*

1**mate** \ˈmāt\ *n* **1 a :** ASSOCIATE, COMPANION **b :** an assistant workman **:** HELPER ⟨plumber's *mate*⟩ **2 :** a deck officer on a merchant ship ranking below the captain **3 a :** either member of a married couple **b :** one of a pair of animals ⟨a dove and his *mate*⟩ **c :** either of two matched objects ⟨the *mate* to a glove⟩

2**mate** *vb* **1 :** to join or fit together **2 a :** to bring or come together as mates; *esp* **:** MARRY **b :** to provide a mate for — **mate with :** to take as a mate

ma·té *or* **ma·te** \ˈmä-ˌtā\ *n* **:** a fragrant beverage made from the leaves and shoots of a So. American holly; *also* **:** these leaves and shoots

1**ma·te·ri·al** \mə-ˈtir-ē-əl\ *adj* **1 :** relating to or consisting of matter **:** PHYSICAL ⟨*material* world⟩ ⟨*material* comforts⟩ **2 a :** IMPORTANT ⟨food is *material* to health⟩ **b :** RELEVANT **3 :** bodily or physical rather than spiritual or intellectual ⟨*material* progress⟩ ⟨*material* needs⟩ — **ma·te·ri·al·i·ty** \-ˌtir-ē-ˈal-ət-ē\ *n* — **ma·te·ri·al·ly** \-ˈtir-ē-ə-lē\ *adv*

2**material** *n* **1 :** the elements or substance of which something is composed or can be made ⟨dress *material*⟩ ⟨building *materials*⟩ **2 :** apparatus and supplies for doing or making something ⟨writing *materials*⟩

ma·te·ri·al·ism \mə-ˈtir-ē-ə-ˌliz-əm\ *n* **1 :** a theory that everything can be explained as being or coming from matter **2 :** a tendency to attach too much importance to physical comfort and well-being — **ma·te·ri·al·ist** \-ē-ə-ləst\ *n or adj* — **ma·te·ri·al·is·tic** \-ˌtir-ē-ə-ˈlis-tik\ *adj*

ma·te·ri·al·ize \mə-ˈtir-ē-ə-ˌlīz\ *vb* **1 :** to give material form and substance to **2 :** to assume bodily form ⟨a ghost *materialized* out of nowhere⟩ **3 a** : to become realized fact **b** : to appear suddenly

ma·té·ri·el *or* **ma·te·ri·el** \mə-ˌtir-ē-ˈel\ *n* : MATERIAL 2

ma·ter·nal \mə-ˈtərn-əl\ *adj* **1** : of or relating to a mother : MOTHERLY **2 a** : related through a mother ⟨*maternal* grandparents⟩ **b** : derived or received from a female parent ⟨*maternal* chromosomes⟩ — **ma·ter·nal·ly** \-ə-lē\ *adv*

ma·ter·ni·ty \mə-ˈtər-nət-ē\ *n, pl* **-ties 1** : the state of being a mother : MOTHERHOOD **2** : motherly character or qualities : MOTHERLINESS

math \ˈmath\ *n* : MATHEMATICS

math·e·mat·i·cal \ˌmath-ə-ˈmat-i-kəl\ *adj* **1** : of, relating to, or according with mathematics **2** : very exact ⟨*mathematical* precision⟩ — **math·e·mat·i·cal·ly** \-i-k(ə-)lē\ *adv*

math·e·ma·ti·cian \ˌmath-(ə-)mə-ˈtish-ən\ *n* : a specialist in mathematics

math·e·mat·ics \ˌmath-ə-ˈmat-iks\ *n* : the science of numbers and their properties, relations, and combinations and of spatial shapes and their structure and measurement

mat·i·nee *or* **mat·i·née** \ˌmat-ə-ˈnā\ *n* : a musical or dramatic performance held in the daytime and esp. in the afternoon

mat·ins \ˈmat-ənz\ *n pl, often cap* **1** : special prayers said between midnight and 4 a.m. **2** : a service of morning prayer

ma·tri·arch \ˈmā-trē-ˌärk\ *n* : a woman who rules a family, group, or state; *esp* : a mother who is head and ruler of her family and descendants — **ma·tri·ar·chal** \ˌmā-trē-ˈär-kəl\ *adj*

ma·tri·ar·chy \ˈmā-trē-ˌär-kē\ *n, pl* **-chies 1** : a family, group, or state governed by a matriarch **2** : a system of social organization in which descent and inheritance are traced through the female line

mat·ri·cide \ˈma-trə-ˌsīd, ˈmā-\ *n* **1** : murder of a mother by her child **2** : one that murders his mother — **mat·ri·cid·al** \ˌma-trə-ˈsīd-əl, ˌmā-\ *adj*

ma·tric·u·late \mə-ˈtrik-yə-ˌlāt\ *vb* : to enroll esp. in a college or university — **ma·tric·u·la·tion** \-ˌtrik-yə-ˈlā-shən\ *n*

mat·ri·mo·ny \ˈma-trə-ˌmō-nē\ *n, pl* **-nies** : MARRIAGE — **mat·ri·mo·ni·al** \ˌma-trə-ˈmō-nē-əl\ *adj* — **mat·ri·mo·ni·al·ly** \-nē-ə-lē\ *adv*

ma·trix \ˈmā-triks\ *n, pl* **ma·tri·ces** \ˈmā-trə-ˌsēz, ˈma-\ *or* **ma·trix·es** \ˈmā-trik-səz\ **1** : the thickened tissue at the base of a fingernail or toenail from which the nail grows **2** : a place or a surrounding or enclosing substance (as a rock) within which something (as a mineral) originates or develops **3** : something (as a mold) that gives form, foundation, or origin to something else enclosed in it

ma·tron \ˈmā-trən\ *n* **1** : a married woman **2** : a woman in charge of the household affairs of an institution **3** : a woman who supervises women prisoners in a police station or jail

ma·tron·ly \-lē\ *adj* : of, resembling, or suitable for a matron

matron of honor : a married woman serving as the principal wedding attendant of a bride

[1]**mat·ter** \ˈmat-ər\ *n* **1 a** : a subject of interest or concern ⟨a *matter* of dispute⟩ **b** : something to be dealt with : AFFAIR ⟨personal *matters* to take care of⟩ **c** : a condition affecting a person or thing unfavorably ⟨what's the *matter* with him⟩ **2 a** : the physical substance of the universe : something that occupies space and has weight **b** : material substance of a particular kind or function ⟨coloring *matter*⟩ **3** : an indefinite amount or quantity ⟨a *matter* of four miles to the next town⟩ **4** : something written or printed **5** : MAIL ⟨first-class *matter*⟩ — **for that matter** : so far as that is concerned

[2]**matter** *vb* **1** : to be of importance : SIGNIFY **2** : to form or discharge pus : SUPPURATE ⟨*mattering* wound⟩

matter of course : something that may be expected as a result of something else

mat·ter–of–fact \ˌmat-ər-ə-ˈfakt\ *adj* : sticking to fact; *esp* : not fanciful : PRACTICAL, COMMONPLACE — **mat·ter–of–fact·ly** *adv*

Mat·thew \ˈmath-yü\ *n* — see BIBLE table

mat·ting \ˈmat-ing\ *n* **1** : material for mats **2** : MATS

mat·tock \ˈmat-ək\ *n* : an implement for digging consisting of a long wooden handle and a steel head one end of which comes to a point or to a cutting edge

mat·tress \ˈma-trəs\ *n* **1** : a fabric case filled with springy material used as a bed or on a bedstead **2** : an inflatable sack for use as a mattress

mat·u·ra·tion \ˌmach-ə-ˈrā-shən\ *n* **1** : the process of becoming mature **2** : the process involving meiosis by which body cells having two sets of chromosomes are transformed into gametes with one set of chromosomes

[1]**ma·ture** \mə-ˈt(y)u̇(ə)r\ *adj* **1** : fully thought out ⟨a *mature* plan⟩ **2 a** : fully grown or developed : ADULT, RIPE **b** : having attained a final or desired state ⟨*mature* wine⟩ **3** : of or relating to a condition of full development ⟨*mature* outlook⟩ **4** : due for payment ⟨the note becomes *mature* in 90 days⟩ — **ma·ture·ly** *adv*

[2]**mature** *vb* **1** : to bring to maturity or completion ⟨*matured* his plans⟩ **2** : to become mature

ma·tu·ri·ty \mə-ˈt(y)u̇r-ət-ē\ *n* **1** : the quality or state of being mature; *esp* : full development **2** : the date when a note becomes due

mat·zo \ˈmät-sə, -ˌsō\ *n, pl* **mat·zoth** *or* **mat·zos** \-səz, -səs, -ˌsōz, -ˌsōs, -ˌsōt(h)\ : unleavened bread eaten at the Passover

maud·lin \ˈmȯd-lən\ *adj* **1** : weakly and overly sentimental **2** : drunk enough to be tearfully silly

[1]**maul** \ˈmȯl\ *n* : a heavy hammer often with a wooden head used esp. for driving wedges or posts

[2]**maul** *vb* **1** : BEAT, BRUISE **2** : to handle roughly — **maul·er** *n*

maun·der \ˈmȯn-dər, ˈmän-\ *vb* **maun·dered**; **maun·der·ing** \-d(ə-)ring\ **1** : to wander slowly and idly **2** : to speak disconnectedly or aimlessly — **maun·der·er** \-dər-ər\ *n*

Maun·dy Thursday \ˌmȯn-dē-, ˌmän-\ *n* : the Thursday before Easter

mau·so·le·um \ˌmȯ-sə-ˈlē-əm, ˌmȯ-zə-\ *n, pl* **-leums** *or* **-lea** \-ˈlē-ə\ [from Greek *Mausōleion*, name of the tomb of Mausolus, satrap of Caria in the 4th century B.C., whose elaborate tomb was one of the Seven Wonders of the ancient world] : a large or fancy tomb

mauve \ˈmōv, ˈmȯv\ *n* : a moderate purple, violet, or lilac

mav·er·ick \ˈmav-(ə-)rik\ *n* **1** : an unbranded range animal; *esp* : a motherless calf **2** : a person who refuses to conform with his group and sets an independent course

ma·vis \ˈmā-vəs\ *n* : an Old World thrush noted for its song

maw \ˈmȯ\ *n* **1** : a receiving organ (as a stomach or a crop) for swallowed food **2** : the throat, gullet, or jaws esp. of a voracious flesh-eating animal

mawk·ish \ˈmȯ-kish\ *adj* **1** : having an insipid often unpleasant taste **2** : MAUDLIN — **mawk·ish·ly** *adv* — **mawk·ish·ness** *n*

max *abbr* maximum
maxi \'mak-sē\ *n* : a long garment (as a skirt, dress, or coat) that extends often to the ankles
max·il·la \mak-'sil-ə\ *n, pl* **max·il·lae** \-'sil-(,)ē, -'sil-,ī\ *or* **maxillas** **1 a** : JAW 1a **b** : an upper jaw esp. of a mammal **c** : either of two bones of the upper jaw that in higher vertebrates and man bear most of the teeth **2** : one of the first or second pair of mouth appendages behind the mandibles in various arthropods — **max·il·lary** \'mak-sə-,ler-ē\ *adj or n*
max·im \'mak-səm\ *n* **1** : a general truth or rule of conduct **2** : a proverbial saying
max·i·mize \'mak-sə-,mīz\ *vb* : to raise to a maximum degree
max·i·mum \'mak-s(ə-)məm\ *n, pl* **maximums** *or* **max·i·ma** \-sə-mə\ **1** : the highest quantity, value, or development **2** : an upper limit allowed by authority — **maximum** *adj*
may \(')mā\ *auxiliary verb, past* **might** \(')mīt\; *pres sing & pl* **may** **1 a** : have permission to ⟨you *may* go now⟩ **b** : be in some degree likely to ⟨you *may* be right⟩ **2** — used to express a wish ⟨long *may* he reign⟩ **3** — used to express purpose ⟨we exercise so that we *may* be strong⟩ or contingency ⟨he'll do his duty come what *may*⟩
May \'mā\ *n* [from Latin *Maius*, after *Maia*, a minor Roman goddess] : the 5th month of the year
Ma·ya \'mī-ə\ *n* : a member of a group of peoples of the Yucatán peninsula and adjacent areas — **Ma·yan** \'mī-ən\ *adj*
may·ap·ple \'mā-,ap-əl\ *n* : a No. American large-leaved woodland herb related to the barberries that has a poisonous rootstock and a single large waxy white flower followed by a yellow egg-shaped berry; *also* : its edible but insipid fruit

mayapple
(up to 18 in. high)

may·be \'mā-bē, 'meb-ē\ *adv* : PERHAPS
May Day \'mā-,dā\ *n* : May 1 celebrated as a springtime festival and in some countries as Labor Day
may·flow·er \'mā-,flau̇(-ə)r\ *n* : any of various spring-blooming plants (as the trailing arbutus, hepatica, or several No. American anemones)
may·fly \-,flī\ *n* : any of a group of slender fragile-winged short-lived adult insects
may·hap \'mā-,hap, mā-'\ *adv* : PERHAPS
may·hem \'mā-,hem, 'mā-əm\ *n* : willful and permanent crippling or disfigurement of any part of the body
mayn't \'mā-ənt, (')mānt\ : may not
may·on·naise \'mā-ə-,nāz, ,mā-ə-'\ *n* : a dressing (as for salads) consisting chiefly of egg yolk, vegetable oil, and vinegar or lemon juice
may·or \'mā-ər, 'me(-)ər\ *n* : the highest official of a city or borough — **may·or·al** \'mā-ə-rəl, 'me-ə-\ *adj*
may·or·al·ty \'mā-ə-rəl-tē, 'mer-əl-\ *n, pl* **-ties** : the office or term of office of a mayor
may·pole \'mā-,pōl\ *n, often cap* : a tall flower-wreathed pole forming a center for May Day sports and dances
may·pop \'mā-,päp\ *n* : a climbing passionflower of the southern U.S.; *also* : its ovoid yellow edible fruit
May queen *n* : a girl chosen queen of a May Day festival
maze \'māz\ *n* : a confusing intricate network of passages
ma·zur·ka \mə-'zər-kə, -'zu̇r-\ *n* **1** : a Polish dance in moderate triple measure **2** : music for the mazurka
mazy \'mā-zē\ *adj* **maz·i·er**; **-est** : resembling a maze in confusing turns and windings
mb *abbr* millibar
MBS *abbr* Mutual Broadcasting System
mc *abbr* megacycle
MC *abbr* master of ceremonies
Md *abbr* Maryland
MD *abbr* **1** doctor of medicine **2** Maryland
mdse *abbr* merchandise
me \(')mē\ *pron, objective case of* I
Me *or* **ME** *abbr* Maine
[1]**mead** \'mēd\ *n* : a fermented drink made of water, honey, malt, and yeast
[2]**mead** *n, archaic* : MEADOW
mead·ow \'med-ō\ *n* : usu. level land with a cultivated or natural cover mainly of grass
mead·ow·lark \-,lärk\ *n* : any of several No. American songbirds largely brown and buff above with a yellow breast bearing a black crescent
meadow saffron *n* : any of a genus of Old World flowers that are related to the lily and have often autumn-borne flowers resembling crocuses and seeds and corms that yield colchicine
mead·ow·sweet \'med-ō-,swēt\ *n* : any of several No. American native or naturalized spireas with pink or white fragrant flowers
mea·ger *or* **mea·gre** \'mē-gər\ *adj* **1** : having little flesh : THIN **2** : lacking richness or strength : INADEQUATE ⟨a *meager* harvest⟩ — **mea·ger·ly** *adv* — **mea·ger·ness** *n*
[1]**meal** \'mēl\ *n* **1** : the food eaten or prepared for eating at one time **2** : the act or time of eating a meal
[2]**meal** *n* **1** : ground seeds of a cereal grass or pulse; *esp* : CORNMEAL **2** : something like meal esp. in texture
meal·time \'mēl-,tīm\ *n* : the usual time at which a meal is served
meal·worm \-,wərm\ *n* : any of various small brownish beetle larvae that live in grain products and are often raised as food for insect-eating animals
mealy \'mē-lē\ *adj* **meal·i·er**; **-est** **1** : being soft, dry, and crumbly **2** : containing meal **3** : covered with fine grains or with flecks (as of color) **4** : MEALYMOUTHED
mealy·bug \'mē-lē-,bəg\ *n* : any of numerous destructive scale insects with a white powdery covering
mealy·mouthed \,mē-lē-'mau̇t͟hd, -'mau̇tht\ *adj* **1** : plausible and insincere in speech **2** : affectedly unwilling to use coarse language
[1]**mean** \'mēn\ *adj* [from Middle English *imene*, from Old English *gemǣne*, probably from the same source as Latin *communis* "common", from which comes English *common*] **1** : of low birth or station : HUMBLE **2** : ORDINARY, INFERIOR ⟨a man of no *mean* ability⟩ **3** : POOR, SHABBY ⟨live in *mean* surroundings⟩ **4** : UNKIND, WICKED **5** : STINGY, MISERLY **6** : SPITE-

FUL, MALICIOUS **7** : of a vicious or troublesome disposition ⟨a *mean* horse⟩ **8** : EXCELLENT ⟨plays a *mean* trumpet⟩ **9** : UNWELL, INDISPOSED — **mean·ly** *adv* — **mean·ness** \'mēn-nəs\ *n*

2**mean** \'mēn\ *vb* **meant** \'ment\; **mean·ing** \'mē-ning\ [from Old English *mǣnen*] **1 a** : to have as a purpose : INTEND ⟨I *mean* to go⟩ **b** : to intend for a particular purpose or use ⟨a book *meant* for children⟩ **2** : to serve to convey, show, or indicate : SIGNIFY ⟨what do his words *mean*⟩ ⟨those clouds *mean* rain⟩ **3** : to be important ⟨health *means* everything to him⟩ — **mean business** : to be in earnest

3**mean** \'mēn\ *n* [from medieval French *meien*, from the adjective *meien* "middle", "median", from Latin *medianus*, from *medius* "middle"] **1** : a middle point between extremes **2 a** : a value that represents a range of values; *esp* : ARITHMETIC MEAN **b** : either of the middle two terms of a proportion **3** *pl* : something by which an end is accomplished or furthered ⟨*means* of production⟩ ⟨use any *means* you can⟩ **4** *pl* : WEALTH ⟨a man of *means*⟩ — **by all means** : without fail : CERTAINLY — **by any means** : in any way : at all — **by means of** : through the use of — **by no means** : not at all : certainly not

4**mean** \'mēn\ *adj* **1** : holding a middle position : INTERMEDIATE **2 a** : lying about midway between extremes **b** : being the mean of a set of values : AVERAGE ⟨*mean* temperature⟩

1**me·an·der** \mē-'an-dər\ *n* **1** : a turn or winding of a stream **2** : a winding path or course

2**meander** *vb* **-dered**; **-der·ing** \-d(ə-)ring\ **1** : to follow a winding or intricate course **2** : to wander aimlessly : RAMBLE

1**mean·ing** \'mē-ning\ *n* **1 a** : the sense one intends to convey esp. by language ⟨do not mistake my *meaning*⟩ **b** : the sense that is conveyed ⟨the poem's *meaning* to me⟩ **2** : INTENT, PURPOSE **3** : intent to convey information : SIGNIFICANCE ⟨a glance full of *meaning*⟩

2**meaning** *adj* : MEANINGFUL, EXPRESSIVE ⟨gave him a *meaning* look⟩

mean·ing·ful \'mē-ning-fəl\ *adj* : having a meaning; *esp* : full of meaning : SIGNIFICANT ⟨a *meaningful* experience⟩ — **mean·ing·ful·ly** \-fə-lē\ *adv*

mean·ing·less \-ləs\ *adj* **1** : lacking sense or significance **2** : lacking motive — **mean·ing·less·ly** *adv* — **mean·ing·less·ness** *n*

1**mean·time** \'mēn-,tīm\ *n* : the intervening time

2**meantime** *adv* : MEANWHILE

1**mean·while** \'mēn-,hwīl\ *n* : MEANTIME

2**meanwhile** *adv* : during the intervening time

meas *abbr* measure

mea·sles \'mē-zəlz\ *n sing or pl* : a contagious virus disease marked by fever and red spots on the skin; *also* : any of several similar diseases (as German measles)

mea·sly \'mēz-(ə-)lē\ *adj* **mea·sli·er**; **-est** **1 a** : infected with measles **b** : similar to measles **2** : contemptibly small or insignificant ⟨fought over a *measly* dime⟩

mea·sur·a·ble \'mezh-(ə-)rə-bəl, 'mezh-ər-bəl, 'māzh-\ *adj* : capable of being measured

1**mea·sure** \'mezh-ər, 'māzh-\ *n* **1 a** : a moderate extent or degree ⟨surprised beyond *measure*⟩ **b** : AMOUNT, EXTENT, DEGREE ⟨succeed in large *measure*⟩ **2 a** : the dimensions, capacity, or quantity of something as fixed by measuring ⟨give full *measure*⟩ **b** : something (as a yardstick or cup) used in measuring **c** : a unit used in measuring ⟨the foot is a *measure* of length⟩ **d** : a system of measuring ⟨metric *measure*⟩ **3** : the act or process of measuring **4 a** : DANCE; *esp* : a stately dance **b** : rhythm or movement in music or poetry : METER, CADENCE **c** : the part of a musical staff between two bars or the group of beats between these bars **5** : an action planned or taken as a means to an end; *esp* : a legislative bill or act

2**measure** *vb* **mea·sured**; **mea·sur·ing** \'mezh-(ə-)ring, 'māzh-\ **1** : to mark or fix in multiples of a specific unit ⟨*measure* off three inches⟩ ⟨*measure* out four cups⟩ **2** : to find out the dimensions, extent, or amount of ⟨*measure* the walk of the house⟩ **3** : ESTIMATE ⟨*measured* the distance with his eye⟩ **4** : to bring into comparison ⟨*measure* your skill against a rival⟩ **5** : to serve as a measure of ⟨a thermometer *measures* temperature⟩ **6** : to have as its measurement ⟨the cloth *measures* 3 yards⟩ — **mea·sur·er** \-ər-ər\ *n*

mea·sured \-ərd\ *adj* **1 a** : regulated or determined by a standard **b** : being slow and steady : EVEN ⟨walk with *measured* steps⟩ **2** : DELIBERATE, CALCULATED ⟨speak with *measured* bluntness⟩ **3** : RHYTHMICAL, METRICAL

mea·sure·less \-ər-ləs\ *adj* : being without or beyond measure : IMMEASURABLE

mea·sure·ment \'mezh-ər-mənt, 'māzh-\ *n* **1** : the act or process of measuring **2** : a figure, extent, or amount obtained by measuring : DIMENSION **3** : a system of measures

measure up *vb* **1** : to have necessary or fitting qualifications **2** : to be the equal (as in ability) — used with *to*

measuring worm *n* : LOOPER 1

meat \'mēt\ *n* **1 a** : FOOD; *esp* : solid food as distinguished from drink **b** : the edible part of something as distinguished from the husk, shell, or other covering **2** : animal and esp. mammal tissue used as food

meat·ball \-,bȯl\ *n* : a small ball of chopped or ground meat

meat–pack·ing \-,pak-ing\ *n* : the wholesale meat industry including slaughtering, processing, and distribution to retailers — **meat–pack·er** *n*

meaty \'mēt-ē\ *adj* **meat·i·er**; **-est** **1** : full of meat : FLESHY **2** : rich in matter for thought : SUBSTANTIAL ⟨a *meaty* book⟩ — **meat·i·ness** *n*

mec·ca \'mek-ə\ *n, often cap* [from *Mecca*, city in Arabia, the birthplace of Muhammad and the goal of Muslim pilgrimages] : a place that attracts esp. a particular group of people ⟨a *mecca* for tourists⟩

mech *abbr* mechanical

1**me·chan·ic** \mi-'kan-ik\ *adj* : of or relating to manual work or skill ⟨*mechanic* arts⟩

2**mechanic** *n* : a manual worker; *esp* : a repairer of machines

me·chan·i·cal \mi-'kan-i-kəl\ *adj* **1 a** : of or relating to machinery ⟨*mechanical* engineering⟩ **b** : made or operated by a machine or machinery ⟨a *mechanical* toy⟩ **2** : done as if by machine : IMPERSONAL ⟨gave a *mechanical* reply⟩ **3** : relating to or according with the principles of mechanics — **me·chan·i·cal·ly** \-i-k(ə-)lē\ *adv*

mechanical advantage *n* : the ratio of the force that performs the useful work of a machine to the force that is applied to the machine

mechanical drawing *n* : a method of drawing using such instruments as compasses, squares, and triangles so as to insure mathematical precision; *also* : a drawing made by this method

me·chan·ics \mi-'kan-iks\ *n sing or pl* **1** : a science that deals with energy and forces and their effect on bodies **2** : the application of mechanics to the making or operation of machines **3** : mechanical or functional details ⟨the *mechanics* of running⟩ ⟨the *mechanics* of writing plays⟩

MEASURES AND WEIGHTS

UNIT	ABBR. OR SYMBOL	EQUIVALENTS IN OTHER UNITS OF SAME SYSTEM	METRIC EQUIVALENT
		length	
mile	mi	5280 feet, 320 rods, 1760 yards	1.609 kilometers
rod	rd	5.50 yards, 16.5 feet	5.029 meters
yard	yd	3 feet, 36 inches	0.914 meters
foot	ft *or* ′	12 inches, 0.333 yards	30.480 centimeters
inch	in *or* ″	0.083 feet, 0.027 yards	2.540 centimeters
		area	
square mile	sq mi *or* mi²	640 acres, 102,400 square rods	2.590 square kilometers
acre	a *or* ac (seldom used)	4840 square yards, 43,560 square feet	0.405 hectares, 4047 square meters
square rod	sq rd *or* rd²	30.25 square yards, 0.006 acres	25.293 square meters
square yard	sq yd *or* yd²	1296 square inches, 9 square feet	0.836 square meters
square foot	sq ft *or* ft²	144 square inches, 0.111 square yards	0.093 square meters
square inch	sq in *or* in²	0.007 square feet, 0.00077 square yards	6.451 square centimeters
		volume	
cubic yard	cu yd *or* yd³	27 cubic feet, 46,656 cubic inches	0.765 cubic meters
cubic foot	cu ft *or* ft³	1728 cubic inches, 0.0370 cubic yards	0.028 cubic meters
cubic inch	cu in *or* in³	0.00058 cubic feet, 0.000021 cubic yards	16.387 cubic centimeters
		weight	
		avoirdupois	
ton	tn (seldom used)		
short ton		20 short hundredweight, 2000 pounds	0.907 metric tons
long ton		20 long hundredweight, 2240 pounds	1.016 metric tons
hundredweight	cwt		
short hundredweight		100 pounds, 0.05 short tons	45.359 kilograms
long hundredweight		112 pounds, 0.05 long tons	50.802 kilograms
pound	lb *or* lb av *also* #	16 ounces, 7000 grains	0.453 kilograms
ounce	oz *or* oz av	16 drams, 437.5 grains	28.349 grams
dram	dr *or* dr av	27.343 grains, 0.0625 ounces	1.771 grams
grain	gr	0.036 drams, 0.002285 ounces	0.0648 grams
		troy	
pound	lb t	12 ounces, 240 pennyweight, 5760 grains	0.373 kilograms
ounce	oz t	20 pennyweight, 480 grains	31.103 grams
pennyweight	dwt *also* pwt	24 grains, 0.05 ounces	1.555 grams
grain	gr	0.042 pennyweight, 0.002083 ounces	0.0648 grams
		apothecaries'	
pound	lb ap	12 ounces, 5760 grains	0.373 kilograms
ounce	oz ap *or* ℥	8 drams, 480 grains	31.103 grams
dram	dr ap *or* ʒ	3 scruples, 60 grains	3.887 grams
scruple	s ap *or*	20 grains, 0.333 drams	1.295 grams
grain	gr	0.05 scruples, 0.002083 ounces, 0.0166 drams	0.0648 grams
		capacity	
		U.S. liquid measure	
gallon	gal	4 quarts (231 cubic inches)	3.785 liters
quart	qt	2 pints (57.75 cubic inches)	0.946 liters
pint	pt	4 gills (28.875 cubic inches)	0.473 liters
gill	gi	4 fluidounces (7.218 cubic inches)	118.291 milliliters
fluidounce	fl oz *or* f ℥	8 fluidrams (1.804 cubic inches)	29.573 milliliters
fluidram	fl dr *or* f ʒ	60 minims (0.225 cubic inches)	3.696 milliliters
minim	min *or* ♏	1/60 fluidram (0.003759 cubic inches)	0.061610 milliliters
		U.S. dry measure	
bushel	bu	4 pecks (2150.42 cubic inches)	35.238 liters
peck	pk	8 quarts (537.605 cubic inches)	8.809 liters
quart	qt	2 pints (67.200 cubic inches)	1.101 liters
pint	pt	½ quart (33.600 cubic inches)	0.550 liters
		British imperial liquid and dry measure	
bushel	bu	4 pecks (2219.36 cubic inches)	0.036 cubic meters
peck	pk	2 gallons (554.84 cubic inches)	0.009 cubic meters
gallon	gal	4 quarts (277.420 cubic inches)	4.545 liters
quart	qt	2 pints (69.355 cubic inches)	1.136 liters
pint	pt	4 gills (34.678 cubic inches)	568.26 cubic centimeters
gill	gi	5 fluidounces (8.669 cubic inches)	142.066 cubic centimeters
fluidounce	fl oz *or* ℥	8 fluidrams (1.7339 cubic inches)	28.416 cubic centimeters
fluidram	fl dr *or* f ʒ	60 minims (0.216734 cubic inches)	3.5516 cubic centimeters
minim	min *or* ♏	1/60 fluidram (0.003612 cubic inches)	0.059194 cubic centimeters

mech·a·nism \'mek-ə-,niz-əm\ *n* **1** : a machine or mechanical device **2 a** : the parts by which a machine operates ⟨the *mechanism* of a watch⟩ **b** : the steps that make up a process or activity ⟨the *mechanism* of democratic government⟩ **3** : the processes involved in or responsible for a natural phenomenon (as evolution or an action or reaction)

mech·a·nize \'mek-ə-,nīz\ *vb* **1** : to make mechanical; *esp* : to replace human or animal labor by machinery **2** : to equip with armed and armored motor-driven vehicles ⟨*mechanized* infantry⟩ — **mech·a·ni·za·tion** \,mek-ə-nə-'zā-shən\ *n* — **mech·a·niz·er** \'mek-ə-,nī-zər\ *n*

me·cop·ter·an \mi-'käp-tə-rən\ *n* : any of a group of primitive insects that have membranous wings with heavy veins, a long beak with biting mouthparts at the tip, and larvae that live in soil — **me·cop·ter·ous** \-rəs\ *adj*

med *abbr* 1 medical 2 medicine 3 medium

med·al \'med-əl\ *n* : a piece of metal often like a coin issued to commemorate a person or event or as an award

med·al·ist *or* **med·al·list** \'med-ə-ləst\ *n* : a recipient of a medal

me·dal·lion \mə-'dal-yən\ *n* **1** : a large medal **2** : something (as a tablet in relief) resembling a large medal

med·dle \'med-əl\ *vb* **med·dled**; **med·dling** \-(ə-)liŋ\ : to busy oneself intrusively or officiously ⟨*meddle* in another's business⟩ — **med·dler** \-(ə-)lər\ *n*

syn MEDDLE, INTERFERE, TAMPER can mean to direct one's attentions intrusively or harmfully. MEDDLE suggests inquisitive, inconsiderate, and unauthorized prying into another's concern; INTERFERE suggests getting in someone's way by meddling, whether intentionally or not; TAMPER implies intervention or experimenting that is wrong or uncalled-for and likely to be harmful

med·dle·some \'med-əl-səm\ *adj* : given to meddling

media *pl of* MEDIUM

me·di·ae·val *var of* MEDIEVAL

me·di·al \'mēd-ē-əl\ *adj* **1** : MEDIAN, MIDDLE **2** : ORDINARY, AVERAGE — **me·di·al·ly** \-ə-lē\ *adv*

1**me·di·an** \'mēd-ē-ən\ *n* : a value in a series below and above which there are an equal number of values

2**median** *adj* **1** : being in the middle or in an intermediate position **2** : relating to or constituting a median

1**me·di·ate** \'mēd-ē-ət\ *adj* : acting through an intermediate agent or agency : not direct — **me·di·ate·ly** *adv*

2**me·di·ate** \'mēd-ē-,āt\ *vb* **1** : to intervene between conflicting parties or viewpoints to promote reconciliation, settlement, or compromise ⟨*mediate* a settlement⟩ ⟨*mediate* a dispute⟩ **2** : to transmit or act as a mediate mechanism or agency — **me·di·a·tion** \,mēd-ē-'ā-shən\ *n*

me·di·a·tor \'mēd-ē-,āt-ər\ *n* : one that mediates — **me·di·a·to·ry** \'mēd-ē-ə-,tōr-ē, -,tȯr-\ *adj* — **me·di·a·tress** \'mēd-ē-,ā-trəs\ *n*

med·ic \'med-ik\ *n* : a person engaged in medical work

med·i·ca·ble \'med-i-kə-bəl\ *adj* : CURABLE, REMEDIABLE — **med·i·ca·bly** \-blē\ *adv*

med·ic·aid \'med-i-,kād\ *n* : a program of medical aid designed for those unable to afford regular medical service and financed by the state and federal governments

med·i·cal \'med-i-kəl\ *adj* : of or relating to the science or practice of medicine — **med·i·cal·ly** \-k(ə-)lē\ *adv*

me·dic·a·ment \mi-'dik-ə-mənt\ *n* : MEDICINE 1

medi·care \'med-i-,ke(ə)r, -,ka(ə)r\ *n* : a government program of medical care esp. for the aged

med·i·cate \'med-ə-,kāt\ *vb* **1** : to treat with medicine **2** : to add a medicinal substance to ⟨*medicate* a soap⟩

med·i·ca·tion \,med-ə-'kā-shən\ *n* **1** : the act or process of medicating **2** : MEDICINE 1

me·dic·i·nal \mə-'dis-(ə-)nəl\ *adj* : tending or used to relieve or cure disease or pain — **medicinal** *n* — **me·dic·i·nal·ly** \-ē\ *adv*

med·i·cine \'med-ə-sən\ *n* **1** : a substance or preparation used in treating disease **2** : a science or art that deals with the prevention, cure, or easing of disease; *esp* : the practice of the physician as distinguished from the surgeon **3** : an object, power, or rite held to give control over natural or magical forces

medicine ball *n* : a large stuffed leather-covered ball used for conditioning exercises

medicine dropper *n* : DROPPER 2

medicine man *n* : a person among primitive peoples believed to be able to cure diseases by potions and charms

medicine show *n* : a traveling show using entertainers to attract a crowd that may buy remedies or nostrums

me·di·e·val \,mēd-ē-'ē-vəl, ,med-\ *adj* : of, relating to, or characteristic of the Middle Ages

me·di·o·cre \,mēd-ē-'ō-kər\ *adj* : of moderate or low quality : ORDINARY

me·di·oc·ri·ty \,mēd-ē-'äk-rət-ē\ *n, pl* **-ties** **1** : the quality or state of being mediocre **2** : a mediocre person

med·i·tate \'med-ə-,tāt\ *vb* **1 a** : to reflect on or muse over : CONTEMPLATE **b** : to engage in contemplation or reflection **2** : INTEND, PLAN ⟨*meditate* a trip abroad⟩ — **med·i·ta·tion** \,med-ə-'tā-shən\ *n* — **med·i·ta·tive** \'med-ə-,tāt-iv\ *adj* — **med·i·ta·tive·ly** *adv*

Med·i·ter·ra·ne·an \,med-ə-tə-'rā-nē-ən, -'rā-nyən\ *adj* : of or relating to the Mediterranean sea or to the lands or peoples around it

Mediterranean fruit fly *n* : a widely distributed two-winged fly with black-and-white markings and a larva destructive to ripening fruit

1**me·di·um** \'mēd-ē-əm\ *n, pl* **me·di·ums** *or* **me·dia** \'mēd-ē-ə\ **1 a** : something that is between or in the middle **b** : a middle condition or degree **2** : a means of doing or conveying something ⟨money is a *medium* of exchange⟩; *esp* : a substance through which a force acts or through which something is transmitted ⟨air is the common *medium* of sound⟩ **3** : a channel (as newspapers, radio, or television) of communication **4** : a person through whom others seek to communicate with the spirits of the dead **5** : a surrounding substance or condition : ENVIRONMENT ⟨slums are a good *medium* for delinquency⟩ **6** : a nutrient system for the artificial cultivation of organisms (as bacteria) or cells

2**medium** *adj* : intermediate in amount, quality, position, or degree

med·lar \'med-lər\ *n* : a small hairy-leaved Eurasian tree related to the apples; *also* : its fruit that resembles a crab apple and is used esp. in preserves

med·ley \'med-lē\ *n, pl* **medleys** **1** : MIXTURE; *esp* : a confused mixture **2** : a musical composition made up of parts from other pieces

me·dul·la \mə-'dəl-ə\ *n, pl* **-dul·las** *or* **-dul·lae** \-'dəl-(,)ē, -,ī\ **1** : MARROW 1 **2** : the inner or deep part of an animal or plant structure **3 :** MEDULLA OBLONGATA **4 :** PITH 1a — **med·ul·lary** \'med-ə-ˌler-ē, 'mej-ə-\ *adj*

medulla ob·lon·ga·ta \-ˌäb-ˌlȯng-'gät-ə\ *n* **:** the somewhat pyramid-shaped hind part of the vertebrate brain that is continuous with the spinal cord

me·du·sa \mi-'d(y)ü-sə, -zə\ *n, pl* **-sae** \-ˌsē, -ˌzē\ *or* **-sas :** JELLYFISH — **me·du·san** \-'d(y)ü-sən, -zən\ *adj or n* — **me·du·soid** \-'d(y)ü-ˌsȯid, -ˌzȯid\ *adj or n*

meed \'mēd\ *n* **:** something deserved or earned **:** REWARD ⟨receive one's *meed* of praise⟩

meek \'mēk\ *adj* **1 :** enduring injury with patience **:** MILD **2 :** lacking spirit or self-assurance **:** HUMBLE — **meek·ly** *adv* — **meek·ness** *n*

meer·schaum \'mi(ə)r-shəm, -ˌshȯm\ *n* [from German, meaning literally "sea foam", a compound of nouns coming from the same sources as English *marine* and *scum* respectively] **1 :** a soft white lightweight mineral resembling a very fine clay used esp. for tobacco pipes **2 :** a tobacco pipe made of meerschaum

1**meet** \'mēt\ *vb* **met** \'met\; **meet·ing 1 :** to come by chance into the presence of **:** ENCOUNTER ⟨*met* an old friend⟩ **2 a :** to approach from different directions ⟨the trains *meet* at the junction⟩ **b :** to touch and join or cross ⟨a fork where two roads *meet*⟩ **3 :** to go where a person or thing is or will be ⟨agreed to *meet* her at school⟩ **4 a :** to become acquainted ⟨the couple *met* at a dance⟩ **b :** to make the acquaintance of ⟨*met* interesting people there⟩ **5 a :** to come together as opponents ⟨the brothers *met* in the finals⟩ **b :** to struggle against **:** OPPOSE ⟨was chosen to *meet* the champion⟩ **6 :** MATCH ⟨tries to *meet* the competitor's price⟩ **7 :** ENDURE ⟨*meet* defeat bravely⟩ **8 :** to come together **:** ASSEMBLE ⟨*meet* for discussion⟩ **9 :** to become noticed by ⟨sounds of revelry *meet* the ear⟩ **10 a :** to conform to or comply with **:** SATISFY ⟨*meets* all requirements⟩ **b :** to pay fully **:** DISCHARGE ⟨*meet* a financial obligation⟩

2**meet** *n* **:** a meeting esp. to engage in a competitive sport ⟨a track *meet*⟩

3**meet** *adj* **:** SUITABLE, PROPER — **meet·ly** *adv*

meet·ing \'mēt-ing\ *n* **1 :** the act of persons or things that meet ⟨a chance *meeting* with a friend⟩ **2 :** a coming together of a number of persons for a specific purpose **:** ASSEMBLY ⟨the monthly club *meeting*⟩ **3 :** an assembly for religious worship ⟨a Quaker *meeting*⟩ **4 :** the place where two things come together **:** JUNCTION

meet·ing·house \-ˌhau̇s\ *n* **:** a building for religious worship

mega- *or* **meg-** *comb form* **1 :** great **:** large ⟨*mega*spore⟩ **2 :** million **:** multiplied by one million ⟨*meg*ohm⟩ ⟨*mega*cycle⟩

mega·cy·cle \'meg-ə-ˌsī-kəl\ *n* **:** one million cycles per second ⟨a radio frequency of 1.6 *megacycles*⟩

meg·a·lo·ma·nia \ˌmeg-ə-lō-'mā-nē-ə, -nyə\ *n* **:** a disorder of mind marked by feelings of great personal power and importance — **meg·a·lo·ma·ni·ac** \-'mā-nē-ˌak\ *adj or n*

meg·a·lop·o·lis \ˌmeg-ə-'läp-ə-ləs\ *n* **1 :** a very large city **2 :** a thickly populated region centering in a large city or embracing several large cities

ə abut	ər further	a back	ā bake
ä cot, cart	au̇ out	ch chin	e less	ē easy
g gift	i trip	ī life	j joke	ng sing	ō flow
ȯ flaw	ȯi coin	th thin	th this	ü loot
u̇ foot	y yet	yü few	yu̇ furious	zh vision

megaphone

mega·phone \'meg-ə-ˌfōn\ *n* **:** a cone-shaped device used to intensify or direct the voice

mega·ton \-ˌtən\ *n* **:** an explosive force equal to that of one million tons of TNT

mei·o·sis \mī-'ō-səs\ *n, pl* **-o·ses** \-'ō-ˌsēz\ **:** the process by which the number of chromosomes in a gamete-producing cell is reduced to one half — **mei·ot·ic** \mī-'ät-ik\ *adj* — **mei·ot·i·cal·ly** \-'ät-i-k(ə-)lē\ *adv*

mel·a·mine \'mel-ə-ˌmēn\ *n* **:** a synthetic resin composed of carbon, hydrogen, and nitrogen and used in molded products, adhesives, and coatings

mel·an·cho·lia \ˌmel-ən-'kō-lē-ə\ *n* **:** a mental disorder characterized by extreme depression, real or imagined physical symptoms, and often hallucinations and delusions

mel·an·chol·ic \ˌmel-ən-'käl-ik\ *adj* **1 :** MELANCHOLY **2 :** affected with or relating to melancholia

1**mel·an·choly** \'mel-ən-ˌkäl-ē\ *n, pl* **-chol·ies** [from Greek *melancholia*, from *melan-*, stem of *melas* "black" and *cholē* "bile"; from the former belief that the condition was caused by an excess of a supposed black bile in the system; compare HUMOR] **:** a sad or gloomy mood or condition

syn MELANCHOLY, DEJECTION, GLOOM can mean lowness of spirits. MELANCHOLY suggests sad or gloomy thoughtfulness sometimes without apparent cause; DEJECTION suggests listlessness stemming from disappointment; GLOOM implies a profound and lasting effect on one afflicted with low spirits ***ant*** exhilaration

2**melancholy** *adj* **1 :** depressed in spirits **:** DEJECTED, SAD **2 :** seriously thoughtful **3 :** causing sadness **:** DEPRESSING, LAMENTABLE

Mel·a·ne·sian \ˌmel-ə-'nē-zhən, -shən\ *n* **:** a member of the dominant native group of Melanesia characterized by dark skin and tightly curled hair— **Melanesian** *adj*

mé·lange \mā-'länzh, -'länj\ *n* **:** MIXTURE, MEDLEY

mel·a·nin \'mel-ə-nən\ *n* **:** a dark brown or black animal or plant pigment that in man makes some skins darker than others

mel·a·nism \'mel-ə-ˌniz-əm\ *n* **:** an exceptionally dark coloring (as of skin, feathers, or hair) of an individual or kind of organism

mel·a·no·ma \ˌmel-ə-'nō-mə\ *n, pl* **-nomas** *also* **-no·ma·ta** \-'nō-mət-ə\ **:** a usu. malignant tumor containing dark pigment

me·lee \'mā-ˌlā, mā-'lā\ *n* **:** a confused fight or struggle; *esp* **:** a hand-to-hand fight among a number of persons

me·lio·rate \'mēl-yə-ˌrāt\ *vb* **:** to make or become better **:** IMPROVE — **me·lio·ra·tion** \ˌmēl-yə-'rā-shən\ *n* — **me·lio·ra·tive** \'mēl-yə-ˌrāt-iv\ *adj*

mel·lif·lu·ous \me-'lif-lə-wəs, mə-\ *adj* **:** smoothly flowing ⟨*mellifluous* speech⟩ — **mel·lif·lu·ous·ly** *adv* — **mel·lif·lu·ous·ness** *n*

mel·lo·phone \'mel-ə-ˌfōn\ *n* **:** an althorn in circular form

mel·low \'mel-ō\ *adj* **1 a :** tender and sweet from ripeness ⟨*mellow* peaches⟩ **b :** well aged and pleasingly mild ⟨a *mellow* wine⟩ **2 :** made gentle by age or experience **3 :** of soft and loamy consistency ⟨*mellow* soil⟩ **4 :** being clear, full, and pure **:** not coarse or rough ⟨a *mellow* sound⟩ — **mellow** *vb* — **mel·low·ly** *adv* — **mel·low·ness** *n*

me·lo·de·on \mə-ˈlōd-ē-ən\ *n* : a small reed organ in which a bellows draws air inward through the reeds

me·lod·ic \mə-ˈläd-ik\ *adj* : of or relating to melody : MELODIOUS — **me·lod·i·cal·ly** \-i-k(ə-)lē\ *adv*

me·lo·di·ous \mə-ˈlōd-ē-əs\ *adj* **1** : constituting a melody : TUNEFUL ⟨*melodious* songs⟩ **2** : of, relating to, or producing melody ⟨*melodious* birds⟩ — **me·lo·di·ous·ly** *adv* — **me·lo·di·ous·ness** *n*

melo·dra·ma \ˈmel-ə-ˌdräm-ə, -ˌdram-\ *n* **1 a** : a very theatrical play in which action and plot predominate over characterization **b** : such plays as a group **2** : melodramatic events or behavior

melo·dra·mat·ic \-drə-ˈmat-ik\ *adj* **1** : of or relating to melodrama **2** : resembling or suitable for melodrama : SENSATIONAL — **melo·dra·mat·i·cal·ly** \-i-k(ə-)lē\ *adv*

mel·o·dy \ˈmel-əd-ē\ *n, pl* **-dies** **1** : a pleasing succession of sounds **2** : a series of musical tones arranged to give a pleasing effect **3** : the leading part in a harmonic composition

mel·on \ˈmel-ən\ *n* : any of various soft-fleshed sweet-flavored many-seeded fruits (as a muskmelon or watermelon) that have a firm rind and are usu. eaten raw

[1]**melt** \ˈmelt\ *vb* **1** : to change from a solid to a liquid state usu. through heat ⟨*melt* sugar⟩ ⟨snow *melts*⟩ **2** : DISSOLVE ⟨sugar *melts* in the mouth⟩ **3** : to grow less : disappear as if by dissolving ⟨clouds *melting* away⟩ **4** : to make or become gentle : SOFTEN ⟨her warm smile *melts* the heart⟩ **5** : to lose distinct outline or shape : BLEND, MERGE — **melt·er** *n*

[2]**melt** *n* : a melted substance

melting point *n* : the temperature at which a solid melts

melting pot *n* **1** : a container capable of withstanding great heat in which something is melted : CRUCIBLE **2** : a place (as a city or country) in which various nationalities or races live together and gradually blend into one community

mel·ton \ˈmelt-ən\ *n* : a smooth heavy woolen cloth with a short nap used for overcoats

mem *abbr* member

mem·ber \ˈmem-bər\ *n* **1** : a part (as an arm, leg, leaf, or branch) of an animal or plant **2** : one of the individuals or units of a group or organization ⟨a club *member*⟩ ⟨UN *members*⟩ **3** : a part of a whole and esp. of a structure ⟨a horizontal *member* in a bridge⟩ **4 a** : either of the parts on opposite sides of the equal sign in a mathematical equation **b** : ELEMENT 2b

mem·ber·ship \-ˌship\ *n* **1** : the state or status of being a member **2** : the body of members

mem·brane \ˈmem-ˌbrān\ *n* : a thin soft pliable sheet or layer esp. of an animal or plant part — **mem·bra·nous** \ˈmem-brə-nəs\ *adj*

me·men·to \mi-ˈment-ō\ *n, pl* **-tos** *or* **-toes** : SOUVENIR

memo \ˈmem-ō\ *n, pl* **mem·os** : MEMORANDUM

mem·oir \ˈmem-ˌwär, -ˌwȯr\ *n* **1 a** : a story of a personal experience **b** : AUTOBIOGRAPHY — usu. used in pl. **c** : BIOGRAPHY **2** : ACCOUNT, REPORT

mem·o·ra·bil·ia \ˌmem-ə-rə-ˈbil-ē-ə\ *n pl* : memorable things; *also* : a record of such things

mem·o·ra·ble \ˈmem-(ə-)rə-bəl\ *adj* : worth remembering : NOTABLE — **mem·o·ra·bly** \-blē\ *adv*

mem·o·ran·dum \ˌmem-ə-ˈran-dəm\ *n, pl* **-dums** *or* **-da** \-də\ **1** : an informal record or communication **2** : a brief written reminder

[1]**me·mo·ri·al** \mə-ˈmōr-ē-əl, -ˈmȯr-\ *adj* : serving to preserve the memory of a person or an event ⟨a *memorial* service⟩ — **me·mo·ri·al·ly** \-ē-ə-lē\ *adv*

[2]**memorial** *n* **1** : something that keeps alive the memory of a person or event; *esp* : MONUMENT **2** : a statement of facts accompanying a petition to a government official

Memorial Day *n* **1** : May 30 formerly observed as a legal holiday in most states of the U.S. in commemoration of war dead **2** : the last Monday in May observed as a legal holiday in most states of the U.S. **3** : CONFEDERATE MEMORIAL DAY

me·mo·ri·al·ize \mə-ˈmōr-ē-ə-ˌlīz, -ˈmȯr-\ *vb* **1** : to address or petition by a memorial **2** : COMMEMORATE

mem·o·rize \ˈmem-ə-ˌrīz\ *vb* : to commit to memory : learn by heart — **mem·o·ri·za·tion** \ˌmem-(ə-)rə-ˈzā-shən\ *n*

mem·o·ry \ˈmem-(ə-)rē\ *n, pl* **-ries** **1 a** : the power or process of recalling what has been learned **b** : the store of things learned and retained ⟨recite from *memory*⟩ **2** : COMMEMORATION ⟨a monument in *memory* of a hero⟩ **3** : something remembered ⟨has pleasant *memories* of the trip⟩ **4** : the time within which past events can be remembered ⟨within the *memory* of living men⟩ **5** : a part in an electronic computing machine into which information can be inserted and extracted when needed

syn MEMORY, REMEMBRANCE, RECOLLECTION, REMINISCENCE can mean something remembered. MEMORY may suggest a treasuring of something intimate or personal ⟨left alone with his *memories*⟩; REMEMBRANCE is likely to imply the pleasantness with which something is remembered; RECOLLECTION implies a conscious and sometimes difficult effort to remember without implying whether the thing remembered is pleasant or not; REMINISCENCE may imply the remoteness in time of an often pleasant memory

men *pl of* MAN

[1]**men·ace** \ˈmen-əs\ *n* : THREAT, DANGER

[2]**menace** *vb* **1** : THREATEN **2** : ENDANGER — **men·ac·ing·ly** \ˈmen-ə-sing-lē\ *adv*

mé·nage \mā-ˈnäzh\ *n* : HOUSEHOLD

me·nag·er·ie \mə-ˈnaj-ə-rē, -ˈnazh-\ *n* **1** : a place where animals are kept and trained esp. for exhibition **2** : a collection of wild animals kept esp. for exhibition

[1]**mend** \ˈmend\ *vb* **1** : to improve in manners or morals : REFORM **2** : to put into good shape or working order again : REPAIR **3** : to improve in health; *also* : HEAL — **mend·er** *n*

[2]**mend** *n* **1** : an act of mending : REPAIR **2** : a mended place — **on the mend** : IMPROVING

men·da·cious \men-ˈdā-shəs\ *adj* : given to falsehood : LYING — **men·da·cious·ly** *adv* — **men·dac·i·ty** \men-ˈdas-ət-ē\ *n*

men·de·le·vi·um \ˌmen-də-ˈlē-vē-əm\ *n* : a radioactive element artificially produced — see ELEMENT table

Men·de·li·an \men-ˈdē-lē-ən\ *adj* : of, relating to, or according with Mendel's laws or the operation of Mendel's laws — **Mendelian** *n*

Men·del's law \ˌmen-dəlz-\ *n* **1** : a principle in genetics: paired inherited units that control the expression of a character (as height or seed color) separate during germ cell formation so that each sperm or egg receives only one member of each pair — called also *law of segregation* **2** : a principle in genetics that has to be modified in cases where two or more genes occur on the same chromosome: the members of two or more different pairs of inherited units are passed on to a germ cell independently of each other and the various sperms and eggs unite according to the laws of chance sometimes resulting in new combinations of inherited units and of the characters they determine — called also *law of independent assortment* **3** : a principle in genetics that has many exceptions: when the two members of a pair of inherited units are different, the expression of the character they control is determined by the dominant one — called also *law of dominance*

men·di·cant \'men-di-kənt\ *n* **1** : BEGGAR; *esp* : one who lives by begging **2** : a member of a religious order originally owning neither personal nor community property : FRIAR — **men·di·can·cy** \-kən-sē\ *n* — **mendicant** *adj*

men·folk \'men-ˌfōk\ *or* **men·folks** \-ˌfōks\ *n pl* : MEN

men·ha·den \men-'hād-ən, mən-\ *n, pl* **-den** *also* **-dens** : a fish that is related to the herring, is found along the Atlantic coast of the U.S., and is used for bait or converted into oil and fertilizer

¹**me·ni·al** \'mē-nē-əl, -nyəl\ *adj* : of, relating to, or suitable for servants — **me·ni·al·ly** \-ē\ *adv*

²**menial** *n* : SERVANT

men·in·ge·al \ˌmen-ən-'jē-əl\ *adj* : of, relating to, or affecting the meninges

men·in·gi·tis \ˌmen-ən-'jīt-əs\ *n* : a disease in which a membrane of the brain or spinal cord becomes inflamed

me·ninx \'mē-ning(k)s, 'men-ing(k)s\ *n, pl* **me·nin·ges** \mə-'nin-(ˌ)jēz\ : any of the three membranes that envelop the brain and spinal cord

me·nis·cus \mə-'nis-kəs\ *n, pl* **me·nis·ci** \-'nis-ˌ(k)ī, -ˌkē\ *also* **me·nis·cus·es** **1** : a lens that is convex on one side and concave on the other **2** : the curved upper surface of a liquid column that is concave when the containing walls are wetted by the liquid and convex when not

meno·pause \'men-ə-ˌpȯz\ *n* : the period of natural stopping of menstruation usu. between the ages of 45 and 50 — **meno·paus·al** \ˌmen-ə-'pȯ-zəl\ *adj*

menservants *pl of* MANSERVANT

men·ses \'men-ˌsēz\ *n pl* : the menstrual flow

men·stru·al \'men(t)-strə(-wə)l\ *adj* **1** : of or relating to menstruation **2** : MONTHLY

men·stru·ate \'men(t)-strə-ˌwāt, 'men-ˌstrāt\ *vb* : to undergo menstruation

men·stru·a·tion \ˌmen(t)-strə-'wā-shən, men-'strā-shən\ *n* : a discharging of blood, secretions, and tissue debris from the uterus at approximately monthly intervals in breeding-age female primates that are not pregnant; *also* : PERIOD 4b

men·su·ra·tion \ˌmen(t)-sə-'rā-shən, ˌmen-chə-\ *n* **1** : the process or art of measuring **2** : the branch of mathematics that deals with the measurement of lengths, areas, and volumes — **men·su·ra·ble** \'men(t)-sə-rə-bəl, 'men-chə-\ *adj*

-ment \mənt\ *n suffix* **1** : result, object, or means of a (specified) action ⟨embank*ment*⟩ ⟨entangle*ment*⟩ ⟨entertain*ment*⟩ **2 a** : action : process ⟨encircle*ment*⟩ ⟨develop*ment*⟩ **b** : place of a (specified) action ⟨encamp*ment*⟩ **3** : state : condition ⟨amaze*ment*⟩

men·tal \'ment-əl\ *adj* **1 a** : of or relating to the mind ⟨*mental* powers⟩ **b** : carried on in the mind ⟨*mental* arithmetic⟩ **2 a** : relating to or affected by a disorder of the mind ⟨a *mental* patient⟩ **b** : intended for the care of persons affected by mental disorders ⟨*mental* hospital⟩ — **men·tal·ly** \-ə-lē\ *adv*

ə abut	ər further	a back	ā bake
ä cot, cart	aů out	ch chin	e less
ē easy	g gift	i trip	ī life
j joke	ng sing	ō flow	ȯ flaw
ȯi coin	th thin	t͟h this	ü loot
ů foot	y yet	yü few	yů furious
zh vision			

mental age *n* : a measure of a child's mental development in terms of the number of years it takes an average child to reach the same level

men·tal·i·ty \men-'tal-ət-ē\ *n, pl* **-ties** : mental power : INTELLIGENCE

men·thol \'men-ˌthȯl, -ˌthōl\ *n* : a white soothing substance from oils of mint

men·tho·lat·ed \'men(t)-thə-ˌlāt-əd\ *adj* : treated with or containing menthol

¹**men·tion** \'men-chən\ *n* : a brief or passing reference to something

²**mention** *vb* **men·tioned**; **men·tion·ing** \'mench-(ə-)ning\ : to refer to or speak about briefly — **men·tion·a·ble** \'mench-(ə-)nə-bəl\ *adj*

men·tor \'men-ˌtȯ(ə)r, 'ment-ər\ *n* : a wise and faithful adviser or teacher

menu \'men-yü, 'mān-\ *n* : a list of dishes served at a meal; *also* : the dishes served

me·ow \mē-'aů\ *n* : the cry of a cat — **meow** *vb*

mer·can·tile \'mər-kən-ˌtēl, -ˌtīl\ *adj* : of or relating to merchants, trade, or commerce

mer·ce·nary \'mər-sə-ˌner-ē\ *n, pl* **-nar·ies** : one that serves merely for wages; *esp* : a soldier hired by a foreign country to fight in its army — **mercenary** *adj*

mer·cer \'mər-sər\ *n, Brit* : a dealer in textile fabrics

mer·cer·ize \'mər-sə-ˌrīz\ *vb* : to treat cotton fiber or fabrics with a chemical so that the fibers are strengthened, take dyes better, and often acquire a sheen

¹**mer·chan·dise** \'mər-chən-ˌdīz, -ˌdīs\ *n* : the goods that are bought and sold in trade : WARES

²**merchandise** \-ˌdīz\ *vb* : to buy and sell : TRADE; *esp* : to try to further sales goods or services by attractive presentation and publicity — **mer·chan·dis·er** *n*

¹**mer·chant** \'mər-chənt\ *n* **1** : a buyer and seller of goods for profit; *esp* : one who carries on trade on a large scale or with foreign countries **2** : STOREKEEPER

²**merchant** *adj* **1** : of, relating to, or used in commerce ⟨*merchant* ship⟩ **2** : of or relating to a merchant marine ⟨*merchant* seamen⟩

mer·chant·man \-mən\ *n* : a ship used in commerce

merchant marine *n* **1** : the commercial shipping of a nation **2** : the personnel of a merchant marine

mer·ci·ful \'mər-si-fəl\ *adj* : having, showing, or disposed to mercy : COMPASSIONATE — **mer·ci·ful·ly** \-f(ə-)lē\ *adv* — **mer·ci·ful·ness** \-fəl-nəs\ *n*

mer·ci·less \'mər-si-ləs\ *adj* : having no mercy : PITILESS ⟨*merciless* slaughter⟩ — **mer·ci·less·ly** *adv* — **mer·ci·less·ness** *n*

¹**mer·cu·ri·al** \(ˌ)mər-'kyůr-ē-əl\ *adj* **1** : of or relating to the planet Mercury **2** : having qualities of eloquence, ingenuity, or thievishness **3** : characterized by rapid and unpredictable change of mood **4** : MERCURIC — **mer·cu·ri·al·ly** \-ē-ə-lē\ *adv*

²**mercurial** *n* : a drug or chemical containing mercury

mer·cu·ric \(ˌ)mər-'kyůr-ik\ *adj* : of, relating to, or containing mercury

mer·cu·ry \'mər-kyə-rē\ *n, pl* **-ries** **1** : MESSENGER, GUIDE **2 a** : a heavy silver-white metallic element that is liquid at ordinary temperatures — called also *quicksilver*; see ELEMENT table **b** : the column of mercury in a thermometer or barometer **3** *cap* : the planet nearest the sun — see PLANET table

mer·cy \'mər-sē\ *n, pl* **mercies** **1** : compassion or forbearance shown to someone (as an offender or adversary) having no claim to kindness **2** : a fortunate circumstance **3** : compassion shown to victims of misfortune

syn MERCY, CLEMENCY, LENIENCY can mean the disposition not to be severe in one's dealings with others. MERCY implies a compassionate or forgiving attitude (as toward an offender or adversary); CLEMENCY implies accustomed mercy or mildness in one responsible for imposing punishments; LENIENCY implies overlooking of mistakes by one not inclined to be severe

mercy killing *n* : the act or practice of killing (as an incurable invalid) for reasons of mercy

[1]**mere** \'mi(ə)r\ *n* : a sheet of standing water : POOL

[2]**mere** *adj, superlative* **mer·est** : being only this and nothing else : nothing more than ⟨a *mere* whisper⟩ ⟨a *mere* child⟩ — **mere·ly** *adv*

mer·e·tri·cious \ˌmer-ə-'trish-əs\ *adj* : attracting by a display of showy but superficial and tawdry charms — **mer·e·tri·cious·ly** *adv* — **mer·e·tri·cious·ness** *n*

mer·gan·ser \(ˌ)mər-'gan(t)-sər\ *n, pl* **-sers** *or* **-ser** : a fish-eating wild duck with a slender hooked beak and a usu. crested head

mergansers (about 23 in. long)

merge \'mərj\ *vb* **1** : to be or cause to be swallowed up or absorbed in something else : MINGLE, BLEND ⟨*merging* traffic⟩ **2** : COMBINE, UNITE ⟨*merge* two business firms into one⟩

merg·er \'mər-jər\ *n* : the combination of two or more business firms into one

me·rid·i·an \mə-'rid-ē-ən\ *n* **1** : the highest point attained : ZENITH **2 a** : an imaginary circle on the earth's surface passing through the north and south poles **b** : the half of such a circle included between the poles **c** : a representation of such a circle or half circle on a globe or map numbered according to the degrees of longitude

me·ringue \mə-'raŋ\ *n* **1** : a mixture of beaten egg white and sugar put on pies or cakes and browned **2** : a shell of baked meringue filled with fruit or ice cream

me·ri·no \mə-'rē-nō\ *n, pl* **-nos** **1** : any of a breed of fine-wooled white sheep producing a heavy fleece of high quality **2** : a soft wool or wool and cotton fabric resembling cashmere **3** : a fine wool and cotton yarn — **merino** *adj*

mer·i·stem \'mer-ə-ˌstem\ *n* : a plant tissue made up of unspecialized cells capable of dividing indefinitely and of producing cells that form the fully developed tissues and organs — **mer·i·ste·mat·ic** \ˌmer-ə-stə-'mat-ik\ *adj*

[1]**mer·it** \'mer-ət\ *n* **1** : the condition or fact of deserving well or ill : DESERT **2** : WORTH, EXCELLENCE ⟨a suggestion having considerable *merit*⟩ **3** : a praiseworthy quality : VIRTUE ⟨an answer that at least had the *merit* of honesty⟩

[2]**merit** *vb* : to earn by service or performance : DESERVE

mer·i·to·ri·ous \ˌmer-ə-'tōr-ē-əs, -'tȯr-\ *adj* : deserving reward or honor : PRAISEWORTHY — **mer·i·to·ri·ous·ly** *adv* — **mer·i·to·ri·ous·ness** *n*

mer·maid \'mər-ˌmād\ *n* [from Middle English, from *mere* "sea", "pool" and *maid*] : an imaginary sea creature usu. represented with a woman's body and a fish's tail

mer·man \-ˌman, -mən\ *n, pl* **mer·men** \-ˌmen, -mən\ : an imaginary sea creature usu. represented with a man's body and a fish's tail

mer·ri·ment \'mer-i-mənt\ *n* : MIRTH, FUN

mer·ry \'mer-ē\ *adj* **mer·ri·er**; **-est** **1** : full of good humor and good spirits : MIRTHFUL **2** : marked by gaiety or festivity ⟨a *merry* Christmas⟩ — **mer·ri·ly** \'mer-ə-lē\ *adv* — **mer·ri·ness** \'mer-ē-nəs\ *n*

mer·ry-an·drew \ˌmer-ē-'an-drü\ *n* : CLOWN, BUFFOON

mer·ry-go-round \'mer-ē-gō-ˌrau̇nd\ *n* **1** : a circular revolving platform fitted with seats and figures of animals on which people sit for a ride **2** : a rapid round of activities : WHIRL ⟨a *merry-go-round* of parties⟩

mer·ry·mak·ing \'mer-ē-ˌmā-king\ *n* **1** : gay or festive activity : MERRIMENT **2** : a festive occasion — **mer·ry·mak·er** \-kər\ *n*

mer·yc·hip·pus \ˌmer-i(k)-'hip-əs\ *n* : any of a genus of extinct American horses of the Miocene

me·sa \'mā-sə\ *n* : a flat-topped hill or small plateau with steep sides

mes·cal \mes-'kal\ *n* **1** : a small spineless cactus covered with jointed tubercles that are used as a stimulant and intoxicant **2 a** : a usu. colorless Mexican liquor distilled esp. from the central leaves of agave plants **b** : a plant from which mescal is produced

mes·ca·line \'mes-kə-ˌlēn\ *n* : a mind-altering chemical that is the active ingredient of the mescal cactus and is sometimes used as a drug

mesdames *pl of* MADAM *or of* MADAME

mesdemoiselles *pl of* MADEMOISELLE

me·seems \mi-'sēmz\ *vb, past* **me·seemed** \-'sēmd\ *archaic* : seems to me

mes·en·tery \'mez-ən-ˌter-ē, 'mes-\ *n, pl* **-ter·ies** : membranous tissue or one of the membranes that envelop the visceral organs (as the intestines) and attach them to the wall of the abdominal cavity — **mes·en·ter·ic** \ˌmez-ən-'ter-ik, ˌmes-\ *adj*

[1]**mesh** \'mesh\ *n* **1** : one of the open spaces formed by the threads of a net or the wires of a sieve or screen **2** : NET, NETWORK **3** : a fabric of open texture with evenly spaced small holes **4** : the coming or fitting together of the teeth of two gears — **meshed** \'mesht\ *adj*

[2]**mesh** *vb* **1** : to catch in or as if in a mesh : ENTANGLE **2** : to fit together : INTERLOCK ⟨*mesh* gears⟩

me·si·al \'mē-zē-əl, -sē-\ *adj* : MIDDLE; *esp* : dividing something (as an animal body) into right and left halves

mes·mer·ism \'mez-mə-ˌriz-əm, 'mes-\ *n* : HYPNOTISM

mes·mer·ize \-mə-ˌrīz\ *vb* **1** : HYPNOTIZE **2** : SPELLBIND, FASCINATE — **mes·mer·iz·er** *n*

meso·derm \'mez-ə-ˌdərm, 'mēz-, 'mēs-, 'mes-\ *n* : the middle layer of cells of an embryonic animal from which most of the muscular, skeletal, and connective tissues develop; *also* : tissue derived from this layer — **meso·der·mal** \ˌmez-ə-'dər-məl, ˌmēz-, ˌmēs-, ˌmes-\ *adj*

meso·hip·pus \ˌmez-ə-'hip-əs, ˌmēz-, ˌmēs-, ˌmes-\ *n* : any of a genus of No. American 3-toed horses that existed in the Oligocene

mes·on \'mez-ˌän, 'mēz-, 'mēs-, 'mes-\ *n* : a particle with a mass between that of the electron and the proton that is either positively or negatively charged or neutral

meso·sphere \'mez-ō-ˌsfi(ə)r, 'mēz-, 'mēs-, 'mes-\ *n* : a layer of the atmosphere above the ionosphere

meso·tho·rax \ˌmez-ō-'thō(ə)r-ˌaks, ˌmēz-, ˌmēs-, ˌmes-, -'thȯ(ə)r-\ *n* : the middle of the three segments of the thorax of an insect

Meso·zo·ic \ˌmez-ə-'zō-ik, ˌmēz-, ˌmēs-, ˌmes-\ *n* : the 4th of the five eras of geologic history marked by the existence of dinosaurs, marine and flying reptiles, and evergreen trees; *also* : the corresponding system of rocks — see GEOLOGIC TIME table — **Mesozoic** *adj*

mes·quite \mәs-ˈkēt, mes-\ *n* : a thorny deep-rooted tree or shrub of the southwestern U.S. and Mexico bearing pods rich in sugar and important as a livestock feed

[1]**mess** \ˈmes\ *n* **1 a** : a quantity of food **b** : a dish of soft or liquid food ⟨a *mess* of porridge⟩ **2 a** : a group of people who regularly eat together **b** : the meal they eat **c** : the place where they eat **3 a** : a confused heap **b** : a state of confusion or disorder

[2]**mess** *vb* **1 a** : to supply with meals **b** : to take meals with a mess **2 a** : to make dirty or untidy : DISARRANGE **b** : BUNGLE ⟨*messed* up the job⟩ **3** : INTERFERE, MEDDLE **4** : PUTTER

mes·sage \ˈmes-ij\ *n* **1** : a communication in writing, in speech, or by signals **2** : a messenger's errand or function

messeigneurs *pl of* MONSEIGNEUR

mes·sen·ger \ˈmes-әn-jәr\ *n* : one who bears a message or does an errand

messenger RNA *n* : an RNA that carries the code for a particular protein from DNA in the nucleus to the ribosome and that acts as a pattern or mold for the formation of that protein

mes·si·ah \mә-ˈsī-ә\ *n* **1** *cap* **a** : the expected king and deliverer of the Jews **b** : Jesus Christ **2** : SAVIOR, DELIVERER

messieurs *pl of* MONSIEUR

mess·mate \ˈmes-ˌmāt\ *n* : a member of a mess esp. on shipboard

Messrs *abbr* messieurs

messy \ˈmes-ē\ *adj* **mess·i·er; -est** : marked by confusion, disorder, or dirt : UNTIDY — **mess·i·ly** \ˈmes-ә-lē\ *adv* — **mess·i·ness** \ˈmes-ē-nәs\ *n*

met *past of* MEET

me·tab·o·lism \mә-ˈtab-ә-ˌliz-әm\ *n* **1** : the sum of the processes by which the living protoplasm in an organism is built up or broken down **2** : the sum of the processes by which a particular substance (as iodine) is handled in the living body — **met·a·bol·ic** \ˌmet-ә-ˈbäl-ik\ *adj* — **me·tab·o·lize** \mә-ˈtab-ә-ˌlīz\ *vb*

meta·car·pal \ˌmet-ә-ˈkär-pәl\ *n* : a metacarpal bone

meta·car·pus \-pәs\ *n* : the part of the hand or forefoot between the carpus and the phalanges — **metacarpal** *adj*

met·al \ˈmet-әl\ *n* **1** : any of various substances (as gold, tin, copper, or bronze) that have a more or less shiny appearance, are good conductors of electricity and heat, are opaque, can be melted, and are usu. capable of being drawn into a wire or hammered into a thin sheet **2** : any of more than three fourths of the chemical elements that exhibit the properties of a metal, typically are crystalline solids, and have atoms that readily lose electrons **3** : METTLE, TEMPER — **metal** *adj*

me·tal·lic \mә-ˈtal-ik\ *adj* **1** : of, relating to, or being a metal **2** : containing or made of metal **3** : HARSH, GRATING ⟨a *metallic* voice⟩

met·al·loid \ˈmet-ә-ˌlȯid\ *n* : an element intermediate in properties between the typical metals and other elements

ә abut	әr further	a back	ā bake	
ä cot, cart	au̇ out	ch chin	e less	ē easy
g gift	i trip	ī life	j joke	ng sing	ō flow
ȯ flaw	ȯi coin	th thin	t͟h this	ü loot
u̇ foot	y yet	yü few	yu̇ furious	zh vision

met·al·lur·gy \ˈmet-ә-ˌlәr-jē\ *n* : the science of extracting metals from their ores, refining them, and preparing them for use — **met·al·lur·gi·cal** \ˌmet-ә-ˈlәr-ji-kәl\ *adj* — **met·al·lur·gist** \ˈmet-ә-ˌlәr-jәst\ *n*

met·al·work \ˈmet-әl-ˌwәrk\ *n* **1** : the process or occupation of making things from metal **2** : work and esp. artistic work made of metal — **met·al·work·er** \-ˌwәr-kәr\ *n* — **met·al·work·ing** \-king\ *n*

met·a·mor·phism \ˌmet-ә-ˈmȯr-ˌfiz-әm\ *n* **1** : METAMORPHOSIS **2** : a change in the structure of rock; *esp* : a change to a more compact and more highly crystalline condition produced by such forces as pressure, heat, and water ⟨marble is produced by the *metamorphism* of limestone⟩ — **met·a·mor·phic** \-ˈmȯr-fik\ *adj*

met·a·mor·phose \-ˌfōz, -ˌfōs\ *vb* : to change or cause to change in form : undergo metamorphosis

met·a·mor·pho·sis \ˌmet-ә-ˈmȯr-fә-sәs\ *n, pl* **-pho·ses** \-fә-ˌsēz\ **1** : a change of form, structure, or substance esp. by witchcraft or magic **2** : a striking alteration in appearance, character, or circumstances **3** : a basic and usu. rather abrupt change in the form and often the habits of an animal that occurs during the transformation of a larva into an adult

meta·phase \ˈmet-ә-ˌfāz\ *n* **1** : the stage of mitosis or meiosis in which the chromosomes are arranged in the center of the dividing cell prior to their separation or splitting and movement to the poles of the cell **2** : METAMORPHISM 2

met·a·phor \ˈmet-ә-ˌfȯ(ә)r, -fәr\ *n* : a figure of speech in which a word or phrase denoting one kind of object or idea is used in place of another to suggest a similarity between them (as in *the ship plows the sea*) — **met·a·phor·i·cal** \ˌmet-ә-ˈfȯr-i-kәl, -ˈfär-\ *adj* — **met·a·phor·i·cal·ly** \-i-k(ә-)lē\ *adv*

met·a·phys·i·cal \ˌmet-ә-ˈfiz-i-kәl\ *adj* **1** : of, relating to, or based on metaphysics **2** : SUPERNATURAL, OCCULT **3** : difficult to understand : ABSTRACT — **met·a·phys·i·cal·ly** \-i-k(ә-)lē\ *adv*

met·a·phys·ics \ˌmet-ә-ˈfiz-iks\ *n* [from medieval Latin *Metaphysica*, the title of Aristotle's work on the subject, so called because it came after (Greek *meta*) the *Physics* (Greek *Physika*) in his collected works] : the part of philosophy concerned with the ultimate causes and underlying nature of things

meta·se·quoia \ˌmet-ә-si-ˈkwȯi-ә\ *n* : any of a genus of fossil and living deciduous coniferous trees related to the pines

meta·tar·sal \ˌmet-ә-ˈtär-sәl\ *n* : a metatarsal bone

meta·tar·sus \-sәs\ *n* : the part of the foot in man or of the hind foot in a four-footed animal between the tarsus and phalanges — **metatarsal** *adj*

meta·tho·rax \ˌmet-ә-ˈthō(ә)r-ˌaks, -ˈthȯ(ә)r-\ *n* : the most posterior of the three segments in the thorax of an insect

met·a·zo·an \ˌmet-ә-ˈzō-әn\ *or* **met·a·zo·on** \-ˈzō-ˌän\ *n* : any of the great group of animals with a body composed of cells forming tissues and organs — **metazoan** *adj*

mete \ˈmēt\ *vb* : to assign by measure ⟨*mete* out punishment⟩

me·te·or \ˈmēt-ē-әr\ *n* : one of the small particles of matter in the solar system observable directly only when it falls into the earth's atmosphere where the heat of friction may cause it to glow brightly for a short time; *also* : the streak of light produced by the passage of a meteor

me·te·or·ic \ˌmēt-ē-ˈȯr-ik, -ˈär-\ *adj* **1** : of or relating to a meteor ⟨a *meteoric* shower⟩ **2** : resembling a meteor esp. in sudden and temporary brilliance

⟨a *meteoric* career⟩ — **me·te·or·i·cal·ly** \-i-k(ə-)lē\ *adv*

me·te·or·ite \'mēt-ē-ə-ˌrīt\ *n* : a meteor that reaches the surface of the earth

me·te·or·oid \-ˌrȯid\ *n* : a meteoric particle in interplanetary space

me·te·o·rol·o·gy \ˌmēt-ē-ə-'räl-ə-jē\ *n* : a science that deals with the atmosphere and its phenomena and with weather and weather forecasting — **me·te·o·ro·log·ic** \ˌmēt-ē-ˌȯr-ə-'läj-ik, -ē-ˌär-, -ē-ər-\ *or* **me·te·o·ro·log·i·cal** \-'läj-i-kəl\ *adj* — **me·te·o·rol·o·gist** \ˌmēt-ē-ə-'räl-ə-jəst\ *n*

[1]**me·ter** \'mēt-ər\ *n* : a systematic rhythm in verse or music

[2]**meter** *n* : a measure of length that is equal to 39.37 inches and is the basis of the metric system — see METRIC SYSTEM table

[3]**meter** *n* : an instrument for measuring and sometimes recording the amount of something ⟨a gas *meter*⟩

meter-kilogram-second *adj* : of, relating to, or being a system of units based on the meter as the unit of length, the kilogram as the unit of mass, and the second as the unit of time — abbr. *mks*

meth·ane \'meth-ˌān\ *n* : an odorless flammable gas that consists of carbon and hydrogen and is produced by decomposition of organic matter in marshes and mines and by distillation

me·thinks \mi-'thing(k)s\ *vb, past* **me·thought** \-'thȯt\ *archaic* : seems to me

meth·od \'meth-əd\ *n* **1** : a regular way or a systematic plan or procedure for doing something ⟨developed a new *method* for making cement⟩ **2** : orderly arrangement : ORDERLINESS ⟨a pupil whose work lacks *method*⟩

me·thod·i·cal \mə-'thäd-i-kəl\ *adj* **1** : marked by or performed or arranged by method or order **2** : habitually following a method : SYSTEMATIC — **me·thod·i·cal·ly** \-k(ə-)lē\ *adv* — **me·thod·i·cal·ness** \-kəl-nəs\ *n*

meth·yl \'meth-əl\ *n* : a chemical radical consisting of carbon and hydrogen

methyl alcohol *n* : a poisonous alcohol used esp. as a solvent and antifreeze

meth·y·lene blue \ˌmeth-ə-ˌlēn-\ *n* : a dye used as a biological stain and as an antidote in cyanide poisoning

me·tic·u·lous \mə-'tik-yə-ləs\ *adj* : extremely or excessively careful in small details — **me·tic·u·lous·ly** *adv* — **me·tic·u·lous·ness** *n*

METO *abbr* Middle East Treaty Organization

me·tre \'mēt-ər\ *chiefly Brit var of* METER

met·ric \'me-trik\ *adj* **1** : of or relating to measurement; *esp* : of, relating to, or based on the metric system **2** : METRICAL 1

met·ri·cal \'me-tri-kəl\ *adj* **1** : of, relating to, or ar-

METRIC SYSTEM

LENGTH

unit	*abbreviation*	*number of meters*	*approximate U.S. equivalent*
myriameter	mym	10,000	6.2 miles
kilometer	km	1,000	0.62 mile
hectometer	hm	100	109.36 yards
dekameter	dam	10	32.81 feet
meter	m	1	39.37 inches
decimeter	dm	0.1	3.94 inches
centimeter	cm	0.01	0.39 inch
millimeter	mm	0.001	0.04 inch

AREA

unit	*abbreviation*	*number of square meters*	*approximate U.S. equivalent*
square kilometer	sq km *or* km²	1,000,000	0.3861 square mile
hectare	ha	10,000	2.47 acres
are	a	100	119.60 square yards
centare	ca	1	10.76 square feet
square centimeter	sq cm *or* cm²	0.0001	0.155 square inch

VOLUME

unit	*abbreviation*	*number of cubic meters*	*approximate U.S. equivalent*
dekastere	das	10	13.10 cubic yards
stere	s	1	1.31 cubic yards
decistere	ds	0.10	3.53 cubic feet
cubic centimeter	cu cm *or* cm³ *also* cc	0.000001	0.061 cubic inch

CAPACITY

unit	*abbreviation*	*number of liters*	*approximate U.S. equivalent* *cubic*	*dry*	*liquid*
kiloliter	kl	1,000	1.31 cubic yards		
hectoliter	hl	100	3.53 cubic feet	2.84 bushels	
dekaliter	dal	10	0.35 cubic foot	1.14 pecks	2.64 gallons
liter	l	1	61.02 cubic inches	0.908 quart	1.057 quarts
deciliter	dl	0.10	6.1 cubic inches	0.18 pint	0.21 pint
centiliter	cl	0.01	0.6 cubic inch		0.338 fluidounce
milliliter	ml	0.001	0.06 cubic inch		0.27 fluidram

MASS AND WEIGHT

unit	*abbreviation*	*number of grams*	*approximate U.S. equivalent*
metric ton	MT *or* t	1,000,000	1.1 tons
quintal	q	100,000	220.46 pounds
kilogram	kg	1,000	2.2046 pounds
hectogram	hg	100	3.527 ounces
dekagram	dag	10	0.353 ounce
gram	g *or* gm	1	0.035 ounce
decigram	dg	0.10	1.543 grains
centigram	cg	0.01	0.154 grain
milligram	mg	0.001	0.015 grain

ranged in meter ⟨*metrical* verse⟩ **2 :** METRIC 1 — **met·ri·cal·ly** \-k(ə-)lē\ *adv*

metric system *n* **:** a decimal system of weights and measures in which the meter is the unit of length and the kilogram is the unit of weight

metric ton *n* **:** a weight of 1000 kilograms or 2204.6 pounds — see METRIC SYSTEM table

met·ro·nome \ˈme-trə-ˌnōm\ *n* **:** an instrument that ticks regularly to help a music student play in exact time

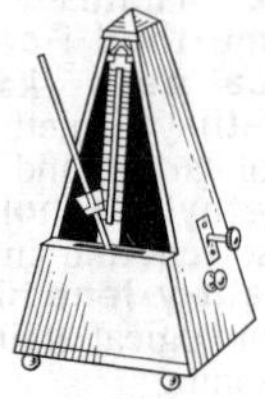
metronome

me·trop·o·lis \mə-ˈträp-(ə-)ləs\ *n* [from Greek *mētropolis*, the mother city of a colony, from *mētr-* (stem of *mētēr* "mother", from the same source as English *mother*) and *polis* "city", "city-state"] **1 :** the chief or capital city of a country, state, or region **2 :** a large or important city **3 :** a principal center of an activity

1**met·ro·pol·i·tan** \ˌme-trə-ˈpäl-ət-ən\ *n* **1 :** the primate of an ecclesiastical province **2 :** one who lives in a metropolis or who exhibits metropolitan manners or customs

2**metropolitan** *adj* **1 :** of, relating to, or characteristic of a metropolis **2 :** constituting a city and the densely populated surrounding areas ⟨*metropolitan* area⟩

met·tle \ˈmet-əl\ *n* **1 :** quality of temperament or disposition **2 :** SPIRIT, ARDOR ⟨the raw troops proved their *mettle* in the assault⟩ — **on one's mettle :** aroused to do one's best

met·tle·some \ˈmet-əl-səm\ *adj* **:** full of mettle **:** SPIRITED

MEV *abbr* million electron volts

1**mew** \ˈmyü\ *n* **:** GULL; *esp* **:** the common European gull

2**mew** *vb* **:** MEOW

3**mew** *n* **:** MEOW

4**mew** *n* **1** *archaic* **:** a cage for hawks **2** *pl, chiefly Brit* **:** stables usu. with living quarters built around a court

5**mew** *vb* **:** to shut up **:** CONFINE

mewl \ˈmyül\ *vb* **:** to cry weakly **:** WHIMPER

Mex *abbr* **1** Mexican **2** Mexico

Mex·i·can \ˈmek-si-kən\ *n* **1 :** a native or inhabitant of Mexico **2 :** a person of Mexican descent — **Mexican** *adj*

Mexican bean beetle *n* **:** a spotted ladybug that feeds on the leaves of beans

mez·za·nine \ˈmez-ə-ˌnēn\ *n* **1 :** a low story between two main stories of a building often in the form of a balcony **2 :** the lowest balcony in a theater or its first few rows

mez·zo for·te \ˌmet-sō-ˈfȯr-ˌtā, ˌme(d)z-ō-, -ˈfȯrt-ē\ *adj or adv* **:** moderately loud — used as a direction in music

mez·zo–so·prano \-sə-ˈpran-ō, -ˈprän-\ *n* **:** a woman's voice between that of the soprano and contralto; *also* **:** a singer having such a voice

mez·zo·tint \ˈmet-sō-ˌtint, ˈme(d)z-ō-\ *n* **:** a process of engraving on copper or steel by scraping or burnishing a roughened surface to produce light and shade; *also* **:** an engraving produced by this process

ə abut	ər further	a back	ā bake	
ä cot, cart	au̇ out	ch chin	e less	ē easy
g gift	i trip	ī life	j joke	ng sing	ō flow
ȯ flaw	ȯi coin	th thin	t͟h this	ü loot
u̇ foot	y yet	yü few	yu̇ furious	zh vision

mf *abbr* mezzo forte

mfd *abbr* manufactured

mfg *abbr* manufacturing

mfr *abbr* manufacturer

mg *abbr* milligram

mgr *abbr* **1** manager **2** monseigneur **3** monsignor

mi \ˈmē\ *n* **:** the 3d note of the diatonic scale

mi *abbr* mile

MI *abbr* Michigan

mi·as·ma \mī-ˈaz-mə, mē-\ *n, pl* **-mas** *or* **-ma·ta** \-mət-ə\ **1 :** a vapor from a swamp formerly believed to cause disease **2 :** a harmful influence or atmosphere

mi·ca \ˈmī-kə\ *n* **:** a silicon-containing mineral that may be separated easily into thin and often somewhat flexible and transparent sheets

Mi·cah \ˈmī-kə\ *n* — see BIBLE table

mice *pl of* MOUSE

Mich *abbr* Michigan

Mich·ael·mas \ˈmik-əl-məs\ *n* **:** September 29

micr- *or* **micro-** *comb form* **1 a :** small **:** minute ⟨*micro*film⟩ **b :** enlarging **:** magnifying or amplifying ⟨*micro*phone⟩ ⟨*micro*scope⟩ **2 :** one millionth part of a (specified) unit ⟨*micro*gram⟩ ⟨*micro*hm⟩

mi·cro \ˈmī-krō\ *adj* **:** MICROSCOPIC

mi·cro·am·pere \ˌmī-krō-ˈam-ˌpi(ə)r\ *n* **:** one millionth of an ampere

mi·crobe \ˈmī-ˌkrōb\ *n* **:** MICROORGANISM, GERM — **mi·cro·bi·al** \mī-ˈkrō-bē-əl\ *or* **mi·cro·bic** \-bik\ *adj*

mi·cro·bi·ol·o·gy \ˌmī-krō-bī-ˈäl-ə-jē\ *n* **:** a branch of biology dealing esp. with microscopic forms of life (as bacteria, protozoans, and viruses) — **mi·cro·bi·o·log·i·cal** \-ˌbī-ə-ˈläj-i-kəl\ *also* **mi·cro·bi·o·log·ic** \-ˈläj-ik\ *adj* — **mi·cro·bi·o·log·i·cal·ly** \-i-k(ə-)lē\ *adv* — **mi·cro·bi·ol·o·gist** \-bī-ˈäl-ə-jəst\ *n*

mi·cro·coc·cus \ˌmī-krə-ˈkäk-əs\ *n* **:** a small spherical bacterium

mi·cro·cosm \ˈmī-krə-ˌkäz-əm\ *n* **:** an individual man or a community thought of as a miniature universe or a world in itself

mi·cro·eco·sys·tem \ˌmī-krō-ˈē-kō-ˌsis-təm\ *n* **:** a small ecosystem (as a rotting log or a puddle of water)

mi·cro·film \ˈmī-krə-ˌfilm\ *n* **:** a film bearing a photographic record (as of printing or a drawing) on a reduced scale — **microfilm** *vb*

mi·cro·gram \-ˌgram\ *n* **:** one millionth of a gram

mi·crom·e·ter \mī-ˈkräm-ət-ər\ *n* **1 :** an instrument used with a telescope or microscope for measuring very small distances **2 :** MICROMETER CALIPER — **mi·crom·e·try** \-ˈkräm-ə-trē\ *n*

micrometer caliper *n* **:** a caliper having a spindle moved by a finely threaded screw for making precise measurements

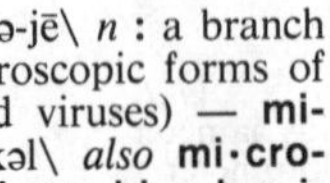
micrometer caliper

mi·cro–mini \ˌmī-krō-ˈmin-ē\ *n* **:** MICROSKIRT

mi·cron \ˈmī-ˌkrän\ *n* **:** one thousandth of a millimeter

mi·cro·or·gan·ism \ˌmī-krō-ˈȯr-gə-ˌniz-əm\ *n* **:** an organism (as a bacterium) of microscopic or less than microscopic size

mi·cro·phone \ˈmī-krə-ˌfōn\ *n* **:** an instrument used in increasing or transmitting sounds; *esp* **:** one used in radio and television to receive sound and convert it into electrical waves

mi·cro·pho·to \ˌmī-krə-ˈfōt-ō\ *n* **:** PHOTOMICROGRAPH

mi·cro·pho·to·graph \-ˈfōt-ə-ˌgraf\ *n* **:** PHOTOMICROGRAPH

mi·cro·scope \'mī-krə-ˌskōp\ *n* **1** : an optical instrument consisting of a lens or a combination of lenses for making enlarged or magnified images of minute objects **2** : an instrument using radiations other than light for making enlarged images of minute objects

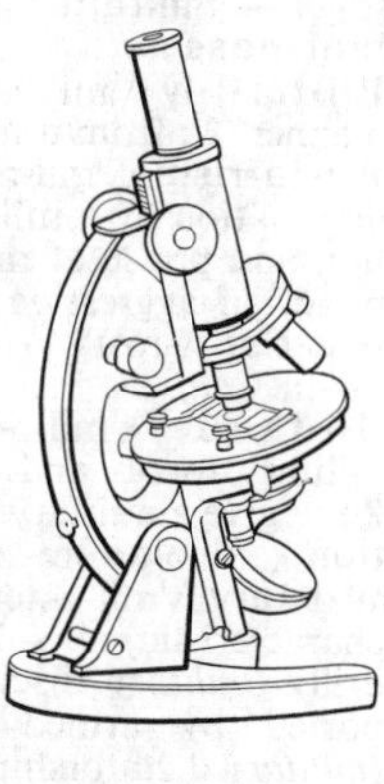
microscope 1

mi·cro·scop·ic \ˌmī-krə-'skäp-ik\ *or* **mi·cro·scop·i·cal** \-'skäp-i-kəl\ *adj* **1** : of, relating to, or conducted with the microscope or microscopy ⟨a *microscopic* examination⟩ **2** : resembling a microscope : able to see very tiny objects ⟨some insects have *microscopic* vision⟩ **3** : able to be seen only through a microscope : very small ⟨a *microscopic* plant⟩ — **mi·cro·scop·i·cal·ly** \-i-k(ə-)lē\ *adv*

mi·cros·co·py \mī-'kräs-kə-pē\ *n* : the use of the microscope : investigation with the microscope — **mi·cros·co·pist** \-pəst\ *n*

mi·cro·skirt \'mī-krə-ˌskərt\ *n* : a very short miniskirt

mi·cro·wave \-ˌwāv\ *n* : a radio wave between 1 and 100 centimeters in wavelength

1**mid** \(')mid\ *adj* **1** : being the part in the middle or midst ⟨in *mid* ocean⟩ ⟨*mid*-August⟩ **2** : occupying a middle position ⟨the *mid* finger⟩

2**mid** \(ˌ)mid\ *prep* : AMID

mid *abbr* middle

mid·brain \'mid-ˌbrān\ *n* : the middle division of the embryonic vertebrate brain or the parts developed from it

mid·day \'mid-ˌdā, -'dā\ *n* : NOON — **midday** *adj*

1**mid·dle** \'mid-əl\ *adj* **1** : equally distant from the ends or sides **2** : being at neither extreme : INTERMEDIATE ⟨of *middle* size⟩ **3** *cap* : constituting an intermediate division or period ⟨*Middle* Paleozoic⟩

2**middle** *n* **1** : a middle part, point, or position : CENTER **2** : WAIST

middle age *n* : the period of life from about 40 to about 60 — **mid·dle-aged** \ˌmid-əl-'ājd\ *adj*

Middle Ages *n pl* : the period of European history from about A.D. 500 to about 1500

middle C *n* : the note designated by the first ledger line below the treble staff and the first above the bass staff

middle class *n* : a social class that occupies a position between the upper class and the lower class and is composed principally of business and professional people, bureaucrats, farmers, and skilled workers

middle-class *adj* : of or relating to the middle class; *esp* : characterized by a high material standard of living, sexual morality, and respect for property

middle ear *n* : a small membrane-lined cavity that is separated from the outer ear by the eardrum and that transmits sound waves from the eardrum to the partition between the middle and inner ears through a chain of tiny bones

Middle Eastern *or* **Mid·east·ern** \(')mid-'ē-stərn\ *adj* : of, relating to, or characteristic of the Middle East or its people

Middle English *n* : the English language of the 12th to 15th centuries

middle finger *n* : the third digit of the hand if the thumb is counted as the first

mid·dle·man \'mid-əl-ˌman\ *n* : INTERMEDIARY, GO-BETWEEN; *esp* : a dealer between the producer of goods and the retailer or the consumer

mid·dle·most \-ˌmōst\ *adj* : MIDMOST

mid·dle-of-the-road \ˌmid-əl-əv-thə-'rōd\ *adj* : standing for or following a course of action midway between extremes; *esp* : being neither liberal nor conservative in politics — **mid·dle-of-the-road·er** \-'rōd-ər\ *n*

mid·dle·weight \'mid-əl-ˌwāt\ *n* : one of average weight; *esp* : a boxer weighing more than 147 but not over 160 pounds

Middle Western *or* **Mid·west·ern** \(')mid-'wes-tərn\ *adj* : of, relating to, or characteristic of the Middle West or its people

1**mid·dling** \'mid-ling, -lən\ *adj* : of medium or moderate size, degree, or quality — **middling** *adv*

2**middling** *n* **1** : any of various commodities of medium quality or size **2** *pl* : a granular product of grain milling; *esp* : a by-product of wheat milling that is used in animal feeds

mid·dy \'mid-ē\ *n, pl* **middies** **1** : MIDSHIPMAN **2** : a loose blouse for women and children with a wide square collar

midge \'mij\ *n* : a very small fly : GNAT

midg·et \'mij-ət\ *n* : an individual much smaller than the usual or typical — **midget** *adj*

midi \'mid-ē\ *n* : a calf-length dress or skirt

mid·land \'mid-lənd, -ˌland\ *n* : the interior or central region of a country — **midland** *adj*

mid·line \-ˌlīn\ *n* : a median line

mid·most \-ˌmōst\ *adj* **1** : being in the exact middle **2** : INNERMOST — **midmost** *adv or n*

mid·night \'mid-ˌnīt\ *n* : 12 o'clock at night — **midnight** *adj*

mid·point \-ˌpȯint\ *n* : a point at or near the center or middle

mid·rib \-ˌrib\ *n* : the central vein or ridge of a leaf or a leaflike part

mid·riff \-ˌrif\ *n* : the middle region of the human torso

mid·ship·man \'mid-ˌship-mən, (')mid-'\ *n* : a student naval officer

mid·ships \'mid-ˌships\ *adv* : AMIDSHIPS

1**midst** \'midst\ *n* **1** : the interior or central part : MIDDLE ⟨in the *midst* of the forest⟩ **2** : the condition of being surrounded ⟨in the *midst* of his troubles⟩

2**midst** \(ˌ)midst\ *prep* : AMID

mid·stream \'mid-'strēm\ *n* : the middle of a stream

mid·sum·mer \-'səm-ər\ *n* **1** : the middle of summer **2** : the summer solstice

1**mid·way** \-ˌwā\ *n* : an avenue at a fair, carnival, or amusement park for concessions and light amusements

2**mid·way** \-ˌwā, -'wā\ *adv or adj* : in the middle of the way or distance : HALFWAY

mid·week \'mid-ˌwēk\ *n* : the middle of the week — **midweek** *adj*

mid·wife \-ˌwīf\ *n* : a woman who helps other women in childbirth — **mid·wife·ry** \-ˌwī-f(ə-)rē\ *n*

mid·win·ter \-'wint-ər\ *n* **1** : the middle of winter **2** : the winter solstice

mid·year \-ˌyi(ə)r\ *n* **1** : the middle of a calendar year or academic year **2** : a midyear examination — **midyear** *adj*

mien \'mēn\ *n* : look, appearance, or bearing esp. as showing mood or personality ⟨a kindly *mien*⟩

1**might** \(')mīt\ *past of* MAY — used as an auxiliary verb to express permission ⟨asked if she *might* leave⟩, possibility ⟨she *might* go, if urged⟩ ⟨thought he *might* try⟩, or a present condition contrary to fact ⟨if you were older, you *might* understand⟩

2might \'mīt\ *n* : power to do something : FORCE ⟨hit the ball with all his *might*⟩

might·i·ly \'mīt-ə-lē\ *adv* **1** : in a mighty manner : VIGOROUSLY **2** : very much

mightn't \'mīt-ənt\ : might not

1mighty \'mīt-ē\ *adj* **might·i·er**; **-est** **1** : having might : POWERFUL, STRONG ⟨a *mighty* army⟩ **2** : done by might : showing great power ⟨*mighty* deeds⟩ **3** : very great ⟨a *mighty* famine⟩ — **might·i·ness** *n*

2mighty *adv* : VERY, EXTREMELY ⟨a *mighty* big man⟩

mi·gnon·ette \,min-yə-'net\ *n* : a garden plant with long spikes of small fragrant greenish white flowers

mi·graine \'mī-,grān\ *n* : a severe headache often restricted to one side of the head and accompanied by nausea and vomiting

mi·grant \'mī-grənt\ *n* : a person, animal, or plant that migrates — **migrant** *adj*

mi·grate \'mī-,grāt\ *vb* **1** : to move from one country, place, or locality to another **2** : to pass usu. periodically from one region or climate to another for feeding or breeding **3** : to extend the habitat gradually from an old into a new region — **mi·gra·tion** \mī-'grā-shən\ *n* — **mi·gra·tion·al** \-sh(ə-)nəl\ *adj*

mi·gra·to·ry \'mī-grə-,tōr-ē, -,tȯr-\ *adj* : of, relating to, or characterized by migration ⟨*migratory* workers⟩ ⟨*migratory* birds⟩

mi·ka·do \mə-'käd-ō\ *n, pl* **-dos** : an emperor of Japan

mike \'mīk\ *n* : MICROPHONE

mil \'mil\ *n* : a unit of length equal to 1/1000 inch used esp. for the diameter of wire

mil *abbr* military

milch \'milk, 'milch, 'milks\ *adj* : giving milk : kept for milk production ⟨a *milch* cow⟩

mild \'mīld\ *adj* **1** : gentle in nature or behavior ⟨a *mild* man⟩ **2** : moderate in action or effect : not strong ⟨a *mild* drug⟩ **3** : TEMPERATE ⟨*mild* weather⟩ — **mild·ly** \'mīl(d)-lē\ *adv* — **mild·ness** \'mīl(d)-nəs\ *n*

1mil·dew \'mil-,d(y)ü\ *n* : a usu. whitish growth produced on organic matter or living plants by fungi; *also* : a fungus producing mildew — **mil·dewy** \-,d(y)ü-ē\ *adj*

2mildew *vb* : to affect with or become affected with mildew

mile \'mīl\ *n* **1** : a unit of measure equal to 5280 feet — called also *statute mile*; see MEASURE table **2** : a unit of measure equal to 6076.115 feet — called also *geographical mile, nautical mile*

mile·age \'mī-lij\ *n* **1** : an allowance for traveling expenses at a certain rate per mile **2** : distance or distance covered in miles **3** : the number of miles that something (as a car or tire) will travel before wearing out

mile·post \'mīl-,pōst\ *n* : a post indicating the distance in miles to a stated place

mil·er \'mī-lər\ *n* : a man or a horse that competes in races of a mile's distance

mile·stone \'mīl-,stōn\ *n* **1** : a stone serving as a milepost **2** : an important point in progress or development

mi·lieu \mēl-'yə(r), -'yü\ *n* : ENVIRONMENT, SETTING

mil·i·tant \'mil-ə-tənt\ *adj* **1** : engaged in warfare : FIGHTING **2** : aggressively active esp. in a cause ⟨a *militant* conservationist⟩ — **mil·i·tan·cy** \-tən-sē\ *n* — **militant** *n* — **mil·i·tant·ly** *adv* — **mil·i·tant·ness** *n*

mil·i·tar·i·ly \,mil-ə-'ter-ə-lē\ *adv* **1** : in a military manner **2** : from a military standpoint

mil·i·ta·rism \'mil-ə-tə-,riz-əm\ *n* **1** : control or domination by a military class **2** : extreme admiration and praise of military virtues and ideals **3** : a policy of aggressive military preparedness — **mil·i·ta·rist** \-rəst\ *n* — **mil·i·ta·ris·tic** \,mil-ə-tə-'ris-tik\ *adj*

mil·i·ta·rize \'mil-ə-tə-,rīz\ *vb* **1** : to equip with military forces and defenses ⟨*militarize* a frontier⟩ **2** : to give a military character to — **mil·i·ta·ri·za·tion** \,mil-ə-t(ə-)rə-'zā-shən\ *n*

1mil·i·tary \'mil-ə-,ter-ē\ *adj* **1** : of, relating to, or characteristic of soldiers, arms, or war ⟨*military* drill⟩ ⟨*military* discipline⟩ **2** : carried on or supported by armed force ⟨*military* government⟩ ⟨*military* dictatorship⟩ **3** : of or relating to the army ⟨*military* and naval affairs⟩ ***syn*** see MARTIAL

2military *n, pl* **military** **1** : ARMED FORCES **2** : military persons; *esp* : army officers

military police *n* : a branch of an army that exercises guard and police functions

mil·i·tate \'mil-ə-,tāt\ *vb* : to have weight or effect : OPERATE ⟨factors *militating* against success⟩

mi·li·tia \mə-'lish-ə\ *n* : a body of citizens with some military training who are called to active duty only in an emergency — **mi·li·tia·man** \-mən\ *n*

1milk \'milk\ *n* **1** : a fluid secreted by the mammary glands of female mammals for the nourishment of their young **2** : a liquid (as a plant juice) resembling milk

2milk *vb* **1** : to draw milk from the breasts or udder of **2** : to draw or yield milk **3** : to draw something from as if by milking; *esp* : to draw excessive profit from ⟨*milk* a business⟩ — **milk·er** *n*

milk·maid \'milk-,mād\ *n* : DAIRYMAID

milk·man \-,man, -mən\ *n* : a man who sells or delivers milk

milk of magnesia : a milk-white liquid preparation of magnesium in water used as a laxative and as a medicine

milk shake *n* : a drink made of milk, a flavoring syrup, and sometimes ice cream mixed thoroughly

milk snake *n* : a common harmless gray or tan snake with black-bordered blotches and an arrow-shaped spot on the head

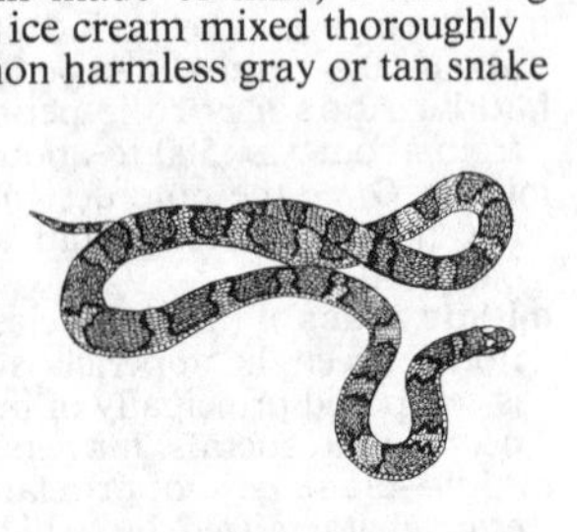

milk snake (between 24 and 36 in. long)

milk·sop \'milk-,säp\ *n* : a timid man or boy : SISSY

milk sugar *n* : LACTOSE

milk tooth *n* : one of the first temporary teeth of a young mammal that in man number 20

milk·weed \'milk-,wēd\ *n* : any of a group of herbs and shrubs with milky juice and flowers usu. in dense clusters

milky \'mil-kē\ *adj* **milk·i·er**; **-est** **1** : resembling milk esp. in color **2** : consisting of or containing milk — **milk·i·ness** *n*

Milky Way *n* **1** : a broad luminous irregular band of light that stretches across the sky and is composed of a vast multitude of faint stars **2** : MILKY WAY GALAXY

Milky Way galaxy *n* : the galaxy of which the solar system is a part and which contains the stars that comprise the Milky Way

[1]**mill** \'mil\ *n* **1** : a building with machinery for grinding grain into flour **2** : a machine used in treating (as by grinding, crushing, stamping, cutting, or finishing) raw material **3** : FACTORY

[2]**mill** *vb* **1** : to process in a mill (as by grinding into flour, meal, or powder or by shaping and dressing with a cutter) **2** : to give a raised rim to ⟨*mill* a coin⟩ **3** : to hit out hard with the fists : SLUG **4** : to move in a circle or in a disorderly eddying mass ⟨cattle *milling* about⟩

[3]**mill** *n* [from Latin *mille* "thousand"; so called because it is worth one thousandth of a dollar] : one tenth of a cent

mill·dam \'mil-ˌdam\ *n* **1** : the dam of a millpond **2** : MILLPOND

mil·le·nary \'mil-ə-ˌner-ē, mə-'len-ə-rē\ *n, pl* **-naries** **1** : a thousand units or things **2** : 1000 years : MILLENNIUM — **millenary** *adj*

mil·len·ni·um \mə-'len-ē-əm\ *n, pl* **-nia** \-ē-ə\ *or* **-ni·ums** **1 a** : a period of 1000 years **b** : a 1000th anniversary or its celebration **2 a** : the thousand years mentioned in Revelation 20 during which holiness is to prevail and Christ is to reign on earth **b** : a period of great happiness — **mil·len·ni·al** \-ē-əl\ *adj*

mill·er \'mil-ər\ *n* **1** : one that operates a mill; *esp* : one that grinds grain into flour **2** : a moth whose wings are covered with powdery dust

mil·let \'mil-ət\ *n* **1** : a grass cultivated for its grain and used as food both for man and for birds and in the U.S. sometimes grown for hay **2** : the seed of a millet

milli- *comb form* : thousandth ⟨*milli*meter⟩

mil·liard \'mil-ˌyärd, 'mil-ē-ˌärd\ *n, Brit* : a thousand millions — see NUMBER table

mil·li·bar \'mil-ə-ˌbär\ *n* : a unit used in measuring atmospheric pressure and in reading the barometer equal to a force of 1000 dynes acting on a square centimeter

mil·li·gram \-ˌgram\ *n* : a weight equal to 1/1000 gram — see METRIC SYSTEM table

mil·li·li·ter \-ˌlēt-ər\ *n* : a measure of capacity equal to 1/1000 liter — see METRIC SYSTEM table

mil·li·me·ter \-ˌmēt-ər\ *n* : a measure of length equal to 1/1000 meter — see METRIC SYSTEM table

mil·li·ner \'mil-ə-nər\ *n* [originally a dealer in various women's accessories commonly made in Milan, Italy; the name is irregularly formed from *Milan*] : a person who designs, makes, trims, or sells women's hats

mil·li·nery \-ˌner-ē\ *n* **1** : women's hats **2** : the business or work of a milliner

mil·lion \'mil-yən\ *n, pl* **millions** *or* **million** **1** — see NUMBER table **2** : a very great number ⟨*millions* of mosquitoes⟩ — **million** *adj* — **millionth** \-yən(t)th\ *adj or n*

mil·lion·aire \ˌmil-yə-'na(ə)r, -'ne(ə)r, 'mil-yə-ˌ\ *n* : one who is worth a million dollars or more

mil·li·pede *or* **mil·le·pede** \'mil-ə-ˌpēd\ *n* : any of numerous myriopods having a long segmented body with a hard covering, two pairs of legs on most apparent segments, and no poison fangs — compare CENTIPEDE

mil·li·sec·ond \'mil-ə-ˌsek-ənd\ *n* : one thousandth of a second

mil·li·volt \-ˌvōlt\ *n* : one thousandth of a volt

mill·pond \'mil-ˌpänd\ *n* : a pond that supplies water for running a mill

mill·race \-ˌrās\ *n* **1** : a canal in which water flows to and from a mill wheel **2** : the current that drives a mill wheel

mill·stone \-ˌstōn\ *n* **1** : either of two circular stones used for grinding a substance (as grain) **2** : a heavy burden

mill·stream \-ˌstrēm\ *n* **1** : a stream whose flow is used to run a mill **2** : the stream in a millrace

mill wheel *n* : a waterwheel that drives a mill

mill·wright \'mil-ˌrīt\ *n* : one who builds mills or sets up their machinery

mi·lo \'mī-lō\ *n* : a small usu. early and drought-resistant grain sorghum

milt \'milt\ *n* : the male reproductive glands of fishes when filled with secretion; *also* : the secretion itself

[1]**mime** \'mīm, 'mēm\ *n* **1** : MIMIC 2 **2** : an ancient play or skit representing scenes from life usu. in a ridiculous manner **3** : PANTOMIME **4** : an actor in a mime

[2]**mime** *vb* **1** : to act in a mime usu. without words **2** : to imitate closely : MIMIC **3** : to act out in the manner of a mime

mim·eo·graph \'mim-ē-ə-ˌgraf\ *n* : a machine for making copies of typewritten or written matter by means of a stencil — **mimeograph** *vb*

mi·met·ic \mə-'met-ik, mī-\ *adj* : relating to, characterized by, or exhibiting mimicry ⟨*mimetic* coloring of a butterfly⟩

[1]**mim·ic** \'mim-ik\ *n* **1** : MIME 4 **2** : one that mimics

[2]**mimic** *adj* **1** : IMITATIVE **2** : IMITATION, MOCK ⟨a *mimic* battle⟩

[3]**mimic** *vb* **mim·icked** \-ikt\; **mim·ick·ing** **1** : to imitate closely : APE **2** : to ridicule by imitation **3** : to resemble by biological mimicry ***syn*** see IMITATE

mim·ic·ry \'mim-i-krē\ *n, pl* **-ries** **1** : the action, art, or an instance of mimicking **2** : a superficial resemblance of one organism to another or to natural objects among which it lives that secures it concealment, protection, or other advantage

mi·mo·sa \mə-'mō-sə, mī-, -zə\ *n* : any of a genus of trees, shrubs, and herbs of warm regions with small white or pink flowers in ball-shaped heads

min *abbr* **1** minimum **2** minute

min·a·ret \ˌmin-ə-'ret\ *n* : a tall slender tower of a mosque from a balcony of which the people are called to prayer

minaret

[1]**mince** \'min(t)s\ *vb* **1** : to cut into very small pieces : HASH **2** : to act, walk, or speak in an unnaturally dainty way ⟨*mince* no words⟩ — **minc·ing·ly** \'min(t)-sing-lē\ *adv*

[2]**mince** *n* : small bits into which something is chopped; *esp* : MINCEMEAT

mince·meat \'min(t)s-ˌmēt\ *n* **1** : minced meat **2** : a finely chopped mixture of ingredients (as raisins, apples, or spices) with or without meat

mince pie *n* : a pie made of mincemeat

[1]**mind** \'mīnd\ *n* **1** : MEMORY, RECOLLECTION ⟨call to *mind*⟩ **2** : the part of a person that feels, perceives, thinks, wills, and esp. reasons **3** : INTENTION, DESIRE ⟨changed his *mind*⟩ **4** : the normal or healthy condition of the mental faculties ⟨lost her *mind*⟩ **5** : OPINION, VIEW ⟨spoke his *mind*⟩ **6** : CHOICE, LIKING ⟨the decision was not at all to his *mind*⟩

[2]**mind** *vb* **1** *chiefly dial* : REMEMBER **2** : to pay attention to : HEED ⟨*mind* what you're doing⟩ ⟨*minds* his own business⟩ **3** : OBEY ⟨*minds* her parents⟩ **4** : to be

bothered by ⟨never *mind* your mistake⟩ ⟨doesn't *mind* the cold⟩ **5** : to be careful about : watch out for ⟨*mind* the broken rung⟩ **6** : to take charge of : TEND ⟨*mind* the children⟩

mind·ed \'mīn-dəd\ *adj* **1** : having a specified kind of mind ⟨narrow-*minded*⟩ **2** : DISPOSED, INCLINED

mind·ful \'mīn(d)-fəl\ *adj* : bearing in mind : HEEDFUL — **mind·ful·ly** \-fə-lē\ *adv*

mind·less \'mīn-dləs\ *adj* : lacking mind or consciousness; *esp* : UNINTELLIGENT — **mind·less·ly** *adv* — **mind·less·ness** *n*

1**mine** \(')mīn\ *adj, archaic* : MY — used before a word beginning with a vowel or *h* ⟨*mine* eyes⟩ ⟨*mine* host⟩ or as a modifier of a preceding noun ⟨mother *mine*⟩

2**mine** \'mīn\ *pron* : my one : my ones

3**mine** \'mīn\ *n* **1** : a pit or tunnel from which minerals (as coal, gold, or diamonds) are taken **2** : a deposit of ore **3** : an underground passage dug beneath an enemy position **4 a** : a charge buried in the ground and set to explode when disturbed (as by an enemy soldier or vehicle) **b** : an explosive charge placed in a case and sunk in the water to sink enemy ships **5** : a rich source ⟨he is a *mine* of information⟩

4**mine** \'mīn\ *vb* **1** : to dig a mine **2** : to obtain from a mine ⟨*mine* coal⟩ **3** : to work in a mine **4** : to dig or form mines under a place **5** : to lay military mines in or under ⟨*mine* a harbor⟩

min·er \'mī-nər\ *n* : one that mines; *esp* : a person who works in a mine

1**min·er·al** \'min-(ə-)rəl\ *n* **1** : a naturally occurring crystalline substance (as diamond or quartz) of definite chemical composition that results from processes other than those of plants and animals **2** : a naturally occurring substance (as ore, sand, petroleum, or water) obtained for man's use usu. from the ground

2**mineral** *adj* **1** : of, relating to, or having the characteristics of a mineral : INORGANIC **2** : containing mineral salts or gases

min·er·al·ize \'min-(ə-)rə-ˌlīz\ *vb* **1** : to transform a metal into an ore **2** : PETRIFY ⟨*mineralized* bones⟩ **3 a** : to impregnate or supply with minerals **b** : to change into mineral form

min·er·al·o·gy \ˌmin-ə-'räl-ə-jē, -'ral-\ *n* : a science that collects and studies facts about minerals — **min·er·al·og·i·cal** \ˌmin-(ə-)rə-'läj-i-kəl\ *adj* — **min·er·al·o·gist** \ˌmin-ə-'räl-ə-jəst, -'ral-\ *n*

mineral oil *n* **1** : an oil (as petroleum) of mineral origin **2** : a refined petroleum oil having no color, odor, or taste that is used as a laxative

mineral water *n* : water naturally or artificially impregnated with mineral salts or gases

mineral wool *n* : any of various lightweight materials that resemble wool in texture, are made from slag, rock, or glass, and are used esp. in heat and sound insulation

min·e·stro·ne \ˌmin-ə-'strō-nē, -'strōn\ *n* : a rich thick vegetable soup with dried beans, macaroni, vermicelli, or similar ingredients

mine·sweep·er \'mīn-ˌswē-pər\ *n* : a warship designed for removing or neutralizing mines

min·gle \'ming-gəl\ *vb* **min·gled**; **min·gling** \-g(ə-)ling\ **1 a** : to bring or combine together or with something else ⟨*mingled* fact with fancy⟩ **b** : to become mingled **2** : to come in contact : ASSOCIATE ⟨*mingles* with all sorts of people⟩

syn MINGLE, MIX, BLEND, COALESCE can mean to put or come together in one mass. MINGLE implies that the elements are still at least somewhat distinguishable; MIX may or may not imply loss of each element's separate identity; BLEND implies that the elements undergo much or complete loss of individuality; COALESCE may suggest an organic unity brought about when like things grow together

mini \'min-ē\ *n* **1** : MINISKIRT **2** : a dress with a miniskirt

1**min·i·a·ture** \'min-ē-ə-ˌchu̇r, 'min-i-ˌchu̇r, -chər\ *n* [from Italian *miniatura* "the art of illuminating manuscripts", "a picture in an illuminated manuscript", from medieval Latin, from Latin *miniare* "to color with red lead", from *minium* "red lead"] **1** : something much smaller than the usual size; *esp* : a copy on a much reduced scale **2** : a very small portrait or painting (as on ivory or metal) **3** : the art of painting miniatures — **min·i·a·tur·ist** \-ˌchu̇r-əst\ *n*

2**miniature** *adj* : very small : represented on a small scale ⟨collects *miniature* books⟩

min·i·a·tur·ize \-ˌchu̇r-ˌīz, -chər-\ *vb* : to design or construct in small size — **min·i·a·tur·i·za·tion** \ˌmin-ē-ə-chu̇r-ə-'zā-shən, ˌmin-i-ˌchu̇r-, -chər-\ *n*

mini·bus \'min-ē-ˌbəs\ *n* : a small bus

min·im \'min-əm\ *n* : either of two units of liquid capacity equal to 1⁄60 fluidram — see MEASURE table

min·i·mal \'min-ə-məl\ *adj* : relating to or being a minimum : LEAST — **min·i·mal·ly** \-mə-lē\ *adv*

min·i·mize \'min-ə-ˌmīz\ *vb* **1** : to make as small as possible ⟨*minimize* the chance of error⟩ **2 a** : to place a low estimate on ⟨*minimized* his losses⟩ **b** : BELITTLE, DISPARAGE ⟨*minimize* his victory⟩

min·i·mum \'min-ə-məm\ *n, pl* **-ma** \-mə\ *or* **-mums** **1** : the least quantity possible or allowable **2** : the lowest degree or amount reached or recorded — **minimum** *adj*

minimum wage *n* : a wage fixed (as by law) as the least that will provide a minimum standard of living

min·ing \'mī-ning\ *n* : the process or business of working mines

min·ion \'min-yən\ *n* **1** : a servile dependent **2** : FAVORITE

mini·skirt \'min-ē-ˌskərt\ *n* : a woman's short skirt with the hemline several inches above the knees — **mini·skirt·ed** \-əd\ *adj*

1**min·is·ter** \'min-ə-stər\ *n* **1 a** : a clergyman officiating or assisting at the administration of a sacrament **b** : a Protestant clergyman **2** : a high government official entrusted with the management of a division of governmental activities **3** : a diplomatic representative

2**minister** *vb* **min·is·tered**; **min·is·ter·ing** \-st(ə-)ring\ : to give aid : SERVE ⟨*minister* to the sick⟩ — **min·is·tra·tion** \ˌmin-ə-'strā-shən\ *n*

min·is·te·ri·al \ˌmin-ə-'stir-ē-əl\ *adj* : of or relating to a minister or ministry

min·is·trant \'min-ə-strənt\ *adj* : serving as a minister — **ministrant** *n*

min·is·try \'min-ə-strē\ *n, pl* **-tries** **1** : the action of ministering **2** : the office, duties, or functions of a minister ⟨study for the *ministry*⟩ **3** : the body of ministers of religion : CLERGY **4** : AGENCY, MEANS **5 a** : the body of ministers governing a nation or state **b** : a government department headed by a minister ⟨*ministry* of foreign affairs⟩ **c** : the building in which a ministry is housed **d** : the office or term of office of a ministry or governmental minister

mink \'miŋk\ *n, pl* **mink** *or* **minks** : any of several slender-bodied mammals resembling the related weasels, having partially webbed feet and a somewhat bushy tail, and living near water; *also* : the soft typically dark brown fur of this animal

mink
(up to 28 in. long)

Minn *abbr* Minnesota

min·now \'min-ō\ *n, pl* **minnows** *or* **minnow** : any of various small freshwater bottom-feeding fish (as the dace or shiner) related to the carps; *also* : any of various similar small fishes

1**mi·nor** \'mī-nər\ *adj* **1** : less in dignity, rank, or quantity ⟨a *minor* poet⟩ ⟨a *minor* injury⟩ **2** : not having attained majority **3 a** : having the 3d, 6th, and sometimes the 7th degrees lowered a semitone ⟨*minor* scale⟩ **b** : based on a minor scale ⟨*minor* key⟩ **4** : of or relating to an academic minor

2**minor** *n* **1** : a person who has not attained majority **2** : a minor musical interval, scale, key, or mode **3 a** : a secondary academic subject **b** : a student studying a minor

3**minor** *vb* : to pursue an academic minor

mi·nor·i·ty \mə-'nȯr-ət-ē, mī-, -'när-\ *n, pl* **-ties** **1** : the state or period of being a legal minor **2** : the smaller number; *esp* : a group having less than the number of votes necessary for control **3** : a part of a population differing from other groups in some characteristics and often discriminated against

min·ster \'min(t)-stər\ *n* **1** : a church attached to a monastery **2** : a large or important church

min·strel \'min(t)-strəl\ *n* **1** : a medieval musical entertainer; *esp* : a singer of verses to the accompaniment of a harp **2 a** : MUSICIAN **b** : POET **3 a** : one of a troupe of performers typically giving a program of Negro melodies and jokes and usu. blacked in imitation of Negroes **b** : a performance by a troupe of minstrels

min·strel·sy \-sē\ *n, pl* **-sies** **1** : the singing and playing of a minstrel **2** : a body of minstrels **3** : a collection of songs or verse

1**mint** \'mint\ *n* **1** : a place where coins, medals, and tokens are made **2** : a great amount

2**mint** *vb* : to convert metal into coin — **mint·er** *n*

3**mint** *n* **1** : any of a family of herbs and shrubs (as basil or rosemary) with square stems, opposite leaves, and commonly 2-lipped flowers; *esp* : one (as peppermint or spearmint) that is fragrant and yields a flavoring oil **2** : a mint-flavored piece of candy

mint·age \'mint-ij\ *n* **1** : the process of minting coins **2** : coins produced by minting **3** : the cost of manufacturing coins

min·u·end \'min-yə-ˌwend\ *n* : a number from which another number is to be subtracted

min·u·et \ˌmin-yə-'wet\ *n* **1** : a slow graceful dance **2** : music for or in the rhythm of a minuet

1**mi·nus** \'mī-nəs\ *prep* **1** : diminished by ⟨seven *minus* four is three⟩ **2** : WITHOUT ⟨*minus* his hat⟩

2**minus** *n* **1** : a negative quantity **2** : LACK, DEFECT

3**minus** *adj* **1** : mathematically negative ⟨plus four and *minus* three is one⟩ **2** : falling low in a specified range ⟨a grade of C *minus*⟩

minus sign *n* : a sign − used esp. to indicate subtraction (as in $8 - 6 = 2$) or a negative quantity (as in $-10°$)

1**min·ute** \'min-ət\ *n* [from Latin *minuta*, short for *minuta pars* "tiny part", from the adjective *minutus* "minute"] **1** : the 60th part of an hour of time or of a degree **2** : the distance one can cover in a minute ⟨10 *minutes* from home to office⟩ **3** : MOMENT **4** *pl* : a brief record of the proceedings of a meeting

2**mi·nute** \mī-'n(y)üt, mə-\ *adj* **1** : very small : TINY **2** : of small importance : PETTY **3** : marked by close attention to details ⟨a *minute* description⟩ — **mi·nute·ly** *adv* — **mi·nute·ness** *n*

min·ute·man \'min-ət-ˌman\ *n* : a member of a group of armed men pledged to take the field at a minute's notice during and immediately before the American Revolution

minute steak \ˌmin-ət-\ *n* : a small thin steak that can be quickly cooked

minx \'miŋ(k)s\ *n* : a saucy girl

Mio·cene \'mī-ə-ˌsēn\ *n* : the epoch of the Tertiary between the Oligocene and Pliocene; *also* : the corresponding system of rocks — **Miocene** *adj*

mir·a·cle \'mir-i-kəl\ *n* **1** : an extraordinary event taken as a sign of the supernatural power of God **2** : an extremely outstanding or unusual event, thing, or accomplishment

miracle drug *n* : a usu. newly discovered drug capable of producing a marked and favorable change in a patient's condition

miracle play *n* : a medieval play showing events from the life of a saint or martyr

mi·rac·u·lous \mə-'rak-yə-ləs\ *adj* **1** : of the nature of a miracle : SUPERNATURAL **2** : resembling a miracle : MARVELOUS **3** : working or able to work miracles — **mi·rac·u·lous·ly** *adv*

mi·rage \mə-'räzh\ *n* : an illusory optical effect that gives the appearance of a pool of water or a mirror in which distant objects are seen inverted and is sometimes seen at sea, in the desert, or over a hot pavement

1**mire** \'mī(ə)r\ *n* **1** : MARSH, BOG **2** : heavy often deep mud or slush

2**mire** *vb* **1 a** : to sink or stick fast in mire **b** : ENTANGLE, INVOLVE **2** : to soil with mud or slush

1**mir·ror** \'mir-ər\ *n* **1** : a glass backed with a reflecting substance (as mercury) **2** : a smooth or polished surface that reflects an image **3** : something that reflects a true likeness or gives a true description

2**mirror** *vb* : to reflect in or as if in a mirror

mirth \'mərth\ *n* : gladness or gaiety accompanied with laughter

mirth·ful \-fəl\ *adj* : full of, expressing, or producing mirth — **mirth·ful·ly** \-fə-lē\ *adv* — **mirth·ful·ness** *n*

miry \'mī(ə)r-ē\ *adj* **mir·i·er**; **-est** **1** : MARSHY, BOGGY **2** : MUDDY, SLUSHY

mis- *prefix* **1 a** : badly : wrongly ⟨*mis*judge⟩ **b** : unfavorably ⟨*mis*esteem⟩ **c** : in a suspicious manner ⟨*mis*doubt⟩ **2** : bad : wrong ⟨*mis*deed⟩ **3** : opposite or lack of ⟨*mis*trust⟩

mis·ad·ven·ture \ˌmis-əd-'ven-chər\ *n* : MISFORTUNE, MISHAP

mis·al·li·ance \ˌmis-ə-'lī-ən(t)s\ *n* : an improper or unsuitable alliance esp. in marriage

mis·an·thrope \'mis-ən-ˌthrōp\ *n* : a person who dislikes and distrusts mankind

mis·an·thro·py \mis-'an(t)-thrə-pē\ *n* : a dislike or hatred of mankind — **mis·an·throp·ic** \ˌmis-ən-'thräp-ik\ *adj* — **mis·an·throp·i·cal·ly** \-'thräp-i-k(ə-)lē\ *adv*

mis·ap·ply \ˌmis-ə-'plī\ *vb* : to apply wrongly — **mis·ap·pli·ca·tion** \ˌmis-ˌap-lə-'kā-shən\ *n*

mis·ap·pre·hend \ˌmis-ˌap-ri-'hend\ *vb* : MISUNDERSTAND — **mis·ap·pre·hen·sion** \-'hen-chən\ *n*

mis·ap·pro·pri·ate \ˌmis-ə-'prō-prē-ˌāt\ *vb* : to appropriate wrongly; *esp* : to take dishonestly for one's

own use — **mis·ap·pro·pri·a·tion** \-ˌprō-prē-ˈā-shən\ *n*
mis·be·got·ten \ˌmis-bi-ˈgät-ən\ *adj* : ILLEGITIMATE
mis·be·have \ˌmis-bi-ˈhāv\ *vb* : to behave badly — **mis·be·hav·ior** \-ˈhā-vyər\ *n*
mis·be·lief \ˌmis-bə-ˈlēf\ *n* : a mistaken or false belief — **mis·be·liev·er** \-ˈlē-vər\ *n*
misc *abbr* miscellaneous
mis·cal·cu·late \(ˈ)mis-ˈkal-kyə-ˌlāt\ *vb* : to calculate wrongly — **mis·cal·cu·la·tion** \ˌmis-ˌkal-kyə-ˈlā-shən\ *n*
mis·call \(ˈ)mis-ˈkȯl\ *vb* : to call by a wrong name
mis·car·riage \mis-ˈkar-ij\ *n* **1** : MISMANAGEMENT; *esp* : a failure in the administration of justice **2 a** : a failure to arrive ⟨*miscarriage* of a letter⟩ **b** : a failure to carry properly ⟨*miscarriage* of a shipment⟩ **3** : the accidental separation of an unborn child from the body of its mother before it is capable of living independently : loss of a child through premature birth — compare ABORTION
mis·car·ry \mis-ˈkar-ē\ *vb* **1** : to have a miscarriage : give birth prematurely **2** : to fail of the intended purpose : go wrong ⟨the plan *miscarried*⟩
mis·cast \(ˈ)mis-ˈkast\ *vb* : to cast in an unsuitable role
mis·ceg·e·na·tion \(ˌ)mis-ˌej-ə-ˈnā-shən, ˌmis-i-jə-ˈnā-\ *n* : marriage or interbreeding between persons of different races
mis·cel·la·ne·ous \ˌmis-ə-ˈlā-ne-əs\ *adj* : consisting of many things of different sorts ⟨a *miscellaneous* collection⟩ ⟨*miscellaneous* tools⟩ — **mis·cel·la·ne·ous·ly** *adv* — **mis·cel·la·ne·ous·ness** *n*
mis·cel·la·ny \ˈmis-ə-ˌlā-nē\ *n, pl* **-nies** **1** : a mixture of various things **2** : a collection of writings : ANTHOLOGY
mis·chance \(ˈ)mis-ˈchan(t)s\ *n* **1** : bad luck not bringing on serious or permanent evils **2** : a piece of bad luck : MISHAP ***syn*** see MISFORTUNE
mis·chief \ˈmis-chəf\ *n* **1** : INJURY, HARM **2** : a person or animal who causes mischief **3** : mischievous conduct or quality ⟨a child gets into *mischief*⟩ ⟨he has *mischief* in his eyes⟩
mis·chie·vous \ˈmis-chə-vəs\ *adj* **1** : harming or intended to do harm ⟨*mischievous* gossip⟩ **2** : causing or tending to cause petty injury or annoyance ⟨a *mischievous* puppy⟩ **3** : showing a spirit of mischief ⟨*mischievous* behavior⟩ — **mis·chie·vous·ly** *adv* — **mis·chie·vous·ness** *n*
mis·con·ceive \ˌmis-kən-ˈsēv\ *vb* : MISJUDGE — **mis·con·cep·tion** \-ˈsep-shən\ *n*
mis·con·duct \(ˈ)mis-ˈkän-(ˌ)dəkt\ *n* **1** : bad management **2** : improper or unlawful behavior — **mis·con·duct** \ˌmis-kən-ˈdəkt\ *vb*
mis·con·struc·tion \ˌmis-kən-ˈstrək-shən\ *n* : the act, the process, or an instance of misconstruing
mis·con·strue \ˌmis-kən-ˈstru\ *vb* : to construe wrongly : MISINTERPRET
mis·count \(ˈ)mis-ˈkau̇nt\ *vb* : to count incorrectly — **miscount** *n*
mis·cre·ant \ˈmis-krē-ənt\ *n* : VILLAIN, SCOUNDREL — **miscreant** *adj*
[1]**mis·cue** \(ˈ)mis-ˈkyü\ *n* **1** : a stroke (as in billiards) in which the cue slips **2** : MISTAKE, SLIP
[2]**miscue** *vb* **1** : to make a miscue **2 a** : to miss a stage cue **b** : to answer a wrong cue

ə abut	ər further	a back	ā bake
ä cot, cart	au̇ out	ch chin	e less	ē easy
g gift	i trip	ī life	j joke	ng sing	ō flow
ȯ flaw	ȯi coin	th thin	t͟h this	ü loot
u̇ foot	y yet	yü few	yu̇ furious	zh vision

mis·deal \(ˈ)mis-ˈdēl\ *vb* **-dealt** \-ˈdelt\; **-deal·ing** \-ˈdē-ling\ : to deal wrongly ⟨*misdeal* cards⟩ — **misdeal** *n*
mis·deed \(ˈ)mis-ˈdēd\ *n* : an immoral or illegal deed
mis·de·mea·nor \ˌmis-di-ˈmē-nər\ *n* **1** : a crime less serious than a felony **2** : MISDEED
mis·di·rect \ˌmis-də-ˈrekt, -dī-\ *vb* : to direct incorrectly — **mis·di·rec·tion** \-ˈrek-shən\ *n*
mis·do·ing \(ˈ)mis-ˈdü-ing\ *n* **1** : WRONGDOING **2** : MISDEED — **mis·do·er** \-ˈdü-ər\ *n*
mi·ser \ˈmī-zər\ *n* [from Latin, meaning "a miserable person", "a wretch"] : a mean grasping person; *esp* : one who lives miserably in order to hoard his wealth
mis·er·a·ble \ˈmiz-ər-bəl, ˈmiz-(ə-)rə-bəl\ *adj* **1 a** : wretchedly deficient or meager ⟨a *miserable* hovel⟩ **b** : causing great discomfort or unhappiness ⟨a *miserable* cold⟩ **2** : extremely poor or unhappy : WRETCHED **3** : PITIFUL, LAMENTABLE — **mis·er·a·ble·ness** *n* — **mis·er·a·bly** \-blē\ *adv*
mi·ser·ly \ˈmī-zər-lē\ *adj* : of, relating to, or characteristic of a miser : GRASPING — **mi·ser·li·ness** *n*
mis·ery \ˈmiz-(ə-)rē\ *n, pl* **-er·ies** **1** : a state of great suffering and want due to poverty or affliction **2** : a source of misery ⟨the *miseries* of prison⟩ **3** : UNHAPPINESS
mis·file \(ˈ)mis-ˈfīl\ *vb* : to file in an incorrect place
mis·fire \(ˈ)mis-ˈfī(ə)r\ *vb* **1** : to have the explosive or propulsive charge fail to ignite at the proper time ⟨the engine *misfired*⟩ **2** : to fail to fire ⟨the gun *misfired*⟩ **3** : to miss an intended effect — **misfire** *n*
mis·fit \ˈmis-ˌfit, (ˈ)mis-ˈfit\ *n* **1** : something that fits badly **2** : a person poorly adjusted to his circumstances
mis·for·tune \mis-ˈfȯr-chən\ *n* **1** : bad fortune esp. of long duration **2** : an unfortunate condition or event : DISASTER

syn MISFORTUNE, MISCHANCE, MISHAP can mean an unlucky turn of events. MISFORTUNE implies resulting distress of some duration; MISCHANCE implies an immediate practical inconvenience; MISHAP commonly implies an inconvenience of no serious or lasting consequence ***ant*** happiness, prosperity

mis·giv·ing \mis-ˈgiv-ing\ *n* : a feeling of doubt or suspicion esp. concerning a future event
mis·gov·ern \(ˈ)mis-ˈgəv-ərn\ *vb* : to govern badly — **mis·gov·ern·ment** \-ər(n)-mənt\ *n*
mis·guide \(ˈ)mis-ˈgīd\ *vb* : to lead astray : MISDIRECT — **mis·guid·ance** \-ˈgīd-ən(t)s\ *n*
mis·han·dle \(ˈ)mis-ˈhan-dəl\ *vb* **1** : to treat roughly : MALTREAT **2** : to manage wrongly
mis·hap \ˈmis-ˌhap, mis-ˈ\ *n* **1** *archaic* : bad luck **2** : an unfortunate accident ***syn*** see MISFORTUNE
mish·mash \ˈmish-ˌmash, -ˌmäsh\ *n* : HODGEPODGE, JUMBLE
mis·in·form \ˌmis-ən-ˈfȯrm\ *vb* : to give false or misleading information to — **mis·in·for·ma·tion** \ˌmis-ˌin-fər-ˈmā-shən\ *n*
mis·in·ter·pret \ˌmis-ən-ˈtər-prət\ *vb* : to understand or explain wrongly — **mis·in·ter·pre·ta·tion** \-ˌtər-prə-ˈtā-shən\ *n*
mis·judge \(ˈ)mis-ˈjəj\ *vb* : to judge wrongly or unjustly — **mis·judg·ment** \-ˈjəj-mənt\ *n*
mis·lay \(ˈ)mis-ˈlā\ *vb* **-laid** \-ˈlād\; **-lay·ing** : to put in a place later forgotten : LOSE
mis·lead \(ˈ)mis-ˈlēd\ *vb* **-led** \-ˈled\; **-lead·ing** : to lead in a wrong direction or into a mistaken action or belief — **misleading** *adj*
mis·like \(ˈ)mis-ˈlīk\ *vb* : DISLIKE — **mislike** *n*
mis·man·age \(ˈ)mis-ˈman-ij\ *vb* : to manage badly or improperly — **mis·man·age·ment** \-mənt\ *n*

mis·match \(')mis-'mach\ *vb* : to match (as in marriage) unsuitably or badly — **mismatch** *n*
mis·mate \(')mis-'māt\ *vb* : to mate unsuitably
mis·name \(')mis-'nām\ *vb* : to name incorrectly : MISCALL
mis·no·mer \mis-'nō-mər\ *n* : a wrong or unsuitable name
mi·sog·a·mist \mə-'säg-ə-məst\ *n* : one who hates marriage — **mi·sog·a·my** \-'säg-ə-mē\ *n*
mi·sog·y·nist \mə-'säj-ə-nəst\ *n* : one who hates or distrusts women — **mi·sog·y·ny** \-nē\ *n*
mis·place \(')mis-'plās\ *vb* **1** : to put in a wrong place ⟨*misplaced* a comma⟩ **2** : MISLAY — **mis·place·ment** \-mənt\ *n*
mis·play \(')mis-'plā\ *n* : a wrong or unskillful play — **misplay** *vb*
mis·print \(')mis-'print\ *vb* : to print incorrectly — **mis·print** \'mis-ˌprint, (')mis-'\ *n*
mis·pro·nounce \ˌmis-prə-'naůn(t)s\ *vb* : to pronounce in a way regarded as incorrect — **mis·pro·nun·ci·a·tion** \-ˌnən(t)-sē-'ā-shən\ *n*
mis·quote \(')mis-'kwōt\ *vb* : to quote incorrectly — **mis·quo·ta·tion** \ˌmis-kwō-'tā-shən\ *n*
mis·read \(')mis-'rēd\ *vb* **-read** \-'red\; **-read·ing** \-'rēd-ing\ **1** : to read incorrectly **2** : to misinterpret in or as if in reading
mis·rep·re·sent \ˌmis-ˌrep-ri-'zent\ *vb* : to give a false or misleading representation of — **mis·rep·re·sen·ta·tion** \(ˌ)mis-ˌrep-ri-ˌzen-'tā-shən\ *n*
¹**mis·rule** \(')mis-'rül\ *vb* : to rule or govern badly
²**misrule** *n* **1** : bad government **2** : DISORDER
¹**miss** \'mis\ *vb* **1** : to fail to hit, catch, reach, or get ⟨*miss* a target⟩ ⟨*miss* the ball⟩ **2** : ESCAPE, AVOID ⟨just *missed* being hurt⟩ **3 a** : to leave out : OMIT ⟨*missed* his lunch⟩ **b** : to fail to attend ⟨*missed* three days of school⟩ **4** : to discover or feel the absence of ⟨*miss* an absent friend⟩ **5** : to fail to understand, sense, or experience ⟨*missed* his meaning⟩ **6** : MISFIRE ⟨the engine *missed*⟩
²**miss** *n* **1** : a failure to reach a desired goal or result **2** : MISFIRE
³**miss** *n* **1 a** — used as a title before the name of an unmarried woman or girl **b** — used to form a title for a girl who represents the thing indicated ⟨*Miss* America⟩ **2** : a young woman or girl ⟨*misses*' dresses⟩ — used as a term of address ⟨*miss*, has the bus left?⟩
Miss *abbr* Mississippi
mis·sal \'mis-əl\ *n* : a book containing the prayers to be said or sung in the Mass during the year
mis·shape \(')mis(h)-'shāp\ *vb* : to shape badly : DEFORM — **mis·shap·en** \-'shā-pən\ *adj*
mis·sile \'mis-əl\ *n* [from Latin, from the past participle *missus* of the verb *mittere* "to let go", "send", and hence applied to a weapon that was not, like a sword, retained in the hand] : an object (as a stone, arrow, artillery shell, bullet, or rocket) that is thrown or projected usu. so as to strike something at a distance; *esp* : GUIDED MISSILE
miss·ing \'mis-ing\ *adj* : ABSENT, LOST ⟨*missing* persons⟩ ⟨*missing* in action⟩
missing link *n* : a hypothetical intermediate form between man and the apes that has not been discovered in the fossil record
mis·sion \'mish-ən\ *n* **1 a** : a group of missionaries **b** : the work of a missionary **c** : a place where a mission or missionary works **2 a** : a group sent to a foreign country to conduct negotiations or to provide training or assistance ⟨trade *mission*⟩ ⟨military *mission*⟩ **b** : a permanent embassy or legation **3** : a task or function assigned or undertaken ⟨his *mission* was to recover the stolen plans⟩ — **mission** *adj*
¹**mis·sion·ary** \'mish-ə-ˌner-ē\ *adj* **1** : relating to, engaged in, or devoted to missions **2** : characteristic of a missionary : ZEALOUS
²**missionary** *n, pl* **-ar·ies** : one sent to spread a religious faith among unbelievers
Mis·sis·sip·pi·an \ˌmis-ə-'sip-ē-ən\ *adj* **1** : of or relating to Mississippi, its people, or the Mississippi river **2** : of, relating to, or being the period of the Paleozoic era between the Devonian and Pennsylvanian or the corresponding system of rocks — **Mississippian** *n*
mis·sive \'mis-iv\ *n* : LETTER, MESSAGE
mis·spell \(')mis-'spel\ *vb* : to spell incorrectly
mis·spend \(')mis-'spend\ *vb* **-spent** \-'spent\; **-spend·ing** : WASTE, SQUANDER ⟨a *misspent* youth⟩
mis·state \(')mis-'stāt\ *vb* : to state incorrectly — **mis·state·ment** \-mənt\ *n*
mis·step \(')mis-'step\ *n* **1** : a wrong step **2** : MISTAKE, BLUNDER
¹**mist** \'mist\ *n* **1** : water in the form of particles floating in the air or falling as fine rain **2** : something that blurs or hinders vision : HAZE, FILM
²**mist** *vb* **1** : to be or become misty **2** : to become dim or blurred
¹**mis·take** \mə-'stāk\ *vb* **mis·took** \-'stůk\; **mis·tak·en** \-'stā-kən\; **mis·tak·ing** **1** : to understand wrongly : MISINTERPRET ⟨*mistook* his meaning⟩ **2** : to estimate incorrectly ⟨*mistook* the strength of the enemy⟩ **3** : to identify wrongly ⟨*mistook* him for another⟩
²**mistake** *n* **1** : a wrong judgment : MISUNDERSTANDING **2** : a wrong action or statement : BLUNDER ***syn*** see ERROR
mis·tak·en \mə-'stā-kən\ *adj* **1** : judging or identifying wrongly : being in error ⟨*mistaken* about the time⟩ **2** : WRONG, INCORRECT ⟨a *mistaken* idea⟩ — **mis·tak·en·ly** *adv*
mis·ter \'mis-tər\ *n* [an altered form of *master*] **1 a** — used as a title before the name of a man or a designation of office and usu. written *Mr.* or in the plural *Messrs.* ⟨*Mr.* President⟩ ⟨*Messrs.* Jones and Smith⟩ **b** — used to form a title for a male representing the thing indicated ⟨*Mr.* Conservative⟩ **2** : SIR — used as a conventional term of address to a man
mis·time \(')mis-'tīm\ *vb* : to time wrongly
mis·tle·toe \'mis-əl-ˌtō\ *n* : a green plant with yellowish flowers and waxy white berries that grows on the branches and trunks of trees

mistletoe

mis·tral \'mis-trəl, mi-'sträl\ *n* : a violent cold dry northerly wind of southern Europe
mis·treat \(')mis-'trēt\ *vb* : to treat badly : ABUSE — **mis·treat·ment** \-mənt\ *n*
mis·tress \'mis-trəs; *in contracted form "Mrs."* ˌmis-əz, -əs, *esp South* ˌmiz-əz, -əs, (ˌ)miz *or before given names* (ˌ)mis\ *n* **1** : a woman who has control or authority like that of a master ⟨the *mistress* of the household⟩ **2** : something personified as female that rules or directs **3** : a woman with whom a man habitually fornicates **4** — used formerly as a title before the name of a woman
mis·tri·al \(')mis-'trī(-ə)l\ *n* : a trial that is void because of an error in the proceedings
¹**mis·trust** \(')mis-'trəst\ *n* : DISTRUST — **mis·trust·ful** \-fəl\ *adj* — **mis·trust·ful·ly** \-fə-lē\ *adv* — **mis·trust·ful·ness** *n*

2mistrust *vb* **1 :** SUSPECT ⟨I *mistrust* his motives⟩ **2 :** to lack confidence in ⟨*mistrusts* his own ability⟩

misty \'mis-tē\ *adj* **mist·i·er; -est 1 :** full of mist ⟨a *misty* valley⟩ **2 :** blurred by or as if by mist ⟨through *misty* eyes⟩ **3 :** VAGUE, INDISTINCT ⟨a *misty* memory⟩ — **mist·i·ly** \-tə-lē\ *adv* — **mist·i·ness** \-tē-nəs\ *n*

mis·un·der·stand \(,)mis-,ən-dər-'stand\ *vb* **-stood** \-'stu̇d\; **-stand·ing 1 :** to fail to understand **2 :** to interpret incorrectly

mis·un·der·stand·ing \-'stan-diŋ\ *n* **:** a failure to understand **:** QUARREL

1mis·use \(')mis-'yüz, mish-'üz\ *vb* **1 :** to use incorrectly **:** MISAPPLY **2 :** ABUSE, MISTREAT — **mis·us·age** \-'(y)ü-sij, -zij\ *n*

2mis·use \(')mis-'yüs, mish-'üs\ *n* **:** incorrect or improper use ⟨*misuse* of public funds⟩

mite \'mīt\ *n* **1 :** any of various tiny animals that are related to the ticks and spiders, often live on plants, animals, and stored foods, and include important carriers of disease **2 :** a very small coin or sum of money **3 :** a very small object or creature

1mi·ter *or* **mi·tre** \'mīt-ər\ *n* **1 :** a high pointed headdress worn by a bishop or abbot in church ceremonies **2 :** MITER JOINT

2miter *or* **mitre** *vb* **mi·tered** *or* **mi·tred; mi·ter·ing** *or* **mi·tring** \'mīt-ə-riŋ\ **1 :** to match or fit together in a miter joint **2 :** to bevel the ends of for making a miter joint

miter joint *n* **:** the joint or corner made by cutting the edges of two boards at an angle and fitting them together

miter joint

mit·i·gate \'mit-ə-,gāt\ *vb* **:** to make less severe ⟨*mitigate* a punishment⟩ ⟨a fact that *mitigates* his guilt⟩ — **mit·i·ga·tion** \,mit-ə-'gā-shən\ *n*

mi·to·chon·dri·on \,mīt-ə-'kän-drē-ən\ *n, pl* **-dria** \-drē-ə\ **:** one of the round or long bodies found in cells that are rich in fats, proteins, and enzymes and are important centers of metabolic processes (as the breakdown and synthesis of carbohydrates, fats, and amino acids) — **mi·to·chon·dri·al** \-drē-əl\ *adj*

mi·to·sis \mī-'tō-səs\ *n, pl* **-to·ses** \-'tō-,sēz\ **1 :** a nuclear process in a dividing cell that results in the formation of two new nuclei with the same number of chromosomes as the parent nucleus **2 :** a cell division in which mitosis occurs — **mi·tot·ic** \-tät-ik\ *adj*

mitt \'mit\ *n* **1 :** MITTEN **2 :** a baseball catcher's or first baseman's glove

mit·ten \'mit-ən\ *n* **:** a covering for the hand and wrist having a separate section for the thumb only

1mix \'miks\ *vb* **1 :** to make into one mass by stirring together **:** BLEND **2 :** to make by blending different things ⟨*mix* a salad dressing⟩ **3 :** to become one mass through blending ⟨oil will not *mix* with water⟩ **4 :** to associate with others on friendly terms ⟨*mixes* well in any company⟩ **5 :** CONFUSE ⟨*mix* up facts⟩ ***syn*** see MINGLE — **mix·er** *n*

2mix *n* **:** MIXTURE; *esp* **:** a commercially prepared mixture of food ingredients

mixed \'mikst\ *adj* **1 a :** made of mingled or blended elements ⟨a *mixed* drink⟩ **b :** combining features of more than one kind ⟨a *mixed* economy⟩ **2 a :** involving persons differing in race, national origin, or religion ⟨a *mixed* marriage⟩ **b :** made up of or involving individuals of both sexes ⟨*mixed* company⟩ ⟨a *mixed* chorus⟩ **c :** containing two or more kinds of organism in abundance ⟨a *mixed* deciduous forest⟩ **3 :** including or accompanied by inconsistent or incompatible elements ⟨a *mixed* blessing⟩ ⟨a *mixed* reaction⟩ **4 :** CROSSBRED

mixed number *n* **:** a number (as $5\,^2/_3$) composed of an integer and a proper fraction — called also *mixed numeral*

mixt *abbr* mixture

mix·ture \'miks-chər\ *n* **1 :** the act or process or an instance of mixing **2 a :** something mixed or being mixed ⟨add eggs to the *mixture*⟩ **b :** a cloth made of thread of different colors **c :** a preparation consisting of two or more ingredients or kinds ⟨a smoking *mixture*⟩ **3 :** the relative proportion of the elements in a mixture **4 :** two or more substances mixed together but not chemically united and not necessarily present in definite proportions ⟨sand mixed with sugar forms a *mixture*⟩

mix–up \'miks-,əp\ *n* **1 :** an instance of confusion ⟨a *mix-up* about who was to meet the train⟩ **2 :** CONFLICT, FIGHT

1miz·zen *or* **miz·en** \'miz-ən\ *n* **1 :** a fore-and-aft sail set on the mizzenmast **2 :** MIZZENMAST

2mizzen *or* **mizen** *adj* **:** of or relating to the mizzenmast ⟨*mizzen* shrouds⟩

miz·zen·mast \-,mast, -məst\ *n* **:** the mast aft or next aft of the mainmast in a ship

mk *abbr* mark

mks *abbr* meter-kilogram-second

ml *abbr* milliliter

mlle *abbr* mademoiselle

mm *abbr* millimeter

mme *abbr* madame

MN *abbr* Minnesota

mnr *abbr* manor

mo *abbr* month

Mo *or* **MO** *abbr* Missouri

1moan \'mōn\ *n* **1 :** a low drawn-out sound indicative of pain or grief **2 :** a sound like a moan

2moan *vb* **1 :** to utter a moan **2 :** COMPLAIN **3 :** to utter with moans

moat \'mōt\ *n* **:** a deep wide trench around the walls of a castle or fortress that is usu. filled with water

1mob \'mäb\ *n* **1 :** the common people **:** MASSES **2 :** a disorderly crowd **:** RABBLE **3 :** a criminal gang

2mob *vb* **mobbed; mob·bing :** to crowd about and attack or annoy

1mo·bile \'mō-bəl, -,bēl, -,bīl\ *adj* **1 :** MOVABLE **2 :** changing quickly in expression ⟨a *mobile* face⟩ **3 :** readily moved ⟨*mobile* troops⟩ **4 :** MIGRATORY ⟨*mobile* workers⟩ **5 :** characterized by movement from one class to another ⟨a *mobile* society⟩ — **mo·bil·i·ty** \mō-'bil-ət-ē\ *n*

2mo·bile \'mō-,bēl\ *n* **:** an artistic structure that is moved easily or that has parts easily moved (as by a current of air)

mo·bi·lize \'mō-bə-,līz\ *vb* **1 :** to put into movement or circulation **2 :** to assemble and make ready for action **:** MARSHAL ⟨*mobilize* army reserves⟩ ⟨the townspeople *mobilized* to fight the fire⟩ — **mo·bi·li·za·tion** \,mō-b(ə-)lə-'zā-shən\ *n*

Mö·bi·us strip \,mə(r)b-ē-əs-'strip, ,māb-\ *n* **:** a continuous surface constructed by holding one end of a rectangle fixed, rotating the opposite end through 180 degrees, and applying it to the first end

mob·ster \'mäb-stər\ *n* **:** a member of a criminal gang

ə abut	ər further	a back	ā bake
ä cot, cart	au̇ out	ch chin	e less
ē easy	g gift	i trip	ī life
j joke	ŋ sing	ō flow	ȯ flaw
ȯi coin	th thin	t͟h this	ü loot
u̇ foot	y yet	yü few	yu̇ furious
zh vision			

moc·ca·sin \'mäk-ə-sən\ *n* **1 a** : a soft leather shoe without a heel and with the sole and sides made of one piece joined on top by a seam to a U-shaped piece across the front **b** : a similar shoe with a separate sole **2** : WATER MOCCASIN

moccasin flower *n* : any of several lady's slippers; *esp* : a woodland orchid of eastern No. America with usu. pink flowers

mo·cha \'mō-kə\ *n* **1** : choice coffee grown in Arabia **2** : a mixture of coffee and chocolate **3** *often cap* : a dark olive brown

1**mock** \'mäk, 'mök\ *vb* **1** : to laugh at scornfully : RIDICULE **2** : DEFY, DISREGARD **3** : to make fun of by mimicking ***syn*** see IMITATE — **mock·er** *n* — **mock·ing·ly** \-ing-lē\ *adv*

2**mock** *n* **1** : an act of mocking : JEER **2** : an object of ridicule

3**mock** *adj* : not real : SHAM ⟨*mock* grief⟩

mock·ery \'mäk-(ə-)rē, 'mök-\ *n*, *pl* **-er·ies** **1** : insulting or contemptuous action or speech **2** : someone or something that is laughed at **3** : an insincere or a poor imitation ⟨the trial was a *mockery* of justice⟩ **4** : ridiculously useless or unsuitable action

mock·ing·bird \'mäk-ing-ˌbərd, 'mök-\ *n* : a songbird of the southern U.S. that is closely related to the catbirds and thrashers and is noted for the sweetness of its song and for its imitations of the notes of other birds

mock orange *n* : a hardy white-flowered shrub

mock–up \'mäk-ˌəp, 'mök-\ *n* : a full-sized scale model built for study, testing, or display ⟨a *mock-up* of an airplane⟩

mod \'mäd\ *adj* : MODERN; *esp* : bold, free, and unconventional in dress, style, or behavior

mod·al \'mōd-əl\ *adj* : relating to or being a grammatical form or category that characteristically expresses a point of view (as concerning desirability, possibility, or necessity) about the being or occurrence of something — **modal** *n*

modal auxiliary *n* : a verb (as *can, must, might, may*) that is characteristically used with a verb of predication and expresses a modal modification

1**mode** \'mōd\ *n* **1** : 2MOOD **2** : a form or manner of expression or acting : WAY ⟨a *mode* of travel⟩ **3** : the most frequent value of a frequency distribution

2**mode** *n* : a prevailing fashion or style

1**mod·el** \'mäd-əl\ *n* **1 a** : a small but exact copy of something ⟨a ship *model*⟩ **b** : a pattern or figure of something to be made ⟨clay *models* for a statue⟩ **2** : a person who sets a good example ⟨a *model* of politeness⟩ **3 a** : a person or thing that serves as an artist's pattern; *esp* : a person who poses for an artist or photographer **b** : a person who wears in the presence of customers garments that are for sale or who poses for ads for merchandise (as clothes) **4** : TYPE, KIND ⟨his car is a late *model*⟩ **5 a** : a description or analogy used to help visualize something (as an atom) that cannot be directly observed **b** : a system constructed of fact and reason that is used to describe mathematically an object or state of affairs ***syn*** see PATTERN

2**model** *vb* **mod·eled** *or* **mod·elled**; **mod·el·ing** *or* **mod·el·ling** \'mäd-(ə-)ling\ **1** : to plan or shape after a pattern ⟨a sports car *modeled* on a racing car⟩ **2** : to make a model : MOLD ⟨*model* a dog in clay⟩ **3** : to act or serve as a model ⟨*model* for an artist⟩ — **mod·el·er** *or* **mod·el·ler** \-(ə-)lər\ *n*

3**model** *adj* **1** : serving as or worthy of being a pattern ⟨a *model* student⟩ **2** : being a miniature representation of something ⟨a *model* airplane⟩

1**mod·er·ate** \'mäd-(ə-)rət\ *adj* **1** : neither very much nor very little : not extreme ⟨*moderate* heat⟩ **2** : avoiding extremes : TEMPERATE ⟨*moderate* in his habits⟩ **3** : REASONABLE, CALM ⟨*moderate* in his protests⟩ **4** : neither very good nor very bad : MEDIOCRE ⟨*moderate* success⟩ **5** : reasonable in price ⟨*moderate* rates⟩ — **mod·er·ate·ly** *adv* — **mod·er·ate·ness** *n*

2**mod·er·ate** \'mäd-ə-ˌrāt\ *vb* **1** : to make or become less violent, severe, or intense **2** : to preside over a meeting

3**mod·er·ate** \'mäd-(ə-)rət\ *n* : one holding moderate views or belonging to a moderate group (as in politics)

moderate breeze *n* : wind having a speed of 13 to 18 miles per hour

moderate gale *n* : wind having a speed of 32 to 38 miles per hour

mod·er·a·tion \ˌmäd-ə-'rā-shən\ *n* **1** : the action of moderating **2** : the quality or state of being moderate : avoidance of extremes ⟨do everything in *moderation*⟩

mod·er·a·to \ˌmäd-ə-'rät-ō\ *adv or adj* : MODERATE — used as a direction in music to indicate tempo

mod·er·a·tor \'mäd-ə-ˌrāt-ər\ *n* **1** : one that moderates **2** : a presiding officer (as of a Presbyterian governing body, a town meeting, or a discussion group) **3** : a substance (as graphite) used for slowing down neutrons in a nuclear reactor — **mod·er·a·tor·ship** \-ˌship\ *n*

1**mod·ern** \'mäd-ərn\ *adj* **1** : of, relating to, or characteristic of the present or the immediate past : CONTEMPORARY **2** : of or relating to the period from about 1500 to the present ⟨*modern* history⟩ — **mo·der·ni·ty** \mə-'dər-nət-ē, mä-\ *n* — **mod·ern·ness** \-ərn-nəs\ *n*

2**modern** *n* : a person of modern times or with modern views

Modern English *n* : the English language of the period from about 1500 to the present

mod·ern·ism \'mäd-ər-ˌniz-əm\ *n* : a modern practice; *esp* : a modern usage, expression, characteristic, or style — **mod·ern·ist** \-nəst\ *n or adj* — **mod·ern·is·tic** \ˌmäd-ər-'nis-tik\ *adj*

mod·ern·ize \'mäd-ər-ˌnīz\ *vb* : to make or become modern; *esp* : to alter to modern tastes and provide with modern equipment ⟨*modernize* an old house⟩ — **mod·ern·i·za·tion** \ˌmäd-ər-nə-'zā-shən\ *n* — **mod·ern·iz·er** \'mäd-ər-ˌnī-zər\ *n*

mod·est \'mäd-əst\ *adj* **1** : having a moderate opinion of one's own good qualities and abilities : not boastful ⟨a *modest* winner⟩ **2** : showing moderation : not excessive ⟨a *modest* request⟩ ⟨a *modest* cottage⟩ **3** : pure in thought, conduct, and dress : DECENT ⟨a *modest* girl⟩ — **mod·est·ly** *adv*

mod·es·ty \'mäd-ə-stē\ *n* : the quality of being modest

mod·i·cum \'mäd-i-kəm, 'mōd-\ *n* : a small amount ⟨anyone with a *modicum* of intelligence should understand it⟩

mod·i·fi·ca·tion \ˌmäd-ə-fə-'kā-shən\ *n* **1 a** : the act of modifying **b** : the state of being modified **2** : QUALIFICATION, LIMITATION ⟨a *modification* of a statement made in haste⟩ **3** : partial alteration ⟨*modification* of plans⟩ **4** : a change in an organism that is caused by the environment and is not inherited

mod·i·fi·er \'mäd-ə-ˌfī(-ə)r\ *n* : a word (as an adjective or adverb) joined to another word to limit or qualify its meaning

mod·i·fy \'mäd-ə-ˌfī\ *vb* **-fied**; **-fy·ing** **1** : to make changes in : ALTER ⟨*modify* a plan⟩ **2** : to lower or reduce in extent or degree : MODERATE **3** : to limit in meaning : QUALIFY ⟨in the phrase "green gloves" "green" *modifies* "gloves"⟩ — **mod·i·fi·a·ble** \-ˌfī-ə-bəl\ *adj*

mod·ish \ˈmōd-ish\ *adj* : FASHIONABLE ***syn*** see STYLISH — **mod·ish·ly** *adv* — **mod·ish·ness** *n*

mod·u·lar arithmetic \ˌmäj-ə-lər-\ *n* : an arithmetic based on a finite set of numbers in which the results of operations are expressed as remainders found by dividing by the modulus — called also *clock arithmetic, finite arithmetic*

mod·u·late \ˈmäj-ə-ˌlāt\ *vb* **1** : to adjust or regulate to a certain proportion; *esp* : to tone down : SOFTEN ⟨*modulated* his voice⟩ **2** : to tune to a key or pitch **3** : to vary a quality of an electric wave in radio and television in accordance with a quality of another electric wave; *esp* : to vary the frequency or amplitude of the carrier wave in accordance with the electric wave that carries the sound or picture **4** : to pass from one musical key to another usu. in a gradual movement — **mod·u·la·tor** \-ˌlāt-ər\ *n* — **mod·u·la·to·ry** \-lə-ˌtōr-ē, -ˌtȯr-\ *adj*

mod·u·la·tion \ˌmäj-ə-ˈlā-shən\ *n* **1** : an action of modulating **2** : the extent or degree by which something is modulated **3** : variation of some quality (as the frequency or amplitude) of the carrier wave in radio or television in accordance with the sound or picture that is to be transmitted

mod·ule \ˈmäj-ül\ *n* **1** : a usu. packaged subassembly of parts (as for an electronic device) **2** : an independent unit of a space vehicle ⟨a propulsion *module*⟩

mod·u·lo \ˈmäj-ə-ˌlō\ *prep* : with respect to a modulus of

mod·u·lus \ˈmäj-ə-ləs\ *n, pl* **-li** \-ˌlī, -ˌlē\ : the cardinal number of a finite set of numbers upon which a particular modular arithmetic is based

mo·gul \ˈmō-(ˌ)gəl, mō-ˈgəl\ *n* [from Persian *mughul*, from Mongolian *Mongol* meaning "a Mongolian"] **1** *or* **moghul** *cap* : a member of a Turkish and Mongolian dynasty that ruled India from the 16th to the 18th century **2** : a great personage : MAGNATE

mo·hair \ˈmō-ˌha(ə)r, -ˌhe(ə)r\ *n* **1** : a fabric or yarn made wholly or in part of the long silky hair of the Angora goat **2** : the hair of the Angora goat

Mo·ham·med·an *var of* MUHAMMADAN

Mo·hawk \ˈmō-ˌhȯk\ *n* : a member of an Iroquoian Amerindian people of the Mohawk river valley, New York

Mo·hi·can \mō-ˈhē-kən\ *n* **1** : a member of an Amerindian people of the upper Hudson river valley **2** *or* **Mo·he·gan** \-ˈhē-gən\ : a member of an Amerindian people of southeastern Connecticut

Mohs' scale \ˈmōz-, ˈmōs-, ˌmō-səz-\ *n* : a scale of hardness for minerals ranging from 1 for the softest to 10 for the hardest

moi·e·ty \ˈmȯi-ət-ē\ *n, pl* **-ties** : one of two equal or approximately equal parts : HALF

moi·ré \mȯ-ˈrā, mwä-\ *or* **moire** *same, or* ˈmȯi(ə)r, ˈmwär\ *n* : a fabric (as silk) having a watered appearance — **moiré** *adj*

moist \ˈmȯist\ *adj* : slightly wet ⟨*moist* earth⟩ — **moist·ly** *adv* — **moist·ness** \ˈmȯis(t)-nəs\ *n*

syn MOIST, DAMP, DANK can mean wet to some degree less than soaking or saturated. MOIST suggests a barely perceptible wetness; DAMP suggests a moderate wetness sometimes disagreeable to contact; DANK usu. suggests an unpleasantly chill and penetrating dampness and often implies mustiness and decay

ə abut	ər further	a back	ā bake
ä cot, cart	au̇ out	ch chin	e less	ē easy
g gift	i trip	ī life	j joke	ng sing	ō flow
ȯ flaw	ȯi coin	th thin	th this	ü loot
u̇ foot	y yet	yü few	yu̇ furious	zh vision

moist·en \ˈmȯis-ən\ *vb* **moist·ened**; **moist·en·ing** \-(ə-)ning\ : to make or become moist — **moist·en·er** \-(ə-)nər\ *n*

mois·ture \ˈmȯis-chər\ *n* : the small amount of liquid that causes moistness : DAMPNESS

mol *abbr* **1** molecular **2** molecule

[1]**mo·lar** \ˈmō-lər\ *n* [from Latin *molaris*, from the adjective *molaris* "grinding", derived from *mola* "mill"] : a tooth with a rounded or flattened surface adapted for grinding : a cheek tooth behind the premolars of a mammal

[2]**molar** *adj* **1** : able or fitted to grind **2** : of or relating to a molar

mo·las·ses \mə-ˈlas-əz\ *n* : a thick brown syrup that is separated from raw sugar in sugar manufacture

[1]**mold** \ˈmōld\ *n* : light rich crumbly earth containing decayed organic matter (as leaves)

[2]**mold** *n* **1** : the frame on, around, or in which something is constructed or shaped ⟨a candle *mold*⟩ ⟨a *mold* for gelatin⟩ **2** : something shaped in a mold ⟨a *mold* of ice cream⟩

[3]**mold** *vb* **1** : to knead into shape ⟨*mold* loaves of bread⟩ **2** : to form or become formed in or as if in a mold — **mold·er** *n*

[4]**mold** *n* : an often fuzzy surface growth of fungus esp. on damp or decaying organic matter; *also* : a fungus that produces mold

[5]**mold** *vb* : to become moldy

mol·der \ˈmōl-dər\ *vb* **mol·dered**; **mol·der·ing** \-d(ə-)ring\ : to crumble into particles

mold·ing \ˈmōl-ding\ *n* **1** : the act or work of a person who molds **2** : an object produced by molding **3** : a strip of material having a shaped surface and used as a decoration (as on a wall or the edge of a table)

moldy \ˈmōl-dē\ *adj* **mold·i·er**; **-est** : consisting of or covered with mold ⟨*moldy* bread⟩ — **mold·i·ness** *n*

[1]**mole** \ˈmōl\ *n* : a small usu. brown and sometimes protruding persistent spot on the skin

[2]**mole** *n* : any of numerous burrowing insect-eating mammals with tiny eyes, concealed ears, and soft fur

[3]**mole** *n* : a heavy masonry structure built in the sea as a breakwater or pier

mole cricket *n* : an insect that is related to the grasshoppers and crickets, has large front legs used for digging, and feeds largely on roots of plants

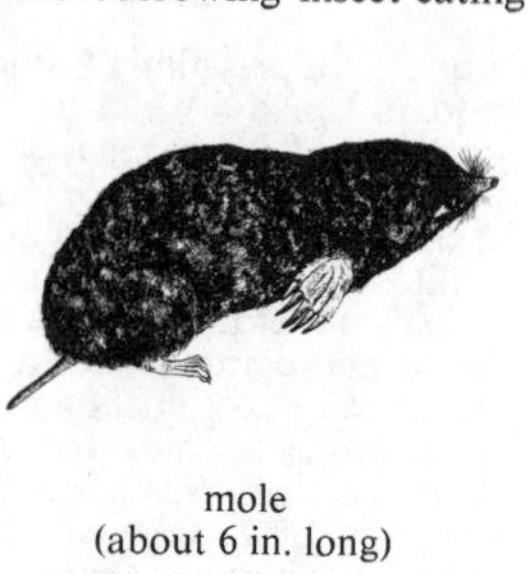

mole
(about 6 in. long)

mo·lec·u·lar \mə-ˈlek-yə-lər\ *adj* **1** : relating to molecules **2** : produced by or consisting of molecules

molecular formula *n* : a chemical formula that gives the total number of atoms of each element present in a molecule

molecular weight *n* : the weight of a molecule equal to the sum of the weights of the atoms contained in it

mol·e·cule \ˈmäl-i-ˌkyül\ *n* **1** : the smallest portion of a substance retaining all the properties of the substance in a mass ⟨a *molecule* of water⟩ ⟨a *molecule* of oxygen⟩ **2** : a very small bit : PARTICLE

mole·hill \'mōl-ˌhil\ *n* **1** : a little ridge of earth thrown up by a mole **2** : an unimportant obstacle

mo·lest \mə-'ləst\ *vb* **1** : to injure or disturb by interfering : ANNOY **2** : to take indecent liberties with — **mo·les·ta·tion** \ˌmō-ˌles-'tā-shən, ˌmäl-ˌes-\ *n* — **mo·lest·er** \mə-'les-tər\ *n*

mol·lie \'mäl-ē\ *n* : any of several brightly colored topminnows often kept in a tropical aquarium

mol·li·fy \'mäl-ə-ˌfī\ *vb* **-fied**; **-fy·ing** **1** : CALM, QUIET **2** : to soothe in temper or disposition : CONCILIATE ***syn*** see PACIFY ***ant*** exasperate — **mol·li·fi·ca·tion** \ˌmäl-ə-fə-'kā-shən\ *n*

mol·lusk *or* **mol·lusc** \'mäl-əsk\ *n* : any of a large phylum of invertebrate animals (as snails or clams) with a soft body lacking segments and usu. enclosed in a shell containing calcium — **mol·lus·can** *also* **mol·lus·kan** \mə-'ləs-kən, mä-\ *adj*

1**mol·ly·cod·dle** \'mäl-ē-ˌkäd-əl\ *n* : a pampered man or boy : SISSY

2**mollycoddle** *vb* **-cod·dled**; **-cod·dling** \-ˌkäd-(ə-)ling\ : CODDLE, PAMPER

1**molt** \'mōlt\ *vb* : to shed hair, feathers, outer skin, or horns with the cast-off parts being replaced by a new growth

2**molt** *n* : the act, process, or period of molting

mol·ten \'mōlt-ən\ *adj* : melted esp. by intense heat

mol·to \'mōl-tō, 'mȯl-\ *adv* : MUCH, VERY — used in music directions

mol wt *abbr* molecular weight

mo·lyb·de·num \-mə-'lib-də-nəm\ *n* : a white metallic element used in steel alloys to give greater strength and hardness — see ELEMENT table

mo·ment \'mō-mənt\ *n* **1** : a small portion of time : INSTANT **2** : a time of importance or success ⟨a great *moment* for him⟩ **3** : IMPORTANCE, CONSEQUENCE ⟨a matter of great *moment*⟩

mo·men·tar·i·ly \ˌmō-mən-'ter-ə-lē\ *adv* **1** : for a moment ⟨the pain eased *momentarily*⟩ **2** : INSTANTLY ⟨he was stunned but recovered *momentarily*⟩ **3** : at any moment ⟨we expect him *momentarily*⟩

mo·men·tary \'mō-mən-ˌter-ē\ *adj* : lasting only a moment

mo·ment·ly \'mō-mənt-lē\ *adv* : MOMENTARILY

mo·men·tous \mō-'ment-əs\ *adj* : very important ⟨a *momentous* decision⟩ — **mo·men·tous·ly** *adv*

mo·men·tum \mō-'ment-əm\ *n, pl* **-men·ta** \-'ment-ə\ *or* **-mentums** : a property of a moving body that determines the length of time required to bring it to rest when under the action of a constant force : the product of the mass of a body and its velocity; *also* : IMPETUS

mon- *or* **mono-** *comb form* **1** : one : single : alone ⟨*mono*plane⟩ **2** : one atom or group ⟨*mon*oxide⟩

Mon *abbr* Monday

mon·arch \'män-ərk, -ˌärk\ *n* **1** : a person who reigns over a kingdom or empire **2** : someone or something likened to a monarch ⟨the oak is the *monarch* of the forest⟩ **3** : a large orange and black migratory American butterfly — called also *monarch butterfly* — **mo·nar·chal** \mə-'när-kəl, mä-\ *or* **mo·nar·chi·al** \-kē-əl\ *adj*

monarch 3
(up to 4 in. across)

mo·nar·chi·cal \mə-'när-ki-kəl, mä-\ *or* **mo·nar·chic** \-'när-kik\ *adj* **1** : of or relating to a monarch or monarchy ⟨*monarchical* government⟩ **2** : favoring monarchism

mon·ar·chism \'män-ər-ˌkiz-əm\ *n* **1** : the principles of monarchy **2** : belief in or support of monarchism — **mon·ar·chist** \-kəst\ *n*

mon·ar·chy \'män-ər-kē\ *n, pl* **-chies** **1** : rule by a monarch **2** : a nation or country having a monarch **3** : a form of government headed by a monarch

mon·as·tery \'män-ə-ˌster-ē\ *n, pl* **-ter·ies** : a building or set of buildings in which a community of religious persons and esp. monks live and work — **mon·as·te·ri·al** \ˌmän-ə-'stir-ē-əl\ *adj*

mo·nas·tic \mə-'nas-tik\ *adj* **1** : of or relating to monks or monasteries **2** : separated from worldly affairs ⟨a *monastic* life⟩ — **monastic** *n* — **mo·nas·ti·cal·ly** \-ti-k(ə-)lē\ *adv*

mo·nas·ti·cism \mə-'nas-tə-ˌsiz-əm\ *n* : the system or practice of living apart from the rest of the world for religious reasons esp. as members of a secluded community

mon·au·ral \(')män-'ȯ-rəl\ *adj* : MONOPHONIC — **mon·au·ral·ly** \-rə-lē\ *adv*

Mon·day \'mən-dē\ *n* [from Old English *mōnandæg*, meaning "day of the moon", a translation of Latin *lunae dies*] : the 2d day of the week

mon·ecious *var of* MONOECIOUS

mon·e·tary \'män-ə-ˌter-ē, 'mən-\ *adj* **1** : of or relating to coinage or currency ⟨*monetary* policy⟩ **2** : of or relating to money : PECUNIARY ⟨*monetary* gifts⟩

mon·e·tize \'män-ə-ˌtīz, 'mən-\ *vb* : to establish as the standard of a currency ⟨*monetize* silver⟩ — **mon·e·ti·za·tion** \ˌmän-ət-ə-'zā-shən, ˌmən-\ *n*

mon·ey \'mən-ē\ *n, pl* **moneys** *or* **mon·ies** \-ēz\ **1 a** : something (as coins or governmental promissory notes) generally accepted as a means of payment **b** : a sum of money **c** : wealth reckoned in terms of money **2** : the 1st, 2d, and 3d place in a horse or dog race ⟨finished in the *money*⟩ — **mon·ey·lend·er** \'mən-ē-ˌlen-dər\ *n*

mon·ey·bags \'mən-ē-ˌbagz\ *n sing or pl* : a wealthy person

money changer *n* : one whose business is the exchanging of kinds or denominations of currency

mon·eyed *or* **mon·ied** \'mən-ēd\ *adj* : having money : WEALTHY

money order *n* : an order purchased at a post office, bank, or express or telegraph office directing another office to pay a specified sum of money to a person or firm named on it

Mon·gol \'mäng-gəl, 'män-ˌgōl\ *n* **1** : a member of one of the Mongoloid peoples of Mongolia **2** : MONGOLIAN 2

Mon·go·lian \män-'gōl-yən\ *n* **1** : a native or inhabitant of Mongolia **2** : the language of the Mongol people — **Mongolian** *adj*

mon·gol·ism \'mäng-gə-ˌliz-əm\ *also* **mon·go·lian·ism** \män-'gōl-yə-ˌniz-əm\ *n* : a birth defect characterized by slanting eyes, a broad short skull, broad hands with short fingers, and mental deficiency

mon·gol·oid \'mäng-gə-ˌlȯid\ *adj* **1** *cap* : of or relating to peoples of northern and eastern Asia and Malaysia and the Eskimos and often the American Indians **2** : affected with mongolism — **mongoloid** *n, often cap*

mon·goose \'män-güs, 'mäng-\ *n, pl* **mon·goos·es** : a small agile Indian mammal that is related to the civet cats and feeds on snakes and rodents

mongoose
(up to 33 in. long)

mon·grel \'məng-grəl, 'mäng-\ *n* **1 :** the offspring of parents of different breeds (as of dogs); *esp* **:** one of uncertain ancestry **2 :** a person or thing of mixed origin — **mongrel** *adj* — **mon·grel·i·za·tion** \ˌməng-grə-lə-'zā-shən, ˌmäng-\ *n* — **mon·grel·ize** \'məng-grə-ˌlīz, 'mäng-\ *vb*

1**mon·i·tor** \'män-ət-ər\ *n* **1 a :** a student appointed to assist a teacher **b :** a person that warns or instructs **c :** one that monitors or is used in monitoring; *esp* **:** a receiver used to view the picture being picked up by a television camera **2 :** any of various large tropical Old World lizards closely related to the iguanas **3 :** a heavily armored warship having low sides and one or more revolving gun turrets and formerly used in coastal operations

2**monitor** *vb* **mon·i·tored; mon·i·tor·ing** \'män-ət-ə-ring, 'män-ə-tring\ **:** to watch, observe, or check for a special purpose ⟨*monitor* a broadcast for sound quality⟩

monk \'məngk\ *n* [from Old English *munuc*, from Greek *monachos*, from *monos* "alone", the source also of English *monastery*] **1 :** a member of a religious order of men taking vows of poverty, chastity, and obedience and living in community under a rule **2 :** a man who renounces the world for religious reasons — **monk·ish** \'məng-kish\ *adj*

1**mon·key** \'məng-kē\ *n, pl* **monkeys 1 :** a primate mammal other than man and usu. also the lemurs and tarsiers; *esp* **:** any of the smaller longer-tailed primates as contrasted with the apes **2 a :** a mischievous child **:** IMP **b :** DUPE — **mon·key·ish** \-kē-ish\ *adj*

2**monkey** *vb* **mon·keyed; mon·key·ing 1 :** to act in a grotesque or mischievous manner **2 :** TRIFLE, MEDDLE

mon·key·shine \'məng-kē-ˌshīn\ *n* **:** a mischievous trick **:** PRANK

monkey wrench *n* **:** a wrench with one fixed and one adjustable jaw at right angles to the handle

monks·hood \'məng(k)s-ˌhu̇d\ *n* **:** a poisonous herb related to the buttercups and having showy hood-shaped white or purplish flowers

mono- — see MON-

mono·chro·mat·ic \ˌmän-ə-krō-'mat-ik\ *adj* **1 :** having or consisting of one color **2 :** consisting of radiation (as light) of a single wavelength — **mono·chro·mat·i·cal·ly** \-'mat-i-k(ə-)lē\ *adv*

mono·chro·ma·tism \-'krō-mə-ˌtiz-əm\ *n* **:** complete color blindness in which all colors appear as shades of gray

mono·chrome \'män-ə-ˌkrōm\ *n* **:** a painting, drawing, or photograph in a single hue — **monochrome** *adj*

mon·o·cle \'män-i-kəl\ *n* **:** an eyeglass for one eye — **mon·o·cled** \-kəld\ *adj*

mon·o·cot \'män-ə-ˌkät\ *also* **mon·o·cot·yl** \-ˌkät-əl\ *n* **:** MONOCOTYLEDON — **monocot** *adj*

mono·cot·y·le·don \ˌmän-ə-ˌkät-ə-'lēd-ən\ *n* **:** any of a group of seed plants (as the palms and grasses) having an embryo with a single cotyledon and usu. parallel-veined leaves and flower parts in groups of three — **mono·cot·y·le·don·ous** \-'lēd-ə-nəs\ *adj*

mon·oe·cious \mə-'nē-shəs, (')män-'ē-\ *adj* **1 :** having male and female sex organs in the same individual **:** HERMAPHRODITIC **2 :** having on the same plant flowers with stamens only and flowers with pistils only — **mon·oe·cism** \mə-'nē-ˌsiz-əm, (')män-'ē-\ *or* **mon·oe·cy** \'män-ˌē-sē\ *n*

mo·nog·a·my \mə-'näg-ə-mē\ *n* **:** marriage with but one person at a time — **mo·nog·a·mist** \-məst\ *n* — **mo·nog·a·mous** \-məs\ *adj*

mono·gram \'män-ə-ˌgram\ *n* **:** an identifying symbol usu. made up of a person's initials — **monogrammed** \-ˌgramd\ *adj*

mono·graph \-ˌgraf\ *n* **:** a scholarly or scientific paper printed in a journal or separately

mon·o·lith \'män-ə-ˌlith\ *n* **1 :** a single great stone often in the form of a monument or column **2 :** something (as a political organization or a social structure) held to be a single massive whole — **mon·o·lith·ic** \ˌmän-ə-'lith-ik\ *adj*

mon·o·logue *or* **mon·o·log** \'män-ə-ˌlȯg\ *n* **1 :** a dramatic sketch performed by one actor **2 :** a literary composition (as a poem) in the form of a soliloquy **3 :** a long speech uttered by one person — **mon·o·logu·ist** \'män-ə-ˌlȯg-əst\ *n*

mono·ma·nia \ˌmän-ə-'mā-nē-ə, -'mā-nyə\ *n* **1 :** mental disorder characterized by deranged thinking in regard to one idea or group of ideas **2 :** excessive concentration on a single object or idea — **mono·ma·ni·ac** \-'mā-nē-ˌak\ *n or adj*

mon·o·mer \'män-ə-mər\ *n* **:** one of the molecular units of a polymer — **mon·o·mer·ic** \ˌmän-ə-'mer-ik\ *adj*

mono·phon·ic \ˌmän-ə-'fän-ik\ *adj* **:** of or relating to sound recording or reproduction involving a single transmission path

mono·plane \'män-ə-ˌplān\ *n* **:** an airplane with one main supporting surface

mo·nop·o·list \mə-'näp-ə-ləst\ *n* **:** one who has a monopoly or favors monopoly

mo·nop·o·lize \mə-'näp-ə-ˌlīz\ *vb* **:** to acquire or have a monopoly of — **mo·nop·o·li·za·tion** \-ˌnäp-ə-lə-'zā-shən\ *n* — **mo·nop·o·liz·er** \-'näp-ə-ˌlī-zər\ *n*

mo·nop·o·ly \mə-'näp-(ə-)lē\ *n, pl* **-lies 1 a :** exclusive ownership or control of a commodity or supply **b :** exclusive possession ⟨has a *monopoly* on bad manners⟩ **2 :** a commodity controlled by one party **3 :** a person or group having a monopoly — **mo·nop·o·lis·tic** \-ˌnäp-ə-'lis-tik\ *adj*

mono·rail \'män-ə-ˌrāl\ *n* **:** a single rail serving as a track for cars that are balanced upon it or suspended from it

mono·sac·cha·ride \ˌmän-ə-'sak-ə-ˌrīd\ *n* **:** a sugar that cannot be split into simpler sugars by reaction with water

mono·syl·la·ble \'män-ə-ˌsil-ə-bəl, ˌmän-ə-'\ *n* **:** a word of one syllable — **mono·syl·lab·ic** \ˌmän-ə-sə-'lab-ik\ *adj*

mono·the·ism \'män-ə-(ˌ)thē-ˌiz-əm\ *n* **:** a doctrine or belief that there is only one deity — **mono·the·ist** \-ˌthē-əst\ *n* — **mono·the·is·tic** \-thē-'is-tik\ *adj*

mono·tone \'män-ə-ˌtōn\ *n* **1 :** a succession of syllables, words, or sentences on one unvaried key or pitch ⟨speak in a *monotone*⟩ **2 :** a single unvaried musical tone **3 a :** sameness of tone or style ⟨a poem written in *monotone*⟩ **b :** sameness of color ⟨engravings in *monotone*⟩ **4 :** a person not able to produce musical intervals properly with the voice

mo·not·o·nous \mə-'nät-(ə-)nəs\ *adj* **1 :** uttered or sounded in one unvarying tone **2 :** tediously unvarying ⟨a *monotonous* voice⟩ — **mo·not·o·nous·ly** *adv* — **mo·not·o·nous·ness** *n*

mo·not·o·ny \mə-'nät-(ə-)nē\ *n, pl* **-nies 1 :** sameness of tone or sound **2 :** lack of variety; *esp* **:** tiresome sameness ⟨the *monotony* of the empty landscape⟩

mono·treme \'män-ə-ˌtrēm\ *n* : any of an order of primitive egg-laying mammals comprising the platypuses and echidnas

mon·ox·ide \mə-'näk-ˌsīd\ *n* : an oxide containing only one oxygen atom in the molecule

mon·sei·gneur \ˌmōn-ˌsān-'yər\ *n, pl* **mes·sei·gneurs** \ˌmā-ˌsān-'yər(z)\ : a French dignitary — used as a title preceding a title of office or rank ⟨*Monseigneur* the Archbishop⟩

mon·sieur \məs(h)-'yə(r), mə-'si(ə)r\ *n, pl* **mes·sieurs** *same, or with z added*\ — used as a title equivalent to *Mister* for a Frenchman

mon·si·gnor \män-'sē-nyər\ *n, pl* **mon·si·gnors** *or* **mon·si·gno·ri** \ˌmän-ˌsēn-'yōr-ē, -'yȯr-\ — used as a title for any of various Roman Catholic clergymen

mon·soon \män-'sün\ *n* **1** : a wind in the Indian ocean and southern Asia that blows from the southwest from April to October and from the northeast from October to April **2** : the rainy season that accompanies the southwest monsoon

1**mon·ster** \'män(t)-stər\ *n* **[**from Latin *monstrum*, meaning first "a portent", "divine warning", and derived from the verb *monstrare* "to show"; the meanings of the Latin and English noun result from the belief that the gods gave warnings to mortals by showing them freaks of nature**]** **1** : an animal or plant of abnormal form or structure **2** : a creature of strange or horrible form **3** : something unusually large **4** : an extremely wicked or cruel person

2**monster** *adj* : very large : ENORMOUS

mon·strance \'män(t)-strən(t)s\ *n* : a vessel in which the consecrated Host is exposed

mon·stros·i·ty \män-'sträs-ət-ē\ *n, pl* **-ties** **1** : the condition of being monstrous **2** : MONSTER

mon·strous \'män(t)-strəs\ *adj* **1** : unusually or excessively great in size : GIGANTIC **2** : very ugly or vicious : HORRIBLE **3** : shockingly wrong or ridiculous **4** : deviating greatly from the natural form or character — **mon·strous·ly** *adv*

syn MONSTROUS, TREMENDOUS, STUPENDOUS, COLOSSAL can mean of very great size. MONSTROUS usu. implies that something is abnormally great in size for its type; TREMENDOUS applies to something that inspires awe or fear by its immense size; STUPENDOUS implies a power to astound with size; COLOSSAL suggests size that is almost unimaginably great

Mont *abbr* Montana

mon·tage \män-'täzh\ *n* : an artistic composition made up of several different kinds of items (as strips of newspaper, pictures, bits of wood) arranged together

month \'mən(t)th\ *n, pl* **months** \'mən(t)s, 'mən(t)ths\ **[**from Old English *mōnath*, from the same source as English *moon;* so called because it was formerly measured by a complete revolution of the moon**]** **1** : one of the 12 portions into which the year is divided **2 a** : MOON 2 **b** : a period of 28 days regarded as the period of revolution of the moon

1**month·ly** \'mən(t)th-lē\ *adj* **1** : occurring, done, produced, or issued every month **2** : computed in terms of one month **3** : lasting a month — **monthly** *adv*

2**monthly** *n, pl* **monthlies** **1** : a monthly periodical **2** *pl* : a menstrual period

mon·u·ment \'män-yə-mənt\ *n* **1** : something that serves as a memorial; *esp* : a building, pillar, stone, or statue commemorating a person or event **2** : a work, saying, or deed that lasts or that is worth preserving ⟨the book is a *monument* of scholarship⟩ **3** : a boundary marker (as a stone) **4** : a natural feature or historic site set aside and maintained by the government as public property

mon·u·men·tal \ˌmän-yə-'ment-əl\ *adj* **1** : serving as a monument **2** : OUTSTANDING ⟨a *monumental* achievement⟩ **3** : relating to or suitable for a monument **4** : very great : COLOSSAL ⟨*monumental* stupidity⟩; *esp* : MASSIVE — **mon·u·men·tal·ly** \-ə-lē\ *adv*

moo \'mü\ *vb* : to make the natural throat noise of a cow : LOW — **moo** *n*

1**mood** \'müd\ *n* : a predominantly emotional state of mind: DISPOSITION ⟨in a good *mood*⟩

syn MOOD, HUMOR can mean a state of mind dominated by a single feeling. MOOD suggests strong emotion that influences one's words and actions for some time; HUMOR generally suggests a more whimsical or changeable emotion

2**mood** *n* : a set of inflectional forms of a verb that show whether the action or state expressed is to be thought of as a fact, a command, or a wish or possibility

moody \'müd-ē\ *adj* **mood·i·er**; **-est** **1** : subject to moods; *esp* : subject to fits of depression or bad temper **2** : expressing a moody state of mind ⟨a *moody* face⟩ — **mood·i·ly** \'müd-ə-lē\ *adv* — **mood·i·ness** \'müd-ē-nəs\ *n*

1**moon** \'mün\ *n* **1 a** : the earth's natural satellite shining by the sun's reflected light that revolves about the earth from west to east and has a diameter of 2160 miles, a mean distance from the earth of about 238,857 miles, and a volume about one forty-ninth that of the earth **b** : SATELLITE 2a **2** : the average period of revolution of the moon about the earth equal to about 29½ days **3** : MOONLIGHT — **moon·less** \-ləs\ *adj*

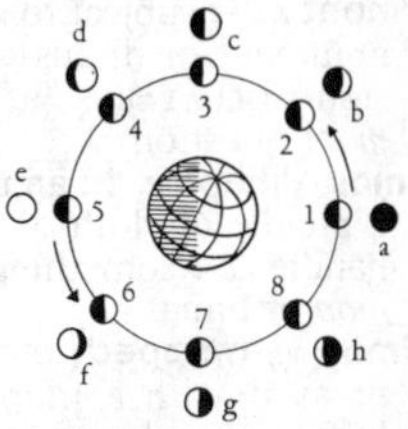

phases of the moon: 1–8 showing the moon in orbit around the earth; a–h corresponding phases as seen from the earth; l, new moon; 3, first quarter; 5, full moon; 7, last quarter; a, new moon; b, waxing crescent; c, half-moon; d, gibbous; e, full moon; f, gibbous; g, half-moon; h, waning crescent

2**moon** *vb* : to spend time in idle thought : DREAM ⟨*moon* away the hours⟩

moon·beam \'mün-ˌbēm\ *n* : a ray of light from the moon

moon·fish \-ˌfish\ *n* : any of various compressed often short deep-bodied silvery or yellowish marine fishes

moon·flow·er \-ˌflau̇(-ə)r\ *n* : a tropical American morning glory with fragrant night-blooming flowers; *also* : any of several related plants

1**moon·light** \-ˌlīt\ *n* : the light of the moon

2**moonlight** *vb* : to hold two jobs at the same time — **moon·light·er** *n*

moon·lit \'mün-ˌlit\ *adj* : lighted by the moon ⟨a *moonlit* night⟩

moon·scape \-ˌskāp\ *n* : the surface of the moon as seen or pictured

moon·shine \-ˌshīn\ *n* **1** : MOONLIGHT **2** : empty talk : NONSENSE **3** : intoxicating liquor; *esp* : illegally distilled corn whiskey — **moon·shin·er** \-ˌshī-nər\ *n*

moon·stone \-ˌstōn\ *n* : a transparent or translucent mineral with a pearly greenish or bluish luster that is a variety of feldspar and is used in jewelry

moon·struck \-ˌstrək\ *adj* **1** : mentally unbalanced **2** : romantically sentimental

[1]**moor** \'mu̇(ə)r\ *n* : an area of open wasteland that is usu. infertile or wet and peaty
[2]**moor** *vb* : to secure or fasten with cables, lines, or anchors ⟨*moor* a boat⟩ — **moor·age** \-ij\ *n*
moor·ing \'mu̇(ə)r-ing\ *n* **1** : a place where a craft can be made fast **2** : a device or line by which a craft is moored
moor·land \'mu̇(ə)r-lənd, -ˌland\ *n* : land consisting of moors
moose \'müs\ *n, pl* **moose** [from its name in some Algonquian language, such as Natick *moos*, derived from *moos-u* "he trims"; from the animal's habit of stripping bark and lower branches from trees] **1** : a large cud-chewing mammal related to the typical deers and found in forested parts of Canada and northern U.S. **2** : ELK 1

moose 1
(about 6 ft. at shoulder)

[1]**moot** \'müt\ *vb* **1** : to bring up for discussion **2** : DEBATE
[2]**moot** *adj* : subject to argument or discussion : DEBATABLE ⟨a *moot* question⟩
[1]**mop** \'mäp\ *n* **1** : an implement for cleaning made of a bundle of cloth or yarn or a sponge fastened to a handle **2** : something resembling a mop ⟨a tangled *mop* of hair⟩
[2]**mop** *vb* **mopped**; **mop·ping** : to wipe or clean with or as if with a mop ⟨*mop* the floor⟩ ⟨*mopped* his brow with a handkerchief⟩
[1]**mope** \'mōp\ *vb* : to be in a dull and dispirited state — **mop·er** *n*
[2]**mope** *n* **1** : a dull listless person **2** *pl* : low spirits : BLUES ⟨a fit of the *mopes*⟩
mop·pet \'mäp-ət\ *n* : a young child
mo·raine \mə-'rān\ *n* : an accumulation of earth and stones deposited by a glacier
[1]**mor·al** \'mȯr-əl, 'mär-\ *adj* **1 a** : of or relating to principles of right and wrong : ETHICAL **b** : expressing or teaching a conception of right behavior ⟨a *moral* poem⟩ **c** : conforming to a standard of right behavior : GOOD ⟨*moral* conduct⟩ ⟨a *moral* man⟩ **d** : capable of right and wrong action ⟨man is a *moral* being⟩ **2** : probable but not proved : VIRTUAL ⟨a *moral* certainty⟩ — **mor·al·ly** \-ə-lē\ *adv*
[2]**moral** *n* **1** : the lesson to be learned from a story or an experience **2** *pl* : moral conduct ⟨men of bad *morals*⟩ **3** *pl* : moral teachings or principles
mo·rale \mə-'ral\ *n* : the mental and emotional condition (as of enthusiasm, spirit, loyalty) of an individual or a group
mor·al·ist \'mȯr-ə-ləst, 'mär-\ *n* **1** : one who moralizes; *esp* : a person who teaches, studies, or points out morals **2** : one who leads a moral life

ə abut	ər further	a back	ā bake
ä cot, cart	au̇ out	ch chin	e less
ē easy	g gift	i trip	ī life
j joke	ng sing	ō flow	ȯ flaw
ȯi coin	th thin	th this	ü loot
u̇ foot	y yet	yü few	yu̇ furious
zh vision			

mor·al·is·tic \ˌmȯr-ə-'lis-tik, ˌmär-\ *adj* **1** : teaching or pointing out morals : MORALIZING ⟨a *moralistic* story⟩ **2** : conventional in morals ⟨a *moralistic* attitude toward the problems of youth⟩ — **mor·al·is·ti·cal·ly** \-ti-k(ə-)lē\ *adv*
mo·ral·i·ty \mə-'ral-ət-ē\ *n, pl* **-ties** **1** : moral quality of character : VIRTUE ⟨judge the *morality* of an action⟩ **2** : moral conduct : MORALS ⟨standards of *morality*⟩ **3** : a system of moral principles
morality play *n* : an allegorical play esp. of the 15th and 16th centuries in which the characters personify moral qualities or abstractions
mor·al·ize \'mȯr-ə-ˌlīz, 'mär-\ *vb* **1** : to explain in a moral sense : draw a moral from **2** : to make moral or morally better **3** : to make moral comments — **mor·al·i·za·tion** \ˌmȯr-ə-lə-'zā-shən, ˌmär-\ *n* — **mor·al·iz·er** \'mȯr-ə-ˌlī-zər, 'mär-\ *n*
mo·rass \mə-'ras\ *n* : MARSH, SWAMP — **mo·rassy** \-'ras-ē\ *adj*
mor·a·to·ri·um \ˌmȯr-ə-'tōr-ē-əm, ˌmär-, -'tȯr-\ *n, pl* **-ri·ums** *or* **-ria** \-ē-ə\ **1** : a legally authorized period of delay in the payment of a debt **2** : BAN, SUSPENSION ⟨a *moratorium* on atomic testing⟩
mo·ray \mə-'rā, 'mȯr-ˌā\ *n* : any of numerous often brightly colored savage voracious eels occurring in warm seas
mor·bid \'mȯr-bəd\ *adj* **1 a** : of, relating to, or characteristic of disease **b** : not healthful : DISEASED ⟨*morbid* condition⟩ **2** : characterized by gloomy or unwholesome ideas or feelings ⟨takes a *morbid* interest in funerals⟩ — **mor·bid·ly** *adv* — **mor·bid·ness** *n*
mor·bid·i·ty \mȯr-'bid-ət-ē\ *n, pl* **-ties** **1** : the quality or state of being morbid **2** : the frequency of diseased individuals in a population
[1]**mor·dant** \'mȯrd-ənt\ *adj* : BITING, SARCASTIC ⟨*mordant* criticism⟩
[2]**mordant** *n* **1** : a chemical that fixes a dye in or on a substance by combining with the dye to form an insoluble compound **2** : a corroding substance used in etching
[3]**mordant** *vb* : to treat with a mordant
[1]**more** \'mō(ə)r, 'mȯ(ə)r\ *adj* **1** : greater in amount or degree ⟨*more* bother than it's worth⟩ ⟨felt *more* pain⟩ **2** : ADDITIONAL, FURTHER ⟨bought *more* apples⟩ ⟨has to read a few *more* pages⟩
[2]**more** *adv* **1** : in addition **2** : to a greater or higher degree — often used with an adjective or adverb to form the comparative ⟨*more* active⟩ ⟨*more* actively⟩
[3]**more** *n* **1** : a greater amount or number ⟨got *more* than he expected⟩ **2** : an additional amount ⟨too full to eat *more*⟩ **3** : additional persons or things ⟨the *more* the merrier⟩
mo·rel \mə-'rel\ *n* : any of several large pitted edible fungi
more·over \mōr-'ō-vər, mȯr-\ *adv* : in addition to what has been said : BESIDES
mo·res \'mȯ(ə)r-ˌāz, 'mō(ə)r-, -ˌēz\ *n pl* **1** : the fixed morally binding customs of a particular group **2** : CUSTOMS, CONVENTIONS
Mor·gan \'mȯr-gən\ *n* : any of an American breed of light horses
mor·ga·nat·ic marriage \ˌmȯr-gə-ˌnat-ik-\ *n* : a marriage between a person of royal or noble rank and a commoner who does not assume the superior partner's rank and whose children do not succeed to the title or inheritance of the parent of superior rank

morel
(up to 4 in. high)

morgue \'mȯrg\ *n* **1 :** a place where the bodies of persons found dead are kept temporarily usu. for identification **2 :** a department of a newspaper where reference material is filed

mor·i·bund \'mȯr-ə-(ˌ)bənd, 'mär-\ *adj* **:** being in a dying state

morn \'mȯrn\ *n* **:** MORNING

morn·ing \'mȯr-ning\ *n* **1 a :** DAWN **b :** the time from sunrise to noon **c :** the time from midnight to noon **2 :** the first or early part ⟨the *morning* of life⟩

morning glory *n* **:** any of various usu. twining plants with showy trumpet-shaped flowers that usu. close by the middle of the day; *also* **:** any of various related plants including herbs, vines, shrubs, or trees with alternate leaves and usu. funnel-shaped flowers

morning sickness *n* **:** nausea on arising usu. associated with early pregnancy

morning star *n* **:** any of the planets Jupiter, Mars, Mercury, Saturn, and esp. Venus when it rises before the sun

Mo·roc·can \mə-'räk-ən\ *adj* **:** of, relating to, or characteristic of Morocco or its people — **Moroccan** *n*

mo·roc·co \mə-'räk-ō\ *n* **:** a fine leather made of goat skins tanned with sumac

mo·ron \'mōr-ˌän, 'mȯr-\ *n* **1 :** a feebleminded person having a potential mental age of between 8 and 12 years and being capable of doing routine work under supervision **2 :** a very stupid person — **mo·ron·ic** \mə-'rän-ik, mȯ-\ *adj*

mo·rose \mə-'rōs\ *adj* **:** SULLEN, GLOOMY — **mo·rose·ly** *adv* — **mo·rose·ness** *n*

mor·pheme \'mȯr-ˌfēm\ *n* **:** a word or a part of a word (as an affix or a base) that contains no smaller unit of meaning — **mor·phe·mic** \mȯr-'fē-mik\ *adj*

mor·phine \'mȯr-ˌfēn\ *n* [after *Morpheus*, Greek god of dreams] **:** a bitter white crystalline habit-forming narcotic made from opium and used esp. to deaden pain

mor·phol·o·gy \mȯr-'fäl-ə-jē\ *n* **1 a :** a branch of biology that deals with the form and structure of animals and plants **b :** the form and structure of an organism or any of its parts **2 :** the part of grammar dealing with word formation and including inflection, derivation, and the formation of compounds **3 :** STRUCTURE, FORM ⟨the *morphology* of rocks⟩ — **mor·pho·log·i·cal** \ˌmȯr-fə-'läj-i-kəl\ *adj* — **mor·pho·log·i·cal·ly** \-i-k(ə-)lē\ *adv* — **mor·phol·o·gist** \mȯr-'fäl-ə-jəst\ *n*

mor·ris \'mȯr-əs, 'mär-\ *n* **:** a vigorous English dance performed by men wearing costumes and bells

mor·ris chair \ˌmȯr-əs-, ˌmär-\ *n* **:** an easy chair with adjustable back and removable cushions

mor·row \'mär-ō, 'mȯr-\ *n* **1** *archaic* **:** MORNING **2 :** the next following day

Morse code \'mȯrs-\ *n* **:** either of two codes consisting of dots and dashes or long and short sounds used for transmitting messages

mor·sel \'mȯr-səl\ *n* **1 :** a small piece of food **:** BITE **2 :** a small quantity or piece

[1]**mor·tal** \'mȯrt-əl\ *adj* **1 :** capable of causing death **:** FATAL ⟨a *mortal* wound⟩ **2 :** subject to death ⟨men are *mortal*⟩ **3 :** extremely hostile ⟨a *mortal* enemy⟩ **4 a :** leading to eternal punishment ⟨a *mortal* sin⟩ **b :** very great, intense, or severe ⟨in *mortal* fear⟩ **5 :** HUMAN ⟨*mortal* limitations⟩ **6 :** of, relating to, or connected with death ⟨*mortal* agony⟩ — **mor·tal·ly** \-ə-lē\ *adv*

[2]**mortal** *n* **:** a human being

mor·tal·i·ty \mȯr-'tal-ət-ē\ *n, pl* **-ties 1 :** the quality or state of being mortal **2 :** the death of large numbers **3 a :** the number of deaths in a given time or place **b :** the ratio of deaths to population

[1]**mor·tar** \'mȯrt-ər\ *n* **1 :** a bowl-shaped container in which substances are pounded or rubbed with a pestle **2 :** a short muzzle-loading cannon used to throw projectiles at high angles

[2]**mortar** *n* **:** a plastic building material (as one made of lime and cement mixed with sand and water) that hardens and is spread between bricks or stones to hold them together — **mortar** *vb*

mor·tar·board \'mȯrt-ər-ˌbōrd, -ˌbȯrd\ *n* **1 :** a board for holding mortar while it is being applied **2 :** an academic cap with a broad projecting square top

mortarboard

[1]**mort·gage** \'mȯr-gij\ *n* **1 :** a transfer of rights to a piece of property usu. as security for the payment of a loan or debt that becomes void when the debt is paid **2 :** the document effecting such a transfer

[2]**mortgage** *vb* **:** to subject to or as if to a mortgage

mort·gag·ee \ˌmȯr-gi-'jē\ *n* **:** a person to whom property is mortgaged

mort·ga·gor \ˌmȯr-gi-'jȯ(ə)r\ *also* **mort·gag·er** \'mȯr-gi-jər\ *n* **:** a person who mortgages his property

mor·ti·cian \mȯr-'tish-ən\ *n* **:** UNDERTAKER

mor·ti·fy \'mȯrt-ə-ˌfī\ *vb* **-fied; -fy·ing 1 :** to subdue bodily appetites through penance and self-denial **2 :** HUMILIATE, SHAME **3 :** to become necrotic or gangrenous — **mor·ti·fi·ca·tion** \ˌmȯrt-ə-fə-'kā-shən\ *n*

[1]**mor·tise** \'mȯrt-əs\ *n* **:** a hole cut in a piece of wood or other material into which another piece fits so as to form a joint

MORSE CODE

AMERICAN MORSE CODE[1]

A ·–	K –·–	U ··–	5 –––
B –···	L —	V ···–	6 ······
C ·· ·	M ––	W ·––	7 ––··
D –··	N –·	X ·–··	8 –····
E ·	O · ·	Y ·· ··	9 –··–
F ·–·	P ·····	Z ··· ·	0 —
G ––·	Q ··–·	1 ·––·	, (comma) ·–·–
H ····	R · ··	2 ··––··	. ··––··
I ··	S ···	3 ···–·	& ····
J –·–·	T –	4 ····–	

INTERNATIONAL CODE[2]

A ·–	N –·	Á ·––·–	8 –––··
B –···	O –––	Ä ·–·–	9 ––––·
C –·–·	P ·––·	É ··–··	0 –––––
D –··	Q ––·–	Ñ ––·––	, (comma) ––··––
E ·	R ·–·	Ö –––·	. ·–·–·–
F ··–·	S ···	Ü ··––	? ··––··
G ––·	T –	1 ·––––	; –·–·–·
H ····	U ··–	2 ··–––	: –––···
I ··	V ···–	3 ···––	' (apostrophe) ·––––·
J ·–––	W ·––	4 ····–	- (hyphen) –····–
K –·–	X –··–	5 ·····	/ –··–·
L ·–··	Y –·––	6 –····	parentheses –·––·–
M ––	Z ––··	7 ––···	underline ··––·–

[1]Formerly used on overland telegraph lines in the U.S. and Canada but largely out of use

[2]Often called the continental code; a modification of this code, with dots only, is used on ocean cables

M

2**mortise** *vb* **1 :** to join or fasten securely esp. by a tenon and mortise **2 :** to cut a mortise in
1**mor·tu·ary** \'mȯr-chə-ˌwer-ē\ *n, pl* **-ar·ies :** a place in which dead bodies are kept until burial
2**mortuary** *adj* **:** of or relating to death or burial
mos *abbr* months
mo·sa·ic \mō-'zā-ik\ *n* **1 :** a surface decoration made by inlaying small pieces of variously colored material to form pictures or patterns **2 :** the process of making mosaics **3 :** something resembling a mosaic; *esp* **:** a virus disease of plants characterized by mottling of the foliage — **mosaic** *adj* — **mo·sa·i·cal·ly** \-'zā-i-k(ə-)lē\ *adv*
Mos·lem \'mäz-ləm, 'mäs-\ *var of* MUSLIM
mosque \'mäsk\ *n* **:** a Muslim place of worship
mos·qui·to \mə-'skēt-ō\ *n, pl* **-toes** *also* **-tos** [from

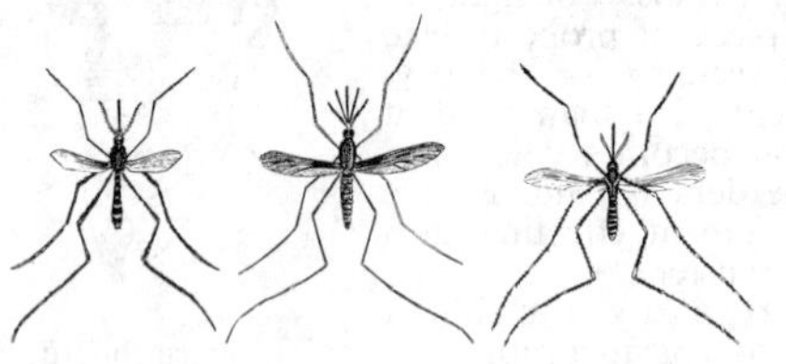

mosquito: 1, culex; 2, anopheles; 3, aëdes

Spanish, meaning literally "little fly", from *mosca* "fly", from Latin *musca*] **:** any of numerous two-winged flies having females with a needlelike proboscis adapted to puncture the skin of animals and to suck the blood — **mos·qui·to·ey** \-'skēt-ə-wē\ *adj*
mosquito net *n* **:** a net for keeping out mosquitoes
moss \'mȯs\ *n* **1 :** any of a class of plants without flowers but with small leafy often tufted stems growing in patches and bearing sex organs at the tip **2 :** any of various plants (as lichens) resembling mosses — **moss·like** \-ˌlīk\ *adj* — **mossy** \'mȯ-sē\ *adj*
1**most** \'mōst\ *adj* **1 :** the majority of ⟨*most* men⟩ **2 :** greatest in quantity, extent, or degree ⟨the *most* ability⟩
2**most** *adv* **1 :** to the greatest or highest degree — often used with an adjective or adverb to form the superlative ⟨*most* active⟩ ⟨*most* actively⟩ **2 :** to a very great degree ⟨a *most* careful driver⟩
3**most** *n* **:** the greatest amount, number, or part
4**most** *adv* **:** ALMOST
-most \ˌmōst\ *adj suffix* **:** most ⟨inner*most*⟩ **:** most toward ⟨head*most*⟩
most·ly \'mōst-lē\ *adv* **:** for the greatest part **:** MAINLY
mote \'mōt\ *n* **:** a small particle **:** SPECK
mo·tel \mō-'tel\ *n* [a word formed by telescoping the two parts of the term *motor hotel*] **:** a building or group of buildings used as a hotel in which the rooms are directly accessible from automobiles
mo·tet \mō-'tet\ *n* **:** a polyphonic choral composition on a sacred text usu. without accompaniment
moth \'mȯth\ *n, pl* **moths** \'mȯthz, 'mȯths\ **1 :** CLOTHES MOTH **2 :** a usu. night-flying insect with a stouter body, duller coloring, and proportionately smaller wings than the related butterflies
moth·ball \'mȯth-ˌbȯl\ *n* **1 :** a ball (as of naphthalene) used to keep moths out of clothing **2** *pl* **:** protective storage ⟨a fleet put in *mothballs* after the war⟩
moth–eat·en \'mȯth-ˌēt-ən\ *adj* **1 :** eaten into by moths **2 :** resembling cloth eaten into by moths
1**moth·er** \'məth-ər\ *n* **1 a :** a female parent **b :** a woman in authority; *esp* **:** the superior of a religious community of women **2 :** an elderly woman **3 :** SOURCE, ORIGIN ⟨necessity is the *mother* of invention⟩ — **moth·er·hood** \-ˌhu̇d\ *n* — **moth·er·less** \-ləs\ *adj*
2**mother** *adj* **1 a :** of or relating to a mother ⟨*mother* love⟩ **b :** being in the relation of a mother to others ⟨a *mother* church⟩ ⟨a *mother* country⟩ **2 :** derived from or as if from one's mother
3**mother** *vb* **moth·ered**; **moth·er·ing** \'məth-(ə-)riŋ\ **:** to be or act as mother to
4**mother** *n* **:** a slimy mass of yeast cells and bacteria that forms on the surface of fermenting alcoholic liquids and is added to wine or cider to produce vinegar
Mother Car·ey's chicken \ˌməth-ər-ˌkar-ēz, -ˌker-\ *n* **:** any of several small petrels; *esp* **:** STORM PETREL
Mother Hub·bard \ˌməth-ər-'həb-ərd\ *n* **:** a loose usu. shapeless dress
moth·er–in–law \'məth-ər(-ə)n-ˌlȯ\ *n, pl* **moth·ers–in–law** \-ər-zən-ˌlȯ\ **:** the mother of one's husband or wife
moth·er·land \'məth-ər-ˌland\ *n* **:** FATHERLAND
moth·er·ly \'məth-ər-lē\ *adj* **1 :** of, relating to, or characteristic of a mother ⟨*motherly* affection⟩ **2 :** resembling a mother ⟨a *motherly* old lady⟩ — **moth·er·li·ness** *n*
moth·er–of–pearl \ˌməth-ər-ə(v)-'pərl\ *n* **:** the hard pearly iridescent substance forming the inner layer of a mollusk shell
Mother's Day n **:** the 2d Sunday in May appointed for the honoring of mothers
mother tongue *n* **1 :** one's native language **2 :** a language from which another language derives
moth flakes *n pl* **:** flakes or crystals of a moth repellent (as paradichlorobenzene)
mo·tif \mō-'tēf\ *n* **1 :** a recurring idea or theme **2 :** a feature in a decoration or design ⟨a flower *motif* in wallpaper⟩
mo·tile \'mōt-əl, 'mō-ˌtīl\ *adj* **:** exhibiting or being capable of movement — **mo·til·i·ty** \mō-'til-ət-ē\ *n*
1**mo·tion** \'mō-shən\ *n* **1 :** a formal proposal made in a deliberative assembly ⟨a *motion* to adjourn⟩ **2 :** an act, process, or instance of changing place **:** MOVEMENT — **mo·tion·less** \-ləs\ *adj* — **mo·tion·less·ly** *adv* — **mo·tion·less·ness** *n*
2**motion** *vb* **mo·tioned**; **mo·tion·ing** \'mō-sh(ə-)niŋ\ **:** to direct or signal by a movement or gesture ⟨*motioned* him to come forward⟩
motion picture *n* **1 :** a series of pictures projected on a screen in rapid succession so as to produce the effect of a continuous picture in which the objects move **2 :** a representation of a story or other subject matter by means of motion pictures
motion sickness *n* **:** sickness induced by motion (as in travel by air, car, or ship) and characterized by nausea
mo·ti·vate \'mōt-ə-ˌvāt\ *vb* **:** to provide with a motive **:** INDUCE — **mo·ti·va·tion** \ˌmōt-ə-'vā-shən\ *n* — **mo·ti·va·tion·al** \-sh(ə-)nəl\ *adv*
1**mo·tive** \'mōt-iv, *2 is also* mō-'tēv\ *n* **1 :** something

ə abut	ər further	a back	ā bake		
ä cot, cart	au̇ out	ch chin	e less	ē easy	
g gift	i trip	ī life	j joke	ŋ sing	ō flow
ȯ flaw	ȯi coin	th thin	th this	ü loot	
u̇ foot	y yet	yü few	yu̇ furious	zh vision	

(as a need or desire) that leads or influences a person to do something ⟨his *motive* in running away was to avoid trouble⟩ **2 :** MOTIF ***syn*** see CAUSE

2motive *adj* **:** of, relating to, or causing motion ⟨*motive* power⟩

1mot·ley \'mät-lē\ *adj* **1 :** having various colors **2 :** of various mixed kinds or parts ⟨a *motley* crowd⟩

2motley *n* **1 a :** a garment of mixed colors worn by a court jester **b :** JESTER, FOOL **2 :** a mixture of diverse elements

mo·to·neu·ron \ˌmōt-ə-'n(y)ü-ˌrän, -'n(y)u̇(ə)r-ˌän\ *n* **:** a motor nerve cell with its processes

1mo·tor \'mōt-ər\ *n* **1 :** a machine that produces motion or power for doing work ⟨a gasoline *motor*⟩ ⟨electric *motors*⟩ **2 :** a motor vehicle (as a car or motorcycle)

2motor *adj* **1 :** causing or imparting motion ⟨*motor* power⟩ **2 a :** of, relating to, or being a nerve or nerve fiber that conducts an impulse to a muscle causing movement ⟨*motor* nerves⟩ **b :** concerned with or involving muscular movement ⟨*motor* areas of the brain⟩ ⟨a *motor* reaction⟩ **3 a :** equipped with or driven by a motor ⟨a *motor* vehicle⟩ **b :** of, relating to, or intended for use in an automobile ⟨a *motor* accident⟩ ⟨a *motor* mechanic⟩

3motor *vb* **:** to travel by automobile

mo·tor·bike \'mōt-ər-ˌbīk\ *n* **:** MOTORCYCLE; *esp* **:** a light motorcycle

mo·tor·boat \-ˌbōt\ *n* **:** a boat propelled by a motor

mo·tor·cade \-ˌkād\ *n* **:** a procession of motor vehicles

mo·tor·car \-ˌkär\ *n* **:** AUTOMOBILE

motor court *n* **:** MOTEL

mo·tor·cy·cle \'mōt-ər-ˌsī-kəl\ *n* **:** a 2-wheeled motor vehicle having one or two saddles and sometimes a third wheel for the support of a sidecar — **motorcycle** *vb* — **mo·tor·cy·clist** \-ˌsī-k(ə-)ləst\ *n*

motor home *n* **:** an automotive vehicle built on a bus or truck chassis and equipped as a complete traveling home

mo·tor·ist \'mōt-ə-rəst\ *n* **:** a person who travels by automobile

mo·tor·ize \'mōt-ə-ˌrīz\ *vb* **1 :** to equip with a motor **2 :** to equip with motor-driven vehicles for transportation ⟨*motorized* troops⟩

mo·tor·man \'mōt-ər-mən\ *n* **:** an operator of a motor-driven vehicle (as a streetcar or a subway train)

mo·tor·truck \'mōt-ər-ˌtrək\ *n* **:** an automotive truck (as for transporting freight)

mot·tle \'mät-əl\ *n* **1 :** a colored spot **2 :** a pattern of colored spots or blotches — **mottle** *vb* — **mot·tled** \-əld\ *adj*

mot·to \'mät-ō\ *n, pl* **mottoes** *also* **mottos** **1 :** a sentence, phrase, or word inscribed on something as suitable to its character or use ⟨a *motto* on a sundial⟩ **2 :** a short expression of a guiding rule of conduct **:** MAXIM

mould \'mōld\ *var of* MOLD

moult \'mōlt\ *var of* MOLT

1mound \'mau̇nd\ *n* **1 :** a small hill or heap of dirt **2 :** the slightly elevated ground on which a baseball pitcher stands

2mound *vb* **:** to form into a mound

1mount \'mau̇nt\ *n* **:** a high hill **:** MOUNTAIN

2mount *vb* **1 a :** RISE, ASCEND **b :** CLIMB ⟨*mount* a ladder⟩ **2 :** to get up onto something ⟨*mount* a platform⟩; *esp* **:** to get astride a horse **3 :** to furnish with riding animals or vehicles ⟨*mounted* infantry⟩ **4 :** to increase rapidly in amount ⟨*mounting* debts⟩ **5 :** to prepare for use or display esp. by fastening in proper position on a support ⟨*mount* a picture on cardboard⟩ ⟨*mount* an engine⟩ **6 :** to furnish with scenery, properties, and costumes ⟨*mount* a play⟩ **7 :** to post as a means of defense or observation ⟨*mount* guard⟩ **8 :** to place in position ⟨*mount* artillery to cover a flank⟩

3mount *n* **1 :** something upon which a person or thing is mounted: as **a :** a jewelry setting **b :** a specimen mounted on a slide for microscopic examination **2 :** SADDLE HORSE

moun·tain \'mau̇nt-ən\ *n* **1 :** a land mass that is higher than a hill **2 :** a great mass or vast number ⟨a *mountain* of mail⟩

mountain ash *n* **:** any of various trees related to the roses and having pinnate leaves and red or orange fruits

moun·tain·eer \ˌmau̇nt-ə-'ni(ə)r\ *n* **1 :** a person who lives in the mountains **2 :** a mountain climber — **mountaineer** *vb*

mountain goat *n* **:** an antelope of the mountains of western No. America that has a thick white hairy coat and slightly curved black horns and closely resembles a goat

mountain laurel *n* **:** a No. American evergreen shrub that is related to the rhododendrons and has glossy leaves and pink or white cup-shaped flowers

mountain lion *n* **:** COUGAR

mountain goat (up to 40 in. at shoulder)

moun·tain·ous \'mau̇nt-(ə-)nəs\ *adj* **1 :** having many mountains ⟨*mountainous* country⟩ **2 :** resembling a mountain esp. in size **:** HUGE ⟨*mountainous* waves⟩

mountain range *n* **:** a series of mountains or mountain ridges closely related in direction and position

mountain sheep *n* **:** any of various wild sheep inhabiting high mountains

moun·tain·side \'mau̇nt-ən-ˌsīd\ *n* **:** the side of a mountain

moun·tain·top \-ˌtäp\ *n* **:** the summit of a mountain

moun·te·bank \'mau̇nt-i-ˌbangk\ *n* **1 :** a person who sells quack medicines from a platform (as at fairs and carnivals) **2 :** a boastful pretender **:** CHARLATAN

mount·ing \'mau̇nt-ing\ *n* **1 :** the act of a person who mounts **2 :** something that serves as a mount **:** SUPPORT ⟨a *mounting* for an engine⟩ ⟨a *mounting* for a diamond⟩

mourn \'mōrn, 'mȯrn\ *vb* **:** to feel or show grief or sorrow; *esp* **:** to grieve over someone's death — **mourn·er** *n*

mourn·ful \'mōrn-fəl, 'mȯrn-\ *adj* **1 :** expressing or full of sorrow **:** SORROWFUL ⟨a *mournful* face⟩ **2 :** causing sorrow **:** SADDENING ⟨a *mournful* story⟩ — **mourn·ful·ly** \-fə-lē\ *adv* — **mourn·ful·ness** *n*

mourn·ing \'mōr-ning, 'mȯr-\ *n* **1 :** the act of sorrowing **2 :** an outward sign (as black clothes or a veil) of grief for a person's death ⟨to wear *mourning*⟩ **3 :** a period of time during which signs of grief are shown — **in mourning :** showing the outward signs and observing the conventions of mourning

mourning cloak *n* **:** a blackish brown butterfly of Europe, Asia, and No. America having a broad yellow border on the wings

mourning dove *n* **:** a wild dove of the U.S. with a mournful cry

1**mouse** \'maůs\ *n, pl* **mice** \'mīs\ **1 :** any of numerous small rodents with pointed snout, rather small ears, elongated body, and slender tail **2 :** a timid or spiritless person

mouse 1
(about 6 in. long)

2**mouse** \'maůz\ *vb* **1 :** to hunt mice **2 :** to search or move slyly **3 :** to move about softly like a mouse

mous·er \'maů-zər\ *n* **:** a cat good at mousing

mousse \'müs\ *n* **:** a light spongy food; *esp* **:** a frozen dessert of sweetened and flavored whipped cream or thin cream and gelatin

mous·tache \'məs-,tash, (,)məs-'\ *n* **1 :** the hair growing on the human upper lip **2 :** hair or bristles about the mouth of a lower animal

mousy *or* **mous·ey** \'maů-sē, -zē\ *adj* **mous·i·er; -est 1 :** resembling or suggesting a mouse ⟨her hair was a *mousy* color⟩ **2 :** QUIET **3 :** TIMID, SHY

1**mouth** \'maůth\ *n, pl* **mouths** \'maůt͟hz, 'maůths\ **1 a :** the opening through which food passes into the body of an animal **b :** the cavity that encloses in the typical vertebrate the tongue, gums, and teeth **2 :** GRIMACE ⟨make a *mouth*⟩ **3 :** an opening likened to a mouth ⟨the *mouth* of a cave⟩ **4 :** the place where a stream enters a larger body of water

2**mouth** \'maůt͟h\ *vb* **1 a :** to speak or utter esp. loudly or pompously **b :** to repeat without understanding or sincerity ⟨*mouth* platitudes⟩ **2 :** to take into the mouth — **mouth·er** *n*

mouthed \'maůt͟hd, 'maůtht\ *adj* **:** having a mouth ⟨large-*mouthed* jar⟩

mouth·ful \'maůth-,fůl\ *n* **1 a :** as much as the mouth will hold **b :** the amount put into the mouth at one time **2 :** a word or phrase that is very long or difficult to say

mouth hook *n* **:** one of a pair of clawlike structures that occur on either side of the mouth opening of some fly larvae and function as jaws

mouth organ *n* **:** HARMONICA

mouth·part \'maůth-,pärt\ *n* **:** a structure or appendage near the mouth

mouth·piece \-,pēs\ *n* **1 :** something placed at or held in the mouth **2 :** a part (as of an instrument) to which the mouth is held ⟨the *mouthpiece* of a trumpet⟩ **3 :** one that expresses another's views **:** SPOKESMAN

mouth·wash \-,wòsh, -,wäsh\ *n* **:** a usu. antiseptic liquid preparation for cleaning the mouth and teeth

mou·ton \'mü-,tän\ *n* **:** processed sheepskin sheared and dyed to resemble beaver or seal

1**mov·a·ble** *or* **move·a·ble** \'mü-və-bəl\ *adj* **1 :** capable of being moved **:** not fixed ⟨*movable* property⟩ **2 :** changing from one date to another ⟨Easter is a *movable* holiday⟩ — **mov·a·bly** \-blē\ *adv*

2**movable** *or* **moveable** *n* **:** a piece of property (as an article of furniture) that can be moved

1**move** \'müv\ *vb* **1 :** to change the place or position of **:** SHIFT ⟨*move* the chair closer⟩ **2 :** to go from one place to another ⟨*move* into the shade⟩ **3 :** to set in motion ⟨*moved* his head⟩ **4 a :** to cause a person to act or decide **:** PERSUADE ⟨*moved* him to change his mind⟩ **b :** to take action **:** ACT **5 :** to affect the feelings of ⟨the sad story *moved* her to tears⟩ **6 :** to propose formally in an assembly ⟨*move* that the meeting adjourn⟩ **7 :** SELL ⟨the store's stock must be *moved*⟩ **8 a :** to change residence ⟨*move* to California⟩ **b :** to change place or position **:** STIR ⟨*moved* around in his chair⟩ **9 :** OPERATE, ACTUATE ⟨*move* the handle to increase pressure⟩ **10 :** PROGRESS, ADVANCE **11 :** to carry on one's life ⟨he *moves* in high circles⟩ **12 :** to go away **:** DEPART ⟨police made the crowd *move* on⟩ **13 :** to transfer a piece in a game (as chess) from one place to another **14 :** to evacuate or cause to evacuate ⟨the medicine *moved* the bowels⟩

2**move** *n* **1 a :** the act of moving a piece in a game **b :** the turn of a player to move **2 a :** a step taken to gain an objective **:** MANEUVER **b :** the action of moving **:** MOVEMENT **c :** a change of residence or location

move·ment \'müv-mənt\ *n* **1 a :** the act or process of moving **b :** an instance or manner of moving ⟨observe the *movement* of a star⟩ **c :** ACTION, ACTIVITY ⟨a great deal of *movement* in the crowd⟩ **2 :** TENDENCY, TREND ⟨a *movement* of prices upward⟩ **3 a :** a series of actions taken by a group to bring about an objective ⟨a *movement* for political reform⟩ **b :** the body of persons taking part in a series of actions ⟨joined the *movement*⟩ **4 :** a mechanical arrangement (as of wheels) for causing motion (as in a clock or watch) **5 a :** RHYTHM, METER **b :** a section of a longer piece of music ⟨a *movement* in a symphony⟩ **6 :** an emptying of the bowels or the matter emptied

mov·er \'mü-vər\ *n* **:** one that moves; *esp* **:** a person or company that moves the belongings of others from one home or place of business to another

mov·ie \'mü-vē\ *n* **1 :** MOTION PICTURE **2** *pl* **:** a showing of a motion picture **3** *pl* **:** the motion-picture industry

mov·ing \'mü-ving\ *adj* **1 :** changing place or position ⟨a *moving* target⟩ **2 :** causing motion or action **3 :** having the power to affect the feelings or sympathies ⟨a *moving* song⟩ **4 :** being or used in a mover's business ⟨a *moving* van⟩ — **mov·ing·ly** \-ving-lē\ *adv*

moving picture *n* **:** MOTION PICTURE

moving staircase *n* **:** ESCALATOR

1**mow** \'maů\ *n* **1 :** a stack of hay or straw esp. in a barn **2 :** the part of a barn where hay or straw is stored

2**mow** \'mō\ *vb* **mowed; mowed** *or* **mown** \'mōn\; **mow·ing 1 :** to cut down with a scythe or machine ⟨*mow* hay⟩ **2 :** to cut the standing herbage from ⟨*mow* a lawn⟩ **3 :** to kill or destroy in great numbers **4 :** to overcome decisively **:** ROUT ⟨*mow* down the other team⟩ — **mow·er** \'mō(-ə)r\ *n*

mp *abbr* melting point

MP *abbr* **1** member of parliament **2** military police

mpg *abbr* miles per gallon

mph *abbr* miles per hour

Mr *abbr* mister

Mrs *abbr* mistress

MS *abbr* **1** manuscript **2** master of science **3** Mississippi

msec *abbr* millisecond

msgr *abbr* monsignor

MSS *abbr* manuscripts

mt *abbr* **1** mount **2** mountain

mtn *abbr* mountain

mu \'myü\ *n* **:** the 12th letter of the Greek alphabet — M or μ

ə abut	ər further		a back	ā bake
ä cot, cart	aů out	ch chin	e less	ē easy
g gift	i trip	ī life	j joke	ng sing	ō flow
ȯ flaw	ȯi coin	th thin	t͟h this	ü loot
ů foot	y yet	yü few	yů furious	zh vision

1much \'məch\ *adj* **more** \'mō(ə)r, 'mȯ(ə)r\; **most** \'mōst\ : great in quantity, amount, extent, or degree ⟨has *much* money⟩ ⟨takes too *much* time⟩
2much *adv* **more**; **most** **1** : to a great degree or extent ⟨*much* happier⟩ **2** : APPROXIMATELY, NEARLY
3much **1** : a great quantity, amount, extent, or degree **2** : something considerable or impressive ⟨not *much* to look at⟩
mu·ci·lage \'myü-s(ə-)lij\ *n* **1** : a jellylike substance esp. from seaweeds that is similar to plant gums **2** : an aqueous solution of a sticky substance (as a gum) used esp. as an adhesive
muck \'mək\ *n* **1** : moist manure **2** : DIRT, FILTH **3 a** : dark highly organic soil **b** : MIRE, MUD — **mucky** \'mək-ē\ *adj*
muck·rak·er \'mək-ˌrā-kər\ *n* : one of a group of writers noted for seeking out and exposing abuses (as graft or corruption) in American business, government, and society at the beginning of the 20th century — **muck·rake** \-ˌrāk\ *vb*
mu·co·sa \myü-'kō-zə\ *n, pl* **-sae** \-(ˌ)zē, -ˌzī\ *or* **-sas** : MUCOUS MEMBRANE — **mu·co·sal** \-zəl\ *adj*
mu·cous \'myü-kəs\ *adj* **1** : of, relating to, or resembling mucus ⟨*mucous* discharges⟩ **2** : secreting or containing mucus ⟨a *mucous* gland⟩
mucous membrane *n* : a membrane rich in mucous glands; *esp* : one lining body passages and cavities which connect directly or indirectly with the outside
mu·cus \'myü-kəs\ *n* **1** : a slippery animal secretion produced esp. by mucous membranes which it moistens and protects **2** : an animal secretion (as of a snail) that resembles mucus — **mu·coid** \-kȯid\ *adj*
mud \'məd\ *n* : soft wet earth
mud dauber *n* : any of various wasps that construct mud cells in which the female places an egg with paralyzed insects or spiders to serve as larval food
mud·dle \'məd-əl\ *vb* **mud·dled**; **mud·dling** \-(ə-)ling\ **1** : CONFUSE, STUPEFY ⟨*muddled* by too much advice⟩ **2** : to mix up confusedly ⟨*muddle* the household accounts⟩ **3** : to think or act in a confused way : BUNGLE ⟨*muddle* through a task⟩ — **muddle** *n* — **mud·dler** \-(ə-)lər\ *n*
1mud·dy \'məd-ē\ *adj* **mud·di·er**; **-est** **1** : filled or covered with mud ⟨a *muddy* pond⟩ ⟨*muddy* shoes⟩ **2** : resembling mud ⟨a *muddy* color⟩ ⟨*muddy* coffee⟩ **3** : not clear or bright : DULL, CLOUDY ⟨a *muddy* complexion⟩ **4** : CONFUSED, MUDDLED ⟨*muddy* thinking⟩ — **mud·di·ness** *n*
2muddy *vb* **mud·dies**; **mud·dy·ing** **1** : to soil or stain with or as if with mud **2** : to make cloudy or dull **3** : CONFUSE
mud·guard \'məd-ˌgärd\ *n* : the fender of a motor vehicle
mud puddle *n* : a small pool of dirty water usu. left by a rainstorm
mud puppy *n* : any of several large American salamanders; *esp* : HELLBENDER
mud turtle *n* : a bottom-dwelling freshwater turtle
1muff \'məf\ *n* : a soft thick cover into which both hands may be thrust for protection from cold
2muff *n* : a bungling performance; *esp* : a failure to hold a ball in attempting a catch — **muff** *vb*
muf·fin \'məf-ən\ *n* : a bread made of egg batter or yeast dough and baked in a small cup-shaped container

muff

muf·fle \'məf-əl\ *vb* **muf·fled**; **muf·fling** \-(ə-)ling\ **1** : to wrap up so as to conceal or protect or to prevent seeing, hearing, or speaking **2** : to deaden the sound of ⟨*muffle* a cry⟩
muf·fler \'məf-lər\ *n* **1** : a scarf for the neck **2** : something that deadens noises; *esp* : a device attached to the exhaust system of an automobile
muf·ti \'məf-tē\ *n* : ordinary clothes when worn by one usu. dressed in a uniform
1mug \'məg\ *n* **1** : a usu. large cylindrical drinking cup **2** : the face or mouth of a person **3** : PUNK, THUG
2mug *vb* **mugged**; **mug·ging** **1** : to make faces : GRIMACE **2** : PHOTOGRAPH; *esp* : to take a police photograph of
3mug *vb* : to attack from behind esp. with intent to rob — **mug·ger** *n*
mug·gy \'məg-ē\ *adj* **mug·gi·er**; **-est** : being warm, damp, and stifling ⟨a *muggy* day in August⟩ — **mug·gi·ness** *n*
Mu·ham·mad·an \mō-'ham-əd-ən, mü-\ *n* : MUSLIM — **Muhammadan** *adj* — **Mu·ham·mad·an·ism** \-ˌiz-əm\ *n*
muk·luk \'mək-ˌlək\ *n* **1** : an Eskimo boot of sealskin or reindeer skin **2** : a boot with a soft leather sole worn over several pairs of socks
mu·lat·to \m(y)u̇-'lat-ō\ *n, pl* **-toes** *or* **-tos** [from Spanish *mulato*, from *mulo* "mule"; so called because the mule is the offspring of parents of two different species] **1** : a person with one Negro and one white parent **2** : a person of mixed white and Negro descent
mul·ber·ry \'məl-ˌber-ē\ *n* **1** : any of a genus of trees with edible usu. purple fruits resembling berries; *also* : the fruit **2** : a dark purple or purplish black
mulch \'məlch\ *n* : a protective covering (as of sawdust, compost, or paper) used on the ground esp. to reduce evaporation, prevent erosion, control weeds, or enrich the soil — **mulch** *vb*
1mulct \'məlkt\ *n* : a fine imposed as a punishment
2mulct *vb* **1** : to punish by a fine **2 a** : DEFRAUD, SWINDLE **b** : to obtain (as money) by fraud, duress, or theft
1mule \'myül\ *n* **1** : a hybrid between a horse and a donkey; *esp* : the offspring of a male donkey and a mare **2** : a very stubborn person **3** : a machine for drawing and twisting fiber into yarn or thread and winding it onto spindles
2mule *n* : a slipper whose upper does not extend around the heel of the foot
mule deer *n* : a long-eared deer of western No. America that is larger and more heavily built than the common whitetail
mule skinner *n* : a driver of mules
mu·le·teer \ˌmyü-lə-'ti(ə)r\ *n* : a driver of mules
mul·ish \'myü-lish\ *adj* : STUBBORN, INFLEXIBLE — **mul·ish·ly** *adv* — **mul·ish·ness** *n*
1mull \'məl\ *vb* : to consider at length : PONDER ⟨*mull* over an idea⟩
2mull *vb* : to sweeten, spice, and heat ⟨*mulled* wine⟩
mul·lein *also* **mul·len** \'məl-ən\ *n* : a tall herb having coarse woolly leaves and spikes of usu. yellow flowers
mul·let \'məl-ət\ *n, pl* **mullet** *or* **mullets** **1** : any of a family of largely gray food fishes — called also *gray mullet* **2** : any of a family of moderate-sized usu. red or golden fishes with two barbels on the chin — called also *red mullet*
multi- *comb form* **1 a** : many : multiple : much ⟨*multi*colored⟩ **b** : more than two ⟨*multi*lateral⟩ ⟨*multi*racial⟩ **2** : many times over ⟨*multi*millionaire⟩
mul·ti·cel·lu·lar \ˌməl-ti-'sel-yə-lər, -ˌtī-\ *adj* : hav-

ing or consisting of many cells — **mul·ti·cel·lu·lar·i·ty** \-ˌsel-yə-ˈlar-ət-ē\ *n*
mul·ti·col·ored \ˌməl-ti-ˈkəl-ərd\ *adj* : having many colors
mul·ti·far·i·ous \ˌməl-tə-ˈfar-ē-əs, -ˈfer-\ *adj* : of various kinds : being many and varied ⟨the *multifarious* complexities of language⟩ — **mul·ti·far·i·ous·ness** *n*
mul·ti·form \ˈməl-tə-ˌfȯrm\ *adj* : having many forms, shapes, or appearances
mul·ti·lat·er·al \ˌməl-ti-ˈlat-ə-rəl, -ˈla-trəl\ *adj* **1** : having many sides **2** : participated in by more than two nations or parties ⟨a *multilateral* treaty⟩ — **mul·ti·lat·er·al·ly** \-ē\ *adv*
mul·ti·mil·lion·aire \-ˌmil-yə-ˈna(ə)r, -ˈne(ə)r, -ˈmil-yə-ˌ\ *n* : a person worth several million dollars
[1]**mul·ti·ple** \ˈməl-tə-pəl\ *adj* : containing or consisting of more than one : MANIFOLD ⟨*multiple* ideas⟩ ⟨*multiple* copies⟩
[2]**multiple** *n* : the product of a quantity by an integer ⟨35 is a *multiple* of 7⟩
multiple fruit *n* : a fruit (as a mulberry) formed from a cluster of flowers
multiple sclerosis *n* : a disease marked by patches of hardened tissue in the brain or spinal cord resulting in partial or complete paralysis and muscular twitching
mul·ti·pli·cand \ˌməl-tə-pli-ˈkand\ *n* : the number that is to be multiplied by another
mul·ti·pli·ca·tion \ˌməl-tə-plə-ˈkā-shən\ *n* **1** : the act or process of multiplying **2** : a mathematical operation that consists of adding a number to itself a specified number of times — **mul·ti·plic·a·tive** \ˌməl-tə-ˈplik-ət-iv, ˈməl-tə-plə-ˌkāt-\ *adj*
multiplicative identity element *n* : an element of a set that when multiplied by any element of the set leaves the element unchanged ⟨the integer 1 is a *multiplicative identity element* in the set of real numbers⟩
multiplicative inverse *n* : the reciprocal of a given number
mul·ti·plic·i·ty \ˌməl-tə-ˈplis-ət-ē\ *n, pl* **-ties** **1** : the quality or state of being multiple or various **2** : a great number ⟨a *multiplicity* of ideas⟩
mul·ti·pli·er \ˈməl-tə-ˌplī(-ə)r\ *n* **1** : one that multiplies **2** : a number by which another number is multiplied
mul·ti·ply \ˈməl-tə-ˌplī\ *vb* **-plied**; **-ply·ing** **1** : to increase in number : make or become more numerous **2** : to find the product of multiplication ⟨*multiply* 7 by 8⟩
mul·ti·pur·pose \ˌməl-ti-ˈpər-pəs, -ˌtī-\ *adj* : having several purposes ⟨*multipurpose* furniture⟩
mul·ti·ra·cial \-ˈrā-shəl\ *adj* : composed of, relating to, or representing various races
mul·ti·stage \ˌməl-ti-ˌstāj\ *adj* : operating in or involving two or more steps or stages ⟨a *multistage* rocket⟩
mul·ti·tude \ˈməl-tə-ˌt(y)üd\ *n* : a great number of things or people

syn MULTITUDE, HOST, CROWD, THRONG can mean a large number of individuals. MULTITUDE applies to a large number, relative or absolute, in describing any group; HOST often suggests the close array or concentration of a multitude; CROWD usu. applies to a group of people and suggests disorder and dense packing together; THRONG suggests milling around by many people gathered together

mul·ti·tu·di·nous \ˌməl-tə-ˈt(y)üd-(ə-)nəs\ *adj* : consisting of a multitude — **mul·ti·tu·di·nous·ly** *adv*
mul·ti·vi·ta·min \ˌməl-ti-ˈvīt-ə-mən\ *adj* : containing several vitamins and esp. all known to be essential to health ⟨a *multivitamin* formula⟩
[1]**mum** \ˈməm\ *adj* : SILENT ⟨keep *mum*⟩
[2]**mum** *n* : CHRYSANTHEMUM
mum·ble \ˈməm-bəl\ *vb* **mum·bled**; **mum·bling** \-b(ə-)liŋ\ **1** : to speak indistinctly usu. with lips partly closed ⟨*mumble* one's words⟩ **2** : to chew gently with closed lips or with little use of the lips ⟨a baby *mumbling* its food⟩ — **mumble** *n* — **mumbler** \-b(ə-)lər\ *n* — **mum·bling·ly** \-bliŋ-lē\ *adv*
mum·mer \ˈməm-ər\ *n* **1** : a person who masks and engages in merry-making (as at Christmas) **2** : ACTOR
mum·mery \ˈməm-ə-rē\ *n, pl* **-mer·ies** **1** : a performance by mummers **2** : a ridiculous or pompous ceremony
mum·mi·fy \ˈməm-i-ˌfī\ *vb* **-fied**; **-fy·ing** **1** : to embalm and dry as a mummy **2** : to dry up like the skin of a mummy : SHRIVEL — **mum·mi·fi·ca·tion** \ˌməm-i-fə-ˈkā-shən\ *n*
mum·my \ˈməm-ē\ *n, pl* **mummies** **1** : a body embalmed for burial in the manner of the ancient Egyptians **2** : an unusually well-preserved body
mumps \ˈməm(p)s\ *n sing or pl* : a contagious virus disease marked by fever and by swelling esp. of salivary glands
munch \ˈmənch\ *vb* : to chew with a crunching sound ⟨*munch* on hard candy⟩ — **munch·er** *n*
mun·dane \ˌmən-ˈdān, ˈmən-ˌ\ *adj* : of or relating to the world : WORLDLY ⟨concerned with *mundane* affairs⟩ — **mun·dane·ly** *adv*
mu·nic·i·pal \myu̇-ˈnis-ə-pəl\ *adj* : of or relating to a municipality ⟨*municipal* government⟩
municipal bond *n* : a bond issued by a local or state government agency and paying interest exempt from federal income tax
mu·nic·i·pal·i·ty \myu̇-ˌnis-ə-ˈpal-ət-ē\ *n, pl* **-ties** : an urban political unit (as a city or town) having powers of self-government
mu·nif·i·cent \myu̇-ˈnif-ə-sənt\ *adj* : extremely liberal in giving : very generous — **mu·nif·i·cence** \-sən(t)s\ *n* — **mu·nif·i·cent·ly** *adv*
mu·ni·tions \myu̇-ˈnish-ənz\ *n pl* : military supplies, equipment, or provisions; *esp* : AMMUNITION — **mu·ni·tion** \-ən\ *vb*
[1]**mu·ral** \ˈmyu̇r-əl\ *adj* **1** : of or relating to a wall **2** : applied directly to a wall ⟨a *mural* painting⟩
[2]**mural** *n* : a mural painting
[1]**mur·der** \ˈmərd-ər\ *n* : the intentional and unlawful killing of a person
[2]**murder** *vb* **mur·dered**; **mur·der·ing** \ˈmərd-(ə-)riŋ\ **1** : to commit murder **2** : to spoil by performing in a wretched manner : MANGLE ⟨*murder* a song⟩ *syn* see KILL — **mur·der·er** \-ər-ər\ *n* — **mur·der·ess** \-ə-rəs\ *n*
mur·der·ous \ˈmərd-(ə-)rəs\ *adj* **1** : marked by or causing murder or bloodshed ⟨*murderous* machine-gun fire⟩ ⟨a *murderous* act⟩ **2** : intending or appearing to intend murder ⟨a *murderous* glance⟩ — **mur·der·ous·ly** *adv*
mu·ri·at·ic acid \ˌmyu̇r-ē-ˌat-ik-\ *n* : HYDROCHLORIC ACID
murk \ˈmərk\ *n* : DARKNESS, GLOOM — **murky** \ˈmər-kē\ *adj* — **murk·i·ness** *n*

mur·mur \'mər-mər\ *n* **1** : a muttered complaint : GRUMBLE **2** : a low indistinct sound ⟨the *murmur* of the wind⟩ **3** : an abnormal heart sound occurring when the heart is disordered in function or structure — **murmur** *vb* — **mur·mur·er** \'mər-mər-ər\ *n*

mur·mur·ous \'mərm-(ə-)rəs\ *adj* : filled with or characterized by murmurs — **mur·mur·ous·ly** *adv*

mur·rain \'mər-ən, 'mə-rən\ *n* : a pestilence or plague esp. of domestic animals

mus *abbr* **1** museum **2** music

mus·cat \'məs-ˌkat, -kət\ *n* : any of several cultivated grapes used in making wine and raisins

mus·ca·tel \ˌməs-kə-'tel\ *n* : a sweet wine made from muscat grapes

mus·cle \'məs-əl\ *n* [from Latin *musculus*, literally "little mouse"; probably so called from the shape and motion of the biceps when flexed] **1 a** : a body tissue consisting of long cells that contract when stimulated **b** : an organ that is essentially a mass of muscle tissue attached at either end to a fixed point and that by contracting moves or checks the movement of a body part **2 a** : muscular strength : BRAWN **b** : effective strength : POWER

mus·cle–bound \'məs-əl-ˌbau̇nd\ *adj* : having some of the muscles abnormally enlarged and lacking in elasticity (as from excessive athletic exercise)

mus·cu·lar \'məs-kyə-lər\ *adj* **1 a** : of, relating to, or constituting muscle **b** : performed by the muscles **2** : having well-developed muscles : STRONG — **mus·cu·lar·i·ty** \ˌməs-kyə-'lar-ət-ē\ *n*

muscular dystrophy *n* : a disease characterized by progressive wasting of muscles

mus·cu·la·ture \'məs-kyə-lə-ˌchu̇r\ *n* : the muscles of the body or of one of its parts

1**muse** \'myüz\ *vb* : PONDER, MEDITATE

2**muse** *n* **1** *cap* : any of the nine sister goddesses of song and poetry and the arts and sciences in Greek mythology **2** : a source of esp. artistic, musical, or literary inspiration

mu·se·um \myu̇-'zē-əm\ *n* [from the Latin form of Greek *mouseion*, literally "shrine of the Muses" (from *mousa* "muse"), and then any place devoted to literary or artistic activity] : a building or part of a building in which are displayed objects of interest in one or more of the arts or sciences

1**mush** \'məsh\ *n* **1** : cornmeal boiled in water **2** : something soft and spongy **3** : insipid sentiment — **mush·i·ness** \-ē-nəs\ *n* — **mush·i·ly** \-ə-lē\ *adv* — **mushy** \-ē\ *adj*

2**mush** *vb* : to travel over snow with a sled drawn by dogs — often used as a command to a dog team

3**mush** *n* : a hike across snow with a dog team

1**mush·room** \'məsh-ˌrüm, -ˌru̇m\ *n* [from French *mousseron*] **1** : a fleshy fruiting body of a fungus that is shaped typically like an umbrella; *esp* : one that is edible **2** : FUNGUS 1

2**mushroom** *adj* **1** : springing up suddenly or multiplying rapidly ⟨*mushroom* growth of suburbs⟩ **2** : shaped like a mushroom

3**mushroom** *vb* : to spring up suddenly or multiply rapidly

mu·sic \'myü-zik\ *n* **1 a** : the art of combining tones so that they are pleasing, expressive, or intelligible **b** : compositions made according to the rules of music **c** : the score of music compositions ⟨did you bring your *music* with you?⟩ **2 a** : sounds that have rhythm, harmony, and melody **b** : an agreeable sound ⟨the *music* of a brook⟩ **3** : PUNISHMENT ⟨must face the *music*⟩

1**mu·si·cal** \'myü-zi-kəl\ *adj* **1 a** : of or relating to music ⟨*musical* instruments⟩ **b** : having the qualities of music ⟨a *musical* voice⟩ **2** : fond of or gifted in music ⟨a *musical* family⟩ **3** : set to or accompanied by music — **mu·si·cal·ly** \-k(ə-)lē\ *adv*

2**musical** *n* : a film or theatrical production consisting of musical numbers and dialogue that develop a plot — called also *musical comedy*

mu·si·cale \ˌmyü-zi-'kal\ *n* : a usu. private social gathering to hear music

music box *n* : a case enclosing an apparatus that plays music mechanically by clockwork

mu·si·cian \myu̇-'zish-ən\ *n* : a composer or performer of music — **mu·si·cian·ship** \-ˌship\ *n*

musk \'məsk\ *n* : a strong-smelling substance obtained usu. from the male musk deer and used in perfume; *also* : an odor of or resembling that of musk — **musky** \'məs-kē\ *adj*

musk deer *n* : a small hornless deer about 3 feet long and 20 inches tall that lives in the high regions of central Asia

mus·keg \'məs-ˌkeg\ *n* : BOG; *esp* : a dense sphagnum bog of northern No. America

mus·kel·lunge \'məs-kə-ˌlənj\ *n*, *pl* **muskellunge** [from an American Indian word meaning "big fish"] : a large No. American pike prized as a sport fish

mus·ket \'məs-kət\ *n* : a usu. muzzle-loading military shoulder firearm with smooth bore

mus·ke·teer \ˌməs-kə-'ti(ə)r\ *n* : a soldier armed with a musket

mus·ket·ry \'məs-kə-trē\ *n*, *pl* **-ries** : small-arms fire

musk·mel·on \'məsk-ˌmel-ən\ *n* : a small round to oval and sometimes ridged melon that is related to the cucumber and has usu. sweet edible green or orange flesh — compare CANTALOUPE

musk–ox \'məsk-ˌäks\ *n* : a heavyset shaggy-coated wild ox confined to Greenland and the barren lands of northern No. America

musk–ox (about 5 ft. at shoulder)

musk·rat \'məs-ˌkrat\ *n*, *pl* **muskrat** *or* **muskrats** : a No. American aquatic rodent with a long scaly tail, webbed hind feet, and dark glossy brown fur; *also* : its fur or pelt

Mus·lim \'məz-ləm, 'mu̇s-\ *n* : a follower of Islam — **Muslim** *adj*

mus·lin \'məz-lən\ *n* : a cotton fabric of plain weave

1**muss** \'məs\ *n* : DISORDER, CONFUSION — **mussy** \-ē\ *adj*

2**muss** *vb* : to make untidy : RUMPLE ⟨*mussed* his hair⟩

mus·sel \'məs-əl\ *n* **1** : an edible saltwater 2-valved mollusk with a long dark shell **2** : any of numerous 2-valved freshwater mollusks of the central U.S. having shells with pearly inner linings

1**must** \məs(t), 'məst\ *auxiliary verb*, *pres & past all persons* **must** **1** : is commanded, requested, or urged to ⟨the train *must* stop⟩ ⟨you *must* read that book⟩ **2** : is compelled, required, or obliged to ⟨leaves *must* fall⟩ ⟨one *must* eat to live⟩ ⟨we *must* be quiet⟩ **3** : is determined to ⟨if you *must* go⟩ **4** : is inferred by reasoning to ⟨it *must* be time⟩ ⟨*must* have lost it⟩ **5** : is certain to ⟨the bus *must* be coming⟩

2**must** \'məst\ *n* : something necessary, required, or indispensable ⟨new shoes are a *must*⟩

mus·tache *var of* MOUSTACHE

mus·ta·chio \(ˌ)məs-'tash-ō, -'täsh-, -ē-ˌō\ *n*, *pl* **-chios** : MOUSTACHE — **mus·ta·chioed** \-ōd, -ē-ˌōd\ *adj*

mus·tang \'məs-ˌtang\ *n* [from American Spanish,

M

mestengo, from Spanish, "animal without an owner", from *mesta* "annual roundup of strays", from medieval Latin (*animalia*) *mixta* "mixed animals"] : the small hardy naturalized horse of the western plains directly descended from horses brought in by the Spaniards; *also* : BRONCO

mus·tard \'məs-tərd\ *n* **1** : a yellow powder of the seeds of a common mustard used in food seasonings or in medicine **2** : any of several yellow-flowered herbs related to the turnips and cabbages

mustard gas *n* : a poisonous gas having violent irritating and esp. blistering effects

mustard plaster *n* : a medicinal plaster containing powdered mustard

1**mus·ter** \'məs-tər\ *vb* **mus·tered**; **mus·ter·ing** \-t(ə-)riŋ\ **1** : to assemble (as troops) for roll call or inspection **2** : to collect and display ⟨all the strength he could *muster*⟩

2**muster** *n* **1** : an act of assembling; *esp* : a formal military inspection or drill **2** : critical examination ⟨work that would never pass *muster*⟩

muster out *vb* : to discharge from service

mustn't \'məs-ənt\ : must not

musty \'məs-tē\ *adj* **must·i·er**; **-est** **1 a** : impaired by damp or mildew : MOLDY **b** : tasting or smelling of damp and decay **2 a** : TRITE, STALE **b** : OUT-OF-DATE, ANTIQUATED — **must·i·ness** *n*

mu·ta·ble \'myüt-ə-bəl\ *adj* **1** : prone to change : INCONSTANT **2 a** : capable of change **b** : capable of or liable to mutation — **mu·ta·bil·i·ty** \ˌmyüt-ə-'bil-ət-ē\ *n*

mu·tant \'myüt-ənt\ *adj* : of, relating to, or produced by mutation — **mutant** *n*

mu·tate \'myü-ˌtāt\ *vb* : to undergo or cause to undergo mutation

mu·ta·tion \myü-'tā-shən\ *n* **1** : a basic alteration : CHANGE **2 a** : an inherited change in genetic material involving either a physical change (as breaking and inverting a part) in a chromosome or a change in the chemical structure of a gene **b** : an individual or strain resulting from mutation

1**mute** \'myüt\ *adj* **1** : having an often correctable inability to speak (as from never having learned speech) **2** : marked by absence of speech ⟨a *mute* appeal for help⟩ **3** : not pronounced : SILENT ⟨the *mute* *b* in *thumb*⟩ ***syn*** see DUMB

2**mute** *n* **1** : a person who cannot or does not speak **2** : a device on a musical instrument that deadens, softens, or muffles its tone **3** : STOP 8

3**mute** *vb* **1** : to muffle or reduce the sound of **2** : to tone down ⟨*muted* his criticism⟩

mu·ti·late \'myüt-ə-ˌlāt\ *vb* **1** : CRIPPLE, MAIM **2** : to make imperfect by cutting or alteration ⟨*mutilate* a play⟩ — **mu·ti·la·tion** \ˌmyüt-ə-'lā-shən\ *n* — **mu·ti·la·tor** \'myüt-ə-ˌlāt-ər\ *n*

mu·ti·neer \ˌmyüt-ə-'ni(ə)r\ *n* : one that mutinies

mu·ti·nous \'myüt-(ə-)nəs\ *adj* **1** : disposed to or in a state of mutiny : REBELLIOUS ⟨a *mutinous* crew⟩ **2** : relating to or constituting mutiny ⟨*mutinous* acts⟩ — **mu·ti·nous·ly** *adv*

mu·ti·ny \'myüt-(ə-)nē\ *n, pl* **-nies** : willful refusal to obey authority; *esp* : military revolt against a superior officer — **mutiny** *vb*

mutt \'mət\ *n* : MONGREL, CUR

mut·ter \'mət-ər\ *vb* **1** : MUMBLE **2** : to murmur complainingly : GRUMBLE — **mutter** *n* — **mut·ter·er** \-ər-ər\ *n*

mut·ton \'mət-ən\ *n* [from French *mouton* "sheep"] : the flesh of a mature sheep

mut·ton·chops \-ˌchäps\ *n pl* : side-whiskers that are narrow at the temple and broad and round by the lower jaws

mu·tu·al \'myü-ch(ə-w)əl\ *adj* **1 a** : given and received in equal amount ⟨*mutual* favors⟩ **b** : having the same relation one to the other ⟨*mutual* enemies⟩ **2** : owned, shared, or enjoyed by two or more at the same time : JOINT ⟨our *mutual* friend⟩ ⟨*mutual* defense⟩ **3** : organized so that the members share in the profits and liabilities ⟨*mutual* savings bank⟩ ⟨*mutual* fund⟩ — **mu·tu·al·ly** \-ē\ *adv*

mu·tu·al·ism \'myü-ch(ə-w)ə-ˌliz-əm\ *n* : association between different kinds of organisms that benefits both

muu·muu \'mü-mü\ *n* : a loose dress of Hawaiian origin for informal wear

1**muz·zle** \'məz-əl\ *n* **1** : the projecting jaws and nose of an animal : SNOUT **2** : a fastening or covering for the mouth of an animal used to prevent eating or biting **3** : the open end of a weapon from which the missile is discharged

2**muzzle** *vb* **muz·zled**; **muz·zling** \'məz-(ə-)liŋ\ **1** : to fit with a muzzle **2** : to prevent free or normal expression by : GAG ⟨the dictator *muzzled* the press⟩

muz·zle–load·er \ˌməz-əl-'(l)ōd-ər\ *n* : a gun that is loaded through the muzzle — **muz·zle–load·ing** \-'(l)ōd-iŋ\ *adj*

mv *abbr* millivolt

MVP *abbr* most valuable player

my \(ˌ)mī, mə\ *adj* : of or relating to me or myself ⟨*my* head⟩ ⟨kept *my* promise⟩ ⟨*my* injuries⟩

my·ce·li·um \mī-'sē-lē-əm\ *n, pl* **-lia** \-lē-ə\ *also* **-li·ums** : the vegetative part of the body of a fungus typically consisting of a mass of interwoven hyphae and often being submerged in another body (as of soil, organic matter, or the tissues of a plant or animal host) — **my·ce·li·al** \-lē-əl\ *adj*

my·col·o·gy \mī-'käl-ə-jē\ *n* **1** : a branch of botany dealing with fungi **2** : fungal life — **my·co·log·i·cal** \ˌmī-kə-'läj-i-kəl\ *adj* — **my·col·o·gist** \mī-'käl-ə-jəst\ *n*

my·e·lin \'mī-ə-lən\ *n* : a soft white somewhat fatty material that forms a thick sheath about certain nerve fibers — **my·e·lin·at·ed** \-lə-ˌnāt-əd\ *adj*

my·na *or* **my·nah** \'mī-nə\ *n* : an Asiatic starling that is black with a white spot on the wings and a pair of flat yellow wattles on the head and is often tamed and taught to pronounce words

my·o·pia \mī-'ō-pē-ə\ *n* : NEARSIGHTEDNESS, SHORTSIGHTEDNESS — **my·o·pic** \-'ōp-ik, -'äp-\ *adj* — **my·o·pi·cal·ly** \-i-k(ə-)lē\ *adv*

myr·ia \'mir-ē-ə, ˌmir-\ *comb form* : ten thousand — used esp. in terms belonging to the metric system

1**myr·i·ad** \'mir-ē-əd\ *n* [from Greek *myriad-*, stem of *myrias*, from *myrioi* (plural adjective) "extremely many", "ten thousand"] **1** : ten thousand **2** : an indefinitely large number ⟨the *myriads* of stars⟩

2**myriad** *adj* : extremely numerous ⟨the *myriad* grains of sand on a beach⟩

myr·ia·me·ter \'mir-ē-ə-ˌmēt-ər\ *n* — see METRIC SYSTEM table

myr·io·pod *or* **myr·ia·pod** \'mir-ē-ə-ˌpäd\ *n* : any of a group of arthropods including the millipedes and centipedes — **myriopod** *adj*

myr·mi·don \'mər-mə-ˌdän, 'mər-məd-ən\ *n* : a subordinate who executes orders without question or pity

myrrh \'mər\ *n* : a brown slightly bitter gum obtained

from African and Arabian trees and used esp. in perfumes or formerly in incense

myr·tle \'mərt-əl\ *n* **1** : a common evergreen shrub of southern Europe with oval to lance-shaped shining leaves, fragrant white or rosy flowers, and black berries **2 a** : any of the family of chiefly tropical shrubs or trees (as eucalyptus or guava) to which the common myrtle belongs **b** : PERIWINKLE

my·self \mī-'self, mə-\ *pron* **1** : the one that is I — used reflexively ⟨I'm going to get *myself* a new suit⟩ or for emphasis ⟨I *myself* will go⟩ **2** : my normal or healthy self ⟨didn't feel *myself* yesterday⟩

mys·te·ri·ous \mis-'tir-ē-əs\ *adj* : containing, suggesting, or implying a mystery : SECRET ⟨the *mysterious* ways of nature⟩ — **mys·te·ri·ous·ly** *adv*

mys·tery \'mis-t(ə-)rē\ *n, pl* **-ter·ies** **1 a** : a religious truth that man cannot fully understand **b** : any of the 15 events (as the Nativity, the Crucifixion, or the Assumption) serving as a subject for meditation during the saying of the rosary **2 a** : something that has not been or cannot be explained ⟨where he went is a *mystery*⟩ **b** : a deep secret ⟨kept his plans a *mystery*⟩ **3** : a piece of fiction dealing with a mysterious crime

mystery play *n* : a medieval play based on scriptural incidents (as the life and death of Jesus Christ)

[1]**mys·tic** \'mis-tik\ *adj* **1** : MYSTICAL **2** : of or relating to magical rites : OCCULT **3** : MYSTERIOUS, AWESOME

[2]**mystic** *n* : a person who seeks direct knowledge of God through contemplation and prayer

mys·ti·cal \'mis-ti-kəl\ *adj* **1** : having a spiritual meaning or reality not discoverable by the senses or intellect **2** : of, relating to, or resulting from communion with God or ultimate reality — **mys·ti·cal·ly** \-k(ə-)lē\ *adv*

mys·ti·cism \'mis-tə-,siz-əm\ *n* **1** : the experience of mystical communion with ultimate reality **2** : the belief that direct knowledge of God or of spiritual truth can be achieved by personal insight and inspiration

mys·ti·fy \'mis-tə-,fī\ *vb* **-fied**; **-fy·ing** **1** : to make obscure or difficult to understand **2** : PERPLEX, BEWILDER ⟨strange actions that *mystified* everyone⟩ ***syn*** see PUZZLE ***ant*** enlighten — **mys·ti·fi·ca·tion** \,mis-tə-fə-'kā-shən\ *n*

mys·tique \mis-'tēk\ *n* : a set of beliefs and attitudes developing around an object or associated with a group : CULT ⟨the *mystique* of mountain climbing⟩

myth \'mith\ *n* [from Greek *mythos*, meaning first "speech", "word", and then "story", "tale"] **1** : a usu. legendary narrative that presents part of the beliefs of a people or explains a practice, belief, or natural phenomenon **2** : a person or thing having only an imaginary existence ⟨the dragon is a *myth*⟩ **3** : a false or unsupported belief

myth·i·cal \'mith-i-kəl\ *also* **myth·ic** \-ik\ *adj* **1** : based on, described in, or being a myth ⟨Hercules is a *mythical* hero⟩ **2** : IMAGINARY, INVENTED — **myth·i·cal·ly** \-i-k(ə-)lē\ *adv*

my·thol·o·gy \mith-'äl-ə-jē\ *n, pl* **-gies** **1** : a body of myths; *esp* : the myths dealing with the gods and heroes of a people ⟨Greek *mythology*⟩ **2** : a branch of knowledge that deals with myth — **myth·o·log·i·cal** \,mith-ə-'läj-i-kəl\ *adj*

myxo·my·cete \,mik-sō-'mī-,sēt, -mī-'\ *n* : SLIME MOLD — **myxo·my·ce·tous** \-mī-'sēt-əs\ *adj*

M

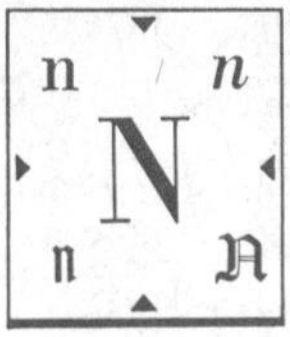

n \'en\ *n, often cap* **1 :** the 14th letter of the English alphabet **2 :** an unspecified quantity ⟨*n* samples of vaccine⟩

-n — see -EN

n *abbr* **1** note **2** noun

N *abbr* **1** north **2** northern

NA *abbr* not available

NAACP *abbr* National Association for the Advancement of Colored People

nab \'nab\ *vb* **nabbed**; **nab·bing 1 :** to seize and take into custody **:** ARREST **2 :** to seize suddenly; *esp* **:** STEAL

na·bob \'nā-ˌbäb\ *n* [from Hindi *nawwāb*] **1 :** a provincial governor of the Mogul empire in India **2 :** a man of great wealth or prominence

na·celle \nə-'sel\ *n* **:** an enclosed shelter on an aircraft for an engine or sometimes for crew

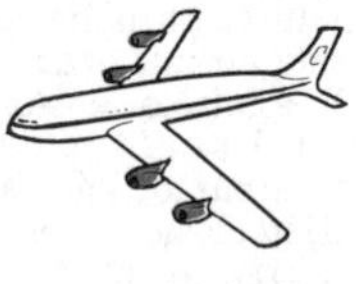

nacelles

na·cre \'nā-kər\ *n* **:** MOTHER-OF-PEARL — **na·cre·ous** \-krē-əs, -k(ə-)rəs\ *adj*

na·dir \'nā-ˌdi(ə)r, 'nād-ər\ *n* [from Arabic *naẓīr* "opposite", in the phrase *naẓīr as-samt* "opposite the zenith"] **1 :** the point of the celestial sphere that is directly opposite the zenith and directly under the observer **2 :** the lowest point ⟨our hopes reached their *nadir*⟩

1**nag** \'nag\ *n* **:** HORSE; *esp* **:** an old or decrepit horse

2**nag** *vb* **nagged**; **nag·ging 1 :** to find fault incessantly **:** COMPLAIN **2 :** to annoy constantly ⟨a *nagging* toothache⟩ — **nag·ger** *n*

Na·hum \'nā-(h)əm\ *n* — see BIBLE table

na·iad \'nā-əd, 'nī-, -ˌad\ *n, pl* **na·iads** *or* **na·ia·des** \-ə-ˌdēz\ **1 :** one of the nymphs in ancient mythology living in lakes, rivers, springs, and fountains **2 :** the aquatic young of a mayfly, dragonfly, damselfly, or stone fly

1**nail** \'nāl\ *n* **1 :** a horny protective sheath or claw at the end of the fingers and toes of man, apes, and many other mammals **2 :** a slender usu. pointed and headed fastener to be pounded in

2**nail** *vb* **1 :** to fasten with or as if with a nail **2 :** CATCH, TRAP ⟨*nail* a thief⟩ — **nail·er** *n*

nail·brush \'nāl-ˌbrəsh\ *n* **:** a small brush for cleaning the hands and fingernails

na·ïve *also* **na·ive** \nä-'ēv\ *adj* **1 :** marked by unaffected simplicity **:** ARTLESS **2 :** showing lack of informed judgment **:** CREDULOUS — **na·ïve·ly** *adv*

na·ïve·té *also* **na·ive·té** \(ˌ)nä-ˌē-və-'tā, nä-'ē-və-ˌ\ *n* **1 :** the quality or state of being naïve **2 :** a naïve remark or action

na·ked \'nā-kəd, *esp South* 'nek-əd\ *adj* **1 :** having no clothes on **:** NUDE **2 a :** lacking a usual or natural covering (as of foliage or feathers) ⟨*naked* hills⟩ **b :** UNSHEATHED ⟨a *naked* sword⟩ **c :** lacking protective enveloping parts (as membranes, scales, or shells) ⟨a *naked* seed⟩ ⟨slugs and other *naked* mollusks⟩ **3 :** PLAIN, UNADORNED ⟨the *naked* truth⟩ **4 :** not aided by artificial means ⟨seen by the *naked* eye⟩ — **na·ked·ly** *adv* — **na·ked·ness** *n*

1**name** \'nām\ *n* **1 :** a word or combination of words by which a person or thing is regularly known **2 :** a descriptive often disparaging word or phrase ⟨called him *names*⟩ **3 :** REPUTATION, FAME ⟨made a *name* for himself⟩ **4 :** appearance as opposed to fact ⟨a friend in *name* only⟩

2**name** *vb* **1 :** to give a name to **:** CALL **2 a :** to mention or identify by name **b :** to accuse by name **3 :** to nominate for office **:** APPOINT ⟨*named* him prime minister⟩ **4 :** to decide upon **:** CHOOSE ⟨*name* the date for a wedding⟩ **5 :** to speak about **:** MENTION ⟨*name* a price⟩ — **nam·er** *n*

3**name** *adj* **1 :** bearing a name ⟨*name* tag⟩ **2 :** having an established reputation ⟨*name* performers⟩ ⟨*name* brands⟩ — **name·a·ble** *also* **nam·a·ble** \'nā-mə-bəl\ *adj*

name·less \'nām-ləs\ *adj* **1 :** having no name **2 :** not marked with a name ⟨a *nameless* grave⟩ **3 :** UNKNOWN, ANONYMOUS ⟨a *nameless* hero⟩ ⟨a *nameless* author⟩ **4 :** not to be described ⟨*nameless* fears⟩ — **name·less·ly** *adv* — **name·less·ness** *n*

name·ly \'nām-lē\ *adv* **:** that is to say ⟨the cat family, *namely*, lions, tigers, and similar animals⟩

name·sake \'nām-ˌsāk\ *n* **:** one that has the same name as another; *esp* **:** one named after another

nan·keen \nan-'kēn\ *also* **nan·kin** \-'kēn, -'kin\ *n* **:** a durable brownish yellow cotton fabric orig. from China

nan·ny goat \'nan-ē-\ *n* **:** a female goat

nano- \'nan-ō, -ə\ *comb form* **:** one billionth part of ⟨*nano*second⟩

Nan·sen bottle \ˌnan(t)-sən-\ *n* **:** a device used in oceanographic studies for collecting water samples at predetermined depths

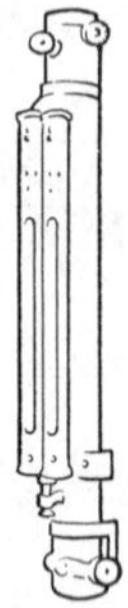

Nansen bottle

1**nap** \'nap\ *vb* **napped**; **nap·ping 1 :** to sleep briefly esp. during the day **:** DOZE **2 :** to be off guard ⟨was caught *napping*⟩

2**nap** *n* **:** a short sleep esp. during the day **:** SNOOZE ⟨takes a *nap* every day after lunch⟩

3**nap** *n* **:** a hairy or downy surface on a woven fabric — **nap·py** \'nap-ē\ *adj*

4**nap** *vb* **napped**; **nap·ping :** to raise a nap on fabric or leather

na·palm \'nā-ˌpäm, -ˌpälm\ *n* **1 :** a thickener used in jelling gasoline (as for incendiary bombs) **2 :** fuel jelled with napalm

nape \'nāp, 'nap\ *n* **:** the back of the neck

naph·tha \'naf-thə, 'nap-thə\ *n* **1 :** PETROLEUM **2 :** any of various volatile often flammable liquid hydrocarbon mixtures used esp. as solvents

naph·tha·lene \-ˌlēn\ *n* **:** a crystalline hydrocarbon usu. obtained by distillation of coal tar and used in chemical manufacture and as a moth repellent

Na·pier's bones \'nā-pē-ərz-\ *n* **:** a set of 11 rods invented by the Scottish mathematician Napier for making numerical calculations

nap·kin \'nap-kən\ *n* **1 :** a small square of cloth or paper used at table to wipe the lips or fingers and protect the clothes **2 :** a small cloth or towel

na·po·leon \nə-'pōl-yən, -'pō-lē-ən\ *n* **1 :** a French 20-franc gold coin **2 :** an oblong pastry with a filling of cream, custard, or jelly between layers of crust

narc *or* **nark** \'närk\ *n* **:** a person (as a government agent) who investigates narcotics violations

nar·cis·sus \när-'sis-əs\ *n, pl* **-cissus** *or* **-cis·sus·es** \-'sis-ə-səz\ *or* **-cis·si** \-'sis-ˌī, -(ˌ)ē\ **:** DAFFODIL; *esp* **:** one whose flowers have a short corona and are usu. borne separately

nar·co·sis \när-'kō-səs\ *n, pl* **-co·ses** \-'kō-ˌsēz\ **:** a state of stupor, unconsciousness, or arrested activity produced by chemicals (as narcotics)

1nar·cot·ic \när-ˈkät-ik\ *n* **1 :** a drug (as opium) that in moderate doses dulls the senses, relieves pain, and induces sleep but in excessive doses causes stupor, coma, or convulsions **2 :** something that soothes, relieves, or lulls

2narcotic *adj* **1 :** having the properties of or yielding a narcotic **2 :** of or relating to narcotics or to their use or to addicts

nar·co·tize \ˈnär-kə-ˌtīz\ *vb* **1 a :** to treat with or subject to a narcotic **b :** to put into a state of narcosis **2 :** to soothe to unconsciousness or unawareness

na·ris \ˈnar-əs, ˈner-\ *n, pl* **na·res** \ˈna(ə)r-(ˌ)ēz, ˈne(ə)r-\ **:** any of the openings of the nose or nasal cavity of a vertebrate

nar·rate \ˈnar-ˌāt, na-ˈrāt\ *vb* **:** RELATE, TELL ⟨*narrate* a story⟩ — **nar·ra·tor** \ˈnar-ˌāt-ər, na-ˈrāt-\ *n*

nar·ra·tion \na-ˈrā-shən, nə-\ *n* **1 :** the act or process or an instance of narrating **2 :** STORY, NARRATIVE — **nar·ra·tion·al** \-sh(ə-)nəl\ *adj*

nar·ra·tive \ˈnar-ət-iv\ *n* **1 :** something (as a story or an account of a series of events) that is narrated **2 :** the art or practice of narration — **narrative** *adj*

syn NARRATIVE, ACCOUNT, RECITAL can mean a statement of facts or events. NARRATIVE implies a series of connected events told or written often in artistic fashion; ACCOUNT suggests a simple repetition of facts; RECITAL may suggest either great detail or mechanical enumeration of seemingly memorized facts in a narrative

1nar·row \ˈnar-ō\ *adj* **1 :** of slender or of less than usual width **2 :** limited in size or scope **:** RESTRICTED **3 a :** not liberal in views **:** PREJUDICED **b :** interpreted or interpreting strictly ⟨a *narrow* view⟩ **4 :** barely sufficient **:** CLOSE ⟨a *narrow* escape⟩ ⟨won by a *narrow* margin⟩ — **nar·row·ly** *adv* — **nar·row·ness** *n*

2narrow *n* **:** a narrow part or passage; *esp* **:** a strait connecting two bodies of water — usu. used in pl.

3narrow *vb* **:** to lessen in width or extent **:** CONTRACT, RESTRICT

nar·row–mind·ed \ˌnar-ō-ˈmīn-dəd\ *adj* **:** INTOLERANT, BIGOTED — **nar·row–mind·ed·ness** *n*

nar·whal \ˈnär-ˌ(h)wäl, ˈnär-wəl\ *n* **:** an arctic sea

narwhal

mammal that is about 20 feet long, is related to the dolphin, and in the male has a long twisted ivory tusk

NASA *abbr* National Aeronautics and Space Administration

1na·sal \ˈnā-zəl\ *n* **:** a nasal consonant or vowel

2nasal *adj* **1 :** of or relating to the nose **2 a :** uttered with the mouth passage closed and the nose passage open ⟨the *nasal* consonants \m\, \n\, and \ng\⟩ **b :** uttered with the nose and mouth passages open ⟨the *nasal* vowels in French⟩ **c :** marked by resonance produced through the nose ⟨speaking in a *nasal* tone⟩ — **na·sal·i·ty** \nā-ˈzal-ət-ē\ *n* — **na·sal·ly** \ˈnā-zə-lē\ *adv*

nasal cavity *n* **:** an incompletely divided chamber that lies between the floor of the skull and the roof of the mouth and functions in the warming and filtering of inhaled air and in the sensing of odors

nas·tur·tium \nə-ˈstər-shəm, na-\ *n* **:** any of a genus of watery-stemmed herbs with showy spurred flowers and 3-seeded fruits

nas·ty \ˈnas-tē\ *adj* **nas·ti·er; -est** **1 :** very dirty or foul **:** FILTHY **2 :** INDECENT, VILE **3 :** DISAGREEABLE ⟨*nasty* weather⟩ **4 :** MEAN, ILL-NATURED ⟨a *nasty* temper⟩ **5 :** DISHONORABLE ⟨a *nasty* trick⟩ **6 :** HARMFUL, DANGEROUS ⟨a *nasty* fall on the ice⟩ — **nas·ti·ly** \-tə-lē\ *adv* — **nas·ti·ness** \-tē-nəs\ *n*

na·tal \ˈnāt-əl\ *adj* **:** of or relating to birth

na·tion \ˈnā-shən\ *n* **1 :** NATIONALITY 3 **2 :** a community of people composed of one or more nationalities usu. with its own territory and government **3 :** the territory of a nation — **na·tion·al·ly** \-ē\ *adv*

1na·tion·al \ˈnash-(ə-)nəl\ *adj* **:** of or relating to a nation ⟨the *national* government⟩

2national *n* **1 :** a citizen or subject of a nation **2 :** an organization (as a labor union) having local units throughout a nation

national bank *n* **:** a commercial bank organized under laws passed by Congress and chartered by the national government

National Guard *n* **:** a militia force recruited by each state, equipped by the federal government, and subject to the call of either

na·tion·al·ism \ˈnash-(ə-)nə-liz-əm\ *n* **:** loyalty and devotion to a nation esp. as expressed in an exalting of one nation above all others with primary emphasis on promotion of its culture and interests

na·tion·al·ist \-ləst\ *n* **1 :** an advocate of nationalism **2** *cap* **:** a member of a group advocating national independence — **nationalist** *adj, often cap* — **na·tion·al·is·tic** \ˌnash-(ə-)nə-ˈlis-tik\ *adj*

na·tion·al·i·ty \ˌnash-ə-ˈnal-ət-ē\ *n, pl* **-ties** **1 :** the fact or state of belonging to a nation ⟨a man of French *nationality*⟩ **2 :** political independence as a nation **3 :** a people having a common origin, tradition, or language and capable of forming or actually constituting a state

na·tion·al·ize \ˈnash-(ə-)nə-ˌlīz\ *vb* **1 :** to make national **:** make a nation of **2 :** to remove from private ownership and place under government control ⟨*nationalize* railroads⟩ — **na·tion·al·i·za·tion** \ˌnash-(ə-)nə-lə-ˈzā-shən\ *n*

na·tion·wide \ˌnā-shən-ˈwīd\ *adj* **:** extending throughout a nation

1na·tive \ˈnāt-iv\ *adj* **1 :** INBORN, NATURAL ⟨*native* shrewdness⟩ **2 :** born in a particular place or country ⟨*native* Americans⟩ **3 :** belonging to a person because of the place or circumstances of his birth ⟨his *native* language⟩ **4 :** grown, produced, or having its origin in a particular region ⟨*native* art⟩ **5 :** occurring in nature **:** not artificially prepared ⟨*native* salt⟩ — **na·tive·ly** *adv*

syn NATIVE, INDIGENOUS, ABORIGINAL can mean belonging to a locality. NATIVE applies to one born or having originated in a place or region; INDIGENOUS applies to species or races and esp. to those that have not been introduced from elsewhere to their present location; ABORIGINAL implies the absence of predecessors in a region and in application to people may suggest a primitive level of civilization ***ant*** alien, foreign

[2]**native** *n* **1 :** one born or reared in a particular place **2 :** an original inhabitant **3 :** something native to or produced in a locality ⟨*native* corn⟩

na·tiv·i·ty \nə-ˈtiv-ət-ē, nā-\ *n, pl* **-ties 1** *cap* **:** the birth of Christ **2** *cap* **:** CHRISTMAS 1 **3 :** the time, place, or manner of being born **:** BIRTH

natl *abbr* national

NATO *abbr* North Atlantic Treaty Organization

nat·ty \ˈnat-ē\ *adj* **nat·ti·er; -est :** trimly neat and tidy **:** SMART — **nat·ti·ly** \ˈnat-ə-lē\ *adv* — **nat·ti·ness** \ˈnat-ē-nəs\ *n*

[1]**nat·u·ral** \ˈnach-(ə-)rəl\ *adj* **1 :** born in or with one **:** INNATE ⟨*natural* ability⟩ **2 :** being such by nature **:** BORN ⟨a *natural* fool⟩ **3 :** born of unmarried parents **:** ILLEGITIMATE ⟨a *natural* son⟩ **4 :** existing or used in or produced by nature ⟨the *natural* woodland flora⟩ ⟨meat is the *natural* food of dogs⟩ **5 :** HUMAN ⟨it is not *natural* to hate your son⟩ **6 :** of, relating to, or conforming to the laws of nature or of the physical world ⟨*natural* causes⟩ **7 :** not made or altered by man ⟨*natural* silk⟩ ⟨a person's *natural* complexion⟩ **8 :** not affected ⟨*natural* manners⟩ **9 :** LIFELIKE ⟨the people in the picture look *natural*⟩ **10 :** having neither sharps nor flats in the key signature or having a sharp or a flat changed in pitch by a natural sign — **nat·u·ral·ness** *n*

[2]**natural** *n* **1 a :** a character ♮ placed on a line or space of the musical staff to nullify the effect of a preceding sharp or flat **b :** a note or tone affected by the natural sign **2 :** one naturally adapted to something ⟨a *natural* at golf⟩ **3 :** AFRO

natural gas *n* **:** gas issuing from the earth's crust through natural openings or bored wells; *esp* **:** a combustible mixture of hydrocarbons and esp. methane used chiefly as a fuel and raw material

natural history *n* **:** the scientific study of peoples, animals, plants, and minerals ⟨a museum of *natural history*⟩

natural immunity *n* **:** inherent genetically determined immunity as distinguished from that acquired by vaccination or by having a disease

nat·u·ral·ist \ˈnach-(ə-)rə-ləst\ *n* **:** a student of natural history; *esp* **:** a field biologist — **naturalist** *adj*

nat·u·ral·ize \-ˌlīz\ *vb* **1 :** to introduce into common use ⟨*naturalize* a foreign word⟩ **2 :** to become or cause to become established as if native ⟨*naturalized* weeds⟩ **3 :** to confer the rights and privileges of citizenship on ⟨*naturalize* a foreign-born person⟩ — **nat·u·ral·i·za·tion** \ˌnach-(ə-)rə-lə-ˈzā-shən\ *n*

nat·u·ral·ly \ˈnach-(ə-)rə-lē, ˈnach-ər-lē\ *adv* **1 :** by natural character or ability ⟨*naturally* timid⟩ **2 :** according to the usual course of things ⟨we *naturally* dislike being hurt⟩ **3 a :** without artificial aid ⟨hair that curls *naturally*⟩ **b :** without affectation ⟨speak *naturally*⟩ **4 :** in a lifelike manner ⟨paints flowers *naturally*⟩

natural number *n* **:** the number 1 or any number (as 3, 12, or 432) obtained by repeatedly adding 1 to it

natural resource *n* **:** something (as a mineral, waterpower source, forest, or kind of animal) that occurs in nature and is valuable to man

natural science *n* **:** a science (as physics, chemistry, or biology) that deals with the basic elements, properties, and behavior of matter, energy, or life in a thoroughly objective way

natural selection *n* **:** a natural process in which individuals or groups best adapted to the conditions under which they live survive and poorly adapted forms are eliminated

na·ture \ˈnā-chər\ *n* **1 :** the basic quality, character, or constitution of a person or thing ⟨the *nature* of steel⟩ **2 :** KIND, SORT ⟨and things of that *nature*⟩ **3 :** DISPOSITION, TEMPERAMENT ⟨behavior quite contrary to his *nature*⟩ **4** *often cap* **:** a power or set of forces thought of as controlling the universe ⟨Mother *Nature*⟩ **5 :** natural feeling esp. as shown in one's attitude toward others ⟨his good *nature* is well known⟩ **6 :** man's native state **:** primitive life ⟨return to *nature*⟩ **7 :** the physical universe ⟨the study of *nature*⟩ **8 :** the physical constitution or drives of an organism ⟨sex is a part of *nature*⟩ **9 :** natural scenery ⟨the beauties of *nature*⟩

naught \ˈnȯt, ˈnät\ *n* **1 a :** NOTHING **b :** NOTHINGNESS **2 :** ZERO — see NUMBER table

naugh·ty \ˈnȯt-ē, ˈnät-\ *adj* **naugh·ti·er; -est :** behaving badly or improperly — **naugh·ti·ly** \ˈnȯt-ə-lē, ˈnät-\ *adv* — **naugh·ti·ness** \ˈnȯt-ē-nəs, ˈnät-\ *n*

nau·sea \ˈnȯ-zē-ə, -shə\ *n* [from Latin, from Greek *nautia, nausia,* meaning originally "seasickness", from *nautēs* "sailor"] **1 :** a stomach distress with distaste for food and an urge to vomit **2 :** extreme disgust

nau·se·ate \ˈnȯ-z(h)ē-ˌāt, -s(h)ē-\ *vb* **:** to affect or become affected with nausea — **nau·se·at·ing·ly** \-ing-lē\ *adv*

nau·seous \ˈnȯ-shəs, ˈnȯ-zē-əs\ *adj* **:** affected with or tending to cause nausea ⟨feel *nauseous*⟩ ⟨a *nauseous* odor⟩ — **nau·seous·ly** *adv*

nau·ti·cal \ˈnȯt-i-kəl\ *adj* **:** of or relating to seamen, navigation, or ships — **nau·ti·cal·ly** \-k(ə-)lē\ *adv*

nautical mile *n* **:** MILE 2

nau·ti·lus \ˈnȯt-ə-ləs\ *n, pl* **-lus·es** *or* **-li** \-ə-ˌlī, -ˌlē\ **1 :** any of a genus of cephalopod mollusks of the So. Pacific and Indian oceans having a spiral chambered shell pearly on the inside **2 :** PAPER NAUTILUS

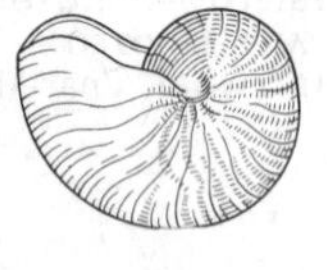

nautilus 1 (shell about 10 in. in diameter)

nav *abbr* **1** naval **2** navigational

Nav·a·ho *or* **Nav·a·jo** \ˈnav-ə-ˌhō, ˈnäv-\ *n* **:** a member of an Amerindian people of northern New Mexico and Arizona

na·val \ˈnā-vəl\ *adj* **1 :** of or relating to a navy or warships ⟨*naval* shipyard⟩ ⟨*naval* officer⟩ **2 :** possessing a navy ⟨a *naval* power⟩

naval stores *n pl* **:** products (as pitch, turpentine, or rosin) obtained from coniferous trees (as pines)

[1]**nave** \ˈnāv\ *n* **:** the hub of a wheel

[2]**nave** *n* **:** the long central main part of a church

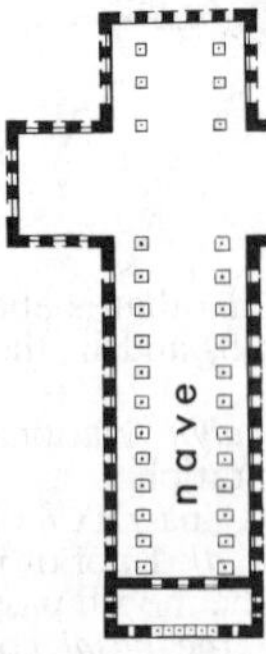

na·vel \ˈnā-vəl\ *n* **:** a depression in the middle of the abdomen marking the point of attachment of the umbilical cord

navel orange *n* **:** a usu. seedless orange with a small secondary fruit resembling a navel at one end

nav·i·ga·ble \ˈnav-i-gə-bəl\

N

adj **1** : deep and wide enough to afford passage to ships **2** : capable of being steered ⟨a *navigable* balloon⟩ — **nav·i·ga·bil·i·ty** \ˌnav-i-gə-ˈbil-ət-ē\ *n*
nav·i·gate \ˈnav-ə-ˌgāt\ *vb* **1 a** : to travel by water **b** : to sail over, on, or through **2 a** : to direct one's course in a ship or aircraft **b** : to control the course of : STEER
nav·i·ga·tion \ˌnav-ə-ˈgā-shən\ *n* **1** : the act or practice of navigating **2** : the science of determining the course of a ship or aircraft — **nav·i·ga·tion·al** \-sh(ə-)nəl\ *adj*
nav·i·ga·tor \ˈnav-ə-ˌgāt-ər\ *n* **1** : an officer on a ship or airplane responsible for its navigation **2** : one who explores by ship
na·vy \ˈnā-vē\ *n, pl* **navies 1** : a fleet of ships **2** : a nation's warships **3** *often cap* : a nation's complete equipment and men for sea warfare **4** : a grayish purplish blue
navy bean *n* : a kidney bean grown esp. for its small white nutritious seeds
navy yard *n* : a naval shore station with facilities for building, equipping, and repairing warships
na·wab \nə-ˈwäb\ *n* : a Muslim prince of India
[1]**nay** \ˈnā\ *adv* **1** : NO **2** : not merely this but also : not only so but ⟨the letter made him happy, *nay*, ecstatic⟩
[2]**nay** *n* **1** : DENIAL, REFUSAL **2 a** : a negative reply or vote **b** : one who votes no
Naz·a·rene \ˌnaz-ə-ˈrēn\ *n* **1** : a native or resident of Nazareth **2** : Jesus Christ — **Nazarene** *adj*
Na·zi \ˈnät-sē, ˈnat-\ *n* : a member of a German fascist party controlling Germany from 1933 to 1945 — **Nazi** *adj* — **Na·zism** \ˈnät-ˌsiz-əm, ˈnat-\ *or* **Na·zi·ism** \-sē-ˌiz-əm\ *n*
NB *abbr* **1** Nebraska **2** northbound
N.B. *abbr* New Brunswick
NBA *abbr* **1** National Basketball Association **2** National Boxing Association
NBC *abbr* National Broadcasting Company
NBS *abbr* National Bureau of Standards
NC *abbr* **1** no charge **2** North Carolina
N.C. *abbr* North Carolina
NCAA *abbr* National Collegiate Athletic Association
NCE *abbr* New Catholic Edition
NCO *abbr* noncommissioned officer
N. Dak. *or* **N.D.** *or* **ND** *abbr* North Dakota
ne- *or* **neo-** *comb form* **1** : new : recent ⟨*Neo*cene⟩ ⟨*neo*phyte⟩ **2** : New World ⟨*Neo*tropical⟩
NE *abbr* northeast
Ne·an·der·thal \nē-ˈan-dər-ˌt(h)ȯl, nā-ˈän-dər-ˌtäl\ *adj* **1** : being, relating to, or resembling Neanderthal man **2** : suggesting a caveman in appearance or behavior — **Ne·an·der·thal·er** \-ər\ *or* **Neanderthal** *n*
Neanderthal man *n* : a prehistoric man intermediate in some respects between modern man and pithecanthropus
Ne·a·pol·i·tan ice cream \ˌnē-ə-ˌpäl-ət-ən\ *n* : a brick of ice cream with layers of different flavors
neap tide *n* : a tide of least range occurring at the 1st and 3d quarters of the moon
[1]**near** \ˈni(ə)r\ *adv* **1** : at, within, or to a short distance or time **2** : NEARLY ⟨*near* dead⟩ **3** : CLOSELY ⟨*near* related⟩
[2]**near** *prep* : close to ⟨standing *near* the door⟩
[3]**near** *adj* **1** : closely related or associated **2 a** : not far away **b** : barely avoided ⟨a *near* disaster⟩ **c** : coming close : NARROW ⟨a *near* miss⟩ **3** : being the closer of two ⟨the *near* side of a hill⟩ **4** : DIRECT, SHORT ⟨*nearest* route⟩ **5** : closely resembling a model or a genuine example ⟨*near* silk⟩ — **near·ly** *adv* — **near·ness** *n*
[4]**near** *vb* : to come near : APPROACH
near·by \ni(ə)r-ˈbī, ˈni(ə)r-ˌ\ *adv or adj* : close at hand
near·sight·ed \ˈni(ə)r-ˈsīt-əd\ *adj* : able to see near things more clearly than distant ones : MYOPIC
near·sight·ed·ness *n* : a visual condition in which the image focuses in front of the retina causing defective vision of distant objects
neat \ˈnēt\ *adj* [from Old French *net*, from Latin *nitidus*, meaning originally "bright", from *nitēre* "to shine"] **1** : not mixed or diluted : STRAIGHT ⟨*neat* brandy⟩ **2** : marked by tasteful simplicity **3** : SKILLFUL, ADROIT **4** : being orderly and clean : TIDY — **neat·ly** *adv* — **neat·ness** *n*
neat's–foot oil \ˈnēts-ˌfu̇t-\ *n* : a pale yellow fatty oil made esp. from the bones of cattle and used chiefly for dressing leather
NEB *abbr* New English Bible
Nebr *or* **Neb** *abbr* Nebraska
neb·u·la \ˈneb-yə-lə\ *n, pl* **-las** *or* **-lae** \-ˌlē, -ˌlī\ **1** : any of many immense bodies of highly rarefied gas or dust in interstellar space **2** : GALAXY — **neb·u·lar** \-lər\ *adj*
nebular hypothesis *n* : a hypothesis in astronomy: the solar system has evolved from a hot gaseous nebula
neb·u·lous \ˈneb-yə-ləs\ *adj* **1** : HAZY, VAGUE **2** : of, relating to, or resembling a nebula — **neb·u·lous·ly** *adv* — **neb·u·lous·ness** *n*
[1]**nec·es·sary** \ˈnes-ə-ˌser-ē\ *adj* **1** : going to happen with no way of preventing it : INEVITABLE **2** : being the only possible result of an argument : CERTAIN **3** : REQUIRED, COMPULSORY ⟨it is *necessary* that you do your homework⟩ **4** : impossible to do without : INDISPENSABLE ⟨food is *necessary* for life⟩ — **nec·es·sar·i·ly** \ˌnes-ə-ˈser-ə-lē\ *adv*
[2]**necessary** *n, pl* **-sar·ies** : something necessary : REQUIREMENT ⟨the *necessaries* of life⟩
ne·ces·si·tate \ni-ˈses-ə-ˌtāt\ *vb* : to make necessary : REQUIRE, COMPEL ⟨sick enough to *necessitate* his staying home⟩ — **ne·ces·si·ta·tion** \-ˌses-ə-ˈtā-shən\ *n*
ne·ces·si·ty \ni-ˈses-ət-ē, -ˈses-tē\ *n, pl* **-ties 1** : very great need of help or relief ⟨call in case of *necessity*⟩ **2** : something badly needed **3** : lack of necessary things : WANT, POVERTY **4** : conditions that cannot be changed ⟨compelled by *necessity*⟩
neck \ˈnek\ *n* **1** : the part of the body connecting the head and the trunk **2** : the part of a garment covering or nearest to the neck **3** : something like a neck in shape or position ⟨the *neck* of a bottle⟩ ⟨a *neck* of land⟩ — **necked** \ˈnekt\ *adj* — **neck and neck** : so nearly equal (as in a race) that one cannot be said to be ahead of the other
neck·er·chief \ˈnek-ər-chəf, -(ˌ)chif, -ˌchēf\ *n, pl* **-chiefs** *also* **-chieves** \-chəfs, -(ˌ)chifs, -ˌchēvz, -ˌchēfs\ : a square of cloth worn folded about the neck like a scarf
neck·lace \ˈnek-ləs\ *n* : an ornament (as a string of beads) worn around the neck
neck·line \-ˌlīn\ *n* : the outline of the neck opening of a garment
neck·piece \-ˌpēs\ *n* : an article of apparel (as a fur scarf) worn about the neck
neck·tie \-ˌtī\ *n* : a narrow length of cloth worn about the neck and tied in front
neck·wear \-ˌwa(ə)r, -ˌwe(ə)r\ *n* : articles (as scarves or neckties) for wear around the neck
nec·ro·man·cy \ˈnek-rə-ˌman(t)-sē\ *n* **1** : the art or practice of conjuring up the spirits of the dead for magical purposes **2** : MAGIC — **nec·ro·man·cer** \-sər\ *n*
ne·cro·sis \nə-ˈkrō-səs, ne-\ *n, pl* **-cro·ses** \-ˈkrō-

ˌsēz\ : usu. local death of body tissue — **ne·crot·ic** \-ˈkrät-ik\ *adj*

nec·tar \ˈnek-tər\ *n* **1** : the drink of the Greek and Roman gods **2** : a sweet liquid secreted by plants that is the chief raw material of honey

nec·tar·ine \ˌnek-tə-ˈrēn\ *n* : a smooth-skinned peach; *also* : a tree producing this fruit

nec·tary \ˈnek-tə-rē\ *n, pl* **-tar·ies** : a plant gland that secretes nectar

née *or* **nee** \ˈnā\ *adj* : BORN — used to identify a woman by her maiden family name ⟨Mrs. Jane Doe, *née* Roe⟩

[1]**need** \ˈnēd\ *n* **1** : necessary duty : OBLIGATION **2 a** : a lack of something necessary, desirable, or useful **b** : a mental or physical requirement for maintaining the normal condition of an organism **3** : something necessary or desired ⟨our daily *needs*⟩ **4** : POVERTY, WANT

[2]**need** *vb* **1** : to be in want **2** : to be in need of : REQUIRE ⟨he *needs* advice⟩ **3** : to be required or obliged ⟨we *need* to look at the facts⟩ ⟨you *need* not answer⟩ **4** : to be necessary ⟨something *needs* to be done⟩

need·ful \ˈnēd-fəl\ *adj* : NECESSARY, REQUISITE — **need·ful·ly** \-fə-lē\ *adv* — **need·ful·ness** *n*

[1]**nee·dle** \ˈnēd-əl\ *n* **1 a** : a slender usu. steel instrument having an eye for thread and used for sewing **b** : a device for carrying thread and making stitches (as in sewing up a wound) **c** : a slender hollow instrument for introducing material into or removing material from the body **2** : a slender indicator on a dial **3 a** : a slender pointed object (as a pointed crystal or an obelisk) **b** : a needle-shaped leaf (as of a pine) **4** : a slender piece of jewel or steel with a rounded tip used in a phonograph to transmit vibrations from the record — **nee·dle·like** \ˈnēd-əl-ˌ(l)īk\ *adj*

[2]**needle** *vb* **nee·dled**; **nee·dling** \ˈnēd-(ə-)liŋ\ : PROD, GOAD; *esp* : to incite to action by repeated gibes — **nee·dler** \-(ə-)lər\ *n* — **nee·dling** *n*

nee·dle·point \ˈnēd-əl-ˌpȯint\ *n* : embroidery done on canvas usu. in simple even stitches across counted threads

need·less \ˈnēd-ləs\ *adj* : UNNECESSARY — **need·less·ly** *adv*

nee·dle·work \ˈnēd-əl-ˌwərk\ *n* : work done with a needle; *esp* : EMBROIDERY

needn't \ˈnēd-ənt\ : need not

needs \ˈnēdz\ *adv* : of necessity : NECESSARILY ⟨must *needs* be recognized⟩

needy \ˈnēd-ē\ *adj* **need·i·er**; **-est** : being in want : very poor — **need·i·ness** *n*

ne'er \(ˈ)ne(ə)r, (ˈ)na(ə)r\ *adv* : NEVER

ne'er-do-well \ˈne(ə)rd-ü-ˌwel, ˈna(ə)rd-\ *n* : an idle worthless person

ne·far·i·ous \ni-ˈfar-ē-əs, -ˈfer-\ *adj* : very wicked : EVIL — **ne·far·i·ous·ly** *adv* — **ne·far·i·ous·ness** *n*

neg *abbr* negative

ne·gate \ni-ˈgāt\ *vb* **1** : to deny the existence or truth of **2** : to cause to be ineffective or invalid

ne·ga·tion \ni-ˈgā-shən\ *n* **1 a** : the action of negating : DENIAL **b** : a negative statement **2** : something that is the opposite of something positive ⟨death is the *negation* of life⟩ — **ne·ga·tion·al** \-sh(ə-)nəl\ *adj*

ə abut · ər further · a back · ā bake · ä cot, cart · aù out · ch chin · e less · ē easy · g gift · i trip · ī life · j joke · ŋ sing · ō flow · ȯ flaw · ȯi coin · th thin · th this · ü loot · ù foot · y yet · yü few · yù furious · zh vision

[1]**neg·a·tive** \ˈneg-ət-iv\ *adj* **1** : marked by denial, prohibition, or refusal ⟨a *negative* reply⟩ **2** : not positive or constructive ⟨a *negative* attitude⟩ ⟨*negative* criticism⟩ **3** : less than zero and opposite in sign to a positive number ⟨*negative* angle⟩ **4 a** : of, being, or relating to electricity of a kind of which the electron is the elementary unit and which predominates in a hard rubber rod after being rubbed with wool ⟨a *negative* charge⟩ **b** : having more electrons than protons ⟨a *negative* particle⟩ **c** : being the part toward which the electric current flows from the external circuit ⟨the *negative* pole of a battery⟩ **5 a** : not affirming the presence of a particular germ or condition ⟨a *negative* TB test⟩ **b** : directed or moving away from a source of stimulation ⟨a *negative* tropism⟩ **6** : having the light and dark parts in approximately inverse order to those of the original photographic subject — **neg·a·tive·ly** *adv* — **neg·a·tive·ness** *n* — **neg·a·tiv·i·ty** \ˌneg-ə-ˈtiv-ət-ē\ *n*

[2]**negative** *n* **1** : a reply that indicates denial or contradiction : REFUSAL **2** : something that is the opposite or negation of something else **3** : an expression (as the word *no*) of negation or denial **4** : a negative number **5** : the side that argues or votes against something in a debate **6** : a negative photographic image on transparent film or plate used for printing positive pictures

[3]**negative** *vb* **1** : to refuse to accept or approve **2** : to vote against **3** : DENY, CONTRADICT

[1]**ne·glect** \ni-ˈglekt\ *vb* **1** : to give little attention or respect to : DISREGARD **2** : to leave undone or unattended to esp. through carelessness — **ne·glect·er** *n*

[2]**neglect** *n* **1** : an act or instance of neglecting something **2** : the condition of being neglected

ne·glect·ful \ni-ˈglekt-fəl\ *adj* : given to neglecting : CARELESS — **ne·glect·ful·ly** \-fə-lē\ *adv*

neg·li·gee *also* **neg·li·gé** \ˌneg-lə-ˈzhā\ *n* **1** : a woman's long flowing dressing gown **2** : informal attire

neg·li·gence \ˈneg-li-jən(t)s\ *n* **1** : the quality or state of being negligent; *esp* : failure to exercise the care that a prudent person usually exercises **2** : an act or instance of negligence

neg·li·gent \-jənt\ *adj* **1** : marked by or given to neglect **2** : failing to exercise proper or normal care — **neg·li·gent·ly** *adv*

neg·li·gi·ble \ˈneg-li-jə-bəl\ *adj* : fit to be neglected or disregarded : TRIFLING — **neg·li·gi·bly** \-blē\ *adv*

ne·go·tia·ble \ni-ˈgō-sh(ē-)ə-bəl\ *adj* : capable of being negotiated; *esp* : capable of being passed from one person to another in return for something of equal value — **ne·go·tia·bil·i·ty** \-ˌgō-sh(ē-)ə-ˈbil-ət-ē\ *n*

ne·go·ti·ate \ni-ˈgō-shē-ˌāt\ *vb* **1 a** : to discuss with another so as to arrive at an agreement **b** : to arrange for or bring about by such conference ⟨*negotiate* a treaty⟩ **2** : to transfer to another in return for something of equal value ⟨*negotiate* a check⟩ **3** : to get through, around, or over successfully ⟨*negotiate* a turn⟩ — **ne·go·ti·a·tion** \-ˌgō-s(h)ē-ˈā-shən\ *n* — **ne·go·ti·a·tor** \-ˈgō-shē-ˌāt-ər\ *n*

neg·ri·tude \ˈneg-rə-ˌt(y)üd, ˈnē-grə-\ *n* : consciousness of and pride in the cultural values that constitute the African heritage

Ne·gro \ˈnē-grō, *esp South* ˈnig-rō\ *n, pl* **Negroes** [from Spanish or Portuguese *negro* "black", from Latin *nigr-*, stem of *niger*] **1** : a member of the black race of mankind distinguished from members of other races by physical features without regard to language or culture; *esp* : a member of a people belonging to the African branch of the black race **2** : a person of Negro ancestry — **Negro** *adj* — **ne·groid** \'nē-ˌgrȯid\ *n or adj, often cap*

Ne·he·mi·ah \ˌnē-(h)ə-'mī-ə\ *n* — see BIBLE table

neigh \'nā\ *vb* : to make the loud prolonged cry of a horse — **neigh** *n*

1**neigh·bor** \'nā-bər\ *n* [from Old English *nēahgebūr*, from *nēah* "near" and *gebūr* "dweller"] **1** : a person who lives near another **2** : a person or thing located near another ⟨Canada is a *neighbor* of the U.S.⟩ **3** : FELLOWMAN

2**neighbor** *vb* **neigh·bored**; **neigh·bor·ing** \-b(ə-)riŋ\ : to be next to or near to ⟨*neighboring* towns⟩

neigh·bor·hood \'nā-bər-ˌhu̇d\ *n* **1** : the quality or state of being neighbors : NEARNESS **2 a** : a place or region near : VICINITY **b** : a number or amount near ⟨cost in the *neighborhood* of $10⟩ **3 a** : the people living near one another **b** : a section lived in by people who consider themselves neighbors

neigh·bor·ly \'nā-bər-lē\ *adj* : of, relating to, or characteristic of neighbors : FRIENDLY — **neigh·bor·li·ness** *n*

1**nei·ther** \'nē-t͟hər, 'nī-\ *pron* : not the one and not the other ⟨*neither* of the two⟩

2**neither** *conj* **1** : both not : equally not ⟨*neither* black nor white⟩ **2** : also not ⟨*neither* did I⟩

3**neither** *adj* : not either ⟨*neither* hand⟩

nek·ton \'nek-tən, -ˌtän\ *n* : strong-swimming aquatic animals whose distribution is essentially independent of wave and current action — **nek·ton·ic** \nek-'tän-ik\ *adj*

nem·a·tode \'nem-ə-ˌtōd\ *n* : any of a major group of elongated cylindrical worms parasitic in animals or plants or living in soil or water — **nematode** *adj*

ne·mer·te·an \ni-'mərt-ē-ən\ *n* : any of a class of often vividly colored marine worms most of which burrow in the mud or sand along seacoasts — **nemertean** *adj*

nem·e·sis \'nem-ə-səs\ *n, pl* **-e·ses** \-ə-ˌsēz\ [from Greek *Nemesis*, goddess of divine retribution, from *nemesis* "righteous indignation"] **1** : one that inflicts punishment or vengeance **2** : an act or instance of just punishment

ne·moph·i·la \ni-'mäf-ə-lə\ *n* : any of a genus of American herbs widely grown for their showy blue usu. spotted flowers

neo- — see NE-

neo·clas·sic \ˌnē-ō-'klas-ik\ *adj* : of or relating to a revival or adaptation of the classical style esp. in literature, art, or music — **neo·clas·si·cal** \-'klas-i-kəl\ *adj* — **neo·clas·si·cism** \-'klas-ə-ˌsiz-əm\ *n*

ne·o·dym·i·um \ˌnē-ō-'dim-ē-əm\ *n* : a metallic element whose oxides are used to color ceramic material violet — see ELEMENT table

neo·lith\'nē-ə-ˌlith\ *n* : a Neolithic stone implement

Neo·lith·ic \ˌnē-ə-'lith-ik\ *adj* : of, relating to, or being the latest period of the Stone Age which is characterized by polished stone implements

ne·ol·o·gism \nē-'äl-ə-ˌjiz-əm\ *n* : a new word or expression — **ne·ol·o·gis·tic** \-ˌäl-ə-'jis-tik\ *adj*

ne·on \'nē-ˌän\ *n* [from Greek, neuter of *neos* "new"] **1** : a colorless odorless gaseous element found in minute amounts in air and used in electric lamps — see ELEMENT table **2 a** : a lamp in which the gas contains a large amount of neon that gives a reddish glow when a current is passed through it **b** : a sign composed of such lamps

ne·o·phyte \'nē-ə-ˌfīt\ *n* **1** : a newly converted person **2** : BEGINNER, NOVICE

neo·plasm \-ˌplaz-əm\ *n* : a new growth of tissue serving no physiologic function : TUMOR — **neo·plas·tic** \ˌnē-ə-'plas-tik\ *adj*

ne·pen·the \nə-'pen(t)-thē\ *n* : a potion used by the ancients to dull pain and sorrow

neph·ew \'nef-yü\ *n* : a son of one's brother or sister

ne·phri·tis \ni-'frīt-əs\ *n* : inflammation of the kidneys — **ne·phrit·ic** \-'frit-ik\ *adj*

nep·o·tism \'nep-ə-ˌtiz-əm\ *n* : favoritism shown to a relative (as in the distribution of political offices)

Nep·tune \'nep-ˌt(y)ün\ *n* — see PLANET table — **Nep·tu·ni·an** \nep-'t(y)ü-nē-ən\ *adj*

nep·tu·ni·um \nep-'t(y)ü-nē-əm\ *n* [from scientific Latin, from Latin *Neptunus* "Neptune", Roman god of the sea] : a radioactive metallic element similar to uranium and obtained in nuclear reactors as a by-product in the production of plutonium — see ELEMENT table

Ne·re·id \'nir-ē-əd\ *n* : any of the sea nymphs held in Greek mythology to be the daughters of the sea-god Nereus

ne·re·is \'nir-ē-əs\ *n, pl* **ne·re·ides** \nə-'rē-ə-ˌdēz\ : any of a genus of usu. large greenish marine annelid worms

ne·rit·ic \nə-'rit-ik\ *adj* : of, relating to, or being the shallow water adjoining the seacoast

ner·va·tion \ˌnər-'vā-shən\ *n* : an arrangement or system of nerves; *also* : VENATION

nerve \'nərv\ *n* **1** : SINEW, TENDON ⟨strain every *nerve*⟩ **2** : one of the stringy bands of nervous tissue connecting the nervous system with other organs and conducting nerve impulses **3 a** : power of endurance or control **b** : BOLDNESS, DARING **c** : IMPUDENCE **4 a** : a sore or sensitive point **b** *pl* : nervous disorganization or collapse : HYSTERIA **5** : a vein in a leaf or in the wing of an insect **6** : the sensitive pulp of a tooth — **nerve** *adj* — **nerved** \'nərvd\ *adj*

nerve cell *n* : NEURON; *also* : a nerve cell body not including its processes

nerve center *n* : CENTER 2b

nerve cord *n* : a cord of nervous tissue

nerve ending *n* : a structure forming an end of a nerve axon that is distant from the cell body

nerve fiber *n* : AXON, DENDRITE

nerve gas *n* : a war gas damaging esp. to the nervous and respiratory systems

nerve impulse *n* : a progressive change in a nerve fiber that follows stimulation and transmits a record of sensation or an instruction to act — called also *nervous impulse*

nerve·less \'nərv-ləs\ *adj* **1** : lacking strength or courage : FEEBLE **2** : showing or having control : not nervous — **nerve·less·ly** *adv*

nerve net *n* : a network of nerve cells apparently continuous one with another and conducting impulses in all directions; *also* : a nervous system (as in a jellyfish) consisting of such a network

nerv·ous \'nər-vəs\ *adj* **1 a** : of, relating to, or composed of neurons **b** : of or relating to the nerves; *also* : originating in or affected by the nerves **2 a** : easily excited or irritated : JUMPY **b** : TIMID, FEARFUL **3** : UNEASY, UNSTEADY — **nerv·ous·ly** *adv* — **nerv·ous·ness** *n*

nervous breakdown *n* **1** : a disorder often characterized by reduced efficiency, depression, tenseness, irritability, susceptibility to fatigue, headache, and ill-defined circulatory or digestive distress **2** : a case of nervous breakdown

nervous system *n* : the bodily system that receives and processes stimuli and transmits impulses to the effector organs and that in vertebrates is made up of brain and spinal cord, nerves, ganglia, and parts of the receptor organs

ner·vure \'nər-vyər\ *n* : a vein in a leaf or in the wing of an insect

nervy \'nər-vē\ *adj* **nerv·i·er; -est 1 a :** BOLD, DARING **b :** IMPUDENT, BRASH ⟨a *nervy* salesman⟩ **2 :** EXCITABLE, NERVOUS — **nerv·i·ness** *n*

-ness \nəs\ *n suffix* : state : condition : quality : degree ⟨good*ness*⟩

1nest \'nest\ *n* **1 a :** a bed or shelter prepared by a bird for its eggs and young **b :** a place where eggs (as of insects, fishes, or turtles) are laid and hatched **2 a :** a place of rest, retreat, or lodging **b :** DEN, HANGOUT **3 :** the occupants or frequenters of a nest ⟨a *nest* of thieves⟩ **4 :** a group of objects made to fit one within another

2nest *vb* **1 :** to build or occupy a nest ⟨robins *nested* in the underbrush⟩ **2 :** to fit compactly together or within one another — **nest·er** *n*

nest egg *n* **1 :** a natural or artificial egg left in a nest to induce a fowl to continue to lay there **2 :** a fund of money set aside as a reserve

nes·tle \'nes-əl\ *vb* **nes·tled; nes·tling** \-(ə-)liŋ\ **1 :** to lie close and snug : CUDDLE **2 :** to settle as if in a nest — **nes·tler** \-(ə-)lər\ *n*

nest·ling \'nest-liŋ\ *n* **1 :** a young bird not yet able to leave the nest **2 :** a young child

1net \'net\ *n* **1 a :** a fabric of open texture made of intersecting threads, cords, ropes, or wires **b :** something made of net; *esp* : a device for catching fish, birds, or insects **2 :** something that traps like a net **3 :** a network of lines, fibers, or figures — **net·ted** \'net-əd\ *adj*

2net *vb* **net·ted; net·ting 1 :** to cover with or as if with a net **2 :** to catch in or as if in a net ⟨*net* fish⟩ **3 :** to hit the ball into the net in a racket game — **net·ter** *n*

3net *adj* **1 :** free from all charges or deductions ⟨*net* profit⟩ **2 :** excluding all tare ⟨*net* weight⟩

4net *vb* **net·ted; net·ting :** to gain or produce as profit : CLEAR ⟨*net* 10 cents⟩

5net *n* : a net amount, profit, weight, or price

Neth *abbr* Netherlands

neth·er \'neth-ər\ *adj* : LOWER

neth·er·most \-ˌmōst\ *adj* : LOWEST

neth·er·world \-ˌwərld\ *n* : the world of the dead

net income *n* : the balance of gross income remaining after deducting related costs, expenses, and losses usu. for a given period

net·ting \'net-iŋ\ *n* **1 :** NETWORK **2 :** the act or process of making a net

nettle

1net·tle \'net-əl\ *n* : any of various coarse herbs with stinging hairs

2nettle *vb* **net·tled; net·tling** \'net-(ə-)liŋ\ **1 :** to sting with nettles **2 :** ANNOY, VEX

net-veined \'net-'vānd\ *adj* : having veins that branch and interlace to form a network ⟨dicotyledons have *net-veined* leaves⟩ — compare PARALLEL-VEINED

ə abut	ər further	a back	ā bake	
ä cot, cart	au̇ out	ch chin	e less	ē easy
g gift	i trip	ī life	j joke	ŋ sing
ō flow	ȯ flaw	ȯi coin	th thin	th this
ü loot	u̇ foot	y yet	yü few	yu̇ furious

zh vision

net·work \-ˌwərk\ *n* **1 :** a fabric or structure of cords or wires that cross at regular intervals **2 :** a system of lines or channels resembling a network **3 :** an interconnected group or system; *esp* : a group of connected radio or television stations

neu·ral \'n(y)u̇r-əl\ *adj* : of, relating to, or involving a nerve or the nervous system

neu·ral·gia \n(y)u̇-'ral-jə\ *n* : acute pain that follows the course of a nerve; *also* : a condition marked by such pain — **neu·ral·gic** \-jik\ *adj*

neu·ri·tis \n(y)u̇-'rīt-əs\ *n* : inflammation of a nerve — **neu·rit·ic** \-'rit-ik\ *adj or n*

neu·ro·crine \'n(y)u̇r-ə-krən, -ˌkrīn, -ˌkrēn\ *adj* : of, relating to, or being a hormonal substance that influences the activity of nerves

neu·ro·hu·mor \ˌn(y)u̇r-ō-'hyü-mər, -'yü-\ *n* : a substance released at a nerve ending that plays a part in transmitting a nerve impulse — **neu·ro·hu·mor·al** \-mə-rəl\ *adj*

neurol *abbr* neurology

neu·rol·o·gist \n(y)u̇-'räl-ə-jəst\ *n* : a specialist in neurology

neu·rol·o·gy \n(y)u̇-'räl-ə-jē\ *n* : the scientific study of the nervous system — **neu·ro·log·i·cal** \ˌn(y)u̇r-ə-'läj-i-kəl\ *or* **neu·ro·log·ic** \-'läj-ik\ *adj*

neu·ron \'n(y)ü-ˌrän, 'n(y)u̇(ə)r-ˌän\ *also* **neu·rone** \-ˌrōn, -ˌōn\ *n* : a grayish or reddish cell with specialized processes that is the fundamental functional unit of nervous tissue — **neu·ro·nal** \'n(y)u̇r-ən-əl, n(y)u̇-'rōn-\ *adj*

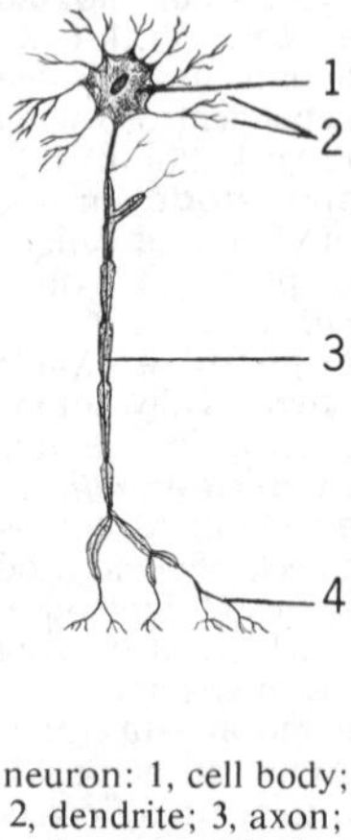

neuron: 1, cell body; 2, dendrite; 3, axon; 4, nerve ending

neu·rop·ter·an \n(y)u̇-'räp-tə-rən\ *n* : any of an order of insects (as an ant lion) having wings with a fine network of veins — **neurop·teran** *adj* — **neu·rop·ter·ous** \-rəs\ *adj*

neu·ro·sis \n(y)u̇-'rō-səs\ *n, pl* **-ro·ses** \-'rō-ˌsēz\ : a nervous disorder that has no obvious physical cause but is sometimes characterized by an upset in a bodily system

neu·ros·po·ra \n(y)u̇-'räs-pə-rə\ *n* : any of a genus of often pink-spored fungi that are destructive in bakeries but important tools of genetic research

1neu·rot·ic \n(y)u̇-'rät-ik\ *adj* : of, relating to, constituting, or affected with neurosis — **neu·rot·i·cal·ly** \-i-k(ə-)lē\ *adv*

2neurotic *n* : an emotionally unstable person or one affected with a neurosis

neut *abbr* neuter

1neu·ter \'n(y)üt-ər\ *adj* **1 :** relating to or being the class of words that ordinarily includes most of those referring to things that are neither male nor female ⟨a *neuter* noun⟩ ⟨the *neuter* gender⟩ **2 :** lacking sex organs; *also* : having imperfectly developed sex organs

2neuter *n* **1 a :** a word or form of the neuter gender **b :** the neuter gender **2 :** WORKER 2

3neuter *vb* : CASTRATE, ALTER

1neu·tral \'n(y)ü-trəl\ *adj* **1 a :** not favoring either side in a quarrel, contest, or war **b :** of or relating to a neutral country **2 :** neither one thing nor the other : MIDDLING **3 :** GRAYISH **4 :** neither acid nor basic **5** : not electrically charged — **neu·tral·ly** \-trə-lē\ *adv*

[2]**neutral** *n* **1** : one that is neutral **2** : a neutral color **3** : a state in which transmission gears are not engaged

neu·tral·ism \'n(y)ü-trə-ˌliz-əm\ *n* : a policy of neutrality in international affairs

neu·tral·ist \'n(y)ü-trə-ləst\ *n* **1** : one that advocates or practices neutrality **2** : one that favors the neutralization of a state or region

neu·tral·i·ty \n(y)ü-'tral-ət-ē\ *n* : the quality or state of being neutral esp. in time of war

neu·tral·ize \'n(y)ü-trə-ˌlīz\ *vb* **1** : to make chemically neutral ⟨*neutralize* an acid with a base⟩ **2** : to destroy the effectiveness of : NULLIFY ⟨*neutralize* an opponent's move⟩ **3** : to make electrically inert by combining equal positive and negative quantities **4** : to make politically neutral ⟨*neutralize* a country⟩ — **neu·tral·i·za·tion** \ˌn(y)ü-trə-lə-'zā-shən\ *n* — **neu·tral·iz·er** \'n(y)ü-trə-ˌlī-zər\ *n*

neu·tri·no \n(y)ü-'trē-nō\ *n, pl* **-nos** : an uncharged particle having a mass less than 1/10 that of the electron

neu·tron \'n(y)ü-ˌträn\ *n* : an uncharged particle that has a mass nearly equal to that of the proton and is present in all known atomic nuclei except the hydrogen nucleus

Nev *abbr* Nevada

né·vé \nā-'vā\ *n* : partially compacted granular snow that forms the surface part of the upper end of a glacier; *also* : a field of granular snow

nev·er \'nev-ər\ *adv* **1** : not ever : at no time ⟨*never* saw him before⟩ ⟨*never* had a sick day in his life⟩ **2** : not in any degree, way, or condition ⟨*never* fear⟩ ⟨*never* the wiser for his frightening experience⟩

nev·er·more \ˌnev-ər-'mō(ə)r, -'mȯ(ə)r\ *adv* : never again

nev·er·the·less \ˌnev-ər-thə-'les\ *adv* : in spite of that : HOWEVER

[1]**new** \'n(y)ü\ *adj* **1** : not old : RECENT, MODERN **2** : not the same as the former : taking the place of one that came before ⟨a *new* teacher⟩ **3** : recently discovered or learned about ⟨*new* lands⟩ ⟨*new* plants and animals⟩ **4** : not formerly known or experienced ⟨*new* feelings⟩ **5** : not accustomed ⟨*new* to her work⟩ **6** : beginning as a repetition of some previous act or thing ⟨the *new* year⟩ **7** : REFRESHED, REGENERATED ⟨vacation made a *new* man of him⟩ **8** : being in a position or place for the first time ⟨a *new* member⟩ — **new·ness** *n*

syn NEW, NOVEL, FRESH can mean having only recently come into existence, notice, or use. NEW may apply to what has not been known or experienced before ⟨he started his *new* job today⟩; NOVEL applies to something not only new but striking or unprecedented; FRESH is likely to suggest continuing signs of newness in something new or signs of preservation in something old ***ant*** old

[2]**new** *adv* : NEWLY, RECENTLY ⟨*new*-mown hay⟩

new·born \'n(y)ü-'bȯrn\ *adj* **1** : recently born **2** : born anew : REBORN

new·com·er \'n(y)ü-ˌkəm-ər\ *n* **1** : one recently arrived **2** : BEGINNER

new·el \'n(y)ü-əl\ *n* **1** : an upright post about which the steps of a circular staircase wind **2** : a post at the foot of a straight stairway or one at a landing

new·fan·gled \'n(y)ü-'fang-gəld\ *adj* : of the newest style : NOVEL ⟨*newfangled* ideas⟩ ⟨a *newfangled* contraption⟩

new–fash·ioned \-'fash-ənd\ *adj* : UP-TO-DATE, MODERN

New·found·land \'n(y)ü-fən-(d)lənd, -ˌ(d)land; n(y)ü-'fau̇n-(d)lənd\ *n* : any of a breed of very large usu. black dogs developed in Newfoundland

Newfoundland

New Hamp·shire \n(y)u̇-'ham(p)-shər, -ˌshi(ə)r\ *n* : any of a breed of single-combed domestic fowls developed chiefly in New Hampshire and noted for heavy winter egg production

New Left *n* : a recent group of political radicals distinguished from older leftist groups by their opposition to all government controls and stress on complete individual freedom — **New Leftist** *adj or n*

new·ly \'n(y)ü-lē\ *adv* **1** : LATELY, RECENTLY ⟨a *newly* married couple⟩ **2** : ANEW, AFRESH ⟨a *newly* furnished house⟩

new·ly·wed \-ˌwed\ *n* : a person recently married

new moon *n* : the moon's phase when it is in conjunction with the sun so that its dark side is toward the earth; *also* : the thin crescent moon seen a few days after the actual occurrence of the new moon phase

news \'n(y)üz\ *n* **1** : a report of recent events or of something unknown ⟨brought him the office *news*⟩ **2** : material reported in a newspaper or news periodical or on a newscast **3** : newsworthy matter

news agency *n* : an organization that supplies news to subscribing newspapers, periodicals, and newscasters

news·boy \-ˌbȯi\ *n* : a person who delivers or sells newspapers

news·cast \-ˌkast\ *n* : a radio or television broadcast of news — **news·cast·er** \-ˌkas-tər\ *n*

news·let·ter \-ˌlet-ər\ *n* : a newspaper of interest chiefly to a special group

news·man \-mən, -ˌman\ *n* : one who gathers or reports the news : REPORTER, CORRESPONDENT

news·pa·per \'n(y)üz-ˌpā-pər\ *n* : a paper that is printed and distributed usu. daily or weekly and contains news, articles of opinion, features, and advertising

news·pa·per·man \-ˌman\ *n* : one who owns or is employed by a newspaper; *esp* : one who writes or edits copy for a newspaper

news·print \'n(y)üz-ˌprint\ *n* : paper made chiefly from wood pulp and used mostly for newspapers

news·reel \-ˌrēl\ *n* : a short motion picture dealing with current events

news·stand \-ˌstand\ *n* : a place where newspapers and magazines are sold

news·wor·thy \-ˌwər-thē\ *adj* : sufficiently interesting to the average person to deserve reporting

newsy \'n(y)ü-zē\ *adj* **news·i·er**; **-est** : filled with news; *esp* : CHATTY ⟨a *newsy* letter⟩

newt \'n(y)üt\ *n* : any of various small salamanders that live mostly in water

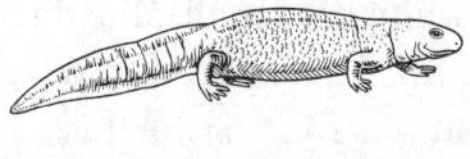

newt (about 4 in. long)

New Testament *n* : the second of the two chief divisions of the Bible — see BIBLE table

new·ton \'n(y)üt-ən\ *n* : a unit of force of such size that under its influence a body whose mass is one kilogram would experience an acceleration of one meter per second per second

New World *n* : the western hemisphere including No. and So. America

New Year *n* **1** : NEW YEAR'S DAY **2** : ROSH HASHANAH

New Year's Day *n* : January 1 observed as a legal holiday

1**next** \'nekst\ *adj* : immediately preceding or following ⟨the *next* page⟩ ⟨the house *next* to ours⟩

2**next** *adv* **1** : in the nearest time, place, or order following ⟨open this package *next*⟩ **2** : at the first time after this to come ⟨when *next* we meet⟩

3**next** *prep* : next to

1**next to** *prep* : immediately following : adjacent to ⟨*next to* the head of his class⟩

2**next to** *adv* : very nearly : ALMOST

Nez Percé \'nez-'pərs, *French* nā-per-sā\ *n* : a member of an Amerindian people of central Idaho and adjacent parts of Washington and Oregon

NFL *abbr* National Football League

Nfld *abbr* Newfoundland

NG *abbr* National Guard

N.H. *or* **NH** *abbr* New Hampshire

NHL *abbr* National Hockey League

ni·a·cin \'nī-ə-sən\ *n* : a vitamin whose deficiency is associated with pellagra and which is found esp. in protein

nib \'nib\ *n* **1** : BILL, BEAK **2** : the point of a pen **3** : a pointed or projecting part

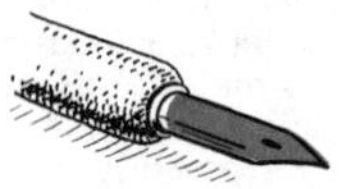

nib 2

nib·ble \'nib-əl\ *vb* **nib·bled**; **nib·bling** \-(ə-)liŋ\ : to bite or chew gently or bit by bit — **nibble** *n* — **nib·bler** \-(ə-)lər\ *n*

nice \'nīs\ *adj* **1** : very particular (as about appearance, manner, or food) : REFINED **2 a** : requiring precise discrimination or delicate treatment ⟨a *nice* distinction⟩ **b** : able to make precise distinctions ⟨a *nice* ear for music⟩ **3** : PLEASING, AGREEABLE ⟨a *nice* time⟩ ⟨a *nice* person⟩ **4** : WELL-BRED, RESPECTABLE — **nice·ly** *adv* — **nice·ness** *n*

ni·ce·ty \'nī-sət-ē, -stē\ *n, pl* **-ties** **1** : a dainty, delicate, or elegant thing ⟨enjoy the *niceties* of life⟩ **2** : a small point : a fine detail ⟨*niceties* of table manners⟩ **3** : careful attention to details : EXACTNESS ⟨*nicety* is needed in making watches⟩ **4** : the point at which a thing is at its best ⟨roasted to a *nicety*⟩

niche \'nich\ *n* **1** : a recess in a wall esp. for a statue **2** : a place, use, or work for which a person is best fitted **3 a** : a habitat supplying the factors necessary for the existence of an organism or species **b** : the ecological role of an organism in a community

1**nick** \'nik\ *n* **1** : a small groove : NOTCH **2** : CHIP ⟨a *nick* in a cup⟩ **3** : the final critical moment ⟨in the *nick* of time⟩

2**nick** *vb* **1** : to make a nick in **2** : to touch lightly : GRAZE ⟨*nicked* by a bullet⟩

1**nick·el** \'nik-əl\ *n* [from German *kupfernickel*, an ore compounded of nickel and arsenic, from *kupfer* "copper" and *nickel* "goblin"; so called because the ore looked like copper, and was thought by the miners to have been bewitched by goblins] **1** : a silver-white hard malleable ductile metallic element that is capable of a high polish, resistant to corrosion, and used chiefly in alloys and as a catalyst — see ELEMENT table **2 a** *also* **nick·le** : the U.S. 5-cent piece made of nickel and copper **b** : five cents

2**nick·el** *vb* **-eled** *or* **-elled**; **-el·ing** *or* **-el·ling** \'nik-(ə-)liŋ\ : to plate with nickel

nick·el·ode·on \,nik-ə-'lōd-ē-ən\ *n* **1** : an early movie theater charging five cents for admission **2** : JUKEBOX

nickel silver *n* : a silver-white alloy of copper, zinc, and nickel

nick·er \'nik-ər\ *vb* **nick·ered**; **nick·er·ing** \-(ə-)riŋ\ : NEIGH, WHINNY — **nicker** *n*

1**nick·name** \'nik-,nām\ *n* **1** : an often descriptive name (as "Shorty" or "Tex") given in addition to the one belonging to an individual **2** : a familiar form of a proper name (as "Billy" for "William")

2**nickname** *vb* : to give a nickname to

nic·o·tine \'nik-ə-,tēn\ *n* : a poisonous substance found in tobacco and used esp. as an insecticide

nic·o·tin·ic acid \,nik-ə-,tin-ik-\ *n* : NIACIN

nic·ti·tat·ing membrane \,nik-tə-,tāt-iŋ\ *n* : a thin membrane found in many animals at the inner angle or beneath the lower lid of the eye and capable of extending across the eyeball

niece \'nēs\ *n* : a daughter of one's brother or sister

nif·ty \'nif-tē\ *adj* **nif·ti·er**; **-est** : FINE, SWELL — **nifty** *n*

Ni·ge·ri·an \nī-'jir-ē-ən\ *adj* : of, relating to, or characteristic of Nigeria or its people — **Nigerian** *n*

nig·gard \'nig-ərd\ *n* : a mean stingy person : MISER — **niggard** *adj*

nig·gard·ly \-lē\ *adj* **1** : STINGY, MISERLY **2** : characteristic of a niggard : SCANTY — **niggardly** *adv*

1**nigh** \'nī\ *adv* **1** : NEAR **2** : NEARLY, ALMOST

2**nigh** *adj* : CLOSE, NEAR

night \'nīt\ *n* **1** : the time between dusk and dawn when there is no sunlight **2** : NIGHTFALL **3** : the darkness of night — **night** *adj*

night blindness *n* : subnormal vision in faint light (as at night) — **night-blind** *adj*

night-blooming cereus *n* : any of several night-blooming cacti; *esp* : a slender sprawling or climbing cactus often grown for its large showy fragrant white flowers

night·cap \'nīt-,kap\ *n* **1** : a cap worn with nightclothes **2** : a drink taken at bedtime **3** : the final race or contest of a day's sports activities

night·clothes \-,klō(th)z\ *n pl* : garments worn in bed

night·club \-,kləb\ *n* : a place of entertainment open in the evening and usu. serving food and liquor, having a floor show, and providing music for dancing

night crawler *n* : EARTHWORM; *esp* : a large earthworm found on the soil surface at night

night·dress \'nīt-,dres\ *n* : NIGHTGOWN

night·fall \-,fȯl\ *n* : the coming of night : DUSK

night·gown \-,gau̇n\ *n* : a long loose garment worn in bed

night·hawk \-,hȯk\ *n* **1** : any of several insect-eating birds that resemble the related whippoorwill **2** : a person who habitually stays up late at night

night·in·gale \'nīt-ən-,gāl\ *n* : any of several Old World thrushes noted for the sweet usu. nocturnal song of the male

night·ly \'nīt-lē\ *adj* **1** : of or relating to the night or every night **2** : happening, done, or produced by night or every night — **nightly** *adv*

night·mare \-,ma(ə)r, -,me(ə)r\ *n* **1** : a frightening or oppressive dream **2** : a frightening or horrible experience — **night·mar·ish** \-,ma(ə)r-ish, -,me(ə)r-\ *adj*

night owl *n* : a person who keeps late hours at night

night·shade \'nīt-ˌshād\ *n* : any of a family of herbs, shrubs, and trees having alternate leaves, clusters of usu. white, yellow, or purple flowers, and fruits that are berries and including many poisonous forms (as belladonna) and important food plants (as the potato, tomato, and eggplant)

nightshade

night·shirt \-ˌshərt\ *n* : a nightgown resembling a shirt

night·stick \-ˌstik\ *n* : a policeman's club

night·time \'nīt-ˌtīm\ *n* : the time from dusk to dawn

nil \'nil\ *n* : NOTHING, ZERO — **nil** *adj*

nim \'nim\ *n* : any of various games in which counters are laid out in one or more piles of agreed numbers, each of two players in turn draws one or more counters, and the object is to take the last counter, force the opponent to take it, or take the most or the fewest counters

nim·ble \'nim-bəl\ *adj* **nim·bler** \-b(ə-)lər\; **-blest** \-b(ə-)ləst\ **1** : quick and light in motion : AGILE ⟨a *nimble* dancer⟩ **2** : quick in understanding and learning : CLEVER ⟨a *nimble* mind⟩ — **nim·ble·ness** \-bəl-nəs\ *n* — **nim·bly** \-blē\ *adv*

nim·bo·stra·tus \ˌnim-bō-'strāt-əs, -'strat-\ *n* : a low dark gray rainy cloud layer

nim·bus \'nim-bəs\ *n, pl* **nim·bi** \-ˌbī, -ˌbē\ *or* **nim·bus·es** **1** : a luminous cloud about a god or goddess when on earth **2** : an indication (as a circle) of radiant light about the head of a drawn or sculptured god or saint **3** : a rain cloud that is of uniform grayness and extends over the entire sky

nin·com·poop \'nin-kəm-ˌpüp, 'ning-\ *n* : FOOL, SIMPLETON

nine \'nīn\ *n* **1** — see NUMBER table **2** : the ninth in a set or series **3** : a baseball team — **nine** *adj or pron*

nine–band·ed armadillo \ˌnīn-ˌban-dəd-\ *n* : a small American armadillo that has nine movable bands of bony plates and ranges from Texas to Paraguay

nine·pin \'nīn-ˌpin\ *n* **1** : a pin used in ninepins **2** *pl* : tenpins played without the headpin

nine·teen \(')nīn(t)-'tēn\ *n* — see NUMBER table — **nineteen** *adj or pron* — **nine·teenth** \-'tēn(t)th\ *adj or n*

nine·ty \'nīnt-ē\ *n, pl* **nineties** — see NUMBER table — **nine·ti·eth** \-ē-əth\ *adj or n* — **ninety** *adj or pron*

nin·ny \'nin-ē\ *n, pl* **ninnies** : FOOL, SIMPLETON

nin·ny·ham·mer \'nin-ē-ˌham-ər\ *n* : NINNY

ninth \'nīn(t)th\ *n, pl* **ninths** — see NUMBER table — **ninth** *adj or adv*

ni·o·bi·um \nī-'ō-bē-əm\ *n* : a lustrous platinum-gray ductile metallic element used in alloys — see ELEMENT table

[1]**nip** \'nip\ *vb* **nipped**; **nip·ping** **1** : to catch hold of and squeeze tightly between two surfaces, edges, or points ⟨the dog *nipped* his ankle⟩ **2** : to cut off by pinching or clipping **3** : to destroy the growth or progress of ⟨*nipped* in the bud⟩ **4** : to make numb with cold : CHILL **5** : SNATCH, STEAL

[2]**nip** *n* **1** : something (as a sharp stinging cold or a pungent flavor) that nips **2** : the act of nipping : PINCH, BITE **3** : a small portion : BIT

[3]**nip** *n* : a small quantity of liquor ⟨takes a *nip* now and then⟩

nip and tuck \ˌnip-ən-'tək\ *adj or adv* : so close that the lead or advantage shifts rapidly from one contestant to another

nip·per \'nip-ər\ *n* **1** : a device (as pincers) for nipping — usu. used in pl. **2** : CHELA **3** *chiefly Brit* : a small boy

nip·ple \'nip-əl\ *n* **1** : the part of the breast from which in the female a baby or young mammal sucks milk **2** : something resembling a nipple; *esp* : the rubber mouthpiece of a baby's nursing bottle

Nip·pon·ese \ˌnip-ə-'nēz, -'nēs\ *adj* : JAPANESE — **Nipponese** *n*

nip·py \'nip-ē\ *adj* **nip·pi·er**; **-est** **1** : NIMBLE, BRISK **2** : CHILLING, BITING ⟨a *nippy* day⟩

nit \'nit\ *n* : the egg of a louse or similar insect; *also* : the insect itself when young

ni·ter *also* **ni·tre** \'nīt-ər\ *n* **1** : POTASSIUM NITRATE **2** : SODIUM NITRATE

nitr- *or* **nitro-** *comb form* **1** : nitrate **2** : nitrogen ⟨*nitr*ide⟩

ni·trate \'nī-ˌtrāt, -trət\ *n* **1** : a salt or ester of nitric acid **2** : nitrate of sodium or potassium used as a fertilizer

ni·tric \'nī-trik\ *adj* : of, relating to, or containing nitrogen

nitric acid *n* : a corrosive liquid nitrogen-containing acid used esp. as an oxidizing agent and in making fertilizers, explosives, and dyes

ni·tri·fi·ca·tion \ˌnī-trə-fə-'kā-shən\ *n* : the process of nitrifying; *esp* : the oxidation (as by bacteria) of ammonium salts to nitrites and then to nitrates

ni·tri·fy \'nī-trə-ˌfī\ *vb* **-fied**; **-fy·ing** **1** : to combine with nitrogen or a nitrogen compound **2** : to subject to or produce by nitrification **3** : to engage or be active in nitrification ⟨*nitrifying* bacteria⟩ — **ni·tri·fi·er** \-ˌfī(-ə)r\ *n*

ni·trite \'nī-ˌtrīt\ *n* : a salt or ester of nitrous acid

ni·tro \'nī-trō\ *n* : any of various nitrated products; *esp* : NITROGLYCERIN

ni·tro·ben·zene \ˌnī-trō-'ben-ˌzēn, -ˌben-'\ *n* : a poisonous insoluble oil made by nitration of benzene and used as a solvent, oxidizing agent, and source of aniline

ni·tro·cel·lu·lose \-'sel-yə-ˌlōs\ *n* : GUNCOTTON

ni·tro·gen \'nī-trə-jən\ *n* : a colorless tasteless odorless gaseous element that constitutes 78 percent of the atmosphere by volume and is a constituent of all living tissues — see ELEMENT table — **ni·trog·e·nous** \nī-'träj-ə-nəs\ *adj*

nitrogen cycle *n* : a continuous series of natural processes by which nitrogen passes from air to soil to organisms and back involving nitrogen fixation, nitrification, decay, and denitrification

nitrogen fixation *n* : the conversion of free nitrogen in the air into combined forms esp. by microorganisms in soil and root nodules and its subsequent release in a form fit for plant use

nitrogen–fixing *adj* : capable of nitrogen fixation ⟨*nitrogen-fixing* bacteria⟩

ni·tro·glyc·er·in *or* **ni·tro·glyc·er·ine** \ˌnī-trō-'glis-(ə-)rən\ *n* : a heavy oily explosive poisonous liquid used chiefly in making dynamites and in medicine to relax blood vessels

ni·trous acid \ˌnī-trəs-\ *n* : an unstable nitrogen-containing acid known only in solution or in the form of its salts

nitrous oxide *n* : a colorless gas that when inhaled produces loss of sensibility to pain and sometimes laughter and is used esp. as an anesthetic in dentistry — called also *laughing gas*

nit·ty–grit·ty \ˌnit-ē-'grit-ē, 'nit-ē-ˌ\ *n* : the actual state of things : what is really true ⟨getting down to the *nitty-gritty*⟩

nit·wit \'nit-,wit\ *n* : a stupid or silly person
N.J. *or* **NJ** *abbr* New Jersey
NL *abbr* National League
N. Mex. *or* **N.M.** *or* **NM** *abbr* New Mexico
[1]**no** \(')nō\ *adv* **1** : in no respect or degree ⟨he is *no* better than he should be⟩ **2** : not so — used to express disagreement or refusal ⟨*no*, I'm not hungry⟩ **3** — used to emphasize a following negative or to introduce a more emphatic or explicit statement ⟨has the right, *no*, the duty, to continue⟩ **4** — used to express surprise, doubt, or disbelief ⟨*no* — you don't say⟩
[2]**no** *adj* **1 a** : not any ⟨he has *no* money⟩ **b** : hardly any : very little ⟨finished in *no* time⟩ **2** : not a ⟨he's *no* expert⟩
[3]**no** \'nō\ *n, pl* **noes** *or* **nos** \'nōz\ **1** : an act or instance of refusing or denying by the use of the word *no* : DENIAL **2 a** : a negative vote or decision **b** *pl* : persons voting in the negative
no *abbr* **1** north **2** number
no·bel·i·um \nō-'bel-ē-əm\ *n* : a radioactive element produced artificially — see ELEMENT table
no·bil·i·ty \nō-'bil-ət-ē\ *n, pl* **-ties 1** : the quality or state of being noble ⟨*nobility* of character⟩ **2** : noble rank ⟨conferred *nobility* on him⟩ **3** : the class or group of nobles ⟨a member of the *nobility*⟩
[1]**no·ble** \'nō-bəl\ *adj* **no·bler** \-b(ə-)lər\; **no·blest** \-b(ə-)ləst\ **1** : FAMOUS, NOTABLE ⟨*noble* deed⟩ **2** : of high birth or exalted rank : ARISTOCRATIC **3** : possessing very high qualities : EXCELLENT ⟨a *noble* hawk⟩ **4** : grand esp. in appearance : IMPOSING ⟨a *noble* edifice⟩ **5** : having or characterized by superiority of mind or character : MAGNANIMOUS ⟨a *noble* nature⟩ **6** : chemically inert or inactive esp. toward oxygen ⟨*noble* metal⟩ — **no·ble·ness** \-bəl-nəs\ *n* — **no·bly** \-blē\ *adv*
[2]**noble** *n* : a person of noble rank or birth
no·ble·man \'nō-bəl-mən\ *n* : a member of the nobility : PEER — **no·ble·wom·an** \-,wu̇m-ən\ *n*
[1]**no·body** \'nō-,bäd-ē, -bəd-ē\ *pron* : no person : not anybody
[2]**nobody** *n, pl* **no·bod·ies** : a person of no importance
noc·tur·nal \näk-'tərn-əl\ *adj* **1** : of, relating to, or occurring in the night ⟨a *nocturnal* journey⟩ **2** : active at night ⟨*nocturnal* insects⟩ — **noc·tur·nal·ly** \-ə-lē\ *adv*
noc·turne \'näk-,tərn\ *n* : a work of art dealing with night; *esp* : a dreamy pensive composition for the piano
[1]**nod** \'näd\ *vb* **nod·ded; nod·ding 1** : to bend the head downward or forward (as in bowing or going to sleep or as a way of answering "yes") **2** : to move up and down ⟨the tulips *nodded* in the breeze⟩ **3** : to show by a nod of the head ⟨*nod* agreement⟩ **4** : to let one's attention lapse for a moment and make an error — **nod·der** *n*
[2]**nod** *n* : the action of nodding
nod·dle \'näd-əl\ *n* : HEAD
nod·dy \'näd-ē\ *n, pl* **noddies** : any of several stout-bodied terns of warm seas
node \'nōd\ *n* **1 a** : a thickened or swollen enlargement (as of a rheumatic joint) **b** : a body part resembling a knot **2** : a point on a stem at which a leaf is inserted — **nod·al** \'nōd-əl\ *adj*

ə abut	ər further	a back	ā bake	
ä cot, cart	au̇ out	ch chin	e less	ē easy
g gift	i trip	ī life	j joke	ng sing	ō flow
ȯ flaw	ȯi coin	th thin	th this	ü loot
u̇ foot	y yet	yü few	yu̇ furious	zh vision

nod·ule \'näj-ül\ *n* **1** : a small rounded mass **2** : a swelling on the root of a legume that contains nitrogen-fixing bacteria — **nod·u·lar** \'näj-ə-lər\ *adj*
no·el \nō-'el\ *n* **1** : a Christmas carol **2** *cap* : the Christmas season
nog·gin \'näg-ən\ *n* **1** : a small mug **2** : a small quantity of drink usu. equivalent to a gill **3** : a person's head
no–good \'nō-'gu̇d\ *adj* : having no worth, use, or chance of success — **no–good** \-,gu̇d\ *n*
no–hit·ter \(')nō-'hit-ər\ *n* : a baseball game in which a pitcher allows the opposition no base hits
[1]**noise** \'nȯiz\ *n* **1** : loud, confused, or senseless shouting or outcry **2 a** : SOUND; *esp* : a loud, harsh, or discordant sound **b** : an unwanted signal in an electronic communication system
[2]**noise** *vb* : to spread by rumor or report ⟨*noised* it about that the troops would be home by Christmas⟩
noise·less \'nȯiz-ləs\ *adj* : making or causing no noise ⟨kittens on *noiseless* feet⟩ — **noise·less·ly** *adv*
noise·mak·er \-,mā-kər\ *n* : one that makes noise; *esp* : a device used to make noise at parties
noise pollution *n* : environmental pollution consisting of annoying or harmful noise — called also *sound pollution*
noi·some \'nȯi-səm\ *adj* **1** : NOXIOUS, UNWHOLESOME ⟨a *noisome* slum⟩ **2** : offensive esp. to the smell : DISGUSTING ⟨*noisome* odors⟩ ⟨*noisome* pig farms⟩ — **noi·some·ly** *adv* — **noi·some·ness** *n*
noisy \'nȯi-zē\ *adj* **nois·i·er; -est 1** : making noise **2** : full of or characterized by noise — **nois·i·ly** \-zə-lē\ *adv* — **nois·i·ness** \-zē-nəs\ *n*
nom *abbr* nominative
no·mad \'nō-,mad\ *n* **1** : a member of a people that has no fixed residence but wanders from place to place **2** : an individual who roams about aimlessly — **nomad** *or* **no·mad·ic** \nō-'mad-ik\ *adj* — **no·mad·ism** \'nō-,mad-,iz-əm\ *n*
no–man's–land \'nō-,manz-,land\ *n* : an unoccupied area between opposing troops
nom de plume \,näm-di-'plüm\ *n, pl* **noms de plume** \,näm(z)-di-\ [a phrase intended by an Englishman as a French translation of *pen name*, but not used by French speakers; from French *nom* "name" and *de* "of" and *plume* "pen"] : PEN NAME
no·men·cla·ture \'nō-mən-,klā-chər\ *n* : a system of terms used in a particular science, discipline, or art; *esp* : the scientific names for plants and animals used in biology
nom·i·nal \'näm-ən-əl\ *adj* **1** : existing in name or form only ⟨the *nominal* head of his party⟩ **2** : very small : TRIFLING ⟨a *nominal* price⟩ — **nom·i·nal·ly** \-ə-lē\ *adv*
nom·i·nate \'näm-ə-,nāt\ *vb* : to choose as a candidate for election, appointment, or honor; *esp* : to propose for office ⟨*nominate* a man for president⟩ — **nom·i·na·tor** \-,nāt-ər\ *n*
nom·i·na·tion \,näm-ə-'nā-shən\ *n* **1** : the act, process, or an instance of nominating **2** : the state of being nominated
nom·i·na·tive \'näm-(ə-)nət-iv\ *adj* : relating to or being a grammatical case marking typically the subject of a verb — **nominative** *n*
nom·i·nee \,näm-ə-'nē\ *n* : a person nominated for an office, duty, or position
nomo·gram \'näm-ə-,gram\ *n* : NOMOGRAPH
nomo·graph \-,graf\ *n* : a graphic representation consisting of several lines marked off to scale and arranged in such a way that by using a straightedge to connect known values on two lines an unknown

value can be read at the point of intersection with another line

non- \(ˈ)nän, ˌnän\ *prefix* : not : reverse of : absence of ⟨*non*resident⟩ ⟨*non*fiction⟩

nonabsorbent
nonabstainer
nonacademic
nonacid
nonactive
nonadhesive
nonadjacent
nonadjustable
nonaggression
nonagreement
nonagricultural
nonalcoholic
nonaquatic
nonathletic
nonattendance
nonautomatic
nonbeliever
nonbelligerent
nonbiting
nonbreakable
nonbusiness
noncaking
noncellular
nonchargeable
noncitizen
nonclassical
nonclerical
nonclinical
nonclotting
noncoercive
noncollectable
noncollegiate
noncombat
noncombustible
noncommercial
noncommunicable
noncompetent
noncompeting
noncompetitive
noncomplementary
noncompliance
noncompressible
nonconclusive
nonconditioned
nonconducting
nonconfidence
nonconflicting
nonconforming
noncongenital
nonconscious
nonconstitutional
nonconstructive
noncontemporary
noncontinuous
noncontradictory
noncontributing
noncontrolled
noncontrolling
noncontroversial
nonconvertible
noncorporate
noncorrosive
noncreative
noncriminal
noncritical
noncrystalline
noncultivated
nondeductible
nondegenerate
nondelivery
nondemocratic
nondenominational
nonderivative
nondestructive
nondevelopment
nondigestible
nondirectional
nondisclosure
nondisjoint
nondistinctive
nondistribution
nondivided
nondocumentary
nondollar
nondomesticated
nondramatic
nondrying
nondurable
noneconomic
noneducational
noneffervescent
nonelastic
nonelective
nonelectric
noneligible
nonempirical
nonethical
nonexclusive
nonexempt
nonexistence
nonexistent
nonexplosive
nonfarm
nonfat
nonfatal
nonfattening
nonfederal
nonfederated
nonfeeding
nonferrous
nonfiction
nonfictional
nonfigurative
nonfinancial
nonfissionable
nonflagellated
nonflammable
nonflowering
nonflying
nonfraternal
nonfreezing
nonfulfillment
nonfunctional
nongaseous
nongenetic
nongovernmental
nonhardy
nonhereditary
nonhistorical
nonhuman
nonidentical
nonidentity
nonimmigrant
nonimmune
nonindustrial
noninflammable
noninflammatory
noninstitutional
noninstructional
nonintegrated
nonintellectual
noninterference
nonintersecting
noninvolvement
nonionized
nonirritating
nonlegal
nonlethal
nonlexical
nonliquid
nonliterary
nonliterate
nonliturgical
nonlocal
nonlogical
nonluminous
nonmagnetic
nonmalignant
nonmalleable
nonmaterial
nonmechanical
nonmedicinal
nonmember
nonmembership
nonmetrical
nonmigratory
nonmilitary
nonmoral
nonmotile
nonmoving
nonmutant
nonnational
nonnative
nonnatural
nonnecessity
nonnegotiable
nonobligatory
nonobservance
nonoccurrence
nonofficial
nonoily
nonoperating
nonorganic
nonorthodox
nonparallel
nonparalytic
nonparasitic
nonparticipant
nonparty
nonpathogenic
nonpayment
nonpecuniary
nonperformance
nonperishable
nonpersistent
nonpersonal
nonphysical
nonpoisonous
nonpolar
nonpolitical
nonporous
nonpossession
nonpractical
nonpregnant
nonprinting
nonproducer
nonprofessional
nonprogressive
nonprotein
nonproven
nonpublic
nonracial
nonradical
nonradioactive
nonrated
nonrational
nonreactive
nonreader
nonreciprocal
nonrecoverable
nonrecurrent
nonreducing
nonregistered
nonregulation
nonreligious
nonrepresentative
nonresidential
nonrestraint
nonrestricted
nonretractile
nonreturnable
nonrevenue
nonreversible
nonrhetorical
nonrotating
nonsalable
nonscientific
nonseasonal
nonsecret
nonsegregated
nonselective
nonsensitive
nonsensuous
nonsexual
nonshrinkable
nonsinkable
nonsocial
nonsolid
nonspatial
nonspeaking
nonspecialized
nonspecific
nonspeculative
nonstaining
nonstationary
nonstatistical
nonstellar
nonstrategic
nonstriated
nonstriker
nonstructural
nonsubscriber
nonsuccess
nonsurgical
nonsymbolic
nonsymmetrical
nontaxable
nontechnical
nontemporal
nonterritorial
nontheatrical
nontoxic
nontransferable
nontransparent
nontropical
nontuberculous
nontypical
nonuniform
nonuniformity
nonuser
nonvariant
nonvenomous
nonvibratory
nonviolation
nonviscous
nonvisual
nonvocal
nonvocational
nonvoluntary
nonvoting
nonwhite
nonworker
nonwoven
nonzero

no·na·ge·nar·i·an \ˌnō-nə-jə-ˈner-ē-ən, ˌnän-ə-\ *n* : a person who is 90 or more but less than 100 years old — **nonagenarian** *adj*

no·na·gon \ˈno-nə-ˌgän, ˈnän-ə-\ *n* : a polygon of nine angles and nine sides

nonce \ˈnän(t)s\ *n* : the one, particular, or present occasion, purpose, or use ⟨for the *nonce*⟩

non·cel·lu·lar \(ˈ)nän-ˈsel-yə-lər\ *adj* : not made up of or divided into cells

non·cha·lant \ˌnän-shə-ˈlänt\ *adj* [from French, from present participle of obsolete *nonchaloir* "to be indifferent", from *non* "not" and Latin *calēre* "to be warm"] : having a confident and easy manner; *esp* : unconcerned about drawing attention to oneself ⟨face a crowd with *nonchalant* ease⟩ — **non·cha·lance** \-ˈlän(t)s\ *n* — **non·cha·lant·ly** *adv*

non·com \ˈnän-ˌkäm\ *n* : NONCOMMISSIONED OFFICER

non·com·bat·ant \ˌnän-kəm-ˈbat-ənt, (ˈ)nän-ˈkäm-bət-ənt\ *n* **1** : a member (as a chaplain) of the armed forces whose duties do not include fighting **2** : CIVILIAN — **noncombatant** *adj*

non·com·mis·sioned officer \ˌnän-kə-ˌmish-ənd-\ *n* : a subordinate officer (as a sergeant) in the armed forces appointed from enlisted personnel

non·com·mit·tal \ˌnän-kə-ˈmit-əl\ *adj* : not telling or showing what a person thinks or has decided ⟨a *noncommittal* answer⟩ — **non·com·mit·tal·ly** \-ə-lē\ *adv*

non·con·duc·tor \ˌnän-kən-ˈdək-tər\ *n* : a substance that conducts heat, electricity, or sound only in very small degree

non·con·form·ist \ˌnän-kən-ˈfȯr-məst\ *n, often cap* : a person who does not conform esp. to an established church — **nonconformist** *adj, often cap* — **non·con·for·mi·ty** \-ˈfȯr-mət-ē\ *n*

non·count noun \(ˈ)nän-ˈkau̇nt-\ *n* : MASS NOUN

non·con·ju·gat·ed \(ˈ)nän-ˈkän-jə-ˌgāt-əd\ *adj* : not in a state of conjugation ⟨*nonconjugated* cells of spirogyra⟩

non·de·script \ˌnän-di-ˈskript\ *adj* : belonging or appearing to belong to no particular class or kind : not easily described — **nondescript** *n*

[1]**none** \ˈnən\ *pron* **1** : not any ⟨*none* of them went⟩ ⟨*none* of it is needed⟩ **2** : not one ⟨*none* of the family⟩ **3** : not any such thing or person ⟨half a loaf is better than *none*⟩

[2]**none** *adv* **1** : by no means : not at all ⟨he finally got there, and *none* too soon⟩ **2** : in no way : to no extent

non·en·ti·ty \nä-ˈnent-ət-ē\ *n, pl* **-ti·ties** **1** : something that does not exist or exists only in the imagination **2** : a person of no importance

non·es·sen·tial \ˌnän-ə-ˈsen-chəl\ *adj* : not necessary or essential — **nonessential** *n*

none·the·less \ˌnən-t͟hə-ˈles\ *adv* : NEVERTHELESS

non·flow·er·ing \(ˈ)nän-ˈflau̇-(ə-)ring\ *adj* : lacking a flowering stage in the life cycle

non·green \ˈnän-ˈgrēn\ *adj* : lacking chlorophyll ⟨*nongreen* plants⟩

no·nil·lion \nō-ˈnil-yən\ *n* — see NUMBER table

non·in·fec·tious \ˌnän-in-ˈfek-shəs\ *adj* : not infectious

non·in·ter·ven·tion \ˌnän-ˌint-ər-ˈven-chən\ *n* **1** : the state or habit of not intervening **2** : refusal or failure to intervene

non·in·tox·i·cat·ing \ˌnän-in-ˈtäk-sə-ˌkāt-ing\ *adj* : not causing intoxication

non·liv·ing \(ˈ)nän-ˈliv-iŋ\ *adj* : not having or characterized by life
non·met·al \(ˈ)nän-ˈmet-əl\ *n* : an element (as carbon or nitrogen) that lacks metallic properties — **non·me·tal·lic** \ˌnän-mə-ˈtal-ik\ *adj*
non·mo·bile \(ˈ)nän-ˈmō-bəl, -ˌbēl, -ˌbīl\ *adj* : not capable of self-produced motion ⟨*nonmobile* eggs fertilized by mobile sperm⟩
non·neg·a·tive \(ˈ)nän-ˈneg-ət-iv\ *adj* : not negative : being either positive or zero ⟨a *nonnegative* integer⟩
non·ob·jec·tive \ˌnän-əb-ˈjek-tiv\ *adj* : intended to represent no natural or actual object or appearance ⟨*nonobjective* art⟩
¹**non·pa·reil** \ˌnän-pə-ˈrel\ *adj* : having no equal : PEERLESS
²**nonpareil** *n* **1** : an individual of unequaled excellence : PARAGON **2** : PAINTED BUNTING
non·par·ti·san \(ˈ)nän-ˈpärt-ə-zən\ *adj* : not partisan; *esp* : free from party ties, bias, or designation ⟨a *nonpartisan* ballot⟩ ⟨a *nonpartisan* committee⟩
non·pay·ment \-ˈpā-mənt\ *n* : failure to pay
non·plus \(ˈ)nän-ˈpləs\ *vb* **non·plussed** *also* **nonplused**; **non·plus·sing** *also* **non·plus·ing** : to cause to be at a loss as to what to say, think, or do : PERPLEX
non·pro·duc·tive \ˌnän-prə-ˈdək-tiv\ *adj* **1** : UNPRODUCTIVE ⟨a *nonproductive* oil well⟩ **2** : not directly productive ⟨*nonproductive* labor⟩
non·prof·it \(ˈ)nän-ˈpräf-ət\ *adj* : not conducted or maintained for the purpose of making a profit ⟨a *nonprofit* organization⟩
non·ran·dom \(ˈ)nän-ˈran-dəm\ *adj* : not governed strictly by chance : following a definite pattern or plan
non·re·new·a·ble \ˌnän-ri-ˈn(y)ü-ə-bəl\ *adj* : not renewable; *esp* : not restored or replaced by natural means ⟨*nonrenewable* resources⟩
non·res·i·dent \(ˈ)nän-ˈrez-əd-ənt, -ə-ˌdent\ *adj* : not living in a particular place — **non·res·i·dence** \-əd-ən(t)s, -ə-ˌden(t)s\ *n* — **nonresident** *n*
non·re·sist·ance \ˌnän-ri-ˈzis-tən(t)s\ *n* : the principles or practice of submission to authority even when unjust or oppressive — **non·re·sist·ant** \-tənt\ *adj*
non·re·stric·tive \ˌnän-ri-ˈstrik-tiv\ *adj* **1** : not serving or tending to restrict **2** : not limiting the reference of the word or phrase modified ⟨a *nonrestrictive* clause⟩
non·rig·id \(ˈ)nän-ˈrij-əd\ *adj* : maintaining form by pressure of contained gas ⟨a *nonrigid* airship⟩
non·sched·uled \nän-ˈskej-üld, -əld\ *adj* : licensed to carry passengers or freight by air without a regular schedule ⟨a *nonscheduled* airline⟩
non·sci·en·tist \-ˈsī-ən-təst\ *n* : a person who is not a scientist or who lacks training in the sciences
non·sec·tar·i·an \ˌnän-sek-ˈter-ē-ən\ *adj* : not having a sectarian character
non·sense \ˈnän-ˌsen(t)s, ˈnän(t)-sən(t)s\ *n* **1** : foolish or meaningless words or actions **2** : things of no importance or value : TRIFLES ⟨don't spend your money on *nonsense*⟩ — **non·sen·si·cal** \(ˈ)nän-ˈsen(t)-si-kəl\ *adj* — **non·sen·si·cal·ly** \-k(ə-)lē\ *adv* — **non·sen·si·cal·ness** \-kəl-nəs\ *n*
non·sked \(ˈ)nän-ˈsked\ *n* : a nonscheduled airline or plane

ə abut	ər further	a back	ā bake	
ä cot, cart	aů out	ch chin	e less	ē easy
g gift	i trip	ī life	j joke	ŋ sing	ō flow
ȯ flaw	ȯi coin	th thin	t͟h this	ü loot
ů foot	y yet	yü few	yů furious	zh vision

non·skid \(ˈ)nän-ˈskid\ *adj* : having the tread specially designed to resist skidding
non·smok·er \-ˈsmō-kər\ *n* : a person who does not smoke tobacco
nonstand *abbr* nonstandard
non·stan·dard \(ˈ)nän-ˈstan-dərd\ *adj* **1** : not standard **2** : not conforming in pronunciation, grammatical construction, idiom, or choice of word to the usage generally characteristic of educated native speakers of the language
non·stop \-ˈstäp\ *adj* : done or made without a stop ⟨a *nonstop* flight to Chicago⟩ — **nonstop** *adv*
non·sup·port \ˌnän(t)-sə-ˈpōrt, -ˈpȯrt\ *n* : failure to support; *esp* : failure to provide legally required financial support
non·tast·er \(ˈ)nän-ˈtā-stər\ *n* : a person unable to taste the chemical phenylthiocarbamide
non·union \(ˈ)nän-ˈyü-nyən\ *adj* **1** : not belonging to a trade union ⟨*nonunion* carpenters⟩ **2** : not recognizing or favoring trade unions or their members ⟨*nonunion* employers⟩
non·vas·cu·lar \-ˈvas-kyə-lər\ *adj* : not vascular ⟨the *nonvascular* plants include the mosses and liverworts⟩
non·vi·a·ble \-ˈvī-ə-bəl\ *adj* : not capable of living, growing, or developing and functioning successfully
non·vi·o·lence \-ˈvī-ə-lən(t)s\ *n* : abstention on principle from violence or the principle of such abstention — **non·vi·o·lent** \-lənt\ *adj*
non·woody \-ˈwůd-ē\ *adj* : not woody ⟨*nonwoody* plants⟩
noo·dle \nüd-əl\ *n* : a food like macaroni but shaped into long flat strips and made with egg — usu. used in pl.
nook \ˈnůk\ *n* **1** : an interior angle or corner formed usu. by two walls ⟨a chimney *nook*⟩ **2** : a sheltered or hidden place ⟨a shady *nook*⟩
noon \ˈnün\ *n* : the middle of the day : 12 o'clock in the daytime — **noon** *adj*
noon·day \-ˌdā\ *n* : NOON
no one *pron* : NOBODY
noon·tide \ˈnün-ˌtīd\ *n* : NOON
noon·time \-ˌtīm\ *n* : NOON
noose \ˈnüs\ *n* : a loop with a running knot that binds closer the more it is drawn
nor \nər, (ˈ)nȯ(ə)r\ *conj* : and not ⟨not for you *nor* for me⟩ — used esp. between two words or phrases preceded by *neither* ⟨neither here *nor* there⟩
nor·adren·a·line \ˌnȯr-ə-ˈdren-ə-lən\ *n* : NOREPINEPHRINE
nor·epi·neph·rine \ˈnȯ(ə)r-ˌep-ə-ˈnef-ˌrēn, -rən\ *n* : a hormone that causes blood vessels to contract and assists in the transmission of nerve impulses in the sympathetic nervous system
norm \ˈnȯrm\ *n* : AVERAGE, STANDARD
¹**nor·mal** \ˈnȯr-məl\ *adj* **1** : conforming to a norm, rule, or principle : REGULAR **2 a** : relating to or marked by average intelligence or development **b** : SOUND, SANE **3 a** : having a concentration of one gram equivalent of solute per liter ⟨a *normal* salt solution⟩ **b** : containing neither basic hydroxl nor acid hydrogen ⟨a *normal* salt⟩ **c** : having a straight-chain structure ⟨a *normal* alcohol⟩ — **nor·mal·cy** \-sē\ *n* — **nor·mal·i·ty** \nȯr-ˈmal-ət-ē\ *n* — **nor·mal·ly** \ˈnȯr-mə-lē\ *adv*
²**normal** *n* **1** : a person or thing that is normal **2** : the usual condition, level, or quantity : AVERAGE
nor·mal·ize \ˈnȯr-mə-ˌlīz\ *vb* : to make normal or average — **nor·mal·i·za·tion** \ˌnȯr-mə-lə-ˈzā-shən\ *n*
normal school *n* : a usu. two-year school for training chiefly elementary teachers

N

Nor·man \'nȯr-mən\ *n* **1** : one of the Scandinavians who conquered Normandy in the 10th century **2** : one of the people of mixed Norman and French blood who conquered England in 1066 **3** : a native or inhabitant of the province of Normandy — **Norman** *adj*

Norse \'nȯrs\ *n* **1** *pl* **Norse a** : SCANDINAVIANS **b** : NORWEGIANS **2 a** : NORWEGIAN 2 **b** : any of the Scandinavian languages — **Norse** *adj*

Norse·man \-mən\ *n* : one of the ancient Scandinavians

1**north** \'nȯrth; *in compounds, as "northeast", also* (')nȯr *esp by seamen*\ *adv* : to or toward the north

2**north** *adj* **1** : situated toward or at the north **2** : coming from the north

3**north** *n* **1 a** : the direction to the left of one facing east **b** : the compass point opposite to south **2** *cap* : regions or countries north of a specified or implied point

North American *adj* : of, relating to, or characteristic of North America or its people — **North American** *n*

north·bound \'nȯrth-ˌbau̇nd\ *adj* : headed north

1**north·east** \nȯrth-'ēst\ *adv* : to or toward the northeast

2**northeast** *n* **1** : the direction between north and east **2** *cap* : regions or countries northeast of a specified or implied point

3**northeast** *adj* **1** : situated toward or at the northeast **2** : coming from the northeast

north·east·er \nȯrth-'ē-stər\ *n* : a storm or strong wind from the northeast

north·east·er·ly \-lē\ *adv or adj* **1** : from the northeast **2** : toward the northeast

north·east·ern \nȯrth-'ē-stərn\ *adj* **1** *often cap* : of, relating to, or characteristic of the Northeast **2** : lying toward or coming from the northeast

North·east·ern·er \-stə(r)-nər\ *n* : a native or inhabitant of a northeastern region (as of the U.S.)

north·east·ward \nȯrth-'ēs-twərd\ *adv or adj* : toward the northeast — **north·east·wards** \-twərdz\ *adv*

north·er \'nȯr-thər\ *n* : a storm or wind coming from the north

1**north·er·ly** \-lē\ *adv or adj* **1** : from the north **2** : toward the north

2**northerly** *n, pl* **-lies** : a wind from the north

north·ern \'nȯr-thə(r)n\ *adj* **1** *often cap* : of, relating to, or characteristic of the North **2** : lying toward or coming from the north — **north·ern·most** \-ˌmōst\ *adj*

North·ern·er \'nȯr-thə(r)-nər\ *n* : a native or inhabitant of the North (as of the U.S.)

northern lights *n pl* : AURORA BOREALIS

north·land \'nȯrth-ˌland, -lənd\ *n, often cap* : land in the north : the north of a country or region

North·man \-mən\ *n* : NORSEMAN

north pole *n, often cap N & P* : the northernmost point of the earth : the northern end of the earth's axis

North Star *n* : the star toward which the northern end of the earth's axis very nearly points — called also *polestar*

north·ward \'nȯrth-wərd\ *adv or adj* : toward the north — **north·wards** \-wərdz\ *adv*

1**north·west** \nȯrth-'west\ *adv* : to or toward the northwest

2**northwest** *n* **1** : the direction between north and west **2** *cap* : regions or countries northwest of a specified or implied point

3**northwest** *adj* **1** : situated toward or at the northwest **2** : coming from the northwest

north·west·er \nȯrth-'wes-tər\ *n* : a storm or wind from the northwest

north·west·er·ly \-lē\ *adv or adj* **1** : from the northwest **2** : toward the northwest

north·west·ern \nȯrth-'wes-tərn\ *adj* **1** *often cap* : of, relating to, or characteristic of the Northwest **2** : lying toward or coming from the northwest

North·west·ern·er \-tə(r)-nər\ *n* : a native or inhabitant of a northwestern region (as of the U.S.)

north·west·ward \nȯrth-'wes-twərd\ *adv or adj* : toward the northwest — **north·west·wards** \-twərdz\ *adv*

Norw *abbr* **1** Norway **2** Norwegian

Nor·we·gian \nȯr-'wē-jən\ *n* **1 a** : a native or inhabitant of Norway **b** : a person of Norwegian descent **2** : the Germanic language of the Norwegian people — **Norwegian** *adj*

nos *pl of* NO

1**nose** \'nōz\ *n* **1 a** : the part of the face that bears the nostrils and covers the forepart of the nasal cavity; *also* : this part together with the nasal cavity **b** : the vertebrate organ of smell **2** : the sense of smell **3** : something (as a point, edge, or projection) like a nose ⟨the *nose* of a plane⟩ — **nosed** \'nōzd\ *adj*

2**nose** *vb* **1** : to detect by or as if by smell : SCENT **2 a** : to push or move with the nose **b** : to touch or rub with the nose : NUZZLE **3** : to defeat by a narrow margin in a contest ⟨the home team barely *nosed* out the visitors⟩ **4** : to search esp. into other peoples' business : PRY **5** : to move ahead slowly or cautiously ⟨the ship *nosed* into her berth⟩

nose·bleed \'nōz-ˌblēd\ *n* : a bleeding from the nose

nose cone *n* : a protective cone constituting the forward end of a rocket or missile

nose dive *n* **1** : a downward nose-first plunge of an airplane **2** : a sudden extreme drop — **nose-dive** *vb*

nose·gay \'nōz-ˌgā\ *n* : a small bunch of flowers : POSY

nose·piece \-ˌpēs\ *n* : a fitting at the lower end of a microscope tube to which the objectives are attached

nos·tal·gia \nä-'stal-jə, nə-\ *n* [from modern Latin, from Greek *nostos* "return home" and *algos* "grief", "pain"] : a wistful yearning for something past or beyond recall — **nos·tal·gic** \-jik\ *adj* — **nos·tal·gi·cal·ly** \-ji-k(ə-)lē\ *adv*

nos·tril \'näs-trəl\ *n* : either of the outer openings of the nose with its adjoining passage; *also* : either fleshy lateral wall of the nose

nos·trum \'näs-trəm\ *n* [from Latin, meaning "our thing", from the neuter of *noster* "our"] **1** : a medicine of secret composition recommended esp. by its preparer **2** : a questionable remedy or scheme : PANACEA

nosy *or* **nos·ey** \'nō-zē\ *adj* **nos·i·er**; **-est** : INQUISITIVE, PRYING — **nos·i·ly** \-zə-lē\ *adv* — **nos·i·ness** \-zē-nəs\ *n*

not \(')nät\ *adv* **1** — used to make negative a word or group of words ⟨the books are *not* here⟩ **2** — used to stand for the negative of a preceding group of words ⟨is sometimes hard to see and sometimes *not*⟩

1**no·ta·ble** \'nōt-ə-bəl\ *adj* **1** : worthy of note : REMARKABLE **2** : DISTINGUISHED, PROMINENT — **no·ta·bly** \-blē\ *adv*

2**notable** *n* : a person of great reputation

no·ta·rize \'nōt-ə-ˌrīz\ *vb* : to make legally authentic through the use of the powers granted to a notary public — **no·ta·ri·za·tion** \ˌnōt-ə-rə-'zā-shən\ *n*

no·ta·ry public \ˌnōt-ə-rē-\ *n, pl* **notaries public** *or* **notary publics** : a public officer who certifies writings (as deeds) as authentic and takes statements — called also *notary*

no·ta·tion \nō-'tā-shən\ *n* **1 :** the act of noting ⟨careful *notation* of the foibles of his time⟩ **2 :** ANNOTATION, NOTE ⟨make *notations* for corrections on the margin⟩ **3 :** a system of marks, signs, figures, or characters used to express facts, quantities, or actions ⟨musical *notation*⟩ — **no·ta·tion·al** \-sh(ə-)nəl\ *adj*

1**notch** \'näch\ *n* **1 :** a V-shaped or rounded indentation in a surface **2 :** a narrow pass between mountains **:** GAP **3 :** DEGREE, STEP

2**notch** *vb* **1 :** to cut or make notches in **2 a :** SCORE **b :** to record a score **:** TALLY

1**note** \'nōt\ *vb* **1 a :** to notice or observe with care **b :** to record or preserve in writing **2 :** to make special mention of **:** NOTICE — **not·er** *n*

2**note** *n* **1 a :** a musical sound **b :** an animal's cry, call, or sound ⟨a bird's *note*⟩ **c :** a special tone of voice ⟨a *note* of fear⟩ **2 a :** MEMORANDUM **b :** a brief and informal record **c :** a written or printed comment or explanation ⟨*notes* in the back of the book⟩ **3 a :** a short informal letter **b :** a formal diplomatic or official communication **4 a :** a written promise to pay **b :** a piece of paper money **5 :** a character in music that by its shape shows the length of time a tone is to be held and by its place on the staff shows the pitch of a tone **6 :** MOOD, QUALITY ⟨a *note* of optimism⟩ **7 a :** REPUTATION, DISTINCTION ⟨a man of *note*⟩ **b :** NOTICE, HEED ⟨take *note* of the exact time⟩

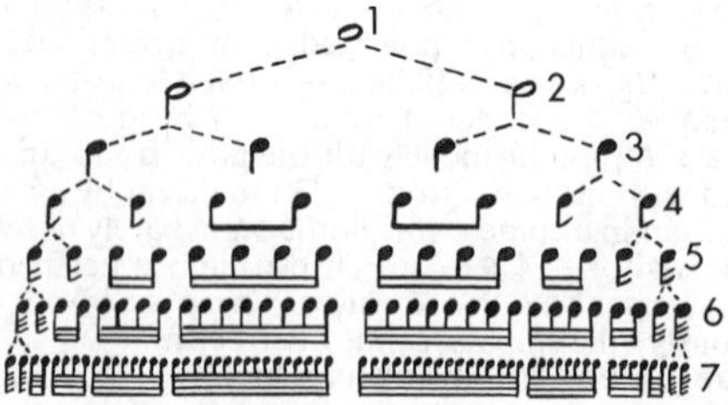

notes 5: 1, whole; 2, half; 3, quarter; 4, eighth; 5, sixteenth; 6, thirty-second; 7, sixty-fourth

note·book \'nōt-ˌbu̇k\ *n* **:** a book for notes or memoranda

not·ed \'nōt-əd\ *adj* **:** well-known and highly regarded **:** FAMOUS ⟨a *noted* scientist⟩ — **not·ed·ly** *adv*

note·wor·thy \'nōt-ˌwər-thē\ *adj* **:** worthy of note **:** REMARKABLE — **note·wor·thi·ness** *n*

1**noth·ing** \'nəth-ing\ *pron* **1 :** not anything ⟨there's *nothing* in the box⟩ **2 :** one of no interest, value, or consequence ⟨she's *nothing* to me⟩ — **nothing doing :** by no means **:** definitely no

2**nothing** *adv* **:** not at all **:** in no degree

3**nothing** *n* **1 a :** something that does not exist **b :** absence of magnitude **:** ZERO **2 :** something of little or no worth or importance — **noth·ing·ness** *n*

ə abut	ər further	a back	ā bake
ä cot, cart	au̇ out	ch chin	e less	ē easy
g gift	i trip	ī life	j joke	ng sing	ō flow
ȯ flaw	ȯi coin	th thin	th this	ü loot
u̇ foot	y yet	yü few	yu̇ furious	zh vision

1**no·tice** \'nōt-əs\ *n* **1 :** WARNING, ANNOUNCEMENT ⟨his footsteps gave *notice* of his coming⟩ **2 :** notification of the ending of an agreement at a specified time **3 :** ATTENTION, HEED **4 :** a written or printed announcement **5 :** a brief published criticism (as of a book)

2**notice** *vb* **1 :** to make mention of **:** remark on **2 :** to take notice of **:** OBSERVE, MARK ⟨*notice* even the smallest details⟩

no·tice·a·ble \'nōt-ə-sə-bəl\ *adj* **1 :** worthy of notice ⟨*noticeable* for its fine coloring⟩ **2 :** capable of being or likely to be noticed ⟨a *noticeable* improvement⟩ — **no·tice·a·bly** \-blē\ *adv*

no·ti·fi·ca·tion \ˌnōt-ə-fə-'kā-shən\ *n* **1 :** the act or an instance of notifying **2 :** written or printed matter that gives notice

no·ti·fy \'nōt-ə-ˌfī\ *vb* **-fied; -fy·ing :** to give notice to **:** inform by a notice — **no·ti·fi·er** \-ˌfī(-ə)r\ *n*

no·tion \'nō-shən\ *n* **1 a :** IDEA, CONCEPTION ⟨have a *notion* of a poem's meaning⟩ **b :** a belief held **:** OPINION **c :** WHIM, FANCY ⟨a sudden *notion* to go home⟩ **2** *pl* **:** small useful articles (as pins, needles, or thread)

no·tion·al \'nō-sh(ə-)nəl\ *adj* **1 :** IMAGINARY, UNREAL **2 :** inclined to foolish or visionary fancies or moods ⟨a *notional* man⟩

no·to·chord \'nōt-ə-ˌkȯrd\ *n* **:** a flexible rod of cells that in the lowest chordates (as lancelets and the lampreys) and in the embryos of the higher vertebrates forms a support for the body

no·to·ri·e·ty \ˌnōt-ə-'rī-ət-ē\ *n, pl* **-ties :** the quality or state of being notorious

no·to·ri·ous \nō-'tōr-ē-əs, -'tȯr-\ *adj* **:** generally known and talked of; *esp* **:** widely and unfavorably known — **no·to·ri·ous·ly** *adv*

1**not·with·stand·ing** \ˌnät-with-'stan-ding, -with-\ *prep* **:** in spite of ⟨he failed *notwithstanding* his skill⟩

2**notwithstanding** *adv* **:** NEVERTHELESS, HOWEVER

3**notwithstanding** *conj* **:** ALTHOUGH

nou·gat \'nü-gət\ *n* **[**from French, from Provençal, from *nougo* "nut"**] :** a candy of nuts or fruit pieces in a sugar paste

nought \'nȯt, 'nät\ *var of* NAUGHT

noun \'nau̇n\ *n* **:** a word that is the name of something that can be talked about (as a person, animal, plant, place, thing, substance, quality, idea, action, or state) and that is typically used in a sentence as subject or object of a verb or as object of a preposition

noun phrase *n* **:** a phrase consisting of a word (as a noun or pronoun) or words that can function as the subject of a sentence or as the object of a verb or preposition

nour·ish \'nər-ish, 'nə-rish\ *vb* **1 :** to promote the growth or development of **2 :** to provide with food **:** FEED ⟨plants *nourished* by rain and soil⟩ **3 :** SUPPORT, MAINTAIN ⟨a friendship *nourished* by trust⟩

nour·ish·ing *adj* **:** giving nourishment **:** NUTRITIOUS ⟨*nourishing* food⟩

nour·ish·ment \'nər-ish-mənt, 'nə-rish-\ *n* **:** something that nourishes **:** NUTRIMENT

Nov *abbr* November

no·va \'nō-və\ *n, pl* **novas** *or* **no·vae** \-(ˌ)vē, -ˌvī\ **:** a star that suddenly increases greatly in brightness and then within a few months or years grows dim again

1**nov·el** \'näv-əl\ *adj* **:** new in conception, kind, or style **:** having no precedent ⟨a *novel* experience⟩ ⟨*novel* costumes⟩ ***syn*** see NEW

2**novel** *n* **:** a long prose narrative that usu. portrays imaginary characters and events

nov·el·ette \ˌnäv-ə-'let\ *n* **:** a brief novel

N

nov·el·ist \'näv-(ə-)ləst\ *n* : a writer of novels
nov·el·ty \'näv-əl-tē\ *n, pl* **-ties** **1** : something new or unusual **2** : the quality or state of being novel : NEWNESS **3** : a small article intended mainly for personal or household adornment
No·vem·ber \nō-'vem-bər\ *n* [from Latin, originally the ninth month of the Roman year, from *novem* "nine"] : the 11th month of the year
no·ve·na \nō-'vē-nə\ *n, pl* **-nas** *or* **-nae** \-(ˌ)nē\ : a Roman Catholic devotion in which prayers are said for the same intention on nine successive days
nov·ice \'näv-əs\ *n* **1** : a new member of a religious order who is preparing to take the vows of religion **2** : one who has no previous training or experience in a field or activity : BEGINNER
no·vi·tiate \nō-'vish-ət\ *n* **1** : the period or state of being a novice **2** : NOVICE **3** : a place where novices are trained
¹now \(')nau̇\ *adv* **1 a** : at the present time ⟨he is busy *now*⟩ **b** : in the time immediately before the present ⟨he left just *now*⟩ **c** : in the time immediately to follow ⟨he will leave *now*⟩ **2** — used with the sense of present time weakened or lost (as to express command or introduce an important point) ⟨*now* this would imply a deliberate act⟩ **3** : SOMETIMES ⟨*now* one and *now* another⟩ **4** : under the present circumstances ⟨*now* what can we do⟩ **5** : at the time referred to ⟨*now* the trouble began⟩
²now *conj* : SINCE
³now \'nau̇\ *n* : the present time : PRESENT
⁴now \'nau̇\ *adj* : of or relating to the present time : EXISTING ⟨the *now* president⟩
now·a·days \'nau̇-(ə-)ˌdāz\ *adv* : at the present time
no·way \'nō-ˌwā\ *or* **no·ways** \-ˌwāz\ *adv* : NOWISE
¹no·where \'nō-ˌhwe(ə)r, -ˌhwa(ə)r, -hwər\ *adv* **1** : not in or at any place **2** : to no place
²nowhere *n* : a place that does not exist ⟨sounds seeming to come from *nowhere*⟩
nowhere near *adv* : not nearly
no·wise \'nō-ˌwīz\ *adv* : in no way : not at all
nox·ious \'näk-shəs\ *adj* : harmful or injurious esp. to health : UNWHOLESOME ⟨*noxious* fumes⟩
noz·zle \'näz-əl\ *n* : a projecting part with an opening that usu. serves as an outlet; *esp* : a short tube on a hose or pipe to direct or control a flow of fluid
NP *abbr* noun phrase
N.S. *abbr* Nova Scotia
-n't \(ə)nt\ *adv comb form* : not ⟨is*n't*⟩
NT *abbr* New Testament
nth \'en(t)th\ *adj* **1** : numbered with an unspecified or indefinitely large ordinal number **2** : EXTREME, UTMOST ⟨to the *nth* degree⟩
NTP *abbr* normal temperature and pressure
nu \'n(y)ü\ *n* : the 13th letter of the Greek alphabet — N or ν
nu·ance \'n(y)ü-ˌän(t)s, n(y)u̇-'\ *n* : a slight shade or degree of difference (as in color, tone, or meaning)
nub \'nəb\ *n* **1** : KNOB, LUMP **2** : GIST, POINT ⟨the *nub* of the story⟩
nub·bin \'nəb-ən\ *n* **1** : a small or imperfect ear of Indian corn; *also* : any small shriveled or undeveloped fruit **2** : a small projecting part
nub·ble \'nəb-əl\ *n* : a small knob or lump — **nub·bly** \'nəb-(ə-)lē\ *adj*
nu·cle·ar \'n(y)ü-klē-ər\ *adj* **1** : of, relating to, or constituting a nucleus (as of a cell) **2** : of, relating to, or utilizing the atomic nucleus, atomic energy, the atom bomb, or atomic power
nuclear energy *n* : ATOMIC ENERGY
nuclear membrane *n* : the boundary of a nucleus
nuclear pile *n* : ATOMIC PILE
nuclear reactor *n* : REACTOR 2
nuclear sap *n* : the ground substance of a cell nucleus
nu·cle·ic acid \n(y)ü-ˌklē-ik-, -ˌklā-\ *n* : any of various acids (as DNA) composed of a sugar or derivative of a sugar, phosphoric acid, and a base and found esp. in cell nuclei
nu·cle·o·lus \n(y)ü-'klē-ə-ləs\ *n, pl* **-li** \-ˌlī\ : a body in a cell nucleus that is rich in RNA
nu·cle·on \'n(y)ü-klē-ˌän\ *n* : a proton or a neutron esp. as part of the atomic nucleus
nu·cle·on·ics \ˌn(y)ü-klē-'än-iks\ *n* : a branch of physical science that deals with nucleons or with all phenomena of the atomic nucleus
nu·cleo·plasm \'n(y)ü-klē-ə-ˌplaz-əm\ *n* : the protoplasm of a nucleus; *esp* : NUCLEAR SAP
nu·cle·us \'n(y)ü-klē-əs\ *n, pl* **-clei** \-klē-ˌī\ *also* **-cle·us·es** [from modern Latin, from Latin, meaning "kernel", being a diminutive of *nux* (stem *nuc-*) "nut"] : a central point, group, or mass of something: as **a** : the small, brighter, and denser part of a galaxy or of the head of a comet **b** : a part of cell protoplasm that contains chromosomes, controls heredity, and is bounded by a nuclear membrane **c** : a mass of gray matter or group of nerve cells in the central nervous system **d** : the positively charged central part of an atom that comprises nearly all of the atomic mass and consists of protons and neutrons except in hydrogen which consists of one proton only
¹nude \'n(y)üd\ *adj* : NAKED, BARE; *esp* : having no clothes on — **nude·ness** *n* — **nu·di·ty** \'n(y)üd-ət-ē\ *n*
²nude *n* **1** : a nude human figure esp. as depicted in art **2** : the condition of being nude ⟨in the *nude*⟩
nudge \'nəj\ *vb* : to touch or push gently; *esp* : to seek the attention of by a push of the elbow — **nudge** *n*
nud·ism \'n(y)ü-ˌdiz-əm\ *n* : the practice of going nude esp. in sexually mixed groups and during periods spent at specially secluded places — **nud·ist** \'n(y)üd-əst\ *n or adj*
nug·get \'nəg-ət\ *n* : a solid lump esp. of precious metal
nui·sance \'n(y)üs-ən(t)s\ *n* : an annoying or troublesome person, thing, or practice
null \'nəl\ *adj* **1** : having no legal or binding force : INVALID, VOID **2** : having no value : INSIGNIFICANT **3** : having no members ⟨the *null* set⟩
null and void *adj* : having no force, binding power, or validity
nul·li·fi·ca·tion \ˌnəl-ə-fə-'kā-shən\ *n* **1** : the act of nullifying : the state of being nullified **2** : the action of a state impeding or attempting to prevent the enforcement within its territory of a federal law of the U.S. — **nul·li·fi·ca·tion·ist** \-sh(ə-)nəst\ *n*
nul·li·fy \'nəl-ə-ˌfī\ *vb* **-fied; -fy·ing** : to make null or valueless; *esp* : ANNUL
num *abbr* number
numb \'nəm\ *adj* **1** : lacking in sensation esp. from cold **2** : lacking in emotion : INDIFFERENT — **numb** *vb* — **numb·ly** *adv* — **numb·ness** *n*
¹num·ber \'nəm-bər\ *n* **1 a** : the total of individual items taken together : AMOUNT ⟨the *number* of people in the room⟩ **b** : an unspecified group : MANY ⟨a *number* of accidents occur on wet roads⟩ **2** : the possibility of being counted ⟨mosquitoes in swarms beyond *number*⟩ **3 a** : a unit (as an integer or irrational number) belonging to a mathematical system and subject to its laws **b** *pl* : ARITHMETIC **4** : a distinction of word form to denote reference to one or more than one ⟨a verb agrees in *number* with its subject⟩ **5 a** : a word or symbol used to represent a

TABLE OF NUMBERS

CARDINAL NUMBERS[1]

NAME[2]	SYMBOL *arabic*	SYMBOL *roman*[3]
zero *or* naught *or* cipher	0	
one	1	I
two	2	II
three	3	III
four	4	IV
five	5	V
six	6	VI
seven	7	VII
eight	8	VIII
nine	9	IX
ten	10	X
eleven	11	XI
twelve	12	XII
thirteen	13	XIII
fourteen	14	XIV
fifteen	15	XV
sixteen	16	XVI
seventeen	17	XVII
eighteen	18	XVIII
nineteen	19	XIX
twenty	20	XX
twenty-one	21	XXI
twenty-two	22	XXII
twenty-three	23	XXIII
twenty-four	24	XXIV
twenty-five	25	XXV
twenty-six	26	XXVI
twenty-seven	27	XXVII
twenty-eight	28	XXVIII
twenty-nine	29	XXIX
thirty	30	XXX
thirty-one *etc*	31	XXXI
forty	40	XL
fifty	50	L
sixty	60	LX
seventy	70	LXX
eighty	80	LXXX
ninety	90	XC
one hundred	100	C
one hundred and one *or* one hundred one *etc*	101	CI
two hundred	200	CC
three hundred	300	CCC
four hundred	400	CD
five hundred	500	D
six hundred	600	DC
seven hundred	700	DCC
eight hundred	800	DCCC
nine hundred	900	CM
one thousand *or* ten hundred *etc*	1,000	M
two thousand *etc*	2,000	MM
five thousand	5,000	$\overline{V}$
ten thousand	10,000	$\overline{X}$
one hundred thousand	100,000	$\overline{C}$
one million	1,000,000	$\overline{M}$

ORDINAL NUMBERS[4]

NAME[5]	SYMBOL[6]
first	1st
second	2d *or* 2nd
third	3d *or* 3rd
fourth	4th
fifth	5th
sixth	6th
seventh	7th
eighth	8th
ninth	9th
tenth	10th
eleventh	11th
twelfth	12th
thirteenth	13th
fourteenth	14th
fifteenth	15th
sixteenth	16th
seventeenth	17th
eighteenth	18th
nineteenth	19th
twentieth	20th
twenty-first	21st
twenty-second	22d *or* 22nd
twenty-third	23d *or* 23rd
twenty-fourth	24th
twenty-fifth	25th
twenty-sixth	26th
twenty-seventh	27th
twenty-eighth	28th
twenty-ninth	29th
thirtieth	30th
thirty-first *etc*	31st
fortieth	40th
fiftieth	50th
sixtieth	60th
seventieth	70th
eightieth	80th
ninetieth	90th
hundredth *or* one hundredth	100th
hundred and first *or* one hundred and first *etc*	101st
two hundredth	200th
three hundredth	300th
four hundredth	400th
five hundredth	500th
six hundredth	600th
seven hundredth	700th
eight hundredth	800th
nine hundredth	900th
thousandth *or* one thousandth	1,000th
two thousandth *etc*	2,000th
five thousandth	5,000th
ten thousandth	10,000th
hundred thousandth *or* one hundred thousandth	100,000th
millionth *or* one millionth	1,000,000th

(*continued on next page*)

[1]The cardinal numbers are used in simple counting or in answer to "how many?" The words for these numbers may be used as nouns (he counted to *twelve*), as pronouns (*twelve* were found), or as adjectives (*twelve* boys).

[2]In formal contexts the numbers one to one hundred and in less formal contexts the numbers one to nine are commonly written out, while larger numbers are given in numerals. In nearly all contexts a number occurring at the beginning of a sentence is usually written out. Except in very formal contexts numerals are invariably used for dates. Arabic numerals from 1,000 to 9,999 are often written without commas (1000; 9999). Year numbers are always written without commas (1783).

[3]The roman numerals are written either in capitals or in lowercase letters.

[4]The ordinal numbers are used to show the order of succession in which such items as names, objects, and periods of time are considered (the *twelfth*) month; the *fourth* row of seats; the *18th* century).

[5]Each of the terms for the ordinal numbers excepting *first* and *second* is used in designating one of a number of parts into which a whole may be divided (a *fourth;* a *sixth;* a *tenth*) and as the denominator in fractions designating the number of such parts constituting a certain portion of a whole (*one fourth; three fifths*). When used as nouns the fractions are usually written as two words, although they are regularly hyphenated as adjectives (a *two-thirds* majority). When fractions are written in numerals, the cardinal symbols are used (1/4, 3/5, 5/6).

[6]The arabic symbols for the cardinal numbers may be read as ordinals in certain contexts (January 1 = January first; 2 Samuel = Second Samuel). The roman numerals are sometimes read as ordinals (Henry IV = Henry the Fourth); sometimes they are written with the ordinal suffixes (XIXth Dynasty).

DENOMINATIONS ABOVE ONE MILLION

American system[1]

NAME	VALUE IN POWERS OF TEN	NUMBER OF ZEROS[2]	NUMBER OF GROUPS OF THREE 0's AFTER 1,000
billion	10^{9}	9	2
trillion	10^{12}	12	3
quadrillion	10^{15}	15	4
quintillion	10^{18}	18	5
sextillion	10^{21}	21	6
septillion	10^{24}	24	7
octillion	10^{27}	27	8
nonillion	10^{30}	30	9
decillion	10^{33}	33	10

British system[1]

NAME	VALUE IN POWERS OF TEN	NUMBER OF ZEROS[2]	POWERS OF 1,000,000
milliard	10^{9}	9	—
billion	10^{12}	12	2
trillion	10^{18}	18	3
quadrillion	10^{24}	24	4
quintillion	10^{30}	30	5
sextillion	10^{36}	36	6
septillion	10^{42}	42	7
octillion	10^{48}	48	8
nonillion	10^{54}	54	9
decillion	10^{60}	60	10

[1]The American system of numeration for denominations above one million was modeled on the French system but more recently the French system has been changed to correspond to the German and British systems. In the American system each of the denominations above 1,000 millions (the American *billion*) is 1,000 times the one preceding (one trillion = 1,000 billions; one quadrillion = 1,000 trillions). In the British system the first denomination above 1,000 millions (the British *milliard*) is 1,000 times the preceding one, but each of the denominations above 1,000 milliards (the British *billion*) is 1,000,000 times the preceding one (one trillion = 1,000,000 billions; one quadrillion = 1,000,000 trillions).

[2]For convenience in reading large numerals the thousands, millions, etc., are usually separated by commas (21,530; 1,155,465) or by half spaces (1 155 465). Serial numbers (as a social security number or the engine number of a car) are often written with hyphens (583-695-20).

mathematical number; *esp* : NUMERAL 1 **b** : a number used to identify or designate ⟨*number* one on the list⟩ ⟨a phone *number*⟩ **6** : a member of a sequence or series ⟨the best *number* on the program⟩ ⟨the March *number* of a magazine⟩ — **by the numbers 1** : in unison to a specific count or cadence **2** : in a mechanical manner

2**number** *vb* **num·bered**; **num·ber·ing** \-b(ə-)riŋ\ **1** : COUNT, ENUMERATE **2** : to claim as part of a total : INCLUDE ⟨I *number* him among my friends⟩ **3** : to restrict to a definite number ⟨the old man's days are *numbered*⟩ **4** : to assign a number to **5** : to comprise in number ⟨our group *numbered* 10 in all⟩ — **num·ber·er** \-bər-ər\ *n*

num·ber·less \'nəm-bər-ləs\ *adj* : too many to count : INNUMERABLE ⟨the *numberless* stars in the sky⟩

number line *n* : a line in which points are matched to numbers

Num·bers \'nəm-bərz\ *n* — see BIBLE table

numb·skull *var of* NUMSKULL

nu·mer·a·ble \'n(y)üm-(ə-)rə-bəl\ *adj* : capable of being counted

nu·mer·al \'n(y)üm-(ə-)rəl\ *n* **1** : a symbol or group of symbols representing a number **2** *pl* : numbers designating by year a student's school or college class that are awarded to him for distinction esp. in sports

nu·mer·ate \'n(y)ü-mə-ˌrāt\ *vb* : ENUMERATE

nu·mer·a·tion \ˌn(y)ü-mə-'rā-shən\ *n* **1** : the act or process or a system or instance of enumeration **2** : the reading in words of numbers expressed by numerals

nu·mer·a·tor \'n(y)ü-mə-ˌrāt-ər\ *n* **1** : the part of a fraction written above the line that signifies the number of parts of the denominator taken **2** : one that counts something

nu·mer·i·cal \n(y)u̇-'mer-i-kəl\ *adj* **1** : of or relating to numbers **2** : denoting a number or expressed in numbers — **nu·mer·i·cal·ly** \-k(ə-)lē\ *adv*

nu·mer·ous \'n(y)üm-(ə-)rəs\ *adj* **1** : consisting of or including a great number ⟨a *numerous* group of people⟩ **2** : of or relating to a great number : MANY ⟨has been late on *numerous* occasions⟩ — **nu·mer·ous·ly** *adv*

nu·mis·mat·ics \ˌn(y)ü-məz-'mat-iks\ *n* : the study or collection of coins, medals, or paper money — **nu·mis·mat·ic** \-ik\ *adj* — **nu·mis·ma·tist** \n(y)ü-'miz-mət-əst\ *n*

num·skull \'nəm-ˌskəl\ *n* : a stupid person : DUNCE

nun \'nən\ *n* : a woman belonging to a religious order; *esp* : one under solemn vows of poverty, chastity, and obedience

nun·cio \'nən(t)-sē-ˌō, 'nu̇n(t)-\ *n, pl* **-ci·os** : a papal emissary to a civil government

nun·nery \'nən-(ə-)rē\ *n, pl* **-ner·ies** : a convent of nuns

1**nup·tial** \'nəp-shəl\ *adj* **1** : of or relating to marriage or a wedding **2** : characteristic of the breeding season

2**nuptial** *n* : MARRIAGE, WEDDING — usu. used in pl.

1**nurse** \'nərs\ *n* **1** : a woman who has the care of a young child **2** : one skilled or trained in caring for the sick or infirm esp. under the supervision of a physician **3** : a worker of a social insect that cares for the young

2**nurse** *vb* **1** : to feed at the breast : SUCKLE **2** : REAR, EDUCATE **3** : to manage with care or economy ⟨*nursed* his small funds⟩ **4** : to care for as a nurse ⟨*nursed* him back to health⟩ **5** : to hold in one's memory ⟨*nurse* a grudge⟩ **6** : to treat with special care ⟨*nursed* his car over the rough road⟩ — **nurs·er** *n*

nurse·maid \'nərs-ˌmād\ *n* : a girl employed to look after children

nurs·ery \'nərs-(ə-)rē\ *n, pl* **-er·ies 1 a** : a child's bedroom **b** : a place where children are temporarily cared for in their parents' absence **2** : a place where plants (as trees or shrubs) are grown for transplanting, for use as stocks in grafting, or for sale

nurs·ery·man \-(ə-)rē-mən\ *n* : a man who keeps or works in a plant nursery

nursery rhyme *n* : a tale in rhymed verse for children

nursery school *n* : a school for children usu. under five years of age

nursery–web spider *n* : any of a family of spiders that typically build webs only for the shelter and protection of the young

nursing bottle *n* : a bottle with a rubber nipple used for feeding a baby

nurs·ling \'nərs-liŋ\ *n* **1** : one that is tended with special care **2** : a nursing child

1**nur·ture** \'nər-chər\ *n* **1** : TRAINING, UPBRINGING **2** : something that nourishes : FOOD

2**nurture** *vb* **nur·tured**; **nur·tur·ing** \'nərch-(ə-)riŋ\ **1** : to supply with nourishment **2** : EDUCATE **3** : to further the development of : FOSTER — **nur·tur·er** \'nər-chər-ər\ *n*

nut \'nət\ *n* [from Old English *hnutu*] **1 a :** a hard-shelled dry fruit (as a peanut in the shell) or seed (as a Brazil nut) with a separable rind or shell and an inner kernel; *also* **:** this kernel **b :** a dry one-seeded fruit (as an acorn, hazelnut, or chestnut) that has a woody outer layer and does not burst open at maturity **2 :** a block of metal with a hole in it that is fastened to a bolt by means of a screw thread within the hole **3 :** the ridge on the upper end of the fingerboard of a stringed instrument over which the strings pass **4 a :** a foolish, eccentric, or crazy person **b :** FANATIC, FAN — **nut·like** \-ˌlīk\ *adj*

nut·crack·er \'nət-ˌkrak-ər\ *n* **1 :** an instrument for cracking the shells of nuts **2 :** a bird related to the crows that lives largely on seeds from the cones of the pine tree

nut·hatch \'nət-ˌhach\ *n* **:** any of a group of small tree-climbing insect-eating birds that are noted for their habit of going down tree trunks headfirst

nuthatch (about 6 in. long)

nut·let \'nət-lət\ *n* **:** a small nut

nut·meg \'nət-ˌmeg\ *n* **1 :** the seed of a tree grown in the East and West Indies and Brazil; *also* **:** this tree **2 :** a spice consisting of ground nutmeg seeds

nu·tria \'n(y)ü-trē-ə\ *n* **1 :** COYPU 1 **2 :** the durable usu. light brown fur of the coypu esp. when plucked and blended to look like beaver

¹**nu·tri·ent** \'n(y)ü-trē-ənt\ *adj* **:** furnishing nourishment

²**nutrient** *n* **:** a nutritive substance or ingredient

nu·tri·ment \'n(y)ü-trə-mənt\ *n* **:** something that nourishes

nu·tri·tion \n(y)u̇-'trish-ən\ *n* **:** the act or process of nourishing or being nourished; *esp* **:** the processes by which an animal or plant takes in and utilizes food substances — **nu·tri·tion·al** \-'trish-(ə-)nəl\ *adj* — **nu·tri·tion·al·ly** \-ē\ *adv*

nu·tri·tion·ist \-'trish-(ə-)nəst\ *n* **:** a specialist in the study of nutrition

nu·tri·tious \n(y)u̇-'trish-əs\ *adj* **:** NOURISHING — **nu·tri·tious·ly** *adv* — **nu·tri·tious·ness** *n*

nu·tri·tive \'n(y)ü-trət-iv\ *adj* **1 :** of or relating to nutrition **2 :** NUTRITIOUS — **nu·tri·tive·ly** *adv*

nuts \'nəts\ *adj* **1 :** ENTHUSIASTIC, KEEN **2 :** CRAZY, DEMENTED

nut·shell \'nət-ˌshel\ *n* **:** the shell of a nut — **in a nutshell :** in a small space **:** in brief

nut·ty \'nət-ē\ *adj* **nut·tier; -est 1 :** containing or suggesting nuts (as in flavor) **2 a :** CRACKBRAINED, ECCENTRIC **b :** CRAZY, INSANE — **nut·ti·ness** *n*

nuz·zle \'nəz-əl\ *vb* **nuz·zled; nuz·zling** \-(ə-)ling\ **1 :** to push or rub with the nose **2 :** to lie close **:** NESTLE

NV *abbr* Nevada

NW *abbr* northwest

N.Y. *or* **NY** *abbr* New York

NYC *abbr* New York City

ny·lon \'nī-ˌlän\ *n* [a word coined from meaningless elements] **1 :** any of numerous strong tough elastic synthetic materials used esp. in textiles and plastics **2** *pl* **:** stockings made of nylon — **nylon** *adj*

nymph \'nim(p)f\ *n, pl* **nymphs 1 :** one of a group of beautiful maidens represented in ancient mythology as dwelling in mountains, forests, meadows, and waters **2 :** any of various immature insects; *esp* **:** a larval insect that has a form resembling the adult and differs chiefly in size

N.Z. *abbr* New Zealand

ə abut	ər further	a back	ā bake	
ä cot, cart	au̇ out	ch chin	e less	ē easy
g gift	i trip	ī life	j joke	ng sing	ō flow
ȯ flaw	ȯi coin	th thin	th this	ü loot
u̇ foot	y yet	yü few	yu̇ furious	zh vision

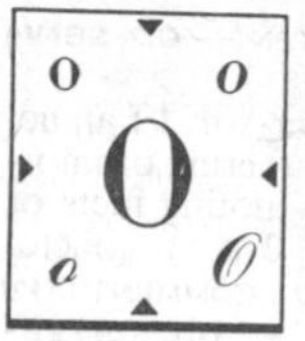

o \'ō\ *n, often cap* **1 :** the 15th letter of the English alphabet **2 :** ZERO
o' *also* **o** \ə\ *prep* **:** OF ⟨one o'clock⟩
O \(')ō\ *var of* OH
O *abbr* ocean
oaf \'ōf\ *n* **:** a stupid or awkward person — **oaf·ish** \'ō-fish\ *adj* — **oaf·ish·ness** *n*
oak \'ōk\ *n, pl* **oaks** *or* **oak 1 :** any of various hardwood timber trees or shrubs closely related to the beech and chestnut and having a rounded one-seeded thin-shelled nut **2 :** the usu. tough hard durable wood of the oak much used for furniture and flooring — **oak** *adj* — **oak·en** \'ō-kən\ *adj*
oa·kum \'ō-kəm\ *n* [from Old English *ācumba*, literally "off-combings", from *ā-* "away" and the root of English *comb*] **:** hemp or jute fiber impregnated with tar or a tar derivative and used in caulking seams and packing joints
oar \'ō(ə)r, 'ȯ(ə)r\ *n* **1 :** a long slender broad-bladed wooden implement for propelling or steering a boat **2 :** OARSMAN — **oared** \'ō(ə)rd, 'ȯ(ə)rd\ *adj*
oar·lock \'ō(ə)r-ˌläk, 'ȯ(ə)r-\ *n* **:** a usu. U-shaped device for holding an oar in place
oars·man \'ō(ə)rz-mən, 'ȯ(ə)rz-\ *n* **:** one who rows a boat
OAS *abbr* Organization of American States
oa·sis \ō-'ā-səs\ *n, pl* **oa·ses** \-'ā-ˌsēz\ **:** a fertile or green area in an arid region
oat \'ōt\ *n* **:** a grain with long spikelets in loose clusters that is widely grown for its seed which is used for human food and for livestock feed — **oat·en** \'ōt-ən\ *adj*

oat

oath \'ōth\ *n, pl* **oaths** \'ōt͟hz, 'ōths\ **1 :** a solemn appeal to God or to some revered person or thing to bear witness to the truth of one's word or the sacredness of a promise ⟨under *oath* to tell the truth⟩ **2 :** a careless or profane use of a sacred name
oat·meal \'ōt-ˌmēl, ōt-'\ *n* **1 :** oats husked and crushed into coarse meal or flattened into flakes **2 :** porridge made from oatmeal
Oba·di·ah \ˌō-bə-'dī-ə\ *n* — see BIBLE table
1**ob·bli·ga·to** \ˌäb-lə-'gät-ō\ *adj* **:** not to be omitted **:** OBLIGATORY — used as a direction in music
2**obbligato** *n, pl* **-gatos** *also* **-ga·ti** \-'gät-ē\ **:** a prominent accompanying part usu. played by a solo instrument ⟨a violin *obbligato*⟩; *also* **:** any accompanying part
ob·du·ra·cy \'äb-d(y)ə-rə-sē, äb-'d(y)u̇r-ə-\ *n, pl* **-cies 1 :** the quality or state of being obdurate **2 :** an instance of being obdurate
ob·du·rate \'äb-d(y)ə-rət, äb-'d(y)u̇r-ət\ *adj* **1 :** HARDHEARTED **2 :** STUBBORN, UNYIELDING — **ob·du·rate·ly** *adv*
obe·di·ence \ō-'bēd-ē-ən(t)s, ə-\ *n* **1 :** an act or instance of obeying **2 :** the quality or state of being obedient
obe·di·ent \-ənt\ *adj* **:** willing or inclined to obey — **obe·di·ent·ly** *adv*
obei·sance \ō-'bā-sən(t)s, -'bē-\ *n* **1 :** a movement of the body made as a sign of respect **:** BOW **2 :** DEFERENCE, HOMAGE
obe·lia \ō-'bēl-yə\ *n* **:** any of a genus of small colonial marine hydroids with colonies branched like trees
ob·e·lisk \'äb-ə-ˌlisk\ *n* [from Greek *obeliskos*, from the diminutive of *obelos* "spit for roasting meat"] **:** a 4-sided pillar that tapers toward the top and ends in a pyramid

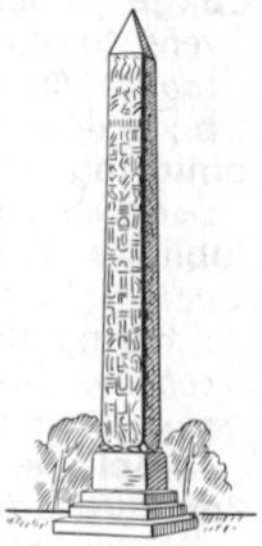

obelisk

obese \ō-'bēs\ *adj* **:** excessively fat — **obe·si·ty** \ō-'bē-sət-ē\ *n*
obey \ō-'bā, ə-\ *vb* **obeyed**; **obey·ing 1 :** to follow the commands or guidance of **2 :** to comply with **:** EXECUTE ⟨*obey* an order⟩
obi \'ō-bē\ *n* **:** a broad sash worn with a Japanese kimono
obit·u·ary \ə-'bich-ə-ˌwer-ē\ *n, pl* **-ar·ies :** a notice of a person's death (as in a newspaper) usu. with a short account of his life — **obituary** *adj*
obj *abbr* **1** object **2** objective
1**ob·ject** \'äb-jikt\ *n* **1 a :** something that may be seen or felt ⟨tables and chairs are *objects*⟩ **b :** something that may be thought about ⟨an *object* of study⟩ **2 :** something that arouses an emotion (as affection, hatred, or pity) ⟨an *object* of envy⟩ **3 :** AIM, PURPOSE ⟨the *object* is to raise money⟩ **4 a :** a noun or noun equivalent denoting someone or something that the action of a verb is directed toward **b :** a noun or noun equivalent in a prepositional phrase — **ob·ject·less** \'äb-jik-tləs\ *adj*
2**ob·ject** \əb-'jekt\ *vb* **1 :** to offer or cite as an objection ⟨*objected* that the price was too high⟩ **2 :** to state one's opposition to or oppose something ⟨*objected* to the plan⟩ — **ob·jec·tor** \-'jek-tər\ *n*
object ball \'äb-jik(t)-\ *n* **:** the ball struck by the cue ball in pool or billiards
ob·jec·tion \əb-'jek-shən\ *n* **1 :** an act of objecting **2 :** a reason for or feeling of disapproval
ob·jec·tion·a·ble \-sh(ə-)nə-bəl\ *adj* **:** arousing objection **:** DISPLEASING, OFFENSIVE ⟨uses *objectionable* language⟩ — **ob·jec·tion·a·bly** \-blē\ *adv*
1**ob·jec·tive** \əb-'jek-tiv\ *adj* **1 :** relating to or being a goal ⟨reached our *objective* point⟩ **2 :** existing outside and independent of the mind ⟨dragons have no *objective* existence⟩ **3 :** treating facts without distortion by personal feelings or prejudices ⟨an *objective* editorial⟩ **4 :** relating to or being a grammatical case marking typically the object of a verb or preposition — **ob·jec·tive·ly** *adv* — **ob·jec·tiv·i·ty** \(ˌ)äb-ˌjek-'tiv-ət-ē, əb-\ *n*
2**objective** *n* **1 :** an aim or end of action **:** GOAL **2 :** the objective case or a word in the objective case **3 :** a lens or system of lenses (as in a microscope) that forms an image of an object — called also *objective lens*
object lesson \'äb-jikt-\ *n* **:** a lesson taught by means of illustrative objects or concrete examples
ob·late \äb-'lāt, 'äb-ˌ\ *adj* **:** flattened or depressed at the poles ⟨the *oblate* shape of the earth⟩
ob·li·gate \'äb-lə-ˌgāt\ *vb* **:** to bring under obligation **:** bind legally or morally ⟨*obligated* to pay taxes⟩
ob·li·ga·tion \ˌäb-lə-'gā-shən\ *n* **1 :** an act of binding oneself to a course of action **2 a :** something (as a promise or contract) that binds one to a course of action **b :** something one is bound to do **3 :** indebtedness for an act of kindness

syn OBLIGATION, DUTY can mean something that ought to be done. OBLIGATION implies the immediacy of something specific that ought to be done; DUTY implies less immediacy but a stronger pull of something general that is demanded on moral grounds ⟨in complying with his three-year *obligation* of military service, he felt he was only doing a citizen's *duty*⟩

oblig·a·to·ry \ə-'blig-ə-ˌtōr-ē, 'äb-li-gə-, -ˌtȯr-\ *adj* : legally or morally binding : REQUIRED
oblige \ə-'blīj\ *vb* **1** : FORCE, COMPEL ⟨laws *oblige* citizens to pay taxes⟩ **2 a** : to bind by a favor ⟨*oblige* an acquaintance by lending him money⟩ **b** : to do something as a favor — **oblig·er** *n*
oblig·ing \ə-'blī-jing\ *adj* : willing to do favors : ACCOMMODATING — **oblig·ing·ly** \-jing-lē\ *adv*
1**oblique** \ō-'blēk, ə-, -'blīk; *military usu* ī\ *adj* **1 a** : INCLINED, SLANTING **b** *of a solid* : having the axis not perpendicular to the base ⟨*oblique* circular cylinder⟩ **2** : not straightforward : INDIRECT ⟨*oblique* accusations⟩ — **oblique·ly** *adv* — **oblique·ness** *n* — **obliq·ui·ty** \-'blik-wət-ē\ *n*
2**oblique** *adv* : at a 45 degree angle ⟨to the right *oblique*, march⟩
oblique angle *n* : an acute or obtuse angle
oblit·er·ate \ə-'blit-ə-ˌrāt\ *vb* : to remove or destroy completely : wipe out ⟨his tracks were *obliterated* by the wind⟩ — **oblit·er·a·tion** \-ˌblit-ə-'rā-shən\ *n*
obliv·i·on \ə-'bliv-ē-ən\ *n* **1** : an act or instance of forgetting **2** : the state of being forgotten
obliv·i·ous \-ē-əs\ *adj* **1** : FORGETFUL **2** : INATTENTIVE, UNAWARE ⟨*oblivious* to the danger⟩ — **obliv·i·ous·ly** *adv* — **obliv·i·ous·ness** *n*
ob·long \'äb-ˌlȯng\ *adj* : longer in one direction than in the other with parallel sides : RECTANGULAR — **oblong** *n*
ob·lo·quy \'äb-lə-kwē\ *n, pl* **-quies** **1** : strong condemnation : CENSURE **2** : bad repute : DISGRACE
ob·nox·ious \äb-'näk-shəs, əb-\ *adj* : extremely disagreeable : OFFENSIVE, REPUGNANT — **ob·nox·ious·ly** *adv* — **ob·nox·ious·ness** *n*
oboe \'ō-bō\ *n* [from Italian, from French *hautbois*,

oboe

literally "high wood"] : a slender conical woodwind instrument with holes and keys that is played by blowing into a reed mouthpiece — **obo·ist** \-(ˌ)bō-əst\ *n*
ob·ovate \(')äb-'ō-ˌvāt\ *adj* : ovate with the base narrower ⟨an *obovate* leaf⟩
obs *abbr* obsolete
ob·scene \äb-'sēn, əb-\ *adj* : deeply offensive to morality or decency : INDECENT — **ob·scene·ly** *adv*
ob·scen·i·ty \-'sen-ət-ē\ *n, pl* **-ties** **1** : the quality or state of being obscene **2** : an obscene word, phrase, or act
1**ob·scure** \äb-'skyu̇(ə)r, əb-\ *adj* **1** : DARK, GLOOMY **2** : REMOTE, HIDDEN ⟨an *obscure* country village⟩ **3** : not readily understood or not clearly expressed : DIFFICULT ⟨an *obscure* book⟩ **4** : not widely known : HUMBLE ⟨an *obscure* poet⟩ **5** : INDISTINCT, FAINT ⟨an *obscure* cry⟩ — **ob·scure·ly** *adv* — **ob·scu·ri·ty** \-'skyu̇r-ət-ē\ *n*
2**obscure** *vb* : to make obscure : HIDE
ob·serv·ance \əb-'zər-vən(t)s\ *n* **1** : a customary practice or ceremony ⟨religious *observances*⟩ **2** : an act or instance of following a custom, rule, or law **3** : an act or instance of noticing : OBSERVATION
ob·serv·ant \-vənt\ *adj* **1** : WATCHFUL, ATTENTIVE **2** : careful or quick in observing : KEEN — **ob·serv·ant·ly** *adv*
ob·ser·va·tion \ˌäb-sər-'vā-shən, -zər-\ *n* **1** : an act or the power of observing **2** : the gathering of information (as for scientific studies) by noting facts or occurrences ⟨weather *observations*⟩ **3 a** : a conclusion drawn from observing : VIEW **b** : COMMENT *syn* see REMARK — **observation** *adj* — **ob·ser·va·tion·al** \-sh(ə-)nəl\ *adj*
ob·serv·a·to·ry \əb-'zər-və-ˌtōr-ē, -ˌtȯr-\ *n, pl* **-ries** **1** : a place or institution equipped with instruments for observation of natural phenomena (as in astronomy) **2** : a place commanding a wide view
ob·serve \əb-'zərv\ *vb* **1** : to comply with : OBEY ⟨*observe* rules⟩ **2** : CELEBRATE 1 **3** : to pay attention to : WATCH ⟨*observe* a parade⟩ **4** : to discover by the senses or by considering mentally : NOTICE ⟨*observed* that the sky was clearing⟩ **5** : to utter as a remark **6** : to make a scientific observation of ⟨*observe* an eclipse⟩ — **ob·serv·a·ble** \-'zər-və-bəl\ *adj* — **ob·serv·a·bly** \-blē\ *adv* — **ob·serv·er** *n*
ob·sess \əb-'ses, äb-\ *vb* : to occupy the mind of intensely or abnormally : HAUNT ⟨*obsessed* by fear⟩
ob·ses·sion \äb-'sesh-ən, əb-\ *n* : a disturbing and often unreasonable idea or feeling that cannot be put out of the mind — **ob·ses·sive** \-'ses-iv\ *adj* — **ob·ses·sive·ly** *adv*
ob·sid·i·an \əb-'sid-ē-ən\ *n* : a dark-colored natural glass formed by the cooling of molten lava
ob·so·les·cent \ˌäb-sə-'les-ənt\ *adj* : going out of use : becoming obsolete — **ob·so·lesce** \-'les\ *vb* — **ob·so·les·cence** \-'les-ən(t)s\ *n*
ob·so·lete \ˌäb-sə-'lēt\ *adj* **1** : no longer in use ⟨an *obsolete* word⟩ **2** : superseded by newer types : OUTMODED ⟨*obsolete* machinery⟩ — **ob·so·lete·ly** *adv* — **ob·so·lete·ness** *n*
ob·sta·cle \'äb-sti-kəl\ *n* : something that stands in the way or opposes : HINDRANCE, OBSTRUCTION
ob·stet·ri·cal \əb-'ste-tri-kəl\ *also* **ob·stet·ric** \-trik\ *adj* : of or relating to childbirth or obstetrics — **ob·stet·ri·cal·ly** \-tri-k(ə-)lē\ *adv*
ob·ste·tri·cian \ˌäb-stə-'trish-ən\ *n* : a physician specializing in obstetrics
ob·stet·rics \əb-'ste-triks\ *n* : a branch of medical science that deals with childbirth and with the care of women before, during, and after this
ob·sti·nate \'äb-stə-nət\ *adj* **1** : clinging to an opinion, purpose, or course in spite of reason, arguments, or persuasion **2** : not easily subdued, remedied, or removed ⟨an *obstinate* fever⟩ — **ob·sti·na·cy** \-nə-sē\ *n* — **ob·sti·nate·ly** *adv*
syn OBSTINATE, DOGGED, STUBBORN can mean fixed or unyielding in a course or purpose. OBSTINATE implies inflexibility or unreasonableness in adhering to a course; DOGGED implies unwearied tenacity or persistence; STUBBORN implies natural fixedness that resists all efforts to wear it down
ob·strep·er·ous \əb-'strep-(ə-)rəs, äb-\ *adj* **1** : uncontrollably noisy **2** : UNRULY — **ob·strep·er·ous·ly** *adv* — **ob·strep·er·ous·ness** *n*
ob·struct \əb-'strəkt\ *vb* **1** : to block or close up by an obstacle **2** : to hinder from passage, action, or operation : IMPEDE **3** : to cut off from sight ⟨a wall *obstructing* the view⟩ — **ob·struc·tive** \-'strək-tiv\ *adj or n* — **ob·struc·tor** \-tər\ *n*
ob·struc·tion \əb-'strək-shən\ *n* **1** : an act of obstructing : the state of being obstructed **2** : something that obstructs : HINDRANCE
ob·struc·tion·ist \-sh(ə-)nəst\ *n* : a person who hinders progress esp. in a legislative body — **ob·struc·tion·ism** \-shə-ˌniz-əm\ *n*
ob·tain \əb-'tān\ *vb* **1** : to gain or acquire usu. by

ə abut	ər further	a back	ā bake	
ä cot, cart	au̇ out	ch chin	e less	ē easy
g gift	i trip	ī life	j joke	ng sing
ō flow	ȯ flaw	ȯi coin	th thin	t͟h this
ü loot	u̇ foot	y yet	yü few	yu̇ furious
zh vision				

planning or effort **2 :** to be generally recognized or established ⟨customs that *obtain* in France⟩ ***syn*** see GET — **ob·tain·a·ble** \-'tā-nə-bəl\ *adj*

ob·trude \əb-'trüd\ *vb* **1 :** to thrust out ⟨the tortoise *obtruded* his head⟩ **2 :** to thrust forward or present without warrant or request ⟨*obtruded* his views on the group⟩ — **ob·trud·er** *n* — **ob·tru·sion** \-'trü-zhən\ *n*

ob·tru·sive \əb-'trü-siv, -ziv\ *adj* **:** inclined to obtrude **:** FORWARD, PUSHING — **ob·tru·sive·ly** *adv* — **ob·tru·sive·ness** *n*

ob·tuse \äb-'t(y)üs\ *adj* **1 :** lacking sharpness or quickness of wit **:** DULL **2 :** being between 90° and 180° ⟨an *obtuse* angle⟩ **3 :** not pointed or sharp **:** BLUNT — **ob·tuse·ly** *adv* — **ob·tuse·ness** *n*

ob·verse \'äb-ˌvərs, äb-'\ *n* **1 :** the side of something (as a coin) bearing the principal design or lettering **2 :** a front or principal surface **3 :** COUNTERPART

ob·vi·ate \'äb-vē-ˌāt\ *vb* **:** to anticipate and take care of beforehand ⟨*obviate* an objection⟩

ob·vi·ous \'äb-vē-əs\ *adj* **:** easily discovered, seen, or understood **:** PLAIN ⟨an *obvious* mistake⟩ — **ob·vi·ous·ly** *adv* — **ob·vi·ous·ness** *n*

oc·a·ri·na \ˌäk-ə-'rē-nə\ *n* **:** a simple wind instrument having an oval body with finger holes and a projecting mouthpiece and giving soft flutelike tones

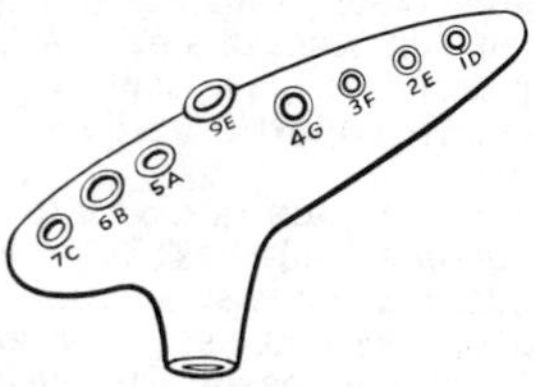

ocarina

occas *abbr* occasionally

[1]oc·ca·sion \ə-'kā-zhən\ *n* **1 :** a favorable opportunity or circumstance **2 :** a state of affairs that provides a ground or reason ⟨an *occasion* for rejoicing⟩ **3 :** an occurrence or condition that brings something about; *esp* **:** the direct cause **4 :** a time at which something happens **5 :** NEED, NECESSITY ⟨have *occasion* to travel⟩ **6 :** a special event or ceremony **:** CELEBRATION

[2]occasion *vb* **oc·ca·sioned**; **oc·ca·sion·ing** \-'kāzh-(ə-)niŋ\ **:** to give occasion to **:** CAUSE

oc·ca·sion·al \ə-'kāzh-(ə-)nəl\ *adj* **1 :** happening or met with now and then ⟨made *occasional* references to the war⟩ **2 :** used or meant for a special occasion ⟨*occasional* verse⟩ — **oc·ca·sion·al·ly** \-ē\ *adv*

Oc·ci·dent \'äk-səd-ənt, -sə-ˌdent\ *n* [from Latin *occident-*, stem of *occidens* "setting" (of heavenly bodies), present participle of *occidere* "to fall down", "set", from *ob-* "toward" and *cadere* "to fall"] **:** WEST 2 — **oc·ci·den·tal** \ˌäk-sə-'dent-əl\ *adj, often cap*

Occidental *n* **1 :** a European and esp. a western European **2 :** a descendant of Europeans

oc·cip·i·tal \äk-'sip-ət-əl\ *adj* **:** of or relating to the back part of the head or skull — **occipital** *n*

occipital bone *n* **:** a compound bone that forms the back part of the skull

oc·clude \ə-'klüd, ä-\ *vb* **1 :** to stop up **:** OBSTRUCT **2 :** to shut in or out **3 :** to take up and hold by absorption or adsorption

oc·clu·sion \ə-'klü-zhən\ *n* **1 :** the act of occluding **:** the state of being occluded **2 :** the coming together of the opposing surfaces of the teeth of the two jaws

oc·cult \ə-'kəlt, ä-\ *adj* **1 :** SECRET, HIDDEN **2 :** beyond understanding **:** MYSTERIOUS **3 :** of or relating to supernatural forces or their effects

oc·cult·ism \ə-'kəl-ˌtiz-əm, ä-\ *n* **:** a belief in or study of supernatural powers and ways of subjecting them to human control — **oc·cult·ist** \-təst\ *n*

oc·cu·pan·cy \'äk-yə-pən-sē\ *n, pl* **-cies 1 :** the act of occupying **2 :** the state of being occupied

oc·cu·pant \'äk-yə-pənt\ *n* **:** one that occupies something or takes or has possession of it

oc·cu·pa·tion \ˌäk-yə-'pā-shən\ *n* **1 :** an activity in which one engages; *esp* **:** one's business or vocation **2 :** the taking possession or holding and controlling of an area or property ⟨*occupation* of a defeated country⟩ — **oc·cu·pa·tion·al** \-sh(ə-)nəl\ *adj*

oc·cu·py \'äk-yə-ˌpī\ *vb* **-pied**; **-py·ing 1 a :** to engage the attention or energies of ⟨*occupy* oneself with reading⟩ **b :** to fill up an extent in space or time ⟨sports *occupied* his spare time⟩ ⟨a liter of water *occupies* 1000 cubic centimeters of space⟩ **2 a :** to take or hold possession of ⟨the troops *occupied* the town⟩ **b :** to reside in ⟨*occupy* an apartment⟩ **3 :** USE ⟨*occupied* his time well⟩ — **oc·cu·pi·er** \-ˌpī(-ə)r\ *n*

oc·cur \ə-'kər\ *vb* **oc·curred**; **oc·cur·ring** \-'kər-iŋ\ **1 :** to be found or met with **:** APPEAR ⟨plants that *occur* in meadows⟩ **2 :** to take place **3 :** to come to mind **:** suggest itself

oc·cur·rence \ə-'kər-ən(t)s, -'kə-rən(t)s\ *n* **1 :** something that happens **:** EVENT **2 :** the action or process of taking place

ocean \'ō-shən\ *n* **1 :** the whole body of salt water that covers nearly three fourths of the surface of the earth **2 :** one of the large bodies of water into which the ocean is divided **3 :** an unlimited space or quantity — **oce·an·ic** \ˌō-shē-'an-ik\ *adj*

ocean·aut \'ō-shə-ˌnȯt\ *n* **:** a scuba diver who lives beneath the surface for a long period and carries on activities both inside and outside an underwater shelter

ocean·og·ra·phy \ˌō-shə-'näg-rə-fē\ *n* **:** a science that deals with the ocean and its phenomena — **ocean·og·ra·pher** \-fər\ *n* — **ocean·o·graph·ic** \ˌō-shə-nə-'graf-ik\ *adj* — **ocean·o·graph·i·cal·ly** \-i-k(ə-)lē\ *adv*

oc·e·lot \'äs-ə-ˌlät, 'ō-sə-\ *n* **:** a medium-sized American wildcat ranging from Texas to Patagonia and having a tawny yellow or grayish coat marked with black

ocelot
(up to 4 ft. long)

ocher *or* **ochre** \'ō-kər\ *n* **1 :** an earthy usu. red or yellow and often impure iron ore used as a pigment **2 :** the color of ocher and esp. of yellow ocher — **och·er·ous** \'ō-k(ə-)rəs\ *or* **ochre·ous** \'ō-k(ə-)rəs, -krē-əs\ *adj*

o'·clock \ə-'kläk\ *adv* **1 :** according to the clock ⟨the time is three *o'clock*⟩ **2 —** used for indicating position or direction as if on a clock dial ⟨an airplane approaching at eleven *o'clock*⟩

Oct *abbr* October

octa- *or* **octo-** *also* **oct-** *comb form* **:** eight ⟨*octa*gon⟩ ⟨*oct*opus⟩ ⟨*oct*ave⟩

oc·ta·gon \'äk-tə-ˌgän\ *n* **:** a plane figure with eight angles and eight sides — **oc·tag·o·nal** \äk-'tag-ən-əl\ *adj* — **oc·tag·o·nal·ly** \-ə-lē\ *adv*

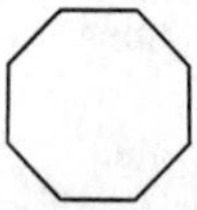
octagon

oc·tane \'äk-ˌtān\ *n* **:** any of several isomeric liquid hydrocarbons

octane number *n* **:** a number that is used to measure or indicate the antiknock properties of a liquid motor fuel and that increases as the likelihood of knocking decreases — called also *octane rating*

oc·tave \'äk-tiv, -təv\ *n* **1 a :** a musical interval em-

octave 1

bracing eight diatonic degrees **b :** a tone or note at this interval **c :** the whole series of notes, tones, or keys within this interval **2 :** a group of eight

oc·ta·vo \äk-'tā-vō, -'täv-ō\ *n, pl* **-vos :** the size of a piece of paper cut eight from a sheet; *also* **:** a book, a page, or paper of this size

oc·tet \äk-'tet\ *n* **1 a :** a musical composition for eight voices or eight instruments **b :** the performers of an octet **2 :** a group or set of eight

oc·til·lion \äk-'til-yən\ *n* — see NUMBER table

Oc·to·ber \äk-'tō-bər\ *n* [from Latin, originally the eighth month of the Roman year, from *octo* "eight"] **:** the 10th month of the year

oc·to·ge·nar·i·an \ˌäk-tə-jə-'ner-ē-ən\ *n* **:** a person who is 80 or more but less than 90 years old

oc·to·pod \'äk-tə-ˌpäd\ *n* **:** any of an order of cephalopod mollusks comprising the octopuses, argonauts, and related 8-armed mollusks — **octopod** *adj* — **oc·top·o·dan** \äk-'täp-əd-ən\ *adj or n* — **oc·top·o·dous** \-əd-əs\ *adj*

oc·to·pus \'äk-tə-pəs\ *n, pl* **-pus·es** *or* **-pi** \-ˌpī, -ˌpē\ **1 :** any of various cephalopod sea mollusks having round the front of the head eight muscular arms with two rows of suckers which hold objects (as its prey) **2 :** something suggestive of an octopus; *esp* **:** a powerful grasping organization with many branches

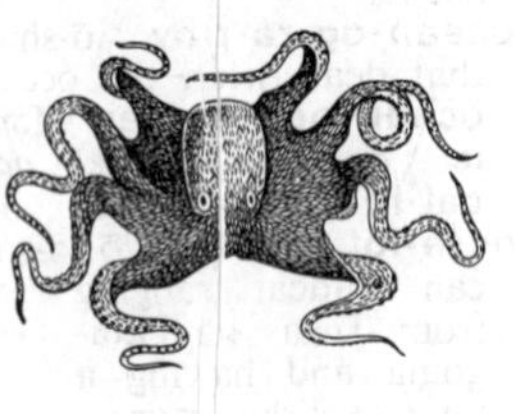

octopus 1 (about 6 ft. from arm tip to arm tip)

¹oc·u·lar \'äk-yə-lər\ *adj* **1 :** of or relating to the eye or the eyesight **2 :** obtained or perceived by the sight **:** VISUAL ⟨*ocular* proof⟩

²ocular *n* **:** EYEPIECE

oc·u·list \'äk-yə-ləst\ *n* **1 :** OPHTHALMOLOGIST **2 :** OPTOMETRIST

odd \'äd\ *adj* **1 :** being only one of a pair or set ⟨an *odd* shoe⟩ ⟨an *odd* chair⟩ **2 a :** not divisible by two without leaving a remainder ⟨1, 3, 5, and 7 are *odd* numbers⟩ **b :** numbered with an odd number ⟨an *odd* year⟩ **3 :** somewhat more than the number mentioned ⟨50 *odd* years ago⟩ **4 :** additional to or apart from what is usual, planned on, or taken into account **:** OCCASIONAL ⟨*odd* jobs⟩ **5 :** not usual or conventional **:** STRANGE ⟨an *odd* way of behaving⟩ — **odd·ly** *adv* — **odd·ness** *n*

odd·ball \-ˌbȯl\ *n* **:** an eccentric person

odd·i·ty \'äd-ət-ē\ *n, pl* **-ties 1 :** an odd person or thing **2 :** the quality or state of being odd

ə abut	ər further	a back	ā bake
ä cot, cart	au̇ out	ch chin	e less
ē easy	g gift	i trip	ī life
j joke	ŋ sing	ō flow	ȯ flaw
ȯi coin	th thin	t͟h this	ü loot
u̇ foot	y yet	yü few	yu̇ furious
zh vision			

odd·ment \'äd-mənt\ *n* **:** something left over **:** REMNANT

odds \'ädz\ *n pl* **1 :** a difference by which one thing is favored over another ⟨the *odds* are in favor of our side⟩ **2 :** an equalizing allowance made to a bettor or contestant believed to have a smaller chance of winning **3 :** DISAGREEMENT, QUARRELING ⟨the brothers were at *odds*⟩

odds and ends *n pl* **:** miscellaneous things **:** ODDMENTS

ode \'ōd\ *n* **:** a lyric poem that expresses a noble feeling in a dignified style

-ode \ˌōd\ *n comb form* **1 :** way **:** path ⟨electr*ode*⟩ **2 :** electrode ⟨di*ode*⟩

odi·ous \'ōd-ē-əs\ *adj* **:** causing or deserving hatred or strong dislike — **odi·ous·ly** *adv* — **odi·ous·ness** *n*

odi·um \'ōd-ē-əm\ *n* **1 :** the condition of being generally hated **2 :** the disgrace or shame attached to something considered hateful or low

odom·e·ter \ō-'däm-ət-ər\ *n* **:** an instrument for measuring distance traversed (as by a vehicle)

odo·nate \'ōd-ə-ˌnāt\ *n* **:** any of an order of insects that live by preying on other animals and comprise the dragonflies and damselflies — **odonate** *adj*

odor \'ōd-ər\ *n* **1 :** a quality of something that stimulates the sense of smell **:** SCENT **2 :** a smell whether pleasant or unpleasant **3 :** REPUTE, FAVOR ⟨in bad *odor*⟩ — **odored** \-ərd\ *adj* — **odor·less** \-ər-ləs\ *adj*

odor·if·er·ous \ˌōd-ə-'rif-(ə-)rəs\ *adj* **:** ODOROUS

odor·ous \'ōd-ə-rəs\ *adj* **:** having or giving off an odor and esp. a sweet odor

od·ys·sey \'äd-ə-sē\ *n, pl* **-seys** [from the *Odyssey*, Greek epic poem attributed to Homer recounting the ten-year wanderings of Odysseus, king of Ithaca] **:** a long wandering or series of travels

oe·do·go·ni·um \ˌēd-ə-'gō-nē-əm\ *n* **:** any of a genus of freshwater green algae with long unbranched filaments

o'er \'ō(ə)r, 'ȯ(ə)r\ *adv or prep* **:** OVER

of \əv, 'əv, 'äv\ *prep* **1 :** from as a point of reckoning ⟨north *of* the lake⟩ **2 a :** from by origin or derivation ⟨a man *of* noble birth⟩ **b :** from as a consequence ⟨died *of* flu⟩ **c :** by as author or doer ⟨the plays *of* Shakespeare⟩ **d :** as experienced by ⟨love *of* a parent for his child⟩ **3 a :** made from ⟨a throne *of* gold⟩ **b :** CONTAINING ⟨a cup *of* water⟩ **4** — used to indicate the whole that includes the part denoted by the preceding word ⟨most *of* the army⟩ **5 a :** CONCERNING ⟨stories *of* his travels⟩ **b :** in respect to ⟨slow *of* speech⟩ **6 :** possessed by **:** belonging to ⟨courage *of* the pioneers⟩ **7** — used to indicate separation ⟨eased *of* pain⟩ **8 :** specified as ⟨the city *of* Rome⟩ **9 :** having as its object ⟨love *of* nature⟩ **10 :** having as a quality or possession ⟨a man *of* courage⟩

OF *abbr* outfield

¹off \'ȯf\ *adv* **1 a :** from or away from a place or position ⟨march *off*⟩ ⟨stood 10 paces *off*⟩ ⟨drove the dogs *off*⟩ **b :** from a course **:** ASIDE ⟨turned *off* into a bypath⟩ **c :** into an unconscious state ⟨dozed *off*⟩ **2 :** so as not to be supported ⟨fell *off*⟩ or covering or enclosing ⟨blew the lid *off*⟩ or attached ⟨the handle came *off*⟩ **3 :** so as to be divided ⟨surface marked *off* into squares⟩ **4 :** so as to be discontinued or completed ⟨shut *off* an engine⟩ ⟨a coat of paint to finish it *off*⟩ **5 :** away from work ⟨take time *off* for lunch⟩

²off \(')ȯf\ *prep* **1 :** away or apart from ⟨*off* the main road⟩; *esp* **:** from a place or situation on ⟨take it *off* the table⟩ **2 :** at the expense of ⟨lived *off* his sister⟩

3 : to seaward of ⟨two miles *off* shore⟩ **4 a** : not now engaged in ⟨*off* duty⟩ **b** : below the usual level of ⟨*off* his game⟩ ⟨a dollar *off* the list price⟩ **5** : diverging or opening from ⟨a path *off* the main walk⟩

3**off** \(ˈ)ȯf\ *adj* **1 a** : more distant ⟨the *off* side of the building⟩ **b** : not left : RIGHT ⟨the *off* horse⟩ **2** : started on the way ⟨*off* on a spree⟩ **3 a** : CANCELED ⟨the game is *off*⟩ **b** : not operating ⟨the light is *off*⟩ **4** : not corresponding to fact : INCORRECT ⟨*off* in his reckoning⟩ **5 a** : POOR, INFERIOR ⟨an *off* grade of oil⟩ **b** : below or down from the normal ⟨stocks were *off*⟩ **c** : not entirely sane : ECCENTRIC **6** : REMOTE, SLIGHT ⟨an *off* chance⟩ **7 a** : spent off duty ⟨reading on his *off* days⟩ **b** : SLACK ⟨*off* season⟩ **8** : different from the typical shade ⟨an *off* yellow⟩ **9** : CIRCUMSTANCED ⟨comfortably *off*⟩

off *abbr* **1** office **2** officer

of·fal \ˈȯ-fəl, ˈäf-əl\ *n* **1** : the waste or by-product of a process; *esp* : the viscera and trimmings of a butchered animal removed in dressing **2** : RUBBISH

1**off·beat** \ˈȯf-ˌbēt\ *n* : the unaccented part of a musical measure

2**offbeat** *adj* : ECCENTRIC, UNUSUAL ⟨offers *offbeat* entertainment⟩

offence *chiefly Brit var of* OFFENSE

of·fend \ə-ˈfend\ *vb* **1** : to commit a wrong; *esp* : SIN **2** : to cause dislike, anger, or annoyance : DISPLEASE — **of·fend·er** *n*

of·fense \ə-ˈfen(t)s, *esp for 2* ˈäf-ˌen(t)s\ *n* **1** : something that offends : NUISANCE **2 a** : the act of attacking : ASSAULT **b** : the side that is attacking in a contest or battle **3 a** : the act of offending **b** : the state of being offended **4 a** : SIN, MISDEED **b** : an infraction of law : CRIME

1**of·fen·sive** \ə-ˈfen(t)-siv\ *adj* **1** : relating to or made or suited for attack ⟨*offensive* weapons⟩ **2** : causing unpleasant sensations ⟨*offensive* smells⟩ **3** : causing displeasure or resentment : INSULTING ⟨an *offensive* remark⟩ — **of·fen·sive·ly** *adv* — **of·fen·sive·ness** *n*

2**offensive** *n* **1** : the act, attitude, or position of an attacking party ⟨on the *offensive*⟩ **2** : ATTACK ⟨launch an *offensive*⟩

1**of·fer** \ˈȯf-ər, ˈäf-\ *vb* **of·fered**; **of·fer·ing** \-(ə-)riŋ\ **1** : to present as an act of worship : SACRIFICE **2** : to present for acceptance or rejection : TENDER ⟨*offer* $10 for the desk⟩ ⟨*offer* fruit for sale⟩ **3 a** : PROPOSE, SUGGEST **b** : to declare one's willingness ⟨*offered* to help me⟩ **4** : to try to make, do, or inflict ⟨*offered* stubborn resistance⟩

2**offer** *n* **1** : PROPOSAL ⟨an *offer* to help⟩ **2** : a price named by one proposing to buy : BID

of·fer·ing *n* **1** : the act of one who offers **2** : something offered; *esp* : a sacrifice offered as a part of worship **3** : a contribution to the support of a church

of·fer·to·ry \ˈȯf-ə(r)-ˌtōr-ē, ˈäf-, -ˌtȯr-\ *n*, *pl* **-ries** **1** *often cap* **a** : the offering of the sacramental bread and wine to God before they are consecrated **b** : a verse from a psalm said or sung at the beginning of the offertory **2 a** : the presentation of the offerings of the congregation in church **b** : the music played or sung during an offertory

off·hand \ˈȯf-ˈhand\ *adv or adj* : without previous thought or preparation beforehand

off·hand·ed \-ˈhan-dəd\ *adj* : OFFHAND — **off·hand·ed·ly** *adv*

of·fice \ˈȯf-əs, ˈäf-\ *n* **1** : a special duty, job, or position; *esp* : a responsible or executive position (as in government) ⟨hold public *office*⟩ ⟨the *office* of chairman⟩ **2** : a prescribed form or service of worship : RITE **3** : a place where a business is transacted or an esp. professional service is supplied ⟨ticket *office*⟩ ⟨a dentist's *office*⟩ **4** : a major government department ⟨British Foreign *Office*⟩ ⟨Patent *Office*⟩

of·fice·hold·er \-ˌhōl-dər\ *n* : one holding a public office

1**of·fi·cer** \ˈȯf-ə-sər, ˈäf-\ *n* **1** : a policeman or other person charged with the enforcement of law **2** : one who holds an office of trust or authority **3 a** : one who holds a position of command in the armed forces; *esp* : COMMISSIONED OFFICER **b** : the master or mate of a merchant or passenger ship

2**officer** *vb* **1** : to furnish with officers **2** : to command or direct as an officer

1**of·fi·cial** \ə-ˈfish-əl\ *n* : one who holds an office : OFFICER

2**official** *adj* **1** : of or relating to an office, position, or trust ⟨*official* duties⟩ **2** : holding an office ⟨an *official* referee⟩ **3** : prescribed or permitted by authority : AUTHORIZED ⟨an *official* American League baseball⟩ **4** : befitting or characteristic of a person in office : FORMAL ⟨an *official* greeting⟩ — **of·fi·cial·ly** \-ˈfish-(ə-)lē\ *adv*

of·fi·cial·dom \ə-ˈfish-əl-dəm\ *n* : officials as a class

of·fi·ci·ate \ə-ˈfish-ē-ˌāt\ *vb* **1** : to perform a ceremony ⟨*officiate* at a wedding⟩ **2** : to act in an official capacity; *esp* : to preside as an officer

of·fi·cious \ə-ˈfish-əs\ *adj* : volunteering one's services where they are not asked for or needed : MEDDLESOME — **of·fi·cious·ly** *adv* — **of·fi·cious·ness** *n*

off·ing \ˈȯf-iŋ, ˈäf-\ *n* **1** : the part of the deep sea seen from the shore **2** : the near or foreseeable future ⟨sees trouble in the *offing*⟩

off·ish \ˈȯf-ish\ *adj* : inclined to be formal, stiff, or aloof in manner — **off·ish·ly** *adv* — **off·ish·ness** *n*

1**off·set** \ˈȯf-ˌset\ *n* **1** : a short prostrate shoot arising from the base of a plant **2** : a pair of abrupt bends by which an object (as a pipe or wall) continues parallel to itself in a different plane **3** : something that serves to compensate or make up for something else

offset 1

2**off·set** \ˈȯf-ˌset, ȯf-ˈ\ *vb* **-set**; **-set·ting** : to compensate for : BALANCE ⟨credits *offset* debits⟩

off·shoot \ˈȯf-ˌshüt\ *n* **1** : a branch of a main stem of a plant **2** : something arising from or branching out of something else ⟨appliances that are *offshoots* of space research⟩

1**off·shore** \ˈȯf-ˈshō(ə)r, -ˈshȯ(ə)r\ *adv* : from the shore : at a distance from the shore

2**off·shore** \ˈȯf-ˌ\ *adj* **1** : coming or moving away from the shore ⟨an *offshore* breeze⟩ **2** : located off the shore ⟨*offshore* islands⟩

off side *adv or adj* : illegally in advance of the ball or puck

off·spring \ˈȯf-ˌspriŋ\ *n*, *pl* **offspring** *also* **off·springs** : the first generation of descendants produced by an animal or plant : YOUNG

off·stage \-ˈstāj\ *adv or adj* : off or away from the stage

oft \ˈȯft\ *adv* : OFTEN ⟨an *oft* neglected factor⟩

of·ten \ˈȯ-fən, ˈȯf-tən\ *adv* : many times : FREQUENTLY

of·ten·times \-ˌtīmz\ *or* **oft·times** \ˈȯf(t)-ˌtīmz\ *adv* : OFTEN

ogle \ˈō-gəl\ *vb* **ogled**; **ogling** \-g(ə-)liŋ\ : to look at in a flirting way — **ogle** *n* — **ogler** \-g(ə-)lər\ *n*

ogre \'ō-gər\ *n* **1 :** a hideous giant of fairy tales and folklore that feeds on human beings : MONSTER **2 :** a dreaded person or object — **ogre·ish** \'ō-g(ə-)rish\ *adj* — **ogress** \'ō-g(ə-)rəs\ *n*

[1]**oh** \(')ō\ *interj* **1** — used to express various emotions (as astonishment, pain, or desire) **2** — used in direct address ⟨*Oh* sir, you forgot your change⟩

[2]**oh** \'ō\ *n* : ZERO

OH *abbr* Ohio

ohm \'ōm\ *n* [named after G. S. *Ohm* (1787–1854), German physicist] : a unit of electric resistance equal to the resistance of a circuit in which a potential difference of one volt produces a current of one ampere — **ohm·ic** \'ō-mik\ *adj*

ohm·me·ter \'ōm-,(m)ēt-ər\ *n* : an instrument for indicating resistance in ohms directly

[1]**-oid** \,ȯid\ *n suffix* : something resembling a (specified) object or having a (specified) quality ⟨planet*oid*⟩

[2]**-oid** *adj suffix* : resembling : having the form or appearance of ⟨petal*oid*⟩

[1]**oil** \'ȯil\ *n* **1 a :** any of numerous greasy combustible and usu. liquid substances from plant, animal, or mineral sources that are soluble in ether but not in water **b :** PETROLEUM **2 :** a substance of oily consistency **3 a :** an artist's paint made with oil **b :** a painting done in oils — **oil** *adj*

[2]**oil** *vb* : to treat, furnish, or lubricate with oil — **oil·er** \'ȯi-lər\ *n*

oil·cloth \'ȯil-,klȯth\ *n* : cloth treated with oil or paint and used for table and shelf coverings

oil gland *n* : a gland (as of the skin) that produces an oily secretion

oil of vitriol : concentrated sulfuric acid

oil of wintergreen : an ester of salicylic acid used as a flavoring

oil·skin \'ȯil-,skin\ *n* **1 :** an oiled waterproof cloth **2 :** an oilskin raincoat **3** *pl* : an oilskin coat and trousers

oil slick *n* : a film of oil floating on water

oily \'ȯi-lē\ *adj* **oil·i·er; -est 1 :** of, relating to, or consisting of oil **2 :** covered with oil : GREASY **3 :** too smooth or suave in manner — **oil·i·ness** *n*

oint·ment \'ȯint-mənt\ *n* : a soft usu. greasy and medicated preparation for application to the skin

Ojib·wa *or* **Ojib·way** \ō-'jib-wā\ *n* : a member of an Amerindian people of the region around Lake Superior

[1]**OK** *or* **okay** \ō-'kā\ *adv or adj* : all right

[2]**OK** *or* **okay** *vb* **OK'd** *or* **okayed; OK'·ing** *or* **okay·ing** : APPROVE

[3]**OK** *or* **okay** *n* : APPROVAL, ENDORSEMENT

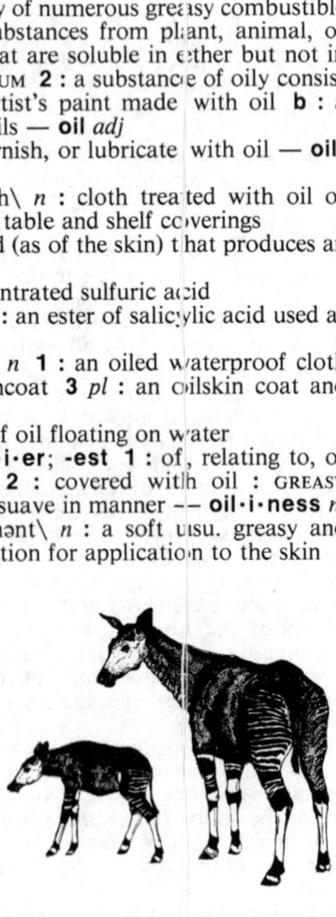

okapis
(about 5 ft. at shoulder)

oka·pi \ō-'käp-ē\ *n* : an African mammal closely related to the giraffe but lacking the long neck

Okla *or* **OK** *abbr* Oklahoma

okra \'ō-krə\ *n* : a tall annual plant related to the hollyhocks and grown for its edible green pods which are used esp. in soups and stews; *also* : these pods

[1]**old** \'ōld\ *adj* **1 a :** dating from the past and esp. the remote past : ANCIENT ⟨*old* traditions⟩ **b :** being of long standing ⟨an *old* friend⟩ **2** *cap* : belonging to an early period in development ⟨*Old* Irish⟩ **3 :** having existed for a specified period of time ⟨a girl three years *old*⟩ **4 :** advanced in years or age ⟨an *old* man⟩ **5 :** FORMER ⟨his *old* teachers⟩ **6 :** showing the effects of time or use : WORN ⟨*old* shoes⟩

syn OLD, ELDERLY, AGED can mean advanced in age. OLD applies broadly to those who have lost their youthful qualities in later years; ELDERLY applies more especially to those who are old but not extremely so; AGED implies extreme old age and suggests its typical feebleness and senility ***ant*** young

[2]**old** *n* : old or earlier time ⟨days of *old*⟩

old·en \'ōl-dən\ *adj* : OLD, ANCIENT

Old English *n* : the language of the English people before about 1100

old–fash·ioned \'ōl(d)-'fash-ənd\ *adj* **1 :** of, relating to, or characteristic of a past era : ANTIQUATED ⟨*old-fashioned* clothes⟩ **2 :** adhering to customs of a past era : CONSERVATIVE

Old French *n* : the French language from the 9th to the 16th century

Old Glory *n* : the flag of the U.S.

old·ish \'ōl-dish\ *adj* : somewhat old

old maid *n* **1 :** SPINSTER 2 **2 :** a prim nervous fussy person **3 :** a card game in which the player holding the odd queen at the end is an "old maid" — **old–maid·ish** \'ōl(d)-'mād-ish\ *adj*

Old Norse *n* : the Germanic language of the Scandinavian peoples prior to about 1350

old·ster \'ōl(d)-stər\ *n* : an old or elderly person

Old Style *n* : a style of reckoning time used before the adoption of the Gregorian calendar

Old Testament *n* : the first of the two chief divisions of the Bible — see BIBLE table

old–time \'ōl(d)-,tīm\ *adj* : of, relating to, or typical of an earlier period

old–tim·er \-'tī-mər\ *n* **1 a :** VETERAN **b :** OLDSTER **2 :** something old-fashioned : ANTIQUE

old wives' tale *n* : a traditional tale or bit of lore (as a superstitious notion)

Old World *n* : the half of the earth to the east of the Atlantic ocean including Europe, Asia, and Africa; *esp* : the continent of Europe

old–world *adj* **1 :** of or relating to the Old World **2 :** OLD-FASHIONED, PICTURESQUE

ole·an·der \'ō-lē-,an-dər\ *n* : a poisonous evergreen shrub often grown for its showy fragrant white, red, or pink flowers

ole·in \'ō-lē-ən\ *n* : the liquid portion of any fat

oleo \'ō-lē-,ō\ *n, pl* **ole·os** : MARGARINE

oleo·mar·ga·rine \,ō-lē-ō-'märj-(ə-)rən, -'märj-ə-,rēn\ *n* : MARGARINE

ol·fac·tion \äl-'fak-shən, ōl-\ *n* : the sense of smell : the act or process of smelling

ol·fac·to·ry \äl-'fak-t(ə-)rē, ōl-\ *adj* : of, relating to, or concerned with the sense of smell

olfactory lobe *n* : a lobe of the brain that projects forward from the lower part of each cerebral hemisphere and is continuous with the olfactory nerve

olfactory nerve *n* : either of a pair of sensory cranial nerves that arise in the nose and conduct odor stimuli to the brain

ol·i·garch \'äl-ə-,gärk\ *n* : a member of an oligarchy

ol·i·gar·chy \-,gär-kē\ *n, pl* **-chies 1 :** a government in which the power is in the hands of a few persons **2 a :** a state governed by an oligarchy **b :** the group of persons holding power in such a state — **ol·i·gar·chic** \ˌäl-ə-'gär-kik\ *or* **ol·i·gar·chi·cal** \-ki-kəl\ *adj*

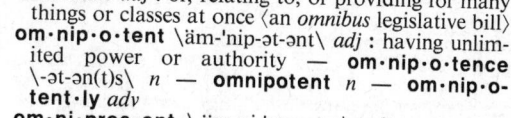

Ol·i·go·cene \'äl-i-gō-ˌsēn\ *n* **:** the epoch of the Tertiary between the Eocene and Miocene; *also* **:** the corresponding system of rocks — **Oligocene** *adj*

ol·ive \'äl-iv\ *n* **1 :** an Old World evergreen tree grown for its fruit **2 :** the edible and oil-yielding fruit of the olive tree **3 :** the dull yellowish green color of the unripe olive — **olive** *adj*

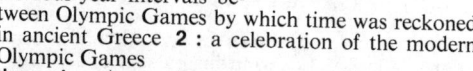

olive: 1, flowering branch; 2, fruit

olive branch *n* **1 :** a branch of the olive tree esp. when used as a symbol of peace **2 :** an offer or gesture of peace or goodwill

ol·iv·ine \'äl-i-ˌvēn\ *n* **:** a mineral that is a complex silicate of magnesium and iron

olym·pi·ad \ə-'lim-pē-ˌad, ō-\ *n, often cap* **1 :** one of the four-year intervals between Olympic Games by which time was reckoned in ancient Greece **2 :** a celebration of the modern Olympic Games

¹**Olym·pi·an** \-pē-ən\ *adj* **1 :** of or relating to the ancient Greek region of Olympia **2 :** of, relating to, or being the Olympic Games

²**Olympian** *n* **:** a participant in Olympic Games

³**Olympian** *adj* **1 :** of or relating to Mount Olympus in Greece **2 :** befitting or characteristic of the gods of Olympus **:** LOFTY

Olym·pic \ə-'lim-pik, ō-\ *adj* **:** OLYMPIAN

Olympic Games *n pl* **1 :** an ancient Greek festival held at Olympia every 4th year and made up of contests in sports, music, and literature **2 :** a revival of the Olympic Games held every 4th year and made up of international athletic contests — called also *Olympics* \-'lim-piks\

om·buds·man \'ȯm-bədz-ˌman\ *n, pl* **om·buds·men** \-ˌmen\ **:** a government official who investigates complaints made by people concerning abuses or arbitrary acts of public officials

omega \ō-'meg-ə, -'mē-gə\ *n* [from Greek *ō mega*, meaning literally "big o"] **1 :** the 24th and last letter of the Greek alphabet — Ω or ω **2 :** LAST, ENDING

om·e·let *also* **om·e·lette** \'äm-(ə-)lət\ *n* **:** eggs beaten with milk or water, cooked without stirring, and folded over

omen \'ō-mən\ *n* **:** an event or sign warning of some future occurrence **:** PORTENT

om·i·cron \'äm-ə-ˌkrän\ *n* [from Greek *o mikron*, meaning literally "small o"] **:** the 15th letter of the Greek alphabet — O or o

om·i·nous \'äm-ə-nəs\ *adj* **:** being or showing an omen; *esp* **:** foretelling evil **:** THREATENING ⟨*ominous* clouds⟩ — **om·i·nous·ly** *adv*

omis·sion \ō-'mish-ən, ə-\ *n* **1 :** something neglected or left undone **2 :** the act of omitting **:** the state of being omitted

omit \ō-'mit, ə-\ *vb* **omit·ted; omit·ting 1 :** to leave out or leave unmentioned ⟨*omitted* his name from the list⟩ **2 :** to fail to perform **:** leave undone **:** NEGLECT ⟨*omitted* to write in her diary that day⟩

¹**om·ni·bus** \'äm-ni-(ˌ)bəs\ *n* **1 :** a public vehicle designed to carry many passengers **:** BUS **2 :** a book containing reprints of a number of works

²**omnibus** *adj* **:** of, relating to, or providing for many things or classes at once ⟨an *omnibus* legislative bill⟩

om·nip·o·tent \äm-'nip-ət-ənt\ *adj* **:** having unlimited power or authority — **om·nip·o·tence** \-ət-ən(t)s\ *n* — **omnipotent** *n* — **om·nip·o·tent·ly** *adv*

om·ni·pres·ent \ˌäm-ni-'prez-ənt\ *adj* **:** present in all places at all times — **om·ni·pres·ence** \-ən(t)s\ *n*

om·ni·scient \äm-'nish-ənt\ *adj* **:** having complete knowledge and wisdom — **om·ni·science** \-ən(t)s\ *n* — **om·ni·scient·ly** *adv*

om·ni·um–gath·er·um \ˌäm-nē-əm-'gath-ə-rəm\ *n* **:** a collection of all sorts of things or persons

om·niv·o·ra \äm-'niv-ə-rə\ *n pl* **:** omnivorous animals

om·ni·vore \'äm-ni-ˌvōr, -ˌvȯr\ *n* **:** one that is omnivorous

om·niv·o·rous \äm-'niv-(ə-)rəs\ *adj* **1 :** feeding on both animal and vegetable substances **2 :** avidly taking in everything as if devouring or consuming — **om·niv·o·rous·ly** *adv* — **om·niv·o·rous·ness** *n*

¹**on** \(')ȯn, (')än\ *prep* **1 a :** over and supported by ⟨the book *on* the table⟩ ⟨stand *on* one foot⟩ **b :** in contact with or near ⟨a fly *on* the wall⟩ ⟨a town *on* the river⟩ **c :** in the direction of ⟨*on* the right⟩ **2 :** ONTO 1 ⟨jumped *on* the horse⟩ ⟨put the notice *on* the bulletin board⟩ **3** — used to indicate someone or something that action or feeling is directed toward ⟨crept up *on* him⟩ ⟨have pity *on* me⟩ ⟨paid *on* account⟩ **4 :** on the basis of ⟨know it *on* good authority⟩ **5 a :** with respect to ⟨agreed *on* a price⟩ **b :** CONCERNING, ABOUT ⟨a book *on* cats⟩ ⟨a satire *on* society⟩ **6 a :** in connection, association, or activity with or with regard to ⟨*on* a committee⟩ ⟨*on* tour⟩ **b :** in a state or process of ⟨*on* fire⟩ ⟨*on* the increase⟩ **7 :** during or at a specified time ⟨came *on* Monday⟩ ⟨every hour *on* the hour⟩ ⟨cash *on* delivery⟩ **8 :** by means of ⟨talking *on* the telephone⟩ **9 :** following in series ⟨loss *on* loss⟩

²**on** \'ȯn, 'än\ *adv* **1 :** in or into a position of contact esp. with an upper surface ⟨put the plates *on*⟩ ⟨has new shoes *on*⟩ **2 :** forward in space, time, or action **:** ONWARD ⟨went *on* home⟩ **3 :** in continuance or succession ⟨and so *on*⟩ **4 :** into operation or a position permitting operation ⟨turn the light *on*⟩

³**on** \'ȯn, 'än\ *adj* **1 a :** OPERATING ⟨the radio is *on*⟩ **b :** placed so as to permit operation ⟨the switch is *on*⟩ **2 :** taking place ⟨the game is *on*⟩ **3 :** PLANNED ⟨has nothing *on* for tonight⟩

¹**once** \'wən(t)s\ *adv* **1 :** one time only ⟨will repeat the question *once*⟩ **2 :** at any one time **:** EVER ⟨if he *once* hesitates, he's lost⟩ **3 :** at some time in the past **:** FORMERLY ⟨*once* lived in luxury⟩ **4 :** by one degree of relationship ⟨cousin *once* removed⟩

²**once** *n* **:** one single time ⟨just this *once*⟩ — **at once 1 :** at the same time **:** SIMULTANEOUSLY ⟨two people talking *at once*⟩ **2 :** IMMEDIATELY ⟨leave *at once*⟩

³**once** *conj* **:** as soon as ⟨*once* that is done, all will be well⟩

on·com·ing \'ȯn-ˌkəm-ing, 'än-\ *adj* **:** APPROACHING ⟨*oncoming* traffic⟩

¹**one** \'wən\ *adj* **1 :** being a single unit or thing ⟨*one* man went⟩ — see NUMBER table **2 :** being one in particular ⟨early *one* morning⟩ **3 a :** being the same in kind or quality ⟨of *one* race⟩ **b :** not divided **:** UNITED **4 :** not definitely fixed or placed ⟨will see you again *one* day⟩

²**one** *pron* **1 :** a single member or specimen ⟨saw *one* of his friends⟩ **2 :** a person in general **:** SOMEBODY ⟨*one* never knows⟩

³**one** *n* **1 :** the number denoting a single unit

2 : the first in a set or series **3 :** a single person or thing

one another *pron* **:** EACH OTHER

one·ness \'wən-nəs\ *n* **1 :** SINGLENESS, UNITY **2 :** SAMENESS, IDENTITY

on·er·ous \'än-ə-rəs, 'ō-nə-\ *adj* **:** BURDENSOME, OPPRESSIVE ⟨an *onerous* task⟩ — **on·er·ous·ly** *adv* — **on·er·ous·ness** *n*

one·self \(,)wən-'self\ *pron* **1 :** one's own self — used reflexively or for emphasis **2 :** one's normal or healthy self

one–sid·ed \'wən-'sīd-əd\ *adj* **1 a :** having or occurring on one side only ⟨a *one-sided* argument⟩ **b :** having one side prominent or more developed **c :** UNEQUAL ⟨a *one-sided* game⟩ **2 :** limited to or favoring one side **:** PARTIAL ⟨a *one-sided* view of the case⟩ — **one–sid·ed·ly** *adv* — **one–sid·ed·ness** *n*

one·time \'wən-,tīm\ *adj* **:** FORMER ⟨a *one-time* boxing champion⟩

one–to–one \,wən-tə-'wən\ *adj* **:** pairing each element of a set with one and only one element of another set ⟨a *one-to-one* correspondence between the real numbers and the points on a straight line⟩

one–way \'wən-'wā\ *adj* **:** moving or allowing movement in only one direction ⟨*one-way* traffic⟩ ⟨a *one-way* ticket⟩

on·go·ing \'ȯn-,gō-ing, 'än-\ *adj* **:** continuously moving forward **:** GROWING

on·ion \'ən-yən\ *n* **:** a widely grown Asiatic herb related to the lilies and having pungent edible bulbs; *also* **:** its bulb

on·look·er \'ȯn-,lu̇k-ər, 'än-\ *n* **:** one that looks on **:** SPECTATOR — **on·look·ing** \-,lu̇k-ing\ *adj*

1on·ly \'ōn-lē\ *adj* **1 :** unquestionably the best **:** PEERLESS ⟨the *only* girl for me⟩ **2 :** alone in its class **:** SOLE ⟨the *only* survivor of the crash⟩

2only *adv* **1 :** as the solo fact or instance **:** EXCLUSIVELY ⟨worked *only* in the mornings⟩ ⟨known *only* to him⟩ **2 :** at the very least ⟨it was *only* too true⟩ **3 :** in the final outcome ⟨it will *only* make you sick⟩ ⟨won the battles, *only* to lose the war⟩ **4 a :** as recently as ⟨*only* last week⟩ **b :** in the immediate past ⟨*only* just talked to her⟩

3only *conj* **:** except that ⟨might play tennis, *only* I'm too tired⟩

on·o·mat·o·poe·ia \,än-ə-,mat-ə-'pē-(y)ə\ *n* **1 :** formation of words in imitation of natural sounds (as *buzz* or *hiss*) **2 :** the use of words whose sound suggests the sense (as in "the rumbling truck") — **on·o·mat·o·poe·ic** \-'pē-ik\ *or* **on·o·mat·o·po·et·ic** \-pō-'et-ik\ *adj*

on·rush \'ȯn-,rəsh, 'än-\ *n* **:** a rushing on

on·set \-,set\ *n* **1 :** ATTACK **2 :** BEGINNING

on·shore \'ȯn-,shōr, 'än-, -,shȯr\ *adj* **:** moving toward the shore ⟨*onshore* winds⟩ — **on·shore** \-'shōr, -'shȯr\ *adv*

on·slaught \'än-,slȯt, 'ȯn-\ *n* **:** a fierce attack

Ont *abbr* Ontario

on·to \'ȯn-tə, 'än-, -tü\ *prep* **1 :** to a position or point on ⟨climbed *onto* the roof⟩ **2 :** into a state of awareness of ⟨I'm *onto* his tricks⟩

1on·ward \'ȯn-wərd, 'än-\ *also* **on·wards** \-wərdz\ *adv* **:** toward or at a point lying ahead in space or time **:** FORWARD ⟨kept moving *onward*⟩

ə abut	ər further	a back	ā bake	
ä cot, cart	au̇ out	ch chin	e less	ē easy
g gift	i trip	ī life	j joke	ng sing	ō flow
ȯ flaw	ȯi coin	th thin	th this	ü loot
u̇ foot	y yet	yü few	yu̇ furious	zh vision

2onward *adj* **:** directed or moving onward

on·yx \'än-iks\ *n* **:** chalcedony with straight parallel alternating bands of color or dyed jet black

oo·dles \'üd-əlz\ *n pl* **:** a great quantity **:** LOT

1ooze \'üz\ *n* **1 :** a soft deposit (as of mud, slime, or shells) esp. on the bottom of a body of water **2 :** MUD, SLIME

2ooze *vb* **1 :** to leak or flow slowly as if through small openings ⟨sap *oozed* from the tree⟩ **2 :** to give off **:** RADIATE ⟨her manner *oozed* confidence⟩

3ooze *n* **:** something that oozes — **oozy** \'ü-zē\ *adj*

op \'äp\ *n* **:** OPTICAL ART

op *abbr* opus

opac·i·ty \ō-'pas-ət-ē\ *n, pl* **-ties :** the quality or state of being opaque

opal \'ō-pəl\ *n* **:** a mineral that is a hydrated amorphous silica softer and less dense than quartz and typically with an iridescent play of colors

opal·es·cent \,ō-pə-'les-ənt\ *adj* **:** having a play of colors like an opal — **opal·esce** \-'les\ *vb* — **opal·es·cence** \-'les-ən(t)s\ *n*

opaque \ō-'pāk\ *adj* **1 :** not transmitting radiant energy and esp. light rays **2 a :** not easily understood **:** OBSCURE **b :** mentally dull **3 :** neither reflecting nor giving off light **:** DARK — **opaque·ly** *adv* — **opaque·ness** *n*

op art *n* **:** OPTICAL ART — **op artist** *n*

ope \'ōp\ *vb* **:** OPEN

1open \'ō-pən\ *adj* **open·er** \'ōp-(ə-)nər\; **open·est** \-(ə-)nəst\ **1 :** permitting passage or access **:** not shut, stopped, or clogged ⟨an *open* door⟩ ⟨*open* books⟩ ⟨*open* pores⟩ **2 a :** not enclosed or covered **:** BARE ⟨an *open* boat⟩ ⟨an *open* fire⟩ ⟨*open* wounds⟩ **b :** LIABLE ⟨*open* to challenge⟩ ⟨*open* to infection⟩ **c :** not completely enclosed by lines ⟨an *open* geometric figure⟩ **3 a :** not secret **:** PUBLIC ⟨*open* dislike⟩ **b :** not secretive **:** FRANK ⟨*open* about his plans⟩ **4 a :** free to the use, entry, or participation of all ⟨an *open* meeting⟩ ⟨an *open* golf tournament⟩ **b :** easy to enter, get through, or see ⟨*open* country⟩ ⟨an *open* woodland⟩ **c :** free from restraints or controls ⟨an *open* economy⟩ **5 :** not snowy ⟨an *open* winter⟩ **6 :** not folded or contracted **:** spread out ⟨an *open* flower⟩ ⟨*open* umbrellas⟩ **7 a :** not decided or settled ⟨an *open* question⟩ **b :** receptive to appeals or ideas **:** RESPONSIVE ⟨an *open* mind⟩ ⟨*open* to suggestion⟩ **8 :** not capable of being judged true or false ⟨$x + 3 = 10$ is an *open* equation⟩ ⟨"It is divisible by 6" is an *open* sentence⟩ — **open·ly** \'ō-pən-lē\ *adv* — **open·ness** \'ō-pən-nəs\ *n*

2open *vb* **opened** \'ō-pənd\; **open·ing** \'ōp-(ə-)ning\ **1 a :** to change or move from a shut condition **:** UNFASTEN, UNCLOSE ⟨*open* a book⟩ ⟨the door *opened*⟩ **b :** to clear of or as if of obstacles ⟨*open* a road blocked with snow⟩ ⟨the clouds *opened*⟩ **c :** to make an opening in ⟨*open* a boil⟩ **d :** to spread out **:** UNFOLD ⟨an *opening* flower⟩ ⟨*open* a napkin⟩ **2 :** to make or become ready for use ⟨*open* a new store⟩ ⟨the office *opens* early⟩ **3 :** to give access ⟨the rooms *open* onto a hall⟩ **4 :** BEGIN, START ⟨*open* fire⟩ ⟨*open* talks⟩ — **open·er** \'ōp-(ə-)nər\ *n*

3open *n* **1 :** open space; *esp* **:** OUTDOORS ⟨go out in the *open*⟩ **2 :** an open contest or tournament

open air *n* **:** OUT-OF-DOORS

open door *n* **:** a policy of giving equal opportunity for trade to all nations — **open–door** *adj*

open–eyed \,ō-pən-'īd\ *adj* **1 :** having the eyes open **2 :** WATCHFUL, ALERT

open·hand·ed \,ō-pən-'han-dəd\ *adj* **:** GENEROUS, LIBERAL — **open·hand·ed·ly** *adv* — **open·hand·ed·ness** *n*

open-heart *adj* : relating to or done on a heart temporarily laid open for inspection and treatment ⟨*open-heart* surgery⟩
open·heart·ed \ˌō-pən-'härt-əd\ *adj* : FRANK, GENEROUS — **open·heart·ed·ly** *adv* — **open·heart·ed·ness** *n*
open-hearth *adj* : being or relating to a process of making steel from pig iron in a furnace that reflects heat from the roof onto the material
open house *n* : usu. informal hospitality or entertainment for all comers; *also* : an occasion devoted to such hospitality
open·ing \'ōp-(ə-)niŋ\ *n* **1** : an act or instance of making or becoming open ⟨the *opening* of a new school⟩ **2** : an open place or span ⟨an *opening* in the woods⟩ **3 a** : BEGINNING, START; *esp* : a series of moves made at the start of a game of chess or checkers **b** : a first performance **4 a** : OCCASION, CHANCE **b** : an opportunity for employment ⟨*openings* for welders and machinists⟩
open-mind·ed \ˌō-pən-'mīn-dəd\ *adj* : open to arguments or ideas : not prejudiced — **open-mind·ed·ly** *adv* — **open-mind·ed·ness** *n*
open·mouthed \ˌō-pən-'mau̇t͟hd, -'mau̇tht\ *adj* **1** : having the mouth wide open **2** : struck with amazement or wonder
open secret *n* : something supposedly secret but in fact generally known
open ses·a·me \ˌō-pən-'ses-ə-mē\ *n* [from *open sesame*, the magical command used by Ali Baba to open the door of the robbers' den in *Ali Baba and the Forty Thieves*] : something that unfailingly brings about a desired end
open shop *n* : an establishment employing both members and nonmembers of a labor union
open·work \'ō-pən-ˌwərk\ *n* : something made or work done so as to show openings through the material — **openwork** *or* **open-worked** \ˌō-pən-'wərkt\ *adj*
[1]**opera** *pl of* OPUS
[2]**op·era** \'äp-(ə-)rə\ *n* : a play set to music and made up of vocal pieces with orchestral accompaniment and orchestral overtures and interludes — **op·er·at·ic** \ˌäp-ə-'rat-ik\ *adj*
op·er·a·ble \'äp-(ə-)rə-bəl\ *adj* **1** : fit, possible, or desirable to use : PRACTICABLE **2** : that can be treated surgically ⟨an *operable* cancer⟩
opera glass *n* : a small binocular adapted for use at the opera — often used in pl.
op·er·ate \'äp-ə-ˌrāt\ *vb* **1** : to perform or cause to perform a function : WORK ⟨the switch *operates* easily⟩ ⟨*operate* a car safely⟩ **2** : to produce an effect ⟨a drug that *operates* quickly⟩ **3** : CONDUCT, MANAGE ⟨*operate* a business⟩ **4** : to perform surgery ⟨*operate* on a tumor⟩
op·er·a·tion \ˌäp-ə-'rā-shən\ *n* **1** : the act, process, method, or result of operating ⟨the *operation* of a drug⟩ **2** : the quality or state of being functional or operative ⟨put a factory into *operation*⟩ **3** : a surgical procedure **4** : a process (as addition or multiplication) of deriving one mathematical expression from others according to a rule **5** : a military or naval action, mission, or maneuver — **op·er·a·tion·al** \-sh(ə-)nəl\ *adj*
operational definition *n* : definition by means of a test, operation, or measurement that is carried out to determine if a particular example fits the defined term
[1]**op·er·a·tive** \'äp-(ə-)rət-iv, 'äp-ə-ˌrāt-\ *adj* **1** : exerting force or influence : OPERATING, WORKING ⟨an *operative* force⟩; *esp* : producing a normal or desired effect **2** : of or relating to manual or mechanical operations ⟨*operative* skills⟩ **3** : engaged in work
[2]**operative** *n* **1** : ARTISAN, MECHANIC **2 a** : SPY **b** : DETECTIVE
op·er·a·tor \'äp-ə-ˌrāt-ər\ *n* **1** : one that operates; *esp* : a person in charge of a telephone switchboard **2** : a shrewd person who knows how to get around regulations or difficulties
op·er·et·ta \ˌäp-ə-'ret-ə\ *n* : a light romantic opera containing spoken dialogue and dancing scenes — **op·er·et·tist** \-'ret-əst\ *n*
oph·thal·mia \äf-'thal-mē-ə, äp-\ *n* : inflammation of the eyeball or of the mucous membrane that lines the inner surface of the eyelid and covers the front part of the eyeball
oph·thal·mic \-mik\ *adj* : of, relating to, or situated near the eye : OCULAR
oph·thal·mol·o·gist \ˌäf-ˌthal-'mäl-ə-jəst, ˌäp-\ *n* : a physician specializing in ophthalmology
oph·thal·mol·o·gy \-jē\ *n* : a branch of medical science dealing with the structure, functions, and diseases of the eye — **oph·thal·mo·log·ic** \(ˌ)äf-ˌthal-mə-'läj-ik, (ˌ)äp-\ *or* **oph·thal·mo·log·i·cal** \-'läj-i-kəl\ *adj*
oph·thal·mo·scope \äf-'thal-mə-ˌskōp, äp-\ *n* : an optical instrument for viewing the inside of the eye
[1]**opi·ate** \'ō-pē-ət, -ˌāt\ *adj* **1** : containing or mixed with opium **2 a** : inducing sleep **b** : causing dullness or inaction
[2]**opiate** *n* **1** : a preparation of or derived from opium; *also* : NARCOTIC 1 **2** : something restful or soothing
opine \ō-'pīn\ *vb* : to have or express an opinion
opin·ion \ə-'pin-yən\ *n* **1** : a belief stronger than an impression but less strong than positive knowledge **2** : a judgment about a person or thing ⟨has a high *opinion* of his doctor⟩ **3** : a formal statement by an expert after careful study
opin·ion·at·ed \-yə-ˌnāt-əd\ *adj* : stubbornly holding to personal opinions
opi·um \'ō-pē-əm\ *n* **1** : a bitter brownish addictive narcotic drug that is the dried juice of the opium poppy **2** : something having an effect like that of opium — **opium** *adj*
opium poppy *n* : an annual Eurasian poppy grown for opium, for its edible oily seeds, and for its showy flowers
opos·sum \(ə-)'päs-əm\ *n, pl* **-sums** *also* **-sum** [from *âpäsûm*, an American Indian word meaning literally "white animal"] : a common marsupial mammal of the eastern U.S. that usu. is active at night and dwells in trees

opossum (about 3 ft. long)

opp *abbr* opposite
op·po·nent \ə-'pō-nənt\ *n* : a person or thing that opposes another : RIVAL, FOE
op·por·tune \ˌäp-ər-'t(y)ün\ *adj* : SUITABLE, TIMELY ⟨an *opportune* moment to act⟩ — **op·por·tune·ly** *adv*
op·por·tun·ism \-'t(y)ü-ˌniz-əm\ *n* : the practice of taking advantage of opportunities or circumstances regardless of principles or consequences

— **op·por·tun·ist** \-nəst\ *n or adj* — **op·por·tu·nis·tic** \-t(y)ü-'nis-tik\ *adj*

op·por·tu·ni·ty \ˌäp-ər-'t(y)ü-nət-ē\ *n, pl* **-ties** **1** : a favorable combination of circumstances, time, and place **2** : a chance for advancement or progress

op·pos·a·ble \ə-'pō-zə-bəl\ *adj* : capable of being placed opposite something else and esp. in a position for grasping ⟨the *opposable* human thumb⟩

op·pose \ə-'pōz\ *vb* **1** : to place opposite or against something to provide resistance, balance, or contrast **2** : to strive against : RESIST

1**op·po·site** \'äp-ə-zət\ *n* : something opposed or contrary

2**opposite** *adj* **1** : set over against something that is at the other end or side of an intervening line or space : FACING: as **a** *of two sides or angles of a quadrilateral* : not adjacent **b** *of two angles formed by the intersection of a pair of lines* : having contact only at the vertex **2 a** : OPPOSED, HOSTILE ⟨*opposite* sides of the question⟩ **b** : as different as possible : CONTRADICTORY ⟨*opposite* meanings⟩ **3** : contrary to one another ⟨went off in *opposite* directions⟩ **4** : being the other of a matching or contrasting pair ⟨the *opposite* sex⟩ — **op·po·site·ly** *adv* — **op·po·site·ness** *n*

3**opposite** *adv* : on opposite sides

4**opposite** *prep* : across from and usu. facing or on the same level with ⟨the house *opposite* ours⟩

op·po·si·tion \ˌäp-ə-'zish-ən\ *n* **1** : a setting opposite or being set opposite **2** : contrary action or condition : RESISTANCE ⟨offer *opposition* to a plan⟩ ⟨the *opposition* of two forces⟩ **3 a** : something (as a team or an enemy force) that opposes **b** *often cap* : a political party opposing the party in power

op·press \ə-'pres\ *vb* **1** : to weigh down : burden in spirit as if with weight ⟨*oppressed* by debts⟩ **2** : to rule cruelly or too severely ⟨a country *oppressed* by a dictator⟩ — **op·pres·sor** \-'pres-ər\ *n*

op·pres·sion \ə-'presh-ən\ *n* **1 a** : the act of oppressing; *esp* : unjust or cruel exercise of authority or power **b** : the state of being oppressed **2** : a sense of heaviness or obstruction in the body or mind — **op·pres·sive** \-'pres-iv\ *adj* — **op·pres·sive·ly** *adv* — **op·pres·sive·ness** *n*

op·pro·bri·ous \ə-'prō-brē-əs\ *adj* **1** : expressing opprobrium : ABUSIVE ⟨*opprobrious* language⟩ **2** : deserving opprobrium : DISGRACEFUL

op·pro·bri·um \-brē-əm\ *n* **1** : something that brings disgrace **2** : disgrace that follows from shameful conduct : INFAMY

opt *abbr* **1** optical **2** optician **3** optional

op·tic \'äp-tik\ *adj* : of or relating to vision or the eye

op·ti·cal \'äp-ti-kəl\ *adj* **1** : relating to optics **2** : OPTIC ⟨an *optical* illusion⟩ — **op·ti·cal·ly** \-k(ə-)lē\ *adv*

optical art *n* : abstract art marked by straight or curved lines or geometric patterns that often give the illusion of motion

op·ti·cian \äp-'tish-ən\ *n* **1** : a maker of or dealer in optical items and instruments **2** : one that grinds eyeglass lenses to prescription and sells glasses

optic lobe *n* : either of a pair of lobes in the midbrain of lower vertebrates (as birds and amphibians) that receive the fibers of the optic nerve

ə abut	ər further	a back	ā bake	
ä cot, cart	aü out	ch chin	e less	ē easy
g gift	i trip	ī life	j joke	ng sing	ō flow
ȯ flaw	ȯi coin	th thin	th this	ü loot
u̇ foot	y yet	yü few	yu̇ furious	zh vision

optic nerve *n* : either of a pair of sensory cranial nerves that transmit visual stimuli from the retina of the eye to the brain

op·tics \'äp-tiks\ *n* : a science that deals with the nature and properties of light and the effects that it undergoes and produces

op·ti·mal \'äp-tə-məl\ *adj* : most desirable or satisfactory — **op·ti·mal·ly** \-mə-lē\ *adv*

op·ti·mism \'äp-tə-ˌmiz-əm\ *n* [from Latin *optimus* "best"] **1** : a doctrine that this is the best possible world **2** : an inclination to be cheerful or hopeful about everything — **op·ti·mist** \-məst\ *n* — **op·ti·mis·tic** \ˌäp-tə-'mis-tik\ *adj* — **op·ti·mis·ti·cal·ly** \-ti-k(ə-)lē\ *adv*

op·ti·mum \'äp-tə-məm\ *n, pl* **-ma** \-mə\ *also* **-mums** : the best or most favorable amount or degree — **optimum** *adj*

op·tion \'äp-shən\ *n* **1 a** : the power or right to choose **b** : a choice made **2** : a right to buy or sell something at a specified price during a specified period **3** : something offered for choice

op·tion·al \'äp-sh(ə-)nəl\ *adj* : permitting a choice : not compulsory ⟨*optional* equipment on a new car⟩ — **op·tion·al·ly** \-ē\ *adv*

op·tom·e·trist \äp-'täm-ə-trəst\ *n* : a specialist in optometry

op·tom·e·try \-trē\ *n* : the profession of examining the eye for defects of vision and prescribing correctional glasses or exercises but not drugs or surgery — **op·to·met·ric** \ˌäp-tə-'me-trik\ *or* **op·to·met·ri·cal** \-tri-kəl\ *adj*

op·u·lent \'äp-yə-lənt\ *adj* **1** : WEALTHY **2** : richly abundant : PROFUSE ⟨*opulent* harvests⟩ ⟨*opulent* foliage⟩; *also* : amply fashioned : LUSH — **op·u·lence** \-lən(t)s\ *n* — **op·u·lent·ly** *adv*

opus \'ō-pəs\ *n, pl* **opera** \'ō-pə-rə, 'äp-ə-\ *also* **opus·es** \'ō-pə-səz\ : WORK; *esp* : a musical composition or set of compositions

or \ər, (ˌ)ȯ(ə)r\ *conj* — used to indicate an alternative ⟨coffee *or* tea⟩ ⟨sink *or* swim⟩

-or \ər, ˌȯ(ə)r, 'ȯ(ə)r\ *n suffix* : one that does a (specified) thing ⟨grant*or*⟩ ⟨elevat*or*⟩

OR *abbr* Oregon

or·a·cle \'ȯr-ə-kəl, 'är-\ *n* **1 a** : a person (as a priestess of ancient Greece) through whom a deity is held to speak **b** : a shrine where a deity speaks through an oracle **c** : an answer or revelation given by an oracle **2 a** : a person giving wise advice **b** : an authoritative or wise opinion

orac·u·lar \ȯ-'rak-yə-lər, ə-\ *adj* **1** : of, relating to, or being an oracle **2** : resembling an oracle in wisdom, solemnity, or obscurity — **orac·u·lar·ly** *adv*

oral \'ōr-əl, 'ȯr-, 'är-\ *adj* **1** : uttered by the mouth : SPOKEN ⟨an *oral* agreement⟩ **2** : of or relating to the mouth ⟨*oral* hygiene⟩ — **oral·ly** \-ə-lē\ *adv*

syn ORAL, VERBAL can mean expressed or communicated in words. ORAL applies only to the spoken word and implies a contrast with written words ⟨an *oral* examination⟩; VERBAL applies to either spoken or written expression and carries an emphasis on words as a medium of communication in contrast with a medium other than verbal ***ant*** written

or·ange \'ȯr-inj, 'är-\ *n* [from French, from Provençal *auranja*, from Arabic *nāranj*, from Persian *nārang*, from Sanskrit *nāraṅga*] **1 a** : a sphere-shaped fruit with a reddish yellow rind and a sweet edible pulp **b** : any of various rather small evergreen citrus trees whose fruits are oranges **2** : a color midway between red and yellow like that of a ripe orange — **orange** *adj*

or·ange·ade \ˌȯr-inj-ˈād, ˌär-\ *n* : a drink made of orange juice, sugar, and water

orange hawkweed *n* : a European plant that is related to the daisies, has bright orange-red flower heads, and is a troublesome weed in northeastern No. America

orang·u·tan *or* **orang·ou·tan** \ə-ˈrang-ə-ˌtang, -ˌtan\ *n* [from Malay *orang hutan*, meaning literally "man of the forest"] : a largely herbivorous and arboreal anthropoid ape of Borneo and Sumatra about two thirds as large as the gorilla

orangutan (about 4½ ft. tall)

orate \ȯ-ˈrāt\ *vb* : to speak in the manner of an oration

ora·tion \ə-ˈrā-shən, ȯ-\ *n* : an elaborate discourse delivered in a formal and dignified manner usu. on some special occasion

or·a·tor \ˈȯr-ət-ər, ˈär-\ *n* **1** : one that delivers an oration **2** : one distinguished as a skilled and powerful public speaker

or·a·tor·i·cal \ˌȯr-ə-ˈtȯr-i-kəl, ˌär-ə-ˈtär-\ *adj* : of, relating to, or characteristic of an orator or oratory — **or·a·tor·i·cal·ly** \-k(ə-)lē\ *adv*

or·a·to·rio \ˌȯr-ə-ˈtōr-ē-ˌō, ˌär-, -ˈtȯr-\ *n, pl* **-ri·os** : a vocal and orchestral work usu. dramatizing a biblical subject without action or scenery

[1]**or·a·to·ry** \ˈȯr-ə-ˌtōr-ē, ˈär-, -ˌtȯr-\ *n, pl* **-ries** : a place for prayer; *esp* : a private chapel

[2]**oratory** *n* **1** : the art of an orator **2** : oratorical language or speeches

orb \ˈȯrb\ *n* : a spherical body (as a heavenly body or an eye) : BALL, GLOBE

[1]**or·bit** \ˈȯr-bət\ *n* [from Latin *orbita* "wheel track", "orbit", from *orbis* "circle", "orb"] **1** : EYE SOCKET **2** : a path described by one body or object as it revolves about another ⟨the *orbit* of the earth about the sun⟩ **3** : range or sphere of activity — **or·bit·al** \-əl\ *adj*

[2]**orbit** *vb* **1** : to revolve in an orbit around ⟨a satellite *orbiting* Mars⟩ **2** : to send up so as to orbit ⟨*orbit* a satellite⟩ — **or·bit·er** *n*

orch *abbr* orchestra

or·chard \ˈȯr-chərd\ *n* [from Old English *ortgeard*, from Latin *hortus* "garden" and Old English *geard* "yard", both from the same prehistoric Indo-European word meaning "enclosed place"] **1** : a place where fruit or nut trees are grown **2** : the trees in an orchard

or·ches·tra \ˈȯr-kə-strə\ *n* [from Greek *orchēstra*, name of the space occupied by the chorus in the ancient Greek theater, literally "dancing place"] **1** : a group of musicians who perform together on instruments and esp. on stringed instruments **2 a** : the space in front of the stage in a theater that is used by an orchestra **b** : the front section of seats on the main floor of a theater

or·ches·tral \ȯr-ˈkes-trəl\ *adj* : of, relating to, or composed for an orchestra ⟨*orchestral* music⟩ ⟨*orchestral* concert⟩

or·ches·trate \ˈȯr-kə-ˌstrāt\ *vb* : to compose or arrange music for an orchestra — **or·ches·tra·tion** \ˌȯr-kə-ˈstrā-shən\ *n*

or·chid \ˈȯr-kəd\ *n* **1** : any of a large family of monocotyledonous plants that have usu. showy 3-petaled flowers with the middle petal enlarged into a lip and differing from the others in shape and color; *also* : its flower **2** : a variable color averaging a light purple

orchid 1

or·chis \ˈȯr-kəs\ *n* : ORCHID; *esp* : a woodland plant having fleshy roots and spikes of purple and white flowers with the lip spurred

ord *abbr* order

or·dain \ȯr-ˈdān\ *vb* **1** : to make a person a Christian minister or priest by a special ceremony **2 a** : ORDER, DECREE **b** : DESTINE

or·deal \ȯr-ˈdēl\ *n* **1** : a primitive method of finding out the guilt or innocence of the accused by requiring him to submit to dangerous or painful tests believed to be under supernatural control ⟨*ordeal* by fire⟩ **2** : a severe trial or experience

[1]**or·der** \ˈȯrd-ər\ *n* **1 a** : a group of people united in some formal way (as by living under the same religious rules or by loyalty to common interests and obligations) ⟨an *order* of monks⟩ ⟨an *order* of knighthood⟩ **b** : the badge or insignia of such an order **c** : a military decoration **2** *pl* : the Christian ministry ⟨in *orders*⟩ **3 a** : a rank or class in society ⟨the lower *orders*⟩ **b** : CLASS, KIND **c** : a group of related plants or animals ranking in taxonomic classification above the family and below the class **4 a** : the arrangement or sequence of objects in space or events in time ⟨the *order* of the seasons⟩ ⟨in alphabetical *order*⟩ **b** : the property or state of being mathematically ordered **c** : the prevailing mode or arrangement ⟨the old *order*⟩ ⟨the *order* of worship⟩ **d** : regular or harmonious arrangement or a condition marked by such an arrangement ⟨kept his room in *order*⟩ **5 a** : the rule of law or authority ⟨restored *order*⟩ **b** : a specific rule or direction : COMMAND **6 a** : a style of building **b** : a type of architectural column with its related parts **7** : condition with regard to functioning or repair ⟨out of *order*⟩ **8 a** : a direction to pay or not to pay money, to buy or sell, or to supply goods or services **b** : goods or items bought or sold ⟨an *order* of ham and eggs⟩ — **in order to** : for the purpose of

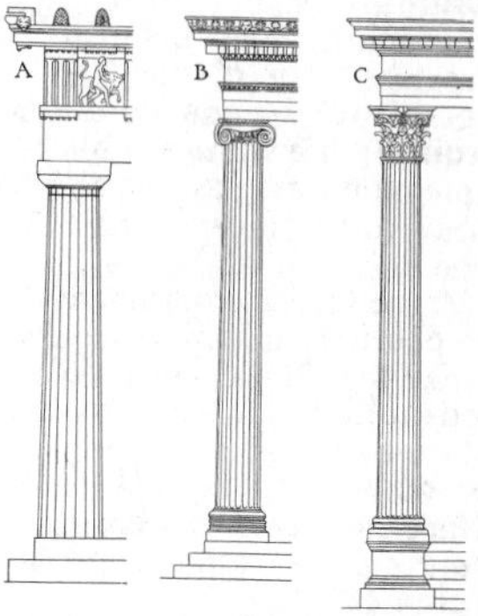

order 6b: A, Doric; B, Ionic; C, Corinthian

[2]**order** *vb* **or·dered**; **or·der·ing** \ˈȯrd-(ə-)ring\ **1** : to put in order : ARRANGE, REGULATE **2** : to give an order to or for ⟨*order* troops to the front⟩ ⟨*order* groceries⟩ — **or·der·er** \ˈȯrd-ər-ər\ *n* — **in order to** *or* **in order that** : for the purpose of — **on the order of** : LIKE ⟨cloth *on the order of* tweed⟩ — **to order** : in fulfillment of an order given ⟨a suit made *to order*⟩

or·dered *adj* : having the property that for any two different elements *a* and *b* either *a* is greater than *b* or *a* is less than *b* ⟨the set of real numbers is *ordered*⟩

ordered pair *n* : a set with two elements in which one element is identified as the first and the other as the second

¹**or·der·ly** \'ȯrd-ər-lē\ *adj* **1 a** : being in order; *esp* : TIDY, NEAT **b** : METHODICAL ⟨an *orderly* girl⟩ **2** : governed by law or system : REGULATED ⟨an *orderly* universe⟩ **3** : well behaved ⟨an *orderly* crowd⟩ — **or·der·li·ness** *n* — **orderly** *adv*

²**orderly** *n, pl* **-lies 1** : a soldier who conveys messages and performs services for an officer **2** : a hospital attendant who does general work

or·di·nal \'ȯrd-(ə-)nəl\ *n* : ORDINAL NUMBER

ordinal number *n* : a number designating the place (as first, fifth, 22d) of an item in an ordered sequence — see NUMBER table

or·di·nance \'ȯrd-(ə-)nən(t)s\ *n* : an authoritative decree, order, or law; *esp* : a regulation of a city or town

¹**or·di·nary** \'ȯrd-ə-ˌner-ē\ *n, pl* **-nar·ies 1** : regular or customary condition or course of things ⟨nothing out of the *ordinary*⟩ **2** *chiefly Brit* : a tavern or eating house serving regular meals

²**ordinary** *adj* **1** : to be expected : NORMAL, USUAL **2** : neither good nor bad : AVERAGE **3** : POOR, INFERIOR — **or·di·nar·i·ly** \ˌȯrd-ə-'ner-ə-lē\ *adv* — **or·di·nar·i·ness** \'ȯrd-ə-ˌner-ē-nəs\ *n*

ordinary life insurance *n* : life insurance for which premiums are payable as long as the insured lives

or·di·nate \'ȯrd-(ə-)nət\ *n* **1** : the distance of a point on a graph above or below the horizontal line **2** : the vertical coordinate on a graph

or·di·na·tion \ˌȯrd-ə-'nā-shən\ *n* : the act of ordaining : the state of being ordained

ord·nance \'ȯrd-nən(t)s\ *n* : military supplies; *esp* : CANNON, ARTILLERY

Or·do·vi·cian \ˌȯrd-ə-'vish-ən\ *n* : the period of the Paleozoic era between the Cambrian and Silurian; *also* : the corresponding system of rocks — **Ordovician** *adj*

or·dure \'ȯr-jər\ *n* : EXCREMENT

ore \'ō(ə)r, 'ȯ(ə)r\ *n* : a mineral containing a constituent for which it is mined and worked ⟨iron *ore*⟩

ore·ad \'ōr-ē-ˌad, 'ȯr-\ *n* : a nymph of mountains and hills

Oreg *or* **Ore** *abbr* Oregon

oreg·a·no \ə-'reg-ə-ˌnō\ *n, pl* **-nos** : a bushy mint used as a seasoning and a source of aromatic oil

org *abbr* organization

or·gan \'ȯr-gən\ *n* **1 a** : a keyboard wind instrument consisting of pipes made to sound by compressed air **b** : REED ORGAN **c** : an instrument in which electronic devices are used to produce or amplify sounds similar to those of an organ **2** : a differentiated animal or plant structure consisting of cells and tissues and performing some specific function — compare SYSTEM **3** : a means of performing some function or accomplishing some end ⟨courts are *organs* of government⟩ **4** : a publication (as a newspaper or magazine) of a special group

or·gan·dy *also* **or·gan·die** \'ȯr-gən-dē\ *n, pl* **-dies** : a fine transparent muslin with a stiff finish

or·gan·elle \ˌȯr-gə-'nel\ *n* : a specialized part of a cell analogous to an organ

ə abut	ər further	a back	ā bake	
ä cot, cart	au̇ out	ch chin	e less	ē easy
g gift	i trip	ī life	j joke	ng sing	ō flow
ȯ flaw	ȯi coin	th thin	t͟h this	ü loot
u̇ foot	y yet	yü few	yu̇ furious	zh vision

or·gan–grind·er \'ȯr-gən-ˌgrīn-dər\ *n* : a traveling street musician who cranks a hand organ

or·gan·ic \ȯr-'gan-ik\ *adj* **1 a** : of, relating to, or arising in a bodily organ **b** : affecting the structure of the organism ⟨an *organic* disease⟩ **2 a** : of, relating to, or derived from living organisms ⟨*organic* matter⟩ **b** : of, relating to, or containing carbon compounds **c** : of, relating to, or dealt with by a branch of chemistry concerned with the carbon compounds of living beings and most other carbon compounds **3 a** : forming an essential part of a whole **b** : ORGANIZED ⟨an *organic* whole⟩ — **or·gan·i·cal·ly** \-i-k(ə-)lē\ *adv*

or·gan·ism \'ȯr-gə-ˌniz-əm\ *n* **1** : an individual living being that carries on the activities of life by means of organs separate in function but mutually dependent : a living person, plant, or animal **2** : something like an organism in having many related parts — **or·gan·is·mic** \ˌȯr-gə-'niz-mik\ *adj*

or·gan·ist \'ȯr-gə-nəst\ *n* : one who plays an organ

or·ga·ni·za·tion \ˌȯrg-(ə-)nə-'zā-shən\ *n* **1** : the act or process of organizing **2** : the condition or manner of being organized **3** : a group of persons organized for some purpose ⟨a business *organization*⟩ — **or·ga·ni·za·tion·al** \-sh(ə-)nəl\ *adj*

or·ga·nize \'ȯr-gə-ˌnīz\ *vb* **1** : to make separate parts into one united whole : form or form into an organization **2** : to put into order : SYSTEMATIZE ⟨*organize* your work⟩ — **or·ga·niz·er** *n*

or·gasm \'ȯr-ˌgaz-əm\ *n* : the climax of sexual excitement typically occurring in coitus

or·gy \'ȯr-jē\ *n, pl* **orgies 1** : secret rites in honor of an ancient Greek or Roman deity usu. celebrated by wild singing and dancing **2** : excessive indulgence in an activity

ori·el \'ōr-ē-əl, 'ȯr-\ *n* : a bay window projecting from a wall and supported by a bracket

oriel

Ori·ent \'ōr-ē-ənt, 'ȯr-, -ē-ˌent\ *n* [from Latin *orient-*, stem of *oriens* "rising" (of heavenly bodies), present participle of *oriri* "to rise"] : EAST; *esp* : the countries of eastern Asia

ori·ent \-ˌent\ *vb* **1 a** : to cause to face toward the east **b** : to set or arrange in a definite position esp. in relation to the points of the compass **2** : to acquaint with a situation or environment ⟨*orient* new students⟩ — **ori·en·ta·tion** \ˌōr-ē-ən-'tā-shən, ˌȯr-, -ē-ˌen-\ *n*

ori·en·tal \ˌōr-ē-'ent-əl, ˌȯr-\ *adj, often cap* : of or relating to the Orient — **ori·en·tal·ly** \-ə-lē\ *adv*

Oriental *n* : a member of one of the peoples of the Orient; *esp* : a Chinese, Japanese, or other Mongoloid

Oriental poppy *n* : an Asiatic perennial poppy widely grown for its very large showy flowers

ori·en·tate \'ōr-ē-ən-ˌtāt, 'ȯr-, -ˌen-\ *vb* : ORIENT

or·i·fice \'ȯr-ə-fəs, 'är-\ *n* : an opening (as a mouth or hole) through which something may pass

orig *abbr* original

ori·ga·mi \ˌȯr-ə-'gäm-ē\ *n* : the Japanese art of folding paper

or·i·gin \'ȯr-ə-jən, 'är-\ *n* **1** : ANCESTRY, PARENTAGE ⟨of French *origin*⟩ **2 a** : rise, beginning, or derivation from a source **b** : primary source or cause **3** : the intersection of the horizontal and vertical axes on a graph

1**orig·i·nal** \ə-'rij-(ə-)nəl\ *n* **:** something from which a copy, reproduction, or translation is made

2**original** *adj* **1 :** relating to or being the origin or beginning **:** FIRST, EARLIEST ⟨the *original* part of an old house⟩ ⟨*original* inhabitants⟩ **2 :** not copied, reproduced, or translated **:** NEW ⟨*original* paintings⟩ ⟨an *original* idea⟩ **3 :** being an original **4 :** independent and creative in thought or action **:** INVENTIVE — **orig·i·nal·ly** \-ē\ *adv*

orig·i·nal·i·ty \ə-,rij-ə-'nal-ət-ē\ *n* **1 :** the quality or state of being original **:** FRESHNESS ⟨the *originality* of an idea⟩ **2 :** the power or ability to think, to act, or to do something in new ways **:** CREATIVITY ⟨an artist of great *originality*⟩

orig·i·nate \ə-'rij-ə-,nāt\ *vb* **1 :** to bring into existence **:** cause to be **:** INITIATE, INVENT **2 :** to come into existence **:** ARISE — **orig·i·na·tion** \-,rij-ə-'nā-shən\ *n* — **orig·i·na·tor** \-'rij-ə-,nāt-ər\ *n*

orig·i·na·tive \ə-'rij-ə-,nāt-iv\ *adj* **:** having ability to originate **:** CREATIVE — **orig·i·na·tive·ly** *adv*

ori·ole \'ōr-ē-,ōl, 'ȯr-\ *n* **[**from French *oriol*, from Latin *aureolus* "golden", from *aurum* "gold"**]** **1 :** any of a family of usu. brightly colored Old World birds related to the crows **2 :** any of a family of New World birds of which the males are usu. black and yellow or orange and the females chiefly greenish or yellowish

or·i·son \'ȯr-ə-sən, 'är-\ *n* **:** PRAYER

1**or·na·ment** \'ȯr-nə-mənt\ *n* **1 :** something that adorns or adds beauty **:** DECORATION **2 :** addition of something that beautifies ⟨applied for *ornament*⟩

2**or·na·ment** \-,ment\ *vb* **:** ADORN, DECORATE — **or·na·men·ta·tion** \,ȯr-nə-mən-'tā-shən, -,men-\ *n*

1**or·na·men·tal** \,ȯr-nə-'ment-əl\ *adj* **:** of, relating to, or serving as ornament — **or·na·men·tal·ly** \-ə-lē\ *adv*

2**ornamental** *n* **:** a decorative object; *esp* **:** a plant cultivated for its beauty rather than for use

or·nate \ȯr-'nāt\ *adj* **:** elaborately or excessively decorated — **or·nate·ly** *adv* — **or·nate·ness** *n*

or·nery \'ȯrn-(ə-)rē, 'än-\ *adj* **or·neri·er; -est :** having an irritable disposition — **or·neri·ness** *n*

ornith *abbr* ornithology

or·ni·thol·o·gy \,ȯr-nə-'thäl-ə-jē\ *n* **:** a branch of zoology dealing with birds — **or·ni·tho·log·i·cal** \,ȯr-,nith-ə-'läj-i-kəl\ *adj* — **or·ni·thol·o·gist** \,ȯr-nə-'thäl-ə-jəst\ *n*

orog·e·ny \ȯ-'räj-ə-nē\ *n, pl* **-nies :** the process of mountain formation — **oro·gen·ic** \,ōr-ə-'jen-ik, ,ȯr-\ *adj*

1**or·phan** \'ȯr-fən\ *n* **:** a child whose parents are dead — **orphan** *adj*

2**orphan** *vb* **or·phaned; or·phan·ing** \'ȯrf-(ə-)niŋ\ **:** to cause to become an orphan ⟨a child *orphaned* by a plane wreck⟩

or·phan·age \'ȯrf-(ə-)nij\ *n* **:** an institution for the care of orphans

or·ris \'ȯr-əs, 'är-\ *n* **:** a European iris with a fragrant rootstock used esp. in perfume and sachet powder; *also* **:** its rootstock

or·ris·root \-,rüt, -,ru̇t\ *n* **:** the rootstock of an orris

orth·odon·tics \,ȯr-thə-'dänt-iks\ *n* **:** a branch of dentistry dealing with irregularities of the teeth and their correction — **orth·odon·tic** \-'dänt-ik\ *adj* — **orth·odon·tist** \-'dänt-əst\ *n*

or·tho·dox \'ȯr-thə-,däks\ *adj* **[**from Greek *orthodoxos*, from *orthos* "straight", "right" and *doxa* "opinion"**]** **1 :** holding established beliefs esp. in religion ⟨an *orthodox* Christian⟩ **2 :** approved as measuring up to some standard **:** USUAL, CONVENTIONAL ⟨*orthodox* dress for a church wedding⟩

Orthodox Judaism *n* **:** Judaism that adheres to biblical law as interpreted in the authoritative rabbinic tradition and seeks to observe all the practices commanded in it

or·tho·doxy \-,däk-sē\ *n, pl* **-dox·ies 1 :** the quality or state of being orthodox **2 :** an orthodox belief or practice

or·thog·ra·phy \ȯr-'thäg-rə-fē\ *n, pl* **-phies 1 :** correct spelling **2 :** a way or style of spelling — **or·tho·graph·ic** \,ȯr-thə-'graf-ik\ *or* **or·tho·graph·i·cal** \-i-kəl\ *adj* — **or·tho·graph·i·cal·ly** \-i-k(ə-)lē\ *adv*

or·tho·pe·dic \,ȯr-thə-'pēd-ik\ *adj* **1 :** of or relating to orthopedics **2 :** marked by deformities or crippling

or·tho·pe·dics \-'pēd-iks\ *n* **:** the correction or prevention of skeletal deformities — **or·tho·pe·dist** \-'pēd-əst\ *n*

or·thop·ter·an \ȯr-'thäp-tə-rən\ *n* **:** any of an order comprising insects with biting mouthparts, two pairs of wings or none, and an incomplete metamorphosis and usu. including the grasshoppers, mantises, and crickets — **orthopteran** *or* **or·thop·ter·ous** \-rəs\ *adj* — **or·thop·ter·on** \-,rän\ *n*

1**-o·ry** \,ōr-ē, ,ȯr-ē, (ə-)rē\ *n suffix, pl* **-ories :** place of or for ⟨observat*ory*⟩

2**-ory** *adj suffix* **:** of, relating to, serving for, or characterized by ⟨prohibit*ory*⟩

oryx \'ōr-iks, 'ȯr-, 'är-\ *n, pl* **oryx·es** *or* **oryx :** a large straight-horned African antelope

Osage \ō-'sāj\ *n* **:** a member of a Siouan Amerindian people of Missouri

oryx
(about 40 in. at shoulder)

os·cil·late \'äs-ə-,lāt\ *vb* **1 :** to swing backward and forward like a pendulum **:** VIBRATE **2 :** to waver between opposing beliefs, feelings, or theories **3 :** to exhibit or cause electrical oscillation — **os·cil·la·to·ry** \ä-'sil-ə-,tōr-ē, -,tȯr-\ *adj*

os·cil·la·tion \,äs-ə-'lā-shən\ *n* **1 :** the act or fact of oscillating **:** VIBRATION **2 :** VARIATION, FLUCTUATION **3 :** a flow of electricity changing periodically from a maximum to a minimum; *esp* **:** a flow periodically changing direction **4 :** a single swing or change of an oscillating body or medium

os·cil·la·tor \'äs-ə-,lāt-ər\ *n* **1 :** one that oscillates **2 :** a device for producing alternating current; *esp* **:** a radio-frequency or audio-frequency generator

os·cil·lo·scope \ä-'sil-ə-,skōp, ə-\ *n* **:** an instrument in which the variations in a fluctuating electrical quantity appear temporarily as visible waves of light on a fluorescent screen

os·cu·late \'äs-kyə-,lāt\ *vb* **:** KISS — **os·cu·la·tion** \,äs-kyə-'lā-shən\ *n*

osier \'ō-zhər\ *n* **1 :** any of various willows with pliable twigs used for furniture and basketry **2 :** a willow rod used in basketry **3 :** any of several American dogwoods — **osier** *adj*

os·mi·um \'äz-mē-əm\ *n* **:** a hard brittle blue-gray or blue-black metallic element with a high melting point that is the heaviest metal known and is used esp. as a catalyst and in hard alloys — see ELEMENT table

os·mo·sis \äs-'mō-səs, äz-\ *n* **:** the passage of material (as a solvent) through a partially permeable membrane (as of a plant or animal cell) from a region of higher to one of lower concentration — **os·mot·ic** \-'mät-ik\ *adj*

os·prey \'äs-prē\ *n, pl* **ospreys :** a large brown and white hawk that feeds on fish

os·si·fy \'äs-ə-,fī\ *vb* **-fied**; **-fy·ing 1 :** to become or change into bone or bony tissue **2 :** to become or make callous or set in one's ways — **os·si·fi·ca·tion** \,äs-ə-fə-'kā-shən\ *n*

os·te·ich·thy·an \,äs-tē-'ik-thē-ən\ *n* : any of a large group of fishes comprising the higher fishes with bony skeletons as distinguished from those (as sharks) with skeletons of cartilage — **osteichthyan** *adj*

os·ten·si·ble \ä-'sten(t)-sə-bəl\ *adj* : shown outwardly : APPARENT — **os·ten·si·bly** \-blē\ *adv*

os·ten·ta·tion \,äs-tən-'tā-shən\ *n* : pretentious or excessive display — **os·ten·ta·tious** \-shəs\ *adj* — **os·ten·ta·tious·ly** *adv* — **os·ten·ta·tious·ness** *n*

os·te·o·path \'äs-tē-ə-,path\ *n* : a practitioner of osteopathy

os·te·op·a·thy \,äs-tē-'äp-ə-thē\ *n* : a system of treating diseases that places emphasis on manipulation esp. of bones but does not exclude other treatment (as the use of medicine and surgery) — **os·te·o·path·ic** \,äs-tē-ə-'path-ik\ *adj*

os·tler *var of* HOSTLER

os·tra·cism \'äs-trə-,siz-əm\ *n* **1 :** a method of temporary banishment by popular vote without trial practiced in ancient Greece **2 :** exclusion by general consent from common privileges or social acceptance

os·tra·cize \'äs-trə-,sīz\ *vb* [from Greek *ostrakizein*, from *ostrakon* "shell", "pottery fragment"; from the use of pieces of broken pottery as secret ballots in the voting] : to exile or exclude by ostracism

os·trich \'äs-trich, 'ȯs-\ *n* **1 :** a large swift-footed 2-toed flightless bird of Africa and Arabia often weighing 300 pounds with valuable wing and tail plumes **2 :** one who tries to avoid danger by refusing to face it

ostrich 1
(about 8 ft. tall)

Os·we·go tea \ä-,swē-gō-\ *n* : a No. American mint with showy bright scarlet irregular flowers

OT *abbr* Old Testament

[1]**oth·er** \'əth-ər\ *adj* **1 a :** being the one (as of two or more) left ⟨broke his *other* arm⟩ **b :** being the ones distinct from those first mentioned ⟨thought the *other* members dull⟩ **2 :** SECOND, ALTERNATE ⟨every *other* day⟩ **3 :** ADDITIONAL ⟨some *other* guests are coming⟩ **4 :** recently past ⟨the *other* evening⟩

[2]**other** *pron* **1 :** remaining one : remaining ones ⟨lift one foot and then the *other*⟩ **2 :** a different or additional one ⟨something or *other*⟩

[3]**other** *adv* : OTHERWISE

oth·er·wise \'ə-thər-,wīz\ *adv* **1 :** in a different way : DIFFERENTLY ⟨could not do *otherwise*⟩ **2 :** in different circumstances ⟨*otherwise* he might have won⟩ **3 :** in other respects ⟨the *otherwise* busy street⟩

oth·er·world \'əth-ər-,wərld\ *n* : a world beyond death

ot·ter \'ät-ər\ *n, pl* **otter** *or* **otters 1 :** any of several aquatic fish-eating mammals that are related to the weasels and minks and have webbed and clawed feet and dark brown fur **2 :** the fur or pelt of an otter

otter 1
(up to 4½ ft. long)

ot·to·man \'ät-ə-mən\ *n, pl* **-mans 1** *cap* : TURK — called also *Ottoman Turk* **2 :** an upholstered footstool — **Ottoman** *adj*

ouch \'au̇ch\ *interj* — used to express sudden pain or displeasure

ought \'ȯt\ *auxiliary verb* — used to express obligation ⟨we *ought* to pay our debts⟩, advisability ⟨you *ought* to take care of yourself⟩, natural expectation ⟨he *ought* to be here by now⟩, or logical consequence ⟨the result *ought* to be infinity⟩

oughtn't \'ȯt-ənt\ : ought not

[1]**ounce** \'au̇n(t)s\ *n* [from medieval French *unce*, from Latin *uncia* "twelfth part" of anything, the source also, through Old English *ynce*, of English *inch*] **1 a :** a unit of weight equal to 1/12 troy pound — see MEASURE table **b :** a unit of weight equal to 1/16 avoirdupois pound **c :** a small quantity **2 :** FLUIDOUNCE

[2]**ounce** *n* : SNOW LEOPARD

our \är, (')au̇(ə)r\ *adj* : of or relating to us or ourselves or ourself ⟨*our* throne⟩ ⟨*our* actions⟩ ⟨*our* being chosen⟩

ours \(')au̇(ə)rz, ärz\ *pron* : our one : our ones

our·selves \är-'selvz, au̇(ə)r-\ *pron* **1 :** our own selves — used reflexively or for emphasis ⟨we amused *ourselves*⟩ ⟨we did it *ourselves*⟩ **2 :** our normal or healthy selves

-ous \əs\ *adj suffix* **1 :** full of : abounding in ⟨clamor*ous*⟩ **2 :** having : possessing the qualities of ⟨poison*ous*⟩

ou·sel *var of* OUZEL

oust \'au̇st\ *vb* : to force or drive out (as from office or from possession of something) : EXPEL

oust·er \'au̇s-tər\ *n* : the act or an instance of ousting

[1]**out** \'au̇t\ *adv* **1 a :** in a direction away from the inside, center, or surface ⟨look *out* of a window⟩ **b :** from among others ⟨picked *out* a hat⟩ **2 :** away from home, business, or usual or proper place ⟨*out* to lunch⟩ ⟨left a word *out*⟩ **3 :** into a state of loss or deprivation ⟨vote the party *out* of office⟩ **4 :** beyond control or possession ⟨let a secret *out*⟩ ⟨lent *out* money⟩ **5 :** into a state of disagreement ⟨friends fall *out*⟩ **6 :** so as to be exhausted, completed, or discontinued ⟨the food ran *out*⟩ ⟨the light burned *out*⟩ **7 a :** in or into the open ⟨the sun came *out*⟩ ⟨let a secret *out*⟩ **b :** ALOUD ⟨cried *out*⟩ **8 —** used as an intensive with numerous verbs ⟨sketch *out* plans⟩ **9 :** so as to put out or be put out in baseball ⟨the catcher threw the runner *out*⟩ ⟨grounded *out* to shortstop⟩

[2]**out** *vb* : to become known ⟨the truth will *out*⟩

[3]**out** *adj* **1 :** situated outside or at a distance ⟨the *out* islands⟩ **2 :** not being in power ⟨the *out* party⟩ **3 :** not successful in reaching base ⟨the batter was *out*⟩ **4 :** directed outward or serving to direct something outward ⟨a letter in the *out* basket⟩

5 : ABSENT, MISSING ⟨a basket with its bottom *out*⟩ 6 : no longer in fashion ⟨argyle socks are *out*⟩

[4]**out** \ˌau̇t\ *prep* **1** : out through ⟨ran *out* the door⟩ **2** : outward along or on ⟨drive *out* the old road⟩

[5]**out** \ˈau̇t\ *n* **1** : one who is out of power **2 a** : the retiring of a batter or base runner in baseball **b** : a player so retired **3** : a ball hit out-of-bounds in tennis or squash **4** : an item that is out of stock **5** : a way of escaping from an embarrassing situation or a difficulty

out- *prefix* : in a manner that goes beyond, surpasses, or excels ⟨*out*maneuver⟩

out–and–out \ˌau̇t-ən-ˈ(d)au̇t\ *adj* : COMPLETE, THOROUGHGOING

out·bid \(ˈ)au̇t-ˈbid\ *vb* **-bid**; **-bid·ding** : to make a higher bid than

[1]**out·board** \ˈau̇t-ˌbōrd, -ˌbȯrd\ *adj* **1** : situated outboard **2** : using an outboard motor

[2]**outboard** *adv* **1** : outside the line of a ship's hull **2** : in a position closer to the wing tips of an airplane

outboard motor *n* : a small internal-combustion engine with propeller attached for mounting at the stern of a small boat

out·bound \ˈau̇t-ˌbau̇nd\ *adj* : outward bound ⟨*outbound* traffic⟩

out·brave \(ˈ)au̇t-ˈbrāv\ *vb* **1** : to face or resist defiantly **2** : to exceed in courage

out·break \ˈau̇t-ˌbrāk\ *n* **1** : a sudden or violent increase of activity or currency ⟨the *outbreak* of war⟩ **2** : something (as an epidemic or revolt) that breaks out

out·breed *vb* **-bred**; **-breed·ing** **1** \ˈau̇t-ˌbrēd\ : to subject to outbreeding **2** \(ˈ)au̇t-ˈ\ : to breed faster than

out·breed·ing \ˈau̇t-ˌbrēd-ing\ *n* : the interbreeding of relatively unrelated individuals

out·build·ing \ˈau̇t-ˌbil-ding\ *n* : a building separate from and smaller than the main one

out·burst \-ˌbərst\ *n* : ERUPTION, OUTBREAK ⟨an *outburst* of anger⟩

out·cast \-ˌkast\ *n* : one who is cast out by society : PARIAH — **outcast** *adj*

out·caste \-ˌkast\ *n* **1** : a Hindu who has been ejected from his caste for violation of its rules **2** : one who has no caste

out·class \(ˈ)au̇t-ˈklas\ *vb* : to surpass so much as to appear of a higher class

out·come \ˈau̇t-ˌkəm\ *n* : final consequence : RESULT

[1]**out·crop** \ˈau̇t-ˌkräp\ *n* **1** : a coming out of bedrock or of an unconsolidated deposit to the surface of the ground **2** : the part of a rock formation that appears at the surface of the ground

[2]**out·crop** \ˈau̇t-ˈkräp\ *vb* : to come to the surface : APPEAR ⟨granite *outcropping* through softer rocks⟩

out·cross·ing \ˈau̇t-ˌkrȯ-sing\ *n* : interbreeding of individuals of different strains but usu. the same breed — **out·cross** \-ˌkrȯs\ *vb or n*

out·cry \ˈau̇t-ˌkrī\ *n* **1** : a loud cry : CLAMOR **2** : a strong protest

out·dat·ed \(ˈ)au̇t-ˈdāt-əd\ *adj* : OBSOLETE

out·dis·tance \-ˈdis-tən(t)s\ *vb* : to go far ahead of (as in a race) : OUTSTRIP

out·do \-ˈdü\ *vb* **-did** \-ˈdid\; **-done** \-ˈdən\; **-do·ing** \-ˈdü-ing\ : EXCEL, SURPASS

out·door \ˌau̇t-ˌdōr, -ˌdȯr\ *also* **out·doors** \-ˌdōrz, -ˌdȯrz\ *adj* **1** : of or relating to the outdoors ⟨an *outdoor* setting⟩ **2** : done outdoors ⟨*outdoor* games⟩ **3** : having no roof and walls ⟨an *outdoor* theater⟩

[1]**out·doors** \(ˈ)au̇t-ˈdō(ə)rz, -ˈdȯ(ə)rz\ *adv* : outside a building : in or into the open air

[2]**outdoors** *n* **1** : the open air **2** : the world away from human dwellings

out·er \ˈau̇t-ər\ *adj* **1** : situated on the outside or farther out ⟨the *outer* wall⟩ **2** : being away from a center ⟨the *outer* solar planets⟩

outer ear *n* : the outer visible portion of the ear that collects and directs sound waves toward the eardrum by way of a canal which extends inward through the temporal bone

out·er·most \ˈau̇t-ər-ˌmōst\ *adj* : farthest out

outer space *n* : SPACE; *esp* : the region beyond the solar system

out·field \ˈau̇t-ˌfēld\ *n* **1** : the part of a baseball field beyond the infield and between the foul lines **2** : the baseball defensive positions comprising right field, center field, and left field — **out·field·er** \-ˌfēl-dər\ *n*

out·fight \(ˈ)au̇t-ˈfīt\ *vb* **-fought** \-ˈfȯt\; **-fight·ing** : to surpass in fighting : DEFEAT

[1]**out·fit** \ˈau̇t-ˌfit\ *n* **1** : the equipment or clothing for some purpose ⟨a camping *outfit*⟩ ⟨a sports *outfit*⟩ **2** : a group of persons working together or associated in the same undertaking ⟨soldiers belonging to the same *outfit*⟩

[2]**outfit** *vb* : to furnish with an outfit : EQUIP ⟨*outfit* an expedition⟩ — **out·fit·ter** *n*

out·flank \(ˈ)au̇t-ˈflangk\ *vb* : to get around the flank of ⟨*outflank* the enemy⟩

out·flow \ˈau̇t-ˌflō\ *n* **1** : a flowing out **2** : something that flows out

out·fox \(ˈ)au̇t-ˈfäks\ *vb* : OUTSMART

out·go \ˈau̇t-ˌgō\ *n, pl* **outgoes** : money spent : OUTLAY

out·go·ing \ˈau̇t-ˌgō-ing\ *adj* **1 a** : going out : DEPARTING ⟨*outgoing* tide⟩ **b** : retiring from a position ⟨the *outgoing* governor⟩ **2** : FRIENDLY, RESPONSIVE ⟨an *outgoing* person⟩

out·grow \(ˈ)au̇t-ˈgrō\ *vb* **-grew** \-ˈgrü\; **-grown** \-ˈgrōn\; **-grow·ing** **1** : to grow faster than **2** : to grow too large for ⟨*outgrew* his clothes⟩

out·growth \ˈau̇t-ˌgrōth\ *n* : OFFSHOOT, BY-PRODUCT

out·guess \(ˈ)au̇t-ˈges\ *vb* : ANTICIPATE, OUTWIT

out·house \ˈau̇t-ˌhau̇s\ *n* : OUTBUILDING; *esp* : an outdoor toilet

out·ing \ˈau̇t-ing\ *n* **1** : an excursion usu. with a picnic **2** : a brief stay or trip in the open ⟨took the baby for an *outing*⟩

out·land·er \ˈau̇t-ˌlan-dər\ *n* : FOREIGNER, STRANGER

out·land·ish \(ˈ)au̇t-ˈlan-dish\ *adj* : of foreign appearance or manner : BIZARRE — **out·land·ish·ly** *adv* — **out·land·ish·ness** *n*

out·last \(ˈ)au̇t-ˈlast\ *vb* : to last longer than : SURVIVE

[1]**out·law** \ˈau̇t-ˌlȯ\ *n* **1** : a person excluded from the protection of the law **2** : a lawless person or a fugitive from the law — **outlaw** *adj*

[2]**outlaw** *vb* **1** : to deprive of the protection of law **2** : to make illegal ⟨*outlaw* war⟩ — **out·law·ry** \ˈau̇t-ˌlȯ-rē\ *n*

out·lay \ˈau̇t-ˌlā\ *n* **1** : the act of spending **2** : an amount spent : PAYMENT

out·let \ˈau̇t-ˌlet, -lət\ *n* **1** : a place or opening through which something is let out : EXIT, VENT **2** : a means of release or satisfaction ⟨an *outlet* for her grief⟩ **3** : a place (as in a wall) at which an electrical device can be plugged into the wiring system **4** : a market for a product or an agency through which a product is marketed

[1]**out·line** \ˈau̇t-ˌlīn\ *n* **1** : a line that traces or forms the outer limits of an object or figure and shows its shape **2 a** : a drawing or picture giving only the outlines of something **b** : this method of drawing **3 a** : a brief summary often in numbered divisions **b** : a brief treatment of a subject : DIGEST

2**outline** *vb* **1** : to draw or trace the outline of **2** : to indicate the main features or parts of
out·live \(ˈ)au̇t-ˈliv\ *vb* : to live longer than : OUTLAST
out·look \ˈau̇t-ˌlu̇k\ *n* **1 a** : a place offering a view **b** : a view from a particular place **2** : POINT OF VIEW **3** : the prospect for the future
out·ly·ing \ˈau̇t-ˌlī-ing\ *adj* : remote from a center or main body ⟨an *outlying* suburb⟩
out·ma·neu·ver \ˌau̇t-mə-ˈn(y)ü-vər\ *vb* **1** : to defeat by more skillful maneuvering **2** : to surpass in maneuvering
out·mod·ed \(ˈ)au̇t-ˈmōd-əd\ *adj* : no longer acceptable, usable, or fashionable ⟨*outmoded* beliefs⟩
out·most \ˈau̇t-ˌmōst\ *adj* : OUTERMOST
out·num·ber \(ˈ)au̇t-ˈnəm-bər\ *vb* : to exceed in number ⟨girls *outnumber* boys in the class⟩
out of *prep* **1 a** (1) : from within to the outside of ⟨walked *out of* the room⟩ (2) — used to indicate a change in quality, state, or form ⟨woke *out of* a deep sleep⟩ **b** (1) : beyond the range or limits of ⟨*out of* sight⟩ (2) : from among ⟨one *out of* four survived⟩ **2** : deprived of : WITHOUT ⟨the store is *out of* bread⟩ ⟨cheated him *out of* his savings⟩ **3** : because of : FROM ⟨came *out of* curiosity⟩ **4** — used to indicate the material, basis, or source ⟨built *out of* old lumber⟩
out–of–bounds \ˌau̇t-ə(v)-ˈbau̇n(d)z\ *adv or adj* : outside the prescribed area of play
out–of–date \ˌau̇t-ə(v)-ˈdāt\ *adj* : OUTMODED, OBSOLETE
out–of–door \ˌau̇t-ə(v)-ˈdō(ə)r, -ˈdȯ(ə)r\ *or* **out–of–doors** \-ˈdō(ə)rz, -ˈdȯ(ə)rz\ *adj* : OUTDOOR
out–of–doors *n* : OUTDOORS
out–of–the–way \ˌau̇t-ə(v)-t͟hə-ˈwā\ *adj* **1** : being off the usual paths ⟨an *out-of-the-way* village⟩ **2** : not commonly found or met : UNUSUAL ⟨the store specializes in *out-of-the-way* books⟩
out·pa·tient \ˈau̇t-ˌpā-shənt\ *n* : a patient who visits a hospital for diagnosis or treatment without residing there — **outpatient** *adj*
out·play \(ˈ)au̇t-ˈplā\ *vb* : to play better than
out·point \-ˈpȯint\ *vb* : to win more points than
out·post \ˈau̇t-ˌpōst\ *n* **1** : a guard stationed at a distance from a military force or camp **2** : the position occupied by an outpost **3** : an outlying frontier settlement
out·pour·ing \ˈau̇t-ˌpōr-ing, -ˌpȯr-\ *n* **1** : the act of pouring out **2** : something that pours out or is poured out **3** : OUTBURST
out·put \-ˌpu̇t\ *n* **1** : the amount produced or able to be produced usu. in a stated time by a man, machine, factory, or industry : PRODUCTION ⟨daily *output* of a factory⟩ **2 a** : power or energy delivered by a machine or system **b** : a point at which something (as power, an electronic signal, or data) comes out
output sentence *n* : a sentence that is the result of a transformation combining two or more basic sentences
1**out·rage** \ˈau̇t-ˌrāj\ *n* [from French, literally "going too far", from *outre* "beyond", "in excess", from Latin *ultra*] **1** : a violent or brutal act **2** : INJURY, INSULT **3** : the resentment aroused by injury or insult
2**outrage** *vb* **1** : to subject to violent injury or abuse **2** : to arouse anger or resentment in

ə abut	ər further	a back	ā bake
ä cot, cart	au̇ out	ch chin	e less	ē easy
g gift	i trip	ī life	j joke	ng sing	ō flow
ȯ flaw	ȯi coin	th thin	t͟h this	ü loot
u̇ foot	y yet	yü few	yu̇ furious	zh vision

out·ra·geous \au̇t-ˈrā-jəs\ *adj* : extremely offensive, insulting, or shameful : SHOCKING — **out·ra·geous·ly** *adv* — **out·ra·geous·ness** *n*
out·rank \(ˈ)au̇t-ˈrangk\ *vb* : to rank higher than : exceed in importance
out·rid·er \ˈau̇t-ˌrīd-ər\ *n* : a mounted attendant
out·rig·ger \ˈau̇t-ˌrig-ər\ *n* **1 a** : a projecting frame

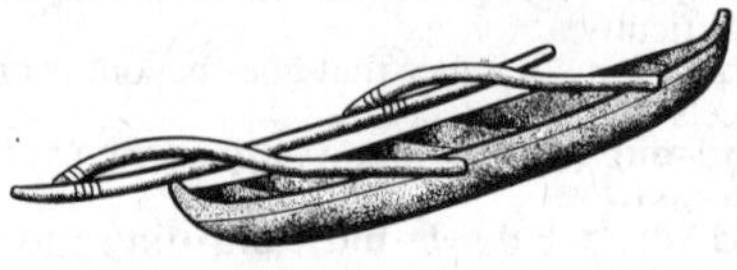

outrigger 1a

attached to the side of a canoe or boat to prevent upsetting **b** : a projecting beam run out from a ship's side to help secure the masts or from a mast to extend a rope or sail **c** : a craft equipped with an outrigger **2** : a projecting frame to support the elevator or tail planes of an airplane or the rotor of a helicopter
1**out·right** \(ˈ)au̇t-ˈrīt\ *adv* **1 a** : in entirety : COMPLETELY ⟨sold *outright*⟩ **b** : without holding back ⟨laughed *outright*⟩ **2** : on the spot : INSTANTANEOUSLY ⟨killed *outright*⟩
2**out·right** \ˈau̇t-ˌrīt\ *adj* **1** : going to the full extent ⟨*outright* persecution⟩ **2** : given without reservation ⟨an *outright* gift⟩
out·run \(ˈ)au̇t-ˈrən\ *vb* **-ran** \-ˈran\; **-run**; **-running** **1** : to run faster than **2** : EXCEED ⟨his needs *outran* his funds⟩
out·sell \-ˈsel\ *vb* **-sold** \-ˈsōld\; **-sell·ing** **1** : to exceed in sales ⟨corn *outsold* beets⟩ **2** : to surpass in selling
out·set \ˈau̇t-ˌset\ *n* : BEGINNING, START
out·shine \(ˈ)au̇t-ˈshīn\ *vb* **-shone** \-ˈshōn\; **-shining** **1** : to shine brighter than **2** : EXCEL, SURPASS
1**out·side** \(ˈ)au̇t-ˈsīd, ˈau̇t-ˌ\ *n* **1** : a place or region beyond an enclosure or boundary **2** : an outer side or surface **3** : the utmost limit or extent ⟨will take a week at the *outside*⟩
2**outside** *adj* **1** : of, relating to, or being on the outside ⟨the *outside* edge⟩ **2** : giving access to the outside ⟨an *outside* door⟩ **3** : coming from outside ⟨*outside* influences⟩ **4** : barely possible : REMOTE ⟨an *outside* chance⟩
3**outside** *adv* : on or to the outside : OUTDOORS ⟨took the dog *outside*⟩
4**outside** *prep* **1** : on or to the outside of ⟨*outside* the house⟩ **2** : beyond the limits of ⟨*outside* the law⟩ **3** : EXCEPT, BESIDES ⟨nobody *outside* a few close friends⟩
outside of *prep* : OUTSIDE
out·sid·er \(ˈ)au̇t-ˈsīd-ər\ *n* : a person who does not belong to a particular group
1**out·size** \ˈau̇t-ˌsīz\ *n* : a size different and esp. larger than the standard
2**outsize** *also* **out·sized** \-ˌsīzd\ *adj* : unusually large or heavy
out·skirts \ˈau̇t-ˌskərts\ *n pl* : the outlying parts of a place or town
out·smart \(ˈ)au̇t-ˈsmärt\ *vb* : OUTWIT
out·spo·ken \au̇t-ˈspō-kən\ *adj* : direct and open in speech or expression : FRANK — **out·spo·ken·ness** \-kən-nəs\ *n*
out·spread \au̇t-ˈspred\ *vb* **-spread**; **-spread·ing** : to spread out : EXTEND — **out·spread** \ˈau̇t-ˌspred\ *adj*
out·stand·ing \au̇t-ˈstan-ding\ *adj* **1 a** : UNPAID

⟨*outstanding* bills⟩ **b :** CONTINUING, UNRESOLVED ⟨problems *outstanding*⟩ **2 :** conspicuous esp. for excellence : DISTINGUISHED, EMINENT ⟨*outstanding* scholar⟩ ***syn*** see PROMINENT ***ant*** commonplace — **out·stand·ing·ly** \au̇t-'stan-ding-lē\ *adv*

out·stay \(')au̇t-'stā\ *vb* **1 :** to stay beyond or longer than ⟨*outstayed* his welcome⟩ **2 :** to surpass in staying power

out·stretch \au̇t-'strech\ *vb* **:** to stretch out : EXTEND

out·strip \au̇t-'strip\ *vb* **1 :** to go faster or farther than ⟨*outstripped* the other runners⟩ **2 a :** EXCEL ⟨*outstripped* all rivals⟩ **b :** EXCEED ⟨demand *outstrips* supply⟩

1**out·ward** \'au̇t-wərd\ *adj* **1 :** moving or directed toward the outside or away from a center ⟨the *outward* journey⟩ **2 :** showing outwardly : EXTERNAL ⟨*outward* signs of fear⟩

2**outward** *or* **out·wards** \-wərdz\ *adv* **:** toward the outside ⟨the city stretches *outward* for miles⟩ ⟨fold it *outward*⟩

out·ward·ly \'au̇t-wərd-lē\ *adv* **:** on the outside : in outward appearance ⟨*outwardly* calm⟩

out·wear \(')au̇t-'wa(ə)r, -'we(ə)r\ *vb* **-wore** \-'wō(ə)r, -'wȯ(ə)r\; **-worn** \-'wōrn, -'wȯrn\; **-wear·ing :** to wear or last longer than ⟨a fabric that *outwears* others⟩

out·weigh \-'wā\ *vb* **:** to exceed in weight, value, or importance

out·wit \au̇t-'wit\ *vb* **:** to get the better of by superior cleverness

1**out·work** \(')au̇t-'wərk\ *vb* **:** to outdo in working

2**out·work** \'au̇t-ˌwərk\ *n* **:** a minor defensive position constructed outside a fortified area

out·worn \(')au̇t-'wōrn, -'wȯrn\ *adj* **:** worn out : OUT-OF-DATE ⟨an *outworn* system⟩

ou·zel \'ü-zəl\ *n* **1 :** a European blackbird **2 :** any of various thrushes or other birds that are related to the ouzel

ova *pl of* OVUM

1**oval** \'ō-vəl\ *adj* [from medieval Latin *ovalis*, from Latin *ovum* "egg"] **1 :** having the shape of an egg **2 :** broadly elliptical

2**oval** *n* **:** an oval figure or object

ova·ry \'ōv-(ə-)rē\ *n, pl* **-ries 1 :** the typically paired female reproductive organ that produces eggs and in vertebrates female sex hormones **2 :** the enlarged rounded part of a flowering plant in which seeds are produced — **ovar·i·an** \ō-'var-ē-ən, -'ver-\ *adj*

ovate \'ō-ˌvāt\ *adj* **:** shaped like an egg esp. with the basal end broader ⟨*ovate* leaves⟩

ova·tion \ō-'vā-shən\ *n* **:** a public expression of praise : enthusiastic applause ⟨received a standing *ovation*⟩

ov·en \'əv-ən\ *n* **:** a heated chamber (as in a stove) for baking, heating, or drying

ov·en·bird \-ˌbərd\ *n* **:** an olive-green American warbler that builds a dome-shaped nest often on the ground

ovenbird
(about 8 in. long)

1**over** \'ō-vər\ *adv* **1 a :** across a barrier or space ⟨fly *over* to London⟩ **b :** in a direction down or forward and down ⟨fell *over*⟩ **c :** across the brim ⟨soup boiled *over*⟩ **d :** so as to bring the underside up ⟨turned his cards *over*⟩ **e :** from one person or side to another ⟨hand it *over*⟩ ⟨won them *over*⟩ **2 :** ACROSS ⟨got his point *over*⟩ **3 a :** beyond a limit ⟨show ran a minute *over*⟩ **b :** in or to excess : EXCESSIVELY ⟨has two cards left *over*⟩ ⟨*over* fond of cake⟩ **4 :** so as to cover the whole surface ⟨windows boarded *over*⟩ **5 a :** THROUGH ⟨read it *over*⟩ **b :** once more : AGAIN ⟨do it *over*⟩

2**over** *prep* **1 :** higher than : ABOVE ⟨towered *over* his mother⟩ **2 a :** above in authority, power, or worth ⟨respected those *over* him⟩ **b :** in front of : ahead of : BEYOND ⟨a big lead *over* the others⟩ **3 :** more than ⟨cost *over* $5⟩ **4 a :** upon esp. so as to cover ⟨laid a blanket *over* the child⟩ **b :** THROUGH ⟨all *over* town⟩ ⟨went *over* his notes⟩ **c :** ALONG ⟨*over* the road⟩ **5 a :** ACROSS ⟨jump *over* a stream⟩ **b :** to or on the other side of ⟨climb *over* the fence⟩ ⟨lives *over* the way⟩ **c :** down from : OFF ⟨fell *over* a cliff⟩ **6 :** DURING ⟨*over* the past 25 years⟩ **7 :** on account of ⟨trouble *over* money⟩ **8 :** by means of ⟨heard the news *over* TV⟩

3**over** *adj* **1 :** having or showing an excess or surplus ⟨the cash was $3 *over* in his books⟩ **2 :** DONE, FINISHED ⟨the day is *over*⟩

over- *prefix* **1 :** so as to exceed or surpass **2 :** excessive : excessively

overabundant	**overextend**	**overproduce**
overambitious	**overfatigued**	**overproduction**
overanxious	**overfeed**	**overprotect**
overbold	**overgenerous**	**overprotective**
overcareful	**overhasty**	**overproud**
overcautious	**overheat**	**overrefined**
overconfidence	**overindulge**	**oversensitive**
overconfident	**overindulgence**	**oversensitiveness**
overconscientious	**overindulgent**	**oversimplification**
overcooked	**overlarge**	**oversimplify**
overcritical	**overlearn**	**oversize**
overcrowd	**overliberal**	**oversized**
overdecorated	**overlong**	**overspecialization**
overeager	**overmodest**	**overspecialize**
overeat	**overnice**	**overstrict**
overemphasis	**overpay**	**oversubtle**
overemphasize	**overpopulate**	**overtax**
overenthusiastic	**overpopulation**	**overtired**
overexcite	**overpraise**	**overtrain**
overexert	**overprice**	**overvalue**
overexertion		**overzealous**

over·abun·dance \ˌō-vər-ə-'bən-dən(t)s\ *n* **:** a supply that is too great : EXCESS, SURFEIT

over·act \ˌō-vər-'akt\ *vb* **:** to exaggerate in acting

over·ac·tive \-'ak-tiv\ *adj* **:** excessively active ⟨an *overactive* thyroid⟩

1**over·age** \ˌō-vər-'āj\ *adj* **:** older than is normal for one's position ⟨*overage* students⟩

2**over·age** \'ōv-(ə-)rij\ *n* **:** SURPLUS, EXCESS

1**over·all** \ˌō-vər-'ȯl\ *adv* **:** as a whole : GENERALLY ⟨we find his work satisfactory, *overall*⟩

2**overall** *adj* **:** including everything ⟨*overall* expenses⟩

over·alls \'ō-vər-ˌȯlz\ *n pl* **:** loose trousers made of strong material usu. with a bib and shoulder straps and worn esp. by workmen

over·arm \'ō-vər-ˌärm\ *adj* **:** done with the arm raised above the shoulder ⟨*overarm* pitching⟩

over·awe \ˌō-vər-'ȯ\ *vb* **:** to restrain or subdue by awe ⟨a mob *overawed* by troops⟩

over·bal·ance \ˌō-vər-'bal-ən(t)s\ *vb* **1 :** to have greater weight or importance than ⟨his good qualities *overbalanced* his shortcomings⟩ **2 :** to lose or cause to lose balance ⟨a boat *overbalanced* by shifting cargo⟩

over·bear \ˌō-vər-'ba(ə)r, -'be(ə)r\ *vb* **-bore** \-'bō(ə)r, -'bȯ(ə)r\; **-borne** \-'bōrn, -'bȯrn\ *also* **-born** \-'bȯrn\; **-bear·ing 1 :** to bear down (as by too much weight) : OVERBURDEN **2 :** to domineer over **3 :** to bear fruit or offspring to excess

over·bear·ing \-'ba(ə)r-ing, -'be(ə)r-\ *adj* : DOMINEERING, ARROGANT — **over·bear·ing·ly** \-ing-lē\ *adv*

over·bid \,ō-vər-'bid\ *vb* **-bid**; **-bid·ding** : to bid too high — **over·bid** \'ō-vər-,bid\ *n*

over·board \'ō-vər-,bōrd, -,bȯrd\ *adv* **1** : over the side of a ship into the water **2** : to extremes ⟨go *overboard* for a new fad⟩

¹**over·bur·den** \,ō-vər-'bərd-ən\ *vb* : to burden too heavily

²**over·bur·den** \'ō-vər-,bərd-ən\ *n* : material overlying a deposit of useful geological materials

¹**over·cast** \,ō-vər-'kast, 'ō-vər-,\ *vb* **-cast**; **-cast·ing** : DARKEN, OVERSHADOW

²**over·cast** \'ō-vər-,kast, ,ō-vər-'\ *adj* : clouded over : GLOOMY ⟨an *overcast* night⟩

over·charge \,ō-vər-'chärj\ *vb* **1** : to charge too much **2** : to fill or load too full ⟨a cannon *overcharged* with powder⟩ — **over·charge** \'ō-vər-,chärj\ *n*

over·cloud \,ō-vər-'klau̇d\ *vb* : to overspread with clouds : DARKEN

over·coat \'ō-vər-,kōt\ *n* : a warm coat worn over indoor clothing

over·come \,ō-vər-'kəm\ *vb* **-came** \-'kām\; **-come**; **-com·ing** **1** : to get the better of : CONQUER ⟨*overcome* an enemy⟩ ⟨*overcome* temptation⟩ **2** : to make helpless or exhausted ⟨was *overcome* by gas⟩

over·do \-'dü\ *vb* **-did** \-'did\; **-done** \-'dən\; **-do·ing** \-'dü-ing\ **1** : to do too much ⟨she *overdoes* it getting ready for a party⟩ **2** : EXAGGERATE ⟨*overdo* praise⟩ **3** : to cook too long ⟨meat that is *overdone*⟩

¹**over·dose** \'ō-vər-,dōs\ *n* : too great a dose — **over·dos·age** \,ō-vər-'dō-sij\ *n*

²**over·dose** \,ō-vər-'dōs\ *vb* : to give an overdose or too many doses to

over·draft \'ō-vər-,draft, -,drȧft\ *n* : an overdrawing of a bank account or the amount overdrawn

over·draw \,ō-vər-'drȯ\ *vb* **-drew** \-'drü\; **-drawn** \-'drȯn\; **-draw·ing** **1** : to draw checks on a bank account for more than the balance in it **2** : EXAGGERATE, OVERSTATE ⟨*overdrew* the dangers in the task⟩

¹**over·dress** \,ō-vər-'dres\ *vb* : to dress too richly for an occasion

²**over·dress** \'ō-vər-,dres\ *n* : a dress worn over another

over·drive \'ō-vər-,drīv\ *n* : an automotive gear mechanism that provides a higher car speed for a specific engine speed than that provided by ordinary high gear

over·due \,ō-vər-'d(y)ü\ *adj* **1 a** : unpaid when due ⟨*overdue* bills⟩ **b** : delayed beyond an appointed time ⟨an *overdue* train⟩ **2** : more than ready ⟨a country *overdue* for governmental reform⟩

over·es·ti·mate \,ō-vər-'es-tə-,māt\ *vb* : to estimate too highly — **over·es·ti·mate** \-mət\ *n* — **over·es·ti·ma·tion** \-,es-tə-'mā-shən\ *n*

over·ex·pose \,ō-vər-ik-'spōz\ *vb* : to expose (as photographic material) for a longer time than is needed or desirable — **over·ex·po·sure** \-'spō-zhər\ *n*

over·fill \,ō-vər-'fil\ *vb* : to fill to overflowing

over·fish \-'fish\ *vb* : to fish to the depletion of a kind of fish or to the detriment of a fishing ground

ə abut	ər further	a back	ā bake
ä cot, cart	au̇ out	ch chin	e less	ē easy
g gift	i trip	ī life	j joke	ng sing	ō flow
ȯ flaw	ȯi coin	th thin	t͟h this	ü loot
u̇ foot	y yet	yü few	yu̇ furious	zh vision

over·flight \'ō-vər-,flīt\ *n* : a flight over an area — **over·fly** \,ō-vər-'flī\ *vb*

¹**over·flow** \,ō-vər-'flō\ *vb* **1** : to cover with or as if with water : INUNDATE **2** : to flow over the brim or top of ⟨the river *overflowed* its banks⟩ **3** : to flow over bounds ⟨the creek *overflows* every spring⟩

²**over·flow** \'ō-vər-,flō\ *n* **1** : a flowing over : FLOOD **2** : something that flows over : SURPLUS **3** : an outlet or receptacle for surplus liquid

over·gar·ment \'ō-vər-,gär-mənt\ *n* : an outer garment

over·graze \,ō-vər-'grāz\ *vb* : to allow animals to graze to the point of damaging the vegetation

over·grow \,ō-vər-'grō\ *vb* **-grew** \-'grü\; **-grown** \-'grōn\; **-grow·ing** **1** : to grow over so as to cover **2** : OUTGROW **3** : to grow excessively — **over·grown** \,ō-vər-'grōn\ *adj* — **over·growth** \'ō-vər-,grōth\ *n*

¹**over·hand** \'ō-vər-,hand\ *adj* **1** : made with the hand brought down from above ⟨an *overhand* blow⟩ **2** : played with the hand downward or inward toward the body ⟨an *overhand* tennis stroke⟩ — **overhand** *adv* — **over·hand·ed** \,ō-vər-'han-dəd\ *adv*

²**overhand** *n* : an overhand stroke (as in tennis)

overhand knot \,ō-vər-,han(d)-\ *n* : a small knot often used to prevent the end of a cord from fraying

¹**over·hang** \'ō-vər-,hang\ *vb* **-hung** \-,həng\; **-hang·ing** \-,hang-ing\ **1** : to jut, project, or be suspended over **2** : to hang over threateningly

²**overhang** *n* : a part that overhangs ⟨the *overhang* of a roof⟩

over·haul \,ō-vər-'hȯl\ *vb* **1** : to make thorough repairs on ⟨*overhaul* an engine⟩ **2** : OVERTAKE ⟨the frigate was *overhauled* by a gunboat⟩ — **overhaul** \'ō-vər-,hȯl\ *n*

¹**over·head** \,ō-vər-'hed\ *adv* : above one's head : ALOFT ⟨geese flying *overhead*⟩

²**over·head** \'ō-vər-,hed\ *adj* **1** : operating or lying above ⟨an *overhead* door⟩ **2** : of or relating to business expense

³**over·head** \'ō-vər-,hed\ *n* **1** : general business expenses (as rent, heat, or lighting) **2** : a stroke in a racket game made above head height : SMASH

over·hear \,ō-vər-'hi(ə)r\ *vb* **-heard** \-'hərd\; **-hear·ing** \-'hi(ə)r-ing\ : to hear without the speaker's knowledge or intention

over·joy \,ō-vər-'jȯi\ *vb* : to fill with great joy

over·kill \,ō-vər-'kil\ *vb* : to obliterate a target with more nuclear force than required — **over·kill** \'ō-vər-,kil\ *n*

over·land \'ō-vər-,land, -lənd\ *adv or adj* : by, on, or across land

over·lap \,ō-vər-'lap\ *vb* : to lap over — **over·lap** \'ō-vər-,lap\ *n*

¹**over·lay** \,ō-vər-'lā\ *vb* **-laid** \-'lād\; **-lay·ing** **1** : to lay or spread over or across **2** : OVERLIE

²**over·lay** \'ō-vər-,lā\ *n* : something (as a veneer on wood) that is overlaid

over·leap \,ō-vər-'lēp\ *vb* **1** : to leap over or across ⟨*overleap* a ditch⟩ **2** : to defeat oneself by going too far

over·lie \,ō-vər-'lī\ *vb* **-lay** \-'lā\; **-lain** \-'lān\; **-ly·ing** \-'lī-ing\ : to lie over or upon

¹**over·load** \,ō-vər-'lōd\ *vb* : to load to excess

²**over·load** \'ō-vər-,lōd\ *n* **1** : an excessive load **2** : the amount that is beyond the proper load

over·look \,ō-vər-'lu̇k\ *vb* **1** : to look over : INSPECT **2 a** : to look down upon from above **b** : to provide a view of from above ⟨the mountain *overlooks* a lake⟩ **3 a** : to fail to see : MISS **b** : to pass over : IGNORE **c** : EXCUSE ⟨*overlook* a beginner's mistakes⟩ **4** : to watch over : SUPERVISE

over·lord \ˈō-vər-ˌlȯrd\ *n* **1** : a lord who has supremacy over other lords **2** : an absolute or supreme ruler

over·ly \ˈō-vər-lē\ *adv* : EXCESSIVELY, TOO

over·mas·ter \ˌō-vər-ˈmas-tər\ *vb* : OVERPOWER, SUBDUE

over·match \ˌō-vər-ˈmach\ *vb* **1** : to be more than a match for : DEFEAT ⟨our troops *overmatched* the enemy⟩ **2** : to match with a superior opponent ⟨a boxer who was badly *overmatched*⟩

[1]**over·much** \ˌō-vər-ˈməch\ *adj or adv* : too much

[2]**over·much** \ˈō-vər-ˌməch\ *n* : too great an amount : EXCESS

[1]**over·night** \ˌō-vər-ˈnīt\ *adv* **1** : on or during the evening or night ⟨stayed away *overnight*⟩ **2** : SUDDENLY ⟨became famous *overnight*⟩

[2]**overnight** *adj* **1** : of, lasting, or staying the night ⟨*overnight* trip⟩ ⟨*overnight* guests⟩ **2** : for use on short trips ⟨an *overnight* bag⟩

[1]**over·pass** \ˌō-vər-ˈpas\ *vb* **1** : to pass across, over, or beyond **2** : SURPASS **3** : DISREGARD, IGNORE

[2]**over·pass** \ˈō-vər-ˌpas\ *n* **1** : a crossing (as of two highways or of a highway and railroad) at different levels usu. by means of a bridge **2** : the upper level of an overpass

over·play \ˌō-vər-ˈplā\ *vb* **1** : EXAGGERATE, OVEREMPHASIZE **2** : to rely too much on the strength of ⟨*overplayed* his hand⟩

over·pop·u·late \-ˈpäp-yə-ˌlāt\ *vb* : to populate too densely

over·pop·u·la·tion \-ˌpäp-yə-ˈlā-shən\ *n* : the condition of being overpopulated; *also* : an excess of population

over·pow·er \ˌō-vər-ˈpau̇(-ə)r\ *vb* **1** : to overcome by superior force : DEFEAT **2** : OVERWHELM ⟨*overpowered* by hunger⟩ — **over·pow·er·ing·ly** \-ˈpau̇r-ing-lē\ *adv*

over·print \ˌō-vər-ˈprint\ *vb* : to print over with something additional — **over·print** \ˈō-vər-ˌprint\ *n*

over·pro·duc·tion \-prə-ˈdək-shən\ *n* : excessive production esp. to the point that supply exceeds demand

over·rate \ˌō-və(r)-ˈrāt\ *vb* : to rate too highly ⟨a book that was *overrated*⟩

over·reach \ˌō-və(r)-ˈrēch\ *vb* **1** : to reach above or beyond : OVERTOP **2** : to defeat oneself by seeking to do or gain too much **3** : OUTWIT, TRICK **4** : to go to excess — **over·reach·er** *n*

over·ride \ˌō-və(r)-ˈrīd\ *vb* **-rode** \-ˈrōd\; **-rid·den** \-ˈrid-ən\; **-rid·ing** \-ˈrīd-ing\ **1 a** : to ride over or across **b** : TRAMPLE **2** : to ride a horse too much or too hard **3** : to set aside : annul by a contrary decision ⟨Congress *overrode* the president's veto⟩

over·ripe \ˌō-və(r)-ˈrīp\ *adj* : passed beyond maturity or ripeness toward decay

over·rule \ˌō-və(r)-ˈrül\ *vb* **1** : to decide against ⟨the chairman *overruled* the suggestion⟩ **2** : to reverse or set aside a decision or ruling made by a lesser authority

[1]**over·run** \ˌō-və(r)-ˈrən\ *vb* **-ran** \-ˈran\; **-run**; **-run·ning** **1** : to run over : OVERSPREAD ⟨a garden *overrun* with weeds⟩ **2** : to trample down ⟨the escaped cattle *overran* the field of wheat⟩ **3** : INFEST ⟨rats *overran* the ship⟩ **4** : to win over and occupy the positions of ⟨the outpost was *overrun* by the enemy⟩ **5** : to run further than : go beyond : EXCEED ⟨*overrun* first base⟩ ⟨the program *overran* the time allowed⟩

[2]**over·run** \ˈō-və(r)-ˌrən\ *n* **1** : an act or instance of overrunning **2** : the amount by which something overruns

over·sea \ˌō-vər-ˈsē, ˈō-vər-ˌ\ *adj or adv* : OVERSEAS

over·seas \-ˈsēz, -ˌsēz\ *adv* : beyond or across the sea : ABROAD — **overseas** *adj*

over·see \ˌō-vər-ˈsē\ *vb* **-saw** \-ˈsȯ\; **-seen** \-ˈsēn\; **-see·ing** **1** : SURVEY, WATCH **2 a** : INSPECT, EXAMINE **b** : SUPERINTEND, SUPERVISE — **over·seer** \ˈō-vər-ˌsi(ə)r, -ˌsē-ər\ *n*

over·sell \ˌō-vər-ˈsel\ *vb* **-sold** \-ˈsōld\; **-sell·ing** : to sell too much to or of

over·shad·ow \-ˈshad-ō\ *vb* **1** : to cast a shadow over : DARKEN **2** : to exceed in importance : OUTWEIGH ⟨the win *overshadowed* his injury⟩

over·shoe \ˈō-vər-ˌshü\ *n* : a protective outer shoe; *esp* : GALOSH

over·shoot \ˌō-vər-ˈshüt\ *vb* **-shot** \-ˈshät\; **-shoot·ing** **1 a** : to pass swiftly beyond ⟨the train *overshot* the platform⟩ **b** : to miss by going beyond ⟨the plane *overshot* the field⟩ **2** : to shoot over or beyond ⟨*overshot* his target⟩

over·shot \ˈō-vər-ˌshät\ *adj* **1** : having the upper jaw extending beyond the lower **2** : moved by water shooting over from above ⟨an *overshot* waterwheel⟩

over·sight \ˈō-vər-ˌsīt\ *n* **1** : the act or duty of overseeing : SUPERVISION ⟨have the *oversight* of a job⟩ **2** : an omission or error resulting from carelessness or haste

over·skirt \-ˌskərt\ *n* : a skirt worn over another skirt

over·sleep \ˌō-vər-ˈslēp\ *vb* **-slept** \-ˈslept\; **-sleep·ing** : to sleep beyond the usual time or beyond the time set for getting up

over·spread \-ˈspred\ *vb* **-spread**; **-spread·ing** : to spread over or above ⟨branches *overspreading* a garden path⟩

over·state \ˌō-vər-ˈstāt\ *vb* : to state in too strong terms : EXAGGERATE — **over·state·ment** \-mənt\ *n*

over·stay \-ˈstā\ *vb* : to stay beyond the time or the limits of ⟨*overstayed* his leave⟩

over·step \ˌō-vər-ˈstep\ *vb* : to step over or beyond : EXCEED ⟨*overstepped* his authority⟩

over·stock \ˌō-vər-ˈstäk\ *vb* : to stock beyond requirements or facilities ⟨*overstock* on canned goods⟩ — **over·stock** \ˈō-vər-ˌstäk\ *n*

over·strung \ˌō-vər-ˈstrəng\ *adj* : too highly strung : too sensitive

over·stuffed \-ˈstəft\ **1** : stuffed too full **2** : covered completely and deeply with upholstery ⟨an *overstuffed* chair⟩

over·sub·scribe \ˌō-vər-səb-ˈskrīb\ *vb* : to subscribe for more of than is available, asked for, or offered for sale ⟨*oversubscribe* a stock issue⟩ — **over·sub·scrip·tion** \-ˈskrip-shən\ *n*

over·sup·ply \ˌō-vər-sə-ˈplī\ *n* : an excessive supply : SURPLUS

overt \ō-ˈvərt, ˈō-ˌ\ *adj* : open to view : not secret — **overt·ly** *adv*

over·take \ˌō-vər-ˈtāk\ *vb* **-took** \-ˈtu̇k\; **-tak·en** \-ˈtā-kən\; **-tak·ing** **1 a** : to catch up with **b** : to catch up with and pass by **2** : to come upon suddenly ⟨a blizzard *overtook* the hunting party⟩

over·throw \ˌō-vər-ˈthrō\ *vb* **-threw** \-ˈthrü\; **-thrown** \-ˈthrōn\; **-throw·ing** **1** : OVERTURN, UPSET ⟨lawn chairs *overthrown* by the gale⟩ **2** : to bring down : DEFEAT ⟨a government *overthrown* by rebels⟩ — **over·throw** \ˈō-vər-ˌthrō\ *n*

over·time \ˈō-vər-ˌtīm\ *n* **1** : time in excess of a set limit; *esp* : working time in excess of a standard day or week **2** : the wage paid for overtime work — **overtime** *adv or adj*

over·tone \ˈō-vər-ˌtōn\ *n* **1** : one of the higher tones that with the fundamental comprise a musical tone

2 : a secondary effect, quality, or meaning : SUGGESTION ⟨the words carried an *overtone* of menace⟩

over·top \ˌō-vər-ˈtäp\ *vb* **1** : to rise above the top of : surpass in height **2** : SURPASS

over·ture \ˈō-vər-ˌchu̇r, -chər\ *n* [from French *ouverture*, literally "opening", from Latin *apertura*] **1** : an opening offer : a first proposal ⟨the enemy made *overtures* for peace⟩ **2 a** : an orchestral introduction to an oratorio, opera, or dramatic work **b** : a composition in the style of an overture for concert performance

over·turn \ˌō-vər-ˈtərn\ *vb* **1** : to turn over or upside down **2** : OVERTHROW, DESTROY — **over·turn** \ˈō-vər-ˌtərn\ *n*

1**over·use** \ˌō-vər-ˈyüz\ *vb* : to use too much ⟨an *overused* phrase⟩

2**over·use** \-ˈyüs\ *n* : too much use

over·view \ˈō-vər-ˌvyü\ *n* : an overall view

over·ween·ing \ˌō-vər-ˈwē-ning\ *adj* **1** : ARROGANT, CONCEITED **2** : EXAGGERATED, IMMODERATE — **over·ween·ing·ly** \-ning-lē\ *adv*

over·weigh \ˌō-vər-ˈwā\ *vb* : to exceed in weight : OVERBALANCE

1**over·weight** \ˈō-vər-ˌwāt, ˌō-vər-ˈ\ *n* **1** : weight above what is required or allowed **2** : bodily weight in excess of what is held normal for one's age, height, and build — **over·weight** \ˌō-vər-ˈ\ *adj*

2**over·weight** \ˌō-vər-ˈwāt\ *vb* : OVERLOAD

over·whelm \ˌō-vər-ˈhwelm\ *vb* **1** : to cover over completely : SUBMERGE ⟨a boat *overwhelmed* by a wave⟩ **2** : to overcome completely : CRUSH ⟨*overwhelmed* by grief⟩ — **over·whelm·ing·ly** \-ˈhwel-ming-lē\ *adv*

over·wind \-ˈwīnd\ *vb* **-wound** \-ˈwau̇nd\; **-winding** : to wind too much

over·work \ˌō-vər-ˈwərk\ *vb* **1** : to work or cause to work too hard or long ⟨*overworked* his horses⟩ **2** : to make excessive use of ⟨*overworked* phrases⟩ — **overwork** *n*

over·wrought \ˌō-və(r)-ˈrȯt\ *adj* **1** : extremely excited : AGITATED ⟨*overwrought* feelings⟩ **2** : decorated to excess : OVERDONE

ovi·duct \ˈō-və-ˌdəkt\ *n* : a tube for the passage of eggs from the ovary of an animal

ovip·a·rous \ō-ˈvip-(ə-)rəs\ *adj* : producing eggs that develop and hatch outside the maternal body

ovi·pos·it \ˈō-və-ˌpäz-ət\ *vb* : to lay eggs — used esp. of insects — **ovi·po·si·tion** \ˌō-və-pə-ˈzish-ən\ *n*

ovi·pos·i·tor \ˈō-və-ˌpäz-ət-ər\ *n* : a specialized organ (as of an insect) for depositing eggs

ovoid \ˈō-ˌvȯid\ *or* **ovoi·dal** \ō-ˈvȯid-əl\ *adj* : OVATE — **ovoid** *n*

ov·u·late \ˈäv-yə-ˌlāt, ˈō-vyə-\ *vb* : to produce eggs or discharge them from an ovary — **ov·u·la·tion** \ˌäv-yə-ˈlā-shən, ˌō-vyə-\ *n*

ovule \ˈō-vyül\ *n* **1** : an outgrowth of the ovary of a seed plant that after fertilization develops into a seed **2** : a small egg; *esp* : one in an early stage of growth — **ov·u·lar** \ˈäv-yə-lər, ˈō-vyə-\ *adj*

ovum \ˈō-vəm\ *n, pl* **ova** \-və\ : EGG 1c

owe \ˈō\ *vb* **1** : to have an emotion or attitude toward someone or something : BEAR ⟨*owes* the boss a grudge⟩ **2 a** : to be under obligation to pay or repay ⟨*owes* me $5⟩ **b** : to be indebted to ⟨*owes* the grocer for supplies⟩ **c** : to be in debt ⟨*owes* for his house⟩

ow·ing \ˈō-ing\ *adj* : due to be paid : OWED ⟨have bills *owing*⟩ ⟨claim no more than is *owing*⟩

owing to *prep* : because of ⟨absent *owing to* illness⟩

owl \ˈau̇l\ *n* : any of an order of birds of prey with large head and eyes, short hooked bill, and strong talons and more or less active at night

owl (up to 10 in. long)

owl·et \ˈau̇-lət\ *n* : a young or small owl

owl·ish \ˈau̇-lish\ *adj* : resembling or suggesting an owl (as in solemnity or appearance of wisdom) — **owl·ish·ly** *adv* — **owl·ish·ness** *n*

1**own** \ˈōn\ *adj* : belonging to oneself or itself ⟨has his *own* room⟩

2**own** *vb* **1** : to have or hold as property : POSSESS **2** : ACKNOWLEDGE, ADMIT ⟨*own* a debt⟩ **3** : CONFESS ⟨*owned* to being scared⟩ ⟨if you break a window, *own* up⟩ — **own·er** \ˈō-nər\ *n* — **own·er·ship** \-ˌship\ *n*

3**own** *pron* : one or ones belonging to oneself — used after a possessive ⟨dog of his *own*⟩ — **on one's own** : without outside help or control ⟨he's *on his own* now⟩ ⟨did the whole thing *on his own*⟩

ox \ˈäks\ *n, pl* **ox·en** \ˈäk-sən\ *also* **ox** **1** : an individual of the common large domestic cattle kept for milk, draft, and meat; *esp* : an adult castrated male **2** : any of the larger hollow-horned cud-chewing mammals (as the domestic ox, buffaloes, and the yak) with even-toed hoofs as distinguished from similar and related but smaller forms (as sheep and goats)

ox·a·late \ˈäk-sə-ˌlāt\ *n* : a salt or ester of oxalic acid

ox·al·ic acid \(ˌ)äk-ˌsal-ik-\ *n* : a poisonous strong organic acid used esp. as a bleaching or cleaning agent and in making dyes

ox·blood \ˈäks-ˌbləd\ *n* : a moderate reddish brown

ox·bow \ˈäks-ˌbō\ *n* **1** : a U-shaped collar worn by a draft ox **2** : a U-shaped bend in a river — **oxbow** *adj*

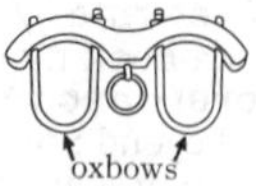

oxbows

ox·cart \ˈäks-ˌkärt\ *n* : a cart drawn by oxen

ox·eye \ˈäk-ˌsī\ *n* : any of several plants related to the asters and having heads with both disk and ray flowers

oxeye daisy *n* : DAISY 1b

ox·ford \ˈäks-fərd\ *n* : a low shoe laced over the instep

ox·heart \ˈäks-ˌhärt\ *n* : any of various large sweet cherries

ox·i·da·tion \ˌäk-sə-ˈdā-shən\ *n* **1** : the process of oxidizing **2** : the state or result of being oxidized — **ox·i·da·tive** \ˈäk-sə-ˌdāt-iv\ *adj*

ox·ide \ˈäk-ˌsīd\ *n* : a compound of oxygen with an element or radical

ox·i·dize \ˈäk-sə-ˌdīz\ *vb* **1** : to combine with oxygen **2** : to dehydrogenate esp. by the action of oxygen **3** : to remove one or more electrons from (an atom, ion, or molecule) **4** : to become oxidized — **ox·i·diz·er** *n*

oxy·acet·y·lene \ˌäk-sē-ə-ˈset-ə-lən, -ˌlēn\ *adj* : of, relating to, or utilizing a mixture of oxygen and acetylene ⟨*oxyacetylene* torch⟩

ox·y·gen \ˈäk-si-jən\ *n* [from French *oxygène*, from Greek *oxys* "sour", "acid" and *geinesthai* "to produce"; so called because it was once thought to be an essential element of all acids] : an element that is a colorless tasteless odorless gas, forms about 21 percent of the atmosphere, is capable of combining with almost all elements, is active in physiological processes, and is essential to combustion — see ELEMENT table

ox·y·gen·ate \'äk-si-jə-ˌnāt, äk-'sij-ə-\ *vb* : to impregnate, combine, or supply with oxygen — **ox·y·gen·a·tion** \ˌäk-si-jə-'nā-shən, (ˌ)äk-ˌsij-ə-\ *n*

oxygen debt *n* : a deficiency of oxygen that develops in the body during periods of intense activity and must be made good when the body returns to rest

oxygen mask *n* : a device worn over the nose and mouth through which oxygen is supplied from a storage tank

oxygen tent *n* : a canopy which can be placed over a bedfast person and within which a flow of oxygen can be maintained

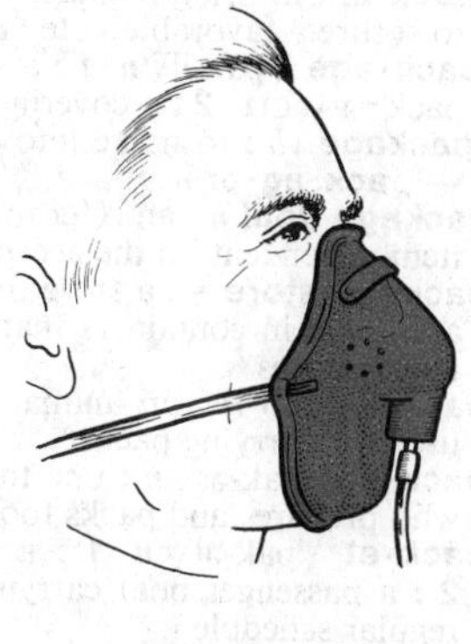

oxygen mask

oxy·he·mo·glo·bin \ˌäk-si-'hē-mə-ˌglō-bən\ *n* : a compound of hemoglobin with oxygen that is the chief means of transportation of oxygen from the air (as in the lungs) by way of the blood to the tissues

oyez \ō-'yā, -'yes, -'yez\ *imperative verb* — used by a court or public crier to gain attention before a proclamation

oys·ter \'ȯi-stər\ *n* : any of various marine mollusks that include important edible shellfish and have a rough irregular shell made up of two hinged parts and closed by a single muscle

oyster bed *n* : a place where oysters grow or are cultivated

oz *abbr* [from Italian *onza*, from Latin *uncia*; see OUNCE] ounce

ozone \'ō-ˌzōn\ *n* [from German *ozon*, from Greek *ozōn*, present participle of *ozein* "to smell"; so called from its sharp odor] **1** : a form of oxygen that is a faintly blue irritating gas with a pungent odor, is generated usu. in dilute form by a silent electric discharge in oxygen or air, and is used esp. in disinfection and deodorization and in oxidation and bleaching **2** : pure and refreshing air

ozo·no·sphere \ō-'zō-nə-ˌsfi(ə)r\ *n* : an atmospheric layer at heights of approximately 20 to 30 miles characterized by high ozone content

O

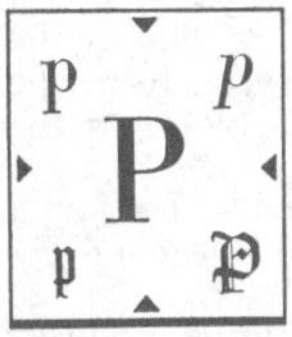

p \'pē\ *n, often cap* : the 16th letter of the English alphabet
p *abbr* **1** page **2** post **3** piano
P *abbr* **1** pedal **2** pressure
pa \'pä, 'pȯ\ *n* : FATHER
Pa *abbr* Pennsylvania
PA *abbr* **1** Pennsylvania **2** public address
pab·u·lum \'pab-yə-ləm\ *n* : FOOD; *esp* : a suspension or solution of nutrients suitable for absorption
Pac *abbr* Pacific
1**pace** \'pās\ *n* **1** : rate of moving or progressing esp. on foot **2** : a manner of going on foot : GAIT; *esp* : a fast 2-beat gait of a horse in which legs on the same side move together **3** : a single step or a measure based on the length of a human step
2**pace** *vb* **1** : to walk with slow measured steps **2** : to go or cover at a pace ⟨*pace* the floor⟩ **3** : to measure by paces **4** : to set or regulate the pace of — **pac·er** *n*
pach·y·derm \'pak-i-ˌdərm\ *n* [from Greek *pachydermos*, "thick-skinned"] : any of various thick-skinned hoofed mammals (as an elephant or a rhinoceros)
pa·cif·ic \pə-'sif-ik\ *adj* **1** : making or suitable to make peace ⟨*pacific* words to end a quarrel⟩ **2** : having a mild and calm nature : PEACEABLE ⟨a quiet *pacific* people⟩ — **pa·cif·i·cal·ly** \-i-k(ə-)lē\ *adv*
Pacific herring *n* : a herring of the northern Pacific ocean
pac·i·fi·er \'pas-ə-ˌfī(-ə)r\ *n* **1** : one that pacifies **2** : a usu. nipple-shaped device for babies to suck or bite upon
pac·i·fism \'pas-ə-ˌfiz-əm\ *n* : opposition to war or violence as a means of settling disputes — **pac·i·fist** \-fəst\ *n*
pac·i·fy \'pas-ə-ˌfī\ *vb* **-fied; -fy·ing** **1** : to ease the anger, agitation, or distress of : SOOTHE ⟨*pacify* a crying child⟩ **2** : to restore to a peaceful state : SETTLE, SUBDUE ⟨*pacify* a country⟩ — **pac·i·fi·ca·tion** \ˌpas-ə-fə-'kā-shən\ *n*

syn PACIFY, MOLLIFY, APPEASE, PLACATE can mean to calm the feelings of. PACIFY suggests the quieting of persons in a state of agitation or hostility; MOLLIFY suggests a soothing of ruffled or hurt feelings; APPEASE suggests quieting anger or averting threats by making concessions often to unreasonable demands; PLACATE suggests changing resentment or bitterness to goodwill ***ant*** anger

1**pack** \'pak\ *n* **1 a** : a bundle arranged for carrying esp. on the back of a man or animal **b** : a group or pile of related objects ⟨a *pack* of cards⟩ **2** : a method of packing ⟨vacuum *pack*⟩ **3** : a group of like persons or animals ⟨a *pack* of thieves⟩ ⟨a wolf *pack*⟩ **4** : a tight mass or group; *esp* : a mass of ice chunks floating on the sea **5** : absorbent material (as gauze pads) used to make compresses, to plug body cavities in order to stop bleeding, and to apply medication ⟨hot *packs* for an infected arm⟩ **6** : a cosmetic paste for the face — **pack** *adj*
2**pack** *vb* **1 a** : to place articles in (as for transportation or storage) ⟨*pack* a suitcase⟩ **b** : to place closely and securely in a container or bundle ⟨*pack* goods⟩ **2 a** : to crowd in : CRAM ⟨people *packed* the hall⟩ **b** : to form into a pack or packs ⟨the ice is *packing* in the gorge⟩ **3** : to fill or cover so as to prevent passage (as of air or steam) ⟨*pack* a joint in a pipe⟩ **4** : to send or go away without ceremony ⟨*pack* a boy off to school⟩ **5** : to transport in packs **6** : CARRY ⟨*pack* a gun⟩ **7** : to process foodstuffs for sale
3**pack** *vb* : to bring together or make up fraudulently to secure a favorable vote ⟨*pack* a jury⟩
1**pack·age** \'pak-ij\ *n* **1** : a small or moderate-sized pack : PARCEL **2** : a covering wrapper or container
2**package** *vb* : to make into or enclose in a package — **pack·ag·er** *n*
package deal *n* : an offer making acceptance of one item dependent on the acceptance of another
package store *n* : a store that sells alcoholic beverages only in containers that may not be opened on the premises
pack animal *n* : an animal (as a horse or donkey) used for carrying packs
pack·er \'pak-ər\ *n* : one that packs; *esp* : a dealer who prepares and packs foods for the market
pack·et \'pak-ət\ *n* **1** : a small bundle or parcel **2** : a passenger boat carrying mail and cargo on a regular schedule
pack·ing·house \'pak-ing-ˌhau̇s\ *n* : an establishment for processing and packing foodstuffs and esp. meat
pack rat *n* : WOOD RAT; *esp* : a large bushy-tailed rodent of the Rocky Mountain area that hoards food and miscellaneous objects

pack rat
(about 15 in. long)

pack·sad·dle \'pak-ˌsad-əl\ *n* : a saddle that supports the load on the back of a pack animal
pack·thread \-ˌthred\ *n* : strong thread or twine used esp. for sewing or tying packs or parcels
pact \'pakt\ *n* : AGREEMENT; *esp* : an international treaty
1**pad** \'pad\ *n* **1 a** : a cushioned part or thing : CUSHION **b** : a piece of material that holds ink for inking a rubber stamp **2 a** : the hairy foot of some mammals (as a fox or hare) **b** : the cushioned thickening of the underside of the toes of some mammals **3** : a floating leaf of a water plant **4** : TABLET 1b **5** : LAUNCHING PAD **6** *slang* **a** : BED **b** : living quarters : HOME
2**pad** *vb* **pad·ded; pad·ding** **1** : to furnish with a pad or padding **2** : to expand with unnecessary or trivial matter ⟨*pad* a speech⟩
3**pad** *vb* **pad·ded; pad·ding** **1** : to go on foot **2** : to move along with a muffled step
pad·ding \'pad-ing\ *n* : material used to pad
1**pad·dle** \'pad-əl\ *n* **1 a** : an implement with a flat blade to propel and steer a small craft (as a canoe) **b** : something (as the flipper of a seal) suggesting a paddle in appearance or action **2 a** : an implement used for stirring, mixing, or beating **b** : a short bat with a broad flat blade used to hit the ball esp. in table tennis **3** : one of the broad boards at the outer rim of a paddle wheel or waterwheel
2**paddle** *vb* **pad·dled; pad·dling** \'pad-(ə-)ling\ **1** : to move or propel by or as if by a paddle **2** : to beat, stir, or punish by or as if by a paddle

ə abut	ər further	a back	ā bake	
ä cot, cart	au̇ out	ch chin	e less	ē easy
g gift	i trip	ī life	j joke	ng sing	ō flow
ȯ flaw	ȯi coin	th thin	t͟h this	ü loot
u̇ foot	y yet	yü few	yu̇ furious	zh vision

[3]**paddle** *vb* **pad·dled**; **pad·dling** \'pad-(ə-)ling\ : to move the hands or feet about in shallow water

pad·dle·fish \'pad-əl-ˌfish\ *n* : a fish of the Mississippi valley about four feet long with a paddle-shaped snout

paddle wheel *n* : a wheel with boards around its circumference used to propel a vessel

pad·dock \'pad-ək\ *n* : an enclosed area for pasturing or exercising animals; *esp* : an enclosure where racehorses are saddled and paraded

pad·dy \'pad-ē\ *n, pl* **paddies** **1** : RICE; *esp* : rice when still growing or when first cut **2** : wet land in which rice is grown

pad·dy wagon \'pad-ē-\ *n* : PATROL WAGON

pad·lock \'pad-ˌläk\ *n* : a removable lock with a hinged bow-shaped piece that snaps in or out of a catch — **padlock** *vb*

pa·dre \'päd-(ˌ)rā, -rē\ *n* [from Spanish, Portuguese, and Italian, literally "father", from Latin *pater*] **1** : PRIEST **2** : a military chaplain

pae·an \'pē-ən\ *n* : a song of joy, praise, or triumph

pa·gan \'pā-gən\ *n* **1** : HEATHEN 1 **2** : an irreligious person — **pagan** *adj* — **pa·gan·ism** \-gə-ˌniz-əm\ *n*

[1]**page** \'pāj\ *n* **1** : a youth being trained for knighthood and in the service of a knight **2** : a youth attending a person of rank **3** : a person employed (as by a hotel) esp. to deliver messages or perform personal services for patrons

[2]**page** *vb* **1** : to serve as a page **2** : to summon by calling out the name of

[3]**page** *n* **1 a** : one side of a printed or written leaf **b** : the entire leaf ⟨a *page* torn from a book⟩ **c** : the matter printed or written on a page ⟨set several *pages* of type⟩ **2 a** : a written record ⟨the *pages* of history⟩ **b** : an event or circumstance worth recording ⟨an exciting *page* in his life⟩

[4]**page** *vb* : to number or mark the pages of

pag·eant \'paj-ənt\ *n* **1** : an elaborate exhibition or spectacle **2** : an entertainment consisting of scenes based on history or legend ⟨a Christmas *pageant*⟩

pag·eant·ry \'paj-ən-trē\ *n, pl* **-ries** **1** : the presentation of pageants : PAGEANTS **2** : splendid display : POMP

pa·go·da \pə-'gōd-ə\ *n* : a Far Eastern tower of several stories erected as a temple or memorial

pagoda

paid *past of* PAY

pail \'pāl\ *n* **1** : a usu. cylindrical container with a handle : BUCKET **2** : PAILFUL

pail·ful \-ˌfu̇l\ *n, pl* **pailfuls** \-ˌfu̇lz\ *or* **pails·ful** \'pālz-ˌfu̇l\ : the quantity held by a pail

[1]**pain** \'pān\ *n* **1** : PUNISHMENT ⟨under *pain* of death⟩ **2 a** : physical suffering associated with disease, injury, or other bodily disorder ⟨a *pain* in his back⟩ ⟨in constant *pain*⟩ **b** : a basic bodily sensation caused by a harmful stimulus, characterized by physical discomfort (as pricking, throbbing, or aching), and typically leading to attempts to escape its source **3** : mental distress : GRIEF **4** *pl* : the throes of childbirth **5** *pl* : great care or effort ⟨took *pains* with his work⟩ — **pain·less** \-ləs\ *adj* — **pain·less·ly** *adv* — **pain·less·ness** *n*

[2]**pain** *vb* **1** : to cause pain in or to : HURT **2** : to give or experience pain

pain·ful \'pān-fəl\ *adj* **1** : feeling or giving pain **2** : PAINSTAKING — **pain·ful·ly** \-fə-lē\ *adv* — **pain·ful·ness** *n*

pain–kill·er \-ˌkil-ər\ *n* : something (as a drug) that relieves pain — **pain–kill·ing** *adj*

pains·tak·ing \'pānz-ˌtā-king\ *adj* : marked by diligent care and effort — **pains·tak·ing·ly** \-king-lē\ *adv*

[1]**paint** \'pānt\ *vb* **1** : to apply paint or a covering or coloring substance to ⟨*paint* a wall⟩ ⟨*paint* the wound with iodine⟩ **2 a** : to represent in lines and colors on a surface by applying pigments ⟨*paint* a picture⟩ **b** : to describe vividly ⟨*paint* a scene in words⟩ **3** : to practice the art of painting

[2]**paint** *n* **1** : MAKEUP; *esp* : a cosmetic to add color **2 a** : a mixture of a pigment and a suitable liquid to form a thin coating when spread on a surface **b** : an applied coating of paint ⟨scrape old *paint* from woodwork⟩

paint·brush \'pānt-ˌbrəsh\ *n* **1** : a brush for applying paint **2** : any of several plants with showy tufted flowers

painted bunting *n* : a brightly colored finch of the southern U.S.

painted turtle *n* : any of several common freshwater turtles that are found chiefly in the eastern U.S. and have a greenish black upper shell with yellow bands and red markings and a yellow lower shell

[1]**paint·er** \'pānt-ər\ *n* : one that paints; *esp* : an artist who paints — **paint·er·ly** \-lē\ *adj*

[2]**pain·ter** \'pānt-ər\ *n* : a line used for securing or towing a boat

[3]**pain·ter** *n, dial* : COUGAR

paint·ing \'pānt-ing\ *n* **1** : a painted work of art **2** : the art or occupation of painting

[1]**pair** \'pa(ə)r, 'pe(ə)r\ *n, pl* **pairs** *also* **pair** **1** : two corresponding things naturally matched or intended to be used together ⟨a *pair* of hands⟩ ⟨a *pair* of gloves⟩ **2** : a thing having two connected corresponding parts ⟨a *pair* of scissors⟩ **3** : a set of two (as two mated animals or two persons in love, engaged, or married) **4** : two individuals (as in a legislature) who hold opposed opinions and agree not to vote on an issue ***syn*** see COUPLE

[2]**pair** *vb* **1** : to make a pair of or arrange in pairs ⟨*paired* her guests⟩ **2** : to form a pair or pairs ⟨*paired* off for the next dance⟩

pais·ley \'pāz-lē\ *adj, often cap* : made with colorful curved abstract figures ⟨a *paisley* shawl⟩ — **paisley** *n*

Pai·ute \'pī-ˌ(y)üt\ *n* : a member of an Amerindian people of Utah, Arizona, Nevada, and California

pa·ja·mas \pə-'jäm-əz, -'jam-\ *n pl* [from Hindi *pājāma* "pair of lightweight trousers", from Persian *pā* "leg" and *jāma* "garment"] : a loose lightweight suit designed for sleeping or lounging

Pak·i·stani \ˌpak-i-'stan-ē, ˌpäk-i-'stän-ē\ *adj* : of, relating to, or characteristic of Pakistan or its people — **Pakistani** *n*

[1]**pal** \'pal\ *n* [from Romany *phral*, *phal* "brother", "friend", from Sanskrit *bhrātṛ*, from the same source as English *brother*] : PARTNER; *esp* : a close friend

[2]**pal** *vb* **palled**; **pal·ling** : to be or become pals

pal·ace \'pal-əs\ *n* [from French *palais*, from Latin *palatium*, from *Palatium*, the name of a hill in Rome on which the emperors' residences were built] **1** : the official residence of a sovereign **2** : a large stately house **3** : a large public building (as for a legislature, court, or governor)

pal·a·din \'pal-əd-ən\ *n* : a knightly supporter of a medieval prince

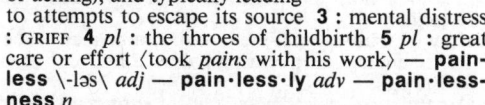

pal·an·quin \ˌpal-ən-'kēn\ *n* : a conveyance usu. for

one person consisting of an enclosed litter carried on the shoulders of men by means of poles

pal·at·a·ble \'pal-ət-ə-bəl\ *adj* **1** : agreeable to the taste **2** : AGREEABLE, ACCEPTABLE — **pal·at·a·bil·i·ty** \,pal-ət-ə-'bil-ət-ē\ *n* — **pal·at·a·bly** \'pal-ət-ə-blē\ *adv*

pal·ate \'pal-ət\ *n* **1** : the roof of the mouth separating the mouth from the nasal cavity **2 a** : the sense of taste **b** : intellectual relish or taste

pa·la·tial \pə-'lā-shəl\ *adj* : of, resembling, or fit for a palace : MAGNIFICENT — **pa·la·tial·ly** \-shə-lē\ *adv*

1**pal·a·tine** \'pal-ə-,tīn\ *adj* **1** : of or relating to a palace : PALATIAL **2 a** : possessing royal privileges **b** : of or relating to a palatine noble

2**palatine** *adj* : of, relating to, or lying near the palate

1**pa·lav·er** \pə-'lav-ər, -'läv-\ *n* **1** : a long parley usu. between persons of different levels of culture **2** : TALK; *esp* : idle or flattering talk

2**palaver** *vb* : to talk esp. at length or idly

1**pale** \'pāl\ *adj* **1 a** : lacking color or intensity of color : not vivid ⟨a *pale* pink⟩ **b** : not having the warm skin color of a person in good health : WAN ⟨became *pale*⟩ **2** : not bright or brilliant : DIM ⟨a *pale* moon⟩ — **pale·ly** \'pāl-lē\ *adv* — **pale·ness** \'pāl-nəs\ *n*

2**pale** *vb* : to make or become pale

3**pale** *vb* : to enclose with pales : FENCE

4**pale** *n* **1** : a stake or picket of a fence or palisade **2** : an enclosed place **3** : territory within clearly marked bounds or under a particular jurisdiction **4** : BOUNDS, LIMITS ⟨beyond the *pale* of decency⟩

pale·face \'pāl-,fās\ *n* : a white person : CAUCASIAN

Pa·le·o·cene \'pā-lē-ə-,sēn\ *n* : the earliest epoch of the Tertiary; *also* : the corresponding system of rocks — **Paleocene** *adj*

pa·le·o·lith \'pā-lē-ə-,lith\ *n* : a Paleolithic stone implement

Pa·leo·lith·ic \,pā-lē-ə-'lith-ik\ *adj* : of, relating to, or being the 2d period of the Stone Age which is characterized by rough or crudely chipped stone implements

paleon *abbr* paleontology

pa·le·on·tol·o·gy \,pā-lē-än-'täl-ə-jē\ *n* : a science dealing with the life of past geological periods as known esp. from fossil remains — **pa·le·on·to·log·i·cal** \-,änt-ə-'läj-i-kəl\ *or* **pa·le·on·to·log·ic** \-'läj-ik\ *adj* — **pa·le·on·tol·o·gist** \-än-'täl-ə-jəst\ *n*

Pa·leo·zo·ic \,pā-lē-ə-'zō-ik\ *n* : the 3d of the five eras of geologic history which is the period of greatest development of nearly all classes of invertebrates except the insects and in the later epochs of which seed-bearing plants, amphibians, and reptiles first appeared; *also* : the corresponding system of rocks — see GEOLOGIC TIME table — **Paleozoic** *adj*

Pal·es·tin·i·an \,pal-ə-'stin-ē-ən, -'stin-yən\ *adj* : of, relating to, or characteristic of Palestine or its people — **Palestinian** *n*

pal·ette \'pal-ət\ *n* **1** : a thin usu. oval board or tablet with a hole for the thumb at one end used by a painter to lay and mix pigments on **2** : the colors put on the palette

pal·frey \'pȯl-frē\ *n, pl* **palfreys** : a saddle horse; *esp* : one suitable for a lady

ə abut	ər further	a back	ā bake
ä cot, cart	aü out	ch chin	e less	ē easy
g gift	i trip	ī life	j joke	ng sing	ō flow
ȯ flaw	ȯi coin	th thin	th this	ü loot
u̇ foot	y yet	yü few	yu̇ furious	zh vision

pal·ing \'pā-ling\ *n* **1** : PALE, PICKET **2** : pales or a fence of pales

1**pal·i·sade** \,pal-ə-'sād\ *n* **1 a** : a stout high fence of stakes esp. for defense **b** : a long strong pointed stake set close with others as a defense **2** : a line of bold cliffs

2**palisade** *vb* : to surround or fortify with palisades

palisade cell *n* : a cell of the palisade layer

palisade layer *n* : a layer of columnlike or cylindrical cells that are rich in chloroplasts, have small intercellular spaces, and are usu. found just beneath the upper epidermis of foliage leaves

1**pall** \'pȯl\ *n* **1** : a heavy cloth covering for a coffin, hearse, or tomb **2** : a chalice cover made of a square piece of stiffened linen **3** : something that covers, darkens, or produces a gloomy effect ⟨a *pall* of smoke⟩

2**pall** *vb* : to become dull or uninteresting : lose the ability to give pleasure

pal·la·di·um \pə-'lād-ē-əm\ *n* : a silver-white ductile malleable metallic element that is used esp. as a catalyst and in alloys — see ELEMENT table

pall·bear·er \'pȯl-,bar-ər, -,ber-\ *n* : a person who attends the coffin at a funeral

pal·let \'pal-ət\ *n* **1** : a straw-filled tick or mattress **2** : a small, hard, or temporary bed

pal·li·ate \'pal-ē-,āt\ *vb* **1** : to make less severe **2** : to cover by excuses and apologies : EXCUSE — **pal·li·a·tion** \,pal-ē-'ā-shən\ *n*

pal·li·a·tive \'pal-ē-,āt-iv\ *adj* : serving to palliate — **palliative** *n* — **pal·li·a·tive·ly** *adv*

pal·lid \'pal-əd\ *adj* : deficient in healthy color : WAN — **pal·lid·i·ty** \pa-'lid-ət-ē\ *n* — **pal·lid·ly** \'pal-əd-lē\ *adv* — **pal·lid·ness** *n*

pal·lor \'pal-ər\ *n* : paleness esp. of the face

1**palm** \'päm, 'pälm\ *n* **1** : any of a family of mostly tropical or subtropical woody trees, shrubs, or vines usu. with a simple but often tall stem topped by a crown of huge feathery or fan-shaped leaves **2 a** : a palm leaf esp. when carried as a symbol of victory or rejoicing **b** : an emblem of success or triumph : HONORS — **palm·like** \-,līk\ *adj*

2**palm** *n* **1** : the under part of the hand between the fingers and the wrist **2** : a rough measure of length based on the width or length of the palm **3** : something (as the blade of a paddle) resembling or corresponding to the palm of the hand

3**palm** *vb* **1** : to conceal in or pick up stealthily with the hand **2** : to impose by fraud ⟨trash *palmed* off on the unwary⟩

pal·mate \'pal-,māt, 'pä(l)m-,āt\ *also* **pal·mat·ed** \-,māt-əd, -,āt-\ *adj* : resembling a hand with the fingers spread

palm·er \'päm-ər, 'päl-mər\ *n* : a person wearing two crossed palm leaves as a sign of his pilgrimage to the Holy Land

pal·met·to \pal-'met-ō\ *n, pl* **-tos** *or* **-toes** : any of several usu. low-growing palms with fan-shaped leaves

palm·ist·ry \'päm-ə-strē, 'päl-mə-\ *n* : the art or practice of reading a person's character or future from the markings on his palms — **palm·ist** \'päm-əst, 'päl-məst\ *n*

Palm Sunday *n* : the Sunday before Easter celebrated in commemoration of Christ's triumphal entry into Jerusalem

palmy \'päm-ē, 'päl-mē\ *adj* **palm·i·er**; **-est** **1** : abounding in or bearing palms **2** : FLOURISHING, PROSPEROUS

pal·o·mi·no \,pal-ə-'mē-nō\ *n, pl* **-nos** : a slender-legged short-bodied horse of a light tan or cream color with lighter mane and tail

palp \'palp\ *n* : PALPUS — **pal·pal** \'pal-pəl\ *adj*

pal·pa·ble \'pal-pə-bəl\ *adj* **1** : capable of being touched or felt : TANGIBLE **2** : easily perceived : NOTICEABLE **3** : easily understood or recognized : OBVIOUS ⟨a *palpable* error⟩ — **pal·pa·bil·i·ty** \ˌpal-pə-'bil-ət-ē\ *n* — **pal·pa·bly** \'pal-pə-blē\ *adv*

pal·pate \'pal-ˌpāt\ *vb* : to examine by touch esp. medically — **pal·pa·tion** \pal-'pā-shən\ *n*

pal·pi·tate \'pal-pə-ˌtāt\ *vb* : to beat rapidly and strongly : THROB, QUIVER ⟨*palpitating* with excitement⟩

pal·pi·ta·tion \ˌpal-pə-'tā-shən\ *n* : an act or instance of palpitating; *esp* : an abnormally rapid beating (as from violent exercise or strong emotion) of the heart

pal·pus \'pal-pəs\ *n, pl* **pal·pi** \-ˌpī, -(ˌ)pē\ : a segmented process on an arthropod mouthpart that functions in sensing by touch or in feeding

pal·sy \'pȯl-zē\ *n* **1** : PARALYSIS **2** : a condition marked by uncontrollable trembling or shaking of the body or a part — **palsy** *vb*

pal·ter \'pȯl-tər\ *vb* **pal·tered**; **pal·ter·ing** \-t(ə-)riŋ\ **1** : to act or speak insincerely **2** : HAGGLE, BARGAIN — **pal·ter·er** \-tər-ər\ *n*

pal·try \'pȯl-trē\ *adj* **pal·tri·er**; **-est** **1** : PETTY, MEAN ⟨a *paltry* trick⟩ **2** : TRIVIAL, WORTHLESS — **pal·tri·ness** *n*

pam *abbr* pamphlet

pam·pa \'pam-pə\ *n, pl* **pampas** \-pəz, -pəs\ : an extensive generally grass-covered plain of So. America

•**pam·per** \'pam-pər\ *vb* **pam·pered**; **pam·per·ing** \-p(ə-)riŋ\ : to treat with extreme or excessive care and attention

pam·phlet \'pam(p)-flət\ *n* : a short printed publication with no cover or a paper cover

pam·phle·teer \ˌpam(p)-flə-'ti(ə)r\ *n* : a writer of pamphlets usu. attacking something or urging a cause — **pamphleteer** *vb*

1**pan** \'pan\ *n* **1 a** : a usu. broad, shallow, and open container for cooking **b** : a vessel or article like a pan ⟨the *pans* of a pair of scales⟩ ⟨a gold miner's screening *pan*⟩ **2** : a basin or depression in the earth ⟨a salt *pan*⟩ **3** : HARDPAN 1

2**pan** *vb* **panned**; **pan·ning** **1** : to wash earthy material in a pan to concentrate bits of metal ⟨*pan* for gold⟩ **2 a** : to yield precious metal in panning **b** : to turn out; *esp* : SUCCEED ⟨a visit that *panned* out⟩ **3** : to criticize severely

Pan *abbr* Panama

pan·a·cea \ˌpan-ə-'sē-ə\ *n* : a remedy for all ills or difficulties : CURE-ALL

pan·a·ma \'pan-ə-ˌmä, -ˌmȯ\ *n, often cap* : a lightweight hat of hand-plaited leaves of a tropical American tree

Pan–Amer·i·can \ˌpan-ə-'mer-ə-kən\ *adj* : of, relating to, or involving the independent republics of No. and So. America

1**pan·cake** \'pan-ˌkāk\ *n* : GRIDDLE CAKE

2**pancake** *vb* : to make or cause to make a pancake landing

pancake landing *n* : a landing in which an airplane is leveled off higher than for a normal landing causing it to stall and drop abruptly

pan·chro·mat·ic \ˌpan-krō-'mat-ik\ *adj* : sensitive to light of all colors in the visible spectrum ⟨*panchromatic* film⟩

pan·cre·as \'paŋ-krē-əs, 'pan-\ *n* : a large compound gland of vertebrates that lies near the stomach and secretes digestive enzymes and the hormone insulin — **pan·cre·at·ic** \ˌpaŋ-krē-'at-ik, ˌpan-\ *adj*

pancreatic duct *n* : the duct leading from the pancreas and opening into the duodenum

pancreatic juice *n* : a clear digestive secretion of pancreatic enzymes that is poured into the duodenum

pan·da \'pan-də\ *n* **1** : a large black-and-white

panda 1 (about 6 ft. long)
panda 2 (about 3½ ft. long)

mammal of Tibet that suggests a bear but is related to the raccoon **2** : a smaller reddish animal related to the panda but resembling the raccoon

pan·da·nus \pan-'dā-nəs, -'dan-əs\ *n* : SCREW PINE

pan·de·mo·ni·um \ˌpan-də-'mō-nē-əm\ *n* **1** : a wild uproar : TUMULT **2** : a wildly riotous place

pan·der \'pan-dər\ *or* **pan·der·er** \-dər-ər\ *n* **1** : a go-between in love intrigues **2** : someone who caters to the weaknesses and base desires of others — **pander** *vb*

pan·di·ag·o·nal \ˌpan-dī-'ag-ən-əl\ *adj* : having the same sum along all possible diagonals ⟨*pandiagonal* magic squares⟩

pane \'pān\ *n* **1 a** : a section or side of something (as a facet of a gem) **b** : one of the sections into which a sheet of postage stamps is divided and which in the U.S. usu. contains 100 stamps **2** : a sheet of glass in or for a window or door

pan·e·gyr·ic \ˌpan-ə-'jir-ik, -'jī-rik\ *n* **1** : a formal speech or writing in praise of someone or something **2** : formal or elaborate praise — **pan·e·gyr·i·cal** \-'jir-i-kəl, -'jī-ri-\ *adj* — **pan·e·gyr·ist** \-'jir-əst, -'jī-rəst\ *n*

1**pan·el** \'pan-əl\ *n* **1 a** : a list or a group of persons summoned as jurors **b** : a group of persons who discuss a topic before an audience **c** : a group of entertainers or guests engaged as players in a quiz or guessing game on a radio or television program **2 a** : a usu. rectangular and sunken or raised section of a door, wall, or ceiling **b** : a unit of construction material (as plywood) made to form part of a surface **c** : a vertical section (as a gore) of cloth **d** : a surface on which instruments or controls are mounted **3 a** : a thin flat piece of wood on which a picture is painted **b** : a painting on such a surface

2**panel** *vb* **-eled** *or* **-elled**; **-el·ing** *or* **-el·ling** : to furnish or decorate with panels

pan·el·ing \'pan-ə-liŋ\ *n* **1** : panels joined in a continuous surface **2** : material for panels

pan·el·ist \'pan-ə-ləst\ *n* : a member of a panel for discussion or entertainment

pan·fish \'pan-ˌfish\ *n* : a small food fish (as a sunfish) usu. taken with hook and line but not sold on the market

pang \'pang\ *n* : a sudden sharp attack of pain or distress ⟨hunger *pangs*⟩

pan·go·lin \pan-'gō-lən\ *n* : any of several Asiatic and African mammals having the body covered with large overlapping horny scales

pangolin
(up to 4 ft. long)

1**pan·han·dle** \'pan-ˌhan-dəl\ *n* : a narrow projection of a larger territory (as a state) ⟨the Texas *Panhandle*⟩

2**panhandle** *vb* **-dled**; **-dling** \-d(ə-)ling\ : to beg for money on the street — **pan·han·dler** \-dlər\ *n*

1**pan·ic** \'pan-ik\ *n* **1** : a sudden overpowering fright esp. without reasonable cause **2** : a sudden widespread fright concerning financial affairs causing hurried selling and a sharp fall in prices — **panic** *adj* — **pan·icky** \'pan-i-kē\ *adj* — **pan·ic–strick·en** \'pan-ik-ˌstrik-ən\ *adj*

2**panic** *vb* **pan·icked** \-ikt\; **pan·ick·ing** : to affect or be affected with panic

pan·i·cle \'pan-i-kəl\ *n* : a loosely branched often pyramid-shaped flower cluster (as of the oat) that is usu. technically a raceme — **pan·i·cled** \-kəld\ *adj* — **pa·nic·u·late** \pa-'nik-yə-lət\ *adj*

pan·nier \'pan-yər\ *n* **1** : a large basket; *esp* : one of wicker carried on the back of an animal or the shoulder of a person **2 a** : either of a pair of hoops formerly used by women to expand their skirts at the hips **b** : an overskirt puffed out at the sides

pan·o·ply \'pan-ə-plē\ *n, pl* **-plies** **1** : a full suit of armor **2** : a protective covering **3** : a magnificent array or display — **pan·o·plied** \-plēd\ *adj*

pan·o·rama \ˌpan-ə-'ram-ə, -'räm-\ *n* **1** : a picture shown a part at a time by being unrolled before the spectator **2** : a full and unobstructed view in every direction **3** : a complete presentation of a subject — **pan·o·ram·ic** \-'ram-ik\ *adj*

pan·pipe \'pan-ˌpīp\ *n* : a wind instrument consisting of a series of short pipes of different lengths bound together with the mouthpieces in a row — often used in pl.

panpipe

pan·sy \'pan-zē\ *n, pl* **pansies** [from French *pensée*, literally "thought"; so called from its being a symbol of remembrance] : a garden plant originated by hybridization of various violets and violas; *also* : its showy velvety 5-petaled flower

pant \'pant\ *vb* **1 a** : to breathe hard or quickly : GASP **b** : to make a throbbing or puffing sound **c** : to progress with panting ⟨the car *panted* up the hill⟩ **2** : to long eagerly : YEARN **3** : to utter with panting ⟨ran up and *panted* out the message⟩ — **pant** *n*

pan·ta·lets *or* **pan·ta·lettes** \ˌpant-ə-'lets\ *n pl* : long drawers with a ruffle at the bottom of each leg formerly worn by women and girls

pan·ta·loon \ˌpant-ə-'lün\ *n* **1** : CLOWN, BUFFOON **2** *pl* : TROUSERS

pan·ther \'pan(t)-thər\ *n, pl* **panthers** *also* **panther** **1** : LEOPARD; *esp* : a leopard of the black color phase **2** : COUGAR **3** : JAGUAR

pant·ie *or* **panty** \'pant-ē\ *n, pl* **pant·ies** : a woman's or child's undergarment covering the lower trunk and made with closed crotch and short legs — usu. used in pl.

panti·hose *or* **panty hose** \'pant-ē-ˌhōz\ *n pl* : a one-piece garment for women combining the function of panties and hose

pan·to·mime \'pant-ə-ˌmīm\ *n* **1** : PANTOMIMIST **2** : a performance in which a story is told by expressive bodily or facial movements **3** : expression of information by bodily or facial movements — **pantomime** *vb* — **pan·to·mim·ic** \ˌpant-ə-'mim-ik\ *adj*

pan·to·mim·ist \'pant-ə-ˌmim-əst, -ˌmīm-\ *n* : an actor or dancer in pantomimes

pan·to·then·ic acid \ˌpant-ə-ˌthen-ik-\ *n* : an oily acid of the vitamin B complex found in all living tissues and necessary for growth

pan·try \'pan-trē\ *n, pl* **pantries** : a small room in which food and dishes are kept

pants \'pan(t)s\ *n pl* **1** : TROUSERS **2** : UNDERPANTS; *esp* : PANTIE

pant·suit \'pant-ˌsüt\ *n* : a woman's outfit consisting usu. of a long jacket and pants made of the same material

pap \'pap\ *n* : soft or bland food for infants or invalids

pa·pa \'päp-ə\ *n* : FATHER

pa·pa·cy \'pā-pə-sē\ *n, pl* **-cies** **1** : the office of pope **2** : the term of a pope's reign **3** *cap* : the government of the Roman Catholic Church of which the pope is the head

pa·pa·in \pə-'pā-ən, -'pī-ən\ *n* : an enzyme in papaya juice used esp. as a meat tenderizer and in medicine

pa·pal \'pā-pəl\ *adj* : of or relating to the pope or the papacy — **pa·pal·ly** \-pə-lē\ *adv*

pa·paw *n* **1** \pə-'pȯ\ : PAPAYA **2** \'päp-ȯ, 'pȯp-\ : a No. American tree related to the custard apple and having purple flowers and a yellow edible fruit; *also* : its fruit

pa·pa·ya \pə-'pī-ə\ *n* : a tropical American tree with large lobed leaves and oblong yellow black-seeded edible fruit; *also* : its fruit

1**pa·per** \'pā-pər\ *n* [from French *papier*, from Latin *papyrus* "papyrus", from Greek *papyros*] **1 a** : a felted sheet made usu. from rags, wood, straw, or bark and used to write or print on, to wrap things in, or to cover walls **b** : a sheet or piece of paper **2** : something written or printed on paper (as a school composition) **3** : a paper container or wrapper ⟨a *paper* of pins⟩ **4** : NEWSPAPER **5 a** : instruments (as negotiable notes) of credit **b** : an official document identifying a person or his position ⟨lost his *papers*⟩ **6** : WALLPAPER

2**paper** *vb* **pa·pered**; **pa·per·ing** \'pā-p(ə-)ring\ : to cover or line with paper and esp. wallpaper ⟨*paper* a room⟩ — **pa·per·er** \-pər-ər\ *n*

3**paper** *adj* **1 a** : of, relating to, or made of paper or

ə abut	ər further	a back	ā bake	
ä cot, cart	aů out	ch chin	e less	ē easy
g gift	i trip	ī life	j joke	ng sing	ō flow
ȯ flaw	ȯi coin	th thin	th this	ü loot
ů foot	y yet	yü few	yů furious	zh vision

paperboard ⟨*paper* carton⟩ ⟨*paper* mills⟩ **b :** PAPERY ⟨nuts with *paper* shells⟩ **2 :** NOMINAL 1

pa·per·back \ˈpā-pər-ˌbak\ *n* **:** a book with a flexible paper binding — **paperback** *adj*

pa·per·board \-ˌbōrd, -ˌbȯrd\ *n* **:** a board made from cellulose fiber (as a mush of waste paper) and used esp. for packaging

paper chromatography *n* **:** a technique for separating substances in a mixture based on the different rates at which they are taken up by and migrate through special paper

paper clip *n* **:** a length of wire bent into flat loops that is used to hold papers together

pa·per·hang·er \-ˌhang-ər\ *n* **:** a person who applies wallpaper to walls esp. as an occupation — **pa·per·hang·ing** \-ˌhang-ing\ *n*

paper money *n* **:** money consisting of government notes and bank notes

paper nautilus *n* **:** an 8-armed mollusk related to the octopus that in the female has two of the arms expanded at the tips to clasp the thin fragile unchambered shell

pa·per·weight \ˈpā-pər-ˌwāt\ *n* **:** an object used to hold down loose papers by its weight

paper work *n* **:** routine clerical or record-keeping work

pa·pery \ˈpā-p(ə-)rē\ *adj* **:** resembling paper in thinness or consistency — **pa·per·i·ness** *n*

pa·pier–mâ·ché \ˌpā-pər-mə-ˈshā, -ma-\ *n* **:** a light strong material of paper pulp with glue and other additives — **papier–mâché** *adj*

pa·pil·la \pə-ˈpil-ə\ *n, pl* **-pil·lae** \-ˈpil-(ˌ)ē, -ˌī\ **:** a small projecting bodily structure (as one of the nubs on the surface of the tongue) that suggests a nipple

pa·poose \pa-ˈpüs, pə-\ *n* **:** a No. American Indian infant

pa·pri·ka \pə-ˈprē-kə, pa-\ *n* **:** a mild red condiment consisting of the dried finely ground fruit of various cultivated sweet peppers; *also* **:** a sweet pepper used for making paprika

pa·py·rus \pə-ˈpī-rəs\ *n, pl* **-rus·es** *or* **-ri** \-(ˌ)rē, -ˌrī\ **1 :** a tall sedge of the Nile valley **2 :** the pith of the papyrus plant esp. when cut in strips and pressed into a writing material **3 :** a writing on or written scroll of papyrus

papyrus 1 (about 15 ft. high)

par \ˈpär\ *n* **1 a :** the fixed value of the monetary unit of one country expressed in terms of the monetary unit of another country **b :** the face value or issuing price of a security ⟨stocks that sell near *par*⟩ **2 :** common level **:** EQUALITY ⟨boys with abilities on a *par*⟩ **3 :** an accepted standard (as of physical condition or health) ⟨not feeling up to *par*⟩ **4 :** the number of golf strokes set as standard for a golf hole or course — **par** *adj*

par *abbr* paragraph

para–ami·no·ben·zo·ic acid \ˈpar-ə-ə-ˌmē-nō-ben-ˌzō-ik-, ˈpar-ə-ˌam-ə-ˌnō-\ *n* **:** a colorless organic acid that is a growth factor of the vitamin B complex

par·a·ble \ˈpar-ə-bəl\ *n* **:** a short simple story illustrating a moral or spiritual truth

pa·rab·o·la \pə-ˈrab-ə-lə\ *n* **1 :** the curve formed by the intersection of a cone with a plane parallel to one of its sides **2 :** a curve like a parabola — **par·a·bol·ic** \ˌpar-ə-ˈbäl-ik\ *adj*

[1]**par·a·chute** \ˈpar-ə-ˌshüt\ *n* [from French, from *para-* "protection against" (derived from words like *parasol* "protection against the sun") and *chute* "fall"] **1 :** a folding umbrella-shaped device of light fabric used esp. for making a safe descent from an airplane **2 :** the tuft of hairs enabling a dandelion seed to float in air

parachute 1

[2]**parachute** *vb* **:** to convey or descend by means of a parachute — **par·a·chut·ist** \-ˌshüt-əst\ *n*

[1]**pa·rade** \pə-ˈrād\ *n* **1 :** pompous show or display **2 :** a ceremonial formation of a body of troops before a superior officer **3 :** a public procession **4 :** a crowd of strolling people ⟨the Easter *parade*⟩

[2]**parade** *vb* **1 a :** to cause to maneuver or march **b :** to march in a parade **2 :** PROMENADE **3 :** to show off **:** DISPLAY ⟨*paraded* his knowledge⟩ — **pa·rad·er** *n*

para·di·chlo·ro·ben·zene \ˌpar-ə-ˌdī-ˌklōr-ə-ˈben-ˌzēn, -ˌklȯr-, -ˌben-ˈ\ *n* **:** a white crystalline chlorinated benzene used chiefly in moth balls

par·a·digm \ˈpar-ə-ˌdīm, -ˌdim\ *n* **1 :** MODEL, PATTERN ⟨a *paradigm* of clear writing⟩ **2 :** an example of a conjugation or declension showing a word in all its inflectional forms — **par·a·dig·mat·ic** \ˌpar-ə-dig-ˈmat-ik\ *adj*

par·a·dise \ˈpar-ə-ˌdīs, -ˌdīz\ *n* [from Greek *paradeisos*, literally "park", from an Old Persian word meaning "a walled enclosure"] **1 :** the garden of Eden **2 :** HEAVEN **3 :** a place or state of bliss

par·a·dox \ˈpar-ə-ˌdäks\ *n* **1 a :** a statement that seems to contradict common sense but may still be true **b :** a self-contradictory statement that at first seems true **2 :** a person or thing with seemingly contradictory qualities or phases — **par·a·dox·i·cal** \ˌpar-ə-ˈdäk-si-kəl\ *adj* — **par·a·dox·i·cal·ly** \-k(ə-)lē\ *adv*

[1]**par·af·fin** \ˈpar-ə-fən\ *n* **:** a flammable waxy mixture of hydrocarbons obtained esp. from distillates of wood, coal, or petroleum and used chiefly in coating and sealing, in candles, and in drugs and cosmetics — **par·af·fin·ic** \ˌpar-ə-ˈfin-ik\ *adj*

[2]**paraffin** *vb* **:** to coat or saturate with paraffin

par·a·gon \ˈpar-ə-ˌgän, -gən\ *n* **:** a model of excellence or perfection

[1]**par·a·graph** \ˈpar-ə-ˌgraf\ *n* **1 :** a part of a writing or speech that develops in an organized manner one point of a subject or gives the words of one speaker **2 :** a short written article (as in a newspaper) complete in one section

[2]**paragraph** *vb* **:** to divide into or write paragraphs — **par·a·graph·er** \ˈpar-ə-ˌgraf-ər\ *n*

par·a·keet *var of* PARRAKEET

par·al·lax \ˈpar-ə-ˌlaks\ *n* **:** the apparent shift in position of an object as seen from two different points not on a straight line with the object

[1]**par·al·lel** \ˈpar-ə-ˌlel\ *adj* [from Greek *parallēlos* from the phrase *para allēlous* "alongside one another"] **1 :** extending in the same direction and being always the same distance apart ⟨train tracks are *parallel*⟩ **2 :** LIKE, SIMILAR ⟨*parallel* situations⟩

[2]**parallel** *n* **1 :** a parallel line, curve, or surface

2 a : one of the imaginary circles on the surface of the earth paralleling the equator and marking latitude **b :** a corresponding line on a globe or map **3 a :** COUNTERPART, EQUAL ⟨his victory is without a *parallel*⟩ **b :** SIMILARITY, LIKENESS **c :** a tracing of similarity ⟨draw a *parallel* between two eras⟩ **4 :** the arrangement of electrical devices in which all positive poles, electrodes, and terminals are joined to one conductor and all negative ones to another

3**parallel** *vb* **1 :** COMPARE **2 :** to correspond to **:** MATCH **3 :** to extend, run, or move in a direction parallel to ⟨the highway *parallels* the river⟩

4**parallel** *adv* **:** in a parallel manner — often used with *with* or *to*

par·al·lel·e·pi·ped \\ˌpar-ə-ˌlel-ə-ˈpī-pəd, -ˈpip-əd\\ *n* **:** a prism whose bases are parallelograms

par·al·lel·ism \\ˈpar-ə-ˌlel-ˌiz-əm\\ *n* **:** the quality or state of being parallel; *esp* **:** similarity of construction of adjacent word groups esp. for rhetorical effect or rhythm

par·al·lel·o·gram \\ˌpar-ə-ˈlel-ə-ˌgram\\ *n* **:** a 4-sided figure whose opposite sides are parallel and equal

par·al·lel–veined \\ˌpar-ə-ˌlel-ˈvānd\\ *adj* **:** having linear veins that do not branch and interlace ⟨monocotyledons have *parallel-veined* leaves⟩ — compare NET-VEINED

pa·ral·y·sis \\pə-ˈral-ə-səs\\ *n, pl* **-y·ses** \\-ə-ˌsēz\\ **:** complete or partial loss of function esp. when involving motion or sensation in a part of the body — **par·a·lyt·ic** \\ˌpar-ə-ˈlit-ik\\ *adj or n*

par·a·lyze \\ˈpar-ə-ˌlīz\\ *vb* **1 :** to affect with paralysis **2 :** to make powerless or unable to act or function ⟨a labor dispute *paralyzed* industry⟩

par·a·me·cium \\ˌpar-ə-ˈmē-sh(ē-)əm, -sē-əm\\ *n, pl* **-cia** \\-sh(ē-)ə, -sē-ə\\ *also* **-ciums** **:** any of a genus of one-celled somewhat slipper-shaped protozoans that move by cilia

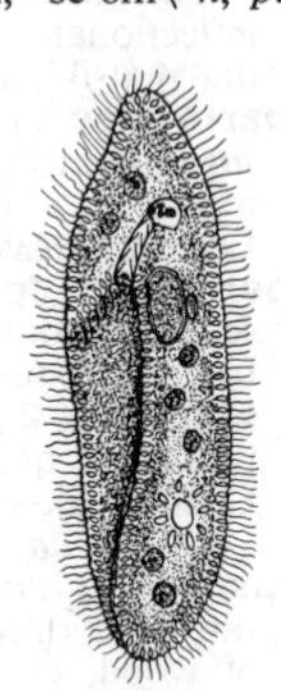

paramecium (magnified 150 times)

par·a·mount \\ˈpar-ə-ˌmau̇nt\\ *adj* **:** superior to all others **:** SUPREME ⟨an event of *paramount* importance⟩ ⟨a *paramount* chief⟩

par·a·noia \\ˌpar-ə-ˈnȯi-ə\\ *n* **1 :** a serious mental disorder marked by feelings of persecution or of distorted ideas of one's own importance usu. without hallucinations **2 :** a tendency toward excessive or irrational suspiciousness and distrustfulness of others — **par·a·noi·ac** \\-ˈnȯi-ˌak, -ˈnȯi-ik\\ *adj or n*

par·a·noid \\ˈpar-ə-ˌnȯid\\ *adj* **1 :** resembling paranoia **2 :** characterized by suspiciousness, feelings of persecution, or an exaggerated sense of one's own importance — **paranoid** *n*

par·a·pet \\ˈpar-ə-pət, -ˌpet\\ *n* **1 :** a wall of earth or stone to protect soldiers **2 :** a low wall or railing at the edge of a platform, roof, or bridge

par·a·pher·na·lia \\ˌpar-ə-fə(r)-ˈnāl-yə\\ *n sing or pl* **1 :** personal belongings **2 :** FURNISHINGS, APPARATUS

1**par·a·phrase** \\ˈpar-ə-ˌfrāz\\ *n* **:** a restatement of a passage or work giving the meaning in another form

2**paraphrase** *vb* **:** to give the meaning in different words — **par·a·phras·er** *n*

ə abut	ər further	a back	ā bake
ä cot, cart	au̇ out	ch chin	e less	ē easy
g gift	i trip	ī life	j joke	ng sing	ō flow
ȯ flaw	ȯi coin	th thin	t͟h this	ü loot
u̇ foot	y yet	yü few	yu̇ furious	zh vision

par·a·site \\ˈpar-ə-ˌsīt\\ *n* **1 :** a person who lives at the expense of another **2 :** an organism living in or on another organism in parasitism **3 :** a person dependent on something else for life or support without making adequate return — **par·a·sit·ic** \\ˌpar-ə-ˈsit-ik\\ *adj*

par·a·sit·ism \\ˈpar-ə-ˌsīt-ˌiz-əm\\ *n* **:** an intimate association between organisms of two or more kinds in which a parasite obtains benefits from a host which it usu. injures

par·a·sit·ize \\ˈpar-ə-sə-ˌtīz, -ˌsīt-ˌīz\\ *vb* **:** to infest or live on or with as a parasite

par·a·si·tol·o·gy \\ˌpar-ə-sə-ˈtäl-ə-jē, -ˌsīt-ˈäl-\\ *n* **:** a branch of biology dealing with parasites and parasitism esp. among animals — **par·a·si·tol·o·gist** \\-jəst\\ *n*

par·a·sol \\ˈpar-ə-ˌsȯl\\ *n* **:** a light umbrella for protection against the sun

parasol mushroom *n* **:** a long-stalked edible woodland mushroom that has white flesh, white gills, and white spores

para·sym·pa·thet·ic \\ˌpar-ə-ˌsim-pə-ˈthet-ik\\ *adj* **:** of, relating to, being, or acting on the parasympathetic nervous system

parasympathetic nervous system *n* **:** the part of the autonomic nervous system that tends to induce secretion, increase the tone and power of contracting of smooth muscle, and cause the expansion of blood vessels — compare SYMPATHETIC NERVOUS SYSTEM

par·a·thi·on \\ˌpar-ə-ˈthī-ən, -ˌän\\ *n* **:** an extremely poisonous insecticide that is a derivative of a sulfur-containing phosphoric acid

par·a·thor·mone \\ˌpar-ə-ˈthȯr-ˌmōn\\ *n* **:** the parathyroid hormone

para·thy·roid \\ˌpar-ə-ˈthī-ˌrȯid\\ *adj* **:** of, relating to, or produced by the parathyroid glands

parathyroid gland *n* **:** any of usu. four small endocrine glands adjacent to or embedded in the thyroid gland that produce a hormone concerned with calcium metabolism

para·troops \\ˈpar-ə-ˌtrüps\\ *n pl* **:** troops trained and equipped to parachute from an airplane — **para·troop** \\-ˌtrüp\\ *adj* — **para·troop·er** \\-ˌtrü-pər\\ *n*

1**para·ty·phoid** \\ˌpar-ə-ˈtī-ˌfȯid, -tī-ˈ\\ *adj* **1 :** resembling typhoid fever **2 :** of or relating to paratyphoid or the organisms that cause it

2**paratyphoid** *n* **:** a disease caused by bacteria, resembling typhoid fever, and occurring as a food poisoning

1**par·cel** \\ˈpär-səl\\ *n* **1 :** PORTION, PART **2 :** a plot of land **3 :** GROUP, LOT **4 :** BUNDLE, PACKAGE

2**parcel** *vb* **par·celed** *or* **par·celled**; **par·cel·ing** *or* **par·cel·ling** \\ˈpär-s(ə-)liŋ\\ **1 :** to divide into parts **:** DISTRIBUTE **2 :** to wrap up into a parcel

parcel post *n* **1 :** a mail service handling parcels **2 :** packages handled by parcel post

parch \\ˈpärch\\ *vb* **1 :** to toast by dry heat **2 :** to dry up **:** shrivel with heat

parch·ment \\ˈpärch-mənt\\ *n* **1 :** the skin of a sheep or goat prepared as a writing material **2 :** a paper like parchment **3 :** something (as a diploma) written on parchment

1**par·don** \\ˈpärd-ən\\ *n* **:** the excusing of an offense without a penalty — **par·don·a·ble** \\ˈpärd-(ə-)nə-bəl\\ *adj* — **par·don·a·bly** \\-blē\\ *adv*

2**pardon** *vb* **par·doned**; **par·don·ing** \\ˈpärd-(ə-)niŋ\\ **1 :** to free from penalty **2 :** to allow an offense to pass without punishment **:** FORGIVE ***syn*** see EXCUSE ***ant*** punish

pare \\ˈpa(ə)r, ˈpe(ə)r\\ *vb* **1 :** to cut or shave off the outside or the ends of ⟨*pare* an apple⟩ ⟨*paring* his nails⟩ **2 :** to reduce as if by paring ⟨*pare* expenses⟩

par·e·gor·ic \ˌpar-ə-ˈgȯr-ik, -ˈgōr-, -ˈgär-\ *n* : tincture of opium and camphor used esp. to relieve pain

pa·ren·chy·ma \pə-ˈreng-kə-mə\ *n* **1** : a tissue of higher plants consisting of thin-walled living cells that remain capable of cell division even when mature, are agents of photosynthesis and storage, and make up much of the substance of leaves and roots and the pulp of fruits as well as parts of stems and supporting structures **2** : the distinctive functional tissue of an animal organ (as a gland) as distinguished from its supporting tissue or framework — **par·en·chym·a·tous** \ˌpar-ən-ˈkim-ət-əs\ *also* **pa·ren·chy·mal** \pə-ˈreng-kə-məl\ *adj*

par·ent \ˈpar-ənt, ˈper-\ *n* **1 a** : one that is a father or mother **b** : an animal or plant that produces offspring **2** : the source or originator of something — **parent** *adj* — **par·ent·hood** \-ˌhu̇d\ *n*

par·ent·age \-ənt-ij\ *n* : descent from parents or ancestors : LINEAGE ⟨a man of noble *parentage*⟩

pa·ren·tal \pə-ˈrent-əl\ *adj* : of, typical of, or being parents ⟨*parental* affection⟩ — **pa·ren·tal·ly** \-ə-lē\ *adv*

pa·ren·the·sis \pə-ˈren(t)-thə-səs\ *n, pl* **-the·ses** \-thə-ˌsēz\ **1** : a word, phrase, or sentence inserted in a passage to explain or comment on it **2** : one of a pair of marks ( ) used to enclose a parenthesis or to group units in a mathematical expression — **par·en·thet·ic** \ˌpar-ən-ˈthet-ik\ *or* **par·en·thet·i·cal** \-ˈthet-i-kəl\ *adj* — **par·en·thet·i·cal·ly** \-i-k(ə-)lē\ *adv*

par ex·cel·lence \ˌpär-ˌek-sə-ˈläns\ *adv or adj* : in the highest degree : PREEMINENTLY

par·fait \pär-ˈfā\ *n* [from French, from *parfait* "perfect", from Latin *perfectus*] **1** : a flavored custard containing whipped cream and syrup frozen without stirring **2** : a dessert made of layers of fruit, syrup, ice cream, and whipped cream

pa·ri·ah \pə-ˈrī-ə\ *n* : a person despised or rejected by society : OUTCAST

par·ing \ˈpa(ə)r-ing, ˈpe(ə)r-\ *n* **1** : the act of cutting away an edge or surface **2** : something pared off

Par·is green \ˌpar-əs-\ *n* : a poisonous bright green powder containing copper and arsenic that is used as a pigment and as an insecticide

par·ish \ˈpar-ish\ *n* **1 a** : a section of a diocese in charge of a priest or minister **b** : the persons who live in such a section and attend the parish church **2** : the members of a church **3** : a division of the state of Louisiana corresponding to a county in other states

pa·rish·io·ner \pə-ˈrish-(ə-)nər\ *n* : a member or resident of a parish

Pa·ri·sian \pə-ˈrizh-ən\ *adj* : of, relating to, or characteristic of Paris or its people — **Parisian** *n*

par·i·ty \ˈpar-ət-ē\ *n, pl* **-ties** : the quality or state of being equal or equivalent : EQUALITY

1**park** \ˈpärk\ *n* **1** : a tract of land around a country house used for recreation (as hunting or riding) **2 a** : a piece of ground in or near a city or town kept as a place of beauty or recreation **b** : an area maintained in its natural state as a public property **3 a** : a space occupied by military vehicles or materials **b** : PARKING LOT **4** : ARENA, STADIUM

2**park** *vb* **1** : to leave a vehicle standing temporarily on a public way or in a parking lot or garage **2** : to set and leave temporarily ⟨*park* your coat here⟩

par·ka \ˈpär-kə\ *n* : a very warm jacket with a hood

parking lot *n* : an outdoor area for parking motor vehicles

park·way \ˈpärk-ˌwā\ *n* : a broad landscaped thoroughfare

par·lance \ˈpär-lən(t)s\ *n* : manner of speech : IDIOM

par·ley \ˈpär-lē\ *vb* **par·leyed**; **par·ley·ing** : CONFER; *esp* : to discuss terms with an enemy — **parley** *n*

par·lia·ment \ˈpär-lə-mənt, ˈpärl-yə-\ *n* **1** : a formal conference on public affairs **2** : the supreme legislative body of various political units ⟨the British *parliament*⟩

par·lia·men·tar·i·an \ˌpär-lə-ˌmen-ˈter-ē-ən, -mən-, ˌpärl-yə-\ *n* : an expert in parliamentary procedure

par·lia·men·ta·ry \-ˈment-ə-rē, -ˈmen-trē\ *adj* **1** : of, relating to, or enacted by a parliament **2** : of or relating to government by a cabinet whose members belong to and are responsible to the legislature **3** : being in accordance with the rules and customs of a parliament or other deliberative body

par·lor \ˈpär-lər\ *n* **1** : a room in a home, hotel, or club used for conversation or the reception of guests **2** : any of various business places ⟨funeral *parlor*⟩ ⟨beauty *parlor*⟩

parlor car *n* : an extra-fare railroad car for day travel equipped with individual chairs

par·lous \ˈpär-ləs\ *adj* **1** : DANGEROUS, RISKY **2** : SHOCKING — **par·lous·ly** *adv*

pa·ro·chi·al \pə-ˈrō-kē-əl\ *adj* **1** : of or relating to a parish **2** : NARROW, PROVINCIAL ⟨a *parochial* attitude⟩ — **pa·ro·chi·al·ism** \-kē-ə-ˌliz-əm\ *n* — **pa·ro·chi·al·ly** \-kē-ə-lē\ *adv*

parochial school *n* : a school maintained by a religious body

par·o·dy \ˈpar-əd-ē\ *n, pl* **-dies** **1** : a literary or musical work in which the style of an author or work is imitated for comic effect **2** : a poor imitation — **par·o·dist** \-əd-əst\ *n* — **parody** *vb*

1**pa·role** \pə-ˈrōl\ *n* **1** : a promise confirmed by a pledge; *esp* : the promise of a prisoner of war to fulfill stated conditions in return for his release **2** : a conditional release of a prisoner before his sentence has expired

2**parole** *vb* : to release on parole — **pa·rol·ee** \pə-ˌrō-ˈlē\ *n*

pa·rot·id \pə-ˈrät-əd, -ˈrōt-\ *adj* : of or relating to the parotid gland

parotid gland *n* : either of a pair of large salivary glands situated below and in front of the ear

par·ox·ysm \ˈpar-ək-ˌsiz-əm\ *n* **1** : a fit, attack, or sudden increase of violence of a disease that occurs at intervals ⟨a *paroxysm* of coughing⟩ **2** : a sudden violent emotion or action ⟨*paroxysms* of rage⟩

par·quet \pär-ˈkā\ *n* **1** : a flooring of parquetry **2** : the lower floor of a theater esp. in front of the balcony

par·que·try \ˈpär-kə-trē\ *n, pl* **-tries** : a patterned wood inlay used esp. for floors

par·ra·keet \ˈpar-ə-ˌkēt\ *n* : any of numerous usu. small slender parrots with a long tapered tail

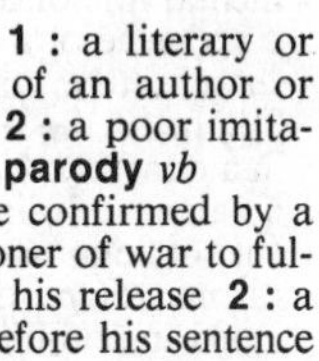
parquetry

1**par·rot** \ˈpar-ət\ *n* **1** : a bright-colored tropical bird of a family characterized by a strong hooked bill, by toes arranged in pairs with two in front and two behind, and often by the ability to mimic speech **2** : a person who repeats words mechanically and without understanding

2**parrot** *vb* : to repeat mechanically

parrot fever *n* : PSITTACOSIS

par·ry \ˈpar-ē\ *vb* **par·ried**; **par·ry·ing** **1** : to ward off : turn aside skillfully ⟨*parry* a blow⟩ **2** : EVADE ⟨*parry* an embarrassing question⟩ — **parry** *n*

parse \ˈpärs, ˈpärz\ *vb* [from Latin *pars orationis*

"part of speech"] **1 :** to analyze a sentence by naming its parts and their relations to each other **2 :** to give the part of speech of a word and explain its relation to other words in a sentence

Par·si \'pär-ˌsē\ *n* : a Zoroastrian descended from Persian refugees settled principally at Bombay

par·si·mo·ny \'pär-sə-ˌmō-nē\ *n* : extreme frugality : STINGINESS — **par·si·mo·ni·ous** \ˌpär-sə-'mō-nē-əs\ *adj* — **par·si·mo·ni·ous·ly** *adv* — **par·si·mo·ni·ous·ness** *n*

pars·ley \'pär-slē\ *n, pl* **parsleys** : a southern European herb related to the carrot and widely grown for its finely divided leaves which are used as a flavoring or garnish

pars·nip \'pär-snəp\ *n* : a European herb related to the carrot and grown for its long white root used as a vegetable; *also* : this root

par·son \'pär-sən\ *n* [from Middle English *persone*, from medieval Latin *persona*, literally "person"; so called because he was the legal "person" representing the parish] **1 :** a minister in charge of a parish **2 :** CLERGYMAN; *esp* : a Protestant pastor

par·son·age \'pär-s(ə-)nij\ *n* : the house provided by a church for its pastor

[1]**part** \'pärt\ *n* **1 a :** one of the portions into which something is divisible **b :** one of the equal units of which something is composed ⟨a fifth *part* for each⟩ **c :** a portion of a plant or animal body : MEMBER, ORGAN ⟨wash the injured *part*⟩ **d :** a vocal or instrumental line or melody in harmony or the score for it **e :** a piece of a machine or apparatus **2 :** a person's share, duty, or function ⟨everyone did his *part*⟩ **3 :** one of the sides in a conflict ⟨take another's *part* in a quarrel⟩ **4 :** DISTRICT, REGION — usu. used in pl. **5 :** an actor's lines or role in a play **6** *pl* : a constituent of character or capacity : ABILITY, TALENT ⟨a man of *parts*⟩ **7 :** the line where the hair is divided in combing

syn PART, SEGMENT, PORTION can mean something less than the whole. PART, a general term, implies only that something is taken away from the whole or regarded separately from the rest; SEGMENT implies separation or marking out along natural lines of cleavage; PORTION implies assignment or allotment from a whole *ant* whole

[2]**part** *vb* **1 :** to separate from or leave someone : go away : DEPART **2 :** to become separated, detached, or broken ⟨the ice *parted*⟩ **3 :** to give up possession or control ⟨wouldn't *part* with his old car⟩ **4 a :** to divide into parts **b :** to separate by combing on each side of a line **c :** SEPARATE, SPLIT

[3]**part** *adv* : PARTLY ⟨was only *part* right⟩

part *abbr* participle

par·take \pär-'tāk, pər-\ *vb* **par·took** \-'tu̇k\; **par·tak·en** \-'tā-kən\; **par·tak·ing** **1 a :** to take a share ⟨*partake* of a meal⟩ **b :** to take part in something ⟨all may *partake* in the ceremony⟩ **2 :** to have some of the qualities of something ⟨the story *partook* of the nature of fantasy⟩ — **par·tak·er** *n*

syn PARTAKE, PARTICIPATE, SHARE can mean to take part together. PARTAKE is likely to apply to the sharing of food and drink; PARTICIPATE suggests an enterprise or activity in which persons work or act as a group; SHARE may imply either things or experiences had in common and implies also a spirit of communion between the persons involved

par·tial \'pär-shəl\ *adj* **1 :** inclined to favor one side over another : BIASED ⟨a *partial* judge⟩ **2 :** fond or too fond of someone or something ⟨*partial* to double milk shakes⟩ **3 :** relating to or being a part rather than the whole ⟨a *partial* eclipse⟩ — **par·tial·ly** \'pärsh-(ə-)lē\ *adv*

par·ti·al·i·ty \ˌpär-shē-'al-ət-ē, pär-'shal-\ *n, pl* **-ties** **1 :** the quality or state of being partial **2 :** a special taste or liking

partial product *n* : one of the products obtained by multiplying successively the multiplicand by each digit of the multiplier

par·tic·i·pant \pər-'tis-ə-pənt, pär-\ *n* : one that participates

par·tic·i·pate \pər-'tis-ə-ˌpāt, pär-\ *vb* : to take part or have a share in something in common with others ⟨*participate* in sports⟩ *syn* see PARTAKE — **par·tic·i·pa·tion** \-ˌtis-ə-'pā-shən\ *n* — **par·tic·i·pa·tor** \-'tis-ə-ˌpāt-ər\ *n*

par·ti·cip·i·al \ˌpärt-ə-'sip-ē-əl\ *adj* : of, relating to, or formed with a participle ⟨*participial* phrase⟩ — **par·ti·cip·i·al·ly** \-ē-ə-lē\ *adv*

par·ti·ci·ple \'pärt-ə-ˌsip-əl\ *n* : a word that functions like an adjective and also shows such features of a verb as tense and voice and the ability to take an object

par·ti·cle \'pärt-i-kəl\ *n* **1 :** one of the minute subdivisions of matter (as a molecule, atom, electron) **2 :** a very small quantity or fragment **3 :** the smallest possible portion

par·ti–col·ored \ˌpärt-ē-'kəl-ərd\ *adj* : showing different colors or tints

[1]**par·tic·u·lar** \pə(r)-'tik-yə-lər\ *adj* **1 :** of or relating to the separate parts of a whole ⟨each *particular* item on the list⟩ **2 :** of or relating to a single person or thing ⟨his *particular* skills⟩ **3 :** SPECIAL ⟨a storm of *particular* violence⟩ **4 :** hard to please : EXACTING ⟨*particular* about his clothes⟩

[2]**particular** *n* : an individual fact, detail, or item — **in particular** : ESPECIALLY, PARTICULARLY

par·tic·u·lar·i·ty \-ˌtik-yə-'lar-ət-ē\ *n, pl* **-ties** **1 :** a minute detail **2 :** attentiveness to detail : EXACTNESS, CARE

par·tic·u·lar·ize \-'tik-yə-lə-ˌrīz\ *vb* : to state in detail : SPECIFY — **par·tic·u·lar·i·za·tion** \-ˌtik-yə-lə-rə-'zā-shən\ *n*

par·tic·u·lar·ly \-'tik-yə-lər-lē\ *adv* **1 :** in a particular manner **2 :** to an unusual degree : ESPECIALLY

[1]**part·ing** \'pärt-ing\ *n* **1 :** SEPARATION, DIVISION **2 :** a place where a division or separation occurs ⟨the *parting* of the ways⟩ **3 :** LEAVE-TAKING ⟨shake hands at *parting*⟩

[2]**parting** *adj* **1 :** DEPARTING ⟨*parting* day⟩ **2 :** serving to divide : SEPARATING ⟨the *parting* strip of a window sash⟩ **3 :** given, taken, or performed at parting ⟨a *parting* kiss⟩

par·ti·san \'pärt-ə-zən\ *n* **1 :** a person who takes the part of another; *esp* : a devoted adherent to a cause **2 :** GUERRILLA — **partisan** *adj* — **par·ti·san·ship** \-ˌship\ *n*

par·ti·tion \pər-'tish-ən, pär-\ *n* **1 :** DIVISION, SEPARATION ⟨*partition* of a defeated country among its conquerors⟩ **2 :** an interior dividing wall **3 :** PART, SECTION — **partition** *vb* — **par·ti·tion·er** \-'tish-(ə-)nər\ *n*

part·ly \'pärt-lē\ *adv* : in some measure or degree : PARTIALLY

part music *n* : vocal music for several voices in independent parts usu. without accompaniment

part·ner \'pärt-nər\ *n* **1 :** one associated in action

ə abut	ər further		a back		ā bake
ä cot, cart	au̇ out	ch chin	e less		ē easy
g gift	i trip	ī life	j joke	ng sing	ō flow
ȯ flaw	ȯi coin	th thin	th this		ü loot
u̇ foot	y yet	yü few	yu̇ furious		zh vision

with another : COLLEAGUE **2** : either of a couple who dance together **3** : one of two or more persons who play together in a game against an opposing side **4** : SPOUSE **5** : a member of a partnership

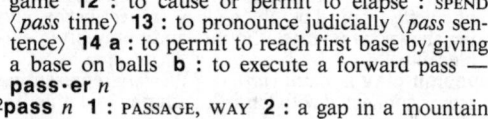

part·ner·ship \'pärt-nər-ˌship\ *n* **1** : the state of being a partner : PARTICIPATION **2** : a business organization owned by two or more persons who agree to share the profits and usu. are individually liable for losses

part of speech : a traditional class of words (as adjectives, adverbs, conjunctions, interjections, nouns, prepositions, pronouns, or verbs) distinguished according to the kind of idea denoted and the function performed in a sentence

partook *past of* PARTAKE

par·tridge \'pär-trij\ *n, pl* **partridge** *or* **par·tridges** : any of several stout-bodied Old World game birds related to the common domestic fowl; *also* : any of various similar and related American birds (as a bobwhite or ruffed grouse)

partridge (up to 14 in. long)

par·tridge·ber·ry \-trij-ˌber-ē\ *n* : an American trailing evergreen plant with rather tasteless scarlet berries

part–song \'pärt-ˌsȯŋ\ *n* : a song consisting of two or more voice parts

par·tu·ri·tion \ˌpärt-ə-'rish-ən\ *n* : CHILDBIRTH

par·ty \'pärt-ē\ *n, pl* **parties** **1** : one side in a dispute or contest ⟨the *parties* to a lawsuit⟩ **2** : a group of persons usu. agreeing on fundamental principles that is organized to influence or direct the policies of a government or to overthrow an established government **3** : PERSON ⟨get the right *party* on the telephone⟩ **4** : a small group engaged in a task ⟨a scouting *party*⟩ **5 a** : a social gathering **b** : entertainment for such a gathering — **party** *adj*

syn PARTY, FACTION can mean a group working together often for political ends. PARTY suggests the relatively large size and settled political principles of an established group; FACTION suggests a group of smaller size and often implies quarrelsome contention or reckless disregard of the public good

par·ve·nu *also* **par·ve·nue** \'pär-və-ˌn(y)ü\ *n* : one who has recently or suddenly risen to wealth or power but has not yet secured the social position appropriate to it — **parvenu** *also* **parvenue** *adj*

Pasch \'pask\ *n* **1** : PASSOVER **2** : EASTER — **paschal** \'pas-kəl\ *adj*

pa·sha \'päsh-ə, pə-'shä\ *n* : a Middle Eastern man (as a governor of the Ottoman Empire) of high rank

1**pass** \'pas\ *vb* **1** : MOVE, PROCEED **2 a** : to go away ⟨the pain will soon *pass*⟩ **b** : DIE ⟨*passed* on yesterday⟩ **3** : to go by or beyond or move past **4** : to go or allow to go across, over, or through ⟨let no one *pass*⟩ **5** : to change or transfer ownership or possession ⟨the throne *passed* to his son⟩ **6** : HAPPEN, OCCUR **7 a** : to secure the approval of a legislative body ⟨the bill *passed* both houses⟩ **b** : to approve officially ⟨*pass* a new law⟩ **8** : to go or allow to go through an examination or course of study successfully ⟨*passed* French⟩ ⟨the teacher *passed* everyone⟩ **9** : to be held or regarded ⟨*passed* for an honest man⟩ **10** : to transfer or become transferred from one person to another ⟨*pass* the butter⟩ ⟨*pass* a football⟩ **11** : to decline to bid, bet, or draw in a card game **12** : to cause or permit to elapse : SPEND ⟨*pass* time⟩ **13** : to pronounce judicially ⟨*pass* sentence⟩ **14 a** : to permit to reach first base by giving a base on balls **b** : to execute a forward pass — **pass·er** *n*

2**pass** *n* **1** : PASSAGE, WAY **2** : a gap in a mountain range

3**pass** *n* **1** : the act or an instance of passing : PASSAGE **2** : ACCOMPLISHMENT, REALIZATION — used in the phrase *come to pass* and *bring to pass* **3** : a state of affairs : CONDITION ⟨have come to a strange *pass*⟩ **4** : a written permission to enter or leave or to move about freely ⟨a railroad *pass*⟩ ⟨a soldier's three-day *pass*⟩ **5** : a moving of the hands over or along something **6** : a transfer of a ball or puck from one player to another; *esp* : FORWARD PASS **7** : BASE ON BALLS **8** : an act of passing in a card game **9** : EFFORT, TRY ⟨make a *pass* at it⟩; *esp* : an attempt at love-making

pass *abbr* **1** passenger **2** passive

pass·a·ble \'pas-ə-bəl\ *adj* **1** : capable of being passed, crossed, or traveled on ⟨*passable* roads⟩ **2** : barely good enough : TOLERABLE ⟨a *passable* imitation⟩ — **pass·a·bly** \-blē\ *adv*

pas·sage \'pas-ij\ *n* **1** : the action or process of passing from one place or condition to another **2 a** : a road, path, channel, or course by which something can pass **b** : CORRIDOR **3 a** : VOYAGE, JOURNEY **b** : a right to travel as a passenger ⟨book *passage* on an airplane⟩ **4** : the enactment of a legislative measure **5** : a usu. brief portion of a written work or speech or of a musical composition

pas·sage·way \-ˌwā\ *n* : PASSAGE 2

pass·book \'pas-ˌbu̇k\ *n* : BANKBOOK

pas·sé \pa-'sā\ *adj* [from French, literally "past", "gone by", from the past participle of *passer* "to pass"] : OUT-OF-DATE, OUTMODED

pas·sen·ger \'pas-ən-jər\ *n* **1** : PASSERBY, WAYFARER **2** : a traveler in a vehicle

passenger pigeon *n* : an extinct but formerly abundant No. American migratory pigeon

pass·er·by \ˌpas-ər-'bī\ *n, pl* **pass·ers·by** \-ərz-\ : one who passes by

1**pass·ing** \'pas-iŋ\ *n* : the act of one that passes or causes to pass; *esp* : DEATH — **in passing** : by the way : PARENTHETICALLY

2**passing** *adj* **1** : going by or past ⟨the *passing* crowd⟩ **2** : lasting only for a short time; *esp* : HASTY, SUPERFICIAL ⟨a *passing* glance⟩ **3** : given on satisfactory completion of an examination or course of study ⟨a *passing* grade⟩

3**passing** *adv* : VERY, EXCEEDINGLY ⟨*passing* fair⟩

pas·sion \'pash-ən\ *n* **1** *often cap* : the sufferings of Christ between the night of the Last Supper and his death **2 a** *pl* : the emotions as distinguished from reason **b** : strong feeling or emotion **3 a** : ardent affection : LOVE **b** : a strong liking ⟨a *passion* for music⟩ **c** : an object of desire or deep interest ⟨bowling is his *passion*⟩

pas·sion·ate \'pash-(ə-)nət\ *adj* **1** : aroused or easily aroused to strong feeling **2** : showing or expressing strong feeling ⟨a *passionate* speech⟩ **3** : strongly affected with sexual desire — **pas·sion·ate·ly** *adv*

pas·sion·flow·er \'pash-ən-ˌflau̇(-ə)r\ *n* [from the fancied resemblance of parts of the flower to the cross, nails, and crown of

passionflower

thorns used in Christ's crucifixion] : any of a genus of chiefly tropical climbing vines or erect herbs having showy symmetrical flowers and pulpy often edible fruits

passion play *n, often cap 1st P* : a play representing scenes connected with Christ's suffering and crucifixion

Passion Sunday *n* : the 5th Sunday in Lent

Pas·sion·tide \'pash-ən-ˌtīd\ *n* : the last two weeks of Lent

Passion Week *n* **1** : HOLY WEEK **2** : the 2d week before Easter

1**pas·sive** \'pas-iv\ *adj* **1 a** : not active but acted upon ⟨*passive* spectators⟩ **b** : indicating that the person or thing represented by the subject is subjected to the action represented by the verb ⟨*was hit* in "he was hit by the ball" is *passive*⟩ **2** : PATIENT, SUBMISSIVE ⟨*passive* surrender to fate⟩ — **pas·sive·ly** *adv* — **pas·sive·ness** *n* — **pas·siv·i·ty** \pa-'siv-ət-ē\ *n*

2**passive** *n* **1** : the passive voice **2** : a passive verb form

passive immunity *n* : immunity acquired by transfer (as by injection of serum from an individual with active immunity) of antibodies

pass·key \'pas-ˌkē\ *n* **1** : a key for opening two or more locks **2** : SKELETON KEY

pass out *vb* : to lose consciousness

Pass·over \'pas-ˌō-vər\ *n* [a translation of Hebrew *Pesaḥ;* from the Lord's passing over the houses of the Israelites when he smote the firstborn in Egypt (Exodus 12:12–14)] : a Jewish holiday celebrated in March or April in commemoration of the liberation of the Hebrews from slavery in Egypt

pass·port \'pas-ˌpōrt, -ˌpȯrt\ *n* **1** : an official document issued to a citizen about to travel abroad authorizing him to leave his own country and requesting protection for him in foreign countries **2** : something that secures admission or acceptance

pass·word \-ˌwərd\ *n* : a word or phrase that must be spoken by a person before he is allowed to pass a guard

1**past** \'past\ *adj* **1 a** : AGO ⟨10 years *past*⟩ **b** : just gone by ⟨for the *past* few months⟩ **2** : having existed or taken place in a period before the present ⟨*past* customs⟩ **3** : of, relating to, or constituting a verb tense that in English is usu. formed by internal vowel change (as in *sang*) or by the addition of a suffix (as in *laughed*) and that expresses elapsed time **4** : no longer serving ⟨a *past* president⟩

2**past** *prep* **1** : BEYOND ⟨*past* 50 years old⟩ ⟨half *past* ten⟩ **2** : in a course by and then beyond ⟨the road goes *past* the house⟩

3**past** *n* **1** : a former time or event **2 a** : PAST TENSE **b** : a verb form in the past tense **3** : a past life or history; *esp* : a past life that is secret or questionable ⟨a man with a *past*⟩

4**past** *adv* : so as to pass by ⟨a deer ran *past*⟩

pas·ta \'päs-tə\ *n* **1** : wheat paste in processed form (as spaghetti) or in the form of fresh dough (as ravioli) **2** : a dish of cooked pasta

1**paste** \'pāst\ *n* **1 a** : a dough rich in fat used for pastry **b** : a candy made by evaporating fruit with sugar or by flavoring a gelatin, starch, or gum arabic preparation **c** : a smooth food product made by evaporation or grinding ⟨almond *paste*⟩ **d** : a shaped dough (as spaghetti or ravioli) prepared from wheat products (as semolina, farina, or flour) **2** : a preparation of flour or starch and water used for sticking things together **3** : a soft plastic substance or mixture **4** : a very brilliant glass used for the manufacture of artificial gems

2**paste** *vb* **1** : to stick on or together by paste **2** : to cover with something pasted on ⟨*paste* a wall with advertising⟩

3**paste** *vb* : to hit hard

paste·board \'pās(t)-ˌbōrd, -ˌbȯrd\ *n* : paperboard of moderate thickness esp. when formed of layers pasted or pressed together

1**pas·tel** \pas-'tel\ *n* **1 a** : a paste made of ground color and used for making crayons **b** : a crayon of such paste **2** : a drawing in pastel **3** : any of various pale or light colors

2**pastel** *adj* **1** : of, relating to, or made with pastels **2** : pale and light in color

pas·tern \'pas-tərn\ *n* : the part of the foot of a horse between the fetlock and the joint at the hoof; *also* : the corresponding part of some other 4-footed animals

pas·teur·i·za·tion \ˌpas-chə-rə-'zā-shən, ˌpas-tə-\ *n* : partial sterilization of a substance and esp. a fluid (as milk) by exposure to heat that destroys objectionable organisms without major alteration of the chemical composition

pas·teur·ize \'pas-chə-ˌrīz, 'pas-tə-\ *vb* [after Louis *Pasteur* (1822–1895), French chemist who invented the process of pasteurization] : to subject to pasteurization

pas·time \'pas-ˌtīm\ *n* : something that helps to make time pass agreeably

past master *n* : one who is experienced : EXPERT

pas·tor \'pas-tər\ *n* : a minister or priest in charge of a church or parish — **pas·tor·ship** \-ˌship\ *n*

1**pas·to·ral** \'pas-t(ə-)rəl\ *adj* **1 a** : of or relating to shepherds or rural life **b** : devoted to or based on livestock raising **2** : of or relating to the pastor of a church

2**pas·to·ral** \'pas-t(ə-)rəl, *3 is often* ˌpas-tə-'räl, -'ral\ *n* **1** : a literary work dealing with shepherds or rural life **2** : a rural picture or scene **3** : PASTORALE

pas·to·rale \ˌpas-tə-'räl, -'ral\ *n* : an instrumental or vocal composition having a pastoral theme

pas·tor·ate \'pas-t(ə-)rət\ *n* **1** : the office, duties, or term of service of a pastor **2** : a body of pastors

past participle *n* : a participle that expresses completed action and that is traditionally one of the principal parts of the verb ⟨*raised* in "Many hands were raised" and *thrown* in "The ball has been thrown" are *past participles*⟩

past perfect *adj* : relating to or being a verb tense formed in English with *had* and expressing an action or state completed at or before a past time spoken of — **past perfect** *n*

past·ry \'pā-strē\ *n, pl* **pastries** **1** : sweet baked goods (as cakes, puffs, or tarts) made of dough or having a crust made of enriched dough **2** : a piece of pastry

past tense *n* : a verb tense expressing action or state in the past

pas·tur·age \'pas-chə-rij\ *n* : PASTURE

1**pas·ture** \'pas-chər\ *n* **1** : plants (as grass) for the feeding esp. of grazing animals **2** : land or a plot of land used for grazing

2**pasture** *vb* **1** : GRAZE **2** : to feed (as cattle) on pasture

1**pas·ty** \'pas-tē\ *n, pl* **pas·ties** : 2PIE 1; *esp* : a meat pie

²pasty \'pā-stē\ *adj* **past·i·er**; **-est** : resembling paste; *esp* : pale and unhealthy in appearance — **past·i·ness** *n*

PA system \pē-'ā-\ *n* : PUBLIC-ADDRESS SYSTEM

¹pat \'pat\ *n* **1** : a light blow esp. with the hand or a flat instrument **2** : a light tapping sound **3** : something (as butter) shaped into a small flat portion

²pat *vb* **pat·ted**; **pat·ting** **1** : to strike lightly with the hand or a flat instrument : strike or beat gently **2** : to flatten, smooth, or shape with pats **3** : to soothe, caress, or show approval with pats **4** : PATTER

³pat *adj* **pat·ter**; **pat·test** **1** : exactly suited : APT, TIMELY ⟨a *pat* answer⟩ **2** : learned exactly ⟨have a lesson down *pat*⟩ **3** : FIRM, UNYIELDING ⟨stand *pat*⟩

pat *abbr* patent

¹patch \'pach\ *n* **1** : a piece of material used to mend or cover a hole, a torn place, or a weak spot **2** : a shield (as of cloth) worn over an injured eye **3** : a small piece : SCRAP **4 a** : a small area or plot distinguished from its surroundings ⟨a *patch* of oats⟩ ⟨a *patch* of blistered skin⟩ **b** : a spot of color : BLOTCH **5** : a piece of cloth worn (as on the shoulder of a uniform) as an ornament or insignia

²patch *vb* **1** : to mend, cover, or fill up a hole or weak spot in **2** : to provide with a patch **3 a** : to make out of patches **b** : to mend or put together esp. hastily or clumsily **c** : SETTLE, ADJUST — usu. used with *up* ⟨*patched* up their differences⟩

patch test *n* : a test for determining a person's sensitivity to an allergy-producing substance made by applying to the unbroken skin small pads soaked with the substance in question

patch·work \'pach-ˌwərk\ *n* **1** : something made up of various parts **2** : pieces of cloth of various colors and shapes sewed together usu. in a pattern — **patchwork** *adj*

patchy \'pach-ē\ *adj* **patch·i·er**; **-est** : consisting of or marked by patches : resembling patchwork

pate \'pāt\ *n* : HEAD; *esp* : the crown of the head — **pat·ed** \'pāt-əd\ *adj*

pa·tel·la \pə-'tel-ə\ *n, pl* **-tel·lae** \-'tel-(ˌ)ē, -ˌī\ *or* **-tellas** : KNEECAP

pat·en \'pat-ən\ *n* **1** : a plate of precious metal for the eucharistic bread **2** : PLATE **3** : a thin disk (as of metal)

¹pat·ent *2 is* 'pat-ənt, 'pāt-; *1 is* 'pat-, *Brit also* 'pāt-\ *adj* **1 a** : PATENTED **b** : of, relating to, or concerned with patents ⟨a *patent* lawyer⟩ **c** : marketed as a proprietary commodity ⟨a *patent* can opener⟩ **2** : PLAIN, OBVIOUS ⟨a *patent* lie⟩ — **pat·ent·ly** *adv*

²pat·ent \'pat-ənt, *Brit also* 'pāt-\ *n* **1** : an official document conferring a right or privilege; *esp* : one granting a writing to an inventor for a term of years the exclusive right to make, use, or sell his invention **2** : the right granted by a patent

³pat·ent *vb* : to secure by patent — **pat·ent·a·ble** \-ə-bəl\ *adj*

pat·en·tee \ˌpat-ən-'tē, *Brit also* ˌpāt-\ *n* : one to whom a patent is granted

pat·ent leather \ˌpat-ən(t)-, *Brit usu* ˌpāt-\ *n* : a leather with a hard smooth glossy surface

patent medicine *n* : a packaged medicine put up for immediate use by the public with a label bearing the name of the medicine, the manufacturer's name, and directions for use

pa·ter·nal \pə-'tərn-əl\ *adj* **1** : FATHERLY **2** : received or inherited from one's father **3** : related through the father ⟨a *paternal* grandfather⟩ — **pa·ter·nal·ly** \-ə-lē\ *adv*

pa·ter·nal·ism \pə-'tərn-ə-ˌliz-əm\ *n* : the principle or practice of governing or of exercising authority (as over a group of employees) in a manner suggesting the care and control exercised by a father over his children — **pa·ter·nal·is·tic** \-ˌtərn-ə-'lis-tik\ *adj*

pa·ter·ni·ty \pə-'tər-nət-ē\ *n* **1** : the state of being a father **2** : origin or descent from a father

pat·er·nos·ter \'pat-ər-ˌnäs-tər\ *n* [from Latin, meaning "our father", the opening words of the Latin version] *often cap* : LORD'S PRAYER

path \'path, 'pȧth\ *n, pl* **paths** \'pat͟hz, 'paths, 'pȧt͟hz, 'pȧths\ **1** : a track made by foot travel specially constructed (as for walking or horseback riding) **2 a** : the way along which something moves : COURSE, ROUTE **b** : a way of life, conduct, or thought — **path·less** \'path-ləs, 'pȧth-\ *adj*

path *or* **pathol** *abbr* pathology

pa·thet·ic \pə-'thet-ik\ *adj* **1** : arousing tenderness, pity, or sorrow **2** : marked by sorrow or melancholy : SAD ⟨a *pathetic* lament⟩ — **pa·thet·i·cal·ly** \-i-k(ə-)lē\ *adv*

path·find·er \'path-ˌfīn-dər, 'pȧth-\ *n* : one that discovers a way and esp. a new route for travelers in unexplored regions

path·o·gen \'path-ə-jən\ *n* : a specific cause (as a bacterium or virus) of disease — **path·o·gen·ic** \ˌpath-ə-'jen-ik\ *adj* — **path·o·ge·nic·i·ty** \-jə-'nis-ət-ē\ *n*

path·o·log·i·cal \ˌpath-ə-'läj-i-kəl\ *or* **path·o·log·ic** \-ik\ *adj* **1** : of or relating to pathology **2** : altered or caused by disease — **path·o·log·i·cal·ly** \-i-k(ə-)lē\ *adv*

pa·thol·o·gist \pə-'thäl-ə-jəst, pa-\ *n* : a specialist in pathology

pa·thol·o·gy \-jē\ *n* **1** : the study of diseases and esp. of the changes produced by them **2** : something abnormal; *esp* : the disorders in structure and function that constitute disease or characterize a particular disease

pa·thos \'pā-ˌthäs\ *n* : an element in life or in artistic representation of it that moves one to pity or compassion

path·way \'path-ˌwā, 'pȧth-\ *n* : PATH, COURSE

pa·tience \'pā-shən(t)s\ *n* **1** : the quality or state of being patient **2** *chiefly Brit* : SOLITAIRE 2

¹pa·tient \'pā-shənt\ *adj* **1** : bearing pains or trials calmly or without complaint **2** : showing calm self-control **3** : not hasty or impetuous **4** : CONSTANT, PERSEVERING ⟨years of *patient* labor⟩ — **pa·tient·ly** *adv*

²patient *n* : an individual awaiting or under medical care and treatment

pat·io \'pat-ē-ˌō, 'pät-\ *n, pl* **-i·os** **1** : COURTYARD; *esp* : an inner court open to the sky **2** : an often paved recreation area that adjoins a dwelling

pa·tois \'pa-ˌtwä\ *n, pl* **patois** \-ˌtwäz\ **1** : DIALECT **2** : illiterate or provincial speech

pa·tri·arch \'pā-trē-ˌärk\ *n* **1 a** : one of the Old Testament fathers of the human race or of the Hebrew people **b** : the father and ruler of a family or tribe **c** : a venerable old man **2** : any of various bishops of highest rank and dignity — **pa·tri·ar·chal** \ˌpā-trē-'är-kəl\ *adj*

pa·tri·ar·chy \'pā-trē-ˌär-kē\ *n, pl* **-chies** **1** : social organization in which the father is head of the clan or family and descent and inheritance are traced in the male line **2** : a society organized according to the principles of patriarchy

pa·tri·cian \pə-'trish-ən\ *n* **1** : a member of one of the original citizen families of ancient Rome **2** : a person of high birth or cultivation : ARISTOCRAT — **patrician** *adj* — **pa·tri·ci·ate** \-'trish-ē-ət\ *n*

P

pat·ri·mo·ny \'pa-trə-ˌmō-nē\ *n, pl* **-nies** **1 a :** an estate inherited from one's father or ancestors **b :** something derived from one's father or ancestors **:** HERITAGE **2 :** an ancient endowment of a church — **pat·ri·mo·ni·al** \ˌpa-trə-'mō-nē-əl\ *adj*

pa·tri·ot \'pā-trē-ət\ *n* **[**originally meaning "fellow countryman", from Greek *patriōtes*, from *patrios* "of one's forefathers", from *patēr* "father"**]** **:** a person who loves his country and zealously supports it

pa·tri·ot·ic \ˌpā-trē-'ät-ik\ *adj* **1 :** inspired by patriotism **2 :** befitting or characteristic of a patriot — **pa·tri·ot·i·cal·ly** \-i-k(ə-)lē\ *adv*

pa·tri·ot·ism \'pā-trē-ə-ˌtiz-əm\ *n* **:** love of one's own country and devotion to its welfare

1**pa·trol** \pə-'trōl\ *n* **1 a :** the action of going the rounds of an area for observation or guard **b :** the person or group performing such an action **2 :** a detachment of men employed for reconnaissance, security, or combat **3 :** a subdivision of a boy scout or girl scout troop

2**patrol** *vb* **pa·trolled**; **pa·trol·ling :** to carry out a patrol or a patrol of — **pa·trol·ler** *n*

pa·trol·man \pə-'trōl-mən\ *n* **:** a policeman assigned to a beat

patrol wagon *n* **:** an enclosed police truck used to carry prisoners

pa·tron \'pā-trən\ *n* **[**from Latin *patronus* "one standing in the role of father", from *pater* "father"**]** **1 :** a person chosen as a special guardian or supporter ⟨a *patron* of poets⟩ **2 :** one who gives generous support or approval ⟨a *patron* of the arts⟩ **3 :** a regular client or customer — **pa·tron·ess** \-trə-nəs\ *n*

pat·ron·age \'pa-trə-nij, 'pā-\ *n* **1 :** the support or influence of a patron **2 :** the trade of customers **3 :** the power to distribute government jobs on a basis other than merit alone

pa·tron·ize \'pā-trə-ˌnīz, 'pa-\ *vb* **1 :** to act as a patron to or of **:** FAVOR, SUPPORT ⟨*patronize* the arts⟩ **2 :** to be condescending toward **3 :** to do business with ⟨*patronize* a store⟩ — **pa·tron·iz·ing·ly** \-ˌnī-zing-lē\ *adv*

patron saint *n* **:** a saint to whom a person, society, church, or place is dedicated

pa·troon \pə-'trün\ *n* **:** the proprietor of a manorial estate in New York or New Jersey granted by the Dutch

1**pat·ter** \'pat-ər\ *vb* **:** to talk glibly or mechanically **:** CHATTER

2**patter** *n* **1 :** JARGON, CANT **2 :** a speech by a street hawker or a circus barker to attract customers **3 :** empty chatter **4 a :** the talk of a comedian or a magician **b :** a comic song or rapid speech introduced into such a song

3**patter** *vb* **1 :** to strike or pat rapidly and repeatedly ⟨rain *pattering* on a roof⟩ **2 :** to run with quick light-sounding steps

4**patter** *n* **:** a quick series of light sounds ⟨the *patter* of little feet⟩

1**pat·tern** \'pat-ərn\ *n* **[**from Middle English *patron* "patron", "patron saint"**]** **1 :** a form or model to be imitated or copied **2 :** something to be used as a guide ⟨a dress *pattern*⟩ **3 :** an artistic form, figure, or design ⟨chintz with a small *pattern*⟩ **4 :** a natural or chance formation or marking ⟨frost *patterns*⟩ **5 :** a set of characteristics that are displayed repeatedly ⟨behavior *patterns*⟩ ⟨the *pattern* of American industry⟩

syn PATTERN, MODEL, IDEAL can mean an example to be followed. PATTERN applies to a carefully worked out design or an example to be followed closely; MODEL often applies to a person or thing that is outstandingly worthy of imitation ⟨a new state law that became regarded as a *model* for other states⟩; IDEAL suggests either a reality or a mental conception that represents the highest attainable standard

2**pattern** *vb* **:** to make or fashion according to a pattern ⟨he *patterned* himself after his hero⟩

pat·ty *also* **pat·tie** \'pat-ē\ *n, pl* **patties** **1 :** a little pie **2 a :** a small flat cake of chopped food ⟨a fish *patty*⟩ **b :** a small flat candy ⟨chocolate-covered mint *patties*⟩

pau·ci·ty \'pò-sət-ē\ *n* **:** smallness of number or quantity **:** SCARCITY ⟨a *paucity* of food⟩ ⟨a *paucity* of experience⟩

paunch \'pònch, 'pänch\ *n* **1 a :** the belly together with its contents **b :** POTBELLY **2 :** RUMEN

paunchy \'pòn-chē\ *adj* **:** having a potbelly — **paunch·i·ness** *n*

pau·per \'pò-pər\ *n* **:** a very poor person; *esp* **:** one supported by charity — **pau·per·ism** \-pə-ˌriz-əm\ *n* — **pau·per·ize** \-ˌrīz\ *vb*

1**pause** \'pòz\ *n* **1 :** a temporary stop or rest **2 :** the sign ⌒ or ⌣ placed over or under a musical note, chord, or rest to indicate that it is to be prolonged **3 :** a reason for pausing ⟨a thought that should give *pause*⟩

2**pause** *vb* **1 :** to stop temporarily **:** HESITATE **2 :** to linger for a time ⟨*pause* on a high note⟩

pa·vane \pə-'vän, -'van\ *n* **:** a stately court dance by couples that was introduced from southern Europe into England in the 16th century

pave \'pāv\ *vb* **:** to lay or cover with material (as stone or concrete) that makes a firm level surface for travel — **pave the way :** to prepare a smooth easy way ⟨inventors who *pave the way* for those who come after⟩

pave·ment \'pāv-mənt\ *n* **1 :** a paved surface (as of a street) **2 :** material used in paving

pa·vil·ion \pə-'vil-yən\ *n* **[**from Old French *paveillon*, from Latin *papilion*, stem of *papilio* "butterfly"; so called from the spreading out of the sections of the top like a butterfly's wings**]** **1 :** a usu. large tent with a peaked or rounded top **2 :** a lightly constructed ornamented building serving as a shelter in a park, garden, or athletic field **3 :** a part of a building projecting from the main part **4 :** a building partly or completely detached from the main building or group of buildings

pav·ing \'pā-ving\ *n* **:** PAVEMENT

1**paw** \'pò\ *n* **:** the foot of a 4-footed animal (as a lion or dog) having claws; *also* **:** the foot of an animal

2**paw** *vb* **1 :** to touch or handle clumsily or rudely ⟨goods *pawed* by customers⟩ **2 :** to touch or strike with a paw **3 :** to scrape or beat with a hoof

pawl \'pòl\ *n* **:** a pivoted tongue or sliding bolt on a machine part that is adapted to fall into notches on another part (as a ratchet wheel) so as to permit motion in only one direction

1**pawn** \'pòn, 'pän\ *n* **1 :** something given as security for a loan **:** PLEDGE **2 :** the state of being pledged ⟨the watch was in *pawn*⟩

2**pawn** *vb* **:** to deposit as security — **pawn·er** *n*

3**pawn** *n* **[**from medieval French *peon*, from medieval Latin *pedon-*, stem of *pedo* "foot soldier", from Latin *ped-*, stem of *pes* "foot"**]** **1 :** one of the chess-

ə abut	ər further	a back	ā bake	
ä cot, cart	aù out	ch chin	e less	ē easy
g gift	i trip	ī life	j joke	ng sing	ō flow
ò flaw	òi coin	th thin	t͟h this	ü loot
ù foot	y yet	yü few	yù furious	zh vision

men of least value **2 :** a person used to further the purposes of another

pawn·bro·ker \'pȯn-ˌbrō-kər, 'pän-\ *n* **:** one who loans money on the security of personal property pledged in his keeping — **pawn·bro·king** \-king\ *n*

Paw·nee \pȯ-'nē, pä-\ *n* **:** a member of an Amerindian people of Nebraska and Kansas

paw·paw *var of* PAPAW

[1]**pay** \'pā\ *vb* **paid** \'pād\ *also in sense 7* **payed; paid; pay·ing** [from Old French *paier*, from Latin *pacare* "to pacify", "appease", from *pac-*, stem of *pax* "peace"] **1 :** to give money in return for services received or for something bought ⟨*pay* the taxi driver⟩ ⟨*pay* for a ticket⟩ **2 :** to discharge a debt ⟨*pay* a tax⟩ **3 :** to get even with ⟨*pay* someone back for an injury⟩ **4 :** to give or offer freely ⟨*pay* a compliment⟩ ⟨*pay* attention⟩ **5 :** to return value or profit ⟨an investment *paying* 5 percent⟩ **6 :** to be worth the effort or pains required ⟨it *pays* to drive carefully⟩ **7 :** to make slack and allow to run out ⟨*pay* out a rope⟩ — **pay·er** \'pā-ər\ *also* **pay·or** \'pā-ər, pā-'ȯ(ə)r\ *n*

[2]**pay** *n* **1 a :** the act of paying **:** PAYMENT **b :** the status of being paid by an employer **:** EMPLOY ⟨in his *pay*⟩ **2 :** something paid; *esp* **:** WAGES, SALARY — **pay** *adj*

pay·a·ble \'pā-ə-bəl\ *adj* **:** that may, can, or must be paid; *esp* **:** DUE ⟨accounts *payable*⟩

pay·check \'pā-ˌchek\ *n* **:** a check in payment of wages or salary

pay dirt *n* **:** earth or ore that yields a profit to a miner

pay·ee \pā-'ē\ *n* **:** one to whom money is or is to be paid

pay·load \'pā-ˌlōd\ *n* **:** something (as cargo, passengers, instruments, or explosives) carried by a vehicle, missile, or rocket in addition to what is necessary for its operation

pay·mas·ter \-ˌmas-tər\ *n* **:** an officer or agent of an employer whose duty it is to pay salaries or wages

pay·ment \'pā-mənt\ *n* **1 :** the act of paying **2 :** money given to discharge a debt ⟨monthly *payments* on a radio⟩ **3 :** PAY ⟨receive *payment* for a day's work⟩

pay·off \'pā-ˌȯf\ *n* **1 :** payment at the outcome of an enterprise ⟨a big *payoff* from an investment⟩ **2 :** the climax of an incident or enterprise ⟨the *payoff* of a story⟩

pay off \-'ȯf\ *vb* **1 :** to pay in full often through small payments made at intervals ⟨*pay off* a mortgage over a 20-year period⟩ **2 :** to take revenge on ⟨*pay off* an enemy⟩ **3 :** to yield returns ⟨investments that *pay off*⟩

pay·roll \'pā-ˌrōl\ *n* **1 :** a list of persons entitled to receive pay with the amounts due to each **2 :** the amount of money necessary to pay those on a payroll

payt *abbr* payment

pay up *vb* **:** to pay in full esp. debts that are overdue

pc *abbr* piece

PC *abbr* **1** percent **2** postcard

pd *abbr* paid

PD *abbr* police department

pea \'pē\ *n, pl* **peas** *also* **pease** \'pēz\ **1 :** a leguminous annual plant widely grown for its pods of protein-rich edible rounded seeds **2 :** the seed of a pea **3 :** a plant (as the sweet pea) related to the pea

pea 1

peace \'pēs\ *n* **1 :** a state of tranquillity or quiet; *esp* **:** freedom from civil disturbance or foreign war **2 :** freedom from disquiet or emotional fears **3 :** harmony in personal relations **4 a :** a state or period of peace between governments **b :** an agreement to end a war

peace·a·ble \'pē-sə-bəl\ *adj* **1 :** inclined toward peace **:** not quarrelsome **2 :** PEACEFUL — **peace·a·bly** \-blē\ *adv*

peace·ful \'pēs-fəl\ *adj* **1 :** PEACEABLE 1 ⟨a *peaceful* man⟩ **2 :** QUIET, TRANQUIL ⟨a *peaceful* countryside⟩; *esp* **:** not at war **3 :** not involving violence or force ⟨settled the conflict by *peaceful* means⟩ — **peace·ful·ly** \-fə-lē\ *adv* — **peace·ful·ness** *n*

peace·mak·er \'pēs-ˌmā-kər\ *n* **:** a person who settles an argument or conflict or stops a fight — **peace·mak·ing** \-king\ *n or adj*

peace·time \-ˌtīm\ *n* **:** a time when a nation is not at war

peach \'pēch\ *n* **1 :** a low spreading Chinese tree related to the plums and cherries that is grown in most temperate areas for its sweet juicy fruit with pulpy white or yellow flesh, thin downy skin, and single rough hard stone; *also* **:** its fruit **2 :** a moderate yellowish pink

pea·cock \'pē-ˌkäk\ *n* **:** a male peafowl distinguished by a small upright tuft on the head and by greatly elongated feathers in the tail mostly tipped with eyelike spots and erected and spread at will in a fan shimmering with iridescent color; *also* **:** PEAFOWL

pea·fowl \-ˌfau̇l\ *n* **:** a very large pheasant of southeastern Asia and the East Indies that is often kept in captivity for its beauty

pea·hen \-ˌhen, -'hen\ *n* **:** a female peafowl

pea jacket \'pē-\ *n* **:** a heavy woolen double-breasted jacket worn chiefly by sailors

[1]**peak** \'pēk\ *n* **1 :** a projecting point or part **2 :** the visor of a cap or hat **3 a :** the top of a hill, ridge, or mountain **b :** an isolated mountain **4 :** the highest level or greatest degree of development ⟨the *peak* of perfection⟩ — **peak** *adj*

[2]**peak** *vb* **:** to come or lead to a peak

peaked *adj* **1** \'pēkt, 'pē-kəd\ **:** having a peak **:** POINTED ⟨a *peaked* roof⟩ **2** \'pē-kəd\ **:** THIN, SICKLY — **peaked·ness** \'pēk(t)-nəs, 'pē-kəd-nəs\ *n*

peal \'pēl\ *n* **1 a :** the loud ringing of bells **b :** a complete set of changes on a set of bells **c :** a set of tuned bells **2 :** a loud sound or series of sounds ⟨a *peal* of laughter⟩ ⟨a *peal* of thunder⟩ — **peal** *vb*

pea·nut \'pē-(ˌ)nət\ *n* **1 :** a low-branching widely cultivated annual legume with showy yellow flowers and pods that ripen underground; *also* **:** this pod or one of the oily edible seeds it contains **2** *pl* **:** a trivial amount

peanut butter *n* **:** a paste made chiefly of ground roasted peanuts

pear \'pa(ə)r, 'pe(ə)r\ *n* **:** a fleshy fruit that usu. tapers toward the stem end; *also* **:** a tree related to the apple that bears pears

[1]**pearl** \'pərl\ *n* **1 a :** a dense usu. shiny body formed of layers of nacre as an abnormal growth within the shell of some mollusks and used as a gem **b :** MOTHER-OF-PEARL **2 :** something like a pearl (as in shape, color, or value) **3 :** a light bluish gray

[2]**pearl** *adj* **1 :** of, relating to, or resembling pearl **2 :** made of pearls

pearl·er \'pər-lər\ *n* **1 :** a person who dives for pearls or who employs pearl divers **2 :** a boat used in pearl fishing

pearly \'pər-lē\ *adj* **pearl·i·er; -est :** resembling pearls or mother-of-pearl

peas·ant \'pez-ənt\ *n* **1 :** a European small farmer or farm laborer **2 :** a member of a similar agricultural class elsewhere

peas·ant·ry \-ən-trē\ *n* **:** a body of peasants

pease *pl of* PEA

peat \'pēt\ *n* **1 :** TURF 2b **2 :** a dark brown or black substance formed when certain plants partly decay in water — **peaty** \'pēt-ē\ *adj*

peat moss *n* **:** SPHAGNUM

1**peb·ble** \'peb-əl\ *n* **:** a small rounded stone — **peb·ble·like** \-əl-ˌ(l)īk\ *adj* — **peb·bly** \-(ə-)lē\ *adj*

2**pebble** *vb* **peb·bled**; **peb·bling** \'peb-(ə-)ling\ **:** to treat so as to produce a rough indented surface ⟨*pebble* leather⟩

pe·can \pi-'kän, -'kan\ *n* **:** a large hickory of the south central U.S.; *also* **:** its edible oblong nut

pec·ca·dil·lo \ˌpek-ə-'dil-ō\ *n, pl* **-loes** *or* **-los :** a slight offense or fault

pec·ca·ry \'pek-ə-rē\ *n, pl* **-ries :** either of two American chiefly tropical mammals resembling but smaller than the related pigs

peccary (about 20 in. at shoulder)

1**peck** \'pek\ *n* **1** — see MEASURE table **2 :** a large quantity ⟨a *peck* of trouble⟩

2**peck** *vb* **1 :** to strike with the bill **:** thrust the beak into **2 :** to strike with a sharp instrument (as a pick) **3 :** to pick up with the bill ⟨a chicken *pecking* corn⟩ **4 :** to bite daintily **:** NIBBLE ⟨*pecked* at his food⟩

3**peck** *n* **1 :** a mark or hole made by pecking **2 :** a quick sharp stroke

peck order *n* **:** a basic pattern of social organization within a flock of poultry in which each bird pecks another lower in the scale without being pecked in return and submits to pecking by one of higher rank — called also *pecking order*

pec·tin \'pek-tən\ *n* **:** any of various water-soluble substances in plant tissues that yield a gel which is the basis of fruit jellies; *also* **:** a commercial product rich in pectins

pec·to·ral \'pek-t(ə-)rəl\ *adj* **:** of, relating to, or situated in, near, or on the chest

pectoral fin *n* **:** either of a pair of fins that correspond in a fish to the forelimbs of a four-footed animal — compare PELVIC FIN

pectoral girdle *n* **:** the bony or cartilaginous arch supporting the forelimbs of a vertebrate

pe·cu·liar \pi-'kyül-yər\ *adj* **1 :** belonging to or characteristic of one person, group, or thing **:** DISTINCTIVE, UNIQUE ⟨a custom *peculiar* to England⟩ **2 :** different from the usual or normal **:** ODD, QUEER ⟨*peculiar* behavior⟩ — **pe·cu·liar·ly** *adv*

pe·cu·li·ar·i·ty \pi-ˌkyü-lē-'ar-ət-ē, -ˌkyül-'yar-\ *n, pl* **-ties 1 :** the quality or state of being peculiar **2 :** a distinguishing characteristic **3 :** ODDITY, QUIRK

pe·cu·ni·ary \pi-'kyü-nē-ˌer-ē\ *adj* **:** of, relating to, or consisting of money ⟨*pecuniary* aid⟩ ⟨*pecuniary* policies⟩

-ped \ˌped\ *or* **-pede** \ˌpēd\ *n comb form* **:** foot ⟨maxilli*ped*⟩ ⟨maxilli*pede*⟩

Ped *abbr* pedal

ped·a·gog·ics \ˌped-ə-'gäj-iks\ *n* **:** PEDAGOGY

ped·a·gogue \'ped-ə-ˌgäg\ *n* **1 :** TEACHER, SCHOOLMASTER; *esp* **:** a dull and pedantic teacher

ped·a·go·gy \'ped-ə-ˌgō-jē, -ˌgäj-ē\ *n* **:** the art, science, or profession of teaching **:** EDUCATION — **ped·a·gog·ic** \ˌped-ə-'gäj-ik\ *or* **ped·a·gog·i·cal** \-i-kəl\ *adj* — **ped·a·gog·i·cal·ly** \-i-k(ə-)lē\ *adv*

1**ped·al** \'ped-əl\ *n* **:** a device (as on a piano, bicycle, or sewing machine) worked by the foot

2**pedal** *adj* **:** of or relating to the foot

3**pedal** *vb* **ped·aled** *also* **ped·alled**; **ped·al·ing** *also* **ped·al·ling** \'ped-(ə-)ling\ **1 :** to use or work the pedals of something **2 :** to ride a bicycle or tricycle

pedal pushers *n pl* **:** women's and girls' calf-length trousers

ped·ant \'ped-ənt\ *n* **1 :** a person who shows off his learning **2 :** a formal unimaginative teacher — **pe·dan·tic** \pi-'dant-ik\ *adj* — **pe·dan·ti·cal·ly** \-i-k(ə-)lē\ *adv*

ped·ant·ry \'ped-ən-trē\ *n, pl* **-ries :** pedantic presentation or application of knowledge or learning

ped·dle \'ped-əl\ *vb* **ped·dled**; **ped·dling** \-(ə-)ling\ **1 :** to travel about esp. from house to house with goods for sale **2 :** to sell from place to place usu. in small quantities **:** HAWK — **ped·dler** *or* **ped·lar** \'ped-lər\ *n*

ped·es·tal \'ped-ə-stəl\ *n* **1 :** the support or foot of a column **2 :** the base of an upright structure (as a vase, lamp, or statue) **3 :** a position of high regard or esteem ⟨placed on a *pedestal* by his children⟩

1**pe·des·tri·an** \pə-'des-trē-ən\ *adj* **1 :** UNIMAGINATIVE, COMMONPLACE **2 a :** going on foot **b :** of or relating to walking — **pe·des·tri·an·ism** \-trē-ə-ˌniz-əm\ *n*

2**pedestrian** *n* **:** a person going on foot **:** WALKER

pe·di·a·tri·cian \ˌpēd-ē-ə-'trish-ən\ *n* **:** a specialist in pediatrics

pe·di·at·rics \ˌpēd-ē-'a-triks\ *n* **:** a branch of medicine dealing with the child, its development, care, and diseases — **pe·di·at·ric** \-trik\ *adj*

ped·i·cure \'ped-i-ˌkyu̇r\ *n* **:** care of the feet, toes, and nails; *also* **:** a single treatment of these parts — **ped·i·cur·ist** \-ˌkyu̇r-əst\ *n*

ped·i·gree \'ped-ə-ˌgrē\ *n* [from medieval French *pie de grue* "foot of a crane"; from the shape made by the lines of a genealogical chart] **1 :** a table or list showing the line of ancestors of a person or animal **2 :** an ancestral line **:** LINEAGE **3 :** purity of breed recorded by a pedigree — **ped·i·greed** \-ˌgrēd\ *adj*

ped·i·ment \'ped-ə-mənt\ *n* **1 :** a triangular space forming the gable of a roof in classic architecture **2 :** a similar form used as a decoration (as over a door)

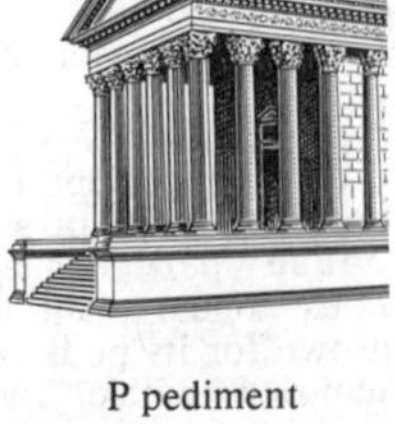

P pediment

pe·dom·e·ter \pi-'däm-ət-ər\ *n* **:** an instrument that measures the distance one covers in walking

pe·dun·cle \'pē-ˌdəng-kəl, pi-'\ *n* **:** a narrow part by which some larger part or the body of an organism is attached; *esp* **:** a stalk that supports a flower cluster — **pe·dun·cu·late** \pi-'dəng-kyə-lət\ *adj*

peek \'pēk\ *vb* **1 :** to look cautiously or briefly

2 : to peer through a crack or hole or from a hiding place — **peek** *n*

¹**peel** \'pēl\ *vb* **1** : to strip off the skin, bark, or rind of ⟨*peel* an apple⟩ **2** : to strip or tear off ⟨*peeled* off his coat⟩ **3 a** : to come off in strips or patches ⟨the paint is *peeling*⟩ **b** : to lose the skin, bark, or rind ⟨his face is *peeling*⟩ — **peel·er** *n*

²**peel** *n* : a skin or rind esp. of a fruit

peel·ing \'pē-ling\ *n* : a peeled-off piece or strip (as of skin or rind)

¹**peep** \'pēp\ *vb* **1** : to utter a feeble shrill sound as of a bird newly hatched : CHEEP **2** : to speak with a small weak voice

²**peep** *n* : a feeble shrill sound : CHEEP

³**peep** *vb* **1** : PEEK, PEER **2** : to show slightly ⟨crocuses *peeping* through the grass⟩

⁴**peep** *n* **1** : the first appearance ⟨the *peep* of dawn⟩ **2** : a brief or furtive look

¹**peep·er** \'pē-pər\ *n* : one that peeps; *esp* : any of various small frogs that peep shrilly in spring

²**peeper** *n* **1** : one that peeps; *esp* : PEEPING TOM **2** : EYE

peep·hole \'pēp-ˌhōl\ *n* : a hole or crack to peep through

peeping Tom \-'täm\ *n* [after *Peeping Tom*, a legendary 11th century inhabitant of Coventry, England, who peeked at Lady Godiva as she rode naked through the streets in order to gain tax relief for the citizens from her husband, the Earl of Mercia] : a person who spies into the windows of private dwellings

peep show *n* : an entertainment consisting of objects or pictures viewed through a small hole usu. fitted with a lens

¹**peer** \'pi(ə)r\ *n* **1** : a person of the same rank or standing as another : EQUAL **2 a** : a member (as a duke, marquess, earl, viscount, or baron) of one of the five ranks of the British nobility **b** : NOBLE 1 — **peer·ess** \'pir-əs\ *n*

²**peer** *vb* **1** : to look closely or curiously ⟨*peer* into a box⟩ **2** : ³PEEP 2 ***syn*** see GAZE

peer·age \'pi(ə)r-ij\ *n* **1** : NOBILITY **2** : a list or register of peers

peer·less \'pi(ə)r-ləs\ *adj* : having no equal : INCOMPARABLE — **peer·less·ly** *adv* — **peer·less·ness** *n*

¹**peeve** \'pēv\ *vb* : to make peevish or resentful : ANNOY, IRRITATE

²**peeve** *n* **1** : a peevish mood **2** : GRUDGE

pee·vish \'pē-vish\ *adj* **1** : FRETFUL, IRRITABLE **2** : STUBBORN — **pee·vish·ly** *adv* — **pee·vish·ness** *n*

syn PEEVISH, FRETFUL, QUERULOUS, CROSS can mean disposed to complain or show discontent. PEEVISH applies to one who shows a childish irritability and expresses petty complaints; FRETFUL suggests constant worrisome complaint, restlessness, and whining peevishness; QUERULOUS implies an often habitual discontent that is shown in whining complaints; CROSS suggests the ill humor of one who is out of sorts

pee·wee \'pē-(ˌ)wē\ *n* : a tiny person or thing

¹**peg** \'peg\ *n* **1** : a small usu. cylindrical pointed piece (as of wood) used esp. to fasten things or to fit into or close holes ⟨a tent *peg*⟩ **2** : a projecting piece used as a support or marker ⟨a clothes *peg*⟩ **3 a** : one of the pins of a stringed instrument that are turned to regulate the pitch **b** : STEP, DEGREE ⟨took him down a *peg*⟩ **4** : THROW ⟨a quick *peg* to first base⟩

²**peg** *vb* **pegged**; **peg·ging 1 a** : to fasten or mark with pegs **b** : to fix or hold (as prices) at a level **2** : to place in a category **3** : THROW **4** : to work steadily and diligently

peg–top \'peg-'täp\ *or* **peg–topped** \-'täpt\ *adj* : wide at the top and narrow at the bottom ⟨*peg-top* trousers⟩

P.E.I. *abbr* Prince Edward Island

Pe·king·ese *or* **Pe·kin·ese** \ˌpē-kən-'ēz, -king-, -'ēs\ *n, pl* **Pekingese** *or* **Pekinese 1 a** : a native or resident of Peking **b** : the Chinese dialect of Peking **2** : any of a Chinese breed of small short-legged dogs with a broad flat face and a profuse long soft coat

Pe·king man \ˌpē-ˌking-\ *n* : an extinct Pleistocene man known from skeletal and cultural remains in cave deposits found in northeastern China

pe·koe \'pē-kō\ *n* : a black tea made from small-sized tea leaves esp. in India and Ceylon

pe·lag·ic \pə-'laj-ik\ *adj* : of, relating to, or living or occurring in the open sea : OCEANIC

pelf \'pelf\ *n* : MONEY, RICHES

pel·i·can \'pel-i-kən\ *n* : any of a genus of large web-footed birds with a very large bill bearing a pouch used to scoop in fish for food

pel·lag·ra \pə-'lag-rə, -'lāg-\ *n* : a disease associated with a diet deficient in niacin and protein and marked by skin rash, disorders of the digestive system, and certain nervous and mental symptoms

pel·let \'pel-ət\ *n* **1** : a little ball (as of food or medicine) **2 a** : a usu. stone ball used as a missile in medieval times **b** : BULLET **c** : a piece of small shot

pel·li·cle \'pel-i-kəl\ *n* : a thin skin or film

pell–mell \'pel-'mel\ *adv* **1** : in confusion or disorder **2** : in great haste ⟨ran *pell-mell* down the street⟩ — **pell–mell** *adj*

pel·lu·cid \pə-'lü-səd\ *adj* **1** : extremely clear or transparent **2** : extremely easy to understand — **pel·lu·cid·ly** *adv* — **pel·lu·cid·ness** *n*

¹**pelt** \'pelt\ *n* : a usu. undressed skin with its hair, wool, or fur

²**pelt** *vb* **1** : to strike with a series of blows, missiles, or words ⟨*pelted* him with snowballs⟩ ⟨*pelted* with questions by reporters⟩ **2** : HURL, THROW **3** : BEAT, DASH ⟨hail *pelting* against a window⟩

³**pelt** *n* **1** : a persistent falling or beating (as of rain or sleet) **2** : a rapid pace or speed — used esp. in the phrase *full pelt*

pel·vic \'pel-vik\ *adj* : of, relating to, or located in or near the pelvis

pelvic fin *n* : either of a pair of fins that correspond in a fish to the hind limbs of a four-footed animal

pelvic girdle *n* : a bony or cartilaginous arch that supports the hind limbs of a vertebrate

pel·vis \'pel-vəs\ *n, pl* **pel·vis·es** *or* **pel·ves** \'pel-ˌvēz\ : a basin-shaped structure in the skeleton of many vertebrates formed by the pelvic girdle and adjoining bones of the spine; *also* : its cavity

Pem·broke \'pem-ˌbrōk, -ˌbru̇k\ *n* : a Welsh corgi of a variety characterized by pointed erect ears, straight legs, and short tail

pem·mi·can \'pem-i-kən\ *n* : dried lean meat pounded fine and mixed with melted fat

¹**pen** \'pen\ *n* **1** : a small enclosure for animals **2** : a small place of confinement or storage

²**pen** *vb* **penned**; **pen·ning** : to shut in a pen

³**pen** *n* **1** : an implement for writing or drawing with ink **2** : the internal horny feather-shaped shell of a squid

⁴**pen** *vb* **penned**; **pen·ning** : to write esp. with a pen

⁵**pen** *n, slang* : PENITENTIARY

pe·nal \'pēn-əl\ *adj* : of or relating to punishment ⟨*penal* laws⟩ ⟨a *penal* colony⟩

pe·nal·ize \'pēn-ə-ˌlīz, 'pen-\ *vb* **1** : to subject to a penalty ⟨*penalize* an athlete for a foul⟩ **2** : to place

P

at a disadvantage : HANDICAP ⟨*penalized* in business by his youth⟩

pen·al·ty \'pen-əl-tē\ *n, pl* **-ties 1 :** punishment for a crime or offense **2 :** something forfeited when a person fails to do what he agreed to do **3 :** disadvantage, loss, or hardship due to some action or condition **4 :** a punishment or handicap imposed for breaking a rule in a sport or game

pen·ance \'pen-ən(t)s\ *n* **1 :** an act showing sorrow or repentance for sin **2 :** a sacrament consisting in repentance for sin, confession to a priest, satisfaction as imposed by the confessor, and absolution

pence *pl of* PENNY

pen·chant \'pen-chənt\ *n* [from French, from the present participle of *pencher* "to lean"] **:** a strong attraction : LIKING

[1]**pen·cil** \'pen(t)-səl\ *n* **1 :** an implement for writing, drawing, or marking consisting of a stick of black or colored material encased in wood, plastic, or metal **2 :** a group of rays of light **3 :** something like a pencil in form or use ⟨an eyebrow *pencil*⟩

[2]**pencil** *vb* **-ciled** *or* **-cilled**; **-cil·ing** *or* **-cil·ling** \'pen(t)-s(ə-)liŋ\ **:** to mark, draw, or write with or as if with a pencil

pen·dant *also* **pen·dent** \'pen-dənt\ *n* **:** something that hangs down esp. as an ornament

pen·dent *or* **pen·dant** \'pen-dənt\ *adj* **1 :** supported from above : HANGING **2 :** jutting out : OVERHANGING **3 :** PENDING

[1]**pend·ing** \'pen-diŋ\ *prep* **:** while awaiting ⟨*pending* a reply⟩

[2]**pending** *adj* **:** not yet decided ⟨questions *pending*⟩

pen·du·lous \'pen-jə-ləs\ *adj* **1 :** suspended so as to swing freely **2 :** DROOPING — **pen·du·lous·ly** *adv*

pen·du·lum \'pen-jə-ləm, -d(y)ə-ləm\ *n* **:** a body suspended from a fixed point so as to swing freely to and fro under the combined action of gravity and momentum ⟨the *pendulum* of a clock⟩

pen·e·tra·ble \'pen-ə-trə-bəl\ *adj* **:** capable of being penetrated — **pen·e·tra·bil·i·ty** \,pen-ə-trə-'bil-ət-ē\ *n*

pen·e·trate \'pen-ə-,trāt\ *vb* **1 a :** to pass into or through **b :** to enter by piercing **2 :** to come to understand **3 :** to move deeply ⟨cries that *penetrated* his heart⟩

pen·e·trat·ing *adj* **1 :** BITING, SHARP ⟨*penetrating* cold⟩ **2 :** ACUTE, DISCERNING ⟨a *penetrating* mind⟩ — **pen·e·trat·ing·ly** \-,trāt-iŋ-lē\ *adv*

pen·e·tra·tion \,pen-ə-'trā-shən\ *n* **1 :** the act or process of penetrating **2 a :** the depth to which something penetrates **b :** the ability to discern deeply and acutely

pen·guin \'pen-gwən, 'peŋ-\ *n* **:** any of various short-legged aquatic birds of the southern hemisphere with the wings reduced to flippers and used in swimming

penguins (about 48 in. tall)

pen·i·cil·lin \,pen-ə-'sil-ən\ *n* **:** any of several antibiotics or a mixture of these produced by penicillia or synthetically and used esp. to prevent multiplication of bacteria

ə abut	ər further	a back	ā bake	
ä cot, cart	au̇ out	ch chin	e less	ē easy
g gift	i trip	ī life	j joke	ŋ sing	ō flow
ȯ flaw	ȯi coin	th thin	t͟h this	ü loot
u̇ foot	y yet	yü few	yu̇ furious	zh vision

pen·i·cil·li·um \-'sil-ē-əm\ *n, pl* **-lia** \-ē-ə\ **:** any of a genus of fungi comprising mostly blue molds found chiefly on moist nonliving organic matter

penin *abbr* peninsula

pen·in·su·la \pə-'nin(t)-sə-lə, -'nin-chə-lə\ *n* [from Latin *paeninsula*, from *paene* "almost" and *insula* "island"] **:** a piece of land nearly surrounded by water or jutting out into the water — **pen·in·su·lar** \-lər\ *adj*

pe·nis \'pē-nəs\ *n, pl* **pe·nes** \'pē-,nēz\ *or* **pe·nis·es :** a male organ of copulation — **pe·ni·al** \-nē-əl\ *adj* — **pe·nile** \-,nīl\ *adj*

pen·i·tence \'pen-ə-tən(t)s\ *n* **:** sorrow for one's sins or faults : REPENTANCE — **pen·i·tent** \-tənt\ *adj* — **pen·i·tent·ly** *adv*

penitent *n* **:** a person who repents or is doing penance

pen·i·ten·tial \,pen-ə-'ten-chəl\ *adj* **:** of or relating to penitence or penance — **pen·i·ten·tial·ly** \-'tench-(ə-)lē\ *adv*

pen·i·ten·tia·ry \,pen-ə-'tench-(ə-)rē\ *n, pl* **-ries :** a prison in which criminals are confined

pen·knife \'pen-,nīf\ *n* [so called from its original use for making and mending quill pens] **:** a small pocketknife

pen·man \'pen-mən\ *n* **1 :** one who is expert in penmanship **2 :** AUTHOR

pen·man·ship \'pen-mən-,ship\ *n* **1 :** the art or practice of writing with the pen **2 :** quality or style of handwriting

Penn *or* **Penna** *abbr* Pennsylvania

pen name *n* **:** an author's pseudonym

pen·nant \'pen-ənt\ *n* **1 :** a flag with a usu. tapering or forked tail that is used esp. for signaling **2 :** a flag that serves as the emblem of championship

pen·nate \'pen-,āt\ *also* **pen·nat·ed** \-,āt-əd\ *adj* **:** PINNATE

pen·ni·less \'pen-i-ləs\ *adj* **:** having no money : very poor

pen·non \'pen-ən\ *n* **1 :** a long streamer usu. with a triangular or forked tail typically attached to the head of a lance as an ensign **2 :** FLAG, PENNANT

Penn·syl·va·nia Dutch \,pen(t)-səl-,vā-nyə-\ *n* **1 :** a people of eastern Pennsylvania whose culture goes back to the German migrations of the 18th century **2 :** the German dialect of the Pennsylvania Dutch — **Pennsylvania Dutchman** *n*

Penn·syl·va·nian \-'vā-nyən\ *adj* **1 :** of or relating to Pennsylvania or its people **2 :** of, relating to, or being the period of the Paleozoic era between the Mississippian and Permian or the corresponding system of rocks — **Pennsylvanian** *n*

pen·ny \'pen-ē\ *n, pl* **pen·nies** \-ēz\ *or* **pence** \'pen(t)s\ **1 a :** a British monetary unit formerly equal to 1/240 pound but now equal to 1/100 pound **b :** a coin representing this unit **2** *pl pennies* **:** CENT **3 :** a sum of money ⟨earn an honest *penny*⟩

penny arcade *n* **:** an amusement center where each device for entertainment may be operated for a small sum

pen·ny·roy·al \,pen-ē-'rȯi(-ə)l, 'pen-i-,rīl\ *n* **:** a European mint with small aromatic leaves; *also* **:** a similar American mint that yields an oil used in folk medicine or to drive away mosquitoes

pen·ny·weight \'pen-ē-,wāt\ *n* — see MEASURE table

pen·ny–wise \-,wīz\ *adj* **:** wise only in small or unimportant matters

pe·nol·o·gy \pi-'näl-ə-jē\ *n* **:** a branch of criminology dealing with prison management and the treatment of offenders — **pe·nol·o·gist** \-jəst\ *n*

pen pal *n* **:** a friend made and kept through correspondence often without any face-to-face acquaintance

¹**pen·sion** \'pen-chən\ *n* **:** a fixed sum paid regularly to a person esp. following his retirement or to his surviving dependents

²**pension** *vb* **pen·sioned; pen·sion·ing** \'pench-(ə-)ning\ **:** to grant a pension to

pen·sion·er \'pench-(ə-)nər\ *n* **:** a person who receives or lives on a pension

pen·sive \'pen(t)-siv\ *adj* **1 :** dreamily thoughtful **:** MUSING **2 :** suggestive of sad thoughtfulness **:** MELANCHOLY — **pen·sive·ly** *adv* — **pen·sive·ness** *n*

pen·stock \'pen-ˌstäk\ *n* **1 :** a sluice or valve for regulating a flow (as of water) **2 :** a conduit or pipe for conducting water

pent \'pent\ *adj* **:** shut up **:** CONFINED ⟨*pent*-up feelings⟩

pen·ta·gon \'pent-i-ˌgän\ *n* **:** a figure of five angles and five sides — **pen·tag·o·nal** \pen-'tag-ən-əl\ *adj*

pen·tam·e·ter \pen-'tam-ət-ər\ *n* **:** a line consisting of five metrical feet

pen·tath·lon \pen-'tath-lən\ *n* **:** an athletic contest in which each contestant participates in five different events

Pen·te·cost \'pent-i-ˌkȯst, -ˌkäst\ *n* **1 :** SHABUOTH **2 :** the 7th Sunday after Easter observed as a church festival in commemoration of the descent of the Holy Spirit on the apostles — **Pen·te·cos·tal** \ˌpent-i-'käs-təl, -'kȯs-\ *adj or n* — **Pen·te·cos·tal·ism** \-ˌiz-əm\ *n*

pent·house \'pent-ˌhau̇s\ *n* **1 :** a sloping roof or a shed attached to a wall or building **2 :** a structure (as an apartment) built on the roof of a building

pen·tose \'pen-ˌtōs\ *n* **:** any of various sugars containing five carbon atoms in the molecule

pent·ste·mon *or* **pen·ste·mon** \pen(t)-'stē-mən, 'pen(t)-stə-\ *n* **:** any of a genus of chiefly American herbs that are related to the snapdragon and have showy blue, purple, red, yellow, or white flowers

pe·nult \'pē-ˌnəlt\ *n* **:** the next to the last syllable of a word

pen·ul·ti·mate \pi-'nəl-tə-mət\ *adj* **1 :** next to the last **2 :** of or relating to a penult — **penultimate** *n* — **pen·ul·ti·mate·ly** *adv*

pen·um·bra \pə-'nəm-brə\ *n, pl* **-brae** \-(ˌ)brē, -ˌbrī\ *or* **-bras 1 :** the partial shadow surrounding a perfect shadow (as in an eclipse) **2 :** the shaded region around the dark central portion of a sunspot — **pen·um·bral** \-brəl\ *adj*

pe·nu·ri·ous \pə-'n(y)u̇r-ē-əs\ *adj* **1 :** marked by or suffering from penury **2 :** extremely or excessively frugal **:** MISERLY — **pe·nu·ri·ous·ly** *adv* — **pe·nu·ri·ous·ness** *n*

pen·u·ry \'pen-yə-rē\ *n* **:** extreme poverty

pe·on \'pē-ˌän, -ən\ *n* **1 :** a member of the landless laboring class in Spanish America **2 :** a person forced to work off a debt — **pe·on·age** \'pē-ə-nij\ *n*

pe·o·ny \'pē-ə-nē\ *n, pl* **-nies :** any of a genus of plants related to the buttercups and widely grown for their large usu. double red, pink, or white flowers

¹**peo·ple** \'pē-pəl\ *n, pl* **people 1** *pl* **:** human beings **2** *pl* **a :** the members of a family **:** KINDRED **b :** ANCESTORS **3** *pl* **:** the mass of a community as distinguished from a special class **4** *pl* **peoples :** a body of persons united by a common culture, tradition, or sense of kinship, and usu. language **5 :** a body of voters **:** ELECTORATE

²**people** *vb* **peo·pled; peo·pling** \'pē-p(ə-)ling\ **1 :** to supply or fill with people **2 :** INHABIT

¹**pep** \'pep\ *n* **:** brisk energy **:** LIVELINESS — **pep·pi·ness** *n* — **pep·py** *adj*

²**pep** *vb* **pepped; pep·ping :** to inject pep into **:** STIMULATE ⟨*pep* him up⟩

pep·lum \'pep-ləm\ *n* **:** a short section attached to the waistline of a blouse, jacket, or dress

¹**pep·per** \'pep-ər\ *n* **1 :** either of two pungent products from the fruit of an East Indian plant used as a condiment and in medicine: **a :** BLACK PEPPER **b :** WHITE PEPPER **2 :** a woody vine with rounded leaves and flowers arranged in a spike that is widely cultivated in the tropics for its red berries from which pepper is prepared **3 :** any of several products similar to pepper that are obtained from close relatives of the pepper **4 :** any of a genus of tropical herbs and shrubs related to the potato and widely cultivated for their many-seeded usu. fleshy-walled fruits; *esp* **:** one of the New World whose fruits are hot peppers or sweet peppers — **pepper** *adj*

pepper 2

²**pepper** *vb* **pep·pered; pep·per·ing** \'pep-(ə-)ring\ **1 :** to sprinkle or season with or as if with pepper **2 :** to shower with missiles (as shot) ⟨mustered by their officers and *peppered* by the enemy⟩

pep·per·corn \'pep-ər-ˌkȯrn\ *n* **:** a dried berry of the East Indian pepper

peppered moth *n* **:** a European moth that typically has white wings with small black specks but often has black wings in areas with heavy air pollution

pep·per·mint \-(ˌ)mint\ *n* **1 :** a fragrant sharp-tasting mint with spikes of small pink flowers **2 :** candy flavored with peppermint

pep·pery \'pep-(ə-)rē\ *adj* **1 :** of, relating to, or having the qualities of pepper **:** HOT, PUNGENT **2 :** having a hot temper **:** TOUCHY **3 :** FIERY, STINGING

pep·sin \'pep-sən\ *n* **1 :** an enzyme secreted by glands in the wall of the stomach that begins the digestion of most proteins **2 :** a preparation of pepsin obtained esp. from the stomach of the hog and used medicinally

pep·tic \'pep-tik\ *adj* **1 :** relating to or promoting digestion **2 :** resulting from the action of digestive juices ⟨a *peptic* ulcer⟩

pep·ti·dase \'pep-tə-ˌdās\ *n* **:** an enzyme that breaks down simple fragments of proteins

pep·tone \'pep-ˌtōn\ *n* **:** any of various water-soluble products of the partial breakdown of proteins

per \(')pər\ *prep* **1 :** by means of **2 :** to or for each ⟨$10 *per* day⟩ **3 :** as indicated by **:** according to ⟨*per* list price⟩

per *abbr* period

¹**per·ad·ven·ture** \'pər-əd-ˌven-chər, 'per-\ *adv, archaic* **:** PERHAPS, POSSIBLY

²**peradventure** *n* **:** DOUBT, CHANCE

per·am·bu·late \pə-'ram-byə-ˌlāt\ *vb* **1 :** to walk over or through **2 :** STROLL, RAMBLE — **per·am·bu·la·tion** \-ˌram-byə-'lā-shən\ *n*

per·am·bu·la·tor \pə-'ram-byə-ˌlāt-ər\ *n* **1 :** one that perambulates **2** *chiefly Brit* **:** a baby carriage

per an·num \(ˌ)pər-'an-əm\ *adv* **:** in or for each year **:** ANNUALLY

per·cale \(ˌ)pər-'kāl, -'kal\ *n* **:** a fine closely woven cotton cloth used esp. for sheeting

per cap·i·ta \(ˌ)pər-'kap-ət-ə\ *adv or adj* **:** by or for each person ⟨*per capita* income⟩

per·ceive \pər-'sēv\ *vb* **1 :** UNDERSTAND, COMPREHEND **2 :** to become aware of through the senses

and esp. through sight — **per·ceiv·a·ble** \-'sē-və-bəl\ *adj* — **per·ceiv·er** *n*
[1]**per·cent** \pər-'sent\ *adv* [from *per* and Latin *centum* "hundred"] : in the hundred : of each hundred
[2]**percent** *n, pl* **percent 1** : one part in a hundred : HUNDREDTH **2** : PERCENTAGE
[3]**percent** *adj* : reckoned on the basis of a whole divided into one hundred parts
per·cent·age \pər-'sent-ij\ *n* **1** : a part of a whole expressed in hundredths **2 a** : PROBABILITY ⟨a gambler who plays the *percentages*⟩ **b** : favorable odds
per cen·tum \pər-'sent-əm\ *n* : PERCENT
per·cep·ti·ble \pər-'sep-tə-bəl\ *adj* : capable of being perceived ⟨a *perceptible* change⟩ — **per·cep·ti·bly** \-blē\ *adv*
per·cep·tion \pər-'sep-shən\ *n* **1** : a result of perceiving : OBSERVATION **2** : the act, process, or power of perceiving; *esp* : awareness of the elements of environment through sensation ⟨color *perception*⟩ **3** : capacity for comprehension : INSIGHT
per·cep·tive \pər-'sep-tiv\ *adj* : capable of or exhibiting keen perception : OBSERVANT
[1]**perch** \'pərch\ *n* **1** : a roost for a bird **2** : a raised seat or position **3 a** : a measure of length equal to a rod **b** : a unit of area equal to a square rod
[2]**perch** *vb* **1** : to place on a perch ⟨*perched* himself on the table⟩ **2** : to alight, settle, or rest on or as if on a perch
[3]**perch** *n, pl* **perch** *or* **perch·es 1** : a small largely olive-green and yellow European freshwater spiny-finned fish; *also* : a closely related American fish **2** : any of numerous fishes related to or resembling the true perches
per·chance \pər-'chan(t)s\ *adv* : PERHAPS, POSSIBLY
per·co·late \'pər-kə-,lāt\ *vb* **1** : to pass or cause to pass through a porous substance (as a powdered drug) esp. for extracting a soluble part : FILTER, SEEP **2** : to prepare coffee in a percolator **3** : to be or become diffused through : PENETRATE — **per·co·la·tion** \,pər-kə-'lā-shən\ *n*
per·co·la·tor \'pər-kə-,lāt-ər\ *n* : one that percolates; *esp* : a coffeepot in which boiling water rising through a tube is repeatedly deflected downward through a perforated basket containing the ground coffee beans to extract their essence
per·cus·sion \pər-'kəsh-ən\ *n* **1** : the act of tapping sharply; *esp* : the striking of a percussion cap so as to set off the charge in a firearm **2** : the act or technique of tapping the surface of a body part to learn the condition of the parts beneath by the sound produced **3** : the striking of sound sharply on the ear
percussion cap *n* : a small cap or container of explosive to be fired by a sharp forceful blow
percussion instrument *n* : a musical instrument sounded by striking
per·cus·sion·ist \pər-'kəsh-(ə-)nəst\ *n* : one who plays percussion instruments
per di·em \(,)pər-'dē-əm, -'dī-\ *adv* : by the day : for each day — **per diem** *adj*
per·di·tion \pər-'dish-ən\ *n* **1** : eternal damnation **2** : HELL
per·e·gri·nate \'per-ə-grə-,nāt\ *vb* : to travel esp. on foot : WALK, TRAVERSE — **per·e·gri·na·tion** \,per-ə-grə-'nā-shən\ *n*

ə abut	ər further	a back	ā bake	
ä cot, cart	au̇ out	ch chin	e less	ē easy
g gift	i trip	ī life	j joke	ng sing	ō flow
ȯ flaw	ȯi coin	th thin	th this	ü loot
u̇ foot	y yet	yü few	yu̇ furious	zh vision

per·e·grine falcon \,per-ə-grən-, -,grēn-\ *n* : a dark swift widely distributed falcon much used in falconry

peregrine falcon (about 17 in. long)

pe·remp·to·ry \pə-'rem(p)-t(ə-)rē\ *adj* **1** : ABSOLUTE, FINAL **2** : POSITIVE, IMPERATIVE ⟨a *peremptory* tone⟩ **3** : DECISIVE, CONCLUSIVE **4** : HAUGHTY, ARROGANT — **pe·remp·to·ri·ly** \-t(ə-)rə-lē\ *adv* — **pe·remp·to·ri·ness** \-t(ə-)rē-nəs\ *n*
[1]**pe·ren·ni·al** \pə-'ren-ē-əl\ *adj* **1** : present at all seasons of the year ⟨*perennial* springs⟩ **2** : persisting for several years usu. with new herbaceous growth from the base each year ⟨*perennial* asters⟩ **3 a** : PERSISTENT, CONSTANT **b** : RECURRENT ⟨a *perennial* problem⟩ — **pe·ren·ni·al·ly** \-ē-ə-lē\ *adv*
[2]**perennial** *n* : a plant that lives for an indefinite number of years
perf *abbr* perfect
[1]**per·fect** \'pər-fikt\ *adj* **1 a** : being entirely without fault or defect : FLAWLESS **b** : ACCURATE, EXACT ⟨a *perfect* circle⟩ ⟨a *perfect* copy⟩ **c** : PURE, TOTAL ⟨*perfect* stillness⟩ **d** : WHOLE, COMPLETE **2** : of an extreme kind : UNMITIGATED ⟨a *perfect* fool⟩ **3** : of, relating to, or being a verb form that expresses an action or state completed at the time of speaking or at a time spoken of **4** : having both stamens and pistil — **per·fect·ness** \-fik(t)-nəs\ *n*
[2]**per·fect** \pər-'fekt, 'pər-fikt\ *vb* **1** : to make perfect **2** : to bring to final form — **per·fect·er** *n*
[3]**per·fect** \'pər-fikt\ *n* **1** : the perfect tense **2** : a verb form in the perfect tense
per·fect·i·ble \pər-'fek-tə-bəl, 'pər-fik-\ *adj* : capable of improvement or perfection — **per·fect·i·bil·i·ty** \pər-,fek-tə-'bil-ət-ē, ,pər-fik-\ *n*
per·fec·tion \pər-'fek-shən\ *n* **1** : the quality or state of being perfect **2** : a perfect quality or thing **3** : an unsurpassable degree of accuracy or excellence ⟨cooked to *perfection*⟩ **4** : the act or process of perfecting
per·fec·tion·ist \-sh(ə-)nəst\ *n* : a person who is not content with anything less than perfection — **perfectionist** *or* **per·fec·tion·is·tic** \-,fek-shə-'nis-tik\ *adj*
per·fect·ly \'pər-fik-(t)lē\ *adv* **1** : in a perfect manner ⟨understand *perfectly*⟩ **2** : QUITE, ALTOGETHER ⟨he was *perfectly* willing⟩
perfect number *n* : an integer that is equal to the sum of all its divisors except itself ⟨28 is a *perfect number* because it is the sum of 1 + 2 + 4 + 7 + 14⟩
perfect square *n* : an integer whose square root is an integer ⟨9 is a *perfect square*⟩
per·fi·dy \'pər-fəd-ē\ *n, pl* **-dies** : the quality or state of being faithless or disloyal : TREACHERY — **per·fid·i·ous** \(,)pər-'fid-ē-əs\ *adj* — **per·fid·i·ous·ly** *adv* — **per·fid·i·ous·ness** *n*
per·fo·rate \'pər-fə-,rāt\ *vb* : to make a hole or series of holes through; *esp* : to make a line of holes to facilitate separation — **per·fo·rate** \'pər-f(ə-)rət, -fə-,rāt\ *adj* — **per·fo·ra·tor** \-fə-,rāt-ər\ *n*
per·fo·ra·tion \,pər-fə-'rā-shən\ *n* **1** : the act or process of perforating **2** : a hole, pattern, or series of holes made by perforating

per·force \pər-ˈfōrs, -ˈfȯrs\ *adv* **:** by force of circumstances or of necessity ⟨he went *perforce*⟩

per·form \pər-ˈfȯrm\ *vb* **1 a :** to carry out **:** DO **b :** ACT, FUNCTION ⟨the car *performs* well⟩ **2 :** to do something requiring special skill ⟨*perform* on the piano⟩ **3 a :** to do in a formal manner or according to prescribed ritual **b :** to give a performance of ⟨*perform* a play⟩ — **per·form·a·ble** \-ˈfȯr-mə-bəl\ *adj* — **per·form·er** *n*

per·form·ance \pər-ˈfȯr-mən(t)s\ *n* **1 a :** the doing of an action **b :** something accomplished **:** DEED, FEAT **2 a :** the action of representing a character in a play **b :** a public presentation ⟨*performance* of a symphony⟩ **3 :** the manner in which something performs ⟨an engine's *performance*⟩

[1]**per·fume** \ˈpər-ˌfyüm, (ˌ)pər-ˈ\ *n* **1 :** the scent of something usu. sweet-smelling **2 :** a substance that emits a pleasant odor; *esp* **:** a fluid preparation (as of floral essences and a fixative) used for scenting

[2]**per·fume** \(ˌ)pər-ˈfyüm, ˈpər-ˌ\ *vb* **:** to fill or impregnate with a pleasing odor (as of flowers) **:** SCENT

per·fum·ery \pə(r)-ˈfyüm-(ə-)rē\ *n, pl* **-er·ies 1 a :** the art or process of making perfume **b :** the products made by a perfumer **2 :** a place where perfumes are prepared

per·func·to·ry \pər-ˈfəŋ(k)-t(ə-)rē\ *adj* **1 :** done mechanically or carelessly ⟨a *perfunctory* inspection⟩ **2 :** lacking in interest or enthusiasm **:** INDIFFERENT — **per·func·to·ri·ly** \-t(ə-)rə-lē\ *adv* — **per·func·to·ri·ness** \-t(ə-)rē-nəs\ *n*

perh *abbr* perhaps

per·haps \pər-ˈ(h)aps, ˈpraps\ *adv* **:** possibly but not certainly **:** MAYBE

per·i·anth \ˈper-ē-ˌan(t)th\ *n* **:** the external part of a flower esp. when not formed into a separate calyx and corolla

per·i·car·di·um \ˌper-ə-ˈkärd-ē-əm\ *n, pl* **per·i·car·dia** \-ē-ə\ **:** the cone-shaped sac of membrane that encloses the heart and the roots of the great blood vessels of vertebrates — **per·i·car·di·al** \-ē-əl\ *adj*

peri·gee \ˈper-ə-(ˌ)jē\ *n* **:** the point nearest the center of a celestial body (as the earth or the moon) reached by an object (as a satellite or vehicle) orbiting it — compare APOGEE

peri·he·lion \ˌper-ə-ˈhēl-yən\ *n* **:** the point in the path of a celestial body (as a planet) that is nearest to the sun

[1]**per·il** \ˈper-əl\ *n* **1 :** exposure to injury, loss, or destruction **2 :** something that imperils **:** RISK ⟨*perils* of the highway⟩ *syn* see DANGER

[2]**peril** *vb* **-iled** *also* **-illed**; **-il·ing** *also* **-il·ling :** IMPERIL

per·il·ous \ˈper-ə-ləs\ *adj* **:** full of or involving peril **:** HAZARDOUS — **per·il·ous·ly** *adv* — **per·il·ous·ness** *n*

pe·rim·e·ter \pə-ˈrim-ət-ər\ *n* **:** the boundary of a closed plane figure or area; *also* **:** the length of such a boundary

pe·ri·od \ˈpir-ē-əd\ *n* **1 :** a punctuation mark . used chiefly to mark the end of a declarative sentence or an abbreviation **2 :** the completion of a cycle, a series of events, or an action **:** CONCLUSION **3 a :** a portion of time marked by some characteristic ⟨a *period* of cool weather⟩ **b :** the interval of time required for a motion or phenomenon to complete a cycle and begin to repeat itself ⟨the *period* of a pendulum⟩ **4 a :** a single cycle of a series of cycles **b :** a single cyclic occurrence of menstruation **5 a :** a chronological division **:** STAGE **b :** a division of geologic time longer than an epoch and shorter than an era **c :** a stage or portion of time in the history of something ⟨the colonial *period*⟩ **6 a :** one of the divisions of the school day **b :** one of the divisions of the playing time of a game **7 :** a series of elements of increasing atomic number as listed in horizontal rows in the periodic table

pe·ri·od·ic \ˌpir-ē-ˈäd-ik\ *adj* **1 :** occurring occasionally or at regular intervals **2 :** consisting of or containing a series of repeated stages **:** CYCLIC ⟨*periodic* vibrations⟩

[1]**pe·ri·od·i·cal** \ˌpir-ē-ˈäd-i-kəl\ *adj* **1 :** PERIODIC 1 **2 :** published at regular intervals — **pe·ri·od·i·cal·ly** \-k(ə-)lē\ *adv*

[2]**periodical** *n* **:** a periodical publication

periodic law *n* **:** a law in chemistry: the elements when arranged in the order of their atomic numbers show a periodic variation in most of their properties

periodic table *n* **:** an arrangement of chemical elements based on the periodic law

peri·os·te·um \ˌper-ē-ˈäs-tē-əm\ *n, pl* **-tea** \-tē-ə\ **:** the membrane of connective tissue that covers all bones except at the surfaces in a joint — **peri·os·te·al** \-tē-əl\ *adj*

per·i·pa·tet·ic \ˌper-ə-pə-ˈtet-ik\ *adj* **:** moving about from place to place **:** ITINERANT ⟨a *peripatetic* preacher⟩

pe·riph·er·al \pə-ˈrif-(ə-)rəl\ *adj* **:** of, relating to, located in, or forming a periphery ⟨*peripheral* vision⟩ — **pe·riph·er·al·ly** \-ē\ *adv*

pe·riph·ery \pə-ˈrif-(ə-)rē\ *n, pl* **-er·ies 1 :** the perimeter of a closed curve **2 :** the boundary or surface of a body **3 :** the outer or outermost part

peri·scope \ˈper-ə-ˌskōp\ *n* **:** a tubular optical instrument containing lenses and mirrors by which an observer (as on a submerged submarine) obtains an otherwise obstructed field of view — **peri·scop·ic** \ˌper-ə-ˈskäp-ik\ *adj*

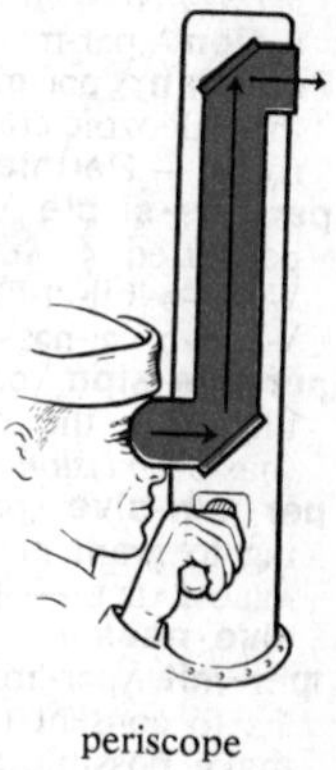

periscope

per·ish \ˈper-ish\ *vb* **:** to pass away completely **:** become destroyed **:** DIE

per·ish·a·ble \-ə-bəl\ *adj* **:** liable to spoil or decay ⟨*perishable* fruit⟩ — **perishable** *n*

per·i·stal·sis \ˌper-ə-ˈstȯl-səs, -ˈstal-\ *n, pl* **-stal·ses** \-ˌsēz\ **:** successive waves of contraction passing along the walls of a hollow muscular structure (as the intestine) and forcing the contents onward — **per·i·stal·tic** \-ˈstȯl-tik, -ˈstal-\ *adj*

per·i·to·ne·um \ˌper-ət-ə-ˈnē-əm\ *n, pl* **-ne·ums** *or* **-nea** \-ˈnē-ə\ **:** the smooth transparent membrane that lines the cavity of the abdomen and encloses the abdominal and pelvic organs — **per·i·to·ne·al** \-ˈnē-əl\ *adj*

per·i·to·ni·tis \ˌper-ət-ə-ˈnīt-əs\ *n* **:** inflammation of the peritoneum

peri·wig \ˈper-i-ˌwig\ *n* **:** WIG

[1]**per·i·win·kle** \ˈper-i-ˌwing-kəl\ *n* **:** a trailing evergreen herb with shiny leathery leaves and single blue or white flowers

[2]**periwinkle** *n* **1 :** any of numerous small edible marine snails of coastal regions **2 :** the shell of a periwinkle

per·jure \ˈpər-jər\ *vb* **per·jured**; **per·jur·ing** \ˈpərj-(ə-)ring\ **:** to make oneself guilty of perjury ⟨he *perjured* himself⟩ — **per·jur·er** \ˈpər-jər-ər\ *n*

per·ju·ry \ˈpərj-(ə-)rē\ *n, pl* **-ries :** an act of swearing to what one knows is untrue

perk \ˈpərk\ *vb* **1 :** to lift quickly, saucily, or alertly

⟨a dog *perking* its ears⟩ **2 :** to smarten one's appearance — **perk up :** to become lively

perky \'pər-kē\ *adj* **perk·i·er; -est :** JAUNTY, LIVELY — **perk·i·ness** *n*

per·lite \'pər-ˌlīt\ *n* **:** glassy volcanic lava of shelly structure that when expanded by heat forms a lightweight material used esp. in concrete and plaster

perm *abbr* permanent

per·ma·frost \'pər-mə-ˌfrȯst\ *n* **:** a permanently frozen layer at variable depth below the earth's surface in frigid regions

1**per·ma·nent** \'pər-mə-nənt\ *adj* **:** lasting or intended to last for a very long time **:** not temporary or changing ⟨a *permanent* address⟩ ⟨the *permanent* population of a city⟩ ***syn*** see LASTING ***ant*** temporary, transitory — **per·ma·nence** \-nən(t)s\ *n* — **per·ma·nen·cy** \-nən-sē\ *n* — **per·ma·nent·ly** *adv* — **per·ma·nent·ness** *n*

2**permanent** *n* **:** a long-lasting hair wave produced by mechanical and chemical means

permanent magnet *n* **:** a magnet that retains its magnetism after removal of the magnetizing force

permanent tooth *n* **:** one of the second set of teeth of a mammal that follow the milk teeth, typically persist into old age, and in man are 32 in number

per·me·a·ble \'pər-mē-ə-bəl\ *adj* **:** having pores or openings that permit liquids or gases to pass through ⟨a *permeable* membrane⟩ ⟨*permeable* limestone⟩ — **per·me·a·bil·i·ty** \ˌpər-mē-ə-'bil-ət-ē\ *n*

per·me·ate \'pər-mē-ˌāt\ *vb* **1 :** to pass through something which has pores or small openings or is of loose texture **:** seep through ⟨water *permeates* sand⟩ **2 :** to spread throughout **:** PERVADE ⟨a room *permeated* with the odor of tobacco⟩ — **per·me·a·tion** \ˌpər-mē-'ā-shən\ *n*

Perm·ian \'pər-mē-ən\ *n* **:** the most recent period of the Paleozoic era; *also* **:** the corresponding system of rocks — **Permian** *adj*

per·mis·si·ble \pər-'mis-ə-bəl\ *adj* **:** that may be permitted **:** ALLOWABLE — **per·mis·si·bil·i·ty** \-ˌmis-ə-'bil-ət-ē\ *n* — **per·mis·si·ble·ness** \-'mis-ə-bəl-nəs\ *n* — **per·mis·si·bly** \-blē\ *adv*

per·mis·sion \pər-'mish-ən\ *n* **1 :** the act of permitting **2 :** the consent of a person in authority ⟨has *permission* to leave⟩

per·mis·sive \pər-'mis-iv\ *adj* **1 :** granting or tending to grant permission **:** ALLOWING **2 :** ALLOWED, ALLOWABLE — **per·mis·sive·ly** *adv* — **per·mis·sive·ness** *n*

1**per·mit** \pər-'mit\ *vb* **per·mit·ted; per·mit·ting** **1 :** to consent to **:** give permission **:** ALLOW **2 :** to make possible **:** give an opportunity ⟨if time *permits*⟩ — **per·mit·ter** *n*

2**per·mit** \'pər-ˌmit, pər-'\ *n* **:** a written statement of permission given by one having authority **:** LICENSE ⟨a *permit* to keep a dog⟩

per·ni·cious \pər-'nish-əs\ *adj* **:** very destructive or injurious ⟨a *pernicious* habit⟩ — **per·ni·cious·ly** *adv* — **per·ni·cious·ness** *n*

pernicious anemia *n* **:** a severe anemia in which the red blood cells decrease in number and increase in size and which is associated with a deficiency of vitamin B_{12}

per·ora·tion \ˌper-ər-'ā-shən\ *n* **:** the last part of a speech

1**per·ox·ide** \pə-'räk-ˌsīd\ *n* **:** an oxide containing a high proportion of oxygen; *esp* **:** HYDROGEN PEROXIDE

2**peroxide** *vb* **:** to bleach with hydrogen peroxide ⟨*peroxided* her hair⟩

perp *abbr* perpendicular

1**per·pen·dic·u·lar** \ˌpər-pən-'dik-yə-lər\ *adj* **1 :** exactly vertical or upright **2 :** being at right angles to a given line or plane — **per·pen·dic·u·lar·ly** \-'dik-yə-lər-lē\ *adv*

2**perpendicular** *n* **:** a perpendicular line, surface, or position

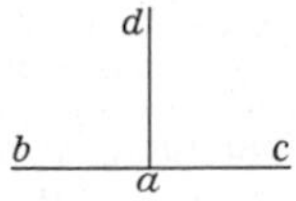

ad, perpendicular; *bc,* horizontal

per·pe·trate \'pər-pə-ˌtrāt\ *vb* **:** to be guilty of doing **:** COMMIT ⟨*perpetrate* a crime⟩ — **per·pe·tra·tion** \ˌpər-pə-'trā-shən\ *n* — **per·pe·tra·tor** \'pər-pə-ˌtrāt-ər\ *n*

per·pet·u·al \pər-'pech-(ə-w)əl\ *adj* **1 :** continuing forever **:** EVERLASTING **2 :** occurring continually **:** CONSTANT — **per·pet·u·al·ly** \-ē\ *adv*

per·pet·u·ate \pər-'pech-ə-ˌwāt\ *vb* **:** to make perpetual or cause to last indefinitely ⟨*perpetuate* a lie⟩ — **per·pet·u·a·tion** \-ˌpech-ə-'wā-shən\ *n* — **per·pet·u·a·tor** \-'pech-ə-ˌwāt-ər\ *n*

per·pe·tu·i·ty \ˌpər-pə-'t(y)ü-ət-ē\ *n, pl* **-ties** **1 :** perpetual existence or duration **2 :** endless time **:** ETERNITY

per·plex \pər-'pleks\ *vb* **1 :** to disturb mentally; *esp* **:** CONFUSE, BEWILDER **2 :** to make intricate or involved **:** COMPLICATE ***syn*** see PUZZLE — **per·plexed** \-'plekst\ *adj* — **per·plexed·ly** \-'plek-səd-lē, -'pleks-tlē\ *adv*

per·plex·i·ty \pər-'plek-sət-ē\ *n, pl* **-ties** **1 :** the state of being perplexed **:** BEWILDERMENT **2 :** something that perplexes

per·qui·site \'pər-kwə-zət\ *n* **1 :** a profit made from one's employment in addition to one's regular pay; *esp* **:** such a profit when expected or promised **2 :** TIP

pers *abbr* **1** person **2** personal

Pers *abbr* **1** Persia **2** Persian

per·se·cute \'pər-si-ˌkyüt\ *vb* **1 :** to harass so as to injure, grieve, or afflict; *esp* **:** to cause to suffer for one's belief **2 :** ANNOY, PESTER — **per·se·cu·tor** \-ˌkyüt-ər\ *n* — **per·se·cu·to·ry** \-kyü-ˌtōr-ē, -ˌtȯr-\ *adj*

per·se·cu·tion \ˌpər-si-'kyü-shən\ *n* **1 :** the act or practice of persecuting **2 :** the condition of being persecuted

per·se·ver·ance \ˌpər-sə-'vir-ən(t)s\ *n* **:** the action, state, or an instance of persevering **:** STEADFASTNESS

per·se·vere \ˌpər-sə-'vi(ə)r\ *vb* **:** to keep at something in spite of difficulties, opposition, or discouragement

per·se·ver·ing \-'vi(ə)r-ing\ *adj* **:** showing perseverance — **per·se·ver·ing·ly** \-ing-lē\ *adv*

Per·sian \'pər-zhən\ *n* **1 :** a native or inhabitant of ancient Persia or modern Iran **2 :** the language of the Persians — **Persian** *adj*

Persian cat *n* **:** a stocky round-headed domestic cat with long and silky fur that is the long-haired cat of shows and fanciers

Persian lamb *n* **:** a pelt obtained from karakul lambs older than those yielding broadtail and characterized by very silky tightly curled fur

per·si·flage \'pər-sə-ˌfläzh, 'per-\ *n* **:** frivolous or lightly jesting talk **:** BANTER

per·sim·mon \pər-'sim-ən\ *n* **1 :** any of a genus of trees with hard fine wood, oblong leaves, and small

ə abut	ər further	a back	ā bake
ä cot, cart	aù out	ch chin	e less	ē easy
g gift	i trip	ī life	j joke	ng sing	ō flow
ȯ flaw	ȯi coin	th thin	th this	ü loot
ù foot	y yet	yü few	yù furious	zh vision

bell-shaped white flowers **2** : the usu. orange several-seeded berry of a persimmon that resembles a plum and is edible when fully ripe

per·sist \pər-'sist, -'zist\ *vb* **1** : to go on resolutely in spite of opposition, warnings, or pleas : PERSEVERE **2** : to last on and on : continue to exist ⟨rain *persisting* for days⟩ — **per·sist·er** *n*

per·sist·ence \pər-'sis-tən(t)s, -'zis-\ *n* **1** : the act or fact of persisting **2** : the quality of being persistent : PERSEVERANCE

per·sist·ent \-tənt\ *adj* **1** : continuing, existing, or acting for a long or longer than usual time ⟨a *persistent* cold⟩ ⟨a *persistent* drug⟩ **2** : DOGGED, TENACIOUS ⟨a *persistent* salesman⟩ — **per·sist·ent·ly** *adv*

per·son \'pər-sən\ *n* [from Latin, meaning at first "a mask", then "a character in a play" (compare the phrase DRAMATIS PERSONAE), and then "any person"; probably borrowed by the early Romans from *phersu* meaning "mask" in the language of their neighbors the Etruscans] **1** : a human being : INDIVIDUAL **2** : CHARACTER, GUISE **3 a** : bodily appearance ⟨kept his *person* neat⟩ **b** : bodily presence ⟨appear in *person*⟩ **4** : reference to the speaker, to one spoken to, or to one spoken of as indicated esp. by means of certain pronouns

per·son·a·ble \'pər-s(ə-)nə-bəl\ *adj* : pleasing in appearance or manner — **per·son·a·ble·ness** *n*

per·son·age \'pər-s(ə-)nij\ *n* **1** : a person of rank or distinction **2** : a character in a book or play

[1]**per·son·al** \'pər-s(ə-)nəl\ *adj* **1** : of, relating to, or belonging to a person : PRIVATE ⟨*personal* property⟩ **2 a** : done in person **b** : proceeding from or directed to a single person **c** : carried on between individuals directly ⟨a *personal* correspondence⟩ **3** : relating to the person or body ⟨your *personal* appearance⟩ **4** : closely related to an individual : INTIMATE **5** : denoting grammatical person

[2]**personal** *n* : a short newspaper paragraph relating to personal matters

per·son·al·i·ty \,pər-sə-'nal-ət-ē\ *n, pl* **-ties** **1** : the state of being a person **2** : the characteristics and traits of a person that make him different from others : INDIVIDUALITY **3** : pleasing qualities of character ⟨lacks *personality*⟩ **4** : a person who has strongly marked qualities ⟨a great stage *personality*⟩ **5** : a slighting or abusive reference to a person ⟨use *personalities* in an argument⟩

per·son·al·ize \'pər-s(ə-)nə-,līz\ *vb* **1** : PERSONIFY **2** : to make personal; *esp* : to mark as belonging to a particular person ⟨*personalized* stationery⟩

per·son·al·ly \'pər-s(ə-)nə-lē\ *adv* **1** : in person ⟨attend to the matter *personally*⟩ **2** : as a person : in personality ⟨*personally* attractive⟩ **3** : for oneself : as far as oneself is concerned ⟨*personally*, I am against it⟩

personal pronoun *n* : a pronoun (as *I*, *you*, or *they*) expressing a distinction of person

per·son·al·ty \'pər-s(ə-)nəl-tē\ *n, pl* **-ties** : personal property as distinguished from real estate

per·son·i·fi·ca·tion \pər-,sän-ə-fə-'kā-shən\ *n* **1** : the act of personifying **2** : an imaginary being thought of as representing a thing or an idea ⟨Uncle Sam is the *personification* of the U.S.⟩ **3** : a perfect example : EMBODIMENT ⟨he is the *personification* of generosity⟩ **4** : a figure of speech in which a lifeless object or abstract quality is spoken of as if alive

per·son·i·fy \pər-'sän-ə-,fī\ *vb* **-fied; -fy·ing** **1** : to think of or represent as a person ⟨*personify* the forces of nature⟩ **2** : to represent in a physical form ⟨the law was *personified* in the sheriff⟩ **3** : to serve as the perfect example of ⟨she *personified* kindness⟩

per·son·nel \,pər-sə-'nel\ *n* : a group of persons employed (as in a public service, a factory, or an office)

[1]**per·spec·tive** \pər-'spek-tiv\ *n* **1** : the art or technique of painting or drawing a scene so that objects in it seem to have depth and distance **2** : the power to understand things in their true relationship to each other **3** : the true relationship of objects or events to one another ⟨view the events of the last year in *perspective*⟩ **4** : the appearance to the eye of objects in respect to their relative distance and positions

[2]**perspective** *adj* : of, relating to, or seen in perspective

per·spi·ca·cious \,pər-spə-'kā-shəs\ *adj* : having or showing keen understanding or discernment — **per·spi·ca·cious·ly** *adv* — **per·spi·cac·i·ty** \-'kas-ət-ē\ *n*

per·spic·u·ous \pər-'spik-yə-wəs\ *adj* **1** : plain to the understanding : CLEAR **2** : expressing oneself clearly — **per·spi·cu·i·ty** \,pər-spə-'kyü-ət-ē\ *n* — **per·spic·u·ous·ly** \pər-'spik-yə-wəs-lē\ *adv* — **per·spic·u·ous·ness** *n*

per·spi·ra·tion \,pər-spə-'rā-shən\ *n* **1** : the act or process of perspiring **2** : a salty fluid secreted by the sweat glands : SWEAT

per·spire \pər-'spī(ə)r\ *vb* : to secrete and emit perspiration : SWEAT

per·suade \pər-'swād\ *vb* : to win over to a belief or to a course of action by argument or earnest request — **per·suad·a·ble** \-'swād-ə-bəl\ *adj* — **per·suad·er** *n*

per·sua·si·ble \-'swā-zə-bəl\ *adj* : capable of being persuaded

per·sua·sion \pər-'swā-zhən\ *n* **1** : the act of persuading **2** : the power or ability to persuade **3** : the state of being persuaded **4** : BELIEF; *esp* : a system of religious beliefs **5** : a group having the same religious beliefs

per·sua·sive \pər-'swā-siv, -ziv\ *adj* : tending to persuade ⟨a *persuasive* speech⟩ — **per·sua·sive·ly** *adv* — **per·sua·sive·ness** *n*

pert \'pərt\ *adj* **1** : saucily free : IMPUDENT **2** : being trim and chic : JAUNTY **3** : LIVELY, VIVACIOUS — **pert·ly** *adv* — **pert·ness** *n*

per·tain \pər-'tān\ *vb* **1** : to belong to a person or thing as a part, quality, or function ⟨duties that *pertain* to an office⟩ **2** : to refer or relate to a person or thing ⟨books *pertaining* to birds⟩

per·ti·na·cious \,pərt-ə-'nā-shəs\ *adj* **1** : holding strongly to an opinion, purpose, or course of action **2** : stubbornly persistent — **per·ti·na·cious·ly** *adv* — **per·ti·na·cious·ness** *n* — **per·ti·nac·i·ty** \-'nas-ət-ē\ *n*

per·ti·nent \'pərt-ə-nənt\ *adj* : having to do with the matter being considered ⟨a *pertinent* suggestion⟩ — **per·ti·nence** \-nən(t)s\ *or* **per·ti·nen·cy** \-nən-sē\ *n* — **per·ti·nent·ly** *adv*

per·turb \pər-'tərb\ *vb* : to disturb greatly esp. in mind : AGITATE — **per·turb·a·ble** \-'tər-bə-bəl\ *adj*

per·tur·ba·tion \,pərt-ər-'bā-shən, ,pər-,tər-\ *n* **1 a** : the action of perturbing **b** : the state of being perturbed **2** : a cause of worry or disquiet — **per·tur·ba·tion·al** \-sh(ə-)nəl\ *adj*

pe·ruke \pə-'rük\ *n* : WIG

pe·rus·al \pə-'rü-zəl\ *n* : the action of perusing

pe·ruse \pə-'rüz\ *vb* : READ; *esp* : to read carefully or thoroughly — **pe·rus·er** *n*

Pe·ru·vi·an bark \pə-,rü-vē-ən-\ *n* : the bark of a cinchona

per·vade \pər-'vād\ *vb* : to spread or become diffused throughout every part of — **per·va·sion** \-'vā-zhən\ *n* — **per·va·sive** \-'vā-siv, -ziv\ *adj* — **per·va·sive·ly** *adv* — **per·va·sive·ness** *n*

per·verse \(,)pər-'vərs, 'pər-,\ *adj* **1** : morally bad : CORRUPT **2** : obstinate in being wrong ⟨a *perverse* reluctance to admit his error⟩ **3** : IRRITABLE, CRANKY — **per·verse·ly** *adv* — **per·verse·ness** *n*

per·ver·sion \pər-'vər-zhən\ *n* **1 a** : the action of perverting **b** : the state of being perverted **2** : a perverted form **3** : abnormal sexual behavior

per·ver·si·ty \pər-'vər-sət-ē\ *n, pl* **-ties** : the quality, state, or an instance of being perverse

1**per·vert** \pər-'vərt\ *vb* **1** : to cause to turn away from what is good or true or right : CORRUPT **2** : to cause to turn aside or away from the correct course ⟨*pervert* justice⟩ **3** : to twist the meaning of : MISINTERPRET — **per·vert·er** *n*

2**per·vert** \'pər-,vərt\ *n* : one that is perverted; *esp* : one given to some form of sexual perversion

per·vi·ous \'pər-vē-əs\ *adj* : capable of being penetrated or permeated ⟨*pervious* soil⟩

Pe·sach \'pā-,säk\ *n* : PASSOVER

pe·se·ta \pə-'sāt-ə\ *n* **1** : the basic monetary unit of Spain **2** : a coin or note representing one peseta

pes·ky \'pes-kē\ *adj* **pes·ki·er**; **-est** : ANNOYING, TROUBLESOME — **pes·ki·ly** \-kə-lē\ *adv* — **pes·ki·ness** \-kē-nəs\ *n*

pe·so \'pā-sō\ *n, pl* **pesos** **1** : an old silver coin of Spain or Spanish America equal to eight reals **2 a** : the basic monetary unit of any of several countries (as Argentina, Mexico, the Republic of the Philippines) **b** : a coin or note representing one peso

pes·si·mism \'pes-ə-,miz-əm\ *n* **1** : an inclination to expect the worst possible outcome **2** : a belief that evil is more common or powerful than good — **pes·si·mist** \-məst\ *n*

pes·si·mis·tic \,pes-ə-'mis-tik\ *adj* **1** : lacking in hope that one's troubles will end or that success or happiness will come : GLOOMY ⟨*pessimistic* about the stock market⟩ **2** : believing in pessimism — **pes·si·mis·ti·cal·ly** \-ti-k(ə-)lē\ *adv*

pest \'pest\ *n* **1** : an epidemic disease with a high mortality; *esp* : PLAGUE **2** : something resembling a pest in destructiveness; *esp* : a plant or animal harmful to man **3** : one that pesters or annoys : NUISANCE

pes·ter \'pes-tər\ *vb* **pes·tered**; **pes·ter·ing** \-t(ə-)riŋ\ : ANNOY, BOTHER

pest·hole \'pest-,hōl\ *n* : a place in which pestilences are common

pest·house \-,hau̇s\ *n* : a shelter or hospital for those infected with a contagious or epidemic disease

pes·ti·cide \'pes-tə-,sīd\ *n* : an agent used to destroy pests — **pes·ti·cid·al** \,pes-tə-'sīd-əl\ *adj*

pes·tif·er·ous \pes-'tif-(ə-)rəs\ *adj* **1** : dangerous to society : PERNICIOUS **2** : carrying or causing infection **3** : ANNOYING, TROUBLESOME

pes·ti·lence \'pes-tə-lən(t)s\ *n* : a contagious or infectious epidemic disease that spreads quickly and has devastating effects; *esp* : BUBONIC PLAGUE

pes·ti·lent \-lənt\ *adj* **1** : dangerous or destructive to life : DEADLY ⟨a *pestilent* drug⟩; *also* : being or conveying a pestilence ⟨a *pestilent* disease⟩ ⟨*pestilent* infections⟩ **2** : harmful or dangerous to society : PERNICIOUS **3** : VEXING, IRRITATING ⟨a *pestilent* child⟩

ə abut ər further a back ā bake
ä cot, cart au̇ out ch chin e less ē easy
g gift i trip ī life j joke ŋ sing ō flow
ȯ flaw ȯi coin th thin th this ü loot
u̇ foot y yet yü few yu̇ furious zh vision

pes·ti·len·tial \,pes-tə-'len-chəl\ *adj* : causing or likely to cause pestilence : PESTILENT

pes·tle \'pes-əl\ *n* : a usu. club-shaped implement for pounding or grinding substances in a mortar — **pestle** *vb*

pestle in a mortar

1**pet** \'pet\ *n* **1** : a domesticated animal kept for pleasure **2** : a pampered child or adult : DARLING

2**pet** *adj* **1** : kept or treated as a pet **2** : expressing fondness or endearment ⟨a *pet* name⟩ **3** : FAVORITE

3**pet** *vb* **pet·ted**; **pet·ting** **1** : FONDLE, CARESS **2** : to treat as a pet : PAMPER **3** : to engage in amorous embracing, caressing, and kissing

4**pet** *n* : a fit of peevishness, sulkiness, or anger

pet·al \'pet-əl\ *n* : one of the often brightly colored modified leaves making up the corolla of a flower — **pet·aled** *or* **pet·alled** \-əld\ *adj* — **pet·al·like** \-əl-,(l)īk\ *adj*

pet cock \'pet-,käk\ *n* : a small faucet or valve (as for letting out air or draining)

pe·ter \'pēt-ər\ *vb* : to become exhausted : FAIL ⟨the stream *peters* out⟩

Pe·ter \'pēt-ər\ *n* — see BIBLE table

pet·i·o·lar \,pet-ē-'ō-lər\ *adj* : relating to or originating from a petiole

pet·i·o·late \'pet-ē-ə-,lāt\ *or* **pet·i·o·lat·ed** \-,lāt-əd\ *adj* : having a petiole

pet·i·ole \'pet-ē-,ōl\ *n* **1** : the stem of a leaf — see LEAF illustration **2** : STALK; *esp* : a narrow segment joining the abdomen and thorax in some insects (as wasps)

pe·tite \pə-'tēt\ *adj* : small and trim of figure

pe·tit four \,pet-ē-'fō(ə)r, -'fȯ(ə)r\ *n, pl* **petits fours** *or* **petit fours** \-ē-'fō(ə)rz, -'fȯ(ə)rz\ : a small frosted cake cut from pound or sponge cake

1**pe·ti·tion** \pə-'tish-ən\ *n* **1** : an earnest request : ENTREATY **2** : a formal written request made to a superior or authority

2**petition** *vb* **pe·ti·tioned**; **pe·ti·tion·ing** \-'tish-(ə-)niŋ\ : to make a request to or for : SOLICIT; *esp* : to make a formal written request — **pe·ti·tion·er** \-'tish-(ə-)nər\ *n*

pet·it jury \'pet-ē-, 'pet-ət-\ *n* : a jury of 12 persons whose duty is to try and decide the facts at issue in a case being tried in a court

petr- *or* **petri-** *or* **petro-** *comb form* : stone : rock ⟨*petro*logy⟩

pet·rel \'pe-trəl\ *n* : any of various long-winged seabirds (as the storm petrel) that fly far from land

Pe·tri dish \,pē-trē-\ *n* : a small shallow dish of thin glass with a loose cover used esp. for cultures in bacteriology

pet·ri·fac·tion \,pe-trə-'fak-shən\ *n* **1** : the process of petrifying or state of being petrified **2** : something that is petrified

pet·ri·fi·ca·tion \,pe-trə-fə-'kā-shən\ *n* : PETRIFACTION

pet·ri·fy \'pe-trə-,fī\ *vb* **-fied**; **-fy·ing** **1** : to convert an organic object into stony material **2** : to make lifeless or inactive : DEADEN **3** : to paralyze with fear, amazement, or awe : STUN

pe·trog·ra·phy \pə-'träg-rə-fē\ *n* : the description and systematic classification of rocks — compare PETROLOGY — **pe·trog·ra·pher** \-fər\ *n* — **pet·ro·graph·ic** \,pe-trə-'graf-ik\ *or* **pet·ro·graph·i·cal** \-i-kəl\ *adj*

pet·rol \'pe-trəl\ *n, Brit* : GASOLINE

pet·ro·la·tum \,pe-trə-'lāt-əm\ *n* : a tasteless, odorless, and oily or greasy substance from petroleum that is used esp. in ointments and dressings

pe·tro·le·um \pə-'trō-lē-əm, -'trōl-yəm\ *n* [from medieval Latin, formed from Greek *petra* "rock" and Latin *oleum* "oil"] : an oily flammable liquid widely distributed in the upper strata of the earth that is a complex mixture mostly of hydrocarbons and is the source of gasoline and lubricants and a major industrial raw material

pe·trol·o·gy \pə-'träl-ə-jē\ *n* : a science that deals with the origin, history, occurrence, structure, chemical composition, and classification of rocks — compare PETROGRAPHY — **pet·ro·log·ic** \ˌpe-trə-'läj-ik\ *or* **pet·ro·log·i·cal** \-i-kəl\ *adj* — **pet·ro·log·i·cal·ly** \-i-k(ə-)lē\ *adv* — **pe·trol·o·gist** \pə-'träl-ə-jəst\ *n*

1**pet·ti·coat** \'pet-ē-ˌkōt\ *n* : a skirt worn under a dress or outer skirt

2**petticoat** *adj* : FEMALE ⟨*petticoat* government⟩

pet·ti·fog \'pet-ē-ˌfȯg, -ˌfäg\ *vb* **-fogged**; **-fog·ging** **1** : to engage in legal trickery **2** : to quibble over insignificant details — **pet·ti·fog·ger** *n* — **pet·ti·fog·gery** \-ˌfȯg-(ə-)rē, -ˌfäg-\ *n*

pet·tish \'pet-ish\ *adj* : FRETFUL, PEEVISH — **pet·tish·ly** *adv* — **pet·tish·ness** *n*

pet·ty \'pet-ē\ *adj* **pet·ti·er**; **-est** [from French *petit* "small", "minor"] **1** : having secondary rank : MINOR ⟨a *petty* prince⟩ **2** : having little or no importance or significance **3** : marked by narrow interests and sympathies : SMALL-MINDED — **pet·ti·ly** \'pet-ə-lē\ *adv* — **pet·ti·ness** \'pet-ē-nəs\ *n*

petty cash *n* : cash kept on hand for payment of minor items

petty officer *n* : an enlisted man in the navy of a rank corresponding to a noncommissioned officer in the army

pet·u·lant \'pech-ə-lənt\ *adj* : marked by ill humor : PEEVISH — **pet·u·lance** \-lən(t)s\ *n* — **pet·u·lant·ly** *adv*

pe·tu·nia \pə-'t(y)ü-nyə\ *n* : any of a genus of tropical American herbs related to the potato and widely grown for their showy funnel-shaped flowers

pew \'pyü\ *n* : one of the benches with backs set in rows in a church

pe·wee \'pē-(ˌ)wē\ *n* : any of various small olive greenish flycatchers

pe·wit \'pē-ˌwit, 'pyü-ət\ *n* : any of several birds: as **a** : LAPWING **b** : PEWEE

pew·ter \'pyüt-ər\ *n* **1** : an alloy of tin usu. with lead sometimes together with copper or antimony **2** : utensils of pewter — **pewter** *adj*

pey·o·te \pā-'ōt-ē\ *or* **pey·otl** \-'ōt-əl\ *n* : MESCAL 1; *also* : a drug obtained from mescal tops

pfen·nig \'fen-ig, -ik\ *n, pl* **pfennigs** *or* **pfen·ni·ge** \'fen-i-gə\ **1** : a unit of value equal to 1/100 deutsche mark **2** : a coin representing one pfennig

pg *abbr* page

pH \pē-'āch\ *n* : a value that can be used in expressing relative acidity and alkalinity

PH *abbr* pinch-hit

pha·e·ton \'fā-ət-ən\ *n* [from French *phaéton*, named after *Phaëthon*, son of the Greek sun god who persuaded his father to let him drive the chariot of the sun, but lost control of the horses with disastrous consequences] : a light four-wheeled carriage

phage \'fāj\ *n* : BACTERIOPHAGE

pha·lanx \'fā-ˌlang(k)s\ *n, pl* **pha·lanx·es** *or* **pha·lan·ges** \fə-'lan-(ˌ)jēz, fā-\ **1 a** : a body of heavily armed infantry of antiquity formed in close deep ranks and files **b** : a body of troops in close array **2** *pl phalanges* : one of the bones of a finger or toe

phal·a·rope \'fal-ə-ˌrōp\ *n* : any of various small shorebirds that resemble sandpipers but have lobed toes and are good swimmers

phal·lus \'fal-əs\ *n, pl* **phal·li** \'fal-ˌī, -ˌē\ *or* **phal·lus·es** **1** : a symbol or representation of the male sex organ **2** : PENIS — **phal·lic** \'fal-ik\ *adj*

phan·tasm \'fan-ˌtaz-əm\ *n* **1** : a deceptive appearance : ILLUSION **2** : GHOST, SPECTER **3** : a figment of the imagination : FANTASY — **phan·tas·mal** \fan-'taz-məl\ *adj*

phantasy *var of* FANTASY

1**phan·tom** \'fant-əm\ *n* **1** : something (as a specter) that seems to be there but does not actually exist : APPARITION **2** : an object of dread or abhorrence **3** : something existing in appearance only ⟨a king with only the *phantom* of authority⟩

2**phantom** *adj* **1** : suggesting or being a phantom **2** : FICTITIOUS, DUMMY ⟨*phantom* voters⟩

phar·aoh \'fe(ə)r-ō, 'fa(ə)r-\ *n, often cap* : a ruler of ancient Egypt — **phar·a·on·ic** \ˌfer-ā-'än-ik, ˌfar-\ *adj, often cap*

pharm *abbr* **1** pharmaceutical **2** pharmacist **3** pharmacy

1**phar·ma·ceu·ti·cal** \ˌfär-mə-'süt-i-kəl\ *or* **phar·ma·ceu·tic** \-'süt-ik\ *adj* : of or relating to pharmacy or pharmacists — **phar·ma·ceu·ti·cal·ly** \-i-k(ə-)lē\ *adv*

2**pharmaceutical** *n* : a pharmaceutical preparation : a medicinal material or product

phar·ma·cist \'fär-mə-səst\ *n* : one skilled or engaged in pharmacy

phar·ma·col·o·gy \ˌfär-mə-'käl-ə-jē\ *n* **1** : the science of drugs esp. as related to their use in medicine **2** : the properties and reactions of drugs esp. with relation to their medical value — **phar·ma·co·log·i·cal** \-kə-'läj-i-kəl\ *or* **phar·ma·co·log·ic** \-'läj-ik\ *adj* — **phar·ma·co·log·i·cal·ly** \-i-k(ə-)lē\ *adv* — **phar·ma·col·o·gist** \-'käl-ə-jəst\ *n*

phar·ma·co·poe·ia *or* **phar·ma·co·pe·ia** \ˌfär-mə-kə-'pē-(y)ə\ *n* **1** : a book describing drugs, chemicals, and medicinal preparations **2** : a collection or stock of drugs

phar·ma·cy \'fär-mə-sē\ *n, pl* **-cies** **1** : the art or practice of mixing drugs according to a doctor's prescription **2 a** : a place where medicines are compounded or dispensed **b** : DRUGSTORE

phar·ynx \'far-ing(k)s\ *n, pl* **pha·ryn·ges** \fə-'rin-(ˌ)jēz\ *also* **phar·ynx·es** : the space in a vertebrate just behind the cavity of the mouth into which the nostrils, Eustachian tubes, esophagus, and trachea open — **phar·yn·ge·al** \ˌfar-ən-'jē-əl, fə-'rin-j(ē-)əl\ *adj*

phase \'fāz\ *n* **1** : the apparent shape of the moon or a planet at any time in its series of changes of illumination ⟨the new moon and the full moon are *phases* of the moon⟩ **2** : a stage or interval in a development or cycle **3** : a physically distinct portion or kind of matter present in a mixed system ⟨the three *phases* ice, water, and steam⟩ — **pha·sic** \'fā-zik\ *adj*

PhD *abbr* doctor of philosophy

pheas·ant \'fez-ənt\ *n, pl* **pheasant** *or* **pheasants** [from Old French *fesan*, from Latin *phasianus*, from *Phasis*, a river in the western Caucasus] : any of numerous large long-tailed brilliantly colored Old World birds that are related to the

pheasant
(about 34 in. long)

domestic fowl and many of which are reared as ornamental or game birds

phe·no·bar·bi·tal \ˌfē-nō-ˈbär-bə-ˌtȯl\ *n* : a crystalline barbiturate drug used as a hypnotic and sedative

phe·nol \ˈfē-ˌnōl, fi-ˈ\ *n* **1** : a caustic poisonous crystalline acidic compound present in coal tar and wood tar that in dilute solution is used as a disinfectant **2** : any of various acidic compounds analogous to phenol and regarded as hydroxyl derivatives of aromatic hydrocarbons — **phe·no·lic** \fi-ˈnō-lik, -ˈnäl-ik\ *adj*

phe·no·lic \fi-ˈnō-lik, -ˈnäl-ik\ *n* : a resin or plastic made by condensation of a phenol with an aldehyde and used esp. for molding and insulating and in coatings and adhesives

phe·nol·phthal·ein \ˌfē-ˌnōl-ˈthal-ē-ən, ˌfēn-əl-, -ˈthal-ˌēn, -ˈthāl-\ *n* : a compound used as a laxative and as an acid-base indicator because its solution is brilliant red in alkalies and is decolorized by acids

phe·nom·e·nal \fi-ˈnäm-ən-əl\ *adj* **1** : of, relating to, or being a phenomenon **2** : EXTRAORDINARY, REMARKABLE — **phe·nom·e·nal·ly** \-ə-lē\ *adv*

phe·nom·e·non \fi-ˈnäm-ə-ˌnän, -nən\ *n, pl* **-na** \-nə, -ˌnä\ *or* **-nons** [from Greek *phainomenon* "that which appears", from the neuter of the present participle of *phainesthai* "to appear"] **1** : an observable fact or event **2** : a fact or feature characteristic of something **3 a** : a rare or significant fact or event **b** *pl phenomenons* : an exceptionally good person, thing, or event : PRODIGY

phe·no·type \ˈfē-nə-ˌtīp\ *n* : the visible characters of an organism resulting from the interaction of genotype and environment — **phe·no·typ·ic** \ˌfē-nə-ˈtip-ik\ *adj*

phen·yl \ˈfen-əl, ˈfēn-\ *n* : a univalent radical derived from benzene by removal of one hydrogen atom — **phe·nyl·ic** \fi-ˈnil-ik\ *adj*

phen·yl·thio·car·ba·mide \ˌfen-əl-ˌthī-ō-ˈkär-bə-ˌmīd\ *n* : a crystalline compound that is tasteless to many persons and extremely bitter to others

phi \ˈfī\ *n, pl* **phis** \ˈfīz\ : the 21st letter of the Greek alphabet — Φ or ϕ

phi·al \ˈfī(-ə)l\ *n* : VIAL

phil- *or* **philo-** *comb form* : loving : having a fondness for ⟨*philo*-German⟩

-phil \ˌfil\ *or* **-phile** \ˌfīl\ *n comb form* : lover : one having a strong attraction to ⟨Franco*phil*⟩ ⟨Russo*phile*⟩ — **-phil** *or* **-phile** *adj comb form*

Phila *abbr* Philadelphia

phi·lan·der \fə-ˈlan-dər\ *vb* **phi·lan·dered**; **phi·lan·der·ing** \-d(ə-)riŋ\ : to make love frivolously : FLIRT — **phi·lan·der·er** \-dər-ər\ *n*

phil·an·throp·ic \ˌfil-ən-ˈthräp-ik\ *adj* : of, relating to, or marked by philanthropy : BENEVOLENT, CHARITABLE — **phil·an·throp·i·cal** \-ˈthräp-i-kəl\ *adj*

phi·lan·thro·py \fə-ˈlan(t)-thrə-pē\ *n, pl* **-pies** **1** : goodwill to fellowmen; *esp* : active effort to promote human welfare **2** : a philanthropic act or gift **3** : an organization devoted to or supported by philanthropy — **phi·lan·thro·pist** \-pəst\ *n*

phi·lat·e·ly \fə-ˈlat-ə-lē\ *n* : the collection and study of postage and imprinted stamps — **phil·a·tel·ic** \ˌfil-ə-ˈtel-ik\ *adj* — **phi·lat·e·list** \-ləst\ *n*

Phi·le·mon \fə-ˈlē-mən, fī-\ *n* — see BIBLE table

ə abut	ər further	a back	ā bake	
ä cot, cart	au̇ out	ch chin	e less	ē easy
g gift	i trip	ī life	j joke	ŋ sing	ō flow
ȯ flaw	ȯi coin	th thin	th this	ü loot
u̇ foot	y yet	yü few	yu̇ furious	zh vision

Phi·lip·pi·ans \fə-ˈlip-ē-ənz\ *n* — see BIBLE table

phil·is·tine \ˈfil-ə-ˌstēn; fə-ˈlis-tən, -ˌtēn\ *n* **1** *cap* : a member of an ancient race that lived in the coastal regions of Palestine **2** *often cap* : a person who is smugly indifferent to art, literature, and cultural values **3** : one who dislikes creative intellectual activity that has no clear practical application — **philistine** *adj* — **phil·is·tin·ism** \-ˌstē-ˌniz-əm; -tə-ˌniz-, -ˌtē-\ *n*

phil·o·den·dron \ˌfil-ə-ˈden-drən\ *n, pl* **-drons** *or* **-dra** \-drə\ : any of various arums grown for their showy often variegated foliage

phi·lol·o·gy \fə-ˈläl-ə-jē\ *n* : LINGUISTICS; *esp* : historical and comparative linguistics — **phil·o·log·i·cal** \ˌfil-ə-ˈläj-i-kəl\ *adj* — **phi·lol·o·gist** \fə-ˈläl-ə-jəst\ *n*

phi·los·o·pher \fə-ˈläs-ə-fər\ *n* **1** : a student of philosophy **2** : a person whose philosophical perspective enables him to meet trouble with fortitude and resignation

philosophers' stone *n* : an imaginary substance once believed to have the power of transmuting base metals into gold

phil·o·soph·ic \ˌfil-ə-ˈsäf-ik\ *adj* **1** : of, relating to, or based on philosophy **2** : calm and patient in face of trouble — **phil·o·soph·i·cal** \-ˈsäf-i-kəl\ *adj* — **phil·o·soph·i·cal·ly** \-i-k(ə-)lē\ *adv*

phi·los·o·phize \fə-ˈläs-ə-ˌfīz\ *vb* **1** : to reason in the manner of a philosopher **2** : to expound a philosophy : MORALIZE — **phi·los·o·phiz·er** *n*

phi·los·o·phy \fə-ˈläs-ə-fē\ *n, pl* **-phies** **1** : the study of the nature of knowledge and existence and the principles of moral and esthetic value **2** : the philosophical teachings or principles of a man or group of men ⟨Greek *philosophy*⟩ **3** : the general principles of a field of study ⟨the *philosophy* of history⟩ **4** : wisdom or insight applied to life itself ⟨a *philosophy* of live and let live⟩

phil·ter *or* **phil·tre** \ˈfil-tər\ *n* : a drug or charm held to make one person love another

phlegm \ˈflem\ *n* **1** : thick mucus secreted in abnormal quantity in the respiratory passages **2 a** : sluggish indifference **b** : cool bravery — **phlegmy** \ˈflem-ē\ *adj*

phleg·mat·ic \fleg-ˈmat-ik\ *adj* : not easily excited or aroused : slow to respond — **phleg·mat·i·cal·ly** \-i-k(ə-)lē\ *adv*

phlo·em \ˈflō-ˌem\ *n* : a vascular tissue of higher plants that transports dissolved food material, contains sieve tubes, and lies mostly external to the cambium — compare XYLEM

phlo·gis·ton \flō-ˈjis-tən\ *n* : the hypothetical principle of fire regarded formerly as a material substance

phlox \ˈfläks\ *n, pl* **phlox** *or* **phlox·es** : any of a genus of American annual or perennial herbs with showy red, purple, white, or variegated flowers

-phobe \ˌfōb\ *n comb form* : one fearing or disliking ⟨Franco*phobe*⟩ — **-pho·bic** \ˈfō-bik, ˈfäb-ik\ *adj comb form*

pho·bia \ˈfō-bē-ə\ *n* : an unreasonable persistent fear of something

phoe·be \ˈfē-bē\ *n* : any of several American flycatchers; *esp* : one of the eastern U.S. that has a slight crest and is plain grayish brown above and yellowish white below

Phoe·ni·cian \fi-ˈnish-ən\ *n* **1** : a native or inhabitant of ancient Phoenicia **2** : the Semitic language of ancient Phoenicia — **Phoenician** *n*

phoe·nix \ˈfē-niks\ *n* : a legendary bird represented by ancient Egyptians as living five or six centuries, burning itself to death, and rising young and fresh from its own ashes

phon- *or* **phono-** *comb form* : sound : voice : speech ⟨*phon*ate⟩ ⟨*phono*graph⟩
pho·na·tion \fō-ˈnā-shən\ *n* : the act or process of producing speech sounds ⟨organs of *phonation*⟩ — **pho·nate** \ˈfō-ˌnāt\ *vb*
1**phone** \ˈfōn\ *n* **1** : EARPHONE **2** : TELEPHONE
2**phone** *vb* : TELEPHONE
3**phone** *n* : a speech sound considered as a physical event without regard to its place in the structure of a language
-phone \ˌfōn\ *n comb form* : sound ⟨homo*phone*⟩ — often in names of musical instruments and sound-transmitting devices ⟨radio*phone*⟩ ⟨xylo*phone*⟩
pho·neme \ˈfō-ˌnēm\ *n* : one of the smallest units of speech that serves to distinguish one utterance from another in a particular language or dialect ⟨\n\ and \t\ in *pin* and *pit* are different *phonemes*⟩
pho·ne·mic \fə-ˈnē-mik\ *adj* **1** : of, relating to, or having the characteristics of a phoneme **2** : being different phonemes ⟨in English \n\ and \ng\ are *phonemic*⟩ — **pho·ne·mi·cal·ly** \-mi-k(ə-)lē\ *adv*
pho·net·ic \fə-ˈnet-ik\ *adj* **1 a** : of or relating to spoken language or speech sounds **b** : of or relating to phonetics **2** : representing speech sounds — **pho·net·i·cal** \-i-kəl\ *adj* — **pho·net·i·cal·ly** \-i-k(ə-)lē\ *adv*
pho·net·ics \fə-ˈnet-iks\ *n* : the study and classification of spoken sounds — **pho·ne·ti·cian** \ˌfō-nə-ˈtish-ən\ *n*
phon·ic \ˈfän-ik\ *adj* **1** : of, relating to, or producing sound **2** : of or relating to speech sounds or to phonics — **phon·i·cal·ly** \-i-k(ə-)lē\ *adv*
phon·ics \ˈfän-iks\ *n* : a method of teaching beginners to read and pronounce words by learning the phonetic value of letters, letter groups, and esp. syllables
pho·no·graph \ˈfō-nə-ˌgraf\ *n* [from Greek *phōnē* "sound" and *graphein* "to write", "record"] : an instrument for reproducing sounds by means of a vibrating needle following a spiral groove on a revolving disc — **pho·no·graph·ic** \ˌfō-nə-ˈgraf-ik\ *adj* — **pho·no·graph·i·cal·ly** \-i-k(ə-)lē\ *adv*
pho·ny *or* **pho·ney** \ˈfō-nē\ *adj* **pho·ni·er; -est** : FALSE, COUNTERFEIT — **pho·ni·ness** *n* — **phony** *or* **phoney** *n*
phosph- *or* **phospho-** *comb form* : phosphorus ⟨*phosph*ide⟩ ⟨*phospho*protein⟩
phos·phate \ˈfäs-ˌfāt\ *n* **1** : a salt of a phosphoric acid **2** : an effervescent drink of carbonated water with a small amount of phosphoric acid or an acid phosphate flavored with fruit syrup
phos·phor \ˈfäs-fər\ *n* : a phosphorescent substance
phos·pho·res·cence \ˌfäs-fə-ˈres-ən(t)s\ *n* **1** : the property of emitting light without easily perceptible heat shown by phosphorus or living organisms (as various bacteria and fungi); *also* : the light so produced **2** : luminescence caused by the absorption of radiations (as X rays or ultraviolet light) and continuing for a noticeable time after these radiations have stopped — **phos·pho·res·cent** \-ənt\ *adj*
phosphoric acid *n* : any of several oxygen-containing acids of phosphorus
phos·pho·rus \ˈfäs-f(ə-)rəs\ *n* **1** : a phosphorescent substance; *esp* : one that glows in the dark **2** : a poisonous chemically active element usu. obtained in the form of waxy disagreeable-smelling crystals that glow in moist air —see ELEMENT table — **phos·phor·ic** \fäs-ˈfȯr-ik, -ˈfär-\ *adj* — **phos·pho·rous** \ˈfäs-f(ə-)rəs; fäs-ˈfōr-əs, -ˈfȯr-\ *adj*
phosphorus cycle *n* : the cycle of phosphorus in living systems and in the environment including both biological and physical processes
phot- *or* **photo-** *comb form* **1** : light ⟨*phot*on⟩ ⟨*photo*graphy⟩ **2** : photograph : photographic ⟨*photo*engraving⟩ **3** : photoelectric ⟨*photo*cell⟩
pho·to \ˈfōt-ō\ *n, pl* **photos** : PHOTOGRAPH — **photo** *vb or adj*
pho·to·chem·is·try \ˌfōt-ō-ˈkem-ə-strē\ *n* : a branch of chemistry that deals with the effect of radiant energy in producing chemical changes — **pho·to·chem·i·cal** \-ˈkem-i-kəl\ *adj*
pho·to·copy \ˈfōt-ə-ˌkäp-ē\ *n* : a photographic reproduction of graphic matter — **photocopy** *vb*
pho·to·elec·tric \ˌfōt-ō-ə-ˈlek-trik\ *adj* : relating to or utilizing any of various electrical effects due to the interaction of light with matter
photoelectric cell *n* : a cell in which variations of light are converted into corresponding variations in an electric current
photoelectric effect *n* : the emission of free electrons from a metal surface when light strikes it
pho·to·elec·tron \ˌfōt-ō-ə-ˈlek-ˌträn\ *n* : an electron released in the photoelectric effect
pho·to·emis·sive \ˌfōt-ō-i-ˈmis-iv\ *adj* : emitting electrons when exposed to radiation (as light)
photo finish *n* : a race finish in which contestants are so close that a photograph of them as they cross the finish line has to be examined to determine the winner
photog *abbr* **1** photographic **2** photography
pho·to·gen·ic \ˌfōt-ə-ˈjen-ik, -ˈjēn-\ *adj* : suitable for being photographed : likely to photograph well ⟨a *photogenic* girl⟩ — **pho·to·gen·i·cal·ly** \-i-k(ə-)lē\ *adv*
1**pho·to·graph** \ˈfōt-ə-ˌgraf\ *n* [from Greek *phōt-*, stem of *phōs* "light" and *graphein* "to write", "record"] : a picture obtained by photography
2**photograph** *vb* : to take a picture of with a camera — **pho·tog·ra·pher** \fə-ˈtäg-rə-fər\ *n*
pho·to·graph·ic \ˌfōt-ə-ˈgraf-ik\ *adj* **1** : relating to, obtained by, or used in photography ⟨*photographic* supplies⟩ **2** : representing nature and human beings with the exactness of a photograph ⟨a painter with a *photographic* technique⟩ — **pho·to·graph·i·cal·ly** \-i-k(ə-)lē\ *adv*
pho·tog·ra·phy \fə-ˈtäg-rə-fē\ *n* : the art or process of producing images on a sensitized surface (as a film) by the action of light or other radiant energy
pho·to·gra·vure \ˌfōt-ə-grə-ˈvyu̇(ə)r\ *n* : a process for making prints from an intaglio plate prepared by photographic methods; *also* : a print produced by photogravure
pho·to·mi·cro·graph \ˌfōt-ə-ˈmī-krə-ˌgraf\ *n* : a photograph of a magnified image of a small object — **pho·to·mi·crog·ra·phy** \-mī-ˈkräg-rə-fē\ *n*
pho·ton \ˈfō-ˌtän\ *n* : a quantum of radiant energy
pho·to·play \ˈfōt-ə-ˌplā\ *n* : MOTION PICTURE 2
pho·to·sphere \-ˌsfi(ə)r\ *n* : the luminous surface of the sun or a star — **pho·to·spher·ic** \ˌfōt-ə-ˈsfi(ə)r-ik, -ˈsfer-\ *adj*
pho·to·syn·the·sis \ˌfōt-ə-ˈsin(t)-thə-səs\ *n* : the process by which plants that contain chlorophyll make carbohydrates from water and from carbon dioxide of the air in the presence of light — **pho·to·syn·thet·ic** \-sin-ˈthet-ik\ *adj*
pho·tot·ro·pism \fō-ˈtä-trə-ˌpiz-əm\ *n* : a tropism in which light is the orienting stimulus — **pho·to·trop·ic** \ˌfōt-ə-ˈträp-ik\ *adj*
phr *abbr* phrase
1**phrase** \ˈfrāz\ *n* **1** : manner of expression : DICTION **2** : a brief expression; *esp* : one commonly used **3** : a musical unit typically two to four measures long and closing with a cadence **4** : a group of two or more grammatically related words that form a

P

sense unit expressing a thought but not containing a subject and predicate ⟨the adverbial prepositional *phrase* "with pleasure" in "accept with pleasure"⟩ ⟨the verb *phrase* "should have gone" in "we should have gone hours ago"⟩ — **phras·al** \ˈfrā-zəl\ *adj* — **phras·al·ly** \-zə-lē\ *adv*

²**phrase** *vb* **1** : to express in words ⟨*phrased* his thoughts well⟩ **2** : to divide into melodic phrases

phra·se·ol·o·gy \ˌfrā-zē-ˈäl-ə-jē\ *n* : manner of speaking and writing : DICTION, STYLE

phras·ing \ˈfrā-zing\ *n* **1** : PHRASEOLOGY **2** : the act, method, or result of grouping notes into musical phrases

phy·lac·tery \fə-ˈlak-t(ə-)rē\ *n, pl* **-ter·ies** **1** : one of two small square leather boxes containing slips inscribed with scripture passages and worn by Jewish men during morning prayers **2** : AMULET

phyl·lo·qui·none \ˌfil-ə-kwin-ˈōn, -ˈkwin-ˌōn\ *n* : a vitamin K that is obtained from alfalfa or made synthetically

phyl·lo·taxy \ˈfil-ə-ˌtak-sē\ *also* **phyl·lo·tax·is** \ˌfil-ə-ˈtak-səs\ *n* : the arrangement of leaves on a stem and in relation to one another

phy·log·e·ny \fī-ˈläj-ə-nē\ *n, pl* **-nies** : the evolutionary development of a group as distinguished from the individual development of an organism — **phy·lo·ge·net·ic** \ˌfī-lō-jə-ˈnet-ik\ *adj*

phy·lum \ˈfī-ləm\ *n, pl* **phy·la** \-lə\ : a group of animals or in some classifications plants sharing one or more characteristics that set them apart from all other animals or plants and forming a primary division of the animal or plant kingdom

phys *abbr* **1** physical **2** physician **3** physics

¹**phys·ic** \ˈfiz-ik\ *n* : a remedy for disease; *esp* : CATHARTIC, PURGATIVE

²**physic** *vb* **phys·icked**; **phys·ick·ing**; **phys·ics** *or* **phys·icks** : to treat with or administer medicine to; *esp* : PURGE

phys·i·cal \ˈfiz-i-kəl\ *adj* **1** : of or relating to nature or the laws of nature **2** : of or relating to material things : not mental or spiritual **3** : of or relating to physics **4** : of or relating to the body : BODILY — **phys·i·cal·ly** \-k(ə-)lē\ *adv*

physical education *n* : instruction in the care and development of the body ranging from simple calisthenic exercises to a course of study in hygiene, gymnastics, and the performance and management of athletic games

physical geography *n* : geography that deals with the exterior physical features and changes of the earth

physical science *n* : the natural sciences (as mineralogy or astronomy) that deal primarily with nonliving materials

physical therapy *n* : the treatment of disease by physical and mechanical means (as massage, exercise, water, or heat) — **physical therapist** *n*

phy·si·cian \fə-ˈzish-ən\ *n* : a person skilled in the art of healing; *esp* : a doctor of medicine

phys·i·cist \ˈfiz-ə-səst\ *n* : a specialist in the science of physics

phys·ics \ˈfiz-iks\ *n* **1** : a science that deals with the phenomena of inanimate matter and motion and includes consideration of mechanics, heat, light, electricity, sound, and nuclear phenomena **2** : physical composition, properties, or processes ⟨the *physics* of sound⟩

phys·i·og·no·my \ˌfiz-ē-ˈä(g)-nə-mē\ *n, pl* **-mies** : the facial features held to show qualities of mind or character

phys·i·og·ra·phy \ˌfiz-ē-ˈäg-rə-fē\ *n* : PHYSICAL GEOGRAPHY — **phys·i·og·ra·pher** \-fər\ *n* — **phys·i·o·graph·ic** \ˌfiz-ē-ə-ˈgraf-ik\ *adj*

physiol *abbr* **1** physiologist **2** physiology

phys·i·o·log·i·cal \ˌfiz-ē-ə-ˈläj-i-kəl\ *or* **phys·i·o·log·ic** \-ˈläj-ik\ *adj* **1** : of, relating to, or affecting physiology **2** : characteristic of healthy or normal physiology — **phys·i·o·log·i·cal·ly** \-i-k(ə-)lē\ *adv*

phys·i·ol·o·gy \ˌfiz-ē-ˈäl-ə-jē\ *n* **1** : a branch of biology dealing with the processes and activities by which life is manifested and which characterize the function of organisms, tissues, and cells **2** : the life processes and activities of an organism or any of its parts or of a particular bodily process — **phys·i·ol·o·gist** \-jəst\ *n*

phys·io·ther·a·py \ˌfiz-ē-ō-ˈther-ə-pē\ *n* : PHYSICAL THERAPY

phy·sique \fə-ˈzēk\ *n* : the build of a person's body : physical constitution

-phyte \ˌfīt\ *n comb form* : plant having a (specified) characteristic or habitat

¹**pi** \ˈpī\ *n, pl* **pis** \ˈpīz\ **1** : the 16th letter of the Greek alphabet — Π or π **2 a** : the symbol π denoting the ratio of the circumference of a circle to its diameter **b** : the ratio itself having a value of approximately 3.1416

²**pi** *n, pl* **pies** : type or type matter that is pied

³**pi** *vb* **pied**; **pi·ing** : to spill or mix up type or type matter

P.I. *abbr* Philippine Islands

pi·a·nis·si·mo \ˌpē-ə-ˈnis-ə-ˌmō\ *adv or adj* : very softly — used as a direction in music

¹**pi·a·no** \pē-ˈän-ō\ *adv or adj* : SOFTLY, QUIETLY — used as a direction in music

²**pi·ano** \pē-ˈan-ō\ *n, pl* **-an·os** [from Italian, short for *pianoforte*, from *piano* "soft" and *forte* "loud"; so called because, unlike earlier keyboard instruments, it could be played with varying degrees of loudness] : a stringed percussion instrument having steel-wire strings that sound when struck by felt-covered hammers operated from a keyboard — **pi·an·ist** \pē-ˈan-əst, ˈpē-ə-nəst\ *n*

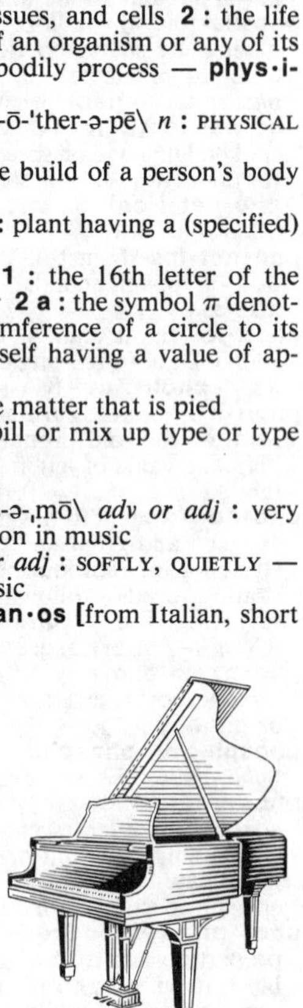
piano

pi·an·o·forte \pē-ˈan-ə-ˌfōrt, -ˌfȯrt, -ˌfȯrt-ē\ *n* : PIANO

pi·az·za \pē-ˈaz-ə, *1 is usu* -ˈat-sə, -ˈät-\ *n, pl* **piazzas** *or* **pi·az·ze** \-ˈat-(ˌ)sā, -ˈät-\ [from Italian, from Latin *platea* "broad street"; see PLACE] **1** : an open square esp. in an Italian town **2 a** : an arched and roofed gallery **b** *chiefly North & Midland* : VERANDA, PORCH

pi·broch \ˈpē-ˌbräk\ *n* : a set of martial or mournful variations for the Scottish bagpipe

pic·a·dor \ˈpik-ə-ˌdȯr\ *n, pl* **picadors** \-ˌdȯrz\ *or* **pic·a·do·res** \ˌpik-ə-ˈdōr-ēz, -ˈdȯr-\ : a horseman in a bullfight who prods the bull with a lance to weaken its neck and shoulder muscles

pic·a·yune \ˌpik-ē-'(y)ün\ *adj* **1** : of small value : PALTRY **2** : PETTY, MEAN
pic·ca·lil·li \ˌpik-ə-'lil-ē\ *n* : a pungent relish of chopped vegetables and spices
pic·co·lo \'pik-ə-ˌlō\ *n, pl* **-los** [from Italian, short for *piccolo flauto* "little flute"] : a small shrill flute pitched an octave higher than the ordinary flute — **pic·co·lo·ist** \-əst\ *n*
1**pick** \'pik\ *vb* **1 a** : to strike or work on (as for piercing, breaking, or denting) with a pointed tool **b** : to move, alter, or form by picking **2 a** : to clear or free from something by or as if by plucking ⟨*pick* meat from a bone⟩ ⟨*picked* the bone clean⟩ **b** : to gather or move by plucking ⟨*pick* berries⟩ ⟨*picked* the dish from the table⟩ **c** : to handle or operate by plucking ⟨*pick* a guitar⟩ **3 a** : CULL ⟨*picked* over the apples and threw away the spoiled ones⟩ **b** : SELECT, CHOOSE ⟨*pick* out a dress⟩ **4** : to steal or pilfer from ⟨*pick* a purse⟩ **5** : PROVOKE ⟨*pick* a quarrel⟩ **6** : to eat sparingly or in a finicky manner **7** : to unlock without a key ⟨*pick* a lock⟩ — **pick·er** *n* — **pick on 1** : TEASE, HARASS **2** : to single out esp. for an unpleasant task
2**pick** *n* **1** : a blow or stroke with a pointed instrument **2 a** : the act or privilege of choosing : CHOICE ⟨take your *pick*⟩ **b** : the best or choicest one ⟨took only the *pick* of the crop⟩
3**pick** *n* **1** : PICKAX **2** : a slender pointed implement for picking or chipping **3** : PLECTRUM
pick·a·back \'pig-ē-ˌbak, 'pik-ə-\ *var of* PIGGYBACK
pickaback plant *n* : an herb that is native to western No. America, has young plants borne at the junction of leaf blade and leaf stem, and is used as a foliage plant
pick·a·nin·ny *or* **pic·a·nin·ny** \'pik-ə-ˌnin-ē, ˌpik-ə-'\ *n, pl* **-nies** : a Negro child — often taken to be offensive
pick·ax *or* **pick·axe** \'pik-ˌaks\ *n* : a heavy tool with a wooden handle and a blade pointed at one or both ends used esp. to loosen or break up soil or rock
picked \'pikt\ *adj* : fit or ready for use : CHOICE ⟨a team of *picked* men⟩
pick·er·el \'pik-(ə-)rəl\ *n, pl* **pickerel** *or* **pickerels** **1** : any of several comparatively small pikes **2** : WALLEYE 2

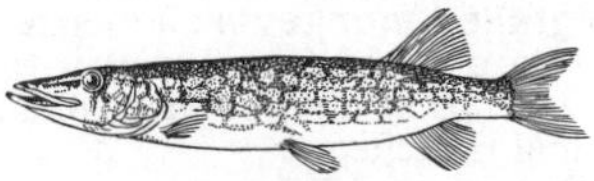

pickerel 1
(up to 30 in. long)

pick·er·el·weed \-ˌwēd\ *n* : an American shallow-water plant having a rootstock which grows in mud, thick arrow-shaped leaves, and blue flowers
1**pick·et** \'pik-ət\ *n* **1** : a pointed stake or post (as for a fence) **2** : a soldier or a group of soldiers posted as a guard against surprise attack **3 a** : a person posted by a labor organization at a place of work where there is a strike **b** : a person posted for a demonstration or protest
2**picket** *vb* **1** : to enclose, fence, or fortify with pickets **2** : to guard with or post as a picket **3** : TETHER **4 a** : to post pickets or act as a picket at ⟨*picket* a factory⟩ **b** : to serve as a picket — **pick·et·er** *n*
1**pick·le** \'pik-əl\ *n* **1** : a bath for preserving or cleaning; *esp* : a brine or vinegar solution in which foods are preserved **2** : a difficult situation : PLIGHT **3** : an article of food (as a cucumber) preserved in brine or vinegar
2**pickle** *vb* **pick·led**; **pick·ling** \'pik-(ə-)liŋ\ : to treat, preserve, or clean in or with a pickle
pick off *vb* **1** : to shoot or bring down one by one **2** : to catch off base with a quick throw ⟨the pitcher *picked off* the runner⟩
pick out *vb* **1 a** : SELECT, CHOOSE **b** : DISTINGUISH ⟨*picked* him *out* in the crowd⟩ **2** : to play the notes of by ear or one by one ⟨*pick out* a tune⟩
pick·pock·et \'pik-ˌpäk-ət\ *n* : a thief who steals from pockets and purses
pick·up \'pik-ˌəp\ *n* **1 a** : a revival of activity ⟨a business *pickup*⟩ **b** : ACCELERATION **2** : a temporary chance acquaintance **3 a** : the conversion of mechanical movements into electrical impulses in the reproduction of sound **b** : a device (as on a phonograph) for making such conversion **4 a** : the reception of sound or an image into a radio or television transmitting apparatus **b** : a device (as a microphone or a television camera) for converting sound or an image into electrical signals **5** : a light truck with an open body and low sides
pick up \-'əp\ *vb* **1 a** : to take hold of and lift ⟨*pick up* your clothes⟩ **b** : to take into a vehicle ⟨the bus *picked up* passengers⟩ **2 a** : to acquire casually, irregularly, or at a bargain ⟨*pick up* a habit⟩ ⟨*picked up* some shirts at the sale⟩ **b** : to strike up an acquaintance with and persuade to accompany esp. for purposes of making love **3** : to bring within range of sight or hearing ⟨a radio that *picks up* foreign broadcasts⟩ **4** : to gather or regain speed, vigor, or activity ⟨failed to *pick up* after his illness⟩
picky \'pik-ē\ *adj* **pick·i·er**; **-est** : FUSSY, FINICKY
1**pic·nic** \'pik-(ˌ)nik\ *n* **1** : an excursion or outing with food usu. taken along and eaten in the open **2** : something pleasant or easy
2**picnic** *vb* **pic·nicked**; **pic·nick·ing** : to go on a picnic — **pic·nick·er** *n*
pi·co- \'pē-kō\ *comb form* : one trillionth part of ⟨*pico*gram⟩
pi·cot \'pē-kō, pē-'\ *n* : one of a series of small loops forming an edging on ribbon or lace
pic·to·gram \'pik-tə-ˌgram\ *n* : PICTOGRAPH
pic·to·graph \-ˌgraf\ *n* **1** : an ancient or prehistoric drawing or painting on a rock wall **2** : one of the symbols belonging to a system of picture writing **3** : a diagram representing statistical data by pictures which can be varied in color, size, or number to indicate change — **pic·to·graph·ic** \ˌpik-tə-'graf-ik\ *adj*
pic·to·ri·al \pik-'tōr-ē-əl, -'tȯr-\ *adj* **1** : of or relating to a painting or drawing ⟨*pictorial* art⟩ **2** : consisting of or illustrated by pictures ⟨*pictorial* magazines⟩ **3** : having the qualities of a picture ⟨*pictorial* reporting⟩ — **pic·to·ri·al·ly** \-ē-ə-lē\ *adv*
1**pic·ture** \'pik-chər\ *n* **1** : a representation made on a surface (as by painting, drawing, or photography) **2** : a vivid description **3** : a state of affairs : SITUATION ⟨a worsening of the economic *picture*⟩ **4 a** : an exact likeness : COPY ⟨the *picture* of his father⟩ **b** : a tangible or visible representation : EMBODIMENT ⟨the *picture* of health⟩ **5 a** : an image on a screen **b** : MOTION PICTURE — **picture** *adj*
2**picture** *vb* **pic·tured**; **pic·tur·ing** **1** : to draw or paint a picture of : DEPICT **2** : to describe vividly **3** : to form a mental image of : IMAGINE
picture graph *n* : PICTOGRAPH 3
pic·tur·esque \ˌpik-chə-'resk\ *adj* **1** : resembling or suitable for a painted picture **2** : CHARMING, QUAINT ⟨*picturesque* customs⟩ — **pic·tur·esque·ly** *adv* — **pic·tur·esque·ness** *n*
picture tube *n* : KINESCOPE 1
picture window *n* : an outsize window designed to frame a view

P

picture writing *n* **1** : the recording of events or messages by pictures representing actions or facts **2** : the record or message represented by picture writing
pid·dling \'pid(-ə)-lən, -ling\ *adj* : TRIVIAL, UNIMPORTANT
pid·gin \'pij-ən\ *n* : a simplified speech used for communication between people with different languages; *esp* : an English-based pidgin used in the Orient
1pie \'pī\ *n* : MAGPIE
2pie *n* **1** : a dish consisting of a pastry crust and a filling (as of fruit or meat) **2** : a layer cake with a thick filling (as of jam or custard)
3pie *var of* PI
1pie·bald \'pī-,bȯld\ *adj* : of two colors; *esp* : blotched with black and white ⟨a *piebald* horse⟩
2piebald *n* : a piebald animal (as a horse)
1piece \'pēs\ *n* **1** : a part cut, torn, or broken from a thing : FRAGMENT ⟨a *piece* of string⟩ **2** : one of a group, set, or mass of things ⟨a *piece* of mail⟩ ⟨a 3-*piece* suite of furniture⟩ ⟨a chess *piece*⟩ **3** : a portion marked off ⟨a *piece* of land⟩ **4** : a single item, example, or instance ⟨a *piece* of news⟩ **5** : a quantity or size in which an article is made for sale or use ⟨buy lumber by the *piece*⟩ **6** : something made, composed, or written ⟨a *piece* of music⟩ ⟨a sculptor's most famous *piece*⟩ **7** : COIN ⟨a 50-cent *piece*⟩ **8** : FIREARM — **of a piece** : ALIKE, UNIFORM, CONSISTENT
2piece *vb* **1** : to repair, renew, or complete by adding pieces : PATCH **2** : to join into a whole ⟨*pieced* their stories together⟩ — **piec·er** *n*
1piece·meal \'pēs-,mēl\ *adv* **1** : one piece at a time : GRADUALLY **2** : in or into pieces : APART
2piecemeal *adj* : done, made, or accomplished piece by piece : GRADUAL
piece of eight : an old Spanish peso of eight reals
piece·work \'pēs-,wərk\ *n* : work paid for at a rate based on the number of articles made rather than the time spent in making them — **piece·work·er** \-,wər-kər\ *n*
pie chart *n* : a circular chart that illustrates quantities or frequencies by radial segments—called also *pie graph*
1pied \'pīd\ *adj* : of two or more colors in blotches : PARTI-COLORED
2pied *past of* PI
pied·mont \'pēd-,mänt\ *adj* : lying or formed at the base of mountains — **piedmont** *n*
pier \'pi(ə)r\ *n* **1** : a support for a bridge span **2** : a structure built out into the water for use as a landing place or walk or to protect or form a harbor **3** : a pillar or structure used to support something **4** : a mass of masonry (as a buttress) used to strengthen a wall
pierce \'pi(ə)rs\ *vb* **1** : to run into or through as a pointed weapon does : STAB **2** : to make a hole through : PERFORATE **3** : to force or make a way into or through something **4** : to penetrate with the eye or mind ⟨*pierced* the darkness⟩ — **pierc·ing·ly** \'pir-sing-lē\ *adv*
pies *pl of* PI *or of* PIE
pi·e·ty \'pī-ət-ē\ *n, pl* **-ties** **1** : the quality or state of being pious : DEVOUTNESS **2** : an act inspired by piety

ə abut ər further a back ā bake
ä cot, cart aů out ch chin e less ē easy
g gift i trip ī life j joke ng sing ō flow
ȯ flaw ȯi coin th thin th this ü loot
ů foot y yet yü few yů furious zh vision

pif·fle \'pif-əl\ *n* : trifling talk or action
1pig \'pig\ *n* **1 a** : a young swine **b** : a wild or domestic swine **2 a** : PORK **b** : PIGSKIN **3** : a casting of metal (as iron or lead) run directly from the smelting furnace into a mold — **pig** *adj*
2pig *vb* **pigged**; **pig·ging** : FARROW
pi·geon \'pij-ən\ *n* **1** : any of numerous birds with a stout body, usu. short legs, and smooth and compact plumage **2** : an easy mark : DUPE
1pi·geon·hole \-,hōl\ *n* **1** : a hole or small place for pigeons to nest **2** : a small open compartment (as in a desk) for keeping letters or papers
2pigeonhole *vb* **1** : to place in or as if in the pigeonhole of a desk : FILE **2** : to assign to a category : CLASSIFY
pi·geon–toed \,pij-ən-'tōd\ *adj* : having the toes turned in
pig·gery \'pig-ə-rē\ *n, pl* **-ger·ies** : a place where pigs are kept
pig·gish \'pig-ish\ *adj* : resembling a pig esp. in greed or dirtiness — **pig·gish·ly** *adv*
pig·gy·back \'pig-ē-,bak\ *adv or adj* **1** : on the back or shoulders **2** : on a railroad flatcar
piggy bank *n* : a coin bank often in the shape of a pig
pig·head·ed \'pig-'hed-əd\ *adj* : OBSTINATE, STUBBORN
pig iron *n* : iron that is the direct product of the blast furnace and when refined yields steel, wrought iron, or ingot iron
pig·ment \'pig-mənt\ *n* **1** : a substance that gives black or white or a color to other materials; *esp* : a powdered substance mixed with a liquid to give color **2** : a natural coloring matter in animals and plants — **pig·men·tary** \-mən-,ter-ē\ *adj* — **pig·ment·ed** \-mənt-əd, -,ment-\ *adj*
pig·men·ta·tion \,pig-mən-'tā-shən, -,men-\ *n* : a coloring with pigment; *esp* : an excessive deposition of bodily pigment
pigmy *var of* PYGMY
pig·pen \'pig-,pen\ *n* **1** : PIGSTY **2** : a dirty place
pig·skin \-,skin\ *n* **1** : the skin of a swine or leather made of it **2** : FOOTBALL 2
pig·sty \-,stī\ *n* : a pen for pigs
pig·tail \-,tāl\ *n* : a tight braid of hair — **pig·tailed** \-,tāld\ *adj*
pigtailed monkey *n* : a monkey of the Malay peninsula and the East Indies with a short slender tail which is held in the shape of a letter S when the animal is excited
piing *pres part of* PI
pi·ka \'pē-kə\ *n* : any of various small short-eared mammals of rocky uplands of Asia and western No. America that are related to the rabbits
1pike \'pīk\ *n* : a sharp point or spike — **piked** \'pīkt\ *adj*
2pike *n, pl* **pike** *or* **pikes** **1** : a large long-bodied and long-snouted freshwater fish valued for food and sport and widely distributed in cool northern waters **2** : any of various fishes related to or similar to the pike
3pike *n* : a long wooden shaft with a pointed steel head formerly used as a weapon by infantry
4pike *n* : TURNPIKE
pik·er \'pī-kər\ *n* **1** : one who does things in a small way or on a small scale **2** : CHEAPSKATE, CHISELER
pike·staff \'pīk-,staf\ *n* : the shaft of a soldier's pike
pi·las·ter \'pī-,las-tər\ *n* : an upright rectangular slightly projecting column that ornaments or helps to support a wall
pil·chard \'pil-chərd\ *n* : any of several marine fishes related to the true herrings with young that are often canned as sardines

1**pile** \'pīl\ *n* : a long slender column usu. of timber, steel, or concrete driven into the ground to carry a load

2**pile** *vb* : to equip or support with piles

3**pile** *n* **1 a** : a quantity of things heaped together **b** : a heap of wood for burning a corpse or a sacrifice **2** : a great amount ⟨has *piles* of money⟩ **3 a** : a vertical series of alternate disks of two dissimilar metals (as copper and zinc) with disks of cloth or paper moistened with an electrolyte between them for producing a current of electricty **b** : a battery made up of cells similarly constructed **4** : REACTOR 2

4**pile** *vb* **1** : to lay or place something in a pile : STACK **2** : to heap in abundance : LOAD ⟨*piled* his plate high⟩ **3** : to move or press forward in a mass : CROWD ⟨*piled* into a car⟩

5**pile** *n* **1** : a coat or surface of usu. short close fine furry hairs **2** : a velvety surface on a textile made of raised loops cut and sheared — **piled** *adj*

6**pile** *n* **1** : HEMORRHOID **2** *pl* : HEMORRHOID 2

pi·le·at·ed woodpecker \ˌpī-lē-ˌāt-əd-\ *n* : a No. American woodpecker that is black with a red crest and white on the wings and sides of the neck

pile driver *n* : a machine for hammering piles into place

pil·fer \'pil-fər\ *vb* **pil·fered**; **pil·fer·ing** \-f(ə-)riŋ\ : to steal articles of small value or in small amounts — **pil·fer·age** \-f(ə-)rij\ *n* — **pil·fer·er** \-fər-ər\ *n*

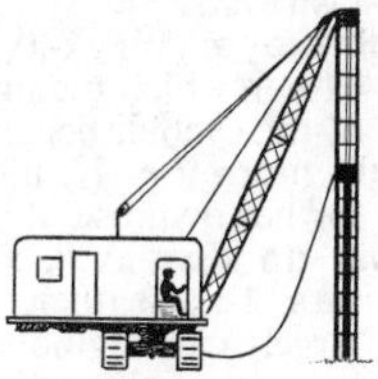
pile driver

pil·grim \'pil-grəm\ *n* [from Old French *peligrin*, from Latin *peregrinus* "foreigner"] **1** : WANDERER, TRAVELER **2** : a person who travels to a shrine or holy place as a devotee **3** *cap* : one of the English colonists founding the first permanent settlement in New England at Plymouth in 1620

pil·grim·age \'pil-grə-mij\ *n* : a journey of a pilgrim — **pilgrimage** *vb*

pil·ing \'pī-liŋ\ *n* **1** : a structure of piles **2** : PILES

pill \'pil\ *n* **1** : medicine in a small rounded mass to be swallowed whole **2** : something (as a baseball or an unpleasant situation) that resembles a pill esp. in shape or distastefulness **3** : an oral contraceptive — usu. used with *the*

pil·lage \'pil-ij\ *vb* : to take booty : PLUNDER, LOOT — **pillage** *n* — **pil·lag·er** *n*

pil·lar \'pil-ər\ *n* **1** : a slender upright support (as for a roof) **2** : a column or shaft standing alone (as for a monument) **3** : something like a pillar : SUPPORT ⟨a *pillar* of society⟩ — **pil·lared** \-ərd\ *adj*

pill·box \'pil-ˌbäks\ *n* **1** : a small usu. shallow box for pills **2** : a small low fortification for machine guns and antitank weapons **3** : a small round brimless hat with a flat crown and straight sides

pill bug *n* : WOOD LOUSE

pil·lion \'pil-yən\ *n* **1** : a cushion or pad placed behind a saddle for an extra rider **2** : a passenger's saddle (as on a motorcycle)

pil·lo·ry \'pil-ə-rē\ *n, pl* **-ries** **1** : a device for publicly punishing offenders that consists of a wooden frame with holes in which the head and hands can be locked **2** : a means for exposing a person to public scorn or ridicule — **pillory** *vb*

1**pil·low** \'pil-ō\ *n* : a support for the head of a person lying down that consists usu. of a bag filled with resilient material (as feathers or sponge rubber)

2**pillow** *vb* **1** : to place on or as if on a pillow **2** : to serve as a pillow for

pil·low·case \-ˌkās\ *n* : a removable covering for a pillow

1**pi·lot** \'pī-lət\ *n* **1 a** : a person who steers a ship **b** : a person qualified to conduct a ship into and out of a port or in specified waters **2** : GUIDE, LEADER **3** : an inclined frame on the front of a locomotive for throwing obstacles off the track **4** : one who flies or is qualified to fly an aircraft **5** : a piece that guides a tool or machine part — **pi·lot·less** \-ləs\ *adj*

2**pilot** *vb* **1** : CONDUCT, GUIDE **2 a** : to direct the navigation of ⟨*pilot* the ship through the canal⟩ **b** : to act as pilot of : FLY

3**pilot** *adj* **1** : serving as a guiding device or an activating or auxiliary unit ⟨a *pilot* light⟩ ⟨a *pilot* parachute⟩ **2** : serving on a small scale as a testing or trial device or unit ⟨a *pilot* factory⟩

pilot balloon *n* : a small unmanned balloon sent up to show the direction and speed of the wind

pilot fish *n* : a spiny-finned fish with narrow body and widely forked tail that often accompanies a shark

pi·lot·house \'pī-lət-ˌhau̇s\ *n* : an enclosed place forward on the upper deck of a ship that shelters the steering gear and the helmsman

pi·men·to \pə-'ment-ō\ *n, pl* **-tos** *or* **-to** : PIMIENTO

pi·mien·to \pə-'ment-ō, pəm-'yent-\ *n, pl* **-tos** : any of various thick-fleshed sweet peppers of mild flavor used esp. as a source of paprika

pim·per·nel \'pim-pər-ˌnel\ *n* : any of a genus of herbs related to the primrose; *esp* : one whose scarlet, white, or purplish flowers close at the approach of rainy or cloudy weather

pim·ple \'pim-pəl\ *n* : a small inflamed swelling of the skin often containing pus : PUSTULE — **pim·pled** \-pəld\ *adj* — **pim·ply** \-p(ə-)lē\ *adj*

1**pin** \'pin\ *n* **1 a** : a piece of wood, metal, or plastic used esp. for fastening articles together or for hanging one article from another **b** : one of the pieces constituting the target in various games (as bowling) **c** : the staff of the flag marking a hole on a golf course **d** : a peg for regulating the tension of the strings of a musical instrument **2 a** : a small pointed piece of wire with a head used esp. for fastening cloth or paper **b** : an ornament or emblem fastened to clothing with a pin **c** : a device (as a hairpin or safety pin) for fastening **3** : LEG ⟨wobbly on his *pins*⟩ **4** : something of small value : TRIFLE ⟨doesn't care a *pin* for her⟩

2**pin** *vb* **pinned**; **pin·ning** **1 a** : to fasten, join, or pierce with or as if with a pin **b** : to hold fixed ⟨*pinned* his opponent against the wall⟩ **2 a** : ATTACH, HANG ⟨*pinned* his hopes on a miracle⟩ **b** : to assign the blame for ⟨*pin* the robbery on him⟩

pin·a·fore \'pin-ə-ˌfōr, -ˌfȯr\ *n* : a low-necked sleeveless apron worn esp. by children

pi·ña·ta \pēn-'yät-ə\ *n* : a decorated pottery jar filled with candies, fruits, and gifts and hung from the ceiling to be broken as part of Mexican Christmas festivities

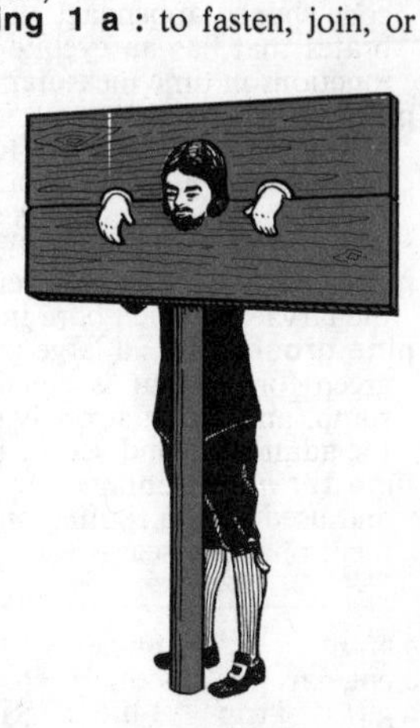
pillory 1

pin·ball machine \'pin-,bȯl-\ *n* : a device in which a ball propelled by a plunger scores points as it rolls down a slanting surface among pins and targets
pince–nez \pan(t)s-'nā\ *n, pl* **pince–nez** \-'nā(z)\ : eyeglasses clipped to the nose by a spring
pin·cer \'pin-chər, 'pin(t)-sər\ *n* **1 a** *pl* : an instrument having two handles and two pivoting jaws and used for gripping things **b** : CHELA **2** : one of two attacking forces advancing one on each side of an enemy position so as to surround and destroy it — **pin·cer·like** \-,līk\ *adj*
¹**pinch** \'pinch\ *vb* **1 a** : to squeeze between the finger and thumb or between the jaws of an instrument **b** : to squeeze painfully **c** : to nip off (a bud) to control flowering or prune the tip of (a young shoot) to induce branching **2** : to make appear thin or shrunken ⟨a face *pinched* with cold⟩ **3** : to practice economy **4** *slang* **a** : STEAL **b** : ARREST **5** : NARROW, TAPER ⟨a skirt *pinched* at the waist⟩
²**pinch** *n* **1 a** : a critical time or point : EMERGENCY ⟨help out in a *pinch*⟩ **b** : painful pressure or stress : HARDSHIP ⟨the *pinch* of hunger⟩ **2 a** : an act of pinching : SQUEEZE **b** : as much as may be taken between the finger and thumb ⟨a *pinch* of salt⟩ **3** *slang* **a** : THEFT **b** : a police raid : ARREST
pinch·cock \'pinch-,käk\ *n* : a clamp used on a flexible tube to regulate the flow of a fluid through it
pinch·er \'pin-chər\ *n* **1** : one that pinches **2** *pl* : PINCER 1a
pinch hitter *n* **1** : a baseball player sent in to bat for another esp. when a hit is needed **2** : a person called upon to do another's work in an emergency — **pinch–hit** \'pinch-'hit\ *vb*
pin curl *n* : a curl made usu. by dampening a strand of hair with water or lotion, coiling it, and securing it by a hairpin or clip
pin·cush·ion \'pin-,ku̇sh-ən\ *n* : a small cushion in which pins may be stuck
¹**pine** \'pīn\ *vb* **1** : to lose vigor, health, or weight through grief, worry, or distress ⟨*pine* away⟩ **2** : LONG, YEARN ⟨*pine* for home⟩
²**pine** *n* **1** : any of a genus of cone-bearing evergreen trees having slender elongated needles and including valuable timber trees as well as many ornamentals **2** : the straight-grained white or yellow usu. durable and resinous wood of a pine — **piny** *or* **pin·ey** \'pī-nē\ *adj*
pin·e·al body \'pin-ē-əl-, 'pī-nē-\ *n* : a small usu. cone-shaped appendage of the brain of most vertebrates that has an eyelike structure in reptiles and functions in time measurement in birds
pine·ap·ple \'pīn-,ap-əl\ *n* [so called from the resemblance of its fruit to a pine cone, formerly called *pineapple*] : a tropical plant with stiff spiny sword-shaped leaves and a short flowering stalk that develops into a fleshy edible fruit; *also* : this fruit
pine beetle *n* : any of several No. American beetles the larvae of which bore in pine trees
pine grosbeak *n* : a large grosbeak of northern evergreen forests that is chiefly gray with the crown, rump, and breast strongly suffused with rosy red in the adult male and yellow in the female
pine tar *n* : tar obtained by distillation of pinewood and used esp. in roofing and soaps and in the treatment of skin diseases

ə abut	ər further	a back	ā bake
ä cot, cart	au̇ out	ch chin	e less	ē easy
g gift	i trip	ī life	j joke	ng sing	ō flow
ȯ flaw	ȯi coin	th thin	t͟h this	ü loot
u̇ foot	y yet	yü few	yu̇ furious	zh vision

pine·wood \'pīn-,wu̇d\ *n* **1** : a wood or growth of pines **2** : PINE 2
pin·feath·er \'pin-,fet͟h-ər\ *n* : an incompletely developed feather just breaking through the skin
ping \'ping\ *n* **1** : a sharp sound like that of a bullet striking **2** : KNOCK 4 — **ping** *vb*
pin·head \'pin-,hed\ *n* : the head of a pin
pin·hole \-,hōl\ *n* : a very small hole
¹**pin·ion** \'pin-yən\ *n* **1** : the end part of a bird's wing; *also* : WING **2** : FEATHER, QUILL — **pin·ioned** \-yənd\ *adj*
²**pinion** *vb* **1** : to restrain a bird from flight esp. by cutting off the pinion of one wing **2** : to disable or restrain by binding the arms
³**pinion** *n* **1** : a gear with a small number of teeth designed to mesh with a larger wheel or rack **2** : the smallest of a train or set of gear wheels
¹**pink** \'pingk\ *vb* **1** : PIERCE, STAB **2 a** : to perforate in an ornamental pattern **b** : to cut a saw-toothed edge on
²**pink** *n* **1** : any of a genus of herbs that have stems with thick nodes and are often grown for their showy flowers borne singly or in clusters **2** : the highest degree ⟨the *pink* of condition⟩
³**pink** *n* : a pale red — **pink** *adj* — **pink·ish** \'ping-kish\ *adj*
pink·eye \'pingk-,ī\ *n* : a painful and infectious disease in which the inner surface of the eyelid and part of the eyeball become pinkish and sore
pin money *n* **1** : money given by a man to his wife for her own use **2** : money for incidental expenses
pin·na \'pin-ə\ *n, pl* **pin·nae** \'pin-(,)ē, -,ī\ *or* **pin·nas** **1** : a feather, wing, fin, or similar part **2** : the largely cartilaginous projecting portion of the external ear — **pin·nal** \'pin-əl\ *adj*
pin·nace \'pin-əs\ *n* **1** : a light sailing ship used largely as a tender **2** : a ship's boat
pin·na·cle \'pin-i-kəl\ *n* **1** : an upright structure (as on a tower) usu. ending in a small spire **2** : a high pointed peak **3** : the summit or highest point of achievement or development
pin·nate \'pin-,āt\ *adj* : resembling a feather esp. in having similar parts arranged on opposite sides of an axis ⟨a *pinnate* leaf⟩ — **pin·nate·ly** *adv*
pi·noch·le \'pē-,nək-əl\ *n* : a card game played with two cards of each suit with 9 the lowest card
pi·ñon \'pin-,yän\ *n, pl* **piñons** *or* **pi·ño·nes** \pin-'yō-ñēz\ : any of various low-growing pines of western No. America with edible seeds
¹**pin·point** \'pin-,pȯint\ *vb* : to locate or determine with precision ⟨*pinpoint* a bombing target⟩
²**pinpoint** *adj* **1** : extremely fine or precise ⟨*pinpoint* accuracy⟩ **2** : located, fixed, or directed with extreme precision
pin·prick \'pin-,prik\ *n* : a small puncture made by or as if by a pin
pins and needles *n pl* : a pricking tingling sensation in a limb recovering from numbness — **on pins and needles** : in a nervous or jumpy state of anticipation
pint \'pīnt\ *n* **1** — see MEASURE table **2** : a pint container
pin·tail \'pin-,tāl\ *n, pl* **pintail** *or* **pintails** : a bird (as a duck or grouse) with long central tail feathers — **pin–tailed** \-,tāld\ *adj*
¹**pin·to** \'pin-tō\ *n, pl* **pintos** *also* **pintoes** : a spotted horse or pony
²**pinto** *adj* : MOTTLED, PIED
pint–size \'pīnt-,sīz\ *or* **pint–sized** \-,sīzd\ *adj* : SMALL, TINY
pin·wale \'pin-,wāl\ *adj* : made with narrow wales ⟨*pinwale* corduroy⟩

pin·wheel \-ˌhwēl\ *n* **1** : a toy consisting of light vanes that revolve at the end of a stick **2** : a fireworks device in the form of a revolving wheel of colored fire

pin·worm \-ˌwərm\ *n* : any of numerous small roundworms that infest the intestines and usu. the cecum of various vertebrates; *esp* : one parasitic in man

1pi·o·neer \ˌpī-ə-'ni(ə)r\ *n* **1** : a person who goes before opening up new ways (as of thought or activity) ⟨*pioneers* of American medicine⟩ **2** : one of the first to settle in an area : COLONIST — **pioneer** *adj*

2pioneer *vb* **1** : to act as a pioneer **2** : to open or prepare for others to follow; *esp* : SETTLE **3** : to originate or take part in the development of something new

pi·ous \'pī-əs\ *adj* **1** : having or showing reverence for God : DEVOUT **2** : marked by sham or hypocrisy ⟨a *pious* fraud⟩ — **pi·ous·ly** *adv* — **pi·ous·ness** *n*

1pip \'pip\ *n* : a disorder of a bird marked by formation of a scale or crust on the tongue; *also* : this scale or crust

2pip *n* **1** : DOT, SPOT ⟨a playing card with two *pips*⟩ **2** : BLIP

3pip *n* **1** : a small fruit seed ⟨apple *pips*⟩ **2** *slang* : something very good

4pip *vb* **pipped**; **pip·ping** **1** : PEEP, CHIRP **2 a** : to break the shell of the egg in hatching **b** : to be broken by a pipping bird ⟨eggs starting to *pip*⟩

1pipe \'pīp\ *n* **1 a** : a musical instrument consisting of a tube of reed, wood, or metal that is played by blowing **b** : a tube producing a musical sound ⟨an organ *pipe*⟩ **c** : BAGPIPE — usu. used in pl. **d** : the whistle, call, or note esp. of a bird or an insect **2** : a long tube used esp. to conduct a substance (as water, steam, or gas) **3 a** : a tube with a small bowl at one end used for smoking tobacco **b** : a toy pipe for blowing bubbles

2pipe *vb* **1 a** : to play on a pipe **b** : to convey orders or direct by signals on a boatswain's pipe **2** : to speak in or have a high shrill tone **3** : to furnish or trim with piping **4** : to convey by or as if by pipes ⟨*pipe* water⟩ — **pip·er** *n*

pipe cleaner *n* : a piece of flexible wire in which tufted fabric is twisted and which is designed to clean the stem of a tobacco pipe

pipe·fish \'pīp-ˌfish\ *n* : any of various long slender fishes that are related to the sea horses and have a tube-shaped snout and an angular body covered with bony plates

pipe·line \-ˌlīn\ *n* **1** : a line of pipe with pumps, valves, and control devices for conveying liquids, gases, or finely divided solids **2** : a channel for information or goods

pipe organ *n* : ORGAN 1a

pi·pette \pī-'pet\ *n* : a device for measuring and transferring small volumes of liquid that typically consists of a narrow glass tube into which the liquid is drawn by suction and retained by closing the upper end — **pipette** *vb*

pip·ing \'pī-piŋ\ *n* **1 a** : the music of a pipe **b** : the producing of shrill pipes ⟨the *piping* of frogs⟩ **2** : a quantity or system of pipes **3** : a narrow decorative fold stitched in seams or along edges

pip·ing hot \ˌpī-piŋ-\ *adj* : very hot

pip·it \'pip-ət\ *n* : any of various small singing birds resembling the lark

pip·kin \'pip-kən\ *n* : a small earthenware or metal pot usu. with a handle

pip·pin \'pip-ən\ *n* : any of numerous apples with usu. yellow or greenish yellow skins strongly flushed with red

pi·quant \'pē-kənt\ *adj* **1** : agreeably stimulating to the palate : PUNGENT **2** : pleasingly exciting ⟨a *piquant* bit of gossip⟩ **3** : having a lively arch charm ⟨a *piquant* face⟩ — **pi·quan·cy** \-kən-sē\ *n* — **pi·quant·ly** *adv*

1pique \'pēk\ *n* **1** : offense taken by one slighted or looked down upon **2** : a fit of resentment

2pique *vb* **1** : to arouse anger or resentment in : IRRITATE; *esp* : to offend by slighting **2** : EXCITE, AROUSE ⟨the package *piqued* her curiosity⟩

pi·qué *or* **pi·que** \pi-'kā, 'pē-ˌ\ *n* : a durable ribbed fabric of cotton, rayon, or silk

pi·ra·cy \'pī-rə-sē\ *n, pl* **-cies** **1** : robbery on the high seas **2** : the unauthorized use of another's production or invention

pi·ra·nha \pə-'ran-yə\ *n* : a small flesh-eating So. American freshwater fish that may attack swimmers

1pi·rate \'pī-rət\ *n* : a person who commits piracy and esp. robbery on the high seas — **pi·rat·i·cal** \pə-'rat-i-kəl, pī-\ *adj* — **pi·rat·i·cal·ly** \-i-k(ə-)lē\ *adv*

2pirate *vb* : to take or appropriate by piracy ⟨*pirate* an invention⟩

pi·rogue \'pē-ˌrōg\ *n* **1** : DUGOUT 1 **2** : a boat like a canoe

pir·ou·ette \ˌpir-ə-'wet\ *n* : a rapid whirling or turning on the toe or ball of one foot — **pirouette** *vb*

pis *pl of* PI

Pi·sces \'pī-(ˌ)sēz, 'pis-ˌēz\ *n* — see ZODIAC table

pis·tach·io \pə-'stash-(ē-ˌ)ō, -'stäsh-\ *n, pl* **-chios** : a small tree that is related to the sumacs and has a fruit containing a greenish edible seed; *also* : its seed

pis·til \'pis-təl\ *n* [from Latin *pistillum* "pestle", the source, via French, of English *pestle;* so called from its shape] : the seed-producing part and female reproductive organ of a flower consisting usu. of stigma, style, and ovary

pis·til·late \'pis-tə-ˌlāt\ *adj* : having pistils; *esp* : having pistils but no stamens

pis·tol \'pis-təl\ *n* : a short firearm aimed and fired with one hand

pis·ton \'pis-tən\ *n* **1** : a sliding piece moved by or moving against fluid pressure that usu. consists of a short cylinder moving within a larger cylinder **2** : a sliding valve in a brass instrument serving when pressed down to lower its pitch

piston ring *n* : a springy split metal ring around a piston for making a tight fit

piston rod *n* : a rod by which a piston is moved or by which it communicates motion

1pit \'pit\ *n* **1** : a hole, shaft, or cavity in the ground ⟨gravel *pit*⟩ **2** : an area set off from and often sunken below adjacent areas: as **a** : an enclosure where animals (as cocks) are set to fight **b** : the space occupied by an orchestra in a theater **3 a** : a hollowed or indented area esp. in the surface of the body ⟨the *pit* of the stomach⟩ **b** : an indented scar (as from a boil)

2pit *vb* **pit·ted**; **pit·ting** **1 a** : to put into or store in a pit **b** : to make pits in; *esp* : to scar with pits **2** : to set into opposition or rivalry ⟨*pitted* himself against the champion⟩ **3** : to become marked with pits

3pit *n* : the stone of a fruit (as the cherry) that is a drupe

4pit *vb* **pit·ted**; **pit·ting** : to remove the pit from ⟨*pitted* dates⟩

pit–a–pat \ˌpit-i-'pat\ *adv or adj* : PITTER-PATTER — **pit–a–pat** *n* — **pit–a–pat** *vb*

1pitch \'pich\ *n* **1** : a dark sticky substance obtained as a residue in the distillation of organic materials (as tars) **2** : resin from various cone-bearing trees

[2]**pitch** *vb* : to cover, smear, or treat with pitch

[3]**pitch** *vb* **1** : to erect and fix firmly in place ⟨*pitch* a tent⟩ **2 a** : THROW, TOSS ⟨*pitch* hay⟩ **b** : to deliver a baseball to a batter **3 a** : to fix or set at a particular pitch or level ⟨*pitch* a tune too high⟩ **b** : SLOPE, INCLINE **4 a** : to fall headlong **b** : to have the bow plunge and rise abruptly ⟨a ship *pitching* in heavy seas⟩ **c** : BUCK 1a ⟨a *pitching* horse⟩ **5** : to play ball as a pitcher

[4]**pitch** *n* **1** : the action or a manner of pitching **2** : slope or degree of slope **3 a** : the distance between one point on a gear tooth or screw thread and the corresponding point on the next tooth or thread **b** : the distance advanced by a propeller in one revolution **4** : a high point : ZENITH ⟨a *pitch* of excitement⟩ **5 a** : highness or lowness of sound **b** : a standard frequency for tuning instruments ⟨the oboe sounded the *pitch*⟩ **6** : a high-pressure sales talk **7** : the delivery of a baseball by a pitcher to a batter — **pitched** \'picht\ *adj*

pitch–black \'pich-'blak\ *adj* : extremely dark or black

pitch·blende \'pich-ˌblend\ *n* : a brown to black mineral that is a source of uranium and radium

pitch–dark \'pich-'därk\ *adj* : extremely dark

pitched battle \'pich(t)-\ *n* : an intensely fought battle in which the opposing forces are locked in close combat

[1]**pitch·er** \'pich-ər\ *n* **1** : a container for holding and pouring liquids that usu. has a lip or spout and a handle **2** : a modified leaf of a pitcher plant in which the hollowed leaf stem and base of the blade form an elongated container for catching and digesting small arthropods (as insects)

[2]**pitcher** *n* : one that pitches; *esp* : a baseball player who pitches

pitcher plant *n* : any of various plants with leaves modified into pitchers

pitch·fork \'pich-ˌfȯrk\ *n* : a usu. long-handled fork used in pitching hay or grain

pitch in *vb* **1** : to begin to work energetically **2** : to contribute to a common task

pitch·out \'pich-ˌau̇t\ *n* **1** : a pitch in baseball deliberately out of reach of the batter to enable the catcher to check or put out a base runner **2** : a lateral pass in football between two backs behind the line of scrimmage

pitch pipe *n* : a small pipe blown to indicate musical pitch

pitchy \'pich-ē\ *adj* **pitch·i·er**; **-est** **1 a** : full of pitch : TARRY **b** : of, relating to, or having the qualities of pitch **2** : PITCH-BLACK

pit·e·ous \'pit-ē-əs\ *adj* : PITIFUL 1 — **pit·e·ous·ly** *adv* — **pit·e·ous·ness** *n*

pit·fall \'pit-ˌfȯl\ *n* **1** : TRAP, SNARE; *esp* : a covered or camouflaged pit used to capture animals or men **2** : a hidden or not easily recognized danger or difficulty

pith \'pith\ *n* **1 a** : a central strand of spongy tissue in the stems of most vascular plants that prob. functions chiefly in storage **b** : the spongy interior of a bone or feather **2** : the essential part : CORE — **pith** *adj*

pith·e·can·thro·pus \ˌpith-i-'kan(t)-thrə-pəs, -kan-'thrō-\ *n, pl* **-thro·pi** \-ˌpī, -ˌpē\ : any of several primitive extinct men intermediate between modern man and the manlike apes and known esp. from skeletal remains from Pliocene deposits in Java — compare PEKING MAN

pithy \'pith-ē\ *adj* **pith·i·er**; **-est** **1** : consisting of or filled with pith **2** : being short and to the point ⟨a *pithy* saying⟩ — **pith·i·ly** \'pith-ə-lē\ *adv* — **pith·i·ness** \'pith-ē-nəs\ *n*

piti·a·ble \'pit-ē-ə-bəl\ *adj* : PITIFUL — **piti·a·ble·ness** *n* — **piti·a·bly** \-blē\ *adv*

pit·i·ful \'pit-i-fəl\ *adj* **1** : arousing pity or sympathy ⟨a *pitiful* orphan⟩ **2** : deserving pitying contempt ⟨a *pitiful* excuse⟩ — **pit·i·ful·ly** \-f(ə-)lē\ *adv*

pit·i·less \'pit-i-ləs\ *adj* : having no pity : MERCILESS — **pit·i·less·ly** *adv* — **pit·i·less·ness** *n*

pit·tance \'pit-ən(t)s\ *n* : a small portion, amount, or allowance esp. of money

pit·ter–pat·ter \'pit-ər-ˌpat-ər, 'pit-ē-ˌpat-\ *n* : a rapid succession of light sounds or beats — **pit·ter–pat·ter** \ˌpit-ər-', ˌpit-ē-'\ *adv or adj* — **pitter–patter** *like adv*\ *vb*

pi·tu·i·tary \pə-'t(y)ü-ə-ˌter-ē\ *adj* : of, relating to, or being the pituitary body — **pituitary** *n*

pituitary body *n* : a small oval endocrine organ attached to the base of the brain that produces various internal secretions that regulate esp. growth and reproduction — called also *pituitary gland*

pit viper *n* : any of a family of mostly New World poisonous snakes with a sensory pit on each side of the head and hollow perforated fangs

[1]**pity** \'pit-ē\ *n* **1** : sympathetic sorrow for one suffering, distressed, or unhappy : COMPASSION **2** : something to be regretted ⟨it's a *pity* you didn't come sooner⟩

[2]**pity** *vb* **pit·ied**; **pity·ing** : to feel pity for — **pit·i·er** *n*

[1]**piv·ot** \'piv-ət\ *n* **1** : a shaft or pin on which something turns **2** : a central member, part, or point

[2]**pivot** *vb* **1** : to turn on or as if on a pivot **2** : to provide with, mount on, or attach by a pivot

piv·ot·al \'piv-ət-əl\ *adj* **1** : of, relating to, or functioning as a pivot **2** : vitally important : CRUCIAL — **piv·ot·al·ly** \-ə-lē\ *adv*

pivot joint *n* : a bodily joint that consists of a bony pivot in a ring of bone and cartilage and permits movement by rotation only

pix·ie *or* **pixy** \'pik-sē\ *n, pl* **pix·ies** : a mischievous sprite or fairy — **pix·ie·ish** \-sē-ish\ *adj*

pizz *abbr* pizzicato

piz·za \'pēt-sə\ *n* : an open pie made typically of thinly rolled bread dough spread with a spiced mixture (as of tomatoes, cheese, and ground meat) and baked

piz·ze·ria \ˌpēt-sə-'rē-ə\ *n* : an establishment where pizzas are made or sold

piz·zi·ca·to \ˌpit-si-'kät-ō\ *adv or adj* : by means of plucking by the fingers instead of bowing — used as a direction in music

pj *abbr* pajama

pk *abbr* **1** park **2** peak **3** peck

pkg *abbr* package

pkwy *abbr* parkway

pl *abbr* **1** place **2** plural

[1]**plac·ard** \'plak-ˌärd, -ərd\ *n* : a notice posted in a public place : POSTER

[2]**placard** *vb* **1** : to post placards on or in **2** : to announce by or as if by posting

pla·cate \'plā-ˌkāt, 'plak-ˌāt\ *vb* : to calm the anger of esp. by concessions : APPEASE ***syn*** see PACIFY ***ant*** enrage

[1]**place** \'plās\ *n* [from medieval French, meaning "open space", from Latin *platea* "broad street",

from Greek *plateia*, feminine of *platys* "broad"] **1 a :** SPACE, ROOM ⟨make a *place* for a newcomer⟩ **b :** a particular location in space : LOCALITY ⟨stopped several days at each *place*⟩ **c :** an inhabited area (as a city or village) ⟨her native *place*⟩ **2 a :** DWELLING **b :** a building, room, or area devoted to a particular purpose ⟨amusement *places*⟩ ⟨a *place* of worship⟩ **3 :** a particular part of something : SPOT ⟨a sore *place* on his shoulder⟩ ⟨lost his *place* in the book⟩ **4 a :** position in an ordering ⟨in the first *place*⟩ **b :** the position next after the winner in a race or contest : SECOND ⟨win, *place*, and show⟩ **c :** the position of a figure in a numeral ⟨12 is a two *place* number⟩ ⟨in 316 the figure 1 is in the tens *place*⟩ **5 a :** suitable or assigned location or situation ⟨not the *place* for an active man⟩ ⟨a servant who knew her *place*⟩ **b :** accommodations for one person ⟨set 12 *places* at table⟩ **c :** space or situation customarily or formerly occupied ⟨paper towels taking the *place* of linen⟩ **6 :** JOB, POSITION ⟨lost her *place* at the office⟩ — **in place :** in the proper place — **out of place 1 :** not in the proper place **2 :** UNSUITABLE, INAPPROPRIATE ⟨his remark was *out of place*⟩

2**place** *vb* **1 :** to put or arrange in a particular place or position **2 a :** to appoint to a position **b :** to find a job or home for ⟨*place* a child for adoption⟩ **3 :** RANK, ESTIMATE ⟨*placed* the value of the estate too high⟩ **4 :** to identify by association ⟨could not *place* the girl when he met her again⟩ **5 :** to give an order for ⟨*place* a bet⟩ **6 :** to come in second in a horse race

place·hold·er \'plās-ˌhōl-dər\ *n* **:** a symbol used in mathematics in the place of a numeral not yet determined

place–kick \-ˌkik\ *n* **:** the kicking of a football placed or held in a stationary position on the ground — **place–kick** *vb*

place·ment \'plās-mənt\ *n* **1 :** an act or instance of placing; *esp* **:** the assignment of a person to a suitable place (as a class in school or a job) **2 a :** the position of a ball for a place-kick **b :** PLACE-KICK

pla·cen·ta \plə-'sent-ə\ *n* **:** the organ in most mammals by which the fetus is joined to the maternal uterus and nourished — **pla·cen·tal** \-'sent-əl\ *adj*

plac·er \'plas-ər\ *n* **:** a deposit of sand or gravel containing particles of valuable mineral (as gold) — **placer miner** *n* — **placer mining** *n*

place value *n* **:** the value of the location of a digit in a number ⟨in 425 the location of the digit 2 has a *place value* of ten while the digit itself indicates that there are two tens⟩

plac·id \'plas-əd\ *adj* **:** PEACEFUL, CALM ⟨a *placid* disposition⟩ — **pla·cid·i·ty** \pla-'sid-ət-ē, plə-\ *n* — **plac·id·ly** \'plas-əd-lē\ *adv*

plack·et \'plak-ət\ *n* **:** a slit or opening in a garment (as a skirt) which closes after the garment has been put on

pla·gia·rism \'plā-jə-ˌriz-əm\ *n* **1 :** an act of plagiarizing **2 :** something plagiarized — **pla·gia·rist** \-rəst\ *n* — **pla·gia·ris·tic** \ˌplā-jə-'ris-tik\ *adj*

pla·gia·rize \'plā-jə-ˌrīz\ *vb* **:** to steal and pass off as one's own the work of another ⟨*plagiarized* a classmate's homework⟩ — **pla·gia·riz·er** *n*

1**plague** \'plāg\ *n* **1 :** a disastrous evil; *esp* **:** a large number of destructive pests ⟨a *plague* of locusts⟩ **2 :** a cause or occasion of annoyance : NUISANCE **3 :** an epidemic disease causing a high rate of mortality : PESTILENCE; *esp* **:** BUBONIC PLAGUE

2**plague** *vb* **1 :** to strike or afflict with or as if with disease, calamity, or evil **2 :** TEASE, TORMENT — **plagu·er** *n*

plaid \'plad\ *n* **1 :** a rectangular length of tartan worn over the shoulder as part of the Scottish national costume **2 :** TARTAN 2 **3 a :** TARTAN 1 **b :** a pattern of unevenly spaced repeated stripes crossing at right angles — **plaid** *adj*

1**plain** \'plān\ *n* **:** a broad area of level or rolling treeless country

2**plain** *adj* **1 a :** lacking ornament : UNDECORATED ⟨her dress was *plain*⟩ **b :** of simple weave or solid color ⟨a *plain* fabric⟩ **2 :** free of added or extra matter : PURE ⟨a glass of *plain* water⟩ **3 :** CLEAR, UNOBSTRUCTED ⟨in *plain* view⟩ **4 a :** clear to the mind ⟨his meaning was *plain*⟩ **b :** FRANK, BLUNT ⟨*plain* speaking⟩ **5 a :** of common or average attainments or status : ORDINARY ⟨*plain* people⟩ **b :** not complex : SIMPLE **c :** not rich or luxurious ⟨*plain* living⟩ **6 :** not handsome or beautiful : HOMELY — **plain·ly** *adv* — **plain·ness** \'plān-nəs\ *n*

3**plain** *adv* **:** in a plain manner

plain·clothes·man \'plān-'klō(th)z-mən, -ˌman\ *n* **:** a police officer who does not wear a uniform on duty : DETECTIVE

plains·man \'plānz-mən\ *n* **:** an inhabitant of plains

plain·song \'plān-ˌsȯng\ *n* **:** rhythmic but not metrical liturgical chant sung in unison in various Christian rites

plain·spo·ken \-'spō-kən\ *adj* **:** speaking or spoken bluntly ⟨a *plainspoken* man⟩

plaint \'plānt\ *n* **1 :** LAMENTATION, WAIL **2 :** PROTEST, COMPLAINT

plain·tiff \'plānt-əf\ *n* **:** the complaining party in a lawsuit

plain·tive \'plānt-iv\ *adj* **:** expressive of suffering or woe : MELANCHOLY — **plain·tive·ly** *adv* — **plain·tive·ness** *n*

1**plait** \'plāt, 'plat\ *n* **1 :** PLEAT **2 :** a usu. flat braid (as of hair)

2**plait** *vb* **1 :** PLEAT 1 **2 a :** BRAID **b :** to make by plaiting — **plait·er** *n*

1**plan** \'plan\ *n* **1 :** a drawing or diagram showing the parts or outline of something **2 :** a method or scheme of acting, doing, or arranging ⟨a civil defense *plan*⟩ ⟨vacation *plans*⟩ **3 :** INTENT, AIM ⟨his *plan* was to stop them at the bridge⟩ — **plan·less** \-ləs\ *adj*

2**plan** *vb* **planned; plan·ning 1 :** to form a plan of or for; *esp* **:** to arrange the parts or details of in advance ⟨*plan* a church⟩ ⟨*plan* a party⟩ **2 :** to have in mind : INTEND **3 :** to make plans — **plan·ner** *n*

pla·nar·ia \plə-'nar-ē-ə, -'ner-\ *n* **:** PLANARIAN; *esp* **:** one of a common freshwater genus

pla·nar·i·an \-ē-ən\ *n* **:** any of an order of small soft-bodied ciliated mostly aquatic flatworms — **planarian** *adj*

planarian (about 1 in. long)

1**plane** \'plān\ *vb* **1 :** to make smooth or even esp. with a plane **2 :** to remove by planing — **plan·er** *n*

2**plane** *n* **:** any of a genus of trees with large 5-lobed leaves and flowers in globe-shaped heads — called also *sycamore*

3**plane** *n* **:** a tool for smoothing or shaping wood

4**plane** *n* **1 a :** a surface any two points of which can be joined by a straight line lying wholly within it **b :** a flat or level surface **2 :** a level of existence or development **3 a :** one of the main supporting surfaces of an airplane **b :** AIRPLANE

5**plane** *adj* **1 :** lacking elevations or depressions : FLAT, LEVEL **2 a :** of, relating to, or dealing with planes ⟨*plane* geometry⟩ **b** : lying within a plane ⟨a closed *plane* curve⟩

plane–po·lar·ized \'plān-'pō-lə-ˌrīzd\ *adj* : vibrating in a single plane ⟨*plane-polarized* light waves⟩

plan·et \'plan-ət\ *n* [from Greek *planēt-*, stem of *planēs*, literally "wanderer"; so called because its position among the fixed stars is constantly changing] : a heavenly body except a comet or meteor that revolves about the sun; *also* : such a body revolving about another star

PLANETS

SYMBOL	NAME	MEAN DISTANCE FROM THE SUN astronomical units	million miles	PERIOD OF REVOLUTION IN DAYS OR YEARS	EQUATORIAL DIAMETER IN MILES
☿	Mercury	0.387	36.0	88.0 d.	3,100
♀	Venus	0.723	67.2	224.7 d.	7,700
⊕	Earth	1.000	92.9	365.26 d.	7,926
♂	Mars	1.524	141.5	687.0 d.	4,200
♃	Jupiter	5.203	483.4	11.86 y.	88,700
♄	Saturn	9.539	886.0	29.46 y.	75,100
⛢	Uranus	19.18	1782.0	84.01 y.	29,200
♆	Neptune	30.06	2792.0	164.8 y.	27,700
♇	Pluto	39.44	3664.0	247.7 y.	3,500?

plan·e·tar·i·um \ˌplan-ə-'ter-ē-əm\ *n, pl* **-i·ums** *or* **-ia** \-ē-ə\ **1** : an optical device to project images of heavenly bodies on a dome-shaped ceiling **2** : a building or room housing a planetarium

plan·e·tary \'plan-ə-ˌter-ē\ *adj* **1 a** : of or relating to a planet **b** : moving like a planet ⟨*planetary* electrons of the atomic nucleus⟩ **2** : GLOBAL, WORLDWIDE ⟨a matter of *planetary* concern⟩

plan·e·tes·i·mal \ˌplan-ə-'tes-ə-məl\ *n* : one of numerous small solid heavenly bodies which may have existed at an early stage of the development of the solar system and from which the planets may have been formed

plan·e·toid \'plan-ə-ˌtȯid\ *n* : a body resembling a planet; *esp* : ASTEROID

1**plank** \'plangk\ *n* **1** : a wide heavy thick board **2** : an item in the platform of a political party

2**plank** *vb* **1** : to cover or floor with planks **2** : to set down forcefully ⟨*planked* the book on the table⟩ **3** : to cook and serve on a board ⟨*planked* steak⟩

plank·ter \'plang(k)-tər\ *n* : a planktonic organism

plank·ton \'plang(k)-tən, -ˌtän\ *n* : the passively floating or weakly swimming animal and plant life of a body of water — **plank·ton·ic** \plang(k)-'tän-ik\ *adj*

pla·no–con·cave \ˌplā-nō-kän-'kāv, -'kän-ˌ\ *adj* : flat on one side and concave on the other

pla·no–con·vex \-kän-'veks, -'kän-ˌ, -kən-'\ *adj* : flat on one side and convex on the other

1**plant** \'plant\ *vb* **1 a** : to put or set in the ground to grow ⟨*plant* seeds⟩ **b** : IMPLANT ⟨*plant* good habits⟩ **2 a** : to cause to become established ⟨*plant* colonies⟩ **b** : to stock or provide with something usu. to grow or increase ⟨*plant* fields to corn⟩ ⟨*plant* a stream with trout⟩ **3 a** : to place or fix in the ground ⟨*planted* stakes to hold the vines⟩ **b** : to place firmly or forcibly ⟨*planted* a blow on his nose⟩ ⟨*planting* herself in his path⟩ **4** : to place or introduce so as to mislead ⟨*plant* a spy in an office⟩ ⟨*plant* a rumor⟩

2**plant** *n* **1** : any of a kingdom of living beings typically lacking the ability to move from place to place under their own power, having no obvious nervous or sensory organs, possessing cellulose cell walls, and often having a body capable of growing indeterminately **2 a** : the land, buildings, and equipment of an organization ⟨the college *plant*⟩ **b** : FACTORY **3** : something or someone planted — **plant·like** \-ˌlīk\ *adj*

1**plan·tain** \'plant-ən\ *n* : any of several common short-stemmed or stemless weedy herbs with parallel-veined leaves and a long spike of tiny greenish flowers

2**plantain** *n* : a banana plant with large greenish starchy fruit that is eaten cooked and is a staple food in the tropics; *also* : this fruit

plan·ta·tion \plan-'tā-shən\ *n* **1** : a group of plants and esp. trees under cultivation **2** : a settlement in a new country or region : COLONY **3** : a planted area; *esp* : an agricultural estate worked by resident labor

plant·er \'plant-ər\ *n* **1** : one that plants or cultivates ⟨a mechanical corn *planter*⟩; *esp* : an owner or operator of a plantation **2** : a container in which ornamental plants are grown

plant food *n* **1** : FOOD 1b **2** : FERTILIZER

plant hormone *n* : an organic substance produced by a plant that influences a plant physiological process elsewhere than at the site of production

plant louse *n* : an aphid or a related insect

plaque \'plak\ *n* **1** : an ornamental brooch; *esp* : an honorary badge **2** : a flat thin piece (as of metal) used for decoration or inscribed as a memorial or marker

plash \'plash\ *n* : SPLASH — **plash** *vb*

plas·ma \'plaz-mə\ *n* **1** : the fluid part of blood, lymph, or milk as distinguished from suspended material **2** : a gas in a highly ionized condition — **plas·mat·ic** \plaz-'mat-ik\ *adj*

1**plas·ter** \'plas-tər\ *n* **1** : a medicated or protective dressing consisting of a film (as of cloth or plastic) spread with a substance that clings to the skin ⟨adhesive *plaster*⟩ **2** : a pasty composition (as of lime, water, and sand) that hardens on drying and is used for coating walls, ceilings, and partitions **3** : PLASTER OF PARIS — **plas·tery** \-t(ə-)rē\ *adj*

2**plaster** *vb* **plas·tered**; **plas·ter·ing** \-t(ə-)ring\ **1 a** : to apply plaster **b** : to cover with or as if with plaster **2** : to apply a plaster to **3** : to stick as if with paste ⟨wet clothes *plastered* to his body⟩ **4** : to affix to or place upon ⟨*plaster* posters to a wall⟩ — **plas·ter·er** \-tər-ər\ *n*

plas·ter·board \'plas-tər-ˌbōrd, -ˌbȯrd\ *n* : a board used in sheets and consisting of fiberboard, paper, or felt over a plaster core

plaster cast *n* : a rigid dressing of gauze impregnated with plaster of paris

plaster of par·is \-'par-əs\ *often cap 2d P* : a white powdery substance made from gypsum that forms a quick-setting paste with water and is used chiefly for casts and molds

1**plas·tic** \'plas-tik\ *adj* [from Greek *plastikos*, from *plassein* "to mold"] **1** : capable of being molded or modeled ⟨*plastic* clay⟩ **2** : marked by or using modeling ⟨sculpture is a *plastic* art⟩ **3** : made or consisting of a plastic — **plas·ti·cal·ly** \-ti-k(ə-)lē\ *adv* — **plas·tic·i·ty** \plas-'tis-ət-ē\ *n*

2**plastic** *n* : a plastic substance; *esp* : any of numerous organic synthetic or processed materials that can be formed into objects, films, or filaments

plastic surgery *n* : surgery concerned with the repair or restoration of lost, injured, or deformed parts of the body — **plastic surgeon** *n*

plas·tid \'plas-təd\ *n* : any of various small bodies of specialized protoplasm in a cell

ə abut	ər further	a back	ā bake	
ä cot, cart	aů out	ch chin	e less	ē easy
g gift	i trip	ī life	j joke	ng sing
ō flow	ȯ flaw	ȯi coin	th thin	t͟h this
ü loot	u̇ foot	y yet	yü few	yu̇ furious
zh vision				

plat \'plat\ *n* **1** : a small plot of ground **2** : a plan or map of an area with lots marked out — **plat** *vb*

1plate \'plāt\ *n* **1 a** : a flat thin piece of material **b** : metal in sheets ⟨steel *plate*⟩ **c** : a thin layer of one metal deposited on another **2 a** : one of the broad metal pieces used in medieval armor **b** : armor made of plates **3** : a usu. flat bony or horny outgrowth forming part of a covering of an animal (as some fishes or reptiles) **4 a** : HOME PLATE **b** : a rubber slab from which a baseball pitcher delivers the ball **5 a** : precious metal; *esp* : silver bullion **b** : domestic hollow ware usu. of or plated with precious metal (as silver) **6 a** : a shallow usu. circular dish **b** : a main food course served on a plate ⟨a *plate* of beans⟩ ⟨a vegetable *plate*⟩ **c** : food and service for one person ⟨a dinner at $10 a *plate*⟩ **d** : a dish or pouch used in taking a collection (as in a church) **7 a** : a flat piece or surface on which something is embossed or engraved ⟨license *plates*⟩ **b** : a page of type prepared for use in printing **c** : a sheet of material (as glass) coated with a light-sensitive photographic emulsion **8 a** : the electrode to which the electrons flow in an electron tube **b** : a metallic grid with its openings filled with active material that forms one of the structural units of an electric storage cell or battery **9** : the part of a denture that bears the teeth and fits to the mouth **10** : a full-page illustration ⟨color *plates*⟩ — **plate-like** \-ˌlīk\ *adj*

2plate *vb* **1** : to cover or equip with plate ⟨*plate* the teapot with silver⟩ **2** : to deposit on a surface ⟨*plate* silver onto copper⟩

pla·teau \pla-'tō, 'pla-ˌ\ *n, pl* **plateaus** *or* **plateaux** \-'tōz, -ˌtōz\ **1** : a usu. large level area raised above adjacent land **2** : a stable level, period, or state

plate·ful \'plāt-ˌfu̇l\ *n, pl* **platefuls** \-ˌfu̇lz\ *also* **plates·ful** \'plāts-ˌfu̇l\ : a quantity to fill a plate

plate glass *n* : fine rolled, ground, and polished sheet glass

plate·let \'plāt-lət\ *n* : a tiny flat body; *esp* : BLOOD PLATELET

plat·form \'plat-ˌfȯrm\ *n* **1** : a declaration of principles and policies esp. of a political party or candidate **2** : a raised flat surface; *esp* : a raised flooring (as for speakers or performers) **3** : a thick sole for a shoe or a shoe with such a sole

plat·ing \'plāt-ing\ *n* **1** : the act or process of covering esp. with metal plate **2** : a coating of metal plates or plate ⟨armor *plating*⟩ ⟨the *plating* wore off the spoons⟩

pla·tin·ic \pla-'tin-ik\ *adj* : of, relating to, or containing platinum

plat·i·num \'plat-(ə-)nəm\ *n* : a heavy precious grayish white ductile malleable metallic element that is used esp. in chemical ware and apparatus, as a catalyst, and in jewelry — see ELEMENT table

platinum blonde *n* **1** : a pale silvery blonde color **2** : a person with platinum blonde hair

plat·i·tude \'plat-ə-ˌt(y)üd\ *n* **1** : the quality or state of being dull or insipid : TRITENESS **2** : a flat or trite remark — **plat·i·tu·di·nous** \ˌplat-ə-'t(y)üd-(ə-)nəs\ *adj*

pla·toon \plə-'tün\ *n* **1** : a subdivision of a military company consisting of two or more squads **2** : a group of football players sent into or withdrawn from the game as a body

platoon sergeant *n* **1** : a noncommissioned officer who is in charge of a platoon **2** : SERGEANT FIRST CLASS

plat·ter \'plat-ər\ *n* **1** : a large plate used esp. for serving meat **2** : a phonograph record

plat·y·pus \'plat-i-pəs, -ˌpu̇s\ *n* [from Greek *platypous* "flat-footed", from *platys* "wide", "flat" and *pous* "foot"] : a small aquatic egg-laying mammal of southern and eastern Australia and Tasmania with a fleshy bill resembling that of a duck, webbed feet, and a broad flattened tail

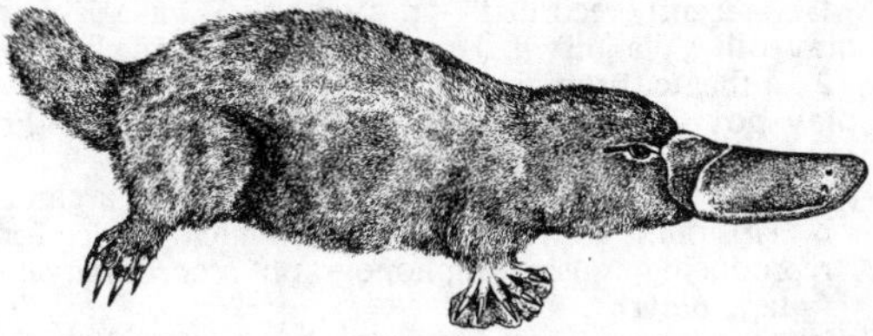

platypus (about 2 ft. long)

plau·dit \'plȯd-ət\ *n* **1** : APPLAUSE **2** : enthusiastic approval

plau·si·ble \'plȯ-zə-bəl\ *adj* **1** : apparently reasonable or worthy of belief ⟨a *plausible* explanation⟩ **2** : seemingly trustworthy : inspiring confidence : PERSUASIVE ⟨a very *plausible* liar⟩ — **plau·si·bil·i·ty** \ˌplȯ-zə-'bil-ət-ē\ *n* — **plau·si·bly** \'plȯ-zə-blē\ *adv*

1play \'plā\ *n* **1** : a brisk handling or using ⟨the *play* of a sword⟩ **2 a** : the conduct, course, or action of a game ⟨rain held up *play*⟩ **b** : a particular act or maneuver in a game **c** : one's turn in a game ⟨it's your *play*⟩ **3 a** : recreational activity; *esp* : the spontaneous activity of children **b** : JEST ⟨said it in *play*⟩ **c** : PUN ⟨a *play* on words⟩ **4** : GAMBLING, GAMING **5 a** : ACTION, CONDUCT ⟨fair *play*⟩ **b** : OPERATION, ACTIVITY **c** : brisk, fitful, or light movement ⟨the light *play* of a breeze⟩ **d** : free or unimpeded motion ⟨a jacket that gave *play* to his shoulders⟩ **e** : scope or opportunity for action ⟨the new job gave *play* to his talents⟩ **6 a** : the stage representation of an action or story **b** : a dramatic composition : DRAMA — **in play** : in a state or position to be legitimately played

2play *vb* **1 a** : to move swiftly or lightly ⟨shadows *playing* on the wall⟩ **b** : to move freely ⟨the shaft *played* in its housing⟩ **2 a** : to treat or behave lightly or without due respect ⟨*play* with a new idea⟩ ⟨*played* me for a fool⟩ **b** : PUN **c** : to trifle with something : TOY ⟨*played* with his pencil⟩ **3** : to take advantage ⟨*play* upon the people's fears⟩ **4** : to discharge in a stream ⟨hoses *playing* on the fire⟩ **5 a** : to engage in sport or recreation and esp. in spontaneous activity for amusement ⟨children *playing*⟩ **b** : to imitate in playing ⟨*play* school⟩ **c** : to take part in ⟨*play* cards⟩ ⟨*play* ball⟩ **d** : to contend against in a game ⟨Pittsburgh *plays* Chicago today⟩ **6 a** : to perform on an instrument ⟨*play* the piano⟩ ⟨*play* waltzes⟩ **b** : to produce music ⟨listen to an organ *playing*⟩ **7** : to be performed ⟨a new show *playing* for one week⟩ ⟨the music began to *play*⟩ **8 a** : ACT, BEHAVE; *esp* : to behave in a particular way ⟨*play* safe⟩ **b** : to perform on or as if on the stage ⟨*play* a part⟩ **c** : to act the part of ⟨*play* the fool⟩ **d** : to put or keep in action ⟨*play* a card in a game⟩ ⟨*play* a fish on a line⟩ **e** : to do for amusement or from mischief ⟨*play* a trick on someone⟩ **f** : CAUSE ⟨the wind *played* havoc with the garden⟩ — **play·a·ble** \'plā-ə-bəl\ *adj* — **play ball** : COOPERATE — **play hooky** \-'hu̇k-ē\ : to stay out of school without permission

play·act·ing \'plā-ˌak-ting\ *n* **1** : performance in

theatrical productions **2** : insincere or artificial behavior
play back \'plā-'bak\ *vb* : to run through a disc or tape recently recorded — **play·back** \-ˌbak\ *n*
play·bill \'plā-ˌbil\ *n* **1** : a poster advertising a play **2** : a theater program
play·boy \-ˌbȯi\ *n* : a man whose chief interest is the pursuit of pleasure
play·er \'plā-ər\ *n* **1 a** : a person who plays a game **b** : MUSICIAN **c** : ACTOR **2** : a mechanical device for reproducing music ⟨a phonograph record *player*⟩ ⟨a tape *player*⟩
player piano *n* : a piano containing a mechanical player
play·fel·low \'plā-ˌfel-ō\ *n* : PLAYMATE
play·ful \-fəl\ *adj* **1** : fond of playing **2** : HUMOROUS, JOCULAR — **play·ful·ly** \-fə-lē\ *adv* — **play·ful·ness** *n*
play·ground \-ˌgrau̇nd\ *n* : a piece of ground used for games and recreation esp. by children
play·house \-ˌhau̇s\ *n* **1** : THEATER **2** : a small house for children to play in
playing card *n* : one of a set of cards marked to show its rank and suit (as spades, hearts, diamonds, or clubs) and used in playing games
play·let \'plā-lət\ *n* : a short play
play·mate \-ˌmāt\ *n* : a companion in play
play–off \'plā-ˌȯf\ *n* **1** : a final contest or series of contests to break a tie **2** : a series of contests played after the end of the regular season to determine a championship

playing cards

play off \-'ȯf\ *vb* : to break a tie by a play-off
play out *vb* **1** : to perform to the end **2 a** : to use up or become used up **b** : TIRE, EXHAUST **3** : UNREEL, UNFOLD
play·pen \'plā-ˌpen\ *n* : a portable enclosure in which a baby or young child may play
play·thing \-ˌthing\ *n* : TOY
play up *vb* : to give emphasis or prominence to
play·wright \'plā-ˌrīt\ *n* : a person who writes plays
plaza \'plaz-ə, 'pläz-\ *n* [from Spanish, from Latin *platea* "broad street"; see PLACE] : a public square in a city or town
plea \'plē\ *n* **1** : a defendant's answer to a lawsuit or to a criminal charge ⟨a *plea* of insanity⟩ ⟨a *plea* of guilty⟩ **2** : something offered as an excuse **3** : an earnest entreaty : APPEAL
plead \'plēd\ *vb* **plead·ed** \'plēd-əd\ *or* **pled** \'pled\; **plead·ing 1** : to argue a case in a court of law **2** : to answer to a claim or charge in a court of law ⟨*plead* not guilty⟩ **3 a** : to argue for or against a claim **b** : to appeal earnestly : IMPLORE **4** : to offer in defense, apology, or excuse ⟨*plead* sickness⟩ — **plead·er** *n*
pleas·ant \'plez-ənt\ *adj* **1** : giving pleasure : AGREEABLE **2** : having or marked by pleasing manners, behavior, or appearance — **pleas·ant·ly** *adv* — **pleas·ant·ness** *n*
pleas·ant·ry \-ən-trē\ *n, pl* **-ries 1** : agreeable playfulness esp. in conversation **2 a** : a humorous act or speech : JEST **b** : a light or casual polite remark

ə abut	ər further	a back	ā bake
ä cot, cart	au̇ out	ch chin	e less	ē easy
g gift	i trip	ī life	j joke	ng sing	ō flow
ȯ flaw	ȯi coin	th thin	th this	ü loot
u̇ foot	y yet	yü few	yu̇ furious	zh vision

please \'plēz\ *vb* **1** : to give pleasure or satisfaction : GRATIFY **2** : to feel the desire or inclination : LIKE ⟨do what you *please*⟩ **3** : to be willing to — usu. used in the imperative to express a polite command or request ⟨*please* come in⟩
pleas·ing \'plē-zing\ *adj* : giving pleasure : AGREEABLE — **pleas·ing·ly** \-zing-lē\ *adv*
plea·sur·a·ble \'plezh-(ə-)rə-bəl, 'plāzh-\ *adj* : GRATIFYING, PLEASANT — **plea·sur·a·bly** \-blē\ *adv*
plea·sure \'plezh-ər, 'plāzh-\ *n* **1** : DESIRE, INCLINATION ⟨what's your *pleasure*⟩ **2** : a state of gratification : ENJOYMENT **3** : a source of delight or joy
[1]**pleat** \'plēt\ *vb* **1** : FOLD; *esp* : to arrange in pleats **2** : BRAID — **pleat·ed** *adj* — **pleat·er** *n*
[2]**pleat** *n* : a fold (as in cloth) made by doubling material over on itself
ple·be·ian \pli-'bē-(y)ən\ *n* **1** : a member of the common people in ancient Rome **2** : one of the common people — **plebeian** *adj*
pleb·i·scite \'pleb-ə-ˌsīt, -sət\ *n* : a popular vote by which the people indicate their wishes on a measure officially submitted to them
ple·cop·ter·id \pli-'käp-tə-rəd\ *n* : STONE FLY — **plecopterid** *adj*
plec·trum \'plek-trəm\ *n, pl* **plec·tra** \-trə\ *or* **plec·trums** : a small thin piece (as of plastic or metal) used to pluck a stringed instrument
[1]**pledge** \'plej\ *n* **1 a** : the handing over of something to another as security for the fulfillment of a promise; *also* : the thing handed over **b** : the state of being held as security ⟨given in *pledge*⟩ **2** : a token, sign, or evidence of something else ⟨shake hands as a *pledge* of friendship⟩ **3 a** : TOAST 3 **b** : a binding promise or agreement ⟨a *pledge* of loyalty⟩ **4** : a gift pledged (as to a charity)
[2]**pledge** *vb* **1** : to give as a pledge; *esp* : to deposit in pledge or pawn **2** : TOAST **3** : to bind by a pledge ⟨*pledged* himself to give $50⟩ **4** : to promise by a pledge ⟨*pledge* money to charity⟩
Pleis·to·cene \'plī-stə-ˌsēn\ *n* : the earlier epoch of the Quaternary; *also* : the corresponding system of rocks — **Pleistocene** *adj*
ple·na·ry \'plē-nə-rē, 'plen-ə-\ *adj* **1** : COMPLETE, FULL ⟨*plenary* powers⟩ **2** : including all entitled to attend ⟨a *plenary* session of an assembly⟩
plen·i·po·ten·tia·ry \ˌplen-ə-pə-'tench-(ə-)rē, -'ten-chē-ˌer-ē\ *n, pl* **-ries** : a person and esp. a diplomatic agent having full power to transact business — **plenipotentiary** *adj*
plen·i·tude \'plen-ə-ˌt(y)üd\ *or* **plent·i·tude** \'plen(t)-ə-\ *n* : the quality or state of being full or plentiful : ABUNDANCE
plen·te·ous \'plent-ē-əs\ *adj* : PLENTIFUL — **plen·te·ous·ly** *adv* — **plen·te·ous·ness** *n*
plen·ti·ful \'plent-i-fəl\ *adj* : existing in plenty : ABUNDANT — **plen·ti·ful·ly** \-fə-lē\ *adv* — **plen·ti·ful·ness** *n*
[1]**plen·ty** \'plent-ē\ *n* **1** : a full or abundant supply : a sufficient number or amount ⟨there will be *plenty* of things to choose from⟩ ⟨got there in *plenty* of time⟩ **2** : ABUNDANCE ⟨times of *plenty*⟩
[2]**plenty** *adj* : PLENTIFUL ⟨food was not too *plenty*⟩ ⟨had *plenty* help⟩
[3]**plenty** *adv* : ABUNDANTLY, QUITE ⟨the game was *plenty* exciting⟩
ple·si·o·saur \'plē-sē-ə-ˌsȯr\ *n* : any of a group of Mesozoic marine reptiles with flattened bodies and limbs modified into paddles
pleu·ra \'plu̇r-ə\ *n, pl* **pleu·rae** \'plu̇(ə)r-ˌē, -ˌī\ *or* **pleuras** : the delicate membrane lining each half of the chest of mammals and folded back over the sur-

face of the lung of the same side — **pleu·ral** \'plu̇r-əl\ *adj*

pleural cavity *n* : the potential space between the two layers of pleura that becomes apparent usu. only in a disordered condition (as a collapsed lung)

pleu·ri·sy \'plu̇r-ə-sē\ *n* : inflammation of the pleura usu. with fever, painful breathing, and coughing

pleu·ro·coc·cus \ˌplu̇r-ə-'käk-əs\ *n, pl* **-coc·cus·es** *or* **-coc·ci** \-'käk-ˌ(s)ī, -'käk-(ˌ)(s)ē\ : PROTOCOCCUS

plex·us \'plek-səs\ *n, pl* **plex·us·es** *or* **plex·us** \-səs, -ˌsüs\ : an interlacing network esp. of blood vessels or nerves

pli·a·ble \'plī-ə-bəl\ *adj* **1** : capable of being bent or folded without damage : FLEXIBLE **2** : easily influenced ⟨a boy too *pliable* for his own good⟩ — **pli·a·bil·i·ty** \ˌplī-ə-'bil-ət-ē\ *n* — **pli·a·bly** \'plī-ə-blē\ *adv*

pli·ant \'plī-ənt\ *adj* **1** : readily yielding without breaking : FLEXIBLE ⟨*pliant* willow twigs⟩ **2** : easily influenced **3** : ADAPTABLE — **pli·an·cy** \-ən-sē\ *n* — **pli·ant·ly** *adv*

pli·ers \'plī(-ə)rz\ *n pl* : a small pincers with jaws for holding small objects or for bending and cutting wire

[1]**plight** \'plīt\ *vb* : to put or give in pledge : ENGAGE — **plight·er** *n*

[2]**plight** *n* : CONDITION, STATE; *esp* : a bad state : PREDICAMENT ⟨in a sorry *plight*⟩

plinth \'plin(t)th\ *n* **1** : the lowest part of the base of an architectural column **2** : a block used as a base (as for a vase)

Pli·o·cene \'plī-ə-ˌsēn\ *n* : the latest epoch of the Tertiary; *also* : the corresponding system of rocks — **Pliocene** *adj*

plod \'pläd\ *vb* **plod·ded**; **plod·ding** **1** : to walk heavily or slowly : TRUDGE **2** : to work or study laboriously : DRUDGE — **plod** *n* — **plod·der** *n* — **plod·ding·ly** \-ing-lē\ *adv*

plop \'pläp\ *vb* **plopped**; **plop·ping** **1** : to make or move with a sound like that of something dropping into water **2** : to set, drop, or throw heavily ⟨*plopped* himself in a chair⟩ — **plop** *n*

[1]**plot** \'plät\ *n* **1** : a small area of ground : LOT **2** : GROUND PLAN **3** : the main story of a literary work **4** : a secret plan; *esp* : an evil or unlawful scheme **5** : CHART, DIAGRAM

[2]**plot** *vb* **plot·ted**; **plot·ting** **1 a** : to make a plot, map, or plan of **b** : to mark, note, or locate on a map or chart ⟨*plot* a ship's position⟩ ⟨*plot* a curve⟩ **2** : to plan esp. secretly : SCHEME — **plot·ter** *n*

plov·er \'pləv-ər, 'plō-vər\ *n, pl* **plover** *or* **plovers** : any of numerous shorebirds differing from the related sandpipers in having shorter and stouter bills

[1]**plow** *or* **plough** \'plau̇\ *n* **1** : an implement to cut, lift, and turn over soil for planting **2** : a device that operates like a plow; *esp* : SNOWPLOW

[2]**plow** *or* **plough** *vb* **1** : to open, break up, or work with a plow ⟨*plow* a furrow⟩ ⟨*plow* a road out with a snowplow⟩ **2** : to move through like a plow cutting the soil ⟨a ship *plowing* the waves⟩ **3** : to go steadily and laboriously : PLOD ⟨*plow* through a report⟩

plow·boy \'plau̇-ˌbȯi\ *n* : a boy who guides a plow or leads the horse drawing it

plow·man \-mən\ *n* **1** : a man who guides a plow **2** : a farm laborer

plow·share \-ˌshe(ə)r, -ˌsha(ə)r\ *n* : the part of a plow that cuts the earth

ploy \'plȯi\ *n* : a trick to embarrass or frustrate an opponent

[1]**pluck** \'plək\ *vb* **1 a** : to pull or pick at, off, or out ⟨*pluck* a flower⟩ **b** : to pluck hair or feathers from ⟨*pluck* a chicken⟩ **2** : to seize and remove forcibly : SNATCH ⟨*plucked* the child from danger⟩ **3** : to play by pulling the strings ⟨*pluck* a guitar⟩ — **pluck·er** *n*

[2]**pluck** *n* **1** : a sharp pull : TUG **2** : the heart, liver, lungs, and windpipe of an animal killed for food **3** : SPIRIT, COURAGE

plucky \'plək-ē\ *adj* **pluck·i·er**; **-est** : COURAGEOUS, BRAVE — **pluck·i·ly** \'plək-ə-lē\ *adv* — **pluck·i·ness** \'plək-ē-nəs\ *n*

P

[1]**plug** \'pləg\ *n* **1** : a piece used to close or fill a hole **2** : a worn-out horse **3** : SPARK PLUG **4** : a device for making an electrical connection by insertion into a receptacle **5** : a flat cake of tightly pressed tobacco leaves **6** : a lure with several hooks used in casting for fish **7** : a piece of favorable publicity

[2]**plug** *vb* **plugged**; **plug·ging** **1** : to stop, make tight, or secure with or as if with a plug ⟨*plug* a gap with an infantry company⟩ **2** : to hit with a bullet : SHOOT **3** : to advertise or publicize insistently **4** : to become plugged — usu. used with *up* — **plug·ger** *n*

plug in *vb* : to make an electric circuit by inserting a plug

plum \'pləm\ *n* [from Old English *plūme*, from Latin *prunum* "fruit of the plum tree"] **1 a** : any of numerous trees and shrubs related to the peach and cherries and having globe-shaped to oval fruits with oblong seeds **b** : the edible smooth-skinned fruit of a plum **2** : a raisin for use in cooking **3** : something very good **4** : a dark reddish purple — **plum·like** \-ˌlīk\ *adj*

plum·age \'plü-mij\ *n* : the entire clothing of feathers of a bird

[1]**plumb** \'pləm\ *n* : a weight used on a line esp. to determine a vertical direction or distance — called also *plumb bob* — **out of plumb** *or* **off plumb** : not vertical or true

[2]**plumb** *adv* **1** : straight down or up : VERTICALLY **2** : DIRECTLY, EXACTLY **3** *chiefly dial* : COMPLETELY, ABSOLUTELY

[3]**plumb** *vb* **1** : to sound, adjust, or test with a plumb ⟨*plumb* a wall⟩ ⟨*plumb* the depth of the well⟩ **2** : to search hidden aspects of : FATHOM ⟨*plumbed* their motives⟩ **3** : to install plumbing

[4]**plumb** *adj* : exactly vertical or true

plum·ba·go \ˌpləm-'bā-gō\ *n* : GRAPHITE

plumb bob *n* : PLUMB

plumb·er \'pləm-ər\ *n* : one that installs, repairs, and maintains plumbing

plumb·ing \'pləm-ing\ *n* **1** : a plumber's occupation or trade **2** : the apparatus (as pipes and fixtures) concerned in the distribution and use of water in a building

plumb line *n* : a line having at one end a weight (as a plumb bob) and serving esp. to determine whether something is vertical or to measure depth

[1]**plume** \'plüm\ *n* **1** : FEATHER; *esp* : a large showy feather **2 a** : a feather or tuft of feathers worn as an ornament **b** : a token of honor or prowess : PRIZE — **plumy** \'plü-mē\ *adj*

[2]**plume** *vb* **1** : to provide or deck with plumes **2** : to pride oneself on or take pride in something ⟨*plumed* himself on his swimming skill⟩ **3** : PREEN ⟨a bird *pluming* itself⟩

[1]**plum·met** \'pləm-ət\ *n* **1** : PLUMB **2** : PLUMB LINE

[2]**plummet** *vb* : to fall sharply and abruptly : PLUNGE

[1]**plump** \'pləmp\ *vb* : to drop, sink, or come in contact suddenly or heavily ⟨*plumped* down into the chair⟩ — **plump for** : to speak out strongly or campaign for ⟨*plump for* a candidate⟩

[2]**plump** *adv* **1** : with a sudden or heavy drop **2** : STRAIGHT, DIRECTLY ⟨ran *plump* into the wall⟩

3**plump** *n* : a sudden plunge or blow

4**plump** *adj* : having a full rounded form : CHUBBY — **plump·ness** *n*

5**plump** *vb* : to make or become plump ⟨*plump* up a pillow⟩

plum pudding *n* : a boiled or steamed pudding containing fruits (as raisins) and usu. rich in fat

plu·mule \'plü-myül\ *n* **1** : the primary bud of a plant embryo **2** : a down feather

plun·der \'plən-dər\ *vb* **plun·dered**; **plun·der·ing** \-d(ə-)riŋ\ : to rob esp. openly and by force (as in a raid) : PILLAGE — **plunder** *n* — **plun·der·er** \-dər-ər\ *n*

1**plunge** \'plənj\ *vb* **1** : to thrust or force quickly and forcibly ⟨*plunged* her hands into the washtub⟩ ⟨*plunging* a knife into the roast⟩ **2** : to leap or dive into water **3** : to move suddenly and sharply downward or forward and downward ⟨the stock market *plunged* after war was declared⟩ **4 a** : to rush with reckless haste ⟨*plunged* into debt⟩; *also* : to bring into an unpleasant state ⟨*plunged* his family into gloom⟩ **b** : to gamble recklessly

2**plunge** *n* : a sudden dive, leap, or rush

plung·er \'plən-jər\ *n* **1** : a person (as a diver or a reckless gambler) that plunges **2 a** : a device (as a piston in a pump) that acts with a plunging motion **b** : a rubber suction cup on a handle used to free plumbing traps and waste outlets

plunk \'pləŋk\ *vb* **1** : to make or cause to make a hollow metallic sound ⟨*plunk* the strings of a banjo⟩ **2** : to drop heavily or suddenly ⟨*plunk* a suitcase on the bench⟩ — **plunk** *n*

plu·ral \'plu̇r-əl\ *adj* : of, relating to, or being a class of grammatical forms used to denote more than one ⟨*plural* nouns⟩ — **plural** *n* — **plu·ral·ly** \-ə-lē\ *adv*

plu·ral·i·ty \plu̇-'ral-ət-ē\ *n, pl* **-ties 1** : the state of being plural or numerous **2** : the greater number or part ⟨a *plurality* of the nations want peace⟩ **3 a** : the fact of being chosen by the voters out of three or more candidates or measures when no one of them obtains more than half the total vote **b** : the excess of the number of votes received by one candidate over another; *esp* : that of the highest over the next highest ⟨win by a *plurality* of 4000 votes⟩

plu·ral·ize \'plu̇r-ə-ˌlīz\ *vb* : to make plural or express in the plural form — **plu·ral·i·za·tion** \ˌplu̇r-ə-lə-'zā-shən\ *n*

1**plus** \'pləs\ *prep* [from Latin meaning "more"] **1** : increased by ⟨4 *plus* 5 is 9⟩ **2** : WITH

2**plus** *n* **1** : an added quantity **2** : a positive factor or quality : ADVANTAGE

3**plus** *adj* **1** : having, receiving, or being in addition ⟨now she is *plus* a kitten⟩ **2** : falling high in a specified range ⟨a grade of C *plus*⟩ **3** : POSITIVE ⟨a *plus* and minus 4⟩

1**plush** \'pləsh\ *n* : a fabric with pile longer and softer than velvet

2**plush** *adj* **1** : made of or like plush **2** : very luxurious ⟨a *plush* home⟩

plus sign *n* : a sign + used esp. in mathematics to indicate addition (as in $8+6=14$) or a positive quantity (as in $+10°$)

Plu·to \'plüt-ō\ *n* : the planet most remote from the sun — see PLANET table

plu·toc·ra·cy \plü-'täk-rə-sē\ *n, pl* **-cies 1** : government by the wealthy **2** : a controlling class of rich men — **plu·to·crat** \'plüt-ə-ˌkrat\ *n* — **plu·to·crat·ic** \ˌplüt-ə-'krat-ik\ *adj*

plu·to·ni·um \plü-'tō-nē-əm\ *n* : a radioactive metallic element that is formed by decay of neptunium and found in minute quantities in pitchblende and that is fissionable to yield atomic energy — see ELEMENT table

1**ply** \'plī\ *n, pl* **plies** : one of the folds, layers, or strands of which something (as yarn or plywood) is made up

2**ply** *vb* **plied**; **ply·ing 1 a** : to use steadily or forcefully ⟨*ply* an ax⟩ **b** : to work at ⟨*plied* his trade⟩ **2** : to keep supplying to ⟨*ply* a guest with food⟩ ⟨*plied* her with questions⟩ **3** : HARASS **4** : to go or travel regularly

Plym·outh Rock \ˌplim-əth-\ *n* : a bird of an American breed of medium-sized single-combed domestic fowl

ply·wood \'plī-ˌwu̇d\ *n* : thin sheets of wood glued together under heat and pressure

plz *abbr* plaza

p.m. *abbr* post meridiem

pmt *abbr* payment

pneu·mat·ic \n(y)u̇-'mat-ik\ *adj* **1** : of, relating to, or using air, wind, or other gas **2** : moved or worked by air pressure ⟨a *pneumatic* drill⟩ **3** : inflated with or adapted for holding compressed air ⟨*pneumatic* tires⟩ — **pneu·mat·i·cal·ly** \-i-k(ə-)lē\ *adv*

pneu·mo·coc·cus \ˌn(y)ü-mə-'käk-əs\ *n, pl* **-coc·ci** \-'käk-ˌ(s)ī, -'käk-(ˌ)(s)ē\ *also* **-coc·cus·es** : the bacterium that causes pneumonia — **pneu·mo·coc·cal** \-'käk-əl\ *or* **pneu·mo·coc·cic** \-'käk-(s)ik\ *adj*

pneu·mo·nia \n(y)u̇-'mō-nyə\ *n* : a disease of the lungs characterized by inflammation and congestion and caused by infection or irritants — compare BRONCHIAL PNEUMONIA, LOBAR PNEUMONIA

pneu·mon·ic \n(y)u̇-'män-ik\ *adj* **1** : of or relating to the lungs **2** : of, relating to, or affected with pneumonia

PO *abbr* post office

1**poach** \'pōch\ *vb* : to cook in simmering liquid ⟨*poached* eggs⟩

2**poach** *vb* : to hunt or fish unlawfully usu. on private property — **poach·er** *n*

pock \'päk\ *n* : a small swelling on the skin like a pimple (as in chicken pox or smallpox); *also* : the scar it leaves — **pock** *vb*

1**pock·et** \'päk-ət\ *n* **1 a** : a small bag carried by a person : PURSE **b** : a small bag open at the top or side inserted in a garment **2** : supply of money : MEANS ⟨out of *pocket*⟩ **3** : RECEPTACLE, CONTAINER; *esp* : a bag at the corner or side of a billiard table **4** : something like a pocket ⟨a *pocket* of ore in a mine⟩ **5** : AIR POCKET

2**pocket** *vb* **1 a** : to put or enclose in a pocket ⟨*pocketed* his change⟩ **b** : to take for one's own use esp. dishonestly ⟨*pocket* the profits⟩ **2** : SUPPRESS ⟨*pocketed* his anger⟩ **3** : to supply with pockets

3**pocket** *adj* **1 a** : small enough to fit in the pocket ⟨a *pocket* dictionary⟩ **b** : SMALL, MINIATURE **2** : carried in or paid from one's pocket ⟨*pocket* money⟩

pock·et·book \'päk-ət-ˌbu̇k\ *n* **1** *usu* **pocket book** : a small esp. paperback book **2 a** : a container for money and personal papers : WALLET **b** : PURSE **c** : HANDBAG 2 **3** : MONEY, INCOME

pock·et·ful \-ˌfu̇l\ *n, pl* **pocketfuls** \-ˌfu̇lz\ *or* **pock·ets·ful** \-əts-ˌfu̇l\ : as much or as many as the pocket will contain

pocket gopher *n* : any of various stocky burrowing No. American rodents with fur-lined cheek pouches

ə abut	ər further	a back	ā bake	
ä cot, cart	au̇ out	ch chin	e less	ē easy
g gift	i trip	ī life	j joke	ŋ sing	ō flow
ȯ flaw	ȯi coin	th thin	t͟h this	ü loot
u̇ foot	y yet	yü few	yu̇ furious	zh vision

pock·et·knife \ˈpäk-ət-ˌnīf\ *n* : a knife with a folding blade to be carried in the pocket

pocket veto *n* : an indirect veto of a legislative bill by an executive through retention of the bill unsigned until after adjournment of the legislature

pock·mark \ˈpäk-ˌmärk\ *n* : the scar left by a pock esp. of smallpox — **pockmark** *vb*

pod \ˈpäd\ *n* **1** : a fruit or seed vessel that splits open when ripe; *esp* : LEGUME **2** : any of various natural protective coverings (as a cocoon) or cases (as for grasshopper eggs) **3** : a streamlined compartment under the wings or fuselage of an airplane used as a container (as for fuel or a jet engine)

POD *abbr* pay on delivery

po·di·um \ˈpōd-ē-əm\ *n, pl* **-diums** *or* **-dia** \-ē-ə\ : a dais esp. for an orchestral conductor

po·em \ˈpō-əm, -ˌem\ *n* : a composition in verse : a piece of poetry communicating to the reader the sense of a complete experience

po·e·sy \ˈpō-ə-zē, -sē\ *n, pl* **-sies** : POETRY

po·et \ˈpō-ət\ *n* [from Latin *poeta*, from Greek *poiētēs*, literally "maker"] : a person who writes poetry — **po·et·ess** \-ət-əs\ *n*

po·et·ic \pō-ˈet-ik\ *adj* **1** : of, relating to, or characteristic of poets or poetry ⟨*poetic* words⟩ **2** : written in verse — **po·et·i·cal** \-i-kəl\ *adj* — **po·et·i·cal·ly** \-k(ə-)lē\ *adv*

poet laureate *n, pl* **poets laureate** *or* **poet laureates** **1** : a poet appointed by an English sovereign as a member of the royal household to write poems for state occasions **2** : a poet regarded by a country or region as its most outstanding

po·et·ry \ˈpō-ə-trē\ *n* **1 a** : VERSE **b** : the productions of a poet : POEMS **2** : writing chosen and arranged to create a specific emotional response through meaning, sound, and rhythm

poi \ˈpȯi\ *n, pl* **poi** *or* **pois** : a Hawaiian food made of cooked taro root pounded to a paste and often fermented

poi·gnant \ˈpȯi-nyənt\ *adj* **1** : SHARP, PIERCING ⟨*poignant* grief⟩ **2** : deeply affecting : TOUCHING — **poi·gnan·cy** \-nyən-sē\ *n* — **poi·gnant·ly** *adv*

poin·ci·ana \ˌpȯin(t)-sē-ˈan-ə\ *n* : any of several showy tropical trees or shrubs with bright orange or red flowers

poin·set·tia \pȯin-ˈset-ē-ə, -ˈset-ə\ *n* : a showy Mexican and So. American plant with tapering scarlet bracts that grow like petals about its small yellow flowers

[1]**point** \ˈpȯint\ *n* **1 a** : an individual detail : ITEM **b** : a distinguishing detail : CHARACTERISTIC **c** : the chief part or meaning ⟨the *point* of the joke⟩ ⟨the *point* at issue in a court of law⟩ **2** : an end to be achieved : PURPOSE ⟨there's no *point* in continuing⟩ **3 a** : a geometric element that has position but no size **b** : a usu. small or precise place : LOCALITY ⟨a starting *point*⟩ **c** : an exact moment **d** : a step, stage, or degree in development or rank ⟨the melting *point* of ice⟩ **4 a** : the usu. sharp or tapering end of something (as a sword or pencil) : TIP **b** : either of two metal pieces in a distributor through which the circuit is made or broken **5** : a projecting piece of land **6 a** : a very small mark : DOT **b** : PUNCTUATION MARK; *esp* : PERIOD **c** : DECIMAL POINT **7 a** : one of the 32 marks indicating direction on a mariner's compass **b** : the difference of 11¼ degrees between two such adjacent points **8 a** : a unit used in giving a value or score **b** : a unit of about 1/72 inch used to measure the size of printing type **9** : the action of pointing — **in point** : RELEVANT, PERTINENT ⟨a case *in point*⟩ — **to the point** : RELEVANT, PERTINENT ⟨a remark that was quite *to the point*⟩

[2]**point** *vb* **1 a** : to furnish with a point **b** : to give force or emphasis to ⟨*point* up a remark⟩ **2** : to fill in the joints of new material ⟨*point* a brick wall⟩ **3 a** : PUNCTUATE **b** : to separate a decimal fraction from an integer by a decimal point ⟨*point* off three decimal places⟩ **4 a** : to direct someone's attention to ⟨*point* out a mistake⟩ **b** : to indicate the position or direction of something (as by the finger) ⟨*point* out a house⟩ **c** : to indicate game by freezing into a rigid position with head and gaze directed toward the object hunted ⟨a dog that *points* well⟩ **5** : to turn, face, or cause to be turned in a particular direction : AIM ⟨*point* a gun⟩ **6** : to indicate the fact or probability of something

point–blank \ˈpȯint-ˈblangk\ *adj* **1** : so close to a target that a missile fired will travel in a straight line to the mark ⟨fired from *point-blank* range⟩ **2** : DIRECT, BLUNT ⟨a *point-blank* refusal⟩ — **point–blank** *adv*

point·ed \ˈpȯint-əd\ *adj* **1** : having a point **2 a** : PERTINENT, TERSE **b** : aimed at a particular person or group ⟨*pointed* remarks⟩ — **point·ed·ness** *n*

point·er \ˈpȯint-ər\ *n* **1** : one that points; *esp* : a rod used to direct attention **2** : a large strong slender smooth-haired hunting dog that hunts by scent and indicates the presence of game by pointing **3** : a useful hint : TIP ⟨*pointers* on how to study⟩

point·less \ˈpȯint-ləs\ *adj* **1** : without a point **2** : devoid of meaning : SENSELESS ⟨a *pointless* remark⟩ — **point·less·ly** *adv* — **point·less·ness** *n*

point of view : a position from which something is considered or evaluated : STANDPOINT

[1]**poise** \ˈpȯiz\ *vb* **1 a** : BALANCE; *esp* : to hold or make firm or steady by balancing **b** : to hold or be suspended without motion in a steady position : HOVER ⟨a bird *poised* in the air⟩ **2** : to put into readiness : BRACE ⟨*poised* for action⟩

[2]**poise** *n* **1** : BALANCE, EQUILIBRIUM **2 a** : calm self-control and composure **b** : a way of carrying oneself : BEARING

[1]**poi·son** \ˈpȯi-zən\ *n* [from Old French, meaning first "a drink", then "a magic potion", and then "poison", from Latin *potion-*, stem of *potio* "drink"] **1** : a substance that if taken up by the body is able to kill, injure, or impair an organism **2** : something destructive or harmful

[2]**poison** *vb* **poi·soned**; **poi·son·ing** \ˈpȯiz-(ə-)ning\ **1 a** : to injure or kill with poison **b** : to treat, taint, or impregnate with poison ⟨*poisoned* the air with its fumes⟩ **2** : to exert a harmful influence on : CORRUPT ⟨*poisoned* their minds⟩ — **poi·son·er** \ˈpȯiz-(ə-)nər\ *n*

[3]**poison** *adj* : POISONOUS ⟨a *poison* plant⟩

poison gas *n* : a poisonous gas or a liquid or a solid giving off poisonous vapors designed (as in chemical warfare) to kill, injure, or disable

poison hemlock *n* : a poisonous herb related to the carrot and having finely divided leaves and white flowers

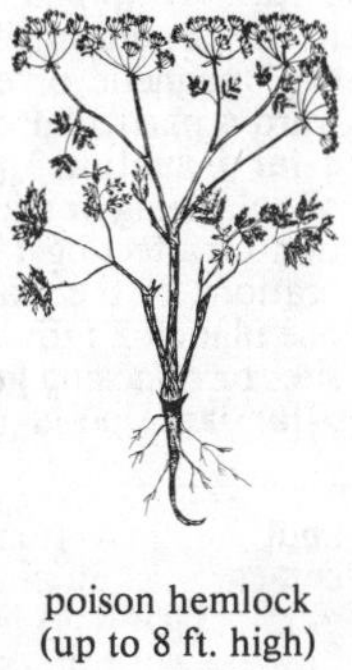

poison hemlock (up to 8 ft. high)

poison ivy *n* : a usu. climbing plant that is related to the sumacs, has leaves mostly with three leaflets, greenish flowers and berries, and foliage and stems that when bruised and touched may cause an itching rash on the skin

P

poison oak *n* : a shrubby poison ivy; *esp* : POISON SUMAC

poi·son·ous \'pȯiz-(ə-)nəs\ *adj* : having the properties or effects of poison : VENOMOUS — **poi·son·ous·ly** *adv*

poison sumac *n* : a swamp shrub related to poison ivy, having compound leaves with 7 to 13 leaflets, and sometimes producing a severe rash on the skin

1**poke** \'pōk\ *n, dial* : BAG, SACK

2**poke** *vb* **1 a** : PROD, JAB **b** : THRUST, STAB **c** : to produce by piercing, stabbing, or jabbing ⟨*poke* a hole⟩ **2** : to stick out : PROJECT **3** : to pry esp. into things that do not concern one ⟨*poked* his nose into our business⟩ **4** : to move slowly : DAWDLE ⟨*poke* along⟩ — **poke fun at** : RIDICULE, MOCK

3**poke** *n* : a quick thrust : JAB

poke bonnet *n* : a woman's bonnet with a projecting brim

1**pok·er** \'pō-kər\ *n* : one that pokes; *esp* : a metal rod for stirring a fire

2**po·ker** \'pō-kər\ *n* : a card game in which a player bets on the value of his hand

poke·weed \'pōk-,wēd\ *n* : an American herb with spikes of white flowers, dark purple juicy berries, a poisonous root, and young shoots sometimes used as potherbs

poky *or* **pok·ey** \'pō-kē\ *adj* **pok·i·er**; **-est** **1** : being small and cramped ⟨a *poky* room⟩ **2** : SLOW — **pok·i·ness** *n*

Pol *abbr* **1** Poland **2** Polish

po·lar \'pō-lər\ *adj* **1** : of or relating to a pole (as of the earth or a magnet); *esp* : coming from or having the characteristics of a polar region ⟨*polar* cold⟩ **2** : diametrically opposite

polar bear *n* : a large creamy-white bear of arctic regions

polar bear
(about 5 ft. at shoulder)

po·lar·i·ty \pō-'lar-ət-ē, pə-\ *n, pl* **-ties** **1** : the quality or condition of being polar : having poles and esp. magnetic or electrical poles **2** : attraction toward a particular object or in a specific direction

po·lar·i·za·tion \,pō-lə-rə-'zā-shən\ *n* **1** : the action of polarizing or state of being polarized; *esp* : the action of affecting radiation (as light) so that the vibrations of the wave assume a definite form (as in one plane) **2** : division or formation into two opposites or opposing groups ⟨a *polarization* of attitudes⟩

po·lar·ize \'pō-lə-,rōz\ *vb* **1** : to cause to undergo polarization **2** : to give polarity to **3** : to become polarized

1**pole** \'pōl\ *n* **1** : a long slender piece of material (as wood or metal) ⟨telephone *poles*⟩ **2** : ROD 2

2**pole** *vb* : to push or propel with a pole — **pol·er** *n*

3**pole** *n* **1** : either end of an axis of a sphere and esp. of the earth's axis **2 a** : one of the two terminals of an electric cell, battery, or dynamo **b** : one of two or more regions in a magnetized body at which the magnetism seems to be concentrated **3** : either end of the spindle-shaped structure formed in dividing cells and along which the chromosomes move

Pole \'pōl\ *n* **1** : a native or inhabitant of Poland **2** : a person of Polish descent

pole bean *n* : a cultivated bean with twining stems that is usu. trained to grow upright on supports

pole·cat \'pōl-,kat\ *n, pl* **polecats** *or* **polecat** **1** : a European flesh-eating mammal related to the weasel **2** : SKUNK

po·lem·ic \pə-'lem-ik\ *n* : an aggressive attack on the opinions or principles of another — **polemic** *or* **po·lem·i·cal** \-'lem-i-kəl\ *adj* — **po·lem·i·cal·ly** \-i-k(ə-)lē\ *adv* — **po·lem·i·cist** \-'lem-ə-səst\ *n*

pole·star \'pōl-,stär\ *n* **1** : NORTH STAR **2** : a directing principle

pole vault *n* : a vault with the aid of a pole; *esp* : a field event consisting of a vault for height over a crossbar — called also *pole jump* — **pole–vault** *vb* — **pole–vault·er** *n*

1**po·lice** \pə-'lēs\ *n, pl* **police** **1** : the department of government concerned with maintenance of public order and safety, enforcement of laws, and the prevention and detection of crimes **2** *pl* : POLICEMEN **3** : a private or military force like police ⟨railroad *police*⟩

2**police** *vb* **1** : to control, regulate, or keep in order by use of police **2** : to make clean and put in order ⟨*police* the area⟩

police dog *n* : GERMAN SHEPHERD

po·lice·man \pə-'lēs-mən\ *n* : a member of a police force — **po·lice·wom·an** \-,wu̇m-ən\ *n*

police state *n* : a state in which the activities of the people are under the arbitrary power of the government often acting through a secret police force

1**pol·i·cy** \'päl-ə-sē\ *n, pl* **-cies** : a course of action selected to guide and determine decisions

2**policy** *n, pl* **-cies** : the document containing the contract (as for life insurance or an annuity) made by an insurance company with a person

pol·i·cy·hold·er \'päl-ə-sē-,hōl-dər\ *n* : a person granted an insurance policy

po·lio \'pō-lē-,ō\ *n* : POLIOMYELITIS — **polio** *adj*

po·lio·my·e·li·tis \,pō-lē-,ō-,mī-ə-'līt-əs\ *n* : an infectious virus disease marked by inflammation of nerve cells in the spinal cord accompanied by fever and often paralysis and wasting of muscles — called also *infantile paralysis*

1**pol·ish** \'päl-ish\ *vb* **1** : to make smooth and glossy usu. by rubbing **2** : to bring to a highly finished state : PERFECT ⟨*polishing* her manners⟩ — **pol·ish·er** *n*

2**polish** *n* **1 a** : a smooth glossy surface : LUSTER **b** : REFINEMENT, CULTURE **2** : the action or process of polishing **3** : a preparation used in polishing

1**Pol·ish** \'pō-lish\ *adj* : of, relating to, or characteristic of Poland, the Poles, or Polish

2**Polish** *n* : the Slavic language of the Poles

polish off *vb* : to dispose of rapidly or completely

po·lite \pə-'līt\ *adj* **1** : REFINED, CULTIVATED ⟨*polite* society⟩ ⟨*polite* forms of address⟩ **2** : showing consideration and courtesy : COURTEOUS — **po·lite·ly** *adv* — **po·lite·ness** *n*

pol·i·tic \'päl-ə-ˌtik\ *adj* **1** : shrewd esp. in promoting a policy **2** : shrewdly tactful ⟨a *politic* answer⟩
po·lit·i·cal \pə-'lit-i-kəl\ *adj* **1** : of or relating to a government or the conduct of government **2** : of or relating to politics **3** : organized in governmental terms ⟨*political* units⟩ — **po·lit·i·cal·ly** \-k(ə-)lē\ *adv*
political science *n* : a social science concerned chiefly with governmental institutions and processes — **political scientist** *n*
pol·i·ti·cian \ˌpäl-ə-'tish-ən\ *n* **1** : a person experienced in the art of government **2** : a person engaged in politics
pol·i·tics \'päl-ə-ˌtiks\ *n sing or pl* **1 a** : POLITICAL SCIENCE **b** : the art of guiding or influencing governmental policy **c** : the art of winning and holding control over a government **2 a** : political affairs or business; *esp* : competition between groups or individuals for power and leadership **b** : political activity esp. as a profession **3** : political opinions
pol·ka \'pōl-kə\ *n* [from Czech, from Polish *Polka* "Polish woman"] : a vivacious couple dance of Bohemian origin with three steps and a hop in duple time — **polka** *vb*
pol·ka dot \'pō-kə-\ *n* : a dot in a textile pattern of evenly spaced dots
[1]**poll** \'pōl\ *n* **1 a** : HEAD **b** : the top or back of the head **2 a** : the casting or recording of votes **b** : the place where votes are cast or recorded — usu. used in pl. ⟨at the *polls*⟩ **3 a** : a questioning of persons to obtain information or opinions to be analyzed **b** : the information so obtained
[2]**poll** *vb* **1 a** : to take and record the votes of **b** : to request each member of to declare his vote individually ⟨*poll* a jury⟩ **2** : to receive votes in an election ⟨the candidate *polled* 10,000 votes⟩ **3** : to question or canvass in a poll **4** : to cast one's vote at a poll — **poll·er** *n*
pol·len \'päl-ən\ *n* : a mass of tiny particles in a seed plant that fertilize the seeds and usu. appear as fine yellow dust — **pollen** *adj*
pollen basket *n* : a flat or hollow area bordered with stiff hairs on the hind leg of a bee in which it carries pollen to the hive or nest

bee with full pollen baskets

pollen grain *n* : one of the microscopic grains of which pollen is made up
pol·len·iz·er \'päl-ə-ˌnī-zər\ *n* **1** : a plant that is a source of pollen **2** : POLLINATOR 1
pollen sac *n* : one of the pouches of a seed plant anther in which pollen is formed
pollen tube *n* : a tube formed by the pollen grain that grows down the style and conveys the sperm nuclei to the embryo sac of a flower
pol·li·nate \'päl-ə-ˌnāt\ *vb* : to place pollen on the stigma of — **pol·li·na·tion** \ˌpäl-ə-'nā-shən\ *n*
pol·li·na·tor \'päl-ə-ˌnāt-ər\ *n* **1** : an agent that pollinates flowers **2** : POLLENIZER 1
pol·li·wog *or* **pol·ly·wog** \'päl-ē-ˌwäg\ *n* : TADPOLE
poll·ster \'pōl-stər\ *n* : one that conducts a poll or compiles data obtained by a poll
poll tax *n* : a tax of a fixed amount per person often payable as a requirement for voting
pol·lut·ant \pə-'lüt-ənt\ *n* : something that pollutes
pol·lute \pə-'lüt\ *vb* : to make impure; *esp* : to contaminate (as a natural resource) with man-made waste ⟨industrial wastes *polluted* the river⟩
pol·lu·tion \pə-'lü-shən\ *n* : the action of polluting : the state of being polluted ⟨air *pollution*⟩ — compare NOISE POLLUTION, THERMAL POLLUTION
po·lo \'pō-lō\ *n* : a game played by teams of players on horseback using mallets with long flexible handles to drive a wooden ball — **po·lo·ist** \'pō-lə-wəst\ *n*
pol·o·naise \ˌpäl-ə-'nāz, ˌpō-lə-\ *n* [from French, from the feminine of *polonais* "Polish"] : a stately 19th century Polish dance
po·lo·ni·um \pə-'lō-nē-əm\ *n* : a radioactive metallic element that emits a helium nucleus to form an isotope of lead — see ELEMENT table
polo shirt *n* : a close-fitting pullover shirt of knitted cotton
pol·troon \päl-'trün\ *n* : COWARD
poly- *comb form* : many : much : MULTI- ⟨*poly*syllable⟩
poly·cy·the·mia \ˌpäl-i-sī-'thē-mē-ə\ *n* : any condition marked by an abnormal increase in the number of circulating red blood cells
poly·eth·yl·ene \ˌpäl-ē-'eth-ə-ˌlēn\ *n* : a lightweight plastic resistant to chemicals and moisture and used esp. in the form of sheets in packaging
po·lyg·a·mous \pə-'lig-ə-məs\ *adj* **1** : of or relating to marriage in which a spouse has more than one mate at one time **2** : having more than one spouse at one time — **po·lyg·a·mist** \-məst\ *n* — **po·lyg·a·my** \-mē\ *n*
pol·y·glot \'päl-i-ˌglät\ *adj* **1** : speaking or writing several languages **2** : containing or composed of several languages — **polyglot** *n*
pol·y·gon \'päl-i-ˌgän\ *n* : a closed plane figure bounded by straight lines — **po·lyg·o·nal** \pə-'lig-ən-əl\ *adj*

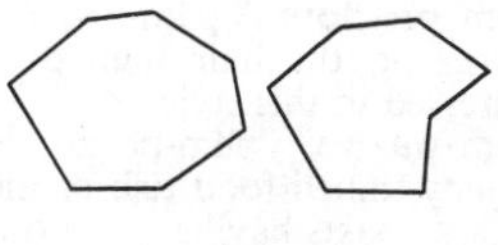
polygons

pol·y·he·dron \ˌpäl-i-'hē-drən\ *n, pl* **-drons** *or* **-dra** \-drə\ : a solid formed by plane faces — **pol·y·he·dral** \-drəl\ *adj*
pol·y·mer \'päl-ə-mər\ *n* : a chemical compound or mixture of compounds that is formed by combination of smaller molecules and consists essentially of repeating structural units — **pol·y·mer·ic** \ˌpäl-ə-'mer-ik\ *adj* — **po·lym·er·i·za·tion** \pə-ˌlim-ə-rə-'zā-shən, ˌpäl-ə-mə-rə-\ *n* — **po·lym·er·ize** \pə-'lim-ə-ˌrīz, 'päl-ə-mə-\ *vb*
Pol·y·ne·sian \ˌpäl-ə-'nē-zhən, -shən\ *n* **1** : a member of any of the native peoples of Polynesia **2** : a group of languages spoken in Polynesia — **Polynesian** *adj*
[1]**pol·y·no·mi·al** \ˌpäl-i-'nō-mē-əl\ *n* : an algebraic expression having two or more terms ⟨the *polynomial* $a^2 + 2ab - b^2$⟩
[2]**polynomial** *adj* : having the character of a polynomial ⟨7023 written as $7(10^3) + 0(10^2) + 2(10^1) + 3(10^0)$ is in *polynomial* form⟩
pol·yp \'päl-əp\ *n* : a coelenterate (as a sea anemone or coral) having a hollow cylinder-shaped body closed and attached at one end and opening at the other by a central mouth surrounded by tentacles armed with minute stinging organs
po·lyph·o·ny \pə-'lif-ə-nē\ *n* : music consisting of two or more independent but harmonious melodies — **pol·y·phon·ic** \ˌpäl-i-'fän-ik\ *adj*
poly·sac·cha·ride \ˌpäl-i-'sak-ə-ˌrīd\ *n* : a carbohydrate that can be broken down into two or more molecules of simple sugars
poly·syl·lab·ic \ˌpäl-i-sə-'lab-ik\ *adj* : having many

syllables; *esp* : having more than three syllables — **poly·syl·lab·i·cal·ly** \-'lab-i-k(ə-)lē\ *adv* — **poly·syl·la·ble** \'päl-i-ˌsil-ə-bəl, ˌpäl-i-'\ *n*
pol·y·tech·nic \ˌpäl-i-'tek-nik\ *adj* : relating to or devoted to instruction in many technical arts or applied sciences ⟨a *polytechnic* school⟩
poly·the·ism \'päl-i-(ˌ)thē-ˌiz-əm\ *n* : belief in or worship of more than one god — **poly·the·ist** \-ˌthē-əst\ *adj or n* — **poly·the·is·tic** \ˌpäl-i-thē-'is-tik\ *adj*
poly·un·sat·u·rat·ed \ˌpäl-ē-ˌən-'sach-ə-ˌrāt-əd\ *adj* : rich in unsaturated chemical bonds ⟨a *polyunsaturated* oil⟩
po·made \pō-'mād, -'mäd\ *n* : a perfumed ointment esp. for the hair or scalp — **pomade** *vb*
pome \'pōm\ *n* : a fleshy fruit (as an apple) consisting of a central core that has usu. five seeds and is surrounded by a thick fleshy outer layer derived from the receptacle
pome·gran·ate \'päm-(ə-)ˌgran-ət, 'pəm-ˌgran-\ *n* : a thick-skinned reddish tart-flavored berry about the size of an orange having many seeds in a crimson pulp; *also* : a tropical Old World tree bearing pomegranates
Pom·er·a·ni·an \ˌpäm-ə-'rā-nē-ən, -nyən\ *n* : any of a breed of very small compact long-haired dogs resembling the spitz — **Pomeranian** *adj*
1**pom·mel** \'pəm-əl, 'päm-\ *n* : the knob on the hilt of a sword or at the front of a saddle
2**pom·mel** \'pəm-əl\ *vb* **-meled** *or* **-melled**; **-mel·ing** *or* **-mel·ling** \-(ə-)liŋ\ : PUMMEL
pomp \'pämp\ *n* **1** : a show of magnificence : SPLENDOR ⟨the *pomp* of a coronation ceremony⟩ **2** : showy display ⟨a person who loves *pomp*⟩
pom·pa·dour \'päm-pə-ˌdōr, -ˌdȯr\ *n* : a style of dressing the hair high over the forehead or hair dressed in this style
pom·pa·no \'päm-pə-ˌnō, 'pəm-\ *n, pl* **-nos** : a spiny-finned food fish of the southern Atlantic and Gulf coasts having a narrow body and forked tail
pom·pon \'päm-ˌpän\ *n* **1** : an ornamental ball or tuft used on clothing, caps, and fancy costumes **2** : a chrysanthemum or dahlia with small rounded flower heads
pomp·ous \'päm-pəs\ *adj* **1** : making a show of importance or dignity ⟨a *pompous* manner⟩ **2** : SELF-IMPORTANT ⟨a *pompous* little man⟩ — **pomp·ous·ly** *adv* — **pomp·ous·ness** *n*
pon·cho \'pän-chō\ *n, pl* **ponchos** **1** : a cloak like a blanket with a slit in the middle for the head **2** : a waterproof garment like a poncho
pond \'pänd\ *n* : a body of water usu. smaller than a lake
pon·der \'pän-dər\ *vb* **pon·dered**; **pon·der·ing** \-d(ə-)riŋ\ : to consider carefully — **pon·der·er** \-dər-ər\ *n*
pon·der·o·sa pine \ˌpän-də-ˌrō-sə-, -zə-\ *n* : a tall timber pine of western No. America with long needles in bundles of 2 to 5; *also* : its strong straight-grained wood
pon·der·ous \'pän-d(ə-)rəs\ *adj* **1** : very heavy **2** : not light or lively : DULL ⟨*ponderous* words⟩ — **pon·der·ous·ly** *adv* — **pon·der·ous·ness** *n*
pond lily *n* : WATER LILY
pond scum *n* **1** : SPIROGYRA; *also* : any of various related algae **2** : a mass of tangled threads of algae in stagnant water
pond·weed \'pänd-ˌwēd\ *n* : any of several water plants with both submerged and floating leaves and spikes of greenish flowers
pone \'pōn\ *n, South & Midland* : CORN PONE
pon·gee \pän-'jē, 'pän-ˌ\ *n* **1** : a thin soft silk fabric of Chinese origin **2** : an imitation of pongee in cotton or rayon
pon·iard \'pän-yərd\ *n* : a slender dagger
pon·tiff \'pänt-əf\ *n* : BISHOP; *esp* : POPE — **pon·tif·i·cal** \pän-'tif-i-kəl\ *adj*
pon·tif·i·cals \pän-'tif-i-kəlz\ *n pl* : the attire worn by a bishop when celebrating a mass
1**pon·tif·i·cate** \pän-'tif-i-kət, -'tif-ə-ˌkāt\ *n* : the office or term of office of a pontiff
2**pon·tif·i·cate** \-'tif-ə-ˌkāt\ *vb* : to speak pompously or dogmatically
pon·toon \pän-'tün\ *n* **1** : a flat-bottomed boat **2** : a float used in building a floating bridge **3** : a float of an airplane
po·ny \'pō-nē\ *n, pl* **ponies** **1** : a horse of any of several breeds of very small stocky animals **2** : a literal translation of a foreign language text; *esp* : one used illegitimately by students in preparing or reciting lessons
Pony Express *n* : a rapid postal and express system across the western U.S. in 1860–61 operating by relays of horses
po·ny·tail \'pō-nē-ˌtāl\ *n* : hair arranged to resemble the tail of a pony
pooch \'püch\ *n, slang* : DOG
poo·dle \'püd-əl\ *n* : any of a breed of active intelligent heavy-coated solid-colored dogs

poodle

pooh \'pü, 'pu̇\ *interj* — used to express disapproval
pooh–pooh \'pü-pü, pü-'pü\ *also* **pooh** \'pü\ *vb* **1** : to express contempt or impatience **2** : DERIDE, SCORN ⟨*pooh-pooh* the idea of ghosts⟩
1**pool** \'pül\ *n* **1** : a small deep body of water **2** : a small body of standing liquid : PUDDLE
2**pool** *n* **1** : the money bet by a number of persons on an event or in a game **2** : a game played on a billiard table having 6 pockets with usu. 15 object balls **3 a** : a common fund for buying or selling esp. securities or commodities **b** : a combination between competing firms for the control of business **4 a** : a readily available supply ⟨a *pool* of talent⟩ ⟨a typing *pool*⟩ **b** : a group sharing in some activity ⟨a car *pool*⟩
3**pool** *vb* : to contribute to a common fund or effort ⟨*pooled* their resources⟩
poop \'püp\ *n* : an enclosed superstructure at the stern of a ship
1**poor** \'pu̇(ə)r, 'pō(ə)r\ *adj* **1** : lacking riches : NEEDY **2** : SCANTY, INSUFFICIENT ⟨a *poor* crop⟩ **3** : not good in quality or workmanship **4** : FEEBLE ⟨*poor* health⟩ **5** : lacking fertility ⟨*poor* land⟩ **6** : UNFAVORABLE, UNCOMFORTABLE ⟨the patient had a *poor* day⟩ **7** : lacking in signs of wealth or good taste ⟨*poor* furnishings⟩ **8** : not efficient or capable

⟨a *poor* carpenter⟩ **9** : worthy of pity or sympathy ⟨the *poor* child hurt herself⟩ — **poor·ness** *n*
[2]**poor** *n pl* : poor people ⟨charity for the *poor*⟩
poor boy *n, chiefly South* : SUBMARINE 2
poor farm *n* : a farm maintained at public expense for the support and employment of needy or dependent persons
poor·house \'pu̇(ə)r-ˌhau̇s, 'pō(ə)r-\ *n* : a place maintained at public expense to house needy or dependent persons
poor·ly \-lē\ *adj* : somewhat ill : INDISPOSED
[1]**pop** \'päp\ *vb* **popped**; **pop·ping** **1** : to burst or cause to burst with a pop ⟨the balloon *popped*⟩ ⟨*pop* corn⟩ **2** : to go, come, push, or enter quickly or unexpectedly ⟨*pop* into bed⟩ ⟨*popped* a candy into her mouth⟩ **3** : to shoot with a gun **4** : to stick out ⟨eyes *popping* with surprise⟩ **5** : to hit a pop fly
[2]**pop** *n* **1** : a sharp explosive sound **2** : a shot from a gun **3** : a flavored carbonated beverage
[3]**pop** *adv* : like or with a pop : SUDDENLY
[4]**pop** *n* : FATHER
[5]**pop** *adj* **1 a** : POPULAR ⟨*pop* music⟩ **b** : of or relating to pop music ⟨a *pop* singer⟩ **2** : of, relating to, or being a mass culture esp. of the young **3** : of, relating to, or influenced by pop art ⟨a *pop* movie⟩
[6]**pop** *n* **1** : a popular song ⟨the top *pops*⟩ **2** : art in which everyday objects (as comic strips or soup cans) are used as subject matter and are often made part of the work — called also *pop art*
pop *abbr* **1** popular **2** population
pop artist *n* : one who produces pop art
pop·corn \'päp-ˌkȯrn\ *n* : an Indian corn with kernels that burst open to form a white starchy mass when heated
pope \'pōp\ *n, often cap* : the head of the Roman Catholic Church
pop-eyed \'päp-'īd\ *adj* : having eyes that bulge
pop fly *n* : a short high fly in baseball
pop·gun \'päp-ˌgən\ *n* : a toy gun for shooting pellets or corks by compressed air
pop·in·jay \'päp-ən-ˌjā\ *n* : a vain talkative thoughtless person
pop·lar \'päp-lər\ *n* **1** : any of a genus of slender quick-growing trees (as an aspen or cottonwood) related to the willows **2** : the wood of a poplar
pop·lin \'päp-lən\ *n* : a strong ribbed fabric in plain weave
pop·over \'päp-ˌō-vər\ *n* : a quick bread made from eggs, milk, and flour which bakes into a hollow shell
pop·per \'päp-ər\ *n* : one that pops; *esp* : a utensil for popping corn
pop·py \'päp-ē\ *n, pl* **poppies** : any of a genus of herbs or shrubs that have milky juice, showy flowers, and a fruit that is a capsule and include one that is the source of opium and several that are grown as ornamentals
pop·u·lace \'päp-yə-ləs\ *n* **1** : the common people : MASSES **2** : POPULATION
pop·u·lar \'päp-yə-lər\ *adj* **1** : of, relating to, or coming from the whole body of people ⟨*popular* government⟩ ⟨*popular* opinion⟩ **2** : suitable to the average person (as in low price or ease of understanding) ⟨*popular* prices⟩ ⟨*popular* science⟩ **3** : generally current : PREVALENT ⟨*popular* opinion⟩ **4** : commonly liked or approved ⟨the most *popular* girl in the class⟩ — **pop·u·lar·i·ty** \ˌpäp-yə-'lar-ət-ē\ *n* — **pop·u·lar·ly** *adv*
pop·u·lar·ize \'päp-yə-lə-ˌrīz\ *vb* : to make popular — **pop·u·lar·i·za·tion** \ˌpäp-yə-lə-rə-'zā-shən\ *n* — **pop·u·lar·iz·er** \'päp-yə-lə-ˌrī-zər\ *n*
pop·u·late \'päp-yə-ˌlāt\ *vb* : to provide with inhabitants : PEOPLE
pop·u·la·tion \ˌpäp-yə-'lā-shən\ *n* **1** : the whole number of inhabitants in a country or region **2** : the act or process of populating **3** : a group of one or more species of organisms inhabiting a particular area or habitat
pop·u·lous \'päp-yə-ləs\ *adj* : thickly populated — **pop·u·lous·ly** *adv* — **pop·u·lous·ness** *n*
por·ce·lain \'pōr-s(ə-)lən, 'pȯr-\ *n* : a hard translucent white ceramic ware used esp. for dishes, dentures, and chemical utensils
porch \'pōrch, 'pȯrch\ *n* **1** : a covered entrance to a building usu. with a separate roof **2** : VERANDA 2
por·cu·pine \'pȯr-kyə-ˌpīn\ *n* : any of various rather large rodents with stiff sharp quills mingled with its hair

porcupine (about 3 ft. long)

porcupine fish *n* : any of various usu. inedible fish that are widespread in tropical seas and have the body covered with spines and the teeth of each jaw fused into a cutting plate
[1]**pore** \'pō(ə)r, 'pȯ(ə)r\ *vb* : to gaze, study, or think long or earnestly ⟨*pore* over a book⟩
[2]**pore** *n* : a tiny opening or space (as in the skin or the soil) — **pored** \'pōrd, 'pȯrd\ *adj*
por·gy \'pȯr-gē\ *n, pl* **porgies** *also* **porgy** : a blue-spotted crimson food fish of the coasts of Europe and America; *also* : any of various other fishes
pork \'pōrk, 'pȯrk\ *n* : the flesh of swine used for food
pork·er \'pōr-kər, 'pȯr-\ *n* : HOG; *esp* : a young pig suitable for use as fresh pork
por·nog·ra·phy \pȯr-'näg-rə-fē\ *n* : pictures or writings describing erotic behavior and intended to cause sexual excitement — **por·no·graph·ic** \ˌpȯr-nə-'graf-ik\ *adj*
po·ros·i·ty \pə-'räs-ət-ē, pōr-'äs-, pȯ-'räs-\ *n, pl* **-ties** : the quality or state of being porous
po·rous \'pōr-əs, 'pȯr-\ *adj* **1** : full of pores **2** : capable of absorbing liquids : permeable to fluids — **po·rous·ly** *adv* — **po·rous·ness** *n*
por·phy·ry \'pȯr-f(ə-)rē\ *n, pl* **-ries** : a rock consisting of feldspar crystals embedded in a compact dark red or purple groundmass — **por·phy·rit·ic** \ˌpȯr-fə-'rit-ik\ *adj*
por·poise \'pȯr-pəs\ *n* [from medieval French *porpois*, literally "pig fish", from Latin *porcus* "pig" and *piscis* "fish"] **1** : any of several small blunt-snouted toothed whales that live and travel in groups **2** : DOLPHIN 1a
por·ridge \'pȯr-ij, 'pär-\ *n* : a soft food made by boiling meal in milk or water until thick ⟨oatmeal *porridge*⟩
por·rin·ger \'pȯr-ən-jər, 'pär-\ *n* : a low metal bowl or cup with a handle
[1]**port** \'pōrt, 'pȯrt\ *n* [from Old English, from Latin *portus*] **1** : a place where ships may ride secure from storms **2** : a harbor where ships take on or discharge cargo **3** : AIRPORT
[2]**port** *n* [from Middle English, "gate", "opening in the side of a ship", from medieval French, "gate", from Latin *porta*] **1** : an opening (as in machinery) for intake or exhaust of a fluid **2** : PORTHOLE
[3]**port** *n* [probably from [1]*port*; so called because the left side of a docked ship usually faced the port town] : the left side of a ship or airplane looking forward — **port** *adj*

[4]**port** *vb* : to turn or put the helm to the left
[5]**port** *n* [from *O Porto*, Portuguese port from which wines were shipped] : a rich sweet wine
Port *abbr* **1** Portugal **2** Portuguese
por·ta·ble \'pōrt-ə-bəl, 'pȯrt-\ *adj* : capable of being carried : easily moved from place to place
[1]**por·tage** \'pōrt-ij, 'pȯrt-; pȯr-'täzh\ *n* **1** : the carrying of boats or goods overland from one body of water to another **2** : a route for such carrying
[2]**portage** *vb* : to go or carry over a portage
por·tal \'pōrt-əl, 'pȯrt-\ *n* : DOOR, GATE, ENTRANCE
port·cul·lis \pōrt-'kəl-əs, pȯrt-\ *n* : a grating at the gateway of a castle or fortress that can be lowered to prevent entrance
por·tend \pȯr-'tend, pōr-\ *vb* : to give a sign or warning of beforehand ⟨the distant thunder *portended* a storm⟩
por·tent \'pȯ(ə)r-ˌtent, 'pō(ə)r-\ *n* : a sign or warning usu. of evil : OMEN
por·ten·tous \pȯr-'tent-əs, pōr-\ *adj* **1** : being a portent : THREATENING **2** : AMAZING, MARVELOUS — **por·ten·tous·ly** *adv* — **por·ten·tous·ness** *n*
[1]**por·ter** \'pōrt-ər, 'pȯrt-\ *n*, *chiefly Brit* : DOORKEEPER
[2]**porter** *n* **1** : one who carries burdens; *esp* : a person employed to carry baggage for patrons at a hotel or terminal **2** : a parlor-car or sleeping-car attendant **3** : a dark heavy ale
por·ter·house \-ˌhau̇s\ *n* : a beefsteak with a large piece of tenderloin on a T-shaped bone
port·fo·lio \pōrt-'fō-lē-ˌō, pȯrt-\ *n*, *pl* **-lios** **1** : a case for carrying papers or drawings **2** : the office and functions of a minister of state or member of a cabinet **3** : the securities held by an investor or a financial house
port·hole \'pōrt-ˌhōl, 'pȯrt-\ *n* **1** : an opening in the side of a ship or airplane **2** : an opening (as in a wall) to shoot through
por·ti·co \'pōrt-i-ˌkō, 'pȯrt-\ *n*, *pl* **-coes** *or* **-cos** **1** : a covered walk **2** : a row of columns supporting a roof around or at the entrance of a building
[1]**por·tion** \'pōr-shən, 'pȯr-\ *n* **1 a** : an individual's share of something ⟨a *portion* of food⟩ **b** : DOWRY **2** : one's lot or fate **3** : an element, section, or division of a whole ***syn*** see PART
[2]**portion** *vb* **por·tioned**; **por·tion·ing** \-sh(ə-)ning\ : APPORTION
port·land cement \ˌpōrt-lən(d)-, ˌpȯrt-\ *n* : a cement made by burning and grinding a mixture usu. of clay and limestone
port·ly \'pōrt-lē, 'pȯrt-\ *adj* **port·li·er**; **-est** : heavy of body : STOUT — **port·li·ness** *n*
port·man·teau \pōrt-'man-tō, pȯrt-\ *n*, *pl* **-teaus** *or* **-teaux** \-tōz\ : TRAVELING BAG
por·trait \'pōr-trət, 'pȯr-, -ˌtrāt\ *n* **1** : a pictorial representation (as a painting or photograph) of a person usu. showing his face **2** : a portrayal in words
por·tray \pōr-'trā, pȯr-\ *vb* **1** : to make a portrait of : DEPICT **2 a** : to describe in words **b** : to play the role of : ENACT — **por·tray·er** *n*
por·tray·al \-'trā(-ə)l\ *n* **1** : the act or process of portraying : REPRESENTATION **2** : PORTRAIT
Por·tu·guese \ˌpōr-chə-'gēz, ˌpȯr-, -'gēs\ *n*, *pl* **Portuguese** **1 a** : a native or inhabitant of Portugal **b** : a person of Portuguese descent **2** : the Romance language of Portugal and Brazil — **Portuguese** *adj*

ə abut	ər further	a back	ā bake
ä cot, cart	au̇ out	ch chin	e less	ē easy
g gift	i trip	ī life	j joke	ng sing	ō flow
ȯ flaw	ȯi coin	th thin	t͟h this	ü loot
u̇ foot	y yet	yü few	yu̇ furious	zh vision

Portuguese man-of-war *n* : any of several large colonial coelenterates having a large crested bladder by means of which the colony floats at the surface of the sea
pos *abbr* positive
[1]**pose** \'pōz\ *vb* **1 a** : to hold or cause to hold a special posture ⟨*posed* for fashion photographers⟩ **b** : to pretend to be what one is not ⟨*pose* as a hero⟩ **2** : to put forth : PROPOSE ⟨*posed* a question⟩
[2]**pose** *n* **1** : a sustained posture; *esp* : one assumed for artistic effect **2** : an assumed attitude ⟨his cheerfulness is a *pose*⟩
[1]**po·ser** \'pō-zər\ *n* : a puzzling or baffling question
[2]**pos·er** \'pō-zər\ *n* : a person who poses
po·seur \pō-'zər\ *n* : one who pretends to be what he is not
posh \'päsh\ *adj* : ELEGANT, FASHIONABLE
[1]**po·si·tion** \pə-'zish-ən\ *n* **1 a** : the manner in which something is placed or arranged **b** : POSTURE **2** : a stand taken on a question **3** : the point or area occupied by a physical object **4 a** : social or official rank **b** : EMPLOYMENT, JOB **c** : a situation that confers advantage or preference ⟨jockeyed for *position* in the race⟩ — **po·si·tion·al** \-'zish-(ə-)nəl\ *adj*
[2]**position** *vb* **po·si·tioned**; **po·si·tion·ing** \-'zish-(ə-)ning\ : to put in proper position
[1]**pos·i·tive** \'päz-ət-iv, 'päz-tiv\ *adj* **1 a** : clearly or definitely stated ⟨*positive* orders⟩ **b** : filled with confidence : CERTAIN ⟨was *positive* he'd win⟩ **2** : of the degree of comparison expressed by the unmodified and uninflected form of an adjective or adverb **3** : definite, accurate, or certain in its action ⟨*positive* traction⟩ **4 a** : having or expressing actual existence, quality, or activity as distinguished from deprivation or deficiency ⟨*positive* change in temperature⟩ **b** : showing light and shade similar in tone to the tones of the original subject ⟨a *positive* photographic image⟩ **c** : being numerically greater than zero ⟨+2 is a *positive* integer⟩ **d** : reckoned or proceeding in a direction taken as that of increase or progress **e** : directed or moving toward a source of stimulation ⟨a *positive* tropism⟩ **5 a** : of, being, or relating to electricity of a kind that predominates in a glass rod after being rubbed with silk ⟨a *positive* charge⟩ **b** : charged with positive electricity : having a deficiency of electrons ⟨a *positive* particle⟩ **c** : being the part from which the current flows to the external circuit ⟨the *positive* pole of a storage battery⟩ **d** : electron-collecting — used of an electrode in an electron tube **6 a** : marked by or indicating agreement or affirmation ⟨a *positive* response⟩ **b** : affirming the presence of what is sought or suspected to be present ⟨*positive* test for blood⟩ — **pos·i·tive·ness** *n*
[2]**positive** *n* **1** : the positive degree or a positive form in a language **2** : a positive photograph or a print from a negative
pos·i·tive·ly \-lē, *2 is often* ˌpäz-ə-'tiv-lē\ *adv* **1** : in a positive manner : so as to be positive **2** : EXTREMELY, REALLY ⟨*positively* rude⟩
pos·i·tron \'päz-ə-ˌträn\ *n* [from *posi*tive and *-tron* (as in *electron*)] : a positively charged particle having the same mass and magnitude of charge as the electron
poss *abbr* possessive
pos·se \'päs-ē\ *n* [from medieval Latin *posse comitatus*, literally "power of the county"] **1** : a force of men called upon by a sheriff to aid him (as in pursuit of a criminal) **2** : a number of people organized to make a search (as for a lost child)
pos·sess \pə-'zes\ *vb* **1 a** : to have and hold as property : OWN **b** : to have as an attribute, knowl-

edge, or skill ⟨*possesses* a keen wit⟩ **2** : to enter into and control firmly : DOMINATE ⟨*possessed* by a demon⟩ ⟨whatever *possessed* you to do such a stupid thing⟩ — **pos·ses·sor** \-'zes-ər\ *n*

pos·ses·sion \pə-'zesh-ən\ *n* **1 a** : the act of possessing or holding as one's own : OWNERSHIP **b** : control of property without regard to ownership **2 a** : something held as one's own **b** : an area under the control of but not formally part of a nation ⟨island *possessions* of the U.S.⟩ **3** : domination by an idea or influence from outside oneself

[1]**pos·ses·sive** \pə-'zes-iv\ *adj* **1** : of, relating to, or being a grammatical case that denotes ownership or a similar relation **2** : showing the desire to possess or keep ⟨a *possessive* attitude⟩ — **pos·ses·sive·ly** *adv* — **pos·ses·sive·ness** *n*

[2]**possessive** *n* **1** : the possessive case **2** : a word in the possessive case

pos·set \'päs-ət\ *n* : a hot drink of sweetened and spiced milk curdled with ale or wine

pos·si·bil·i·ty \ˌpäs-ə-'bil-ət-ē\ *n, pl* **-ties 1** : the state or fact of being possible **2** : something possible

pos·si·ble \'päs-ə-bəl\ *adj* **1** : being something that can be done or brought about ⟨a task *possible* only to skilled workmen⟩ **2** : being something that may or may not occur ⟨plan against *possible* dangers⟩ **3** : ALLOWABLE, PERMITTED ⟨*possible* to see the patient now⟩ **4** : able or fitted to be or to become ⟨a *possible* site for a camp⟩

pos·si·bly \-blē\ *adv* **1** : by possible means : by any possibility ⟨not *possibly* true⟩ **2** : PERHAPS ⟨may *possibly* recover⟩

pos·sum \'päs-əm\ *n* : OPOSSUM

[1]**post** \'pōst\ *n* **1** : a piece of timber or metal fixed upright esp. as a support : PILLAR **2** : a pole or stake set up as a marker ⟨the starting *post*⟩ **3** : a metallic device (as on a battery) used in connecting up an electrical circuit

[2]**post** *vb* **1 a** : to fix notices to or on a suitable place (as a bulletin board) **b** : to publish or announce by or as if by a notice ⟨*posted* the students' grades⟩ **2** : to forbid persons from entering or using by putting up warning notices ⟨*post* a trout stream⟩ **3** : SCORE ⟨*posted* a 72 for the round⟩

[3]**post** *n* **1** *chiefly Brit* : POST OFFICE 1 **2** *chiefly Brit* : the mail handled by the post **3** *chiefly Brit* : a single dispatch of mail

[4]**post** *vb* **1** : to ride or travel with haste : HURRY **2** : MAIL **3** : to transfer a bookkeeping item from a book of original entry to a ledger **4** : to make familiar with a subject : INFORM

[5]**post** *n* **1 a** : the place at which a soldier is stationed; *esp* : a sentry's beat or station **b** : a station or task to which anyone is assigned **c** : a place to which troops are assigned : CAMP **d** : a local subdivision of a veterans' organization **2** : an office or position to which a person is appointed **3** : TRADING POST, SETTLEMENT

[6]**post** *vb* **1** : to station in a given place ⟨*post* a guard⟩ **2** : to put up as security ⟨*post* a bond⟩

post- *prefix* **1 a** : after : later ⟨*post*date⟩ **b** : behind : following ⟨*post*lude⟩ **2** : subsequent to : later than ⟨*post*graduate⟩

post·age \'pō-stij\ *n* : the charge fixed by law for carrying an article by mail

postage stamp *n* : a government stamp used on mail to show that postage has been paid

post·al \'pō-stəl\ *adj* : of or relating to the mails or to the post office

postal card *n* : POSTCARD; *esp* : one with a government postage stamp printed on it and sold by a post office

postal service *n* : POST OFFICE 1

post·card \'pōs(t)-ˌkärd\ *n* : a card on which a message may be written and that may be mailed without an envelope

post chaise *n* : a usu. closed 4-wheeled carriage for two to four persons

post·date \(')pōs(t)-'dāt\ *vb* **1** : to date with a date later than that of execution ⟨*postdate* a check⟩ **2** : to follow in time

post·er \'pō-stər\ *n* **1** : a notice or advertisement to be posted in a public place **2** : a person who posts such notices ⟨a bill *poster*⟩

[1]**pos·te·ri·or** \pō-'stir-ē-ər, pä-\ *adj* **1** : later in time : SUBSEQUENT **2** : situated behind or toward the back — **pos·te·ri·or·ly** *adv*

[2]**posterior** *n* : the hinder parts of the body; *esp* : BUTTOCKS

pos·ter·i·ty \pä-'ster-ət-ē\ *n* **1** : the offspring of one ancestor : DESCENDANTS **2** : all future generations : future time ⟨leave a record for *posterity*⟩

pos·tern \'pōs-tərn, 'päs-\ *n* **1** : a back door or gate **2** : a private or side entrance or way — **postern** *adj*

post exchange *n* : a store at a military post that sells to military personnel and authorized civilians

[1]**post·grad·u·ate** \(')pōst-'graj-ə-wət, -ˌwāt\ *adj* : GRADUATE 2

[2]**postgraduate** *n* : a student continuing his education after graduation

post·haste \'pōst-'hāst\ *adv* : with great speed : in great haste ⟨sent *posthaste* for the doctor⟩

post·hole \'pōst-ˌhōl\ *n* : a hole for a post and esp. a fence post

post·hu·mous \'päs-chə-məs\ *adj* **1** : born after the death of the father ⟨a *posthumous* son⟩ **2** : published after the death of the author ⟨a *posthumous* novel⟩ **3** : following or occurring after one's death ⟨*posthumous* fame⟩ ⟨a *posthumous* award⟩ — **post·hu·mous·ly** *adv*

pos·til·ion *or* **pos·til·lion** \pō-'stil-yən\ *n* : a person who rides as a guide on the left-hand horse of a pair drawing a coach

post·lude \'pōst-ˌlüd\ *n* : a closing piece of music; *esp* : an organ solo at the end of a church service

post·man \'pōs(t)-mən, -ˌman\ *n* : MAILMAN

post·mark \-ˌmärk\ *n* : a mark officially canceling the postage stamp on a piece of mail and giving the date and place of sending — **postmark** *vb*

post·mas·ter \-ˌmas-tər\ *n* : a person in charge of a post office

postmaster general *n, pl* **postmasters general** : an official in charge of a national post office department or postal service

post·me·rid·i·an \ˌpōs(t)-mə-'rid-ē-ən\ *adj* : occurring after noon

post me·ri·di·em \-'rid-ē-əm\ *adj* : POSTMERIDIAN

post·mis·tress \'pōs(t)-ˌmis-trəs\ *n* : a woman in charge of a post office

[1]**post·mor·tem** \pōs(t)-'mȯrt-əm\ *adj* : occurring after death

[2]**postmortem** *n* : an examination of a dead body esp. to determine the cause of death — called also *postmortem examination*

post·na·tal \(')pōs(t)-'nāt-əl\ *adj* : subsequent to birth; *also* : of or relating to a newborn child ⟨*postnatal* care⟩ — **post·na·tal·ly** \-ə-lē\ *adv*

post office *n* **1** : a government department handling the transmission of mail **2** : a local branch of a post office department handling the mail for a particular place

post·paid \'pōs(t)-'pād\ *adv* : with postage paid by the sender

post·pone \pōs(t)-'pōn\ *vb* : to hold back the doing

of until a later time — **post·pone·ment** \-mənt\ *n* — **post·pon·er** *n*

post road *n* : a road over which mail is carried

post·script \'pō(s)-ˌskript\ *n* : a note or series of notes added at the end of a letter, article, or book

pos·tu·lant \'päs-chə-lənt\ *n* : a person admitted to a religious house as a probationary candidate for membership

1**pos·tu·late** \'päs-chə-ˌlāt\ *vb* : to claim as true : assume as a postulate or axiom ⟨*postulates* that all men are created equal⟩ — **pos·tu·la·tion** \ˌpäs-chə-'lā-shən\ *n*

2**pos·tu·late** \'päs-chə-lət, -ˌlāt\ *n* : a statement or claim assumed to be true esp. as the basis of a process of reasoning

1**pos·ture** \'päs-chər\ *n* **1** : the position or bearing of the body or a body part ⟨erect *posture*⟩ **2** : state with reference to something else ⟨a country's defense *posture*⟩ — **pos·tur·al** \-chə-rəl\ *adj*

2**posture** *vb* : to assume a posture : POSE; *esp* : to strike a pose for effect — **pos·tur·er** *n*

post·war \'pōst-'wȯ(ə)r\ *adj* : of, relating to, or being a period after a war

po·sy \'pō-zē\ *n, pl* **posies** **1** : a brief motto **2 a** : FLOWER **b** : a bunch of flowers : BOUQUET

1**pot** \'pät\ *n* **1 a** : a rounded usu. metal or earthen container ⟨cooking *pot*⟩ ⟨watering *pot*⟩ ⟨flower *pot*⟩ **b** : the quantity held by a pot ⟨a *pot* of tea⟩ **2** : an enclosed framework for catching fish or lobsters **3 a** : a large quantity or sum **b** : the total of the bets at stake at one time **4** : RUIN, DETERIORATION ⟨business went to *pot*⟩ **5** *slang* : MARIJUANA

2**pot** *vb* **pot·ted**; **pot·ting** **1** : to preserve in a sealed pot, jar, or can **2** : to plant or grow in a pot

po·ta·ble \'pōt-ə-bəl\ *adj* : suitable for drinking — **po·ta·bil·i·ty** \ˌpōt-ə-'bil-ət-ē\ *n* — **po·ta·ble·ness** \'pōt-ə-bəl-nəs\ *n*

pot·ash \'pät-ˌash\ *n* [so called from its originally being produced by evaporating leached wood ashes in iron pots] **1 a** : potassium carbonate esp. from wood ashes **b** : POTASSIUM HYDROXIDE **2** : potassium or a potassium compound esp. as used in agriculture or industry

po·tas·si·um \pə-'tas-ē-əm\ *n* : a silver-white soft light low-melting metallic element that occurs abundantly in nature esp. combined in minerals — see ELEMENT table

potassium bromide *n* : a crystalline salt used as a sedative and in photography

potassium carbonate *n* : a white salt used in making glass and soap

potassium chloride *n* : a crystalline salt used as a fertilizer

potassium hydroxide *n* : a white solid that forms a very alkaline and caustic solution in water and is used in making soap and as a reagent

potassium iodide *n* : a crystalline salt used in photography and in medicine

potassium nitrate *n* : a crystalline salt used in making gunpowder, in preserving meat, and in medicine

potassium permanganate *n* : a dark purple salt used as an oxidizer and disinfectant

potassium sulfate *n* : a salt present in seawater and minerals that is used esp. as a fertilizer and in the manufacture of chemicals

ə abut	ər further	a back	ā bake	
ä cot, cart	au̇ out	ch chin	e less	ē easy
g gift	i trip	ī life	j joke	ng sing	ō flow
ȯ flaw	ȯi coin	th thin	t͟h this	ü loot
u̇ foot	y yet	yü few	yu̇ furious	zh vision

po·ta·to \pə-'tāt-ō\ *n, pl* **-toes** **1** : SWEET POTATO **2 a** : an erect American herb widely cultivated as a vegetable crop **b** : the edible starchy tuber of the potato

potato 2a

potato beetle *n* : a black-and-yellow striped beetle that feeds on the leaves of the potato — called also *potato bug*

potato chip *n* : a thin slice of potato fried in deep fat

pot·bel·ly \'pät-ˌbel-ē\ *n* **1** : an enlarged, swollen, or protruding abdomen **2** : a stove with a bulging body — **pot·bel·lied** \-ēd\ *adj*

po·ten·cy \'pōt-ən-sē\ *n, pl* **-cies** : the quality or state of being potent ⟨vitamins of high *potency*⟩; *esp* : power to bring about a certain result

po·tent \'pōt-ənt\ *adj* **1** : having or wielding force, authority, or influence : POWERFUL **2 a** : EFFECTIVE ⟨a *potent* vaccine⟩; *esp* : very effective **b** : rich in a constituent : STRONG ⟨*potent* tea⟩ **3** : able to copulate — **po·tent·ly** *adv*

po·ten·tate \'pōt-ən-ˌtāt\ *n* : a person who wields controlling power : SOVEREIGN

1**po·ten·tial** \pə-'ten-chəl\ *adj* : capable of becoming real : POSSIBLE ⟨aware of the *potential* dangers in a scheme⟩ — ***syn*** see LATENT ***ant*** active, actual — **po·ten·tial·ly** \-'tench-(ə-)lē\ *adv*

2**potential** *n* **1 a** : something that can develop or become actual : POSSIBILITY **b** : POTENTIALITY **2** : the condition of electrical charge at one place in relation to the charge at another place such that a current tends to flow between the two places when there is a difference between the amount of the charges

potential energy *n* : the amount of energy a thing (as a weight raised to a height or a coiled spring) has because of its position or because of the arrangement of its parts

po·ten·ti·al·i·ty \pə-ˌten-chē-'al-ət-ē\ *n, pl* **-ties** **1** : the ability to develop or to come into existence **2** : POTENTIAL 1a

pot·ful \'pät-ˌfu̇l\ *n* : the quantity held by a pot

poth·er \'pät͟h-ər\ *n* : DISTURBANCE, FUSS

pot·herb \'pät-ˌ(h)ərb\ *n* : an herb whose leaves or stems are boiled for use as greens; *also* : one (as mint) used to season food

pot·hole \-ˌhōl\ *n* : a large pit or hole (as in a road surface)

pot·hook \-ˌhu̇k\ *n* : an S-shaped hook for hanging pots over an open fire

po·tion \'pō-shən\ *n* : DRINK, DOSE; *esp* : a dose of a liquid medicine or poison

pot·luck \'pät-'lək\ *n* : a regular meal for which no special preparations have been made ⟨invited the guest to stay and take *potluck*⟩

pot marigold *n* : a common European annual garden plant widely grown esp. for ornament

pot·pie \'pät-'pī\ *n* : meat or fowl stew served with a crust or dumplings

pot·pour·ri \ˌpō-pu̇-'rē\ *n* **1** : a jar of flower petals and spices used for scent **2** : a miscellaneous collection : MEDLEY

pot roast *n* : a piece of meat (as beef) cooked by braising usu. on top of the stove

pot·shot \'pät-ˌshät\ *n* : a shot taken in a casual manner or at an easy target

pot·tage \'pät-ij\ *n* : a thick soup of vegetables or vegetables and meat

[1]**pot·ter** \'pät-ər\ *n* : one that makes pottery

[2]**potter** *vb* : PUTTER — **pot·ter·er** *n*

potter's clay *n* : clay suitable for making pottery — called also *potter's earth*

potter's field *n* : a public burial place for paupers, unknown persons, and criminals

potter's wheel *n* : a horizontal disk revolving on a spindle and carrying the clay being shaped by a potter

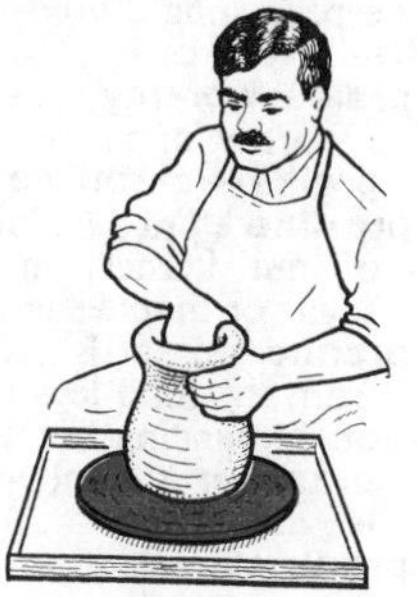

potter's wheel

pot·tery \'pät-ə-rē\ *n, pl* **-ter·ies** **1** : a place where ceramic objects are made **2** : the art of the potter : CERAMICS **3** : ware made usu. from clay that is shaped while moist and soft and hardened by heat; *esp* : coarser ware so made

[1]**pouch** \'pau̇ch\ *n* **1** : BAG, SACK; *esp* : one with a drawstring, lock, clasp, or zipper ⟨tobacco *pouch*⟩ ⟨mail *pouch*⟩ **2** : a structure in the form of a bag or sac; *esp* : one for carrying the young on the abdomen of a female marsupial (as a kangaroo or opossum) — **pouched** \'pau̇cht\ *adj*

[2]**pouch** *vb* : to put or form into or as if into a pouch

poul·tice \'pōl-təs\ *n* : a soft usu. heated and often medicated mass spread on cloth and applied to sores or other lesions — **poultice** *vb*

poul·try \'pōl-trē\ *n* : domesticated birds kept for eggs or meat

poul·try·man \-mən\ *n* : one that raises or deals in poultry

pounce \'pau̇n(t)s\ *vb* **1** : to swoop down on and seize something ⟨a cat waiting to *pounce*⟩ **2** : to make an abrupt assault or approach ⟨salesman *pounced* on me immediately⟩ — **pounce** *n*

[1]**pound** \'pau̇nd\ *n, pl* **pounds** *also* **pound** [from Old English *pund*, from Latin *pondo*, from the root of *pendere* "to weigh", literally "to hang"] **1** : a unit of weight equal to 16 ounces — see MEASURE table **2 a** : the basic monetary unit of the United Kingdom — called also *pound sterling* **b** : a basic monetary unit of another country (as Turkey, Lebanon, or Israel)

[2]**pound** *vb* **1** : to reduce to powder or pulp by beating **2 a** : to strike heavily or repeatedly ⟨*pound* the piano⟩ **b** : to produce by pounding ⟨*pound* out a tune on the piano⟩ **c** : DRIVE ⟨*pound* a nail⟩ **3** : to move heavily ⟨the horses *pounded* along the lane⟩ — **pound·er** *n*

[3]**pound** *n* : an act or sound of pounding

[4]**pound** *n* **1** : a public enclosure for stray or unlicensed animals ⟨the dog *pound*⟩ **2 a** : a trap or enclosure for animals or fish **b** : an establishment selling live lobsters

pour \'pō(ə)r, 'pȯ(ə)r\ *vb* **1** : to flow or to cause to flow in a stream ⟨*pour* the tea⟩ ⟨tears *pouring* down her cheeks⟩ **2** : to let loose something without restraint : express freely **3** : to rain very hard — **pour·er** *n*

[1]**pout** \'pau̇t\ *vb* **1** : to show displeasure by thrusting out the lips **2** : SULK

[2]**pout** *n* **1** : an act of pouting **2** *pl* : a fit of bad humor

pov·er·ty \'päv-ərt-ē\ *n* **1** : the state of being poor : lack of money or material possessions : WANT **2** : SCARCITY, LACK **3** : lack of fertility ⟨*poverty* of the soil⟩

pov·er·ty–strick·en \-,strik-ən\ *adj* : very poor : DESTITUTE

[1]**pow·der** \'pau̇d-ər\ *n* **1 a** : dry material made up of fine particles **b** : a medicinal or cosmetic preparation in this form **2** : a solid explosive used in gunnery or blasting

[2]**powder** *vb* **1** : to sprinkle or cover with or as if with powder **2** : to reduce to or become powder — **pow·der·er** \-ər-ər\ *n*

powder blue *n* : a pale blue

powder horn *n* : a flask for carrying gunpowder; *esp* : one made of the horn of an ox or cow

pow·dery \'pau̇d-ə-rē\ *adj* **1 a** : resembling or consisting of powder **b** : easily reduced to powder : CRUMBLY **2** : covered with or as if with powder : DUSTY

powdery mildew *n* : a parasitic fungus producing abundant powdery spores on the host; *also* : a plant disease caused by such a fungus

[1]**pow·er** \'pau̇(-ə)r\ *n* **1 a** : CONTROL, AUTHORITY ⟨in the *power* of his enemies⟩ **b** : one having such power; *esp* : a sovereign state **2** : ability to act or do ⟨lose the *power* of speech⟩ **3 a** : physical might **b** : mental strength **4** : the number of times as indicated by an exponent a number occurs as a factor in a product; *also* : the product obtained by raising a number to a power ⟨10^3, or 10·10·10, is the 3d power of 10⟩ **5 a** : force or energy that is or can be applied to work ⟨electric *power*⟩ **b** : the time rate at which work is done or energy emitted or transferred **6** : MAGNIFICATION 2

syn POWER, ENERGY, STRENGTH can mean the ability to exert effort or force. POWER, a general term, applies broadly to ability to act, whether latent or actually exerted; ENERGY applies to stored-up power that can be expended in work; STRENGTH implies the presence of power residing in someone or something as the result of health, good materials, or sound construction

[2]**power** *adj* : relating to, supplying, using, or run by power ⟨a *power* drill⟩ ⟨*power* failure⟩

[3]**power** *vb* : to supply with power

pow·er·boat \'pau̇(-ə)r-'bōt\ *n* : MOTORBOAT

power dive *n* : a dive of an airplane accelerated by the power of the engine — **power–dive** *vb*

pow·er·ful \'pau̇(-ə)r-fəl\ *adj* : full of or having power or influence : STRONG, EFFECTIVE — **pow·er·ful·ly** \-f(ə-)lē\ *adv*

pow·er·house \'pau̇(-ə)r-,hau̇s\ *n* **1** : a building in which electric power is generated **2** : a source of power, energy, or influence **3** : a person or thing having unusual strength or energy

pow·er·less \'pau̇(-ə)r-ləs\ *adj* **1** : lacking power, force, or energy **2** : lacking authority to act — **pow·er·less·ly** *adv* — **pow·er·less·ness** *n*

power plant *n* : POWERHOUSE 1

pow·wow \'pau̇-,wau̇\ *n* **1** : a No. American Indian medicine man **2 a** : a No. American Indian ceremony (as for victory in war) **b** : a conference with an Indian leader or group **3 a** : a noisy gathering **b** : a meeting for discussion — **powwow** *vb*

pox \'päks\ *n* : a disease (as smallpox, chicken pox, or syphilis) that causes eruptions on the skin

pp *abbr* **1** pages **2** pianissimo

PP *abbr* past participle

ppd *abbr* **1** postpaid **2** prepaid

PPS *abbr* [for Latin *post postscriptum*, literally "after postscript"] additional postscript

PQ *abbr* Province of Quebec

pr *abbr* **1** pair **2** price

PR *abbr* Puerto Rico

prac·ti·ca·ble \'prak-ti-kə-bəl\ *adj* **1** : capable of being done, put into practice, or accomplished : FEASIBLE ⟨an interesting but not *practicable* idea⟩ **2** : USABLE ⟨a *practicable* weapon⟩ — **prac·ti·ca·bil·i·ty** \ˌprak-ti-kə-ˈbil-ət-ē\ *n* — **prac·ti·ca·bly** \ˈprak-ti-kə-blē\ *adv*

prac·ti·cal \ˈprak-ti-kəl\ *adj* **1** : of, relating to, or manifested in practice or action ⟨for *practical* purposes⟩ **2** : being such in practice or effect : VIRTUAL ⟨a *practical* failure⟩ **3** : capable of being put to use or account : USEFUL **4** : inclined to action rather than planning or thinking ⟨a *practical* mind⟩ — **prac·ti·cal·i·ty** \ˌprak-ti-ˈkal-ət-ē\ *n*

practical joke *n* : a joke turning on something done rather than said; *esp* : a trick played on a person — **practical joker** *n*

prac·ti·cal·ly \ˈprak-ti-k(ə-)lē\ *adv* **1** : REALLY, ACTUALLY ⟨a clever but *practically* worthless scheme⟩ **2** : by experience or experiment **3** : to all practical purposes though not absolutely ⟨a *practically* inert gas⟩ **4** : NEARLY, ALMOST ⟨*practically* friendless⟩

practical nurse *n* : a professional nurse who does not have the qualifications of a registered nurse; *esp* : one trained and licensed to provide routine care for the sick

1**prac·tice** *or* **prac·tise** \ˈprak-təs\ *vb* **1** : to perform or work at repeatedly so as to become skilled ⟨*practice* his act⟩ **2** : to carry out : APPLY ⟨*practices* what he preaches⟩ **3** : to do or perform often, customarily, or habitually ⟨*practice* politeness⟩ **4** : to be professionally engaged in ⟨*practice* medicine⟩ — **prac·tic·er** *n*

2**practice** *also* **practise** *n* **1 a** : actual performance or application **b** : a repeated or customary action ⟨it was his *practice* to rise early⟩ **c** : the usual way of doing something ⟨local *practice*⟩ **2 a** : systematic exercise for gaining skill ⟨*practice* makes perfect⟩ **b** : skill acquired by practice ⟨get in *practice*⟩ **3 a** : the exercise of a profession ⟨the *practice* of law⟩ **b** : a professional business ⟨the doctor sold his *practice*⟩

prac·ticed *or* **prac·tised** \ˈprak-təst\ *adj* **1** : EXPERIENCED, SKILLED **2** : learned by practice

prac·ti·tio·ner \prak-ˈtish-(ə-)nər\ *n* : a person who practices a profession and esp. law or medicine

prae·tor \ˈprēt-ər\ *n* : an ancient Roman magistrate ranking below a consul and having chiefly judicial functions

1**prae·to·ri·an** \prē-ˈtōr-ē-ən, -ˈtȯr-\ *adj* **1** : of or relating to a Roman praetor **2** *often cap* : of, relating to, or being the bodyguard of a Roman emperor ⟨the *praetorian* guard⟩

2**praetorian** *n*, *often cap* : a member of the praetorian guard

prag·mat·ic \prag-ˈmat-ik\ *also* **prag·mat·i·cal** \-i-kəl\ *adj* : concerned with practical rather than intellectual or artistic matters — **prag·mat·i·cal·ly** \-i-k(ə-)lē\ *adv*

prag·ma·tism \ˈprag-mə-ˌtiz-əm\ *n* **1** : a practical approach to problems and affairs **2** : a doctrine that truth is to be tested by the practical consequences of belief — **prag·ma·tist** \-mət-əst\ *adj or n*

prai·rie \ˈpre(ə)r-ē\ *n* : a large area of level or rolling grassland

prairie chicken *n* : a grouse of the Mississippi valley with a patch of bare inflatable skin on the neck

ə abut ər further a back ā bake
ä cot, cart aủ out ch chin e less ē easy
g gift i trip ī life j joke ng sing ō flow
ȯ flaw ȯi coin th thin t͟h this ü loot
ủ foot y yet yü few yủ furious zh vision

prairie dog *n* : a buff or grayish American burrowing rodent related to the marmots and living in colonies

prairie dog (about 15 in. long)

prairie schooner *n* : a covered wagon used by pioneers in cross-country travel

prairie wolf *n* : COYOTE

praise \ˈprāz\ *vb* **1** : to express approval : COMMEND **2** : to glorify esp. in song : WORSHIP — **praise** *n* — **prais·er** *n*

praise·wor·thy \-ˌwər-t͟hē\ *adj* : worthy of praise : LAUDABLE — **praise·wor·thi·ness** *n*

pra·line \ˈprä-ˌlēn, ˈprā-\ *n* : a candy of nut kernels in boiled brown sugar or maple sugar

prance \ˈpran(t)s\ *vb* **1** : to spring from the hind legs or move by so doing **2** : to ride on a prancing horse **3** : SWAGGER — **prance** *n* — **pranc·er** \ˈpran(t)-sər\ *n* — **pranc·ing·ly** \-sing-lē\ *adv*

prank \ˈprangk\ *n* : a playful or mischievous act : TRICK ⟨Halloween *pranks*⟩ — **prank·ish** \ˈprang-kish\ *adj* — **prank·ish·ness** *n*

prank·ster \ˈprang(k)-stər\ *n* : a player of pranks

pra·se·o·dym·i·um \ˌprā-zē-ō-ˈdim-ē-əm\ *n* : a yellowish white metallic element used chiefly in the form of its salts in coloring glass greenish yellow — see ELEMENT table

prate \ˈprāt\ *vb* : to talk long and idly : CHATTER — **prate** *n* — **prat·er** *n* — **prat·ing·ly** \ˈprāt-ing-lē\ *adv*

prat·fall \ˈprat-ˌfȯl\ *n* : a fall on the buttocks

pra·tique \pra-ˈtēk\ *n* : clearance given an incoming ship by the health authority of a port

prat·tle \ˈprat-əl\ *vb* **prat·tled**; **prat·tling** \-(ə-)ling\ : PRATE, BABBLE — **prattle** *n* — **prat·tler** \-(ə-)lər\ *n*

prawn \ˈprȯn, ˈprän\ *n* : any of numerous widely distributed edible crustaceans resembling shrimps and having large compressed abdomens; *also* : SHRIMP

pray \ˈprā\ *vb* **1** : ENTREAT, IMPLORE ⟨*prayed* the king for land⟩ — often used to introduce a request ⟨*pray* tell me the time⟩ **2** : to address God with adoration, confession, pleading, or thanksgiving

prayer \ˈpra(ə)r, ˈpre(ə)r\ *n* **1** : the act or practice of praying to God ⟨a moment of silent *prayer*⟩ **2 a** : a supplication or expression addressed to God ⟨a *prayer* of thanksgiving⟩ **b** : an earnest request or wish : PLEA **3** : a religious service consisting chiefly of prayers ⟨had regular family *prayers*⟩ **4** : words used in praying ⟨a book of *prayers*⟩

prayer·ful \-fəl\ *adj* **1** : given to or marked by prayer : DEVOUT **2** : EARNEST — **prayer·ful·ly** \-fə-lē\ *adv* — **prayer·ful·ness** *n*

praying mantis *n* : MANTIS

pre- *prefix* **1 a** : earlier than : before ⟨*pre*historic⟩ **b** : preparatory or prerequisite to ⟨*pre*medical⟩ **2** : in advance : beforehand ⟨*pre*pay⟩ **3** : in front of : anterior to ⟨*pre*molar⟩

preach \ˈprēch\ *vb* **1 a** : to deliver a sermon : utter publicly **b** : to set forth in a sermon ⟨*preach* the gospel⟩ **2** : to urge publicly : ADVOCATE ⟨*preach* patience⟩

preach·er \ˈprē-chər\ *n* : one that preaches; *esp* : MINISTER

pre·am·ble \ˈprē-ˌam-bəl\ *n* **1** : an introductory statement; *esp* : the introductory part of a constitution or statute that usu. states the reasons for and intent of the law **2** : an introductory fact or circumstance : PRELIMINARY

P

pre·ar·range \ˌprē-ə-ˈrānj\ *vb* : to arrange beforehand — **pre·ar·range·ment** \-mənt\ *n*

Pre·cam·bri·an \(ˈ)prē-ˈkam-brē-ən\ *n* : the earliest era of geological history; *also* : the corresponding system of rocks — **Precambrian** *adj*

pre·car·i·ous \pri-ˈkar-ē-əs, -ˈker-\ *adj* **1** : dependent on unknown conditions or chance circumstances **2** : dangerously lacking in security or stability ⟨*precarious* health⟩ — **pre·car·i·ous·ly** *adv* — **pre·car·i·ous·ness** *n*

pre·cau·tion \pri-ˈkȯ-shən\ *n* **1** : care taken in advance : FORESIGHT **2** : a measure taken beforehand to prevent harm or secure good ⟨take *precautions* against fire⟩ — **pre·cau·tion·ary** \-shə-ˌner-ē\ *adj*

pre·cede \pri-ˈsēd\ *vb* : to be, go, or come before (as in rank, position, or time)

prec·e·dence \ˈpres-əd-ən(t)s, pri-ˈsēd-\ *or* **prec·e·den·cy** \-ən-sē\ *n* **1** : the act or fact of preceding **2** : PRIORITY, PREFERENCE

[1]**pre·ce·dent** \pri-ˈsēd-ənt, ˈpres-əd-\ *adj* : prior in time, order, arrangement, or significance

[2]**prec·e·dent** \ˈpres-əd-ənt\ *n* **1** : an earlier occurrence of something similar **2** : something that may serve as an example or rule to be followed in the future

pre·ced·ing \pri-ˈsēd-ing\ *adj* : going before : PREVIOUS

pre·cept \ˈprē-ˌsept\ *n* : a command or principle intended as a general rule of action

pre·cep·tor \pri-ˈsep-tər, ˈprē-ˌ\ *n* **1** : TEACHER, TUTOR **2** : the principal of a school

pre·ces·sion \prē-ˈsesh-ən\ *n* : a comparatively slow circling of the rotation axis of a spinning body about another line intersecting it — **pre·cess** \-ˈses\ *vb*

pre·cinct \ˈprē-ˌsing(k)t\ *n* **1** : an administrative district esp. of a town or city ⟨a police *precinct*⟩ ⟨an electoral *precinct*⟩ **2** : a surrounding or enclosed area ⟨within the *precincts* of the college⟩

pre·cious \ˈpresh-əs\ *adj* **1** : of great value or high price ⟨diamonds and other *precious* stones⟩ **2** : highly esteemed or cherished ⟨*precious* memories⟩ **3** : too refined : AFFECTED ⟨*precious* language⟩ — **pre·cious·ly** *adv* — **pre·cious·ness** *n*

prec·i·pice \ˈpres-ə-pəs\ *n* : a very steep or overhanging place (as the face of a cliff)

[1]**pre·cip·i·tate** \pri-ˈsip-ə-ˌtāt\ *vb* **1 a** : to throw violently : HURL **b** : to fall headlong **2 a** : to move or urge on with haste or violence **b** : to bring on abruptly **3 a** : to separate or cause to separate from solution or suspension **b** : to cause vapor to condense and fall or deposit or to condense from a vapor and fall as rain or snow — **pre·cip·i·ta·tor** \-ˌtāt-ər\ *n*

[2]**pre·cip·i·tate** \pri-ˈsip-ət-ət, -ə-ˌtāt\ *n* : a usu. solid substance separated from a solution or suspension by chemical or physical change

[3]**pre·cip·i·tate** \pri-ˈsip-ət-ət\ *adj* : HASTY, RASH ⟨a *precipitate* attack⟩ — **pre·cip·i·tate·ly** *adv* — **pre·cip·i·tate·ness** *n*

pre·cip·i·ta·tion \pri-ˌsip-ə-ˈtā-shən\ *n* **1** : HASTE, RASHNESS **2** : the process of precipitating or of forming a precipitate **3** : a deposit on the earth of hail, mist, rain, sleet, or snow

pre·cip·i·tous \pri-ˈsip-ət-əs\ *adj* **1 a** : steep like a precipice **b** : having precipices ⟨a *precipitous* trail⟩ **2** : falling very quickly : very rapid **3** : SUDDEN, RASH ⟨a *precipitous* act⟩ — **pre·cip·i·tous·ly** *adv* — **pre·cip·i·tous·ness** *n*

pré·cis \prā-ˈsē, ˈprā-(ˌ)sē\ *n, pl* **pré·cis** \-ˈsēz, -(ˌ)sēz\ : a concise summary of essential points

pre·cise \pri-ˈsīs\ *adj* **1** : exactly or sharply defined or stated **2** : very exact : ACCURATE ⟨*precise* scales⟩ ⟨his *precise* time of arrival⟩ **3** : clear and sharp in enunciation : DISTINCT ⟨*precise* speech⟩ **4** : strictly conforming to rules or customs ⟨*precise* daily habits⟩ *syn* see CORRECT *ant* loose — **pre·cise·ly** *adv* — **pre·cise·ness** *n*

[1]**pre·ci·sion** \pri-ˈsizh-ən\ *n* : the quality or state of being precise : EXACTNESS, ACCURACY

[2]**precision** *adj* **1** : adapted for extremely accurate measurement or operation ⟨a *precision* gauge⟩ **2** : marked by precision ⟨*precision* drilling⟩

pre·clude \pri-ˈklüd\ *vb* : to make impossible or ineffectual : PREVENT ⟨his actions *precluded* him from winning⟩ ⟨*preclude* escape⟩

pre·co·cious \pri-ˈkō-shəs\ *adj* [from Latin *praecoc-*, stem of *praecox*, meaning literally "ripening early", from *prae-* "pre-" and *coquere* "to cook", "ripen"] : exhibiting mature qualities or abilities at an unusually early age ⟨a *precocious* child⟩ — **pre·co·cious·ly** *adv* — **pre·co·cious·ness** *n* — **pre·coc·i·ty** \-ˈkäs-ət-ē\ *n*

pre·con·ceive \ˌprē-kən-ˈsēv\ *vb* : to form an opinion of beforehand ⟨*preconceived* notions about foreign lands⟩ — **pre·con·cep·tion** \-ˈsep-shən\ *n*

pre·con·cert·ed \ˌprē-kən-ˈsərt-əd\ *adj* : arranged or agreed upon in advance

pre·cook \(ˈ)prē-ˈku̇k\ *vb* : to cook partially or entirely before final cooking or reheating

pre·cur·sor \pri-ˈkər-sər, ˈprē-ˌ\ *n* : FORERUNNER, PREDECESSOR

pre·da·cious *or* **pre·da·ceous** \pri-ˈdā-shəs\ *adj* : PREDATORY

pre·date \(ˈ)prē-ˈdāt\ *vb* : ANTEDATE

pre·da·tion \pri-ˈdā-shən\ *n* : a mode of life in which food is primarily obtained by killing and consuming animals

pred·a·tor \ˈpred-ət-ər\ *n* : a predatory organism; *esp* : a predatory animal or bird

pred·a·to·ry \ˈpred-ə-ˌtōr-ē, -ˌtȯr-\ *adj* **1** : of, relating to, or marked by plundering ⟨*predatory* raids⟩ **2** : living by predation ⟨*predatory* animals⟩

pred·e·ces·sor \ˈpred-ə-ˌses-ər, ˈprēd-\ *n* : one that precedes; *esp* : a person who has held a position or office before another

pre·des·ti·na·tion \(ˌ)prē-ˌdes-tə-ˈnā-shən\ *n* **1 a** : the act of predestining **b** : the state of being predestined **2** : the doctrine that God has predestined some persons to eternal happiness and others to eternal punishment

pre·des·tine \(ˈ)prē-ˈdes-tən\ *vb* : to destine, decree, determine, appoint, or settle beforehand esp. by divine decree

pre·de·ter·mine \ˌprēd-i-ˈtər-mən\ *vb* **1** : PREDESTINE **2** : to determine or settle beforehand ⟨meet at a *predetermined* place⟩ — **pre·de·ter·mi·na·tion** \-ˌtər-mə-ˈnā-shən\ *n*

pre·dic·a·ment \pri-ˈdik-ə-mənt\ *n* : a difficult, perplexing, or trying situation : FIX

[1]**pred·i·cate** \ˈpred-i-kət\ *n* : the part of a sentence or clause that expresses what is said about the subject and that usu. consists of a verb with or without objects, complements, or adverbial modifiers — **pred·i·ca·tive** \ˈpred-i-kət-iv, ˈpred-ə-ˌkāt-\ *adj* — **pred·i·ca·tive·ly** *adv*

[2]**predicate** *adj* : belonging to the predicate; *esp* : completing the meaning of a linking verb ⟨*hot* in "the sun is hot" is a *predicate* adjective⟩ — compare ATTRIBUTIVE

[3]**pred·i·cate** \ˈpred-ə-ˌkāt\ *vb* **1** : AFFIRM, DECLARE **2** : to assert to be a quality ⟨*predicate* sweetness of sugar⟩ **3** : BASE, FOUND ⟨a proposal *predicated* on belief in equality⟩ — **pred·i·ca·tion** \ˌpred-ə-ˈkā-shən\ *n*

pre·dict \pri-ˈdikt\ *vb* : to declare in advance : foretell on the basis of observation, experience, or reasoning ***syn*** see FORETELL — **pre·dict·a·ble** \-ˈdik-tə-bəl\ *adj* — **pre·dict·a·bly** \-blē\ *adv*

pre·dic·tion \pri-ˈdik-shən\ *n* **1** : an act of predicting **2** : something predicted : FORECAST — **pre·dic·tive** \-ˈdik-tiv\ *adj*

pre·di·gest \ˌprēd-ī-ˈjest, ˌprēd-ə-\ *vb* : to subject to predigestion ⟨*predigest* food for babies and invalids⟩

pre·di·ges·tion \-ˈjes-chən\ *n* : artificial partial digestion of food esp. by chemical means for use in illness or impaired digestion

pred·i·lec·tion \ˌpred-ə-ˈlek-shən, ˌprēd-\ *n* : INCLINATION, PREFERENCE

pre·dis·pose \ˌprēd-is-ˈpōz\ *vb* : to dispose in advance : make susceptible : INCLINE — **pre·dis·po·si·tion** \ˌprē-ˌdis-pə-ˈzish-ən\ *n*

pre·dom·i·nant \pri-ˈdäm-ə-nənt\ *adj* : having superior strength, influence, or authority : PREVAILING ⟨the *predominant* color in a painting⟩ — **pre·dom·i·nance** \-nən(t)s\ *n* — **pre·dom·i·nant·ly** *adv*

pre·dom·i·nate \pri-ˈdäm-ə-ˌnāt\ *vb* **1** : to be predominant : PREVAIL **2** : to exceed others in number ⟨cottages *predominated*⟩ — **pre·dom·i·na·tion** \-ˌdäm-ə-ˈnā-shən\ *n*

pre·em·i·nent \prē-ˈem-ə-nənt\ *adj* : having supreme rank, dignity, or importance : OUTSTANDING — **pre·em·i·nence** \-nən(t)s\ *n* — **pre·em·i·nent·ly** *adv*

pre·empt \prē-ˈem(p)t\ *vb* **1 a** : to settle upon (as public land) with the right to purchase before others **b** : to take by such a right **2** : to take before someone else can : APPROPRIATE ⟨*preempt* a seat at the stadium⟩ — **pre·emp·tion** \-ˈem(p)-shən\ *n* — **pre·emp·tive** \-ˈem(p)-tiv\ *adj* — **pre·emp·tor** \-tər\ *n*

preen \ˈprēn\ *vb* **1** : to trim or dress with the bill **2** : to dress or smooth oneself up : PRIMP — **preen·er** *n*

pre·ex·ist \ˌprē-ig-ˈzist\ *vb* : to exist before something else

pre·ex·ist·ence \-ˈzis-tən(t)s\ *n* : existence in a former state or previous to something else; *esp* : existence of the soul before its union with the body — **pre·ex·ist·ent** \-tənt\ *adj*

pref *abbr* preface

pre·fab \(ˈ)prē-ˈfab, ˈprē-ˌ\ *n* : a prefabricated structure

pre·fab·ri·cate \(ˈ)prē-ˈfab-ri-ˌkāt\ *vb* : to fabricate the parts of something at a factory so that it can be built merely by putting together the parts — **pre·fab·ri·ca·tion** \ˌprē-ˌfab-ri-ˈkā-shən\ *n*

1**pref·ace** \ˈpref-əs\ *n* : the introductory remarks of a speaker or author : PROLOGUE

2**preface** *vb* **1** : to make introductory remarks : say or write as a preface ⟨a note *prefaced* to the manuscript⟩ **2** : to introduce by or begin with a preface

pre·fect \ˈprē-ˌfekt\ *n* **1** : a high official or magistrate (as of ancient Rome or France) **2** : a student monitor in some schools

pre·fec·ture \ˈprē-ˌfek-chər\ *n* **1** : the office or term of office of a prefect **2** : the district governed by a prefect — **pre·fec·tur·al** \prē-ˈfek-chə-rəl\ *adj*

pre·fer \pri-ˈfər\ *vb* **pre·ferred**; **pre·fer·ring** **1** : to choose or esteem above another ⟨*prefer* dark clothes⟩ **2** : to present for action or consideration ⟨*prefer* charges against a thief⟩

pref·er·a·ble \ˈpref-(ə-)rə-bəl, ˈpref-ər-bəl\ *adj* : worthy to be preferred : more desirable — **pref·er·a·bil·i·ty** \ˌpref-(ə-)rə-ˈbil-ət-ē\ *n* — **pref·er·a·ble·ness** \ˈpref-(ə-)rə-bəl-nəs, -ər-bəl-nəs\ *n* — **pref·er·a·bly** \-blē\ *adv*

pref·er·ence \ˈpref-ərn(t)s, ˈpref-(ə-)rən(t)s\ *n* **1 a** : the act of preferring **b** : the state of being preferred **2** : the power or opportunity of choosing ⟨gave him his *preference*⟩ **3** : one that is preferred : FAVORITE **4** : the act of giving advantages to some over others ⟨show *preference*⟩

pref·er·en·tial \ˌpref-ə-ˈren-chəl\ *adj* **1** : of or relating to preference **2** : showing preference ⟨*preferential* treatment⟩ **3** : creating or employing preference ⟨a *preferential* tariff⟩ **4** : permitting the showing of order of preference (as of candidates in an election) ⟨a *preferential* ballot⟩ — **pref·er·en·tial·ly** \-ˈrench-(ə-)lē\ *adv*

pre·fer·ment \pri-ˈfər-mənt\ *n* **1** : advancement or promotion in dignity, office, or station **2** : a position or office of honor or profit

pre·fig·ure \(ˈ)prē-ˈfig-yər, *esp Brit* -ˈfig-ər\ *vb* **1** : to show, suggest, or announce by an antecedent type, image, or likeness ⟨other religions *prefigured* the Christian Easter⟩ **2** : FORESEE — **pre·fig·u·ra·tion** \(ˌ)prē-ˌfig-(y)ə-ˈrā-shən\ *n* — **pre·fig·ure·ment** \(ˈ)prē-ˈfig-yər-mənt, *esp Brit* -ˈfig-ər-\ *n*

1**pre·fix** \ˈprē-ˌfiks, prē-ˈ\ *vb* : to place in front as a prefix ⟨*prefix* a syllable to a word⟩

2**pre·fix** \ˈprē-ˌfiks\ *n* : a sound or sequence of sounds or in writing a letter or sequence of letters attached to the beginning of a word to produce a derivative word

preg·nan·cy \ˈpreg-nən-sē\ *n, pl* **-cies** : the state of being pregnant : GESTATION

preg·nant \ˈpreg-nənt\ *adj* **1** : containing unborn young within the uterus **2** : full of ideas : INVENTIVE ⟨a *pregnant* mind⟩ — **preg·nant·ly** *adv*

pre·heat \(ˈ)prē-ˈhēt\ *vb* : to heat beforehand ⟨*preheat* the oven to 400 degrees⟩

pre·hen·sile \prē-ˈhen(t)-səl\ *adj* : adapted for grasping esp. by wrapping around ⟨a *prehensile* tail⟩

pre·his·tor·ic \ˌprē-(h)is-ˈtȯr-ik, -ˈtär-\ *adj* : of, relating to, or existing in times before written history ⟨*prehistoric* man⟩ — **pre·his·tor·i·cal** \-i-kəl\ *adj* — **pre·his·tor·i·cal·ly** \-i-k(ə-)lē\ *adv*

pre·his·to·ry \(ˈ)prē-ˈhis-t(ə-)rē\ *n* : the study of prehistoric man — **pre·his·to·ri·an** \ˌprē-(h)is-ˈtōr-ē-ən, -ˈtȯr-\ *n*

pre·judge \(ˈ)prē-ˈjəj\ *vb* : to judge before full and sufficient examination — **pre·judg·ment** \-ˈjəj-mənt\ *n*

1**prej·u·dice** \ˈprej-əd-əs\ *n* **1** : injury or damage due to a judgment or action of another **2 a** : preconceived judgment or opinion **b** : a favoring or dislike of something without just grounds or before sufficient knowledge **c** : an irrational attitude of hostility directed against an individual, a group, or a race

2**prejudice** *vb* **1** : to injure or damage by a judgment or action **2** : to cause to have prejudice : BIAS ⟨the incident *prejudiced* them against her⟩

prej·u·di·cial \ˌprej-ə-ˈdish-əl\ *adj* : tending to injure or impair : DETRIMENTAL

prel·a·cy \ˈprel-ə-sē\ *n, pl* **-cies** **1** : the office or dignity of a prelate **2** : the whole body of prelates **3** : episcopal church government

prel·ate \ˈprel-ət\ *n* : a high-ranking clergyman (as a bishop)

1**pre·lim·i·nary** \pri-ˈlim-ə-ˌner-ē\ *n, pl* **-nar·ies** : something preliminary; *esp* : a minor boxing or wrestling match preceding the main event

2**preliminary** *adj* : preceding the main part or item : INTRODUCTORY — **pre·lim·i·nar·i·ly** \-ˌlim-ə-ˈner-ə-lē\ *adv*

pre·lit·er·ate \(ˈ)prē-ˈlit-ə-rət, -ˈli-trət\ *adj* **1** : existing before the use of writing **2** : not yet having attained a level of cultural development characterized by use of a written language

1**prel·ude** \ˈprel-ˌyüd, ˈprā-ˌlüd\ *n* **1** : an introductory performance, action, or event : INTRODUCTION ⟨the wind was a *prelude* to the storm⟩ **2 a** : a musical section or movement introducing the theme or serving as an introduction to an opera or oratorio **b** : a short musical piece (as an organ solo) played at the beginning of a church service

2**prelude** *vb* : to give, play, or serve as a prelude

pre·ma·ture \ˌprē-mə-ˈt(y)u̇(ə)r, -ˈchu̇(ə)r\ *adj* : happening, coming, existing, or done before the proper or usual time; *esp* : born after a gestation period of less than 37 weeks ⟨*premature* babies⟩ — **pre·ma·ture·ly** *adv*

pre·med·i·cal \(ˈ)prē-ˈmed-i-kəl\ *adj* : preceding and preparing for the professional study of medicine

pre·med·i·tate \pri-ˈmed-ə-ˌtāt, ˈprē-\ *vb* : to think about and plan beforehand ⟨*premeditated* murder⟩ — **pre·med·i·ta·tion** \pri-ˌmed-ə-ˈtā-shən, ˌprē-\ *n*

1**pre·mier** \pri-ˈm(y)i(ə)r; ˈprē-mē-ər, ˈprem-ē-\ *adj* [from French, from Latin *primarius* (the direct source of English *primary*), from *primus* "first"] **1** : first in position, rank, or importance : PRINCIPAL **2** : first in time : EARLIEST

2**premier** *n* : the chief minister of government : PRIME MINISTER — **pre·mier·ship** \-ˌship\ *n*

1**pre·miere** \pri-ˈmye(ə)r, -ˈmi(ə)r\ *n* : a first performance or exhibition ⟨*premiere* of a play⟩

2**premiere** *adj* : OUTSTANDING, CHIEF ⟨the nation's *premiere* author⟩

1**prem·ise** \ˈprem-əs\ *n* **1** : a proposition assumed as a basis of argument or inference **2** *pl* **a** : a tract of land with the buildings thereon **b** : a building or part of a building usu. with its grounds

2**premise** *vb* **1** : to set forth beforehand as introductory : POSTULATE **2** : to offer as a premise

1**pre·mi·um** \ˈprē-mē-əm\ *n* **1 a** : a reward for an act **b** : a sum over and above a regular price or a face or par value **c** : something given free or at a reduced price with the purchase of a product or service **2** : the amount paid for a contract of insurance **3** : a high or extra value ⟨put a *premium* on accuracy⟩ — **at a premium** : usually valuable esp. because of demand ⟨housing was *at a premium*⟩

2**premium** *adj* : of high quality, value, or price

1**pre·mo·lar** \(ˈ)prē-ˈmō-lər\ *adj* : situated in front of or preceding the molar teeth; *also* : being or relating to the premolars

2**premolar** *n* : any of the double-pointed grinding teeth which occur between the canines and the true molars and of which in man there are two on each side of each jaw — called also *biscuspid*

pre·mo·ni·tion \ˌprē-mə-ˈnish-ən, ˌprem-ə-\ *n* **1** : a previous warning or notice : FOREWARNING **2** : PRESENTIMENT — **pre·mon·i·to·ry** \pri-ˈmän-ə-ˌtōr-ē, -ˌtȯr-\ *adj*

pre·na·tal \(ˈ)prē-ˈnāt-əl\ *adj* : occurring or existing before birth ⟨*prenatal* care⟩

pre·oc·cu·pied \prē-ˈäk-yə-ˌpīd\ *adj* **1** : lost in thought : ENGROSSED **2** : already occupied

pre·oc·cu·py *vb* **-pied; -py·ing 1** \prē-ˈäk-yə-ˌpī\ : to engage the attention of beforehand **2** \(ˈ)prē-\ : to take possession of before another — **pre·oc·cu·pa·tion** \(ˌ)prē-ˌäk-yə-ˈpā-shən\ *n*

pre·or·dain \ˌprē-ȯr-ˈdān\ *vb* : FOREORDAIN — **pre·or·di·na·tion** \(ˌ)prē-ˌȯrd-ə-ˈnā-shən\ *n*

prep *abbr* preposition

prep·a·ra·tion \ˌprep-ə-ˈrā-shən\ *n* **1** : the action or process of making ready in advance **2** : a state of being prepared : READINESS **3** : a preparatory act or measure **4** : something prepared ⟨a medicinal *preparation*⟩

pre·par·a·to·ry \pri-ˈpar-ə-ˌtōr-ē, -ˌtȯr-\ *adj* : preparing or serving to prepare for something : INTRODUCTORY

preparatory school *n* **1** : a usu. private school preparing students primarily for college **2** *Brit* : a private elementary school preparing students primarily for public schools

pre·pare \pri-ˈpa(ə)r, -ˈpe(ə)r\ *vb* **1** : to make or get ready ⟨*prepared* her for the shocking news⟩ ⟨*prepare* for a test⟩ **2** : to put together : COMPOUND ⟨*prepare* a prescription⟩ — **pre·par·er** *n*

pre·par·ed·ness \pri-ˈpar-əd-nəs, -ˈper-; -ˈpa(ə)rd-nəs, -ˈpe(ə)rd-\ *n* : the quality or state of being prepared; *esp* : a state of readiness for war

pre·pay \(ˈ)prē-ˈpā\ *vb* **pre·paid** \-ˈpād\; **pre·pay·ing** : to pay or pay for in advance — **pre·pay·ment** \-ˈpā-mənt\ *n*

pre·pon·der·ance \pri-ˈpän-d(ə-)rən(t)s\ *n* : a superiority in weight, power, importance, or numbers

pre·pon·der·ant \-d(ə-)rənt\ *adj* **1** : outweighing others : PREDOMINANT **2** : having greater frequency — **pre·pon·der·ant·ly** *adv*

pre·pon·der·ate \pri-ˈpän-də-ˌrāt\ *vb* : to exceed in weight, power, importance, or numbers — **pre·pon·der·a·tion** \-ˌpän-də-ˈrā-shən\ *n*

prep·o·si·tion \ˌprep-ə-ˈzish-ən\ *n* [from Latin *praepositus*, past participle stem of *praeponere* "to put in front", from *prae-* "pre-" and *ponere* "to put"] : a linguistic form that combines with a noun or pronoun to form a phrase that typically has an adverbial, adjectival, or substantival relation to another word ⟨*with* in "the girl with red hair" is a *preposition*⟩ — **prep·o·si·tion·al** \-ˈzish-(ə-)nəl\ *adj*

pre·pos·sess \ˌprē-pə-ˈzes\ *vb* **1** : PREOCCUPY **2** : to influence beforehand; *esp* : to move to a favorable opinion beforehand

pre·pos·sess·ing *adj* : tending to create a favorable impression : ATTRACTIVE ⟨a *prepossessing* appearance⟩

pre·pos·ses·sion \ˌprē-pə-ˈzesh-ən\ *n* **1** : an attitude, belief, or impression formed beforehand : PREJUDICE **2** : PREOCCUPATION

pre·pos·ter·ous \pri-ˈpäs-t(ə-)rəs\ *adj* : contrary to nature, reason, or common sense : ABSURD — **pre·pos·ter·ous·ly** *adv* — **pre·pos·ter·ous·ness** *n*

pre·puce \ˈprē-ˌpyüs\ *n* : FORESKIN

pre·re·cord \ˌprē-ri-ˈkȯrd\ *vb* : to record (as a radio or television program) in advance of presentation or use

pre·req·ui·site \(ˈ)prē-ˈrek-wə-zət\ *n* : something required beforehand or necessary as a preliminary ⟨the course is a *prerequisite* for advanced study⟩ — **prerequisite** *adj*

pre·rog·a·tive \pri-ˈräg-ət-iv\ *n* : a superior privilege or advantage; *esp* : a right attached to an office, rank, or status ⟨a royal *prerogative*⟩ ⟨a woman's *prerogative* to change her mind⟩

pres *abbr* **1** present **2** president

1**pres·age** \ˈpres-ij\ *n* **1** : OMEN **2** : FOREBODING, PRESENTIMENT

2**pres·age** \ˈpres-ij, pri-ˈsāj\ *vb* **1** : to give an omen or warning of : PORTEND **2** : FORETELL, PREDICT

pres·by·ter \'prez-bət-ər, 'pres-\ *n* : a member of the governing body of an early Christian church — **pres·byt·er·ate** \prez-'bit-ə-rət, pres-\ *n*

pres·by·te·ri·an \ˌprez-bə-'tir-ē-ən, ˌpres-\ *adj, often cap* [from *presbyter* "elder", from Latin, "elder", "priest", from Greek *presbyteros*, from the comparative of *presbys* "old man"] : characterized by a system of representative governing councils of ministers and elders — **Presbyterian** *n* — **Pres·by·te·ri·an·ism** \-ē-ə-ˌniz-əm\ *n*

pres·by·tery \'prez-bə-ˌter-ē, 'pres-\ *n, pl* **-ter·ies** **1** : the part of a church reserved for the officiating clergy **2** : a ruling body in presbyterian churches consisting of the ministers and representative elders from congregations within a district **3** : the jurisdiction of a presbytery **4** : the house of a Roman Catholic parish priest

pre·school \'prē-'skül\ *adj* : of, relating to, or being the period in a child's life from infancy to the age of five or six that ordinarily precedes attendance at elementary school

pre·science \'prēsh-(ē-)ən(t)s, 'presh-\ *n* : foreknowledge of events — **pre·scient** \-(ē-)ənt\ *adj* — **pre·scient·ly** *adv*

pre·scribe \pri-'skrīb\ *vb* **1** : to lay down as a guide, direction, or rule of action : ORDAIN ⟨*prescribed* a way of life⟩ **2** : to order or direct the use of something as a remedy ⟨the doctor *prescribed* rest⟩ — **pre·scrib·er** *n*

pre·scrip·tion \pri-'skrip-shən\ *n* **1 a** : the establishment of a claim of title to something usu. by use for a fixed period **b** : the right or title thus acquired **2** : the action of prescribing rules or directions **3 a** : a written direction or order for the preparation and use of a medicine **b** : a medicine prescribed — **pre·scrip·tive** \-'skrip-tiv\ *adj* — **pre·scrip·tive·ly** *adv*

pres·ence \'prez-ən(t)s\ *n* **1** : the fact or state of being present ⟨no one noticed his *presence*⟩ **2** : the part of space within someone's immediate vicinity ⟨felt awkward in her *presence*⟩ **3** : BEARING, APPEARANCE ⟨a stately *presence*⟩ **4** : something present ⟨a ghostly *presence* in the room⟩

presence of mind : self-control in an emergency

¹**pres·ent** \'prez-ənt\ *n* : something presented
syn PRESENT, GIFT, DONATION can mean something given. Of the three terms PRESENT most often implies a personal expression of affection; GIFT applies more broadly to anything given without thought of return; DONATION usu. applies to a gift made to a public, religious, or charitable organization and often presented publicly in the name of the donor

²**pre·sent** \pri-'zent\ *vb* **1 a** : to bring or introduce into the presence of someone **b** : to bring before the public ⟨*present* a play⟩ **c** : to introduce one person formally to another **2** : to make a gift to ⟨*presented* him with a watch⟩ **3** : to give or bestow formally ⟨*present* a medal⟩ **4** : to make an accusation against someone ⟨*present* a charge⟩ **5** : DISPLAY, SHOW **6** : to submit for consideration or action ⟨*present* a plan⟩ *syn* see GIVE — **pre·sent·er** *n*

³**pres·ent** \'prez-ənt\ *adj* **1** : now existing or in progress **2** : being in view, at hand, or under consideration ⟨all the pupils were *present*⟩ ⟨the *present* writer⟩ **3** : of, relating to, or being a verb tense that expresses present time or the time of speaking

⁴**pres·ent** \'prez-ənt\ *n* **1** *pl* : the document containing these words ⟨know all men by these *presents*⟩ **2 a** : PRESENT TENSE **b** : a verb form in the present tense **3** : the present time

pre·sent·a·ble \pri-'zent-ə-bəl\ *adj* **1** : capable of being presented ⟨whipped the speech into *presentable* form⟩ **2** : being in condition to be seen or inspected ⟨made the room *presentable*⟩ — **pre·sent·a·bly** \-blē\ *adv*

pre·sen·ta·tion \ˌprē-ˌzen-'tā-shən, ˌprez-ən-\ *n* **1** : the act of presenting **2 a** : something presented : GIFT **b** : something set forth for attention (as a play or a sales demonstration) — **pre·sen·ta·tion·al** \-sh(ə-)nəl\ *adj*

pres·ent–day \ˌprez-ənt-ˌdā\ *adj* : now existing or occurring : CURRENT

pre·sen·ti·ment \pri-'zent-ə-mənt\ *n* : a feeling that something will or is about to happen

pres·ent·ly \'prez-ənt-lē\ *adv* **1** *archaic* : at once **2** : before long : SOON ⟨*presently* they arrived⟩ **3** : at the present time : NOW ⟨*presently* we have none⟩

pre·sent·ment \pri-'zent-mənt\ *n* **1** : the act of presenting; *esp* : the act of offering a promissory note for payment **2 a** : the act of presenting to view or consciousness **b** : something presented

pres·ent participle \ˌprez-ənt-\ *n* : a participle that expresses present action, that in English is formed with the suffix *-ing*, and that indicates action in progress

present perfect tense *n* : a tense formed in English with *have* and expressing action or state completed at the time of speaking

present tense *n* : a tense that expresses action or state in the present time and is used of what is true at the time of speaking or of what is habitual or characteristic or is always or necessarily true

¹**pre·ser·va·tive** \pri-'zər-vət-iv\ *adj* : having the power of preserving

²**preservative** *n* : a preservative substance or agent

¹**pre·serve** \pri-'zərv\ *vb* **1** : to keep safe from harm, decay, or destruction : PROTECT ⟨*preserve* the republic⟩ **2** : to keep up : MAINTAIN ⟨*preserve* silence⟩ **3** : to prepare (as by canning or pickling) for future use ⟨*preserve* beets⟩ — **pre·serv·a·ble** \-'zər-və-bəl\ *adj* — **pres·er·va·tion** \ˌprez-ər-'vā-shən\ *n* — **pre·serv·er** *n*

²**preserve** *n* **1** : fruit canned or made into jams or jellies ⟨strawberry *preserves*⟩ **2** : an area restricted for the protection and preservation of natural resources (as animals and trees)

pre·side \pri-'zīd\ *vb* **1 a** : to occupy the place of authority **b** : to act as chairman ⟨*preside* over a meeting⟩ **2** : to exercise guidance or control ⟨*presided* over the destinies of the empire⟩ **3** : to occupy a featured position ⟨*presided* at the organ⟩

pres·i·den·cy \'prez-əd-ən-sē, 'prez-dən-; 'prez-ə-ˌden(t)-sē\ *n, pl* **-cies** : the office or term of office of a president

pres·i·dent \'prez-əd-ənt, 'prez-dənt, 'prez-ə-ˌdent\ *n* **1** : a person who presides over a meeting **2** : the chief officer of a corporation, institution, or organization **3** : the chief executive officer or the chief of state in a republic — **pres·i·den·tial** \ˌprez-ə-'den-chəl\ *adj*

¹**press** \'pres\ *n* **1** : CROWD, THRONG **2** : an apparatus or machine for exerting pressure (as for shaping material, extracting liquid, or drilling) **3** : CLOSET **4** : an act of pressing : PRESSURE **5** : the smoothed and creased condition of a freshly pressed garment

6 a : PRINTING PRESS **b** : the act or process of printing ⟨go to *press*⟩ **c** : a printing or publishing establishment **7 a** : the gathering and publishing of news : JOURNALISM **b** : newspapers, news periodicals, and often news broadcasting **c** : comment or notice in newspapers and periodicals ⟨got a good *press*⟩

[2]**press** *vb* **1** : to act upon by steady pushing : SQUEEZE **2** : FORCE, COMPEL ⟨*pressed* by business to return⟩ **3 a** : to squeeze so as to force out the juice or contents of ⟨*press* oranges⟩ **b** : to squeeze out ⟨*press* juice from grapes⟩ **4** : to flatten out or smooth by bearing down upon; *esp* : to smooth by ironing ⟨*press* a tie⟩ **5** : to urge or present strongly or forcefully ⟨*pressed* him to attend⟩ ⟨*presses* his claim⟩ **6** : EMBRACE **7 a** : to crowd closely : MASS ⟨reporters *pressed* around the celebrity⟩ **b** : to force or push one's way ⟨*presses* forward through the throng⟩ **8** : to seek urgently : CONTEND ⟨*pressed* for higher salaries⟩ — **press·er** *n*

[3]**press** *vb* : to force into service esp. in the army or navy : IMPRESS

press agent *n* : an agent employed to gain publicity

press conference *n* : an interview given by a public figure to a group of newsmen

press·ing \'pres-iŋ\ *adj* : urgently important : CRITICAL — **press·ing·ly** \-iŋ-lē\ *adv*

press·man \'pres-mən, -ˌman\ *n* : an operator of a press and esp. a printing press

pres·sure \'presh-ər\ *n* **1 a** : the action of pressing ⟨done by slow steady *pressure*⟩ **b** : the condition of being pressed ⟨kept under *pressure*⟩ **2 a** : a painful feeling of weight or burden : OPPRESSION, DISTRESS **b** : a burdensome or restricting force or influence ⟨the *pressure* of taxes⟩ ⟨the *pressures* of modern life⟩ **3 a** : the action of a force against an opposing force **b** : the force exerted over a surface divided by its area **c** : ELECTROMOTIVE FORCE **4** : URGENCY

pressure cooker *n* : a utensil for cooking or preserving of foods by means of steam under pressure — **pressure-cook** \ˌpresh-ər-'kůk\ *vb*

pressure point *n* : a point where a blood vessel runs near a bone and can be compressed (as to check bleeding) by pressure against the bone

pres·sur·ize \'presh-ə-ˌrīz\ *vb* : to maintain near-normal atmospheric pressure in ⟨*pressurize* an airplane cabin⟩ — **pres·sur·i·za·tion** \ˌpresh-ə-rə-'zā-shən\ *n*

pres·ti·dig·i·ta·tion \ˌpres-tə-ˌdij-ə-'tā-shən\ *n* : SLEIGHT OF HAND — **pres·ti·dig·i·ta·tor** \-'dij-ə-ˌtāt-ər\ *n*

pres·tige \pre-'stēzh, -'stēj\ *n* : importance in the estimation of others : STANDING — **pres·ti·gious** \-'stij-əs\ *adj* — **pres·ti·gious·ly** *adv* — **pres·ti·gious·ness** *n*

pres·to \'pres-tō\ *adv or adj* **1** : at once : QUICKLY ⟨a wave of the hand and, *presto*, it's gone⟩ **2** : at a rapid tempo — used as a direction in music

pre·sume \pri-'züm\ *vb* **1** : to undertake without leave or justification : DARE ⟨*presume* to question the authority of a superior⟩ **2** : to suppose to be true without proof ⟨our law *presumes* all persons charged with crime to be innocent until they are proved guilty⟩ **3** : to act or behave boldly without reason for doing so; *esp* : to take liberties ⟨*presume* upon a brief acquaintance to ask favors⟩ — **pre·sum·a·ble** \-'zü-mə-bəl\ *adj* — **pre·sum·a·bly** \-blē\ *adv*

pre·sump·tion \pri-'zəm(p)-shən\ *n* **1** : presumptuous attitude or conduct : AUDACITY **2 a** : strong grounds for believing something to be so in spite of lack of proof **b** : a conclusion reached on strong grounds : something believed to be so but not proved

pre·sump·tive \-'zəm(p)-tiv\ *adj* **1** : giving grounds for belief ⟨*presumptive* evidence⟩ **2** : based on probability ⟨the heir *presumptive*⟩ — **pre·sump·tive·ly** *adv*

pre·sump·tu·ous \pri-'zəm(p)-ch(ə-w)əs\ *adj* : overstepping due bounds : taking liberties — **pre·sump·tu·ous·ly** *adv* — **pre·sump·tu·ous·ness** *n*

pre·sup·pose \ˌprē-sə-'pōz\ *vb* : to suppose beforehand : take for granted ⟨a book that *presupposes* wide knowledge in its readers⟩ — **pre·sup·po·si·tion** \(ˌ)prē-ˌsəp-ə-'zish-ən\ *n*

pre·tend \pri-'tend\ *vb* **1** : to hold out the appearance of being, possessing, or performing : PROFESS ⟨*pretend* friendship⟩ **2** : to make believe : feign an action, part, or role ⟨*pretend* to be a bear⟩ **3** : to put in a claim ⟨*pretend* to a throne⟩

pre·tend·er \pri-'ten-dər\ *n* : one that pretends; *esp* : a person who claims a throne without right

pre·tense *or* **pre·tence** \'prē-ˌten(t)s, pri-'\ *n* **1** : a claim usu. not supported by fact **2** : DISPLAY, SHOW; *esp* : dishonest show ⟨free from *pretense*⟩ **3** : ATTEMPT ⟨no *pretense* at completeness⟩ **4** : pretended intention : PRETEXT **5** : false show : SIMULATION ⟨a *pretense* of illness⟩

pre·ten·sion \pri-'ten-chən\ *n* **1** : PRETEXT **2** : PRETENSE 1 **3** : PRETENTIOUSNESS, VANITY

pre·ten·tious \-chəs\ *adj* **1** : making or having claims esp. as to excellence or worth : SHOWY ⟨living in a *pretentious* style⟩ **2** : making demands on one's skill, ability, or means : AMBITIOUS ⟨*pretentious* plans⟩ — **pre·ten·tious·ly** *adv* — **pre·ten·tious·ness** *n*

pret·er·it *or* **pret·er·ite** \'pret-ə-rət\ *adj* : of, relating to, or being a verb tense that indicates action in the past without reference to duration, continuance, or repetition — **preterit** *n*

pre·ter·nat·u·ral \ˌprēt-ər-'nach-(ə-)rəl\ *adj* : beyond or above the natural : inexplicable by ordinary means — **pre·ter·nat·u·ral·ly** \-'nach(ə-)rə-lē, -'nach-ər-lē\ *adv*

pre·text \'prē-ˌtekst\ *n* : an intent or motive put forward in order to conceal a real intent or motive

[1]**pret·ty** \'prit-ē, 'pu̇rt-\ *adj* **pret·ti·er**; **-est** [originally meaning "wily", "clever", from Old English *prættig*, from *prætt* "trick"] : delicately or gracefully attractive to the eye or ear ⟨*pretty* tunes⟩ — **pret·ti·ly** \'prit-ə-lē, 'pu̇rt-\ *adv* — **pret·ti·ness** \'prit-ē-nəs, 'pu̇rt-\ *n*

[2]**pret·ty** \ˌpu̇rt-ē, pərt-ē (*unstressed* pərt-), ˌprit-ē\ *adv* : in some degree : MODERATELY ⟨*pretty* big⟩

[3]**pretty** *like* [1]\ *n, pl* **pretties** : a pretty person or thing

pret·zel \'pret-səl\ *n* : a brittle, glazed and salted, and usu. twisted cracker

prev *abbr* previous

pre·vail \pri-'vāl\ *vb* **1** : to win a victory : TRIUMPH **2** : to be or become effective **3** : to urge successfully ⟨*prevailed* upon him to sing⟩ **4** : to be frequent : PREDOMINATE ⟨west winds *prevail* here⟩ **5** : to be in use or fashion : PERSIST ⟨customs that *prevail* in France⟩

pre·vail·ing *adj* **1** : having superior force or influence **2 a** : most frequent ⟨*prevailing* winds⟩ **b** : generally current : COMMON — **pre·vail·ing·ly** \-'vā-liŋ-lē\ *adv*

prev·a·lent \'prev(-ə)-lənt\ *adj* : generally or widely accepted, practiced, or favored : WIDESPREAD — **prev·a·lence** \-lən(t)s\ *n* — **prev·a·lent·ly** *adv*

pre·var·i·cate \pri-'var-ə-ˌkāt\ *vb* : to deviate from the truth : LIE — **pre·var·i·ca·tion** \-ˌvar-ə-'kā-shən\ *n* — **pre·var·i·ca·tor** \-'var-ə-ˌkāt-ər\ *n*

pre·vent \pri-'vent\ *vb* : to keep from happening, acting, or succeeding : HINDER, STOP ⟨*prevent* accidents⟩ ⟨rain *prevented* the plane from taking off⟩ — **pre·vent·a·ble** *also* **pre·vent·i·ble** \-ə-bəl\ *adj* — **pre·ven·tion** \-'ven-chən\ *n*

pre·ven·ta·tive \pri-'vent-ət-iv\ *adj or n* : PREVENTIVE

1**pre·ven·tive** \pri-'vent-iv\ *n* : something that prevents; *esp* : something used to prevent disease

2**preventive** *adj* : devoted to, concerned with, or undertaken for prevention ⟨*preventive* measures⟩ ⟨*preventive* medicine⟩

1**pre·view** \'prē-ˌvyü\ *vb* : to view or show in advance

2**preview** *n* **1** : an advance showing, viewing, or announcement ⟨a *preview* of an art exhibit⟩ **2** *also* **pre·vue** \-ˌvyü\ : a showing of bits from a motion picture advertised for future appearance

pre·vi·ous \'prē-vē-əs\ *adj* : PRECEDING, EARLIER ⟨the *previous* lesson⟩ — **pre·vi·ous·ly** *adv*

previous to *prep* : prior to : BEFORE

pre·war \'prē-'wȯ(ə)r\ *adj* : occurring or existing before a war

1**prey** \'prā\ *n* **1** : an animal hunted or killed by another animal for food **2** : a person that is helpless or unable to resist attack : VICTIM **3** : the act or habit of preying

2**prey** *vb* **1** : to raid for booty **2** : to seize and devour something as prey **3** : to have a harmful or wasting effect ⟨fears that *prey* on the mind⟩ — **prey·er** *n*

prf *abbr* proof

1**price** \'prīs\ *n* **1** : the quantity of one thing and esp. money that is exchanged or demanded in exchange for another **2** : a reward for the capture or death of a person ⟨an outlaw with a *price* on his head⟩ **3** : the cost at which something is obtainable ⟨victory at any *price*⟩

syn PRICE, CHARGE, FEE can mean payment exacted for something. PRICE usu. implies purchase of goods or commodities; CHARGE applies to what is paid for services (as delivery or postage); FEE applies to a charge fixed (as by law or an institution) for a service or privilege ⟨tuition *fees*⟩

2**price** *vb* **1** : to set a price on **2** : to ask the price of **3** : to drive by raising prices excessively ⟨*priced* themselves out of the market⟩ — **pric·er** *n*

price·less \'prīs-ləs\ *adj* **1** : having a value beyond any price : INVALUABLE **2** : very amusing or absurd ⟨a *priceless* remark⟩

1**prick** \'prik\ *n* **1** : a mark or shallow hole made by a pointed instrument **2** : a pointed instrument or part **3** : an instance of pricking **4** : the sensation of being pricked

2**prick** *vb* **1 a** : to pierce slightly with a sharp point **b** : to feel or cause a pricking sensation **2** : to cause to feel guilt or remorse ⟨his conscience *pricked* him⟩ **3** : to urge on a horse with spurs **4** : to point forward or upward ⟨the dog's ears *pricked* up at the sound⟩ — **prick up one's ears** : to listen intently

prick·er \'prik-ər\ *n* **1** : one that pricks **2** : PRICKLE, THORN

1**prick·le** \'prik-əl\ *n* **1** : a fine sharp projection; *esp* : a sharp pointed process of the bark or outer protective layer of a plant **2** : a prickling sensation

2**prickle** *vb* **prickled**; **prick·ling** \'prik-(ə-)liŋ\ **1** : to prick lightly **2** : TINGLE

ə abut	ər further		a back	ā bake
ä cot, cart	au̇ out	ch chin	e less	ē easy
g gift	i trip	ī life	j joke	ŋ sing	ō flow
ȯ flaw	ȯi coin	th thin	t͟h this	ü loot
u̇ foot	y yet	yü few	yu̇ furious	zh vision

prick·ly \'prik-lē\ *adj* **prick·li·er**; **-est** **1** : full of or covered with prickles ⟨*prickly* plants⟩ **2** : PRICKING, STINGING, TINGLING ⟨a *prickly* sensation⟩ — **prick·li·ness** *n*

prickly heat *n* : an inflammation around the sweat ducts with pimples, itching, and tingling

prickly pear *n* **1** : any of numerous flat-jointed often prickly cacti **2** : the pear-shaped edible pulpy fruit of a prickly pear

1**pride** \'prīd\ *n* **1** : the quality or state of being proud **2** : proud or disdainful behavior or treatment **3** : something that is a source of pride ⟨his car is his chief *pride*⟩ **4** : a company of lions

syn PRIDE, VANITY, CONCEIT can mean inordinate self-esteem. PRIDE may imply an exalted opinion of oneself often bolstered by a lower opinion of others; VANITY implies a preoccupation with one's appearance or accomplishments; CONCEIT implies an openly displayed and often inflated feeling of superiority ***ant*** humility

2**pride** *vb* : to indulge in pride : PLUME ⟨*pride* oneself on one's skill⟩

priest \'prēst\ *n* [from Old English *prēost*, from Latin *presbyter* "elder", "priest"; see PRESBYTERIAN] : a person who has the authority to conduct religious rites — **priest·ess** \'prē-stəs\ *n*

priest·hood \'prēst-ˌhu̇d\ *n* **1** : the office, dignity, or status of a priest **2** : the whole group of priests

priest·ly \'prēst-lē\ *adj* **priest·li·er**; **-est** **1** : of or relating to a priest or the priesthood **2** : characteristic of or befitting a priest — **priest·li·ness** *n*

prig \'prig\ *n* : a person who offends or irritates others by a too careful or rigid observance of niceties — **prig·gery** \'prig-ə-rē\ *n* — **prig·gish** \'prig-ish\ *adj* — **prig·gish·ly** *adv* — **prig·gish·ness** *n*

prim \'prim\ *adj* **prim·mer**; **-mest** : very or excessively formal and precise (as in conduct or dress) ⟨a *prim* old lady⟩ — **prim·ly** *adv* — **prim·ness** *n*

prim *abbr* primary

pri·ma·cy \'prī-mə-sē\ *n, pl* **-cies** **1** : the state of being first (as in time, place, or rank) **2** : the office, status, or dignity of a bishop of the highest rank

pri·ma don·na \ˌprim-ə-'dän-ə, ˌprē-mə-\ *n, pl* **prima donnas** **1** : a principal female singer (as in an opera) **2** : a self-centered, vain, or temperamental person

pri·mal \'prī-məl\ *adj* **1** : ORIGINAL, PRIMITIVE **2** : first in importance : CHIEF

pri·mar·i·ly \prī-'mer-ə-lē\ *adv* **1** : FUNDAMENTALLY **2** : in the first place : ORIGINALLY

1**pri·mary** \'prī-ˌmer-ē, 'prīm-(ə-)rē\ *adj* **1 a** : first in time or development : INITIAL, PRIMITIVE ⟨the *primary* meaning of a word⟩ **b** : not derived or derivable from or dependent on something else ⟨a *primary* source of information⟩ **c** : coming before and usu. preparatory to something else ⟨*primary* school⟩ **2 a** : of first rank, importance, or value : CHIEF **b** : BASIC, FUNDAMENTAL ⟨man's *primary* duty⟩ **c** : being the strongest degree of stress **3** : of, relating to, or being one of the principal quills of a bird's wing borne on the outer joint **4** : of, relating to, or being the inducing current or its circuit in an induction coil or transformer

2**primary** *n, pl* **-mar·ies** **1** : a planet as distinguished from its satellites **2** : a primary quill or feather **3** : any of a set of colors (as red, yellow, or blue) from which all other colors may be derived — called also *primary color* **4** : an election in which voters select party candidates for political office **5** : PRIMARY COIL

primary coil *n* : the coil through which the inducing current passes in an induction coil or transformer

pri·mate \'prī-ˌmāt *or esp for 1* -mət\ *n* **1** : a bishop or archbishop having highest status in a district, nation, or church **2** : any of an order of mammals comprising man, apes, monkeys, and related forms (as lemurs and tarsiers)

[1]**prime** \'prīm\ *n* **1** : the first part : earliest stage **2** : the most active, thriving, or successful stage or period ⟨the *prime* of life⟩ **3** : the best part : PICK ⟨the *prime* of the flock⟩ **4** : PRIME NUMBER **5** : the symbol ′

[2]**prime** *adj* **1** : first in time : ORIGINAL **2** : of, relating to, or being a prime number **3** : first in rank, quality, or importance ⟨*prime* beef⟩ — **prime·ly** *adv* — **prime·ness** *n*

[3]**prime** *vb* **1** : to apply a first color, coating, or preparation to **2** : to put into working order by filling or charging with something ⟨*prime* a pump with water⟩ **3** : to instruct beforehand : COACH

prime meridian *n* : the meridian of 0° longitude from which other longitudes are reckoned east and west

prime minister *n* : the chief minister of a ruler or state : the chief executive of a parliamentary government — **prime ministry** *n*

prime number *n* : an integer other than 0 or $+1$ that is not divisible by any other integers except ± 1 and $\pm$ itself

[1]**prim·er** \'prim-ər, *esp Brit* 'prī-mər\ *n* **1** : a small book for teaching children to read **2** : a small introductory book on a subject

[2]**prim·er** \'prī-mər\ *n* **1** : a device (as a cap, tube, or wafer) that is ignited first and thus ignites an explosive charge **2** : PRIMING

pri·me·val \prī-'mē-vəl\ *adj* [from Latin *primaevus*, from *primus* "first" and *aevum* "age"] : of or relating to the earliest ages : PRIMITIVE — **pri·me·val·ly** \-və-lē\ *adv*

prim·ing \'prī-ming\ *n* **1** : the explosive used in priming a charge **2** : the material used in priming a surface

[1]**prim·i·tive** \'prim-ət-iv\ *adj* **1** : ORIGINAL, PRIMARY **2 a** : of or relating to the earliest age or period ⟨*primitive* forests⟩ ⟨the *primitive* church⟩ **b** : closely resembling an ancient ancestor ⟨a *primitive* fish⟩ **3** : of, relating to, or characteristic of a relatively simple people or culture ⟨*primitive* society⟩ ⟨*primitive* building techniques⟩ **4 a** : SELF-TAUGHT **b** : produced by a self-taught artist — **prim·i·tive·ly** *adv* — **prim·i·tive·ness** *n*

[2]**primitive** *n* **1** : something primitive **2 a** : an artist or a work of art of an early period **b** : a self-taught artist or one of his works **3** : a member of a primitive people

pri·mo·gen·i·ture \ˌprī-mō-'jen-ə-ˌchu̇r, -'jen-i-chər\ *n* **1** : the state of being the firstborn child of two parents **2** : an exclusive right of inheritance belonging to the eldest son

pri·mor·di·al \prī-'mȯrd-ē-əl\ *adj* **1** : first created or developed : PRIMEVAL **2** : FUNDAMENTAL, PRIMARY — **pri·mor·di·al·ly** \-ē-ə-lē\ *adv*

primp \'primp\ *vb* : to dress, adorn, or arrange in a careful or finicky manner

prim·rose \'prim-ˌrōz\ *n* **1** : any of a genus of herbs with large leaves arranged at the base of the stem and showy variously colored flowers borne in clusters on leafless stalks **2** : EVENING PRIMROSE

primrose yellow *n* : a light to moderate yellow

prin *abbr* principal

prince \'prin(t)s\ *n* [from Old French, from Latin *princeps* "leader", "head of state", literally "one who takes the first part", from *primus* "first" and *capere* "to take"] **1 a** : MONARCH, KING **b** : the ruler of a principality **2** : a male member of a royal family; *esp* : a son of the king **3** : a nobleman of high rank **4** : a person of high standing in his class or profession

prince consort *n, pl* **princes consort** : the husband of a reigning queen

prince·ling \'prin(t)s-ling\ *n* : a petty prince

prince·ly \'prin(t)s-lē\ *adj* **prince·li·er**; **-est** **1** : of or relating to a prince : ROYAL **2** : befitting a prince : NOBLE, MAGNIFICENT ⟨a *princely* sum⟩

prin·cess \'prin(t)-səs, 'prin-ˌses, prin-'ses\ *n* **1** : a female member of a royal family; *esp* : a daughter of a sovereign **2** : the wife of a prince

princess royal *n, pl* **prin·cess·es royal** : the eldest daughter of a sovereign

[1]**prin·ci·pal** \'prin(t)-sə-pəl\ *adj* **1** : most important or influential : CHIEF **2** : of, relating to, or being principal or a principal — **prin·ci·pal·ly** \-pə-lē\ *adv*

[2]**principal** *n* **1 a** : a chief or head man or woman **b** : the head of a school **c** : one who employs another to act for him **d** : a participant in a crime **2** : a sum used to earn interest

prin·ci·pal·i·ty \ˌprin(t)-sə-'pal-ət-ē\ *n, pl* **-ties** : the territory or jurisdiction of a prince

principal parts *n pl* : a series of verb forms from which all others can be derived including in English the present infinitive, the past tense, and the past participle

principal square root *n* : the positive square root of a number

prin·ci·ple \'prin(t)-sə-pəl\ *n* **1** : a fundamental law or doctrine **2 a** : a rule or code of conduct **b** : devotion to right principles ⟨a man of *principle*⟩ **3** : the laws or facts of nature underlying the working of an artificial device ⟨the *principle* of magnetism⟩ **4 a** : a primary source : ORIGIN **b** : an underlying faculty or endowment ⟨curiosity is a *principle* of human nature⟩ **5** : a constituent that gives a substance its essential qualities ⟨quinine is the active *principle* of cinchona bark⟩

prin·ci·pled \-pəld\ *adj* : based on or marked by principle ⟨high-*principled*⟩

prink \'pringk\ *vb* : PRIMP — **prink·er** *n*

[1]**print** \'print\ *n* **1 a** : a mark made by pressure : IMPRESSION **b** : something impressed with a print or formed in a mold ⟨a *print* of butter⟩ **2** : a device or instrument for impressing or forming a print **3 a** : printed state ⟨put a manuscript into *print*⟩ **b** : printed matter **c** : printed letters : TYPE **4** : a copy made by printing (as from a photographic negative) **5 a** : cloth with a pattern applied by printing **b** : an article of such cloth

[2]**print** *vb* **1 a** : to impress something in or on another **b** : to produce impressions with a relief surface (as type or a plate) **c** : to impress a surface with a design by pressure ⟨*print* wallpaper⟩ **2** : to publish in printed form ⟨*print* a newspaper⟩ **3** : to write in unconnected letters like those made by a printing press **4** : to make a positive picture on a sensitized photographic surface

print·a·ble \'print-ə-bəl\ *adj* **1** : capable of being printed or printed from **2** : worthy or fit to be published

printed circuit *n* : a circuit for electronic apparatus made by depositing conductive material on an insulating surface

print·er \'print-ər\ *n* **1** : a person whose business or occupation is printing **2** : a device used for printing

printer's devil *n* : an apprentice in a printing office

print·ing \'print-ing\ *n* **1** : reproduction in printed form **2** : the art, practice, or business of a printer **3** : IMPRESSION 4b

printing press *n* : a machine that produces printed copies

print·out \'print-,au̇t\ *n* : a printed record produced automatically (as by a computer); *also* : the producing of such a record

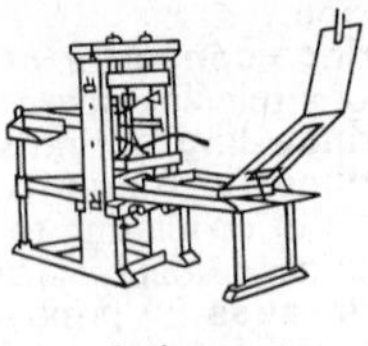
printing press

1**pri·or** \'prī(-ə)r\ *n* **1** : the deputy head of an abbey **2** : the head of a monastic house, province, or order — **pri·or·ess** \'prī-ə-rəs\ *n*

2**prior** *adj* **1** : earlier in time or order **2** : taking precedence in importance or value

pri·or·i·ty \prī-'ȯr-ət-ē, -'är-\ *n, pl* **-ties** **1** : the quality or state of coming before another in time, importance, or rank **2** : order of preference based on urgency or importance; *esp* : a preferential rating that allocates rights to goods and services in limited supply ⟨in time of war top *priority* is given to military requirements⟩

prior to *prep* : in advance of : BEFORE

pri·o·ry \'prī-(ə-)rē\ *n, pl* **-ries** : a religious house under a prior or prioress

prism \'priz-əm\ *n* **1** : a solid whose ends are similar, equal, and parallel polygons and whose faces are parallelograms **2** : a solid body usu. of glass or crystal and often three-sided that causes light passing through to deviate and break up into rays of rainbow colors **3** : a decorative glass pendant

prism 2

pris·mat·ic \priz-'mat-ik\ *adj* **1** : relating to, resembling, or constituting a prism **2** : formed by refraction of light through a transparent prism ⟨*prismatic* colors⟩ **3** : highly colored : BRILLIANT — **pris·mat·i·cal·ly** \-i-k(ə-)lē\ *adv*

pris·on \'priz-ən\ *n* **1** : a state of confinement esp. for criminals ⟨sentenced to *prison*⟩ **2** : a building or group of buildings for the confinement of criminals

pris·on·er \'priz-(ə-)nər\ *n* : a person under restraint, confinement, or custody; *esp* : one in prison

pris·tine \'pris-,tēn\ *adj* : ORIGINAL, PRIMITIVE; *esp* : having the purity or freshness of the original state

prith·ee \'prith-ē, 'prith-\ *interj, archaic* — used to express a request

pri·va·cy \'prī-və-sē\ *n, pl* **-cies** **1** : the condition of being apart from company or observation : SECLUSION ⟨the *privacy* of the home⟩ **2** : SECRECY ⟨talk in *privacy*⟩

1**pri·vate** \'prī-vət\ *adj* **1** : belonging to, concerning, or reserved for the use of a particular person or group : not public ⟨*private* property⟩ **2 a** : offering privacy : SECLUDED ⟨a *private* office⟩ **b** : not publicly known : SECRET ⟨*private* agreements⟩ **3** : not holding public office or employment ⟨a *private* citizen⟩ **4** : not under public control ⟨a *private* school⟩ — **pri·vate·ly** *adv* — **pri·vate·ness** *n*

2**private** *n* : a person of low or lowest rank in an organized group (as a police or fire department); *esp* : an enlisted man in the army ranking just below a private first class — **in private** : SECRETLY ⟨would like to speak to you *in private*⟩

1**pri·va·teer** \,prī-və-'ti(ə)r\ *n* **1** : an armed private ship commissioned to raid the ships of an enemy **2** : the commander or one of the crew of a privateer — **pri·va·teers·man** \-'ti(ə)rz-mən\ *n*

2**privateer** *vb* : to cruise in or as a privateer

private first class *n* : an enlisted man in the army ranking just below a corporal

pri·va·tion \prī-'vā-shən\ *n* : the state of being deprived esp. of what is needed for existence : WANT

priv·et \'priv-ət\ *n* : a shrub that is related to the olive, has small white flowers, and is widely used for hedges

1**priv·i·lege** \'priv(-ə)-lij\ *n* : a right or liberty granted as a benefit, advantage, or favor; *esp* : one attached to a position or an office

2**privilege** *vb* : to grant a privilege to ⟨was *privileged* to meet the president⟩

priv·i·ly \'priv-ə-lē\ *adv* : SECRETLY

1**privy** \'priv-ē\ *adj* **1** : WITHDRAWN, PRIVATE ⟨a *privy* place⟩ **2** : sharing in a secret ⟨*privy* to the conspiracy⟩

2**privy** *n, pl* **priv·ies** **1** : a small building without plumbing used as a toilet **2** : TOILET 2b

1**prize** \'prīz\ *n* **1** : something won or to be won in a contest **2** : something exceptionally desirable

2**prize** *adj* **1 a** : awarded a prize **b** : awarded as a prize **2** : outstanding of its kind ⟨a *prize* idiot⟩

3**prize** *vb* **1** : to estimate the value of : RATE **2** : to value highly : ESTEEM

4**prize** *n* **1** : something taken by force or threat; *esp* : property lawfully captured in time of war **2** : an act of capturing or taking; *esp* : the wartime capture of a ship and its cargo at sea

5**prize** *vb* : to press, force, or move with or as if with a lever : PRY

prize·fight \'prīz-,fīt\ *n* : a contest between professional boxers for pay — **prize·fight·er** \-ər\ *n* — **prize·fight·ing** \-ing\ *n*

prize·win·ner \-,win-ər\ *n* : a winner of a prize — **prize·win·ning** \-,win-ing\ *adj*

1**pro** \'prō\ *n, pl* **pros** \'prōz\ **1** : a favorable argument or piece of evidence ⟨*pros* and cons⟩ **2** : the affirmative position or one holding it

2**pro** *adv* : on the affirmative side

3**pro** *n or adj* : PROFESSIONAL

1**pro-** *prefix* : located in front of or at the front of : anterior to ⟨*pro*thorax⟩

2**pro-** *prefix* **1** : taking the place of : substituting for **2** : favoring : supporting : championing ⟨*pro*-American⟩

prob *abbr* **1** probably **2** problem

prob·a·bil·i·ty \,präb-ə-'bil-ət-ē\ *n, pl* **-ties** **1** : the quality, state, or degree of being probable : LIKELIHOOD **2** : something probable **3** : a measure of the relative frequency of occurrence of an event ⟨the *probability* of a coin coming up heads is ½⟩

prob·a·ble \'präb-ə-bəl\ *adj* **1** : likely though not certain to be true ⟨a *probable* explanation⟩ **2** : likely to happen or to have happened ⟨the *probable* outcome of the game⟩ — **prob·a·bly** \'präb-ə-blē, 'präb-lē\ *adv*

1**pro·bate** \'prō-,bāt\ *n* **1** : proof before a probate court that the last will and testament of a deceased person is genuine **2** : judicial determination of the validity of a will

2**probate** *vb* : to establish by probate as genuine and valid

probate court *n* : a court that probates wills and administers estates of deceased persons

pro·ba·tion \prō-'bā-shən\ *n* **1** : critical testing and evaluation **2 a** : subjection of an individual to a period of testing and trial to determine his fitness (as for a job or school) **b** : the suspending of a convicted offender's sentence during good behavior under the supervision of a probation officer **c** : a period of being subject to probation — **pro·ba·tion·al** \-sh(ə-)nəl\ *adj* — **pro·ba·tion·ary** \-shə-ˌner-ē\ *adj*

pro·ba·tion·er \-sh(ə-)nər\ *n* : a person (as a new student nurse or a released convict) who is undergoing probation

probation officer *n* : an officer appointed to supervise convicted offenders on probation

1**probe** \'prōb\ *n* **1** : a slender instrument esp. for examining a cavity (as a wound) **2** : a device used to penetrate or send back information from outer space **3** : a searching examination; *esp* : an inquiry to discover evidence of wrongdoing ⟨a legislative *probe*⟩

2**probe** *vb* **1** : to examine with or as if with a probe **2** : to investigate thoroughly — **prob·er** *n*

pro·bi·ty \'prō-bət-ē\ *n* : HONESTY, UPRIGHTNESS

1**prob·lem** \'präb-ləm\ *n* **1 a** : a question for inquiry, consideration, or solution **b** : a proposition in mathematics stating something to be done **2 a** : an intricate unsettled question **b** : a source of perplexity or trouble

2**problem** *adj* **1** : dealing with a problem of human conduct or social justice ⟨a *problem* play⟩ **2** : difficult to deal with ⟨a *problem* child⟩

prob·lem·at·ic \ˌpräb-lə-'mat-ik\ *or* **prob·lem·at·i·cal** \-'mat-i-kəl\ *adj* : having the nature of a problem : difficult and uncertain : PUZZLING — **prob·lem·at·i·cal·ly** \-i-k(ə-)lē\ *adv*

pro·bos·cis \prə-'bäs-əs\ *n, pl* **-bos·cis·es** *also* **-bos·ci·des** \-'bäs-ə-ˌdēz\ **1** : the trunk of an elephant; *also* : a long, flexible, or prominent snout or nose **2** : a long sometimes extensible tubular process of the mouth region of an invertebrate (as a mosquito or butterfly)

pro·caine \'prō-ˌkān\ *n* : a drug resembling cocaine and used as a local anesthetic

pro·ce·dure \prə-'sē-jər\ *n* **1** : a manner or method of proceeding in a process or a course of action ⟨observance of legal *procedure*⟩ **2** : an action or series of actions — **pro·ce·dur·al** \-'sēj-(ə-)rəl\ *adj*

pro·ceed \prō-'sēd, prə-\ *vb* **1** : to come forth from a source : ISSUE **2 a** : to continue after a pause or interruption **b** : to go on in an orderly regulated way **3 a** : to carry on an action, process, or movement **b** : to be in process ⟨the job *proceeds* well⟩ **4** : to move along a course

pro·ceed·ing *n* **1** : PROCEDURE **2** *pl* : EVENTS, HAPPENINGS ⟨talked over the day's *proceedings*⟩ **3** : a suit or action at law **4** : AFFAIR, TRANSACTION **5** *pl* : an official record of things said or done

pro·ceeds \'prō-ˌsēdz\ *n pl* : the total amount or the profit arising from an investment, transaction, tax, or business : RETURN

1**proc·ess** \'präs-ˌes, 'prōs-, -əs\ *n, pl* **proc·ess·es** \-ˌes-əz, -ə-səz, -ə-ˌsēz\ **1 a** : PROGRESS, ADVANCE ⟨in the *process* of time⟩ **b** : something going on : PROCEEDING **2** : a series of actions, operations, or changes leading to an end or result ⟨the *process* of growth⟩ ⟨a manufacturing *process*⟩ **3 a** : the procedure in a legal action ⟨due *process* of law⟩ **b** : a legal summons or writ used by a court to enforce its authority **4** : a prominent or projecting bodily part : OUTGROWTH ⟨a bony *process*⟩

2**process** *vb* : to subject to a special process (as in manufacturing) — **proc·es·sor** \-ˌes-ər, -ə-sər, -ə-ˌsȯr\ *n*

3**process** *adj* : treated or made by a special process ⟨*process* cheese⟩

pro·ces·sion \prə-'sesh-ən\ *n* **1** : PROGRESSION **2** : a group of individuals moving along in an orderly way : PARADE ⟨a funeral *procession*⟩

1**pro·ces·sion·al** \prə-'sesh-(ə-)nəl\ *n* : a hymn sung during a church procession

2**processional** *adj* : of, relating to, or moving in a procession

pro·claim \prō-'klām\ *vb* : to announce publicly : DECLARE ⟨*proclaim* a holiday⟩ — **pro·claim·er** *n*

proc·la·ma·tion \ˌpräk-lə-'mā-shən\ *n* **1** : the action of proclaiming ⟨*proclamation* of a new law⟩ **2** : something proclaimed

pro·cliv·i·ty \prō-'kliv-ət-ē\ *n, pl* **-ties** : TENDENCY, INCLINATION ⟨a marked *proclivity* toward laziness⟩

pro·con·sul \(')prō-'kän(t)-səl\ *n* **1** : a governor or military commander of an ancient Roman province **2** : an administrator of a colony or occupied area — **pro·con·sul·ar** \-s(ə-)lər\ *adj*

pro·cras·ti·nate \prə-'kras-tə-ˌnāt\ *vb* : to keep postponing something supposed to be done — **pro·cras·ti·na·tion** \-ˌkras-tə-'nā-shən\ *n* — **pro·cras·ti·na·tor** \-'kras-tə-ˌnāt-ər\ *n*

pro·cre·ate \'prō-krē-ˌāt\ *vb* : to beget or bring forth offspring : REPRODUCE — **pro·cre·a·tion** \ˌprō-krē-'ā-shən\ *n*

proc·tor \'präk-tər\ *n* : SUPERVISOR, MONITOR; *esp* : one appointed to supervise students (as at an examination) — **proctor** *vb*

proc·u·ra·tor \'präk-yə-ˌrāt-ər\ *n* : a Roman provincial administrator

pro·cure \prə-'kyu̇(ə)r\ *vb* **1** : to get possession of : OBTAIN **2** : to bring about : ACHIEVE ***syn*** see GET — **pro·cur·a·ble** \-'kyu̇r-ə-bəl\ *adj* — **pro·cure·ment** \-'kyu̇(ə)r-mənt\ *n*

1**prod** \'präd\ *vb* **prod·ded; prod·ding** **1** : to thrust a pointed or blunt instrument into : POKE, PRICK **2** : to incite to action : STIR ⟨*prodding* him to finish the job⟩ — **prod·der** *n*

2**prod** *n* **1** : an instrument used to prod **2** : an incitement to act

prod *abbr* production

1**prod·i·gal** \'präd-i-gəl\ *adj* **1** : recklessly extravagant ⟨a *prodigal* spender⟩ **2** : WASTEFUL, LAVISH ⟨*prodigal* entertainment⟩ — **prod·i·gal·i·ty** \ˌpräd-ə-'gal-ət-ē\ *n* — **prod·i·gal·ly** \'präd-i-g(ə-)lē\ *adv*

2**prodigal** *n* : SPENDTHRIFT

pro·di·gious \prə-'dij-əs\ *adj* **1** : exciting amazement or wonder **2** : huge in bulk, quantity, or degree : ENORMOUS — **pro·di·gious·ly** *adv* — **pro·di·gious·ness** *n*

prod·i·gy \'präd-ə-jē\ *n, pl* **-gies** **1** : something (as a comet) out of the ordinary course of nature **2** : an amazing event, thing, or deed ⟨his pitching was a *prodigy* of skill⟩ **3** : a highly gifted or precocious person ⟨a child *prodigy*⟩

1**pro·duce** \prə-'d(y)üs\ *vb* **1** : to offer to view or notice : EXHIBIT ⟨*produce* evidence⟩ **2** : to give birth or rise to ⟨a tree *producing* good fruit⟩ **3** : to present to the public ⟨*produce* a play⟩ **4** : FORM, MAKE; *esp* : MANUFACTURE **5** : to accrue or cause to accrue : YIELD ⟨income-*producing* investments⟩ **6** : to bring about : CAUSE ⟨a call that *produced* results⟩ — **pro·duc·i·ble** \-'d(y)ü-sə-bəl\ *adj*

2**prod·uce** \'präd-ˌüs, 'prōd-, -ˌyüs\ *n* **1** : something produced **2** : fresh fruits and vegetables

pro·duc·er \prə-'d(y)ü-sər\ *n* **1** : one that produces; *esp* : one that grows agricultural products or manufactures articles **2** : a person who supervises or finances a stage or screen production or radio or television program **3** : an organism (as a green plant) that manufactures its food from simple inorganic substances

prod·uct \'präd-(ˌ)əkt\ *n* **1** : the number or expression resulting from the multiplication of two or more numbers or expressions **2** : something produced **3** : PRODUCTION 3

pro·duc·tion \prə-ˈdək-shən\ *n* **1 a** : PRODUCT 2 **b** : a literary or artistic work **c** : a work presented on the stage or screen or over the air **2 a** : the act or process of producing **b** : the making of goods available for human wants **3** : total output ⟨steel *production* rose sharply⟩

pro·duc·tive \prə-ˈdək-tiv\ *adj* **1** : having the power to produce esp. in abundance ⟨*productive* fishing waters⟩ **2** : effective in bringing about a production ⟨an age *productive* of great men⟩ **3** : yielding or furnishing results **4** : yielding or devoted to the production of wealth — **pro·duc·tive·ly** *adv* — **pro·duc·tive·ness** *n* — **pro·duc·tiv·i·ty** \(ˌ)prō-ˌdək-ˈtiv-ət-ē, ˌpräd-(ˌ)ək-\ *n*

product set *n* : CARTESIAN PRODUCT

prof \ˈpräf\ *n, slang* : PROFESSOR

[1]**pro·fane** \prō-ˈfān\ *vb* [from Latin *profanus*, from *pro-* "in front of" (i.e., outside) and *fanum* "temple"] **1** : to violate or treat with irreverence, abuse, or contempt : DESECRATE **2** : to put to a wrong, unworthy, or vulgar use : DEBASE — **prof·a·na·tion** \ˌpräf-ə-ˈnā-shən, ˌprō-fə-\ *n* — **pro·fan·er** *n*

[2]**profane** *adj* **1** : not concerned with religion or religious purposes : SECULAR ⟨*profane* affairs⟩ **2** : not holy because unconsecrated, impure, or defiled : UNSANCTIFIED **3** : serving to debase or defile what is holy : BLASPHEMOUS ⟨*profane* language⟩ — **profane·ly** *adv* — **pro·fane·ness** \-ˈfān-nəs\ *n*

pro·fan·i·ty \prō-ˈfan-ət-ē\ *n, pl* **-ties** **1** : the quality or state of being profane **2** : profane language

pro·fess \prə-ˈfes\ *vb* **1 a** : to declare openly or freely ⟨*profess* confidence in a friend's honesty⟩ **b** : PRETEND, CLAIM ⟨*professed* to be a gentleman⟩ **2** : to confess one's faith in or allegiance to ⟨*profess* Christianity⟩ **3** : to follow as a calling ⟨*profess* the law⟩

pro·fessed \-ˈfest\ *adj* **1** : openly declared whether truly or falsely ⟨a *professed* hater of lies⟩ **2** : having taken the vows of religious order

pro·fess·ed·ly \prə-ˈfes-əd-lē, -ˈfest-lē\ *adv* **1** : according to one's own declaration **2** : SUPPOSEDLY

pro·fes·sion \prə-ˈfesh-ən\ *n* **1** : the act of taking the vows of a religious community **2** : an open declaration of a belief, faith, or opinion **3** : an avowed religious faith **4 a** : a calling requiring specialized knowledge and academic preparation **b** : the body of persons engaged in a profession ***syn*** see TRADE

[1]**pro·fes·sion·al** \prə-ˈfesh-(ə-)nəl\ *adj* **1 a** : of, relating to, or characteristic of a profession ⟨his work had a *professional* polish⟩ **b** : engaged in a profession **2 a** : participating for money in an activity often engaged in by amateurs ⟨*professional* golfers⟩ **b** : engaged in by professionals rather than amateurs ⟨*professional* football⟩ **3** : following a line of conduct as though it were a profession ⟨a *professional* patriot⟩ — **pro·fes·sion·al·ly** \-ē\ *adv*

[2]**professional** *n* **1** : one that engages in a profession **2** : one that engages in professional sports or activities

pro·fes·sor \prə-ˈfes-ər\ *n* **1** : one that professes or avows ⟨a *professor* of Christianity⟩ **2** : a faculty member of the highest academic rank at a university or college — **pro·fes·so·ri·al** \ˌprō-fə-ˈsōr-ē-əl, ˌpräf-ə-, -ˈsȯr-\ *adj* — **pro·fes·so·ri·al·ly** \-ē-ə-lē\ *adv*

pro·fes·sor·ate \prə-ˈfes-ə-rət\ *n* : the office, term of office, or position of a professor

pro·fes·sor·ship \prə-ˈfes-ər-ˌship\ *n* : the office, duties, or position of an academic professor

prof·fer \ˈpräf-ər\ *vb* **prof·fered**; **prof·fer·ing** \ˈpräf-(ə-)riŋ\ : to offer for acceptance : TENDER — **proffer** *n*

pro·fi·cient \prə-ˈfish-ənt\ *adj* : skilled through practice : EXPERT ***syn*** see SKILLFUL — **pro·fi·cien·cy** \-ən-sē\ *n* — **pro·fi·cient·ly** *adv*

pro·file \ˈprō-ˌfīl\ *n* **1** : a head or face represented or seen in a side view **2** : OUTLINE, CONTOUR **3** : a vertical section of soil that shows the various zones

[1]**prof·it** \ˈpräf-ət\ *n* **1** : a valuable return : GAIN **2** : the excess of returns over expenses; *esp* : the excess of the selling price of goods over their cost — **prof·it·less** \-ləs\ *adj*

[2]**profit** *vb* **1** : to be of use or advantage : BENEFIT **2** : to derive benefit : GAIN ⟨*profit* by experience⟩

prof·it·a·ble \ˈpräf-ət-ə-bəl, ˈpräf-tə-bəl\ *adj* : yielding profits : USEFUL, LUCRATIVE ***syn*** see BENEFICIAL ***ant*** unprofitable — **prof·it·a·bly** \-blē\ *adv*

prof·i·teer \ˌpräf-ə-ˈti(ə)r\ *n* : one who makes an unreasonable profit esp. on the sale of goods during an emergency — **profiteer** *vb*

prof·li·gate \ˈpräf-li-gət\ *adj* **1** : loose in character or morals : DISSIPATED **2** : extremely wasteful : PRODIGAL — **prof·li·ga·cy** \-gə-sē\ *n* — **profligate** *n* — **prof·li·gate·ly** *adv*

pro·found \prə-ˈfau̇nd\ *adj* **1** : intellectually deep : SCHOLARLY **2** : coming from or situated at a depth : DEEP-SEATED **3** : deeply felt : INTENSE ⟨*profound* regret⟩ — **pro·found·ly** *adv* — **pro·found·ness** \-ˈfau̇n(d)-nəs\ *n*

pro·fun·di·ty \prə-ˈfən-dət-ē\ *n, pl* **-ties** **1** : intellectual depth **2** : something profound or obscure

pro·fuse \prə-ˈfyüs\ *adj* **1** : pouring forth liberally ⟨*profuse* in their thanks⟩ **2** : exhibiting great abundance — **pro·fuse·ly** *adv* — **pro·fuse·ness** *n*

pro·fu·sion \prə-ˈfyü-zhən\ *n* **1** : profuse or lavish expenditure **2** : ABUNDANCE, PLENTY ⟨a *profusion* of flowers⟩

prog·e·ny \ˈpräj-ə-nē\ *n, pl* **-nies** : DESCENDANTS, CHILDREN, OFFSPRING

prog·no·sis \präg-ˈnō-səs\ *n, pl* **-no·ses** \-ˈnō-ˌsēz\ **1** : the act or art of forecasting esp. the course of a disease **2** : the prospects for recovery given by prognosis

prog·nos·tic \präg-ˈnäs-tik\ *n* **1** : something that foretells : OMEN **2** : PROGNOSTICATION, PROPHECY — **prognostic** *adj*

prog·nos·ti·cate \präg-ˈnäs-tə-ˌkāt\ *vb* : to foretell from signs or symptoms : PREDICT, PROPHESY — **prog·nos·ti·ca·tor** \-ˌkāt-ər\ *n*

prog·nos·ti·ca·tion \(ˌ)präg-ˌnäs-tə-ˈkā-shən\ *n* **1** : an indication in advance : SIGN **2** : FORECAST

[1]**pro·gram** \ˈprō-ˌgram, -grəm\ *n* **1** : a brief statement or written outline of something (as a concert or play) **2** : PERFORMANCE ⟨a television *program*⟩ **3** : a plan of action **4** : a sequence of coded instructions for a computer

[2]**program** *vb* **pro·grammed** *or* **pro·gramed** \-ˌgramd, -grəmd\; **pro·gram·ming** *or* **pro·gram·ing** **1** : to arrange or furnish a program of or for : SCHEDULE **2** : to provide with a program ⟨*program* a computer⟩ — **pro·gram·mer** *n*

programmed instruction *n* : instruction through information given in small steps with each requiring a correct response by the learner before going on to the next step

program music *n* : music that is inspired by or that describes something other than a musical idea or thing

[1]**prog·ress** \'präg-rəs, -ˌres, *chiefly Brit* 'prō-ˌgres\ *n* **1** : a royal or official journey or tour **2** : a forward movement : ADVANCE ⟨the *progress* of a ship⟩ **3** : progressive growth or advancement ⟨the *progress* of science⟩

[2]**pro·gress** \prə-'gres\ *vb* **1** : to move forward : PROCEED **2** : to develop to a higher, better, or more advanced stage

pro·gres·sion \prə-'gresh-ən\ *n* **1** : the action of progressing or moving forward ⟨a snail's manner of *progression*⟩ **2** : a continuous and connected series ⟨the *progression* of scenes in a play⟩ **3** : a sequence of numbers in which each term is related to its predecessor by a uniform law **4** : succession of musical chords — **pro·gres·sion·al** \-'gresh-(ə-)nəl\ *adj*

[1]**pro·gres·sive** \prə-'gres-iv\ *adj* **1 a** : of, relating to, or characterized by progress or progression **b** : gradually increasing : GRADUATED ⟨*progressive* income tax⟩ **2 a** : moving forward or onward : ADVANCING ⟨the *progressive* movements of the hands of a clock⟩ **b** : increasing in extent or severity ⟨a *progressive* disease⟩ **3 a** : favoring or striving for progress (as in politics or education) **b** : ADVANCED, MODERN ⟨*progressive* education⟩ **4** : of, relating to, or being a verb form that expresses action or state in progress at the time of speaking or a time spoken of — **pro·gres·sive·ly** *adv* — **pro·gres·sive·ness** *n*

[2]**progressive** *n* : a progressive person; *esp* : one believing in moderate political change and social improvement by governmental action

pro·hib·it \prō-'hib-ət\ *vb* **1** : to forbid by authority ⟨*prohibit* all-day parking⟩ **2 a** : to prevent from doing something **b** : to make impossible ⟨the high walls *prohibit* escape⟩

pro·hi·bi·tion \ˌprō-ə-'bish-ən\ *n* **1** : the act of prohibiting **2** : an order forbidding something **3** : the forbidding by law of the sale and sometimes the manufacture of alcoholic beverages

pro·hi·bi·tion·ist \-'bish-(ə-)nəst\ *n* : a person who is in favor of prohibiting the manufacture and sale of alcoholic beverages

pro·hib·i·tive \prō-'hib-ət-iv\ *adj* : serving or tending to prohibit ⟨*prohibitive* prices⟩

[1]**proj·ect** \'präj-ˌekt, -ikt\ *n* **1** : PLAN, SCHEME, PROPOSAL **2** : a planned undertaking **3** : a group of houses or apartment buildings constructed and arranged according to a single plan; *esp* : one built with government help to provide low-cost housing

[2]**pro·ject** \prə-'jekt\ *vb* **1** : to devise in the mind : DESIGN ⟨*project* civic improvements⟩ **2** : to throw or cast forward **3** : to stick out or cause to protrude ⟨a stone jetty *projecting* into the bay⟩ **4** : to cause to spread in space or fall upon a surface ⟨*project* a beam of light⟩ ⟨*project* motion pictures on a screen⟩

pro·jec·tile \prə-'jek-təl\ *n* **1** : a body projected by external force and continuing in motion by its own inertia; *esp* : a missile for a weapon **2** : a self-propelling weapon (as a guided missile)

pro·jec·tion \prə-'jek-shən\ *n* **1 a** : a method of representing a curved surface (as the earth) on a flat one (as a map) **b** : the process of projecting an object or design on a surface **c** : the picture or design so formed **2** : the act of throwing or shooting forward : EJECTION **3** : the forming of a plan : SCHEMING **4 a** : a jutting out **b** : a part that juts out **5** : a prediction based on a current trend

pro·jec·tion·ist \-sh(ə-)nəst\ *n* : a person who operates a motion-picture projector or television equipment

pro·jec·tor \prə-'jek-tər\ *n* **1** : one that plans a project; *esp* : PROMOTOR **2** : an optical instrument or machine for projecting an image or pictures upon a surface

pro·leg \'prō-ˌleg\ *n* : a fleshy leg on an abdominal segment of some insect larvae

[1]**pro·le·tar·i·an** \ˌprō-lə-'ter-ē-ən\ *n* : a member of the proletariat

[2]**proletarian** *adj* : of or relating to the proletariat

pro·le·tar·i·at \ˌprō-lə-'ter-ē-ət, -'tar-\ *n, pl* **proletariat** **1** : the lowest social or economic class of a community **2** : industrial workers who sell their labor to live

pro·lif·er·ate \prə-'lif-ə-ˌrāt\ *vb* : to grow or increase rapidly — **pro·lif·er·a·tion** \-ˌlif-ə-'rā-shən\ *n*

pro·lif·ic \prə-'lif-ik\ *adj* **1** : producing young or fruit abundantly ⟨a *prolific* orchard⟩ **2** : highly inventive : PRODUCTIVE ⟨a *prolific* mind⟩ **3** : causing fruitfulness : characterized by fruitfulness ⟨a *prolific* growing season⟩ ***syn*** see FERTILE ***ant*** barren, unfruitful — **pro·lif·i·cal·ly** \-'lif-i-k(ə-)lē\ *adv*

pro·lix \prō-'liks, 'prō-(ˌ)liks\ *adj* : continued or drawn out too long (as by too many words) — **pro·lix·i·ty** \prō-'lik-sət-ē\ *n*

pro·logue \'prō-ˌlȯg\ *n* **1** : the preface or introduction to a literary or dramatic work **2** : the actor speaking a prologue **3** : an introductory or preceding act or event

pro·long \prə-'lȯng\ *vb* : to make longer than usual : continue or lengthen in time, extent, or range ⟨a *prolonged* whistle of a train⟩ ⟨*prolong* a boundary line⟩

pro·lon·ga·tion \(ˌ)prō-ˌlȯng-'gā-shən\ *n* **1** : a lengthening in space or time **2** : something that prolongs or is prolonged

prom \'präm\ *n* [short for *promenade*] : an often formal dance given by a high school or college class

[1]**prom·e·nade** \ˌpräm-ə-'nād, -'näd\ *n* **1** : a leisurely walk or ride esp. in a public place for pleasure or display **2** : a place for strolling **3** : a ceremonious march opening a formal ball

[2]**promenade** *vb* **1** : to take or go on a promenade **2** : to walk about in or on ⟨*promenading* the sun deck⟩

pro·me·thi·um \prə-'mē-thē-əm\ *n* : a metallic element obtained as a fission product of uranium or from neutron-irradiated neodymium — see ELEMENT table

prom·i·nence \'präm-ə-nən(t)s\ *n* **1** : the quality, state, or fact of being prominent : DISTINCTION ⟨a person of *prominence*⟩ **2** : something (as a mountain) that is prominent **3** : a mass of gas resembling a cloud that arises from the chromosphere of the sun

prom·i·nent \-nənt\ *adj* **1** : standing out or projecting beyond a surface or line **2** : readily noticeable **3** : NOTABLE, EMINENT — **prom·i·nent·ly** *adv*

syn PROMINENT, CONSPICUOUS, OUTSTANDING can mean compelling notice or attention. PROMINENT may apply to an object that stands out from its surroundings or to a person with qualities that mark him as superior; CONSPICUOUS applies chiefly to what is so obvious or striking that the eye or mind cannot miss it ⟨*conspicuous* bravery⟩ ⟨*conspicuous* clothes⟩; OUTSTANDING implies superiority (as in performance) over others of the same kind

prom·is·cu·i·ty \ˌpräm-əs-'kyü-ət-ē, (ˌ)prō-ˌmis-\ *n, pl* **-ties** **1** : a miscellaneous mixture of persons or things **2** : promiscuous sexual behavior

P

pro·mis·cu·ous \prə-'mis-kyə-wəs\ *adj* **1** : composed of all sorts of persons and things **2** : not restricted to one person or class ⟨give *promiscuous* praise⟩; *esp* : not restricted to one sexual partner **3** : HAPHAZARD, IRREGULAR ⟨*promiscuous* eating habits⟩ — **pro·mis·cu·ous·ly** *adv* — **pro·mis·cu·ous·ness** *n*

[1]**prom·ise** \'präm-əs\ *n* **1** : a statement assuring someone that the person making the statement will do or not do something : PLEDGE ⟨a *promise* to pay⟩ **2** : something promised **3** : a ground for hope or expectation ⟨give *promise* of success⟩ ⟨the boy shows *promise*⟩

[2]**promise** *vb* **1 a** : to engage to do, bring about, or provide ⟨*promise* aid⟩ ⟨*promise* to pay⟩ **b** : to tell as a promise ⟨*promised* her he'd be on time⟩ **c** : to make a promise **2** : to suggest beforehand : FORETOKEN ⟨dark clouds *promising* rain⟩ — **prom·is·er** \'präm-ə-sər\ *or* **prom·i·sor** \ˌpräm-ə-'sȯ(ə)r\ *n*

promised land *n* [from the land of Canaan promised to Abraham and his descendants (Genesis 17:8; Exodus 3:8)] : a better place or state that one hopes to reach

prom·is·ing \'präm-ə-sing\ *adj* : giving hope or assurance (as of success) ⟨a *promising* pupil⟩ — **prom·is·ing·ly** \-sing-lē\ *adv*

prom·is·so·ry \'präm-ə-ˌsōr-ē, -ˌsȯr-\ *adj* : containing a promise esp. to pay ⟨a *promissory* note⟩

prom·on·to·ry \'präm-ən-ˌtōr-ē, -ˌtȯr-\ *n, pl* **-ries** : a high point of land or rock jutting out into a body of water : HEADLAND

pro·mote \prə-'mōt\ *vb* **1** : to advance in position, rank, or honor : ELEVATE ⟨*promote* pupils to a higher grade⟩ **2** : to contribute to the growth, success, or development of : FURTHER ⟨good food *promotes* health⟩ **3** : to take the first steps in organizing (as a business)

pro·mot·er \prə-'mōt-ər\ *n* : one that promotes; *esp* : one who finances a sporting event

pro·mo·tion \prə-'mō-shən\ *n* **1** : advancement in position or rank **2** : the act of furthering the growth or development of something — **pro·mo·tion·al** \-sh(ə-)nəl\ *adj*

[1]**prompt** \'präm(p)t\ *vb* **1** : to move to action : CAUSE ⟨curiosity *prompted* him to ask the question⟩ **2** : to remind of something forgotten or poorly learned (as by suggesting the next few words in a speech) ⟨*prompt* an actor⟩ **3** : SUGGEST, INSPIRE ⟨pride *prompted* the act⟩

[2]**prompt** *adj* **1 a** : being ready and quick as occasion demands ⟨*prompt* to answer⟩ **b** : PUNCTUAL ⟨*prompt* in arriving⟩ **2** : performed readily or immediately ⟨*prompt* assitance⟩ — **prompt·ly** *adv* — **prompt·ness** *n*

prompt·er \'präm(p)-tər\ *n* : a person who reminds another of the words to be spoken next (as in a play)

promp·ti·tude \'präm(p)-tə-ˌt(y)üd\ *n* : the quality or habit of being prompt : PROMPTNESS

prom·ul·gate \'präm-əl-ˌgāt; prō-'məl-, 'prō-(ˌ)\ *vb* : to declare openly or officially : PROCLAIM ⟨*promulgate* a new law⟩ — **prom·ul·ga·tion** \ˌpräm-əl-'gā-shən, ˌprō-(ˌ)məl-\ *n*

pron *abbr* **1** pronoun **2** pronunciation

prone \'prōn\ *adj* **1** : having a tendency or inclination : DISPOSED ⟨*prone* to laziness⟩ **2 a** : lying face downward ⟨shoot from a *prone* position⟩ **b** : not erect : lying flat or prostrate ⟨the wind blew the trees *prone*⟩ — **prone·ness** \'prōn-nəs\ *n*

prong \'prȯng, 'präng\ *n* **1** : a tine of a fork **2** : a slender pointed or projecting part (as of an antler) — **pronged** \'prȯngd, 'prängd\ *adj*

prong·horn \'prȯng-ˌhȯrn, 'präng-\ *n, pl* **pronghorn** *also* **pronghorns** : a cud-chewing mammal of treeless parts of western No. America resembling an antelope

pronghorn (about 3 ft. at shoulder)

pro·nom·i·nal \prō-'näm-ən-əl\ *adj* **1** : of, relating to, or being a pronoun **2** : resembling a pronoun in identifying or specifying without describing ⟨the *pronominal* adjective *this* in "this dog"⟩ — **pro·nom·i·nal·ly** \-ə-lē\ *adv*

pro·noun \'prō-ˌnau̇n\ *n* : a word that is used as a substitute for a noun and refers to persons or things named, asked for, or understood in the context

pro·nounce \prə-'nau̇n(t)s\ *vb* **1** : to declare officially or solemnly ⟨the minister *pronounced* them man and wife⟩ ⟨the judge *pronounced* sentence⟩ **2** : to assert as an opinion ⟨*pronounce* the book a success⟩ **3** : to utter the sounds of : speak aloud ⟨practice *pronouncing* foreign words⟩; *esp* : to say or speak correctly ⟨she can't *pronounce* his name⟩ — **pro·nounc·er** *n*

pro·nounced \-'nau̇n(t)st\ *adj* : strongly marked : DECIDED ⟨a *pronounced* change for the better⟩ — **pro·nounc·ed·ly** \-'nau̇n(t)-səd-lē\ *adv*

pro·nounce·ment \prə-'nau̇n(t)s-mənt\ *n* : a usu. formal declaration or announcement

pro·nun·ci·a·tion \prə-ˌnən(t)-sē-'ā-shən\ *n* : the act or manner of pronouncing something

[1]**proof** \'prüf\ *n* **1 a** : evidence of truth or correctness ⟨gave *proof* of his statement⟩ **b** : a test to find out or show the facts or truth ⟨put his theory to the *proof*⟩ **2 a** : an impression (as from type) taken for correction or examination **b** : a test photographic print made from a negative **3** : alcoholic content (as of a beverage) indicated by a number that is about twice the percent by volume of alcohol present ⟨whiskey of 90 *proof* is about 45% alcohol⟩

[2]**proof** *adj* : designed for or successful in repelling, resisting, or withstanding ⟨*proof* against tampering⟩ — usu. used in combination ⟨shock*proof*⟩ ⟨water*proof*⟩

proof·read \'prüf-ˌrēd\ *vb* : to read and make corrections (as in printer's proof) ⟨*proofread* a composition⟩ — **proof·read·er** *n*

[1]**prop** \'präp\ *n* : something that props : SUPPORT

[2]**prop** *vb* **propped**; **prop·ping** **1 a** : to hold up or keep from falling or slipping by placing something under or against ⟨*prop* up a broken chair⟩ **b** : to support by placing against something ⟨*propped* his rake against the tree⟩ **2** : SUSTAIN, STRENGTHEN ⟨*propped* up by his faith in times of crisis⟩

[3]**prop** *n* : PROPERTY 5

[4]**prop** *n* : PROPELLER

prop *abbr* **1** property **2** proprietor

prop·a·gan·da \ˌpräp-ə-'gan-də, ˌprō-pə-\ *n* : the spreading of ideas, information, or rumor to help or injure a cause or the ideas, facts, or allegations so spread — **prop·a·gan·dist** \-dəst\ *n* — **prop·a·gan·dis·tic** \-ˌgan-ˈdis-tik\ *adj*

prop·a·gan·dize \-ˈgan-ˌdīz\ *vb* **1** : to spread propaganda **2** : to influence or attempt to influence by propaganda

prop·a·gate \ˈpräp-ə-ˌgāt\ *vb* **1** : to reproduce or increase by sexual or asexual means : MULTIPLY ⟨*propagate* an apple by grafting⟩ **2** : to cause to affect a greater number or greater area — **prop·a·ga·tion** \ˌpräp-ə-ˈgā-shən\ *n*

pro·pane \ˈprō-ˌpān\ *n* : a heavy flammable gaseous hydrocarbon found in crude petroleum and natural gas and used esp. as fuel and in the chemical industry

pro·pel \prə-ˈpel\ *vb* **pro·pelled**; **pro·pel·ling** **1** : to push or drive usu. forward or onward ⟨a bicycle is *propelled* by pedals⟩ **2** : to urge ahead : IMPEL ⟨a man *propelled* by ambition⟩

[1]**pro·pel·lant** *or* **pro·pel·lent** \-ˈpel-ənt\ *adj* : capable of or used for propelling

[2]**propellant** *also* **propellent** *n* : something that propels: as **a** : an explosive for propelling projectiles **b** : fuel plus an oxidizing agent used by a rocket engine

pro·pel·ler \prə-ˈpel-ər\ *n* : one that propels; *esp* : a device consisting of a hub with twisted radiating blades that can be revolved by a motor or engine and is used esp. for propelling airplanes and ships

pro·pen·si·ty \prə-ˈpen(t)-sət-ē\ *n, pl* **-ties** : a natural talent or liking : BENT ⟨a *propensity* for drawing⟩

prop·er \ˈpräp-ər\ *adj* **1** : SUITABLE, RIGHT, FIT **2** : appointed for the liturgy of a particular day **3** : belonging characteristically to a group or individual : PECULIAR ⟨diseases *proper* to the tropics⟩ **4** : limited to a specified thing, place, or idea ⟨outside the city *proper*⟩ **5** : strictly accurate : CORRECT **6** : strictly following social rules : GENTEEL

proper adjective *n* : an adjective formed from a proper noun

proper fraction *n* : a fraction in which the numerator is less or of lower degree than the denominator

prop·er·ly \ˈpräp-ər-lē\ *adv* **1** : in a suitable or fit manner ⟨behave *properly* in church⟩ **2** : in accordance with fact : CORRECTLY ⟨*properly* labeled goods⟩ ⟨*properly* speaking, whales are not fish⟩

proper noun *n* : a noun that designates a particular being, place, or thing and does not take a limiting modifier — called also *proper name*

prop·er·tied \ˈpräp-ərt-ēd\ *adj* : owning property and esp. much property

prop·er·ty \ˈpräp-ərt-ē\ *n, pl* **-ties** **1** : a special quality or characteristic of something ⟨the associative *property* of addition⟩ : a quality or attribute common to all things called by the same name ⟨sweetness is a *property* of sugar⟩ **2** : something (as land, goods, or money) that is owned **3** : a piece of real estate with or without a structure on it ⟨a business *property*⟩ **4** : OWNERSHIP **5** : an article to be used in a play or motion picture other than scenery or costumes — **prop·er·ty·less** \-ē-ləs\ *adj*

pro·phase \ˈprō-ˌfāz\ *n* : the first stage of mitosis or meiosis in which chromosomes become visible as threads

proph·e·cy \ˈpräf-ə-sē\ *n, pl* **-cies** **1** : the work or revelation of a prophet **2** : the foretelling of the future ⟨the gift of *prophecy*⟩ **3** : something foretold : PREDICTION

proph·e·sy \ˈpräf-ə-ˌsī\ *vb* **-sied**; **-sy·ing** **1 a** : to speak or write as a prophet **b** : to utter by divine inspiration **2** : FORETELL, PREDICT ⟨*prophesy* bad weather⟩ — **proph·e·si·er** \-ˌsī(-ə)r\ *n*

proph·et \ˈpräf-ət\ *n* **1** : a person who declares publicly a message that he believes has been divinely inspired **2** : one who foretells future events **3** : an effective spokesman ⟨a *prophet* of the revolution⟩ — **proph·et·ess** \-ət-əs\ *n*

pro·phet·ic \prə-ˈfet-ik\ *adj* **1** : of, relating to, or characteristic of a prophet or prophecy ⟨*prophetic* insight⟩ **2** : foretelling events : PREDICTIVE ⟨a *prophetic* statement⟩ — **pro·phet·i·cal** \-ˈfet-i-kəl\ *adj* — **pro·phet·i·cal·ly** \-i-k(ə-)lē\ *adv*

Proph·ets \ˈpräf-əts\ *n pl* : the second part of the Jewish scriptures — compare HAGIOGRAPHA, LAW

pro·pi·ti·ate \prō-ˈpish-ē-ˌāt\ *vb* : to gain or regain the favor or goodwill of : CONCILIATE — **pro·pi·ti·a·tion** \-ˌpish-ē-ˈā-shən\ *n* — **pro·pi·ti·a·tor** \-ˈpish-ē-ˌāt-ər\ *n* — **pro·pi·tia·to·ry** \-ˈpish-(ē-)ə-ˌtōr-ē, -ˌtȯr-\ *adj*

pro·pi·tious \prə-ˈpish-əs\ *adj* **1** : favorably disposed ⟨the fates are *propitious*⟩ **2** : of good omen : PROMISING ⟨*propitious* signs⟩ **3** : likely to produce good results : OPPORTUNE ⟨the *propitious* moment for asking a favor⟩ — **pro·pi·tious·ness** *n*

pro·po·nent \prə-ˈpō-nənt\ *n* : one who argues in favor of something : ADVOCATE

[1]**pro·por·tion** \prə-ˈpōr-shən, -ˈpȯr-\ *n* **1** : the size, number, or amount of one thing or group as compared to the size, number, or amount of another ⟨the *proportion* of boys to girls in our class is three to one⟩ **2** *pl* : the length and width or length, breadth, and height : DIMENSIONS ⟨the *proportions* of this room are good⟩ **3** : a balanced or pleasing arrangement ⟨out of *proportion*⟩ **4** : fair or just share ⟨each did his *proportion* of the work⟩ **5** : a statement of the equality of two ratios (as $4/2 = 10/5$)

[2]**proportion** *vb* **-tioned**; **-tion·ing** \-sh(ə-)niŋ\ **1** : to adjust a part or thing in size relative to other parts or things **2** : to make the parts of harmonious or symmetrical

pro·por·tion·al \prə-ˈpōr-sh(ə-)nəl, -ˈpȯr-\ *adj* **1 a** : PROPORTIONATE ⟨wages *proportional* to ability⟩ **b** : having the same or a constant ratio **2** : determined with reference to proportions ⟨*proportional* representation in a legislature⟩ — **pro·por·tion·al·i·ty** \-ˌpōr-shə-ˈnal-ət-ē, -ˌpȯr-\ *n* — **pro·por·tion·al·ly** \-ˈpōr-sh(ə-)nə-lē, -ˈpȯr-\ *adv*

pro·por·tion·ate \prə-ˈpōr-sh(ə-)nət, -ˈpȯr-\ *adj* : being in proportion — **pro·por·tion·ate·ly** *adv*

pro·pos·al \prə-ˈpō-zəl\ *n* **1** : an act of putting forward something for consideration **2 a** : something proposed : SUGGESTION **b** : OFFER; *esp* : an offer of marriage

pro·pose \prə-ˈpōz\ *vb* **1** : to offer for consideration or discussion : SUGGEST ⟨*propose* terms of peace⟩ **2** : to make plans : INTEND ⟨*propose* to buy a new house⟩ **3** : to offer as a toast : suggest drinking to ⟨*propose* a toast⟩ **4** : NAME, NOMINATE ⟨*proposed* him for membership⟩ **5** : to make an offer of marriage — **pro·pos·er** *n*

prop·o·si·tion \ˌpräp-ə-ˈzish-ən\ *n* **1** : something offered for consideration or acceptance : PROPOSAL **2** : a statement to be proved or explained **3** : a project for action : UNDERTAKING

pro·pound \prə-ˈpau̇nd\ *vb* : to offer for consideration : PROPOSE — **pro·pound·er** *n*

[1]**pro·pri·e·tary** \prə-ˈprī-ə-ˌter-ē\ *n, pl* **-tar·ies** **1** : one to whom a proprietary colony is granted **2** : a body of proprietors **3** : PATENT MEDICINE

[2]**proprietary** *adj* **1** : of, relating to, or characteristic of a proprietor ⟨*proprietary* rights⟩ **2** : made and marketed by one having the exclusive right to manufacture and sell **3** : privately owned and managed ⟨a *proprietary* clinic⟩

proprietary colony *n* : a colony granted to a proprietary with full powers of government
pro·pri·e·tor \prə-'prī-ət-ər\ *n* **1** : a possessor of property : OWNER **2** : PROPRIETARY 1 — **pro·pri·e·tor·ship** \-ˌship\ *n* — **pro·pri·e·tress** \-'prī-ə-trəs\ *n*
pro·pri·e·ty \prə-'prī-ət-ē\ *n, pl* **-ties 1** : the quality or state of being proper **2** : correctness in manners or behavior : POLITENESS **3** *pl* : the rules and customs of polite society
prop root *n* : a root that braces or supports a plant
pro·pul·sion \prə-'pəl-shən\ *n* **1** : the action or process of propelling **2** : something that propels — **pro·pul·sive** \-'pəl-siv\ *adj*
pro ra·ta \(')prō-'rāt-ə, -'rät-ə\ *adv* : according to share : PROPORTIONATELY — **pro rata** *adj*
pro·rate \(')prō-'rāt\ *vb* : to divide or distribute proportionately — **pro·ra·tion** \prō-'rā-shən\ *n*
pros *pl of* PRO
pro·sa·ic \prō-'zā-ik\ *adj* **1 a** : characteristic of prose as distinguished from poetry : FACTUAL **b** : DULL, UNIMAGINATIVE **2** : belonging to the everyday world : COMMONPLACE — **pro·sa·i·cal·ly** \-'zā-ə-k(ə-)lē\ *adv*
pro·scribe \prō-'skrīb\ *vb* **1** : to put outside the protection of the law : OUTLAW **2** : to condemn or forbid as harmful : PROHIBIT — **pro·scrip·tion** \-'skrip-shən\ *n* — **pro·scrip·tive** \-'skrip-tiv\ *adj*
prose \'prōz\ *n* [from Latin *prosa*, from feminine of *prorsus*, *prosus* "going straight ahead", contraction of *proversus* "turned forward"; so called in contrast to *versus* "verse" (literally "turning"), which turns back to repeat a metrical pattern] **1 a** : the ordinary language of men in speaking or writing **b** : a literary medium distinguished from poetry by its closer correspondence to the patterns of everyday speech **2** : a prosaic style, quality, character, or state — **prose** *adj*
pros·e·cute \'präs-i-ˌkyüt\ *vb* **1** : to follow up to the end : keep at ⟨*prosecute* a war⟩ **2** : to carry on a legal action against an accused person to prove his guilt — **pros·e·cut·a·ble** \-ˌkyüt-ə-bəl\ *adj*
prosecuting attorney *n* : DISTRICT ATTORNEY
pros·e·cu·tion \ˌpräs-i-'kyü-shən\ *n* **1** : the act or process of prosecuting; *esp* : the institution and carrying on of a criminal suit in court **2** : the party by whom criminal proceedings are prosecuted
pros·e·cu·tor \'präs-i-ˌkyüt-ər\ *n* : a person who institutes a criminal prosecution; *esp* : DISTRICT ATTORNEY
¹**pros·e·lyte** \'präs-ə-ˌlīt\ *n* : a new convert : NEOPHYTE
²**proselyte** *vb* **1** : to convert to a religion, belief, or party **2** : to recruit members
pros·e·ly·tize \'präs-ə-lə-ˌtīz\ *vb* : PROSELYTE
pro·sim·i·an \(')prō-'sim-ē-ən\ *n* : a lower primate (as a lemur) — **prosimian** *adj*
pros·o·dy \'präs-əd-ē\ *n, pl* **-dies 1** : the study of versification **2** : a particular system, theory, or style of versification
¹**pros·pect** \'präs-ˌpekt\ *n* **1** : a wide view **2** : the act of looking forward : ANTICIPATION **3** : something awaited or expected : POSSIBILITY **4 a** : a potential buyer **b** : a candidate or a person likely to become a candidate ⟨a presidential *prospect*⟩

ə abut   ər further   a back   ā bake
ä cot, cart   aù out   ch chin   e less   ē easy
g gift   i trip   ī life   j joke   ng sing   ō flow
ò flaw   òi coin   th thin   th this   ü loot
ù foot   y yet   yü few   yù furious   zh vision

²**prospect** *vb* : to explore an area esp. for mineral deposits — **pros·pec·tor** \-ˌpek-tər\ *n*
pro·spec·tive \prə-'spek-tiv, 'präs-ˌpek-\ *adj* **1** : likely to come about : EXPECTED ⟨the *prospective* benefits of a law⟩ **2** : likely to be or become ⟨a *prospective* bride⟩ — **pro·spec·tive·ly** *adv*
pro·spec·tus \prə-'spek-təs, prä-\ *n, pl* **pro·spec·tus·es** : a printed statement describing an enterprise and distributed to prospective investors
pros·per \'präs-pər\ *vb* **pros·pered**; **pros·per·ing** \-p(ə-)riŋ\ **1** : SUCCEED; *esp* : to succeed financially **2** : FLOURISH, THRIVE **3** : to cause to prosper
pros·per·i·ty \prä-'sper-ət-ē\ *n* : the state of being prosperous; *esp* : economic well-being
pros·per·ous \'präs-p(ə-)rəs\ *adj* **1** : marked by success or economic well-being **2** : FLOURISHING — **pros·per·ous·ly** *adv* — **pros·per·ous·ness** *n*
pros·tate \'präs-ˌtāt\ *also* **pros·tat·ic** \prä-'stat-ik\ *adj* : of or relating to or being the prostate gland
prostate gland *n* : a partly muscular partly glandular body about the base of the male urethra in mammals
¹**pros·ti·tute** \'präs-tə-ˌt(y)üt\ *vb* : to devote to corrupt or unworthy purposes : DEBASE ⟨*prostitute* one's talent⟩
²**prostitute** *n* : a woman who engages in sexual intercourse for money
pros·ti·tu·tion \ˌpräs-tə-'t(y)ü-shən\ *n* **1** : the acts or practices of a prostitute **2** : the state of being prostituted : DEBASEMENT
¹**pros·trate** \'präs-ˌtrāt\ *adj* **1 a** : lying face down (as in adoration or submission) **b** : lying flat and stretched out **2** : lacking in vitality or will : OVERCOME
²**prostrate** *vb* **1** : to throw or put into a prostrate position **2** : to make helpless or exhausted : OVERCOME
pros·tra·tion \prä-'strā-shən\ *n* **1** : the act of assuming or state of being in a prostrate position **2** : complete physical or mental exhaustion : COLLAPSE
prosy \'prō-zē\ *adj* **pros·i·er**; **-est 1** : PROSAIC **2** : TEDIOUS
Prot *abbr* Protestant
prot·ac·tin·i·um \ˌprōt-ˌak-'tin-ē-əm\ *n* : a shiny metallic radioactive element of relatively short life — see ELEMENT table
pro·tag·o·nist \prō-'tag-ə-nəst\ *n* : the leading character in a drama, novel, or story
pro·te·an \'prōt-ē-ən\ *adj* [from *Proteus*, a sea god of Greek mythology who could change his shape at will] : easily taking different shapes or roles ⟨the *protean* amoeba⟩
pro·tect \prə-'tekt\ *vb* : to cover or defend from injury or destruction : GUARD
pro·tec·tion \prə-'tek-shən\ *n* **1 a** : the act of protecting ⟨under his *protection*⟩ **b** : the state of being protected **2** : a person or thing that protects **3** : the freeing of the producers of a country from foreign competition by high duties on foreign goods — **pro·tec·tive** \-'tek-tiv\ *adj* — **pro·tec·tive·ly** *adv*
protective coloration *n* : coloration by which an organism appears less visible or less attractive to predators
pro·tec·tor \prə-'tek-tər\ *n* **1 a** : one that protects : GUARDIAN **b** : a device used to prevent injury : GUARD **2** : one having the care of a commonwealth or of a kingdom during the king's minority : REGENT
pro·tec·tor·ate \prə-'tek-t(ə-)rət\ *n* **1 a** : government by a protector **b** : the rank, office, or period of rule of a protector **2 a** : the relationship of authority assumed by one state over another **b** : the dependent state in a protectorate

pro·té·gé \'prōt-ə-ˌzhā\ *n* [from French, from past participle of *protéger* "to protect"] : a person under the care and protection of another

pro·tein \'prō-ˌtēn, 'prōt-ē-ən\ *n* : any of numerous naturally occurring substances that consist of chains of amino acids and are essential constituents of all living cells — **pro·tein·a·ceous** \ˌprō-ˌtē-'nā-shəs, ˌprōt-ē-ə-'nā-\ *adj*

pro tem·po·re \prō-'tem-pə-rē\ *adv* : for the present : TEMPORARILY ⟨chairman *pro tempore*⟩

Prot·ero·zo·ic \ˌprät-ə-rə-'zō-ik, ˌprōt-\ *n* : the 2d of the five eras of geologic history that perhaps exceeds in length all of subsequent geological time and is marked by rocks which contain a few fossils indicating the existence of annelid worms and algae; *also* : the corresponding system of rocks — see GEOLOGIC TIME table — **Proterozoic** *adj*

[1]**pro·test** \'prō-ˌtest\ *n* : a complaint, objection, or display of unwillingness or disapproval

[2]**pro·test** \prə-'test\ *vb* **1** : to declare solemnly : ASSERT ⟨*protested* his innocence⟩ **2 a** : to make a protest against ⟨*protested* the higher tax rate⟩ **b** : to object strongly ⟨*protest* against a ruling⟩

prot·es·tant \'prät-əs-tənt, *2 is also* prə-'tes-\ *n* **1** *cap* : a member of one of the Christian churches that separated from the Roman Catholic church in the 16th century or of a church deriving from them **2** : one who protests — **protestant** *adj, often cap* — **Prot·es·tant·ism** \'prät-əs-tənt-ˌiz-əm\ *n*

prot·es·ta·tion \ˌprät-əs-'tā-shən, ˌprō-ˌtes-\ *n* **1** : the act of protesting **2** : a solemn declaration

pro·tho·rax \(')prō-'thōr-ˌaks, -'thȯr-\ *n* : the first segment of the thorax of an insect — **pro·tho·rac·ic** \ˌprō-thə-'ras-ik\ *adj*

pro·tist \'prōt-əst\ *n* : any of a group or in some classifications a kingdom of one-celled or noncellular organisms comprising bacteria, protozoans, various algae and fungi, and sometimes viruses — **pro·tis·tan** \prō-'tis-tən\ *adj or n*

pro·to·coc·cus \ˌprōt-ə-'käk-əs\ *n* : any of a genus of globe-shaped and mostly terrestrial green algae

pro·to·col \'prōt-ə-ˌkȯl\ *n* **1** : an original copy or record of a document or transaction **2** : a code of diplomatic or military etiquette

pro·ton \'prō-ˌtän\ *n* : an elementary particle identical with the nucleus of the hydrogen atom that along with neutrons is a constituent of all other atomic nuclei and carries a positive charge numerically equal to the negative charge of an electron — **pro·ton·ic** \prō-'tän-ik\ *adj*

pro·to·plan·et \ˌprōt-ō-'plan-ət\ *n* : a whirling mass of gas rotating about a sun that according to one theory is the source of a planet

pro·to·plasm \'prōt-ə-ˌplaz-əm\ *n* : a complex of protein, various organic and inorganic substances, and water that makes up the living nucleus, cytoplasm, plastids, and mitochondria of the cell and is considered the physical basis of life — **pro·to·plas·mic** \ˌprōt-ə-'plaz-mik\ *adj*

pro·to·plast \'prōt-ə-ˌplast\ *n* : the nucleus, cytoplasm, and plasma membrane of a cell considered as a living unit

pro·to·type \'prōt-ə-ˌtīp\ *n* **1** : an original model on which something is patterned **2** : an individual that exhibits the essential features of a later individual or group

pro·to·zo·an \ˌprōt-ə-'zō-ən\ *n* [from Greek *prōtos* "first" and *zōion* "animal", the source of English *zoology*] : any of a phylum or group of minute animals that are not divided into cells and have varied structure and physiology and often complex life cycles — **protozoan** *adj*

pro·to·zo·ol·o·gy \-zō-'äl-ə-jē\ *n* : a branch of zoology dealing with protozoans — **pro·to·zo·ol·o·gist** \-jəst\ *n*

pro·tract \prō-'trakt\ *vb* **1** : PROLONG **2** : to lay down the lines and angles of with scale and protractor : PLOT — **pro·trac·tion** \-'trak-shən\ *n*

pro·trac·tor \prō-'trak-tər\ *n* **1** : one that protracts **2** : an instrument for laying down and measuring angles that is used in drawing and plotting

pro·trude \prō-'trüd\ *vb* : to stick out or cause to stick out : PROJECT — **pro·tru·sion** \-'trü-zhən\ *n*

pro·tu·ber·ance \prō-'t(y)ü-b(ə-)rən(t)s\ *n* **1** : the quality or state of being protuberant **2** : something protuberant : BULGE

pro·tu·ber·ant \-b(ə-)rənt\ *adj* : bulging beyond the surrounding surface : PROMINENT — **pro·tu·ber·ant·ly** *adv*

proud \'prau̇d\ *adj* **1 a** : having or displaying excessive self-esteem ⟨a *proud* manner⟩ **b** : much pleased : EXULTANT ⟨*proud* parents of a hero⟩ **c** : having proper self-respect ⟨too *proud* to beg⟩ **2** : MAGNIFICENT, GLORIOUS ⟨a *proud* record⟩ **3** : VIGOROUS, SPIRITED ⟨a *proud* steed⟩ — **proud·ly** *adv*

prov *abbr* province

prove \'prüv\ *vb* **proved**; **proved** *or* **prov·en** \'prü-vən\; **prov·ing** **1** : to test by an experiment or a standard **2 a** : to show the truth or validity of by evidence or demonstration **b** : to check the correctness of (as an arithmetic problem) **3** : to show the genuineness of : VERIFY ⟨*prove* a will⟩ **4** : to turn out esp. after trial or test ⟨the new automobile engine *proved* to be impractical⟩ — **prov·a·ble** \'prü-və-bəl\ *adj*

Pro·ven·çal \ˌpräv-ən-'säl\ *n* **1** : a native or inhabitant of Provence **2** : a Romance language spoken in southeastern France — **Provençal** *adj*

prov·en·der \'präv-ən-dər\ *n* **1** : dry food for domestic animals : FEED **2** : FOOD

prov·erb \'präv-ˌərb\ *n* : a brief popular saying or maxim : ADAGE

pro·ver·bi·al \prə-'vər-bē-əl\ *adj* **1** : of, relating to, or resembling a proverb ⟨*proverbial* wisdom⟩ **2** : commonly spoken of ⟨the *proverbial* beginner's luck⟩ — **pro·ver·bi·al·ly** \-bē-ə-lē\ *adv*

Prov·erbs \'präv-ˌərbz\ *n* — see BIBLE table

pro·vide \prə-'vīd\ *vb* [from Latin *providēre*, literally "to see ahead", from *pro-* and *vidēre* "to see"] **1** : to take precautionary measures ⟨*provide* against a possible scarcity⟩ **2** : to state as a condition : STIPULATE ⟨the contract *provided* for 10 paid holidays⟩ **3** : to supply what is needed for sustenance or support ⟨*provides* for a large family⟩ **4** : SUPPLY, YIELD ⟨cows *provide* milk⟩ — **pro·vid·er** *n*

pro·vid·ed \prə-'vīd-əd\ *conj* : on condition : IF — sometimes followed by *that*

prov·i·dence \'präv-əd-ən(t)s, -ə-ˌden(t)s\ *n* **1 a** *often cap* : divine guidance or care **b** *cap* : God conceived as the power sustaining and guiding human destiny **2** : the quality or state of being provident : PRUDENCE

prov·i·dent \-əd-ənt, -ə-ˌdent\ *adj* **1** : making provision for the future : PRUDENT **2** : FRUGAL, SAVING — **prov·i·dent·ly** *adv*

prov·i·den·tial \ˌpräv-ə-'den-chəl\ *adj* **1** : of, relating to, or determined by Providence ⟨a *providential* plan⟩ **2** : FORTUNATE, TIMELY ⟨a *providential* escape⟩ — **prov·i·den·tial·ly** \-'dench-(ə-)lē\ *adv*

prov·ince \'präv-ən(t)s\ *n* **1 a** : a country or region brought under the control of the ancient Roman government **b** : a usu. large administrative division of a country **c** *pl* : all of a country except the capital or chief city **2** : the jurisdiction of an archbishop or metropolitan or of a religious provincial **3** : proper or appropriate business or scope : SPHERE ⟨a legal question outside the physician's *province*⟩

[1]**pro·vin·cial** \prə-'vin-chəl\ *n* **1** : the superior of a province of a religious order **2** : a person living in or coming from a province **3** : a provincial person

[2]**provincial** *adj* **1** : of, relating to, or coming from a province **2 a** : limited in outlook : NARROW **b** : lacking the polish of urban society : UNSOPHISTICATED **3** : of or relating to a style (as in furniture) marked by simple design and plain decoration — **pro·vin·ci·al·i·ty** \-,vin-chē-'al-ət-ē\ *n* — **pro·vin·cial·ly** \-'vinch-(ə-)lē\ *adv*

pro·vin·cial·ism \prə-'vin-chə-,liz-əm\ *n* **1** : a dialectal or local word, phrase, or idiom **2** : the quality or state of being provincial

proving ground *n* : a place for scientific testing; *esp* : an area used for testing weapons

[1]**pro·vi·sion** \prə-'vizh-ən\ *n* **1 a** : the act or process of providing ⟨*provision* of transportation for the trip⟩ **b** : a measure taken beforehand : PREPARATION ⟨make *provision* for emergencies⟩ **2** : a stock of materials or supplies; *esp* : a stock of food — usu. used in pl. **3** : STIPULATION, CONDITION ⟨a constitutional *provision*⟩

[2]**provision** *vb* **pro·vi·sioned**; **pro·vi·sion·ing** \-'vizh-(ə-)ning\ : to supply with provisions

pro·vi·sion·al \prə-'vizh-(ə-)nəl\ *adj* : serving for the time being : TEMPORARY, TENTATIVE ⟨a *provisional* government⟩ ⟨*provisional* arrangements⟩ — **pro·vi·sion·al·ly** \-ē\ *adv*

pro·vi·so \prə-'vī-zō\ *n, pl* **-sos** *or* **-soes** **1** : a sentence or clause in a legal document in which a condition is stated **2** : a conditional stipulation : PROVISION ⟨released with the *proviso* that he behave⟩

prov·o·ca·tion \,präv-ə-'kā-shən\ *n* **1** : the act of provoking : INCITEMENT **2** : something that provokes

pro·voc·a·tive \prə-'väk-ət-iv\ *adj* : serving or tending to provoke ⟨*provocative* comments⟩ — **pro·voc·a·tive·ly** *adv* — **pro·voc·a·tive·ness** *n*

pro·voke \prə-'vōk\ *vb* **1** : to arouse to action or feeling; *esp* : to excite to anger **2** : to bring about : stir up ⟨*provoke* an argument⟩

pro·vok·ing \-'vō-king\ *adj* : causing mild anger : ANNOYING ⟨a *provoking* delay⟩ — **pro·vok·ing·ly** \-king-lē\ *adv*

pro·vost \'prō-,vōst, 'präv-əst, *before "marshal" often* ,prō-vō\ *n* **1** : the chief dignitary of a collegiate or cathedral chapter **2** : a high administrative officer (as in a university)

provost marshal *n* : a military police chief

prow \'praů\ *n* **1** : the bow of a ship **2** : a projecting front part

prow·ess \'praů-əs\ *n* **1** : distinguished bravery; *esp* : military valor and skill **2** : extraordinary ability

prowl \'praůl\ *vb* **1** : to move about or wander stealthily like a wild beast seeking prey **2** : to roam over in a predatory manner ⟨*prowl* the streets⟩ — **prowl** *n* — **prowl·er** *n*

prowl car *n* : SQUAD CAR

prox·im·i·ty \präk-'sim-ət-ē\ *n* : NEARNESS

proxy \'präk-sē\ *n, pl* **prox·ies** **1** : authority held by one person to act for another (as in voting) **2 a** : a person holding authority to act for another **b** : a written paper giving a person such authority — **proxy** *adj*

prude \'prüd\ *n* : a person who is exaggeratedly or affectedly modest in speech, behavior, and dress and is oversensitive to violations of rules of behavior — **prud·ish** \'prüd-ish\ *adj* — **prud·ish·ly** *adv* — **prud·ish·ness** *n*

pru·dence \'prüd-ən(t)s\ *n* **1** : the ability to govern and discipline oneself by the use of reason **2** : skill and good judgment in the management of affairs

pru·dent \-ənt\ *adj* **1** : FORESIGHTED, WISE **2** : shrewd in the management of practical affairs **3** : DISCREET **4** : FRUGAL — **pru·dent·ly** *adv*

pru·den·tial \prü-'den-chəl\ *adj* **1** : of, relating to, or resulting from prudence **2** : using prudence — **pru·den·tial·ly** \-chə-lē\ *adv*

prud·ery \'prüd-(ə-)rē\ *n, pl* **-er·ies** **1** : the quality or state of being prudish **2** : a prudish remark or act

[1]**prune** \'prün\ *n* : a plum dried or capable of drying without fermentation

[2]**prune** *vb* **1** : to cut off the dead or unwanted parts of a woody plant ⟨*prune* the hedge⟩ **2 a** : to reduce by eliminating unnecessary or unwanted matter ⟨*prune* an essay⟩ ⟨*prune* a budget⟩ **b** : to remove as unnecessary — **prun·er** *n*

pru·ri·ent \'průr-ē-ənt\ *adj* : having or revealing indecent desires or thoughts : LEWD — **pru·ri·ence** \-ē-ən(t)s\ *n* — **pru·ri·ent·ly** *adv*

Prus·sian \'prəsh-ən\ *adj* : of, relating to, or characteristic of Prussia or its people — **Prussian** *n*

prus·sic acid \,prəs-ik-\ *n* : a poisonous volatile acid used in fumigating and in the chemical industry

[1]**pry** \'prī\ *vb* **pried**; **pry·ing** : to look closely : PEER; *esp* : to search inquisitively into other people's affairs — **pry·ing·ly** \-ing-lē\ *adv*

[2]**pry** *n, pl* **pries** : a person that pries

[3]**pry** *vb* **pried**; **pry·ing** **1** : to raise, move, or pull apart with a lever : PRIZE ⟨*pry* off a tight lid⟩ **2** : to extract, detach, or open with difficulty ⟨*pry* a secret out of him⟩

[4]**pry** *n* : a tool for prying

PS *abbr* **1** [for Latin *postscriptum*, literally "something written afterward"] postscript **2** public school

psalm \'säm, 'sälm\ *n* [from Greek *psalmos*, from *psallein* "to pluck a string"; so called from the harp originally used to accompany the psalms of David in the Old Testament] **1** : a sacred song or poem **2** *cap* : one of the hymns that make up the Old Testament Book of Psalms

psalm·ist \-əst\ *n* : a writer or composer of psalms

psalm·o·dy \-əd-ē\ *n, pl* **-dies** **1** : the art or practice of singing psalms in worship **2** : a collection of psalms

Psalms \'sämz, 'sälmz\ *n* — see BIBLE table

Psal·ter \'sȯl-tər\ *n* **1** : the Book of Psalms **2** : a collection of Psalms

psal·tery *also* **psal·try** \'sȯl-t(ə-)rē\ *n, pl* **-ter·ies** *also* **-tries** : an ancient stringed musical instrument resembling the zither

pseud- *or* **pseudo-** *comb form* : false : sham : spurious ⟨*pseudo*classic⟩

pseu·do \'süd-ō\ *adj* : SHAM, FEIGNED, SPURIOUS

pseu·do·nym \'süd-ə-,nim\ *n* : a fictitious name; *esp* : PEN NAME

pseu·do·pod \'süd-ə-,päd\ *n* : PSEUDOPODIUM — **pseu·dop·o·dal** \sü-'däp-əd-əl\ *adj*

pseu·do·po·di·um \,süd-ə-'pōd-ē-əm\ *n, pl* **pseu·do·po·dia** \-ē-ə\ : a part of a cell that is temporarily protruded by moving cytoplasm (as in the amoeba) and that helps to move the cell and to take in its food — **pseu·do·po·di·al** \-ē-əl\ *adj*

pshaw \ˈshȯ\ *interj* — used to express irritation, contempt, or disbelief

psi \ˈsī\ *n* : the 23d letter of the Greek alphabet — Ψ or ψ

psit·ta·co·sis \ˌsit-ə-ˈkō-səs\ *n* : an infectious disease of birds caused by a rickettsia, marked by diarrhea and wasting, and communicable to man

psych- *or* **psycho-** *comb form* : mind : mental processes and activities ⟨*psycho*analysis⟩

psych *abbr* psychology

psy·che \ˈsī-kē\ *n* **1** : SOUL, SELF **2** : MIND

[1]**psy·che·del·ic** \ˌsī-kə-ˈdel-ik\ *adj* **1 a** : of, relating to, or being a drug that radically alters the mind or mental processes usu. only temporarily ⟨LSD is a *psychedelic* drug that often causes hallucinations⟩ **b** : relating to the taking of psychedelic drugs **2 a** : imitating the effect of psychedelic drugs ⟨*psychedelic* art⟩ **b** : very bright; *esp* : FLUORESCENT ⟨*psychedelic* colors⟩

[2]**psychedelic** *n* : a psychedelic drug

psy·chi·a·try \sə-ˈkī-ə-trē, sī-\ *n* : a branch of medicine that deals with mental, emotional, or behavioral disorders — **psy·chi·at·ric** \ˌsī-kē-ˈa-trik\ *adj* — **psy·chi·a·trist** \sə-ˈkī-ə-trəst, sī-\ *n*

[1]**psy·chic** \ˈsī-kik\ *adj* **1** : of or relating to the psyche **2** : not physical; *esp* : not to be explained by knowledge of natural laws **3** : sensitive to influences or forces supposedly exerted from beyond the natural world — **psy·chi·cal** \-ki-kəl\ *adj* — **psy·chi·cal·ly** \-ki-k(ə-)lē\ *adv*

[2]**psychic** *n* : a person (as a medium) apparently sensitive to nonphysical forces

psy·cho·anal·y·sis \ˌsī-kō-ə-ˈnal-ə-səs\ *n, pl* **-y·ses** \-ˌsēz\ : a method of explaining and treating disorders that emphasizes the importance of the patient's talking freely about himself while under treatment and esp. about early childhood memories and experiences and about his dreams — **psy·cho·an·a·lyst** \-ˈan-ə-ləst\ *n* — **psy·cho·an·a·lyt·ic** \-ˌan-ə-ˈlit-ik\ *or* **psy·cho·an·a·lyt·i·cal** \-ˈlit-i-kəl\ *adj* — **psy·cho·an·a·lyt·i·cal·ly** \-i-k(ə-)lē\ *adv* — **psy·cho·an·a·lyze** \-ˈan-ə-ˌlīz\ *vb*

psychol *abbr* **1** psychologist **2** psychology

psy·cho·log·i·cal \ˌsī-kə-ˈläj-i-kəl\ *also* **psy·cho·log·ic** \-ˈläj-ik\ *adj* **1 a** : of or relating to psychology **b** : MENTAL **2** : intended to influence the will or mind ⟨*psychological* warfare⟩ — **psy·cho·log·i·cal·ly** \-i-k(ə-)lē\ *adv*

psy·chol·o·gy \sī-ˈkäl-ə-jē\ *n, pl* **-gies** [from Greek *psychē* "soul"] **1** : the science or study of mind and behavior **2** : the mental or behavioral characteristics of an individual or group — **psy·chol·o·gist** \-jəst\ *n*

psy·cho·path \ˈsī-kə-ˌpath\ *n* : a mentally ill or unstable person; *esp* : one who has a poorly balanced and antisocial personality and is unable to perceive or accept his social responsibilities and moral obligations

psy·cho·pa·thol·o·gy \ˌsī-kō-pə-ˈthäl-ə-jē\ *n* : the study of mental disorders from the point of view of psychology; *also* : a disordered psychological or behavioral state — **psy·cho·path·o·log·i·cal** \-ˌpath-ə-ˈläj-i-kəl\ *adj*

psy·cho·sis \sī-ˈkō-səs\ *n, pl* **-cho·ses** \-ˈkō-ˌsēz\ : fundamental lasting mental disorder characterized by defective or lost contact with reality — **psy·chot·ic** \-ˈkät-ik\ *adj or n*

psy·cho·ther·a·py \ˌsī-kō-ˈther-ə-pē\ *n* : treatment of mental or emotional disorder or of related bodily ills by psychological means — **psy·cho·ther·a·pist** \-pəst\ *n*

Psy·cho·zo·ic \ˌsī-kə-ˈzō-ik\ *adj* : QUATERNARY

psy·chrom·e·ter \sī-ˈkräm-ət-ər\ *n* : an instrument for measuring the water vapor in the atmosphere by means of the difference in the readings of two thermometers when one of them is kept wet so that it is cooled by evaporation

psy·chro·phil·ic \ˌsī-krō-ˈfil-ik\ *adj* : thriving at relatively low temperatures ⟨*psychrophilic* bacteria⟩ — **psy·chro·phile** \ˈsī-krō-ˌfīl\ *n*

pt *abbr* **1** part **2** pint **3** point

PT *abbr* physical training

PTA *abbr* Parent-Teacher Association

ptar·mi·gan \ˈtär-mi-gən\ *n, pl* **ptarmigans** *or* **ptarmigan** : any of various grouses of northern regions with completely feathered feet

ptarmigan (up to 15 in. long)

P T boat \(ˈ)pē-ˈtē-\ *n* : a high-speed 60- to 100-foot motorboat usu. equipped with torpedoes, machine guns, and depth charges

PTC *abbr* phenylthiocarbamide

pter·an·o·don \tə-ˈran-ə-ˌdän\ *n* : any of a genus of Cretaceous flying reptiles with a wingspread of up to 25 feet

pte·rid·o·phyte \tə-ˈrid-ə-ˌfīt\ *n* : any of a division of vascular plants that have roots, stems, and leaves, lack flowers or seeds, and comprise the ferns and related forms

pter·o·dac·tyl \ˌter-ə-ˈdak-təl\ *n* [from Greek *pteron* "wing" and *daktylos* "finger"] : an extinct flying reptile having a featherless membrane extending from the body along the arms and forming the supporting surface of the wings

pter·o·saur \ˈter-ə-ˌsȯr\ *n* : PTERODACTYL

Ptol·e·ma·ic model \ˌtäl-ə-ˌmā-ik-\ *n* : a model of planetary motions according to which the earth is at the center with the sun, moon, and planets revolving around it

pto·maine \ˈtō-ˌmān, tō-ˈ\ *n* : any of various organic compounds formed by the action of putrefactive bacteria on nitrogenous matter

ptomaine poisoning *n* : food poisoning caused usu. by bacteria or bacterial products

PTV *abbr* public television

pty·a·lin \ˈtī-ə-lən\ *n* : an enzyme found in the saliva of many animals that helps change starch into sugar

pub \ˈpəb\ *n, chiefly Brit* : PUBLIC HOUSE

pub *abbr* public

pu·ber·ty \ˈpyü-bərt-ē\ *n* **1** : the condition of being or the period of becoming first capable of reproducing sexually **2** : the age at which puberty occurs often interpreted legally as 14 in boys and 12 in girls — **pu·ber·tal** \-bərt-əl\ *adj*

pu·bic \ˈpyü-bik\ *adj* : of, relating to, or situated near the pubis

pu·bis \ˈpyü-bəs\ *n, pl* **pu·bes** \-(ˌ)bēz\ : the front and lower of the three principal bones composing each hipbone

[1]**pub·lic** \ˈpəb-lik\ *adj* **1 a** : of, relating to, or affecting all the people ⟨*public* law⟩ **b** : GOVERNMENTAL ⟨*public* education⟩ ⟨the *public* prosecutor⟩ **c** : relating to or engaged in the service of the community or nation ⟨*public* life⟩ **2** : of or relating to community interests as opposed to private affairs : SOCIAL **3** : devoted to the general welfare : HUMANITARIAN ⟨his *public* spirit⟩ **4** : open to or shared by all ⟨a *public* meeting⟩ ⟨the *public* library⟩ **5 a** : generally known ⟨the story became *public*⟩ **b** : WELL=

KNOWN, PROMINENT ⟨a *public* figure⟩ — **pub·lic·ly** *adv*

2**public** *n* **1 :** a place accessible or visible to the public ⟨seen in *public*⟩ **2 :** the people as a whole **:** POPULACE ⟨a lecture open to the *public*⟩ **3 :** a particular group of people ⟨a writer's *public*⟩

public address system *n* **:** an apparatus including one or more loudspeakers for reproducing sound so that it may be heard by a large audience in an auditorium or out of doors

pub·li·can \'pəb-li-kən\ *n* **:** a provincial tax collector for the ancient Romans

pub·li·ca·tion \ˌpəb-lə-'kā-shən\ *n* **1 :** the act or process or an instance of publishing **2 :** a published work

public house *n* **1 :** INN, HOTEL **2** *chiefly Brit* **:** a licensed saloon or bar

pub·li·cist \'pəb-lə-səst\ *n* **1 a :** an expert in international law **b :** an expert or commentator on public affairs **2 :** PRESS AGENT

pub·lic·i·ty \(ˌ)pə-'blis-ət-ē\ *n* **1 :** the condition of being public or publicly known **2 :** ADVERTISING; *esp* **:** information with a news value designed to further the interests of a place, person, or cause **3 a :** an action that gains public attention **b :** the attention so gained ⟨he likes *publicity*⟩

pub·li·cize \'pəb-lə-ˌsīz\ *vb* **:** to give publicity to **:** ADVERTISE

public relations *n* **1 :** the business of creating public goodwill for a person, firm, or institution **2 :** the degree of understanding and goodwill achieved

public school *n* **1 :** a select endowed British school that gives a liberal education and prepares students for the universities **2 :** an elementary or secondary school maintained by a local government

public servant *n* **:** a governmental official or employee

public service *n* **1 :** the business of supplying a commodity (as electricity or gas) or service (as transportation) to any or all members of a community **2 :** governmental employment; *esp* **:** CIVIL SERVICE

public television *n* **:** television whose programs do not broadcast commercial messages

public utility *n* **:** a business organization performing a public service and subject to special governmental regulation

public works *n pl* **:** works (as schools, highways, or docks) constructed with public funds for public use

pub·lish \'pəb-lish\ *vb* **1 :** to make generally known **:** make public announcement of **2 a :** to produce or release for publication; *esp* **:** PRINT **b :** to issue the work of ⟨*publish* a poet⟩ — **pub·lish·a·ble** \-ə-bəl\ *adj*

pub·lish·er \-ər\ *n* **:** one that publishes; *esp* **:** one that issues and offers for sale printed matter (as books, periodicals, or newspapers)

1**puck** \'pək\ *n* **:** a mischievous sprite **:** HOBGOBLIN

2**puck** *n* **:** a rubber disk used in ice hockey

1**puck·er** \'pək-ər\ *vb* **puck·ered; puck·er·ing** \-(ə-)ring\ **:** to contract into folds or wrinkles ⟨*puckered* his brow⟩

2**pucker** *n* **:** a fold or wrinkle caused by puckering — **puck·ery** \'pək-(ə-)rē\ *adj*

pud·ding \'pu̇d-ing\ *n* **1 :** a boiled or baked soft food usu. with a cereal base ⟨corn *pudding*⟩ **2 :** a soft, spongy, or thick creamy dessert ⟨bread *pudding*⟩

pudding stone *n* **:** conglomerate rock

1**pud·dle** \'pəd-əl\ *n* **1 :** a very small pool of usu. dirty or muddy water **2 :** an earthy mixture (as of clay, sand, and gravel) worked while wet into a compact mass that becomes impervious to water when dry

2**puddle** *vb* **pud·dled; pud·dling** \'pəd-(ə-)ling\ **1 :** to make muddy or turbid **:** MUDDLE **2 :** to make a puddle of (as clay) **3 :** to cover with puddles — **pud·dler** \-(ə-)lər\ *n*

pudgy \'pəj-ē\ *adj* **pudg·i·er; -est :** short and plump **:** CHUBBY — **pudg·i·ness** *n*

pu·eb·lo \pü-'eb-lō, pyü-\ *n, pl* **pueblos** [from Spanish, "people", "village", from Latin *populus* "people"] **1 :** an Indian village of Arizona or New Mexico consisting of flat-roofed stone or adobe houses joined in groups sometimes several stories high **2** *cap* **:** a member of any of several Amerindian peoples of Arizona and New Mexico

pu·er·ile \'pyu̇(-ə)r-əl, -ˌīl\ *adj* **:** CHILDISH, SILLY ⟨*puerile* remarks⟩ — **pu·er·il·i·ty** \ˌpyu̇(-ə)r-'il-ət-ē\ *n*

Puer·to Ri·can \ˌpwert-ə-'rē-kən, ˌpōrt-, ˌpȯrt-\ *adj* **:** of, relating to, or characteristic of Puerto Rico or its people — **Puerto Rican** *n*

1**puff** \'pəf\ *vb* **1 a :** to blow in short gusts **b :** to exhale forcibly **c :** to breathe hard **:** PANT ⟨*puffed* as he climbed the hill⟩ **d :** to emit or blow by or as if by puffs ⟨*puffed* at his pipe⟩ ⟨a breeze *puffed* the clouds away⟩ **2 :** to swell or become swollen with or as if with air or gas **:** INFLATE ⟨the sprained ankle *puffed* up⟩ ⟨*puffed* up with pride⟩

2**puff** *n* **1 a :** an act or instance of puffing **:** WHIFF, GUST **b :** a cloud (as of smoke or steam) emitted in a puff **2 :** a light pastry that rises high in baking **3 a :** a slight swelling **b :** a small fluffy pad for applying cosmetic powder **c :** a quilted bed covering — **puff·i·ness** \'pəf-ē-nəs\ *n* — **puffy** \'pəf-ē\ *adj*

puff adder *n* **:** HOGNOSE SNAKE

puff·ball \'pəf-ˌbȯl\ *n* **:** any of various mostly edible globe-shaped fungi that discharge ripe spores in a cloud resembling smoke when they are disturbed

puff·er \'pəf-ər\ *n* **1 :** one that puffs **2 :** any of various fishes that can inflate their bodies with air

puf·fin \'pəf-ən\ *n* **:** any of several short-necked seabirds related to the auk that have a deep grooved bill marked with different colors

puffin
(about 13 in. long)

pug \'pəg\ *n* **1 :** a small sturdy compact dog with a close coat, tightly curled tail, and broad wrinkled face **2 :** PUG NOSE

pu·gi·list \'pyü-jə-ləst\ *n* **:** 1BOXER — **pu·gi·lis·tic** \ˌpyü-jə-'lis-tik\ *adj*

pug·na·cious \ˌpəg-'nā-shəs\ *adj* **:** QUARRELSOME, BELLIGERENT — **pug·na·cious·ly** *adv* — **pug·nac·i·ty** \-'nas-ət-ē\ *n*

pug nose *n* **:** a nose with a slightly concave bridge and flattened nostrils — **pug-nosed** \'pəg-'nōzd\ *adj*

puis·sance \'pwis-ən(t)s, 'pyü-ə-sən(t)s\ *n* **:** STRENGTH, POWER — **puis·sant** \-ənt, -sənt\ *adj*

pule \'pyül\ *vb* **:** WHINE, WHIMPER ⟨a *puling* infant⟩

1**pull** \'pu̇l\ *vb* **1 :** to separate forcibly from a natural or firm attachment ⟨*pull* a tooth⟩ ⟨*pull* up carrots⟩ **2 a :** to exert force upon so as to cause or tend to

ə abut		ər further	a back		ā bake
ä cot, cart		au̇ out	ch chin	e less	ē easy
g gift	i trip	ī life	j joke	ng sing	ō flow
ȯ flaw		ȯi coin	th thin	th this	ü loot
u̇ foot	y yet	yü few	yu̇ furious		zh vision

cause motion toward the force ⟨*pull* a wagon⟩ ⟨*pull* at a rope⟩ **b** : to stretch repeatedly ⟨*pull* taffy⟩ **c** : to strain by stretching ⟨*pull* a tendon⟩ **d** : MOVE ⟨the car *pulled* out of the driveway⟩ **3** : to draw apart : TEAR **4** : REMOVE ⟨*pull* a crankshaft⟩ ⟨*pulled* the pitcher in the third inning⟩ **5** : to bring into the open ⟨*pulled* a knife⟩ **6** : COMMIT **7** : ATTRACT ⟨*pull* customers⟩ — **pull·er** *n* — **pull oneself together** : to regain one's self-possession — **pull one's leg** : to deceive someone playfully : HOAX — **pull together** : to work in harmony : COOPERATE

2**pull** *n* **1 a** : the act or an instance of pulling **b** : the force exerted in pulling ⟨a long *pull* uphill⟩ **2** : special influence ⟨got his job through *pull*⟩ **3** : a device for pulling ⟨a drawer *pull*⟩ **4** : a force that attracts, compels, or influences : ATTRACTION ⟨the *pull* of gravity⟩

pul·let \'pu̇l-ət\ *n* : a young hen; *esp* : a hen of the common fowl less than a year old

pul·ley \'pu̇l-ē\ *n, pl* **pulleys** : a small wheel with a grooved rim used with a rope or chain to change the direction of or to increase a pulling force

Pull·man \'pu̇l-mən\ *n* : a railroad passenger car with specially comfortable furnishings; *esp* : SLEEPING CAR

1**pull·over** \ˌpu̇l-ˌō-vər\ *adj* : put on by being pulled over the head

2**pull·over** \'pu̇l-ˌō-vər\ *n* : a pullover garment

pull through *vb* : to help through or to survive a dangerous or difficult period or situation

pul·mo·nary \'pu̇l-mə-ˌner-ē, 'pəl-\ *adj* **1** : relating to or associated with the lungs **2** : carried on by the lungs

pulmonary artery *n* : an artery that conveys venous blood from the heart to the lungs

pulmonary circulation *n* : the passage of blood from the right side of the heart through arteries to the lungs where it picks up oxygen and is returned to the left side of the heart by veins

pulmonary vein *n* : a vein that returns oxygen-rich blood from the lungs to the heart

1**pulp** \'pəlp\ *n* **1 a** : the soft juicy or fleshy part of a fruit or vegetable ⟨the *pulp* of an apple⟩ **b** : a mass of vegetable matter from which the moisture has been pressed **2** : the soft sensitive tissue that fills the central cavity of a tooth **3** : a material prepared by chemical or mechanical means chiefly from wood but also from other materials (as rags) and used in making paper and cellulose products **4** : pulpy state ⟨beat him to a *pulp*⟩ **5** : a magazine or book on rough-surfaced paper and often dealing with sensational material

2**pulp** *vb* : to make or become pulpy — **pulp·er** *n*

pul·pit \'pu̇l-ˌpit\ *n* **1** : an elevated platform or high desk used in preaching or conducting a worship service **2** : the preaching profession **3** : a position as a preacher

pulp·wood \'pəlp-ˌwu̇d\ *n* : wood (as of aspen, hemlock, pine, or spruce) used in making pulp for paper

pulpy \'pəl-pē\ *adj* **pulp·i·er**; **-est** : resembling or consisting of pulp — **pulp·i·ness** *n*

pul·que \'pül-ˌkā\ *n* : a fermented drink made in Mexico from the juice of a maguey

pul·sate \'pəl-ˌsāt\ *vb* : to expand and contract in a rhythmic manner : throb rhythmically : BEAT

pul·sa·tion \ˌpəl-'sā-shən\ *n* : pulsating movement or action (as of an artery); *also* : a single throb of such movement

1**pulse** \'pəls\ *n* : the edible seeds of several leguminous crops (as peas, beans, or lentils); *also* : a plant yielding pulse

2**pulse** *n* **1** : a regular throbbing caused in the arteries by the contractions of the heart **2 a** : rhythmical beating or throbbing **b** : BEAT, THROB **3 a** : a transient variation of a quantity (as electrical current) whose value is normally constant **b** : an electromagnetic wave or a sound wave of brief duration

3**pulse** *vb* : THROB, BEAT

pul·ver·ize \'pəl-və-ˌrīz\ *vb* **1** : to reduce or become reduced (as by beating or grinding) into a powder or dust **2** : to demolish as if by pulverizing : SMASH

pu·ma \'p(y)ü-mə\ *n, pl* **pumas** *also* **puma** : COUGAR

pum·ice \'pəm-əs\ *n* : a volcanic glass full of cavities and very light in weight used esp. in powder form for smoothing and polishing — called also *pumice stone*

pum·mel \'pəm-əl\ *vb* **-meled** *or* **-melled**; **-mel·ing** *or* **-mel·ling** : POUND, BEAT, THUMP

1**pump** \'pəmp\ *n* : a device that raises, transfers, or compresses fluids esp. by suction or pressure or both

2**pump** *vb* **1** : to raise, transfer, or compress by means of a pump ⟨*pump* up water⟩ **2** : to free (as from water or air) by the use of a pump ⟨*pump* a boat dry⟩ **3** : to fill by means of a pump ⟨*pump* up a tire⟩ **4** : to draw, force, or drive onward in the manner of a pump ⟨the heart *pumps* blood into the arteries⟩ **5** : to move up and down like a pump handle ⟨*pump* the hand of a friend⟩ **6 a** : to subject to persistent questioning to find out something **b** : to draw out by such questioning — **pump·er** *n*

3**pump** *n* : a low shoe gripping the foot chiefly at the toe and heel

pum·per·nick·el \'pəm-pər-ˌnik-əl\ *n* : a dark coarse somewhat sour rye bread

pump·kin \'pəng-kən, 'pəm(p)-kən\ *n* **1** : the usu. round deep yellow fruit of a vine related to the squashes and cucumber and widely used as food; *also* : a fruit (as a crookneck squash) of a closely related vine **2** : a usu. hairy prickly vine that produces pumpkins

pump·kin·seed \-ˌsēd\ *n* : a small brilliantly colored No. American freshwater sunfish or the related bluegill

pun \'pən\ *n* : the humorous use of a word in such a way as to suggest different meanings or of words having the same sound but different meanings — **pun** *vb*

1**punch** \'pənch\ *vb* **1 a** : PROD, POKE **b** : DRIVE, HERD ⟨*punch* cattle⟩ **2 a** : to strike with the fist **b** : to press, strike, or activate by or as if by punching ⟨*punch* a typewriter⟩ **3** : to pierce or stamp with a punch — **punch·er** *n*

2**punch** *n* **1** : a quick blow with or as if with the fist **2** : effective force ⟨the team was well trained but lacked *punch*⟩

3**punch** *n* : a tool or machine for piercing, cutting, or stamping or for driving a nail

4**punch** *n* : a drink made of various and usu. many ingredients and often flavored with wine or liquor

punched card *or* **punch card** *n* : a data card with holes punched in particular positions each with its own meaning for use in electrically operated tabulating or accounting equipment or computers

pun·cheon \'pən-chən\ *n* : a large cask of varying capacity

punc·til·io \ˌpəng(k)-'til-ē-ˌō\ *n, pl* **-i·os** **1** : a nice detail of conduct in a ceremony or in observance of a code **2** : careful observance of forms (as in social conduct)

punc·til·i·ous \-ē-əs\ *adj* : marked by exact accordance with the details of codes or conventions — **punc·til·i·ous·ly** *adv* — **punc·til·i·ous·ness** *n*

punc·tu·al \'pəng(k)-chə-wəl\ *adj* : acting or habitually acting at an appointed time or at a regularly scheduled time : PROMPT — **punc·tu·al·i·ty** \ˌpəŋ(k)-chə-ˈwal-ət-ē\ *n* — **punc·tu·al·ly** \ˈpəŋ(k)-chə-wə-lē\ *adv*

punc·tu·ate \ˈpəŋ(k)-chə-ˌwāt\ *vb* **1** : to mark or divide with punctuation marks **2** : to interrupt at intervals ⟨a speech *punctuated* by a harsh cough⟩

punc·tu·a·tion \ˌpəŋ(k)-chə-ˈwā-shən\ *n* : the act, practice, or system of inserting punctuation marks in written matter to clarify the meaning and separate structural units

punctuation mark *n* : any of various standardized marks or signs used in punctuation

[1]**punc·ture** \ˈpəŋ(k)-chər\ *n* **1** : the act of puncturing **2** : a hole or a narrow wound resulting from puncturing ⟨a slight *puncture* of the skin⟩ ⟨a tire *puncture*⟩

[2]**puncture** *vb* **1** : to pierce with a point ⟨a nail *punctured* the tire⟩ **2** : to suffer a puncture of ⟨*punctured* his tire on a nail⟩ **3** : to become punctured ⟨worn tires *puncture* easily⟩ **4** : to make useless or absurd as if by a puncture ⟨*puncture* an argument⟩

pun·gent \ˈpən-jənt\ *adj* **1** : sharply stimulating to the mind ⟨*pungent* criticism⟩ ⟨*pungent* wit⟩ **2** : causing a sharp or irritating sensation; *esp* : ACRID — **pun·gen·cy** \-jən-sē\ *n* — **pun·gent·ly** *adv*

pun·ish \ˈpən-ish\ *vb* **1** : to cause to suffer pain or loss of freedom or privileges for an offense committed : CHASTISE ⟨*punish* criminals with imprisonment⟩ **2** : to inflict punishment for ⟨*punish* treason with death⟩ **3** : to deal with or handle severely or roughly ⟨badly *punished* by his opponent⟩ — **pun·ish·a·ble** \-ə-bəl\ *adj* — **pun·ish·er** *n*

pun·ish·ment \ˈpən-ish-mənt\ *n* **1 a** : the act of punishing **b** : the state or fact of being punished ⟨persons undergoing *punishment*⟩ **2** : the penalty for a fault or crime ⟨the *punishment* for speeding⟩ **3** : severe, rough, or disastrous treatment

pu·ni·tive \ˈpyü-nət-iv\ *adj* **1** : of or relating to punishment or penalties ⟨*punitive* law⟩ **2** : intended to inflict punishment ⟨a *punitive* expedition against outlaws⟩ — **pu·ni·tive·ly** *adv* — **pu·ni·tive·ness** *n*

[1]**punk** \ˈpəŋk\ *adj* : very poor in quality : BAD, MISERABLE

[2]**punk** *n* **1** : wood so decayed as to be dry, crumbly, and useful for tinder **2** : a dry spongy substance prepared from fungi and used to ignite fuses esp. of fireworks

[1]**punt** \ˈpənt\ *n* : a long narrow flat-bottomed boat with square ends usu. propelled with a pole

[2]**punt** *vb* **1** : to propel by pushing with a pole against the bottom of a body of water **2** : to go boating in a punt

[3]**punt** *vb* : to kick a football before it touches the ground when dropped from the hands — **punt·er** *n*

[4]**punt** *n* : the act or an instance of punting a ball

pu·ny \ˈpyü-nē\ *adj* **pu·ni·er**; **-est** : slight or inferior in power, size, or importance : WEAK — **pu·ni·ness** *n*

pup \ˈpəp\ *n* **1** : PUPPY **2** : one of the young of various animals (as seals)

pu·pa \ˈpyü-pə\ *n, pl* **pu·pae** \-(ˌ)pē, -ˌpī\ *or* **pupas** : the stage of an insect (as a bee, moth, or beetle) having complete metamorphosis that occurs between the larva and the adult, is usu. enclosed in a cocoon or case, and undergoes internal changes by which structures of the larva are replaced by those of the adult — **pu·pal** \ˈpyü-pəl\ *adj*

ə abut		ər further	a back	ā bake
ä cot, cart		au̇ out	ch chin	e less	ē easy
g gift	i trip	ī life	j joke	ng sing	ō flow
ȯ flaw		ȯi coin	th thin	t͟h this	ü loot
u̇ foot	y yet	yü few	yu̇ furious	zh vision

pu·par·i·um \pyü-ˈpar-ē-əm, -ˈper-\ *n, pl* **pu·par·ia** \-ē-ə\ : the outer shell covering some insect pupae (as of a fly) and formed from the skin of the larva

pu·pate \ˈpyü-ˌpāt\ *vb* : to become a pupa : pass through a pupal stage — **pu·pa·tion** \pyü-ˈpā-shən\ *n*

[1]**pu·pil** \ˈpyü-pəl\ *n* **1** : a child or young person in school or in the charge of a tutor : STUDENT **2** : one who has been taught or influenced by a person of fame or distinction : DISCIPLE

[2]**pupil** *n* : the usu. round opening in the iris of the eye that contracts and expands according to the degree of light

pu·pil·age *or* **pu·pil·lage** \ˈpyü-pə-lij\ *n* : the state or period of being a pupil

pup·pet \ˈpəp-ət\ *n* **1** : a small figure of a human being or animal often made with jointed limbs and moved by hand or by strings or wires **2** : DOLL 1 **3** : a person or a government whose acts are controlled by an outside force or influence

pup·pe·teer \ˌpəp-ə-ˈti(ə)r\ *n* : one who manipulates puppets

pup·py \ˈpəp-ē\ *n, pl* **puppies** : a young domestic dog; *esp* : one less than a year old

pur·blind \ˈpər-ˌblīnd\ *adj* **1** : partly blind **2** : lacking in insight or understanding

[1]**pur·chase** \ˈpər-chəs\ *vb* : to get by paying money for : BUY ⟨*purchase* a house⟩ — **pur·chas·a·ble** \-chə-sə-bəl\ *adj* — **pur·chas·er** *n*

[2]**purchase** *n* **1** : an act or instance of purchasing **2** : something purchased **3** : a secure hold, grasp, or place to stand ⟨could not get a *purchase* on the ledge⟩

pure \ˈpyu̇(ə)r\ *adj* **1** : not mixed with anything else : free from everything that might taint, alter, or lower the quality ⟨*pure* water⟩ ⟨*pure* French⟩ **2** : free from sin or guilt; *esp* : CHASTE **3** : nothing other than : SHEER ⟨*pure* nonsense⟩ **4** : ABSTRACT, THEORETICAL ⟨*pure* science⟩ ⟨*pure* mathematics⟩ **5 a** : of unmixed ancestry **b** : breeding true for one or more characters

pure·blood \-ˌbləd\ *or* **pure–blood·ed** \-ˈbləd-əd\ *adj* : of unmixed ancestry : PUREBRED — **pure·blood** *n*

pure·bred \-ˈbred\ *adj* : bred from members of a recognized breed, strain, or kind without crossbreeding over many generations — **pure·bred** \-ˌbred\ *n*

[1]**pu·ree** \pyu̇-ˈrā, -ˈrē\ *n* **1** : a paste or thick liquid usu. made by rubbing cooked food through a sieve **2** : a thick soup having pureed vegetables as a base

[2]**puree** *vb* **pu·reed**; **pu·ree·ing** : to boil soft and then rub through a sieve

pure line *n* : an essentially genetically pure strain (as of corn plants) usu. formed by repeated inbreeding — **pure–line** *adj*

pure·ly \ˈpyu̇(ə)r-lē\ *adv* **1** : without admixture of anything injurious or foreign **2** : MERELY, SOLELY **3** : CHASTELY, INNOCENTLY **4** : COMPLETELY

[1]**pur·ga·tive** \ˈpər-gət-iv\ *adj* : tending to purge or act as a laxative

[2]**purgative** *n* : a purgative medicine

pur·ga·to·ry \ˈpər-gə-ˌtōr-ē, -ˌtȯr-\ *n, pl* **-ries** : an intermediate state after death in which according to Roman Catholic doctrine the souls of those who die in God's grace are purified of their sins by suffering

[1]**purge** \ˈpərj\ *vb* **1** : CLEANSE, PURIFY; *esp* : to

remove sin or guilt from **2** : to have or cause vigorous and usu. repeated evacuation of the bowels ⟨*purged* him with drugs⟩ — **purg·er** *n*

2**purge** *n* **1** : an act or instance of purging **2** : something that purges; *esp* : PURGATIVE

pu·ri·fy \'pyu̇r-ə-ˌfī\ *vb* **-fied**; **-fy·ing** : to make or become pure : free from impurities — **pu·ri·fi·ca·tion** \ˌpyu̇r-ə-fə-'kā-shən\ *n* — **pu·ri·fi·er** \-ˌfī(-ə)r\ *n*

Pu·rim \'pu̇r-(ˌ)im, pu̇r-'\ *n* [from Hebrew *pūrīm*, literally "the lots", from the casting of lots by Haman to destroy the Jews (Esther 9:24–26)] : a Jewish holiday celebrated in February or March in commemoration of the deliverance of the Jews from the massacre plotted by Haman

pur·ism \'pyu̇(ə)r-ˌiz-əm\ *n* : rigid adherence to or insistence on nicety esp. in use of words — **pur·ist** \-əst\ *n*

pu·ri·tan \'pyu̇r-ət-ən\ *n* **1** *cap* : a member of a 16th and 17th century Protestant group in England and New England opposing many traditional customs of the Church of England **2** : one who practices or preaches a stricter moral code than that which prevails — **puritan** *adj, often cap* — **pu·ri·tan·i·cal** \ˌpyu̇r-ə-'tan-i-kəl\ *adj* — **pu·ri·tan·ism** \'pyu̇r-ət-ə-ˌniz-əm\ *n, often cap*

pu·ri·ty \'pyu̇r-ət-ē\ *n* **1** : the quality or state of being pure : freedom from impurities **2** : freedom from guilt or sin **3** : freedom from inappropriate linguistic or stylistic elements

1**purl** \'pərl\ *vb* : to invert the stitches in knitting

2**purl** *n* **1** : a purling stream **2** : a gentle murmur

3**purl** *vb* **1** : EDDY, SWIRL **2** : to make a murmuring sound

pur·lieu \'pərl-ˌyü\ *n* **1** : an outlying or adjacent district **2** : ENVIRONS

pur·loin \(ˌ)pər-'lȯin, 'pər-ˌ\ *vb* : STEAL, FILCH — **pur·loin·er** *n*

1**pur·ple** \'pər-pəl\ *adj* : of the color purple

2**purple** *n* **1** : a color midway between red and blue **2** : imperial or regal rank or power : high station

3**purple** *vb* **pur·pled**; **pur·pling** \'pər-p(ə-)ling\ : to turn purple

pur·plish \'pər-p(ə-)lish\ *adj* : somewhat purple

1**pur·port** \'pər-ˌpōrt, -ˌpȯrt\ *n* **1** : meaning conveyed, professed, or implied : IMPORT **2** : SUBSTANCE, GIST

2**pur·port** \(ˌ)pər-'pōrt, -'pȯrt\ *vb* : to give the impression of being : CLAIM, PROFESS ⟨*purports* to be a physician⟩

pur·pose \'pər-pəs\ *n* **1** : something set up as an end to be attained : INTENTION, AIM **2** : an object or result achieved ⟨worked to little *purpose*⟩ — **pur·pose·ful** \-fəl\ *adj* — **pur·pose·ful·ly** \-fə-lē\ *adv* — **pur·pose·ful·ness** \-fəl-nəs\ *n* — **pur·pose·less** \-pəs-ləs\ *adj* — **on purpose** : by intent : INTENTIONALLY

pur·pose·ly \'pər-pəs-lē\ *adv* : with a deliberate purpose : INTENTIONALLY

purr \'pər\ *n* : a low murmur typical of a contented cat — **purr** *vb*

1**purse** \'pərs\ *n* **1** : a small receptacle (as a wallet) for money; *esp* : a woman's pocketbook **2** : RESOURCES, FUNDS **3** : a sum of money offered as a prize or present

2**purse** *vb* **1** : to put into a purse **2** : PUCKER, KNIT ⟨*pursed* lips⟩

purs·er \'pər-sər\ *n* : an official on a ship who keeps accounts and attends to passengers

purs·lane \'pər-slən, -ˌslān\ *n* : a fleshy-leaved trailing plant with tiny bright yellow flowers that is a common troublesome weed but is sometimes eaten as a potherb or used in salads

pur·su·ance \pər-'sü-ən(t)s\ *n* : the act of pursuing or carrying out ⟨in *pursuance* of his plans⟩

pur·su·ant to \-ənt-\ *prep* : in conformance to : according to

pur·sue \pər-'sü\ *vb* [from Old French *poursuir*, from Latin *prosequi* (the source of English *prosecute*), from *pro-* "forward" and *sequi* "to follow"] **1** : to follow in order to overtake and capture or destroy **2** : to try to obtain or accomplish : SEEK ⟨*pursue* pleasure⟩ **3** : to proceed along : FOLLOW ⟨*pursue* a northerly course⟩ **4** : to engage in : PRACTICE ⟨*pursue* a hobby⟩ **5** : HARASS, HAUNT ⟨*pursued* by fear⟩ — **pur·su·er** *n*

pur·suit \pər-'süt\ *n* **1** : the act of pursuing **2** : an activity that one engages in : OCCUPATION

pur·vey \(ˌ)pər-'vā, 'pər-ˌ\ *vb* **pur·veyed**; **pur·vey·ing** : to supply (as provisions) usu. as a business — **pur·vey·ance** \-ən(t)s\ *n* — **pur·vey·or** \-ər\ *n*

pus \'pəs\ *n* : thick cloudy usu. yellowish white fluid matter formed at a place of inflammation and infection (as an abscess) and containing white blood cells, tissue debris, and microorganisms

1**push** \'pu̇sh\ *vb* **1** : to press against with force in order to drive or impel **2** : to thrust forward, downward, or outward **3** : to press or urge forward ⟨*push* the job to completion⟩ **4** : to bear hard upon so as to involve in difficulty ⟨was *pushed* for time⟩

2**push** *n* **1** : a vigorous advance against obstacles **2** : a sudden thrust : SHOVE **3** : a steady application of physical force in a direction away from the body exerting it

push button *n* : a small button or knob that when pushed operates something esp. by closing an electric circuit

push–button *adj* : using or dependent on complex automatic mechanisms ⟨*push-button* warfare⟩ ⟨a *push-button* civilization⟩

push·cart \'pu̇sh-ˌkärt\ *n* : a cart pushed by hand

push·er \'pu̇sh-ər\ *n* **1** : one that pushes **2** : an illicit peddler of narcotics

push·over \'pu̇sh-ˌō-vər\ *n* **1** : an opponent easy to defeat or incapable of resistance **2** : someone unable to resist an attraction or appeal **3** : something easily done : SNAP

pu·sil·lan·i·mous \ˌpyü-sə-'lan-ə-məs\ *adj* : COWARDLY

1**puss** \'pu̇s\ *n* **1** : CAT **2** : GIRL

2**puss** *n, slang* : FACE

1**pussy** \'pu̇s-ē\ *n, pl* **puss·ies** **1** : PUSS **2** : a catkin of the pussy willow

2**pus·sy** \'pəs-ē\ *adj* **pus·si·er**; **-est** : full of or resembling pus

pussy·foot \'pu̇s-ē-ˌfu̇t\ *vb* **1** : to tread or move warily or stealthily **2** : to keep from committing oneself : HEDGE

pussy willow \ˌpu̇s-ē-\ *n* : a willow having large cylindrical silky catkins

pussy willow

pus·tu·lar \'pəs-chə-lər\ *adj* **1** : of, relating to, marked by, or resembling pustules ⟨a *pustular* eruption on the skin⟩ **2** : covered with elevations resembling pustules ⟨a *pustular* leaf⟩

pus·tule \'pəs-chül\ *n* **1** : a small elevation of the skin having an inflamed base and containing pus **2** : a small elevation resembling a pimple or blister

1**put** \'pu̇t\ *vb* **put**; **put·ting** **1 a** : to place in or move into a position or relationship ⟨*put* the book down⟩ **b** : to throw with an overhand pushing motion ⟨*put* the shot⟩ **c** : to bring into a state ⟨*put* it to use⟩ ⟨*put* the matter right⟩ **2 a** : to cause to undergo something ⟨*put* him to death⟩ **b** : IMPOSE, INFLICT ⟨*put* a special tax on luxuries⟩ **3** : to set before one for judgment or decision (as by a formal vote) ⟨*put* the motion⟩ **4** : EXPRESS, TRANSLATE ⟨*put* his feelings in words⟩ ⟨*put* the poem into English⟩ **5 a** : to devote or urge to an activity or end ⟨*put* his mind to the problem⟩ ⟨*put* them to work⟩ **b** : INVEST ⟨*put* his money in the company⟩ **6 a** : ESTIMATE ⟨*put* the time at about eleven⟩ **b** : ATTACH, ATTRIBUTE ⟨*puts* a high value on friendship⟩ **7** : GO, PROCEED ⟨the ship *put* to sea⟩ — **put forth 1** : to bring into action : EXERT **2** : to produce or send out by growth ⟨*put forth* leaves⟩ — **put forward** : PROPOSE ⟨*put forward* a theory⟩ — **put in mind** : REMIND — **put to it** : to give difficulty to ⟨was *put to it* to keep up⟩

2**put** *n* : a throw made with an overhand pushing motion

3**put** *adj* : FIXED, SET ⟨stay *put* until I come back⟩

put about *vb* : to change course or direction

put across *vb* : to gain or communicate successfully ⟨*put across* a plan⟩

put by *vb* : to lay aside : SAVE ⟨have money *put by* for an emergency⟩

put down *vb* **1** : to bring to an end by force : SUPPRESS ⟨*put down* a riot⟩ **2** : to write down (as in a list) **3** : BELITTLE, CRITICIZE

put in *vb* **1** : to make or make as a request, offer, or declaration ⟨*put in* a plea of guilty⟩ ⟨*put in* for a job at the store⟩ **2** : to spend at some activity or place ⟨*put in* six hours at the office⟩ **3** : PLANT ⟨*put in* a crop⟩ **4** : to enter a harbor or port ⟨the freighter *put in* for overnight⟩

put off *vb* **1** : REPEL ⟨was *put off* by his appearance⟩ **2** : DELAY, DEFER ⟨*put off* his visit to the dentist⟩ **3** : to rid oneself of ⟨*put off* his coat⟩

put–on \'pu̇t-ˌȯn, -ˌän\ *n* **1** : PRETENSE, SHOW **2** : an elaborate joke

put on \-'ȯn, -'än\ *vb* **1 a** : to dress oneself in : DON **b** : ADOPT ⟨*put on* airs⟩ **c** : FEIGN ⟨*put on* a show of anger⟩ **2** : EXAGGERATE, OVERSTATE ⟨he's *putting* it *on* when he makes such claims⟩ **3** : PERFORM, PRODUCE ⟨*put on* an entertaining act⟩ **4** : KID, FOOL ⟨you're *putting* me *on*⟩ — **put–on** *adj*

put·out \'pu̇t-ˌau̇t\ *n* : the retiring of a base runner or batter in baseball

put out \-'au̇t\ *vb* **1** : EXERT, USE ⟨*put out* all his strength to move the piano⟩ **2** : EXTINGUISH ⟨*put* the fire *out*⟩ **3** : PRODUCE **4** : IRRITATE, PROVOKE ⟨his father was *put out* by his failure⟩ **5** : to cause to be out (as in baseball) **6** : to set out from shore

put over *vb* : to put across ⟨*put over* a deception⟩

pu·tre·fac·tion \ˌpyü-trə-'fak-shən\ *n* **1** : the rotting of organic matter **2** : the state of being putrefied : CORRUPTION — **pu·tre·fac·tive** \-'fak-tiv\ *adj*

pu·tre·fy \'pyü-trə-ˌfī\ *vb* **-fied**; **-fy·ing** : to make or become putrid : DECOMPOSE, ROT

pu·tres·cent \pyü-'tres-ənt\ *adj* : becoming putrid : ROTTING — **pu·tres·cence** \-ən(t)s\ *n*

pu·trid \'pyü-trəd\ *adj* **1 a** : being in a state of putrefaction : ROTTEN ⟨*putrid* meat⟩ **b** : characteristic of putrefaction : FOUL ⟨a *putrid* odor⟩ **2** : CORRUPT, VILE

putt \'pət\ *n* : a golf stroke made to cause the ball to roll into or near the hole — **putt** *vb*

ə abut	ər further	a back	ā bake
ä cot, cart	au̇ out	ch chin	e less	ē easy
g gift	i trip	ī life	j joke	ng sing	ō flow
ȯ flaw	ȯi coin	th thin	t͟h this	ü loot
u̇ foot	y yet	yü few	yu̇ furious	zh vision

put·tee \ˌpə-'tē, pu̇-; 'pət-ē\ *n* **1** : a cloth strip wrapped around the leg from ankle to knee **2** : a leather legging

1**put·ter** \'pu̇t-ər\ *n* : one that puts

2**putt·er** \'pət-ər\ *n* : a golf club used in putting

3**put·ter** \'pət-ər\ *vb* : to work at random : TINKER — **put·ter·er** \-ər-ər\ *n*

put through *vb* : to carry to a conclusion ⟨*put through* a number of reforms⟩

1**put·ty** \'pət-ē\ *n, pl* **putties** : a soft cement used in fastening glass in sashes and stopping cracks in woodwork

2**putty** *vb* **put·tied**; **put·ty·ing** : to cement or seal up with putty

put up *vb* **1 a** : to prepare for later use ⟨*put up* a lunch⟩; *esp* : CAN ⟨*put up* peaches⟩ **b** : to put away out of use ⟨*put up* your sword⟩ **2 a** : to nominate for election **b** : to offer for public sale ⟨*puts* his possessions *up* for auction⟩ **3** : to give or obtain food and shelter : LODGE ⟨*put* him *up* overnight⟩ **4** : BUILD, ERECT **5** : to carry on ⟨*put up* a struggle⟩ **6** : to make available ⟨*put up* a prize for the best essay⟩ — **put up to** : INCITE, INSTIGATE — **put up with** : TOLERATE, ENDURE

1**puz·zle** \'pəz-əl\ *vb* **puz·zled**; **puz·zling** \-(ə-)liŋ\ **1** : to confuse the understanding of : BEWILDER **2** : to solve with difficulty or ingenuity ⟨*puzzled* out the mystery⟩ — **puz·zler** \-(ə-)lər\ *n*

syn PUZZLE, PERPLEX, MYSTIFY can mean to frustrate the understanding of. PUZZLE implies a complication that is hard to understand or explain; PERPLEX adds a suggestion of worry or disturbance; MYSTIFY implies the thoroughness of one's puzzlement

2**puzzle** *n* **1** : the state of being puzzled : PERPLEXITY **2 a** : something that puzzles **b** : a question, problem, or device designed for testing ingenuity

puz·zle·ment \'pəz-əl-mənt\ *n* **1** : the state of being puzzled : PERPLEXITY **2** : PUZZLE 2

pyg·my \'pig-mē\ *n, pl* **pygmies** [from Greek *Pygmaios,* meaning literally "one an ell long", from *pygmē* "ell" (the distance from the elbow to the knuckles), literally "fist"] **1** *cap* : one of a small people of equatorial Africa ranging under five feet in height **2** : a person or thing very small for its kind : DWARF — **pygmy** *adj*

py·ja·mas \pə-'jä-məz\ *chiefly Brit var of* PAJAMAS

py·lon \'pī-ˌlän, -lən\ *n* **1** : a usu. massive gateway; *esp* : an ancient Egyptian one composed of two flat-topped pyramids and a crosspiece **2** : a tower for supporting a long span of wire **3** : a post or tower marking a prescribed course of flight for an airplane

py·lo·rus \-'lōr-əs, -'lȯr-\ *n, pl* **-lo·ri** \-'lōr-ˌī, -'lȯr-, -ˌē\ [from Greek *pylōros,* meaning literally "gatekeeper"] : the opening in a vertebrate from the stomach into the intestine — **py·lo·ric** \pī-'lōr-ik, pə-, -'lȯr-\ *adj*

py·or·rhea \ˌpī-ə-'rē-ə\ *n* : a pussy inflammation of the sockets of the teeth leading usu. to loosening of the teeth

pyr- *or* **pyro-** *comb form* : fire : heat ⟨*pyro*technic⟩

1**pyr·a·mid** \'pir-ə-ˌmid\ *n* **1** : a massive structure built esp. in ancient Egypt that usu. has a square base and four triangular faces meeting at a point and contains tombs **2** : something that resembles a pyramid in shape or organization ⟨the

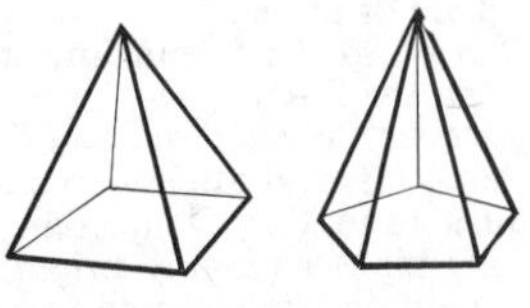

pyramids 3

social *pyramid*⟩ **3** : a solid having a polygon for its base and for its sides three or more triangles that meet to form the vertex — **py·ram·i·dal** \pə-'ram-əd-əl, ˌpir-ə-'mid-əl\ *adj*

²**pyramid** *vb* : to build up in the form of a pyramid

pyre \'pī(ə)r\ *n* : a combustible heap for burning a dead body as a funeral rite; *also* : a pile of material to be burned

py·re·thrum \pī-'rē-thrəm, -'reth-rəm\ *n* **1** : any of several chrysanthemums that have finely divided often aromatic leaves and include ornamentals as well as important sources of insecticides **2** : an insecticide consisting of the dried heads of some Old World pyrethrums

pyr·i·dox·ine \ˌpir-ə-'däk-ˌsēn, -sən\ *n* : a crystalline alcohol of the vitamin B_6 group found esp. in cereals

py·rite \'pī-ˌrīt\ *n* : a mineral that consists of iron combined with sulfur, has a pale brass-yellow color and metallic luster, and is used esp. in making sulfuric acid

py·rites \pə-'rīt-ēz, pī-; 'pī-ˌrīts\ *n, pl* **pyrites** : any of various metallic-looking sulfides of which pyrite is the commonest

py·ro·ma·nia \ˌpī-rō-'mā-nē-ə, -nyə\ *n* : a compulsive urge to start fires — **py·ro·ma·ni·ac** \-nē-ˌak\ *n*

py·rom·e·ter \pī-'räm-ət-ər\ *n* : an instrument for measuring temperatures esp. when above the range of mercurial thermometers

py·ro·tech·nics \ˌpī-rə-'tek-niks\ *n pl* **1 a** : the art of making fireworks **b** : the making or use of fireworks **c** : fireworks or a display of fireworks **2** : a spectacular display (as of oratory) — **py·ro·tech·ni·cal** \-ni-kəl\ *or* **pyrotechnic** \-nik\ *adj*

py·rox·ene \pī-'räk-ˌsēn\ *n* : any of various silicate minerals that usu. contain magnesium or iron

py·rox·y·lin \pī-'räk-sə-lən\ *n* : a flammable substance resembling cotton that is produced chemically from cellulose and used in the manufacture of various products (as celluloid, lacquer, and some explosives)

Py·thag·o·re·an numbers \pə-ˌthag-ə-ˌrē-ən-, pī-\ *n pl* : any set of three positive integers (as 3, 4, 5) that satisfy the equation $x^2 + y^2 = z^2$

py·thon \'pī-ˌthän, -thən\ *n* [named after *Python*, a monstrous serpent killed by Apollo] : a large constrictor (as a boa); *esp* : any of an Old World genus including the largest recent snakes

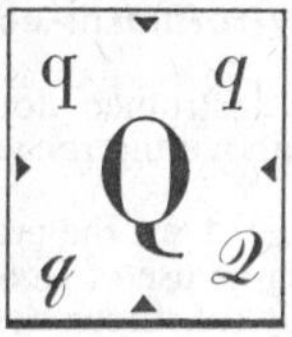

q \'kyü\ *n, often cap* : the 17th letter of the English alphabet
q *abbr* **1** quart **2** question
Q *abbr* queen
QED *abbr* [for Latin *quod erat demonstrandum*] which was to be demonstrated
qr *abbr* **1** quarter **2** quire
qt *abbr* quart
q.t. *abbr* quiet
[1]**quack** \'kwak\ *vb* : to make the characteristic cry of a duck
[2]**quack** *n* : a cry made by or as if by quacking
[3]**quack** *n* **1** : a person who pretends to have medical skill **2** : CHARLATAN — **quack** *adj* — **quack·ery** \'kwak-(ə-)rē\ *n* — **quack·ish** \'kwak-ish\ *adj*
[1]**quad** \'kwäd\ *n* : QUADRANGLE
[2]**quad** *n* : QUADRUPLET
quad·ran·gle \'kwäd-ˌrang-gəl\ *n* **1** : QUADRILATERAL **2 a** : a 4-sided enclosure esp. when surrounded by buildings **b** : the buildings enclosing a quadrangle — **qua·dran·gu·lar** \kwä-'drang-gyə-lər\ *adj*
quad·rant \'kwäd-rənt\ *n* **1** : an instrument for measuring altitudes (as in astronomy or surveying) **2** : an arc of 90° : one quarter of a circle

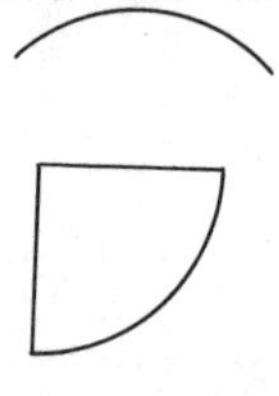
quadrants 2

qua·drat·ic \kwä-'drat-ik\ *adj* : involving terms of second degree at most — **quadratic** *n*
quadratic equation *n* : an equation containing one term in which the unknown is squared and no term in which it is raised to a higher power
qua·dren·ni·al \kwä-'dren-ē-əl\ *adj* **1** : consisting of or lasting for four years **2** : occurring or being done every four years — **qua·dren·ni·al·ly** \-ē-ə-lē\ *adv*
quadri- *or* **quadr-** *or* **quadru-** *comb form* **1** : four ⟨*quadri*lingual⟩ **2** : fourth ⟨*quadri*centennial⟩
quad·ri·ceps \'kwäd-rə-ˌseps\ *n* : the great extensor muscle of the front of the thigh
[1]**quad·ri·lat·er·al** \ˌkwäd-rə-'lat-ə-rəl, -'la-trəl\ *adj* : having four sides
[2]**quadrilateral** *n* : a plane figure of four sides and four angles
qua·drille \kwä-'dril, k(w)ə-\ *n* : a square dance for four couples or music for this dance
qua·dril·lion \kwä-'dril-yən\ *n* — see NUMBER table
quad·ri·par·tite \ˌkwäd-rə-'pär-ˌtīt\ *adj* **1** : consisting of four parts ⟨a *quadripartite* vault⟩ **2** : shared by four parties ⟨a *quadripartite* agreement⟩
qua·droon \kwä-'drün\ *n* : a person of quarter Negro ancestry
quad·ru·ped \'kwäd-rə-ˌped\ *n* : an animal having four feet — **quadruped** *or* **qua·dru·pe·dal** \kwä-'drü-pəd-əl, ˌkwäd-rə-'ped-\ *adj*
[1]**qua·dru·ple** \kwä-'drüp-əl, -'drəp-; 'kwäd-rəp-\ *vb* **qua·dru·pled**; **qua·dru·pling** \-(ə-)ling\ : to make or become four times as great or as many
[2]**quadruple** *adj* **1** : having four units or members **2** : being four times as great or as many **3** : marked by four beats per measure ⟨*quadruple* time⟩ — **quadruple** *n*

ə abut	ər further	a back	ā bake
ä cot, cart	aù out	ch chin	e less	ē easy
g gift	i trip	ī life	j joke	ng sing	ō flow
ȯ flaw	ȯi coin	th thin	t͟h this	ü loot
ù foot	y yet	yü few	yù furious	zh vision

qua·drup·let \kwä-'drəp-lət, -'drüp-; 'kwäd-rəp-\ *n* **1** : one of four offspring born at one birth **2** : a combination of four of a kind
quaff \'kwäf, 'kwaf\ *vb* : to drink deeply or repeatedly — **quaff** *n*
quag·gy \'kwag-ē, 'kwäg-\ *adj* **quag·gi·er**; **-est** **1** : BOGGY, MARSHY **2** : FLABBY, YIELDING
quag·mire \'kwag-ˌmī(ə)r, 'kwäg-\ *n* : soft miry land : BOG, MARSH
qua·hog \'kwō-ˌhȯg, 'k(w)ō-, -ˌhäg\ *n* : a round thick-shelled American clam
[1]**quail** \'kwāl\ *n, pl* **quail** *or* **quails** : any of various game birds related to the common fowl: as **a** : a stocky short-winged Old World migratory bird occurring in many varieties **b** : any of various small American birds; *esp* : BOBWHITE
[2]**quail** *vb* : to lose courage : retreat fearfully : COWER
quaint \'kwānt\ *adj* : unusual or different in character or appearance : ODD; *esp* : pleasingly old-fashioned or unfamiliar — **quaint·ly** *adv* — **quaint·ness** *n*
[1]**quake** \'kwāk\ *vb* **1** : to shake or vibrate usu. from shock or instability **2** : to tremble or shudder usu. from cold or fear
[2]**quake** *n* : a shaking or trembling; *esp* : EARTHQUAKE
quak·er \'kwā-kər\ *n* **1** : one that quakes **2** *cap* : FRIEND 4 — **Quak·er·ism** \-kə-ˌriz-əm\ *n*
qual·i·fi·ca·tion \ˌkwäl-ə-fə-'kā-shən\ *n* **1** : the act or an instance of qualifying **2** : the state of being qualified **3 a** : a special skill, knowledge, or ability that fits a person for a particular work or position : FITNESS **b** : a condition that must be complied with (as to attain a privilege)
qual·i·fied \'kwäl-ə-ˌfīd\ *adj* **1** : having the necessary qualifications : FITTED ⟨*qualified* to lead men⟩ **2** : limited or modified in some way ⟨*qualified* agreement⟩ — **qual·i·fied·ly** \-ˌfī(-ə)d-lē\ *adv*
qual·i·fi·er \-ˌfī(-ə)r\ *n* **1** : a person or thing that satisfies requirements **2** : a word or word group that limits the meaning of another word or word group : MODIFIER
qual·i·fy \'kwäl-ə-ˌfī\ *vb* **-fied**; **-fy·ing** **1 a** : to make less general or more restricted : MODIFY ⟨*qualify* a statement⟩ **b** : to make less harsh or strict : MODERATE **c** : to alter the strength or flavor of ⟨*qualify* a liquor⟩ **d** : to limit the meaning of (as a noun) **2** : to characterize by naming an attribute : DESCRIBE **3 a** : to fit by training, skill, or ability for a special purpose ⟨his skills *qualified* him for the job⟩ **b** : CERTIFY, LICENSE ⟨*qualified* to practice law⟩
qual·i·ta·tive \'kwäl-ə-ˌtāt-iv\ *adj* : of, relating to, or involving quality or kind ⟨*qualitative* change⟩ — **qual·i·ta·tive·ly** *adv*
qual·i·ty \'kwäl-ət-ē\ *n, pl* **-ties** **1 a** : peculiar and essential character : NATURE **b** : an inherent feature : PROPERTY ⟨hardness is a *quality* of steel⟩ **2** : degree of excellence : GRADE ⟨a fine *quality* of yarn⟩ **3** : social status : RANK **4** : a distinguishing attribute : CHARACTERISTIC **5** : TIMBRE
qualm \'kwäm, 'kwälm, 'kwȯm\ *n* **1** : a sudden attack of illness, faintness, or nausea **2** : a sudden fear or misgiving **3** : a feeling of doubt or hesitation in matters of conscience ⟨had no *qualms* about lying⟩ — **qualmy** \-ē\ *adj*

syn QUALM, SCRUPLE, COMPUNCTION can mean an uneasy feeling about a morally questionable course of action. QUALM implies a sickening fear that one is violating one's conscience or better judgment; SCRUPLE implies doubt of the rightness of an act on grounds of principle; COMPUNCTION implies a spontaneous feeling that one is inflicting a wrong or injustice on someone

qualm·ish \-ish\ *adj* **1 a** : feeling qualms : NAUSEATED, QUEASY **b** : overly scrupulous : SQUEAMISH ⟨*qualmish* about dissecting a frog⟩ **2** : of, relating to, or producing qualms — **qualm·ish·ly** *adv* — **qualm·ish·ness** *n*

quan·da·ry \ˈkwän-d(ə-)rē\ *n, pl* **-ries** : a state of confusion or doubt : DILEMMA

quan·ti·ta·tive \ˈkwänt-ə-ˌtāt-iv\ *adj* : of, relating to, or involving the measurement of quantity — **quan·ti·ta·tive·ly** *adv* — **quan·ti·ta·tive·ness** *n*

quan·ti·ty \ˈkwänt-ət-ē\ *n, pl* **-ties 1 a** : an indefinite amount or number **b** : a great amount or number ⟨buys food in *quantity*⟩ **2 a** : the character of something that makes it possible to measure or number it **b** : the subject of a mathematical operation

quan·tum \ˈkwänt-əm\ *n, pl* **quan·ta** \ˈkwänt-ə\ : one of the very small parcels into which many forms of energy are subdivided

quantum mechanics *n* : a general mathematical theory dealing with the interactions of matter and radiation in terms of observable quantities only — **quantum mechanical** *adj*

quantum number *n* : one of a set of numbers used to define the quantum state of an electron in a system (as an atom or a molecule) or of the electronic system as a whole

quantum theory *n* : a branch of physical theory based on the concept of the subdivision of radiant energy into quanta

[1]**quar·an·tine** \ˈkwȯr-ən-ˌtēn, ˈkwär-\ *n* [from Italian *quarantina* "period of 40 days", from French *quarantaine*, from *quarante* "forty", from Latin *quadraginta*] **1** : a term during which a ship arriving in port and suspected of carrying contagious disease is forbidden contact with the shore **2** : a restriction upon the activities or movements of persons or the transport of goods that is designed to prevent the spread of disease or pests **3** : the period during which a person with a contagious disease is under quarantine **4** : a place (as a hospital) where persons are kept in quarantine — **quar·an·tin·a·ble** \-ˌtē-nə-bəl\ *adj*

[2]**quarantine** *vb* : to detain in or exclude by quarantine : ISOLATE

[1]**quar·rel** \ˈkwȯr(-ə)l, ˈkwär(-ə)l\ *n* **1** : a cause of dispute or complaint **2** : DISAGREEMENT, FIGHT; *esp* : an angry dispute ***syn*** see DISPUTE

[2]**quarrel** *vb* **-reled** *or* **-relled**; **-rel·ing** *or* **-rel·ling 1** : to find fault : CAVIL ⟨*quarrel* with his lot⟩ **2** : to contend or dispute actively : SQUABBLE — **quar·rel·er** *or* **quar·rel·ler** *n*

quar·rel·some \ˈkwȯr(-ə)l-səm, ˈkwär(-ə)l-\ *adj* : apt or inclined to quarrel : CONTENTIOUS — **quar·rel·some·ly** *adv* — **quar·rel·some·ness** *n*

[1]**quar·ry** \ˈkwȯr-ē, ˈkwär-\ *n, pl* **quarries 1** : the object of a chase : GAME; *esp* : game hunted with hawks **2** : PREY

[2]**quarry** *n, pl* **quarries** : an open excavation usu. for obtaining building stone, slate, or limestone

[3]**quarry** *vb* **quar·ried**; **quar·ry·ing 1** : to dig or take from or as if from a quarry **2** : to make a quarry in — **quar·ri·er** *n*

quart \ˈkwȯrt\ *n* **1** — see MEASURE table **2** : a vessel or measure having a capacity of one quart

[1]**quar·ter** \ˈkwȯrt-ər\ *n* **1** : one of four equal parts **2** : a unit (as of weight or length) that equals one fourth of some larger unit **3 a** : any of four 3-month divisions of a year **b** : a school term of about 12 weeks **c** : a coin worth a fourth of a dollar **d** : the sum of 25 cents **e** : one limb of a 4-limbed animal or carcass with the parts near it ⟨a *quarter* of beef⟩ **f** : a fourth part of the moon's period ⟨a moon in its first *quarter*⟩ **g** : one of the four equal parts into which the playing time of some games is divided **4** : someone or something (as a place, direction, or group) not specified ⟨expecting trouble from another *quarter*⟩ **5 a** : a particular division or district of a city ⟨the foreign *quarter*⟩ **b** : an assigned station esp. of a crewman ⟨call to *quarters*⟩ **c** *pl* : living accommodations : LODGING **6** : MERCY; *esp* : a refraining from destroying a defeated enemy **7** : the stern area of a ship's side — **at close quarters** : at close range or in immediate contact

[2]**quarter** *vb* **1 a** : to divide into four equal parts **b** : to separate into parts ⟨peel and *quarter* an orange⟩ **c** : DISMEMBER ⟨the traitor was hanged and *quartered*⟩ **2** : to provide with or occupy a lodging

[3]**quarter** *adj* : consisting of or equal to a quarter

quar·ter·back \ˈkwȯrt-ər-ˌbak\ *n* : an offensive football back who calls the signals and directs the offensive play of his team — **quarterback** *vb*

quarter day *n, chiefly Brit* : the day which begins a quarter of the year and on which a quarterly payment falls due

quar·ter·deck \ˈkwȯrt-ər-ˌdek\ *n* **1** : the stern area of a ship's upper deck **2** : a part of a naval vessel set aside for ceremonial and official use

quarterdeck 1

quarter horse *n* : an alert stocky muscular horse capable of high speed for short distances and of great endurance under the saddle

quarter hour *n* **1** : 15 minutes **2** : any of the quarter points of an hour

[1]**quar·ter·ly** \ˈkwȯrt-ər-lē\ *adv* : at 3-month intervals ⟨interest compounded *quarterly*⟩

[2]**quarterly** *adj* : coming during or at the end of each 3-month interval ⟨*quarterly* premium⟩ ⟨*quarterly* meeting⟩

[3]**quarterly** *n, pl* **-lies** : a periodical published four times a year

quar·ter·mas·ter \ˈkwȯrt-ər-ˌmas-tər\ *n* **1** : a petty officer who attends to a ship's steering and signals **2** : an army officer responsible for the clothing and subsistence of a body of troops

quarter note *n* : a musical note equal in time to ¼ of a whole note

quarter section *n* : a tract of land half a mile square and containing 160 acres in the U.S. government system of land surveying

quar·ter·staff \ˈkwȯrt-ər-ˌstaf\ *n* : a long stout staff formerly used as a weapon

quar·tet *also* **quar·tette** \kwȯr-ˈtet\ *n* **1 a** : a musical composition for four instruments or voices **b** : the performers of a quartet **2** : a group or set of four

quar·to \ˈkwȯrt-ō\ *n, pl* **quartos 1 a** : the size of a piece of paper cut four from a sheet **b** : a page of this size **2** : a book printed on quarto pages

quartz \ˈkwȯrts\ *n* : a common mineral consisting of silica that is often found in the form of colorless transparent crystals but is sometimes (as in amethysts, agates, and jaspers) brightly colored

quartz·ite \ˈkwȯrt-ˌsīt\ *n* : a compact granular rock composed of quartz and derived from sandstone

qua·sar \ˈkwā-ˌzär, -ˌsär\ *n* : any of the very distant starlike celestial objects that emit intense blue and ultraviolet light and powerful radio waves

1**quash** \\'kwäsh, 'kwȯsh\\ *vb* **:** to make void by judicial action ⟨*quash* an indictment⟩
2**quash** *vb* **:** to suppress or extinguish completely **:** QUELL ⟨*quash* a rebellion⟩
qua·si \\'kwā-ˌzī, -ˌsī; 'kwäz-ē\\ *adj or adv* **:** in some sense or degree **:** SEEMING ⟨a *quasi* bargain⟩ ⟨*quasi*-historical⟩ ⟨*quasi*-officially⟩
Qua·ter·na·ry \\'kwät-ər-ˌner-ē, kwə-'tər-nə-rē\\ *adj* **:** of, relating to, or being the geological period from the end of the Tertiary to the present time or the corresponding system of rocks — **Quaternary** *n*
qua·train \\'kwä-ˌtrān\\ *n* **:** a unit or group of four lines of verse
1**qua·ver** \\'kwā-vər\\ *vb* **qua·vered; qua·ver·ing** \\'kwāv-(ə-)ring\\ **1 :** TREMBLE, SHAKE ⟨*quavering* nervously⟩ **2 :** TRILL **3 :** to utter sound in trembling unsteady tones ⟨a voice that *quavered*⟩ **4 :** to speak or sing with a quavering voice — **qua·ver·ing·ly** \\'kwāv-(ə-)ring-lē\\ *adv* — **qua·very** \\'kwāv-(ə-)rē\\ *adj*
2**quaver** *n* **1 :** EIGHTH NOTE **2 :** TRILL 1 **3 :** a trembling vibrating sound
quay \\'kē, 'k(w)ā\\ *n* **:** a paved bank or a solid artificial place for loading and unloading ships
Que *abbr* Quebec
quea·sy *also* **quea·zy** \\'kwē-zē\\ *adj* **quea·si·er; -est 1 :** full of doubt **:** UNSETTLED **2 a :** causing nausea ⟨*queasy* motion⟩ **b :** NAUSEOUS **3 a :** causing uneasiness **b :** DELICATE, SQUEAMISH ⟨a *queasy* conscience⟩ **c :** ill at ease ⟨*queasy* about his debts⟩ — **quea·si·ly** \\-zə-lē\\ *adv* — **quea·si·ness** \\-zē-nəs\\ *n*
1**queen** \\'kwēn\\ *n* **1 :** the wife or widow of a king **2 :** a female monarch **3 a :** a woman eminent in rank, power, or attractions ⟨a society *queen*⟩ **b :** something regarded as female and having supremacy in a specified field ⟨*queen* of the ocean liners⟩ **c :** an attractive girl or woman; *esp* **:** a beauty contest winner **4 :** the most privileged chess piece **5 :** a playing card bearing the figure of a queen **6 :** the fertile fully developed female of social bees, ants, and termites whose function is to lay eggs — **queen·dom** \\-dəm\\ *n* — **queen·like** \\-ˌlīk\\ *adj* — **queen·li·ness** \\-lē-nəs\\ *n* — **queen·ly** \\-lē\\ *adv or adj*
2**queen** *vb* **1 a :** to act like a queen **b :** to assume a superior attitude **:** put on airs ⟨she *queened* it over her friends⟩ **2 :** to become or promote to a queen in chess
Queen Anne's lace \\-'anz-\\ *n* **:** WILD CARROT
queen mother *n* **:** the widowed mother of a reigning king
1**queer** \\'kwi(ə)r\\ *adj* **1 a :** ODD, STRANGE **b :** ECCENTRIC, CRAZY **2** *slang* **:** COUNTERFEIT ⟨*queer* money⟩ **3 :** not quite well **:** QUEASY — **queer·ish** \\-ish\\ *adj* — **queer·ly** *adv* — **queer·ness** *n*
2**queer** *vb* **1 :** to spoil the effect or success of **:** DISRUPT ⟨*queered* his plans⟩ **2 :** to put or get into an embarrassing or unfavorable situation ⟨*queered* himself with the teacher⟩
quell \\'kwel\\ *vb* **1 :** to put down **:** SUPPRESS ⟨*quell* a riot⟩ **2 :** QUIET, PACIFY ⟨*quell* fears⟩ — **quell·er** *n*
quench \\'kwench\\ *vb* **1 :** to put out **:** EXTINGUISH ⟨*quench* a lamp⟩ **2 :** SUBDUE, SUPPRESS ⟨*quench* hatred⟩ **3 :** DESTROY ⟨*quench* rebellion⟩ **4 :** RELIEVE, SATISFY ⟨*quench* thirst⟩ — **quench·a·ble** \\'kwen-chə-bəl\\ *adj* — **quench·er** *n*
quer·u·lous \\'kwer-(y)ə-ləs\\ *adj* **1 :** habitually complaining **:** CAPTIOUS **2 :** expressing complaint **:** WHINING ⟨a *querulous* voice⟩ ***syn*** see PEEVISH — **quer·u·lous·ly** *adv* — **quer·u·lous·ness** *n*
1**que·ry** \\'kwi(ə)r-ē, 'kwe(ə)r-\\ *n, pl* **queries :** QUESTION, INQUIRY
2**query** *vb* **que·ried; que·ry·ing 1 :** to put as a question ⟨*queried* the matter to his teacher⟩ **2 :** to ask questions about or of ⟨*queried* a statement⟩ ⟨*queried* the professor⟩
1**quest** \\'kwest\\ *n* **1 :** an act or instance of seeking **2 a :** PURSUIT, SEARCH ⟨in *quest* of game⟩ **b :** a chivalrous expedition in medieval romance
2**quest** *vb* **1 :** to go on a quest **:** SEEK **2 :** to search for **:** PURSUE **3 :** to ask for **:** DEMAND
1**ques·tion** \\'kwes-chən\\ *n* **1 a :** an interrogative expression **b :** a subject or aspect in dispute or open for discussion **:** ISSUE, PROBLEM **c :** a subject or point of debate or a proposition to be voted on in a meeting ⟨put the *question* to the members⟩ **2 a :** an act or instance of asking **:** INQUIRY **b :** OBJECTION, DISPUTE ⟨obey without *question*⟩ **c :** CHANCE, POSSIBILITY ⟨no *question* of escape⟩
2**question** *vb* **1 a :** to ask questions of or about **b :** INQUIRE ⟨a *questioning* mind⟩ **2 :** CROSS-EXAMINE ⟨*question* a witness⟩ **3 a :** DOUBT, DISPUTE ⟨*question* a decision⟩ **b :** to subject to analysis **:** EXAMINE — **ques·tion·er** *n* — **ques·tion·ing·ly** \\-chə-ning-lē\\ *adv*
ques·tion·a·ble \\'kwes-chə-nə-bəl\\ *adj* **1 :** open to doubt, question, or challenge **:** not certain or exact ⟨milk of *questionable* purity⟩ ⟨a *questionable* decision⟩ **2 :** suspected of being immoral, crude, false, or unsound **:** DUBIOUS ⟨*questionable* motives⟩ — **ques·tion·a·bly** \\-blē\\ *adv*
question mark *n* **:** a punctuation mark ? used chiefly at the end of a sentence to indicate a direct question
ques·tion·naire \\ˌkwes-chə-'na(ə)r, -'ne(ə)r\\ *n* **:** a set of questions to be asked of a number of persons usu. in order to gather statistics (as on opinions, facts, or knowledge)
quet·zal \\ket-'säl, -'sal\\ *n, pl* **quet·zals** *or* **quet·za·les** \\-'säl-ās\\ **:** a Central American bird with narrow crest and brilliant plumage and in the male tail feathers often over two feet in length

quetzal
(about 38 in. long)

1**queue** \\'kyü\\ *n* [from French, meaning literally "tail", from Latin *cauda*] **1 :** a pigtail usu. worn hanging at the back of the head **2 :** a line esp. of persons or vehicles ⟨a *queue* waiting at a ticket window⟩
2**queue** *vb* **queued; queu·ing** *or* **queue·ing 1 :** to arrange or form in a queue **2 :** to line up or wait in a queue ⟨the crowd *queued* up for tickets⟩ — **queu·er** *n*

ə abut	ər further	a back	ā bake	
ä cot, cart	au̇ out	ch chin	e less	ē easy
g gift	i trip	ī life	j joke	ng sing	ō flow
ȯ flaw	ȯi coin	th thin	<u>th</u> this	ü loot
u̇ foot	y yet	yü few	yu̇ furious	zh vision

[1]quib·ble \'kwib-əl\ *n* **1 :** a statement that evades, shifts from, or obscures the real point at issue **2 :** a minor objection or criticism

[2]quibble *vb* **quib·bled; quib·bling** \'kwib-(ə-)ling\ **1 :** to evade the issue : HEDGE **2 a :** to criticize on trivial grounds : CARP **b :** to quarrel about trivial matters : BICKER — **quib·bler** \-(ə-)lər\ *n*

[1]quick \'kwik\ *adj* **1** *archaic* : not dead : LIVING, ALIVE **2 a :** fast in understanding, thinking, or learning : mentally keen **b :** reacting with speed and sensitivity **c :** aroused immediately and intensely ⟨*quick* temper⟩ **d :** fast in development or occurrence ⟨a *quick* series of events⟩ ⟨gave a *quick* look⟩ **e :** marked by speed, readiness, or promptness of action or physical movement ⟨walked with *quick* steps⟩ ⟨made a *quick* job of it⟩ — **quick** *adv* — **quick·ly** *adv* — **quick·ness** *n*

[2]quick *n* **1 :** living persons ⟨the *quick* and the dead⟩ **2 :** a very sensitive area of flesh (as under a fingernail) **3 :** the inmost sensibilities ⟨hurt to the *quick* by the remark⟩ **4 :** the very center of something : HEART ⟨the *quick* of the matter⟩

quick bread *n* : a bread made with a leavening agent that permits immediate baking

quick·en \'kwik-ən\ *vb* **quick·ened; quick·en·ing** \-(ə-)ning\ **1 a :** to make or become alive : REVIVE ⟨warm spring days that *quickened* the earth⟩ **b :** AROUSE, STIMULATE ⟨curiosity *quickened* her interest⟩ **2 :** to increase in speed : HASTEN, ACCELERATE ⟨*quickened* her steps⟩ ⟨her pulse *quickened* at the sight⟩ **3 a :** to begin growth and development ⟨seeds *quickening* in the soil⟩ **b :** to reach the stage of fetal growth at which motion is begun

quick–freeze \'kwik-'frēz\ *vb* **-froze** \-'frōz\ ; **-frozen** \-'frō-zən\; **-freez·ing :** to freeze food for preservation so rapidly that the natural juices and flavor are not lost

quick·ie \'kwik-ē\ *n* : something done or made in a hurry or in less than the usual time

quick·lime \'kwik-,līm\ *n* : a caustic white substance obtained by heating limestone or seashells, consisting mostly of calcium and oxygen, and used esp. in building (as in mortar and cement), in agriculture, and in the chemical industry

quick·sand \-,sand\ *n* : a deep mass of loose sand mixed with water into which heavy objects sink

quick·sil·ver \-,sil-vər\ *n* : MERCURY 2a

quick–tem·pered \-'tem-pərd\ *adj* : easily angered : IRASCIBLE

quick–wit·ted \-'wit-əd\ *adj* : quick in perception and understanding : mentally alert — **quick–wit·ted·ness** *n*

quid \'kwid\ *n* : a cut or wad of something chewable ⟨a *quid* of tobacco⟩

qui·es·cent \kwī-'es-ənt, kwē-\ *adj* : being at rest : INACTIVE, MOTIONLESS ***syn*** see LATENT — **qui·es·cence** \-ən(t)s\ *n* — **qui·es·cent·ly** *adv*

[1]qui·et \'kwī-ət\ *n* : the quality or state of being quiet : TRANQUILLITY — **on the quiet :** in a secretive manner

[2]quiet *adj* **1 a :** marked by little or no motion, activity, or noise : CALM **b :** GENTLE, EASYGOING ⟨a *quiet* temperament⟩ **c :** UNDISTURBED ⟨*quiet* reading⟩ **d :** enjoyed in peace and relaxation ⟨a *quiet* cup of tea⟩ **2 :** not colorful or showy : CONSERVATIVE ⟨*quiet* clothes⟩ **3 :** hidden from public view : SECLUDED ⟨a *quiet* nook⟩ — **quiet** *adv* — **qui·et·ly** *adv* — **qui·et·ness** *n*

[3]quiet *vb* : to make or become quiet — **qui·et·er** *n*

qui·e·tude \'kwī-ə-,t(y)üd\ *n* : TRANQUILLITY, QUIETNESS

qui·e·tus \kwī-'ēt-əs\ *n* **1 :** a final freeing from something (as a debt, an office or duty, or life) **2 :** something that quiets or represses ⟨put the *quietus* on a scandal⟩ **3 :** a state of inactivity

quill \'kwil\ *n* **1 a :** the hollow horny barrel of a feather **b :** one of the large stiff feathers of the wing or tail **2 :** one of the hollow sharp spines of a porcupine or hedgehog **3 :** a pen made from a feather

[1]quilt \'kwilt\ *n* **1 :** a bed cover made of two layers of cloth filled with wool, cotton, or down **2 :** something quilted or like a quilt

[2]quilt *vb* **1 a :** to fill, pad, or line like a quilt **b :** to stitch, sew, or cover with lines or patterns like those used in quilts **c :** to fasten between two pieces of material **2 :** to stitch or sew in layers with padding in between — **quilt·er** *n*

quilt·ing *n* **1 :** the process of quilting **2 :** quilted material or material used for quilts

quince \'kwin(t)s\ *n* : the fruit of an Asiatic tree that resembles a hard-fleshed yellow apple and is used esp. for marmalade, jelly, and preserves; *also* : this tree

quince

qui·nine \'kwī-,nīn, *Brit* kwin-'ēn\ *n* : a bitter white crystalline substance from cinchona bark used in medicine esp. against malaria; *also* : a salt of quinine

quinine water *n* : a carbonated beverage flavored with a small amount of quinine, lemon, and lime

Quin·qua·ge·si·ma \,kwing-kwə-'jes-ə-mə, -'jā-zə-\ *n* : the Sunday before Lent

quin·quen·ni·al \kwin-'kwen-ē-əl\ *adj* **1 :** consisting of or lasting for five years **2 :** occurring or done every five years — **quinquennial** *n* — **quin·quen·ni·al·ly** \-ē-ə-lē\ *adv*

quin·sy \'kwin-zē\ *n* : a severe inflammation of the throat or adjacent parts with swelling and fever

quint \'kwint\ *n* : QUINTUPLET

quin·tal \'kwint-əl\ *n* **1 :** HUNDREDWEIGHT **2** — see METRIC SYSTEM table

quin·tes·sence \kwin-'tes-ən(t)s\ *n* **1 :** the purest form of something **2 :** the most perfect type or example ⟨manners that were the *quintessence* of courtesy⟩ — **quint·es·sen·tial** \,kwint-ə-'sen-chəl\ *adj*

quin·tet \kwin-'tet\ *n* **1 a :** a musical composition for five instruments or voices **b :** the performers of a quintet **2 :** a group or set of five

quin·til·lion \kwin-'til-yən\ *n* — see NUMBER table

[1]quin·tu·ple \kwin-'t(y)üp-əl, -'təp-; 'kwint-əp-\ *adj* **1 :** having five units or members **2 :** being five times as great or as many — **quintuple** *n*

[2]quintuple *vb* **quin·tu·pled; quin·tu·pling** \-(ə-)ling\ : to make or become five times as great or as many

quin·tup·let \kwin-'təp-lət, -'t(y)üp-; 'kwint-əp-\ *n* **1 :** a group of five **2 :** one of five offspring born at one birth

quip \'kwip\ *n* **1 :** a clever remark : GIBE **2 :** a witty or funny saying — **quip** *vb*

quire \'kwī(ə)r\ *n* : a group of 24 or sometimes 25 sheets of paper of the same size and quality

quirk \'kwərk\ *n* **1 :** a sudden turn, twist, or curve (as a flourish in writing) **2 :** a peculiar trait : MANNERISM — **quirky** \'kwər-kē\ *adj*

quirt \'kwərt\ *n* : a riding whip with a short handle and a rawhide lash

quis·ling \'kwiz-ling\ *n* [after Vidkun *Quisling* (1887–1945), Norwegian politician who collaborated with the Germans in World War II] : a traitor who collaborates with the invaders of his country esp. by serving in a puppet government

1**quit** \'kwit\ *adj* : released from obligation, charge, or penalty : FREE ⟨*quit* of debt⟩

2**quit** *vb* **quit** *also* **quit·ted**; **quit·ting** **1 :** to make full payment to or for : REPAY ⟨*quit* a debt⟩ **2 :** CONDUCT ⟨the boys *quit* themselves like men⟩ **3 a :** to depart from : LEAVE **b :** to bring to an end : ABANDON **c :** to give up : RESIGN ⟨*quit* a job⟩ **4 :** to admit defeat : SURRENDER — **quit·ter** *n*

quite \'kwīt\ *adv* **1 :** COMPLETELY, WHOLLY ⟨not *quite* all⟩ **2 :** to an extreme : POSITIVELY ⟨not *quite* sure⟩ **3 :** to a considerable extent : RATHER ⟨*quite* near⟩

quits \'kwits\ *adj* : even or equal with another (as by repaying a debt, returning a favor, or retaliating for an injury)

quit·tance \'kwit-ən(t)s\ *n* **1 a :** discharge from a debt or an obligation **b :** a document certifying quittance **2 :** something given in return : RECOMPENSE

1**quiv·er** \'kwiv-ər\ *n* **1 :** a case for carrying arrows **2 :** the arrows in a quiver

2**quiver** *vb* **quiv·ered**; **quiv·er·ing** \'kwiv-(ə-)ring\ : to move with a slight trembling motion ⟨tall grass *quivering* in the breeze⟩

3**quiver** *n* : the act or action of quivering : TREMOR

quix·ot·ic \kwik-'sät-ik\ *adj* [from Don *Quixote*, hero of the novel *Don Quixote de la Mancha* by Cervantes] : impractically idealistic : ROMANTIC — **quix·ot·i·cal·ly** \-'sät-i-k(ə-)lē\ *adv*

1**quiz** \'kwiz\ *n, pl* **quiz·zes** **1 :** a person who ridicules or mocks **2 :** the act or action of quizzing; *esp* : a short oral or written test

2**quiz** *vb* **quizzed**; **quiz·zing** **1 :** to make fun of : MOCK **2 :** to question closely : EXAMINE — **quizzer** *n*

quiz·zi·cal \'kwiz-i-kəl\ *adj* **1 :** slightly eccentric : ODD ⟨a *quizzical* old man⟩ **2 :** BANTERING, TEASING ⟨a *quizzical* remark⟩ **3 :** QUESTIONING, INQUISITIVE ⟨a *quizzical* look⟩ — **quiz·zi·cal·ly** \-k(ə-)lē\ *adv*

quoin \'k(w)ȯin\ *n* : a solid exterior angle (as of a building) or one of the blocks forming it

quoit \'kwāt, 'k(w)ȯit\ *n* **1 :** a ring of iron or circle of rope to be thrown over a peg in a game **2** *pl* : a game played with quoits

quo·rum \'kwōr-əm, 'kwȯr-\ *n* : the number of members of an organization required to be present when business is conducted

quot *abbr* quotation

quo·ta \'kwōt-ə\ *n* **1 :** a proportional part or share; *esp* : the share or proportion assigned to each member of a group **2 :** the number or amount constituting a quota

quot·a·ble \'kwōt-ə-bəl\ *adj* : fit for or worth quoting

quo·ta·tion \kwō-'tā-shən\ *n* **1 :** something quoted; *esp* : a passage referred to or repeated **2 :** the act or process of quoting **3 a :** the naming or publishing of current prices of securities or commodities **b :** the prices so named or published

quotation mark *n* : one of a pair of punctuation marks " " or ' ' used chiefly to indicate the beginning and the end of a direct quotation

1**quote** \'kwōt\ *vb* **1 :** to speak or write a passage from another usu. with acknowledgment ⟨*quote* Shakespeare⟩ **2 :** to cite in illustration ⟨*quote* cases⟩ **3 :** to name the current price of a commodity, stock, or bond **4 :** to set off a passage by quotation marks

2**quote** *n* **1 :** QUOTATION **2 :** QUOTATION MARK

quoth \(')kwōth\ *vb past, archaic* : SAID — used chiefly in the first and third persons and placed before the subject

quo·tient \'kwō-shənt\ *n* [from Latin *quotiens* "how many times", from *quot* "how many"; so called from its being the answer to the question "How many times does the divisor go into the dividend?"] : the number resulting from the division of one number by another

ə abut	ər further	a back	ā bake
ä cot, cart	aů out	ch chin	e less	ē easy
g gift	i trip	ī life	j joke	ng sing	ō flow
ȯ flaw	ȯi coin	th thin	t͟h this	ü loot
u̇ foot	y yet	yü few	yu̇ furious	zh vision

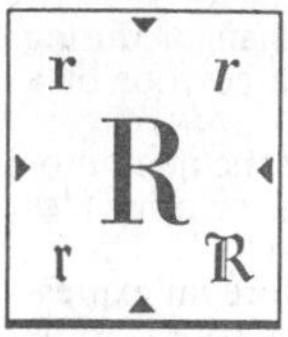

r \'är\ *n, often cap* : the 18th letter of the English alphabet
r *abbr* **1** right **2** river
R *abbr* **1** radius **2** Republican **3** runs scored **4** rural
¹**rab·bet** \'rab-ət\ *n* : a groove or recess cut in the edge or face of a surface esp. to receive the edge of another surface (as a panel)
²**rabbet** *vb* **1** : to cut a rabbet in **2** : to join the edges of by a rabbet
rab·bi \'rab-ˌī\ *n* [from Hebrew *rabbī* "my master", from *rabh* "master" with the suffix *-ī* "my"] **1** : MASTER, TEACHER — used as a term of address for Jewish religious leaders **2** : a professionally trained and ordained leader of a Jewish congregation — **rab·bin·ic** \rə-'bin-ik, ra-\ *or* **rab·bin·i·cal** \-i-kəl\ *adj*
rab·bin·ate \'rab-ə-nət, -ˌnāt\ *n* **1** : the office or tenure of a rabbi **2** : a group of rabbis
rab·bit \'rab-ət\ *n, pl* **rabbits** *also* **rabbit** : a small long-eared burrowing mammal differing from the related hares esp. in producing naked young; *also* : its pelt — **rabbit** *vb*

rabbit
(about 17 in. long)

rabbit ears *n pl* : an indoor antenna (as for a television set) consisting of two extendible rods
rabbit punch *n* : a short chopping blow to the back of the neck or the base of the skull
rab·ble \'rab-əl\ *n* **1** : a noisy and unruly crowd : MOB **2** : a body of people looked down upon as ignorant and disorderly
rab·ble–rous·er \-ˌraù-zər\ *n* : one that stirs up the masses of the people esp. to hatred or violence
rab·id \'rab-əd\ *adj* **1** : extremely violent : FURIOUS **2** : extremely enthusiastic : AVID ⟨a *rabid* sports fan⟩ **3** : affected with rabies ⟨a *rabid* dog⟩ — **rab·id·ly** *adv* — **rab·id·ness** *n*
ra·bies \'rā-bēz\ *n* : an acute virus disease of the central nervous system of warm-blooded animals transmitted by the bite of a rabid animal and always fatal when untreated — called also *hydrophobia*
rac·coon \ra-'kün\ *n, pl* **raccoon** *or* **raccoons** : a small flesh-eating mammal of No. America that is chiefly gray, has a bushy ringed tail, and lives chiefly in trees; *also* : its pelt

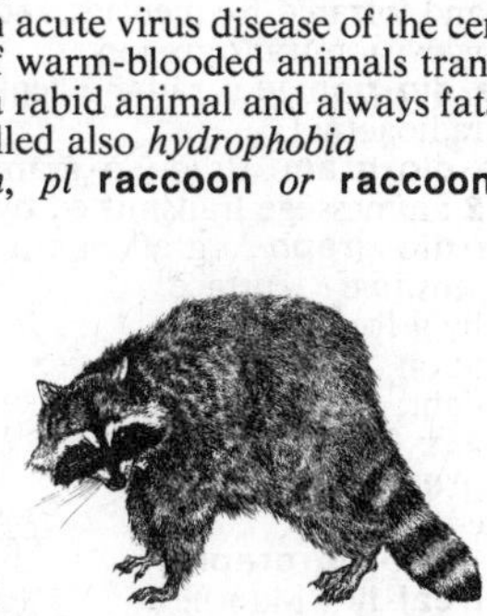

raccoon
(up to 36 in. long)

¹**race** \'rās\ *n* **1** : a strong or rapid current of water or the channel for such a current; *esp* : a current of water used industrially (as in mining or for turning a mill wheel) **2 a** : a contest of speed **b** : a contest for a desired goal ⟨the *race* for the governorship⟩ **3** : a track or channel in which something rolls or slides; *esp* : a groove for the balls in a bearing
²**race** *vb* **1** : to run in a race **2** : to go, move, or drive at top speed or out of control **3** : to engage in a race with ⟨*race* the champion⟩ **4** : to speed an idling engine
³**race** *n* **1 a** : a group of people of common ancestry or stock **b** : one of the three, four, or five primary divisions commonly recognized in mankind and based on readily observed traits (as skin color) that are transmitted by heredity ⟨the Caucasian *race*⟩ **c** : MANKIND ⟨the human *race*⟩ **2** : a group of individuals within a species capable of interbreeding; *also* : a taxonomic category (as a subspecies or breed) that represents such a group
race·course \'rās-ˌkōrs, -ˌkȯrs\ *n* : RACETRACK
race·horse \-ˌhȯrs\ *n* : a horse bred or kept for racing
ra·ceme \rā-'sēm\ *n* : a simple flower cluster (as of the lily of the valley) with a long axis bearing flowers on short stems in succession toward the apex — **rac·e·mose** \'ras-ə-ˌmōs, rā-'sē-\ *adj*

raceme

rac·er \'rā-sər\ *n* **1** : one that races **2** : any of various slender active American snakes; *esp* : a common blacksnake
race·track \'rās-ˌtrak\ *n* : a usu. oval course on which races are run
ra·chis \'rā-kəs, 'rak-əs\ *n, pl* **ra·chis·es** *also* **rach·i·des** \'rak-ə-ˌdēz, 'rā-kə-\ **1 a** : the main axis of a flower cluster **b** : the main stalk of a compound leaf — see LEAF illustration **2** : the part of the shaft of a feather more distant from the point of attachment
ra·cial \'rā-shəl\ *adj* **1** : of or relating to race **2** : existing or occurring between human races ⟨*racial* tensions⟩ — **ra·cial·ly** \-shə-lē\ *adv*
ra·cial·ism \'rā-shə-ˌliz-əm\ *n* : RACISM — **ra·cial·ist** \'rāsh-(ə-)ləst\ *n* — **ra·cial·is·tic** \ˌrā-shə-'lis-tik\ *adj*
rac·ism \'rā-ˌsiz-əm\ *n* **1** : belief that certain races of men are by birth and nature superior to others **2 a** : discrimination against the members of one or more races based upon racism **b** : race hatred and discrimination — **rac·ist** \'rā-səst\ *n or adj*
¹**rack** \'rak\ *n* **1 a** : a framework for holding fodder **b** : a framework on a vehicle for carrying loose produce (as hay or grain) **2** : an instrument of torture on which a body is stretched **3** : a framework, stand, or grating on or in which articles are placed ⟨clothes *rack*⟩ ⟨bicycle *rack*⟩ ⟨baggage *rack*⟩ **4** : a bar with teeth on one face for meshing with those of a pinion — **on the rack** : under great mental or emotional stress
²**rack** *vb* **1** : to torture on the rack **2** : to cause to suffer torture, pain, or anguish ⟨*racked* by a cough⟩ **3** : to stretch or strain violently **4** : to place (as pool balls) in a rack
¹**rack·et** *also* **rac·quet** \'rak-ət\ *n* **1** : a light bat consisting of a net stretched in an oval open frame ⟨a tennis *racket*⟩ **2** : PADDLE 2b

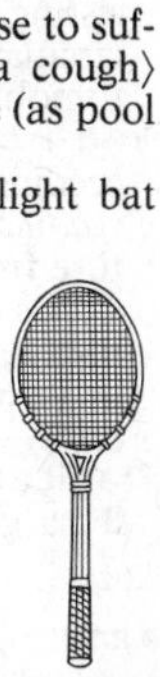

racket 1

²**racket** *n* **1** : confused clattering noise : DIN **2 a** : a dishonest scheme; *esp* : one for obtaining money by cheating or threats **b** *slang* : OCCUPATION
³**racket** *vb* : to make a racket
rack·e·teer \ˌrak-ə-'ti(ə)r\ *n* : one who extorts money or advantages by threats, blackmail, or unlawful interference with business or employment — **racketeer** *vb*
rack up *vb* : SCORE ⟨*racked* 30 points *up* in the first half⟩
ra·coon *var of* RACCOON

rac·quets \'rak-əts\ *n* : a game for two or four played with ball and racket on a 4-walled court

[1]**racy** \'rā-sē\ *adj* **rac·i·er**; **-est** **1 a** : full of zest or vigor : LIVELY ⟨brisk, *racy* prose⟩ **b** : sharply stimulating : PUNGENT ⟨*racy* satire⟩ **2** : slightly indecent or improper : SUGGESTIVE ⟨*racy* stories⟩ — **rac·i·ly** \-sə-lē\ *adv* — **rac·i·ness** \-sē-nəs\ *n*

[2]**racy** *adj* : being long-bodied and lean ⟨a *racy* whippet⟩

rad *abbr* **1** radio **2** radius

ra·dar \'rā-ˌdär\ *n* [from the beginning letters of *ra*dio *d*etecting *a*nd *r*anging] : a device that sends out a powerful beam of radio waves that when reflected back to it from a distant object indicate the position and direction of motion of the object — **ra·dar·man** \-mən, -ˌman\ *n*

ra·dar·scope \-ˌskōp\ *n* : the part of a radar apparatus on which the spots of light appear that indicate the position and direction of motion of a distant object

[1]**ra·di·al** \'rād-ē-əl\ *adj* **1** : arranged or having parts arranged like rays coming from a common center **2** : relating to, placed like, or moving along a bodily radius **3** : of, relating to, or arranged like a radius — **ra·di·al·ly** \-ē-ə-lē\ *adv*

[2]**radial** *n* : a radial part

radial symmetry *n* : the condition of having similar parts regularly arranged around a central axis ⟨*radial symmetry* of the starfish⟩

ra·di·ance \'rād-ē-ən(t)s\ *also* **ra·di·an·cy** \-ən-sē\ *n, pl* **-anc·es** *or* **-an·cies** : the quality or state of being radiant : BRILLIANCE

ra·di·ant \'rād-ē-ənt\ *adj* **1** : giving out or reflecting light ⟨the *radiant* sun⟩ ⟨a *radiant* jewel⟩ **2** : expressing love, confidence, or happiness ⟨a *radiant* bride⟩ **3** : emitted or transmitted by radiation ⟨*radiant* heat⟩ — **ra·di·ant·ly** *adv*

radiant energy *n* : energy (as heat waves, light waves, radio waves, X rays) transmitted in the form of electromagnetic waves

[1]**ra·di·ate** \'rād-ē-ˌāt\ *vb* **1** : to send out rays of or as if of light **2** : to proceed in a direct line from or toward a center **3** : to send out in or as if in rays ⟨stars *radiate* energy⟩ ⟨*radiates* good health⟩

[2]**ra·di·ate** \-ē-ət\ *adj* : having rays or radial parts

ra·di·a·tion \ˌrād-ē-'ā-shən\ *n* **1** : the action or process of radiating; *esp* : the process of emitting radiant energy in the form of waves or particles **2** : something that is radiated; *esp* : energy radiated in the form of waves or particles — **ra·di·a·tion·al** \-sh(ə-)nəl\ *adj*

ra·di·a·tor \'rād-ē-ˌāt-ər\ *n* **1** : a heating device consisting of pipes through which hot water or steam circulates **2** : a device for cooling water (as of an automobile engine) that circulates through it

[1]**rad·i·cal** \'rad-i-kəl\ *adj* **1** : of, relating to, or proceeding from a root **2** : BASIC, FUNDAMENTAL ⟨*radical* differences⟩ **3 a** : marked by a sharp departure from the usual or traditional : DRASTIC **b** : desirous of making extreme changes in existing views, habits, conditions, or institutions **c** : of, relating to, or being political radicals — **rad·i·cal·ly** \-k(ə-)lē\ *adv* — **rad·i·cal·ness** *n*

[2]**radical** *n* **1** : ROOT 5 **2** : a person who is radical **3** : a group of atoms that is replaceable by a single atom and is capable of remaining unchanged during a series of reactions **4 a** : the indicated root of a mathematical expression **b** : RADICAL SIGN

rad·i·cal·ism \'rad-i-kə-ˌliz-əm\ *n* **1** : the quality or state of being radical **2** : the doctrines or principles of radicals

radical sign *n* : the sign √ placed before an expression in mathematics to indicate that its root is to be extracted

rad·i·cand \ˌrad-ə-'kand\ *n* : the expression under a radical sign

radii *pl of* RADIUS

[1]**ra·dio** \'rād-ē-ˌō\ *n, pl* **ra·di·os** [short for *radiotelegraphy* "telegraphy by rays", from Latin *radius* "spoke", "ray"] **1** : the sending or receiving of signals by means of electric waves without a connecting wire ⟨*radio* includes television and radar⟩ **2** : a radio message **3** : a radio receiving set **4** : the radio broadcasting industry

[2]**radio** *adj* **1** : of, relating to, or operated by radiant energy and esp. by the electric frequencies used in radio **2** : of, relating to, or used in radio or a radio set

[3]**radio** *vb* **1** : to send or communicate by radio **2** : to send a radio message to

radio- *comb form* **1** : radiant energy : radiation ⟨*radio*active⟩ **2** : radioactive ⟨*radio*carbon⟩

ra·dio·ac·tive \ˌrād-ē-ō-'ak-tiv\ *adj* : of, caused by, exhibiting, or employing radioactivity — **ra·dio·ac·tive·ly** *adv*

ra·dio·ac·tiv·i·ty \-ˌak-'tiv-ət-ē\ *n* : the property possessed by some elements (as uranium) of spontaneously emitting rays by the disintegration of the nuclei of atoms

radio astronomy *n* : astronomy dealing with electromagnetic radiations of radio frequency received from outside the earth's atmosphere — **radio astronomer** *n*

radio beacon *n* : a radio transmitting station that transmits special radio signals for use (as on a landing field) in determining the direction or position of those receiving them

ra·dio·car·bon \ˌrād-ē-ō-'kär-bən\ *n* : radioactive carbon; *esp* : CARBON 14

radio frequency *n* : any of the electromagnetic wave frequencies intermediate between audio frequencies and infrared frequencies and used esp. in radio and television transmission

ra·dio·gen·ic \ˌrād-ē-ō-'jen-ik\ *adj* : produced by radioactivity

ra·dio·gram \'rād-ē-ō-ˌgram\ *n* **1** : RADIOGRAPH **2** : a message transmitted by radiotelegraphy

ra·dio·graph \-ˌgraf\ *n* : a picture produced on a sensitive surface by a form of radiation other than light; *esp* : X RAY 2 — **ra·dio·graph·ic** \ˌrād-ē-ō-'graf-ik\ *adj* — **ra·dio·graph·i·cal·ly** \-i-k(ə-)lē\ *adv* — **ra·di·og·ra·phy** \ˌrād-ē-'äg-rə-fē\ *n*

ra·dio·iso·tope \ˌrād-ē-ō-'ī-sə-ˌtōp\ *n* : a radioactive isotope

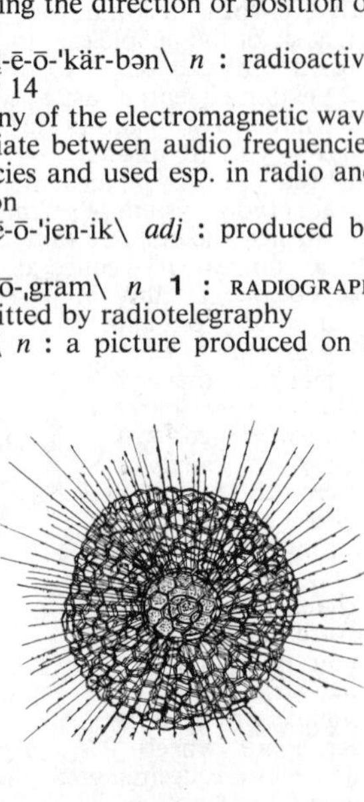

radiolarian
(magnified 150 times)

ra·di·o·lar·i·an \ˌrād-ē-ō-'lar-ē-ən, -'ler-\ *n* : any of a large order of marine protozoans with radiating threadlike pseudopodia and a skeleton containing silica

ra·di·om·e·ter \ˌrād-ē-ˈäm-ət-ər\ *n* : an instrument for measuring the intensity of radiant energy — **ra·dio·met·ric** \ˌrād-ē-ō-ˈme-trik\ *adj* — **ra·di·om·e·try** \-ˈäm-ə-trē\ *n*

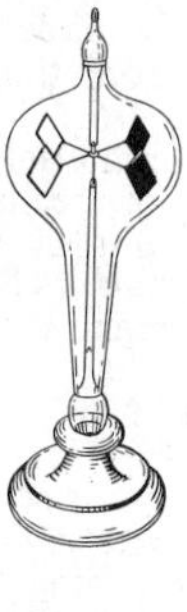
radiometer

ra·dio·phone \ˈrād-ē-ə-ˌfōn\ *n* : RADIOTELEPHONE

ra·dio·sonde \ˈrād-ē-ō-ˌsänd\ *n* : a miniature radio transmitter that is carried (as by a balloon) aloft with instruments for broadcasting data on the humidity, temperature, and pressure

ra·dio·tel·e·graph \ˌrād-ē-ō-ˈtel-ə-ˌgraf\ *n* : WIRELESS TELEGRAPHY — **ra·dio·te·leg·ra·phy** \-tə-ˈleg-rə-fē\ *n*

ra·dio·tel·e·phone \-ˈtel-ə-ˌfōn\ *n* : a telephone that utilizes radio waves wholly or partly instead of connecting wires — **ra·dio·te·leph·o·ny** \-tə-ˈlef-ə-nē, -ˈtel-ə-ˌfō-nē\ *n*

radio telescope *n* : a radio receiver-antenna combination used for observation in radio astronomy

ra·dio·ther·a·py \ˌrad-ē-ō-ˈther-ə-pē\ *n* : the treatment of disease by means of X rays or radioactive substances — **ra·dio·ther·a·pist** \-pəst\ *n*

ra·dio–ul·na \ˌrād-ē-ō-ˈəl-nə\ *n* : a bone of some lower vertebrates (as the toad) equivalent to the combined radius and ulna of higher forms

radio wave *n* : an electromagnetic wave with radio frequency

rad·ish \ˈrad-ish, ˈred-\ *n* : a pungent fleshy root usu. eaten raw; *also* : a plant related to the cabbage and having roots that are radishes

ra·di·um \ˈrād-ē-əm\ *n* : an intensely radioactive shining white metallic element that occurs in combination in minute quantities in minerals (as pitchblende) and is used chiefly in luminous materials and in the treatment of cancer — see ELEMENT table

ra·di·us \ˈrād-ē-əs\ *n, pl* **-dii** \-ē-ˌī\ *also* **-di·us·es** [from Latin, originally meaning "a rod", then "the spoke of a wheel", "ray", "radius"] **1** : the anterior and thicker and shorter bone of the human forearm or of the corresponding part of the forelimb of vertebrates above fishes **2 a** : a line extending from the center of a circle or sphere to the circumference or surface **b** : a circular area determined by a given radius ⟨deer may wander within a *radius* of several miles⟩ **3** : a radial part or plane

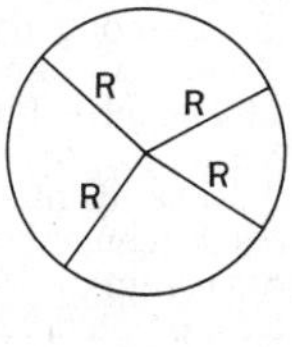

R radii 2a

ra·don \ˈrā-ˌdän\ *n* : a heavy radioactive gaseous element formed by disintegration of radium — see ELEMENT table

raf·fia \ˈraf-ē-ə\ *n* : fiber from a palm of Madagascar with compound leaves used esp. for baskets and hats

raff·ish \ˈraf-ish\ *adj* **1** : vulgarly crude or flashy ⟨*raffish* language⟩ **2** : carelessly unconventional : DISREPUTABLE — **raff·ish·ly** *adv* — **raff·ish·ness** *n*

¹raf·fle \ˈraf-əl\ *n* : a lottery in which the prize is won by one of the persons buying chances

²raffle *vb* **raf·fled**; **raf·fling** \ˈraf-(ə-)ling\ : to dispose of by a raffle ⟨*raffle* off a turkey⟩

¹raft \ˈraft\ *n* **1** : logs or timbers fastened together to serve as a means of transportation on water **2** : a flat buoyant structure for support or transportation on water

²raft *vb* **1** : to transport or move in or by means of a raft **2** : to make into a raft

³raft *n* : a large amount

raf·ter \ˈraf-tər\ *n* : a usu. sloping timber supporting a roof

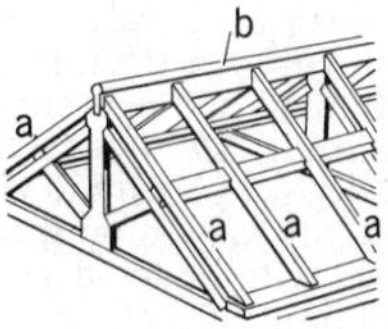

a rafters, *b* ridgepole

rag \ˈrag\ *n* **1** : a waste or worn piece of cloth **2** *pl* : shabby or tattered clothing ⟨dressed in *rags*⟩

rag·a·muf·fin \ˈrag-ə-ˌməf-ən\ *n* : a ragged often disreputable person; *esp* : a poorly clothed often dirty child

¹rage \ˈrāj\ *n* **1 a** : violent and uncontrolled anger : FURY **b** : a fit of violent anger **2** : violent action (as of wind or sea) **3** : CRAZE, FAD ⟨the current *rage* for decorated sweat shirts⟩

²rage *vb* **1** : to be in a rage **2** : to be in tumult **3** : to prevail uncontrollably ⟨an epidemic was *raging*⟩ ⟨*raging* seas⟩

rag·ged \ˈrag-əd\ *adj* **1** : having an irregular edge or outline : JAGGED ⟨*ragged* cliffs⟩ **2 a** : torn or worn to or as if to tatters ⟨a *ragged* dress⟩ ⟨run *ragged*⟩ **b** : wearing tattered clothes — **rag·ged·ly** *adv* — **rag·ged·ness** *n*

rag·lan \ˈrag-lən\ *n* : a loose overcoat with sleeves sewn in by seams slanted from the underarm to the neck

rag·man \ˈrag-ˌman\ *n* : a collector of or dealer in rags and waste

ra·gout \ra-ˈgü\ *n* : a highly seasoned meat stew with vegetables

rag·time \ˈrag-ˌtīm\ *n* **1** : musical rhythm in which the melody has the accented notes falling on beats that are not usu. accented **2** : music with ragtime rhythm

rag·weed \ˈrag-ˌwēd\ *n* : any of various chiefly No. American weedy herbs related to the daisies and producing pollen irritating to the eyes and nasal passages of some persons

ragweed

rah \ˈrä, ˈrȯ\ *interj* : HURRAH — used esp. to cheer a team on ⟨*rah, rah,* team⟩

¹raid \ˈrād\ *n* [from Scottish dialect, from Old English *rād*, meaning literally "a ride", "the act of riding", the same word which in southern English became *road*] **1** : a sudden attack or invasion **2** : a daring, sudden, or stealthy act to gain something ⟨a *raid* on the icebox⟩

²raid *vb* : to make a raid on — **raid·er** *n*

¹rail \ˈrāl\ *n* **1 a** : a bar extending from one post or support to another and serving as a guard or barrier **b** : RAILING **2 a** : a bar of rolled steel forming a track for wheeled vehicles **b** : TRACK 2b **c** : RAILROAD

²rail *vb* : to provide with a railing : FENCE

³rail *n, pl* **rails** *or* **rail** : any of a family of small wading birds related to the cranes

⁴rail *vb* : to scold or complain in harsh, bitter, or abusive language — **rail·er** *n*

rail
(about 16 in. long)

rail·ing \'rā-liŋ\ *n* **1** : a barrier (as a fence or balustrade) consisting of rails and their supports **2** : material for rails : RAILS

rail·lery \'rā-lə-rē\ *n, pl* **-ler·ies** **1** : good-natured ridicule : BANTER **2** : JEST

1**rail·road** \'rāl-,rōd\ *n* **1** : a permanent road having a line of rails fixed to ties and laid on a roadbed and providing a track for cars **2** : a company owning a railroad and operating equipment on it

2**railroad** *vb* **1 a** : to transport by railroad **b** : to work for a railroad company **2 a** : to push through hastily or without careful consideration **b** : to convict with undue haste and by means of false charges or insufficient evidence — **rail·road·er** *n*

rail·way \'rāl-,wā\ *n* : RAILROAD; *esp* : a railroad operating with light equipment or within a small area

rai·ment \'rā-mənt\ *n* : CLOTHING, GARMENTS

1**rain** \'rān\ *n* **1 a** : water falling in drops from clouds **b** : the falling of such water **2 a** : RAINSTORM **b** *pl* : the rainy season **3** : rainy weather ⟨a week of *rain*⟩ **4** : a heavy fall of particles or bodies : BARRAGE ⟨a *rain* of protests⟩ — **rain·less** \-ləs\ *adj*

2**rain** *vb* **1** : to fall as water in drops from the clouds **2** : to send down rain **3** : to fall like rain ⟨ashes *rained* from the volcano⟩ **4** : to send like rain ⟨the boxers *rained* blows on each other⟩

rain·bow \'rān-,bō\ *n* **1** : an arc or circle showing the colors of the spectrum and formed by refraction and reflection of the sun's rays in raindrops, spray, or mist **2** : a multicolored array ⟨a *rainbow* of colors⟩

rainbow trout *n* : a large stout-bodied usu. brightly marked trout native to western No. America — called also *rainbow*

rain·coat \'rān-,kōt\ *n* : a coat of waterproof or water-resistant material

rain·fall \-,fȯl\ *n* **1** : a fall of rain **2** : amount of precipitation ⟨an annual *rainfall* of 20 inches⟩

rain forest *n* : a usu. tropical woodland with a high annual rainfall and lofty trees forming a continuous canopy

rain gauge *n* : an instrument for measuring rainfall

rain·mak·ing \'rān-,mā-kiŋ\ *n* : the act or process of attempting to produce rain by artificial means — **rain·mak·er** \-kər\ *n*

rain·proof \-'prüf\ *adj* : protecting or protected against rain

rain·storm \-,stȯrm\ *n* : a storm of or with rain

rain·wa·ter \-,wȯt-ər, -,wät-\ *n* : water falling or fallen as rain

rainy \'rā-nē\ *adj* **rain·i·er**; **-est** : having much rain : SHOWERY ⟨a *rainy* season⟩

rainy day *n* : a period of want or need ⟨set a little aside for a *rainy day*⟩

1**raise** \'rāz\ *vb* **1** : to cause to rise : LIFT ⟨*raise* a window⟩ ⟨*raise* dust⟩ **2** : to stir up : AROUSE, INCITE ⟨*raise* a rebellion⟩ **3 a** : BUILD, ERECT **b** : to place higher in rank or dignity : ELEVATE **4** : COLLECT ⟨*raise* funds⟩ **5 a** : to foster the growth and development of : GROW, REAR ⟨*raise* a crop for market⟩ ⟨*raise* pigs on slop⟩ **b** : to bring up a child ⟨boys *raised* in the city⟩ **6** : to give voice to ⟨*raise* a cheer⟩ **7** : to bring up for consideration or debate ⟨*raise* an issue⟩ **8 a** : to increase the strength, intensity, or pitch of ⟨*raised* his voice⟩ **b** : to increase the amount or rate of ⟨*raise* the rent⟩ **c** : to multiply a quantity by itself a specified number of times **d** : to increase a bid or bet **9** : to make light and porous ⟨*raise* dough⟩ — **rais·er** *n*

syn RAISE, LIFT, HOIST can mean to bring to a higher position or plane. RAISE often suggests a suitable or intended higher position to which something is brought; LIFT implies exertion of effort in bringing something material or immaterial to a higher plane; HOIST implies the use of mechanical means in raising something heavy ***ant*** lower

2**raise** *n* **1** : an act of raising or lifting **2 a** : an increase in the amount of a bet or bid **b** : an increase in pay

rai·sin \'rā-zən\ *n* : a grape usu. of a special type dried for food

ra·ja *or* **ra·jah** \'räj-ə\ *n* [from Hindi *rājā*, from Sanskrit *rājan* "king", from an Indo-European root meaning "to rule", the source of English *reign, regal, rule*] : an Indian or Malay prince or chief

1**rake** \'rāk\ *n* **1** : a long-handled garden tool having a bar with teeth or prongs **2** : a machine for gathering hay

2**rake** *vb* **1** : to gather together with or as if with a rake **2** : to search through : RANSACK ⟨*rake* the records for evidence⟩ **3** : to sweep the length of esp. with gunfire ⟨the guns *raked* the enemy's ship⟩ — **rak·er** *n*

3**rake** *n* : a person who is loose in morals and conduct : LIBERTINE

rake–off \'rāk-,ȯf\ *n* : an often unlawful commission or profit received by one party in a business deal

1**rak·ish** \'rā-kish\ *adj* : of, relating to, or characteristic of a rake : DISSOLUTE — **rak·ish·ly** *adv* — **rak·ish·ness** *n*

2**rakish** *adj* **1** : having a smart stylish appearance suggestive of speed ⟨a *rakish* ship⟩ **2** : SHOWY, SPORTY ⟨*rakish* clothes⟩ — **rak·ish·ly** *adv* — **rak·ish·ness** *n*

1**ral·ly** \'ral-ē\ *vb* **ral·lied**; **ral·ly·ing** **1** : to bring together for a common purpose : UNITE ⟨*rallied* his friends to help the cause⟩ **2** : to arouse from a state of weakness : RECOVER, REVIVE ⟨*rallied* his strength for a second try⟩ ⟨the medicine *rallied* the fainting girl⟩ **3** : to join in a rally

2**rally** *n, pl* **rallies** **1** : the action of rallying **2** : a mass meeting intended to arouse group enthusiasm **3** : a series of strokes interchanged between players (as in tennis) before a point is won

1**ram** \'ram\ *n* **1** : a male sheep **2** : BATTERING RAM **3** : a pointed beak on the prow of a ship for piercing an enemy ship **4** : a guided piece for exerting pressure or for driving something by impact

2**ram** *vb* **rammed**; **ram·ming** **1** : to strike or strike against with violence : CRASH **2** : to rush violently or forcibly ⟨*ram* through traffic⟩ **3** : to force in, down, or through by or as if by driving or pressing ⟨*ram* a bill through congress⟩ — **ram·mer** *n*

1**ram·ble** \'ram-bəl\ *vb* **ram·bled**; **ram·bling** \-b(ə-)liŋ\ **1 a** : to move aimlessly from place to place : WANDER, ROAM **b** : to explore idly **2** : to talk or write aimlessly **3** : to grow or extend irregularly

2**ramble** *n* : a leisurely aimless walk

ram·bler \'ram-blər\ *n* **1** : one that rambles **2** : a climbing rose with rather small often double flowers in large clusters

ram·bunc·tious \ram-'bəŋ(k)-shəs\ *adj* : marked by unrestrained exuberance : UNRULY, WILD — **ram·bunc·tious·ly** *adv* — **ram·bunc·tious·ness** *n*

ram·i·fi·ca·tion \,ram-ə-fə-'kā-shən\ *n* **1 a** : the act or process of branching **b** : arrangement of branches (as on a plant) **2** : BRANCH, OFFSHOOT **3** : OUTGROWTH, CONSEQUENCE ⟨the *ramifications* of a problem⟩

ram·i·fy \'ram-ə-ˌfī\ *vb* **-fied; -fy·ing** : to spread out or split up into branches or divisions

[1]**ramp** \'ramp\ *vb* : to move or act furiously : STORM

[2]**ramp** *n* : a sloping passage or roadway connecting different levels

[1]**ram·page** \'ram-ˌpāj, (')ram-'\ *vb* : to rush wildly about : STORM

[2]**ram·page** \'ram-ˌpāj\ *n* : a fit of violent, riotous, or reckless action or behavior — **ram·pa·geous** \ram-'pā-jəs\ *adj*

ram·pant \'ram-pənt, -ˌpant\ *adj* **1** : marked by a menacing wildness, extravagance, or absence of restraint **2** : unchecked in growth or spread ⟨a *rampant* disease⟩ — **ram·pan·cy** \-pən-sē\ *n* — **ram·pant·ly** *adv*

ram·part \'ram-ˌpärt, -pərt\ *n* : a broad embankment raised as a fortification or protective barrier

[1]**ram·rod** \'ram-ˌräd\ *n* **1** : a rod for ramming home the charge in a muzzle-loading firearm **2** : a cleaning rod for small arms

[2]**ramrod** *adj* : severely stiff

ram·shack·le \'ram-ˌshak-əl\ *adj* : DILAPIDATED, RICKETY

ran *past of* RUN

[1]**ranch** \'ranch\ *n* **1** : an establishment for the grazing and rearing of horses, cattle, or sheep **2** : a farm devoted to a specialty ⟨a fruit *ranch*⟩

[2]**ranch** *vb* : to live or work or raise livestock on a ranch

ranch·er \'ran-chər\ *n* : one who owns or works on a ranch

ran·che·ro \ran-'che(ə)r-ō, rän-\ *n, pl* **-ros** : RANCHER

ranch house *n* : a one-story house usu. with a low-pitched roof

ran·cid \'ran(t)-səd\ *adj* : having a disagreeable smell or taste typical of decomposed oil or fat ⟨*rancid* butter⟩ — **ran·cid·i·ty** \ran-'sid-ət-ē\ *n* — **ran·cid·ness** \'ran(t)-səd-nəs\ *n*

ran·cor \'rang-kər\ *n* : intense hatred or spite — **ran·cor·ous** \-k(ə-)rəs\ *adj* — **ran·cor·ous·ly** *adv*

R & B *abbr* rhythm and blues

R & D *abbr* research and development

[1]**ran·dom** \'ran-dəm\ *n* : a haphazard course — **at random** : without definite aim, direction, rule, or method

[2]**random** *adj* **1** : lacking a definite plan, purpose, or pattern ⟨a *random* arrangement⟩ **2** : having a definite and esp. an equal probability of occurring ⟨*random* number⟩ — **random** *adv* — **ran·dom·ize** \'ran-də-ˌmīz\ *vb* — **ran·dom·ly** *adv* — **ran·dom·ness** *n*

random error *n* : a statistical error due wholly to chance — compare SYSTEMATIC ERROR

rang *past of* RING

[1]**range** \'rānj\ *n* **1 a** : a series of things in a line : ROW ⟨a *range* of mountains⟩ **b** : a group of individuals in one rank : CLASS, ORDER **2** : a cooking stove that has an oven **3 a** : open land over which livestock may roam and feed **b** : the region throughout which a kind of organism or ecological community naturally occurs **4** : the act of ranging about **5 a** : the maximum distance a projectile or vehicle can travel **b** : a place where shooting is practiced **6** : the distance or extent included, covered, or used : SCOPE **7 a** : a variation between limits ⟨a great *range* in prices⟩ **b** : the difference between the least and greatest of a set of values

[2]**range** *vb* **1** : to set in a row or in proper order **2 a** : to rove over or through : ROAM **b** : to sail or pass along **3** : to raise livestock on a range **4** : to find or give the elevation necessary for shooting at a target **5** : to vary within limits ⟨the temperature *ranged* from 50° to 90°⟩

rang·er \'rān-jər\ *n* **1** : FOREST RANGER **2** : an animal that ranges **3** : a soldier trained in close-range fighting and raiding tactics

rangy \'rān-jē\ *adj* **rang·i·er; -est** **1** : able to range for considerable distances **2** : being tall and slender ⟨*rangy* cattle⟩ **3** : having room for ranging : SPACIOUS — **rang·i·ness** *n*

ra·ni *or* **ra·nee** \rä-'nē\ *n* : an Indian queen : a raja's wife

[1]**rank** \'rangk\ *adj* **1** : strong and vigorous and usu. coarse in growth ⟨*rank* weeds⟩ ⟨*rank* meadows⟩ **2** : offensively crude or coarse **3** : unpleasantly strong-smelling : RANCID, FOUL ⟨smoke from a *rank* cigar⟩ **4** : EXTREME, UTTER ⟨*rank* dishonesty⟩ — **rank·ly** *adv* — **rank·ness** *n*

[2]**rank** *n* **1** : ROW, SERIES ⟨*ranks* of houses⟩ **2** : a line of soldiers ranged side by side **3** *pl* : a group of individuals classed together ⟨in the *ranks* of the unemployed⟩ **4** : relative position or order : STANDING ⟨his *rank* was fifth in points scored⟩ **5** : official grade or status (as in the army or navy) ⟨the *rank* of general⟩ **6** : position in regard to merit ⟨a musician of the highest *rank*⟩ **7** : high social position ⟨a man of *rank*⟩ **8** *pl* : RANK AND FILE ⟨he rose from the *ranks*⟩

[3]**rank** *vb* **1** : to arrange in lines or in a regular formation **2** : to determine the relative position of : RATE **3** : to rate above : OUTRANK ⟨a captain *ranks* a lieutenant⟩ — **rank·er** *n*

rank and file *n* **1** : the enlisted men of an armed force **2** : the members of an organization or society other than the leaders

rank·ing \'rang-king\ *adj* **1** : FOREMOST ⟨the *ranking* poet⟩ **2** : being high or next to highest in seniority ⟨the *ranking* committee member⟩

ran·kle \'rang-kəl\ *vb* **ran·kled; ran·kling** \-k(ə-)ling\ **1** : to cause anger, irritation, or deep bitterness **2** : to cause resentment or bitterness in : irritate deeply ⟨*rankled* by a rival's success⟩

ran·sack \'ran-ˌsak, (')ran-'\ *vb* [from Old Norse *rannsaka*, from *rann* "house" and a common Germanic root which is the source of English *seek*] : to search thoroughly : RUMMAGE; *esp* : to search through and rob — **ran·sack·er** *n*

[1]**ran·som** \'ran(t)-səm\ *n* [from Old French *rançon*, from Latin *redemption-*, stem of *redemptio*, "buying back", "redemption"] **1** : money paid or demanded for the freedom of a captive **2** : the act of ransoming

[2]**ransom** *vb* : to free from captivity or punishment by paying a ransom — **ran·som·er** *n*

[1]**rant** \'rant\ *vb* **1** : to talk noisily, excitedly, or wildly ⟨*rant* and rave in anger⟩ **2** : to scold violently — **rant·er** *n*

[2]**rant** *n* : ranting speech : bombastic extravagant language

[1]**rap** \'rap\ *n* **1** : a sharp blow or knock **2** *slang* **a** : the blame for an action ⟨took the *rap*⟩ **b** : a criminal charge ⟨a murder *rap*⟩

[2]**rap** *vb* **rapped; rap·ping** **1** : to give a quick sharp blow : KNOCK ⟨*rap* on the door⟩ **2** : to utter suddenly with force ⟨*rap* out an order⟩

[3]**rap** *n, slang* : TALK, CONVERSATION

[4]**rap** *vb* **rapped; rap·ping** *slang* : to talk freely and frankly

ra·pa·cious \rə-'pā-shəs\ *adj* **1** : excessively greedy : RAVENOUS **2** : living on prey : PREDATORY — **ra-**

pa·cious·ly *adv* — **ra·pa·cious·ness** *n* — **ra·pac·i·ty** \-'pas-ət-ē\ *n*

1**rape** \'rāp\ *n* : a European herb that is related to the cabbage and is grown as a forage crop and for its seeds which are used as a source of oil and as a bird food

2**rape** *vb* **1** *archaic* : to take away by force **2** : to commit rape on : RAVISH — **rap·er** *n* — **rap·ist** \'rā-pəst\ *n*

3**rape** *n* **1** : a seizing by force **2** : sexual intercourse with a woman against her will

1**rap·id** \'rap-əd\ *adj* : very fast : SWIFT— **ra·pid·i·ty** \rə-'pid-ət-ē, ra-\ *n* — **rap·id·ly** *adv* — **rap·id·ness** *n*

2**rapid** *n* : a part of a river where the current flows fast over rocks — usu. used in pl.

rap·id–fire \ˌrap-əd-'fī(ə)r\ *adj* **1** : capable of firing shots in rapid succession **2** : marked by rapidity, liveliness, or sharpness ⟨*rapid-fire* questions⟩

rapid transit *n* : fast public passenger transportation (as by subway) in urban areas

ra·pi·er \'rā-pē-ər\ *n* : a straight 2-edged sword with a narrow pointed blade

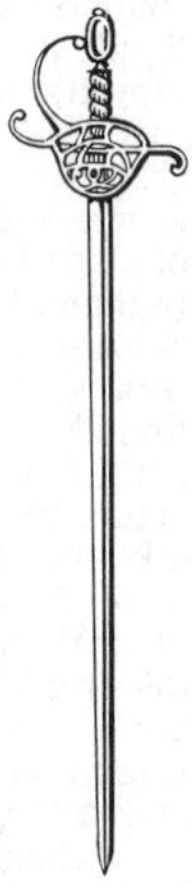

rapier

rap·ine \'rap-ən\ *n* : the seizing and carrying away of something by force : PILLAGE, PLUNDER

rap·port \ra-'pō(ə)r, -'pȯ(ə)r\ *n* : a friendly relationship between people that makes communication possible or easy ⟨an actor able to establish *rapport* with his audience⟩

rap·proche·ment \ˌrap-ˌrōsh-'män\ *n* : the establishment or a state of cordial relations

rap·scal·lion \rap-'skal-yən\ *n* : RASCAL, SCAMP

rapt \'rapt\ *adj* : carried away with delight or interest : ENRAPTURED, ENGROSSED ⟨a *rapt* audience⟩ ⟨listened with *rapt* attention⟩ — **rapt·ly** *adv* — **rapt·ness** \'rap(t)-nəs\ *n*

rap·ture \'rap-chər\ *n* : a deep joyous feeling : ECSTASY — **rap·tur·ous** \-chə-rəs\ *adj* — **rap·tur·ous·ly** *adv* — **rap·tur·ous·ness** *n*

1**rare** \'ra(ə)r, 're(ə)r\ *adj, of meat* : not cooked through ⟨*rare* roast beef⟩

2**rare** *adj* **1** : not thick or dense : THIN ⟨*rare* atmosphere at high altitudes⟩ **2** : unusually fine : EXCELLENT, SPLENDID ⟨a woman of *rare* charm⟩ **3** : UNCOMMON, INFREQUENT ⟨one of his *rare* appearances on television⟩ **4** : valuable because of scarcity ⟨a collection of *rare* books⟩ — **rare·ness** *n*

syn RARE, SCARCE can mean being in short supply. RARE usu. applies to an object or quality of which only a few examples are to be found and which is therefore esp. cherished or valued ⟨a *rare* gem⟩; SCARCE may apply to something that for the time being is in too short supply to meet the demand for it ⟨food was *scarce* that winter⟩ ***ant*** commonplace

rare·bit \'ra(ə)r-bət, 're(ə)r-\ *n* : WELSH RABBIT

rare earth *n* : any of a series of metallic elements that includes the elements with atomic numbers 58 through 71, usu. lanthanum, and sometimes yttrium and scandium, that have similar properties — called also *rare-earth element*

rar·e·fac·tion \ˌrar-ə-'fak-shən, ˌrer-\ *n* : the act or process of rarefying : the state of being rarefied — **rar·e·fac·tion·al** \-sh(ə-)nəl\ *adj*

rar·e·fy *also* **rar·i·fy** \'rar-ə-ˌfī, 'rer-\ *vb* **-fied**; **-fy·ing** : to make or become thin, porous, or less dense

rare·ly \'ra(ə)r-lē, 're(ə)r-\ *adv* **1** : not often : SELDOM **2** : with rare skill : EXCELLENTLY **3** : UNUSUALLY

rar·ing \'ra(ə)r-ing, 're(ə)r-\ *adj* : full of enthusiasm or eagerness ⟨all set and *raring* to go⟩

rar·i·ty \'rar-ət-ē, 'rer-\ *n, pl* **-ties** **1** : the quality, state, or fact of being rare : THINNESS ⟨the *rarity* of the atmosphere⟩ **2** : SCARCITY ⟨the *rarity* of genius⟩ **3** : someone or something rare ⟨black pearls are *rarities*⟩

ras·cal \'ras-kəl\ *n* **1** : a mean, unprincipled, or dishonest person : ROGUE **2** : a mischievous person : IMP

ras·cal·i·ty \ra-'skal-ət-ē\ *n, pl* **-ties** : the act, actions, or character of a rascal

ras·cal·ly \'ras-kə-lē\ *adj* : of or characteristic of a rascal ⟨a *rascally* trick⟩ — **rascally** *adv*

1**rash** \'rash\ *adj* **1** : being too hasty in speech or action or in making decisions **2** : showing a careless disregard for consequences : RECKLESS ⟨a *rash* act⟩ ⟨regret a *rash* promise⟩ — **rash·ly** *adv* — **rash·ness** *n*

2**rash** *n* : a breaking out of the skin with red spots (as in measles) : ERUPTION

rash·er \'rash-ər\ *n* : a thin slice of bacon or ham cut for broiling or frying

1**rasp** \'rasp\ *vb* **1** : to rub with or as if with a rough file ⟨*rasp* off a rough edge⟩ ⟨snails *rasping* at leaves⟩ **2** : to grate harshly upon : IRRITATE ⟨a *rasping* voice⟩ **3** : to speak or utter in a grating tone **4** : to produce a grating sound — **rasp·er** *n*

2**rasp** *n* **1** : a coarse file with cutting points instead of lines **2 a** : an act of rasping **b** : a rasping sound, sensation, or effect — **raspy** \'ras-pē\ *adj*

rasp·ber·ry \'raz-ˌber-ē, -b(ə-)rē\ *n* **1 a** : any of various black or red edible berries that consist of numerous small drupes on a fleshy receptacle and are rounder and smaller than the related blackberries **b** : a bramble that bears raspberries **2** : a sound of contempt made by sticking out the tongue and expelling air forcibly so as to make it vibrate

1**rat** \'rat\ *n* **1** : a scaly-tailed gnawing rodent distinguished from the mouse chiefly by its larger size and by differences in the teeth **2** : a person who deserts a cause or betrays his fellows

2**rat** *vb* **rat·ted**; **rat·ting** **1** : to desert or inform on one's associates : SQUEAL **2** : to catch or hunt rats

rat·a·ble *or* **rate·a·ble** \'rāt-ə-bəl\ *adj* : capable of being rated, estimated, or apportioned — **rat·a·bly** \-blē\ *adv*

ratch \'rach\ *n* : RATCHET

ratch·et \'rach-ət\ *n* **1** : a mechanism that consists of a bar or wheel having inclined teeth into which a pawl drops so as to allow motion in one direction only **2** : PAWL

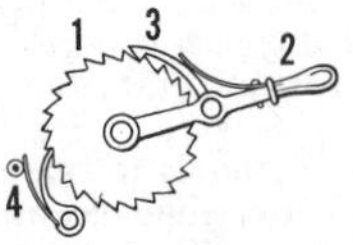

ratchet wheel: 1, wheel; 2, reciprocating lever; 3, pawl for communicating motion; 4, pawl for preventing backward motion

ratchet wheel *n* : a toothed wheel held in position or turned by a pawl

1**rate** \'rāt\ *vb* : to scold violently : BERATE

2**rate** *n* **1** : estimated value : VALUATION **2 a** : a fixed ratio between two things ⟨a *rate* of exchange⟩ **b** : a charge, payment, or price fixed according to a ratio, scale, or standard ⟨tax *rate*⟩ **3 a :** a quantity, amount, or degree of something measured in relationship to something else **b :** an amount of payment or charge based on another amount ⟨interest at the *rate* of six percent⟩ **4 :** relative condition or quality : CLASS — **at any rate :** in any case : at least

³**rate** *vb* **1 :** CONSIDER, REGARD ⟨*rated* a good pianist⟩ **2 :** to set an estimate on : EVALUATE ⟨*rate* houses for tax purposes⟩ **3 :** to determine the rank, class, or position of : assign to a rank or class : GRADE ⟨*rate* a seaman⟩ ⟨*rate* a ship⟩ **4 :** to have a rating or rank : be classed ⟨*rates* high in his class⟩ **5 :** to set a rate on **6 :** to be qualified for : DESERVE ⟨*rate* a promotion⟩ — **rat·er** *n*

rath·er \'ra<u>th</u>-ər, 'rə<u>th</u>-, 'rä<u>th</u>-\ *adv* **1 :** more willingly : PREFERABLY ⟨I would *rather* not go⟩ **2 :** on the contrary : INSTEAD ⟨things did not turn out well; *rather*, they turned out very badly⟩ **3 :** more exactly : more properly : with better reason ⟨my father, or, *rather*, my stepfather⟩ ⟨to be pitied *rather* than blamed⟩ **4 :** SOMEWHAT ⟨*rather* cold today⟩

rat·i·fy \'rat-ə-ˌfī\ *vb* **-fied; -fy·ing :** to approve and accept formally : CONFIRM ⟨*ratify* a treaty⟩ ⟨*ratify* the decision of a subordinate⟩ — **rat·i·fi·ca·tion** \ˌrat-ə-fə-'kā-shən\ *n* — **rat·i·fi·er** \'rat-ə-ˌfī(-ə)r\ *n*

rat·ing \'rāt-ing\ *n* **1 a :** a classification according to grade or rank **b :** a naval specialist classification **2 :** a relative estimate or evaluation ⟨credit *rating*⟩

ra·tio \'rā-shō, -shē-ˌō\ *n, pl* **ra·tios 1 :** a fixed or approximate relation in number, quantity, or degree between things or to another thing ⟨the *ratio* of eggs to butter in a cake⟩ ⟨women outnumbered men in the *ratio* of three to one⟩ **2 :** the quotient of one quantity divided by another ⟨the *ratio* of 6 to 3 may be expressed as 6:3, $6/3$, and 2⟩

¹**ra·tion** \'rash-ən, 'rā-shən\ *n* **1 a :** a food allowance for one day **b :** FOOD, PROVISIONS, DIET — usu. used in pl. ⟨had to pack supplies and *rations* on their backs⟩ **2 :** a share esp. as determined by supply or allotment by authority ⟨wartime meat *ration*⟩

²**ration** *vb* **ra·tioned; ra·tion·ing** \'rash-(ə-)ning, 'rāsh-\ **1 :** to supply with rations ⟨*ration* cattle⟩ **2 a :** to distribute or allot as a ration ⟨the government *rationed* gas⟩ **b :** to use or allot sparingly ⟨her doctor *rationed* her sugar intake⟩

¹**ra·tio·nal** \'rash-(ə-)nəl\ *adj* **1 a :** having reason or understanding ⟨*rational* beings⟩ **b :** being reasonable : SANE ⟨*rational* behavior⟩ **2 :** relating to or involving rational numbers ⟨a *rational* fraction⟩ — **ra·tio·nal·i·ty** \ˌrash-ə-'nal-ət-ē\ *n* — **ra·tio·nal·ly** \'rash-(ə-)nə-lē\ *adv*

²**rational** *n* **:** something rational; *esp* **:** a rational number or fraction

ra·tio·nale \ˌrash-ə-'nal\ *n* **:** a basic reason or explanation for something

ra·tio·nal·ism \'rash-(ə-)nə-ˌliz-em\ *n* **:** the theory or practice of guiding one's actions and opinions solely by what seems reasonable — **ra·tio·nal·ist** \-ləst\ *n* — **rationalist** *or* **ra·tio·nal·is·tic** \ˌrash-(ə-)nə-'lis-tik\ *adj* — **ra·tio·nal·is·ti·cal·ly** \-ti-k(ə-)lē\ *adv*

ra·tio·nal·ize \'rash-(ə-)nə-ˌlīz\ *vb* **1 :** to free a mathematical equation from irrational expressions **2 a :** to provide a rational explanation of ⟨*rationalize* a myth⟩ **b :** to justify unreasonable actions or views by seemingly reasonable motives ⟨*rationalized* his dislike of his brother⟩ — **ra·tio·nal·i·za·tion** \ˌrash-(ə-)nə-lə-'zā-shən\ *n*

rational number *n* **:** a number expressible as an integer or the quotient of two integers

rat·line \'rat-lən\ *n* **:** one of the small cross ropes attached to the shrouds of a ship so as to form the steps of a rope ladder

ratlines

rat·tan \ra-'tan, rə-\ *n* [from Malay *rotan*] **1 a :** a climbing palm with very long tough stems **b :** a part of one of these stems used esp. for walking sticks and wickerwork **2 :** a rattan cane or switch

rat·ter \'rat-ər\ *n* **:** one that catches rats; *esp* **:** a rat-catching dog or cat

¹**rat·tle** \'rat-əl\ *vb* **rat·tled; rat·tling** \-(ə-)ling\ **1 :** to make or cause to make a rattle **2 :** to chatter continuously and aimlessly **3 :** to say or do in a brisk lively fashion ⟨*rattled* off the answers⟩ **4 :** to disturb the composure of : UPSET ⟨*rattled* the speaker with a barrage of questions⟩

²**rattle** *n* **1 :** a series of short sharp sounds : CLATTER ⟨the *rattle* of hail on a roof⟩ **2 :** a device (as a toy) for making a rattling sound **3 :** a rattling organ at the end of a rattlesnake's tail made up of horny joints **4 :** a noise in the throat caused by air passing through mucus esp. at the approach of death

rat·tler \'rat-(ə-)lər\ *n* **:** RATTLESNAKE

rat·tle·snake \'rat-əl-ˌsnāk\ *n* **:** any of various poisonous American snakes having at the end of the tail horny interlocking joints that rattle when shaken

rattlesnake (up to 7 ft. long)

rat·tle·trap \-ˌtrap\ *n* **:** something rattly or rickety; *esp* **:** an old car — **rattletrap** *adj*

rat·tling \'rat-(ə-)ling\ *adj* **:** LIVELY, BRISK ⟨a *rattling* argument⟩ — **rat·tling·ly** \'rat-ling-lē\ *adv*

rat·tly \'rat-(ə-)lē\ *adj* **:** likely to rattle : making a rattle ⟨a *rattly* old car⟩

rat·ty \'rat-ē\ *adj* **rat·ti·er; -est 1 :** infested with or suggestive of rats **2 :** resembling a rat esp. in shabbiness or meanness

rau·cous \'rö-kəs\ *adj* **1 :** disagreeably harsh or strident ⟨a *raucous* voice⟩ **2 :** boisterously disorderly ⟨a *raucous* party⟩ — **rau·cous·ly** *adv* — **rau·cous·ness** *n*

¹**rav·age** \'rav-ij\ *n* **1 :** an act or practice of ravaging **2 :** damage resulting from ravaging : DEVASTATION, RUIN

²**ravage** *vb* **1 :** to lay waste : PLUNDER **2 :** DESTROY, RUIN ⟨body *ravaged* by disease⟩ — **rav·ag·er** *n*

¹**rave** \'rāv\ *vb* **1 :** to talk wildly in or as if in delirium **2 :** to speak or utter with extreme enthusiasm or violence ⟨*raved* out his denunciation⟩ — **rav·er** *n*

²**rave** *n* **:** an extravagantly favorable criticism

¹**rav·el** \'rav-əl\ *vb* **-eled** *or* **-elled; -el·ing** *or* **-el·ling** \-(ə-)ling\ **1 :** to separate or undo the texture of : UNRAVEL, FRAY **2 :** to make plain : SIMPLIFY ⟨*ravel* out a problem⟩ — **rav·el·er** *or* **rav·el·ler** \-(ə-)lər\ *n*

²**ravel** *n* **:** something that is raveled

rav·el·ing *or* **rav·el·ling** \'rav(-ə)-ling, -lən\ *n* **:** something raveled or frayed; *esp* **:** a thread raveled out of a fabric

1ra·ven \'rā-vən\ *n* : a glossy black bird of northern regions that is about two feet long, is related to the crow, and has pointed throat feathers

2raven *adj* : of the color or glossy sheen of the raven

rav·en·ous \'rav-ə-nəs\ *adj* : very eager for food, satisfaction, or gratification : GREEDY, RAPACIOUS — **rav·en·ous·ly** *adv* — **rav·en·ous·ness** *n*

raven
(about 25 in. long)

ra·vine \rə-'vēn\ *n* : a small narrow steep-sided valley larger than a gully, smaller than a canyon, and usu. worn by running water : a deep gorge

rav·i·o·li \ˌrav-ē-'ō-lē\ *n pl* : little shells of dough usu. containing chopped meat or cheese that are usu. boiled and served with a spicy tomato sauce

rav·ish \'rav-ish\ *vb* **1** : to seize and take away by violence **2** : to carry away with delight : ENRAPTURE **3** : RAPE **4** : PLUNDER, ROB — **rav·ish·er** *n*

rav·ish·ing \'rav-i-shing\ *adj* : unusually attractive or pleasing — **rav·ish·ing·ly** \-shing-lē\ *adv*

1raw \'rȯ\ *adj* **raw·er** \'rȯ(-ə)r\; **raw·est** \'rȯ-əst\ **1** : not cooked ⟨a *raw* carrot⟩ **2 a** : being in or nearly in the natural state ⟨*raw* furs⟩ : not processed or manufactured ⟨*raw* milk⟩ ⟨*raw* data⟩ **b** : not diluted or blended ⟨*raw* alcohol⟩ **3** : having the skin scraped or torn off ⟨a *raw* wound⟩ **4 a** : lacking experience or understanding : GREEN ⟨a *raw* recruit⟩ **b** : VULGAR, CRUDE ⟨a *raw* story⟩ **5** : disagreeably damp or cold — **raw·ly** \'rȯ-lē\ *adv* — **raw·ness** *n*

2raw *n* : a raw place or state

raw·boned \'rȯ-'bōnd\ *adj* : extremely thin : GAUNT

raw deal *n* : an instance of unfair treatment

1raw·hide \'rȯ-ˌhīd\ *n* **1** : untanned cattle skin **2** : a whip of untanned hide

2rawhide *vb* **-hid·ed**; **-hid·ing** : to whip or drive with or as if with a rawhide

raw material *n* : natural resources (as petroleum or grain) from which useful things can be produced

1ray \'rā\ *n* : any of numerous flat broad fishes (as a skate) that live on the sea bottom and have their eyes on the upper surface of their bodies and the tail long and narrow

2ray *n* [from medieval French *rai*, from Latin *radius* "spoke", "ray"] **1 a** : one of the lines of light that appear to radiate from a bright object **b** : a thin beam of radiant energy (as heat) **c** : a stream of particles (as electrons) traveling in the same line **2 a** : any of a group of lines coming from a common center **b** : HALF LINE **3** : a plant or animal structure that resembles a ray; *esp* : a band of tissue extending radially in a woody plant stem and usu. storing food or conducting raw material **4** : a tiny bit : TRACE ⟨not even a *ray* of hope⟩

rayed \'rād\ *adj* : having rays or ray flowers

ray flower *n* : one of the flowers with a strap-shaped corolla in the head of a composite plant (as an aster)

ə abut	ər further	a back	ā bake
ä cot, cart	au̇ out	ch chin	e less	ē easy
g gift	i trip	ī life	j joke	ng sing	ō flow
ȯ flaw	ȯi coin	th thin	t͟h this	ü loot
u̇ foot	y yet	yü few	yu̇ furious	zh vision

ray·on \'rā-ˌän\ *n* **1** : a smooth textile fiber made from cellulosic material by extrusion through minute holes **2** : a rayon yarn, thread, or fabric

raze \'rāz\ *vb* : to utterly destroy by tearing down : DEMOLISH ⟨*razed* the building⟩

ra·zor \'rā-zər\ *n* : a sharp cutting instrument used esp. to shave off hair — **razor** *adj*

ra·zor·back \-ˌbak\ *n* : a thin-bodied long-legged half-wild mongrel hog chiefly of the southeastern U.S.

razz \'raz\ *vb* : to tease mockingly : KID

RBC *abbr* red blood cells; red blood count

RBI *abbr* runs batted in

RC *abbr* **1** Red Cross **2** Roman Catholic

rd *abbr* **1** road **2** rod

RD *abbr* rural delivery

re \'rā\ *n* : the 2d note of the diatonic scale

re- \(ˈ)rē *before* ˈ-*stressed syll*, (ˌ)rē *before* ˌ-*stressed syll*, ˌrē *before unstressed syll*\ *prefix* **1** : again : anew ⟨*re*tell⟩ **2** : back : backward ⟨*re*call⟩

reaccommodate
reacquire
readapt
readdress
readjust
readmission
readmit
readopt
reaffirm
realign
reanalysis
reanalyze
reanimation
reapplication
reapply
reappoint
reappointment
reapportionment
reappraisal
reappraise
rearrest
reassail
reassemble
reassembly
reassess
reassign
reattach
reattack
reawake
reawaken
rebaptism
rebaptize
rebid
reboil
reburial
rebury
recarbonize
rechannel
recharge
recharter
recheck
reclean
recolor
recomb
recombine
recommission
recompile
recompress
recompression
recompute
reconceive
reconcentrate
reconception
recondensation
recondense
reconnect
reconquer
reconquest
reconsecrate
reconsecration
reconsult
reconsultation
recontact
recontaminate
recontamination
recontract
reconvene
recook
recopy
recouple
recross
recut
recycle
rededicate
redefine
redeliver
redelivery
redeposit
redevelop
redeveloper
redigest
redigestion
redip
rediscover
rediscovery
redispose
redissolve
redistill
redistribute
redistribution
redraft
redraw
reeligible
reembodiment
reembody
reemerge
reemit
reemission
reemphasis
reemphasize
reenlist
reenlistment
reenter
reequip
reestablish
reestablishment
reevaluate
reexamination
reexamine
reexchange
reface
refasten
refigure
refilm
refilter
refinance
refind
refix
refloat
refly
refreeze
refurnish
regather
regild
regive
reglue
regrade
regrind
regrow
regrowth
rehandle
rehear
reheat
reimpose
reimposition
reincorporate
reinsert
reintroduce
reinvasion
relearn
reletter
relight
reload
remanufacture
remarry
remelt
remix
remold
rename
reoccupy
reordination
reorient
reorientate
repack
repaint
rephotograph
replay
reprice
reprocess
repurchase
reread
rerecord
reroll
resaw
resay
rescore
reseal
reseat
resell
reset
resettle
resew
reshow
resow
respell
restaff
restage
restock
restraighten
restrengthen
restrike
restring
restructure
restudy
restyle
resubmit
resummon
resupply
resurface
resurvey
resynthesis
resynthesize
retaste
retell
rethink
retrack
retrain
retransmission
retransmit
reverify
revisit
rewash
reweave
rewed
reweigh
reweld
rewind

re *abbr* **1** reference **2** regarding

1**reach** \'rēch\ *vb* **1 a :** to stretch out : EXTEND ⟨*reached* out his arms⟩ **b :** to attempt to grasp something with or as if with the hand ⟨*reached* for a knife⟩ **2 :** to go as far as ⟨the shadow *reached* the wall⟩ **3 a :** to arrive at : come to ⟨*reached* home late⟩ **b :** ACHIEVE ⟨*reached* an understanding⟩ **4 :** to communicate with ⟨tried to *reach* you by phone⟩ **5 :** to make an impression on : INFLUENCE ⟨couldn't *reach* his own son⟩ — **reach·a·ble** \'rē-chə-bəl\ *adj* — **reach·er** *n*

2**reach** *n* **1 :** the action or an act of reaching **2 a :** the distance or extent of reaching or of ability to reach **b :** the ability to understand : COMPREHENSION, RANGE ⟨the subject was beyond his *reach*⟩ **3 :** a continuous unbroken stretch or expanse

re·act \rē-'akt\ *vb* **1 :** to exert a return influence — often used with *on* or *upon* **2 :** to act or behave in response ⟨*reacted* violently to his suggestion⟩ **3 :** to act in opposition to a force or influence — usu. used with *against* ⟨*reacted* against unfair treatment⟩ **4 :** to move or tend in a reverse direction ⟨prices *reacted* strongly after a brief drop⟩ **5 :** to undergo or make undergo chemical reaction

re–act \(')rē-'akt\ *vb* **:** to act or perform again

re·act·ant \rē-'ak-tənt\ *n* **:** a chemically reacting substance

re·ac·tion \rē-'ak-shən\ *n* **1 a :** the act or process or an instance of reacting **b :** tendency toward a former esp. outmoded political or social order or policy **2 :** bodily response to or activity aroused by a stimulus; *esp* **:** the response (as in vaccinations) of tissues to a foreign substance **3 :** the force that a body subjected to the action of a force from another body exerts in the opposite direction **4 a :** chemical transformation or change : the action between atoms or molecules to form one or more new substances **b :** a process involving change in atomic nuclei — **re·ac·tion·al** \-sh(ə-)nəl\ *adj* — **re·ac·tion·al·ly** \-ē\ *adv*

1**re·ac·tion·ary** \rē-'ak-shə-ˌner-ē\ *adj* **:** relating to, marked by, or favoring esp. political reaction

2**reactionary** *n, pl* **-ar·ies :** a reactionary person

re·ac·ti·vate \(')rē-'ak-tə-ˌvāt\ *vb* **:** to make or become activated again — **re·ac·ti·va·tion** \(ˌ)rē-ˌak-tə-'vā-shən\ *n*

re·ac·tive \rē-'ak-tiv\ *adj* **1 :** of or relating to reaction **2 :** reacting or tending to react — **re·ac·tive·ly** *adv* — **re·ac·tive·ness** *n* — **re·ac·tiv·i·ty** \(ˌ)rē-ˌak-'tiv-ət-ē\ *n*

re·ac·tor \rē-'ak-tər\ *n* **1 :** one that reacts; *esp* **:** one that reacts positively to a foreign substance (as in a test for a disease) **2 :** an apparatus in which a chain reaction of fissionable material is initiated and controlled — called also *nuclear reactor*

1**read** \'rēd\ *vb* **read** \'red\; **read·ing** \'rēd-iŋ\ **1 a :** to go over systematically by sight or touch to take in and understand the meaning of letters or symbols **b :** to study the movements of (a speaker's lips) and so understand what is being said **c :** to utter aloud the words represented by written matter **d :** to understand the written form of ⟨*reads* French⟩ **2 :** to learn from what one has seen or found in writing or printing ⟨*read* that she got married⟩ ⟨*read* about his promotion⟩ **3 :** to utter aloud by or as if by reading **4 :** to make a study of ⟨*read* law⟩ **5 a :** to interpret the meaning or significance of ⟨*read* palms⟩ **b :** FORETELL, PREDICT **6 :** to put into something a meaning that may or may not actually be there ⟨he *read* fear in her eyes⟩ **7 :** INDICATE ⟨thermometer *reads* zero⟩ **8 :** to consist of specific words, phrases, or symbols ⟨the passage *reads* differently in older versions⟩ — **read·a·bil·i·ty** \ˌrēd-ə-'bil-ət-ē\ *n* — **read·a·ble** \'rēd-ə-bəl\ *adj* — **read·a·ble·ness** *n* — **read·a·bly** \-blē\ *adv* — **read between the lines :** to understand more than is directly stated — **read the riot act 1 :** to give an order or warning to cease something **2 :** to give a severe reprimand

2**read** \'red\ *adj* **:** taught or informed by reading ⟨a well-*read* man⟩ ⟨widely *read* in history⟩

read·er \'rēd-ər\ *n* **1 :** one that reads **2 :** a book for instruction and practice esp. in reading

read·er·ship \-ˌship\ *n* **1 :** the office or position of a reader **2 :** the mass or a particular group of readers

read·ing \'rēd-iŋ\ *n* **1 :** material to be read or for reading **2 :** something that is registered (as on a gauge) ⟨the thermometer *reading* was 70 degrees⟩ **3 :** a particular interpretation or performance ⟨gave an excellent *reading* of the role⟩

1**ready** \'red-ē\ *adj* **read·i·er** \-ē-ər\; **-est 1 :** PREPARED ⟨dinner is *ready*⟩ **2 :** on the verge of : ABOUT ⟨*ready* to cry⟩ **3 :** WILLING ⟨*ready* to give aid⟩ **4 :** PROMPT ⟨a *ready* answer⟩ **5 :** AVAILABLE, HANDY ⟨*ready* money⟩ — **read·i·ly** \'red-ə-lē\ *adv* — **read·i·ness** \'red-ē-nəs\ *n*

2**ready** *vb* **read·ied; ready·ing :** to make ready

ready–made \ˌred-ē-'mād\ *adj* **1 :** made beforehand for general sale ⟨*ready-made* suit⟩ **2 :** lacking individuality : COMMONPLACE ⟨*ready-made* ideas⟩

re·agent \rē-'ā-jənt\ *n* **:** one that reacts or induces a reaction; *esp* **:** a substance that takes part in or brings about a particular chemical reaction

1**re·al** \'rē(-ə)l\ *adj* **1 :** of, relating to, or constituting fixed, permanent, or immovable things (as lands, houses, or fixtures) ⟨*real* property⟩ **2 a :** not artificial or fake : GENUINE ⟨*real* gold⟩ **b :** not imaginary : ACTUAL ⟨a story from *real* life⟩ — **re·al·ness** *n*

2**real** *adv* **:** VERY ⟨we had a *real* good time⟩

3**re·al** \rā-'äl\ *n, pl* **re·als** *or* **re·ales** \-'äl-ās\ **:** a silver coin formerly used in Spain and Portugal

real estate *n* **:** property in houses and land

real image *n* **:** an image of an object formed by rays of light coming to a focus

re·al·ism \'rē-ə-ˌliz-əm\ *n* **1 :** the belief that objects we perceive through our senses are real and have an existence outside our own minds **2 :** the tendency to see situations or difficulties in the light of facts and to deal with them practically **3 :** the representation in literature and art of things as they are in life — **re·al·ist** \-ləst\ *n*

re·al·is·tic \ˌrē-ə-'lis-tik\ *adj* **1 :** true to life or nature ⟨a *realistic* painting⟩ **2 :** having or showing an inclination to face facts and to deal with them sensibly ⟨a *realistic* approach⟩ — **re·al·is·ti·cal·ly** \-ti-k(ə-)lē\ *adv*

re·al·i·ty \rē-'al-ət-ē\ *n, pl* **-ties 1 :** actual existence ⟨doubt the *reality* of sea serpents⟩ **2 :** someone or something real or actual ⟨the *realities* of life⟩ **3 :** the characteristic of being true to life or to fact

re·al·ize \'rē-ə-ˌlīz\ *vb* **1 :** to make actual : ACCOMPLISH ⟨*realize* a lifelong ambition⟩ **2 :** to convert into money ⟨*realized* his assets⟩ **3 :** to bring or get by sale, investment, or effort : GAIN ⟨*realize* a profit⟩ **4 :** to be aware of ⟨*realized* his danger⟩ — **re·al·iz·a·ble** \'rē-ə-ˌlī-zə-bəl\ *adj* — **re·al·i·za·tion** \ˌrē-ə-lə-'zā-shən\ *n* — **re·al·iz·er** \'rē-ə-ˌlī-zər\ *n*

re·al·ly \'rē-(ə-)lē\ *adv* **1 :** in reality : ACTUALLY ⟨didn't *really* mean what she said⟩ **2 :** UNQUESTIONABLY, TRULY ⟨a *really* beautiful day⟩

realm \'relm\ *n* **1 :** KINGDOM **2 :** field of influence or activity : DOMAIN ⟨the *realm* of fancy⟩

real number *n* **:** a number (as -2, 3, $7/8$, $.25$, $\sqrt{2}$, π) that is rational or irrational

Re·al·tor \'rē(-ə)l-tər\ *n* : a real estate agent who is a member of the National Association of Real Estate Boards

re·al·ty \'rē(-ə)l-tē\ *n, pl* **-ties** : REAL ESTATE

1**ream** \'rēm\ *n* **1** : a quantity of paper being variously 480, 500, or 516 sheets **2** : a great amount — usu. used in pl. ⟨*reams* of notes⟩

2**ream** *vb* **1** : to widen the opening of a hole **2** : to shape, enlarge, or clean a hole with a reamer

ream·er \'rē-mər\ *n* **1** : a rotating tool with cutting edges for enlarging or shaping a hole **2** : a juice extractor with a ridged and pointed center rising from a shallow dish

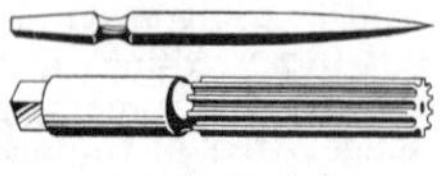

reamers 1

re·an·i·mate \(')rē-'an-ə-ˌmāt\ *vb* : to give life to anew : REVIVE

reap \'rēp\ *vb* **1 a** : to cut with a sickle, scythe, or reaping machine **b** : to gather by so cutting : HARVEST **2** : to gain as a reward ⟨*reap* the benefit of hard work⟩

reap·er \'rē-pər\ *n* : one that reaps; *esp* : a machine for reaping grain

re·ap·pear \ˌrē-ə-'pi(ə)r\ *vb* : to appear again — **re·ap·pear·ance** \-'pir-ən(t)s\ *n*

1**rear** \'ri(ə)r\ *vb* **1** : to erect by building : CONSTRUCT ⟨*reared* a temple⟩ **2 a** : to raise upright **b** : to rise high ⟨skyscrapers *rearing* above the city⟩ **c** : to rise up on the hind legs ⟨the horse *reared* in fright⟩ **3 a** : to breed and raise ⟨*rear* cattle⟩ **b** : to bring up a person

2**rear** *n* **1** : the unit (as of an army) or area farthest from the enemy **2** : BUTTOCKS **3** : the space or position at the back ⟨the *rear* of a building⟩

3**rear** *adj* : being at the back

rear admiral *n* : a commissioned officer in the navy ranking just below a vice admiral

rear guard *n* : a military detachment detailed to bring up and protect the rear of a main body or force

re·arm \(')rē-'ärm\ *vb* : to arm again esp. with new or better weapons — **re·ar·ma·ment** \-'är-mə-mənt\ *n*

rear·most \'ri(ə)r-ˌmōst\ *adj* : farthest in the rear

re·ar·range \ˌrē-ə-'rānj\ *vb* : to arrange again esp. in a different way

1**rear·ward** \'ri(ə)r-wərd\ *adj* **1** : located at, near, or toward the rear **2** : directed toward the rear : BACKWARD — **rear·ward·ly** *adv*

2**rearward** *also* **rear·wards** \-wərdz\ *adv* : at, near, or toward the rear : BACKWARD

1**rea·son** \'rēz-ən\ *n* [from Old French *raison*, from Latin *ration-*, stem of *ratio*, literally "reckoning", "computation"] **1 a** : a statement offered in explanation or justification ⟨asked to give a *reason* for his absence⟩ **b** : a rational ground or motive ⟨*reasons* for thinking life may exist on Mars⟩ **c** : the thing that makes some fact intelligible : CAUSE ⟨the *reason* for the tides⟩ **2 a** : the power of thinking esp. in orderly logical ways : INTELLIGENCE ⟨used *reason* to solve the problem⟩ **b** : SANITY ⟨afraid she would lose her *reason*⟩ ***syn*** see CAUSE — **within reason** : within reasonable limits — **with reason** : with good cause : JUSTIFIABLY

ə abut	ər further	a back	ā bake	
ä cot, cart	au̇ out	ch chin	e less	ē easy
g gift	i trip	ī life	j joke	ng sing	ō flow
ȯ flaw	ȯi coin	th thin	t͟h this	ü loot
u̇ foot	y yet	yü few	yu̇ furious	zh vision

2**reason** *vb* **rea·soned**; **rea·son·ing** \'rēz-(ə-)niŋ\ **1** : to talk persuasively or to present reasons in order to cause a change of mind ⟨*reason* with someone⟩ **2 a** : to use one's reason or to think in a logical way or manner **b** : to state, formulate, or conclude by use of reason ⟨*reasoned* that both statements couldn't be true⟩

rea·son·a·ble \'rēz-(ə-)nə-bəl\ *adj* **1 a** : agreeable to reason ⟨a *reasonable* theory⟩ **b** : not extreme or excessive : MODERATE ⟨a *reasonable* request⟩ **c** : INEXPENSIVE ⟨*reasonable* rates⟩ **2** : having the faculty of reason : RATIONAL ⟨believed man to be a *reasonable* animal⟩ — **rea·son·a·bil·i·ty** \ˌrēz-(ə-)nə-'bil-ət-ē\ *n* — **rea·son·a·ble·ness** \'rēz-(ə-)nə-bəl-nəs\ *n* — **rea·son·a·bly** \-blē\ *adv*

rea·son·ing *n* **1** : the use of reason; *esp* : the drawing of conclusions through the use of reason **2** : the reasons used in and the proofs that result from thought : ARGUMENT

re·as·sur·ance \ˌrē-ə-'shu̇r-ən(t)s\ *n* : the action of reassuring : the state of being reassured

re·as·sure \ˌrē-ə-'shu̇(ə)r\ *vb* **1** : to assure anew **2** : to restore to confidence **3** : to insure anew

re·ata \rē-'at-ə, -'ät-\ *n* : LARIAT

reave \'rēv\ *vb* **reaved** *or* **reft** \'reft\; **reav·ing** *archaic* : PLUNDER, ROB — **reav·er** *n*

1**re·bate** \'rē-ˌbāt, ri-'\ *vb* : to make a rebate of : give as a rebate — **re·bat·er** *n*

2**re·bate** \'rē-ˌbāt\ *n* : a return of a portion of a payment : ABATEMENT

1**reb·el** \'reb-əl\ *adj* : REBELLIOUS

2**rebel** *n* : one who rebels or participates in a rebellion

3**re·bel** \ri-'bel\ *vb* **re·belled**; **re·bel·ling** **1 a** : to oppose or resist authority or control **b** : to renounce and resist by force the authority of one's government **2** : to feel or exhibit anger or revulsion

re·bel·lion \ri-'bel-yən\ *n* **1** : opposition to one in authority or dominance **2 a** : open defiance of or resistance to an established government **b** : an instance of such defiance or resistance : REVOLT, UPRISING

re·bel·lious \ri-'bel-yəs\ *adj* **1** : engaged in rebellion **2** : inclined to resist or disobey authority : INSUBORDINATE — **re·bel·lious·ly** *adv* — **re·bel·lious·ness** *n*

re·bind \(')rē-'bīnd\ *vb* **-bound** \-'bau̇nd\; **-binding** : to bind anew or again

re·birth \(')rē-'bərth\ *n* **1** : a new or second birth **2** : RENAISSANCE, REVIVAL

re·born \(')rē-'bȯrn\ *adj* : born again : REVIVED

1**re·bound** \ri-'bau̇nd\ *vb* **1** : to spring back on striking something **2** : to recover from setback or frustration

2**re·bound** \'rē-ˌbau̇nd, ri-'\ *n* **1 a** : a springing back : RECOIL **b** : an upward leap or movement ⟨a *rebound* in prices⟩ **2 a** : a basketball or hockey puck that rebounds **b** : the act of taking a basketball rebound **3** : an immediate spontaneous reaction to setback, frustration, or crisis ⟨is on the *rebound* after her losses⟩

re·branch \(')rē-'branch\ *vb* : to branch again

re·broad·cast \(')rē-'brȯd-ˌkast\ *vb* **-cast** *also* **-cast·ed**; **-cast·ing** **1** : to broadcast again a radio or television program being simultaneously received from another source **2** : to repeat a broadcast at a later time — **rebroadcast** *n*

1**re·buff** \ri-'bəf\ *vb* **1** : SNUB **2** : to drive or beat back

2**rebuff** *n* **1** : an abrupt refusal to meet an advance or offer : SNUB **2** : a sharp check : SETBACK

re·build \(')rē-'bild\ *vb* **-built** \-'bilt\; **-build·ing** **1** : to restore to a previous state by repairing **2** : to make extensive changes in : REMODEL **3** : to build again ⟨planned to *rebuild* after the fire⟩

1**re·buke** \ri-'byük\ *vb* : to scold or criticize sharply : REPRIMAND — **re·buk·er** *n*

syn REBUKE, CHIDE, ADMONISH can mean to voice criticism of. REBUKE usu. applies to a sharp and stern expression of disapproval intended to put an immediate stop to bad conduct; CHIDE implies somewhat less severity in taking to task; ADMONISH implies still less severity in administering a gentle and friendly warning to one who is called on to mend his ways

2**rebuke** *n* : REPRIMAND, REPROOF

re·bus \'rē-bəs\ *n* [from Latin, meaning "by things" (ablative plural of *res* "thing")] : a representation of words or syllables by pictures of objects whose names resemble the intended words or syllables in sound; *also* : a riddle or puzzle made up of such pictures or symbols

rebus

re·but \ri-'bət\ *vb* **re·but·ted**; **re·but·ting** **1** : to contradict or oppose by formal argument, plea, or contrary proof **2** : to expose the falsity of : REFUTE ⟨*rebuts* a long-accepted doctrine⟩ — **re·but·ta·ble** \-'bət-ə-bəl\ *adj*

re·but·tal \ri-'bət-əl\ *n* : the act of rebutting; *also* : argument or proof that rebuts

rec *abbr* **1** record **2** recreation

re·cal·ci·trance \ri-'kal-sə-trən(t)s\ *or* **re·cal·ci·tran·cy** \-trən-sē\ *n* : the state of being recalcitrant

re·cal·ci·trant \-trənt\ *adj* **1** : obstinately defiant of authority or restraint **2** : not responsive to handling or treatment — **recalcitrant** *n*

1**re·call** \ri-'kȯl\ *vb* **1 a** : to ask or order to come back **b** : to bring back to mind **2** : CANCEL, REVOKE ⟨*recalled* the order⟩ — **re·call·a·ble** \-'kȯ-lə-bəl\ *adj*

2**re·call** \ri-'kȯl, 'rē-ˌ\ *n* **1** : a summons to return **2** : the right or procedure by which an official may be removed from office by vote of the people **3** : remembrance of what has been learned or experienced **4 a** : the act of revoking **b** : the possibility of being revoked ⟨the matter is beyond *recall*⟩

re·cant \ri-'kant\ *vb* : to withdraw or repudiate a statement of opinion or belief formally and publicly — **re·can·ta·tion** \ˌrē-ˌkan-'tā-shən\ *n*

1**re·cap** \(')rē-'kap\ *vb* **re·capped**; **re·cap·ping** : to cement, mold, and vulcanize a strip of rubber upon the tread of a worn automobile tire

2**re·cap** \'rē-ˌkap\ *n* : a recapped tire

3**re·cap** \ri-'kap, 'rē-ˌ\ *vb* **re·capped**; **re·cap·ping** : RECAPITULATE ⟨now, to *recap* the news⟩

4**re·cap** \'rē-ˌkap, ri-'\ *n* : RECAPITULATION ⟨a *recap* of the news highlights⟩

re·ca·pit·u·late \ˌrē-kə-'pich-ə-ˌlāt\ *vb* : to repeat briefly : SUMMARIZE — **re·ca·pit·u·la·tion** \-ˌpich-ə-'lā-shən\ *n*

re·cap·ture \(')rē-'kap-chər\ *n* **1** : the act of retaking : the fact of being retaken : RECOVERY **2** : something that is captured again — **recapture** *vb*

re·cast \(')rē-'kast\ *vb* **-cast**; **-cast·ing** : to cast again ⟨*recast* a cannon⟩ ⟨*recast* a play⟩ — **re·cast** \(')rē-'kast, 'rē-ˌ\ *n*

recd *abbr* received

re·cede \ri-'sēd\ *vb* **1 a** : to move back or away : WITHDRAW ⟨the *receding* tide⟩ **b** : to slant backward ⟨a *receding* forehead⟩ **2** : to grow less : DIMINISH ⟨*receded* in importance⟩

1**re·ceipt** \ri-'sēt\ *n* **1** : RECIPE **2** : the act or process of receiving **3** : something received — usu. used in pl. **4** : a writing acknowledging the receiving of goods or money

2**receipt** *vb* **1** : to give a receipt for or acknowledge the receipt of **2** : to mark as paid ⟨*receipt* a bill⟩

re·ceiv·a·ble \ri-'sē-və-bəl\ *adj* **1** : capable of being received **2** : subject to call for payment ⟨accounts *receivable*⟩

re·ceiv·a·bles \-bəlz\ *n pl* : amounts of money receivable

re·ceive \ri-'sēv\ *vb* **1** : to take or get something that is given, paid, or sent ⟨*receive* the money⟩ ⟨*receive* a letter⟩ **2** : WELCOME, GREET ⟨*receive* friends⟩ **3** : to hold a reception ⟨*receive* from four to six o'clock⟩ **4** : to undergo or be subjected to (an experience or treatment) ⟨*receive* a shock⟩ **5** : to change incoming radio waves into sounds or pictures

re·ceiv·er \ri-'sē-vər\ *n* **1** : a person appointed to take control of property that is involved in a lawsuit or of a business that is bankrupt or is being reorganized **2 a** : an apparatus for receiving radio or television broadcasts **b** : the portion of a telegraphic or telephonic apparatus that converts the electric currents or waves into visible or audible signals **3** : an offensive football player who may catch a forward pass

re·ceiv·er·ship \-ˌship\ *n* **1** : the office or function of a receiver **2** : the state of being in the hands of a receiver

re·cen·cy \'rē-sən-sē\ *n* : the quality or state of being recent

re·cent \'rē-sənt\ *adj* **1 a** : of or relating to a time not long past ⟨*recent* history⟩ **b** : having lately appeared or come into existence : NEW, FRESH ⟨*recent* events⟩ **2** *cap* : of, relating to, or being the present epoch of the Quaternary which is dated from the close of the Pleistocene — **re·cent·ly** *adv* — **re·cent·ness** *n*

re·cep·ta·cle \ri-'sep-ti-kəl\ *n* **1** : something used to receive and contain smaller objects : CONTAINER **2** : the enlarged end of the flower stalk upon which the floral organs are borne **3** : an electrical fitting (as a socket) into which another fitting may be pushed or screwed for making an electrical connection

re·cep·tion \ri-'sep-shən\ *n* **1** : the act or process of receiving, welcoming, or accepting ⟨a warm *reception*⟩ **2** : a social gathering ⟨a wedding *reception*⟩ **3** : the receiving of a radio or television broadcast

re·cep·tion·ist \-sh(ə-)nəst\ *n* : an office employee who is usu. a woman and who greets callers, answers questions, and arranges appointments

re·cep·tive \ri-'sep-tiv\ *adj* **1** : able or inclined to receive esp. ideas **2** : able to receive and transmit stimuli : SENSORY — **re·cep·tive·ly** *adv* — **re·cep·tive·ness** *n* — **re·cep·tiv·i·ty** \ˌrē-ˌsep-'tiv-ət-ē, ri-\ *n*

re·cep·tor \ri-'sep-tər\ *n* : a cell or group of cells that receives stimuli : SENSE ORGAN

1**re·cess** \'rē-ˌses, ri-'\ *n* **1** : a hidden, secret, or secluded place **2 a** : a space or little hollow set back (as from the main line of a coast or mountain range) **b** : ALCOVE **3** : a stopping for a time of business or procedure; *esp* : a brief period for relaxation between class or study periods of a school day

2**recess** *vb* **1** : to put into a recess ⟨*recessed* lighting⟩ **2** : to make a recess in **3** : to interrupt for or take a recess

re·ces·sion \ri-'sesh-ən\ *n* **1** : the act or fact of receding or withdrawing **2** : a departing procession (as of clergy and choir at the end of a church service) **3** : a downward turn in business activity; *also* : the period of such a downward turn

re·ces·sion·al \ri-'sesh-nəl, -ən-əl\ *n* : a hymn or musical piece at the conclusion of a service or program; *also* : RECESSION 2

[1]**re·ces·sive** \ri-'ses-iv\ *adj* **1** : tending to go back : RECEDING **2** : not expressed in the organism if a contrasting dominant gene or a gene determining a contrasting dominant trait is present — **re·ces·sive·ly** *adv* — **re·ces·sive·ness** *n*

[2]**recessive** *n* : a recessive character or factor or an organism possessing one or more such characters

rec·i·pe \'res-ə-(,)pē\ *n* [from Latin, meaning "take", the imperative form of *recipere* "to take", "receive"] **1** : PRESCRIPTION 3a **2** : a set of instructions for making something (as a food dish) from various ingredients ⟨a *recipe* for strawberry shortcake⟩ **3** : method of procedure ⟨a *recipe* for happiness⟩

re·cip·i·ent \ri-'sip-ē-ənt\ *n* : one that receives ⟨the *recipient* of many honors⟩ — **recipient** *adj*

[1]**re·cip·ro·cal** \ri-'sip-rə-kəl\ *adj* **1** : done or felt equally by both sides ⟨*reciprocal* affection⟩ **2** : related to each other in such a way that one completes the other or is the equivalent of the other : mutually corresponding — **re·cip·ro·cal·ly** \-k(ə-)lē\ *adv*

[2]**reciprocal** *n* **1** : something in a reciprocal relationship to another **2** : one of a pair of numbers (as 9, 1/9; 2/3, 3/2) whose product is one

re·cip·ro·cate \ri-'sip-rə-,kāt\ *vb* **1** : to give and take mutually : EXCHANGE **2** : to make a return for something ⟨*reciprocate* a favor⟩ **3** : to move forward and backward alternately ⟨a *reciprocating* piston⟩ — **re·cip·ro·ca·tion** \-,sip-rə-'kā-shən\ *n* — **re·cip·ro·ca·tor** \-'sip-rə-,kāt-ər\ *n*

rec·i·proc·i·ty \,res-ə-'präs-ət-ē\ *n*, *pl* **-ties** **1** : mutual dependence, cooperation, or exchange between persons, groups, or states **2** : international policy by which special commercial advantages are granted to one country in return for special advantages granted by another

re·cir·cu·late \(')rē-'sər-kyə-,lāt\ *vb* : to circulate again (as through a system or cycle) ⟨*recirculate* unburned gases to reduce pollution⟩

re·cit·al \ri-'sīt-əl\ *n* **1** : a reciting of something; *esp* : a story told in detail ⟨the *recital* of his troubles⟩ **2** : a program of one kind of music ⟨a piano *recital*⟩ **3** : a public performance by pupils (as music or dancing pupils) ***syn*** see NARRATIVE — **re·cit·al·ist** \-ə-ləst\ *n*

rec·i·ta·tion \,res-ə-'tā-shən\ *n* **1** : an enumeration or telling in detail **2** : the act or an instance of reading or repeating aloud esp. publicly **3** : a student's oral reply to questions

rec·i·ta·tive \,res-(ə-)tə-'tēv\ *n* : a style of singing without a fixed rhythm that imitates speech and is used for dialogue and narrative in operas and oratorios; *also* : a passage in this style — **recitative** *adj*

re·cite \ri-'sīt\ *vb* **1** : to repeat from memory or read aloud publicly ⟨*recite* a poem⟩ **2** : to give a detailed narration of **3** : to answer (as a teacher) questions about a lesson — **re·cit·er** *n*

reck·less \'rek-ləs\ *adj* : marked by lack of caution : IRRESPONSIBLE, WILD — **reck·less·ly** *adv* — **reck·less·ness** *n*

reck·on \'rek-ən\ *vb* **reck·oned**; **reck·on·ing** \-(ə-)ning\ **1 a** : COUNT, COMPUTE ⟨*reckon* the days till Christmas⟩ **b** : to estimate by calculation ⟨*reckon* the height of a building⟩ **2** : CONSIDER, REGARD ⟨was *reckoned* among the leaders⟩ **3** *chiefly dial* : THINK, SUPPOSE **4** : to count on : DEPEND ⟨*reckon* on support⟩ — **reck·on·er** \-(ə-)nər\ *n*

reck·on·ing *n* **1** : the act or an instance of computing or calculating **2** : calculation of a ship's position **3** : a settling of accounts ⟨day of *reckoning*⟩

re·claim \ri-'klām\ *vb* **1** : to recall from wrong or improper conduct : REFORM ⟨*reclaim* sinners⟩ **2** : to alter from an undesirable or uncultivated state ⟨*reclaim* swampland for agriculture⟩ **3** : to obtain from a waste product or by-product : RECOVER ⟨*reclaimed* wool⟩ — **re·claim·a·ble** \-'klā-mə-bəl\ *adj* — **re·claim·er** *n*

rec·la·ma·tion \,rek-lə-'mā-shən\ *n* : the act or process of reclaiming : the state of being reclaimed

re·cline \ri-'klīn\ *vb* **1** : to lean or cause to lean backwards **2** : REPOSE, LIE ⟨*reclining* on the sofa⟩

rec·luse \'rek-,lüs, ri-'klüs\ *n* : a person (as a hermit) who lives away from others — **re·clu·sive** \ri-'klü-siv, -ziv\ *adj*

rec·og·ni·tion \,rek-ig-'nish-ən, ,rek-əg-\ *n* **1** : the act of recognizing **2** : special attention or notice **3** : acknowledgment of something done or given ⟨got a medal in *recognition* of bravery⟩ **4** : formal acknowledgment of the political existence of a government or nation

re·cog·ni·zance \ri-'käg-nə-zən(t)s, -'kän-ə-\ *n* : a recorded legal promise to do something (as to appear in court)

rec·og·nize \'rek-ig-,nīz, 'rek-əg-\ *vb* **1** : to know and remember upon seeing ⟨*recognize* a person⟩ **2** : to consent to admit : ACKNOWLEDGE ⟨*recognized* her own faults⟩ **3** : to take approving notice of ⟨*recognize* an act of bravery by the award of a medal⟩ **4** : to acknowledge acquaintance with ⟨*recognize* someone with a nod⟩ **5** : to acknowledge as entitled to be heard at a meeting ⟨the chair *recognizes* the delegate from Illinois⟩ **6** : to grant diplomatic recognition to ⟨*recognized* the new government⟩ — **rec·og·niz·a·bil·i·ty** \,rek-ig-,nī-zə-'bil-ət-ē, ,rek-əg-\ *n* — **rec·og·niz·a·ble** \'rek-ig-,nī-zə-bəl, 'rek-əg-\ *adj* — **rec·og·niz·a·bly** \-,nī-zə-blē\ *adv*

[1]**re·coil** \ri-'kȯil\ *vb* **1 a** : to fall back under pressure : RETREAT **b** : to shrink back ⟨*recoil* in horror⟩ **2** : to spring back to or as if to a starting point ⟨the compressed spring *recoiled* upon release⟩ ⟨the big gun *recoiled* upon firing⟩

[2]**re·coil** \ri-'kȯil, 'rē-,\ *n* **1** : the act or action or an instance of recoiling **2** : the distance through which something (as a spring) recoils

re·coil·less \ri-'kȯil-ləs, 'rē-,\ *adj* : having a minimum of recoil ⟨a *recoilless* gun⟩

re–col·lect \,rē-kə-'lekt\ *vb* : to collect again; *esp* : RALLY, RECOVER

rec·ol·lect \,rek-ə-'lekt\ *vb* **1** : to recall to mind : REMEMBER **2** : to remind oneself of something temporarily forgotten

rec·ol·lec·tion \,rek-ə-'lek-shən\ *n* **1** : the action or power of recalling to mind : REMEMBRANCE **2** : something recalled to the mind ***syn*** see MEMORY

re·com·bi·na·tion \,rē-,käm-bə-'nā-shən\ *n* : the formation of new combinations of genes

re·com·bine \,rē-kəm-'bīn\ *vb* **1** : to combine again **2** : to submit to genetic recombination

rec·om·mend \,rek-ə-'mend\ *vb* **1** : to make a statement in praise of; *esp* **:** to endorse as fit, worthy, or competent ⟨*recommend* a person for a position⟩ **2 :** to put forward or suggest as one's advice, as one's choice, or as having one's support ⟨*recommend* that the matter be dropped⟩ **3 :** to cause to receive favorable attention ⟨a man *recommended* by his good manners⟩ — **rec·om·mend·a·ble** \-'men-də-bəl\ *adj* — **rec·om·mend·er** *n*

rec·om·men·da·tion \ˌrek-ə-mən-'dā-shən, -ˌmen-\ *n* **1 :** the act of recommending **2 :** something that recommends ⟨a written *recommendation*⟩ **3 :** a thing or course of action recommended

re·com·mit \ˌrē-kə-'mit\ *vb* **1 :** to refer (as a bill) again to a committee **2 :** to commit again — **re·com·mit·ment** \-mənt\ *n* — **re·com·mit·tal** \-'mit-əl\ *n*

rec·om·pense \'rek-əm-ˌpen(t)s\ *vb* **:** to give compensation to or for **:** REPAY, PAY — **recompense** *n*

rec·on·cile \'rek-ən-ˌsīl\ *vb* **1 :** to make friendly again ⟨*reconcile* friends who have quarreled⟩ **2 :** SETTLE, ADJUST ⟨*reconcile* differences⟩ **3 :** to make agree ⟨a story that cannot be *reconciled* with the facts⟩ **4 :** to cause to submit or to accept **:** make content ⟨*reconciled* himself to the loss⟩ — **rec·on·cil·a·ble** \ˌrek-ən-'sī-lə-bəl, 'rek-ən-ˌ\ *adj* — **rec·on·cile·ment** \'rek-ən-ˌsīl-mənt\ *n* — **rec·on·cil·er** *n* — **rec·on·cil·i·a·tion** \ˌrek-ən-ˌsil-ē-'ā-shən\ *n* — **rec·on·cil·ia·to·ry** \ˌrek-ən-'sil-yə-ˌtōr-ē, -ˌtȯr-\ *adj*

rec·on·dite \'rek-ən-ˌdīt, ri-'kän-\ *adj* **1** *archaic* **:** hidden from sight **:** CONCEALED **2 :** difficult to understand **:** DEEP ⟨a *recondite* subject⟩ — **rec·on·dite·ly** *adv* — **rec·on·dite·ness** *n*

re·con·di·tion \ˌrē-kən-'dish-ən\ *vb* **:** to restore to good condition ⟨a *reconditioned* used car⟩

re·con·firm \ˌrē-kən-'fərm\ *vb* **1 :** to confirm again **2 :** to establish more strongly — **re·con·fir·ma·tion** \(ˌ)rē-ˌkän-fər-'mā-shən\ *n*

re·con·nais·sance \ri-'kän-ə-zən(t)s\ *n* **:** a preliminary survey of an area to gain information; *esp* **:** an exploratory military survey of enemy territory

re·con·noi·ter \ˌrē-kə-'nȯit-ər, ˌrek-ə-\ *vb* **:** to make a reconnaissance; *esp* **:** to survey in preparation for military action ⟨*reconnoiter* enemy territory⟩

re·con·sid·er \ˌrē-kən-'sid-ər\ *vb* **:** to consider again esp. with a view to change or reversal — **re·con·sid·er·a·tion** \-ˌsid-ə-'rā-shən\ *n*

re·con·sti·tute \(')rē-'kän(t)-stə-ˌt(y)üt\ *vb* **:** to restore to a former condition by adding water

re·con·struct \ˌrē-kən-'strəkt\ *vb* **:** to construct again **:** REBUILD, REMODEL

re·con·struc·tion \ˌrē-kən-'strək-shən\ *n* **1 a :** the action of reconstructing **:** the state of being reconstructed **b** *often cap* **:** the reorganization and reestablishment of the seceded states in the Union after the American Civil War **2 :** something reconstructed

re·con·ver·sion \ˌrē-kən-'vər-zhən\ *n* **:** conversion back to a previous state

re·con·vert \-'vərt\ *vb* **:** to convert back

1**re·cord** \ri-'kȯrd\ *vb* **1 a :** to set down in writing **b :** to deposit an authentic official copy of ⟨*record* a deed⟩ **c :** to register permanently ⟨events *recorded* in history⟩ **d :** INDICATE, READ ⟨the thermometer *recorded* 90°⟩ **2 :** to cause (as sound or visual images) to be registered (as on a phonograph disc or magnetic tape) in reproducible form **3 :** to admit of being recorded or reproduced ⟨a voice that *records* well⟩ **4 :** to give evidence of

2**rec·ord** \'rek-ərd, -ˌȯrd\ *n* **1 :** the state or fact of being recorded ⟨on *record*⟩ ⟨a matter of *record*⟩ **2 a :** something that recalls or relates past events **b :** an official writing that records the proceedings or acts of a group, organization, or official **c :** an authentic official copy of a document **3 a :** the known or recorded facts regarding something or someone ⟨his school *record*⟩ **b :** an attested top performance ⟨broke the high jump *record*⟩ **4 :** something on which sound or visual images have been recorded for later reproduction; *esp* **:** a disc with a spiral groove carrying recorded sound for phonograph reproduction

3**rec·ord** \'rek-ərd\ *adj* **:** setting a record **:** outstanding among other like things ⟨a *record* crop⟩ ⟨*record* prices⟩

re·cord·er \ri-'kȯrd-ər\ *n* **1 :** a person or device that records **2 :** a municipal judge with criminal and sometimes limited civil jurisdiction **3 :** a flute with eight finger holes in which the sound is produced by air blown through a flue in the mouthpiece

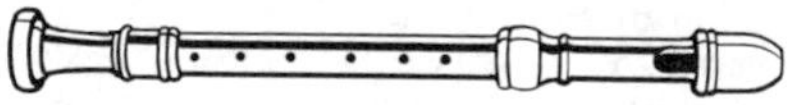

recorder 3

re·cord·ing \ri-'kȯrd-ing\ *n* **:** RECORD 4

rec·ord player \'rek-ərd-\ *n* **:** an electronic instrument for playing phonograph records

1**re·count** \ri-'kau̇nt\ *vb* **:** to relate in detail **:** NARRATE ⟨*recount* an adventure⟩

2**re·count** \(')rē-'kau̇nt\ *vb* **:** to count again

3**re·count** \'rē-ˌkau̇nt, (')rē-'\ *n* **:** a second or fresh count (as of election votes)

re·coup \ri-'küp\ *vb* **1 :** to make up for **:** RECOVER ⟨*recoup* a loss⟩ **2 :** REIMBURSE, COMPENSATE ⟨*recoup* a person for losses⟩ — **re·coup·a·ble** \-'kü-pə-bəl\ *adj* — **re·coup·ment** \-'küp-mənt\ *n*

re·course \'rē-ˌkōrs, -ˌkȯrs, ri-'\ *n* **1 :** a turning for assistance or protection ⟨have *recourse* to the law⟩ **2 :** a source of help or strength **:** RESORT

re·cov·er \ri-'kəv-ər\ *vb* **-cov·ered; -cov·er·ing** \-'kəv-(ə-)ring\ [from medieval French *recoverer*, from Latin *recuperare*, from which more directly, bypassing French, comes English *recuperate*] **1 :** to get back **:** REGAIN ⟨*recover* a lost wallet⟩ ⟨*recovered* his breath⟩ **2 :** to bring back to normal position or condition ⟨stumbled, then *recovered* himself⟩ **3 :** to make up for ⟨*recover* lost time⟩ **4 :** to obtain something useful by separating it from a source (as ore or waste) **:** RECLAIM ⟨*recover* gold from gravel⟩ **5 :** to regain health, consciousness, or self-control — **re·cov·er·a·ble** \-'kəv-(ə-)rə-bəl\ *adj*

re–cov·er \(')rē-'kəv-ər\ *vb* **:** to cover again or anew

re·cov·ery \ri-'kəv-(ə-)rē\ *n, pl* **-er·ies :** the act or process or an instance of recovering; *esp* **:** return to a former normal state (as of health or spirits)

recovery room *n* **:** a hospital room equipped for meeting emergencies following surgery or childbirth

1**rec·re·ant** \'rek-rē-ənt\ *adj* **1 :** crying for mercy **:** COWARDLY **2 :** unfaithful to duty or allegiance

2**recreant** *n* **1 :** COWARD **2 :** BETRAYER, DESERTER

rec·re·ate \'rek-rē-ˌāt\ *vb* **1 :** to give new life or freshness to **2 :** to take recreation — **rec·re·a·tive** \-ˌāt-iv\ *adj*

re–cre·ate \ˌrē-krē-'āt\ *vb* **:** to create anew esp. in the imagination — **re–cre·a·tion** \-'ā-shən\ *n* — **re–cre·a·tive** \-'āt-iv\ *adj*

rec·re·a·tion \ˌrek-rē-'ā-shən\ *n* **1 :** refreshment of strength and spirits after toil **:** DIVERSION **2 :** a means of refreshment or diversion (as a game or exercise) — **rec·re·a·tion·al** \-sh(ə-)nəl\ *adj*

re·crim·i·nate \ri-'krim-ə-ˌnāt\ *vb* **1 :** to make a return charge against an accuser **2 :** to retort bitterly

— **re·crim·i·na·tion** \-ˌkrim-ə-'nā-shən\ *n* — **re·crim·i·na·to·ry** \-'krim-ə-nə-ˌtōr-ē, -ˌtȯr-\ *adj*

re·cru·desce \ˌrē-krü-'des\ *vb* : to break out or become active again

re·cru·des·cence \-'des-ən(t)s\ *n* : a renewal or breaking out again esp. of something unhealthful or dangerous — **re·cru·des·cent** \-ənt\ *adj*

[1]**re·cruit** \ri-'krüt\ *n* [from French *recrute* "fresh growth", "new levy of soldiers", from medieval French *recroistre* "to grow up again", from Latin *recrescere*, from *re-* and *crescere* "to grow"] **1** : a newcomer to a field or activity; *esp* : a newly enlisted or drafted member of the armed forces **2** : an enlisted man of the lowest rank in the army

[2]**recruit** *vb* **1 a** : to increase the membership of an organization by enlisting new members **b** : to secure the services of : ENGAGE ⟨*recruited* new teachers⟩ **2** : REPLENISH ⟨*recruited* his finances⟩ **3** : to restore or increase the health, vigor, or intensity of — **re·cruit·er** *n* — **re·cruit·ment** \-'krüt-mənt\ *n*

rect *abbr* **1** rectangle **2** rectangular

rect·an·gle \'rek-ˌtang-gəl\ *n* : a parallelogram all of whose angles are right angles

rect·an·gu·lar \rek-'tang-gyə-lər\ *adj* **1** : having a flat surface shaped like a rectangle **2 a** : crossing, lying, or meeting at a right angle **b** : having lines or surfaces that meet at right angles ⟨*rectangular* coordinates⟩

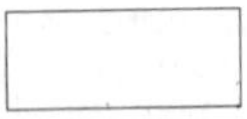
rectangle

rectangular solid *n* : a prism whose faces and bases are rectangles

rec·ti·fy \'rek-tə-ˌfī\ *vb* **-fied**; **-fy·ing** **1** : to set right : REMEDY **2** : to purify (as alcohol) esp. by repeated or fractional distillation **3** : to convert (an alternating current) into a direct current ***syn*** see CORRECT — **rec·ti·fi·a·ble** \-ˌfī-ə-bəl\ *adj* — **rec·ti·fi·ca·tion** \ˌrek-tə-fə-'kā-shən\ *n* — **rec·ti·fi·er** \'rek-tə-ˌfī(-ə)r\ *n*

rec·ti·lin·e·ar \ˌrek-tə-'lin-ē-ər\ *adj* **1** : moving in, being in, or forming a straight line ⟨*rectilinear* motion⟩ **2** : marked by straight lines

rec·ti·tude \'rek-tə-ˌt(y)üd\ *n* **1** : STRAIGHTNESS **2** : moral integrity : RIGHTEOUSNESS

rec·tor \'rek-tər\ *n* **1** : a clergyman in charge of a church or parish **2** : the priest in charge of certain Roman Catholic religious houses for men **3** : the head of a university or school

rec·to·ry \'rek-t(ə-)rē\ *n, pl* **-ries** : a rector's residence

rec·tum \'rek-təm\ *n, pl* **rectums** *or* **rec·ta** \-tə\ : the last part of the intestine linking the colon to the anus — **rec·tal** \-təl\ *adj*

re·cum·ben·cy \ri-'kəm-bən-sē\ *n* : recumbent position : REPOSE

re·cum·bent \-bənt\ *adj* **1** : RESTING **2** : lying down — **re·cum·bent·ly** *adv*

re·cu·per·ate \ri-'k(y)ü-pə-ˌrāt\ *vb* : to get back : RECOVER; *esp* : to regain health or strength — **re·cu·per·a·tion** \-ˌk(y)ü-pə-'rā-shən\ *n* — **re·cu·per·a·tive** \ri-'k(y)ü-pə-ˌrāt-iv, -p(ə-)rət-\ *adj*

re·cur \ri-'kər\ *vb* **re·curred**; **re·cur·ring** **1** : to go or come back in thought or discussion **2** : to come again into the mind **3** : to occur or appear again — **re·cur·rence** \-'kər-ən(t)s, -'kə-rən(t)s\ *n*

ə abut	ər further	a back	ā bake	
ä cot, cart	au̇ out	ch chin	e less	ē easy
g gift	i trip	ī life	j joke	ng sing	ō flow
ȯ flaw	ȯi coin	th thin	t͟h this	ü loot
u̇ foot	y yet	yü few	yu̇ furious	zh vision

re·cur·rent \ri-'kər-ənt, -'kə-rənt\ *adj* **1** : returning from time to time : RECURRING ⟨a *recurrent* fever⟩ **2** : running or turning back in direction ⟨a *recurrent* vein⟩ — **re·cur·rent·ly** *adv*

re·curved \(ˈ)rē-'kərvd\ *adj* : curved backward or inward ⟨*recurved* insect antennae⟩

re·cy·cle \(ˈ)rē-'sī-kəl\ *vb* : to process (as liquid body waste, glass, or cans) in order to regain materials for human use

[1]**red** \'red\ *adj* **red·der**; **red·dest** **1** : of the color red **2 a** : flushed esp. with anger or embarrassment **b** : BLOODSHOT ⟨eyes *red* from weeping⟩ **3 a** : advocating radical social or political change esp. by force **b** : COMMUNIST **c** : of or relating to the U.S.S.R. or a Communist country — **red·ly** *adv* — **red·ness** *n*

[2]**red** *n* **1** : a color whose hue resembles that of blood or the ruby **2** : one that is of a red or reddish color **3** : a pigment or dye that colors red **4 a** : REVOLUTIONARY **b** *cap* : COMMUNIST **5** : the condition of showing a loss ⟨in the *red*⟩

red alga *n* : an alga having predominantly red pigmentation

red·bird \'red-ˌbərd\ *n* : any of several birds (as a cardinal, several tanagers, or the bullfinch) with predominantly red plumage

red blood cell *n* : one of the hemoglobin-containing cells that carry oxygen to the tissues and are responsible for the red color of vertebrate blood — called also *red blood corpuscle, red corpuscle*

red–blood·ed \'red-'bləd-əd\ *adj* : ENERGETIC, VIGOROUS

red·breast \-ˌbrest\ *n* : a bird (as a robin) with a reddish breast

red·cap \-ˌkap\ *n* : a baggage porter (as at a railroad station)

red–car·pet \-'kär-pət\ *adj* : marked by ceremonial courtesy ⟨*red-carpet* treatment⟩

red cedar *n* : an American juniper with fragrant close-grained red wood; *also* : its wood

red cell *n* : RED BLOOD CELL

red clover *n* : a Eurasian clover with globe-shaped heads of reddish purple flowers widely grown as a hay, forage, and cover crop

red·coat \'red-ˌkōt\ *n* : a British soldier esp. during the Revolutionary War

red cross *n* : a red-colored cross on a white background used as a badge for hospitals and for members of an international organization that helps the suffering esp. in war or disaster areas

red deer *n* : the common deer of temperate Europe and Asia related to but smaller than the elk

red deer (about 4 ft. at shoulder)

red·den \'red-ən\ *vb* **red·dened**; **red·den·ing** \-(ə-)ning\ : to make or become red or reddish; *esp* : BLUSH

red·dish \'red-ish\ *adj* : somewhat red — **red·dish·ness** *n*

re·dec·o·rate \(ˈ)rē-'dek-ə-ˌrāt\ *vb* : to freshen or change a decorative scheme — **re·dec·o·ra·tion** \(ˌ)rē-ˌdeck-ə-'rā-shən\ *n*

re·deem \ri-'dēm\ *vb* **1** : to buy or win back **2 a** : to free from captivity esp. by paying a ransom **b** : to free from the penalties of sin **3** : to change for the better : REFORM ⟨sinners not easily *redeemed*⟩ **4** : to remove the obligation of by payment ⟨the government *redeems* savings bonds⟩ **5** : to make good : FULFILL ⟨*redeem* a promise⟩ — **re·deem·a·ble** \-'dē-mə-bəl\ *adj*

re·deem·er \ri-'dē-mər\ *n* : a person who redeems; *esp, cap* : Jesus Christ

re·demp·tion \ri-'dem(p)-shən\ *n* : the act or process or an instance of redeeming — **re·demp·tion·al** \-sh(ə-)nəl\ *adj* — **re·demp·tive** \-'dem(p)-tiv\ *adj*

re·de·sign \ˌrēd-i-'zīn\ *vb* : to revise in appearance, function, or content — **redesign** *n*

re·de·vel·op·ment \ˌrēd-i-'vel-əp-mənt\ *n* : the act or process of redeveloping; *esp* : renovation of a blighted area

red fox *n* : a common fox with orange-red to dusky reddish brown fur

red giant *n* : a very large star with a comparatively low surface temperature — compare WHITE DWARF

red fox
(up to 3½ ft. long)

red–green blindness *n* : a form of color blindness in which the spectrum is seen in tones of yellow and blue — called also *red-green color blindness*

red–hand·ed \'red-'han-dəd\ *adv or adj* : in the act of committing a crime or misdeed

red·head \-ˌhed\ *n* **1** : a person having red hair **2** : an American duck related to the canvasback but having in the male a brighter reddish head and shorter bill

red herring *n* **1** : a herring cured by salting and slow smoking to a dark brown color **2** : a diversion intended to distract attention from the real issue

red–hot \'red-'hät\ *adj* **1** : glowing red with heat **2** : marked by intense emotion, enthusiasm, or energy ⟨a *red-hot* political campaign⟩ **3** : FRESH, NEW ⟨*red-hot* news⟩

re·di·rect \ˌrēd-ə-'rekt, ˌrē-(ˌ)dī-\ *vb* : to change the course or direction of — **re·di·rec·tion** \-'rek-shən\ *n*

re·dis·trict \(')rē-'dis-(ˌ)trikt\ *vb* : to divide anew into districts; *esp* : to revise the legislative districts of

red lead *n* : a red oxide of lead used in storage-battery plates, in glass and ceramics, and as a paint pigment

red–let·ter *adj* [from the practice of marking holy days in red letters in church calendars] : memorable esp. in a happy or joyful way ⟨a *red-letter* day⟩

red maple *n* : a common American maple with reddish twigs and rather soft wood

red marrow *n* : reddish bone marrow that is the seat of blood-cell production

re·do \(')rē-'dü\ *vb* **-did** \-'did\; **-done** \-'dən\; **-do·ing** \-'dü-iŋ\ : to do over or again; *esp* : REDECORATE

red oak *n* : any of numerous American oaks with acorns that take two years to mature

red·o·lence \'red-ə-lən(t)s\ *n* **1** : the quality or state of being redolent **2** : SCENT, AROMA

red·o·lent \-lənt\ *adj* **1** : exuding fragrance : AROMATIC **2** : full of a specified fragrance or odor : SCENTED ⟨a room *redolent* of tobacco smoke⟩ — **red·o·lent·ly** *adv*

re·dou·ble \(')rē-'dəb-əl\ *vb* **1** : to make or become doubled (as in size, amount, or degree) ⟨*redoubled* his efforts⟩ **2** : to double back ⟨the fox *redoubled* on his tracks⟩ **3** : to double again

re·doubt·a·ble \ri-'daůt-ə-bəl\ *adj* : arousing fear or dread : FORMIDABLE ⟨a *redoubtable* warrior⟩ — **re·doubt·a·bly** \-blē\ *adv*

re·dound \ri-'daůnd\ *vb* : to become reflected back esp. so as to bring credit or discredit : have a result or effect ⟨actions that *redound* to a man's credit⟩

red pepper *n* : CAYENNE PEPPER

red·poll \'red-ˌpōl\ *n* : any of several small finches in which the males usu. have a red or rosy crown

[1]**re·dress** \ri-'dres\ *vb* **1** : to set (as a wrong) right : make amends for : REMEDY, RELIEVE **2** : to correct or amend the faults of

[2]**re·dress** \ri-'dres, 'rē-ˌ\ *n* **1 a** : relief from distress **b** : means or possibility of seeking a remedy **2** : compensation for wrong or loss **3** : an act or instance of redressing

red shift *n* : displacement of a spectrum esp. of a distant star or galaxy toward longer wavelengths

red·skin \'red-ˌskin\ *n* : a No. American Indian

red snapper *n* : any of several reddish sea fishes including some esteemed for food or sport

red soil *n* : any of a group of soils that develop in a warm temperate moist climate under deciduous or mixed forests and are characterized by several zones resting on a red zone consisting of soil material carried downward from the upper layers

red spider *n* : any small web-spinning mite that attacks forage and crop plants

red spruce *n* : a cone-bearing tree of eastern No. America that is an important source of lumber and pulp wood

red·start \'red-ˌstärt\ *n* **1** : a small red-tailed European thrush **2** : an American fly-catching warbler

red tape *n* : official routine or procedure that results in delay or inaction

red tide *n* : seawater discolored and made toxic by the presence of large numbers of dinoflagellates

re·duce \ri-'d(y)üs\ *vb* **1 a** : to diminish in size, amount, extent, or number ⟨*reduce* the number of accidents⟩; *esp* : to lose weight by dieting **b** : to undergo meiosis **2** : to bring to a specified state or condition ⟨*reduce* anarchy to order⟩ **3 a** : to bring to a systematic form or character ⟨*reduce* language to writing⟩ **b** : to become converted or equated ⟨their differences *reduced* to a question of semantics⟩ **4 a** : to lower in grade or rank : DEMOTE **b** : to lower in condition or status ⟨*reduced* to panhandling⟩ **c** : to diminish in strength or intensity **5** : to change the form of an arithmetic expression without changing the value ⟨*reduce* a fraction to its lowest terms⟩ **6** : to break down (as by crushing or grinding) ⟨*reduce* stone to powder⟩ **7 a** : DEOXIDIZE **b** : to combine with or subject to the action of hydrogen **c** : to add one or more electrons to (an atom or ion or molecule) — **re·duc·er** *n* — **re·duc·i·bil·i·ty** \-ˌd(y)ü-sə-'bil-ət-ē\ *n* — **re·duc·i·ble** \-'d(y)ü-sə-bəl\ *adj* — **re·duc·i·bly** \-blē\ *adv*

re·duc·tion \ri-'dək-shən\ *n* **1** : the act or process of reducing : the state of being reduced **2 a** : the amount by which something is reduced in price **b** : something made by reducing **3** : MEIOSIS; *esp* : halving of the chromosome number in the first meiotic division — **re·duc·tion·al** \-sh(ə-)nəl\ *adj* — **re·duc·tive** \-'dək-tiv\ *adj*

reduction division *n* : the first division of meiosis in which chromosome reduction occurs; *also* : MEIOSIS

R

re·dun·dan·cy \ri-'dən-dən-sē\ *n, pl* **-cies** **1 :** the quality or state of being redundant **2 a :** unnecessary repetition : PROLIXITY **b :** an act or instance of needless repetition
re·dun·dant \ri-'dən-dənt\ *adj* **1 :** exceeding what is necessary or normal **2 :** using or having more words than necessary : REPETITIOUS — **re·dun·dant·ly** *adv*
re·du·pli·cate \ri-'d(y)ü-pli-ˌkāt, 'rē-\ *vb* **:** to make or perform again : COPY — **re·du·pli·cate** \-kət\ *adj*
re·du·pli·ca·tion \ri-ˌd(y)ü-pli-'kā-shən, ˌrē-\ *n* **:** an act or instance of doubling or repeating : DUPLICATION — **re·du·pli·ca·tive** \ri-'d(y)ü-pli-ˌkāt-iv, 'rē-\ *adj* — **re·du·pli·ca·tive·ly** *adv*
red·wing \'red-ˌwing\ *n* **1 :** a red-winged European thrush **2 :** REDWING BLACKBIRD
red·wing blackbird *or* **red–winged blackbird** \ˌred-ˌwing(d)-\ *n* **:** a No. American blackbird of which the adult male is black with a patch of bright scarlet on the wing
red·wood \'red-ˌwu̇d\ *n* **1 :** a tree yielding a red dye or having red or reddish wood **2 :** a tall cone-bearing timber tree of California; *also* **:** its light durable brownish red wood
re·echo \(')rē-'ek-ō\ *vb* **:** to echo back : REVERBERATE
reed \'rēd\ *n* **1 a :** any of various tall grasses having slender often prominently jointed stems and growing esp. in wet areas **b :** a stem of such a grass **c :** a growth or mass of reeds **2 :** a musical instrument made of the hollow joint of a plant **3 a :** a thin elastic strip (as of cane, wood, metal, or plastic) fastened at one end to the mouthpiece of a musical instrument (as a clarinet) or to a fixture (as a reed block) over an air opening (as in an accordion) and set in vibration by an air current (as the breath) **b :** a reed instrument ⟨the *reeds* of an orchestra⟩

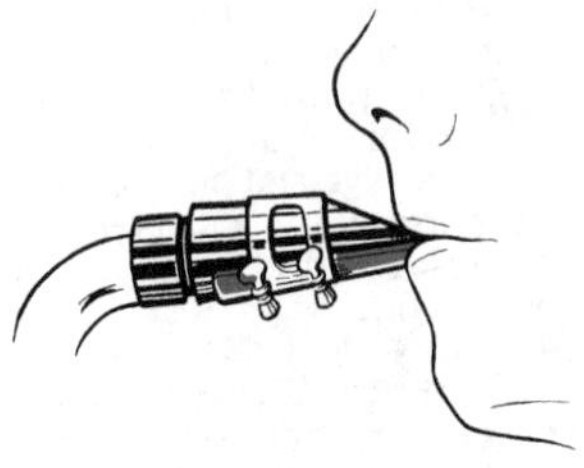
reed 3a

reed organ *n* **:** a keyboard wind instrument in which the wind acts on a set of metal reeds
re·ed·u·cate \(')rē-'ej-ə-ˌkāt\ *vb* **:** to train again; *esp* **:** to rehabilitate through education — **re·ed·u·ca·tion** \(ˌ)rē-ˌej-ə-'kā-shən\ *n*
reedy \'rēd-ē\ *adj* **reed·i·er; -est** **1 :** abounding in or covered with reeds ⟨a *reedy* marsh⟩ **2 :** made of or resembling reeds; *esp* **:** SLENDER, FRAIL ⟨*reedy* arms⟩ **3 :** having the tone quality of a reed instrument ⟨a *reedy* tenor voice⟩ — **reed·i·ly** \'rēd-ə-lē\ *adv* — **reed·i·ness** \'rēd-ē-nəs\ *n*
[1]**reef** \'rēf\ *n* **1 :** a part of a sail taken in or let out in regulating size **2 :** the reduction in sail area made by reefing
[2]**reef** *vb* **1 :** to reduce the area of (a sail) by rolling or folding a portion **2 :** to lower or bring inboard (a spar) wholly or partially

ə abut	ər further	a back	ā bake	
ä cot, cart	au̇ out	ch chin	e less	ē easy
g gift	i trip	ī life	j joke	ng sing	ō flow
ȯ flaw	ȯi coin	th thin	t͟h this	ü loot
u̇ foot	y yet	yü few	yu̇ furious	zh vision

[3]**reef** *n* **:** a chain of rocks or ridge of sand at or near the surface of water
[1]**reef·er** \'rē-fər\ *n* **1 :** one that reefs **2 :** a close-fitting usu. double-breasted jacket of thick cloth
[2]**reefer** *n* **:** a marijuana cigarette
[1]**reek** \'rēk\ *n* **1 :** VAPOR, FOG **2 :** a strong or disagreeable fume or odor
[2]**reek** *vb* **1 :** to emit smoke or vapor **2 a :** to have a strong or unpleasant smell **b :** to be unpleasantly or strongly permeated — **reeky** \'rē-kē\ *adj*
[1]**reel** \'rēl\ *n* **1 a :** a revolvable device on which something flexible is wound **b :** a device consisting of a crank-operated revolvable cylinder on which a line is wound and which is set on the handle of a fishing pole and used for winding up or letting out the line **c :** a narrow flanged spool for photographic film or magnetic tape **2 :** a quantity of something wound on a reel **3 :** a frame for drying clothes usu. having radial arms on a vertical pole
[2]**reel** *vb* **1 :** to wind upon or as if upon a reel **2 :** to draw (as a fish) by reeling a line **3 :** to wind or turn a reel — **reel·a·ble** \'rē-lə-bəl\ *adj* — **reel·er** *n*
[3]**reel** *vb* **1 a :** to whirl around ⟨*reeling* in a dance⟩ **b :** to be in a whirl ⟨heads *reeling* with excitement⟩ **2 :** to give way : fall back : WAVER ⟨soldiers *reeling* in defeat⟩ **3 :** to stagger or sway dizzily
[4]**reel** *n* **:** a reeling motion
[5]**reel** *n* **:** a lively Scottish-Highland dance or its music
re·elect \ˌrē-ə-'lekt\ *vb* **:** to elect for another term in office — **re·elec·tion** \-'lek-shən\ *n*
reel off *vb* **1 :** to recite fluently ⟨*reeled off* some impressive statistics⟩ **2 :** to cover or traverse with seeming ease ⟨*reeled off* a four-minute mile⟩
re·en·act \ˌrē-ə-'nakt\ *vb* **1 :** to enact again **2 :** to perform again — **re·en·act·ment** \-'nak(t)-mənt\ *n*
re·en·force \ˌrē-ən-'fōrs, -'fȯrs\ *var of* REINFORCE
re·en·ter \(')rē-'ent-ər\ *vb* **:** to enter again
re·en·trance \(')rē-'en-trən(t)s\ *n* **:** REENTRY
re·en·try \(')rē-'en-trē\ *n* **1 :** a second or new entry **2 :** the action of reentering the earth's atmosphere after travel in space
reeve \'rēv\ *n* **:** a medieval English manor officer responsible chiefly for enforcing the discharge of feudal obligations
ref \'ref\ *n* **:** REFEREE 2
ref *abbr* reference
re·fash·ion \(')rē-'fash-ən\ *vb* **:** to make over : ALTER
re·fec·to·ry \ri-'fek-t(ə-)rē\ *n, pl* **-ries** **:** a dining hall esp. in a monastery or convent
refectory table *n* **:** a long narrow table with heavy legs
re·fer \ri-'fər\ *vb* **re·ferred; re·fer·ring** [from Latin *referre*, literally "to carry back", from *re-* and *ferre* "to carry", from the same prehistoric source as English *bear*] **1 :** to place in a certain class so far as cause, relationship, or source is concerned ⟨*referred* the defeat to poor training⟩ **2 :** to send or direct to some person or place for treatment, help, or information ⟨*refer* a boy to a dictionary⟩ **3 :** to go for information, advice, or aid ⟨*refer* to the dictionary for the meaning of a word⟩ **4 :** to have relation or connection : RELATE ⟨the asterisk *refers* to a footnote⟩ **5 :** to submit or hand over to someone else ⟨*refer* a patient to a specialist⟩ **6 :** to direct attention : make reference — **ref·er·a·ble** \'ref-(ə-)rə-bəl, ri-'fər-ə-\ *adj* — **re·fer·rer** \ri-'fər-ər\ *n*
[1]**ref·er·ee** \ˌref-ə-'rē\ *n* **1 :** a person to whom a matter is referred for investigation and report or for settlement **2 :** a sports official usu. having final authority in administering a game

²**referee** *vb* **-eed**; **-ee·ing** : to act or supervise as a referee

ref·er·ence \'ref-ərn(t)s, 'ref-(ə-)rən(t)s\ *n* **1** : the act of referring or consulting **2** : a bearing on a matter : RELATION ⟨with *reference* to what was said⟩ **3 a** : a remark referring to something : ALLUSION ⟨made *reference* to our agreement⟩ **b** : a sign or indication referring a reader to another passage or book **c** : consultation of sources of information ⟨volumes for ready *reference*⟩ **4 a** : a person to whom inquiries as to character or ability can be made **b** : a statement of the qualifications of a person seeking employment or appointment given by someone familiar with them **c** : a book, passage, or document to which a reader is referred

reference mark *n* : a conventional mark (as *, †, or ‡) placed in written or printed text to direct the reader's attention esp. to a footnote

ref·er·en·dum \,ref-ə-'ren-dəm\ *n, pl* **-da** \-də\ *or* **-dums** : the principle or practice of submitting to popular vote a measure passed upon or proposed by a legislative body or by popular initiative; *also* : a vote on a measure so submitted

ref·er·ent \'ref-(ə-)rənt\ *n* : something that refers or is referred to; *esp* : the thing a word stands for — **referent** *adj*

re·fer·ral \ri-'fər-əl\ *n* : the act or an instance of referring

¹**re·fill** \(')rē-'fil\ *vb* : to fill or become filled again — **re·fill·a·ble** \-'fil-ə-bəl\ *adj*

²**re·fill** \'rē-,fil\ *n* : a new or fresh supply of something ⟨a *refill* for a ball-point pen⟩

re·fine \ri-'fīn\ *vb* **1** : to come or bring to a pure state ⟨*refine* sugar⟩ **2** : to make or become improved or perfected esp. by pruning or polishing **3** : to free from what is coarse, vulgar, or uncouth **4** : to make improvement by introducing subtleties or distinctions ⟨*refined* upon the older methods⟩ — **re·fin·er** *n*

re·fined \ri-'fīnd\ *adj* **1** : freed from impurities : PURE ⟨*refined* sugar⟩ **2** : WELL-BRED, CULTURED ⟨very *refined* manners⟩ **3** : carried to a fine point : SUBTLE ⟨*refined* measurements⟩

re·fine·ment \ri-'fīn-mənt\ *n* **1** : the action or process of refining **2** : the quality or state of being refined : CULTIVATION **3 a** : a refined feature or method ⟨*refinements* in dress and behavior⟩ **b** : a contrivance or device intended to improve or perfect

re·fin·ery \ri-'fīn-(ə-)rē\ *n, pl* **-er·ies** : an establishment for refining metals, oil, or sugar

re·fin·ish \(')rē-'fin-ish\ *vb* : to give (as furniture) a new surface — **re·fin·ish·er** *n*

re·fit \(')rē-'fit\ *vb* **re·fit·ted**; **re·fit·ting** : to get ready for use again ⟨*refit* a ship for service⟩ — **refit** \'rē-,fit, (')rē-'\ *n*

re·flect \ri-'flekt\ *vb* **1** : to bend or throw back waves of light, sound, or heat ⟨a polished surface *reflects* light⟩ **2** : to give back an image or likeness of as if by a mirror **3** : to bring as a result ⟨the boy's scholarship *reflects* credit on his school⟩ **4** : to cast reproach or blame ⟨our bad conduct *reflects* upon our training⟩ **5** : to think seriously and carefully : MEDITATE

reflecting telescope *n* : REFLECTOR 2

re·flec·tion \ri-'flek-shən\ *n* **1** : an instance of reflecting; *esp* : the return of light or sound waves from a surface **2** : the production of an image by or as if by a mirror **3** : an image given back by a reflecting surface — **re·flec·tion·al** \-sh(ə-)nəl\ *adj*

re·flec·tive \ri-'flek-tiv\ *adj* **1** : capable of reflecting light, images, or sound waves **2** : marked by reflection : THOUGHTFUL **3** : of, relating to, or caused by reflection — **re·flec·tive·ly** *adv* — **re·flec·tive·ness** *n* — **re·flec·tiv·i·ty** \,rē-,flek-'tiv-ət-ē, ri-\ *n*

re·flec·tor \ri-'flek-tər\ *n* **1** : one that reflects; *esp* : a polished surface for reflecting light or heat **2** : a telescope in which the principal focusing element is a mirror

¹**re·flex** \'rē-,fleks\ *n* **1 a** : reflected heat, light, or color **b** : a mirrored image **2 a** : an automatic and usu. inborn response to a stimulus in which a nerve impulse passes from the point of stimulation to a nerve center and thence to the point of action (as a muscle or gland) without reaching the level of consciousness — compare HABIT **b** *pl* : the power of acting or responding with adequate speed ⟨an athlete with great *reflexes*⟩

²**reflex** *adj* **1** *or* **re·flexed** \-,flekst\ : bent, turned, or directed back : REFLECTED **2** : produced in reaction, resistance, or return **3** *of an angle* : being between 180° and 360° **4** : of, relating to, or produced by a reflex of the nervous system ⟨*reflex* action⟩ — **re·flex·ly** *adv*

reflex arc *n* : the complete nervous path involved in a reflex

reflex camera *n* : a camera in which the image formed by a lens is reflected onto a screen for focusing and composition

re·flex·ion \ri-'flek-shən\ *chiefly Brit var of* REFLECTION

¹**re·flex·ive** \ri-'flek-siv\ *adj* **1** : directed or turned back upon itself **2** : of, relating to, or being an action directed back upon the doer or the grammatical subject ⟨*myself* in "I hurt myself" is a *reflexive* pronoun⟩ — **re·flex·ive·ly** *adv* — **re·flex·ive·ness** *n* — **re·flex·iv·i·ty** \,rē-,flek-'siv-ət-ē, ri-\ *n*

²**reflexive** *n* : a reflexive pronoun or verb

re·flux \'rē-,fləks\ *n* : a flowing back : EBB

re·for·est \(')rē-'fȯr-əst, -'fär-\ *vb* : to renew forest cover on by seeding or planting — **re·for·es·ta·tion** \(,)rē-,fȯr-ə-'stā-shən, -,fär-\ *n*

¹**re·form** \ri-'fȯrm\ *vb* **1** : to make better by removal of faults ⟨*reform* a prisoner⟩ **2** : to correct or improve one's own character or habits — **re·form·a·ble** \-'fȯr-mə-bəl\ *adj*

²**reform** *n* **1** : improvement in what is bad or corrupt **2** : a removal or correction of an abuse, a wrong, or errors

re–form \(')rē-'fȯrm\ *vb* : to form again or anew ⟨water decomposes to *re-form* hydrogen and oxygen⟩

ref·or·ma·tion \,ref-ər-'mā-shən\ *n* **1** : the act of reforming : the state of being reformed **2** *cap* : a 16th century religious movement marked by rejection or modification of much of Roman Catholic doctrine and practice and establishment of the Protestant churches — **ref·or·ma·tion·al** \-sh(ə-)nəl\ *adj*

re·for·ma·tive \ri-'fȯr-mət-iv\ *adj* : tending or inclined to reform

¹**re·for·ma·to·ry** \ri-'fȯr-mə-,tōr-ē, -,tȯr-\ *adj* : REFORMATIVE ⟨*reformatory* measures⟩

²**reformatory** *n, pl* **-ries** : a penal institution to which young or first offenders or women are committed for training and reformation

re·form·er \ri-'fȯr-mər\ *n* : one that works for or urges reform

Reform Judaism *n* : a 19th and 20th century development of Judaism marked by rationalization of belief, simplification of many observances, and affirmation of the religious rather than national character of Judaism

reform school *n* : a reformatory for boys or girls

re·fract \ri-'frakt\ *vb* : to subject to refraction

refracting telescope *n* : REFRACTOR

re·frac·tion \ri-'frak-shən\ *n* : the bending of a ray when it passes slantwise from one medium into another in which its speed is different (as when light passes from air into water) — **re·frac·tive** \-'frak-tiv\ *adj*

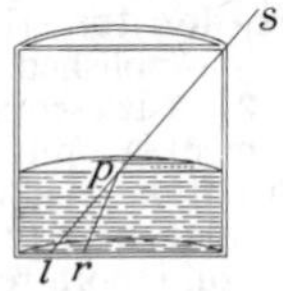

refraction: ray of light *sp* passing from air into water at *p* is refracted from *pl* to *pr*

re·frac·tor \ri-'frak-tər\ *n* : a telescope whose principal focusing element is a lens

re·frac·to·ry \ri-'frak-t(ə-)rē\ *adj* **1** : resisting control or authority : STUBBORN ⟨a *refractory* boy⟩ **2** : resistant to treatment : UNRESPONSIVE **3** : capable of enduring high temperatures — **re·frac·to·ri·ly** \-t(ə-)rə-lē\ *adv* — **re·frac·to·ri·ness** \-t(ə-)rē-nəs\ *n*

1**re·frain** \ri-'frān\ *vb* : to hold oneself back : restrain oneself ⟨*refrain* from laughing⟩

2**refrain** *n* : a regularly repeated phrase or verse esp. at the end of each stanza of a poem or song : CHORUS

re·fresh \ri-'fresh\ *vb* **1** : to restore strength and animation to : REVIVE ⟨sleep *refreshes* the body⟩ ⟨*refreshing* his memory by looking at his notes⟩ **2** : to restore or maintain by renewing supply

re·fresh·en \-'fresh-ən\ *vb* : REFRESH

re·fresh·er \ri-'fresh-ər\ *n* **1** : something that refreshes **2** : REMINDER **3** : review or instruction designed esp. to keep one abreast of professional developments

re·fresh·ing *adj* : serving to refresh; *esp* : agreeably stimulating because of freshness or newness ⟨her sense of humor is very *refreshing*⟩

re·fresh·ment \ri-'fresh-mənt\ *n* **1** : the act of refreshing : the state of being refreshed **2 a** : something that refreshes **b** *pl* : a light meal : LUNCH ⟨*refreshments* will be served after the meeting⟩

refrig *abbr* refrigeration

re·frig·er·ant \ri-'frij-(ə-)rənt\ *n* : a substance (as ice, ammonia, or carbon dioxide) used in refrigeration

re·frig·er·ate \ri-'frij-ə-ˌrāt\ *vb* : to make or keep cold or cool; *esp* : to freeze or chill food for preservation — **re·frig·er·a·tion** \-ˌfrij-ə-'rā-shən\ *n*

re·frig·er·a·tor \ri-'frij-ə-ˌrāt-ər\ *n* : a cabinet or room for keeping articles (as food) cool esp. by means of ice or a mechanical device

reft *past of* REAVE

re·fu·el \(')rē-'fyü-əl\ *vb* : to provide with or take on fresh fuel

ref·uge \'ref-ˌyüj\ *n* **1** : shelter or protection from danger or distress **2** : a place that provides shelter or protection ⟨wildlife *refuges*⟩

ref·u·gee \ˌref-yu̇-'jē\ *n* : a person who flees for safety esp. to a foreign country

re·ful·gence \ri-'fu̇l-jən(t)s, -'fəl-\ *n* : a radiant or resplendent quality or state : BRILLIANCE — **re·ful·gent** \-jənt\ *adj*

1**re·fund** \ri-'fənd, 'rē-ˌfənd\ *vb* : to return money in restitution or repayment — **re·fund·a·ble** \-ə-bəl\ *adj*

2**re·fund** \'rē-ˌfənd\ *n* **1** : the act of refunding **2** : a sum refunded

3**re·fund** \(')rē-'fənd\ *vb* : to fund a debt again or anew

ə abut	ər further	a back	ā bake
ä cot, cart	au̇ out	ch chin	e less
ē easy	g gift	i trip	ī life
j joke	ng sing	ō flow	ȯ flaw
ȯi coin	th thin	th this	ü loot
u̇ foot	y yet	yü few	yu̇ furious
zh vision			

re·fur·bish \ri-'fər-bish\ *vb* : to brighten or freshen up : RENOVATE ⟨*refurbish* an old house⟩ — **re·fur·bish·ment** \-mənt\ *n*

re·fus·al \ri-'fyü-zəl\ *n* **1** : the act of refusing or denying **2** : the opportunity or right of refusing or taking before others

1**re·fuse** \ri-'fyüz\ *vb* **1** : to decline to accept : REJECT ⟨*refused* the money⟩ **2 a** : to show or express positive unwillingness : fail deliberately ⟨*refused* to act⟩ **b** : DENY ⟨was *refused* entrance⟩ **3** : to withhold acceptance, compliance, or permission ***syn*** see DECLINE — **re·fus·er** *n*

2**ref·use** \'ref-ˌyüs, -ˌyüz\ *n* : worthless material : TRASH, GARBAGE

ref·u·ta·tion \ˌref-yu̇-'tā-shən\ *n* : the act or process of refuting : DISPROOF

re·fute \ri-'fyüt\ *vb* : to prove wrong by argument or evidence : show to be false ⟨*refute* the testimony of a witness⟩ — **re·fut·a·ble** \ri-'fyüt-ə-bəl, 'ref-yət-\ *adj* — **re·fut·a·bly** \-blē\ *adv* — **re·fut·er** \ri-'fyüt-ər\ *n*

reg *abbr* regular

re·gain \ri-'gān\ *vb* **1** : to gain or get again : get back ⟨*regained* his health⟩ **2** : to get back to : reach again ⟨*regain* the shore⟩

re·gal \'rē-gəl\ *adj* [from Latin *regalis*, from *reg-*, stem of *rex* "king", from a root meaning "to rule"] **1** : of, relating to, or suitable for a king **2** : of notable excellence or magnificence : SPLENDID — **re·gal·i·ty** \ri-'gal-ət-ē\ *n* — **re·gal·ly** \'rē-gə-lē\ *adv*

re·gale \ri-'gāl\ *vb* **1** : to treat or entertain sumptuously or agreeably **2** : to feast oneself : FEED — **re·gale·ment** \-mənt\ *n*

re·ga·lia \ri-'gāl-yə\ *n sing or pl* **1** : the emblems and symbols (as the crown and scepter) of royalty **2** : the insignia of an office or order **3** : special dress : FINERY

1**re·gard** \ri-'gärd\ *n* **1 a** : CONSIDERATION, CONCERN ⟨little *regard* for others' feelings⟩ **b** : LOOK, GAZE **2 a** : the worth or estimation in which something is held **b** (1) : a feeling of respect and affection : ESTEEM ⟨a high *regard* for his teacher⟩ (2) *pl* : friendly greetings implying such feeling ⟨give him my *regards*⟩ **3** : REFERENCE, RESPECT ⟨this is in *regard* to your unpaid balance⟩ **4** : an aspect to be taken into consideration : a particular matter or point ⟨nothing to worry about in that *regard*⟩

2**regard** *vb* **1** : to pay attention to **2 a** : to show respect or consideration for **b** : to hold in high esteem **3** : to look at steadily or attentively **4** : to take into consideration or account **5** : to relate to **6** : to think of : look upon ⟨*regarded* him as a friend⟩ — **as regards** : with respect to : REGARDING

re·gard·ful \ri-'gärd-fəl\ *adj* **1** : HEEDFUL, OBSERVANT **2** : full or expressive of regard or respect : RESPECTFUL — **re·gard·ful·ly** \-fə-lē\ *adv* — **re·gard·ful·ness** *n*

re·gard·ing *prep* : CONCERNING

1**re·gard·less** \ri-'gärd-ləs\ *adj* : having or taking no regard or heed : HEEDLESS, CARELESS ⟨*regardless* of the consequences⟩ — **re·gard·less·ly** *adv* — **re·gard·less·ness** *n*

2**regardless** *adv* : despite everything

re·gat·ta \ri-'gät-ə, -'gat-\ *n* : a rowing, speedboat, or sailing race or a series of such races

re·gen·cy \'rē-jən-sē\ *n, pl* **-cies** **1** : the office, jurisdiction, or government of a regent or body of regents **2** : the period of rule of a regent or body of regents

1**re·gen·er·ate** \ri-'jen-(ə-)rət\ *adj* : REGENERATED; *esp* : spiritually reborn or converted — **re·gen·er·ate·ly** *adv* — **re·gen·er·ate·ness** *n*

[2]**re·gen·er·ate** \ri-'jen-ə-ˌrāt\ *vb* **1** : to cause to be reborn spiritually **2** : to reform completely in character and habits **3** : to generate or produce anew; *esp* : to renew (a lost or damaged body part) by a new growth of tissue **4** : to give new life to : REVIVE ⟨land *regenerated* by rotation of crops⟩ **5** : to increase the amplification of (radio signals) by electron tubes in which a part of the outgoing current acts upon the incoming signal so as to increase the amplification — **re·gen·er·a·tor** \-ˌrāt-ər\ *n*

re·gen·er·a·tion \ri-ˌjen-ə-'rā-shən, ˌrē-\ *n* : an act or the process of regenerating : the state of being regenerated; *esp* : spiritual renewal or revival

re·gen·er·a·tive \ri-'jen-ə-ˌrāt-iv\ *adj* **1** : of, relating to, or marked by regeneration **2** : tending to regenerate

re·gent \'rē-jənt\ *n* **1** : one who governs a kingdom during the childhood, absence, or disability of the sovereign **2** : a member of a governing board (as of a state university) — **regent** *adj*

reg·i·cide \'rej-ə-ˌsīd\ *n* **1** : one who kills a king or assists in his death **2** : the killing of a king — **reg·i·cid·al** \ˌrej-ə-'sīd-əl\ *adj*

re·gime *also* **ré·gime** \rā-'zhēm, ri-\ *n* **1 a** : REGIMEN 1 **b** : a regular pattern of occurrence or action **2 a** : a method of rule or management **b** : a form of government or administration; *esp* : a governmental or social system ⟨a totalitarian *regime*⟩ **c** : a period of rule of a regime ⟨during the last *regime*⟩

reg·i·men \'rej-ə-mən, 'rezh-ə-\ *n* **1** : a systematic course of treatment ⟨a strict dietary *regimen*⟩ **2** : GOVERNMENT, RULE

[1]**reg·i·ment** \'rej-(ə-)mənt\ *n* : a military unit consisting of a variable number of units (as battalions) — **reg·i·men·tal** \ˌrej-ə-'ment-əl\ *adj* — **reg·i·men·tal·ly** \-ə-lē\ *adv*

[2]**reg·i·ment** \'rej-ə-ˌment\ *vb* **1** : to organize rigidly esp. for the sake of regulation or control **2** : to subject to order or uniformity — **reg·i·men·ta·tion** \ˌrej-ə-mən-'tā-shən, -ˌmen-\ *n*

reg·i·men·tals \ˌrej-ə-'ment-əlz\ *n pl* **1** : a regimental uniform **2** : military dress

re·gion \'rē-jən\ *n* **1** : an administrative area, division, or district **2 a** : an often indefinitely bounded part, portion, or area ⟨the darker *regions* of the night sky⟩ **b** : VICINITY ⟨had a pain in the *region* of the heart⟩ **c** : a broad continuous area (as of the earth) usu. having a uniform natural environment ⟨arctic *regions*⟩

re·gion·al \'rēj-(ə-)nəl\ *adj* **1** : of, relating to, or characteristic of a region ⟨*regional* branches of a company⟩ **2** : affecting a particular region : LOCALIZED ⟨*regional* pain⟩ — **re·gion·al·ly** \-ē\ *adv*

re·gion·al·ism \'rēj-(ə-)nə-ˌliz-əm\ *n* **1** : consciousness of and loyalty to a distinct region **2** : emphasis on regional locale and characteristics in art or literature — **re·gion·al·ist** \-ləst\ *n or adj* — **re·gion·al·is·tic** \ˌrēj-(ə-)nə-'lis-tik\ *adj*

[1]**reg·is·ter** \'rej-ə-stər\ *n* **1 a** : a written record or list containing regular entries of items or details **b** : a book for such a record ⟨a *register* of deeds⟩ ⟨*register* of voters⟩ **2** : a device (as in a floor or wall) usu. with a grille and shutters that regulates the flow of heated air from a furnace **3** : a part of the range of a human voice or a musical instrument comprising tones similarly produced or of the same quality **4 a** : an automatic device registering a number or a quantity **b** : a number or quantity registered by such a device

[2]**register** *vb* **reg·is·tered**; **reg·is·ter·ing** \-st(ə-)riŋ\ **1 a** : to make or secure official entry of in a register : RECORD ⟨*register* a will⟩ **b** : to enroll formally esp. as a voter or student **c** : to record automatically : INDICATE ⟨the thermometer *registered* zero⟩ **2** : to secure special protection for (a piece of mail) by prepayment of a fee **3** : to convey by expression and bodily movements alone ⟨his face *registered* surprise⟩ **4** : to make or convey an impression ⟨his name didn't *register* with me⟩

[3]**register** *n* : REGISTRAR

registered nurse *n* : a graduate trained nurse who has been licensed to practice by a state authority

reg·is·trant \'rej-ə-strənt\ *n* : one that registers or is registered

reg·is·trar \'rej-ə-ˌsträr\ *n* : an official recorder or keeper of records

reg·is·tra·tion \ˌrej-ə-'strā-shən\ *n* **1** : an act or the fact of registering **2** : an entry in a register **3** : the number of individuals registered : ENROLLMENT **4** : a document certifying an act of registering ⟨automobile *registration*⟩

reg·is·try \'rej-ə-strē\ *n, pl* **-tries** **1** : ENROLLMENT, REGISTRATION **2** : a place of registration **3** : an official record book or an entry in one

re·gress \ri-'gres\ *vb* : to go or cause to go back esp. to a former level or condition — **re·gres·sor** \-'gres-ər\ *n*

re·gres·sion \ri-'gresh-ən\ *n* : an act or the fact of regressing : RETROGRESSION

re·gres·sive \ri-'gres-iv\ *adj* : of, relating to, or tending toward regression — **re·gres·sive·ly** *adv* — **re·gres·sive·ness** *n*

[1]**re·gret** \ri-'gret\ *vb* **re·gret·ted**; **re·gret·ting** **1 a** : to mourn the loss or death of **b** : to miss poignantly **2** : to be keenly sorry for **3** : to experience regret — **re·gret·ta·ble** \-'gret-ə-bəl\ *adj* — **re·gret·ta·bly** \-blē\ *adv* — **re·gret·ter** *n*

[2]**regret** *n* **1** : sorrow aroused by circumstances beyond one's power to remedy **2 a** : an expression of sorrow or disappointment **b** *pl* : a note politely declining an invitation — **re·gret·ful** \-'gret-fəl\ *adj* — **re·gret·ful·ly** \-fə-lē\ *adv* — **re·gret·ful·ness** *n*

re·group \(')rē-'grüp\ *vb* : to form into a new grouping ⟨in order to subtract 129 from 531 *regroup* 531 into 5 hundreds, 2 tens, and 11 ones⟩ — **re·group·ment** \-mənt\ *n*

[1]**reg·u·lar** \'reg-yə-lər\ *adj* [from Latin *regularis* "according to rule", from *regula* "rule", "ruler" (straightedge), from *regere* "to rule", "make straight"] **1** : belonging to a religious order ⟨*regular* clergy⟩ **2 a** : formed, built, arranged, or ordered according to an established rule, law, principle, or type **b** : being both equilateral and equiangular ⟨a *regular* polygon⟩ **c** : perfectly symmetrical or even; *esp* : radially symmetrical ⟨*regular* flowers⟩ **3 a** : ORDERLY, METHODICAL **b** : recurring or functioning at fixed or uniform intervals **4 a** : following or conforming to established or prescribed usages, rules, or discipline ⟨a *regular* Democrat⟩ **b** : COMPLETE, UNMITIGATED ⟨a *regular* scoundrel⟩ **c** : conforming to the normal or usual manner of inflection ⟨*regular* verbs⟩ **5** : of, relating to, or being a permanent standing army ⟨a *regular* army⟩ — **reg·u·lar·i·ty** \ˌreg-yə-'lar-ət-ē\ *n* — **reg·u·lar·ly** \'reg-yə-lər-lē\ *adv*

[2]**regular** *n* **1** : a member of the regular clergy **2** : a soldier in a regular army **3** : a player on an athletic team who usu. starts every game

reg·u·lar·ize \'reg-yə-lə-ˌrīz\ *vb* : to make regular — **reg·u·lar·iz·er** *n*

regular pyramid *n* : a pyramid having a regular polygon for a base and an altitude that intersects the base in its center

regular tetrahedron *n* : a pyramid all of whose faces and base are congruent equilateral triangles

reg·u·late \'reg-yə-ˌlāt\ *vb* **1 a** : to govern or direct according to rule **b** : to bring under the control of law or constituted authority **2** : to make regular ⟨*regulated* his habits⟩ **3** : to adjust so as to work accurately or regularly ⟨*regulate* a clock⟩ — **reg·u·la·tor** \-ˌlāt-ər\ *n* — **reg·u·la·to·ry** \-lə-ˌtōr-ē, -ˌtȯr-\ *adj*

[1]**reg·u·la·tion** \ˌreg-yə-'lā-shən\ *n* **1** : the act of regulating : the state of being regulated **2 a** : an authoritative rule dealing with details of procedure ⟨safety *regulations*⟩ **b** : a rule or order having the force of law

[2]**regulation** *adj* : prescribed by or conforming to regulations ⟨a *regulation* cap of a nurse⟩ ⟨a *regulation* baseball⟩

re·gur·gi·tate \(')rē-'gər-jə-ˌtāt\ *vb* : to throw or be thrown back or out again ⟨*regurgitate* undigested food⟩ — **re·gur·gi·ta·tion** \(ˌ)rē-ˌgər-jə-'tā-shən\ *n*

re·ha·bil·i·tate \ˌrē-(h)ə-'bil-ə-ˌtāt\ *vb* **1** : to restore to a former status **2 a** : to restore to a state of efficiency, good management, or repair **b** : to restore to a condition of health or useful and constructive activity ⟨*rehabilitate* criminals⟩ — **re·ha·bil·i·ta·tion** \-ˌbil-ə-'tā-shən\ *n* — **re·ha·bil·i·ta·tive** \-'bil-ə-ˌtāt-iv\ *adj*

re·hash \(')rē-'hash\ *vb* : to present or use (as an argument) again in another form without substantial change or improvement — **re·hash** \'rē-ˌhash\ *n*

re·hears·al \ri-'hər-səl\ *n* **1** : a private performance or practice session preparatory to a public appearance **2** : a practice exercise : TRIAL

re·hearse \ri-'hərs\ *vb* **1 a** : to say again : REPEAT **b** : to recount in order : ENUMERATE **2 a** : to practice (a play or scene) for public performance **b** : to train or make proficient (as actors) by rehearsal **3** : to engage in a rehearsal — **re·hears·er** *n*

re·hy·drate \(')rē-'hī-ˌdrāt\ *vb* : to restore or regain fluid lost in dehydration — **re·hy·dra·tion** \ˌrē-ˌhī-'drā-shən\ *n*

reichs·mark \'rīks-ˌmärk\ *n pl* **reichsmarks** *also* **reichsmark** : the German mark from 1925 to 1948

[1]**reign** \'rān\ *n* **1** : the authority or rule of a sovereign **2** : the time during which a sovereign reigns

[2]**reign** *vb* **1** : to possess or exercise sovereign power : RULE **2** : to exercise authority or hold sway in the manner of a monarch **3** : to be predominant or prevalent

reign of terror : a period marked by violence usu. committed by those in power that produces terror among the people involved

re·im·burse \ˌrē-əm-'bərs\ *vb* [from *re-* and obsolete *imburse* "to put in one's purse", from medieval French *embourser*, from *en-* and *bourse* "purse"] : to pay back : REPAY — **re·im·burs·a·ble** \-'bər-sə-bəl\ *adj* — **re·im·burse·ment** \-'bərs-mənt\ *n*

[1]**rein** \'rān\ *n* **1** : a line or strap fastened to a bit on each side for controlling an animal (as a horse) — usu. used in pl. **2 a** : a restraining influence : CHECK ⟨kept his son under a tight *rein*⟩ **b** : controlling or guiding power ⟨seized the *reins* of government⟩ **3** : complete freedom : SCOPE — usu. used in the phrase *give rein to*

[2]**rein** *vb* : to check, control, or stop by or as if by reins

re·in·car·nate \ˌrē-ən-'kär-ˌnāt\ *vb* : to give a new or different body or form to

re·in·car·na·tion \(ˌ)rē-ˌin-ˌkär-'nā-shən\ *n* **1** : the action of reincarnating : the state of being reincarnated **2** : rebirth in new bodies or forms of life; *esp* : a rebirth of a soul in a new human body

rein·deer \'rān-ˌdi(ə)r\ *n, pl* **reindeer** *also* **reindeers** : any of several large deer of northern regions having antlers in both sexes and including some used as meat and draft animals

reindeer moss *n* : a gray, tufted, and much-branched lichen of northern and arctic regions important as reindeer food

reindeer moss (up to 4 in. high)

re·in·force \ˌrē-ən-'fōrs, -'fȯrs\ *vb* **1** : to strengthen with new force, assistance, material, or support ⟨*reinforce* a wall⟩ ⟨*reinforce* an argument⟩ **2** : to strengthen with additional troops or ships — **re·in·forc·er** *n*

re·in·force·ment \ˌrē-ən-'fōrs-mənt, -'fȯrs-\ *n* **1** : the action of reinforcing : the state of being reinforced **2** : something that reinforces

re·in·state \ˌrē-ən-'stāt\ *vb* : to restore to a former position, condition, or capacity ⟨*reinstate* an official⟩ — **re·in·state·ment** \-mənt\ *n*

re·in·ter·pret \ˌrē-ən-'tər-prət\ *vb* : to interpret again; *esp* : to give a new or different interpretation to — **re·in·ter·pre·ta·tion** \-ˌtər-prə-'tā-shən\ *n*

re·in·vest \ˌrē-ən-'vest\ *vb* : to invest again or anew — **re·in·vest·ment** \-'ves(t)-mənt\ *n*

re·is·sue \(')rē-'ish-ü\ *vb* : to issue again ⟨*reissued* the book in one volume⟩ — **reissue** *n*

re·it·er·ate \rē-'it-ə-ˌrāt\ *vb* : to say or do over again or repeatedly — **re·it·er·a·tion** \(ˌ)rē-ˌit-ə-'rā-shən\ *n* — **re·it·er·a·tive** \rē-'it-ə-ˌrāt-iv, -rət-\ *adj* — **re·it·er·a·tive·ly** *adv* — **re·it·er·a·tive·ness** *n*

[1]**re·ject** \ri-'jekt\ *vb* **1** : to refuse to acknowledge, believe, or receive **2** : to throw away as useless or unsatisfactory **3** : to refuse to grant or consider ***syn*** see DECLINE

[2]**re·ject** \'rē-ˌjekt\ *n* : a rejected person or thing

re·jec·tion \ri-'jek-shən\ *n* **1** : the action of rejecting : the state of being rejected **2** : something rejected

re·joice \ri-'jȯis\ *vb* **1** : to give joy to : GLADDEN ⟨news that *rejoices* the heart⟩ **2** : to feel joy or great delight ⟨*rejoice* over a friend's good fortune⟩ — **re·joic·er** *n* — **re·joic·ing·ly** \-'jȯi-sing-lē\ *adv*

re·joic·ing \-'jȯi-sing\ *n* **1** : the action of one that rejoices **2** : an instance, occasion, or expression of joy

re·join *vb* **1** \(')rē-'jȯin\ : to join again : return to ⟨*rejoined* his family after a week in camp⟩ **2** \ri-\ : to say as an answer : REPLY

re·join·der \ri-'jȯin-dər\ *n* : REPLY; *esp* : an answer to a reply

re·ju·ve·nate \ri-'jü-və-ˌnāt\ *vb* : to make young or youthful again : give new vigor to — **re·ju·ve·na·tion** \-ˌjü-və-'nā-shən\ *n* — **re·ju·ve·na·tor** \-'jü-və-ˌnāt-ər\ *n*

re·kin·dle \(')rē-'kin-dəl\ *vb* : to kindle again

rel *abbr* religion

[1]**re·lapse** \ri-'laps\ *n* : a relapsing; *esp* : a recurrence of illness after a period of improvement

[2]**relapse** *vb* : to slip or fall back into a former worse state — **re·laps·er** *n*

re·late \ri-'lāt\ *vb* **1** : to give an account of : NAR-

ə abut	ər further	a back	ā bake	
ä cot, cart	aů out	ch chin	e less	ē easy
g gift	i trip	ī life	j joke	ng sing	ō flow
ȯ flaw	ȯi coin	th thin	t͟h this	ü loot
ů foot	y yet	yü few	yů furious	zh vision

RATE ⟨*relate* a story⟩ **2** : to show or establish a relationship between ⟨*relate* cause and effect⟩ **3** : to have relationship or connection : REFER **4** : to have meaningful social relationships — **re·lat·a·ble** \-'lāt-ə-bəl\ *adj* — **re·lat·er** *n*

re·lat·ed *adj* **1** : having relationship **2** : belonging to the same group on the basis of known or determinable qualities ⟨pneumonia and *related* diseases⟩ **3 a** : having a common ancestry ⟨bees and the *related* wasps⟩ **b** : belonging to the same family by blood or marriage ⟨*related* to the queen⟩

re·la·tion \ri-'lā-shən\ *n* **1** : the act of telling or recounting : ACCOUNT **2** : CONNECTION, RELATIONSHIP ⟨the *relation* of master to servant⟩ **3** : a related person : RELATIVE **4** : REFERENCE, RESPECT ⟨in *relation* to⟩ **5 a** : the state of being mutually or reciprocally interested (as in social or commercial matters) **b** *pl* : DEALINGS, AFFAIRS ⟨good trade *relations*⟩ **c** *pl* : INTERCOURSE — **re·la·tion·al** \-sh(ə-)nəl\ *adj*

re·la·tion·ship \-shən-,ship\ *n* **1** : the state or character of being related or interrelated ⟨language *relationships*⟩ **2 a** : KINSHIP **b** : a specific instance or type of this ⟨family *relationships*⟩

1**rel·a·tive** \'rel-ət-iv\ *n* **1** : a word referring grammatically to an antecedent **2** : an individual connected with another by blood or marriage

2**relative** *adj* **1 a** : introducing a subordinate clause that qualifies an expressed or implied antecedent ⟨*relative* pronoun⟩ **b** : introduced by such a connective ⟨*relative* clause⟩ **2** : RELEVANT, PERTINENT ⟨questions *relative* to the topic⟩ **3** : not absolute or independent : COMPARATIVE ⟨lived in *relative* isolation⟩ **4** : having the same key signature — used of major and minor keys and scales — **rel·a·tive·ly** *adv* — **rel·a·tive·ness** *n*

relative error *n* : the ratio of an error in a measured or calculated quantity to the magnitude of that quantity

relative humidity *n* : the ratio of the amount of water vapor actually present in the air to the greatest amount possible at the same temperature

rel·a·tiv·i·ty \,rel-ə-'tiv-ət-ē\ *n* **1** : the quality or state of being relative; *esp* : dependence on something else **2** : a theory which deals with phenomena resulting from velocities comparable to that of light relative to an observer, high accelerations, and gravitational fields — **rel·a·tiv·ist** \'rel-ət-iv-əst\ *n* — **rel·a·tiv·is·tic** \,rel-ət-iv-'is-tik\ *adj* — **rel·a·tiv·is·ti·cal·ly** \-ti-k(ə-)lē\ *adv*

re·la·tor \ri-'lāt-ər\ *n* : one that relates : NARRATOR

re·lax \ri-'laks\ *vb* **1** : to make or become less tense or rigid : SLACKEN, EASE ⟨*relaxed* his attention⟩ **2** : to make or become less severe or stringent ⟨*relax* discipline⟩ **3** : to cast off social restraint, nervous tension, or attitude of anxiety or suspicion **4** : to seek rest or recreation ⟨*relaxed* at the beach⟩ — **re·lax·er** *n*

1**re·lax·ant** \-'lak-sənt\ *adj* : producing relaxation

2**relaxant** *n* : a relaxing agent; *esp* : a drug that induces muscular relaxation

re·lax·a·tion \,rē-,lak-'sā-shən, ri-\ *n* : the act or fact of relaxing : the state of being relaxed; *esp* : the lengthening that characterizes inactive muscle

re·laxed \ri-'lakst\ *adj* **1** : lacking in precision or strictness **2** : set at rest or at ease **3** : easy of manner : INFORMAL — **re·laxed·ly** \-'lak-səd-lē, -'laks-tlē\ *adv* — **re·laxed·ness** \-'lak-səd-nəs, -'laks(t)-nəs\ *n*

1**re·lay** \'rē-,lā\ *n* **1** : a fresh supply (as of horses or men) arranged to relieve others at various stages esp. of a journey or race **2 a** : a race between teams in which each team member covers a specified portion of the course **b** : one of the divisions of a relay **3** : an electromagnetic device in which the opening or closing of one circuit operates another device (as a switch in another circuit) **4** : the act of passing along by stages; *also* : one of such stages

2**re·lay** \'rē-,lā, ri-'lā\ *vb* **re·layed**; **re·lay·ing** **1 a** : to place or dispose in relays **b** : to provide with relays **2** : to pass along by relays

3**re·lay** \(')rē-'lā\ *vb* **-laid** \-'lād\; **-lay·ing** : to lay again

1**re·lease** \ri-'lēs\ *vb* **1** : to set free from restraint, confinement, or servitude **2** : to relieve from something that holds, burdens, or oppresses ⟨*released* from his promise⟩ **3** : to give up in favor of another : RELINQUISH ⟨*release* a claim to property⟩ **4** : to give permission for publication, performance, exhibition, or sale of at a specified date — **re·leas·a·bil·i·ty** \-,lē-sə-'bil-ət-ē\ *n* — **re·leas·a·ble** \-'lē-sə-bəl\ *adj* — **re·leas·er** *n*

2**release** *n* **1** : relief or deliverance from sorrow, suffering, or trouble **2 a** : a discharge from an obligation (as a debt) **b** : a relinquishment of a right or claim **c** : a document embodying a release **3** : the act or an instance of liberating or freeing : a letting go (as from physical restraint) **4** : the state of being freed **5** : a device adapted to hold or release a mechanism as required **6 a** : the act of permitting performance or publication **b** : the matter released

rel·e·gate \'rel-ə-,gāt\ *vb* **1** : EXILE, BANISH **2** : to remove or dismiss to a less important or prominent place ⟨*relegate* some old books to the attic⟩ **3** : to refer or hand over for decision or carrying out — **rel·e·ga·tion** \,rel-ə-'gā-shən\ *n*

re·lent \ri-'lent\ *vb* **1** : to become less severe, harsh, or strict **2** : to let up : SLACKEN

re·lent·less \-ləs\ *adj* : mercilessly hard or harsh — **re·lent·less·ly** *adv* — **re·lent·less·ness** *n*

rel·e·vance \'rel-ə-vən(t)s\ *also* **rel·e·van·cy** \-vən-sē\ *n, pl* **-vanc·es** *also* **-van·cies** : relation to the matter at hand : PERTINENCE

rel·e·vant \-vənt\ *adj* : having something to do with the case being considered : PERTINENT ⟨a *relevant* question⟩ — **rel·e·vant·ly** *adv*

re·li·a·ble \ri-'lī-ə-bəl\ *adj* : suitable or fit to be relied on : DEPENDABLE — **re·li·a·bil·i·ty** \-,lī-ə-'bil-ət-ē\ *n* — **re·li·a·ble·ness** \-'lī-ə-bəl-nəs\ *n* — **re·li·a·bly** \-blē\ *adv*

re·li·ance \ri-'lī-ən(t)s\ *n* **1** : the act of relying **2** : the condition or attitude of one who relies : DEPENDENCE **3** : something or someone relied on

re·li·ant \-ənt\ *adj* : having reliance on something or someone : TRUSTING — **re·li·ant·ly** *adv*

rel·ic \'rel-ik\ *n* **1** : an object venerated because of association with a saint or martyr **2** : something left behind after decay, disintegration, or disappearance ⟨*relics* of ancient cities⟩

rel·ict \'rel-ikt\ *n* : WIDOW

re·lief \ri-'lēf\ *n* **1 a** : removal or lightening of something oppressive, painful, or distressing **b** : aid in the form of money or necessities for the poor, aged, or handicapped **c** : military assistance to a post or force in extreme danger **d** : means of breaking monotony or boredom : DIVERSION **2 a** : release from duty **b** : one that takes the place of another on duty **3** : legal remedy or redress **4 a** : projection

relief 4b

from the background (as of figures in sculpture or of mountains on a relief map) : sharpness of outline **b** : a work of art with such raised figures **c** : the appearance of projection above the background given in drawing and painting by lines and shading **5** : the elevations or inequalities of a land surface

relief map *n* : a map or model in which inequalities of surface are shown in relief

re·lieve \ri-'lēv\ *vb* **1** : to bring or give relief wholly or partly from a burden, pain, discomfort, or trouble ⟨*relieve* the distress of the poor⟩ **2** : to release from a post or duty esp. by taking the place of ⟨*relieve* a sentry⟩ **3** : to take away the sameness or monotony of ⟨black dress *relieved* by a white collar⟩ **4** : to put or stand out in relief : give prominence to or set off by contrast (as in sculpture or painting) — **re·liev·er** *n*

re·li·gion \ri-'lij-ən\ *n* **1 a** : the service and worship of God or the supernatural **b** : belief in or devotion to religious faith or observance **c** : the state of a religious **2** : a set or system of religious attitudes, beliefs, and practices **3** : a cause, principle, or system of beliefs held to with ardor and faith

[1]**re·li·gious** \ri-'lij-əs\ *adj* **1 a** : devoted to God or to the powers or principles believed to govern life ⟨a very *religious* person⟩ **b** : belonging to a religious order ⟨a *religious* house⟩ **2** : of or relating to religion ⟨*religious* beliefs⟩ **3** : DEPENDABLE, FAITHFUL ⟨performed his duties with *religious* regularity⟩ — **re·li·gious·ly** *adv* — **re·li·gious·ness** *n*

[2]**religious** *n, pl* **religious** : a member of a religious order

re·lin·quish \ri-'ling-kwish\ *vb* **1** : to withdraw or retreat from : ABANDON **2 a** : to desist from **b** : to release a claim to or possession or control of : RENOUNCE ⟨*relinquish* a claim⟩ **3** : to let go of : RELEASE ⟨*relinquished* his grip⟩ — **re·lin·quish·ment** \-mənt\ *n*

rel·i·quary \'rel-ə-ˌkwer-ē\ *n, pl* **-quar·ies** : a small box or shrine in which sacred relics are kept

[1]**rel·ish** \'rel-ish\ *n* [from Middle English *reles* "aftertaste", "taste", from Old French *relais* "something left behind", from *relaissier* "to leave behind"] **1** : a pleasing appetizing taste **2** : a small bit added for flavor : DASH **3** : personal liking ⟨a *relish* for hard work⟩ **4** : keen enjoyment of food or of anything ⟨ate with *relish*⟩ **5** : a highly seasoned sauce (as of pickles or mustard) eaten with other food to add flavor

[2]**relish** *vb* **1** : to add relish to **2** : to be pleased or gratified by : ENJOY **3** : to eat or drink with pleasure — **rel·ish·a·ble** \-ə-bəl\ *adj*

re·live \(')rē-'liv\ *vb* : to live again or over again; *esp* : to experience again in imagination

re·lo·cate \(')rē-'lō-ˌkāt, ˌrē-lō-'kāt\ *vb* **1** : to locate again **2** : to move to a new location ⟨*relocate* a factory⟩ — **re·lo·ca·tion** \ˌrē-lō-'kā-shən\ *n*

re·luc·tance \ri-'lək-tən(t)s\ *n* : the quality or state of being reluctant

re·luc·tant \ri-'lək-tənt\ *adj* : HESITANT, UNWILLING ⟨*reluctant* to answer⟩ — **re·luc·tant·ly** *adv*

re·ly \ri-'lī\ *vb* **re·lied**; **re·ly·ing** **1** : to have confidence : TRUST **2** : to be dependent : COUNT ⟨a man you can *rely* on⟩

[1]**re·main** \ri-'mān\ *vb* **1 a** : to be a part not destroyed, taken, or used up ⟨little *remained* after the fire⟩ **b** : to be something yet to be shown, done, or treated : have yet ⟨that *remains* to be proved⟩ **2** : to stay in the same place or with the same person or group; *esp* : to stay behind **3** : to continue unchanged ⟨the weather *remained* cold⟩

[2]**remain** *n* **1** : a remaining part or trace — usu. used in pl. **2** *pl* : writings left unpublished at a writer's death **3** *pl* : a dead body

re·main·der \ri-'mān-dər\ *n* **1** : a remaining group, part, or trace **2** : the number left after a subtraction **3** : the final undivided part after division that is less than the divisor

re·make \(')rē-'māk\ *vb* **-made** \-'mād\; **-mak·ing** : to make anew or in a different form — **re·make** \'rē-ˌmāk\ *n*

[1]**re·mand** \ri-'mand\ *vb* **1** : to send back a case to a lower court for further action **2** : to return to custody pending trial or for further detention

[2]**remand** *n* : the act of remanding : the state of being remanded ⟨sent back on *remand*⟩

[1]**re·mark** \ri-'märk\ *vb* **1** : to take notice of : OBSERVE ⟨*remarked* her strange manner⟩ **2** : to express as an observation or comment : SAY **3** : to make an observation or comment

[2]**remark** *n* **1** : the act of remarking : NOTICE **2** : mention of that which deserves attention or notice **3** : an expression of opinion or judgment

syn REMARK, OBSERVATION, COMMENT can mean something said to express an opinion. REMARK usu. implies a passing thought or casual judgment; OBSERVATION implies the more carefully considered opinion that follows on having examined the thing spoken of; COMMENT is likely to apply to a remark or observation made by way of explanation, interpretation, or criticism

re·mark·a·ble \ri-'mär-kə-bəl\ *adj* **1** : worthy of being or likely to be noticed **2** : UNCOMMON, EXTRAORDINARY — **re·mark·a·ble·ness** *n* — **re·mark·a·bly** \-blē\ *adv*

re·mar·riage \(')rē-'mar-ij\ *n* : a second or later marriage

re·match \(')rē-'mach, 'rē-ˌ\ *n* : a second match between the same contestants or teams

re·mea·sure \(')rē-'mezh-ər, -'māzh-\ *vb* : to measure again

re·me·di·a·ble \ri-'mēd-ē-ə-bəl\ *adj* : capable of being remedied — **re·me·di·a·ble·ness** *n* — **re·me·di·a·bly** \-blē\ *adv*

re·me·di·al \ri-'mēd-ē-əl\ *adj* : intended to remedy or improve ⟨*remedial* measures⟩ ⟨*remedial* reading courses⟩ — **re·me·di·al·ly** \-ē-ə-lē\ *adv*

[1]**rem·e·dy** \'rem-əd-ē\ *n, pl* **-dies** **1** : a medicine or treatment that cures or relieves **2** : something that corrects an evil, rights a wrong, or makes up for a loss

[2]**remedy** *vb* **-died**; **-dy·ing** : to provide or serve as a remedy for : RELIEVE

re·mem·ber \ri-'mem-bər\ *vb* **-bered**; **-ber·ing** \-b(ə-)ring\ **1** : to bring to mind or think of again **2 a** : to keep in mind for attention or consideration **b** : REWARD ⟨*remembered* her in his will⟩ **3** : to retain in the memory **4** : to convey greetings from — **re·mem·ber·a·ble** \-b(ə-)rə-bəl\ *adj* — **re·mem·ber·er** \-bər-ər\ *n*

re·mem·brance \ri-'mem-brən(t)s\ *n* **1** : the act of remembering **2** : something remembered ⟨a vivid *remembrance*⟩ **3** : something (as a souvenir) that brings to mind **4** *pl* : GREETINGS ***syn*** see MEMORY

re·mind \ri-'mīnd\ *vb* : to put in mind of something : cause to remember ⟨*remind* a child that it is bedtime⟩ — **re·mind·er** *n*

ə abut	ər further	a back	ā bake	
ä cot, cart	aù out	ch chin	e less	ē easy
g gift	i trip	ī life	j joke	ng sing	ō flow
ȯ flaw	ȯi coin	th thin	th this	ü loot
ù foot	y yet	yü few	yù furious	zh vision

rem·i·nisce \ˌrem-ə-ˈnis\ *vb* : to indulge in reminiscence

rem·i·nis·cence \ˌrem-ə-ˈnis-ən(t)s\ *n* **1** : a recalling or telling of a past experience ⟨a *reminiscence* of early childhood⟩ **2** *pl* : an account of one's memorable experiences ***syn*** see MEMORY

rem·i·nis·cent \-ənt\ *adj* **1** : of or relating to reminiscence : indulging in reminiscence **2** : that reminds one (as of something seen or known before) ⟨painted in a style *reminiscent* of Van Gogh⟩

re·miss \ri-ˈmis\ *adj* **1** : negligent in the performance of work or duty : CARELESS **2** : showing neglect or inattention : LAX — **re·miss·ly** *adv* — **re·miss·ness** *n*

re·mis·si·ble \ri-ˈmis-ə-bəl\ *adj* : that may be forgiven ⟨*remissible* sins⟩ — **re·mis·si·bly** \-blē\ *adv*

re·mis·sion \ri-ˈmish-ən\ *n* : the act or process of remitting

re·mit \ri-ˈmit\ *vb* **re·mit·ted**; **re·mit·ting** **1 a** : to release from the guilt or penalty of : PARDON ⟨*remit* sins⟩ **b** : to refrain from exacting ⟨*remit* a penalty⟩ **c** : to give relief from suffering **2 a** : to lay aside a mood or disposition partly or wholly **b** : to desist from **c** : to let slacken : RELAX **3** : to submit or refer for consideration, judgment, decision, or action **4** : to restore or consign to a former status or condition **5** : POSTPONE, DEFER **6** : to send money esp. in payment **7** : to lessen in intensity or severity often temporarily : MODERATE ⟨the fever had *remitted*⟩ — **remit** *n* — **re·mit·ment** \-ˈmit-mənt\ *n* — **re·mit·ta·ble** \-ˈmit-ə-bəl\ *adj* — **re·mit·ter** *n*

re·mit·tal \ri-ˈmit-əl\ *n* : REMISSION

re·mit·tance \ri-ˈmit-ən(t)s\ *n* **1** : a sending (as of money or bills) esp. to a distance **2** : money sent esp. in payment

rem·nant \ˈrem-nənt\ *n* **1** : something that remains or is left over ⟨a *remnant* of cloth⟩ **2** : a surviving trace ⟨*remnants* of a great civilization⟩

re·mod·el \(ˈ)rē-ˈmäd-əl\ *vb* : to alter the structure of : partly rebuild

re·mon·strance \ri-ˈmän(t)-strən(t)s\ *n* : an act or instance of remonstrating : PROTEST

re·mon·strant \-strənt\ *adj* : vigorously objecting or opposing — **remonstrant** *n* — **re·mon·strant·ly** *adv*

re·mon·strate \ri-ˈmän-ˌstrāt\ *vb* : to plead in opposition to something : speak in reproof ⟨*remonstrate* with a pupil for being disorderly⟩

rem·o·ra \ˈrem-ə-rə\ *n* : a fish having the front upper fin converted into a disk on the head by means of which it clings to other fishes and to ships — **rem·o·rid** \-rəd\ *adj*

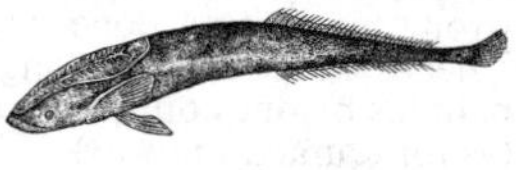

remora
(about 2 ft. long)

re·morse \ri-ˈmȯrs\ *n* : a deep regret arising from a sense of guilt for past wrongs : SELF-REPROACH

re·morse·ful \-fəl\ *adj* : arising from or marked by remorse — **re·morse·ful·ly** \-fə-lē\ *adv* — **re·morse·ful·ness** *n*

re·morse·less \-ləs\ *adj* : being without remorse : MERCILESS — **re·morse·less·ly** *adv* — **re·morse·less·ness** *n*

re·mote \ri-ˈmōt\ *adj* **1** : far off in place or time : not near or recent ⟨*remote* countries⟩ ⟨*remote* ages⟩ **2** : OUT-OF-THE-WAY, SECLUDED ⟨a *remote* valley⟩ **3** : not closely connected or related **4** : not obvious or striking : SLIGHT ⟨a *remote* likeness⟩ **5** : APART, ALOOF ⟨kept himself *remote* from the dispute⟩ **6** : operated or operating from a distance ⟨*remote* control⟩ — **re·mote·ly** *adv* — **re·mote·ness** *n*

1**re·mount** \(ˈ)rē-ˈmau̇nt\ *vb* : to mount again

2**re·mount** \ˈrē-ˌmau̇nt, (ˈ)rē-ˈ\ *n* : a fresh horse to take the place of one disabled or exhausted

re·mov·a·ble \ri-ˈmü-və-bəl\ *adj* : capable of being removed — **re·mov·a·bil·i·ty** \-ˌmü-və-ˈbil-ət-ē\ *n* — **re·mov·a·ble·ness** \-ˈmü-və-bəl-nəs\ *n* — **re·mov·a·bly** \-blē\ *adv*

re·mov·al \ri-ˈmü-vəl\ *n* : the act of removing : the fact of being removed

1**re·move** \ri-ˈmüv\ *vb* **1 a** : to change or cause to change to another location, position, station, or residence **b** : to go away **2 a** : to move by lifting, pushing aside, or taking away or off **b** : to yield to being so moved ⟨this cap should *remove* easily⟩ **3** : to dismiss from office **4** : ELIMINATE — **re·mov·er** *n*

2**remove** *n* **1** : REMOVAL; *esp* : MOVE 2c **2 a** : a distance or interval separating one thing from another **b** : a degree or stage of separation ⟨at one *remove*⟩

re·moved \ri-ˈmüvd\ *adj* **1** : far away : DISTANT ⟨a town far *removed* from cities⟩ **2** : being a generation older or younger ⟨the children of your first cousin are your first cousins once *removed*⟩

re·mu·ner·ate \ri-ˈmyü-nə-ˌrāt\ *vb* : to pay an equivalent to for a service, loss, or expense : RECOMPENSE — **re·mu·ner·a·tor** \-ˌrāt-ər\ *n* — **re·mu·ner·a·to·ry** \-ˈmyü-nə-rə-ˌtōr-ē, -ˌtȯr-\ *adj*

re·mu·ner·a·tion \ri-ˌmyü-nə-ˈrā-shən\ *n* **1** : an act or fact of remunerating **2** : something that remunerates : RECOMPENSE

re·mu·ner·a·tive \ri-ˈmyü-nə-ˌrāt-iv\ *adj* **1** : serving to remunerate **2** : PROFITABLE ⟨made a highly *remunerative* investment⟩ — **re·mu·ner·a·tive·ly** *adv* — **re·mu·ner·a·tive·ness** *n*

Re·nais·sance \ˌren-ə-ˈsän(t)s, -ˈzän(t)s\ *n* **1** : the movement or period in Europe between the 14th and 17th centuries marked by a revival of interest in the classical arts and literature and by the beginnings of modern science **2** *often not cap* : a movement or period marked by a vigorous revival

re·nal \ˈrēn-əl\ *adj* : of, relating to, or located in or near the kidneys

re·name \(ˈ)rē-ˈnām\ *vb* : to give a new name to ⟨*renaming* numbers when adding⟩

re·nas·cence \ri-ˈnas-ən(t)s, -ˈnās-\ *n, often cap* : RENAISSANCE — **re·nas·cent** \-ənt\ *adj*

rend \ˈrend\ *vb* **rent** \ˈrent\ *also* **rend·ed**; **rend·ing** **1** : to remove from place by force : WREST **2** : to split or tear apart or in pieces by force **3** : to tear (the hair or clothing) as a sign of anger, grief, or despair **4** : to affect as if splitting or tearing ⟨silence *rent* by a scream⟩

ren·der \ˈren-dər\ *vb* **ren·dered**; **ren·der·ing** \-d(ə-)riŋ\ **1** : DELIVER, GIVE ⟨*render* judgment⟩ **2** : to melt down : extract by heating ⟨*render* lard⟩ **3** : to give up : SURRENDER ⟨*rendered* his life⟩ **4** : to give in return ⟨*render* thanks⟩ **5** : to present a statement of ⟨*render* a bill⟩ **6** : to cause to be or become ⟨*render* a person helpless⟩ **7** : FURNISH, CONTRIBUTE ⟨*render* aid⟩ **8** : PRESENT, PERFORM ⟨*render* a song⟩ ⟨*render* a salute⟩ **9** : TRANSLATE ⟨*render* Latin into English⟩ — **ren·der·a·ble** \-d(ə-)rə-bəl\ *adj* — **ren·der·er** \-dər-ər\ *n*

1**ren·dez·vous** \ˈrän-di-ˌvü, -dā-\ *n, pl* **ren·dez·vous** \-ˌvüz\ [from French, from *rendez vous* "present yourself"] **1 a** : a place appointed for assembling or meeting **b** : a place of popular resort : HAUNT **2** : an appointed meeting

2**rendezvous** *vb* **ren·dez·voused** \-ˌvüd\; **ren·dez·vous·ing** \-ˌvü-iŋ\; **ren·dez·vouses** \-ˌvüz\ : to come or bring together at a rendezvous

ren·di·tion \ren-'dish-ən\ *n* : an act or result of rendering : TRANSLATION, PERFORMANCE, INTERPRETATION

1**ren·e·gade** \'ren-i-ˌgād\ *n* : a deserter from one faith, cause, or allegiance to another

2**renegade** *adj* : TRAITOROUS, APOSTATE

re·nege \ri-'nig, -'neg, -'nēg, -'näg\ *vb* **1** : to violate a rule in a card game by failing to follow suit when able **2** : to go back on a promise — **re·neg·er** *n*

re·ne·go·ti·ate \ˌrē-ni-'gō-shē-ˌāt\ *vb* : to negotiate again; *esp* : to readjust by negotiation to eliminate or recover excessive profits — **re·ne·go·tia·ble** \-sh(ē-)ə-bəl\ *adj* — **re·ne·go·ti·a·tion** \-ˌgō-s(h)ē-'ā-shən\ *n*

re·new \ri-'n(y)ü\ *vb* **1** : to restore to freshness or vigor ⟨strength *renewed* by a night's rest⟩ **2** : to restore to existence ⟨*renew* the splendor of a palace⟩ **3** : to do or make again ⟨*renew* a complaint⟩ **4** : to begin again : RESUME ⟨*renewed* efforts to make peace⟩ **5** : to put in a fresh supply of : REPLACE ⟨*renew* the water in a tank⟩ **6** : to grant or obtain an extension of : continue in force for a fresh period ⟨*renew* a lease⟩ ⟨*renew* a subscription⟩ — **re·new·er** *n*

re·new·a·ble \ri-'n(y)ü-ə-bəl\ *adj* : capable of being renewed; *esp* : capable of being replaced by natural ecological cycles or sound management procedures ⟨*renewable* resources like water, wildlife, forests, and grasslands⟩ — **re·new·a·bil·i·ty** \-ˌn(y)ü-ə-'bil-ət-ē\ *n*

re·new·al \ri-'n(y)ü-əl\ *n* **1** : the act of renewing : the state of being renewed **2** : something renewed

ren·net \'ren-ət\ *n* **1** : the contents of the stomach esp. of an unweaned calf or the lining membrane of the stomach used for curdling milk **2** : something used to curdle milk; *esp* : RENNIN

ren·nin \'ren-ən\ *n* : a stomach enzyme that curdles milk

re·nom·i·nate \(ˈ)rē-'näm-ə-ˌnāt\ *vb* : to nominate again esp. for a succeeding term — **re·nom·i·na·tion** \(ˌ)rē-ˌnäm-ə-'nā-shən\ *n*

re·nounce \ri-'nau̇n(t)s\ *vb* **1** : to give up, abandon, or resign usu. by formal declaration ⟨*renounced* the throne⟩ **2** : to refuse further to follow, obey, or recognize : REPUDIATE ⟨*renounced* his allegiance⟩ — **re·nounce·ment** \-mənt\ *n* — **re·nounc·er** *n*

ren·o·vate \'ren-ə-ˌvāt\ *vb* : to make like new again : restore to good condition — **ren·o·va·tion** \ˌren-ə-'vā-shən\ *n* — **ren·o·va·tor** \'ren-ə-ˌvāt-ər\ *n*

re·nown \ri-'nau̇n\ *n* : a state of being widely acclaimed and highly honored : FAME

re·nowned \-'nau̇nd\ *adj* : having renown : CELEBRATED

1**rent** \'rent\ *n* [from Old French *rente* "income from property", from *rendre* "to render", "yield"] : money paid for the use of property : a periodic payment made by a tenant to the owner for the possession and use of real property — **for rent** : available for use or service at a price

2**rent** *vb* **1** : to take and hold property under an agreement to pay rent **2** : to grant the possession and enjoyment of for rent : LET **3** : to be for rent ⟨the room *rents* for $20 a week⟩ — **rent·a·ble** \-ə-bəl\ *adj* — **rent·er** *n*

3**rent** *past of* REND

4**rent** *n* [from Middle English *renten* "to rend", alteration of *renden*] **1** : an opening made by or as if by rending **2** : an act or instance of rending

1**rent·al** \'rent-əl\ *n* **1** : an amount paid or collected as rent **2** : an act of renting

2**rental** *adj* **1** : of, relating to, or available for rent ⟨a *rental* car⟩ **2** : dealing in rental property ⟨a *rental* agency⟩

rental library *n* : a commercially operated library (as in a store) that lends books at a fixed charge per book per day

re·num·ber \(ˈ)rē-'nəm-bər\ *vb* : to number again or differently

re·nun·ci·a·tion \ri-ˌnən(t)-sē-'ā-shən\ *n* : the act or practice of renouncing — **re·nun·ci·a·tive** \-'nən(t)-sē-ˌāt-iv\ *adj* — **re·nun·ci·a·to·ry** \-sē-ə-ˌtōr-ē, -ˌtȯr-\ *adj*

re·open \(ˈ)rē-'ō-pən\ *vb* **1** : to open again **2** : to take up again : RESUME

1**re·or·der** \(ˈ)rē-'ȯrd-ər\ *vb* **1** : REORGANIZE **2** : to place a reorder

2**reorder** *n* : an order like a previous order from the same supplier

re·or·ga·ni·za·tion \(ˌ)rē-ˌȯrg-(ə-)nə-'zā-shən\ *n* : the act of reorganizing : the state of being reorganized; *esp* : the financial reconstruction of a business concern

re·or·ga·nize \(ˈ)rē-'ȯr-gə-ˌnīz\ *vb* : to organize again or anew; *esp* : to bring about a reorganization (as of a business concern) — **re·or·ga·niz·er** *n*

Rep *abbr* **1** Representative **2** Republic **3** Republican

re·pack·age \(ˈ)rē-'pak-ij\ *vb* : to package again or anew

1**re·pair** \ri-'pa(ə)r, -'pe(ə)r\ *vb* : GO ⟨*repair* to an inner office⟩

2**repair** *vb* **1** : to restore to a good condition : REMEDY **2** : to make up for : compensate for ⟨*repair* an injustice⟩ — **re·pair·a·ble** \-'par-ə-bəl, -'per-\ *adj* — **re·pair·er** \-ər\ *n*

3**repair** *n* **1** : the action or process of repairing ⟨make *repairs*⟩ **2** : the result of repairing ⟨a tire with three *repairs*⟩ **3** : good or sound condition ⟨a house in *repair*⟩ **4** : condition with respect to soundness or need of repairing ⟨a house in bad *repair*⟩

re·pair·man \-'pa(ə)r-ˌman, -'pe(ə)r-, -mən\ *n* : one whose occupation is making repairs ⟨TV *repairman*⟩

rep·a·ra·ble \'rep-(ə-)rə-bəl\ *adj* : capable of being repaired

rep·a·ra·tion \ˌrep-ə-'rā-shən\ *n* **1** : the action or process of repairing or restoring : the state of being repaired or restored **2** : a making amends for a wrong or injury done : COMPENSATION **3** : the amends made for a wrong or injury; *esp* : money paid (as by one country to another) in compensation (as for damages in war)

re·par·a·tive \ri-'par-ət-iv\ *adj* : of, relating to, or serving to repair

rep·ar·tee \ˌrep-ər-'tē\ *n* **1** : a clever witty reply **2** : the making of such replies

re·past \ri-'past\ *n* : MEAL, FEAST

re·pa·tri·ate \(ˈ)rē-'pā-trē-ˌāt, -'pa-\ *vb* : to send or bring back to one's own country or to the country of which one is a citizen ⟨*repatriate* prisoners of war⟩ — **re·pa·tri·ate** \-trē-ət, -trē-ˌāt\ *n* — **re·pa·tri·a·tion** \(ˌ)rē-ˌpā-trē-'ā-shən, -ˌpa-\ *n*

re·pay \(ˈ)rē-'pā\ *vb* **-paid** \-'pād\; **-pay·ing** **1** : to pay back ⟨he's already been *repaid*⟩ ⟨*repay* a loan⟩ **2** : to make return payment or requital ⟨a lending bank requires proof of ability to *repay*⟩ — **re·pay·a·ble** \-'pā-ə-bəl\ *adj* — **re·pay·ment** \-'pā-mənt\ *n*

re·peal \ri-'pēl\ *vb* : REVOKE, ANNUL; *esp* : to do away with by legislative enactment ⟨*repeal* a law⟩ — **repeal** *n* — **re·peal·a·ble** \-'pē-lə-bəl\ *adj* — **re·peal·er** *n*

[1]**re·peat** \ri-'pēt\ *vb* **1 a** : to say or state again : REITERATE **b** : to say over from memory : RECITE **c** : to say after another **d** : to tell to others ⟨*repeat* gossip⟩ **2** : to make, do, or perform again ⟨*repeat* a mistake⟩ — **re·peat·a·ble** \-ə-bəl\ *adj* — **repeat oneself** : to say or do the same thing more than once

[2]**re·peat** \ri-'pēt, 'rē-ˌ\ *n* **1** : the act of repeating **2** : something repeated

re·peat·ed \ri-'pēt-əd\ *adj* : done or happening again and again : FREQUENT — **re·peat·ed·ly** *adv*

re·peat·er \ri-'pēt-ər\ *n* **1** : a watch that strikes the time when a spring is pressed **2** : a firearm that fires several times without reloading **3** : an habitual violator of the laws **4** : a student repeating a class or course

repeating decimal *n* : a decimal in which after a certain point a particular digit or sequence of digits repeats itself indefinitely

re·pel \ri-'pel\ *vb* **re·pelled**; **re·pel·ling** **1 a** : to drive back : REPULSE **b** : to fight against : RESIST **2** : to turn away : REJECT ⟨*repelled* the suggestion⟩ **3 a** : to be incapable of adhering to, mixing with, taking up, or holding ⟨a fabric that *repels* water⟩ **b** : to force away or apart or tend to do so by mutual action at a distance ⟨two like electrical charges *repel* each other⟩ **4** : to cause aversion : DISGUST — **re·pel·ler** *n*

re·pel·lant \ri-'pel-ənt\ *adj or n* : REPELLENT

[1]**re·pel·lent** \-ənt\ *adj* **1** : serving or tending to drive away or ward off **2** : arousing aversion or disgust : REPULSIVE — **re·pel·len·cy** \-ən-sē\ *n* — **re·pel·lent·ly** *adv*

[2]**repellent** *n* : something that repels; *esp* : a substance employed to prevent insect attacks

re·pent \ri-'pent\ *vb* **1** : to feel sorrow for one's sin and determine to do what is right **2** : to feel sorry for or dissatisfied with something one has done : REGRET — **re·pent·er** *n*

re·pent·ance \ri-'pent-ən(t)s\ *n* : a feeling of regret for something done or said; *esp* : regret or sorrow for sin

re·pent·ant \-ənt\ *adj* : feeling or showing repentance — **re·pent·ant·ly** *adv*

re·peo·ple \(')rē-'pē-pəl\ *vb* **1** : to people anew **2** : to stock again (as with animals)

re·per·cus·sion \ˌrē-pər-'kəsh-ən, ˌrep-ər-\ *n* **1** : a reflection of sound : REVERBERATION **2** : a reaction to something done or said — **re·per·cus·sive** \-'kəs-iv\ *adj*

rep·er·toire \'rep-ə(r)-ˌtwär\ *n* **1** : a list or supply of dramas, operas, pieces, or parts that a company or person is prepared to perform **2** : a supply of skills, devices, or expedients possessed by a person

rep·er·to·ry \'rep-ə(r)-ˌtōr-ē, -ˌtȯr-\ *n, pl* **-ries** **1** : a stock or store of something : COLLECTION **2** : REPERTOIRE

rep·e·ti·tion \ˌrep-ə-'tish-ən\ *n* **1** : the act or an instance of repeating **2** : the fact of being repeated **3** : something repeated

rep·e·ti·tious \-'tish-əs\ *adj* : marked by repetition; *esp* : tediously repeating — **rep·e·ti·tious·ly** *adv* — **rep·e·ti·tious·ness** *n*

re·pet·i·tive \ri-'pet-ət-iv\ *adj* : REPETITIOUS — **re·pet·i·tive·ly** *adv* — **re·pet·i·tive·ness** *n*

re·phrase \(')rē-'frāz\ *vb* : to phrase over again in a different form

re·pine \ri-'pīn\ *vb* **1** : to feel or express dejection or discontent : COMPLAIN **2** : to wish discontentedly — **re·pin·er** *n*

repl *abbr* **1** replace **2** replacement

re·place \ri-'plās\ *vb* **1** : to put back in a proper or former place ⟨*replace* a card in a file⟩ **2** : to take the place of : SUPPLANT ⟨paper money has *replaced* gold coins⟩ **3** : to fill the place of : supply an equivalent for ⟨*replace* a broken dish⟩ — **re·place·a·ble** \-'plā-sə-bəl\ *adj*

re·place·ment \-'plās-mənt\ *n* **1** : the act of replacing : the state of being replaced **2** : one that replaces another

replacement set *n* : a set of elements any one of which may be used to replace a given variable or placeholder in a mathematical expression (as an equation)

re·plant \(')rē-'plant\ *vb* **1** : to set a plant to grow again or anew **2** : to provide with new plants ⟨*replanted* the park⟩

re·plen·ish \ri-'plen-ish\ *vb* : to fill again : bring back to a condition of being full or complete — **re·plen·ish·er** *n* — **re·plen·ish·ment** \-ish-mənt\ *n*

re·plete \ri-'plēt\ *adj* **1** : filled to capacity : FULL; *esp* : full of food **2** : fully supplied or provided ⟨a book *replete* with illustrations⟩ **3** : COMPLETE — **re·plete·ness** *n*

re·ple·tion \ri-'plē-shən\ *n* **1** : the act of eating to excess : the state of being fed to excess : SURFEIT **2** : the condition of being filled up or overcrowded **3** : fulfillment of a need or desire : SATISFACTION

rep·li·ca \'rep-li-kə\ *n* **1** : a close reproduction or facsimile esp. by the maker of the original **2** : COPY, DUPLICATE

[1]**rep·li·cate** \'rep-lə-ˌkāt\ *vb* : DUPLICATE, REPEAT

[2]**rep·li·cate** \-li-kət\ *n* : one of several identical experiments, procedures, or samples

rep·li·ca·tion \ˌrep-lə-'kā-shən\ *n* : precise copying or reproduction; *also* : an act or process of this

[1]**re·ply** \ri-'plī\ *vb* **re·plied**; **re·ply·ing** **1 a** : to respond in words or writing **b** : to give as an answer **2** : to do something in response; *esp* : to return an attack — **re·pli·er** \-'plī(-ə)r\ *n*

[2]**reply** *n, pl* **replies** : something said, written, or done in answer or response

re·pop·u·late \(')rē-'päp-yə-ˌlāt\ *vb* : to populate anew with one or more kinds of living organisms ⟨an ecologically devastated area that will be *repopulated* very slowly⟩ — **re·pop·u·la·tion** \(ˌ)rē-ˌpäp-yə-'lā-shən\ *n*

[1]**re·port** \ri-'pōrt, -'pȯrt\ *n* **1 a** : common talk : RUMOR **b** : FAME, REPUTATION **2** : a usu. detailed account or statement ⟨a *report* of a fire⟩ ⟨wrote a *report* of the meeting⟩ **3** : an explosive noise ⟨the *report* of a gun⟩

[2]**report** *vb* **1** : to give an account (as of an incident or of one's activities) **2** : to give an account of in a newspaper article ⟨*report* a baseball game⟩ **3** : to make a charge of misconduct against ⟨*report* a schoolmate⟩ **4** : to present oneself ⟨*report* for duty⟩ ⟨*report* at the office⟩ **5** : to make known to the proper authorities ⟨*report* a fire⟩ **6** : to return or present (as a matter officially referred to a committee) with conclusions and recommendations — **re·port·a·ble** \-ə-bəl\ *adj*

report card *n* : a report containing a student's grades that is regularly sent by a school to the student's parents or guardian

re·port·ed·ly \ri-'pōrt-əd-lē, -'pȯrt-\ *adv* : according to report

re·port·er \ri-'pōrt-ər, -'pȯrt-\ *n* : a person who reports; *esp* : one employed by a newspaper, magazine, or radio or television station to gather, write, or report news — **rep·or·to·ri·al** \ˌrep-ər-ˈtōr-ē-əl, ˌrēp-, -ˈtȯr-\ *adj* — **rep·or·to·ri·al·ly** \-ē-ə-lē\ *adv*

1**re·pose** \ri-ˈpōz\ *vb* **1** : to place unquestioningly : SET ⟨*repose* trust in a friend⟩ **2** : to place for control, management, or use

2**repose** *vb* **1** : to lay at rest : put in a restful position ⟨*reposed* his head on a cushion⟩ **2** : to lie at rest : take rest ⟨*reposing* on the couch⟩

3**repose** *n* **1** : a state of resting after exertion or strain; *esp* : rest in sleep **2** : CALM, PEACE **3** : cessation or absence of activity, movement, or animation ⟨a face in *repose*⟩

re·pose·ful \ri-ˈpōz-fəl\ *adj* : full of repose : QUIET — **re·pose·ful·ly** \-fə-lē\ *adv* — **re·pose·ful·ness** *n*

re·po·si·tion \ˌrē-pə-ˈzish-ən\ *vb* : to change or restore the position of

re·pos·i·to·ry \ri-ˈpäz-ə-ˌtōr-ē, -ˌtȯr-\ *n, pl* **-ries** : a place or container where something is deposited or stored

re·pos·sess \ˌrē-pə-ˈzes\ *vb* : to regain or retake possession of — **re·pos·ses·sion** \-ˈzesh-ən\ *n*

rep·re·hend \ˌrep-ri-ˈhend\ *vb* : to voice disapproval of : CENSURE, REPRIMAND

rep·re·hen·si·ble \ˌrep-ri-ˈhen(t)-sə-bəl\ *adj* : worthy of or deserving blame or censure — **rep·re·hen·si·ble·ness** *n* — **rep·re·hen·si·bly** \-blē\ *adv*

rep·re·hen·sion \-ˈhen-chən\ *n* : the act of reprehending : CONDEMNATION, REPROOF — **rep·re·hen·sive** \-ˈhen(t)-siv\ *adj*

rep·re·sent \ˌrep-ri-ˈzent\ *vb* **1** : to present a picture, image, or likeness of : PORTRAY ⟨this picture *represents* a scene at court⟩ **2** : to serve as a sign or symbol of ⟨the flag *represents* our country⟩ **3 a** : to take the place of in some respect **b** : to act for or in the place of (as in a legislative body) **4** : to describe as having a specified character or quality ⟨*represented* himself as being poor⟩ **5** : to serve as a specimen, example, or instance of — **rep·re·sent·a·ble** \-ə-bəl\ *adj* — **rep·re·sent·er** *n*

rep·re·sen·ta·tion \ˌrep-ri-ˌzen-ˈtā-shən\ *n* **1** : an artistic likeness or image **2** : a sign or symbol of something **3** : the act or action of representing or state of being represented (as in a legislative body) — **rep·re·sen·ta·tion·al** \-sh(ə-)nəl\ *adj*

1**rep·re·sen·ta·tive** \ˌrep-ri-ˈzent-ət-iv\ *adj* **1** : serving to represent **2** : standing or acting for another esp. through delegated authority **3** : of, based upon, or being a government in which the people are represented by persons chosen from among them usu. by election **4** : serving as a typical or characteristic example ⟨a *representative* housewife⟩ — **rep·re·sen·ta·tive·ly** *adv* — **rep·re·sen·ta·tive·ness** *n*

2**representative** *n* **1** : a typical example of a group, class, or quality : SPECIMEN **2** : one that represents another or others : DELEGATE, AGENT; *esp* : a member of the house of representatives of the U.S. Congress or a state legislature

re·press \ri-ˈpres\ *vb* **1** : to check by or as if by pressure **2** : to hold in by self-control ⟨*repressed* his anger⟩ **3** : to put down by force : SUBDUE **4** : to prevent the natural or normal expression, activity, or development of **5** : to exclude from consciousness ⟨*repressed* past painful experiences⟩ — **re·pres·sive** \-ˈpres-iv\ *adj* — **re·pres·sive·ly** *adv* — **re·pres·sive·ness** *n* — **re·pres·sor** \-ˈpres-ər\ *n*

ə abut	ər further	a back	ā bake	
ä cot, cart	au̇ out	ch chin	e less	ē easy
g gift	i trip	ī life	j joke	ng sing
ō flow	ȯ flaw	ȯi coin	th thin	th this
ü loot	u̇ foot	y yet	yü few	yu̇ furious
zh vision				

re·pressed *adj* **1** : subjected to or marked by usu. excessive repression **2** : characterized by restraint

re·pres·sion \ri-ˈpresh-ən\ *n* **1** : the act of repressing : the state of being repressed **2** : a psychological process by which unacceptable wishes or impulses are kept from conscious awareness

1**re·prieve** \ri-ˈprēv\ *vb* **1** : to delay the punishment of (as a condemned prisoner) **2** : to give relief or deliverance to for a time

2**reprieve** *n* **1 a** : the act of reprieving : the state of being reprieved **b** : a formal temporary suspension of the execution of a sentence **2** : a temporary escape

1**rep·ri·mand** \ˈrep-rə-ˌmand\ *n* : a severe or formal reproof

2**reprimand** *vb* : to reprove severely and esp. officially : CENSURE

1**re·print** \(ˈ)rē-ˈprint\ *vb* : to print again — **re·print·er** *n*

2**re·print** \ˈrē-ˌprint\ *n* **1** : a new or additional printing without change in the text **2** : a separately printed text or excerpt

re·pri·sal \ri-ˈprī-zəl\ *n* **1** : the use of force short of war by one nation against another in retaliation for damage or loss suffered ⟨economic *reprisals*⟩ **2** : an act of retaliation esp. in war

1**re·proach** \ri-ˈprōch\ *n* **1 a** : a cause or occasion of blame, discredit, or disgrace **b** : DISCREDIT, DISGRACE **2** : the act or action of reproaching : REBUKE — **re·proach·ful** \-fəl\ *adj* — **re·proach·ful·ly** \-fə-lē\ *adv* — **re·proach·ful·ness** *n*

2**reproach** *vb* **1** : to utter a reproach to : find fault with : blame for a mistake or failure ⟨*reproached* him for his cowardice⟩ **2** : to bring into discredit — **re·proach·a·ble** \-ˈprō-chə-bəl\ *adj* — **re·proach·er** *n* — **re·proach·ing·ly** \-ˈprō-ching-lē\ *adv*

1**rep·ro·bate** \ˈrep-rə-ˌbāt\ *vb* : to reject as unworthy or evil : CONDEMN — **rep·ro·ba·tion** \ˌrep-rə-ˈbā-shən\ *n* — **rep·ro·ba·tive** \ˈrep-rə-ˌbāt-iv\ *adj* — **rep·ro·ba·to·ry** \-bə-ˌtōr-ē, -ˌtȯr-\ *adj*

2**reprobate** *adj* **1** : foreordained to damnation : CONDEMNED **2** : morally abandoned : CORRUPT, DEPRAVED

3**reprobate** *n* : a reprobate person

re·pro·duce \ˌrē-prə-ˈd(y)üs\ *vb* **1 a** : to give rise to new individuals of the same kind **b** : to cause to exist again or anew ⟨*reproduce* water from steam⟩ **c** : to imitate closely ⟨sound-effects men can *reproduce* the sound of thunder⟩ **d** : to present again **e** : to make an image or copy of **f** : to translate a recording into sound **2** : to undergo reproduction ⟨her voice *reproduces* well⟩ **3** : to produce offspring — **re·pro·duc·er** *n* — **re·pro·duc·i·bil·i·ty** \-ˌd(y)ü-sə-ˈbil-ət-ē\ *n* — **re·pro·duc·i·ble** \-ˈd(y)ü-sə-bəl\ *adj*

re·pro·duc·tion \ˌrē-prə-ˈdək-shən\ *n* **1** : the act or process of reproducing; *esp* : the process by which plants and animals give rise to offspring **2** : something reproduced : COPY

re·pro·duc·tive \ˌrē-prə-ˈdək-tiv\ *adj* : of, relating to, capable of, or concerned with reproduction — **re·pro·duc·tive·ly** *adv* — **re·pro·duc·tive·ness** *n* — **re·pro·duc·tiv·i·ty** \-ˌdək-ˈtiv-ət-ē\ *n*

re·proof \ri-ˈprüf\ *n* : censure for a fault : REBUKE

re·prove \ri-ˈprüv\ *vb* **1** : to administer a rebuke to : SCOLD **2** : to express disapproval of : CENSURE, CONDEMN — **re·prov·er** *n*

rept *abbr* report

1**rep·tile** \'rep-təl, -ˌtīl\ *n* [from Latin, literally "creeping thing", from *repere* "to creep"] **1** : any of a class of air-breathing vertebrates (as the alligators, crocodiles, lizards, snakes, and turtles) that have a bony skeleton and a body usu. covered with scales or bony plates **2** : a groveling or despicable person

2**reptile** *adj* : characteristic of a reptile : REPTILIAN

1**rep·til·i·an** \rep-'til-ē-ən\ *adj* : of, relating to, or resembling reptiles

2**reptilian** *n* : REPTILE 1

re·pub·lic \ri-'pəb-lik\ *n* [from French *république*, from Latin *res publica*, literally "public thing", "commonwealth"] **1 a** : a government having a chief of state who is not a monarch and who is usu. a president **b** : a political unit having such a form of government **2 a** : a government in which supreme power resides in a body of citizens entitled to vote and is exercised by elected officers and representatives responsible to them **b** : a political unit (as a nation) having such a form of government **3** : a political and territorial unit of the U.S.S.R. or Yugoslavia

1**re·pub·li·can** \ri-'pəb-li-kən\ *adj* **1 a** : of, relating to, or having the characteristics of a republic **b** : favoring, supporting, or advocating a republic **2** *cap* **a** : DEMOCRATIC-REPUBLICAN **b** : of, relating to, or constituting a political party in the U.S. usu. associated with business, financial, and some agricultural interests and with favoring a restricted governmental role in social and economic life

2**republican** *n* **1** : one that favors or supports a republican form of government **2** *cap* **a** : a member of a political party advocating republicanism **b** : a member of the Republican party of the U.S.

re·pub·li·can·ism \ri-'pəb-li-kə-ˌniz-əm\ *n* **1** : adherence to or sympathy for a republican form of government **2** : the principles or theory of republican government **3** *cap* : the principles, policy, or practices of the Republican party of the U.S.

re·pu·di·ate \ri-'pyüd-ē-ˌāt\ *vb* **1** : to divorce or separate formally from a woman **2** : to refuse to have anything to do with : DISOWN ⟨*repudiated* his son and heir⟩ **3 a** : to refuse to accept **b** : to reject as untrue, unjust, or unworthy ⟨*repudiate* a charge of favoritism⟩ ⟨*repudiated* his former friends⟩ **4** : to refuse to acknowledge or pay — **re·pu·di·a·tion** \-ˌpyüd-ē-'ā-shən\ *n* — **re·pu·di·a·tor** \-'pyüd-ē-ˌāt-ər\ *n*

re·pug·nance \ri-'pəg-nən(t)s\ *n* : deep-rooted dislike : AVERSION, LOATHING

re·pug·nant \-nənt\ *adj* **1** : CONTRARY, INCOMPATIBLE ⟨punishments *repugnant* to the spirit of the law⟩ **2** : DISTASTEFUL, REPULSIVE — **re·pug·nant·ly** *adv*

1**re·pulse** \ri-'pəls\ *vb* **1** : to drive or beat back : REPEL ⟨*repulse* an attack⟩ **2** : to cause repulsion in : DISGUST ⟨*repulsed* at the sight⟩

2**repulse** *n* **1** : REBUFF, REJECTION **2** : the action of repelling an attacker : the fact of being repelled

re·pul·sion \ri-'pəl-shən\ *n* **1** : the action of repulsing : the state of being repulsed **2** : the force with which bodies, particles, or like forces repel one another **3** : a feeling of aversion : REPUGNANCE

re·pul·sive \ri-'pəl-siv\ *adj* **1** : tending or serving to repulse **2** : arousing aversion or disgust — **re·pul·sive·ly** *adv* — **re·pul·sive·ness** *n*

rep·u·ta·ble \'rep-yət-ə-bəl\ *adj* : having a good reputation : RESPECTED — **rep·u·ta·bil·i·ty** \ˌrep-yət-ə-'bil-ət-ē\ *n* — **rep·u·ta·bly** \'rep-yət-ə-blē\ *adv*

rep·u·ta·tion \ˌrep-yə-'tā-shən\ *n* **1** : overall quality or character as seen or judged by people in general ⟨has a bad *reputation*⟩ **2** : recognition by other people of some characteristic or ability ⟨the *reputation* of being clever⟩ **3** : good name : a place in public esteem ⟨lost her *reputation*⟩ **4** : FAME ⟨ worldwide *reputation*⟩

1**re·pute** \ri-'pyüt\ *vb* : SUPPOSE, BELIEVE, CONSIDER ⟨*reputed* to be a millionaire⟩

2**repute** *n* **1** : REPUTATION ⟨know a man by *repute*⟩ **2** : FAME, NOTE ⟨a scientist of *repute*⟩

re·put·ed \ri-'pyüt-əd\ *adj* **1** : having repute ⟨a highly *reputed* lawyer⟩ **2** : popularly supposed ⟨a *reputed* success⟩ — **re·put·ed·ly** *adv*

req *abbr* require

1**re·quest** \ri-'kwest\ *n* **1** : an asking for something **2** : something asked for **3** : the condition of being requested ⟨tickets are available upon *request*⟩ **4** : DEMAND ⟨in great *request*⟩

2**request** *vb* **1** : to make a request to or of **2** : to ask for — **re·quest·er** *n*

req·ui·em \'rek-wē-əm, 'rā-kwē-\ *n* [from Latin, accusative case of *requies* "rest"; from the opening words of the mass: *Requiem aeternam dona eis* "Eternal rest grant to them"] **1** : a mass for a dead person; *also* : a musical setting for such a mass **2** : a musical service or hymn in honor of the dead

re·quire \ri-'kwī(ə)r\ *vb* **1** : ORDER, COMMAND ⟨the law *requires* drivers to observe traffic lights⟩ **2** : to call for : NEED ⟨a trick that *requires* skill⟩

re·quire·ment \-mənt\ *n* **1** : something (as a condition or quality) required ⟨comply with all *requirements*⟩ **2** : NECESSITY, NEED

req·ui·site \'rek-wə-zət\ *adj* : REQUIRED, NEEDFUL — **requisite** *n* — **req·ui·site·ness** *n*

1**req·ui·si·tion** \ˌrek-wə-'zish-ən\ *n* **1** : the act of requiring or demanding **2** : an authoritative or formal demand or application ⟨a *requisition* for supplies⟩

2**requisition** *vb* **-si·tioned**; **-si·tion·ing** \-'zish-(ə-)ning\ : to make a requisition for ⟨*requisition* fresh supplies⟩

re·quit·al \ri-'kwīt-əl\ *n* **1** : the act or action of requiting : the state of being requited **2** : something given in requital

re·quite \ri-'kwīt\ *vb* **1 a** : to make return for : REPAY **b** : to make retaliation for : AVENGE **2** : to make return to for a benefit or service or for an injury — **re·quit·er** *n*

re·ra·di·ate \(ˈ)rē-'rād-ē-ˌāt\ *vb* : to radiate anew : dissipate by radiating ⟨the ground *reradiates* the heat obtained from the sun⟩ — **re·ra·di·a·tion** \ˌrē-ˌrād-ē-'ā-shən\ *n*

1**re·run** \(ˈ)rē-'rən\ *vb* : to run again or anew

2**re·run** \'rē-ˌrən, (ˈ)rē-\ *n* : the act or action or an instance of rerunning; *esp* : presentation of a movie or television program after its first run

re·sale \'rē-ˌsāl, (ˈ)rē-'\ *n* : the act or an instance of selling again

re·scind \ri-'sind\ *vb* **1** : to make void : ANNUL, CANCEL ⟨*rescind* a contract⟩ **2** : REPEAL ⟨*rescind* a law⟩ — **re·scind·er** *n*

re·scis·sion \ri-'sizh-ən\ *n* : an act of rescinding

res·cue \'res-kyü\ *vb* : to free from confinement, danger, or evil : SAVE — **res·cue** *n* — **res·cu·er** *n*

re·search \ri-'sərch, 'rē-\ *n* **1** : careful or diligent search **2** : studious inquiry or examination; *esp* : investigation or experimentation aimed at the discovery and interpretation of facts, revision of accepted theories or laws in the light of new facts, or practical application of such new or revised theories or laws — **research** *vb* — **re·search·er** *n*

re·seed \(ˈ)rē-'sēd\ *vb* : to sow seed on again or anew

re·sem·blance \ri-'zem-blən(t)s\ *n* **1 a** : the quality or state of resembling : SIMILARITY **b** : a point of likeness **2** : REPRESENTATION, IMAGE

re·sem·ble \ri-ˈzem-bəl\ *vb* **-bled**; **-bling** \-b(ə-)liŋ\ : to be like or similar to ⟨he *resembles* his father⟩

re·sent \ri-ˈzent\ *vb* : to feel or express annoyance or ill will over

re·sent·ful \-fəl\ *adj* **1** : full of resentment : inclined to resent **2** : caused or marked by resentment — **re·sent·ful·ly** \-fə-lē\ *adv* — **re·sent·ful·ness** *n*

re·sent·ment \ri-ˈzent-mənt\ *n* : a feeling of indignant displeasure at something regarded as a wrong, insult, or injury

res·er·va·tion \ˌrez-ər-ˈvā-shən\ *n* **1** : the act of reserving **2** : an arrangement to have something (as a hotel room or a seat on a plane) held for one's use **3** : something reserved for a special use; *esp* : a tract of public lands so reserved ⟨an Indian *reservation*⟩ **4** : a limiting condition : EXCEPTION ⟨agree without *reservations*⟩

1**re·serve** \ri-ˈzərv\ *vb* **1** : to keep in store for future or special use **2** : to retain or hold over to a future time or place : DEFER **3** : to arrange to have set aside and held for one's use ⟨*reserve* a hotel room⟩ **4** : to set or have set aside or apart

2**reserve** *n* **1** : something stored or available for future use : STOCK ⟨oil *reserves*⟩ **2 a** : military forces withheld or available for later decisive use — usu. used in pl. **b** : the military forces of a country not part of the regular services **c** : RESERVIST **3** : a tract set apart : RESERVATION **4** : restraint, closeness, or caution in one's words and behavior **5** : money or its equivalent kept in hand or set apart usu. to meet obligations ⟨gold *reserves*⟩ **6** : SUBSTITUTE ⟨the *reserves* of the football team⟩

re·served \ri-ˈzərvd\ *adj* **1** : restrained in words and actions **2** : kept or set apart or aside for future or special use — **re·serv·ed·ly** \-ˈzər-vəd-lē\ *adv* — **re·served·ness** \-ˈzər-vəd-nəs, -ˈzərv(d)-nəs\ *n*

re·serv·ist \ri-ˈzər-vəst\ *n* : a member of a military reserve

res·er·voir \ˈrez-ə(r)v-ˌwär, -ə(r)v-ˌ(w)ȯr\ *n* **1** : a place where something is kept in store; *esp* : an artificial lake where water is collected and kept in quantity for use **2** : an extra supply : RESERVE

re·shape \(ˈ)rē-ˈshāp\ *vb* : to give a new form to

re·shuf·fle \(ˈ)rē-ˈshəf-əl\ *vb* **1** : to shuffle again **2** : to reorganize usu. by redistribution of existing elements — **reshuffle** *n*

re·side \ri-ˈzīd\ *vb* **1** : to dwell permanently or continuously ⟨*reside* in St. Louis⟩ **2** : to be present as an element, quality, or right ⟨the power of veto *resides* in the president⟩ — **re·sid·er** *n*

res·i·dence \ˈrez-əd-ən(t)s, -ə-ˌden(t)s\ *n* **1** : the act or fact of residing in a place as a dweller or in discharge of a duty ⟨physicians in *residence* in a hospital⟩ ⟨*residence* abroad⟩ **2 a** : the place where one lives **b** : the status of a legal resident **3 a** : the period during which a person resides in a place **b** : a period of active study, research, or teaching at a college or university

res·i·den·cy \ˈrez-əd-ən-sē, -ə-ˌden(t)-\ *n, pl* **-cies** **1** : a usu. official place of residence **2** : a territorial unit in which a political resident exercises authority **3** : a period of advanced resident training esp. in a medical specialty

1**res·i·dent** \ˈrez-əd-ənt, -ə-ˌdent\ *adj* **1** : living in a place for some length of time : RESIDING **2** : living in a place while discharging official duties ⟨a *resident* physician of a hospital⟩ **3** : not migratory ⟨*resident* birds⟩

2**resident** *n* **1** : one who resides in a place **2** : a diplomatic agent exercising authority in a protected state **3** : a person (as a physician) serving a residency

res·i·den·tial \ˌrez-ə-ˈden-chəl\ *adj* **1** : used as a residence or by residents ⟨a *residential* hotel⟩ **2** : adapted to or occupied by residences ⟨a *residential* section⟩ **3** : of or relating to residence or residences — **res·i·den·tial·ly** \-ˈdench-(ə-)lē\ *adv*

1**re·sid·u·al** \ri-ˈzij-(ə-w)əl\ *adj* : being or active as a residue : left over — **re·sid·u·al·ly** \-ē\ *adv*

2**residual** *n* : a residual product, substance, or result

res·i·due \ˈrez-ə-ˌd(y)ü\ *n* **1** : whatever remains after a part is taken, set apart, or lost : REMNANT, REMAINDER **2** : the part of an estate remaining after the payment of all debts and bequests

re·sign \ri-ˈzīn\ *vb* **1** : to give up by a formal or official act ⟨*resign* an office⟩ **2** : to give up an office or position **3** : to submit or give oneself over calmly or patiently ⟨*resigned* herself to the disappointment⟩ — **re·sign·er** *n*

res·ig·na·tion \ˌrez-ig-ˈnā-shən\ *n* **1 a** : an act of resigning **b** : a letter or written statement that gives notice of this act **2** : the quality or the feeling of a person who is resigned : quiet or patient submission or acceptance

re·signed \ri-ˈzīnd\ *adj* : submitting patiently (as to loss, sorrow, or misfortune) : UNCOMPLAINING — **re·sign·ed·ly** \-ˈzī-nəd-lē\ *adv* — **re·sign·ed·ness** \-ˈzī-nəd-nəs\ *n*

re·sil·ience \ri-ˈzil-yən(t)s\ *or* **re·sil·ien·cy** \-yən-sē\ *n* **1** : the ability of a body to rebound, recoil, or resume its original size and shape after being compressed, bent, or stretched : ELASTICITY **2** : the ability to recover from or adjust to misfortune or change

re·sil·ient \-yənt\ *adj* **1** : capable of withstanding shock without permanent deformation or rupture **2** : SPRINGY ⟨*resilient* turf⟩ **3** : tending to recover readily from fatigue or depression — **re·sil·ient·ly** *adv*

res·in \ˈrez-ən\ *n* **1** : any of various usu. transparent or translucent and yellowish to brown organic substances (as rosin) that are obtained from plant secretions, are soluble in organic solvents but not in water, and are used chiefly in varnishes, printing inks, plastics, and sizes and in medicine **2** : any of various synthetic products with some of the physical properties of natural resins that are used chiefly as plastics — **res·in·ous** \-ə-nəs\ *adj*

re·sist \ri-ˈzist\ *vb* **1** : to withstand the force or effect of ⟨*resist* disease⟩ ⟨silver *resists* acids⟩ **2** : to exert oneself to check or defeat **3** : to exert force in opposition — **re·sist·er** *n*

re·sist·ance \ri-ˈzis-tən(t)s\ *n* **1 a** : an act or instance of resisting : OPPOSITION **b** : a means of resisting **2** : the ability to resist **3** : an opposing or retarding force **4** : the opposition offered by a body or substance to the passage through it of a steady electric current **5** : a source of resistance **6** *often cap* : an underground organization of a conquered country engaging in sabotage and secret operations against occupation forces and collaborators

re·sist·ant \-tənt\ *adj* : giving or capable of resistance

re·sist·i·bil·i·ty \ri-ˌzis-tə-ˈbil-ət-ē\ *n* **1** : the quality or state of being resistible **2** : the ability to resist

re·sist·i·ble \ri-ˈzis-tə-bəl\ *adj* : capable of being resisted

re·sis·tive \ri-'zis-tiv\ *adj* : marked by resistance

re·sis·tiv·i·ty \ri-ˌzis-'tiv-ət-ē\ *n, pl* **-ties** **1** : capacity for resisting : RESISTANCE **2** : the longitudinal electrical resistance of a uniform rod of unit length and unit cross-sectional area : the reciprocal of conductivity

re·sist·less \ri-'zist-ləs\ *adj* **1** : IRRESISTIBLE **2** : offering no resistance — **re·sist·less·ly** *adv* — **re·sist·less·ness** *n*

re·sis·tor \ri-'zis-tər\ *n* : a device offering electrical resistance

res·o·lute \'rez-ə-ˌlüt\ *adj* **1** : marked by firm determination : RESOLVED **2** : BOLD, STEADY — **res·o·lute·ly** *adv* — **res·o·lute·ness** *n*

res·o·lu·tion \ˌrez-ə-'lü-shən\ *n* **1 a** : the act or process of reducing to simpler form **b** : the act of answering : SOLVING **c** : the act of determining **2** : the process or capability of making distinguishable individual parts, closely adjacent optical images, or sources of light **3 a** : something that is resolved **b** : DETERMINATION **4** : a formal expression of the opinion, will, or intent of a group

¹re·solve \ri-'zälv, -'zölv\ *vb* **1 a** : to break up or separate into component parts **b** : to distinguish between or make adjacent parts independently visible ⟨a telescope with good *resolving* power⟩ **2 a** : to clear up : DISPEL ⟨*resolve* doubts⟩ **b** : to find an answer or solution to **3** : to reach a decision about : DETERMINE, DECIDE **4** : to declare or decide by a formal resolution and vote — **re·solv·a·ble** \-'zäl-və-bəl, -'zöl-\ *adj* — **re·solv·er** *n*

²resolve *n* **1** : something resolved : DETERMINATION, RESOLUTION **2** : firmness of purpose

re·solved \ri-'zälvd, -'zölvd\ *adj* : DETERMINED, RESOLUTE — **re·solv·ed·ly** \-'zäl-vəd-lē, -'zöl-\ *adv*

res·o·nance \'rez-ə-nən(t)s\ *n* **1** : the quality or state of being resonant **2 a** : a prolonging or increasing of sound in a vibrating body or system caused by waves from another body vibrating at nearly the same rate caused by a relatively small periodic stimulus of the same or nearly the same period as the natural vibration period of the system (as frequency) **b** : the state of adjustment that produces resonance in a mechanical or electrical system ⟨two circuits in *resonance* with each other⟩ **3 a** : the intensification and enriching of a musical tone by supplementary vibration **b** : a vibrating quality of a voice sound

res·o·nant \-nənt\ *adj* **1** : continuing to sound : RINGING, ECHOING **2** : of, relating to, or showing resonance **3** : intensified and enriched by resonance — **res·o·nant·ly** *adv*

res·o·nate \'rez-ə-ˌnāt\ *vb* **1** : to produce or exhibit resonance **2** : REECHO, RESOUND

res·o·na·tor \-ˌnāt-ər\ *n* : something (as a device for increasing the resonance of a musical instrument) that resounds or resonates

¹re·sort \ri-'zört\ *n* **1 a** : someone or something that is looked to for help : REFUGE, RESOURCE ⟨a last *resort*⟩ **b** : RECOURSE ⟨have *resort* to force⟩ **2 a** : frequent, habitual, or general visiting **b** : a frequently visited place **c** : a place providing recreation and entertainment esp. to vacationers

²resort *vb* **1** : to go esp. frequently or habitually : REPAIR **2** : to have recourse ⟨*resort* to violence⟩ — **re·sort·er** *n*

re·sound \ri-'zaùnd\ *vb* **1** : to become filled with sound : REVERBERATE **2 a** : to sound loudly **b** : to sound or utter in full resonant tones **3** : to become renowned **4** : to extol loudly or widely : CELEBRATE ⟨his fame *resounded* far and wide⟩

re·sound·ing *adj* **1** : RESONATING, RESONANT **2 a** : impressively sonorous ⟨*resounding* name⟩ **b** : EMPHATIC, UNEQUIVOCAL ⟨a *resounding* success⟩ — **re·sound·ing·ly** \-'zaùn-ding-lē\ *adv*

re·source \'rē-ˌsōrs, -ˌzōrs, -ˌsörs, -ˌzörs, ri-'\ *n* **1** : a new or a reserve source of supply or support **2** *pl* : a usable stock or supply (as of money, products, power, or energy) ⟨natural *resources*⟩ **3** : the possibility of relief or recovery ⟨left helpless without *resource*⟩ **4** : the ability to meet and handle situations : RESOURCEFULNESS **5** : a means of handling a situation or of getting out of difficulty

re·source·ful \-fəl\ *adj* : able to meet situations : capable of devising ways and means — **re·source·ful·ly** \-fə-lē\ *adv* — **re·source·ful·ness** *n*

¹re·spect \ri-'spekt\ *n* **1** : a relation to or concern with something usu. specified : REFERENCE ⟨with *respect* to your last letter⟩ **2 a** : high or special regard : ESTEEM **b** : the quality or state of being esteemed : HONOR **c** *pl* : expressions of respect or deference ⟨paid his *respects*⟩ **3** : PARTICULAR, DETAIL ⟨perfect in all *respects*⟩

²respect *vb* **1 a** : to consider worthy of high regard : ESTEEM **b** : to refrain from interfering with ⟨*respected* their privacy⟩ **2** : to have reference to : CONCERN — **re·spect·er** *n*

re·spect·a·ble \ri-'spek-tə-bəl\ *adj* **1** : worthy of respect : REPUTABLE **2** : decent or correct in character or behavior : PROPER ⟨a *respectable* woman⟩ **3** : fair in size, quality, or quantity ⟨a *respectable* amount⟩ **4** : fit to be seen : PRESENTABLE ⟨*respectable* clothes⟩ — **re·spect·a·bil·i·ty** \-ˌspek-tə-'bil-ət-ē\ *n* — **re·spect·a·ble·ness** \-'spek-tə-bəl-nəs\ *n* — **re·spect·a·bly** \-blē\ *adv*

re·spect·ful \ri-'spekt-fəl\ *adj* : marked by or showing respect or deference — **re·spect·ful·ly** \-fə-lē\ *adv* — **re·spect·ful·ness** *n*

re·spect·ing *prep* : CONCERNING

re·spec·tive \ri-'spek-tiv\ *adj* **1** : PARTIAL, DISCRIMINATIVE **2** : relating individually to each of several persons ⟨their *respective* homes⟩ — **re·spec·tive·ness** *n*

re·spec·tive·ly \ri-'spek-tiv-lē\ *adv* : as relating to each : each in the order given

re·spell \(ˈ)rē-'spel\ *vb* : to spell again or in another way; *esp* : to spell out according to a phonetic system ⟨*respelled* pronunciations⟩

res·pi·ra·tion \ˌres-pə-'rā-shən\ *n* **1 a** : the placing (as by breathing) of air or dissolved gases in contact with the circulating fluid of a many-celled organism **b** : a single complete act of breathing **2** : the physical and chemical processes by which an organism supplies its cells and tissues with the oxygen needed for metabolism and relieves them of the carbon dioxide formed — **res·pi·ra·tion·al** \-sh(ə-)nəl\ *adj*

res·pi·ra·tor \'res-pə-ˌrāt-ər\ *n* **1** : a device covering the mouth or nose esp. to prevent the inhalation of harmful vapors **2** : a device used in artificial respiration

res·pi·ra·to·ry \'res-p(ə-)rə-ˌtōr-ē, ri-'spī-rə-, -ˌtör-\ *adj* : of or relating to respiration or the organs of respiration ⟨*respiratory* diseases⟩

respiratory system *n* : a system of organs functioning in respiration that in air-breathing vertebrates consists of the lungs with their nerves and blood vessels, the organs by which the lungs connect with the outside air, and usu. the muscles and parts of the skeleton concerned with support and with emptying and filling the lungs

re·spire \ri-'spī(ə)r\ *vb* : to engage in respiration; *esp* : BREATHE

res·pite \'res-pət\ *n* **1** : a temporary delay : POST-

PONEMENT; *esp* : REPRIEVE 1b **2** : an interval of rest or relief ⟨a *respite* from toil⟩

re·splen·dent \ri-ˈsplen-dənt\ *adj* : shining brilliantly : LUSTROUS — **re·splen·dence** \-dən(t)s\ *n* — **re·splen·den·cy** \-dən-sē\ *n* — **re·splen·dent·ly** *adv*

re·spond \ri-ˈspänd\ *vb* **1** : to say something in return : make an answer **2** : to react esp. favorably in response ⟨*respond* to surgery⟩

re·sponse \ri-ˈspän(t)s\ *n* **1** : the act of replying : ANSWER **2** : words said or sung by the people or choir in a religious service **3** : a reaction of an organism to stimulation

re·spon·si·bil·i·ty \ri-ˌspän(t)-sə-ˈbil-ət-ē\ *n, pl* **-ties** **1** : the quality or state of being responsible **2** : RELIABILITY, TRUSTWORTHINESS **3** : something for which one is responsible

re·spon·si·ble \ri-ˈspän(t)-sə-bəl\ *adj* **1** : liable to be called upon to give satisfaction (as for losses or misdeeds) : ANSWERABLE ⟨*responsible* for the damage⟩ **2** : able to fulfill one's obligations : TRUSTWORTHY, RELIABLE ⟨he proved *responsible*⟩ **3** : requiring a person to take charge of or be trusted with important matters ⟨a *responsible* job⟩ **4** : able to choose for oneself between right and wrong — **re·spon·si·ble·ness** *n* — **re·spon·si·bly** \-blē\ *adv*

re·spon·sive \ri-ˈspän(t)-siv\ *adj* **1** : giving response : ANSWERING ⟨*responsive* glance⟩ **2** : quick to respond or react sympathetically : SENSITIVE **3** : using responses ⟨*responsive* worship⟩ — **re·spon·sive·ly** *adv* — **re·spon·sive·ness** *n*

1**rest** \ˈrest\ *n* **1** : REPOSE, SLEEP **2 a** : freedom from activity **b** : a state of motionlessness or inactivity **3** : a place for resting or lodging **4 a** : a silence in music equivalent in duration to a note of the same name **b** : a character representing such a silence **5** : something used for support ⟨a chin *rest* for a violin⟩

rests: w, whole; h, half; q, quarters; e, eighth; s, sixteenth; t, thirty-second

2**rest** *vb* **1 a** : to get rest by lying down : SLEEP **b** : to give rest to ⟨*rest* yourself on the couch⟩ **c** : to lie dead **2** : to refrain from work or activity **3** : to place or be placed for or as if for support ⟨*rested* his foot on the rail⟩ **4 a** : to remain for action or accomplishment ⟨the outcome *rests* with him alone⟩ **b** : DEPEND ⟨the success of the flight *rests* on the wind⟩ **5** : to stop voluntarily the introduction of evidence in a law case ⟨the defense *rests*⟩

3**rest** *n* : something that is left over or behind : REMAINDER — used with *the*

re·state \(ˈ)rē-ˈstāt\ *vb* : to state again or in another way — **re·state·ment** \-mənt\ *n*

res·tau·rant \ˈres-t(ə-)rənt, -tə-ˌränt\ *n* [from French, from the present participle of the verb *restaurer* "to restore"] : a public eating place

res·tau·ra·teur \ˌres-tə-rə-ˈtər\ *also* **res·tau·ran·teur** \-ˌrän-\ *n* : the operator or proprietor of a restaurant

rest·ful \ˈrest-fəl\ *adj* **1** : giving rest ⟨a *restful* chair⟩ **2** : giving a feeling of rest : QUIET ⟨a *restful* scene⟩ — **rest·ful·ly** \-fə-lē\ *adv* — **rest·ful·ness** *n*

rest home *n* : SANATORIUM

rest house *n* : a building used for shelter by travelers

rest·ing *adj* : DORMANT ⟨a *resting* spore⟩

res·ti·tu·tion \ˌres-tə-ˈt(y)ü-shən\ *n* : the restoring of something to its rightful owner or the giving of an equivalent (as for loss or damage)

res·tive \ˈres-tiv\ *adj* **1** : stubbornly resisting control : BALKY ⟨a *restive* horse⟩ **2** : fidgeting about : UNEASY ⟨the crowd grew *restive*⟩ — **res·tive·ly** *adv* — **res·tive·ness** *n*

rest·less \ˈrest-ləs\ *adj* **1** : being without rest : giving no rest **2** : finding no rest or sleep : UNEASY ⟨a *restless* night⟩ **3** : never resting or settled : always moving — **rest·less·ly** *adv* — **rest·less·ness** *n*

re·stock \(ˈ)rē-ˈstäk\ *vb* : to stock again : provide new stock ⟨*restocked* the stream with trout⟩

res·to·ra·tion \ˌres-tə-ˈrā-shən\ *n* **1** : an act of restoring or the condition of being restored **2** : something that is restored; *esp* : a representation or reconstruction of the original form (as of a fossil or a building)

1**re·stor·a·tive** \ri-ˈstōr-ət-iv, -ˈstȯr-\ *adj* : of or relating to restoration; *esp* : having power to restore — **re·stor·a·tive·ly** *adv* — **re·stor·a·tive·ness** *n*

2**restorative** *n* : something that serves to restore to consciousness or health

re·store \ri-ˈstō(ə)r, -ˈstȯ(ə)r\ *vb* **1** : to give back : RETURN ⟨*restored* the purse to its owner⟩ **2** : to put or bring back into existence or use ⟨*restore* harmony to the club⟩ **3** : to bring back to or put back into a former or original state : RENEW; *esp* : RECONSTRUCT **4** : to put again in possession of something ⟨*restore* the king to the throne⟩ — **re·stor·a·ble** \-ˈstōr-ə-bəl, -ˈstȯr-\ *adj* — **re·stor·er** *n*

re·strain \ri-ˈstrān\ *vb* **1 a** : to prevent from doing something **b** : CURB, REPRESS ⟨*restrained* his anger⟩ **c** : to limit, restrict, or keep under control ⟨*restrain* trade⟩ **2** : to deprive of liberty; *esp* : to place under arrest or restraint — **re·strain·a·ble** \-ˈstrā-nə-bəl\ *adj* — **re·strain·er** *n*

re·strained \ri-ˈstrānd\ *adj* : marked by restraint : being without excess or extravagance : DISCIPLINED — **re·strain·ed·ly** \-ˈstrā-nəd-lē\ *adv*

re·straint \ri-ˈstrānt\ *n* **1** : the act of restraining : the state of being restrained ⟨held in *restraint*⟩ **2** : a means of restraining : a restraining force or influence **3** : control over one's behavior : RESERVE ⟨showed *restraint* in his choice of clothing⟩

re·strict \ri-ˈstrikt\ *vb* **1** : to confine within bounds : RESTRAIN **2** : to place under restrictions as to use — **re·strict·ed** *adj* — **re·strict·ed·ly** *adv*

re·stric·tion \ri-ˈstrik-shən\ *n* **1** : something (as a law or rule) that restricts **2** : an act of restricting : the condition of being restricted

re·stric·tive \ri-ˈstrik-tiv\ *adj* **1** : serving or tending to restrict **2** : limiting the reference of a modified word or phrase ⟨a *restrictive* clause⟩ — **restrictive** *n* — **re·stric·tive·ly** *adv* — **re·stric·tive·ness** *n*

rest room *n* : a room or suite of rooms providing personal facilities (as toilets)

1**re·sult** \ri-ˈzəlt\ *vb* [from Latin *resultare* "to rebound", from *re-* and *saltare* "to jump"] **1** : to come about as an effect ⟨disease *results* from infection⟩ **2** : to end as an effect : FINISH ⟨the disease *results* in death⟩

2**result** *n* **1** : something that results as a consequence, issue, or conclusion **2** : a beneficial or tangible effect ⟨this method gets *results*⟩ — **re·sult·ful** \-fəl\ *adj* — **re·sult·less** \-ləs\ *adj*

[1]**re·sult·ant** \ri-'zəlt-ənt\ *adj* : derived from or resulting from something else : being a resultant — **re·sult·ant·ly** *adv*
[2]**resultant** *n* **1** : something that results : OUTCOME **2 a** : a single force equal to two or more other forces and therefore exerting an effect on a body equivalent to that which would be produced by the joint action of the forces that it equals **b** : a vector equal to a given set of vectors
re·sume \ri-'züm\ *vb* **1** : to take again : occupy again ⟨*resume* your seats⟩ **2** : to begin again or go back to (as after an interruption) ⟨*resumed* the game the next day⟩
ré·su·mé *or* **re·su·me** \'rez-ə-ˌmā\ *n* : a summing up : SUMMARY ⟨a *résumé* of the news⟩; *esp* : a short account of one's career and qualifications prepared by an applicant for a position
re·sump·tion \ri-'zəm(p)-shən\ *n* : the action of resuming ⟨*resumption* of work⟩
re·sur·gence \ri-'sər-jən(t)s\ *n* : a rising again into life, activity, or prominence — **re·sur·gent** \-jənt\ *adj*
res·ur·rect \ˌrez-ə-'rekt\ *vb* **1** : to raise from the dead : bring back to life **2** : to bring to view or into use again ⟨*resurrect* an old song⟩
res·ur·rec·tion \ˌrez-ə-'rek-shən\ *n* **1 a** *cap* : the rising of Christ from the dead **b** *often cap* : the rising again to life of all the human dead before the final judgment **2** : RESURGENCE, REVIVAL — **res·ur·rec·tion·al** \-sh(ə-)nəl\ *adj*
re·sus·ci·tate \ri-'səs-ə-ˌtāt\ *vb* : to revive from apparent death or from unconsciousness — **re·sus·ci·ta·tion** \-ˌsəs-ə-'tā-shən\ *n* — **re·sus·ci·ta·tive** \-'səs-ə-ˌtāt-iv\ *adj*
re·sus·ci·ta·tor \ri-'səs-ə-ˌtāt-ər\ *n* : an apparatus that delivers oxygen or a mixture of oxygen and carbon dioxide for respiration and is used to relieve asphyxia
ret \'ret\ *vb* **ret·ted**; **ret·ting** : to soak so as to loosen the fiber from the woody tissue ⟨*ret* flax⟩
[1]**re·tail** \'rē-ˌtāl, *esp for 2 also* ri-'\ *vb* **1 a** : to sell in small quantities **b** : to sell directly to the consumer ⟨*retail* groceries⟩ ⟨these shoes *retail* for $20⟩ **2** : TELL, RETELL — **re·tail·er** *n*
[2]**re·tail** \'rē-ˌtāl\ *n* : the sale of commodities or goods in small quantities directly to consumers — **at retail 1** : at a retailer's price **2** : [4]RETAIL
[3]**re·tail** \'rē-ˌtāl\ *adj* : of, relating to, or engaged in the sale of commodities at retail ⟨*retail* trade⟩
[4]**re·tail** \'rē-ˌtāl\ *adv* **1** : in small quantities **2** : from a retailer
re·tain \ri-'tān\ *vb* **1 a** : to keep in possession or use ⟨*retain* knowledge⟩ **b** : to keep in pay or in one's service; *esp* : to employ by paying a retainer ⟨*retain* an attorney⟩ **2** : to hold secure or intact ⟨lead *retains* heat⟩
[1]**re·tain·er** \ri-'tā-nər\ *n* : a fee paid (as to a lawyer) for advice or services or for a claim upon his services in case of need
[2]**retainer** *n* **1** : one that retains **2** : a servant or follower in a wealthy household
[1]**re·take** \(')rē-'tāk\ *vb* **-took** \-'tu̇k\; **-tak·en** \-'tā-kən\; **-tak·ing** : to take again; *esp* : to photograph again
[2]**re·take** \'rē-ˌtāk\ *n* : a second photographing or photograph
re·tal·i·ate \ri-'tal-ē-ˌāt\ *vb* : to return (as an injury) in kind : to get revenge — **re·tal·i·a·tion** \-ˌtal-ē-'ā-shən\ *n* — **re·tal·i·a·tive** \-'tal-ē-ˌāt-iv\ *adj* — **re·tal·ia·to·ry** \-'tal-yə-ˌtōr-ē, -ˌtȯr-\ *adj*
re·tard \ri-'tärd\ *vb* : to slow up : keep back : HINDER ***syn*** see DELAY ***ant*** advance, further — **re·tard·er** *n*
re·tard·ate \ri-'tär-ˌdāt\ *n* : one who is mentally retarded
re·tar·da·tion \ˌrē-ˌtär-'dā-shən\ *n* **1** : an act or instance of retarding **2** : the extent to which something is retarded **3** : an abnormal slowness esp. of mental or bodily development
re·tard·ed \ri-'tärd-əd\ *adj* : showing developmental retardation
retch \'rech, *Brit* 'rēch\ *vb* **1** : VOMIT **2** : to strain to vomit
re·ten·tion \ri-'ten-chən\ *n* **1** : the act of retaining : the state of being retained **2** : power of retaining : RETENTIVENESS **3** : something retained
re·ten·tive \ri-'tent-iv\ *adj* **1** : having ability to retain ⟨a *retentive* memory⟩ **2** : having a good memory ⟨a *retentive* person⟩ — **re·ten·tive·ly** *adv* — **re·ten·tive·ness** *n*
ret·i·cent \'ret-ə-sənt\ *adj* **1** : inclined to be silent or secretive : UNCOMMUNICATIVE **2** : restrained in expression or presentation ***syn*** see SILENT ***ant*** frank — **ret·i·cence** \-sən(t)s\ *n* — **ret·i·cen·cy** \-sən-sē\ *n* — **ret·i·cent·ly** *adv*
re·tic·u·lar \ri-'tik-yə-lər\ *adj* : RETICULATE
[1]**re·tic·u·late** \-lət\ *adj* : resembling a net — **re·tic·u·late·ly** *adv*
[2]**re·tic·u·late** \-ˌlāt\ *vb* **1** : to divide, mark, or construct so as to form a network **2** : to become reticulated
re·tic·u·la·tion \ri-ˌtik-yə-'lā-shən\ *n* : a reticulate formation : NETWORK
ret·i·cule \'ret-i-ˌkyül\ *n* : a woman's drawstring bag used esp. as a carryall
ret·i·na \'ret-ə-nə\ *n*, *pl* **retinas** *or* **ret·i·nae** \-ə-ˌnē, -ˌnī\ : the sensory membrane that lines the eye, receives the image formed by the lens, and is connected with the brain by the optic nerve — **ret·i·nal** \-nəl\ *adj*
ret·i·nue \'ret-ə-ˌn(y)ü\ *n* : the body of retainers who follow a distinguished person : SUITE
re·tire \ri-'tī(ə)r\ *vb* **1** : WITHDRAW, RETREAT **2** : to withdraw esp. for privacy **3** : to give up or cause to give up one's position or occupation **4** : to go to bed **5** : to withdraw from circulation ⟨*retire* bonds⟩ **6** : to put out a batter or side in baseball
re·tired *adj* **1** : QUIET, HIDDEN, SECRET ⟨a *retired* spot in the woods⟩ **2** : withdrawn from active duties or business **3** : received by or due to a person who has retired ⟨*retired* pay⟩
re·tire·ment \ri-'tī(ə)r-mənt\ *n* : an act of retiring : the state of being retired; *esp* : withdrawal from one's position or occupation
re·tir·ing \ri-'tī(ə)r-ing\ *adj* : RESERVED, SHY — **re·tir·ing·ly** \-ing-lē\ *adv* — **re·tir·ing·ness** *n*
re·tool \(')rē-'tül\ *vb* : to equip anew with new or different tools ⟨*retool* a factory for making a new product⟩
[1]**re·tort** \ri-'tȯrt\ *vb* **1** : to answer back : reply angrily or sharply **2** : to reply to an argument with a counter argument
[2]**retort** *n* : a quick, witty, or cutting reply; *esp* : one that turns the first speaker's words against him
[3]**re·tort** \ri-'tȯrt, 'rē-ˌ\ *n* : a vessel in which substances are distilled or decomposed by heat
re·touch \(')rē-'təch\ *vb* : to touch up; *esp* : to alter (as a photographic negative) in order to produce a more desir-

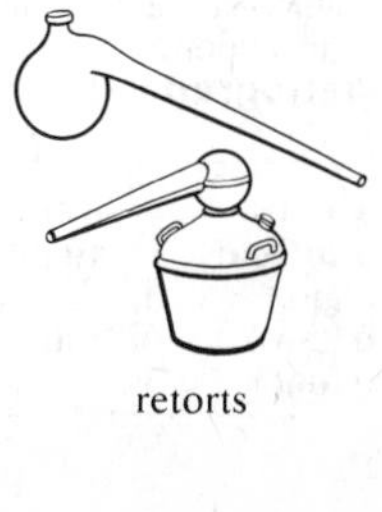
retorts

able appearance — **re·touch** \'rē-ˌtəch, (')rē-'\ *n* — **re·touch·er** \(')rē-'təch-ər\ *n*

re·trace \(')rē-'trās\ *vb* : to trace again or back

re·tract \ri-'trakt\ *vb* **1** : to draw or pull back or in ⟨a cat can *retract* its claws⟩ **2** : to take back (as an offer, a statement, or an accusation) : WITHDRAW, DISAVOW — **re·tract·a·ble** \-'trak-tə-bəl\ *adj*

re·trac·tile \ri-'trak-təl, -ˌtīl\ *adj* : capable of being drawn back or in ⟨the *retractile* claws of a cat⟩ — **re·trac·til·i·ty** \ˌrē-ˌtrak-'til-ət-ē\ *n*

re·trac·tion \ri-'trak-shən\ *n* **1** : a statement retracting something previously said or published **2** : an act of retracting : the state of being retracted **3** : the ability to retract

re·trac·tor \ri-'trak-tər\ *n* : one that retracts; *esp* : a muscle that draws an organ or part in or back

1re·tread \(')rē-'tred\ *vb* **re·tread·ed**; **re·tread·ing** : to provide (a worn pneumatic tire) with a new tread

2re·tread \'rē-ˌtred\ *n* **1** : a new tread on a tire **2** : a retreaded tire

1re·treat \ri-'trēt\ *n* **1 a** : an act or process of withdrawing esp. from what is difficult, dangerous, or disagreeable **b** : the usu. forced withdrawal of troops **c** : a signal for retreating **d** : a signal given by bugle at the beginning of a military flag-lowering ceremony **e** : a military flag-lowering ceremony **2** : a place of privacy or safety : REFUGE

2retreat *vb* **1** : to make a retreat **2** : to slope backward

re·trench \ri-'trench\ *vb* **1** : to cut down : REDUCE **2** : to reduce expenses : ECONOMIZE — **re·trench·ment** \-mənt\ *n*

re·tri·al \(')rē-'trī(-ə)l\ *n* : a second trial, experiment, or test

ret·ri·bu·tion \ˌre-trə-'byü-shən\ *n* : something given in payment for an offense : PUNISHMENT

re·trib·u·tive \ri-'trib-yət-iv\ *adj* : of, relating to, or marked by retribution ⟨*retributive* justice⟩ — **re·trib·u·tive·ly** *adv*

re·trib·u·to·ry \-yə-ˌtōr-ē, -ˌtȯr-\ *adj* : RETRIBUTIVE

re·triev·al \ri-'trē-vəl\ *n* **1** : an act or process of retrieving **2** : possibility of being retrieved or of recovering

re·trieve \ri-'trēv\ *vb* **1 a** : to find and bring in killed or wounded game **b** : to get and bring back **2** : to recover, restore, repair, or make good ⟨*retrieve* a damaged reputation⟩ — **re·triev·a·ble** \-'trē-və-bəl\ *adj*

re·triev·er \ri-'trē-vər\ *n* : one that retrieves; *esp* : a vigorous active medium-sized dog having a heavy water-resistant coat and used esp. for retrieving game

retro- *prefix* **1** : backward : back ⟨*retro*-rocket⟩ **2** : situated behind ⟨*retro*choir⟩

ret·ro·ac·tive \ˌre-trō-'ak-tiv\ *adj* : intended to apply or take effect at a date in the past ⟨a *retroactive* pay raise⟩ — **ret·ro·ac·tive·ly** *adv*

re·tro·fire \'re-trō-ˌfī(-ə)r\ *vb* : to ignite a retro-rocket — **retrofire** *n*

1ret·ro·grade \'re-trə-ˌgrād\ *adj* **1** : going or inclined to go from a better to a worse state : DEGENERATING **2** : having a backward direction, motion, or tendency

2retrograde *vb* **1** : to go back : RETREAT ⟨a glacier *retrogrades*⟩ **2** : to decline to a worse condition — **ret·ro·gra·da·tion** \ˌre-trō-grā-'dā-shən, -grə-\ *n*

ret·ro·gress \ˌre-trə-'gres\ *vb* : to move backward; *esp* : to revert to an earlier, lower, or less specialized state or condition — **ret·ro·gres·sion** \-'gresh-ən\ *n*

ret·ro·gres·sive \-'gres-iv\ *adj* : marked by or tending to retrogression — **ret·ro·gres·sive·ly** *adv*

ret·ro–rock·et \'re-trō-ˌräk-ət\ *n* : an auxiliary rocket (as on an airplane or space vehicle) that produces thrust in a direction opposite to or at an oblique angle to the motion of the object in order to slow it down

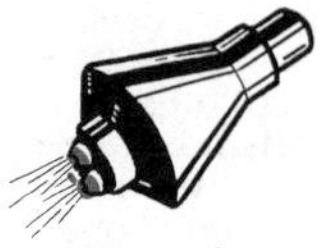

retro-rockets

ret·ro·spect \'re-trə-ˌspekt\ *n* : a looking back on things past : a thinking of past events

ret·ro·spec·tion \ˌre-trə-'spek-shən\ *n* **1** : the act or power of recalling the past **2** : a review of past events

ret·ro·spec·tive \ˌre-trə-'spek-tiv\ *adj* **1** : of, relating to, characteristic of, or given to retrospection **2** : affecting things past : RETROACTIVE — **ret·ro·spec·tive·ly** *adv*

1re·turn \ri-'tərn\ *vb* **1** : to come or go back **2** : REPLY, ANSWER **3** : to make (as a report) officially by submitting a statement ⟨the jury *returned* a verdict⟩ **4** : to elect to office ⟨a candidate *returned* by a large majority⟩ **5** : to bring, carry, send, or put back : RESTORE ⟨*return* a book to the library⟩ **6** : to bring in (as profit) : YIELD **7** : REPAY ⟨*return* borrowed money⟩ **8** : to send or say in response or reply ⟨*return* thanks⟩ — **re·turn·er** *n*

2return *n* **1** : the act of coming back to or from a place or condition **2 a** : a report of the results of balloting — usu. used in pl. ⟨election *returns*⟩ **b** : a filled-out income tax form ⟨*returns* must be postmarked on or before April 15⟩ **3** : a means for conveying something (as water) back to its starting point **4** : the profit from labor, investment, or business : YIELD **5 a** : the act of returning something to a former place, condition, or ownership **b** : something returned **6 a** : the act of returning a ball to an opponent **b** : the run of a football after a kick by the other team

3return *adj* : played, delivered, or given in return ⟨a *return* call⟩ ⟨a *return* game⟩

re·turn·a·ble \ri-'tər-nə-bəl\ *adj* : that may or must be returned ⟨*returnable* bottles⟩

re·turn·ee \ri-ˌtər-'nē\ *n* : one who returns; *esp* : one returning to the U.S. after military service abroad

re·uni·fy \(')rē-'yü-nə-ˌfī\ *vb* : to restore unity to — **re·uni·fi·ca·tion** \(ˌ)rē-ˌyü-nə-fə-'kā-shən\ *n*

re·union \(')rē-'yü-nyən\ *n* **1** : the act of reuniting : the state of being reunited **2** : a reuniting of persons after separation ⟨a class *reunion*⟩

re·unite \ˌrē-yü-'nīt\ *vb* : to come or bring together again after a separation

re·use \(')rē-'yüz\ *vb* : to use again — **re·us·a·ble** \-'yü-zə-bəl\ *adj* — **re·use** \-'yüs\ *n*

1rev \'rev\ *n* : a revolution of a motor

2rev *vb* **revved**; **rev·ving** : to speed an idling engine by pumping the accelerator ⟨*rev* up a motor⟩

rev *abbr* revolution

Rev *abbr* Reverend

re·val·u·ate \(')rē-'val-yə-ˌwāt\ *vb* : REVALUE — **re·val·u·a·tion** \(ˌ)rē-ˌval-yə-'wā-shən\ *n*

re·val·ue \(')rē-'val-yü\ *vb* : to make a new valuation of : REAPPRAISE

ə abut	ər further	a back	ā bake	
ä cot, cart	au̇ out	ch chin	e less	ē easy
g gift	i trip	ī life	j joke	ng sing	ō flow
ȯ flaw	ȯi coin	th thin	t͟h this	ü loot
u̇ foot	y yet	yü few	yu̇ furious	zh vision

re·vamp \(ˈ)rē-ˈvamp\ *vb* **1** : RENOVATE, RECONSTRUCT **2** : to work over : REVISE
re·veal \ri-ˈvēl\ *vb* **1** : to make known : DIVULGE ⟨*reveal* a secret⟩ **2** : to show plainly : DISPLAY — **re·veal·er** *n*
rev·eil·le \ˈrev-ə-lē\ *n* [from French *réveillez* "wake up!"] : a signal sounded at about sunrise on a bugle or drum to call soldiers or sailors to duty
[1]**rev·el** \ˈrev-əl\ *vb* **-eled** *or* **-elled**; **-el·ing** *or* **-el·ling** \ˈrev-(ə-)liŋ\ **1** : to take part in a revel : be noisy in a festive manner **2** : to take great delight in something ⟨*reveling* in success⟩ — **rev·el·er** *or* **rev·el·ler** \-(ə-)lər\ *n*
[2]**revel** *n* : a noisy or merry celebration
rev·e·la·tion \ˌrev-ə-ˈlā-shən\ *n* **1** : an act of revealing or communicating divine truth **2 a** : an act of revealing to view **b** : something that is revealed; *esp* : an enlightening or astonishing disclosure
Rev·e·la·tion \ˌrev-ə-ˈlā-shən\ *n* — see BIBLE table
re·vel·a·to·ry \ri-ˈvel-ə-ˌtōr-ē, -ˌtȯr-\ *adj* : of, relating to, or characteristic of revelation
rev·el·ry \ˈrev-əl-rē\ *n, pl* **-ries** : boisterous merrymaking : REVELING
[1]**re·venge** \ri-ˈvenj\ *vb* **1** : to inflict injury in return for an injury received **2** : to avenge for a wrong done ⟨able to *revenge* himself on his former persecutors⟩ — **re·veng·er** *n*
[2]**revenge** *n* **1** : an act or instance of revenging **2** : a desire to repay injury for injury **3** : an opportunity for getting satisfaction — **re·venge·ful** \-fəl\ *adj* — **re·venge·ful·ly** \-fə-lē\ *adv* — **re·venge·ful·ness** *n*
rev·e·nue \ˈrev-ə-ˌn(y)ü\ *n* **1** : the income from an investment **2** : the income that a government collects for public use **3** : the income produced by a given source
rev·e·nu·er \ˈrev-ə-ˌn(y)ü-ər\ *n* : a revenue officer or boat
re·ver·ber·ant \ri-ˈvər-b(ə-)rənt\ *adj* : REVERBERATING — **re·ver·ber·ant·ly** *adv*
re·ver·ber·ate \ri-ˈvər-bə-ˌrāt\ *vb* : RESOUND, ECHO — **re·ver·ber·a·tion** \-ˌvər-bə-ˈrā-shən\ *n*
re·vere \ri-ˈvi(ə)r\ *vb* : to show devotion and honor to : regard with reverence
[1]**rev·er·ence** \ˈrev-(ə-)rən(t)s, ˈrev-ərn(t)s\ *n* **1** : honor or respect felt or shown : DEFERENCE **2** : a gesture of respect (as a bow) **3** : the state of being revered or honored
[2]**reverence** *vb* : to regard or treat with reverence
[1]**rev·er·end** \ˈrev-(ə-)rənd, ˈrev-ərnd\ *adj* **1** : worthy of reverence : REVERED ⟨these *reverend* halls⟩ **2** — used as a title for clergymen and some female religious ⟨the *Reverend* Mr. Doe⟩ ⟨the *Reverend* John Doe⟩ ⟨the *Reverend* Mother Superior⟩
[2]**reverend** *n* : a member of the clergy
rev·er·ent \ˈrev-(ə-)rənt, ˈrev-ərnt\ *adj* : very respectful : showing reverence — **rev·er·ent·ly** *adv*
rev·er·en·tial \ˌrev-ə-ˈren-chəl\ *adj* **1** : proceeding from or expressing reverence ⟨*reverential* awe⟩ **2** : inspiring reverence — **rev·er·en·tial·ly** \-ˈrench-(ə-)lē\ *adv*
rev·er·ie *or* **rev·ery** \ˈrev-(ə-)rē\ *n, pl* **-er·ies** **1** : DAYDREAM **2** : the condition of being lost in thought
re·vers·al \ri-ˈvər-səl\ *n* : an act or the process of reversing
[1]**re·verse** \ri-ˈvərs\ *adj* **1** : opposite or contrary to a previous or normal condition ⟨*reverse* order⟩ **2** : acting or operating in a manner contrary to the usual **3** : bringing about reverse movement ⟨*reverse* gear⟩ — **re·verse·ly** *adv*
[2]**reverse** *vb* **1** : to turn completely about or upside down or inside out **2 a** : to overthrow or set aside a legal decision by a contrary decision **b** : to change to the contrary ⟨*reverse* a policy⟩ **3 a** : to go or cause to go in the opposite direction **b** : to put (as a car) into reverse — **re·vers·er** *n*
[3]**reverse** *n* **1** : something directly contrary to something else : OPPOSITE **2** : an act or instance of reversing; *esp* : a change for the worse **3** : the back part of something **4** : a gear that reverses something
[1]**re·vers·i·ble** \ri-ˈvər-sə-bəl\ *adj* **1** : capable of being reversed or of reversing ⟨a *reversible* chemical reaction⟩ **2 a** : having two finished usable sides ⟨*reversible* fabric⟩ **b** : wearable with either side out ⟨*reversible* coat⟩ — **re·vers·i·bil·i·ty** \-ˌvər-sə-ˈbil-ət-ē\ *n* — **re·vers·i·bly** \-ˈvər-sə-blē\ *adv*
[2]**reversible** *n* : a reversible cloth or garment
re·ver·sion \ri-ˈvər-zhən\ *n* **1** : a right of future possession (as of property or a title) **2 a** : an act or the process of returning (as to a former condition) **b** : a product of reversion **c** : return toward some ancestral type : THROWBACK **3** : an act or instance of turning the opposite way : the state of being so turned
re·vert \ri-ˈvərt\ *vb* **1** : to come or go back ⟨*revert* to savagery⟩ **2** : to undergo reversion — **re·vert·er** *n* — **re·vert·i·ble** \-ˈvərt-ə-bəl\ *adj*
[1]**re·view** \ri-ˈvyü\ *n* **1** : a formal military inspection **2** : a general survey **3** : an act of inspecting or examining **4 a** : a critical evaluation (as of a book or play) **b** : a magazine devoted chiefly to reviews and essays **5 a** : a retrospective view or survey **b** : renewed study of material previously studied **6** : REVUE
[2]**review** *vb* **1** : to look at a thing again : study or examine again ⟨*review* a lesson⟩; *esp* : to reexamine judicially **2** : to make a formal inspection of (as troops) **3** : to give a criticism of (as a book or play) **4** : to look back on ⟨*review* accomplishments⟩ — **re·view·er** *n*
re·vile \ri-ˈvīl\ *vb* **1** : to subject to verbal abuse **2** : to use abusive language : RAIL — **re·vile·ment** \-mənt\ *n* — **re·vil·er** *n*
[1]**re·vise** \ri-ˈvīz\ *vb* **1** : to look over again in order to correct or improve ⟨*revise* a manuscript⟩ **2** : to make a new, amended, improved, or up-to-date version or arrangement of ⟨*revise* a dictionary⟩ — **re·vis·er** *or* **re·vi·sor** \-ˈvī-zər\ *n*
[2]**re·vise** \ˈrē-ˌvīz, ri-ˈ\ *n* : an act of revising : REVISION
Revised Standard Version *n* : a revision of the American Standard Version of the Bible published in 1946 and 1952
Revised Version *n* : a British revision of the Authorized Version of the Bible published in 1881 and 1885
re·vi·sion \ri-ˈvizh-ən\ *n* **1** : an act of revising (as a manuscript) **2** : a revised version — **re·vi·sion·ary** \-ˈvizh-ə-ˌner-ē\ *adj*
re·vi·tal·ize \(ˈ)rē-ˈvīt-ə-ˌlīz\ *vb* : to give new life or vigor to — **re·vi·tal·i·za·tion** \(ˌ)rē-ˌvīt-ə-lə-ˈzā-shən\ *n*
re·viv·al \ri-ˈvī-vəl\ *n* **1** : a reviving of interest (as in art, literature, or religion) **2** : a new publication or presentation (as of a book or play) **3** : a renewed flourishing ⟨a *revival* of business⟩ **4** : a meeting or series of meetings conducted by a preacher to arouse religious emotions or to make converts
re·viv·al·ism \-ˈvī-və-ˌliz-əm\ *n* : the often highly emotional spirit or methods characteristic of religious revivals
re·viv·al·ist \-ˈvī-və-ləst\ *n* : one who conducts revivals
re·vive \ri-ˈvīv\ *vb* **1** : to bring back or come back to

life, consciousness, or activity : make or become fresh or strong again **2** : to bring back into use ⟨trying to *revive* an old fashion⟩ — **re·viv·er** *n*

rev·o·ca·ble \'rev-ə-kə-bəl\ *adj* : capable of being revoked

rev·o·ca·tion \ˌrev-ə-'kā-shən\ *n* : an act or instance of revoking

1**re·voke** \ri-'vōk\ *vb* **1** : to put an end to (as a law, order, or privilege) by withdrawing, repealing, or canceling : ANNUL ⟨*revoke* a driver's license for speeding⟩ **2** : to renege in cards — **re·vok·er** *n*

2**revoke** *n* : an act or instance of revoking in a card game

1**re·volt** \ri-'vōlt\ *vb* **1** : to renounce allegiance or subjection (as to a government) : REBEL **2** : to experience or cause to experience disgust or shock — **re·volt·er** *n*

2**revolt** *n* **1** : an act or instance of revolting **2** : a renunciation of allegiance to a government or other legitimate authority; *esp* : INSURRECTION

re·volt·ing *adj* : extremely offensive : DISGUSTING — **re·volt·ing·ly** \-'vōl-ting-lē\ *adv*

rev·o·lu·tion \ˌrev-ə-'lü-shən\ *n* **1 a** : the action by a celestial body of going round in an orbit or elliptic course **b** : the time taken to complete one such circuit **2** : completion of a course (as of years) : CYCLE **3 a** : the action or motion of revolving : a turning round a center or axis : ROTATION **b** : a single complete turn (as of a wheel or a phonograph record) **4 a** : a sudden, radical, or complete change **b** : a fundamental change in political organization; *esp* : the overthrow of one government and the substitution of another by the governed

rev·o·lu·tion·ary \-shə-ˌner-ē\ *adj* **1 a** : of, relating to, or constituting a revolution ⟨*revolutionary* war⟩ **b** : tending to or promoting revolution **c** : RADICAL, EXTREMIST **2** *cap* : of or relating to the American Revolution — **revolutionary** *n*

rev·o·lu·tion·ist \ˌrev-ə-'lü-sh(ə-)nəst\ *n* **1** : a person who takes part in a revolution **2** : a person who believes in revolution as a means of change — **revolutionist** *adj*

rev·o·lu·tion·ize \-shə-ˌnīz\ *vb* **1** : to overthrow the established government of **2** : to cause a person to become a revolutionist **3** : to change fundamentally or completely ⟨an invention that *revolutionized* the industry⟩ — **rev·o·lu·tion·iz·er** *n*

re·volve \ri-'välv, -'vȯlv\ *vb* **1** : to consider at length **2 a** : to go round or cause to go round in an orbit **b** : to turn round on or as if on an axis : ROTATE **3** : RECUR **4** : to move in response to or dependence on a specified agent ⟨whole household *revolves* about the baby⟩ — **re·volv·a·ble** \-'väl-və-bəl, -'vȯl-\ *adj*

re·volv·er \ri-'väl-vər, -'vȯl-\ *n* : a handgun with a cylinder of usu. six chambers brought successively into line with the barrel and discharged with the same hammer

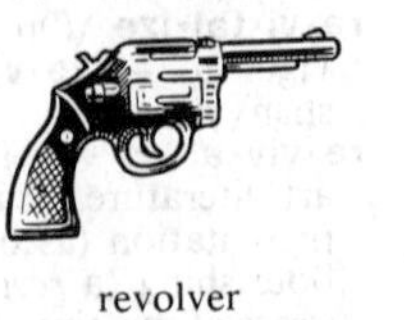
revolver

re·volv·ing *adj* : tending to revolve or recur; *esp* : recurrently available ⟨*revolving* credit⟩

re·vue \ri-'vyü\ *n* : a theatrical production consisting typically of brief often satirical sketches and songs

re·vul·sion \ri-'vəl-shən\ *n* **1** : a strong pulling or drawing away : WITHDRAWAL **2 a** : a sudden or strong reaction or change **b** : a sense of complete dislike : REPUGNANCE — **re·vul·sive** \-'vəl-siv\ *adj*

re·wake \(')rē-'wāk\ *or* **re·wak·en** \-'wā-kən\ *vb* : to waken again or anew

1**re·ward** \ri-'wȯrd\ *vb* **1** : to give a reward to or for **2** : RECOMPENSE — **re·ward·a·ble** \-ə-bəl\ *adj* — **re·ward·er** *n*

2**reward** *n* : something given or offered in return for a service; *esp* : money offered for the return of something lost or stolen or for the capture of a criminal

re·weigh \(')rē-'wā\ *vb* : to weigh again or anew

re·word \(')rē-'wərd\ *vb* : to restate in different words

re·work \(')rē-'wərk\ *vb* : to work again or anew: as **a** : REVISE, REWRITE **b** : to process (as used material) for further use

1**re·write** \(')rē-'rīt\ *vb* **-wrote** \-'rōt\; **-writ·ten** \-'rit-ən\ *also* **-writ** \-'rit\; **-writ·ing** \-'rīt-ing\ **1** : to write over again esp. in a different form **2** : to put material turned in by a reporter into form for publication in a newspaper — **re·writ·er** \-'rīt-ər\ *n*

2**re·write** \'rē-ˌrīt\ *n* : something (as a newspaper article) rewritten

rey·nard \'rān-ərd, 'ren-\ *n, often cap* : FOX

re·zone \(')rē-'zōn\ *vb* : to alter the zoning of

RF *abbr* radio frequency

RFD *abbr* rural free delivery

RH *abbr* right hand

rhap·so·dize \'rap-sə-ˌdīz\ *vb* : to speak or write in the style of a rhapsody

rhap·so·dy \'rap-səd-ē\ *n, pl* **-dies** **1** : a written or spoken expression of extravagant praise or ecstasy **2** : a musical composition of irregular form — **rhap·sod·ic** \rap-'säd-ik\ *or* **rhap·sod·i·cal** \-i-kəl\ *adj* — **rhap·sod·i·cal·ly** \-i-k(ə-)lē\ *adv*

rhea \'rē-ə\ *n* : any of several large flightless three-toed So. American birds that are smaller than the African ostrich

rhea
(about 4 ft. tall)

rhe·ni·um \'rē-nē-əm\ *n* : a rare heavy hard silvery white metallic element that is used in catalysts and thermocouples — see ELEMENT table

rhe·o·stat \'rē-ə-ˌstat\ *n* : a resistor for regulating an electric current by means of variable resistances — **rhe·o·stat·ic** \ˌrē-ə-'stat-ik\ *adj*

rhe·sus monkey \ˌrē-səs-\ *n* : a pale brown Indian monkey frequently used in medical research

rhesus monkey
(about 33 in. long)

rhet·o·ric \'ret-ə-rik\ *n* [from Greek *rhētorikē*, originally meaning "(the art) of the orator", from *rhētōr* "orator"] **1** : the art of speaking or writing effectively **2** : the study or application of the principles and rules of composition **3 a** : skill in the effective use of speech **b** : insincere or grandiloquent language — **rhet·o·ri·cian** \ˌret-ə-'rish-ən\ *n*

rhe·tor·i·cal \ri-'tȯr-i-kəl, -'tär-\ *adj* **1 a** : of, relating to, or dealing with rhetoric ⟨*rhetorical* studies⟩ **b** : used solely for rhetorical effect ⟨a *rhetorical* question⟩ **2** : using rhetoric; *esp* : GRANDILOQUENT ⟨*rhetorical* speeches⟩ — **rhe·tor·i·cal·ly** \-k(ə-)lē\ *adv*

rheum \'rüm\ *n* **1** : a watery discharge from the mucous membranes esp. of the eyes or nose **2** : a condition (as a cold) marked by a rheum — **rheumy** \'rü-mē\ *adj*

[1]**rheu·mat·ic** \rü-'mat-ik\ *adj* : of, relating to, characteristic of, or affected with rheumatism — **rheu·mat·i·cal·ly** \-'mat-i-k(ə-)lē\ *adv*

[2]**rheumatic** *n* : one affected with rheumatism

rheumatic fever *n* : an acute disease esp. of young people characterized by fever, by inflammation and pain in and around the joints, and by inflammation of the membranes surrounding the heart and the heart valves

rheu·ma·tism \'rü-mə-ˌtiz-əm\ *n* : any of various conditions characterized by inflammation or pain in muscles, joints, or fibrous tissue

Rh factor \är-'āch-\ *n* : an inherited substance present in the red blood cells and capable of inducing intense antigenic reactions

rhine·stone \'rīn-ˌstōn\ *n* : a brilliant colorless imitation diamond that is made usu. of glass or paste

Rhine wine \'rīn-\ *n* : a typically light-bodied dry white wine produced in the Rhine valley; *also* : a similar wine made elsewhere

rhi·no \'rī-nō\ *n, pl* **rhino** *or* **rhinos** : RHINOCEROS

rhi·noc·er·os \rī-'näs-(ə-)rəs\ *n, pl* **-er·os·es** *or* **-eros** [from Greek *rhinokerōs*, from *rhin-*, stem of *rhis* "nose", and *keras* "horn"] : a large thick-skinned three-toed plant-eating mammal of Africa and Asia that has one or two heavy upright horns on the snout

rhinoceros
(over 6 ft. at shoulder)

rhi·zoid \'rī-ˌzȯid\ *n* : a structure (as a hypha of a fungus) that functions like a root

rhi·zome \'rī-ˌzōm\ *n* : a somewhat elongated, often thickened, and usu. horizontal underground plant stem that produces shoots above and roots below

Rh–negative \ˌär-ˌāch-\ *adj* : lacking Rh factor in the red blood cells

rho \'rō\ *n* : the 17th letter of the Greek alphabet — Ρ or ρ

Rhode Is·land Red \rō-ˌdī-lən(d)-\ *n* : any of an American breed of domestic fowls with rich brownish red plumage

rho·di·um \'rōd-ē-əm\ *n* : a white hard ductile metallic element used in alloys with platinum — see ELEMENT table

rho·do·den·dron \ˌrōd-ə-'den-drən\ *n* [from Greek, from *rhodon* "rose" and *dendron* "tree"] : any of a genus of widely grown shrubs and trees with alternate leaves and showy flowers; *esp* : one with leathery evergreen leaves as distinguished from a deciduous azalea

rhom·boid \'räm-ˌbȯid\ *n* : a parallelogram in which the angles are oblique and adjacent sides are unequal — **rhomboid** *adj* — **rhom·boi·dal** \räm-'bȯid-əl\ *adj*

rhom·bus \'räm-bəs\ *n, pl* **rhom·bus·es** *or* **rhom·bi** \-ˌbī, -ˌbē\ : a parallelogram having the sides equal

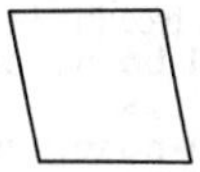

rhombus

Rh–positive \ˌär-ˌāch-\ *adj* : containing Rh factor in the red blood cells

rhu·barb \'rü-ˌbärb\ *n* **1** : a plant related to buckwheat that has broad green leaves borne on thick juicy pinkish stems often used for food **2** : a heated dispute or controversy ⟨the pitcher got into a *rhubarb* with the umpire⟩

rhumba *var of* RUMBA

[1]**rhyme** \'rīm\ *n* **1 a** : similarity in final sounds of two or more words or lines of verse **b** : one of two or more words having this similarity in sound **2 a** : rhyming verse **b** : a composition in verse that rhymes

[2]**rhyme** *vb* **1 a** : to make rhymes : put into rhyme **b** : to compose rhyming verse **2** : to end in syllables that rhyme ⟨*rhymed* verse⟩ **3** : to cause to rhyme : use as rhyme ⟨*rhymed* "moon" with "June"⟩ — **rhym·er** *n*

rhyme scheme *n* : the arrangement of rhymes in a stanza or a poem

rhy·o·lite \'rī-ə-ˌlīt\ *n* : a very acid volcanic rock that is the lava form of granite

rhythm \'rith-əm\ *n* **1 a** : a flow of rising and falling sounds in language that is produced in verse by a regular recurrence of stressed and unstressed syllables : CADENCE **b** : a particular example or form of rhythm ⟨iambic *rhythm*⟩ **2 a** : a flow of sound in music marked by accented beats coming at regular intervals **b** : a particular or characteristic pattern of rhythm ⟨waltz *rhythm*⟩ **3** : a movement or activity in which some action or element recurs regularly ⟨the *rhythm* of breathing⟩ — **rhyth·mic** \'rith-mik\ *or* **rhyth·mi·cal** \-mi-kəl\ *adj* — **rhyth·mi·cal·ly** \-mi-k(ə-)lē\ *adv*

rhythm and blues *n* : popular music with elements of blues and Negro folk music

R.I. *or* **RI** *abbr* Rhode Island

[1]**rib** \'rib\ *n* **1 a** : one of the paired curved bony or partly cartilaginous rods that are joined to the spinal column, stiffen the walls of the body of most vertebrates, and protect the viscera **b** : a cut of meat including a rib **2** : something (as a structural member of a ship or airplane) resembling a rib in shape or function **3 a** : a major vein of an insect's wing or of a leaf **b** : one of the ridges in some knitted or woven fabrics

[2]**rib** *vb* **ribbed**; **rib·bing** **1** : to furnish or enclose with ribs **2** : to form ribs in a fabric in knitting or weaving — **rib·ber** *n*

[3]**rib** *vb* **ribbed**; **rib·bing** : to poke fun at : KID — **rib·ber** *n*

rib·ald \'rib-əld\ *adj* **1** : CRUDE, OFFENSIVE ⟨*ribald* language⟩ **2** : characterized by or using broad indecent humor — **rib·ald·ry** \-əl-drē\ *n*

rib·bon \'rib-ən\ *n* **1 a** : a narrow usu. closely woven strip of decorative fabric (as silk) used esp. for trimming or for tying or decorating packages **b** : a piece of usu. multicolored ribbon worn as a military decoration or as a symbol of a medal **c** : a strip of colored ribbon given as a token of a place won in competition **2 a** : a long narrow strip resembling a ribbon ⟨fastened with long *ribbons* of steel⟩ **b** : a board framed into the studs to support the ceiling or floor joists **c** : a strip of inked fabric (as in a typewriter) **3** : TATTER, SHRED — usu. used in pl. ⟨torn to *ribbons*⟩ — **rib·bon·like** \-ˌlīk\ *adj*

rib cage *n* : the bony enclosing wall of the chest consisting chiefly of the ribs and their connecting parts

ri·bo·fla·vin \ˌrī-bə-ˈflā-vən\ *n* : a growth-promoting substance of the vitamin B complex occurring both free (as in milk) and combined (as in liver)

ri·bo·nu·cle·ic acid \ˌrī-bō-n(y)u̇-ˌklē-ik-, -ˌklā-\ *n* : RNA

ri·bose nucleic acid \ˈrī-ˌbōs-\ *n* : RNA

ri·bo·some \ˈrī-bə-ˌsōm\ *n* : one of numerous small RNA-containing granules in the cell that are sites of protein synthesis

rice \ˈrīs\ *n, pl* **rice** **1** : an annual grass widely grown in warm wet areas for its seed that is used esp. for food **2** : the seed or grain of rice

rice

rice·bird \ˈrīs-ˌbərd\ *n* : any of several small birds common in rice fields; *esp* : BOBOLINK

ric·er \ˈrī-sər\ *n* : a kitchen utensil in which soft foods (as boiled potatoes) are pressed through a perforated container

rice rat *n* : a native rat of the southeastern U.S. that is smaller than the rat found commonly in houses

rich \ˈrich\ *adj* **1** : possessing or controlling great wealth : WEALTHY **2 a** : having high value ⟨a *rich* harvest⟩ **b** : COSTLY, SUMPTUOUS ⟨*rich* robes⟩ **3 a** : abundantly supplied with some usu. desirable quality or thing ⟨a land *rich* in resources⟩ **b** : of pleasingly strong odor ⟨*rich* perfumes⟩ **c** : highly productive : FRUITFUL, FERTILE ⟨a *rich* mine⟩ ⟨*rich* soils⟩ **d** : containing much seasoning, fat, or sugar ⟨*rich* food⟩ **e** : high in combustible content ⟨a *rich* fuel mixture⟩ **4 a** : vivid and deep in color ⟨*rich* red⟩ **b** : full and mellow in tone and quality ⟨*rich* voice⟩ **5** : AMUSING, LAUGHABLE — **rich·ness** *n*

rich·en \ˈrich-ən\ *vb* **rich·ened**; **rich·en·ing** \-(ə-)ning\ : to make rich or richer

rich·es \ˈrich-əz\ *n pl* [from Middle English *richesse, riches*, not originally a plural, but a singular meaning "richness", "wealth", from French *richesse*, from *riche* "rich"] : things that make one rich : WEALTH

rich·ly \ˈrich-lē\ *adv* **1** : in a rich manner ⟨*richly* dressed⟩ **2** : in full measure : AMPLY ⟨*richly* deserved the praise she received⟩

Rich·ter scale \ˈrik-tər-\ *n* : a logarithmic scale for expressing the intensity of an earthquake in terms of the energy dissipated in it

1**rick** \ˈrik\ *n* : a stack or pile (as of hay or grain) in the open air

2**rick** *vb* : to pile (as hay) in ricks

rick·ets \ˈrik-əts\ *n* : a children's disease marked esp. by soft and deformed bones and caused by inadequate vitamin D

rick·ett·sia \rik-ˈet-sē-ə\ *n, pl* **-si·as** *or* **-si·ae** \-sē-ˌē, -sē-ˌī\ : any of various microorganisms that live in cells and include agents causing serious diseases (as typhus) — **rick·ett·si·al** \-sē-əl\ *adj*

rick·ety \ˈrik-ət-ē\ *adj* **1** : affected with rickets **2** : feeble in the joints ⟨a *rickety* old man⟩ **3** : DILAPIDATED, SHAKY ⟨a *rickety* wagon⟩

rick·ey \ˈrik-ē\ *n, pl* **rickeys** : a drink containing liquor, lime juice, sugar, and soda water; *also* : a similar drink without liquor

rick·rack *or* **ric·rac** \ˈrik-ˌrak\ *n* : a flat braid woven to form zigzags and used esp. as trimming on clothing

rick·sha *or* **rick·shaw** \ˈrik-ˌshȯ\ *n* : JINRIKISHA

1**ric·o·chet** \ˈrik-ə-ˌshā, *Brit also* -ˌshet\ *n* **1** : a glancing rebound (as of a bullet off a flat surface) **2** : an object that ricochets

2**ricochet** *vb* **-cheted** \-ˌshād\ *or* **-chet·ted** \-ˌshet-əd\; **-chet·ing** \-ˌshā-ing\ *or* **-chet·ting** \-ˌshet-ing\ : SKIP, GLANCE, REBOUND ⟨bullets *ricocheted* off the wall⟩

rid \ˈrid\ *vb* **rid** *also* **rid·ded**; **rid·ding** : to make free : RELIEVE — often used in the phrase *be rid of* or *get rid of* ⟨glad to be *rid* of such a troublesome task⟩ ⟨got *rid* of some junk⟩

rid·a·ble *or* **ride·a·ble** \ˈrīd-ə-bəl\ *adj* **1** : fit for riding ⟨a battered but still *ridable* bicycle⟩ **2** : fit for riding over ⟨a *ridable* road⟩

rid·dance \ˈrid-ən(t)s\ *n* : the act of ridding : the state of being rid of

1**rid·dle** \ˈrid-əl\ *n* **1** : a mystifying, misleading, or puzzling question posed as a problem to be solved or guessed : CONUNDRUM **2** : something or someone difficult to understand ⟨doctors working to solve the many *riddles* of cancer⟩

2**riddle** *vb* **rid·dled**; **rid·dling** \ˈrid-(ə-)ling\ **1** : to find the solution of a riddle or mystery **2** : to set a riddle for : MYSTIFY **3** : to speak in riddles or set forth a riddle — **rid·dler** \-(ə-)lər\ *n*

3**riddle** *n* : a coarse sieve (as for ashes)

4**riddle** *vb* **1** : to sift or separate with or as if with a riddle **2 a** : to fill full of holes so as to make like a riddle ⟨a boat *riddled* with shot⟩ **b** : to damage or corrupt as if by filling with holes ⟨a police force *riddled* by graft⟩

1**ride** \ˈrīd\ *vb* **rode** \ˈrōd\; **rid·den** \ˈrid-ən\; **rid·ing** \ˈrīd-ing\ **1 a** : to go or be carried along on an animal's back or on or in a conveyance (as a boat, automobile, or airplane) **b** : to sit on and control so as to be carried along ⟨*ride* a bicycle⟩ **2 a** : to be supported and usu. carried along by ⟨a ship *riding* the waves⟩ ⟨the bearings *ride* on a cushion of grease⟩ **b** : to float at anchor **c** : to remain afloat through : SURVIVE ⟨*ride* out a storm⟩ **3** : to be supported on a bearing point or surface **4 a** : to convey in or as if in a vehicle : give a ride to ⟨*rode* the child on his back⟩ **b** : to function as a means of conveyance ⟨the car *rides* well⟩ **5 a** : to torment by constant nagging or teasing : HARASS ⟨*ride* a man about his faults⟩ **b** : OBSESS, OPPRESS ⟨*ridden* by fears⟩ **6** : to depend on something ⟨all our hopes *ride* on his success⟩ — **ride roughshod over** : to treat with disdain or abuse

2**ride** *n* **1** : an act of riding; *esp* : a trip on horseback or by vehicle ⟨a *ride* in the country⟩ **2** : a way (as a road or path) for riding **3** : a mechanical device (as at an amusement park) for riding on **4** : a means of transportation ⟨needs a *ride* to work⟩

rid·er \ˈrīd-ər\ *n* **1** : one that rides **2 a** : an addition to a document often attached on a separate piece of paper **b** : an additional clause often dealing with an unrelated subject attached to a bill during its passage through a lawmaking body — **rid·er·less** \-ləs\ *adj*

1**ridge** \ˈrij\ *n* **1** : a raised body part (as along the backbone) **2** : a range of hills or mountains **3** : a raised strip (as of plowed ground) **4** : the line made where two sloping surfaces come together ⟨the *ridge* of a roof⟩

2**ridge** *vb* : to form into or extend in ridges

ridge·pole \'rij-ˌpōl\ *n* **1** : the highest horizontal timber in a sloping roof to which the upper ends of the rafters are fastened **2** : a horizontal support for the top of a tent

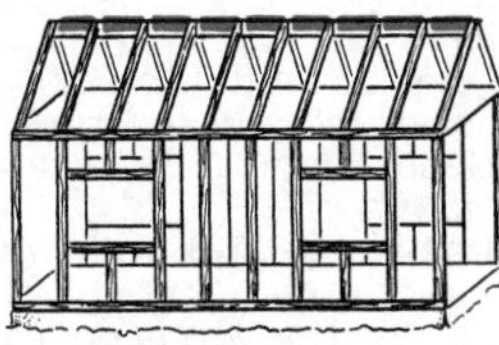

ridgepole 1

ridgy \'rij-ē\ *adj* : having or rising in ridges

1**rid·i·cule** \'rid-ə-ˌkyül\ *n* : the act of making fun of someone or something : DERISION

2**ridicule** *vb* : to make fun of — **rid·i·cul·er** *n*

ri·dic·u·lous \rə-'dik-yə-ləs\ *adj* : arousing or deserving ridicule : ABSURD, PREPOSTEROUS — **ri·dic·u·lous·ly** *adv* — **ri·dic·u·lous·ness** *n*

rid·ing \'rīd-ing\ *adj* **1** : used for or when riding ⟨*riding* horse⟩ **2** : operated by a rider ⟨a *riding* lawn mower⟩

rife \'rīf\ *adj* **1** : WIDESPREAD, PREVALENT ⟨lands where famine is *rife*⟩ **2** : ABOUNDING ⟨the air was *rife* with rumors⟩ — **rife·ly** *adv*

1**rif·fle** \'rif-əl\ *n* **1 a** : a shallow extending across a stream bed and causing broken water **b** : a stretch of water flowing over a riffle **2** : a small wave or succession of small waves : RIPPLE **3** : the act or process of shuffling (as cards)

2**riffle** *vb* **rif·fled**; **rif·fling** \'rif-(ə-)ling\ **1** : to form, flow over, or move in riffles **2** : to ruffle slightly : RIPPLE **3 a** : to flip or leaf through hastily **b** : to shuffle playing cards by separating the deck into two parts and sliding the thumbs along the edges so the cards intermix

riff·raff \'rif-ˌraf\ *n* **1 a** : disreputable persons **b** : RABBLE **2** : REFUSE, RUBBISH — **riffraff** *adj*

1**ri·fle** \'rī-fəl\ *vb* **ri·fled**; **ri·fling** \-f(ə-)ling\ **1** : to ransack esp. with the intent to steal **2** : to steal and carry away — **ri·fler** \-f(ə-)lər\ *n*

2**rifle** *vb* **ri·fled**; **ri·fling** \-f(ə-)ling\ : to cut spiral grooves into the bore of ⟨*rifled* arms⟩

3**rifle** *n* **1 a** : a weapon with a rifled bore that is de-

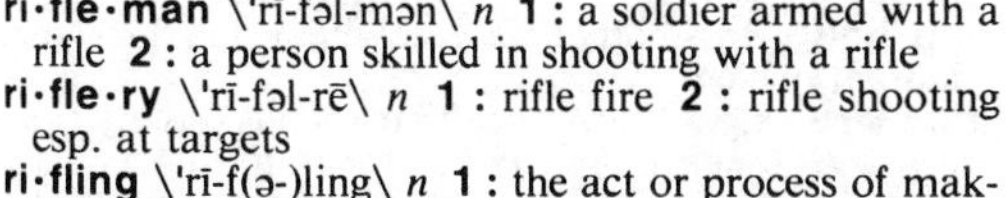

rifle 1a

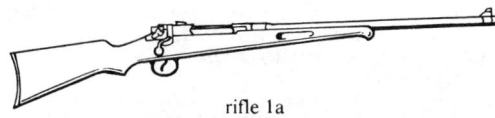

signed to be fired from the shoulder **b** : a rifled artillery piece **2** *pl* : a body of soldiers armed with rifles

4**rifle** *vb* **ri·fled**; **ri·fling** \-f(ə-)ling\ : to hit or throw a ball with great force

ri·fle·man \'rī-fəl-mən\ *n* **1** : a soldier armed with a rifle **2** : a person skilled in shooting with a rifle

ri·fle·ry \'rī-fəl-rē\ *n* **1** : rifle fire **2** : rifle shooting esp. at targets

ri·fling \'rī-f(ə-)ling\ *n* **1** : the act or process of making spiral grooves **2** : a system of spiral grooves in the bore of a gun causing a projectile when fired to rotate about its longer axis

1**rift** \'rift\ *n* **1 a** : an opening made by splitting or separation : CLEFT, FISSURE, CREVASSE **b** : a normal geological fault **2 a** : a break in normally friendly relations : BREACH **b** : a disagreement or dispute causing such a break

2**rift** *vb* : CLEAVE, DIVIDE, SPLIT

1**rig** \'rig\ *vb* **rigged**; **rig·ging** **1** : to fit out (as a ship) with rigging **2** : CLOTHE, DRESS **3** : to furnish with gear : EQUIP

2**rig** *n* **1** : the distinctive shape, number, and arrangement of sails and masts of a ship ⟨a schooner *rig*⟩ **2** : EQUIPAGE; *esp* : a carriage with its horse **3** : DRESS, CLOTHING **4** : tackle, equipment, or machinery fitted for a specified purpose ⟨oil-drilling *rig*⟩

3**rig** *vb* **rigged**; **rig·ging** : to manipulate or control usu. by deceptive or dishonest means ⟨*rig* an election⟩

rig·ger \'rig-ər\ *n* **1** : one that rigs **2** : a ship of a specified rig ⟨square-*rigger*⟩

rig·ging \'rig-ing, -ən\ *n* **1** : the lines and chains used aboard a ship esp. in working sail and supporting masts and spars **2** : TACKLE, GEAR

1**right** \'rīt\ *adj* **1** : RIGHTEOUS, UPRIGHT **2** : being in accordance with what is just, good, or proper ⟨*right* conduct⟩ **3 a** : agreeable to a standard **b** : conforming to facts or truth : CORRECT ⟨*right* answer⟩ **4** : SUITABLE, APPROPRIATE ⟨*right* man for the job⟩ ⟨*right* tool⟩ **5** : STRAIGHT ⟨*right* line⟩ **6** : GENUINE, REAL **7 a** : of, relating to, situated on, or being the side of the body which is away from the heart and on which the hand is stronger and more skilled in most people ⟨*right* leg⟩ **b** : located nearer to the right side of the body ⟨the *right* arm of his chair⟩ **8** : having its axis perpendicular to the base ⟨*right* cone⟩ ⟨*right* circular cylinder⟩ **9** : of, relating to, or constituting the principal or more prominent side of an object ⟨*right* side out⟩ **10** : acting or judging in accordance with truth or fact ⟨time proved him *right*⟩ **11** : physically or mentally well ⟨did not feel *right*⟩ **12** : most favorable or desired : PREFERABLE — **right·ness** *n*

2**right** *n* **1** : qualities (as devotion to duty and obedience to lawful authority) that together constitute the ideal of moral propriety **2** : something to which one has a just claim — often used in pl. ⟨mineral *rights*⟩ ⟨film *rights* of the novel⟩ **3** : something that one may properly claim as due **4** : the cause of truth or justice **5** : the right side or the part on the right side **6 a** : the true account or correct interpretation **b** : the quality or state of being factually correct **7** : the members of a European legislative body sitting to the right of the presiding officer and holding more conservative political views than other members **8** *cap* : political conservatives or reactionaries; *also* : their beliefs — **by rights** : with reason or justice : PROPERLY — **to rights** : into proper order

3**right** *adv* **1** : according to right ⟨live *right*⟩ **2** : EXACTLY, PRECISELY ⟨*right* at his fingertips⟩ **3** : in a suitable, proper, or desired manner ⟨hold your pen *right*⟩ **4** : in a direct line or course ⟨go *right* home⟩ **5** : according to fact or truth : TRULY ⟨guess *right*⟩ ⟨heard *right*⟩ **6 a** : all the way ⟨windows *right* to the floor⟩ **b** : COMPLETELY **7** : IMMEDIATELY ⟨*right* after lunch⟩ **8** : EXTREMELY, VERY ⟨*right* pleasant day⟩

4**right** *vb* **1 a** : to relieve from wrong **b** : JUSTIFY, VINDICATE **2 a** : to adjust or restore to the proper state or condition **b** : to bring or restore to an upright position **3** : to become upright — **right·er** *n*

right angle *n* : the angle bounded by two lines perpendicular to each other — **right–an·gled** \'rīt-'ang-gəld\ *or* **right–an·gle** \-gəl\ *adj*

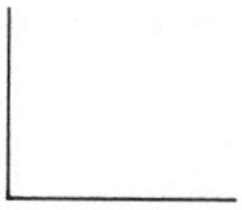

right angle

right circular cone *n* : CONE 2a

righ·teous \'rī-chəs\ *adj* **1** : acting rightly : UPRIGHT **2 a** : according to what is right ⟨*righteous* actions⟩ **b** : arising from an outraged sense of justice or morality ⟨*righteous* indignation⟩ — **righ·teous·ly** *adv* — **righ·teous·ness** *n*

right·ful \'rīt-fəl\ *adj* **1** : JUST, EQUITABLE **2** : having a just or legally enforceable claim : LEGITIMATE ⟨*rightful* owner⟩ **3** : held by right or just claim : LEGAL ⟨*rightful* authority⟩ — **right·ful·ly** \-fə-lē\ *adv* — **right·ful·ness** *n*

right–hand \ˌrīt-ˌhand\ *adj* **1** : situated on the right **2** : RIGHT-HANDED **3** : chiefly relied on ⟨*right-hand* man⟩

right–hand·ed \'rīt-'han-dəd\ *adj* **1** : using the right hand more easily than the left **2** : done or made with or for the right hand **3** : having or moving with a clockwise turn or twist — **right–hand·ed·ly** *or* **right–hand·ed** *adv* — **right–hand·ed·ness** *n* — **right–hand·er** \-'han-dər\ *n*

right·ist \'rīt-əst\ *n, often cap* : a conservative or reactionary in politics — **rightist** *adj, often cap*

right·ly \'rīt-lē\ *adv* **1** : FAIRLY, JUSTLY **2** : PROPERLY, FITLY **3** : CORRECTLY, EXACTLY

right–mind·ed \'rīt-'mīn-dəd\ *adj* : inclined to do what is right

right–of–way \ˌrīt-ə(v)-'wā\ *n* **1** : a legal right of passage over another person's ground **2 a** : the area over which a right-of-way exists **b** : the strip of land over which is built a public road **c** : the land occupied by a railroad esp. for its main line **d** : the land used by a public utility (as for a transmission line) **3** : the right of certain traffic to proceed ahead of other traffic

right prism *n* : a prism all of whose lateral faces are rectangles

right–to–work law \ˌrī(t)-tə-'wərk-\ *n* : a law that prohibits the union shop in its jurisdiction

right triangle *n* : a triangle having a right angle

right·ward \'rīt-wərd\ *also* **right·wards** \-wərdz\ *adv* : toward or on the right — **rightward** *adj*

rig·id \'rij-əd\ *adj* **1** : lacking flexibility : STIFF, HARD **2 a** : inflexibly set : UNYIELDING **b** : strictly observed : SCRUPULOUS **3** : precise and accurate in procedure — **ri·gid·i·ty** \rə-'jid-ət-ē\ *n* — **rig·id·ly** \'rij-əd-lē\ *adv* — **rig·id·ness** *n*

rig·ma·role \'rig-(ə)mə-ˌrōl\ *n* **1** : confused or meaningless talk **2** : a complex and often unnecessary procedure

rig·or \'rig-ər\ *n* **1 a** : harsh strictness : the quality of being unyielding : SEVERITY **b** : an act or instance of strictness or severity **2** : a shuddering caused by a chill **3** : a condition that makes life difficult or uncomfortable; *esp* : extreme cold **4** : strict precision : EXACTNESS ⟨logical *rigor*⟩

rig·or mor·tis \ˌrig-ər-'mȯrt-əs\ *n* : temporary rigidity of muscles occurring after death

rig·or·ous \'rig-(ə-)rəs\ *adj* **1** : exercising or favoring rigor : very strict **2** : marked by extremes of temperature or climate : HARSH, SEVERE **3** : scrupulously accurate : PRECISE — **rig·or·ous·ly** *adv* — **rig·or·ous·ness** *n*

rile \'rīl\ *vb* **1** : ROIL 1 **2** : to make angry

¹rill \'ril\ *n* : a very small brook

²rill \'ril\ *or* **rille** \'ril, 'ril-ə\ *n* : a long narrow valley on the moon's surface

¹rim \'rim\ *n* **1 a** : the outer often curved or circular edge or border of something **b** : BRINK **2** : the outer part of a wheel joined to the hub usu. by spokes — **rim·less** \-ləs\ *adj*

²rim *vb* **rimmed**; **rim·ming** **1** : to furnish with a rim : serve as a rim for : BORDER **2** : to run around the rim of ⟨his putt *rimmed* the cup⟩ **3** : to form or show a rim

¹rime \'rīm\ *n* **1** : FROST 2 **2** : an accumulation of granular ice tufts on objects that resembles frost in appearance but is formed from supercooled fog or cloud **3** : CRUST 3a, INCRUSTATION — **rimy** \'rī-mē\ *adj*

²rime *vb* : to cover with or as if with rime

³rime, rim·er *var of* RHYME, RHYMER

rind \'rīnd\ *n* : the bark of a tree; *also* : a usu. hard or tough outer layer (as the skin of a fruit)

rin·der·pest \'rin-dər-ˌpest\ *n* : an acute virus disease of cattle and sometimes sheep and goats

¹ring \'ring\ *n* **1** : a circular band for holding, connecting, hanging, or pulling or for packing or sealing **2** : a circular band usu. of precious metal worn on the finger **3 a** : a circular line, figure, or object **b** : an encircling arrangement ⟨a *ring* of suburbs⟩ **c** : a circular or spiral course **4 a** : an often circular space for exhibitions or competitions; *esp* : such a space at a circus **b** : a square enclosure in which boxers or wrestlers compete **c** : PRIZEFIGHTING **5** : ANNUAL RING **6** : a combination of persons for a selfish and often corrupt purpose — **ringed** \'ringd\ *adj* — **ring·like** \'ring-ˌlīk\ *adj*

²ring *vb* **1** : to place or form a ring around : ENCIRCLE **2** : to provide with a ring **3** : to throw a ring over (the mark) in a game where curved objects (as horseshoes) are tossed at a mark **4** : to form or take the shape of a ring

³ring *vb* **rang** \'rang\; **rung** \'rəng\; **ring·ing** \'ring-ing\ **1** : to sound clearly and resonantly when struck ⟨church bells *ringing*⟩ ⟨swords *rang* on helmets⟩ **2** : to cause to sound esp. by striking ⟨*rang* the bell⟩ **3** : to announce by or as if by ringing ⟨*ring* an alarm⟩ ⟨*ring* in the new year⟩ **4** : to sound loudly ⟨cheers *rang* out⟩ **5 a** : to be filled with reverberating sound : RESOUND ⟨the whole hall *rang* with their cheers⟩ **b** : to have a sensation of being filled with a humming sound ⟨his ears were *ringing*⟩ **6** : to be filled with talk or report ⟨the whole land *rang* with his fame⟩ **7** : to have a sound or character expressive of some quality ⟨a story that *rings* true⟩ **8 a** : to summon esp. by bell **b** : to call on the telephone **9** : to cause a device to register ⟨*ring* a cash register⟩ ⟨*ring* a time clock⟩ — often used with *up* ⟨*rang* up a sale⟩ — **ring a bell** : to arouse a response ⟨no, that name doesn't *ring a bell*⟩

⁴ring *n* **1** : a set of bells **2** : a clear resonant sound made by or as if by vibrating metal **3** : resonant tone : SONORITY **4** : a loud sound continued, repeated, or reverberated **5** : a sound or character expressive of some particular quality ⟨a story with the *ring* of truth⟩ **6 a** : the act or an instance of ringing **b** : a telephone call

ring·bolt \'ring-ˌbōlt\ *n* : a bolt with a ring through a loop at one end

¹ring·er \'ring-ər\ *n* **1** : one that sounds esp. by ringing **2 a** : one that enters a competition under false representations **b** : one that strongly resembles another

²ringer *n* : a quoit or horsehoe that falls right over a peg

ring finger *n* : the third finger of the left hand counting the index finger as one

ring·lead·er \'ring-ˌlēd-ər\ *n* : a leader esp. of a group of troublemakers

ring·let \'ring-lət\ *n* **1** *archaic* : a small ring or circle **2** : CURL; *esp* : a long curl of hair

ring·mas·ter \'ring-ˌmas-tər\ *n* : one in charge of performances in a ring (as of a circus)

ring–necked pheasant *n* : an Old World pheasant with a white neck ring widely introduced in temperate regions as a game bird

ring·side \'ring-ˌsīd\ *n* : the area just outside a ring esp. in which a contest occurs — **ringside** *adj*

ring stand *n* : a metal stand consisting of an upright rod on a substantial base used with rings and clamps for supporting laboratory apparatus

ring–tailed \'ring-'tāld\ *adj* : having a tail marked with rings of differing colors

ring·worm \-ˌwərm\ *n* : a contagious skin disease caused by fungi and characterized by ring-shaped discolored patches

rink \'ringk\ *n* **1** : a sheet of ice designed for curling, ice hockey, or ice-skating **2** : an enclosure for roller-skating

¹rinse \'rin(t)s\ *vb* [from medieval French *rincer*, probably from a Latin verb *recentiare* meaning "to freshen", from Latin *recent-*, stem of *recens* "fresh", "recent"] **1** : to cleanse with liquid (as water) **2** : to treat (hair) with a rinse **3** : to remove (as dirt or impurities) by washing lightly or in water only — **rins·er** *n*

²rinse *n* **1** : the act or process of rinsing **2 a** : liquid used for rinsing **b** : a solution that temporarily tints hair

¹ri·ot \'rī-ət\ *n* **1 a** : public violence, tumult, or disorder **b** : a tumultuous disturbance of the public peace by three or more persons assembled together **2** : a random or disorderly profusion esp. of color **3** : something or someone wildly amusing ⟨he was a *riot* at the party⟩

²riot *vb* : to create or engage in a riot — **ri·ot·er** *n*

riot act *n* : a vigorous reproof, reprimand, or warning — used in the phrase *read the riot act*

ri·ot·ous \'rī-ət-əs\ *adj* **1** : ABUNDANT, EXUBERANT ⟨a *riotous* display of colors⟩ **2 a** : of the nature of a riot : TURBULENT **b** : participating in riot — **ri·ot·ous·ly** *adv* — **ri·ot·ous·ness** *n*

¹rip \'rip\ *vb* **ripped**; **rip·ping** **1** : to tear or split apart or open **2** : to saw or split wood with the grain **3** : to slash or slit with or as if with a sharp blade **4** : to rush headlong — **rip·per** *n*

²rip *n* : a rent made by ripping : TEAR

³rip *n* : a body of water made rough by the meeting of opposing currents or by passing over an irregular bottom

⁴rip *n* **1** : a worn-out worthless horse **2** : a person who is loose in morals and conduct : LIBERTINE, RAKE

rip cord *n* : a cord or wire pulled by a jumper to release a pilot parachute which lifts the main parachute out of its container

ripe \'rīp\ *adj* **1** : fully grown and developed : MATURE **2** : having mature knowledge, understanding, or judgment **3** : far advanced in years ⟨a *ripe* old age⟩ **4** : SUITABLE, READY ⟨*ripe* for action⟩ **5** : brought by aging to full flavor or the best state : MELLOW ⟨*ripe* cheese⟩ — **ripe·ly** *adv* — **ripe·ness** *n*

rip·en \'rī-pən\ *vb* **rip·ened**; **rip·en·ing** \'rīp-(ə-)ning\ : to grow or make ripe — **rip·en·er** \-(ə-)nər\ *n*

rip off \'rip-'ȯf\ *vb, slang* : ROB, steal — **rip–off** \-ˌȯf\ *n, slang*

ri·poste \ri-'pōst\ *n* **1** : a fencer's quick return thrust **2** : a quick retort — **riposte** *vb*

rip·ping \'rip-ing\ *adj* : EXCELLENT, SWELL

¹rip·ple \'rip-əl\ *vb* **rip·pled**; **rip·pling** \-(ə-)ling\ **1 a** : to become lightly ruffled or covered with small waves **b** : to flow in small waves **2** : to stir up small waves on ⟨wind *rippling* water⟩ **3** : to impart a wavy motion or appearance to ⟨the athlete *rippled* his arm muscles⟩ — **rip·pler** \-(ə-)lər\ *n*

²ripple *n* **1 a** : the ruffling of the surface of water **b** : a small wave **2** : a sound like that of rippling water

rip–roar·ing \'rip-'rōr-ing, -'rȯr-\ *adj* : noisily excited or exciting : BOISTEROUS

rip·saw \'rip-ˌsȯ\ *n* : a coarse-toothed saw for cutting wood in the direction of the grain

¹rise \'rīz\ *vb* **rose** \'rōz\; **ris·en** \'riz-ən\; **ris·ing** \'rī-zing\ **1 a** : to get up esp. from lying, kneeling, or sitting **b** : to get up from sleep or from one's bed **2** : to return from death **3** : to take up arms ⟨*rise* in rebellion⟩ **4** : to appear above the horizon ⟨sun *rises* at six⟩ ⟨land *rose* to starboard⟩ **5 a** : to move upward : ASCEND ⟨smoke *rises*⟩ **b** : to extend upward ⟨hill *rises* to a great height⟩ **6** : to swell in size or volume ⟨the river was *rising*⟩ ⟨bread dough *rises*⟩ **7 a** : to become heartened or elated ⟨their spirits *rose*⟩ **b** : to increase in intensity ⟨felt his anger *rising*⟩ **8 a** : to attain a higher rank or position ⟨*rose* to colonel⟩ **b** : to increase in quantity or number ⟨steel production *rose* sharply⟩ **9 a** : to come about : HAPPEN ⟨an ugly rumor had *risen*⟩ **b** : to have a source : ORIGINATE ⟨river *rises* in the hills⟩ **10** : to exert oneself to meet a challenge ⟨always *rose* to the occasion⟩

R

²rise \'rīz\ *n* **1** : an act of rising : a state of being risen **2** : BEGINNING, ORIGIN **3** : the distance or elevation of one point above another **4** : the amount of an increase (as in number, volume, price, value, or rate) **5 a** : an upward slope **b** : a spot higher than surrounding ground **6** : an irritated or angry reaction ⟨got a *rise* out of him⟩

ris·er \'rī-zər\ *n* **1** : one that rises (as from sleep) ⟨an early *riser*⟩ **2** : the upright member between two stair treads

ris·i·bil·i·ty \ˌriz-ə-'bil-ət-ē\ *n, pl* **-ties** **1** : the ability or inclination to laugh — often used in pl. **2** : LAUGHTER, MERRIMENT

ris·i·ble \'riz-ə-bəl\ *adj* **1** : able or inclined to laugh **2** : arousing laughter : FUNNY **3** : relating to or used in laughter ⟨*risible* muscles⟩

¹risk \'risk\ *n* **1** : possibility of loss or injury : PERIL **2 a** : the chance of loss or the perils to a person or thing that is insured **b** : a person or thing that is a hazard to an insurer ⟨a poor *risk*⟩ ⟨a good *risk*⟩ *syn* see DANGER

²risk *vb* **1** : to expose to hazard or danger ⟨*risked* his life⟩ **2** : to take the risk or danger of ⟨*risked* breaking his neck⟩ — **risk·er** *n*

risky \'ris-kē\ *adj* **risk·i·er**; **-est** : attended with risk or danger : HAZARDOUS — **risk·i·ness** *n*

ris·qué \ri-'skā\ *adj* : verging on impropriety or indecency

rit *or* **ritard** *abbr* ritardando

ri·tar·dan·do \ri-ˌtär-'dän-dō, ˌrē-\ *adv or adj* : with a gradual slackening in tempo — used as a direction in music — **ritardando** *n*

rite \'rīt\ *n* **1 a** : a prescribed form for a ceremony **b** : LITURGY **2** : a ceremonial act or action

¹rit·u·al \'rich-(ə-w)əl\ *adj* **1** : of or relating to rites or a ritual ⟨a *ritual* dance⟩ **2** : according to religious law or social custom ⟨*ritual* purity⟩ — **rit·u·al·ly** \-ē\ *adv*

²ritual *n* **1** : an established form for a ceremony **2 a** : ritual observance; *esp* : a system of rites **b** : a ceremonial act or action **c** : a formal and customarily repeated act or series of acts

rit·u·al·ism \-ˌiz-əm\ *n* **1** : the use of ritual **2** : excessive devotion to ritual — **rit·u·al·is·tic** \ˌrich-(ə-w)əl-'is-tik\ *adj*

ritzy \'rit-sē\ *adj* **ritz·i·er; -est** **1** : ostentatiously smart : FASHIONABLE **2** : SNOBBISH

riv *abbr* river

[1]**ri·val** \'rī-vəl\ *n* [from Latin *rivalis* "one using the same stream as another", "rival in love", from *rivus* "stream"] **1 a** : one of two or more striving to reach or obtain that which only one can possess : COMPETITOR **b** : one who tries to excel **2** : one that equals another in desired qualities : PEER

[2]**rival** *adj* : of, relating to, or being a rival : having the same pretensions or claims

[3]**rival** *vb* **-valed** *or* **-valled; -val·ing** *or* **-val·ling** \'rīv-(ə-)ling\ **1** : to be in competition with **2** : to strive to equal or excel **3** : EQUAL, MATCH ⟨manufacture linens that *rival* the world's best⟩

ri·val·ry \'rī-vəl-rē\ *n, pl* **-ries** : the act of rivaling : the state of being a rival : COMPETITION

rive \'rīv\ *vb* **rived** \'rīvd\; **riv·en** \'riv-ən\ *also* **rived; riv·ing** \'rī-ving\ **1** : to tear apart : REND **2** : SPLIT, CLEAVE

riv·er \'riv-ər\ *n* **1** : a natural stream of water larger than a brook or creek **2** : a large stream : copious flow ⟨a *river* of oil⟩ ⟨shed *rivers* of blood⟩

riv·er·bed \-ˌbed\ *n* : the channel occupied or formerly occupied by a river

riv·er·boat \-ˌbōt\ *n* : a boat for use on a river

river mink *n* : the skin of a muskrat esp. when processed to resemble mink

riv·er·side \'riv-ər-ˌsīd\ *n* : the side or bank of a river

[1]**riv·et** \'riv-ət\ *n* : a headed pin or bolt of metal used for uniting two or more pieces by passing the shank through a hole in each piece and then beating or pressing down the plain end so as to make a second head

[2]**rivet** *vb* **1** : to fasten with or as if with rivets **2** : to attract and hold (as the attention) completely — **riv·et·er** *n*

riv·u·let \'riv-(y)ə-lət\ *n* : a small stream

rm *abbr* **1** ream **2** room

RN *abbr* registered nurse

RNA \ˌär-en-'ā\ *n* : any of various ribonucleic acids that occur esp. in cytoplasm and are associated with the control of cellular chemical activities

[1]**roach** \'rōch\ *n, pl* **roach** *also* **roach·es** : a silver-white greenish-backed European freshwater fish related to the carp

[2]**roach** *n* : COCKROACH

road \'rōd\ *n* **1** : a place less enclosed than a harbor where ships may ride at anchor — often used in pl. **2 a** : an open way for vehicles, persons, and animals; *esp* : one lying outside an urban district **b** : ROADBED 2 **3** : ROUTE, PATH **4** : RAILWAY, RAILROAD

road·bed \'rōd-ˌbed\ *n* **1** : the foundation of a road or railroad **2** : the part of the surface of a road traveled by vehicles

road·block \-ˌbläk\ *n* **1 a** : a barricade at a point on a road that can be covered by heavy fire from a defending army **b** : a road barricade set up by law-enforcement officers **2** : an obstruction in a road

road hog *n* : a driver who obstructs others esp. by occupying part of another's traffic lane

road·house \'rōd-ˌhau̇s\ *n* : a nightclub usu. outside city limits

ə abut	ər further	a back	ā bake
ä cot, cart	au̇ out	ch chin	e less	ē easy
g gift	i trip	ī life	j joke	ng sing	ō flow
ȯ flaw	ȯi coin	th thin	t͟h this	ü loot
u̇ foot	y yet	yü few	yu̇ furious	zh vision

road·run·ner \'rōd-ˌrən-ər\ *n* : a swift-running long-tailed bird of the southwestern U.S.

roadrunner
(about 22 in. long)

road·side \'rōd-ˌsīd\ *n* : the strip of land along a road : the side of a road — **roadside** *adj*

road·stead \'rōd-ˌsted\ *n* : ROAD 1

road·ster \'rōd-stər\ *n* **1** : a light horse for driving or riding **2** : an open automobile with one cross seat

road·way \'rōd-ˌwā\ *n* **1 a** : the strip of land over which a road passes **b** : ROAD; *esp* : ROADBED 2 **2** : a railroad right-of-way **3** : the part of a bridge used by vehicles

roam \'rōm\ *vb* : to go or go over from place to place aimlessly : WANDER ⟨*roam* the hills⟩ ⟨cattle *roaming* in search of water⟩ — **roam·er** *n*

[1]**roan** \'rōn\ *adj* : having basic color (as black, red, or brown) mixed with white hairs ⟨*roan* horse⟩

[2]**roan** *n* **1** : an animal (as a horse) with a roan coat **2** : the color of a roan horse

[1]**roar** \'rō(ə)r, 'rȯ(ə)r\ *vb* **1** : to utter or emit a loud prolonged sound **2** : to laugh loudly — **roar·er** \'rōr-ər, 'rȯr-\ *n*

[2]**roar** *n* **1 a** : the deep cry of a wild beast **b** : a loud deep cry (as of pain or anger) **2** : a loud continuous confused sound ⟨the *roar* of the crowd⟩

roar·ing \'rōr-ing, 'rȯr-\ *adj* : THRIVING, BOOMING ⟨a *roaring* fire⟩ ⟨a *roaring* frontier town⟩

[1]**roast** \'rōst\ *vb* **1** : to cook by exposing to dry heat (as in an oven or before a fire) **2** : to dry and parch by exposure to heat ⟨*roast* coffee⟩ ⟨*roast* chestnuts⟩

[2]**roast** *n* **1** : a piece of meat roasted or suitable for roasting **2** : an outing at which food is roasted (as before as open fire)

[3]**roast** *adj* : ROASTED ⟨*roast* beef⟩

roast·er \'rō-stər\ *n* **1** : one that roasts; *esp* : a usu. covered pan for roasting meat **2** : something (as a chicken) of a size or kind suitable for roasting

rob \'räb\ *vb* **robbed; rob·bing** **1 a** : to take something away from a person or place by force, threat, stealth, or trickery ⟨*rob* a store⟩ ⟨*rob* a safe⟩ ⟨*rob* an old woman⟩ **b** : to commit robbery : STEAL **2 a** : to deprive of something due, expected, or desired **b** : to withhold unjustly or injuriously — **rob·ber** *n* — **rob·bery** \'räb-(ə-)rē\ *n*

robber fly *n* : any of various predacious flies that usu. are covered with coarse bristly hair and have a slender body and long legs

[1]**robe** \'rōb\ *n* **1 a** : a long loose garment used for ceremonial occasions or as a symbol of office or profession **b** : a loose garment replacing outer garments for informal wear **2** : a covering or wrap for the lower body

[2]**robe** *vb* **1** : to clothe, invest, or cover with or as if with a robe **2** : to put on a robe

rob·in \'räb-ən\ *n* **1** : a small European thrush with yellowish red throat and breast **2** : a large No. American thrush with grayish upperparts, streaked throat, and chiefly dull reddish breast and underparts

ro·bot \'rō-ˌbät\ *n* [from Czech, from *robota* "forced labor"] **1 a** : a mechanism made in human form that performs mechanically complex acts (as walking or talking) like those of a person **b :** an efficient, insensitive, often brutalized person **2 :** an automatic apparatus that performs functions ordinarily ascribed to human beings or operates with what appears to be almost human intelligence esp. in guidance or control of other mechanisms ⟨a *robot* factory⟩

ro·bust \rō-'bəst, 'rō-ˌ\ *adj* **1 :** being strong and vigorously healthy **:** STURDY **2 :** requiring strength or vigor ⟨*robust* work⟩ — **ro·bust·ly** *adv* — **ro·bust·ness** *n*

roc \'räk\ *n* **:** a fabulous bird of oriental folklore so huge that it carries off elephants to feed its young

Ro·chelle salt \rō-ˌshel-\ *n* **:** a hydrated crystalline salt of potassium and sodium that is a mild purgative

[1]**rock** \'räk\ *vb* **1 :** to move back and forth as in a cradle **2 a :** to sway or cause to sway back and forth **b** (1) **:** DAZE, STUN (2) **:** DISTURB, UPSET

[2]**rock** *n* **1 :** a rocking movement **2 :** ROCK 'N' ROLL

[3]**rock** *n* **1 :** a large mass of stone often forming a cliff, promontory, or peak **2 :** consolidated or unconsolidated solid mineral matter **3 :** something (as a support or refuge) like a rock in firmness — **on the rocks 1 :** in or into a state of destruction or wreckage ⟨a marriage *on the rocks*⟩ **2 :** on ice cubes ⟨bourbon *on the rocks*⟩

rock·bound \'räk-'bau̇nd\ *adj* **:** fringed, surrounded, or covered with rocks

rock crystal *n* **:** transparent quartz

rock·er \'räk-ər\ *n* **1 a :** a curving piece of wood or metal on which an object (as a cradle) rocks **b :** a structure or device (as a chair) that rocks upon rockers **2 :** a mechanism that works with a rocking motion

[1]**rock·et** \'räk-ət\ *n* [from Italian *rocchetta*, from the diminutive of *rocca* "distaff"] **1 :** a firework that is shot into the air by rearward discharge of gases liberated by combustion and there bursts into a shower of sparks **2 :** a jet engine that carries its own oxygen for burning the fuel and is therefore able to run without the oxygen of the air — called also *rocket engine* **3 :** a rocket-propelled object (as a missile or bomb)

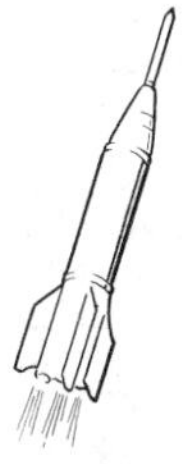

rocket 3

[2]**rocket** *vb* **1 :** to convey by means of a rocket ⟨*rocket* a satellite into orbit⟩ **2 :** to rise up swiftly, spectacularly, and with force **3 :** to travel rapidly in or as if in a rocket

rock·et·ry \'räk-ə-trē\ *n* **:** the study of, experimentation with, or use of rockets

rocket ship *n* **:** a rocket-propelled spaceship

rock garden *n* **:** a garden laid out among rocks or decorated with rocks

rocking chair *n* **:** a chair mounted on rockers

rocking horse *n* **:** a toy horse mounted on rockers

rock lobster *n* **:** SPINY LOBSTER

rock 'n' roll \ˌräk-ən-'rōl\ *n* **:** popular music characterized by a fast tempo, strong beat, and much repetition; *also* **:** improvisational dancing associated with this music

rock–ribbed \'räk-'ribd\ *adj* **1 :** ROCKY **2 :** firmly inflexible (as in doctrine)

rock salt *n* **:** common salt in large crystals or masses

rock·weed \'räk-ˌwēd\ *n* **:** FUCUS

rock wool *n* **:** a fibrous material resembling wool made by blowing a jet of steam through molten rock or through slag and used chiefly for heat and sound insulation

[1]**rocky** \'räk-ē\ *adj* **rock·i·er; -est 1 :** abounding in or consisting of rocks **2 :** difficult to impress or affect — **rock·i·ness** *n*

[2]**rocky** *adj* **rock·i·er; -est 1 :** UNSTABLE, WOBBLY **2 :** physically upset **:** UNWELL — **rock·i·ness** *n*

Rocky Mountain sheep *n* **:** BIGHORN

Rocky Mountain spotted fever *n* **:** an acute rickettsial disease marked by chills, fever, exhaustion, pains in muscles and joints, and a red to purple eruption and transmitted by the bite of a tick

ro·co·co \rə-'kō-kō\ *adj* **:** of or relating to a style of artistic expression common in the 18th century marked by fanciful curved forms — **rococo** *n*

rod \'räd\ *n* **1 a :** a straight slender stick or bar ⟨a curtain *rod*⟩ **b :** a pole with a line and usu. a reel attached for fishing **2 a :** a unit of length — see MEASURE table **b :** a square rod **3 :** any of the rod-shaped sensory bodies in the retina responsive to faint light **4** *slang* **:** PISTOL — **rod·less** \-ləs\ *adj* — **rod·like** \-ˌlīk\ *adj*

rode *past of* RIDE

ro·dent \'rōd-ənt\ *n* [from Latin *rodent-*, stem of *rodens* "one that gnaws", from present participle of *rodere* "to gnaw"] **:** any of an order of relatively small gnawing mammals (as mice, squirrels, or beavers) — compare LAGOMORPH — **rodent** *adj*

ro·deo \'rōd-ē-ˌō, rə-'dā-ō\ *n, pl* **-de·os** [from Spanish, from *rodear* "to surround", from Latin *rota* "wheel"] **1 :** ROUNDUP 1 **2 :** an exhibition featuring cowboy skills (as riding and roping)

rod·o·mon·tade \ˌräd-ə-mən-'tād, ˌrōd-\ *n* **:** vain boasting or bluster — **rodomontade** *adj*

[1]**roe** \'rō\ *n, pl* **roe** *or* **roes :** DOE

[2]**roe** *n* **:** the eggs of a fish esp. while still bound together in a membrane

roe·buck \'rō-ˌbək\ *n, pl* **roebuck** *or* **roebucks :** ROE DEER; *esp* **:** the male roe deer

roe deer *n* **:** a small active deer of Europe and Asia that has erect antlers forked at the tip and is reddish brown in summer and grayish in winter

roe deer
(about 2½ ft. at shoulder)

roent·gen ray \ˌrent-gən-, ˌrənt-, -jən-\ *n, often cap 1st R* **:** X RAY

Ro·ga·tion Day \rō-'gā-shən\ *n* **:** one of the days of prayer esp. for the harvest observed on the three days before Ascension Day and by Roman Catholics also on April 25

rog·er \'räj-ər\ *interj* — used esp. in radio and signaling to indicate that a message has been received and understood

[1]**rogue** \'rōg\ *n* **1 a :** an idle, wandering, or disorderly person (as a vagabond) **b :** a worthless, dishonest, or unprincipled person **:** KNAVE, SCOUNDREL **c :** a pleasantly mischievous individual **:** SCAMP **2 :** a vicious or lazy animal — **rogu·ish** \'rō-gish\ *adj* — **rogu·ish·ly** *adv* — **rogu·ish·ness** *n*

[2]**rogue** *adj* **:** being vicious, destructive, and solitary ⟨*rogue* elephants⟩

rogu·ery \'rō-g(ə-)rē\ *n, pl* **-er·ies :** the practices of a rogue: as **a :** CHEATING, FRAUD **b :** playful trickery **:** MISCHIEVOUSNESS

rogues' gallery *n* **:** a file kept by the police of photographs of persons arrested as criminals

roil \ˈrȯil, *2 is also* ˈrīl\ *vb* **1 :** to make cloudy or muddy by stirring up sediment ⟨*roil* the water of a brook⟩ **2 :** to rouse the temper of : stir up : VEX, ANGER

roily \ˈrȯi-lē\ *adj* **roil·i·er; -est 1 :** full of sediment or dregs : MUDDY **2 :** TURBULENT

rois·ter \ˈrȯi-stər\ *vb* **rois·tered; rois·ter·ing** \-st(ə-)riŋ\ : to engage in noisy revelry : CAROUSE — **rois·ter·er** \-stər-ər\ *n*

role *also* **rôle** \ˈrōl\ *n* [from French, "actor's part", literally "roll", from Latin *rotula*, diminutive of *rota* "wheel"; so called from the roll on which the actor's part was written] **1 a :** a character assigned or assumed **b :** a part played by an actor or singer ⟨a starring *role*⟩ **2 :** FUNCTION ⟨the *role* of enzymes in digestion⟩

1**roll** \ˈrōl\ *n* **1 a :** a written document that may be rolled up : SCROLL **b :** an official list esp. of members of a body (as a legislative body) ⟨call the *roll*⟩ **2 a :** a quantity (as of fabric or paper) rolled up to form a single package **b :** a food preparation rolled up for cooking or serving; *esp* : a small piece of baked bread dough **c :** paper money folded or rolled

2**roll** *vb* **1 a :** to move by turning over and over on a surface without sliding **b :** to turn over and over **c :** to move about or as if about an axis or point ⟨clouds *rolling* by⟩ **2 a :** to put a wrapping around **b :** to form into a ball or roll **3 :** to make smooth, even, or compact with or as if with a roller **4 a :** to move on rollers or wheels **b :** to begin operating or moving ⟨the new shop finally got *rolling*⟩ **5 a :** to sound with a full reverberating tone or with a continuous beating sound ⟨*roll* a drum⟩ ⟨thunder *rolled*⟩ **b :** to utter with a trill ⟨*rolled* his *r*'s⟩ **6 :** to luxuriate in an abundant supply ⟨*rolling* in money⟩ **7 :** ELAPSE, PASS ⟨time *rolled* by⟩ **8 :** to flow in a continuous stream ⟨money was *rolling* in⟩ **9 :** to have a wavy surface ⟨a *rolling* prairie⟩ **10 :** to move with a side-to-side sway : ROCK ⟨the ship heaved and *rolled*⟩

3**roll** *n* **1 :** a heavy echoing sound or a series of such sounds ⟨a drum *roll*⟩ **2 :** a rolling movement or an action or process involving such movement ⟨a *roll* of the dice⟩; *esp* : a swaying or side-to-side movement

roll bar *n* : an overhead metal bar in an automobile that is designed to protect riders in case of a turnover

roll call *n* : the action of calling off a list of names (as for checking attendance); *also* : a time for a roll call to be made

1**roll·er** \ˈrō-lər\ *n* **1 a :** a revolving cylinder over or on which something is moved or which is used to press, shape, or smooth something **b :** a rod on which something (as a map) is rolled up **c :** a small wheel (as of a roller skate) **2 :** a long heavy wave on the sea **3 :** a tumbler pigeon

2**rol·ler** \ˈrō-lər\ *n* : a canary with a soft trilling song

roller bearing *n* : a bearing in which a revolving part turns on rollers held in a circular frame or cage

roll·er coast·er \ˈrō-lər-ˌkō-stər, ˈrō-lē-ˌkō-\ *n* : an elevated railway (as in an amusement park) constructed with sharp curves and steep inclines on which cars roll

ə abut   ər further   a back   ā bake
ä cot, cart   au̇ out   ch chin   e less   ē easy
g gift   i trip   ī life   j joke   ŋ sing   ō flow
ȯ flaw   ȯi coin   th thin   t͟h this   ü loot
u̇ foot   y yet   yü few   yu̇ furious   zh vision

roller skate *n* : a skate that has wheels instead of a runner — **roller–skate** *vb*

rol·lick \ˈräl-ik\ *vb* : to move or behave in a carefree joyous manner : FROLIC — **rollick** *n* — **rol·lick·ing** *adj*

roller skates

rolling pin *n* : a cylinder (as of wood) for rolling out dough

rolling stock *n* : wheeled vehicles owned or used by a railroad or motor carrier

ro·ly–po·ly \ˌrō-lē-ˈpō-lē\ *n, pl* **-lies 1 :** a pudding made of rolled-out dough spread with a filling, rolled up into a cylinder shape, and baked or steamed **2 :** a short stout person or thing — **roly–poly** *adj*

Rom *abbr* **1** Roman **2** Romania **3** Romanian

1**Ro·man** \ˈrō-mən\ *n* **1 a :** a native or resident of Rome **b :** a citizen of the Roman Empire **2 :** ROMAN CATHOLIC — often taken to be offensive **3** *not cap* : roman letters or type

2**Roman** *adj* **1 :** of or relating to ancient or modern Rome, the people of Rome, or the empire of which Rome was the original capital ⟨*Roman* law⟩ **2 :** LATIN **3** *not cap* : UPRIGHT — used of numbers and letters whose capital forms are modeled on ancient Roman inscriptions **4 :** of or relating to the see of Rome or the Roman Catholic Church

Roman candle *n* : a cylindrical firework that discharges at intervals balls or stars of fire

Roman Catholic *adj* : of or relating to the body of Christians having a hierarchy under the pope, a liturgy centered in the Mass, and a body of dogma formulated by the church as the infallible interpreter of revealed truth — **Roman Catholic** *n* — **Roman Catholicism** *n*

1**ro·mance** \rō-ˈman(t)s, ˈrō-ˌ\ *n* **1 a :** a medieval tale based on legend, chivalric love and adventure, and the supernatural **b :** an adventure novel **c :** a love story **2 :** a love affair **3 :** the adventurous or glamorous attractiveness of something ⟨the *romance* of the old West⟩

2**romance** *vb* **1 :** to exaggerate or invent detail or incident **2 a :** to entertain romantic thoughts or ideas **b :** to carry on a love affair with

Ro·mance \rō-ˈman(t)s, ˈrō-ˌ\ *adj* : of, relating to, or being the languages (as French, Italian, or Spanish) developed from Latin

Ro·ma·ni·an \ru̇-ˈmā-nē-ən, rō-\ *n* **1 :** a native or inhabitant of Romania **2 :** the Romance language of the Romanians — **Romanian** *adj*

roman numeral *n, often cap R* : a numeral in a system of notation based on the ancient Roman system — see NUMBER table

Ro·mans \ˈrō-mənz\ *n* — see BIBLE table

1**ro·man·tic** \rō-ˈmant-ik\ *adj* **1 a :** of, relating to, or resembling a romance ⟨*romantic* writing⟩ **b :** not factual : IMAGINARY ⟨a too *romantic* report of his adventure⟩ **2 a :** IMPRACTICAL, UNREALISTIC **b** *often cap* : of, relating to, or exhibiting romanticism **3 :** having a strong emotional or imaginative appeal or association ⟨a *romantic* spot⟩ **4 :** of, relating to, or associated with love ⟨*romantic* episodes in her past⟩ — **ro·man·ti·cal·ly** \-i-k(ə-)lē\ *adv*

2**romantic** *n* : a romantic person, trait, or component

ro·man·ti·cism \rō-ˈmant-ə-ˌsiz-əm\ *n* **1 :** the quality or state of being romantic **2** *often cap* : a literary, artistic, and philosophical movement marked chiefly by an emphasis on the imagination and emotions — **ro·man·ti·cist** \-səst\ *n, often cap*

ro·man·ti·cize \rō-ˈmant-ə-ˌsīz\ *vb* **1** : to make romantic : present romantically **2** : to hold romantic ideas — **ro·man·ti·ci·za·tion** \-ˌmant-ə-sə-ˈzā-shən\ *n*

Rom·a·ny \ˈräm-ə-nē, ˈrō-mə-\ *n* **1** : GYPSY 1 **2** : the Indic language of the Gypsies — **Romany** *adj*

[1]**romp** \ˈrämp\ *n* **1** : one that romps; *esp* : a romping girl or woman **2** : boisterous play : FROLIC

[2]**romp** *vb* : to play in a boisterous manner : FROLIC

romp·er \ˈräm-pər\ *n* **1** : one that romps **2** : a child's one-piece garment with the lower part shaped like bloomers — usu. used in pl.

rood \ˈrüd\ *n* **1** : CROSS, CRUCIFIX **2** : any of various units of land area; *esp* : a British unit equal to ¼ acre

[1]**roof** \ˈrüf, ˈru̇f\ *n, pl* **roofs** \ˈrüfs, ˈru̇fs, ˈrüvz, ˈru̇vz\ **1** : the upper covering part of a building **2** : something (as the vaulted upper boundary of the mouth) resembling a roof in form, position, or function — **roofed** \ˈrüft, ˈru̇ft\ *adj* — **roof·less** \ˈrüf-ləs, ˈru̇f-\ *adj* — **roof·like** \-ˌlīk\ *adj*

[2]**roof** *vb* **1** : to cover with or as if with a roof **2** : to provide a roof with a protective exterior — **roof·er** *n*

roof·ing *n* : material for a roof

roof·top \ˈrüf-ˌtäp, ˈru̇f-\ *n* : ROOF; *esp* : the outer surface of a usu. flat roof ⟨sunning themselves on the *rooftop*⟩

roof·tree \-ˌtrē\ *n* : RIDGEPOLE

[1]**rook** \ˈru̇k\ *n* : a common Old World gregarious bird about the size and color of the related American crow

[2]**rook** *vb* : to defraud by cheating or swindling

[3]**rook** *n* [from medieval French *roc*, from Arabic *rukhkh*, from Persian *rukh*] : a chess piece that can move parallel to the sides of the board across any number of unoccupied squares — called also *castle*

rook·ery \ˈru̇k-ə-rē\ *n, pl* **-er·ies** **1** : the breeding place of a colony of rooks or of some other birds or mammals; *also* : the colony itself **2** : a crowded dilapidated tenement or group of dwellings : WARREN

rook·ie \ˈru̇k-ē\ *n* : RECRUIT, BEGINNER

[1]**room** \ˈrüm, ˈru̇m\ *n* **1** : unoccupied area : SPACE ⟨*room* to turn the car⟩ **2** : a partitioned part of the inside of a building **3** : the people in a room **4** *pl* : LODGINGS, APARTMENT **5** : opportunity or occasion for something : CHANCE ⟨*room* for improvement⟩

[2]**room** *vb* : to provide with or occupy lodgings

room·er \ˈrü-mər, ˈru̇m-ər\ *n* : LODGER

room·ful \ˈrüm-ˌfu̇l, ˈru̇m-\ *n, pl* **roomfuls** \-ˌfu̇lz\ *or* **rooms·ful** \ˈrümz-ˌfu̇l, ˈru̇mz-\ **1** : as much or as many as a room will hold **2** : the persons or objects in a room

rooming house *n* : a house where rooms are provided and let

room·mate \ˈrüm-ˌmāt, ˈru̇m-\ *n* : one of two or more persons occupying the same room

roomy \ˈrü-mē, ˈru̇m-ē\ *adj* **room·i·er**; **-est** : having plenty of room : SPACIOUS — **room·i·ness** *n*

[1]**roost** \ˈrüst\ *n* **1** : PERCH **2** : a place where birds customarily roost

[2]**roost** *vb* : to settle on or as if on a roost : PERCH

roost·er \ˈrü-stər\ *n* : an adult male domestic fowl : an adult male bird

[1]**root** \ˈrüt, ˈru̇t\ *n* **1 a** : the usu. underground part of a seed plant body that absorbs and stores substances necessary to the plant's growth and often serves to anchor and support it **b** : an underground plant part esp. when fleshy and edible **2 a** : the part of a tooth within the socket **b** : the enlarged basal part of a hair within the skin **c** : the basal or central part of a bodily structure or that by which it is attached ⟨nerve *roots*⟩ ⟨the *root* of a fingernail⟩ **3 a** : an original cause or quality : SOURCE ⟨the *roots* of violence⟩ **b** : an underlying support or base : BASIS ⟨the *roots* of the mountains⟩ **c** : the essential core : HEART ⟨get to the *root* of the matter⟩ **4 a** : a number that when taken as a factor an indicated number of times gives a specified number ⟨2 is a 4th *root* of 16⟩ **b** : a solution of a polynomial equation in one unknown **5** : a word or part of a word from which other words are derived by adding a prefix or suffix — **root·ed** \-əd\ *adj* — **root·less** \-ləs\ *adj* — **root·like** \-ˌlīk\ *adj*

[2]**root** *vb* **1 a** : to form or enable to form roots **b** : to fix or become fixed by or as if by roots : take root **2** : to remove altogether often by force ⟨*root* out dissenters⟩

[3]**root** *vb* **1** : to turn up or dig in the earth with the snout **2** : to poke or dig about

[4]**root** \ˈrüt\ *vb* **1** : to applaud noisily : CHEER **2** : to encourage or lend support to someone or something ⟨*rooted* for the reform candidate⟩ — **root·er** *n*

root beer *n* : a sweetened effervescent or carbonated beverage flavored with extracts of roots and herbs

root cap *n* : a protective cap of cells that forms a terminal cover in most root tips

root hair *n* : one of the threadlike outgrowths near the tip of a rootlet that function in absorption of water and minerals

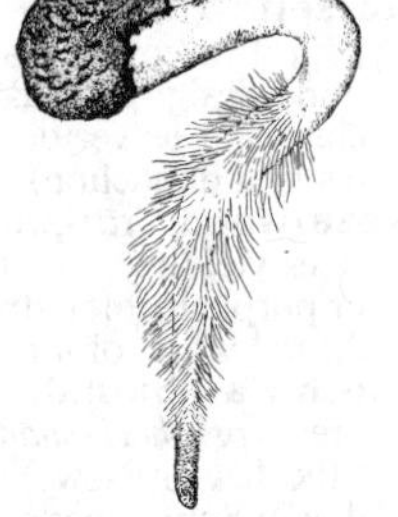

root hairs on bean rootlet (magnified 2 times)

root·let \ˈrüt-lət, ˈru̇t-\ *n* : a small root

root·stock \-ˌstäk\ *n* : an underground part of a plant resembling a rhizome

[1]**rope** \ˈrōp\ *n* **1 a** : a large stout cord of strands (as of fiber or wire) twisted or braided together **b** : a length of material (as rope or rawhide) suitable for a use; *esp* : LARIAT **c** : a hangman's noose **2** : a row or string consisting of things united by or as if by braiding, twining, or threading ⟨a *rope* of daisies⟩

[2]**rope** *vb* **1 a** : to bind, fasten, or tie with a rope or cord **b** : to set off or divide by a rope ⟨*rope* off the street⟩ **c** : LASSO **2** : to draw as if with a rope : LURE **3** : to take the form of or twist in the manner of rope — **rop·er** *n*

rope·walk \-ˌwȯk\ *n* : a place where rope is made

rope·walk·er \-ˌwȯ-kər\ *n* : an acrobat that walks on a rope high in the air

ropy \ˈrō-pē\ *adj* **rop·i·er**; **-est** **1** : capable of being drawn into a sticky thread : VISCOUS **2** : resembling rope : STRINGY, SINEWY ⟨*ropy* muscles⟩ — **rop·i·ness** *n*

Roque·fort \ˈrōk-fərt\ *trademark* — used for a cheese made in France of ewe's milk and ripened in caves by a greenish blue mold

ro·sa·ry \ˈrōz-(ə-)rē\ *n, pl* **-ries** **1** : a string of beads used in counting prayers esp. of the Roman Catholic rosary **2** *often cap* : a Roman Catholic devotion consisting of meditation on usu. five sacred mysteries during recitation of five decades of Hail Marys of which each is preceded by the Lord's Prayer and followed by the Gloria Patri

[1]**rose** *past of* RISE

R

[2]**rose** \'rōz\ *n* **1 a :** any of a genus of usu. prickly trailing or shrubby woody plants with pinnate leaves and showy often fragrant flowers having five petals in the wild state but being often double in cultivation **b :** the flower of a rose **2 :** a variable color averaging a moderate purplish red — **rose·like** \-ˌlīk\ *adj*

rose 1b

[3]**rose** *adj* **1 :** of, relating to, resembling, or used for the rose **2 :** of the color rose

ro·se·ate \'rō-zē-ət, -zē-ˌāt\ *adj* **1 :** resembling a rose esp. in color ⟨*roseate* cheeks⟩ **2 :** overly optimistic : viewed favorably ⟨a *roseate* outlook on life⟩ — **ro·se·ate·ly** *adv*

rose–breast·ed grosbeak \ˌrōz-ˌbres-təd-\ *n* **:** a grosbeak of eastern No. America that in the male is chiefly black and white with the breast and lining of the wings rose red and in the female is a streaky grayish brown with the lining of the wings orange

rose·bush \'rōz-ˌbu̇sh\ *n* **:** a shrubby rose

rose–col·ored \'rōz-ˌkəl-ərd\ *adj* **1 :** having a rose color **2 :** OPTIMISTIC

rose mallow *n* **:** a usu. rosy-flowered hibiscus or hollyhock

rose·mary \'rōz-ˌmer-ē\ *n* [an alteration of Middle English *rosmarine*, from Latin *ros marinus*, meaning literally "dew of the sea"] **:** a fragrant shrubby mint used in cookery and in perfumery

ro·sette \rō-'zet\ *n* **1 :** an ornament (as of cloth or paper) resembling a rose **2 :** a disk of foliage or a floral design used as a decorative motif **3 :** a circular cluster of leaves developed on a plant either basally (as in a dandelion) or at the apex (as in palms)

rose·wood \'rōz-ˌwu̇d\ *n* **1 :** any of various tropical trees yielding valuable cabinet woods of a dark red or purplish color streaked and variegated with black **2 :** the wood of a rosewood

Rosh Ha·sha·nah \ˌrōsh-(h)ə-'shō-nə\ *n* [from Hebrew *rōsh hash-shānāh*, literally "head of the year"] **:** the Jewish New Year observed as a religious holiday in September or October

[1]**ros·in** \'räz-ən, 'ro̊z-\ *n* **:** a translucent amber-colored to almost black brittle resin obtained esp. from pine trees and used in making varnish, paper size, soap, and soldering flux and on violin bows — **ros·in·ous** \-ə-nəs\ *adj*

[2]**rosin** *vb* **:** to rub (as the bow of a violin) with rosin

ros·ter \'räs-tər\ *n* **:** a list usu. of personnel **:** ROLL; *esp* **:** one assigning duties

ros·trum \'räs-trəm\ *n, pl* **rostrums** *or* **ros·tra** \-trə\ [from Latin *Rostra*, the name of the speakers' platform in the ancient Roman forum, from the plural of *rostrum* "beak"; so called because the platform was decorated with the beaks of captured warships] **1 :** a stage or platform for public speaking **2 :** a bodily part or process (as a snout) suggesting a bird's bill — **ros·tral** \-trəl\ *adj* — **ros·trate** \-ˌtrāt\ *adj*

rosy \'rō-zē\ *adj* **ros·i·er; -est 1 a :** of the color rose **b :** having a rosy complexion **:** BLOOMING **c :** BLUSHING **2 :** characterized by or tending to promote optimism ⟨*rosy* prospects⟩ — **ros·i·ly** \-zə-lē\ *adv* — **ros·i·ness** \-zē-nəs\ *n*

[1]**rot** \'rät\ *vb* **rot·ted; rot·ting 1 a :** to undergo decomposition from the action of bacteria or fungi **b :** to become unsound or weak (as from use or chemical action) **2 a :** to go to ruin **:** DETERIORATE **b :** to become morally corrupt **:** DEGENERATE **3 :** to cause to decompose or deteriorate with rot

[2]**rot** *n* **1 a :** the process of rotting **:** the state of being rotten **b :** something rotten or rotting **2 a :** a disease of plants or animals marked by the breaking down of tissue **b :** an area of broken-down tissue ⟨pruned the *rot* from the tree trunk⟩ **3 :** NONSENSE — often used interjectionally

[1]**ro·ta·ry** \'rōt-ə-rē\ *adj* **1 a :** turning on an axis like a wheel ⟨a *rotary* blade⟩ **b :** taking place about an axis ⟨*rotary* motion⟩ **2 :** having a blade that turns on an axis ⟨a *rotary* lawn mower⟩ **3 :** characterized by rotation

[2]**rotary** *n, pl* **-ries 1 :** a rotary machine **2 :** a road junction formed around a central circle about which traffic moves in one direction only

ro·tate \'rō-ˌtāt\ *vb* **1 :** to turn or cause to turn about an axis or a center **:** REVOLVE ⟨the earth *rotates*⟩ **2 a :** to do or cause to do something in turn ⟨*rotate* on the night shift⟩ **b :** to pass in a series ⟨the seasons *rotate*⟩ **3 :** to cause to grow in rotation ⟨*rotate* alfalfa and corn⟩ — **ro·tat·a·ble** \-ˌtāt-ə-bəl\ *adj*

syn ROTATE, ALTERNATE can mean to succeed or cause to succeed each other in turn. ROTATE applies to two or more persons or things and implies a series of indefinite length ⟨all the soldiers in the company work in the kitchen on a *rotating* basis⟩; ALTERNATE applies to only two and does not so strongly imply continuity ⟨the weather *alternated* between sunshine and storms⟩

ro·ta·tion \rō-'tā-shən\ *n* **1 a :** the act of rotating esp. on or as if on an axis **b :** one complete turn **2 :** return or succession in a series (as of different successive crops on one field) — **ro·ta·tion·al** \-sh(ə-)nəl\ *adj*

ro·ta·tor \'rō-ˌtāt-ər\ *n* **:** one that rotates or causes rotation

ro·ta·to·ry \'rōt-ə-ˌtōr-ē, -ˌto̊r-\ *adj* **1 :** of, relating to, or producing rotation **2 :** occurring in rotation

ROTC *abbr* Reserve Officers' Training Corps

rote \'rōt\ *n* **1 :** the use of memory usu. with little intelligence ⟨learn by *rote*⟩ **2 :** routine or repetition carried out mechanically or without understanding

ro·ti·fer \'rōt-ə-fər\ *n* **:** any of a class of minute aquatic animals having at one end a disk with circles of cilia which in motion look like revolving wheels

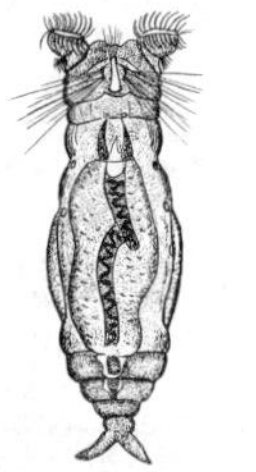

rotifer (magnified 100 times)

ro·tis·ser·ie \rō-'tis-(ə-)rē\ *n* **1 :** a restaurant specializing in broiled and barbecued meats **2 :** an appliance fitted with a spit on which food is rotated before or over a source of heat

ro·tor \'rōt-ər\ *n* **1 :** a part that revolves in a stationary part (as in an electrical machine) **2 :** a complete system of more or less horizontal rotating blades that supplies all or a major part of the force supporting an aircraft in flight ⟨the *rotor* of a helicopter⟩

rot·ten \'rät-ən\ *adj* **1 :** having rotted **:** PUTRID, UNSOUND ⟨*rotten* wood⟩ **2 :** morally corrupt **3 :** extremely unpleasant or inferior — **rot·ten·ly** *adv* — **rot·ten·ness** \-ən-(n)əs\ *n*

rot·ten·stone \'rät-ən-ˌstōn\ *n* : a decomposed siliceous limestone used for polishing
ro·tund \rō-'tənd\ *adj* **1** : marked by roundness : ROUNDED **2** : FULL, SONOROUS ⟨*rotund* voices⟩ **3** : PLUMP, CHUBBY ⟨a *rotund* little man⟩ — **ro·tun·di·ty** \rō-'tən-dət-ē\ *n* — **ro·tund·ly** \rō-'tən-dlē\ *adv* — **ro·tund·ness** \rō-'tən(d)-nəs\ *n*
ro·tun·da \rō-'tən-də\ *or* **ro·ton·da** \-'tän-\ *n* **1** : a round building; *esp* : one covered by a dome **2 a** : a large round room **b** : a large central area (as in a hotel)
rou·ble *var of* RUBLE
roué \rü-'ā\ *n* : a man devoted to a life of sensual pleasure : DEBAUCHEE, RAKE
¹rouge \'rüzh, *esp South* 'rüj\ *n* [from French, from the adjective meaning "red"] **1** : any of various cosmetics to color the cheeks or lips red **2** : a red powder consisting essentially of an oxide of iron used in polishing glass, metal, or gems and as a pigment
²rouge *vb* **1** : to apply rouge to **2** : to use rouge
¹rough \'rəf\ *adj* **1 a** : having an uneven surface : not smooth **b** : covered with or made up of coarse and often shaggy hair or bristles ⟨a *rough*-coated terrier⟩ ⟨a *rough* unshaven face⟩ **2 a** : difficult to travel over or through : STORMY, TEMPESTUOUS ⟨a *rough* sea⟩ **b** : characterized by harshness, violence, or force ⟨*rough* treatment⟩ **3 a** : harsh to the ear **b** : crude in style or expression **c** : crude in behavior : UNCOUTH **4** : marked by incompleteness or inexactness ⟨a *rough* draft⟩ ⟨*rough* estimate⟩ — **rough·ish** \'rəf-ish\ *adj* — **rough·ly** *adv* — **rough·ness** *n*
²rough *n* **1** : uneven ground covered with high grass, brush, and stones; *esp* : such ground bordering a golf fairway **2 a** : something in a crude, unfinished, or preliminary state **b** : broad outline : general terms ⟨problems discussed in the *rough*⟩ **3** : RUFFIAN, TOUGH
³rough *vb* **1** : ROUGHEN **2** : MANHANDLE, BEAT ⟨*roughed* up by hoodlums⟩ **3** : to shape, make, or indicate in a rough or preliminary way ⟨*rough* out a plan⟩ — **rough it** : to live without modern conveniences
rough·age \'rəf-ij\ *n* : coarse bulky food (as bran) having much indigestible matter
¹rough·cast \'rəf-ˌkast\ *n* : a rough model
²roughcast *vb* **-cast**; **-cast·ing** : to shape or form roughly
rough·dry \'rəf-'drī\ *vb* : to dry laundry without smoothing or ironing — **roughdry** *adj*
rough·en \'rəf-ən\ *vb* **rough·ened**; **rough·en·ing** \-(ə-)ning\ : to make or become rough
rough·hew \'rəf-'hyü\ *vb* **-hewed**; **-hewed** *or* **-hewn** \-'hyün\; **-hew·ing** **1** : to hew (as timber) coarsely without smoothing or finishing **2** : to form crudely : ROUGHCAST
rough·house \'rəf-ˌhaüs\ *n* : violence or rough boisterous play esp. among occupants of a room — **rough·house** \-ˌhaüs, -ˌhaüz\ *vb*
rough·neck \'rəf-ˌnek\ *n* : a rough or uncouth person; *esp* : ROWDY, TOUGH
rough·rid·er \'rəf-'rīd-ər\ *n* : one who breaks horses to the saddle or who rides untrained horses
rough·shod \-'shäd\ *adj* : shod with calked shoes ⟨a *roughshod* horse⟩
rou·lette \rü-'let\ *n* **1** : a gambling game in which players bet on which compartment of a revolving wheel a small ball will come to rest in **2** : a toothed wheel or disk used to make a series of dots or small holes — **roulette** *vb*
Rou·ma·ni·an \rü-'mā-nē-ən\ *var of* ROMANIAN
¹round \'raünd\ *adj* [from Old French *roont*, from Latin *rotundus*, a derivative of *rota* "wheel"] **1 a** : SPHERICAL, CIRCULAR **b** : CYLINDRICAL **c** : having a curved outline **2** : PLUMP, SHAPELY **3 a** : COMPLETE, FULL ⟨a *round* dozen⟩ ⟨a *round* ton⟩ **b** : approximately correct; *esp* : exact only to a specific decimal ⟨3.1416 is a *round* number for the value of π⟩ **c** : AMPLE, LARGE ⟨a good *round* sum⟩ **4** : done or made by going through a series of points with a return to the starting point ⟨a *round* trip⟩ — **round·ish** \'raün-dish\ *adj* — **round·ly** *adv* — **round·ness** \'raün(d)-nəs\ *n*
²round *adv* : AROUND
³round \(ˈ)raünd\ *prep* **1** : AROUND **2** : all during : THROUGHOUT ⟨*round* the year⟩
⁴round \'raünd\ *n* **1** : something (as a circle, globe, or ring) that is round **2** : ROUND DANCE 1 **3** : a vocal composition in which three or four voices follow each other around and sing the same melody and words **4** : a rung of a ladder or a chair **5** : a circling path or course **6** : a route or circuit habitually covered : a series of customary calls or stops ⟨the watchman made his *rounds*⟩ **7** : a drink apiece served at one time to each person in a group ⟨a *round* of cocktails⟩ **8** : a sequence of recurring routine or repetitive actions or events ⟨a *round* of parties⟩ **9 a** : one shot fired by a weapon or by each man in a military unit **b** : one unit of ammunition **10** : a unit of play in a contest or game ⟨a *round* of golf⟩ ⟨a boxing match of 15 *rounds*⟩ **11** : an outburst of applause **12** : a cut of beef esp. between the rump and the lower leg **13** : a rounded or curved part — **in the round** **1** : in full sculptured form unattached to a background **2** : with an inclusive or comprehensive view or representation **3** : with a center stage surrounded by an audience on all sides ⟨theater *in the round*⟩
⁵round \'raünd\ *vb* **1 a** : to make round **b** : to become round, plump, or shapely **c** : to pronounce a sound with rounding of the lips **2 a** : to go around ⟨*rounded* the curve⟩ **b** : to pass part way around **3** : ENCIRCLE, ENCOMPASS **4** : to bring to completion : FINISH ⟨*round* out a career⟩ **5** : to express as a round number esp. by dropping decimal figures to the right of a specified number of places and increasing the final remaining figure by 1 if the first digit dropped is 5 or greater ⟨*round* off to three decimal places⟩ **6** : to follow a winding course : BEND ⟨jockeys *rounding* into the homestretch⟩
¹round·about \'raün-də-ˌbaüt\ *n* **1** : an indirect route : DETOUR **2** *Brit* : MERRY-GO-ROUND **3** : a short close-fitting jacket worn by men and boys esp. in the 19th century
²round·about \ˌraün-də-'baüt\ *adj* : not direct : CIRCUITOUS
round dance *n* **1** : a folk dance in which participants form a ring and move in a prescribed direction **2** : a ballroom dance in which couples progress around the room **3** : a series of movements performed by a bee and indicating that a source of food is nearby
roun·de·lay \'raün-də-ˌlā\ *n* **1** : a simple song with refrain **2** : a poem with a refrain recurring frequently or at fixed intervals
round·house \'raünd-ˌhaüs\ *n* **1** : a circular building for housing and repairing locomotives **2** : a cabin or apartment on the stern of a quarterdeck **3** : a blow in boxing delivered with a wide swing **4** : a slow wide curve in baseball
round robin *n* **1 a** : a written petition or protest whose signers affix their signatures in a circle so as not to indicate who signed first **b** : a letter sent in turn to the members of a group each of whom signs and forwards it sometimes after adding comment

2 : a tournament in which every contestant meets every other contestant in turn
round–shoul·dered \ˈrau̇n(d)-ˈshōl-dərd\ *adj* : having the shoulders stooping or rounded
round steak *n* : a steak cut from the whole round
round table *n* **1** : a meeting of a group of persons for discussion of questions of mutual interest **2** : the persons meeting at a round table
round·up \ˈrau̇n-ˌdəp\ *n* **1** : the gathering together of cattle on the range by riding around them and driving them in **2** : a gathering together of scattered persons or things **3** : SUMMARY, RÉSUMÉ ⟨a *roundup* of the day's news⟩
round up \ˈrau̇n-ˈdəp\ *vb* **1** : to collect cattle by means of a roundup **2** : to gather in or bring together
round·worm \ˈrau̇nd-ˌwərm\ *n* : a nematode worm; *also* : a related round-bodied unsegmented worm as distinguished from a flatworm
1**rouse** \ˈrau̇z\ *vb* **1** : to arouse or become aroused from or as if from sleep : AWAKEN **2** : to become stirred **3** : to stir up : EXCITE
2**rouse** *n* : an act or instance of rousing; *esp* : an excited stir
rous·ing \ˈrau̇-ziŋ\ *adj* **1** : EXCITING, STIRRING ⟨a *rousing* speech⟩ **2** : BRISK, LIVELY ⟨a *rousing* cheer⟩
roust·about \ˈrau̇-stə-ˌbau̇t\ *n* **1** : one who does heavy unskilled labor; *esp* : a laborer in an oil field **2 a** : DECKHAND **b** : LONGSHOREMAN **3** : a circus worker who erects and dismantles tents
1**rout** \ˈrau̇t\ *vb* **1** : to poke around with the snout : ROOT **2** : to search haphazardly : RUMMAGE **3** : to find or bring to light esp. with difficulty : DISCOVER **4** : to scoop out with or as if with a gouging tool **5 a** : to expel by force : EJECT ⟨*routed* out of their homes⟩ **b** : to cause to emerge esp. from bed : drag out
2**rout** *n* **1** : a state of wild confusion and disorderly retreat **2 a** : a disastrous defeat : DEBACLE **b** : an act or instance of routing
3**rout** *vb* **1** : to disorganize or defeat completely **2** : to drive out : DISPEL
1**route** \ˈrüt, ˈrau̇t\ *n* **1** : a course of action toward an intended goal ⟨decide on the best *route* to peace⟩ **2** : an established, selected, or assigned course of travel ⟨a mailman's *route*⟩
2**route** *vb* **1** : to send, forward, or transport by a certain route ⟨*route* traffic around the city⟩ **2** : to arrange and direct the course of procedure of (as a series of operations in a factory)
route·man \-mən, -ˌman\ *n* : one who sells or makes deliveries on an assigned route
1**rou·tine** \rü-ˈtēn\ *n* **1** : a regular or customary course of procedure **2** : an often repeated speech or formula **3** : a fixed piece of entertainment often repeated : ACT; *esp* : a theatrical number
2**routine** *adj* **1** : COMMONPLACE, ORDINARY **2** : of, relating to, or in accordance with established procedure ⟨*routine* inspection⟩ — **rou·tine·ly** *adv*
rove \ˈrōv\ *vb* **1** : to move aimlessly : ROAM ⟨*rove* about the country⟩ **2** : to wander through or over ⟨*rove* the seas⟩
1**ro·ver** \ˈrō-vər\ *n* : PIRATE
2**rov·er** \ˈrō-vər\ *n* **1** : a random or long-distance mark in archery — usu. used in pl. **2** : WANDERER, ROAMER
1**row** \ˈrō\ *vb* **1** : to propel a boat by means of oars **2** : to move by or as if by the propulsion of oars **3** : to be equipped with a specified number of oars **4 a** : to participate in a rowing match **b** : to compete against in rowing **c** : to pull an oar in a crew **5** : to transport in or as if in a boat propelled by oars — **row·er** \ˈrō(-ə)r\ *n*
2**row** *n* : an act or instance of rowing
3**row** *n* **1** : a number of objects in an orderly series or sequence **2** : WAY, STREET **3 a** : a continuous strip usu. running horizontally or parallel to a base line **b** : a horizontal arrangement of items **c** : a line of cultivated plants
4**row** \ˈrau̇\ *n* : a noisy disturbance or quarrel : BRAWL
5**row** \ˈrau̇\ *vb* : to engage in a row : FIGHT, QUARREL
row·boat \ˈrō-ˌbōt\ *n* : a boat designed to be rowed by oars
1**row·dy** \ˈrau̇d-ē\ *adj* **row·di·er**; **row·di·est** : coarse or boisterous in behavior : ROUGH — **row·di·ness** *n* — **row·dy·ish** \-ē-ish\ *adj* — **row·dy·ism** \-ē-ˌiz-əm\ *n*

rowboat

2**rowdy** *n, pl* **rowdies** : a rowdy person : TOUGH
1**row·el** \ˈrau̇(-ə)l\ *n* : a revolving disk at the end of a spur with sharp points for goading a horse
2**rowel** *vb* **-eled** *or* **-elled**; **-el·ing** *or* **-el·ling** : to goad with or as if with a rowel : SPUR
row house \ˈrō-\ *n* : one of a series of houses connected by common sidewalls and forming a continuous group
row·lock \ˈräl-ək, ˈrō-ˌläk\ *n, chiefly Brit* : OARLOCK
roy·al \ˈrȯi(-ə)l\ *adj* [from French, from Latin *regalis*; see REGAL] **1 a** : of kingly ancestry **b** : of, relating to, or subject to the crown **c** : being in the Crown's service ⟨*Royal* Navy⟩ **2** : suitable for royalty : MAGNIFICENT ⟨a *royal* welcome⟩ **3** : established or chartered by the Crown ⟨a *royal* colony⟩ — **roy·al·ly** \ˈrȯi-ə-lē\ *adv*
royal blue *n* : a variable color averaging a vivid purplish blue
roy·al·ist \ˈrȯi-ə-ləst\ *n* **1** : a supporter (as during a time of civil war) of a king **2** : a believer in monarchy as a system of government — **royalist** *adj*
royal jelly *n* : a highly nutritious secretion from glands in the pharynx of the honeybee that is fed to all very young larvae and continuously to queen larvae
royal palm *n* : a tall graceful American palm widely planted as an ornamental tree in tropical regions
roy·al·ty \ˈrȯi(-ə)l-tē\ *n, pl* **-ties 1 a** : royal status or power : SOVEREIGNTY **b** : a right or privilege of a sovereign (as a percentage of gold or silver taken from mines) **2** : regal character or bearing : NOBILITY **3 a** : persons of royal lineage **b** : a person of royal rank **c** : a privileged class **4 a** : a share of the product or profit reserved by the grantor esp. of an oil or mining lease **b** : a payment made to the owner of a patent or copyright for the use of it
RP *abbr* relief pitcher
rpm *abbr* revolutions per minute
rps *abbr* revolutions per second
RR *abbr* **1** railroad **2** rural route
RS *abbr* right side
RSV *abbr* Revised Standard Version
RSVP *abbr* [for French *répondez s'il vous plaît* "reply if you please"] please reply
rt *abbr* right
rte *abbr* route

ə abut	ər further	a back	ā bake	
ä cot, cart	au̇ out	ch chin	e less	ē easy
g gift	i trip	ī life	j joke	ŋ sing	ō flow
ȯ flaw	ȯi coin	th thin	th this	ü loot
u̇ foot	y yet	yü few	yu̇ furious	zh vision

[1]**rub** \'rəb\ *vb* **rubbed; rub·bing 1 a :** to move (as the palm of the hand) along the surface of a body or object with pressure ⟨*rubbed* his back⟩ **b :** to fret or chafe with friction ⟨the new shoes *rubbed*⟩ **c :** to cause discontent, irritation, or anger : ANNOY, IRRITATE ⟨*rubbed* me the wrong way⟩ **2 a :** to apply or spread by rubbing ⟨*rub* ointment on his chest⟩ **b :** to remove by rubbing : ERASE ⟨*rub* out an error⟩ **c :** to bring into reciprocal back-and-forth or rotary contact ⟨*rubbed* his hands together⟩

[2]**rub** *n* **1 a :** OBSTACLE, DIFFICULTY ⟨that's the *rub*⟩ **b :** something that hurts the feelings (as a gibe, sarcasm, or harsh criticism) **c :** something that mars or upsets serenity **2 :** the application of friction with pressure : RUBBING ⟨an alcohol *rub*⟩

[1]**rub·ber** \'rəb-ər\ *n* **1 a :** one that rubs **b :** an instrument or object (as a rubber eraser) used in rubbing, polishing, scraping, or cleaning **c :** something that prevents rubbing or chafing **2 a :** an elastic substance obtained by coagulating the milky juice of various tropical plants **b :** any of various synthetic substances that resemble or are used in place of natural rubber **3 :** something made of or resembling rubber: as **a :** a rubber overshoe **b :** PLATE 4b — **rub·ber·like** \-ˌlīk\ *adj* — **rub·bery** \'rəb-(ə-)rē\ *adj*

[2]**rubber** *n* **1 :** a contest that consists of an odd number of games and is won by the side that takes a majority (as two out of three) **2 :** an extra game played to determine the winner of a tie

rub·ber·ize \'rəb-ə-ˌrīz\ *vb* **:** to coat or impregnate with rubber or a rubber preparation

rubber plant *n* **:** a tall tropical Asian fig tree that is often dwarfed in pots as a house plant

rub·ber–stamp \ˌrəb-ər-'stamp\ *vb* **:** to approve, endorse, or dispose of as a matter of routine without serious consideration

rubber tree *n* **:** a So. American tree that is a source of rubber and is cultivated in plantations; *also* **:** any tree that yields rubber

rub·bing \'rəb-ing\ *n* **:** an image of a raised, indented, or textured surface obtained by placing paper over it and rubbing the paper (as with charcoal or graphite)

rubbing alcohol *n* **:** a watery solution of an alcohol used externally esp. to soothe or refresh

rub·bish \'rəb-ish\ *n* **:** useless waste or rejected matter : TRASH — **rub·bishy** \'rəb-i-shē\ *adj*

rub·ble \'rəb-əl\ *n* **1 :** rough stone as it comes from the quarry **2 :** rough broken stones or bricks used in coarse masonry or in filling courses of walls; *also* **:** RUBBLEWORK **3 :** a mass of rough irregular pieces

rub·ble·work \'rəb-əl-ˌwərk\ *n* **:** masonry of unsquared or rudely squared stones that are irregular in size and shape

rub·down \'rəb-ˌdau̇n\ *n* **:** a brisk rubbing of the body (as after a bath)

ru·bid·i·um \rü-'bid-ē-əm\ *n* **:** a soft silvery metallic element that decomposes water with violence and bursts into flame spontaneously in air — see ELEMENT table

ru·ble \'rü-bəl\ *n* **1 :** the basic monetary unit of the U.S.S.R. **2 :** a coin representing one ruble

ru·bric \'rü-brik\ *n* **1 :** an authoritative rule; *esp* **:** a rule for conduct of a liturgical service **2 :** an established rule or custom — **rubric** *or* **ru·bri·cal** \-bri-kəl\ *adj*

ru·by \'rü-bē\ *n, pl* **rubies 1 :** a precious stone that is a deep red corundum **2 a :** the dark red color of the ruby **b :** something resembling a ruby in color — **ruby** *adj*

ruck·sack \'rək-ˌsak, 'ru̇k-\ *n* **:** KNAPSACK

ruck·us \'rək-əs, 'rü-kəs\ *n* **:** ROW, DISTURBANCE

rud·der \'rəd-ər\ *n* **:** a flat movable piece of wood or metal attached vertically to the stern of a boat or to the tail of an aircraft for steering it

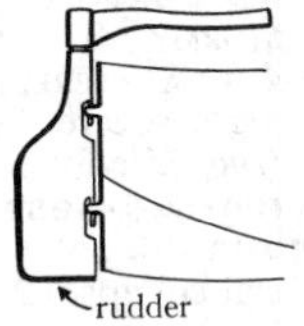

rudder

rud·dy \'rəd-ē\ *adj* **rud·di·er; -est 1 :** having a healthy reddish color **2 :** RED, REDDISH — **rud·di·ly** \'rəd-ə-lē\ *adv* — **rud·di·ness** \'rəd-ē-nəs\ *n*

rude \'rüd\ *adj* **1 :** being in a rough or unfinished state **:** CRUDE **2 :** lacking refinement, delicacy, or culture : UNCOUTH **3 :** offensive in manner or action : DISCOURTEOUS, IMPOLITE **4 :** FORCEFUL, ABRUPT ⟨a *rude* awakening⟩ — **rude·ly** *adv* — **rude·ness** *n*

ru·di·ment \'rüd-ə-mənt\ *n* **1 :** a basic principle or element or a fundamental skill — usu. used in pl. ⟨the *rudiments* of chess⟩ **2 a :** something unformed or undeveloped : BEGINNING — usu. used in pl. **b :** a body part so deficient in size or structure as to prevent its performing its normal function — **ru·di·men·tal** \ˌrüd-ə-'ment-əl\ *adj* — **ru·di·men·ta·ri·ness** \-'ment-ə-rē-nəs, -'men-trē-\ *n* — **ru·di·men·ta·ry** \ˌrüd-ə-'ment-ə-rē, -'men-trē\ *adj*

[1]**rue** \'rü\ *vb* **rued; ru·ing :** to feel penitence, remorse, or regret for

[2]**rue** *n* **:** REGRET, SORROW

[3]**rue** *n* **:** a woody herb with yellow flowers, a strong smell, and bitter-tasting leaves

rue·ful \'rü-fəl\ *adj* **1 :** arousing pity or sympathy : PITIABLE ⟨a *rueful* tale⟩ **2 :** MOURNFUL, REGRETFUL ⟨took defeat with a *rueful* smile⟩ — **rue·ful·ly** \-fə-lē\ *adv* — **rue·ful·ness** *n*

[1]**ruff** \'rəf\ *n* **1 :** a wheel-shaped stiff collar worn by men and women of the late 16th and early 17th centuries **2 :** a fringe of long hairs or feathers growing around or on the neck — **ruffed** \'rəft\ *adj*

[2]**ruff** *n* **:** the act of trumping

[3]**ruff** *vb* **:** TRUMP

ruffed grouse \'rəft-\ *n* **:** a No. American grouse with tufts of shiny black feathers on the sides of the neck

ruffed grouse
(about 18 in. long)

ruf·fi·an \'rəf-ē-ən\ *n* **:** a brutal cruel fellow : TOUGH — **ruffian** *adj* — **ruf·fi·an·ism** \-ē-ə-ˌniz-əm\ *n* — **ruf·fi·an·ly** \-ē-ən-lē\ *adj*

[1]**ruf·fle** \'rəf-əl\ *vb* **ruf·fled; ruf·fling** \'rəf-(ə-)ling\ **1 a :** to disturb the smoothness of : ROUGHEN ⟨*ruffle* the waters of a pond⟩ **b :** TROUBLE, VEX ⟨*ruffled* her composure⟩ **2 :** to erect (as feathers) in or like a ruff **3 a :** to flip through the pages of a book **b :** to shuffle cards rapidly **4 :** to make into a ruffle

[2]**ruffle** *n* **1 :** a state or cause of irritation **2 :** an unevenness or disturbance of surface : RIPPLE **3 a :** a strip of fabric gathered or pleated on one edge **b :** [1]RUFF 2 — **ruf·fly** \'rəf-(ə-)lē\ *adj*

[3]**ruffle** *n* **:** a low vibrating drumbeat that is less loud that a roll

rug \'rəg\ *n* **1 :** a piece of thick heavy fabric usu. with a nap or pile used as a floor covering **2 :** a floor mat of an animal pelt **3 :** a lap robe

rug·by \'rəg-bē\ *n, often cap* [named after *Rugby* School in Rugby, England, where it originated] **:** a

R

football game played by teams of 15 players and marked by continuous play

rug·ged \ˈrəg-əd\ *adj* **1 :** having a rough uneven surface : JAGGED ⟨*rugged* mountains⟩ **2 :** TURBULENT, STORMY **3 :** HARDY, STURDY ⟨*rugged* pioneers⟩ **4 a :** AUSTERE, STERN **b :** COARSE, RUDE **5 :** presenting a severe test of ability, stamina, or resolution ⟨*rugged* course of training⟩ — **rug·ged·ly** *adv* — **rug·ged·ness** *n*

1ru·in \ˈrü-ən\ *n* **1 :** physical, moral, economic, or social collapse **2 a** *archaic* **:** the state of being ruined **b :** the remains of something destroyed — usu. used in pl. ⟨the *ruins* of a city⟩ **3 :** a cause of destruction ⟨drink was his *ruin*⟩ **4 :** the action of destroying, laying waste, or wrecking **5 :** a ruined building, person, or object

2ruin *vb* **1 :** to reduce to ruins : DEVASTATE **2 a :** to damage irreparably **b :** BANKRUPT, IMPOVERISH — **ru·in·er** *n*

ru·in·a·tion \ˌrü-ə-ˈnā-shən\ *n* **:** RUIN, DESTRUCTION

ru·in·ous \ˈrü-ə-nəs\ *adj* **1 :** RUINED, DILAPIDATED **2 :** causing or tending to cause ruin : DESTRUCTIVE — **ru·in·ous·ly** *adv*

1rule \ˈrül\ *n* **1 a :** a prescribed guide for conduct or action **b :** the laws laid down by the founder of a religious order **c :** an accepted procedure, custom, or habit **d :** a legal precept or doctrine **e :** REGULATION, BYLAW **2 a :** a statement of a fact or relationship generally found to hold good **b :** a generally prevailing quality, state, or mode ⟨fair weather was the *rule* yesterday⟩ **c :** a regulating principle ⟨the *rules* of harmony⟩ **3 a :** the exercise of authority or control : DOMINION **b :** a period of such rule : REIGN ⟨during the *rule* of King George III⟩ **4 :** RULER 2

2rule *vb* **1 a :** to exercise authority or power over : GOVERN, CONTROL **b :** to have great influence over : DOMINATE **2 :** to declare authoritatively; *esp* **:** to lay down a legal rule **3 :** to mark with lines drawn along or as if along the straight edge of a ruler **4 a :** to exercise supreme authority **b :** PREDOMINATE, PREVAIL ***syn*** see GOVERN

rule·less \ˈrül-ləs\ *adj* **:** not restrained or regulated by law

rule of thumb 1 : a rough measurement or calculation **2 :** a judgment based on practical experience rather than on scientific knowledge

rule out *vb* **1 :** EXCLUDE, ELIMINATE **2 :** to make impossible : PREVENT

rul·er \ˈrü-lər\ *n* **1 :** one that rules; *esp* **:** SOVEREIGN **2 :** a smooth-edged strip (as of wood or metal) used as a guide in drawing lines or for measuring

1rul·ing \ˈrü-liŋ\ *n* **:** an official or authoritative decision or interpretation (as by a judge on a point of law)

2ruling *adj* **1 :** exerting power or authority **2 :** CHIEF, PREDOMINATING ⟨his *ruling* ambition⟩

rum \ˈrəm\ *n* **1 :** an alcoholic liquor made from molasses or sugar cane **2 :** alcoholic liquor

Rum *abbr* **1** Rumania **2** Rumanian

Ru·ma·ni·an \rů-ˈmā-nē-ən\ *var of* ROMANIAN

rum·ba \ˈrəm-bə, ˈrům-\ *n* **:** a Cuban Negro dance or an imitation of it

1rum·ble \ˈrəm-bəl\ *vb* **rum·bled; rum·bling** \-b(ə-)liŋ\ **1 :** to make a low heavy rolling sound ⟨thunder *rumbled* in the distance⟩ **2 :** to move with a low reverberating sound **3 :** to speak or utter in a low rolling tone

2rumble *n* **:** a low heavy continuous reverberating often muffled sound

rumble seat *n* **:** a folding seat in the back of an automobile (as a coupe or roadster) not covered by the top

ru·men \ˈrü-mən\ *n, pl* **ru·mi·na** \-mə-nə\ *or* **rumens :** the large first compartment of the stomach of a cud-chewing mammal in which cellulose is broken down by the action of microorganisms and in which food is stored prior to chewing

1ru·mi·nant \ˈrü-mə-nənt\ *n* **:** a cud-chewing mammal

2ruminant *adj* **1 a :** chewing the cud **b :** of or relating to a group of even-toed hoofed mammals (as sheep, giraffes, deer, and camels) that chew the cud and have a complex 3- or 4-chambered stomach **2 :** given to or engaged in contemplation : MEDITATIVE — **ru·mi·nant·ly** *adv*

ru·mi·nate \ˈrü-mə-ˌnāt\ *vb* [from Latin *ruminare*, literally "to chew the cud", from *rumen* "gullet"] **1 :** to engage in contemplation : MUSE, MEDITATE **2 :** to chew the cud : bring up and chew again what has been chewed slightly and swallowed — **ru·mi·na·tion** \ˌrü-mə-ˈnā-shən\ *n* — **ru·mi·na·tive** \ˈrü-mə-ˌnāt-iv\ *adj* — **ru·mi·na·tive·ly** *adv* — **ru·mi·na·tor** \-ˌnāt-ər\ *n*

1rum·mage \ˈrəm-ij\ *n* **:** a thorough search esp. among a confusion of objects or into every section

2rummage *vb* **1 :** to make a thorough or active search esp. by moving about, turning over, or looking through the contents of a place or receptacle ⟨*rummage* through an attic⟩ **2 :** to discover by searching : hunt out ⟨*rummaged* up what they needed for costumes⟩

rummage sale *n* **:** a sale of donated articles usu. by a church or charitable organization

rum·my \ˈrəm-ē\ *n* **:** a card game in which each player tries to be the first to assemble all of his cards in groups of three or more

1ru·mor \ˈrü-mər\ *n* **1 :** talk or opinion widely current but having no known source : HEARSAY **2 :** a statement or report current without known authority for its truth

2rumor *vb* **ru·mored; ru·mor·ing** \ˈrüm-(ə-)riŋ\ **:** to tell or spread by rumor

rump \ˈrəmp\ *n* **1 :** the back part of an animal's body where the hips and thighs join generally including the buttocks **2 :** a cut of beef between the loin and round

rum·ple \ˈrəm-pəl\ *vb* **rum·pled; rum·pling** \-p(ə-)liŋ\ **1 :** WRINKLE, CRUMPLE ⟨*rumple* the bedclothes⟩ **2 :** to make unkempt : MUSS ⟨*rumpled* his hair⟩

rum·pus \ˈrəm-pəs\ *n* **:** DISTURBANCE, FRACAS

rumpus room *n* **:** a room usu. in the basement of a home set apart for games, parties, and recreation

1run \ˈrən\ *vb* **ran** \ˈran\; **run; run·ning 1 a :** to go faster than a walk; *esp* **:** to go steadily by springing steps so that both feet leave the ground for an instant in each step **b :** to move at a fast gallop ⟨*running* horses⟩ **c :** FLEE, RETREAT, ESCAPE ⟨dropped his gun and *ran*⟩ **2 a :** to move freely about at will ⟨let his chickens *run* loose⟩ **b :** ROAM, ROVE ⟨caught cold *running* around without a coat⟩ **3 a :** to go or cause to go rapidly or hurriedly : HASTEN **b :** to do or accomplish something by or as if by running ⟨*run* errands⟩ **4 a :** to contend in a race **b :** to enter or put forward as a contestant in an election contest ⟨*ran* for mayor⟩ **5 a :** to move on or as if on wheels : GLIDE ⟨file drawers *running* on ball bearings⟩ **b** : to roll forward rapidly or freely **c** : to ravel lengthwise ⟨stockings guaranteed not to *run*⟩ **6** : to sing or play a musical passage quickly ⟨*run* up the scale⟩ **7 a** : to go back and forth ⟨a ferry *runs* to the island every hour⟩ **b** : to migrate or move in schools; *esp* : to ascend a river to spawn ⟨shad are *running* in the river⟩ **8** : FUNCTION, OPERATE **9 a** : to continue in force or operation ⟨the contract has two years to *run*⟩ **b** : to accompany as an obligation or right **10** : to pass into a specified condition ⟨*run* into debt⟩ **11 a** : to move as a fluid : FLOW **b** : MELT, FUSE **c** : to spread out : DISSOLVE ⟨colors guaranteed not to *run*⟩ **d** : to discharge a fluid ⟨a *running* sore⟩ **12 a** : to develop rapidly in a specific direction **b** : to tend to develop a specified quality or feature ⟨they *run* to big noses in that family⟩ **13 a** : EXTEND ⟨the boundary line *runs* east⟩ **b** : to go back **c** : to be in a certain form or expression ⟨the letter *runs* as follows⟩ or order of succession ⟨house numbers *run* in odd numbers⟩ **14 a** : to occur persistently : RECUR ⟨thoughts *running* through his mind⟩ **b** : to exist or occur in a continuous range of variation **c** : to play on a stage a number of successive days or nights ⟨the play *ran* for six months⟩ **15 a** : to spread or pass quickly from point to point ⟨chills *ran* up his spine⟩ **b** : to be current : CIRCULATE ⟨speculation *ran* rife⟩ **16 a** : to bring to a specified condition by or as if by running ⟨*ran* himself to death⟩ **b** : TRACE ⟨*ran* the rumor to its source⟩ **17** : to slip through or past ⟨*run* a blockade⟩ **18 a** : to cause to penetrate or enter : THRUST ⟨*ran* a splinter into his toe⟩ **b** : STITCH **c** : to cause to pass : LEAD ⟨*run* a wire in from the antenna⟩ **d** : to cause to collide ⟨*ran* his head into a post⟩ **e** : SMUGGLE **19** : to cause to pass lightly or quickly over, along, or into something ⟨*ran* his eye down the list⟩ **20 a** : to cause or allow to go in a specified manner or direction ⟨*ran* his car off the road⟩ ⟨*run* out the beam from the ship's side⟩ **b** : to carry on : MANAGE ⟨*run* a factory⟩ **21 a** : to flow with ⟨streets *ran* blood⟩ **b** : CONTAIN, ASSAY ⟨the ore *runs* high in silver⟩ **22** : to make oneself liable to : INCUR ⟨*ran* the risk of discovery⟩ **23** : to mark out ⟨*run* a contour line on a map⟩ : DRAW **24** : to permit charges to accumulate before settling ⟨*run* an account⟩ **25** : PRINT ⟨*run* the advertisement for three days⟩ **26** : to lead winning cards of (a suit) successively — **run across** : to meet with or discover by chance — **run foul of** : to collide with ⟨*ran foul of* a hidden reef⟩ : run into conflict with or hostility to ⟨*run foul of* the law⟩ — **run into 1** : to mount up to ⟨a boat like that one *runs into* money⟩ **2 a** : to collide with **b** : ENCOUNTER, MEET — **run riot 1** : to act wildly or without restraint **2** : to occur in profusion — **run short** : to become insufficient ⟨drinking water was *running short*⟩

²**run** *n* **1 a** : an act or the action of running : continued rapid movement ⟨broke into a *run*⟩ **b** : a fast gallop **c** : a migrating of fish **d** : fish migrating esp. to spawn **e** : a running race ⟨a mile *run*⟩ **f** : a score made in baseball by a base runner reaching home plate **2 a** *chiefly Midland* : CREEK 2 **b** : something that flows in the course of an operation or during a particular time ⟨the first *run* of maple sap⟩ **3 a** : the horizontal distance from one point to another **b** : general tendency or direction **4** : a continuous series esp. of things of identical or similar sort: as **a** : a rapid scale passage in vocal or instrumental music **b** : the act of making a number of successful consecutive shots or strokes ⟨a *run* of 20 in billiards⟩ **c** : an unbroken course of theatrical performances **d** : sudden heavy demands from depositors, creditors, or customers ⟨a *run* on a bank⟩ **5** : the quantity of work turned out in a continuous operation **6** : the usual or normal kind ⟨average *run* of college graduates⟩ **7 a** : the distance covered in a period of continuous traveling or sailing ⟨logged the day's *run*⟩ **b** : regular course : TRIP ⟨the bus makes four *runs* daily⟩ **c** : freedom of movement in or access to a place or area ⟨has the *run* of his friend's house⟩ **8 a** : a way, track, or path frequented by animals **b** : an enclosure for livestock where they may feed or exercise **9 a** : an inclined course (as for skiing) **b** : a track or guide on which something runs **10** : a ravel in a knitted fabric (as in hosiery) caused by the breaking of stitches — **run·less** \'rən-ləs\ *adj*

run·about \'rən-ə-ˌbau̇t\ *n* **1** : one who wanders about : STRAY **2** : a light open wagon, roadster, or motorboat

run·a·gate \'rən-ə-ˌgāt\ *n* **1** : FUGITIVE, RUNAWAY **2** : VAGABOND

run·around \'rən-ə-ˌrau̇nd\ *n* : deceptive or delaying action esp. in response to a request

¹**run·away** \'rən-ə-ˌwā\ *n* **1** : FUGITIVE **2** : the act of running away out of control; *also* : a horse that is running out of control

²**runaway** *adj* **1** : running away : FUGITIVE **2** : accomplished by elopement or during flight ⟨a *runaway* marriage⟩ **3** : won by or having a long lead ⟨a *runaway* victory⟩ **4** : subject to uncontrolled changes ⟨*runaway* inflation⟩

run away \ˌrən-ə-'wā\ *vb* **1** : FLEE, DESERT **2** : to leave home **3** : to run out of control : STAMPEDE, BOLT

run·down \'rən-ˌdau̇n\ *n* : an item by item report : SUMMARY

run–down \'rən-'dau̇n\ *adj* **1** : being in poor repair : DILAPIDATED **2** : being in poor health **3** : completely unwound ⟨a *run-down* clock⟩

run down \'rən-'dau̇n\ *vb* **1 a** : to collide with and knock down **b** : to run against and cause to sink **2 a** : to chase until exhausted or captured **b** : to find by search : trace the source of **3** : DISPARAGE **4** : to cease to operate because of the exhaustion of motive power **5** : to deteriorate in physical condition

rune \'rün\ *n* **1** : one of the characters of an alphabet used by the Germanic peoples from about the 3d to the 13th centuries **2** : a mystic utterance or inscription **3** : a Finnish or Old Norse poem — **ru·nic** \'rü-nik\ *adj*

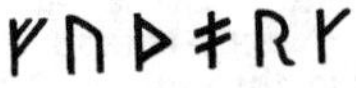
runes 1

¹**rung** *past part of* RING

²**rung** \'rəŋ\ *n* **1 a** : a rounded part placed as a crosspiece between the legs of a chair **b** : one of the crosspieces of a ladder **2** : LEVEL, POSITION, RANK ⟨the lowest *rung* of the social scale⟩

run–in \'rən-ˌin\ *n* : ALTERCATION, QUARREL

run·ner \'rən-ər\ *n* **1 a** : one that runs : RACER **b** : a football player in possession of a live ball **2** : MESSENGER **3 a** : either of the longitudinal pieces on which a sled or sleigh slides **b** : the part of a skate that slides on the ice : BLADE **c** : the support of a drawer or a sliding door **4 a** : a slender creeping branch of a plant; *esp* : STOLON **b** : a plant that forms or spreads by runners **5 a** : a long narrow carpet for a hall or staircase **b** : a narrow decorative cloth cover for a table or dresser top

run·ner–up \'rən-ər-ˌəp\ *n, pl* **runners–up** : the competitor in a contest that finishes next to the winner

1run·ning \ˈrən-iŋ\ *adj* **1 :** FLUID, RUNNY **2 :** INCESSANT, CONTINUOUS ⟨a *running* battle⟩ **3 :** measured in a straight line ⟨cost of lumber per *running* foot⟩ **4 :** FLOWING, CURSIVE ⟨a *running* hand in writing⟩ **5 :** initiated or performed while running or with a running start ⟨a *running* leap⟩ **6 :** fitted or trained for running ⟨a *running* track⟩ ⟨a *running* horse⟩

2running *adv* **:** in succession **:** CONSECUTIVELY

running board *n* **:** a footboard esp. at the side of an automobile

running knot *n* **:** a knot that slips along the line round which it is tied

running light *n* **:** one of the lights carried by a ship under way at night or on the wing and fuselage of an airplane

running mate *n* **:** a candidate running for a subordinate office (as of vice-president) who is paired with the candidate for the top office on the same ticket

run·ny \ˈrən-ē\ *adj* **run·ni·er; -est :** having a tendency to run; *esp* **:** secreting mucus ⟨watery eyes and *runny* nose⟩

run·off \ˈrən-ˌȯf\ *n* **1 :** water that is removed from soil by natural drainage **2 :** a final contest to decide a previously indecisive contest or series of contests

run off \ˈrən-ˈȯf\ *vb* **1 :** to produce by a printing press **2 :** to cause to be run or played to a finish **3 :** to steal (as cattle) by driving away **4 :** to run away — **run off with :** to carry off **:** STEAL

run–of–the–mill \ˌrən-ə(v)-t͟hə-ˈmil\ *adj* **:** not outstanding in quality or rarity **:** AVERAGE

1run–on \ˈrən-ˈȯn, -ˈän\ *adj* **:** continuing without rhetorical pause from one line of verse into another

2run–on \ˈrən-ˌȯn, -ˌän\ *n* **:** something (as a dictionary entry) that is run on

run on \ˈrən-ˈȯn, -ˈän\ *vb* **1 :** CONTINUE **2 :** to talk or narrate at length **3 :** to continue matter in type without a break or a new paragraph **4 :** to place or add (as an entry in a dictionary) at the end of a paragraphed item

run–on sentence *n* **:** a sentence formed with a comma fault

run out *vb* **1 :** to come to an end **:** EXPIRE ⟨the lease *runs out* next month⟩ **2 :** to become exhausted or used up **:** FAIL — **run out of :** to use up the available supply of

run over *vb* **1 :** OVERFLOW **2 :** to exceed a limit **3 :** to go over, examine, repeat, or rehearse quickly **4 :** to collide with, knock down, and often drive over

runt \ˈrənt\ *n* **:** an unusually small person or animal — **runt·i·ness** \-ē-nəs\ *n* — **runty** \-ē\ *adj*

run through *vb* **1 :** PIERCE **2 :** to spend or consume wastefully and rapidly ⟨*ran through* his inheritance in no time⟩

run·way \ˈrən-ˌwā\ *n* **1 :** RUN 8 **2 :** an artificially surfaced strip of ground on a landing field for the landing and takeoff of airplanes **3 :** a support (as a track, pipe, or trough) on which something runs

ru·pee \rü-ˈpē, ˈrü-(ˌ)pē\ *n* [from Hindi *rūpaiyā*, from Sanskrit *rūpya* "coined silver", from *rūpa* "shape", "beauty"] **1 :** the basic monetary unit of India, Pakistan, and Ceylon **2 :** a coin representing one rupee

1rup·ture \ˈrəp-chər\ *n* **1 :** a break in peaceful relations; *esp* **:** open hostility or war between nations **2 :** a breaking or tearing apart (as of body tissue) or the resulting state **3 :** HERNIA

ə abut	ər further	a back	ā bake
ä cot, cart	aú out	ch chin	e less	ē easy
g gift	i trip	ī life	j joke	ŋ sing	ō flow
ȯ flaw	ȯi coin	th thin	t͟h this	ü loot
ú foot	y yet	yü few	yú furious	zh vision

2rupture *vb* **1 :** to part by violence **:** BREAK **2 :** to produce a rupture in **3 :** to have a rupture

ru·ral \ˈrúr-əl\ *adj* **:** of or relating to the country, country people or life, or agriculture

rural free delivery *n* **:** the free delivery of mail on routes in country districts — called also *rural delivery*

rural route *n* **:** a route in a rural free delivery area

ruse \ˈrüs, ˈrüz\ *n* **:** a deceptive stratagem **:** TRICK

1rush \ˈrəsh\ *n* **:** any of various often tufted marsh plants with cylinder-shaped often hollow stems used in chair seats and mats

2rush *vb* **1 :** to move forward, progress, or act with haste or eagerness or without preparation **2 :** to act as carrier of a football in a running play **3 :** to push or impel on or forward with speed or violence **4 :** to perform in a short time or at high speed **5 :** ATTACK, CHARGE **6 :** to lavish attention on **:** COURT — **rush·er** *n*

3rush *n* **1 a :** a violent forward motion ⟨a *rush* of wind⟩ **b :** ATTACK, ONSET **2 :** a burst of activity, productivity, or speed **3 :** an eager migration of people usu. to a new place and in search of wealth ⟨gold *rush*⟩ **4 :** the act of carrying a football during a game **:** running play

4rush *adj* **:** requiring or marked by special speed or urgency ⟨*rush* orders⟩

rusk \ˈrəsk\ *n* **:** a sweet or plain bread baked, sliced, and baked again until dry and crisp

Russ \ˈrəs\ *n, pl* **Russ** *or* **Russ·es :** RUSSIAN — **Russ** *adj*

Russ *abbr* Russia

rus·set \ˈrəs-ət\ *n* **1 :** coarse homespun usu. reddish brown cloth **2 :** a variable color averaging a strong brown **3 :** any of various late-ripening apples that have rough russet skins and keep well in winter — **russet** *adj*

Rus·sian \ˈrəsh-ən\ *n* **1 a :** one of the people of Russia **b :** a person of Russian descent **2 :** a Slavic language of the Russian people that is the official language of the U.S.S.R. — **Russian** *adj*

Russian wolfhound *n* **:** BORZOI

Rus·so- *comb form* **1** \ˌrəs-ə, ˈrəs-, -ō\ **:** Russia **:** Russians ⟨*Russo*phobia⟩ **2** \ˈrəs(h)-ō, ˌrəs(h)-\ **:** Russian and ⟨*Russo*-Japanese⟩

1rust \ˈrəst\ *n* [from Old English *rūst*, from a common prehistoric Germanic noun derived from the root of English *red*] **1 a :** a reddish brittle coating chiefly of oxide formed on iron esp. when chemically attacked by moist air **b :** a comparable coating produced on other metals by corrosion **2 a :** any of numerous destructive diseases of plants caused by fungi and marked by reddish brown spots **b :** any of an order of parasitic fungi that cause plant rusts **3 :** a strong reddish brown

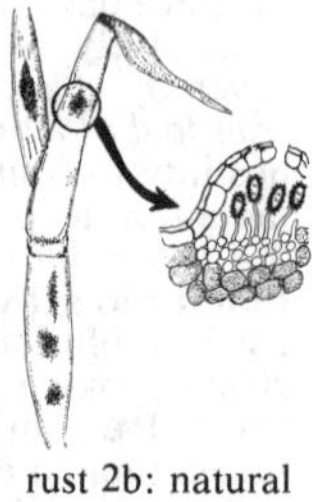

rust 2b: natural size on wheat; magnified to show spores

2rust *vb* **1 :** to form or cause to form rust **:** become oxidized ⟨iron *rusts*⟩ **2 :** to weaken or degenerate or cause to degenerate esp. from inaction, lack of use, or passage of time

1rus·tic \ˈrəs-tik\ *adj* **1 :** of, relating to, or suitable for the country **:** RURAL ⟨*rustic* sports⟩ **2 :** AWKWARD, BOORISH ⟨*rustic* manners⟩ **3 :** PLAIN, SIMPLE — **rus·ti·cal·ly** \-ti-k(ə-)lē\ *adv* — **rus·tic·i·ty** \ˌrəs-ˈtis-ət-ē\ *n*

2rustic *n* **:** an inhabitant of a rural area; *esp* **:** an unsophisticated one

[1]**rus·tle** \'rəs-əl\ *vb* **rus·tled**; **rus·tling** \'rəs-(ə-)liŋ\ **1** : to make or cause to make a rustle ⟨*rustled* the papers in his hand⟩ **2** : to get something by energetic activity ⟨*rustle* up some food⟩ **3** : to steal (as cattle) from the range — **rus·tler** \'rəs-(ə-)lər\ *n*

[2]**rustle** *n* : a quick succession or confusion of small sounds ⟨the *rustle* of leaves⟩

rust·proof \'rəst-'prüf\ *adj* : protected against rusting

rusty \'rəs-tē\ *adj* **rust·i·er**; **-est** **1** : affected by or as if by rust; *esp* : stiff with or as if with rust **2** : weakened and slow through lack of practice or old age **3** : of the color rust — **rust·i·ly** \-tə-lē\ *adv* — **rust·i·ness** \-tē-nəs\ *n*

[1]**rut** \'rət\ *n* : a state of sexual excitement esp. in the male deer; *also* : a period in which rut occurs

[2]**rut** *vb* **rut·ted**; **rut·ting** : to be in or enter into a state of rut

[3]**rut** *n* **1** : a track worn by a wheel or by habitual passage **2** : a usual or fixed practice : a regualr course; *esp* : a monotonous routine ⟨his teaching has fallen into a *rut*⟩ — **rut·ty** \'rət-ē\ *adj*

[4]**rut** *vb* **rut·ted**; **rut·ting** : to make a rut in : FURROW

ru·ta·ba·ga \ˌrüt-ə-'bā-gə, -'beg-ə\ *n* : a turnip with a very large yellowish root

Ruth \'rüth\ *n* — see BIBLE table

ru·the·ni·um \rü-'thē-nē-əm\ *n* : a hard brittle grayish rare metallic element used in hardening platinum alloys — see ELEMENT table

ruth·less \'rüth-ləs\ *adj* [from *ruth* "pity", from middle English, from *ruen* "to rue"] : having no pity : MERCILESS, CRUEL — **ruth·less·ly** *adv* — **ruth·less·ness** *n*

-ry \rē\ *n suffix, pl* **-ries** : -ERY ⟨wizard*ry*⟩ ⟨citizen*ry*⟩

ry *abbr* railway

rya \'rē-ə, 'rē-ä\ *n* : a Scandanavian rug with a deep resilient comparatively flat pile

rye \'rī\ *n* **1** : a hardy annual cereal grass widely grown for grain and as a cover crop; *also* : its seeds **2** : whiskey distilled from rye or from rye and malt

rye bread *n* : bread made wholly or partly from rye flour

s \'es\ *n, often cap* **1 :** the 19th letter of the English alphabet **2 :** a grade rating a student's work as satisfactory

[1]**-s** \s *after a voiceless consonant sound,* z *after a voiced consonant sound or a vowel sound*\ *n pl suffix* **1** — used to form the plural of most nouns that do not end in *s, z, sh,* or *ch* or in *y* following a consonant ⟨head*s*⟩ ⟨book*s*⟩ ⟨boy*s*⟩ ⟨belief*s*⟩, to form the plural of proper nouns that end in *y* following a consonant ⟨Mary*s*⟩, and with or without a preceding apostrophe to form the plural of abbreviations, numbers, letters, and symbols used as nouns ⟨MC*s*⟩ ⟨4*s*⟩ ⟨#*s*⟩ ⟨B'*s*⟩ **2** — used to form adverbs denoting usual or repeated action or state ⟨always at home Sunday*s*⟩ ⟨goes to school night*s*⟩

[2]**-s** *vb suffix* — used to form the third person singular present of most verbs that do not end in *s, z, sh,* or *ch* or in *y* following a consonant ⟨fall*s*⟩ ⟨take*s*⟩ ⟨play*s*⟩

-'s \s *after voiceless consonant sounds other than* s, sh, ch; z *after vowel sounds and voiced consonant sounds other than* z, zh, j; əz *after* s, sh, ch, z, zh, j\ *n suffix or pron suffix* — used to form the possessive of singular nouns ⟨boy'*s*⟩, of plural nouns not ending in *s* ⟨children'*s*⟩, of some pronouns ⟨anyone'*s*⟩, and of word groups functioning as nouns ⟨the man in the corner'*s* hat⟩ or pronouns ⟨someone else'*s*⟩

[1]**'s** *like* -'s\ *vb* **1 :** IS ⟨she'*s* here⟩ **2 :** HAS ⟨he'*s* seen them⟩ **3 :** DOES ⟨what'*s* he want?⟩

[2]**'s** \s\ *pron* **:** US — used with *let* ⟨let'*s*⟩

s *abbr* second

S *abbr* **1** sentence **2** south **3** southern

SA *abbr* **1** Salvation Army **2** South Africa

Sab·bath \'sab-əth\ *n* **1 :** the 7th day of the week observed from Friday evening to Saturday evening as a day of rest and worship by Jews and some Christians **2 :** the day of the week (as among Christians) set aside in a religion for rest and worship

sab·bat·i·cal \sə-'bat-i-kəl\ *or* **sab·bat·ic** \-'bat-ik\ *adj* **1 :** of or relating to the Sabbath ⟨*sabbatical* candles⟩ **2 :** being a recurring period of rest or renewal ⟨*sabbatical* leave⟩

sa·ber *or* **sa·bre** \'sā-bər\ *n* **:** a cavalry sword with a curved blade

sa·ber–toothed tiger \ˌsā-bər-ˌtüth(t)-\ *n* **:** any of various large prehistoric cats with very long curved upper canine teeth — called also *saber-toothed cat*

saber-toothed tiger
(about 6 ft. long)

Sa·bine \'sā-ˌbīn\ *n* **:** a member of an ancient Italic people conquered by Rome in 290 B.C. — **Sabine** *adj*

Sa·bin vaccine \'sā-bən-\ *n* [named after Albert B. *Sabin* (born 1906), American virologist] **:** a polio vaccine that is taken by mouth

sa·ble \'sā-bəl\ *n, pl* **sable** *or* **sables** **1 :** the color black **2 a :** a flesh-eating mammal of northern Europe and Asia related to the martens and valued for its soft rich brown fur **b :** the fur or pelt of a sable — **sable** *adj*

sable 2a
(up to 30 in. long)

[1]**sab·o·tage** \'sab-ə-ˌtäzh\ *n* [from French, from *saboter* "to botch", "sabotage", literally "to clatter with wooden shoes", from *sabot* "wooden shoe"] **1 :** destruction of an employer's property or the hindering of work by discontented workmen **2 :** destructive or obstructive action carried on by enemy agents or sympathizers to hinder a nation's war effort

[2]**sabotage** *vb* **:** to practice sabotage on **:** WRECK

sab·o·teur \ˌsab-ə-'tər, -'tu̇r\ *n* **:** a person who commits sabotage

sac \'sak\ *n* **:** a pouch in an animal or plant often containing a fluid — **sac·like** \-ˌlīk\ *adj*

SAC *abbr* Strategic Air Command

sac·cha·ride \'sak-ə-ˌrīd\ *n* **:** a simple sugar, combination of sugars, or polymerized sugar

sac·cha·rin \'sak-(ə-)rən\ *n* **:** a very sweet white coal tar derivative that is used as a calorie-free sweetener

sac·cha·rine \'sak-ə-rən\ *adj* [from Greek *sakcharon* "sugar", from Sanskrit *śarkarā* "gravel", "sugar"] **1 a :** of, relating to, or resembling that of sugar ⟨*saccharine* taste⟩ **b :** yielding or containing sugar ⟨*saccharine* fluids⟩ **2 :** overly or ingratiatingly sweet ⟨a *saccharine* smile⟩

sac·er·do·tal \ˌsas-ər-'dōt-əl\ *adj* **:** PRIESTLY — **sac·er·do·tal·ly** \-ə-lē\ *adv*

sac fungus *n* **:** ASCOMYCETE

sa·chem \'sā-chəm\ *n* **:** a No. American Indian chief

sa·chet \sa-'shā\ *n* [from French, diminutive of *sac* "bag"] **:** a small bag containing a perfumed powder for scenting clothes and linens

[1]**sack** \'sak\ *n* **1 :** a flexible container (as of jute or paper) **:** BAG **2 :** SACKFUL **3 :** DISMISSAL — usu. used with *get* or *give* **4 :** BUNK, BED — **sack·like** \-ˌlīk\ *adj*

[2]**sack** *vb* **1 :** to put in a sack **2 :** DISMISS, FIRE

[3]**sack** *n* **:** a dry strong white wine formerly imported to England from the south of Europe

[4]**sack** *n* **:** the plundering of a captured town

[5]**sack** *vb* **1 :** to plunder after capture **2 :** PILLAGE, LOOT

sack·cloth \'sak-ˌklȯth\ *n* **1 :** coarse cloth for sacks **:** SACKING **2 :** a garment of sackcloth worn as a sign of mourning or penitence

sack coat *n* **:** a man's jacket with a straight unfitted back

sack·ful \'sak-ˌfu̇l\ *n, pl* **sackfuls** \-ˌfu̇lz\ *or* **sacks·ful** \'saks-ˌfu̇l\ **:** the quantity that fills a sack

sack·ing \'sak-ing\ *n* **:** strong coarse cloth (as burlap) from which sacks are made

sac·ral \'sak-rəl, 'sā-krəl\ *adj* **:** of, relating to, or lying near the sacrum

sac·ra·ment \'sak-rə-mənt\ *n* **1 :** a formal religious act that is a sign or symbol of a spiritual reality; *esp* **:** one instituted by Jesus Christ as a means of grace **2** *cap* **:** BLESSED SACRAMENT — **sac·ra·men·tal** \ˌsak-rə-'ment-əl\ *adj* — **sac·ra·men·tal·ly** \-ə-lē\ *adv*

sa·cred \'sā-krəd\ *adj* **1 :** set apart in honor of someone (as a god) ⟨a mountain *sacred* to Jupiter⟩

ə abut	ər further	a back	ā bake	
ä cot, cart	au̇ out	ch chin	e less	ē easy
g gift	i trip	ī life	j joke	ng sing
ō flow	ȯ flaw	ȯi coin	th thin	t͟h this
ü loot	u̇ foot	y yet	yü few	yu̇ furious
zh vision				

2 : HOLY ⟨the *sacred* name of Jesus⟩ 3 : RELIGIOUS ⟨*sacred* songs⟩ 4 : not to be violated or misused ⟨a *sacred* right⟩ ⟨his *sacred* word⟩ — **sa·cred·ly** *adv* — **sa·cred·ness** *n*

1sac·ri·fice \'sak-rə-ˌfīs, -fəs\ *n* 1 : an act of offering something precious to God or a god; *esp* : the killing of a victim on an altar 2 : something offered in sacrifice 3 : a giving up of something esp. for the sake of someone else; *also* : something so given up 4 : loss of profit ⟨sell goods at a *sacrifice*⟩

2sac·ri·fice \-ˌfīs\ *vb* 1 : to offer or perform as a sacrifice 2 : to give up for the sake of something else ⟨*sacrificed* his free time to help⟩ 3 : to sell at a loss 4 : to make a sacrifice hit — **sac·ri·fic·er** *n*

sacrifice fly *n* : an outfield fly in baseball caught by a fielder after which a base runner scores

sacrifice hit *n* : a bunt in baseball that allows a runner to advance one base while the batter is put out

sac·ri·fi·cial \ˌsak-rə-'fish-əl\ *adj* : of or relating to sacrifice — **sac·ri·fi·cial·ly** \-ə-lē\ *adv*

sac·ri·lege \'sak-rə-lij\ *n* : theft or violation of something sacred — **sac·ri·le·gious** \ˌsak-rə-'lij-əs, -'lē-jəs\ *adj* — **sac·ri·le·gious·ly** *adv* — **sac·ri·le·gious·ness** *n*

sac·ris·tan \'sak-rə-stən\ *n* 1 : a church officer in charge of the sacristy 2 : SEXTON

sac·ris·ty \'sak-rə-stē\ *n, pl* **-ties** : VESTRY 1a

sac·ro·sanct \'sak-rō-ˌsang(k)t\ *adj* : SACRED, INVIOLABLE — **sac·ro·sanc·ti·ty** \ˌsak-rō-'sang(k)-tət-ē\ *n*

sac·rum \'sak-rəm, 'sāk-\ *n, pl* **sac·ra** \-rə\ : the part of the vertebral column that is directly connected with or forms a part of the pelvis and in man consists of five united vertebrae

sad \'sad\ *adj* **sad·der**; **sad·dest** 1 : filled with or expressing grief or unhappiness ⟨*sad* at the loss of his dog⟩ ⟨*sad* songs⟩ 2 : causing grief or unhappiness : DEPRESSING ⟨*sad* news⟩ — **sad·ly** *adv*

sad·den \'sad-ən\ *vb* **sad·dened**; **sad·den·ing** \-(ə-)ning\ : to make or become sad

1sad·dle \'sad-əl\ *n* 1 a : a padded and leather-covered seat for a horseback rider b : a comparable part of a harness c : a bicycle or motorcycle seat 2 : a ridge connecting two higher land elevations 3 : a cut of meat consisting of both sides of the back including the loins 4 : something like a saddle in shape, position, or use; *esp* : a support for an object — **in the saddle** : in control or command

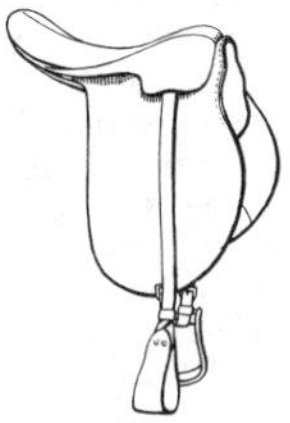
saddle 1a

2saddle *vb* **sad·dled**; **sad·dling** \'sad-(ə-)ling\ 1 : to put a saddle on 2 : ENCUMBER, BURDEN

sad·dle·bag \'sad-əl-ˌbag\ *n* : a large pouch carried hanging from a saddle or over the rear wheel of a bicycle or motorcycle

sad·dle·bow \-ˌbō\ *n* : the arch in the front of a saddle

saddle horse *n* : a horse suited for or trained for riding

sad·dler \'sad-lər\ *n* : one that makes, repairs, or sells horse equipment (as saddles)

sad·dlery \'sad-lə-rē, 'sad-əl-rē\ *n, pl* **-dler·ies** : the work, articles of trade, or shop of a saddler

saddle shoe *n* : an oxford-style shoe having a saddle of contrasting color or leather

saddle sore *n* 1 : a sore on the back of a horse from an ill-fitting saddle 2 : an irritation or sore on parts of the rider's body chafed by the saddle

sad·dle·tree \'sad-əl-ˌtrē\ *n* : the frame of a saddle

sad·ism \'sād-ˌiz-əm, 'sad-\ *n* 1 : a perversion in which sexual pleasure depends upon hurting another 2 : excessive cruelty — **sad·ist** \-əst\ *n* — **sa·dis·tic** \sə-'dis-tik, sā-\ *adj*

sad·ness \'sad-nəs\ *n* : the quality, state, or fact of being sad

sa·fa·ri \sə-'fär-ē, -'far-\ *n, pl* **-ris** [from Arabic *safarīy* "of a trip"] : a hunting expedition esp. in eastern Africa

1safe \'sāf\ *adj* 1 : freed or secure from danger, harm, or loss 2 : successful in reaching base in baseball 3 : affording safety 4 : not threatening danger : HARMLESS ⟨*safe* medicine⟩ 5 a : CAUTIOUS ⟨a *safe* policy⟩ b : TRUSTWORTHY, RELIABLE ⟨a *safe* guide⟩ — **safe·ly** *adv* — **safe·ness** *n*

2safe *n* : a receptacle to keep articles (as provisions or valuables) safe

safe–de·pos·it box \ˌsāf-di-'päz-ət-\ *n* : a box (as in the vault of a bank) for the safe storage of valuables

1safe·guard \'sāf-ˌgärd\ *n* : something that protects and gives safety : DEFENSE

2safeguard *vb* : to make safe or secure : PROTECT

safe·keep·ing \'sāf-'kē-ping\ *n* : PROTECTION, CUSTODY

safe·ty \'sāf-tē\ *n, pl* **safeties** 1 : the state of being safe : SECURITY 2 : a protective device (as on a pistol) to prevent accidental operation 3 a : a football play in which the ball is downed by the offensive team behind its own goal line and which counts two points for the defensive team b : a defensive football back who plays deepest

safety glass *n* : glass that resists shattering and is formed of two sheets of glass with a sheet of transparent plastic between them

safety island *n* : an area within a roadway from which vehicles are excluded

safety match *n* : a match that can be struck only on a specially prepared surface

safety pin *n* : a pin made in the form of a clasp with a guard covering its point

safety razor *n* : a razor with a guard for the blade to prevent deep cuts

safety valve *n* 1 : a valve that opens automatically (as when steam pressure becomes too great) 2 : an outlet for pent-up energy or emotion

saf·flow·er \'saf-ˌlau̇(-ə)r\ *n* : a widely grown Old World herb related to the daisies that has large orange or red flower heads yielding a dyestuff and seeds rich in edible oil

safflower oil *n* : a polyunsaturated edible oil obtained from the seeds of the safflower

saf·fron \'saf-rən\ *n* 1 a : a purple-flowered crocus whose deep orange dried stigmas are used esp. to color and flavor foods b : the dried usu. powdered stigmas of saffron 2 : a moderate orange to orange yellow

saf·ra·nine *or* **saf·ra·nin** \'saf-rə-ˌnēn, -nən\ *n* : any of various usu. red synthetic dyes

1sag \'sag\ *vb* **sagged**; **sag·ging** 1 : to droop or sink below the normal or right level 2 : to lose firmness, resiliency, or vigor ⟨spirits *sagging* from overwork⟩

2sag *n* 1 : a sagging part or area ⟨the *sag* in a rope⟩ 2 : an instance or amount of sagging

sa·ga \'säg-ə\ *n* 1 : a tale of historic or legendary figures and events of Norway and Iceland 2 : a story of heroic deeds

sa·ga·cious \sə-'gā-shəs\ *adj* : quick and shrewd in understanding and judgment — **sa·ga·cious·ness** *n* — **sa·gac·i·ty** \-'gas-ət-ē\ *n*

sag·a·more \'sag-ə-ˌmōr, -ˌmȯr\ *n* 1 : an Algon-

S

quian Indian chief subordinate to a sachem **2 :** SACHEM
1**sage** \'sāj\ *adj* **:** WISE, PRUDENT ⟨*sage* advice⟩ — **sage·ly** *adv* — **sage·ness** *n*
2**sage** *n* **:** a very wise man
3**sage** *n* **1 :** a mint with grayish green aromatic leaves used esp. in flavoring meats; *also* **:** any of several related plants **2 :** SAGEBRUSH
sage·brush \'sāj-ˌbrəsh\ *n* **:** a common plant related to the daisies and having a bitter juice and an odor like a sage that is widespread on plains of the western U.S.; *also* **:** any of several related plants
Sag·it·tar·i·us \ˌsaj-ə-'ter-ē-əs, ˌsag-\ *n* — see ZODIAC table
sa·go \'sā-gō\ *n, pl* **sagos :** a dry granulated or powdered starch prepared from the pith of a sago palm
sago palm *n* **:** any of a genus of tall pinnate-leaved East Indian palms that yield sago
sa·gua·ro \sə-'(g)wär-ō\ *n, pl* **-ros :** a cactus of desert regions of the southwestern U.S. and Mexico that has a spiny branched trunk of up to 60 feet and bears white flowers and edible fruit

saguaro

said *past of* SAY
1**sail** \'sāl, *as last element in compounds often* səl\ *n* **1 a :** a usu. rectangular or triangular piece of fabric (as canvas) by means of which wind is used to propel a ship through water **b :** the sails of a ship ⟨under full *sail*⟩ **c** *pl usu* **sail :** a ship with sails **2 :** something like a sail ⟨the *sail* of an iceboat⟩ **3 :** a journey or trip by ship
2**sail** *vb* **1 a :** to travel by a sailing craft **b :** to travel or begin a journey by water ⟨*sailed* for England on the first steamer⟩ **c :** to pass over by ship ⟨*sail* the seas⟩ **d :** to function in sailing ⟨a boat that *sails* well⟩ **e :** to manage the sailing of **2 :** to move or glide along in a manner suggesting a ship under sail ⟨*sailed* into the room⟩ **3 :** to go at something eagerly ⟨*sailed* into his dinner⟩
sail·boat \'sāl-ˌbōt\ *n* **:** a boat equipped with sails
sail·cloth \-ˌklȯth\ *n* **:** a heavy canvas used esp. for sails and tents
sail·fish \-ˌfish\ *n* **:** any of a genus of large sea fishes related to the swordfish but having teeth, scales, and a very large dorsal fin
sail·or \'sā-lər\ *n* **1 a :** a person who sails **:** SEAMAN **b :** a person considered with respect to his ability to withstand seasickness ⟨a poor *sailor*⟩ **2 :** a stiff straw hat with a low flat crown and straight circular brim
sail·plane \'sāl-ˌplān\ *n* **:** a glider designed to rise in an upward current of air
1**saint** \'sānt; *when a name follows* (ˌ)sānt *or* sənt\ *n* **1 :** a holy and godly person; *esp* **:** one who is canonized **2 :** a person who is sweet-tempered, self-sacrificing, and righteous
2**saint** \'sānt\ *vb* **:** CANONIZE
Saint Ag·nes's Eve \sānt-ˌag-nə-səz-'ēv\ *n* **:** the night of January 20 when a woman is traditionally held to have a revelation of her future husband
Saint An·drew's cross \-ˌan-ˌdrüz-\ *n* **:** a cross shaped like the letter X

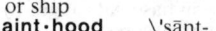

ə abut	ər further	a back	ā bake
ä cot, cart	aů out	ch chin	e less	ē easy
g gift	i trip	ī life	j joke	ng sing	ō flow
ȯ flaw	ȯi coin	th thin	t͟h this	ü loot
ů foot	y yet	yü few	yů furious	zh vision

Saint Ber·nard \ˌsānt-bər-'närd\ *n* **:** any of a Swiss alpine breed of tall powerful dogs formerly used in aiding lost travelers

Saint Bernard

saint·ed \'sānt-əd\ *adj* **:** SAINTLY
Saint El·mo's fire \-ˌel-mōz-\ *n* **:** a luminous discharge of electricity sometimes seen in stormy weather at prominent points on an airplane or ship
saint·hood \'sānt-ˌhůd\ *n* **1 :** the quality or state of being a saint **2 :** SAINTS
saint·ly \'sānt-lē\ *adj* **saint·li·er; -est :** relating to, resembling, or befitting a saint **:** HOLY — **saint·li·ness** *n*
Saint Pat·rick's Day \sānt-'pa-triks-\ *n* **:** March 17 celebrated in honor of St. Patrick and observed as a legal holiday in Ireland in commemoration of his death
saint·ship \'sānt-ˌship\ *n* **:** SAINTHOOD 1
Saint Val·en·tine's Day \-'val-ən-ˌtīnz-\ *n* **:** February 14 observed as a time for sending valentines
Saint Vi·tus's dance \-ˌvīt-əs(-əz)-\ *n* **:** CHOREA
saith \(')seth, 'sā-əth\ *archaic pres 3d sing of* SAY
1**sake** \'sāk\ *n* **1 :** END, PURPOSE ⟨for the *sake* of argument⟩ **2 :** GOOD, ADVANTAGE ⟨the *sake* of his country⟩
2**sa·ke** *or* **sa·ki** \'säk-ē\ *n* **:** a Japanese alcoholic drink of fermented rice usu. served hot
sa·laam \sə-'läm\ *n* **[**from Arabic *salām*, formula of greeting, meaning literally "peace"**] :** a ceremonial greeting in the East performed by bowing very low with the palm on the forehead — **salaam** *vb*
sal·a·ble *or* **sale·a·ble** \'sā-lə-bəl\ *adj* **1 :** fit to be sold **2 :** easy to sell — **sal·a·bil·i·ty** \ˌsā-lə-'bil-ət-ē\ *n*
sal·ad \'sal-əd\ *n* **1 :** green vegetables (as lettuce, chicory, endive) often with tomato, cucumber, or radish served with dressing **2 :** a cold dish (as of meat, shellfish, fruit, or vegetables served singly or in combinations) with a dressing
sal·a·man·der \'sal-ə-ˌman-dər\ *n* **1 :** a mythical being having the power to endure fire without harm **2 :** any of an order of amphibians superficially resembling lizards but scaleless and covered with a soft moist skin — **sal·a·man·drine** \ˌsal-ə-'man-drən\ *adj*
sa·la·mi \sə-'läm-ē\ *n* **:** highly seasoned sausage of pork and beef
sal am·mo·ni·ac \ˌsal-ə-'mō-nē-ˌak\ *n* **:** AMMONIUM CHLORIDE
sal·a·ried \'sal-(ə-)rēd\ *adj* **:** receiving or yielding a salary ⟨a *salaried* position⟩
sal·a·ry \'sal-(ə-)rē\ *n, pl* **-ries :** money paid regularly for work or services **:** STIPEND
sale \'sāl\ *n* **1 :** the act of selling; *esp* **:** the exchange of property for a price **2 :** availability for purchase — usu. used in the phrases *for sale* and *on sale* **3 :** AUCTION **4 :** a selling of goods at bargain prices **5** *pl* **a :** the business of selling **b :** gross receipts ⟨*sales* were up during the year⟩
sales·man \'sālz-mən\ *n* **:** a person whose occupation is selling — **sales·man·ship** \-ˌship\ *n* — **sales·wom·an** \'sālz-ˌwům-ən\ *n*
sales tax *n* **:** a tax levied on the sale of goods and services and collected by the seller

sal·i·cin \'sal-ə-sən\ *n* : a bitter white substance in the bark and leaves of several willows and poplars that was formerly used in medicine

sal·i·cyl·ic acid \ˌsal-ə-ˌsil-ik-\ *n* : an organic acid used esp. in the form of salts to relieve pain and fever and in the treatment of rheumatism

1**sa·lient** \'sāl-yənt, 'sā-lē-ənt\ *adj* **1** : projecting outward ⟨a *salient* angle⟩ **2** : OUTSTANDING — **salient·ly** *adv*

2**salient** *n* : something that projects outward; *esp* : a projecting part of a line of defense

1**sa·line** \'sā-ˌlēn, -ˌlīn\ *adj* **1** : consisting of or containing salt ⟨a *saline* solution⟩ **2** : of, relating to, or resembling salt : SALTY ⟨a *saline* taste⟩ ⟨*saline* compounds⟩ — **sa·lin·i·ty** \sā-'lin-ət-ē, sə-\ *n*

2**sa·line** *1 usu* sə-'lēn, *2 & 3 usu* 'sā-ˌlēn *or* 'sā-ˌlīn\ *n* **1** : a natural deposit of common salt or other soluble salt **2** : a metallic salt; *esp* : a salt of potassium, sodium, or magnesium with a cathartic action **3** : a saline solution

sa·li·va \sə-'lī-və\ *n* : a secretion of water, protein, salts, and often a starch-splitting enzyme secreted into the mouth by salivary glands

sal·i·vary \'sal-ə-ˌver-ē\ *adj* : of or relating to saliva or the glands that secrete it; *esp* : producing or carrying saliva

salivary glands *n pl* : any of various glands that discharge saliva into the mouth cavity

sal·i·vate \'sal-ə-ˌvāt\ *vb* : to secrete saliva esp. in large amounts — **sal·i·va·tion** \ˌsal-ə-'vā-shən\ *n*

Salk vaccine \'sȯ(l)k-\ *n* [named after Jonas *Salk* (born 1914), American physician] : a polio vaccine that contains inactivated virus and is administered by injection

1**sal·low** \'sal-ō\ *adj* : of a grayish greenish yellow color ⟨*sallow* complexion⟩ — **sal·low·ish** \'sal-ə-wish\ *adj* — **sal·low·ness** \'sal-ō-nəs\ *n*

2**sallow** *vb* : to make sallow

1**sal·ly** \'sal-ē\ *n, pl* **sallies** **1** : an action of rushing or bursting forth; *esp* : a sortie of besieged troops upon the attackers **2** : a witty remark : QUIP **3** : EXCURSION, JAUNT

2**sally** *vb* **sal·lied**; **sal·ly·ing** **1** : to leap out or burst forth suddenly **2** : to set out : DEPART ⟨*sallied* forth to see the town⟩

salm·on \'sam-ən\ *n, pl* **salmon** *also* **salmons** **1** : any of various large soft-finned food fishes with pinkish or reddish flesh that live in oceans or large lakes and swim up streams to lay eggs **2** : SALMON PINK — **salmon** *adj* — **salm·on·oid** \'sam-ə-ˌnȯid\ *adj or n*

salmon 1
(up to 3 ft. long)

sal·mo·nel·la \ˌsal-mə-'nel-ə\ *n, pl* **-nellas** *or* **-nella** *also* **-nel·lae** \-'nel-(ˌ)ē, -ˌī\ : any of a genus of rod-shaped bacteria that cause various disorders in man and warm-blooded animals

salmon pink *n* : a strong yellowish pink

sa·lon \sə-'län\ *n* **1** : an elegant apartment or living room **2** : a reception held in a salon **3 a** : an art gallery **b** : an annual exhibition of art **4** : a stylish business establishment

sa·loon \sə-'lün\ *n* **1** : a public room for socializing esp. on a ship **2** : BARROOM

sal·si·fy \'sal-sə-fē, -ˌfī\ *n, pl* **-fies** : a purple-flowered herb related to the daisies that is grown for its long fleshy edible root

sal soda \'sal-'sōd-ə\ *n* : a hydrated carbonate of sodium used in washing and bleaching textiles — called also *washing soda*

1**salt** \'sȯlt\ *n* **1 a** : a crystalline compound that is the chloride of sodium used esp. for seasoning or preserving food and in the chemical industry — called also *common salt* **b** : a compound formed by replacement of part or all of the hydrogen of an acid by a metal or by a radical acting like a metal **2** *pl* **a** : a mineral or saline mixture (as Epsom salts) used as a laxative or cathartic **b** : SMELLING SALTS **3** : an element that gives zest : FLAVOR **4** : SAILOR **5** : SALTCELLAR

2**salt** *vb* : to treat, preserve, flavor, or supply with salt (as a mine)

3**salt** *adj* **1 a** : SALINE, SALTY ⟨*salt* water⟩ **b** : being or inducing one of the four basic taste sensations **2** : cured or seasoned with salt : SALTED ⟨*salt* pork⟩ — **salt·ness** *n*

salt away *vb* : to lay away safely : SAVE

salt·cel·lar \'sȯlt-ˌsel-ər\ *n* : a small vessel for holding salt at table

salt flat *n* : an area of salt-encrusted land left by evaporation of water (as from a former lake)

sal·tine \sȯl-'tēn\ *n* : a square crisp salted cracker

salt lick *n* : LICK 3

salt marsh *n* : flat land subject to overflow by salt water — **salt–marsh** *adj*

salt·pe·ter \'sȯlt-'pēt-ər\ *n* **1** : POTASSIUM NITRATE **2** : a chemical that is the nitrate of sodium and is used esp. as a fertilizer

salt·shak·er \-ˌshā-kər\ *n* : a container with a perforated top for sprinkling salt

salt water *n* : water containing salt in solution; *esp* : the water of the ocean and of certain seas and lakes — **salt·wa·ter** *adj*

salty \'sȯl-tē\ *adj* **salt·i·er**; **-est** **1** : seasoned with or containing salt : tasting of or like salt **2** : smacking of the sea or nautical life **3** : EARTHY, RACY ⟨*salty* talk⟩ — **salt·i·ness** *n*

sa·lu·bri·ous \sə-'lü-brē-əs\ *adj* : favorable to or promoting health ***syn*** see HEALTHFUL — **sa·lu·bri·ous·ly** *adv* — **sa·lu·bri·ous·ness** *n*

sal·u·tary \'sal-yə-ˌter-ē\ *adj* **1** : promoting health **2** : producing a beneficial effect ⟨*salutary* advice⟩ — **sal·u·tar·i·ness** *n*

sal·u·ta·tion \ˌsal-yə-'tā-shən\ *n* **1** : an expression of greeting, goodwill, or courtesy **2** : the word or phrase of greeting (as *Gentlemen* or *Dear Sir*) that conventionally begins a letter — **sal·u·ta·tion·al** \-sh(ə-)nəl\ *adj*

sa·lu·ta·to·ri·an \sə-ˌlüt-ə-'tōr-ē-ən, -'tȯr-\ *n* : the graduating student usu. second highest in rank who gives the salutatory address

1**sa·lu·ta·to·ry** \sə-'lüt-ə-ˌtōr-ē, -ˌtȯr-\ *adj* : expressing salutations or welcome

2**salutatory** *n, pl* **-ries** : a salutatory address at a commencement

1**sa·lute** \sə-'lüt\ *vb* **1** : to greet with courteous words or a bow **2 a** : to honor by a conventional military ceremony **b** : to show respect and recognition to by assuming a prescribed position ⟨*salute* an officer⟩ — **sa·lut·er** *n*

2**salute** *n* **1** : GREETING, SALUTATION **2 a** : a sign or ceremony (as a kiss or bow) of goodwill, compliment, or respect **b** : the formal position assumed by a person saluting a superior

1**sal·vage** \'sal-vij\ *n* **1** : money paid for saving a wrecked or endangered ship or its cargo or passengers **2** : the act of saving a ship or possessions in danger of being lost **3** : something saved or recovered (as from a wreck or fire)

[2]**salvage** *vb* : to rescue or save esp. from wreckage or ruin — **sal·vage·a·ble** \-ə-bəl\ *adj* — **sal·vag·er** *n*

sal·va·tion \sal-'vā-shən\ *n* **1** : the saving of a person from sin **2** : the saving from danger or evil ⟨the *salvation* of a country⟩ **3** : something that saves ⟨the medicine was his *salvation*⟩

[1]**salve** \'sav, 'sȧv\ *n* : a healing ointment or agency

[2]**salve** *vb* : to ease or soothe with or as if with a salve

sal·ver \'sal-vər\ *n* : a serving tray

sal·via \'sal-vē-ə\ *n* : SAGE 1; *esp* : a scarlet-flowered sage widely grown for ornament

sal·vo \'sal-vō\ *n, pl* **salvos** *or* **salvoes** **1** : a discharge of one gun after another in a battery **2 a** : a simultaneous discharge of two or more guns at the same target or as a salute **b** : the release all at once of a rack of bombs or rockets **3** : a sudden burst (as of cheers)

sa·mar·i·um \sə-'mer-ē-əm, -'mar-\ *n* : a pale gray lustrous metallic element — see ELEMENT table

[1]**same** \'sām\ *adj* **1** : resembling in every respect ⟨gave him the *same* answer as before⟩ **2** : being one without addition, change, or discontinuance : IDENTICAL, UNCHANGED **3** : so alike as to be indistinguishable : COMPARABLE ⟨on the *same* day last year⟩

[2]**same** *pron* : the same one or ones

same·ness \'sām-nəs\ *n* **1** : the quality or state of being the same : IDENTITY **2** : MONOTONY, UNIFORMITY

sam·o·var \'sam-ə-ˌvär\ *n* [from Russian, meaning literally "self-boiler"] : an urn with a spigot at its base used esp. in Russia to boil water for tea

sam·pan \'sam-ˌpan\ *n* : a flat-bottomed Chinese skiff usu. propelled by oars

sampan

[1]**sam·ple** \'sam-pəl\ *n* [from medieval French *essample* "example", "sample", from Latin *exemplum*] **1** : a part or item that shows the quality or nature of the whole or group **2** : a part (as of a statistical population) used for investigating the properties of the whole

[2]**sample** *vb* **sam·pled**; **sam·pling** \-p(ə-)ling\ : to judge the quality of by a sample : TEST ⟨*sampled* her jams⟩

[1]**sam·pler** \'sam-plər\ *n* : a piece of needlework typically having letters or verses embroidered on it in various stitches as an example of skill

[2]**sampler** *n* **1** : one that collects or examines samples **2** : a collection of samples

sample space *n* : the set of all possible outcomes of a statistical experiment (as tossing a pair of dice)

Sam·u·el \'sam-yə(-wə)l\ *n* — see BIBLE table

sam·u·rai \'sam-(y)ə-ˌrī\ *n, pl* **samurai** : a Japanese knight

san·a·tar·i·um \ˌsan-ə-'ter-ē-əm\ *n, pl* **-i·ums** *or* **-ia** \-ē-ə\ : SANATORIUM

san·a·to·ri·um \ˌsan-ə-'tōr-ē-əm, -'tȯr-\ *n, pl* **-riums** *or* **-ria** \-ē-ə\ : an establishment for the care and treatment esp. of convalescents or the chronically ill

sanc·ti·fy \'sang(k)-tə-ˌfī\ *vb* **-fied**; **-fy·ing** **1** : to set apart as sacred : CONSECRATE **2** : to make free from sin : PURIFY — **sanc·ti·fi·ca·tion** \ˌsang(k)-tə-fə-'kā-shən\ *n*

sanc·ti·mo·ni·ous \ˌsang(k)-tə-'mō-nē-əs\ *adj* : hypocritically devout — **sanc·ti·mo·ni·ous·ly** *adv* — **sanc·ti·mo·ni·ous·ness** *n*

[1]**sanc·tion** \'sang(k)-shən\ *n* **1** : a measure used to enforce a law or rule **2** : official permission or approval

[2]**sanction** *vb* **sanc·tioned**; **sanc·tion·ing** \-sh(ə-)ning\ : RATIFY, PERMIT

sanc·ti·ty \'sang(k)-tət-ē\ *n, pl* **-ties** **1** : HOLINESS, SAINTLINESS **2** : SACREDNESS ⟨the *sanctity* of an oath⟩

sanc·tu·ary \'sang(k)-chə-ˌwer-ē\ *n, pl* **-ar·ies** **1** : a holy or sacred place **2** : a building or room for religious worship **3** : the most sacred part of a place of worship **4** : a refuge for wildlife **5 a** : a place of refuge **b** : protection afforded by a sanctuary

sanc·tum \'sang(k)-təm\ *n, pl* **sanctums** *also* **sanc·ta** \-tə\ **1** : a sacred place **2** : a place where one is free from intrusion ⟨an editor's *sanctum*⟩

[1]**sand** \'sand\ *n* **1 a** : loose granular material resulting from the disintegration of rocks **b** : soil containing 85 percent or more of sand and not more than 10 percent of clay **2** : a tract, region, or deposit of sand; *esp* : BEACH — often used in pl. **3 a** : the sand in an hourglass **b** *pl* : the moments of a lifetime

[2]**sand** *vb* **1** : to sprinkle with sand **2** : to add sand to **3** : to smooth by rubbing with sandpaper — **sand·er** *n*

san·dal \'san-dəl\ *n* : a shoe consisting of a sole strapped to the foot

san·dal·wood \-ˌwu̇d\ *n* : the close-grained fragrant yellowish heartwood of an Asiatic tree much used in carving and cabinetwork; *also* : the tree itself

[1]**sand·bag** \'san(d)-ˌbag\ *n* **1** : a bag filled with sand and used as ballast or as part of a fortification wall or of a temporary dam **2** : a small bag of sand used as a weapon

[2]**sandbag** *vb* **1** : to bank, stop up, or weight with sandbags **2** : to hit or stun with a sandbag

sand·bank \-ˌbangk\ *n* : a deposit of sand

sand·bar \-ˌbär\ *n* : a ridge of sand formed in water by tides or currents

sand·blast \-ˌblast\ *vb* : to engrave, cut, or clean with a high-velocity stream of sand — **sand·blast·er** *n*

sand·box \'san(d)-ˌbäks\ *n* : a box for holding sand esp. for children to play in

sandbox tree *n* : a tropical American tree having a seed capsule that bursts with a loud report when dry and scatters the seeds

sand·bur \'san(d)-ˌbər\ *n* : any of several weeds of waste places with spiky fruit

sand dollar *n* : a flat circular sea urchin that lives chiefly in shallow water and on sandy bottoms

sand dollar (about 3 in. across)

sand flea *n* **1** : a flea found in sandy places **2** : BEACH FLEA

sand·glass \'san(d)-ˌglas\ *n* : an hourglass containing sand

sand·hog \'sand-ˌhȯg, -ˌhäg\ *n* : a laborer who works in a caisson in driving underwater tunnels

sand lizard *n* : any of several lizards that are common in sandy arid regions

sand·lot \'san-ˌdlät\ *n* : a vacant lot esp. when used for unorganized boys' sports — **sandlot** *adj* — **sand·lot·ter** *n*

sand·man \'san(d)-ˌman\ *n* : the genie of folklore who makes children sleepy supposedly by sprinkling sand in their eyes

ə abut	ər further	a back	ā bake	
ä cot, cart	au̇ out	ch chin	e less	ē easy
g gift	i trip	ī life	j joke	ng sing
ō flow	ȯ flaw	ȯi coin	th thin	t͟h this
ü loot	u̇ foot	y yet	yü few	yu̇ furious
zh vision				

sand·pa·per \-ˌpā-pər\ *n* : paper with abrasive material (as sand) glued on one side and used for smoothing and polishing — **sandpaper** *vb*

sand·pile \-ˌpīl\ *n* : a pile of sand esp. for children to play in

sand·pip·er \-ˌpī-pər\ *n* : any of numerous small shorebirds distinguished from the related plovers chiefly by the longer and soft-tipped bill

sand·stone \ˈsan(d)-ˌstōn\ *n* : a sedimentary rock consisting of usu. quartz sand united by a natural cement

sand·storm \-ˌstȯrm\ *n* : a storm of wind (as in a desert) that drives clouds of sand

1**sand·wich** \ˈsan-ˌ(d)wich\ *n* [named after John Montagu, 4th Earl of *Sandwich* (1718–1792), English diplomat, its supposed inventor] **1** : one or more slices of bread or a roll with a filling or spread (as of meat, cheese, or peanut butter) **2** : something resembling a sandwich

2**sandwich** *vb* **1** : to insert between two or more things ⟨plastic *sandwiched* between layers of glass to make safety glass⟩ **2** : to make a place for : CROWD

sandwich man *n* : one who advertises or pickets a place of business by wearing an advertising board in front of him and another behind him

sandy \ˈsan-dē\ *adj* **sand·i·er**; **-est** **1** : consisting of, containing, or sprinkled with sand **2** : of a yellowish gray color

sane \ˈsān\ *adj* **1** : mentally sound and healthy **2** : RATIONAL, SENSIBLE — **sane·ly** *adv* — **sane·ness** \ˈsān-nəs\ *n*

sang *past of* SING

san·gui·nary \ˈsang-gwə-ˌner-ē\ *adj* **1** : BLOODTHIRSTY, MURDEROUS **2** : BLOODY

san·guine \ˈsang-gwən\ *adj* **1 a** : having the color of blood **b** : RUDDY ⟨a *sanguine* complexion⟩ **2** : SANGUINARY 1 **3** : CHEERFUL, HOPEFUL ⟨a *sanguine* disposition⟩ **4** : CONFIDENT, OPTIMISTIC ⟨*sanguine* of success⟩ — **san·guine·ly** *adv* — **san·guin·i·ty** \san(g)-ˈgwin-ət-ē\ *n*

san·i·tar·i·um \ˌsan-ə-ˈter-ē-əm\ *n, pl* **-i·ums** *or* **-ia** \-ē-ə\ : SANATORIUM

san·i·tary \ˈsan-ə-ˌter-ē\ *adj* **1** : of or relating to health : HYGIENIC ⟨*sanitary* laws⟩ **2** : free from filth, infection, or dangers to health — **san·i·tar·i·ly** \ˌsan-ə-ˈter-ə-lē\ *adv*

sanitary napkin *n* : a disposable absorbent pad in a gauze covering used to absorb uterine flow (as during menstruation)

san·i·ta·tion \ˌsan-ə-ˈtā-shən\ *n* : the study and use of sanitary measures for the prevention of disease

san·i·ty \ˈsan-ət-ē\ *n* : the quality or state of being sane

San Jo·se scale \ˌsan-ə-ˌzā-\ *n* : a scale insect naturalized in the U.S. and a most damaging pest to fruit trees

sank *past of* SINK

sans \(ˌ)sanz\ *prep* : WITHOUT

san·se·vie·ria \ˌsan(t)-sə-ˈvir-ē-ə\ *n* : any of a genus of tropical Old World herbs with mottled or striped sword-shaped leaves

San·skrit \ˈsan-ˌskrit\ *n* : an ancient Indic language that is the classical language of India and of Hinduism

San·ta Claus \ˈsant-ə-ˌklȯz, ˈsant-ē-\ *n* [from Dutch *Sinterklaas*, alteration of *Sint Nikolaas* "Saint Nicholas"] : the spirit of Christmas personified as a fat jolly old man in a red suit who distributes toys to children

1**sap** \ˈsap\ *n* **1** : the fluid part of a plant; *esp* : a watery solution that circulates through a vascular plant **2** : VITALITY **3** : a foolish gullible person

2**sap** *vb* **sapped**; **sap·ping** **1** : UNDERMINE **2** : to weaken gradually ⟨the extreme heat *sapped* his strength⟩

sa·pi·ence \ˈsā-pē-ən(t)s, ˈsap-ē-\ *n* : WISDOM, SAGENESS

sa·pi·ent \-ənt\ *adj* : WISE, DISCERNING — **sa·pi·ent·ly** *adv*

sap·ling \ˈsap-ling\ *n* : a young tree

sap·o·dil·la \ˌsap-ə-ˈdil-ə\ *n* : a tropical American evergreen tree with hard reddish wood, an edible brownish berry, and a latex that yields chicle

sa·pon·i·fi·ca·tion \sə-ˌpän-ə-fə-ˈkā-shən\ *n* : the hydrolysis of a fat by alkali to form a soap and glycerol

sa·pon·i·fy \sə-ˈpän-ə-ˌfī\ *vb* **-fied**; **-fy·ing** : to subject to or undergo saponification

sap·per \ˈsap-ər\ *n* : a soldier who constructs field fortifications or who lays, detects, and disarms mines

sap·phire \ˈsaf-ˌī(ə)r\ *n* **1** : a typically blue precious stone that is a variety of corundum **2** : a deep purplish blue — **sapphire** *adj*

sap·py \ˈsap-ē\ *adj* **sap·pi·er**; **-est** **1** : full of sap **2 a** : foolishly sentimental **b** : SILLY — **sap·pi·ness** *n*

sap·ro·phyte \ˈsap-rə-ˌfīt\ *n* : an organism and esp. a plant living on dead or decaying organic matter — **sap·ro·phyt·ic** \ˌsap-rə-ˈfit-ik\ *adj* — **sap·ro·phyt·i·cal·ly** \-ˈfit-i-k(ə-)lē\ *adv*

sap·suck·er \ˈsap-ˌsək-ər\ *n* : any of various small American woodpeckers

sap·wood \-ˌwu̇d\ *n* : the outer portion of wood that lies between the cambium and the heartwood

sa·ran \sə-ˈran\ *n* : a tough, flexible, waterproof, and chemically resistant plastic

sa·ra·pe \sə-ˈräp-ē\ *n* : a woolen blanket worn by Spanish-American men as a cloak or poncho

sar·casm \ˈsär-ˌkaz-əm\ *n* **1** : a cutting remark : a bitter rebuke **2** : the use of sarcasms often ironically *syn* see IRONY

sar·cas·tic \sär-ˈkas-tik\ *adj* **1** : given to sarcasm **2** : containing sarcasm ⟨a *sarcastic* remark⟩ — **sar·cas·ti·cal·ly** \-ti-k(ə-)lē\ *adv*

sar·co·ma \sär-ˈkō-mə\ *n* : a malignant tumor arising in connective tissue or striated muscle — **sar·com·a·tous** \sär-ˈkäm-ət-əs, -ˈkōm-\ *adj*

sar·coph·a·gus \sär-ˈkäf-ə-gəs\ *n, pl* **-gi** \-ˌgī, -ˌjī\ *or* **-gus·es** [from Greek *sarkophagos*, literally "flesh eater"] : a stone coffin; *esp* : one exposed to view in the open air or in a tomb

sar·dine \sär-ˈdēn\ *n, pl* **sardines** *also* **sardine** : any of various young very small fish often preserved in oil for food

sar·don·ic \sär-ˈdän-ik\ *adj* : SCORNFUL, MOCKING — **sar·don·i·cal·ly** \-ˈdän-i-k(ə-)lē\ *adv*

sard·on·yx \sär-ˈdän-iks, ˈsärd-ə-niks\ *n* : onyx having layers of carnelian

sar·gas·so \sär-ˈgas-ō\ *n, pl* **-sos** **1** : GULFWEED, SARGASSUM **2** : a mass of floating vegetation and esp. sargassums

sar·gas·sum \sär-ˈgas-əm\ *n* : any of a genus of branching brown algae with lateral outgrowths differentiated as leafy segments, air bladders, or spore-bearing structures

sa·ri *or* **sa·ree** \ˈsär-ē\ *n* : a garment of Hindu women that consists of a long cloth draped around the body and head or shoulder

sari

sa·rong \sə-'ròng, -'räng\ *n* : a loose skirt made of a long strip of cloth wrapped loosely around the body and worn by men and women of the Malay archipelago and the Pacific islands

sar·sa·pa·ril·la \ˌsas-(ə-)pə-'ril-ə, ˌsärs-\ *n* **1** : the dried roots of any of several tropical American woody plants used esp. as a flavoring; *also* : a plant yielding sarsaparilla **2** : a sweetened carbonated beverage flavored chiefly with sassafras and an oil from birch

sar·to·ri·al \sär-'tōr-ē-əl, -'tòr-\ *adj* : of or relating to a tailor or tailored clothes — **sar·to·ri·al·ly** \-ē-ə-lē\ *adv*

[1]**sash** \'sash\ *n* : a broad band (as of silk) worn around the waist or over the shoulder

[2]**sash** *n, pl* **sash** *or* **sash·es** **1** : the framework in which panes of glass are set in a window or door **2** : the movable part of a window

Sask *abbr* Saskatchewan

sas·sa·fras \'sas-(ə-)ˌfras\ *n* : a tall eastern No. American tree related to the laurel and having fragrant yellow flowers and blue-black berries; *also* : its dried root bark used esp. in medicine or as a flavoring agent

sassafras

sassy \'sas-ē\ *adj* **sass·i·er; -est** : SAUCY

sat *past of* SIT

sat *abbr* **1** saturate **2** saturated **3** saturation

Sat *abbr* Saturday

Sa·tan \'sāt-ən\ *n* : DEVIL 1 — **sa·tan·ic** \sə-'tan-ik, sā-\ *adj* — **sa·tan·i·cal·ly** \-'tan-i-k(ə-)lē\ *adv*

satch·el \'sach-əl\ *n* : a small bag usu. of leather or heavy cloth with a flat bottom for carrying clothes or books

sate \'sāt\ *vb* **1** : to fill esp. with food beyond desire : GLUT **2** : to satisfy fully

sa·teen \sa-'tēn\ *n* : a glossy cotton fabric resembling satin

sat·el·lite \'sat-ə-ˌlīt\ *n* **1** : a servile follower **2 a** : a celestial body orbiting another of larger size **b** : a man-made vehicle intended to orbit a celestial body (as the earth or the moon) **3** : a subordinate or dependent person or thing; *esp* : a country dominated or controlled by a more powerful country — **satellite** *adj*

[1]**sa·tiate** \'sā-sh(ē-)ət\ *adj* : SATIATED

[2]**sa·ti·ate** \'sā-shē-ˌāt\ *vb* : SATE — **sa·ti·a·tion** \ˌsā-s(h)ē-'ā-shən\ *n*

sa·ti·e·ty \sə-'tī-ət-ē\ *n* : FULLNESS, GLUT

sat·in \'sat-ən\ *n* : a fabric (as of silk) with smooth lustrous face and dull back — **satin** *adj* — **sat·iny** \'sat-ə-nē\ *adj*

sat·in·et *or* **sat·in·ette** \ˌsat-ə-'net\ *n* : a usu. thin silk satin

sat·in·wood \'sat-ən-ˌwu̇d\ *n* **1** : a hard yellowish brown wood with a satiny luster **2** : a tree yielding satinwood; *esp* : an East Indian tree related to mahogany

sat·ire \'sa-ˌtī(ə)r\ *n* **1** : a literary work holding up human vices and follies to ridicule or scorn **2** : biting wit or sarcasm used to expose and discredit vice or folly — **sa·tir·ic** \sə-'tir-ik\ *or* **sa·tir·i·cal** \-'tir-i-kəl\ *adj* — **sa·tir·i·cal·ly** \-i-k(ə-)lē\ *adv*

sat·i·rist \'sat-ə-rəst\ *n* : a satirical writer

sat·i·rize \-ˌrīz\ *vb* : to censure or ridicule by means of satire

sat·is·fac·tion \ˌsat-əs-'fak-shən\ *n* **1 a** : the quality or state of being satisfied **b** : a cause of satisfaction : GRATIFICATION **2 a** : compensation for a loss or injury : RESTITUTION **b** : PUNISHMENT **3** : ASSURANCE

sat·is·fac·to·ry \ˌsat-əs-'fak-t(ə-)rē\ *adj* : sufficient or adequate to satisfy — **sat·is·fac·to·ri·ly** \-t(ə-)rə-lē\ *adv* — **sat·is·fac·to·ri·ness** \-t(ə-)rē-nəs\ *n*

sat·is·fy \'sat-əs-ˌfī\ *vb* **-fied; -fy·ing** **1 a** : to carry out the terms of ⟨*satisfy* a contract⟩ **b** : to meet an obligation ⟨*satisfy* a debt⟩ **2 a** : to make happy : PLEASE **b** : to gratify to the full : APPEASE ⟨*satisfied* his hunger⟩ **3** : CONVINCE ⟨*satisfied* that he is innocent⟩ **4** : FULFILL, MEET ⟨*satisfy* the requirements for graduation⟩ — **sat·is·fi·a·ble** \-ˌfī-ə-bəl\ *adj* — **sat·is·fy·ing·ly** \-ˌfī-ing-lē\ *adv*

sa·trap \'sā-ˌtrap, 'sa-\ *n* [from Greek *satrapēs*, from Old Persian *xshathrapāvan*, literally "protector of the dominion"] **1** : the governor of a province in ancient Persia **2** : a subordinate ruler; *esp* : a petty tyrant

sat·u·rate \'sach-ə-ˌrāt\ *vb* **1** : to treat, furnish, or charge with something to the point where no more can be absorbed, dissolved, or retained ⟨water *saturated* with salt⟩ ⟨air *saturated* with water vapor⟩ **2** : to infuse thoroughly or cause to be pervaded : STEEP *syn* see SOAK — **sat·u·ra·bil·i·ty** \ˌsach-(ə-)rə-'bil-ət-ē\ *n* — **sat·u·ra·ble** \'sach-(ə-)rə-bəl\ *adj* — **sat·u·ra·tor** \'sach-ə-ˌrāt-ər\ *n*

sat·u·rat·ed \'sach-ə-ˌrāt-əd\ *adj* **1** : steeped in moisture : SOAKED **2 a** : being the most concentrated solution that can exist in the presence of an excess of the dissolved substance **b** : being a compound that does not tend to unite directly with another compound **3** : not diluted with white ⟨a *saturated* color⟩

sat·u·ra·tion \ˌsach-ə-'rā-shən\ *n* **1** : the act or process of saturating **2** : the state of being saturated

Sat·ur·day \'sat-ərd-ē\ *n* [from Old English *sæterndæg*, translation of Latin *Saturni dies* "day of Saturn"] : the 7th day of the week

Sat·urn \'sat-ərn\ *n* : the planet 6th in order from the sun — see PLANET table

sat·ur·na·lia \ˌsat-ər-'nāl-yə\ *n sing or pl* **1** *cap* : the festival of the ancient Roman god Saturn beginning on Dec. 17 **2** : an unrestrained often licentious celebration : ORGY — **sat·ur·na·lian** \-yən\ *adj*

sat·ur·nine \'sat-ər-ˌnīn\ *adj* : GLOOMY, SULLEN

sa·tyr \'sāt-ər, 'sat-\ *n* **1** : a forest god in Greek mythology having the ears and tail of a horse or goat and given to boisterous pleasures **2** : a lustful man

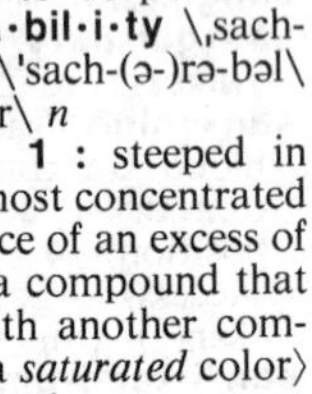

satyr 1

[1]**sauce** \'sòs, *3 is usu* 'sas\ *n* **1** : an often fluid relish for food : DRESSING **2** : stewed or canned fruit **3** : impudent language or actions

[2]**sauce** \'sòs, *2 is usu* 'sas\ *vb* **1** : to add sauce to : SEASON **2** : to be rude or impudent to

sauce·pan \'sòs-ˌpan\ *n* : a small cooking pan with a handle

sau·cer \'sò-sər\ *n* **1** : a small round shallow dish in which a cup is set **2** : something like a saucer esp. in shape

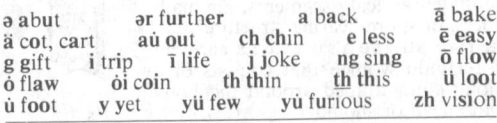

ə abut	ər further	a back	ā bake
ä cot, cart	au̇ out	ch chin	e less	ē easy
g gift	i trip	ī life	j joke	ng sing	ō flow
ȯ flaw	ȯi coin	th thin	th this	ü loot
u̇ foot	y yet	yü few	yu̇ furious	zh vision

saucy \'sas-ē *also* 'sȯs-ē\ *adj* **sauc·i·er; -est** **1 :** BOLD, IMPUDENT **2 :** PERT **3 :** SMART, TRIM ⟨a *saucy* ship⟩ — **sauc·i·ly** \-ə-lē\ *adv* — **sauc·i·ness** \-ē-nəs\ *n*

Sau·di Arabian \ˌsau̇d-ē-\ *adj* **:** of, relating to, or characteristic of Saudi Arabia or its people — **Saudi Arabian** *n*

sau·er·kraut \'sau̇(-ə)r-ˌkrau̇t\ *n* [from German, literally "sour cabbage"] **:** finely cut cabbage fermented in brine

sau·na \'sau̇-nə\ *n* **:** a Finnish steam bath

saun·ter \'sȯnt-ər, 'sänt-\ *vb* **:** to walk along in an idle or leisurely manner **:** STROLL — **saunter** *n* — **saun·ter·er** \-ər-ər\ *n*

sau·ri·an \'sȯr-ē-ən\ *n* **:** any of a group of reptiles including the lizards and in some classifications the crocodiles and various extinct forms (as the dinosaurs) — **saurian** *adj*

sau·sage \'sȯ-sij\ *n* **1 :** highly seasoned minced meat (as pork) usu. stuffed in casings **2 :** a roll of sausage meat in a casing

S. Aust *abbr* South Australia

[1]**sau·té** \sȯ-'tā, sō-\ *n* **:** a sautéed dish — **sauté** *adj*

[2]**sauté** *vb* **sau·téed** *or* **sau·téd; sau·té·ing :** to fry in shallow fat

sau·terne \sō-'tərn, -'te(ə)rn\ *n* **:** a semisweet golden table wine

[1]**sav·age** \'sav-ij\ *adj* [from French *sauvage*, from Latin *silvaticus*, literally "of the woods", from *silva* "wood"] **1 :** not tamed **:** WILD **2 :** CRUEL, FEROCIOUS **3 a :** PRIMITIVE **b :** UNCIVILIZED, RUDE — **sav·age·ly** *adv* — **sav·age·ness** *n*

[2]**savage** *n* **1 :** a person of a primitive society **2 :** a brutal person

sav·age·ry \'sav-ij-(ə-)rē\ *n, pl* **-ries 1 :** savage disposition or action **:** CRUELTY **2 :** the state of being savage

sa·van·na *or* **sa·van·nah** \sə-'van-ə\ *n* **:** a grassland containing scattered trees

sa·vant \sa-'vänt, -'vän; 'sav-ənt\ *n* **:** SCHOLAR

[1]**save** \'sāv\ *vb* **1 a :** to deliver from sin **b :** to rescue or deliver from danger or harm **c :** to keep from injury, destruction, or loss **2 :** to put by as a store or reserve **3 a :** to make unnecessary **:** AVOID ⟨*save* an hour's waiting⟩ **b :** to prevent an opponent from scoring or winning **4 :** MAINTAIN, PRESERVE ⟨*save* appearances⟩ **5 a :** to put by money **b :** ECONOMIZE — **sav·er** *n*

[2]**save** *n* **1 :** a play that prevents an opponent from scoring or winning **2 :** a game that has been saved

[3]**save** \(ˌ)sāv\ *prep* **:** EXCEPT ⟨no hope *save* one⟩

[1]**sav·ing** \'sā-ving\ *n* **1 :** the act of rescuing ⟨the *saving* of lives⟩ **2 a :** something saved ⟨made a *saving* of 50 percent⟩ **b** *pl* **:** money saved over a period of time

[2]**saving** *adj* **1 :** ECONOMICAL, THRIFTY **2 :** making up for something **:** COMPENSATING ⟨a *saving* sense of humor⟩

[3]**saving** *prep* **1 :** EXCEPT, SAVE **2 :** without disrespect to

[4]**saving** *conj* **:** EXCEPT

savings account *n* **:** an account (as in a bank) on which interest is usu. paid and from which withdrawals can be made usu. only by presentation of a passbook or by written authorization

savings bank *n* **:** a bank that receives and invests savings and pays interest to depositors

savings bond *n* **:** a registered U.S. bond issued in denominations of $25 to $1000

sav·ior *or* **sav·iour** \'sāv-yər\ *n* **:** one that saves from danger or destruction; *esp, cap* **:** Jesus Christ

[1]**sa·vor** \'sā-vər\ *n* **1 :** the taste and odor of something ⟨the *savor* of roast meat⟩ **2 :** a distinctive quality **:** SMACK — **sa·vor·less** \-ləs\ *adj*

[2]**savor** *vb* **sa·vored; sa·vor·ing** \'sāv-(ə-)ring\ **1 :** to have a specified smell or quality **:** SMACK **2 :** to give flavor to **:** SEASON **3 :** to taste or smell with pleasure **:** RELISH — **sa·vor·er** \'sā-vər-ər\ *n*

[1]**sa·vory** \'sāv-(ə-)rē\ *adj* **sa·vor·i·er; -est :** pleasing to the taste or smell **:** APPETIZING ⟨*savory* sausages⟩ — **sa·vor·i·ness** *n*

[2]**sa·vo·ry** \'sāv-(ə-)rē\ *n, pl* **-ries :** any of a genus of mints used in cookery as seasonings

[1]**sav·vy** \'sav-ē\ *vb* **sav·vied; sav·vy·ing** *slang* **:** COMPREHEND, UNDERSTAND

[2]**savvy** *n, slang* **:** pratical grasp **:** SHREWDNESS ⟨political *savvy*⟩

[1]**saw** *past of* SEE

[2]**saw** \'sȯ\ *n* **1 :** a hand or power tool with a tooth-edged blade used for cutting hard material **2 :** a machine that mounts a saw (as a band saw or circular saw)

[3]**saw** *vb* **sawed** \'sȯd\; **sawed** *or* **sawn** \'sȯn\; **saw·ing :** to cut or shape with a saw

[4]**saw** *n* **:** a common saying **:** PROVERB

saw·buck \'sȯ-ˌbək\ *n* **1 :** SAWHORSE **2** *slang* **:** a 10-dollar bill

saw·dust \'sȯ-(ˌ)dəst\ *n* **:** dust or fine particles of wood made by a saw in cutting

sawed–off \'sȯd-'ȯf\ *adj* **1 :** having an end sawed off ⟨a *sawed-off* shotgun⟩ **2 :** being of less than average height ⟨a *sawed-off* little guy⟩

saw·fish \'sȯ-ˌfish\ *n* **:** any of several mostly tropical rays with a long flattened snout bearing a row of stout toothlike structures along each edge

saw·fly \-ˌflī\ *n* **:** any of numerous insects that are related to the wasps and bees and usu. have in the female a pair of organs for making slits in leaves or stems into which she lays her eggs

saw grass *n* **:** a sedge with sharply toothed leaves

saw·horse \'sȯ-ˌhȯrs\ *n* **:** a frame or rack on which wood is rested while being sawed

saw·mill \-ˌmil\ *n* **:** a mill or machine for sawing logs

saw·tooth \-ˌtüth\ *n* **:** a tooth of a saw or one of the teeth of an animal or machine shaped or arranged like the teeth of a saw

saw–toothed \-'tütht\ *adj* **:** having an edge or outline like the teeth of a saw

saw·yer \'sȯ-yər\ *n* **:** a person who saws timber

sax \'saks\ *n* **:** SAXOPHONE

sax·horn \'saks-ˌhȯrn\ *n* **:** one of a family of valved conical-bore brass-wind instruments of full even tone and large compass

sax·i·frage \'sak-sə-frij, -ˌfrāj\ *n* **:** any of a genus of plants with showy 5-parted flowers and usu. with leaves growing in tufts close to the ground

sax·o·phone \'sak-sə-ˌfōn\ *n* [from French, from Adolphe *Sax* (1814–1894), Belgian maker of musical instruments, and Greek *phōnē* "sound"] **:** a wind instrument with reed mouthpiece, curved conical metal tube, and finger keys — **sax·o·phon·ist** \-ˌfō-nəst\ *n*

sax·tu·ba \'saks-'t(y)ü-bə\ *n* **:** a bass saxhorn

[1]**say** \'sā\ *vb* **said** \'sed\; **say·ing** \'sā-ing\; **says** \'sez\ **1 a :** to express in words **:** STATE **b :** to state as opinion or belief **:** DECLARE ⟨*said* to be the best you can get⟩ **2 a :** UTTER, PRONOUNCE **b :** RECITE, REPEAT ⟨*said* his prayers⟩ **3 :** INDICATE, SHOW ⟨the clock *says* five minutes after

saxophone

twelve⟩ ⟨a glance that *said* all that was necessary⟩ — **say·er** \'sā-ər\ *n*

2**say** *n* **1** : an expression of opinion ⟨had his *say*⟩ **2** : the power to decide or help decide ⟨had no *say* in the matter⟩

3**say** *adv* **1** : ABOUT, APPROXIMATELY ⟨the property is worth, *say*, four million dollars⟩ **2** : for example : AS ⟨if we compress any gas, *say* oxygen⟩

say·ing \'sā-ing\ *n* : something frequently said : PROVERB, SAW

say–so \'sā-,sō\ *n* **1 a** : one's unsupported word or assurance ⟨couldn't be convicted on one man's *say-so*⟩ **b** : an authoritative judgment ⟨acted on the doctors' *say-so*⟩ **2** : a right of final decision : AUTHORITY ⟨an affair in which I have no *say-so*⟩

sb *abbr* substantive

SB *abbr* **1** bachelor of science **2** stolen base

sc *abbr* science

Sc *abbr* Scots

S.C. *or* **SC** *abbr* South Carolina

1**scab** \'skab\ *n* **1 a** : scabies of domestic animals **b** : any of various plant diseases characterized by crusted spots **2** : a crust of hardened blood and serum over a wound **3** : a worker who takes the place of a striking worker

2**scab** *vb* **scabbed**; **scab·bing** **1** : to become covered with a scab **2** : to act as a scab

scab·bard \'skab-ərd\ *n* : a sheath for a sword, dagger, or bayonet

scab·by \'skab-ē\ *adj* **scab·bi·er**; **-est** **1 a** : covered with or full of scabs ⟨*scabby* skin⟩ **b** : diseased with scab ⟨a *scabby* animal⟩ **2** : MEAN, CONTEMPTIBLE ⟨a *scabby* trick⟩

sca·bies \'skā-bēz\ *n, pl* **scabies** : an itch or mange caused by mites living as parasites under the skin

scads \'skadz\ *n pl* : a great quantity ⟨*scads* of money⟩

scaf·fold \'skaf-əld, -,ōld\ *n* **1** : an elevated platform built as a support for workmen **2** : a platform on which a criminal is executed

scaf·fold·ing \-əl-ding, -,ōl-\ *n* **1** : a system of scaffolds **2** : materials for scaffolds

scag \'skag\ *n, slang* : HEROIN

1**sca·lar** \'skā-lər\ *adj* **1** : arranged like a ladder : GRADUATED ⟨*scalar* chain of authority⟩ ⟨*scalar* cells⟩ **2** : describable by a number that can be represented by a point on a scale ⟨*scalar* quantity⟩

2**scalar** *n* **1** : a quantity fully described by a number — compare VECTOR **2** : a scalar number

sca·lare \skə-'la(ə)r-ē, -'le(ə)r-\ *n* : a black and silver So. American fish popular in aquariums

scal·a·wag \'skal-i-,wag\ *n* **1** : RASCAL **2** : a white Southerner acting as a Republican in the time of reconstruction after the Civil War

1**scald** \'skȯld\ *vb* **1** : to burn with or as if with hot liquid or steam ⟨*scalded* his hands⟩ **2 a** : to subject to the action of boiling water or steam ⟨*scald* dishes⟩ **b** : to bring to a temperature just below the boiling point ⟨*scald* milk⟩ **3** : SCORCH

2**scald** *n* : an injury to the body caused by scalding

scald·ing \'skȯl-ding\ *adj* **1** : causing the sensation of scalding or burning **2** : BOILING ⟨*scalding* water⟩ **3** : SCORCHING ⟨the *scalding* sun⟩ **4** : BITING, SCATHING ⟨a series of *scalding* editorials⟩

1**scale** \'skāl\ *n* [from Old Norse *skāl* "bowl", "scale", from the same Germanic root as English *shell*] **1 a** : either pan of a balance **b** : BALANCE — usu. used in pl. **2** : a device for weighing ⟨a bathroom *scale*⟩

2**scale** *vb* **1** : to weigh in scales **2** : to have a specified weight

3**scale** *n* [from medieval French *escale*, borrowed from a word in some Germanic language formed from the same root as English *shell*] **1** : one of the small rigid flattened plates forming an outer covering on the body esp. of a fish or reptile **2** : a small thin part or structure suggesting a fish scale: as **a** : a modified leaf covering a bud of a seed plant **b** : a small dry flake of skin ⟨dandruff *scales*⟩ **3** : SCALE INSECT **4** : a thin layer, coating, or incrustation forming esp. on metal (as iron) ⟨boiler *scale*⟩ — **scaled** \'skāld\ *adj* — **scale·less** \'skāl-ləs\ *adj* — **scale·like** \'skāl-,līk\ *adj*

4**scale** *vb* **1** : to remove scale or the scales from ⟨*scale* a boiler⟩ ⟨*scale* fish⟩ **2** : to take off in scales or thin layers ⟨*scale* the bark off a tree⟩ **3** : to come off in scales or shed scales : FLAKE **4** : to throw a flat object so as to sail in air or skip on water ⟨*scaling* cards into a hat⟩

5**scale** *n* [from Latin *scala* "ladder", from *scandere* "to climb", the source of English *ascend* and *descend*] **1 a** : a series of spaces marked by lines and used to measure distances or to register something (as the height of the mercury in a thermometer) **b** : a divided line on a map or chart indicating the length (as an inch) used to represent a larger unit of measure (as a mile) **c** : an instrument consisting of a strip (as of wood, plastic, or metal) with spaces graduated and numbered on its surface for measuring or laying off distances or dimensions **2** : a basis for a system of numbering ⟨the decimal *scale*⟩ **3** : a graduated series ⟨the *scale* of prices⟩ **4** : the size of a picture, plan, or model of a thing in proportion to the size of the thing itself **5** : a relative size or degree ⟨do things on a large *scale*⟩ **6** : a standard by which something can be measured or judged **7** : a graduated series of tones going up or down in pitch

6**scale** *vb* **1** : to climb by or as if by means of a ladder : SURMOUNT ⟨*scale* a wall⟩ ⟨*scale* a cliff⟩ **2 a** : to arrange in a graded series ⟨*scale* a test⟩ **b** : to measure by or as if by a scale **c** : to make, regulate, or estimate according to a rate or standard ⟨*scale* down a budget⟩ — **scal·er** *n*

scaled \'skāld\ *adj* : furnished with or adjusted to a scale ⟨a *scaled* line⟩

scale insect *n* : any of numerous small insects that are related to the plant lice, include many destructive plant pests, and have winged males, degenerated scale-covered females attached to the host plant, and young that suck the juices of plants

scale insects on tree branch (less than one inch across)

sca·lene \'skā-,lēn, skā-'\ *adj* : having the sides unequal

scale·pan \'skāl-,pan\ *n* : a pan of a scale for weighing

scal·lion \'skal-yən\ *n* : a young onion pulled before the bulb has enlarged

1**scal·lop** \'skäl-əp, 'skal-\ *n* **1 a** : any of a family of marine bivalve mollusks with the shell radially ribbed **b** : the adductor muscle of a scallop as an article of food **2** : a scallop-shell valve or a similarly shaped dish used for baking **3** : one of a continuous series of

ə abut   ər further   a back   ā bake
ä cot, cart   au̇ out   ch chin   e less   ē easy
g gift   i trip   ī life   j joke   ng sing   ō flow
ȯ flaw   ȯi coin   th thin   t͟h this   ü loot
u̇ foot   y yet   yü few   yu̇ furious   zh vision

rounded or angular projections forming a border (as on lace)

2**scallop** *vb* **1 :** to bake in a sauce usu. covered with seasoned bread or cracker crumbs ⟨*scalloped* potatoes⟩ **2 :** to shape, cut, or edge in scallops

1**scalp** \'skalp\ *n* **1 :** the part of the skin and flesh of the head usu. covered with hair **2 :** a part of the human scalp cut or torn from an enemy esp. as a token of victory

2**scalp** *vb* **1 :** to remove the scalp from **2 a :** to buy and sell so as to make small quick profits ⟨*scalp* stocks⟩ **b :** to buy and resell at greatly increased prices ⟨*scalp* theater tickets⟩ — **scalp·er** *n*

scal·pel \'skal-pəl, skal-'pel\ *n* **:** a small straight thin-bladed knife used esp. in surgery

scaly \'skā-lē\ *adj* **scal·i·er; -est 1 a :** covered with, composed of, or rich in scale or scales **b :** FLAKY ⟨soft *scaly* stone⟩ **2 :** infested with scale insects

1**scamp** \'skamp\ *n* **:** RASCAL

2**scamp** *vb* **:** to perform in a hasty, neglectful, or imperfect manner **:** SKIMP ⟨*scamp* one's work⟩

scam·per \'skam-pər\ *vb* **scam·pered; scam·per·ing** \-p(ə-)ring\ **:** to run lightly and playfully about — **scamper** *n*

scan \'skan\ *vb* **scanned; scan·ning 1 :** to read or mark verses so as to show metrical structure **2 a :** to examine intensively ⟨*scanned* their faces⟩ **b :** to make a wide sweeping search of ⟨*scanning* the field with binoculars⟩ **c :** to look through or over hastily ⟨*scanned* the headlines⟩ **3 a :** to move across in successive lines in reproducing a television image ⟨the electron beam *scans* the face of the picture tube⟩ **b :** to direct a succession of radar beams over in searching for a target — **scan** *n* — **scan·ner** *n*

Scand *abbr* 1 Scandinavia 2 Scandinavian

scan·dal \'skan-dəl\ *n* **1 :** an offense against faith or morals that causes another to sin **2 :** loss of or damage to reputation caused by actual or apparent violation of morality or propriety **:** DISGRACE ⟨his behavior brought *scandal* on the school⟩ **3 :** something that causes a general feeling of shame ⟨the slum is a *scandal*⟩ **4 :** talk that injures a person's good name ⟨untouched by *scandal*⟩

scan·dal·ize \'skan-də-ˌlīz\ *vb* **1 :** to speak falsely or maliciously of **2 :** to offend the moral sense of **:** SHOCK ⟨her actions *scandalized* the neighbors⟩

scan·dal·ous \'skan-d(ə-)ləs\ *adj* **1 :** DEFAMATORY ⟨a *scandalous* story⟩ **2 :** offensive to propriety or morality **:** SHOCKING ⟨*scandalous* behavior⟩ — **scan·dal·ous·ly** *adv*

Scan·di·na·vi·an \ˌskan-də-'nā-vē-ən\ *adj* **:** of, relating to, or characteristic of Scandinavia or its people — **Scandinavian** *n*

scan·di·um \'skan-dē-əm\ *n* **:** a white metallic element — see ELEMENT table

scan·sion \'skan-chən\ *n* **:** the scanning of verse to show its meter

1**scant** \'skant\ *adj* **1 a :** barely or scarcely sufficient; *esp* **:** not quite coming up to a stated measure ⟨a *scant* cup of milk⟩ **b :** lacking in amplitude or quantity **:** MEAGER, SCANTY **2 :** having a small or insufficient supply ⟨*scant* of breath⟩ — **scant·ly** *adv*

2**scant** *vb* **:** SKIMP, STINT

scant·ling \'skant-ling, -lən\ *n* **:** a small piece of lumber; *esp* **:** one of the upright pieces in the frame of a house

scanty \'skant-ē\ *adj* **scant·i·er; -est :** scant esp. in size or amount **:** barely enough ⟨*scanty* nourishment⟩ ⟨*scanty* bikinis⟩ — **scant·i·ly** \'skant-ə-lē\ *adv* — **scant·i·ness** \'skant-ē-nəs\ *n*

scape \'skāp\ *n* **1 :** a leafless flower stalk (as in the tulip) that begins at or beneath the surface of the ground **2 :** the shaft of a column **3 :** the shaft of an animal part (as an antenna or a feather)

-scape \ˌskāp\ *n comb form* **:** a (specified) type of scene; *also* **:** a pictorial representation of (such a scene) ⟨painted sea*scapes*⟩

scape·goat \'skāp-ˌgōt\ *n* **:** a person or thing bearing the blame for others

scape·grace \-ˌgrās\ *n* **:** an incorrigible rascal

scap·u·la \'skap-yə-lə\ *n, pl* **-lae** \-ˌlē, -ˌlī\ *or* **-las :** SHOULDER BLADE

1**scap·u·lar** \'skap-yə-lər\ *n* **1 :** a long wide band of cloth with an opening for the head worn front and back over the shoulders as part of a monastic habit **2 :** a pair of small cloth squares joined by shoulder tapes and worn under the clothing on the breast and back esp. for religious purposes

2**scapular** *adj* **:** of or relating to the shoulder or the scapula

1**scar** \'skär\ *n* **1 a :** a mark remaining after injured tissue has healed **b :** a mark (as on furniture) resembling a scar **c :** a mark on a stem where a leaf or fruit has separated **2 :** a lasting moral or emotional injury

2**scar** *vb* **scarred; scar·ring** *vb* **1 :** to mark with or form a scar **2 :** to do lasting injury to ⟨a child *scarred* by neglect⟩ **3 :** to become scarred

scar·ab \'skar-əb\ *n* **1 :** a large black or nearly black dung beetle regarded by the ancient Egyptians as symbolic of resurrection and immortality; *also* **:** any of various related beetles **2 :** an ornament or a gem made to represent a scarab

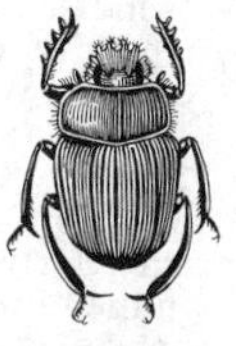

scarab 1 (about one inch long)

scar·a·bae·us \ˌskar-ə-'bē-əs\ *n, pl* **-bae·us·es** *or* **-baei** \-'bē-ˌī\ **:** SCARAB

scarce \'ske(ə)rs, 'ska(ə)rs\ *adj* **:** deficient in quantity or number **:** not plentiful or abundant ⟨food is *scarce*⟩ ***syn*** see RARE ***ant*** abundant — **scarce·ly** *adv* — **scarce·ness** *n*

scar·ci·ty \'sker-sət-ē, 'skar-\ *n, pl* **-ties :** the quality or condition of being scarce **:** a very small supply

1**scare** \'ske(ə)r, 'ska(ə)r\ *vb* **1 :** to frighten suddenly **:** ALARM **2 :** to become scared ⟨she *scared* easily⟩

2**scare** *n* **1 :** a sudden fright **2 :** a widespread state of alarm **:** PANIC

scare·crow \'ske(ə)r-ˌkrō, 'ska(ə)r-\ *n* **1 :** an object usu. suggesting a human figure that is set up to scare birds away from crops **2 :** a skinny or ragged person

scare up *vb* **:** to bring to light or get together with considerable labor or difficulty

scarf \'skärf\ *n, pl* **scarves** \'skärvz\ *or* **scarfs** \'skärfs\ **1 :** a broad band of cloth worn about the shoulders, around the neck, over the head, or about the waist **2 :** RUNNER 5b

scarf·skin \'skärf-ˌskin\ *n* **:** CUTICLE, EPIDERMIS; *esp* **:** that about the base of a nail

scar·i·fy \'skar-ə-ˌfī, 'sker-\ *vb* **-fied; -fy·ing 1 :** to make scratches or small cuts in **:** wound superficially ⟨*scarify* skin for vaccination⟩ ⟨*scarify* seeds to help them germinate⟩ **2 :** to lacerate the feelings of **:** FLAY

scar·la·ti·na \ˌskär-lə-'tē-nə\ *n* **:** a usu. mild scarlet fever

scar·let \'skär-lət\ *n* **1 :** scarlet cloth or clothes **2 :** a bright red — **scarlet** *adj*

scarlet fever *n* **:** a contagious disease marked by fever, inflammation of the nose, throat, and mouth, and a red rash

scarlet ibis *n* **:** an ibis of South and Central America that is an intense scarlet with black-tipped wings

S

scarlet runner *n* : a tropical American high-climbing bean with large bright red flowers and red-and-black seeds

scarlet tanager *n* : a common American tanager of which the male is scarlet with black wings

1**scarp** \'skärp\ *n* **1** : the side of a ditch below the parapet of a fortification **2 a** : a line of cliffs produced by faulting or erosion **b** : a low steep slope along a beach caused by wave erosion

2**scarp** *vb* : to cut so as to form a scarp

scar tissue *n* : connective tissue forming a scar

scary *also* **scar·ey** \'ske(ə)r-ē, 'ska(ə)r-\ *adj* **scar·i·er**; **-est** **1** : causing fright : ALARMING ⟨a *scary* movie⟩ **2** : easily scared : TIMID **3** : SCARED, FRIGHTENED ⟨*scary* feeling⟩

1**scat** \'skat\ *vb* **scat·ted**; **scat·ting** **1** : to go away quickly — often used interjectionally to drive away an animal (as a cat) **2** : to move fast : SCOOT

2**scat** *n* : jazz singing with nonsense syllables

3**scat** *vb* **scat·ted**; **scat·ting** : to improvise nonsense syllables to an instrumental accompaniment : sing scat

1**scathe** \'skāth\ *n* : HARM, INJURY — **scathe·less** \-ləs\ *adj*

2**scathe** *vb* **1** : to do harm to : INJURE; *esp* : SCORCH, SEAR **2** : to attack with withering accusations

scath·ing \'skā-thing\ *adj* : bitterly severe ⟨*scathing* rebuke⟩ — **scath·ing·ly** \-thing-lē\ *adv*

scat·ter \'skat-ər\ *vb* **1** : to cause to separate widely ⟨wind *scattered* the dry leaves⟩ **2** : to distribute irregularly ⟨*scattered* his toys all over the house⟩ **3** : to sow widely and at random **4** : to diffuse or disperse (a beam of radiation) in a random manner **5** : to separate from each other and go in different directions ⟨the crowd *scattered*⟩ **6** : to occur or fall irregularly or at random ⟨lakes *scattered* everywhere in the hills⟩

scat·ter·brain \'skat-ər-ˌbrān\ *n* : a giddy heedless person incapable of concentration — **scat·ter·brained** \-ˌbrānd\ *adj*

1**scat·ter·ing** \'skat-ə-ring\ *n* **1** : an act or process in which something scatters or is scattered **2** : something scattered; *esp* : a small number or quantity placed or found here and there ⟨a *scattering* of visitors⟩

2**scattering** *adj* **1** : going in various directions **2** : found or placed far apart and in no order

scatter rug *n* : a rug of such a size that several can be used (as to fill vacant places) in a room

scav·enge \'skav-inj\ *vb* : to salvage usable material from what has been discarded

scav·en·ger \'skav-ən-jər\ *n* **1** : someone or something that scavenges **2** : an organism that feeds habitually on refuse or carrion

ScD *abbr* doctor of science

sce·nar·io \sə-'nar-ē-ˌō, -'ner-, -'när-\ *n, pl* **-i·os** **1 a** : an outline or synopsis of a play **b** : the libretto of an opera **2** : SCREENPLAY

sce·nar·ist \-'nar-əst, -'ner-, -'när-\ *n* : a writer of scenarios

scene \'sēn\ *n* [from Latin *scena* "stage", from Greek *skēnē* "tent", "hut", and then the temporary building erected for actors' changes of costumes which came to form a background for a dramatic performance] **1 a** : a division of an act during which there is no change of scene or break in time **b** : a single situation or unit of dialogue in a play ⟨a famous fight *scene*⟩ **c** : a motion picture or television episode or sequence **2 a** : a stage setting ⟨change *scenes*⟩ **b** : a view or sight having pictorial quality ⟨a winter *scene*⟩ **3 a** : the place and time of the action in a play or story **b** : the place of an occurrence or action : LOCALE ⟨*scene* of a riot⟩ **4** : a show of unbecoming behavior ⟨made a *scene*⟩ **5** *slang* **a** : sphere of activity ⟨the drug *scene*⟩ **b** : SITUATION ⟨the *scene* got heavy when the cops arrived⟩ — **behind the scenes** **1** : out of public view : in secret ⟨decisions reached *behind the scenes*⟩ **2** : in a position to see or control the hidden workings ⟨the man *behind the scenes*⟩

scen·ery \'sēn-(ə-)rē\ *n* **1** : the painted scenes or hangings and accessories used on a theater stage **2** : a picturesque view or landscape ⟨mountain *scenery*⟩

scene–steal·er \'sēn-ˌstē-lər\ *n* : an actor who diverts attention to himself when he is not intended to be the center of attraction

sce·nic \'sē-nik\ *adj* **1** : of or relating to the stage, a stage setting, or stage representation ⟨*scenic* effects⟩ **2** : of or relating to natural scenery ⟨a *scenic* route⟩ **3** : representing an action, event, or episode in pictured form ⟨*scenic* wallpaper⟩

1**scent** \'sent\ *vb* **1 a** : SMELL ⟨the dog *scented* a rabbit⟩ **b** : to get a hint of ⟨*scent* trouble⟩ **2** : to fill with an odor : PERFUME ⟨*scent* a handkerchief⟩

2**scent** *n* **1 a** : an odor left by an animal **b** : a course of pursuit or discovery ⟨throw them off the *scent*⟩ **c** : a characteristic or particular and usu. agreeable odor **2 a** : sense of smell ⟨a keen *scent*⟩ **b** : power of detection ⟨a *scent* for heresy⟩ **3** : HINT, INKLING ⟨a *scent* of trouble⟩ **4** : PERFUME 2 **5** : an odorous lure for an animal

scent·ed *adj* : having scent; *esp* : PERFUMED

scep·ter \'sep-tər\ *n* **1** : a staff or baton carried by a sovereign as an emblem of authority **2** : royal or imperial authority : SOVEREIGNTY — **scep·tered** \-tərd\ *adj*

scep·tic \'skep-tik\ *var of* SKEPTIC

sch *abbr* school

1**sched·ule** \'skej-ül, -əl, *Canad also* 'shej-, *Brit usu* 'shed-yül\ *n* **1 a** : a written or printed list, catalog, or inventory ⟨a *schedule* of social events⟩ **b** : TIMETABLE ⟨a plane *schedule*⟩ ⟨a *schedule* for completion of the school⟩ **2** : PROGRAM, AGENDA ⟨my *schedule* for tomorrow⟩

2**schedule** *vb* **1** : to place in a schedule ⟨*schedule* a meeting⟩ **2** : to make a schedule of ⟨*scheduled* his income and debts⟩

schee·lite \'shā-ˌlīt\ *n* : a mineral that is a source of tungsten

sche·mat·ic \ski-'mat-ik\ *adj* : of, relating to, or forming a scheme, plan, or diagram : DIAGRAMMATIC — **sche·mat·i·cal·ly** \-'mat-i-k(ə-)lē\ *adv*

sche·ma·tize \'skē-mə-ˌtīz\ *vb* : to form or form into a scheme or systematic arrangement

1**scheme** \'skēm\ *n* **1** : a graphic sketch or outline **2** : a concise statement in an outline, table, or list **3** : a plan or program of action ⟨a new *scheme* for better insurance coverage⟩; *esp* : a crafty or secret one ⟨a *scheme* to seize control⟩ **4** : a systematic or organized design ⟨color *scheme* of a room⟩ ⟨his whole *scheme* of life⟩

2**scheme** *vb* **1** : to form a scheme for **2** : to form plans; *esp* : to engage in intrigue : PLOT — **schem·er** *n*

schem·ing \'skē-ming\ *adj* : given to forming schemes; *esp* : shrewdly devious and contriving

Schick test \'shik-\ *n* : a test to determine whether an individual is susceptible to diphtheria

schism \'siz-əm, 'skiz-\ *n* **1 a** : DIVISION, SEPARATION **b** : lack of harmony : DISCORD **2** : formal division in or separation from a church or religious body

[1]**schis·mat·ic** \s(k)iz-'mat-ik\ *n* : one who creates or takes part in schism

[2]**schismatic** *adj* : of, relating to, or guilty of schism

schist \'shist\ *n* : a metamorphic rock that can be split along approximately parallel planes

schiz·oid \'skit-ˌsȯid\ *adj* : characterized by, resulting from, or suggestive of a split personality — **schizoid** *n*

schiz·o·phre·nia \ˌskit-sə-'frē-nē-ə\ *n* : a mental disorder marked by loss of contact with environment and by personality disintegration — **schiz·o·phren·ic** \-'fren-ik\ *adj or n*

schle·miel \shlə-'mēl\ *n, slang* : an unlucky bungler : CHUMP

schmaltz *or* **schmalz** \'shmȯlts\ *n* : sentimental or florid music or art — **schmaltzy** \'shmȯlt-sē\ *adj*

schnau·zer \'shnaůt-sər\ *n* : any of a breed of terriers with a long head, small ears, and wiry coat

schnauzer

schol·ar \'skäl-ər\ *n* **1** : one who attends a school or studies under a teacher : PUPIL **2 a** : one who has done advanced study in a special field **b** : a learned person **3** : a holder of a scholarship — **schol·ar·ly** \-lē\ *adj*

schol·ar·ship \-ˌship\ *n* **1** : money given (as by a college) to a student to help pay for further education **2** : the character, qualities, or attainments of a scholar : LEARNING

scho·las·tic \skə-'las-tik\ *adj* : of or relating to schools or scholars — **scho·las·ti·cal·ly** \-ti-k(ə-)lē\ *adv*

[1]**school** \'skül\ *n* [from Old English *scōl*, from Greek *scholē*, literally "leisure", then "discussion", a favorite leisure-time occupation of the ancient Greeks, then "lecture", "school"] **1 a** : a place or establishment for teaching and learning ⟨public *schools*⟩ ⟨a music *school*⟩ **b** : SCHOOLHOUSE **c** : the students or students and teachers of a school ⟨a *school* outing⟩ ⟨the whole *school* was sick⟩ **d** : a session of school ⟨missed *school* yesterday⟩ **2** : persons holding the same opinions and beliefs or accepting the same intellectual methods or leadership ⟨the radical *school* of economists⟩ **3** : a faculty or division within an institution of higher learning devoted to teaching, study, and research in a particular field of knowledge : COLLEGE ⟨*school* of law⟩ ⟨graduate *school*⟩

[2]**school** *vb* : TEACH, TRAIN; *esp* : to drill in or habituate to something ⟨*school* himself in patience⟩

[3]**school** *n* : a large number of aquatic animals of one kind (as bass) swimming together

school·bag \'skül-ˌbag\ *n* : a bag for carrying schoolbooks and school supplies

school board *n* : a board in charge of local public schools

school·book \'skül-ˌbu̇k\ *n* : a school textbook

school·boy \-ˌbȯi\ *n* : a boy attending school

school bus *n* : a vehicle for transporting children to and from school

school·child \-ˌchīld\ *n* : a child attending school

school·fel·low \-ˌfel-ō\ *n* : SCHOOLMATE

school·girl \-ˌgərl\ *n* : a girl attending school

school·house \-ˌhaůs\ *n* : a building used as a school

school·ing *n* **1** : instruction in school : EDUCATION **2** : the cost of instruction and maintenance at school

school·marm \'skül-ˌmä(r)m\ *or* **school·ma'am** \-ˌmäm\ *n* **1** : a woman schoolteacher esp. in an old rural or small-town school **2** : a person who exhibits characteristics (as excessive attention to bookish matters) attributed to schoolteachers

school·mas·ter \-ˌmas-tər\ *n* : a male schoolteacher

school·mate \-ˌmāt\ *n* : a school companion

school·mis·tress \-ˌmis-trəs\ *n* : a woman schoolteacher

school·room \-ˌrüm, -ˌru̇m\ *n* : CLASSROOM

school·teach·er \-ˌtē-chər\ *n* : a person who teaches in a school

school·time \-ˌtīm\ *n* : the time for beginning a session of school or during which school is held

school·work \-ˌwərk\ *n* : lessons done in classes at school or assigned to be done at home

school·yard \-ˌyärd\ *n* : the playground of a school

schoo·ner \'skü-nər\ *n* **1** : a fore-and-aft rigged ship with two or more masts **2** : a large tall glass (as for beer) **3** : PRAIRIE SCHOONER

schot·tische \'shät-ish, shä-'tēsh\ *n* **1** : a round dance similar to the polka but slower **2** : music for the schottische

Schroe·ding·er equation \ˌshrād-ing-ər-\ *n* : an equation that describes the wave nature of elementary particles

schuss \'shu̇s, 'shüs\ *n* **1** : a straight high-speed run on skis **2** : a straight downhill skiing course — **schuss** *vb*

schwa \'shwä\ *n* [from German, from Hebrew *shĕwā*] **1** : an unstressed vowel that is the usual sound of the first and last vowels of the English word *America* **2** : the symbol ə commonly used for a schwa and sometimes also for a similarly articulated stressed vowel (as in *cut*)

sci *abbr* science

sci·at·ic \sī-'at-ik\ *adj* **1** : of, relating to, or situated near the hip **2** : of, relating to, or caused by sciatica

sci·at·i·ca \sī-'at-i-kə\ *n* : pain along the course of a sciatic nerve esp. in the back of the thigh; *also* : pain in or near the hips

sciatic nerve *n* : a nerve that runs down the back of the thigh and is the largest nerve in the body

sci·ence \'sī-ən(t)s\ *n* [from Latin, "knowledge", from *scire* "to know"] **1 a** : a branch of systematized knowledge that is an object of study ⟨the *science* of theology⟩; *esp* : one of the natural sciences ⟨chemistry is a *science*⟩ **b** : something (as a sport or technique) that may be studied or learned like a science **2** : knowledge covering general truths or the operation of general laws esp. as obtained and tested through the scientific method ⟨application of the laws of *science* to a study of atomic nuclei⟩

science fiction *n* : fiction that deals with the effect of actual or imagined science on society or individuals

sci·en·tif·ic \ˌsī-ən-'tif-ik\ *adj* : of, relating to, or exhibiting the methods or principles of science — **sci·en·tif·i·cal·ly** \-'tif-i-k(ə-)lē\ *adv*

scientific method *n* : principles and procedures for the pursuit of knowledge involving the finding and stating of a problem, the collection of data through observation and experiment, and the making and testing of hypotheses

scientific notation *n* : the representation of numbers as the product of a decimal between 1 and 10 and a power of 10

sci·en·tist \'sī-ən-təst\ *n* : a person versed in science and esp. natural science : a scientific investigator

scim·i·tar \'sim-ət-ər, -ə-ˌtär\ *n* : a sword with a curved blade used chiefly in Muhammadan countries

S

scin·til·la \sin-'til-ə\ *n* [from Latin, literally "spark", the source of English *scintillate*] : IOTA, TRACE
scin·til·late \'sint-ə-ˌlāt\ *vb* **1** : to give off sparks **2** : to flash or gleam as if throwing off sparks ⟨eyes *scintillating* with anger⟩ — **scin·til·lant** \-lənt\ *adj* — **scin·til·la·tion** \ˌsint-ə-'lā-shən\ *n*
sci·on \'sī-ən\ *n* **1** : a detached living portion of a plant that is joined to a stock in grafting and yields aerial parts **2** : DESCENDANT, CHILD ⟨a *scion* of a royal stock⟩
¹scis·sor \'siz-ər\ *n* : SCISSORS
²scissor *vb* : to cut with scissors or shears
scis·sors \'siz-ərz\ *n sing or pl* : a cutting instrument having two blades so fastened together that the sharp edges slide against each other
scissors kick *n* : a swimming kick in which the legs move like scissors
sclera \'skler-ə\ *n* : the dense fibrous white or bluish white tissue that covers that portion of the eyeball not covered by the cornea
scle·ro·sis \sklə-'rō-səs\ *n* : a usu. pathological hardening of tissue esp. from increase of connective tissue
¹scle·rot·ic \sklə-'rät-ik\ *adj* **1** : being or relating to the sclera **2** : of, relating to, or affected with sclerosis
²sclerotic *n* : SCLERA
¹scoff \'skäf, 'skȯf\ *n* : an expression of scorn, derision, or contempt
²scoff *vb* : JEER, RIDICULE ⟨*scoffed* at his efforts⟩ — **scoff·er** *n*
¹scold \'skōld\ *n* : a person who scolds constantly
²scold *vb* **1** : to find fault noisily ⟨*scolding* at each other instead of reasoning together⟩ **2** : to rebuke severely or angrily ⟨*scolded* the press for emphasizing violence⟩
sconce \'skän(t)s\ *n* : a candlestick or group of candlesticks mounted on a plaque and fastened to a wall
scone \'skōn, 'skän\ *n* **1** : a quick bread usu. made with oatmeal or barley flour and baked on a griddle **2** : a quick bread made with baking powder and sometimes eggs, sugar, and raisins and baked in an oven
¹scoop \'sküp\ *n* **1 a** : a large shovel (as for shoveling coal) **b** : a tool or utensil shaped like a shovel for digging into a soft substance and lifting out a portion ⟨a flour *scoop*⟩ **c** : a round utensil with a handle for dipping out soft food (as ice cream) **d** : a small tool for cutting or gouging **2** : an act or the action of scooping : a motion made with or as if with a scoop **3 a** : the amount held by a scoop ⟨a *scoop* of ice cream⟩ **b** : a hole made by scooping **4 a** : information of immediate interest ⟨what's the *scoop*⟩ **b** : BEAT 5 — **scoop·ful** \-ˌfu̇l\ *n*
²scoop *vb* **1** : to take out or up with or as if with a scoop **2** : to make hollow : dig out **3** : BEAT 5b — **scoop·er** *n*
scoot \'sküt\ *vb* : to go suddenly and swiftly : DART — **scoot** *n*
scoot·er \'sküt-ər\ *n* **1** : a vehicle consisting of a narrow base mounted between two tandem wheels and guided by a handle attached to the front wheel **2** : MOTOR SCOOTER
¹scope \'skōp\ *n* **1** : space or opportunity for action or thought ⟨full *scope* for the exercise of his talents⟩ **2** : extent covered, reached, or viewed : RANGE ⟨a subject broad in *scope*⟩
²scope *n* : any of various instruments for viewing: as **a** : MICROSCOPE **b** : TELESCOPE **c** : OSCILLOSCOPE **d** : RADARSCOPE
sco·pol·amine \skō-'päl-ə-ˌmēn\ *n* : a poisonous substance found in some plants related to the potato and used as a truth serum or as a sedative
scor·bu·tic \skȯr-'byüt-ik\ *adj* : of, relating to, or resembling scurvy; *also* : diseased with scurvy
¹scorch \'skȯrch\ *vb* **1 a** : to burn on the surface ⟨*scorch* a roast⟩ **b** : to burn so as to brown, dry, or shrivel ⟨lawns *scorched* by summer suns⟩ **2** : to hurt or embarrass usu. with sarcasm ***syn*** see SINGE
²scorch *n* **1** : a result of scorching **2** : a browning of plant tissues usu. from disease or heat
scorched earth *n* : land stripped of anything that could be of use to an invading enemy force
scorch·er \'skȯr-chər\ *n* : someone or something that scorches; *esp* : a very hot day
¹score \'skō(ə)r, 'skȯ(ə)r\ *n, pl* **scores** *or* **score** **1 a** : TWENTY **b** : a group of 20 things — often used in combination with a cardinal number ⟨five*score*⟩ **2** : a line made with or as if with a sharp instrument **3** : a record of points made or lost (as in a game) **4** : an obligation or injury kept in mind for requital ⟨had some old *scores* to settle⟩ **5 a** : REASON, GROUND ⟨felt tired but didn't leave on that *score*⟩ **b** : SUBJECT, TOPIC ⟨his ideas on the *score* of love⟩ **6** : a musical composition in written or printed notation **7** : a number expressing accomplishment (as in a test) or quality (as of a product) ⟨had a *score* of 80 out of a possible 100⟩ **8** : the stark inescapable facts of a situation ⟨we won't know what the *score* is until the laboratory results are in⟩ — **score·less** \'skō(ə)r-ləs, 'skȯ(ə)r-\ *adj*
²score *vb* **1 a** : to set down in an account : RECORD **b** : to keep score in a game or contest **2** : to mark with lines, grooves, scratches, or notches **3** : BERATE, SCOLD **4 a** : to make a score in or as if in a game : TALLY ⟨*score* a run⟩ **b** : to enable to make a score ⟨*scored* the man on second base with a single⟩ **c** : ACHIEVE, WIN ⟨*scored* a big success⟩ **5** : GRADE, MARK **6** : to orchestrate or arrange for performance — **scor·er** *n*
score·board \'skōr-ˌbōrd, 'skȯr-ˌbȯrd\ *n* : a large board for displaying the score of a game or match
score·card \-ˌkärd\ *n* : a card for recording the score (as of a game)
score·keep·er \-ˌkē-pər\ *n* : a person appointed to record the score during the progress of a game or contest
sco·ria \'skōr-ē-ə, 'skȯr-\ *n, pl* **-ri·ae** \-ē-ˌē, -ē-ˌī\ : rough cindery lava
¹scorn \'skȯrn\ *n* **1** : bitter contempt **2** : an object of extreme disdain, contempt, or derision
²scorn *vb* **1** : to hold in scorn ⟨was *scorned* as an incompetent⟩ **2** : to refuse because of scorn : DISDAIN ⟨*scorned* to reply to the charge⟩ — **scorn·er** *n*
scorn·ful \'skȯrn-fəl\ *adj* : feeling or showing scorn ***syn*** see CONTEMPTUOUS — **scorn·ful·ly** \-fə-lē\ *adv*
Scor·pio \'skȯr-pē-ˌō\ *n* — see ZODIAC table
scor·pi·on \'skȯr-pē-ən\ *n* **1** : any of an order of arachnids having an elongated body and a narrow

scorpion 1 (about 7 in. long)

ə abut	ər further	a back	ā bake	
ä cot, cart	au̇ out	ch chin	e less	ē easy
g gift	i trip	ī life	j joke	ng sing	ō flow
ȯ flaw	ȯi coin	th thin	t͟h this	ü loot
u̇ foot	y yet	yü few	yu̇ furious	zh vision

segmented tail with a venomous sting at the tip **2 :** something that stirs a person to action

scorpion fly *n* **:** any of a group of primitive insects having membranous wings and a long beak with biting mouthparts at the tip

Scot \'skät\ *n* **1 :** a native or inhabitant of Scotland **2 :** a person of Scotch descent

Scot *abbr* **1** Scotland **2** Scottish

scotch \'skäch\ *vb* **1 :** to injure so as to make temporarily harmless **2 :** to stamp out **:** CRUSH ⟨*scotch* a rebellion⟩; *esp* **:** to end decisively by showing the falsity of ⟨*scotch* a rumor⟩

[1]**Scotch** \'skäch\ *adj* **:** of, relating to, or characteristic of Scotland or its people

[2]**Scotch** *n* **1 Scotch** *pl* **:** the people of Scotland **2 :** whiskey distilled in Scotland esp. from barley

Scotch·man \'skäch-mən\ *n* **:** a male Scot **:** a man of Scotch descent — **Scotch·wom·an** \-ˌwu̇m-ən\ *n*

Scotch terrier *n* **:** SCOTTISH TERRIER

sco·ter \'skōt-ər\ *n, pl* **scoters** *or* **scoter :** any of several sea ducks of northern coasts of Europe and No. America

scot–free \'skät-'frē\ *adj* [from *scot*, "a charge to be paid", from Old Norse *skot* "shot", from the same source as English *shot*] **:** completely free from obligation, harm, or penalty ⟨get off *scot-free*⟩

[1]**Scots** \'skäts\ *adj* **:** SCOTCH

[2]**Scots** *n* **:** the English language of Scotland

Scots·man \'skäts-mən\ *n* **:** SCOTCHMAN

scot·tie \'skät-ē\ *n* **1** *cap* **:** SCOTCHMAN **2 :** SCOTTISH TERRIER

[1]**Scot·tish** \'skät-ish\ *adj* **:** SCOTCH

[2]**Scottish** *n* **:** SCOTS

Scottish terrier *n* **:** any of an old Scottish breed of terrier with short legs, large head, small erect ears, broad deep chest, and a thick rough coat

scoun·drel \'skau̇n-drəl\ *n* **:** a mean worthless person **:** VILLAIN — **scoun·drel·ly** \-drə-lē\ *adj*

[1]**scour** \'skau̇(ə)r\ *vb* **1 :** to move about or through quickly esp. in search ⟨*scoured* the woods for the missing boys⟩ **2 :** to examine minutely and rapidly ⟨*scoured* the legal documents⟩ — **scour·er** *n*

[2]**scour** *vb* **1 a :** to rub hard with a rough material in order to clean **b :** to remove by rubbing hard and washing ⟨*scour* spots from the stove⟩ **2 :** to free from foreign matter or impurities by or as if by washing **3 :** to wear away (as by water) **:** ERODE ⟨a stream *scouring* its banks⟩ — **scour·er** *n*

[3]**scour** *n* **:** an action or result of scouring

[1]**scourge** \'skərj\ *n* **1 :** WHIP, LASH **2 a :** someone or something that is an instrument of punishment or criticism **b :** AFFLICTION

[2]**scourge** *vb* **1 :** to whip severely **:** FLOG **2 :** to subject to affliction **:** DEVASTATE ⟨a region *scourged* by malaria⟩

scouring rush *n* **:** EQUISETUM

[1]**scout** \'skau̇t\ *vb* [from medieval French *escouter* "to listen", from Latin *auscultare*] **1 :** to go about and observe in search of information **:** RECONNOITER ⟨*scout* an area for minerals⟩ ⟨*scouted* around the enemy position⟩ **2 a :** to make a search ⟨*scout* about for firewood⟩ **b :** to find by searching ⟨*scouted* up the necessary materials⟩

[2]**scout** *n* **1 :** the act or an instance of scouting **:** RECONNAISSANCE **2 a :** one sent to obtain information and esp. to reconnoiter in war **b :** a person who searches for talented newcomers ⟨a baseball *scout*⟩ **3 a :** BOY SCOUT **b :** GIRL SCOUT **4 :** FELLOW, GUY ⟨he's a good *scout*⟩

[3]**scout** *vb* **1 :** to make fun of **:** MOCK **2 :** to reject scornfully as absurd ⟨*scout* a theory⟩

scout·ing \'skau̇t-ing\ *n* **1 :** the action of one that scouts **2 :** the activities of the various boy scout and girl scout movements

scout·mas·ter \'skau̇t-ˌmas-tər\ *n* **:** the leader of a band of scouts and esp. of a troop of boy scouts

scow \'skau̇\ *n* **:** a large flat-bottomed boat with broad square ends used chiefly for transporting sand, gravel, or refuse

[1]**scowl** \'skau̇l\ *vb* **1 :** to make a frowning expression of displeasure **2 :** to exhibit or express with a scowl ⟨he *scowled* his disappointment⟩ — **scowl·er** *n*

[2]**scowl** *n* **:** a facial expression of displeasure **:** FROWN

[1]**scrab·ble** \'skrab-əl\ *vb* **scrab·bled; scrab·bling** \-(ə-)ling\ **1 :** to scratch or scrape about frantically with hands or paws **2 :** SCRAMBLE **3 :** to struggle by or as if by scraping or scratching ⟨*scrabble* for a living⟩ — **scrab·bler** \-(ə-)lər\ *n*

[2]**scrabble** *n* **:** an act or instance of scrabbling

scrag \'skrag\ *n* **:** a rawboned or scrawny person or animal

scrag·gly \'skrag-(ə-)lē\ *adj* **scrag·gli·er; -est :** RAGGED, UNKEMPT ⟨a *scraggly* beard⟩

scrag·gy \'skrag-ē\ *adj* **scrag·gi·er; -est 1 :** ROUGH, JAGGED ⟨*scraggy* cliffs⟩ **2 :** being lean and long **:** SCRAWNY ⟨his *scraggy* withered neck⟩

scram \'skram\ *vb* **scrammed; scram·ming :** to go away at once ⟨*scram*, you're not wanted⟩

scram·ble \'skram-bəl\ *vb* **scram·bled; scram·bling** \-b(ə-)ling\ **1 :** to move or climb hastily on all fours **2 :** to strive or struggle for something ⟨*scramble* for front seats⟩ ⟨*scrambled* out of the path of the bus⟩ **3 a :** to toss or mix together **:** JUMBLE ⟨bad weather *scrambled* the air schedules⟩ **b :** to cook the mixed whites and yolks of eggs by stirring them while frying — **scramble** *n* — **scram·bler** \-b(ə-)lər\ *n*

S

[1]**scrap** \'skrap\ *n* **1** *pl* **:** fragments of discarded or leftover food **2 :** a small bit **:** FRAGMENT ⟨*scraps* of cloth⟩ ⟨not a *scrap* of truth in the story⟩ **3 :** material discarded as worthless ⟨buy *scrap*⟩

[2]**scrap** *vb* **scrapped; scrap·ping 1 :** to break up into scrap ⟨*scrap* a battleship⟩ **2 :** to discard as worthless ⟨*scrap* outworn methods⟩

[3]**scrap** *adj* **:** being in the form of scraps or fragments

[4]**scrap** *n* **:** QUARREL, FIGHT

[5]**scrap** *vb* **scrapped; scrap·ping :** QUARREL, FIGHT — **scrap·per** *n*

scrap·book \'skrap-ˌbu̇k\ *n* **:** a book of blank pages for mementos (as clippings and pictures)

[1]**scrape** \'skrāp\ *vb* **1 a :** to remove by repeated strokes of an edged tool ⟨*scrape* off rust⟩ **b :** to clean or smooth by rubbing with an edged tool or abrasive **2 a :** to rub or cause to rub so as to make a grating noise **b :** to damage or injure by dragging against a rough surface ⟨*scrape* a fender⟩ **3 a :** to gather with difficulty and little by little ⟨*scrape* together a few dollars⟩ **b :** to barely get by ⟨*scraped* through with low marks⟩ — **scrap·er** *n*

[2]**scrape** *n* **1 a :** the act or process of scraping **b :** a sound, mark, or injury made by scraping ⟨a *scrape* on his leg⟩ **2 :** a bow made by drawing back the foot **3 :** a disagreeable predicament

scrap·ing \'skrā-ping\ *n* **:** something scraped off or together — usu. used in pl.

scrap·ple \'skrap-əl\ *n* **:** a seasoned mush of meat scraps and cornmeal set in a mold and served in fried slices

scrap·py \'skrap-ē\ *adj* **scrap·pi·er; -est 1 :** QUARRELSOME **2 :** aggressive and determined in spirit — **scrap·pi·ness** *n*

[1]**scratch** \'skrach\ *vb* **1 :** to scrape, rub, or mar with or as if with the claws or nails **2 :** to make a living by hard work and saving **3 :** to write or draw esp.

hastily or carelessly : SCRAWL **4** : ERASE, CANCEL ⟨*scratch* a name from a list⟩ ⟨*scratch* several entries from the contest⟩ **5** : to make a thin grating sound ⟨this pen *scratches*⟩ — **scratch·er** *n*

²**scratch** *n* **1 a** : an act or sound of scratching **b** : a mark (as a line) or injury made by scratching **2 a** : the line from which contestants start in a race **b** : NOTHING ⟨start from *scratch*⟩ **3** : satisfactory condition or performance ⟨not up to *scratch*⟩

³**scratch** *adj* : intended for chance or casual action or use and usu. of less than the best quality ⟨*scratch* team⟩

scratch hit *n* : a batted ball not solidly hit or cleanly fielded yet credited to the batter as a base hit

scratch test *n* : a test for allergic susceptibility made by rubbing an extract of an allergy-producing substance into small breaks or scratches in the skin

scratchy \'skrach-ē\ *adj* **scratch·i·er**; **-est** **1** : likely to scratch or irritate : PRICKLY ⟨*scratchy* undergrowth⟩ ⟨*scratchy* woolens⟩ **2** : making a scratching noise **3** : marked or made with scratches ⟨a *scratchy* surface⟩ ⟨*scratchy* handwriting⟩ **4** : uneven in quality : RAGGED ⟨played a *scratchy* game of golf⟩ — **scratch·i·ly** \'skrach-ə-lē\ *adv* — **scratch·i·ness** \'skrach-ē-nəs\ *n*

scrawl \'skrȯl\ *vb* : to write or draw awkwardly, hastily, or carelessly : SCRIBBLE — **scrawl** *n* — **scrawly** \'skrȯ-lē\ *adj*

scraw·ny \'skrȯ-nē\ *adj* **scraw·ni·er**; **-est** : ill-nourished : SKINNY ⟨*scrawny* cattle⟩ — **scraw·ni·ness** *n*

¹**scream** \'skrēm\ *vb* **1** : to cry out, sound, or utter loudly and shrilly ⟨*screaming* with rage⟩ ⟨the saw *screamed* through the wood⟩ ⟨*screamed* a curse at the enemy⟩ **2** : to produce or give a vivid, startling, or alarming effect or expression ⟨a *screaming* red⟩ ⟨headlines that *screamed* the news⟩

²**scream** *n* **1** : a loud shrill prolonged cry or noise ⟨*screams* of terror⟩ **2** : one that provokes screams of laughter ⟨she's a *scream* when she gets going⟩

scream·er \'skrē-mər\ *n* : someone or something that screams

scream·ing·ly \'skrē-ming-lē\ *adv* : to an extreme degree ⟨a *screamingly* funny movie⟩

¹**screech** \'skrēch\ *vb* **1** : to make an outcry usu. in terror or pain **2** : to make a sound like a screech ⟨the car *screeched* to a halt⟩ — **screech·er** *n*

²**screech** *n* **1** : a shrill harsh cry usu. expressing pain or terror **2** : a sound like a screech ⟨*screech* of brakes⟩

screech owl *n* : any of numerous small New World owls that have two tufts of feathers on the head and plumage with blackish streaks

¹**screen** \'skrēn\ *n* **1** : a device or partition used to hide or protect ⟨a wire-mesh window *screen*⟩ **2** : something that serves to shelter, protect, or conceal ⟨a *screen* of fighter planes⟩ **3** : a sieve or perforated material set in a frame and used for separating finer parts from coarser parts (as of sand) **4 a** : a flat surface upon which a picture or series of pictures is projected; *also* : the surface upon which the image appears in a television or radar receiver **b** : the motion-picture industry ⟨a star of stage and *screen*⟩

²**screen** *vb* **1** : to guard from injury or danger **2 a** : to shelter, protect, or separate with or as if with a screen **b** : to pass through a screen to separate the fine part from the coarse ⟨*screen* gravel⟩ **c** : to remove by or as if by a screen ⟨*screens* out much harmful radiation⟩ **d** : to examine systematically in order to separate into groups or to select or eliminate ⟨carefully *screened* all applicants⟩ **3** : to provide with a screen ⟨*screen* a porch⟩ **4** : to project on a screen ⟨*screen* a movie⟩

screen·ing \'skrē-ning\ *n* **1** *pl* : material (as fine coal) separated out by passage through or retention on a screen **2** : a mesh (as of metal or plastic) used esp. for screens

screen·play \'skrēn-ˌplā\ *n* : the written form of a story prepared for film production

screen·writ·er \-ˌrīt-ər\ *n* : a writer of screenplays

¹**screw** \'skrü\ *n* **1 a** : a simple machine consisting of a spirally grooved solid cylinder and a correspondingly grooved cylindrical hollow part into which it fits **b** : a nail-shaped or rod-shaped metal piece with a spiral groove and a slotted or recessed head used for fastening pieces of solid material together **2 a** : something having the shape of a screw : SPIRAL **b** : the act of screwing tight : TWIST **c** : a screw-shaped device (as a corkscrew) **3** : SCREW PROPELLER — **screw·like** \-ˌlīk\ *adj*

²**screw** *vb* **1 a** : to attach, fasten, or close with a screw ⟨*screw* a hinge to a door⟩ **b** : to operate, tighten, or adjust with a screw ⟨*screw* up a sagging beam with a jack⟩ **c** : to turn or twist on a screwlike thread ⟨*screw* on a lid⟩ **2** : to twist out of shape ⟨a face *screwed* up in pain⟩ **3** : to increase in amount or capability ⟨*screwed* up his nerve⟩ — **screw·er** *n*

¹**screw·ball** \'skrü-ˌbȯl\ *n* **1** : a baseball pitch having reverse spin and a break in opposite direction to a curve **2** : a whimsical, eccentric, or crazy person

²**screwball** *adj* : crazily eccentric or whimsical ⟨*screwball* ideas⟩

screw cap *n* : a cap that screws onto the threaded top of a container

screw·driv·er \'skrü-ˌdrī-vər\ *n* : a tool for turning screws

screw eye *n* : a screw having a head in the form of a loop

screw·fly \'skrü-ˌflī\ *n* : the adult of a screwworm

screw pine *n* : any of a genus of tropical plants with slender stems, often huge prop roots, and crowns of swordlike leaves — called also *pandanus*

screw propeller *n* : a device consisting of a hub with twisted radiating blades that is used for propelling airplane or ships

screw·worm \'skrü-ˌwərm\ *n* : the grub of a two-winged fly of warm parts of America that develops esp. in sores or wounds of mammals

screwy \'skrü-ē\ *adj* **screw·i·er**; **-est** **1** : crazily absurd, eccentric, or unusual ⟨knew something was *screwy*⟩ **2** : CRAZY, INSANE ⟨completely *screwy* people⟩

scrib·ble \'skrib-əl\ *vb* **scrib·bled**; **scrib·bling** \-(ə-)ling\ : to write or draw hastily or carelessly — **scribble** *n* — **scrib·bler** \'skrib-lər\ *n*

¹**scribe** \'skrīb\ *n* **1** : a scholar of the Jewish law in New Testament times **2 a** : an official or public secretary or clerk **b** : a copier of manuscripts

²**scribe** *vb* : to mark or make by cutting or scratching with a pointed instrument ⟨*scribe* a line on metal⟩

¹**scrim·mage** \'skrim-ij\ *n* **1** : a confused fight : SCUFFLE **2 a** : the play between two football teams that begins with the snap of the ball **b** : practice play between a team's squads (as in football)

²**scrimmage** *vb* : to take part in a scrimmage — **scrim·mag·er** *n*

scrimp \'skrimp\ *vb* **1** : to make too small, short, or scanty : SKIMP **2** : to be frugal : ECONOMIZE

scrip \'skrip\ *n* **1** : a document showing that the holder or bearer is entitled to something (as stock or land) **2** : currency issued for temporary use in an emergency

script \'skript\ *n* **1 a** : something written : TEXT **b** : the written text of a stage play, screenplay, or broadcast **2** : letters and figures written by hand : HANDWRITING

scrip·to·ri·um \skrip-'tōr-ē-əm, -'tȯr-\ *n, pl* **-ria** \-ē-ə\ : a copying room in a medieval monastery set apart for the scribes

scrip·tur·al \'skrip-chə-rəl\ *adj* : of, relating to, or being in accordance with a sacred writing; *esp* : BIBLICAL — **scrip·tur·al·ly** \-rə-lē\ *adv*

scrip·ture \'skrip-chər\ *n* **1** *cap* : the books of the Old and New Testaments or of either of them : BIBLE — often used in pl. **2** *often cap* : a passage from the Bible **3** : the sacred writings of a religion

script·writ·er \'skript-ˌrīt-ər\ *n* : one that writes scripts for motion pictures or for radio or television programs

scriv·e·ner \'skriv-(ə-)nər\ *n* : a professional copyist or writer : SCRIBE

scrod \'skräd\ *n* : a young fish (as a cod or haddock); *esp* : one split and boned for cooking

scrof·u·la \'skrȯf-yə-lə, 'skräf-\ *n* : tuberculosis of the lymph glands esp. in the neck — **scrof·u·lous** \-ləs\ *adj*

scroll \'skrōl\ *n* **1** : a roll of paper or parchment providing a writing surface; *esp* : one on which something is written or engraved **2** : an ornament resembling a loosely or partly rolled scroll

scroll·work \-ˌwərk\ *n* : ornamental work (as in metal or wood) having a scroll or scrolls as its chief feature

scrooge \'skrüj\ *n, often cap* : a miserly person

scro·tum \'skrōt-əm\ *n, pl* **scro·ta** \'skrōt-ə\ *or* **scro·tums** : the external pouch that in most mammals contains the testes — **scro·tal** \'skrōt-əl\ *adj*

scrounge \'skrau̇nj\ *vb* **1** : to collect by or as if by foraging ⟨*scrounge* around for firewood⟩ **2** : to get by coaxing or persuasion ⟨*scrounge* a dollar from a friend⟩ — **scroung·er** *n*

1**scrub** \'skrəb\ *n* **1** : vegetation consisting chiefly of or a tract covered with stunted trees or shrubs **2** : a usu. inferior domestic animal of mixed or unknown parentage **3 a** : a person of insignificant size or social standing **b** : a player not belonging to the first team — **scrub** *adj*

2**scrub** *vb* **scrubbed**; **scrub·bing** : to rub hard in cleaning or washing ⟨*scrub* clothes⟩ — **scrub·ber** *n*

3**scrub** *n* : an act or instance of scrubbing

scrub·by \'skrəb-ē\ *adj* **scrub·bi·er**; **-est** **1** : inferior in size or quality : STUNTED ⟨*scrubby* cattle⟩ **2** : covered with or consisting of scrub

scruff \'skrəf\ *n* : the loose skin of the back of the neck : NAPE

scruffy \-ē\ *adj* **scruff·i·er**; **-est** : SHABBY

scrump·tious \'skrəm(p)-shəs\ *adj* : DELIGHTFUL, EXCELLENT

scrunch \'skrənch\ *vb* **1 a** : CRUNCH, CRUSH, CRUMPLE ⟨*scrunch* a paper cup⟩ **b** : to make or move with a crunching sound ⟨cinders *scrunching* under foot⟩ **2** : CROUCH, SQUEEZE

1**scru·ple** \'skrü-pəl\ *n* **1** — see MEASURE table **2** : a tiny part or quantity

2**scruple** *n* [from Latin *scrupulus*, literally "small sharp stone"; so called from the discomfort caused by such a stone in one's sandal] **1** : an ethical consideration or principle that makes one uneasy or inhibits action **2** : the quality or state of being scrupulous ⟨acted without *scruple*⟩ ***syn*** see QUALM

3**scruple** *vb* **scru·pled**; **scru·pling** \-p(ə-)liŋ\ : to have scruples

scru·pu·lous \'skrü-pyə-ləs\ *adj* : full of or having scruples : STRICT — **scru·pu·lous·ly** *adv* — **scru·pu·lous·ness** *n*

scru·ti·nize \'skrüt-ə-nīz\ *vb* : to examine very closely or critically : INSPECT

scru·ti·ny \'skrüt-(ə-)nē\ *n, pl* **-nies** : a searching study, inquiry, or inspection : EXAMINATION

scu·ba \'sk(y)ü-bə\ *n* [from the initials of the words *self-contained underwater breathing apparatus*] : an apparatus used for breathing while swimming under water

1**scud** \'skəd\ *vb* **scud·ded**; **scud·ding** : to move or run swiftly ⟨clouds *scudding* across the sky⟩

2**scud** *n* **1** : the act of scudding **2** : light clouds driven by the wind

1**scuff** \'skəf\ *vb* **1** : to scrape the feet in walking : SHUFFLE ⟨*scuffed* his feet on the ground⟩ ⟨*scuffed* along the path⟩ **2** : to become rough or scratched through wear ⟨soft leather *scuffs* easily⟩

2**scuff** *n* : a noise or act of scuffing

scuf·fle \'skəf-əl\ *vb* **scuf·fled**; **scuf·fling** \-(ə-)liŋ\ **1** : to struggle in a confused way at close quarters **2 a** : to move with a quick shuffling gait : SCURRY **b** : SCUFF — **scuffle** *n*

1**scull** \'skəl\ *n* **1 a** : an oar used at the stern of a boat to propel it forward **b** : one of a pair of short oars **2** : a boat usu. for racing propelled by one or more pairs of sculls

2**scull** *vb* : to propel a boat by a scull or sculls — **scull·er** *n*

scul·lery \'skəl-(ə-)rē\ *n, pl* **-ler·ies** : a room for cleaning and storing dishes and culinary utensils, washing vegetables, and similar domestic work

scul·lion \'skəl-yən\ *n* : a kitchen helper

scul·pin \'skəl-pən\ *n, pl* **sculpins** *also* **sculpin** : any of numerous spiny large-headed broad-mouthed usu. scaleless fishes often having one or more venomous spines on the dorsal fin; *esp* : one of the southern California coast esteemed for food and sport

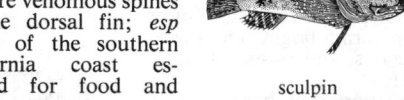

sculpin
(up to 15 in. long)

sculpt \'skəlpt\ *vb* : CARVE, SCULPTURE

sculp·tor \'skəlp-tər\ *n* : one that sculptures — **sculp·tress** \-trəs\ *n*

1**sculp·ture** \'skəlp-chər\ *n* **1** : the act, process, or art of carving or cutting hard materials, modeling plastic materials, or casting molten metals into works of art **2 a** : work produced by sculpture **b** : a piece of such work — **sculp·tur·al** \-chə-rəl\ *adj*

2**sculpture** *vb* **1 a** : to make sculptures : CARVE **b** : to adorn with sculpture ⟨*sculpture* a tomb⟩ **2** : to work as a sculptor

scum \'skəm\ *n* **1 a** : extraneous matter or impurities risen to or formed on the surface of a liquid **b** : a slimy coating esp. on stagnant water **2** : the lowest class : RABBLE — **scum·my** \'skəm-ē\ *adj*

scup·per \'skəp-ər\ *n* : an opening in the bulwarks of a boat through which water drains overboard

scup·per·nong \-ˌnȯŋ, -ˌnäŋ\ *n* : a large yellowish green plum-flavored grape

scur·ri·lous \'skər-ə-ləs, 'skə-rə-\ *adj* **1** : being vulgar and evil : LOW ⟨*scurrilous* crooks⟩ **2** : containing

S

obscenities or coarse abuse ⟨*scurrilous* attacks on his character⟩ — **scur·ril·i·ty** \skə-'ril-ət-ē\ *n* — **scur·ri·lous·ly** \'skər-ə-ləs-lē, 'skə-rə-\ *adv*
scur·ry \'skər-ē, 'skə-rē\ *vb* **scur·ried**; **scur·ry·ing** : to move briskly : SCAMPER — **scurry** *n*
1**scur·vy** \'skər-vē\ *adj* **scur·vi·er**; **-est** : CONTEMPTIBLE, MEAN ⟨*scurvy* tricks⟩
2**scurvy** *n* : a deficiency disease caused by lack of vitamin C that was once common among sailors on long voyages
scut \'skət\ *n* : a short erect tail (as of a rabbit)
scutch·eon \'skəch-ən\ *n* : ESCUTCHEON
1**scut·tle** \'skət-əl\ *n* : a metal pail for carrying coal
2**scuttle** *n* : a small opening (as in the deck of a ship or the roof of a house) with a lid or cover
3**scuttle** *vb* **scut·tled**; **scut·tling** \'skət-(ə-)ling\ **1** : to sink by cutting holes or by opening valves to let in water ⟨*scuttle* a ship⟩ **2** : to injure or end by a deliberate act ⟨*scuttle* a conference⟩
4**scuttle** *vb* **scut·tled**; **scut·tling** \'skət-(ə-)ling\ : SCURRY
5**scuttle** *n* **1** : a quick shuffling pace **2** : a short swift run
scut·tle·butt \'skət-əl-ˌbət\ *n* : RUMOR, GOSSIP
scythe \'sīth\ *n* : an implement consisting of a curved blade on a long curved handle for mowing grass or grain by hand
SD *abbr* **1** South Dakota **2** standard deviation
S. Dak. *or* **S.D.** *abbr* South Dakota
SE *abbr* southeast
sea \'sē\ *n* **1 a** : a great body of salty water that covers much of the earth; *also* : the waters of the earth as distinguished from the land and air **b** : a body of salt water less extensive than an ocean ⟨the Mediterranean *sea*⟩ **c** : OCEAN **d** : an inland body of water either salt or fresh ⟨the *Sea* of Galilee⟩ **2** : rough water : a heavy swell or wave ⟨a high *sea* swept the deck⟩ **3** : something suggesting the sea (as in vastness) ⟨a golden *sea* of wheat⟩ **4** : the seafaring life ⟨hoped to make a career of the *sea*⟩ **5** : any of several dark areas on the moon — **sea** *adj* — **at sea** **1** : on the sea; *esp* : on a sea voyage **2** : LOST, BEWILDERED — **to sea** : to or upon the open sea
sea anemone *n* : any of numerous usu. solitary polyps that suggest a flower in form, bright and varied colors, and cluster of tentacles

sea anemone
(about 3 in. tall)

sea·bag \'sē-ˌbag\ *n* : a cylindrical canvas bag used esp. by a sailor for gear (as clothes)
sea bass *n* : a food and sport fish of the Atlantic coast of the U.S. that is smaller and more active than the related groupers
sea·bed \'sē-ˌbed\ *n* : the floor of a sea or ocean
Sea·bee \'sē-(ˌ)bē\ *n* : a member of a construction battalion of the U.S. Navy
sea·bird \'sē-ˌbərd\ *n* : a bird (as a gull or albatross) frequenting the open ocean
sea·board \'sē-ˌbōrd, -ˌbȯrd\ *n* : SEACOAST; *esp* : the country bordering a seacoast — **seaboard** *adj*

ə abut	ər further	a back	ā bake
ä cot, cart	aů out	ch chin	e less
ē easy	g gift	i trip	ī life
j joke	ng sing	ō flow	ȯ flaw
ȯi coin	th thin	th this	ü loot
ů foot	y yet	yü few	yů furious
zh vision			

sea breeze *n* : a breeze blowing inland from the sea
sea·coast \'sē-ˌkōst\ *n* : the shore of the sea
sea cow *n* : any of several large swimming mammals (as the manatee) that feed on seaweed
sea cucumber *n* : any of a class of echinoderms having a long flexible tough muscular body

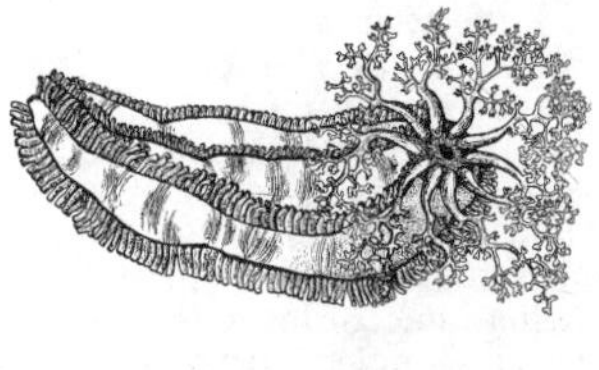

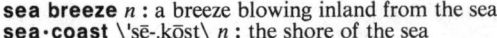

sea cucumber
(about 5 in. long)

sea dog *n* **1 a** : any of several seals **b** : DOGFISH **2** : a veteran sailor
sea eagle *n* : any of various eagles that feed largely on fish
sea·far·er \'sē-ˌfar-ər, -ˌfer-\ *n* : a person who travels over the ocean : MARINER
sea·far·ing \-ˌfar-ing, -ˌfer-\ *n* : a traveling over the sea as work or recreation — **seafaring** *adj*
sea·food \-ˌfüd\ *n* : edible marine fish and shellfish
sea·go·ing \-ˌgō-ing\ *adj* : adapted or used for sea travel ⟨*seagoing* ships⟩
sea green *n* **1** : a moderate green or bluish green **2** : a moderate yellow green
sea gull *n* : GULL; *esp* : one frequenting the sea
sea horse *n* **1** : a fabled animal half horse and half fish **2 a** : WALRUS **b** : a small long-snouted fish that is covered with bony plates and has a head suggestive of a horse's head
1**seal** \'sēl\ *n, pl* **seals** *also* **seal** **1** : any of numerous marine flesh-eating mammals chiefly of cold regions with limbs modified into webbed flippers adapted primarily to swimming **2 a** : the soft dense fur of a seal **b** : leather made from the skin of a seal

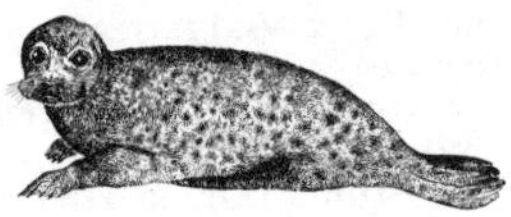

seal 1
(up to 6 ft. long)

2**seal** *vb* : to hunt seals — **seal·er** *n*
3**seal** *n* **1** : a device with a cut or raised design or figure that can be pressed or stamped into paper or wax to form a mark (as for certifying a signature or authenticating a document) **2** : a usu. ornamental adhesive stamp that may be used to close a letter or package ⟨Christmas *seals*⟩ **3 a** : something (as a pledge) that makes safe or secure ⟨under *seal* of secrecy⟩ **b** : a closure that can be opened only by breaking or tearing **c** : a tight and perfect closure ⟨test the *seal* of the jars⟩ **d** : something that closes tightly ⟨the water *seal* of a toilet⟩
4**seal** *vb* **1** : to mark with a seal ⟨*seal* a deed⟩ **2** : to close or make fast with or as if with a seal ⟨the sheriff *sealed* the premises⟩ ⟨ice *sealed* the ships into the harbor⟩ **3** : to determine finally and irrevocably ⟨his answer *sealed* our fate⟩ — **seal·er** *n*
sea–lane \'sē-ˌlān\ *n* : an established sea route
seal·ant \'sē-lənt\ *n* : a sealing agent ⟨radiator *sealant*⟩
sea legs *n* : bodily adjustment to the motion of a ship at sea indicated esp. by ability to walk steadily and by freedom from seasickness
sea lettuce *n* : ULVA
sea level *n* : the height of the surface of the sea midway between the average high and low tides
sea lily *n* : any of a class of echinoderms having usu. a cup-shaped body with five or more feathery arms

sealing wax *n* : a resinous composition that is plastic when warm and is used for sealing (as letters, dry cells, or cans)
sea lion *n* : any of several large Pacific eared seals
seal·skin \'sēl-ˌskin\ *n* **1** : the fur or pelt of a fur seal **2** : a garment (as a coat) of sealskin — **sealskin** *adj*
[1]**seam** \'sēm\ *n* **1** : the fold, line, or groove made by sewing together or joining two edges or two pieces of material ⟨the *seams* of a dress⟩ ⟨the *seams* of a boat⟩ **2 a** : a raised or depressed line (as of scarring) : GROOVE, FURROW, WRINKLE **b** : a layer or stratum (as of mineral) between distinctive layers ⟨coal *seams*⟩ — **seam·less** \-ləs\ *adj*
[2]**seam** *vb* **1** : to join with a seam **2** : to mark with a line, scar, or wrinkle ⟨creeks *seam* the valley⟩ ⟨a face *seamed* with age⟩
sea·man \'sē-mən\ *n* **1** : SAILOR, MARINER **2** : an enlisted man in the navy ranking just below a petty officer third class
seaman apprentice *n* : an enlisted man in the navy ranking below a seaman
seaman recruit *n* : an enlisted man in the navy of the lowest rank
sea·man·ship \'sē-mən-ˌship\ *n* : the art or skill of handling, working, and navigating a ship
sea mew *n* : SEA GULL
sea mile *n* : MILE 2
sea mink *n* : either of two whitings of the Atlantic coast of No. America
sea monster *n* **1** : a large sea animal **2** : a fabulous monster of the sea often described as eating men but not proved to exist
sea·mount \'sē-ˌmau̇nt\ *n* : a submarine mountain
seam·stress \'sēm(p)-strəs\ *n* : a woman who sews esp. for a living
seamy \'sē-mē\ *adj* **seam·i·er**; **-est** **1** : having or showing seams ⟨*seamy* ledges⟩ **2** : less pleasing or presentable : WORSE ⟨the *seamy* side of life⟩ — **seam·i·ness** *n*
sé·ance \'sā-ˌän(t)s\ *n* **1** : a meeting for discussion : SESSION **2** : a spiritualist meeting
sea otter *n* : a large marine otter of northern Pacific coasts nearly exterminated for its valuable fur

sea otter
(about 4 ft. long)

sea·plane \'sē-ˌplān\ *n* : an airplane designed to take off from and land on the water
sea·port \-ˌpōrt, -ˌpȯrt\ *n* : a port, harbor, or town accessible to seagoing ships
[1]**sear** \'si(ə)r\ *vb* **1** : to cause withering or drying : PARCH, SHRIVEL ⟨harsh winds that *sear* and burn⟩ **2 a** : to burn, scorch, or injure with or as if with sudden application of intense heat **b** : to brown the surface of quickly in cooking ⟨*sear* a pot roast⟩
[2]**sear** *n* : a mark or scar left by searing
[1]**search** \'sərch\ *vb* **1 a** : to go through or look carefully and thoroughly in an effort to find or discover ⟨*search* a room⟩ ⟨*search* for a lost child⟩ **b** : to look in the pockets or the clothing of for something hidden ⟨*search* an arrested man⟩ **2** : to find or come to know by or as if by careful investigation or scrutiny ⟨*searching* out every weakness in his adversary's argument⟩ — **search·er** *n* — **search·ing·ly** \'sər-ching-lē\ *adv*
[2]**search** *n* : an act of searching : an attempt to get, find, or seek out
search·light \'sərch-ˌlīt\ *n* **1** : an apparatus for projecting a beam of light; *also* : a beam of light projected by it **2** : FLASHLIGHT 2
search warrant *n* : a warrant authorizing a search of a specified place (as a house) for stolen goods or unlawful possessions (as burglars' tools)
sea·scape \'sē-ˌskāp\ *n* **1** : a view of the sea **2** : a picture representing a scene at sea
sea scout *n* : one enrolled in the Boy Scouts of America program that provides training for older boys in seamanship and water activities
sea serpent *n* : a large marine animal resembling a snake often reported to have been seen but never proved to exist
sea·shell \'sē-ˌshel\ *n* : the shell of a marine animal and esp. a mollusk
sea·shore \-ˌshōr, -ˌshȯr\ *n* : land adjacent to the sea : SEACOAST
sea·sick \-ˌsik\ *adj* : affected with or suggestive of seasickness
sea·sick·ness \-nəs\ *n* : motion sickness experienced on the water
sea·side \'sē-ˌsīd\ *n* : country adjacent to the sea : SEASHORE
sea slug *n* : a marine gastropod mollusk that has no shell in the adult stage
[1]**sea·son** \'sē-zən\ *n* [from Old French *saison*, from Latin *sation-*, stem of *satio* "act of sowing", from the same prehistoric root as English *seed*] **1 a** : a suitable or natural time or occasion ⟨a *season* for all things⟩ **b** : a usu. brief period of time ⟨willing to wait a *season*⟩ **c** : a particular point in a period or in the course of events ⟨visitors at all *seasons*⟩ **2 a** : a period of the year associated with some recurrent phenomenon or activity ⟨during the rainy *season*⟩ ⟨a long breeding *season*⟩ **b** : one of the four quarters into which the year is commonly divided — compare AUTUMN, SPRING, SUMMER, WINTER **c** : a period of the year associated with a particular event (as a holiday) or phase of human activity (as sport or business) ⟨the Christmas *season*⟩ ⟨the baseball *season*⟩ — **in season** **1** : at the right or fitting time **2 a** : in a state or at the stage of greatest fitness (as for eating) ⟨peaches are *in season*⟩ **b** : proper or legal to take by hunting or fishing — **out of season** : not in season ⟨fined for hunting *out of season*⟩
[2]**season** *vb* **sea·soned**; **sea·son·ing** \'sēz-(ə-)ning\ **1** : to make pleasant to the taste by adding seasoning ⟨a perfectly *seasoned* stew⟩ **2 a** : to make or become suitable for use (as by aging or drying) ⟨*season* lumber⟩ **b** : to make fit by experience ⟨*seasoned* veterans⟩ — **sea·son·er** \'sēz-(ə-)nər\ *n*
sea·son·a·ble \'sēz-(ə-)nə-bəl\ *adj* : TIMELY ⟨a *seasonable* frost⟩ ⟨*seasonable* advice⟩ — **sea·son·a·bly** \-blē\ *adv*
sea·son·al \'sēz-(ə-)nəl\ *adj* : of, relating to, or restricted to a particular season ⟨*seasonal* industries⟩ ⟨*seasonal* activity⟩ — **sea·son·al·ly** \-ē\ *adv*
sea·son·ing \'sēz-(ə-)ning\ *n* : something (as a spice or herb) that seasons
season ticket *n* : a ticket (as to all of a club's games) valid for a specified season
sea star *n* : STARFISH
[1]**seat** \'sēt\ *n* **1 a** : something (as a chair) intended to be sat in or on **b** : the part of something on which one rests in sitting ⟨*seat* of the trousers⟩ ⟨a chair *seat*⟩ **c** : the part of the body on which a person sits : BUTTOCKS **2 a** : a seating accommodation ⟨his *seat* at table⟩ ⟨had three *seats* for the game⟩ **b** : a right of sitting usu. as a member ⟨a *seat* in the senate⟩

S

c : MEMBERSHIP ⟨a *seat* on the stock exchange⟩ **3** : a place or area where something is situated or centered ⟨the *seat* of the pain⟩ ⟨*seats* of higher learning⟩; *esp* : a place (as a capital city) from which authority is exercised ⟨the new *seat* of the government⟩ **4** : posture in or way of sitting esp. on horseback **5** : a part or surface on which another part or surface rests ⟨valve *seat*⟩ — **seat·ed** \-əd\ *adj*

[2]**seat** *vb* **1 a** : to place in or on a seat ⟨*seat* a guest⟩ **b** : to provide seats for ⟨a theater *seating* 1000 persons⟩ **2** : to repair the seat of or provide a new seat for ⟨*seating* chairs⟩ — **seat·er** *n*

seat belt *n* : straps (as in an automobile or airplane) designed to hold a person steady in a seat

SEA·TO \'sē-tō\ *abbr* Southeast Asia Treaty Organization

sea urchin *n* : any of a class of echinoderms enclosed in shells that are usu. flattened and globe-shaped and covered with movable spines

sea·wall \'sē-ˌwȯl\ *n* : a wall or embankment to protect the shore from erosion or to act as a breakwater

[1]**sea·ward** \-wərd\ *also* **sea·wards** \-wərdz\ *adv or adj* : toward the sea

[2]**seaward** *n* : the direction or side away from land and toward the open sea

sea·wa·ter \'sē-ˌwȯt-ər, -ˌwät-\ *n* : water in or from the sea

sea·way \-ˌwā\ *n* **1** : a moderate or rough sea ⟨caught in a *seaway*⟩ **2** : a ship's headway **3 a** : a route for travel on the sea **b** : an ocean traffic lane **4** : a deep inland waterway that admits ocean shipping

sea·weed \-ˌwēd\ *n* : a plant growing in the sea; *esp* : a marine alga (as a kelp)

sea·wor·thy \-ˌwər-thē\ *adj* : fit or safe for a sea voyage ⟨a *seaworthy* ship⟩ — **sea·wor·thi·ness** *n*

se·ba·ceous \si-'bā-shəs\ *adj* : of, relating to, or secreting fatty material

sebaceous gland *n* : one of the skin glands that secrete an oily lubricating substance into the hair follicles

sec *abbr* **1** secant **2** second **3** secretary **4** section

se·cant \'sē-ˌkant, -kənt\ *n* **1** : a straight line cutting a curve at two or more points **2** : a trigonometric function that for an acute angle in a right triangle is the ratio of the hypotenuse to the side adjacent to the angle

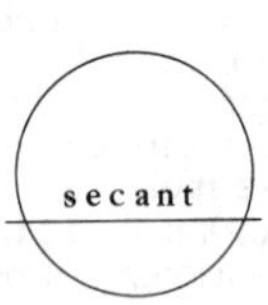

se·cede \si-'sēd\ *vb* : to withdraw from an organization (as a nation, church, or political party)

se·ces·sion \si-'sesh-ən\ *n* **1** : the act of seceding : a formal withdrawal **2** *often cap* : the withdrawal of the 11 southern states from the Union at the start of the Civil War — **se·ces·sion·ism** \-'sesh-ə-ˌniz-əm\ *n* — **se·ces·sion·ist** \-'sesh-(ə-)nəst\ *n*

se·clude \si-'klüd\ *vb* **1** : to keep away from others : make inaccessible ⟨*secluded* themselves with a few old friends⟩ **2** : to shut away : SCREEN, ISOLATE ⟨a cottage *secluded* by dense forests⟩

se·clud·ed *adj* **1** : screened or hidden from view ⟨a *secluded* valley⟩ **2** : living in seclusion : SOLITARY ⟨*secluded* monks⟩ — **se·clud·ed·ness** *n*

se·clu·sion \si-'klü-zhən\ *n* **1** : the act of secluding : the state of being secluded **2** : a secluded or isolated place — **se·clu·sive** \-'klü-siv, -ziv\ *adj*

[1]**sec·ond** \'sek-ənd\ *adj* **1** — see NUMBER table **2** : next to the first in time, order, or importance ⟨*second* violin⟩ ⟨*second* place⟩ **3** : ALTERNATE, OTHER ⟨elects a mayor every *second* year⟩ **4** : resembling or suggesting a prototype : ANOTHER ⟨a *second* Cato⟩ — **second** *adv* — **sec·ond·ly** *adv*

[2]**second** *n* **1 a** — see NUMBER table **b** : one next after the first in time, order, or importance **2** : one who assists or supports another (as in a duel or prizefight) **3** : a musical interval embracing two diatonic degrees **4** : an inferior or flawed article (as of merchandise) **5** : the act of seconding a motion **6** : SECOND BASE **7** : the second gear or speed in an automotive vehicle **8** *pl* : a second helping of food

[3]**second** *n* [so called from its being the second subdivision of a unit, as a minute is the first] **1** : the 60th part of a minute of time or of a degree **2** : INSTANT, MOMENT ⟨said he'd be back in a *second*⟩

[4]**second** *vb* **1** : to give support or encouragement to : ASSIST **2** : to endorse that it may be debated or voted on ⟨*second* a motion⟩ — **sec·ond·er** *n*

[1]**sec·ond·ary** \'sek-ən-ˌder-ē\ *adj* **1 a** : of second rank, importance, or value ⟨*secondary* streams⟩ **b** : of, relating to, or constituting the second strongest of the three or four degrees of stress ⟨the fourth syllable of *basketball team* carries *secondary* stress⟩ **2 a** : derived from something original, primary, or basic **b** : or of relating to the induced current or its circuit in an induction coil or transformer ⟨a *secondary* coil⟩ ⟨*secondary* voltage⟩ **3 a** : of, relating to, or being a second order or stage in a sequence or series **b** : intermediate between elementary and collegiate ⟨*secondary* school⟩ — **sec·ond·ar·i·ly** \ˌsek-ən-'der-ə-lē\ *adv*

[2]**secondary** *n, pl* **-ar·ies** **1** : a defensive football backfield **2** : any of the quill feathers of the forearm of a bird

secondary sex characteristic *n* : a bodily or mental peculiarity that appears in members of one sex at puberty or at the breeding season and is not directly concerned with reproduction

second base *n* : the base that must be touched second by a base runner in baseball or the position of the player defending the area around it — **second baseman** *n*

second class *n* : the second and usu. next to highest group in a classification

second–class *adj* **1** : of or relating to a second class **2 a** : INFERIOR, MEDIOCRE **b** : socially or economically deprived

second–degree burn *n* : a burn characterized by pain, blistering, and superficial destruction of the dermis accompanied by the accumulation of blood and fluid in the tissues beneath the burned area

second fiddle *n* : a person who fills a subordinate or secondary role or function

second growth *n* : forest trees that come up naturally after removal of the first growth by cutting or by fire

sec·ond–guess \ˌsek-ən-'ges\ *vb* **1** : to think out alternative strategies or explanations for after the event **2 a** : OUTGUESS **b** : PREDICT — **sec·ond–guess·er** *n*

sec·ond·hand \ˌsek-ən(d)-'hand\ *adj* **1** : not original : taken from someone else ⟨*secondhand* information⟩ **2** : not new : having had a previous owner ⟨a *secondhand* car⟩ **3** : selling used goods ⟨a *secondhand* store⟩ — **secondhand** *adv*

second lieutenant *n* : a commissioned officer (as in the army) of the lowest rank

sec·ond–rate \ˌsek-ən-ˈ(d)rāt\ *adj* : of second or inferior quality or value : MEDIOCRE
se·cre·cy \ˈsē-krə-sē\ *n, pl* **-cies** **1** : the habit or practice of keeping secrets : SECRETIVENESS **2** : the quality or state of being hidden or concealed
[1]**se·cret** \ˈsē-krət\ *adj* **1 a** : hidden or kept from knowledge or view **b** : working in secret as a spy or detective : UNDERCOVER ⟨a *secret* agent⟩ **2** : SECLUDED ⟨a *secret* valley⟩ — **se·cret·ly** *adv*
[2]**secret** *n* **1 a** : something that cannot be explained : MYSTERY **b** : something kept from the knowledge of others or shared only confidentially with a few **2** : a secret condition or place : SECRECY ⟨conspired in *secret*⟩ **3** : something taken to be a key to a desired end ⟨the *secret* of longevity⟩
sec·re·tar·i·at \ˌsek-rə-ˈter-ē-ət\ *n* **1** : the clerical staff of an organization **2** : the administrative department of a governmental organization ⟨the United Nations *secretariat*⟩
sec·re·tary \ˈsek-rə-ˌter-ē\ *n, pl* **-tar·ies** **1** : a person employed to handle correspondence and routine or detail work for a superior **2** : an officer of a business corporation or society who has charge of the correspondence and records **3** : a government official in charge of the affairs of a department ⟨*Secretary* of State⟩ **4** : a writing desk with a top section for books — **sec·re·tar·i·al** \ˌsek-rə-ˈter-ē-əl\ *adj*
secretary–general *n, pl* **secretaries–general** : a principal administrative officer ⟨*secretary-general* of the United Nations⟩
[1]**se·crete** \si-ˈkrēt\ *vb* : to produce and give off a secretion ⟨glands that *secrete* saliva⟩
[2]**se·crete** \si-ˈkrēt, ˈsē-krət\ *vb* : to deposit or conceal in a hiding place ⟨*secrete* stolen goods⟩
se·cre·tion \si-ˈkrē-shən\ *n* **1** : a concealing or hiding of something **2 a** : the act or process of secreting **b** : a product of glandular activity; *esp* : one (as a hormone or enzyme) that performs a specific useful function in the organism
se·cre·tive \ˈsē-krət-iv, si-ˈkrēt-\ *adj* : disposed to secrecy or concealment : not frank or open — **se·cre·tive·ly** *adv* — **se·cre·tive·ness** *n*
secret police *n* : a police organization operating mostly in secrecy and esp. for the political purposes of its government and often using terroristic methods
sect \ˈsekt\ *n* **1 a** : a dissenting or schismatic religious body; *esp* : one regarded as extreme or heretical **b** : a religious denomination **2 a** : a group adhering to a distinctive doctrine or to a leader **b** : PARTY, FACTION
sect *abbr* section
[1]**sec·tar·i·an** \sek-ˈter-ē-ən\ *adj* **1** : of, relating to, or characteristic of a sect or sectarian **2** : limited in character or scope : of narrow interests ⟨a *sectarian* mind⟩ — **sec·tar·i·an·ism** \-ē-ə-ˌniz-əm\ *n*
[2]**sectarian** *n* **1** : a member of a sect **2** : a narrow or bigoted person
[1]**sec·tion** \ˈsek-shən\ *n* **1** : a part cut off or separated ⟨a *section* of an orange⟩ **2 a** : a part of a written work ⟨a *section* of a chapter⟩ **b** : a distinct component part of a newspaper ⟨sports *section*⟩ **3** : the appearance that a thing has or would have if cut straight through ⟨a drawing of a gun in *section*⟩ **4** : a piece of land one square mile in area forming one of the 36 subdivisions of a township **5** : a distinct part of an area, community, or group of people ⟨a suburban *section*⟩ **6** : a part of a permanent railroad way under the care of a particular set of men **7** : one of several component parts (as of a bookcase) that may be assembled or reassembled **8** : a division of an orchestra composed of one class of instruments ⟨brass *section*⟩
[2]**section** *vb* **sec·tioned**; **sec·tion·ing** \-sh(ə-)ning\ **1** : to cut or separate into or become cut or separated into parts or sections **2** : to represent in sections (as by a drawing)
sec·tion·al \ˈsek-sh(ə-)nəl\ *adj* **1 a** : of or relating to a section **b** : local or regional in character ⟨*sectional* interests⟩ **2** : consisting of or divided into sections ⟨*sectional* furniture⟩ — **sec·tion·al·ly** \-ē\ *adv*
sec·tion·al·ism \ˈsek-sh(ə-)nə-ˌliz-əm\ *n* : excessive devotion to the interests of a region
section gang *n* : a gang or crew of track workers employed to maintain a railroad section
sec·tor \ˈsek-tər\ *n* **1** : the part of a circle included between two radii **2** : an area assigned to a military commander to defend **3** : a distinctive part (as of an economy) ⟨the industrial *sector*⟩
sec·u·lar \ˈsek-yə-lər\ *adj* **1 a** : of or relating to the worldly or temporal ⟨*secular* concerns⟩ **b** : not religious ⟨*secular* music⟩ **c** : not ecclesiastical or clerical ⟨*secular* courts⟩ ⟨*secular* landowners⟩ **2** : of or relating to clergy not belonging to a religious order ⟨a *secular* priest⟩ — **sec·u·lar·ly** *adv*
sec·u·lar·ism \-lə-ˌriz-əm\ *n* : indifference to or rejection or exclusion of religion and religious considerations — **sec·u·lar·ist** \-rəst\ *n* — **secularist** *or* **sec·u·lar·is·tic** \ˌsek-yə-lə-ˈris-tik\ *adj*
sec·u·lar·ize \ˈsek-yə-lə-ˌrīz\ *vb* **1** : to make secular **2** : to transfer from ecclesiastical to civil or lay use, possession, or control — **sec·u·lar·i·za·tion** \ˌsek-yə-lə-rə-ˈzā-shən\ *n*
[1]**se·cure** \si-ˈkyu̇(ə)r\ *adj* [from Latin *securus*, literally "free from care", from *se-*, prefix denoting separation, and *cura* "care"] **1** : easy in mind : CONFIDENT ⟨*secure* in the knowledge that help was near⟩ **2 a** : affording safety : SAFE ⟨*secure* hideaway⟩ ⟨*secure* against attack⟩ **b** : TRUSTWORTHY, DEPENDABLE ⟨*secure* foundation⟩ **3** : ASSURED, CERTAIN ⟨victory is *secure*⟩ — **se·cure·ly** *adv* — **se·cure·ness** *n*
[2]**secure** *vb* **1 a** : to relieve from exposure to danger : make safe : GUARD, SHIELD ⟨*secure* a supply line from enemy raids⟩ **b** : to assure payment of ⟨*secure* a note by a collateral security⟩ **2 a** : to take into custody : hold fast ⟨*secure* a prisoner⟩ **b** : to fasten tightly ⟨*secure* a door⟩ **3** : ACQUIRE, OBTAIN ⟨*secure* employment⟩ ***syn*** see GET
se·cure·ment \si-ˈkyu̇(ə)r-mənt\ *n* : the act or process of making secure
se·cu·ri·ty \si-ˈkyu̇r-ət-ē\ *n, pl* **-ties** **1** : the state of being secure : SAFETY ⟨*security* against aggression⟩ **2** : something given as a pledge of payment ⟨*security* for a loan⟩ **3** : an evidence of debt or of property (as a stock certificate or bond) ⟨government *securities*⟩ **4** : something that secures : PROTECTION; *esp* : measures taken to guard against espionage or sabotage ⟨a senate committee concerned with internal *security*⟩
se·dan \si-ˈdan\ *n* **1** : a portable often covered chair that is designed to carry one person and is borne on poles by two men **2** : an enclosed automobile that seats four to seven persons including the driver in a single compartment and has a permanent top
se·date \si-ˈdāt\ *adj* : QUIET, STAID, SOBER ⟨*sedate* manners⟩ ⟨too *sedate* for her age⟩ — **se·date·ly** *adv* — **se·date·ness** *n*
[1]**sed·a·tive** \ˈsed-ət-iv\ *adj* : tending to calm, moderate, or relieve tension or irritability
[2]**sedative** *n* : a sedative agent or drug
sed·en·tary \ˈsed-ən-ˌter-ē\ *adj* **1** : not migratory

S

: SETTLED ⟨*sedentary* birds⟩ **2** : doing or requiring much sitting ⟨a *sedentary* job⟩

sedge \'sej\ *n* : any of a family of usu. tufted marsh plants differing from the related grasses in having solid stems — **sedgy** \'sej-ē\ *adj*

sed·i·ment \'sed-ə-mənt\ *n* **1** : the material from a liquid that settles to the bottom **2** : material (as stones and sand) deposited by water, wind, or glaciers — **sed·i·ment** \-ˌment\ *vb*

sed·i·men·ta·ry \ˌsed-ə-'ment-ə-rē, -'men-trē\ *adj* **1** : of, relating to, or containing sediment ⟨*sedimentary* deposits⟩ **2** : formed by or from deposits of sediment ⟨limestone and sandstone are *sedimentary* rocks⟩

sed·i·men·ta·tion \ˌsed-ə-mən-'tā-shən, -ˌmen-\ *n* : the action or process of depositing sediment : SETTLING

se·di·tion \si-'dish-ən\ *n* : incitement of resistance to or of insurrection against lawful authority

se·di·tious \-'dish-əs\ *adj* : of, relating to, or inciting sedition ⟨*seditious* statements⟩ — **se·di·tious·ly** *adv* — **se·di·tious·ness** *n*

se·duce \si-'d(y)üs\ *vb* **1** : to persuade to disobedience or disloyalty **2** : to lead astray ⟨*seduced* into crime⟩ **3** : to persuade to have sexual relations esp. for the first time — **se·duc·er** *n* — **se·duc·tion** \-'dək-shən\ *n*

se·duc·tive \si-'dək-tiv\ *adj* : tending to seduce : ALLURING, TEMPTING — **se·duc·tive·ly** *adv* — **se·duc·tive·ness** *n*

sed·u·lous \'sej-ə-ləs\ *adj* : diligent in application or pursuit — **sed·u·lous·ly** *adv*

se·dum \'sēd-əm\ *n* : any of a genus of fleshy-leaved herbs with clusters of yellow, white, or pink flowers

¹**see** \'sē\ *vb* **saw** \'sȯ\; **seen** \'sēn\; **see·ing** \'sē-ing\ **1 a** : to perceive with the eyes or have the power of sight ⟨*see* a bird⟩ ⟨a person who cannot *see*⟩ **b** : to give or pay attention ⟨*see*, the bus is coming⟩ **2 a** : to have experience of : UNDERGO ⟨had *seen* something of life⟩ **b** : to know or determine by investigation ⟨*see* what's wrong with the car⟩ **3** : to perceive the meaning or importance of : UNDERSTAND ⟨I *see* what you mean⟩ **4 a** : to take care of : provide for ⟨*see* him through⟩ **b** : to make sure ⟨*see* that order is kept⟩ **5 a** : to call on : VISIT ⟨*see* a sick friend⟩ **b** : to grant an interview to : RECEIVE ⟨the president will *see* you⟩ **6** : ACCOMPANY, ESCORT ⟨*see* the girls home⟩ — **see one's way** : to find a course of action possible or reasonable ⟨couldn't *see his way* to lending me a ten⟩ — **see to** : to take care of ⟨*saw to* the children's education⟩ — **see to it** : to make certain ⟨*see to it* you're home by supper⟩

²**see** *n* **1** : the city in which a bishop's church is located **2** : the jurisdiction of a bishop : DIOCESE

see·a·ble \'sē-ə-bəl\ *adj* : capable of being seen

¹**seed** \'sēd\ *n, pl* **seed** *or* **seeds** **1 a** : the grains of plants used for sowing **b** : the fertilized ripened ovule of a flowering plant containing an embryo and capable normally of producing a new plant; *also* : a plant structure (as a spore or small dry fruit) capable of producing a new plant **2** : MILT, SEMEN **3** : DESCENDANTS ⟨the *seed* of David⟩ **4** : a source of development or growth : GERM ⟨sowed the *seeds* of discord⟩ — **seed** *adj* — **seed·ed** \-əd\ *adj* — **seed·ed·ness** *n* — **seed·like** \'sēd-ˌlīk\ *adj* — **go to seed** *or* **run to seed** : to lose vitality or effectiveness : DECAY

²**seed** *vb* **1 a** : PLANT, SOW ⟨*seed* a field⟩ **b** : to bear or shed seeds ⟨weeds that *seed* freely⟩ **c** : to remove seeds from ⟨*seed* raisins⟩ **2** : to supply with nuclei (as of crystallization or condensation); *esp* : to treat (a cloud) with solid particles to convert water droplets into ice crystals in an attempt to produce rain **3** : to schedule tournament players or teams so that superior ones will not meet in early rounds ⟨was *seeded* second in the state tournament⟩

seed·bed \'sēd-ˌbed\ *n* : soil or a bed of soil prepared for planting seed

seed·case \-ˌkās\ *n* : a dry hollow fruit (as a pod) enclosing seeds

seed coat *n* : the hardened outer protective cover of a seed

seed·eat·er \'sēd-ˌēt-ər\ *n* : a bird (as a finch) whose diet consists basically of seeds

seed·er \'sēd-ər\ *n* **1** : a machine for planting or sowing seeds **2** : a device for seeding fruit

seed leaf *n* : COTYLEDON

seed·less \'sēd-ləs\ *adj* : having no seeds ⟨*seedless* grapes⟩

seed·ling \-ling\ *n* **1** : a plant grown from seed **2** : a young plant; *esp* : a tree smaller than a sapling — **seedling** *adj*

seed plant *n* : a plant that bears seeds : SPERMATOPHYTE

seed·pod \'sēd-ˌpäd\ *n* : POD 1

seedy \'sēd-ē\ *adj* **seed·i·er**; **-est** **1** : containing or full of seeds ⟨a *seedy* fruit⟩ **2** : inferior in condition or quality ⟨*seedy* clothes⟩ — **seed·i·ness** *n*

see·ing \'sē-ing\ *conj* : in view of the fact that

seek \'sēk\ *vb* **sought** \'sȯt\; **seek·ing** **1** : to resort to : go to ⟨*seek* the shade on a sunny day⟩ **2 a** : to go in search of : look for ⟨*seek* out the culprit⟩ **b** : to try to discover ⟨*seek* the truth⟩ **3** : to ask for : REQUEST ⟨*seeks* advice⟩ **4** : to try to acquire or gain : aim at ⟨*seeking* public office⟩ **5** : to make an attempt : TRY ⟨*seek* to find a way⟩ ⟨*sought* to improve his work⟩— **seek·er** *n*

seem \'sēm\ *vb* **1 a** : to give the impression of being : APPEAR ⟨the request *seems* reasonable⟩ **b** : to appear to a person's own mind or opinion ⟨can't *seem* to solve the problem⟩ **2** : to appear to exist ⟨there *seems* no reason for worry⟩

seem·ing \'sē-ming\ *adj* : apparent on superficial view ⟨suspicious of his *seeming* enthusiasm⟩ — **seem·ing·ly** \-ming-lē\ *adv*

seem·ly \'sēm-lē\ *adj* **seem·li·er**; **-est** **1** : good-looking : HANDSOME, ATTRACTIVE **2** : conventionally proper ⟨*seemly* behavior⟩ **3** : suited to the occasion, purpose, or person : FIT ⟨a *seemly* reply⟩ — **seem·li·ness** *n* — **seemly** *adv*

see out *vb* : to continue with until the end : FINISH ⟨*see out* one's education⟩

seep \'sēp\ *vb* : to flow or pass slowly through fine pores or small openings : OOZE ⟨water had *seeped* in through a crack in the ceiling⟩

seep·age \'sē-pij\ *n* **1** : the process of seeping : OOZING **2** : a quantity of fluid that has seeped through porous material

seer \'si(ə)r, *esp for 1 also* 'sē-ər\ *n* **1** : someone or something that sees **2** : a person who foresees or foretells events

seer·suck·er \'si(ə)r-ˌsək-ər\ *n* : a light fabric of linen, cotton, or rayon usu. striped and slightly puckered

¹**see·saw** \'sē-ˌsȯ\ *n* **1 a** : an alternating up-and-down or backward-and-forward motion or

ə abut	ər further	a back	ā bake	
ä cot, cart	au̇ out	ch chin	e less	ē easy
g gift	i trip	ī life	j joke	ng sing	ō flow
ȯ flaw	ȯi coin	th thin	t͟h this	ü loot
u̇ foot	y yet	yü few	yu̇ furious	zh vision

movement **b** : a contest or struggle in which now one side now the other has the lead **2 a** : a game in which two children or groups of children ride on opposite ends of a plank balanced in the middle so that one end goes up as the other goes down **b** : the plank used in seesaw — **seesaw** *adj*

seesaw 2b

2**seesaw** *vb* **see·sawed**; **see·saw·ing** **1** : to ride on a seesaw **2** : to move like a seesaw

seethe \'sēth\ *vb* **1** : BOIL, STEW **2** : to churn or foam as if boiling ⟨the river rapids *seethed*⟩ **3** : to be in a state of great excitement or upset ⟨was *seething* with rage⟩

1**seg·ment** \'seg-mənt\ *n* **1** : any of the parts into which a thing is divided or naturally separates : SECTION, DIVISION **2 a** : a part cut off from a geometrical figure (as a circle or sphere) by a line or plane; *esp* : the part of a circle bounded by a chord and an arc of that circle **b** : a part of a straight line included between two points — called also *line segment* *syn* see PART — **seg·ment·ed** \-ˌment-əd, -mənt-\ *adj*

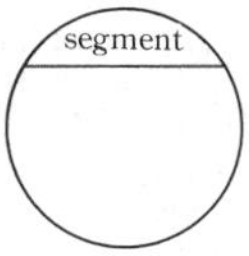

2**seg·ment** \'seg-ˌment\ *vb* : to separate into segments

seg·men·ta·tion \ˌseg-mən-'tā-shən, -ˌmen-\ *n* : the process of dividing into segments; *esp* : the formation of many cells from a single cell (as in a developing egg)

se·go \'sē-gō\ *n, pl* **segos** : the bulb of the sego lily

sego lily *n* : a western No. American herb with bell-shaped flowers white within and largely green without and an edible bulb

seg·re·gate \'seg-ri-ˌgāt\ *vb* [from Latin *segregare*, from *se-*, prefix denoting separation, and *greg-*, stem of *grex* "herd", "flock"] **1** : to separate or set apart from others : ISOLATE; *esp* : to separate by races **2** : to separate from the general mass and collect together (as in crystallization)

seg·re·ga·tion \ˌseg-ri-'gā-shən\ *n* **1** : the act or process of segregating : the state of being segregated **2** : the separation or isolation of a race, class, or ethnic group (as by restriction to an area or by separate schools)

seg·re·ga·tion·ist \-sh(ə-)nəst\ *n* : an advocate of segregation esp. of races

sei·gneur \sān-'yər\ *n, often cap* : LORD, SEIGNIOR

sei·gnior \sān-'yō(ə)r\ *n* : a man of rank or authority; *esp* : the feudal lord of a manor

sei·gniory *or* **sei·gnory** \'sān-yə-rē\ *n, pl* **-gnior·ies** *or* **-gnor·ies** : the territory of a lord : DOMAIN

1**seine** \'sān\ *n* : a large fishing net kept hanging vertically in the water by weights and floats

2**seine** *vb* : to fish with or catch with a seine — **sein·er** *n*

seism \'sī-zəm\ *n* : EARTHQUAKE

seis·mic \'sīz-mik, 'sīs-\ *adj* : of, subject to, or caused by an earthquake or an artificially produced earth vibration

seismo- *comb form* : earthquake : vibration ⟨*seismo*graph⟩

seis·mo·gram \'sīz-mə-ˌgram, 'sīs-\ *n* : the record of an earth tremor made by a seismograph

seis·mo·graph \-ˌgraf\ *n* : an apparatus for recording the intensity, direction, and duration of earthquakes or similar vibrations of the ground — **seis·mo·graph·ic** \ˌsīz-mə-'graf-ik, ˌsīs-\ *adj* — **seis·mog·ra·phy** \sīz-'mäg-rə-fē, sīs-\ *n*

seis·mol·o·gy \sīz-'mäl-ə-jē, sīs-\ *n* : a science that deals with earthquakes and with artificially produced vibrations of the earth — **seis·mo·log·i·cal** \ˌsīz-mə-'läj-i-kəl, ˌsīs-\ *adj* — **seis·mol·o·gist** \sīz-'mäl-ə-jəst, sīs-\ *n*

seize \'sēz\ *vb* **1** : to take possession of by force ⟨*seize* a fortress⟩ **2** : to take hold of suddenly or with force : CLUTCH ⟨*seized* her in his arms⟩ **3** : UNDERSTAND, COMPREHEND ⟨*seize* an idea quickly⟩ **4** : to take prisoner : ARREST **5** : to bind together by lashing (as with small cord) ⟨*seize* two ropes⟩ **6** : to attack or overwhelm suddenly (as with fever) — **seiz·er** *n* — **seize on** *or* **seize upon** : to take immediate advantage or make immediate use of : CLUTCH

sei·zure \'sē-zhər\ *n* **1** : the act of seizing : the state of being seized **2** : a sudden attack (as of disease) : FIT

sel *abbr* **1** select **2** selection

se·lag·i·nel·la \sə-ˌlaj-ə-'nel-ə\ *n* : any of a genus of mossy lower vascular plants

selaginella (about 2 in. high)

sel·dom \'sel-dəm\ *adv* : not often : RARELY

1**se·lect** \sə-'lekt\ *adj* **1** : chosen from a number or group by fitness or preference ⟨a *select* group⟩ **2** : of special value or excellence : SUPERIOR, CHOICE ⟨a *select* hotel⟩ — **se·lect·ness** *n*

2**select** *vb* : to take by preference from a number or group : pick out : CHOOSE

se·lec·tion \sə-'lek-shən\ *n* **1** : the act of selecting : the state of being selected ⟨*selection* of the best entry was difficult⟩ ⟨cheered his *selection* as athlete of the year⟩ **2 a** : one that is selected : CHOICE **b** : a collection of selected things **3** : any natural or artificial process that tends to prevent some individuals or groups of organisms from surviving and propagating while allowing others to do so

se·lec·tive \sə-'lek-tiv\ *adj* **1** : of or relating to selection : selecting or tending to select ⟨*selective* shoppers⟩ **2** : of, relating to, or constituting the ability of a radio circuit or apparatus to respond to a specific frequency without interference — **se·lec·tiv·i·ty** \si-ˌlek-'tiv-ət-ē, ˌsē-\ *n*

se·lect·man \sə-'lek(t)-ˌman, -mən; -ˌlek(t)-'man\ *n* : one of a board of town officials elected annually in some of the New England states

se·lec·tor \sə-'lek-tər\ *n* : someone or something that selects

sel·e·nite \'sel-ə-ˌnīt\ *n* : a variety of gypsum occurring in transparent crystals or crystalline masses

se·le·ni·um \sə-'lē-nē-əm\ *n* : a nonmetallic element that varies in electrical conductivity with the intensity of its illumination and is used in electronic devices — see ELEMENT table

sel·e·nog·ra·phy \ˌsel-ə-'näg-rə-fē\ *n* : the science of the physical features of the moon

1**self** \'self\ *pron* : MYSELF, HIMSELF, HERSELF

⟨check payable to *self*⟩ ⟨accommodations for *self* and wife⟩

²**self** \'self\ *n*, *pl* **selves** \'selvz\ **1 :** a person regarded as an individual apart from everyone else ⟨a man's *self*⟩ **2 :** a particular side of a person's character ⟨his better *self*⟩ **3 :** personal interest or advantage ⟨without thought of *self*⟩

self- \'self *before '-stressed syllable*, ˌself *before ˌ-stressed or unstressed syllable*\ *comb form* **1 a :** oneself or itself ⟨*self*-loving⟩ **b :** of oneself or itself ⟨*self*-abasement⟩ **c :** by oneself or itself ⟨*self*-propelled⟩ **2 a :** to, with, for, or toward oneself or itself ⟨*self*-consistent⟩ ⟨*self*-addressed⟩ ⟨*self*-satisfaction⟩ **b :** of or in oneself or itself inherently ⟨*self*-evident⟩ **c :** from or by means of oneself or itself ⟨*self*-fertile⟩

self–act·ing \'self-'ak-ting\ *adj* **:** acting or capable of acting of or by itself **:** AUTOMATIC

self–ad·dressed \ˌself-ə-'drest, 'self-'ad-ˌrest\ *adj* **:** addressed for return to the sender ⟨*self-addressed* envelope⟩

self–ad·mi·ra·tion \ˌself-ˌad-mə-'rā-shən\ *n* **:** SELF-CONCEIT

self–ap·point·ed \ˌself-ə-'pȯint-əd\ *adj* **:** appointed by oneself usu. without qualifications ⟨a *self-appointed* censor⟩

self–as·ser·tion \ˌself-ə-'sər-shən\ *n* **1 :** the act of asserting oneself or one's own rights or claims **2 :** the act of asserting one's superiority over others — **self–as·sert·ive** \-'sərt-iv\ *adj*

self–as·sur·ance \ˌself-ə-'shu̇r-ən(t)s\ *n* **:** SELF-CONFIDENCE

self–as·sured \-'shu̇rd\ *adj* **:** SELF-CONFIDENT

self–aware·ness \ˌself-ə-'wa(ə)r-nəs, -'we(ə)r-\ *n* **:** an awareness of one's own personality or individuality

self–cen·tered \'self-'sent-ərd\ *adj* **:** interested chiefly in one's own self **:** SELFISH — **self–cen·tered·ly** *adv* — **self–cen·tered·ness** *n*

self–con·ceit \ˌself-kən-'sēt\ *n* **:** an exaggerated opinion of one's own qualities or abilities **:** VANITY — **self–con·ceit·ed** \-əd\ *adj*

self–con·fessed \ˌself-kən-'fest\ *adj* **:** openly acknowledged ⟨a *self-confessed* gambler⟩

self–con·fi·dence \'self-'kän-fəd-ən(t)s, -fə-ˌden(t)s\ *n* **:** confidence in oneself and in one's powers and abilities — **self–con·fi·dent** \-fəd-ənt, -fə-ˌdent\ *adj* — **self–con·fi·dent·ly** *adv*

self–con·scious \'self-'kän-chəs\ *adj* **:** uncomfortably conscious of oneself as an object of the observation of others **:** ill at ease — **self–con·scious·ly** *adv* — **self–con·scious·ness** *n*

self–con·tained \ˌself-kən-'tānd\ *adj* **1 :** sufficient or complete in itself **2 a :** showing self-control **b :** formal and reserved in manner — **self–con·tain·ment** \-'tān-mənt\ *n*

self–con·trol \ˌself-kən-'trōl\ *n* **:** control over one's own impulses, emotions, or acts — **self–con·trolled** \-'trōld\ *adj*

self–de·feat·ing \ˌself-di-'fēt-ing\ *adj* **:** acting to defeat its own purpose

self–de·fense \ˌself-di-'fen(t)s\ *n* **:** the act of defending oneself, one's property, or a close relative

self–de·ni·al \ˌself-di-'nī(-ə)l\ *n* **:** the act of refraining from gratifying one's own desires

ə abut	ər further	a back	ā bake
ä cot, cart	au̇ out	ch chin	e less
ē easy	g gift	i trip	ī life
j joke	ng sing	ō flow	ȯ flaw
ȯi coin	th thin	th this	ü loot
u̇ foot	y yet	yü few	yu̇ furious
zh vision			

self–de·struc·tion \ˌself-di-'strək-shən\ *n* **:** destruction of oneself or itself; *esp* **:** SUICIDE — **self–de·struc·tive** \-'strək-tiv\ *adj*

self–de·ter·mi·na·tion \ˌself-di-ˌtər-mə-'nā-shən\ *n* **1 :** the act or power of deciding things for oneself **2 :** determination by the people of a territorial unit of the form of government they will have

self–di·rect·ed \ˌself-də-'rek-təd, -dī-\ *adj* **:** directed by oneself; *esp* **:** not motivated by an outside force or agency ⟨a *self-directed* personality⟩

self–doubt \'self-'dau̇t\ *n* **:** a lack of faith in oneself — **self–doubt·ing** \-ing\ *adj*

self–ed·u·cat·ed \'self-'ej-ə-ˌkāt-əd\ *adj* **:** educated by one's own efforts without formal instruction

self–em·ployed \ˌself-im-'plȯid\ *adj* **:** earning income directly from one's own business, trade, or profession rather than as salary or wages from an employer

self–es·teem \ˌself-ə-'stēm\ *n* **1 :** SELF-RESPECT **2 :** SELF-CONCEIT

self–ev·i·dent \'self-'ev-əd-ənt, -ə-ˌdent\ *adj* **:** evident without proof or argument

self–ex·plan·a·to·ry \ˌself-ik-'splan-ə-ˌtōr-ē, -ˌtȯr-\ *adj* **:** understandable without explanation

self–ex·pres·sion \ˌself-ik-'spresh-ən\ *n* **:** the expression of one's own personality ⟨found a form of *self-expression* in music⟩

self–fer·tile \'self-'fərt-əl\ *adj* **:** fertile by means of its own pollen or sperm — **self–fer·til·i·ty** \ˌself-(ˌ)fər-'til-ət-ē\ *n*

self–fer·til·i·za·tion \ˌself-ˌfərt-ə-lə-'zā-shən\ *n* **:** fertilization by pollen or sperm from the same individual — **self–fer·til·ize** \'self-'fərt-ə-ˌlīz\ *vb*

self–gov·ern·ment \'self-'gəv-ər(n)-mənt\ *n* **1 :** SELF-CONTROL **2 :** government by action of the people making up a community; *esp* **:** democratic government — **self–gov·erned** \-'gəv-ərnd\ *adj* — **self–gov·ern·ing** \-ər-ning\ *adj*

self–hard·en·ing \'self-'härd-(ə-)ning\ *adj* **:** hardening by itself or without quenching after heating ⟨*self-hardening* steel⟩

self–heal \'self-ˌhēl\ *n* **:** a low-growing blue-flowered mint supposed to have healing properties

self–help \'self-'help\ *n* **:** the act of providing for or helping oneself without dependence on others

self–im·por·tance \ˌself-im-'pȯrt-ən(t)s\ *n* **:** an exaggerated estimate of one's own importance **:** SELF-CONCEIT — **self–im·por·tant** \-ənt\ *adj* — **self–im·por·tant·ly** *adv*

self–im·posed \ˌself-im-'pōzd\ *adj* **:** imposed on one by oneself **:** voluntarily assumed ⟨went into a *self-imposed* exile in his later years⟩

self–in·crim·i·na·tion \ˌself-in-ˌkrim-ə-'nā-shən\ *n* **:** incrimination of oneself; *esp* **:** the giving of evidence or answering of questions the tendency of which would be to subject one to criminal prosecution

self–in·duced \ˌself-in-'d(y)üst\ *adj* **1 :** induced by oneself or itself **2 :** produced by self-induction ⟨a *self-induced* voltage⟩

self–in·duc·tion \-'dək-shən\ *n* **:** induction of an electromotive force in a circuit by a varying current in the same circuit

self–in·dul·gence \ˌself-in-'dəl-jən(t)s\ *n* **:** excessive gratification of one's own appetites, desires, or whims — **self–in·dul·gent** \-jənt\ *adj* — **self–in·dul·gent·ly** *adv*

self–in·flict·ed \ˌself-in-'flik-təd\ *adj* **:** inflicted by oneself ⟨a *self-inflicted* wound⟩

self–in·ter·est \'self-'in-trəst, -'int-ə-rəst\ *n* **1 :** one's own interest or advantage ⟨our *self-interest* demands that we act now⟩ **2 :** a concern for one's own advantage and well-being ⟨a generosity motivated by *self-interest*⟩

self·ish \'sel-fish\ *adj* : taking care of one's own desires or advantage without regard for the interests of others — **self·ish·ly** *adv* — **self·ish·ness** *n*

self·less \'self-ləs\ *adj* : having or showing no concern for self : UNSELFISH — **self·less·ly** *adv* — **self·less·ness** *n*

self–made \'self-'mād\ *adj* **1** : made by oneself or itself **2** : raised from poverty or obscurity by one's own efforts ⟨*self-made* man⟩

self–per·pet·u·at·ing \ˌself-pər-'pech-ə-ˌwāt-ing\ *adj* : capable of continuing or renewing itself indefinitely ⟨a *self-perpetuating* board of trustees⟩

self–pity \'self-'pit-ē\ *n* : pity for oneself — **self–pity·ing** \-ē-ing\ *adj*

self–pol·li·nate \'self-'päl-ə-ˌnāt\ *vb* : to undergo or cause to undergo self-pollination

self–pol·li·na·tion \ˌself-ˌpäl-ə-'nā-shən\ *n* : pollination in which the pollen is from the same flower or sometimes from a genetically identical flower

self–por·trait \'self-'pōr-trət, -'pȯr-, -ˌtrāt\ *n* : a portrait of oneself done by oneself

self–pos·sessed \ˌself-pə-'zest\ *adj* : having or showing self-possession : CALM

self–pos·ses·sion \-'zesh-ən\ *n* : control of one's emotions or reactions : COMPOSURE

self–pres·er·va·tion \ˌself-ˌprez-ər-'vā-shən\ *n* : the keeping of oneself from destruction, injury, or loss

self–pro·claimed \ˌself-prō-'klāmd\ *adj* : based on one's own say-so ⟨a *self-proclaimed* genius⟩

self–pro·duced \ˌself-prə-'d(y)üst\ *adj* : produced by oneself or itself

self–pro·pelled \ˌself-prə-'peld\ *adj* : containing within itself the means for its own propulsion

self–pro·pel·ling \-'pel-ing\ *adj* : SELF-PROPELLED

self–pro·tec·tive \ˌself-prə-'tek-tiv\ *adj* : serving or tending to protect oneself

self–re·gard \ˌself-ri-'gärd\ *n* **1** : regard for or consideration of oneself or one's own interests **2** : SELF-RESPECT

self–reg·is·ter·ing \'self-'rej-ə-st(ə-)ring\ *adj* : registering automatically ⟨a *self-registering* barometer⟩

self–reg·u·lat·ing \'self-'reg-yə-ˌlāt-ing\ *adj* : regulating oneself; *esp* : AUTOMATIC ⟨a *self-regulating* mechanism⟩ — **self–reg·u·la·tion** \ˌself-ˌreg-yə-'lā-shən\ *n*

self–re·li·ance \ˌself-ri-'lī-əns\ *n* : reliance upon one's own efforts and abilities — **self–re·li·ant** \-ənt\ *adj*

self–re·proach \ˌself-ri-'prōch\ *n* : the act of blaming or accusing oneself

self–re·spect \ˌself-ri-'spekt\ *n* **1** : a proper respect for oneself as a human being **2** : regard for one's own standing or position — **self–re·spect·ing** \-'spek-ting\ *adj*

self–re·straint \ˌself-ri-'strānt\ *n* : restraint imposed on oneself : SELF-CONTROL

self–righ·teous \'self-'rī-chəs\ *adj* : convinced of one's own righteousness — **self–righ·teous·ly** *adv* — **self–righ·teous·ness** *n*

self–right·ing \'self-'rīt-ing\ *adj* : capable of righting itself when capsized ⟨a *self-righting* boat⟩

self–ris·ing \'self-'rī-zing\ *adj* : rising without the use of leaven ⟨*self-rising* flour⟩

self–sac·ri·fice \'self-'sak-rə-ˌfīs, -fəs\ *n* : sacrifice of oneself or one's interest for others or for a cause or ideal — **self–sac·ri·fic·ing** \-ˌfī-sing\ *adj*

self·same \'self-ˌsām\ *adj* : exactly the same : IDENTICAL

self–sat·is·fac·tion \ˌself-ˌsat-əs-'fak-shən\ *n* : a usu. smug satisfaction with oneself or one's position or achievements

self–sat·is·fied \'self-'sat-əs-ˌfīd\ *adj* : feeling or showing self-satisfaction

self–seal·ing \'self-'sē-ling\ *adj* : capable of sealing itself (as after puncture) ⟨a *self-sealing* tire⟩

self–seek·er \'self-'sē-kər\ *n* : a person who is interested only in his own advantage or pleasure — **self–seek·ing** \-king\ *n or adj*

self–ser·vice \'self-'sər-vəs\ *n* : the serving of oneself (as in a cafeteria or supermarket) with things to be paid for at a cashier's desk usu. upon leaving — **self–service** *adj*

self–start·er \'self-'stärt-ər\ *n* : a more or less automatic attachment for starting an internal-combustion engine

self–styled \'self-'stīld\ *adj* : called by oneself ⟨*self-styled* experts⟩

self–suf·fi·cient \ˌself-sə-'fish-ənt\ *adj* **1** : able to take care of oneself without outside help : INDEPENDENT **2** : having an extreme confidence in one's own ability or worth : HAUGHTY

self–sup·port \ˌself-sə-'pōrt, -'pȯrt\ *n* : independent support of oneself or itself — **self–sup·port·ing** \-ing\ *adj*

self–taught \'self-'tȯt\ *adj* **1** : having knowledge or skills acquired by one's own efforts without formal instruction **2** : learned by oneself ⟨*self-taught* understanding of music⟩

self–treat·ment \'self-'trēt-mənt\ *n* : medication of oneself or treatment of one's ailment without medical supervision

self–will \'self-'wil\ *n* : stubborn adherence to one's own desires or ideas : OBSTINACY — **self–willed** \-'wild\ *adj*

self–wind·ing \'self-'wīn-ding\ *adj* : not needing to be wound by hand : winding by itself ⟨a *self-winding* watch⟩

sell \'sel\ *vb* **sold** \'sōld\; **sell·ing** [from Old English *sellen*, meaning originally simply "to give", "hand over"] **1** : to betray a person or duty ⟨the traitors *sold* their king to the enemy⟩ **2** : to give in exchange esp. for money ⟨he *sold* me his car⟩ ⟨*sells* his services to the highest bidder⟩ **3 a** : to find buyers : be bought ⟨that model didn't *sell* very well⟩ **b** : to be for sale ⟨they *sell* for $15 apiece⟩ **4 a** : to make acceptable, believable, or desirable by persuasion ⟨the President couldn't *sell* his program to Congress⟩ **b** : to bring around to a favorable way of thinking ⟨tried to *sell* me on his idea⟩ — **sell·a·ble** \'sel-ə-bəl\ *adj* — **sell·er** *n* — **sell short** : to underestimate the ability, strength, or importance of ⟨made the mistake of *selling* his rival *short*⟩

sell·out \'sel-ˌau̇t\ *n* **1** : the act or an instance of selling out **2** : a performance or exhibition for which all seats are sold

sell out \-'au̇t\ *vb* **1** : to dispose of all of one's goods by sale **2** : to betray one's cause or associates

selt·zer \'selt-sər\ *n* : an artificially prepared water containing carbon dioxide

sel·vage *or* **sel·vedge** \'sel-vij\ *n* : the edge of cloth so woven that it will not ravel

selves *pl of* SELF

sem *abbr* seminary

se·man·tic \si-'mant-ik\ *adj* **1** : of or relating to meaning in language **2** : of or relating to semantics — **se·man·ti·cal·ly** \-'mant-i-k(ə-)lē\ *adv*

se·man·tics \si-'mant-iks\ *n* : the study of meanings and changes of meaning — **se·man·ti·cist** \si-'mant-ə-səst\ *n*

[1]**sem·a·phore** \'sem-ə-ˌfōr, -ˌfȯr\ *n* **1** : an apparatus for visual signaling (as by the position of one or

S

more movable arms) **2 :** a system of visual signaling by two flags held one in each hand

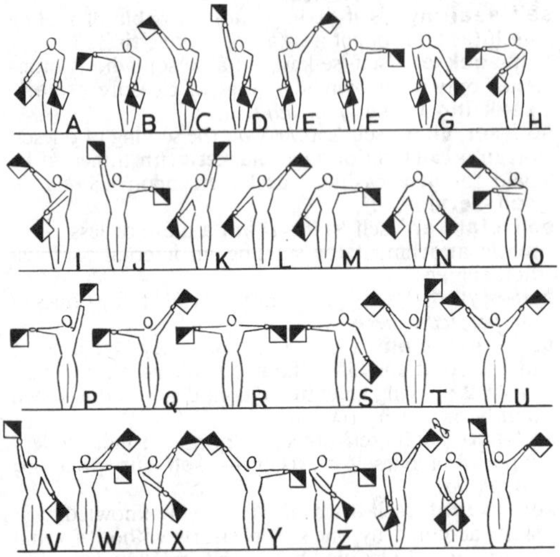

semaphore 2

²**semaphore** *vb* **:** to signal by or as if by semaphore

sem·blance \'sem-blən(t)s\ *n* **1 :** outward appearance **2 :** LIKENESS, IMAGE

se·men \'sē-mən\ *n, pl* **sem·i·na** \'sem-ə-nə\ *or* **semens :** a viscid whitish fluid of the male reproductive tract containing the spermatozoa

se·mes·ter \sə-'mes-tər\ *n* **:** one of two terms of about 18 weeks each into which an academic year is divided

semi- \ˌsem-i, 'sem-, -ˌī\ *prefix* **1 a :** precisely half of ⟨*semi*circle⟩ **b :** half in quantity or value **:** half of or occurring halfway through a specified period of time ⟨*semi*annual⟩ **2 :** to some extent **:** partly **:** incompletely ⟨*semi*tropical⟩ **3 :** partial **:** incomplete ⟨*semi*darkness⟩

semi·an·nu·al \ˌsem-ē-'an-y(ə-w)əl, ˌsem-ˌī-\ *adj* **:** occurring twice a year ⟨*semiannual* dividend on stock⟩ — **semi·an·nu·al·ly** \-ē\ *adv*

semi·aquat·ic \-ə-'kwät-ik, -'kwat-\ *adj* **:** chiefly aquatic; *esp* **:** growing in or adjacent to water (as in moist lowlands)

semi·ar·id \-'ar-əd\ *adj* **:** characterized by light rainfall; *esp* **:** having from about 10 to about 20 inches of annual precipitation

semi·au·to·mat·ic \-ˌȯt-ə-'mat-ik\ *adj* **:** not fully automatic — **semiautomatic** *n* — **semi·au·to·mat·i·cal·ly** \-'mat-i-k(ə-)lē\ *adv*

semi·cir·cle \'sem-i-ˌsər-kəl\ *n* **:** half of a circle — **semi·cir·cu·lar** \ˌsem-i-'sər-kyə-lər\ *adj*

semicircular canal *n* **:** any of the loop-shaped tubular parts in the inner ear of vertebrates that together are concerned with the sense of bodily balance

semi·civ·i·lized \ˌsem-i-'siv-ə-ˌlīzd, ˌsem-ˌī-\ *adj* **:** partly civilized

semi·clas·si·cal \-'klas-i-kəl\ *adj* **1 :** having some of the characteristics of the classical; *esp* **:** of or relating to a musical composition that acts as a bridge between classical and popular music **2 :** of or relating to a classical musical composition that has become generally popular

semi·co·lon \'sem-i-ˌkō-lən\ *n* **:** a punctuation mark ; used chiefly to separate independent clauses not joined by a conjunction or to separate phrases and clauses containing commas

semi·con·duc·tor \ˌsem-i-kən-'dək-tər, ˌsem-ˌī-\ *n* **:** a solid (as germanium) whose electrical conductivity is between that of a conductor and that of an insulator — **semi·con·duct·ing** \-tiŋ\ *adj*

semi·dark·ness \-'därk-nəs\ *n* **:** partial darkness

semi·di·vine \-də-'vīn\ *adj* **:** more than mortal but not fully divine

¹**semi·fi·nal** \ˌsem-i-'fīn-əl\ *adj* **1 :** being next to the last in an elimination tournament ⟨*semifinal* pairings⟩ **2 :** of or participating in a semifinal

²**semi·fi·nal** \'sem-i-ˌfīn-əl\ *n* **:** a semifinal match or round — **semi·fi·nal·ist** \ˌsem-i-'fīn-ə-ləst\ *n*

semi·flu·id \ˌsem-i-'flü-əd, ˌsem-ˌī-\ *adj* **:** having the qualities of both a fluid and a solid **:** VISCOUS ⟨fluid and *semifluid* greases⟩

semi·for·mal \ˌsem-i-'fȯr-məl, ˌsem-ˌī-\ *adj* **:** being or suitable for an occasion of moderate formality ⟨a *semiformal* dinner⟩ ⟨*semiformal* gowns⟩

semi·gloss \'sem-i-ˌgläs, 'sem-ˌī-, -ˌglȯs\ *adj* **:** having a low luster ⟨*semigloss* paint⟩

¹**semi·month·ly** \ˌsem-i-'mən(t)th-lē, ˌsem-ˌī-\ *adj* **:** occurring twice a month

²**semimonthly** *n* **:** a semimonthly publication

³**semimonthly** *adv* **:** twice a month

sem·i·nal \'sem-ən-əl\ *adj* **:** of, relating to, or consisting of seed or semen — **sem·i·nal·ly** \-ə-lē\ *adv*

sem·i·nar \'sem-ə-ˌnär\ *n* **1 :** a course of study pursued by a group of advanced students doing original research under a professor and exchanging results at meetings **2 :** a meeting of a seminar or a room for such meetings **3 :** a meeting for giving and discussing information **:** CONFERENCE ⟨a sales *seminar*⟩

sem·i·nar·i·an \ˌsem-ə-'ner-ē-ən\ *n* **:** a student in a seminary esp. of the Roman Catholic Church

sem·i·nary \'sem-ə-ˌner-ē\ *n, pl* **-nar·ies :** an educational institution; *esp* **:** an institution for training clergymen

Sem·i·nole \'sem-ə-ˌnōl\ *n* **:** a member of an Amerindian people of Florida

semi·of·fi·cial \ˌsem-ē-ə-'fish-əl, ˌsem-ˌī-\ *adj* **:** having some official authority or standing ⟨a *semiofficial* statement⟩

semi·per·ma·nent \ˌsem-i-'pər-mə-nənt, ˌsem-ˌī-\ *adj* **1 :** permanent in some respects **2 :** lasting for an indefinite time

semi·per·me·a·ble \-'pər-mē-ə-bəl\ *adj* **:** partially but not freely or wholly permeable; *esp* **:** permeable to some usu. small molecules but not to other usu. larger particles — **semi·per·me·a·bil·i·ty** \-ˌpər-mē-ə-'bil-ət-ē\ *n*

semi·pre·cious \-'presh-əs\ *adj* **:** of less commercial value than precious ⟨*semiprecious* gemstones⟩

semi·pri·vate \-'prī-vət\ *adj* **:** shared with only one or a few others ⟨a *semiprivate* room in a hospital⟩

semi·pro \'sem-i-ˌprō, 'sem-ˌī-\ *adj or n* **:** SEMIPROFESSIONAL

semi·pro·fes·sion·al \ˌsem-i-prə-'fesh-(ə-)nəl, ˌsem-ˌī-\ *adj* **1 :** engaging in an activity for pay or gain but not as a full-time occupation **2 :** engaged in by semiprofessional players ⟨*semiprofessional* baseball⟩ — **semiprofessional** *n*

semi·re·li·gious \-ri-'lij-əs\ *adj* **:** somewhat religious in character

ə abut	ər further	a back	ā bake	
ä cot, cart	au̇ out	ch chin	e less	ē easy
g gift	i trip	ī life	j joke	ŋ sing	ō flow
ȯ flaw	ȯi coin	th thin	t͟h this	ü loot
u̇ foot	y yet	yü few	yu̇ furious	zh vision

semi·skilled \-'skild\ *adj* : having or requiring less training than skilled labor and more than unskilled labor
semi·soft \-'sȯft\ *adj* : moderately soft; *esp* : firm but easily cut ⟨*semisoft* cheese⟩
semi·sol·id \-'säl-əd\ *adj* : having the qualities of both a solid and a liquid — **semisolid** *n*
semi·sweet \-'swēt\ *adj* : slightly sweetened ⟨*semisweet* chocolate⟩
Sem·ite \'sem-,īt\ *n* : a member of any of a group of peoples of southwestern Asia chiefly represented by the Jews and Arabs
Se·mit·ic \sə-'mit-ik\ *adj* : of or relating to the Semites; *esp* : JEWISH
semi·tone \'sem-i-,tōn, 'sem-,ī-\ *n* **1** : the tone at a half step **2** : HALF STEP
semi·trail·er \'sem-i-,trā-lər, 'sem-,ī-\ *n* : a freight trailer that when attached is supported at its forward end by the truck tractor; *also* : a semitrailer with attached tractor
semi·trop·ic \,sem-i-'träp-ik, ,sem-,ī-\ *adj* : SUBTROPICAL — **semi·trop·i·cal** \-i-kəl\ *adj*
¹**semi·week·ly** \-'wē-klē\ *adj* : occurring twice a week — **semiweekly** *adv*
²**semiweekly** *n* : a semiweekly publication
sem·o·li·na \,sem-ə-'lē-nə\ *n* : the purified middlings of hard wheat used for macaroni, spaghetti, or vermicelli
sen *abbr* **1** senate **2** senator
sen·ate \'sen-ət\ *n* [from Latin *senatus*, literally "council of elders", from *sen-*, stem of *senex* "old", "old man"] **1 a** : the supreme council of the ancient Roman republic and empire **b** : the higher branch of some bicameral legislatures **2** : an official law-making group or council
sen·a·tor \'sen-ət-ər\ *n* : a member of a senate
sen·a·to·ri·al \,sen-ə-'tōr-ē-əl, -'tȯr-\ *adj* : of or relating to a senator or a senate ⟨*senatorial* office⟩
send \'send\ *vb* **sent** \'sent\; **send·ing** **1** : to cause to go : DISPATCH ⟨*sent* the pupil home⟩ ⟨*sent* a message⟩; *esp* : to drive or propel physically ⟨*sent* the ball into right field⟩ ⟨*send* a rocket to the moon⟩ **2** : to cause to happen or occur ⟨asked the Lord to *send* some rain⟩ **3** : to have an agent, order, or request go or be transmitted ⟨*send* out for coffee⟩ ⟨*sent* away for a pair of skates⟩ ⟨*sent* for their price list⟩; *esp* : to transmit an order or request to come or return ⟨the principal *sent* for the boy⟩ **4** : to put or bring into a certain condition ⟨her request *sent* him into a rage⟩ — **send·er** *n* — **send packing** : to send off roughly or in disgrace ⟨if he comes in here just to fool around, I'll *send* him *packing*⟩
send–off \'send-,ȯf\ *n* : a demonstration of goodwill and enthusiasm for the beginning of a new venture (as a trip or a new business)
Sen·e·ca \'sen-i-kə\ *n* : a member of an Iroquoian Amerindian people of western New York
sen·e·schal \'sen-ə-shəl\ *n* : an agent or bailiff who managed a lord's estate in feudal times
se·nile \'sēn-,īl, 'sen-\ *adj* **1** : of or relating to old age **2** : having infirmities associated with old age
se·nil·i·ty \si-'nil-ət-ē\ *n* : the quality or state of being senile; *esp* : the physical and mental infirmity of old age
¹**se·nior** \'sē-nyər\ *n* [from Latin, comparative of *senex* "old", "old man"] **1** : a person who is older or of higher rank than another **2** : a student in his final year of high school or college before graduation
²**senior** *adj* **1** : OLDER — used chiefly to distinguish a father from a son with the same name **2** : higher in standing or rank ⟨*senior* partner⟩ **3** : of or relating to seniors in an educational institution
senior chief petty officer *n* : a petty officer in the navy ranking just below a master chief petty officer
se·nior·i·ty \sēn-'yȯr-ət-ē, -'yär-\ *n* **1** : the quality or state of being senior : PRIORITY **2** : a privileged status attained by length of service
senior master sergeant *n* : a noncommissioned officer in the air force ranking just below a chief master sergeant
sen·na \'sen-ə\ *n* **1** : CASSIA 2; *esp* : one used medicinally **2** : the dried leaflets of various cassias used as a purgative
se·nor *or* **se·ñor** \sān-'yō(ə)r\ *n, pl* **senors** *or* **se·ño·res** \-'yōr-ās, -'yȯr-\ — used for or by a Spanish speaker as a title equivalent to *Mister*
se·no·ra *or* **se·ño·ra** \sān-'yōr-ə, -'yȯr-\ *n* — used for or by a Spanish speaker as a title equivalent to *Mrs.*
se·no·ri·ta *or* **se·ño·ri·ta** \,sān-yə-'rēt-ə\ *n* — used for or by a Spanish speaker as a title equivalent to *Miss*
sen·sa·tion \sen-'sā-shən, sən-\ *n* **1 a** : awareness (as of noise or heat) or a mental process (as seeing, hearing, or smelling) due to stimulation of a sense organ **b** : an indefinite bodily feeling ⟨a *sensation* of buoyancy⟩ **2 a** : a state of excited interest or feeling ⟨the announcement caused a *sensation*⟩ **b** : a cause of such excitement ⟨the play was a *sensation*⟩
sen·sa·tion·al \-sh(ə-)nəl\ *adj* **1** : of or relating to sensation or the senses **2** : arousing an intense and usu. superficial interest or emotional reaction ⟨*sensational* news⟩ **3** : exceedingly or unexpectedly excellent or great ⟨he made a *sensational* diving catch⟩ — **sen·sa·tion·al·ly** \-ē\ *adv*
¹**sense** \'sen(t)s\ *n* **1 a** : the power to perceive by means of sense organs **b** : a specialized function or mechanism (as sight, hearing, smell, taste, or touch) by means of which an animal is sensitive to one or more stimuli ⟨the pain *sense*⟩ **2** : a particular sensation or kind or quality of sensation ⟨a good *sense* of balance⟩ **3** : AWARENESS, CONSCIOUSNESS ⟨a *sense* of danger⟩ **4** : intellectual appreciation ⟨a *sense* of humor⟩ **5** : INTELLIGENCE, JUDGMENT; *esp* : good judgment **6** : good reason or excuse ⟨no *sense* in waiting⟩ **7** : MEANING; *esp* : one of the meanings a word can have **8** : IMPORT, INTENTION ⟨get the *sense* of the speaker's words⟩
²**sense** *vb* **1** : to perceive by the senses **2** : to be or become conscious of ⟨*sense* danger⟩
sense·less \'sen(t)s-ləs\ *adj* **1** : UNCONSCIOUS ⟨knocked *senseless*⟩ **2** : FOOLISH, STUPID **3** : POINTLESS, MEANINGLESS ⟨a *senseless* act⟩ — **sense·less·ly** *adv* — **sense·less·ness** *n*
sense organ *n* : a bodily structure capable of being affected by a stimulus (as heat or sound waves) in such a manner as to activate nerve fibers to convey impulses to the central nervous system
sen·si·bil·i·ty \,sen(t)-sə-'bil-ət-ē\ *n, pl* **-ties** **1** : ability to receive sensations : SENSITIVENESS **2** : the emotion or feeling of which a person is capable ⟨a woman of acute *sensibility*⟩
sen·si·ble \'sen(t)-sə-bəl\ *adj* **1** : capable of being perceived by the senses or by reason or understanding ⟨*sensible* impressions⟩ **2** : capable of receiving sense impressions ⟨*sensible* to pain⟩ **3** : AWARE ⟨made *sensible* of his mistakes⟩ **4** : showing or containing good sense or reason : REASONABLE ⟨a *sensible* arrangement⟩ — **sen·si·bly** \-blē\ *adv*
sen·si·tive \'sen(t)-sət-iv, 'sen(t)-stiv\ *adj* **1** : responsive to stimuli **2** : easily or strongly affected or hurt ⟨a *sensitive* child⟩ **3 a** : capable of indicating minute differences : DELICATE ⟨*sensitive* scales⟩ **b** : readily affected or changed by various agents or

causes (as light or mechanical shock) **c :** high in radio sensitivity — **sen·si·tive·ly** *adv* — **sen·si·tive·ness** *n*

sensitive plant *n* **:** any of several mimosas having leaves that fold or droop when touched

sen·si·tiv·i·ty \ˌsen(t)-sə-ˈtiv-ət-ē\ *n, pl* **-ties** **1 :** the quality or state of being sensitive **2 :** the degree to which a radio receiving set responds to incoming waves

sen·si·tize \ˈsen(t)-sə-ˌtīz\ *vb* **1 :** to make or become sensitive **2 :** to make allergic

sen·sor \ˈsen-ˌsȯr, ˈsen(t)-sər\ *n* **:** a device that responds to a physical stimulus (as heat, light, or a particular motion) and transmits a resulting impulse (as for operating a control)

sen·so·ry \ˈsen(t)s-(ə-)rē\ *adj* **1 :** of or relating to sensation or to the senses **2 :** conveying nerve impulses from the sense organs ⟨*sensory* neuron⟩

sen·su·al \ˈsench-(ə-)wəl\ *adj* **1 :** SENSORY 1 **2 :** relating to the pleasing of the senses **3 :** devoted to the pleasures of the senses — **sen·su·al·i·ty** \ˌsen-chə-ˈwal-ət-ē\ *n* — **sen·su·al·ly** \ˈsench-(ə-)wə-lē\ *adv*

sen·su·al·ism \ˈsench-(ə-)wə-ˌliz-əm\ *n* **:** preoccupation with sensual matters — **sen·su·al·ist** \-ləst\ *n*

sen·su·ous \ˈsench-(ə-)wəs\ *adj* **1 :** having to do with the senses or with things perceived by the senses ⟨*sensuous* pleasure⟩ **2 :** highly susceptible to influence through the senses — **sen·su·ous·ly** *adv* — **sen·su·ous·ness** *n*

sent *past of* SEND

[1]**sen·tence** \ˈsent-ən(t)s\ *n* [from Latin *sententia*, literally "feeling", "opinion", from *sentire* "to feel"] **1 a :** JUDGMENT 2; *esp* **:** one formally pronounced by a court in a criminal proceeding and specifying the punishment **b :** the punishment so imposed ⟨serve a *sentence* for robbery⟩ **2 a :** a grammatically self-contained speech unit that expresses an assertion, a question, a command, a wish, or an exclamation **b :** a mathematical or logical statement (an as equation) in words or symbols — **sen·ten·tial** \sen-ˈten-chəl\ *adj* — **sen·ten·tial·ly** \-chə-lē\ *adv*

[2]**sentence** *vb* **1 :** to pronounce sentence on ⟨the judge will *sentence* him today⟩ **2 :** to condemn to a specified punishment ⟨*sentenced* him to die⟩

sen·ten·tious \sen-ˈten-chəs\ *adj* **1 :** being concise and forceful **:** PITHY **2 :** containing, using, or inclined to use high-sounding empty phrases or pompous sayings ⟨*sententious* writers⟩

sen·tient \ˈsen-ch(ē-)ənt\ *adj* **:** capable of feeling **:** conscious of sense impressions ⟨the lowest of *sentient* creatures⟩ — **sen·tience** \-ch(ē-)ən(t)s\ *n*

sen·ti·ment \ˈsent-ə-mənt\ *n* **1 a :** a thought or attitude influenced by feeling ⟨a strong religious *sentiment*⟩ **b :** OPINION **2 :** feelings of affection or nostalgia

sen·ti·men·tal \ˌsent-ə-ˈment-əl\ *adj* **1 :** influenced strongly by sentiment **2 :** primarily affecting the emotions **3 :** having an excess of sentiment or sensibility — **sen·ti·men·tal·ly** \-ə-lē\ *adv*

sen·ti·men·tal·ism \-ə-ˌliz-əm\ *n* **1 :** the disposition to favor or indulge in sentiment **2 :** an excessively sentimental idea or statement — **sen·ti·men·tal·ist** \-ləst\ *n*

sen·ti·men·tal·i·ty \ˌsent-ə-ˌmen-ˈtal-ət-ē, -mən-\ *n, pl* **-ties** **1 :** the quality or state of being sentimental esp. to excess **2 :** a sentimental idea or its expression

sen·ti·nel \ˈsent-(ə-)nəl\ *n* **:** SENTRY, GUARD

sen·try \ˈsen-trē\ *n, pl* **sen·tries** **:** a person and esp. a soldier standing guard

se·pal \ˈsēp-əl, ˈsep-\ *n* **:** one of the modified leaves comprising a flower calyx

sep·a·ra·ble \ˈsep-(ə-)rə-bəl\ *adj* **:** capable of being separated or distinguished — **sep·a·ra·bil·i·ty** \ˌsep-(ə-)rə-ˈbil-ət-ē\ *n* — **sep·a·ra·bly** \ˈsep-(ə-)rə-blē\ *adv*

[1]**sep·a·rate** \ˈsep-ə-ˌrāt\ *vb* **1 a :** to set or keep apart ⟨*separate* the pages with a slip of paper⟩ **b :** to make a distinction between **:** DISTINGUISH ⟨*separate* religion from magic⟩ **c :** SORT ⟨*separate* mail⟩ **d :** to disperse in space or time **:** SCATTER ⟨widely *separated* homesteads⟩ **2 :** to sever contractual relations with **:** DISCHARGE ⟨*separated* from the army⟩ **3 :** to isolate the constituent parts of ⟨*separate* milk⟩ **4 :** to become divided or detached **:** come apart **5 :** to cease to be or live together **6 :** to go in different directions **7 :** to become isolated from a mixture

[2]**sep·a·rate** \ˈsep-(ə-)rət\ *adj* **1 :** not connected **:** not united or associated ⟨two *separate* apartments⟩ **2 :** divided from each other **3 :** relating to one only **:** not shared ⟨live in *separate* rooms⟩ **4 :** SINGLE, PARTICULAR ⟨the *separate* pieces of a puzzle⟩ — **sep·a·rate·ly** *adv* — **sep·a·rate·ness** *n*

sep·a·ra·tion \ˌsep-ə-ˈrā-shən\ *n* **1 :** the act or process of separating **:** the state of being separated **2 a :** a point or line of division **b :** an intervening space **:** GAP **3 a :** a formal separating of husband and wife by agreement but without divorce **b :** termination of a contractual relationship (as employment or military service)

sep·a·rat·ist \ˈsep(-ə)-rət-əst\ *n* **:** a person who favors separation (as from a church or party) — **sep·a·rat·ism** \-rə-ˌtiz-əm\ *n* — **separatist** *adj*

sep·a·ra·tor \ˈsep-ə-ˌrāt-ər\ *n* **:** one that separates; *esp* **:** a device for separating liquids (as cream from milk) of different specific gravities or liquids from solids

[1]**se·pia** \ˈsē-pē-ə\ *n* **1 :** a brown pigment from the ink of cuttlefishes **2 :** a brownish gray

[2]**sepia** *adj* **1 :** of the color sepia **2 :** made of or done in sepia ⟨*sepia* print⟩

se·poy \ˈsē-ˌpȯi\ *n* **:** a native of India employed as a soldier in the service of a European power

sep·sis \ˈsep-səs\ *n, pl* **sep·ses** \ˈsep-ˌsēz\ **:** a poisoned condition resulting from the spread of bacteria or their poisonous products from a center of infection

Sept *abbr* September

Sep·tem·ber \sep-ˈtem-bər, səp-\ *n* [from Latin, originally the seventh month of the Roman year, from *septem* "seven"] **:** the 9th month of the year

sep·tet *also* **sep·tette** \sep-ˈtet\ *n* **1 :** a musical composition for seven instruments or voices **2 :** a group or set of seven; *esp* **:** the musicians that perform a septet

sep·tic \ˈsep-tik\ *adj* **1 :** of, relating to, or causing putrefaction **2 :** relating to or characteristic of sepsis

septic tank *n* **:** a tank in which the solid sewage is disintegrated by bacteria

sep·til·lion \sep-ˈtil-yən\ *n* — see NUMBER table

sep·tu·a·ge·nar·i·an \sep-ˌt(y)ü-ə-jə-ˈner-ē-ən, ˌsep-tə-wə-jə-\ *n* **:** a person who is 70 or more but less than 80 years old — **septuagenarian** *adj*

Sep·tu·a·ges·i·ma \ˌsep-tə-wə-ˈjes-ə-mə\ *n* **:** the 3d Sunday before Lent

sep·tum \'sep-təm\ *n, pl* **sep·ta** \-tə\ *also* **sep·tums** : a dividing wall or membrane esp. between bodily spaces or masses of soft tissue — **sep·tal** \-təl\ *adj*

[1]**sep·ul·cher** *or* **sep·ul·chre** \'sep-əl-kər\ *n* **1** : a place of burial : TOMB **2** : a receptacle for religious relics esp. in an altar

[2]**sepulcher** *or* **sepulchre** *vb* **-chered** *or* **-chred**; **-cher·ing** *or* **-chring** \-k(ə-)ring\ : to place in a sepulcher : BURY, ENTOMB

se·pul·chral \sə-'pəl-krəl\ *adj* **1** : of or relating to burial, the grave, or monuments to the dead ⟨a *sepulchral* stone⟩ **2** : DISMAL, GLOOMY

sep·ul·ture \'sep-əl-ˌchu̇r\ *n* **1** : BURIAL **2** : SEPULCHER

se·quel \'sē-kwəl\ *n* **1** : an event that follows or comes afterward : RESULT **2** : a book that continues a story begun in another

se·quence \'sē-kwən(t)s, -ˌkwen(t)s\ *n* **1 a** : a continuous or connected series **b** : a part of a motion picture consisting of several shots or scenes ⟨the fight *sequence* in a spy movie⟩ **2** : order of succession ⟨the *sequence* of events⟩ **3 a** : CONSEQUENCE, RESULT **b** : a subsequent development

se·quent \-kwənt\ *adj* : following in time or as an effect — **sequent** *n*

se·ques·ter \si-'kwes-tər\ *vb* **se·ques·tered**; **se·ques·ter·ing** \-t(ə-)ring\ **1** : to set apart : REMOVE **2** : to take custody of (as personal property) until a demand is satisfied

se·ques·trate \si-'kwes-ˌtrāt\ *vb* : CONFISCATE

se·ques·tra·tion \ˌsē-kwəs-'trā-shən, si-ˌkwes-\ *n* : the act of sequestering : the state of being sequestered

se·quin \'sē-kwən\ *n* : a spangle used as an ornament on clothes

se·quined *or* **se·quinned** \-kwənd\ *adj* : ornamented with or as if with sequins

se·quoia \si-'kwȯi-ə\ *n* : either of two huge cone-bearing California trees that reach a height of over 300 feet: **a** : GIANT SEQUOIA **b** : REDWOOD 2

ser *abbr* series

sera *pl of* SERUM

se·ra·glio \sə-'ral-yō\ *n, pl* **-glios** : HAREM 1a

serape *var of* SARAPE

ser·aph \'ser-əf\ *n, pl* **ser·a·phim** \-ə-ˌfim\ *or* **ser·aphs** [from Hebrew *śĕrāphīm*, plural, "seraphs"] : an angel of a very high order — **se·raph·ic** \sə-'raf-ik\ *adj*

Serb \'sərb\ *n* : a native or inhabitant of Serbia

Ser·bi·an \'sər-bē-ən\ *adj* : of, relating to, or characteristic of Serbia or its people

Ser·bo–Cro·atian \ˌsər-bō-krō-'ā-shən\ *n* : the Slavic language of the Serbs and Croats

sere \'si(ə)r\ *adj* : dried up : WITHERED ⟨*sere* deserts⟩

[1]**ser·e·nade** \ˌser-ə-'nād\ *n* : music as sung or played at night under the window of a lady

[2]**serenade** *vb* : to entertain with or perform a serenade — **ser·e·nad·er** *n*

ser·en·dip·i·ty \ˌser-ən-'dip-ət-ē\ *n* : the gift of finding valuable or agreeable things not looked for

se·rene \sə-'rēn\ *adj* **1** : BRIGHT, CLEAR ⟨*serene* skies⟩ **2** : QUIET, CALM ⟨a *serene* manner⟩ — **se·rene·ly** *adv*

se·ren·i·ty \sə-'ren-ət-ē\ *n* : the quality or state of being serene : PEACEFULNESS

serf \'sərf\ *n* : a member of a servile feudal class bound to the soil and subject to the will of his lord — **serf·dom** \-dəm\ *n*

serge \'sərj\ *n* : woolen cloth woven with raised diagonal ribs

ser·geant \'sär-jənt\ *n* [from Middle English, literally "servant", from Old French *sergent*, from Latin *servient-*, stem of *serviens*, present participle of *servire* "to serve"] **1** : a police officer ranking in the U.S. just below captain or sometimes lieutenant **2** : a noncommissioned officer in the army ranking just below a staff sergeant

sergeant at arms *n* : an officer of a court of law or a lawmaking body appointed to keep order

sergeant first class *n* : a noncommissioned officer in the army ranking just below a master sergeant

sergeant major *n, pl* **sergeants major** *or* **sergeant majors 1** : a noncommissioned officer (as in the army) serving as chief enlisted assistant in a headquarters **2** : a noncommissioned officer in the army of the highest enlisted rank

[1]**se·ri·al** \'sir-ē-əl\ *adj* **1** : consisting of or arranged in a series, rank, or row ⟨*serial* order⟩ **2** : appearing in parts or numbers that follow regularly ⟨a *serial* story⟩ — **se·ri·al·ly** \-ē-ə-lē\ *adv*

[2]**serial** *n* **1** : a work appearing (as in a magazine or on television) in installments **2** : one installment of a serial work — **se·ri·al·ist** \'sir-ē-ə-ləst\ *n*

se·ri·al·ize \'sir-ē-ə-ˌlīz\ *vb* : to arrange or publish in serial form

serial number *n* : a number indicating place in a series and used as a means of identification

se·ries \'si(ə)r-(ˌ)ēz\ *n, pl* **series 1** : a number of things or events arranged in order and connected by being alike in some way ⟨a concert *series*⟩ ⟨a *series* of talks⟩ **2** : a division of rock formations smaller than a system comprising rocks deposited during an epoch **3** : an arrangement of the parts of or elements in an electric circuit whereby the whole current passes through each part or element without branching **4** : a group of successive coordinate sentence elements joined together ⟨an a, b, and c *series*⟩ — **in series** : in a serial arrangement

S

ser·if \'ser-əf\ *n* : any of the short lines crossing the upper and lower ends of the strokes of a printed letter

se·ri·ous \'sir-ē-əs\ *adj* **1** : thoughtful or subdued in appearance or manner **2 a** : requiring much thought or work ⟨*serious* study⟩ **b** : of or relating to a matter of importance ⟨a *serious* novel⟩ **3** : not joking or trifling : EARNEST **4** : DANGEROUS, HARMFUL ⟨a *serious* injury⟩ — **se·ri·ous·ly** *adv* — **se·ri·ous·ness** *n*

se·ri·ous–mind·ed \ˌsir-ē-əs-'mīn-dəd\ *adj* : having a serious disposition or trend of thought — **se·ri·ous–mind·ed·ly** *adv* — **se·ri·ous–mind·ed·ness** *n*

ser·mon \'sər-mən\ *n* **1** : a public speech usu. by a clergyman for the purpose of giving religious instruction **2** : a serious talk to a person about his conduct — **ser·mon·ize** \-mə-ˌnīz\ *vb*

se·rous \'sir-əs\ *adj* : of, relating to, resembling, or producing serum; *esp* : of thin watery constitution

ser·pent \'sər-pənt\ *n* : SNAKE; *esp* : a large snake

[1]**ser·pen·tine** \'sər-pən-ˌtēn, -ˌtīn\ *adj* **1** : of or resembling a serpent **2** : winding or turning one way and another ⟨a *serpentine* path⟩

[2]**serpentine** *n* : a mineral consisting essentially of a hydrous silicate of magnesium usu. having a dull green color and often a mottled appearance

ser·rate \sə-'rāt, 'ser-ˌāt\ *or* **ser·rat·ed** \sə-'rāt-əd, 'ser-ˌāt-\ *adj* : having a saw-toothed edge ⟨a *serrate* leaf⟩ ⟨a *serrated* knife⟩

ser·ried \'ser-ēd\ *adj* : crowded or pressed together

se·rum \'sir-əm\ *n, pl* **serums** *or* **se·ra** \'sir-ə\ : the watery portion of an animal fluid (as blood) remaining after coagulation; *esp* : immune blood serum that contains specific immune bodies ⟨antitoxin *serum*⟩ — **se·ral** \'sir-əl\ *adj*

serum sickness *n* : an allergic reaction to the injection of foreign serum
serv *abbr* service
ser·vant \'sər-vənt\ *n* : someone or something that serves others; *esp* : a person hired to perform household or personal services
[1]**serve** \'sərv\ *vb* **1 a** : to be a servant : ATTEND **b** : to give the service and respect due **c** : WORSHIP ⟨*serve* God⟩ **d** : to work through or perform a term of service esp. in the army or navy **e** : to put in : SPEND ⟨*serve* a two-year sentence⟩ **2 a** : to officiate as a clergyman or priest **b** : to assist as server at mass **3 a** : to be of use : answer a purpose ⟨the tree *serves* as shelter⟩ **b** : BENEFIT ⟨machines that *serve* man⟩ **c** : to be favorable, opportune, or convenient ⟨when the time *serves*⟩ **d** : to be enough for ⟨a pie that will *serve* eight people⟩ **e** : to hold an office : perform a duty or function ⟨*serve* on a jury⟩ **4 a** : to help persons to foods (as at a table or counter) **b** : to set out portions of food or drink **5 a** : to furnish or supply with something needed or desired **b** : to wait on customers **6** : to make a serve (as in tennis) **7** : to treat or act toward in a specified way ⟨he *served* me ill⟩ **8** : DELIVER, EXECUTE ⟨*serve* a summons⟩ — **serve one right** : to be a just return for what one is or does
[2]**serve** *n* : the act of putting the ball or shuttlecock in play (as in tennis or badminton)
serv·er \'sər-vər\ *n* **1** : a person who serves food or drink **2** : the player who puts a ball in play **3** : something (as a tray) used in serving food or drink
[1]**ser·vice** \'sər-vəs\ *n* **1** : the occupation or function of serving ⟨in active *service*⟩; *esp* : employment as a servant ⟨entered the duke's *service*⟩ **2 a** : the work or action performed by one that serves ⟨gives good and quick *service*⟩ **b** : HELP, USE, BENEFIT ⟨be of *service* to them⟩ **3** : a religious ceremony or rite ⟨the burial *service*⟩ **4 a** : the act of serving **b** : a helpful act : good turn ⟨did him a *service*⟩ **c** : useful labor that does not produce goods — usu. used in pl. ⟨charge for professional *services*⟩ **d** : SERVE **5** : a set of dishes or silverware ⟨a coffee *service*⟩ **6 a** : a branch of public employment or the people working in it ⟨the consular *service*⟩ **b** : a nation's armed forces ⟨called into the *service*⟩ **7** : a facility supplying some public demand or maintenance and repair of something ⟨bus *service*⟩ ⟨television sales and *service*⟩ — **service** *adj* — **at one's service** : ready to serve one : available for use ⟨promised her that he was *at her service*⟩ ⟨placed a car *at his service*⟩
[2]**service** *vb* : to perform services for : repair or provide maintenance for ⟨*service* cars⟩
ser·vice·a·ble \'sər-və-sə-bəl\ *adj* **1** : prepared for or capable of service : USEFUL **2** : wearing well in use ⟨*serviceable* shoes⟩ — **ser·vice·a·bil·i·ty** \ˌsər-və-sə-'bil-ət-ē\ *n*
service club *n* **1** : a club of business or professional men or women organized for their common benefit and active in community service **2** : a recreation center for enlisted men provided by one of the armed services
ser·vice·man \'sər-vəs-ˌman, -mən\ *n* : a male member of the armed forces
service module *n* : a space vehicle module containing propellant tanks, fuel cells, and the main rocket engine
service station *n* : GAS STATION
ser·vile \'sər-vəl, -ˌvīl\ *adj* **1** : of or befitting a slave ⟨*servile* work⟩ ⟨*servile* flattery⟩ **2** : lacking spirit or independence : SUBMISSIVE — **ser·vile·ly** \-və(l)-lē, -ˌvīl-lē\ *adv* — **ser·vile·ness** \-vəl-nəs, -ˌvīl-\ *n* — **ser·vil·i·ty** \(ˌ)sər-'vil-ət-ē\ *n*
serv·ing \'sər-viŋ\ *n* : a helping of food ⟨another *serving* of meat⟩
ser·vi·tor \'sər-vət-ər\ *n* : a male servant
ser·vi·tude \'sər-və-ˌt(y)üd\ *n* : a state of subjection to another that constitutes or resembles slavery or serfdom
ser·vo·mech·a·nism \'sər-vō-ˌmek-ə-ˌniz-əm\ *n* : an automatic device (as a thermostat) for automatically correcting the performance of a mechanism
ses·a·me \'ses-ə-mē\ *n* **1** : an East Indian annual hairy herb; *also* : its small somewhat flat seeds used as a source of oil and a flavoring agent **2** : OPEN SESAME
sesqui- *comb form* : one and a half times ⟨*sesqui*centennial⟩
ses·qui·cen·ten·ni·al \ˌses-kwi-sen-'ten-ē-əl\ *n* : a 150th anniversary or its celebration — **sesquicentennial** *adj*
ses·sile \'ses-əl, -ˌīl\ *adj* **1** : attached directly by the base and not raised upon a stalk ⟨a *sessile* leaf⟩ **2** : permanently attached and not free to move about : SEDENTARY ⟨*sessile* polyps⟩
ses·sion \'sesh-ən\ *n* **1** : a single meeting (as of a court, lawmaking body, or school) **2** : a whole series of meetings ⟨congress was in *session* for ten months⟩ **3** : the time during which a court, congress, or school meets ⟨a summer *session*⟩
[1]**set** \'set\ *vb* **set**; **set·ting** **1** : to cause to sit **2** : to give (a fowl) eggs to hatch or provide (eggs) with suitable conditions for hatching **3 a** : to put or fix in a place, condition, or position ⟨*set* a dish on the table⟩ ⟨*set* a trap⟩ ⟨*set* a watch⟩ ⟨*set* down opinions on paper⟩ **b** : to arrange or put into a desired and esp. a normal position ⟨*set* a broken bone⟩ **4** : to direct with fixed attention ⟨had *set* his heart on going home⟩ **5** : to cause to be, become, or do ⟨slaves were *set* free⟩ **6** : FIX, SETTLE ⟨*set* a price⟩ ⟨*set* a wedding day⟩ **7 a** : to establish as the best performance ⟨*set* a record for the mile⟩ **b** : to furnish as a pattern or model ⟨*set* an example of generosity⟩ **8 a** : to put in order for immediate use ⟨*set* the table⟩ **b** : to provide (as words or verses) with music **c** : to put pieces of type together for printing : put something into type **9** : to wave, curl, or arrange hair by wetting and drying **10** : to fix in a setting or frame ⟨*set* diamonds in a ring⟩ **11** : VALUE, RATE ⟨*set* the loss at $2000⟩ **12** : to put and fix in a direction ⟨*set* our faces toward home once more⟩ **13** : to fix firmly : make immobile ⟨*set* his jaw in determination⟩ **14** : to become or cause to become firm or solid ⟨the jelly is *setting*⟩ ⟨*set* cement⟩ **15** : to form and bring (fruit or seed) to maturity **16** : to cover and warm eggs to hatch them ⟨the hen has been *setting* for several days⟩ **17** : to pass below the horizon : go down ⟨the sun *sets*⟩ **18** : START ⟨*set* to work⟩ **19** : to have a specified direction in motion : FLOW ⟨a current that *sets* to the north⟩ — **set about** : to begin to do — **set aside** **1** : DISCARD **2** : RESERVE, SAVE **3** : ANNUL, OVERRULE ⟨the verdict was *set aside* by the court⟩ — **set eyes on** : to catch sight of : SEE ⟨loved her from the minute he *set eyes on* her⟩ — **set forth** **1** : to make known ⟨*set forth* an idea⟩ **2** : to start out on a jour-

ə abut	ər further	a back	ā bake	
ä cot, cart	aù out	ch chin	e less	ē easy
g gift	i trip	ī life	j joke	ŋ sing	ō flow
ȯ flaw	ȯi coin	th thin	t͟h this	ü loot
ù foot	y yet	yü few	yù furious	zh vision

ney : set out — **set one's hand to** : to set about doing : UNDERTAKE — **set store by** : to consider valuable or trustworthy ⟨*set store by* religion as the way to happiness⟩ — **set upon** : to attack with violence : ASSAULT

[2]**set** *adj* **1** : INTENT, DETERMINED ⟨*set* upon going⟩ **2** : fixed by authority ⟨a *set* rule⟩ **3** : STUBBORN, OBSTINATE ⟨an old man very *set* in his ways⟩ **4 a** : FIXED, RIGID ⟨a *set* smile⟩ **b** : BUILT-IN ⟨a *set* tub for washing⟩ **5** : PREPARED, READY ⟨all *set* to go⟩

[3]**set** *n* **1** : the act or action of setting : the condition of being set **2** : a number of persons or things of the same kind that belong or are used together ⟨the social *set*⟩ ⟨a *set* of dishes⟩ **3** : DIRECTION, COURSE ⟨*set* of the wind⟩ **4** : form or carriage of the body or of its parts ⟨the *set* of his shoulders⟩ **5** : an artificial setting for a scene of a play or motion picture **6** : a group of tennis games **7** : a collection of mathematical elements (as numbers or points) **8** : an electronic apparatus ⟨a television *set*⟩

se·ta \'sēt-ə\ *n, pl* **se·tae** \'sē-ˌtē\ : a slender usu. rigid or bristly and springy organ or part of an animal or plant

set·back \'set-ˌbak\ *n* : a checking of progress ⟨production suffered a severe *setback*⟩

set down *vb* **1** : to cause to sit down : SEAT **2** : to place at rest on a surface or on the ground **3** : to land (an airplane) on the ground or water **4** : to put in writing

set in *vb* **1** : to become prevalent or settled ⟨winter *set in* early⟩ **2** : to set to work : begin to function

set off *vb* **1 a** : to show up by contrast ⟨her pale face *sets off* her dark eyes⟩ **b** : to set apart : make distinct or outstanding ⟨commas used to *set off* words in a series⟩ **2** : to cause to explode **3** : to start out on a course or a journey ⟨*set off* for home⟩

set out *vb* **1** : to begin with a definite purpose : UNDERTAKE ⟨deliberately *set out* to win⟩ **2** : to start out on a course, a journey, or a career

set·screw \'set-ˌskrü\ *n* : a screw screwed through one part tightly upon or into another part to keep both parts securely fastened to each other

set·tee \se-'tē\ *n* **1** : a long seat with a back **2** : a medium-sized sofa with arms and a back

set·ter \'set-ər\ *n* **1** : someone or something that sets ⟨brick*setter*⟩ **2** : a large long-coated bird dog trained to stand stiffly and point on finding game

set theory *n* : a branch of mathematics that deals with the nature and relations of sets — **set–theoretic** *adj*

set·ting \'set-ing\ *n* **1** : the manner, position, or direction in which something is set ⟨change a thermostat *setting*⟩ **2** : the frame or bed in which a gem is set **3** : the background (as time and place) of the action of a story or play : SCENERY, SURROUNDINGS **4** : the articles of tableware required for setting a place at table **5** : a batch of eggs for incubation

[1]**set·tle** \'set-əl\ *n* : a wooden bench with arms, a high solid back, and an enclosed foundation

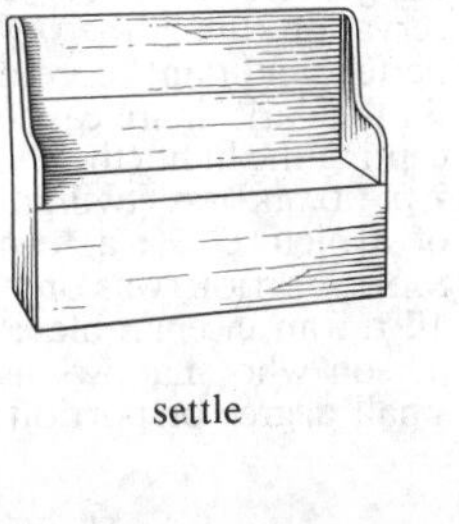

settle

[2]**settle** *vb* **set·tled**; **set·tling** \'set-(ə-)ling\ **1** : to place so as to stay ⟨*settled* himself in a chair⟩ **2 a** : to establish residence in : COLONIZE ⟨*settled* the West⟩ **b** : to make one's home ⟨*settle* in the country⟩ **3 a** : to sink gradually to a lower level ⟨the house *settled*⟩ **b** : to sink in a liquid ⟨sediment *settles* to the bottom⟩ **4 a** : to make quiet : CALM ⟨crocheting *settles* her nerves⟩ **b** : to take up an ordered or stable life ⟨marry and *settle* down⟩ **5** : DECIDE ⟨*settle* the question⟩ **6 a** : to make or arrange for final disposition of ⟨*settle* an estate⟩ **b** : to pay in full ⟨*settle* a bill⟩ **7** : to adjust differences ⟨*settle* a quarrel⟩

set·tle·ment \'set-əl-mənt\ *n* **1** : the act of settling : the condition of being settled **2** : final payment (as of a bill) **3 a** : a place or region newly settled **b** : a small village **4** : an institution providing various community services to people in a crowded part of a city — called also *settlement house*

set·tler \'set-(ə-)lər\ *n* : a person who settles in a new region : COLONIST

set·up \'set-ˌəp\ *n* : the way in which something is set up : ORGANIZATION, ARRANGEMENT

set up \-'əp\ *vb* **1** : to place in position ⟨*set up* a target⟩ **2** : to make (a loud noise) with the voice ⟨*set up* a shout⟩ **3 a** : ERECT ⟨*set up* a building⟩ **b** : to assemble the parts of ⟨*set up* a printing press⟩ **4 a** : FOUND, INAUGURATE ⟨*set up* a school⟩ **b** : to put in operation as a way of living ⟨*set up* housekeeping⟩ or a means of livelihood ⟨*set up* shop in a new neighborhood⟩

sev·en \'sev-ən\ *n* **1** — see NUMBER table **2** : the seventh in a set or series ⟨the *seven* of hearts⟩ — **seven** *adj or pron*

S

seven seas *n pl* : all the waters or oceans of the world ⟨had sailed the *seven seas*⟩

sev·en·teen \ˌsev-ən-'tēn\ *n* — see NUMBER table — **seventeen** *adj or pron* — **sev·en·teenth** \-'tēn(t)th\ *adj or n*

seventeen–year locust *n* : a cicada of the U.S. with a life of seventeen years in the North and of thirteen years in the South of which the greatest part is spent as a wingless underground nymph that feeds on roots and finally emerges from the soil to become a short-lived winged adult

sev·enth \'sev-ən(t)th\ *n* **1** — see NUMBER table **2** : a musical interval embracing seven diatonic degrees — **seventh** *adj or adv*

sev·en·ty \'sev-ən-tē\ *n, pl* **-ties** — see NUMBER table — **sev·en·ti·eth** \-tē-əth\ *adj or n* — **seventy** *adj or pron*

sev·er \'sev-ər\ *vb* **sev·ered**; **sev·er·ing** \-(ə-)ring\ **1** : to put or keep apart : DIVIDE; *esp* : to cut off or through ⟨his finger was *severed* in the accident⟩ ⟨the rope *severed* in three places⟩ **2** : to come or break apart — **sev·er·a·ble** \'sev-(ə-)rə-bəl\ *adj*

[1]**sev·er·al** \'sev-(ə-)rəl\ *adj* **1 a** : separate or distinct from one another : DIFFERENT ⟨federal union of the *several* states⟩ **b** : PARTICULAR, RESPECTIVE ⟨specialists in their *several* fields⟩ **2** : being more than two but not very many ⟨*several* persons⟩ — **sev·er·al·ly** \-ē\ *adv*

[2]**several** *pron* : an indefinite number more than two and fewer than many ⟨*several* of the guests⟩

sev·er·ance \'sev-(ə-)rən(t)s\ *n* : the act or process of severing : the state of being severed

se·vere \sə-'vi(ə)r\ *adj* **1** : serious in feeling or manner : GRAVE, AUSTERE **2** : very strict : HARSH **3** : not using unnecessary ornament : PLAIN **4** : inflicting pain, distress, or hardship : GRIEVOUS ⟨*severe* wounds⟩ ⟨a *severe* winter⟩ **5** : requiring great effort ⟨*severe* test⟩ — **se·vere·ly** *adv* — **se·vere·ness** *n*

se·ver·i·ty \sə-'ver-ət-ē\ *n, pl* **-ties** : the quality or state of being severe ⟨*severity* of the winter⟩ ⟨the *severity* of his illness⟩

sew \'sō\ *vb* **sewed**; **sewn** \'sōn\ *or* **sewed**; **sew·ing 1 :** to join or fasten by stitches made with a flexible thread or filament ⟨*sews* on the button⟩ **2 :** to work with needle and thread

sew·age \'sü-ij\ *n* **:** waste liquids or waste matter carried off by sewers

¹**sew·er** \'sō(-ə)r\ *n* **:** one that sews

²**sew·er** \'sü-ər, 'su̇(-ə)r\ *n* **:** a covered usu. underground passage to carry off water and sewage

sew·er·age \'sü-ə-rij, 'su̇(-ə)r-ij\ *n* **1 :** SEWAGE **2 :** the removal and disposal of sewage and surface water by sewers **3 :** a system of sewers

sew·ing \'sō-ing\ *n* **1 :** the act, method, or occupation of one that sews **2 :** material that has been or is to be sewed

sew up *vb* **1 :** to get exclusive use or control of **:** MONOPOLIZE **2 :** to make certain of the support or cooperation of ⟨*sew up* most of the delegates⟩

sex \'seks\ *n* **1 :** either of two divisions of organisms distinguished respectively as male and female **2 :** the sum of the structural, functional, and behavioral peculiarities of living beings that are ultimately related to reproduction by two interacting parents and that serve to distinguish males and females **3 :** sexual activity

sex- *or* **sexi-** *comb form* **:** six ⟨*sexi*valent⟩ ⟨*sex*partite⟩

sex·a·ge·nar·i·an \ˌsek-sə-jə-'ner-ē-ən\ *n* **:** a person who is 60 or more but less than 70 years old — **sexagenarian** *adj*

sex cell *n* **:** an egg cell or a sperm cell

sex chromosome *n* **:** one of usu. a pair of chromosomes that are usu. similar in one sex but different in the other sex and are concerned with the inheritance of sex

sex hormone *n* **:** a hormone that affects the growth or function of the reproductive organs or the development of secondary sex characteristics

sex–linked \'seks-ˌling(k)t\ *adj* **1 :** located in a sex chromosome ⟨a *sex-linked* gene⟩ **2 :** controlled by a sex-linked gene ⟨a *sex-linked* character⟩ — **sex–link·age** \-ˌling-kij\ *n*

sex·tant \'sek-stənt\ *n* **:** an instrument for measuring altitudes of celestial bodies from a moving ship or airplane

sextant

sex·tet *also* **sex·tette** \sek-'stet\ *n* **1 :** a musical composition for six instruments or voices **2 :** a group or set of six

sex·til·lion \sek-'stil-yən\ *n* — see NUMBER table

sex·ton \'sek-stən\ *n* **:** an official of a church who takes care of church buildings and property

¹**sex·tu·ple** \sek-'st(y)üp-əl, -'stəp-; 'sek-stəp-\ *adj* **1 :** having six units or members **2 :** being six times as great or as many — **sextuple** *n*

²**sextuple** *vb* **sex·tu·pled**; **sex·tu·pling** \-(ə-)ling\ **:** to make or become six times as much or as many

sex·tup·let \sek-'stəp-lət, -'st(y)üp-; 'sek-stəp-\ *n* **1 :** a combination of six of a kind **2 :** one of six offspring born at one birth

sex·u·al \'sek-sh(ə-w)əl\ *adj* **1 :** of or relating to sex or the sexes ⟨*sexual* differences⟩ **2 :** having or involving sex ⟨*sexual* reproduction⟩ ⟨*sexual* spores⟩ — **sex·u·al·i·ty** \ˌsek-shə-'wal-ət-ē\ *n* — **sex·u·al·ly** \'sek-shə-(wə-)lē\ *adv*

sexy \'sek-sē\ *adj* **sex·i·er**; **-est :** sexually exciting **:** EROTIC — **sex·i·ness** *n*

sf *or* **sfz** *abbr* sforzando

SF *abbr* **1** sacrifice fly **2** science fiction

sfor·zan·do \sfȯrt-'sän-dō\ *adj* **:** ACCENTED — used of a single note or chord as a direction in music

SG *abbr* surgeon general

sgt *abbr* sergeant

sh *abbr* share

shab·by \'shab-ē\ *adj* **shab·bi·er**; **-est 1 a :** threadbare and faded from wear ⟨*shabby* clothes⟩ **b :** ill kept **:** DILAPIDATED ⟨a *shabby* neighborhood⟩ **2 :** dressed in worn clothes **3 :** MEAN, UNFAIR ⟨*shabby* treatment⟩ — **shab·bi·ly** \'shab-ə-lē\ *adv* — **shab·bi·ness** \'shab-ē-nəs\ *n*

Sha·bu·oth \shə-'vü-ˌōt(h), -ˌōs\ *n* **:** a Jewish holiday celebrated in May or June to commemorate the revelation of the Ten Commandments at Mt. Sinai and in biblical times as a harvest festival

shack \'shak\ *n* **:** HUT, SHANTY

¹**shack·le** \'shak-əl\ *n* **1 :** something (as a manacle or fetter) that confines the legs or arms **2 :** something that checks or prevents free action as if by fetters ⟨the *shackles* of superstition⟩ **3 :** a usu. U-shaped part or device (as a clevis) for making something secure

²**shackle** *vb* **shack·led**; **shack·ling** \'shak-(ə-)ling\ **1 a :** to bind with shackles **b :** to make fast with a shackle **2 :** to deprive of freedom of action **:** HINDER ⟨*shackled* by poverty⟩ — **shack·ler** \-(ə-)lər\ *n*

shad \'shad\ *n, pl* **shad :** any of several deep-bodied food fishes that are closely related to the herrings but ascend rivers in the spring to spawn

¹**shade** \'shād\ *n* **1 a :** partial darkness caused by interception of light **b :** relative obscurity or retirement **2 :** space sheltered from light or heat and esp. from the sun **3** *pl* **:** the shadows that gather as darkness falls **4 :** SPIRIT, GHOST **5 a :** something that intercepts or shelters from light, sun, or heat **b :** a device partially covering a lamp so as to reduce glare **c :** an adjustable screen usu. on a roller used to shut out or regulate light **6 :** the representation in painting or drawing of the effect of shade **7 :** a dark color **:** a special variety of a color **:** the degree of darkness or lightness of a color ⟨four *shades* of brown⟩ ⟨maroon is a *shade* of red⟩ **8 :** a minute difference or variation ⟨*shades* of meaning⟩ — **shade·less** \-ləs\ *adj*

²**shade** *vb* **1 :** to shelter from light or heat **2 :** to mark with degrees of light or color ⟨*shade* a drawing⟩ **3 :** to undergo or show slight differences or variations of color, value, or meaning ⟨the point where religion *shades* into politics⟩ — **shad·er** *n*

shade tree *n* **:** a tree (as the American elm) grown primarily to produce shade

¹**shad·ow** \'shad-ō\ *n* **1 :** shade within certain bounds ⟨the valley was in *shadow*⟩ **2 :** a reflected image (as in a mirror) **3 :** shelter from danger or observation ⟨under the *shadow* of the flag⟩ **4 a :** an imperfect and faint representation **b :** IMITATION, COPY **5 :** the dark figure cast on a surface by a body intercepting the light ⟨the *shadow* of a man⟩ **6 :** PHANTOM **7** *pl* **:** DARKNESS ⟨twilight *shadows*⟩ **8 :** a shaded part of a picture **9 :** a form without substance **:** REMNANT, VESTIGE ⟨was only a *shadow* of his former self⟩ **10 a :** an inseparable companion or follower **b :** a person who shadows as a spy or detective **11 :** a small degree or portion **:** TRACE ⟨not a *shadow* of a

ə abut	ər further	a back	ā bake	
ä cot, cart	au̇ out	ch chin	e less	ē easy
g gift	i trip	ī life	j joke	ng sing	ō flow
ȯ flaw	ȯi coin	th thin	t͟h this	ü loot
u̇ foot	y yet	yü few	yu̇ furious	zh vision

doubt⟩ **12** : a gloomy influence — **shad·ow·less** \-ləs\ *adj* — **shad·ow·like** \-ˌlīk\ *adj*

[2]**shadow** *vb* **1 a** : to cast a shadow on **b** : to cast gloom over : CLOUD ⟨sadness *shadowed* his face⟩ **2** : to represent or indicate obscurely or faintly : FORESHADOW **3** : to follow esp. secretly : TRAIL **4** : to pass gradually or by degrees ⟨the hills *shadowing* into darkness⟩ — **shad·ow·er** \ˈshad-ə-wər\ *n*

shad·ow·box \ˈshad-ō-ˌbäks\ *vb* : to box with an imaginary opponent esp. as a form of training — **shad·ow·box·ing** *n*

shad·owy \ˈshad-ə-wē\ *adj* **1** : of or resembling a shadow : UNREAL ⟨*shadowy* dreams of glory⟩ **2** : SHADY 1 ⟨a *shadowy* path⟩ **3** : DIM ⟨the *shadowy* area between good and bad⟩

shady \ˈshād-ē\ *adj* **shad·i·er**; **-est** **1** : casting a shadow : giving shade **2** : sheltered from the sun's rays ⟨a *shady* grove⟩ **3** : QUESTIONABLE, DISREPUTABLE ⟨a *shady* deal⟩ — **shad·i·ly** \ˈshād-ə-lē\ *adv* — **shad·i·ness** \ˈshād-ē-nəs\ *n*

shaft \ˈshaft\ *n, pl* **shafts** \ˈshaf(t)s, *in sense 3 also* ˈshavz\ **1 a** : the long handle of a weapon (as a spear) **b** : SPEAR, LANCE **2 a** : the slender stem of an arrow **b** : ARROW **3** : POLE; *esp* : one of two poles between which a horse is hitched to pull a vehicle **4** : a narrow beam of light **5** : something suggestive of the shaft of an arrow or spear ⟨the *shaft* or trunk of a tree⟩ **6** : the handle of a tool **7** : a tall monument (as a column) **8** : a vertical opening or passage through the floors of a building ⟨an air *shaft*⟩ **9** : a commonly cylindrical bar used to support rotating pieces or to transmit power or motion by rotation **10** : a vertical or inclined opening of uniform and limited cross section made for finding or mining ore, raising water, or ventilating underground workings **11** : the midrib of a feather

[1]**shag** \ˈshag\ *n* **1 a** : a shaggy tangled mass or covering **b** : long coarse or matted fiber or nap **2** : a strong coarse tobacco cut into fine shreds

[2]**shag** *vb* **shagged**; **shag·ging** **1** : to retrieve a ball **2** : to catch a ball

shag·bark \ˈshag-ˌbärk\ *n* : a hickory with a gray shaggy outer bark that peels off in long strips

shag·gy \ˈshag-ē\ *adj* **shag·gi·er**; **-est** **1** : covered with or made up of long, coarse, or tangled growth ⟨a dog with a *shaggy* coat⟩ ⟨*shaggy* garden hedges⟩ **2** : having a rough or hairy surface — **shag·gi·ly** \ˈshag-ə-lē\ *adv*

shah \ˈshä, ˈshȯ\ *n* : the sovereign of Iran

[1]**shake** \ˈshāk\ *vb* **shook** \ˈshu̇k\; **shak·en** \ˈshā-kən\; **shak·ing** **1** : to move irregularly to and fro : QUIVER, TREMBLE ⟨*shaking* with cold⟩ **2** : to become unsteady : TOTTER **3** : to cause to move in a quick jerky manner **4** : to free oneself from ⟨*shake* off a cold⟩ **5** : to cause to waver : WEAKEN ⟨*shake* one's faith⟩ **6** : to dislodge by quick jerky movements ⟨*shake* the dust from a blanket⟩ **7** : to clasp (hands) in greeting or as a sign of goodwill or agreement — **shak·a·ble** *or* **shake·a·ble** \ˈshā-kə-bəl\ *adj* — **shake a leg** : to hurry up

[2]**shake** *n* **1** : an act of shaking **2** *pl* : a condition of trembling (as from chill) **3** : something produced by shaking; *esp* : MILK SHAKE **4** : a very brief period of time : INSTANT ⟨ready in two *shakes*⟩ **5** : [3]DEAL 2 ⟨a fair *shake*⟩ **6** : a long shingle usu. split from a piece of log

shake·down \ˈshāk-ˌdau̇n\ *adj* : designed to test a new ship or airplane under operating conditions and to familiarize the crew with it ⟨*shakedown* cruise⟩

shak·er \ˈshā-kər\ *n* : a utensil or machine used in shaking ⟨a salt *shaker*⟩

shake–up \ˈshāk-ˌəp\ *n* : an act or instance of shaking up; *esp* : an extensive and often drastic reorganization ⟨lost his job in an office *shake-up*⟩

shake up \-ˈəp\ *vb* **1** : to jar by or as if by a physical shock ⟨the collision *shook* both drivers *up*⟩ ⟨the news *shook* her *up*⟩ **2** : to effect an extensive and often drastic reorganization of ⟨the new president *shook* things *up* in the office⟩

shako \ˈshak-ō, ˈshāk-\ *n, pl* **shak·os** *or* **shak·oes** : a stiff military cap with a high crown and plume

shako

shaky \ˈshā-kē\ *adj* **shak·i·er**; **-est** **1 a** : lacking stability ⟨*shaky* in his belief⟩ **b** : lacking in authority or reliability : QUESTIONABLE **2** : marked by shaking : TREMBLING **3** : easily shaken : UNSOUND ⟨a *shaky* fence⟩ ⟨*shaky* arguments⟩ — **shak·i·ly** \-kə-lē\ *adv*

shale \ˈshāl\ *n* : a rock that is formed by the consolidation of clay, mud, or silt, has a finely layered structure, and splits easily

shall \shəl, (ˈ)shal\ *auxiliary verb, past* **should** \shəd, (ˈ)shu̇d\; *pres sing & pl* **shall** **1** : am or are going to or expecting to ⟨I *shall* write today⟩ **2** : is or are compelled to : MUST ⟨they *shall* not pass⟩

shal·lop \ˈshal-əp\ *n* : a small open boat propelled by oars or sails

shal·low \ˈshal-ō\ *adj* **1** : having little depth **2** : lacking intellectual depth — **shal·low·ly** *adv* — **shal·low·ness** *n*

shallows *n pl* : a shallow place or area in a body of water

shalt \shəlt, (ˈ)shalt\ *archaic pres 2d sing of* SHALL

[1]**sham** \ˈsham\ *n* **1** : HOAX **2** : something resembling an article of personal or household linen and used in place of or over it **3** : IMITATION, COUNTERFEIT

[2]**sham** *vb* **shammed**; **sham·ming** : PRETEND, FEIGN

[3]**sham** *adj* : FALSE, PRETENDED ⟨*sham* battle⟩

sham·ble \ˈsham-bəl\ *vb* **sham·bled**; **sham·bling** \-b(ə-)ling\ : to walk awkwardly with dragging feet : SHUFFLE — **shamble** *n*

sham·bles \ˈsham-bəlz\ *n sing or pl* : a place or scene of slaughter or destruction

[1]**shame** \ˈshām\ *n* **1** : a painful emotion caused by consciousness of having done something wrong, improper, or immodest **2** : DISHONOR, DISGRACE **3** : something that brings strong regret, disgrace, or reproach

[2]**shame** *vb* **1** : to bring shame to : DISGRACE **2** : to cause to feel shame **3** : to force by causing to feel guilty ⟨they were *shamed* into confessing⟩

shame·faced \ˈshām-ˈfāst\ *adj* **1** : MODEST, SHY **2** : ASHAMED — **shame·faced·ly** \-ˈfā-səd-lē, -ˈfāst-lē\ *adv*

shame·ful \ˈshām-fəl\ *adj* **1** : bringing shame : DISGRACEFUL ⟨*shameful* behavior⟩ **2** : arousing the feeling of shame : INDECENT ⟨a *shameful* sight⟩ — **shame·ful·ly** \-fə-lē\ *adv*

shame·less \ˈshām-ləs\ *adj* **1** : having no shame **2** : showing lack of shame : DISGRACEFUL — **shame·less·ly** *adv* — **shame·less·ness** *n*

[1]**sham·poo** \sham-ˈpü\ *vb* **1** : to wash the hair with soap and water or with a special preparation **2** : to wash or clean a rug or upholstery with soap or a dry-cleaning preparation — **sham·poo·er** *n*

[2]**shampoo** *n, pl* **shampoos** **1** : an act or instance of shampooing **2** : a preparation used in shampooing

sham·rock \ˈsham-ˌräk\ *n* [from Irish Gaelic *seamrōg*, diminutive of *seamar* "clover"] : any of several plants (as a wood sorrel or some clovers) having leaves with three leaflets and used as a national emblem by the Irish

S

shang·hai \shang-ˈhī\ *vb* **shang·haied**; **shang·hai·ing** [from Shanghai, China; from the former use of such methods to secure crews for ships bound for the Orient] **1** : to make helpless (as by drugs or alcohol) and put on a ship as a sailor **2** : to put by deceit or force into a place of detention

shank \ˈshangk\ *n* **1 a** : the part of the leg between the knee and the ankle in man or the corresponding part in various other vertebrates **b** : a cut of meat from usu. the upper part of a leg **2 a** : the straight shaft of a nail, pin, or fishhook **b** : the narrow part of the sole of a shoe beneath the instep **3** : a part of a tool that connects the acting part with a part by which it is held or moved ⟨the *shank* of a drill⟩ ⟨the *shank* of a key⟩

shan't \(ˈ)shant, (ˈ)shånt\ : shall not

shan·ty \ˈshant-ē\ *n, pl* **shanties** : a small roughly built shelter or dwelling : HUT

[1]**shape** \ˈshāp\ *vb* **1** : FORM, CREATE; *esp* : to give a particular form or shape to **2** : to fashion (as a garment) by a pattern **3** : DEVISE, PLAN **4** : to make fit for : ADAPT, ADJUST ⟨learned to *shape* his aims to his abilities⟩ **5** : to take on or approach a definite form : DEVELOP ⟨plans were *shaping* up⟩ — **shap·er** *n*

[2]**shape** *n* **1** : external appearance : FORM **2** : bodily contour esp. of the trunk : FIGURE ⟨worried about losing her *shape*⟩ **3** : definite form and arrangement ⟨a plan now taking *shape*⟩ **4** : something having a particular form **5** : CONDITION ⟨in excellent *shape* for his age⟩ — **shaped** \ˌshāpt\ *adj*

shape·less \ˈshāp-ləs\ *adj* **1** : having no definite shape **2 a** : deprived of usual or normal shape : MISSHAPEN **b** : not shapely — **shape·less·ly** *adv* — **shape·less·ness** *n*

shape·ly \ˈshāp-lē\ *adj* **shape·li·er**; **-est** : having a regular or pleasing shape : TRIM — **shape·li·ness** *n*

shard \ˈshärd\ *n* : a piece or fragment of something brittle (as pottery)

[1]**share** \ˈshe(ə)r, ˈsha(ə)r\ *n* **1** : a portion belonging to, due to, or contributed by an individual **2** : the part allotted or belonging to one of a number owning something together **3** : any of the equal portions or interests into which the property of a corporation is divided

[2]**share** *vb* **1** : to divide and distribute in shares **2** : to use, experience, or enjoy with others **3** : to give or be given a share : take a part ⟨*share* in planning the program⟩ ***syn*** see PARTAKE — **shar·er** *n*

share·crop·per \ˈshe(ə)r-ˌkräp-ər, ˈsha(ə)r-\ *n* : a farmer who works land for a landlord in return for a share of the value of the crop — **share·crop** \-ˌkräp\ *vb*

share·hold·er \-ˌhōl-dər\ *n* : one that owns a share in a joint fund or property; *esp* : STOCKHOLDER

[1]**shark** \ˈshärk\ *n* : any of numerous rather large marine fishes that are mostly active predators and are of economic importance esp. for their large livers which are a source of oil and for their hides from which leather is made

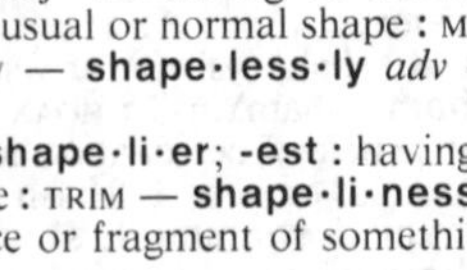
shark
(up to 40 ft. long)

[2]**shark** *n* **1** : a greedy crafty person who takes advantage of the needs of others ⟨a loan *shark*⟩ **2** : a person who excels esp. in a particular line ⟨a *shark* at arithmetic⟩

shark·skin \ˈshärk-ˌskin\ *n* **1** : the hide of a shark or leather made from it **2** : a smooth durable material in twill or basket weave with small woven designs

[1]**sharp** \ˈshärp\ *adj* **1 a** : having a thin keen edge or fine point ⟨a *sharp* knife⟩ **b** : briskly cold : NIPPING ⟨*sharp* biting wind⟩ **2 a** : keen in intellect : QUICK-WITTED ⟨a *sharp* student⟩ **b** : keen in perception ⟨*sharp* eyes⟩ **c** : keen in attention to one's own interest **3 a** : BRISK, ENERGETIC **b** : EAGER ⟨a *sharp* appetite⟩ **c** : capable of acting or reacting strongly; *esp* : CAUSTIC **4** : SEVERE, HARSH ⟨*sharp* criticism⟩ **5** : having a strong odor or flavor ⟨*sharp* cheese⟩ **6 a** : terminating in a point or edge ⟨*sharp* features⟩ ⟨*sharp* mountain peaks⟩ **b** : involving an abrupt change in direction ⟨a *sharp* turn⟩ **c** : clear in outline or detail : DISTINCT **d** : set forth with clarity and distinctness ⟨*sharp* contrast⟩ **7 a** : higher by a half step ⟨tone of G *sharp*⟩ **b** : higher than the true pitch **8** : STYLISH, DRESSY — **sharp·ly** *adv* — **sharp·ness** *n*

syn SHARP, KEEN, ACUTE can mean displaying mental agility. SHARP may imply either clever resourcefulness or questionable trickiness ⟨a *sharp* trader⟩; KEEN may suggest quickness and zest ⟨a *keen* student of history⟩; ACUTE implies a penetrating intellect well able to make subtle distinctions ⟨*acute* reasoning⟩ ***ant*** dull

[2]**sharp** *vb* **1** : to raise in pitch esp. by a half step **2** : to sing or play above the true pitch

[3]**sharp** *adv* **1** : in a sharp manner : SHARPLY **2** : PRECISELY, EXACTLY ⟨4 o'clock *sharp*⟩

[4]**sharp** *n* : a musical note or tone one half step higher than a specified note or tone; *also* : a character # on a line or space of the staff indicating such a note or tone

sharp·en \ˈshär-pən\ *vb* **sharp·ened**; **sharp·en·ing** \ˈshärp-(ə-)ning\ : to make or become sharp or sharper — **sharp·en·er** \ˈshärp-(ə-)nər\ *n*

sharp·er \ˈshär-pər\ *n* : CHEAT, SWINDLER

sharp–eyed \ˈshärp-ˈīd\ *adj* : having keen sight; *also* : keen in observing or penetrating

sharp·ie *or* **sharpy** \ˈshär-pē\ *n, pl* **sharp·ies** : a long narrow shallow-draft boat with one or two masts that bear a triangular sail

sharp·shoot·er \ˈshärp-ˌshüt-ər\ *n* : one skilled in shooting : a good marksman — **sharp·shoot·ing** \-ˌshüt-ing\ *n*

sharp–wit·ted \-ˈwit-əd\ *adj* : having or showing a quick keen mind

[1]**shat·ter** \ˈshat-ər\ *vb* **1** : to dash or burst violently into fragments : break at once into pieces **2** : to damage badly : RUIN, WRECK ⟨his health had been *shattered*⟩ ⟨*shattered* hopes⟩

[2]**shatter** *n* : FRAGMENT, SHRED ⟨an armful of dishes lay in *shatters*⟩

shat·ter·proof \ˌshat-ər-ˈprüf\ *adj* : made so as not to shatter ⟨*shatterproof* glass⟩

[1]**shave** \ˈshāv\ *vb* **shaved**; **shaved** *or* **shav·en** \ˈshā-vən\; **shav·ing** **1 a** : to cut or pare off by means of an edged instrument ⟨*shaved* his beard⟩ **b** : to remove hair close to the skin with a razor ⟨has to *shave* every day⟩ **2** : to make bare or smooth by cutting the hair from ⟨had his head *shaved*⟩ **3** : to cut off closely ⟨a lawn *shaven* close⟩ **4** : to cut off thin slices from (as with a plane) ⟨*shaved* the edge of the board⟩ **5** : to pass close to : skim along or near the surface of with or without touching

[2]**shave** *n* **1** : any of various tools for shaving or cut-

ting thin slices **2 :** an act or process of shaving esp. the beard **3 :** a narrow escape ⟨a close *shave*⟩

shav·er \'shā-vər\ *n* **1 :** one that shaves; *esp* : an electric-powered razor **2 :** BOY, YOUNGSTER

shave·tail \'shāv-ˌtāl\ *n* **1 :** an untrained mule **2 :** a newly appointed second lieutenant — usu. used disparagingly

shav·ing \'shā-ving\ *n* **1 :** the act of one that shaves **2 :** something shaved off ⟨wood *shavings*⟩

[1]**shawl** \'shȯl\ *n* : a square or oblong piece of woven or knitted fabric used esp. by women as a loose covering for the head or shoulders

[2]**shawl** *vb* : to wrap in or as if in a shawl

Shaw·nee \shȯ-'nē, shä-\ *n* : a member of an Algonquian Amerindian people ranging through most of the states east of the Mississippi and south of the Great Lakes

shay \'shā\ *n, chiefly dial* : CHAISE 1

[1]**she** \(')shē\ *pron* : that female one ⟨*she* is my wife⟩

[2]**she** \'shē\ *n* : a female person or animal ⟨*she*-cat⟩

sheaf \'shēf\ *n, pl* **sheaves** \'shēvz\ *also* **sheafs** \'shēfs\ **1 :** a bundle of stalks and ears of grain **2 :** something resembling or suggesting a sheaf of grain ⟨*sheaf* of arrows⟩ ⟨*sheaf* of papers⟩ — **sheaf-like** \'shēf-ˌlīk\ *adj*

[1]**shear** \'shi(ə)r\ *vb* **sheared**; **sheared** *or* **shorn** \'shōrn, 'shȯrn\; **shear·ing 1 :** to cut the hair or wool from : CLIP ⟨*shearing* sheep⟩ **2 :** to deprive of by or as if by cutting off ⟨*shorn* of his power⟩ **3 :** to become divided under the action of a shear ⟨bolt may *shear* off⟩ — **shear·er** *n*

[2]**shear** *n* : an action or force that causes or tends to cause two parts of a body to slide on each other in a direction parallel to their plane of contact

shears \'shi(ə)rz\ *n pl* : a cutting tool like large scissors

sheath \'shēth\ *n, pl* **sheaths** \'shēt͟hz, 'shēths\ **1 :** a case for a blade (as of a knife) **2 :** a covering esp. of an anatomical structure like a sheath in form or use

sheathe \'shēt͟h\ *vb* **1 :** to put into or as if into a sheath **2 :** to encase or cover with something that protects ⟨*sheathe* a ship's bottom with copper⟩ — **sheath·er** *n*

sheath·ing \'shē-t͟hing, -thing\ *n* : material used to sheathe something; *esp* : the first covering of boards or of waterproof material on the outside wall of a frame house or on a timber roof

sheath knife *n* : a knife having a fixed blade and designed to be carried in a sheath

[1]**sheave** \'shiv, 'shēv\ *n* : a grooved wheel : PULLEY

[2]**sheave** \'shēv\ *vb* : to gather and bind into a sheaf

she·bang \shi-'bang\ *n* : AFFAIR, CONCERN ⟨blew up the whole *shebang*⟩

[1]**shed** \'shed\ *vb* **shed**; **shed·ding 1 :** to pour forth or down esp. in drops ⟨*shed* tears⟩ **2 :** to cause to flow from a cut or wound ⟨*shed* blood⟩ **3 :** to spread abroad : DIFFUSE ⟨the sun *sheds* light and heat⟩ **4 :** to throw off ⟨the duck's plumage *sheds* water⟩ **5 a :** to cast aside or let fall some natural covering ⟨a snake *sheds* its skin⟩ ⟨the cat is *shedding*⟩ **b :** to rid oneself of : DISCARD ⟨*shed* excess weight⟩ — **shed·der** *n*

[2]**shed** *n* : a slight structure built for shelter or storage

she'd \(ˌ)shēd\ : she had : she would

sheen \'shēn\ *n* : subdued shininess of surface : LUSTER ⟨the *sheen* of satin⟩

sheep \'shēp\ *n, pl* **sheep 1 :** any of a genus of cud-chewing mammals related to the goats but stockier and lacking a beard in the male; *esp* : one long domesticated esp. for its flesh and wool **2 :** one that is timid, defenseless, or easily led — **sheep** *adj*

sheep·cote \-ˌkōt, -ˌkät\ *n, chiefly Brit* : SHEEPFOLD

sheep–dip \-ˌdip\ *n* : a liquid preparation of toxic chemicals into which sheep are plunged esp. to destroy external parasites

sheep dog *n* : a dog used or trained to tend, drive, or guard sheep

sheep dog

sheep·fold \'shēp-ˌfōld\ *n* : a pen or shelter for sheep

sheep·herd·er \'shēp-ˌhərd-ər\ *n* : a worker in charge of sheep — **sheep·herd·ing** \-ˌhərd-ing\ *n*

sheep·ish \'shē-pish\ *adj* **1 :** resembling a sheep in meekness, stupidity, or timidity **2 :** embarrassed by consciousness of a fault — **sheep·ish·ly** *adv*

sheep·shear·ing \'shēp-ˌshi(ə)r-ing\ *n* **1 :** the act of shearing sheep **2 :** the time or season for shearing sheep — **sheep·shear·er** \-ˌshir-ər\ *n*

sheep·skin \-ˌskin\ *n* **1 :** the skin of a sheep or leather prepared from it **2 :** DIPLOMA

[1]**sheer** \'shi(ə)r\ *adj* **1 :** very thin or transparent ⟨*sheer* stockings⟩ **2 a :** UNQUALIFIED, UTTER ⟨*sheer* nonsense⟩ **b :** taken or acting apart from everything else ⟨by *sheer* force⟩ **3 :** very steep : being almost straight up and down ⟨a *sheer* drop to the sea⟩ — **sheer·ly** *adv*

[2]**sheer** *adv* **1 :** ALTOGETHER, COMPLETELY **2 :** PERPENDICULARLY

[3]**sheer** *vb* : to deviate from a course : SWERVE

[4]**sheer** *n* : a turn, deviation, or change in the course of a ship

[1]**sheet** \'shēt\ *n* **1 :** a broad piece of cloth; *esp* : an oblong of usu. linen or cotton cloth used as an article of bedding next to the person **2 a :** a usu. rectangular piece of paper **b** *pl* : the unbound pages of a book **c :** a newspaper, periodical, or occasional publication **d :** the unseparated postage stamps printed by one impression of a plate on a single piece of paper **3 :** a broad expanse or surface of something ⟨*sheet* of ice⟩ **4 :** a portion of something that is thin in comparison to its length and breadth

[2]**sheet** *vb* : to cover with a sheet : SHROUD

[3]**sheet** *n* **1 :** a rope or chain that regulates the angle at which a sail is set in relation to the wind **2** *pl* : the spaces at either end of an open boat not occupied by thwarts

sheet erosion *n* : erosion that removes surface material more or less evenly from an extensive area

sheet·ing \'shēt-ing\ *n* : material in the form of sheets or suitable for forming into sheets

sheet lightning *n* : lightning in diffused or sheet form

sheet metal *n* : metal in the form of a sheet

sheet music *n* : music printed on large unbound sheets of paper

sheikh *or* **sheik** \'shēk, *for 1 also* 'shāk *and* 'shīk\ *n* [from Arabic *shaykh*] **1 :** an Arab chief **2** *usu sheik* : a man supposed to be irresistibly attractive to romantic young women — **sheik·dom** \-dəm\ *n*

shek·el \'shek-əl\ *n* [from Hebrew *sheqel*] **1 :** an ancient unit of weight or value; *esp* : a Hebrew unit equal to about 252 grains troy **2 :** a coin weighing one shekel

shel·drake \'shel-ˌdrāk\ *n* **1 :** any of several Old World ducks; *esp* : a common mostly black-and-white European duck slightly larger than the mallard **2 :** MERGANSER

S

shelf \'shelf\ *n, pl* **shelves** \'shelvz\ **1 a :** a thin flat usu. long and narrow piece of material (as of wood or glass) fastened horizontally (as on a wall) to hold objects **b :** the contents of a shelf **2 a :** a sandbank or ledge of rocks usu. partially submerged **b :** a flat projecting layer of rock — **shelf·like** \'shelf-ˌlīk\ *adj* — **on the shelf :** in a state of inactivity or uselessness

shelf fungus *n* **:** a fungus that forms shelflike fruiting bodies

1**shell** \'shel\ *n* **1 a :** a hard rigid outer covering of an animal (as a turtle or beetle) **b :** the outer covering of an egg and esp. of a bird's egg **c :** the outer covering of a nut, fruit, or seed esp. when hard or tough **2 a :** shell material or shells esp. of mollusks **b :** a shell-bearing mollusk **3 a :** a framework or exterior structure **b :** an edible case for holding a filling ⟨a pastry *shell*⟩ **4 :** a narrow light racing boat propelled by one or more oarsmen **5 :** any of the spaces occupied by the orbits of a group of electrons of approximately equal energy surrounding the nucleus of an atom **6 a :** a hollow projectile for cannon containing an explosive bursting charge **b :** a metal or paper case which holds the explosive charge and shot or bullet used in small arms — **shelly** \'shel-ē\ *adj*

2**shell** *vb* **1 a :** to remove from a natural enclosing cover (as a shell or husk) **:** SHUCK ⟨*shell* peas⟩ **b :** to remove the grains from (as an ear of Indian corn) **2 :** to throw or shoot shells at, upon, or into **:** BOMBARD **3 :** to fall out of the pod or husk

she'll \(ˌ)shēl, shil\ **:** she shall **:** she will

1**shel·lac** \shə-'lak\ *n* **1 :** purified lac **2 :** a preparation of lac dissolved in alcohol and used in filling wood or as a varnish

2**shellac** *vb* **shel·lacked**; **shel·lack·ing** **1 :** to coat or treat with shellac **2 :** to defeat decisively

shel·lack·ing \shə-'lak-ing\ *n* **:** a sound drubbing ⟨took a *shellacking* in last year's election⟩

shell·bark \'shel-ˌbärk\ *n* **:** SHAGBARK

shell bean *n* **:** a bean grown primarily for its edible seeds; *also* **:** these seeds

shelled \'sheld\ *adj* **1 :** having or encased in a shell **2 a :** taken from the shell ⟨*shelled* oysters⟩ **b :** removed from the cob ⟨*shelled* corn⟩

shell·fish \'shel-ˌfish\ *n* **:** an aquatic invertebrate animal with a shell; *esp* **:** an edible mollusk or crustacean

shell shock *n* **:** a nervous condition appearing in soldiers exposed to modern warfare — **shell–shock** \'shel-ˌshäk\ *vb*

1**shel·ter** \'shel-tər\ *n* **1 :** something that covers or affords protection **:** a means or place of protection ⟨an air raid *shelter*⟩ ⟨fallout *shelter*⟩ **2 :** the state of being covered and protected **:** REFUGE ⟨take *shelter* from a storm⟩

2**shelter** *vb* **shel·tered**; **shel·ter·ing** \-t(ə-)ring\ **1 :** to constitute or provide a shelter for **:** PROTECT **2 :** to place under shelter or protection **3 :** to take shelter — **shel·ter·er** \-tər-ər\ *n*

shelve \'shelv\ *vb* **1 :** to furnish with shelves ⟨*shelve* a closet⟩ **2 :** to place on a shelf ⟨*shelve* books⟩ **3 :** to put aside temporarily or permanently ⟨*shelve* a bill⟩ **4 :** to slope in a formation like a shelf **:** INCLINE — **shelv·er** *n*

ə abut   ər further   a back   ā bake
ä cot, cart   au̇ out   ch chin   e less   ē easy
g gift   i trip   ī life   j joke   ng sing   ō flow
ȯ flaw   ȯi coin   th thin   th this   ü loot
u̇ foot   y yet   yü few   yu̇ furious   zh vision

shelv·ing \'shel-ving\ *n* **1 :** material for shelves **2 :** SHELVES

1**shep·herd** \'shep-ərd\ *n* **1 :** a man who tends and guards sheep **2 :** PASTOR — **shep·herd·ess** \-ərd-əs\ *n*

2**shepherd** *vb* **1 :** to tend as a shepherd **2 :** to guide or guard in the manner of a shepherd ⟨*shepherd* tourists through a museum⟩

shepherd dog *n* **:** SHEEP DOG

sher·bet \'shər-bət\ *n* [from Turkish *şerbet*, from Persian *sharbat*, from Arabic *sharbah* "drink"] **1 :** a cooling drink of sweetened and diluted fruit juice **2 :** a water ice with milk, egg white, or gelatin added

sher·iff \'sher-əf\ *n* [from Old English *scīrgerēfa*, from *scīr* "shire", "county" and *gerēfa* "government agent", the source of English *reeve*] **:** an important official of a county charged primarily with judicial duties (as executing the orders of courts)

sher·ry \'sher-ē\ *n, pl* **sherries** **:** a fortified wine with a distinctive nutty flavor

she's \(ˌ)shēz\ **:** she is **:** she has

Shet·land pony \ˌshet-lən(d)-\ *n* **:** any of a breed of small stocky shaggy hardy ponies

Shetland pony

Shetland sheepdog *n* **:** any of a breed of dogs resembling miniature collies with an abundant long coat

shib·bo·leth \'shib-ə-ləth, -ˌleth\ *n* [from Hebrew *shibbōleth* "stream"; from the use of this word as a test to distinguish Gileadites from Ephraimites, who pronounced it *sibbōleth* (Judges 12:5,6)] **:** CATCHWORD, SLOGAN

1**shield** \'shēld\ *n* **1 :** a broad piece of defensive armor carried on the arm **2 :** one (as a person, part, or device) that protects or defends **:** DEFENSE **3 :** ESCUTCHEON

2**shield** *vb* **1 :** to cover with or as if with a shield **2 :** to cut off from observation **:** HIDE ⟨*shield* your eyes from the sun⟩

1**shift** \'shift\ *vb* **1 :** to exchange for or replace by another **:** CHANGE **2 a :** to change the place, position, or direction of **:** MOVE **b :** to make a change in place, position, or direction **c :** to change the gear rotating the transmission shaft of an automobile **3 :** to get along **:** MANAGE ⟨left the others to *shift* for themselves⟩

2**shift** *n* **1 :** a means or device for effecting an end **:** SCHEME **2 :** the act of shifting **3 :** a change in direction ⟨a *shift* in the wind⟩ **4 :** a change in place or position **5 a :** a group who work together in alternation with other groups **b :** the period during which a group of workers is working **6 :** GEARSHIFT

shift·less \'shift-ləs\ *adj* **:** lacking in ambition or incentive **:** LAZY — **shift·less·ly** *adv*

shifty \'shif-tē\ *adj* **shift·i·er**; **-est** **1 :** given to deception, evasion, or fraud **:** TRICKY **2 :** indicative of a tricky nature ⟨*shifty* eyes⟩ — **shift·i·ly** \-tə-lē\ *adv*

shi·gel·la \shə-'gel-ə\ *n* **:** any of a genus of bacteria that cause dysenteries in man and animals

shil·le·lagh *also* **shil·la·lah** \shə-'lā-lē\ *n* **:** CUDGEL, CLUB

shil·ling \'shil-iŋ\ *n* **1 a :** a former British monetary unit equal to 12 pence or 1/20 pound **b :** a coin representing this unit **2 :** a unit of value equal to 1/20 pound and a corresponding coin in any of several countries in or formerly in the British Commonwealth **3 :** any of several early American coins **4 a :** the basic monetary unit of British East Africa **b :** a coin representing this unit

1**shil·ly–shal·ly** \'shil-ē-ˌshal-ē\ *adj* **:** IRRESOLUTE, VACILLATING

2**shilly–shally** *n* **:** INDECISION, IRRESOLUTION

3**shilly–shally** *vb* **shil·ly–shal·lied; shil·ly–shal·ly·ing :** to show hesitation or lack of decisiveness **:** VACILLATE

shim·mer \'shim-ər\ *vb* **shim·mered; shim·mer·ing** \-(ə-)riŋ\ **:** to shine with a wavering light **:** GLIMMER ⟨leaves *shimmering* in the sunshine⟩ — **shimmer** *n*

1**shim·my** \'shim-ē\ *n, pl* **shimmies 1 :** a jazz dance characterized by a shaking of the body from the shoulders down **2 :** an abnormal vibration esp. in the front wheels of an automobile

2**shimmy** *vb* **shim·mied; shim·my·ing 1 :** to shake or quiver in or as if in dancing a shimmy **2 :** to vibrate abnormally

1**shin** \'shin\ *n* **:** the front part of the leg below the knee

2**shin** *vb* **shinned; shin·ning :** to climb by moving oneself along alternately with the arms or hands and legs ⟨*shin* up a tree⟩

shin·bone \'shin-'bōn, -ˌbōn\ *n* **:** the inner and larger of the two bones of the vertebrate hind limb between the knee and the ankle

shin·dig \'shin-ˌdig\ *n* **:** a festive occasion; *esp* **:** a usu. large or lavish party

1**shine** \'shīn\ *vb* **shone** \'shōn\ *or* **shined; shin·ing 1 :** to send out rays of light **2 :** to be bright by reflection of light **:** GLEAM **3 :** to exhibit unusual talent or powers ⟨*shine* in conversation⟩ **4 :** to make bright by polishing ⟨*shined* his shoes every day⟩

2**shine** *n* **1 :** brightness caused by the emission of light **2 :** brightness caused by the reflection of light **:** LUSTER **3 :** BRILLIANCE, SPLENDOR **4 :** fair weather **:** SUNSHINE ⟨will go, rain or *shine*⟩ **5 :** LIKING, FANCY ⟨took a *shine* to him⟩ **6 :** a polish given to shoes

shin·er \'shī-nər\ *n* **1 :** one that shines **2 :** a silvery fish; *esp* **:** any of numerous small freshwater American fishes related to the carp **3 :** a black eye

1**shin·gle** \'shiŋ-gəl\ *n* **1 :** a small thin piece of building material (as of wood or a composition of asbestos) for laying in overlapping rows as a covering for the roof or sides of a building **2 :** a small signboard **3 :** a woman's short haircut — **shin·gle·like** \-gəl-ˌlīk\ *adj*

2**shingle** *vb* **shin·gled; shin·gling** \-g(ə-)liŋ\ **1 :** to cover with or as if with shingles **2 :** to bob and shape the hair in a shingle

shin·gles \'shiŋ-gəlz\ *n* **:** a virus disease marked by inflammation of one or more ganglia and by pain and skin eruption usu. along the course of a single nerve

shin·ing \'shī-niŋ\ *adj* **1 :** giving forth or reflecting a steady light **:** GLOWING **2 :** having a distinguished quality **:** ILLUSTRIOUS ⟨a *shining* example of integrity⟩ ***syn*** see BRIGHT — **shin·ing·ly** \'shī-niŋ-lē\ *adv*

shining willow *n* **:** a common No. American shrubby willow with shiny lance-shaped leaves

1**shin·ny** \'shin-ē\ *n* **:** the variation of hockey played with a curved stick and a ball or block of wood by schoolboys

2**shinny** *vb* **shin·nied; shin·ny·ing :** SHIN 1

shiny \'shī-nē\ *adj* **shin·i·er; -est 1 :** bright in appearance **:** GLITTERING, POLISHED ⟨*shiny* kitchenware⟩ **2 :** rubbed or worn smooth ⟨*shiny* old clothes⟩

1**ship** \'ship\ *n* **1 :** a large seagoing boat **2 :** a ship's crew **3 :** AIRSHIP, AIRPLANE **4 :** ROCKET SHIP, SPACESHIP

2**ship** *vb* **shipped; ship·ping 1 :** to place or receive on board a ship for transportation by water **2 :** to cause to be transported ⟨*ship* grain by rail⟩ **3 :** to take into a ship or boat ⟨*ship* oars⟩ **4 :** to sign on as a crew member of a ship

-ship \ˌship\ *n suffix* **1 :** state **:** condition **:** quality ⟨friend*ship*⟩ **2 :** office **:** dignity **:** profession ⟨lord*ship*⟩ ⟨author*ship*⟩ **3 :** art **:** skill ⟨horseman*ship*⟩ **4 :** something showing, exhibiting, or embodying a quality or state ⟨member*ship*⟩ ⟨town*ship*⟩ **5 :** one entitled to a (specified) rank, title, or appellation ⟨his Lord*ship*⟩

ship biscuit *n* **:** HARDTACK — called also *ship bread*

ship·board \'ship-ˌbōrd, -ˌbȯrd\ *n* **1 :** the side of a ship **2 :** SHIP ⟨met on *shipboard*⟩

ship·build·er \-ˌbil-dər\ *n* **:** one who designs or builds ships — **ship·build·ing** \-diŋ\ *n*

ship·mas·ter \-ˌmas-tər\ *n* **:** the master or commander of a ship other than a warship

ship·mate \-ˌmāt\ *n* **:** a fellow sailor

ship·ment \-mənt\ *n* **1 :** the act or process of shipping **2 :** the goods shipped

ship·pa·ble \'ship-ə-bəl\ *adj* **:** suitable for shipping

ship·per \'ship-ər\ *n* **:** one that sends goods by any form of conveyance

ship·ping \'ship-iŋ\ *n* **1 :** the body of ships in one place or belonging to one port or country **2 :** the act or business of one that ships

ship·shape \'ship-'shāp\ *adj* **:** TRIM, TIDY

ship·worm \-ˌwərm\ *n* **:** any of various long-bodied marine clams that resemble worms, burrow in submerged wood, and damage wharf piles and wooden ships

1**ship·wreck** \-ˌrek\ *n* **1 :** a wrecked ship or its parts **:** WRECKAGE **2 :** the destruction or loss of a ship **3 :** total loss or failure **:** RUIN

2**shipwreck** *vb* **1 :** to cause to experience shipwreck **2 :** to destroy a ship by grounding or foundering

ship·wright \'ship-ˌrīt\ *n* **:** a carpenter skilled in ship construction and repair

ship·yard \-ˌyärd\ *n* **:** a place where ships are built or repaired

shire \'shī(ə)r, *in place-name compounds* ˌshi(ə)r, shər\ *n* **:** a territorial division of England usu. identical with a county

shirk \'shərk\ *vb* **:** to evade the performance of an obligation ⟨some worked, others *shirked*⟩ — **shirk·er** *n*

shirr \'shər\ *vb* **1 :** to draw cloth together in a shirring **2 :** to bake eggs removed from the shell until set

shirr·ing \'shər-iŋ\ *n* **:** a decorative gathering (as of cloth) made by drawing up the material along two or more parallel lines of stitching

shirt \'shərt\ *n* **:** a garment for the upper part of the body usu. having a collar, sleeves, a front opening, and a tail long enough to be tucked inside trousers or a skirt **b :** UNDERSHIRT

shirt·ing \'shərt-iŋ\ *n* **:** fabric suitable for shirts

shirt·waist \'shərt-ˌwāst\ *n* **:** a woman's tailored garment (as a dress or blouse) with details copied from men's shirts

1**shiv·er** \'shiv-ər\ *n* **:** one of the small pieces into which a brittle thing is broken by sudden violence

2**shiver** *vb* **shiv·ered; shiv·er·ing** \'shiv-(ə-)riŋ\ **:** to break into many small pieces **:** SHATTER

3**shiver** *vb* **shiv·ered; shiv·er·ing** \'shiv-(ə-)riŋ\ **:** to undergo trembling (as from cold or fear)

[4]**shiver** *n* : an instance of shivering : TREMBLE

shiv·ery \'shiv-(ə-)rē\ *adj* **1** : characterized by shivers : TREMULOUS ⟨felt *shivery* before the interview⟩ **2** : causing shivers ⟨a *shivery* winter's day⟩ ⟨*shivery* ghost stories⟩

[1]**shoal** \'shōl\ *adj* : SHALLOW ⟨*shoal* water⟩

[2]**shoal** *n* **1** : a shallow place in a body of water (as the sea or a river) **2** : a sandbank or sandbar that makes the water shallow

[3]**shoal** *vb* : to become shallow

shoat \'shōt\ *n* : a young hog usu. less than one year old

[1]**shock** \'shäk\ *n* : a bunch of sheaves of grain or stalks of Indian corn set upright in a field

[2]**shock** *vb* : to collect into shocks

[3]**shock** *n* **1** : the sudden violent collision of bodies in combat ⟨the *shock* of battle⟩ **2** : a violent shake or jar : CONCUSSION ⟨an earthquake *shock*⟩ **3** : a sudden or violent agitation of the mind or feelings **4** : a state of greatly reduced vitality associated with reduced blood volume and pressure and caused usu. by severe esp. crushing injuries, hemorrhage, or burns **5** : sudden stimulation of the nerves and convulsive contraction of the muscles caused by the discharge of electricity through the animal body

[4]**shock** *vb* **1** : to strike with surprise, terror, horror, or disgust ⟨visitors were *shocked* by the city's slums⟩ **2** : to subject to the action of an electrical discharge **3** : to drive into or out of by or as if by a shock ⟨*shocked* the public into action⟩ — **shock·er** *n*

[5]**shock** *n* : a thick bushy mass (as of hair)

shock absorber *n* : a device for absorbing the energy of sudden impulses or shocks in machinery or structures (as springs of automobiles)

shock·ing *adj* : extremely startling and offensive ⟨a *shocking* crime⟩ ⟨*shocking* behavior⟩ — **shock·ing·ly** \-iŋ-lē\ *adv*

shock wave *n* **1** : BLAST 5c **2** : a compressional wave formed whenever the speed of a body exceeds the speed of sound

shod \'shäd\ *adj* **1** : wearing shoes **2** : furnished or equipped with a shoe

[1]**shod·dy** \'shäd-ē\ *n* : a fabric made from reclaimed wool

[2]**shoddy** *adj* **shod·di·er**; **-est** **1** : made of shoddy **2** : hastily or poorly done : INFERIOR **3** : SHABBY — **shod·di·ly** \'shäd-ə-lē\ *adv*

[1]**shoe** \'shü\ *n* **1** : an outer covering for the human foot usu. made of leather with a thick or stiff sole and an attached heel **2 a** : HORSESHOE **b** : the runner of a sled **c** : the part of a brake that presses on the wheel of a vehicle **3** : the outside casing of an automobile tire

[2]**shoe** *vb* **shod** \'shäd\ *also* **shoed** \'shüd\; **shoe·ing** **1** : to furnish with a shoe or shoes **2** : to cover for protection, strength, or ornament

shoe·black \'shü-ˌblak\ *n* : BOOTBLACK

shoe·horn \-ˌhȯrn\ *n* : a curved piece (as of horn, wood, or metal) to aid in slipping on a shoe

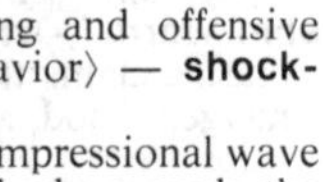

shoehorn

shoe·lace \-ˌlās\ *n* : a lace or string for fastening a shoe

shoe·mak·er \-ˌmā-kər\ *n* : one whose business is selling or repairing shoes

ə abut	ər further	a back	ā bake	
ä cot, cart	aù out	ch chin	e less	ē easy
g gift	i trip	ī life	j joke	ŋ sing	ō flow
ȯ flaw	ȯi coin	th thin	t͟h this	ü loot
ù foot	y yet	yü few	yù furious	zh vision

shoe·string \-ˌstriŋ\ *n* **1** : SHOELACE **2** : a small or barely adequate amount of money or capital ⟨start a business on a *shoestring*⟩

shoe tree *n* : a foot-shaped device for inserting in a shoe to preserve its shape

sho·gun \'shō-gən, -ˌgün\ *n* : one of a line of military governors ruling Japan until the revolution of 1867-68

shone *past of* SHINE

shoo \'shü\ *vb* : to scare, drive, or send away by or as if by crying *shoo*

shook *past or chiefly dial past part of* SHAKE

[1]**shoot** \'shüt\ *vb* **shot** \'shät\; **shoot·ing** **1 a** : to let fly or cause to be driven forward with force ⟨*shoot* an arrow⟩ **b** : to cause a missile to be driven forth from : DISCHARGE ⟨*shoot* a gun⟩ **c** : to cause an engine or weapon to discharge a missile ⟨*shoot* at a target⟩ **2 a** : to propel with the thumb ⟨*shoot* marbles⟩ **b** : to propel (as a ball or puck) toward a goal; *esp* : to score by shooting ⟨*shoot* a basket⟩ **c** : PLAY ⟨*shoot* a round of golf⟩ ⟨*shoot* craps⟩ **3 a** : to strike with a missile esp. from a bow or gun; *esp* : to wound or kill with a missile discharged from a firearm ⟨*shoot* deer⟩ **b** : to remove or destroy by use of firearms ⟨*shoot* off a lock⟩ **4** : to push or slide into or out of a fastening ⟨*shot* the door bolt⟩ **5** : to throw or cast esp. suddenly or with force ⟨*shoot* flour into bins⟩ ⟨*shot* him a meaningful look⟩ **6** : to set off : DETONATE, IGNITE ⟨*shoot* off fireworks⟩ **7 a** : to push or thrust forward usu. abruptly or swiftly ⟨lizards *shooting* out their tongues⟩ **b** : DEVELOP, MATURE ⟨boys *shooting* up into manhood⟩ **8 a** : to go or pass rapidly and precipitately ⟨*shot* out of his office⟩ ⟨the pain *shot* down his arm⟩ **b** : to pass swiftly along ⟨*shoot* the rapids in a canoe⟩ **c** : to stream out suddenly : SPURT ⟨blood *shot* out of the wound⟩ **9 a** : to take the altitude of ⟨*shoot* the sun with a sextant⟩ **b** : to take a picture of : PHOTOGRAPH **c** : to film a scene ⟨the director is ready to *shoot*⟩ — **shoot·er** *n* — **shoot at** *or* **shoot for** : to aim at : strive for — **shoot the works** : to put forth all one's efforts

[2]**shoot** *n* **1 a** : the aerial part of a plant : a new growth of a plant branch esp. when developed from a single bud **b** : OFFSHOOT **2 a** : an act or the action of shooting **b** : a hunting trip or party ⟨a duck *shoot*⟩ **c** : a shooting match ⟨skeet *shoot*⟩

syn SHOOT, BRANCH, BOUGH, LIMB can mean an outgrowth from a plant's main stem or from one of its divisions. SHOOT applies chiefly to a young undeveloped outgrowth from a bud; BRANCH suggests the dividing and spreading of a well developed outgrowth; BOUGH often suggests the foliage and flowers of a branch in bloom; LIMB applies usu. to a large branch growing directly out of a tree trunk or produced by a forking of the trunk

shooting star *n* : a meteor appearing as a temporary streak of light in the night sky

[1]**shop** \'shäp\ *n* **1** : a workman's place of business **2** : a building or room stocked with merchandise for sale : STORE **3** : FACTORY, MILL **4 a** : a school laboratory equipped for instruction in manual arts **b** : the art or science of working with tools and machinery **5** : SHOPTALK

[2]**shop** *vb* **shopped**; **shop·ping** **1** : to examine goods or services with intent to buy or in search of the best buy **2** : to make a search : HUNT ⟨*shopped* around for the best-qualified man⟩

shop·keep·er \'shäp-ˌkē-pər\ *n* : STOREKEEPER

shop·lift·er \-ˌlif-tər\ *n* : a thief who steals merchandise on display in stores — **shop·lift·ing** \-tiŋ\ *n*

shop·per \'shäp-ər\ *n* **1 :** one that shops **2 :** one whose occupation is shopping as an agent for customers or for an employer

shopping center *n* **:** a group of retail and service stores located in a suburban area and provided with extensive parking space

shop·talk \'shäp-ˌtȯk\ *n* **:** the jargon or subject matter peculiar to an occupation or a special area of interest

shop·worn \-ˌwōrn, -ˌwȯrn\ *adj* **:** faded, soiled, or impaired by remaining too long in a store ⟨sells *shopworn* merchandise at a discount⟩

[1]**shore** \'shō(ə)r, 'shȯ(ə)r\ *n* **:** the land bordering a usu. large body of water

syn SHORE, BEACH, BANK can mean the land bordering on a body of water. SHORE, a general term, applies to land lying along the edge of a lake, a river, or esp. a sea; BEACH usu. applies to a stretch of shore covered by sand or pebbles, and often suggests a place for bathing and sunning; BANK applies esp. to the steeply rising edge of a stream or river

[2]**shore** *vb* **:** to give support to **:** BRACE

[3]**shore** *n* **:** a prop or support placed beneath or against something to support it

shores

shore·bird \-ˌbərd\ *n* **:** any of a group of birds that frequent the seashore

shore·line \-ˌlīn\ *n* **:** the line where a body of water touches the shore

shore patrol *n* **:** a branch of a navy that exercises guard and police functions

shorn *past part of* SHEAR

[1]**short** \'shȯrt\ *adj* **1 a :** having little length **b :** not tall **:** LOW **2 a :** not extended in time **:** BRIEF ⟨a *short* life⟩ **b :** limited in distance ⟨a *short* walk⟩ **3 :** not retentive ⟨a *short* memory⟩ **4 a :** being a syllable or speech sound of relatively brief duration **b :** being the member of a pair of similarly spelled vowel or vowel-containing sounds that is descended from an originally short vowel ⟨*short a* in *fat*⟩ ⟨*short i* in *sin*⟩ **5 a :** not coming up to a measure or requirement **:** INSUFFICIENT ⟨in *short* supply⟩ ⟨his cash was three dollars *short*⟩ **b :** not reaching far enough ⟨*short* of the target⟩ **c :** inherently or basically weak ⟨*short* on brains⟩ **6 :** ABRUPT, CURT ⟨*short* tempers⟩ **7 :** containing or cooked with shortening **:** CRISP, FRIABLE ⟨*short* piecrust⟩ **8 :** ABBREVIATED ⟨*doc* is *short* for *doctor*⟩ — **short·ish** \-ish\ *adj* — **in short order :** QUICKLY, EFFICIENTLY

[2]**short** *adv* **1 :** ABRUPTLY, SUDDENLY ⟨he stopped *short*⟩ **2 :** at some point before a goal or limit aimed at ⟨the arrow fell *short*⟩

[3]**short** *n* **1 :** a short syllable **2** *pl* **:** a by-product of wheat milling that includes the germ, fine bran, and some flour **3 :** something that is shorter than the usual or regular length **4** *pl* **a :** knee-length or less than knee-length trousers **b :** short underpants **5 :** SHORT CIRCUIT — **in short :** by way of summary **:** BRIEFLY

[4]**short** *vb* **:** SHORT-CIRCUIT

short·age \'shȯrt-ij\ *n* **:** a lack in the amount needed **:** DEFICIT ⟨a *shortage* in the accounts⟩

short·bread \'shȯrt-ˌbred\ *n* **:** a thick cookie made of flour, sugar, and much shortening

short·cake \-ˌkāk\ *n* **1 :** a crisp and often unsweetened biscuit or cookie **2 :** a dessert made of usu. very short baking-powder-biscuit dough baked and spread with sweetened fruit

short·change \-'chānj\ *vb* **:** to give less than the correct amount of change to

short circuit *n* **:** a connection of comparatively low resistance accidentally or intentionally made between points in an electric circuit between which the resistance is normally much greater

short–cir·cuit \'shȯrt-'sər-kət\ *vb* **:** to make a short circuit in or have a short circuit

short·com·ing \shȯrt-'kəm-ing\ *n* **:** DEFICIENCY, DEFECT, FAULT

short·cut \'shȯrt-ˌkət\ *n* **1 :** a route more direct than that usu. taken **2 :** a quicker way of doing something

short division *n* **:** mathematical division in which the successive steps are performed without writing out the remainders

short·en \'shȯrt-ən\ *vb* **short·ened**; **short·en·ing** \-(ə-)ning\ **:** to make or become short or shorter — **short·en·er** \-(ə-)nər\ *n*

short·en·ing \'shȯrt-(ə-)ning\ *n* **1 :** a making or becoming short or shorter **2 :** an edible fat (as butter or lard) used in baking

short·hand \'shȯrt-ˌhand\ *n* **:** a method of writing rapidly by substituting characters, abbreviations, or symbols for letters, words, or phrases **:** STENOGRAPHY — **shorthand** *adj*

short·hand·ed \-'han-dəd\ *adj* **:** short of the regular or necessary number of people

short·horn \'shȯrt-ˌhȯrn\ *n* **:** a short-horned animal; *esp* **:** one of a short-horned breed of cattle

short–horned grasshopper \ˌshȯrt-ˌhȯrn(d)-\ *n* **:** any of a family of grasshoppers with short antennae

short hundredweight *n* **:** HUNDREDWEIGHT 1

short–lived \'shȯrt-'līvd, -'livd\ *adj* **:** not living or lasting long ⟨*short-lived* happiness⟩

short·ly \'shȯrt-lē\ *adv* **1 :** in a few words **:** BRIEFLY ⟨put it *shortly*⟩ **2 a :** in a short time **:** SOON ⟨will arrive *shortly*⟩ **b :** at a short interval ⟨*shortly* after⟩

short·ness \'shȯrt-nəs\ *n* **:** the quality or state of being short ⟨*shortness* of breath⟩

short shrift *n* **1 :** a brief respite from death **2 :** little consideration ⟨gave the matter *short shrift*⟩

short·sight·ed \'shȯrt-'sīt-əd\ *adj* **1 :** NEARSIGHTED, MYOPIC **2 :** characterized by lack of foresight — **short·sight·ed·ly** *adv* — **short·sight·ed·ness** *n*

short–spo·ken \-'spō-kən\ *adj* **:** CURT

short·stop \'shȯrt-ˌstäp\ *n* **:** the baseball player stationed between second and third base

short–tem·pered \-'tem-pərd\ *adj* **:** having a quick temper **:** easily angered

short·wave \-'wāv\ *n* **:** a radio wave of 60-meter wavelength or less used esp. in long-distance broadcasting

Sho·sho·ni *also* **Sho·sho·ne** \shə-'shō-nē\ *n* **:** a member of a group of Amerindian peoples in California, Colorado, Idaho, Nevada, Utah, and Wyoming

[1]**shot** \'shät\ *n* **1 a :** an action of shooting **b :** a directed discharge of a gun or cannon **c :** a stroke or throw at a goal ⟨the last *shot* in the game⟩ **d :** an injection of something (as a medicine or antibody) into the body ⟨penicillin *shots*⟩ **2 a** *pl* **shot :** something propelled by shooting; *esp* **:** small lead or steel pellets forming a charge for a shotgun **b :** a metal ball that is put for distance **3 :** the distance that a missile is or can be thrown **:** RANGE, REACH

⟨not within rifle *shot*⟩ **4 :** one that shoots : MARKSMAN ⟨he is a good *shot*⟩ **5 a :** ATTEMPT, TRY ⟨take another *shot* at the puzzle⟩ **b :** CHANCE ⟨the horse was a 10 to 1 *shot*⟩ **6 :** a remark so directed as to have telling effect **7 a :** PHOTOGRAPH **b :** a single sequence of a motion picture or a television program shot by one camera without interruption : SCENE **8 :** a single drink of liquor

[2]**shot** *past of* SHOOT

[3]**shot** *adj* **1 :** having contrasting and changeable color effects that react varyingly to dyes : IRIDESCENT ⟨blue silk *shot* with silver⟩ **2 :** reduced to a state of ruin, prostration, or uselessness ⟨his nerves were *shot*⟩ ⟨tires are *shot*⟩

shot·gun \ˈshät-ˌgən\ *n* **:** a gun with a smooth bore used to fire small shot at short range

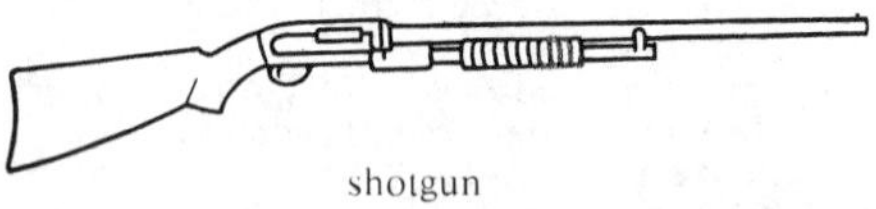

shotgun

shot put *n* **:** a field event consisting in putting the shot for distance — **shot–put·ter** \-ˌpu̇t-ər\ *n*

should \shəd, (ˈ)shu̇d\ *past of* SHALL — used as an auxiliary verb to express (1) condition or possibility ⟨if you *should* see him, tell him this⟩, (2) obligation or propriety ⟨you *should* brush your teeth regularly⟩, (3) futurity from the point of view in the past ⟨thought I *should* soon be released⟩, (4) what is probable or expected ⟨they started early and *should* be here soon⟩, and (5) politeness in softening a request or assertion ⟨I *should* like some coffee⟩ ⟨so it *should* seem⟩

[1]**shoul·der** \ˈshōl-dər\ *n* **1 :** the part of the body of a person or animal where the arm or foreleg joins the body **2 :** a cut of meat including the upper joint of the foreleg and adjacent parts **3 :** the part of a garment at the wearer's shoulder **4 :** a part or projection resembling a human shoulder ⟨*shoulder* of a hill⟩ **5 :** either edge of a road; *esp* **:** the part of a road outside of the traveled way

[2]**shoulder** *vb* **shoul·dered**; **shoul·der·ing** \-d(ə-)riŋ\ **1 :** to push or thrust with the shoulder : JOSTLE ⟨*shouldered* his way through the crowd⟩ **2 a :** to place or bear on the shoulder ⟨*shouldered* the knapsack⟩ **b :** to assume the burden or responsibility of ⟨*shoulder* the blame⟩

shoulder blade *n* **:** the flat triangular bone of the shoulder jointed to the bone of the upper arm

shoulder strap *n* **1 :** a strap worn over the shoulder to hold up a garment **2 :** a strip worn on the shoulder of a military uniform to show rank

should·est \ˈshu̇d-əst\ *archaic past 2d sing of* SHALL

shouldn't \ˈshu̇d-ənt\ **:** should not

shouldst \(ˈ)shu̇dst\ *archaic past 2d sing of* SHALL

[1]**shout** \ˈshau̇t\ *vb* **1 :** to utter a sudden loud cry ⟨*shouted* with delight⟩ **2 :** to utter in a loud voice ⟨*shouted* insults at each other⟩ — **shout·er** *n*

[2]**shout** *n* **:** a loud cry or call

[1]**shove** \ˈshəv\ *vb* **1 :** to push with steady force **2 :** to push carelessly or rudely ⟨*shove* a person out of the way⟩ — **shov·er** *n* — **shove off 1 :** to move away from shore by pushing **2 :** to set out : DEPART

[2]**shove** *n* **:** an act or instance of shoving : a forceful push

[1]**shov·el** \ˈshəv-əl\ *n* **1 :** an implement consisting of a plate or scoop attached to a long handle used for lifting and throwing loose material (as snow, earth, grain, or coal) **2 :** SHOVELFUL ⟨toss up a *shovel* of earth⟩

[2]**shovel** *vb* **-eled** *or* **-elled**; **-el·ing** *or* **-el·ling** \ˈshəv-(ə-)liŋ\ **1 :** to take up and throw with a shovel **2 :** to dig or clean out with a shovel **3 :** to throw or convey roughly or in the mass as if with a shovel ⟨*shovels* food into his mouth⟩

shov·el·er *or* **shov·el·ler** \ˈshəv-(ə-)lər\ *n* **1 :** one that shovels **2 :** any of several river ducks having a large and very broad bill

shov·el·ful \ˈshəv-əl-ˌfu̇l\ *n, pl* **shovelfuls** \-ˌfu̇lz\ *or* **shov·els·ful** \-əlz-ˌfu̇l\ **:** the amount held by a shovel

[1]**show** \ˈshō\ *vb* **showed**; **shown** \ˈshōn\ *or* **showed**; **show·ing 1 :** to place in sight : DISPLAY **2 :** REVEAL ⟨*showed* himself a coward⟩ **3 :** GRANT, BESTOW ⟨the king *showed* no mercy⟩ **4 :** TEACH, INSTRUCT ⟨*showed* her how to knit⟩ **5 :** PROVE ⟨the result *showed* that he was right⟩ **6 :** DIRECT, USHER, GUIDE ⟨*show* a visitor to the door⟩ **7 :** APPEAR ⟨anger *showed* in his face⟩ **8 :** to be noticeable ⟨the patch hardly *shows*⟩ **9 :** to be third or at least third in a horse race

[2]**show** *n* **1 :** a demonstrative display ⟨a *show* of strength⟩ **2 a :** a false semblance : PRETENSE ⟨he made a *show* of friendship⟩ **b :** a more or less true appearance of something : SIGN ⟨a *show* of reason⟩ **c :** an impressive display **3 :** something exhibited esp. for wonder or ridicule : SPECTACLE **4 a :** a theatrical presentation **b :** a radio or television program **5 :** ENTERPRISE, AFFAIR ⟨he ran the whole *show*⟩ **6 :** third place at the finish of a horse race

show·boat \ˈshō-ˌbōt\ *n* **:** a river steamboat containing a theater and carrying a troupe of actors to give plays at river communities

show·case \-ˌkās\ *n* **:** a glass case or box to display and protect wares in a store or articles in a museum

show·down \-ˌdau̇n\ *n* **:** the final settlement of a contested issue

[1]**show·er** \ˈshau̇(-ə)r\ *n* **1 a :** a fall of rain of short duration **b :** a like fall of sleet, hail, or snow **2 :** something resembling a rain shower ⟨a *shower* of sparks from a bonfire⟩ ⟨a *shower* of tears⟩ **3 :** a party given by friends who bring gifts often of a particular kind ⟨attended a linen *shower* for the bride⟩ **4 :** SHOWER BATH

[2]**shower** *vb* **1 :** to rain or fall in or as if in a shower **2 :** to bathe in a shower bath **3 :** to wet copiously (as with water) in a spray, fine stream, or drops **4 :** to give in abundance ⟨*showered* her with gifts⟩

shower bath *n* **1 :** a bath in which water is sprayed on the person **2 :** the apparatus that provides a shower bath

show·ing \ˈshō-iŋ\ *n* **1 :** an act of putting something on view : DISPLAY, EXHIBITION ⟨a *showing* of fall millinery⟩ **2 :** PERFORMANCE, RECORD ⟨the team made a good *showing*⟩

show·man \ˈshō-mən\ *n* **1 :** the producer of a theatrical show **2 :** a person having a sense or knack for dramatization or visual effectiveness — **show·man·ship** \-ˌship\ *n*

show–off \ˈshō-ˌȯf\ *n* **1 :** the act of showing off **2 :** one that shows off

show off \-ˈȯf\ *vb* **1 :** to display proudly **2 :** to seek to attract attention by conspicuous behavior

ə abut	ər further	a back	ā bake	
ä cot, cart	au̇ out	ch chin	e less	ē easy
g gift	i trip	ī life	j joke	ŋ sing	ō flow
ȯ flaw	ȯi coin	th thin	t͟h this	ü loot
u̇ foot	y yet	yü few	yu̇ furious	zh vision

show·piece \\-ˌpēs\\ *n* : a prime or outstanding example used for exhibition

show·place \\-ˌplās\\ *n* : a place (as an estate or building) that is frequently exhibited or is regarded as an example of beauty or excellence

show·room \\-ˌrüm, -ˌru̇m\\ *n* : a room used for the display of merchandise or of samples

show up *vb* **1** : to reveal the true nature of : EXPOSE ⟨*showed up* his ignorance⟩ **2** : ARRIVE ⟨he *showed up* late⟩

showy \\ˈshō-ē\\ *adj* **show·i·er**; **-est** **1** : making an attractive show : STRIKING ⟨*showy* blossoms⟩ **2** : OSTENTATIOUS, GAUDY — **show·i·ly** \\ˈshō-ə-lē\\ *adv* — **show·i·ness** \\ˈshō-ē-nəs\\ *n*

shrap·nel \\ˈshrap-nəl\\ *n, pl* **shrapnel** **1** : a projectile that consists of a case provided with a powder charge and a large number of usu. lead balls and is exploded in flight **2** : bomb, mine, or shell fragments

1**shred** \\ˈshred\\ *n* **1** : a long narrow strip cut or torn off : SCRAP ⟨*shreds* of cloth⟩ **2** : a small amount : BIT ⟨not a *shred* of truth in the accusation⟩

2**shred** *vb* **shred·ded**; **shred·ding** **1** : to cut or tear into shreds **2** : to break up into shreds — **shred·der** *n*

shrew \\ˈshrü\\ *n* **1** : any of numerous small mammals related to the moles but having a long pointed snout, very small eyes, and velvety fur **2** : a woman who scolds or quarrels constantly

shrew 1
(about 3 in. long)

shrewd \\ˈshrüd\\ *adj* : marked by cleverness, discernment, or sagacity : ASTUTE ⟨*shrewd* observer⟩ — **shrewd·ly** *adv* — **shrewd·ness** *n*

shrew·ish \\ˈshrü-ish\\ *adj* : ILL-TEMPERED, SCOLDING — **shrew·ish·ly** *adv*

1**shriek** \\ˈshrēk\\ *vb* **1** : to utter a loud shrill sound **2** : to cry out in a high-pitched voice : SCREECH **3** : to utter with a shriek or sharply and shrilly

2**shriek** *n* **1** : a shrill usu. wild or involuntary cry **2** : a sound like a shriek ⟨a *shriek* of escaping steam⟩

shrift \\ˈshrift\\ *n, archaic* : the confession of sins to a priest or the hearing of a confession by a priest

shrike \\ˈshrīk\\ *n* : any of numerous usu. largely gray or brownish singing birds that have a strong notched bill hooked at the tip, feed chiefly on insects, and often impale their prey on thorns

1**shrill** \\ˈshril\\ *vb* : to utter or emit an acute piercing sound : SCREAM

2**shrill** *adj* **1** : having or emitting a sharp high-pitched tone or sound : PIERCING ⟨a *shrill* whistle⟩ **2** : accompanied by sharp high-pitched sounds or cries ⟨*shrill* gaiety⟩ — **shrill** *adv* — **shril·ly** \\ˈshril-lē\\ *adv*

3**shrill** *n* : a shrill sound

1**shrimp** \\ˈshrimp\\ *n, pl* **shrimp** *or* **shrimps** **1** : any of numerous small mostly marine crustaceans related to the lobsters and having a long slender body, compressed abdomen, and long legs **2** : a very small or puny person or thing

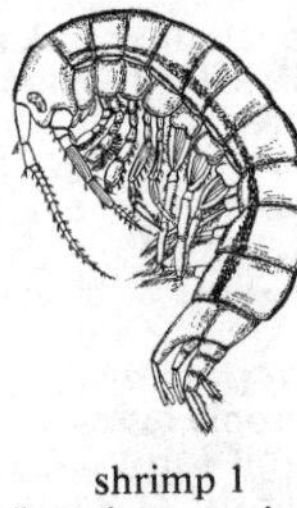

shrimp 1
(less than one inch long)

2**shrimp** *vb* : to fish for or catch shrimp

shrimp plant *n* : a widely cultivated tropical American shrubby plant having spikes of whitish flowers and overlapping reddish brown bracts

shrine \\ˈshrīn\\ *n* **1** : a case or box for sacred relics (as the bones of a saint) **2** : the tomb of a holy person (as a saint) **3** : a place or object that is considered sacred ⟨Westminster Abbey is a *shrine* for tourists⟩

1**shrink** \\ˈshringk\\ *vb* **shrank** \\ˈshrangk\\ *also* **shrunk** \\ˈshrəngk\\; **shrunk**; **shrink·ing** **1** : to contract or curl up the body or part of it : HUDDLE, COWER ⟨*shrink* in horror⟩ **2** : to become or cause to become smaller or more compacted (as from heat or melting) ⟨the sweater *shrank* when it was washed⟩ ⟨meat *shrinks* in cooking⟩ **3** : to lessen in value : DWINDLE ⟨their fortune *shrank* during the depression⟩ **4** : to draw back ⟨*shrink* from a quarrel⟩ — **shrink·a·ble** \\ˈshring-kə-bəl\\ *adj* — **shrink·er** *n*

2**shrink** *n* : the act of shrinking

shrink·age \\ˈshring-kij\\ *n* **1** : the act or process of shrinking **2** : the amount lost by shrinkage

shrive \\ˈshrīv\\ *vb* **shrived** *or* **shrove** \\ˈshrōv\\; **shriv·en** \\ˈshriv-ən\\ *or* **shrived**; **shriv·ing** \\ˈshrī-ving\\ **1** : to hear the confession of and administer the sacrament of penance to : PARDON **2** : to confess one's sins esp. to a priest

shriv·el \\ˈshriv-əl\\ *vb* **-eled** *or* **-elled**; **-el·ing** *or* **-el·ling** \\-(ə-)ling\\ **1** : to wrinkle esp. with a loss of moisture **2** : to reduce or become reduced to inanition, helplessness, or inefficiency

1**shroud** \\ˈshrau̇d\\ *n* **1** : burial garment : WINDING-SHEET **2** : something that covers, screens, or guards ⟨a *shroud* of secrecy⟩ **3** : one of the ropes leading usu. in pairs from a ship's masthead to give lateral support to the mast

shrouds 3

2**shroud** *vb* **1** : to cover with a shroud **2** : to veil under another appearance ⟨*shrouded* in mystery⟩

Shrove·tide \\ˈshrōv-ˌtīd\\ *n* : the period of three days immediately preceding Ash Wednesday

Shrove Tuesday \\ˈshrōv-\\ *n* : the Tuesday before Ash Wednesday

shrub \\ˈshrəb\\ *n* : a low usu. several-stemmed woody plant — compare HERB, TREE

shrub·bery \\ˈshrəb-(ə-)rē\\ *n, pl* **-ber·ies** : a planting or growth of shrubs

shrub·by \\ˈshrəb-ē\\ *adj* **shrub·bi·er**; **-est** **1** : consisting of or covered with shrubs **2** : resembling a shrub

shrug \\ˈshrəg\\ *vb* **shrugged**; **shrug·ging** : to raise or draw in the shoulders esp. to express lack of interest or dislike — **shrug** *n*

shrug off *vb* : to brush aside : MINIMIZE

shrunk·en \\ˈshrəng-kən\\ *adj* **1** : that has diminished or contracted esp. in size or value ⟨*shrunken* dollar⟩ **2** : that has been subjected to a shrinking process ⟨*shrunken* human heads⟩

1**shuck** \\ˈshək\\ *n* **1** : the outer covering of a nut or of Indian corn **2** : the shell of an oyster or clam

2**shuck** *vb* : to strip of shucks

1**shud·der** \\ˈshəd-ər\\ *vb* **shud·dered**; **shud·der·ing** \\-(ə-)ring\\ **1** : to tremble or shake (as with fear, horror, or aversion) : SHIVER ⟨*shuddered* to think of the accident⟩ ⟨*shudder* from cold⟩ **2** : QUIVER ⟨the train slowed up and *shuddered* to a halt⟩

2**shudder** *n* : an act of shuddering : TREMOR

1**shuf·fle** \'shəf-əl\ *vb* **shuf·fled**; **shuf·fling** \-(ə-)ling\ **1 :** to mix in a mass confusedly : JUMBLE ⟨odds and ends *shuffled* in a drawer⟩ **2 :** to put or thrust aside or under cover **3 a :** to mix cards to change their order in the pack **b :** to move about, back and forth, or from one place to another : SHIFT ⟨constantly *shuffling* chairs⟩ **4 a :** to move the feet by sliding along or dragging back and forth without lifting **b :** to perform a dance with a dragging sliding step — **shuf·fler** \-(ə-)lər\ *n*

2**shuffle** *n* **1 a :** an act of shuffling **b :** a right or turn to shuffle cards **2 :** a dragging sliding movement

shuf·fle·board \'shəf-əl-ˌbōrd, -ˌbȯrd\ *n* **1 :** a game

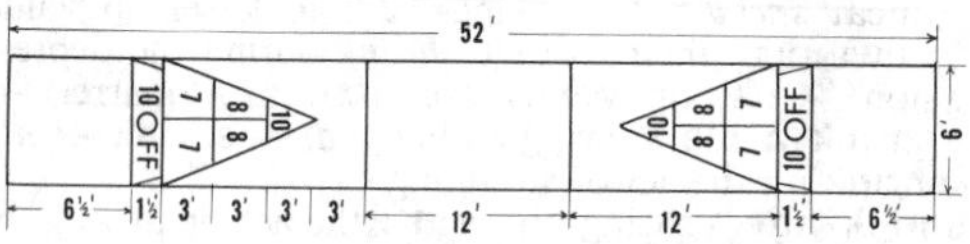

shuffleboard 2

in which players use long-handled cues to shove wooden disks into scoring areas of a diagram marked on a smooth surface **2 :** the diagram on which shuffleboard is played

shun \'shən\ *vb* **shunned**; **shun·ning :** to avoid deliberately and esp. habitually — **shun·ner** *n*

1**shunt** \'shənt\ *vb* **:** to turn off to one side : SHIFT; *esp* **:** to switch (as a train) from one track to another — **shunt·er** *n*

2**shunt** *n* **:** a means or mechanism for turning or thrusting aside; *esp* **:** a conductor joining two points in an electrical circuit so as to form a path through which a portion of the current may pass

shush \'shəsh\ *n* **:** a sibilant sound uttered to demand silence — **shush** *vb*

shut \'shət\ *vb* **shut**; **shut·ting 1 :** to close or become closed ⟨*shut* the door⟩ ⟨*shut* his eyes⟩ **2 :** to forbid entrance to or passage to or from : BAR **3 :** to hold within limits by or as if by enclosure : IMPRISON ⟨*shut* up in a stalled elevator⟩

shut·down \'shət-ˌdau̇n\ *n* **:** a temporary or permanent ending of an activity ⟨the strike forced a *shutdown* at the factory⟩

shute *var of* CHUTE

shut–in \ˌshət-ˌin\ *adj* **:** confined by illness or incapacity — **shut–in** \'shət-ˌin\ *n*

shut·off \'shət-ˌȯf\ *n* **1 :** something that shuts off **2 :** INTERRUPTION, STOPPAGE

shut·out \'shət-ˌau̇t\ *n* **:** a game or contest in which one side fails to score

shut out \-'au̇t\ *vb* **1 :** to keep out : EXCLUDE **2 :** to prevent an opponent from scoring in a game or contest

1**shut·ter** \'shət-ər\ *n* **1 :** one that shuts **2 :** a usu. movable cover for a window **3 :** the part of a camera that opens and closes to expose the film

2**shutter** *vb* **:** to close with or by shutters

shut·ter·bug \-ˌbəg\ *n* **:** a photography enthusiast

1**shut·tle** \'shət-əl\ *n* **1 a :** an instrument used in weaving to carry the thread back and forth from side to side through the threads that run lengthwise **b :** a thread holder for the lower thread of a sewing machine that carries the lower thread through a loop of the upper thread to make a stitch **2 :** a vehicle that goes back and forth regularly over a specified route ⟨a *shuttle* bus⟩ ⟨a *shuttle* train⟩

2**shuttle** *vb* **shut·tled**; **shut·tling** \-(ə-)ling\ **1 :** to move or travel back and forth frequently **2 :** to move by or as if by a shuttle

shut·tle·cock \'shət-əl-ˌkäk\ *n* **:** an object of cork stuck with feathers or of molded plastic that is struck with rackets and played back and forth in badminton

shut up *vb* **1 :** to cause a person to stop talking **2 :** to cease writing or speaking

1**shy** \'shī\ *adj* **shi·er** *or* **shy·er** \'shī(-ə)r\; **shi·est** *or* **shy·est** \'shī-əst\ **1 a :** easily frightened : TIMID **b :** having a hesitant retiring manner : BASHFUL **2 :** DEFICIENT, LACKING ⟨*shy* of ready cash⟩ — **shy·ly** \'shī-lē\ *adv* **shy·ness** \'shī-nəs\ *n*

syn SHY, BASHFUL, DIFFIDENT can mean disinclined to assert oneself in company. SHY suggests hesitance in or avoidance of the give and take of social contact; BASHFUL suggests the frightened shyness characteristic of some children and socially awkward adolescents; DIFFIDENT implies a tendency to withdraw from people because of lack of self-confidence ***ant*** obtrusive

2**shy** *vb* **shied**; **shy·ing 1 :** to draw back in sudden dislike or distaste : RECOIL ⟨*shied* from publicity⟩ **2 :** to start suddenly aside through fright or alarm ⟨the horse *shied* at a blowing paper⟩

3**shy** *n, pl* **shies :** a sudden start aside (as of a horse)

shy·ster \'shī-stər\ *n* **:** an unscrupulous lawyer or politician

si \'sē\ *n* **:** the 7th note of the diatonic scale : TI

S. I. *abbr* **1** Sandwich Islands **2** Staten Island (N.Y.)

1**Si·a·mese** \ˌsī-ə-'mēz, -'mēs\ *adj* **:** of, relating to, or characteristic of Thailand, the Thais, or their language

2**Siamese** *n, pl* **Siamese 1 :** THAI 1 **2 :** THAI 2

Siamese cat *n* **:** a slender blue-eyed short-haired domestic cat with pale body and darker ears, paws, tail, and face

Siamese cat

Siamese twin *n* [so called after Chang and Eng, a pair of such twins born in Siam (now Thailand) and widely exhibited before their death in 1874] **:** either of a pair of human or animal twins born joined together

Si·be·ri·an \sī-'bir-ē-ən\ *adj* **:** of, relating to, or characteristic of Siberia or its people — **Siberian** *n*

Siberian husky *n* **:** any of a breed of medium-sized compact dogs developed as sled dogs and resembling the Alaskan malamutes

1**sib·i·lant** \'sib-ə-lənt\ *adj* **:** having, containing, or producing the sound of or a sound resembling that of the *s* or the *sh* in *sash*

2**sibilant** *n* **:** a sibilant speech sound (as English \s\, \z\, \sh\, \zh\, \ch (=tsh)\, or \j (=dzh)\)

sib·ling \'sib-ling\ *n* **:** one of the offspring of a pair of parents : a brother or sister without regard to sex

sib·yl \'sib-əl\ *n, often cap* **1 :** any of several ancient prophetesses **2 :** a female prophet

Si·cil·ian \sə-'sil-yən\ *adj* **:** of, relating to, or characteristic of Sicily or its people — **Sicilian** *n*

sick \'sik\ *adj* **1 a :** affected with disease or ill health

ə abut	ər further	a back	ā bake	
ä cot, cart	au̇ out	ch chin	e less	ē easy
g gift	i trip	ī life	j joke	ng sing	ō flow
ȯ flaw	ȯi coin	th thin	th this	ü loot
u̇ foot	y yet	yü few	yu̇ furious	zh vision

: AILING **b** : of, relating to, or intended for use in sickness ⟨*sick* pay⟩ ⟨a *sick* ward⟩ **c** : NAUSEATED, QUEASY ⟨*sick* at his stomach⟩ **2 a** : sickened by strong emotion (as shame or fear) **b** : SATIATED, SURFEITED ⟨*sick* of flattery⟩ **c** : depressed and longing for something ⟨*sick* at heart⟩ **3** : mentally or emotionally unsound or disordered ⟨*sick* thoughts⟩

sick bay *n* : a compartment in a ship used as a hospital

sick·bed \'sik-ˌbed\ *n* : the bed of a sick person

sick·en \'sik-ən\ *vb* **sick·ened**; **sick·en·ing** \-(ə-)ning\ : to make or become sick — **sick·en·er** \-(ə-)nər\ *n*

sick·en·ing *adj* : causing sickness : NAUSEATING — **sick·en·ing·ly** \'sik-(ə-)ning-lē\ *adv*

sick·ish \'sik-ish\ *adj* **1** : somewhat nauseated : QUEASY **2** : somewhat sickening ⟨a *sickish* odor⟩ — **sick·ish·ly** *adv*

sick·le \'sik-əl\ *n* **1** : an agricultural tool consisting of a curved metal blade with a short handle **2** : a cutting mechanism (as of a combine) consisting of a bar with a series of cutters

sickle cell *n* : an abnormal red blood cell of crescent shape

sickle–cell anemia *n* : a chronic anemia that occurs esp. in Negroes and is characterized by sickle cells in the circulating blood

sick·ly \'sik-lē\ *adj* **sick·li·er**; **-est** **1** : somewhat unwell; *esp* : habitually or often ailing **2** : produced by or associated with sickness ⟨a *sickly* complexion⟩ ⟨a *sickly* appetite⟩ **3** : producing or tending to sickness ⟨a *sickly* climate⟩ **4 a** : LANGUID, PALE ⟨a *sickly* flame⟩ **b** : lacking in vigor : WEAK ⟨a *sickly* plant⟩ — **sick·li·ly** \-lə-lē\ *adv*

sick·ness \'sik-nəs\ *n* **1** : ill health : ILLNESS **2** : a specific disease : MALADY **3** : NAUSEA

sick·room \'sik-ˌrüm, -ˌru̇m\ *n* : a room in which a person is confined by sickness

[1]**side** \'sīd\ *n* **1 a** : the right or left part of the trunk or wall of the body ⟨struck him in the *side*⟩ **b** : the entire right or left half of the animal body ⟨a *side* of beef⟩ **2** : a place, space, or direction away from or beyond a center point or line ⟨set it to one *side*⟩ **3** : a surface forming a border or face of an object ⟨swim to the *side* of the pool⟩ **4** : an outer portion of a thing considered as facing in a particular direction ⟨the upper *side*⟩ **5** : a slope or declivity of a hill or ridge **6 a** : a bounding line of a geometrical figure ⟨*side* of a square⟩ **b** : one of the surfaces that delimit a solid **c** : either surface of a thin object ⟨one *side* of a record⟩ **7** : a body of partisans or contestants ⟨victory for neither *side*⟩ **8** : a line of descent traced through either parent **9** : an aspect or part of something held to be contrasted with some other aspect or part ⟨the better *side* of his nature⟩ — **on the side** **1** : in addition to the main portion ⟨an order of french fries *on the side*⟩ **2** : in addition to a principal occupation ⟨selling insurance *on the side*⟩

[2]**side** *adj* **1** : of, relating to, or situated on the side ⟨*side* window⟩ **2** : directed toward or from the side ⟨*side* thrust⟩ ⟨*side* wind⟩ **3 a** : in addition to or secondary to something primary : INCIDENTAL ⟨*side* issue⟩ **b** : additional to the main portion ⟨*side* order of french fries⟩

[3]**side** *vb* **1** : to take sides : join or form sides ⟨*sided* with the rebels⟩ **2** : to furnish with sides or siding ⟨*side* a house⟩

side arm *n* : a weapon (as a sword, revolver, or bayonet) worn at the side or in the belt

side·board \'sīd-ˌbōrd, -ˌbȯrd\ *n* : a piece of dining-room furniture with drawers and compartments for dishes, silverware, and table linen

side·burns \'sīd-ˌbərnz\ *n pl* : hair growing on the side of the face in front of the ears

side·car \-ˌkär\ *n* : a one-wheeled car attached to the side of a motorcycle

sid·ed \'sīd-əd\ *adj* : having sides often of a specified number or kind ⟨glass-*sided*⟩ ⟨4-*sided* figures⟩

side dish *n* : food served in addition to the main course in a separate dish

side effect *n* : a secondary and usu. adverse effect ⟨worried about the *side effects* of the new drug⟩

side·kick \'sīd-ˌkik\ *n* : a person closely associated with another as subordinate or partner

side·light \-ˌlīt\ *n* **1** : light from the side **2** : incidental or additional information **3** : the red light on the port bow or the green light on the starboard bow carried by ships under way at night

side·line \-ˌlīn\ *n* **1** : a line at right angles to a goal line or end line and marking a side of a field of play **2 a** : a line of goods sold in addition to one's principal line **b** : a business or activity pursued in addition to one's regular occupation ⟨repaired television sets as a *sideline*⟩ **3** : the standpoint of persons not immediately participating or concerned ⟨watch from the *sidelines*⟩

[1]**side·long** \-ˌlȯng\ *adv* **1** : OBLIQUELY, SIDEWAYS ⟨glanced *sidelong* at him⟩ **2** : on the side ⟨lay it *sidelong*⟩

[2]**sidelong** *adj* **1** : lying or inclining to one side : SLANTING **2 a** : directed to one side ⟨*sidelong* looks⟩ **b** : indirect rather than straightforward

side·piece \'sīd-ˌpēs\ *n* : a piece contained in or forming the side of something

si·de·re·al \sī-'dir-ē-əl\ *adj* **1** : of or relating to the stars or constellations **2** : measured by the apparent motion of fixed stars ⟨*sidereal* time⟩ ⟨a *sidereal* day⟩

sid·er·ite \'sid-ə-ˌrīt\ *n* : a natural carbonate of iron that is a valuable iron ore

side·sad·dle \'sīd-ˌsad-əl\ *n* : a saddle for women in which the rider sits with both legs on the same side of the horse — **sidesaddle** *adv*

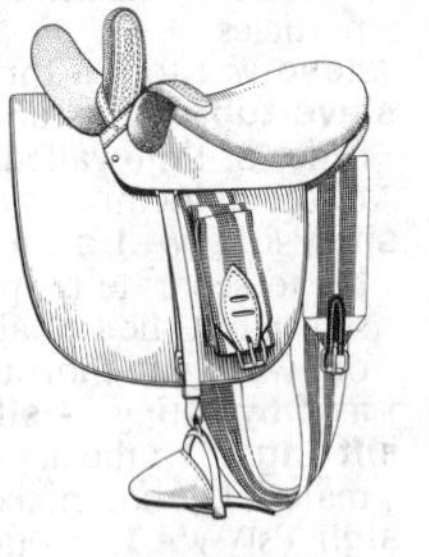

sidesaddle

side·show \-ˌshō\ *n* : a minor show offered in addition to a main exhibition ⟨a circus *sideshow*⟩

side·slip \-ˌslip\ *vb* : to skid sideways — **sideslip** *n*

side·spin \-ˌspin\ *n* : a rotary motion that causes a ball to revolve horizontally

side·step \'sīd-ˌstep\ *vb* **1** : to take a side step **2** : to avoid by a step to the side ⟨*sidestepped* the punch⟩ **3** : to avoid meeting issues : EVADE ⟨adept at *sidestepping* awkward questions⟩

side step *n* **1** : a step aside (as in boxing to avoid a blow) **2** : a step taken sideways (as in climbing on skis)

side·stroke \-ˌstrōk\ *n* : a stroke made by a swimmer while lying on his side in which the arms are moved without breaking water while the legs do a scissors kick

side·swipe \-ˌswīp\ *vb* : to strike with a glancing blow along the side ⟨*sideswiped* a parked car⟩

[1]**side·track** \-ˌtrak\ *n* : SIDING 1

[2]**sidetrack** *vb* **1** : to transfer from a main railroad line to a siding ⟨*sidetrack* a train⟩ **2** : to turn aside from a main purpose or use

side·walk \'sīd-ˌwȯk\ *n* : a usu. paved walk for pedestrians at the side of a street

side·wall \-ˌwȯl\ *n* **1** : a wall forming the side of something **2** : the side of an automotive tire between the tread shoulder and the rim bead
side·ward \-wərd\ *or* **side·wards** \-wərdz\ *adv or adj* : toward the side
side·ways \ˈsīd-ˌwāz\ *adv or adj* **1** : from one side **2** : with one side forward **3** : toward one side
side·wind·er \-ˌwīn-dər\ *n* **1** : a heavy swinging blow from the side **2** : a small rattlesnake of the southwestern U.S. that moves over sand by thrusting its body diagonally forward in flat loops using its neck as an anchor
side·wise \-ˌwīz\ *adv or adj* : SIDEWAYS
sid·ing \ˈsīd-ing\ *n* **1** : a short railroad track connected with the main track by switches at one or more places **2** : material (as boards or metal pieces) used to cover the outside walls of frame buildings
si·dle \ˈsīd-əl\ *vb* **si·dled**; **si·dling** \-(ə-)ling\ : to go or move with one side foremost
siege \ˈsēj\ *n* [from Old French, "military blockade", literally "act of sitting", from Latin *sedēre* "to sit"] **1** : a military blockade of a fortified place **2** : a continued attempt to gain possession of something **3** : a persistent attack (as of illness) ⟨a *siege* of the flu⟩
si·en·na \sē-ˈen-ə\ *n* : an earthy substance that is brownish yellow when raw and orange red or reddish brown when burnt and is used as a pigment
si·er·ra \sē-ˈer-ə\ *n* [from Spanish, literally "saw", from Latin *serra*] : a range of mountains esp. with jagged peaks
si·es·ta \sē-ˈes-tə\ *n* [from Spanish, from Latin *sexta* (*hora*) "noon", literally "sixth hour"] : an afternoon nap or rest
[1]**sieve** \ˈsiv\ *n* : a device with meshes or perforations through which finer particles of a mixture (as of ashes, flour, or sand) are passed to separate them from coarser ones, through which the liquid is drained from liquid-containing material, or through which soft materials are forced for reduction to fine particles
[2]**sieve** *vb* : to put through a sieve : SIFT
sieve tube *n* : a tube that consists of an end-to-end series of thin-walled living cells and is characteristic of the phloem
sift \ˈsift\ *vb* **1 a** : to put through a sieve ⟨*sift* flour⟩ **b** : to separate by putting through a sieve **2 a** : to screen out the valuable or good : SELECT **b** : to study or investigate thoroughly : PROBE **3** : to scatter by or as if by sifting — **sift·er** *n*
sift·ing *n* **1** : the act or process of sifting **2** *pl* : sifted material ⟨bran mixed with *siftings*⟩
sigh \ˈsī\ *vb* **1** : to take a deep audible breath (as in weariness or grief) **2** : to make a sound like sighing ⟨wind *sighing* in the branches⟩ **3** : GRIEVE, YEARN ⟨*sighing* for the days of his youth⟩ **4** : to express by sighs — **sigh** *n*
[1]**sight** \ˈsīt\ *n* **1** : something that is seen : SPECTACLE **2 a** : a thing that is worth seeing **b** : something ludicrous or disorderly in appearance **3** : the process, power, or function of seeing; *esp* : the animal sense of which the eye is the receptor organ and by which the position, shape, and color of objects are perceived **4** : the act of looking at or beholding **5 a** : INSPECTION, PERUSAL ⟨this letter is for your *sight* only⟩ **b** : VIEW, GLIMPSE **6 a** : a perceiving of an object by the eye **b** : the range of vision ⟨stay out of my *sight*⟩ **7** : a device (as a small metal bead on a gun barrel) that aids the eye in aiming or in determining the direction of an object
[2]**sight** *adj* : based on recognition or comprehension without previous study ⟨*sight* translation⟩
[3]**sight** *vb* **1** : to get sight of **2** : to look at through or as if through a sight **3** : to aim by means of sights
sight·ed \ˈsīt-əd\ *adj* : having sight ⟨clear-*sighted*⟩
sight·less \ˈsīt-ləs\ *adj* : lacking sight : BLIND — **sight·less·ness** *n*
sight·ly \ˈsīt-lē\ *adj* **1** : pleasing to the sight : HANDSOME **2** : affording a good view ⟨a *sightly* location overlooking the valley⟩ — **sight·li·ness** *n*
sight–read \ˈsīt-ˌrēd\ *vb* **-read** \-ˌred\; **-read·ing** \-ˌrēd-ing\ : to read a foreign language or perform music without previous preparation or study
sight–see·ing \ˈsīt-ˌsē-ing\ *n* : the act or pastime of seeing places of interest — **sight–seeing** *adj* — **sight·se·er** \ˈsīt-ˌsē-ər, -ˌsi(-ə)r\ *n*
sight unseen *adv* : without inspection or appraisal ⟨bought it *sight unseen*⟩
sig·ma \ˈsig-mə\ *n* : the 18th letter of the Greek alphabet — Σ or σ or ς
[1]**sign** \ˈsīn\ *n* **1 a** : a motion or gesture by which a thought is expressed or a command made known ⟨made a *sign* that he was ready⟩ **b** : something that stands for something else : SYMBOL ⟨made a peace *sign*⟩ **2** : a mark having a conventional meaning and used in place of words or to represent a complex notion **3** : one of the 12 divisions of the zodiac **4 a** : a character (as a flat or sharp) used in musical notation **b** : a character (as ÷ or $\sqrt{\ }$) indicating a mathematical operation; *also* : one of two characters + and − characterizing a number as positive or negative **5 a** : a lettered board or other display used to identify or advertise something ⟨a "For Sale" *sign*⟩ **b** : a posted command, warning, or direction ⟨road *signs*⟩ **6 a** : something that serves to indicate the presence or existence of something : TOKEN ⟨no *sign* of life⟩ ⟨first *signs* of spring⟩ **b** : PRESAGE, OMEN **c** : an objective evidence of plant or animal disease — compare SYMPTOM
[2]**sign** *vb* **1 a** : to place a sign upon **b** : to represent or indicate by a sign **2** : to affix a signature to **3** : to communicate by making a sign **4** : to hire by getting the signature of ⟨*sign* him on⟩ — **sign·er** *n*
[1]**sig·nal** \ˈsig-nəl\ *n* **1 a** : an act, event, or word that serves to start some action **b** : something that incites to action ⟨one blow was the *signal* for a general fight⟩ **2** : a sound or gesture made to give warning or command **3** : an object placed to convey notice or warning ⟨a traffic *signal*⟩ **4 a** : the message, sound, or effect transmitted in electronic communication (as radio or television) **b** : a radio wave or electric current that transmits a message or effect (as in radio or television)
[2]**signal** *vb* **-naled** *or* **-nalled**; **-nal·ing** *or* **-nal·ling 1** : to notify by a signal **2** : to communicate by signals — **sig·nal·er** *n*
[3]**signal** *adj* **1** : distinguished from the ordinary : OUTSTANDING ⟨*signal* achievement⟩ **2** : used in signaling ⟨*signal* beacon⟩ — **sig·nal·ly** \-nə-lē\ *adv*
sig·nal·ize \ˈsig-nə-ˌlīz\ *vb* : to make conspicuous : DISTINGUISH
sig·na·ture \ˈsig-nə-ˌchu̇r, -chər\ *n* **1** : the name of a person written with his own hand **2** : a notation used in music to indicate the key or the time **3** : a tune, musical number, or sound effect or in television a characteristic title or picture used to identify a program, entertainer, or orchestra

sign·board \'sīn-ˌbōrd, -ˌbȯrd\ *n* : a board bearing a notice or sign

sig·net \'sig-nət\ *n* : a seal used in place of a signature on a document

sig·nif·i·cance \sig-'nif-i-kən(t)s\ *n* **1** : MEANING **2** : IMPORTANCE, CONSEQUENCE

sig·nif·i·cant \-kənt\ *adj* **1** : having meaning : SUGGESTIVE, EXPRESSIVE **2** : suggesting or containing a disguised or special meaning **3** : IMPORTANT, WEIGHTY **4** : of, relating to, or being significant figures — **sig·nif·i·cant·ly** *adv*

significant figures *n pl* : the figures of a number beginning with the first figure to the left that is not zero and ending with the last figure to the right that is not zero or is a zero that is considered to be exact — called also *significant digits*

sig·ni·fi·ca·tion \ˌsig-nə-fə-'kā-shən\ *n* **1** : a signifying by signs esp. to convey meaning **2** : MEANING, IMPORT

sig·ni·fi·er \'sig-nə-ˌfī(-ə)r\ *n* : one that signifies : SIGN

sig·ni·fy \'sig-nə-ˌfī\ *vb* **-fied**; **-fy·ing** **1** : MEAN, DENOTE **2** : to show esp. by a conventional token (as word, signal, or gesture) : make known **3** : to have significance or importance

sign language *n* : a system of hand gestures used for communication by the deaf or by people speaking different languages

sign of the cross : a gesture of the hand forming a cross esp. on forehead, shoulders, and breast to profess Christian faith or invoke divine protection or blessing

sign·post \'sīn-ˌpōst\ *n* : a post with a sign on it to direct travelers

si·lage \'sī-lij\ *n* : fodder converted into succulent feed for livestock through fermentation (as in a silo)

[1]**si·lence** \'sī-lən(t)s\ *n* **1** : the state of keeping or being silent **2** : absence of sound or noise : STILLNESS **3** : absence of mention : SECRECY

[2]**silence** *vb* **1** : to stop the noise or speech of : reduce to silence **2** : to restrain from expression : SUPPRESS

si·lenc·er \'sī-lən-sər\ *n* : one that silences; *esp* : a silencing device for small arms

si·lent \'sī-lənt\ *adj* **1** : making no utterance : MUTE, SPEECHLESS ⟨stood *silent* before his accusers⟩ **2** : indisposed to speak : TACITURN ⟨she is a very *silent* girl⟩ **3** : free from sound or noise : STILL **4** : performed or borne without utterance : UNSPOKEN ⟨*silent* disapproval⟩ ⟨*silent* grief⟩ **5 a** : making no mention ⟨history is *silent* about this man⟩ **b** : INACTIVE; *esp* : taking no active part in the conduct of a business ⟨*silent* partner⟩ **6** : UNPRONOUNCED ⟨*silent b* in *doubt*⟩ — **si·lent·ly** *adv*

syn SILENT, RETICENT, TACITURN can mean not inclined to talk. SILENT suggests avoidance of saying more than is necessary, whether in general or on some particular occasion; RETICENT implies a reluctance to speak esp. about one's personal affairs; TACITURN implies a temperamental dislike of talking to others at all and is apt to suggest sullenness and unsociability ***ant*** talkative

silent butler *n* : a receptacle with hinged lid for collecting table crumbs and the contents of ash trays

[1]**sil·hou·ette** \ˌsil-ə-'wet\ *n* [from French; named after Étienne de *Silhouette* (1709–1767) French controller general of finances, whose petty economies were much resented] **1** : a drawing or cutout of the outline of an object filled in with black; *esp* : a profile portrait of this kind **2** : characteristic shape of an object (as an airplane) seen or as if seen against the light

[2]**silhouette** *vb* **1** : to represent by a silhouette **2** : to project upon a background like a silhouette

sil·i·ca \'sil-i-kə\ *n* : the dioxide of silicon occurring in crystalline, amorphous, and impure forms (as in quartz, opal, and sand)

sil·i·cate \'sil-i-kət, 'sil-ə-ˌkāt\ *n* : a compound formed from silica and any of various oxides of metals and used esp. in building materials (as bricks)

si·li·ceous *also* **si·li·cious** \sə-'lish-əs\ *adj* : of, relating to, or containing silica or a silicate

sil·i·con \'sil-i-kən, 'sil-ə-ˌkän\ *n* [from *silica* (from Latin *silic-*, stem of *silex* "flint", "quartz") with the ending found in *carbon*, a closely related element] : a nonmetallic element that occurs combined as the most abundant element next to oxygen in the earth's crust and is used esp. in alloys — see ELEMENT table

silicon carbide *n* : a hard brittle crystalline compound of silicon and carbon used as an abrasive

silicon dioxide *n* : SILICA

sil·i·cone \'sil-ə-ˌkōn\ *n* : any of various polymeric organic silicon compounds obtained as oily or greasy substances or plastics and used esp. for water-resistant and heat-resistant lubricants, varnishes, binders, and electric insulators

sil·i·co·sis \ˌsil-ə-'kō-səs\ *n* : a disease of the lungs marked by scar tissue in the lungs and shortness of breath and caused by prolonged inhaling of silica dusts

silk \'silk\ *n* **1** : a fine continuous protein fiber produced by various insect larvae usu. for cocoons; *esp* : a lustrous tough elastic fiber produced by silkworms and used for textiles **2 a** : thread, yarn, or fabric made from silk **b** : a garment of silk **3** : a silky material or filament (as that produced by a spider) ⟨milkweed *silk*⟩; *esp* : the styles of an ear of Indian corn — **silk** *adj*

S

silk cotton *n* : the silky or cottony covering of seeds of a silk-cotton tree; *esp* : KAPOK

silk–cotton tree *n* : any of various tropical trees having large fruits with the seeds enveloped by silk cotton

silk·en \'sil-kən\ *adj* **1** : made or consisting of silk **2** : resembling silk esp. in soft lustrous smoothness

silk moth *n* : the silkworm moth

silk·worm \'silk-ˌwərm\ *n* : a moth larva that spins a large amount of strong silk in constructing its cocoon; *esp* : the rough wrinkled hairless yellowish caterpillar of an Asiatic moth grown as a source of silk

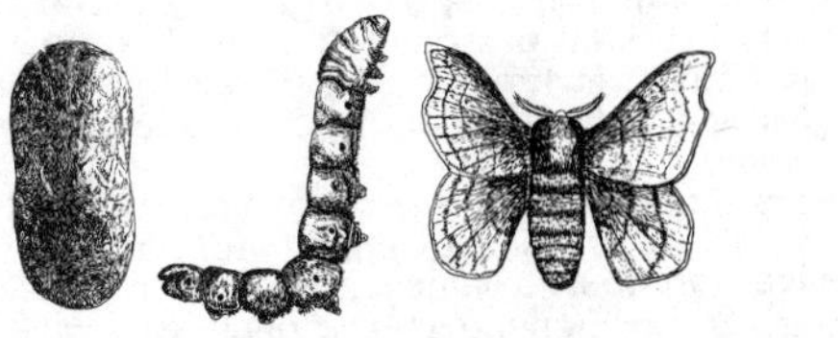

silkworm: left, cocoon; center, larva; right, adult female

silky \'sil-kē\ *adj* **silk·i·er**; **-est** **1** : SILKEN **2** : having or covered with fine soft hairs, plumes, or scales — **silk·i·ly** \-kə-lē\ *adv*

sill \'sil\ *n* **1** : a horizontal supporting piece (as a timber) at the base of a structure (as of a house or bridge) **2** : the horizontal member at the base of a window **3** : the timber or stone at the foot of a door : THRESHOLD

sil·ly \'sil-ē\ *adj* **sil·li·er; -est** [from Middle English *sely* meaning originally "happy", then "innocent", then "feeble", "pathetic"] **1** : weak in intellect : FOOLISH **2** : contrary to reason : ABSURD **3** : TRIFLING, FRIVOLOUS — **sil·li·ly** \'sil-ə-lē\ *adv* — **sil·li·ness** \'sil-ē-nəs\ *n*

si·lo \'sī-lō\ *n, pl* **silos** **1** : a trench, pit, or esp. a tall cylinder (as of wood or concrete) used for making and storing silage **2** : a deep bin for housing a missile underground

silo 1

1silt \'silt\ *n* **1** : loose sedimentary material with rock particles usu. 1/20 millimeter or less in diameter; *also* : soil containing 80 percent or more of such silt and less than 12 percent of clay **2** : a deposit of sediment (as by a river) — **silty** \'sil-tē\ *adj*

2silt *vb* : to become or make choked, obstructed, or covered with silt

Si·lu·ri·an \sī-'lu̇r-ē-ən, sə-\ *n* : the period of the Paleozoic era between the Ordovician and Devonian marked by the beginning of coral-reef building and the appearance of very large crustaceans; *also* : the corresponding system of rocks — **Silurian** *adj*

silvan *var of* SYLVAN

1sil·ver \'sil-vər\ *n* **1** : a white ductile and malleable metallic element that takes a high polish and has the highest thermal and electric conductivity of any substance — see ELEMENT table **2 a** : coin made of silver **b** : articles (as tableware) made of or plated with silver **3** : a medium gray

2silver *adj* **1** : relating to, made of, or yielding silver ⟨*silver* jewelry⟩ ⟨*silver* ore⟩ **2** : SILVERY 1

3silver *vb* **sil·vered; sil·ver·ing** \'silv-(ə-)riŋ\ **1 a** : to cover with silver (as by electroplating) **b** : to coat with a substance (as a metal) resembling silver ⟨*silver* a glass with an amalgam⟩ **2** : to give a silvery appearance to — **sil·ver·er** \'sil-vər-ər\ *n*

silver bromide *n* : a compound that is extremely sensitive to light and is much used in the preparation of photographic emulsions

silver chloride *n* : a compound sensitive to light and used esp. for photographic emulsions

sil·ver·fish \'sil-vər-,fish\ *n* **1** : any of various silvery fishes (as a tarpon) **2** : any of various small primitive wingless insects; *esp* : one found in houses and sometimes injurious to sized papers or starched clothes

silver fox *n* : a color phase of the common red fox in which the pelt is black tipped with white

silver iodide *n* : a compound that is sensitive to light and is used in photography, rainmaking, and medicine

silver nitrate *n* : a chemical compound that is used esp. in photography and in medicine

silver plate *n* **1** : a plating of silver **2** : domestic flatware and hollow ware made of or plated with silver

sil·ver·smith \'sil-vər-,smith\ *n* : a person who makes articles of silver

sil·ver·ware \-,wa(ə)r, -,we(ə)r\ *n* : SILVER PLATE 2

sil·very \'silv-(ə-)rē\ *adj* **1** : having the white lustrous sheen of silver **2** : containing or consisting of silver

sim *abbr* simile

Sim·chas To·rah \,sim-häs-'tōr-ə, -'tȯr-\ *n* : a Jewish holiday observed in October or November in celebration of the completion of the annual reading of the Torah

1sim·i·an \'sim-ē-ən\ *adj* : of, relating to, or resembling monkeys or apes

2simian *n* : MONKEY, APE

sim·i·lar \'sim-ə-lər\ *adj* **1** : marked by correspondence or resemblance **2** : not differing in shape but only in size or position ⟨*similar* triangles⟩ — **sim·i·lar·ly** *adv*

sim·i·lar·i·ty \,sim-ə-'lar-ət-ē\ *n, pl* **-ties** **1** : the quality or state of being similar : RESEMBLANCE **2** : a point in which things are similar : CORRESPONDENCE

sim·i·le \'sim-ə-(,)lē\ *n* : a figure of speech in which things different in kind or quality are compared by the use of the word *like* or *as* (as in *eyes like stars*)

si·mil·i·tude \sə-'mil-ə-,t(y)üd\ *n* **1** : a visible likeness : IMAGE **2** : an imaginative comparison **3** : SIMILARITY

sim·mer \'sim-ər\ *vb* **sim·mered; sim·mer·ing** \-(ə-)riŋ\ **1** : to stew gently below or just at the boiling point **2** : to be at the point of violently expressing one's feelings ⟨*simmered* with fury at the insult⟩ — **simmer** *n*

si·mo·nize \'sī-mə-,nīz\ *vb* : to polish with or as if with wax

si·mo·ny \'sī-mə-nē, 'sim-ə-\ *n* : the buying or selling of a church office

si·moom \sə-'müm, sī-\ *or* **si·moon** \-'mün\ *n* : a hot dry violent wind laden with dust from Asian and African deserts

1sim·per \'sim-pər\ *vb* **sim·pered; sim·per·ing** \-p(ə-)riŋ\ : to smile in a foolish affected manner — **sim·per·er** \-pər-ər\ *n*

2simper *n* : a simpered smile : SMIRK

sim·ple \'sim-pəl\ *adj* **sim·pler** \-p(ə-)lər\; **sim·plest** \-p(ə-)ləst\ [from Old French, "plain", "uncomplicated", from Latin *simplus*, literally "one-fold", from the roots found in English *same* and *fold* respectively] **1** : free from guile or vanity : INNOCENT **2** : of humble origin ⟨*simple* folks⟩ **3** : lacking in education, experience, or intelligence **4 a** : free from complexity or complications ⟨a *simple* melody⟩ ⟨neat *simple* clothing⟩ **b** : consisting of only one main clause and no subordinate clauses ⟨*simple* sentence⟩ **5** : not compound ⟨a *simple* eye⟩ ⟨*simple* interest⟩ **6 a** : not subdivided into branches or leaflets ⟨*simple* leaf⟩ **b** : developing from a single ovary ⟨*simple* fruits⟩ **7** : UTTER, ABSOLUTE ⟨the *simple* truth⟩ **8** : STRAIGHTFORWARD, EASY ⟨a *simple* explanation⟩ **9** : having a relatively small and uncomplicated molecule ⟨*simple* sugars⟩ — **sim·ple·ness** \-pəl-nəs\ *n*

syn SIMPLE, EASY can mean presenting no great difficulty. SIMPLE implies freedom from problematical complexity or subtlety ⟨*simple* arithmetic⟩; EASY applies more broadly to anything that is gotten without great effort or application ⟨won an *easy* victory⟩ ***ant*** complicated, difficult

simple event *n* : one of the set of possible outcomes of a statistical experiment

simple fraction *n* : a fraction having whole numbers for the numerator and denominator — compare COMPLEX FRACTION

simple fracture *n* : a breaking of a bone in such a way that the skin is not broken and bone fragments do not protrude

ə abut	ər further	a back	ā bake	
ä cot, cart	au̇ out	ch chin	e less	ē easy
g gift	i trip	ī life	j joke	ŋ sing
ō flow	ȯ flaw	ȯi coin	th thin	th this
ü loot	u̇ foot	y yet	yü few	yu̇ furious
zh vision				

simple interest *n* : interest paid or computed on the original principal only of a loan or on the amount of an account

simple machine *n* : any of six elementary mechanisms having the elements of which all machines are composed and comprising the lever, the wheel and axle, the pulley, the inclined plane, the wedge, and the screw

sim·ple·mind·ed \\ˌsim-pəl-ˈmīn-dəd\\ *adj* **1** : not subtle **2** : FOOLISH

simplest form *n* : LOWEST TERMS

sim·ple·ton \\ˈsim-pəl-tən\\ *n* : a person lacking in common sense

sim·plic·i·ty \\sim-ˈplis-ət-ē\\ *n, pl* **-ties** **1** : the quality or state of being simple **2** : HONESTY, STRAIGHTFORWARDNESS **3 a** : directness or clarity of expression **b** : PLAINNESS **4** : FOLLY, SILLINESS

sim·pli·fy \\ˈsim-plə-ˌfī\\ *vb* **-fied**; **-fy·ing** : to make simple or simpler — **sim·pli·fi·ca·tion** \\ˌsim-plə-fə-ˈkā-shən\\ *n* — **sim·pli·fi·er** \\ˈsim-plə-ˌfī(-ə)r\\ *n*

sim·ply \\ˈsim-plē\\ *adv* **1 a** : CLEARLY ⟨stated the directions *simply*⟩ **b** : PLAINLY ⟨*simply* dressed⟩ **c** : DIRECTLY, CANDIDLY ⟨told the story as *simply* as a child would⟩ **2 a** : MERELY, SOLELY ⟨eats *simply* to keep alive⟩ **b** : REALLY, TRULY ⟨*simply* marvelous⟩

sim·u·late \\ˈsim-yə-ˌlāt\\ *vb* : to give the appearance or effect of : IMITATE — **sim·u·la·tor** \\-ˌlāt-ər\\ *n*

sim·u·la·tion \\ˌsim-yə-ˈlā-shən\\ *n* **1** : the act or process of simulating **2** : a sham object : COUNTERFEIT

si·mul·ta·ne·ous \\ˌsī-məl-ˈtā-nē-əs\\ *adj* **1** : existing or occurring at the same time : COINCIDENT **2** : satisfied by the same values of the variables ⟨*simultaneous* equations⟩ — **si·mul·ta·ne·ous·ly** *adv*

[1]**sin** \\ˈsin\\ *n* **1** : an offense against God **2** : MISDEED, FAULT

[2]**sin** *vb* **sinned**; **sin·ning** : to commit a sin

sin *abbr* sine

[1]**since** \\(ˈ)sin(t)s\\ *adv* **1** : from a definite past time until now ⟨has stayed there ever *since*⟩ **2** : before the present time : AGO ⟨long *since* dead⟩ **3** : after a time in the past : SUBSEQUENTLY ⟨has *since* become rich⟩

[2]**since** *prep* : from or after a specified time in the past ⟨improvements made *since* 1928⟩ ⟨has been happy *since* then⟩

[3]**since** *conj* **1** : at a time or times in the past after or later than ⟨has held two jobs *since* he graduated⟩ **2** : from the time in the past when ⟨ever *since* he was a child⟩ **3** : in view of the fact that : BECAUSE ⟨*since* it was raining he wore a hat⟩

sin·cere \\sin-ˈsi(ə)r\\ *adj* **1** : TRUSTWORTHY, STRAIGHTFORWARD ⟨a *sincere* friend⟩ ⟨a *sincere* interest in study⟩ **2** : GENUINE, REAL ⟨a *sincere* work of art⟩ ***syn*** see HONEST ***ant*** insincere — **sin·cere·ly** *adv* — **sin·cer·i·ty** \\-ˈser-ət-ē\\ *n*

sine \\ˈsīn\\ *n* : a function that for an acute angle in a right triangle is the ratio of the side opposite the angle to the hypotenuse

si·ne·cure \\ˈsī-ni-ˌkyu̇r, ˈsin-i-\\ *n* : an office or position that requires little or no work

sin·ew \\ˈsin-yü, ˈsin-ü\\ *n* **1** : TENDON; *esp* : one dressed for use as a cord or thread **2** : solid resilient strength : POWER

sin·ewy \\ˈsin-(y)ə-wē\\ *adj* **1** : full of sinews : TOUGH, STRINGY ⟨*sinewy* meat⟩ **2** : STRONG ⟨*sinewy* arms⟩

sin·ful \\ˈsin-fəl\\ *adj* : marked by or full of sin : WICKED — **sin·ful·ly** \\-fə-lē\\ *adv* — **sin·ful·ness** *n*

[1]**sing** \\ˈsing\\ *vb* **sang** \\ˈsang\\ *or* **sung** \\ˈsəng\\; **sung**; **sing·ing** \\ˈsing-ing\\ **1 a** : to produce musical sounds by means of the voice ⟨*sing* for joy⟩ **b** : to utter with musical sounds ⟨*sing* a song⟩ **c** : CHANT, INTONE ⟨*sing* mass⟩ **2** : to make pleasing musical sounds ⟨birds *singing* at dawn⟩ **3** : to make a slight shrill sound ⟨a kettle *singing* on the stove⟩ **4** : to express vividly and enthusiastically ⟨*sing* her praises⟩ **5** : BUZZ, RING ⟨ears *singing* from the sudden descent⟩ **6** : to act on or affect by singing ⟨*sing* a baby to sleep⟩ ⟨*sing* the blues away⟩ **7** : to call aloud : cry out ⟨*sing* out when you find them⟩ — **sing·a·ble** \\ˈsing-ə-bəl\\ *adj*

[2]**sing** *n* : a singing esp. in company ⟨a community *sing*⟩

sing *abbr* singular

[1]**singe** \\ˈsinj\\ *vb* **singed** \\ˈsinjd\\; **singe·ing** \\ˈsin-jing\\ : to burn superficially or lightly; *esp* : to remove hair, down, or fuzz from usu. by passing briefly over a flame

syn SINGE, SCORCH, CHAR can mean to burn less than completely. SINGE suggests a very light burning (as from passing quickly over a flame) usu. of hair, down, or fuzz; SCORCH suggests a superficial burning serious enough to change the color and flavor or texture of the affected part; CHAR suggests an even more serious burning that reduces a usu. outside area to carbon or cinder

[2]**singe** *n* : a slight burn : SCORCH

[1]**sing·er** \\ˈsing-ər\\ *n* : one that sings

[2]**sing·er** \\ˈsin-jər\\ *n* : one that singes

[1]**sin·gle** \\ˈsing-gəl\\ *adj* **1** : UNMARRIED **2** : being alone : being the only one **3** : consisting of one ⟨*single* standard⟩ ⟨holds to a *single* ideal⟩ **4** : having but one whorl of petals or ray flowers ⟨a *single* rose⟩ **5 a** : consisting of a separate whole : INDIVIDUAL ⟨each *single* citizen⟩ **b** : of, relating to, or involving only one person **6** : FRANK, HONEST ⟨a *single* devotion⟩ **7** : UNBROKEN, UNDIVIDED ⟨a *single* world⟩ **8** : engaged in man to man ⟨fight in *single* combat⟩ **9** : designed for the use of one person or family only ⟨a *single* house⟩ — **sin·gle·ness** *n*

[2]**single** *n* **1** : a separate individual person or thing **2** : a hit in baseball that enables a batter to reach first base safely **3** *pl* : a game (as of tennis or golf) between two players

[3]**single** *vb* **sin·gled**; **sin·gling** \\ˈsing-g(ə-)ling\\ **1** : to select or distinguish (a person or thing) from a number or group ⟨*single* out the runt of the litter⟩ **2** : to make a single in baseball

sin·gle–breast·ed \\ˌsing-gəl-ˈbres-təd\\ *adj* : having a center closing with one row of buttons and no lap ⟨*single-breasted* coat⟩

single file *n* : a line of persons or things arranged one behind another — **single file** *adv*

sin·gle–hand·ed \\ˌsing-gəl-ˈhan-dəd\\ *adj* **1** : managed or done by one person or with one hand **2** : working alone : lacking help — **sin·gle–hand·ed·ly** *adv*

sin·gle–heart·ed \\-ˈhärt-əd\\ *adj* : characterized by sincerity and unity of purpose — **sin·gle–heart·ed·ly** *adv*

sin·gle–mind·ed \\-ˈmīn-dəd\\ *adj* **1** : SINCERE, SINGLE-HEARTED **2** : having one overriding purpose — **sin·gle–mind·ed·ly** *adv*

sin·gle·stick \\ˈsing-gəl-ˌstik\\ *n* **1** : fighting or fencing with a one-handed wooden stick or sword **2** : the weapon used in singlestick

sin·glet \\ˈsing-glət\\ *n, chiefly Brit* : an athletic jersey : UNDERSHIRT

sin·gle·tree \\ˈsing-gəl-(ˌ)trē\\ *n* : WHIFFLETREE

sin·gly \\ˈsing-g(ə-)lē\\ *adv* **1** : by or with oneself : INDIVIDUALLY **2** : SINGLE-HANDEDLY

[1]**sing·song** \\ˈsing-ˌsȯng\\ *n* : a monotonous rhythm or a monotonous rise and fall of pitch

[2]**singsong** *adj* : having a monotonous cadence or rhythm

1**sin·gu·lar** \'sing-gyə-lər\ *adj* **1 a** : of or relating to a separate person or thing : INDIVIDUAL **b** : of, relating to, or constituting a word form denoting one person, thing, or instance **c** : of or relating to a single instance or to something considered by itself **2 a** : EXCEPTIONAL **b** : UNIQUE **3** : PECULIAR ⟨holding *singular* views of civic responsibility⟩ — **sin·gu·lar·ly** *adv*

2**singular** *n* : something that is singular; *esp* : the singular number, the inflectional form denoting it, or a word in that form

sin·gu·lar·i·ty \ˌsing-gyə-'lar-ət-ē\ *n, pl* **-ties** **1** : the quality or state of being singular **2** : something that is singular : PECULIARITY

sin·is·ter \'sin-ə-stər\ *adj* [from Latin meaning "inauspicious", literally "being on the left side", omens appearing on the left being regarded as unfavorable] **1** : singularly evil or productive of evil : BAD **2** : of or relating to the left **3** : threatening evil, harm, or danger : OMINOUS — **sin·is·ter·ly** *adv*

1**sink** \'singk\ *vb* **sank** \'sangk\ *or* **sunk** \'səngk\; **sunk**; **sink·ing** **1 a** : to move or cause to move downward usu. so as to be submerged or swallowed up ⟨feet *sinking* into deep mud⟩ ⟨*sink* a ship⟩ **b** : to descend gradually lower and lower ⟨the sun *sank* behind the hills⟩ **2** : to lessen in amount or intensity **3** : to fall to or into an inferior status (as of quality, worth, or number) : DECLINE ⟨*sink* into decay⟩ **4 a** : to penetrate or cause to penetrate ⟨*sank* his ax into the tree⟩ **b** : to become absorbed ⟨the water *sank* into the dry ground⟩ **5** : to form by digging or boring ⟨*sink* a well⟩ **6** : INVEST ⟨*sank* a million dollars in the new company⟩ — **sink·a·ble** \'sing-kə-bəl\ *adj*

2**sink** *n* **1 a** : CESSPOOL **b** : SEWER **2** : a stationary basin for washing (as in a kitchen) connected with a drain and usu. a water supply **3** : a place where vice, corruption, or evil collect **4** : a depression in the land surface; *esp* : one having a saline lake with no outlet

sink·er \'sing-kər\ *n* **1** : one that sinks; *esp* : a weight for sinking a line or net **2** : DOUGHNUT

sink·hole \'singk-ˌhōl\ *n* : a hollow place in which drainage collects

sinking fund *n* : a fund set up for paying off the principal of a debt when it falls due

sin·ner \'sin-ər\ *n* : one that sins

Si·no- \'sī-nō\ *comb form* **1** : Chinese ⟨*Sino*phile⟩ **2** : Chinese and ⟨*Sino*-Soviet⟩

sin·ter \'sint-ər\ *vb* : to cause to become a coherent nonporous mass by heating without melting

sin·u·os·i·ty \ˌsin-yə-'wäs-ət-ē\ *n, pl* **-ties** **1** : the quality or state of being sinuous **2** : something that is sinuous : winding turn

sin·u·ous \'sin-yə-wəs\ *adj* : of a serpentine or wavy form : WINDING — **sin·u·ous·ly** *adv*

si·nus \'sī-nəs\ *n* : CAVITY, HOLLOW; *esp* : any of several cavities in the skull mostly communicating with the nostrils

si·nus·i·tis \ˌsī-nə-'sīt-əs\ *n* : inflammation of a sinus

Siou·an \'sü-ən\ *n* **1** : a language stock of central and eastern No. America **2** : a member of a group of Amerindian peoples speaking Siouan languages

ə abut	ər further	a back	ā bake	
ä cot, cart	aù out	ch chin	e less	ē easy
g gift	i trip	ī life	j joke	ng sing	ō flow
ȯ flaw	ȯi coin	th thin	th this	ü loot
ù foot	y yet	yü few	yù furious	zh vision

Sioux \'sü\ *n, pl* **Sioux** \'sü(z)\ **1** : DAKOTA **2** : SIOUAN

1**sip** \'sip\ *vb* **sipped**; **sip·ping** **1** : to drink in small quantities or little by little **2** : to take sips from : TASTE — **sip·per** *n*

2**sip** *n* **1** : the act of sipping **2** : a small amount taken by sipping

1**si·phon** \'sī-fən\ *n* **1 a** : a bent tube through which a liquid can be drawn by means of air pressure up and over the edge of one container and into another container at a lower level **b** *usu* **sy·phon** : a bottle for holding carbonated water under pressure that is driven out through a bent tube in its neck **2** : any of various tubular organs in animals and esp. mollusks used for drawing in or ejecting fluids

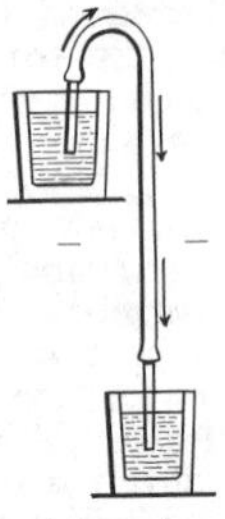
siphon 1a

2**siphon** *vb* **si·phoned**; **si·phon·ing** \'sīf-(ə-)ning\ : to draw off or pass off by or as if by a siphon

si·phon·ap·ter·ous \ˌsī-fə-'nap-tə-rəs\ *adj* : of or relating to the fleas

sir \(')sər\ *n* [from Middle English, alteration of *sire*, from Old French, from Latin *senior* "elder", "senior"] **1** : a man entitled to be addressed as *sir* — used as a title before the given name of a knight or baronet **2** : a title of respect used in addressing a man without using his name

1**sire** \'sī(ə)r\ *n* **1** : FATHER **2** *archaic* : FOREFATHER **3** : the male parent of an animal and esp. of a domestic animal

2**sire** *vb* : BEGET, PROCREATE — used esp. of domestic animals

si·ren \'sī-rən\ *n* **1** *often cap* : one of a group of womanlike creatures in Greek mythology that lured mariners to destruction by their singing **2** : a seductive or alluring woman **3** : a device often electrically operated for producing a loud shrill fluctuating warning sound ⟨ambulance *siren*⟩ **4** : any of a genus of eel-shaped amphibians with small forelimbs and permanent external gills as well as lungs

sir·loin \'sər-ˌlȯin\ *n* : a cut of meat and esp. of beef from the part of the hindquarter just in front of the round

si·roc·co \sə-'räk-ō\ *n, pl* **-cos** **1 a** : a hot dust-laden wind from the Libyan desert that blows on the northern Mediterranean coast **b** : a warm moist oppressive southeast wind on the northern Mediterranean coast **2** : a hot or warm wind of cyclonic origin

sirup *var of* SYRUP

si·sal \'sī-səl, -zəl\ *n* **1** : a strong durable white fiber used to make ropes and twine **2** : a widely grown West Indian agave whose leaves yield sisal

sis·sy \'sis-ē\ *n, pl* **sissies** **1** : an effeminate man or boy **2** : a timid or cowardly person — **sissy** *adj*

1**sis·ter** \'sis-tər\ *n* **1** : a female person or animal related to another person or animal having one or both parents in common **2** *often cap* : a member of a religious society of women : NUN **3 a** : a woman related to another by a common tie or interest **b** : one having similar characteristics to another ⟨botany, a *sister* of zoology⟩ **4** *chiefly Brit* : NURSE

2**sister** *adj* : having or suggesting the relationship of a sister ⟨*sister* ships⟩

sis·ter·hood \'sis-tər-ˌhu̇d\ *n* **1** : the state of being a sister **2** : a community or society of sisters; *esp* : a society of women religious

sis·ter–in–law \'sis-t(ə-)rən-ˌlȯ, -tərn-ˌlȯ\ *n, pl* **sis·ters–in–law** \-tər-zən-\ **1** : the sister of one's spouse **2** : the wife of one's brother

sis·ter·ly \'sis-tər-lē\ *adj* : of, relating to, or having the characteristics of a sister — **sisterly** *adv*

sit \'sit\ *vb* **sat** \'sat\; **sit·ting** **1 a** : to rest upon the buttocks or haunches ⟨*sit* in a chair⟩ **b** : to cause thus to rest : SEAT ⟨*sat* him down to write a letter⟩ **c** : PERCH, ROOST **2** : to provide seats or seating room for ⟨car will *sit* six people⟩ **3** : to occupy a place as a member of an official body ⟨*sit* in Congress⟩ **4** : to hold a session **5** : to cover eggs for hatching : BROOD **6** : to pose for a portrait or photograph : serve as a model **7** : to lie or rest in any condition or location ⟨the vase *sits* on the table⟩ ⟨house *sits* well back from the road⟩ **8** : to remain inactive ⟨the car *sits* in the garage⟩ **9** : BABY-SIT — **sit on** : to hold deliberations concerning — **sit on one's hands** : to fail to take action — **sit pretty** : to be in a highly favorable situation — **sit tight** : to maintain one's position without change

sit–down \'sit-ˌdau̇n\ *n* : a strike in which the workers stop work and refuse to leave their places of employment — called also *sit-down strike*

site \'sīt\ *n* **1** : local position (as of a building, town, or monument) **2** : the place or scene of something ⟨famous battle *sites*⟩ ⟨good camp *site*⟩

sit–in \'sit-ˌin\ *n* : an act of occupying seats (as in a restaurant or office) as a means of organized protest

Sit·ka spruce \ˌsit-kə-\ *n* : a tall spruce of the northern Pacific coast with thin reddish brown bark and flat needles

sit·ter \'sit-ər\ *n* : one that sits; *esp* : BABY-SITTER

[1]**sit·ting** \'sit-ing\ *n* **1** : an act of one that sits; *esp* : a single occasion of continuous sitting ⟨finished the portrait in one *sitting*⟩ **2 a** : a brooding over eggs for hatching **b** : SETTING 5 **3** : SESSION ⟨*sitting* of the legislature⟩

[2]**sitting** *adj* : used in or for sitting ⟨a *sitting* position⟩

sitting duck *n* : an easy or defenseless target (as for attack or criticism)

sitting room *n* : LIVING ROOM

sit·u·ate \'sich-ə-ˌwāt\ *vb* : to place in a site or situation : LOCATE

sit·u·at·ed \-ˌwāt-əd\ *adj* **1** : LOCATED **2** : placed in certain circumstances ⟨not rich but comfortably *situated*⟩

sit·u·a·tion \ˌsich-ə-'wā-shən\ *n* **1 a** : the way in which something is placed in relation to its surroundings **b** : SITE **2 a** : position or place of employment : POST, JOB **b** : position in life : STATUS **3** : position with respect to conditions and circumstances ⟨military *situation*⟩ ⟨the *situation* seemed to call for a general retreat⟩

six \'siks\ *n* **1** — see NUMBER table **2** : the sixth in a set or series — **six** *adj or pron* — **at sixes and sevens** : in disorder : CONFUSED

six–gun \'siks-ˌgən\ *n* : a 6-chambered revolver

six·pence \'siks-pən(t)s, *US also* -ˌpen(t)s\ *n* : the sum of six pence; *also* : a coin representing six pence

six–shoot·er \'sik(s)-'shüt-ər\ *n* : SIX-GUN

six·teen \(')siks-'tēn\ *n* — see NUMBER table — **sixteen** *adj or pron* — **six·teenth** \-'tēn(t)th\ *adj or n*

sixteenth note *n* : a musical note with the time value of one sixteenth of a whole note

sixth \'siks(t)th\ *n* **1** — see NUMBER table **2** : a musical interval embracing six diatonic degrees — **sixth** *adj or adv* — **sixth·ly** \-lē\ *adv*

sixth sense *n* : a keen intuitive power

six·ty \'sik-stē\ *n, pl* **sixties** — see NUMBER table — **six·ti·eth** \-stē-əth\ *adj or n* — **sixty** *adj or pron*

siz·a·ble *or* **size·a·ble** \'sī-zə-bəl\ *adj* : fairly large : CONSIDERABLE — **siz·a·bly** \-blē\ *adv*

[1]**size** \'sīz\ *n* **1** : physical magnitude, extent, or bulk **2 a** : the measurements of a thing **b** : relative aggregate amount **3** : one of a series of graduated measures esp. of manufactured articles (as of clothing)

[2]**size** *vb* **1** : to make a particular size **2** : to arrange, grade, or classify according to size

[3]**size** *n* : a gluey material (as a preparation of glue, flour, varnish, or resins) used for filling the pores in a surface (as of plaster), as a stiffener (as of fabric), or as an adhesive

[4]**size** *vb* : to apply size to

[5]**size** *adj* : SIZED ⟨medium-*size*⟩

sized \'sīzd\ *adj* **1** : having a specified size or bulk ⟨a small-*sized* house⟩ **2** : arranged or adjusted according to size

size up *vb* : to form a judgment of ⟨*size up* a situation⟩

siz·ing \'sī-zing\ *n* : [3]SIZE

siz·zle \'siz-əl\ *vb* **siz·zled**; **siz·zling** \-(ə-)ling\ : to make a hissing sound in or as if in burning or frying — **sizzle** *n* — **siz·zler** \-(ə-)lər\ *n*

[1]**skate** \'skāt\ *n* : any of numerous rays with broadly developed fins

[2]**skate** *n* **1 a** : a metallic runner that has a frame usu. shaped to fit the sole of a shoe to which it is attached and that is used for gliding on ice **b** : a fixed combination of shoe and skate **2** : ROLLER SKATE

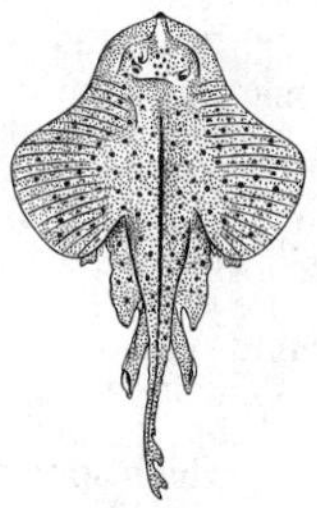
skate (about 1½ ft. long)

[3]**skate** *vb* **1** : to glide along on skates propelled by the alternate action of the legs **2** : to slip or glide as if on skates — **skat·er** *n*

skate·board \'skāt-ˌbōrd, -ˌbȯrd\ *n* : a short and narrow board mounted on roller-skate wheels — **skate·board·er** \-ər\ *n* — **skate·board·ing** \-ing\ *n*

skeet \'skēt\ *n* : trapshooting in which clay targets are thrown in such a way as to simulate the angle of flight of a flushed game bird

skein \'skān\ *also* **skean** *or* **skeane** \'skān\ *n* : a looped length of yarn or thread put up in a loose twist after it is taken from the reel

skel·e·tal \'skel-ət-əl\ *adj* : of, relating or attached to, forming, or resembling a skeleton ⟨*skeletal* muscles⟩ ⟨the *skeletal* system⟩

[1]**skel·e·ton** \'skel-ət-ən\ *n* **1** : a usu. rigid supporting or protecting structure or framework of an organism; *esp* : the bony or sometimes cartilaginous framework supporting the soft tissues and protecting the internal organs of a vertebrate (as a fish or man) **2** : an emaciated person or animal **3** : something forming a structural framework

[2]**skeleton** *adj* : of, consisting of, or resembling a skeleton ⟨a *skeleton* hand⟩ ⟨a *skeleton* crew⟩

skeleton key *n* : a key made to open many locks

skep·tic \'skep-tik\ *n* : a person slow to believe or ready to question : DOUBTER

skep·ti·cal \-ti-kəl\ *adj* : relating to or marked by doubt — **skep·ti·cal·ly** \-k(ə-)lē\ *adv*

skep·ti·cism \'skep-tə-ˌsiz-əm\ *n* : an attitude of doubt

[1]**sketch** \'skech\ *n* **1 a** : a rough drawing representing the chief features of an object or scene and often made as a preliminary study **b** : a tentative draft (as for a literary work) **2** : a brief description or outline **3** : a short theatrical piece having a single scene; *esp* : a comic vaudeville act

[2]**sketch** *vb* **1** : to make a sketch, rough draft, or outline of **2** : to draw or paint sketches — **sketch·er** *n*

S

sketch·book \'skech-ˌbu̇k\ *n* : a book of or for sketches

sketchy \'skech-ē\ *adj* **sketch·i·er**; **-est** **1** : of the nature of a sketch : roughly outlined **2** : lacking completeness, clearness, or substance : SLIGHT, VAGUE

1**skew** \'skyü\ *vb* **1** : to take a slanting course : move or turn aside : TWIST, SWERVE **2** : to distort from a true value or symmetrical form ⟨*skewed* the facts to fit his theory⟩

2**skew** *adj* **1 a** : set, placed, or running obliquely to something else **b** : neither parallel nor intersecting ⟨*skew* lines⟩ **2** : ASYMMETRICAL

3**skew** *n* : a deviation from a straight line : SLANT

1**skew·er** \'skyü-ər, 'skyu̇(-ə)r\ *n* **1** : a long pin for keeping meat in form while roasting or for holding small pieces of meat and vegetables for broiling **2** : something shaped or used like a meat skewer

2**skewer** *vb* : to fasten or pierce with or as if with a skewer

skew·ness \'skyü-nəs\ *n* : lack of straightness or symmetry

1**ski** \'skē\ *n, pl* **skis** *or* **ski** [from Norwegian, from Old Norse *skīth*, literally "stick"] : one of a pair of narrow strips of wood, metal, or plastic curving upward in front that are fastened to the feet and used for traveling over snow or water

2**ski** *vb* **skied**; **ski·ing** : to glide on skis — **ski·er** *n*

ski boot *n* : a heavy usu. reinforced leather shoe for use with skis

1**skid** \'skid\ *n* **1** : a log or plank for supporting something (as above the ground) ⟨put a boat on *skids*⟩ **2** : one of the logs, planks, or rails along or on which something heavy is rolled or slid **3** : a device placed under a carriage wheel to prevent its turning : DRAG **4** : a runner used as part of the landing gear of an airplane or helicopter **5** : the act of skidding : SLIDE

2**skid** *vb* **skid·ded**; **skid·ding** **1** : to haul along, slide, hoist, or store on skids **2** : to slide without rotating ⟨the wheels *skidded* as we went down the hill⟩ **3** : to fail to grip the roadway; *esp* : to slip sideways on the road ⟨the car *skidded* on an icy road⟩ ⟨studded snow tires to prevent *skidding*⟩

skid row \-'rō\ *n* : a district of cheap saloons and cheap rooming houses frequented by migrant workers, vagrants, and alcoholics

skiff \'skif\ *n* **1** : a small light sailing ship **2** : a light rowboat **3** : a small fast motorboat

ski·ing *n* : the art or sport of gliding or jumping on skis

ski jump *n* **1** : a jump made by a person wearing skis **2** : a steeply inclined course or track leveled off at its lower end from which a skier makes a jump — **ski jump** *vb*

ski lift *n* : a power-driven conveyor for transporting skiers or sightseers up a long slope or mountainside

skill \'skil\ *n* **1** : ability or dexterity that comes from training or practice **2 a** : a particular art or science ⟨achievements of medical *skill*⟩ **b** : a developed or acquired ability : ACCOMPLISHMENT ⟨*skills* of swimming and diving⟩

skilled \'skild\ *adj* **1** : having skill : EXPERT ⟨a *skilled* mason⟩ **2** : requiring skill and training ⟨a *skilled* trade⟩

skil·let \'skil-ət\ *n* : a frying pan

skill·ful *or* **skil·ful** \'skil-fəl\ *adj* **1** : having or displaying skill ⟨*skillful* debater⟩ **2** : accomplished with skill ⟨*skillful* defense⟩ — **skill·ful·ly** \-fə-lē\ *adv* — **skill·ful·ness** *n*

syn SKILLFUL, PROFICIENT, EXPERT can mean showing good ability in a specified activity. SKILLFUL suggests adroitness in performance or execution; PROFICIENT implies the competence that comes with training and practice; EXPERT implies the highest degree of proficiency, often in something that requires special knowledge ***ant*** unskillful

1**skim** \'skim\ *vb* **skimmed**; **skim·ming** **1 a** : to clear a liquid of scum or floating substance : remove (as film or scum) from the surface of a liquid **b** : to remove cream from by skimming **2** : to glance through (as a book) for the chief ideas or the plot **3** : to throw so as to ricochet along the surface of water **4** : to pass swiftly or lightly over : glide or skip along, above, or near a surface

2**skim** *n* **1** : a thin layer, coating, or film **2** : the act of skimming **3** : something skimmed; *esp* : SKIM MILK

3**skim** *adj* : having been skimmed

skim·mer \'skim-ər\ *n* **1** : one that skims; *esp* : a flat perforated scoop or spoon used for skimming **2** : any of several long-winged seabirds related to the terns that fly with the lower mandible in the water so as to skim out small sea animals

skim milk *also* **skimmed milk** *n* : milk from which the cream has been taken

skimp \'skimp\ *vb* **1** : to give insufficient or barely sufficient attention or effort to or funds for : SCAMP **2** : to save by or as if by skimping : SCRIMP

skimpy \'skim-pē\ *adj* **skimp·i·er**; **-est** : barely adequate : SCANTY — **skimp·i·ly** \-pə-lē\ *adv* — **skimp·i·ness** \-pē-nəs\ *n*

1**skin** \'skin\ *n* **1 a** : HIDE, PELT **b** : a sheet of parchment or vellum made from a hide **c** : BOTTLE 1b **2 a** : the external usu. tough and flexible covering layer of an animal body; *also* : the 2-layered tissue of which this is formed in a vertebrate **b** : an outer or surface layer ⟨a sausage *skin*⟩ ⟨apple *skins*⟩ **3** : the life or physical well-being of a person ⟨made sure to save his *skin*⟩ — **skin·less** \-ləs\ *adj* — **skinned** \'skind\ *adj*

2**skin** *vb* **skinned**; **skin·ning** **1** : to cover or become covered with or as if with skin **2** : to strip, scrape, or rub off the skin of ⟨*skin* a rabbit⟩ ⟨*skinned* his knee⟩ **3** : CHEAT, FLEECE **4 a** : to climb or descend ⟨*skin* up and down a rope⟩ **b** : to pass or get by with scant room to spare — **skin·ner** *n*

skin-deep \'skin-'dēp\ *adj* **1** : as deep as the skin **2** : SUPERFICIAL

skin dive *vb* : to swim deep below the surface of water with a face mask and flippers and with or without a portable breathing device — **skin diver** *n*

skin·flint \'skin-ˌflint\ *n* : a person who is very hard and grasping in money matters : MISER

skin game *n* : a swindling game or trick

skin graft *n* : skin transferred from a donor area to grow new skin at a place denuded (as by burning)

skink \'skiŋk\ *n* : any of a family of mostly small lizards with small scales

skin·ny \'skin-ē\ *adj* **skin·ni·er**; **-est** **1** : resembling skin : MEMBRANOUS ⟨a *skinny* layer⟩ **2** : very thin : LEAN, EMACIATED — **skin·ni·ness** *n*

skin·tight \'skin-'tīt\ *adj* : closely fitted to the figure

1**skip** \'skip\ *vb* **skipped**; **skip·ping** **1 a** : to move or proceed with leaps and bounds : CAPER **b** : to bound or cause to bound off one point after another ⟨*skipping* stones⟩ **c** : to leap over lightly and nimbly

2 : to leave hurriedly or secretly ⟨*skip* town⟩ **3 a** : to pass over or omit (as an interval, item, or step) ⟨*skipped* the dull parts of the book⟩ **b** : to omit or cause to omit a grade in school in advancing to the next **c** : to fail to attend ⟨*skipped* the meeting⟩
[2]**skip** *n* **1 a** : a light bounding step **b** : a gait composed of alternating hops and steps **2** : an act of omission or the thing omitted
ski pants *n pl* : pants for skiing that are ribbed or close-fitted at the ankle
ski pole *n* : a metal-pointed pole fitted with a strap for the hand at the top and an encircling disk set a little above the point and used as an aid in skiing
[1]**skip·per** \'skip-ər\ *n* **1** : one that skips **2** : any of numerous small stout-bodied insects of swift erratic flight that differ from the typical butterflies in the veins of the wings and the form of the antennae
[2]**skipper** *n* [from Dutch *schipper*, from *schip* "ship", from the same source as English *ship*] : the master of a ship; *esp* : the master of a fishing, small trading, or pleasure boat
[1]**skir·mish** \'skər-mish\ *n* **1** : a minor fight between small bodies of troops **2** : a minor dispute or contest
[2]**skirmish** *vb* **1** : to engage in a skirmish **2** : to search about (as for supplies) — **skir·mish·er** *n*
[1]**skirt** \'skərt\ *n* **1 a** : a free hanging part of a garment extending from the waist down **b** : a separate free hanging garment for women and girls covering the body from the waist down **c** : either of two flaps on a saddle covering the bars on which the stirrups are hung **2** *pl* : OUTSKIRTS **3** : a part or attachment serving as a rim, border, or edging
[2]**skirt** *vb* **1 a** : to go or pass around or about; *esp* : to go around or keep away from in order to avoid danger or discovery **b** : to evade or miss by a narrow margin **2** : to be, lie, or move along an edge, border, or margin — **skirt·er** *n*
ski run *n* : a slope or trail suitable for skiing
skit \'skit\ *n* : a satirical or humorous story or sketch; *esp* : a sketch included in a dramatic performance (as a revue)
ski tow *n* **1** : a power-driven conveyor for pulling skiers to the top of a slope **2** : SKI LIFT
skit·ter \'skit-ər\ *vb* : to glide or skip lightly or quickly : skim along a surface
skit·tish \'skit-ish\ *adj* **1** : lively or frisky in action : CAPRICIOUS **2** : easily frightened : RESTIVE ⟨a *skittish* horse⟩ **3** : COY, BASHFUL — **skit·tish·ly** *adv* — **skit·tish·ness** *n*
skit·tles \'skit-əlz\ *n pl* : a form of ninepins that sometimes uses wooden disks instead of balls
skiv·vy \'skiv-ē\ *n, pl* **skivvies** : underwear consisting of shorts and a collarless short-sleeved pullover — usu. used in pl.
skoal \'skōl\ *n* : TOAST, HEALTH — often used interjectionally
skul·dug·gery *or* **skull·dug·gery** \ˌskəl-'dəg-(ə-)rē\ *n, pl* **-ger·ies** : underhanded or unscrupulous behavior : DISHONESTY, TRICKERY
skulk \'skəlk\ *vb* **1** : to move in a stealthy or furtive manner : SNEAK **2** : to hide or conceal oneself from cowardice or fear or with treacherous intent ***syn*** see LURK — **skulk·er** *n*
skull \'skəl\ *n* **1** : the bony framework of the vertebrate head **2** : the seat of understanding or intelligence : MIND — **skulled** \'skəld\ *adj*
skull and cross·bones \-'krȯs-ˌbōnz\ *n* : a representation of a human skull over crossbones formerly pictured on pirates' flags and now used as a warning of danger to life
skull·cap \'skəl-ˌkap\ *n* : a close-fitting cap; *esp* : a light cap without brim for indoor wear
[1]**skunk** \'skəngk\ *n, pl* **skunks** *also* **skunk** **1** : any of various common black-and-white New World mammals related to the weasels and ejecting a fluid with a pungent and offensive odor when startled **2** : an obnoxious person

skunk 1
(up to 28 in. long)

[2]**skunk** *vb* : to defeat decisively; *esp* : to shut out in a game
skunk cabbage *n* : an ill-smelling broad-leaved American marsh herb
sky \'skī\ *n, pl* **skies** **1** : the upper atmosphere that constitutes an apparent great vault or arch over the earth : FIRMAMENT **2** : HEAVEN 2a **3** : WEATHER, CLIMATE ⟨the weatherman predicts sunny *skies* for tomorrow⟩
sky blue *n* : a variable color averaging a pale to light blue
sky·cap \-ˌkap\ *n* : one employed to carry hand luggage at an airport
sky·div·ing \-ˌdī-ving\ *n* : the sport of jumping from an airplane and executing various body maneuvers before pulling the rip cord of a parachute — **sky diver** *n*
sky–high \'skī-'hī\ *adv or adj* **1 a** : high into the air **b** : to a high level or degree **2** : in an enthusiastic manner **3** : to bits : APART **4** : EXORBITANTLY
sky·jack·er \-ˌjak-ər\ *n* : a person who takes possession of a flying airplane (as by coercing the pilot at gunpoint)
[1]**sky·lark** \-ˌlärk\ *n* : a common Old World lark that sings as it rises in almost perpendicular flight
[2]**skylark** *vb* : to play wild boisterous pranks : FROLIC — **sky·lark·er** *n*
sky·light \'skī-ˌlīt\ *n* : a window or group of windows in a roof or ceiling
sky·line \-ˌlīn\ *n* **1** : the line where earth and sky or water and sky seem to meet : HORIZON **2** : an outline against the sky ⟨a *skyline* of tall buildings⟩
sky map *n* : a chart showing the positions of celestial bodies
[1]**sky·rock·et** \'skī-ˌräk-ət\ *n* : [1]ROCKET 1
[2]**skyrocket** *vb* **1** : to shoot up abruptly ⟨costs have *skyrocketed*⟩ **2** : to cause to rise or increase abruptly and rapidly
sky·scrap·er \'skī-ˌskrā-pər\ *n* : a very tall building
sky·ward \'skī-wərd\ *adv or adj* **1** : toward the sky ⟨gaze *skyward*⟩ **2** : UPWARD
sky·way \-ˌwā\ *n* **1** : a route used by airplanes : AIR LANE **2** : an elevated highway
sky·writ·ing \-ˌrīt-ing\ *n* : writing formed in the sky by means of a visible substance (as smoke) emitted from an airplane — **sky·writ·er** \-ˌrīt-ər\ *n*
slab \'slab\ *n* **1** : a thick plate or slice (as of stone, wood, or bread) **2** : the outside piece cut from a log in squaring it
slab·ber \'slab-ər\ *vb* **slab·bered**; **slab·ber·ing** \-(ə-)ring\ : SLOBBER, DROOL — **slabber** *n*
[1]**slack** \'slak\ *adj* **1** : CARELESS, NEGLIGENT **2** : marked by sluggishness or lack of energy ⟨*slack* pace⟩ **3 a** : not tight : not tense or taut : RELAXED ⟨*slack* rope⟩ **b** : lacking in firmness : WEAK, SOFT ⟨*slack* control⟩ **4** : not busy : SLOW ⟨*slack* season⟩ — **slack·ly** *adv* — **slack·ness** *n*
[2]**slack** *vb* **1 a** : to be or become slack or negligent in performing or doing **b** : LESSEN, MODERATE **2** : to

shirk or evade work or duty **3 :** LOOSEN **4 a :** to cause to abate **b :** SLAKE 4

3**slack** *n* **1 :** cessation in movement or flow **2 :** a part of something that hangs loose without strain ⟨take up the *slack* of a rope⟩ **3** *pl* **:** trousers esp. for casual wear **4 :** a dull season or period **:** LULL

slack·en \'slak-ən\ *vb* **slack·ened**; **slack·en·ing** \-(ə-)ning\ **1 :** to make or become less active **:** slow up **:** MODERATE, RETARD ⟨*slacken* speed⟩ **2 :** to make less taut **:** LOOSEN ⟨*slacken* sail⟩ **3 :** to become negligent

slack·er \'slak-ər\ *n* **:** one who shirks work or evades an obligation

slag \'slag\ *n* **1 :** waste left after the melting of ores and the separation of the metal from them **2 :** volcanic lava resembling cinders — **slag·gy** \'slag-ē\ *adj*

slain *past part of* SLAY

slake \'slāk, *3 & 4 are also* 'slak\ *vb* **1** *archaic* **:** ABATE, MODERATE **2 :** to relieve or satisfy with water or liquid **:** QUENCH ⟨*slaked* his thirst⟩ **3 :** to become slaked ⟨lime may *slake* spontaneously in moist air⟩ **4 :** to cause (lime) to heat and crumble by treatment with water

slaked lime *n* **:** LIME 2

sla·lom \'släl-əm\ *n* **1 :** skiing in a zigzag or wavy course between upright poles **2 :** a race against time over such a course

1**slam** \'slam\ *n* **:** the winning of all or all but one of the tricks of a hand in bridge

2**slam** *vb* **slammed**; **slam·ming** **1 :** to strike or beat hard **2 :** to shut forcibly and noisily **:** BANG **3 :** to set or slap down violently or noisily **4 :** to make a banging noise **5 :** to criticize harshly ⟨senators *slam* foreign policy⟩

3**slam** *n* **1 :** a heavy impact **2 a :** a noisy violent closing **b :** a banging noise esp. from the slamming of a door **3 :** a cutting or violent criticism

slam–bang \'slam-'bang\ *adv or adj* **1 :** with noisy violence **2 :** HEADLONG, RECKLESSLY

1**slan·der** \'slan-dər\ *n* **1 :** the utterance of false charges or misrepresentations which defame and damage another's reputation **2 :** a false and defamatory oral statement about a person — **slan·der·ous** \-d(ə-)rəs\ *adj* — **slan·der·ous·ly** *adv* — **slan·der·ous·ness** *n*

2**slander** *vb* **slan·dered**; **slan·der·ing** \-d(ə-)ring\ **:** to utter slander against **:** DEFAME — **slan·der·er** \-dər-ər\ *n*

slang \'slang\ *n* **1 :** language peculiar to a particular group, trade, or pursuit ⟨baseball *slang*⟩ **2 :** an informal nonstandard vocabulary composed typically of coinages, arbitrarily changed words, and extravagant, forced, or facetious figures of speech — **slang** *adj*

slangy \'slang-ē\ *adj* **slang·i·er**; **-est** **1 :** of, relating to, or being slang **:** containing slang **2 :** addicted to the use of slang — **slang·i·ly** \'slang-ə-lē\ *adv* — **slang·i·ness** \'slang-ē-nəs\ *n*

1**slant** \'slant\ *vb* **1 :** to turn or incline from a straight line or a level **:** SLOPE **2 :** to interpret or present in accordance with a special viewpoint **:** SKEW ⟨*slanted* news⟩

syn SLANT, SLOPE, LEAN can mean to diverge or cause to diverge from a vertical or horizontal line. Of the three SLANT carries most strongly the implication of a noticeable divergence ⟨gusts drove the rain *slanting* by the window⟩; SLOPE applies most often to a side of an elevation (as a hill or roof) and suggests lack of steepness; LEAN carries the implication of a directed or induced bending ⟨*leaned* forward to get a better look⟩

2**slant** *n* **1 :** a slanting direction, line, or plane **:** SLOPE **2 :** something that slants **3 :** a way of looking at something ⟨get a new *slant* on the problem⟩ — **slant** *adj*

slant height *n* **:** the length of a line segment lying in the lateral surface of a right circular cone

slant·ways \'slant-,wāz\ *adv* **:** SLANTWISE

slant·wise \-,wīz\ *adv or adj* **:** so as to slant **:** in a slanting direction or position

1**slap** \'slap\ *n* **1 :** a quick sharp blow esp. with the open hand **2 :** a noise suggesting that of a slap

2**slap** *vb* **slapped**; **slap·ping** **1 a :** to strike with or as if with the open hand **b :** to make a sound like that of slapping **2 :** to put, place, or throw with careless haste or force ⟨*slapped* down his paper⟩

3**slap** *adv* **:** DIRECTLY, SMACK

slap·dash \'slap-,dash, -'dash\ *adv or adj* **:** in a slipshod manner **:** HAPHAZARD; *also* **:** HASTILY

slap·jack \'slap-,jak\ *n* **1 :** GRIDDLE CAKE **2 :** a card game in which each player tries to be the first to slap his hand on any jack that appears face up

slap·stick \-,stik\ *n* **1 :** a device made of two flat sticks so fastened as to make a loud noise when used to strike a person **2 :** comedy stressing farce and horseplay — **slapstick** *adj*

1**slash** \'slash\ *vb* **1 :** to cut by sweeping and aimless blows **:** GASH **2 :** to whip or strike with or as if with a cane **3 :** to criticize without mercy **4 :** to cut slits in (as a skirt) to reveal a color beneath **5 :** to reduce sharply **:** CUT ⟨*slash* prices⟩ — **slash·er** *n*

2**slash** *n* **1 :** a long cut or stroke made by slashing **2 :** an ornamental slit in a garment **3 :** a sharp reduction ⟨budget *slash*⟩

slat \'slat\ *n* **:** a thin narrow flat strip of wood, plastic, or metal ⟨the *slats* of a blind⟩ — **slat·ted** \'slat-əd\ *adj*

1**slate** \'slāt\ *n* **1 :** a fine-grained and usu. bluish gray rock formed by compression of shales or other rocks that splits readily into thin layers or plates and is used esp. for roofing and blackboards; *also* **:** a piece of this dressed for use **2 :** a tablet of material (as slate) used for writing on **3 :** something (as events or a list of candidates) recorded or made public as if written on a slate **4 a :** a dark purplish gray **b :** a gray similar in color to common roofing slate — **slate** *adj* — **slate·like** \-,līk\ *adj*

2**slate** *vb* **1 :** to cover with slate or a slatelike substance ⟨*slate* a roof⟩ **2 :** to register or schedule on or as if on a slate ⟨*slate* a meeting⟩ — **slat·er** *n*

slat·tern \'slat-ərn\ *n* **:** an untidy slovenly woman — **slat·tern·ly** \-lē\ *adj or adv*

slaty \'slāt-ē\ *adj* **:** of, containing, or characteristic of slate

1**slaugh·ter** \'slȯt-ər\ *n* **1 :** the act of killing; *esp* **:** the butchering of livestock for market **2 :** destruction of human lives in battle **:** CARNAGE

2**slaughter** *vb* **1 :** to kill an animal for food **:** BUTCHER **2 :** to kill ruthlessly or in large numbers **:** MASSACRE — **slaugh·ter·er** \'slȯt-ər-ər\ *n*

slaugh·ter·house \'slȯt-ər-,hau̇s\ *n* **:** an establishment where animals are butchered

Slav \'släv, 'slav\ *n* **:** a person speaking a Slavic language as his native tongue

1**slave** \'slāv\ *n* **[**from medieval Latin *sclavus*, from *Sclavus* Slav; from the reduction to slavery of many

Slavic peoples of central Europe in the Middle Ages] **1 :** a person held in servitude as the property of another **2 :** a person who has lost control of himself and is dominated by something or someone ⟨a *slave* to drink⟩ **3 :** DRUDGE, TOILER — **slave** *adj*

2**slave** *vb* **:** to work like a slave **:** DRUDGE

slave driver *n* **1 :** a supervisor of slaves at work **2 :** a harsh taskmaster

slave·hold·er \ˈslāv-ˌhōl-dər\ *n* **:** an owner of slaves — **slave·hold·ing** \-diŋ\ *adj or n*

1**slav·er** \ˈslav-ər, ˈslāv-\ *vb* **slav·ered; slav·er·ing** \-(ə-)riŋ\ **:** DROOL, SLOBBER

2**slaver** *n* **:** a saliva drooling from the mouth

3**slav·er** \ˈslāv-ər\ *n* **:** a person or ship engaged in the slave trade

slav·ery \ˈslāv-(ə-)rē\ *n* **1 :** DRUDGERY, TOIL **2 a :** the state of being a slave **:** SERVITUDE **b :** the practice of slaveholding

1**Slav·ic** \ˈslav-ik, ˈsläv-\ *adj* **:** of, relating to, or characteristic of the Slavs or their languages

2**Slavic** *n* **:** a branch of the Indo-European language family including Bulgarian, Czech, Polish, Serbo-Croatian, Slovene, Russian, and Ukrainian

slav·ish \ˈslā-vish\ *adj* **1 :** of or characteristic of a slave **:** SERVILE **2 :** lacking in independence or originality esp. of thought ⟨*slavish* imitators⟩ — **slav·ish·ly** *adv* — **slav·ish·ness** *n*

1**Sla·von·ic** \slə-ˈvän-ik\ *adj* **:** SLAVIC

2**Slavonic** *n* **:** SLAVIC

slaw \ˈslȯ\ *n* **:** COLESLAW

slay \ˈslā\ *vb* **slew** \ˈslü\; **slain** \ˈslān\; **slay·ing :** to put to death violently ***syn*** see KILL — **slay·er** *n*

slea·zy \ˈslē-zē, ˈslā-\ *adj* **slea·zi·er; -est 1 :** not firmly or closely woven **:** FLIMSY **2 :** made carelessly of inferior material **:** SHODDY — **slea·zi·ly** \-zə-lē\ *adv* — **slea·zi·ness** \-zē-nəs\ *n*

1**sled** \ˈsled\ *n* **1 :** a vehicle on runners for conveying loads esp. over snow or ice **:** SLEDGE **2 :** a sled used by children for coasting on snow-covered slopes

2**sled** *vb* **sled·ded; sled·ding :** to ride or carry on a sled or sleigh — **sled·der** *n*

sled dog *n* **:** a dog trained to draw a sledge esp. in the Arctic regions

1**sledge** \ˈslej\ *n* **:** SLEDGEHAMMER

2**sledge** *n* **:** a vehicle with low runners that is used for transporting loads esp. over snow or ice

3**sledge** *vb* **:** to travel with or transport on a sledge

sledge·ham·mer \ˈslej-ˌham-ər\ *n* **:** a large heavy hammer usu. used with both hands — **sledgehammer** *adj or vb*

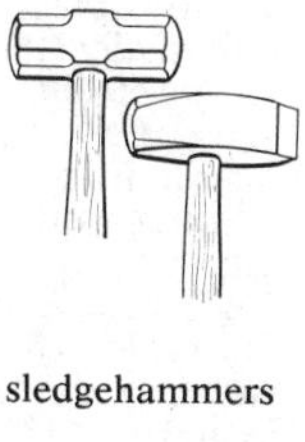

sledgehammers

1**sleek** \ˈslēk\ *vb* **1 :** to make or become sleek **2 :** to cover up **:** gloss over

2**sleek** *adj* **1 a :** smooth and glossy as if polished ⟨*sleek* dark hair⟩ **b :** having a smooth healthy well-groomed look ⟨*sleek* cattle grazing⟩ **2 :** having a prosperous air **:** THRIVING — **sleek·ly** *adv* — **sleek·ness** *n*

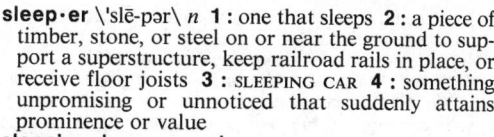

1**sleep** \ˈslēp\ *n* **1 :** the natural periodic suspension of consciousness during which the powers of the body are restored **2 :** a state resembling sleep: as **a :** a state of inactivity like sleep **b :** DEATH; *also* **:** TRANCE, COMA — **sleep·like** \-ˌlīk\ *adj*

2**sleep** *vb* **slept** \ˈslept\; **sleep·ing 1 :** to rest or be in a state of sleep **2 :** to have sexual relations **3 :** to get rid of or spend in or by sleep ⟨*slept* away his cares⟩ **4 :** to provide sleeping space for ⟨the boat *sleeps* six⟩

sleep·er \ˈslē-pər\ *n* **1 :** one that sleeps **2 :** a piece of timber, stone, or steel on or near the ground to support a superstructure, keep railroad rails in place, or receive floor joists **3 :** SLEEPING CAR **4 :** something unpromising or unnoticed that suddenly attains prominence or value

sleeping bag *n* **:** a bag usu. water-repellent and warmly lined or padded to sleep in outdoors

sleeping car *n* **:** a railroad passenger car having berths for sleeping

sleeping sickness *n* **1 :** a serious disease found in much of tropical Africa and transmitted by tsetse flies **2 :** any of various virus diseases of which lethargy or sleepiness is a major symptom

sleep·less \ˈslēp-ləs\ *adj* **1 :** not able to sleep **2 :** affording no sleep **3 :** unceasingly alert or active — **sleep·less·ly** *adv* — **sleep·less·ness** *n*

sleep·walk·er \ˈslēp-ˌwȯ-kər\ *n* **:** one that walks in his sleep **:** SOMNAMBULIST — **sleep·walk·ing** \-kiŋ\ *n*

sleepy \ˈslē-pē\ *adj* **sleep·i·er; -est 1 :** having an inclination to sleep **:** ready to fall asleep **2 :** quietly inactive **:** DULL ⟨a *sleepy* village⟩ — **sleep·i·ly** \-pə-lē\ *adv* — **sleep·i·ness** \-pē-nəs\ *n*

syn SLEEPY, SOMNOLENT, DROWSY can mean experiencing an urge or tendency to sleep. SLEEPY, the most general term, may imply no more than the consciousness of an urge to sleep ⟨*sleepy* after a long day⟩; SOMNOLENT is more likely to suggest the sluggishness or inertia of one who is sleepy or less than fully conscious by inclination ⟨a *somnolent* pupil⟩; DROWSY suggests most strongly the signs (as very sluggish reactions and dulled consciousness) of a sleeping tendency that is heavily upon one ⟨a sedative that left him *drowsy*⟩ ***ant*** wakeful

sleepy·head \ˈslē-pē-ˌhed\ *n* **:** a sleepy person

1**sleet** \ˈslēt\ *n* **1 :** partly frozen rain **:** a mixture of rain and snow **2 :** the icy coating formed by freezing rain **:** GLAZE — **sleety** \ˈslēt-ē\ *adj*

2**sleet** *vb* **:** to shower sleet

sleeve \ˈslēv\ *n* **1 :** the part of a garment covering the arm **2 :** something like a sleeve in shape or use; *esp* **:** a tubular part fitting over another part — **sleeved** \ˈslēvd\ *adj* — **sleeve·less** \ˈslēv-ləs\ *adj*

1**sleigh** \ˈslā\ *n* **:** a vehicle on runners used for transporting persons or goods over snow or ice

2**sleigh** *vb* **:** to drive or travel in a sleigh

sleight \ˈslīt\ *n* **1 a :** deceitful craftiness **:** CUNNING **b :** TRICK, STRATAGEM **2 :** DEXTERITY, SKILL

sleight of hand 1 : skill and dexterity esp. in juggling or magical tricks **2 :** a magical or juggling trick requiring sleight of hand

slen·der \ˈslen-dər\ *adj* **1 :** THIN, SLIM **2 :** limited or inadequate in amount **:** MEAGER ⟨a *slender* income⟩ — **slen·der·ly** *adv* — **slen·der·ness** *n*

slen·der·ize \-də-ˌrīz\ *vb* **:** to make slender

1**sleuth** \ˈslüth\ *n* [short for *sleuthhound*, from Middle English *sloth, sleuth* "track", "trail", from Old Norse *slōth*] **:** DETECTIVE

2**sleuth** *vb* **:** to act as a detective

sleuth·hound \-ˌhau̇nd\ *n* **:** a dog that tracks by scent; *esp* **:** BLOODHOUND

1**slew** \ˈslü\ *past of* SLAY

2**slew** *var of* SLUE

3**slew** *n* **:** a large number **:** LOT

1**slice** \ˈslīs\ *n* **1 :** a thin flat piece cut from something ⟨a *slice* of bread⟩ **2 :** a spatula or knife with wedge-shaped blade ⟨fish *slice*⟩ **3 :** a flight of a ball (as in golf) that veers to the right of a right-handed player and to the left of a left-handed player

2**slice** *vb* **1 a :** to cut with or as if with a knife

b : to cut into slices **2** : to hit a ball so that a slice results — **slic·er** *n*

1**slick** \'slik\ *vb* : to make sleek or smooth

2**slick** *adj* **1 a** : having a smooth surface : SLIPPERY ⟨a *slick* road⟩ **b** : GLIB, TRITE **2 a** : characterized by subtlety or nimble wit : CLEVER; *esp* : TRICKY **b** : DEFT, SKILLFUL — **slick·ly** *adv* — **slick·ness** *n*

3**slick** *n* : something that is smooth or slippery; *esp* : a smooth patch of water covered with a film of oil

slick·er \'slik-ər\ *n* **1** : a long loose raincoat often of oilskin or plastic **2** : a sly clever tricky person

1**slide** \'slīd\ *vb* **slid** \'slid\; **slid·ing** \'slīd-ing\ **1 a** : to move or cause to move smoothly over a surface : GLIDE, SLIP ⟨*slide* a dish across the table⟩ ⟨the pen *slides* smoothly over the paper⟩ **b** : to coast on snow or ice **2** : to slip and fall by a loss of footing, balance, or support ⟨the package *slid* from the heap⟩ **3 a** : to move or pass smoothly and easily ⟨the dog *slid* through the brush⟩ **b** : to move, pass, or put so as not to be noticed ⟨*slid* quietly into his seat⟩ ⟨time *slid* by⟩

2**slide** *n* **1** : the act or motion of sliding **2** : a loosened mass that slides ⟨a rock *slide*⟩ **3 a** : an inclined surface down which a person or thing slides **b** : something (as a cover for an opening) that operates or adjusts by sliding **4 a** : a transparent picture or image that can be projected on a screen **b** : a small glass plate for holding an object to be examined under a microscope

slid·er \'slīd-ər\ *n* : one that slides or operates a slide

slide rule *n* : an instrument consisting in its simple

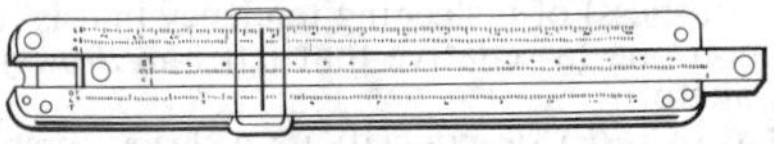

slide rule

form of a ruler with a graduated scale along its movable middle and used for rapid calculation

slide·way \'slīd-ˌwā\ *n* : a way along which something slides

1**slight** \'slīt\ *adj* **1 a** : having a slim or delicate build : not stout or massive **b** : lacking in strength or substance : FLIMSY, FRAIL **c** : lacking weight, solidity, or importance : TRIVIAL **2** : small of its kind or in amount : SCANTY, MEAGER — **slight·ly** *adv* — **slight·ness** *n*

2**slight** *vb* **1** : to treat with disdain or discourteous indifference **2** : to perform or attend to carelessly and inadequately

3**slight** *n* **1** : an act or an instance of slighting **2** : a humiliating discourtesy

slight·ing *adj* : characterized by disregard or disrespect : DISPARAGING ⟨a *slighting* remark⟩ — **slight·ing·ly** \-ing-lē\ *adv*

1**slim** \'slim\ *adj* **slim·mer**; **slim·mest** **1** : of small diameter or thickness in proportion to the height or length : SLENDER **2 a** : inferior in quality or amount : SLIGHT **b** : SCANTY, SMALL — **slim·ly** *adv* — **slim·ness** *n*

2**slim** *vb* **slimmed**; **slim·ming** : to make or become slender

slime \'slīm\ *n* **1** : soft moist earth or clay; *esp* : sticky slippery mud **2** : a soft slippery substance; *esp* : a skin secretion (as of a slug or catfish)

slime mold *n* : any of a group of organisms that consist of a mobile mass of protoplasm, reproduce by spores, and have been classified with the protozoans but are now usu. placed with the plants

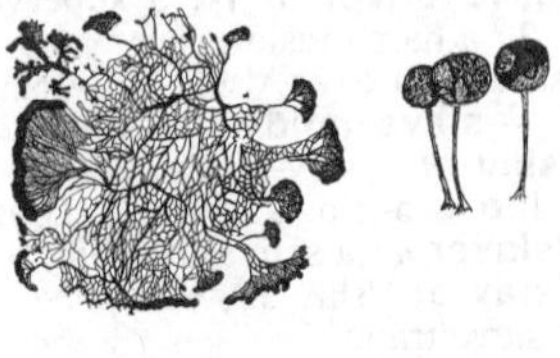

slime mold: left, protoplasmic mass; right, spore cases (magnified 10 times)

slimy \'slī-mē\ *adj* **slim·i·er**; **-est** **1 a** : of, relating to, or resembling slime : VISCOUS **b** : covered with or yielding slime **2** : VILE, OFFENSIVE — **slim·i·ly** \-mə-lē\ *adv* — **slim·i·ness** \-mē-nəs\ *n*

1**sling** \'sling\ *vb* **slung** \'sləng\; **sling·ing** \'sling-ing\ **1** : to toss casually or forcibly : FLING **2** : to throw with a sling — **sling·er** \'sling-ər\ *n*

2**sling** *n* : a slinging or hurling of or as if of a missile

3**sling** *n* **1 a** : a short strap with strings fastened to its ends that is whirled round to throw something (as a stone) **b** : SLINGSHOT **2** : something (as a rope or chain) used to hoist, lower, support, or carry something; *esp* : a hanging bandage suspended from the neck to support an arm or hand

4**sling** *vb* **slung** \'sləng\; **sling·ing** \'sling-ing\ **1** : to put in or move or support with a sling **2** : to cause to become suspended

sling·shot \'sling-ˌshät\ *n* : a forked stick with an elastic band attached for shooting small stones

slink \'slingk\ *vb* **slunk** \'sləngk\; **slink·ing** : to move or go stealthily : creep along (as in fear or shame)

slinky \'sling-kē\ *adj* **slink·i·er**; **-est** **1** : stealthily quiet ⟨*slinky* movements⟩ **2** : following the lines of the figure in a gracefully flowing manner ⟨women wearing *slinky* dresses⟩

1**slip** \'slip\ *vb* **slipped**; **slip·ping** **1 a** : to move easily and smoothly : SLIDE ⟨*slip* the knife into its sheath⟩ **b** : to move or place quietly or stealthily : STEAL ⟨*slipped* from the room⟩ **c** : to pass without being noted or used ⟨let the opportunity *slip*⟩ **2 a** : to get away from : ELUDE ⟨*slipped* his pursuers⟩ **b** : to free from : SHED ⟨the dog *slipped* his collar⟩ **c** : to escape the attention of ⟨*slipped* his mind⟩ **d** : to express or become expressed unintentionally or casually ⟨the secret *slipped* out⟩ **e** : to let loose or let go of ⟨*slip* a dog from a leash⟩ **f** : to cause to slide open : RELEASE, DISENGAGE ⟨*slip* a bolt⟩ **g** : to let a knitting stitch pass from one needle to another without working a new stitch **3 a** : to slide out of place, away from a support, or from one's grasp ⟨the dish *slipped* to the floor⟩ **b** : to slide so as to fall or lose balance ⟨*slip* on a grease spot⟩ **c** : to cause to slide esp. in putting, passing, or inserting easily or quickly ⟨*slip* into a coat⟩ **d** : DISLOCATE ⟨*slipped* his shoulder⟩ **e** : to fail to progress or hold normally from or as if from sliding ⟨the loose belt continued to *slip*⟩ **4** : to fall from some level or standard (as of conduct or activity) usu. gradually or by degrees ⟨the market *slipped* from an earlier high⟩ — **slip something over** : to get the better of another by trickery

2**slip** *n* **1 a** : a sloping ramp that extends out into the water and serves for landing or repairing ships **b** : a ship's berth between two piers **2** : the act or an instance of departing secretly or hurriedly **3 :** a mistake in judgment, policy, or procedure : BLUNDER, MISSTEP **4 :** the act or an instance of slipping down or out of place ⟨a *slip* on the ice⟩ **5 a :** an undergarment made in dress length with shoulder straps **b :** PILLOWCASE

³slip *n* **1 :** a small shoot or twig cut for planting or grafting : CUTTING **2 a :** a long narrow strip of material **b :** a piece of paper used for a memorandum or record ⟨sales *slip*⟩

⁴slip *vb* **slipped; slip·ping :** to take cuttings from a plant

slip·cov·er \ˈslip-ˌkəv-ər\ *n* **:** a removable protective covering for an article of furniture

slip·knot \-ˌnät\ *n* **:** a knot that slips along a line around which it is made

slip·page \ˈslip-ij\ *n* **1 :** an act, instance, or process of slipping **2 :** a loss in transmission of power

slipped disk *n* **:** a protrusion of one of the disks of cartilage between vertebrae with pressure on spinal nerves resulting in low back pain

slip·per \ˈslip-ər\ *n* **:** a light low shoe without laces that is easily slipped on or off — **slip·pered** \-ərd\ *adj*

slip·pery \ˈslip-(ə-)rē\ *adj* **slip·per·i·er; -est** **1 :** having a surface smooth enough to cause one to slide or lose one's hold ⟨a *slippery* floor⟩ **2 :** not worthy of trust : TRICKY, UNRELIABLE — **slip·per·i·ness** *n*

slip ring *n* **:** a metal ring that transmits electricity between the armature and the brushes of a device (as a generator)

slip·shod \ˈslip-ˈshäd\ *adj* **:** very careless : SLOVENLY ⟨contempt for makeshift methods and *slipshod* work⟩

slip·stick \ˈslip-ˌstik\ *n* **:** SLIDE RULE

slip·stream \ˈslip-ˌstrēm\ *n* **:** the stream of air driven aft by the propeller of an aircraft

slip–up \ˈslip-ˌəp\ *n* **1 :** MISTAKE **2 :** MISCHANCE

¹slit \ˈslit\ *vb* **slit; slit·ting 1 a :** to make a slit in : SLASH **b :** to cut off or away : SEVER **2 :** to cut into long narrow strips — **slit·ter** *n*

²slit *n* **:** a long narrow cut or opening — **slit** *adj* — **slit·like** \-ˌlīk\ *adj*

slith·er \ˈslith-ər\ *vb* **slith·ered; slith·er·ing** \-(ə-)riŋ\ **1 :** to slide or cause to slide on or as if on a loose gravelly surface **2 :** to slip or slide like a snake

slith·ery \-ə-rē\ *adj* **:** having a slippery surface, texture, or quality

slit trench *n* **:** a narrow trench for shelter in battle from bomb and shell fragments

¹sliv·er \ˈsliv-ər\ *n* **:** a long slender piece cut or torn off : SPLINTER

²sliver *vb* **sliv·ered; sliv·er·ing** \ˈsliv-(ə-)riŋ\ **:** to cut or form into slivers : SPLINTER

slob \ˈsläb\ *n* **:** a slovenly or boorish person

¹slob·ber \ˈsläb-ər\ *vb* **slob·bered; slob·ber·ing** \-(ə-)riŋ\ **1 :** to let saliva or liquid dribble from the mouth : DROOL **2 :** to show feeling to excess : GUSH — **slob·ber·er** \-ər-ər\ *n*

²slobber *n* **1 :** dripping saliva **2 :** silly excessive show of feeling — **slob·bery** \ˈsläb-(ə-)rē\ *adj*

sloe \ˈslō\ *n* **:** the tart bluish black globe-shaped fruit of the blackthorn; *also* : BLACKTHORN 1

sloe–eyed \ˈslō-ˈīd\ *adj* **1 :** having soft dark bluish or purplish black eyes **2 :** having slanted eyes

sloe gin *n* **:** a sweet reddish liqueur flavored chiefly with sloes

slog \ˈsläg\ *vb* **slogged; slog·ging 1 :** to hit hard : BEAT **2 :** to plod or work doggedly on — **slog·ger** *n*

slo·gan \ˈslō-gən\ *n* [from Scottish Gaelic *sluagh ghairm* "army cry"] **1 :** a word or phrase that calls to battle **2 :** a word or phrase used by a party, a group, or a business to attract attention

sloop \ˈslüp\ *n* **:** a sailing boat with one mast and a fore-and-aft mainsail and jib

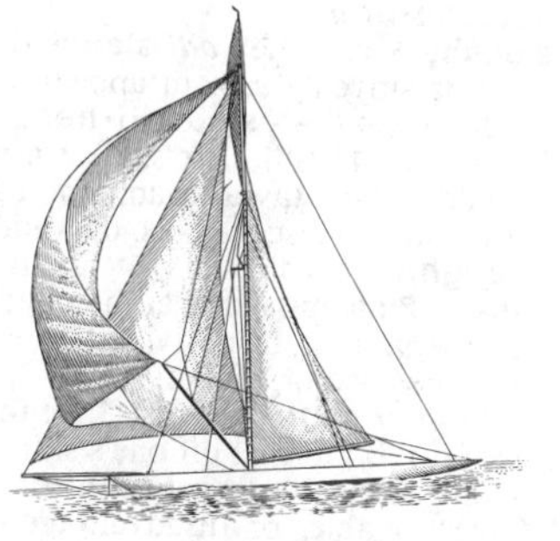
sloop

¹slop \ˈsläp\ *n* **1 :** soft mud : SLUSH **2 :** thin tasteless drink or liquid food — usu. used in pl. **3 :** liquid spilled or splashed **4 a :** food waste (as garbage) or a thin gruel fed to animals **b :** excreted body waste — usu. used in pl.

²slop *vb* **slopped; slop·ping 1 :** to spill on or over ⟨*slop* milk from a glass⟩ ⟨*slopped* her dress with gravy⟩ **2 :** to feed slop to ⟨*slop* the pigs⟩ **3 :** to behave or deal with in a sloppy manner ⟨*slop* about the house⟩

¹slope \ˈslōp\ *adj* **:** SLANTING, SLOPING

²slope *vb* **:** to take a slanting direction : give a slant to : INCLINE *syn* see SLANT — **slop·er** *n*

³slope *n* **1 :** ground that forms a natural or artificial incline **2 :** upward or downward slant or inclination or degree of slant **3 :** the part of a continent draining to a particular ocean

slop·py \ˈsläp-ē\ *adj* **slop·pi·er; -est 1 a :** wet so as to spatter easily : SLUSHY **b :** wet with or as if with something slopped over **2 :** SLOVENLY, CARELESS **3 :** excessively sentimental — **slop·pi·ly** \ˈsläp-ə-lē\ *adv* — **slop·pi·ness** \ˈsläp-ē-nəs\ *n*

¹slosh \ˈsläsh\ *n* **1 :** SLUSH **2 :** the slap or splash of liquid

²slosh *vb* **1 :** to flounder through or splash about in or with water, mud, or slush **2 :** to move with a splashing motion

¹slot \ˈslät\ *n* **:** a long narrow opening, groove, or passage : SLIT, NOTCH

²slot *vb* **slot·ted; slot·ting :** to cut a slot in

slot car *n* **:** a toy racing car that fits into a groove and is guided electrically by remote control

sloth \ˈslȯth, ˈslōth\ *n* [from Middle English *slouth*, from *slow* with the same suffix found in *warmth*] **1 :** INDOLENCE, LAZINESS **2 :** any of several slow-moving mammals of Central and So. America that are related to the armadillos, live in trees, and feed on leaves, shoots, and fruits

sloth 2
(about 20 in. long)

sloth·ful \-fəl\ *adj* **:** LAZY, SLUGGISH, INDOLENT — **sloth·ful·ly** \-fə-lē\ *adv* — **sloth·ful·ness** *n*

slot machine *n* **1 :** a machine whose operation is begun when a coin is dropped into a slot **2 :** a coin-

S

operated gambling machine that pays off according to the matching of symbols on wheels spun by a handle

¹**slouch** \'sl‌au̇ch\ *n* **1 :** an awkward, lazy, or incompetent person **2 :** a gait or posture characterized by ungainly stooping of head and shoulders

²**slouch** *vb* **:** to walk with or assume a slouch — **slouch·er** *n*

slouchy \'slau̇-chē\ *adj* **slouch·i·er; -est :** slouching or slovenly esp. in appearance — **slouch·i·ly** \-chə-lē\ *adv* — **slouch·i·ness** \-chē-nəs\ *n*

¹**slough** *n* **1** \'slü *also* 'slau̇\ **:** a wet and marshy or muddy place (as a swamp or backwater) **2** \'slau̇ *also* 'slü\ **:** a discouraged, degraded, or dejected state

²**slough** *or* **sluff** \'sləf\ *n* **1 :** the cast-off skin of a snake **2 :** a mass of dead tissue (as in a wound or ulcer) separating from living tissue **3 :** something that may be shed or cast off

³**slough** *or* **sluff** \'sləf\ *vb* **1 a :** to cast off or become cast off **b :** to cast off one's skin or dead tissue from living tissue **c :** to get rid of or discard as irksome, objectionable, or disadvantageous **2 :** to crumble slowly and fall away

Slo·vak \'slō-ˌväk, -ˌvak\ *n* **1 :** a member of a Slavic people of eastern Czechoslovakia **2 :** the Slavic language of the Slovak people — **Slovak** *adj* — **Slo·vak·i·an** \slō-'väk-ē-ən, -'vak-\ *adj or n*

slov·en \'sləv-ən\ *n* **:** a slovenly person **:** SLOB

Slo·vene \'slō-ˌvēn\ *n* **1 a :** a member of a southern Slavic group of people usu. classed with the Serbs and Croats and living in Yugoslavia **b :** a native or inhabitant of Slovenia **2 :** the language of the Slovenes — **Slovene** *adj* — **Slo·ve·ni·an** \slō-'vē-nē-ən\ *adj or n*

slov·en·ly \'sləv-ən-lē\ *adj* **1 a :** untidy esp. in dress or person **b :** lazily slipshod **2 :** characteristic of a sloven — **slov·en·li·ness** *n* — **slovenly** *adv*

¹**slow** \'slō\ *adj* **1 a :** mentally dull **:** STUPID **b :** naturally inert or sluggish **2 a :** unwilling to take prompt action **b :** not easily aroused or excited **3 a :** moving, flowing, or proceeding without speed or at less than usual speed ⟨*slow* traffic⟩ ⟨a *slow* stream⟩ **b :** not vigorous or active ⟨a *slow* fire⟩ **c :** taking place at a low rate or over a considerable period of time ⟨*slow* growth⟩ **4 :** having qualities that hinder or stop rapid progress or action ⟨a *slow* racetrack⟩ **5 a :** registering behind or below what is correct ⟨the clock is *slow*⟩ **b :** that is behind the time at a specified time or place **6 :** lacking in activity or liveliness ⟨a *slow* market⟩ — **slow·ish** \'slō-ish\ *adj* — **slow·ly** *adv* — **slow·ness** *n*

²**slow** *adv* **:** SLOWLY

³**slow** *vb* **:** to make or go slow or slower

slow·down \'slō-ˌdau̇n\ *n* **:** a slowing down

slow motion *n* **:** action in a projected motion picture apparently taking place at a speed much slower than that of the photographed action

slow·poke \'slō-ˌpōk\ *n* **:** a very slow person

sludge \'sləj\ *n* **1 :** MUD, MIRE **2 :** a muddy or slushy mass, deposit, or sediment; *esp* **:** precipitated solid matter produced by water and sewage treatment processes — **sludgy** \'sləj-ē\ *adj*

¹**slue** \'slü\ *var of* SLOUGH

²**slue** *vb* **:** to turn, twist, or swing about esp. out of a course **:** VEER

ə abut ər further a back ā bake ä cot, cart au̇ out ch chin e less ē easy g gift i trip ī life j joke ng sing ō flow ȯ flaw ȯi coin th thin th this ü loot u̇ foot y yet yü few yu̇ furious zh vision

³**slue** *n* **:** an act or instance of or the position attained by sluing

⁴**slue** *var of* SLEW

¹**slug** \'sləg\ *n* **1 :** SLUGGARD **2 :** any of numerous long and wormlike chiefly terrestrial mollusks that are closely related to the land snails but have only a rudimentary shell or none **3 :** a smooth soft larva of a sawfly or moth that creeps like a snail

²**slug** *n* **1 a :** a small piece of shaped metal (as a bullet) **b :** a metal disk used in place of a coin in a coin-operated machine **2 :** a single drink of liquor **:** SHOT

³**slug** *n* **:** a heavy blow esp. with the fist

⁴**slug** *vb* **slugged; slug·ging :** to strike heavily with or as if with the fist or a bat — **slug·ger** *n*

slug·gard \'sləg-ərd\ *n* **:** an habitually lazy person — **sluggard** *adj* — **slug·gard·ly** \-lē\ *adj*

slug·gish \'sləg-ish\ *adj* **:** slow and inactive in movement or reaction by habit or condition — **slug·gish·ly** *adv* — **slug·gish·ness** *n*

¹**sluice** \'slüs\ *n* **1 :** an artificial passage for water with a gate for controlling its flow or changing its direction **2 :** a body of water held back by a gate or a stream flowing through a gate **3 :** a device (as a floodgate) for controlling the flow of water **4 :** a channel that carries off surplus water **5 :** a long inclined trough (as for floating logs to a sawmill)

²**sluice** *vb* **1 :** to draw off by or through a sluice **2 a :** to wash with or in water running through or from a sluice **b :** DRENCH, FLUSH

sluice·way \'slüs-ˌwā\ *n* **:** an artificial channel into which water is let by a sluice

¹**slum** \'sləm\ *n* **:** a thickly populated section esp. of a city marked by crowding, dirty run-down housing, and generally wretched living conditions

²**slum** *vb* **slummed; slum·ming :** to visit slums esp. out of curiosity or for pleasure — **slum·mer** *n*

slum·ber \'sləm-bər\ *vb* **slum·bered; slum·ber·ing** \-b(ə-)riŋ\ **1 :** to sleep usu. lightly **2 :** to lie dormant **:** be inactive ⟨a *slumbering* volcano⟩ — **slumber** *n* — **slum·ber·er** \-bər-ər\ *n*

slum·ber·ous *or* **slum·brous** \'sləm-b(ə-)rəs\ *adj* **1 :** SLEEPY, SOMNOLENT **2 :** inviting slumber **:** SOPORIFIC

slum·lord \'sləm-ˌlȯrd\ *n* **:** a landlord who receives unusually large profits from renting substandard properties

¹**slump** \'sləmp\ *vb* **1 :** to drop or slide down suddenly **:** COLLAPSE **2 :** to assume a drooping posture or carriage **:** SLOUCH **3 :** to fall off sharply

²**slump** *n* **:** a marked or sustained decline esp. in economic activity or prices

slung *past of* SLING

slunk *past of* SLINK

¹**slur** \'slər\ *vb* **slurred; slur·ring 1 a :** to slide or slip over without due mention, consideration, or emphasis **b :** to perform hurriedly **:** SKIMP **2 :** to sing or play successive musical notes of different pitch in a smooth or connected manner **3 :** to speak indistinctly usu. as a result of carelessness or haste

²**slur** *n* **1 a :** a curved line ‿ or ⁀ connecting notes to be sung or played without a break **b :** the combination of two or more slurred tones **2 :** a slurring manner of speech

³**slur** *vb* **slurred; slur·ring 1 :** to cast aspersions upon **:** DISPARAGE **2 :** to make indistinct **:** OBSCURE **3 :** to slip so as to cause a slur

⁴**slur** *n* **1 a :** ASPERSION, CALUMNY **b :** REPROACH, STIGMA **2 :** a blurred spot in printed matter **:** SMUDGE

slurp \'slərp\ *vb* **:** to eat or drink noisily or with a sucking sound — **slurp** *n*

slush \'sləsh\ *n* **1 :** partly melted or watery snow **2 :** soft mud **:** MIRE **3 :** RUBBISH, DRIVEL

slushy \'sləsh-ē\ *adj* **slush·i·er; -est** : full of or resembling slush ⟨a *slushy* road⟩ ⟨soft *slushy* ice⟩ — **slush·i·ness** *n*

slut \'slət\ *n* **1** : a slovenly woman : SLATTERN **2** : a lewd woman; *esp* : PROSTITUTE — **slut·tish** \'slət-ish\ *adj* — **slut·tish·ly** *adv* — **slut·tish·ness** *n*

sly \'slī\ *adj* **sli·er** *also* **sly·er** \'slī(-ə)r\; **sli·est** *also* **sly·est** \'slī-əst\ **1 a** : artfully cunning : CRAFTY **b** : SECRETIVE, FURTIVE **2** : lightly mischievous : ROGUISH *syn* see CUNNING *ant* candid, straightforward — **sly·ly** *adv* — **sly·ness** *n* — **on the sly** : FURTIVELY

sm *abbr* small

SM *abbr* master of science

[1]**smack** \'smak\ *n* **1** : characteristic or perceptible taste or flavor **2** : a small quantity

[2]**smack** *vb* : to have a flavor, trace, or suggestion ⟨the roast *smacks* of thyme⟩ ⟨such actions *smack* of treachery⟩

[3]**smack** *vb* **1** : to close and open the lips noisily esp. in eating **2** : to kiss usu. loudly or boisterously **3** : to make or give a smack ⟨*smacked* the cat from the table⟩

[4]**smack** *n* **1** : a quick sharp noise made by rapidly opening and closing the lips **2** : a loud kiss **3** : a sharp slap or blow

[5]**smack** *adv* : in a square and sharp manner : DIRECTLY ⟨it hit him *smack* in the face⟩

[6]**smack** *n* : a sailing ship (as a sloop or cutter) used chiefly in coasting and fishing

[7]**smack** *n, slang* : HEROIN

smack–dab \'smak-'dab\ *adv, dial* : SQUARELY, EXACTLY

[1]**small** \'smȯl\ *adj* **1** : little in size **2** : few in numbers or members ⟨a *small* crowd⟩ **3** : little in amount ⟨a *small* supply⟩ **4** : not very much ⟨*small* success⟩ **5** : UNIMPORTANT ⟨a *small* matter⟩ **6** : operating on a limited scale ⟨*small* dealers⟩ **7** : GENTLE, SOFT ⟨a *small* voice⟩ **8** : not generous : MEAN ⟨a *small* nature⟩ **9** : made up of small units **10** : HUMBLE, MODEST ⟨a *small* beginning⟩ **11** : HUMILIATED, HUMBLED ⟨felt very *small* to be caught cheating⟩ — **small·ish** \'smȯ-lish\ *adj* — **small·ness** *n*

[2]**small** *adv* **1** : in or into small pieces ⟨cut the meat *small*⟩ **2** : in a small manner ⟨most businesses begin *small*⟩

[3]**small** *n* : a part smaller and esp. narrower than the remainder ⟨the *small* of the back⟩

small arm *n* : a firearm fired while held in the hands

small calorie *n* : CALORIE 1a

small change *n* **1** : coins of low denominations **2** : something trifling or petty

small–fry \'smȯl-ˌfrī\ *adj* **1** : MINOR, UNIMPORTANT **2** : of or relating to children : CHILDISH

small game *n* : birds and small mammals (as rabbits) hunted for sport

small intestine *n* : the part of the intestine that lies between the stomach and colon, consists of duodenum, jejunum, and ileum, secretes digestive enzymes, and is the chief seat of the absorption of digested nutrients

small–mind·ed \'smȯl-'mīn-dəd\ *adj* **1** : having narrow interests, sympathies, or outlook **2** : typical of a small-minded person : PETTY — **small–mind·ed·ly** *adv* — **small–mind·ed·ness** *n*

small·mouth black bass \'smȯl-ˌmau̇th-\ *n* : a black bass that lives chiefly in cool clear rivers and lakes and is bronze green above and lighter below — called also *smallmouth bass*

small·pox \'smȯl-ˌpäks\ *n* : an acute contagious virus disease marked by fever and skin eruption

small talk *n* : light or casual conversation

[1]**smart** \'smärt\ *vb* **1** : to cause or feel a sharp stinging pain **2** : to feel or endure distress, remorse, or embarrassment ⟨*smart* under criticism⟩

[2]**smart** *adj* **1** : causing smarting : STINGING **2** : marked by forceful activity or vigorous strength **3** : BRISK, SPIRITED **4 a** : mentally alert : BRIGHT ⟨a *smart* teacher⟩ **b** : sharp in scheming : SHREWD **5 a** : WITTY, CLEVER **b** : PERT, SAUCY ⟨a *smart* retort⟩ **6 a** : stylish or elegant in dress or appearance **b** : SOPHISTICATED **c** : FASHIONABLE — **smart·ly** *adv* — **smart·ness** *n*

[3]**smart** *adv* : SMARTLY

[4]**smart** *n* : a smarting pain; *esp* : a stinging local pain

smart al·eck \'smärt-ˌal-ik, -ˌel-\ *n* : a conceited person who obnoxiously tries to be witty or clever — **smart–al·ecky** \-ˌal-ə-kē, -ˌel-\ *or* **smart–aleck** *adj*

smart·en \'smärt-ən\ *vb* **smart·ened; smart·en·ing** \-(ə-)ning\ **1** : to make smart or smarter : SPRUCE, FRESHEN ⟨*smartened* himself for the party⟩ **2** : to make or become more alert ⟨*smarten* up, young man⟩

smart set *n* : extremely fashionable society

smarty *or* **smart·ie** \'smärt-ē\ *n, pl* **smart·ies** : SMART ALECK

[1]**smash** \'smash\ *vb* **1** : to break into pieces by violence : SHATTER ⟨*smash* down a door⟩ ⟨the dish *smashed* on the floor⟩ **2** : to drive, throw, or move violently esp. with a destructive effect ⟨the ball *smashed* through the window⟩ **3** : to destroy utterly : WRECK **4** : to go to pieces suddenly : COLLAPSE — **smash·er** *n*

[2]**smash** *n* **1 a** : a smashing blow or attack **b** : a hard overhand stroke (as in tennis) **2** : the condition of being smashed **3 a** : the action or sound of smashing; *esp* : a wreck due to collision : CRASH **b** : utter collapse : RUIN; *esp* : BANKRUPTCY **4** : a striking success : HIT ⟨the new play is a *smash*⟩

smash·up \'smash-ˌəp\ *n* **1** : a complete collapse **2** : a destructive collision of motor vehicles

smat·ter·ing \'smat-ə-ring\ *n* **1** : superficial piecemeal knowledge ⟨had a *smattering* of French⟩ **2** : a small scattered number

[1]**smear** \'smi(ə)r\ *n* **1** : a spot made by or as if by an oily or sticky substance : SMUDGE **2** : material smeared on a surface; *esp* : material prepared for microscopic examination by smearing on a slide **3** : a usu. unsubstantiated charge or accusation

[2]**smear** *vb* **1 a** : to spread or daub with something oily or sticky **b** : to spread over a surface **2 a** : to stain, smudge, or dirty by or as if by smearing **b** : to blacken the reputation of **3** : to obliterate or blur by or as if by smearing — **smear·er** *n*

smear·case *or* **smier·case** \'smi(ə)r-ˌkās\ *n, chiefly Midland* : COTTAGE CHEESE

smear word *n* : an epithet intended to smear a person or group

smeary \'smi(ə)r-ē\ *adj* **smear·i·er; -est** **1** : SMEARED **2** : liable to cause smears

[1]**smell** \'smel\ *vb* **smelled** \'smeld\ *or* **smelt** \'smelt\; **smell·ing** **1** : to get the odor or scent of through stimuli affecting certain sense organs of the nose **2** : to detect or become aware of as if by the sense of smell ⟨he *smelled* trouble⟩ **3** : to use the sense of smell **4 a** : to have or give forth an odor **b** : to give off a suggestion of something and esp. of something unwholesome or evil ⟨the plan *smells* of trickery⟩ — **smell·er** *n* — **smell a rat** : to have a suspicion of something wrong

[2]**smell** *n* **1 a** : the process or power of smelling **b** : the special sense concerned with detecting odor

S

2 : the property of a thing that affects the organs of smell : ODOR **3** : a pervading quality : AURA ⟨the *smell* of adventure⟩ **4** : an act of smelling
smelling salts *n pl* : a strong-smelling preparation of ammonia in water used to relieve faintness
smelly \'smel-ē\ *adj* **smell·i·er**; **-est** : having a smell and esp. a bad smell
1**smelt** \'smelt\ *n, pl* **smelts** *or* **smelt** : any of several very small food fishes of coastal or fresh waters that resemble and are related to the trout

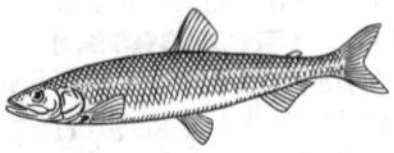
smelt
(up to 15 in. long)

2**smelt** *vb* : to melt or fuse as ore usu. in order to separate the metal : REFINE, REDUCE
smelt·er \'smel-tər\ *n* : one that smelts: **a** : a worker in or an owner of a smeltery **b** *or* **smelt·ery** \-t(ə-)rē\ : an establishment for smelting
smid·gen *or* **smid·geon** *or* **smid·gin** \'smij-ən\ *n* : a small amount : BIT
1**smile** \'smīl\ *vb* **1** : to have, produce, or exhibit a smile **2 a** : to look with amusement or ridicule ⟨*smiled* at his own folly⟩ **b** : to be propitious or agreeable ⟨the weather *smiled* on our plans⟩ **3** : to express by a smile — **smil·er** *n* — **smil·ing·ly** \'smī-ling-lē\ *adv*
2**smile** *n* : a change of facial expression in which the eyes brighten and the lips curve slightly upward esp. in expression of amusement, pleasure, approval, or sometimes scorn — **smile·less** \'smīl-ləs\ *adj* — **smile·less·ly** *adv*
smirch \'smərch\ *vb* **1** : to make dirty, stained, or discolored esp. by smearing with something that soils **2** : to bring discredit or disgrace on — **smirch** *n*
smirk \'smərk\ *vb* : to smile in an affected manner : SIMPER — **smirk** *n*
smirky \'smər-kē\ *adj* : SMIRKING
smite \'smīt\ *vb* **smote** \'smōt\; **smit·ten** \'smit-ən\ *or* **smote**; **smit·ing** \'smīt-ing\ **1** : to strike sharply or heavily esp. with the hand or a hand weapon **2 a** : to kill or injure by smiting **b** : to attack or afflict suddenly and injuriously ⟨*smitten* by disease⟩ **3** : to affect like a sudden hard blow ⟨*smitten* with terror⟩ — **smit·er** \'smīt-ər\ *n*
smith \'smith\ *n* **1** : a worker in metals : BLACKSMITH **2** : MAKER — often used in combination ⟨gun*smith*⟩ ⟨tune*smith*⟩
smith·er·eens \,smith-ə-'rēnz\ *n pl* [from Irish Gaelic *smidirín*, diminutive of *smiodar* "fragment"] : FRAGMENTS, BITS
smithy \'smith-ē, 'smith-\ *n, pl* **smith·ies** : the workshop of a smith
1**smock** \'smäk\ *n* **1** *archaic* : a woman's undergarment; *esp* : CHEMISE **2** : a light loose garment worn usu. over regular clothing for protection from dirt
2**smock** *vb* : to embroider or shirr with smocking
smock·ing \'smäk-ing\ *n* : a decorative embroidery or shirring made by gathering cloth in regularly spaced round tucks
smog \'smäg\ *n* [from a blend of *smoke* and *fog*] : a fog made heavier and darker by smoke and chemical fumes — **smog·gy** \'smäg-ē\ *adj*

ə abut	ər further	a back	ā bake
ä cot, cart	au̇ out	ch chin	e less	ē easy
g gift	i trip	ī life	j joke	ng sing	ō flow
ȯ flaw	ȯi coin	th thin	th this	ü loot
u̇ foot	y yet	yü few	yu̇ furious	zh vision

1**smoke** \'smōk\ *n* **1 a** : the gas of burning organic materials (as coal, wood, or tobacco) made visible by small particles of carbon **b** : a suspension of solid or liquid particles in a gas **2** : a mass or column of smoke **3** : fume or vapor often resulting from the action of heat on moisture **4** : something of little substance, permanence, or value **5** : something that obscures **6** : something to smoke (as a cigarette) — **smoke·like** \-,līk\ *adj*
2**smoke** *vb* **1 a** : to emit or exhale smoke **b** : to emit excessive smoke **2 a** : to inhale and exhale the fumes of a burning substance (as tobacco) **b** : to use in smoking ⟨*smoke* a pipe⟩ ⟨*smoke* a cigar⟩ **3 a** : to drive away by smoke **b** : to blacken or discolor with smoke **c** : to cure by exposure to smoke ⟨*smoked* meat⟩ ⟨*smoked* cheese⟩ **d** : to stupefy (as bees) by smoke
smoke·house \'smōk-,hau̇s\ *n* : a building where meat or fish is cured by means of dense smoke
smoke jumper *n* : a forest-fire fighter who parachutes to locations otherwise difficult to reach
smoke·less \'smōk-ləs\ *adj* : producing or containing little or no smoke ⟨*smokeless* powder⟩
smok·er \'smō-kər\ *n* **1** : one that smokes **2** : a railroad car or compartment in which smoking is allowed **3** : an informal social gathering
smoke screen *n* : a screen of or as if of smoke to hinder observation or detection
smoke·stack \'smōk-,stak\ *n* : a chimney or funnel through which smoke and gases are discharged
smoke tree *n* : a small shrubby tree related to the sumac and often grown for its large clusters of tiny flowers suggesting a cloud of smoke
smoky \'smō-kē\ *adj* **smok·i·er**; **-est** **1** : emitting smoke esp. in large quantities ⟨*smoky* stoves⟩ **2** : resembling or suggestive of smoke ⟨a *smoky* flavor⟩ **3** : filled with or darkened by smoke ⟨a *smoky* room⟩ — **smok·i·ly** \-kə-lē\ *adv* — **smok·i·ness** \-kē-nəs\ *n*
smoky quartz *n* : CAIRNGORM
1**smol·der** *or* **smoul·der** \'smōl-dər\ *n* : a slow smoky fire
2**smolder** *or* **smoulder** *vb* **smol·dered** *or* **smoul·dered**; **smol·der·ing** *or* **smoul·der·ing** \-d(ə-)ring\ **1** : to burn sluggishly with smoke and usu. without flame ⟨fire was *smoldering* in the grate⟩ **2 a** : to exist in a state of suppressed activity ⟨a *smoldering* rebellion⟩ **b** : to indicate a suppressed emotion ⟨eyes *smoldering* with anger⟩
smooch \'smüch\ *vb* : KISS, PET — **smooch** *n*
1**smooth** \'smüth\ *adj* **1 a** : having a continuous even surface : not rough ⟨a *smooth* skin⟩ **b** : being without hairs or projections **c** : causing no resistance to sliding **2** : free from obstacles or difficulties ⟨a *smooth* path⟩ **3** : even and uninterrupted in flow or flight **4** : insincerely flattering : INGRATIATING ⟨a *smooth* salesman⟩ **5 a** : SERENE, EQUABLE ⟨a *smooth* disposition⟩ **b** : AMIABLE, COURTEOUS **6** : not sharp or acid : BLAND ⟨a *smooth* sherry⟩ — **smooth·ly** *adv* — **smooth·ness** *n*
2**smooth** *vb* **1** : to make smooth **2 a** : to free from what is harsh or disagreeable : POLISH ⟨*smoothed* out his style⟩ **b** : SOOTHE **3** : to minimize (as a fault) in order to allay ill will : PALLIATE ⟨*smoothed* things over with apologies⟩ **4** : to free from obstruction or difficulty ⟨*smoothed* the way for a quick settlement of the dispute⟩ **5** : to cause to lie evenly and in order : PREEN ⟨*smooths* down her hair⟩ — **smooth·er** *n*
smooth·bore \'smüth-'bō(ə)r, -'bȯ(ə)r\ *adj* : having a smooth-surfaced bore ⟨*smoothbore* firearms⟩ — **smooth·bore** \-,bō(ə)r, -,bȯ(ə)r\ *n*

smooth·en \'smü-thən\ *vb* : to make or become smooth

smooth muscle *n* : muscle made up of spindle-shaped cells with single nuclei and no cross striations that is typical of visceral organs, occurs esp. in sheets and rings, and is not under voluntary control — called also *involuntary muscle;* compare STRIATED MUSCLE

smooth–tongued \'smüth-'təŋd\ *adj* : ingratiating in speech : insincerely flattering

smoothy *or* **smooth·ie** \'smü-thē\ *n, pl* **smooth·ies 1 a** : a person with polished manners **b** : a man with an ingratiating manner toward women **2** : a smooth-tongued person

smor·gas·bord \'smȯr-gəs-ˌbȯrd, -ˌbōrd\ *n* : a luncheon or supper buffet offering a large variety of foods and dishes

smote *past of* SMITE

smoth·er \'sməth-ər\ *vb* **smoth·ered; smoth·er·ing** \-(ə-)riŋ\ **1 a** : to overcome by depriving of air or exposing to smoke or fumes : SUFFOCATE **b** : to prevent the development or activity of ⟨*smother* a child with too much care⟩ **2** : to become suffocated **3 a** : to cover up : SUPPRESS ⟨*smother* a yawn⟩ **b** : to overlay thickly ⟨steak *smothered* with mushrooms⟩

1**smudge** \'sməj\ *vb* **1 a** : to make a smudge on **b** : to soil as if by smudging **2** : to smoke or protect by a smudge **3** : to make a smudge or become smudged

2**smudge** *n* **1 a** : a blurry spot or streak : SMEAR **b** : STAIN **2** : a fire made to smoke (as for protecting fruit from frost) — **smudg·i·ly** \'sməj-ə-lē\ *adv* — **smudg·i·ness** \'sməj-ē-nəs\ *n* — **smudgy** \'sməj-ē\ *adj*

smug \'sməg\ *adj* **smug·ger; smug·gest** : highly self-satisfied : COMPLACENT — **smug·ly** *adv* — **smug·ness** *n*

smug·gle \'sməg-əl\ *vb* **smug·gled; smug·gling** \-(ə-)liŋ\ **1** : to export or import secretly and unlawfully esp. to avoid paying duty ⟨*smuggle* jewels⟩ **2** : to take, bring, or introduce secretly or stealthily — **smug·gler** \'sməg-lər\ *n*

1**smut** \'smət\ *vb* **smut·ted; smut·ting 1** : to stain, taint, or affect with smut **2** : to become affected by smut

2**smut** *n* **1** : matter that soils or blackens; *esp* : a particle of soot **2** : any of various destructive diseases of plants caused by fungi that transform plant organs (as seeds) into dark masses of spores; *also* : a fungus causing a smut **3** : obscene or indecent language or matter

smut·ty \'smət-ē\ *adj* **smut·ti·er; -est 1** : soiled or tainted with smut ⟨a *smutty* face⟩ **2** : affected with smut fungus **3** : OBSCENE, INDECENT ⟨*smutty* jokes⟩ — **smut·ti·ly** \'smət-ə-lē\ *adv* — **smut·ti·ness** \'smət-ē-nəs\ *n*

snack \'snak\ *n* : a light meal : LUNCH

snack bar *n* : a public eating place where snacks are served usu. at a counter

1**snag** \'snag\ *n* **1** : a stump or stub of a tree branch esp. when embedded under water and not visible from the surface **2** : an uneven or broken projection from a smooth or finished surface ⟨caught her stocking on a *snag*⟩ **3** : a concealed or unexpected difficulty or hindrance ⟨the negotiations hit a *snag*⟩ — **snag·gy** \'snag-ē\ *adj*

2**snag** *vb* **snagged; snag·ging** : to catch on or as if on a snag

snag·gle·tooth \'snag-əl-ˌtüth\ *n* : an irregular, broken, or projecting tooth — **snag·gle·toothed** \ˌsnag-əl-'tütht\ *adj*

snail \'snāl\ *n* **1** : a gastropod mollusk esp. when having an external spiral shell into which it can withdraw **2** : a slow-moving person or thing

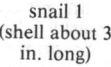

snail 1 (shell about 3 in. long)

1**snake** \'snāk\ *n* **1** : any of numerous limbless long-bodied reptiles that eat large insects or small mammals and birds **2** : a despicable or treacherous person — **snake·like** \-ˌlīk\ *adj*

2**snake** *vb* **1** : to crawl or move sinuously, silently, or secretly **2** : to move (as logs) by dragging

snake·bite \'snāk-ˌbīt\ *n* : the bite of a snake and esp. a venomous snake

snake in the grass 1 : a lurking or unsuspected danger **2** : a secretly faithless friend

snake plant *n* : SANSEVIERIA

snake·skin \'snāk-ˌskin\ *n* : the skin of a snake or leather made from it

snaky \'snā-kē\ *adj* **snak·i·er; -est 1** : of or resembling a snake **2** : abounding in snakes — **snak·i·ly** \-kə-lē\ *adv*

1**snap** \'snap\ *vb* **snapped; snap·ping 1 a** : to make a sudden closing of the jaws : seize something sharply with the mouth ⟨fish *snapping* at the bait⟩ **b** : to grasp at something eagerly ⟨*snapped* at the chance to travel⟩ **c** : to take possession of promptly and decisively ⟨*snap* up a bargain⟩ **2** : to speak sharply or irritably ⟨*snap* at a questioner⟩ **3 a** : to break or break apart suddenly esp. with a sharp sound ⟨the twig *snapped*⟩ ⟨*snapped* the bone in two⟩ **b** : to give way or cause to give way suddenly under stress ⟨his nerve *snapped*⟩ **c** : to bring to a sudden end ⟨*snapped* the opposing team's winning streak⟩ **4** : to make or cause to make a sharp or crackling sound ⟨*snap* a whip⟩ **5 a** : to close or fit in place with an abrupt movement ⟨the lid *snapped* shut⟩ **b** : to put into or remove from a position by a sudden movement or with a snapping sound ⟨*snap* off a switch⟩ **c** : to close by means of snaps or fasteners ⟨*snapped* up her dress⟩ **6** : FLASH ⟨her eyes *snapped* in anger⟩ **7 a** : to act or be acted upon with snap ⟨*snapped* to attention⟩ **b** : to put a football in play esp. by passing or handing backward between the legs **c** : to take a snapshot of

2**snap** *n* **1** : an abrupt closing (as of the mouth in biting or of scissors in cutting); *esp* : a biting or snatching with the teeth or jaws **2** : something that is easy and presents no problems : CINCH **3** : a small amount : BIT ⟨don't care a *snap*⟩ **4 a** : a sudden snatching at something **b** : a quick short movement **c** : a sudden sharp breaking **5** : a sound made by snapping something ⟨shut the book with a *snap*⟩ **6** : a sudden interval of harsh weather ⟨cold *snap*⟩ **7** : a catch or fastening that closes or locks with a click ⟨*snap* of a bracelet⟩ **8** : a thin brittle cookie **9** : SNAPSHOT **10 a** : ENERGY **b** : SMARTNESS, SNAPPINESS **11** : an act or instance of snapping a football ⟨fumbled the *snap* from center⟩

3**snap** *adj* **1** : made suddenly or without deliberation ⟨a *snap* judgment⟩ **2** : shutting or fastening with a click or by means of a device that snaps ⟨*snap* lock⟩ **3** : unusually easy ⟨*snap* course⟩

snap·back \'snap-ˌbak\ *n* **1** : a football snap **2** : a sudden rebound or recovery

snap back \-'bak\ *vb* : to make a quick or vigorous recovery ⟨*snap back* after an illness⟩

snap bean *n* : a bean grown primarily for its young pods usu. used broken in pieces as a cooked vegetable

S

snap·drag·on \'snap-ˌdrag-ən\ *n* : any of several garden plants having showy white, crimson, or yellow 2-lipped flowers

snapdragon

snap·per \'snap-ər\ *n, pl* **snappers** *also* **snapper** **1 a** : something that snaps **b** : SNAPPING TURTLE **2 a** : any of a large family of active flesh-eating fishes of warm seas important as food and sport fishes **b** : any of several immature fishes (as the young of the bluefish) that resemble a snapper

snapping turtle *n* : any of several large edible American aquatic turtles with powerful jaws and a strong musky odor

snap·pish \'snap-ish\ *adj* **1** : marked by snapping irritable speech : IRASCIBLE ⟨a *snappish* disposition⟩ **2** : inclined to bite ⟨a *snappish* dog⟩ — **snap·pish·ly** *adv* — **snap·pish·ness** *n*

snap·py \'snap-ē\ *adj* **snap·pi·er**; **-est** **1** : SNAPPISH **2** : QUICK, SUDDEN ⟨make it *snappy*⟩ **3 a** : LIVELY **b** : briskly cold **c** : STYLISH, SMART ⟨a *snappy* dresser⟩ — **snap·pi·ly** \'snap-ə-lē\ *adv* — **snap·pi·ness** \'snap-ē-nəs\ *n*

snap·shot \'snap-ˌshät\ *n* : a casual photograph usu. taken by an amateur with a hand-held camera

1**snare** \'sna(ə)r, 'sne(ə)r\ *n* **1** : a trap often consisting of a noose for catching small animals or birds **2** : something by which one is entangled, trapped, or deceived **3** : one of the catgut strings or metal spirals of a snare drum

2**snare** *vb* **1** : to capture or entangle by or as if by use of a snare **2** : to win or attain by skillful or deceptive maneuvers — **snar·er** *n*

snare drum *n* : a small double-headed drum with one or more snares stretched across its lower head

1**snarl** \'snärl\ *n* **1** : a tangle esp. of hairs or thread : KNOT **2** : a tangled situation ⟨a traffic *snarl*⟩

2**snarl** *vb* : to get into a tangle

3**snarl** *vb* **1** : to growl with a snapping or gnashing of teeth **2** : to express anger in surly language **3** : to utter with a snarl — **snarl·er** *n*

4**snarl** *n* : a surly angry growl

1**snatch** \'snach\ *vb* **1** : to seize or try to seize something quickly or suddenly **2** : to grasp or take suddenly or hastily : GRAB — **snatch·er** *n*

2**snatch** *n* **1** : a snatching at or of something **2** : a brief opportune period ⟨slept in *snatches*⟩ **3** : something brief, fragmentary, or hurried

snaz·zy \'snaz-ē\ *adj* **snaz·zi·er**; **-est** : conspicuously or flashily attractive ⟨a *snazzy* tie⟩

1**sneak** \'snēk\ *vb* **1** : to go stealthily or furtively : SLINK **2** : to put, bring, or take in a furtive or sly manner *syn* see LURK

2**sneak** *n* **1** : a person who acts in a stealthy, furtive, or sly manner **2** : the act or an instance of sneaking

3**sneak** *adj* **1** : carried on secretly : CLANDESTINE **2** : SURPRISE ⟨a *sneak* attack⟩

sneak·er \'snē-kər\ *n* **1** : one that sneaks **2** : a usu. canvas sports shoe with a pliable rubber sole

sneak·ing \'snē-king\ *adj* **1** : FURTIVE, UNDERHAND **2** : not openly expressed as if something to be ashamed of ⟨a *sneaking* suspicion⟩ — **sneak·ing·ly** \-king-lē\ *adv*

ə abut	ər further	a back	ā bake
ä cot, cart	aù out	ch chin	e less	ē easy
g gift	i trip	ī life	j joke	ng sing	ō flow
ȯ flaw	ȯi coin	th thin	th this	ü loot
ù foot	y yet	yü few	yù furious	zh vision

sneaky \'snē-kē\ *adj* **sneak·i·er**; **-est** : marked by stealth, furtiveness, or slyness — **sneak·i·ly** \-kə-lē\ *adv* — **sneak·i·ness** \-kē-nəs\ *n*

1**sneer** \'sni(ə)r\ *vb* **1** : to smile or laugh with facial expressions of scorn or contempt **2** : to speak or write in a scornfully jeering manner — **sneer·er** *n*

2**sneer** *n* : a sneering expression or remark

sneeze \'snēz\ *vb* : to make a sudden violent spasmodic audible expiration of breath — **sneeze** *n* — **sneez·er** *n* — **sneeze at** : to treat lightly : DESPISE

1**snick** \'snik\ *vb* : to cut slightly : NICK

2**snick** *n* : a cutting or clicking noise

1**snick·er** \'snik-ər\ *or* **snig·ger** \'snig-ər\ *vb* **snickered** *or* **snig·gered**; **snick·er·ing** *or* **snig·ger·ing** \-(ə-)ring\ : to laugh in a slight, covert, or partly suppressed manner : TITTER

2**snicker** *or* **snigger** *n* : an act or sound of snickering

snide \'snīd\ *adj* **1** : MEAN, LOW ⟨a *snide* trick⟩ **2** : slyly disparaging : INSINUATING ⟨*snide* remarks⟩

sniff \'snif\ *vb* **1** : to draw air audibly up the nose **2** : to show or express disdain or scorn ⟨*sniffed* at menial jobs⟩ **3** : to smell or take by inhalation through the nose : INHALE ⟨*sniff* perfume⟩ **4** : to detect by or as if by smelling ⟨*sniff* out trouble⟩ — **sniff** *n* — **sniff·er** *n*

sniff·ish \'snif-ish\ *adj* : inclined to sniff haughtily : SCORNFUL, DISDAINFUL ⟨a *sniffish* aristocrat⟩ — **sniff·ish·ly** *adv* — **sniff·ish·ness** *n*

1**snif·fle** \'snif-əl\ *vb* **snif·fled**; **snif·fling** \-(ə-)ling\ **1** : to sniff repeatedly : SNUFFLE **2** : to speak with or as if with sniffling — **snif·fler** \-(ə-)lər\ *n*

2**sniffle** *n* **1** : an act or sound of sniffling **2** *pl* : a head cold marked by nasal discharge

sniffy \'snif-ē\ *adj* : SNIFFISH — **sniff·i·ly** \'snif-ə-lē\ *adv* — **sniff·i·ness** \'snif-ē-nəs\ *n*

1**snip** \'snip\ *n* **1** : a small piece that is snipped off : FRAGMENT **2** : an act or sound of snipping **3** : a rude person; *esp* : MINX

2**snip** *vb* **snipped**; **snip·ping** : to cut or cut off with or as if with shears or scissors; *esp* : to clip suddenly or by bits

1**snipe** \'snīp\ *n, pl* **snipes** *or* **snipe** : any of several long-billed game birds esp. of marshy areas that resemble the related woodcocks

snipe
(about 12 in. long)

2**snipe** *vb* **1** : to shoot at exposed individuals of an enemy's forces esp. when not in action from a usu. concealed point of vantage **2** : to aim a carping or snide attack — **snip·er** *n*

snip·pet \'snip-ət\ *n* : a small part, piece, or thing

snip·py \'snip-ē\ *adj* **snip·pi·er**; **-est** **1** : SHORT-TEMPERED, SNAPPISH **2** : unduly brief or curt **3** : putting on airs — **snip·pi·ness** *n*

snips \'snips\ *n pl* : hand shears used esp. for cutting sheet metal ⟨tin *snips*⟩

snitch \'snich\ *vb* **1** : INFORM, TATTLE ⟨always *snitching* on someone⟩ **2** : to take by stealth; *esp* : PILFER ⟨*snitched* a dime from his sister⟩ — **snitch·er** *n*

sniv·el \'sniv-əl\ *vb* **-eled** *or* **-elled**; **-el·ing** *or* **-el·ling** \-(ə-)ling\ **1** : to run at the nose **2** : to snuff mucus up the nose audibly : SNUFFLE **3** : to cry or whine with snuffling **4** : to speak or act in a whining or weakly emotional manner — **sniv·el·er** \-(ə-)lər\ *n*

snob \'snäb\ *n* **1** : one who obviously imitates, fawningly admires, or vulgarly seeks association with those of higher status than himself **2 :** one who looks down upon those he regards as inferior to himself

snob appeal *n* **:** the appeal (as from high price, rarity, or foreign origin) that a product has for a person of snobbish tastes

snob·bery \'snäb-(ə-)rē\ *n* **:** snobbish conduct

snob·bish \'snäb-ish\ *adj* **:** characteristic of or befitting a snob — **snob·bish·ly** *adv* — **snob·bish·ness** *n* — **snob·bism** \'snäb-ˌiz-əm\ *n*

snob·by \'snäb-ē\ *adj* **snob·bi·er**; **-est :** SNOBBISH

snood \'snüd\ *n* **:** a net or fabric bag for confining a woman's hair pinned or tied on at the back of the head

[1]**snoop** \'snüp\ *vb* **:** to look or pry esp. in a sneaking or meddlesome manner — **snoop·er** *n*

[2]**snoop** *n* **:** one that snoops **:** SNOOPER

snoop·er·scope \'snü-pər-ˌskōp\ *n* **:** a device utilizing infrared radiation for enabling a person to see an object obscured (as by darkness)

snoopy \'snü-pē\ *adj* **snoop·i·er**; **-est :** given to snooping esp. for personal information about others

snoot \'snüt\ *n* **1 :** SNOUT **2 :** NOSE

snooty \'snüt-ē\ *adj* **snoot·i·er**; **-est :** haughtily contemptuous **:** SNOBBISH — **snoot·i·ly** \'snüt-ə-lē\ *adv* — **snoot·i·ness** \'snüt-ē-nəs\ *n*

snooze \'snüz\ *vb* **:** to take a nap **:** DOZE — **snooze** *n* — **snooz·er** *n*

snore \'snō(ə)r, 'snȯ(ə)r\ *vb* **:** to breathe during sleep with a rough hoarse noise — **snore** *n* — **snor·er** *n*

[1]**snor·kel** \'snȯr-kəl\ *n* [from German *schnorchel*, from a dialect word meaning "snout", from *schnorchen* "to snore"] **1 :** a tube or tubes that can be extended above the surface of the water to supply air to and remove exhaust from a submerged submarine **2 :** a tube used by swimmers for breathing with the head under water

snorkel 2

[2]**snorkel** *vb* **:** to swim submerged using a snorkel

[1]**snort** \'snȯrt\ *vb* **1 :** to force air violently through the nose with a rough harsh sound **2 :** to express scorn, anger, indignation, or surprise by a snort — **snort·er** *n*

[2]**snort** *n* **1 :** an act or sound of snorting **2 :** a drink of usu. straight liquor taken in one swallow

snout \'snau̇t\ *n* **1 a :** a long projecting nose or muzzle (as of a pig) **b :** a front part of the head of an animal **c :** the human nose esp. when large or grotesque **2 :** something resembling a snout — **snout·ed** \-əd\ *adj*

snout beetle *n* **:** WEEVIL

[1]**snow** \'snō\ *n* **1 a :** small white crystals of frozen water formed directly from the water vapor of the air **b :** a fall of snow crystals **:** a mass of snow crystals fallen to earth **2 a :** a congealed or crystallized substance resembling snow in appearance ⟨carbon dioxide *snow*⟩ **b :** small transient light or dark spots on a television or radar screen

snow 1a

[2]**snow** *vb* **1 :** to fall or cause to fall in or as snow **2 :** to cover, shut in, or imprison with or as if with snow

[1]**snow·ball** \'snō-ˌbȯl\ *n* **1 :** a round mass of snow pressed or rolled together **2 :** a viburnum widely grown for its ball-shaped clusters of white sterile flowers

[2]**snowball** *vb* **1 :** to throw snowballs at **2 :** to increase or expand at a rapidly accelerating rate

snow·bird \'snō-ˌbərd\ *n* **:** any of several small birds (as a junco) seen chiefly in winter

snow–blind \-ˌblīnd\ *or* **snow–blind·ed** \-'blīn-dəd\ *adj* **:** affected with snow blindness

snow blindness *n* **:** inflammation and inability to tolerate light caused by exposure of the eyes to ultraviolet rays reflected from snow or ice

snow·bound \'snō-'bau̇nd\ *adj* **:** shut in or blockaded by snow

snow·cap \-ˌkap\ *n* **:** a covering cap of snow (as on a mountain peak) — **snow·capped** \-ˌkapt\ *adj*

snow·drift \-ˌdrift\ *n* **:** a bank of drifted snow

snow·drop \-ˌdräp\ *n* **:** an early-blooming European plant that bears nodding white flowers and is related to the amaryllis

snow·fall \-ˌfȯl\ *n* **1 :** a fall of snow **2 :** the amount of snow that falls in a single storm or in a given period

snow fence *n* **:** a barrier stretched across the path of prevailing winds to deflect drifting snow

snow·field \'snō-ˌfēld\ *n* **:** a broad level expanse of snow; *esp* **:** a mass of perennial snow (as at the head of a glacier)

snow·flake \-ˌflāk\ *n* **:** a flake or crystal of snow

snow leopard *n* **:** a large cat of central Asia with a long heavy pelt blotched with brownish black in summer and almost pure white in winter

snow machine *n* **:** a device that produces snow esp. for skiing

snow·man \'snō-ˌman\ *n* **:** snow shaped to resemble a person

snow·mo·bile \'snō-mō-ˌbēl\ *n* **:** any of various automotive vehicles for travel on snow — **snow·mo·bil·er** \-ˌbē-lər\ *n* — **snow·mo·bil·ing** \-ˌbē-ling\ *n*

snow·plow \'snō-ˌplau̇\ *n* **:** any of various devices used for clearing away snow

[1]**snow·shoe** \-ˌshü\ *n* **:** a light oval wooden frame strung with thongs that is attached to the foot to enable a person to walk on soft snow without sinking

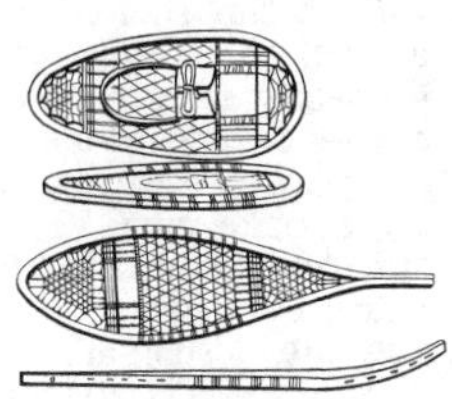
snowshoes

[2]**snowshoe** *vb* **snow·shoed**; **snow·shoe·ing :** to travel on snowshoes

snowshoe rabbit *n* **:** a rather large northern No. American rabbit with heavily furred hind feet and a coat that is brown in summer but usu. white in winter — called also *snowshoe hare*

snow·slide \'snō-ˌslīd\ *n* **:** the slipping down of a mass of snow (as on a mountain slope)

snow·storm \-ˌstȯrm\ *n* **:** a storm of falling snow

snow·suit \-ˌsüt\ *n* **:** a one-piece or two-piece lined garment worn by children

snow tire *n* : an automobile tire with a tread designed to give added traction on snow

snow under *vb* **1** : to overwhelm esp. in excess of capacity to absorb or deal with something **2** : to defeat by a large margin

snow–white \'snō-'hwīt\ *adj* : white as snow

snowy \'snō-ē\ *adj* **snow·i·er**; **-est** **1 a** : marked by snow ⟨a *snowy* day⟩ **b** : covered with snow ⟨*snowy* mountaintops⟩ **2** : whitened by or as if by snow ⟨an orchard *snowy* with apple blossoms⟩ **3** : SNOW-WHITE — **snow·i·ly** \'snō-ə-lē\ *adv* — **snow·i·ness** \'snō-ē-nəs\ *n*

snowy owl *n* : a large chiefly arctic owl that is white or white spotted with brown

1**snub** \'snəb\ *vb* **snubbed**; **snub·bing** **1** : to check or stop with a cutting reply : REBUKE **2 a** : to check (as a line) suddenly while running out esp. by turning around a fixed object (as a post) **b** : to check the motion of by snubbing a line **3** : to slight deliberately **4** : to extinguish by stubbing ⟨*snub* out a cigarette⟩ — **snub·ber** *n*

2**snub** *n* : an act or an instance of snubbing; *esp* : REBUFF

3**snub** *or* **snubbed** \'snəbd\ *adj* : BLUNT, STUBBY — **snub·ness** *n*

snub·by \'snəb-ē\ *adj* **snub·bi·er**; **-est** : SNUB-NOSED

snub–nosed \'snəb-'nōzd\ *adj* : having a stubby and usu. slightly turned-up nose

1**snuff** \'snəf\ *n* : the charred part of a candlewick

2**snuff** *vb* **1** : to cut or pinch off the snuff of a candle so as to brighten the light **2** : EXTINGUISH ⟨*snuff* out a candle⟩ ⟨*snuff* out a life⟩

3**snuff** *vb* **1** : to draw forcibly through or into the nostrils **2** : to sniff inquiringly

4**snuff** *n* : the act of snuffing : SNIFF

5**snuff** *n* : powdered tobacco esp. for snuffing up the nose — **up to snuff** : in good shape

snuff·box \'snəf-ˌbäks\ *n* : a small box for snuff

1**snuff·er** \'snəf-ər\ *n* **1** : a device somewhat like a pair of scissors for cropping and holding the snuff of a candle — usu. used in pl. **2** : a device for extinguishing candles

2**snuffer** *n* : one that snuffs or sniffs

1**snuf·fle** \'snəf-əl\ *vb* **snuf·fled**; **snuf·fling** \-(ə-)liŋ\ **1** : to snuff or sniff usu. audibly and repeatedly **2** : to breathe through an obstructed nose with a sniffing sound **3** : WHINE — **snuf·fler** \-(ə-)lər\ *n*

2**snuffle** *n* : the sound made in snuffling

1**snug** \'snəg\ *adj* **snug·ger**; **snug·gest** **1 a** : SEAWORTHY **b** : TRIM, NEAT **c** : fitting closely and comfortably ⟨a *snug* coat⟩ **2** : enjoying or affording warm secure shelter and comfort : COZY ⟨a *snug* little alcove⟩ **3** : fairly large : AMPLE ⟨a *snug* fortune⟩ **4** : SECRETED, CONCEALED — **snug** *adv* — **snug·ly** *adv* — **snug·ness** *n*

2**snug** *vb* **snugged**; **snug·ging** **1** : SNUGGLE **2** : to make snug

snug·gery \'snəg-(ə-)rē\ *n, pl* **-ger·ies** : a snug place; *esp* : DEN

snug·gle \'snəg-əl\ *vb* **snug·gled**; **snug·gling** \-(ə-)liŋ\ **1** : to curl up comfortably or cozily : CUDDLE **2** : to draw close esp. for comfort or in affection : NESTLE

ə abut	ər further	a back	ā bake	
ä cot, cart	aů out	ch chin	e less	ē easy
g gift	i trip	ī life	j joke	ŋ sing
ō flow	ȯ flaw	ȯi coin	th thin	t͟h this
ü loot	ů foot	y yet	yü few	yů furious
zh vision				

1**so** \(')sō\ *adv* **1 a** : in a manner or way that is indicated or suggested ⟨said he'd attend and did *so*⟩ ⟨it *so* happened that all were wrong⟩ **b** : in the same manner or way : ALSO ⟨worked hard and *so* did she⟩ **c** : SUBSEQUENTLY, THEN ⟨and *so* home and to bed⟩ **2 a** : to an indicated or suggested extent or degree or way ⟨had never been *so* happy⟩ **b** : to a great extent or degree : VERY, EXTREMELY ⟨he loved her *so*⟩ **c** : to a definite but unspecified extent or degree ⟨can only do *so* much in a day⟩ **d** : most certainly : INDEED ⟨you did *so* do it⟩ **3** : for a reason that has just been stated : THEREFORE ⟨the witness is biased and *so* unreliable⟩

2**so** *conj* **1 a** : with the result that ⟨her diction is good, *so* every word is clear⟩ **b** : in order that ⟨be quiet *so* he can sleep⟩ — often followed by *that* **2** : provided that — often preceded by *just* **3** : for that reason ⟨don't want to go, *so* I won't⟩

3**so** \'sō\ *adj* **1** : conforming with actual facts : TRUE ⟨said things that were not *so*⟩ **2** : marked by a definite order ⟨his books are always just *so*⟩

4**so** \ˌsō, 'sō\ *pron* **1** : such as has been specified : the same ⟨became chairman and remained *so*⟩ **2** : approximately that ⟨20 years or *so*⟩

5**so** \'sō\ *n* : 1SOL

so *abbr* south

SO *abbr* strikeout

1**soak** \'sōk\ *vb* **1 a** : to remain steeping in liquid (as water) **b** : to place in a medium (as liquid) to wet or as if to wet thoroughly **2 a** : to enter or pass through something by or as if by pores or interstices : PERMEATE **b** : to penetrate or affect the mind or feelings **3 a** : to extract by or as if by steeping ⟨*soak* the dirt out⟩ **b** : to levy an exorbitant charge against ⟨*soaked* the taxpayers⟩ **4** : to draw in by or as if by suction or absorption ⟨*soaked* up the sunshine⟩ — **soak·er** *n*

syn SOAK, SATURATE, STEEP, DRENCH can mean to seep through or be permeated (as with water). SOAK suggests immersion in a liquid so that the substance absorbs and holds liquid to the point of becoming totally wetted, softened, or dissolved ⟨letting dirty clothes *soak*⟩; SATURATE suggests absorption to a point where no more can be absorbed; STEEP implies the complete immersion of something that is soaked, usu. so that its essence is dissolved into the liquid ⟨letting tea *steep*⟩; DRENCH implies a thorough wetting esp. by rainwater

2**soak** *n* **1** : the act or process of soaking : the state of being soaked **2** : DRUNKARD

so–and–so \'sō-ən-ˌsō\ *n, pl* **so–and–sos** \-ən-ˌsōz\ : an unnamed or unspecified person or thing

1**soap** \'sōp\ *n* **1** : a substance that is usu. made by the action of alkali on fat, dissolves in water, and is used for washing **2** : a salt of a fatty acid — **soap·less** \-ləs\ *adj* — **soap·mak·ing** \-ˌmā-kiŋ\ *n*

2**soap** *vb* : to rub soap over or into

soap·ber·ry \'sōp-ˌber-ē\ *n* : any of a genus of mostly tropical trees having simple pinnate leaves and a fruit that is a globe-shaped or 2- to 3-lobed berry

soap·box \-ˌbäks\ *n* **1** : a box for soap **2** : an improvised platform used by a spontaneous or informal orator — **soapbox** *adj*

soap opera *n* [so called from its frequently being sponsored by soap manufacturers] : a radio or television serial drama performed usu. on a daytime commercial program

soap·stone \'sōp-ˌstōn\ *n* : a soft stone having a soapy feel and composed essentially of talc, chlorite, and often some magnetite

soap·suds \-ˌsədz\ *n pl* : SUDS 1
soap·wort \-ˌwərt, -ˌwȯrt\ *n* : BOUNCING BET
soapy \ˈsō-pē\ *adj* **soap·i·er**; **-est** **1** : smeared with or full of soap ⟨a *soapy* face⟩ **2** : containing or combined with soap ⟨*soapy* ammonia⟩ **3** : resembling or having the qualities of soap — **soap·i·ly** \-pə-lē\ *adv* — **soap·i·ness** \-pē-nəs\ *n*
1**soar** \ˈsō(ə)r, ˈsȯ(ə)r\ *vb* **1 a** : to fly aloft or about **b** : to sail or hover in the air often at a great height : GLIDE **2 a** : to move upward in position or status : RISE **b** : to ascend to a higher or more exalted level **3** : to rise to majestic stature : TOWER ⟨*soaring* cloud-draped peaks⟩ — **soar·er** *n*
2**soar** *n* : the act of soaring : upward flight
1**sob** \ˈsäb\ *vb* **sobbed**; **sob·bing** **1** : to weep with heavings of the chest or with catching in the throat **2** : to bring about by sobbing ⟨*sobbed* himself to sleep⟩ **3 a** : to make a sound like that of sobbing ⟨the wind *sobbed* through the trees⟩ **b** : to utter with sobs ⟨*sobbed* out her story⟩
2**sob** *n* **1** : an act of sobbing **2** : a sound of or like that of sobbing
1**so·ber** \ˈsō-bər\ *adj* **so·ber·er** \-bər-ər\; **so·ber·est** \-b(ə-)rəst\ **1 a** : sparing or temperate esp. in the use of food and drink **b** : not drunk **2** : being gravely or earnestly thoughtful in character or demeanor : SERIOUS, SOLEMN **3** : subdued in tone or color **4** : not affected by emotion or prejudice : well balanced ⟨*sober* decision⟩ — **so·ber·ly** \-bər-lē\ *adv* — **so·ber·ness** *n*
2**sober** *vb* **so·bered**; **so·ber·ing** \-b(ə-)ring\ : to make or become sober
so·bri·e·ty \sə-ˈbrī-ət-ē\ *n* : the quality or state of being sober
so·bri·quet \ˈsō-bri-ˌkā\ *n* : a fanciful name or epithet : NICKNAME
soc *abbr* social
so–called \ˈsō-ˈkȯld\ *adj* : commonly or popularly but often inaccurately so termed ⟨his *so-called* friend⟩
soc·cer \ˈsäk-ər\ *n* [formed by shortening and alteration of *association football*, so called from the *Football Association*, founded in 1863 in England to standardize the rules of football] : a football game with 11 players on a side in which a round ball is advanced by kicking or by propelling it with any part of the body except the hands and arms
so·cia·bil·i·ty \ˌsō-shə-ˈbil-ət-ē\ *n*, *pl* **-ties** **1** : the quality or state of being sociable : AFFABILITY **2** : the act or an instance of being sociable
1**so·cia·ble** \ˈsō-shə-bəl\ *adj* **1** : inclined to seek or enjoy companionship : AFFABLE, FRIENDLY ⟨*sociable* people⟩ **2** : conducive to friendliness or pleasant social relations — **so·cia·ble·ness** *n* — **so·cia·bly** \-blē\ *adv*
2**sociable** *n* : an informal gathering for sociability and frequently a special activity or interest
1**so·cial** \ˈsō-shəl\ *adj* **1 a** : marked by, devoted to, or engaged in for sociability ⟨*social* events⟩ ⟨her *social* life⟩ **b** : SOCIABLE **2 a** : naturally living or growing in groups or communities ⟨bees are *social* insects⟩ **b** : tending to form cooperative and interdependent relationships with one's fellows ⟨man is a *social* being⟩ **3** : of or relating to human society, the interaction of the group and its members, and the welfare of these members ⟨*social* institutions⟩ **4 a** : of, relating to, or based on rank in a particular society ⟨different *social* circles⟩ **b** : of or relating to fashionable society ⟨a *social* leader⟩ **5** : SOCIALIST
2**social** *n* : SOCIABLE
social climber *n* : one who attempts to gain a higher social position or acceptance in fashionable society
so·cial·ism \ˈsō-shə-ˌliz-əm\ *n* : any of various economic and political theories or social systems based on collective or governmental ownership and administration of the means of production and distribution of goods — **so·cial·ist** \ˈsōsh-(ə-)ləst\ *n* — **socialist** *or* **so·cial·is·tic** \ˌsō-shə-ˈlis-tik\ *adj* — **so·cial·is·ti·cal·ly** \-ti-k(ə-)lē\ *adv*
so·cial·ite \ˈsō-shə-ˌlīt\ *n* : a person prominent in fashionable society
so·ci·al·i·ty \ˌsō-shē-ˈal-ət-ē\ *n*, *pl* **-ties** **1** : SOCIABILITY **2** : the tendency to associate with one's fellows or to form social groups
so·cial·ize \ˈsō-shə-ˌlīz\ *vb* **1** : to make social; *esp* : to train so as to develop the qualities essential to group living **2** : to adapt to social needs and uses **3** : to regulate according to the theory or practice of socialism **4** : to take part in the social life around one — **so·cial·i·za·tion** \ˌsō-shə-lə-ˈzā-shən\ *n* — **so·cial·iz·er** \ˈsō-shə-ˌlī-zər\ *n*
so·cial·ly \ˈsōsh-(ə-)lē\ *adv* **1** : in a social manner ⟨*socially* popular⟩ **2** : with respect to society ⟨*socially* inferior⟩
social science *n* **1** : a science that deals with human society or its elements (as family, state, or race) and with man's institutions and relationships in an organized community **2** : a science (as economics or political science) dealing with a particular phase or aspect of human society — **social scientist** *n*
social security *n* **1** : the principle or practice of public provision for the economic security and social welfare of the individual and his family **2** *often cap* : a U.S. government program established in 1935 to include old-age and survivors insurance, contributions to state unemployment insurance, and old-age assistance
social studies *n pl* : the studies dealing with human relationships and the functioning of society (as history, civics, economics, and geography)
social work *n* : the art, practice, or profession of extending the benefits of organized society esp. through assistance of the economically underprivileged and the socially maladjusted — **social worker** *n*
1**so·ci·e·ty** \sə-ˈsī-ət-ē\ *n*, *pl* **-ties** [from Latin *societas*, from *socius* "companion", "associate"] **1** : companionship with one's fellows : COMPANY **2** : the social order or community life considered as a system within which the individual lives ⟨rural *society*⟩ **3** : people in general ⟨the benefit of *society*⟩ **4** : an association of persons for some purpose ⟨a mutual benefit *society*⟩ **5** : a part of a community regarded as a unit distinguished by common interests or standards; *esp* : the group or set of fashionable persons **6** : a system of interdependent organisms or biological units — **so·ci·e·tal** \-ət-əl\ *adj*
2**society** *adj* : of, relating to, or characteristic of fashionable society
sociol *abbr* sociology
so·ci·ol·o·gy \ˌsō-sē-ˈäl-ə-jē, -shē-\ *n* : the science of society, social institutions, and social relationships — **so·ci·o·log·i·cal** \-ə-ˈläj-i-kəl\ *adj* — **so·ci·o·log·i·cal·ly** \-ə-ˈläj-i-k(ə-)lē\ *adv* — **so·ci·ol·o·gist** \-ˈäl-ə-jəst\ *n*
1**sock** \ˈsäk\ *n*, *pl* **socks** *or* **sox** \ˈsäks\ : a knitted or woven covering for the foot usu. extending above the ankle and sometimes to the knee
2**sock** *vb* : to hit, strike, or apply forcefully : deliver a blow
3**sock** *n* : a vigorous or violent blow : PUNCH
sock·et \ˈsäk-ət\ *n* : an opening or hollow that receives and holds something ⟨the eye *socket*⟩ ⟨light-bulb *socket*⟩

[1]**sod** \'säd\ *n* **1 a** : TURF 1 **b** : the grass and herb covered surface of the ground **2** : one's native land

[2]**sod** *vb* **sod·ded**; **sod·ding** : to cover with sod or turfs

so·da \'sōd-ə\ *n* **1 a** : SODIUM CARBONATE **b** : SODIUM BICARBONATE **c** : SODIUM HYDROXIDE **2 a** : SODA WATER **b** : a sweet drink consisting of soda water, flavoring, and often ice cream

soda cracker *n* : a cracker leavened with bicarbonate of soda and cream of tartar

soda fountain *n* **1** : an apparatus for drawing soda water **2** : the equipment and counter for the preparation and serving of carbonated drinks, sodas, sundaes, and ice cream

soda jerk *n* : one who dispenses carbonated drinks and ice cream at a soda fountain

so·da·list \'sōd-ə-ləst, sō-'dal-\ *n* : a member of a sodality

so·dal·i·ty \sō-'dal-ət-ē\ *n, pl* **-ties** : an organized society or fellowship; *esp* : a devotional or charitable association of Roman Catholic laity

soda pop *n* : a bottled soft drink consisting of soda water with added flavoring and a sweet syrup

soda water *n* : a beverage consisting of water highly charged with carbonic acid gas

[1]**sod·den** \'säd-ən\ *adj* **1** *archaic* : cooked by stewing : BOILED **2 a** : dull or lacking in expression ⟨*sodden* features⟩ **b** : SLUGGISH, UNIMAGINATIVE ⟨*sodden* minds⟩ **3** : heavy with moisture : SOAKED, SATURATED ⟨*sodden* ground⟩ — **sod·den·ly** *adv* — **sod·den·ness** \-ən-(n)əs\ *n*

[2]**sodden** *vb* : to make or become sodden

sod house *n* : a house built of turfs laid in horizontal layers

so·di·um \'sōd-ē-əm\ *n* : a soft waxy silver-white metallic element chemically very active and found abundantly in nature always in combination — see ELEMENT table

sodium benzoate *n* : a sodium salt used chiefly as a food preservative

sodium bicarbonate *n* : a white crystalline weakly alkaline salt used esp. in baking powders, fire extinguishers, and medicine

sodium carbonate *n* **1** : a salt used in making glass, soaps, and chemicals **2** : SAL SODA

sodium chloride *n* : SALT 1a

sodium citrate *n* : a salt used in medicine esp. to prevent clotting of blood

sodium hydroxide *n* : a white brittle solid that is a strong caustic base used esp. in making soap, rayon, and paper and in bleaching

sodium hyposulfite *n* **1** : SODIUM THIOSULFATE **2** : a crystalline water-soluble salt used esp. in dyeing and bleaching

sodium nitrate *n* : a crystalline salt found in crude form in Chile and used as a fertilizer, in curing meat, and in the preparation of other chemicals (as nitric acid)

sodium peroxide *n* : a compound used as an oxidizing and bleaching agent

sodium thio·sul·fate \-ˌthī-ō-'səl-ˌfāt\ *n* : a hygroscopic crystalline substance used esp. as a photographic fixing agent and a reducing or bleaching agent — called also *hypo*

sodium-vapor lamp *n* : an electric lamp (as for lighting highways) that contains sodium vapor and electrodes between which a light-giving discharge takes place

so·fa \'sō-fə\ *n* [from Arabic *ṣuffah* "long bench"] : a long upholstered seat usu. with arms and a back and often convertible into a bed

soft \'sȯft\ *adj* **1 a** : having a pleasing, comfortable, or soothing quality or effect : GENTLE, MILD ⟨*soft* breezes⟩ **b** : pleasing to the ear : melodious and quiet in pitch or volume ⟨*soft* voices⟩ **c** : not bright or glaring ⟨*soft* lighting⟩ **d** : demanding little effort : EASY ⟨a *soft* job⟩ **e** : smooth or delicate in appearance or texture ⟨a *soft* silk⟩ ⟨*soft* flowing lines⟩ **2 a** : having a mild gentle nature : DOCILE **b** : lacking in strength or vigor : unfit for prolonged exertion or severe stress : FEEBLE ⟨*soft* from good living⟩ **c** : weak or deficient mentally **d** : advocating or being a moderate or conciliatory policy ⟨took a *soft* stand toward the rebels⟩ **3 a** : yielding to physical pressure : COMPRESSIBLE, MALLEABLE ⟨a *soft* mattress⟩ ⟨*soft* metals such as lead⟩ **b** : relatively lacking in hardness ⟨*soft* wood⟩ **4** : gently or gradually curved or rounded : not harsh or jagged ⟨a range of *soft* hills⟩ **5** : sounding as in *ace* and *gem* respectively — used of *c* and *g* **6 a** : lacking substances (as calcium and magnesium salts) that prevent lathering of soap ⟨*soft* water⟩ **b** : containing no alcohol ⟨*soft* drinks⟩ **7** : having relatively low penetrating power ⟨*soft* X rays⟩ **8** : occurring at such a speed and under such circumstances as to avoid destructive impact ⟨*soft* landing of a spacecraft on the moon⟩ — **soft·ly** *or* **soft** *adv* — **soft·ness** \'sȯf(t)-nəs\ *n*

soft·ball \'sȯf(t)-ˌbȯl\ *n* **1** : a game resembling baseball but played on a smaller diamond with a ball larger and softer than a baseball **2** : the ball used in softball

soft-boiled \-'bȯild\ *adj* : lightly boiled so that the contents are only partly coagulated ⟨*soft-boiled* eggs⟩

soft coal *n* : BITUMINOUS COAL

soft·en \'sȯ-fən\ *vb* **soft·ened**; **soft·en·ing** \'sȯf-(ə-)ning\ **1** : to make or become soft or softer **2** : to impair the strength or resistance of ⟨*soften* up a sales prospect⟩ — **soft·en·er** \'sȯf-(ə-)nər\ *n*

soft·heart·ed \-'härt-əd\ *adj* : emotionally responsive : SYMPATHETIC, TENDER — **soft·heart·ed·ly** *adv* — **soft·heart·ed·ness** *n*

soft-shell \'sȯf(t)-ˌshel\ *or* **soft-shelled** \-'sheld\ *adj* : having a soft or fragile shell esp. as a result of recent shedding

soft-shoe \'sȯf(t)-'shü\ *adj* : of or relating to tap dancing done in soft-soled shoes without metal taps

soft soap *n* **1** : a semifluid soap **2** : FLATTERY

soft-soap \'sȯf(t)-'sōp\ *vb* : to soothe or coax with flattery — **soft-soap·er** *n*

soft·wood \'sȯft-ˌwu̇d\ *n* **1** : the wood of a cone-bearing tree including both soft and hard woods **2** : a tree that yields softwood

softy \'sȯf-tē\ *n, pl* **soft·ies** **1** : a silly or sentimental person **2** : WEAKLING

sog·gy \'säg-ē\ *adj* **sog·gi·er**; **-est** : saturated or heavy with water or moisture : SOAKED, SODDEN — **sog·gi·ly** \'säg-ə-lē\ *adv* — **sog·gi·ness** \'säg-ē-nəs\ *n*

[1]**soil** \'sȯil\ *vb* : to make or become dirty or corrupt

[2]**soil** *n* **1 a** : SOILAGE, STAIN **b** : moral defilement : CORRUPTION **2** : something that soils or pollutes

[3]**soil** *n* **1** : firm land : EARTH **2** : the loose surface material of the earth in which plants grow **3** : COUNTRY, LAND **4** : a medium in which something may take root and grow ⟨slums are fertile *soil* for crime⟩

soil·age \'sȯi-lij\ *n* : the act of soiling : the condition of being soiled
soil auger *n* : an auger for taking soil samples
soil bank *n* : land retired from crop cultivation and planted with soil-building crops under a government plan that pays farmers for taking part in the program
soil conservation *n* : management of soil designed to obtain the highest possible yields while improving and protecting the soil
soil creep *n* : slow movement of earth materials down a slope under the influence of gravitation
soil·less \'sȯil-ləs\ *adj* : carried on without soil ⟨*soilless* agriculture⟩
soil profile *n* : PROFILE 3
soil science *n* : the science of soils — **soil scientist** *n*
soi·ree *or* **soi·rée** \swä-'rā\ *n* : an evening party or reception
1**so·journ** \'sō-,jərn, sō-'\ *n* : a temporary stay
2**sojourn** *vb* : to stay as a temporary resident : STOP ⟨*sojourned* for a month at a resort⟩ — **so·journ·er** *n*
1**sol** \'sōl\ *n* : the 5th note of the diatonic scale
2**sol** \'säl, 'sȯl\ *n* : a fluid colloidal system
1**sol·ace** \'säl-əs\ *n* **1** : comfort in times of grief or anxiety : CONSOLATION **2** : a source of comfort
2**solace** *vb* **1** : to give solace to : CONSOLE **2** : to make cheerful : DIVERT **3** : ALLAY, SOOTHE — **sol·ac·er** *n*
so·lar \'sō-lər\ *adj* **1** : of, derived from, or relating to the sun **2** : measured by the earth's course in relation to the sun ⟨*solar* time⟩ ⟨*solar* year⟩ **3** : produced or operated by the action of the sun's light or heat ⟨a *solar* battery⟩ ⟨a *solar* furnace⟩; *also* : utilizing the sun's rays
solar flare *n* : a sudden temporary outburst of energy from a small area of the sun's surface
solar house *n* : a house equipped with glass areas and so planned as to utilize the sun's rays extensively in heating
so·lar·i·um \sō-'lar-ē-əm, -'ler-\ *n, pl* **-ia** \-ē-ə\ *also* **-i·ums** : a room exposed to the sun (as for treatment of illness)
solar plexus *n* **1** : a nerve plexus in the abdomen behind the stomach that contains ganglia distributing nerve fibers to the viscera **2** : the pit of the stomach
solar still *n* : a device that converts salt water or contaminated water into drinking water by vaporization by the sun's rays and condensation
solar system *n* : the sun and the planets, asteroids, comets, and meteors that revolve around it
solar wind \-'wind\ *n* : the continuous ejection of particles from the sun's surface
sold *past of* SELL
1**sol·der** \'säd-ər, 'sȯd-\ *n* : a metal or metallic alloy used when melted to join metallic surfaces; *esp* : an alloy of lead and tin so used
2**solder** *vb* **sol·dered**; **sol·der·ing** \'säd-(ə-)riŋ, 'sȯd-\ **1** : to unite or repair with solder ⟨*solder* wires together⟩ ⟨*solder* a leak⟩ **2** : to become joined or renewed by or as if by the use of solder — **sol·der·er** \-ər-ər\ *n*
soldering iron *n* : a metal device for applying heat in soldering
1**sol·dier** \'sōl-jər\ *n* **1** : a person in military service usu. as an enlisted man or woman **2** : a worker in a cause **3** : a member of a caste of wingless individuals with large heads and jaws among termites and some ants — **sol·dier·ly** \-lē\ *adj* — **sol·dier·ship** \-,ship\ *n*
2**soldier** *vb* : to serve as or act like a soldier
soldier of fortune : one who follows a military career wherever there is promise of profit, adventure, or pleasure
sol·diery \'sōl-jə-rē\ *n, pl* **-dier·ies** : a body of soldiers
1**sole** \'sōl\ *n* **1** : the undersurface of a foot **2** : the part of footwear on which the sole of the foot rests — **soled** \'sōld\ *adj*
2**sole** *vb* : to furnish with a sole ⟨*sole* shoes⟩
3**sole** *n* : any of a family of small-mouthed flatfishes having reduced fins and small closely set eyes and including valued food fishes
4**sole** *adj* **1** : having no companion : ALONE **2 a** : having no sharer ⟨*sole* owner⟩ **b** : being the only one **3** : functioning independently and without assistance or interference ⟨the *sole* judge⟩ **4** : belonging exclusively to the one person, unit, or group named ⟨given *sole* authority⟩ — **sole·ness** *n*
sol·e·cism \'säl-ə-,siz-əm, 'sō-lə-\ *n* [from Greek *soloikos* "speaking incorrectly", literally "inhabitant of Soloi", from *Soloi*, a city in ancient Cilicia where a substandard form of Greek was often heard] **1** : an ungrammatical combination of words in a sentence **2** : a breach of etiquette or decorum — **sol·e·cis·tic** \,säl-ə-'sis-tik, ,sō-lə-\ *adj*
sole·ly \'sō(l)-lē\ *adv* **1** : without another : SINGLY, ALONE **2** : EXCLUSIVELY, ENTIRELY ⟨done *solely* for money⟩
sol·emn \'säl-əm\ *adj* **1** : celebrated with religious rites or ceremony : SACRED **2** : FORMAL, STATELY ⟨*solemn* procession⟩ **3** : done or made seriously and thoughtfully ⟨*solemn* promise⟩ **4** : GRAVE, SOBER ⟨*solemn* faces⟩ — **so·lem·ni·ty** \sə-'lem-nət-ē\ *n* — **sol·emn·ly** \'säl-əm-lē\ *adv* — **sol·emn·ness** \'säl-əm-nəs\ *n*
sol·em·nize \'säl-əm-,nīz\ *vb* **1** : to observe or honor with solemnity **2** : to perform with pomp or ceremony; *esp* : to celebrate a marriage with religious rites **3** : to make solemn : DIGNIFY — **sol·em·ni·za·tion** \,säl-əm-nə-'zā-shən\ *n*
so·le·noid \'sō-lə-,nȯid\ *n* : a coil of wire commonly in the form of a long cylinder that when carrying a current acts as a magnet
sole·plate \'sōl-,plāt\ *n* : the undersurface of a flatiron
sole·print \-,print\ *n* : a print of the sole of the foot; *esp* : one made in the manner of a fingerprint and used for the identification of an infant
soli *pl of* SOLO
so·lic·it \sə-'lis-ət\ *vb* **1** : BEG, ENTREAT; *esp* : to approach with a request or plea **2** : to appeal for ⟨*solicited* the help of his neighbors⟩ **3 a** : to entice or lure esp. into evil **b** : to accost a man for immoral purposes — **so·lic·i·ta·tion** \-,lis-ə-'tā-shən\ *n*
so·lic·i·tant \sə-'lis-ət-ənt\ *n* : one who solicits
so·lic·i·tor \sə-'lis-ət-ər\ *n* **1** : one that solicits **2** : a British lawyer **3** : the chief law officer of a municipality, county, or government department
so·lic·i·tous \sə-'lis-ət-əs\ *adj* **1** : full of concern or fears : APPREHENSIVE **2** : anxiously willing : EAGER **3** : extremely careful — **so·lic·i·tous·ly** *adv* — **so·lic·i·tous·ness** *n*
so·lic·i·tude \sə-'lis-ə-,t(y)üd\ *n* **1** : the state of being solicitous : ANXIETY **2** : excessive care or attention
1**sol·id** \'säl-əd\ *adj* **1 a** : having an interior filled with matter : not hollow **b** : written as one word without a hyphen ⟨a *solid* compound⟩ **c** : not interrupted ⟨for three *solid* hours⟩ **2** : having, involving, or dealing with three dimensions or with solids ⟨*solid* geometry⟩ **3 a** : not loose or spongy : COMPACT ⟨a *solid* mass of rock⟩ **b** : neither gaseous nor liquid : HARD, RIGID ⟨*solid* ice⟩ **4** : of good substan-

S

tial quality or kind ⟨*solid* comfort⟩ ⟨*solid* reasons⟩ **5 :** UNANIMOUS, UNITED ⟨*solid* for pay increases⟩ **6 a :** thoroughly dependable : RELIABLE ⟨a *solid* citizen⟩ **b :** serious in purpose or character ⟨*solid* reading⟩ **7 a :** entirely of one metal or containing the minimum of alloy necessary to impart hardness ⟨*solid* gold⟩ **b :** of a single color or tone — **solid** *adv* — **sol·id·ly** *adv* — **sol·id·ness** *n*

[2]**solid** *n* **1 :** a geometrical figure or element (as a cube or sphere) having three dimensions **2 :** a solid substance : a substance that does not flow perceptibly under moderate stress

sol·i·dar·i·ty \ˌsäl-ə-ˈdar-ət-ē\ *n, pl* **-ties :** community of interests, objectives, or standards in a group

so·lid·i·fi·ca·tion \sə-ˌlid-ə-fə-ˈkā-shən\ *n* **:** an act or instance of solidifying : the condition of being solidified

so·lid·i·fy \sə-ˈlid-ə-ˌfī\ *vb* **-fied; -fy·ing :** to make or become solid, compact, or hard

so·lid·i·ty \sə-ˈlid-ət-ē\ *n, pl* **-ties 1 :** the quality or state of being solid **2 :** moral, mental, or financial soundness

sol·id–state \ˌsäl-əd-ˌstāt\ *adj* **1 :** relating to the properties, structure, or reactivity of solid material **2 :** not using electron tubes ⟨a *solid-state* radio⟩

so·lil·o·quist \sə-ˈlil-ə-kwəst\ *n* **:** one who soliloquizes

so·lil·o·quize \-ˌkwīz\ *vb* **:** to utter a soliloquy : talk to oneself — **so·lil·o·quiz·er** *n*

so·lil·o·quy \sə-ˈlil-ə-kwē\ *n, pl* **-quies 1 :** the act of talking to oneself **2 :** a dramatic monologue that gives the illusion of being a series of unspoken thoughts

sol·i·taire \ˈsäl-ə-ˌta(ə)r, -ˌte(ə)r\ *n* **1 :** a single gem (as a diamond) set alone **2 :** a card game played by one person alone

[1]**sol·i·tary** \ˈsäl-ə-ˌter-ē\ *adj* **1 :** all alone ⟨a *solitary* traveler⟩ **2 :** seldom visited : LONELY **3 :** being the only one : SOLE ⟨*solitary* example⟩ **4 :** growing or living alone : not forming part of a group or cluster ⟨flowers terminal and *solitary*⟩ ⟨the *solitary* wasps⟩ — **sol·i·tar·i·ly** \ˌsäl-ə-ˈter-ə-lē\ *adv* — **sol·i·tar·i·ness** \ˈsäl-ə-ˌter-ē-nəs\ *n*

[2]**solitary** *n, pl* **-tar·ies :** one who lives or seeks to live a solitary life : RECLUSE, HERMIT

sol·i·tude \ˈsäl-ə-ˌt(y)üd\ *n* **1 :** the quality or state of being alone or remote from society : SECLUSION, LONELINESS **2 :** a lonely place (as a desert)

[1]**so·lo** \ˈsō-lō\ *n, pl* **solos** [from Italian, from *solo* "alone", from Latin *solus*] **1** *or pl* **so·li** \ˈsō-(ˌ)lē\ **a :** a musical composition for a single voice or instrument with or without accompaniment **b :** the featured part of a concerto or similar work **2 :** an action in which there is only one performer

[2]**solo** *adv or adj* **:** without a companion : ALONE

[3]**solo** *vb* **:** to perform a solo; *esp* **:** to fly solo in an airplane

so·lo·ist \ˈsō-lə-wəst, -ˌlō-əst\ *n* **:** one who performs a solo

so·lon \ˈsō-lən, -ˌlän\ *n* [after *Solon*, 6th century B.C. Athenian lawgiver] **1 :** a wise and skillful lawgiver **2 :** a member of a legislative body

so long \sō-ˈlȯŋ\ *interj* — used to express goodbye or farewell

ə abut	ər further	a back	ā bake	
ä cot, cart	aü out	ch chin	e less	ē easy
g gift	i trip	ī life	j joke	ŋ sing	ō flow
ȯ flaw	ȯi coin	th thin	th this	ü loot
ů foot	y yet	yü few	yů furious	zh vision

so long as *conj* **1 :** during and up to the end of the time that : WHILE **2 :** provided that

sol·stice \ˈsäl-stəs, ˈsōl-, ˈsȯl-\ *n* **1 :** the point in the apparent path of the sun at which the sun is farthest from the equator either north or south **2 :** the time of the sun's passing a solstice which occurs on June 22d to begin summer in the northern hemisphere and on December 22d to begin winter in the northern hemisphere

sol·u·bil·i·ty \ˌsäl-yə-ˈbil-ət-ē\ *n, pl* **-ties 1 :** the quality or state of being soluble **2 :** the amount of a substance that will dissolve in a given amount of another substance

sol·u·bi·lize \ˈsäl-yə-bə-ˌlīz\ *vb* **:** to make soluble or increase the solubility of

sol·u·ble \ˈsäl-yə-bəl\ *adj* **1 a :** capable of being dissolved in a fluid ⟨sugar is *soluble* in water⟩ **b :** EMULSIFIABLE ⟨a *soluble* oil⟩ **2 :** capable of being solved or explained : SOLVABLE ⟨a *soluble* problem⟩ — **sol·u·ble·ness** *n* — **sol·u·bly** \-blē\ *adv*

sol·ute \ˈsäl-ˌyüt\ *n* **:** a dissolved substance

so·lu·tion \sə-ˈlü-shən\ *n* **1 a :** an act or process of solving **b :** an answer to a problem : EXPLANATION **c :** SOLUTION SET **d :** a member of a solution set **2 a :** an act or the process by which a solid, liquid, or gaseous substance is uniformly mixed with a liquid or sometimes a gas or solid **b :** a typically liquid uniform mixture formed by the process of solution **c :** the condition of being dissolved **d :** a liquid containing a dissolved substance

solution set *n* **:** a set of values that satisfy an equation; *also* **:** TRUTH SET

solv·a·ble \ˈsäl-və-bəl, ˈsȯl-\ *adj* **:** capable of being solved — **solv·a·bil·i·ty** \ˌsäl-və-ˈbil-ət-ē, ˌsȯl-\ *n*

solve \ˈsälv, ˈsȯlv\ *vb* **:** to find a solution for

sol·ven·cy \ˈsäl-vən-sē, ˈsȯl-\ *n, pl* **-cies :** the quality or state of being solvent

[1]**sol·vent** \-vənt\ *adj* **1 :** able to pay all legal debts **2 :** dissolving or able to dissolve ⟨*solvent* fluids⟩ — **sol·vent·ly** *adv*

[2]**solvent** *n* **1 :** a usu. liquid substance capable of dissolving or dispersing one or more other substances **2 :** something that provides a solution

So·ma·li \sō-ˈmäl-ē\ *n* **:** a member of a people chiefly of Somaliland and apparently of mixed Mediterranean and negroid stock — **Somali** *adj*

so·mat·ic \sō-ˈmat-ik\ *adj* **1 :** of, relating to, or affecting the body esp. as distinguished from the germ plasm or the psyche **2 :** of or relating to the wall of the body

somatic cell *n* **:** any cell of an animal or plant other than a germ cell

som·ber *or* **som·bre** \ˈsäm-bər\ *adj* **1 :** so shaded as to be dark and gloomy **2 :** GRAVE, MELANCHOLY ⟨a *somber* mood⟩ **3 :** dull or dark colored — **som·ber·ly** *or* **som·bre·ly** *adv* — **som·ber·ness** *or* **som·bre·ness** *n*

som·bre·ro \səm-ˈbre(ə)r-ō, säm-\ *n, pl* **-ros** [from Spanish, from *sombra* "shade"] **:** a high-crowned hat with a very wide brim worn esp. in the Southwest and Mexico

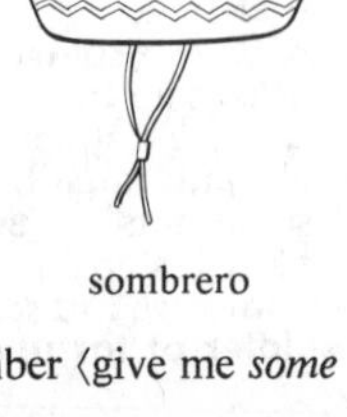

sombrero

[1]**some** \ˈsəm *or, for 2b, without stress*\ *adj* **1 :** being one unknown, undetermined, or unspecified unit or thing ⟨*some* person knocked⟩ **2 a :** being one, a part, or an unspecified number of something (as a class or group) named or implied ⟨*some* gems are hard⟩ **b :** being of an unspecified amount or number ⟨give me *some*

water⟩ ⟨have *some* apples⟩ **3** : worthy of notice or consideration ⟨that was *some* party⟩

2**some** \'səm\ *pron* **1** : some one among a number ⟨*some* of these days⟩ **2** : one indeterminate quantity, portion, or number as distinguished from the rest ⟨*some* of the milk⟩ ⟨*some* of the apples⟩

3**some** \'səm, ˌsəm\ *adv* : ABOUT ⟨*some* eighty houses⟩

1**-some** \səm\ *adj suffix* : characterized by a (specified) thing, quality, state, or action ⟨awe*some*⟩ ⟨burden*some*⟩

2**-some** \səm\ *n suffix* : group of (so many) members and esp. persons ⟨four*some*⟩

some·body \'səm-ˌbäd-ē, -bəd-\ *pron* **1** : one or some person of no certain or known identity ⟨did *somebody* knock?⟩ **2** : a person of position or importance ⟨wanted to be *somebody*⟩

some·day \'səm-ˌdā\ *adv* : at some future time

some·how \'səm-ˌhau̇\ *adv* : in one way or another not known or designated : by some means

some·one \-(ˌ)wən\ *pron* : SOMEBODY

some·place \-ˌplās\ *adv* : SOMEWHERE

som·er·sault \'səm-ər-ˌsȯlt\ *n* : a leap or roll in which a person turns his heels over his head — **somersault** *vb*

som·er·set \-ˌset\ *n or vb* : SOMERSAULT

1**some·thing** \'səm(p)-thiŋ\ *pron* **1 a** : some undetermined or unspecified thing **b** : some thing not remembered or immaterial ⟨the twelve *something* train⟩ **2** : some definite but not specified thing ⟨*something* to live for⟩ **3** : an important person or thing ⟨decided to make *something* of himself⟩

2**something** *adv* **1** : in some degree : SOMEWHAT **2** : EXTREMELY ⟨swears *something* awful⟩

1**some·time** \'səm-ˌtīm\ *adv* **1** : at some time in the future ⟨I'll do it *sometime*⟩ **2** : at some unspecified or uncertain point of time ⟨*sometime* last night⟩

2**sometime** *adj* : FORMER, LATE ⟨*sometime* mayor⟩

some·times \'səm-ˌtīmz, (ˌ)səm-'\ *adv* : at times : now and then : OCCASIONALLY

some·way \'səm-ˌwā\ *also* **some·ways** \-ˌwāz\ *adv* : in some way : SOMEHOW

1**some·what** \-ˌhwät, -ˌhwət, (ˌ)səm-'\ *pron* **1** : some indefinite or unspecified part, amount, or degree : SOMETHING **2** : one having a character, quality, or nature to some extent ⟨*somewhat* of a connoisseur⟩

2**somewhat** *adv* : in some degree or measure : SLIGHTLY ⟨*somewhat* relieved⟩

1**some·where** \'səm-ˌhwe(ə)r, -ˌhwa(ə)r, -hwər\ *adv* **1** : in, at, or to a place unknown or unspecified **2** : APPROXIMATELY ⟨*somewhere* about nine o'clock⟩

2**somewhere** *n* : an undetermined or unnamed place

some·wheres \-ˌhwe(ə)rz, -ˌhwa(ə)rz, -hwərz\ *adv, chiefly dial* : SOMEWHERE

som·nam·bu·lism \säm-'nam-byə-ˌliz-əm\ *n* : a state of sleep in which motor acts (as walking) are performed; *also* : actions characteristic of this state — **som·nam·bu·list** \-ləst\ *n*

som·no·lence \'säm-nə-lən(t)s\ *n* : DROWSINESS, SLEEPINESS

som·no·lent \-lənt\ *adj* : showing indications of not being fully awake ***syn*** see SLEEPY

son \'sən\ *n* **1 a** : a male offspring esp. of human beings **b** : a male adopted child **c** : a male descendant — usu. used in pl. **2** *cap* : the second person of the Trinity

so·nar \'sō-ˌnär\ *n* : an apparatus that detects the presence and location of submerged objects (as submarines) by reflected vibrations

so·na·ta \sə-'nät-ə\ *n* : an instrumental musical composition typically of three or four movements in contrasting rhythms and keys

song \'sȯŋ\ *n* **1** : the act or art of singing **2** : poetical composition : POETRY **3 a** : a short musical composition of words and music **b** : a collection of such compositions **4 a** : a melody for a lyric poem or ballad **b** : a poem easily set to music **5** : a small amount ⟨can be bought for a *song*⟩ — **song·book** \-ˌbu̇k\ *n*

song·bird \-ˌbərd\ *n* : a bird that sings

song·fest \-ˌfest\ *n* : an informal session of group singing of popular or folk songs

song·ful \-fəl\ *adj* : given to singing : MELODIOUS — **song·ful·ly** \-fə-lē\ *adv* — **song·ful·ness** *n*

Song of Sol·o·mon \-'säl-ə-mən\ — see BIBLE table

song sparrow *n* : a common sparrow of eastern No. America noted for its sweet cheerful song

song·ster \'sȯŋ-stər\ *n* : one skilled in song : a man that sings — **song·stress** \-strəs\ *n*

song·writ·er \-ˌrīt-ər\ *n* : a person who composes words or music or both esp. for popular songs

son·ic \'sän-ik\ *adj* **1** : utilizing, produced by, or relating to sound waves ⟨*sonic* altimeter⟩ **2** : of, relating to, or being the speed of sound in air that is about 741 miles per hour at sea level

sonic boom *n* : a sound resembling an explosion produced when a pressure wave formed at the nose of an aircraft traveling at supersonic speed reaches the ground

sonic depth finder *n* : an instrument for determining the depth of a body of water or of an object below the surface by means of sound waves

son-in-law \'sən-ən-ˌlȯ\ *n, pl* **sons-in-law** \'sənzən-\ : the husband of one's daughter

son·net \'sän-ət\ *n* : a poem of 14 lines usu. in iambic pentameter rhyming according to a prescribed scheme

son·ne·teer \ˌsän-ə-'ti(ə)r\ *n* : a writer of sonnets

son·ny \'sən-ē\ *n, pl* **sonnies** : a young boy — used chiefly as a term of address

so·nom·e·ter \sə-'näm-ət-ər\ *n* : an instrument for demonstrating the mathematical relations of musical tones that consists of a single string stretched on a board and a movable bridge

so·nor·i·ty \sə-'nȯr-ət-ē, -'när-\ *n, pl* **-ties** **1** : the quality or state of being sonorous : RESONANCE **2** : a sonorous tone or speech

so·no·rous \sə-'nōr-əs, -'nȯr-; 'sän-ə-rəs\ *adj* **1** : producing sound (as when struck) **2** : full or loud in sound : RESONANT **3** : imposing or impressive in effect or style — **so·no·rous·ly** *adv* — **so·no·rous·ness** *n*

soon \'sün\ *adv* **1** : before long : without undue time lapse ⟨*soon* after sunrise⟩ **2** : PROMPTLY, SPEEDILY ⟨as *soon* as possible⟩ **3** : before the usual time **4** : READILY, WILLINGLY ⟨would as *soon* do it now⟩

soot \'su̇t, 'sət\ *n* : a black substance that is formed by combustion, rises in fine particles, and adheres to the sides of the chimney or pipe conveying the smoke; *esp* : the fine powder consisting chiefly of carbon that colors smoke

sooth \'süth\ *n, archaic* : TRUTH, REALITY

soothe \'sü*th*\ *vb* **1 a** : to please by or as if by attention or concern : PLACATE **b** : RELIEVE, ALLEVIATE **2** : to bring comfort, solace, or reassurance

sooth·say·er \'süth-ˌsā-ər\ *n* : a person who claims to foretell events — **sooth·say·ing** \-ˌsā-iŋ\ *n*

sooty \'su̇t-ē, 'sət-\ *adj* **soot·i·er; -est** **1 a** : of, relating to, or producing soot **b** : soiled with soot **2** : of the color of soot — **soot·i·ly** \'su̇t-ə-lē, 'sət-\ *adv* — **soot·i·ness** \'su̇t-ē-nəs, 'sət-\ *n*

1**sop** \'säp\ *n* **1** *chiefly dial* : a piece of food dipped or steeped in a liquid (as bread dipped in milk or gravy) **2** : a bribe, gift, or gesture for pacifying or winning favor

2**sop** *vb* **sopped; sop·ping 1 a :** to steep or dip in or as if in liquid **b :** to wet thoroughly : SOAK ⟨*sop* a floor with soapy water⟩ **2 :** to mop up (as water)

sop *abbr* soprano

soph·ism \'säf-ˌiz-əm\ *n* : an unsound misleading argument that on the surface seems reasonable

soph·ist \'säf-əst\ *n* : one who argues by the use of sophisms

so·phis·tic \sə-'fis-tik\ *or* **so·phis·ti·cal** \-ti-kəl\ *adj* : being clever and subtle but misleading — **so·phis·ti·cal·ly** \-ti-k(ə-)lē\ *adv*

1**so·phis·ti·cate** \sə-'fis-tə-ˌkāt\ *vb* : to cause to become sophisticated — **so·phis·ti·ca·tion** \-ˌfis-tə-'kā-shən\ *n*

2**so·phis·ti·cate** \sə-'fis-ti-kət, -tə-ˌkāt\ *n* : a sophisticated person

so·phis·ti·cat·ed \-tə-ˌkāt-əd\ *adj* **1 :** not in a natural, pure, or original state : ADULTERATED ⟨a *sophisticated* oil⟩ **2 a :** deprived of native or original simplicity **b :** highly complicated : COMPLEX ⟨*sophisticated* instruments⟩ **c :** WORLDLY-WISE, KNOWING ⟨a *sophisticated* young lady⟩ **3 a :** finely experienced and aware ⟨a *sophisticated* observer of the political scene⟩ **b :** intellectually appealing ⟨a *sophisticated* novel⟩ — **so·phis·ti·cat·ed·ly** *adv*

soph·ist·ry \'säf-ə-strē\ *n, pl* **-ries :** deceptively subtle reasoning or argumentation

soph·o·more \'säf(-ə)-ˌmōr, -ˌmȯr\ *n* : a student in his second year at a college or secondary school

soph·o·mor·ic \ˌsäf-ə-'mōr-ik, -'mȯr-\ *adj* **1 :** of, relating to, or characteristic of a sophomore **2 :** being conceited and overconfident of knowledge but poorly informed and immature

1**sop·o·rif·ic** \ˌsäp-ə-'rif-ik, ˌsō-pə-\ *adj* **1 :** causing or tending to cause sleep **2 :** of, relating to, or characterized by sleepiness or lethargy ⟨*soporific* old men⟩

2**soporific** *n* : a soporific agent or drug

sop·ping \'säp-ing\ *adj* : thoroughly wet : wet through : SOAKING

sop·py \'säp-ē\ *adj* **sop·pi·er; -est 1 :** soaked through : SATURATED **2 :** very wet

1**so·prano** \sə-'pran-ō, -'prän-\ *n, pl* **-pran·os** [from Italian, from *sopra* "above", from Latin *supra*] **1 :** the highest voice part in 4-part mixed harmony **2 :** the highest singing voice **3 :** a singer with a soprano voice

2**soprano** *adj* **1 :** relating to the soprano voice or part **2 :** having a high range ⟨*soprano* sax⟩

sor·cer·er \'sȯrs(-ə)-rər\ *n* : a person who practices sorcery : WIZARD — **sor·cer·ess** \-rəs\ *n*

sor·cery \'sȯrs(-ə)-rē\ *n, pl* **-cer·ies :** the use of power gained from the assistance or control of evil spirits : WITCHCRAFT

sor·did \'sȯrd-əd\ *adj* **1 :** DIRTY, FILTHY ⟨*sordid* surroundings⟩ **2 :** marked by baseness or grossness : VILE ⟨*sordid* motives⟩ **3 :** MISERLY, NIGGARDLY, COVETOUS — **sor·did·ly** *adv* — **sor·did·ness** *n*

1**sore** \'sō(ə)r, 'sȯ(ə)r\ *adj* **1 a :** causing pain or distress ⟨*sore* news⟩ **b :** painfully sensitive : TENDER ⟨*sore* muscles⟩ **c :** hurt or inflamed so as to be or seem painful ⟨*sore* runny eyes⟩ **2 :** attended by difficulties, hardship, or exertion ⟨a *sore* subject⟩ **3 :** ANGERED, VEXED ⟨she's *sore* at me⟩ — **sore·ness** *n*

2**sore** *n* **1 :** a sore spot on the body; *esp* : one (as an ulcer) with the tissues broken and usu. infected **2 :** a source of pain or vexation : AFFLICTION

3**sore** *adv* : SORELY

sore·head \'sō(ə)r-ˌhed, 'sȯ(ə)r-\ *n* : a person easily angered or disgruntled — **sorehead** *or* **sore·head·ed** \-'hed-əd\ *adj*

sore·ly \-lē\ *adv* : in a sore manner : PAINFULLY, SEVERELY, EXTREMELY

sor·ghum \'sȯr-gəm\ *n* **1 :** any of a genus of Old World tropical grasses similar to Indian corn in habit; *esp* : one cultivated for grain, forage, or syrup — compare SORGO **2 :** syrup from sorgo

sorghum 1

sor·go \'sȯr-gō\ *n, pl* **sorgos :** a sorghum grown primarily for its sweet juice from which syrup is made but also used for fodder and silage

so·ror·i·ty \sə-'rȯr-ət-ē, -'rär-\ *n, pl* **-ties** [from medieval Latin *sororitas* "sisterhood", from Latin *soror* "sister"] : a club of girls or women esp. at a college

1**sor·rel** \'sȯr-əl, 'sär-\ *n* **1 :** an animal (as a horse) of a sorrel color **2 :** a brownish orange to light brown

2**sorrel** *n* : any of various plants (as wood sorrel) with sour juice

1**sor·row** \'sär-ō, 'sȯr-\ *n* **1 a :** sadness or anguish due to loss (as of something loved) **b :** a cause of grief or sadness **2 :** CONTRITION, REPENTANCE

2**sorrow** *vb* : to feel or express sorrow : GRIEVE

sor·row·ful \-fəl\ *adj* **1 :** full of or marked by sorrow **2 :** expressive of or causing sorrow — **sor·row·ful·ly** \-fə-lē\ *adv* — **sor·row·ful·ness** *n*

sor·ry \'sär-ē, 'sȯr-\ *adj* **sor·ri·er; -est 1 :** feeling sorrow, regret, or penitence **2 :** MOURNFUL, SAD **3 :** inspiring sorrow, pity, scorn, or ridicule : WRETCHED — **sor·ri·ly** \'sär-ə-lē, 'sȯr-\ *adv* — **sor·ri·ness** \'sär-ē-nəs, 'sȯr-\ *n*

1**sort** \'sȯrt\ *n* **1 :** a group set up on the basis of any characteristic in common : CLASS **2 :** a number of things used together : SET, SUIT **3 :** method or manner of acting : WAY, MANNER **4 a :** general character or disposition **b :** PERSON, INDIVIDUAL ⟨he's not a bad *sort*⟩ — **of sorts** *or* **of a sort :** of an inconsequential or mediocre quality ⟨a poet *of sorts*⟩ — **out of sorts 1 :** out of temper : IRRITABLE **2 :** not well

2**sort** *vb* **1 :** to put in a certain place or rank according to kind, class, or nature : CLASSIFY ⟨*sort* mail⟩ ⟨*sort* out socks by color⟩ **2** *archaic* : HARMONIZE, AGREE — **sort·a·ble** \'sȯrt-ə-bəl\ *adj* — **sort·er** *n*

sor·tie \'sȯrt-ē, sȯr-'tē\ *n* **1 :** a sudden issuing of troops from a defensive position against the enemy : SALLY **2 :** one mission or attack by a single plane — **sortie** *vb*

sort of *adv* : to a moderate degree : RATHER

so·rus \'sōr-əs, 'sȯr-\ *n, pl* **so·ri** \'sōr-ˌī, 'sȯr-, -(ˌ)ē\ : one of the dots on the underside of a fertile fern frond consisting of a cluster of spores

SOS \ˌes-(ˌ)ō-'es\ *n* : an internationally recognized signal of distress in radio code · · · – – – · · · used esp. by ships calling for help

1**so–so** \'sō-'sō\ *adv* : TOLERABLY, PASSABLY

2**so–so** *adj* : neither very good nor very bad : MIDDLING

sot \'sät\ *n* : a habitual drunkard

sot·to vo·ce \ˌsät-ō-'vō-chē\ *adv or adj* [from Italian, literally "under the voice"] **1 :** under the breath

ə abut	ər further	a back		ā bake
ä cot, cart	aù out	ch chin	e less	ē easy
g gift	i trip ī life	j joke	ng sing	ō flow
ȯ flaw	ȯi coin	th thin	t͟h this	ü loot
u̇ foot	y yet	yü few	yu̇ furious	zh vision

: in an undertone; *also* : PRIVATELY **2** : very softly ⟨play the finale *sotto voce*⟩

sou \'sü\ *n* : a French bronze coin of the period before 1914 worth 5 centimes

sou·bri·quet \'sō-bri-ˌkā, 'sü-\ *var of* SOBRIQUET

[1]**souf·flé** \sü-'flā\ *n* [from French, from the past participle of *souffler* "to blow up", "inflate"] : a delicate spongy hot dish lightened in baking by stiffly beaten egg whites ⟨cheese *soufflé*⟩

[2]**soufflé** *or* **souf·fléed** \-'flād\ *adj* : puffed by or in cooking ⟨*soufflé* omelet⟩

sough \'səf, 'sau̇\ *vb* : to make a moaning or sighing sound — **sough** *n*

sought *past of* SEEK

[1]**soul** \'sōl\ *n* **1** : the spiritual part of man believed to give life to his body and in many religions regarded as immortal **2 a** : man's moral and emotional nature ⟨felt his *soul* rebel against cruelty⟩ **b** : spiritual force : FERVOR **3** : the essential part of something **4** : the moving spirit : LEADER ⟨the *soul* of an enterprise⟩ **5** : EMBODIMENT ⟨he was the *soul* of honor⟩ **6** : a human being : PERSON ⟨a kind *soul*⟩ **7** : a disembodied spirit **8** : the qualities that are essential to or characteristic of the cultural heritage of black Americans — **souled** \'sōld\ *adj*

[2]**soul** *adj* **1** : of, relating to, or characteristic of black Americans or their culture ⟨*soul* food⟩ ⟨*soul* music⟩ **2** : intended for or controlled by blacks ⟨*soul* radio stations⟩

soul·ful \-fəl\ *adj* : full of or expressing feeling or emotion — **soul·ful·ly** \-fə-lē\ *adv* — **soul·ful·ness** *n*

soul·less \'sōl-ləs\ *adj* : having no soul or no greatness or nobleness of mind or feeling — **soul·less·ly** *adv*

soul–search·ing \'sōl-ˌsər-ching\ *n* : examination of one's conscience esp. with regard to motives and values

[1]**sound** \'sau̇nd\ *adj* **1** : free from flaw, defect, or decay **2** : not diseased or weak : HEALTHY ⟨a *sound* mind in a *sound* body⟩ **3** : SOLID, FIRM ⟨a building of *sound* construction⟩ **4** : STABLE **5** : not faulty : VALID, RIGHT ⟨a *sound* argument⟩ **6** : showing good sense : WISE ⟨*sound* advice⟩ **7** : HONORABLE, HONEST ⟨*sound* principles⟩ **8** : THOROUGH ⟨a *sound* beating⟩ **9** : UNDISTURBED, DEEP ⟨a *sound* sleep⟩ — **sound·ly** *adv* — **sound·ness** \'sau̇n(d)-nəs\ *n*

[2]**sound** *adv* : SOUNDLY ⟨*sound* asleep⟩

[3]**sound** *n* **1 a** : the sensation of hearing **b** : a particular auditory impression : NOISE, TONE **c** : the energy of vibration that causes the sensation of hearing **2 a** : one of the noises that together make up human speech ⟨the *sound* of *th* in *this*⟩ **b** : a sequence of spoken noises ⟨*-cher* of *teacher* and *-ture* of *creature* have the same *sound*⟩ **3 a** : meaningless noise **b** : impression conveyed : IMPORT, IMPLICATION ⟨the excuse has a suspicious *sound*⟩ **4** : hearing distance : EARSHOT ⟨within *sound* of my voice⟩

[4]**sound** *vb* **1 a** : to make or cause to make a sound **b** : RESOUND **c** : to give a summons by sound **2** : to put into words : VOICE **3 a** : to make known : PROCLAIM **b** : to order, signal, or indicate by a sound **4** : to make or convey an impression : SEEM ⟨*sounds* incredible⟩ **5** : to examine by causing to emit sounds ⟨*sound* the lungs⟩ — **sound·a·ble** \'sau̇n-də-bəl\ *adj*

[5]**sound** *n* : a long passage of water that is wider than a strait and often connects two larger bodies of water or forms a channel between the mainland and an island

[6]**sound** *vb* **1 a** : to measure the depth of (as with a sounding line) : FATHOM **b** : to look into or investigate the possibility **2** : to try to find out the views or intentions of : PROBE ⟨*sounded* him out on the idea⟩ **3** : to dive down suddenly ⟨a *sounding* whale⟩

sound barrier *n* : the sudden large increase in resistance that the air offers to an airplane whose speed nears the speed of sound

sound·board \'sau̇n(d)-ˌbōrd, -ˌbȯrd\ *n* **1** : a thin resonant board so placed in a musical instrument as to reinforce its tones by sympathetic vibration **2** : SOUNDING BOARD 1a

soundboard 1 (of a piano)

sound effects *n pl* : effects that are imitative of sounds called for in the script of a play, radio or television program, or motion picture

sound·er \'sau̇n-dər\ *n* : one that sounds; *esp* : an electromagnetic device in a telegraph receiver that makes clicking sounds from which the message can be interpreted

[1]**sound·ing** \'sau̇n-ding\ *n* **1 a** : measurement by sounding **b** : the depth so sounded **2** : measurement of atmospheric conditions at various heights **3** : a probe, test, or sampling of opinion or intention

[2]**sounding** *adj* **1** : RESONANT, SONOROUS **2** : HIGH-SOUNDING — **sound·ing·ly** \-ding-lē\ *adv*

sounding board *n* **1 a** : a structure behind or over a pulpit, rostrum, or platform to give distinctness and sonority to sound uttered from it **b** : a device or agency that helps spread opinions or utterances **2** : SOUNDBOARD 1

sounding line *n* : a line, wire, or cord weighted at one end for sounding

sound·less \'sau̇n-dləs\ *adj* : making no sound : SILENT — **sound·less·ly** *adv*

sound off *vb* **1** : to count cadence while marching **2** : to voice one's opinions freely and vigorously

sound pollution *n* : NOISE POLLUTION

sound·proof \'sau̇n(d)-'prüf\ *adj* : designed to prevent sound from entering or leaving — **soundproof** *vb*

sound track *n* : the area on a motion-picture film that carries the sound record

sound truck *n* : a truck equipped with a loudspeaker

sound wave *n* : a disturbance that travels away from a vibrating object through a material (as air) and that when reaching a person's ear is perceived as sound

[1]**soup** \'süp\ *n* **1** : a liquid food with a meat, fish, or vegetable stock as a base and often containing pieces of solid food **2** : something having or suggesting the consistency of soup (as a heavy fog or nitroglycerin)

[2]**soup** *vb* : to increase the power or efficiency of ⟨*soup* up an engine⟩ — **souped–up** \'süpt-'əp\ *adj*

soupy \'sü-pē\ *adj* **soup·i·er**; **-est** **1** : having the consistency of soup **2** : densely foggy or cloudy

[1]**sour** \'sau̇(ə)r\ *adj* **1** : having an acid or tart taste ⟨*sour* as vinegar⟩ **2 a** : having undergone a usu. acid fermentation ⟨*sour* milk⟩ **b** : indicating decay : PUTRID ⟨a *sour* odor⟩ **3** : UNPLEASANT, DISAGREEABLE ⟨a *sour* look⟩ ⟨played a *sour* note⟩ **4** : acid in reaction ⟨*sour* soil⟩ — **sour·ish** \-ish\ *adj* — **sour·ly** *adv* — **sour·ness** *n*

[2]**sour** *n* **1 a** : something sour **b** : the primary taste sensation produced by acid stimuli **2** : a cocktail made with liquor, lemon or lime juice, sugar, and sometimes soda water

[3]**sour** *vb* : to become or make sour

sour ball *n* : a spherical piece of hard candy having a tart flavor

source \'sōrs, 'sȯrs\ *n* **1** : the point of origin of a stream of water : FOUNTAINHEAD **2 a** : force that gives rise to something : CAUSE ⟨a *source* of strength⟩ **b** : a point of origin **c** : a person or a publication that supplies information; *esp* : a firsthand document or primary reference work

sour·dough \'sau̇(ə)r-ˌdō\ *n* **1** : a leaven of dough in which fermentation is active **2** : an old-time prospector in Alaska or northwestern Canada

sour grapes *n pl* : the belittling of something that has proven unattainable

sour gum *n* : a timber tree of the eastern U.S. with bluish black fruits and close-grained grayish wood

sou·sa·phone \'sü-zə-ˌfōn\ *n* : a large circular tuba with a flaring adjustable bell

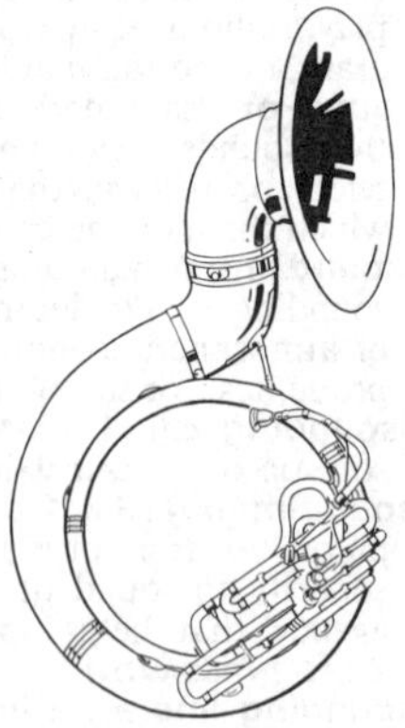
sousaphone

¹souse \'sau̇s\ *vb* **1** : PICKLE **2 a** : to plunge in liquid : IMMERSE **b** : to wet thoroughly : DRENCH **3** : to make or become drunk : INEBRIATE

²souse *n* **1** : something pickled; *esp* : seasoned and chopped pork trimmings, fish, or shellfish **2** : an act of sousing : WETTING **3** : an habitual drunkard

sou·tane \sü-'tän, -'tan\ *n* : CASSOCK

¹south \'sau̇th; *in compounds, as "southwest", also* (')sau̇ *esp by seamen*\ *adv* : to or toward the south

²south *adj* **1** : situated toward or at the south **2** : coming from the south

³south *n* **1 a** : the direction to the right of one facing east **b** : the compass point opposite to north **2** *cap* : regions or countries south of a specified or implied point

South African *adj* : of, relating to, or characteristic of the Republic of South Africa or its people — **South African** *n*

South American *adj* : of, relating to, or characteristic of South America or its people — **South American** *n*

south·bound \'sau̇th-ˌbau̇nd\ *adj* : headed south

¹south·east \sau̇th-'ēst\ *adv* : to or toward the southeast

²southeast *n* **1** : the direction between south and east **2** *cap* : regions or countries southeast of a specified or implied point

³southeast *adj* **1** : situated toward or at the southeast **2** : coming from the southeast

south·east·er \sau̇th-'ē-stər\ *n* : a storm, strong wind, or gale coming from the southeast

south·east·er·ly \-lē\ *adv or adj* **1** : from the southeast **2** : toward the southeast

south·east·ern \sau̇th-'ē-stərn\ *adj* **1** *often cap* : of, relating to, or characteristic of the Southeast **2** : lying toward or coming from the southeast — **south·east·ern·most** \-ˌmōst\ *adj*

South·east·ern·er \-stə(r)-nər\ *n* : a native or inhabitant of a southeastern region (as of the U.S.)

south·east·ward \sau̇th-'ēs-twərd\ *adv or adj* : toward the southeast — **south·east·wards** \-twərdz\ *adv*

south·er \'sau̇-thər\ *n* : a southerly wind

south·er·ly \'səth-ər-lē\ *adv or adj* **1** : from the south **2** : toward the south

south·ern \'səth-ərn\ *adj* **1** *often cap* : of, relating to, or characteristic of the South **2** : lying toward or coming from the south — **south·ern·most** \-ˌmōst\ *adj*

South·ern·er \'səth-ə(r)-nər\ *n* : a native or inhabitant of the South (as of the U.S.)

southern lights *n pl* : AURORA AUSTRALIS

south·ern·ly \'səth-ərn-lē\ *adj* **1** : coming from the south **2** : headed south

south·land \'sau̇th-ˌland, -lənd\ *n, often cap* : land in the south : the south of a country or region

south·paw \'sau̇th-ˌpȯ\ *n* : LEFT-HANDER; *esp* : a left-handed baseball pitcher — **southpaw** *adj*

south pole *n, often cap S & P* : the southernmost point of the earth : the southern end of the earth's axis

south·ward \'sau̇th-wərd\ *adv or adj* : toward the south — **south·wards** \-wərdz\ *adv*

¹south·west \sau̇th-'west\ *adv* : to or toward the southwest

²southwest *n* **1** : the direction between south and west **2** *cap* : regions or countries southwest of a specified or implied point

³southwest *adj* **1** : situated toward or at the southwest **2** : coming from the southwest

south·west·er \sau̇th-'wes-tər\ *n* : a storm or wind from the southwest

south·west·er·ly \-lē\ *adv or adj* **1** : from the southwest **2** : toward the southwest

south·west·ern \sau̇th-'wes-tərn\ *adj* **1** *often cap* : of, relating to, or characteristic of the Southwest **2** : lying toward or coming from the southwest — **south·west·ern·most** \-ˌmōst\ *adj*

South·west·ern·er \-tə(r)-nər\ *n* : a native or inhabitant of a southwestern region (as of the U.S.)

south·west·ward \sau̇th-'wes-twərd\ *adv or adj* : toward the southwest — **south·west·wards** \-twərdz\ *adv*

sou·ve·nir \'sü-və-ˌni(ə)r, ˌsü-və-'\ *n* : something that serves as a reminder : MEMENTO, REMEMBRANCE

sou'·west·er \sau̇-'wes-tər\ *n* **1** : a long oilskin coat worn esp. at sea during stormy weather **2** : a waterproof hat with a wide slanting brim longer in back than in front

sou'wester 2

¹sov·er·eign \'säv-(ə-)rən, 'säv-ərn, 'səv-\ *n* **1** : a person, body of persons, or a state possessing sovereignty; *esp* : a monarch exercising supreme authority in a state **2** : a British gold coin no longer issued worth 1 pound sterling

²sovereign *adj* **1** : CHIEF, HIGHEST ⟨our *sovereign* interest⟩ ⟨a citizen's *sovereign* duty⟩ **2** : supreme in power or authority ⟨a *sovereign* prince⟩ **3** : having independent authority ⟨a *sovereign* state⟩ — **sov·er·eign·ly** *adv*

sov·er·eign·ty \-tē\ *n, pl* **-ties** **1** : the condition of being sovereign or a sovereign **2 a** : supreme power esp. over a politically organized unit : DOMINION **b** : freedom from external control : AUTONOMY **3** : one that is sovereign; *esp* : an autonomous state

¹so·vi·et \'sō-vē-ˌet, -ət, 'säv-ē-\ *n* [from Russian *sovet* "council", from Old Russian *sŭvětŭ*, from *sŭ-* "with", "together" and *větŭ* "council"] **1 a** : one of the representative councils of workers, peasants, or soldiers formed during the Russian revolution

ə abut	ər further	a back	ā bake	
ä cot, cart	au̇ out	ch chin	e less	ē easy
g gift	i trip	ī life	j joke	ng sing
ō flow	ȯ flaw	ȯi coin	th thin	th this
ü loot	u̇ foot	y yet	yü few	yu̇ furious
zh vision				

b : one of a hierarchy of governing councils in the U.S.S.R. **2** *cap* **a** : the U.S.S.R. **b** *pl* : the people and esp. the political and military leaders of the U.S.S.R.

2**soviet** *adj* **1** : of, relating to, or organized on the basis of soviets ⟨a *soviet* republic⟩ **2** *cap* : of or relating to the U.S.S.R.

so·vi·et·ize \-ˌīz\ *vb, often cap* **1** : to bring under Soviet control **2** : to force into conformity with Soviet cultural patterns or governmental policies — **so·vi·et·i·za·tion** \ˌsō-vē-ˌet-ə-'zā-shən, ˌsäv-ē-, -ət-\ *n, often cap*

1**sow** \'saů\ *n* : an adult female swine

2**sow** \'sō\ *vb* **sowed**; **sown** \'sōn\ *or* **sowed**; **sowing** **1 a** : to plant seed for growth esp. by scattering **b** : PLANT 1a **c** : to strew with or as if with seed **d** : to introduce into a selected environment : IMPLANT **2** : to set in motion : FOMENT ⟨*sow* suspicion⟩ **3** : to spread abroad : DISPERSE, DISSEMINATE — **sow·er** \'sō(-ə)r\ *n*

sow bug \'saů-\ *n* : WOOD LOUSE

sox *pl of* SOCK

soy \'sȯi\ *n* **1** : a Chinese and Japanese sauce made from soybeans fermented in brine **2** : SOYBEAN

soya \'sȯi-(y)ə\ *n* [from Dutch *soja*, from Japanese *shōyu* "soy"] : SOYBEAN

soy·bean \'sȯi-'bēn, -ˌbēn\ *n* : a hairy annual Asiatic legume widely grown for its oil-rich and protein-rich edible seeds and for forage and soil improvement; *also* : its seed

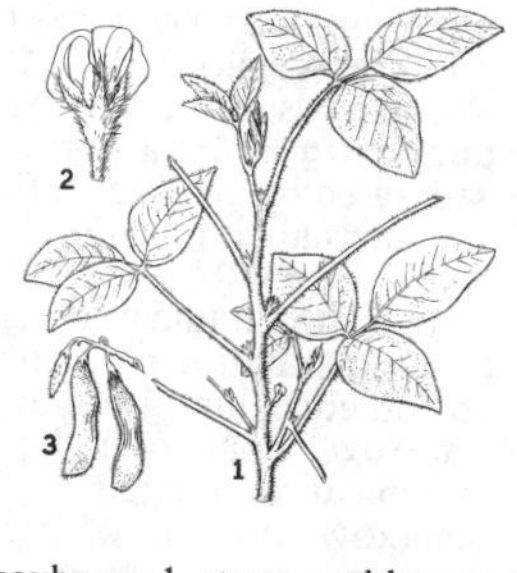

soybean: 1, stems and leaves; 2, flower; 3, seed pods

sp *abbr* **1** special **2** species **3** specimen **4** spelling

Sp *abbr* **1** Spain **2** Spanish

spa \'spä, 'spȯ\ *n* [from *Spa*, mineral spring and health resort in Belgium] **1 a** : a mineral spring **b** : a resort with mineral springs **2** : a fashionable resort or hotel

1**space** \'spās\ *n* **1** : a period or duration of time **2 a** : a limited extent in one, two, or three dimensions : DISTANCE, AREA, VOLUME **b** : an extent set apart or available ⟨parking *space*⟩ ⟨floor *space*⟩ **3** : one of the degrees between or above or below the lines of a musical staff **4** : a boundless three-dimensional extent in which objects and events occur and have relative position and direction **5** : the region beyond the earth's atmosphere **6** : a blank area separating words or lines **7** : accommodations on a public vehicle

2**space** *vb* : to place at intervals or arrange with space between

space age *n* : the period of history beginning with the launching of the first satellite into orbit around the earth

space·craft \'spās-ˌkraft\ *n* : SPACESHIP

space·flight \-ˌflīt\ *n* : flight beyond the earth's atmosphere

space heater *n* : a device for heating an enclosed space; *esp* : an often portable device that heats the space in which it is located and has no external heating ducts

space·man \'spās-ˌman\ *n* **1** : one who travels outside the earth's atmosphere **2** : a person engaged in any of various fields bearing on flight through outer space

space medicine *n* : a branch of medicine concerned with the physiologic and biologic effects on the human body of flight beyond the earth's atmosphere

space·port \'spās-ˌpōrt, -ˌpȯrt\ *n* : an installation for testing and launching rockets, missiles, and satellites

space·ship \'spās(h)-ˌship\ *n* : a vehicle designed to operate outside the earth's atmosphere

space station *n* : a manned artificial satellite designed for a fixed orbit about the earth and to serve as a base (as for the refueling of spaceships or launching of missiles)

space suit *n* : a suit with air supply and provisions to make life in free space possible for its wearer

space suit

spac·ing \'spā-sing\ *n* **1** : an arrangement in space **2 a** : SPACE **b** : the distance between any two objects in a usu. regularly arranged series

spa·cious \'spā-shəs\ *adj* **1** : vast or ample in extent : ROOMY ⟨a *spacious* hall⟩ **2** : large or magnificent in scale : EXPANSIVE — **spa·cious·ly** *adv* — **spa·cious·ness** *n*

1**spade** \'spād\ *n* [from Old English *spadu*] **1** : a tool for turning soil that resembles a shovel, is adapted for being pushed into the ground with the foot, and has a heavy usu. flat blade **2** : a spade-shaped instrument

2**spade** *vb* : to dig with or use a spade

3**spade** *n* [from Italian *spada* or Spanish *espada* "broad sword", both from Latin *spatha*, from Greek *spathē* "blade", from the same source as Old English *spadu* "spade for digging"] **1** : a black figure resembling an inverted heart with a short stem at the bottom used to distinguish a suit of playing cards **2** : a card of the suit bearing spades

spade·work \'spād-ˌwərk\ *n* **1** : work done with the spade **2** : the hard plain preliminary drudgery in any undertaking

spa·ghet·ti \spə-'get-ē\ *n* [from Italian, from plural of *spaghetto* "little string", diminutive of *spago* "string"] : a food made chiefly of semolina paste dried in the form of thin solid strings

spake \'spāk\ *archaic past of* SPEAK

1**span** \'span\ *archaic past of* SPIN

2**span** *n* **1 a** : the distance from the end of the thumb to the end of the little finger of a spread hand **b** : an English unit of length equal to 9 inches **2 a** : a limited space of time ⟨*span* of life⟩ **b** : the spread of an arch, beam, truss, or girder from one support to another **c** : the portion extended to form a span **3** : the amount grasped in a single mental performance ⟨memory *span*⟩

3**span** *vb* **spanned**; **span·ning** **1 a** : to measure by or as if by the hand with fingers and thumb extended **b** : MEASURE **2 a** : to reach or extend across ⟨a bridge *spans* the river⟩ **b** : to place or construct a span over : BRIDGE

4**span** *n* : a pair of animals (as mules) driven together

Span *abbr* Spanish

1**span·gle** \'spang-gəl\ *n* **1** : a small piece of shining metal or plastic used for ornamentation esp. on dresses **2** : a small glittering object

2**spangle** *vb* **span·gled**; **span·gling** \'spang-g(ə-)ling\ : to set or sprinkle with or as if with spangles

Span·iard \'span-yərd\ *n* : a native or inhabitant of Spain

span·iel \'span-yəl\ *n* [from medieval French *espaignol*, literally "Spaniard"] **1** : any of numerous small or medium-sized mostly short-legged dogs usu. having long wavy hair and large drooping ears **2** : a cringing fawning person

Span·ish \'span-ish\ *n* **1** : the Romance language of the largest part of Spain and of the countries colonized by Spaniards **2 Spanish** *pl* : the people of Spain — **Spanish** *adj*

Spanish American *n* **1** : a native or inhabitant of one of the countries of America in which Spanish is the national language **2** : a resident of the U.S. whose native language is Spanish and whose culture is of Spanish origin — **Spanish–American** *adj*

Spanish moss *n* : a plant related to the pineapple that forms hanging tufts of grayish green filaments on trees in the southern U.S. and the West Indies

spank \'spangk\ *vb* : to strike esp. on the buttocks usu. with the open hand — **spank** *n*

spank·ing \'spang-king\ *adj* : moving with a quick, lively pace : BRISK, LIVELY ⟨a *spanking* wind⟩

span·ner \'span-ər\ *n* **1** *chiefly Brit* : WRENCH **2** : a wrench having a jaw or socket to fit a nut or head of a bolt, a pipe, or hose coupling; *esp* : one having a tooth or pin in its jaw to fit a hole or slot in an object

1**spar** \'spär\ *n* **1** : a stout rounded wood or metal piece (as a mast, boom, or yard) used to support sail rigging **2** : one of the main lengthwise members of the wing of an airplane that carry the ribs

spars 1

2**spar** *vb* **sparred**; **spar·ring** **1 a** : BOX **b** : to engage in a practice or exhibition bout of boxing **2** : SKIRMISH, WRANGLE

3**spar** *n* : any of various nonmetallic somewhat lustrous minerals usu. able to be split readily in certain directions

1**spare** \'spa(ə)r, 'spe(ə)r\ *vb* **1** : to show mercy to : be lenient ⟨*spare* a prisoner⟩ **2** : to relieve of the necessity of doing or undergoing something : EXEMPT ⟨be *spared* the labor⟩ **3** : to refrain from : AVOID ⟨*spare* no cost⟩ **4** : to use frugally ⟨*spare* the rod and spoil the child⟩ **5 a** : to give up as not strictly needed ⟨unable to *spare* a dollar⟩ **b** : to have left over or as margin ⟨time to *spare*⟩

2**spare** *adj* **1** : not being used; *esp* : held for emergency use ⟨a *spare* tire⟩ **2** : being over and above what is needed : SUPERFLUOUS ⟨*spare* time⟩ **3** : not liberal or ample : SPARING ⟨a *spare* diet⟩ **4** : somewhat thin ⟨of *spare* build⟩ **5** : not abundant or plentiful : SCANTY — **spare·ly** *adv* — **spare·ness** *n*

3**spare** *n* **1** : a spare or duplicate piece or part **2** : the knocking down of all 10 pins with the first 2 bowls of a frame in bowling or the score made by this action

spare·ribs \'spa(ə)r-ˌ(r)ibz, 'spe(ə)r-\ *n pl* : a cut of pork ribs separated from the bacon strip

spar·ing \'spa(ə)r-ing, 'spe(ə)r-\ *adj* **1** : tending to save; *esp* : FRUGAL **2** : MEAGER, SCANTY — **sparing·ly** \-ing-lē\ *adv*

1**spark** \'spärk\ *n* **1 a** : a small particle of a burning substance **b** : a hot glowing particle struck from a larger mass; *esp* : one heated by friction ⟨produce a *spark* by striking steel on flint⟩ **2 a** : a luminous electrical discharge of very short duration between two conductors **b** : the electrical discharge in a spark plug **c** : the mechanism controlling the discharge in a spark plug **3** : SPARKLE, FLASH **4** : something that sets off a sudden force ⟨the *spark* that set off the rebellion⟩ **5** : a latent particle capable of growth or developing : GERM ⟨not a *spark* of life⟩

2**spark** *vb* **1 a** : to throw out or produce sparks : SPARKLE **b** : to flash or fall like sparks ⟨fireflies *sparked* in the darkness⟩ **2 a** : to set off in a burst of activity : ACTIVATE **b** : to subject to the effect of an electrical spark **3** : to stir to activity ⟨the captain *sparked* his team to victory⟩ — **spark·er** *n*

3**spark** *n* **1** : a foppish young man : GALLANT **2** : LOVER, BEAU

4**spark** *vb* : WOO, COURT — **spark·er** *n*

1**spar·kle** \'spär-kəl\ *vb* **spar·kled**; **spar·kling** \-k(ə-)ling\ **1 a** : to throw out sparks **b** : to shine as if throwing out sparks : GLISTEN **2** : to perform brilliantly **3** : EFFERVESCE ⟨*sparkling* wine⟩ **4** : to become lively or animated

2**sparkle** *n* **1** : a little spark : SCINTILLATION ⟨the *sparkle* of a diamond⟩ **2** : the quality of sparkling **3 a** : ANIMATION, LIVELINESS ⟨the *sparkle* of a witty play⟩ **b** : EFFERVESCENCE

spar·kler \'spär-klər\ *n* **1** : DIAMOND **2** : a firework that throws off brilliant sparks on burning

spark plug *n* **1** : a part that carries two electrodes separated by an air gap, fits into the cylinder head of an internal-combustion engine, and produces the spark for combustion **2** : one that initiates or gives impetus to an undertaking

sparring partner *n* : one with whom a boxer spars for practice during training

spar·row \'spar-ō\ *n* **1** : any of several small dull singing birds related to the finches; *esp* : ENGLISH SPARROW **2** : any of various finches (as the song sparrow) resembling the true sparrows

sparrow hawk *n* : any of various small hawks or falcons

sparse \'spärs\ *adj* : not thickly grown or settled — **sparse·ly** *adv* — **sparse·ness** *n* — **spar·si·ty** \'spär-sət-ē\ *n*

1**Spar·tan** \'spärt-ən\ *n* **1** : a native or inhabitant of ancient Sparta **2** : a person of great courage and fortitude

2**Spartan** *adj* **1** : of or relating to Sparta in ancient Greece **2 a** : marked by strict self-discipline and avoidance of comfort and luxury ⟨*Spartan* simplicity⟩ **b** : undaunted by pain or danger ⟨*Spartan* courage⟩

spasm \'spaz-əm\ *n* **1** : a sudden uncontrolled muscular contraction **2** : a sudden violent and temporary effort or emotion

spas·mod·ic \spaz-'mäd-ik\ *adj* **1** : relating to or affected or characterized by spasm ⟨*spasmodic* movements⟩ **2** : acting or proceeding fitfully : INTERMITTENT ⟨*spasmodic* interest⟩ **3** : subject to outbursts of emotional excitement : EXCITABLE — **spas·mod·i·cal·ly** \-'mäd-i-k(ə-)lē\ *adv*

1**spas·tic** \'spas-tik\ *adj* **1** : of, relating to, or characterized by spasm ⟨*spastic* colon⟩ **2** : suffering from spastic paralysis

2**spastic** *n* : one suffering from spastic paralysis

spastic paralysis *n* : paralysis with rigidly contracted muscles

ə abut	ər further	a back	ā bake	
ä cot, cart	au̇ out	ch chin	e less	ē easy
g gift	i trip	ī life	j joke	ng sing	ō flow
ȯ flaw	ȯi coin	th thin	t͟h this	ü loot
u̇ foot	y yet	yü few	yu̇ furious	zh vision

[1]**spat** \'spat\ *past of* SPIT
[2]**spat** *n, pl* **spat** *or* **spats** : a young oyster or oysters
[3]**spat** *n* : a cloth or leather gaiter covering the instep and ankle
[4]**spat** *n* **1** : a brief petty quarrel : DISPUTE **2** : a sound like that of rain falling in large drops
[5]**spat** *vb* **spat·ted**; **spat·ting** **1** : to quarrel pettily or briefly : DISPUTE **2** : to strike with a sound like that of rain falling in large drops
spate \'spāt\ *n* **1** : FRESHET, FLOOD **2 a** : a large number or amount **b** : a sudden or strong outburst : RUSH
spa·tial \'spā-shəl\ *adj* : of, relating to, or occupying space — **spa·ti·al·i·ty** \ˌspā-shē-'al-ət-ē\ *n* — **spa·tial·ly** \'spāsh-(ə-)lē\ *adv*
[1]**spat·ter** \'spat-ər\ *vb* **1 a** : to splash with or as if with a liquid **b** : to soil or spot by splashing **2** : to scatter by splashing ⟨*spatter* mud⟩ **3 a** : to spurt forth in scattered drops **b** : to drop with a sound like rain
[2]**spatter** *n* **1** : the act or noise of spattering : the state of being spattered **2 a** : a drop or splash spattered on something **b** : a small number or quantity : SPRINKLE ⟨a *spatter* of rain⟩ ⟨a *spatter* of applause⟩
spat·u·la \'spach-ə-lə\ *n* : a flat thin usu. metal implement that resembles a knife and is used esp. for spreading or mixing soft substances, scooping, or lifting
spav·in \'spav-ən\ *n* : a disorder of horses characterized by bony enlargement of the hock and associated with strain — **spav·ined** \-ənd\ *adj*
[1]**spawn** \'spȯn, 'spän\ *vb* [from Old French *espandre* "to spread out", "expand", from Latin *expandere*] **1** : to produce or deposit eggs or spawn **2** : to bring forth : GENERATE **3** : to produce young esp. in large numbers — **spawn·er** *n*
[2]**spawn** *n* **1** : the eggs of aquatic animals (as fishes or oysters) that lay many small eggs **2** : PRODUCT, OFFSPRING; *also* : offspring produced in large quantities
spay \'spā\ *vb* : to remove the ovaries of (a female animal)
SPCA *abbr* Society for the Prevention of Cruelty to Animals
SPCC *abbr* Society for the Prevention of Cruelty to Children
speak \'spēk\ *vb* **spoke** \'spōk\; **spo·ken** \'spō-kən\; **speak·ing** **1** : to utter words with the ordinary voice : TALK **2** : to utter by means of words ⟨*speak* the truth⟩ **3** : to address a gathering **4** : to mention in speech or writing **5** : to carry a meaning as if by speech ⟨his clothes *spoke* of poverty⟩ **6** : to make a natural or characteristic sound **7** : to use or be able to use in talking ⟨*speak* French⟩ — **speak·a·ble** \'spē-kə-bəl\ *adj* — **speak for** **1** : to speak in behalf of : represent the opinions of **2** : to apply for : CLAIM — **speak to** : REPROVE, REBUKE — **speak well for** : to be evidence in favor of — **speak with** : to talk to
speak·easy \'spēk-ˌē-zē\ *n* : a place where alcoholic drinks are illegally sold
speak·er \'spē-kər\ *n* **1 a** : one that speaks **b** : one who makes a public speech **c** : one who acts as a spokesman **2** : the presiding officer of a deliberative assembly ⟨*Speaker* of the House of Representatives⟩ **3** : LOUDSPEAKER
speak·er·ship \-ˌship\ *n* : the position of speaker esp. of a legislative body
speak·ing \'spē-king\ *adj* **1** : highly significant or expressive : ELOQUENT ⟨*speaking* eyes⟩ **2** : STRIKING, FAITHFUL ⟨a *speaking* resemblance⟩
speak out *vb* **1** : to speak loudly and distinctly **2** : to speak freely ⟨*spoke out* on the issues⟩
speak up *vb* : to speak out
[1]**spear** \'spi(ə)r\ *n* **1** : a thrusting or throwing weapon with long shaft and sharp head or blade **2** : a sharp-pointed instrument with barbs used in spearing fish **3** : SPEARMAN — **spear·like** \-ˌlīk\ *adj*
[2]**spear** *vb* **1** : to pierce or strike with or as if with a spear **2** : to thrust with or as if with a spear — **spear·er** *n*
[3]**spear** *n* : a usu. young blade, shoot, or sprout (as of grass)
[1]**spear·head** \'spi(ə)r-ˌhed\ *n* **1** : the sharp-pointed head of a spear **2** : a leading element, force, or influence (as in an attack, drive, or enterprise)
[2]**spearhead** *vb* : to serve as leader or leading element of ⟨*spearhead* the attack⟩
spear·man \'spi(ə)r-mən\ *n* : one (as a soldier) armed with a spear
spear·mint \-ˌmint, -mənt\ *n* : a common mint grown for flavoring and esp. for its aromatic oil
spe·cial \'spesh-əl\ *adj* **1 a** : distinguished by some unusual quality ⟨a *special* occasion⟩ **b** : regarded with particular favor ⟨a *special* friend⟩ **2** : PECULIAR, UNIQUE ⟨a *special* case⟩ **3** : ADDITIONAL, EXTRA ⟨a *special* edition⟩ **4** : designed for a particular purpose or occasion ⟨a *special* diet⟩ — **special** *n* — **spe·cial·ly** \'spesh-(ə-)lē\ *adv*
special delivery *n* : messenger delivery of mail matter made ahead of the regular carrier delivery for an extra fee
spe·cial·ist \'spesh-(ə-)ləst\ *n* **1** : one who devotes himself to a special occupation or branch of learning ⟨an eye *specialist*⟩ **2** : any of six enlisted ranks in the army corresponding to the ranks of corporal through sergeant major — **specialist** *or* **spe·cial·is·tic** \ˌspesh-ə-'lis-tik\ *adj*
spe·ci·al·i·ty \ˌspesh-ē-'al-ət-ē\ *n, pl* **-ties** **1** : a special mark or quality **2** : a special object or class of objects **3 a** : a special aptitude or skill **b** : a particular occupation or branch of learning
spe·cial·i·za·tion \ˌspesh-(ə-)lə-'zā-shən\ *n* **1** : a making or becoming specialized **2 a** : structural adaptation of a body part to a particular function or of an organism for life in a particular environment **b** : a body part or an organism adapted by specialization
spe·cial·ize \'spesh-ə-ˌlīz\ *vb* **1** : to concentrate one's efforts in a special activity or field ⟨*specialize* in French⟩ **2** : to undergo specialization
spe·cial·ty \'spesh-əl-tē\ *n, pl* **-ties** **1** : a distinctive mark or quality **2** : a special object or class of objects; *esp* : a product of a special kind or of special excellence ⟨pancakes were the cook's *specialty*⟩ **3** : something in which one specializes or has special knowledge
spe·cie \'spē-shē, -sē\ *n* : money in coin esp. of gold or silver
spe·cies \'spē-(ˌ)shēz, -(ˌ)sēz\ *n, pl* **species** [from Latin, "appearance", "kind", from the root of *specere* "to look" found in English *spectator*, *inspect*, *aspect*] **1** : a class of individuals with common qualities and a common name : KIND, SORT **2** : a category of biological classification ranking below the genus, composed of related organisms or populations capable of interbreeding, and designated by a binomial scientific name
spec·i·fi·a·ble \'spes-ə-ˌfī-ə-bəl\ *adj* : capable of being specified
[1]**spe·cif·ic** \spi-'sif-ik\ *adj* **1** : of, relating to, or constituting a species **2** : PARTICULAR, ACTUAL, EXACT ⟨a *specific* date⟩ ⟨*specific* directions for assembling a machine⟩ **3** : having a unique relation to something: as **a** : exerting a usu. causative or curative influence

⟨quinine is *specific* for malaria⟩ **b :** capable of reacting with but one chemical substance (as an antibody or antigen) or with a chemical substance in but one way — **spe·cif·i·cal·ly** \-'sif-i-k(ə-)lē\ *adv* — **spec·i·fic·i·ty** \ˌspes-ə-'fis-ət-ē\ *n*

²**specific** *n* **1 :** something peculiarly adapted to a purpose or use; *esp* **:** a drug or remedy specific for a particular disease **2 a :** a characteristic quality or trait **b** *pl* **:** DETAILS, PARTICULARS ⟨stop talking in general terms and get down to *specifics*⟩

spec·i·fi·ca·tion \ˌspes-(ə-)fə-'kā-shən\ *n* **1 :** the act or process of specifying **2 a :** a detailed precise presentation of something or of a plan or proposal for something — usu. used in pl. ⟨the architect's *specifications* for a new building⟩ **b :** a single item in such a detailed presentation

specific gravity *n* **:** the ratio of the weight of a volume of a substance to the weight of an equal volume of some other substance taken as the standard which is water for solids and liquids and air or hydrogen for gases

specific heat *n* **:** the heat in calories required to raise the temperature of one gram of a substance one degree centigrade

spec·i·fy \'spes-ə-ˌfī\ *vb* **-fied; -fy·ing 1 :** to name or state explicitly or in detail ⟨*specify* the reason for absence⟩ **2 :** to include as an item in a specification ⟨*specify* oak flooring⟩ — **spec·i·fi·er** \-ˌfī(-ə)r\ *n*

spec·i·men \'spes-ə-mən\ *n* **1 :** an item or part typical of a group or whole **:** SAMPLE **2 :** SORT, INDIVIDUAL ⟨a tough *specimen*⟩

spe·cious \'spē-shəs\ *adj* **:** apparently but not really fair, just, or right ⟨a *specious* argument⟩ — **spe·cious·ly** *adv* — **spe·cious·ness** *n*

¹**speck** \'spek\ *n* **1 :** a small discoloration or spot esp. from dirt or decay **2 :** BIT, PARTICLE **3 :** something marked or marred with specks

²**speck** *vb* **:** to produce specks on or in ⟨a washing *specked* with soot⟩

¹**speck·le** \'spek-əl\ *n* **:** a little speck

²**speckle** *vb* **speck·led; speck·ling** \'spek-(ə-)liŋ\ **1 :** to mark with speckles **2 :** to be distributed in or on like speckles ⟨small lakes *speckled* the land⟩

specs \'speks\ *n pl* **1 :** GLASS 2b **2 :** SPECIFICATIONS

spec·ta·cle \'spek-ti-kəl\ *n* **1 a :** something exhibited to view as unusual, notable, or entertaining; *esp* **:** an eye-catching or dramatic public display **b :** an object of curiosity or contempt ⟨made a *spectacle* of herself at the party⟩ **2** *pl* **:** GLASS 2b

spec·ta·cled \-kəld\ *adj* **1 :** having or wearing spectacles **2 :** having markings suggesting a pair of spectacles

¹**spec·tac·u·lar** \spek-'tak-yə-lər\ *adj* **:** of, relating to, or constituting a spectacle **:** STRIKING, SENSATIONAL — **spec·tac·u·lar·ly** *adv*

²**spectacular** *n* **:** something (as an elaborate television show) that is spectacular

spec·ta·tor \'spek-ˌtāt-ər, spek-'\ *n* **:** one who looks on or watches **:** ONLOOKER — **spectator** *adj*

spec·ter *or* **spec·tre** \'spek-tər\ *n* **1 :** a visible disembodied spirit **:** GHOST **2 :** something that haunts or disturbs the mind

spec·tral \'spek-trəl\ *adj* **1 :** of, relating to, or suggesting a specter **:** GHOSTLY **2 :** of, relating to, or made by a spectrum ⟨*spectral* color⟩

ə abut	ər further	a back	ā bake	
ä cot, cart	aù out	ch chin	e less	ē easy
g gift	i trip	ī life	j joke	ŋ sing	ō flow
ȯ flaw	ȯi coin	th thin	th this	ü loot
ù foot	y yet	yü few	yù furious	zh vision

spec·tro·gram \'spek-trə-ˌgram\ *n* **:** a photograph or diagram of a spectrum

spec·tro·graph \'spek-trə-ˌgraf\ *n* **:** an apparatus for dispersing radiation into a spectrum and photographing or mapping the spectrum — **spec·tro·graph·ic** \ˌspek-trə-'graf-ik\ *adj* — **spec·tro·graph·i·cal·ly** \-'graf-i-k(ə-)lē\ *adv*

spec·trom·e·ter \spek-'träm-ət-ər\ *n* **1 :** an instrument used in determining the index of refraction **2 :** a spectroscope fitted for measurements of the spectra observed with it

spec·tro·scope \'spek-trə-ˌskōp\ *n* **:** any of various instruments for forming and examining spectra — **spec·tro·scop·ic** \ˌspek-trə-'skäp-ik\ *adj* — **spec·tro·scop·i·cal·ly** \-'skäp-i-k(ə-)lē\ *adv* — **spec·tros·co·pist** \spek-'träs-kə-pəst\ *n* — **spec·tros·co·py** \-pē\ *n*

spec·trum \'spek-trəm\ *n, pl* **spec·tra** \-trə\ *or* **spec·trums 1 a :** a series of colors formed when a beam of white light is dispersed (as by passing through a prism) so that the component waves are arranged in the order of their wavelengths from red continuing through orange, yellow, green, blue, indigo, and violet **b :** a series of radiations arranged in regular order according to some varying characteristic (as wavelength) — compare ELECTROMAGNETIC SPECTRUM **2 :** a continuous sequence or range ⟨a wide *spectrum* of political opinions⟩

spec·u·late \'spek-yə-ˌlāt\ *vb* **1 a :** to meditate on or ponder a subject **:** REFLECT **b :** to think or theorize about something in which evidence is too slight for certainty to be reached **2 :** to assume a business risk in hope of gain; *esp* **:** to buy or sell in expectation of profiting from market fluctuations — **spec·u·la·tion** \ˌspek-yə-'lā-shən\ *n* — **spec·u·la·tive** \'spek-yə-lət-iv, -ˌlāt-\ *adj* — **spec·u·la·tive·ly** *adv* — **spec·u·la·tor** \-ˌlāt-ər\ *n*

speech \'spēch\ *n* **1 a :** the communication or expression of thoughts in spoken words **b :** CONVERSATION **2 a :** something that is spoken **b :** a public discourse **3 a :** LANGUAGE, DIALECT **b :** an individual manner or style of speaking **4 :** the power of expressing or communicating thoughts by speaking

speech area *n* **:** a brain center associated with the motor control of speech

speech·less \'spēch-ləs\ *adj* **1 :** lacking or deprived of the power of speaking **2 :** not speaking for a time **:** SILENT ⟨*speechless* with surprise⟩ ***syn*** see DUMB — **speech·less·ly** *adv* — **speech·less·ness** *n*

¹**speed** \'spēd\ *n* **1** *archaic* **:** prosperity in an undertaking **:** SUCCESS **2 a :** the act or state of moving swiftly **:** SWIFTNESS **b :** rate of motion **:** VELOCITY **3 :** swiftness or rate of performance or action **:** QUICKNESS **4 :** a transmission gear in automotive vehicles ⟨shift to low *speed*⟩ **5 :** a form or derivative of amphetamine

²**speed** *vb* **sped** \'sped\ *or* **speed·ed; speed·ing 1** *archaic* **a :** to prosper in an undertaking **b :** to help to succeed **:** AID **2 a :** to make haste **b :** to go or drive at excessive or illegal speed **3 :** to move, work, or take place faster **:** ACCELERATE **4 a :** to cause to move quickly **:** HASTEN **b :** to wish Godspeed to **c :** to increase the speed of **:** ACCELERATE ⟨*speeded* up the engine⟩

³**speed** *adj* **:** of, relating to, or regulating speed

speed·boat \'spēd-ˌbōt\ *n* **:** a fast launch or motorboat

speed·er \'spēd-ər\ *n* **:** one that speeds; *esp* **:** a person who exceeds the legal speed limit

speed·i·ly \'spēd-ə-lē\ *adv* **1 :** RAPIDLY, QUICKLY **2 :** PROMPTLY, SOON

speed limit *n* **:** the maximum speed permitted by law in a given area under specified circumstances

speed·om·e·ter \spi-'däm-ət-ər\ *n* **1 :** an instrument that measures speed **2 :** an instrument that both measures speed and records distance traveled

speed·ster \'spēd-stər\ *n* **:** one that speeds or is capable of great speed

speed·way \'spēd-ˌwā\ *n* **1 :** a road on which more than ordinary speed is allowed **2 :** a racecourse for motor vehicles

speed·well \'spēd-ˌwel\ *n* **:** any of a genus of creeping plants with mostly oblong toothed leaves and blue or white flowers

speedy \'spēd-ē\ *adj* **speed·i·er; -est :** FAST, SWIFT ⟨hope you have a *speedy* recovery from your illness⟩ — **speed·i·ness** *n*

[1]**spell** \'spel\ *n* **1 a :** a spoken word or form of words believed to have magic power **:** INCANTATION **b :** a state of enchantment **2 :** a strong compelling influence or attraction

[2]**spell** *vb* **:** to put under a spell **:** BEWITCH

[3]**spell** *vb* **spelled** \'speld, 'spelt\; **spell·ing 1 :** to read or discern slowly and with difficulty **2 a :** to name, write, or print the letters of in order **b :** to be the letters of ⟨*c-a-t spells* "cat"⟩ **3 :** MEAN, SIGNIFY ⟨another drought may *spell* famine⟩ **4 :** to form words with letters

[4]**spell** *vb* **spelled** \'speld\; **spell·ing 1 :** to take the place of for a time **:** RELIEVE ⟨if we can *spell* each other we won't get tired⟩ **2 :** to allow an interval of rest to **:** REST

[5]**spell** *n* **1 :** one's turn at work **2 :** a period spent in a job or occupation **3 a :** a short period of time **b :** a stretch of a specified type of weather **4 :** a period of bodily or mental distress or disorder **:** ATTACK, FIT ⟨a *spell* of coughing⟩ ⟨fainting *spell*⟩

spell·bind \'spel-ˌbīnd\ *vb* **-bound** \-ˌbau̇nd\; **-bind·ing :** to hold by or as if by a spell **:** FASCINATE

spell·bind·er \-ˌbīn-dər\ *n* **:** a speaker of compelling eloquence

spell·bound \-'bau̇nd\ *adj* **:** ENTRANCED, FASCINATED ⟨the speaker held them *spellbound*⟩

spell·er \'spel-ər\ *n* **1 :** one who spells words **2 :** a book with exercises for teaching spelling

spell·ing \'spel-iŋ\ *n* **:** the forming of words from letters according to accepted usage; *also* **:** the letters composing a word

spelling bee *n* **:** a spelling contest that proceeds by the elimination of each contestant who misspells a word

spell out *vb* **:** to make very explicit or emphatic ⟨each one's duties were *spelled out* in detail⟩

spelt \'spelt\ *chiefly Brit past of* SPELL

spe·lunk·er \spi-'ləŋ-kər, 'spē-ˌ\ *n* **:** one who makes a hobby of exploring caves — **spe·lunk·ing** \-kiŋ\ *n*

spend \'spend\ *vb* **spent** \'spent\; **spend·ing** [from Old English *spendan*, from Latin *expendere* "to expend", literally "to weigh out"] **1 :** to use up or pay out **:** EXPEND **2 a :** to wear out **:** EXHAUST **b :** to consume wastefully **:** SQUANDER **3 :** to cause or permit to elapse **:** PASS **4 :** to make use of **:** EMPLOY, OCCUPY — **spend·er** *n*

spend·a·ble \'spen-də-bəl\ *adj* **:** available for spending

spending money *n* **:** money for small personal expenses

spend·thrift \'spen(d)-ˌthrift\ *n* **:** one who spends lavishly or wastefully — **spendthrift** *adj*

spent \'spent\ *adj* **1 :** used up **:** CONSUMED **2 :** drained of energy or effectiveness **:** EXHAUSTED

sperm \'spərm\ *n, pl* **sperm** *or* **sperms 1 a :** SEMEN **b :** a male gamete **2 :** a product (as oil) of the sperm whale

sper·ma·ce·ti \ˌspər-mə-'sēt-ē, -'set-\ *n* **:** a waxy solid obtained from the oil of some sea-dwelling mammals (as the sperm whale) and used in ointments, cosmetics, and candles

sper·ma·tid \'spər-mət-əd\ *n* **:** one of the cells produced in meiosis that form spermatozoa

sper·ma·to·gen·e·sis \ˌspər-mət-ə-'jen-ə-səs, (ˌ)spər-ˌmat-\ *n, pl* **-gen·e·ses** \-ə-ˌsēz\ **:** the process of male gamete formation including meiosis and formation of spermatozoa

sper·mat·o·phyte \(ˌ)spər-'mat-ə-ˌfīt\ *n* **:** any of a group of higher plants comprising those that produce seeds and including the gymnosperms and angiosperms — **sper·mat·o·phyt·ic** \-ˌmat-ə-'fit-ik\ *adj*

sper·ma·to·zo·on \ˌspər-mət-ə-'zō-ˌän, (ˌ)spər-ˌmat-ə-'zō-ən\ *n, pl* **-zoa** \-'zō-ə\ **:** a motile male gamete of an animal usu. with rounded or elongate head and a long posterior flagellum — called also *sperm cell* **sper·ma·to·zo·al** \-'zō-əl\ *adj*

sperm oil *n* **:** a pale yellow oil from the sperm whale used esp. as a lubricant

sperm whale *n* **:** a large toothed whale with a closed cavity in the head containing a fluid mixture of spermaceti and oil

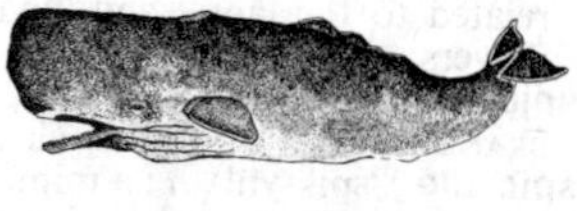

sperm whale
(up to 65 ft. long)

[1]**spew** \'spyü\ *vb* **:** to pour forth **:** VOMIT — **spew·er** *n*

[2]**spew** *n* **:** matter that is spewed

sp gr *abbr* specific gravity

sphag·num \'sfag-nəm\ *n* **1 :** any of a large genus of mosses that grow only in wet acid areas **2 :** a mass of sphagnum plants

sphal·er·ite \'sfal-ə-ˌrīt\ *n* **:** a widely distributed ore of zinc composed essentially of the sulfide of zinc

sphagnum 1
(about 3 in. high)

sphere \'sfi(ə)r\ *n* **1 a :** a globular body **:** BALL, GLOBE **b :** a surface all points of which are equally distant from a center; *also* **:** the space enclosed by such a surface **2 :** natural, normal, or proper place; *esp* **:** social order or rank **3 :** a field or range of influence or significance **:** PROVINCE — **spher·ic** \'sfi(ə)r-ik, 'sfer-\ *adj* — **sphe·ric·i·ty** \sfir-'is-ət-ē\ *n*

sphere of influence : an area within which the interests of one nation are paramount

spher·i·cal \'sfir-i-kəl, 'sfer-\ *adj* **1 :** having the form of a sphere or of one of its segments **2 :** relating to or dealing with a sphere or its properties — **spher·i·cal·ly** \-k(ə-)lē\ *adv*

sphe·roid \'sfi(ə)r-ˌȯid, 'sfe(ə)r-\ *n* **:** a figure resembling a flattened sphere — **sphe·roi·dal** \sfir-'ȯid-əl\ *adj*

spher·u·lite \'sfir-(y)ə-ˌlīt, 'sfer-\ *n* **:** a usu. spherical crystalline body of radiating crystal fibers found in vitreous volcanic rocks

sphinc·ter \'sfiŋ(k)-tər\ *n* **:** a muscular ring surrounding and able to contract or close a bodily opening

sphinx \'sfing(k)s\ *n* **1 a** : a monster in ancient Greek mythology having typically a lion's body, wings, and the head and bust of a woman **b** : a person whose character, motives, or feelings are enigmatic **2** : an ancient Egyptian image having the body of a lion and the head of a man, ram, or hawk **3** : HAWKMOTH — called also *sphinx moth*

sphinx 2

sphyg·mo·ma·nom·e·ter \ˌsfig-mō-mə-'näm-ət-ər\ *n* : an instrument for measuring blood pressure and esp. arterial blood pressure

[1]**spice** \'spīs\ *n* **1** : any of various aromatic plant products (as pepper or nutmeg) used to season or flavor foods **2** : something that gives zest or relish **3** : a pungent or fragrant odor : PERFUME

[2]**spice** *vb* : to season with or as if with spices

spice·bush \'spīs-ˌbu̇sh\ *n* : an aromatic shrub related to the laurel and having small early yellow flowers

spick–and–span \ˌspik-ən-'span\ *adj* **1** : FRESH, BRAND-NEW **2** : spotlessly clean and neat

spic·ule \'spik-yül\ *n* : a minute slender pointed usu. hard body; *esp* : one of the minute calcium- or silica-containing bodies that support the tissues of various invertebrates

spicy \'spī-sē\ *adj* **spic·i·er**; **-est** **1** : having the quality, flavor, or fragrance of spice **2** : producing or abounding in spices **3** : KEEN, ZESTFUL **4** : somewhat scandalous or salacious — **spic·i·ly** \-sə-lē\ *adv* — **spic·i·ness** \-sē-nəs\ *n*

spi·der \'spīd-ər\ *n* [from Middle English *spithre*, literally "spinner", from old English *spinnan* "to spin"] **1** : any of an order of arachnids having a body with two main divisions, four pairs of walking legs, and two or more pairs of abdominal organs for spinning threads of silk used in making cocoons for their eggs, nests for themselves, or webs for catching their prey **2** : a cast-iron frying pan orig. made with short feet to stand among coals on the hearth

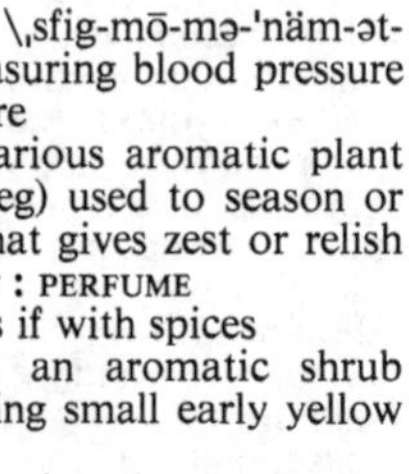
spider 1
(about one inch long)

spider crab *n* : any of numerous crabs with extremely long legs and nearly triangular bodies

spi·der·web \'spīd-ər-ˌweb\ *n* **1** : the silken web spun by most spiders and used as a resting place and a trap for small prey **2** : something like a spiderweb in appearance or function

spi·dery \'spīd-ə-rē\ *adj* **1** : resembling a spider; *also* : long and thin like the legs of a spider **2** : resembling a spiderweb **3** : full of spiders

[1]**spiel** \'spēl\ *vb* : to talk volubly or perfunctorily — **spiel·er** *n*

[2]**spiel** *n* : voluble mechanical often extravagant talk

spiffy \'spif-ē\ *adj* **spiff·i·er**; **-est** : fine looking : SMART

spig·ot \'spig-ət, 'spik-ət\ *n* **1** : a pin or peg used to stop the vent in a cask **2** : FAUCET

[1]**spike** \'spīk\ *n* **1** : a very large nail **2 a** : one of a row of pointed irons placed (as on the top of a wall) to prevent passage **b** : one of several metal projections set in the sole and heel of a shoe to improve traction in sports **3** : an unbranched antler of a young deer **4** : a pointed element (as in a graph)

[2]**spike** *vb* **1** : to fasten or furnish with spikes **2 a** : to disable a muzzle-loading cannon temporarily by driving a spike into the vent **b** : to suppress or block completely : QUASH **3** : to pierce or impale with or on a spike **4** : to add alcohol or liquor to a drink

[3]**spike** *n* **1** : an ear of grain **2** : a long usu. rather narrow flower cluster in which the blossoms grow close to the central stem

spiked \'spīkt\ *adj* **1 a** : bearing ears of grain **b** : having a spiky inflorescence ⟨*spiked* flowers⟩ **2** : SPIKY

spike·let \'spīk-lət\ *n* : a small or secondary spike; *esp* : one of the small few-flowered spikes that occur in grasses and sedges

spike·nard \'spīk-ˌnärd\ *n* **1** : a fragrant ointment of the ancients **2** : an East Indian aromatic plant from which spikenard may have been derived

spiky \'spī-kē\ *adj* **spik·i·er**; **-est** **1** : resembling a spike : POINTED **2** : having spikes

spile \'spīl\ *n* **1** : a large stake driven into the ground to support a superstructure : PILE **2** : a small plug used to stop the vent of a cask : BUNG **3** : a spout inserted in a tree to draw off sap — **spile** *vb*

[1]**spill** \'spil\ *vb* **spilled** \'spild, 'spilt\ *also* **spilt** \'spilt\; **spill·ing** **1** : to cause blood to flow **2 a** : to cause or allow accidentally or unintentionally to fall, flow, or run out **b** : to fall or run out so as to be lost or wasted **3** : to throw off or out ⟨a horse *spilled* him⟩ **4** : to let out : DIVULGE ⟨*spilled* the secret⟩ — **spill·a·ble** \'spil-ə-bəl\ *adj*

[2]**spill** *n* **1** : an act or instance of spilling; *esp* : a fall from a horse or vehicle **2** : something spilled **3** : SPILLWAY

[3]**spill** *n* **1** : a small metallic rod or pin **2** : a small roll or twist of paper or slip of wood for lighting a fire **3** : a roll or cone of paper serving as a container **4** : a peg for plugging a hole : SPILE

spill·age \'spil-ij\ *n* **1** : the act or process of spilling **2** : the quantity that spills

spill·way \'spil-ˌwā\ *n* : a passage for surplus water to run over or around a dam or similar obstruction

[1]**spin** \'spin\ *vb* **spun** \'spən\; **spin·ning** **1** : to draw out and twist into yarn or thread ⟨*spin* flax⟩ **2 a** : to produce by drawing out and twisting fibers ⟨*spin* thread⟩ **b** : to form threads or a web or cocoon by ejecting from the body a sticky rapidly hardening fluid **3 a** : to revolve rapidly : GYRATE **b** : to be dizzy : feel as if turning rapidly **4** : to cause to whirl : TWIRL ⟨*spin* a top⟩ **5 a** : to extend to great length : PROLONG **b** : to make up with the imagination ⟨*spin* a yarn⟩ **6** : to move swiftly on wheels or in a vehicle **7** : to shape into threadlike form in manufacture

[2]**spin** *n* **1 a** : the act of spinning or twirling something **b** : whirling motion imparted by spinning : rapid rotation **c** : a short trip in a vehicle ⟨go for a *spin*

ə abut	ər further	a back	ā bake	
ä cot, cart	au̇ out	ch chin	e less	ē easy
g gift	i trip	ī life	j joke	ng sing	ō flow
ȯ flaw	ȯi coin	th thin	th this	ü loot
u̇ foot	y yet	yü few	yu̇ furious	zh vision

around the block⟩ **2 a :** a plunging descent or downward spiral **b :** a mental whirl or state of confusion

spin·ach \'spin-ich\ *n* : a potherb widely grown for its edible leaves

spi·nal \'spīn-əl\ *adj* **1 :** of, relating to, or situated near the backbone **2 :** of, relating to, or affecting the spinal cord

spinal column *n* : the axial skeleton of the trunk and tail of a vertebrate that consists of a jointed series of vertebrae enclosing and protecting the spinal cord — called also *backbone*

spinal cord *n* : the cord of nervous tissue that extends from the brain along the back in the cavity of the spinal column, gives off the spinal nerves and carries nerve impulses to and from the brain

spinal nerve *n* : any of the paired nerves which arise from the spinal cord and pass to various parts of the trunk and limbs and of which there are normally 31 pairs in man

[1]**spin·dle** \'spin-dəl\ *n* **1 :** a round stick with tapered ends used to form and twist the yarn in hand spinning **2 :** something shaped like a spindle (as a figure along which the chromosomes are distributed during mitosis) **3 a :** a slender rod ⟨the *spindles* of a chair⟩ **b :** the part of an axle on which the wheel turns

[2]**spindle** *vb* **spin·dled**; **spin·dling** \'spin-d(ə-)ling\ : to form a long slender stalk usu. without flower or fruit

spin·dling \'spin-d(ə-)ling\ *adj* : being long or tall and thin and usu. feeble or frail ⟨*spindling* stems⟩

spin·dly \'spin-d(ə-)lē\ *adj* **spin·dli·er**; **-est** : SPINDLING

spin·drift \'spin-ˌdrift\ *n* : spray blown from waves

spine \'spīn\ *n* **1 a :** SPINAL COLUMN **b :** something resembling a spinal column **c :** the back of a book **2 :** a stiff pointed process; *esp* : one on a plant that is a modified leaf or leaf part

spi·nel \spə-'nel\ *n* : a hard crystalline mineral consisting of an oxide of magnesium and aluminum that varies from colorless to ruby-red to black and is used as a gem

spine·less \'spīn-ləs\ *adj* **1 :** free from spines, thorns, or prickles **2 a :** having no spinal column : INVERTEBRATE **b :** lacking courage or strength of character — **spine·less·ly** *adv* — **spine·less·ness** *n*

spin·et \'spin-ət\ *n* **1 :** a small upright piano **2 :** a small electronic organ

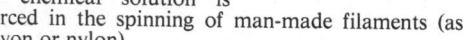

spin·na·ker \'spin-i-kər\ *n* : a large triangular sail set on a long light pole and used when running before the wind

spinnaker

spin·ner \'spin-ər\ *n* **1** : one that spins **2 :** a fishing lure that revolves when drawn through the water

spin·ner·et \ˌspin-ə-'ret\ *n* **1 :** an organ esp. of a spider or caterpillar for producing threads of silk from the secretion of silk glands **2** *or* **spin·ner·ette :** a small metal plate, thimble, or cap with fine holes through which a cellulose or chemical solution is forced in the spinning of man-made filaments (as rayon or nylon)

spinning jen·ny \'spin-ing-ˌjen-ē\ *n* : an early multiple-spindle machine for spinning wool or cotton

spinning wheel *n* : a small domestic hand-driven or foot-driven machine for spinning yarn or thread in which a wheel drives a single spindle

spi·nose \'spī-ˌnōs\ *adj* : SPINY 1 — **spi·nose·ly** *adv*

spi·nous \'spī-nəs\ *adj* : SPINY

spin·ster \'spin(t)-stər\ *n* **1 :** a woman whose occupation is to spin **2 :** an unmarried woman; *esp* : a woman past the common age for marrying or one who seems unlikely to marry — **spin·ster·hood** \-ˌhu̇d\ *n* — **spin·ster·ish** \-st(ə-)rish\ *adj*

spin·thar·i·scope \spin-'thar-ə-ˌskōp\ *n* : an instrument consisting of a fluorescent screen and a magnifying lens system for visual detection of alpha rays

spiny \'spī-nē\ *adj* **spin·i·er**; **-est 1 :** covered or armed with spines or sometimes with prickles or thorns **2 :** abounding with difficulties, obstacles, or annoyances : THORNY — **spin·i·ness** *n*

spiny anteater *n* : ECHIDNA

spiny lobster *n* : an edible crustacean distinguished from the related true lobster by the simple unenlarged first pair of legs and by the spiny carapace

spiny–skinned \ˌspī-nē-'skind\ *adj* : having a skin covered with knobs or spines

spir·a·cle \'spir-i-kəl, 'spī-ri-\ *n* : a breathing hole (as of a whale or of an insect) — **spi·rac·u·lar** \spə-'rak-yə-lər, spī-\ *adj*

[1]**spi·ral** \'spī-rəl\ *adj* **1 a :** winding around a center or pole and gradually receding from or approaching it ⟨*spiral* curve of a watch spring⟩ **b :** HELICAL ⟨*spiral* form of the thread of a screw⟩ **c :** of, relating to, or resembling a spiral ⟨a flat *spiral* coil of rope⟩ ⟨a *spiral* staircase⟩ **2 :** advancing to higher levels through a series of cyclical movements — **spi·ral·ly** \-rə-lē\ *adv*

[2]**spiral** *n* **1 a :** the path of a point in a plane moving around a central point while continuously receding from or approaching it **b :** a three-dimensional curve (as a helix) turning about an axis **2 :** a single turn or coil in a spiral object **3 :** something having a spiral form **4 :** a continuously spreading and accelerating increase or decrease ⟨wage-price *spiral*⟩

[3]**spiral** *vb* **-raled** *or* **-ralled**; **-ral·ing** *or* **-ral·ling** **1 :** to move in a spiral course **2 :** to form into a spiral

[1]**spire** \'spī(ə)r\ *n* **1 :** a slender tapering blade or stalk (as of grass) **2 :** a sharp pointed tip (as of a tree or antler) **3 a :** a pointed roof esp. of a tower **b :** STEEPLE — **spired** \'spī(ə)rd\ *adj*

[2]**spire** *vb* : to shoot up like a spire

[3]**spire** *n* **1 a :** SPIRAL **b :** COIL **2 :** the upper part of a spiral mollusk shell

[4]**spire** *vb* : to rise upward in a spiral

spi·rea *or* **spi·raea** \spī-'rē-ə\ *n* : any of a genus of shrubs related to the roses and having small perfect white or pink flowers in dense clusters

spi·ril·lum \spī-'ril-əm\ *n, pl* **-ril·la** \-'ril-ə\ : any of a genus of long curved flagellate bacteria; *also* : any spiral thread-shaped bacterium (as a spirochete)

[1]**spir·it** \'spir-ət\ *n* [from Latin *spiritus*, literally "breath", from the same root as *spirare* "to blow", "breathe" seen in English *respiration*] **1 :** a life-giving force; *esp* : a force within man held to endow his body with life, energy, and power : SOUL **2 a** *cap* : HOLY SPIRIT **b :** a supernatural being : GHOST, DEVIL **c :** a supernatural being that enters into and controls a person **3 :** MOOD, DISPOSITION ⟨in good *spirits*⟩ **4 :** mental vigor or animation : VIVACITY ⟨answered with *spirit*⟩ **5 :** real meaning or intention ⟨the *spirit* of the law⟩ **6 :** an emotion, frame of mind, or inclination governing one's actions ⟨said in a *spirit* of fun⟩ ⟨school *spirit*⟩ **7 :** PERSON ⟨a bold *spirit*⟩ **8 a :** a distilled alcoholic liquor — usu. used in pl.

S

b : an alcoholic solution of a volatile substance — often used in pl. ⟨*spirits* of camphor⟩
²**spirit** *vb* **1** : to put energy or life into : ANIMATE, ENCOURAGE **2** : to carry off or convey secretly or mysteriously
spir·it·ed \'spir-ət-əd\ *adj* : full of spirit, courage, or energy : LIVELY, ANIMATED — **spir·it·ed·ly** *adv*
spir·it·less \'spir-ət-ləs\ *adj* : lacking animation, cheerfulness, or courage : DEPRESSED — **spir·it·less·ly** *adv* — **spir·it·less·ness** *n*
¹**spir·i·tu·al** \'spir-ich-(ə-w)əl\ *adj* **1** : of, relating to, or consisting of spirit : not bodily or material ⟨man's *spiritual* needs⟩ **2** : ecclesiastical rather than lay or temporal : RELIGIOUS **3** : related or joined in spirit ⟨*spiritual* home⟩ ⟨*spiritual* heir⟩ **4** : of or relating to supernatural beings — **spir·i·tu·al·ly** \-ē\ *adv* — **spir·i·tu·al·ness** *n*
²**spiritual** *n* : a Negro religious song esp. of the southern U.S. usu. of a deeply emotional character
spir·i·tu·al·ism \'spir-ich-(ə-w)ə-,liz-əm\ *n* **1** : the view that spirit is a prime element of reality **2 a** : a belief that the spirits of the dead communicate with the living **b** *cap* : a religious movement emphasizing spiritualism — **spir·i·tu·al·ist** \-ləst\ *n, often cap* — **spir·i·tu·al·is·tic** \,spir-ich-(ə-w)ə-'lis-tik\ *adj*
spir·i·tu·al·i·ty \,spir-ich-ə-'wal-ət-ē\ *n* **1** : sensitivity or attachment to religious values **2** : the quality or state of being spiritual
spir·i·tu·ous \'spir-ich-(ə-w)əs\ *adj* : containing or impregnated with distilled alcohol ⟨*spirituous* liquors⟩ — **spir·i·tu·os·i·ty** \,spir-ich-ə-'wäs-ət-ē\ *n*
spi·ro·chete *or* **spi·ro·chaete** \'spī-rə-,kēt\ *n* : any of a group of slender spirally undulating bacteria including one causing syphilis
spi·ro·gy·ra \,spī-rə-'jī-rə\ *n* : any of a genus of freshwater green algae with spiral bands of chlorophyll
¹**spit** \'spit\ *n* **1** : a slender pointed rod for holding meat over a fire **2** : a small point of land esp. of sand or gravel running into a body of water
²**spit** *vb* **spit·ted**; **spit·ting** : to fix on or as if on a spit
³**spit** *vb* **spit** *or* **spat** \'spat\; **spit·ting** **1 a** : to eject saliva from the mouth : EXPECTORATE **b** : to express by or as if by spitting : make a spitting sound ⟨the cat *spat* angrily⟩ ⟨*spitting* a contemptuous reply⟩ ⟨the wire *spat* and crackled⟩ **2 a** : to give off usu. briskly or vigorously : EMIT ⟨the fire *spat* sparks⟩ **b** : to rain or snow in flurries — **spit·ter** *n*
⁴**spit** *n* **1 a** : SALIVA **b** : the act of spitting **2** : a frothy secretion produced by spittlebugs **3** : perfect likeness ⟨the boy was the *spit* of his father⟩
spit and polish *n* : extreme attention to cleanliness, orderliness, smartness of appearance, and ceremony esp. at the expense of efficiency
spit curl *n* : a spiral curl that is usu. pressed flat against the forehead, temple, or cheek
¹**spite** \'spīt\ *n* : petty ill will or malice with a wish to irritate, annoy, or thwart — **in spite of** : in defiance or contempt of : DESPITE, NOTWITHSTANDING ⟨went ahead *in spite of* the difficulties⟩
²**spite** *vb* **1** : to treat maliciously (as by shaming or thwarting) **2** : ANNOY, OFFEND ⟨did it to *spite* me⟩
spite·ful \'spīt-fəl\ *adj* : filled with or showing spite : MALICIOUS — **spite·ful·ly** \-fə-lē\ *adv* — **spite·ful·ness** *n*
spit·fire \'spit-,fī(ə)r\ *n* : a quick-tempered or highly emotional person
spit·tle \'spit-əl\ *n* **1** : SALIVA **2** : ⁴SPIT 2
spit·tle·bug \-,bəg\ *n* : any of numerous leaping bugs that produce froth in the immature stages
spittle insect *n* : SPITTLEBUG
spit·toon \spi-'tün\ *n* : a receptacle for spit
spitz \'spits\ *n* : any of several stocky heavy-coated dogs with erect ears and a heavily furred tail tightly recurved over the back

spitz

¹**splash** \'splash\ *vb* **1 a** : to strike or move through a liquid or semifluid substance and cause it to move and scatter roughly ⟨*splash* water⟩ ⟨*splash* through mud⟩ **b** : to wet or soil by dashing water or mud on : SPATTER ⟨*splashed* by a passing car⟩ **c** : to cause to soil something by splashing ⟨*splashed* mud on her shoes⟩ **2** : to make a splashing sound (as in falling or moving) ⟨a brook *splashing* over rocks⟩ **3** : to spread or scatter like a splashed liquid ⟨a painting *splashed* with color⟩ — **splash·er** *n*
²**splash** *n* **1 a** : splashed material **b** : a spot or daub from or as if from splashed liquid **2** : the sound or action of splashing **3** : a vivid impression created esp. by doing something spectacular or striking — **splash·i·ly** \'splash-ə-lē\ *adv* — **splash·i·ness** \'splash-ē-nəs\ *n* — **splashy** \'splash-ē\ *adj*
splash·down \'splash-,daun\ *n* : the landing of a manned spacecraft in the ocean
splat \'splat\ *n* : a single flat thin usu. vertical member of a back of a chair
splat·ter \'splat-ər\ *vb* : SPATTER — **splatter** *n*
splatter erosion *n* : erosion caused by the unequal splatter of soil (as on a hill) when hit by raindrops or hail
¹**splay** \'splā\ *vb* **1** : to spread out : EXPAND **2** : to make or become slanting
²**splay** *n* **1** : a slope or bevel esp. of the sides of a door or window **2** : SPREAD, EXPANSION
³**splay** *adj* : turned outward
spleen \'splēn\ *n* **1** : a ductless organ containing many blood vessels, located near the stomach or intestine of most vertebrates, and concerned with final destruction of blood cells, storage of blood, and production of lymphocytes **2** : ANGER, MALICE, SPITE
splen·did \'splen-dəd\ *adj* [from Latin *splendidus*, from *splendēre* "to shine"] **1** : possessing or displaying splendor : SHINING, BRILLIANT **2** : ILLUSTRIOUS, GRAND **3** : EXCELLENT — **splen·did·ly** *adv* — **splen·did·ness** *n*
splen·dif·er·ous \splen-'dif-(ə-)rəs\ *adj* **1** : SPLENDID **2** : deceptively splendid — **splen·dif·er·ous·ly** *adv* — **splen·dif·er·ous·ness** *n*
splen·dor \'splen-dər\ *n* **1** : great brightness or luster : BRILLIANCE ⟨the *splendor* of the sun⟩ **2** : sumptuous display or ceremonial : MAGNIFICENCE, POMP — **splen·dor·ous** *also* **splen·drous** \-d(ə-)rəs\ *adj*
sple·net·ic \spli-'net-ik\ *adj* : marked by bad temper, malevolence, or spite — **sple·net·i·cal·ly** \-'net-i-k(ə-)lē\ *adv*
sple·nic \'splē-nik, 'splen-ik\ *adj* : of, relating to, or located in the spleen

1**splice** \'splīs\ *vb* **1** : to unite (as two ropes) by weaving the strands together **2** : to unite (as rails or timbers) by lapping the ends together and making them fast — **splic·er** *n*

2**splice** *n* : a joining or joint made by splicing

1**splint** \'splint\ *or* **splent** \'splent\ *n* **1** : a thin strip of wood interwoven with others in caning **2** : SPLINTER **3** : material or a device used to protect and immobilize a body part (as a broken arm)

splice

2**splint** *vb* : to support and immobilize with or as if with a splint or splints

splint bone *n* : one of the slender rudimentary bones in the limb of a horse

1**splin·ter** \'splint-ər\ *n* **1 a** : a thin piece split or torn off lengthwise : SLIVER **b** : a small jagged particle **2** : a group or faction broken away from a parent body — **splinter** *adj* — **splin·tery** \'splint-ə-rē\ *adj*

2**splinter** *vb* : to divide or break into splinters

1**split** \'split\ *vb* **split**; **split·ting** **1 a** : to divide lengthwise usu. along a grain or seam or by layers : CLEAVE ⟨wood that *splits* easily⟩ ⟨*split* slate into shingles⟩ **b** : to separate the parts of by inserting something ⟨*split* an infinitive⟩ **2 a** : to tear or break apart : BURST **b** : to subject (an atom or atomic nucleus) to artificial disintegration esp. by fission **c** : to affect as if by breaking up or tearing apart : SHATTER **3 a** : to divide between individuals : SHARE ⟨the winning team *split* the prize⟩ **b** : to divide into factions, parties, or groups **c** : to mark a ballot or cast a vote for candidates of different parties — **split·ter** *n* — **split hairs** : to make overly fine or trivial distinctions

2**split** *n* **1** : a narrow break made by or as if by splitting : CRACK **2** : the act or process of splitting : DIVISION **3** : the feat of lowering oneself to the floor or leaping into the air with the legs extended in a straight line and in opposite directions

3**split** *adj* **1** : divided by or as if by splitting ⟨a *split* lip⟩ ⟨*split* families⟩ **2** : HETEROZYGOUS

split infinitive *n* : an infinitive having a modifier between the *to* and the verbal (as in "to really start")

split–lev·el \'split-'lev-əl\ *adj* : divided vertically so that the floor level of rooms in one part is about midway between the levels of two successive stories in an adjoining part ⟨*split-level* house⟩ — **split–level** \-,lev-əl\ *n*

split personality *n* : a personality structure composed of two or more separate and distinct personalities

split second *n* : a fractional part of a second : FLASH

splotch \'spläch\ *n* : BLOTCH, SPOT — **splotch** *vb* — **splotchy** \'spläch-ē\ *adj*

1**splurge** \'splərj\ *n* : a showy display

2**splurge** *vb* **1** : to make a splurge **2** : to indulge oneself extravagantly ⟨*splurged* on a steak and a sundae⟩

1**splut·ter** \'splət-ər\ *n* **1** : a confused noise (as of hasty speaking) **2** : a splashing or sputtering sound — **splut·tery** \'splət-ə-rē\ *adj*

2**splutter** *vb* **1** : to make a noise as if spitting **2** : to speak or utter hastily and confusedly — **splut·ter·er** \-ər-ər\ *n*

1**spoil** \'spȯil\ *n* **1 a** : plunder taken from an enemy in war or a victim in robbery : LOOT **b** : public offices made the property of a successful party — usu. used in pl. **c** : something won usu. by effort or skill : PREY ⟨the *spoils* of the hunt⟩ **2** : PLUNDERING, SPOLIATION

2**spoil** *vb* **spoiled** \'spȯild, 'spȯilt\ *or* **spoilt** \'spȯilt\; **spoil·ing** **1** : DESPOIL, PILLAGE, ROB **2 a** : to damage seriously : RUIN ⟨a crop *spoiled* by floods⟩ **b** : to impair the quality or effect of ⟨a quarrel *spoiled* the celebration⟩ **c** : to decay or lose freshness, value, or usefulness usu. through being kept too long **3** : to damage the disposition or character of by pampering **4** : to have an eager desire ⟨*spoiling* for a fight⟩ — **spoil·a·ble** \'spȯi-lə-bəl\ *adj* — **spoil·er** *n*

spoil·age \'spȯi-lij\ *n* **1** : the act or process of spoiling **2** : something spoiled or wasted **3** : loss by spoilage

spoil·sport \'spȯil-,spōrt, -,spȯrt\ *n* : one who spoils the sport or pleasure of others

1**spoke** \'spōk\ *past & archaic past part of* SPEAK

2**spoke** *n* **1 a** : one of the small bars extending from the hub of a wheel to support the rim **b** : something resembling the spoke of a wheel **2** : a rung of a ladder

3**spoke** *vb* : to furnish with or as if with spokes

spo·ken \'spō-kən\ *adj* **1** : delivered by word of mouth : UTTERED ⟨the *spoken* word⟩ **2** : speaking in (such) a manner — used in combination ⟨soft-*spoken*⟩ ⟨plain*spoken*⟩

spoke·shave \'spōk-,shāv\ *n* : a two-handled tool that is used for planing curved pieces of wood

spokes·man \'spōks-mən\ *n* : a person who speaks as a representative of another person or of a group

spo·li·a·tion \,spō-lē-'ā-shən\ *n* : the act of plundering : the state of being plundered esp. in war — **spo·li·a·tor** \'spō-lē-,āt-ər\ *n*

spon·dee \'spän-,dē\ *n* : a metrical foot consisting of two accented syllables (as in *tom-tom*) — **spon·da·ic** \spän-'dā-ik\ *adj*

1**sponge** \'spənj\ *n* **1 a** : a springy porous mass of fibers that forms the internal skeleton of any of a group of colonial marine animals and is able when wetted to absorb water; *also* : a piece of this material or of a natural or synthetic product with similar properties used esp. for cleaning **b** : any of a phylum of primitive aquatic animals that are essentially double-walled cell colonies and permanently attached as adults **2** : a pad (as of folded gauze) used in surgery and medicine (as to remove discharges or apply medication) **3** : one who lives upon others : SPONGER **4 a** : raised dough **b** : a metal (as platinum) obtained in porous form usu. by reduction without fusion ⟨titanium *sponge*⟩

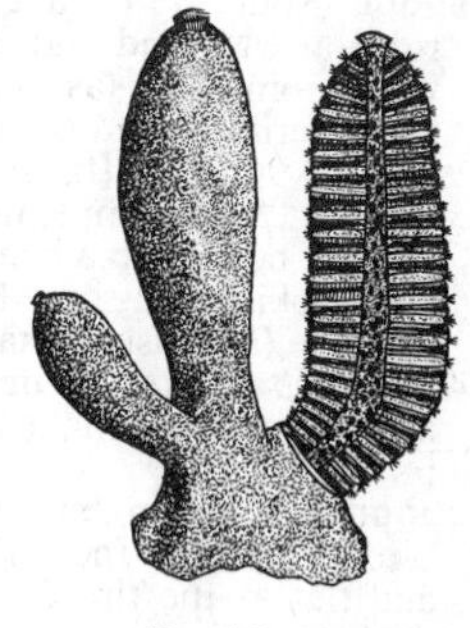
sponge 1b: right branch in cross section (magnified 1½ times)

2**sponge** *vb* **1 a** : to cleanse, wipe, or moisten with or as if with a sponge **b** : to erase or destroy with or as if with a sponge **2** : to absorb with or as if with or like a sponge **3** : to get something from or live on another by imposing on hospitality or good nature **4** : to dive or dredge for sponges — **spong·er** *n*

spon·gin \'spən-jən\ *n* : a protein that is the chief constituent of flexible fibers in sponge skeletons

spongy \'spən-jē\ *adj* **spong·i·er**; **-est** : resembling a sponge in appearance or absorbency : soft and full of holes or moisture : not firm or solid — **spong·i·ness** *n*

S

spongy layer *n* : a layer of loosely and irregularly arranged chlorophyll-bearing cells that fills the part of a leaf between the palisade layer and the lower epidermis

1**spon·sor** \ˈspän(t)-sər\ *n* [from Latin, "bondsman", from *spondēre* "to pledge", "promise"] **1** : a person who takes the responsiblity for some other person or thing ⟨agreed to be his *sponsor* at the club⟩ **2** : GODPARENT **3 a** : a person or an organization that pays for or plans and carries out a project or activity **b** : one that pays the cost of a radio or television program — **spon·sor·ship** \-ˌship\ *n*

2**sponsor** *vb* **spon·sored**; **spon·sor·ing** \ˈspän(t)s-(ə-)riŋ\ : to be or stand sponsor for

spon·ta·ne·i·ty \ˌspänt-ə-ˈnē-ət-ē, -ˈnā-\ *n* **1** : the quality or state of being spontaneous **2** : spontaneous action or movement

spon·ta·ne·ous \spän-ˈtā-nē-əs\ *adj* **1** : done, said, or produced freely and naturally ⟨*spontaneous* laughter⟩ **2** : acting or taking place without external force, cause, or influence — **spon·ta·ne·ous·ly** *adv* — **spon·ta·ne·ous·ness** *n*

spontaneous combustion *n* : a bursting into flame of combustible material through heat produced within itself by chemical action (as oxidation)

spontaneous generation *n* : the bringing into existence of living organisms from lifeless matter

1**spoof** \ˈspüf\ *vb* **1** : DECEIVE, HOAX **2** : to make good-natured fun of ⟨a skit *spoofing* big business⟩

2**spoof** *n* **1** : HOAX, DECEPTION **2** : a light amiable takeoff : PARODY

1**spook** \ˈspük\ *n* : GHOST, SPECTER — **spook·ish** \ˈspü-kish\ *adj*

2**spook** *vb* : to make or become frightened : SCARE

spooky \ˈspü-kē\ *adj* **spook·i·er**; **-est** **1** : relating to, resembling, or suggesting spooks ⟨a very *spooky* movie⟩ ⟨*spooky* houses⟩ **2** : NERVOUS, SKITTISH ⟨a *spooky* horse⟩ — **spook·i·ness** *n*

spool \ˈspül\ *n* **1** : a cylinder which has a rim or ridge at each end and usu. a hollow center and on which something (as thread, wire, or tape) is wound **2** : material wound on a spool — **spool** *vb*

1**spoon** \ˈspün\ *n* [from Old English *spān* "chip of wood"] **1** : an implement that consists of a small shallow bowl with a handle and is used esp. in eating and cooking **2** : something that resembles a spoon in shape (as a usu. metal or shell fishing lure)

2**spoon** *vb* **1** : to take up and usu. transfer in or as if in a spoon **2** : to make love by kissing and caressing : NECK

spoon·bill \ˈspün-ˌbil\ *n* **1** : any of several wading birds related to the ibises that have the bill broad and flat at the tip **2** : any of several broad-billed ducks

spoon bread *n, chiefly South & Midland* : soft bread made of cornmeal mixed with milk, eggs, shortening, and leavening and served with a spoon

spoo·ner·ism \ˈspü-nə-ˌriz-əm\ *n* : a transposition of usu. initial sounds of two or more words (as in *tons of soil* for *sons of toil*)

spoon–feed \ˈspün-ˌfēd\ *vb* **-fed** \-ˌfed\; **-feeding** : to feed by means of a spoon

spoon·ful \ˈspün-ˌfu̇l\ *n, pl* **spoonfuls** \-ˌfu̇lz\ *or* **spoons·ful** \ˈspünz-ˌfu̇l\ : as much as a spoon can hold; *esp* : TEASPOONFUL

ə abut	ər further	a back	ā bake
ä cot, cart	au̇ out	ch chin	e less
ē easy	g gift	i trip	ī life
j joke	ŋ sing	ō flow	ȯ flaw
ȯi coin	th thin	th this	ü loot
u̇ foot	y yet	yü few	yu̇ furious
zh vision			

1**spoor** \ˈspu̇(ə)r, ˈspō(ə)r, ˈspȯ(ə)r\ *n* : a track or trail esp. of a wild animal

2**spoor** *vb* : to track something by a spoor

spo·rad·ic \spə-ˈrad-ik\ *adj* : occurring occasionally, singly, or in scattered instances : SEPARATE, ISOLATED ⟨*sporadic* outbreaks of disease⟩ — **spo·rad·i·cal·ly** \-ˈrad-i-k(ə-)lē\ *adv*

spo·ran·gi·um \spə-ˈran-jē-əm\ *n, pl* **-gia** \-jē-ə\ : a sac or case within which usu. asexual spores are produced

1**spore** \ˈspō(ə)r, ˈspȯ(ə)r\ *n* : a primitive usu. one-celled body produced by plants and some lower animals and capable of developing either directly or after fusion with another spore into a new individual in some cases unlike the parent — **spored** \ˈspōrd, ˈspȯrd\ *adj*

2**spore** *vb* : to produce or reproduce by spores

spore case *n* : SPORANGIUM

spore sac *n* : SPORANGIUM

spo·ro·phyll *or* **spo·ro·phyl** \ˈspōr-ə-ˌfil, ˈspȯr-\ *n* : a spore-bearing and usu. greatly modified leaf (as a stamen or carpel)

spo·ro·phyte \-ˌfīt\ *n* : the individual or generation of a plant having alternating sexual and asexual generations that bears asexual spores — compare GAMETOPHYTE — **spo·ro·phyt·ic** \ˌspōr-ə-ˈfit-ik, ˌspȯr-\ *adj*

spo·ro·zo·an \ˌspōr-ə-ˈzō-ən, ˌspȯr-\ *n* : any of a large group of strictly parasitic protozoans (as the parasites causing malaria) that have a life cycle usu. involving both asexual and sexual generations often in different hosts — **spo·ro·zo·al** \-ˈzō-əl\ *adj* — **sporozoan** *adj* — **spo·ro·zo·on** \-ˈzō-ˌän\ *n*

spor·ran \ˈspȯr-ən, ˈspär-\ *n* : a pouch of skin with the hair or fur on that is worn in front of the kilt by Highlanders in full dress

sporran

1**sport** \ˈspōrt, ˈspȯrt\ *vb* [from Middle English *sporten*, short for *disporten* "to disport"] **1 a** : to amuse oneself : FROLIC **b** : to engage in a sport **2** : to speak or act in jest or mockingly : TRIFLE **3** : to make usu. ostentatious display of : show off ⟨*sport* a new hat⟩ **4** : to deviate or vary abruptly from type : MUTATE

2**sport** *n* **1 a** : a source of diversion : RECREATION **b** : physical activity engaged in for pleasure; *esp* : a particular activity (as hunting or an athletic game) so engaged in **2 a** : PLEASANTRY, JEST **b** : MOCKERY, DERISION ⟨his friends made *sport* of him⟩ **3 a** : something tossed or driven about in or as if in play ⟨the battered boat became the *sport* of wind and waves⟩ **b** : LAUGHINGSTOCK, BUTT **4 a** : SPORTSMAN ⟨was a good *sport* about losing⟩ **b** : a person devoted to a gay easy life **5** : a variant individual esp. when caused by mutation

3**sport** *or* **sports** \ˈspōrts, ˈspȯrts\ *adj* : of, relating to, or suitable for sport ⟨*sport* fish⟩ ⟨*sport* coats⟩

sport·ing \ˈspōrt-iŋ, ˈspȯrt-\ *adj* **1** : used or suitable for sport **2** : marked by or calling for sportsmanship **3** : involving such risk as a sports contender may expect to take or encounter ⟨a *sporting* chance⟩

sport·ive \ˈspōrt-iv, ˈspȯrt-\ *adj* : PLAYFUL, FROLICSOME, MERRY — **sport·ive·ly** *adv* — **sport·ive·ness** *n*

sports car *n* : a low fast usu. 2-seat automobile

sports·cast \'spōrts-ˌkast, 'spȯrts-\ *n* : a broadcast dealing with sports events — **sports·cast·er** *n*
sports·man \'spōrts-mən, 'spȯrts-\ *n* **1** : a person who engages in or is interested in sports and esp. outdoor sports **2** : a person who is fair and generous and a good loser and a graceful winner — **sports·man·like** \-ˌlīk\ *adj* — **sports·man·ly** \-lē\ *adj* — **sports·wom·an** \-ˌwu̇m-ən\ *n*
sports·man·ship \-mən-ˌship\ *n* : skill in or devotion to sports; *esp* : conduct befitting a good sportsman
sports·wear \-ˌwa(ə)r, -ˌwe(ə)r\ *n* : clothes suitable for engaging in or watching sports
sports·writ·er \-ˌrīt-ər\ *n* : one who writes about sports esp. for a newspaper
sporty \'spōrt-ē, 'spȯrt-\ *adj* **sport·i·er**; **-est** : notably gay : FLASHY, SHOWY — **sport·i·ly** \'spōrt-ə-lē, 'spȯrt-\ *adv* — **sport·i·ness** \'spōrt-ē-nəs, 'spȯrt-\ *n*
spor·u·la·tion \ˌspōr-(y)ə-'lā-shən, ˌspȯr-\ *n* : formation of or division into spores — **spor·u·late** \'spōr-(y)ə-ˌlāt, 'spȯr-\ *vb*
¹**spot** \'spät\ *n* **1** : a blemish or stain on character or reputation : FAULT **2 a** : a small area visibly different (as in color, finish, or material) from the surrounding area **b** : an area marred or marked (as by dirt) **c** : a small well-defined diseased surface area (as in measles) **3 a** : a small quantity or amount **b** : a small or particular place or extent of space ⟨a good *spot* for a picnic⟩ ⟨a sore *spot*⟩ **4 a** : a particular position (as in an organization or on a program) **b** : a position usu. of difficulty or embarrassment ⟨the question put him in a *spot*⟩ — **on the spot 1** : at once : IMMEDIATELY **2** : at the place of action **3** : in difficulty or danger
²**spot** *vb* **spot·ted**; **spot·ting 1** : to mark or mar with or as if with spots : STAIN, BLEMISH ⟨a *spotted* reputation⟩ ⟨white *spots* so easily⟩ **2 a** : to single out : IDENTIFY, DETECT ⟨*spot* a friend⟩ ⟨*spot* an opportunity⟩ **b** : to locate precisely ⟨*spot* an enemy's position⟩ **3 a** : to lie or occur at intervals in or on ⟨slopes *spotted* with plowed fields⟩ **b** : to place at intervals or in a desired spot **4** : to remove spots from — **spot·ta·ble** \'spät-ə-bəl\ *adj*
³**spot** *adj* **1** : being, originating, or done on the spot or in or for a particular spot ⟨*spot* coverage of the news⟩ **2 a** : paid out upon delivery ⟨*spot* cash⟩ **b** : broadcast between scheduled programs ⟨*spot* announcements⟩ **3** : made at random or restricted to a few places or instances ⟨a *spot* check⟩
spot–check \'spät-ˌchek\ *vb* : to make a spot check
spot·less \'spät-ləs\ *adj* : free from spot or blemish : immaculately clean or pure — **spot·less·ly** *adv* — **spot·less·ness** *n*
spot·light \'spät-ˌlīt\ *n* **1 a** : a projected spot of light used to illuminate something (as a person on the stage) brilliantly **b** : conspicuous public notice **2** : a light designed to direct a narrow intense beam of light on a small area — **spotlight** *vb*
spot·ted \'spät-əd\ *adj* **1 a** : marked with spots **b** : SULLIED, TARNISHED **2** : accompanied by an eruption ⟨a *spotted* fever⟩ **3** : SPOTTY 2
spot·ter \'spät-ər\ *n* **1** : one that makes, applies, or removes spots **2** : one that keeps watch : OBSERVER
spot·ty \'spät-ē\ *adj* **spot·ti·er**; **-est 1** : marked with spots : SPOTTED **2** : lacking uniformity (as in quality or quantity) : UNEVEN ⟨*spotty* attendance⟩ — **spot·ti·ly** \'spät-ə-lē\ *adv* — **spot·ti·ness** \'spät-ē-nəs\ *n*
spouse \'spau̇s, 'spau̇z\ *n* : a married person : HUSBAND, WIFE
¹**spout** \'spau̇t\ *vb* **1** : to eject (as liquid) in a stream or jet ⟨wells *spouting* oil⟩ **2** : to speak or utter readily, pompously, and at length **3** : to issue with force or in a jet : SPURT ⟨blood *spouted* from the wound⟩ — **spout·er** *n*
²**spout** *n* **1** : a tube, pipe, or hole through which something (as rainwater) spouts **2** : a jet of liquid; *esp* : WATERSPOUT
spp *abbr* species
¹**sprain** \'sprān\ *n* **1** : a sudden or violent twist or wrench of a joint with stretching or tearing of ligaments **2** : a sprained condition
²**sprain** *vb* : to subject to sprain
sprat \'sprat\ *n* : a small European herring closely related to the common herring; *also* : a small or young herring or similar fish (as an anchovy)
sprawl \'sprȯl\ *vb* **1** : to creep or clamber awkwardly **2** : to lie or sit with arms and legs spread out **3** : to spread or cause to spread out irregularly or awkwardly — **sprawl** *n*
¹**spray** \'sprā\ *n* **1** : a usu. flowering branch or shoot or an arrangement of these **2** : something (as an ornament) resembling a spray
²**spray** *n* **1** : water flying in small drops or particles blown from waves or thrown up by a waterfall **2 a** : a jet of vapor or finely divided liquid **b** : a device (as an atomizer or sprayer) by which a spray is dispersed or applied
³**spray** *vb* **1** : to scatter or let fall in a spray **2** : to throw spray on or into — **spray·er** *n*
spray gun *n* : a device for spraying liquids (as paints and pesticides)
¹**spread** \'spred\ *vb* **spread**; **spread·ing 1 a** : to open or expand over a larger area ⟨*spread* out a map⟩ **b** : to stretch out : EXTEND ⟨*spread* her arms wide⟩ **2 a** : SCATTER, STREW ⟨*spread* fertilizer⟩ **b** : to distribute over a period or among a group ⟨*spread* the work to be done⟩ **c** : to apply on a surface ⟨*spread* butter on bread⟩ **d** : COVER, OVERLAY ⟨*spread* a floor with carpet⟩ **e** : to prepare or furnish for dining : SET ⟨*spread* a table⟩ **f** : SERVE ⟨*spread* a banquet⟩ **3 a** : to become or cause to become circulated or widely known ⟨the news *spread* rapidly⟩ **b** : to extend the range or incidence of ⟨*spread* a disease⟩ **4** : to stretch or move apart ⟨*spreads* his fingers⟩ — **spread·er** *n*
²**spread** *n* **1 a** : the act or process of spreading ⟨the *spread* of education⟩ **b** : extent of spreading ⟨the *spread* of a bird's wings⟩ **2 a** : EXPANSE **b** : a prominent display in a periodical **3 a** : a food to be spread on bread or crackers **b** : a sumptuous meal : FEAST **c** : a cloth cover for a table or bed **4** : distance between two points : GAP
spread–ea·gle \'spred-ˌē-gəl\ *vb* **spread–ea·gled**; **spread–ea·gling** \-g(ə-)liŋ\ **1** : to stand, move, or stretch out with arms and legs spread wide **2** : STRADDLE
spree \'sprē\ *n* : an unrestrained indulgence in or outburst of an activity ⟨went on a buying *spree*⟩ ⟨a drinking *spree*⟩
sprig \'sprig\ *n* **1** : a small shoot : TWIG **2** : an ornament resembling a sprig, stemmed flower, or leaf
spright·ly \'sprīt-lē\ *adj* **spright·li·er**; **-est** : marked by a gay lightness and liveliness — **spright·li·ness** *n*
¹**spring** \'spriŋ\ *vb* **sprang** \'spraŋ\ *or* **sprung** \'sprəŋ\; **sprung**; **spring·ing** \'spriŋ-iŋ\ **1 a** : DART, SHOOT **b** : to be resilient or elastic **c** : to move by elastic force ⟨the lid *sprang* shut⟩ **d** : to become warped **2** : to issue with speed and force or as a stream **3 a** *of vegetation* : to become established or produce new growth — often used with *up* ⟨fresh grass is *springing* up⟩ **b** : to issue by

birth or descent **c :** to come into being : ARISE ⟨hope *springs* eternal⟩ **4 a :** to make a leap or series of leaps **b :** to jump up suddenly **5 a :** SPLIT, CRACK ⟨wind *sprang* the mast⟩ **b :** to undergo the opening of a leak **6 :** to cause to operate suddenly ⟨*spring* a trap⟩ **7 :** to produce or disclose suddenly or unexpectedly ⟨*sprung* a surprise on us⟩ — **spring·er** \'spring-ər\ *n*

2**spring** *n* **1 a :** a source of supply; *esp* : a source of water issuing from the ground **b :** an ultimate source esp. of action or motion **2 a :** the season between winter and summer comprising in the northern hemisphere usu. the months of March, April, and May or as reckoned astronomically extending from the March equinox to the June solstice **b :** a time or season of growth or development **3 :** an elastic body or device that recovers its original shape when released after being distorted **4 a :** the act or an instance of leaping up or forward : BOUND **b :** capacity for springing : RESILIENCE, BOUNCE

spring·board \'spring-ˌbōrd, -ˌbȯrd\ *n* **1 :** a flexible board usu. secured at one end and used for gymnastic stunts or diving **2 :** a point of departure ⟨a *springboard* to political success⟩

spring·er spaniel \ˌspring-ər-\ *n* **:** a medium-sized sporting dog of either of two breeds used chiefly for finding and flushing small game

spring fever *n* **:** a lazy or restless feeling often associated with the onset of spring

spring·let \'spring-lət\ *n* **:** a little spring : STREAMLET

spring peeper *n* **:** a small brown tree toad of the eastern U.S. and Canada with a shrill piping call

spring peeper
(about one inch long)

spring tide *n* **:** a greater than usual tide occurring at each new moon and full moon

spring·time \'spring-ˌtīm\ *n* **:** the season of spring

spring·wood \-ˌwu̇d\ *n* **:** the softer more porous portion of an annual ring of wood that develops early in the growing season — compare SUMMERWOOD

springy \'spring-ē\ *adj* **spring·i·er; -est :** having an elastic quality : RESILIENT ⟨walks with a *springy* step⟩ — **spring·i·ly** \'spring-ə-lē\ *adv* — **spring·i·ness** \'spring-ē-nəs\ *n*

1**sprin·kle** \'spring-kəl\ *vb* **sprin·kled; sprin·kling** \-k(ə-)ling\ **1 :** to scatter in drops or particles **2 a :** to scatter over or at intervals in or among **b :** to wet lightly **3 :** to rain lightly in scattered drops — **sprin·kler** \-k(ə-)lər\ *n*

2**sprinkle** *n* **1 :** the act or an instance of sprinkling; *esp* : a light rain **2 :** SPRINKLING

ə abut	ər further	a back	ā bake
ä cot, cart	au̇ out	ch chin	e less	ē easy
g gift	i trip	ī life	j joke	ng sing	ō flow
ȯ flaw	ȯi coin	th thin	t͟h this	ü loot
u̇ foot	y yet	yü few	yu̇ furious	zh vision

sprinkler system *n* **:** a system for protecting a building against fire in which overhead pipes convey an extinguishing liquid (as water) to heat-activated outlets

sprin·kling \'spring-kling\ *n* **:** a limited quantity or amount; *esp* : SCATTERING

1**sprint** \'sprint\ *vb* **:** to run at top speed esp. for a short distance — **sprint·er** *n*

2**sprint** *n* **1 :** the act or an instance of sprinting **2 :** DASH 5b

sprit \'sprit\ *n* **:** a spar that crosses a fore-and-aft sail diagonally

sprite \'sprīt\ *n* **1 :** a disembodied spirit **2 a :** ELF, FAIRY **b :** an elfish person

sprit·sail \'sprit-ˌsāl, -səl\ *n* **:** a sail extended by a sprit

sprock·et \'spräk-ət\ *n* **1 :** a projection on the rim of a wheel shaped so as to interlock with the links of a chain **2 :** a wheel having sprockets

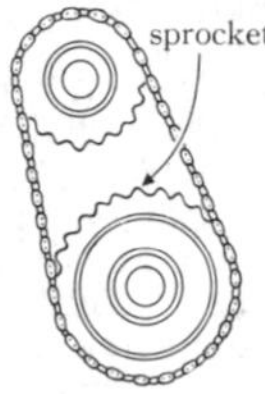

1**sprout** \'sprau̇t\ *vb* **1 :** to send out new growth **2 :** to grow rapidly **3 :** to cause to sprout

2**sprout** *n* **1 :** SHOOT 1a; *esp* **:** a young shoot (as from a seed or root) **2** *pl* **:** BRUSSELS SPROUTS

1**spruce** \'sprüs\ *n* **1 :** any of a genus of pyramid-shaped evergreen trees related to the pines and having soft light wood **2 :** the wood of a spruce

2**spruce** *adj* **:** neat or smart in appearance : TRIM — **spruce·ly** *adv* — **spruce·ness** *n*

3**spruce** *vb* **:** to make or make oneself spruce ⟨*spruce* up a room⟩ ⟨*spruce* up a bit before dinner⟩

sprung *past of* SPRING

spry \'sprī\ *adj* **spri·er** *or* **spry·er** \'sprī(-ə)r\; **spri·est** *or* **spry·est** \'sprī-əst\ **:** vigorously active : SPRIGHTLY ⟨a *spry* old gentleman⟩ — **spry·ly** *adv* — **spry·ness** *n*

1**spud** \'spəd\ *n* **1 :** a tool or device (as for digging, lifting, or cutting) combining the characteristics of spade and chisel **2 :** POTATO

2**spud** *vb* **spud·ded; spud·ding :** to dig with a spud

1**spume** \'spyüm\ *n* **:** frothy matter on liquids : FOAM, SCUM — **spu·mous** \'spyü-məs\ *adj* — **spumy** \'spyü-mē\ *adj*

2**spume** *vb* **:** FROTH, FOAM

spu·mo·ni *or* **spu·mo·ne** \spu̇-'mō-nē\ *n* **:** ice cream in layers of different colors, flavors, and textures often with candied fruits and nuts

spun *past of* SPIN

spun glass *n* **:** FIBER GLASS

spunk \'spəngk\ *n* **:** SPIRIT, PLUCK

spunky \'spəng-kē\ *adj* **spunk·i·er; -est :** full of spunk : SPIRITED — **spunk·i·ly** \-kə-lē\ *adv* — **spunk·i·ness** \-kē-nəs\ *n*

1**spur** \'spər\ *n* **1 a :** a pointed device secured to a rider's heel and used to urge the horse **b** *pl* **:** recognition for achievement **2 :** a goad to action : STIMULUS **3 a :** a stiff sharp projecting part (as a broken branch of a tree or a horny process on a cock's leg) **b :** a hollow projecting part of a corolla or calyx (as in larkspur or columbine) **4 :** a ridge that extends from the side of a mountain **5 :** a short wooden brace of a post **6 :** a railroad track diverging from a main line — **on the spur of the moment :** on hasty impulse

2**spur** *vb* **spurred; spur·ring 1 :** to urge a horse on with spurs **2 :** INCITE, STIMULATE

spu·ri·ous \'spyu̇r-ē-əs\ *adj* **:** not genuine or authentic : FALSE, COUNTERFEIT — **spu·ri·ous·ly** *adv* — **spu·ri·ous·ness** *n*

[1]**spurn** \'spərn\ *vb* **1** : to kick aside **2** : to reject or thrust aside with disdain or contempt — **spurn·er** *n*
[2]**spurn** *n* **1** : KICK **2** : disdainful rejection
spurred \'spərd\ *adj* **1** : wearing spurs **2** : having one or more spurs ⟨a *spurred* violet⟩
[1]**spurt** \'spərt\ *n* : a brief burst of increased effort or activity
[2]**spurt** *vb* : to make a spurt
[3]**spurt** *vb* **1** : to gush forth : SPOUT **2** : SQUIRT
[4]**spurt** *n* : a sudden gush : JET
sput·nik \'spu̇t-nik, 'spət-\ *n* : SATELLITE 2b
[1]**sput·ter** \'spət-ər\ *vb* **1** : to spit or squirt particles of food or saliva noisily from the mouth **2** : to speak or utter hastily or explosively in confusion or excitement ⟨*sputtered* out his protests⟩ **3** : to make explosive popping sounds ⟨the motor *sputtered* and died⟩ — **sput·ter·er** \-ər-ər\ *n*
[2]**sputter** *n* : the act or sound of sputtering
spu·tum \'sp(y)üt-əm\ *n, pl* **spu·ta** \-ə\ : material that is spit out and made up of saliva and mucous discharges from the respiratory passages
[1]**spy** \'spī\ *vb* **spied**; **spy·ing** **1** : to watch, inspect, or examine secretly : act as a spy **2** : to catch sight of : SEE ⟨*spied* a friend in the crowd⟩
[2]**spy** *n, pl* **spies** **1** : one that watches the conduct of others esp. in secret **2** : a person who tries secretly to obtain information for one country in the territory of another usu. hostile country
spy·glass \'spī-ˌglas\ *n* : a small telescope
sq *abbr* square
squab \'skwäb\ *n, pl* **squabs** *or* **squab** : a fledgling bird; *esp* : a fledgling pigeon about four weeks old
[1]**squab·ble** \'skwäb-əl\ *n* : a noisy quarrel usu. over trifles
[2]**squabble** *vb* **squab·bled**; **squab·bling** \'skwäb-(ə-)ling\ : to quarrel noisily and to no purpose : WRANGLE — **squab·bler** \-(ə-)lər\ *n*
squad \'skwäd\ *n* **1** : a small organized group of military personnel; *esp* : a tactical unit that can be easily directed in the field **2** : a small group engaged in a common effort or occupation ⟨a football *squad*⟩
squad car *n* : a police car connected by shortwave radiophone with headquarters
squad·ron \'skwäd-rən\ *n* : any of several units of military organization
squal·id \'skwäl-əd\ *adj* **1** : marked by filthiness and degradation from neglect or poverty **2** : morally debased : SORDID — **squal·id·ly** *adv* — **squal·id·ness** *n*
[1]**squall** \'skwȯl\ *vb* : to cry out raucously : SCREAM — **squall·er** *n*
[2]**squall** *n* **1** : a raucous cry **2** : SQUAWK
[3]**squall** *n* **1** : a sudden violent wind often with rain or snow **2** : a short-lived commotion
[4]**squall** *vb* : to blow a squall
squally \'skwȯ-lē\ *adj* **squall·i·er**; **-est** : marked by squalls : GUSTY, STORMY
squal·or \'skwäl-ər\ *n* : the quality or state of being squalid
squan·der \'skwän-dər\ *vb* **squan·dered**; **squan·der·ing** \-d(ə-)ring\ : to spend extravagantly or wastefully — **squan·der·er** \-dər-ər\ *n*
[1]**square** \'skwa(ə)r, 'skwe(ə)r\ *n* **1** : an instrument having at least one right angle and two straight edges used to lay out or test right angles **2** : a rectangle with all four sides equal **3** : any of the quadrilateral spaces marked out on a board for playing games **4** : the product of a number multiplied by itself **5 a** : an open place or area formed at the meeting of two or more streets **b** : BLOCK 7 — **on the square** **1** : at right angles **2** : in a fair open manner : HONESTLY — **out of square** : not at an exact right angle

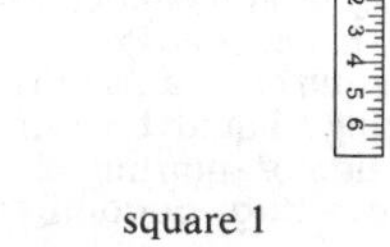

square 1

[2]**square** *adj* **1 a** : having four sides of equal measure and four right angles ⟨a *square* array⟩ **b** : forming a right angle ⟨*square* corner⟩ **2** : raised to the second power **3 a** : of a shape suggesting strength and solidity ⟨*square* jaw⟩ ⟨*square* shoulders⟩ **b** : rectangular and equal-sided in section ⟨*square* tower⟩ **c** : having a rectangular rather than curving outline **4 a** : converted from a linear unit into a square unit of area having the same length of side : SQUARED ⟨a *square* foot⟩ **b** : being of a specified length in each of two equal dimensions ⟨10 feet *square*⟩ **5 a** : exactly adjusted : well made **b** : JUST, FAIR **c** : leaving no balance : SETTLED **d** : TIED ⟨the golfers were all *square* at the end of the 6th hole⟩ **e** : SUBSTANTIAL, SATISFYING ⟨three *square* meals a day⟩ — **square·ly** *adv* — **square·ness** *n* — **squar·ish** \'skwa(ə)r-ish, 'skwe(ə)r-\ *adj*
[3]**square** *vb* **1** : to form with right angles, straight edges, and flat surfaces : make square or rectangular ⟨*square* a timber⟩ **2** : to bring to a right angle ⟨*squared* his shoulders⟩ **3 a** : to multiply (a number) by itself **b** : to find a square equal in area to ⟨*square* a circle⟩ **4** : to agree or make agree ⟨his story does not *square* with the facts⟩ **5** : BALANCE, SETTLE ⟨*square* an account⟩ **6** : to mark off into squares **7** : BRIBE, FIX **8** : to take a fighting stance ⟨the two *squared* off⟩
square away *vb* : to put in order or readiness
square dance *n* : a dance for four couples who form a hollow square — **square dancer** *n* — **square dancing** *n*
square knot *n* : a knot made of two reverse half-knots and typically used to join the ends of two cords
square measure *n* : a unit or system of units for measuring area — see MEASURE table, METRIC SYSTEM table
square number *n* : a number (as 1, 4, or 9) that is the square of an integer
square–rigged \'skwa(ə)r-'rigd, 'skwe(ə)r-\ *adj* : having the principal sails extended on yards fastened to the masts horizontally and at their center
square–rig·ger \-'rig-ər\ *n* : a square-rigged ship

square-rigger

square root *n* : either of the numbers that when squared yields a given number ⟨either +3 or −3 is the *square root* of 9⟩

square shooter *n* : a just or honest person
[1]**squash** \'skwäsh\ *vb* **1** : to press or beat into a pulp or a flat mass : CRUSH ⟨*squash* a beetle⟩ **2** : to put down : SUPPRESS, SQUELCH **3** : SQUEEZE, PRESS ⟨*squashed* into the seat⟩ — **squash·er** *n*
[2]**squash** *n* **1** : the sudden fall of a heavy soft body or the sound of such a fall **2** : a squelching sound **3** : a crushed mass **4** : SQUASH RACQUETS
[3]**squash** *n, pl* **squash·es** *or* **squash** : a fruit of any of various widely grown vines that is used esp. as a vegetable and for livestock feed; *also* : a plant that bears squashes
squash bug *n* : a large black American bug injurious to squash vines
squash racquets *n* : a game played in a 4-wall court with a racket and a rubber ball
squashy \'skwäsh-ē\ *adj* **squash·i·er**; **-est** : easily squashed : SOFT — **squash·i·ly** \'skwäsh-ə-lē\ *adv* — **squash·i·ness** \'skwäsh-ē-nəs\ *n*
[1]**squat** \'skwät\ *vb* **squat·ted**; **squat·ting** **1** : to sit or cause (oneself) to sit on one's haunches or heels **2** : to occupy land as a squatter **3** : CROUCH, COWER ⟨*squatting* hare⟩
[2]**squat** *n* **1** : the act of squatting **2** : a squatting posture
[3]**squat** *adj* **squat·ter**; **squat·test** **1** : CROUCHING **2** : low to the ground **3** : being short and thick — **squat·ly** *adv* — **squat·ness** *n*
squat·ter \'skwät-ər\ *n* **1** : one that squats **2 a** : one that settles on land without right or title or payment of rent **b** : one that settles on public land under government regulation with the purpose of acquiring title
squat·ty \'skwät-ē\ *adj* **squat·ti·er**; **-est** : SQUAT, THICKSET
squaw \'skwȯ\ *n* : an American Indian woman
[1]**squawk** \'skwȯk\ *vb* **1** : to utter a harsh abrupt scream **2** : to complain or protest loudly or vehemently — **squawk·er** *n*
[2]**squawk** *n* **1** : a harsh abrupt scream **2** : a noisy complaint
squaw·root \'skwȯ-ˌrüt, -ˌru̇t\ *n* : a No. American herb that is parasitic on oak and hemlock and has a thick stem with yellow fleshy scales
[1]**squeak** \'skwēk\ *vb* **1** : to make a short shrill cry or noise **2** : to pass, succeed, or win by a narrow margin ⟨barely *squeaked* by⟩ **3** : to utter in a shrill piping tone
[2]**squeak** *n* **1** : a sharp shrill cry or sound **2** : ESCAPE ⟨a close *squeak*⟩ — **squeaky** \'skwē-kē\ *adj*
[1]**squeal** \'skwēl\ *vb* **1** : to make a shrill cry or noise **2 a** : to turn informer **b** : COMPLAIN, PROTEST **3** : to utter with or as if with a squeal — **squeal·er** *n*
[2]**squeal** *n* : a shrill sharp cry or noise
squea·mish \'skwē-mish\ *adj* **1 a** : easily nauseated : QUEASY **b** : affected with nausea : NAUSEATED **2** : easily shocked or disgusted — **squea·mish·ly** *adv* — **squea·mish·ness** *n*
squee·gee \'skwē-ˌjē\ *n* : a blade of leather or rubber set on a handle and used for spreading or wiping liquid material on, across, or off a surface (as a window) — **squeegee** *vb*
[1]**squeeze** \'skwēz\ *vb* **1 a** : to exert pressure esp. on opposite sides of : COMPRESS **b** : to extract or emit under pressure ⟨*squeeze* juice from a lemon⟩ **c** : to force or thrust by compression : CROWD ⟨*squeezed* into the car⟩ **2 a** : to extort money, goods, or services from ⟨*squeezed* their tenants mercilessly⟩ **b** : to reduce the amount of ⟨rising costs *squeezed* profits⟩ **3** : to gain or win by a narrow margin — **squeez·er** *n*
[2]**squeeze** *n* **1 a** : an act or instance of squeezing : COMPRESSION **b** : HANDCLASP **2** : financial pressure
squeeze bottle *n* : a bottle of flexible plastic that dispenses its contents by being pressed
[1]**squelch** \'skwelch\ *n* **1** : a sound of or as if of semifluid matter under suction ⟨the *squelch* of mud⟩ **2** : a retort that silences an opponent
[2]**squelch** *vb* **1 a** : to fall or stamp on so as to crush **b** : to completely suppress : QUELL, SILENCE **2** : to emit or cause to emit a sucking sound **3** : to splash through water, slush, or mire — **squelch·er** *n*
squib \'skwib\ *n* **1 a** : a small firecracker **b** : a broken firecracker that burns out with a fizz **2** : a short humorous or satiric writing or speech
squid \'skwid\ *n, pl* **squid** *or* **squids** : any of numerous 10-armed cephalopod mollusks with a long tapered body, a fin on each side, and usu. a slender internal chitinous support
squig·gle \'skwig-əl\ *n* : a short wavy twist or line : CURLICUE
[1]**squint** \'skwint\ *adj* : affected with cross-eye
[2]**squint** *vb* **1 a** : to look in a squint-eyed manner **b** : to be cross-eyed **2** : to look or peer with eyes partly closed — **squint·er** *n*
[3]**squint** *n* : inability to direct both eyes to the same object due to a fault of the muscles of the eyeball; *also* : SQUINTING — **squinty** \'skwint-ē\ *adj*
squint–eyed \'skwint-'īd\ *adj* **1** : having eyes that are partly closed **2** : looking askance (as in envy or malice)
[1]**squire** \'skwī(ə)r\ *n* [from medieval French *esquier*, from Latin *scutarius* "one armed with a shield", from *scutum* "shield"] **1** : one who bears the shield or armor of a knight **2 a** : a male attendant **b** : GALLANT, ESCORT **3 a** : a member of the British gentry ranking below a knight and above a gentleman **b** : an owner of a country estate **c** : JUSTICE OF THE PEACE
[2]**squire** *vb* : to attend as a squire or escort
squirm \'skwərm\ *vb* **1** : to twist about like an eel or a worm **2** : to feel acutely embarrassed — **squirmy** \'skwər-mē\ *adj*
squir·rel \'skwər(-ə)l, 'skwə-rəl\ *n, pl* **squirrels** *also* **squirrel** [from medieval French *esquireul*, from Latin *sciurus*, from Greek *skiouros*, from *skia* "shadow" and *oura* "tail"] **1** : any of various small or medium-sized rodents; *esp* : one with a long bushy tail and strong hind legs adapted to leaping from branch to branch **2** : the fur of a squirrel

squirrel 1
(about 12 in. long)

[1]**squirt** \'skwərt\ *vb* : to come forth, drive, or eject in a sudden rapid stream : SPURT
[2]**squirt** *n* **1 a** : an instrument (as a syringe) for squirting a liquid **b** : a small quick stream : JET **c** : the action of squirting **2** : an impudent youngster
squirting cucumber *n* : a Mediterranean plant

ə abut	ər further	a back	ā bake	
ä cot, cart	au̇ out	ch chin	e less	ē easy
g gift	i trip	ī life	j joke	ng sing	ō flow
ȯ flaw	ȯi coin	th thin	t͟h this	ü loot
u̇ foot	y yet	yü few	yu̇ furious	zh vision

related to the cucumber and having a fruit that bursts when ripe forcibly ejecting the seeds
squishy \'skwish-ē\ *adj* : being soft, yielding, and damp
Sr *abbr* **1** senior **2** sister
SS *abbr* **1** steamship **2** Sunday school
S-shaped \'es(h)-ˌshāpt\ *adj* : having the shape of a capital S
ssp *abbr* subspecies
SSR *abbr* Soviet Socialist Republic
SSS *abbr* Selective Service System
SST *abbr* supersonic transport
-st — see -EST
st *abbr* **1** saint **2** strait **3** street
St *abbr* stratus
sta *abbr* station
[1]**stab** \'stab\ *n* **1** : a wound produced by a pointed weapon **2** : a thrust of a pointed weapon **3** : EFFORT, TRY
[2]**stab** *vb* **stabbed**; **stab·bing** **1** : to wound or pierce by or as if by the thrust of a pointed weapon **2** : THRUST, DRIVE — **stab·ber** *n*
sta·bil·i·ty \stə-'bil-ət-ē\ *n, pl* **-ties** **1** : the quality, state, or degree of being stable **2** : the property of a body that causes it to return to its original condition when disturbed (as in balance) **3** : resistance to chemical change or to physical disintegration
sta·bi·lize \'stā-bə-ˌlīz\ *vb* **1** : to make or become stable, steadfast, or firm **2** : to hold steady (as by means of a stabilizer) — **sta·bi·li·za·tion** \ˌstā-bə-lə-'zā-shən\ *n*
sta·bi·liz·er \'stā-bə-ˌlī-zər\ *n* : one (as a chemical or a device) that stabilizes something; *esp* : a fixed surface for stabilizing the motion of an airplane
[1]**sta·ble** \'stā-bəl\ *n* [from Latin *stabulum*, literally "place for standing", from *stare* "to stand"] **1** : a building in which domestic animals are sheltered and fed; *esp* : such a building having stalls or compartments ⟨horse *stable*⟩ **2** **a** : the racehorses of one owner **b** : a group of athletes (as boxers) under one management — **sta·ble·man** \-mən, -ˌman\ *n*
[2]**stable** *vb* **sta·bled**; **sta·bling** \-b(ə-)ling\ : to put, keep, or live in or as if in a stable
[3]**stable** *adj* **sta·bler** \-b(ə-)lər\; **sta·blest** \-b(ə-)ləst\ [from Latin *stabilis*, literally "capable of standing", from *stare* "to stand"] **1** **a** : firmly established : FIXED, STEADFAST ⟨a *stable* community⟩ **b** : not changing or fluctuating : UNVARYING ⟨a *stable* income⟩ **2** : steady in purpose : CONSTANT ⟨*stable* personalities⟩ **3** **a** : designed so as to develop forces that restore the original condition when disturbed from a condition of equilibrium or steady motion ⟨a *stable* airplane⟩ **b** : able to resist alteration in chemical, physical, or biological properties ⟨a *stable* compound⟩ ⟨*stable* emulsions⟩ — **sta·bly** \-b(ə-)lē\ *adv*
sta·ble·ness \'stā-bəl-nəs\ *n* : STABILITY
sta·bler \-b(ə-)lər\ *n* : one that keeps a stable
stacc *abbr* staccato
stac·ca·to \stə-'kät-ō\ *adj* [from Italian, literally "detached", from past participle of *staccare* "to detach", from Old French *destachier*, the source of English *detach*] **1** : cut short or apart in performing : DISCONNECTED ⟨*staccato* notes⟩ **2** : ABRUPT, DISJOINTED — **staccato** *adv* — **staccato** *n*
[1]**stack** \'stak\ *n* **1** : a large usu. conical pile (as of hay, straw, or grain) **2** : an orderly pile of objects usu. one on top of the other ⟨a *stack* of dishes⟩ **3** : a vertical pipe for carrying off smoke or vapor : CHIMNEY, SMOKESTACK **4** **a** : a rack with shelves for storing books **b** *pl* : the part of a library in which books are stored in racks **5** : three or more rifles arranged together to stand in the form of a pyramid
[2]**stack** *vb* : to arrange in or form a stack : PILE ⟨*stacked* the dishes on the table⟩ — **stack·er** *n*
stack up *vb* : to measure up : COMPARE ⟨see how you *stack up* against the champion⟩
sta·di·um \'stād-ē-əm\ *n, pl* **-dia** \-ē-ə\ *or* **-di·ums** **1** : a course for footraces in ancient Greece with tiers of seats for spectators **2** *pl usu stadiums* : a large usu. unroofed building with tiers of seats for spectators at modern sports events
[1]**staff** \'staf\ *n, pl* **staffs** \'stafs\ *or* **staves** \'stavz, 'stāvz\ **1** **a** : a pole, stick, rod, or bar used as a support or as a sign of authority ⟨a flag hanging limp on its *staff*⟩ **b** : the long handle of a weapon (as a lance or pike) **c** : CLUB, CUDGEL **2** : something that props or sustains ⟨bread is the *staff* of life⟩ **3** : the five horizontal lines with their spaces on which music is written **4** *pl staffs* **a** : a group of persons serving as assistants to or employees under a chief ⟨a hospital *staff*⟩ **b** : a group of officers or aides appointed to assist a civil executive or commanding officer **c** : military officers not eligible for operational command but having administrative duties — **staff** *adj*
[2]**staff** *vb* : to supply with a staff or with workers
staff·er \'staf-ər\ *n* : a member of a staff and esp. a newspaper staff
staff sergeant *n* : a noncommissioned officer ranking in the army just below a sergeant first class and in the air force just below a technical sergeant
[1]**stag** \'stag\ *n, pl* **stag** *or* **stags** **1** : an adult male red deer : the male of various large deer **2** **a** : a social gathering of men only **b** : a man who attends a dance or party unaccompanied by a woman
[2]**stag** *adj* : intended or suitable for men only ⟨a *stag* party⟩
[1]**stage** \'stāj\ *n* **1** **a** : one of the horizontal levels into which a structure is divisible **b** : a floor of a building **c** : a shelf or layer esp. as one of a series **d** : any of the levels attained by a river above an arbitrary zero point ⟨flood *stage*⟩ **2** **a** : a raised platform (as a scaffold or landing stage) **b** : a part of a theater including the acting area **c** : the small platform on which an object is placed for microscopic examination **3** **a** : a center of attention : scene of action **b** : the theatrical profession or art **4** **a** : a stopping place esp. for a stagecoach providing fresh horses and refreshments **b** : the distance between stopping places in a journey **c** : a degree of advance attained (as in a process or undertaking) ⟨an early *stage* of a disease⟩ **d** : one of the distinguishable periods of the growth and development of a plant or animal ⟨the larval *stage* of a beetle⟩; *also* : an individual in such a stage **e** : one complete process or step in a sequential or recurrent activity **5** : STAGECOACH **6** : a propulsion unit in a rocket with its own fuel and containers ⟨a three-*stage* missile⟩ — **on the stage** : in or into the acting profession
[2]**stage** *vb* : to produce or show publicly on or as if on the stage ⟨*stages* two plays each year⟩ ⟨*stage* a track meet⟩
stage·coach \'stāj-ˌkōch\ *n* : a horse-drawn passenger and mail coach running on a regular schedule between established stops
stage fright *n* : nervousness felt at appearing before an audience
stage·hand \'stāj-ˌhand\ *n* : a stage worker who handles scenery, properties, or lights
stage manager *n* : a person who is in charge of the stage and physical aspects of a theatrical production
stage·struck \'stāj-ˌstrək\ *adj* : fascinated by the stage; *esp* : urgently desirous of becoming an actor
stage whisper *n* : a loud whisper by an actor audible

to the spectators but supposed not to be heard by persons on the stage

1**stag·ger** \'stag-ər\ *vb* **stag·gered**; **stag·ger·ing** \-(ə-)riŋ\ **1 a :** to move unsteadily from side to side as if about to fall : REEL **b :** to cause to reel or totter **2 a :** to begin to doubt and waver : become less confident **b :** to cause to doubt, waver, or hesitate **3 :** to place or arrange in a zigzag or alternate but regular way — **stag·ger·er** \-ər-ər\ *n*

2**stagger** *n* **1** *pl* **:** a disease of domestic mammals and birds marked by reeling, unsteady movements, and falling **2 :** a reeling or unsteady gait or stance

stag·ger·ing *adj* **:** serving to stagger : ASTONISHING, OVERWHELMING — **stag·ger·ing·ly** \'stag-(ə-)riŋ-lē\ *adv*

stag·hound \'stag-ˌhau̇nd\ *n* **:** a hound formerly used in hunting large animals (as the stag)

stag·ing \'stā-jiŋ\ *n* **1 :** SCAFFOLDING **2 :** the putting of a play on the stage **3 :** the assembling of troops or supplies in a particular place

stag·nant \'stag-nənt\ *adj* **1 :** not flowing in a current or stream : MOTIONLESS **2 :** DULL, INACTIVE — **stag·nan·cy** \-nən-sē\ *n* — **stag·nant·ly** *adv*

stag·nate \'stag-ˌnāt\ *vb* **:** to be or become stagnant — **stag·na·tion** \stag-'nā-shən\ *n*

1**staid** \'stād\ *adj* **1 :** SETTLED, FIXED ⟨a *staid* opinion⟩ **2 :** GRAVE, SERIOUS — **staid·ly** *adv* — **staid·ness** *n*

2**staid** *past of* STAY

1**stain** \'stān\ *vb* **1 :** to soil or discolor esp. in spots **2 :** to give color to (as by dyeing) : TINGE **3 a :** to taint with guilt, vice, or corruption **b :** to bring reproach on — **stain·a·ble** \'stā-nə-bəl\ *adj* — **stain·er** *n*

2**stain** *n* **1 :** a soiled or discolored spot **2 :** a taint of guilt : STIGMA **3 :** a preparation (as of dye or pigment) used in staining; *esp* **:** one capable of penetrating the pores of wood — **stain·less** \'stān-ləs\ *adj* — **stain·less·ly** *adv*

stained glass *n* **:** glass colored or stained for use in windows

stainless steel *n* **:** steel alloyed with chromium and highly resistant to stain, rust, and corrosion

stair \'sta(ə)r, 'ste(ə)r\ *n* **1 :** a series of steps or flights of steps for passing from one level to another — often used in pl. ⟨ran down the *stairs*⟩ **2 :** one step of a stairway

stair·case \-ˌkās\ *n* **:** a flight of stairs with the supporting framework, casing, and balusters

stair·way \-ˌwā\ *n* **:** one or more flights of stairs usu. with landings to pass from one level to another

stair·well \-ˌwel\ *n* **:** a vertical shaft around which stairs are located

1**stake** \'stāk\ *n* **1 :** a pointed piece (as of wood) driven or to be driven into the ground esp. as a marker or support **2 a :** a post to which a person is bound for execution by burning **b :** execution by burning at a stake **3 a :** something that is staked for gain or loss **b :** the prize in a contest **c :** an interest or share in a commercial venture **4 :** GRUBSTAKE — **at stake :** at issue : in a position to be lost or won

2**stake** *vb* **1 a :** to mark the limits of by stakes ⟨*stake* out a mining claim⟩ **b :** to tie to a stake **c :** to fasten up or support (as plants) with stakes **2 a :** BET, HAZARD **b :** to back financially; *esp* **:** GRUBSTAKE

ə abut	ər further	a back	ā bake	
ä cot, cart	au̇ out	ch chin	e less	ē easy
g gift	i trip	ī life	j joke	ŋ sing	ō flow
ȯ flaw	ȯi coin	th thin	t͟h this	ü loot
u̇ foot	y yet	yü few	yu̇ furious	zh vision

sta·lac·tite \stə-'lak-ˌtīt\ *n* [from Greek *stalaktos* "dripping" (adjective)] **:** a deposit of calcium carbonate resembling an icicle hanging from the roof or sides of a cavern

sta·lag·mite \stə-'lag-ˌmīt\ *n* [from Greek *stalagmos* "a dripping"] **:** a deposit like an inverted stalactite found on the floor of a cave

1**stale** \'stāl\ *adj* **1 :** tasteless, unpleasant, or unwholesome from age ⟨*stale* food⟩ **2 :** tedious from familiarity ⟨*stale* news⟩ **3 :** WEAK, INEFFECTIVE ⟨felt *stale* and listless after his illness⟩ — **stale·ly** \'stāl-lē\ *adv* — **stale·ness** *n*

2**stale** *vb* **:** to make or become stale

1**stale·mate** \'stāl-ˌmāt\ *n* **1 :** a drawing position in chess in which only the king can move and although not in check can move only into check **2 :** a drawn contest : DEADLOCK

2**stalemate** *vb* **:** to bring into a stalemate

1**stalk** \'stȯk\ *vb* **1 a :** to hunt stealthily ⟨a *stalking* cat⟩ ⟨*stalk* deer⟩ **b :** to cover an area in stalking prey **2 :** to walk with haughty or pompous bearing ⟨*stalked* out of the room⟩ — **stalk·er** *n*

2**stalk** *n* **1 :** the act of stalking **2 :** a stalking gait

3**stalk** *n* **1 :** a plant stem; *esp* **:** the main stem of an herbaceous plant **2 :** a slender upright or supporting or connecting structure — **stalked** \'stȯkt\ *adj* — **stalk·less** \'stȯk-ləs\ *adj* — **stalk·like** \-ˌlīk\ *adj*

stalk·ing–horse \'stȯ-kiŋ-ˌhȯrs\ *n* **1 :** a horse or a figure like a horse behind which a hunter stalks game **2 :** something used to mask a purpose

1**stall** \'stȯl\ *n* **1 :** a compartment for a domestic animal in a stable or barn **2 a :** a seat in the chancel of a church with back and sides wholly or partly enclosed **b** *Brit* **:** a front orchestra seat in a theater **3 :** a booth, stand, or counter at which articles are displayed for sale

2**stall** *vb* **1 :** to put into or keep in a stall **2 a :** to bring or come to a standstill ⟨*stalled* the car⟩ **b :** to cause (an airplane or airfoil) to go into a stall

3**stall** *n* **:** the condition of an airfoil or airplane operating so that there is a breakdown of airflow and loss of lift with a tendency to drop

4**stall** *n* **:** a ruse to deceive or delay

5**stall** *vb* **:** to hold off, divert, or delay by evasion or deception

stal·lion \'stal-yən\ *n* **:** a male horse; *esp* **:** one kept primarily as a stud

1**stal·wart** \'stȯl-wərt\ *adj* **:** STOUT, STURDY — **stal·wart·ly** *adv*

2**stalwart** *n* **1 :** a stalwart person **2 :** an unwavering supporter (as in politics)

sta·men \'stā-mən\ *n, pl* **stamens** *also* **sta·mi·na** \'stā-mə-nə, 'stam-ə-\ **:** an organ of a flower that consists of an anther and a filament and produces the pollen

stam·i·na \'stam-ə-nə\ *n* **:** VIGOR, ENDURANCE

sta·mi·nate \'stā-mə-nət, 'stam-ə-, -ˌnāt\ *adj* **:** having stamens; *esp* **:** having stamens but no pistils

1**stam·mer** \'stam-ər\ *vb* **stam·mered**; **stam·mer·ing** \-(ə-)riŋ\ **:** to speak or utter with involuntary stops and repetitions — **stam·mer·er** \-ər-ər\ *n*

2**stammer** *n* **:** an act or instance of stammering

1**stamp** \'stamp; *1b & 2 are also* 'stämp\ *vb* **1 a :** to pound or crush with a heavy instrument **b :** to strike or beat forcibly with the bottom of the foot **c :** to extinguish or destroy by or as if by stamping with the foot **2 :** to walk heavily or noisily **3 a :** IMPRESS, IMPRINT ⟨*stamp* the bill *paid*⟩ **b :** to attach a stamp to ⟨*stamp* a letter⟩ **4 :** to form with a stamp or die **5 :** CHARACTERIZE — **stamp·er** *n*

2**stamp** *n* **1 :** a device or instrument for stamping

2 : the impression or mark made by stamping **3** : a distinctive character, indication, or mark ⟨*stamp* of genius⟩ **4** : the act of stamping **5 a** : a stamped or printed paper affixed in evidence that a tax has been paid **b** : POSTAGE STAMP

[1]**stam·pede** \stam-'pēd\ *n* [from American Spanish *estampida*, from Spanish, "loud noise", "crash", from *estampar* "to stamp"] **1** : a wild headlong rush or flight of frightened animals **2** : a mass movement of people at a common impulse

[2]**stampede** *vb* **1** : to run away or cause (as cattle) to run away in panic **2** : to act together or cause to act together suddenly and without thought

stance \'stan(t)s\ *n* : way of standing or being placed : POSTURE

[1]**stanch** \'stȯnch, 'stänch\ *vb* : to stop the flow of ⟨*stanch* tears⟩; *also* : to stop the flow of blood from (a wound) — **stanch·er** *n*

[2]**stanch** *var of* STAUNCH

[1]**stan·chion** \'stan-chən\ *n* **1** : an upright bar, post, or support **2** : a device that fits loosely around an animal's neck and limits forward and backward motion (as in a stall)

[2]**stanchion** *vb* : to provide with stanchions or secure with a stanchion

[1]**stand** \'stand\ *vb* **stood** \'stu̇d\; **stand·ing** **1 a** : to support oneself on the feet in an erect position **b** : to rise to one's feet **2** : to take up or maintain a usu. specified position or posture ⟨*stand* aside⟩ ⟨where do we *stand* on this question⟩ **3** : to be firm and steadfast in support or opposition **4** : to be in a particular state or situation ⟨*stands* accused⟩ **5** *chiefly Brit* : to be a candidate : RUN **6 a** : to rest, remain, or set upright on a base or lower end ⟨the spade *stood* in the sod⟩ **b** : to occupy a place or location ⟨a house *standing* on a knoll⟩ **7 a** : to remain stationary or inactive ⟨rainwater *standing* in stagnant pools⟩ **b** : to remain in effect ⟨the order *stands*⟩ **8** : to exist in a definite form ⟨you must take or leave his offer as it *stands*⟩ **9 a** : to endure or undergo successfully : BEAR ⟨*stand* pain⟩ ⟨the building *stood* the pressure of the storm⟩ **b** : to submit to ⟨*stand* trial⟩ **10** : to pay for ⟨*stand* drinks⟩ — **stand·er** *n* — **stand by** : to be or remain present, available, or loyal to — **stand for 1** : to be a symbol for : REPRESENT **2** : to put up with : PERMIT — **stand pat** : to oppose or resist change

[2]**stand** *n* **1** : an act or instance of stopping or staying in one place **2 a** : a halt for defense or resistance **b** : a stop made to give a theatrical performance **3 a** : a place or post where one stands **b** : a position esp. with respect to an issue **4 a** : the place occupied by a witness testifying in court **b** : a tier of seats for spectators of an outdoor sport or spectacle **c** : a raised platform (as for a speaker) **5** : a small often open-air structure for a small retail business **6** : a support (as a rack or table) on or in which something may be placed ⟨umbrella *stands*⟩ **7** : a group of plants growing in a continuous area ⟨a good *stand* of wheat⟩

[1]**stan·dard** \'stan-dərd\ *n* **1 a** : a figure adopted as an emblem by an organized body of people ⟨the eagle was the Roman legion's *standard*⟩ **b** : the personal flag of the ruler of a state **2 a** : something set up by authority or by general consent as a rule for measuring or as a model ⟨a *standard* of weight⟩ ⟨*standards* of good manners⟩ **b** : the basis of value in a monetary system ⟨gold *standard*⟩ **3** : a structure that serves as a support ⟨a lamp *standard*⟩

[2]**standard** *adj* **1** : constituting or conforming to a standard established by law or custom ⟨*standard* weight⟩ **2** : regularly and widely used ⟨*standard* practice in the trade⟩ **3** : having recognized and permanent value ⟨*standard* reference work⟩

stan·dard–bear·er \-,bar-ər, -,ber-\ *n* **1** : one that bears a standard or banner **2** : the leader of an organization or movement

stan·dard·bred \-,bred\ *n* : any of an American breed of light trotting and pacing horses bred for speed and noted for endurance

standard conditions *n pl* : a temperature of 0°C and a pressure of 760 millimeters of mercury employed esp. in comparison of gas volumes

standard deviation *n* : the square root of the arith-

S

STANDARD TIME IN 50 PLACES THROUGHOUT THE WORLD WHEN IT IS 12:00 NOON IN NEW YORK

CITY	TIME	CITY	TIME
[1]Amsterdam, Netherlands	6:00 P.M.	Montreal, Quebec	12:00 NOON
Anchorage, Alaska	7:00 A.M.	[1]Moscow, U.S.S.R.	8:00 P.M.
Bangkok, Thailand	12:00 MIDNIGHT	Ottawa, Ontario	12:00 NOON
Berlin, Germany	6:00 P.M.	[1]Paris, France	6:00 P.M.
Bombay, India	10:30 P.M.	Peking, China	1:00 A.M. next day
[1]Brussels, Belgium	6:00 P.M.	Perth, Australia	1:00 A.M. next day
Buenos Aires, Argentina	2:00 P.M.	Rio de Janeiro, Brazil	2:00 P.M.
Calcutta, India	10:30 P.M.	Rome, Italy	6:00 P.M.
Cape Town, So. Africa	7:00 P.M.	Saint John's, Newfoundland	1:30 P.M.
Chicago, Ill.	11:00 A.M.	Salt Lake City, Utah	10:00 A.M.
Delhi, India	10:30 P.M.	San Francisco, Calif.	9:00 A.M.
Denver, Colo.	10:00 A.M.	San Juan, Puerto Rico	1:00 P.M.
Djakarta, Indonesia	12:00 MIDNIGHT	Santiago, Chile	1:00 P.M.
Halifax, Nova Scotia	1:00 P.M.	Shanghai, China	1:00 A.M. next day
Hong Kong	1:00 A.M. next day	Singapore	12:30 A.M. next day
Honolulu, Hawaii	7:00 A.M.	Stockholm, Sweden	6:00 P.M.
Istanbul, Turkey	7:00 P.M.	Sydney, Australia	3:00 A.M. next day
Juneau, Alaska	9:00 A.M.	Tehran, Iran	8:30 P.M.
Karachi, Pakistan	10:00 P.M.	Tokyo, Japan	2:00 A.M. next day
[1]London, England	6:00 P.M.	Toronto, Ontario	12:00 NOON
Los Angeles, Calif.	9:00 A.M.	Vancouver, British Columbia	9:00 A.M.
[1]Madrid, Spain	6:00 P.M.	[1]Vladivostok, U.S.S.R.	3:00 A.M. next day
Manila, Philippines	1:00 A.M. next day	Washington, D.C.	12:00 NOON
Mexico City, Mexico	11:00 A.M.	Wellington, New Zealand	5:00 A.M. next day
[1]Montevideo, Uruguay	2:00 P.M.	Winnipeg, Manitoba	11:00 A.M.

[1]Time in Great Britain, Ireland, France, Spain, Netherlands, Belgium, Uruguay, and the U.S.S.R. is one hour in advance of the standard meridians.

metic mean of the squares of differences between the arithmetic mean of a frequency distribution and the values of the variable

stan·dard·ize \'stan-dər-ˌdīz\ *vb* : to compare with or bring into conformity with a standard — **stan·dard·i·za·tion** \ˌstan-dərd-ə-'zā-shən\ *n*

standard of living : the necessities, comforts, and luxuries that a person or group is accustomed to

standard time *n* : the time established by law or by general usage over a region or country

stand·by \'stan(d)-ˌbī\ *n* : one available or to be relied upon esp. in emergencies

stand by \-'bī\ *vb* **1** : to be present **2** : to be or to get ready to act

stand·ee \stan-'dē\ *n* : one who occupies standing room

stand–in \'stan-ˌdin\ *n* **1** : someone employed to occupy an actor's place while lights and camera are readied **2** : SUBSTITUTE

stand in \-'din\ *vb* : to act as a stand-in

1**stand·ing** \'stan-ding\ *adj* **1** : upright on the feet or base : ERECT ⟨*standing* grain⟩ **2 a** : not flowing : STAGNANT **b** : remaining at the same level, degree, or amount for an indeterminate period ⟨*standing* offer⟩ **c** : continuing in existence or use indefinitely : PERMANENT ⟨a *standing* army⟩ ⟨*standing* committees⟩ **3** : done from a standing position ⟨*standing* jump⟩

2**standing** *n* **1** : the action or position of one that stands **2** : DURATION ⟨a quarrel of long *standing*⟩ **3 a** : position or comparative rank **b** : good reputation ⟨people of *standing* in the community⟩

standing room *n* : space available for spectators or passengers to stand in after all seats are filled

standing wave *n* : a vibration of a body or physical system in which the amplitude varies from place to place, is constantly zero at fixed points, and has maxima at other points

stand·off \'stan-ˌdȯf\ *n* : TIE, DRAW, DEADLOCK

stand·off·ish \stan-'dȯ-fish\ *adj* : COOL, ALOOF

stand·out \'stan-ˌdau̇t\ *n* : one that is prominent or conspicuous esp. because of excellence

stand out \-'dau̇t\ *vb* **1** : to appear as if in relief : PROJECT **2** : to be prominent or conspicuous

stand·point \'stan(d)-ˌpȯint\ *n* : a position from which objects or principles are viewed and according to which they are compared and judged

stand·still \-ˌstil\ *n* : a state marked by absence of motion or activity : STOP ⟨business was at a *standstill*⟩

stand up *vb* **1** : to remain sound and intact **2** : to fail to keep an appointment with — **stand up for** : DEFEND — **stand up to 1** : to meet fairly and fully **2** : to face boldly

stank *past of* STINK

stan·za \'stan-zə\ *n* : a division of a poem consisting of a series of lines arranged together in a usu. recurring pattern of meter and rhyme — **stan·za·ic** \stan-'zā-ik\ *adj*

staph·y·lo·coc·cus \ˌstaf-ə-lō-'käk-əs\ *n, pl* **-coc·ci** \-'käk-ˌ(s)ī, -(ˌ)(s)ē\ : any of various spherical bacteria that occur esp. in irregular clusters and include parasites of skin and mucous membranes — **staph·y·lo·coc·cal** \-'käk-əl\ *adj* — **staph·y·lo·coc·cic** \-'käk-(s)ik\ *adj*

1**sta·ple** \'stā-pəl\ *n* **1** : a U-shaped piece of metal usu. with sharp points to be driven into a surface to hold something (as a hook, rope, or wire) **2** : a U-shaped piece of thin wire to be driven through papers and bent over at the ends to fasten them together or to be driven through thin material to fasten it to something else

2**staple** *vb* **sta·pled**; **sta·pling** \-p(ə-)ling\ : to fasten with staples

3**staple** *n* **1** : a chief commodity or product of a place **2 a** : something in widespread and constant use or demand **b** : the sustaining or principal element : SUBSTANCE **3** : RAW MATERIAL **4** : textile fiber (as wool or rayon) of relatively short length that when spun and twisted forms a yarn rather than a filament

4**staple** *adj* **1** : used, needed, or enjoyed constantly usu. by many individuals **2** : produced regularly or in large quantities **3** : PRINCIPAL, CHIEF ⟨*staple* crop⟩

sta·pler \'stā-plər\ *n* : a device that staples

1**star** \'stär\ *n* **1** : any natural luminous body visible in the sky except a planet, satellite, comet, or meteor; *esp* : a self-luminous gaseous celestial body (as the sun) of great mass whose shape is usu. spheroidal and whose size may be as small as the earth or larger than the earth's orbit **2 a** : a planet or a configuration of the planets that is held in astrology to influence one's destiny or fortune — usu. used in pl. **b** : FORTUNE, FAME **3 a** : a conventional figure with five or more points that represents or resembles a star; *esp* : ASTERISK **b** : an often star-shaped ornament or medal worn as a badge of honor, authority, or rank or as the insignia of an order **4 a** : the principal member of a theatrical or operatic company ⟨*star* of stage, screen, and radio⟩ **b** : an outstandingly talented performer ⟨football *stars*⟩ — **star·like** \-ˌlīk\ *adj*

2**star** *vb* **starred**; **star·ring 1** : to sprinkle or adorn with stars **2 a** : to mark with a star as being superior **b** : to mark with an asterisk **3** : to present in the role of a star **4** : to play the most prominent or important role ⟨will produce and *star* in a new play⟩ **5** : to perform outstandingly ⟨*starred* at shortstop in the series⟩

3**star** *adj* **1** : of, relating to, or being a star **2** : being of outstanding excellence : PREEMINENT ⟨*star* athlete⟩ ⟨our *star* salesman⟩

1**star·board** \'stär-bərd\ *n* : the right side of a ship or airplane looking forward

2**starboard** *vb* : to turn or put (a helm or rudder) to the right

3**starboard** *adj* : of, relating to, or situated to starboard

1**starch** \'stärch\ *vb* : to stiffen with or as if with starch

2**starch** *n* **1** : a white odorless tasteless granular or powdery complex carbohydrate that is the chief storage form of carbohydrate in plants, is an important foodstuff, and is used also in adhesives and sizes, in laundering, and in pharmacy and medicine **2** : a stiff formal manner : FORMALITY **3** : resolute vigor : ENERGY

starchy \'stär-chē\ *adj* **starch·i·er**; **-est 1** : containing, consisting of, or resembling starch **2** : consisting of or marked by formality or stiffness — **starch·i·ness** *n*

star·dom \'stärd-əm\ *n* **1** : the status or position of a star **2** : a body of stars

1**stare** \'sta(ə)r, 'ste(ə)r\ *vb* **1** : to look fixedly often with wide-open eyes ⟨*stare* at a stranger⟩ **2** : to show oneself conspicuously ⟨the brilliance of *staring* colors⟩ ***syn*** see GAZE — **star·er** *n*

2**stare** *n* : the act or an instance of staring

ə abut	ər further	a back		ā bake
ä cot, cart	au̇ out	ch chin	e less	ē easy
g gift	i trip	ī life	j joke	ng sing	ō flow
ȯ flaw	ȯi coin	th thin	t͟h this	ü loot
u̇ foot	y yet	yü few	yu̇ furious	zh vision

star·fish \'stär-,fish\ *n* : any of a class of echinoderms having a body of usu. five arms radially arranged about a central disk and feeding largely on mollusks (as oysters)

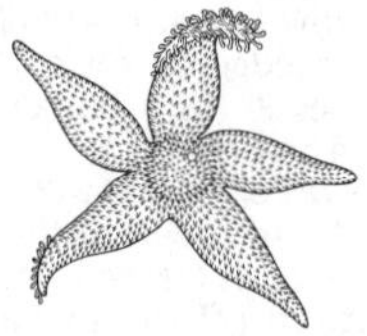

starfish
(about 4 in. across)

star·gaze \-,gāz\ *vb* **1** : to gaze at stars **2** : to stare absentmindedly : DAYDREAM

star·gaz·er \-,gā-zər\ *n* **1** : ASTROLOGER **2** : ASTRONOMER

¹stark \'stärk\ *adj* **1** : STRONG, ROBUST **2 a** : STIFF, MOTIONLESS ⟨*stark* in death⟩ **b** : UNBENDING, STRICT ⟨*stark* discipline⟩ **3** : SHEER, UTTER ⟨*stark* nonsense⟩ **4 a** : BARREN, DESOLATE ⟨a *stark* landscape⟩ **b** : having few or no ornaments : BARE **5** : HARSH, UNADORNED ⟨*stark* realism⟩ — **stark·ly** *adv*

²stark *adv* : WHOLLY, ABSOLUTELY ⟨*stark* mad⟩

star·less \'stär-ləs\ *adj* : being without stars and esp. visible stars

star·let \-lət\ *n* : a young movie actress being coached and publicized for starring roles

star·light \-,līt\ *n* : the light given by the stars

star·ling \'stär-ling\ *n* : any of a family of usu. dark gregarious birds; *esp* : a dark brown or in summer glossy greenish black European bird naturalized and often a pest in the U.S.

star·lit \'stär-,lit\ *adj* : lighted by the stars

starred \'stärd\ *adj* **1** : adorned with or as if with stars **2** : marked with or having the shape of a star **3** : affected in fortune by the stars

star·ry \'stär-ē\ *adj* **star·ri·er**; **-est** **1** : adorned with stars ⟨*starry* heavens⟩ **2** : of, relating to, or consisting of the stars : STELLAR ⟨*starry* light⟩ **3** : shining like stars : SPARKLING ⟨*starry* eyes⟩ **4** : having parts arranged like the rays of a star : STELLATE

Stars and Bars *n sing or pl* : the first flag of the Confederate States of America

Stars and Stripes *n sing or pl* : the flag of the United States

star–span·gled \'stär-,spang-gəld\ *adj* : studded with stars

¹start \'stärt\ *vb* **1** : to move suddenly and sharply : react with a quick involuntary movement **2** : to come or bring into being, activity, or operation ⟨who *started* the rumor⟩ ⟨*started* a camp for young boys⟩ ⟨fire *started* in the cellar⟩ ⟨the game *started* late⟩ **3** : to seem to protrude : PROTRUDE ⟨his eyes *started* from their sockets⟩ **4** : to become or cause to become loosened or forced out of place **5** : to set out : BEGIN ⟨*start* to school⟩ **6** : to be or cause to be a participant in a game or contest **7** : to cause to move, act, or operate ⟨*start* the motor⟩

²start *n* **1 a** : a quick involuntary bodily reaction **b** : a brief and sudden action or movement **c** : a sudden impulse or outburst **2** : a beginning of movement, activity, or development ⟨get an early *start*⟩ **3** : a lead or handicap at the beginning of a race or competition **4** : a place of beginning

start·er \'stärt-ər\ *n* **1** : one who initiates or sets going; *esp* : an official who gives the signal to begin a race **2** : one that enters a competition; *esp* : one that begins a competition

star·tle \'stärt-əl\ *vb* **star·tled**; **star·tling** \-(ə-)ling\ **1** : to move or jump suddenly as in surprise or alarm **2** : to frighten suddenly and usu. not seriously — **startle** *n*

star·tling *adj* : causing a momentary fright, surprise, or astonishment — **star·tling·ly** \'stärt-(ə-)ling-lē\ *adv*

star·va·tion \stär-'vā-shən\ *n* : the act or an instance of starving : the state of being starved

starve \'stärv\ *vb* [from Old English *steorfan* "to die"] **1** : to suffer or die or cause to suffer or die from lack of food **2** : to suffer or die or cause to suffer or die from deprivation ⟨a child *starving* for affection⟩

starve·ling \-ling\ *n* : one thin and weakened by or as if by lack of food

¹stash \'stash\ *vb* : to store in a usu. secret place for future use

²stash *n* **1** : a hiding place **2** : something stored or hidden away

¹state \'stāt\ *n* **1** : manner or condition of being ⟨water in the gaseous *state*⟩ ⟨*state* of readiness⟩ **2** : condition of mind or temperament ⟨in a highly nervous *state*⟩ **3** : elaborate or luxurious style of living : formal dignity ⟨travel in *state*⟩ **4 a** : a politically organized body of people usu. occupying a definite territory; *esp* : one that is sovereign **b** : the political organization of such a body of people **5** : one of the constituent units of a nation having a federal government ⟨the United *States* of America⟩ **6** : the territory of a state — **state·less** \-ləs\ *adj*

²state *adj* **1** : suitable or used for ceremonial or formal occasions ⟨*state* robes⟩ **2** : of or relating to a national state or to a constituent state of a federal government **3** : GOVERNMENTAL ⟨*state* secrets⟩

³state *vb* **1** : to set by regulation or authority ⟨at *stated* times⟩ **2** : to express in words ⟨*state* an opinion⟩

State flower *n* : a flowering plant selected as the floral emblem of a state of the U.S.

state·hood \'stāt-,hu̇d\ *n* : the condition of being a state; *esp* : the condition or status of one of the states of the U.S.

state·house \-,hau̇s\ *n* : the building in which a state legislature sits

state·ly \'stāt-lē\ *adj* **state·li·er**; **-est** : marked by lofty or imposing dignity — **state·li·ness** *n*

state·ment \'stāt-mənt\ *n* **1** : the act or process of stating **2 a** : something stated : REPORT, ASSERTION **b** : PROPOSITION 2 **3** : a brief summarized record of a financial account ⟨a monthly bank *statement*⟩

state·room \'stāt-,rüm, -,ru̇m\ *n* : a private room on a ship or on a railroad car

state·side \'stāt-,sīd\ *adj* : of or relating to the United States as regarded from outside its continental limits

states·man \'stāts-mən\ *n* : a person engaged in fixing the policies and conducting the affairs of a government; *esp* : one having unusual wisdom in such matters — **states·man·like** \-,līk\ *adj* — **states·man·ly** \-lē\ *adj* — **states·man·ship** \-,ship\ *n*

state·wide \'stāt-'wīd\ *adj* : including all parts of a state ⟨a *statewide* spelling contest⟩

¹stat·ic \'stat-ik\ *adj* **1** : exerting force by reason of weight alone without motion ⟨*static* load⟩ **2** : of or relating to bodies at rest or forces in equilibrium **3** : characterized by a lack of movement, animation, or progression **4** : of, relating to, producing, or being stationary charges of electricity (as those produced by friction or induction) **5** : of, relating to, or caused by radio static

²static *n* : disturbing effects produced in a radio or television receiver by atmospheric or electrical disturbances

¹sta·tion \'stā-shən\ *n* **1** : the place or position in which something or someone stands or is assigned to stand or remain **2** : a regular stopping place : DEPOT

S

⟨drove him to the bus *station*⟩ **3 a** : a post or sphere of duty or occupation **b** : a stock farm or ranch of Australia or New Zealand **4** : STANDING, RANK ⟨a woman of high *station*⟩ **5** : a place for specialized observation and study of scientific phenomena ⟨a biological *station*⟩ ⟨a weather *station*⟩ **6** : a place established to provide a public service ⟨police *station*⟩ ⟨fire *station*⟩ ⟨power *station*⟩ **7** : a complete assemblage of radio or television equipment for transmitting or receiving

²**station** *vb* **sta·tioned**; **sta·tion·ing** \'stā-sh(ə-)niŋ\ : to assign to or set in a station or position : POST

sta·tion·ary \'stā-shə-ˌner-ē\ *adj* **1** : fixed in a station, course, or mode : IMMOBILE ⟨a *stationary* laundry tub⟩ **2** : unchanging in condition : STABLE ⟨a *stationary* population⟩

station break *n* : a pause in a radio or television broadcast for announcement of the identity of the network or station

sta·tio·ner \'stā-sh(ə-)nər\ *n* : one that sells stationery

sta·tio·nery \'stā-shə-ˌner-ē\ *n* **1** : materials (as paper, pens, and ink) for writing or typing **2** : letter paper usu. accompanied with matching envelopes

station wagon *n* : an automobile that has an interior longer than a sedan's, has one or more rear seats readily lifted out or folded to facilitate light trucking, and usu. has a door at the rear end

sta·tis·tic \stə-'tis-tik\ *n* : a single term or datum in a collection of statistics

stat·is·ti·cian \ˌstat-ə-'stish-ən\ *n* : one versed in or engaged in compiling statistics

sta·tis·tics \stə-'tis-tiks\ *n sing or pl* : a branch of mathematics dealing with the collection, analysis, interpretation, and presentation of masses of numerical data; *also* : a collection of such numerical data — **sta·tis·ti·cal** \-'tis-ti-kəl\ *adj* — **sta·tis·ti·cal·ly** \-ti-k(ə-)lē\ *adv*

sta·tor \'stāt-ər\ *n* : a stationary part in a machine in or about which a rotor revolves

stat·u·ary \'stach-ə-ˌwer-ē\ *n, pl* **-ar·ies** **1** : SCULPTURE **2** : a collection of statues — **statuary** *adj*

stat·ue \'stach-ü\ *n* : a likeness (as of a person or animal) sculptured, modeled, or cast in a solid substance (as marble or bronze)

stat·u·esque \ˌstach-ə-'wesk\ *adj* : resembling a statue esp. in well-proportioned or massive dignity

stat·u·ette \ˌstach-ə-'wet\ *n* : a small statue

stat·ure \'stach-ər\ *n* **1** : natural height (as of a person) in an upright position **2** : quality or status gained by growth, development, or achievement

sta·tus \'stāt-əs, 'stat-\ *n* **1** : position or rank in relation to others : STANDING **2** : CONDITION, SITUATION ⟨the economic *status* of a country⟩

sta·tus quo \ˌstāt-əs-'kwō, ˌstat-\ *n* : the existing state of affairs

stat·ute \'stach-üt, -ət\ *n* : a law enacted by the legislative branch of a government

statute mile *n* : MILE 1

stat·u·to·ry \'stach-ə-ˌtōr-ē, -ˌtȯr-\ *adj* **1** : of, relating to, or of the nature of a statute **2** : fixed by statute **3** : punishable by statute

¹**staunch** *var of* STANCH

²**staunch** \'stȯnch, 'stänch\ *adj* **1 a** : WATERTIGHT, SOUND ⟨a *staunch* ship⟩ **b** : strongly built : SUBSTANTIAL ⟨*staunch* foundations⟩ **2** : steadfast in loyalty or principle ⟨a *staunch* friend⟩ — **staunch·ly** *adv*

¹**stave** \'stāv\ *n* **1** : a wooden stick **2** : one of the narrow strips of wood or narrow iron plates placed edge to edge to form the sides, covering, or lining of a vessel (as a barrel or cask) or structure **3** : STANZA **4** : STAFF 3

²**stave** *vb* **staved** *or* **stove** \'stōv\; **stav·ing** **1** : to break in the staves of (a cask) **2** : to smash a hole in ⟨*stave* in a boat⟩

stave off *vb* : to ward or fend off ⟨*stave off* trouble⟩

staves *pl of* STAFF

¹**stay** \'stā\ *n* : a strong rope or wire used to steady or brace something (as a mast)

²**stay** *vb* : to fasten or brace with stays

³**stay** *vb* **stayed** \'stād\ *or* **staid** \'stād\; **stay·ing** **1** : to stop going forward : PAUSE **2** : to continue in a place or condition : REMAIN ⟨*stayed* at home⟩ **3** : to stand firm **4** : to take up residence : LODGE ⟨*stayed* in a hotel⟩ **5** : WAIT, DELAY **6** : to last out (as a race) **7** : CHECK, HALT ⟨*stay* an execution⟩ **8** : ALLAY, PACIFY

⁴**stay** *n* **1** : the action of halting : the state of being stopped **2** : a residence or sojourn in a place

⁵**stay** *n* **1 a** : something that serves as a prop : SUPPORT **b** : a thin firm strip (as of whalebone, steel, or plastic) used for stiffening a garment (as a corset) or part (as a shirt collar) **2** : a corset stiffened with stays — usu. used in pl.

⁶**stay** *vb* : to provide physical or moral support for

stay·sail \'stā-ˌsāl, -səl\ *n* : a fore-and-aft sail hoisted on a stay

stead \'sted\ *n* **1** : ADVANTAGE, SERVICE ⟨his knowledge of French stood him in good *stead*⟩ **2** : the office, place, or function of someone or something else ⟨acted in his brother's *stead*⟩

stead·fast \'sted-ˌfast\ *adj* **1 a** : firmly fixed in place **b** : not subject to change ⟨a *steadfast* purpose⟩ **2** : firm in belief, determination, or adherence : LOYAL ⟨*steadfast* friends⟩ — **stead·fast·ly** *adv* — **stead·fast·ness** \-ˌfas(t)-nəs\ *n*

¹**steady** \'sted-ē\ *adj* **stead·i·er**; **-est** **1 a** : firm in position : FIXED **b** : direct or sure in movement : UNFALTERING ⟨took *steady* aim⟩ **2 a** : REGULAR, UNIFORM ⟨a *steady* pace⟩ **b** : not fluctuating or varying widely ⟨*steady* prices⟩ **3 a** : not easily moved or upset : RESOLUTE **b** : constant in feeling, principle, purpose, or attachment : DEPENDABLE **c** : not given to dissipation or disorderly behavior : SOBER ⟨*steady* habits⟩ — **stead·i·ly** \'sted-ə-lē\ *adv* — **stead·i·ness** \'sted-ē-nəs\ *n*

²**steady** *vb* **stead·ied**; **steady·ing** : to make, keep, or become steady

³**steady** *adv* **1** : in a steady manner : STEADILY **2** : on the course set — used as a direction to the helmsman of a ship

⁴**steady** *n, pl* **stead·ies** : one that is steady; *esp* : a boyfriend or girl friend with whom one goes steady

steady state *n* **1** : a dynamically balanced condition of a system or process that when once established tends to persist **2** : a state of physiological equilibrium esp. in regard to a metabolic activity — **steady–state** *adj*

steady–state theory *n* : a theory in astronomy that states that the universe has always existed and has always been expanding

steak \'stāk\ *n* **1 a** : a slice of meat cut from a fleshy part of a beef carcass **b** : a similar slice of a specified meat other than beef **2** : a cross-section slice of a large fish (as salmon)

[1]steal \'stēl\ *vb* **stole** \'stōl\; **sto·len** \'stō-lən\; **steal·ing** **1** : to come or go secretly, gradually, or quietly ⟨*stole* out of the room⟩ **2 a** : to take and carry away without right and with intent to keep the property of another : ROB **b** : to take entirely to oneself or beyond one's proper share ⟨*steal* the show⟩ **3 a** : SMUGGLE **b** : to accomplish or get in a concealed or unobserved manner ⟨*steal* a nap⟩ **4 a** : to seize, gain, or win by trickery, skill, or daring ⟨a basketball player adept at *stealing* the ball from his opponents⟩ **b** : to gain a base in baseball by running without the aid of a hit or an error — **steal·er** *n*

[2]steal *n* **1** : the act or an instance of stealing **2** : something offered or purchased at a low price : BARGAIN

stealth \'stelth\ *n* : sly or secret action

stealthy \'stel-thē\ *adj* **stealth·i·er**; **-est** **1** : slow, deliberate, and secret in action or character **2** : intended to escape observation : FURTIVE

[1]steam \'stēm\ *n* **1 a** : the invisible vapor into which water is converted when heated to the boiling point **b** : the mist formed by the condensation on cooling of water vapor **2 a** : water vapor kept under pressure so as to supply energy for heating, cooking, or mechanical work **b** : the power so generated **3 a** : driving force : POWER ⟨arrived under their own *steam*⟩ **b** : emotional tension ⟨let off a little *steam*⟩

[2]steam *vb* **1** : to rise or pass off as vapor **2** : to give off steam or vapor **3** : to move or travel by or as if by the power of steam ⟨*steamed* up the river⟩ **4** : to be angry : BOIL ⟨was *steaming* over the insult⟩ **5** : to expose to the action of steam (as for softening or cooking) ⟨*steamed* clams⟩

steam·boat \'stēm-ˌbōt\ *n* : a boat propelled by steam power

steam engine *n* : an engine driven by steam; *esp* : a reciprocating engine having a piston driven in a closed cylinder by steam

steam·er \'stē-mər\ *n* **1** : a vessel in which something is steamed **2 a** : a ship propelled by steam **b** : an engine, machine, or vehicle operated by steam

steam fitter *n* : one that installs or repairs equipment (as steam pipes) for heating, ventilating, or refrigerating systems — **steam fitting** *n*

steam iron *n* : a pressing iron with a compartment holding water that is converted to steam by the iron's heat and emitted through holes in the bottom onto the fabric being pressed

[1]steam·roll·er \'stēm-'rō-lər\ *n* **1** : a steam-driven road roller **2** : a power or force that crushes opposition

[2]steamroller *also* **steam·roll** \-'rōl\ *vb* **1** : to crush with a steamroller **2** : to overwhelm by greatly superior force

steam·ship \'stēm-ˌship\ *n* : STEAMER 2a

steam shovel *n* : a power shovel operated by steam

steam turbine *n* : a turbine that is driven by the pressure of steam discharged at high velocity against the turbine vanes

steamy \'stē-mē\ *adj* **steam·i·er**; **-est** : consisting of, characterized by, or full of steam — **steam·i·ly** \-mə-lē\ *adv*

ste·ap·sin \stē-'ap-sən\ *n* : a fat-digesting enzyme in pancreatic juice

ste·a·rate \'stē-ə-ˌrāt\ *n* : a salt or ester of stearic acid

ste·ar·ic acid \stē-ˌar-ik-\ *n* : a white crystalline acid obtained by saponifying tallow or other hard fats containing stearin

ste·a·rin \'stē-ə-rən\ *n* **1** : an ester of glycerol and stearic acid that is a chief component of beef fat **2** *also* **ste·a·rine** \-rən, -ˌrēn\ : the solid portion of a fat

steed \'stēd\ *n* : HORSE; *esp* : a spirited horse

[1]steel \'stēl\ *n* **1** : hard and tough iron that contains carbon as an essential alloying constituent and is distinguished from cast iron by its malleability and lower carbon content **2 a** : a thrusting or cutting weapon **b** : an instrument (as a fluted round rod with a handle) for sharpening knives **c** : a piece of steel for striking sparks from flint **3** : a hard cold quality characteristic of steel ⟨a man of *steel*⟩

[2]steel *vb* **1** : to overlay, point, or edge with steel **2 a** : to cause to resemble steel **b** : to fill with resolution or determination

[3]steel *adj* **1** : made of or resembling steel **2** : of or relating to the production of steel

steel·head \'stēl-ˌhed\ *n* : a large silvery western No. American seagoing trout that ascends rivers to breed and is usu. classified with a race of rainbow trout

steel wool *n* : an abrasive material composed of long fine steel shavings and used esp. for scouring and burnishing

steel·work \'stēl-ˌwərk\ *n* **1** : work in steel **2** *pl* : an establishment where steel is made — **steel·work·er** \-ˌwər-kər\ *n*

steely \'stē-lē\ *adj* **steel·i·er**; **-est** **1** : made of steel **2** : resembling steel (as in hardness or color) — **steel·i·ness** *n*

steel·yard \'stēl-ˌyärd\ *n* : a balance on which something to be weighed is hung from the shorter arm of a lever and is balanced by a weight that slides along the longer arm which is marked with a scale

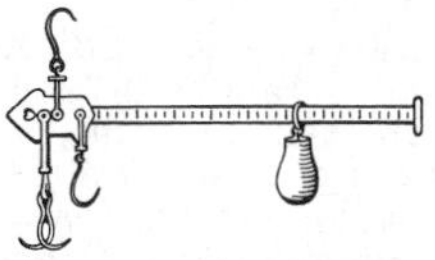

steelyard

[1]steep \'stēp\ *adj* **1** : making a large angle with the plane of the horizon : almost perpendicular **2** : being or characterized by a very rapid decline or increase **3** : too great or high : EXTREMES ⟨*steep* prices⟩ — **steep·ly** *adv*

[2]steep *n* : a precipitous place

[3]steep *vb* **1 a** : to soak in a liquid (as for softening, bleaching, or extracting a flavor) at a temperature under the boiling point ⟨*steep* tea⟩ **b** : to undergo the process of soaking in a liquid **2** : to saturate with or subject thoroughly to ⟨*steeped* in learning⟩ ***syn*** see SOAK

steep·en \'stē-pən\ *vb* **steep·ened**; **steep·en·ing** \'stēp-(ə-)ning\ : to make or become steeper

stee·ple \'stē-pəl\ *n* **1** : a tall structure usu. having a small spire at the top and surmounting a church tower **2** : a church tower — **stee·pled** \-pəld\ *adj*

stee·ple·chase \'stē-pəl-ˌchās\ *n* **1** : a cross-country race by horsemen **2** : a race over a course obstructed by obstacles (as hedges, walls, or hurdles) — **stee·ple·chas·er** \-ˌchā-sər\ *n*

stee·ple·jack \-ˌjak\ *n* : one who works on smokestacks, towers, or steeples

[1]steer \'sti(ə)r\ *n* : a domestic bull castrated before sexual maturity; *esp* : a young ox being raised for beef

[2]steer *vb* **1** : to direct the course or the course of : GUIDE ⟨*steer* by the stars⟩ ⟨*steer* a boat⟩ ⟨*steer* a conversation⟩ **2** : to set and hold to (a course) **3** : to pursue a course of action **4** : to be subject to guidance ⟨an automobile that *steers* well⟩ — **steer·a·ble** \'stir-ə-bəl\ *adj* — **steer·er** \'stir-ər\ *n* — **steer clear** : to keep entirely away ⟨*steer clear* of arguments⟩

S

steer·age \'sti(ə)r-ij\ *n* **1** : the act or practice of steering; *also* : DIRECTION **2** : a section in a passenger ship for passengers paying the lowest fares

steers·man \'sti(ə)rz-mən\ *n* : one who steers : HELMSMAN

steg·o·sau·rus \,steg-ə-'sȯr-əs\ *n* : any of a genus of large armored dinosaurs of the Upper Jurassic rocks of Colorado and Wyoming

stein \'stīn\ *n* **1** : an earthenware mug esp. for beer **2** : the quantity of beer that a stein holds

stel·lar \'stel-ər\ *adj* **1** : of or relating to the stars ⟨*stellar* light⟩ **2 a** : of or relating to a theatrical or film star : LEADING, PRINCIPAL ⟨a *stellar* role⟩ **b** : OUTSTANDING ⟨a *stellar* performance⟩

1**stem** \'stem\ *n* **1 a** : the main axis of a plant that develops buds and shoots instead of roots **b** : a plant part (as a petiole or stipe) that supports another **2** : the bow or prow of a ship **3** : a line of ancestry : STOCK **4** : the part of an inflected word that remains unchanged throughout an inflection **5** : something felt to resemble a plant stem: as **a** : the short perpendicular line extending from the head of a musical note **b** : the part of a tobacco pipe from the bowl outward **c** : a spindle of a mechanical part — **stem·less** \-ləs\ *adj* — **from stem to stern** : THROUGHOUT, THOROUGHLY

2**stem** *vb* **stemmed**; **stem·ming** : to make headway against (as an adverse tide, current, or wind)

3**stem** *vb* **stemmed**; **stem·ming** **1** : to have or trace an origin or development : DERIVE ⟨illness that *stems* from an accident⟩ **2** : to remove the stem from — **stem·mer** *n*

4**stem** *vb* **stemmed**; **stem·ming** **1** : to stop, check, or restrain by or as if by damming **2** : to become checked or stanched

stem cutting *n* : a piece of a plant stem or branch used in propagation

1**stemmed** \'stemd\ *adj* : having a stem

2**stemmed** *adj* : having the stem removed ⟨*stemmed* berries⟩

stench \'stench\ *n* : an extremely disagreeable smell : STINK

1**sten·cil** \'sten(t)-səl\ *n* **1** : a piece of material (as a sheet of paper, thin wax, or woven fabric) perforated with lettering or a design through which ink or paint is forced onto a surface to be printed **2** : a pattern, design, or print produced by means of a stencil

2**stencil** *vb* **-ciled** *or* **-cilled**; **-cil·ing** *or* **-cil·ling** \-s(ə-)liŋ\ **1** : to produce by stencil **2** : to mark or paint with a stencil

steno \'sten-ō\ *n, pl* **sten·os** : STENOGRAPHER

ste·nog·ra·pher \stə-'näg-rə-fər\ *n* **1** : a writer of shorthand **2** : one employed chiefly to take and transcribe dictation

ste·nog·ra·phy \-fē\ *n* : the art or process of writing in shorthand — **sten·o·graph·ic** \,sten-ə-'graf-ik\ *adj* — **sten·o·graph·i·cal·ly** \-'graf-i-k(ə-)lē\ *adv*

sten·to·ri·an \sten-'tōr-ē-ən, -'tȯr-\ *adj* : extremely loud ⟨a *stentorian* voice⟩

1**step** \'step\ *n* **1** : a rest for the foot in ascending or descending : STAIR, RUNG **2 a** : an advance or movement made by raising the foot and bringing it down elsewhere **b** : a combination of foot or foot and body movements constituting a unit or a repeated pattern **3** : manner of walking : STRIDE ⟨know a man by his *step*⟩ **4** : FOOTPRINT **5** : the sound of a footstep **6** : the space passed over in one step **7** : a short distance ⟨only a *step* away⟩ **8** : the height of one stair **9** *pl* : COURSE, WAY ⟨directed his *steps* down the path⟩ **10 a** : a degree, grade, or rank in a scale ⟨one *step* nearer graduation⟩ **b** : a stage in a process **11** : an action, proceeding, or measure often occurring as one in a series ⟨took *steps* to correct the situation⟩ **12** : a musical scale degree — **step·like** \-,līk\ *adj* — **stepped** \'stept\ *adj*

2**step** *vb* **stepped**; **step·ping** **1 a** : to move or take by raising the foot and bringing it down elsewhere or by moving each foot in succession ⟨*step* three paces⟩ ⟨*stepped* ashore⟩ **b** : DANCE **2 a** : to go or traverse on foot : WALK ⟨*step* outside⟩ **b** : to move briskly ⟨the horse *stepped* along⟩ ⟨kept up *stepping*⟩ **3** : to press down with the foot ⟨*step* on a nail⟩ **4** : to come as if at a single step ⟨*step* into a good job⟩ **5** : to measure by steps ⟨*step* off 50 yards⟩ — **step·per** *n*

step·broth·er \'step-,brəth-ər\ *n* : a son of one's stepparent by a former marriage

step–by–step \,step-bə-'step\ *adj* : marked by successive degrees usu. of limited extent : GRADUAL

step·child \'step-,chīld\ *n* : a child of one's wife or husband by a former marriage

step·daugh·ter \-,dȯt-ər\ *n* : a daughter of one's wife or husband by a former marriage

step down \'step-'daủn\ *vb* **1** : to give up a position **2** : to lower the voltage of (a current) by means of a transformer — **step–down** \-,daủn\ *adj*

step·fa·ther \'step-,fäth-ər\ *n* : the husband of one's mother by a subsequent marriage

step–in \'step-,in\ *n* **1** : an article of clothing that is put on by being stepped into **2** *pl* : a woman's brief panties

step·lad·der \-,lad-ər\ *n* : a portable set of steps with a hinged frame for steadying

step·moth·er \-,məth-ər\ *n* : the wife of one's father by a subsequent marriage

step out *vb* **1** : to go away from a place usu. for a short distance and for a short time ⟨*stepped out* for a walk⟩ **2** : to lead an active social life

step·par·ent \'step-,par-ənt, -,per-\ *n* : the husband or wife of one's mother or father by a subsequent marriage

steppe \'step\ *n* : dry usu. rather level predominantly grass-covered land in regions of wide temperature range (as in southeastern Europe and parts of Asia)

step·ping–stone \'step-iŋ-,stōn\ *n* **1** : a stone on which to step (as in crossing a stream) **2** : a means of progress or advancement ⟨a *stepping-stone* to success⟩

step rocket *n* : a multistage rocket whose sections are fired successively

step·sis·ter \'step-,sis-tər\ *n* : a daughter of one's stepparent by a former marriage

step·son \-,sən\ *n* : a son of one's husband or wife by a former marriage

step up *vb* **1** : to increase the voltage of (a current) by means of a transformer **2** : to increase, augment, or advance ⟨*step up* production⟩

-ster \stər\ *n comb form* **1** : one that does or handles or operates ⟨spin*ster*⟩ ⟨tap*ster*⟩ ⟨team*ster*⟩ **2** : one that makes or uses ⟨song*ster*⟩ ⟨pun*ster*⟩ **3** : one that is associated with or participates in ⟨game*ster*⟩ ⟨gang*ster*⟩ **4** : one that is ⟨young*ster*⟩

stere \'sti(ə)r, 'ste(ə)r\ *n* — see METRIC SYSTEM table

ster·eo \'ster-ē-,ō\ *n* [short for *stereophonic reproduction*, from Greek *stereos* "solid" and *phōnē* "sound"] **1** : stereophonic reproduction **2** : a stereophonic sound system — **stereo** *adj*

ster·e·o·phon·ic \ˌster-ē-ə-'fän-ik\ *adj* : giving, relating to, or constituting a three-dimensional effect of reproduced sound

ster·e·op·ti·con \ˌster-ē-'äp-ti-kən\ *n* : a projector for transparent slides

ster·e·o·scope \'ster-ē-ə-ˌskōp\ *n* : an optical instrument that blends two slightly different pictures of the same subject to produce a three-dimensional effect — **ster·e·o·scop·ic** \ˌster-ē-ə-'skäp-ik\ *adj* — **ster·e·o·scop·i·cal·ly** \-'skäp-i-k(ə-)lē\ *adv*

ster·e·o·type \'ster-ē-ə-ˌtīp\ *n* **1** : a solid metal printing plate made by casting molten metal in a mold made from the original type **2** : something conforming to a general pattern and lacking individual distinguishing marks or qualities — **stereotype** *vb*

ster·e·o·typed \-ˌtīpt\ *adj* : repeated without variation : lacking originality

ster·ile \'ster-əl\ *adj* **1** : not able to bear fruit, crops, or offspring : not fertile ⟨*sterile* soil⟩ **2** : free from living organisms and esp. microorganisms ⟨*sterile* dressing for a wound⟩ — **ste·ril·i·ty** \stə-'ril-ət-ē\ *n*

ster·il·ize \'ster-ə-ˌlīz\ *vb* : to make sterile : free from living organisms (as bacteria) — **ster·il·i·za·tion** \ˌster-ə-lə-'zā-shən\ *n* — **ster·il·iz·er** \'ster-ə-ˌlī-zər\ *n*

1**ster·ling** \'stər-ling\ *n* [from the phrase *pound sterling*, the British monetary pound, but meaning originally "a pound by weight of sterlings", from Middle English *sterling* "silver penny"] **1** : British money **2** : sterling silver or articles of it

2**sterling** *adj* **1** : of or relating to British sterling **2 a** : having a fixed standard of purity usu. 925 parts of silver with 75 parts of copper ⟨*sterling* silver⟩ **b** : made of sterling silver **3** : conforming to the highest standard ⟨a man of *sterling* quality⟩

1**stern** \'stərn\ *adj* **1** : hard and severe in nature or manner ⟨a *stern* judge⟩ **2** : not inviting or attractive : FORBIDDING, GRIM **3** : showing severity : HARSH **4** : STOUT, RESOLUTE ⟨*stern* resolve⟩ — **stern·ly** *adv* — **stern·ness** \'stərn-nəs\ *n*

2**stern** *n* **1** : the rear end of a boat **2** : a hinder or rear part

ster·num \'stər-nəm\ *n, pl* **sternums** *or* **ster·na** \-nə\ : a compound ventral bone or cartilage connecting the ribs in front in most vertebrates above the fishes — called also *breastbone*

stern–wheel·er \'stərn-'hwē-lər\ *n* : a paddle-wheel steamer having a stern wheel instead of side wheels

steth·o·scope \'steth-ə-ˌskōp\ *n* : an instrument used for listening to sounds produced in the body and esp. in the chest

stethoscope

ste·ve·dore \'stē-və-ˌdōr, -ˌdȯr\ *n* : a person whose work is to load and unload boats in port — **stevedore** *vb*

1**stew** \'st(y)ü\ *vb* **1** : to boil slowly : SIMMER **2** : to become agitated or worried : FRET

2**stew** *n* **1** : food (as meat with vegetables) prepared by slow boiling **2** : a state of excitement, worry, or confusion ⟨in a *stew* over nothing⟩

stew·ard \'st(y)ü-ərd, 'st(y)u̇(-ə)rd\ *n* [from Old English *stīweard*, from *stig* "hall", "sty" and *weard* "keeper", "warder"] **1** : a manager of a large household, estate, or organization **2 a** : a person employed to supervise the provision and distribution of food (as on a ship) **b** : a worker who serves and attends the needs of passengers (as on a train, airplane, or ship) — **stew·ard·ess** \-əs\ *n*

stew·ard·ship \-ˌship\ *n* : the office, duties, and obligations of a steward

1**stick** \'stik\ *n* **1** : a cut or broken branch or twig esp. when dry and dead **2** : a long slender piece of wood : CLUB, STAFF **3** : WALKING STICK **4** : an implement used for striking or propelling an object in a game **5 a** : something like a stick in shape, origin, or use ⟨a *stick* of dynamite⟩ **b** : an airplane lever operating the elevators and ailerons **c** : the gearshift lever of an automobile **6** : a person who is dull, stiff, and lifeless **7** *pl* : remote or rural districts ⟨way out in the *sticks*⟩

2**stick** *vb* **stuck** \'stək\; **stick·ing** **1 a** : PIERCE, STAB **b** : to kill by piercing **2** : to cause to penetrate ⟨*stuck* a needle in her finger⟩ **3** : FASTEN, ATTACH ⟨*stuck* a flower in his buttonhole⟩ **4** : to push out, up, or under ⟨*stuck* out his hand⟩ **5** : to put or set in a specified place or position ⟨*stuck* his cap on his head⟩ **6** : to adhere to a surface ⟨snowflakes *stuck* on the windowpane⟩ **7** : to halt the movement or action of **8** : BAFFLE, STUMP ⟨were all *stuck* by his question⟩ **9 a** : CHEAT, DEFRAUD **b** : to saddle with something disadvantageous or disagreeable ⟨*stuck* with the job of cleaning up⟩ **10** : to hold to something firmly by or as if by adhesion ⟨car *stuck* in mud⟩ **11 a** : to remain in a place, situation, or environment **b** : CLING **12 a** : to become blocked, wedged, or jammed **b** : to be unable to proceed through fear or scruple **13** : PROJECT, PROTRUDE ⟨a football player with his hair *sticking* out from under his helmet⟩

stick around *vb* : to stay or wait about : LINGER

stick·er \'stik-ər\ *n* **1** : something that pierces with a point **2 a** : something that adheres (as a bur) or causes adhesion (as glue) **b** : a slip of paper with gummed back that adheres to a surface — **stick·er·like** \-ˌlīk\ *adj*

stick insect *n* : any of various usu. wingless insects that are distantly related to the mantises and have a long round body resembling a stick

stick–in–the–mud \'stik-ən-t͟hə-ˌməd\ *n* : one who is slow, old-fashioned, or unprogressive

stick·le \'stik-əl\ *vb* **stick·led**; **stick·ling** \-(ə-)ling\ **1** : to fight for something esp. stubbornly and often on insufficient grounds **2** : to feel often excessive scruples — **stick·ler** \-(ə-)lər\ *n*

stick·le·back \'stik-əl-ˌbak\ *n* : any of numerous small scaleless fishes having two or more free spines on the back

stick out *vb* **1** : to be conspicuous **2** : to put up with : ENDURE ⟨*stuck out* the winter in the old cabin⟩

stick·pin \'stik-ˌpin\ *n* : an ornamental pin worn in a necktie

stick·tight \-ˌtīt\ *n* : BUR MARIGOLD

stick up \'stik-'əp\ *vb* : to rob at the point of a gun — **stick·up** \-ˌəp\ *n*

sticky \'stik-ē\ *adj* **stick·i·er**; **-est** **1 a** : ADHESIVE, GLUEY **b** : coated with a sticky substance **2** : HUMID, MUGGY **3** : tending to stick ⟨*sticky* valve⟩ — **stick·i·ly** \'stik-ə-lē\ *adv* — **stick·i·ness** \'stik-ē-nəs\ *n*

stiff \'stif\ *adj* **1** : not easily bent : RIGID **2 a** : lacking in normal or usual suppleness or mobility ⟨*stiff* muscles⟩ ⟨*stiff* valves⟩ **b** : not flowing easily : THICK, HEAVY ⟨beat egg whites until *stiff*⟩ **3 a** : FIRM, RESOLUTE **b** : formally reserved in manner **4** : hard fought ⟨a *stiff* fight⟩ **5 a** : exerting great force : STRONG, VIGOROUS ⟨*stiff* wind⟩ **b** : POTENT

⟨a *stiff* dose⟩ **6 a :** HARSH, SEVERE ⟨a *stiff* penalty⟩ **b :** difficult to do or cope with ⟨a *stiff* task⟩ **7 :** EXPENSIVE, STEEP ⟨a *stiff* price⟩ — **stiff·ly** *adv* — **stiff·ness** *n*

stiff·en \'stif-ən\ *vb* **stiff·ened; stiff·en·ing** \-(ə-)ning\ **:** to make or become stiff or stiffer — **stiff·en·er** \-(ə-)nər\ *n*

sti·fle \'stī-fəl\ *vb* **sti·fled; sti·fling** \-f(ə-)ling\ **1 a :** to kill by depriving of or die from lack of oxygen or air **b :** to smother by or as if by depriving of air ⟨*stifle* a fire⟩ **2 :** to keep in check by deliberate effort **:** REPRESS ⟨*stifle* his anger⟩ — **sti·fling·ly** \-f(ə-)ling-lē\ *adv*

stig·ma \'stig-mə\ *n, pl* **stig·ma·ta** \stig-'mät-ə, 'stig-mət-ə\ *or* **stigmas 1 a :** a mark of shame or discredit **:** STAIN **b :** an identifying mark or characteristic; *esp* **:** a specific diagnostic sign of a disease **2** *pl* **:** bodily marks or pains resembling the wounds of the crucified Christ **3 :** the part of the pistil of a flower which receives the pollen grains and on which they germinate **4 :** a minute spot due to hemorrhage that occurs in certain diseases — **stig·mat·ic** \stig-'mat-ik\ *adj*

stig·ma·tize \'stig-mə-,tīz\ *vb* **:** to mark with a stigma; *esp* **:** to describe or identify as disgraceful or shameful

stil·bite \'stil-,bīt\ *n* **:** a mineral consisting of a hydrous silicate of aluminum, calcium, and sodium in sheaflike aggregations of crystals

stile \'stīl\ *n* **1 :** a step or set of steps for passing over a fence or wall **2 :** TURNSTILE

sti·let·to \stə-'let-ō\ *n, pl* **-tos** *or* **-toes 1 :** a slender dagger **2 :** a pointed instrument for piercing holes for eyelets or embroidery

1still \'stil\ *adj* **1 a :** MOTIONLESS **b :** not carbonated ⟨*still* wine⟩ **c :** of, relating to, or being an ordinary photograph as distinguished from a motion picture **2 :** uttering no sound **:** QUIET **3 a :** CALM, TRANQUIL **b :** PEACEFUL — **still·ness** *n*

2still *vb* **1 a :** ALLAY, CALM **b :** SETTLE **2 :** to make or become still **:** QUIET

3still *adv* **1 :** without motion ⟨sit *still*⟩ **2 :** up to this or that time ⟨*still* lived there⟩ ⟨drink it while it's *still* hot⟩ **3 :** in spite of that **:** NEVERTHELESS ⟨those who take the greatest care *still* make mistakes⟩ **4 :** EVEN, YET ⟨won *still* another tournament⟩

4still *n* **1 :** QUIET, SILENCE **2 :** a still photograph

5still *n* **1 :** DISTILLERY **2 :** apparatus used in distillation

still·born \'stil-'bȯrn\ *adj* **:** dead at birth

still life *n, pl* **still lifes :** a picture of predominantly inanimate objects

stilly \'stil-ē\ *adj* **still·i·er; -est :** STILL

stilt \'stilt\ *n* **1 :** one of two poles each with a rest or strap for the foot used to elevate the wearer above the ground in walking **2 :** a pile or post serving as one of the supports of a structure above ground or water level

stilt·ed \'stil-təd\ *adj* **:** stiffly formal **:** not easy and natural ⟨a *stilted* speech⟩

stim·u·lant \'stim-yə-lənt\ *n* **1 :** an agent (as a drug) that temporarily increases the physiological activity or efficiency of a tissue or organ **2 :** STIMULUS ⟨a *stimulant* to trade⟩ — **stimulant** *adj*

stim·u·late \-,lāt\ *vb* **1 :** to make active or more active **:** ANIMATE, AROUSE ⟨*stimulate* industry⟩ **2 :** to act toward as a physiological stimulus or stimulant — **stim·u·la·tion** \,stim-yə-'lā-shən\ *n*

stim·u·lus \'stim-yə-ləs\ *n, pl* **-li** \-,lī, -,lē\ [from Latin, literally "prick", "goad"] **1 :** something that rouses or incites to activity **:** INCENTIVE ⟨new *stimuli* to commerce and agriculture⟩ **2 :** an influence that acts to alter bodily activity (as by exciting a sensory organ) ⟨heat, light, and sound are common physical *stimuli*⟩

1sting \'sting\ *vb* **stung** \'stəng\; **sting·ing** \'sting-ing\ **1 a :** to prick painfully esp. with a sharp or poisonous process ⟨*stung* by a bee⟩ **b :** to affect with or feel sharp, quick, and usu. burning pain or smart ⟨hail *stung* their faces⟩ **2 :** to cause to suffer acutely ⟨*stung* with remorse⟩ **3 :** OVERCHARGE, CHEAT ⟨got *stung* on the deal⟩ **4 :** to use a stinger

2sting *n* **1 a :** the act of stinging **b :** a wound or pain caused by or as if by stinging **2 :** STINGER 2 — **sting·less** \'sting-ləs\ *adj*

sting·er \'sting-ər\ *n* **1 :** one that stings; *esp* **:** a sharp blow or remark **2 :** a sharp organ of offense and defense (as of a bee or scorpion) usu. adapted to wound by piercing and injecting a poisonous secretion

sting·ray \'sting-,rā\ *n* **:** any of numerous rays with

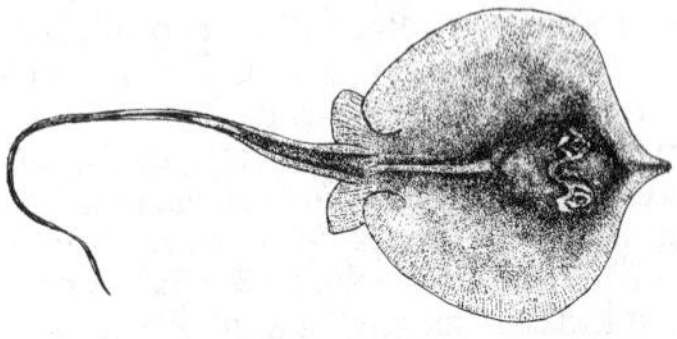

stingray
(about 5 ft. across)

one or more large sharp barbed spines near the base of the whiplike tail

stin·gy \'stin-jē\ *adj* **stin·gi·er; -est 1 :** not generous or liberal **:** sparing or scant in giving or spending **2 :** SCANTY, MEAGER ⟨*stingy* portion⟩ — **stin·gi·ly** \-jə-lē\ *adv* — **stin·gi·ness** \-jē-nəs\ *n*

1stink \'stingk\ *vb* **stank** \'stangk\ *or* **stunk** \'stəngk\; **stunk; stink·ing 1 :** to give forth or cause to have a strong and offensive smell ⟨*stink* up a room⟩ **2 :** to be offensive or of very poor quality — **stink·er** *n*

2stink *n* **1 :** a strong offensive odor **:** STENCH **2 :** a public outcry against something offensive ⟨raised a *stink* about gambling⟩ — **stinky** \'sting-kē\ *adj*

stink·bug \'stingk-,bəg\ *n* **:** any of various true bugs that emit a disagreeable odor

1stint \'stint\ *vb* **1 :** to limit in share or portion **:** cut short in amount ⟨*stint* the children's milk⟩ **2 :** to be sparing or frugal — **stint·er** *n*

2stint *n* **1 :** RESTRAINT, LIMITATION ⟨donated money without *stint*⟩ **2 :** a definite quantity of work assigned

stipe \'stīp\ *n* **:** a short plant stalk; *esp* **:** one supporting a fern frond or the cap of a mushroom

sti·pend \'stī-,pend, -pənd\ *n* **:** a fixed sum of money paid periodically for services or to defray expenses

stip·ple \'stip-əl\ *vb* **stip·pled; stip·pling** \-(ə-)ling\ **1 :** to engrave by means of dots **2 :** to depict (as in paint or ink) by small short touches that together produce an even or softly graded shadow — **stipple** *n* — **stip·pler** \-(ə-)lər\ *n*

stip·u·late \'stip-yə-ˌlāt\ *vb* : to make an agreement or arrange as part of an agreement; *esp* : to demand or insist on as a condition in an agreement
stip·u·la·tion \ˌstip-yə-'lā-shən\ *n* **1** : an act of stipulating **2** : something stipulated; *esp* : a condition required as part of an agreement
stip·ule \'stip-yül\ *n* : either of a pair of small leaflike parts at the base of the leaf in many plants — see LEAF illustration
[1]**stir** \'stər\ *vb* **stirred**; **stir·ring** **1 a** : to make or cause to make an esp. slight movement or change of position **b** : to disturb the quiet of : AGITATE **2** : to mix, dissolve, or make esp. by a continued circular movement **3** : to rouse to activity : INCITE, QUICKEN ⟨his emotions *stirred*⟩ ⟨*stirred* the fire⟩ ⟨*stir* up trouble⟩ **4** : to be active or busy ⟨not a creature was *stirring*⟩ — **stir·rer** *n*
[2]**stir** *n* **1 a** : a state of disturbance, agitation, or activity **b** : widespread notice and discussion : IMPRESSION **2 a** : a slight movement **b** : a stirring movement
stir·ring \'stər-ing\ *adj* : ROUSING, INSPIRING ⟨a *stirring* song⟩
stir·rup \'stər-əp, 'stə-rəp\ *n* **1** : either of a pair of small light frames often of metal hung by straps from a saddle and used as a support for the foot of a horseback rider **2** : the innermost of the chain of small bones in the ears of a mammal
[1]**stitch** \'stich\ *n* **1** : a local sharp and sudden pain esp. in the side **2 a** : one in-and-out movement of a threaded needle in sewing or embroidering **b** : a portion of thread left in the material after one stitch **3** : a single loop of thread or yarn around a knitting needle or crochet hook **4** : a series of stitches **5** : a method of stitching — **in stitches** : in a state of uncontrollable laughter
[2]**stitch** *vb* **1 a** : to join with or as if with stitches **b** : to make, mend, or decorate with or as if with stitches **2** : to do needlework : SEW — **stitch·er** *n*
stoat \'stōt\ *n* : the European ermine esp. in its brown summer coat
stob \'stäb\ *n, chiefly dial* : STAKE, POST
[1]**stock** \'stäk\ *n* **1 a** : STUMP **b** *archaic* : a log or block of wood **2 a** : something without life or consciousness **b** : a dull, stupid, or lifeless person **3** *pl* : a timber frame with holes to contain the feet or feet and hands of an offender undergoing public punishment **4** : the wooden part by which a rifle or shotgun is held during firing **5 a** : the main stem of a plant : TRUNK **b** : a plant or plant part that will yield mostly underground parts in a graft **6 a** : the original (as a man, race, or language) from which others derive : SOURCE **b** : ANCESTRY, LINEAGE **7 a** : the equipment or goods of an establishment **b** : farm animals : LIVESTOCK **8 a** : the capital that a firm employs in the conduct of business **b** : the ownership element of a corporation divided into shares giving to the owners an interest in its assets and earnings and usu. voting power ⟨ten shares of *stock*⟩ **9** : any of a genus of herbaceous or shrubby plants related to the mustard and having clusters of usu. sweet-scented flowers **10** : a wide band or scarf worn about the neck esp. by some clergymen **11 a** : liquid in which meat, fish, or vegetables have been simmered and which is used as a basis for soup, stew, or gravy **b** : RAW MATERIAL **12** : confidence placed in one **13** : the production and presentation of plays by a stock company
[2]**stock** *vb* **1** : to fit to or with a stock **2 a** : to provide with or acquire stock or a stock ⟨*stock* up on food⟩ **b** : to procure or keep a stock of ⟨a store that *stocks* only the finest goods⟩
[3]**stock** *adj* **1** : kept regularly in stock ⟨comes in *stock* sizes⟩ ⟨a *stock* model⟩ **2** : commonly used or brought forward : STANDARD ⟨the *stock* answer⟩
[1]**stock·ade** \stä-'kād\ *n* **1** : a line of stout posts set firmly to form a defense **2 a** : an enclosure or pen made with posts and stakes **b** : an enclosure in which prisoners are kept
[2]**stockade** *vb* : to fortify or surround with a stockade
stock·bro·ker \'stäk-ˌbrō-kər\ *n* : one that executes orders to buy and sell securities
stock car *n* **1** : an automotive vehicle of a model and type kept in stock for regular sales **2** : a racing car having the basic chassis of a commercially produced assembly-line model
stock company *n* **1** : a corporation whose capital is represented by stock **2** : a theatrical company attached to a repertory theater
stock exchange *n* **1** : a place where the buying and selling of shares of stock is conducted **2** : an association of stockbrokers
stock·hold·er \'stäk-ˌhōl-dər\ *n* : an owner of stocks
stock·ing \'stäk-ing\ *n* : a close-fitting usu. knit covering for the foot and leg
stocking cap *n* : a long knitted cone-shaped cap usu. with a tassel or pompon on the top
stock market *n* : STOCK EXCHANGE 1
stock·pile \'stäk-ˌpīl\ *n* : a reserve supply esp. of something essential accumulated within a country for use during a shortage — **stockpile** *vb*
stock·room \-ˌrüm, -ˌrům\ *n* : a storage place for supplies or goods used in a business
stock–still \-'stil\ *adj* : very still : MOTIONLESS
stocky \'stäk-ē\ *adj* **stock·i·er**; **-est** : compact, sturdy, and relatively thick in build : THICKSET — **stock·i·ly** \'stäk-ə-lē\ *adv*
stock·yard \'stäk-ˌyärd\ *n* : a yard in which livestock are kept temporarily for slaughter, market, or shipping
stodgy \'stäj-ē\ *adj* **stodg·i·er**; **-est** **1** : moving in a slow plodding way esp. as a result of physical bulkiness **2** : having no excitement or interest : DULL, BORING **3** : extremely old-fashioned in attitude or outlook — **stodg·i·ly** \'stäj-ə-lē\ *adv*
[1]**sto·ic** \'stō-ik\ *n* : one who appears or claims to be indifferent to pleasure or pain
[2]**stoic** *or* **sto·i·cal** \'stō-i-kəl\ *adj* : indifferent to pleasure or pain — **sto·i·cal·ly** \-i-k(ə-)lē\ *adv*
stoke \'stōk\ *vb* **1** : to stir up or tend ⟨*stoke* the fire⟩ **2** : to supply with fuel ⟨*stoke* a furnace⟩
stoke·hold \-ˌhōld\ *n* **1** : the space in front of the boilers of a ship from which the furnaces are fed **2** : a room containing a ship's boilers
stoke·hole \-ˌhōl\ *n* **1** : the mouth to the grate of a furnace **2** : STOKEHOLD
stok·er \'stō-kər\ *n* **1** : one that tends a furnace; *esp* : one that tends a ship's steam boiler **2** : a machine for feeding a fire
[1]**stole** *past of* STEAL
[2]**stole** \'stōl\ *n* **1** : a long narrow band worn around the neck by bishops and priests and over the left shoulder by deacons in ceremonies **2** : a long wide scarf or similar covering worn by women usu. across the shoulders
stolen *past part of* STEAL
stol·id \'stäl-əd\ *adj* : having or expressing little or no sensibility : not easily aroused or excited — **stol·id·ly** *adv*
sto·lon \'stō-lən, -ˌlän\ *n* **1** : a horizontal branch from the base of a plant that produces new plants from buds at its tip or nodes (as in the strawberry) **2** : an extension of the body wall (as of a hydrozoan) forming buds that reproduce the organism

sto·ma \'stō-mə\ *n, pl* **sto·ma·ta** \-mət-ə\ *also* **stomas** : a small opening giving passage to moisture and gases through the epidermis of a leaf

1**stom·ach** \'stəm-ək, -ik\ *n* **1 a** : a pouch of the vertebrate alimentary canal into which food goes for further mixing and digestion after it leaves the mouth and passes down the throat; *also* : a cavity with a similar function in an invertebrate animal **b** : the part of the body that contains the stomach : BELLY, ABDOMEN **2 a** : desire for food caused by hunger : APPETITE **b** : INCLINATION, DESIRE ⟨no *stomach* for a quarrel⟩ — **stomach** *adj*

2**stomach** *vb* : to bear without overt reaction or resentment : put up with ⟨could not *stomach* the smell⟩

stom·ach·ache \-,āk\ *n* : pain in or in the region of the stomach

stomp \'stämp\ *vb* **1** : to strike or beat forcibly with the bottom of the foot **2** : to bring down heavily or forcibly ⟨*stomping* his foot⟩ **3** : to walk heavily or noisily ⟨angrily *stomping* around the house⟩ — **stomp** *n* — **stomp·er** *n*

1**stone** \'stōn\ *n* **1** : earth or mineral matter hardened in a mass **2** : a piece of rock not as fine as gravel ⟨throw *stones*⟩ **3** : rock used as a material esp. for building **4** : a piece of rock used for some special purpose (as for a monument at a grave) **5** : JEWEL, GEM ⟨precious *stones*⟩ **6** : CALCULUS 1 **7** : a hard stony seed or one (as of a plum) enclosed in a stony cover **8** *pl usu* **stone** : any of various units of weight; *esp* : a British unit equal to 14 pounds

2**stone** *vb* **1** : to hurl stones at; *esp* : to kill by hitting with stones **2** : to remove the stones of (a fruit) — **ston·er** *n*

3**stone** *adj* : of, relating to, or made of stone

Stone Age *n* : the first known period of prehistoric human culture characterized by the use of stone tools

stone–blind \'stōn-'blīnd\ *adj* : totally blind

stone–broke \-'brōk\ *adj* : completely broke

stone·crop \-,kräp\ *n* : SEDUM; *esp* : a mossy evergreen creeping sedum with pungent leaves

stone·cut·ter \-,kət-ər\ *n* **1** : a person who cuts, carves, or dresses stone **2** : a machine for dressing stone — **stone·cut·ting** \-,kət-ing\ *n*

stone–deaf \-'def\ *adj* : totally deaf

stone fly *n* : any of an order of 4-winged insects with aquatic gilled nymphs used by anglers for bait

stone·ma·son \'stōn-,mā-sən\ *n* : a mason who builds with stone

stone·ware \-,wa(ə)r, -,we(ə)r\ *n* : an opaque glazed or unglazed pottery that is well vitrified and nonporous

stone·work \-,wərk\ *n* **1** : a structure or part built of stone : MASONRY **2** : the shaping, preparation, or setting of stone — **stone·work·er** \-,wər-kər\ *n*

stony *also* **ston·ey** \'stō-nē\ *adj* **ston·i·er**; **-est** : abounding in or having the nature of stone : ROCKY

stood *past of* STAND

stooge \'stüj\ *n* **1** : an actor who usu. by asking questions prepares the way for a principal comedian's jokes **2** : one who slavishly follows or serves another — **stooge** *vb*

stool \'stül\ *n* **1 a** : a seat without back or arms **b** : FOOTSTOOL **2 a** : a seat used while defecating or urinating **b** : a discharge of fecal matter

ə abut	ər further		a back	ā bake
ä cot, cart	au̇ out	ch chin	e less	ē easy
g gift	i trip	ī life	j joke	ng sing	ō flow
ȯ flaw	ȯi coin	th thin	th this	ü loot
u̇ foot	y yet	yü few	yu̇ furious	zh vision

stool pigeon *n* **1** : a pigeon used as a decoy to draw others within a net **2** : a person acting as a spy or informer for the police

1**stoop** \'stüp\ *vb* **1** : to bend down or over **2** : to carry the head and shoulders or the upper part of the body bent forward **3** : to do something that is beneath one : degrade or debase oneself ⟨*stoop* to lying⟩

2**stoop** *n* **1** : an act of bending the body forward **2** : a temporary or habitual forward bend of the back and shoulders

3**stoop** *n* : a porch, platform, entrance stairway, or small veranda at a house door

1**stop** \'stäp\ *vb* **stopped**; **stop·ping** **1** : to close an opening by filling or blocking it : PLUG ⟨nose *stopped* up by a cold⟩ **2** : CHECK, RESTRAIN ⟨*stopped* him from going⟩ **3** : to halt the movement or progress of ⟨*stop* the car⟩ **4** : to instruct one's banker not to honor or pay ⟨*stop* payment on a check⟩ **5** : to regulate the pitch of (as a violin string) by pressing with the finger **6** : to come to an end : cease activity or operation **7** : to make a visit ⟨*stopping* with friends for a week⟩

2**stop** *n* **1** : CESSATION, END **2 a** : a graduated set of organ pipes of like kind and tone quality **b** : STOP KNOB **3** : something that impedes, obstructs, or brings to a halt : IMPEDIMENT, OBSTACLE **4** : a device for arresting or limiting motion ⟨door was held open by a *stop*⟩ **5** : the act of stopping : the state of being stopped **6** : a halt in a journey : STAY **7** *chiefly Brit* : any of several punctuation marks **8** : a consonant in the articulation of which there is a stage (as in the *p* of *apt* or the *g* of *tiger*) when the breath passage is completely closed

3**stop** *adj* : serving to stop : designed to stop ⟨*stop* line⟩ ⟨*stop* signal⟩ ⟨*stop* valve⟩

stop·cock \'stäp-,käk\ *n* : a cock for stopping or regulating flow (as through a pipe)

stop·gap \'stäp-,gap\ *n* : something that fills a gap : a temporary substitute or expedient

stop knob *n* : one of the handles by which an organist draws or shuts off a particular stop

stop·light \'stäp-,līt\ *n* **1** : a light on the rear of a motor vehicle that is illuminated when the driver presses the brake pedal **2** : TRAFFIC SIGNAL

stop·over \'stäp-,ō-vər\ *n* **1** : a stop at an intermediate point in one's journey **2** : a stopping place on a journey

stop·page \'stäp-ij\ *n* : the act of stopping : the state of being stopped

1**stop·per** \'stäp-ər\ *n* **1** : one that brings to a halt : CHECK **2** : one that closes, shuts, or fills up; *esp* : something used to plug an opening

2**stopper** *vb* : to close or secure with or as if with a stopper

stop·ple \'stäp-əl\ *n* : STOPPER — **stopple** *vb*

stop·watch \'stäp-,wäch\ *n* : a watch having a hand that can be started and stopped at will for exact timing (as of a race)

stor·a·ble \'stōr-ə-bəl, 'stȯr-\ *adj* : that may be stored ⟨*storable* commodities⟩

stor·age \'stōr-ij, 'stȯr-\ *n* **1** : space or a place for storing **2 a** : the act of storing : the state of being stored **b** : the price charged for storing something

storage cell *n* : a cell or connected group of cells that converts chemical energy into electrical energy by reversible chemical reactions and that may be recharged by passing a current through it in the direction opposite to that of its discharge — called also *storage battery*

1**store** \'stō(ə)r, 'stȯ(ə)r\ *vb* **1** : FURNISH, SUPPLY ⟨*store* a ship with provisions⟩ **2** : to lay away : AC-

CUMULATE ⟨*store* vegetables for winter use⟩ **3 a :** to deposit in a place (as a warehouse) for safekeeping or disposal ⟨*stored* her furniture until she found a new apartment⟩ **b :** to record information in a device (as a computer)

2**store** *n* **1** *pl* **:** accumulated supplies (as of food) ⟨a ship's *stores*⟩ **2 :** something stored **:** STOCK ⟨a *store* of good jokes⟩ **3 :** a place where goods are sold **:** SHOP **4 :** VALUE, IMPORTANCE ⟨a family that set great *store* by tradition⟩ — **in store :** in readiness

3**store** *adj* **:** purchased from a store **:** READY-MADE ⟨*store* clothes⟩ ⟨*store* bread⟩

store·house \'stō(ə)r-ˌhau̇s, 'stȯ(ə)r-\ *n* **1 :** a building for storing goods **2 :** an abundant supply or source

store·keep·er \-ˌkē-pər\ *n* **1 :** one who is in charge of stores **2 :** one who keeps a store or shop

store·room \-ˌrüm, -ˌru̇m\ *n* **:** a room for the storing of goods or supplies

store·wide \-'wīd\ *adj* **:** including all or most merchandise in a store ⟨a *storewide* sale⟩

1**sto·ried** \'stōr-ēd, 'stȯr-\ *adj* **1 :** decorated with designs representing scenes from story or history ⟨a *storied* tapestry⟩ **2 :** having an interesting history **:** celebrated in story or history ⟨a *storied* castle⟩

2**storied** *or* **sto·reyed** \'stōr-ēd, 'stȯr-\ *adj* **:** having stories ⟨a two-*storied* house⟩

stork \'stȯrk\ *n* **:** any of various large mostly Old World wading birds related to the herons and having a long stout bill

stork (up to 4 ft. long)

1**storm** \'stȯrm\ *n* **1 a :** a disturbance of the atmosphere accompanied by wind and usu. by rain, snow, hail, sleet, or thunder and lightning **b :** a heavy fall of rain, snow, or hail **c :** wind having a speed of 64 to 72 miles per hour **2 :** a disturbed or agitated state **:** a sudden or violent commotion **3 :** a heavy discharge of objects or actions ⟨fired a *storm* of arrows at the castle⟩ **4 :** a tumultuous outburst ⟨a *storm* of protest⟩ **5 :** a violent assault on a defended position ⟨taken by *storm*⟩

2**storm** *vb* **1 a :** to blow with violence **b :** to rain, hail, snow, or sleet heavily **2 :** to attack by storm ⟨*stormed* ashore at zero hour⟩ ⟨*storm* the fort⟩ **3 :** to show violent emotion **:** RAGE ⟨*storming* at the unusual delay⟩ **4 :** to rush about violently ⟨the mob *stormed* through the streets⟩

storm petrel *n* **:** a small sooty black white-marked petrel frequenting the north Atlantic and Mediterranean

stormy \'stȯr-mē\ *adj* **storm·i·er; -est 1 :** relating to, characterized by, or indicative of a storm ⟨a *stormy* day⟩ ⟨*stormy* skies⟩ **2 :** marked by turmoil or fury ⟨a *stormy* conference⟩ — **storm·i·ly** \-mə-lē\ *adv* — **storm·i·ness** \-mē-nəs\ *n*

1**sto·ry** \'stōr-ē, 'stȯr-\ *n, pl* **stories 1 a :** an account of incidents or events **b :** ANECDOTE **2 a :** a fictional narrative shorter than a novel; *esp* **:** SHORT STORY **b :** the plot of a narrative or dramatic work **3 :** a widely circulated rumor **4 :** LIE, FALSEHOOD **5 :** a news article or broadcast

2**story** *or* **sto·rey** \'stōr-ē, 'stȯr-\ *n, pl* **stories** *or* **storeys :** a set of rooms or an area making up one floor level of a building

stoup \'stüp\ *n* **1 :** a container (as a large glass or tankard) for beverages **2 :** a basin for holy water at the entrance of a church

1**stout** \'stau̇t\ *adj* **1 :** strong of character **:** BRAVE, BOLD **2 :** physically or materially strong **:** STURDY, VIGOROUS **3 :** FORCEFUL **4 :** bulky in body **:** THICKSET — **stout·ish** \-ish\ *adj* — **stout·ly** *adv*

2**stout** *n* **:** a heavy-bodied dark brew made with roasted malt and a relatively high percentage of hops

stout·en \'stau̇t-ən\ *vb* **stout·ened; stout·en·ing** \-(ə-)niŋ\ **:** to make or become stout

stout·heart·ed \'stau̇t-'härt-əd\ *adj* **:** COURAGEOUS, BOLD — **stout·heart·ed·ly** *adv*

1**stove** \'stōv\ *n* **1 :** an apparatus that burns fuel or uses electricity to provide heat (as for cooking or heating) **2 :** KILN

2**stove** *past of* STAVE

stove·pipe \'stōv-ˌpīp\ *n* **1 :** a metal pipe for carrying off smoke from a stove **2 :** a tall silk hat

stow \'stō\ *vb* **1 :** to put away **:** STORE **2 :** ARRANGE, PACK **3 :** LOAD **4 :** to cram in ⟨*stow* away a meal⟩

stow·age \'stō-ij\ *n* **1 a :** an act or process of stowing **b :** goods stowed or to be stowed **2 :** storage capacity **3 :** a place for storage

stow·away \'stō-ə-ˌwā\ *n* **:** one who stows away **:** an unregistered passenger

stow away \ˌstō-ə-'wā\ *vb* **:** to secrete oneself aboard a vehicle as a means of obtaining transportation

STP *n* **:** a powerful hallucinogenic drug that is chemically related to amphetamine

1**strad·dle** \'strad-əl\ *vb* **strad·dled; strad·dling** \-(ə-)liŋ\ **1 :** to stand, sit, or walk with the legs wide apart; *esp* **:** to sit astride **2 :** to favor or seem to favor two apparently opposite sides ⟨*straddle* an issue⟩ — **strad·dler** \-(ə-)lər\ *n*

2**straddle** *n* **1 :** the act or position of one that straddles **2 :** a noncommittal or equivocal position

strafe \'strāf\ *vb* **:** to fire upon at close range and esp. with machine guns from low-flying airplanes ⟨*strafed* the village⟩ — **straf·er** *n*

strag·gle \'strag-əl\ *vb* **strag·gled; strag·gling** \-(ə-)liŋ\ **1 :** to wander from the direct course or way **:** ROVE, STRAY **2 :** to trail off from others of its kind **:** spread out irregularly or scatteringly — **strag·gler** \-(ə-)lər\ *n*

1**straight** \'strāt\ *adj* **1 :** free from curves, bends, angles, or irregularities ⟨*straight* hair⟩ ⟨*straight* timber⟩ **2 a :** holding to a direct or proper course or method ⟨*straight* thinker⟩ **b :** CANDID, FRANK ⟨a *straight* answer⟩ **3 a :** JUST, VIRTUOUS ⟨*straight* dealings⟩ **b :** properly ordered or arranged ⟨set the kitchen *straight*⟩ **4 a :** not modified **:** UNMIXED, UNDILUTED ⟨*straight* whiskey⟩ **b :** not varying or modified ⟨*straight* pay⟩ ⟨works on *straight* time⟩ **c :** being the only form of remuneration ⟨a salesman on *straight* commission⟩ **5 :** making no exceptions in one's support of a party ⟨vote a *straight* ticket⟩ — **straight·ness** *n*

2**straight** *adv* **:** in a straight manner, course, or line

1**straight·away** \'strāt-ə-ˌwā\ *adj* **1 :** proceeding in a straight line **:** continuous in direction **:** STRAIGHTFORWARD **2 :** IMMEDIATE ⟨made a *straightaway* reply⟩

2**straightaway** *n* **:** the straight part of a closed racecourse **:** STRETCH

3**straight·away** \ˌstrāt-ə-'wā\ *adv* **:** without hesitation or delay **:** IMMEDIATELY

straight·edge \'strāt-ˌej\ *n* **:** a bar or piece of wood, metal, or plastic with a straight edge for testing straight lines and surfaces or drawing straight lines

straight·en \'strāt-ən\ *vb* **straight·ened; straight·en·ing** \-(ə-)niŋ\ **1 :** to make or become straight **2 :** to put in order ⟨*straighten* up a room⟩ ⟨*straightened* out my accounts⟩ — **straight·en·er** \-(ə-)nər\ *n*

straight face *n* : a face giving no evidence of emotion and esp. of merriment — **straight–faced** \'strāt-'fāst\ *adj*

[1]**straight·for·ward** \(')strāt-'fȯr-wərd\ *also* **straight·for·wards** \-wərdz\ *adv* : in a straightforward manner

[2]**straightforward** *adj* **1** : proceeding in a straight course or manner : DIRECT **2** : OUTSPOKEN, CANDID ⟨a *straightforward* reply⟩ — **straight·for·ward·ly** *adv* — **straight·for·ward·ness** *n*

straight line *n* : the path of a point moving always in the same direction

straight·way \'strāt-,wā, -'wā\ *adv* : IMMEDIATELY, FORTHWITH

[1]**strain** \'strān\ *n* **1 a** : LINEAGE, ANCESTRY **b** : a group of animals or plants that are physiologically but usu. not structurally distinct ⟨a high-yielding *strain* of winter wheat⟩ **2 a** : inherited or inherent character, quality, or disposition ⟨a *strain* of madness in the family⟩ **b** : TRACE, STREAK ⟨a *strain* of sadness⟩ **3** : TUNE, AIR **4** : the general tone of an utterance or of a course of action or conduct

[2]**strain** *vb* **1 a** : to draw tight : cause to clasp firmly **b** : to stretch to maximum extension and tautness **2 a** : to exert oneself to the utmost : STRIVE **b** : to injure or undergo injury by overuse, misuse, or excessive pressure ⟨*strained* his heart by overwork⟩ ⟨*strained* his back by lifting⟩ **3** : HUG **4 a** : to pass or cause to pass through or as if through a strainer : FILTER **b** : to remove by straining ⟨*strain* lumps out of the gravy⟩ **5** : to stretch beyond a proper limit ⟨*strain* the truth⟩

[3]**strain** *n* **1** : an act of straining or the condition of being strained **2** : bodily injury from excessive tension, effort, or use ⟨heart *strain*⟩; *esp* : one resulting from a wrench or twist and involving undue stretching of muscles or ligaments ⟨back *strain*⟩

strained \'strānd\ *adj* **1** : FORCED ⟨a *strained* smile⟩ **2** : pushed by antagonism near to open conflict ⟨*strained* relations between countries⟩

strain·er \'strā-nər\ *n* : one that strains; *esp* : a device (as a screen, sieve, or filter) to retain solid pieces while a liquid passes through

[1]**strait** \'strāt\ *adj* : LIMITED, STRAITENED — **strait·ly** *adv*

[2]**strait** *n* **1 a** : a comparatively narrow passageway connecting two large bodies of water — often used in pl. **b** : ISTHMUS **2** : a situation of perplexity or distress : DIFFICULTY, NEED ⟨in dire *straits*⟩

strait·en \'strāt-ən\ *vb* **strait·ened**; **strait·en·ing** \-(ə-)ning\ : to subject to distress, privation, or deficiency : limit or restrict esp. in resources ⟨in *straitened* circumstances⟩

strait·jack·et *or* **straight·jack·et** \'strāt-,jak-ət\ *n* : a cover or overgarment of strong material (as canvas) used to bind the body and esp. the arms closely in restraining a violent prisoner or patient

strait·laced *or* **straight·laced** \'strāt-'lāst\ *adj* : extremely strict or narrow in manners, morals, or outlook

strake \'strāk\ *n* : a continuous band of hull planking or plates on a ship; *also* : the width of such a band

[1]**strand** \'strand\ *n* : the land bordering a body of water : SHORE, BEACH

[2]**strand** *vb* **1** : to run aground : BEACH **2** : to leave in a strange or an unfavorable place esp. without funds or means to depart ⟨*stranded* in a strange city⟩

[3]**strand** *n* **1** : one of the threads, strings, or wires twisted to make a cord, rope, or cable **2** : an elongated or twisted and plaited body resembling a rope ⟨a *strand* of pearls⟩ ⟨a *strand* of hair⟩

[4]**strand** *vb* **1** : to form (as a rope) from strands **2** : to play out, twist, or arrange in a strand

strange \'strānj\ *adj* [originally meaning "foreign", from Old French *estrange*, from Latin *extraneus* "coming from outside", from *extra* "outside"] **1** : of or relating to some other person or place ⟨the cuckoo lays her eggs in a *strange* nest⟩ **2** : exciting surprise or wonder because not usual : UNACCOUNTABLE, QUEER ⟨*strange* clothes⟩ **3** : UNFAMILIAR ⟨*strange* surroundings⟩ **4** : ill at ease : SHY ⟨feels *strange* on his first day in school⟩ — **strange·ly** *adv* — **strange·ness** *n*

strang·er \'strān-jər\ *n* **1** : one who is strange **2 a** : FOREIGNER **b** : GUEST, VISITOR **c** : a person with whom one is unacquainted

stran·gle \'strang-gəl\ *vb* **stran·gled**; **stran·gling** \-g(ə-)ling\ **1** : to choke to death by squeezing the throat **2** : to cause (someone or something) to stifle, choke, or suffocate **3** : to become strangled — **stran·gler** \-g(ə-)lər\ *n*

stran·gle·hold \'strang-gəl-,hōld\ *n* **1** : a wrestling hold by which one's opponent is choked **2** : a force or influence that chokes or suppresses freedom of development or expression

stran·gu·la·tion \,strang-gyə-'lā-shən\ *n* **1** : an act or process of strangling **2** : the state of being strangled

[1]**strap** \'strap\ *n* **1** : a band, plate, or loop of metal for binding objects together or for clamping an object in position **2 a** : a narrow usu. flat strip of a flexible material and esp. leather used variously (as for securing, holding together, or wrapping) **b** : something made of a strap forming a loop ⟨boot *strap*⟩ **3** : a strip of leather used for flogging **4** : STROP

[2]**strap** *vb* **strapped**; **strap·ping** **1** : to secure with or attach by means of a strap **2** : to beat or punish with a strap **3** : STROP

strap·less \'strap-ləs\ *adj* : having no strap; *esp* : made or worn without shoulder straps ⟨*strapless* evening gown⟩

strap·ping \'strap-ing\ *adj* : having a vigorously sturdy constitution : ROBUST

strata *pl of* STRATUM

strat·a·gem \'strat-ə-jəm\ *n* **1** : a trick in war for deceiving and outwitting the enemy **2** : a cleverly contrived trick or scheme

stra·te·gic \strə-'tē-jik\ *adj* **1** : of, relating to, or marked by strategy ⟨*strategic* value of the position⟩ ⟨a *strategic* retreat⟩ **2 a** : important in strategy : required for the conduct of war ⟨*strategic* materials⟩ **b** : of great importance within an integrated whole or to a planned effect ⟨emphasized *strategic* points⟩ **3** : designed or trained to strike an enemy at the sources of his power ⟨*strategic* bomber⟩ — **stra·te·gi·cal** \-ji-kəl\ *adj* — **stra·te·gi·cal·ly** \-ji-k(ə-)lē\ *adv*

strat·e·gist \'strat-ə-jəst\ *n* : one skilled in strategy

strat·e·gy \'strat-ə-jē\ *n, pl* **-gies** [from Greek *stratēgia* "generalship", from *stratēgos* "general", from *stratos* "army" and *agein* "to lead"] **1** : the science and art of employing the political, economic, psychological, and military forces of a country so as to support adopted policies in peace or war; *esp* : the science and art of military command exercised to meet the enemy in combat under advantageous

ə abut	ər further	a back	ā bake	
ä cot, cart	aů out	ch chin	e less	ē easy
g gift	i trip	ī life	j joke	ng sing	ō flow
ȯ flaw	ȯi coin	th thin	th this	ü loot
ů foot	y yet	yü few	yů furious	zh vision

conditions **2** : a careful plan or method : a clever stratagem **3** : the art of devising or employing plans or stratagems toward a goal

strat·i·fy \'strat-ə-ˌfī\ *vb* **-fied**; **-fy·ing** **1** : to form, deposit, or arrange in strata ⟨a society *stratified* by custom⟩ **2** : to become arranged in strata — **strat·i·fi·ca·tion** \ˌstrat-ə-fə-'kā-shən\ *n*

stra·tig·ra·phy \strə-'tig-rə-fē\ *n* : geology that deals with the origin, composition, distribution, and succession of strata

stra·to·cu·mu·lus \ˌstrāt-ō-'kyü-myə-ləs, ˌstrat-\ *n* : stratified cumulus consisting of large balls or rolls of dark cloud which often cover the whole sky esp. in winter

strato·sphere \'strat-ə-ˌsfi(ə)r\ *n* : an upper portion of the atmosphere more than seven miles above the earth where temperature changes little and clouds of water never form

stra·tum \'strāt-əm, 'strat-\ *n*, *pl* **stra·ta** \-ə\ *also* **stra·tums** **1** : a layer of a substance; *esp* : one having parallel layers of other kinds lying above or below or both above and below it ⟨a rock *stratum*⟩ ⟨a *stratum* of earth⟩ ⟨deep *stratum* of the skin⟩ **2** : a stage of historical or cultural development **3** : a level of society comprised of persons of the same or similar social, economic, or cultural status

stra·tus \'strāt-əs, 'strat-\ *n*, *pl* **stra·ti** \'strāt-ˌī, 'strat-\ : a cloud form extending horizontally over a relatively large area at an altitude of from 2000 to 7000 feet

1**straw** \'strȯ\ *n* **1 a** : stalks of grain after threshing **b** : any dry stalky plant residue ⟨pea *straw*⟩ ⟨pine *straw*⟩ **2** : a dry coarse stem esp. of a cereal **3 a** : something of small worth or significance : TRIFLE ⟨not worth a *straw*⟩ **b** : something too insubstantial to provide support or help in a desperate situation ⟨clutch at any *straw* in a crisis⟩ **4** : a prepared tube for sucking up a beverage — **strawy** \'strȯ(-)i\ *adj*

2**straw** *adj* **1** : made of straw ⟨a *straw* rug⟩ **2** : of the pale yellow color of straw

straw·ber·ry \'strȯ-ˌber-ē, -b(ə-)rē\ *n* : an edible juicy red pulpy fruit of a low herb with white flowers and long slender runners; *also* : this plant — **strawberry** *adj*

strawberry

strawberry begonia *n* : an eastern Asiatic saxifrage with round leaves and clusters of red and white flowers

straw boss *n* : a foreman of a small gang of workmen

straw vote *n* : an unofficial vote (as taken at a chance gathering) to indicate the relative strength of opposing candidates or issues

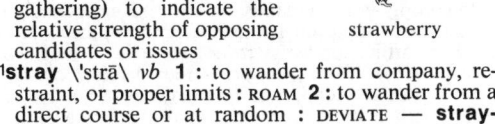

1**stray** \'strā\ *vb* **1** : to wander from company, restraint, or proper limits : ROAM **2** : to wander from a direct course or at random : DEVIATE — **stray·er** *n*

2**stray** *n* : a person or animal that strays

3**stray** *adj* **1** : WANDERING ⟨a *stray* cow⟩ **2** : occurring at random or as detached individuals : SCATTERED, INCIDENTAL ⟨a few *stray* hairs⟩

1**streak** \'strēk\ *n* **1** : a line or mark of a different color or texture from its background : STRIPE **2** : the color of the fine powder of a mineral obtained by scratching or rubbing against a hard white surface **3 a** : a narrow band of light **b** : a lightning bolt **4 a** : TRACE, STRAIN ⟨*streak* of stubbornness⟩ **b** : a brief run (as of luck) **c** : a consecutive series ⟨winning *streak*⟩ **5** : a narrow layer ⟨a *streak* of fat in bacon⟩

2**streak** *vb* **1** : to make streaks on or in **2** : to move swiftly : RUSH ⟨*streaked* through the streets⟩

streaky \'strē-kē\ *adj* **streak·i·er**; **-est** **1** : marked with streaks **2** : VARIABLE, UNRELIABLE — **streak·i·ness** *n*

1**stream** \'strēm\ *n* **1 a** : a body of running water (as a river or brook) flowing on the earth **b** : a body of flowing liquid ⟨a *stream* of blood⟩ **2 a** : a steady succession ⟨a *stream* of words⟩ **b** : a continuous moving procession ⟨a *stream* of cars⟩ **3** : an unbroken flow (as of gas or particles of matter) **4** : a ray or beam of light

2**stream** *vb* **1** : to flow or cause to flow in or as if in a stream **2 a** : to exude a bodily fluid profusely ⟨face *streaming* with sweat⟩ **b** : to become saturated **3** : to trail out at full length ⟨hair *streaming* in the wind⟩ **4** : to pour in large numbers ⟨the people *streamed* into the hall⟩

stream·er \'strē-mər\ *n* **1 a** : a flag that streams in the wind; *esp* : PENNANT **b** : a long narrow wavy strip like or suggesting a banner floating in the wind **2** *pl* : AURORA BOREALIS

stream·let \'strēm-lət\ *n* : a small stream

stream·line \-ˈlīn, -ˌlīn\ *vb* **1** : to design or construct with a contour for decreasing resistance to motion through water or air or as if for this purpose **2** : to bring up to date : MODERNIZE **3** : to make simpler or more efficient

stream·lined \-ˈlīnd, -ˌlīnd\ *also* **streamline** *adj* **1** : contoured to reduce resistance to motion through water or air or as if for this purpose **2** : stripped of everything unnecessary : SIMPLIFIED **3** : MODERNIZED

street \'strēt\ *n* [from Old English *strǣt*, from Latin *strata (via)* "paved (way)", from *stratus*, past participle of *sternere* " to lay flat"] **1 a** : a thoroughfare esp. in a city, town, or village usu. including sidewalks and being wider than an alley or lane **b** : the part of a street reserved for vehicles **c** : a thoroughfare with abutting property ⟨lived on Maple *Street*⟩ **2** : the people occupying property on a street ⟨the whole *street* was excited⟩

street·car \'strēt-ˌkär\ *n* : a vehicle on rails used primarily for transporting passengers and operating on city streets

strength \'streng(k)th\ *n* **1** : the quality or state of being strong : inherent power **2** : SOLIDITY, TOUGHNESS **3** : power of resisting attack : IMPREGNABILITY **4 a** : degree of potency of effect or of concentration ⟨the *strength* of a solution⟩ **b** : intensity of light, color, sound, or odor **5** : force as measured in numbers ⟨army at full *strength*⟩ **6** : SUPPORT ⟨has enough *strength* in the senate to pass the bill⟩ ***syn*** see POWER

strength·en \'streng(k)-thən\ *vb* **strength·ened**; **strength·en·ing** \'streng(k)th-(ə-)ning\ : to make or become stronger — **strength·en·er** \-(ə-)nər\ *n*

strength·less \'streng(k)th-ləs\ *adj* : having no strength

stren·u·ous \'stren-yə-wəs\ *adj* **1 a** : vigorously active : ENERGETIC **b** : FERVENT, ZEALOUS ⟨*strenuous* protest⟩ **2** : marked by or calling for energy or stamina : ARDUOUS ⟨*strenuous* tasks⟩ — **stren·u·ous·ly** *adv*

strep \'strep\ *n* : STREPTOCOCCUS

strep·to·coc·cus \ˌstrep-tə-'käk-əs\ *n*, *pl* **strep·to·coc·ci** \-'käk-ˌ(s)ī, -(ˌ)(s)ē\ : any of various mostly parasitic spherical bacteria that occur in pairs or chains and include some that cause disease in man and domestic animals

strep·to·my·ces \ˌstrep-tə-'mī-ˌsēz\ *n*, *pl* **strep-**

tomyces *or* **strep·to·my·cetes** \-'mī-ˌsēts, -mī-'; -mī-'sēt-(ˌ)ēz\ : any of a genus of mostly soil bacteria including some that form antibiotics as by-products of their metabolism

strep·to·my·cin \ˌstrep-tə-'mī-sən\ *n* : an antibiotic produced by a soil streptomyces and used esp. in the treatment of tuberculosis

[1]**stress** \'stres\ *n* **1 a** : mutual force or action between adjacent surfaces of bodies caused by external force (as tension or shear) **b** : a force that tends to distort a body **c** : a factor that induces bodily or mental tension and may be a factor in disease causation **d** : a state of tension resulting from a stress **2** : EMPHASIS, WEIGHT ⟨lay *stress* on a point⟩ **3** : intensity of utterance given to a speech sound, syllable, or word **4** : ACCENT 4 — **stress·less** \-ləs\ *adj*

[2]**stress** *vb* **1** : ACCENT ⟨*stress* the first syllable⟩ **2** : to subject to physical stress **3** : to lay stress on : EMPHASIZE

stress·ful \'stres-fəl\ *adj* : full of or subject to stress — **stress·ful·ly** \-fə-lē\ *adv*

stress mark *n* : a mark used with (as before, after, or over) a written syllable in the respelling of a word to show that this syllable is to be stressed when spoken : ACCENT MARK

[1]**stretch** \'strech\ *vb* **1** : to extend (as one's limbs or body) in a reclining position ⟨*stretched* himself out on the bed⟩ **2** : to reach out ⟨*stretched* forth his arm⟩ **3 a** : to extend in length or breadth or both : SPREAD **b** : to extend over a continuous period **4** : to draw up (one's body) from a cramped, stooping, or relaxed position ⟨awoke and *stretched* himself⟩ **5** : to pull taut **6 a** : to enlarge or distend esp. by force **b** : STRAIN **7** : to cause to reach or continue ⟨*stretch* a wire between two posts⟩ **8** : to extend often unduly the scope or meaning of ⟨*stretch* the truth⟩ **9** : to become extended without breaking — **stretch·a·ble** \'strech-ə-bəl\ *adj*

[2]**stretch** *n* **1 a** : an exercise of something beyond ordinary or normal limits ⟨*stretch* of the imagination⟩ **b** : an extension of the scope or application of something **2** : the extent to which something may be stretched **3** : the act of stretching : the state of being stretched **4 a** : an extent in length or area ⟨a broad *stretch* of open country⟩ **b** : a continuous period of time ⟨silent for a *stretch*⟩ **5** : a walk to relieve fatigue **6** : a term of imprisonment **7** : either of the straight sides of a racecourse; *esp* : HOMESTRETCH **8** : the capacity for being stretched : ELASTICITY

[3]**stretch** *adj* : easily stretched : ELASTIC ⟨*stretch* socks⟩ ⟨*stretch* ski pants⟩

stretch·er \'strech-ər\ *n* **1** : one that stretches; *esp* : a device or machine for stretching or expanding something ⟨placed curtains on the *stretcher*⟩ **2** : a litter (as of canvas) for carrying a disabled or dead person

stretch·er–bear·er \-ˌbar-ər, -ˌber-\ *n* : one who carries one end of a stretcher

strew \'strü\ *vb* **strewed**; **strewed** *or* **strewn** \'strün\; **strew·ing** **1** : to spread (as seeds or flowers) by scattering **2** : to cover by or as if by scattering something over or on **3** : to spread abroad : DISSEMINATE

stri·at·ed \'strī-ˌāt-əd\ *adj* : marked with lines, bands, or grooves — **stri·a·tion** \strī-'ā-shən\ *n*

ə abut	ər further	a back	ā bake	
ä cot, cart	au̇ out	ch chin	e less	ē easy
g gift	i trip	ī life	j joke	ng sing	ō flow
ȯ flaw	ȯi coin	th thin	th this	ü loot
u̇ foot	y yet	yü few	yu̇ furious	zh vision

striated muscle *n* : muscle that is made up of usu. elongated cells with many nuclei and with alternate light and dark cross striations, is typical of the muscles which move the vertebrate skeleton, and is mostly under voluntary control — compare SMOOTH MUSCLE

strick·en \'strik-ən\ *adj* **1** : hit or wounded by or as if by a missile **2** : afflicted with disease, misfortune, or sorrow

strict \'strikt\ *adj* **1** : permitting no evasion or escape ⟨under *strict* orders⟩ **2 a** : inflexibly maintained or adhered to : COMPLETE, ABSOLUTE ⟨*strict* secrecy⟩ **b** : rigorously conforming to principle or to a norm ⟨a *strict* Catholic⟩ **3** : EXACT, PRECISE — **strict·ly** *adv* — **strict·ness** \'strik(t)-nəs\ *n*

stric·ture \'strik-chər\ *n* **1** : an abnormal narrowing of a bodily passage; *also* : the narrowed part **2** : an adverse criticism : CENSURE

[1]**stride** \'strīd\ *vb* **strode** \'strōd\; **strid·den** \'strid-ən\; **strid·ing** \'strīd-ing\ **1** : to move over, through, or along with or as if with long measured steps **2** : to take a very long step **3** : to step over — **strid·er** \'strīd-ər\ *n*

[2]**stride** *n* **1** : a step or the distance covered by a step **2** : an act or manner of progressing on foot : way of striding **3** : a stage of progress : ADVANCE ⟨the *strides* made in the control of tuberculosis⟩

stri·dent \'strīd-ənt\ *adj* **1** : harsh sounding : GRATING **2** : SHRILL — **stri·dent·ly** *adv*

strid·u·late \'strij-ə-ˌlāt\ *vb* : to make a shrill creaking noise by rubbing together special bodily structures — used esp. of male insects (as crickets or grasshoppers) — **strid·u·la·tion** \ˌstrij-ə-'lā-shən\ *n*

strife \'strīf\ *n* **1** : bitter sometimes violent conflict or dissension ⟨political *strife*⟩ **2** : an act of contention : FIGHT, STRUGGLE

[1]**strike** \'strīk\ *vb* **struck** \'strək\; **struck** *also* **strick·en** \'strik-ən\; **strik·ing** \'strī-king\ **1** : to take a course : GO ⟨*strike* across the field⟩ **2 a** : to deliver a stroke, blow, or thrust : HIT **b** : to attack or seize esp. with fangs or claws ⟨*struck* by a snake⟩ **3** : to come into contact or collision with : COLLIDE **4** : to remove or cancel with or as if with a stroke of the pen ⟨*struck* out a word in the text⟩ **5** : to lower, take down, or take apart ⟨*strike* a flag⟩ ⟨*strike* camp⟩ **6 a** : to indicate or become indicated by a clock, bell, or chime **b** : to indicate by sounding **7** : to pierce or penetrate or to cause to pierce or penetrate **8** : to make a military attack : FIGHT ⟨*strike* for freedom⟩ **9** : to seize the bait ⟨a fish *struck*⟩ **10** : to take root or cause to take root : GERMINATE ⟨some plant cuttings *strike* quickly⟩ **11** : to stop work in order to force an employer to comply with demands **12** : to make a beginning : LAUNCH ⟨the orchestra *struck* into another waltz⟩ **13** : to afflict suddenly ⟨*struck* down at the height of his career⟩ **14 a** : to bring into forceful contact **b** : to fall on ⟨sunlight *strikes* his face⟩ **15 a** : to affect with a mental or emotional state or a strong emotion ⟨*struck* by her beauty⟩ **b** : to produce by stamping with a die or punch ⟨*strike* a medal⟩ **c** : to cause to ignite by friction ⟨*strike* a match⟩ **16** : to produce by or as if by playing a musical instrument ⟨*strike* a chord on the piano⟩ **17 a** : to occur to **b** : to appear to **c** : to make a strong impression on : IMPRESS **18** : to come to ⟨*strike* the main road⟩ **19** : to take on : ASSUME ⟨*strike* a pose⟩ **20** : to mark off : DRAW ⟨*strike* an arc with a compass⟩

[2]**strike** *n* **1** : an act or instance of striking **2 a** : a

work stoppage by a body of workers to force an employer to comply with demands **b** : a temporary stoppage of activities in protest against an act or condition **3** : a pull on a line by a fish in striking **4** : a stroke of good luck; *esp* : a discovery of a valuable mineral deposit **5 a** : a pitched baseball recorded against a batter **b** : DISADVANTAGE, HANDICAP ⟨started the job with two *strikes* against him⟩ **6** : an act or instance of knocking down all the bowling pins with the first bowl **7** : a military attack; *esp* : an air attack on a single objective

strike·bound \'strīk-ˌbau̇nd\ *adj* : subjected to a strike ⟨a *strikebound* factory⟩

strike·break·er \-ˌbrā-kər\ *n* : a person hired to help break up a strike of workmen

strike·break·ing \-king\ *n* : action designed to break up a strike

strike off *vb* : to produce in an effortless manner ⟨*strike off* a poem for the occasion⟩

strike·out \'strīk-ˌau̇t\ *n* : an out in baseball resulting from a batter's being charged with three strikes

strike out \-'au̇t\ *vb* **1** : to retire or be retired by a strikeout **2** : to enter upon a course of action ⟨*struck out* on his own after graduation⟩

strike·over \'strīk-ˌō-vər\ *n* : an act or instance of striking a typewriter character on a spot already occupied by another character

strik·er \'strī-kər\ *n* **1** : the hammer of the striking mechanism of a clock or watch **2** : a worker on strike

strike up *vb* **1** : to begin or cause to begin to sing or play or to be sung or played ⟨*strike up* the band⟩ **2** : to cause to begin ⟨*strike up* a conversation⟩

strike zone *n* : the area (as from the armpits to the tops of the knees of a batter in his natural stance) over home plate through which a pitched baseball must pass to be called a strike

strik·ing \'strī-king\ *adj* : REMARKABLE, IMPRESSIVE ⟨a *striking* costume⟩ ⟨a *striking* resemblance⟩ — **strik·ing·ly** \-king-lē\ *adv*

[1]**string** \'string\ *n* **1** : a small cord used to bind, fasten, or tie **2** : a thin tough plant structure; *esp* : the fiber connecting the halves of a bean pod **3 a** : the gut or wire cord of a musical instrument **b** *pl* : the stringed instruments of an orchestra **4 a** : a group of objects threaded on a string ⟨a *string* of pearls⟩ **b** : a series of things arranged in or as if in a line ⟨a *string* of automobiles⟩ **c** : the animals and esp. horses belonging to or used by one individual **5** : a group of players ranked according to skill or proficiency ⟨third *string* of a football squad⟩ **6** : SUCCESSION, SEQUENCE **7** *pl* : contingent conditions or obligations ⟨an agreement with no *strings* attached⟩

[2]**string** *vb* **strung** \'strəng\; **string·ing** \'string-ing\ **1 a** : to equip with strings **b** : to tune the strings of **2 a** : to thread on or as if on a string ⟨*string* beads⟩ **b** : to tie, hang, or fasten with string **3** : to hang by the neck ⟨*strung* up from a high tree⟩ **4** : to remove the strings of ⟨*string* beans⟩ **5 a** : to extend or stretch like a string ⟨*string* wires from tree to tree⟩ **b** : to set out in a line or series

string along *vb* **1** : to go along : AGREE ⟨*string along* with the majority⟩ **2** : DECEIVE, FOOL ⟨would *string* him *along* with false promises⟩

string bass *n* : DOUBLE BASS

string bean *n* : SNAP BEAN

stringed instrument \'stringd-\ *n* : a musical instrument (as a violin, harp, or piano) sounded by plucking or striking or by drawing a bow across tense strings

strin·gent \'strin-jənt\ *adj* **1** : TIGHT, CONSTRICTED **2** : marked by rigor, strictness, or severity esp. with regard to rule or standard — **strin·gen·cy** \-jən-sē\ *n* — **strin·gent·ly** *adv*

string·er \'string-ər\ *n* **1** : one that strings **2** : a long horizontal piece of wood or metal used for support or strengthening in a building (as under a floor)

string·ing \'string-ing\ *n* : the gut, silk, or nylon with which a racket is strung

stringy \'string-ē\ *adj* **string·i·er**; **-est** : containing, consisting of, or resembling fibrous matter or a string ⟨*stringy* root⟩ ⟨*stringy* hair⟩ — **string·i·ness** *n*

[1]**strip** \'strip\ *vb* **stripped** \'stript\ *also* **stript**; **strip·ping** **1 a** : to remove clothing, covering, or surface matter from **b** : to remove (as clothing) from a person : UNDRESS **c** : SKIN, PEEL ⟨*strip* bark from a tree⟩ **2** : to divest of honors, privileges, or functions **3 a** : to remove extraneous or superficial matter from ⟨a prose style *stripped* to the bones⟩ **b** : to remove furniture, equipment, or accessories from **4** : PLUNDER, SPOIL ⟨troops *stripped* the captured town⟩ **5** : to make bare or clear (as by cutting or grazing) **6** : DISMANTLE, DISASSEMBLE **7** : to tear or damage the screw thread of (as a bolt or nut) — **strip·per** *n*

[2]**strip** *n* **1** : a long narrow piece or area ⟨*strips* of bacon⟩ ⟨a *strip* of land⟩ **2** : AIRSTRIP

strip–crop·ping \'strip-ˌkräp-ing\ *n* : the growing of a cultivated crop (as corn) in strips alternating with strips of a sod-forming crop (as hay) arranged to follow land contours and minimize erosion — **strip–crop** \-ˌkräp\ *vb*

[1]**stripe** \'strīp\ *n* : a stroke or blow with a rod or lash

[2]**stripe** *n* **1** : a line or long narrow section differing in color or texture from parts adjoining **2 a** : a piece of braid (as on the sleeve) to indicate military rank or length of service **b** : CHEVRON — **stripe·less** \'strīp-ləs\ *adj*

[3]**stripe** *vb* : to make stripes on or variegate with stripes

striped \'strīpt, 'strī-pəd\ *adj* : having stripes or streaks

striped muscle *n* : STRIATED MUSCLE

strip·ling \'strip-ling\ *n* : a youth just passing from boyhood to manhood

strive \'strīv\ *vb* **strove** \'strōv\ *also* **strived** \'strīvd\; **striv·en** \'striv-ən\ *or* **strived**; **striv·ing** \'strī-ving\ **1** : to struggle in opposition : CONTEND **2** : to devote serious effort or energy : ENDEAVOR ⟨*strive* to win⟩ — **striv·er** \'strī-vər\ *n*

strobe \'strōb\ *n* : STROBOSCOPE

stro·bo·scope \'strō-bə-ˌskōp\ *n* : an instrument for determining speeds of rotation or frequencies of vibration by means of a rapidly flashing light that illuminates an object intermittently — **stro·bo·scop·ic** \ˌstrō-bə-'skäp-ik\ *adj*

strode *past of* STRIDE

[1]**stroke** \'strōk\ *vb* **1** : to rub gently in one direction **2** : CARESS — **strok·er** *n*

[2]**stroke** *n* **1** : the act of striking; *esp* : a blow with a weapon or implement **2** : a single unbroken movement; *esp* : one of a series of repeated or to-and-fro movements **3** : a striking of the ball in a game; *esp* : a striking or attempt to strike the ball that constitutes the scoring unit in golf **4** : a sudden action or process producing an impact or unexpected result ⟨*stroke* of lightning⟩ ⟨*stroke* of luck⟩ **5** : APOPLEXY **6** : one of a series of propelling movements against a resisting medium ⟨*stroke* of an oar⟩ **7** : a delicate or clever touch in a narrative, description, or construction **8** : the movement or the distance of the movement in either direction of a mechanical part (as a

piston rod) having a reciprocating motion **9 :** the sound of a bell being struck **10 a :** a mark made by a single movement of a tool ⟨a *stroke* of the pen⟩ **b :** one of the lines of a letter of the alphabet ***syn*** see BLOW

[3]**stroke** *vb* **1 :** to mark or cancel with a line **2 :** HIT ⟨gently *stroked* the ball toward the hole⟩

stroll \'strōl\ *vb* **:** to walk in a leisurely or idle manner **:** RAMBLE — **stroll** *n*

stroll·er \'strō-lər\ *n* **1 :** one that strolls **2 :** a wheeled seat in which a baby may be pushed

strong \'strȯng\ *adj* **strong·er** \'strȯng-gər\; **strong·est** \'strȯng-gəst\ **1 :** marked by great physical power **:** ROBUST **2 :** having moral or intellectual power **3 :** having great resources (as of wealth) **4 :** of a specified number ⟨an army ten thousand *strong*⟩ **5 :** FORCEFUL, COGENT ⟨*strong* arguments⟩ **6 a :** not mild or weak **:** INTENSE ⟨*strong* beer⟩ ⟨a *strong* red⟩ **b :** ionizing freely in solution ⟨*strong* acids and bases⟩ **7 :** magnifying by refracting greatly ⟨*strong* lens⟩ **8 :** moving with rapidity or force ⟨*strong* wind⟩ **9 :** ARDENT, ZEALOUS ⟨*strong* advocates of peace⟩ **10 :** able to withstand stress **:** not easily subdued or taken ⟨a *strong* fort⟩ **11 :** well established **:** FIRM ⟨*strong* traditions⟩ **12 :** having an offensive or intense odor or flavor **:** RANK **13 :** of, relating to, or constituting a verb or verb conjugation that forms the past tense by a change in the root vowel and the past participle usu. by the addition of *-en* with or without change of the root vowel (as *strive, strove, striven* or *drink, drank, drunk*) — **strong** *adv* — **strong·ly** \'strȯng-lē\ *adv*

strong·box \'strȯng-ˌbäks\ *n* **:** a strongly made container for money or valuables

strong breeze *n* **:** wind having a speed of 25 to 31 miles per hour

strong gale *n* **:** wind having a speed of 47 to 54 miles per hour

strong·hold \'strȯng-ˌhōld\ *n* **:** a fortified place **:** FORTRESS

stron·tium \'strän-ch(ē-)əm, 'stränt-ē-əm\ *n* **:** a soft malleable metallic element occurring only in combination — see ELEMENT table

strontium 90 *n* **:** a heavy radioactive isotope of strontium having the mass number 90 that is present in the fallout from nuclear explosions

[1]**strop** \'sträp\ *n* **:** STRAP; *esp* **:** a usu. leather band for sharpening a razor

[2]**strop** *vb* **stropped**; **strop·ping :** to sharpen on a strop ⟨*strop* a razor⟩

stro·phe \'strō-fē\ *n* **:** a division of a poem **:** STANZA — **stroph·ic** \'sträf-ik, 'strō-fik\ *adj*

strove *past & chiefly dial past part of* STRIVE

struck *past of* STRIKE

struc·tur·al \'strək-chə-rəl\ *adj* **1 :** of, relating to, or affecting structure ⟨*structural* defects⟩ **2 :** used or formed for use in construction ⟨*structural* steel⟩ — **struc·tur·al·ly** \-rə-lē\ *adv*

structural formula *n* **:** an expanded molecular formula showing the arrangement within the molecule of atoms and of bonds

[1]**struc·ture** \'strək-chər\ *n* **1 :** the action of building **:** CONSTRUCTION **2 :** something constructed **3 :** manner of construction **:** the arrangement or relationship of elements (as particles, parts, or organs) in a substance, body, or system ⟨soil *structure*⟩ ⟨the *structure* of a plant⟩ ⟨molecular *structure*⟩ ⟨social *structure*⟩ ⟨the *structure* of a language⟩ — **struc·ture·less** \-ləs\ *adj*

[2]**structure** *vb* **struc·tured**; **struc·tur·ing :** to form into a structure **:** ORGANIZE

stru·del \'s(h)trüd-əl\ *n* **:** a pastry made of thin dough rolled up with filling and baked

[1]**strug·gle** \'strəg-əl\ *vb* **strug·gled**; **strug·gling** \-(ə-)liŋ\ **1 :** to make violent strenuous efforts against opposition **:** STRIVE **2 :** to proceed with difficulty or with great effort ⟨*struggled* through the snow⟩ — **strug·gler** \-(ə-)lər\ *n*

[2]**struggle** *n* **1 :** a violent effort or exertion **2 :** CONTEST, STRIFE

struggle for existence : competition (as for food, space, or light) of members of a natural population that tends to eliminate weaker or less efficient individuals and thereby to increase the chance of the stronger or more efficient to pass on their traits

strum \'strəm\ *vb* **strummed**; **strum·ming :** to play on a stringed instrument by brushing the strings with the fingers — **strum·mer** *n*

strung *past of* STRING

[1]**strut** \'strət\ *vb* **strut·ted**; **strut·ting 1 :** to walk with a stiff proud gait **2 :** to parade (as clothes) with a show of pride — **strut·ter** *n*

[2]**strut** *n* **1 :** a bar or brace to resist pressure in the direction of its length **2 :** a pompous step or walk

strych·nine \'strik-ˌnīn, -nən, -ˌnēn\ *n* **:** a bitter poison obtained from certain plants and used in rat poison and medicinally as a tonic and stimulant

[1]**stub** \'stəb\ *n* **1 :** STUMP 1b **2 a :** a pen with a short blunt nib **b :** a short part left after a larger part has been broken off or used up ⟨pencil *stub*⟩ **3 a :** a small part of a check kept as a record of the contents of the check **b :** the part of a ticket returned to the user

[2]**stub** *vb* **stubbed**; **stub·bing 1 :** to extinguish (as a cigarette) by crushing **2 :** to strike (as one's toe) against an object

stub·ble \'stəb-əl\ *n* **1 :** the stem ends of herbaceous plants and esp. grains remaining attached to the soil after harvest **2 :** a rough surface or growth resembling stubble — **stub·bly** \-(ə-)lē\ *adj*

stub·born \'stəb-ərn\ *adj* **1 a :** having a firm idea or purpose **:** DETERMINED **b :** hard to convince, persuade, or move ⟨*stubborn* as a mule⟩ **2 :** done or continued in an obstinate or persistent manner ⟨*stubborn* refusal⟩ **3 :** difficult to handle, manage, or treat ⟨*stubborn* hair⟩ ***syn*** see OBSTINATE ***ant*** pliant (sense 2) — **stub·born·ly** *adv* — **stub·born·ness** \-ərn-(n)əs\ *n*

stub·by \'stəb-ē\ *adj* **stub·bi·er**; **-est :** resembling a stub esp. in shortness and broadness ⟨*stubby* fingers⟩ — **stub·bi·ness** *n*

stuc·co \'stək-ō\ *n, pl* **stuccos** *or* **stuccoes :** a plaster used to cover exterior walls or ornament interior walls — **stucco** *vb*

stuck *past of* STICK

stuck–up \'stək-'əp\ *adj* **:** CONCEITED, SELF-IMPORTANT

[1]**stud** \'stəd\ *n* **1 :** a group of animals and esp. horses kept primarily for breeding **2 :** a male animal (as a stallion) kept for breeding

[2]**stud** *n* **1 :** one of the smaller uprights in the framing of the walls of a building **2 a :** a boss, rivet, or nail with a large head used for ornament or protection **b :** a solid button with a shank or eye on the back inserted through an eyelet in a garment as a fastener or ornament **c :** a metal pin projecting from the tread of a snow tire to improve traction

[3]**stud** *vb* **stud·ded; stud·ding 1 :** to furnish with studs **2 :** to adorn, cover, or protect with studs **3 :** to set a place or thing with a number of prominent objects ⟨water *studded* with islands⟩

stud *abbr* student

stu·dent \'st(y)üd-ənt\ *n* **1 :** LEARNER, SCHOLAR; *esp* **:** one who attends a school or college **2 :** one who studies **:** an attentive and systematic observer ⟨a *student* of life⟩

student council *n* **:** a group of students elected by their fellow students to represent them in student government

student government *n* **:** the organization and management of student life, activities, or discipline by various student organizations in a school or college

stud·ied \'stəd-ēd\ *adj* **1 :** carefully considered or prepared **:** THOUGHTFUL ⟨his judgments were always *studied* and fair⟩ **2 :** DELIBERATE, INTENTIONAL ⟨a *studied* insult⟩ — **stud·ied·ly** *adv* — **stud·ied·ness** *n*

stu·dio \'st(y)üd-ē-,ō\ *n, pl* **-di·os 1 :** the working place of an artist **2 :** a place where motion pictures are made **3 :** a place for the transmission of radio or television programs

stu·di·ous \'st(y)üd-ē-əs\ *adj* **1 :** given to or concerned with study ⟨a *studious* boy⟩ ⟨*studious* habits⟩ **2 :** marked by purposeful diligence **:** EARNEST ⟨made a *studious* effort to obey the rules⟩ — **stu·di·ous·ly** *adv* — **stu·di·ous·ness** *n*

[1]**study** \'stəd-ē\ *n, pl* **stud·ies** [from Latin *studium* "zeal", "enthusiasm", from *studēre* "to be eager"] **1 :** a state of contemplation **:** REVERIE **2 a :** application of the mind to acquire knowledge **b :** a careful examination or analysis of something **c :** a report or publication based on a study **3 :** a building or room devoted to study or literary pursuits **4 a :** a branch or department of learning **:** SUBJECT **b :** the activity or work of a student

[2]**study** *vb* **stud·ied; study·ing 1 :** to engage in study or the study of ⟨*studied* hard⟩ ⟨liked to *study* literature⟩ **2 :** to consider attentively or in detail esp. with the intent of fixing in the mind or of appraising ⟨*study* a part in a play⟩ ⟨committee *studied* several plans before making recommendations⟩

study hall *n* **1 :** a room in a school where students can study **2 :** a period in a student's day set aside for study and homework

[1]**stuff** \'stəf\ *n* **1 :** materials, supplies, or equipment used in various activities **2 a :** writing, discourse, or ideas often of little or temporary worth **b :** actions or talk of a particular and often objectionable kind ⟨how do they get away with such *stuff*⟩ **3 a :** an aggregate of matter ⟨volcanic rock is curious *stuff*⟩ **b :** matter of a particular kind often unspecified ⟨sold tons of the *stuff*⟩ **4 a :** fundamental material **:** SUBSTANCE ⟨*stuff* of greatness⟩ ⟨*stuff* of manhood⟩ **b :** subject matter ⟨a teacher who knows her *stuff*⟩ **5 :** special knowledge or capability ⟨a person who has the *stuff* will do well here⟩

[2]**stuff** *vb* **1 a :** to fill by or as if by packing things in **:** CRAM **b :** to eat gluttonously **c :** to fill with a stuffing **d :** to stop up **:** PLUG **e :** to fill with ideas or information **2 :** to put or push into something esp. carelessly or casually ⟨*stuffed* the clothes into the drawer⟩ — **stuff·er** *n*

stuff·ing \'stəf-ing\ *n* **:** material used to stuff something; *esp* **:** a seasoned mixture used to stuff meat or poultry

stuffy \'stəf-ē\ *adj* **stuff·i·er; -est 1 :** SULLEN, ILL-HUMORED **2 a :** lacking fresh air ⟨a *stuffy* room⟩ **b :** stuffed or choked up ⟨had a *stuffy* feeling in his head⟩ **3 :** DULL, STODGY **4 :** narrowly inflexible in standards of conduct **:** SELF-RIGHTEOUS — **stuff·i·ly** \'stəf-ə-lē\ *adv* — **stuff·i·ness** \'stəf-ē-nəs\ *n*

stul·ti·fy \'stəl-tə-,fī\ *vb* **-fied; -fy·ing 1 :** to cause to appear or be stupid, foolish, or absurdly illogical **2 :** to make worthless or useless

stum·ble \'stəm-bəl\ *vb* **stum·bled; stum·bling** \-b(ə-)ling\ **1 a :** to trip in walking or running **b :** to walk unsteadily **2 :** to speak or act in a blundering or clumsy manner **3 :** to come or happen unexpectedly or by chance ⟨*stumbled* onto the ruins of an old fort⟩ — **stumble** *n* — **stum·bler** \-b(ə-)lər\ *n* — **stum·bling·ly** \-b(ə-)ling-lē\ *adv*

stum·bling block \'stəm-bling\ *n* **1 :** an impediment to belief or understanding **2 :** an obstacle to progress

[1]**stump** \'stəmp\ *n* **1 a :** the base of a bodily part (as an arm or leg) remaining after the rest is removed **b :** the part of a plant and esp. a tree remaining attached to the root after the top is cut off **2 :** a part remaining after the rest is worn away or lost **:** STUB **3 :** a place or occasion for political public speaking

[2]**stump** *vb* **1 a :** STUB 2 **b :** to walk or walk over heavily or clumsily **2 a :** CHALLENGE, DARE **b :** PERPLEX, CONFOUND **3 :** to go about making political speeches or supporting a cause ⟨*stump* the state for a candidate⟩ — **stump·er** *n*

stumpy \'stəm-pē\ *adj* **stump·i·er; -est 1 :** full of stumps **2 :** being short and thick **:** SQUAT

stun \'stən\ *vb* **stunned; stun·ning 1 :** to make senseless or dizzy by or as if by a blow **2 :** BEWILDER, STUPEFY ⟨*stunned* by the news⟩ — **stun** *n*

stung *past of* STING

stunk *past of* STINK

stun·ner \'stən-ər\ *n* **:** one that stuns; *esp* **:** an unusually attractive person

stun·ning \'stən-ing\ *adj* **1 :** tending or able to stupefy or bewilder ⟨a *stunning* blow⟩ **2 :** strikingly lovely or pleasing ⟨a *stunning* dress⟩ — **stun·ning·ly** \-ing-lē\ *adv*

[1]**stunt** \'stənt\ *vb* **:** to hinder the normal growth of **:** DWARF

[2]**stunt** *n* **:** an unusual or difficult feat performed or undertaken usu. to gain attention or publicity

[3]**stunt** *vb* **:** to perform stunts

stu·pe·fy \'st(y)ü-pə-,fī\ *vb* **-fied; -fy·ing 1 :** to make stupid, dull, or numb by or as if by drugs **2 :** ASTONISH, BEWILDER — **stu·pe·fac·tion** \,st(y)ü-pə-'fak-shən\ *n* — **stu·pe·fi·er** \'st(y)ü-pə-,fī(-ə)r\ *n*

stu·pen·dous \st(y)u̇-'pen-dəs\ *adj* **:** stupefying or amazing esp. because of great size or height ⟨*stupendous* gorges⟩ ***syn*** see MONSTROUS — **stu·pen·dous·ly** *adv* — **stu·pen·dous·ness** *n*

stu·pid \'st(y)ü-pəd\ *adj* **1 a :** slow of mind **:** DENSE **b :** UNTHINKING, FOOLISH **2 a :** dulled in feeling or sensation **:** TORPID **b :** incapable of feeling or sensation **3 :** marked by or resulting from dullness **:** SENSELESS ⟨a *stupid* mistake⟩ **4 :** DREARY, BORING ⟨a *stupid* plot⟩ — **stu·pid·ly** *adv* — **stu·pid·ness** *n*

stu·pid·i·ty \st(y)u̇-'pid-ət-ē\ *n, pl* **-ties 1 :** the quality or state of being stupid **2 :** something (as an idea or act) that is stupid

stu·por \'st(y)ü-pər\ *n* **1 :** a condition characterized by great dulling or suspension of sense or feeling ⟨drunken *stupor*⟩ **2 :** a state of extreme apathy or torpor resulting often from stress or shock

stur·dy \'stərd-ē\ *adj* **stur·di·er; -est 1 :** firmly built or made ⟨a *sturdy* ship⟩ **2 :** HARDY, ROBUST ⟨*sturdy* peasants⟩ **3 :** FIRM, RESOLUTE ⟨*sturdy* self-reliance⟩ — **stur·di·ly** \'stərd-ə-lē\ *adj* — **stur·di·ness** \'stərd-ē-nəs\ *n*

S

stur·geon \'stər-jən\ *n* : any of various usu. large long-bodied fishes that have a thick skin with rows of bony plates and are valued for their flesh and esp. for their roe which is made into caviar

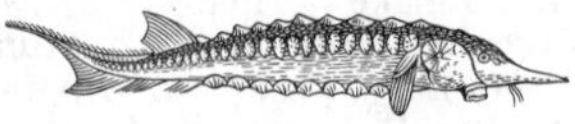

sturgeon
(up to 18 ft. long)

[1]**stut·ter** \'stət-ər\ *vb* : to speak or utter with spasmodic repetition as a result of excitement or impediment — **stut·ter·er** \-ər-ər\ *n*

[2]**stutter** *n* **1** : an act or instance of stuttering **2** : a speech impediment involving stuttering

[1]**sty** \'stī\ *n, pl* **sties** *also* **styes** \'stīz\ : a pen or enclosed housing for swine

[2]**sty** *or* **stye** \'stī\ *n, pl* **sties** *or* **styes** \'stīz\ : an inflamed swelling of a skin gland on the edge of an eyelid

[1]**style** \'stīl\ *n* [from Latin *stilus*, originally "pointed stake"] **1 a** : an instrument used by the ancients in writing on waxed tablets **b** : the shadow-producing pin of a sundial **c** : a slender continuation of a plant ovary bearing a stigma at its end **2** : a mode of expression; *esp* : one characteristic of an individual, period, school, or nation ⟨ornate *style*⟩ **3** : the custom or plan followed in spelling, capitalization, punctuation, and typographic arrangement and display **4 a** : a manner or method of acting or performing esp. in accordance with a standard **b** : a fashionable manner or mode **c** : overall excellence, skill, or grace in performance, manner, or appearance — **style·less** \'stīl-ləs\ *adj*

[2]**style** *vb* **1** : NAME, CALL ⟨*styles* himself a scientist⟩ **2 a** : to cause to conform to a customary style **b** : to design and make in accord with the prevailing mode ⟨*style* hats⟩ — **styl·er** *n*

styl·ish \'stī-lish\ *adj* : having style; *esp* : conforming to current fashion — **styl·ish·ly** *adv* — **styl·ish·ness** *n*

syn STYLISH, MODISH, FASHIONABLE, CHIC can mean conforming to the choice and usage of those who set a vogue. STYLISH implies a following of a passing fad that is prevalent at the moment; MODISH implies conformity with the latest style; FASHIONABLE is more likely to imply conformance with an established and generally accepted fashion; CHIC may not imply up-to-dateness so much as an effectiveness in style that takes a knack

styl·ist \'stī-ləst\ *n* **1** : a master or model of style; *esp* : a writer or speaker eminent in matters of style **2** : one who develops, designs, or advises on styles — **sty·lis·tic** \stī-'lis-tik\ *adj* — **sty·lis·ti·cal·ly** \-ti-k(ə-)lē\ *adv*

styl·ize \'stīl-,īz\ *vb* : to represent or design according to a style or pattern rather than according to nature

sty·lus \'stī-ləs\ *n, pl* **sty·li** \'stīl-,ī\ *also* **sty·lus·es** \'stī-lə-səz\ **1** : STYLE 1c **2** : an instrument for writing or marking **3** : a phonograph needle

styp·tic \'stip-tik\ *adj* : tending to contract or bind; *esp* : tending to check bleeding — **styptic** *n*

sty·rene \'stī(ə)r-,ēn\ *n* : a fragrant liquid hydrocarbon used chiefly in making synthetic rubber, resins, and plastics

sua·sion \'swā-zhən\ *n* : the act of influencing or persuading — **sua·sive** \'swā-siv, -ziv\ *adj* — **sua·sive·ly** *adv* — **sua·sive·ness** *n*

suave \'swäv\ *adj* : persuasively pleasing : smoothly polite and agreeable — **suave·ly** *adv* — **suave·ness** *n* — **suav·i·ty** \'swäv-ət-ē\ *n*

[1]**sub** \'səb\ *n* : SUBSTITUTE

[2]**sub** *vb* **subbed**; **sub·bing** : to act as a substitute

[3]**sub** *n* : SUBMARINE

sub- \'səb, ,səb\ *prefix* **1** : under : beneath : below ⟨*sub*soil⟩ ⟨*sub*aqueous⟩ **2 a** : subordinate : secondary ⟨*sub*station⟩ **b** : subordinate portion of : subdivision of ⟨*sub*committee⟩ ⟨*sub*topic⟩ ⟨*sub*species⟩ **3** : with repetition of a process described in a simple verb so as to form, stress, or deal with subordinate parts or relations ⟨*sub*let⟩ ⟨*sub*contract⟩ **4 a** : less than completely, perfectly, or typically : somewhat ⟨*sub*dominant⟩ **b** : bordering upon ⟨*sub*arctic⟩

sub·al·pine \,səb-'al-,pīn\ *adj* **1** : of or relating to the region about the foot and lower slopes of the Alps **2** *cap* : of, relating to, or growing on upland slopes near timberline

sub·ant·arc·tic \,səb-ant-'ärk-tik, -'ärt-ik\ *adj* : of, relating to, or being a region just outside the antarctic circle

sub·aque·ous \,səb-'ā-kwē-əs, -'ak-wē-\ *adj* : formed, occurring, or existing in or under water

sub·arc·tic \-'ärk-tik, -'ärt-ik\ *adj* : of, relating to, or being regions immediately outside of the arctic circle or regions similar to these in climate or conditions of life

sub·as·sem·bly \,səb-ə-'sem-blē\ *n* : an assembled unit designed to be incorporated with other units in a finished product

sub·atom·ic \,səb-ə-'täm-ik\ *adj* : of or relating to the inside of the atom or particles smaller than atoms

sub·com·mit·tee \'səb-kə-,mit-ē\ *n* : a subdivision of a committee usu. organized for a specific purpose

[1]**sub·con·scious** \,səb-'kän-chəs\ *adj* **1** : existing in the mind but not immediately available to consciousness **2** : imperfectly conscious ⟨a *subconscious* state⟩ — **sub·con·scious·ly** *adv*

[2]**subconscious** *n* : the mental activities just below the limit of consciousness

sub·con·ti·nent \'səb-'känt-(ə-)nənt\ *n* **1** : a large landmass (as Greenland) smaller than any of the usu. recognized continents **2** : a major subdivision of a continent — **sub·con·ti·nen·tal** \,səb-,känt-ə-'nent-əl\ *adj*

sub·con·tract \'səb-'kän-,trakt\ *n* : a contract between a party to an original contract and a third party who usu. agrees to supply work or materials required in the original contract — **sub·con·tract** \,səb-'kän-,trakt, ,səb-kən-'trakt\ *vb* — **sub·con·trac·tor** \,səb-'kän-,trak-tər, ,səb-kən-'\ *n*

sub·cu·ta·ne·ous \,səb-kyü-'tā-nē-əs\ *adj* : being, living, used, or made under the skin ⟨*subcutaneous* fat⟩ ⟨a *subcutaneous* needle⟩ ⟨*subcutaneous* parasite⟩ — **sub·cu·ta·ne·ous·ly** *adv*

sub·di·vide \,səb-də-'vīd\ *vb* **1** : to divide the parts of into more parts **2** : to divide into several parts; *esp* : to divide a tract of land into building lots — **sub·di·vi·sion** \,səb-də-'vizh-ən, 'səb-də-,\ *n*

sub·dom·i·nant \,səb-'däm-ə-nənt\ *n* **1** : something dominant to an inferior or partial degree **2** : the 4th tone of the major or minor scale (as F in the scale of C) — **subdominant** *adj*

sub·due \səb-'d(y)ü\ *vb* **1** : to conquer and bring

into subjection : VANQUISH **2 :** to bring under control or into order : CURB **3 :** to reduce the intensity or degree of ⟨*subdued* light⟩ — **sub·du·er** *n*

sub·en·try \'səb-ˌen-trē\ *n* : an entry made under a more general entry

sub·freez·ing \'səb-'frē-zing\ *adj* : lower than is required to produce freezing

sub·group \'səb-ˌgrüp\ *n* : a group usu. of individuals sharing some common quality that distinguishes them from other members of a major group to which they belong

sub·head \'səb-ˌhed\ *or* **sub·head·ing** \-ing\ *n* **1 :** a heading of a subdivision (as in an outline) **2 :** a subordinate caption or title

subj *abbr* subject

[1]**sub·ject** \'səb-jikt\ *n* **1 a :** one subject to a monarch and governed by his law **b :** one who owes allegiance to a sovereign power or state **2 a :** a department of knowledge or learning **b :** an individual (as a person or plant) that is studied or experimented on **c :** something concerning which something is said or done ⟨the *subject* of an essay⟩ **3 :** a noun phrase about which something is stated by the predicate

[2]**subject** *adj* **1 :** owing obedience or allegiance to the dominion of another **2 a :** EXPOSED, LIABLE ⟨a valley *subject* to floods⟩ **b :** PRONE, DISPOSED **3 :** CONDITIONAL, CONTINGENT ⟨*subject* to approval⟩

[3]**sub·ject** \səb-'jekt\ *vb* **1 a :** to bring under control or dominion : SUBJUGATE **b :** to make amenable to the discipline and control of a superior **2 a :** to make liable : PREDISPOSE **b :** to make accountable : SUBMIT **3 :** to cause to undergo or submit to : EXPOSE — **sub·jec·tion** \səb-'jek-shən\ *n*

sub·jec·tive \səb-'jek-tiv\ *adj* **1 :** of, relating to, or being a subject **2 :** of, relating to, or arising within one's self or mind in contrast to what is outside : PERSONAL — **sub·jec·tive·ly** *adv* — **sub·jec·tiv·i·ty** \(ˌ)səb-ˌjek-'tiv-ət-ē\ *n*

sub·join \(ˌ)səb-'jȯin\ *vb* : ANNEX, APPEND

sub·ju·gate \'səb-jə-ˌgāt\ *vb* **1 :** to force to submit to control and governance : MASTER **2 :** to bring into slavery — **sub·ju·ga·tion** \ˌsəb-jə-'gā-shən\ *n* — **sub·ju·ga·tor** \'səb-jə-ˌgāt-ər\ *n*

[1]**sub·junc·tive** \səb-'jəng(k)-tiv\ *adj* : of, relating to, or being the grammatical mood that represents a denoted act or state not as fact but as contingent or possible or viewed emotionally (as with doubt or desire) ⟨the *subjunctive* mood⟩

[2]**subjunctive** *n* : the subjunctive mood of a verb or a verb in this mood

sub·lease \'səb-'lēs\ *n* : a lease by a tenant of part or all of leased premises to another person — **sublease** *vb*

sub·let \'səb-'let\ *vb* **sub·let**; **sub·let·ting** **1 :** to lease or rent all or part of a leased or rented property **2 :** SUBCONTRACT

[1]**sub·li·mate** \'səb-lə-ˌmāt\ *vb* **1 :** to cause to sublime ⟨*sublimate* sulfur⟩ **2 :** to direct the energy of (desires and impulses) from a lower to a higher level — **sub·li·ma·tion** \ˌsəb-lə-'mā-shən\ *n*

[2]**sub·li·mate** \'səb-lə-ˌmāt, -mət\ *n* : a chemical product obtained by sublimation

[1]**sub·lime** \sə-'blīm\ *vb* **1 :** to pass from a solid to a gaseous state on heating and back to solid form on cooling without apparently passing through a liquid state; *also* : to release or purify by such action ⟨*sublime* sulfur from a mixture⟩ **2 :** to make finer or more worthy — **sub·lim·er** *n*

[2]**sublime** *adj* **1 :** lofty, grand, or exalted in thought, expression, or manner **2 :** inspiring awe : SOLEMN — **sub·lime·ly** *adv* — **sub·lime·ness** *n*

sub·lim·i·nal \(ˌ)səb-'lim-ən-əl\ *adj* **1 :** inadequate to produce a sensation or a perception ⟨*subliminal* stimuli⟩ **2 :** existing or functioning outside the area of conscious awareness ⟨the *subliminal* mind⟩ ⟨*subliminal* techniques in advertising⟩ — **sub·lim·i·nal·ly** \-'lim-ən-ə-lē\ *adv*

sub·lim·i·ty \sə-'blim-ət-ē\ *n, pl* **-ties** **1 :** something sublime **2 :** the quality or state of being sublime

sub·ma·chine gun \ˌsəb-mə-'shēn-ˌgən\ *n* : a lightweight automatic or semiautomatic portable firearm

sub·mar·gin·al \ˌsəb-'märj-(ə-)nəl\ *adj* **1 :** located near or beneath a margin or a marginal structure **2 :** less than marginal; *esp* : inadequate for some end or use ⟨farming *submarginal* land⟩ — **sub·mar·gin·al·ly** \-ē\ *adv*

[1]**sub·ma·rine** \'səb-mə-ˌrēn, ˌsəb-mə-'\ *adj* : being, acting, or growing under water esp. in the sea ⟨*submarine* plants⟩

[2]**submarine** *n* **1 :** a naval vessel designed for undersea operations **2 :** a sandwich made from a long roll split lengthwise and filled with various foods (as meat, cheese, tomatoes, and lettuce)

[3]**submarine** *vb* : to make an attack upon or to sink by means of a submarine

sub·ma·rin·er \'səb-mə-ˌrē-nər, ˌsəb-mə-'\ *n* : a crewman of a submarine

sub·merge \səb-'mərj\ *vb* **1 :** to put under or plunge into water ⟨the whale *submerged*⟩ **2 :** to cover or become covered with or as if with water ⟨floods *submerged* the town⟩ — **sub·mer·gence** \-'mər-jən(t)s\ *n* — **sub·merg·i·ble** \-'mər-jə-bəl\ *adj*

sub·merse \səb-'mərs\ *vb* : SUBMERGE — **sub·mer·sion** \-'mər-zhən\ *n*

[1]**sub·mers·i·ble** \səb-'mər-sə-bəl\ *adj* : capable of submerging

[2]**submersible** *n* : a submergible boat : SUBMARINE

sub·mi·cro·scop·ic \ˌsəb-ˌmī-krə-'skäp-ik\ *adj* : too small to be seen in an ordinary light microscope

sub·min·i·a·ture \ˌsəb-'min-ē-ə-ˌchu̇r, -'min-i-ˌchu̇r, -chər\ *adj* : very small ⟨*subminiature* electronic equipment⟩

sub·mis·sion \səb-'mish-ən\ *n* **1 :** an act of submitting something (as for consideration, inspection, or comment) **2 :** the condition of being submissive, humble, or compliant **3 :** an act of submitting to the authority or control of another

sub·mis·sive \-'mis-iv\ *adj* : inclined or willing to submit to others — **sub·mis·sive·ly** *adv*

sub·mit \səb-'mit\ *vb* **sub·mit·ted**; **sub·mit·ting** **1 :** to give over or leave to the judgment or approval of someone else : REFER ⟨*submit* an issue to arbitration⟩ **2 :** to subject to a process or practice **3 :** to put forward as an opinion, reason, or idea **4 :** to yield to power or authority : SURRENDER ***syn*** see YIELD ***ant*** resist, withstand

sub·nor·mal \ˌsəb-'nȯr-məl\ *adj* : falling below what is normal — **sub·nor·mal·i·ty** \ˌsəb-nȯr-'mal-ət-ē\ *n* — **sub·nor·mal·ly** \ˌsəb-'nȯr-mə-lē\ *adv*

sub·nu·cle·ar \ˌsəb-'n(y)ü-klē-ər\ *adj* : being or relating to the particles (as nucleons and mesons) that make up the atomic nucleus or particles that are produced from such particles

sub·or·bit·al \ˌsəb-'ȯr-bət-əl\ *adj* : being or involving less than one orbit ⟨*suborbital* flight⟩

[1]**sub·or·di·nate** \sə-'bȯrd-(ə-)nət\ *adj* **1 :** placed in or occupying a lower class or rank : INFERIOR **2 :** submissive to or controlled by authority **3 a :** of, relating to, or being a clause that functions as a noun, adjective, or adverb **b :** grammatically subordinating — **sub·or·di·nate·ly** *adv* — **sub·or·di·nate·ness** *n*

²**subordinate** *n* : one that is subordinate

³**sub·or·di·nate** \sə-'bȯrd-ə-ˌnāt\ *vb* : to make subordinate — **sub·or·di·na·tion** \-ˌbȯrd-ə-'nā-shən\ *n* — **sub·or·di·na·tive** \-'bȯrd-ə-ˌnāt-iv\ *adj*

sub·phy·lum \'səb-ˌfī-ləm\ *n* : a primary division of a phylum

sub·plot \'səb-ˌplät\ *n* : a subordinate plot in fiction or drama

¹**sub·poe·na** \sə-'pē-nə\ *n* [from Latin *sub poena* "under penalty", opening words of the writ] : a writ commanding a person designated in it to appear in court under a penalty for failure to appear

²**subpoena** *vb* **-naed** \-nəd\; **-na·ing** : to serve with or summon by a writ of subpoena

sub·po·lar \ˌsəb-'pō-lər\ *adj* : not quite polar : SUBARCTIC, SUBANTARCTIC

sub·scribe \səb-'skrīb\ *vb* **1** : to sign one's name or a document usu. to indicate consent to, obligation by, or approval or awareness of something written **2** : to pledge payment of (as a sum of money) over one's signature ⟨*subscribed* $100 to the building fund⟩ **3 a** : to enter one's name for a publication or service **b** : to receive a periodical or service regularly on order ⟨*subscribe* to a newspaper⟩ — **sub·scrib·er** *n*

sub·script \'səb-ˌskript\ *n* : a distinguishing symbol or letter immediately below or below and to the right or left of another written character — **subscript** *adj*

sub·scrip·tion \səb-'skrip-shən\ *n* **1** : an act or instance of subscribing **2** : an amount or thing that is subscribed **3** : a purchase of future issues of a periodical

sub·sense \'səb-ˌsen(t)s\ *n* : a subordinate division of a sense (as in a dictionary)

sub·se·quent \'səb-si-kwənt, -sə-ˌkwent\ *adj* : following in time, order, or place : SUCCEEDING — **sub·se·quence** \-sə-ˌkwen(t)s, -si-kwən(t)s\ *n* — **subsequent** *n* — **sub·se·quent·ly** \-ˌkwent-lē, -kwənt-\ *adv* — **sub·se·quent·ness** \-ˌkwent-, -kwənt-\ *n*

sub·ser·vi·ent \səb-'sər-vē-ənt\ *adj* **1** : useful in an inferior capacity : SUBORDINATE **2** : SUBMISSIVE, SERVILE — **sub·ser·vi·ence** \-ən(t)s\ *n* — **sub·ser·vi·en·cy** \-ən-sē\ *n* — **sub·ser·vi·ent·ly** *adv*

sub·set \'səb-ˌset\ *n* : a mathematical set each of whose elements is also an element of a more inclusive set

sub·side \səb-'sīd\ *vb* **1** : to sink or fall to the bottom : SETTLE **2** : to tend downward : DESCEND ⟨the flood *subsided* slowly⟩ **3** : to become quiet or less : ABATE ⟨as the fever *subsides*⟩ ⟨his anger *subsided*⟩ — **sub·sid·ence** \səb-'sīd-ən(t)s, 'səb-səd-\ *n*

¹**sub·sid·i·ary** \səb-'sid-ē-ˌer-ē\ *adj* **1 a** : furnishing aid or support : AUXILIARY ⟨*subsidiary* details⟩ **b** : of secondary importance ⟨*subsidiary* streams⟩ **2** : of, relating to, or being a subsidy ⟨*subsidiary* payments⟩ — **sub·sid·i·ar·i·ly** \-ˌsid-ē-'er-ə-lē\ *adv*

²**subsidiary** *n, pl* **-ar·ies** : one that is subsidiary; *esp* : a company wholly controlled by another

sub·si·dize \'səb-sə-ˌdīz, -zə-\ *vb* : to aid or furnish with a subsidy — **sub·si·di·za·tion** \ˌsəb-səd-ə-'zā-shən, ˌsəb-zəd-\ *n*

ə abut	ər further	a back	ā bake	
ä cot, cart	aù out	ch chin	e less	ē easy
g gift	i trip	ī life	j joke	ng sing
ō flow	ȯ flaw	ȯi coin	th thin	th this
ü loot	ù foot	y yet	yü few	yù furious
zh vision				

sub·si·dy \'səb-səd-ē, -zəd-\ *n, pl* **-dies** : a grant or gift esp. of money; *esp* : a grant by a government to a private person or company or to another government to assist an enterprise advantageous to the public

sub·sist \səb-'sist\ *vb* **1** : to have or continue to have existence : BE, PERSIST **2** : to receive maintenance (as food and clothing) : LIVE

sub·sist·ence \səb-'sis-tən(t)s\ *n* **1 a** : real being : EXISTENCE **b** : CONTINUATION, PERSISTENCE **2 a** : means of subsisting **b** : the minimum (as of food and shelter) necessary to support life — **sub·sist·ent** \-tənt\ *adj*

sub·soil \'səb-ˌsȯil\ *n* : a layer of weathered material that lies just under the surface soil

sub·son·ic \ˌsəb-'sän-ik\ *adj* **1** : of, relating to, or being a speed less than that of sound in air **2** : moving, capable of moving, or utilizing air currents moving at a subsonic speed

sub·spe·cies \'səb-ˌspē-(ˌ)shēz, -(ˌ)sēz\ *n* : a subdivision of a species; as **a** : a category in biological classification that ranks immediately below a species and designates a physically distinguishable and geographically separate group whose members are capable of interbreeding with those of other subspecies of the same species where their ranges overlap **b** : a named subdivision (as a race or variety) of a biological species — **sub·spe·cif·ic** \ˌsəb-spi-'sif-ik\ *adj*

sub·stance \'səb-stən(t)s\ *n* **1 a** : essential nature : ESSENCE ⟨divine *substance*⟩ **b** : the fundamental or essential part, quality, or import ⟨the *substance* of his speech⟩ **2 a** : physical material from which something is made **b** : matter of particular or definite chemical constitution **3** : PROPERTY, WEALTH ⟨a man of *substance*⟩

substand *abbr* substandard

sub·stan·dard \ˌsəb-'stan-dərd\ *adj* **1** : deviating from or falling short of a standard or norm **2** : conforming to a pattern of linguistic usage existing within a speech community but not that of the prestige group in that community

sub·stan·tial \səb-'stan-chəl\ *adj* **1 a** : existing as or in substance : MATERIAL ⟨*substantial* life⟩ **b** : not illusory : REAL ⟨the *substantial* world⟩ **c** : IMPORTANT, ESSENTIAL ⟨*substantial* differences⟩ **2 a** : ample to satisfy and nourish ⟨a *substantial* diet⟩ **b** : possessed of means : WELL-TO-DO ⟨a *substantial* farmer⟩ **c** : considerable in quantity : significantly large ⟨earned a *substantial* wage⟩ ⟨sent *substantial* reinforcements⟩ **d** : well and sturdily built ⟨*substantial* buildings⟩ — **sub·stan·ti·al·i·ty** \-ˌstan-chē-'al-ət-ē\ *n* — **sub·stan·tial·ly** \-'stanch-(ə-)lē\ *adv*

sub·stan·ti·ate \səb-'stan-chē-ˌāt\ *vb* **1** : to provide evidence for : PROVE ⟨*substantiated* his claims⟩ **2** : to give substance or body to : EMBODY — **sub·stan·ti·a·tion** \-ˌstan-chē-'ā-shən\ *n*

¹**sub·stan·tive** \'səb-stən-tiv\ *n* : a word or word group functioning syntactically as a noun — **sub·stan·ti·val** \ˌsəb-stən-'tī-vəl\ *adj* — **sub·stan·ti·val·ly** \-və-lē\ *adv*

²**substantive** *adj* **1** : of, relating to, or being something real or independent **2** : having the function of a grammatical substantive ⟨a *substantive* clause⟩ **3** : considerable in amount or numbers : SUBSTANTIAL **4** : creating and defining rights and duties ⟨*substantive* law⟩ — **sub·stan·tive·ly** *adv* — **sub·stan·tive·ness** *n*

sub·sta·tion \'səb-ˌstā-shən\ *n* **1** : a subsidiary station in which electric current is transformed **2** : a station subordinate to another station (as a post-office branch)

1sub·sti·tute \ˈsəb-stə-ˌt(y)üt\ *n* : a person or thing that takes the place of another — **substitute** *adj*

2substitute *vb* : to put in the place of another : REPLACE — **sub·sti·tu·tion** \ˌsəb-stə-ˈt(y)ü-shən\ *n*

sub·stra·tum \ˈsəb-ˌstrāt-əm, -ˌstrat-\ *n* **1** : an underlying support : FOUNDATION **2** : a layer beneath the surface soil : SUBSOIL

sub·struc·ture \ˈsəb-ˌstrək-chər\ *n* : FOUNDATION, GROUNDWORK

sub·teen \ˈsəb-ˈtēn\ *n* : a girl under 13 years of age

sub·ter·fuge \ˈsəb-tər-ˌfyüj\ *n* : a device (as a plan or trick) used to avoid some unpleasant circumstance (as to escape blame) : a deceptive evasion

sub·ter·ra·ne·an \ˌsəb-tə-ˈrā-nē-ən\ *or* **sub·ter·ra·ne·ous** \-nē-əs\ *adj* **1** : being, living, or operating under the surface of the earth **2** : existing or working in secret : HIDDEN — **sub·ter·ra·ne·an·ly** *adv*

sub·ti·tle \ˈsəb-ˌtīt-əl\ *n* **1** : a secondary or explanatory title **2** : a printed statement or fragment of dialogue appearing on the screen between the scenes of a silent motion picture or appearing as a translation at the bottom of the screen during the scenes — **subtitle** *vb*

sub·tle \ˈsət-əl\ *adj* **sub·tler** \ˈsət-(ə-)lər\; **sub·tlest** \ˈsət-(ə-)ləst\ **1 a** : DELICATE, ELUSIVE ⟨a *subtle* fragrance⟩ **b** : difficult to understand or distinguish : OBSCURE ⟨*subtle* differences in vowel sounds⟩ **2** : marked by insight and sensitivity : PERCEPTIVE ⟨a *subtle* mind⟩ **3 a** : WILY, DEVIOUS, ARTFUL ⟨*subtle* flattery⟩ **b** : INSIDIOUS 2 ⟨a *subtle* poison⟩ — **sub·tle·ness** \ˈsət-əl-nəs\ *n* — **sub·tly** \ˈsət-lē, ˈsət-əl-(l)ē\ *adv*

sub·tle·ty \ˈsət-əl-tē\ *n, pl* **-ties** **1** : the quality or state of being subtle **2** : something subtle; *esp* : a fine distinction

sub·ton·ic \ˌsəb-ˈtän-ik\ *n* : LEADING TONE

sub·top·ic \ˈsəb-ˌtäp-ik\ *n* : a subdivision of a topic

sub·tract \səb-ˈtrakt\ *vb* : to take away by deducting : perform a subtraction ⟨*subtract* 5 from 9⟩ — **sub·tract·er** *n*

sub·trac·tion \səb-ˈtrak-shən\ *n* **1** : an act or instance of subtracting **2** : the operation of deducting one number from another

sub·trac·tive \-ˈtrak-tiv\ *adj* **1** : tending to subtract **2** : constituting or involving subtraction

sub·tra·hend \ˈsəb-trə-ˌhend\ *n* : a number that is to be subtracted from a minuend

sub·trop·i·cal \ˌsəb-ˈträp-i-kəl\ *also* **sub·trop·ic** \-ˈträp-ik\ *adj* : of, relating to, or being the regions bordering on the tropical zone

sub·trop·ics \-ˈträp-iks\ *n pl* : subtropical regions

sub·urb \ˈsəb-ˌərb\ *n* **1 a** : an outlying part of a city or town **b** : a smaller community adjacent to a city **2** *pl* : the residential area adjacent to a city or large town — **sub·ur·ban** \sə-ˈbər-bən\ *adj or n*

sub·ur·ban·ite \sə-ˈbər-bə-ˌnīt\ *n* : a person who lives in the suburbs

sub·ver·sion \səb-ˈvər-zhən\ *n* : the act of subverting : the state of being subverted; *esp* : a systematic attempt to overthrow or undermine a government or political system by persons working secretly within the country involved — **sub·ver·sive** \-ˈvər-siv, -ziv\ *adj or n* — **sub·ver·sive·ly** *adv*

sub·vert \səb-ˈvərt\ *vb* **1** : to overturn or overthrow from the foundation : RUIN **2** : to undermine the morals, allegiance, or faith of : CORRUPT — **sub·vert·er** *n*

sub·way \ˈsəb-ˌwā\ *n* **1** : an underground passage **2** : a usu. electric underground railway

suc·ceed \sək-ˈsēd\ *vb* **1 a** : to come next after another in possession of an office or estate; *esp* : to inherit sovereignty **b** : to follow after another in order **2** : to turn out well : be successful ***syn*** see FOLLOW — **suc·ceed·er** *n*

suc·cess \sək-ˈses\ *n* **1 a** : degree or measure of succeeding **b** : a favorable completion of an undertaking **c** : the gaining of wealth, favor, or eminence **2** : a person or thing that succeeds

suc·cess·ful \-fəl\ *adj* **1** : resulting or ending in success **2** : gaining or having gained success — **suc·cess·ful·ly** \-fə-lē\ *adv* — **suc·cess·ful·ness** *n*

suc·ces·sion \sək-ˈsesh-ən\ *n* **1** : the order, action, or right of succeeding to a throne, title, or property **2 a** : a repeated following of one person or thing after another **b** : an ecological process in which a group of plants or animals is replaced by a series of other different groups **3** : a number of persons or things that follow one after another — **suc·ces·sion·al** \-ˈsesh-(ə-)nəl\ *adj* — **suc·ces·sion·al·ly** \-ē\ *adv*

suc·ces·sive \sək-ˈses-iv\ *adj* : following in succession or serial order : CONSECUTIVE — **suc·ces·sive·ly** *adv* — **suc·ces·sive·ness** *n*

suc·ces·sor \sək-ˈses-ər\ *n* : one that follows; *esp* : one who succeeds to a throne, title, estate, or office

suc·cinct \(ˌ)sək-ˈsiŋ(k)t, sə-ˈsiŋ(k)t\ *adj* : marked by brevity and compactness of expression : CONCISE, TERSE — **suc·cinct·ly** *adv* — **suc·cinct·ness** *n*

1suc·cor \ˈsək-ər\ *n* : AID, HELP, RELIEF

2succor *vb* : to go to the aid of (one in want or distress) : RELIEVE — **suc·cor·er** *n*

suc·co·tash \ˈsək-ə-ˌtash\ *n* : lima or shell beans and green corn cooked together

suc·cu·lent \-lənt\ *adj* **1 a** : full of juice : JUICY **b** : having fleshy tissues designed to conserve moisture ⟨*succulent* plants⟩ **2** : full of vitality, freshness, or richness — **suc·cu·lence** \-lən(t)s\ *n* — **suc·cu·lent·ly** *adv*

suc·cumb \sə-ˈkəm\ *vb* **1** : to yield to superior strength or force or overpowering appeal or desire **2** : to cease to exist : DIE

1such \(ˈ)səch\ *adj* **1 a** : of a kind or character to be indicated or suggested ⟨bag *such* as a doctor carries⟩ **b** : having a quality to a degree to be indicated ⟨his excitement was *such* that he shouted⟩ **2** : having a quality already specified ⟨deeply moved by *such* acts of kindness⟩ **3** : of the same class, type, or sort : SIMILAR ⟨established 20 *such* clinics throughout the state⟩ **4** : so great : so remarkable ⟨*such* a storm⟩ ⟨*such* courage⟩

2such *pron* **1** : such a person or thing ⟨he had a plan if it may be called *such*⟩ **2** : someone or something stated, implied, or exemplified ⟨*such* was the result⟩ ⟨*such* were the Romans⟩ **3** : someone or something of the same kind ⟨ships and planes and *such*⟩

3such *adv* **1** : to such a degree : so ⟨*such* tall buildings⟩ ⟨*such* a fine person⟩ **2** : ESPECIALLY, VERY ⟨hasn't been in *such* good spirits lately⟩

1such·like \ˈsəch-ˌlīk\ *adj* : of the kind : SIMILAR

2suchlike *pron* : someone or something of the same sort : a similar person or thing

1suck \ˈsək\ *vb* **1 a** : to draw in liquid or draw liquid from by movements of the mouth ⟨*suck* venom from a snakebite⟩ **b** : to draw milk from a breast or udder with the mouth **c** : to consume by applying the lips or tongue to ⟨*suck* a lollipop⟩ **d** : to apply the mouth to in the manner of a child sucking the breast ⟨*sucked* his bruised finger⟩ **2** : to take something in or up or remove something from by or as if by suction ⟨plants *sucking* moisture from the soil⟩ ⟨a well *sucked* dry by constant pumping⟩

2suck *n* **1** : the act of sucking **2** : a sucking movement or force

suck·er \'sək-ər\ *n* **1** : one that sucks **2** : a person who is easily deceived or tricked **3** : a part of an animal's body used for sucking or for clinging by suction **4** : any of numerous freshwater fishes related to the carps but having usu. thick soft lips for sucking in food **5** : a secondary shoot from the roots or lower part of a plant **6** : LOLLIPOP

suck·le \'sək-əl\ *vb* **suck·led**; **suck·ling** \-(ə-)liŋ\ **1** : to nurse at the breast or udder **2** : to bring up : NOURISH

suck·ling \'sək-liŋ\ *n* : a young unweaned mammal

su·crase \'sü-ˌkrās\ *n* : an enzyme that splits sucrose into glucose and fructose

su·crose \'sü-ˌkrōs\ *n* : a sweet crystalline sugar obtained esp. from sugarcane or sugar beets

suc·tion \'sək-shən\ *n* **1** : the act or process of sucking **2 a** : the action or process of drawing something (as liquid or dust) into a space (as a vacuum cleaner or a pump) by partially exhausting the air in the space **b** : force so exerted

suction cup *n* : a cup of glass or of a flexible material (as rubber) in which a partial vacuum is produced when applied to a surface

Su·da·nese \ˌsüd-ə-'nēz, -'nēs\ *adj* : of, relating to, or characteristic of Sudan or its people — **Sudanese** *n*

sud·den \'səd-ən\ *adj* **1 a** : happening or coming quickly and unexpectedly ⟨*sudden* shower⟩ **b** : come upon unexpectedly ⟨*sudden* turn in the road⟩ **c** : ABRUPT, STEEP ⟨*sudden* descent to the sea⟩ **2** : marked by or showing hastiness : RASH ⟨*sudden* decision⟩ **3** : made or brought about in a short time : PROMPT ⟨*sudden* cure⟩ — **sud·den·ly** *adv* — **sud·den·ness** \'səd-ən-(n)əs\ *n* — **all of a sudden** : sooner than was expected : SUDDENLY

sudden death *n* : a period of play to break a tie in a game or contest that terminates it the moment one side scores

¹suds \'sədz\ *n pl* **1 a** : soapy water esp. when frothy **b** : the froth on soapy water **2** *slang* : BEER

²suds *vb* **1** : to wash in suds **2** : to form suds

sudsy \'səd-zē\ *adj* **suds·i·er**; **-est** : full of suds : FROTHY, FOAMY

sue \'sü\ *vb* **1** : to seek justice from a person by bringing a legal action **2** : to make a request or application : PLEAD — usu. used with *for* or *to* ⟨the weaker nation *sued* for peace⟩ — **su·er** *n*

suede *or* **suède** \'swād\ *n* [from *suede gloves*, part translation of French *gants de Suède*, literally "gloves of Sweden"] **1** : leather with a napped surface **2** : a cloth fabric finished with a nap to simulate suede

su·et \'sü-ət\ *n* : the hard fat about the kidneys and loins in beef and mutton

suf·fer \'səf-ər\ *vb* **suf·fered**; **suf·fer·ing** \-(ə-)riŋ\ **1** : to feel or endure pain **2** : EXPERIENCE, UNDERGO ⟨*suffer* a defeat⟩ **3** : to bear loss or damage ⟨his business *suffered* during his illness⟩ **4** : ALLOW, PERMIT — **suf·fer·a·ble** \'səf-(ə-)rə-bəl\ *adj* — **suf·fer·a·ble·ness** *n* — **suf·fer·a·bly** \-blē\ *adv* — **suf·fer·er** \'səf-ər-ər\ *n*

suf·fer·ance \'səf-(ə-)rən(t)s\ *n* **1** : consent or approval implied by a lack of interference or failure to enforce a prohibition **2** : power or ability to endure ⟨beyond *sufferance*⟩

ə abut	ər further	a back	ā bake
ä cot, cart	aù out	ch chin	e less
ē easy	g gift	i trip	ī life
j joke	ŋ sing	ō flow	ȯ flaw
ȯi coin	th thin	t͟h this	ü loot
ù foot	y yet	yü few	yù furious
zh vision			

suf·fer·ing *n* **1** : the state or experience of one that suffers **2** : PAIN, HARDSHIP

suf·fice \sə-'fīs\ *vb* **1** : to meet or satisfy a need : be sufficient **2** : to be competent or capable **3** : to be enough for

suf·fi·cien·cy \sə-'fish-ən-sē\ *n, pl* **-cies** **1** : sufficient means to meet one's needs **2** : the quality or state of being sufficient : ADEQUACY

suf·fi·cient \sə-'fish-ənt\ *adj* : enough to meet the needs of a situation or a proposed end — **suf·fi·cient·ly** *adv*

¹suf·fix \'səf-ˌiks\ *n* : an affix occurring at the end of a word — **suf·fix·al** \-ˌik-səl\ *adj* — **suf·fix·less** \-ˌiks-ləs\ *adj*

²suf·fix \'səf-ˌiks, (ˌ)sə-'fiks\ *vb* : to attach as a suffix — **suf·fix·a·tion** \ˌsəf-ˌik-'sā-shən\ *n*

suf·fo·cate \'səf-ə-ˌkāt\ *vb* **1 a** : to stop the breath of (as by strangling or asphyxiation) **b** : to deprive of oxygen : distress by want of cool fresh air **2** : to be or become suffocated; *esp* : to die or suffer from lack of breathable air — **suf·fo·ca·tion** \ˌsəf-ə-'kā-shən\ *n*

suf·frage \'səf-rij\ *n* **1** : a vote given in deciding a disputed question or in electing a person to office **2 a** : the right of voting : FRANCHISE **b** : the exercise of such right

suf·frag·ette \ˌsəf-ri-'jet\ *n* : a woman who advocates suffrage for her sex

suf·frag·ist \'səf-ri-jəst\ *n* : one who advocates extension of suffrage esp. to women

suf·fuse \sə-'fyüz\ *vb* : to spread over or through in the manner of fluid or light ⟨a blush *suffused* the girl's cheeks⟩ — **suf·fu·sion** \-'fyü-zhən\ *n* — **suf·fu·sive** \-'fyü-siv, -ziv\ *adj*

¹sug·ar \'shu̇g-ər\ *n* **1** : a sweet substance that consists wholly or mostly of sucrose, is colorless or white when pure, is obtained commercially from sugarcane or sugar beet and some other plants, is a source of dietary carbohydrate, and is used as a sweetener and preservative of other foods **2** : any of various water-soluble compounds that vary widely in sweetness and comprise the simpler carbohydrates

²sugar *vb* **sug·ared**; **sug·ar·ing** \'shu̇g-(ə-)riŋ\ **1** : to mix, cover, or sprinkle with sugar **2** : to make something less hard to take or bear : SWEETEN ⟨*sugar* advice with flattery⟩ **3** : to change to crystals of sugar ⟨candy or icing *sugars* when cooked too long⟩

sugar beet *n* : a white-rooted beet grown for the sugar in its roots

sugar bush *n* : woods in which sugar maples predominate

sug·ar·cane \'shu̇g-ər-ˌkān\ *n* : a stout tall tropical grass that has broad leaves and a jointed stem from the juice of which sugar is made

sug·ar·coat \ˌshu̇g-ər-'kōt\ *vb* **1** : to coat with sugar **2** : to make attractive or agreeable on the surface ⟨*sugarcoat* an unpleasant truth⟩

sug·ar·house \'shu̇g-ər-ˌhau̇s\ *n* : a building where sugar is made or refined; *esp* : one where maple sap is boiled in the making of maple syrup and maple sugar

sug·ar·loaf \-ˌlōf\ *n* **1** : refined sugar molded into a cone **2** : a hill or mountain shaped like a sugarloaf — **sugarloaf** *adj*

sugar maple *n* : a maple of eastern No. America with 3-lobed to 5-lobed leaves, hard close-grained wood that is much used for cabinetwork, and sap that is the chief source of maple syrup and maple sugar

sugar orchard *n, chiefly New Eng* : SUGAR BUSH

sug·ar·plum \'shu̇g-ər-ˌpləm\ *n* : a round piece of candy : BONBON
sug·ary \'shu̇g-ə-rē\ *adj* **1** : containing, resembling, or tasting of sugar **2** : cloyingly sweet : SENTIMENTAL
sug·gest \sə(g)-'jest\ *vb* **1 a** : to put (as a thought, plan, or desire) into a person's mind **b** : to propose as an idea or possibility ⟨*suggest* going for a walk⟩ **2** : to call to mind through close connection or association ⟨that smoke *suggests* a forest fire⟩ — **sug·gest·er** *n*
sug·gest·i·ble \sə(g)-'jes-tə-bəl\ *adj* : easily influenced by suggestion — **sug·gest·i·bil·i·ty** \-ˌjes-tə-'bil-ət-ē\ *n*
sug·ges·tion \sə(g)-'jes-chən\ *n* **1 a** : the act or process of suggesting **b** : something suggested **2 a** : the process by which one thought leads to another esp. through association of ideas **b** : a means or process of influencing attitudes and behavior hypnotically **3** : a slight indication : TRACE
sug·ges·tive \sə(g)-'jes-tiv\ *adj* **1 a** : giving a suggestion : INDICATIVE **b** : full of suggestions : PROVOCATIVE ⟨*suggestive* commentary⟩ **c** : stirring mental associations : EVOCATIVE **2** : suggesting or tending to suggest something improper or indecent : RISQUÉ — **sug·ges·tive·ly** *adv* — **sug·ges·tive·ness** *n*
su·i·cide \'sü-ə-ˌsīd\ *n* **1 a** : the act of taking one's own life voluntarily **b** : ruin of one's own interests ⟨risking scandal and political *suicide*⟩ **2** : one that commits or attempts suicide — **su·i·cid·al** \ˌsü-ə-'sīd-əl\ *adj*
su·i·cid·ol·o·gy \ˌsü-ə-ˌsīd-'äl-ə-jē\ *n* : the study of suicide and suicide prevention
[1]**suit** \'süt\ *n* **1** : an action or process in a court for enforcing a right or claim **2** : an act or instance of suing or seeking by entreaty : APPEAL; *esp* : COURTSHIP **3** : a number of things used together : SET **4 a** : an outer costume of two or more pieces **b** : a costume to be worn for a special purpose or under particular conditions ⟨gym *suit*⟩ **5 a** : all the cards of one kind (as spades or hearts) in a pack of playing cards **b** : all the dominoes bearing the same number
[2]**suit** *vb* **1** : ACCORD, AGREE ⟨position *suits* with his abilities⟩ **2** : to be appropriate or satisfactory **3** : to outfit with clothes : DRESS **4** : ACCOMMODATE, ADAPT ⟨*suit* the action to the word⟩ **5 a** : to be proper for : BEFIT **b** : to be becoming to **6** : to meet the needs or desires of
suit·a·ble \'süt-ə-bəl\ *adj* **1** : adapted to a use or purpose ⟨food *suitable* for human consumption⟩ **2** : satisfying propriety : PROPER ⟨clothes *suitable* to the occasion⟩ **3** : CAPABLE, QUALIFIED ⟨looking for a *suitable* replacement⟩ ***syn*** see FIT ***ant*** unsuitable — **suit·a·bil·i·ty** \ˌsüt-ə-'bil-ət-ē\ *n* — **suit·a·ble·ness** \'süt-ə-bəl-nəs\ *n* — **suit·a·bly** \-blē\ *adv*
suit·case \'süt-ˌkās\ *n* : a rigid flat rectangular traveling bag
suite \'swēt, *2c is also* 'süt\ *n* **1** : the personal staff accompanying a ruler, diplomat, or dignitary on official business **2** : a group of things forming a unit or constituting a collection : SET: as **a** : a group of rooms occupied as a unit : APARTMENT **b** : an instrumental composition in a number of related usu. descriptive movements **c** : a set of matched furniture ⟨a bedroom *suite*⟩
suit·or \'süt-ər\ *n* **1** : one that petitions or entreats : PLEADER **2** : a party to a suit at law **3** : one who courts a woman or seeks to marry her
Suk·koth \'su̇k-ˌōt(h), -ˌōs\ *n* : a Jewish holiday celebrated in September or October as a harvest festival of thanksgiving and to commemorate the temporary shelters used by the Jews during their wanderings in the wilderness
sul·fa \'səl-fə\ *adj* : of or relating to sulfanilamide or the sulfa drugs
sul·fa·di·a·zine \ˌsəl-fə-'dī-ə-ˌzēn\ *n* : a sulfa drug used esp. in the treatment of meningitis, pneumonia, and intestinal infections
sulfa drug *n* : any of various synthetic bacteria-inhibiting drugs that are closely related chemically to sulfanilamide
sul·fa·mer·a·zine \ˌsəl-fə-'mer-ə-ˌzēn\ *n* : a sulfa drug with uses similar to those of sulfadiazine
sul·fa·nil·a·mide \ˌsəl-fə-'nil-ə-ˌmīd, -məd\ *n* : a crystalline compound that is the parent compound of most of the sulfa drugs
sul·fate \'səl-ˌfāt\ *n* : a salt or ester of sulfuric acid
sul·fide *or* **sul·phide** \'səl-ˌfīd\ *n* : a compound of sulfur with one or more other elements : a salt or ester of hydrogen sulfide
sul·fur *or* **sul·phur** \'səl-fər\ *n* : a nonmetallic element that occurs either free or combined esp. in nature, is a constituent of proteins, exists in several forms including yellow crystals, and is used esp. in the chemical and paper industries, in rubber vulcanization, and in medicine for treating skin diseases — see ELEMENT table
sulfur cycle *n* : the natural cycle involving the incorporation of sulfur into protein, its release from decomposed animals and plants, and its conversion by bacteria into a form usable by living organisms
sulfur dioxide *n* : a heavy strong-smelling gas used esp. in making sulfuric acid, in bleaching, as a preservative, and as a refrigerant
sul·fu·ric *or* **sul·phu·ric** \ˌsəl-'fyu̇(ə)r-ik\ *adj* : of, relating to, or containing sulfur
sulfuric acid *n* : a heavy corrosive oily strong acid that is colorless when pure and is a vigorous oxidizing and dehydrating agent
sul·fu·rous *or* **sul·phu·rous** \'səl-f(y)ə-rəs\ *adj* **1** : of, relating to, or dealing with the fire of hell : INFERNAL **2** : FIERY, INFLAMED ⟨*sulfurous* sermon⟩ **3** : PROFANE, BLASPHEMOUS — **sul·fu·rous·ly** *adv* — **sul·fu·rous·ness** *n*
[1]**sulk** \'səlk\ *vb* : to be moodily silent or ill-humored : nurse a grievance
[2]**sulk** *n* **1** : the state of one sulking — often used in pl. ⟨a case of the *sulks*⟩ **2** : a sulky mood or spell ⟨was in a *sulk*⟩
[1]**sulky** \'səl-kē\ *adj* **sulk·i·er**; **-est** **1** : inclined to sulk : given to fits of sulking **2** : DISCONTENTED, GLOOMY ⟨a *sulky* voice⟩ — **sulk·i·ly** \-kə-lē\ *adv* — **sulk·i·ness** \-kē-nəs\ *n*
[2]**sulky** *n, pl* **sulk·ies** : a light 2-wheeled 1-horse vehicle that has a seat for the driver only and that is used in harness racing
sul·len \'səl-ən\ *adj* **1 a** : gloomily or resentfully silent or repressed : not sociable **b** : suggesting a sullen state : LOWERING ⟨*sullen* refusal⟩ **2** : dull or somber in sound or color **3** : DISMAL, GLOOMY — **sul·len·ly** *adv* — **sul·len·ness** \'səl-ən-(n)əs\ *n*
sul·ly \'səl-ē\ *vb* **sul·lied**; **sul·ly·ing** : to make or become soiled or tarnished : SMIRCH
sul·phur–bot·tom whale \ˌsəl-fər-ˌbät-əm-\ *n* : BLUE WHALE
sul·tan \'səlt-ən\ *n* : a king or sovereign esp. of a Muslim state
sul·tana \ˌsəl-'tan-ə\ *n* **1** : a female member of a sultan's family; *esp* : a sultan's wife **2** : a pale yellow seedless grape grown for raisins and wine; *also* : its raisin **3** : a plant related to the jewelweeds and cultivated for its rich scarlet, pink, or white flowers
sul·tan·ate \'səlt-ə-ˌnāt\ *n* **1** : the office, dignity, or

power of a sultan **2 :** a state or country governed by a sultan

sul·try \'səl-trē\ *adj* **sul·tri·er; -est 1 :** very hot and humid **2 :** burning hot ⟨*sultry* sun⟩ **3 :** SENSUAL, VOLUPTUOUS — **sul·tri·ly** \-trə-lē\ *adv* — **sul·tri·ness** \-trē-nəs\ *n*

[1]**sum** \'səm\ *n* **1 :** an indefinite or specified amount of money **2 :** the whole amount : AGGREGATE **3 a :** EPITOME, SUMMARY **b :** GIST **4 a :** the result of adding numbers ⟨*sum* of 5 and 7 is 12⟩ **b :** a problem in arithmetic

[2]**sum** *vb* **summed; sum·ming 1 :** to calculate the sum of : COUNT **2 :** to reach a sum : AMOUNT — usu. used with *to* **3 :** SUMMARIZE — usu. used with *up*

su·mac *or* **su·mach** \'s(h)ü-ˌmak\ *n* **1 :** any of a genus of trees, shrubs, and woody vines with feathery compound leaves turning to brilliant red in autumn and spikes or loose clusters of red or whitish berries — compare POISON IVY, POISON OAK **2 :** a material used in tanning and dyeing made of the leaves and other parts of sumac

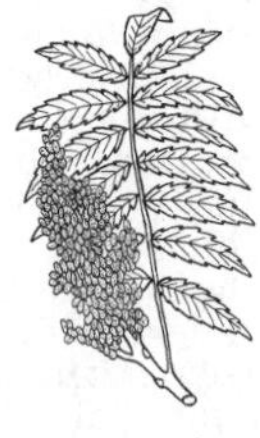
sumac 1

Su·mer·i·an \sů-'mer-ē-ən, -'mir-\ *n* **1 :** a native of Sumer **2 :** the language of the Sumerians surviving as a literary language after the rise of Akkadian — **Sumerian** *adj*

sum·ma·rize \'səm-ə-ˌrīz\ *vb* **1 :** to tell in or reduce to a summary **2 :** to make a summary — **sum·ma·ri·za·tion** \ˌsəm-ə-rə-'zā-shən\ *n* — **sum·ma·riz·er** \'səm-ə-ˌrī-zər\ *n*

[1]**sum·ma·ry** \'səm-ə-rē\ *adj* **1 :** expressing or covering the main points briefly : CONCISE ⟨a *summary* account⟩ **2 :** done without delay or formality : quickly carried out ⟨a *summary* procedure⟩ — **sum·mar·i·ly** \(ˌ)sə-'mer-ə-lē, 'səm-ə-rə-lē\ *adv*

[2]**summary** *n, pl* **-ries :** a concise statement of the main ideas (as of a book)

sum·ma·tion \(ˌ)sə-'mā-shən\ *n* **1 :** the act or process of forming a sum : ADDITION **2 :** SUM, TOTAL **3 :** a final part of an argument reviewing points made and expressing conclusions — **sum·ma·tion·al** \-sh(ə-)nəl\ *adj*

[1]**sum·mer** \'səm-ər\ *n* **1 a :** the season between spring and autumn including usu. the months of June, July, and August or as calculated astronomically extending from the June solstice to the September equinox **b :** the warmer half of the year **2 :** YEAR ⟨a girl of 16 *summers*⟩ **3 :** a time of fulfillment

[2]**summer** *vb* **sum·mered; sum·mer·ing** \'səm-(ə-)riŋ\ **1 :** to pass the summer **2 :** to keep or carry through the summer; *esp* : to provide with pasture during the summer

sum·mer·sault *var of* SOMERSAULT

summer school *n* **:** a school or school session conducted in summer esp. to enable students to accelerate progress, to make up credits lost through absence or failure, or to round out professional education

summer squash *n* **:** any of various garden squashes closely related to the typical pumpkins and used as a vegetable while immature

ə abut ər further a back ā bake
ä cot, cart aů out ch chin e less ē easy
g gift i trip ī life j joke ŋ sing ō flow
ȯ flaw ȯi coin th thin t͟h this ü loot
ů foot y yet yü few yů furious zh vision

sum·mer·time \'səm-ər-ˌtīm\ *n* **:** the summer season or a period like summer

sum·mer·wood \-ˌwůd\ *n* **:** the harder less porous portion of an annual ring of wood that develops late in the growing season — compare SPRINGWOOD

sum·mery \'səm-ə-rē\ *adj* **:** of, resembling, or fit for summer

sum·mit \'səm-ət\ *n* **1 :** TOP, APEX; *esp* : the highest point (as of a mountain) **2 :** the highest degree : PINNACLE **3 :** the highest level (as of officials) ⟨called a *summit* conference⟩

sum·mon \'səm-ən\ *vb* **1 :** to issue a call to convene : CONVOKE **2 :** to command by service of a summons to appear in court **3 :** to send for : CALL ⟨*summon* a physician⟩ **4 :** to call forth : AROUSE ⟨*summon* up enough courage to act⟩ — **sum·mon·er** *n*

[1]**sum·mons** \'səm-ənz\ *n, pl* **sum·mons·es 1 :** the act of summoning; *esp* : a call by authority to appear at a place named or to attend to some duty **2 :** a warning or notice to appear in court **3 :** a call, signal, or knock that summons

[2]**summons** *vb* **:** SUMMON 2

sump \'səmp\ *n* **:** a pit or reservoir serving as a receptacle or as a drain for fluids

sump·tu·ous \'səm(p)-chə-wəs\ *adj* **:** involving large expense : LAVISH, LUXURIOUS ⟨a *sumptuous* feast⟩ — **sump·tu·ous·ly** *adv* — **sump·tu·ous·ness** *n*

sum total *n* **1 :** a total arrived at through the counting of sums **2 :** total result : TOTALITY ⟨the *sum total* of weeks of discussion was a deadlock⟩

[1]**sun** \'sən\ *n* **1 a :** the luminous celestial body around which the planets revolve, from which they receive heat and light, and which has a mean distance from the earth of 93,000,000 miles and a diameter of 864,000 miles **b :** a celestial body like the sun **2 :** the heat or light radiated from the sun : SUNSHINE **3 :** one resembling the sun usu. in brilliance **4 :** the rising or setting of the sun ⟨from *sun* to *sun*⟩ — **in the sun :** in the public eye

[2]**sun** *vb* **sunned; sun·ning 1 :** to expose to or as if to the rays of the sun **2 :** to sun oneself

Sun *abbr* Sunday

sun·baked \'sən-ˌbākt\ *adj* **1 :** baked by exposure to sunshine ⟨*sunbaked* bricks⟩ **2 :** heated, parched, or compacted esp. by excessive sunlight ⟨*sunbaked* beaches of southern Africa⟩

sun·bath \'sən-ˌbath, -ˌbȧth\ *n* **:** exposure to sunlight or a sunlamp

sun·bathe \-ˌbāt͟h\ *vb* **:** to take a sunbath — **sun·bath·er** \-ˌbā-t͟hər\ *n*

sun·beam \-ˌbēm\ *n* **:** a ray of sunlight

sun·bon·net \-ˌbän-ət\ *n* **:** a woman's bonnet with a wide brim framing the face and usu. a ruffle at the back to protect the neck from the sun

[1]**sun·burn** \-ˌbərn\ *vb* **1 :** to burn or discolor by the sun **2 :** to cause or undergo sunburn

[2]**sunburn** *n* **:** a skin inflammation caused by overexposure to sunlight

sun·burst \'sən-ˌbərst\ *n* **1 :** a burst of sunlight esp. through a break in the clouds **2 :** a representation of a sun surrounded by rays

sun·dae \'sən-dē\ *n* **:** a portion of ice cream served with topping (as crushed fruit, syrup, or nuts)

Sun·day \'sən-dē\ *n* **:** the 1st day of the week : the Christian Sabbath

Sunday school *n* **:** a school held on Sunday for religious education

sun deck *n* **:** a ship's deck or a roof or terrace used for sunning

sun·der \'sən-dər\ *vb* **sun·dered; sun·der·ing** \-d(ə-)riŋ\ **:** to break or force apart or in two : sever esp. with violence

sun·di·al \'sən-ˌdī(-ə)l\ *n* : a device to show the time of day by the position of the shadow cast on a plate or disk typically by an upright pin

sundial

sun·down \-ˌdau̇n\ *n* : SUNSET
sun·down·er \-ˌdau̇-nər\ *n, Austral* : TRAMP, HOBO
sun·dries \'sən-drēz\ *n pl* : miscellaneous small articles or items
sun·dry \'sən-drē\ *adj* : MISCELLANEOUS, SEVERAL, VARIOUS ⟨for *sundry* reasons⟩
sun·fast \'sən-ˌfast\ *adj* : resistant to fading by sunlight ⟨*sunfast* dyes⟩
sun·fish \-ˌfish\ *n* **1** : a large sea fish with a very deep, short, and flat body, high fins, and a small mouth **2** : any of a family of American freshwater fishes that are related to the perches and usu. have a deep compressed body and metallic coloration
sun·flow·er \-ˌflau̇(-ə)r\ *n* : any of a genus of tall herbs related to the daisies that are often grown for their showy yellow-rayed flower heads and for their oil-rich seeds
sung *past of* SING
sun·glass·es \'sən-ˌglas-əz\ *n pl* : glasses to protect the eyes from the sun
sunk *past of* SINK
sunk·en \'səng-kən\ *adj* **1** : SUBMERGED ⟨*sunken* ships⟩ **2** : fallen in : HOLLOW ⟨*sunken* cheeks⟩ **3 a** : lying in a depression ⟨*sunken* garden⟩ **b** : constructed below the general floor level ⟨*sunken* living room⟩
sun·lamp \'sən-ˌlamp\ *n* : an electric lamp designed to emit radiation of wavelengths from ultraviolet to infrared
sun·less \'sən-ləs\ *adj* : lacking sunshine
sun·light \-ˌlīt\ *n* : the light of the sun : SUNSHINE
sun·lit \-ˌlit\ *adj* : lighted by or as if by the sun
sun·ny \'sən-ē\ *adj* **sun·ni·er**; **-est 1** : bright with sunshine ⟨*sunny* day⟩ ⟨*sunny* room⟩ **2** : MERRY, BRIGHT, CHEERFUL ⟨*sunny* smile⟩ — **sun·ni·ly** \'sən-ə-lē\ *adv* — **sun·ni·ness** \'sən-ē-nəs\ *n*
sun·rise \'sən-ˌrīz\ *n* **1** : the apparent rising of the sun above the horizon; *also* : the accompanying atmospheric effects (as color) **2** : the time at which the sun rises
sun·set \-ˌset\ *n* **1** : the apparent descent of the sun below the horizon; *also* : the accompanying atmospheric effects **2** : the time at which the sun sets
sun·shine \-ˌshīn\ *n* **1 a** : the sun's light or direct rays **b** : the warmth and light given by the sun's rays **2** : something that radiates warmth, cheer, or happiness — **sun·shiny** \-ˌshī-nē\ *adj*
sun·spot \-ˌspät\ *n* : one of the dark spots that appear from time to time on the sun's surface and are usu. visible only with the telescope
sun·stroke \-ˌstrōk\ *n* : heatstroke caused by direct exposure to the sun
sun·tan \-ˌtan\ *n* : a browning of the skin from exposure to the rays of the sun — **sun·tanned** \-ˌtand\ *adj*
sun time *n* : the time of day reckoned by the daily apparent motion of the sun or by a sundial
sun·up \'sən-ˌəp\ *n* : SUNRISE
1**sun·ward** \-wərd\ *or* **sun·wards** \-wərdz\ *adv* : toward the sun
2**sunward** *adj* : facing the sun
1**sup** \'səp\ *vb* **supped**; **sup·ping** : to take or drink in swallows or gulps
2**sup** *n* : a mouthful of liquid : SIP
3**sup** *vb* **supped**; **sup·ping 1** : to eat the evening meal **2** : to make one's supper — used with *on* or *off* ⟨*supped* on roast beef⟩
sup *abbr* **1** supplement **2** supply
1**su·per** \'sü-pər\ *n* **1** : a supernumerary actor **2** : SUPERINTENDENT, SUPERVISOR
2**super** *adj* **1** : very good **2** : very large or powerful : GREAT — **super** *adv*
super- *prefix* **1 a** : over and above : higher in quantity, quality, or degree than : more than ⟨*super*human⟩ **b** : exceeding or so as to exceed a norm ⟨*super*heat⟩ **c** : surpassing all or most others of its kind ⟨*super*highway⟩ **2 a** : situated or placed above, on, or at the top of ⟨*super*tower⟩ **b** : next above or higher ⟨*super*tonic⟩
su·per·a·ble \'sü-p(ə-)rə-bəl\ *adj* : capable of being overcome or conquered : SURMOUNTABLE — **su·per·a·ble·ness** *n* — **su·per·a·bly** \-blē\ *adv*
su·per·abun·dant \-ə-'bən-dənt\ *adj* : more than ample : EXCESSIVE — **su·per·abun·dance** \-dən(t)s\ *n* — **su·per·abun·dant·ly** *adv*
su·per·an·nu·ate \ˌsü-pər-'an-yə-ˌwāt\ *vb* **1** : to retire and pension because of age or infirmity **2** : to become retired or antiquated — **su·per·an·nu·a·tion** \-ˌan-yə-'wā-shən\ *n*
su·per·an·nu·at·ed *adj* **1** : too old or outmoded for work or use **2** : retired on a pension
su·perb \su̇-'pərb\ *adj* **1** : MAJESTIC, NOBLE **2** : RICH, SUMPTUOUS **3** : of supreme excellence or beauty — **su·perb·ly** *adv* — **su·perb·ness** *n*

S

su·per·charg·er \'sü-pər-ˌchär-jər\ *n* : a device (as a blower or compressor) for increasing the volume air charge of an internal-combustion engine or for pressurizing the cabin of an airplane — **su·per·charge** \-ˌchärj\ *vb*
su·per·cil·i·ous \ˌsü-pər-'sil-ē-əs\ *adj* : haughtily contemptuous : SNOOTY, SNOBBISH — **su·per·cil·i·ous·ly** *adv* — **su·per·cil·i·ous·ness** *n*
su·per·con·duc·tiv·i·ty \ˌsü-pər-ˌkän-ˌdək-'tiv-ət-ē\ *n* : a complete disappearance of electrical resistance in various metals at temperatures near absolute zero
su·per·cool \ˌsü-pər-'kül\ *vb* : to cool below the freezing point without solidification or crystallization
su·per·fi·cial \ˌsü-pər-'fish-əl\ *adj* **1 a** : of or relating to a surface **b** : situated on or near or affecting only the surface **2** : concerned only with the obvious or apparent : not profound or thorough : SHALLOW — **su·per·fi·ci·al·i·ty** \-ˌfish-ē-'al-ət-ē\ *n* — **su·per·fi·cial·ly** \-'fish-(ə-)lē\ *adv* — **su·per·fi·cial·ness** \-'fish-əl-nəs\ *n*
su·per·fine \ˌsü-pər-'fīn\ *adj* **1** : overly refined or nice **2** : extremely fine **3** : of high quality or grade
su·per·flu·ous \su̇-'pər-flə-wəs\ *adj* : exceeding what is sufficient or necessary : EXTRA — **su·per·flu·i·ty** \ˌsü-pər-'flü-ət-ē\ *n* — **su·per·flu·ous·ly** \su̇-'pər-flə-wəs-lē\ *adv* — **su·per·flu·ous·ness** *n*
su·per·heat \ˌsü-pər-'hēt\ *vb* **1 a** : to heat a liquid above the boiling point without converting into vapor **b** : to heat (steam) to a higher temperature than the normal boiling point of water **2** : to heat very much or excessively
su·per·high·way \ˌsü-pər-'hī-ˌwā\ *n* : a broad highway designed for high-speed traffic
su·per·hu·man \-'hyü-mən, -'yü-\ *adj* **1** : being above the human : DIVINE **2** : exceeding normal human power, size, or capability : HERCULEAN ⟨*superhuman* effort⟩ — **su·per·hu·man·ly** *adv*
su·per·im·pose \ˌsü-pər-im-'pōz\ *vb* : to place or lay over or above something — **su·per·im·pos·a·ble** \-'pō-zə-bəl\ *adj* — **su·per·im·po·si·tion** \-ˌim-pə-'zish-ən\ *n*

su·per·in·tend \ˌsü-p(ə-)rin-ˈtend\ *vb* : to have or exercise the charge and oversight of : DIRECT

su·per·in·tend·ence \-ˈten-dən(t)s\ *or* **su·per·in·tend·en·cy** \-dən-sē\ *n, pl* **-enc·es** *or* **-en·cies** : the act, duty, or office of superintending or overseeing

su·per·in·tend·ent \-dənt\ *n* : a person who oversees or manages something ⟨a building *superintendent*⟩ ⟨*superintendent* of schools⟩

[1]**su·pe·ri·or** \su̇-ˈpir-ē-ər\ *adj* **1** : situated higher up : UPPER **2 a** : of higher rank, quality, or importance **b** : greater in quantity or numbers **3** : courageously or serenely indifferent ⟨*superior* to pain⟩ **4 a** : excellent of its kind : BETTER **b** : affecting or assuming an air of superiority : SUPERCILIOUS ⟨a *superior* smile⟩ **5** : covering or including more things ⟨a genus is *superior* to a species⟩ — **su·pe·ri·or·i·ty** \-ˌpir-ē-ˈȯr-ət-ē, -ˈär-\ *n* — **su·pe·ri·or·ly** \-ˈpir-ē-ər-lē\ *adv*

[2]**superior** *n* **1** : one who is above another in rank, station, or office; *esp* : the head of a religious house or order **2** : one that surpasses another in quality or merit

superior vena cava *n* : a large vein that returns blood from the head and forelimbs to the heart

su·per·ja·cent \ˌsü-pər-ˈjā-sənt\ *adj* : lying above or upon : OVERLYING ⟨*superjacent* rocks⟩

[1]**su·per·la·tive** \su̇-ˈpər-lət-iv\ *adj* **1** : of, relating to, or being the degree of grammatical comparison that denotes an extreme or unsurpassed level or extent **2** : surpassing all others : SUPREME ⟨a *superlative* performance⟩ — **su·per·la·tive·ly** *adv* — **su·per·la·tive·ness** *n*

[2]**superlative** *n* **1** : the superlative degree or a superlative form in a language **2** : the superlative or utmost degree of something : ACME **3** : something that is superlative

su·per·man \ˈsü-pər-ˌman\ *n* : a man with superhuman physical, mental, or spiritual powers

su·per·mar·ket \-ˌmär-kət\ *n* : a self-service retail market selling foods and household merchandise

su·per·nal \su̇-ˈpərn-əl\ *adj* **1 a** : being or coming from on high : HEAVENLY **b** : LOFTY, ETHEREAL ⟨*supernal* strains of melody⟩ **2** : located or originating in the sky — **su·per·nal·ly** \-nə-lē\ *adv*

su·per·nat·u·ral \ˌsü-pər-ˈnach-(ə-)rəl\ *adj* **1** : of or relating to an order of existence beyond the visible observable universe; *esp* : of or relating to God or a god, demigod, spirit, or infernal being **2 a** : departing from what is usual or normal esp. so as to appear to transcend the laws of nature **b** : attributed to a supernormal agency (as a ghost or spirit) — **supernatural** *n* — **su·per·nat·u·ral·ly** \-ˈnach-(ə-)rə-lē, -ˈnach-ər-lē\ *adv*

su·per·nor·mal \-ˈnȯr-məl\ *adj* **1** : exceeding the normal or average **2** : being beyond natural human powers

su·per·no·va \-ˈnō-və\ *n* : a star that is a nova in which the maximum luminosity may reach 100 million times that of the sun

[1]**su·per·nu·mer·ary** \ˌsü-pər-ˈn(y)ü-mə-ˌrer-ē\ *adj* : exceeding the stated, prescribed, or needed number : EXTRA, SUPERFLUOUS

[2]**supernumerary** *n, pl* **-ar·ies** **1** : a supernumerary person or thing **2** : an actor employed to play a small usu. nonspeaking part

ə abut	ər further		a back		ā bake
ä cot, cart	au̇ out	ch chin	e less		ē easy
g gift	i trip	ī life	j joke	ng sing	ō flow
ȯ flaw	ȯi coin	th thin	t͟h this		ü loot
u̇ foot	y yet	yü few	yu̇ furious		zh vision

su·per·phos·phate \ˌsü-pər-ˈfäs-ˌfāt\ *n* : a soluble mixture of phosphates used as fertilizer

su·per·pose \ˌsü-pər-ˈpōz\ *vb* : to place or lay over or above another esp. so as to coincide ⟨congruent triangles can be *superposed*⟩ — **su·per·po·si·tion** \-pə-ˈzish-ən\ *n*

su·per·sat·u·rate \ˌsü-pər-ˈsach-ə-ˌrāt\ *vb* : to add to beyond saturation

su·per·scribe \ˈsü-pər-ˌskrīb\ *vb* : to write or engrave on the top or outside; *esp* : to write (as a name or address) on the outside or cover of

su·per·script \-ˌskript\ *n* : a distinguishing symbol or letter written immediately above or above and to the side of another character — **superscript** *adj*

su·per·scrip·tion \ˌsü-pər-ˈskrip-shən\ *n* **1** : the act of superscribing **2** : something superscribed on something else : INSCRIPTION; *esp* : ADDRESS

su·per·sede \ˌsü-pər-ˈsēd\ *vb* [from Latin *supersedēre* "to sit on top of", from *super-* "above" and *sedēre* "to sit"] **1** : to force out of use as inferior ⟨new methods have *superseded* the older ones⟩ **2** : to take the place, room, or position of : REPLACE **3** : to displace in favor of another : SUPPLANT — **su·per·sed·er** *n* — **su·per·se·dure** \-ˈsē-jər\ *n*

su·per·sen·si·tive \-ˈsen(t)-sət-iv, -ˈsen(t)-stiv\ *adj* : HYPERSENSITIVE — **su·per·sen·si·tive·ness** *n*

su·per·ses·sion \ˌsü-pər-ˈsesh-ən\ *n* : the act of superseding : the state of being superseded : SUPERSEDURE — **su·per·ses·sive** \-ˈses-iv\ *adj*

su·per·son·ic \-ˈsän-ik\ *adj* **1** : of, being, or relating to speeds from one to five times the speed of sound in air **2** : moving, capable of moving, or utilizing air currents moving at supersonic speed ⟨a *supersonic* airplane⟩ — **su·per·son·i·cal·ly** \-i-k(ə-)lē\ *adv* — **su·per·son·ics** \-iks\ *n*

su·per·sti·tion \ˌsü-pər-ˈstish-ən\ *n* **1** : beliefs or practices resulting from ignorance, fear of the unknown, or trust in magic or chance **2** : an unreasoning fear of nature, the unknown, or God resulting from superstition — **su·per·sti·tious** \-ˈstish-əs\ *adj* — **su·per·sti·tious·ly** *adv* — **su·per·sti·tious·ness** *n*

su·per·struc·ture \ˈsü-pər-ˌstrək-chər\ *n* : something built upon an underlying or more fundamental base — **su·per·struc·tur·al** \-ˌstrək-chə-rəl\ *adj*

su·per·ton·ic \ˌsü-pər-ˈtän-ik\ *n* : the second tone of the musical scale

su·per·vene \ˌsü-pər-ˈvēn\ *vb* : to take place as an additional, accidental, or unlooked-for development — **su·per·ve·nience** \-ˈvē-nyən(t)s\ *n* — **su·per·ve·nient** \-nyənt\ *adj* — **su·per·ven·tion** \-ˈven-chən\ *n*

su·per·vise \ˈsü-pər-ˌvīz\ *vb* : SUPERINTEND, OVERSEE — **su·per·vi·sion** \ˌsü-pər-ˈvizh-ən\ *n*

su·per·vi·sor \ˈsü-pər-ˌvī-zər\ *n* : one that supervises; *esp* : an administrative officer in charge of a business, government, or school unit or operation — **su·per·vi·so·ry** \ˌsü-pər-ˈvīz-(ə-)rē\ *adj*

su·pine \su̇-ˈpīn\ *adj* **1** : lying on the back or with the face upward **2** : showing mental or moral slackness : SLUGGISH, LAZY — **su·pine·ly** *adv* — **su·pine·ness** \-ˈpīn-nəs\ *n*

sup·per \ˈsəp-ər\ *n* **1** : the evening meal when dinner is taken at midday **2** : refreshments served late in the evening esp. at a social gathering

sup·plant \sə-ˈplant\ *vb* **1** : to take the place of another esp. by force or treachery **2 a** : to root out and supply a substitute for ⟨efforts to *supplant* the vernacular⟩ **b** : to gain the place of esp. by reason of superior excellence or power — **sup·plan·ta·tion** \sə-ˌplan-ˈtā-shən\ *n* — **sup·plant·er** \sə-ˈplant-ər\ *n*

[1]**sup·ple** \'səp-əl\ *adj* **sup·pler** \'səp-(ə-)lər\; **sup·plest** \'səp-(ə-)ləst\ **1** : readily adaptable to new situations ⟨a *supple* mind⟩ **2 a** : capable of being bent or folded without creases or breaks : PLIANT ⟨*supple* leather⟩ **b** : able to bend or twist with ease and grace : LIMBER ⟨*supple* legs of a dancer⟩ — **sup·ple·ness** \-əl-nəs\ *n*

[2]**supple** *vb* **sup·pled**; **sup·pling** \'səp-(ə-)ling\ : to make supple

[1]**sup·ple·ment** \'səp-lə-mənt\ *n* **1** : something that supplies a want or makes an addition ⟨diet *supplements*⟩ **2** : an arc or angle that when added to a given arc or angle equals 180 degrees — **sup·ple·men·tal** \ˌsəp-lə-'ment-əl\ *adj*

[2]**sup·ple·ment** \'səp-lə-ˌment\ *vb* : to add to ⟨*supplements* his income by doing odd jobs⟩

sup·ple·men·ta·ry \ˌsəp-lə-'ment-ə-rē, -'men-trē\ *adj* : added as a supplement : ADDITIONAL

supplementary angles *n pl* : two angles whose sum is 180 degrees

[1]**sup·pli·ant** \'səp-lē-ənt\ *n* : one who supplicates

[2]**suppliant** *adj* : BESEECHING, IMPLORING — **sup·pli·ant·ly** *adv*

sup·pli·cant \'səp-li-kənt\ *n* : one who supplicates — **supplicant** *adj* — **sup·pli·cant·ly** *adv*

sup·pli·cate \'səp-lə-ˌkāt\ *vb* **1** : to make a humble entreaty; *esp* : to pray to God **2** : to ask earnestly and humbly : BESEECH — **sup·pli·ca·tion** \ˌsəp-lə-'kā-shən\ *n*

[1]**sup·ply** \sə-'plī\ *vb* **sup·plied**; **sup·ply·ing** **1** : to add as a supplement **2 a** : to provide for : SATISFY **b** : to provide or furnish with : AFFORD **c** : to satisfy the needs or wishes of — **sup·pli·er** \-'plī(-ə)r\ *n*

[2]**supply** *n*, *pl* **supplies** **1 a** : the quantity or amount (as of a commodity) needed or available **b** : PROVISIONS, STORES — usu. used in pl. **2** : the act or process of filling a want or need : PROVISION **3** : the quantities of goods or services offered for sale at a particular time or at one price

[1]**sup·port** \sə-'pōrt, -'pȯrt\ *vb* **1** : to endure bravely or quietly : BEAR **2 a** : to promote the interests or cause of **b** : to uphold or defend as valid or right : ADVOCATE **c** : to argue or vote for **d** : ASSIST, HELP **e** : to act with a star actor **f** : SUBSTANTIATE, VERIFY **3** : to pay the costs of : MAINTAIN **4 a** : to hold up or in position or serve as a foundation or prop for **b** : to maintain the price of a commodity at a high level by purchases or loans **5** : to keep something going : SUSTAIN — **sup·port·a·ble** \-ə-bəl\ *adj* — **sup·port·a·ble·ness** *n* — **sup·port·a·bly** \-blē\ *adv*

[2]**support** *n* **1** : the act or process of supporting : the condition of being supported **2** : one that supports

sup·port·er \sə-'pōrt-ər, -'pȯrt-\ *n* : one that supports; *esp* : ADHERENT, ADVOCATE

sup·pose \sə-'pōz\ *vb* **1** : to take as true or as a fact for the sake of argument ⟨*suppose* a fire should break out⟩ **2** : to hold as an opinion : BELIEVE ⟨they *supposed* they were on the right bus⟩ **3** : CONJECTURE, OPINE ⟨who do you *suppose* will win⟩

sup·posed \sə-'pōzd\ *adj* **1 a** : BELIEVED **b** : mistakenly believed : IMAGINED **2** : EXPECTED — used in the phrase *be supposed to* ⟨was *supposed* to be here by now⟩ — **sup·pos·ed·ly** \-'pō-zəd-lē\ *adv*

sup·po·si·tion \ˌsəp-ə-'zish-ən\ *n* **1** : something that is supposed : HYPOTHESIS **2** : the act of supposing — **sup·po·si·tion·al** \-'zish-(ə-)nəl\ *adj* — **sup·po·si·tion·al·ly** *adv*

sup·pos·i·tive \sə-'päz-ət-iv\ *adj* : SUPPOSED — **sup·pos·i·tive·ly** *adv*

sup·press \sə-'pres\ *vb* **1** : to put down by authority or force : SUBDUE ⟨*suppress* a rebellion⟩ **2 a** : to keep from being known ⟨tried to *suppress* the news⟩ **b** : to stop the publication or circulation of ⟨*suppresses* the magazine⟩ **3 a** : to exclude from consciousness : REPRESS **b** : to keep from giving vent to ⟨*suppressed* a giggle⟩ **4 a** : to restrain from a usual course or action : HALT ⟨*suppress* a hemorrhage⟩ **b** : to inhibit the growth or development of : STUNT — **sup·press·i·ble** \-ə-bəl\ *adj* — **sup·pres·sion** \-'presh-ən\ *n* — **sup·pres·sive** \-'pres-iv\ *adj* — **sup·pres·sor** \-'pres-ər\ *n*

sup·pu·rate \'səp-yə-ˌrāt\ *vb* : to form or give off pus — **sup·pu·ra·tion** \ˌsəp-yə-'rā-shən\ *n* — **sup·pu·ra·tive** \'səp-yə-ˌrāt-iv\ *adj*

supra- *prefix* **1** : SUPER- 2a ⟨*supra*orbital⟩ **2** : transcending ⟨*supra*molecular⟩

su·pra·na·tion·al \ˌsü-prə-'nash-(ə-)nəl\ *adj* : transcending national boundaries or authority

[1]**su·pra·re·nal** \-'rēn-əl\ *adj* : situated above or anterior to the kidneys; *esp* : ADRENAL

[2]**suprarenal** *n* : ADRENAL GLAND

su·prem·a·cist \sü-'prem-ə-səst\ *n* : an advocate of group supremacy ⟨a white *supremacist*⟩

su·prem·a·cy \sü-'prem-ə-sē\ *n*, *pl* **-cies** **1** : the quality or state of being supreme **2** : supreme authority or power

su·preme \sü-'prēm\ *adj* [from Latin *supremus*, superlative of *superus* "upper", from *super* "over", "above"] **1** : highest in rank or authority **2** : highest in degree or quality **3** : ULTIMATE, FINAL ⟨*supreme* sacrifice⟩ — **su·preme·ly** *adv* — **su·preme·ness** *n*

Supreme Being *n* : [2]GOD

supreme court *n* : the highest court of the U.S. consisting of a chief justice and eight associate justices; *also* : a similar body in many states

supt *abbr* superintendent

sur- *prefix* : over : SUPER- ⟨*sur*print⟩ ⟨*sur*tax⟩

sur·cease \'sər-ˌsēs, (ˌ)sər-'\ *n* : CESSATION; *esp* : a temporary respite or end

[1]**sur·charge** \'sər-ˌchärj\ *vb* **1 a** : OVERCHARGE **b** : to charge an extra fee **2** : OVERLOAD **3** : to mark a new denomination figure or a surcharge on a stamp

[2]**surcharge** *n* **1** : an additional tax or charge **2** : an excessive load or burden **3 a** : an overprint on a stamp; *esp* : one that alters the denomination **b** : a stamp bearing such an overprint

sur·cin·gle \'sər-ˌsing-gəl\ *n* : a belt, band, or girth passing around the body of a horse to bind a saddle or pack fast to the horse's back

sur·coat \'sər-ˌkōt\ *n* : an outer coat or cloak; *esp* : a tunic worn over armor

[1]**sure** \'shu̇(ə)r\ *adj* [from French *sur*, from Latin *securus* "secure"; see SECURE] **1** : firmly established : STEADFAST **2** : RELIABLE, TRUSTWORTHY **3** : ASSURED, CONFIDENT **4** : admitting of no doubt : CERTAIN **5 a** : bound to happen : INEVITABLE ⟨*sure* disaster⟩ **b** : DESTINED, BOUND ⟨he is *sure* to win⟩ — **sure·ness** *n* — **for sure** : without doubt : with certainty — **to be sure** **1** : SURELY, CERTAINLY **2** : ADMITTEDLY

[2]**sure** *adv* : SURELY

sure·fire \-'fī(ə)r\ *adj* : certain to get results : DEPENDABLE

sure·foot·ed \-'fu̇t-əd\ *adj* : not liable to stumble or fall — **sure·foot·ed·ness** *n*

sure·ly \'shu̇(ə)r-lē\ *adv* **1 a** : with assurance : CONFIDENTLY **b** : without doubt : CERTAINLY ⟨slowly but *surely*⟩ **2** : INDEED, REALLY — often used as an intensive ⟨I *surely* am tired this afternoon⟩

S

sure·ty \'shu̇r-ət-ē, 'shu̇(ə)rt-ē\ *n, pl* **sureties** **1 :** sure knowledge : CERTAINTY **2 :** a formal engagement (as a pledge) for the fulfillment of an undertaking : GUARANTEE **3 :** one who assumes legal liability for the debt, default, or failure in duty of another — **sure·ty·ship** \-ē-,ship\ *n*

surf \'sərf\ *n* **1 :** the swell of the sea that breaks upon the shore **2 :** the foam, splash, and sound of breaking waves

1**sur·face** \'sər-fəs\ *n* **1 :** the outside of an object or body **2 :** a plane or curved two-dimensional locus of points ⟨*surface* of a sphere⟩ **3 :** the external or superficial aspect of something — **surface** *adj*

2**surface** *vb* **1 a :** to give a surface to ⟨*surface* a road⟩ **b :** to plane or make smooth (as lumber) **2 :** to come to the surface ⟨the submarine *surfaced*⟩ — **sur·fac·er** *n*

surface tension *n* **:** a condition that exists at the surface of a liquid by reason of intermolecular forces about the individual surface molecules and is manifested by properties resembling those of an elastic skin under tension

sur·fac·ing \'sər-fə-sing\ *n* **:** material forming or used to form a surface

surf·board \'sərf-,bōrd, -,bȯrd\ *n* **:** a buoyant board used in surf-riding — **surfboard** *vb* — **surf·board·er** *n*

surf·boat \-,bōt\ *n* **:** a boat for use in heavy surf

1**sur·feit** \'sər-fət\ *n* **1 :** an overabundant supply : EXCESS **2 :** an intemperate indulgence in something (as food or drink) **3 :** disgust caused by excess : SATIETY

2**surfeit** *vb* **:** to feed, supply, or indulge to the point of surfeit : CLOY

surf–rid·ing \'sərf-,rīd-ing\ *n* **:** the sport of riding the surf on a surfboard

surg *abbr* **1** surgeon **2** surgery **3** surgical

1**surge** \'sərj\ *vb* **1 :** to rise and fall in or as if in waves **2 :** to rise suddenly to an abnormal value — used esp. of current or voltage

2**surge** *n* **1 :** a swelling, rolling, or sweeping forward like that of a wave **2 :** a large wave or billow : SWELL **3 :** a transient sudden rise of current in an electrical circuit

sur·geon \'sər-jən\ *n* **:** a physician who specializes in surgery

sur·gery \'sərj-(ə-)rē\ *n, pl* **-ger·ies** [from Old French *cirurgie, cirurgerie,* from Latin *chirurgia,* from Greek *cheirourgia,* from *cheir* "hand" and *ergon* "work"] **1 :** medical science concerned with the correction of physical defects, the repair and healing of injuries, and the treatment of diseased conditions esp. by operations **2 :** work done by a surgeon : OPERATION **3 :** a room or area where surgery is performed

sur·gi·cal \'sər-ji-kəl\ *adj* **:** of, relating to, or associated with surgeons or surgery — **sur·gi·cal·ly** \-k(ə-)lē\ *adv*

sur·ly \'sər-lē\ *adj* **sur·li·er; -est :** ILL-NATURED, CROSS, DISAGREEABLE ⟨answered in a *surly* tone of voice⟩ — **sur·li·ness** *n*

1**sur·mise** \sər-'mīz\ *vb* **:** to imagine or infer on slight grounds : GUESS

2**sur·mise** \sər-'mīz, 'sər-,\ *n* **:** a thought or idea based on scanty evidence : CONJECTURE

ə abut · ər further · a back · ā bake · ä cot, cart · au̇ out · ch chin · e less · ē easy · g gift · i trip · ī life · j joke · ng sing · ō flow · ȯ flaw · ȯi coin · th thin · th this · ü loot · u̇ foot · y yet · yü few · yu̇ furious · zh vision

sur·mount \sər-'mau̇nt\ *vb* **1 :** to rise superior to : OVERCOME ⟨*surmount* an obstacle⟩ **2 :** to get to the top of : CLIMB **3 :** to stand or lie at the top of : CROWN — **sur·mount·a·ble** \-ə-bəl\ *adj*

sur·name \'sər-,nām\ *n* **1 :** an added name : NICKNAME **2 :** a family name — **surname** *vb*

sur·pass \sər-'pas\ *vb* **1 :** to be greater, better, or stronger than : EXCEED **2 :** to go beyond the reach, powers, or capacity of — **sur·pass·a·ble** \-ə-bəl\ *adj*

sur·plice \'sər-pləs\ *n* **:** a loose white tunic worn at service by a clergyman, altar boy, or choir member

sur·plus \'sər-(,)pləs\ *n* **1 :** the amount that exceeds what is required or necessary : EXCESS **2 :** an excess of receipts over disbursements — **surplus** *adj*

sur·plus·age \-ij\ *n* **1 :** SURPLUS 1 **2 :** excessive or nonessential matter

1**sur·prise** \sə(r)-'prīz\ *n* **1 a :** an attack made without warning **b :** an act or an instance of coming upon someone unexpectedly : a taking unawares **2 :** something that surprises **3 :** the state of being surprised : ASTONISHMENT

2**surprise** *vb* **1 a :** to attack unexpectedly **b :** to capture by an unexpected attack **2 :** to take unawares : come upon unexpectedly **3 :** to bring about or obtain by a taking unawares **4 :** to strike with wonder or amazement because unexpected

sur·pris·ing \sə(r)-'prī-zing\ *adj* **:** ASTONISHING, AMAZING — **sur·pris·ing·ly** \-'prī-zing-lē\ *adv*

1**sur·ren·der** \sə-'ren-dər\ *vb* **sur·ren·dered; sur·ren·der·ing** \-d(ə-)ring\ **1 :** to give over to the power, control, or possession of another esp. under compulsion **2 :** to give oneself over to something ***syn*** see YIELD

2**surrender** *n* **:** the giving of oneself or something into the power of another person or thing

sur·rep·ti·tious \,sər-əp-'tish-əs, ,sə-rəp-\ *adj* **:** done, made, or acquired by stealth : CLANDESTINE, STEALTHY — **sur·rep·ti·tious·ly** *adv* — **sur·rep·ti·tious·ness** *n*

sur·rey \'sər-ē, 'sə-rē\ *n, pl* **surreys** [from *Surrey,* county in England] **:** a 4-wheel 2-seated horse-drawn pleasure carriage

surrey

sur·ro·gate \'sər-ə-,gāt, 'sə-rə-, -gət\ *n* **1 :** DEPUTY, SUBSTITUTE **2 :** a local judicial officer in some states having probate jurisdiction

1**sur·round** \sə-'rau̇nd\ *vb* **:** to enclose on all sides : ENCIRCLE, ENCOMPASS

2**surround** *n* **:** something (as a border or edging) that surrounds

sur·round·ings \sə-'rau̇n-dingz\ *n pl* **:** the circumstances, conditions, or objects by which one is surrounded : ENVIRONMENT

sur·tax \'sər-,taks\ *n* **:** an additional tax over and above a general tax

sur·veil·lance \sər-'vā-lən(t)s\ *n* **:** close watch ⟨kept under constant *surveillance*⟩

sur·veil·lant \-lənt\ *n* **:** one that exercises surveillance

1**sur·vey** \sər-'vā, 'sər-,\ *vb* **sur·veyed; sur·vey·ing 1 :** to look over and examine closely **2 :** to determine the form, extent, and position of a piece of land **3 :** to view or study as a whole : make a survey of

2**sur·vey** \'sər-,vā, sər-'\ *n, pl* **surveys 1 :** the action or an instance of surveying **2 :** something that is surveyed **3 :** a careful examination to learn certain facts ⟨a *survey* of the school system⟩ **4 :** a history or description that covers a large subject briefly ⟨a *survey* of world history⟩ **5 :** the process of determining and making a record of the outline, measurements, and position of any part of the earth's surface esp. by use of geometry and trigonometry **6 :** a measured plan and description (as of a portion of land or of a road)

sur·vey·ing \sər-'vā-iŋ\ *n* **:** the occupation of a surveyor; *esp* **:** the branch of mathematics that teaches the art of measuring and representing the earth's surface accurately

sur·vey·or \sər-'vā-ər\ *n* **:** one that surveys; *esp* **:** one whose occupation is surveying land

sur·viv·al \sər-'vī-vəl\ *n* **1 :** a living or continuing longer than another or beyond something **2 :** one that survives

survival of the fittest : NATURAL SELECTION

sur·vive \sər-'vīv\ *vb* **1 :** to remain alive or in existence **:** live on **2 :** to remain alive after the death of ⟨his son *survived* him⟩ **3 :** to continue to exist or live after ⟨*survived* the flood⟩ — **sur·vi·vor** \-'vī-vər\ *n*

sus·cep·ti·bil·i·ty \sə-ˌsep-tə-'bil-ət-ē\ *n, pl* **-ties 1 :** the quality or state of being susceptible; *esp* **:** lack of ability to resist some extraneous agent (as a pathogen or drug) **:** SENSITIVITY **2 a :** a susceptible temperament or constitution **b** *pl* **:** FEELINGS, SENSIBILITIES

sus·cep·ti·ble \sə-'sep-tə-bəl\ *adj* **1 :** capable of submitting to an action, process, or operation ⟨a theory *susceptible* to proof⟩ **2 :** open, subject, or unresistant to some stimulus, influence, or agency ⟨persons *susceptible* to colds⟩ **3 :** IMPRESSIONABLE — **sus·cep·ti·ble·ness** *n* — **sus·cep·ti·bly** \-blē\ *adv*

1sus·pect \'səs-ˌpekt, sə-'spekt\ *adj* **:** regarded with suspicion **:** SUSPECTED

2sus·pect \'səs-ˌpekt\ *n* **:** one who is suspected

3sus·pect \sə-'spekt\ *vb* **1 :** to have doubts of **:** DISTRUST **2 :** to believe it possible or likely that a person is guilty on little or no evidence **3 :** to imagine to be or be true, likely, or probable **:** SURMISE

sus·pend \sə-'spend\ *vb* **1 :** to bar temporarily from any privilege or office ⟨*suspend* a student from school⟩ **2 a :** to stop or do away with for a time **:** WITHHOLD ⟨*suspend* publication⟩ **b :** to defer on specified conditions ⟨*suspend* sentence on an offender⟩ ⟨*suspend* judgment⟩ **3 :** to cease for a time from operation or activity **4 a :** HANG; *esp* **:** to hang so as to be free on all sides except at the point of support ⟨*suspend* a ball by a thread⟩ **b :** to keep from falling or sinking through the action of some force (as buoyancy) that opposes gravity ⟨dust *suspended* in the air⟩

sus·pend·er \sə-'spen-dər\ *n* **1 :** one that suspends **2 a :** one of two supporting bands worn across the shoulders to support trousers, skirt, or belt — usu. used in pl. ⟨a pair of *suspenders*⟩ **b** *Brit* **:** GARTER

sus·pense \sə-'spen(t)s\ *n* **1 :** temporary cessation **:** SUSPENSION **2 a :** mental uncertainty **:** ANXIETY **b :** a pleasurable excitement produced by a story or play as to its outcome **3 :** the state of being undecided — **sus·pense·ful** \-fəl\ *adj*

sus·pen·sion \sə-'spen-chən\ *n* **1 a :** temporary removal from office or privileges **b :** temporary withholding (as of belief or decision) **c :** temporary relaxation of a law or rule **2 :** the act of hanging **:** the state of being hung **3 a :** the state of a substance when its particles are mixed with but undissolved in a fluid or solid; *also* **:** a substance in this state **b :** a system consisting of a solid dispersed in a solid, liquid, or gas usu. in particles of larger than colloidal size **4 :** something suspended **5 a :** a device by which something is suspended **b :** the system of devices (as springs) supporting the upper part of a vehicle on the axles

suspension bridge *n* **:** a bridge that has its roadway suspended from two or more cables usu. passing over towers and securely anchored at the ends

sus·pen·sive \sə-'spen(t)-siv\ *adj* **:** of, relating to, or marked by suspense or suspension

1sus·pi·cion \sə-'spish-ən\ *n* **1 :** the act or an instance of suspecting or being suspected **2 :** a feeling that something is wrong without definite evidence **3 :** a slight touch or trace ⟨just a *suspicion* of garlic⟩ ***syn*** see DOUBT ***ant*** credence

2suspicion *vb* **sus·pi·cioned; sus·pi·cion·ing** \-'spish-(ə-)niŋ\ *chiefly substand* **:** SUSPECT

sus·pi·cious \sə-'spish-əs\ *adj* **1 :** tending to arouse suspicion **:** QUESTIONABLE **2 :** disposed to suspect **:** DISTRUSTFUL **3 :** indicative of suspicion ⟨a *suspicious* glance⟩ — **sus·pi·cious·ly** *adv* — **sus·pi·cious·ness** *n*

sus·tain \sə-'stān\ *vb* **1 :** to give support or relief to **2 :** to supply with sustenance **:** NOURISH **3 :** to keep up **:** PROLONG **4 :** to support the weight of **:** CARRY **5 :** to buoy up **6 a :** to bear up under **:** ENDURE **b :** RECEIVE, UNDERGO ⟨*sustained* a serious wound⟩ **7 a :** to support as true, legal, or just **b :** to allow or admit as valid ⟨the court *sustained* the motion⟩ **8 :** PROVE, CONFIRM — **sus·tain·a·ble** \-'stā-nə-bəl\ *adj* — **sus·tain·er** *n*

sus·te·nance \'səs-tə-nən(t)s\ *n* **1 a :** means of support, maintenance, or subsistence **b :** FOOD, NOURISHMENT **2 :** the act of sustaining **:** the state of being sustained; *esp* **:** a supplying with the necessaries of life **3 :** something that gives support, endurance, or strength

1su·ture \'sü-chər\ *n* **1 a :** a strand or fiber used to sew parts of the living body; *also* **:** a stitch made with this **b :** the act or process of sewing with sutures **2 :** the line of union in an immovable joint (as between the bones of the skull); *also* **:** such a joint

2suture *vb* **su·tured; su·tur·ing** \'süch-(ə-)riŋ\ **:** to unite, close, or secure with sutures ⟨*suture* a wound⟩

svelte \'sfelt\ *adj* **1 a :** SLENDER, LITHE **b :** having clean lines **:** SLEEK **2 :** URBANE, SUAVE — **svelte·ly** *adv* — **svelte·ness** *n*

Sw *or* **Swed** *abbr* **1** Sweden **2** Swedish

SW *abbr* southwest

S.W.A. *abbr* South West Africa

1swab \'swäb\ *n* **1 a :** MOP; *esp* **:** a yarn mop **b :** a wad of absorbent material usu. wound around one end of a small stick and used for applying medication or for removing material (as from a wound or lesion); *also* **:** a specimen taken with a swab **c :** a sponge attached to a long handle for cleaning the bore of a firearm **2 a :** a useless or contemptible person **b :** SAILOR, GOB

2swab *vb* **swabbed; swab·bing :** to use a swab on

swab·ber \'swäb-ər\ *n* **1 :** one that swabs **2 :** SWAB

swad·dle \'swäd-əl\ *vb* **swad·dled; swad·dling** \-(ə-)liŋ\ **1 a :** to wrap an infant with swaddling clothes **b :** SWATHE, ENVELOP **2 :** RESTRAIN, RESTRICT

swaddling clothes *n pl* **:** narrow strips of cloth wrapped around an infant to restrict movement

swag \'swag\ *n* **:** goods acquired by unlawful means

1swage \'swāj, 'swej\ *n* **:** a tool used by workers in metals for shaping their work by holding it on the work or the work on it and striking with a hammer

[2]**swage** *vb* : to shape by means of a swage
[1]**swag·ger** \'swag-ər\ *vb* **swag·gered**; **swag·ger·ing** \-(ə-)ring\ **1** : to conduct oneself in an arrogant or superciliously pompous manner; *esp* : to walk with an air of overbearing self-confidence **2** : BOAST, BRAG — **swag·ger·er** \-ər-ər\ *n* — **swag·ger·ing·ly** \-(ə-)ring-lē\ *adv*
[2]**swagger** *n* : an act or instance of swaggering
swag·man \'swag-mən\ *n, chiefly Austral* : TRAMP, HOBO
Swa·hi·li \swä-'hē-lē\ *n* **1** : a member of a Bantu-speaking people of Zanzibar and the adjacent coast of Africa **2** : a Bantu language that is a trade and governmental language over much of East Africa and in the Congo region
swain \'swān\ *n* **1** : RUSTIC, PEASANT; *esp* : SHEPHERD **2** : a male admirer or suitor
[1]**swal·low** \'swäl-ō\ *n* **1** : any of a family of small long-winged migratory birds that are noted for their graceful flight and have usu. a deeply forked tail **2** : any of several swifts that superficially resemble swallows

swallow 1 (about 7 in. long)

[2]**swallow** *vb* **1 a** : to take into the stomach through the mouth and throat **b** : to perform the actions used in swallowing something ⟨cleared his throat and *swallowed* before answering⟩ **2** : to envelop or take in as if by swallowing **3** : to accept without question, protest, or resentment ⟨a hard story to *swallow*⟩ **4** : to take back : RETRACT ⟨had to *swallow* his words⟩ **5** : to keep from expressing or showing : REPRESS ⟨*swallowed* his anger⟩ **6** : to utter (as words) indistinctly — **swal·low·er** \'swäl-ə-wər\ *n*
[3]**swallow** *n* **1** : an act of swallowing **2** : an amount that can be swallowed at one time
swal·low·tail \'swäl-ō-,tāl\ *n* **1** : a deeply forked and tapering tail (as of a swallow) **2** : any of various large butterflies with the hind wing drawn out into a process resembling a tail — **swal·low–tailed** \,swäl-ō-'tāld\ *adj*
swam *past of* SWIM
swa·mi \'swäm-ē\ *n* **1** : a Hindu ascetic or religious teacher — used as a title **2** : PUNDIT
[1]**swamp** \'swämp, 'swȯmp\ *n* : wet spongy land or a tract of this often partially covered with water and usu. overgrown with shrubs and trees — **swamp·land** \-,land\ *n*
[2]**swamp** *vb* **1 a** : to cause to capsize in water or fill with water and sink **b** : to fill with or as if with water : SUBMERGE **2** : OVERWHELM ⟨was *swamped* with work⟩
swamp buggy *n* : a vehicle (as a boat driven by an airplane propeller) designed to travel over swampy terrain
swamp loosestrife *n* : a woody marsh herb of eastern No. America that has clusters of magenta flowers and colonizes the edge of open water in swamps and bogs
swampy \'swäm-pē, 'swȯm-\ *adj* : of, relating to, or resembling a swamp — **swamp·i·ness** *n*

ə abut	ər further	a back	ā bake
ä cot, cart	au̇ out	ch chin	e less
ē easy	g gift	i trip	ī life
j joke	ng sing	ō flow	ȯ flaw
ȯi coin	th thin	t͟h this	ü loot
u̇ foot	y yet	yü few	yu̇ furious
zh vision			

swan \'swän\ *n, pl* **swans** *also* **swan** : any of various heavy-bodied long-necked mostly pure white aquatic birds related to but larger than the geese
[1]**swank** \'swangk\ *vb* : to show off : SWAGGER
[2]**swank** *n* **1** : PRETENTIOUSNESS, SWAGGER **2** : ELEGANCE
[3]**swank** *or* **swanky** \'swang-kē\ *adj* **swank·er** *or* **swank·i·er**; **-est 1** : characterized by showy display : OSTENTATIOUS **2** : fashionably elegant : SMART — **swank·i·ly** \'swang-kə-lē\ *adv* — **swank·i·ness** \-kē-nəs\ *n*
swans·down \'swänz-,dau̇n\ *n* **1** : the very soft white down of the swan **2** : a heavy cotton flannel with a thick nap on the face
swan song *n* **1** : a song that a dying swan is said to sing **2** : a farewell appearance or final act or pronouncement
swap \'swäp\ *vb* **swapped**; **swap·ping** : to give in exchange : make an exchange : BARTER, TRADE — **swap** *n*
sward \'swȯrd\ *n* : the grassy surface of land : TURF
[1]**swarm** \'swȯrm\ *n* **1** : a great number of honeybees emigrating together from a hive in company with a queen to start a new colony elsewhere; *also* : a colony of honeybees settled in a hive **2** : a large number (as of people) massed together and usu. in motion
[2]**swarm** *vb* **1** : to form and depart from a hive in a swarm **2** : to migrate, move, or gather in a swarm : THRONG **3** : to contain or fill with a swarm : TEEM ⟨the picnic area was *swarming* with ants⟩
swar·thy \'swȯr-t͟hē, -thē\ *adj* **swar·thi·er**; **-est** : of a dark color, complexion, or cast — **swar·thi·ness** *n*
[1]**swash** \'swäsh\ *n* **1 a** : a body of splashing water **b** : a narrow channel of water lying within a sandbank or between a sandbank and the shore **2** : a dashing of water against or upon something **3** : a bar over which the sea washes **4** : SWAGGER
[2]**swash** *vb* **1** : BLUSTER, SWAGGER **2** : to make violent noisy movements **3** : to move with a splashing sound
swash·buck·ler \'swäsh-,bək-lər\ *n* : a boasting soldier or blustering daredevil — **swash·buck·le** \-,bək-əl\ *vb* — **swash·buck·ling** \-,bək-ling\ *adj or n*
swas·ti·ka \'swäs-ti-kə, swä-'stē-kə\ *n* [from Sanskrit *svastika*, from *svasti* "well-being", from *su-* "well" and the root *as* "to be", from the same source as English *is*] : a symbol or ornament in the form of a cross with the ends of the arms extended at right angles all in the same rotary direction
swat \'swät\ *vb* **swat·ted**; **swat·ting** : to hit with a quick hard blow — **swat** *n* — **swat·ter** *n*
swatch \'swäch\ *n* **1** : a sample piece (as of fabric) or a collection of samples **2** : PATCH ⟨*swatches* of hair⟩
swath \'swäth, 'swȯth\ *or* **swathe** \'swät͟h, 'swȯt͟h, 'swāt͟h\ *n* **1 a** : the sweep of a scythe or machine in mowing or the path cut in one course **b** : a row of cut grain or grass **2** : a long broad strip or belt **3** : a space devastated as if by a scythe
[1]**swathe** \'swät͟h, 'swȯt͟h, 'swāt͟h\ *vb* **1** : to bind, wrap, or swaddle with or as if with a bandage **2** : ENVELOP — **swath·er** *n*
[2]**swathe** \'swät͟h, 'swȯt͟h, 'swāt͟h\ *or* **swath** \'swät͟h, 'swäth, 'swȯt͟h, 'swȯth\ *n* : a band used in swathing
[1]**sway** \'swā\ *vb* **1 a** : to swing or cause to swing slowly back and forth from a base or pivot **b** : to move gently from an upright to a leaning position **2** : to fluctuate or veer between one point, position, or opinion and another **3** : to exert a guiding or controlling influence upon — **sway·er** *n*

²**sway** *n* **1 :** the action or an instance of swaying or of being swayed : an oscillating, fluctuating, or sweeping motion **2 :** an inclination or deflection caused by or as if by swaying **3 a :** a controlling force or influence **b :** sovereign power : DOMINION, RULE

sway·back \'swā-'bak\ *n* : a sagging or abnormally hollow back (as of a horse) — **sway·backed** \-'bakt\ *adj*

swear \'swa(ə)r, 'swe(ə)r\ *vb* **swore** \'swō(ə)r, 'swȯ(ə)r\; **sworn** \'swōrn, 'swȯrn\; **swear·ing** **1 :** to utter or take solemnly an oath **2 a :** to assert as true or promise under oath **b :** to assert or promise emphatically or earnestly **3 a :** to administer an oath to ⟨the witness was *sworn*⟩ **b :** to bind by an oath ⟨*swore* him to secrecy⟩ **4 :** to take an oath **5 :** to use profane or obscene language — **swear·er** *n* — **swear by :** to place great confidence in — **swear off :** to vow to abstain from : RENOUNCE ⟨*swear off* smoking⟩

swear in *vb* : to induct into office by administration of an oath

swear·word \'swa(ə)r-ˌwərd, 'swe(ə)r-\ *n* : a profane or obscene word

¹**sweat** \'swet\ *vb* **sweat** *or* **sweat·ed**; **sweat·ing** **1 :** to give off perceptible salty moisture through the pores of the skin : PERSPIRE **2 :** to give off or cause to give off moisture **3 :** to collect drops of moisture ⟨stones *sweat* at night⟩ **4 a :** to work so hard that one perspires : TOIL ⟨*sweat* over a lesson⟩ **b :** to undergo anxiety or mental distress **5 :** to soak with sweat ⟨*sweat* a collar⟩ **6 :** to get rid of or lose by perspiring ⟨*sweat* off weight⟩ ⟨*sweat* out a fever⟩ **7 :** to drive hard : OVERWORK; *esp* : to force to work hard at low wages and under bad conditions ⟨a factory that *sweats* its employees⟩

²**sweat** *n* **1 :** hard work : DRUDGERY **2 :** fluid excreted from the sweat glands of the skin : PERSPIRATION **3 :** moisture issuing from or gathering in drops on a surface

sweat·er \'swet-ər\ *n* **1 :** one that sweats or causes sweating **2 :** a knitted or crocheted jacket or pullover

sweat gland *n* : a gland of the skin that secretes perspiration and opens by a minute pore in the skin

sweat out *vb* : to endure or wait through the course of

sweat pants *n pl* : pants having a drawstring waist and elastic cuffs at the ankle that are worn esp. by athletes in warming up

sweat shirt *n* : a loose collarless usu. long-sleeved pullover of heavy cotton jersey

sweat·shop \'swet-ˌshäp\ *n* : a shop or factory in which workers are employed for long hours at low wages and under unhealthy conditions

sweaty \'swet-ē\ *adj* **sweat·i·er**; **-est** **1 :** wet or stained with or smelling of sweat **2 :** causing sweat ⟨a *sweaty* day⟩ ⟨*sweaty* work⟩ — **sweat·i·ly** \'swet-ə-lē\ *adv* — **sweat·i·ness** \'swet-ē-nəs\ *n*

swede \'swēd\ *n* **1** *cap* **a :** a native or inhabitant of Sweden **b :** a person of Swedish descent **2 :** RUTABAGA

Swed·ish \'swēd-ish\ *n* **1 :** the Germanic language spoken in Sweden and a part of Finland **2 Swedish** *pl* : the people of Sweden — **Swedish** *adj*

¹**sweep** \'swēp\ *vb* **swept** \'swept\; **sweep·ing** **1 a :** to remove from a surface with or as if with a broom or brush **b :** to remove or take with a single continuous forceful action **c :** to drive or carry along with irresistible force **2 a :** to clean with or as if with a broom or brush **b :** to move across or along swiftly, violently, or overwhelmingly ⟨a storm *swept* across the plains⟩ **c :** to win an overwhelming victory in or on ⟨*sweep* the elections⟩ ⟨*swept* the western states⟩ **3 :** to touch in passing with a swift continuous movement **4 :** to go with stately or sweeping movements ⟨*swept* into the room⟩ **5 :** to trace the outline of a curve **6 :** to cover the entire range of **7 :** to move or extend in a wide curve or range — **sweep·er** *n*

²**sweep** *n* **1 :** a long pole pivoted on a post and used to raise and lower a bucket (as in a well) **2 a :** an act or instance of sweeping; *esp* : a clearing out or away with or as if with a broom **b :** an overwhelming victory (as the winning of all the contests or prizes in a competition) **3 a :** a movement of great range and force **b :** a curving or circular course or line **c :** the compass of a sweeping movement : SCOPE **d :** a broad extent ⟨a wide *sweep* of sage and mesquite lay before us⟩ **4 :** CHIMNEY SWEEP **5 :** SWEEPSTAKES

¹**sweep·ing** *n* **1 :** the act or action of one that sweeps ⟨gave the room a good *sweeping*⟩ **2** *pl* : things collected by sweeping : REFUSE

²**sweeping** *adj* **1 a :** moving or extending in a wide curve or over a wide area **b :** having a curving line or form **2 a :** EXTENSIVE ⟨*sweeping* reforms⟩ **b :** INDISCRIMINATE ⟨*sweeping* generalizations⟩ — **sweep·ing·ly** \'swē-ping-lē\ *adv*

sweep second hand *n* : a long second hand on a timepiece that is read from the same dial as the minute hand

sweep·stakes \'swēp-ˌstāks\ *also* **sweep·stake** \-ˌstāk\ *n, pl* **sweepstakes** **1 a :** a race or contest in which the entire prize may be awarded to the winner; *esp* : a horse race in which the stakes are made up at least in part of the entry fees or money contributed by the owners of the horses **b :** CONTEST, COMPETITION **2 :** any of various lotteries

¹**sweet** \'swēt\ *adj* **1 a :** pleasing to the taste **b :** being or inducing the one of the four basic taste sensations that is typically induced by table sugar **c :** having a relatively large sugar content **2 a :** pleasing to the mind or feelings : AGREEABLE **b :** marked by gentle good humor or kindliness **c :** FRAGRANT **d :** delicately pleasing to the ear or eye **e :** CLOYING, SACCHARINE **3 :** much loved : DEAR **4 a :** not sour or rancid : not decaying or stale : WHOLESOME ⟨*sweet* milk⟩ **b :** not salt or salted : FRESH ⟨*sweet* water⟩ **c :** free from excessive acidity ⟨*sweet* soil⟩ **d :** free from noxious gases and odors — **sweet·ish** \-ish\ *adj* — **sweet·ish·ly** *adv* — **sweet·ly** *adv* — **sweet·ness** *n* — **sweet on :** in love with

²**sweet** *adv* : SWEETLY

³**sweet** *n* **1 a :** a food (as a candy or preserve) having a high sugar content **b** *Brit* : DESSERT **2 :** a sweet taste sensation **3 :** a pleasant or gratifying experience, possession, or state **4 :** DARLING

sweet basil *n* : a mint with clusters of white flowers tinged with purple and leaves used in cooking

sweet·bread \'swēt-ˌbred\ *n* : the thymus or pancreas esp. of a young animal used as food

sweet·bri·er \-ˌbrī(-ə)r\ *n* : an Old World rose with stout recurved prickles and white to deep rosy pink single flowers — called also *eglantine*

sweet clover *n* : any of a genus of tall erect legumes widely grown for soil improvement or hay

sweet corn *n* : an Indian corn with kernels containing much sugar when immature

sweet·en \'swēt-ən\ *vb* **sweet·ened**; **sweet·en·ing** \'swēt-(ə-)ning\ : to make or become sweet — **sweet·en·er** \'swēt-(ē-)nər\ *n*

sweet·en·ing *n* **1 :** the act or process of making sweet **2 :** something that sweetens

sweet fennel *n* : FENNEL

sweet gum *n* : a No. American tree with palm-shaped lobed leaves, hard wood, and a long-stemmed woody fruit resembling a bur; *also* : its wood

sweet gum

sweet·heart \'swēt-ˌhärt\ *n* **1** : DARLING **2** : LOVER

sweet·meat \-ˌmēt\ *n* **1** : a candied or crystallized fruit **2** : CANDY

sweet pea *n* : a garden plant with slender climbing stems and large fragrant flowers; *also* : its flower

sweet pepper *n* : a large mild-flavored thick-walled pepper; *also* : a plant related to the potato bearing this

sweet potato *n* **1** : a tropical vine related to the morning glory with variously shaped leaves and purplish flowers; *also* : its large sweet starchy tuberous root that is cooked and eaten as a vegetable **2** : OCARINA

sweet·shop \'swēt-ˌshäp\ *n, chiefly Brit* : a candy store

sweet sorghum *n* : SORGO

sweet tooth *n* : a craving or fondness for sweet food

sweet wil·liam \swēt-'wil-yəm\ *n, often cap W* : a widely grown Eurasian pink with often showily variegated flowers borne in flat clusters on erect stalks

1**swell** \'swel\ *vb* **swelled**; **swelled** *or* **swol·len** \'swō-lən\; **swell·ing** **1 a** : to expand or distend abnormally esp. by internal pressure or growth ⟨a *swollen* tree trunk⟩ ⟨the sprained ankle *swelled* badly⟩ **b** : to increase in size, number, or intensity **c** : to form a bulge or rounded elevation **2** : to fill or become filled with pride and arrogance **3** : to fill or become filled with emotion

2**swell** *n* **1a** : the condition of being protuberant **b** : a rounded elevation **2** : a long often massive crestless wave or succession of waves **3 a** : a gradual increase and decrease of the loudness of a musical sound **b** : a sign indicating a swell **c** : a device used in an organ for controlling loudness **4 a** : a person dressed in the height of fashion **b** : a person of high social position or outstanding competence

3**swell** *adj* **1** : STYLISH, FASHIONABLE **2** : EXCELLENT, FIRST-RATE

swell·ing \'swel-ing\ *n* **1** : something that is swollen; *esp* : an abnormal localized enlargement on the body **2** : the condition of being swollen

1**swel·ter** \'swel-tər\ *vb* **swel·tered**; **swel·ter·ing** \-t(ə-)ring\ : to suffer, sweat, or be faint from heat

2**swelter** *n* : a state of oppressive heat

swel·ter·ing *adj* : oppressively hot — **swel·ter·ing·ly** \-t(ə-)ring-lē\ *adv*

swept *past of* SWEEP

swept–back \'swep(t)-'bak\ *adj* : slanting toward the tail of an airplane to form an acute angle with the body ⟨*swept-back* wings⟩

swerve \'swərv\ *vb* : to turn aside suddenly from a straight line or course — **swerve** *n*

1**swift** \'swift\ *adj* **1** : moving or capable of moving with great speed **2** : occurring suddenly or within a very short time **3** : quick to respond ⟨*swift* to doubt⟩ — **swift·ly** *adv* — **swift·ness** \'swif(t)-nəs\ *n*

2**swift** *adv* : SWIFTLY ⟨*swift*-flowing⟩

3**swift** *n* : any of numerous small and usu. sooty black birds that are related to the hummingbirds and have long narrow wings

1**swig** \'swig\ *n* : a quantity drunk at one time

2**swig** *vb* **swigged**; **swig·ging** : to drink in long gulps — **swig·ger** *n*

1**swill** \'swil\ *vb* **1** : WASH, DRENCH **2** : to drink great drafts of : consume freely, greedily, or to excess **3** : to feed (as a pig) with swill — **swill·er** *n*

2**swill** *n* **1** : food for animals (as swine) composed of edible refuse mixed with liquid **2** : GARBAGE, REFUSE **3** : SWIG

1**swim** \'swim\ *vb* **swam** \'swam\; **swum** \'swəm\; **swim·ming** **1 a** : to move through water by natural means (as the action of limbs, fins, or tail) **b** : to move quietly and smoothly : GLIDE **2 a** : to float on or in or be covered with or as if with a liquid ⟨meat *swimming* in gravy⟩ **b** : to experience or suffer from or as if from dizziness ⟨his head *swam* in the stuffy room⟩ **3** : to cross by propelling oneself through water (*swim* a stream) — **swim·ma·ble** \'swim-ə-bəl\ *adj* — **swim·mer** *n*

2**swim** *n* **1** : an act or period of swimming **2** : the main current of activity ⟨be in the *swim*⟩

swim·ming *adj* : marked by, adapted to, or used in or for swimming

swim·ming·ly \'swim-ing-lē\ *adv* : very well : SPLENDIDLY

swim·suit \'swim-ˌsüt\ *n* : BATHING SUIT

1**swin·dle** \'swin-dəl\ *vb* **swin·dled**; **swin·dling** \-d(ə-)ling\ : to obtain money or property from by fraud or deceit : DEFRAUD — **swin·dler** \-d(ə-)lər\ *n*

2**swindle** *n* : an act or instance of swindling : FRAUD

swine \'swīn\ *n, pl* **swine** [from Old English *swīn*, from the Latin adjective *suinus* "of swine", from *sus* "swine", from the same source as English *sow*] **1** : any of a family of stout-bodied short-legged hoofed mammals with a thick bristly skin and a long snout; *esp* : a domesticated animal derived from the European wild boar and widely raised for meat **2** : a contemptible person

swine·herd \-ˌhərd\ *n* : one who tends swine

1**swing** \'swing\ *vb* **swung** \'swəng\; **swing·ing** \'swing-ing\ **1 a** : to wield with a sweep or flourish ⟨*swing* an ax⟩ **b** : to cause to sway to and fro or turn on an axis **c** : to face or move in another direction **2 a** : to hang or be hung so as to permit swaying or turning **b** : to die by hanging **c** : to move freely to and fro from or rotate about a point of suspension ⟨the door *swung* open⟩ **d** : to hang freely from a support **e** : to shift or fluctuate between extremes ⟨the market *swung* sharply downward⟩ **3** : to handle successfully : MANAGE **4** : to play or sing in the style of swing music **5 a** : to move along rhythmically **b** : to start up in a smooth vigorous manner **c** : to hit at something with a sweeping movement **6** : to be lively and up-to-date ⟨London really *swings*⟩ — **swing·a·ble** \'swing-ə-bəl\ *adj* — **swing·a·bly** \-blē\ *adv* — **swing·er** \'swing-ər\ *n*

2**swing** *n* **1** : an act of swinging **2 a** : a regular to-and-fro movement of or as if of a suspended body **b** : a steady pulsing rhythm (as in poetry or music) **c** : dancing to swing music **d** : a repeated shifting from one condition, form, or position to another **3** : the distance through which something swings ⟨a pendulum with a 12-inch *swing*⟩ **4** : a swinging seat usu. hung by overhead ropes **5** : a curving course or outline or one beginning and ending at the same point ⟨took a *swing* through the hills⟩ **6** : a style of jazz in which the melody is freely interpreted and improvised on by the individual players within a steadily maintained and usu. lively rhythm — **swing** *adj*

swin·ish \'swī-nish\ *adj* **:** of, suggesting, or befitting swine **:** BEASTLY — **swin·ish·ly** *adv* — **swin·ish·ness** *n*

1**swipe** \'swīp\ *n* **:** a strong sweeping blow

2**swipe** *vb* **1 :** to strike or wipe with a sweeping motion **2 :** SNATCH, PILFER

1**swirl** \'swərl\ *n* **1 :** a whirling mass or motion **:** EDDY **2 :** whirling confusion **3 :** a twisting shape or mark

2**swirl** *vb* **1 :** to move with or pass in a swirl **2 :** to be marked with or arranged in swirls **3 :** to cause to swirl — **swirl·ing·ly** \'swər-ling-lē\ *adv*

1**swish** \'swish\ *vb* **:** to make, move, or strike with a rustling or hissing sound — **swish·ing·ly** \-ing-lē\ *adv*

2**swish** *n* **1 :** a prolonged hissing sound (as of a whip cutting the air) or a light sweeping or rustling sound (as of silk in friction) **2 :** a swishing movement — **swishy** \-ē\ *adj*

Swiss \'swis\ *n* **1** *pl* **Swiss a :** a native or inhabitant of Switzerland **b :** a person of Swiss descent **2** *often not cap* **:** a fine sheer cotton fabric often with raised dots orig. made in Switzerland **3 :** a mild elastic hard cheese with large holes — **Swiss** *adj*

Swiss chard *n* **:** CHARD

1**switch** \'swich\ *n* **1 :** a slender flexible whip, rod, or twig **2 :** an act or an instance of switching **3 :** a tuft of long hairs at the end of the tail of an animal (as a cow) **4 :** a device designed to turn a locomotive or train from one track to another **5 :** a device for making, breaking, or changing the connections in an electrical circuit **6 :** a strand of added or artificial hair used in some coiffures

2**switch** *vb* **1 :** to strike or whip with or as if with a switch **2 :** to lash from side to side ⟨a cat *switching* his tail⟩ **3 :** to turn, shift, or change by operating a switch ⟨*switch* a train onto a siding⟩ ⟨*switch* off the light⟩ **4 :** to change one for another ⟨*switched* to a new barber⟩ — **switch·er** *n*

switch·back \'swich-ˌbak\ *n* **:** a zigzag road or arrangement of tracks for overcoming a steep grade

switch·blade \-ˌblād\ *n* **:** a pocketknife having the blade spring-operated so that pressure on a release catch causes it to fly open

switch·board \-ˌbōrd, -ˌbȯrd\ *n* **:** an apparatus (as in a telephone exchange) consisting of a panel on which are mounted electric switches so arranged that a number of circuits may be connected, combined, and controlled

switch·man \-mən\ *n* **:** one who attends a railroad switch

switch·yard \-ˌyärd\ *n* **:** a place where railroad cars are switched from one track to another and trains are made up

Switz *abbr* Switzerland

1**swiv·el** \'swiv-əl\ *n* **:** a device joining two parts so that one or both can pivot freely

2**swivel** *vb* **-eled** *or* **-elled**; **-el·ing** *or* **-el·ling** \'swiv-(ə-)ling\ **:** to turn on or as if on a swivel

swivel chair *n* **:** a chair that swivels on its base

swiz·zle stick \'swiz-əl-\ *n* **:** a stick used to stir mixed drinks

swob *var of* SWAB

swollen *past part of* SWELL

1**swoon** \'swün\ *vb* **1 :** FAINT **2 :** to drift or fade imperceptibly — **swoon·er** *n* — **swoon·ing·ly** \'swü-ning-lē\ *adv*

2**swoon** *n* **1 :** a partial or total loss of consciousness **2 :** a dazed enraptured state

1**swoop** \'swüp\ *vb* **1 :** to descend or pounce suddenly like a hawk attacking its prey **2 :** SNATCH

2**swoop** *n* **:** an act or instance of swooping

swoosh \'swüsh, 'swu̇sh\ *vb* **:** to make, move, or discharge with a rushing sound — **swoosh** *n*

swop *var of* SWAP

sword \'sōrd, 'sȯrd\ *n* **1 :** a weapon having a long usu. sharp-pointed and sharp-edged blade **2 :** something that kills or punishes as effectively as a sword **3 :** military power or the use of it **:** WAR — **sword-like** \-ˌlīk\ *adj*

sword·fish \'sōrd-ˌfish, 'sȯrd-\ *n* **:** a very large ocean food fish having a long swordlike beak formed by the bones of the upper jaw

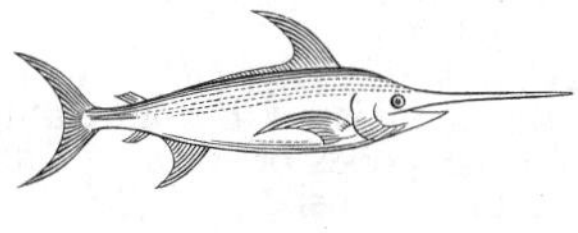
swordfish
(about 10 ft. long)

sword·play \-ˌplā\ *n* **:** the art or skill of using a sword esp. in fencing

swords·man \'sōrdz-mən, 'sȯrdz-\ *n* **1 :** one who fights with a sword **2 :** one skilled in the use of the sword **:** FENCER

swords·man·ship \-ˌship\ *n* **:** SWORDPLAY

sword·tail \'sōrd-ˌtāl, 'sȯrd-\ *n* **:** a small brightly marked Central American fish often kept in the tropical aquarium and bred in many colors

swore *past of* SWEAR

sworn *past part of* SWEAR

swum *past part of* SWIM

swung *past of* SWING

syc·a·more \'sik-ə-ˌmōr, -ˌmȯr\ *n* **1 :** a common fig tree of Egypt and Asia Minor **2 :** a Eurasian maple with yellow flowers in long clusters **3 :** 2PLANE; *esp* **:** a large spreading American plane tree with light-brown flaky bark and round fruits like buttons

sycamore 3

syc·o·phant \'sik-ə-fənt\ *n* **:** a servile self-seeking flatterer **:** PARASITE — **syc·o·phan·cy** \-fən-sē\ *n* — **syc·o·phan·tic** \ˌsik-ə-'fant-ik\ *adj* — **syc·o·phan·ti·cal·ly** \-'fant-i-k(ə-)lē\ *adv*

sy·e·nite \'sī-ə-ˌnīt\ *n* **:** an igneous rock composed chiefly of feldspar

syll *abbr* syllable

syl·lab·ic \sə-'lab-ik\ *adj* **1 :** of, relating to, or denoting syllables ⟨*syllabic* accent⟩ **2 :** characterized by distinct enunciation or separation of syllables — **syl·lab·i·cal·ly** \-i-k(ə-)lē\ *adv*

syl·lab·i·ca·tion \sə-ˌlab-ə-'kā-shən\ *n* **:** the forming of syllables **:** the division of words into syllables — **syl·lab·i·cate** \-'lab-ə-ˌkāt\ *vb*

syl·lab·i·fi·ca·tion \sə-ˌlab-ə-fə-'kā-shən\ *n* **:** SYLLABICATION

syl·lab·i·fy \sə-'lab-ə-ˌfī\ *vb* **-fied**; **-fy·ing :** to form or divide into syllables

1**syl·la·ble** \'sil-ə-bəl\ *n* [from Greek *syllabē*, from *syllambanein* "to combine", from *syn-* "with", "together" and *lambanein* "to take"] **1 :** a unit of spoken language that consists of one or more vowel sounds alone or with one or more consonant sounds preceding or following **2 :** one or more letters (as *syl, la,* and *ble*) in a word (as *syl·la·ble*) usu. set off from the rest of the word by a centered dot or a hyphen and treated as guides to hyphenation at the end of a line

[2]**syllable** *vb* **syl·la·bled; syl·la·bling** \-b(ə-)liŋ\ : to express or utter in syllables

syl·la·bus \'sil-ə-bəs\ *n, pl* **-bi** \-ˌbī, -ˌbē\ *or* **-bus·es** : a summary outline (as of a course of study)

syl·lo·gism \'sil-ə-ˌjiz-əm\ *n* **1** : a brief form for stating an argument from the general to the particular that consists of two statements and a conclusion that must be true if these two statements are true ⟨"all lawbreakers deserve punishment; the man is a lawbreaker; therefore the man deserves punishment" is a *syllogism*⟩ **2** : deductive reasoning — **syl·lo·gis·tic** \ˌsil-ə-'jis-tik\ *adj* — **syl·lo·gis·ti·cal·ly** \-ti-k(ə-)lē\ *adv*

sylph \'silf\ *n* **1** : an imaginary spirit inhabiting the air **2** : a slender graceful woman — **sylph·like** \-ˌlīk\ *adj*

syl·van \'sil-vən\ *adj* **1 a** : living or located in the woods or forest **b** : of, relating to, or characteristic of the woods or forest **2** : abounding in woods or trees : WOODED

sym *abbr* symbol

sym·bi·ont \'sim-ˌbī-ˌänt, -bē-\ *n* : an organism living in symbiosis; *esp* : the smaller member of a symbiotic pair

sym·bi·o·sis \ˌsim-ˌbī-'ō-səs, -bē-\ *n, pl* **-o·ses** \-'ō-ˌsēz\ : the living together in intimate association or close union of two unlike organisms esp. when mutually beneficial — **sym·bi·ot·ic** \-'ät-ik\ *adj* — **sym·bi·ot·i·cal·ly** \-i-k(ə-)lē\ *adv*

sym·bol \'sim-bəl\ *n* **1** : something that stands for something else; *esp* : something concrete that represents or suggests another thing that cannot in itself be represented or visualized ⟨the cross is the *symbol* of Christianity⟩ **2** : a letter, character, or sign used (as to represent a quantity, position, relationship, direction, or something to be done) instead of a word or group of words ⟨the sign + is the *symbol* for addition⟩ *syn* see EMBLEM

sym·bol·ic \sim-'bäl-ik\ *or* **sym·bol·i·cal** \-i-kəl\ *adj* **1** : of, relating to, or using symbols or symbolism ⟨a *symbolic* meaning⟩ ⟨*symbolic* art⟩ **2** : having the function or significance of a symbol — **sym·bol·i·cal·ly** \-i-k(ə-)lē\ *adv*

sym·bol·ism \'sim-bə-ˌliz-əm\ *n* **1** : the art or practice of using symbols (as in art or literature) **2** : a system of symbols or representations

sym·bol·ist \-ləst\ *n* **1** : a user of symbols or symbolism (as in artistic expression) **2** : an expert in the interpretation or explication of symbols — **symbolist** *or* **sym·bol·is·tic** \ˌsim-bə-'lis-tik\ *adj*

sym·bol·ize \'sim-bə-ˌlīz\ *vb* **1** : to serve as a symbol of : TYPIFY ⟨a lion *symbolizes* courage⟩ **2** : to use symbols : represent by a symbol or set of symbols — **sym·bol·i·za·tion** \ˌsim-bə-lə-'zā-shən\ *n* — **sym·bol·iz·er** \'sim-bə-ˌlī-zər\ *n*

sym·met·ri·cal \sə-'me-tri-kəl\ *or* **sym·met·ric** \-trik\ *adj* : having, involving, or exhibiting symmetry — **sym·met·ri·cal·ly** \-tri-k(ə-)lē\ *adv* — **sym·met·ri·cal·ness** \-kəl-nəs\ *n*

sym·me·try \'sim-ə-trē\ *n, pl* **-tries** **1 a** : balanced proportions **b** : beauty of form arising from balanced proportions **2** : correspondence in size, shape, and relative position of parts arranged on opposite sides of a dividing line or plane or about a center or axis

ə abut	ər further	a back	ā bake
ä cot, cart	au̇ out	ch chin	e less	ē easy
g gift	i trip	ī life	j joke	ŋ sing	ō flow
ȯ flaw	ȯi coin	th thin	t͟h this	ü loot
u̇ foot	y yet	yü few	yu̇ furious	zh vision

sym·pa·thet·ic \ˌsim-pə-'thet-ik\ *adj* **1** : existing or operating through an affinity, interdependence, or mutual association **2 a** : appropriate to one's mood or disposition : CONGENIAL ⟨a *sympathetic* environment⟩ **b** : favorably impressed or inclined ⟨*sympathetic* with their aims⟩ **c** : marked by kindly or pleased appreciation **3** : given to or arising from sympathy, compassion, friendliness, and sensitivity to others ⟨a *sympathetic* personality⟩ **4 a** : of or relating to the sympathetic nervous system **b** : mediated by or acting on the sympathetic nerves — **sym·pa·thet·i·cal·ly** \-i-k(ə-)lē\ *adv*

sympathetic nervous system *n* : the part of the autonomic nervous system that tends to depress secretion, decrease the tone and contractility of smooth muscle, and cause the contraction of blood vessels — compare PARASYMPATHETIC NERVOUS SYSTEM

sympathetic vibration *n* : a vibration produced in one body by vibrations of exactly the same period in a neighboring body

sym·pa·thize \'sim-pə-ˌthīz\ *vb* **1** : to react or respond in sympathy **2 a** : to share in some distress, suffering, or grief **b** : to express sympathy **3** : to be in accord with something **4** : to approve and foster the policies of a group without total commitment ⟨*sympathize* with a subversive party⟩ — **sym·pa·thiz·er** *n*

sym·pa·thy \'sim-pə-thē\ *n, pl* **-thies** [from Greek *sympatheia*, from *syn-* "with" and *pathos* "feelings", "experience"] **1** : a relationship between persons or things wherein whatever affects one similarly affects the other **2 a** : inclination to think or feel alike : emotional or intellectual accord forming a bond of goodwill **b** : tendency to favor or support ⟨republican *sympathies*⟩ **3** : the act of or capacity for entering into or sharing the feelings or interests of another

sym·phon·ic \sim-'fän-ik\ *adj* **1** : HARMONIOUS **2** : of, relating to, or suggesting a symphony or symphony orchestra — **sym·phon·i·cal·ly** \-i-k(ə-)lē\ *adv*

sym·pho·ny \'sim(p)-fə-nē\ *n, pl* **-nies** **1** : harmonious arrangement (as of sound or color) **2 a** : a usu. long and complex sonata for symphony orchestra **b** : something resembling a symphony in complexity or variety

symphony orchestra *n* : a large orchestra that plays symphonic works

sym·po·si·um \sim-'pō-zē-əm, -zh(ē-)əm\ *n, pl* **-sia** \-zē-ə, -zh(ē-)ə\ *or* **-si·ums** [from Greek *symposion* "feast", "drinking party", from *syn-* "together" and a root meaning "to drink"] **1** : a meeting at which several speakers deliver short addresses on a topic or on related topics and which may be followed by group discussion **2 a** : a collection of opinions on a subject **b** : DISCUSSION

symp·tom \'sim(p)-təm\ *n* **1** : a change in the structure or functioning of an organism indicating the presence of disease; *esp* : one (as headache) perceptible only to the individual affected — compare SIGN **2** : INDICATION, SIGN, TRACE — **symp·tom·less** \-ləs\ *adj*

symp·tom·at·ic \ˌsim(p)-tə-'mat-ik\ *adj* **1 a** : being a symptom (as of disease) ⟨*symptomatic* of smallpox⟩ **b** : concerned with or affecting symptoms ⟨*symptomatic* medicine⟩ **2** : CHARACTERISTIC, INDICATIVE — **symp·tom·at·i·cal·ly** \-i-k(ə-)lē\ *adv*

syn *abbr* synonym

syn·a·gogue *or* **syn·a·gog** \'sin-ə-ˌgäg\ *n* [from Greek *synagōgē*, literally "assembly", from *syn-* "together" and *agein* "to lead"] **1** : a Jewish congregation **2** : the house of worship and communal center of a Jewish congregation — **syn·a·gog·al** \ˌsin-ə-'gäg-əl\ *adj*

syn·apse \'sin-ˌaps\ *n* : the point at which a nervous impulse passes from one neuron to another

syn·chro·nism \'sin(g)-krə-ˌniz-əm\ *n* **1** : the quality or state of being synchronous **2** : chronological arrangement of historical events and personages so as to indicate coincidence or coexistence — **syn·chro·nis·tic** \ˌsin(g)-krə-'nis-tik\ *adj*

syn·chro·nize \'sin(g)-krə-ˌnīz\ *vb* **1** : to happen at the same time : agree in time **2** : to cause to agree in time : represent, arrange, or tabulate according to dates or time ⟨*synchronize* the events of European history⟩ **3** : to make (as two gears) synchronous in operation — **syn·chro·ni·za·tion** \ˌsin(g)-krə-nə-'zā-shən\ *n* — **syn·chro·niz·er** \'sin(g)-krə-ˌnī-zər\ *n*

syn·chro·nous \'sin(g)-krə-nəs\ *adj* **1** : happening or existing at the same time : SIMULTANEOUS ⟨*synchronous* meetings⟩ **2** : working, moving, or occurring together at the same rate and at the proper time with respect to each other ⟨*synchronous* beat of a bird's wings⟩; *esp* : having the same period and phase ⟨*synchronous* vibration⟩ — **syn·chro·nous·ly** *adv* — **syn·chro·nous·ness** *n*

syn·cline \'sin-ˌklīn\ *n* : a trough of stratified rock in which the beds dip toward each other from either side — compare ANTICLINE

syn·co·pate \'sin(g)-kə-ˌpāt\ *vb* **1 a** : to shorten or produce by syncope **b** : to cut short : CLIP, ABBREVIATE **2** : to modify or affect (musical rhythm) by syncopation — **syn·co·pa·tor** \-ˌpāt-ər\ *n*

syn·co·pa·tion \ˌsin(g)-kə-'pā-shən\ *n* **1** : a temporary displacement of the regular metrical accent in music caused typically by stressing the weak beat **2** : a syncopated rhythm, passage, or dance step — **syn·co·pa·tive** \'sin(g)-kə-ˌpāt-iv\ *adj*

syn·co·pe \'sin(g)-kə-(ˌ)pē\ *n* **1** : FAINT, SWOON **2** : the loss of one or more sounds or letters in the interior of a word (as *fo'c'sle* from *forecastle*)

[1]**syn·di·cate** \'sin-di-kət\ *n* **1** : an association of persons officially authorized to undertake some duty or negotiate some business **2** : a loose association of racketeers in control of organized crime **3** : a business concern that sells materials for publication in a number of newspapers or periodicals simultaneously **4** : a group of newspapers under one management

[2]**syn·di·cate** \'sin-də-ˌkāt\ *vb* **1** : to subject to or manage as a syndicate **2** : to sell (as a cartoon) to a publication syndicate **3** : to unite to form a syndicate — **syn·di·ca·tion** \ˌsin-də-'kā-shən\ *n* — **syn·di·ca·tor** \'sin-də-ˌkāt-ər\ *n*

syn·drome \'sin-ˌdrōm\ *n* : a group of signs and symptoms that occur together and characterize a particular abnormality

syn·er·gism \'sin-ər-ˌjiz-əm\ *n* : cooperative action of separate agencies such that the total effect is greater than the sum of the effects taken independently — **syn·er·gist** \-jəst\ *n*

syn·er·gis·tic \ˌsin-ər-'jis-tik\ *adj* : of, relating to, or able to function in synergism ⟨a *synergistic* reaction⟩ ⟨*synergistic* drugs⟩

syn·od \'sin-əd\ *n* **1** : an ecclesiastical assembly or council: **a** : the governing assembly of an Episcopal province **b** : a Presbyterian governing body ranking above the presbytery **c** : a regional or national organization of Lutheran congregations **2** : a group assembled (as for consultation) : MEETING, CONVENTION ⟨a *synod* of cooks⟩ — **syn·od·al** \'sin-əd-əl\ *adj* — **syn·od·i·cal** \sə-'näd-i-kəl\ *adj*

syn·od·ic month \sə-ˌnäd-ik-\ *n* : the average period of recurrence of the phases of the moon equal to 29½ days

syn·o·nym \'sin-ə-ˌnim\ *n* **1** : one of two or more words of the same language that have the same or nearly the same meaning in some or all senses **2** : a symbolic or figurative name — **syn·o·nym·i·ty** \ˌsin-ə-'nim-ət-ē\ *n*

syn·on·y·mize \-ˌmīz\ *vb* : to give or analyze the synonyms of a word

syn·on·y·mous \sə-'nän-ə-məs\ *adj* **1** : having the character of a synonym **2** : alike in meaning or significance — **syn·on·y·mous·ly** *adv*

syn·on·y·my \-mē\ *n, pl* **-mies 1 a** : the study or discrimination of synonyms **b** : a list or collection of synonyms often defined and discriminated from each other **2** : the quality or state of being synonymous

syn·op·sis \sə-'näp-səs\ *n, pl* **-op·ses** \-'äp-ˌsēz\ : a condensed statement or outline (as of a narrative or treatise) : SUMMARY, ABSTRACT — **syn·op·tic** \sə-'näp-tik\ *adj*

syn·tac·tic \sin-'tak-tik\ *adj* : of, relating to, or according to the rules of syntax — **syn·tac·ti·cal** \-ti-kəl\ *adj* — **syn·tac·ti·cal·ly** \-ti-k(ə-)lē\ *adv*

syn·tax \'sin-ˌtaks\ *n* **1** : a connected or orderly system or arrangement **2 a** : the way in which words are put together to form phrases, clauses, or sentences **b** : the part of grammar dealing with this

syn·the·sis \'sin(t)-thə-səs\ *n, pl* **-the·ses** \-thə-ˌsēz\ **1** : the composition or combination of parts or elements so as to form a whole; *esp* : the production of a substance by union of chemically simpler substances **2 a** : the combining of often diverse conceptions into a coherent whole **b** : the complex so formed **c** : deductive reasoning from general principles or causes to particular effects — **syn·the·sist** \-səst\ *n*

syn·the·size \-ˌsīz\ *vb* : to combine or produce by synthesis — **syn·the·siz·er** *n*

[1]**syn·thet·ic** \sin-'thet-ik\ *adj* **1** : of or relating to synthesis **2** : produced artificially : MAN-MADE ⟨*synthetic* rubber⟩: **a** : produced only by chemical means : not found in nature ⟨*synthetic* fibers such as rayon⟩ **b** : made to substitute for or imitate a natural substance ⟨*synthetic* milk⟩ — **syn·thet·i·cal·ly** \-'thet-i-k(ə-)lē\ *adv*

[2]**synthetic** *n* : a product of chemical synthesis

syph·i·lis \'sif-(ə-)ləs\ *n* : a chronic contagious usu. venereal disease caused by a spirochete and if untreated marked by a series of three stages extending over many years — **syph·i·lit·ic** \ˌsif-ə-'lit-ik\ *adj or n*

sy·phon *var of* SIPHON

Syr·i·ac \'sir-ē-ˌak\ *n* **1** : a literary language based on an eastern Aramaic dialect and used as the literary and liturgical language by several eastern Christian churches **2** : Aramaic spoken by Christian communities — **Syriac** *adj*

Syr·i·an \'sir-ē-ən\ *adj* : of, relating to, or characteristic of Syria or its people — **Syrian** *n*

sy·rin·ga \sə-'ring-gə\ *n* : MOCK ORANGE

[1]**sy·ringe** \sə-'rinj\ *n* [from Greek *syring-*, stem of *syrinx* "panpipe", "tube"] : a device used to inject fluids into or withdraw them from the body or its cavities — **sy·ringe·like** \-ˌlīk\ *adj*

[2]**syringe** *vb* : to irrigate or cleanse with or as if with a syringe

syr·up \'sər-əp, 'sir-əp, 'sə-rəp\ *n* **1** : a thick sticky solution of sugar and water often flavored or medicated **2** : the concentrated juice of a fruit or plant — **syr·upy** \-ē\ *adj*

syst *abbr* system

S

sys·tem \'sis-təm\ *n* **1 a :** a group of objects or units so combined as to form a whole and work, function, or move interdependently and harmoniously ⟨railroad *system*⟩ ⟨steam heating *systems*⟩ ⟨a park *system*⟩ **b :** a body considered as a functioning whole ⟨a *system* weakened by disease⟩ **c :** a group of bodily organs that together carry on one or more vital functions ⟨the nervous *system*⟩ **d :** a particular form of societal organization ⟨the capitalist *system*⟩ **e :** a major division of rocks usu. greater than a series **2 a :** an organized set of doctrines or principles usu. designed to explain the ordering or functioning of some whole **b :** a scheme or method of governing or arranging **:** a method of procedure or classification ⟨a numeration *system*⟩ ⟨taxonomic *systems*⟩ **3 :** regular method or order ⟨it takes *system* to run a school⟩ — **sys·tem·less** \-ləs\ *adj*

sys·tem·at·ic \ˌsis-tə-'mat-ik\ *adj* **1 :** relating to or forming a system ⟨*systematic* thought⟩ **2 :** presented or formulated as a system **:** SYSTEMATIZED **3 a :** methodical in procedure or plan ⟨*systematic* investigation⟩ ⟨*systematic* scholar⟩ **b :** carried on or acting with thoroughness or persistency ⟨*systematic* attacks on his credibility⟩ — **sys·tem·at·i·cal** \-'mat-i-kəl\ *adj* — **sys·tem·at·i·cal·ly** \-i-k(ə-)lē\ *adv* — **sys·tem·at·ic·ness** \-ik-nəs\ *n*

systematic error *n* **:** an error (as one caused by an incorrect ruler) in data that is due to the method of measurement or observation and not due to chance

sys·tem·a·tize \'sis-tə-mə-ˌtīz\ *vb* **:** to make into or arrange according to a system — **sys·tem·a·ti·za·tion** \ˌsis-tə-mət-ə-'zā-shən\ *n* — **sys·tem·a·tiz·er** \'sis-tə-mə-ˌtī-zər\ *n*

sys·tem·ic \sis-'tem-ik\ *adj* **:** of, relating to, or common to a system; *esp* **:** of or relating to the body as a whole ⟨a *systemic* disease⟩

systemic circulation *n* **:** the part of the blood circulation concerned with distribution of blood to the tissues as distinguished from the part concerned with gaseous exchange in the lungs

sys·to·le \'sis-tə-(ˌ)lē\ *n* **:** the contraction of the heart by which the blood is forced onward and the circulation kept up — **sys·tol·ic** \sis-'täl-ik\ *adj*

ə abut	ər further	a back	ā bake	
ä cot, cart	au̇ out	ch chin	e less	ē easy
g gift	i trip	ī life	j joke	ng sing	ō flow
ȯ flaw	ȯi coin	th thin	th this	ü loot
u̇ foot	y yet	yü few	yu̇ furious	zh vision

t \'tē\ *n, often cap* : the 20th letter of the English alphabet — **to a T** : PRECISELY, EXACTLY
t *abbr* **1** teaspoon **2** temperature **3** tenor **4** ton
't \t\ *pron* : IT ⟨*'t*will do⟩
T *abbr* **1** tablespoon **2** tense
[1]**tab** \'tab\ *n* **1 a** : a short projection used as an aid in filing, pulling, or hanging **b** : a small insert ⟨license plate *tab*⟩ **c** : APPENDAGE, EXTENSION **2 a** : SURVEILLANCE, WATCH ⟨keep *tab* on the situation⟩ **b** : BILL, CHECK ⟨paid the *tab*⟩
[2]**tab** *vb* **tabbed**; **tab·bing** **1** : to furnish or ornament with tabs **2** : to single out : DESIGNATE ⟨*tabbed* as a bright prospect by pro football scouts⟩
tab·ard \'tab-ərd\ *n* **1** : a cloak worn by a knight over his armor and emblazoned with his arms **2** : a herald's cape or coat displaying his lord's arms

tabard 2

tab·by \'tab-ē\ *n, pl* **tabbies** **1** : a domestic cat with a gray or tawny coat striped and mottled with black **2** : a female cat
tab·er·na·cle \'tab-ər-ˌnak-əl\ *n* **1 a** *often cap* : a tent sanctuary used by the Israelites during the Exodus **b** : a dwelling place **2** : a locked box fixed to the altar and used for bread consecrated at Mass **3** : a house of worship
[1]**ta·ble** \'tā-bəl\ *n* **1** : TABLET 1a **2 a** : a piece of furniture consisting of a smooth flat slab fixed on legs **b** : FOOD, FARE ⟨sets a good *table*⟩ **c** : a group of people assembled at a table **3 a** : a systematic arrangement of data in rows or columns for ready reference ⟨*table* of weights⟩ ⟨multiplication *table*⟩ **b** : a condensed enumeration : LIST ⟨*table* of contents⟩ **4** : TABLELAND
[2]**table** *vb* **ta·bled**; **ta·bling** \-b(ə-)liŋ\ **1** : TABULATE **2** : to remove a parliamentary motion from consideration indefinitely **3** : to put on a table
tab·leau \'tab-ˌlō, tab-'lō\ *n, pl* **tableaus** *or* **tab·leaux** \-ˌlōz, -'lōz\ : a lifelike representation of a scene or event by a group of persons who remain silent and motionless
ta·ble·cloth \'tā-bəl-ˌklȯth\ *n* : a covering spread over a dining table before the places are set
ta·ble d'hôte \ˌtäb-əl-'dōt, ˌtab-\ *n* **1** : a meal served to all guests of a hotel at a stated hour and fixed price **2** : a complete meal of several courses offered in a restaurant or hotel at a fixed price
ta·ble·land \'tā-bəl-ˌ(l)and\ *n* : PLATEAU
table salt *n* : salt for use at the table and in cooking : SALT 1a
ta·ble·spoon \'tā-bəl-ˌspün\ *n* **1** : a large spoon used for serving rather than eating food **2** : TABLESPOONFUL
ta·ble·spoon·ful \ˌtā-bəl-'spün-ˌfu̇l, 'tā-bəl-ˌ\ *n, pl* **-spoonfuls** \-ˌfu̇lz\ *or* **-spoons·ful** \-'spünz-ˌfu̇l, -ˌspünz-\ **1** : as much as a tablespoon can hold **2** : a unit of measure used esp. in cookery equal to one half fluidounce or three teaspoonfuls
table sugar *n* : purified sugar usu. in granular form : SUCROSE
tab·let \'tab-lət\ *n* **1 a** : a flat slab suited for an inscription **b** : a group of sheets of writing paper glued together at one edge **2 a** : a compressed or molded block of a solid material : CAKE **b** : a small usu. disk-shaped mass of medicated material ⟨aspirin *tablet*⟩
table talk *n* : informal conversation
table tennis *n* : a table game resembling tennis played with wooden paddles and a small hollow plastic ball
ta·ble·ware \'tā-bəl-ˌwa(ə)r, -ˌwe(ə)r\ *n* : utensils (as of china, glass, or silver) for table use
[1]**tab·loid** \'tab-ˌlȯid\ *adj* : compressed or condensed into small scope ⟨*tabloid* information⟩
[2]**tabloid** *n* : a newspaper about half the page size of an ordinary newspaper
[1]**ta·boo** *or* **ta·bu** \ta-'bü, tə-\ *adj* [from *tabu*, a word in a South Sea Island language] : prohibited by a taboo
[2]**taboo** *or* **tabu** *n, pl* **taboos** *or* **tabus** **1** : a prohibition against touching, saying, or doing something on pain of immediate harm **2** : a prohibition imposed by social custom
[3]**taboo** *or* **tabu** *vb* : to place under a taboo
ta·bor \'tā-bər\ *n* : a small drum with one head used to accompany a pipe played by the same person — **ta·bor·er** \-bər-ər\ *n*

tabor

tab·u·lar \'tab-yə-lər\ *adj* **1** : having a flat surface **2 a** : arranged or entered in a table **b** : computed by means of a table — **tab·u·lar·ly** *adv*
tab·u·late \'tab-yə-ˌlāt\ *vb* : to put into tabular form — **tab·u·la·tion** \ˌtab-yə-'lā-shən\ *n*
tab·u·la·tor \'tab-yə-ˌlāt-ər\ *n* **1** : a business machine that sorts and selects information from marked or perforated cards **2** : a device on a typewriter or biller for arranging data in columns
ta·chis·to·scope \tə-'kis-tə-ˌskōp\ *n* : an apparatus for the brief exposure of visual stimuli (as objects, figures, colors, or letters)
ta·chom·e·ter \tə-'käm-ət-ər\ *n* : a device for indicating speed of rotation
tac·it \'tas-ət\ *adj* **1** : expressed without words or speech **2** : implied but not actually expressed ⟨*tacit* consent⟩ — **tac·it·ly** *adv* — **tac·it·ness** *n*
tac·i·turn \'tas-ə-ˌtərn\ *adj* : habitually silent ***syn*** see SILENT ***ant*** garrulous — **tac·i·tur·ni·ty** \ˌtas-ə-'tər-nət-ē\ *n* — **tac·i·turn·ly** \'tas-ə-ˌtərn-lē\ *adv*
[1]**tack** \'tak\ *n* **1** : a small short sharp-pointed nail usu. with a broad flat head for fastening some light object or material to a surface ⟨carpet *tack*⟩ **2 a** : a rope used to hold in place the forward lower corner of the lowest sail on a square-rigged mast **b** : the lower forward corner of a fore-and-aft sail **3 a** : the direction a ship is sailing as shown by the way the sails are trimmed : the run of a ship as trimmed in one way ⟨on the port *tack*⟩ **b** : a change of course from one tack to another **4** : a zigzag movement on land **5** : a course or method of action ⟨he is on the wrong *tack*⟩ **6** : a slight or temporary sewing or fastening
[2]**tack** *vb* **1** : to fasten or attach esp. with tacks **2** : to join in a slight or hasty manner **3** : to add as a supplement **4 a** : to change the direction of a sailing ship by shifting the sails **b** : to change from one tack to another **5 a** : to follow a zigzag course **b** : to modify one's policy or an attitude abruptly — **tack·er** *n*
tack·i·ness \'tak-ē-nəs\ *n* : the quality or state of being tacky
[1]**tack·le** \'tak-əl\ *n* **1** : a set of the equipment used in

an activity : GEAR ⟨fishing *tackle*⟩ **2 a** : a ship's rigging **b** : an assemblage of ropes and pulleys arranged to gain mechanical advantage for hoisting or pulling **3 a** : the act or an instance of tackling **b** : a football lineman who lines up inside the end

tackle 2b

[2]tackle *vb* **tack·led**; **tack·ling** \'tak-(ə-)ling\ **1** : HARNESS ⟨*tackle* up the horses⟩ **2 a** : to seize, take hold of, or grapple with esp. in order to stop or subdue **b** : to seize and throw down or stop in football **3** : to set about dealing with ⟨*tackle* a problem⟩ — **tack·ler** \-(ə-)lər\ *n*

[1]tacky \'tak-ē\ *adj* **tack·i·er**; **-est** : barely sticky to the touch : ADHESIVE ⟨*tacky* varnish⟩

[2]tacky *adj* **tack·i·er**; **-est** **1** : SHABBY, SEEDY **2** : marked by lack of style or good taste : DOWDY

ta·co \'täk-ō\ *n, pl* **tacos** \-ōz, -ōs\ : a tortilla rolled up with or folded over a filling

tact \'takt\ *n* : a keen understanding of how to act in getting along with others; *esp* : the ability to deal with others without offending them — **tact·less** \'tak-tləs\ *adj* — **tact·less·ly** *adv* — **tact·less·ness** *n*

tact·ful \'takt-fəl\ *adj* : having or showing tact — **tact·ful·ly** \-fə-lē\ *adv* — **tact·ful·ness** *n*

tac·tic \'tak-tik\ *n* **1** : a method of employing forces in combat **2** : a planned action or maneuver for accomplishing an end

tac·ti·cal \'tak-ti-kəl\ *adj* **1 a** : of or relating to combat tactics **b** : of or relating to air attack in close support of friendly ground forces ⟨*tactical* air force⟩ **2 a** : of or relating to small-scale actions serving a larger purpose **b** : skillful in planning or maneuvering — **tac·ti·cal·ly** \-k(ə-)lē\ *adv*

tac·ti·cian \tak-'tish-ən\ *n* : one skilled in tactics

tac·tics \'tak-tiks\ *n sing or pl* **1 a** : the science and art of disposing and maneuvering forces in combat **b** : the art or skill of employing available means to accomplish an end **2** : a system or mode of procedure

tac·tile \'tak-təl, -ˌtīl\ *adj* : of, relating to, or perceptible through the sense of touch — **tac·til·i·ty** \tak-'til-ət-ē\ *n*

tad \'tad\ *n* : BOY

tad·pole \'tad-ˌpōl\ *n* [from Middle English *taddepol*, from *tadde* "toad" and *pol* "head"] : an aquatic larval frog or toad typically having a long tail, rounded body, and gills

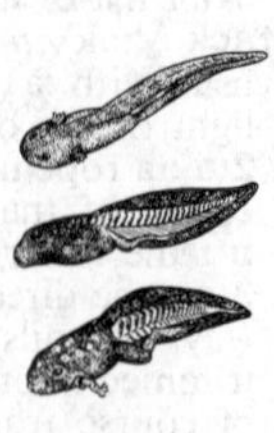

tadpole in successive stages of development

taf·fe·ta \'taf-ət-ə\ *n* : a crisp plain-woven lustrous fabric of various fibers used esp. for women's clothing

taff·rail \'taf-ˌrāl, -rəl\ *n* : the rail around the stern of a ship

taf·fy \'taf-ē\ *n, pl* **taffies** : a candy usu. of molasses or brown sugar boiled and pulled until porous and light-colored

[1]tag \'tag\ *n* **1** : a loose hanging piece of cloth : TATTER **2** : a metal or plastic binding on an end of a shoelace **3 a** : a brief quotation used for emphasis or effect **b** : TAG LINE **4** : a marker used for identification or classification ⟨price *tag*⟩

[2]tag *vb* **tagged**; **tag·ging** **1** : to provide or mark with or as if with a tag **2** : to follow closely and persistently **3 a** : LABEL 3 **b** : to distinguish (as part of an organism or the organism as a whole) by introducing a labeled atom

[3]tag *n* **1** : a children's game in which one player is it and chases the others and tries to make one of them it by touching him **2** : an act or instance of touching a runner with the ball in baseball

[4]tag *vb* **tagged**; **tag·ging** **1** : to touch in a game of tag **2** : to put out in baseball by touching with the ball

tag·along \'tag-ə-ˌlȯng\ *n* : one that persistently and often annoyingly follows the lead of another

tag board *n* : a strong cardboard

tag line *n* : a final line (as in a joke); *esp* : one that serves to clarify a point

tag up *vb* : to touch a base in baseball before running after a fly ball is caught

tai·ga \tī-'gä\ *n* : swampy northern forest of cone-bearing trees beginning where the tundra ends

[1]tail \'tāl\ *n* **1** : the rear end or a lengthened growth from the rear end of the body of an animal **2** : something resembling an animal's tail ⟨*tail* of a kite⟩ ⟨*tail* of a comet⟩ **3** : the back, last, lower, or inferior part of something; *esp* : the reverse of a coin **4** : a spy (as a detective) who follows someone **5** : the rear part of an airplane consisting of horizontal and vertical stabilizing surfaces with attached control surfaces **6** : the trail of a fugitive in flight ⟨posse on his *tail*⟩ — **tailed** \'tāld\ *adj* — **tail·less** \'tāl-ləs\ *adj* — **tail·like** \'tāl-ˌlīk\ *adj*

[2]tail *adj* **1** : being at the rear ⟨*tail* gunner⟩ **2** : coming from the rear

[3]tail *vb* **1** : to make or furnish with a tail **2 a** : to follow or be drawn behind like a tail **b** : to follow closely to observe : SHADOW

tail·board \-ˌbōrd, -ˌbȯrd\ *n* : TAILGATE

[1]tail·gate \'tāl-ˌgāt\ *n* : a board at the back end of a vehicle (as a station wagon) that can be let down for loading and unloading

[2]tailgate *vb* : to drive dangerously close behind another vehicle

tail·light \'tāl-ˌlīt\ *n* : a red warning light mounted at the rear of a vehicle

[1]tai·lor \'tā-lər\ *n* [from French *tailleur*, literally "cutter", from *tailler* "to cut"] : a person whose occupation is making or altering outer garments

[2]tailor *vb* **1** : to make or fashion as the work of a tailor **2** : to make or adapt to suit a special need or purpose — **tai·lored** \-lərd\ *adj* — **tai·lor·ing** *n*

tai·lor–made \ˌtā-lər-'mād\ *adj* **1** : made by or as if by a tailor; *esp* : marked by precise fit and simplicity of style **2** : made or seeming to have been made to suit a particular need

tail·piece \'tāl-ˌpēs\ *n* **1** : a piece added at the end **2** : a triangular piece to which the strings of a stringed instrument are fastened **3** : an ornament placed below the text matter of a page (as at the end of a chapter)

tail pipe *n* **1** : the pipe discharging the exhaust gases from the muffler of an automotive engine **2** : the part of a jet engine that carries the exhaust gases rearward

tail·spin \'tāl-ˌspin\ *n* : a spiral dive or plunge by an airplane

tail wind *n* : a wind moving in the same general direction as a ship or aircraft

[1]taint \'tānt\ *vb* **1** : to touch or affect slightly with something bad **2** : SPOIL, DECAY

ə abut	ər further	a back	ā bake	
ä cot, cart	aù out	ch chin	e less	ē easy
g gift	i trip	ī life	j joke	ng sing	ō flow
ȯ flaw	ȯi coin	th thin	th this	ü loot
ù foot	y yet	yü few	yù furious	zh vision

[2]**taint** *n* **1** : a trace of decay : STAIN **2** : a contaminating influence — **taint·less** \-ləs\ *adj*

[1]**take** \'tāk\ *vb* **took** \'tu̇k\; **tak·en** \'tā-kən\; **tak·ing** **1** : to lay hold of : GRASP ⟨*take* my hand⟩ **2** : CAPTURE ⟨*take* a fort⟩ **3** : WIN ⟨*take* first prize⟩ **4** : to get possession of (as by buying or capturing) ⟨*took* several trout with hook and line⟩ **5** : to seize and affect suddenly ⟨*taken* with a fever⟩ **6** : CHARM, DELIGHT ⟨was much *taken* with his new acquaintance⟩ **7** : EXTRACT ⟨*take* material from an encyclopedia⟩ **8** : REMOVE, SUBTRACT ⟨*take* 78 from 112⟩ **9** : to put an end to (as life) **10** : to find out by testing or examining ⟨*take* a patient's temperature⟩ **11** : SELECT, CHOOSE **12** : ASSUME ⟨*take* office⟩ **13** : ABSORB ⟨this cloth *takes* dye well⟩ **14** : to be affected by : CONTRACT ⟨*took* cold⟩ **15** : ACCEPT, FOLLOW ⟨*take* my advice⟩ **16** : to introduce into one's body ⟨*take* medicine⟩ **17 a** : to submit to ⟨*took* his punishment like a man⟩ **b** : WITHSTAND ⟨*takes* a punch well⟩ **18** : to subscribe for **19** : UNDERSTAND ⟨*take* a nod to mean *yes*⟩ **20** : FEEL ⟨*take* pride in one's work⟩ ⟨*take* offense⟩ **21** : to be formed or used with ⟨a noun that *takes* an *s* in the plural⟩ ⟨this verb *takes* an object⟩ **22** : CONVEY, CONDUCT, CARRY ⟨*take* a parcel to the post office⟩ **23 a** : to avail oneself of ⟨*take* a vacation⟩ **b** : to proceed to occupy ⟨*take* a chair⟩ **24** : NEED, REQUIRE ⟨this job *takes* a lot of time⟩ **25** : to obtain an image or copy of ⟨*take* a photograph⟩ ⟨*take* fingerprints⟩ **26** : to set out to make, do, or perform ⟨*take* a walk⟩ ⟨*took* on a new assignment⟩ **27** : to have effect ⟨the vaccination *took*⟩ **28** : to betake oneself ⟨*take* to the hills⟩ — **take advantage of** **1** : to use to advantage : profit by **2** : to impose upon : EXPLOIT — **take after** **1** : to take as an example : FOLLOW **2** : to look like : RESEMBLE ⟨*takes after* his father⟩ **3** : CHASE ⟨*took after* him with a bat⟩ — **take care** : to be careful — **take care of** : to attend to or provide for the needs, operation, or treatment of — **take effect** **1** : to become operative **2** : to produce a result as expected or intended : be effective — **take for** : to suppose to be; *esp* : to suppose mistakenly to be — **take for granted** : to assume as true, real, or expected — **take hold** : to become attached or established — **take in vain** : to use a name profanely or without proper respect — **take part** : JOIN, PARTICIPATE, SHARE — **take place** : HAPPEN, OCCUR — **take stock** : INVENTORY, ASSESS — **take the floor** : to rise (as in a meeting) to make an address — **take to** : to be drawn or attracted to

[2]**take** *n* **1** : an act or the action of taking **2** : something taken : PROCEEDS, CATCH 1 **3 a** : a scene filmed or televised at one time without stopping the camera **b** : a sound recording made during a single recording period **4** : a bodily reaction that indicates a successful inoculation esp. against smallpox **5** : mental response or reaction

take back *vb* : RETRACT, WITHDRAW ⟨would not *take back* what he had said⟩

take·down \'tāk-ˌdau̇n\ *n* : the action or an act of taking down — **take·down** \-ˌdau̇n\ *adj*

take down \-'dau̇n\ *vb* **1 a** : to pull to pieces **b** : DISASSEMBLE **2** : to lower the spirit or vanity of : HUMBLE **3 a** : to write down **b** : to record by mechanical means

take–home pay \'tāk-ˌhōm-\ *n* : the part of gross salary or wages remaining after deductions (as of income-tax withholding, retirement insurance payments, or union dues)

take in *vb* **1 a** : to draw into a smaller compass ⟨*take in* a slack line⟩ **b** : to make smaller by enlarging seams or tucks ⟨*take in* a coat⟩ **2 a** : to receive as a guest or inmate **b** : to give shelter to **3** : to receive work into one's house to be done for pay ⟨*take in* washing⟩ **4** : to include within fixed limits ⟨the camp *took in* several acres⟩ **5** : ATTEND ⟨*take in* a movie⟩ **6** : PERCEIVE, COMPREHEND ⟨paused to *take* the situation *in*⟩ **7** : CHEAT, DECEIVE ⟨*taken in* by a hard luck story⟩

taken *past part of* TAKE

take·off \'tāk-ˌȯf\ *n* **1** : IMITATION; *esp* : PARODY **2 a** : a rise or leap from a surface in making a jump or flight or an ascent in an airplane **b** : an action of starting out **3** : a spot at which one takes off

take off \-'ȯf\ *vb* **1 a** : REMOVE ⟨*take* your hat *off*⟩ **b** : to take away : DEDUCT ⟨*take off* 10 percent⟩ **2** : RELEASE ⟨*take* the brake *off*⟩ **3** : to omit or withhold from service owed or from time being spent (as at one's occupation) ⟨*took* two weeks *off* in August⟩ **4 a** : to copy from an original : REPRODUCE **b** : MIMIC **5 a** : to start off or away : set out ⟨*took off* without delay⟩ **b** : to leave the surface : begin flight ⟨planes *took off* every minute⟩

take on *vb* **1** : to engage with as an opponent **2** : ENGAGE, HIRE ⟨*took on* more workmen⟩ **3** : to assume or acquire (as an appearance or quality) as one's own ⟨*take on* weight⟩ ⟨*take on* dignity with age⟩ **4** : to show one's feelings esp. of grief or anger in a demonstrative way ⟨don't *take on* so⟩

take out \'tāk-'au̇t\ *vb* **1** : to remove by cleansing **2** : to find release for : EXPEND ⟨*took out* her anger on me⟩ **3** : to conduct or escort into the open or to a public entertainment **4** : to take as an equivalent in another form ⟨*took* the debt *out* in goods⟩ **5** : to obtain from the proper authority ⟨*take out* a charter⟩ **6** : to start on a course : set out — **take-out** \-ˌau̇t\ *n*

take over \'tāk-'ō-vər\ *vb* : to assume control or possession of or responsibility for something ⟨*took over* the government⟩ — **take·over** \-ˌō-vər\ *n*

take up *vb* **1** : to remove by lifting or pulling up **2** : to begin : UNDERTAKE ⟨*took up* swimming⟩ **3** : to pull up or in so as to tighten or to shorten ⟨*take up* the slack in the rope⟩ — **take up with** : to begin to associate with

tak·ing \'tā-king\ *adj* **1** : ATTRACTIVE **2** : CONTAGIOUS

tak·ings \'tā-kingz\ *n pl* : receipts esp. of money : PROFIT

talc \'talk\ *n* : a soft mineral that consists of a silicate of magnesium, is usu. whitish, greenish, or grayish with a soapy feel, and occurs in flaky, granular, or fibrous masses

tal·cum powder \'tal-kəm-\ *n* : a usu. mildly antiseptic powder composed of perfumed talc for sprinkling or rubbing over the skin (as after bathing)

tale \'tāl\ *n* **1** : an oral relation or recital ⟨a *tale* of woe⟩ **2** : a story about an imaginary event ⟨a fairy *tale*⟩ **3** : a false story : LIE **4** : a piece of harmful gossip ⟨spread *tales* about him⟩ **5** : a number of things taken together : TOTAL ⟨the whole *tale* of plays presented this season⟩

tale·bear·er \-ˌbar-ər, -ˌber-\ *n* : one that spreads gossip, scandal, or idle rumors : GOSSIP — **tale-bear·ing** \-ing\ *adj or n*

tal·ent \'tal-ənt\ *n* [from Greek *talanton*; senses 2 to 4 are due to the parable of the talents in Matthew 25:14–30] **1** : an ancient unit of weight and money value (as a unit of Palestine and Syria equal to 3000 shekels or a Greek unit equal to 6000 drachmas) **2** : the natural endowments of a person **3** : a special often creative or artistic aptitude **4** : persons of talent in a field or activity ⟨trying to recruit new *talent*⟩ ***syn*** see ABILITY — **tal·ent·ed** \-ən-təd\ *adj*

talent scout *n* : a person engaged in discovering and recruiting people with special talents

talent show *n* : a show consisting of a series of individual performances (as singing) by amateurs who may be selected for special recognition as performing talent

ta·ler \'täl-ər\ *n* : any of numerous silver coins issued by various German states from the 15th to the 19th centuries

tal·is·man \'tal-əs-mən, -əz-\ *n, pl* **talismans** : a ring or stone carved with symbols and believed to have magical powers : CHARM

1**talk** \'tȯk\ *vb* **1** : to deliver or express in speech : UTTER ⟨*talk* sense⟩ **2** : to make the subject of conversation or discourse : DISCUSS ⟨*talk* business⟩ **3** : to influence, affect, or cause by talking ⟨*talked* them into agreeing⟩ **4 a** : to use for conversing or communicating ⟨*talk* sign language⟩ **b** : to express or exchange ideas by means of spoken words **5 a** : GOSSIP **b** : to reveal secret information ⟨tried to make the suspect *talk*⟩ — **talk·er** *n* — **talk back** : to answer impertinently

2**talk** *n* **1** : the act or an instance of talking : SPEECH **2** : a way of speaking : LANGUAGE **3** : pointless or fruitless discussion **4** : a formal discussion, negotiation, or exchange of views : CONFERENCE **5** : RUMOR, GOSSIP **6** : the topic of interested comment, conversation, or gossip ⟨she is the *talk* of the village⟩

talk·a·tive \'tȯ-kət-iv\ *adj* : fond of talking — **talk·a·tive·ness** *n*

syn TALKATIVE, GARRULOUS, VOLUBLE can mean fond of talking. TALKATIVE implies a readiness to engage in talk or conversation; GARRULOUS suggests a rambling often foolish and tedious talkativeness; VOLUBLE suggests a ready, rapid, and seemingly unending flow of speech ***ant*** silent

talk·ie \'tȯ-kē\ *n* : a motion picture with synchronized sound effects

talking book *n* : a phonograph recording of a reading of a book or magazine designed chiefly for the use of the blind

talk·ing–to \'tȯ-king-ˌtü\ *n* : SCOLDING

talk over *vb* : DISCUSS

tall \'tȯl\ *adj* **1 a** : great in stature or height **b** : of a specified height ⟨five feet *tall*⟩ **2 a** : large in amount, extent, or degree ⟨*tall* order to fill⟩ **b** : IMPROBABLE ⟨*tall* story⟩ ***syn*** see HIGH ***ant*** short — **tall** *adv* — **tall·ness** *n*

tal·lith \'täl-əs, -ət(h)\ *n* : a shawl with fringed corners traditionally worn over the head or shoulders by Jewish men during morning prayers

tal·low \'tal-ō\ *n* : the white nearly tasteless melted and solidified fat of cattle and sheep used chiefly in soap, margarine, candles, and lubricants

1**tal·ly** \'tal-ē\ *n, pl* **tallies** **1** : a device for recording business transactions **2 a** : a reckoning or recorded account **b** : a total recorded **3** : a score or point made (as in a game) **4 a** : a part that corresponds to another : COMPLEMENT **b** : CORRESPONDENCE, AGREEMENT

2**tally** *vb* **tal·lied**; **tal·ly·ing** **1** : to keep a reckoning of : COUNT **2** : to make a tally : SCORE **3** : MATCH, AGREE

tal·ly·ho \ˌtal-ē-'hō\ *n, pl* **tallyhos** : a call of a huntsman at sight of the fox

tally mark *n* : one of a group of lines or marks drawn for the purpose of counting

Tal·mud \'täl-ˌmu̇d, 'tal-məd\ *n* : the authoritative body of Jewish tradition

tal·on \'tal-ən\ *n* : the claw of an animal and esp. of a bird of prey

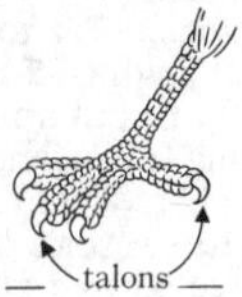
talons

1**ta·lus** \'tā-ləs\ *n* : rock debris at the base of a cliff

2**talus** *n, pl* **ta·li** \'tā-ˌlī\ **1** : ANKLEBONE **2** : the entire ankle

ta·ma·le \tə-'mäl-ē\ *n* : ground meat seasoned usu. with chili, rolled in cornmeal dough, wrapped in corn husks, and steamed

tam·a·rack \'tam-ə-ˌrak\ *n* : an American larch; *also* : its wood

tam·a·rind \'tam-ə-ˌrind, -rənd\ *n* : a tropical tree related to the pea and having hard yellowish wood, feathery pinnate leaves, and red-striped yellow flowers; *also* : its pod which has an acid pulp used for preserves or in drinks

tam·bou·rine \ˌtam-bə-'rēn\ *n* : a small drum; *esp* : a shallow one-headed drum with loose metal disks at the sides played by shaking, striking with the hand, or rubbing with the thumb

tambourine

1**tame** \'tām\ *adj* **1** : reduced from a state of wildness esp. so as to be useful to man : DOMESTICATED **2** : made docile and submissive : SUBDUED **3** : lacking spirit, zest, or interest : INSIPID — **tame·ly** *adv* — **tame·ness** *n*

2**tame** *vb* **1 a** : to make or become tame **b** : to subject land to cultivation **2** : HUMBLE, SUBDUE ⟨*tamed* her temper⟩ — **tam·a·ble** *or* **tame·a·ble** \'tā-mə-bəl\ *adj* — **tam·er** *n*

tam–o'–shan·ter \'tam-ə-ˌshant-ər\ *n* [after *Tam o'-Shanter*, hero of the poem of that name by Robert Burns] : a Scottish cap with a tight headband, wide flat circular crown, and usu. a pompon

tamp \'tamp\ *vb* **1** : to fill up above a blasting charge with material (as sand) ⟨*tamp* a drill hole⟩ **2** : to drive in or down by a succession of blows — **tamp·er** *n*

tam·per \'tam-pər\ *vb* **tam·pered**; **tam·per·ing** \-p(ə-)ring\ **1** : to use underhand or improper methods (as bribery) ⟨*tamper* with a witness⟩ **2 a** : to interfere so as to cause a weakening or change for the worse **b** : to try foolish or dangerous experiments ***syn*** see MEDDLE — **tam·per·er** \-pər-ər\ *n*

1**tan** \'tan\ *vb* **tanned**; **tan·ning** **1** : to convert into leather esp. by treatment with an infusion of tannin-rich bark ⟨*tan* hides⟩ **2** : to make or become tan or brown esp. by exposure to the sun ⟨a well-*tanned* skin⟩ **3** : THRASH, WHIP

2**tan** *n* **1** : TANBARK **2** : a brown color imparted to the skin by exposure to the sun or weather **3** : a light yellowish brown

3**tan** *adj* **tan·ner**; **tan·nest** : of the color tan

tan *abbr* tangent

tan·a·ger \'tan-i-jər\ *n* : any of a family of American birds related to the finches that have brightly colored males and are largely unmusical

tan·bark \'tan-ˌbärk\ *n* : bark rich in tannin that is used in tanning

1**tan·dem** \'tan-dəm\ *n* [from Latin, an adverb meaning "at last", "at length", used in English as if it meant "lengthwise"] **1 a** : a 2-seated carriage drawn by horses harnessed one before the other

b : TANDEM BICYCLE **2** : a group of two or more arranged one behind the other or used or acting in conjunction

2tandem *adv or adj* : one behind another

tandem bicycle *n* : a bicycle for two or more persons sitting tandem

tang \'tang\ *n* **1** : a projecting part on a knife, file, or sword to connect with the handle **2 a** : a sharp distinctive often lingering flavor **b** : a pungent odor — **tanged** \'tangd\ *adj* — **tangy** \'tang-ē\ *adj*

1tan·gent \'tan-jənt\ *adj* : touching a curve or surface at only one point in the given location ⟨a straight line *tangent* to a curve⟩

2tangent *n* **1** : the mathematical function that for an acute angle in a right triangle is the ratio of the side opposite to the side adjacent **2** : a tangent line, curve, or surface **3** : an abrupt change of course : DIGRESSION ⟨went off on a *tangent* and never got to the point⟩ — **tan·gen·tial** \tan-'jen-chəl\ *adj* — **tan·gen·tial·ly** \-'jench-(ə-)lē\ *adv*

tan·ger·ine \'tan-jə-ˌrēn\ *n* : a mandarin of a variety that is grown commercially in the U.S., in Japan, and in southern Africa; *also* : its fruit

1tan·gi·ble \'tan-jə-bəl\ *adj* **1** : capable of being touched **2** : capable of being understood and appreciated ⟨*tangible* benefits⟩ — **tan·gi·bil·i·ty** \ˌtan-jə-'bil-ət-ē\ *n* — **tan·gi·ble·ness** \'tan-jə-bəl-nəs\ *n* — **tan·gi·bly** \-blē\ *adv*

2tangible *n* : something tangible; *esp* : a tangible asset

1tan·gle \'tang-gəl\ *vb* **tan·gled**; **tan·gling** \-g(ə-)ling\ **1** : to make or become involved so as to hamper or embarrass : be or become entangled ⟨hopelessly *tangled* in argument⟩ **2** : to twist or become twisted together into a mass hard to straighten out again : ENTANGLE

2tangle *n* **1** : a tangled twisted mass (as of vines) confusedly interwoven : SNARL **2** : a complicated or confused state or condition

tan·go \'tang-gō\ *n, pl* **tangos** **1** : a Spanish-American ballroom dance marked by a variety of steps and postures **2** : music for the tango in moderate duple time with dotted and syncopated rhythm — **tango** *vb*

tan·gram \'tang-grəm, 'tan(g)-ˌgram\ *n* : a Chinese puzzle made by cutting a square of thin material into a number of pieces which can be recombined into many different figures

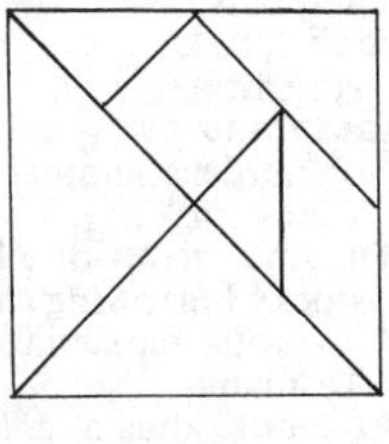

tangram

1tank \'tangk\ *n* **1** : a usu. large receptacle for holding, transporting, or storing liquids **2** : an enclosed heavily armed and armored combat vehicle supported and steered by endless-belt treads

2tank *vb* : to place, store, or treat in a tank

tan·kard \'tang-kərd\ *n* : a tall one-handled drinking vessel; *esp* : a silver or pewter mug with a lid

tank·er \'tang-kər\ *n* **1** : a boat fitted with tanks for carrying liquid in bulk **2** : a vehicle (as a truck or trailer) on which a tank is mounted to carry liquids

tan·ner \'tan-ər\ *n* : a person who tans hides

tan·nery \'tan-(ə-)rē\ *n, pl* **tan·ner·ies** : a place where tanning is carried on

tan·nic acid \ˌtan-ik-\ *n* : TANNIN

tan·nin \'tan-ən\ *n* : any of various substances from plants (as the oak or sumac) used in tanning and dyeing, in inks, and as astringents

tan·ning *n* **1** : the art or process by which a skin is tanned **2** : a browning of the skin by exposure to sun **3** : WHIPPING, FLOGGING

tan·sy \'tan-zē\ *n, pl* **tansies** : any of a genus of mostly weedy herbs related to the daisies; *esp* : one with finely cut leaves, aromatic odor, and very bitter taste

tan·ta·lize \'tant-ə-ˌlīz\ *vb* [from *Tantalus*, a king in Greek mythology who for his sins was punished in the lower world by being condemned to stand in water up to the chin and beneath fruit-laden branches with water and fruit receding at each attempt to drink or eat] : to tease or torment by or as if by presenting something desirable to the view but continually keeping it out of reach — **tan·ta·liz·er** *n* — **tan·ta·liz·ing·ly** \-ˌlī-zing-lē\ *adv*

tan·ta·lum \'tant-ə-ləm\ *n* : a hard ductile gray-white acid-resisting metallic element found combined in rare minerals and used esp. in making chemical apparatus and processing equipment — see ELEMENT table

tan·ta·mount \'tant-ə-ˌmau̇nt\ *adj* : equal in value, meaning, or effect ⟨a statement *tantamount* to an admission of guilt⟩

tan·trum \'tan-trəm\ *n* : a fit of bad temper

1tap \'tap\ *n* **1** : COCK, FAUCET **2** : the procedure of removing fluid from a container or cavity by tapping **3** : a tool for forming an internal screw thread **4** : an intermediate point in an electric circuit where a connection may be made — **on tap** **1** : ready to be drawn ⟨ale *on tap*⟩ **2** : on hand : AVAILABLE

2tap *vb* **tapped**; **tap·ping** **1** : to release or cause to flow by piercing or by drawing a plug from a container or cavity ⟨*tap* wine from a cask⟩ **2 a** : to pierce so as to let out or draw off a fluid ⟨*tap* maple trees⟩ **b** : to draw from or upon ⟨*tap* the nation's resources⟩ **3 a** : to connect into a telephone or telegraph wire to get information **b** : to connect into an electrical circuit — **tap·per** *n*

3tap *vb* **tapped**; **tap·ping** **1** : to strike or cause to strike lightly esp. with a slight sound ⟨*tapping* the desk with his pencil⟩ ⟨*tap* on a window⟩ ⟨*tapping* his foot⟩ **2** : to make or produce by repeated light blows ⟨a woodpecker *tapped* a hole in the tree⟩ **3** : to repair a shoe by putting a half sole on — **tapper** *n*

4tap *n* **1** : a light usu. audible blow or its sound **2** : HALF SOLE **3** : a small metal plate for the sole or heel of a shoe (as for tap dancing)

tap dance *n* : a dance tapped out audibly with the feet — **tap–dance** *vb* — **tap dancer** *n* — **tap dancing** *n*

1tape \'tāp\ *n* **1** : a narrow band of woven fabric **2** : a string stretched breast-high above the finishing line of a race **3** : a narrow flexible strip or band ⟨cash register *tape*⟩ **4** : MAGNETIC TAPE

2tape *vb* **1** : to fasten, tie, bind, cover, or support with tape **2** : to measure with a tape measure **3** : TAPE-RECORD

tape measure *n* : a tape marked off usu. in inches and used for measuring

1ta·per \'tā-pər\ *n* **1 a** : a long waxed wick used esp. for lighting lamps, pipes, or fires **b** : a slender candle **c** : a feeble light **2 a** : a tapering form or figure **b** : gradual lessening of thickness, diameter, or width in an elongated object **c** : a gradual decrease

2taper *vb* **ta·pered**; **ta·per·ing** \-p(ə-)ring\ **1** : to make or become gradually smaller toward one end **2** : to diminish gradually

tape–re·cord \ˌtāp-ri-'kȯrd\ *vb* : to make a recording of sounds on magnetic tape ⟨*tape-record* a concert⟩ — **tape recorder** *n* — **tape recording** *n*

taper off *vb* : to stop or diminish gradually

tap·es·try \'tap-ə-strē\ *n, pl* **-tries** : a heavy decorative fabric used esp. as a wall hanging or furniture covering — **tap·es·tried** \-strēd\ *adj*

tape·worm \'tāp-,wərm\ *n* : a flatworm with a segmented body that is parasitic when adult in the intestine of vertebrates

tapeworm (up to 20 ft. long)

tap·i·o·ca \,tap-ē-'ō-kə\ *n* : grains or flakes of starch obtained from the cassava root and used esp. in puddings and as a thickening in liquid foods

ta·pir \'tā-pər\ *n, pl* **tapir** *or* **tapirs** : any of several large hoofed mammals of tropical America, Malaya, and Sumatra that have a long flexible snout, a very short tail, and stout legs

tap·room \'tap-,rüm, -,rům\ *n* : BARROOM

tap·root \-,rüt, -,růt\ *n* : a large strong root that grows vertically downward and gives off small lateral roots — compare FIBROUS ROOT

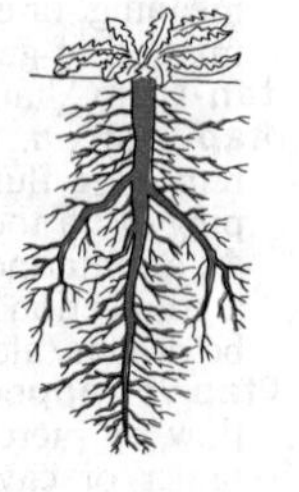
taproot

taps \'taps\ *n sing or pl* [probably an alteration of earlier *taptoo* "tattoo"] **1** : the last bugle call at night blown as a signal that lights are to be put out **2** : a similar call blown at military funerals and memorial services

[1]**tar** \'tär\ *n* : a dark usu. thick sticky liquid obtained by distillation of wood, coal, or peat

[2]**tar** *vb* **tarred**; **tar·ring** : to treat or smear with or as if with tar

[3]**tar** *n* [by shortening from *tarpaulin*] : SEAMAN, SAILOR

ta·ran·tu·la \tə-'ranch-(ə-)lə, -'rant-ə-lə\ *n* **1** : a large European spider whose bite was once thought to cause an uncontrollable desire to dance **2** : any of a family of large hairy American spiders that are mostly rather sluggish and nearly harmless to man although having a sharp bite

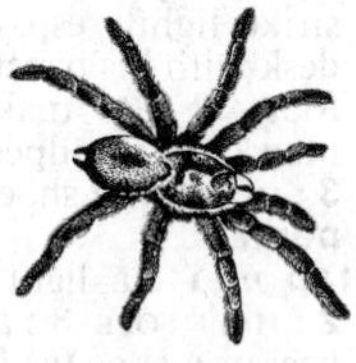
tarantula 2 (about 2 in. long)

tar·dy \'tärd-ē\ *adj* **tar·di·er**; **-est** **1** : moving slowly : SLUGGISH **2** : not on time : LATE — **tar·di·ly** \'tärd-ə-lē\ *adv* — **tar·di·ness** \'tärd-ē-nəs\ *n*

[1]**tare** \'ta(ə)r, 'te(ə)r\ *n* **1** : VETCH; *also* : its seed **2** : a weed of grainfields esp. of biblical times

[2]**tare** *n* : a deduction of weight made to allow for the weight of a container or vehicle — **tare** *vb*

tar·get \'tär-gət\ *n* **1 a** : a mark to shoot at **b** : an object of ridicule or criticism **c** : a goal to be achieved : OBJECTIVE **2** : the surface usu. of platinum or tungsten upon which the cathode rays within an X-ray tube are focused and from which the X rays are emitted

tar·iff \'tar-əf\ *n* **1 a** : a schedule of duties imposed by a government on imported or in some countries exported goods **b** : a duty or rate of duty imposed in such a schedule **2** : a schedule of rates or charges of a business or public utility

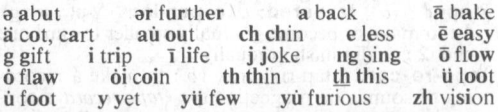

tarn \'tärn\ *n* : a small mountain lake

[1]**tar·nish** \'tär-nish\ *vb* **1** : to make or become dull, dim, or discolored ⟨silver *tarnishes*⟩ **2** : to bring disgrace or cast doubt upon ⟨a *tarnished* reputation⟩ — **tar·nish·a·ble** \-ə-bəl\ *adj*

[2]**tarnish** *n* **1** : tarnished condition **2** : a surface film (as of oxide or sulfide) formed or deposited in tarnishing ⟨hard to get all the *tarnish* off silver⟩

ta·ro \'tär-ō, 'tar-, 'ter-\ *n, pl* **taros** : a plant grown throughout the tropics for its edible starchy tuberous rootstocks; *also* : this rootstock

tar·pau·lin \tär-'pȯ-lən, 'tär-pə-\ *n* : waterproof material and esp. canvas used to protect exposed objects

tar·pon \'tär-pən\ *n, pl* **tarpon** *or* **tarpons** : a large silvery sport fish common off the Florida coast

[1]**tar·ry** \'tar-ē\ *vb* **tar·ried**; **tar·ry·ing** **1** : DELAY, LINGER **2** : to stay in or at a place : SOJOURN

[2]**tar·ry** \'tär-ē\ *adj* : of, resembling, or covered with tar

[1]**tar·sal** \'tär-səl\ *adj* : of or relating to the tarsus

[2]**tarsal** *n* : a tarsal part (as a bone or cartilage)

tar·sus \'tär-səs\ *n, pl* **tar·si** \-,sī, -,sē\ **1** : the part of the foot of a vertebrate between the metatarsus and the leg : ANKLE; *also* : the small bones that support this part of the limb **2** : the shank of a bird's leg **3** : the part of the limb of an arthropod (as an insect) most distant from the body

[1]**tart** \'tärt\ *adj* **1** : agreeably sharp to the taste : pleasantly acid **2** : BITING, CAUSTIC ⟨*tart* words⟩ — **tart·ly** *adv* — **tart·ness** *n*

[2]**tart** *n* : a small pie or pastry shell containing jelly, custard, or fruit

tar·tan \'tärt-ən\ *n* **1** : a plaid textile design of Scottish origin usu. distinctively patterned to designate a clan **2** : a fabric or garment with tartan design

tar·tar \'tärt-ər\ *n* **1** : a substance consisting essentially of cream of tartar found in the juice of grapes and deposited in wine casks as a reddish crust or sediment **2** : a hard crust of saliva, food residue, and various calcium salts that forms on the teeth

tar·tar sauce *or* **tar·tare sauce** \,tärt-ər-\ *n* : mayonnaise with chopped pickles, olives, capers, and parsley

task \'task\ *n* : a piece of assigned work : DUTY, FUNCTION

task·mas·ter \-,mas-tər\ *n* : one that imposes a task or burdens another with labor — **task·mis·tress** \-,mis-trəs\ *n*

Tas·ma·ni·an devil \taz-,mā-nē-ən-\ *n* : a powerful stocky burrowing carnivorous marsupial of Tasmania

Tasmanian devil (about 3 ft. long)

[1]**tas·sel** \'tas-əl *also esp of corn* 'täs-, 'tȯs-\ *n* **1** : a hanging ornament made of a bunch of cords fastened at one end **2** : something resembling a tassel; *esp* : the terminal male flower cluster of Indian corn

[2]**tassel** *vb* **-seled** *or* **-selled**; **-sel·ing** *or* **-sel·ling** \-(ə-)ling\ : to adorn with or put forth tassels

[1]**taste** \'tāst\ *vb* **1** : EXPERIENCE, UNDERGO ⟨*taste* the joy of flying⟩ **2** : to test the flavor of something by taking a little into the mouth **3** : to eat or drink esp. in small quantities **4** : to perceive

or recognize by or as if by the sense of taste ⟨can *taste* the onion in it⟩ **5** : to have a specific flavor ⟨this milk *tastes* sour⟩

[2]**taste** *n* **1 a** : a small amount tasted **b** : a small sample of experience ⟨first *taste* of battle⟩ **2** : the sense that perceives and distinguishes the sweet, sour, bitter, or salty quality of a dissolved substance and is mediated by receptors in the taste buds of the tongue **3 a** : the quality of a dissolved substance perceptible to the sense of taste **b** : a complex sensation resulting from usu. combined stimulation of the senses of taste, smell, and touch : FLAVOR **4** : individual preference : INCLINATION **5 a** : critical judgment or appreciation of beauty or excellence ⟨a man of *taste*⟩ **b** : aesthetic quality : STYLE ⟨in bad *taste*⟩

taste bud *n* : any of the sensory organs by means of which taste is perceived and which lie chiefly in the tongue

taste·ful \'tāst-fəl\ *adj* : having, showing, or conforming to good taste — **taste·ful·ly** \-fə-lē\ *adv* — **taste·ful·ness** *n*

taste·less \'tāst-ləs\ *adj* **1** : lacking flavor : FLAT, INSIPID **2** : not having or showing good taste ⟨*tasteless* decorations⟩ — **taste·less·ly** *adv* — **taste·less·ness** *n*

tast·er \'tā-stər\ *n* : one that tastes: as **a** : a person who has the duty of tasting food or drink prepared for another person esp. to test for poison **b** : a person who is able to taste the chemical phenylthiocarbamide

tasty \'tā-stē\ *adj* **tast·i·er**; **-est** **1** : pleasing to the taste : SAVORY **2** : TASTEFUL — **tast·i·ly** \-stə-lē\ *adv* — **tast·i·ness** \-stē-nəs\ *n*

tat \'tat\ *vb* **tat·ted**; **tat·ting** : to work at or make by tatting

tat·ter \'tat-ər\ *n* **1** : a part torn and left hanging : SHRED **2** *pl* : tattered clothing : RAGS — **tatter** *vb*

tat·tered \'tat-ərd\ *adj* **1** : wearing ragged clothes ⟨a *tattered* barefoot boy⟩ **2** : torn in shreds : RAGGED ⟨*tattered* flag⟩

tat·ting \'tat-ing\ *n* **1** : a delicate handmade lace formed usu. by looping and knotting with a single thread and a small shuttle **2** : the act or process of making tatting

[1]**tat·tle** \'tat-əl\ *vb* **tat·tled**; **tat·tling** \-(ə-)ling\ **1** : CHATTER, PRATTLE **2** : BLAB, GOSSIP

[2]**tattle** *n* **1** : idle talk : CHATTER **2** : GOSSIP

tat·tler \'tat-(ə-)lər\ *n* : TATTLETALE

tat·tle·tale \'tat-əl-,tāl\ *n* : one that tattles : INFORMER

[1]**tat·too** \ta-'tü\ *n*, *pl* **tattoos** [from earlier *taptoo*, from Dutch *taptoe*, from the phrase *tap toe*! "taps shut!", i.e. "no more drinking"] **1** : a call sounded shortly before taps as notice to go to quarters **2** : a rapid rhythmic rapping ⟨the horse's hoofs beat a *tattoo* on the road⟩

[2]**tattoo** *n* : an indelible mark or figure fixed upon the body by insertion of pigment under the skin or by production of scars

[3]**tattoo** *vb* : to mark or color the skin with a tattoo ⟨*tattooed* a flag on his chest⟩ — **tat·too·er** *n*

tau \'tau̇, 'tȯ\ *n* : the 19th letter of the Greek alphabet — Τ or τ

taught *past of* TEACH

taunt \'tȯnt, 'tänt\ *vb* : to reproach or challenge in a mocking or insulting manner : jeer at — **taunt** *n* — **taunt·er** *n* — **taunt·ing·ly** \-ing-lē\ *adv*

taupe \'tōp\ *n* [from French, literally "mole"] : a brownish gray

Tau·rus \'tȯr-əs\ *n* — see ZODIAC table

taut \'tȯt\ *adj* **1 a** : tightly drawn : not slack ⟨*taut* rope⟩ **b** : HIGH-STRUNG, TENSE ⟨*taut* nerves⟩ **2** : kept in proper order or condition ⟨a *taut* ship⟩ ***syn*** see TIGHT ***ant*** slack — **taut·ly** *adv* — **taut·ness** *n*

tau·tol·o·gy \tȯ-'täl-ə-jē\ *n*, *pl* **-gies** : needless repetition of an idea, statement, or word; *also* : an instance of such repetition ⟨"a beginner who has just started" is a *tautology*⟩ — **tau·to·log·i·cal** \,tȯt-ə-'läj-i-kəl\ *adj*

tav·ern \'tav-ərn\ *n* **1** : an establishment where alcoholic liquors are sold to be drunk on the premises **2** : INN

taw \'tȯ\ *n* **1** : a marble used as a shooter **2** : the line from which players shoot at marbles

taw·dry \'tȯd-rē, 'täd-\ *adj* **taw·dri·er**; **-est** : cheap and gaudy in appearance or quality ⟨wearing *tawdry* finery⟩ — **taw·dri·ly** \-rə-lē\ *adv* — **taw·dri·ness** \-rē-nəs\ *n*

[1]**taw·ny** \'tȯ-nē, 'tän-ē\ *adj* **taw·ni·er**; **-est** : of the color tawny — **taw·ni·ness** *n*

[2]**tawny** *n*, *pl* **tawnies** : a brownish orange to light brown color

[1]**tax** \'taks\ *vb* **1** : to levy a tax on **2** : to call to account : CENSURE ⟨*taxed* him with neglect of his duty⟩ **3** : to make rigorous demands upon : STRAIN ⟨*taxed* his strength⟩ — **tax·a·ble** \'tak-sə-bəl\ *adj* — **tax·er** *n*

[2]**tax** *n* **1** : a charge usu. of money imposed by authority upon persons or property for public purposes **2** : something (as an effort or duty) that makes heavy demands : STRAIN

tax·a·tion \tak-'sā-shən\ *n* **1** : the action of taxing; *esp* : the imposition of taxes **2** : income obtained from taxes

[1]**taxi** \'tak-sē\ *n*, *pl* **tax·is** \-sēz\ *also* **tax·ies** **1** : TAXICAB **2** : a boat or airplane carrying passengers for a fare

[2]**taxi** *vb* **tax·ied**; **taxi·ing** *or* **taxy·ing**; **tax·is** \-sēz\ *or* **tax·ies** **1** : to go or transport by taxi **2** : to go at low speed along the surface of the ground ⟨the plane *taxied* into the wind⟩ ⟨*taxied* the plane to the hangar⟩

taxi·cab \'tak-sē-,kab\ *n* [from earlier *taximeter cab*, from *taximeter* "instrument for automatically determining the fare of a hired vehicle", from Latin *taxa* "tax", "charge"] : an automobile that carries passengers for a fare usu. determined by the distance traveled and often shown by a meter

tax·i·der·my \'tak-sə-,dər-mē\ *n* : the art of preparing, stuffing, and mounting skins of animals — **tax·i·der·mic** \,tak-sə-'dər-mik\ *adj* — **tax·i·der·mist** \'tak-sə-,dər-məst\ *n*

tax·is \'tak-səs\ *n*, *pl* **tax·es** \'tak-,sēz\ : reflex movement by a freely motile organism in relation to a source of stimulation (as a light or a temperature or chemical gradient); *also* : a reflex reaction involving such movement — compare TROPISM

taxon *abbr* taxonomy

tax·on·o·my \tak-'sän-ə-mē\ *n* **1** : the study of scientific classification **2** : CLASSIFICATION; *esp* : orderly classification of plants and animals according to their natural relationships — **tax·o·nom·ic** \,tak-sə-'näm-ik\ *adj* — **tax·on·o·mist** \tak-'sän-ə-məst\ *n*

tax·pay·er \'taks-,pā-ər\ *n* : one that pays or is liable for a tax

TB \(')tē-'bē\ *n* : TUBERCULOSIS

TBA *abbr* to be announced

tbs *abbr* tablespoon

TD *abbr* touchdown

tea \'tē\ *n* [from Chinese *t'e* (in the dialect of Amoy)] **1 a** : a shrub that has lance-shaped leaves and fragrant

T

white flowers and is grown mainly in China, Japan, India, and Ceylon **b** : the leaves and leaf buds of the tea prepared for use in beverages **c** : an aromatic beverage prepared from tea by steeping in boiling water **2** : any of various plants used like tea or an infusion from their leaves used medicinally or as a beverage ⟨sage *tea*⟩ **3 a** : a late afternoon serving of tea and a light meal **b** : a party or reception at which tea is served

tea 1a

tea bag *n* : a cloth or filter-paper bag holding enough tea for an individual serving

tea·ber·ry \'tē-ˌber-ē\ *n* : CHECKERBERRY

teach \'tēch\ *vb* **taught** \'tȯt\; **teach·ing** **1** : to assist in learning how to do something : show how ⟨*teach* a child to read⟩ **2** : to guide the studies of : INSTRUCT ⟨*teach* a class⟩ **3** : to give lessons in : instruct pupils in ⟨*teach* music⟩ **4** : to be a teacher **5** : to cause to learn : cause to know the consequences of an action ⟨*taught* by experience⟩

teach·a·ble \'tē-chə-bəl\ *adj* **1** : capable of being taught; *esp* : apt and willing to learn **2** : well adapted for use in teaching ⟨a *teachable* textbook⟩ — **teach·a·bil·i·ty** \ˌtē-chə-'bil-ət-ē\ *n*

teach·er \'tē-chər\ *n* : one that teaches; *esp* : one whose occupation is to instruct

teach–in \'tēch-ˌin\ *n* : an extended meeting of college students and faculty members for lectures, debates, and discussions esp. on U.S. foreign policy

teach·ing *n* **1** : the act, practice, or profession of a teacher **2** : something taught; *esp* : DOCTRINE

tea·cup \'tē-ˌkəp\ *n* : a cup usu. of less than 8-oz. capacity used with a saucer for hot beverages

tea·cup·ful \-ˌfu̇l\ *n, pl* **-cupfuls** \-ˌfu̇lz\ *or* **-cups·ful** \-ˌkəps-ˌfu̇l\ : as much as a teacup can hold

teak \'tēk\ *n* [from Portuguese *teca*, from Malayalam, a language of southern India] **1** : a tall East Indian timber tree **2** : the hard durable yellowish brown wood of a teak — called also *teak·wood* \-ˌwu̇d\

tea·ket·tle \'tē-ˌket-əl\ *n* : a covered kettle with a handle and spout for boiling water

teal \'tēl\ *n, pl* **teal** *or* **teals** : any of several small short-necked river ducks of Europe and America

teal
(about 15 in. long)

[1]**team** \'tēm\ *n* **1 a** : two or more draft animals harnessed to the same vehicle or implement **b** : one or more animals with harness and attached vehicle **2** : a number of persons associated together in work or activity : CREW, GANG

[2]**team** *vb* **1** : to yoke or join in a team **2** : to haul with or drive a team **3** : to form a team ⟨*team* up together⟩

team·mate \'tēm-ˌmāt\ *n* : a fellow member of a team

team·ster \'tēm(p)-stər\ *n* : one who drives a team or motortruck

team·work \'tēm-ˌwərk\ *n* : the work or activity of a number of persons acting together as a unit

tea·pot \'tē-ˌpät\ *n* : a vessel with a spout for brewing and serving tea

[1]**tear** \'ti(ə)r\ *n* **1** : a drop of the salty liquid that keeps the eye and the inner eyelids moist **2** : a transparent drop of fluid or hardened fluid matter (as resin) — **teary** \'ti(ə)r-ē\ *adj*

[2]**tear** *vb* : to shed tears

[3]**tear** \'ta(ə)r, 'te(ə)r\ *vb* **tore** \'tō(ə)r, 'tȯ(ə)r\; **torn** \'tōrn, 'tȯrn\; **tear·ing** **1 a** : to separate or pull apart by force ⟨*tore* a page from the book⟩ **b** : LACERATE ⟨*tear* the skin⟩ **2** : to divide or disrupt by the pull of contrary forces ⟨a mind *torn* by doubts⟩ **3** : to remove by force ⟨children *torn* from their mothers⟩ **4** : to cause by force or violent means ⟨the raging waters *tore* a hole in the wall⟩ **5** : to move or act with violence, haste, or force ⟨went *tearing* down the street⟩ — **tear·er** *n*

[4]**tear** \'ta(ə)r, 'te(ə)r\ *n* **1 a** : the act of tearing **b** : damage from being torn; *esp* : a torn place ⟨mending a *tear* in her skirt⟩ **2 a** : a hurried pace : HURRY **b** : SPREE ⟨go on a *tear*⟩

tear·drop \'ti(ə)r-ˌdräp\ *n* **1** : [1]TEAR 1 **2** : something shaped like a dropping tear

tear·ful \'ti(ə)r-fəl\ *adj* : flowing with, accompanied by, or causing tears — **tear·ful·ly** \-fə-lē\ *adv*

tear gas *n* : a substance that blinds the eyes with tears

tear gland *n* : an almond-sized gland located near the eye and secreting tears

tea·room \'tē-ˌrüm, -ˌru̇m\ *n* : a small restaurant serving light meals

[1]**tease** \'tēz\ *vb* **1 a** : to disentangle and lay parallel by combing or carding ⟨*tease* wool⟩ **b** : TEASEL **2 a** : to annoy persistently : PESTER, TORMENT **b** : TANTALIZE — **teas·er** *n*

[2]**tease** *n* **1 a** : the act of teasing **b** : the state of being teased **2** : one that teases

[1]**tea·sel** *or* **tea·zel** *or* **tea·zle** \'tē-zəl\ *n* **1** : an Old World prickly herb with flower heads covered with stiff hooked bracts **2 a** : a dried flower head of the teasel used to raise a nap on woolen cloth **b** : a wire substitute for the teasel

[2]**teasel** *vb* **tea·seled** *or* **tea·selled**; **tea·sel·ing** *or* **tea·sel·ling** \'tēz-(ə-)liŋ\ : to raise a nap on cloth with teasels

tea·spoon \'tē-ˌspün, -'spün\ *n* **1** : a small spoon used esp. for eating soft foods and stirring beverages **2** : TEASPOONFUL

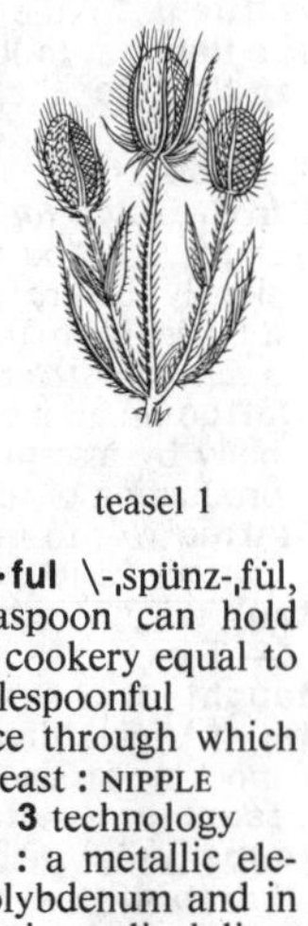
teasel 1

tea·spoon·ful \-ˌfu̇l\ *n, pl* **-spoonfuls** \-ˌfu̇lz\ *or* **-spoons·ful** \-ˌspünz-ˌfu̇l, -'spünz-\ **1** : as much as a teaspoon can hold **2** : a unit of measure used esp. in cookery equal to $1\frac{1}{3}$ fluidrams or one third of a tablespoonful

teat \'tit, 'tēt\ *n* : the protuberance through which milk is drawn from an udder or breast : NIPPLE

tech *abbr* **1** technical **2** technically **3** technology

tech·ne·tium \tek-'nē-sh(ē-)əm\ *n* : a metallic element obtained by bombarding molybdenum and in the fission of uranium and used esp. in medical diagnosis — see ELEMENT table

ə abut	ər further	a back	ā bake
ä cot, cart	au̇ out	ch chin	e less	ē easy
g gift	i trip	ī life	j joke	ŋ sing	ō flow
ȯ flaw	ȯi coin	th thin	th this	ü loot
u̇ foot	y yet	yü few	yu̇ furious	zh vision

tech·nic \'tek-nik, *for 1 also* tek-'nēk\ *n* **1** : TECHNIQUE 1 **2** *pl* : TECHNOLOGY 1a

tech·ni·cal \'tek-ni-kəl\ *adj* **1 a** : having special knowledge esp. of a mechanical or scientific subject ⟨*technical* experts⟩ **b** : marked by specialization ⟨*technical* language⟩ **2** : of or relating to a particular subject; *esp* : of or relating to a practical subject organized on scientific principles ⟨*technical* training⟩ **3** : existing by application of the laws or rules ⟨a *technical* knockout⟩ **4** : of or relating to technique ⟨*technical* skill⟩ — **tech·ni·cal·ly** \-k(ə-)lē\ *adv*

tech·ni·cal·i·ty \,tek-nə-'kal-ət-ē\ *n, pl* **-ties** **1** : the quality or state of being technical **2** : something technical

technical sergeant *n* : a noncommissioned officer in the air force ranking just below a master sergeant

tech·ni·cian \tek-'nish-ən\ *n* : a person skilled in the details or techniques of a subject, art, or occupation

tech·nique \tek-'nēk\ *n* **1 a** : the manner in which details are treated (as by a writer) or basic physical movements are used (as by a dancer) **b** : ability in such treatment or use ⟨faultless piano *technique*⟩ **2 a** : technical methods esp. in scientific research ⟨laboratory *technique*⟩ **b** : a method of accomplishing a desired aim ⟨a *technique* for handling complaints⟩

tech·nol·o·gy \tek-'näl-ə-jē\ *n, pl* **-gies** **1 a** : applied science **b** : a technical method of achieving a practical purpose **2** : the means employed to provide objects for human sustenance and comfort — **tech·no·log·i·cal** \,tek-nə-'läj-i-kəl\ *adj* — **tech·nol·o·gist** \tek-'näl-ə-jəst\ *n*

ted·dy bear \'ted-ē-\ *n* : a stuffed toy bear

te·dious \'tēd-ē-əs, 'tē-jəs\ *adj* : tiresome because of length or dullness : BORING — **te·dious·ly** *adv* — **te·dious·ness** *n*

te·di·um \'tēd-ē-əm\ *n* : the quality or state of being tedious : BOREDOM

1**tee** \'tē\ *n* **1** : the area from which a golf ball is struck in starting play on a hole **2** : a small mound or peg on which a golf ball is set to be struck

2**tee** *vb* **teed**; **tee·ing** **1** : to place on a tee ⟨*teed* up the ball⟩ **2 a** : to drive a golf ball from a tee **b** : BEGIN, START ⟨the speaker *teed* off with an attack on crime⟩

teem \'tēm\ *vb* : to become filled to overflowing : ABOUND ⟨lakes *teem* with fish⟩

teen \'tēn\ *adj* : TEEN-AGE

teen–age \'tēn-,āj\ *or* **teen–aged** \-,ājd\ *adj* : of, being, or relating to people in their teens

teen–ag·er \-,ā-jər\ *n* : a person in his teens

teens \'tēnz\ *n pl* **1** : the numbers 13 through 19; *esp* : the years 13 through 19 in a lifetime or century **2** : TEEN-AGERS

tee·ny \'tē-nē\ *adj* **tee·ni·er**; **-est** : TINY

teeny·bop·per \'tē-nē-,bäp-ər\ *n* : a person in his early teens

tee·pee *var of* TEPEE

tee shirt *var of* T-SHIRT

tee·ter \'tēt-ər\ *vb* **1 a** : to move unsteadily : WOBBLE ⟨*teetered* on the edge and fell over the side⟩ **b** : WAVER **2** : SEESAW — **teeter** *n*

tee·ter·board \-,bōrd, -,bȯrd\ *n* **1** : SEESAW 2b **2** : a board placed on a raised support so that a person standing on one end of the board is thrown into the air if another person jumps on the opposite end

teeth *pl of* TOOTH

teethe \'tēth\ *vb* : to cut one's teeth : grow teeth

teg·u·ment \'teg-yə-mənt\ *n* : INTEGUMENT — **teg·u·men·ta·ry** \,teg-yə-'ment-ə-rē, -'men-trē\ *adj*

tel *abbr* **1** telegram **2** telephone

tele- *or* **tel-** *comb form* **1** : at a distance ⟨*tele*gram⟩ ⟨*tele*pathy⟩ **2** : television ⟨*tele*cast⟩

tele·cast \'tel-i-,kast\ *vb* **telecast** *also* **tele·cast·ed**; **tele·cast·ing** : to broadcast by television — **telecast** *n* — **tele·cast·er** *n*

tel·e·gen·ic \,tel-ə-'jen-ik, -'jēn-\ *adj* : suitable for television broadcast — **tel·e·gen·i·cal·ly** \-i-k(ə-)lē\ *adv*

tel·e·gram \'tel-ə-,gram, *South also* -grəm\ *n* : a message sent by telegraph

1**tel·e·graph** \-,graf\ *n* : an apparatus, system, or process for communication at a distance by electric transmission of coded signals over wire — **tel·e·graph·ic** \,tel-ə-'graf-ik\ *adj* — **tel·e·graph·i·cal·ly** \-'graf-i-k(ə-)lē\ *adv*

2**telegraph** *vb* **1** : to send by or as if by telegraph ⟨*telegraphed* a message⟩ ⟨*telegraph* flowers⟩ **2** : to send a telegram to ⟨*telegraphed* home for money⟩ — **te·leg·ra·pher** \tə-'leg-rə-fər\ *n*

te·leg·ra·phy \tə-'leg-rə-fē\ *n* : the use or operation of a telegraph apparatus or system

1**tel·e·me·ter** \'tel-ə-,mēt-ər\ *n* : an electrical apparatus for measuring something (as pressure, speed, or temperature), transmitting the result esp. by radio to a distant station, and there indicating the measurement — **tel·e·met·ric** \,tel-ə-'me-trik\ *adj* — **tel·e·met·ri·cal·ly** \-tri-k(ə-)lē\ *adv* — **te·lem·e·try** \tə-'lem-ə-trē\ *n*

2**telemeter** *vb* : to transmit by telemeter

te·lep·a·thy \tə-'lep-ə-thē\ *n* : apparent communication from one mind to another without speech or signs — **tel·e·path·ic** \,tel-ə-'path-ik\ *adj* — **tel·e·path·i·cal·ly** \-'path-i-k(ə-)lē\ *adv*

1**tel·e·phone** \'tel-ə-,fōn\ *n* : an instrument for reproducing sounds (as of the human voice) transmitted from a distance over wires by means of electricity

2**telephone** *vb* **1** : to communicate by telephone **2** : to send by telephone **3** : to speak to by telephone — **tel·e·phon·er** *n*

tel·e·phon·ic \,tel-ə-'fän-ik\ *adj* **1** : conveying sound to a distance **2** : of, relating to, or conveyed by telephone

te·leph·o·ny \tə-'lef-ə-nē, 'tel-ə-,fō-\ *n* : the use or operation of an apparatus for transmission of sounds between widely removed points with or without connecting wires

tele·pho·to \,tel-ə-'fōt-ō\ *adj* : of or relating to telephotography : TELEPHOTOGRAPHIC; *esp* : being a camera lens designed to give a large image of a distant object

tele·pho·tog·ra·phy \,tel-ə-fə-'täg-rə-fē\ *n* **1** : FACSIMILE 2 **2** : the photography of distant objects usu. by a camera provided with a telephoto lens or mounted in place of the eyepiece of a telescope — **tele·pho·to·graph·ic** \-,fōt-ə-'graf-ik\ *adj*

tele·play \'tel-ə-,plā\ *n* : a play written for television

tele·print·er \'tel-ə-,print-ər\ *n* : TELETYPEWRITER

1**tel·e·scope** \'tel-ə-,skōp\ *n* **1** : a usu. tubular optical instrument for viewing distant objects and esp. heavenly bodies by means of the refraction of light rays through a lens or the reflection of light rays by a concave mirror **2** : any of various tubular magnifying optical instruments **3** : RADIO TELESCOPE

2**telescope** *vb* **1** : to slide or cause to slide one within another like the cylindrical sections of a hand telescope **2** : to force a way into or enter another lengthwise as the result of collision **3** : COMPRESS, CONDENSE

tel·e·scop·ic \,tel-ə-'skäp-ik\ *adj* **1** : of, with, or relating to a telescope **2** : seen or discoverable only by a telescope ⟨*telescopic* stars⟩ **3** : able to discern

T

objects at a distance : FARSEEING **4** : having parts that telescope — **tel·e·scop·i·cal·ly** \-i-k(ə-)lē\ *adv*

tel·e·thon \'tel-ə-ˌthän\ *n* : a long television program usu. to solicit funds for a charity

tele·type·writ·er \ˌtel-ə-'tīp-ˌrīt-ər\ *n* : a printing telegraph recording like a typewriter

tele·typ·ist \'tel-ə-ˌtī-pəst\ *n* : one that operates a teletypewriter

tele·view \'tel-ə-ˌvyü\ *vb* : to observe or watch by means of a television receiver — **tele·view·er** *n*

tel·e·vise \'tel-ə-ˌvīz\ *vb* : to pick up and usu. to broadcast by television ⟨*televised* the ball game⟩

tel·e·vi·sion \'tel-ə-ˌvizh-ən\ *n* **1** : an electronic system of transmitting images of fixed or moving objects together with sound over a wire or through space by apparatus that converts light and sound into electrical waves and reconverts them into visible light rays and audible sound **2** : a television receiving set **3** : the television broadcasting industry

television tube *n* : KINESCOPE 1

tell \'tel\ *vb* **told** \'tōld\; **tell·ing** **1** : COUNT, ENUMERATE **2 a** : to relate in detail : NARRATE ⟨*tell* a story⟩ **b** : SAY, UTTER ⟨*tell* a lie⟩ **3 a** : to make known : REVEAL ⟨*tell* a secret⟩ **b** : to express in words ⟨can't *tell* you how pleased we are⟩ **4** : to report to : INFORM **5** : ORDER, DIRECT ⟨*told* her to wait⟩ **6** : to ascertain by observing : find out ⟨can *tell* the man's honest⟩ **7** : to act as a talebearer ⟨*tell* on a cheater⟩ **8** : to have a marked effect ⟨the pressure began to *tell* on him⟩ **9** : EVIDENCE, INDICATE ⟨smiles *telling* of success⟩

tell·er \'tel-ər\ *n* **1** : one that relates or communicates ⟨a *teller* of tales⟩ **2** : a person who counts votes (as in a legislative body) **3** : a bank employee who receives and pays out money

tell·ing \'tel-iŋ\ *adj* : producing a marked effect : EFFECTIVE ⟨a *telling* argument⟩ — **tell·ing·ly** \-iŋ-lē\ *adv*

¹**tell·tale** \'tel-ˌtāl\ *n* **1** : TALEBEARER, INFORMER **2** : an outward sign : INDICATION

²**telltale** *adj* : INFORMING, REVEALING ⟨*telltale* fingerprints⟩

tel·lu·ri·um \tə-'lu̇r-ē-əm\ *n* : an element that resembles selenium and sulfur in properties and that occurs in crystalline form, in a dark amorphous form, or combined with metals — see ELEMENT table

te·lo·phase \'tē-lə-ˌfāz, 'tel-ə-\ *n* **1** : the final stage of mitosis in which separate nuclei form **2** : the final stage of the first or second division of meiosis

te·mer·i·ty \tə-'mer-ət-ē\ *n* : RASHNESS, BOLDNESS

temp *abbr* temperature

¹**tem·per** \'tem-pər\ *vb* **tem·pered**; **tem·per·ing** \-p(ə-)riŋ\ **1** : MODERATE, SOFTEN ⟨the mountains *temper* the wind⟩ **2** : to control by reducing : SUBDUE ⟨*temper* one's anger⟩ **3** : to bring to the desired consistency or texture ⟨*temper* modeling clay⟩ **4** : to bring (as steel) to the desired hardness by heating and cooling **5** : to be or become tempered

²**temper** *n* **1** : characteristic tone : TREND, TENDENCY ⟨the *temper* of the times⟩ **2** : the state of a substance with respect to certain desired qualities (as hardness, elasticity, or workability) ⟨*temper* of a knife blade⟩ **3 a** : a characteristic cast of mind or state of feeling : DISPOSITION **b** : calmness of mind : COMPOSURE ⟨lost his *temper*⟩ **c** : state of feeling or frame of mind at a particular time **d** : a state of anger **e** : a proneness to anger ⟨he has a hot *temper*⟩

ə abut	ər further	a back	ā bake
ä cot, cart	au̇ out	ch chin	e less	ē easy
g gift	i trip	ī life	j joke	ŋ sing	ō flow
ȯ flaw	ȯi coin	th thin	t͟h this	ü loot
u̇ foot	y yet	yü few	yu̇ furious	zh vision

tem·pera \'tem-pə-rə\ *n* : a process of painting in which an albuminous or colloidal medium is employed as a vehicle instead of oil

tem·per·a·ment \'tem-p(ə-)rə-mənt\ *n* **1** : characteristic mode of emotional response ⟨nervous *temperament*⟩ **2** : excessive sensitiveness or irritability

tem·per·a·men·tal \ˌtem-p(ə-)rə-'ment-əl\ *adj* **1** : of or relating to temperament ⟨*temperamental* peculiarities⟩ **2** : HIGH-STRUNG, EXCITABLE ⟨a *temperamental* opera singer⟩ — **tem·per·a·men·tal·ly** \-ə-lē\ *adv*

tem·per·ance \'tem-p(ə-)rən(t)s\ *n* **1** : moderation in action, thought, or feeling : RESTRAINT **2** : habitual moderation in the indulgence of the appetites or passions; *esp* : moderation in or abstinence from the use of intoxicating drink

tem·per·ate \'tem-p(ə-)rət\ *adj* **1** : not excessive or extreme **2** : moderate in satisfying one's needs or desires **3** : moderate in the use of liquor **4** : marked by self-control : RESTRAINED ⟨*temperate* speech⟩ **5** : having or associated with a moderate climate — **tem·per·ate·ly** *adv* — **tem·per·ate·ness** *n*

temperate zone *n*, *often cap T & Z* : the area or region between the tropic of Cancer and the arctic circle or between the tropic of Capricorn and the antarctic circle

tem·per·a·ture \'tem-pər-ˌchu̇r, 'tem-p(ə-)rə-ˌchu̇r, -chər\ *n* **1** : the degree of hotness or coldness of something (as air, water, or the body) as shown by a thermometer **2** : FEVER ⟨have a *temperature*⟩

temperature inversion *n* : an increase of temperature with height through a layer of air

tem·pered \'tem-pərd\ *adj* **1** : having a particular kind of temper ⟨a bad-*tempered* boy⟩ **2** : brought to the desired state (as of hardness, toughness, or flexibility) ⟨*tempered* steel⟩ ⟨*tempered* glass⟩ **3** : MODERATED ⟨justice *tempered* with mercy⟩

tem·pest \'tem-pəst\ *n* **1** : a violent wind; *esp* : one accompanied by rain, hail, or snow **2** : a violent commotion : UPROAR

tem·pes·tu·ous \tem-'pes-chə-wəs\ *adj* : VIOLENT, STORMY — **tem·pes·tu·ous·ly** *adv* — **tem·pes·tu·ous·ness** *n*

¹**tem·ple** \'tem-pəl\ *n* **1** : a building for worship **2** *often cap* : one of three successive national sanctuaries in ancient Jerusalem

²**temple** *n* : the flattened space on each side of the forehead of man and some other mammals

tem·po \'tem-pō\ *n*, *pl* **tem·pi** \-(ˌ)pē\ *or* **tempos** **1** : the rate of speed at which a musical piece or passage is to be played or sung **2** : rate of motion or activity : PACE

tem·po·ral \'tem-p(ə-)rəl\ *adj* **1** : of or relating to time as opposed to eternity **2 a** : of or relating to earthly life **b** : of or relating to secular concerns — **tem·po·ral·ly** \-ē\ *adv*

tem·po·ral bone \ˌtem-p(ə-)rəl-\ *n* : a compound bone of the side of the human skull

tem·po·rary \'tem-pə-ˌrer-ē\ *adj* : not permanent : lasting for a time only — **tem·po·rar·i·ly** \ˌtem-pə-'rer-ə-lē\ *adv*

tem·po·rize \'tem-pə-ˌrīz\ *vb* **1** : to act to suit the time or occasion : COMPROMISE **2** : to draw out negotiations so as to gain time : DELAY — **tem·po·ri·za·tion** \ˌtem-pə-rə-'zā-shən\ *n* — **tem·po·riz·er** \'tem-pə-ˌrī-zər\ *n*

tempt \'tem(p)t\ *vb* **1** : to entice to do wrong by promise of pleasure or gain **2** : to arouse to action or anger : PROVOKE **3** : to risk the dangers of **4** : to induce to do something : INCITE ⟨*tempted* him into a rash act⟩ — **tempt·a·ble** \'tem(p)-tə-bəl\ *adj* — **tempt·er** *n* — **tempt·ress** \'tem(p)-trəs\ *n*

temp·ta·tion \tem(p)-'tā-shən\ *n* **1** : the act of tempting : the state of being tempted esp. to evil **2** : something tempting

tempt·ing \'tem(p)-ting\ *adj* : ALLURING, ENTICING — **tempt·ing·ly** \-ting-lē\ *adv*

ten \'ten\ *n* **1** — see NUMBER table **2** : the tenth in a set or series ⟨the *ten* of hearts⟩ **3** : something having ten units or members **4** : the number in the second decimal place to the left of the decimal point in arabic numerals — **ten** *adj or pron*

ten *abbr* tenor

ten·a·ble \'ten-ə-bəl\ *adj* : capable of being held, maintained, or defended ⟨retreated when the position became no longer *tenable*⟩ — **ten·a·bil·i·ty** \,ten-ə-'bil-ət-ē\ *n* — **ten·a·ble·ness** \'ten-ə-bəl-nəs\ *n* — **ten·a·bly** \-blē\ *adv*

te·na·cious \tə-'nā-shəs\ *adj* **1 a** : not easily pulled apart : COHESIVE, TOUGH ⟨a *tenacious* metal⟩ **b** : tending to adhere to another substance : STICKY ⟨*tenacious* burs⟩ **2 a** : holding fast or tending to hold fast : PERSISTENT, STUBBORN ⟨*tenacious* of his rights⟩ **b** : RETENTIVE ⟨a *tenacious* memory⟩ — **te·na·cious·ly** *adv* — **te·na·cious·ness** *n* — **te·nac·i·ty** \tə-'nas-ət-ē\ *n*

ten·an·cy \'ten-ən-sē\ *n, pl* **-cies** **1 a** : the temporary possession or occupancy of another's property **b** : the period of such occupancy or possession **2** : the ownership of property

[1]**ten·ant** \'ten-ənt\ *n* **1** : one who occupies property of another esp. for rent **2** : DWELLER, OCCUPANT

[2]**tenant** *vb* : to hold or occupy as a tenant : INHABIT

ten·ant·ry \'ten-ən-trē\ *n* **1** : the condition of being a tenant **2** : a group of tenants (as on an estate)

[1]**tend** \'tend\ *vb* **1** : to pay attention ⟨*tend* strictly to business⟩ **2** : to take care of : CULTIVATE **3** : to have charge of as caretaker or overseer **4** : to manage or superintend the operation of ⟨*tend* a machine⟩

[2]**tend** *vb* **1** : to move or turn in a certain direction : LEAD ⟨the road *tends* to the right⟩ **2** : to have a tendency : be likely ⟨a boy who *tends* to slouch⟩

tend·en·cy \'ten-dən-sē\ *n, pl* **-cies** **1** : direction or approach toward something **2** : INCLINATION, BENT

[1]**ten·der** \'ten-dər\ *adj* **1** : having a soft or yielding texture ⟨*tender* steak⟩ **2 a** : physically weak : DELICATE ⟨a *tender* plant⟩ **b** : IMMATURE, YOUNG ⟨children of *tender* years⟩ **3** : FOND, LOVING ⟨a *tender* look⟩ **4** : showing care : CONSIDERATE ⟨he was *tender* of her feelings⟩ **5** : GENTLE, MILD **6** : sensitive to touch : easily hurt ⟨a *tender* scar⟩ **7** : demanding careful and sensitive handling : TICKLISH ⟨a *tender* subject⟩ — **ten·der·ly** *adv* — **ten·der·ness** *n*

[2]**tend·er** \'ten-dər\ *n* **1** : one that tends or takes care **2 a** : a ship employed (as to supply provisions) to attend other ships **b** : a boat that carries passengers or freight between shore and a larger ship **3** : a vehicle attached to a locomotive for carrying a supply of fuel and water

[3]**ten·der** *n* **1** : an offer of money in payment of a debt **2** : an offer or proposal made for acceptance; *esp* : a bid for a contract **3** : something that may by law be offered in payment; *esp* : MONEY

[4]**ten·der** *vb* **ten·dered**; **ten·der·ing** \-d(ə-)ring\ **1** : to make a tender of ⟨*tender* the amount of rent⟩ **2** : to present for acceptance ⟨*tendered* his resignation⟩

ten·der·foot \'ten-dər-,fu̇t\ *n, pl* **-feet** \-,fēt\ *also* **-foots** **1** : a person who is not hardened to a rough out-of-door life; *esp* : a newcomer in a recent settlement (as on a frontier) **2** : a beginning boy or girl scout

ten·der·heart·ed \,ten-dər-'härt-əd\ *adj* : easily moved to love, pity, or sorrow : COMPASSIONATE

ten·der·ize \'ten-də-,rīz\ *vb* : to make tender ⟨*tenderize* meat⟩ — **ten·der·i·za·tion** \,ten-də-rə-'zā-shən\ *n* — **ten·der·iz·er** \'ten-də-,rī-zər\ *n*

ten·der·loin \'ten-dər-,lȯin\ *n* : a strip of tender meat on each side of the backbone of beef or pork

ten·don \'ten-dən\ *n* : a tough cord or band of fibrous connective tissue that links a muscle to some other part (as a bone) and transmits the force exerted by the muscle

ten·dril \'ten-drəl\ *n* **1** : a leaf, stipule, or stem modified into a slender spirally coiling sensitive organ serving to attach a plant to its support **2** : something that curls like a tendril ⟨*tendrils* of hair⟩ — **ten·driled** *or* **ten·drilled** \-drəld\ *adj*

1080 *also* **ten–eighty** \ten-'āt-ē\ *n* : a poisonous substance used to kill rodents

ten·e·ment \'ten-ə-mənt\ *n* **1 a** : a house used as a dwelling : RESIDENCE **b** : APARTMENT, FLAT **c** : TENEMENT HOUSE **2** : DWELLING, HABITATION

tenement house *n* : APARTMENT BUILDING; *esp* : one housing poorer families

ten·et \'ten-ət\ *n* : a widely held principle, belief, or doctrine; *esp* : one held in common by members of a group or profession

ten·fold \'ten-,fōld, -'fōld\ *adj* **1** : having 10 units or members **2** : 10 times as much or as many — **tenfold** *adv*

Tenn *abbr* Tennessee

ten·nis \'ten-əs\ *n* : a game played with rackets and a light elastic ball by two players or two pairs of players on a level court divided by a low net

tennis shoe *n* : SNEAKER

[1]**ten·on** \'ten-ən\ *n* : a projecting part in a piece of material (as wood) for insertion into a mortise to make a joint

[2]**tenon** *vb* **1** : to unite by a tenon **2** : to cut or fit for insertion in a mortise

ten·or \'ten-ər\ *n* **1** : the general drift of something spoken or written : PURPORT, INTENT ⟨the *tenor* of the book⟩ **2 a** : the highest natural adult male voice **b** : one that performs a tenor part **3** : a continuance in a course, movement, or activity : TREND ⟨the *tenor* of his life⟩ — **tenor** *adj*

ten·pen·ny nail \,ten-,pen-ē-\ *n* : a nail 3 inches long

ten·pin \'ten-,pin\ *n* **1** : a large bottle-shaped bowling pin **2** *pl* : a bowling game using 10 tenpins and a large ball

[1]**tense** \'ten(t)s\ *n* [from medieval French *tens*, literally "time", from Latin *tempus*] **1** : a distinction of form in a verb to express distinctions of time **2** : a particular inflectional form or set of inflectional forms of a verb expressing a specific time distinction

[2]**tense** *adj* [from Latin *tensus*, past participle of *tendere* "to stretch"] **1** : stretched tight : made taut ⟨*tense* muscles⟩ **2** : feeling or showing nervous tension : HIGH-STRUNG ***syn*** see TIGHT — **tense·ly** *adv* — **tense·ness** *n*

[3]**tense** *vb* : to make or become tense ⟨he *tensed* up and played a poor game⟩

ten·sile \'ten(t)-səl, 'ten-,sīl\ *adj* **1** : capable of tension : DUCTILE **2** : of or relating to tension

ten·sion \'ten-chən\ *n* **1 a** : the act or action of stretching or the state or degree of being stretched to

stiffness : TAUTNESS ⟨*tension* of a muscle⟩ **b** : STRESS 1c **2 a** : inner striving, unrest, or imbalance often with physiological indications of emotion **b** : a state of latent hostility or opposition between individuals or groups : strained relations **3** : VOLTAGE ⟨a high-*tension* wire⟩
ten·si·ty \'ten(t)-sət-ē\ *n* : TENSENESS
ten·sor \'ten(t)-sər, 'ten-,sȯr\ *n* : a muscle that stretches a part
[1]**tent** \'tent\ *n* **1** : a collapsible shelter (as of canvas) stretched over or under poles and used as temporary housing **2 a** : something that resembles a tent or that serves as a shelter **b** : a canopy or enclosure placed over the head and shoulders to retain medicinal vapors or oxygen administered ⟨was in an oxygen *tent*⟩ **c** : the web of a tent caterpillar

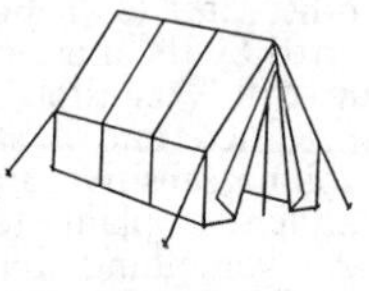
tent

[2]**tent** *vb* **1** : to live or lodge in a tent **2** : to cover with or as if with a tent
ten·ta·cle \'tent-i-kəl\ *n* **1** : one of the long flexible processes usu. about the head or mouth of an animal (as a worm or fish) used esp. for feeling, grasping, or handling **2** : something suggesting a tentacle; *esp* : a sensitive hair on a plant — **ten·ta·cled** \-kəld\ *adj* — **ten·tac·u·lar** \ten-'tak-yə-lər\ *adj*
ten·ta·tive \'tent-ət-iv\ *adj* **1** : not fully worked out or developed : PROVISIONAL, TEMPORARY ⟨*tentative* plans⟩ ⟨a *tentative* hypothesis⟩ **2** : HESITANT, UNCERTAIN ⟨a *tentative* smile⟩ — **ten·ta·tive·ly** *adv*
tent caterpillar *n* : any of several destructive caterpillars that live in groups and construct large silken webs on trees
ten·ter \'tent-ər\ *n* : a frame or endless track with hooks or clips along two sides that is used for drying and stretching cloth
ten·ter·hook \-,hu̇k\ *n* : a sharp hooked nail used esp. for fastening cloth on a tenter — **on tenterhooks** : in a state of uneasiness, strain, or suspense
tenth \'ten(t)th\ *n* **1** — see NUMBER table **2** : one of 10 equal parts of something **3** : the one numbered 10 in a countable series — **tenth** *adj or adv*
ten·u·ous \'ten-yə-wəs\ *adj* **1** : not dense : RARE ⟨a *tenuous* fluid⟩ **2** : not thick : SLENDER ⟨a *tenuous* rope⟩ **3** : having little substance or strength : FLIMSY, WEAK ⟨*tenuous* arguments⟩ — **te·nu·i·ty** \te-'n(y)ü-ət-ē, tə-\ *n* — **ten·u·ous·ly** \'ten-yə-wəs-lē\ *adv*
ten·ure \'ten-yər\ *n* **1** : the act, right, manner, or term of holding something (as real property, a position, or an office) **2** : GRASP, HOLD — **ten·ur·i·al** \te-'nyu̇r-ē-əl\ *adj* — **ten·ur·i·al·ly** \-ē-ə-lē\ *adv*
te·pee \'tē-(,)pē\ *n* : a conical tent usu. of skins used by some American Indians
tep·id \'tep-əd\ *adj* : moderately warm : LUKEWARM ⟨a *tepid* bath⟩

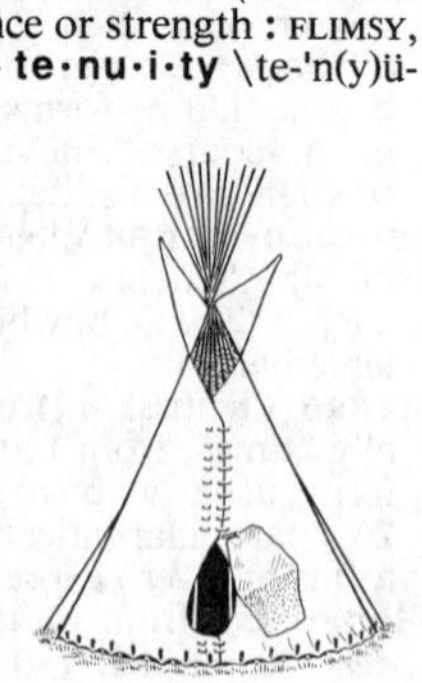
tepee

ə abut	ər further	a back	ā bake
ä cot, cart	au̇ out	ch chin	e less
ē easy	g gift	i trip	ī life
j joke	ng sing	ō flow	ȯ flaw
ȯi coin	th thin	th this	ü loot
u̇ foot	y yet	yü few	yu̇ furious
zh vision			

te·qui·la \tə-'kē-lə\ *n* : a Mexican liquor made by redistilling mescal
ter *abbr* terrace
ter·bi·um \'tər-bē-əm\ *n* : a metallic element of the rare-earth group — see ELEMENT table
te·re·do \tə-'rēd-ō\ *n, pl* **-re·dos** *or* **-red·i·nes** \-'red-ə-,nēz\ : SHIPWORM
[1]**term** \'tərm\ *n* **1** : END, LIMIT **2** : a limited or definite extent of time esp. as fixed by law, custom, or some recurrent phenomenon ⟨the governor served two *terms*⟩ ⟨ready for the new school *term*⟩ **3** *pl* : provisions determining the nature and scope of something and esp. of an agreement : CONDITIONS ⟨could not accept their *terms*⟩ **4 a** : a word or expression that has a precise meaning in some uses or is peculiar to a particular field ⟨legal *terms*⟩ **b** *pl* : diction of a specified kind ⟨spoke in glowing *terms* of their prospects⟩ **5 a** : a mathematical expression connected with another by a plus or minus sign **b** : an element (as a numerator) of a fraction or proportion **6** *pl* **a** : mutual relationship : FOOTING ⟨on good *terms*⟩ **b** : AGREEMENT, CONCORD ⟨came to *terms* with his father⟩ — **in terms of** : with respect to
[2]**term** *vb* : to apply a term to : CALL, NAME
[1]**ter·ma·gant** \'tər-mə-gənt\ *n* : an overbearing quarrelsome woman : SHREW
[2]**termagant** *adj* : noisily quarrelsome
[1]**ter·mi·nal** \'tər-mən-əl\ *adj* **1 a** : of or relating to an end, extremity, boundary, or terminus ⟨*terminal* pillar⟩ **b** : growing at the end of a branch or stem ⟨*terminal* bud⟩ **2** : of or relating to a term **3** : occurring at or constituting the end of a period or series : CONCLUDING — **ter·mi·nal·ly** \-ə-lē\ *adv*
[2]**terminal** *n* **1** : a part that forms the end **2** : a device attached to the end of a wire for making electrical connections **3 a** : either end of a carrier line (as a railroad or shipping line) with its facilities **b** : a freight or passenger station ⟨a bus *terminal*⟩ **c** : a town at the end of a carrier line : TERMINUS
ter·mi·nate \'tər-mə-,nāt\ *vb* **1 a** : to bring or come to an end : CLOSE **b** : to form the conclusion of **2** : to serve as a limit to : BOUND **3** : to extend to a limit (as a point or line); *esp* : to reach a terminus — **ter·mi·na·ble** \-mə-nə-bəl\ *adj* — **ter·mi·na·tion** \,tər-mə-'nā-shən\ *n* — **ter·mi·na·tor** \'tər-mə-,nāt-ər\ *n*
ter·mi·nat·ing decimal *n* : a decimal that is expressible with a finite number of figures
ter·mi·nol·o·gy \,tər-mə-'näl-ə-jē\ *n, pl* **-gies** : the special terms or expressions used in a business, art, science, or subject ⟨the *terminology* of law⟩
ter·mi·nus \'tər-mə-nəs\ *n, pl* **-ni** \-,nī, -,nē\ *or* **-nus·es** **1** : final goal : finishing point **2** : a post or stone marking a boundary **3 a** : either end of a transportation line or travel route **b** : the station or the town or city at such a place : TERMINAL
ter·mite \'tər-,mīt\ *n* : any of a group of pale-colored soft-bodied social insects that have winged sexual forms, wingless sterile workers, and often soldiers, feed on wood, and include some very destructive to wooden structures and trees — called also *white ant*
tern \'tərn\ *n* : any of numerous sea gulls that are smaller and slenderer in body and bill than typical gulls and have narrower wings, often forked tails, black cap, and white body
ter·pin hy·drate \,tər-pən-'hī-,drāt\ *n* : a compound derived from various resinous oils and used esp. in cough medicine

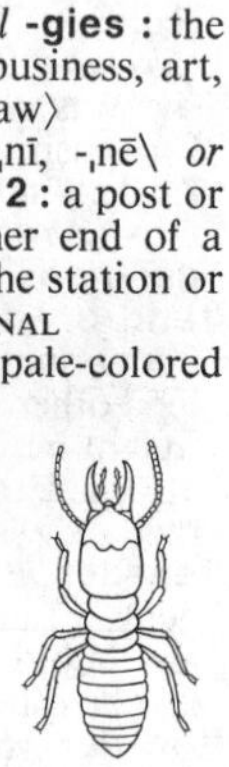
termite (less than one inch long)

terr *abbr* territory

[1]**ter·race** \'ter-əs\ *n* **1 a :** a flat roof or open platform : BALCONY, DECK **b :** a relatively level paved or planted area adjoining a building **2 :** a raised embankment or one of a series of banks or ridges formed in a slope to conserve moisture and soil for agriculture **3 :** a row of houses on raised ground or a sloping site

[2]**terrace** *vb* **:** to make into a terrace or supply with terraces

ter·ra-cot·ta \ˌter-ə-'kät-ə\ *n, pl* **terra–cottas** [from Italian, meaning literally "baked earth"] **1 :** a glazed or unglazed fired earthenware **2 :** a brownish orange

ter·ra fir·ma \-'fər-mə\ *n* **:** dry land **:** solid ground

ter·rain \tə-'rān\ *n* **:** the surface features of a tract of land ⟨a rough *terrain*⟩

ter·ra·pin \'ter-ə-pən, 'tar-\ *n* **:** any of various edible No. American turtles living in fresh or brackish water

ter·rar·i·um \tə-'rar-ē-əm, -'rer-\ *n, pl* **-ia** \-ē-ə\ *or* **-i·ums :** a usually glass-enclosed box for keeping and observing small animals and plants

ter·res·tri·al \tə-'res-trē-əl\ *adj* **1 a :** of or relating to the earth or its inhabitants ⟨*terrestrial* magnetism⟩ **b :** mundane in scope or character **:** not heavenly **2 a :** of or relating to land as distinct from air or water ⟨*terrestrial* transportation⟩ **b :** living on or in or growing from land ⟨*terrestrial* plants⟩ ⟨*terrestrial* birds⟩

ter·ri·ble \'ter-ə-bəl\ *adj* **1 :** causing terror or awe **:** FEARFUL, DREADFUL ⟨a *terrible* disaster⟩ **2 a :** hard to bear usu. because of excess of some quality ⟨*terrible* cold⟩ **b :** very bad or extremely unpleasant ⟨had a *terrible* time⟩ **c :** of notably inferior quality ⟨did a *terrible* job on the painting⟩ — **ter·ri·bly** \-blē\ *adv*

ter·ri·er \'ter-ē-ər\ *n* **:** any of various usu. small dogs orig. used by hunters to dig for small game and engage the quarry underground or drive it out

terrier

ter·rif·ic \tə-'rif-ik\ *adj* **1 :** TERRIBLE, FRIGHTFUL ⟨*terrific* destruction⟩ **2 :** EXTRAORDINARY, ASTOUNDING ⟨*terrific* speed⟩; *esp* **:** TREMENDOUS ⟨a *terrific* explosion⟩ **3 :** unusually fine **:** MAGNIFICENT ⟨the party was *terrific*⟩ — **ter·rif·i·cal·ly** \-i-k(ə-)lē\ *adv*

ter·ri·fy \'ter-ə-ˌfī\ *vb* **-fied; -fy·ing :** to fill with or move to some action by terror — **ter·ri·fy·ing·ly** \-ˌfī-ing-lē\ *adv*

ter·ri·to·ri·al \ˌter-ə-'tōr-ē-əl, -'tȯr-\ *adj* **1 a :** of or relating to territory ⟨*territorial* claims⟩ **b** *often cap* **:** of or relating to all or any of the territories of the U.S. ⟨a *territorial* government⟩ **2 :** organized primarily for territorial defense ⟨a *territorial* army⟩ **3 :** of, relating to, or exhibiting territoriality ⟨*territorial* birds⟩ — **territorial** *n* — **ter·ri·to·ri·al·ly** \ˌter-ə-'tōr-ē-ə-lē, -'tȯr-\ *adv*

ter·ri·to·ri·al·i·ty \ˌter-ə-ˌtōr-ē-'al-ət-ē, -ˌtȯr-\ *n* **:** the pattern of behavior associated with the defense of a male animal's territory

ter·ri·to·ry \'ter-ə-ˌtōr-ē, -ˌtȯr-\ *n, pl* **-ries 1 a :** a geographical area belonging to or under the jurisdiction of a government often having a degree of self-government **b :** a part of the U.S. not included within any state but organized with a separate legislature **2 a :** an assigned area ⟨a salesman's *territory*⟩ **b :** an area that is occupied and defended by a male bird or mammal

ter·ror \'ter-ər\ *n* **1 :** a state of intense fear **2 a :** a cause of fear or anxiety **b :** an appalling person or thing

ter·ror·ism \'ter-ər-ˌiz-əm\ *n* **:** systematic use of terror esp. as a means of keeping or gaining control of a government — **ter·ror·ist** \-ər-əst\ *adj or n*

ter·ror·ize \'ter-ər-ˌīz\ *vb* **1 :** to fill with terror or anxiety **2 :** to coerce by threat or violence — **ter·ror·i·za·tion** \ˌter-ər-ə-'zā-shən\ *n*

ter·ry \'ter-ē\ *n, pl* **terries :** an absorbent fabric with a loose pile of uncut loops

terse \'tərs\ *adj* [from Latin *tersus*, meaning "clean", "neat", from the past participle of *tergere* "to wipe off", the source of English *detergent*] **:** using as few words as possible without loss of force or clearness **:** being brief and effective — **terse·ly** *adv* — **terse·ness** *n*

ter·ti·ary \'tər-shē-ˌer-ē\ *adj* **1 :** of 3d rank, importance, or value **2** *cap* **:** of, relating to, or being the first period of the Cenozoic era or the corresponding system of rocks marked by the formation of high mountains (as the Alps and Himalayas) and the dominance of mammals on land

Tertiary *n* **:** the Tertiary period or system of rocks

[1]**test** \'test\ *n* **1 :** a critical examination, observation, or evaluation **:** TRIAL ⟨put his courage to the *test*⟩ **2 :** a procedure, reaction, or reagent used to identify or differentiate something ⟨a *test* for starch⟩ ⟨a series of allergy *tests*⟩ **3 :** an examination (as in a school) intended to determine factual knowledge or acquired skill or sometimes intelligence, capacities, or aptitudes

[2]**test** *vb* **1 :** to put to test or proof **:** TRY ⟨*test* his strength⟩ **2 a :** to undergo a test ⟨actors *testing* for roles in the play⟩ **b :** to achieve a rating on the basis of tests ⟨the sample *tested* high in gold⟩ **3 :** to use tests as a means of analysis or diagnosis ⟨*test* for copper⟩ — **test·a·ble** \'tes-tə-bəl\ *adj*

[3]**test** *n* **:** a firm or rigid outer covering (as a shell) of many invertebrates

tes·ta \'tes-tə\ *n, pl* **tes·tae** \-ˌtē, -ˌtī\ **:** the hard outer coat of a seed

tes·ta·ment \'tes-tə-mənt\ *n* **1** *cap* **:** either of the two chief divisions of the Bible; *esp* **:** NEW TESTAMENT **2 a :** a tangible proof or tribute **:** EVIDENCE, WITNESS **b :** an expression of conviction **:** CREDO **3 :** a legal instrument by which a person determines the disposition of his property after his death **:** WILL — **tes·ta·men·ta·ry** \ˌtes-tə-'ment-ə-rē, -'men-trē\ *adj*

tes·ta·tor \'tes-ˌtāt-ər, te-'stāt-\ *n* **:** a person who leaves a will in force at his death — **tes·ta·trix** \te-'stā-triks\ *n*

test·ed \'tes-təd\ *adj* **:** subjected to or qualified through testing ⟨time-*tested* principles⟩ ⟨tuberculin-*tested* cattle⟩

[1]**tes·ter** \'tēs-tər, 'tes-\ *n* **:** a canopy over a bed, pulpit, or altar

[2]**test·er** \'tes-tər\ *n* **:** one that tests

tes·ti·cle \'tes-ti-kəl\ *n* **:** TESTIS

tes·ti·fy \'tes-tə-ˌfī\ *vb* **-fied; -fy·ing 1 :** to make a solemn statement of what is personally known or believed to be true **:** give evidence ⟨*testify* in court⟩ **2 :** to give outward proof **:** serve as a sign of

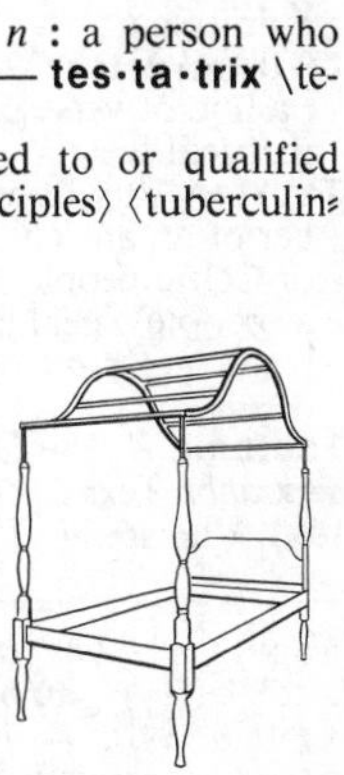
tester

⟨smiles *testifying* contentment⟩ — **tes·ti·fi·er** \-ˌfī(-ə)r\ *n*

1**tes·ti·mo·ni·al** \ˌtes-tə-ˈmō-nē-əl\ *adj* **1** : being a testimonial **2** : expressive of appreciation or esteem ⟨a *testimonial* dinner⟩

2**testimonial** *n* **1 a** : an endorsement of a product or service ⟨writing *testimonials* for patent medicines⟩ **b** : a character reference : letter of recommendation **2** : an expression of appreciation : TRIBUTE

tes·ti·mo·ny \ˈtes-tə-ˌmō-nē\ *n, pl* **-nies** **1** : evidence based on observation or knowledge : authoritative evidence ⟨according to the *testimony* of historians⟩ ⟨his life is *testimony* of his worth⟩ **2** : a solemn declaration usu. made orally by a witness under oath **3** : an open acknowledgment or profession (as of religious experience)

tes·tis \ˈtes-təs\ *n, pl* **tes·tes** \ˈtes-ˌtēz\ : a male reproductive gland

test pilot *n* : a pilot employed to put new aircraft through severe tests

test tube *n* : a tube of thin glass closed at one end and used esp. in chemistry and biology

tes·ty \ˈtes-tē\ *adj* **tes·ti·er**; **-est** : easily annoyed : IRRITABLE

tet·a·nus \ˈtet-ə-nəs\ *n* **1** : an infectious disease characterized esp. by stiffness of the neck muscles with locking of the jaws and caused by the toxin of a bacterium **2** : prolonged contraction of a muscle resulting from rapidly repeated motor nerve impulses

1**tête-à-tête** \ˌtāt-ə-ˈtāt\ *adv* [from French, literally "head to head"] : face to face : PRIVATELY

2**tête-à-tête** *n* : a private conversation between two persons

3**tête-à-tête** *adj* : being face to face : PRIVATE

1**teth·er** \ˈteth-ər\ *n* : a line by which an animal is fastened so as to restrict its range

2**tether** *vb* **teth·ered**; **teth·er·ing** \ˈteth-(ə-)riŋ\ : to fasten or restrain by a tether

tet·ra \ˈte-trə\ *n* : any of various small brightly colored So. American fishes often bred in the tropical aquarium

tetra- *or* **tetr-** *comb form* : four : having four : having four parts

tet·ra·chlo·ride \ˌte-trə-ˈklōr-ˌīd, -ˈklȯr-\ *n* : a chloride containing four atoms of chlorine

tet·ra·chord \ˈte-trə-ˌkȯrd\ *n* : a diatonic series of four tones : half an octave

tet·ra·eth·yl lead \ˌte-trə-ˌeth-əl-ˈled\ *n* : a heavy oily poisonous liquid used as an antiknock agent

tet·ra·he·dron \ˌte-trə-ˈhē-drən\ *n, pl* **-drons** *or* **-dra** \-drə\ : a polyhedron of four faces — **tet·ra·he·dral** \-drəl\ *adj*

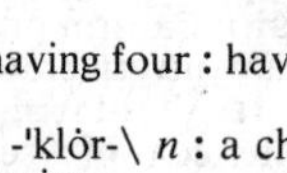
tetrahedron

te·tram·e·ter \te-ˈtram-ət-ər\ *n* : a line of verse consisting of four metrical feet

Teu·ton \ˈt(y)üt-ən\ *n* **1** : a member of an ancient prob. Germanic or Celtic people **2** : a member of a people speaking a Germanic language; *esp* : GERMAN — **Teu·ton·ic** \t(y)ü-ˈtän-ik\ *adj*

Teutonic *n* : the Germanic languages

Tex *abbr* Texas

text \ˈtekst\ *n* **1** : the original written or printed words and form of a literary work **2 a** : the main body of printed or written matter on a page **b** : the principal part of a book exclusive of front and back matter **3 a** : a passage of Scripture chosen for the subject of a sermon **b** : a subject on which one writes or speaks : THEME, TOPIC **4** : TEXTBOOK ⟨a history *text* for high schools⟩

text·book \ˈteks(t)-ˌbu̇k\ *n* : a book used in the study of a subject; *esp* : one that presents the principles of a subject and is used as a basis of instruction

tex·tile \ˈtek-ˌstīl, -stəl\ *n* : CLOTH 1; *esp* : a woven or knit cloth — **textile** *adj*

tex·tu·al \ˈteks-ch(ə-w)əl\ *adj* : of, relating to, or based on a text ⟨*textual* error⟩ — **tex·tu·al·ly** \-ē\ *adv*

tex·ture \ˈteks-chər\ *n* **1 a** : the structure, feel, and appearance of a textile that result from the kind and arrangement of its threads ⟨a silk with a smooth lustrous *texture*⟩ **b** : similar qualities dependent on the nature and arrangement of the constituent parts of a substance ⟨rock with a very fine *texture*⟩ **2** : an essential or identifying part or quality ⟨the unmistakable *texture* of his writing⟩ — **tex·tured** \-chərd\ *adj*

TGIF *abbr* thank God it's Friday

-th — see -ETH

Thai \ˈtī\ *n* **1** : a native or inhabitant of Thailand **2** : the official language of Thailand — **Thai** *adj*

thal·li·um \ˈthal-ē-əm\ *n* : a poisonous metallic element resembling lead in physical properties — see ELEMENT table

thal·lo·phyte \ˈthal-ə-ˌfīt\ *n* : any of a large group of plants having single-celled sex organs or sex organs of which all cells give rise to gametes and including the algae, fungi, and lichens — **thal·lo·phyt·ic** \ˌthal-ə-ˈfit-ik\ *adj*

than \thən, (ˈ)than\ *conj* **1** : when compared to the way, extent, or degree in or to which ⟨10 is less *than* 20⟩ ⟨older *than* I am⟩ ⟨easier said *than* done⟩ **2** : different from in kind, manner, or identity — often used with *other* or *else* ⟨adults other *than* parents⟩ ⟨anywhere else *than* at home⟩

thane \ˈthān\ *n* **1** : THEGN **2** : a Scottish feudal lord

thank \ˈthaŋk\ *vb* **1** : to express gratitude to ⟨*thanked* her for the present⟩ ⟨*thank* you for the loan⟩ **2** : to hold responsible ⟨had only himself to *thank* for his loss⟩

thank·ful \ˈthaŋk-fəl\ *adj* **1** : conscious of benefit received **2** : expressive of thanks **3** : well pleased : GLAD ***syn*** see GRATEFUL ***ant*** thankless — **thank·ful·ly** \-fə-lē\ *adv* — **thank·ful·ness** *n*

thank·less \ˈthaŋk-ləs\ *adj* **1** : not expressing or feeling gratitude : UNGRATEFUL **2** : not likely to obtain thanks : UNAPPRECIATED ⟨a *thankless* job⟩ — **thank·less·ly** *adv* — **thank·less·ness** *n*

thanks \ˈthaŋks\ *n pl* **1** : kindly or grateful thoughts : GRATITUDE ⟨express my *thanks* for their kindness⟩ **2** : an expression of gratitude ⟨return *thanks* before the meal⟩ ⟨many *thanks*⟩

thanks·giv·ing \thaŋ(k)s-ˈgiv-iŋ\ *n* **1** : the act of giving thanks **2** : a prayer expressing gratitude **3** *cap* : THANKSGIVING DAY

Thanksgiving Day *n* : the 4th Thursday in November observed as a legal holiday for public thanksgiving to God

1**that** \(ˈ)that\ *pron, pl* **those** \(ˈ)thōz\ **1 a** : the person, thing, or idea indicated, mentioned, or understood from the situation ⟨*that* is my father⟩ **b** : the one, kind, or thing specified as follows ⟨the purest water is *that* produced by distillation⟩ **2** : the one farther away or less immediately under observation ⟨*those* are elms and these are maples⟩

ə abut	ər further	a back	ā bake	
ä cot, cart	au̇ out	ch chin	e less	ē easy
g gift	i trip	ī life	j joke	ng sing
ō flow	ȯ flaw	ȯi coin	th thin	th this
ü loot	u̇ foot	y yet	yü few	yu̇ furious
zh vision				

2**that** *adj, pl* **those** **1 :** being the one specified or understood ⟨*that* boy did it⟩ **2 :** the farther away or less immediately under observation or discussion ⟨this chair or *that* one⟩

3**that** \thət, (,)that\ *conj* **1 a** — used to introduce a noun clause serving esp. as the subject or object of a verb or as a predicate nominative ⟨*that* he has succeeded is undeniable⟩ ⟨said *that* he was afraid⟩ ⟨the reason for his absence is *that* he is ill⟩ **b** — used to introduce a subordinate clause that modifies a noun or adjective or is in apposition with a noun ⟨certain *that* this is true⟩ ⟨the certainty *that* this is true⟩ ⟨the fact *that* you are here⟩ **2 a** — used alone or after *so* or *in order* to introduce a subordinate clause expressing purpose ⟨saved money so *that* he could buy a bicycle⟩ **b** — used to introduce an exclamatory clause expressing a wish ⟨oh, *that* she were here⟩ **3** — used to introduce a subordinate clause expressing a reason ⟨delighted *that* you could come⟩ **4** — used esp. after an expression including the word *so* or *such* to introduce a subordinate clause expressing result ⟨worked so hard *that* he became exhausted⟩

4**that** \thət, (,)that\ *pron* **1 :** WHO, WHOM, WHICH ⟨the girl *that* smiled⟩ ⟨the man *that* you spoke to⟩ ⟨the house *that* Jack built⟩ **2 :** at, in, or on which : by, to, or with which ⟨each year *that* the lectures are given⟩

5**that** \'that\ *adv* **:** to such an extent ⟨need a nail about *that* long⟩

1**thatch** \'thach\ *vb* **:** to cover with or as if with thatch

2**thatch** *n* **:** a plant material (as straw) for use as roofing

1**thaw** \'thȯ\ *vb* **1 :** to melt or cause to melt : reverse the effect of freezing ⟨ice on the pond is *thawing*⟩ **2 a :** to become so warm or mild as to melt ice or snow ⟨it *thawed* early this year⟩ **b :** to recover from chilling ⟨the skiers *thawed* out in front of the fire⟩ **3 :** to grow less cold or reserved in manner : become more friendly ⟨their relations *thawed*⟩

2**thaw** *n* **1 :** the action, fact, or process of thawing **2 :** a warmth of weather sufficient to thaw ice

THC \ˌtē-ˌāch-'sē\ *n* **:** a liquid derived from hemp plant resin that is an intoxicant in marijuana

1**the** \thə (*esp before consonant sounds*), thē (*before vowel sounds*); *1e is often* 'thē\ *definite article* **1 a :** that or those previously mentioned or clearly understood ⟨put *the* cat out⟩ **b :** that unique one : that one existing as only one at a time ⟨*the* Lord⟩ ⟨*the* sky⟩ ⟨*the* sun⟩ **c :** that or those near in space, time, or thought ⟨news of *the* day⟩ **d :** that or those best known to the speaker or writer or to the hearer or reader ⟨*the* President⟩ ⟨*the* courts will decide⟩ **e :** that or those considered best, most typical, or most worth singling out ⟨*the* poet of his day⟩ ⟨my friend Adams is not one of *the* Adamses⟩ **f :** any one typical of or standing for an entire class so named ⟨courtesy distinguishes *the* gentleman⟩ ⟨good for *the* soul⟩ **2 :** MY, YOUR, HIS, HER, ITS, OUR, THEIR, ONE'S ⟨grabbed him by *the* collar⟩ ⟨how's *the* family⟩ ⟨*the* ankle is better today⟩ **3 :** EACH, EVERY ⟨80 crackers to *the* box⟩ **4 a :** that which is ⟨an essay on *the* sublime⟩ **b :** those that are ⟨*the* Greeks⟩ ⟨*the* wise⟩ ⟨*the* aristocracy⟩

2**the** *adv* **1 :** than before : than otherwise ⟨none *the* wiser for attending⟩ **2 a :** to what extent ⟨*the* sooner the better⟩ **b :** to that extent ⟨the sooner *the* better⟩

the·a·ter *or* **the·a·tre** \'thē-ət-ər\ *n* **[**from Greek *theatron*, literally "a place for viewing", from *theasthai* "to contemplate", the source also of English *theory***]** **1 :** a building or area for dramatic performances or for showing motion pictures **2 :** a place like a theater in form or use; *esp* **:** a room often with rising tiers of seats for assemblies (as for a lecture) **3 :** a place of enactment of significant events or action ⟨a *theater* of war⟩ **4 :** dramatic literature or performance ⟨a course in American *theater*⟩

the·a·ter·go·er \-ˌgō(-ə)r\ *n* **:** a person who frequently goes to the theater

the·at·ri·cal \thē-'a-tri-kəl\ *adj* **1 :** of or relating to the theater or the presentation of plays ⟨*theatrical* costume⟩ **2 :** marked by pretense or artificiality of emotion : not natural and simple : SHOWY ⟨*theatrical* acceptance speech⟩ — **the·at·ri·cal·ly** \-k(ə-)lē\ *adv*

the·at·ri·cals \-kəlz\ *n pl* **:** the performance of plays ⟨amateur *theatricals*⟩

thee \(')thē\ *pron, objective case of* THOU

theft \'theft\ *n* **:** the act of stealing

thegn \'thān\ *n* **:** a free retainer of an Anglo-Saxon lord

their \thər, (,)the(ə)r, (,)tha(ə)r\ *adj* **:** of or relating to them or themselves ⟨*their* clothes⟩ ⟨*their* deeds⟩ ⟨*their* being seen⟩

theirs \'the(ə)rz, 'tha(ə)rz\ *pron* **:** their one : their ones ⟨the house is *theirs*⟩ ⟨these books are *theirs*⟩ ⟨*theirs* are on the table⟩

the·ism \'thē-ˌiz-əm\ *n* **:** belief in the existence of a god or gods; *esp* **:** belief in the existence of God as creator and ruler of the universe — **the·ist** \'thē-əst\ *n* — **the·is·tic** \thē-'is-tik\ *adj*

them \(th)əm, (')them\ *pron, objective case of* THEY

theme \'thēm\ *n* **1 :** a subject of discourse, artistic representation, or musical composition **2 :** a written exercise : COMPOSITION — **the·mat·ic** \thi-'mat-ik\ *adj*

them·selves \thəm-'selvz, them-\ *pron* **1 :** those identical ones that are they ⟨nations that govern *themselves*⟩ ⟨they *themselves* were present⟩ ⟨*themselves* busy, they dislike idleness in others⟩ **2 :** their normal or healthy selves ⟨more than a week before they were *themselves* again⟩

1**then** \(')then\ *adv* **1 :** at that time ⟨it was *then* believed the world was flat⟩ **2 :** soon after that ⟨walked to the door, *then* turned⟩ **3 a :** following next after in order **b :** in addition : BESIDES **4 a :** in that case **b :** according to that ⟨your mind is made up, *then*⟩ **c :** as it appears ⟨the cause, *then*, is established⟩ **d :** as a necessary consequence ⟨if you were there, *then* you saw him⟩

2**then** \'then\ *n* **:** that time ⟨wait until *then*⟩

3**then** \'then\ *adj* **:** existing or acting at or belonging to the time mentioned ⟨the *then* king⟩

thence \'then(t)s, 'then(t)s\ *adv* **1 :** from that place **2 :** from that fact or circumstance : THEREFROM

thence·forth \-ˌfōrth, -ˌfȯrth\ *adv* **:** from that time forward : THEREAFTER

thence·for·ward \then(t)s-'fȯr-wərd, then(t)s-\ *also* **thence·for·wards** \-wərdz\ *adv* **:** onward from that place or time : THENCEFORTH

the·oc·ra·cy \thē-'äk-rə-sē\ *n, pl* **-cies** **1 :** government of a country by officials regarded as divinely guided **2 :** a country governed by a theocracy — **the·o·crat** \'thē-ə-ˌkrat\ *n* — **the·o·crat·ic** \ˌthē-ə-'krat-ik\ *adj*

the·od·o·lite \thē-'äd-ə-ˌlīt\ *n* **:** a surveyor's instrument for measuring horizontal and vertical angles — **the·od·o·lit·ic** \-ˌäd-ə-'lit-ik\ *adj*

the·ol·o·gy \thē-'äl-ə-jē\ *n, pl* **-gies** **1 :** the study and interpretation of religious faith, practice, and experience **2 :** a system of religious beliefs — **the·o·lo·gian** \ˌthē-ə-'lō-jən\ *n* — **the·o·log·i·cal** \-'läj-i-kəl\ *adj*

the·o·rem \'thē-ə-rəm\ *n* **1** : a formula or proposition (as in geometry) that has been or is to be proved from other formulas or propositions **2** : an idea accepted or proposed as a demonstrable truth

the·o·ret·i·cal \ˌthē-ə-'ret-i-kəl\ *also* **the·o·ret·ic** \-'ret-ik\ *adj* **1 a** : relating to or having the character of theory : ABSTRACT **b** : confined to theory or speculation : SPECULATIVE ⟨*theoretical* mechanics⟩ **2** : given to or skilled in theorizing **3** : existing only in theory : HYPOTHETICAL — **the·o·ret·i·cal·ly** \-'ret-i-k(ə-)lē\ *adv*

the·o·rist \'thē-ə-rəst\ *n* : a person that theorizes

the·o·rize \-ˌrīz\ *vb* : to form a theory : SPECULATE — **the·o·riz·er** *n*

the·o·ry \'thē-ə-rē, 'thi(-ə)r-ē\ *n, pl* **-ries** **1** : the general or abstract principles of a body of fact, a science, or an art ⟨music *theory*⟩ **2** : a general principle or body of principles offered to explain phenomena ⟨wave *theory* of light⟩ **3** : a hypothesis assumed for the sake of argument or investigation **4** : abstract thought : SPECULATION

ther·a·peu·tic \ˌther-ə-'pyüt-ik\ *adj* : of, relating to, or dealing with healing and esp. with remedies for diseases : MEDICINAL

ther·a·peu·tics \-'pyüt-iks\ *n* : a branch of medical science dealing with the use of remedies

ther·a·pist \'ther-ə-pəst\ *n* : one specializing in therapy; *esp* : a person trained in methods of treatment and rehabilitation other than the use of drugs or surgery

ther·a·py \'ther-ə-pē\ *n, pl* **-pies** : therapeutic treatment of bodily, mental, or social disorders or maladjustment

¹**there** \'tha(ə)r, 'the(ə)r\ *adv* **1** : in or at that place ⟨stand over *there*⟩ **2** : to or into that place : THITHER ⟨went *there* every year for vacation⟩ **3** : at that point or stage ⟨*there* the plot thickens⟩ **4** : in that matter, respect, or relation ⟨*there* you have a choice⟩ **5** — used interjectionally to express satisfaction, approval, soothing, or defiance ⟨*there*, I'm through⟩

²**there** \(ˌ)tha(ə)r, (ˌ)the(ə)r, thər\ *pron* — used as a function word to introduce a sentence or clause in which the subject comes after the verb ⟨*there* shall come a time⟩

³**there** *like* ¹\ *n* : that place : that point ⟨get away from *there*⟩ ⟨you take it from *there*⟩

there·abouts *or* **there·about** \ˌthar-ə-'bau̇t(s), ˌther-\ *adv* **1** : near that place or time **2** : near that number, degree, or quantity ⟨fifty people or *thereabouts*⟩

there·af·ter \thar-'af-tər, ther-\ *adv* : after that

there·at \-'at\ *adv* **1** : at that place **2** : at that occurrence : on that account

there·by \tha(ə)r-'bī, the(ə)r-\ *adv* **1** : by that : by that means ⟨make a friend *thereby*⟩ **2** : connected with or with reference to that ⟨*thereby* hangs a tale⟩

there·for \-'fȯ(ə)r\ *adv* : for or in return for that ⟨issued bonds *therefor*⟩

there·fore \'tha(ə)r-ˌfōr, 'the(ə)r-, -ˌfȯr\ *adv* : for that reason : CONSEQUENTLY

there·from \tha(ə)r-'frəm, the(ə)r-, -'främ\ *adv* : from that or it ⟨learned much *therefrom*⟩

there·in \thar-'in, ther-\ *adv* **1** : in or into that place, time, or thing ⟨the world and all *therein*⟩ **2** : in that particular or respect ⟨*therein* they disagreed⟩

there·of \-'əv, -'äv\ *adv* **1** : of that or it ⟨took the bread and ate *thereof*⟩ **2** : from that cause or particular : THEREFROM ⟨a wound so deep that he died *thereof*⟩

there·on \-'ȯn, -'än\ *adv* : on that ⟨a table with a vase set *thereon*⟩

there·to \tha(ə)r-'tü, the(ə)r-\ *adv* : to that ⟨signed his name *thereto*⟩

there·to·fore \'thart-ə-ˌfōr, 'thert-, -ˌfȯr\ *adv* : up to that time

there·un·to \thar-'ən-tü, ther-\ *adv, archaic* : THERETO

there·upon \'thar-ə-ˌpȯn, 'ther-, -ˌpän\ *adv* **1** : on that matter : THEREON ⟨they disagreed *thereupon*⟩ **2** : THEREFORE **3** : immediately after that : at once ⟨pressed the button and *thereupon* the bell rang⟩

there·with \tha(ə)r-'with, the(ə)r-, -'with\ *adv* : with that ⟨led a simple life and was happy *therewith*⟩

there·with·al \'tha(ə)r-with-ˌȯl, 'the(ə)r-, -ˌȯl\ *adv* : THEREWITH

therm *abbr* thermometer

¹**ther·mal** \'thər-məl\ *adj* : of, relating to, caused by, or conserving heat : WARM, HOT ⟨*thermal* underwear⟩ — **ther·mal·ly** \-mə-lē\ *adv*

²**thermal** *n* : a rising body of warm air

thermal pollution *n* : the discharge of liquid (as waste from a factory) into a natural body of water at a higher temperature than the surrounding ecosystem

therm·is·tor \'thər-ˌmis-tər\ *n* : an electrical resistor made of a material whose resistance varies sharply in a known manner with the temperature

ther·mo·cline \'thər-mə-ˌklīn\ *n* : a layer of water in a body of water (as a lake) separating an upper warmer lighter oxygen-rich zone from a lower colder heavier oxygen-poor zone

ther·mo·cou·ple \'thər-mə-ˌkəp-əl\ *n* : a thermoelectric couple used to measure temperature differences

ther·mo·dy·nam·ics \ˌthər-mō-dī-'nam-iks\ *n* : physics that deals with the mechanical action or relations of heat — **ther·mo·dy·nam·ic** \-ik\ *adj*

ther·mo·elec·tric \ˌthər-mō-i-'lek-trik\ *adj* : of or relating to phenomena involving relations between the temperature and the electrical condition in a metal or in contacting metals

thermoelectric couple *n* : a union of two conductors (as bars or wires of dissimilar metals joined at their extremities) for producing a thermoelectric current

ther·mo·graph \'thər-mə-ˌgraf\ *n* : a self-recording thermometer

ther·mom·e·ter \thə(r)-'mäm-ət-ər\ *n* : an instrument for measuring temperature commonly by means of the expansion or contraction of mercury or alcohol as indicated by its rise or fall in a thin glass tube alongside a numbered scale — **ther·mo·met·ric** \ˌthər-mə-'me-trik\ *adj* — **ther·mo·met·ri·cal·ly** \-tri-k(ə-)lē\ *adv*

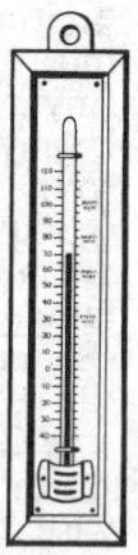

ther-mom-eter

ther·mo·nu·cle·ar \ˌthər-mō-'n(y)ü-klē-ər\ *adj* **1** : of or relating to the transformations in the nucleus of atoms of low atomic weight (as hydrogen) that require a very high temperature (as in the hydrogen bomb or in the sun) ⟨*thermonuclear* reaction⟩ ⟨*thermonuclear* weapon⟩ **2** : of, utilizing, or relating to a thermonuclear bomb ⟨*thermonuclear* war⟩

ther·mo·reg·u·la·tor \ˌthər-mō-'reg-yə-ˌlāt-ər\ *n* : a device for the regulation of temperature : THERMOSTAT

ther·mos \'thər-məs\ *n* : VACUUM BOTTLE
ther·mo·sphere \'thər-mə-,sfi(ə)r\ *n* : the part of the earth's atmosphere that begins at about 50 miles above the earth's surface, extends to outer space, and is characterized by a steadily increasing temperature with height
ther·mo·stat \'thər-mə-,stat\ *n* : an automatic device for regulating temperature (as of a heating system) — **ther·mo·stat·ic** \,thər-mə-'stat-ik\ *adj* — **ther·mo·stat·i·cal·ly** \-i-k(ə-)lē\ *adv*
the·sau·rus \thi-'sȯr-əs\ *n, pl* **-sau·ri** \-'sȯr-,ī, -,ē\ *or* **-sau·rus·es** : a dictionary of synonyms
these *pl of* THIS
the·sis \'thē-səs\ *n, pl* **the·ses** \'thē-,sēz\ **1** : a proposition to be proved or advanced without proof : HYPOTHESIS **2** : a dissertation embodying results of original research; *esp* : one written by a candidate for an academic degree
Thes·sa·lo·nians \,thes-ə-'lō-nyənz\ *n* — see BIBLE table
the·ta \'thāt-ə\ *n* : the 8th letter of the Greek alphabet — Θ *or* θ
thews \'th(y)üz\ *n pl* : MUSCLES, SINEWS
they \(')thā\ *pron* : those ones ⟨*they* dance well⟩
they'd \(,)thād\ : they had : they would
they'll \(,)thā(ə)l, thel\ : they shall : they will
they're \thər, (,)th(ə)r, ,thā-ər\ : they are
they've \(,)thāv\ : they have
thi- *or* **thio-** *comb form* : sulfur ⟨*thi*amine⟩
thi·a·mine \'thī-ə-,mēn, -mən\ *or* **thi·a·min** \-mən\ *n* : a vitamin of the B complex essential to normal metabolism and nerve function and widely distributed in plants and animals — called also *vitamin* B_1
¹**thick** \'thik\ *adj* **1** : having or being of relatively great depth or extent from one surface to its opposite ⟨*thick* plank⟩ **2** : heavily built : THICKSET **3 a** : close-packed : DENSE ⟨*thick* forest⟩ **b** : NUMEROUS **c** : VISCOUS ⟨*thick* syrup⟩ **4** : marked by haze, fog, or mist ⟨*thick* weather⟩ **5** : measuring in thickness ⟨12 inches *thick*⟩ **6** : imperfectly articulated : INDISTINCT ⟨*thick* speech⟩ **7** : OBTUSE, STUPID **8** : INTIMATE **9** : EXCESSIVE — **thick·ish** \-ish\ *adj* — **thick·ly** *adv*
²**thick** *n* **1** : the most crowded or active part ⟨in the *thick* of battle⟩ **2** : the part of greatest thickness
³**thick** *adv* : THICKLY
thick and thin *n* : every difficulty and obstacle ⟨stood by his friend through *thick and thin*⟩
thick·en \'thik-ən\ *vb* **thick·ened**; **thick·en·ing** \-(ə-)ning\ **1** : to make or become thick, dense, or viscous **2** : to grow complicated or keen ⟨the plot *thickens*⟩ — **thick·en·er** \-(ə-)nər\ *n*
thick·en·ing *n* **1** : the act of making or becoming thick **2** : something used to thicken (as flour in a gravy)
thick·et \'thik-ət\ *n* : a thick usu. restricted growth of shrubbery, small trees, or underbrush
thick·head·ed \'thik-'hed-əd\ *adj* : STUPID
thick·ness \'thik-nəs\ *n* **1** : the quality or state of being thick **2** : the smallest of three dimensions ⟨length, width, and *thickness*⟩ **3** : the thick part of something **4** : LAYER, SHEET ⟨a single *thickness* of canvas⟩
thick·set \'thik-'set\ *adj* **1** : closely placed or planted **2** : of short stout build : STOCKY
thick–skinned \-'skind\ *adj* **1** : having a thick skin **2** : CALLOUS, INSENSITIVE
thief \'thēf\ *n, pl* **thieves** \'thēvz\ : one that steals — **thiev·ish** \'thē-vish\ *adj* — **thiev·ish·ly** *adv* — **thiev·ish·ness** *n*
thieve \'thēv\ *vb* : STEAL, ROB
thiev·ery \'thēv-(ə-)rē\ *n, pl* **-er·ies** : the action of stealing : THEFT
thigh \'thī\ *n* : the part of the vertebrate hind limb extending from the hip to the knee and supported by a single large bone
thigh·bone \-'bōn, -,bōn\ *n* : FEMUR
thig·mot·ro·pism \thig-'mä-trə-,piz-əm\ *n* : a tropism in which contact (as with a rigid surface) is the orienting factor
thim·ble \'thim-bəl\ *n* [from Middle English *thymbyl*, from Old English *thȳmel* "covering for the thumb", from *thūma* "thumb"] : a cap or cover used in sewing to protect the finger that pushes the needle
thin \'thin\ *adj* **thin·ner**; **thin·nest** **1** : having little extent from one surface to its opposite ⟨*thin* paper⟩ **2** : not dense in arrangement or distribution ⟨*thin* hair⟩ **3** : not well fleshed **4** : more rarefied than normal ⟨*thin* air⟩ **5** : lacking substance or strength ⟨*thin* broth⟩ ⟨*thin* excuse⟩ **6** : somewhat feeble, shrill, and lacking in resonance ⟨*thin* voice⟩ — **thin** *vb* — **thin·ly** *adv* — **thin·ness** \'thin-nəs\ *n*
syn THIN, LEAN, GAUNT can mean not having abundant flesh. THIN applies to a person having no excess flesh or fat and often less than is desirable for good health; LEAN suggests the spareness of flesh of one that is not plump and may further suggest an athlete's tough, wiry frame that has little excess flesh; GAUNT suggests a bony, emaciated appearance and may imply undernourishment ***ant*** fat, stout
thine \'thīn\ *pron, archaic* : thy one : thy ones
thing \'thing\ *n* **1 a** : a matter of concern : AFFAIR ⟨many *things* to do⟩ **b** *pl* : state of affairs ⟨*things* are improving⟩ **c** : SITUATION ⟨look at this *thing* another way⟩ **d** : EVENT, CIRCUMSTANCE ⟨that shooting was a terrible *thing*⟩ **e** : something one does well or likes to do : SPECIALTY ⟨do your *thing*⟩ **2 a** : DEED, ACT, ACCOMPLISHMENT ⟨do great *things*⟩ **b** : a product of work or activity ⟨likes to build *things*⟩ **c** : the aim of effort or activity ⟨the *thing* is to get well⟩ **3 a** : a distinct item or object; *esp* : a tangible object **b** : an inanimate object **4 a** *pl* : POSSESSIONS, EFFECTS ⟨pack your *things*⟩ **b** : an article of clothing ⟨not a *thing* to wear⟩ **5 a** : DETAIL, POINT ⟨checks every little *thing*⟩ **b** : a material or substance of a specified kind ⟨avoid starchy *things*⟩ **6** : IDEA, NOTION ⟨says the first *thing* he thinks of⟩ **7** : INDIVIDUAL; *esp* : PERSON ⟨poor little *thing*⟩
think \'thingk\ *vb* **thought** \'thȯt\; **think·ing** **1** : to form or have in the mind **2 a** : to have as an opinion : BELIEVE ⟨*think* it's so⟩ **b** : to regard as : CONSIDER ⟨*think* the rule unfair⟩ **3** : to reflect on : PONDER ⟨*think* the matter over⟩ **4** : to call to mind : REMEMBER ⟨never *thought* to ask⟩ **5** : to form a mental picture of **6** : to exercise the powers of judgment, conception, or inference : REASON **7** : to have a view or opinion ⟨*thinks* of himself as a poet⟩ **8** : to have concern ⟨*think* of just yourself⟩ **9** : EXPECT, SUSPECT — **think·a·ble** \'thing-kə-bəl\ *adj* — **think·er** *n* — **think·ing** *adj*
think tank *n* : an institute, corporation, or group organized for broad research esp. on technological or social problems
thin·ner \'thin-ər\ *n* : one that thins; *esp* : a volatile liquid (as turpentine) used to thin paint
thin–skinned \'thin-'skind\ *adj* **1** : having a thin skin or rind **2** : unduly susceptible to criticism or insult : TOUCHY
thio- — see THI-
¹**third** \'thərd\ *adj* **1 a** — see NUMBER table **b** : next after the second in time, order, or importance

2 : being one of three equal parts of something — **third** *adv* — **third·ly** *adv*

2**third** *n* **1** — see NUMBER table **2 :** one of three equal parts of something **3 :** the musical interval embracing three diatonic degrees **4 :** the third gear or speed of an automotive vehicle **5 :** one next after a second in time, order, or importance

third base n **:** the base that must be touched third by a base runner in baseball or the position of the player defending the area around it — **third baseman** *n*

third class *n* **:** the class next below second class in a classification — **third–class** *adj*

third degree *n* **:** severe or brutal treatment of a prisoner by the police in order to get an admission

third–degree burn *n* **:** a burn in which there is destruction of the whole thickness of the skin and sometimes of deeper tissues with loss of fluid and often shock

third eyelid *n* **:** NICTITATING MEMBRANE

1**thirst** \thərst\ *n* **1 a :** a feeling of dryness in the mouth and throat associated with a desire for liquids **b :** the bodily condition (as of dehydration) that induces this **2 :** an ardent desire **:** CRAVING, LONGING

2**thirst** *vb* **1 :** to feel thirsty **:** suffer thirst **2 :** to have a vehement desire **:** CRAVE

thirsty \'thər-stē\ *adj* **thirst·i·er; -est 1 a :** feeling thirst **b :** needing moisture **:** PARCHED ⟨*thirsty* land⟩ **2 :** having a strong desire **:** AVID ⟨*thirsty* for knowledge⟩ — **thirst·i·ly** \-stə-lē\ *adv*

thir·teen \ˌthər(t)-'tēn\ *n* — see NUMBER table — **thirteen** *adj or pron* — **thir·teenth** \-'tēn(t)th\ *adj or n*

thir·ty \'thərt-ē\ *n, pl* **thirties 1** — see NUMBER table **2** *pl* **:** the numbers 30 to 39; *esp* **:** the years 30 to 39 in a lifetime or century —**thir·ti·eth** \-ē-əth\ *n or adj* — **thirty** *adj or pron*

1**this** \(')this\ *pron, pl* **these** \(')thēz\ **1 :** the person, thing, or idea present or near in place, time, or thought, or just mentioned ⟨*these* are my hands⟩ **2 :** the one nearer or more immediately under observation ⟨*this* is iron and that is tin⟩

2**this** *adj, pl* **these 1 :** being the one present or near in place, time, or thought, or just mentioned ⟨*this* book is mine⟩ ⟨early *this* morning⟩ ⟨friends all *these* years⟩ **2 :** the nearer at hand or more immediately under observation or discussion ⟨*this* car or that one⟩ ⟨considers *these* colors preferable to those⟩

3**this** \'this\ *adv* **:** to the degree or extent indicated by something immediately present ⟨didn't expect to wait *this* long⟩

this·tle \'this-əl\ *n* **:** any of various prickly plants related to the daisies but distinguished by often showy heads of mostly tubular flowers — **this·tly** \'this-(ə-)lē\ *adj* — **thistle·like** \-əl-ˌlīk\ *adj*

thistle

this·tle·down \-əl-ˌdau̇n\ *n* **:** the down from the ripe flower head of a thistle

1**thith·er** \'thith-ər\ *adv* **:** to that place **:** THERE

2**thither** *adj* **:** being on the other and farther side **:** more remote

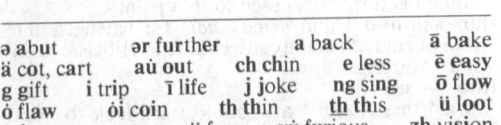

ə abut ər further a back ā bake
ä cot, cart au̇ out ch chin e less ē easy
g gift i trip ī life j joke ng sing ō flow
ȯ flaw ȯi coin th thin th this ü loot
u̇ foot y yet yü few yu̇ furious zh vision

tho *var of* THOUGH

thole \'thōl\ *also* **thole·pin** \-ˌpin\ *n* **:** a pin set in the gunwale of a boat as a pivot for an oar

thong \'thȯng\ *n* **1 :** a strip of leather used esp. for fastening something **2 :** a sandal held on the foot by a thong fitting between the toes

tho·rax \'thōr-ˌaks, 'thȯr-\ *n, pl* **tho·rax·es** *or* **tho·ra·ces** \'thōr-ə-ˌsēz, 'thȯr-\ **1 :** the part of the body of a mammal between the neck and the abdomen; *also* **:** its cavity in which the heart and lungs lie **2 :** the middle of the three chief divisions of the body of an insect — **tho·rac·ic** \thə-'ras-ik\ *adj*

tho·ri·um \'thōr-ē-əm, 'thȯr-\ *n* **:** a radioactive metallic element that occurs combined in minerals — see ELEMENT table

thorn \'thȯrn\ *n* **1 :** a woody plant bearing sharp processes (as briers, prickles, or spines); *esp* **:** HAWTHORN **2 :** a sharp rigid process on a plant; *esp* **:** one that is a short, rigid, sharp-pointed, and leafless branch **3 :** something or someone that causes distress or irritation — **thorned** \'thȯrnd\ *adj* — **thorn·less** \'thȯrn-ləs\ *adj* — **thorn·like** \-ˌlīk\ *adj*

thorny \'thȯr-nē\ *adj* **thorn·i·er; -est 1 :** full of or covered with thorns **:** SPINY **2 :** DIFFICULT, TRYING ⟨a *thorny* problem⟩ — **thorn·i·ness** *n*

tho·ron \'thōr-ˌän, 'thȯr-\ *n* **:** a gaseous radioactive isotope of radon formed from thorium

thor·ough \'thər-ō, 'thə-rō\ *adj* **1 :** EXHAUSTIVE, DETAILED, COMPLETE ⟨a *thorough* search⟩ ⟨*thorough* study⟩ ⟨*thorough* success⟩ **2 :** careful about detail **:** PAINSTAKING ⟨a *thorough* workman⟩ — **thor·ough·ly** *adv* — **thor·ough·ness** *n*

1**thor·ough·bred** \-ˌbred\ *adj* **1 :** bred from the best blood through a long line **:** PUREBRED ⟨*thoroughbred* dogs⟩ **2** *cap* **:** of, relating to, or being a member of the Thoroughbred breed of horses **3 :** marked by high-spirited grace and elegance ⟨a *thoroughbred* lady⟩

2**thoroughbred** *n* **1** *cap* **:** any of an English breed of light speedy horses kept chiefly for racing **2 :** a purebred or pedigreed animal **3 :** a person of sterling qualities

Thoroughbred 1

thor·ough·fare \-ˌfa(ə)r, -ˌfe(ə)r\ *n* **1 :** a street or road open at both ends **2 :** a main road **:** a busy street

thor·ough·go·ing \ˌthər-ə-'gō-ing, ˌthə-rə-\ *adj* **:** THOROUGH

those *pl of* THAT

thou \(')thau̇\ *pron, archaic* **:** the person addressed

thou *abbr* thousand

1**though** \'thō\ *adv* **:** HOWEVER, NEVERTHELESS ⟨not for long, *though*⟩

2**though** \(ˌ)thō\ *conj* **1 :** in spite of the fact that ⟨*though* it was raining, he went hiking⟩ **2 :** even if **:** even supposing ⟨determined to tell the truth *though* he should die for it⟩

1**thought** *past of* THINK

2**thought** \'thȯt\ *n* **1 :** the act or process of thinking **2 :** serious consideration **:** careful attention ⟨give *thought* to the future⟩ **3 :** power of thinking and esp. of reasoning and judging **4 :** power of imagining or comprehending ⟨beauty beyond *thought*⟩ **5 :** a product of thinking (as an idea, fancy, or invention) ⟨idle *thoughts*⟩ ⟨a pleasing *thought*⟩ **6 :** a slight amount : BIT ⟨add just a *thought* more salt to the stew⟩

thought·ful \'thȯt-fəl\ *adj* **1 a :** absorbed in thought : MEDITATIVE **b :** marked by careful reasoned thinking ⟨*thoughtful* essay⟩ **2 :** MINDFUL, HEEDFUL; *esp* : attentive to the needs of others — **thought·ful·ly** \-fə-lē\ *adv* — **thought·ful·ness** *n*

thought·less \'thȯt-ləs\ *adj* **1 a :** insufficiently alert : CARELESS **b :** RECKLESS, RASH **2 :** devoid of thought : INSENSATE **3 :** lacking concern for others : INCONSIDERATE — **thought·less·ly** *adv*

thou·sand \'thau̇-zən(d)\ *n, pl* **thousands** *or* **thousand** **1** — see NUMBER table **2 :** the number in the 4th decimal place to the left of the decimal point in arabic numerals **3 :** a very large or indefinitely great number ⟨a movie with a cast of *thousands*⟩ — **thousand** *adj*

thou·sand–leg·ger \ˌthau̇-zən(d)-'leg-ər\ *n* : MILLIPEDE — called also *thousand-legged worm*

thou·sandth \'thau̇-zən(t)th\ *n* **1 :** one of 1000 equal parts of something **2 :** the one numbered 1000 in a countable series — see NUMBER table — **thousandth** *adj*

thrall \'thrȯl\ *n* **1 :** SLAVE, SERF **2 :** a state of complete absorption or servitude : SLAVERY — **thralldom** *or* **thral·dom** \'thrȯl-dəm\ *n*

thrash \'thrash\ *vb* **1 :** THRESH 1 **2 a :** to beat soundly or strike about with or as if with a stick or whip : FLOG **b :** DEFEAT **3 :** to swing, beat, or stir about in the manner of a rapidly moving flail ⟨*thrashing* his arms⟩ **4 :** to go over again and again ⟨*thrash* the matter over in his mind⟩ ⟨*thrash* out a plan⟩ — **thrash** *n*

¹**thrash·er** \'thrash-ər\ *n* : one that thrashes or threshes

²**thrasher** *n* : any of numerous long-tailed American singing birds that resemble thrushes

¹**thread** \'thred\ *n* **1 :** a thin continuous filament ⟨the spider's sticky *thread*⟩; *esp* : a textile cord made by twisting together strands of spun fiber ⟨silk *thread*⟩ **2 :** something suggesting a filament ⟨a *thread* of light⟩ **3 :** the ridge or groove that winds around a screw **4 :** a line of reasoning or train of thought ⟨lost the *thread* of his story⟩ — **thread·like** \-ˌlīk\ *adj*

²**thread** *vb* **1 :** to put a thread in working position in ⟨*thread* a needle⟩ **2 :** to pass through in the manner of a thread ⟨*thread* a pipe with a wire⟩ **3 :** to make one's way through or between : wind a way ⟨*threading* narrow alleys⟩ **4 :** to put together on a thread : STRING ⟨*thread* beads⟩ **5 :** to interweave with or as if with threads : INTERSPERSE ⟨dark hair *threaded* with silver⟩ **6 :** to form a screw thread on or in — **thread·er** *n*

thread·bare \'thred-ˌba(ə)r, -ˌbe(ə)r\ *adj* **1 :** having the nap worn off so that the thread shows : SHABBY ⟨*threadbare* rug⟩ **2 :** TRITE, HACKNEYED ⟨*threadbare* subject⟩

thready \'thred-ē\ *adj* **thread·i·er; -est** **1 :** consisting of or bearing fibers or filaments ⟨a *thready* bark⟩ **2 :** lacking in fullness or vigor : THIN ⟨a *thready* voice⟩ ⟨a *thready* pulse⟩

threat \'thret\ *n* **1 :** an expression of an intent to do harm **2 :** something that threatens ⟨spring rains bring a *threat* of floods⟩

threat·en \'thret-ən\ *vb* **threat·ened; threat·en·ing** \-(ə-)ning\ **1 :** to utter threats : make threats against ⟨*threaten* trespassers⟩ **2 :** to give warning of by a threat or sign ⟨clouds *threatening* rain⟩ **3 :** to give signs of trouble to come — **threat·en·ing·ly** \-(ə-)ning-lē\ *adv*

three \'thrē\ *n* **1** — see NUMBER table **2 :** the third in a set or series **3 :** something having three units or members — **three** *adj or pron*

3–D \'thrē-'dē\ *n* : the three-dimensional form or a picture produced in it

three–deck·er \'thrē-'dek-ər\ *n* **1 :** a ship having three decks **2 :** a sandwich with three slices of bread and two layers of filling

three–di·men·sion·al *adj* **1 :** of, relating to, or having three dimensions **2 :** giving the illusion of depth or varying distances

three·fold \'thrē-ˌfōld, -'fōld\ *adj* **1 :** having three units or members **2 :** being three times as great or as many — **threefold** *adv*

three–hand·ed \-'han-dəd\ *adj* : played or to be played by three players ⟨*three-handed* bridge⟩

three·pence \'threp-ən(t)s, 'thrip-, 'thrəp-, *US also* 'thrē-ˌpen(t)s\ *n, pl* **threepence** *or* **three·penc·es** **1 :** the sum of three usu. British pennies **2 :** a coin worth three pennies

three·pen·ny \'threp-(ə-)nē, 'thrip-, 'thrəp-, *US also* 'thrē-ˌpen-ē\ *adj* **1 :** costing or worth threepence **2 :** of little value : POOR

three R's *n pl* : the fundamentals taught in elementary school; *esp* : reading, writing, and arithmetic

three·score \'thrē-'skō(ə)r, -'skȯ(ə)r\ *adj* : SIXTY

three·some \'thrē-səm\ *n* : a group of three persons or things

three–toed sloth \ˌthrē-ˌtōd-\ *n* : any of a genus of sloths having three claws on each front foot

thren·o·dy \'thren-əd-ē\ *n, pl* **-dies** : a song of lamentation or sorrow : DIRGE

thresh \'thrash, 'thresh\ *vb* **1 :** to separate seed from a harvested plant mechanically : beat out grain from straw **2 :** THRASH ⟨*thresh* over a problem⟩ ⟨*threshed* about in his bed⟩

thresh·er \-ər\ *n* **1 a :** a person who threshes **b :** THRESHING MACHINE **2 :** a large common shark having a long curved upper lobe on its tail with which it is said to thresh the water to round up the fish on which it feeds

thresher 2 (up to 25 ft. long)

threshing machine *n* : a machine for separating grain or seeds from straw

thresh·old \'thresh-ˌ(h)ōld\ *n* **1 :** the sill of a door **2 a :** GATE, DOOR, ENTRANCE **b :** BEGINNING, OUTSET ⟨at the *threshold* of an adventure⟩ **3 :** the point or level at which a physiological or psychological effect begins to be produced ⟨the *threshold* of hearing⟩

threw *past of* THROW

thrice \'thrīs\ *adv* **1 :** three times **2 :** to a high degree

thrift \'thrift\ *n* [from Old Norse, "prosperity", from *thrīfask*, "to thrive"] **1 :** economical management : FRUGALITY **2 :** healthy vigorous growth (as of a plant) **3 :** a tufted stemless herb having heads of pink or white flowers growing on mountains and seacoasts

thrift·less \-ləs\ *adj* : WASTEFUL, IMPROVIDENT

thrift shop *n* : a shop selling secondhand articles that is often run for charitable purposes

thrifty \'thrif-tē\ *adj* **thrift·i·er; -est** **1 :** inclined to save : SAVING **2 :** thriving through industry and frugality : PROSPEROUS **3 :** thriving in health and growth ⟨*thrifty* cattle⟩ ***syn*** see FRUGAL ***ant*** thriftless — **thrift·i·ly** \-tə-lē\ *adv*

thrill \'thril\ *vb* **1 a :** to experience or cause to experience a sudden sharp feeling of excitement **b** : to feel an intense emotional response ⟨*thrill* to splendid sights⟩ **2** : VIBRATE, TREMBLE ⟨voice *thrilling* with emotion⟩ — **thrill** *n*

thrill·er \-ər\ *n* : one that thrills; *esp* : a work of fiction or drama marked by the use of a high degree of action, intrigue, adventure, or suspense

thrips \'thrips\ *n, pl* **thrips** : any of an order of small to tiny sucking insects most of which feed often destructively on plant juices

thrive \'thrīv\ *vb* **throve** \'thrōv\ *or* **thrived**; **thriven** \'thriv-ən\ *also* **thrived**; **thriv·ing** \'thrī-ving\ **1** : to grow vigorously : do well **2** : to gain in wealth or possessions : PROSPER, FLOURISH — **thriv·er** \'thrī-vər\ *n* — **thriv·ing·ly** \-ving-lē\ *adv*

throat \'thrōt\ *n* **1** : the part of the neck in front of the spinal column; *also* : the passage through it to the stomach and lungs **2** : something resembling the throat esp. in being an entrance, a passageway, or a narrowed part ⟨the *throat* of a vase⟩ — **throat·ed** \-əd\ *adj*

throaty \'thrōt-ē\ *adj* **throat·i·er**; **-est** **1** : uttered or produced from low in the throat ⟨a *throaty* voice⟩ **2** : heavy, thick, and deep as if from the throat ⟨*throaty* notes of a horn⟩ — **throat·i·ly** \'thrōt-ə-lē\ *adv*

throb \'thräb\ *vb* **throbbed**; **throb·bing** **1** : to pulsate or pound with abnormal force or rapidity : PALPITATE **2** : to beat or vibrate rhythmically — **throb** *n*

throe \'thrō\ *n* **1** : PANG, SPASM — usu. used in pl. ⟨death *throes*⟩ ⟨*throes* of childbirth⟩ **2** *pl* : a hard or painful struggle ⟨a state in the *throes* of revolution⟩

throm·bo·sis \thräm-'bō-səs\ *n, pl* **-bo·ses** \-'bō-ˌsēz\ : the formation or presence of a blood clot within a blood vessel during life

throm·bus \'thräm-bəs\ *n, pl* **throm·bi** \-ˌbī, -ˌbē\ : a clot of blood formed within a blood vessel and remaining attached to its place of origin — compare EMBOLUS

throne \'thrōn\ *n* **1** : the chair of state of a high dignitary ⟨the king's *throne*⟩ ⟨*throne* of the bishop⟩ **2** : royal power and dignity : SOVEREIGNTY ⟨loyal to the *throne*⟩ — **throne** *vb*

1throng \'thrȯng\ *n* **1** : a multitude of assembled persons : CROWD **2** : a crowding together of many individuals ***syn*** see MULTITUDE

2throng *vb* **thronged**; **throng·ing** \'thrȯng-ing\ **1** : to crowd upon or into ⟨*throng* a stadium⟩ **2** : to crowd together in great numbers ⟨thousands *thronged* to hear him speak⟩

thros·tle \'thräs-əl\ *n* : THRUSH

1throt·tle \'thrät-əl\ *vb* **throt·tled**; **throt·tling** \-(ə-)ling\ **1** : CHOKE, STRANGLE **2 a** : to obstruct the flow of fuel to an engine by closing a valve **b** : to reduce the speed of by this means ⟨*throttled* down the engine⟩ — **throt·tler** \-(ə-)lər\ *n*

2throttle *n* **1** : THROAT 1 **2 a** : a valve controlling the volume of steam or fuel delivered to an engine **b** : a lever controlling this valve

1through *also* **thru** \(')thrü\ *prep* **1 a** : in at one side and out at the opposite side of ⟨drove *through* the town⟩ **b** : by way of ⟨left *through* the window⟩ **c** : in the midst of : AMONG ⟨highway *through* the trees⟩ **2 a** : by means of ⟨succeeded *through* perseverance⟩ **b** : because of ⟨failed *through* ignorance⟩ **3** : over the whole surface or extent of ⟨all *through* the country⟩ ⟨*through* the school⟩ **4 a** : from the beginning to the end of : DURING ⟨*through* the summer⟩ **b** : to and including ⟨Monday *through* Friday⟩

2through *also* **thru** \'thrü\ *adv* **1 a** : from one end or side to the other ⟨his arm was pierced *through*⟩ **b** : over the whole distance ⟨shipped *through* to Des Moines⟩ **2 a** : from beginning to end ⟨read the book *through* at one sitting⟩ **b** : to completion, conclusion, or accomplishment ⟨see it *through*⟩ **3** : to the core : COMPLETELY ⟨he was wet *through*⟩ **4** : into the open : OUT ⟨break *through*⟩

3through *also* **thru** \'thrü\ *adj* **1** : admitting free or continuous passage : DIRECT ⟨a *through* road⟩ **2 a** : going from point of origin to destination without change or reshipment ⟨a *through* train⟩ **b** : of or relating to such movement ⟨a *through* ticket⟩ **3** : initiated at and destined for points outside a local zone ⟨*through* traffic⟩ **4** : FINISHED ⟨he is *through* with the job⟩

1through·out \thrü-'au̇t\ *adv* **1** : in or to every part : EVERYWHERE ⟨of one color *throughout*⟩ **2** : during the whole time or action : from beginning to end ⟨remained loyal *throughout*⟩

2throughout *prep* **1** : in or to every part of ⟨*throughout* the house⟩ **2** : during the whole time of ⟨*throughout* the evening⟩

through·way *var of* THRUWAY

throve *past of* THRIVE

1throw \'thrō\ *vb* **threw** \'thrü\; **thrown** \'thrōn\; **throw·ing** **1 a** : to propel through the air esp. with a quick forward motion of the arm ⟨*threw* the ball over the fence⟩ **b** : DIRECT ⟨*threw* a glance at her mother⟩ **2** : to cause to fall ⟨the wrestler *threw* his opponent⟩ ⟨a horse shied and *threw* his rider⟩ **3** : to put suddenly in a certain condition or position ⟨was *thrown* out of work⟩ **4** : to put on or take off hastily ⟨*throw* on a coat⟩ **5** : to move quickly ⟨*throw* in reinforcements⟩ **6** : to move to an open or closed position ⟨*throw* a switch⟩ **7** : to act as host for : put on ⟨*throw* a party⟩ **8** : to lose (a game or contest) intentionally ⟨paid to *throw* the fight⟩ — **throw·er** \'thrō(-ə)r\ *n*

syn THROW, TOSS, FLING, HURL can mean to propel (as with the arm) swiftly. THROW, a general term, implies no more than propulsion by some force ⟨*thrown* out of the car⟩; TOSS suggests a light or aimless propulsion ⟨*tossed* a coin⟩; FLING suggests vigor in throwing and may in addition suggest a sometimes careless or emotional lack of conscious control ⟨some took off their hats and *flung* them up in the air⟩; HURL suggests a throwing with strong force ⟨wind *hurling* waves against the shore⟩

2throw *n* **1** : an act of throwing, hurling, or flinging **2** : a method of throwing an opponent in wrestling or judo **3** : the distance a missile is or may be thrown ⟨a stone's *throw*⟩ **4** : a loose covering (as for a sofa) **5** : a woman's light wrap

throw away *vb* **1** : to get rid of : DISCARD ⟨*threw away* old clothes⟩ **2** : SQUANDER, WASTE ⟨careful not to *throw away* his money⟩

throw·back \'thrō-ˌbak\ *n* : reversion to an earlier type or phase — **throw back** \-'bak\ *vb*

throw out *vb* **1** : to throw away : DISCARD ⟨when it broke, she *threw* it *out*⟩ **2** : EJECT, EXPEL ⟨*thrown out* of the game for arguing⟩

throw up *vb* **1** : to build hurriedly **2** : VOMIT **3** : to mention repeatedly by way of reproach ⟨*throw up* a past mistake⟩

thru *var of* THROUGH

ə abut	**ər** further	**a** back	**ā** bake
ä cot, cart	**au̇** out	**ch** chin	**e** less	**ē** easy
g gift	**i** trip	**ī** life	**j** joke	**ng** sing	**ō** flow
ȯ flaw	**ȯi** coin	**th** thin	**th** this	**ü** loot
u̇ foot	**y** yet	**yü** few	**yu̇** furious	**zh** vision

thrum *vb* **thrummed**; **thrum·ming** **1** : to play or pluck a stringed instrument idly : STRUM **2** : to sound with a monotonous hum : recite tiresomely or monotonously — **thrum** *n*

thrush \'thrəsh\ *n* : any of a large family of small or medium-sized birds that are mostly of a plain color often with spotted underparts and include many excellent singers

1**thrust** \'thrəst\ *vb* **thrust**; **thrust·ing** **1** : to push or drive with force : SHOVE ⟨*thrust* his way through the crowd⟩ **2** : to cause to enter or pierce something by pushing ⟨*thrust* a dagger into his heart⟩ **3** : to push forth : EXTEND ⟨*thrust* out roots⟩ **4** : to press or force the acceptance of upon someone ⟨*thrust* new responsibilities upon him⟩

2**thrust** *n* **1 a** : a push or lunge with a pointed weapon **b** : a military assault ⟨made a *thrust* deep into enemy positions⟩ **2** : the sideways pressure of one part of a structure against another part (as of an arch against an abutment) **3 a** : the force exerted endwise through a propeller shaft to give forward motion **b** : the forwardly directed reaction force produced by a high-speed jet of fluid discharged rearward from a nozzle (as in a jet airplane or a rocket) **4 a** : a forward or upward push **b** : a movement (as by a group of people) in a specified direction

thru·way *or* **through·way** \'thrü-ˌwā\ *n* : EXPRESSWAY

thud \'thəd\ *n* **1** : BLOW **2** : a dull sound : THUMP — **thud** *vb*

thug \'thəg\ *n* : GANGSTER, KILLER

thu·li·um \'th(y)ü-lē-əm\ *n* : a metallic element of the rare-earth group — see ELEMENT table

1**thumb** \'thəm\ *n* **1 a** : the short thick first digit of the human hand next to the forefinger **b** : the corresponding digit in lower animals **2** : the part of a glove or mitten that covers the thumb

2**thumb** *vb* **1** : to leaf through with the thumb : TURN ⟨*thumb* the pages of a book⟩ **2** : to request or obtain a ride in a passing automobile by signaling with the thumb

1**thumb·nail** \'thəm-ˌnāl, -'nāl\ *n* : the nail of the thumb

2**thumb·nail** \ˌthəm-ˌnāl\ *adj* : CONCISE, BRIEF ⟨a *thumbnail* sketch⟩

thumb·screw \'thəm-ˌskrü\ *n* **1** : a screw having a head that may be turned by the thumb and forefinger **2** : an instrument of torture for compressing the thumb by a screw

thumb·tack \-ˌtak\ *n* : a tack with a broad flat head for pressing into a board or wall with the thumb

thump \'thəmp\ *vb* **1** : to strike or beat with something thick or heavy so as to cause a dull sound **2** : POUND, KNOCK — **thump** *n*

1**thun·der** \'thən-dər\ *n* **1** : the loud sound that follows a flash of lightning and is caused by sudden expansion of the air in the path of the electrical discharge **2** : BANG, RUMBLE ⟨the *thunder* of guns⟩

2**thunder** *vb* **thun·dered**; **thun·der·ing** \-d(ə-)riŋ\ **1 a** : to produce thunder ⟨it *thundered*⟩ **b** : to produce a sound like thunder ⟨horses *thundered* down the road⟩ **2** : ROAR, SHOUT — **thun·der·er** \-dər-ər\ *n*

thun·der·bolt \'thən-dər-ˌbōlt\ *n* : a single discharge of lightning with the accompanying thunder

thun·der·clap \-ˌklap\ *n* **1** : a crash of thunder **2** : something sharp, loud, or sudden

thun·der·cloud \-ˌklau̇d\ *n* : a dark storm cloud that produces lightning and thunder

thun·der·head \-ˌhed\ *n* : a rounded mass of cumulus cloud often appearing before a thunderstorm

thunder lizard *n* : BRONTOSAURUS

thun·der·ous \'thən-d(ə-)rəs\ *adj* **1** : producing thunder **2** : making or accompanied by a noise like thunder ⟨*thunderous* applause⟩ — **thun·der·ous·ly** *adv*

thun·der·show·er \'thən-dər-ˌshau̇(-ə)r\ *n* : a shower accompanied by lightning and thunder

thun·der·storm \-ˌstȯrm\ *n* : a storm accompanied by lightning and thunder

thun·der·struck \-ˌstrək\ *adj* : stunned as if struck by a thunderbolt : ASTONISHED

Thur *or* **Thurs** *abbr* Thursday

thu·ri·ble \'th(y)u̇r-ə-bəl, 'thər-\ *n* : CENSER

thu·ri·fer \-ə-fər\ *n* : one who carries a censer

Thu·rin·gian \th(y)u̇-'rin-j(ē-)ən\ *adj* : of, relating to, or characteristic of Thuringia or its people — **Thuringian** *n*

Thurs·day \'thərz-dē\ *n* [from Old English *thunresdæg*, *thūrsdæg*, meaning "day of Thor", from *Thunor*, *Thūr* "Thor", god of thunder] : the 5th day of the week

thus \'t͟həs\ *adv* **1** : in this or that manner or way **2** : to this degree or extent : so ⟨a mild winter *thus* far⟩ **3** : becuase of this or that : HENCE **4** : as an example

thwack \'thwak\ *vb* : to strike with or as if with something flat or heavy : WHACK — **thwack** *n*

1**thwart** \'thwȯrt, *naut often* 'thȯrt\ *adv* : ATHWART

2**thwart** *adj* : situated or placed across something else : TRANSVERSE, OBLIQUE

3**thwart** *vb* **1** : to stand in the way of : hinder by opposing **2** : BLOCK, DEFEAT ***syn*** see FRUSTRATE — **thwart·er** *n*

4**thwart** *n* : a rower's seat extending athwart a boat

thy \(ˌ)t͟hī\ *adj*, *archaic* : of or relating to thee or thyself esp. as possessor or agent or as object of an action — used esp. in biblical or poetic language

thyme \'tīm, 'thīm\ *n* : any of a genus of mints with small pungent aromatic leaves; *esp* : one grown for use in seasoning and formerly in medicine

thy·mine \'thī-ˌmēn\ *n* : a base regularly present in DNA

thy·mus \'thī-məs\ *n*, *pl* **thy·mus·es** *or* **thy·mi** \-ˌmī\ : a glandular structure at the base of the neck that is needed for adequate formation of antibodies in most young vertebrates but tends to disappear or become rudimentary in the adult

1**thy·roid** \'thī-ˌrȯid\ *adj* [from Greek *thyreoeidēs* "shield-shaped" (applied to the thyroid cartilage), from *thyreos* "oblong shield", from *thyra* "door"] : of, relating to, or being a thyroid gland

2**thyroid** *n* **1** : THYROID GLAND **2** : a preparation of mammalian thyroid gland used medicinally

thyroid gland *n* : a large endocrine gland of most vertebrates that lies at the base of the neck and produces an iodine-containing hormone which affects esp. growth, development, and metabolic rate

thy·rox·in *also* **thy·rox·ine** \thī-'räk-sən, -ˌsēn\ *n* : the hormone of the thyroid gland or a preparation or derivative of this used to treat thyroid disorders

thy·sa·nop·ter·an \ˌthī-sə-'näp-tə-rən\ *n* : THRIPS — **thysanopteran** *adj* — **thy·sa·nop·ter·ous** \-rəs\ *adj*

thy·self \t͟hī-'self\ *pron*, *archaic* : YOURSELF

ti \'tē\ *n* : the 7th note of the diatonic scale

ti·ara \tē-'ar-ə, -'er-, -'är-\ *n* **1** : a 3-tiered crown worn by the pope **2** : a decorative band or semicircular ornament for the head for formal wear by women

Ti·bet·an \tə-'bet-ən\ *n* **1** : a member of the Mongoloid native race of Tibet **2** : the language of the Tibetan people — **Tibetan** *adj*

T

tib·ia \'tib-ē-ə\ *n, pl* **-i·ae** \-ē-ˌē, -ē-ˌī\ *also* **-i·as** : SHINBONE — **tib·i·al** \-ē-əl\ *adj*
tib·io·fib·u·la \ˌtib-ē-ō-'fib-yə-lə\ *n* : a single bone that replaces the tibia and fibula in a frog or toad
tic \'tik\ *n* : local and habitual twitching of particular muscles esp. of the face
¹**tick** \'tik\ *n* **1** : any of numerous bloodsucking arachnids that are larger than the related mites, attach themselves to warm-blooded vertebrates to feed, and include important carriers of infectious diseases **2** : any of several usu. wingless bloodsucking parasitic dipterous insects

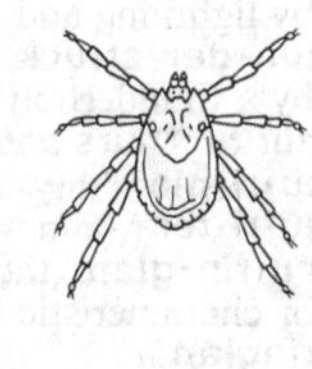

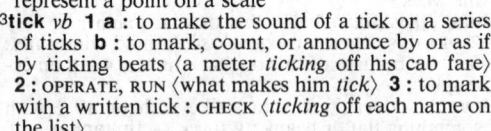

tick 1 (less than one inch long)

²**tick** *n* **1** : a light rhythmic audible tap or beat ⟨the *tick* of a clock⟩ **2** : a small spot or mark used to direct attention to something, to check an item on a list, or to represent a point on a scale
³**tick** *vb* **1 a** : to make the sound of a tick or a series of ticks **b** : to mark, count, or announce by or as if by ticking beats ⟨a meter *ticking* off his cab fare⟩ **2** : OPERATE, RUN ⟨what makes him *tick*⟩ **3** : to mark with a written tick : CHECK ⟨*ticking* off each name on the list⟩
⁴**tick** *n* **1 a** : the fabric case of a mattress, pillow, or bolster **b** : a mattress consisting of a tick and its filling **2** : TICKING
⁵**tick** *n* : CREDIT, TRUST ⟨bought on *tick*⟩
tick·er \'tik-ər\ *n* **1** : WATCH **2** : a telegraphic receiving instrument that automatically prints off stock quotations or news on a paper ribbon **3** *slang* : HEART
¹**tick·et** \'tik-ət\ *n* [from French *étiquette*, from medieval French *estiquier* "to attach", from Dutch *steken* "to stick", from the same source as English *stick*] **1** : TAG, LABEL ⟨price *ticket*⟩ **2** : a summons or warning issued to a traffic offender ⟨got a *ticket* for speeding⟩ **3** : a document or token showing that a fare or admission fee has been paid **4** : a list of candidates for nomination or election **5** : a slip or card recording a transaction or undertaking or giving instructions ⟨sales *ticket*⟩ ⟨repair *ticket*⟩
²**ticket** *vb* **1** : to attach a ticket to : LABEL **2** : to serve with a traffic ticket
tick·ing \'tik-ing\ *n* : a strong linen or cotton fabric used in upholstering and as a covering for mattresses and pillows
tick·le \'tik-əl\ *vb* **tick·led**; **tick·ling** \-(ə-)ling\ **1** : to have a tingling or prickling sensation ⟨my back *tickles*⟩ **2 a** : to excite or stir up agreeably : PLEASE ⟨food that *tickles* the palate⟩ **b** : to provoke to laughter or merriment : AMUSE ⟨the audience was *tickled* by his jokes⟩ **3** : to touch a body part lightly so as to excite the surface nerves and cause uneasiness, laughter, or spasmodic movements — **tickle** *n* — **tick·ler** \'tik-(ə-)lər\ *n*
tick·lish \'tik-(ə-)lish\ *adj* **1** : sensitive to tickling **2** : TOUCHY, OVERSENSITIVE ⟨*ticklish* about his baldness⟩ **3** : requiring delicate handling ⟨a *ticklish* subject⟩ — **tick·lish·ly** *adv* — **tick·lish·ness** *n*
tick·tack·toe *also* **tic–tac–toe** \ˌtik-ˌtak-'tō\ *n* : a game in which two players alternately put crosses and zeros in compartments of a figure formed by two vertical lines crossing two horizontal lines and each tries to get a row of three crosses or three zeros before the opponent does

ə abut	ər further	a back	ā bake
ä cot, cart	aů out	ch chin	e less
ē easy	g gift	i trip	ī life
j joke	ng sing	ō flow	ȯ flaw
ȯi coin	th thin	t͟h this	ü loot
ů foot	y yet	yü few	yů furious
zh vision			

tid·al \'tīd-əl\ *adj* : of or relating to tides : periodically rising and falling or flowing and ebbing ⟨*tidal* waters⟩
tidal wave *n* **1** : an unusually high sea wave that sometimes follows an earthquake **2** : an unusual rise of water alongshore due to strong winds
tid·bit \'tid-ˌbit\ *n* **1** : a choice morsel of food **2** : a choice or pleasing bit (as of news)
tid·dle·dy·winks *or* **tid·dly·winks** \'tid-əl-(d)ē-ˌwing(k)s, 'tid-lē-ˌwing(k)s\ *n* : a game the object of which is to snap small disks from a flat surface into a small container
¹**tide** \'tīd\ *n* [originally meaning "time", from Old English *tīd*] **1** : the alternate rising and falling of the surface of the ocean that occurs twice a day and is caused by the gravitational attraction of the sun and moon occurring unequally on different parts of the earth **2** : the flow of the incoming or outgoing tide ⟨carried away by the *tide*⟩ **3** : something that fluctuates like the tides of the sea ⟨the *tides* of fortune⟩

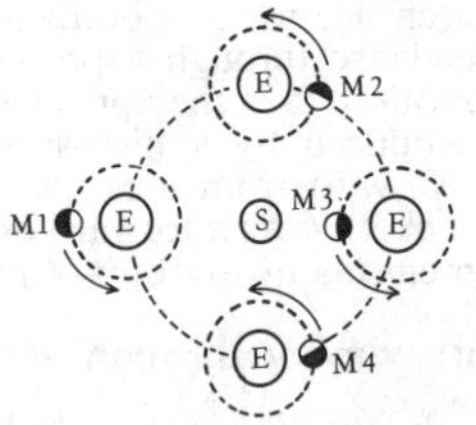

tides 1: M1 and M3, position of moon at spring tides; M2 and M4, moon at neap tides

²**tide** *vb* : to enable to overcome or endure a difficulty ⟨money to *tide* him over the emergency⟩
tide·land \'tīd-ˌland, -lənd\ *n* : land overflowed during flood tide
tide·wa·ter \-ˌwȯt-ər, -ˌwät-\ *n* **1** : water overflowing land at flood tide **2** : low-lying coastal land
tid·ings \'tīd-ingz\ *n pl* : NEWS ⟨good *tidings*⟩
¹**ti·dy** \'tīd-ē\ *adj* **ti·di·er**; **-est** **1** : well ordered and cared for : NEAT, ORDERLY **2** : LARGE, SUBSTANTIAL ⟨a *tidy* price⟩
²**tidy** *vb* **ti·died**; **ti·dy·ing** **1** : to put in order ⟨*tidy* up a room⟩ **2** : to make things tidy ⟨*tidying* up after supper⟩
³**tidy** *n, pl* **tidies** : a piece of fancywork used to protect the back, arms, or headrest of a chair or sofa from wear or soiling
¹**tie** \'tī\ *n* **1** : a line, ribbon, or cord used for fastening, uniting, or drawing something closed; *esp* : SHOELACE **2 a** : a structural element (as a beam) holding two pieces together **b** : one of the transverse supports to which railroad rails are fastened **3** : a connecting link : a bond of kinship or affection ⟨family *ties*⟩ **4** : a curved line that joins two musical notes indicating the same pitch used to denote a single tone sustained through the time value of the two **5** : an equality in number : DEADLOCK ⟨the game ended in a *tie*⟩ **6** : NECKTIE
²**tie** *vb* **tied**; **ty·ing** \'tī-ing\ *or* **tie·ing** **1 a** : to fasten, attach, or close by means of a tie ⟨*tied* the horse to a tree⟩ ⟨*tied* his shoes⟩ **b** : to form a knot or bow in ⟨*tie* your scarf⟩ **2** : to unite musical notes by a tie **3** : to restrain or constrain the acts of ⟨responsibilities *tied* him down⟩ **4 a** : to make or have an equal score with in a contest ⟨the two teams *tied* for first place⟩ **b** : to come up with something equal to : EQUAL ⟨*tied* the score⟩

tie–dye·ing \'tī-ˌdī-ing\ *n* : a hand method of ornamenting textiles by tying portions of the fabric or yarn so that they will not absorb the dye — **tie–dye** \-ˌdī\ *vb* — **tie–dyed** *adj*

[1]**tier** \'ti(ə)r\ *n* : a row, rank, or layer of articles; *esp* : one of two or more rows arranged one above another — **tiered** \'ti(ə)rd\ *adj*

[2]**tier** *vb* **1** : to place or arrange in tiers **2** : to rise in tiers

[3]**ti·er** \'tī(-ə)r\ *n* : a person or thing that ties

tie–up \'tī-ˌəp\ *n* **1** : a suspension of traffic or business **2** : CONNECTION, ASSOCIATION

tie up \-'əp\ *vb* **1** : to attach, fasten, or bind securely **2 a** : to use in such a manner as to make unavailable for other purposes ⟨money *tied up* in stocks⟩ **b** : to restrain from operation or progress ⟨traffic was *tied up* for miles⟩ **3** : DOCK ⟨the ferry *ties up* at the south slip⟩ **4** : to place in or assume a relationship with something else ⟨this *ties up* with what you said before⟩

tiff \'tif\ *n* : a petty quarrel

ti·ger \'tī-gər\ *n, pl* **tigers** *also* **tiger** **1 a** : a large Asiatic flesh-eating mammal related to the domestic cat and having a tawny coat transversely striped with black **b** : any of several large wildcats (as the jaguar or cougar) **c** : TIGER CAT 2 **2** : a fierce person or quality ⟨aroused the *tiger* in him⟩

tiger 1a
(up to 5 ft. at shoulder)

tiger beetle *n* : any of numerous active predaceous beetles having larvae that tunnel in the soil

tiger cat *n* **1** : any of various wildcats (as the ocelot) of moderate size and variegated coloration **2** : a striped or sometimes blotched tabby cat

ti·ger·ish \'tī-g(ə-)rish\ *adj* : of or resembling a tiger : FIERCE

tiger lily *n* : a common Asiatic lily widely grown for its nodding orange-colored flowers densely spotted with black or purple

tiger moth *n* : any of a family of stout-bodied moths usu. with broad striped or spotted wings

tiger shark *n* : a large brown or gray shark of warm seas that is often a man-eater

[1]**tight** \'tīt\ *adj* **1** : so close in structure as not to permit passage of a fluid or light ⟨a *tight* roof⟩ **2 a** : fixed very firmly in place ⟨loosen a *tight* jar cover⟩ **b** : TAUT ⟨*tight* drumhead⟩ **c** : fitting too closely for comfort or free movement ⟨*tight* shoes⟩ **3** : difficult to get through or out of : TRYING ⟨in a *tight* corner⟩ **4 a** : firm in control ⟨kept a *tight* hand on all his affairs⟩ **b** : STINGY, MISERLY **5** : packed or compressed to the limit ⟨*tight* formation⟩ **6** : low in supply : SCARCE ⟨*tight* loan money⟩ **7** : DRUNK — **tight·ly** *adv* — **tight·ness** *n*

syn TIGHT, TAUT, TENSE can mean drawn or stretched to the limit. TIGHT may imply a binding or constricting encirclement; TAUT suggests pulling (as of a rope) until there is no give or slack; TENSE adds to TAUT the suggestion of strain impairing normal functioning ***ant*** loose

[2]**tight** *adv* **1** : TIGHTLY, FIRMLY, HARD ⟨door was shut *tight*⟩ **2** : SOUNDLY ⟨sleep *tight*⟩

tight·en \'tīt-ən\ *vb* **tight·ened**; **tight·en·ing** \-(ə-)ning\ : to make or become tight or tighter — **tight·en·er** \-(ə-)nər\ *n*

tight·fist·ed \'tīt-'fis-təd\ *adj* : MISERLY, STINGY

tight–lipped \-'lipt\ *adj* : TACITURN, SILENT

tight·rope \'tīt-ˌrōp\ *n* : a rope or wire stretched taut for acrobats to perform on

tights \'tīts\ *n pl* : a skintight garment covering the body esp. from the waist down

tight·wad \'tīt-ˌwäd\ *n* : a stingy person

tight·wire \-ˌwī(ə)r\ *n* : a tightrope made of wire

ti·gress \'tī-grəs\ *n* : a female tiger

tike *var of* TYKE

til·de \'til-də\ *n* : a mark ~ placed esp. over the letter *n* (as in Spanish *señor*) to denote a sound that is approximately \ny\

tile \'tīl\ *n* [from Old English *tigele*, from Latin *tegula*, from *tegere* "to cover", from the same prehistoric root as English *thatch*] **1** *pl* **tiles** *or* **tile** **a** : a flat or curved piece of fired clay, stone, or concrete used esp. for roofs, floors, or walls **b** : a hollow or a concave earthenware or concrete piece used for a drain **2** : a surface of tiles **3** : a thin piece of resilient material (as linoleum or rubber) for covering floors or walls — **tile** *vb* — **til·er** *n*

til·ing \'tī-ling\ *n* **1** : the act of one who tiles **2 a** : TILES **b** : a surface of tiles

[1]**till** \təl, (ˌ)til\ *prep or conj* : UNTIL

[2]**till** \'til\ *vb* : to work by plowing, sowing, and raising crops from : CULTIVATE — **till·a·ble** \-ə-bəl\ *adj*

[3]**till** \'til\ *n* : a receptacle (as a drawer) for money

till·age \'til-ij\ *n* **1** : the process of tilling land **2** : cultivated land

[1]**till·er** \'til-ər\ *n* : one that tills : CULTIVATOR

[2]**til·ler** \'til-ər\ *n* : a lever used to turn the rudder of a boat from side to side

til·ler·man \'til-ər-mən\ *n* : one in charge of a tiller

[1]**tilt** \'tilt\ *vb* **1** : to cause to slope : INCLINE **2** : to engage in a tilt : JOUST — **tilt·er** *n*

[2]**tilt** *n* **1** : an exercise on horseback in which two combatants charging with lances try to unhorse each other : JOUST **2** : an encounter (as with words) bringing about a sharp collision **3** : SPEED ⟨at full *tilt*⟩ **4** : the act of tilting : the state or position of being tilted

tilth \'tilth\ *n* **1** : cultivation of the soil **2** : cultivated land : TILLAGE **3** : the state of being tilled

[1]**tim·ber** \'tim-bər\ *n* **1** : wood for use in making something **2** : a usu. large piece of squared or dressed wood **3** : wooded land or growing trees constituting a source of timber — **timber** *adj*

[2]**timber** *vb* **tim·bered**; **tim·ber·ing** \'tim-b(ə-)ring\ : to frame, cover, or support with timbers

tim·bered \'tim-bərd\ *adj* **1** : made of or covered with timber **2** : having walls framed by exposed timbers

tim·ber·land \'tim-bər-ˌland\ *n* : wooded land

tim·ber·line \-ˌlīn\ *n* : the upper limit of tree growth in mountains or high latitudes

timber wolf *n* : a large usu. gray No. American wolf extinct over much of the eastern and southern parts of its range

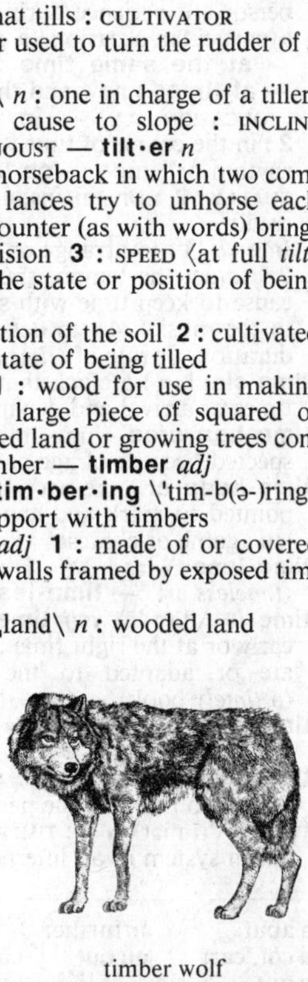

timber wolf
(about 3 ft. at shoulder)

tim·bre \'tam-bər, 'tim-\ *n* **1** : the distinctive quality given to a sound by its overtones **2** : the tone distinctive of a singing voice or a musical instrument

tim·brel \'tim-brəl\ *n* : a small hand drum or tambourine

[1]**time** \'tīm\ *n* **1 a** : the period during which an action, process, or condition exists or continues : DURATION **b** : LEISURE ⟨*time* for reading⟩ **2** : the point or period when something occurs : OCCASION ⟨remember the *time* you entered the pie-eating contest⟩ **3** : an appointed or customary moment or hour for something to happen, begin, or end ⟨arrived on *time*⟩ **4 a** : an historical period : AGE ⟨in grandfather's *time*⟩ **b** : conditions at present or at some specified period ⟨*times* are hard⟩ ⟨move with the *times*⟩ **c** : the present time ⟨issues of the *time*⟩ **5** : a prison sentence ⟨doing *time* for robbery⟩ **6** : the grouping of the beats of music : RHYTHM ⟨keep *time* with the music⟩ **7 a** : a moment, hour, day, or year as indicated by a clock or calendar ⟨what *time* is it⟩ **b** : any of various systems for reckoning time **8 a** : one of a series of recurring instances or repeated actions ⟨told him many *times*⟩ **b** *pl* : multiplied instances ⟨five *times* greater⟩ **c** : TURN ⟨three *times* at bat⟩ **9** : a person's experience during a specified period or on a particular occasion ⟨a good *time*⟩ **10** : TIME-OUT — **at the same time** : HOWEVER, NEVERTHELESS — **at times** : now and then — **from time to time** : OCCASIONALLY — **in time 1** : early enough **2** : in the course of time : EVENTUALLY **3** : in correct rhythm or tempo — **on time 1** : PUNCTUAL, PUNCTUALLY **2** : on an installment payment plan : on credit

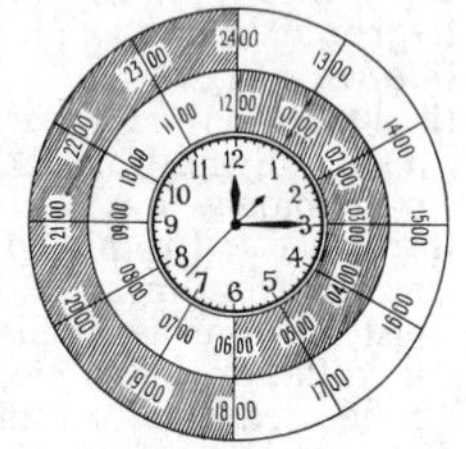

time 7b: a standard 12-hour dial surrounded by bands to show equivalent 24-hour time

[2]**time** *vb* **1** : to arrange or set the time of : SCHEDULE **2** : to set the tempo, speed, or duration of **3** : to cause to keep time with something ⟨*timed* his steps to the music⟩ **4** : to determine or record the time, duration, or rate of ⟨*timed* the race⟩

time clock *n* : a clock that mechanically records the times of arrival and departure of workers

time–hon·ored \'tīm-ˌän-ərd\ *adj* : honored or respected because of age or long-established usage

time·keep·er \-ˌkē-pər\ *n* **1** : TIMEPIECE **2** : one appointed to mark and announce the time in an athletic game or contest

time·less \-ləs\ *adj* **1** : UNENDING **2** : AGELESS ⟨*timeless* art⟩ — **time·less·ly** *adv*

time·ly \'tīm-lē\ *adj* **time·li·er**; **-est 1** : coming early or at the right time : OPPORTUNE **2** : appropriate or adapted to the times or the occasion ⟨a *timely* book⟩ — **time·li·ness** *n*

time–out \'tīm-'aüt\ *n* : a suspension of play in an athletic game

time·piece \'tīm-ˌpēs\ *n* : a device (as a clock or watch) to measure the passage of time

tim·er \'tī-mər\ *n* **1** : TIMEPIECE **2** : a device in the ignition system of an internal-combustion engine that causes the spark to be produced in the cylinder at the correct time **3** : a device (as a clock) that indicates by an audible signal the end of an interval of time or that automatically starts or stops a device

times \ˌtīmz\ *prep* : multiplied by ⟨two *times* seven is fourteen⟩

time·ta·ble \'tīm-ˌtā-bəl\ *n* **1** : a table of departure and arrival times of trains, buses, or airplanes **2** : a list showing a planned order or sequence

time·worn \-ˌwōrn, -ˌwȯrn\ *adj* : worn or impaired by time : HACKNEYED, STALE ⟨a *timeworn* joke⟩

time zone *n* : a geographical region within which the same standard time is used

tim·id \'tim-əd\ *adj* : feeling or showing a lack of courage or self-confidence : FEARFUL, SHY — **ti·mid·i·ty** \tə-'mid-ət-ē\ *n* — **tim·id·ly** \'tim-əd-lē\ *adv*

tim·ing \'tī-ming\ *n* **1** : selection for maximum effect of the precise moment for beginning or doing something **2** : observation and recording (as by a stopwatch) of the elapsed time of an act, action, or process

tim·o·rous \'tim-ə-rəs\ *adj* : TIMID, FEARFUL — **tim·o·rous·ly** *adv* — **tim·o·rous·ness** *n*

tim·o·thy \'tim-ə-thē\ *n* : a European grass with long round spikes widely grown for hay

Tim·o·thy \'tim-ə-thē\ *n* — see BIBLE table

tim·pa·ni \'tim-pə-nē\ *n pl* : a set of two or three kettledrums played by one performer — **tim·pa·nist** \-nəst\ *n*

[1]**tin** \'tin\ *n* **1** : a bluish white lustrous crystalline metallic element that is malleable and ductile at ordinary temperatures and that is used as a protective coating in tinfoil and in soft solders and alloys — see ELEMENT table **2 a** : a box, can, pan, vessel, or a sheet made of tinplate **b** *chiefly Brit* : a sealed can holding food — **tin** *adj*

[2]**tin** *vb* **tinned**; **tin·ning 1** : to cover or plate with tin or an alloy of tin **2** *chiefly Brit* : to put up or pack in tins : CAN

tinct *abbr* tincture

tinc·ture \'ting(k)-chər\ *n* **1** : a substance that colors, dyes, or stains **2** : a slight admixture : TRACE **3** : an alcoholic solution of a medicinal substance ⟨*tincture* of iodine⟩

tin·der \'tin-dər\ *n* : a very flammable substance that can be used as kindling

tin·der·box \-ˌbäks\ *n* : a metal box for holding tinder and usu. a flint and steel for striking a spark

tine \'tīn\ *n* : a slender pointed projecting part : PRONG ⟨the *tines* of a fork⟩

tin·foil \'tin-ˌfȯil\ *n* : a thin metal sheeting usu. of aluminum or tin-lead alloy

ting \'ting\ *n* : a high-pitched sound (as from a light stroke on a glass) — **ting** *vb*

tinge \'tinj\ *vb* **tinged**; **tinge·ing** *or* **ting·ing** \'tin-jing\ **1** : to color slightly : TINT ⟨green *tinged* with blue⟩ **2** : to affect or modify with a slight odor or taste ⟨meat *tinged* with garlic⟩ — **tinge** *n*

tin·gle \'ting-gəl\ *vb* **tin·gled**; **tin·gling** \'ting-g(ə-)ling\ : to feel or cause a ringing, stinging, prickling, or thrilling sensation ⟨the story *tingles* with suspense⟩ ⟨made our toes *tingle*⟩ ⟨trumpets *tingled* in their ears⟩ — **tingle** *n* — **tin·gly** \'ting-g(ə-)lē\ *adj*

[1]**tin·ker** \'ting-kər\ *n* **1** : a usu. itinerant mender of household utensils (as pots and pans) **2** : an unskilled mender : BUNGLER

[2]**tinker** *vb* **tin·kered**; **tin·ker·ing** \'ting-k(ə-)ring\ : to work in the manner of a tinker; *esp* : to repair or adjust something in an unskilled or experimental manner ⟨*tinkering* with his radio⟩ — **tin·ker·er** \-kər-ər\ *n*

tin·kle \'ting-kəl\ *vb* **tin·kled**; **tin·kling** \-k(ə-)ling\

1 : to make or emit a tinkle 2 : to cause to make a tinkle — **tinkle** *n*

tin·ny \'tin-ē\ *adj* **tin·ni·er**; **-est** 1 : resembling or suggestive of tin : LIGHT, CHEAP 2 : thin in tone : METALLIC ⟨a *tinny* voice⟩

tin·plate \'tin-'plāt\ *n* : thin sheet iron or steel coated with tin — **tin–plate** *vb*

1**tin·sel** \'tin(t)-səl\ *n* 1 : a thread, strip, or sheet of metal, paper, or plastic used to produce a glittering and sparkling appearance (as in fabrics, yarns, or decorations) 2 : something superficially attractive but of little real worth

2**tinsel** *adj* 1 : made of or covered with tinsel 2 : cheaply gaudy : TAWDRY

3**tinsel** *vb* **tin·seled** *or* **tin·selled**; **tin·sel·ing** *or* **tin·sel·ling** \'tin(t)-s(ə-)liŋ\ 1 : to adorn with tinsel 2 : to impart a superficial brightness to

tin·smith \'tin-ˌsmith\ *n* : a worker who makes or repairs things of tin

tint \'tint\ *n* 1 : a slight or pale coloring : TINGE ⟨white without a *tint* of yellow⟩ 2 : a light color or shade ⟨pale *tints* of red⟩ — **tint** *vb* — **tint·er** *n*

tin·ware \'tin-ˌwa(ə)r, -ˌwe(ə)r\ *n* : articles of tinplate

ti·ny \'tī-nē\ *adj* **ti·ni·er**; **-est** : very small or diminutive : MINUTE — **ti·ni·ness** *n*

1**tip** \'tip\ *n* 1 : the pointed or rounded end of something : END 2 : a small piece or part serving as an end, cap, or point — **tip·less** \-ləs\ *adj*

2**tip** *vb* **tipped**; **tip·ping** 1 : to furnish with a tip 2 : to cover or adorn the tip of

3**tip** *vb* **tipped**; **tip·ping** 1 : OVERTURN, UPSET ⟨*tipped* over a glass⟩ 2 : LEAN, SLANT, TILT ⟨the bench *tips* on the uneven floor⟩ 3 : to raise and tilt forward in salute ⟨*tipped* his hat⟩

4**tip** *n* : the act or an instance of tipping : TILT

5**tip** *n* : a light touch or blow : TAP

6**tip** *vb* **tipped**; **tip·ping** 1 : to strike lightly : TAP 2 : to hit a baseball a glancing blow with the edge of a bat

7**tip** *vb* **tipped**; **tip·ping** 1 : to give a gratuity to ⟨*tip* a waitress⟩ 2 : to give gratuities ⟨never *tipped*⟩

8**tip** *n* : a gift or small sum of money given for a service performed or anticipated : GRATUITY

9**tip** *n* : an item of authoritative or confidential information ⟨a *tip* on a sure winner in a horse race⟩

10**tip** *vb* **tipped**; **tip·ping** : to give information or advice about or to often in a secret or confidential manner ⟨*tipped* off as to what would happen⟩

ti·pi \'tē-(ˌ)pē\ *var of* TEPEE

tip–off \'tip-ˌof\ *n* : WARNING, TIP

tip·per \'tip-ər\ *n* : one that tips

tip·pet \'tip-ət\ *n* 1 : a long hanging part of a garment (as on a sleeve or cape) 2 : a shoulder cape usu. with hanging ends

tip·ple \'tip-əl\ *vb* **tip·pled**; **tip·pling** \-(ə-)liŋ\ : to drink intoxicating liquor esp. frequently in small amounts — **tipple** *n* — **tip·pler** \-(ə-)lər\ *n*

tip·sy \'tip-sē\ *adj* **tip·si·er**; **-est** : unsteady, staggering, or foolish from the effects of alcohol : somewhat drunk

1**tip·toe** \'tip-ˌtō, -'tō\ *n* 1 : the tip of a toe 2 : the ends of the toes

2**tiptoe** *adv* : on or as if on tiptoe ⟨walk *tiptoe*⟩

3**tiptoe** *adj* 1 : marked by standing or walking on tiptoe 2 : CAUTIOUS, STEALTHY ⟨a *tiptoe* approach⟩

4**tiptoe** *vb* : to stand, raise oneself, or walk on or as if on tiptoe

1**tip–top** \'tip-'täp, -ˌtäp\ *n* : the highest point : SUMMIT

2**tip–top** *adj* : EXCELLENT, FIRST-RATE ⟨in *tip-top* shape⟩ — **tip–top** *adv*

ti·rade \tī-'rād, 'tī-ˌ\ *n* : a long violent usu. abusive speech

1**tire** \'tī(ə)r\ *vb* 1 : to become weary 2 : to exhaust or greatly decrease the physical strength of 3 : to wear out the patience or attention of : BORE

syn TIRE, WEARY, FATIGUE, EXHAUST can mean to make disinclined or unable to continue because of loss of strength or patience. TIRE, the most general term, implies depletion of strength or patience without in itself suggesting to what degree; WEARY implies a point reached at which one feels unable to endure more of the same thing ⟨*wearied* with unending complaints⟩; FATIGUE suggests a high degree of tiredness brought on by excessive effort or long strain; EXHAUST suggests an utter using up of energy that leaves both body and mind incapable of further effort

2**tire** *n* 1 : a metal hoop forming the tread of a wheel 2 : a rubber cushion that is filled with compressed air and that encircles a wheel ⟨automobile *tires*⟩

1**tired** \'tī(ə)rd\ *adj* : FATIGUED, WEARY — **tired·ly** *adv* — **tired·ness** *n*

2**tired** *adj* : having tires

tire·less \'tī(ə)r-ləs\ *adj* : UNTIRING — **tire·less·ly** *adv*

tire·some \'tī(ə)r-səm\ *adj* : WEARISOME, TEDIOUS — **tire·some·ly** *adv*

tis·sue \'tish-ü\ *n* [from Old French *tissu*, from the past participle of *tistre* "to weave", from Latin *texere*, the source of English *textile*] 1 : a fine lightweight often sheer fabric 2 : MESH, NETWORK, WEB ⟨a *tissue* of lies⟩ 3 : a piece of soft absorbent paper used esp. as a handkerchief or for removing cosmetics 4 : a mass or layer of cells usu. of one kind that together with the substance uniting or enclosing them form the basic structural materials of a plant or an animal — compare ORGAN; CONNECTIVE TISSUE, EPITHELIUM, PARENCHYMA

tissue paper *n* : a thin gauzy paper usu. used to wrap delicate articles

1**tit** \'tit\ *n* : TEAT

2**tit** *n* 1 : TITMOUSE 2 : any of various small plump often long-tailed birds

ti·tan \'tīt-ən\ *n* 1 *cap* : one of a family of giants overthrown by the Olympian gods 2 : one of gigantic size, power, or achievement

ti·tan·ic \tī-'tan-ik\ *adj* : of great magnitude, force, or power : COLOSSAL

ti·ta·ni·um \tī-'tā-nē-əm, tə-\ *n* : a silvery gray light strong metallic element found combined in various minerals and used in alloys (as steel) — see ELEMENT table

titanium dioxide *n* : an oxide of titanium used esp. as a white pigment

tit·bit \'tit-ˌbit\ *var of* TIDBIT

1**tithe** \'tīth\ *vb* 1 : to pay or give a tithe 2 : to levy a tithe on — **tith·er** *n*

2**tithe** *n* [from Old English *teogotha* "tenth", from the source of Old English *tīen* "ten"] : a tenth part paid in kind or money as a voluntary contribution or as a tax esp. for the support of a religious establishment

tit·il·late \'tit-ə-ˌlāt\ *vb* 1 : TICKLE 2 : to excite pleasurably — **tit·il·la·tion** \ˌtit-ə-'lā-shən\ *n*

tit·lark \'tit-ˌlärk\ *n* : PIPIT

1**ti·tle** \'tīt-əl\ *n* 1 a : RIGHT, PRIVILEGE; *esp* : the elements constituting legal ownership b : the instrument (as a deed) that is evidence of a right 2 : the distinguishing name of a written, printed, or filmed production or of a musical composition or a work of art 3 : an appellation of dignity or honor attached to a person or family ⟨a *title* of nobility⟩ 4 : CHAMPIONSHIP 2 ⟨won the batting *title*⟩ ⟨will defend his heavyweight *title*⟩

[2]**title** *vb* **ti·tled; ti·tling** \'tīt-(ə-)liŋ\ **:** to designate or call by a title
ti·tled \'tīt-əld\ *adj* **:** having a title esp. of nobility
ti·tle·hold·er \'tīt-əl-ˌhōl-dər\ *n* **:** one that holds a title; *esp* **:** CHAMPION
title page *n* **:** a page of a book bearing the title
title role *n* **:** a part or character that gives a play or movie its name
ti·tlist \'tīt-(ə-)ləst\ *n* **:** TITLEHOLDER
tit·mouse \'tit-ˌmau̇s\ *n, pl* **tit·mice** \-ˌmīs\ **:** any of numerous small tree-dwelling and insect-eating birds that are related to the nuthatches but have longer tails
tit–tat–toe \ˌti-ˌta(t)-'tō\ *var of* TICKTACKTOE
tit·ter \'tit-ər\ *vb* **1 :** to give vent to partly suppressed laughter **2 :** to laugh in a nervous manner esp. at a high pitch — **titter** *n*
tit·tle \'tit-əl\ *n* **1 :** a point or small sign (as the dot over an *i*) used as a diacritical mark in writing or printing **2 :** a very small part
tit·tle–tat·tle \'tit-əl-ˌtat-əl\ *n* **:** GOSSIP, PRATTLE — **tittle–tattle** *vb*
tit·u·lar \'tich-ə-lər\ *adj* **1 :** existing in title only **:** NOMINAL ⟨the *titular* head of a nation⟩ **2 :** of, relating to, or constituting a title — **tit·u·lar·ly** *adv*
Ti·tus \'tīt-əs\ *n* — see BIBLE table
tiz·zy \'tiz-ē\ *n, pl* **tizzies :** a highly excited and distracted state of mind
TL *abbr* throws left
tn *abbr* **1** ton **2** town
TN *abbr* Tennessee
tnpk *abbr* turnpike
TNT \ˌtē-ˌen-'tē\ *n* **:** a high explosive
[1]**to** \tə, tu̇, (')tü\ *prep* **1 a :** in the direction of ⟨walked *to* school⟩ ⟨on the way *to* town⟩ **b :** close against **:** ON ⟨applied polish *to* the table⟩ **c :** as far as ⟨stripped *to* the waist⟩ **2 a :** for the purpose of **:** FOR ⟨came *to* our aid⟩ **b :** in honor of ⟨a toast *to* the bride⟩ **c :** so as to become or bring about ⟨broken *to* pieces⟩ ⟨beaten *to* death⟩ **3 a :** BEFORE ⟨ten minutes *to* five⟩ **b :** UNTIL ⟨from eight *to* five⟩ **4 a :** being a part or accessory of ⟨the trousers *to* this suit⟩ ⟨a key *to* the door⟩ **b :** with the accompaniment of ⟨sang *to* the music⟩ **5 a :** in a relation of likeness or unlikeness with ⟨similar *to* that one⟩ ⟨inferior *to* the other⟩ **b :** in accordance with ⟨add salt *to* taste⟩ **c :** within the range of ⟨*to* my knowledge⟩ **d :** contained, occurring, or included in ⟨400 *to* the box⟩ **6 a :** as regards ⟨agreeable *to* everyone⟩ ⟨attitude *to* our friends⟩ **b :** affecting as the receiver or beneficiary of an action ⟨spoke *to* his father⟩ ⟨gave it *to* me⟩ **c :** for no one except ⟨had a room *to* himself⟩ **7** — used to indicate that the following verb is an infinitive ⟨wants *to* go⟩ ⟨something *to* do⟩ and often used by itself at the end of a clause to stand for an infinitive ⟨knows more than he seems *to*⟩ ⟨don't want *to*⟩
[2]**to** \'tü\ *adv* **1 :** in the direction toward ⟨run *to* and fro⟩ **2 :** into contact, position, or attachment esp. with a frame ⟨snapped her purse *to*⟩ ⟨wind blew the door *to*⟩ **3 :** to the matter or business at hand ⟨the boxers set *to* with a flurry of blows⟩ ⟨if we all fall *to* the job will soon be done⟩ **4 :** to a state of consciousness or awareness ⟨brings her *to* with smelling salts⟩

ə abut	ər further	a back	ā bake
ä cot, cart	au̇ out	ch chin	e less
ē easy	g gift	i trip	ī life
j joke	ŋ sing	ō flow	ȯ flaw
ȯi coin	th thin	t͟h this	ü loot
u̇ foot	y yet	yü few	yu̇ furious
zh vision			

toad \'tōd\ *n* **:** any of numerous tailless leaping amphibians that as compared with the related frogs are generally land-dwelling in habit, squatter and shorter in build and with weaker hind limbs, and rough, dry, and warty rather than smooth and moist of skin

toad (up to 4 in. long)

toad·stool \-ˌstül\ *n* **:** a fungus having an umbrella-shaped cap **:** MUSHROOM; *esp* **:** one that is poisonous or inedible
[1]**toady** \'tōd-ē\ *n, pl* **toad·ies :** a person who flatters or fawns upon another in the hope of receiving favors
[2]**toady** *vb* **toad·ied; toady·ing :** to behave as a toady — **toady·ism** \-ē-ˌiz-əm\ *n*
to–and–fro \ˌtü-ən-'frō\ *adj* **:** forward and backward
[1]**toast** \'tōst\ *vb* **1 :** to make crisp, hot, and brown by heat ⟨*toast* bread⟩ **2 :** to warm thoroughly **:** become toasted ⟨*toasted* his feet by the fire⟩
[2]**toast** *n* **1 :** sliced toasted bread browned on both sides by heat **2 a :** a person whose health is drunk or something in honor of which persons drink **b :** a highly admired person ⟨the *toast* of the town⟩ **3 :** an act of proposing or of drinking a toast
[3]**toast** *vb* **:** to propose or drink to as a toast
toast·er \'tō-stər\ *n* **:** an electrical appliance for toasting
toast·mas·ter \'tōs(t)-ˌmas-tər\ *n* **:** one that presides at a banquet and introduces the after-dinner speakers
to·bac·co \tə-'bak-ō\ *n, pl* **-cos 1 :** any of a genus of chiefly American plants related to the potato and having sticky foliage and tubular flowers; *esp* **:** a tall erect annual So. American herb grown for its leaves **2 :** the leaves of cultivated tobacco prepared for use in smoking or chewing or as snuff

tobacco 1: 1, flowering stem and leaves; 2, magnified flower

tobacco mosaic *n* **:** any of a complex of virus diseases of tobacco and related plants
to·bac·co·nist \tə-'bak-ə-nəst\ *n* **:** a dealer in tobacco esp. at retail
[1]**to·bog·gan** \tə-'bäg-ən\ *n* **:** a long flat-bottomed light sled made without runners and curved up at the front
[2]**toboggan** *vb* **1 :** to coast on a toboggan **2 :** to decline suddenly and sharply (as in value)
to·coph·er·ol \tō-'käf-ə-ˌrȯl, -ˌrōl\ *n* **:** any of several related compounds with varying degrees of vitamin E activity
toc·sin \'täk-sən\ *n* **1 :** an alarm bell or the ringing of it **2 :** a warning signal
[1]**to·day** \tə-'dā\ *adv* **1 :** on or for this day **2 :** at the present time **:** NOWADAYS
[2]**today** *n* **:** the present day, time, or age
tod·dle \'täd-əl\ *vb* **tod·dled; tod·dling** \-(ə-)liŋ\ **:** to walk with short tottering steps in the manner of a young child — **toddle** *n* – **tod·dler** \-(ə-)lər\ *n*
tod·dy \'täd-ē\ *n, pl* **toddies 1 :** the sap of various mostly East Indian palms often fermented to form an alcoholic liquor **2 :** a hot drink consisting of an alcoholic liquor, water, sugar, and spices

to–do \tə-'dü\ *n, pl* **to–dos** \-'düz\ : BUSTLE, STIR, COMMOTION

1**toe** \'tō\ *n* **1 a :** one of the jointed parts of the front end of a vertebrate foot **b :** the front end or part of a foot or hoof **c :** the forepart of something worn on the foot **2 :** something that is felt to resemble the toe of a foot esp. in form or position ⟨the *toe* of Italy⟩

2**toe** *vb* **toed; toe·ing 1 :** to furnish with a toe ⟨*toe* off a sock in knitting⟩ **2 :** to touch, reach, or drive with the toe ⟨*toe* a football⟩ **3 :** to drive slantwise ⟨*toe* a nail⟩ **4 :** to stand or walk so that the toes assume an indicated position or direction ⟨*toe* in⟩ — **toe the line :** to conform rigorously to a rule or standard

toed \'tōd\ *adj* **1 :** having a toe or such or so many toes ⟨*5-toed*⟩ **2 :** driven obliquely ⟨a *toed* nail⟩

toe·hold \'tō-,hōld\ *n* **:** a small foothold **:** a slight footing

1**toe·nail** \'tō-,nāl, -'nāl\ *n* **:** a nail of a toe

2**toenail** *vb* **:** to fasten by toed nails **:** TOE

tof·fee *or* **tof·fy** \'täf-ē\ *n, pl* **toffees** *or* **toffies :** candy of brittle but tender texture made by boiling sugar and butter together

tog \'täg\ *vb* **togged; tog·ging :** to put togs on **:** DRESS ⟨*togged* out in the latest fashion⟩

to·ga \'tō-gə\ *n* **1 :** the loose outer garment worn in public by citizens of ancient Rome **2 :** a professional, official, or academic gown — **to·gaed** \-gəd\ *adj*

toga 1

to·geth·er \tə-'geth-ər\ *adv* **1 :** in or into one group, body, or place ⟨gathered *together*⟩ **2 :** in or into association, union, or contact with each other ⟨in business *together*⟩ ⟨the doors banged *together*⟩ **3 a :** at one time ⟨they all cheered *together*⟩ **b :** in succession **:** without intermission ⟨work for hours *together*⟩ **4 a :** in or by combined effort **:** JOINTLY ⟨worked *together* to clear the road⟩ **b :** in or into agreement ⟨get *together* on a plan⟩ **5 :** considered as a whole **:** in the aggregate ⟨gave more than all the others *together*⟩ — **to·geth·er·ness** *n*

1**tog·gle** \'täg-əl\ *n* **1 :** a crosspiece attached to the end of or to a loop in a rope, chain, or belt to prevent slipping or to serve as a fastening or as a grip for tightening ⟨used a stick as a *toggle* in tightening a rope⟩ **2 :** TOGGLE JOINT

2**toggle** *vb* **tog·gled; tog·gling** \'täg-(ə-)ling\ **1 :** to fasten with or as if with a toggle **2 :** to furnish with a toggle

toggle joint *n* **:** a device consisting of two bars jointed together end to end but not in line so that when a force is applied to the joint tending to straighten it pressure will be exerted on the parts fixed at the ends of the bars

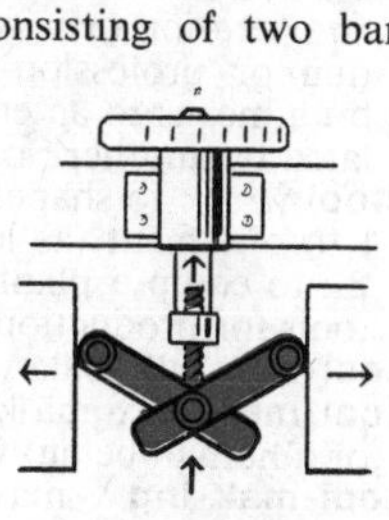
toggle joint

togs \'tägz\ *n pl* **:** CLOTHING; *esp* **:** a set of clothes and accessories for a specified use ⟨riding *togs*⟩ ⟨ski-ing *togs*⟩

1**toil** \'tȯil\ *n* **:** long hard tiring labor **:** DRUDGERY

2**toil** *vb* **1 :** to work hard and long **:** LABOR **2 :** to proceed with laborious effort **:** PLOD ⟨*toiling* up a steep hill⟩ ***syn*** see WORK — **toil·er** *n*

3**toil** *n* **:** something that involves or holds one fast **:** SNARE, TRAP ⟨in the *toils* of the law⟩

toi·let \'tȯi-lət\ *n* **1 :** the act or process of dressing and grooming oneself **2 a :** BATHROOM **b :** a fixture for defecation and urination; *esp* **:** WATER CLOSET

toilet paper *n* **:** a thin soft sanitary absorbent paper for bathroom use chiefly after evacuation

toi·let·ry \'tȯi-lə-trē\ *n, pl* **-ries :** an article or preparation (as a soap, lotion, cosmetic, or cologne) used in grooming

toilet water *n* **:** a perfumed liquid for use in or after a bath or as a skin freshener

toil·some \'tȯil-səm\ *adj* **:** attended with toil or fatigue **:** LABORIOUS

toil·worn \-,wōrn, -,wȯrn\ *adj* **:** showing the effects of or worn out by long hard work

to·ken \'tō-kən\ *n* **1 :** an outward sign ⟨*tokens* of his grief⟩ **2 :** something (as an act, gesture, or object) that serves as a sign or symbol **3 a :** SOUVENIR, KEEPSAKE **b :** INDICATION ⟨a mere *token* of future benefits⟩ **4 :** a piece resembling a coin issued as money or for a particular use ⟨bus *token*⟩ ***syn*** see EMBLEM

told *past of* TELL

tol·er·a·ble \'täl-(ə-)rə-bəl, 'täl-ər-bəl\ *adj* **1 :** capable of being borne or endured **2 :** moderately good or agreeable **:** PASSABLE — **tol·er·a·bly** \-blē\ *adv*

tol·er·ance \'täl(-ə)-rən(t)s\ *n* **1 :** capacity to endure or adapt to an unfavorable environmental factor **2 :** sympathy or indulgence for beliefs or practices differing from one's own **3 :** the allowable deviation from a standard — **tol·er·ant** \-rənt\ *adj* — **tol·er·ant·ly** *adv*

tol·er·ate \'täl-ə-,rāt\ *vb* **1 :** to allow something to be done or to exist without making a move to stop it **:** put up with **:** ENDURE **2 :** to show tolerance toward ⟨plants that *tolerate* drought⟩ ⟨*tolerate* a drug⟩ — **tol·er·a·tion** \,täl-ə-'rā-shən\ *n* — **tol·er·a·tive** \'täl-ə-,rāt-iv\ *adj*

1**toll** \'tōl\ *n* **1 :** a tax paid for a privilege (as the use of a highway or bridge) **2 :** a charge paid for a service (as placing a long-distance telephone call) **3 :** a ruinous price; *esp* **:** cost in life or health

2**toll** *vb* **1 a :** to announce or summon by the sounding of a bell **b :** to announce by striking ⟨the clock *tolled* six⟩ **2 :** to sound with slow measured strokes

3**toll** *n* **:** the sound of a tolling bell

toll·booth \'tōl-,büth\ *n* **:** a booth where tolls are paid

toll bridge *n* **:** a bridge at which a toll is charged for crossing

toll call *n* **:** a long-distance telephone call at charges above a local rate

toll·gate \'tōl-,gāt\ *n* **:** a point where vehicles stop to pay toll

tom \'täm\ *n* **1 :** the male of various animals: as **a :** TOMCAT **b :** TURKEY-COCK **2** *cap* **:** UNCLE TOM

tom·a·hawk \'täm-i-,hȯk\ *n* **:** a light ax used as a weapon by No. American Indians — **toma·hawk** *vb*

tomahawk

to·ma·to \tə-'māt-ō, -'mät-\ *n, pl* **-toes** [from Spanish *tomate*, from Nahuatl (the language of the Aztecs) *tomatl*] **1 :** any of a genus of So. American herbs related to the potato; *esp* **:** one widely grown for its edible fruits **2 :** the usu. large, rounded, and red or yellow pulpy berry of a tomato

tomb \'tüm\ *n* **1** : GRAVE **2** : a house, chamber, or vault for the dead

tom·boy \'täm-ˌbȯi\ *n* : a girl of boyish behavior — **tom·boy·ish** \-ish\ *adj* — **tom·boy·ish·ness** *n*

tomb·stone \'tüm-ˌstōn\ *n* : GRAVESTONE

tom·cat \'täm-ˌkat\ *n* : a male cat

tome \'tōm\ *n* : a usu. large or scholarly book

to·men·tose \tō-'men-ˌtōs, 'tō-mən-\ *adj* : covered with densely matted hairs ⟨a *tomentose* leaf⟩

tom·fool·ery \täm-'fül-(ə-)rē\ *n* : foolish behavior : NONSENSE

[1]**to·mor·row** \tə-'mär-ō, -'mȯr-\ *adv* : on or for the day after today

[2]**tomorrow** *n* **1** : the day after the present **2** : FUTURE 1a ⟨the world of *tomorrow*⟩

tom–tom \'täm-ˌtäm, 'təm-ˌtəm\ *n* [from Hindi *ṭamṭam*, an imitation of its sound] : a small-headed drum commonly beaten with the hands

ton \'tən\ *n, pl* **tons** *also* **ton 1** — see MEASURE table **2** : METRIC TON

ton·al \'tōn-əl\ *adj* : of or relating to a musical tone — **ton·al·ly** \-ə-lē\ *adv*

to·nal·i·ty \tō-'nal-ət-ē\ *n, pl* **-ties 1** : tonal quality; *esp* : the character of a musical composition dependent on its key or on the relation of its tones and chords to a keynote **2** : the arrangement or interrelation of color tones of a picture

[1]**tone** \'tōn\ *n* [from Greek *tonos*, literally "tension", then "musical pitch", which depends on the tension of the string producing it; from the same prehistoric root meaning "to stretch" as English *tense*] **1 a** : quality of vocal or musical sound **b** : a sound of definite pitch **c** : pitch or inflection of voice esp. as an individual characteristic or a linguistic device ⟨a shrill *tone*⟩ **2** : a style or manner of speaking or writing ⟨reply in a friendly *tone*⟩ **3** : general character, quality, or trend ⟨the depressing *tone* of his thoughts⟩ **4 a** : color quality or value : a tint or shade of color ⟨decorated in soft *tones*⟩ **b** : a color that modifies another ⟨gray with a blue *tone*⟩ **5 a** : a healthy state of the body or any of its parts **b** : RESILIENCY **6** : the general usu. harmonious effect in painting of light and shade with color ⟨a picture that has *tone*⟩

[2]**tone** *vb* **1** : to give a particular intonation or inflection to **2** : to impart tone to : STRENGTHEN ⟨medicine to *tone* up the system⟩ **3** : to soften, blend, or harmonize in color, appearance, or sound ⟨*toned* down his voice⟩ — **ton·er** *n*

tone language *n* : a language (as Chinese) in which variations in tone distinguish words of different meaning that would otherwise sound alike

tongs \'tängz, 'tȯngz\ *n pl* : any of numerous grasping devices consisting commonly of two pieces joined at one end by a pivot or hinged like scissors

[1]**tongue** \'təng\ *n* **1** : a fleshy movable process of the floor of the mouth in most vertebrates that bears sensory organs and small glands and functions esp. in taking and swallowing food and in man as a speech organ — see LARYNX illustration **2** : the flesh of a tongue (as of the ox or sheep) used as food **3** : the power of communication through speech ⟨hold your *tongue*⟩ **4 a** : LANGUAGE; *esp* : a spoken language ⟨her native *tongue*⟩ **b** : manner or quality of utterance ⟨smooth *tongue*⟩ **5 a** : a movable pin in a buckle **b** : a swinging inner part that strikes the sides as a bell is swung **c** : the flap under the lacing of a shoe **6** : a projecting ridge (as on one edge of a board) — **tongue·less** \-ləs\ *adj* — **tongue·like** \-ˌlīk\ *adj*

[2]**tongue** *vb* **tongued**; **tongu·ing** \'təng-ing\ **1** : to touch or lick with or as if with the tongue **2** : to cut a tongue on ⟨*tongue* a board⟩ **3** : to articulate notes on a wind instrument by means of the tongue

tongue in cheek *adv or adj* : with insincerity, irony, or whimsical exaggeration

tongue–lash \'təng-ˌlash\ *vb* : CHIDE, REPROVE — **tongue–lash·ing** *n*

tongue–tied \-ˌtīd\ *adj* : unable to speak clearly or freely usu. from abnormal shortness of the membrane under the tongue or from shyness

tongue twister *n* : an utterance (as *she sells seashells*) that is difficult to articulate because of a succession of similar consonants

[1]**ton·ic** \'tän-ik\ *adj* **1** : improving physical or mental tone : INVIGORATING **2** : relating to or based on the first tone of a scale ⟨*tonic* chord⟩ ⟨*tonic* harmony⟩

[2]**tonic** *n* **1** : a tonic medication **2** : the first degree of a major or minor scale

[1]**to·night** \tə-'nīt\ *adv* : on this present night or the night following this present day

[2]**tonight** *n* : the present or the coming night

ton·nage \'tən-ij\ *n* **1** : a duty on ships based on tons carried **2** : ships in terms of their carrying capacity in tons **3** : total weight in tons shipped, carried, or mined

ton·sil \'tän(t)-səl\ *n* : either of a pair of masses of spongy tissue that lie one on each side of the throat at the back of the mouth

ton·sil·lec·to·my \ˌtän(t)-sə-'lek-tə-mē\ *n, pl* **-mies** : the surgical removal of the tonsils

ton·sil·li·tis \-'līt-əs\ *n* : inflammation of the tonsils

ton·so·ri·al \tän-'sōr-ē-əl, -'sȯr-\ *adj* : of or relating to a barber or his work ⟨*tonsorial* parlor⟩

ton·sure \'tän-chər\ *n* [from Latin *tonsura*, literally "the act of shearing", from *tonsus*, past participle of *tondēre* "to shear"] **1** : the Roman Catholic or Eastern rite of admission to the clerical state by the clipping or shaving of the head **2** : the shaven crown or patch worn by monks and many clerics — **ton·sured** \-chərd\ *adj*

too \(')tü\ *adv* **1** : ALSO, BESIDES ⟨sell the house and furniture *too*⟩ **2** : EXCESSIVELY ⟨the dress was *too* short⟩ **3** : to a regrettable degree ⟨this has gone *too* far⟩ **4** : VERY ⟨only *too* glad to help⟩

took *past of* TAKE

[1]**tool** \'tül\ *n* **1** : an instrument (as a hammer, saw, wrench) used or worked by hand or by a machine **2 a** : an instrument or apparatus used in performing an operation or necessary in the practice of a vocation or profession ⟨a scholar's books are *tools*⟩ **b** : a means to an end **3** : a person used or manipulated by another : DUPE

[2]**tool** *vb* **1** : to shape, form, or finish with a tool; *esp* : to ornament (as leather) by means of hand tools **2** : to equip a plant or industry with machines and tools for production

tool·box \'tül-ˌbäks\ *n* : a chest for tools

tool·mak·er \-ˌmā-kər\ *n* : one (as an animal species or a human being) who makes tools

tool·mak·ing \-ˌmā-king\ *n* : the act, process, or art of making tools

toot \'tüt\ *vb* **1** : to sound a short blast ⟨a horn *tooted*⟩ **2** : to blow or sound an instrument esp. so as to produce short blasts ⟨*toot* a whistle⟩ — **toot** *vb* — **toot·er** *n*

ə abut	ər further		a back		ā bake
ä cot, cart	au̇ out	ch chin	e less		ē easy
g gift	i trip	ī life	j joke	ng sing	ō flow
ȯ flaw	ȯi coin	th thin	t͟h this		ü loot
u̇ foot	y yet	yü few	yu̇ furious		zh vision

tooth \'tüth\ *n, pl* **teeth** \'tēth\ **1 a :** one of the hard

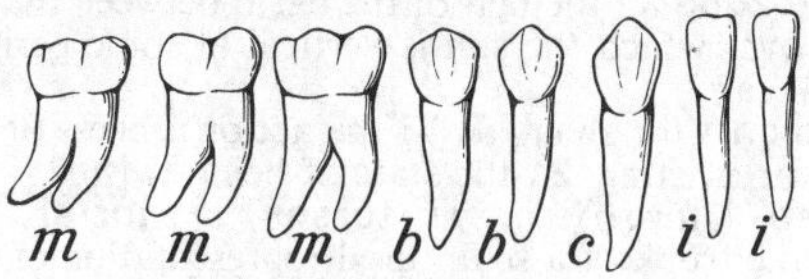

teeth 1a: m, molars; b, bicuspids; c, canine; i, incisors

bony structures borne esp. on the jaws of vertebrates and used for seizing and chewing food and as weapons **b :** any of various usu. hard and sharp processes esp. about the mouth of an invertebrate **2 :** TASTE, LIKING ⟨a *tooth* for sweets⟩ **3 a :** a projection like the tooth of an animal in shape, arrangement, or action ⟨the *tooth* of a saw⟩ **b :** one of the projections on the rim of a cogwheel **:** COG **4 a :** something that injures, tortures, devours, or destroys ⟨in the *teeth* of a wind⟩ **b** *pl* **:** effective means of enforcement ⟨put *teeth* in the new law⟩ — **tooth·less** \'tüth-ləs\ *adj* — **tooth·like** \-ˌlīk\ *adj*

tooth·ache \'tüth-ˌāk\ *n* **:** pain in or about a tooth

tooth·brush \-ˌbrəsh\ *n* **:** a brush for cleaning the teeth

toothed \'tütht\ *adj* **1 :** provided with teeth or such or so many teeth **2 :** NOTCHED, JAGGED

toothed whale *n* **:** any of a group of whales with numerous simple cone-shaped teeth

tooth·paste \'tüth-ˌpāst\ *n* **:** a paste dentifrice

tooth·pick \-ˌpik\ *n* **:** a pointed instrument (as a small flat tapering splinter) used for clearing the teeth of substances lodged between them

tooth powder *n* **:** a dentifrice in powder form

tooth·some \'tüth-səm\ *adj* **:** pleasing to the taste **:** DELICIOUS ⟨*toothsome* delicacies⟩

toothy \'tü-thē\ *adj* **tooth·i·er; -est :** having or showing prominent teeth ⟨a *toothy* grin⟩ — **tooth·i·ly** \-thə-lē\ *adv*

1**top** \'täp\ *n* **1 a :** the highest point, level, or part of something ⟨the *top* of the hill⟩ **b :** the upper end, edge or surface ⟨the *top* of the page⟩ ⟨filled the glass to the *top*⟩ **2 :** the stalk and leaves of a plant and esp. of one with edible roots ⟨beet *tops*⟩ **3 :** an integral part serving as an upper piece, lid, or covering ⟨pajama *top*⟩ ⟨put the *top* on the jar⟩ **4 :** a platform high up on the lower mast of a ship serving to spread the topmost rigging **5 :** the highest position or rank **:** ACME ⟨reached the *top* of his profession⟩ **6 :** a forward spin given to a ball by striking it on or near the top — **topped** \'täpt\ *adj*

2**top** *vb* **topped; top·ping 1 :** to remove or cut the top of ⟨*top* a tree⟩ **2 a :** to cover with a top **:** provide, form, or serve as a top **b :** to supply with a decorative finish or a final touch ⟨*topped* off the sundae with nuts⟩ **3 a :** to be or become higher than ⟨*tops* the previous record⟩ **b :** to be superior to **:** EXCEL, SURPASS ⟨*topped* his team in hits⟩ **4 :** to go over the top of ⟨the horse *topped* the barrier⟩ **5 :** to strike above the center ⟨*top* a golf ball⟩

3**top** *adj* **:** of, relating to, or at the top **:** HIGHEST, UPPERMOST

4**top** *n* **:** a commonly cylindrical or nearly cone-shaped child's toy that has a point on which it is made to spin

to·paz \'tō-ˌpaz\ *n* **1 :** a hard mineral consisting of a silicate of aluminum and occurring in crystals of various colors with the yellow variety being the one usu. cut and prized as a gem **2 :** a gem (as a yellow sapphire) resembling the true topaz

top·coat \'täp-ˌkōt\ *n* **:** a lightweight overcoat

top·er \'tō-pər\ *n* **:** a heavy drinker; *esp* **:** DRUNKARD

1**top·gal·lant** \(ˈ)täp-'gal-ənt, tə-'gal-\ *adj* **:** of or relating to a part next above the topmast

2**topgallant** *n* **:** a topgallant mast or sail

top hat *n* **:** a man's tall-crowned hat

top–heavy \'täp-ˌhev-ē\ *adj* **:** having the top part too heavy for the lower part **:** lacking in stability

top·ic \'täp-ik\ *n* **1 :** a heading in an outlined argument or exposition **2 :** the subject of a discourse or a section of it **:** THEME

top·i·cal \'täp-i-kəl\ *adj* **1 :** local or designed for local application ⟨a *topical* anesthetic⟩ **2 a :** of or relating to topics ⟨*topical* outline⟩ **b :** referring to the topics of the day or place ⟨*topical* allusions⟩ — **top·i·cal·ly** \-k(ə-)lē\ *adv*

topic sentence *n* **:** a sentence that states the main thought of a paragraph

top·knot \'täp-ˌnät\ *n* **:** a crest of feathers or hair on the top of the head

top·mast \-ˌmast, -məst\ *n* **:** the mast next above the lower mast and topmost in a fore-and-aft rig

top·min·now \-ˌmin-ō\ *n* **:** any of a large family of small surface-feeding fishes that produce living young instead of eggs

top·most \-ˌmōst\ *adj* **:** highest of all **:** UPPERMOST

top–notch \-'näch\ *adj* **:** of the highest quality **:** FIRST-RATE ⟨a *top-notch* performance⟩

to·pog·ra·pher \tə-'päg-rə-fər\ *n* **:** one skilled in topography

top·o·graph·ic \ˌtäp-ə-'graf-ik, ˌtō-pə-\ *adj* **:** TOPOGRAPHICAL 1

top·o·graph·i·cal \-'graf-i-kəl\ *adj* **1 :** of, relating to, or concerned with topography ⟨*topographical* engineer⟩ **2 :** showing the topography of a particular locality ⟨*topographical* map⟩ — **top·o·graph·i·cal·ly** \-k(ə-)lē\ *adv*

to·pog·ra·phy \tə-'päg-rə-fē\ *n* **1 :** the art or practice of detailing on maps or charts natural and man-made features of a place or region esp. so as to show elevations **2 :** the outline of a surface including its relief and the position of its natural and man-made features

to·pol·o·gy \tə-'päl-ə-jē\ *n* **:** a branch of mathematics that investigates the properties of geometric figures that do not change when the shape of the figure is subjected to continuous deformation or distortion — **top·o·log·i·cal** \ˌtäp-ə-'läj-i-kəl, ˌtō-pə-\ *adj* — **to·pol·o·gist** \tə-'päl-ə-jəst\ *n*

top·ping \'täp-ing\ *n* **:** a flavorful addition (as of sauce or nuts) served on top of a dessert

top·ple \'täp-əl\ *vb* **top·pled; top·pling** \-(ə-)ling\ **1 :** to fall from or as if from being top-heavy ⟨he *toppled* out of the tree⟩ **2 :** to cause to fall **:** OVERTURN ⟨the storm *toppled* many trees⟩

top·sail \'täp-ˌsāl, -səl\ *also* **top·s'l** \-səl\ *n* **1 :** the sail next above the lowermost sail on a mast in a square-rigged ship **2 :** the sail set above and sometimes on the gaff in a fore-and-aft rigged ship

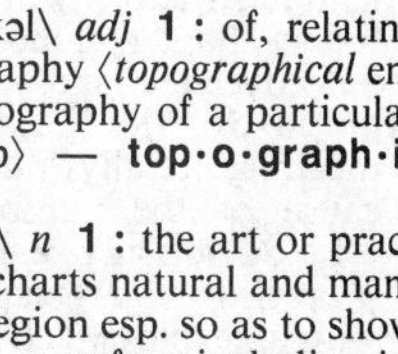

T topsail 2

top·side \'täp-'sīd\ *adv* **:** on deck

top·sides \-ˌsīdz\ *n pl* **:** the top portion of the outer surface of a ship on each side above the waterline

top·soil \-ˌsȯil\ *n* **:** surface soil

[1]**top·sy–tur·vy** \ˌtäp-sē-ˈtər-vē\ *adv* **1** : upside down **2** : in utter confusion or disorder
[2]**topsy–turvy** *adj* : turned upside down : totally disordered
toque \ˈtōk\ *n* : a woman's small hat usu. without a brim
tor \ˈtȯ(ə)r\ *n* : a high craggy hill
torch \ˈtȯrch\ *n* **1** : a flaming light made of something that burns brightly (as resinous wood) and usu. carried in the hand **2** : something (as wisdom or knowledge) likened to a torch as giving light or guidance **3** : any of various portable devices for producing a hot flame — compare BLOWTORCH **4** *chiefly Brit* : FLASHLIGHT — **torch·bear·er** \-ˌbar-ər, -ˌber-\ *n* — **torch·light** \-ˌlīt\ *n*

torch 3

tore *past of* TEAR
tor·e·a·dor \ˈtȯr-ē-ə-ˌdȯr\ *n* : BULLFIGHTER
to·re·ro \tə-ˈre(ə)r-ō\ *n, pl* **-ros** : BULLFIGHTER
[1]**tor·ment** \ˈtȯr-ˌment\ *n* **1** : extreme pain or anguish of body or mind : AGONY **2** : a source of vexation or pain
[2]**tor·ment** \tȯr-ˈment, ˈtȯr-ˌ\ *vb* **1** : to cause severe suffering of body or mind to : DISTRESS **2** : to cause worry or vexation to : HARASS — **tor·men·tor** \-ˈment-ər, -ˌment-\ *n*
torn *past part of* TEAR
tor·na·do \tȯr-ˈnād-ō\ *n, pl* **-does** *or* **-dos** : a violent destructive whirling wind accompanied by a funnel-shaped cloud that progresses in a narrow path over the land
[1]**tor·pe·do** \tȯr-ˈpēd-ō\ *n, pl* **-does** [from Latin, meaning literally "numbness", applied to the fish because of the numbness produced by its shock] **1** : ELECTRIC RAY **2 a** : a submarine mine **b** : a self-propelling cigar-shaped submarine projectile filled with an explosive charge that is released from a ship against another **3 a** : a charge of explosive enclosed in a container or case **b** : a small firework that explodes when thrown against a hard object
[2]**torpedo** *vb* : to hit with or destroy by or as if by a torpedo ⟨*torpedoed* an enemy cruiser⟩ ⟨*torpedoed* the contract talks⟩
torpedo boat *n* : a small very fast thinly plated boat for discharging torpedoes
tor·pid \ˈtȯr-pəd\ *adj* **1** : having lost motion or the power of exertion or feeling : DORMANT ⟨a bear *torpid* in his winter sleep⟩ **2** : sluggish in functioning or acting ⟨a *torpid* mind⟩ — **tor·pid·ly** *adv*
tor·por \ˈtȯr-pər\ *n* **1** : temporary loss or suspension of motion or feeling : extreme sluggishness ⟨the *torpor* of bears in winter⟩ **2** : DULLNESS, APATHY
tor·rent \ˈtȯr-ənt, ˈtär-\ *n* **1** : a violent or rushing stream of a liquid ⟨a *torrent* of rain⟩ **2** : a raging flood : a tumultuous outpouring ⟨a *torrent* of abuse⟩
tor·ren·tial \tȯ-ˈren-chəl, tə-\ *adj* : relating to or having the character of a torrent ⟨*torrential* rains⟩ — **tor·ren·tial·ly** \-ˈrench-(ə-)lē\ *adv*
tor·rid \ˈtȯr-əd, ˈtär-\ *adj* **1 a** : parched with heat esp. of the sun : HOT ⟨*torrid* sands⟩ **b** : giving off intense heat : SCORCHING **2** : ARDENT, PASSIONATE ⟨*torrid* love letters⟩ — **tor·rid·ly** *adv*
torrid zone *n* : the belt of the earth between the tropics over which the sun is vertical at some period of the year
tor·sion \ˈtȯr-shən\ *n* **1** : the act or process of turning or twisting **2** : the state of being twisted
tor·so \ˈtȯr-sō\ *n, pl* **torsos** *or* **tor·si** \-ˌsē\ **1** : the trunk of a sculptured representation of a human body; *esp* : the trunk of a statue whose head and limbs are mutilated **2** : the human trunk
tor·ti·lla \tȯr-ˈtē-(y)ə\ *n* : a round flat cake of unleavened cornmeal bread
tor·toise \ˈtȯrt-əs\ *n* : TURTLE; *esp* : a land turtle
[1]**tor·toise·shell** \ˈtȯrt-əs(h)-ˌshel\ *n* **1** : a mottled horny substance that covers the bony shell of some sea turtles and is used in inlaying and in making various ornamental articles **2** : any of several showy butterflies
[2]**tortoiseshell** *adj* : made of or resembling tortoiseshell esp. in spotted brown and yellow coloring
tor·to·ni \tȯr-ˈtō-nē\ *n* : ice cream made of heavy cream sometimes with minced almonds, chopped maraschino cherries, or various flavoring ingredients
tor·tu·ous \ˈtȯrch-(ə-)wəs\ *adj* **1** : marked by repeated twists, bends, or turns : WINDING ⟨a *tortuous* stream⟩ **2** : confusingly roundabout ⟨the *tortuous* workings of government⟩ — **tor·tu·ous·ly** *adv*
[1]**tor·ture** \ˈtȯr-chər\ *n* **1** : the infliction of intense pain esp. to punish or obtain a confession **2 a** : anguish of body or mind : AGONY **b** : something that causes agony or pain
[2]**torture** *vb* **tor·tured**; **tor·tur·ing** \ˈtȯrch-(ə-)ring\ **1** : to punish or coerce by inflicting excruciating pain **2** : to cause intense suffering to : TORMENT **3** : to twist or wrench out of shape : DISTORT — **tor·tur·er** \ˈtȯr-chər-ər\ *n*
tor·tur·ous \ˈtȯrch-(ə-)rəs\ *adj* : causing torture : cruelly painful — **tor·tur·ous·ly** *adv*
To·ry \ˈtōr-ē, ˈtȯr-\ *n, pl* **Tories** **1** : CONSERVATIVE 1b **2** : an American upholding the cause of the British Crown during the American Revolution : LOYALIST **3** *often not cap* : an extreme conservative esp. in politics and economics — **Tory** *adj*
toss \ˈtȯs, ˈtäs\ *vb* **1** : to keep throwing here and there or backward and forward : cause to pitch or roll ⟨waves *tossed* the ship about⟩ **2** : to throw with a quick light motion ⟨*toss* a ball into the air⟩ **3** : to lift with a sudden motion ⟨*toss* the head⟩ **4** : to pitch or bob about rapidly ⟨the light canoe is *tossing* on the waves⟩ **5** : to be restless : fling oneself about ⟨*tossed* in his sleep⟩ **6** : to stir or mix lightly ⟨*toss* a salad⟩ ***syn*** see THROW — **toss** *n*
toss·pot \-ˌpät\ *n* : DRUNKARD
toss–up \-ˌəp\ *n* **1** : a tossing of a coin to determine a chance **2** : an even chance
tot \ˈtät\ *n* : a small child : TODDLER
tot *abbr* total
[1]**to·tal** \ˈtōt-əl\ *adj* **1** : of or relating to the whole of something ⟨a *total* eclipse⟩ **2** : making up the whole : ENTIRE **3** : COMPLETE, UTTER ⟨*total* ruin⟩ **4** : making use of every means to carry out a planned program ⟨*total* war⟩
[2]**total** *n* **1** : a product of addition : SUM **2** : an entire quantity : AMOUNT
[3]**total** *vb* **to·taled** *or* **to·talled**; **to·tal·ing** *or* **to·tal·ling** **1** : to add up : COMPUTE ⟨*total* these numbers⟩ **2** : to amount to : NUMBER ⟨gifts *totaled* $120⟩
to·tal·i·tar·i·an \tō-ˌtal-ə-ˈter-ē-ən\ *adj* : of or relating to a political regime based on subordination of the individual to the state and strict control of all aspects of life esp. by coercive measures —

totalitarian *n* — **to·tal·i·tar·i·an·ism** \-ē-ə-ˌniz-əm\ *n*
to·tal·i·ty \tō-'tal-ət-ē\ *n, pl* **-ties** **1** : an aggregate amount : SUM, WHOLE **2** : the quality or state of being total : ENTIRETY
to·tal·ize \'tōt-ə-ˌlīz\ *vb* **1** : to add up : TOTAL **2** : to express as a whole : SUMMARIZE
to·tal·ly \'tōt-ə-lē\ *adv* **1** : in a total manner : WHOLLY **2** : as a whole
tote \'tōt\ *vb* : to carry by hand : PACK, HAUL — **tot·er** *n*
to·tem \'tōt-əm\ *n* : an object (as an animal or plant) or representation of an object serving as the emblem of a family or clan and often as a reminder of its ancestry — **to·tem·ic** \tō-'tem-ik\ *adj*
totem pole *n* : a pole carved and painted with totemic symbols that is erected before the houses of some northwest coast Indians

totem pole

tot·ter \'tät-ər\ *vb* **1 a** : to tremble or rock as if about to fall : SWAY **b** : to become unstable : threaten to collapse **2** : to move unsteadily : STAGGER, WOBBLE — **totter** *n* — **tot·tery** \-ə-rē\ *adj*
tou·can \'tü-ˌkan, tü-'\ *n* : any of a family of fruit-eating birds of tropical America with brilliant coloring and a very large bill

toucan (about 24 in. long)

¹touch \'təch\ *vb* **1** : to feel or handle (as with fingers or hands) **2 a** : to bring or come into or be in contact with something ⟨*touch* a match to the kindling⟩ **b** : to come near to or have a common boundary with something : ADJOIN ⟨New Hampshire just *touches* on the ocean⟩ **c** : to come near to being something mentioned ⟨his acts *touched* on treason⟩ **3 a** : to hit lightly ⟨*touch* a horse with the spur⟩ **b** : to affect physically ⟨no bleach would *touch* the stain⟩ ⟨plants *touched* by frost⟩ **4 a** : to lay hands on (as in taking, using, or examining) ⟨wouldn't *touch* the money⟩ ⟨don't *touch* the exhibits⟩ **b** : to act on or tamper with so as to damage in some way or degree ⟨a gray old building *touched* and warped by sun and wind⟩; *esp* : HARM ⟨swore he hadn't *touched* the child⟩ **c** : to make use of esp. as food or drink ⟨never *touches* meat⟩ **5** : to speak or write of something briefly or casually : mention in passing ⟨barely *touched* on domestic politics⟩ **6** : to relate or be of concern to : affect the interest of ⟨a matter that *touches* every parent⟩ **7 a** : to be or become disordered in mind **b** : to move emotionally ⟨*touched* by his friend's regard⟩ **8** : to make a usu. brief or incidental stop in port ⟨*touched* at several coastal towns⟩ **9** : to rival in quality or value : stand comparison with ⟨the new mattress doesn't *touch* the old one for comfort⟩ **10** : to induce to give or lend ⟨*touched* him for a loan⟩ **11** : to mark or change slightly (as in color or aspect) ⟨lips *touched* with a smile⟩ — **touch·a·ble** \-ə-bəl\ *adj* — **touch·er** *n*
²touch *n* **1** : a light stroke, tap, or blow **2** : the act or fact of touching or being touched **3 a** : the special sense by which light pressure is perceived ⟨soft to the *touch*⟩ **b** : a particular sensation conveyed by this sense ⟨the soft *touch* of silk⟩ **4** : a state of contact or communication ⟨keeping in *touch* with friends⟩ **5 a** : manner of touching or striking esp. the keys of a keyboard ⟨a firm *touch* on the piano⟩ **b** : skillful or distinctive manner or method ⟨the *touch* of a master⟩ **6** : a characteristic or distinguishing trait or quality ⟨a classic *touch* distinguishes his writing⟩ **7 a** : a small amount : TRACE ⟨a *touch* of spring in the air⟩ **b** : a trivial or transitory attack ⟨a *touch* of fever⟩
touch·down \'təch-ˌdau̇n\ *n* : the act of scoring American football by being lawfully in possession of the ball on, above, or behind an opponent's goal line when the ball is declared dead
touch·ing \'təch-ing\ *adj* : arousing tenderness or compassion : PATHETIC — **touch·ing·ly** \-ing-lē\ *adv*
touch–me–not \'təch-mē-ˌnät\ *n* : JEWELWEED
touch·stone \'təch-ˌstōn\ *n* **1** : a black stone formerly used to test the purity of gold and silver by the streak left on the stone when rubbed by the metal **2** : a test or criterion for judging something
touch up *vb* : to improve or perfect by small additional strokes or alterations ⟨*touched up* the portrait⟩
touchy \'təch-ē\ *adj* **touch·i·er**; **-est** **1** : acutely sensitive or irritable ⟨a *touchy* swelling⟩ **2** : calling for tact, care, or caution in treatment ⟨a *touchy* subject⟩
¹tough \'təf\ *adj* **1** : able to undergo great strain : flexible and not brittle ⟨*tough* fibers⟩ **2** : not easily chewed ⟨*tough* meat⟩ **3** : able to stand hard work and hardship : ROBUST ⟨a *tough* body⟩ **4 a** : hard to influence : STUBBORN ⟨a *tough* bargainer⟩ **b** : very difficult ⟨a *tough* problem⟩ **5** : hardened in vice : ROWDY, LAWLESS ⟨a *tough* neighborhood⟩ **6** : free from softness or sentimentality : firm and uncompromising ⟨a *tough* approach to delinquency⟩ — **tough·ly** *adv* — **tough·ness** *n*
²tough *n* : a tough person; *esp* : ROWDY
tough·en \'təf-ən\ *vb* **tough·ened**; **tough·en·ing** \'təf-(ə-)ning\ : to make or become tough
tou·pee \tü-'pā\ *n* : a small wig for a bald spot
¹tour \'tu̇(ə)r, *1 is also* 'tau̇(ə)r\ *n* **1** : a period under some orderly schedule ⟨military *tour* of duty⟩ **2** : a trip or excursion usu. ending at the point of beginning ⟨a *tour* of the city⟩
²tour *vb* : to make a tour of : travel as a tourist
tour·ist \'tu̇r-əst\ *n* : one who travels for pleasure — **tourist** *adj*
tourist class *n* : economy accommodation on a ship, airplane, or train
tourist court *n* : MOTEL
tourist home *n* : a house in which rooms are available for rent to transients
tour·ma·line \'tu̇r-mə-lən, -ˌlēn\ *n* : a mineral of variable color that is a complex silicate and makes a gem of great beauty when transparent
tour·na·ment \'tu̇r-nə-mənt, 'tər-\ *n* **1** : a contest of skill and courage between armored knights fighting with blunted lances or swords **2** : a series of athletic contests, sports events, or games for a championship ⟨a tennis *tournament*⟩
tour·ney \'tu̇(ə)r-nē\ *n, pl* **tourneys** : TOURNAMENT
tour·ni·quet \'tu̇r-ni-kət, 'tər-\ *n* : a device (as a tight bandage or a piece of rubber tubing) to check bleeding or blood flow
¹tou·sle \'tau̇-zəl\ *vb* **tou·sled**; **tou·sling** \'tau̇z-(ə-)ling\ : DISHEVEL, RUMPLE
²tousle *n* : a tangled mass or condition
¹tout \'tau̇t\ *vb* **1** : to solicit or canvass for patronage, trade, votes, or support **2 a** *chiefly Brit* : to spy about at racing stables and tracks to get information to be used in betting **b** : to provide tips on racehorses

[2]**tout** *n* **1 :** a person who solicits business **2 :** a person who gives tips or solicits bets on a racehorse
[3]**tout** *vb* **:** to praise or publicize insistently or excessively
[1]**tow** \'tō\ *vb* **:** to draw or pull along behind : HAUL
[2]**tow** *n* **1 :** an act or instance of towing or the fact or condition of being towed **2 :** a line or rope for towing **3 :** something (as a tugboat or barge) that tows or is towed — **in tow 1 :** in the state or course of being towed **2 :** under guidance or protection : in the position of a follower ⟨had a good-looking girl *in tow*⟩
[3]**tow** *n* **1 :** short broken fiber from flax, hemp, or jute used for yarn, twine, or stuffing **2 :** yarn or cloth made of tow
tow·age \'tō-ij\ *n* **1 :** the act of towing **2 :** the price paid for towing
[1]**to·ward** \'tō(-ə)rd, 'tȯ(-ə)rd\ *also* **to·wards** \'tō(-ə)rdz, 'tȯ(-ə)rdz\ *adj* **:** coming soon : IMMINENT ⟨a battle was *toward*⟩
[2]**to·ward** *or* **to·wards** \(')tō(-ə)rd(z), (')tȯ(-ə)rd(z), tə-'wȯrd(z), (')twȯrd(z)\ *prep* **1 :** in the direction of ⟨driving *toward* town⟩ **2 a :** along a course leading to ⟨efforts *toward* reconciliation⟩ **b :** in relation to ⟨attitude *toward* life⟩ **3 :** so as to face ⟨his back was *toward* me⟩ ⟨turn the chair *toward* the window⟩ **4 :** not long before ⟨*toward* noon⟩ **5 :** to provide part of the payment for ⟨save *toward* his education⟩
tow·boat \'tō-,bōt\ *n* **1 :** TUGBOAT **2 :** a compact shallow-draft boat for pushing tows of barges on inland waterways
[1]**tow·el** \'taů(-ə)l\ *n* **:** a cloth or piece of absorbent paper for wiping or drying
[2]**towel** *vb* **-eled** *or* **-elled; -el·ing** *or* **-el·ling :** to rub or dry with or use a towel
tow·el·ing *or* **tow·el·ling** \'taů-(ə-)ling\ *n* **:** material for towels
[1]**tow·er** \'taů(-ə)r\ *n* **1 :** a building or structure typically higher than its diameter and high relative to its surroundings that may stand apart (as a campanile) or be attached (as a church belfry) to a larger structure and that may be of skeleton framework (as an observation or transmission tower) **2 :** a towering citadel : FORTRESS — **tow·ered** \'taů(-ə)rd\ *adj*
[2]**tower** *vb* **:** to reach or rise to a great height
tow·er·ing \'taů-(ə-)ring\ *adj* **1 :** impressively high or great : IMPOSING ⟨*towering* skyscrapers⟩ **2 :** reaching a high point of intensity : OVERWHELMING ⟨a *towering* rage⟩ **3 :** going beyond proper bounds : EXCESSIVE ⟨*towering* ambitions⟩
tow·head \'tō-,hed\ *n* **:** a person having soft whitish hair
to·whee \tō-'(h)ē, -'hwē; 'tō-,hē, 'tō-(,)ē\ *n* **:** any of numerous American finches; *esp* **:** one of eastern No. America having the male black, white, and reddish
tow·line \'tō-,līn\ *n* **:** a line used in towing
town \'taůn\ *n* [from Old English *tūn* "enclosure", "village", "town"] **1 a :** a compactly settled area as distinguished from surrounding rural territory; *esp* **:** one larger than a village but smaller than a city **b :** CITY **c :** an English village having a periodic fair or market **2 a :** the city or urban life as contrasted with the country **b :** TOWNSPEOPLE **3 :** a New England territorial and political unit usu. containing both rural and urban areas under a single town government — **town** *adj*
town clerk *n* **:** an official who keeps the town records
town crier *n* **:** a town officer who makes public proclamations
town hall *n* **:** a public building used for town-government offices and meetings
town meeting *n* **:** a meeting of inhabitants or taxpayers constituting the legislative authority of a town
towns·folk \'taůnz-,fōk\ *n pl* **:** TOWNSPEOPLE
town·ship \'taůn-,ship\ *n* **1 a :** TOWN 3 **b :** a unit of local government in some northeastern and north central states **2 :** a division of territory in surveys of U.S. public land containing 36 sections or 36 square miles
towns·man \'taůnz-mən\ *n* **1 :** a native or resident of a town or city **2 :** a fellow citizen of a town — **towns·wom·an** \-,wům-ən\ *n*
towns·peo·ple \-,pē-pəl\ *n pl* **1 :** the inhabitants of a town or city : TOWNSMEN **2 :** town-dwelling or town-bred persons
tow·path \'tō-,path, -,påth\ *or* **towing path** *n* **:** a path (as along a canal) traveled by men or animals towing boats
tow·rope \'tō-,rōp\ *n* **:** a line used in towing
tow truck *n* **:** WRECKER 4
tox·e·mia \täk-'sē-mē-ə\ *n* **:** a disorder caused by toxic substances in the blood — **tox·e·mic** \-mik\ *adj*
tox·ic \'täk-sik\ *adj* [from Latin *toxicum* "poison", from Greek *toxikon* "poison smeared on arrows", from *toxa* "bow and arrows"] **1 :** of, relating to, or caused by a poison or toxin **2 :** POISONOUS — **tox·ic·i·ty** \täk-'sis-ət-ē\ *n*
tox·i·col·o·gy \,täk-sə-'käl-ə-jē\ *n* **:** a science that deals with poisons and their antidotes — **tox·i·col·o·gist** \-jəst\ *n*
tox·in \'täk-sən\ *n* **:** a complex substance produced by a living organism (as a bacterium) that is very poisonous when introduced directly into the tissues but is usu. destroyed in digestion when taken by mouth and that typically induces antibody formation — compare ANTITOXIN, TOXOID
tox·in–an·ti·tox·in \'täk-sən-'ant-i-,täk-sən\ *n* **:** a mixture of a toxin and its antitoxin used esp. formerly in immunizing against a disease (as diphtheria)
tox·oid \'täk-,sȯid\ *n* **:** a toxin (as of tetanus) treated so as to destroy its poisonous effects while leaving it still capable of causing the formation of antibodies when injected into the body
[1]**toy** \'tȯi\ *n* **1 :** something of small or no real value or importance : TRIFLE **2 :** something for a child to play with **3 :** something tiny; *esp* **:** an animal of a breed or variety characterized by exceptionally small size — **toy** *adj* — **toy·like** \-,līk\ *adj*
[2]**toy** *vb* **:** to amuse oneself as if with a toy : PLAY, TRIFLE ⟨*toy* with an idea⟩
toy·on \'tȯi-,än\ *n* **:** an ornamental evergreen shrub of the No. American Pacific coast that is related to the rose and has white flowers succeeded by persistent bright red berries
tp *abbr* township
tpke *abbr* turnpike
tr *abbr* trill
TR *abbr* throws right
[1]**trace** \'trās\ *n* **1 :** a mark or line left by something that has passed : TRAIL, FOOTPRINT **2 :** a sign or evidence of some past thing : VESTIGE ⟨*traces* of the ancient culture⟩ **3 :** something traced or drawn (as a line) **4 :** a minute amount or indication ⟨a *trace* of red⟩

[2]**trace** *vb* **1 a :** DELINEATE, SKETCH **b :** to form (as letters or figures) carefully or painstakingly **c :** to copy by following the lines or letters as seen through a transparent superimposed sheet ⟨*traced* the drawing⟩ **d :** to make a graphic instrumental record of ⟨*trace* the heart action⟩ **2 a :** to follow the footprints, track, or trail of **b :** to study out or follow the development and progress of in detail or step by step ⟨*traced* his ancestry⟩

[3]**trace** *n* **:** either of two straps, chains, or lines of a harness for attaching a horse to something (as a vehicle) to be drawn

trace·a·ble \'trā-sə-bəl\ *adj* **1 :** capable of being traced **2 :** ATTRIBUTABLE, DUE ⟨a failure *traceable* to laziness⟩

trace element *n* **:** a chemical element used by an organism in minute quantities in its physiological processes

trac·er \'trā-sər\ *n* **1 a :** a person who traces missing persons or property **b :** an inquiry sent out in tracing a shipment lost in transit **2 :** a draftsman who traces designs, patterns, or markings **3 a :** ammunition containing a chemical composition to mark the flight of projectiles by a trail of smoke or fire **b :** a substance and esp. a labeled element or atom used to trace the course of a chemical or biological process

trac·ery \'trās-(ə-)rē\ *n, pl* **-er·ies 1 :** architectural ornamental work with branching lines **2 :** a decorative interlacing of lines ⟨frost formed a *tracery* on the window⟩

tracery 1

tra·chea \'trā-kē-ə\ *n, pl* **-che·ae** \-kē-,ē, -kē-,ī\ *also* **-che·as 1 :** the main trunk of the system of tubes by which air passes to and from the lungs in vertebrates — see LARYNX illustration **2 :** one of the air-conveying tubules forming the respiratory system of most insects and many other arthropods — **tra·che·al** \-kē-əl\ *adj*

tra·che·id \'trā-kē-əd\ *n* **:** a long tubular cell that has tapering closed ends and thickened walls, is found in the xylem, and functions in transport of water and solutions and in support

trac·ing \'trā-sing\ *n* **1 :** the act of one that traces **2 :** something that is traced

[1]**track** \'trak\ *n* **1 a :** detectable evidence (as the wake of a ship, a line of footprints, or a wheel rut) that something has passed **b :** a path made by repeated footfalls **:** TRAIL **2 a :** a course laid out esp. for running **b :** the parallel rails of a railroad **3 a :** a sequence of events **:** a train of ideas **:** SUCCESSION **b :** awareness of a fact or progression ⟨lose *track* of the time⟩ **4 a :** the width of a wheeled vehicle from wheel to wheel **b :** either of two endless metal belts on which a vehicle (as a tank or bulldozer) travels **5 :** track-and-field sports; *esp* **:** those performed on a running track — **in one's tracks :** where one is at the moment **:** on the spot ⟨the shot dropped the deer *in its tracks*⟩

[2]**track** *vb* **1 :** to follow the tracks or traces of **:** TRAIL **2 :** to trace by following the signs or course of ⟨*track* a missile with radar⟩ **3 :** to pass over **:** TRAVERSE ⟨*track* the wilderness⟩ **4 :** to make tracks upon or with ⟨*track* up the floor with muddy feet⟩ ⟨*track* mud all over the floor⟩ — **track·er** *n*

track-and-field \,trak-ən-'fēld\ *adj* **:** of or relating to a sport performed on a racing track or on the adjacent field

track·lay·ing \'trak-,lā-ing\ *adj* **:** of, relating to, or being a vehicle moving on an endless chain or segmented metal belt

track·less \'trak-ləs\ *adj* **:** having no track **:** UNTROD ⟨*trackless* forests⟩

[1]**tract** \'trakt\ *n* **:** a pamphlet or leaflet intended to draw attention or gain support for something (as a political or religious movement)

[2]**tract** *n* **1 a :** an indefinite stretch esp. of land ⟨broad *tracts* of prairie⟩ **b :** a defined area esp. of land ⟨garden *tract*⟩ **2 :** a system of body parts or organs that serves some special purpose ⟨the digestive *tract*⟩

trac·ta·ble \'trak-tə-bəl\ *adj* **1 :** easily led, taught, or controlled **:** DOCILE ⟨*tractable* horse⟩ **2 :** easily handled, managed, or wrought **:** MALLEABLE ⟨*tractable* metal⟩ — **trac·ta·bil·i·ty** \,trak-tə-'bil-ət-ē\ *n* — **trac·ta·bly** \'trak-tə-blē\ *adv*

trac·tion \'trak-shən\ *n* **1 :** the act of drawing **:** the state of being drawn **2 a :** the drawing of a vehicle by motive power **b :** the motive power employed in drawing a vehicle **3 :** the adhesive friction of a body on a surface on which it moves (as of a wheel on a rail)

trac·tor \'trak-tər\ *n* **1 :** a four-wheeled or tracklaying rider-controlled vehicle used esp. for drawing farm implements **2 :** a short truck with no body used in combination with a trailer for hauling freight

[1]**trade** \'trād\ *n* **1 :** the business or work in which one engages regularly **:** OCCUPATION **2 :** an occupation requiring manual or mechanical skill **3 :** the persons engaged in an occupation, business, or industry **4 :** the business of buying and selling or bartering commodities **:** COMMERCE; *also* **:** TRAFFIC, MARKET **5 :** an act or instance of trading **:** TRANSACTION; *esp* **:** an exchange of property without use of money **6 :** a firm's customers **:** CLIENTELE

syn TRADE, CRAFT, PROFESSION can mean a pursuit followed as an occupation or means of livelihood and requiring some degree of technical knowledge or skill. TRADE applies chiefly to work involving skilled manual or mechanical labor; CRAFT more strongly suggests training or skill and sometimes creativity required by more specialized work ⟨a cabinetmaker's *craft*⟩; PROFESSION generally applies to a pursuit that requires prolonged study and training in preparation

[2]**trade** *vb* **1 a :** to give in exchange for another commodity **:** BARTER **b :** to make an exchange of **2 a :** to engage in the exchange, purchase, or sale of goods **b :** to make one's purchases **:** SHOP ⟨*trade* at a new store⟩

[3]**trade** *adj* **1 :** of, relating to, or used in trade ⟨*trade* problems⟩ **2 :** intended for persons in a business or industry ⟨a *trade* journal⟩

trade-in \'trād-,in\ *n* **:** something given in trade usu. as part payment of the price of another

trade in \-'in\ *vb* **:** to turn in as usu. part payment for a purchase ⟨*trade* an old car *in* on a new one⟩

trade·mark \-,märk\ *n* **:** a device (as a word) pointing distinctly to the origin or ownership of merchandise to which it is applied and legally reserved to the exclusive use of the owner as maker or seller — **trademark** *vb*

trade name *n* **1 :** the name by which an article is called in its own trade **2 :** a name that is given by a manufacturer or merchant to a product to distinguish it as made or sold by him and that may be used and protected as a trademark **3 :** the name under which a firm does business

trad·er \'trād-ər\ *n* **1 :** a person who trades **2 :** a ship engaged in trade

trade school *n* : a secondary school teaching the skilled trades

trades·man \'trādz-mən\ *n* **1** : one who runs a retail store : SHOPKEEPER **2** : a workman in a skilled trade : CRAFTSMAN

trades·peo·ple \-ˌpē-pəl\ *n pl* : TRADESMEN

trade union *n* : LABOR UNION — **trade unionist** *n*

trade wind *n* : a wind blowing almost continually in the same course, from northeast to southwest in a belt north of the equator and from southeast to northwest in one south of the equator

trading post *n* : a station or store of a trader or trading company established in a sparsely settled region

trading stamp *n* : a printed stamp of value given as a premium to a retail customer to be accumulated and redeemed in merchandise

tra·di·tion \trə-'dish-ən\ *n* **1** : the handing down of information, beliefs, or customs from one generation to another **2** : a belief or custom handed down by tradition — **tra·di·tion·al** \-'dish-(ə-)nəl\ *adj* — **tra·di·tion·al·ly** \-ē\ *adv*

tra·duce \trə-'d(y)üs\ *vb* : SLANDER — **tra·duc·er** *n*

[1]**traf·fic** \'traf-ik\ *n* **1** : the business of carrying passengers or goods ⟨the tourist *traffic*⟩ **2** : the business of buying and selling : TRADE, COMMERCE **3** : DEALINGS, FAMILIARITY ⟨*traffic* with the enemy⟩ **4 a** : the persons or goods carried by train, boat, or airplane or passing along a road, river, or air route **b** : the motions or activity of travelers or carriers along a route ⟨heavy holiday *traffic*⟩

[2]**traffic** *vb* **traf·ficked**; **traf·fick·ing** : to carry on traffic : TRADE, DEAL — **traf·fick·er** *n*

traffic circle *n* : ROTARY 2

traffic signal *n* : a signal (as a system of colored lights) for controlling traffic

tra·ge·di·an \trə-'jēd-ē-ən\ *n* **1** : a writer of tragedies **2** : an actor of tragic roles

trag·e·dy \'traj-əd-ē\ *n, pl* **-dies** **1** : a serious drama having a sorrowful or disastrous conclusion **2** : a disastrous event : CALAMITY

trag·ic \'traj-ik\ *adj* **1** : of, marked by, or expressive of tragedy **2** : dealing with or treated in tragedy ⟨the *tragic* hero⟩ **3** : DEPLORABLE, LAMENTABLE ⟨war is a *tragic* thing⟩ ⟨a *tragic* accident⟩ — **trag·i·cal·ly** \-i-k(ə-)lē\ *adv*

[1]**trail** \'trāl\ *vb* **1** : to drag or draw along behind ⟨the horse *trailed* its reins⟩ **2** : to lag behind ⟨*trailed* in the race⟩ **3** : to carry or bring along ⟨disliked to *trail* his sister around with him⟩ **4** : to follow in the tracks of : PURSUE ⟨dogs *trailing* a fox⟩ **5** : to hang or let hang so as to touch the ground ⟨a *trailing* skirt⟩ **6** : to grow to such a length as to hang down or rest on or creep over the ground ⟨*trailing* vines⟩ **7** : to form a trail ⟨smoke *trailed* from the chimney⟩ **8** : DWINDLE ⟨the sound *trailed* off⟩

[2]**trail** *n* **1** : something that trails or is trailed ⟨a *trail* of smoke⟩ **2** : a trace or mark left by something that has passed or been drawn along ⟨a *trail* of blood⟩ **3 a** : a track made by passage through a wilderness : a beaten path **b** : a marked path through a forest or mountainous region

trail·er \'trā-lər\ *n* **1** : a vehicle designed to be hauled **2** : a vehicle designed to serve wherever parked as a dwelling or as a place of business

ə abut	ər further	a back	ā bake
ä cot, cart	aů out	ch chin	e less	ē easy
g gift	i trip	ī life	j joke	ng sing	ō flow
ȯ flaw	ȯi coin	th thin	t͟h this	ü loot
u̇ foot	y yet	yü few	yu̇ furious	zh vision

trailer camp *n* : an area where house trailers are congregated — called also *trailer court*, *trailer park*

trailing arbutus *n* : the common No. American arbutus

[1]**train** \'trān\ *n* **1** : a part of a gown that trails behind the wearer **2** : a number of followers or attendants : RETINUE **3** : a moving file of persons, vehicles, or animals ⟨wagon *train*⟩ **4 a** : a connected series ⟨*train* of thought⟩ **b** : accompanying circumstances : AFTERMATH ⟨war brings many evils in its *train*⟩ **5** : a series of moving machine parts (as gears) for transmitting and modifying motion **6** : a connected line of railroad cars with or without a locomotive ⟨a freight *train*⟩ ⟨a passenger *train*⟩

[2]**train** *vb* **1** : to direct the growth of usu. by bending, pruning, and tying ⟨*train* a plant⟩ **2** : to teach in an art, profession, or trade ⟨*trained* him in the law⟩ ⟨*trained* several generations of long-distance runners⟩ **3** : to make ready for a test of skill ⟨spent two months *training* for the fight⟩ **4** : to aim at a target : bring to bear ⟨*trained* the gun on the enemy positions⟩ **5** : to undergo instruction, discipline, or drill ⟨children *trained* at home⟩ — **train·a·ble** \'trā-nə-bəl\ *adj* — **train·ee** \trā-'nē\ *n* — **train·er** \'trā-nər\ *n*

train·ing \'trā-ning\ *n* **1** : the course followed by one who trains or is being trained ⟨take nursing *training*⟩ **2** : the condition of one who has trained for a test or contest ***syn*** see EDUCATION

train oil \'trān-\ *n* : oil from a marine animal (as a whale)

traipse \'trāps\ *vb* : to walk or trudge about — **traipse** *n*

trait \'trāt\ *n* : a distinguishing quality (as of personality or physical makeup) : PECULIARITY ***syn*** see CHARACTERISTIC

trai·tor \'trāt-ər\ *n* [from French *traitre*, from Latin *traditor*, from *tradere* "to betray", literally "to hand over", from *trans-* "across" and *dare* "to give"] **1** : one who betrays another's trust or is false to an obligation or duty **2** : one who commits treason

trai·tor·ous \'trāt-ə-rəs, 'trā-trəs\ *adj* **1** : guilty or capable of treason **2** : constituting treason

tra·jec·to·ry \trə-'jek-t(ə-)rē\ *n, pl* **-ries** : the curve that a body (as a planet in its orbit, a projectile, or a rocket) describes in space

tram \'tram\ *n* **1** : a cart or wagon running on rails (as in a mine) **2** *chiefly Brit* : STREETCAR **3** : the carriage of an overhead conveyor

[1]**tram·mel** \'tram-əl\ *n* **1** : a net for catching birds or fish **2** : something impeding activity, progress, or freedom : RESTRAINT — usu. used in pl. **3** : an adjustable pothook for a fireplace crane

[2]**trammel** *vb* **-meled** *or* **-melled**; **-mel·ing** *or* **-mel·ling** **1** : to catch or hold in or as if in a net : ENMESH **2** : to prevent or impede the free play of : CONFINE

[1]**tramp** \'tramp, *1 & 2 are also* 'trämp\ *vb* **1** : to walk heavily **2** : to tread on forcibly and repeatedly : TRAMPLE **3** : to travel or wander through on foot ⟨*tramp* the streets⟩ — **tramp·er** *n*

[2]**tramp** \'tramp, *3 is also* 'trämp\ *n* **1** : a begging or thieving vagrant **2** : a walking trip : HIKE **3** : the succession of sounds made by the beating of marching feet **4** : a ship not making regular trips but taking cargo to any port

tram·ple \'tram-pəl\ *vb* **tram·pled**; **tram·pling** \-p(ə-)ling\ **1** : to tramp or tread heavily so as to bruise, crush, or injure **2** : to tread underfoot : stamp on **3** : to inflict pain, injury, or loss by ruthless or heartless treatment ⟨*trampled* on his feelings⟩ ⟨*trampled* over their weaker rivals⟩ — **trample** *n* — **tram·pler** \-p(ə-)lər\ *n*

tram·po·line \ˌtram-pə-ˈlēn\ *n* : a resilient canvas sheet or web supported by springs in a metal frame used as a springboard in tumbling

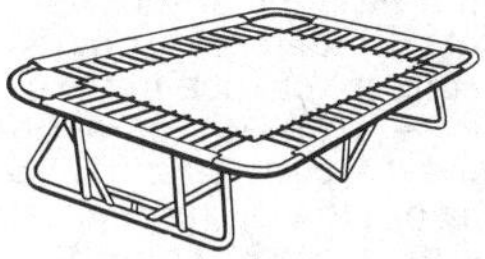

trampoline

tram·way \ˈtram-ˌwā\ *n* **1** : a road or way for trams **2** *Brit* : a streetcar line

trance \ˈtran(t)s\ *n* **1** : a state of partly suspended animation or inability to function : STUPOR **2** : a sleeplike state (as of deep hypnosis) **3** : a state of profound abstraction or absorption : ECSTASY

tran·quil \ˈtran(g)-kwəl\ *adj* : free from disturbance or turmoil : QUIET — **tran·quil·ly** \-kwə-lē\ *adv*

tran·quil·ize *or* **tran·quil·lize** \-kwə-ˌlīz\ *vb* : to make or become tranquil or relaxed; *esp* : to ease the mental tension and anxiety of usu. by means of drugs

tran·quil·iz·er \-ˌlī-zər\ *n* : one that tranquilizes; *esp* : a drug used to reduce anxiety and tension

tran·quil·li·ty *or* **tran·quil·i·ty** \tran(g)-ˈkwil-ət-ē\ *n* : the quality or state of being tranquil

trans- *prefix* **1** : on or to the other side of : across : beyond ⟨*trans*atlantic⟩ **2** : so or such as to change or transfer ⟨*trans*literate⟩ ⟨*trans*ship⟩

trans *abbr* **1** transitive **2** transportation

trans·act \tran(t)s-ˈakt, tranz-\ *vb* **1** : to carry through : bring about : NEGOTIATE ⟨*transact* a sale of property⟩ **2** : to carry on : CONDUCT ⟨*transact* business⟩ — **trans·ac·tor** \-ˈak-tər\ *n*

trans·ac·tion \-ˈak-shən\ *n* **1** : an act, process, or instance of transacting **2 a** : something transacted; *esp* : a business deal **b** *pl* : the record of the meeting of a society : PROCEEDINGS

trans·at·lan·tic \ˌtran(t)s-ət-ˈlant-ik, ˌtranz-\ *adj* : extending across or situated beyond the Atlantic ocean

tran·scend \tran-ˈsend\ *vb* **1** : to rise above or go beyond the limits of : EXCEED **2** : SURPASS ⟨a poem *transcending* all others⟩

tran·scend·ence \-ˈsen-dən(t)s\ *also* **tran·scend·en·cy** \-dən-sē\ *n* : the quality or state of being transcendent

tran·scend·ent \-dənt\ *adj* : exceeding usual limits

tran·scen·den·tal \ˌtran-ˌsen-ˈdent-əl, ˌtran(t)-sən-\ *adj* : TRANSCENDENT — **tran·scen·den·tal·ly** \-ə-lē\ *adv*

trans·con·ti·nen·tal \ˌtran(t)s-ˌkänt-ə-ˈnent-əl\ *adj* **1** : extending or going across a continent ⟨*transcontinental* railroad⟩ **2** : situated on the farther side of a continent

tran·scribe \tran-ˈskrīb\ *vb* **1 a** : to make a written copy of **b** : to make a copy of (dictated or recorded matter) in longhand or on a typewriter **2** : to represent speech sounds by means of phonetic symbols : to record for later broadcast **3** : to make a musical transcription of **4** : to broadcast by electrical transcription — **tran·scrib·er** *n*

tran·script \ˈtran-ˌskript\ *n* **1** : a written, printed, or typed copy **2** : an official copy (as of a student's educational record)

tran·scrip·tion \tran-ˈskrip-shən\ *n* **1** : an act, process, or instance of transcribing **2** : COPY, TRANSCRIPT **3 a** : an arrangement of a musical composition for some instrument or voice other than the original **b** : radio broadcasting from a phonograph record or magnetic tape; *also* : the record or tape itself

tran·sept \ˈtran-ˌsept\ *n* : the part forming the arms of a cross-shaped church

[1]**trans·fer** \tran(t)s-ˈfər, ˈtran(t)s-ˌ\ *vb* **trans·ferred**; **trans·fer·ring** **1 a** : to convey from one person, place, or situation to another : TRANSPORT **b** : to cause to pass from one to another : TRANSMIT **2** : to make over the possession or ownership of : CONVEY **3** : to print or otherwise copy from one surface to another by contact ⟨*transfer* the designs onto china⟩ **4** : to move to a different place, region, or situation; *esp* : to withdraw from one educational institution to enroll at another **5** : to change from one vehicle or transportation line to another — **trans·fer·a·ble** \tran(t)s-ˈfər-ə-bəl\ *adj* — **trans·fer·al** \-ˈfər-əl\ *n*

[2]**trans·fer** \ˈtran(t)s-ˌfər\ *n* **1** : conveyance of right, title, or interest in real or personal property from one person to another **2** : an act, process, or instance of transferring : TRANSFERENCE **3** : a person or thing that transfers or is transferred **4** : a graphic image transferred by contact from one surface to another **5** : a place where a transfer is made (as of trains to ferries) **6** : a ticket entitling a passenger on a public conveyance to continue his journey on another route

trans·fer·ence \tran(t)s-ˈfər-ən(t)s\ *n* : an act, process, or instance of transferring : TRANSFER

transfer RNA \ˈtran(t)s-ˌfər-\ *n* : a relatively small RNA molecule that functions in the transfer of a particular amino acid to the site of protein synthesis

trans·fig·u·ra·tion \(ˌ)tran(t)s-ˌfig-(y)ə-ˈrā-shən\ *n* **1** : a change of form or appearance; *esp* : a glorifying or exalting change **2** *cap* **a** : the supernatural change in the appearance of Jesus on the mountain **b** : a church festival on August 6 commemorating this

trans·fig·ure \tran(t)s-ˈfig-yər, *esp Brit* -ˈfig-ər\ *vb* **1** : to change the form or appearance of : METAMORPHOSE **2** : to make bright or radiant : EXALT, GLORIFY

trans·fix \tran(t)s-ˈfiks\ *vb* **1** : to pierce through with or as if with a pointed weapon : IMPALE **2** : to hold motionless by or as if by piercing ⟨*transfixed* him with a stare⟩

[1]**trans·form** \tran(t)s-ˈfȯrm\ *vb* **1 a** : to change in composition, structure, or character : CONVERT ⟨a caterpillar *transformed* into a butterfly⟩ **b** : to change in outward appearance ⟨city streets *transformed* by snow⟩ **2** : to substitute for or change (a mathematical expression) into another in accord with a mathematical rule **3** : to change (a current) in potential (as from high voltage to low) or in type (as from alternating to direct) — **trans·form·a·tive** \-ˈfȯr-mət-iv\ *adj*

[2]**trans·form** \ˈtran(t)s-ˌfȯrm\ *n* : a linguistic structure (as a sentence) which is derived from another structure or structures by means of a transformation ⟨"they ate and drank" is a *transform* of "they ate" and "they drank"⟩

trans·for·ma·tion \ˌtran(t)s-fər-ˈmā-shən\ *n* **1** : an act, process, or instance of transforming or being transformed **2** : a rule for changing one linguistic structure (as a sentence) into another ⟨"is he at home?" is derived from "he is at home" by means of the question *transformation*⟩ — **trans·for·ma·tion·al** \-sh(ə-)nəl\ *adj*

trans·form·er \tran(t)s-ˈfȯr-mər\ *n* : a device for changing an electric current into one of higher or lower voltage without changing the current energy

trans·fuse \tran(t)s-ˈfyüz\ *vb* **1 a** : to cause to pass from one to another **b** : PERMEATE **2** : to transfer (as blood) into a vein of a man or animal

trans·fu·sion \-ˈfyü-zhən\ *n* **1** : the passing of one thing into another **2** : a transferring into a vein of a person or animal ⟨blood *transfusion*⟩

trans·gress \tran(t)s-'gres, tranz-\ *vb* **[**from Latin *transgress-*, past participle stem of *transgredi*, from *trans-* and *gradi* "to step"**]** **1 :** to go beyond limits set by : VIOLATE ⟨*transgress* the divine law⟩ **2 :** to pass beyond or go over a limit or boundary **3 :** to violate a command or law : SIN — **trans·gres·sor** \-'gres-ər\ *n*

trans·gres·sion \-'gresh-ən\ *n* **:** an act, process, or instance of transgressing; *esp* **:** violation of a law, command, or duty

tran·ship *var of* TRANSSHIP

1**tran·sient** \'tran-chənt\ *adj* **1 :** not lasting or staying long ⟨a hotel accepts *transient* guests⟩ **2 :** changing in form or appearance : SHIFTING ⟨a *transient* scene⟩ — **tran·sient·ly** *adv*

2**transient** *n* **1 :** a transient guest **2 :** a person traveling about usu. in search of work

tran·sis·tor \tran-'zis-tər, -'sis-\ *n* **[**from *tran*sfer and re*sistor*; so called from its transferring an electrical signal across a resistor**]** **1 :** an electronic device that is similar to the electron tube in use and that consists of a small block of a semiconductor (as germanium) with at least three electrodes **2 :** a radio having transistors — called also *transistor radio*

tran·sis·tor·ize \-tə-ˌrīz\ *vb* **:** to equip with transistors

1**tran·sit** \'tran(t)s-ət, 'tranz-\ *n* **1 :** an act, process, or instance of passing through or over : PASSAGE **2 :** conveyance of persons or things from one place to another ⟨goods lost in *transit*⟩ **3 :** local transportation of people by public conveyance or a system of such transportation **4 a :** passage of a celestial body over the meridian of a place or through the field of a telescope **b :** passage of a smaller body across the disk of a larger ⟨the *transit* of Venus across the sun⟩ **5 :** a surveyor's instrument for measuring angles

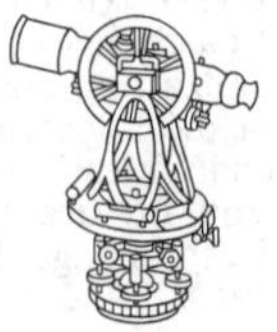
transit 5

2**transit** *vb* **:** to pass or cause to pass over, through, or across

tran·si·tion \tran(t)s-'ish-ən, tranz-\ *n* **1 :** a passing from one state, stage, place, or subject to another : CHANGE ⟨*transition* from war to peacetime⟩ **2 :** a musical passage leading from one section of a piece to another — **tran·si·tion·al** \-'ish-(ə-)nəl\ *adj* — **tran·si·tion·al·ly** \-ē\ *adv*

tran·si·tive \'tran(t)s-ət-iv, 'tranz-\ *adj* **1 :** characterized by having or containing a direct object ⟨a *transitive* verb⟩ **2 :** TRANSITIONAL — **tran·si·tive·ly** *adv*

tran·si·to·ry \'tran(t)s-ə-ˌtōr-ē, 'tranz-, -ˌtȯr-\ *adj* **:** lasting only a short time : SHORT-LIVED, TEMPORARY — **tran·si·to·ri·ly** \ˌtran(t)s-ə-'tōr-ə-lē, ˌtranz-, -'tȯr-\ *adv*

trans·late \tran(t)s-'lāt, tranz-\ *vb* **1 :** to bear or change from one place, state, form, or appearance to another : TRANSFER, TRANSFORM ⟨*translate* plans into action⟩ **2 :** to convey to heaven or to a nontemporal condition without death **3 :** to turn from one language into another ⟨*translated* into English⟩ — **trans·lat·a·ble** \-'lāt-ə-bəl\ *adj* — **trans·la·tor** \-'lāt-ər\ *n*

ə abut ər further a back ā bake
ä cot, cart au̇ out ch chin e less ē easy
g gift i trip ī life j joke ng sing ō flow
ȯ flaw ȯi coin th thin th this ü loot
u̇ foot y yet yü few yu̇ furious zh vision

trans·la·tion \-'lā-shən\ *n* **1 :** an act, process, or instance of translating **2 :** the product of translating ⟨a *translation* of the Bible⟩

trans·lit·er·ate \tran(t)s-'lit-ə-ˌrāt, tranz-\ *vb* **:** to represent or spell in the characters of another alphabet — **trans·lit·er·a·tion** \-ˌlit-ə-'rā-shən\ *n*

trans·lu·cent \tran(t)s-'lü-sənt, tranz-\ *adj* **1 :** shining or glowing through : LUMINOUS ⟨*translucent* rays of the sun⟩ **2 :** admitting and diffusing light so that objects beyond cannot be clearly distinguished ⟨frosted glass is *translucent*⟩ — **trans·lu·cence** \-sən(t)s\ *or* **trans·lu·cen·cy** \-sən-sē\ *n* — **trans·lu·cent·ly** *adv*

trans·mi·gra·tion \ˌtran(t)s-ˌmī-'grā-shən, ˌtranz-\ *n* **1 :** the changing of one's home from one country to another : MIGRATION **2 :** the passing of a soul into another body after death

trans·mis·si·ble \tran(t)s-'mis-ə-bəl, tranz-\ *adj* **:** capable of being transmitted ⟨*transmissible* diseases⟩

trans·mis·sion \-'mish-ən\ *n* **1 :** an act, process, or instance of transmitting something **2 :** the passage of radio waves in the space between transmitting and receiving stations **3 :** the mechanism by which the power that gives motion to a car is transmitted from the engine to the axle **4 :** something transmitted

trans·mit \tran(t)s-'mit, tranz-\ *vb* **trans·mit·ted; trans·mit·ting** **1 a :** to send or transfer from one person or place to another : FORWARD **b :** to convey by or as if by inheritance **c :** to convey abroad or to another ⟨*transmit* a disease⟩ **2 a :** to cause to pass or be conveyed through space or a medium : to admit the passage of ⟨glass *transmits* light⟩ **b :** to send out a signal either by radio waves or over a wire — **trans·mit·ta·ble** \-'mit-ə-bəl\ *adj* — **trans·mit·tal** \-'mit-əl\ *n*

trans·mit·ter \-'mit-ər\ *n* **1 :** one that transmits ⟨a *transmitter* of disease⟩ **2 :** the instrument in a telegraph system that sends out messages **3 :** the part of a telephone that includes the mouthpiece and a mechanism that picks up sound waves and sends them over the wire **4 :** the apparatus that sends out radio or television signals or the building in which it is housed

trans·mu·ta·tion \ˌtran(t)s-myu̇-'tā-shən, ˌtranz-\ *n* **:** an act or instance of transmuting or being transmuted; *esp* **:** conversion of one element into another either naturally or artificially

trans·mute \tran(t)s-'myüt, tranz-\ *vb* **1 :** to change or alter in form, appearance, or nature : CONVERT **2 :** to subject (as an element or a base metal) to transmutation — **trans·mut·a·ble** \-'myüt-ə-bəl\ *adj*

trans·oce·an·ic \(ˌ)tran(t)s-ˌō-shē-'an-ik, (ˌ)tranz-\ *adj* **1 :** lying or dwelling beyond the ocean **2 :** crossing or extending across the ocean ⟨*transoceanic* cables⟩

tran·som \'tran(t)-səm\ *n* **1 :** a horizontal crossbar in a window, over a door, or between a door and a window or fanlight above it **2 :** a window above a door or other window built on and commonly hinged to a transom

transom
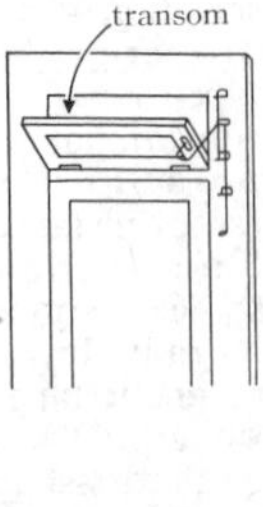

tran·son·ic *also* **trans–son·ic** \tran(t)s-'sän-ik, tran-'sän-\ *adj* **:** being or relating to a speed approximating the speed of sound in air — often used of aeronautical speeds between 600 and 900 miles per hour

trans·pa·cif·ic \ˌtran(t)s-pə-'sif-ik\ *adj* : crossing or extending across or situated beyond the Pacific ocean

trans·par·en·cy \tran(t)s-'par-ən-sē, -'per-\ *n, pl* **-cies 1** : the quality or state of being transparent **2** : a picture or design on glass, thin cloth, paper, or film viewed by light shining through it or by projection

trans·par·ent \-ənt\ *adj* **1 a** : transmitting light so that bodies lying beyond are entirely visible **b** : fine or sheer enough to be seen through ⟨*transparent* gauze⟩ **2** : easily detected or seen through : OBVIOUS ⟨*transparent* falsehood⟩ — **trans·par·ent·ly** *adv*

tran·spi·ra·tion \ˌtran(t)s-pə-'rā-shən\ *n* : the act or process or an instance of transpiring; *esp* : the passage of watery vapor from a living body through a membrane or pores — compare PERSPIRATION

tran·spire \tran(t)s-'pī(ə)r\ *vb* **1** : to pass off or give passage to (a fluid) through small openings; *esp* : to excrete watery vapor through a membrane or pores **2** : to become known or apparent : come to light ⟨their secrets never *transpired*⟩ **3** : to come to pass : OCCUR ⟨what *transpired* at the meeting⟩

1**trans·plant** \tran(t)s-'plant\ *vb* **1** : to lift and reset a plant in another soil or situation **2** : to remove from one place and settle or introduce elsewhere : TRANSPORT **3** : to transfer (an organ or tissue) from one part or individual to another — **trans·plan·ta·tion** \ˌtran(t)s-ˌplan-'tā-shən\ *n* — **trans·plant·er** \tran(t)s-'plant-ər\ *n*

2**trans·plant** \'tran(t)s-ˌplant\ *n* **1** : the act or process of transplanting **2** : something transplanted

trans·po·lar \(')tran(t)s-'pō-lər\ *adj* : going or extending across either of the polar regions

1**trans·port** \tran(t)s-'pōrt, -'pȯrt\ *vb* **1** : to convey from one place to another : CARRY **2** : ENRAPTURE ⟨*transported* with delight⟩ **3** : to send to a penal colony overseas — **trans·port·a·ble** \-ə-bəl\ *adj* — **trans·port·er** *n*

2**trans·port** \'tran(t)s-ˌpōrt, -ˌpȯrt\ *n* **1** : strong or intensely pleasurable emotion : ECSTASY, RAPTURE ⟨*transports* of joy⟩ **2 a** : a ship for carrying soldiers or military equipment **b** : a truck or plane used to transport persons or goods **3** : someone or something transported

trans·por·ta·tion \ˌtran(t)s-pər-'tā-shən\ *n* **1** : an act, process, or instance of transporting or being transported **2** : means of conveyance or travel from one place to another **3** : public conveyance of passengers or goods esp. as a commercial enterprise

trans·pose \tran(t)s-'pōz\ *vb* **1** : to change the relative place or normal order of : alter the sequence of ⟨*transpose* letters to change the spelling⟩ **2** : to write or perform (a musical composition) in a different key **3** : to bring (a term) from one side of an algebraic equation to the other with change of sign — **trans·pos·a·ble** \-'pō-zə-bəl\ *adj* — **trans·po·si·tion** \ˌtran(t)s-pə-'zish-ən\ *n*

trans·ship \tran-'ship, tran(t)s-\ *vb* : to transfer for further transportation from one ship or conveyance to another — **trans·ship·ment** \-mənt\ *n*

tran·sub·stan·ti·a·tion \ˌtran(t)-səb-ˌstan-chē-'ā-shən\ *n* **1** : an act or instance of changing or being changed into another substance **2** : the change in the consecrated bread and wine at Mass in substance but not in appearance to the body and blood of Christ

1**trans·ver·sal** \tran(t)s-'vər-səl, tranz-\ *adj* : TRANSVERSE ⟨*transversal* line⟩ — **trans·ver·sal·ly** \-sə-lē\ *adv*

2**transversal** *n* : a line that intersects a system of lines

trans·verse \tran(t)s-'vərs, tranz-\ *adj* : lying or being across : set crosswise ⟨the *transverse* pieces in a window frame⟩ — **trans·verse·ly** *adv*

transverse wave *n* : a wave in which the vibrating element moves in a direction perpendicular to the direction in which the wave advances

1**trap** \'trap\ *n* **1** : a device (as a snare or pitfall) for catching animals; *esp* : one that holds by springing shut suddenly **2** : something by which one is caught or stopped unawares **3 a** : a device for hurling clay pigeons into the air **b** : a hazard on a golf course consisting of a depression containing sand **4** : a light usu. one-horse carriage with springs **5 a** : any of various devices for preventing passage of something often while allowing other matter to proceed **b** : a device for drains or sewers consisting of a bend or partitioned chamber in which the liquid forms a seal to prevent the passage of sewer gas **6** *pl* : PERCUSSION INSTRUMENTS

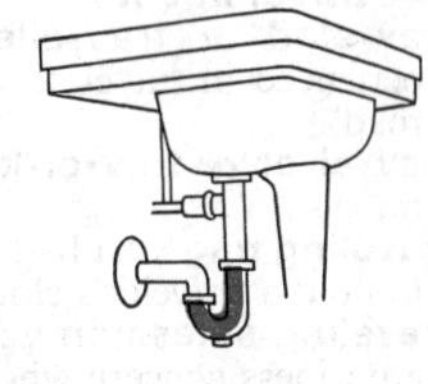
trap 5b

2**trap** *vb* **trapped**; **trap·ping 1 a** : to catch in or as if in a trap : ENSNARE **b** : to place in a restricted position : CONFINE **2** : to provide with a trap **3** : to engage in trapping animals (as for fur) — **trap·per** *n*

3**trap** *or* **trap·rock** \'trap-'räk\ *n* : any of various dark-colored fine-grained igneous rocks used esp. in road making

trap·door \'trap-'dō(ə)r, -'dȯ(ə)r\ *n* : a lifting or sliding door covering an opening in a roof, ceiling, or floor

trap-door spider *n* : any of various spiders that build silk-lined underground nests topped with a hinged lid

tra·peze \tra-'pēz\ *n* : a gymnastic or acrobatic device consisting of a short horizontal bar suspended at a height by two parallel ropes

trap·e·zoid \'trap-ə-ˌzȯid\ *n* : a 4-sided plane figure having only two sides parallel — **trap·e·zoi·dal** \ˌtrap-ə-'zȯid-əl\ *adj*

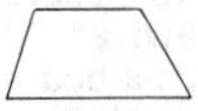
trapezoid

trap·line \'trap-ˌlīn\ *n* : a line or series of traps; *also* : the route along which such a line of traps is set

trap·pings \'trap-ingz\ *n pl* **1** : CAPARISON 1 **2** : outward decoration or dress : ORNAMENTS

trap·shoot·ing \'trap-ˌshüt-ing\ *n* : shooting at clay pigeons sprung into the air from a trap — **trap-shoot·er** \-ˌshüt-ər\ *n*

trash \'trash\ *n* **1** : something worth little or nothing : JUNK, RUBBISH **2** : a worthless or disreputable person — **trashy** \'trash-ē\ *adj*

trash farming *n* : a method of cultivation in which the soil is loosened by methods that leave chopped-up vegetation and stubble on or near the surface to check erosion and serve as a mulch

tra·vail \trə-'vāl, 'trav-ˌāl\ *n* **1** : work esp. of a painful or laborious nature : TOIL **2** : a piece of work : TASK **3** : AGONY, TORMENT — **travail** *vb*

1**trav·el** \'trav-əl\ *vb* **-eled** *or* **-elled**; **-el·ing** *or* **-el·ling** \-(ə-)ling\ [from Middle English *travailen* "to undergo travail" from Old French *travaillier*, from Latin *tripalium* "instrument of torture", from *tri-* and *palus* "stake"] **1** : to journey from place to place or to a distant place **2** : to journey from place to place selling or taking orders **3** : to move or advance from one place to another ⟨the pain *traveled* all the way up his arm⟩ **4** : to journey through or

over : TRAVERSE ⟨this road can be *traveled* only on horseback⟩
²**travel** *n* **1 a** : the act of traveling : PASSAGE **b** : JOURNEY, TRIP — often used in pl. **2** : the number traveling : TRAFFIC
travel agency *n* : an agency engaged in selling, arranging, or furnishing information about personal transportation or travel — called also *travel bureau* — **travel agent** *n*
trav·eled *or* **trav·elled** \'trav-əld\ *adj* **1** : experienced in travel **2** : used by travelers ⟨a *traveled* road⟩
trav·el·er *or* **trav·el·ler** \'trav-(ə-)lər\ *n* : one that travels
traveling bag *n* : a bag carried by hand and designed to hold a traveler's clothing and personal articles
traveling salesman *n* : a traveling representative of a business concern who solicits orders
trav·el·ogue *also* **trav·el·og** \'trav-ə-ˌlȯg\ *n* : a usu. illustrated lecture on travel
travel trailer *n* : a trailer (sense 2) small enough to be towed by a car
tra·vers·al \trə-'vər-səl\ *n* : the act or an instance of traversing
¹**trav·erse** \'trav-ərs\ *n* : something that crosses or lies across
²**tra·verse** \trə-'vərs\ *vb* **1** : to pass through, across, or over **2** : to move back and forth or from side to side ⟨the guard *traversed* the patrol area⟩
³**trav·erse** \'trav-(ˌ)ərs, trə-'vərs\ *adj* : lying across : TRANSVERSE
trav·es·ty \'trav-ə-stē\ *n, pl* **-ties** **1** : a burlesque and usu. grotesque translation or imitation **2** : an inferior imitation or likeness ⟨a *travesty* of justice⟩ — **travesty** *vb*
tra·vois \trə-'vȯi, 'trav-ˌȯi\ *also* **tra·voise** \-'vȯiz, -ˌȯiz\ *n, pl* **tra·vois** \-'vȯiz, -ˌȯiz\ *also* **tra·vois·es** \-'vȯi-zəz, -ˌȯi-zəz\ : a vehicle used by Indians of the Great Plains consisting of two trailing poles serving as shafts and bearing a platform or net for the load
¹**trawl** \'trȯl\ *vb* : to fish or catch with a trawl
²**trawl** *n* **1** : a large cone-shaped net dragged along the sea bottom in fishing **2** : a long heavy fishline to which several hooks are attached in series
trawl·er \'trȯ-lər\ *n* **1** : a person who trawls **2** : a boat used for trawling
tray \'trā\ *n* : an open receptacle with flat bottom and low rim for holding, carrying, or exhibiting articles
treach·er·ous \'trech-(ə-)rəs\ *adj* **1** : guilty of or inclined to treachery **2** : giving a false appearance of safety ⟨*treacherous* quicksand⟩ — **treach·er·ous·ly** *adv*
treach·ery \'trech-(ə-)rē\ *n, pl* **-er·ies** **1** : violation of allegiance or of faith and confidence : TREASON **2** : an act of treason
trea·cle \'trē-kəl\ *n, chiefly Brit* : MOLASSES
¹**tread** \'tred\ *vb* **trod** \'träd\; **trod·den** \'träd-ən\ *or* **trod**; **tread·ing** **1 a** : to step or walk on or over **b** : to walk along : FOLLOW **2** : to beat or press with the feet : TRAMPLE **3 a** : to form by treading : BEAT ⟨*tread* a path⟩ **b** : to execute by stepping or dancing ⟨*tread* a measure⟩ — **tread·er** *n* — **tread water** : to keep the body nearly upright in the water and the head above water by a treading motion of the feet usu. aided by the hands

ə abut	ər further	a back	ā bake
ä cot, cart	au̇ out	ch chin	e less	ē easy
g gift	i trip	ī life	j joke	ng sing	ō flow
ȯ flaw	ȯi coin	th thin	th this	ü loot
u̇ foot	y yet	yü few	yu̇ furious	zh vision

²**tread** *n* **1** : a mark made by or as if by treading **2** : the action, manner, or sound of treading or stepping **3 a** : the part of a sole that touches the ground **b** : the part of a wheel that bears on a road or rail; *esp* : the thickened face of an automobile tire **4** : the horizontal part of a step
¹**trea·dle** \'tred-əl\ *n* : a lever or other device pressed by the foot to drive a machine
²**treadle** *vb* **trea·dled**; **trea·dling** \'tred-(ə-)ling\ : to operate a treadle on a machine
tread·mill \'tred-ˌmil\ *n* **1** : a device moved by persons treading on steps set around the rim of a wide wheel or by animals walking on an endless belt **2** : a wearisome or monotonous routine
trea·son \'trē-zən\ *n* **1** : the betrayal of a trust **2** : the offense of attempting to overthrow the government of the state to which one owes allegiance or to bring about its defeat in war
trea·son·a·ble \'trēz-(ə-)nə-bəl\ *adj* : relating to, consisting of, or involving treason — **trea·son·a·bly** \-blē\ *adv*
trea·son·ous \'trēz-(ə-)nəs\ *adj* : TREASONABLE
¹**trea·sure** \'trezh-ər, 'trāzh-\ *n* [from Old French *tresor*, from Latin *thesaurus*, from Greek *thēsauros*] **1** : wealth (as money, jewels, or precious metals) stored up or hoarded ⟨buried *treasure*⟩ **2** : something of great worth or value
²**treasure** *vb* **trea·sured**; **trea·sur·ing** \-(ə-)ring\ **1** : to collect and store up (something of value) for future use : HOARD **2** : to hold or keep as precious : CHERISH — **trea·sur·a·ble** \-(ə-)rə-bəl\ *adj*
trea·sur·er \'trezh-(ə-)rər, 'trāzh-\ *n* : a person trusted with charge of a treasure or a treasury; *esp* : an officer of a club, business, or government who has charge of money taken in and paid out
treasure trove \'trezh-ər-ˌtrōv, 'trāzh-\ *n* **1** : treasure found buried in the ground or hidden away and of unknown ownership **2** : a discovery or something discovered that is full of things to be treasured
trea·sury \'trezh-(ə-)rē, 'trāzh-\ *n, pl* **trea·sur·ies** **1 a** : a place in which stores of wealth are kept **b** : the place of deposit and disbursement of collected funds **2** *cap* : a governmental department in charge of finances **3** : a repository for treasures ⟨a *treasury* of poems⟩
¹**treat** \'trēt\ *vb* **1** : to discuss terms of accommodation or settlement : NEGOTIATE ⟨*treat* with the enemy⟩ **2 a** : to deal with a matter esp. in writing : DISCOURSE ⟨books *treating* of crime⟩ **b** : to deal with : HANDLE **3 a** : to bear the expense of another's entertainment **b** : to provide with free food, entertainment, or enjoyment **4 a** : to behave or act toward : USE ⟨*treat* a horse cruelly⟩ **b** : to regard and deal with in a specified manner ⟨*treat* as confidential⟩ **5** : to care for or deal with medically or surgically **6** : to subject to some action (as of a chemical) ⟨*treat* soil with lime⟩
²**treat** *n* **1** : an entertainment (as a picnic) given without expense to those invited **2** : a source esp. when unexpected of pleasure or amusement ⟨the *treat* of seeing him again⟩ ⟨served ice cream and cookies afterward as a *treat* for the kids⟩
trea·tise \'trēt-əs\ *n* : a book or an article treating a subject systematically ⟨a *treatise* on war⟩
treat·ment \'trēt-mənt\ *n* **1** : the act or manner or an instance of treating someone or something : HANDLING, USAGE **2** : a substance or technique used in treating ⟨a beauty *treatment*⟩
trea·ty \'trēt-ē\ *n, pl* **treaties** : an agreement or arrangement made by negotiation; *esp* : a contract between two or more states or sovereigns
¹**tre·ble** \'treb-əl\ *n* **1 a** : the highest of the four voice

parts in vocal music : SOPRANO **b** : a singer or instrument taking this part **2** : a high-pitched or shrill voice, tone, or sound **3** : the upper half of the musical pitch range

2**treble** *adj* **1 a** : having three parts **b** : triple in number or amount **2 a** : relating to or having the range of a musical treble ⟨*treble* voice⟩ **b** : high-pitched : SHRILL

3**treble** *vb* **tre·bled**; **tre·bling** \ˈtreb-(ə-)liŋ\ : to make or become three times the size, amount, or number ⟨*treble* its weight⟩

treble clef *n* **1** : a clef that places G above middle C on the second line of the staff **2** : TREBLE STAFF

treble staff *n* : the musical staff carrying the treble clef

1**tree** \ˈtrē\ *n* **1 a** : a perennial woody plant with a single main stem usu. of considerable height that bears branches and foliage mostly near the top **b** : a shrub or herb of treelike form ⟨rose *trees*⟩ ⟨a banana *tree*⟩ **2** : a piece of wood (as a bar or pole) usu. dressed and fitted for a particular use or forming part of a structure or implement **3** : something in the form of a tree ⟨family *tree*⟩ — **tree·less** \-ləs\ *adj* — **tree·like** \-ˌlīk\ *adj*

2**tree** *vb* **treed**; **tree·ing** **1 a** : to drive to or up a tree ⟨*treed* by a bull⟩ **b** : to bring to bay : CORNER **2** : to furnish or fit with a tree ⟨*tree* an axle⟩

tree farm *n* : an area of forest land managed to ensure continuous commercial production — **tree farmer** *n*

tree fern *n* : a tropical fern with a woody stalk and a crown of large often feathery fronds

tree frog *n* : any of a family of tailless tree-dwelling amphibians (as the spring peeper)

tree of heaven : an ailanthus widely grown as a shade and ornamental tree

tree ring *n* : ANNUAL RING

tree toad *n* : TREE FROG

tre·foil \ˈtrē-ˌfȯil, ˈtref-ˌȯil\ *n* **1 a** : CLOVER **b** : any of several herbs related to the clovers and having leaves with three leaflets **2** : an ornament or symbol in the form of a 3-parted leaf

trefoil 2

1**trek** \ˈtrek\ *n* **1** *chiefly southern Africa* : an organized migration of a group of settlers by ox wagon **2** : a slow or difficult journey or migration

2**trek** *vb* **trekked**; **trek·king** [from South African Dutch, from Dutch *trekken* "to pull", "haul", "migrate"] **1** *chiefly southern Africa* : to migrate by ox wagon or in a train of such wagons **2** : to make one's way arduously

1**trel·lis** \ˈtrel-əs\ *n* : a frame of latticework used esp. as a screen or a support for climbing plants

2**trellis** *vb* **1** : to provide with or train on a trellis ⟨*trellis* a vine⟩ **2** : to cross or interlace on or through : INTERWEAVE

trem·a·tode \ˈtrem-ə-ˌtōd\ *n* : any of a class of parasitic flatworms including the flukes — **trematode** *adj*

1**trem·ble** \ˈtrem-bəl\ *vb* **trem·bled**; **trem·bling** \-b(ə-)liŋ\ **1** : to shake involuntarily (as with fear or cold) : SHIVER **2** : to move, sound, pass, or come to pass as if shaken or tremulous **3** : to be affected with fear or doubt ⟨*tremble* for the safety of a friend⟩ — **trem·bler** \-b(ə-)lər\ *n*

2**tremble** *n* **1** : a fit or spell of involuntary shaking or quivering **2** : a tremor or series of tremors

trem·bly \ˈtrem-b(ə-)lē\ *adj* : marked by trembling : TREMULOUS

tre·men·dous \tri-ˈmen-dəs\ *adj* **1** : such as may excite trembling or arouse dread, awe, or terror : DREADFUL **2** : astonishing by reason of extreme size, power, greatness, or excellence ***syn*** see MONSTROUS — **tre·men·dous·ly** *adv*

trem·o·lo \ˈtrem-ə-ˌlō\ *n, pl* **-los** **1** : the rapid reiteration of a musical tone or of alternating tones to produce a tremulous effect **2** : a mechanical device in an organ for causing a tremulous effect

trem·or \ˈtrem-ər\ *n* **1** : a trembling or shaking usu. from weakness or disease **2** : a quivering or vibratory motion (as of the earth or a leaf) **3** : a feeling of uncertainty or insecurity

trem·u·lous \ˈtrem-yə-ləs\ *adj* **1** : characterized by or affected with trembling or tremors ⟨*tremulous* hands⟩ **2** : affected with timidity : TIMOROUS ⟨a shy *tremulous* girl⟩ **3** : such as is caused by a tremulous state ⟨a *tremulous* smile⟩

1**trench** \ˈtrench\ *n* **1 a** : a long narrow cut in land : DITCH **b** : a long narrow depression in an ocean floor **2** : a long ditch protected by a bank of earth thrown before it that is used to shelter soldiers

2**trench** *vb* **1** : to protect with or as if with a trench **2** : to cut a trench in : DITCH **3** : to come close : VERGE ⟨his answer *trenched* on impudence⟩

tren·chant \ˈtren-chənt\ *adj* **1** : having a sharp edge or point : CUTTING ⟨a *trenchant* blade⟩ ⟨*trenchant* sarcasm⟩ **2** : sharply clear : PENETRATING ⟨a *trenchant* analysis of a situation⟩ **3** : mentally energetic — **tren·chant·ly** *adv*

trench coat *n* **1** : a waterproof overcoat with a removable lining **2** : a loose double-breasted raincoat with deep pockets, belt, and straps on the shoulders

1**tren·cher** \ˈtren-chər\ *n* : a usu. wooden platter for serving food

2**trench·er** \ˈtren-chər\ *n* : one that digs trenches

tren·cher·man \-mən\ *n* **1** : a hearty eater **2** *archaic* : HANGER-ON, SPONGER

trench mouth *n* [so called from its having been common among soldiers in the trenches during World War I] : a destructive infectious inflammation of the mouth

1**trend** \ˈtrend\ *vb* **1** : to extend in a general direction **2** : to show a tendency : INCLINE

2**trend** *n* **1** : general direction taken ⟨easterly *trend* of the shoreline⟩ **2 a** : a prevailing tendency or inclination : DRIFT **b** : a general movement : SWING **c** : a current style or preference

trep·i·da·tion \ˌtrep-ə-ˈdā-shən\ *n* : a state of alarm : FEAR

1**tres·pass** \ˈtres-pəs, -ˌpas\ *n* **1** : a violation of morals; *esp* : SIN **2** : an unlawful act committed on the person, property, or rights of another

2**trespass** *vb* **1** : ERR, SIN **2** : to commit a trespass; *esp* : to enter unlawfully upon the land of another — **tres·pass·er** *n*

tress \ˈtres\ *n* **1** : a long lock of hair **2** *pl* : the long unbound hair of a woman

tres·tle \ˈtres-əl\ *n* **1** : a braced frame consisting usu. of a horizontal piece with spreading legs at each end that supports something (as a tabletop or drawing board) **2** : a braced framework of timbers or steel for carrying a road or railroad over a depression

trey \ˈtrā\ *n, pl* **treys** : a card or dice with three spots

tri- *prefix* **1** : three : having three elements or parts ⟨*tri*motor⟩ **2** : into three ⟨*tri*sect⟩ **3** : thrice ⟨*tri*weekly⟩ : every third ⟨*tri*monthly⟩

tri·ad \ˈtrī-ˌad, -əd\ *n* : a union or group of three usu. closely related persons or things

[1]**tri·al** \'trī(-ə)l\ *n* **1** : the action or process of trying or putting to the proof : TEST **2** : formal examination before a competent tribunal of the matter in issue in a civil or criminal case **3** : a test of faith, patience, or stamina **4** : a tryout or experiment to test quality, value, or usefulness **5** : ATTEMPT, EFFORT

[2]**trial** *adj* **1** : of, relating to, or used in a trial **2** : made or done as a test or experiment **3** : used or tried out in a test or experiment

tri·an·gle \'trī-ˌang-gəl\ *n* **1** : a polygon having three

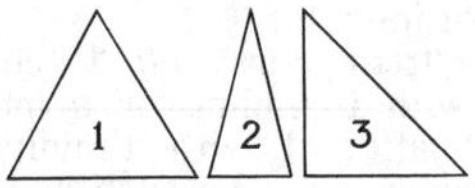

triangles 1: 1, equilateral; 2, isosceles; 3, right-angled

sides **2** : a musical percussion instrument made of a steel rod bent into the form of a triangle open at one angle **3** : a drafting instrument consisting of a thin flat right-angled triangle

tri·an·gu·lar \trī-'ang-gyə-lər\ *adj* **1 a** : of, relating to, or having the form of a triangle **b** : having a triangular base or principal surface ⟨*triangular* table⟩ ⟨*triangular* pyramid⟩ **2** : of, relating to, or involving three parts or persons ⟨a *triangular* business deal⟩ ⟨a *triangular* love affair⟩ — **tri·an·gu·lar·i·ty** \(ˌ)trī-ˌang-gyə-'lar-ət-ē\ *n* — **tri·an·gu·lar·ly** \trī-'ang-gyə-lər-lē\ *adv*

triangular numbers *n pl* : numbers (as 1, 3, 6, 10, 15) that are of the general form $\frac{2(n+1)}{2}$ where $n = 1, 2, 3, \ldots$ and represent the number of dots in the figures formed starting with one dot and adding successive rows to form triangles each row of which has one more dot than the preceding

tri·an·gu·la·tion \(ˌ)trī-ˌang-gyə-'lā-shən\ *n* : the measurement of the elements necessary to determine the network of triangles into which any part of the earth's surface is divided in surveying

Tri·as·sic \trī-'as-ik\ *n* : the earliest period of the Mesozoic era; *also* : the corresponding system of rocks — **Triassic** *adj*

trib *abbr* tributary

trib·al \'trī-bəl\ *adj* : of, relating to, or characteristic of a tribe ⟨*tribal* customs⟩ ⟨*tribal* chiefs⟩ — **trib·al·ly** \-bə-lē\ *adv*

tribe \'trīb\ *n* **1** : a usu. primitive social group comprising numerous families, clans, or generations **2** : a group of persons having a common character, occupation, or interest **3** : a group of closely related animals or strains within a breed

tribes·man \'trībz-mən\ *n* : a member of a tribe

tribes·wom·an \-ˌwu̇m-ən\ *n* : a female member of a tribe

trib·u·la·tion \ˌtrib-yə-'lā-shən\ *n* **1** : distress or suffering resulting from oppression, persecution, or affliction **2** : a trying experience

tri·bu·nal \trī-'byün-əl, trib-'yün-\ *n* **1** : the seat of a judge **2** : a court of justice **3** : something that decides or determines ⟨the *tribunal* of public opinion⟩

trib·une \'trib-ˌyün, trib-'yün\ *n* **1** : a Roman official with the function of protecting the plebeian citizen from arbitrary action by patrician magistrates **2** : a defender of the people esp. against arbitrary abuse of authority — **trib·une·ship** \-ˌship\ *n*

[1]**trib·u·tary** \'trib-yə-ˌter-ē\ *adj* **1** : paying tribute to another : SUBJECT **2** : paid or owed as tribute **3** : CONTRIBUTORY **4** : flowing into a larger stream or a lake

[2]**tributary** *n, pl* **-tar·ies** **1** : a ruler or state that pays tribute **2** : a stream feeding a larger stream or a lake

trib·ute \'trib-ˌyüt, -yət\ *n* **1 a** : a payment made by one ruler or nation to another to show submission or to secure peace or protection **b** : a tax to raise money for a tribute **c** : the obligation to pay tribute ⟨nations under *tribute*⟩ **2** : a gift or service showing respect, gratitude, or affection ⟨floral *tribute*⟩; *esp* : PRAISE, CREDIT ⟨pay *tribute* to her achievements⟩

[1]**trice** \'trīs\ *vb* : to haul up or in and lash or secure with a small rope ⟨*trice* the sail⟩

[2]**trice** *n* : a brief space of time : INSTANT — used chiefly in the phrase *in a trice*

tri·ceps \'trī-ˌseps\ *n, pl* **tri·ceps·es** *also* **triceps** : a muscle that arises from three heads; *esp* : the great extensor muscle along the back of the upper arm

tri·cer·a·tops \trī-'ser-ə-ˌtäps\ *n* : a large plant-eating Cretaceous dinosaur with three horns, a bony hood or crest on the neck, and hoofed toes

tri·chi·na \trə-'kī-nə\ *n, pl* **-nae** \-(ˌ)nē\ *also* **-nas** **1** : a small slender nematode worm that in the larval state is parasitic in the voluntary muscles of flesh-eating mammals (as man and hog) **2** : TRICHINOSIS — **trich·i·nous** \'trik-ə-nəs, trə-'kī-nəs\ *adj*

trich·i·no·sis \ˌtrik-ə-'nō-səs\ *n, pl* **-no·ses** \-'nō-ˌsēz\ : a disease caused by trichinae that is contracted esp. by eating raw or undercooked infested food

tri·chop·ter·an \trik-'äp-tə-rən\ *n* : CADDIS FLY — **trichopteran** *or* **tri·chop·ter·ous** \-rəs\ *adj*

[1]**trick** \'trik\ *n* **1 a** : a crafty procedure or practice meant to deceive or defraud **b** : a mischievous act : PRANK **c** : an indiscreet or childish action **d** : a dexterous or ingenious feat designed to puzzle or amuse ⟨a juggler's *tricks*⟩ **2** : an habitual peculiarity of behavior or manner **3 a** : a quick or artful way of getting a result : KNACK **b** : a technical device ⟨the *tricks* of stage technique⟩ **4** : the cards played in one round of a card game often used as a scoring unit **5** : a turn of duty : a working shift

[2]**trick** *adj* : of or relating to or involving tricks or trickery ⟨*trick* photography⟩ ⟨*trick* dice⟩

[3]**trick** *vb* **1** : to deceive by cunning or artifice : CHEAT **2** : to dress or adorn esp. fancifully or ornately ⟨*tricked* out in a gaudy uniform⟩

trick·ery \'trik-(ə-)rē\ *n, pl* **-er·ies** : the use of tricks to deceive or defraud

trick·le \'trik-əl\ *vb* **trick·led**; **trick·ling** \-(ə-)ling\ **1** : to issue or fall in drops **2** : to flow in a thin gentle stream — **trickle** *n*

trick·ster \'trik-stər\ *n* : one who tricks or cheats

tricky \'trik-ē\ *adj* **trick·i·er**; **-est** **1** : of or characteristic of a trickster : SLY **2** : requiring skill, aptitude, or caution : DELICATE ⟨a *tricky* puzzle⟩

[1]**tri·col·or** \'trī-ˌkəl-ər\ *n* : a flag of three colors ⟨the French *tricolor*⟩

[2]**tricolor** *or* **tri·col·ored** \-ˌkəl-ərd\ *adj* : having or using three colors

tri·cot \'trē-kō, 'trī-kət\ *n* : a plain warp-knitted fabric (as for underwear) of nylon, wool, rayon, silk, or cotton

tri·cy·cle \'trī-ˌsik-əl\ *n* : a 3-wheeled vehicle propelled by pedals, hand levers, or a motor

tri·dent \'trīd-ənt\ *n* [from Latin *trident-*, stem of

ə abut	ər further	a back	ā bake	
ä cot, cart	au̇ out	ch chin	e less	ē easy
g gift	i trip	ī life	j joke	ng sing	ō flow
ȯ flaw	ȯi coin	th thin	t͟h this	ü loot
u̇ foot	y yet	yü few	yu̇ furious	zh vision

tridens, from *tri-* + *dens* "tooth"] : a 3-pronged spear — **trident** *adj*

tried \'trīd\ *adj* : found good, faithful, or trustworthy through experience or testing

tri·en·ni·al \(')trī-'en-ē-əl\ *adj* **1** : consisting of or lasting for three years **2** : occurring or being done every three years — **triennial** *n* — **tri·en·ni·al·ly** \-ē-ə-lē\ *adv*

[1]**tri·fle** \'trī-fəl\ *n* **1** : something of little value or importance; *esp* : an insignificant amount (as of money) **2** : a dessert of sponge cake spread with jam or jelly covered with a custard and whipped cream

[2]**trifle** *vb* **tri·fled**; **tri·fling** \-f(ə-)liŋ\ **1 a** : to talk in a jesting or mocking manner with intent to mislead **b** : to act in a heedless or frivolous manner : PLAY **2** : to waste time : DALLY **3** : to spend or waste in trifling or on trifles **4** : to handle something idly : TOY — **tri·fler** \-f(ə-)lər\ *n*

tri·fling \'trī-fliŋ\ *adj* **1** : lacking in significance or seriousness : FRIVOLOUS ⟨*trifling* talk⟩ **2** : of little value : TRIVIAL ⟨a *trifling* gift⟩

trig \'trig\ *n* : TRIGONOMETRY

[1]**trig·ger** \'trig-ər\ *n* : a movable lever attached to a catch that when released by pressure allows a mechanism to go into action; *esp* : the part of the lock of a firearm that releases the hammer and so fires the gun — **trigger** *adj* — **trig·gered** \-ərd\ *adj*

[2]**trigger** *vb* **trig·gered**; **trig·ger·ing** \-(ə-)riŋ\ **1** : to fire by pulling a mechanical trigger ⟨*trigger* a rifle⟩ **2** : to initiate, actuate, or set in motion as if by pulling a trigger

trig·o·no·met·ric \ˌtrig-ə-nə-'me-trik\ *adj* : of, relating to, or in accordance with trigonometry — **trig·o·no·met·ri·cal** \-tri-kəl\ *adj* — **trig·o·no·met·ri·cal·ly** \-tri-k(ə-)lē\ *adv*

trigonometric function *n* : one of a group of functions (as the sine) based on ratios between pairs of sides of a right-angled triangle

trig·o·nom·e·try \ˌtrig-ə-'näm-ə-trē\ *n* [from Greek *trigōnon* "triangle" (from *tri-* and *gōnia* "angle") and *metron* "measure"] : the study of the properties of triangles and trigonometric functions and of their applications

tri·lat·er·al \(')trī-'lat-ə-rəl, -'la-trəl\ *adj* : having three sides — **tri·lat·er·al·ly** \-ē\ *adv*

[1]**trill** \'tril\ *n* **1 a** : the alternation of two musical tones a scale degree apart **b** : VIBRATO **2** : WARBLE **3** : the rapid vibration of one speech organ against another (as of the tip of the tongue against the ridge just above and behind the upper front teeth)

[2]**trill** *vb* **1** : to utter as or with a trill **2** : to play or sing with a trill : QUAVER

tril·lion \'tril-yən\ *n* — see NUMBER table — **trillion** *adj* — **tril·lionth** \-yən(t)th\ *adj* — **trillionth** *n*

tril·li·um \'tril-ē-əm\ *n* : any of a genus of herbs related to the lily and having an erect stem bearing a whorl of three leaves and a large solitary 3-petaled flower

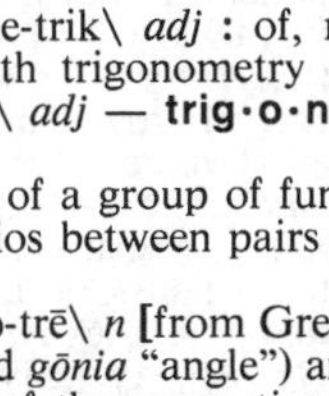

trillium

tri·lo·bate \(')trī-'lō-ˌbāt\ *or* **tri·lo·bat·ed** \-ˌbāt-əd\ *or* **tri·lobed** \'trī-'lōbd\ *adj* : having three lobes ⟨a *trilobate* leaf⟩

tri·lo·bite \'trī-lə-ˌbīt\ *n* : any of a group of extinct Paleozoic marine arthropods having a segmented body divided by longitudinal furrows on the back into three lobes — **trilobite** *or* **tri·lo·bit·ic** \ˌtrī-lə-'bit-ik\ *adj*

tril·o·gy \'tril-ə-jē\ *n, pl* **-gies** : a series of three literary or musical compositions that are closely related and develop a single theme although each individual work is complete

[1]**trim** \'trim\ *vb* **trimmed**; **trim·ming** **1 a** : to embellish with ribbons, lace, or ornaments : ADORN ⟨*trim* a Christmas tree⟩ **b** : to arrange a display of goods in ⟨*trim* a shop window⟩ **2** : to defeat resoundingly **3 a** : to make trim and neat esp. by cutting or clipping **b** : to free of excess or extraneous matter by or as if by cutting ⟨*trim* a budget⟩ **4 a** : to cause (a ship or boat) to assume a desirable position in the water by arrangement of ballast, cargo, or passengers **b** : to adjust to a desired position ⟨*trim* a sail⟩ ⟨*trim* an airplane⟩ ⟨*trim* a surfboard⟩ **5** : to maintain neutrality between opposing parties — **trim·mer** *n*

[2]**trim** *adj* **trim·mer**; **trim·mest** : neat, orderly, and compact in line or structure ⟨*trim* houses⟩ ⟨a *trim* figure⟩ — **trim·ly** *adv* — **trim·ness** *n*

[3]**trim** *adv* : TRIMLY

[4]**trim** *n* **1** : the readiness of a person or thing for action or use : FITNESS **2 a** : material used for ornament or trimming **b** : the woodwork in the finish of a building esp. around openings **c** : the interior furnishings of an automobile **3 a** : the position of a ship or boat esp. with reference to the horizontal **b** : the relation between the plane of a sail and the direction of the ship **4** : something that is trimmed off or cut out

trim·e·ter \'trim-ət-ər\ *n* : a line consisting of three metrical feet

trim·ming \'trim-iŋ\ *n* **1** : the action of one that trims **2** : BEATING, DEFEAT **3** : something that trims, ornaments, or completes ⟨the *trimming* on a hat⟩ ⟨roast turkey and all the *trimmings*⟩ **4** *pl* : parts removed by trimming

tri·month·ly \(')trī-'mən(t)th-lē\ *adj* : occurring every three months

trin·i·ty \'trin-ət-ē\ *n, pl* **-ties** **1** *cap* : the unity of Father, Son, and Holy Spirit as three persons in one Godhead **2** : TRIAD

Trinity Sunday *n* : the 8th Sunday after Easter

Trin·i·ty·tide \'trin-ət-ē-ˌtīd\ *n* : the season of the church year between Trinity Sunday and Advent

trin·ket \'triŋ-kət\ *n* **1** : a small ornament (as a jewel or ring) **2** : a thing of little value : TRIFLE

[1]**tri·no·mi·al** \trī-'nō-mē-əl\ *n* **1** : a polynomial of three terms **2** : a name in biological classification consisting of three terms of which the first denotes the genus, the second the species, and the third the particular variety or subspecies named by the combination

[2]**trinomial** *adj* **1** : consisting of three terms **2** : of or relating to trinomials

trio \'trē-ō\ *n, pl* **tri·os** **1 a** : a musical composition for three voice parts or three instruments **b** : the performers of a musical trio **2** : a group or set of three

tri·ode \'trī-ˌōd\ *n* : an electron tube with three electrodes

[1]**trip** \'trip\ *vb* **tripped**; **trip·ping** **1** : to move (as in dancing or walking) with light quick steps **2** : to catch one's foot while walking or running : cause to stumble **3 a** : to make or cause to make a mistake : SLIP, BLUNDER **b** : to catch in a misstep, fault, or blunder ⟨questions designed to *trip* him up⟩ **4** : to put (as a mechanism) into operation usu. by release of a catch or detent

[2]**trip** *n* **1** : an act of causing another to lose footing **2 a** : VOYAGE, JOURNEY ⟨a *trip* to Europe⟩ **b** : a brief round having a specific aim or recurring regularly

⟨a *trip* to the dentist's⟩ ⟨the milkman's daily *trip*⟩ **3** : ERROR, MISSTEP **4** : a quick light step **5 a** : the action of tripping mechanically **b** : a device (as a catch) for tripping a mechanism **6** : an intense visionary experience undergone by a person who has taken a drug (as LSD)

tri·par·tite \(ˈ)trī-ˈpär-ˌtīt\ *adj* **1** : having three parts **2** : having three corresponding parts or copies **3** : made between or involving three parties — **tri·par·tite·ly** *adv*

tripe \ˈtrīp\ *n* **1** : stomach tissue of a cud-chewing animal (as the ox) for use as food **2** : something poor, worthless, or offensive : TRASH

trip–ham·mer \ˈtrip-ˌham-ər\ *n* : a massive hammer raised by machinery and then tripped to fall on the work below

[1]tri·ple \ˈtrip-əl\ *vb* **tri·pled**; **tri·pling** \ˈtrip-(ə-)liŋ\ **1** : to make or become three times as great or as many : multiply by three **2** : to make a triple

[2]triple *n* **1 a** : a triple sum, quantity, or number **b** : a combination, group, or series of three **2** : a hit that enables a batter to reach third base safely

[3]triple *adj* **1** : having three units or members **2** : being three times as great or as many **3** : three times repeated

triple play *n* : a play in baseball or softball by which three base runners are put out

triple point *n* : a point on a diagram indicating temperature and pressure at which the gaseous, liquid, and solid phases of a substance are in equilibrium

tri·plet \ˈtrip-lət\ *n* **1** : a combination, set, or group of three **2** : one of three offspring born at one birth **3** : a group of three notes played in the time of two of the same value

[1]tri·plex \ˈtrip-ˌleks, ˈtrī-ˌpleks\ *adj* : TRIPLE

[2]triplex *n* : something that is triplex

[1]trip·li·cate \ˈtrip-li-kət\ *adj* : made in three identical copies

[2]triplicate *n* **1** : one of three like things **2** : three copies all alike ⟨typed in *triplicate*⟩

[3]trip·li·cate \ˈtrip-lə-ˌkāt\ *vb* : to make triple or provide in triplicate

tri·ply \ˈtrip-(ə-)lē\ *adv* : in a triple degree, amount, or manner

tri·pod \ˈtrī-ˌpäd\ *n* **1** : something (as a container or stool) resting on three legs **2** : a three-legged stand (as for a camera) — **tripod** *or* **trip·o·dal** \ˈtrip-əd-əl, ˈtrī-ˌpäd-\ *adj*

trip·per \ˈtrip-ər\ *n* **1** *chiefly Brit* : EXCURSIONIST **2** : a tripping device or mechanism

trip·ping·ly \ˈtrip-ing-lē\ *adv* : NIMBLY; *also* : FLUENTLY

tri·reme \ˈtrī-ˌrēm\ *n* : an ancient galley having three banks of oars

tri·sect \ˈtrī-ˌsekt, trī-ˈ\ *vb* : to divide into three usu. equal parts — **tri·sec·tion** \ˈtrī-ˌsek-shən, trī-ˈ\ *n* — **tri·sec·tor** \ˈtrī-ˌsek-tər, trī-ˈ\ *n*

tri·syl·lab·ic \ˌtrī-sə-ˈlab-ik\ *adj* : having three syllables — **tri·syl·lab·i·cal·ly** \-ˈlab-i-k(ə-)lē\ *adv* — **tri·syl·la·ble** \ˈtrī-ˌsil-ə-bəl, (ˈ)trī-ˈ\ *n*

trite \ˈtrīt\ *adj* [from Latin *tritus*, meaning literally "rubbed", "worn away"] : so common that the novelty has worn off : STALE, HACKNEYED ⟨a *trite* remark⟩ — **trite·ly** *adv* — **trite·ness** *n*

trit·i·um \ˈtrit-ē-əm, ˈtrish-ē-\ *n* : a radioactive isotope of hydrogen with atoms of three times the mass of ordinary light hydrogen atoms

tri·ton \ˈtrīt-ən\ *n* : any of various large sea snails with a heavy cone-shaped shell; *also* : the shell of a triton

[1]trit·u·rate \ˈtrich-ə-ˌrāt\ *vb* **1** : CRUSH, GRIND **2** : to reduce to a fine powder by rubbing or grinding — **trit·u·ra·tion** \ˌtrich-ə-ˈrā-shən\ *n* — **trit·u·ra·tor** \ˈtrich-ə-ˌrāt-ər\ *n*

[2]trit·u·rate \ˈtrich-ə-rət\ *n* : a triturated substance

[1]tri·umph \ˈtrī-əm(p)f\ *n* **1** : an ancient Roman ceremonial honoring a victorious general **2** : joy or exultation of victory or success **3 a** : a military victory or conquest **b** : any notable success

[2]triumph *vb* **1** : to celebrate victory or success often boastfully or exultingly **2** : to obtain victory : WIN

tri·um·phal \trī-ˈəm(p)-fəl\ *adj* : of, relating to, or used in a triumph

tri·um·phant \trī-ˈəm(p)-fənt\ *adj* **1** : CONQUERING, VICTORIOUS **2** : rejoicing for or celebrating victory : EXULTANT — **tri·um·phant·ly** *adv*

tri·um·vir \trī-ˈəm-vər\ *n* : one of a commission or ruling body of three esp. in ancient Rome

tri·um·vi·rate \-və-rət\ *n* **1** : the office or term of office of a triumvir **2** : government by three persons who share authority and responsibility **3** : a group of three persons who share power or office

triv·et \ˈtriv-ət\ *n* **1** : a three-legged stand or support; *esp* : one for holding a kettle near the fire **2** : an ornamental metal plate on very short legs used under a hot dish to protect the table

triv·ia \ˈtriv-ē-ə\ *n sing or pl* : unimportant matters : TRIFLES

triv·i·al \ˈtriv-ē-əl\ *adj* [from Latin *trivialis* "found everywhere", "commonplace," "trivial", from *trivium* "crossroads", from *tri-* and *via* "way"] **1** : ORDINARY, COMMONPLACE **2** : of little worth or importance : INSIGNIFICANT ⟨a *trivial* mistake⟩ — **triv·i·al·ly** \-ē-ə-lē\ *adv*

triv·i·al·i·ty \ˌtriv-ē-ˈal-ət-ē\ *n*, *pl* **-ties** **1** : the quality or state of being trivial **2** : something trivial : TRIFLE

[1]tri·week·ly \(ˈ)trī-ˈwē-klē\ *adj* **1** : occurring or appearing three times a week **2** : occurring or appearing every three weeks — **triweekly** *adv*

[2]triweekly *n* : a triweekly publication

trl *abbr* trail

tro·chee \ˈtrō-(ˌ)kē\ *n* : a metrical foot consisting of one accented syllable followed by one unaccented syllable (as in *hungry*) — **tro·cha·ic** \trō-ˈkā-ik\ *adj*

trod *past of* TREAD

trodden *past part of* TREAD

[1]troll \ˈtrōl\ *vb* **1 a** : to sing the parts of (as a round or catch) in succession **b** : to sing loudly or in a jovial manner **2** : to speak or recite in a rolling voice **3** : to angle or angle for with a hook and line drawn through the water — **troll·er** *n*

[2]troll *n* **1** : a lure or a line with its lure and hook used in trolling **2** : a song sung in parts successively : ROUND

[3]troll *n* : a fabled dwarf or giant inhabiting caves or hills

trol·ley *or* **trol·ly** \ˈträl-ē\ *n*, *pl* **trolleys** *or* **trollies** **1 a** : a device for carrying current from a wire to an electrically driven vehicle **b** : TROLLEY CAR **2** : a wheeled carriage running on an overhead rail or track

trolley bus *n* : a bus powered by electric power from two overhead wires

trolley car *n* : a streetcar that runs on tracks and gets its electric power through a trolley

ə abut	ər further	a back	ā bake	
ä cot, cart	au̇ out	ch chin	e less	ē easy
g gift	i trip	ī life	j joke	ng sing	ō flow
ȯ flaw	ȯi coin	th thin	<u>th</u> this	ü loot
u̇ foot	y yet	yü few	yu̇ furious	zh vision

trom·bone \träm-'bōn, (,)trəm-\ *n* [from Italian,

trombone

literally "large trumpet", from *tromba* "trumpet"] : a brass wind instrument that has a cupped mouthpiece, that consists of a long cylindrical metal tube bent twice upon itself and ending in a bell, and that has a movable slide with which to vary the pitch — **trom·bon·ist** \-'bō-nəst\ *n*

1**troop** \'trüp\ *n* **1 a :** a group of soldiers **b :** armed forces : SOLDIERS — usu. used in pl. **2 :** a collection of beings or things : COMPANY **3 :** a unit of boy or girl scouts under a leader

2**troop** *vb* : to move or gather in crowds

troop·er \'trü-pər\ *n* **1 :** CAVALRYMAN **2 a :** a mounted policeman **b :** a state policeman

troop·ship \'trüp-,ship\ *n* : a ship for carrying troops : TRANSPORT

troph·ic \'träf-ik, 'trō-fik\ *adj* **1 :** of or relating to nutrition : NUTRITIONAL **2 :** 3TROPIC

tro·phy \'trō-fē\ *n, pl* **trophies 1 :** something taken in battle or conquest esp. as a memorial ⟨Indians took scalps as *trophies*⟩ **2 :** something given to commemorate a victory or as an award for achievement ⟨won the big golf *trophy*⟩ **3 :** SOUVENIR, MEMENTO — **tro·phied** \-fēd\ *adj*

1**trop·ic** \'träp-ik\ *n* [from Greek *tropikos* "of the solstice", from *tropē* "turn"; so called because they mark the turning points in the sun's apparent annual motion] **1 :** either of the two parallels of the earth's latitude that are approximately 23½ degrees north of the equator and approximately 23½ degrees south of the equator **2** *pl, often cap* : the region lying between the two tropics

2**tropic** *adj* : of, relating to, or occurring in the tropics : TROPICAL

3**tropic** *adj* : of, relating to, or characteristic of tropism or of a tropism

trop·i·cal \'träp-i-kəl\ *adj* : of, located in, or used in the tropics — **trop·i·cal·ly** \-k(ə-)lē\ *adv*

tropical aquarium *n* : an aquarium kept at a uniform warmth and used esp. for tropical fish

tropical fish *n* : any of various small usu. showy fishes of exotic origin often kept in the tropical aquarium

tropic of Cancer : the parallel of latitude that is 23½ degrees north of the equator and is the northernmost latitude reached by the overhead sun

tropic of Capricorn : the parallel of latitude that is 23½ degrees south of the equator and is the southernmost latitude reached by the overhead sun

tro·pism \'trō-,piz-əm, 'träp-,iz-\ *n* : involuntary orientation by an organism or one of its parts that involves turning or curving and is a positive or negative response to a source of stimulation; *also* : a reflex reaction involving such movement — **tro·pis·tic** \trō-'pis-tik, trä-\ *adj*

tro·po·sphere \'trō-pə-,sfi(ə)r, 'träp-ə-\ *n* : the portion of the atmosphere which is below the stratosphere and in which generally temperature decreases rapidly with altitude and clouds form — **tro·po·spher·ic** \,trō-pə-'sfi(ə)r-ik, ,träp-ə-, -'sfer-\ *adj*

1**trot** \'trät\ *n* **1 :** a moderately fast gait of a 4-legged animal (as a horse) in which a front foot and the opposite hind foot move at the same time **2 :** a jogging gait of man that falls between a walk and a run

2**trot** *vb* **trot·ted; trot·ting 1 a :** to ride, drive, or go at a trot **b :** to cause to go at a trot **2 :** to proceed briskly : HURRY

1**troth** \'trȯth, 'träth, 'trōth\ *n* **1 :** loyal or pledged faithfulness : FIDELITY **2 :** one's pledged word

2**troth** \'träth, 'trȯth, 'trōth\ *vb* : PLEDGE, BETROTH

trot·ter \'trät-ər\ *n* : one that trots; *esp* : a standardbred horse trained for harness racing

trou·ba·dour \'trü-bə-,dōr, -,dȯr\ *n* : a poet-musician of medieval France and Italy

1**trou·ble** \'trəb-əl\ *vb* **trou·bled; trou·bling** \'trəb-(ə-)ling\ **1 a :** to agitate or become agitated mentally or spiritually : WORRY, DISTURB **b :** to produce physical disorder in : AFFLICT ⟨*troubled* with deafness⟩ **c :** to put to exertion or inconvenience ⟨can I *trouble* you for the salt⟩ **2 :** to put into confused motion ⟨wind *troubled* the sea⟩ **3 :** to make an effort : take pains ⟨do not *trouble* to come⟩

2**trouble** *n* **1 a :** the quality or state of being troubled : MISFORTUNE ⟨help people in *trouble*⟩ **b :** an instance of distress or annoyance **2 :** civil disorder or agitation ⟨labor *trouble*⟩ **3 :** EXERTION, PAINS ⟨took the *trouble* to call⟩ **4 a :** a condition of physical distress : DISEASE, AILMENT ⟨heart *trouble*⟩ **b :** MALFUNCTION ⟨engine *trouble*⟩ ⟨*trouble* with the plumbing⟩

trou·ble·mak·er \'trəb-əl-,mā-kər\ *n* : a person who causes dissension

trou·ble·some \-səm\ *adj* **1 :** giving trouble or anxiety : VEXATIOUS ⟨a *troublesome* infection⟩ **2 :** DIFFICULT, BURDENSOME — **trou·ble·some·ly** *adv*

trou·blous \'trəb-ləs\ *adj* **1 :** full of trouble : AFFLICTED **2 :** causing trouble : TURBULENT

trough \'trȯf\ *n, pl* **troughs** \'trȯfs, 'trȯvz\ **1 :** a long shallow receptacle for the drinking water or feed of domestic animals **2 :** a conduit, drain, or channel for water; *esp* : a gutter along the eaves **3 :** a long and narrow or shallow depression (as between waves or hills)

trounce \'trau̇n(t)s\ *vb* **1 :** to thrash or punish severely : FLOG, CUDGEL **2 :** to defeat decisively

1**troupe** \'trüp\ *n* : COMPANY, TROOP; *esp* : a group of performers on the stage

2**troupe** *vb* **1 :** to travel in a troupe **2 :** to perform as a member of a theatrical troupe — **troup·er** *n*

trou·sers \'trau̇-zərz\ *n pl* [an alteration, influenced by *drawers*, of earlier *trouse*, from Scotch Gaelic *triubhas*] : an outer garment extending from the waist to the ankle and covering each leg separately

trous·seau \'trü-,sō\ *n, pl* **trous·seaux** \-,sōz\ *or* **trous·seaus :** the personal possessions of a bride

trout \'trau̇t\ *n, pl* **trout** *also* **trouts 1 :** any of various fishes mostly smaller than the related salmons, restricted to cool clear fresh waters, and highly regarded as table and game fish **2 :** any of various fishes that resemble the true trouts

1**trow·el** \'trau̇(-ə)l\ *n* **1 :** a small hand tool consisting of a flat blade with a handle used for spreading and smoothing mortar or plaster **2 :** a small hand tool with a curved blade used by gardeners

2**trowel** *vb* **-eled** *or* **-elled; -el·ing** *or* **-el·ling :** to smooth, mix, or apply with a trowel

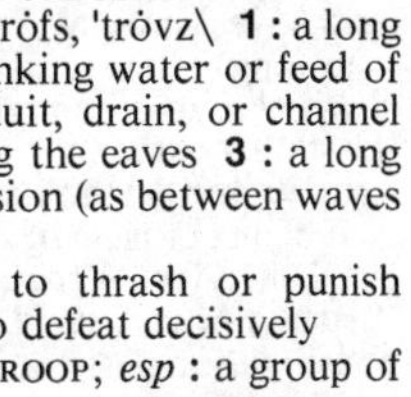

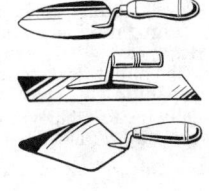

trowels

troy \'trȯi\ *adj* : expressed in troy weight

troy weight *n* : a series of units of weight based on a pound of 12 ounces and the ounce of 20 pennyweights or 480 grains — see MEASURE table

T

tru·ant \'trü-ənt\ *n* [from Old French, meaning "vagrant", "beggar"] : one who shirks duty; *esp* : one who stays out of school without permission — **tru·an·cy** \-ən-sē\ *n* — **truant** *adj*
truant officer *n* : a school officer whose duty is to investigate and deal with cases of truancy
truce \'trüs\ *n* **1** : an interruption of warfare by mutual agreement : ARMISTICE **2** : a temporary rest : RESPITE
[1]**truck** \'trək\ *vb* : to exchange goods : BARTER
[2]**truck** *n* **1** : BARTER **2** : goods for barter or for small trade **3** : close association : DEALINGS **4** : payment of wages in goods instead of cash **5 a** : small articles of little value **b** : RUBBISH
[3]**truck** *n* **1** : a small wooden cap at the top of a flagpole or mast **2** : a vehicle (as a small flat-topped car on wheels, a two-wheeled barrow with long handles, or a strong heavy wagon or automobile) for carrying heavy articles **3 a** : a swiveling carriage with springs and one or more pairs of wheels used to carry an end of a railroad car or a locomotive **b** : an automotive vehicle equipped with a swiveling device for hauling a trailer
[4]**truck** *vb* : to transport on or by truck
truck·er \'trək-ər\ *n* **1** : one whose business is transporting goods by truck **2** : a truck driver
truck farm *n* : a farm growing vegetables for market — **truck farmer** *n*
truck garden *n* : a garden where vegetables are raised for market
truck·ing \'trək-ing\ *n* : the process or business of transporting goods on trucks
truck·le \'trək-əl\ *vb* **truck·led**; **truck·ling** \'trək-(ə-)ling\ : to yield to the will of another : SUBMIT ⟨*truckle* to a conqueror⟩ — **truck·ler** \-(ə-)lər\ *n*
truckle bed *n* : TRUNDLE BED
truc·u·lent \'trək-yə-lənt\ *adj* **1** : FIERCE, SAVAGE **2** : BELLIGERENT, PUGNACIOUS — **truc·u·lence** \-lən(t)s\ *n* — **truc·u·lent·ly** *adv*
[1]**trudge** \'trəj\ *vb* **1** : to walk or march steadily and usu. laboriously **2** : to walk or march along or over — **trudg·er** *n*
[2]**trudge** *n* : a long tiring walk : TRAMP
trud·gen stroke \'trəj-ən-\ *n* : a swimming stroke in which a double overarm motion is combined with a scissors kick
[1]**true** \'trü\ *adj* **1** : FAITHFUL, LOYAL **2** : that can be relied on : CERTAIN **3** : corresponding to fact or actuality : ACCURATE, CORRECT **4** : SINCERE ⟨*true* friendship⟩ **5 a** : properly so called ⟨lichens have no *true* stems⟩ **b** : TYPICAL ⟨the *true* cats⟩ **6** : placed or formed accurately ⟨a *true* square⟩ **7** : RIGHTFUL, LEGITIMATE ⟨the *true* owner⟩ ⟨our *true* king⟩
[2]**true** *n* **1** : TRUTH, REALITY — usu. used with *the* **2** : the quality or state of being accurate (as in alignment or adjustment) — used in the phrases *in true* and *out of true*
[3]**true** *vb* **trued**; **true·ing** *also* **tru·ing** : to make level, square, balanced, or concentric : bring to desired mechanical accuracy or form
[4]**true** *adv* **1** : TRUTHFULLY **2** : ACCURATELY ⟨the bullet flew straight and *true*⟩
true–blue \'trü-'blü\ *adj* : marked by unswerving loyalty (as to a party) : highly faithful
true bug *n* : BUG 1b

ə abut	ər further	a back	ā bake
ä cot, cart	aù out	ch chin	e less
ē easy	g gift	i trip	ī life
j joke	ng sing	ō flow	ȯ flaw
ȯi coin	th thin	th this	ü loot
ù foot	y yet	yü few	yù furious
zh vision			

true seal *n* : HAIR SEAL
truf·fle \'trəf-əl, 'trüf-\ *n* : the usu. dark wrinkled edible underground fruiting body of a European fungus; *also* : this fungus
tru·ism \'trü-,iz-əm\ *n* : an obvious truth
tru·ly \'trü-lē\ *adv* **1** : SINCERELY **2** : TRUTHFULLY **3** : ACCURATELY
[1]**trump** \'trəmp\ *n* : TRUMPET : the sound of a trumpet ⟨till the last *trump* blows⟩
[2]**trump** *n* **1 a** : a card of a suit any of whose cards will win over a card that is not a trump **b** : the suit whose cards are trumps for a particular hand — often used in pl. **2** : a dependable and exemplary person
[3]**trump** *vb* **1** : to take with a trump ⟨*trump* a trick⟩ **2** : to play a trump
trumped–up \'trəm(p)t-'əp\ *adj* : fraudulently concocted : FALSE ⟨*trumped-up* charges⟩
trum·pery \'trəm-p(ə-)rē\ *n*, *pl* **-per·ies** : trivial or useless articles : things of no value — **trumpery** *adj*
[1]**trum·pet** \'trəm-pət\ *n* **1** : a wind instrument consisting of a long cylindrical metal tube commonly once or twice curved and ending in a bell **2** : a trumpet player **3** : a funnel-shaped instrument (as a megaphone or a diaphragm horn) for collecting, directing, or intensifying sound ⟨an ear *trumpet*⟩ **4** : a penetrating cry (as of an elephant)

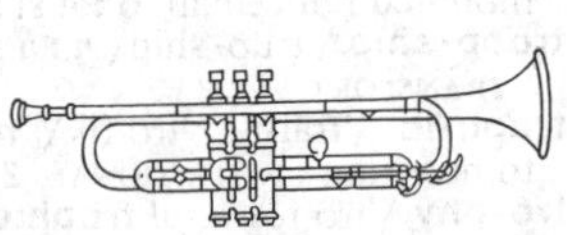
trumpet 1

[2]**trumpet** *vb* **1** : to blow a trumpet **2** : to sound or proclaim on or as if on a trumpet ⟨*trumpeted* the news⟩
trumpet creeper *n* : a No. American woody vine with pinnate leaves and large red trumpet-shaped flowers — called also *trumpet vine*
trum·pet·er \'trəm-pət-ər\ *n* **1** : a trumpet player **2 a** : any of several large long-legged long-necked So. American birds related to the cranes and often kept to protect poultry **b** : a rare pure white No. American wild swan noted for its sonorous voice — called also *trumpeter swan*
[1]**trun·cate** \'trən(g)-,kāt\ *vb* : to shorten by or as if by cutting off — **trun·ca·tion** \,trən(g)-'kā-shən\ *n*
[2]**trun·cate** \'trən(g)-,kāt\ *adj* : having the end square or blunt ⟨a *truncate* leaf⟩
trun·cat·ed \-,kāt-əd\ *adj* : cut short : CURTAILED
[1]**trun·cheon** \'trən-chən\ *n* **1** : a shattered spear or lance **2 a** *obs* : CLUB, BLUDGEON **b** : a policeman's billy
[2]**truncheon** *vb*, *archaic* : to beat with a truncheon
[1]**trun·dle** \'trən-dəl\ *n* **1 a** : a small wheel or roller **b** : CIRCLET, HOOP **2** : a low-wheeled cart or truck
[2]**trundle** *vb* **trun·dled**; **trun·dling** \'trən-d(ə-)ling\ : to propel by causing to rotate : ROLL ⟨*trundled* a wheelbarrow⟩ — **trun·dler** \-d(ə-)lər\ *n*
trundle bed *n* : a low bed usu. on casters that can be slid under a higher bed — called also *truckle bed*
[1]**trunk** \'trəngk\ *n* **1 a** : the main stem of a tree apart from branches or roots **b** : the body of a person or lower animal apart from the head and limbs **c** : the main or basal part of something ⟨*trunk* of an artery⟩ **2 a** : a box or chest for holding clothes or other goods esp. for traveling **b** : the enclosed space usu. in the rear of an automobile for carrying articles (as luggage) **3** : PROBOSCIS; *esp* : the long muscular nose of an elephant **4** *pl* : men's shorts ⟨boxing *trunks*⟩
[2]**trunk** *adj* **1** : being or relating to a main line of a system (as of a railroad, pipeline, or canal) **2** : being or

relating to the circuit between two telephone exchanges ⟨*trunk* call⟩ ⟨*trunk* operator⟩

trunk hose *n pl* : short full breeches reaching about halfway down the thigh worn chiefly in the late 16th and early 17th centuries

1truss \'trəs\ *vb* **1 a** : to secure tightly : BIND ⟨they *trussed* up their victim⟩ **b** : to arrange for cooking by binding close the wings or legs of ⟨*truss* a turkey⟩ **2** : to support, strengthen, or stiffen by a truss

2truss *n* **1** : a rigid framework of beams, bars, or rods ⟨a *truss* for a roof⟩ **2** : a device worn to hold a hernia in place

1trust \'trəst\ *n* **1 a** : assured reliance on the character, ability, strength, or truth of someone or something **b** : one in which confidence is placed **2 a** : dependence on something future or contingent : HOPE **b** : reliance on future payment for goods delivered : CREDIT **3 a** : a legal right or interest in property that one does not actually own ⟨income received under a *trust* established by his father⟩ **b** : property held or managed by one person or concern (as a bank or trust company) for the benefit of another **c** : a combination of firms or corporations formed by a legal agreement; *esp* : one that reduces or threatens to reduce competition **4 a** : something (as a public office) committed to one to be used or cared for in the interest of another **b** : CARE, CUSTODY

2trust *vb* **1 a** : to place confidence : DEPEND ⟨*trust* in God⟩ ⟨*trust* to luck⟩ **b** : to be confident : HOPE **2** : to commit or place in one's care or keeping : ENTRUST **3 a** : to rely on the truthfulness or accuracy of : BELIEVE **b** : to place confidence in : rely on **c** : to hope or expect confidently ⟨*trusted* to find oil on the land⟩ **4** : to sell to in confidence of later payment : extend credit to — **trust·er** *n*

trust company *n* : a corporation and esp. a bank organized to act as a trustee

trust·ee \ˌtrəs-'tē\ *n* **1** : a person to whom property is legally committed in trust **2** : a country charged with the supervision of a trust territory

trust·ee·ship \-ˌship\ *n* **1** : the office or function of a trustee **2** : supervisory control by one or more countries over a trust territory

trust·ful \'trəst-fəl\ *adj* : full of trust : CONFIDING — **trust·ful·ly** \-fə-lē\ *adv*

trust·ing \'trəs-ting\ *adj* : having trust, faith, or confidence : TRUSTFUL — **trust·ing·ly** \-ting-lē\ *adv*

trust territory *n* : a non-self-governing territory placed under an administrative authority by the Trusteeship Council of the United Nations

trust·wor·thy \'trəst-ˌwər-t͟hē\ *adj* : worthy of confidence : DEPENDABLE — **trust·wor·thi·ly** \-t͟hə-lē\ *adv* — **trust·wor·thi·ness** \-t͟hē-nəs\ *n*

1trusty \'trəs-tē\ *adj* **trust·i·er**; **-est** : TRUSTWORTHY

2trusty \'trəs-tē, ˌtrəs-'tē\ *n, pl* **trust·ies** : a trusty or trusted person; *esp* : a convict considered trustworthy and allowed special privileges

truth \'trüth\ *n, pl* **truths** \'trüt͟hz, 'trüths\ **1** : TRUTHFULNESS, HONESTY **2** : a judgment, proposition, or statement that is or is accepted as true ⟨the *truths* of science⟩ **3 a** : the state of being true : FACT **b** : the body of real things, events, and facts : ACTUALITY **4** : the property of being in accord with what is, has been, or must be — **in truth** : in fact : ACTUALLY, REALLY

truth·ful \'trüth-fəl\ *adj* : telling or disposed to tell the truth — **truth·ful·ly** \-fə-lē\ *adv* — **truth·ful·ness** *n*

truth set *n* : a set of the elements that can be substituted to make an open sentence true

1try \'trī\ *vb* **tried**; **try·ing** **1 a** : to examine or investigate judicially **b** : to conduct the trial of **2 a** : to put to test or trial **b** : to test to the limit or breaking point : STRAIN ⟨*tries* his patience⟩ **3** : to melt down and procure in a pure state : RENDER ⟨*try* out whale oil from blubber⟩ **4** : to make an effort to do : ENDEAVOR

2try *n, pl* **tries** : an experimental trial : ATTEMPT

try·ing \'trī-ing\ *adj* : causing distress or annoyance

try on *vb* : to put on in order to test the fit

try out \'trī-'au̇t\ *vb* : to participate in competition esp. for a position on an athletic team or a part in a play — **try·out** \-ˌau̇t\ *n*

tryp·sin \'trip-sən\ *n* : an enzyme from pancreatic juice that helps to digest protein — **tryp·tic** \'trip-tik\ *adj*

tryp·sin·o·gen \trip-'sin-ə-jən\ *n* : the inactive form of trypsin present in the pancreas

tryst \'trist, 'trīst\ *n* **1** : an agreement (as between lovers) to meet **2** : an appointed meeting or meeting place

tsar \'zär, '(t)sär\ *var of* CZAR

tset·se \'(t)set-sē, 'tet-, '(t)sēt-, 'tēt-\ *n, pl* **tsetse** *or* **tseses** : any of a genus of two-winged flies mostly of Africa south of the Sahara desert that by biting convey a tiny parasitic one-celled animal causing a fatal sickness in cattle and sleeping sickness in man — called also *tsetse fly*

T–shirt \'tē-ˌshərt\ *n* : a collarless short-sleeved cotton undershirt for men; *also* : a cotton or wool jersey outer shirt of similar design

tsp *abbr* teaspoon

T square *n* : a ruler with a crosspiece or head at one end used in making parallel lines

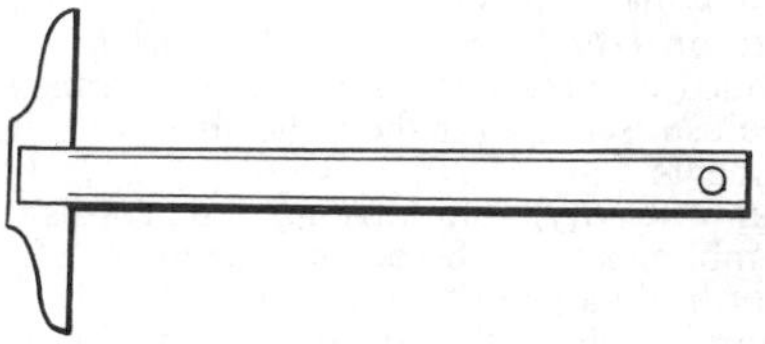

T square

1tub \'təb\ *n* **1** : a wide low vessel orig. formed with wooden staves, round bottom, and hoops **2** : an old or slow boat **3 a** : BATHTUB **b** : BATH ⟨a hot *tub*⟩ **4** : the amount that a tub will hold

2tub *vb* **tubbed**; **tub·bing** : to wash or bathe in a tub

tu·ba \'t(y)ü-bə\ *n* : a large low-pitched brass wind instrument with a cup-shaped mouthpiece

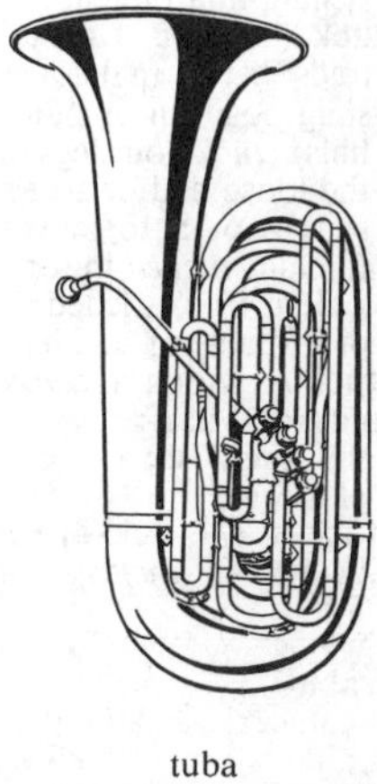

tuba

tub·by \'təb-ē\ *adj* **tub·bi·er**; **-est** : PUDGY, FAT

tube \'t(y)üb\ *n* **1 a** : a hollow elongated cylinder; *esp* : one to convey fluids **b** : a slender channel within a plant or animal body : DUCT **2** : a round metal container from which a paste is dispensed by squeezing **3** : TUNNEL **4** *Brit* : SUB-

WAY **5 :** INNER TUBE **6 :** ELECTRON TUBE **7 :** VACUUM TUBE **8 :** TELEVISION — **tubed** \'t(y)übd\ *adj* — **tube·like** \'t(y)üb-ˌlīk\ *adj*

tube foot *n* **:** one of the small flexible tubular processes of most echinoderms that are extensions of the water-vascular system used esp. in locomotion and grasping

tube·less \'t(y)üb-ləs\ *adj* **:** lacking a tube; *esp* **:** being a pneumatic tire that does not depend on an inner tube to keep it airtight

tu·ber \'t(y)ü-bər\ *n* **:** a plant stem or shoot growing underground and bearing buds or eyes — compare BULB, CORM

tu·ber·cle \'t(y)ü-bər-kəl\ *n* **1 :** a small knobby prominence or outgrowth esp. on a plant or animal **:** NODULE **2 :** a small diseased growth in an organ or the skin; *esp* **:** one caused by tuberculosis

tu·ber·cu·lar \t(y)u̇-'bər-kyə-lər\ *adj* **1 :** relating to, resembling, or constituting a tubercle **2 :** characterized by tubercular lesions ⟨*tubercular* leprosy⟩ **3 :** of, relating to, or affected with tuberculosis **:** TUBERCULOUS ⟨*tubercular* meningitis⟩

tu·ber·cu·lin \t(y)u̇-'bər-kyə-lən\ *n* **:** a sterile liquid containing substances from the causative agent of tuberculosis that is used in its diagnosis

tuberculin test *n* **:** a test for past or present tubercular infection

tu·ber·cu·lo·sis \t(y)u̇-ˌbər-kyə-'lō-səs\ *n* **:** a communicable disease of some vertebrates caused by a bacillus and typically marked by wasting, fever, and formation of cheesy tubercles that in man primarily occur in the lungs — **tu·ber·cu·lous** \t(y)u̇-'bər-kyə-ləs\ *adj*

tube·rose \'t(y)üb-ˌrōz; 't(y)ü-bə-ˌrōz, -bə-ˌrōs\ *n* **:** a Mexican bulbous herb grown for its spike of fragrant white flowers

tu·ber·os·i·ty \ˌt(y)ü-bə-'räs-ət-ē\ *n, pl* **-ties :** a rounded prominence; *esp* **:** such a prominence on a bone usu. serving for the attachment of muscles or ligaments

tu·ber·ous \'t(y)ü-b(ə-)rəs\ *adj* **1 a :** consisting of or resembling a tuber **b :** bearing tubers **2 :** of, relating to, or being a plant tuber

tub·ing \'t(y)ü-biŋ\ *n* **1 :** material in the form of a tube **2 :** a series or system of tubes

tu·bu·lar \'t(y)ü-byə-lər\ *adj* **1 :** having the form of or consisting of a tube **2 :** made or provided with tubes

tu·bule \'t(y)ü-byül\ *n* **:** a small tube; *esp* **:** a long slender anatomical channel

1**tuck** \'tək\ *vb* **1 a :** to pull up or draw together into folds **b :** to make a tuck in **2 :** to put or fit into a snug position or place ⟨cottage *tucked* away in the hills⟩ ⟨*tuck* your legs out of the way⟩ **3 a :** to push in the loose end of so as to hold tightly ⟨*tuck* in your shirt⟩ **b :** to cover by tucking in bedclothes ⟨a child *tucked* in for the night⟩

2**tuck** *n* **1 :** a stitched fold (as in a garment) **2 :** an act or instance of tucking

3**tuck** *n* **:** VIGOR, ENERGY

1**tuck·er** \'tək-ər\ *n* **1 :** someone who or something that tucks **2 :** a piece of lace or cloth in the neckline of a dress

2**tucker** *vb* **tuck·ered**; **tuck·er·ing** \'tək-(ə-)riŋ\ **:** EXHAUST ⟨*tuckered* out by the hard work⟩

ə abut	ər further	a back	ā bake	
ä cot, cart	au̇ out	ch chin	e less	ē easy
g gift	i trip	ī life	j joke	ŋ sing	ō flow
ȯ flaw	ȯi coin	th thin	t͟h this	ü loot
u̇ foot	y yet	yü few	yu̇ furious	zh vision

Tues *abbr* Tuesday

Tues·day \'t(y)üz-dē\ *n* [from Old English *tīwesdæg*, meaning "day of Tiu", from *Tīw* "Tiu", god of war] **:** the 3d day of the week

tuf·fet \'təf-ət\ *n* **1 :** TUFT 1a **2 :** a low seat

1**tuft** \'təft\ *n* **1 a :** a small cluster of long flexible outgrowths (as hairs or feathers) **b :** a bunch of soft fluffy threads cut off short and used as ornament **2 :** CLUMP, CLUSTER ⟨a *tuft* of grass⟩

2**tuft** *vb* **1 :** to provide or adorn with a tuft **2 :** to make firm by stitching at intervals and sewing on tufts ⟨*tuft* a mattress⟩

1**tug** \'təg\ *vb* **tugged**; **tug·ging** **1 a :** to pull hard **b :** to move by pulling hard **:** DRAG, HAUL **2 :** to struggle in opposition **:** CONTEND **3 :** to tow with a tugboat — **tug·ger** *n*

2**tug** *n* **1 a :** a harness trace **b :** a rope or chain used for pulling **2 a :** an act or instance of tugging **:** PULL **b :** a struggle between opposing individuals or forces **3 :** TUGBOAT

tug·boat \'təg-ˌbōt\ *n* **:** a strongly built powerful boat used for towing and pushing

tugboat

tug–of–war \ˌtəg-ə(v)-'wȯ(ə)r\ *n, pl* **tugs–of–war** **1 :** a struggle for supremacy **2 :** an athletic contest in which two teams pull against each other at opposite ends of a rope

tu·i·tion \t(y)u̇-'ish-ən\ *n* **1 :** the act or profession of teaching **:** INSTRUCTION ⟨20 students under her *tuition*⟩ **2 :** the price of or payment for instruction ⟨an increase in *tuition* at the university⟩

tu·la·re·mia \ˌt(y)ü-lə-'rē-mē-ə\ *n* **:** an infectious bacterial disease of rodents, man, and some domestic animals transmitted esp. by the bites of insects

tu·lip \'t(y)ü-ləp\ *n* [from Turkish *tülbend* "turban"; so called from the shape of the flower] **:** any of a genus of Eurasian bulbous herbs related to the lily, having linear or broadly lance-shaped leaves, and widely grown for their showy flowers; *also* **:** the flower or bulb of a tulip

tulip tree *n* **:** a tall No. American timber tree with large greenish yellow tulip-shaped flowers and soft white wood used esp. for cabinetwork; *also* **:** its wood

tulle \'tül\ *n* **:** a sheer often stiffened silk, rayon, or nylon net used chiefly for veils, evening dresses, or ballet costumes

1**tum·ble** \'təm-bəl\ *vb* **tum·bled**; **tum·bling** \-b(ə-)liŋ\ **1 a :** to perform gymnastic feats of rolling and turning **b :** to turn end over end in falling or flight **2 a :** to fall suddenly and helplessly **b :** to suffer a sudden decline, downfall, or defeat **:** COLLAPSE **3 :** to move or go hurriedly and confusedly ⟨people came *tumbling* out of the burning building⟩ **4 :** to come to understand **5 a :** to throw or push and cause to tumble **b :** to toss about or together into a confused mass **c :** to dry clothes in a dryer ⟨wash in warm water and *tumble* dry⟩

2**tumble** *n* **1 :** a disorderly state or collection **2 :** an act or instance of tumbling

tum·ble·bug \'təm-bəl-ˌbəg\ *n* **:** a large stout-bodied beetle that rolls dung into small balls, buries them in the ground, and lays its eggs in them

tum·ble·down \ˌtəm-bəl-ˌdau̇n\ *adj* **:** DILAPIDATED, RAMSHACKLE

tum·bler \'təm-blər\ *n* **1 :** one that tumbles **2 :** a pigeon that habitually somersaults backward in flight **3 :** a drinking glass without foot or stem

4 : a movable part in a lock that must be adjusted (as by a key) before the bolt can be thrown

tum·ble·weed \'təm-bəl-ˌwēd\ *n* : a plant that breaks away from its roots in autumn and is blown about by the wind

tum·bling *n* : the skill, practice, or sport of executing gymnastic tumbles

tum·brel *or* **tum·bril** \'təm-brəl\ *n* : a farmer's cart used during the French Revolution to carry condemned persons to the guillotine

tu·mid \'t(y)ü-məd\ *adj* **1** : marked by swelling : SWOLLEN, ENLARGED ⟨*tumid* flesh⟩ **2** : BOMBASTIC, TURGID ⟨*tumid* speech⟩

tum·my \'təm-ē\ *n, pl* **tummies** : STOMACH 1b

tu·mor \'t(y)ü-mər\ *n* : a swollen part; *esp* : an abnormal mass of tissue that arises usu. without obvious cause from apparently normal tissue cells and possesses no physiologic function — **tu·mor·ous** \-mə-rəs\ *adj*

tump·line \'təmp-ˌlīn\ *n* : a sling formed by a strap slung over the forehead or chest used for carrying a pack on the back or in hauling loads

tu·mult \'t(y)ü-ˌməlt\ *n* **1** : violent and disorderly commotion or disturbance with uproar and confusion ⟨the *tumult* of the sea⟩ **2** : violent agitation of mind

tu·mul·tu·ous \t(y)u̇-'məl-chə-wəs, -chəs\ *adj* : marked by tumult and esp. by violent or overwhelming turbulence or upheaval — **tu·mul·tu·ous·ly** *adv*

tu·mu·lus \'t(y)ü-myə-ləs\ *n, pl* **-li** \-ˌlī, -ˌlē\ : an artificial hillock or mound usu. over an ancient grave : BARROW

tun \'tən\ *n* **1** : a large cask for liquids and esp. wine **2** : the capacity of a tun as a varying liquid measure; *esp* : a measure of 252 gallons

tu·na \'t(y)ü-nə\ *n, pl* **tuna** *or* **tunas** : any of several mostly large active sea fishes (as an albacore or bonito) related to the mackerels and valued for food and sport

tun·a·ble *also* **tune·a·ble** \'t(y)ü-nə-bəl\ *adj* : capable of being tuned

tun·dra \'tən-drə, 'tu̇n-\ *n* [from Russian, probably from Finnish *tunturi* "arctic hill" or Lapp *tundar* "hill"] : a treeless plain of arctic and subarctic regions

1**tune** \'t(y)ün\ *n* **1** : a succession of pleasing musical tones : MELODY **2** : correct musical pitch or consonance ⟨the piano was not in *tune*⟩ **3** : AGREEMENT, HARMONY ⟨in *tune* with the times⟩ **4** : general attitude ⟨changed his *tune* after reading the report⟩ **5** : AMOUNT, EXTENT ⟨a subsidy to the *tune* of $5,000,000⟩

2**tune** *vb* **1** : to come or bring into harmony : ATTUNE **2** : TUNE IN ⟨*tune* a radio⟩ **3** : to adjust in musical pitch ⟨*tune* a piano⟩ **4** : to adjust for precise functioning ⟨*tune* an engine⟩

tune·ful \'t(y)ün-fəl\ *adj* : MELODIOUS, MUSICAL — **tune·ful·ly** \-fə-lē\ *adv*

tune in *vb* : to adjust a radio or television receiver to respond to waves of a particular frequency so as to receive the material that is broadcast ⟨*tune in* a radio⟩ ⟨*tune in* a station⟩ ⟨*tune in* to a program⟩

tune out *vb* : to adjust a radio or television receiver so as not to receive (an unwanted signal) ⟨*tune out* a program⟩

tun·er \'t(y)ü-nər\ *n* **1** : someone who tunes ⟨piano *tuner*⟩ **2** : something used for tuning; *esp* : the part of a receiving set consisting of the circuit used to adjust resonance

tune–up \'t(y)ün-ˌəp\ *n* : a general adjustment to ensure efficient functioning ⟨a motor *tune-up*⟩

tung \'təng\ *n* : any of several trees whose seeds yield a drying oil; *esp* : a Chinese tree widely grown in warm regions

tung·sten \'təng(k)-stən\ *n* [from Swedish, from *tung* "heavy" and *sten* "stone"] : a gray-white heavy ductile hard metallic element that is used esp. for electrical purposes and in hardening alloys (as steel) — called also *wolfram*; see ELEMENT table

tu·nic \'t(y)ü-nik\ *n* **1** : a simple belted knee-length or longer slip-on garment worn by ancient Greeks and Romans **2** : a blouse or jacket reaching to or just below the hips **3** : an enclosing or covering anatomical structure

tu·ni·cate \'t(y)ü-ni-kət, -nə-ˌkāt\ *n* : any of a major group of marine chordates with a reduced nervous system and an outer covering

tuning fork *n* : a 2-pronged metal instrument that gives a fixed tone when struck

1**tun·nel** \'tən-əl\ *n* : an enclosed passage (as a tube or conduit); *esp* : one underground (as under an obstruction or in a mine) — **tun·nel·like** \-əl-ˌ(l)īk\ *adj*

2**tunnel** *vb* **-neled** *or* **-nelled**; **-nel·ing** *or* **-nel·ling** : to make or use a tunnel or form a tunnel in

tun·ny \'tən-ē\ *n, pl* **tunnies** *also* **tunny** : TUNA

tu·pe·lo \'t(y)ü-pə-ˌlō\ *n, pl* **-los** **1** : BLACK GUM; *also* : any of several related trees **2** : the pale soft easily worked wood of a tupelo

tup·pence *var of* TWOPENCE

tur·ban \'tər-bən\ *n* **1** : a headdress worn esp. by Muslims and made of a cap around which is wound a long cloth **2** : a woman's close-fitting brimless hat — **turbaned** *or* **tur·banned** \-bənd\ *adj*

turban 1

tur·bid \'tər-bəd\ *adj* **1 a** : having the sediment stirred up ⟨*turbid* stream⟩ **b** : heavy with smoke or mist : DENSE **2** : CONFUSED, MUDDLED ⟨*turbid* thought⟩ — **tur·bid·i·ty** \ˌtər-'bid-ət-ē\ *n* — **tur·bid·ly** \'tər-bəd-lē\ *adv*

1**tur·bi·nate** \'tər-bə-nət\ *adj* **1** : shaped like an inverted cone or a child's top ⟨a *turbinate* shell⟩ **2** : of, relating to, or being the thin bony or cartilaginous plates on the walls of the nasal passages — **tur·bi·nat·ed** \-ˌnāt-əd\ *adj*

2**turbinate** *n* : a turbinate bone or cartilage

tur·bine \'tər-bən, -ˌbīn\ *n* [from Latin *turbin-*, stem of *turbo* "top", "whirlwind"] : an engine whose central driving shaft is fitted with vanes whirled around by the pressure of water or hot gases (as steam or exhaust gases)

tur·bo·jet \'tər-bō-ˌjet\ *n* : an airplane powered by turbojet engines

turbojet engine *n* : an airplane propulsion system in which the power developed by a turbine is used to drive a compressor that supplies air to a burner and hot gases from the burner pass through the turbine and to a rearward-directed thrust-producing exhaust nozzle

tur·bo·prop \'tər-bō-ˌpräp\ *n* : an airplane powered by turbo-propeller engines

tur·bo–pro·pel·ler engine \ˌtər-bō-prə-'pel-ər-\ *n* : a jet engine having a turbine-driven propeller and designed to produce thrust principally by means of a propeller although additional thrust is usu. obtained from the hot exhaust gases which issue in a jet

tur·bot \'tər-bət\ *n, pl* **turbot** *also* **turbots** **1** : a large brownish European flatfish highly esteemed as a food fish **2 :** any of various flatfishes resembling the turbot

tur·bu·lence \'tər-byə-lən(t)s\ *also* **tur·bu·len·cy** \-lən-sē\ *n* **1 :** the quality or state of being turbulent **2 :** irregular atmospheric motion esp. when characterized by up and down currents

tur·bu·lent \-lənt\ *adj* **1 :** causing unrest, violence, or disturbance **2 :** characterized by agitation or tumult : TEMPESTUOUS — **tur·bu·lent·ly** *adv*

tu·reen \tə-'rēn, tyü-\ *n* **:** a deep bowl from which food is served at table ⟨soup *tureen*⟩

turf \'tərf\ *n, pl* **turfs** \'tərfs\ *or* **turves** \'tərvz\ **1 a :** the upper layer of soil bound by grass and plant roots into a thick mat **b :** a piece of turf **2 a :** PEAT **b :** a piece of peat dried for fuel **3 a :** a track or course for horse racing **b :** the sport or business of horse racing — **turfy** \'tər-fē\ *adj*

tur·gid \'tər-jəd\ *adj* **1 :** being in a state of distension : SWOLLEN ⟨*turgid* limbs⟩; *esp* **:** exhibiting turgor **2 :** excessively embellished in style or language : BOMBASTIC, POMPOUS — **tur·gid·ly** *adv*

tur·gor \'tər-gər, -,gȯr\ *n* **:** the normal state of firmness and tension typical of living cells

Turk \'tərk\ *n* **1 :** a member of any of numerous Asian peoples speaking Turkic languages who live in the region ranging from the Adriatic to the Sea of Okhotsk **2 :** a native or inhabitant of Turkey

Turk *abbr* **1** Turkey **2** Turkish

tur·key \'tər-kē\ *n* [from *Turkey*; from confusion with the guinea fowl, supposed to be imported from Turkish territory] **1 :** a large American bird that is related to the common fowl, is of wide range in No. America, and is domesticated in most parts of the world **2 :** FAILURE, FLOP ⟨the new play was a *turkey*⟩

turkey 1 (about 4 ft. long)

turkey buzzard *n* **:** an American vulture common in So. and Central America and in the southern U.S. — called also *turkey vulture*

tur·key–cock \'tər-kē-,käk\ *n* **1 :** a male turkey — called also *tom, turkey-gob·bler* \,tər-kē-'gäb-lər\ **2 :** a strutting pompous person

[1]**Turk·ish** \'tər-kish\ *adj* **:** of, relating to, or characteristic of Turkey, the Turks, or Turkish

[2]**Turkish** *n* **:** the language of Turkey

Turkish towel *n* **:** a towel made of cotton terry cloth

tur·moil \'tər-,mȯil\ *n* **:** an utterly confused or extremely agitated state or condition

[1]**turn** \'tərn\ *vb* **1 a :** to move or cause to move around an axis or center : ROTATE, REVOLVE ⟨wheels *turning* slowly⟩ ⟨*turn* a crank⟩ **b :** to operate or cause to operate by so turning ⟨*turn* a key in a lock⟩ **2 :** to have as a center (as of interest) or a decisive factor ⟨the story *turns* about the adventures of a poor boy⟩ **3 :** to execute by revolving ⟨*turn* handsprings⟩ **4 :** to alter or reverse in position usu. by moving through an arc ⟨*turned* the paper over⟩ ⟨*turn* a collar⟩ **5 :** DISTURB, UPSET ⟨everything *turned* topsy-turvy⟩ ⟨*turned* her stomach⟩ **6 :** to injure by a sudden twist : WRENCH ⟨*turned* her ankle⟩ **7 :** to take or cause to take or move in another direction ⟨*turned* the flood into an old stream bed⟩ ⟨the road *turns* to the left⟩ ⟨*turned* his car around⟩ ⟨when the tide *turns*⟩ **8 :** to pass with a change of direction ⟨*turn* a corner⟩ **9 :** to alter from a previous or anticipated course ⟨these few votes *turned* the election⟩ **10 :** to bring to bear : TRAIN ⟨*turn* a weapon on an enemy⟩ **11 :** to direct or point usu. toward or away from something ⟨the light *turned* toward the gate⟩ ⟨*turned* his thoughts homeward⟩ **12 :** to seek out as a source of something ⟨*turn* to a friend for help⟩ **13 a :** to change or cause to change ⟨water *turned* to ice⟩ ⟨*turn* wild land into fruitful farms⟩ ⟨*turn* traitor⟩ **b :** to cause to spoil : SOUR ⟨*turned* milk⟩ **c :** to change in color ⟨leaves *turning* in the fall⟩ **14 :** TRANSLATE, PARAPHRASE **15 :** to make on a lathe — **turn·er** *n* — **turn one's hand** *or* **turn a hand :** to set to work : apply oneself usefully — **turn tail :** to run away : FLEE — **turn the trick :** to bring about the desired result or effect — **turn turtle :** CAPSIZE, OVERTURN

[2]**turn** *n* **1 :** the action or an act of turning ⟨each *turn* of the wheel⟩ **2 a :** a change or changing of direction or position ⟨an illegal left *turn*⟩ ⟨*turn* of the tide⟩ **b :** a place where something turns : BEND, CURVE ⟨at the *turn* of the road⟩ **c :** a change or changing of condition or trend ⟨took a *turn* for the better⟩ ⟨a *turn* in the weather⟩ **3 :** a short walk or ride ⟨took a *turn* through the park⟩ **4 :** an act affecting another ⟨did me a bad *turn*⟩ ⟨do a good *turn* daily⟩ **5 a :** a period of action or activity : SPELL ⟨a *turn* as guard⟩ **b :** place or appointed time in a succession or scheduled order ⟨waited his *turn* at the dentist's⟩ ⟨take *turns*⟩ **6 a :** distinctive quality or character ⟨a neat *turn* of phrase⟩ **b :** the form in accord with which something is fashioned : CAST ⟨a peculiar *turn* of mind⟩ **c :** a single round (as of a rope) **d :** a special adaptive twist or interpretation ⟨gave the old tale a new *turn*⟩ **7 :** particular or special aptitude or skill : BENT ⟨a *turn* for languages⟩ — **at every turn :** CONSTANTLY, CONTINUOUSLY — **to a turn :** precisely right : PERFECTLY

turn·about \'tərn-ə-,bau̇t\ *n* **:** a change or reversal of direction, trend, policy, or role

turn away *vb* **:** to refuse admittance or acceptance to : send away ⟨all the seats were sold and a large crowd was *turned away*⟩

turn back *vb* **1 :** to go in the reverse direction : RETURN ⟨*turned back* for home⟩ **2 :** to stop the advance of : CHECK ⟨*turned back* the enemy⟩

turn·buck·le \'tərn-,bək-əl\ *n* **:** a link with a screw thread at one or both ends used for tightening a rod or stay by pulling together the ends that it connects

turn·coat \'tərn-,kōt\ *n* **:** one who forsakes his party or principles : TRAITOR

turn down *vb* **1 :** to fold or double down **2 :** to reduce in height or intensity by turning a control ⟨*turn down* the lights⟩ **3 :** REJECT ⟨*turned down* his application for a job⟩

turn in *vb* **1 :** to give up or hand over ⟨*turn in* extra supplies⟩ **2 :** to inform on : BETRAY ⟨*turned* his accomplice *in* to the police⟩ **3 :** DO ⟨*turned in* a fine job⟩ **4 :** to go to bed

tur·nip \'tər-nəp\ *n* **:** either of two herbs related to cabbage and having thick roots eaten as a vegetable or fed to stock: **a :** one with hairy leaves and usu. white and flattened roots **b :** RUTABAGA

turn·key \'tərn-,kē\ *n* **:** one who has charge of a prison's keys : JAILER

turn·off \'tərn-,ȯf\ *n* **:** a place where one turns off

turn off \-'ȯf\ *vb* **1 :** to turn aside or aside from

ə abut	ər further	a back	ā bake	
ä cot, cart	au̇ out	ch chin	e less	ē easy
g gift	i trip	ī life	j joke	ng sing	ō flow
ȯ flaw	ȯi coin	th thin	t͟h this	ü loot
u̇ foot	y yet	yü few	yu̇ furious	zh vision

something ⟨*turned off* into a side road⟩ **2 :** to stop the functioning or flow of by or as if by turning a control ⟨*turn off* the light⟩

turn on *vb* **1 :** to cause to function or flow by or as if by turning a control ⟨*turn* the water *on*⟩ ⟨*turn on* the lights⟩ ⟨*turned on* all of her charm⟩ **2 :** to experience or become aware of normally repressed psychic elements esp. as a result of taking a drug (as LSD)

turn·out \'tərn-ˌau̇t\ *n* **1 :** an act of turning out **2 :** a gathering of people for a special purpose **3 :** a widened space (as in a highway) for vehicles to pass or park

turn out \-'au̇t\ *vb* **1 :** to put out of some shelter **:** EVICT **2 :** to empty of contents **:** CLEAN **3 :** to make with rapidity or regularity ⟨factory that *turns out* shoes⟩ **4 :** to equip, dress, or finish in a careful or elaborate way **5 :** to turn off ⟨who *turned out* the lights?⟩ **6 :** to prove ultimately to be ⟨it *turned out* that he was her brother⟩

1**turn·over** \'tərn-ˌō-vər\ *n* **1 :** an act or result of turning over; *esp* **:** UPSET **2 :** a reorganization esp. of personnel **3 :** a pie or tart with one half of the crust turned over the other **4 :** the number of employees hired in a given time to replace those leaving or discharged

2**turn·over** \ˌtərn-ˌō-vər\ *adj* **:** capable of being turned over ⟨*turnover* cuffs⟩

turn over \-'ō-vər\ *vb* **1 a :** to shift in position ⟨*turned over* in bed⟩ ⟨*turned* the canoe *over*⟩ **b :** ROTATE ⟨engines *turning over* slowly⟩ **2 a :** to examine or search by shifting item by item often slowly or idly ⟨*turning over* old letters⟩ **b :** to examine in the mind **:** meditate on ⟨*turned over* the problem in search of a solution⟩ **3 :** to hand over **:** TRANSFER ⟨*turned over* his duties to an assistant⟩

turn·pike \'tərn-ˌpīk\ *n* **1 :** a toll road; *esp* **:** a toll expressway **2 :** a main road

turn·spit \-ˌspit\ *n* **:** one that turns a spit

turn·stile \-ˌstīl\ *n* **:** a post with arms pivoted on the top set in a passageway so that persons can pass through only on foot one by one

turn·ta·ble \-ˌtā-bəl\ *n* **1 :** a revolving platform with a track for turning wheeled vehicles **2 :** a rotating platform that carries a phonograph record

turn up *vb* **1 :** to bring or come to light usu. unexpectedly or after being lost ⟨the papers will *turn up*⟩ **2 :** to raise or increase by or as if by adjusting a control ⟨*turn up* the heat⟩ **3 a :** to turn out to be ⟨*turned up* missing⟩ **b :** to put in an appearance ⟨*turned up* half an hour late⟩ — **turn up one's nose :** to show scorn or disdain ⟨*turned up his nose* at every suggestion they made⟩

tur·pen·tine \'tər-pən-ˌtīn\ *n* **1 :** a mixture of oil and resin obtained from various cone-bearing trees (as some pines and firs) **2 :** an essential oil obtained from turpentines by distillation and used esp. as a solvent and thinner (as of paint)

tur·pi·tude \'tər-pə-ˌt(y)üd\ *n* **:** inherent baseness **:** DEPRAVITY ⟨moral *turpitude*⟩

tur·quoise \'tər-ˌk(w)ȯiz\ *n* [from medieval French *turquoyse*, literally "Turkish (stone)", from *Turc* "Turk"] **1 :** a blue, bluish green, or greenish gray mineral containing copper and aluminum, taking a high polish, and sometimes valued as a gem **2 :** a light greenish blue

tur·ret \'tər-ət, 'tə-rət\ *n* **1 :** a little tower often at a corner of a building **2 a :** a gunner's fixed or movable enclosure in an airplane **b :** a revolving structure (as on a tank) in which guns are mounted

1**tur·tle** \'tərt-əl\ *n* [from Old English *turtla*, from Latin *turtur*, a name imitating the call of the bird] *archaic* **:** TURTLEDOVE

2**turtle** *n, pl* **turtles** *also* **turtle** [modification of French *tortue*, the source also of English *tortoise*] **:** any of an order of land, freshwater, and marine reptiles with a toothless horny beak and a bony shell which encloses the trunk and into which the head, limbs, and tail usu. may be withdrawn

turtle
(about 6 in. long)

tur·tle·dove \'tərt-əl-ˌdəv\ *n* **:** any of several small wild pigeons esp. of an Old World genus noted for cooing

tur·tle·neck \-ˌnek\ *n* **1 :** a high close-fitting turnover collar used esp. for sweaters **2 :** a sweater with a turtleneck

turves *pl of* TURF

tush \'təsh\ *n* **:** a long pointed tooth **:** TUSK — **tushed** \'təsht\ *adj*

1**tusk** \'təsk\ *n* **1 :** a long greatly enlarged tooth (as of an elephant, walrus, or boar) that projects when the mouth is closed and serves for digging food or as a weapon **2 :** a tooth-shaped part — **tusked** \'təskt\ *adj*

2**tusk** *vb* **:** to dig up or gash with a tusk

tusk·er \'təs-kər\ *n* **:** an animal with tusks; *esp* **:** a male elephant with two normally developed tusks

1**tus·sle** \'təs-əl\ *vb* **tus·sled**; **tus·sling** \'təs-(ə-)ling\ **:** to struggle roughly **:** SCUFFLE

2**tussle** *n* **:** a physical contest or struggle **:** SCUFFLE

tus·sock \'təs-ək\ *n* **:** a compact tuft esp. of grass or sedge

tussock moth *n* **:** any of numerous dull-colored moths commonly with wingless females

tut *a* t-*sound made by suction rather than explosion; often read as* 'tət\ *or* **tut–tut** *interj* — used to express disapproval or disbelief

tu·te·lage \'t(y)üt-ə-lij\ *n* **1 :** an act of guarding or protecting **:** GUARDIANSHIP **2 :** INSTRUCTION

tu·te·lary \'t(y)üt-ə-ˌler-ē\ *adj* **1 :** having the guardianship of a person or a thing ⟨*tutelary* goddess⟩ **2 :** of or relating to a guardian ⟨*tutelary* authority⟩

1**tu·tor** \'t(y)üt-ər\ *n* **1 :** a person charged with the instruction and guidance of another; *esp* **:** a private teacher **2 :** a college or university teacher ranking below an instructor — **tu·tor·ship** \-ˌship\ *n*

2**tutor** *vb* **:** to teach usu. individually

tu·to·ri·al \t(y)ü-'tōr-ē-əl, -'tȯr-\ *adj* **:** of, relating to, or involving a tutor

tux \'təks\ *n* **:** TUXEDO

tux·e·do \ˌtək-'sēd-ō\ *n, pl* **-dos** *or* **-does** [from *Tuxedo* Park, N.Y., society resort] **1 :** a single-breasted or double-breasted usu. black or blackish blue jacket **2 :** semiformal evening dress for men

TV \(')tē-'vē\ *n* **:** TELEVISION

TVA *abbr* Tennessee Valley Authority

twad·dle \'twäd-əl\ *n* **:** silly idle talk **:** DRIVEL

twain \'twān\ *n* **1 :** TWO **2 :** COUPLE, PAIR

1**twang** \'twang\ *n* **1 :** a harsh quick ringing sound like that of a plucked bowstring **2 :** nasal speech or resonance

2**twang** *vb* **twanged**; **twang·ing** \'twang-ing\ **1 :** to sound or cause to sound with a twang **2 :** to speak with a nasal intonation

tweak \'twēk\ *vb* **:** to pinch and pull with a sudden jerk and twist **:** TWITCH — **tweak** *n*

tweed \'twēd\ *n* **1 :** a rough woolen fabric made usu. in twill weaves **2** *pl* **:** tweed clothing; *esp* **:** a tweed suit

[1]**tweet** \'twēt\ *n* : a chirping note
[2]**tweet** *vb* : CHIRP
tweeze \'twēz\ *vb* : to pluck or remove with tweezers
tweez·ers \'twē-zərz\ *n pl* [from obsolete *tweeze* "a case for small implements", an alteration of earlier *etwee*, from French *étui*] : a small metal instrument that consists of two legs joined at one end, is usu. held between the thumb and forefinger, and is used for plucking, holding, or manipulating
twelfth \'twelfth\ *n* — see NUMBER table — **twelfth** *adj or adv*
Twelfth Day *n* : EPIPHANY
Twelfth Night *n* **1** : the eve preceding Epiphany **2** : the evening of Epiphany
twelve \'twelv\ *n* **1** — see NUMBER table **2** *cap* : the twelve original disciples of Jesus **3** : the 12th in a set or series — **twelve** *adj or pron*
twelve·month \-,mən(t)th\ *n* : YEAR
twen·ti·eth \'twent-ē-əth\ *n* — see NUMBER table — **twentieth** *adj*
twen·ty \'twent-ē\ *n, pl* **twenties** — see NUMBER table — **twenty** *adj or pron*
twen·ty–twen·ty \,twent-ē-'twent-ē\ *adj* : having normal visual acuity — often written 20/20
twice \'twīs\ *adv* : two times ⟨*twice* absent⟩ ⟨*twice* as large⟩
twid·dle \'twid-əl\ *vb* **twid·dled**; **twid·dling** \-(ə-)ling\ : to rotate lightly or idly : TWIRL ⟨*twiddle* one's thumbs⟩ — **twiddle** *n*
twig \'twig\ *n* : a small shoot or branch — **twig·gy** \'twig-ē\ *adj*
twi·light \'twī-,līt\ *n* : the light from the sky between full night and sunrise or between sunset and full night — **twilight** *adj*
[1]**twill** \'twil\ *n* **1** : a fabric with a twill weave **2** : a textile weave that produces a pattern of diagonal lines or ribs
[2]**twill** *vb* : to make (cloth) with a twill weave
[1]**twin** \'twin\ *adj* **1** : born with one other or as a pair at one birth ⟨*twin* brother⟩ ⟨*twin* girls⟩ **2 a** : made up of two similar, related, or connected members or parts **b** : being one of a pair ⟨*twin* city⟩
[2]**twin** *n* **1** : either of two offspring produced at a birth **2** : one of two persons or things closely related to or resembling each other
[3]**twin** *vb* **twinned**; **twin·ning** **1** : to bring together in close association : COUPLE **2** : to bring forth twins
[1]**twine** \'twīn\ *n* : a strong string of two or more strands twisted together
[2]**twine** *vb* **1 a** : to twist together : WEAVE **b** : INTERLACE **2 a** : to coil or cause to coil about a support **b** : EMBRACE
twinge \'twinj\ *n* **1** : a sudden sharp stab of pain **2** : a moral or emotional pang
[1]**twin·kle** \'twing-kəl\ *vb* **twin·kled**; **twin·kling** \-k(ə-)ling\ **1** : to shine or cause to shine with a flickering or sparkling light **2** : to appear bright with merriment **3** : to move or flutter rapidly — **twin·kler** \-k(ə-)lər\ *n*
[2]**twinkle** *n* **1** : a wink of the eyelids **2** : the instant's duration of a wink : TWINKLING **3** : SPARKLE, FLICKER — **twin·kly** \-k(ə-)lē\ *adj*
twin·kling *n* **1** \'twing-k(ə-)ling\ : a winking of the eye **2** \-kling\ : INSTANT
[1]**twirl** \'twərl\ *vb* **1** : to revolve or cause to revolve rapidly : SPIN, WHIRL ⟨*twirl* a baton⟩ **2** : to pitch in a baseball game **3** : CURL, TWIST ⟨*twirled* his moustache⟩ — **twirl·er** *n*
[2]**twirl** *n* **1** : an act of twirling **2** : COIL, WHORL
[1]**twist** \'twist\ *vb* **1** : to unite by winding one thread, strand, or wire around another **2** : TWINE, COIL **3 a** : to turn so as to sprain or hurt ⟨*twisted* my ankle⟩ **b** : to alter the meaning of : PERVERT ⟨*twisted* the facts⟩ **c** : CONTORT ⟨*twisted* his face into a grin⟩ **d** : to pull off, rotate, or break by a turning force ⟨*twisted* a small branch off the tree⟩ **4** : to follow a winding course : SNAKE
[2]**twist** *n* **1** : a thread, yarn, or cord formed by twisting two or more strands together **2** : an act of twisting : the state of being twisted **3 a** : a turning aside : DEFLECTION **b** : DISTORTION, WRENCH **4 a** : an unexpected turn or development **b** : VARIATION ⟨an old story with a new *twist*⟩
twist·er \'twis-tər\ *n* **1** : one that twists **2** : TORNADO
twit \'twit\ *vb* **twit·ted**; **twit·ting** : to subject to light ridicule or reproach : RALLY ⟨*twitted* the girl on her vanity⟩
[1]**twitch** \'twich\ *vb* **1** : to move or pull with a sudden motion : JERK **2** : QUIVER
[2]**twitch** *n* **1** : an act of twitching **2 a** : a short sharp contraction of muscle fibers **b** : a slight jerk of a body part
[1]**twit·ter** \'twit-ər\ *vb* **1** : to utter successive chirping noises **2 a** : to talk in a chattering fashion **b** : GIGGLE, TITTER **3** : to tremble or cause to tremble with agitation : FLUTTER
[2]**twitter** *n* **1** : a trembling agitation : QUIVER **2** : the chirping of birds **3** : a light chattering : GABBLE
two \'tü\ *n, pl* **twos** **1** — see NUMBER table **2** : the second in a set or series — **two** *adj or pron*
two–bit \,tü-,bit\ *adj* **1** : of the value of two bits **2** : PETTY, SMALL-TIME ⟨a *two-bit* gangster⟩
two bits *n sing or pl* **1** : the value of a quarter of a dollar **2** : something of small worth or importance
two–dimensional *adj* **1** : having two dimensions **2** : lacking depth of characterization ⟨*two-dimensional* fiction⟩
two–faced \'tü-'fāst\ *adj* **1** : having two faces **2** : DOUBLE-DEALING, FALSE — **two–faced·ly** \-'fā-səd-lē, -'fāst-lē\ *adv*
two–fist·ed \-'fis-təd\ *adj* : VIRILE, VIGOROUS
two·fold \-,fōld, -'fōld\ *adj* **1** : having two units or members **2** : twice as much or as many — **twofold** *adv*
2, 4–D \,tü-,fōr-'dē, -,fȯr-\ *n* : a white organic compound used as a weed killer
two–hand·ed \'tü-'han-dəd\ *adj* **1** : used with both hands **2** : requiring two persons ⟨a *two-handed* saw⟩
two·pence \'təp-ən(t)s, *US also* 'tü-,pen(t)s\ *n* : the sum of two pence
two·some \'tü-səm\ *n* : a group of two persons or things
two–step \'tü-,step\ *n* **1** : a ballroom dance executed in march or polka time **2** : a piece of music for the two-step — **two–step** *vb*
two–time \-,tīm\ *vb* : DOUBLE-CROSS
two–winged fly \,tü-,wingd-\ *n* : any of a large order of insects including the true flies (as the housefly, mosquitoes, gnats, and related forms) and usu. having the fore wings functional and the posterior reduced to halteres
TX *abbr* Texas
ty·coon \tī-'kün\ *n* [from Japanese *taikun*, from Chinese *ta*[4] "great" and *chün*[1] "ruler"] **1** : SHOGUN **2** : a businessman of exceptional wealth and power
tying *pres part of* TIE
tyke \'tīk\ *n* **1** : DOG, CUR **2** : a small child

ə abut	ər further	a back	ā bake	
ä cot, cart	au̇ out	ch chin	e less	ē easy
g gift	i trip	ī life	j joke	ng sing	ō flow
ȯ flaw	ȯi coin	th thin	t͟h this	ü loot
u̇ foot	y yet	yü few	yu̇ furious	zh vision

tympani *n pl* : TIMPANI

tym·pan·ic \tim-'pan-ik\ *adj* **1** : of or relating to the middle ear or the eardrum **2** : resembling a drum

tympanic membrane *n* : EARDRUM

tym·pa·num \'tim-pə-nəm\ *n, pl* **-na** \-nə\ *also* **-nums 1 a** : EARDRUM **b** : MIDDLE EAR **2** : a thin tense membrane covering an organ of hearing or of sound-production of an insect

1**type** \'tīp\ *n* **1 a** : a person or thing believed to foreshadow or symbolize another **b** : one having qualities of a higher category : MODEL **2 a** : a rectangular block usu. of metal bearing a relief character from which an inked print is made **b** : a collection of such blocks or the letters printed from them **3 a** : general form or character common to a number of individuals that distinguishes them as an identifiable class ⟨horses of draft *type*⟩ **b** : a particular kind, class, or group ⟨a seedless *type* of orange⟩ **c** : something distinguishable as a variety : SORT ⟨reactions of this *type*⟩

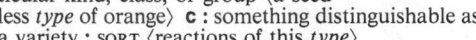

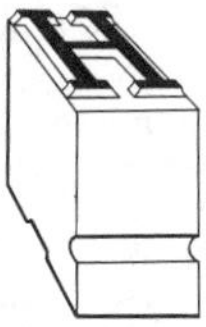

type 2a

2**type** *vb* **1** : TYPIFY **2** : TYPEWRITE **3** : to identify as belonging to a type

type·cast \'tīp-,kast\ *vb* **1** : to cast an actor in a part calling for the same characteristics as those possessed by the actor himself **2** : to cast an actor repeatedly in the same type of role

type·set·ter \-,set-ər\ *n* : one that sets printing type — **type·set·ting** \-,set-ing\ *adj or n*

type·write \'tīp-,rīt\ *vb* : to write with a typewriter

type·writ·er \-,rīt-ər\ *n* **1** : a machine for writing in characters similar to those produced by printer's type by means of keyboard-operated types striking through an inked ribbon **2** : TYPIST

type·writ·ing \-,rīt-ing\ *n* **1** : the act or study of or skill in using a typewriter **2** : the printing done with a typewriter

1**ty·phoid** \'tī-,fȯid, (')tī-'\ *adj* : of, relating to, or being typhoid

2**typhoid** *n* : a communicable bacterial disease marked esp. by fever, diarrhea, weakness, headache, and intestinal inflammation — called also *typhoid fever*

ty·phoon \tī-'fün\ *n* : a cyclone occurring in the region of the Philippines or the China sea

ty·phus \'tī-fəs\ *n* : a severe infectious disease marked by high fever, stupor alternating with delirium, intense headache, and a dark red rash and transmitted esp. by body lice — called also *typhus fever*

typ·i·cal \'tip-i-kəl\ *adj* **1** : being or having the nature of a type ⟨*typical* species⟩ **2** : combining or exhibiting the essential characteristics of a group ⟨*typical* suburban house⟩ — **typ·i·cal·ly** \-k(ə-)lē\ *adv*

typ·i·fy \'tip-ə-,fī\ *vb* **-fied**; **-fy·ing 1** : ILLUSTRATE, REPRESENT **2** : to have or embody the essential or main characteristics of

typ·ist \'tī-pəst\ *n* : one who typewrites

ty·pog·ra·pher \tī-'päg-rə-fər\ *n* : a specialist in the choice and arrangement of type matter : PRINTER

ty·pog·ra·phy \-fē\ *n* : the style, arrangement, or appearance of letterpress matter — **ty·po·graph·ic** \,tī-pə-'graf-ik\ *adj*

ty·ran·ni·cal \tə-'ran-i-kəl, tī-\ *also* **ty·ran·nic** \-'ran-ik\ *adj* : of, relating to, or characteristic of a tyrant or tyranny : DESPOTIC — **ty·ran·ni·cal·ly** \-'ran-i-k(ə-)lē\ *adv*

tyr·an·nize \'tir-ə-,nīz\ *vb* : to act as a tyrant

ty·ran·no·sau·rus \tə-,ran-ə-'sȯr-əs, tī-\ *n* : a very large American flesh-eating dinosaur of the Cretaceous having small forelegs and walking on its hind legs

tyr·an·nous \'tir-ə-nəs\ *adj* : marked by tyranny; *esp* : unjustly severe — **tyr·an·nous·ly** *adv*

tyr·an·ny \'tir-ə-nē\ *n, pl* **-nies 1 a** : a government in which absolute power is vested in a single ruler **b** : the office, authority, and administration of such a ruler **2** : arbitrary and despotic government; *esp* : rigorous, cruel, and oppressive government **3** : a tyrannical act ⟨the petty *tyrannies* of a foreman⟩

ty·rant \'tī-rənt\ *n* **1** : an absolute ruler unrestrained by law or constitution **2 a** : a ruler who exercises absolute power oppressively or brutally **b** : one resembling such a tyrant in the harsh use of authority or power

tyrant flycatcher *n* : any of a family of large American flycatchers with a flattened bill usu. hooked at the tip

tyre *chiefly Brit var of* TIRE

ty·ro \'tī-rō\ *n, pl* **tyros** : a beginner in learning

tzar \'zär, '(t)sär\ *var of* CZAR

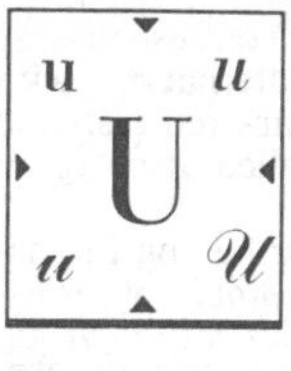

u \ˈyü\ *n, often cap* : the 21st letter of the English alphabet

u *abbr* unit

U *abbr* university

UAR *abbr* United Arab Republic

ubiq·ui·tous \yu̇-ˈbik-wət-əs\ *adj* : existing or being everywhere at the same time : OMNIPRESENT — **ubiq·ui·tous·ly** *adv* — **ubiq·ui·tous·ness** *n* — **ubiq·ui·ty** \-wət-ē\ *n*

U–boat \ˈyü-ˈbōt\ *n* : a German submarine

ud·der \ˈəd-ər\ *n* **1** : a large bag-shaped organ consisting of two or more mammary glands each provided with a nipple **2** : a mammary gland

UFO \ˌyü-(ˌ)ef-ˈō, ˈyü-fō\ *abbr* unidentified flying object

ugh *often read as* ˈəg\ *interj* — used for various sounds that express disgust or horror

ug·li·fy \ˈəg-li-ˌfī\ *vb* **-fied**; **-fy·ing** : to make ugly

ug·ly \ˈəg-lē\ *adj* **ug·li·er**; **-est** [from Middle English *uglike* "frightful", from Old Norse *uggligr*, from *ugga* "to fear"] **1** : offensive or unpleasant esp. to the sight : UNSIGHTLY, HIDEOUS ⟨an *ugly* smell⟩ **2** : morally offensive or objectionable : REPULSIVE ⟨*ugly* habits⟩ **3 a** : likely to cause inconvenience or discomfort : TROUBLESOME ⟨an *ugly* situation⟩ **b** : SURLY, QUARRELSOME ⟨an *ugly* disposition⟩ — **ug·li·ness** *n*

ugly duckling *n* : an unpromising child or thing actually capable of developing into a person or thing worthy of attention or respect

UHF *abbr* ultrahigh frequency

UK *abbr* United Kingdom

ukase \yü-ˈkās\ *n* : an edict esp. of a Russian emperor or government

Ukrai·ni·an \yü-ˈkrā-nē-ən\ *n* **1** : a native or inhabitant of the Ukraine **2** : the language of the Ukrainian people — **Ukrainian** *adj*

uku·le·le \ˌyü-kə-ˈlā-lē\ *n* [from Hawaiian, literally "flea"] : a usu. 4-stringed small guitar popularized in Hawaii

ukulele

ul·cer \ˈəl-sər\ *n* **1** : a slow-healing open sore in which tissue breaks down **2** : something that festers and corrupts

ul·cer·ate \ˈəl-sə-ˌrāt\ *vb* : to cause or become affected with an ulcer ⟨an *ulcerated* wound⟩ — **ul·cer·a·tion** \ˌəl-sə-ˈrā-shən\ *n*

ul·cer·ous \ˈəls-(ə-)rəs\ *adj* **1** : of or marked by ulceration ⟨*ulcerous* lesions⟩ **2** : affected with an ulcer : ULCERATED

ul·na \ˈəl-nə\ *n, pl* **ulnas** *or* **ul·nae** \-ˌnē, -ˌnī\ [scientific Latin, from Latin, "elbow", from the same prehistoric source as English *ell* and *el*bow] : the inner of the two bones of the forearm or a corresponding part of the forelimb of vertebrates above fishes — **ul·nar** \-nər\ *adj*

ul·ster \ˈəl-stər\ *n* : a long loose heavy overcoat

ult *abbr* ultimo

ul·te·ri·or \ˌəl-ˈtir-ē-ər\ *adj* **1** : situated beyond or on the farther side ⟨*ulterior* regions⟩ **2** : lying farther away in time ⟨immediate or *ulterior* measures⟩ **3** : going beyond what is openly said or shown : HIDDEN ⟨*ulterior* motives⟩ — **ul·te·ri·or·ly** *adv*

ul·ti·ma \ˈəl-tə-mə\ *n* : the last syllable of a word

ul·ti·mate \ˈəl-tə-mət\ *adj* **1 a** : most remote in space or time : FARTHEST ⟨*ultimate* reaches of the universe⟩ **b** : last in a progression : FINAL **c** : EXTREME, UTMOST ⟨the *ultimate* sacrifice⟩ **2 a** : ABSOLUTE, SUPREME ⟨*ultimate* truths⟩ **b** : finally reckoned ⟨the *ultimate* damage of the hurricane⟩ **3 a** : BASIC, FUNDAMENTAL ⟨*ultimate* reality⟩ **b** : incapable of further analysis, division, or separation : ELEMENTAL ⟨*ultimate* particles of matter⟩ **4** : MAXIMUM ⟨*ultimate* speed of an airplane⟩ — **ultimate** *n* — **ul·ti·mate·ly** *adv* — **ul·ti·mate·ness** *n*

ul·ti·ma·tum \ˌəl-tə-ˈmāt-əm, -ˈmät-\ *n, pl* **-tums** *or* **-ta** \-ə\ : a final condition or demand; *esp* : one whose rejection will bring about an end of negotiations and a resort to direct action

ul·ti·mo \ˈəl-tə-ˌmō\ *adj* : of or occurring the month preceding the present

ul·tra \ˈəl-trə\ *adj* : going beyond others or beyond due limit : EXTREME ⟨an *ultra* leftist⟩ — **ultra** *n*

ultra- *prefix* **1** : beyond : on the other side ⟨*ultra*violet⟩ **2** : beyond the range or limits of : transcending : SUPER- ⟨*ultra*microscopic⟩ ⟨*ultra*sonic⟩ **3** : beyond what is ordinary, proper, or moderate : excessively ⟨*ultra*modern⟩

ul·tra·high frequency \ˌəl-trə-ˌhī-\ *n* : any radio frequency in the range between 300 and 3000 megacycles — abbr. *uhf*

ul·tra·ma·rine \ˌəl-trə-mə-ˈrēn\ *n* **1** : a deep blue pigment **2** : a vivid blue

ul·tra·mod·ern \ˌəl-trə-ˈmäd-ərn\ *adj* : extremely or excessively modern in idea, style, or tendency — **ul·tra·mod·ern·ist** \-ər-nəst\ *n*

ul·tra·short \-ˈshȯrt\ *adj* : very short; *esp* : having a wavelength below 10 meters

ul·tra·son·ic \-ˈsän-ik\ *adj* : having a frequency above the human ear's ability to hear — **ul·tra·son·i·cal·ly** \-ˈsän-i-k(ə-)lē\ *adv*

ul·tra·sound \ˈəl-trə-ˌsau̇nd\ *n* : vibrations of the same physical nature as sound but with frequencies above the range of human hearing

ul·tra·vi·o·let \ˌəl-trə-ˈvī-ə-lət\ *adj* **1** : situated beyond the visible spectrum at its violet end and having a wavelength shorter than those of visible light but longer than those of X rays **2** : relating to, producing, or employing ultraviolet radiation — **ultraviolet** *n*

ul·va \ˈəl-və\ *n* : any of a genus of green marine algae with a thin flat edible thallus — called also *sea lettuce*

ulva (about 6 in. high)

um·bel \ˈəm-bəl\ *n* : a flat-topped or ball-shaped flower cluster (as in the carrot) in which the stalks of the individual flowers all grow from one point on the main stem like the ribs of an umbrella — **um·beled** *or* **um·belled** \-bəld\ *adj* — **um·bel·late** \ˈəm-bə-ˌlāt, ˌəm-ˈbel-ət\ *adj*

um·ber \ˈəm-bər\ *n* **1** : a brown earth valued as a pigment **2** : a moderate to dark brown or yellowish brown — **umber** *adj*

um·bil·i·cal \ˌəm-ˈbil-i-kəl\ *adj* : of, relating to, or adjacent to the navel

umbilical cord *n* : a cord arising from the navel that connects the fetus with the placenta

um·bil·i·cus \ˌəm-ˈbil-i-kəs\ *n, pl* **-bil·i·ci** \-ˈbil-ə-

ə abut	ər further	a back	ā bake	
ä cot, cart	au̇ out	ch chin	e less	ē easy
g gift	i trip	ī life	j joke	ng sing	ō flow
ȯ flaw	ȯi coin	th thin	t͟h this	ü loot
u̇ foot	y yet	yü few	yu̇ furious	zh vision

ˌkī, -ˌkē, -ˌsī\ *or* **-bil·i·cus·es 1 :** a depression in the abdominal wall at the point of attachment of the umbilical cord **2 :** HILUM

um·bra \ˈəm-brə\ *n, pl* **umbras** *or* **um·brae** \-(ˌ)brē, -ˌbrī\ **1 :** a shaded area **2 :** the conical part of the shadow of a celestial body excluding all light from the primary souce **3 :** the central dark part of a sunspot

um·brage \ˈəm-brij\ *n* **:** RESENTMENT, OFFENSE ⟨take *umbrage* at a remark⟩ — **um·bra·geous** \ˌəm-ˈbrā-jəs\ *adj*

um·brel·la \ˌəm-ˈbrel-ə\ *n* [from Italian *ombrella*, "parasol", "umbrella", from Latin *umbella*, diminutive of *umbra* "shade"] **1 :** a collapsible canopy for protection against weather consisting of fabric stretched over hinged ribs radiating from a center pole; *esp* **:** a small one for carrying in the hand **2 :** something (as part of an organism) resembling an umbrella in shape or function

umbrella tree *n* **:** an American magnolia having large leaves clustered at the ends of the branches

Um·bri·an \ˈəm-brē-ən\ *n* **:** a member of a people of ancient Italy occupying Umbria — **Umbrian** *adj*

umi·ak \ˈü-mē-ˌak\ *n* **:** an open Eskimo boat

um·laut \ˈüm-ˌlau̇t, ˈüm-\ *n* **1 :** the change of a vowel brought about by a succeeding sound **2 :** a diacritical mark ¨ placed esp. over a German vowel to indicate umlaut

umiak

um·pire \ˈəm-ˌpī(ə)r\ *n* [from Middle English *oumpere*, an altered form of earlier *noumpere* (the phrase *a noumpere* being understood as *an oumpere*), from medieval French *nomper* "not matched", "not paired" (i.e., not being one of the opposing parties), from *non-* "not" and *per* "equal", from Latin *par*] **1 :** one having authority to decide a controversy or question between parties **2 :** an official in a sport (as baseball) who rules on plays — **umpire** *vb*

ump·teen \ˌəm(p)-ˈtēn\ *adj* **:** indefinitely numerous ⟨*umpteen* million things to do⟩

¹un- \ˌən, ˈən\ *prefix* **1 :** not **:** IN-, NON- ⟨*un*skilled⟩ ⟨*un*dressed⟩ ⟨*un*kindness⟩ **2 :** opposite of **:** contrary to ⟨*un*constitutional⟩ ⟨*un*believing⟩ ⟨*un*rest⟩

unabsorbed
unacademic
unaccented
unaccentuated
unacceptable
unaccepted
unacclimated
unaccredited
unacquainted
unadapted
unadjusted
unadmirable
unadventurous
unadvertised
unadvisable
unaesthetic
unaffiliated
unafraid
unaged
unaggressive
unaided
unaimed
unaired
unalike
unallied
unaltered
unambiguous
unambitious
unanchored
unanimated
unannounced
unanswered
unanticipated
unapologetic
unapparent
unappeased
unappetizing
unappreciated
unappreciative
unapproved
unarmored
unarticulated
unartistic
unashamed
unaspiring
unassailed
unassisted
unassociated
unattainable
unattempted
unattended
unattractive
unauthenticated
unauthorized
unavailable
unavenged
unawakened
unawed
unbaked
unbaptized
unbeautiful
unblamed
unbleached
unblemished
unblinking
unborrowed
unbought
unbranded
unbreakable
unbridgeable
unbrotherly
unbruised
unbrushed
unburied
unburned
unburnished
unburnt
uncalibrated
uncalled
uncanceled
uncapitalized
uncared-for
uncaring
uncaught
uncensored
uncensured
unchallenged
unchambered
unchanged
unchanging
unchaperoned
unchecked
unchristened
unciliated
unclaimed
uncleaned
unclear
uncleared
unclouded
uncluttered
uncoiled
uncollectable
uncollected
uncolored
uncombed
uncombined
uncompensated
uncomplaining
uncompleted
uncomplicated
unconcealed
unconfined
unconfirmed
unconnected
unconquered
unconsecrated
unconsolidated
uncontaminated
uncontested
uncontrolled
unconverted
unconvinced
unconvincing
uncooked
uncooperative
uncoordinated
uncorrected
uncorrupted
uncountable
uncourteous
uncredited
uncrowded
uncultivated
uncultured
uncurbed
uncured
uncurious
undamaged
undamped
undated
undazzled
undecayed
undecked
undeclared
undecorated
undefeated
undefended
undefiled
undefinable
undefined
undelayed
undemanding
undemocratic
undenominational
undependable
undeserved
undeserving
undesired
undetected
undetermined
undeterred
undeveloped
undigested
undignified
undiluted
undiminished
undimmed
undiplomatic
undiscerning
undisciplined
undisclosed
undiscovered
undiscriminating
undisguised
undismayed
undisputed
undissolved
undistinguished
undisturbed
undivided
undomesticated
undramatic
undreamed
undreamt
undrinkable
uneager
uneaten
uneconomic
unedifying
uneducated
unembarrassed
unemotional
unemphatic
unenclosed
unendorsed
unendurable
unenforced
unengaged
unenlarged
unenterprising
unentertaining
unenthusiastic
unequipped
unethical
unexaggerated
unexamined
unexceptional
unexcited
unexciting
unexpanded
unexpended
unexperienced
unexpired
unexplainable
unexplained
unexploded
unexplored
unexposed
unexpressed
unexpurgated
unextinguished
unfaltering
unfashionable
unfathomable
unfavorable
unfed
unfeminine
unfenced
unfermented
unfertilized
unfilled
unfiltered
unflagging
unflattering
unflavored
unforced
unforeseen
unforested
unforgivable
unforgiving
unframed
unfree
unfrosted
unfrozen
unfulfilled
unfurnished
ungentle
ungentlemanly
unglazed
ungoverned
ungraded
ungrammatical
unguided
unhampered
unhanged
unhardened
unharmed
unhatched
unheeded
unheeding
unheroic
unhesitating
unhindered
unhomogenized
unhonored
unhoused
unhurt
unidentified
unidiomatic
unilluminated
unimaginable
unimaginably
unimaginative
unimpaired
unimpeded
unimportant
unimposing
unimpressionable
unimpressive
unincorporated
uninfected
uninflected
uninfluenced
uninformed
uninhabitable
uninhabited
uninitiated
uninjured
uninspired
uninspiring
unintended
uninteresting
uninvested
uninvited
unjointed
unjustifiable
unjustified
unlabeled
unladylike
unlamented
unleavened
unlicensed
unlighted
unlikable
unlined
unlit
unlivable
unlobed
unlovable
unloved
unloving
unmagnetized
unmanageable
unmanufactured
unmapped
unmarked
unmarketable
unmarried
unmated
unmeasured
unmentioned
unmindful
unmixed
unmodified
unmotivated
unmounted
unmusical
unnameable
unnamed
unneighborly
unnoticeable
unnoticed
unobjectionable
unobliging
unobservant
unobserved
unobserving
unobstructed
unobtainable
unopened
unopposed
unpaid
unpainted
unpalatable
unpardonable
unpardoned
unpatriotic
unpaved
unperceived
unperceiving
unperceptive
unperformed
unperturbed
unpitied
unpitying
unplanned
unplanted
unplayable
unpleasing
unpledged
unplowed
unpoetic
unpolarized
unpolished
unpolled
unpolluted
unposed
unpowered
unprejudiced
unpremeditated
unprepared
unprepossessing
unprescribed
unpressed
unpretending
unpretty
unprinted
unprocessed
unproductive
unprogressive
unprompted
unprotected
unproved
unproven
unprovided
unprovoked
unpruned

unpunished
unpure
unquenchable
unquenched
unquestioned
unransomed
unrated
unratified
unready
unreal
unrealistic
unrealized
unreasonable
unreasoned
unreasoning
unrecognizable
unrecognized
unreconciled
unrecorded
unredeemable
unredeemed
unrefined
unreformed
unregimented
unregistered
unregulated
unrehearsed
unrelated
unreliable
unrelieved
unreligious
unremarkable
unremembered
unrepaired
unrepealed
unrepentant
unreported
unrepresented
unrequited
unresistant
unresisted
unresisting
unresolved
unresponsive
unrestful
unrestricted
unreturnable
unreturned
unrevealed
unrewarded
unrewarding
unrhymed
unrhythmic
unrinsed
unripened
unromantic
unsafe
unsaid
unsaintly
unsalable
unsalaried
unsalted
unsanctified
unsanctioned
unsanitary
unsaponified
unsatisfactory
unsatisfied
unsatisfying
unscarred
unscented
unsealed
unseasoned
unseaworthy
unsecured
unseeded
unseeing
unselected
unsentimental
unseparated
unserved
unsexual
unshaded
unshadowed
unshakable
unshaken
unshapely
unshaved
unshaven
unshed
unsheltered
unshielded
unshorn
unshrinkable
unshrinking
unshut
unsigned
unsingable
unsinkable
unsized
unskillful
unslaked
unsmiling
unsociable
unsoiled
unsold
unsoldierly
unsolicited
unsolicitous
unsolvable
unsolved
unsorted
unsown
unspecialized
unspecified
unspent
unspoiled
unspoken
unsportsmanlike
unsquared
unstained
unsterilized
unstinted
unstinting
unstrained
unstratified
unstriated
unstriped
unstructured
unsubdued
unsubstantiated
unsuited
unsullied
unsupervised
unsupportable
unsupported
unsuppressed
unsure
unsureness
unsurpassable
unsurpassed
unsuspected
unsuspecting
unsustained
unsweetened
unsympathetic
unsystematic
untainted
untalented
untamed
untanned
untapped
untarnished
untaxed
unteachable
untenable
untended
untested
unthanked
unthankful
untheatrical
unthoughtful
unthrifty
untilled
untired
untiring
untouched
untracked
untrained
untranslated
untraveled
untraversed
untreated
untrimmed
untrod
untrodden
untroubled
untrustworthy
unusable
unuttered
unvaried
unvarying
unveiled
unventilated
unverified
unvulcanized
unwanted
unwarranted
unwashed
unwatched
unwatered
unwavering
unweaned
unwearable
unwearying
unweathered
unwed
unweeded
unweighted
unwelcome
unwelded
unwished
unwitnessed
unwomanly
unwon
unwooded
unworkable
unworked
unworn
unworried
unwounded
unwoven
unwrinkled

[2]**un-** *prefix* **1** : do the opposite of : reverse (a specified action) : DE- 1a, DIS- 1a ⟨*un*bend⟩ ⟨*un*dress⟩ ⟨*un*fold⟩ **2 a** : deprive of : remove a specified thing from : free or release from ⟨*un*frock⟩ ⟨*un*hand⟩ ⟨*un*bosom⟩ **b** : cause to cease to be ⟨*un*man⟩ **3** : completely ⟨*un*loose⟩

UN *abbr* United Nations

un·abashed \\ˌən-ə-ˈbasht\\ *adj* : not abashed — **un·abashed·ly** \\-ˈbasht-lē, -ˈbash-əd-lē\\ *adv*

un·abat·ed \\ˌən-ə-ˈbāt-əd\\ *adj* : not abated : at full strength or force — **un·abat·ed·ly** *adv*

un·able \\ˌən-ˈā-bəl\\ *adj* : not able : INCAPABLE

ə abut ər further a back ā bake
ä cot, cart au̇ out ch chin e less ē easy
g gift i trip ī life j joke ng sing ō flow
ȯ flaw ȯi coin th thin t͟h this ü loot
u̇ foot y yet yü few yu̇ furious zh vision

un·abridged \\ˌən-ə-ˈbrijd\\ *adj* **1** : not abridged : COMPLETE ⟨an *unabridged* reprint of a novel⟩ **2** : complete of its class : not based on one larger ⟨an *unabridged* dictionary⟩

un·ac·com·mo·dat·ed \\ˌən-ə-ˈkäm-ə-ˌdāt-əd\\ *adj* : not accommodated : UNPROVIDED

un·ac·com·pa·nied \\ˌən-ə-ˈkəmp-(ə-)nēd\\ *adj* : not accompanied; *esp* : being without instrumental accompaniment

un·ac·count·a·ble \\ˌən-ə-ˈkau̇nt-ə-bəl\\ *adj* **1** : INEXPLICABLE, STRANGE **2** : not to be called to account : not responsible — **un·ac·count·a·bly** \\-blē\\ *adv*

un·ac·count·ed \\-ˈkau̇nt-əd\\ *adj* : not accounted : UNEXPLAINED — often used with *for* ⟨their absence was *unaccounted* for⟩

un·ac·cus·tomed \\ˌən-ə-ˈkəs-təmd\\ *adj* **1** : UNUSUAL, UNFAMILIAR ⟨*unaccustomed* scenes⟩ **2** : not used : not habituated ⟨*unaccustomed* to travel⟩

un·adorned \\ˌən-ə-ˈdȯrnd\\ *adj* : not adorned : lacking embellishment or decoration : SIMPLE

un·adul·ter·at·ed \\ˌən-ə-ˈdəl-tə-ˌrāt-əd\\ *adj* : PURE, UNMIXED ⟨*unadulterated* foods⟩ ⟨*unadulterated* genius⟩

un·ad·vised \\ˌən-əd-ˈvīzd\\ *adj* : ILL-ADVISED — **un·ad·vis·ed·ly** \\-ˈvī-zəd-lē\\ *adv*

un·af·fect·ed \\ˌən-ə-ˈfek-təd\\ *adj* **1** : not influenced or changed mentally, physically, or chemically **2** : free from affectation : GENUINE — **un·af·fect·ed·ly** *adv* — **un·af·fect·ed·ness** *n*

un·alien·a·ble \\ˌən-ˈāl-yə-nə-bəl, -ˈā-lē-ə-nə-\\ *adj* : INALIENABLE

un·aligned \\ˌən-ə-ˈlīnd\\ *adj* : not associated with any one of competing international blocs ⟨*unaligned* nations⟩

un·al·loyed \\ˌən-ə-ˈlȯid\\ *adj* : not alloyed : UNMIXED, PURE ⟨*unalloyed* metals⟩ ⟨*unalloyed* happiness⟩

un·al·ter·a·ble \\ˌən-ˈȯl-t(ə-)rə-bəl\\ *adj* : not capable of being altered or changed ⟨*unalterable* resolve⟩ ⟨*unalterable* hatred⟩ — **un·al·ter·a·ble·ness** *n* — **un·al·ter·a·bly** \\-blē\\ *adv*

un–Amer·i·can \\ˌən-ə-ˈmer-ə-kən\\ *adj* : not American : not characteristic of or consistent with American customs, principles, or traditions — **un–Amer·i·can·ism** \\-kə-ˌniz-əm\\ *n*

un·an·chor \\ˌən-ˈang-kər\\ *vb* : to loosen from an anchor

unan·i·mous \\yu̇-ˈnan-ə-məs\\ *adj* [from Latin *unanimus*, from *unus* "one" and *animus* "mind"] **1** : being of one mind : agreeing completely ⟨the councilors were *unanimous* in their approval of the report⟩ **2** : assented to by all ⟨a *unanimous* vote⟩ — **una·nim·i·ty** \\ˌyü-nə-ˈnim-ət-ē\\ *n* — **unan·i·mous·ly** \\yu̇-ˈnan-ə-məs-lē\\ *adv*

un·an·swer·a·ble \\ˌən-ˈan(t)s-(ə-)rə-bəl\\ *adj* : not answerable; *esp* : IRREFUTABLE ⟨the arguments were *unanswerable*⟩

un·ap·peal·ing \\ˌən-ə-ˈpē-ling\\ *adj* : not appealing : UNATTRACTIVE

un·ap·peas·a·ble \\ˌən-ə-ˈpē-zə-bəl\\ *adj* : not to be appeased : IMPLACABLE — **un·ap·peas·a·bly** \\-blē\\ *adv*

un·apt \\ˌən-ˈapt\\ *adj* **1** : UNSUITABLE, INAPPROPRIATE ⟨an *unapt* quotation⟩ **2** : not accustomed and not likely ⟨*unapt* to run from danger⟩ **3** : INEPT, DULL, BACKWARD ⟨*unapt* students⟩ — **un·apt·ly** *adv* — **un·apt·ness** \\-ˈap(t)-nəs\\ *n*

un·arm \\ˌən-ˈärm\\ *vb* : DISARM

un·armed \\-ˈärmd\\ *adj* : not armed or armored

un·asked \\ˌən-ˈaskt\\ *adj* **1** : not asked ⟨*unasked* questions⟩ **2** : not asked for ⟨*unasked* advice⟩

un·as·sail·a·ble \ˌən-ə-ˈsā-lə-bəl\ *adj* : not assailable : not liable to doubt, attack, or question — **un·as·sail·a·bly** \-blē\ *adv*

un·as·sert·ive \ˌən-ə-ˈsərt-iv\ *adj* : not assertive : MODEST, SHY

un·as·sum·ing \ˌən-ə-ˈsü-miŋ\ *adj* : not putting on airs : MODEST, RETIRING — **un·as·sum·ing·ly** \-miŋ-lē\ *adv* — **un·as·sum·ing·ness** *n*

un·at·tached \ˌən-ə-ˈtacht\ *adj* **1** : not attached **2** : not married or engaged

un·avail·ing \ˌən-ə-ˈvā-liŋ\ *adj* : of no avail : not successful : FUTILE — **un·avail·ing·ly** \-liŋ-lē\ *adv*

un·avoid·a·ble \ˌən-ə-ˈvȯid-ə-bəl\ *adj* : not avoidable : INEVITABLE — **un·avoid·a·bly** \-blē\ *adv*

[1]**un·aware** \ˌən-ə-ˈwa(ə)r, -ˈwe(ə)r\ *adv* : UNAWARES

[2]**unaware** *adj* : not aware : IGNORANT — **un·aware·ness** *n*

un·awares \-ˈwa(ə)rz, -ˈwe(ə)rz\ *adv* **1** : without warning : by surprise ⟨taken *unawares*⟩ **2** : without knowing : UNINTENTIONALLY

un·backed \ˌən-ˈbakt\ *adj* **1** : not supported or encouraged **2** : having no back

un·bal·ance \ˌən-ˈbal-ən(t)s\ *vb* : to put out of balance

un·bal·anced \-ən(t)st\ *adj* **1** : not in equilibrium **2** : mentally disordered or deranged **3** : not adjusted so as to make credits equal to debits ⟨an *unbalanced* account⟩

un·bar \ˌən-ˈbär\ *vb* **-barred**; **-bar·ring** : to remove a bar from : UNBOLT

un·bear·a·ble \ˌən-ˈbar-ə-bəl, -ˈber-\ *adj* : greater than can be borne ⟨*unbearable* pain⟩ — **un·bear·a·bly** \-blē\ *adv*

un·beat·a·ble \-ˈbēt-ə-bəl\ *adj* : not capable of being defeated

un·beat·en \-ˈbēt-ən\ *adj* **1** : not pounded, beaten, or whipped **2** : UNDEFEATED

un·be·com·ing \ˌən-bi-ˈkəm-iŋ\ *adj* : not becoming ⟨an *unbecoming* dress⟩; *esp* : UNSUITABLE, IMPROPER ⟨conduct *unbecoming* an officer⟩ — **un·be·com·ing·ly** \-iŋ-lē\ *adv* — **un·be·com·ing·ness** *n*

un·be·known \ˌən-bi-ˈnōn\ *or* **un·be·knownst** \-ˈnōn(t)st\ *adj* : happening without one's knowledge : UNKNOWN ⟨events *unbeknown* to me⟩

un·be·lief \ˌən-bə-ˈlēf\ *n* : the withholding or absence of belief : DOUBT

un·be·liev·a·ble \-ˈlē-və-bəl\ *adj* : too improbable for belief — **un·be·liev·a·bly** \-blē\ *adv*

un·be·liev·er \-ˈlē-vər\ *n* **1** : one who does not believe : DOUBTER **2** : one who does not believe in a particular religious faith : INFIDEL — **un·be·liev·ing** \-ˈlē-viŋ\ *adj* — **un·be·liev·ing·ly** \-viŋ-lē\ *adv*

un·bend \ˌən-ˈbend\ *vb* **-bent** \-ˈbent\; **-bend·ing** **1** : to free from being bent : make or become straight **2** : to unfasten (as sails) from the spars **3** : to make or become less stiff or more affable : RELAX

un·bend·ing \ˌən-ˈben-diŋ\ *adj* **1** : INFLEXIBLE, RESOLUTE ⟨*unbending* in the performance of his duty⟩ **2** : formal and distant in manner : ALOOF

un·bi·ased \ˌən-ˈbī-əst\ *adj* : free from bias ⟨*unbiased* estimate⟩; *esp* : UNPREJUDICED, IMPARTIAL

un·bid·den \ˌən-ˈbid-ən\ *also* **un·bid** \-ˈbid\ *adj* : not bidden : UNASKED, UNINVITED

un·bind \ˌən-ˈbīnd\ *vb* **-bound** \-ˈbau̇nd\; **-bind·ing** **1** : UNTIE, UNFASTEN, LOOSE **2** : to set free : RELEASE

un·blush·ing \ˌən-ˈbləsh-iŋ\ *adj* **1** : not blushing **2** : SHAMELESS, UNABASHED ⟨an *unblushing* account of his escapades⟩ — **un·blush·ing·ly** \-iŋ-lē\ *adv*

un·bolt \ˌən-ˈbōlt\ *vb* : to open or unfasten by withdrawing a bolt

un·bolt·ed \-ˈbōl-təd\ *adj* : not sifted ⟨*unbolted* flour⟩

un·born \ˌən-ˈbȯrn\ *adj* : not born; *esp* : still to appear : FUTURE ⟨*unborn* generations⟩

un·bos·om \ˌən-ˈbu̇z-əm\ *vb* **1** : to give expression to : DISCLOSE, REVEAL **2** : to disclose one's thoughts or feelings

un·bound \ˌən-ˈbau̇nd\ *adj* **1 a** : not fastened or tied up ⟨*unbound* hair⟩ **b** : not confined ⟨*unbound* spirit⟩ **2** : not having the leaves fastened together ⟨an *unbound* book⟩

un·bound·ed \-ˈbau̇n-dəd\ *adj* : having no bounds or limits ⟨*unbounded* space⟩ ⟨*unbounded* enthusiasm⟩

un·bowed \ˌən-ˈbau̇d\ *adj* **1** : not bowed down ⟨*unbowed* heads⟩ **2** : UNSUBDUED ⟨*unbowed* by failure⟩

un·braid \ˌən-ˈbrād\ *vb* : to separate the strands of : UNRAVEL

un·branched \ˌən-ˈbrancht\ *adj* : free from or not divided into branches ⟨a straight *unbranched* trunk⟩ ⟨a leaf with *unbranched* veins⟩

un·bri·dled \ˌən-ˈbrīd-əld\ *adj* **1** : not confined by a bridle **2** : UNRESTRAINED, UNGOVERNED ⟨*unbridled* enthusiasm⟩

un·bro·ken \ˌən-ˈbrō-kən\ *adj* **1** : not damaged : WHOLE **2** : not subdued or tamed ⟨an *unbroken* colt⟩ **3** : not interrupted : CONTINUOUS ⟨an *unbroken* row of trees⟩ ⟨*unbroken* sleep⟩

un·buck·le \ˌən-ˈbək-əl\ *vb* : to unfasten the buckle of (as a belt)

un·built \ˌən-ˈbilt\ *adj* **1** : not built : not yet constructed **2** : not built on ⟨an *unbuilt* plot⟩

un·bur·den \ˌən-ˈbərd-ən\ *vb* **1** : to free or relieve from a burden **2** : to relieve oneself of : cast off

un·but·ton \ˌən-ˈbət-ən\ *vb* : to unfasten the buttons of (as a garment)

un·but·toned \-ənd\ *adj* **1 a** : not buttoned **b** : not provided with buttons **2** : not under constraint

un·cage \ˌən-ˈkāj\ *vb* : to release from or as if from a cage

un·called–for \ˌən-ˈkȯld-ˌfȯr\ *adj* : not called for : not needed or wanted ⟨an *uncalled-for* remark⟩

un·can·ny \ˌən-ˈkan-ē\ *adj* **1** : seeming to have a supernatural character or origin : MYSTERIOUS **2** : being beyond what is normal or expected : suggesting supernatural powers ⟨an *uncanny* sense of direction⟩ — **un·can·ni·ly** \-ˈkan-ə-lē\ *adv*

un·cap \ˌən-ˈkap\ *vb* : to remove a cap or covering from

un·ceas·ing \ˌən-ˈsē-siŋ\ *adj* : never ceasing : CONTINUOUS, INCESSANT — **un·ceas·ing·ly** \-ˈsē-siŋ-lē\ *adv*

un·cer·e·mo·ni·ous \ˌən-ˌser-ə-ˈmō-nē-əs\ *adj* : acting without or lacking ordinary courtesy — **un·cer·e·mo·ni·ous·ly** *adv*

un·cer·tain \ˌən-ˈsərt-ən\ *adj* **1** : not determined or fixed ⟨an *uncertain* quantity⟩ **2** : subject to chance or change : not dependable ⟨an *uncertain* temper⟩ **3** : not sure ⟨*uncertain* of the truth⟩ **4** : not definitely known ⟨a fire of *uncertain* origin⟩ — **un·cer·tain·ly** *adv* — **un·cer·tain·ness** \-ən-(n)əs\ *n* — **un·cer·tain·ty** \-ən-tē\ *n*

un·chain \ˌən-ˈchān\ *vb* : to free by or as if by removing a chain : set loose

un·change·a·ble \ˌən-ˈchān-jə-bəl\ *adj* : not changing or to be changed : IMMUTABLE — **un·change·a·ble·ness** *n* — **un·change·a·bly** \-blē\ *adv*

un·charged \ˌən-ˈchärjd\ *adj* : having no electric charge

U

un·char·i·ta·ble \ˌən-ˈchar-ət-ə-bəl\ *adj* : not charitable; *esp* : severe in judging others — **un·char·i·ta·ble·ness** *n* — **un·char·i·ta·bly** \-blē\ *adv*
un·chart·ed \ˌən-ˈchärt-əd\ *adj* : not recorded or plotted on a map, chart, or plan : UNKNOWN ⟨vast *uncharted* wastes⟩
un·chaste \ˌən-ˈchāst\ *adj* : not chaste : lacking in chastity — **un·chas·ti·ty** \-ˈchas-tət-ē\ *n*
un·chris·tian \ˌən-ˈkris-chən\ *adj* **1** : not of the Christian faith **2 a** : contrary to the Christian spirit or character **b** : BARBAROUS, UNCIVILIZED
un·civ·il \ˌən-ˈsiv-əl\ *adj* **1** : not civilized : BARBAROUS **2** : lacking in courtesy : ILL-MANNERED, IMPOLITE
un·civ·i·lized \ˌən-ˈsiv-ə-ˌlīzd\ *adj* **1** : not civilized : BARBAROUS **2** : remote from civilization : WILD
un·clad \ˌən-ˈklad\ *adj* : not clothed : UNDRESSED, NAKED
un·clasp \ˌən-ˈklasp\ *vb* : to release from a clasp
un·clas·si·fied \ˌən-ˈklas-ə-ˌfīd\ *adj* : not classified; *esp* : not subject to a security classification
un·cle \ˈəng-kəl\ *n* **1** : the brother of one's father or mother **2** : the husband of one's aunt
un·clean \ˌən-ˈklēn\ *adj* **1** : morally or spiritually impure **2** : prohibited by ritual law for use or contact **3** : DIRTY, FILTHY — **un·clean·ness** \-ˈklēn-nəs\ *n*
un·clean·ly \ˌən-ˈklen-lē\ *adj* : morally or physically unclean — **un·clean·li·ness** *n*
un·clench \ˌən-ˈklench\ *vb* : to open from a clenched position : RELAX ⟨*unclenched* his hands⟩
Un·cle Sam \ˌəng-kəl-ˈsam\ *n* [from a jocular interpretation of the letters *U.S.* stamped on casks of meat supplied to the U.S. Army during the War of 1812 as referring to Samuel Wilson, inspector of provisions for the Army] **1** : the U.S. government personified **2** : the American nation or people
Uncle Tom *n* : a black eager to win the approval of whites and willing to cooperate with them
un·clinch \ˌən-ˈklinch\ *vb* : UNCLENCH
un·cloak \ˌən-ˈklōk\ *vb* **1** : to remove a cloak or cover from **2** : REVEAL, UNMASK
un·close \ˌən-ˈklōz\ *vb* : OPEN
un·clothe \ˌən-ˈklōth\ *vb* : to strip of clothes or a covering
un·coil \ˌən-ˈkȯil\ *vb* : to release or become released from a coiled state : UNWIND
un·com·fort·a·ble \ˌən-ˈkəm(p)(f)-tə-bəl, -ˈkəm(p)-fərt-ə-bəl\ *adj* **1** : causing discomfort ⟨an *uncomfortable* chair⟩ **2** : feeling discomfort : UNEASY — **un·com·fort·a·bly** \-blē\ *adv*
un·com·mit·ted \ˌən-kə-ˈmit-əd\ *adj* : not committed; *esp* : not pledged to a particular belief, allegiance, or program
un·com·mon \ˌən-ˈkäm-ən\ *adj* **1** : not ordinarily encountered : UNUSUAL ⟨not *uncommon* to catch a cold⟩ **2** : REMARKABLE, EXCEPTIONAL ⟨has *uncommon* ability⟩ — **un·com·mon·ly** *adv* — **un·com·mon·ness** \-ən-nəs\ *n*
un·com·mu·ni·ca·tive \ˌən-kə-ˈmyü-nə-ˌkāt-iv, -ni-kət-\ *adj* : not inclined to talk or give out information : RESERVED
un·com·pli·men·ta·ry \ˈən-ˌkäm-plə-ˈment-ə-rē, -ˈmen-trē\ *adj* : not complimentary ⟨an *uncomplimentary* remark⟩

ə abut	ər further	a back	ā bake
ä cot, cart	aù out	ch chin	e less	ē easy
g gift	i trip	ī life	j joke	ng sing	ō flow
ȯ flaw	ȯi coin	th thin	th this	ü loot
ù foot	y yet	yü few	yù furious	zh vision

un·com·pro·mis·ing \ˌən-ˈkäm-prə-ˌmī-zing\ *adj* : not making or accepting a compromise : making no concessions : UNYIELDING — **un·com·pro·mis·ing·ly** \-zing-lē\ *adv*
un·con·cern \ˌən-kən-ˈsərn\ *n* **1** : lack of care or interest : INDIFFERENCE ⟨*unconcern* for world problems⟩ **2** : freedom from excessive concern or anxiety
un·con·cerned \-ˈsərnd\ *adj* **1** : not involved : not having a part or interest **2** : not anxious or upset : free of worry — **un·con·cern·ed·ly** \-ˈsər-nəd-lē\ *adv* — **un·con·cern·ed·ness** \-nəd-nəs\ *n*
un·con·di·tion·al \ˌən-kən-ˈdish-(ə-)nəl\ *adj* : not limited : ABSOLUTE, UNQUALIFIED ⟨*unconditional* surrender⟩ — **un·con·di·tion·al·ly** \-ē\ *adv*
un·con·di·tioned \-ˈdish-ənd\ *adj* **1** : not subject to conditions or limitations **2** : not dependent on learning : INHERENT
un·con·quer·a·ble \ˌən-ˈkäng-k(ə-)rə-bəl\ *adj* : incapable of being conquered or overcome — **un·con·quer·a·bly** \-blē\ *adv*
un·con·scio·na·ble \ˌən-ˈkänch-(ə-)nə-bəl\ *adj* **1** : not being in accordance with what is right or just : UNREASONABLE, EXCESSIVE **2** : not guided or controlled by conscience — **un·con·scio·na·bly** \-blē\ *adv*
¹**un·con·scious** \ˌən-ˈkän-chəs\ *adj* **1** : having lost consciousness ⟨knocked *unconscious* by a fall⟩ **2** : not aware ⟨*unconscious* of having made a mistake⟩ **3** : not realized : not consciously done ⟨an *unconscious* mistake⟩ ⟨*unconscious* humor⟩ — **un·con·scious·ly** *adv* — **un·con·scious·ness** *n*
²**unconscious** *n* : the part of one's mental life of which one is not conscious but which is often a powerful force in determining behavior
un·con·sid·ered \ˌən-kən-ˈsid-ərd\ *adj* **1** : not considered or worth consideration **2** : not resulting from consideration or study ⟨*unconsidered* opinions⟩
un·con·sti·tu·tion·al \ˈən-ˌkän(t)-stə-ˈt(y)üsh-(ə-)nəl\ *adj* : not according to or consistent with the constitution of a state or society — **un·con·sti·tu·tion·al·i·ty** \-ˌt(y)ü-shə-ˈnal-ət-ē\ *n* — **un·con·sti·tu·tion·al·ly** \-ˈt(y)üsh-(ə-)nə-lē\ *adv*
un·con·trol·la·ble \ˌən-kən-ˈtrō-lə-bəl\ *adj* : incapable of being controlled : UNGOVERNABLE — **un·con·trol·la·bly** \-blē\ *adv*
un·con·ven·tion·al \ˌən-kən-ˈvench-(ə-)nəl\ *adj* : not conventional : not bound by or in accordance with convention ⟨*unconventional* behavior⟩ — **un·con·ven·tion·al·i·ty** \-ˌven-chə-ˈnal-ət-ē\ *n* — **un·con·ven·tion·al·ly** \-ˈvench-(ə-)nə-lē\ *adv*
un·cork \ˌən-ˈkȯrk\ *vb* **1** : to draw a cork from **2 a** : to release from a sealed or pent-up state ⟨*uncork* a surprise⟩ **b** : to let go : RELEASE ⟨*uncork* a wild pitch⟩
un·count·ed \ˌən-ˈkaùnt-əd\ *adj* **1** : not counted ⟨a stack of *uncounted* bills⟩ **2** : INNUMERABLE ⟨*uncounted* millions of people⟩
un·cou·ple \ˌən-ˈkəp-əl\ *vb* **-cou·pled**; **-cou·pling** \-ˈkəp-(ə-)ling\ **1** : to loose hunting dogs to seek game **2** : DISCONNECT ⟨*uncouple* railroad cars⟩
un·couth \ˌən-ˈküth\ *adj* [from Middle English, meaning "strange", "unfamiliar", from Old English *uncūth*, literally "unknown"] **1** : strange, awkward, and clumsy in shape or appearance **2** : vulgar in conduct or speech : RUDE
un·cov·er \ˌən-ˈkəv-ər\ *vb* **1** : to make known : DISCLOSE, REVEAL ⟨*uncover* a plot⟩ **2** : to expose to view by removing some covering ⟨*uncover* the ruins of an ancient city⟩ **3** : to take the cover from ⟨*uncover* the box⟩ **4 a** : to remove the hat from **b** : to take off one's hat as a token of respect

un·cov·ered \-'kəv-ərd\ *adj* : not covered or supplied with a covering

un·cre·at·ed \ˌən-krē-'āt-əd\ *adj* **1** : not existing by creation : ETERNAL **2** : not yet created

un·crit·i·cal \ˌən-'krit-i-kəl\ *adj* **1** : not critical : lacking in discrimination **2** : showing lack or improper use of critical standards or procedures — **un·crit·i·cal·ly** \-k(ə-)lē\ *adv*

un·cross \ˌən-'krȯs\ *vb* : to change from a crossed position ⟨*uncrossed* his legs⟩

un·crown \ˌən-'krau̇n\ *vb* : to take the crown from : DEPOSE, DETHRONE

un·crys·tal·lized \ˌən-'kris-tə-ˌlīzd\ *adj* : not crystallized

unc·tion \'əng(k)-shən\ *n* **1** : the act of anointing as a rite of consecration or healing **2** : exaggerated earnestness of language or manner

unc·tu·ous \'əng(k)-ch(ə-w)əs\ *adj* **1** : being like an ointment esp. in smooth greasy texture or appearance : OILY **2** : full of unction in speech and manner; *esp* : insincerely smooth — **unc·tu·ous·ly** *adv* — **unc·tu·ous·ness** *n*

un·curl \ˌən-'kərl\ *vb* : to make or become straightened out from a curled or coiled position

un·cut \ˌən-'kət\ *adj* **1** : not cut down or cut into **2** : not shaped by cutting ⟨an *uncut* diamond⟩ **3** : not having the folds of the leaves slit ⟨*uncut* books⟩ **4** : not abridged or curtailed ⟨the *uncut* version of the movie⟩

un·daunt·ed \ˌən-'dȯnt-əd, -'dänt-\ *adj* : not discouraged or dismayed : FEARLESS — **un·daunt·ed·ly** *adv*

un·de·ceive \ˌən-di-'sēv\ *vb* : to free from deception, illusion, or error

un·de·cid·ed \-'sīd-əd\ *adj* **1** : not yet decided : not settled ⟨the question is still *undecided*⟩ **2** : not having decided : uncertain what to do ⟨still *undecided* about it⟩ — **un·de·cid·ed·ly** *adv*

un·de·mon·stra·tive \ˌən-di-'män(t)-strət-iv\ *adj* : restrained or reserved in expression of feeling : not effusive

un·de·ni·a·ble \ˌən-di-'nī-ə-bəl\ *adj* **1** : plainly true : INCONTESTABLE **2** : unquestionably excellent or genuine ⟨an applicant with *undeniable* references⟩ — **un·de·ni·a·bly** \-blē\ *adv*

[1]**un·der** \'ən-dər\ *adv* **1** : in or into a position below or beneath something ⟨the duck surfaced, then went *under* again⟩ **2** : below some quantity, level, or norm ⟨ten dollars or *under*⟩ — often used in combination ⟨*under*played his part⟩ **3** : in or into a state of subjection, subordination, or unconsciousness ⟨snowed *under* in the election⟩ ⟨the ether put him *under*⟩ **4** : so as to be covered or hidden ⟨turned *under* by the plow⟩

[2]**un·der** \ˌən-dər\ *prep* **1 a** : lower than and overhung, surmounted, or sheltered by ⟨*under* sunny skies⟩ ⟨*under* a tree⟩ **b** : below the surface of ⟨swimming *under* water⟩ **c** : in or into a position covered or concealed by ⟨the moon went *under* a cloud⟩ ⟨wearing a sweater *under* his jacket⟩ **2 a** : subject to the authority or guidance of ⟨served *under* the general⟩ **b** : with the guarantee of ⟨*under* the royal seal⟩ **c** : controlled, limited, or oppressed by ⟨*under* quarantine⟩ ⟨collapsed *under* the strain⟩ **d** : subject to the action or effect of ⟨*under* an anesthetic⟩ **3** : within the group or designation of ⟨*under* this heading⟩ **4 a** : less or lower than (as in size, amount, or rank) ⟨all weights *under* 12 ounces⟩ ⟨nobody *under* a colonel⟩ **b** : below the standard or required degree of ⟨*under* legal age⟩

[3]**un·der** \'ən-dər\ *adj* **1 a** : lying or placed below, beneath, or on the ventral side — often used in combination ⟨the sea's *under*currents⟩ **b** : facing or protruding downward — often used in combination ⟨*under*surface of a leaf⟩ **2** : lower in rank or authority : SUBORDINATE ⟨*under* bookkeepers⟩ **3** : lower than usual, proper, or desired in amount, quality, or degree ⟨*under* dose of medicine⟩

un·der·achiev·er \ˌən-dər-ə-'chē-vər\ *n* : a student who fails to do as well as he can

un·der·ac·tive \ˌən-dər-'ak-tiv\ *adj* : having an abnormally low degree of activity ⟨*underactive* thyroid gland⟩

un·der·age \ˌən-dər-'āj\ *adj* : of less than mature or legal age

[1]**un·der·arm** \'ən-dər-ˌärm\ *adj* **1** : placed under or on the underside of the arm ⟨*underarm* seams⟩ **2** : UNDERHAND ⟨an *underarm* toss⟩ — **underarm** *n*

[2]**underarm** *adv* : with an underarm motion

un·der·bel·ly \'ən-dər-ˌbel-ē\ *n* : the under surface of a body or mass ⟨*underbelly* of a bomber⟩; *also* : a vulnerable area ⟨the *underbelly* of the enemy's defences⟩

un·der·bid \ˌən-dər-'bid\ *vb* **-bid**; **-bid·ding** **1** : to bid less than a competing bidder **2** : to bid too low (as in cards) — **un·der·bid·der** *n*

un·der·bred \ˌən-dər-'bred\ *adj* **1** : marked by lack of good breeding : ILL-BRED **2** : of inferior or mixed breed ⟨an *underbred* dog⟩

un·der·brush \'ən-dər-ˌbrəsh\ *n* : shrubs and small trees growing among large trees : UNDERGROWTH

un·der·car·riage \-ˌkar-ij\ *n* **1** : a supporting framework (as of an automobile) **2** : the landing gear of an airplane

un·der·charge \ˌən-dər-'chärj\ *vb* : to charge too little ⟨was *undercharged* by the salesclerk⟩ — **un·der·charge** \'ən-dər-ˌchärj\ *n*

un·der·class·man \ˌən-dər-'klas-mən\ *n* : a member of the freshman or sophomore class

un·der·clothes \'ən-dər-ˌklō(th)z\ *n pl* : UNDERWEAR

un·der·cloth·ing \-ˌklō-thing\ *n* : UNDERWEAR

un·der·coat \-ˌkōt\ *n* **1** : a coat or jacket formerly worn under another **2** : a growth of short hair or fur partly concealed by a longer growth **3** : a coat of paint under another **4** : UNDERCOATING — **undercoat** *vb*

un·der·coat·ing \-ˌkōt-ing\ *n* : a special waterproof coating applied to the undersurfaces of a vehicle esp. for protection against rust and corrosion

un·der·cool \ˌən-dər-'kül\ *vb* **1** : to cool less than required for some specified purpose **2** : SUPERCOOL

un·der·cov·er \-'kəv-ər\ *adj* : acting or executed in secret ⟨*undercover* scheme⟩; *esp* : employed or engaged in spying or secret investigation ⟨*undercover* agent⟩

un·der·cur·rent \'ən-dər-ˌkər-ənt, -ˌkə-rənt\ *n* : a current below the upper currents or surface ⟨*undercurrents* of water⟩ ⟨an *undercurrent* of public opinion⟩

[1]**un·der·cut** \ˌən-dər-'kət\ *vb* **-cut**; **-cut·ting** **1** : to cut away the under part of or beneath something often so as to leave an overhang ⟨*undercut* a vein of ore⟩ **2** : to offer to sell at lower prices than or to work for lower wages than ⟨*undercut* a competitor⟩ **3** : to strike so as to give a backspin or elevation to the shot ⟨a tennis player *undercutting* the ball⟩

[2]**un·der·cut** \'ən-dər-ˌkət\ *n* : the action or result of undercutting

un·der·de·vel·oped \ˌən-dər-di-'vel-əpt\ *adj* **1** : not normally or adequately developed ⟨*underdeveloped* muscles⟩ **2** : failing to reach a potential level of economic development ⟨the *underdeveloped* nations⟩

un·der·do \ˌən-dər-'dü\ *vb* **-did** \-'did\; **-done** \-'dən\; **-do·ing** \-'dü-iŋ\ : to do less thoroughly than one can; *esp* : to cook rare — **underdone** *adj*
un·der·dog \'ən-dər-ˌdȯg\ *n* : the loser or predicted loser in a struggle
un·der·draw·ers \-ˌdrȯ(-ə)rz\ *n pl* : UNDERPANTS
un·der·es·ti·mate \ˌən-dər-'es-tə-ˌmāt\ *vb* **1** : to estimate as being less than the actual size, quantity, or number ⟨*underestimate* the cost of a new building⟩ **2** : to place too low a value on : UNDERRATE ⟨*underestimate* an opponent⟩ — **un·der·es·ti·mate** \-mət\ *n* — **un·der·es·ti·ma·tion** \-ˌes-tə-'mā-shən\ *n*
un·der·ex·pose \ˌən-dər-ik-'spōz\ *vb* : to expose for less time than is needed ⟨the film was *underexposed*⟩ — **un·der·ex·po·sure** \-'spō-zhər\ *n*
un·der·feed \ˌən-dər-'fēd\ *vb* **-fed** \-'fed\; **-feed·ing** **1** : to feed with too little food **2** : to feed with fuel from the underside
un·der·foot \-'fu̇t\ *adv* **1** : under the feet ⟨flowers trampled *underfoot*⟩ **2** : close about one's feet : in the way ⟨a puppy always *underfoot*⟩
un·der·gar·ment \'ən-dər-ˌgär-mənt\ *n* : a garment to be worn under another
un·der·gird \ˌən-dər-'gərd\ *vb* : to make secure : brace up : STRENGTHEN ⟨a life *undergirded* by religion⟩
un·der·go \ˌən-dər-'gō\ *vb* **-went** \-'went\; **-gone** \-'gȯn, -'gän\; **-go·ing** \-'gō-iŋ\ **1** : to submit or be subjected to : ENDURE ⟨*undergo* an operation⟩ **2** : to pass through : EXPERIENCE ⟨*undergoing* a change⟩
un·der·grad·u·ate \-'graj-ə-wət, -ˌwāt\ *n* : a student at a college or university who has not been granted a degree
1**un·der·ground** \ˌən-dər-'grau̇nd\ *adv* **1** : beneath the surface of the earth **2** : in or into hiding or secret operation ⟨the party went *underground*⟩
2**un·der·ground** \'ən-dər-ˌgrau̇nd\ *adj* **1** : being, growing, operating, or situated below the surface of the ground ⟨an *underground* stream⟩ **2 a** : conducted by secret means ⟨an *underground* resistance movement⟩ **b** : subversive of accepted values ⟨the *underground* press⟩
3**un·der·ground** \'ən-dər-ˌgrau̇nd\ *n* **1** : a space under the surface of the ground; *esp* : SUBWAY **2** : a secret political movement or group; *esp* : an organized body working in secret to overthrow a government or an occupying power
un·der·growth \'ən-dər-ˌgrōth\ *n* : low growth on the floor of a forest including seedlings and saplings, shrubs, and herbs
1**un·der·hand** \'ən-dər-ˌhand\ *adv* **1** : in an underhand or secret manner **2** : with an underhand motion ⟨throw *underhand*⟩
2**underhand** *adj* **1** : marked by secrecy and deception : not honest and aboveboard : SLY ⟨*underhand* methods⟩ **2** : performed with the hand kept below the level of the shoulder ⟨an *underhand* pitch⟩
un·der·hand·ed \ˌən-dər-'han-dəd\ *adj or adv* : UNDERHAND — **un·der·hand·ed·ly** *adv* — **un·der·hand·ed·ness** *n*
un·der·lay \ˌən-dər-'lā\ *vb* **-laid** \-'lād\; **-lay·ing** **1** : to cover, line, or cross the bottom of : give support to on the underside or below ⟨shingles *underlaid* with tar paper⟩ **2** : to raise or support by something laid under — **un·der·lay** \'ən-dər-ˌlā\ *n*
un·der·lie \ˌən-dər-'lī\ *vb* **-lay** \-'lā\; **-lain** \-'lān\; **-ly·ing** \-'lī-iŋ\ **1** : to lie or be situated under **2** : to form the foundation of : SUPPORT ⟨ideas *underlying* the revolution⟩
un·der·line \'ən-dər-ˌlīn, ˌən-dər-'\ *vb* **1** : to draw a line under : UNDERSCORE **2** : EMPHASIZE — **un·der·line** \'ən-dər-ˌlīn\ *n*
un·der·ling \'ən-dər-liŋ\ *n* : one who is under the orders of another : SUBORDINATE, INFERIOR
un·der·ly·ing \ˌən-dər-ˌlī-iŋ\ *adj* **1** : lying under or below ⟨the *underlying* rock is shale⟩ **2** : FUNDAMENTAL, BASIC ⟨*underlying* principles⟩
un·der·mine \ˌən-dər-'mīn\ *vb* **1** : to dig out or wear away the supporting earth beneath ⟨*undermine* a wall⟩ **2** : to weaken or wear away secretly or gradually ⟨*undermine* a government⟩
un·der·most \'ən-dər-ˌmōst\ *adj* : lowest in relative position — **undermost** *adv*
1**un·der·neath** \ˌən-dər-'nēth\ *prep* **1** : directly under ⟨stowed *underneath* the floor⟩ **2** : under subjection to ⟨life *underneath* a tyrant⟩
2**underneath** *adv* **1** : under or below an object or a surface : BENEATH ⟨soaked through his jacket to the shirt *underneath*⟩ **2** : on the lower side ⟨a pot blackened *underneath*⟩
un·der·nour·ished \ˌən-dər-'nər-isht, -'nə-risht\ *adj* : supplied with insufficient nourishment for health and growth — **un·der·nour·ish·ment** \-'nər-ish-ment, -'nə-rish-\ *n*
un·der·pants \'ən-dər-ˌpan(t)s\ *n pl* : short or long pants worn under an outer garment
un·der·part \-ˌpärt\ *n* **1** : a part lying on the lower side esp. of a bird or mammal **2** : a subordinate or auxiliary part or role
un·der·pass \-ˌpas\ *n* : a passage underneath something (as for a road passing under another road)
un·der·pay \ˌən-dər-'pā\ *vb* **-paid** \-'pād\; **-pay·ing** : to pay too little
un·der·pin \-'pin\ *vb* **1** : to form part of, strengthen, or replace the foundation of ⟨*underpin* a structure⟩ **2** : SUPPORT, SUBSTANTIATE ⟨*underpin* a thesis with evidence⟩
un·der·pin·ning \'ən-dər-ˌpin-iŋ\ *n* **1** : the material and construction (as a foundation) used for support of a structure **2** : SUPPORT, PROP **3** : a person's legs — usu. used in pl.
un·der·play \ˌən-dər-'plā\ *vb* : to treat or handle with restraint; *esp* : to play a role with subdued force
un·der·priv·i·leged \-'priv-(ə-)lijd\ *adj* : having fewer economic and social privileges than others : POOR
un·der·pro·duc·tion \-prə-'dək-shən\ *n* : the production of less than enough to satisfy the demand or of less than the usual supply
un·der·rate \ˌən-də(r)-'rāt\ *vb* : to rate too low : UNDERVALUE
un·der·score \'ən-dər-ˌskōr, -ˌskȯr\ *vb* **1** : to draw a line under : UNDERLINE **2** : EMPHASIZE — **underscore** *n*
1**un·der·sea** \ˌən-dər-ˌsē\ *adj* **1** : being or carried on under the sea or under the surface of the sea ⟨*undersea* oil deposits⟩ ⟨*undersea* warfare⟩ **2** : designed for use under the surface of the sea ⟨*undersea* fleet⟩
2**un·der·sea** \ˌən-dər-'sē\ *or* **un·der·seas** \-'sēz\ *adv* : under the sea : beneath the surface of the sea
un·der·sec·re·tary \ˌən-dər-'sek-rə-ˌter-ē\ *n* : a secretary immediately under a principal secretary ⟨*undersecretary* of state⟩

ə abut	ər further	a back	ā bake	
ä cot, cart	au̇ out	ch chin	e less	ē easy
g gift	i trip	ī life	j joke	ŋ sing	ō flow
ȯ flaw	ȯi coin	th thin	t͟h this	ü loot
u̇ foot	y yet	yü few	yu̇ furious	zh vision

un·der·sell \-'sel\ *vb* **-sold** \-'sōld\; **-sell·ing** : to sell articles cheaper than ⟨*undersell* a competitor⟩

un·der·shirt \'ən-dər-ˌshərt\ *n* : a collarless undergarment for the upper body

un·der·shoot \ˌən-dər-'shüt\ *vb* **-shot** \-'shät\; **-shoot·ing** **1** : to shoot short of or below ⟨an archer *undershooting* the target⟩ **2** : to fall short of in landing an airplane ⟨*undershot* the runway⟩

un·der·shot \ˌən-dər-ˌshät\ *adj* **1** : having the lower incisor teeth or lower jaw projecting beyond the upper when the mouth is closed **2** : moved by water passing beneath ⟨*undershot* wheel⟩

un·der·side \'ən-dər-ˌsīd, ˌən-dər-'\ *n* : the side or surface lying underneath

un·der·signed \'ən-dər-ˌsīnd\ *n, pl* **undersigned** : one who signs his name at the end of a document ⟨the *undersigned* testifies⟩ ⟨the *undersigned* all agree to the following conditions⟩

un·der·sized \ˌən-dər-'sīzd\ *adj* : smaller than is usual or standard ⟨*undersized* fruit⟩

un·der·skirt \'ən-dər-ˌskərt\ *n* : a skirt worn under an outer skirt; *esp* : PETTICOAT

un·der·slung \ˌən-dər-'sləng\ *adj* **1** : suspended so as to extend below the axles ⟨an *underslung* automobile frame⟩ **2** : having a low center of gravity

un·der·stand \ˌən-dər-'stand\ *vb* **-stood** \-'stu̇d\; **-stand·ing** **1** : to grasp the meaning of : COMPREHEND **2** : to have thorough acquaintance with ⟨*understand* the arts⟩ **3** : GATHER, INFER ⟨I *understand* that he will come today⟩ **4** : INTERPRET, EXPLAIN ⟨*understand* the letter to be a refusal⟩ **5** : to have a sympathetic attitude ⟨his wife doesn't *understand* about these things⟩ **6** : to accept as settled ⟨it is *understood* that I will pay⟩ **7** : to supply in thought as if expressed ⟨"to be married" is commonly *understood* after the word *engaged*⟩ — **un·der·stand·a·ble** \-'stan-də-bəl\ *adj* — **un·der·stand·a·bly** \-blē\ *adv*

[1]**un·der·stand·ing** \ˌən-dər-'stan-ding\ *n* **1** : knowledge and ability to judge : INTELLIGENCE ⟨a man of *understanding*⟩ **2 a** : agreement of opinion or feeling ⟨had never been much *understanding* between the brothers⟩ **b** : a mutual agreement informally or tacitly entered into ⟨an *understanding* between two nations over trade⟩

[2]**understanding** *adj* : endowed with understanding : TOLERANT, SYMPATHETIC ⟨she seems very *understanding*⟩ — **un·der·stand·ing·ly** \-'stan-ding-lē\ *adv*

un·der·state \ˌən-dər-'stāt\ *vb* **1** : to represent as less than is the case ⟨*understate* taxable income⟩ **2** : to state with restraint esp. for greater effect — **un·der·state·ment** \-mənt\ *n*

un·der·stood \ˌən-dər-'stu̇d\ *adj* **1** : fully comprehended **2** : agreed upon often tacitly : IMPLICIT

un·der·study \'ən-dər-ˌstəd-ē\ *vb* : to study another actor's part in order to be his substitute in an emergency — **understudy** *n*

un·der·sur·face \-ˌsər-fəs\ *n* : UNDERSIDE

un·der·take \ˌən-dər-'tāk\ *vb* **-took** \-'tu̇k\; **-tak·en** \-'tā-kən\ **1** : to take upon oneself as a task : enter upon ⟨*undertake* a journey⟩ **2** : to put oneself under obligation : AGREE, CONTRACT ⟨*undertake* to deliver a package⟩

un·der·tak·er \'ən-dər-ˌtā-kər\ *n* : a person whose business is to prepare the dead for burial and to take charge of funerals

un·der·tak·ing *2 is* 'ən-dər-ˌtā-king, *other senses are also* ˌən-dər-'\ *n* **1** : the act of a person who undertakes something **2** : the business of an undertaker **3** : something undertaken

un·der–the–count·er *adj* : UNLAWFUL, ILLICIT ⟨*under-the-counter* sale of drugs⟩

un·der·tone \'ən-dər-ˌtōn\ *n* **1** : a low or subdued tone **2** : a subdued color as seen through and modifying another color

un·der·tow \-ˌtō\ *n* : a current beneath the surface of the water that moves away from or along the shore while the surface water above it moves toward the shore

un·der·val·ue \ˌən-dər-'val-yü\ *vb* **1** : to value below the real worth **2** : to set little value on — **un·der·val·u·a·tion** \-ˌval-yə-'wā-shən\ *n*

un·der·wa·ter \ˌən-dər-ˌwȯt-ər, -ˌwät-\ *adj* : lying, growing, worn, or operating below the surface of the water — **un·der·wa·ter** \-'wȯt-, -'wät-\ *adv*

under way *adv* **1** : in or into motion ⟨a ship getting *under way*⟩ **2** : in progress : AFOOT ⟨preparations are *under way*⟩

un·der·wear \'ən-dər-ˌwa(ə)r, -ˌwe(ə)r\ *n* : clothing or an article of clothing worn next to the skin and under other clothing

un·der·weight \ˌən-dər-'wāt\ *n* : weight below what is normal, average, or necessary — **underweight** *adj*

un·der·wood \'ən-dər-ˌwu̇d\ *n* : UNDERBRUSH

un·der·world \'ən-dər-ˌwərld\ *n* **1** : the place of departed souls : HADES **2** : the side of the earth opposite to one **3** : a social sphere below the level of ordinary life; *esp* : the world of organized crime

un·der·write \'ən-də(r)-ˌrīt\ *vb* **-wrote** \-ˌrōt\; **-writ·ten** \-ˌrit-ən\; **-writ·ing** \-ˌrīt-ing\ **1** : to write under or at the end of something else **2** : to set one's name to and thereby become answerable for a designated loss or damage ⟨*underwrite* an insurance policy⟩ **3** : to subscribe to : agree to ⟨refused to *underwrite* the government's foreign policy⟩ **4 a** : to undertake the sale of and agree to purchase on a fixed date any remaining unsold ⟨*underwrite* an issue of bonds⟩ **b** : to guarantee financial support of ⟨*underwriting* artistic enterprises⟩ — **un·der·writ·er** *n*

un·de·sir·a·ble \ˌən-di-'zī-rə-bəl\ *adj* : not desirable : UNWANTED — **un·de·sir·a·bil·i·ty** \-ˌzī-rə-'bil-ət-ē\ *n* — **undesirable** *n* — **un·de·sir·a·ble·ness** \-'zī-rə-bəl-nəs\ *n* — **un·de·sir·a·bly** \-blē\ *adv*

un·de·vi·at·ing \ˌən-'dē-vē-ˌāt-ing\ *adj* : keeping a true course : UNSWERVING

un·dies \'ən-dēz\ *n pl* : UNDERWEAR; *esp* : women's underwear

un·di·rect·ed \ˌən-də-'rek-təd, -ˌdī-\ *adj* : not directed ⟨*undirected* efforts⟩

un·do \ˌən-'dü\ *vb* **-did** \-'did\; **-done** \-'dən\; **-do·ing** **1** : to make or become unfastened or loosened : OPEN, UNTIE ⟨*undo* a knot⟩ **2** : to make of no effect or as if not done : NULLIFY, REVERSE ⟨subtraction *undoes* addition⟩ **3 a** : to ruin the worldly means, reputation, or hopes of ⟨his stubbornness *undid* him⟩ ⟨*undone* by greed⟩ **b** : to disturb the composure of : UPSET — **un·do·er** *n*

un·do·ing \-'dü-ing\ *n* **1** : LOOSING, UNFASTENING **2 a** : RUIN ⟨drugs led to his *undoing*⟩ **b** : a cause of ruin ⟨a woman who was to prove his *undoing*⟩ **3** : ANNULMENT, REVERSAL

un·done \-'dən\ *adj* : not done : not performed or finished : NEGLECTED

un·doubt·ed \ˌən-'dau̇t-əd\ *adj* : not doubted or open to doubt : CERTAIN ⟨*undoubted* proof of guilt⟩ — **un·doubt·ed·ly** *adv*

un·drape \ˌən-'drāp\ *vb* : UNCOVER, UNVEIL

[1]**un·dress** \ˌən-'dres\ *vb* : to remove the clothes or covering of : STRIP, DISROBE

²**undress** *n* **1** : informal dress **2** : NUDITY
un·dressed \-'drest\ *adj* **1** : partially, improperly, or informally clothed **2** : not fully processed or finished ⟨*undressed* hides⟩ **3** : not cared for or tended ⟨an *undressed* wound⟩ ⟨*undressed* fields⟩
un·due \ˌən-'d(y)ü\ *adj* **1** : not due : not yet payable **2 a** : INAPPROPRIATE, UNSUITABLE ⟨*undue* behavior⟩ **b** : exceeding or violating propriety or fitness : EXCESSIVE ⟨*undue* elegance⟩
un·du·lant \'ən-jə-lənt, 'ən-d(y)ə-\ *adj* : UNDULATING
undulant fever *n* : a persistent human bacterial disease marked by fluctuating fever, pain and swelling in the joints, and great weakness
un·du·late \'ən-jə-ˌlāt, 'ən-d(y)ə-\ *vb* [from Latin *undulare*, from *unda* "wave"] **1** : to form or move in waves : FLUCTUATE **2** : to rise and fall in volume, pitch, or cadence **3** : to present a wavy appearance
un·du·la·tion \ˌən-jə-'lā-shən, ˌən-d(y)ə-\ *n* **1** : the action of undulating **2** : a wavy appearance or form : WAVINESS
un·du·ly \ˌən-'d(y)ü-lē\ *adv* : in an undue manner; *esp* : EXCESSIVELY ⟨*unduly* upset⟩
un·dy·ing \ˌən-'dī-ing\ *adj* : not dying : IMMORTAL, PERPETUAL ⟨*undying* gratitude⟩ ⟨whose poems won her *undying* fame⟩
un·earned \ˌən-'ərnd\ *adj* : not gained by labor, service, or skill ⟨*unearned* income⟩
un·earth \ˌən-'ərth\ *vb* **1** : to drive or draw from the earth : dig up ⟨*unearth* buried treasure⟩ **2** : to bring to light : DISCOVER ⟨*unearth* a secret⟩
un·earth·ly \-lē\ *adj* **1** : not of or belonging to the earth ⟨*unearthly* terrain⟩ **2** : SUPERNATURAL, WEIRD, TERRIFYING ⟨an *unearthly* scream⟩ — **un·earth·li·ness** *n*
un·easy \ˌən-'ē-zē\ *adj* **1** : not easy in manner : AWKWARD ⟨*uneasy* among strangers⟩ **2** : disturbed by pain or worry : RESTLESS ⟨rain made the crew *uneasy*⟩ — **un·eas·i·ly** \-'ēz-(ə-)lē\ *adv* — **un·eas·i·ness** \-'ē-zē-nəs\ *n*
un·ed·u·cat·ed \ˌən-'ej-ə-ˌkāt-əd\ *adj* : seriously deficient in education and esp. in formal schooling ***syn*** see IGNORANT ***ant*** educated
un·em·ploy·a·ble \ˌən-im-'plȯi-ə-bəl\ *adj* : not capable of being employed; *esp* : not capable of holding a job — **unemployable** *n*
un·em·ployed \-'plȯid\ *adj* **1** : not being used ⟨*unemployed* tools⟩ **2** : not engaged in a gainful occupation ⟨*unemployed* workers⟩
un·em·ploy·ment \-'plȯi-mənt\ *n* : the state of being out of work
un·end·ing \ˌən-'en-ding\ *adj* : ENDLESS — **un·end·ing·ly** \-ding-lē\ *adv*
un·equal \ˌən-'ē-kwəl\ *adj* **1 a** : not of the same measurement, quantity, or number as another **b** : not like or not the same as another in degree, worth, or status ⟨two pieces of *unequal* workmanship⟩ **2** : not uniform : VARIABLE, UNEVEN **3** : badly balanced or matched ⟨an *unequal* fight⟩ **4** : INADEQUATE, INSUFFICIENT ⟨timber *unequal* to the strain⟩ — **un·equal·ly** \-kwə-lē\ *adv*
un·equaled \-kwəld\ *adj* : not equaled : UNPARALLELED
un·equiv·o·cal \ˌən-i-'kwiv-ə-kəl\ *adj* : leaving no doubt : CLEAR, UNAMBIGUOUS ⟨an *unequivocal* refusal⟩ — **un·equiv·o·cal·ly** \-k(ə-)lē\ *adv*

ə abut	ər further	a back	ā bake
ä cot, cart	au̇ out	ch chin	e less	ē easy
g gift	i trip	ī life	j joke	ng sing	ō flow
ȯ flaw	ȯi coin	th thin	t͟h this	ü loot
u̇ foot	y yet	yü few	yu̇ furious	zh vision

un·err·ing \ˌən-'e(ə)r-ing, -'ər-\ *adj* : making no errors : CERTAIN, UNFAILING — **un·err·ing·ly** \-ing-lē\ *adv*
UNESCO \yu̇-'nes-kō\ *abbr* United Nations Educational, Scientific, and Cultural Organization
un·es·sen·tial \ˌən-ə-'sen-chəl\ *adj* : not essential
un·even \ˌən-'ē-vən\ *adj* **1** : not even : not level or smooth : RUGGED, RAGGED ⟨large *uneven* teeth⟩ ⟨*uneven* handwriting⟩ **2** : varying from the straight or parallel **3** : not uniform : IRREGULAR ⟨*uneven* combustion⟩ **4** : varying in quality ⟨an *uneven* performance⟩ — **un·even·ly** *adv* — **un·even·ness** \-vən-nəs\ *n*
un·event·ful \ˌən-i-'vent-fəl\ *adj* : not eventful : lacking interesting or noteworthy happenings ⟨an *uneventful* vacation⟩ — **un·event·ful·ly** \-fə-lē\ *adv*
un·ex·am·pled \ˌən-ig-'zam-pəld\ *adj* : having no example or parallel : UNPRECEDENTED
un·ex·cep·tion·a·ble \ˌən-ik-'sep-sh(ə-)nə-bəl\ *adj* : not open to objection or criticism : beyond reproach : UNIMPEACHABLE
un·ex·pect·ed \ˌən-ik-'spek-təd\ *adj* : not expected : UNFORESEEN ⟨an *unexpected* happening⟩ — **un·ex·pect·ed·ly** *adv*
un·fail·ing \ˌən-'fā-ling\ *adj* **1** : CONSTANT, UNFLAGGING ⟨*unfailing* support⟩ **2** : EVERLASTING, INEXHAUSTIBLE ⟨an *unfailing* supply⟩ **3** : INFALLIBLE ⟨the *unfailing* mark of an amateur⟩ — **un·fail·ing·ly** \-ling-lē\ *adv*
un·fair \ˌən-'fa(ə)r, -'fe(ə)r\ *adj* **1** : marked by injustice, partiality, or deception : UNJUST, DISHONEST ⟨an *unfair* trial⟩ **2** : not equitable in business dealings ⟨*unfair* to organized labor⟩ — **un·fair·ly** *adv* — **un·fair·ness** *n*
un·faith·ful \ˌən-'fāth-fəl\ *adj* **1** : not adhering to vows, allegiance, or duty : DISLOYAL **2** : not faithful to marriage vows **3** : INACCURATE, UNTRUSTWORTHY — **un·faith·ful·ly** \-fə-lē\ *adv* — **un·faith·ful·ness** *n*
un·fa·mil·iar \ˌən-fə-'mil-yər\ *adj* **1** : not well known : STRANGE ⟨an *unfamiliar* place⟩ **2** : not well acquainted ⟨*unfamiliar* with the subject⟩ — **un·fa·mil·iar·i·ty** \-ˌmil-'yar-ət-ē, -ˌmil-ē-'ar-\ *n*
un·fas·ten \ˌən-'fas-ən\ *vb* : to make or become loose : UNDO, DETACH, UNTIE ⟨*unfasten* a belt⟩
un·feel·ing \ˌən-'fē-ling\ *adj* **1** : lacking feeling : INSENSATE **2** : lacking kindness or sympathy : HARDHEARTED, CRUEL — **un·feel·ing·ly** \-ling-lē\ *adv*
un·feigned \ˌən-'fānd\ *adj* : not counterfeit or hypocritical : GENUINE ⟨*unfeigned* curiosity⟩ — **unfeigned·ly** \-'fā-nəd-lē, -'fān-dlē\ *adv*
un·fet·ter \ˌən-'fet-ər\ *vb* : to free from fetters ⟨*unfetter* the prisoner⟩ ⟨*unfetter* the mind from prejudice⟩
un·fin·ished \ˌən-'fin-isht\ *adj* : not finished; *esp* : not brought to the final desired state ⟨*unfinished* furniture⟩
¹**un·fit** \ˌən-'fit\ *adj* **1** : not adapted to a purpose : UNSUITABLE ⟨food *unfit* for human consumption⟩ **2** : INCAPABLE, INCOMPETENT ⟨eliminated *unfit* candidates by examination⟩ **3** : physically or mentally unsound ⟨*unfit* for army service⟩
²**unfit** *vb* : to make unfit : DISABLE, DISQUALIFY
un·flap·pa·ble \ˌən-'flap-ə-bəl\ *adj* : not easily upset or panicked : unusually calm
un·fledged \ˌən-'flejd\ *adj* **1** : not feathered or ready for flight **2** : IMMATURE, CALLOW
un·flinch·ing \ˌən-'flin-ching\ *adj* : not flinching or shrinking : STEADFAST — **un·flinch·ing·ly** \-ching-lē\ *adv*

un·fold \ˌən-ˈfōld\ *vb* **1 a** : to spread or cause to spread or straighten out from a folded position or arrangement **b** : UNWRAP **2 a** : BLOSSOM **b** : DEVELOP **3** : to open out or cause to open out gradually to the view or understanding

un·for·get·ta·ble \ˌən-fər-ˈget-ə-bəl\ *adj* : not to be forgotten : lasting in memory — **un·for·get·ta·bly** \-blē\ *adv*

un·formed \ˌən-ˈfȯrmd\ *adj* **1** : not arranged in regular shape, order, or relations; *esp* : SHAPELESS **2** : UNDEVELOPED, IMMATURE ⟨an *unformed* character⟩

1**un·for·tu·nate** \ˌən-ˈfȯrch-(ə-)nət\ *adj* **1 a** : not fortunate : UNLUCKY **b** : marked or accompanied by or resulting in misfortune ⟨an *unfortunate* experience⟩ ⟨*unfortunate* investments⟩ **2 a** : UNSUITABLE, INFELICITOUS ⟨an *unfortunate* choice of words⟩ **b** : DEPLORABLE ⟨an *unfortunate* lack of taste⟩ — **un·for·tu·nate·ly** *adv*

2**unfortunate** *n* : an unfortunate person

un·found·ed \ˌən-ˈfau̇n-dəd\ *adj* : lacking a sound basis : GROUNDLESS ⟨an *unfounded* accusation⟩

un·fre·quent·ed \ˌən-frē-ˈkwent-əd; ˌən-ˈfrē-kwənt-\ *adj* : not often visited or traveled over

un·friend·ly \ˌən-ˈfren-dlē\ *adj* **1** : not friendly or kind : HOSTILE ⟨an *unfriendly* greeting⟩ **2** : not favorable ⟨an *unfriendly* environment⟩ — **un·friend·li·ness** *n*

un·fruit·ful \ˌən-ˈfrüt-fəl\ *adj* **1** : not bearing fruit or offspring **2** : not producing a desired result ⟨*unfruitful* efforts⟩ — **un·fruit·ful·ly** \-fə-lē\ *adv*

un·furl \ˌən-ˈfərl\ *vb* : to loose from a furled state : open or spread : UNFOLD ⟨*unfurl* sails⟩ ⟨*unfurl* a flag⟩

un·gain·ly \ˌən-ˈgān-lē\ *adj* : CLUMSY, AWKWARD — **un·gain·li·ness** *n*

un·god·ly \ˌən-ˈgäd-lē, -ˈgȯd-\ *adj* **1 a** : IMPIOUS, IRRELIGIOUS **b** : SINFUL, WICKED **2** : OUTRAGEOUS ⟨gets up at an *ungodly* hour⟩ — **un·god·li·ness** *n*

un·gov·ern·a·ble \ˌən-ˈgəv-ər-nə-bəl\ *adj* : not capable of being governed, guided, or restrained ⟨an *ungovernable* temper⟩ — **un·gov·ern·a·bly** \-blē\ *adv*

un·grace·ful \ˌən-ˈgrās-fəl\ *adj* : not graceful : AWKWARD — **un·grace·ful·ly** \-fə-lē\ *adv* — **un·grace·ful·ness** *n*

un·gra·cious \ˌən-ˈgrā-shəs\ *adj* **1** : not courteous : RUDE **2** : not pleasing : DISAGREEABLE — **un·gra·cious·ly** *adv* — **un·gra·cious·ness** *n*

un·grate·ful \ˌən-ˈgrāt-fəl\ *adj* **1** : not thankful for favors **2** : not pleasing : DISAGREEABLE ⟨an *ungrateful* task⟩ — **un·grate·ful·ly** \-fə-lē\ *adv* — **un·grate·ful·ness** *n*

un·ground·ed \ˌən-ˈgrau̇n-dəd\ *adj* **1** : UNFOUNDED, BASELESS **2** : not instructed or informed

un·guard·ed \ˌən-ˈgärd-əd\ *adj* **1** : vulnerable to attack : UNPROTECTED **2** : free from guile or wariness : DIRECT, INCAUTIOUS — **un·guard·ed·ly** *adv*

un·guent \ˈən(g)-gwənt, ˈən-jənt\ *n* : a soothing or healing salve : OINTMENT

1**un·gu·late** \ˈəng-gyə-lət\ *adj* **1** : having hoofs **2** : of or relating to the ungulates

2**ungulate** *n* : any of a group consisting of the hoofed mammals and including the ruminants, swine, horses, tapirs, rhinoceroses, elephants, and hyraxes

un·hal·lowed \ˌən-ˈhal-ōd\ *adj* : UNCONSECRATED, UNHOLY

un·hand \ˌən-ˈhand\ *vb* : to remove the hand from : let go

un·hand·some \ˌən-ˈhan(t)-səm\ *adj* **1** : not handsome; *esp* : not beautiful : HOMELY **2** : lacking in courtesy or taste : UNBECOMING ⟨*unhandsome* behavior⟩ — **un·hand·some·ly** *adv*

un·handy \ˌən-ˈhan-dē\ *adj* **1** : hard to handle : INCONVENIENT **2** : lacking in skill or dexterity : AWKWARD — **un·hand·i·ness** *n*

un·hap·py \ˌən-ˈhap-ē\ *adj* **1** : not fortunate : UNLUCKY ⟨the result of an *unhappy* mistake⟩ **2** : not cheerful : SAD, MISERABLE **3** : INAPPROPRIATE ⟨an *unhappy* color combination⟩ — **un·hap·pi·ly** \-ˈhap-ə-lē\ *adv* — **un·hap·pi·ness** \-ˈhap-i-nəs\ *n*

un·har·ness \ˌən-ˈhär-nəs\ *vb* : to divest of harness

un·health·ful \ˌən-ˈhelth-fəl\ *adj* : not conducive to good health

un·healthy \-ˈhel-thē\ *adj* **1** : UNHEALTHFUL ⟨an *unhealthy* climate⟩ **2** : not in good health : SICKLY, DISEASED **3 a** : RISKY, UNSOUND **b** : BAD, INJURIOUS — **un·health·i·ly** \-thə-lē\ *adv* — **un·health·i·ness** \-thē-nəs\ *n*

un·heard \ˌən-ˈhərd\ *adj* **1** : not perceived by the ear **2** : not given a hearing

un·heard–of \-ˌəv, -ˌäv\ *adj* : previously unknown : UNPRECEDENTED

un·hinge \ˌən-ˈhinj\ *vb* **1** : to remove (as a door) from the hinges **2** : to make unstable : UNSETTLE, DISRUPT ⟨a mind *unhinged* by grief⟩

un·hitch \ˌən-ˈhich\ *vb* : to free from being hitched

un·ho·ly \ˌən-ˈhō-lē\ *adj* : not holy : PROFANE, WICKED — **un·ho·li·ness** *n*

un·hook \ˌən-ˈhu̇k\ *vb* **1** : to remove from a hook **2** : to unfasten by disengaging a hook

un·horse \ˌən-ˈhȯrs\ *vb* : to dislodge from a horse : OVERTHROW, UNSEAT

un·hur·ried \-ˈhər-ēd, -ˈhə-rēd\ *adj* : not hurried : LEISURELY

uni·cam·er·al \ˌyü-ni-ˈkam(-ə)-rəl\ *adj* : having or consisting of a single legislative chamber

UNICEF \ˈyü-nə-ˌsef\ *abbr* United Nations Children's Fund

uni·cel·lu·lar \-ˈsel-yə-lər\ *adj* : having or consisting of a single cell

uni·corn \ˈyü-nə-ˌkȯrn\ *n* [from Latin *unicornis*, from *uni-* and *cornu* "horn"] : a fabulous animal generally depicted with the body and head of a horse and a single horn in the middle of the forehead

unicorn

uni·cy·cle \ˈyü-ni-ˌsī-kəl\ *n* : a vehicle having a single wheel and usu. propelled by pedals

uni·di·rec·tion·al \ˌyü-ni-də-ˈrek-sh(ə-)nəl, -dī-\ *adj* : having, moving in, or responsive in a single direction ⟨a *unidirectional* current⟩ ⟨a *unidirectional* microphone⟩

1**uni·form** \ˈyü-nə-ˌfȯrm\ *adj* **1** : having always the same form, manner, or degree : not varying or variable ⟨*uniform* temperature⟩ **2** : of the same form with others : conforming to one rule ⟨*uniform* ceremonies in the churches⟩ — **uni·form·ly** *adv* — **uni·form·ness** *n*

2**uniform** *vb* : to clothe with a uniform

3**uniform** *n* : uniform dress worn by members of a particular group (as an army or a police force)

uni·for·mi·tar·i·an·ism \ˌyü-nə-ˌfȯr-mə-ˈter-ē-ə-ˌniz-əm\ *n* : a geological doctrine that states that the knowledge of existing processes in nature can help to explain geological changes in the past

uni·for·mi·ty \ˌyü-nə-ˈfȯr-mət-ē\ *n*, *pl* **-ties** : the quality or state or an instance of being uniform

uni·fy \ˈyü-nə-ˌfī\ *vb* **-fied**; **-fy·ing** : to make into a unit or a coherent whole : UNITE — **uni·fi·ca·tion** \ˌyü-nə-fə-ˈkā-shən\ *n*

U

uni·lat·er·al \ˌyü-ni-ˈlat-ə-rəl, -ˈla-trəl\ *adj* **1** : of, relating to, having, or affecting one side only ⟨*unilateral* paralysis⟩ **2** : done or undertaken by only one of two or more parties ⟨*unilateral* disarmament⟩ — **uni·lat·er·al·ly** \-ē\ *adv*

un·im·peach·a·ble \ˌən-im-ˈpē-chə-bəl\ *adj* : not impeachable : not liable to accusation : IRREPROACHABLE ⟨an *unimpeachable* reputation⟩ ⟨information from an *unimpeachable* source⟩ — **un·im·peach·a·bly** \-blē\ *adv*

un·im·proved \-ˈprüvd\ *adj* : not tilled, built upon, or otherwise improved for use ⟨*unimproved* land⟩ ⟨*unimproved* roads⟩

un·in·hib·it·ed \ˌən-in-ˈhib-ət-əd\ *adj* : free from inhibition; *esp* : boisterously informal — **un·in·hib·it·ed·ly** *adv*

un·in·tel·li·gent \-ˈtel-ə-jənt\ *adj* : lacking intelligence : UNWISE, STUPID — **un·in·tel·li·gent·ly** *adv*

un·in·tel·li·gi·ble \-ˈtel-ə-jə-bəl\ *adj* : incapable of being understood : OBSCURE — **un·in·tel·li·gi·bly** \-blē\ *adv*

un·in·ten·tion·al \ˌən-in-ˈtench-(ə-)nəl\ *adj* : not intentional — **un·in·ten·tion·al·ly** \-ē\ *adv*

un·in·ter·est·ed \ˌən-ˈin-trəs-təd, -ˈint-ə-rəs-\ *adj* **1** : having no interest in ⟨*uninterested* in tennis⟩ **2** : not having the mind or feelings engaged : not having the curiosity or sympathy aroused

un·in·ter·rupt·ed \ˌən-ˌint-ə-ˈrəp-təd\ *adj* : not interrupted : CONTINUOUS — **un·in·ter·rupt·ed·ly** *adv*

union \ˈyü-nyən\ *n* **1 a** : an act or instance of uniting two or more things into one ⟨the *union* of Scotland and England⟩ ⟨*union* of a man and woman in marriage⟩ **b** : a unified condition : COMBINATION, JUNCTION ⟨the *union* of art and science to tackle modern problems⟩ **2 a** : something (as a nation or a confederation of nations) formed by a combining of parts or members **b** : LABOR UNION **c** : the set of all elements that belong to one or both of two sets **3 a** : a device emblematic of national unity borne on a flag **b** : the upper inner corner of a flag **4 a** : a device for connecting parts (as of a machine) **b** : a coupling for pipes

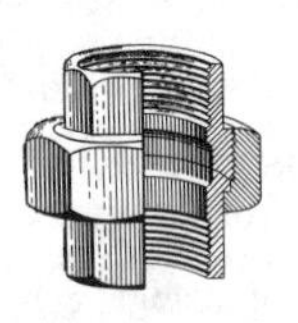

union 4b, partly cut away

Union *adj* : of, relating to, or being the side favoring the federal union in the U.S. Civil War ⟨the *Union* army⟩

union·ism \ˈyü-nyə-ˌniz-əm\ *n* **1** : the principle or policy of forming or adhering to a union **2** *cap* : adherence to the policy of a firm federal union prior to or during the U.S. Civil War **3** : the principles, theory, or system of trade unions — **union·ist** \-nyə-nəst\ *n, often cap*

union·ize \ˈyü-nyə-ˌnīz\ *vb* : to cause to become a member of or subject to the rules of a labor union : form into a labor union — **union·i·za·tion** \ˌyü-nyə-nə-ˈzā-shən\ *n*

union jack *n* **1** : a flag consisting of the part of a national flag that signifies union; *esp* : a U.S. flag consisting of a blue field with one white star for each state **2** *cap U & J* : the national flag of the United Kingdom

ə abut　ər further　a back　ā bake
ä cot, cart　aù out　ch chin　e less　ē easy
g gift　i trip　ī life　j joke　ng sing　ō flow
ȯ flaw　ȯi coin　th thin　th this　ü loot
ù foot　y yet　yü few　yù furious　zh vision

union suit *n* : an undergarment with shirt and drawers in one piece

unique \yù-ˈnēk\ *adj* **1** : being the only one of its kind **2** : very unusual : NOTABLE **3** : being the one and only possible result of one or more mathematical operations ⟨a *unique* solution⟩; *also* : having only one possible result ⟨addition of integers is *unique*⟩ — **unique·ly** *adv* — **unique·ness** *n*

uni·sex \ˈyü-ni-ˌseks\ *adj* : common to males and females ⟨*unisex* clothing⟩

uni·sex·u·al \ˌyü-ni-ˈsek-sh(ə-w)əl\ *adj* : having only male or only female reproductive organs

uni·son \ˈyü-nə-sən, -zən\ *n* **1** : sameness or identity in pitch **2** : the condition of being tuned or sounded at the same pitch or at an octave ⟨sing in *unison* rather than in harmony⟩ **3** : exact agreement : ACCORD ⟨all are in *unison* on the next move⟩

1**unit** \ˈyü-nət\ *n* **1 a** (1) : the first and least natural number : ONE (2) : a single quantity regarded as a whole in calculation **b** : the number occupying the position immediately to the left of the decimal point in the Arabic system of numerals **2** : a definite quantity (as of length, time, or value) adopted as a standard of measurement ⟨the franc is the *unit* of French currency⟩ **3 a** : a single thing or person or group that is a constituent of a whole **b** : a piece or complex of apparatus serving to perform one particular function ⟨a train drawn by two diesel *units*⟩ **c** : a part of a school course focusing on a central theme and making use of resources from numerous subject areas and the pupils' own experience

2**unit** *adj* : being a unit of ⟨*unit* length⟩ ⟨*unit* angle⟩

uni·tar·i·an \ˌyü-nə-ˈter-ē-ən\ *n, often cap* : one who believes that the deity exists only in one person — **unitarian** *adj, often cap* — **uni·tar·i·an·ism** \-ē-ə-ˌniz-əm\ *n, often cap*

uni·tary \ˈyü-nə-ˌter-ē\ *adj* **1 a** : of or relating to a unit **b** : based on or characterized by unity or units **2** : having the character of a unit : UNDIVIDED, WHOLE

unite \yù-ˈnīt\ *vb* **1 a** : to put or come together to form a single unit **b** : to cause to adhere **c** : to link by a legal or moral bond **2** : to become one or as if one ⟨two elements *unite* to form a compound⟩ **3** : to join in action : act as if one ⟨*unite* in prayer⟩ ***syn*** see JOIN ***ant*** disunite — **unit·er** *n*

unit·ed \yù-ˈnīt-əd\ *adj* **1** : made one : COMBINED **2** : relating to or produced by joint action ⟨gave their *united* consent⟩ **3** : being in agreement : HARMONIOUS ⟨a *united* family⟩ — **unit·ed·ly** *adv*

unit·ize \ˈyü-nət-ˌīz\ *vb* : to convert into a unit

uni·ty \ˈyü-nət-ē\ *n, pl* **-ties** **1** : the quality or state of being one : SINGLENESS, ONENESS **2** : CONCORD, HARMONY **3** : continuity without change **4** : a definite mathematical quantity or combination of quantities taken as one or for which 1 is made to stand in a calculation **5** : reference of all the parts of an artistic or literary composition to a single main idea : singleness of effect or style

1**uni·valve** \ˈyü-ni-ˌvalv\ *adj* : having or consisting of one valve

2**univalve** *n* : a univalve mollusk shell or a mollusk having such a shell

uni·ver·sal \ˌyü-nə-ˈvər-səl\ *adj* **1** : including or covering all or a whole without limit or exception ⟨*universal* human traits⟩ **2** : present or existent everywhere or under all conditions ⟨as *universal* as air⟩ ⟨*universal* cultural patterns⟩ **3 a** : embracing a major part or the greatest portion ⟨*universal* practices⟩ **b** : comprehensively broad and versatile ⟨a *universal* genius⟩ **4** : adapted or adjustable to meet varied requirements (as of use, shape, or size)

⟨a *universal* wrench⟩ — **uni·ver·sal·ly** \-s(ə-)lē\ *adv* — **uni·ver·sal·ness** \-səl-nəs\ *n*
universal donor *n* : a person with type O blood
uni·ver·sal·i·ty \ˌyü-nə-(ˌ)vər-'sal-ət-ē\ *n* : the quality or state of being universal (as in range, occurrence, or appeal)
uni·ver·sal·ize \-'vər-sə-ˌlīz\ *vb* : to make universal : GENERALIZE — **uni·ver·sal·i·za·tion** \-ˌvər-sə-lə-'zā-shən\ *n*
universal joint *n* : a shaft coupling capable of transmitting rotation from one shaft to another not in a straight line with it

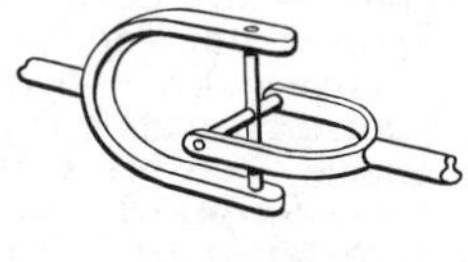
universal joint

universal recipient *n* : a person with type AB blood
uni·verse \'yü-nə-'vərs\ *n* **1** : the whole body of things observed or postulated : COSMOS **2 a** : MILKY WAY GALAXY **b** : an aggregate of stars comparable to the Milky Way galaxy
uni·ver·si·ty \ˌyü-nə-'vər-sət-ē, -'vər-stē\ *n, pl* **-ties** : an institution of higher learning authorized to grant degrees in various special fields (as law, medicine, and theology) as well as in the arts and sciences generally
un·just \ˌən-'jəst\ *adj* : characterized by injustice : deficient in justice and fairness : WRONGFUL — **un·just·ly** *adv* — **un·just·ness** \-'jəs(t)-nəs\ *n*
un·kempt \ˌən-'kem(p)t\ *adj* **1 a** : not combed ⟨*unkempt* hair⟩ **b** : deficient in order or neatness of person : DISHEVELED **2** : ROUGH, UNPOLISHED
un·kind \ˌən-'kīnd\ *adj* : deficient in kindness or sympathy : HARSH, CRUEL — **un·kind·ly** *adv* — **un·kind·ness** \-'kīn(d)-nəs\ *n*
un·kind·ly \-'kīn-dlē\ *adj* : UNKIND — **un·kind·li·ness** *n*
un·know·a·ble \ˌən-'nō-ə-bəl\ *adj* : not knowable
un·know·ing \ˌən-'nō-ing\ *adj* : not knowing — **un·know·ing·ly** \-ing-lē\ *adv*
[1]**un·known** \ˌən-'nōn\ *adj* : not known; *also* : having an unknown value ⟨*unknown* quantity⟩
[2]**unknown** *n* : something that is unknown and usu. to be discovered; *esp* : an unknown quantity usu. symbolized in mathematics by one of the last letters of the alphabet
un·lace \ˌən-'lās\ *vb* : to loose by undoing a lacing
un·lade \ˌən-'lād\ *vb* **1** : to take the load or cargo from **2** : DISCHARGE, UNLOAD
un·lash \ˌən-'lash\ *vb* : to untie the lashing of : LOOSE, UNDO
un·latch \ˌən-'lach\ *vb* **1** : to open or loose by lifting the latch **2** : to become loosed or opened
un·law·ful \ˌən-'lȯ-fəl\ *adj* : not lawful : contrary to law : ILLEGAL — **un·law·ful·ly** \-f(ə-)lē\ *adv* — **un·law·ful·ness** \-fəl-nəs\ *n*
un·learn \ˌən-'lərn\ *vb* : to put out of one's knowledge or memory
un·learned *adj* **1** \ˌən-'lər-nəd\ : not learned : UNEDUCATED, ILLITERATE ⟨a good but *unlearned* man⟩ **2** \-'lərnd\ : not learned by study : not known ⟨lessons *unlearned* by many⟩ **3** \-'lərnd\ : not learned by previous experience ⟨breathing is *unlearned* behavior⟩
un·leash \ˌən-'lēsh\ *vb* : to free from or as if from a leash ⟨*unleash* a dog⟩ ⟨the storm *unleashed* its fury⟩
un·less \(ˌ)ən-'les\ *conj* : except on the condition that : if not ⟨will fail *unless* he works harder⟩
un·let·tered \ˌən-'let-ərd\ *adj* **1** : not educated **2** : ILLITERATE ***syn*** see IGNORANT

[1]**un·like** \ˌən-'līk\ *prep* **1** : different from ⟨feeling completely *unlike* a hero⟩ **2** : not characteristic of ⟨it was *unlike* him to be inquisitive⟩ **3** : in a different manner from ⟨behaving *unlike* his associates⟩
[2]**unlike** *adj* **1** : marked by dissimilarity : DIFFERENT ⟨people are all *unlike*⟩ **2** : UNEQUAL ⟨contributed *unlike* amounts⟩ — **un·like·ness** *n*
un·like·li·hood \-'lī-klē-ˌhu̇d\ *n* : IMPROBABILITY
un·like·ly \-'lī-klē\ *adj* **1** : not likely : IMPROBABLE ⟨an *unlikely* story⟩ **2** : likely to fail : UNPROMISING ⟨an *unlikely* place for fishing⟩ — **un·like·li·ness** *n*
un·lim·ber \ˌən-'lim-bər\ *vb* : to prepare for action
un·lim·it·ed \ˌən-'lim-ət-əd\ *adj* **1** : lacking any controls ⟨*unlimited* freedom⟩ **2** : BOUNDLESS, INFINITE ⟨an *unlimited* expanse of ocean⟩ ⟨there is an *unlimited* number of natural numbers⟩ **3** : not bounded by exceptions : UNDEFINED
un·link \ˌən-'lingk\ *vb* : to unfasten the links of : SEPARATE, DISCONNECT
un·list·ed \ˌən-'lis-təd\ *adj* : not appearing on a list ⟨an *unlisted* telephone number⟩
un·load \ˌən-'lōd\ *vb* **1 a** : to take away or off : REMOVE ⟨*unload* cargo from a hold⟩ **b** : to take a load from ⟨*unload* a ship⟩; *also* : to relieve or set free : UNBURDEN ⟨*unload* your mind of worries⟩ **2** : to get rid of or be relieved of a load or burden ⟨the ship is *unloading* now⟩ **3** : to sell in volume : DUMP ⟨*unload* surplus goods⟩
un·lock \ˌən-'läk\ *vb* **1** : to open or unfasten through release of a lock ⟨*unlock* the door⟩ ⟨the chest won't *unlock*⟩ **2** : RELEASE ⟨*unlock* a flood of emotions⟩ **3** : DISCLOSE, REVEAL ⟨scientists *unlocking* the secrets of nature⟩
un·looked–for \ˌən-'lu̇kt-ˌfȯr\ *adj* : UNEXPECTED
un·loose \ˌən-'lüs\ *vb* **1** : to relax the strain of ⟨*unloose* a grip⟩ **2** : to release from or as if from restraints : set free ⟨*unloosed* a flood of complaints⟩
un·loos·en \ˌən-'lü-sən\ *vb* : UNLOOSE
un·love·ly \ˌən-'ləv-lē\ *adj* : having no charm or appeal : not amiable : DISAGREEABLE ⟨an *unlovely* disposition⟩
un·lucky \ˌən-'lək-ē\ *adj* **1** : marked by adversity or failure **2** : likely to bring misfortune **3** : producing dissatisfaction : REGRETTABLE — **un·luck·i·ly** \-'lək-ə-lē\ *adv* — **un·luck·i·ness** \-'lək-ē-nəs\ *n*
un·make \ˌən-'māk\ *vb* **-made** \-'mād\; **-mak·ing** **1** : to cause to disappear : DESTROY **2** : to deprive of rank or office : DEPOSE
un·man \ˌən-'man\ *vb* **1** : to deprive of manly courage **2** : to deprive of men
un·man·ly \-'man-lē\ *adj* : not manly : as **a** : being of weak character : COWARDLY **b** : EFFEMINATE — **un·man·li·ness** *n*
un·manned \ˌən-'mand\ *adj* : having no men aboard ⟨*unmanned* spacecraft⟩
un·man·ner·ly \ˌən-'man-ər-lē\ *adj* : RUDE, IMPOLITE — **un·man·ner·li·ness** *n* — **unmannerly** *adv*
un·mask \ˌən-'mask\ *vb* **1** : to strip of a mask or a disguise : EXPOSE ⟨*unmask* a traitor⟩ **2** : to take off one's own disguise (as at a masquerade)
un·mean·ing \ˌən-'mē-ning\ *adj* : having no meaning : SENSELESS
un·men·tion·a·ble \ˌən-'mənch-(ə-)nə-bəl\ *adj* : not fit or proper to be talked about
un·mer·ci·ful \ˌən-'mər-si-fəl\ *adj* : not merciful : MERCILESS, CRUEL — **un·mer·ci·ful·ly** \-f(ə-)lē\ *adv*
un·mis·tak·a·ble \ˌən-mə-'stā-kə-bəl\ *adj* : not capable of being mistaken or misunderstood : CLEAR, OBVIOUS — **un·mis·tak·a·bly** \-blē\ *adv*
un·mit·i·gat·ed \ˌən-'mit-ə-ˌgāt-əd\ *adj* **1** : not softened or lessened ⟨the heat was *unmitigated*⟩

2 : ABSOLUTE, DOWNRIGHT ⟨an *unmitigated* liar⟩ ⟨*unmitigated* impudence⟩
un·moor \ˌən-ˈmu̇(ə)r\ *vb* : to loose from or cast off moorings
un·mor·al \ˌən-ˈmȯr-əl, -ˈmär-\ *adj* : having no moral quality or relation : being neither moral nor immoral — **un·mor·al·ly** \-ə-lē\ *adv*
un·moved \ˌən-ˈmüvd\ *adj* **1** : not moved : remaining in the same place **2** : FIRM, RESOLUTE, UNSHAKEN ⟨*unmoved* in his purpose⟩ **3** : not disturbed emotionally ⟨*unmoved* by the sad news⟩
un·muf·fle \ˌən-ˈməf-əl\ *vb* : to free from something that muffles
un·muz·zle \ˌən-ˈməz-əl\ *vb* : to remove a muzzle from
un·nat·u·ral \ˌən-ˈnach-(ə-)rəl\ *adj* **1** : not being in accordance with nature or consistent with a normal course of events **2 a** : not according with normal feelings or behavior : PERVERSE, ABNORMAL **b** : ARTIFICIAL, CONTRIVED — **un·nat·u·ral·ly** \-ˈnach-(ə-)rə-lē, -ˈnach-ər-lē\ *adv* — **un·nat·u·ral·ness** \-ˈnach-(ə-)rəl-nəs\ *n*
un·nec·es·sar·i·ly \ˌən-ˌnes-ə-ˈser-ə-lē\ *adv* **1** : not by necessity ⟨spent money *unnecessarily*⟩ **2** : to an unnecessary degree ⟨an *unnecessarily* harsh punishment⟩
un·nec·es·sary \ˌən-ˈnes-ə-ˌser-ē\ *adj* : not necessary
un·nerve \ˌən-ˈnərv\ *vb* : to deprive of nerve, courage, or self-control
un·num·bered \ˌən-ˈnəm-bərd\ *adj* **1** : INNUMERABLE **2** : not having an identifying number ⟨*unnumbered* page⟩
un·ob·tru·sive \ˌən-əb-ˈtrü-siv, -ziv\ *adj* : not obtrusive or aggressive : INCONSPICUOUS — **un·ob·tru·sive·ly** *adv*
un·oc·cu·pied \ˌən-ˈäk-yə-ˌpīd\ *adj* **1** : not busy : UNEMPLOYED **2** : not occupied : EMPTY
un·of·fi·cial \ˌən-ə-ˈfish-əl\ *adj* : not official — **un·of·fi·cial·ly** \-ˈfish-(ə-)lē\ *adv*
un·or·ga·nized \ˌən-ˈȯr-gə-ˌnīzd\ *adj* : not subjected to organization: as **a** : not formed or brought into an ordered whole **b** : not organized into unions ⟨*unorganized* labor⟩
un·or·tho·dox \ˌən-ˈȯr-thə-ˌdäks\ *adj* : not orthodox : not usual ⟨a boxer with an *unorthodox* style of fighting⟩
un·owned \ˌən-ˈōnd\ *adj* : not owned : not belonging to anybody
un·pack \ˌən-ˈpak\ *vb* **1** : to separate and remove things packed **2** : to open and remove the contents of ⟨*unpack* a trunk⟩
un·paired \ˌən-ˈpa(ə)rd, -ˈpe(ə)rd\ *adj* **1** : not paired; *esp* : not matched or mated ⟨an *unpaired* shoe⟩ **2** : situated centrally on the body ⟨an *unpaired* fin⟩
un·par·al·leled \ˌən-ˈpar-ə-ˌleld\ *adj* : having no parallel; *esp* : having no equal or match : UNSURPASSED
un·par·lia·men·ta·ry \ˌən-ˌpär-lə-ˈment-ə-rē, -ˌpärl-yə-, -ˈmen-trē\ *adj* : contrary to parliamentary practice
un·pile \ˌən-ˈpīl\ *vb* : to take or disentangle from a pile
un·pin \ˌən-ˈpin\ *vb* : to remove a pin from : UNFASTEN

ə abut	ər further	a back	ā bake	
ä cot, cart	au̇ out	ch chin	e less	ē easy
g gift	i trip	ī life	j joke	ng sing	ō flow
ȯ flaw	ȯi coin	th thin	t͟h this	ü loot
u̇ foot	y yet	yü few	yu̇ furious	zh vision

un·pleas·ant \ˌən-ˈplez-ənt\ *adj* : not pleasant : not amiable or agreeable : DISPLEASING — **un·pleas·ant·ly** *adv* — **un·pleas·ant·ness** *n*
un·plumbed \ˌən-ˈpləmd\ *adj* **1** : not tested or measured with a plumb line **2** : not explored in depth, intensity, or significance ⟨many *unplumbed* possibilities⟩
un·po·lit·i·cal \ˌən-pə-ˈlit-i-kəl\ *adj* : not interested or engaged in politics
un·pop·u·lar \ˌən-ˈpäp-yə-lər\ *adj* : not popular : viewed or received unfavorably : disliked by many people — **un·pop·u·lar·i·ty** \-ˌpäp-yə-ˈlar-ət-ē\ *n*
un·prec·e·dent·ed \ˌən-ˈpres-ə-ˌdent-əd\ *adj* : having no precedent : NOVEL
un·pre·dict·a·ble \ˌən-pri-ˈdik-tə-bəl\ *adj* : not predictable — **un·pre·dict·a·bil·i·ty** \-ˌdik-tə-ˈbil-ət-ē\ *n* — **un·pre·dict·a·bly** \-ˈdik-tə-blē\ *adv*
un·pre·ten·tious \ˌən-pri-ˈten-chəs\ *adj* : not pretentious : not showy or pompous : SIMPLE, MODEST ⟨pleasant but *unpretentious* homes⟩ — **un·pre·ten·tious·ly** *adv*
un·prin·ci·pled \ˌən-ˈprin(t)-sə-pəld\ *adj* : lacking moral principles : UNSCRUPULOUS
un·print·a·ble \ˌən-ˈprint-ə-bəl\ *adj* : unfit to be printed
un·pro·fessed \ˌən-prə-ˈfest\ *adj* : not professed ⟨an *unprofessed* aim⟩
un·pro·fes·sion·al \ˌən-prə-ˈfesh-(ə-)nəl\ *adj* : not professional; *esp* : not conforming to the standards of one's profession — **un·pro·fes·sion·al·ly** \-ē\ *adv*
un·prof·it·a·ble \ˌən-ˈpräf-ət-ə-bəl, -ˈpräf-tə-bəl\ *adj* : not profitable : USELESS — **un·prof·it·a·bly** \-blē\ *adv*
un·prom·is·ing \ˌən-ˈpräm-ə-sing\ *adj* : appearing unlikely to prove worthwhile or result favorably — **un·prom·is·ing·ly** \-sing-lē\ *adv*
un·qual·i·fied \ˌən-ˈkwäl-ə-ˌfīd\ *adj* **1** : not fit : not having required qualifications ⟨*unqualified* for the job⟩ **2** : not modified or restricted by reservations ⟨an *unqualified* denial⟩ — **un·qual·i·fied·ly** \-ˌfī(-ə)d-lē\ *adv*
un·ques·tion·a·ble \ˌən-ˈkwes-chə-nə-bəl\ *adj* **1** : acknowledged as beyond question or doubt ⟨an *unquestionable* legal authority⟩ **2** : not questionable : INDISPUTABLE ⟨*unquestionable* evidence⟩ — **un·ques·tion·a·bly** \-blē\ *adv*
un·ques·tion·ing \-chə-ning\ *adj* : not questioning : accepting without examination or hesitation ⟨*unquestioning* obedience⟩ — **un·ques·tion·ing·ly** \-ning-lē\ *adv*
un·qui·et \ˌən-ˈkwī-ət\ *adj* **1** : not quiet : AGITATED, TURBULENT **2** : physically, emotionally, or mentally restless : UNEASY — **un·qui·et·ly** *adv* — **un·qui·et·ness** *n*
un·quote \ˈən-ˌkwōt\ *vb* : to state that the matter preceding is quoted
un·rav·el \ˌən-ˈrav-əl\ *vb* **1** : to separate the threads of : DISENTANGLE ⟨*unravel* a snarl⟩ **2** : SOLVE ⟨*unravel* a mystery⟩ **3** : to become unraveled
un·read \ˌən-ˈred\ *adj* **1** : not read ⟨an *unread* book⟩ **2** : not well informed through reading : UNEDUCATED
un·read·a·ble \ˌən-ˈrēd-ə-bəl\ *adj* **1** : too dull or unattractive to read ⟨a long, *unreadable* essay⟩ **2** : ILLEGIBLE ⟨*unreadable* handwriting⟩
un·re·al·i·ty \ˌən-rē-ˈal-ət-ē\ *n* **1 a** : the quality or state of being unreal : NONEXISTENCE ⟨an air of *unreality* about the place⟩ **b** : something unreal, insubstantial, or visionary : FIGMENT **2** : ineptitude in dealing with reality
un·rea·son·ing \ˌən-ˈrēz-(ə-)ning\ *adj* : not reasoning; *esp* : not using or showing the use of reason as a

guide or control ⟨*unreasoning* fear⟩ ⟨the *unreasoning* beasts⟩

un·reel \ˌən-ˈrēl\ *vb* : to unwind from or as if from a reel

un·re·gen·er·ate \ˌən-ri-ˈjen-(ə-)rət\ *adj* : not at peace with God : SINFUL, WICKED

un·re·lent·ing \ˌən-ri-ˈlent-ing\ *adj* **1** : not softening or yielding in determination : HARD, STERN **2** : not letting up or weakening in vigor or pace ⟨his *unrelenting* struggle⟩ — **un·re·lent·ing·ly** \-ing-lē\ *adv*

un·re·mit·ting \ˌən-ri-ˈmit-ing\ *adj* : not stopping : UNCEASING, PERSEVERING

un·re·served \ˌən-ri-ˈzərvd\ *adj* **1** : not held in reserve : not kept back ⟨*unreserved* enthusiasm⟩ **2** : having or showing no reserve in manner or speech — **un·re·serv·ed·ly** \-ˈzər-vəd-lē\ *adv*

un·rest \ˌən-ˈrest\ *n* : lack of rest : a disturbed or uneasy state : TURMOIL

un·re·strained \ˌən-ri-ˈstrānd\ *adj* **1** : not restrained : IMMODERATE, UNCONTROLLED ⟨*unrestrained* praise⟩ **2** : free of constraint : SPONTANEOUS

un·re·straint \-ˈstrānt\ *n* : lack of restraint

un·rig \ˌən-ˈrig\ *vb* : to strip of rigging ⟨*unrig* a ship⟩

un·righ·teous \ˌən-ˈrī-chəs\ *adj* **1** : not righteous : SINFUL, WICKED **2** : UNJUST, UNMERITED — **un·righ·teous·ly** *adv* — **un·righ·teous·ness** *n*

un·ripe \ˌən-ˈrīp\ *adj* : not ripe : IMMATURE ⟨*unripe* fruit⟩

un·ri·valed *or* **un·ri·valled** \ˌən-ˈrī-vəld\ *adj* : having no rival : INCOMPARABLE, UNEQUALED

un·roll \ˌən-ˈrōl\ *vb* **1** : to unwind a roll of : open out ⟨*unroll* a carpet⟩ **2** : DISPLAY, DISCLOSE **3** : to become unrolled or spread out : UNFOLD ⟨a great vista of lofty mountains *unrolled* before their eyes⟩

un·roof \ˌən-ˈrüf, -ˈru̇f\ *vb* : to strip off the roof or covering of

un·round \ˌən-ˈrau̇nd\ *vb* : to pronounce a sound without, or with decreased, rounding of the lips — **un·round·ed** *adj*

UN·RRA \ˌən-ˌrä\ *abbr* United Nations Relief and Rehabilitation Administration

un·ruf·fled \ˌən-ˈrəf-əld\ *adj* **1** : not upset or agitated ⟨a speaker *unruffled* by jeers⟩ **2** : not ruffled : SMOOTH ⟨*unruffled* water⟩

un·ruly \ˌən-ˈrü-lē\ *adj* : not yielding readily to rule or restraint : UNCONTROLLABLE ⟨an *unruly* temper⟩ ⟨an *unruly* horse⟩

un·sad·dle \ˌən-ˈsad-əl\ *vb* **1** : to remove the saddle from a horse **2** : UNHORSE

un·sat·u·rat·ed \ˌən-ˈsach-ə-ˌrāt-əd\ *adj* **1** : capable of absorbing or dissolving more of something ⟨an *unsaturated* salt solution⟩ **2** : able to form a new product by direct chemical combination with another substance; *esp* : containing double or triple bonds between carbon atoms ⟨an *unsaturated* acid⟩ — **un·sat·u·ra·tion** \-ˌsach-ə-ˈrā-shən\ *n*

un·saved \ˌən-ˈsāvd\ *adj* : not saved; *esp* : not rescued from eternal punishment

un·sa·vory \ˌən-ˈsāv(-ə)-rē\ *adj* **1** : having little or no taste **2** : having a bad taste or smell **3** : morally offensive ⟨an *unsavory* reputation⟩

un·say \ˌən-ˈsā\ *vb* **-said** \-ˈsed\; **-say·ing** \-ˈsā-ing\ : to take back something said : RETRACT, WITHDRAW

un·scathed \ˌən-ˈskāt͟hd\ *adj* : wholly unharmed : not injured

un·schooled \ˌən-ˈsküld\ *adj* : not schooled : UNTAUGHT, UNTRAINED

un·sci·en·tif·ic \ˈən-ˌsī-ən-ˈtif-ik\ *adj* **1** : not used in scientific work **2** : not according with the principles and methods of science — **un·sci·en·tif·i·cal·ly** \-ˈtif-i-k(ə-)lē\ *adv*

un·scram·ble \ˌən-ˈskram-bəl\ *vb* **1** : to separate into original components : RESOLVE, CLARIFY ⟨trying to *unscramble* the jumble of recent events⟩ **2** : to restore to intelligible form ⟨*unscramble* a radio message⟩

un·screw \ˌən-ˈskrü\ *vb* **1** : to draw the screws from **2** : to loosen or withdraw by turning ⟨*unscrew* a cover⟩

un·scru·pu·lous \ˌən-ˈskrü-pyə-ləs\ *adj* : not scrupulous : UNPRINCIPLED — **un·scru·pu·lous·ly** *adv* — **un·scru·pu·lous·ness** *n*

un·seal \ˌən-ˈsēl\ *vb* : to break or remove the seal of : OPEN

un·search·a·ble \ˌən-ˈsər-chə-bəl\ *adj* : not to be searched or explored : INSCRUTABLE — **un·search·a·bly** \-blē\ *adv*

un·sea·son·a·ble \ˌən-ˈsēz-(ə-)nə-bəl\ *adj* : not seasonable : happening or coming at the wrong time : UNTIMELY — **un·sea·son·a·bly** \-blē\ *adv*

un·seat \ˌən-ˈsēt\ *vb* **1** : to throw from one's seat esp. on horseback **2** : to dislodge from a place or position; *esp* : to remove from political office

un·seem·ly \ˌən-ˈsēm-lē\ *adj* : not seemly : UNBECOMING, INDECENT ⟨*unseemly* bickering in public⟩ — **unseemly** *adv*

un·seen \ˌən-ˈsēn\ *adj* : not seen or perceived : INVISIBLE

un·seg·re·gat·ed \ˌən-ˈseg-ri-ˌgāt-əd\ *adj* : not segregated; *esp* : free from racial segregation

un·self·ish \ˌən-ˈsel-fish\ *adj* : not selfish : GENEROUS — **un·self·ish·ly** *adv* — **un·self·ish·ness** *n*

un·set·tle \ˌən-ˈset-əl\ *vb* : to move or loosen from a settled state : make or become displaced or disturbed

un·set·tled \-əld\ *adj* **1** : not settled : not fixed (as in position or character) ⟨*unsettled* weather⟩ **2** : not calm : DISTURBED ⟨*unsettled* waters⟩ **3** : not decided in mind : UNDETERMINED ⟨*unsettled* what to do⟩ **4** : not paid ⟨an *unsettled* account⟩; *also* : not disposed of according to law ⟨an *unsettled* estate⟩ **5** : not occupied by settlers ⟨an *unsettled* region⟩

U

un·shaped \ˌən-ˈshāpt\ *adj* **1** : not shaped; *esp* : not dressed or finished to final form ⟨an *unshaped* timber⟩ **2** : imperfect in form or formulation ⟨*unshaped* ideas⟩

un·shap·en \ˌən-ˈshā-pən\ *adj* : UNSHAPED

un·sheathe \ˌən-ˈshēt͟h\ *vb* : to draw from or as if from a sheath or scabbard ⟨*unsheathe* a sword⟩

un·ship \ˌən-ˈship\ *vb* **1** : to remove from a ship **2** : to remove or become removed from position ⟨*unship* an oar⟩

un·shod \ˌən-ˈshäd\ *adj* **1** : BAREFOOT **2** : not shod ⟨an *unshod* horse⟩

un·sight·ly \ˌən-ˈsīt-lē\ *adj* : unpleasant to the sight : UGLY ⟨an *unsightly* scar⟩ — **un·sight·li·ness** *n*

un·skilled \ˌən-ˈskild\ *adj* **1** : not skilled; *esp* : not skilled in a specified branch of work : lacking technical training **2** : not requiring skill ⟨*unskilled* jobs⟩ **3** : marked by lack of skill ⟨an *unskilled* painting⟩

un·sling \ˌən-ˈsling\ *vb* **-slung** \-ˈsləŋ\; **-sling·ing** \-ˈsling-ing\ **1** : to remove from being slung **2** : to take off the slings of esp. aboard ship : release from slings

un·snap \ˌən-ˈsnap\ *vb* : to loosen or free by or as if by undoing a snap

un·snarl \ˌən-ˈsnärl\ *vb* : to disentangle a snarl in

un·so·cial \ˌən-ˈsō-shəl\ *adj* **1** : not social : not seeking or given to association **2** : ANTISOCIAL

un·so·phis·ti·cat·ed \ˌən(t)-sə-ˈfis-tə-ˌkāt-əd\ *adj* **1 a** : not sophisticated; *esp* : not worldly-wise ⟨was still innocent and *unsophisticated*⟩ **b** : lacking adornment or complexity of structure : PLAIN, SIM-

PLE ⟨*unsophisticated* buildings⟩ **2** : not changed or corrupted : GENUINE ⟨*unsophisticated* loyalty⟩ — **un·so·phis·ti·ca·tion** \-ˌfis-tə-ˈkā-shən\ *n*

un·sought \ˌən-ˈsȯt\ *adj* : not sought : not searched for or asked for : not obtained by effort ⟨*unsought* honors⟩

un·sound \ˌən-ˈsau̇nd\ *adj* **1** : not healthy or whole **2** : not mentally normal : not wholly sane **3** : not firmly made, placed, or fixed **4** : not valid or true : INVALID, SPECIOUS ⟨*unsound* reasoning⟩ — **un·sound·ly** *adv* — **un·sound·ness** \-ˈsau̇n(d)-nəs\ *n*

un·spar·ing \ˌən-ˈspa(ə)r-ing, -ˈspe(ə)r-\ *adj* **1** : not merciful or forgiving : HARD, RUTHLESS **2** : not frugal : LIBERAL, PROFUSE — **un·spar·ing·ly** \-ing-lē\ *adv*

un·speak·a·ble \ˌən-ˈspē-kə-bəl\ *adj* **1** : impossible to express in words ⟨*unspeakable* beauty of the sunset⟩ **2** : extremely bad ⟨*unspeakable* conduct⟩ — **un·speak·a·bly** \-blē\ *adv*

un·sphere \ˌən-ˈsfi(ə)r\ *vb* : to remove (as a planet) from a sphere

un·spot·ted \ˌən-ˈspät-əd\ *adj* : not spotted : free from spot or stain; *esp* : free from moral stain

un·sta·ble \ˌən-ˈstā-bəl\ *adj* **1** : not stable : not firm or fixed : FLUCTUATING, IRREGULAR **2** : FICKLE, WAVERING ⟨*unstable* beliefs⟩; *also* : lacking effective emotional control ⟨an *unstable* person⟩ **3** : readily changing in chemical composition or physical state or properties ⟨an *unstable* emulsion⟩; *esp* : tending to decompose spontaneously ⟨an *unstable* atomic nucleus⟩

un·steady \ˌən-ˈsted-ē\ *adj* : not steady : UNSTABLE — **un·stead·i·ly** \-ˈsted-əl-ē\ *adv* — **un·stead·i·ness** \-ˈsted-ē-nəs\ *n*

un·stick \ˌən-ˈstik\ *vb* **-stuck** \-ˈstək\; **-stick·ing** : to release from being stuck or bound

un·stint·ing·ly \ˌən-ˈstint-ing-lē\ *adv* : FREELY, GENEROUSLY ⟨gave *unstintingly* of his time⟩

un·stop \ˌən-ˈstäp\ *vb* **1** : to free from an obstruction : OPEN **2** : to remove a stopper from

un·strap \ˌən-ˈstrap\ *vb* : to remove or loosen a strap from

un·stressed \ˌən-ˈstrest\ *adj* : not stressed; *esp* : not bearing a stress or accent

un·string \ˌən-ˈstring\ *vb* **-strung** \-ˈstrəng\; **-string·ing** \-ˈstring-ing\ **1** : to loosen or remove the strings of **2** : to remove from a string ⟨*unstrung* her beads⟩ **3** : to make weak, disordered, or unstable ⟨*unstrung* by bad news⟩

un·stud·ied \ˌən-ˈstəd-ēd\ *adj* : not studied or planned with a certain effect in mind : NATURAL, UNFORCED ⟨moved with an *unstudied* grace⟩

un·sub·stan·tial \ˌən(t)-səb-ˈstan-chəl\ *adj* : lacking substance, firmness, or strength — **un·sub·stan·ti·al·i·ty** \-ˌstan-chē-ˈal-ət-ē\ *n*

un·suc·cess·ful \ˌən(t)-sək-ˈses-fəl\ *adj* : not successful : not meeting with or producing success — **un·suc·cess·ful·ly** \-fə-lē\ *adv*

un·suit·a·ble \ˌən-ˈsüt-ə-bəl\ *adj* : not suitable or fitting : UNBECOMING, INAPPROPRIATE — **un·suit·a·bly** \-blē\ *adv*

un·sung \ˌən-ˈsəng\ *adj* **1** : not sung **2** : not celebrated in song or verse ⟨*unsung* heroes⟩

un·swerv·ing \ˌən-ˈswər-ving\ *adj* **1** : not swerving or turning aside **2** : STEADY ⟨*unswerving* loyalty⟩

un·sym·met·ri·cal \ˌən(t)-sə-ˈme-tri-kəl\ *adj* : not symmetrical : ASYMMETRIC — **un·sym·met·ri·cal·ly** \-tri-k(ə-)lē\ *adv*

un·tan·gle \ˌən-ˈtang-gəl\ *vb* **1** : to remove a tangle from : DISENTANGLE **2** : to straighten out : RESOLVE ⟨*untangle* financial difficulties⟩

un·taught \ˌən-ˈtȯt\ *adj* **1** : not instructed or trained : IGNORANT **2** : NATURAL, SPONTANEOUS

un·teth·er \ˌən-ˈteth-ər\ *vb* : to free from a tether

un·think·a·ble \ˌən-ˈthing-kə-bəl\ *adj* : not to be thought of or considered as possible ⟨cruelty *unthinkable* in a decent human being⟩

un·think·ing \-king\ *adj* **1** : not thinking : INATTENTIVE, THOUGHTLESS **2** : not having the power of thought — **un·think·ing·ly** *adv*

un·thought–of \ˌən-ˈthȯt-ˌəv, -ˌäv\ *adj* : not thought of : not considered : not imagined

un·thread \ˌən-ˈthred\ *vb* **1** : to draw or take out a thread from **2** : to loosen the threads or connections of **3** : to make one's way through ⟨*unthread* a maze⟩

un·throne \ˌən-ˈthrōn\ *vb* : to remove from or as if from a throne

un·ti·dy \ˌən-ˈtīd-ē\ *adj* **1** : not neat : CARELESS **2 a** : not neatly organized or carried out **b** : marked by a lack of neatness — **un·ti·di·ly** \-ˈtīd-ə-lē\ *adv* — **un·ti·di·ness** \-ˈtīd-ē-nəs\ *n*

un·tie \ˌən-ˈtī\ *vb* **-tied**; **-ty·ing** *or* **-tie·ing** **1** : to free from something that ties or fastens : UNBIND ⟨*untie* a horse⟩ **2 a** : to undo the knotted parts of ⟨*untied* her scarf⟩ **b** : DISENTANGLE, RESOLVE ⟨*untie* a traffic jam⟩ **3** : to become loosened or unbound ⟨the strings *untied* easily⟩

[1]**un·til** \(ˌ)ən-ˌtil, -təl\ *prep* : up to the time of ⟨stayed *until* morning⟩

[2]**until** *conj* **1** : up to the time that ⟨played *until* it got dark⟩ **2** : to the point or degree that ⟨ran *until* he was breathless⟩

un·time·ly \ˌən-ˈtīm-lē\ *adj* **1** : occurring or done before the due, natural, or proper time : too early : PREMATURE ⟨*untimely* death⟩ **2** : INOPPORTUNE, UNSEASONABLE ⟨an *untimely* joke⟩ ⟨*untimely* frost⟩

un·ti·tled \ˌən-ˈtīt-əld\ *adj* **1** : having no title esp. of nobility **2** : not named ⟨an *untitled* novel⟩

un·to \ˈən-tə, -tü\ *prep* : TO

un·told \ˌən-ˈtōld\ *adj* **1** : not told : not revealed ⟨*untold* secrets⟩ ⟨a story yet *untold*⟩ **2** : not counted : VAST, NUMBERLESS ⟨*untold* resources⟩

[1]**un·touch·a·ble** \ˌən-ˈtəch-ə-bəl\ *adj* **1 a** : forbidden to the touch **b** : exempt from criticism or control **2** : lying beyond the reach

[2]**untouchable** *n* : one that is untouchable; *esp* : a member of the lowest social class in India having in traditional Hindu belief the quality of defiling by contact a member of a higher caste

un·to·ward \-ˈtō(-ə)rd, -ˈtȯ(-ə)rd\ *adj* **1** : difficult to manage : STUBBORN, WILLFUL ⟨an *untoward* child⟩ **2** : INCONVENIENT, TROUBLESOME ⟨an *untoward* accident⟩

un·tried \ˌən-ˈtrīd\ *adj* **1** : not tested or proved by experience or trial ⟨*untried* soldiers⟩ **2** : not tried in court ⟨a backlog of *untried* cases⟩

un·true \ˌən-ˈtrü\ *adj* **1** : not faithful : DISLOYAL **2** : not according with a standard of correctness : not level or exact **3** : not according with the facts : FALSE — **un·tru·ly** \-ˈtrü-lē\ *adv*

un·truth \ˌən-ˈtrüth\ *n* **1** : lack of truthfulness : FALSITY **2** : something that is untrue : FALSEHOOD

un·truth·ful \ˌən-ˈtrüth-fəl\ *adj* : not containing or telling the truth : FALSE, INACCURATE ⟨*untruthful* report⟩ — **un·truth·ful·ly** \-fə-lē\ *adv* — **un·truth·ful·ness** *n*

un·tuck \ˌən-ˈtək\ *vb* : to release from a tuck or from being tucked up

un·tu·tored \ˌən-ˈt(y)üt-ərd\ *adj* : UNTAUGHT, UNLEARNED, IGNORANT

un·twine \ˌən-ˈtwīn\ *vb* **1** : to unwind the twisted or tangled parts of : DISENTANGLE **2** : to remove by unwinding **3** : to become disentangled or unwound

un·twist \ˌən-ˈtwist\ *vb* **1** : to separate the twisted parts of : UNTWINE **2** : to become untwined

un·used \ˌən-ˈyüzd, *in the phrase* "*unused to*" *usually* -ˈyüs(t)\ *adj* **1** : not habituated : UNACCUSTOMED **2** : not used: as **a** : FRESH, NEW **b** : not being in use : IDLE **c** : not consumed : ACCRUED

un·usu·al \ˌən-ˈyüzh-(ə-w)əl\ *adj* : not usual : UNCOMMON, RARE — **un·usu·al·ly** \-ē\ *adv* — **un·usu·al·ness** *n*

un·ut·ter·a·ble \ˌən-ˈət-ə-rə-bəl\ *adj* **1** : not capable of being pronounced **2** : not capable of being put into words : INEXPRESSIBLE ⟨*unutterable* sorrow⟩ — **un·ut·ter·a·bly** \-blē\ *adv*

un·val·ued \ˌən-ˈval-yüd\ *adj* **1** : not important or prized : DISREGARDED **2** : not appraised

un·var·nished \ˌən-ˈvär-nisht\ *adj* **1** : not varnished **2** : not heightened or exaggerated : PLAIN ⟨the *unvarnished* truth⟩

un·veil \ˌən-ˈvāl\ *vb* **1 a** : to remove a veil or covering from ⟨*unveil* a statue⟩ **b** : DISCLOSE, REVEAL ⟨*unveiled* plans for a new housing complex⟩ **2** : to remove a veil; *esp* : to reveal oneself

un·voiced \ˌən-ˈvȯist\ *adj* **1** : not verbally expressed : UNSPOKEN **2** : VOICELESS 2

un·war·rant·a·ble \ˌən-ˈwȯr-ənt-ə-bəl, -ˈwär-\ *adj* : not justifiable : INEXCUSABLE

un·wary \ˌən-ˈwa(ə)r-ē, -ˈwe(ə)r-\ *adj* : not alert : easily fooled or surprised : HEEDLESS, GULLIBLE — **un·war·i·ly** \-ˈwar-ə-lē, -ˈwer-\ *adv* — **un·war·i·ness** \-ˈwar-ē-nəs, -ˈwer-\ *n*

un·wea·ried \ˌən-ˈwi(ə)r-ēd\ *adj* : not tired or jaded : FRESH

un·well \ˌən-ˈwel\ *adj* : being in poor health : AILING, SICK

un·wept \ˌən-ˈwept\ *adj* : not mourned : UNLAMENTED ⟨died *unwept* and unsung⟩

un·whole·some \ˌən-ˈhōl-səm\ *adj* : detrimental to physical, mental, or moral well-being : UNHEALTHY

un·wieldy \ˌən-ˈwēl-dē\ *adj* : not easily handled or managed because of size or weight : AWKWARD, CUMBERSOME ⟨an *unwieldy* tool⟩

un·will·ing \ˌən-ˈwil-iŋ\ *adj* : not willing — **un·will·ing·ly** *adv* — **un·will·ing·ness** *n*

un·wind \ˌən-ˈwīnd\ *vb* **-wound** \-ˈwau̇nd\; **-wind·ing** **1 a** : to cause to uncoil : wind off **b** : to become uncoiled or disentangled **2** : to make or become free of tension : RELAX ⟨wanted to *unwind* after a hard day⟩

un·wise \ˌən-ˈwīz\ *adj* : not wise : FOOLISH — **un·wise·ly** *adv*

un·wit·ting \ˌən-ˈwit-iŋ\ *adj* **1** : not intended : INADVERTENT **2** : not knowing : UNAWARE — **un·wit·ting·ly** \-iŋ-lē\ *adv*

un·wont·ed \ˌən-ˈwȯnt-əd, -ˈwōnt-\ *adj* : being out of the ordinary : RARE, UNUSUAL

un·world·ly \ˌən-ˈwərl-(d)lē\ *adj* **1** : not of this world; *esp* : SPIRITUAL **2** : not wise in the ways of the world — **un·world·li·ness** *n*

un·worn \ˌən-ˈwōrn, -ˈwȯrn\ *adj* : not worn : NEW

un·wor·thy \ˌən-ˈwər-t͟hē, ˈən-\ *adj* **1** : DISHONORABLE **2** : not meritorious : not worthy : UNDESERVING — **un·wor·thi·ly** \-t͟hə-lē\ *adv* — **un·wor·thi·ness** \-t͟hē-nəs\ *n*

un·wrap \ˌən-ˈrap\ *vb* : to remove the wrapping from

un·writ·ten \ˌən-ˈrit-ən\ *adj* **1** : not put in writing : ORAL, TRADITIONAL ⟨an *unwritten* code⟩ **2** : containing no writing : BLANK ⟨*unwritten* pages⟩

un·yield·ing \ˌən-ˈyēl-diŋ\ *adj* **1** : marked by lack of softness or flexibility **2** : marked by firmness or stubbornness

un·yoke \ˌən-ˈyōk\ *vb* **1** : to free from a yoke ⟨*unyoke* oxen⟩ **2** : SEPARATE, DISCONNECT

un·zip \ˌən-ˈzip\ *vb* : to open by means of a zipper

[1]**up** \ˈəp\ *adv* **1 a** : in or to a higher position or level : away from the center of the earth ⟨held *up* his hand⟩ **b** : from beneath a surface (as ground or water) ⟨pulling *up* weeds⟩ **c** : from below the horizon ⟨watched the moon come *up*⟩ **d** : in or into an upright position ⟨stand *up*⟩ **e** : out of bed ⟨stayed *up* late⟩ **2** : with greater intensity ⟨speak *up*⟩ **3 a** : in or into a better or more advanced state ⟨worked his way *up* in the world⟩ **b** : in or into a state of greater intensity or activity ⟨stir *up* a fire⟩ **4 a** : into existence, evidence, or knowledge ⟨the missing ring turned *up*⟩ **b** : into consideration ⟨brought the matter *up*⟩ **5** : into possession or custody ⟨gave himself *up*⟩ **6** : ENTIRELY, COMPLETELY ⟨eat it *up*⟩ ⟨the house burned *up*⟩ **7** : ASIDE, BY ⟨lay *up* supplies⟩ ⟨put his car *up* for the winter⟩ **8** : into a state of closure or confinement ⟨button *up* your coat⟩ ⟨seal *up* a package⟩ **9 a** : so as to arrive or approach ⟨came *up* the drive⟩ **b** : so as to be even with, overtake, or arrive at ⟨catch *up*⟩ ⟨keep *up* with the times⟩ **10** : in or into parts ⟨tear *up* paper⟩ ⟨blow *up* a bridge⟩ **11** : to a stop ⟨pull *up*⟩ ⟨drew *up* at the curb⟩ **12 a** : in advance ⟨went one *up* on his opponent⟩ **b** : for each side ⟨score was 15 *up*⟩

[2]**up** *adj* **1 a** : risen above the horizon ⟨the sun was *up*⟩ **b** : being out of bed **c** : relatively high ⟨the river is *up*⟩ ⟨prices are *up*⟩ **d** : RAISED, LIFTED ⟨windows are *up*⟩ **e** : BUILT ⟨the house is *up* but not finished⟩ **f** : grown above a surface ⟨the corn is *up*⟩ **g** : moving, inclining, or directed upward ⟨the *up* escalator⟩ **2 a** : marked by agitation, excitement, or activity ⟨was eager to be *up* and doing⟩ **b** : READY; *esp* : highly prepared ⟨the team was *up* for the game⟩ **c** : going on : taking place ⟨find out what is *up*⟩ **3** : EXPIRED, ENDED ⟨your time is *up*⟩ **4** : well informed ⟨always *up* on the news⟩ **5** : being ahead or in advance of an opponent ⟨was three games *up* in the series⟩ **6 a** : presented for or under consideration ⟨*up* for reelection⟩ **b** : charged before a court ⟨was *up* for robbery⟩ — **up to 1** : capable of performing or dealing with ⟨feels *up to* her role⟩ **2** : engaged in ⟨what is he *up to*⟩ **3** : being the responsibility of ⟨it's *up to* me⟩

[3]**up** *vb* **upped** *or in 1* **up**; **upped**; **up·ping**; **ups** *or in 1* **up** **1** : to act abruptly or surprisingly ⟨*up* and left town⟩ **2** : to rise from a lying or sitting position **3** : to move or cause to move upward : ASCEND, RAISE ⟨*upped* the prices⟩

[4]**up** \(ˌ)əp, ˈəp\ *prep* **1** : to, toward, or at a higher point of ⟨*up* the hill⟩ **2 a** : toward the source of ⟨going *up* the river⟩ **b** : toward the northern part of ⟨sailed *up* the coast⟩ **c** : to, toward, or in the inner part of ⟨stuck *up* a dead end street⟩ **3** : ALONG ⟨walking *up* the street⟩

[5]**up** \ˈəp\ *n* **1** : an upward course or slope **2** : a period or state of prosperity or success ⟨had had his *ups* and downs⟩

up–and–down \ˌəp-ən-ˈdau̇n\ *adj* **1** : marked by alternate upward and downward movement, action, or surface **2** : PERPENDICULAR

[1]**up·beat** \ˈəp-ˌbēt\ *n* : an unaccented beat in a musical measure; *esp* : the last beat of the measure

[2]**upbeat** *adj* : OPTIMISTIC, CHEERFUL ⟨a story with an *upbeat* ending⟩

up·braid \ˌəp-ˈbrād\ *vb* : to criticize, reproach, or scold severely or vehemently

up·bring·ing \'əp-ˌbring-ing\ *n* : the process of bringing up and training

up·com·ing \ˌəp-ˌkəm-ing\ *adj* : FORTHCOMING, APPROACHING

1**up–coun·try** \ˌəp-ˌkən-trē\ *adj* : of or relating to the interior of a country or a region — **up–coun·try** \'əp-\ *n*

2**up–coun·try** \ˌəp-'kən-trē\ *adv* : to or in the interior of a country or a region

up·date \ˌəp-'dāt\ *vb* : to bring up to date

up·draft \'əp-ˌdraft, -ˌdráft\ *n* : an upward movement of gas (as air)

up·end \ˌəp-'end\ *vb* : to set, stand, or rise on end

1**up·grade** \'əp-ˌgrād\ *n* **1** : an upward grade or slope **2** : INCREASE, RISE ⟨crime has been on the *upgrade*⟩; *esp* : a rise toward a better state or position ⟨trade is on the *upgrade*⟩

2**up·grade** \-ˌgrād\ *vb* : to raise to a higher grade or position

up·growth \'əp-ˌgrōth\ *n* **1** : the process of growing up : upward growth : DEVELOPMENT **2** : a product or result of upward growth or development

up·heav·al \ˌəp-'hē-vəl\ *n* **1** : the action or an instance of upheaving esp. of part of the earth's crust **2** : an instance of violent agitation or change ⟨student *upheavals*⟩

up·heave \ˌəp-'hēv\ *vb* **-heaved**; **-heav·ing** : to heave or lift up from beneath

1**up·hill** \'əp-'hil\ *adv* **1** : upward on a hill or incline **2** : against difficulties

2**up·hill** \ˌəp-ˌhil\ *adj* **1** : situated on elevated ground **2** : going up : ASCENDING **3** : DIFFICULT, LABORIOUS ⟨an *uphill* struggle⟩

up·hold \ˌəp-'hōld\ *vb* **-held** \-'held\; **-hold·ing** **1** : to give support to **2 a** : to keep elevated **b** : to lift up — **up·hold·er** *n*

up·hol·ster \ˌəp-'hōl-stər\ *vb* **-stered**; **-ster·ing** \-st(ə-)ring\ : to furnish with upholstery — **up·hol·ster·er** \-stər-ər\ *n*

up·hol·stery \-st(ə-)rē\ *n*, *pl* **-ster·ies** [from obsolete *upholster* "upholsterer", from Middle English *upholdester* (from *upholden* "to uphold", "maintain" and *-ster*) and 2*-y*] : materials (as fabric, padding, and springs) used to make a soft covering esp. for a seat

UPI *abbr* United Press International

up·keep \'əp-ˌkēp\ *n* : the act or cost of maintaining in good condition : MAINTENANCE

up·land \'əp-lənd, -ˌland\ *n* : high land esp. at some distance from the sea — **upland** *adj*

1**up·lift** \ˌəp-'lift\ *vb* **1** : to lift up : ELEVATE **2** : to improve the condition of esp. spiritually, socially, or intellectually

2**up·lift** \'əp-ˌlift\ *n* **1** : an act, process, or result of uplifting; *esp* : the uplifting of a part of the earth's surface **2** : moral or social improvement or a movement to make such improvement **3** : influences intended to uplift

up·most \'əp-ˌmōst\ *adj* : UPPERMOST

up·on \ə-'pòn, -'pän, -pən\ *prep* : ON

1**up·per** \'əp-ər\ *adj* **1** : higher in physical position, rank, or order **2** : being the smaller and more restricted branch of a bicameral legislature **3** *cap* : of, relating to, or being a later geologic period or formation **4** : being toward the interior : further inland ⟨the *upper* Amazon⟩ **5** : NORTHERN ⟨*upper* New York state⟩

2**upper** *n* **1** : the parts of a shoe or boot above the sole **2** : an upper tooth or denture **3** : an upper berth

up·per·case \ˌəp-ər-'kās\ *adj* : CAPITAL — **upper-case** *n*

upper class *n* : a social class having the highest status in a society — **upper–class** *adj*

up·per·class·man \ˌəp-ər-'klas-mən\ *n* : a junior or senior in a college or high school

upper crust *n* : the highest social class or group

up·per·cut \'əp-ər-ˌkət\ *n* : a swinging blow (as in boxing) directed upward with a bent arm — **upper-cut** *vb*

upper hand *n* : MASTERY, ADVANTAGE

up·per·most \'əp-ər-ˌmōst\ *adv* : in or into the highest or most prominent position — **uppermost** *adj*

up·per·part \-ˌpärt\ *n* : a part lying on the upper side (as of a bird)

up·pish \'əp-ish\ *adj* : UPPITY

up·pi·ty \'əp-ət-ē\ *adj* : putting on airs of superiority : ARROGANT

up·raise \ˌəp-'rāz\ *vb* : to raise or lift up : ELEVATE

1**up·right** \'əp-ˌrīt\ *adj* **1 a** : ERECT, VERTICAL ⟨an *upright* posture⟩ **b** : having the main axis or a main part perpendicular **2** : living by high moral principles : HONORABLE ***syn*** see HONEST ***ant*** unprincipled — **up·right·ness** *n*

2**upright** *n* **1** : an upright or vertical position **2** : something upright

upright piano *n* : a piano whose strings run vertically

up·rise \ˌəp-'rīz\ *vb* **-rose** \-'rōz\; **-ris·en** \-'riz-ən\; **-ris·ing** \-'rī-zing\ **1** : to rise to a higher position **2** : to get up (as from sleep or a sitting position)

upright piano

up·ris·ing \'əp-ˌrī-zing\ *n* : an act or instance of rising up; *esp* : INSURRECTION, REVOLT

up·roar \'əp-ˌrōr, -ˌròr\ *n* : a state of commotion, excitement, or violent disturbance

up·roar·i·ous \ˌəp-'rōr-ē-əs, -'ròr-\ *adj* **1** : marked by uproar **2** : extremely funny — **up·roar·i·ous·ly** *adv*

up·root \ˌəp-'rüt, -'rút\ *vb* : to remove by or as if by pulling up by the roots ⟨*uproot* a vine⟩ ⟨refugees *uprooted* by war⟩

1**up·set** \ˌəp-'set\ *vb* **-set**; **-set·ting** **1** : to force or be forced out of the usual position : OVERTURN, CAPSIZE **2 a** : to disturb emotionally **b** : to make somewhat ill **3 a** : to throw into disorder : DISARRANGE **b** : to defeat unexpectedly

2**up·set** \'əp-ˌset\ *n* **1** : an act or result of upsetting : a state of being upset **2 a** : a minor physical disorder ⟨a stomach *upset*⟩ **b** : an emotional disturbance

up·shot \'əp-ˌshät\ *n* : final result : OUTCOME

up·side \'əp-ˌsīd\ *n* : the upper side or part

up·side down \ˌəp-ˌsīd-'daůn\ *adv* **1** : with the upper and the lower parts reversed in position **2** : in or into great disorder — **upside–down** *adj*

up·si·lon \'yüp-sə-ˌlän, 'əp-\ *n* : the 20th letter of the Greek alphabet — Υ or υ

up·stage \ˌəp-'stāj\ *vb* : to steal the show from ⟨children *upstaging* veteran performers⟩

1**up·stairs** \'əp-'sta(ə)rz, -'ste(ə)rz\ *adv* **1** : up the stairs : to or on a higher floor **2** : to or at a high altitude or higher position

ə abut	ər further	a back	ā bake	
ä cot, cart	aů out	ch chin	e less	ē easy
g gift	i trip	ī life	j joke	ng sing	ō flow
ò flaw	òi coin	th thin	t͟h this	ü loot
ů foot	y yet	yü few	yů furious	zh vision

[2]**up·stairs** \'əp-ˌ\ *adj* : of or relating to the upper floors

[3]**up·stairs** \'əp-', 'əp-ˌ\ *n* : the part of a building above the ground floor

up·stand·ing \ˌəp-'stan-diŋ\ *adj* **1** : ERECT **2** : HONEST, STRAIGHTFORWARD

up·start \'əp-ˌstärt\ *n* : a person who has risen suddenly (as from a low position to wealth or power); *esp* : one who claims more personal importance than he deserves

up·state \'əp-ˌstāt\ *adj* : of, relating to, or characteristic of a part of a state away from a large city and esp. to the north — **upstate** *n*

up·stream \'əp-'strēm\ *adv* : at or toward the source of a stream : against the current ⟨salmon swimming *upstream* to spawn⟩

up·stroke \'əp-ˌstrōk\ *n* : an upward stroke (as of a pen)

up·surge \'əp-ˌsərj\ *n* : a rapid or sudden rise ⟨an *upsurge* of popularity⟩

up·sweep \'əp-ˌswēp\ *vb* **-swept** \-ˌswept\; **-sweep·ing** : to sweep upward : curve or slope upward — **upsweep** *n*

up·swept \'əp-ˌswept\ *adj* : swept upward ⟨*upswept* hairdo⟩

up·swing \'əp-ˌswiŋ\ *n* : an upward swing; *esp* : a marked increase or rise (as in activity)

up·take \'əp-ˌtāk\ *n* **1** : UNDERSTANDING, COMPREHENSION ⟨quick on the *uptake*⟩ **2** : an act or instance of absorbing and incorporating esp. into a living organism

up·thrust \'əp-ˌthrəst\ *n* : an upward thrust; *esp* : an uplift of part of the earth's crust

up·tight \'əp-'tīt\ *adj* : showing signs of tension or uneasiness : APPREHENSIVE

up·tilt \ˌəp-'tilt\ *vb* : to tilt upward

up to *prep* **1** : as far as a designated part or place ⟨sank *up to* his hips⟩ **2** : to or in fulfillment of ⟨write *up to* the standard⟩ **3 a** : to the limit of ⟨come in sizes *up to* 10⟩ **b** : as many or as much as ⟨carry *up to* 10 tons⟩ **4** : UNTIL, TILL ⟨from dawn *up to* dusk⟩

up–to–date \ˌəp-tə-'dāt\ *adj* **1** : extending up to the present time ⟨*up–to–date* maps⟩ **2** : abreast of the times (as in style or technique) : MODERN — **up–to–date·ness** *n*

up·town \'əp-'tau̇n\ *adv* : toward, to, or in the upper part of a town — **up·town** \-ˌtau̇n\ *adj*

up·trend \'əp-ˌtrend\ *n* : a tendency upward

[1]**up·turn** \'əp-ˌtərn, ˌəp-'\ *vb* **1** : to turn up or over ⟨an *upturned* boat⟩ **2** : to turn or direct upward ⟨*upturned* faces⟩

[2]**up·turn** \'əp-ˌtərn\ *n* : an upward turn (as toward better conditions or higher prices)

[1]**up·ward** \'əp-wərd\ *or* **up·wards** \-wərdz\ *adv* **1** : in a direction from lower to higher ⟨the land rises *upward*⟩ **2** : toward a higher or better condition ⟨worked his way *upward* in the business⟩ **3** : toward a greater amount or higher number, degree, or rate ⟨prices shot *upward*⟩

[2]**upward** *adj* : directed toward or situated in a higher place or level : ASCENDING — **up·ward·ly** *adv*

upwards of *also* **upward of** *adv* : more than : in excess of ⟨*upwards of* half a million people⟩

up·well \ˌəp-'wel\ *vb* : to well up

up·well·ing \-iŋ\ *n* : the movement of deeper cooler and often nutrient-rich layers of ocean water to the surface

up·wind \'əp-'wind\ *adv or adj* : in the direction from which the wind is blowing

ura·ni·nite \yu̇-'rā-nə-ˌnīt\ *n* : a mineral that is a black oxide of uranium, contains also various metals (as thorium and lead), and is the chief ore of uranium

ura·ni·um \yu̇-'rā-nē-əm\ *n* [scientific Latin, from *Uranus*, the planet, which was discovered only a few years before the element] : a silvery heavy radioactive metallic element that is found esp. in pitchblende and uraninite and exists naturally as a mixture of three isotopes of mass number 234, 235, and 238 — see ELEMENT table

uranium hexafluoride *n* : a compound used in the gaseous diffusion process for the separation of uranium 235 from ordinary uranium

uranium 235 *n* : a light isotope of uranium of mass number 235 that when bombarded with neutrons undergoes rapid fission into smaller atoms with the release of neutrons and atomic energy

Ura·nus \'yu̇r-ə-nəs, yu̇-'rā-\ *n* — see PLANET table

ur·ban \'ər-bən\ *adj* : of, relating to, characteristic of, or constituting a city ⟨*urban* life⟩ ⟨an *urban* area⟩

ur·bane \ˌər-'bān\ *adj* : notably polite : smoothly courteous — **ur·ban·i·ty** \-'bān-ət-ē\ *n*

ur·ban·ite \'ər-bə-ˌnīt\ *n* : one living in a city

ur·ban·ize \'ər-bə-ˌnīz\ *vb* **1** : to cause to take on urban characteristics ⟨*urbanized* areas⟩ **2** : to impart an urban way of life to — **ur·ban·i·za·tion** \ˌər-bə-nə-'zā-shən\ *n*

ur·chin \'ər-chən\ *n* [from medieval French *herichon*, from Latin *ericius*] : a mischievous boy

-ure *n suffix* **1** : act : process : being ⟨expos*ure*⟩ **2** : office : function; *also* : body performing (such) a function ⟨legislat*ure*⟩

urea \yu̇-'rē-ə\ *n* : a soluble nitrogen-containing compound that is the chief solid component of mammalian urine

ure·mia \yu̇-'rē-mē-ə\ *n* : accumulation in the blood of substances usu. passed off in the urine resulting in a severe toxic condition — **ure·mic** \-mik\ *adj*

ure·ter \'yu̇r-ət-ər\ *n* : a duct that carries urine from a kidney to the bladder or cloaca

ure·thra \yu̇-'rē-thrə\ *n*, *pl* **-thras** *or* **-thrae** \-(ˌ)thrē\ : the canal that in most mammals carries off the urine from the bladder and in the male serves also as a genital duct — **ure·thral** \-thrəl\ *adj*

[1]**urge** \'ərj\ *vb* **1** : to present, advocate, or demand something earnestly ⟨continually *urging* reform⟩ **2 a** : to try to persuade or sway ⟨*urge* a guest to stay longer⟩ **b** : to serve as a motive or reason for **3** : to press or impel to some course or activity (as greater speed) ⟨*urge* on a runner⟩

[2]**urge** *n* **1** : the act or process of urging **2** : a force or impulse that urges; *esp* : a continuing impulse toward an activity or goal

ur·gent \'ər-jənt\ *adj* **1 a** : calling for immediate attention : PRESSING ⟨*urgent* appeals⟩ **b** : conveying a sense of urgency ⟨an *urgent* manner⟩ **2** : urging insistently — **ur·gen·cy** \-jən-sē\ *n* — **ur·gent·ly** *adv*

uric \'yu̇r-ik\ *adj* : of, relating to, or found in urine

uric acid *n* : a white odorless nitrogen-containing acid that is present in small quantity in mammalian urine but is the chief excretory product for the elimination of nitrogen in birds and many lower forms

uri·nal \'yu̇r-ən-əl\ *n* : a receptacle for urine

uri·nal·y·sis \ˌyu̇r-ə-'nal-ə-səs\ *n*, *pl* **uri·nal·y·ses** \-ə-ˌsēz\ : the analysis of urine

uri·nary \'yu̇r-ə-ˌner-ē\ *adj* **1** : relating to, occurring in, or constituting the organs concerned with the formation and discharge of urine **2** : of, relating to, or used for urine

uri·nate \'yu̇r-ə-ˌnāt\ *vb* : to discharge urine — **uri·na·tion** \ˌyu̇r-ə-'nā-shən\ *n*

urine \'yu̇r-ən\ *n* : waste material that is secreted by the kidney, is rich in end products of protein metabolism, and is usu. a yellowish liquid in mammals but semisolid in birds and reptiles

urn \'ərn\ *n* **1** : a vessel that has the form of a vase on a pedestal and often is used for preserving the ashes of the dead **2** : a closed vessel usu. with a spigot for serving a hot beverage ⟨coffee *urn*⟩

uro·style \'yu̇r-ə-ˌstīl\ *n* : a bony rod made of fused vertebrae that forms the end of the spinal column of a frog or toad

us \(ˈ)əs\ *pron, objective case of* WE

US *abbr* United States

USA *abbr* **1** United States Army **2** United States of America

us·a·ble \'yü-zə-bəl\ *adj* : suitable or fit for use ⟨*usable* waste⟩

USAF *abbr* United States Air Force

us·age \'yü-sij, -zij\ *n* **1 a** : customary practice or procedure **b** : the way in which words and phrases are actually used **2 a** : the action or mode of using : USE ⟨increasing *usage* of the nation's highways⟩ **b** : manner of treating ⟨rough *usage*⟩

USCG *abbr* United States Coast Guard

¹use \'yüs\ *n* **1 a** : the act or practice of employing something : APPLICATION ⟨put knowledge to *use*⟩ **b** : the fact or state of being used ⟨a dish in daily *use*⟩ **c** : way of using ⟨the proper *use* of tools⟩ **2 a** : the privilege or benefit of using something **b** : the ability or power to use something (as a limb or faculty) **3 a** : a particular service or end : OBJECT, FUNCTION ⟨no *use* in crying all the time⟩ **b** : the quality of being suitable for employment : USEFULNESS ⟨old clothes that are still of some *use*⟩ **c** : the occasion or need to employ ⟨took only what he had *use* for⟩ **4** : ESTEEM, LIKING ⟨had no *use* for modern art⟩

²use \'yüz\ *vb* **used** \'yüzd, *in the phrase "used to" usually* 'yüs(t)\; **us·ing** \'yü-zing\ **1** : to put into action or service : EMPLOY ⟨pronunciations *used* by different people⟩ **2** : to consume or take regularly ⟨never *uses* tobacco⟩ **3** : to carry out a purpose or action by means of : UTILIZE ⟨*use* tact⟩ **4** : to expend or consume by putting to use ⟨likes to *use* wine in cooking⟩ **5** : to behave toward : TREAT ⟨*used* the prisoners cruelly⟩ **6** — used in the past with *to* to indicate a former practice, fact, or state ⟨claims winters *used* to be harder⟩ ⟨how they *used* to fight as children⟩ — **us·er** \'yü-zər\ *n*

used \'yüzd, *in the phrase "used to" usually* 'yüs(t)\ *adj* **1** : employed in accomplishing something ⟨a much *used* excuse⟩ **2** : that has been used; *esp* : SECONDHAND ⟨*used* car⟩ **3** : ACCUSTOMED, HABITUATED ⟨*used* to flying⟩

use·ful \'yüs-fəl\ *adj* **1** : capable of being put to use : USABLE ⟨a rock makes a *useful* substitute for a hammer⟩ ⟨*useful* scraps of material⟩ **2** : VALUABLE, PRODUCTIVE ⟨a *useful* invention⟩ ⟨*useful* ideas⟩ ⟨*useful* arts⟩ — **use·ful·ly** \-fə-lē\ *adv* — **use·ful·ness** *n*

use·less \'yüs-ləs\ *adj* : having or being of no use : WORTHLESS — **use·less·ly** *adv* — **use·less·ness** *n*

¹ush·er \'əsh-ər\ *n* [originally meaning "doorkeeper", from medieval French *ussier*, from Latin *ostiarius*, from *ostium* "door", from *os* "mouth"] : a person who escorts other persons to seats (as in a theater or at a wedding)

²usher *vb* **ush·ered**; **ush·er·ing** \'əsh-(ə-)ring\ **1** : to conduct to a place **2** : INAUGURATE, INTRODUCE ⟨*usher* in a new era⟩

USMC *abbr* United States Marine Corps

USN *abbr* United States Navy

USS *abbr* United States Ship

USSR *abbr* Union of Soviet Socialist Republics

usu·al \'yüzh-(ə-w)əl\ *adj* : done, found, or used in the ordinary course of events : NORMAL, REGULAR ⟨charged less than his *usual* fee⟩ ⟨took the *usual* route to work⟩ ⟨the *usual* color of the fallow deer⟩ — **usu·al·ly** \-ē\ *adv*

syn USUAL, CUSTOMARY, HABITUAL, ACCUSTOMED can mean familiar or expected through frequent or regular repetition. USUAL suggests something that occurs so frequently that it seems in no way strange or conspicuous ⟨a cat of the *usual* size⟩; CUSTOMARY implies conformity with individual or social practices or conventions ⟨*customary* courtesies⟩; HABITUAL is commonly applied to what has settled by long repetition into a habit ⟨his *habitual* morning walk⟩; ACCUSTOMED suggests something that, though not so strongly ingrained as settled habit, is noticed and expected of someone by others ⟨her *accustomed* graciousness⟩

usu·rer \'yü-zhər-ər\ *n* : one who lends money esp. at an excessively high rate of interest

usu·ri·ous \yu̇-'zhu̇r-ē-əs\ *adj* : practicing, involving, or constituting usury ⟨*usurious* interest⟩

usurp \yu̇-'sərp, -'zərp\ *vb* : to seize and hold by force or without right ⟨*usurp* a throne⟩

usu·ry \'yüzh-(ə-)rē\ *n, pl* **usuries** **1** : the lending of money with an interest charge for its use **2** : an excessive rate or amount of interest charged; *esp* : interest above an established legal rate

UT *abbr* Utah

uten·sil \yu̇-'ten(t)-səl\ *n* **1** : an instrument or container used in a household and esp. a kitchen **2** : an article serving a useful purpose ⟨writing *utensils*⟩

uter·us \'yüt-ə-rəs\ *n, pl* **uteri** \-ˌrī, -ˌrē\ *also* **uter·us·es** : an organ in female mammals for containing and usu. for nourishing the young during development previous to birth — called also *womb* — **uter·ine** \-rən, -ˌrīn\ *adj*

util·i·tar·i·an \yu̇-ˌtil-ə-'ter-ē-ən\ *adj* **1** : of or relating to utility **2** : aiming at usefulness rather than beauty ⟨*utilitarian* furniture⟩

¹util·i·ty \yu̇-'til-ət-ē\ *n, pl* **-ties** **1** : the quality or state of being useful : USEFULNESS **2** : something useful or designed for use **3 a** : PUBLIC UTILITY **b** : a public service or a commodity provided by a public utility; *esp* : equipment or a piece of equipment (as plumbing in a house) to provide such or a similar service

²utility *adj* **1** : capable of serving as a substitute in various roles or positions ⟨*utility* infielder⟩ **2** : being of a usable but inferior grade ⟨*utility* beef⟩ **3** : serving primarily for usefulness rather than beauty : UTILITARIAN **4** : designed for general use ⟨*utility* bag⟩

uti·lize \'yüt-ə-ˌlīz\ *vb* : to make use of : convert to use — **uti·li·za·tion** \ˌyüt-ə-lə-'zā-shən\ *n*

ut·most \'ət-ˌmōst\ *adj* [from Middle English, an alteration of *utmest*, from Old English *ūtmest* "outermost", from *ūt* "out"] **1** : situated at the farthest or most distant point **2** : of the greatest or highest degree, quantity, number, or amount ⟨a matter of the *utmost* urgency⟩ — **utmost** *n*

uto·pia \yu̇-ˈtō-pē-ə\ *n* [from *Utopia*, imaginary ideal country in *Utopia* by Sir Thomas More, from Greek *ou* "not", "no" and *topos* "place"] **1** *often cap* : a place of ideal perfection esp. in laws, government, and social conditions **2** : an impractical scheme for social improvement — **uto·pi·an** \-pē-ən\ *adj or n*

¹**ut·ter** \ˈət-ər\ *adj* : ABSOLUTE, TOTAL ⟨an *utter* impossibility⟩ ⟨*utter* strangers⟩ — **ut·ter·ly** *adv*

²**utter** *vb* [from Middle English *uttren*, from *utter* "outside", from Old English *ūtor*, comparative of *ūt* "out"] **1** : to send forth usu. as a sound ⟨*uttered* a laugh⟩ **2** : to express in words ⟨forced to *utter* the truth⟩

ut·ter·ance \ˈət-ə-rən(t)s\ *n* **1** : something uttered; *esp* : an oral or written statement **2** : the action of uttering with the voice : SPEECH **3** : power, style, or manner of speaking

ut·ter·most \ˈət-ər-ˌmōst\ *adj* : EXTREME, UTMOST — **uttermost** *n*

uvu·la \ˈyü-vyə-lə\ *n, pl* **-las** *or* **-lae** \-ˌlē, -ˌlī\ [from medieval Latin, diminutive of Latin *uva* "grape", "cluster of grapes", "uvula"] : the fleshy lobe hanging down from the back part of the roof of the mouth — **uvu·lar** \-lər\ *adj*

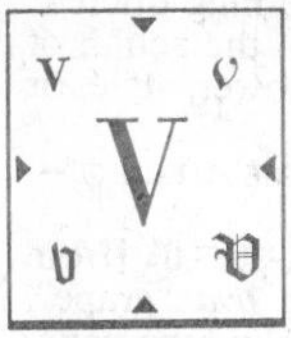

v \'vē\ *n, often cap* **1** : the 22d letter of the English alphabet **2** : the roman numeral 5
v *abbr* **1** verb **2** verse **3** volume
V *abbr* victory
Va *or* **VA** *abbr* Virginia
va·can·cy \'vā-kən-sē\ *n, pl* **-cies** **1 a** : a vacating of an office, post, or property **b** : the time such office or property is vacant **2** : a vacant office, post, or tenancy ⟨two *vacancies* in a building⟩ **3** : empty space ⟨stare into *vacancy*⟩ **4** : the state of being vacant
va·cant \'vā-kənt\ *adj* **1** : being without an occupant : not used ⟨a *vacant* room⟩ ⟨a *vacant* chair⟩ **2** : free from business or care : LEISURE ⟨a few *vacant* hours⟩ **3** : BRAINLESS, FOOLISH ⟨a *vacant* stare⟩ — **va·cant·ly** *adv*
va·cate \'vā-ˌkāt, vā-'\ *vb* **1** : to make void : ANNUL ⟨*vacate* an agreement⟩ **2** : to make vacant : leave empty ⟨*vacate* a building⟩
¹**va·ca·tion** \vā-'kā-shən, və-\ *n* **1** : a period during which activity (as of a school) is suspended **2** : a period spent away from home or business in travel or recreation ⟨had a restful *vacation* at the beach⟩
²**vacation** *vb* **-tioned**; **-tion·ing** \-sh(ə-)niŋ\ : to take or spend a vacation ⟨*vacation* in July⟩
va·ca·tion·er \-sh(ə-)nər\ *n* : VACATIONIST
va·ca·tion·ist \-sh(ə-)nəst\ *n* : a person taking a vacation
vac·ci·nate \'vak-sə-ˌnāt\ *vb* : to inoculate (a person) with cowpox virus in order to produce immunity to smallpox; *also* : to administer a vaccine to usu. by injection — **vac·ci·na·tor** \-ˌnāt-ər\ *n*
vac·ci·na·tion \ˌvak-sə-'nā-shən\ *n* **1** : the act of vaccinating **2** : the scar left by vaccinating
vac·cine \vak-'sēn, 'vak-ˌ\ *n* [from Latin *vaccinus* "of cows", from *vacca* cow; so called because originally produced from cows] : a preparation of killed microorganisms, living attenuated organisms, or living fully infectious organisms that is administered to produce or artificially increase immunity to a particular disease
vac·il·late \'vas-ə-ˌlāt\ *vb* **1** : FLUCTUATE, OSCILLATE ⟨a *vacillating* stock market⟩ **2** : to incline first to one course or opinion and then to another : WAVER — **vac·il·lat·ing·ly** \-ˌlāt-iŋ-lē\ *adv* — **vac·il·la·tion** \ˌvas-ə-'lā-shən\ *n* — **vac·il·la·tor** \'vas-ə-ˌlāt-ər\ *n* — **vac·il·la·to·ry** \-lə-ˌtōr-ē, -ˌtȯr-\ *adj*
va·cu·i·ty \va-'kyü-ət-ē, və-\ *n, pl* **-ties** **1** : an empty space **2 a** : EMPTINESS, HOLLOWNESS **b** : vacancy of mind **3** : a senseless or foolish remark
vac·u·ole \'vak-yə-ˌwōl\ *n* : a usu. fluid-filled cavity in tissues or in the protoplasm of an individual cell — **vac·u·o·lar** \ˌvak-yə-'wō-lər\ *adj*
vac·u·ous \'vak-yə-wəs\ *adj* **1** : EMPTY **2** : STUPID, INANE — **vac·u·ous·ly** *adv* — **vac·u·ous·ness** *n*
¹**vac·u·um** \'vak-yə(-wə)m, -yüm\ *n, pl* **-u·ums** *or* **-ua** \-yə-wə\ [from Latin, from neuter of *vacuus* "empty", "vacant"] **1 a** : a perfectly empty space **b** : a space partially exhausted (as to the highest degree possible) by artificial means (as an air pump) **c** : a degree of rarefaction below atmospheric pressure **2** : a device creating or utilizing a partial vacuum; *esp* : VACUUM CLEANER

ə abut	ər further	a back	ā bake
ä cot, cart	aù out	ch chin	e less	ē easy
g gift	i trip	ī life	j joke	ŋ sing	ō flow
ȯ flaw	ȯi coin	th thin	th this	ü loot
ù foot	y yet	yü few	yù furious	zh vision

²**vacuum** *adj* : of, containing, producing, or utilizing a partial vacuum
³**vacuum** *vb* : to use a vacuum device (as a cleaner) upon
vacuum bottle *n* : a cylindrical container with a vacuum between an inner and an outer wall used to keep liquids hot or cold
vacuum cleaner *n* : an electrical appliance for cleaning (as floors, carpets, or upholstery) by suction
vac·u·um–packed \ˌvak-yə(-wə)m-'pakt, -yüm-\ *adj* : having much of the air removed before being sealed ⟨*vacuum-packed* coffee cans⟩
vacuum tube *n* : an electron tube from which the air has been removed
¹**vag·a·bond** \'vag-ə-ˌbänd\ *adj* **1** : moving from place to place without a fixed home : WANDERING ⟨*vagabond* minstrels⟩ **2** : of, relating to, or characteristic of a wanderer
²**vagabond** *n* : one who leads a vagabond life; *esp* : TRAMP
va·ga·ry \'vā-gə-rē; və-'ge(ə)r-ē, -'ga(ə)r-\ *n, pl* **-ries** : an odd or eccentric idea or action : CAPRICE
va·gi·na \və-'jī-nə\ *n, pl* **-nae** \-(ˌ)nē\ *or* **-nas** : a canal that leads from the uterus to the external opening of the genital canal — **vag·i·nal** \'vaj(ə-)nəl\ *adj*
va·gran·cy \'vā-grən-sē\ *n, pl* **-cies** **1** : VAGARY **2** : the state or action of being vagrant
¹**va·grant** \'vā-grənt\ *n* : an idle wanderer : TRAMP
²**vagrant** *adj* **1** : wandering aimlessly **2** : having no fixed course : RANDOM ⟨*vagrant* thoughts⟩
vague \'vāg\ *adj* **1** : not clearly expressed or meaningful ⟨*vague* accusations⟩ **2** : not clearly felt or understood ⟨a *vague* longing⟩ **3** : not thinking or expressing one's thoughts clearly ⟨*vague* about dates and places⟩ **4** : not sharply outlined : INDISTINCT — **vague·ly** *adv* — **vague·ness** *n*
vain \'vān\ *adj* **1** : WORTHLESS ⟨*vain* promises⟩ **2** : not succeeding : FUTILE ⟨a *vain* attempt⟩ **3** : proud of one's looks or abilities : CONCEITED — **vain·ly** *adv* — **vain·ness** \'vān-nəs\ *n* — **in vain** : to no purpose : without success
vain·glo·ry \'vān-ˌglōr-ē, -ˌglȯr-\ *n* **1** : too great pride in oneself and one's achievements **2** : vain display or show : VANITY — **vain·glo·ri·ous** \(')vān-'glōr-ē-əs, -'glȯr-\ *adj* — **vain·glo·ri·ous·ly** *adv* — **vain·glo·ri·ous·ness** *n*
val·ance \'val-ən(t)s, 'vāl-\ *n* : a short drapery or wood or metal frame across the top of a window or windows
vale \'vāl\ *n* : VALLEY, DALE

val·e·dic·to·ri·an \ˌval-ə-ˌdik-'tōr-ē-ən, -'tȯr-\ *n* : the student usu. of the highest rank in a graduating class who delivers the valedictory oration at commencement
¹**val·e·dic·to·ry** \-'dik-t(ə-)rē\ *adj* [from Latin *valedicere* "to say farewell", from *vale* "farewell", literally "be healthy!" and *dicere* "to say"] : of or relating to leave-taking : FAREWELL; *esp* : given at a leave-taking ceremony (as a school commencement)
²**valedictory** *n, pl* **-ries** : a valedictory oration or statement
val·en·tine \'val-ən-ˌtīn\ *n* **1** : a sweetheart chosen or complimented on St. Valentine's Day **2** : a gift or greeting sent or given on St. Valentine's Day
Valentine Day *or* **Valentine's Day** *n* : SAINT VALENTINE'S DAY
va·le·ri·an \və-'lir-ē-ən\ *n* **1** : any of a genus of

herbs mostly with flat-topped clusters of flowers and roots and rootstock which have medicinal properties **2** : a drug consisting of the dried roots and rootstocks of a widely cultivated Old World heliotrope

val·et \'val-ət, va-'lā\ *n* : a male servant or hotel employee who takes care of a man's clothes and performs personal services

[1]**val·iant** \'val-yənt\ *adj* **1** : boldly brave : COURAGEOUS ⟨a *valiant* leader⟩ **2** : VALOROUS, HEROIC ⟨*valiant* fighting⟩ — **val·iant·ly** *adv* — **val·iant·ness** *n*

[2]**valiant** *n* : a valiant person

val·id \'val-əd\ *adj* **1** : founded on truth or fact : WELL-GROUNDED ⟨*valid* reasons⟩ **2** : binding in law : SOUND ⟨a *valid* contract⟩ — **va·lid·i·ty** \və-'lid-ət-ē\ *n* — **val·id·ly** *adv*

val·i·date \'val-ə-ˌdāt\ *vb* **1** : to make valid **2** : CONFIRM, SUBSTANTIATE — **val·i·da·tion** \ˌval-ə-'dā-shən\ *n*

va·lise \və-'lēs\ *n* : TRAVELING BAG

val·ley \'val-ē\ *n, pl* **valleys** : a long depression between ranges of hills or mountains

val·or \'val-ər\ *n* : personal bravery in combat ***syn*** see COURAGE

val·or·ous \'val-ə-rəs\ *adj* **1** : possessing or showing valor : BRAVE ⟨*valorous* men⟩ **2** : marked by or performed with valor ⟨*valorous* feats⟩ — **val·or·ous·ly** *adv*

[1]**val·u·a·ble** \'val-yə(-wə)-bəl\ *adj* **1 a** : having monetary value **b** : worth a great deal of money **2** : having value : of great use or service — **val·u·a·ble·ness** *n* — **val·u·a·bly** \-blē\ *adv*

[2]**valuable** *n* : a possession (as a jewel) of high monetary value — usu. used in pl. ⟨kept her *valuables* in a safe⟩

val·u·a·tion \ˌval-yə-'wā-shən\ *n* **1** : the act or process of valuing : APPRAISAL **2** : the estimated or determined value

[1]**val·ue** \'val-yü\ *n* **1** : a fair return or equivalent in goods, services, or money for something exchanged **2** : the amount of money something will bring **3** : relative worth, utility, or importance : degree of excellence **4 a** : a numerical quantity assigned or computed **b** : the sound or sounds answering to a letter or orthographic item ⟨the *value* of *a* in *ate*⟩ **5** : the relative duration of a musical note **6** : relative lightness or darkness of a color : LUMINOSITY **7** : something valuable or desirable **8** : DENOMINATION 4

[2]**value** *vb* **1 a** : to estimate the monetary worth of : APPRAISE ⟨*value* a necklace⟩ **b** : to rate in usefulness, importance, or worth : EVALUATE **2** : to consider or rate highly : PRIZE ⟨*valued* his friendship⟩ — **val·u·er** \-yə-wər\ *n*

valve \'valv\ *n* **1** : a structure esp. in a bodily channel (as a vein) that regulates passage of material or movement of a fluid by opening and closing **2 a** : a mechanical device by which the flow of liquid, gas, or loose material in bulk may be started, stopped, or regulated by a movable part; *also* : the movable part of such a device **b** : a device in a brass wind instrument for quickly varying the tube length in order to change the fundamental tone by some definite interval **c** *chiefly Brit* : ELECTRON TUBE **3** : one of the distinct and usu. movably jointed pieces of which the shell of some shell-bearing animals (as bivalve mollusks) consists **4** : one of the segments or pieces into which a ripe seed capsule or pod separates — **valved** \'valvd\ *adj*

val·vu·lar \'val-vyə-lər\ *adj* **1** : resembling or functioning as a valve; *also* : opening by valves **2** : of or relating to a valve esp. of the heart

[1]**vamp** \'vamp\ *n* : the part of a shoe or boot covering the forepart of the foot and sometimes also the toe or the back seam of the upper

[2]**vamp** *vb* : to provide with a vamp

vam·pire \'vam-ˌpī(ə)r\ *n* **1** : the body of a dead person believed to come from the grave at night and suck the blood of persons asleep **2** : one who lives by preying on others **3** : any of various bats reputed to feed on blood: as **a** : any of several large So. and Central American insect-eating bats **b** : any of various So. American bats that feed on blood and are dangerous to man and domestic animals esp. as vectors of disease (as rabies) **c** : a large harmless Old World bat (as a fruit bat)

[1]**van** \'van\ *n* [short for *vanguard*, from French *avant-garde*, literally "fore-guard"] : VANGUARD

[2]**van** *n* [short for *caravan*] **1** : a usu. closed wagon or truck for transporting goods or animals **2** *chiefly Brit* : a closed railroad freight or baggage car

va·na·di·um \və-'nād-ē-əm\ *n* : a grayish malleable metallic element found combined in minerals and used esp. to form alloys (as of steel) — see ELEMENT table

Van Al·len radiation belt \van-'al-ən-, vən-\ *n* : a belt of high-energy charged particles that surrounds the earth in the outer atmosphere

van·dal \'van-dəl\ *n* **1** *cap* : one of a Germanic people overrunning Gaul, Spain, and northern Africa in the 4th and 5th centuries A.D., and in 455 sacking Rome **2** : one who destroys, damages, or defaces property — **vandal** *adj, often cap*

van·dal·ism \'van-də-ˌliz-əm\ *n* : willful or malicious destruction or defacement of property

van·dal·ize \-ˌlīz\ *vb* : to subject to vandalism : DAMAGE, DESTROY

Van de Graaff generator \ˌvan-də-ˌgraf-\ *n* : a generator of high voltages in which electric charges on a moving belt are transferred to a hollow sphere

vane \'vān\ *n* **1** : a movable device attached to something high to show which way the wind is blowing **2 a** : a flat or curved surface attached to an axis and moved by wind or water ⟨the *vanes* of a windmill⟩ **b** : a device revolving similarly in water or air ⟨the *vanes* of a propeller⟩ **3** : the web or flat expanded part of a feather — **vaned** \'vānd\ *adj*

van·guard \'van-ˌgärd\ *n* **1** : the troops moving at the head of an army **2** : the forefront of an action or movement or those in the forefront

va·nil·la \və-'nil-ə\ *n* **1** : any of a genus of tropical American climbing orchids **2** : the long pod of a vanilla that yields a commercially important flavoring extract; *also* : this extract

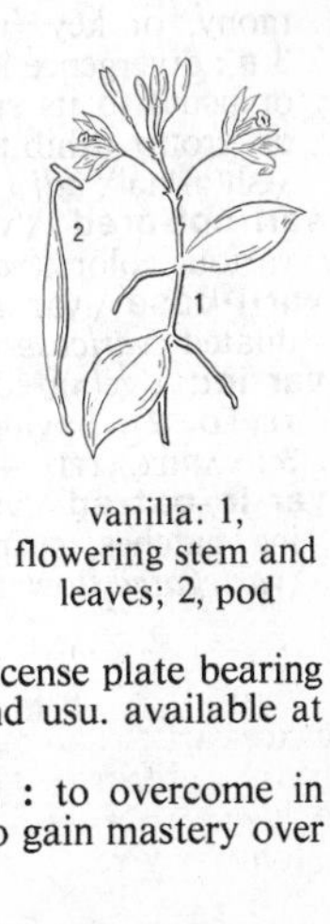

vanilla: 1, flowering stem and leaves; 2, pod

van·ish \'van-ish\ *vb* **1** : to pass quickly from sight : DISAPPEAR **2** : to pass completely from existence — **van·ish·er** *n*

van·i·ty \'van-ət-ē\ *n, pl* **-ties** **1** : something vain **2 a** : WORTHLESSNESS, EMPTINESS **b** : FUTILITY **c** : inflated pride in oneself or one's appearance : CONCEIT **3 a** : [3]COMPACT 1 **b** : DRESSING TABLE ***syn*** see PRIDE ***ant*** modesty

vanity plate *n* : an automobile license plate bearing distinctive letters or numbers and usu. available at extra cost

van·quish \'van(g)-kwish\ *vb* **1** : to overcome in battle : subdue completely **2** : to gain mastery over : DEFEAT — **van·quish·er** *n*

van·tage \'vant-ij\ *n* **1** : superiority in a contest **2** : a position giving advantage or a comprehensive view

vap·id \'vap-əd\ *adj* : FLAT, UNINTERESTING ⟨a *vapid* remark⟩ — **vap·id·ly** *adv*

va·por \'vā-pər\ *n* **1** : fine particles of matter (as fog or smoke) floating in the air and clouding it **2** : a substance in a gaseous state; *esp* : such a substance that is liquid under ordinary conditions **3** : something insubstantial or fleeting

va·por·ize \'vā-pə-ˌrīz\ *vb* : to turn from a liquid or solid into vapor — **va·por·i·za·tion** \ˌvā-pə-rə-'zā-shən\ *n*

va·por·iz·er \'vā-pə-ˌrī-zər\ *n* : a device that vaporizes something (as a medicated liquid)

vapor pressure *n* : the pressure exerted by a vapor that is in equilibrium with its solid or liquid form

va·que·ro \vä-'ke(ə)r-ō\ *n, pl* **-ros** [from Spanish, from *vaca* "cow", from Latin *vacca*] : COWBOY

var *abbr* variant

1**var·i·a·ble** \'ver-ē-ə-bəl, 'var-\ *adj* **1 a** : able or apt to vary : CHANGEABLE ⟨*variable* winds⟩ **b** : FICKLE, INCONSTANT **2** : not true to type : ABERRANT ⟨a *variable* species of wheat⟩ **3** : having the characteristics of a variable — **var·i·a·bil·i·ty** \ˌver-ē-ə-'bil-ət-ē, ˌvar-\ *n* — **var·i·a·ble·ness** \'ver-ē-ə-bəl-nəs, 'var-\ *n* — **var·i·a·bly** \-blē\ *adv*

2**variable** *n* **1** : something variable **2 a** : a quantity that may assume any one of a set of values **b** : a mathematical symbol representing a variable

variable star *n* : a star whose brightness changes usu. in more or less regular periods

var·i·ance \'ver-ē-ən(t)s, 'var-\ *n* **1** : variation or degree of variation : DEVIATION ⟨yearly *variance* in crops⟩ **2** : DISSENSION, DISPUTE **3** : the square of the standard deviation — **at variance** : not in harmony or agreement

1**var·i·ant** \'ver-ē-ənt, 'var-\ *adj* **1** : differing from others of its kind or class and esp. from others regarded as normal or typical **2** : being one of two or more similar but not identical forms with the same meaning ⟨a *variant* spelling⟩

2**variant** *n* : a variant individual; *esp* : one of two or more different spellings or pronunciations of the same word

var·i·a·tion \ˌver-ē-'ā-shən, ˌvar-\ *n* **1 a** : the act, process, or an instance of varying **b** : the state or fact of being varied **c** : the extent to which or range in which a thing varies **2** : the repetition of a musical theme with modifications in rhythm, tune, harmony, or key ⟨*variations* on a theme by Haydn⟩ **3 a** : divergence in characteristics from those typical or usual to its species or group **b** : an individual or group exhibiting variation — **var·i·a·tion·al** \-sh(ə-)nəl\ *adj*

vari·col·ored \'ver-i-ˌkəl-ərd, 'var-\ *adj* : having various colors ⟨*varicolored* marble⟩

var·i·cose \'var-ə-ˌkōs\ *adj* : abnormally swollen or dilated ⟨*varicose* veins⟩

var·ied \'ve(ə)r-ēd, 'va(ə)r-\ *adj* **1** : CHANGED, ALTERED **2** : having many forms or types : DIVERSE **3** : VARIEGATED — **var·ied·ly** *adv*

var·ie·gat·ed \'ver-(ē-)ə-ˌgāt-əd, 'var-\ *adj* **1** : having patches, stripes, or marks of different colors ⟨*variegated* flowers⟩ **2** : full of variety ⟨a *variegated* career⟩ — **var·ie·ga·tion** \ˌver-(ē-)ə-'gā-shən, ˌvar-\ *n*

va·ri·e·ty \və-'rī-ət-ē\ *n, pl* **-ties** **1** : the quality or state of having different forms or types : DIVERSITY **2** : a number or collection of different things : ASSORTMENT ⟨the store stocked a *variety* of goods⟩ **3 a** : something differing from others of the same general kind **b** : any of various groups of plants or animals within a species that are distinguished from other groups by characteristics not constant enough or too trivial to distinguish species **4** : entertainment consisting of successive unrelated performances (as dances, skits, or acrobatic feats)

var·i·ous \'ver-ē-əs, 'var-\ *adj* **1** : of differing kinds : DIVERSIFIED ⟨*various* enterprises use metals⟩ ⟨his *various* responsibilities⟩ **2** : differing one from another : UNLIKE ⟨animals as *various* as cat and mouse⟩ **3** : being of an indefinite number : SEVERAL ⟨stop at *various* towns⟩ — **var·i·ous·ly** *adv* — **var·i·ous·ness** *n*

var·let \'vär-lət\ *n* **1** *archaic* : ATTENDANT **2** : a low fellow

var·nish \'vär-nish\ *n* **1 a** : a liquid preparation that is applied like paint and dries to a hard lustrous typically transparent coating **b** : the covering or glaze given by the application of varnish **2** : outside show : GLOSS — **varnish** *vb*

var·si·ty \'vär-sət-ē, -stē\ *n, pl* **-ties** [from a British pronunciation of obsolete *versity*, short for *university*] : a major team representing a university, college, school, or club — **varsity** *adj*

varve \'värv\ *n* : a pair of layers of alternately finer and coarser silt or clay believed to comprise an annual cycle of deposition in a body of still water

vary \'ve(ə)r-ē, 'va(ə)r-\ *vb* **var·ied**; **vary·ing** **1** : to make a usu. minor or partial change in ⟨the rule must not be *varied*⟩ **2** : to give variety to : DIVERSIFY ⟨*vary* a diet⟩ ⟨a program *varied* to avoid monotony⟩ **3** : to exhibit or undergo change ⟨*varying* skies⟩ ⟨the accuracy of the several chapters *varies* greatly⟩ **4 a** : to be different ⟨laws *vary* from state to state⟩ **b** : to diverge structurally or physiologically from typical members of a group — **vary·ing·ly** \-ing-lē\ *adv*

varying hare *n* : any of several hares having white fur in winter

vas·cu·lar \'vas-kyə-lər\ *adj* : of, relating to, containing, or being anatomical vessels

varying hare (up to 18 in. long): left, in winter coat; right, in summer coat

vascular bundle *n* : a unit of the vascular system of a higher plant consisting usu. of xylem and phloem together with parenchyma cells and fibers

vascular plant *n* : a plant having a specialized conducting system that includes xylem and phloem

vascular ray *n* : a band of tissue in vascular plants that is derived from cambium and conducts food and water radially

vas de·fer·ens \'vas-'def-ə-rənz\ *n, pl* **va·sa de·fer·en·tia** \ˌvā-zə-ˌdef-ə-'ren-ch(ē-)ə\ : a spermatic duct esp. of a higher vertebrate

vase \'vās, 'vāz\ *n* : an ornamental usu. round vessel deeper than it is wide

vas·sal \'vas-əl\ *n* **1** : a person under the protection

ə abut	ər further	a back	ā bake	
ä cot, cart	aü out	ch chin	e less	ē easy
g gift	i trip	ī life	j joke	ng sing	ō flow
ȯ flaw	ȯi coin	th thin	th this	ü loot
u̇ foot	y yet	yü few	yu̇ furious	zh vision

of a feudal lord to whom he has sworn allegiance **2** : one in a dependent or subordinate position — **vassal** *adj*

vas·sal·age \-ə-lij\ *n* **1** : the state of being a vassal **2** : homage and loyalty due a lord from his vassal **3** : the state of being dependent or subservient

vast\'vast\ *adj* : very great in extent, size, amount, degree, or intensity — **vast·ly** *adv* — **vast·ness** \'vas(t)-nəs\ *n*

vasty \'vas-tē\ *adj* **vast·i·er**; **-est** : VAST, IMMENSE

vat \'vat\ *n* : a large vessel (as a cistern, tub, or barrel) esp. for liquids

vau·de·ville \'vȯd(-ə)-vəl, 'vōd-, -ˌvil\ *n* : light theatrical entertainment featuring variety acts

1**vault** \'vȯlt\ *n* **1 a** : an arched masonry structure usu. forming a ceiling or roof **b** : an arch or dome suggesting a vault ⟨the blue *vault* of the sky⟩ **2** : a room or compartment for storage or safekeeping ⟨a bank *vault*⟩ **3 a** : a burial chamber **b** : a usu. metal or concrete case in which a casket is enclosed at burial

vault 1a

2**vault** *vb* : to form or cover with or as if with a vault : ARCH

3**vault** *vb* : to leap or leap over using the hands or a pole — **vault·er** *n*

4**vault** *n* : an act of vaulting : LEAP

vault·ing \'vȯl-ting\ *adj* : too pretentious : ARROGANT ⟨a *vaulting* ambition⟩

vaunt \'vȯnt, 'vänt\ *vb* : BRAG, BOAST — **vaunt** *n* — **vaunt·er** *n* — **vaunt·ing·ly** \-ing-lē\ *adv*

vb *abbr* verb

VC *abbr* Vietcong

VD *abbr* venereal disease

've \v, əv\ *vb* : HAVE ⟨we'*ve* been there⟩

veal \'vēl\ *n* : the flesh of a young calf

vec·tor \'vek-tər\ *n* **1** : a quantity that has magnitude, direction, and sense **2** : an organism (as an insect) that transmits a pathogen

ve·da·lia \və-'dāl-yə\ *n* : a predaceous Australian ladybug widely used in controlling scale insects

veep \'vēp\ *n* : VICE-PRESIDENT

veer \'vi(ə)r\ *vb* : to change direction or course — **veer** *n*

vee·ry \'vi(ə)r-ē\ *n, pl* **veeries** : a tawny brown thrush common in woodlands of the eastern U.S.

veg *abbr* vegetable

1**veg·e·ta·ble** \'vej-tə-bəl, 'vej-ət-ə-bəl\ *adj* : of, relating to, produced by, or derived from plants ⟨the *vegetable* kingdom⟩ ⟨*vegetable* growth⟩ ⟨*vegetable* oils⟩

2**vegetable** *n* **1** : PLANT 1; *esp* : a herbaceous plant used for food **2** : an edible part of a plant eaten with the main part of the meal

vegetable color *n* : a coloring matter of plant origin

vegetable dye *n* : a natural dye obtained from a plant

1**veg·e·tar·i·an** \ˌvej-ə-'ter-ē-ən\ *n* : one who lives solely upon plants and plant products or excludes meat from the diet

2**vegetarian** *adj* **1** : of or relating to vegetarians **2** : consisting wholly of vegetables ⟨a *vegetarian* diet⟩

veg·e·tate \'vej-ə-ˌtāt\ *vb* : to live or grow in the manner of a plant; *esp* : to do little but eat and grow

veg·e·ta·tion \ˌvej-ə-'tā-shən\ *n* **1** : the act or process of vegetating **2** : inert existence **3** : plant life or cover (as of an area)

veg·e·ta·tive \'vej-ə-ˌtāt-iv\ *adj* : of, relating to, or involving propagation by other than sexual means — **veg·e·ta·tive·ly** *adv*

ve·he·ment \'vē-ə-mənt\ *adj* **1** : marked by great force or energy ⟨a *vehement* wind⟩ **2 a** : intensely emotional : PASSIONATE, FERVID **b** : forcefully expressing feelings ⟨*vehement* denunciations⟩ — **ve·he·mence** \-mən(t)s\ *n* — **ve·he·ment·ly** *adv*

ve·hi·cle \'vē-ˌ(h)ik-əl\ *n* **1** : a medium through which something is transmitted, expressed, or achieved ⟨newspapers are *vehicles* of ideas⟩ ⟨turpentine is a *vehicle* for paint⟩ **2** : something used to transport persons or goods : CONVEYANCE ⟨space *vehicle*⟩

ve·hic·u·lar \vē-'hik-yə-lər\ *adj* **1** : of, relating to, or designed for vehicles **2** : serving as a vehicle

1**veil** \'vāl\ *n* **1 a** : a length of cloth or net worn esp. by women over the head and shoulders or over the face **b** : a concealing curtain or cover of cloth **c** : something (as darkness or a membrane) that covers or obscures like a veil ⟨a *veil* of secrecy⟩ **2** : the vows or life of a nun ⟨take the *veil*⟩

2**veil** *vb* : to cover with or as if with a veil

veil·ing \'vā-ling\ *n* **1** : VEIL **2** : material for veils

1**vein** \'vān\ *n* **1** : a fissure in rock filled with mineral matter ⟨a *vein* of gold⟩ **2 a** : one of the tubular branching vessels that carry blood from the capillaries toward the heart **b** : one of the vascular bundles forming the framework of a leaf **c** : one of the thickened ribs that stiffen the wings of an insect **3** : CHANNEL ⟨underground water *veins*⟩ **4** : a wavy band or streak (as of a different color or texture) ⟨a marble with greenish *veins*⟩ **5 a** : a distinctive manner : STYLE ⟨writing in the classic *vein*⟩ **b** : a pervading element or quality : STRAIN ⟨a *vein* of humor in her character⟩

2**vein** *vb* : to form veins in or mark with veins

vein·ing \'vā-ning\ *n* : a pattern of veins : VENATION

veld *or* **veldt** \'felt, 'velt\ *n* [from South African Dutch, from Dutch, "field", from the same source as English *field*] : open grassland esp. of southern Africa usu. with scattered shrubs or trees

vel·lum \'vel-əm\ *n* **1** : a fine-grained lambskin, kidskin, or calfskin prepared esp. for writing on or for binding books **2** : a strong cream-colored paper resembling vellum — **vellum** *adj*

ve·loc·i·pede \və-'läs-ə-ˌpēd\ *n* : a light wheeled vehicle propelled by the rider; *esp* : TRICYCLE

velocipede

ve·loc·i·ty \və-'läs-ət-ē, -'läs-tē\ *n, pl* **-ties** **1** : quickness of motion : SPEED **2** : rate of motion or action

ve·lour *or* **ve·lours** \və-'lu̇(ə)r\ *n, pl* **velours** \-'lu̇(ə)rz\ : a usu. heavy fabric resembling velvet

ve·lum \'vē-ləm\ *n* : a membrane or anatomical partition likened to a veil or curtain; *esp* : SOFT PALATE

vel·vet \'vel-vət\ *n* **1** : a silk or synthetic fabric with a thick soft pile of short erect threads **2** : the soft vascular skin covering the developing antler of a deer — **velvet** *adj*

vel·ve·teen \ˌvel-və-'tēn\ *n* : a cotton fabric imitating velvet

vel·vety \'vel-vət-ē\ *adj* : soft and smooth like velvet

ve·na ca·va \ˌvē-nə-'kā-və\ *n, pl* **ve·nae ca·vae** \ˌvē-nē-'kā-(ˌ)vē\ : one of the large veins by which the blood is returned to the right atrium of the heart in an air-breathing vertebrate

ve·nal \'vēn-əl\ *adj* **1** : willing to take bribes : open to corrupt influences **2** : influenced by bribery : CORRUPT ⟨*venal* conduct⟩ ⟨*venal* magistrates⟩ — **ve·nal·i·ty** \vi-'nal-ət-ē\ *n* — **ve·nal·ly** \'vēn-ə-lē\ *adv*

ve·na·tion \vā-'nā-shən, vē-\ *n* : an arrangement or system of veins ⟨the *venation* of the hand⟩ ⟨the *venation* of a leaf⟩

vend \'vend\ *vb* : to offer for sale; *esp* : PEDDLE — **vend·er** \'ven-dər\ *or* **ven·dor** \'ven-dər, ven-'dȯ(ə)r\ *n*

ven·det·ta \ven-'det-ə\ *n* : a feud in which the relatives of a murdered man try to take vengeance by killing the murderer or his relatives

vending machine *n* : a slot machine for vending merchandise

1**ve·neer** \və-'ni(ə)r\ *n* [from German *furnier*, from *furnieren* "to veneer", from French *fournir* "to furnish", the source of English *furnish*] **1 a** : a thin sheet of a material; *esp* : a layer of a valuable or beautiful wood glued to an inferior wood **b** : any of the thin layers bonded together to form plywood **2** : a protective or ornamental facing (as of brick or stone) **3** : a superficial or false show : GLOSS

2**veneer** *vb* : to cover with a veneer

ven·er·a·ble \'ven-ər(-ə)-bəl, 'ven-rə-\ *adj* **1** : deserving to be venerated — used as a religious title **2** : deserving honor or respect **3** : very old — **ven·er·a·bil·i·ty** \,ven-(ə-)rə-'bil-ət-ē\ *n* — **ven·er·a·bly** \'ven-ər(-ə)-blē, 'ven-rə-\ *adv*

ven·er·ate \'ven-ə-,rāt\ *vb* : to regard with reverence or with admiration and deference — **ven·er·a·tor** \-,rāt-ər\ *n*

ven·er·a·tion \,ven-ə-'rā-shən\ *n* **1 a** : the act of venerating **b** : the state of being venerated ⟨*veneration* of saints⟩ **2** : a feeling of reverence or deep respect : DEVOTION

ve·ne·re·al \və-'nir-ē-əl\ *adj* : of or relating to sexual intercourse or to diseases transmitted by it ⟨a *venereal* infection⟩

venereal disease *n* : a contagious disease (as syphilis) that is typically acquired in sexual intercourse

Ve·ne·tian \və-'nē-shən\ *adj* : of, relating to, or characteristic of Venice or its people — **Venetian** *n*

ve·ne·tian blind \və-,nē-shən-\ *n* : a blind having thin horizontal slats that can be set to overlap to keep out light or tipped to let light come in

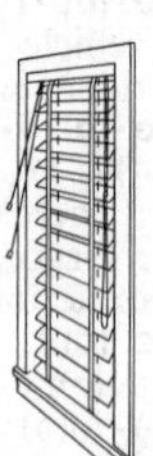

venetian blind

Ven·e·zu·e·lan \,ven-ə-zə-'wā-lən\ *adj* : of, relating to, or characteristic of Venezuela or its people — **Venezuelan** *n*

ven·geance \'ven-jən(t)s\ *n* : punishment inflicted in return for an injury or offense

venge·ful \'venj-fəl\ *adj* : filled with a desire for revenge — **venge·ful·ly** \-fə-lē\ *adv* — **venge·ful·ness** *n*

ve·ni·al \'vē-nē-əl\ *adj* : not being a great offense : FORGIVABLE, EXCUSABLE ⟨a *venial* sin⟩

ve·ni·re \və-'nī(ə)r-ē, -'ni(ə)r-\ *n* : a writ summoning persons to serve as jurors

ve·ni·re·man \-mən\ *n* : a juror summoned by a venire

ə abut	ər further	a back	ā bake	
ä cot, cart	aů out	ch chin	e less	ē easy
g gift	i trip	ī life	j joke	ng sing	ō flow
ȯ flaw	ȯi coin	th thin	th this	ü loot
ů foot	y yet	yü few	yů furious	zh vision

ven·i·son \'ven-ə-sən, -ə-zən\ *n, pl* **venisons** *also* **venison** : the flesh of a deer

Venn diagram \'ven-\ *n* : a diagram using circles or ellipses to represent relations between and operations on sets

ven·om \'ven-əm\ *n* **1** : poison secreted by an animal (as a snake, scorpion, or bee) and transmitted usu. by biting or stinging **2** : MALICE, SPITE

ven·om·ous \'ven-ə-məs\ *adj* **1** : filled with venom : POISONOUS **2** : SPITEFUL, MALIGNANT ⟨*venomous* words⟩ **3** : secreting and using venom ⟨*venomous* snakes⟩ — **ven·om·ous·ly** *adv* — **ven·om·ous·ness** *n*

ve·nous \'vē-nəs\ *adj* : of, relating to, or full of veins ⟨a *venous* rock⟩ ⟨a *venous* system⟩ — **ve·nous·ly** *adv*

1**vent** \'vent\ *vb* **1 a** : to provide with an outlet **b** : to serve as an outlet for ⟨chimneys *vent* smoke⟩ **c** : to let out at a vent **2** : to give expression to ⟨*vented* his anger⟩

2**vent** *n* : OUTLET; *esp* : an opening (as the anus or a flue) for the escape of a gas or liquid or for the relief of pressure

3**vent** *n* : a slit in a garment and esp. in the lower part of a seam

ven·ti·late \'vent-ə-,lāt\ *vb* **1** : to discuss freely and openly : make public ⟨*ventilate* a complaint⟩ **2 a** : to expose to air and esp. to a current of fresh air **b** : to provide with ventilation ⟨*ventilated* by powerful fans⟩

ven·ti·la·tion \,vent-ə-'lā-shən\ *n* **1** : the act or process of ventilating **2** : circulation of air ⟨a room with good *ventilation*⟩ **3** : a system or means of providing fresh air

ven·ti·la·tor \'vent-ə-,lāt-ər\ *n* : one that ventilates; *esp* : a contrivance for introducing fresh air or expelling foul or stagnant air

ventilator

ven·tral \'ven-trəl\ *adj* **1** : of or relating to the belly : ABDOMINAL **2** : of or relating to or located on or near the surface of the body that in man is the front but in most other animals is the lower surface ⟨a fish's *ventral* fins⟩ — **ven·tral·ly** \-trə-lē\ *adv*

ven·tri·cle \'ven-tri-kəl\ *n* **1** : a chamber of the heart which receives blood from a corresponding atrium and from which blood is forced into the arteries **2** : one of the communicating cavities in the brain that are continuous with the central canal of the spinal cord

ven·tric·u·lar \ven-'trik-yə-lər\ *adj* : of, relating to, or being a ventricle or a digestive cavity

ven·tril·o·quism \ven-'tril-ə-,kwiz-əm\ *n* [from Latin *ventriloquus* "ventriloquist", from *venter* "belly" and *loqui* "to speak"; so called from the belief that the voice is produced from the ventriloquist's stomach] : the production of the voice in such a manner that the sound appears to come from a source other than the vocal organs of the speaker — **ven·tril·o·quist** \-kwəst\ *n*

1**ven·ture** \'ven-chər\ *vb* **ven·tured**; **ven·tur·ing** \'vench-(ə-)ring\ **1** : to expose to hazard : RISK ⟨*ventured* more than he could afford⟩ **2** : to face the risks and dangers of : BRAVE ⟨*venture* the storm⟩ **3** : to offer at the risk of rebuff or censure ⟨*venture* an opinion⟩ ⟨*venture* to disagree⟩ **4** : to proceed despite danger : DARE — **ven·tur·er** \'vench-ər-ər\ *n*

2**venture** *n* : an undertaking involving chance, risk, or danger; *esp* : a speculative business enterprise

ven·ture·some \'ven-chər-səm\ *adj* **1** : disposed to

take risks : DARING **2** : RISKY, DANGEROUS ***syn*** see ADVENTUROUS ***ant*** circumspect — **ven·ture·some·ness** *n*

ven·tur·ous \'vench-(ə-)rəs\ *adj* : VENTURESOME

ven·ue \'ven-yü\ *n* **1** : the place in which the events leading to a legal action took place **2** : the place in which a trial is held

ven·ule \'ven-yül\ *n* : a small vein; *esp* : one of the minute veins connecting blood capillaries with larger veins

Ve·nus \'vē-nəs\ *n* — see PLANET table

Venus flower basket *or* **Ve·nus's–flower–basket** \ˌvē-nə-səz-\ *n* : a tubular or cornucopia-shaped sponge with a delicate glassy silica-containing skeleton

Ve·nu·sian \vi-'n(y)ü-zhən\ *adj* : of or relating to the planet Venus

Ve·nus's–fly·trap \ˌvē-nə-səz-'flī-ˌtrap\ *n* : an insect-eating plant that grows along the Carolina coast and has the leaf apex modified into an insect trap

Venus's-flytrap (up to one ft. high)

ve·ra·cious \və-'rā-shəs\ *adj* **1** : TRUTHFUL, HONEST **2** : ACCURATE, TRUE — **ve·ra·cious·ly** *adv*

ve·rac·i·ty \və-'ras-ət-ē\ *n, pl* **-ties** **1** : TRUTHFULNESS **2** : ACCURACY, CORRECTNESS

ve·ran·da *or* **ve·ran·dah** \və-'ran-də\ *n* **1** : PORCH **2** : a long roofed gallery extending along one or more sides of a building

verb \'vərb\ *n* : a word that is usu. the grammatical center of a predicate and expresses an act, occurrence, or mode of being and that in various languages is inflected (as for agreement with the subject or for tense)

[1]**ver·bal** \'vər-bəl\ *adj* **1** : of, relating to, or consisting of words **2** : of, relating to, or formed from a verb ⟨a *verbal* adjective⟩ **3** : spoken rather than written ⟨a *verbal* contract⟩ **4** : VERBATIM ***syn*** see ORAL — **ver·bal·ly** \-bə-lē\ *adv*

[2]**verbal** *n* : a word that combines characteristics of a verb with those of a noun or adjective

ver·bal·ize \'vər-bə-ˌlīz\ *vb* : to express in words

verbal noun *n* : a noun derived directly from a verb or verb stem and in some uses having the meaning and constructions of a verb

ver·ba·tim \(ˌ)vər-'bāt-əm\ *adv or adj* : in the same words : word for word : LITERAL ⟨a *verbatim* translation⟩

ver·be·na \(ˌ)vər-'bē-nə\ *n* : any of numerous plants often grown in gardens for their showy spikes of white, pink, red, or blue flowers

verbena

ver·bi·age \'vər-bē-ij\ *n* **1** : excess of words in proportion to meaning or content : WORDINESS **2** : DICTION, WORDING ⟨concise military *verbiage*⟩

ver·bose \(ˌ)vər-'bōs\ *adj* : using more words than are needed — **ver·bose·ly** *adv* — **ver·bose·ness** *n* — **ver·bos·i·ty** \-'bäs-ət-ē\ *n*

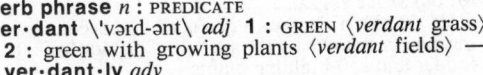

verb phrase *n* : PREDICATE

ver·dant \'vərd-ənt\ *adj* **1** : GREEN ⟨*verdant* grass⟩ **2** : green with growing plants ⟨*verdant* fields⟩ — **ver·dant·ly** *adv*

ver·dict \'vər-(ˌ)dikt\ *n* **1** : the decision of a jury on the matter submitted to them in trial **2** : OPINION, JUDGMENT

ver·di·gris \'vərd-ə-ˌgrēs, -ˌgris\ *n* : a green or greenish blue poisonous pigment produced by the action of acetic acid on copper or found on brass surfaces exposed to weather

ver·dure \'vər-jər\ *n* **1** : the greenness of growing vegetation **2** : green vegetation

[1]**verge** \'vərj\ *n* **1** : a staff carried as an emblem of authority or office **2 a** : something that borders, limits, or bounds : EDGE, BOUNDARY ⟨the *verge* of the sea⟩ **b** : BRINK, THRESHOLD ⟨on the *verge* of bankruptcy⟩

[2]**verge** *vb* **1** : to border on : TOUCH **2** : to be on the verge ⟨conduct that *verges* on treason⟩

[3]**verge** *vb* **1** : to move or extend in some direction or toward some condition : INCLINE **2** : to be in transition or change

verg·er \'vər-jər\ *n* **1** *chiefly Brit* : an attendant that carries a verge (as before a bishop or justice) **2** : a minor church official

ver·i·fi·a·ble \'ver-ə-ˌfī-ə-bəl\ *adj* : capable of being verified — **ver·i·fi·a·bly** \-blē\ *adv*

ver·i·fy \'ver-ə-ˌfī\ *vb* **-fied**; **-fy·ing** **1** : to prove to be true or correct : CONFIRM **2** : to check or test the accuracy of — **ver·i·fi·ca·tion** \ˌver-ə-fə-'kā-shən\ *n* — **ver·i·fi·er** \'ver-ə-ˌfī(-ə)r\ *n*

ver·i·ly \'ver-ə-lē\ *adv* : in fact : CERTAINLY

ver·i·ta·ble \'ver-ət-ə-bəl\ *adj* : ACTUAL, TRUE — **ver·i·ta·bly** \-blē\ *adv*

ver·i·ty \'ver-ət-ē\ *n, pl* **-ties** **1** : the quality or state of being true or real : TRUTH, REALITY **2** : a true fact or statement **3** : HONESTY, VERACITY

ver·mi·cel·li \ˌvər-mə-'chel-ē, -'sel-\ *n* : a food like spaghetti but of smaller diameter

ver·mic·u·lite \(ˌ)vər-'mik-yə-ˌlīt\ *n* : any of numerous minerals that are usu. altered micas whose granules expand greatly at high temperatures to give a lightweight absorbent heat-resistant material used esp. in seedbeds and as insulation

ver·mi·form appendix \'vər-mə-ˌfȯrm-\ *n* : the intestinal appendix

ver·mil·ion *or* **ver·mil·lion** \vər-'mil-yən\ *n* **1** : a bright red pigment; *esp* : one that is a sulfide of mercury **2** : a vivid reddish orange

ver·min \'vər-mən\ *n, pl* **vermin** : small common harmful animals (as fleas or mice) that are difficult to control

ver·mouth \vər-'müth\ *n* : a white wine flavored with aromatic herbs

[1]**ver·nac·u·lar** \və(r)-'nak-yə-lər\ *adj* **1** : using, being, or relating to a native language or dialect rather than a literary, cultured, or foreign language **2** : of, relating to, or used in the normal spoken form of a language : not literary or learned

[2]**vernacular** *n* **1** : a vernacular language **2** : the mode of expression of a group or class **3** : a common name of a plant or animal as distinguished from the taxonomic name

ver·nal \'vərn-əl\ *adj* **1** : of, relating to, or occurring in the spring ⟨the *vernal* equinox⟩ ⟨*vernal* sunshine⟩ **2** : fresh or new like the spring : YOUTHFUL

ver·ni·er \'vər-nē-ər\ *n* : a short scale made to slide along the divisions of a graduated instrument for indicating parts of divisions

ve·ron·i·ca \və-'rän-i-kə\ *n* : SPEEDWELL

ver·sa·tile \'vər-sət-əl\ *adj* : able to do many different kinds of things ⟨a *versatile* musician⟩ — **ver·sa·til·i·ty** \ˌver-sə-'til-ət-ē\ *n*

verse \'vərs\ *n* [from Latin *versus*, literally "turning", then "row", "verse", from the turning of the plow in making rows of furrows; compare PROSE] **1** : a line of metrical writing **2 a** : light or inferior poetry **b** : POETRY ⟨Elizabethan *verse*⟩ **c** : POEM ⟨read the group some of her *verses*⟩ **3** : STANZA **4** : one of the short divisions into which a chapter of the Bible is traditionally divided

versed \'vərst\ *adj* : made familiar by study or experience : SKILLED ⟨*versed* in science⟩

ver·si·fi·ca·tion \ˌvər-sə-fə-'kā-shən\ *n* **1** : the making of verses **2** : metrical arrangement of poetry : PROSODY

ver·si·fy \'vər-sə-ˌfī\ *vb* **-fied**; **-fy·ing** : to compose or turn into verse — **ver·si·fi·er** \-ˌfī(-ə)r\ *n*

ver·sion \'vər-zhən\ *n* **1** : a translation esp. of the Bible ⟨the Douay *version*⟩ ⟨the King James *version*⟩ **2** : an account or description from one point of view esp. as contrasted with another ⟨her *version* of what happened⟩ **3** : a form or variation of another thing ⟨a stage *version* of the novel⟩

ver·sus \'vər-səs, -səz\ *prep* : AGAINST ⟨John Doe *versus* Richard Roe⟩

vert *abbr* vertical

ver·te·bra \'vərt-ə-brə\ *n, pl* **-brae** \-(ˌ)brē, -ˌbrā\ *or* **-bras** : one of the bony or cartilaginous segments composing the spinal column

ver·te·bral \'vərt-ə-brəl, (ˌ)vər-'tē-brəl\ *adj* : of, relating to, or made up of vertebrae : SPINAL — **ver·te·bral·ly** \-brə-lē\ *adv*

vertebral column *n* : SPINAL COLUMN

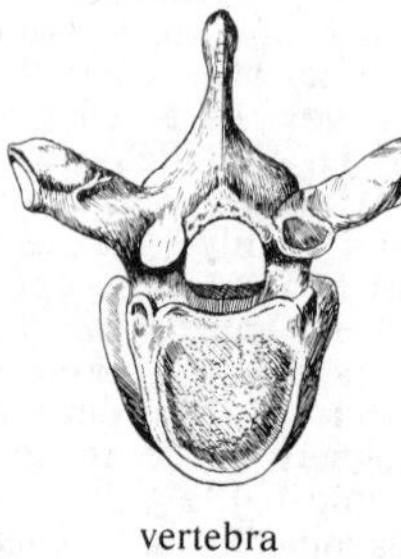

vertebra

1ver·te·brate \'vərt-ə-brət, -ˌbrāt\ *adj* **1** : having a spinal column **2** : of or relating to the vertebrates

2vertebrate *n* : any of a group of chordate animals with a segmented spinal column (as in mammals, birds, reptiles, amphibians, and fishes) or a notochord (as in the lamprey) persisting in the adult and with a tubular nervous system arranged along the back and divided into a brain and spinal cord

ver·tex \'vər-ˌteks\ *n, pl* **ver·ti·ces** \'vərt-ə-ˌsēz\ *also* **ver·tex·es** **1 a** : the point opposite to and farthest from the base in a figure **b** : the common endpoint of the sides of an angle **2** : ZENITH 1 **3** : the highest point : SUMMIT, APEX

1ver·ti·cal \'vərt-i-kəl\ *adj* **1** : directly overhead **2** : perpendicular to the plane of the horizon : UPRIGHT — **ver·ti·cal·ly** \-k(ə-)lē\ *adv*

2vertical *n* **1** : something (as a line or plane) that is vertical **2** : a vertical direction

vertical angle *n* : one of two angles that have the same vertex and are on opposite sides of two intersecting straight lines

vertical file *n* : a collection esp. of pamphlets maintained (as in a library) for reference

ver·ti·go \'vərt-i-ˌgō\ *n, pl* **vertigoes** *or* **ver·tig·i·nes** \(ˌ)vər-'tij-ə-ˌnēz\ : DIZZINESS, GIDDINESS

verve \'vərv\ *n* **1** : spirited enthusiasm : LIVELINESS, VIVACITY **2** : ENERGY, VITALITY

ə abut	ər further	a back	ā bake
ä cot, cart	au̇ out	ch chin	e less	ē easy
g gift	i trip	ī life	j joke	ng sing	ō flow
ȯ flaw	ȯi coin	th thin	t͟h this	ü loot
u̇ foot	y yet	yü few	yu̇ furious	zh vision

1very \'ver-ē\ *adj* **ver·i·er**; **-est** [from Middle English *verray*, literally "truly", from *verray* "true", from Old French *verai*, from Latin *verac-*, stem of *verax* "truthful", the source of English *veracious*] **1 a** : EXACT, PRECISE ⟨*very* heart of the city⟩ **b** : exactly suitable or necessary ⟨the *very* thing for the purpose⟩ **2** : ABSOLUTE, UTTER ⟨the *veriest* fool alive⟩ **3** : MERE, BARE ⟨the *very* thought terrified him⟩ **4** : SELFSAME, IDENTICAL ⟨the *very* man I saw⟩ **5** — used as an intensive ⟨the *very* dogs refused the food⟩

2very *adv* **1** : to a high degree : EXCEEDINGLY ⟨a *very* hot day⟩ **2** : in actual fact : TRULY ⟨told the *very* same story⟩

very high frequency *n* : a radio frequency in the range between 30 and 300 megacycles — abbr. *vhf*

ves·i·cle \'ves-i-kəl\ *n* **1** : a small cavity, cyst, or blister usu. filled with fluid **2** : a small cavity esp. in mineral or rock

1ves·per \'ves-pər\ *n* **1** *cap* : EVENING STAR **2** : a vesper bell **3** *archaic* : EVENING

2vesper *adj* : of or relating to vespers or the evening

ves·pers \'ves-pərz\ *n pl, often cap* : a late afternoon or evening worship service

ves·sel \'ves-əl\ *n* **1** : a hollow utensil (as a hogshead, bottle, kettle, cup, or bowl) for holding something **2** : a water craft bigger than a rowboat; *esp* : SHIP **3** : a tube or canal (as a vein or artery) in which a body fluid is contained and conveyed or circulated

1vest \'vest\ *vb* **1 a** : to give a right, authority, or title to some person or body ⟨powers *vested* in the presidency⟩ **b** : to become legally vested ⟨title *vests* in the purchaser⟩ **2 a** : CLOTHE; *esp* : to clothe in vestments **b** : to put on vestments

2vest *n* **1 a** : a man's sleeveless garment worn esp. under a coat **b** : a similar garment for women **2** : a protective garment worn on active military duty or in or on the water **3** : a knitted undershirt for women

ves·tal \'ves-təl\ *n* **1** : a virgin consecrated to the Roman goddess Vesta and to keeping the sacred fire burning on her altar — called also *vestal virgin* **2** : a chaste woman — **vestal** *adj*

vest·ee \ve-'stē\ *n* **1** : DICKEY **2** : VEST 1b

ves·ti·bule \'ves-tə-ˌbyül\ *n* **1** : a passage or room between the outer door and the interior of a building : LOBBY **2** : an enclosed entrance at the end of a railway passenger car — **ves·tib·u·lar** \ve-'stib-yə-lər\ *adj*

ves·tige \'ves-tij\ *n* **1** : a visible sign or trace left by something vanished or lost **2** : a small and imperfectly developed bodily part or organ that remains from one more fully developed in an earlier stage of the individual, in a past generation, or in closely related forms — **ves·ti·gial** \ve-'stij-(ē-)əl\ *adj* — **ves·ti·gial·ly** \-ē\ *adv*

vest·ment \'ves(t)-mənt\ *n* : GARMENT; *esp* : a ceremonial garment worn by a person officiating at a religious service

ves·try \'ves-trē\ *n, pl* **vestries** **1 a** : a room in a church building for sacred furnishings (as vestments) **b** : a room used for church meetings and classes **2** : an elective body administering the business affairs of an Episcopal parish

ves·try·man \-mən\ *n* : a member of a vestry

ves·ture \'ves-chər\ *n* : CLOTHING, APPAREL

1vet \'vet\ *n* : VETERINARIAN, VETERINARY

2vet *adj or n* : VETERAN

vetch \'vech\ *n* : any of a genus of herbaceous twining plants related to the pea that include valuable fodder and soil-building plants

vet·er·an \'vet-ə-rən, 've-trən\ *n* **1** : a person who has had long experience in something and esp. in war **2** : a former member of the armed forces — **veteran** *adj*

Veterans Day *n* : a day set aside in commemoration of the end of hostilities in 1918 and 1945: **a** : November 11 formerly observed as a legal holiday in the U.S. **b** : the fourth Monday in October observed as a legal holiday in the U.S. **c** : November 11 observed as a legal holiday in Canada

vet·er·i·nar·i·an \ˌvet-(ə-)rən-'er-ē-ən, ˌve-trən-\ *n* : one qualified and authorized to treat diseases and injuries of animals

1**vet·er·i·nary** \'vet-(ə-)rən-ˌer-ē, 've-trən-\ *adj* : of, relating to, or being the medical care of animals ⟨*veterinary* medicine⟩

2**veterinary** *n, pl* **-naries** : VETERINARIAN

1**ve·to** \'vēt-ō\ *n, pl* **vetoes** [from Latin, a verb form meaning "I forbid"] **1** : an authoritative prohibition **2 a** : a power of one branch of a government to forbid something attempted by another; *esp* : the power of a chief executive to prevent a measure passed by a legislature from becoming law **b** : the exercise of such authority **c** : a power possessed by members of some bodies (as the U. N. Security Council) to prohibit action by the body

2**veto** *vb* : PROHIBIT; *esp* : to use one's power of veto — **ve·to·er** *n*

vex \'veks\ *vb* **vexed** *also* **vext**; **vex·ing** **1 a** : to bring trouble, distress, or agitation to **b** : ANNOY, HARASS **2** : to debate or discuss at length ⟨a *vexed* question⟩

vex·a·tion \vek-'sā-shən\ *n* **1** : the quality or state of being vexed : IRRITATION **2** : the act of vexing : ANNOYANCE **3** : a source of trouble or worry

vex·a·tious \-shəs\ *adj* : causing vexation : ANNOYING, DISTRESSING — **vex·a·tious·ly** *adv* — **vex·a·tious·ness** *n*

VFD *abbr* volunteer fire department

VFW *abbr* Veterans of Foreign Wars

VHF *abbr* very high frequency

vi *abbr* verb intransitive

VI *abbr* Virgin Islands

via \ˌvī-ə, ˌvē-ə\ *prep* : by way of ⟨go *via* the northern route⟩

vi·a·ble \'vī-ə-bəl\ *adj* **1** : capable of living **2** : capable of growing or developing ⟨*viable* seeds⟩ ⟨*viable* eggs⟩ **3** : capable of being put into practice : WORKABLE ⟨seeking a *viable* solution to the problem⟩ — **vi·a·bil·i·ty** \ˌvī-ə-'bil-ət-ē\ *n*

vi·a·duct \'vī-ə-ˌdəkt\ *n* : a bridge with high supporting towers or piers for carrying a road or railroad over something (as a gorge or a highway)

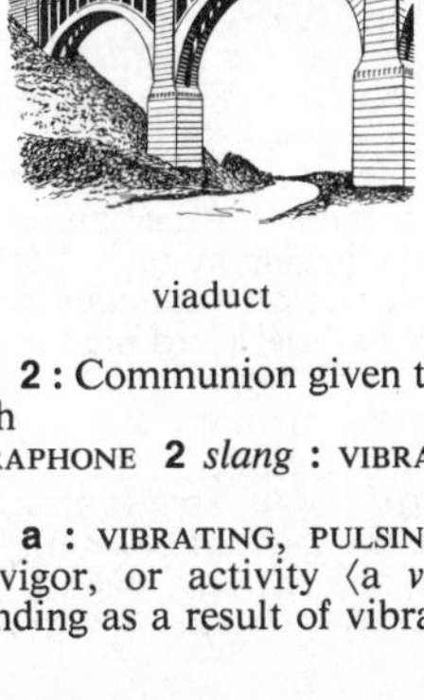

viaduct

vi·al \'vī(-ə)l\ *n* : a small vessel (as for medicines or chemicals)

vi·and \'vī-ənd\ *n* **1** : an article of food **2** *pl* : PROVISIONS, FOOD

vi·at·i·cum \vī-'at-i-kəm, vē-\ *n, pl* **-cums** *or* **-ca** \-kə\ **1** : money or provisions for a journey **2** : Communion given to a person in danger of death

vibes \'vībz\ *n pl* **1** : VIBRAPHONE **2** *slang* : VIBRATIONS

vi·brant \'vī-brənt\ *adj* **1 a** : VIBRATING, PULSING **b** : pulsating with life, vigor, or activity ⟨a *vibrant* personality⟩ **2** : sounding as a result of vibration : RESONANT — **vi·bran·cy** \-brən-sē\ *n* — **vi·brant·ly** *adv*

vi·bra·phone \'vī-brə-ˌfōn\ *n* : a percussion instrument resembling the xylophone but having metal bars and motor-driven resonators for sustaining the tone and producing a vibrato — **vi·bra·phon·ist** \-ˌfō-nəst\ *n*

vibraphone

vi·brate \'vī-ˌbrāt\ *vb* **1** : to swing or move back and forth ⟨a *vibrating* pendulum⟩ **2** : to set in vibration **3** : to produce a quivering effect or sound ⟨mandolin strings *vibrate* when plucked⟩ **4** : THRILL ⟨hearts *vibrating* with joy⟩ **5** : FLUCTUATE ⟨*vibrating* between two choices⟩

vi·bra·tion \vī-'brā-shən\ *n* **1 a** : the action of vibrating : motion or a movement to and fro : OSCILLATION ⟨the *vibration* of a pendulum⟩ **b** : the state of being vibrated **2** : a periodic motion of the particles of an elastic body or medium rapidly to and fro (as when a stretched cord is pulled or struck and produces a musical tone or when particles of air transmit sounds to the ear) **3** : a quivering or trembling motion ⟨*vibration* of a house caused by a passing truck⟩ **4** *pl* : a distinctive usu. emotional atmosphere capable of being sensed : a feeling or impression that someone or something gives off ⟨good *vibrations*⟩ — **vi·bra·tion·al** \-sh(ə-)nəl\ *adj*

vi·bra·to \vē-'brät-ō\ *n, pl* **-tos** : a slightly trembling effect given to vocal or instrumental tone by slight and rapid variations in pitch

vi·bra·tor \'vī-ˌbrāt-ər\ *n* **1** : one that vibrates or causes vibration **2** : an electromagnetic device that converts low direct current to pulsating direct current or alternating current

vi·bra·to·ry \'vī-brə-ˌtōr-ē, -ˌtȯr-\ *adj* : consisting in, capable of, or causing vibration

vi·bur·num \vī-'bər-nəm\ *n* : any of a genus of widely distributed shrubs or trees with simple leaves and white or rarely pink flowers in broad clusters

vic·ar \'vik-ər\ *n* **1** : AGENT; *esp* : an administrative deputy **2** : an Episcopal clergyman having charge of a dependent parish — **vic·ar·ship** \-ˌship\ *n*

vic·ar·age \'vik-ə-rij\ *n* : a vicar's residence

vi·car·i·ous \vī-'ker-ē-əs, -'kar-\ *adj* **1** : serving or acting for another **2** : done or suffered for the benefit of someone else ⟨*vicarious* sacrifice⟩ **3** : experienced through sympathetic sharing in the experience of another ⟨took *vicarious* pleasure in his son's victory⟩ — **vi·car·i·ous·ly** *adv* — **vi·car·i·ous·ness** *n*

vice \'vīs\ *n* **1 a** : moral depravity or corruption : WICKEDNESS **b** : a moral fault or failing **2** : BLEMISH, DEFECT **3** : an undesirable behavior pattern in a domestic animal

vice- \(ˈ)vīs, ˌvīs\ *prefix* : one that takes the place of ⟨*vice*-consul⟩

vice admiral *n* : a commissioned officer in the navy ranking just below an admiral

vi·cen·ni·al \vī-'sen-ē-əl\ *adj* : occurring once every 20 years

vice–pres·i·dent \'vīs-'prez-əd-ənt, -'prez-dənt, -ə-ˌdent\ *n* : an official (as of a government) whose rank is next below that of the president and who takes the place of the president when necessary — **vice–pres·i·den·cy** \-'prez-əd-ən-sē, -'prez-dən-sē, -ə-ˌden-sē\ *n*

vice·re·gal \-'rē-gəl\ *adj* : of or relating to a viceroy or viceroyalty — **vice·re·gal·ly** \-gə-lē\ *adv*

vice·roy \'vīs-ˌrȯi\ *n* **1** : the governor of a country or province who represents his sovereign **2** : a showy American butterfly resembling but smaller than the monarch — **vice·roy·ship** \-ˌship\ *n*

viceroy 2
(up to 3 in. across)

vice·roy·al·ty \ˈvīs-ˌrȯi(-ə)l-tē\ *n* : the office, jurisdiction, or term of service of a viceroy

vi·ce ver·sa \ˌvī-si-ˈvər-sə, (ˈ)vīs-ˈvər-\ *adv* : with the order reversed : CONVERSELY

vic·i·nage \ˈvis-ə-nij\ *n* : NEIGHBORHOOD, VICINITY

vi·cin·i·ty \və-ˈsin-ət-ē\ *n, pl* **-ties 1** : the quality or state of being near : PROXIMITY **2** : a surrounding area or district

vi·cious \ˈvish-əs\ *adj* **1 a** : given to vice : WICKED **b** : of the nature of vice : IMMORAL ⟨*vicious* conduct⟩ **2** : DEFECTIVE, FAULTY **3** : dangerously aggressive ⟨a *vicious* dog⟩ **4** : MALICIOUS, SPITEFUL ⟨*vicious* slander⟩ — **vi·cious·ly** *adv* — **vi·cious·ness** *n*

vicious circle *n* : a situation or condition that endlessly repeats itself (as when a cause produces an effect which in turn produces the original cause)

vi·cis·si·tude \və-ˈsis-ə-ˌt(y)üd, vī-\ *n* : a change from one thing to another; *esp* : an irregular, unexpected, or surprising change ⟨the *vicissitudes* of the weather⟩

vic·tim \ˈvik-təm\ *n* **1** : a living being offered as a sacrifice in a religious rite **2** : an individual injured or killed (as by disease or accident) **3** : a person cheated, fooled, or damaged by someone else or by some impersonal force ⟨a *victim* of the system⟩

vic·tim·ize \ˈvik-tə-ˌmīz\ *vb* : to make a victim of esp. by deception : CHEAT — **vic·tim·i·za·tion** \ˌvik-tə-mə-ˈzā-shən\ *n* — **vic·tim·iz·er** \ˈvik-tə-ˌmī-zər\ *n*

vic·tor \ˈvik-tər\ *n* : one that defeats an enemy or opponent : WINNER

vic·to·ria \vik-ˈtōr-ē-ə, -ˈtȯr-\ *n* : a low four-wheeled carriage with a folding top and a raised seat in front for the driver

victoria

vic·to·ri·ous \vik-ˈtōr-ē-əs, -ˈtȯr-\ *adj* : having won a victory : CONQUERING ⟨a *victorious* army⟩ ⟨*victorious* strategy⟩ — **vic·to·ri·ous·ly** *adv* — **vic·to·ri·ous·ness** *n*

vic·to·ry \ˈvik-t(ə-)rē\ *n, pl* **-ries 1** : the overcoming of an enemy or opponent **2** : achievement of success in a struggle

[1]**vict·ual** \ˈvit-əl\ *n* **1** : food usable by man **2** *pl* : supplies of food : PROVISIONS

[2]**victual** *vb* **-ualed** *or* **-ualled**; **-ual·ing** *or* **-ual·ling 1** : to supply with food **2** : to lay in provisions

vict·ual·ler *or* **vict·ual·er** \ˈvit-ə-lər\ *n* : one that furnishes provisions (as to an army or a ship)

ə abut	ər further	a back	ā bake	
ä cot, cart	aù out	ch chin	e less	ē easy
g gift	i trip	ī life	j joke	ng sing
ō flow	ȯ flaw	ȯi coin	th thin	th this
ü loot	ù foot	y yet	yü few	yù furious
zh vision				

vi·cu·ña *or* **vi·cu·na** \vī-ˈk(y)ü-nə, vi-ˈkün-yə\ *n* **1** : a wild cud-chewing animal of the Andes that is related to the domesticated llama and alpaca **2 a** : the wool from the vicuña's fine lustrous undercoat **b** : a fabric made of vicuña wool

vicuña 1
(about 2½ ft. at shoulder)

[1]**vid·eo** \ˈvid-ē-ˌō\ *adj* : relating to or used in the transmission or reception of the television image ⟨*video* channel⟩

[2]**video** *n* : TELEVISION

vid·eo·tape \ˈvid-ē-ō-ˌtāp\ *vb* : to make a recording on magnetic tape of a television program — **videotape** *n*

vie \ˈvī\ *vb* **vied**; **vy·ing** \ˈvī-ing\ : to strive for superiority : CONTEND — **vi·er** \ˈvī(-ə)r\ *n*

Vi·en·nese \ˌvē-ə-ˈnēz, -ˈnēs\ *adj* : of, relating to, or characteristic of Vienna or its people — **Viennese** *n*

Viet·cong \vē-ˈet-ˈkäng, -ˈkȯng\ *n, pl* **Vietcong** : an adherent of the Vietnamese communist movement supported by North Vietnam and engaged esp. in guerrilla warfare in South Vietnam

Viet·nam·ese \vē-ˌet-nə-ˈmēz, -ˈmēs\ *n, pl* **Vietnamese 1** : a native or inhabitant of Vietnam **2** : the official language of Vietnam — **Vietnamese** *adj*

[1]**view** \ˈvyü\ *n* **1 a** : the act of seeing or examining : INSPECTION **b** : SURVEY **2** : OPINION, JUDGMENT ⟨state his *views*⟩ **3** : SCENE, PROSPECT **4** : extent or range of vision : SIGHT ⟨the planes passed out of *view*⟩ **5** : AIM, INTENTION ⟨studied hard with a *view* to winning honors⟩ **6** : a pictorial representation : SKETCH — **in view of** : in regard to : in consideration of

[2]**view** *vb* **1** : SEE, BEHOLD **2** : to look at attentively : SCRUTINIZE **3** : to survey or examine mentally : CONSIDER ⟨*view* all sides of a question⟩

view·er \-ər\ *n* : one that views; *esp* : an optical device used in viewing

view·point \ˈvyü-ˌpȯint\ *n* : POINT OF VIEW

vig·il \ˈvij-əl\ *n* **1 a** : the day before a religious feast **b** : prayers or devotional services held in the evening or at night — usu. used in pl. **2 a** : the act of keeping awake when sleep is customary **b** : a period of wakefulness **3** : an act of guarding : WATCH ⟨the soldiers kept *vigil* all night⟩

vig·i·lant \ˈvij-ə-lənt\ *adj* : alertly watchful esp. to avoid danger — **vig·i·lance** \-lən(t)s\ *n* — **vig·i·lant·ly** *adv*

vig·i·lan·te \ˌvij-ə-ˈlant-ē\ *n* : a member of a local volunteer committee organized to suppress and punish crime

vi·gnette \vin-ˈyet\ *n* **1** : a small decorative design or picture placed on or just before a title page or at the beginning or end of a chapter **2** : a picture that shades off gradually into the surrounding ground **3** : a brief word picture : SKETCH

vig·or \ˈvig-ər\ *n* **1** : active strength or energy of body or mind **2** : INTENSITY, FORCE ⟨trees growing with *vigor*⟩

vig·or·ous \ˈvig-(ə-)rəs\ *adj* **1** : having vigor : ROBUST ⟨*vigorous* youth⟩ ⟨a *vigorous* plant⟩ **2** : done with force and energy ⟨a *vigorous* protest⟩ — **vig·or·ous·ly** *adv* — **vig·or·ous·ness** *n*

Vi·king \'vī-king\ *n* : one of the pirate Northmen plundering the coasts of Europe in the 8th to 10th centuries

vil *abbr* village

vile \'vīl\ *adj* **1** : of little worth or account **2 a** : morally base : WICKED ⟨*vile* deeds⟩ **b** : physically repulsive : FOUL ⟨*vile* living quarters⟩ **3** : DISGUSTING, CONTEMPTIBLE ⟨a *vile* temper⟩ — **vile** *adv* — **vile·ly** \'vīl-lē\ *adv* — **vile·ness** *n*

vil·i·fy \'vil-ə-ˌfī\ *vb* **-fied**; **-fy·ing** : to utter slanderous and abusive statements against : DEFAME — **vil·i·fi·ca·tion** \ˌvil-ə-fə-'kā-shən\ *n* — **vil·i·fi·er** \'vil-ə-ˌfī(-ə)r\ *n*

vil·la \'vil-ə\ *n* **1** : a country estate **2** : the rural or suburban residence of a person of wealth

vil·lage \'vil-ij\ *n* **1** : a settlement usu. larger than a hamlet and smaller than a town **2** : the residents of a village

vil·lag·er \'vil-ij-ər\ *n* : an inhabitant of a village

vil·lain \'vil-ən\ *n* **1** : VILLEIN **2** : an evil person : SCOUNDREL — **vil·lain·ess** \'vil-ə-nəs\ *n*

vil·lain·ous \'vil-ə-nəs\ *adj* **1** : befitting a villain : DEPRAVED **2** : highly objectionable : WRETCHED — **vil·lain·ous·ly** *adv* — **vil·lain·ous·ness** *n*

vil·lainy \'vil-ə-nē\ *n, pl* **-lain·ies 1 a** : villainous conduct **b** : a villainous act **2** : villainous character : WICKEDNESS

vil·lein \'vil-ən, 'vil-ˌān, vil-'ān\ *n* **1** : a free peasant **2** : an unfree peasant having the status of a slave to his feudal lord but being free in his legal relations with others

vil·lous \'vil-əs\ *adj* : having soft long hairs ⟨leaves *villous* underneath⟩

vil·lus \'vil-əs\ *n, pl* **vil·li** \'vil-ˌī, -(ˌ)ē\ **1** : one of the tiny finger-shaped processes of the mucous membrane of the small intestine that function in the absorption of nourishment **2** : any of the fine straight soft hairs on plants

vim \'vim\ *n* : robust energy and enthusiasm : VITALITY

vin·cu·lum \'ving-kyə-ləm\ *n, pl* **-lums** *or* **-la** \-lə\ : a straight horizontal mark placed over two or more members of a compound mathematical expression as a symbol of grouping (as in $a - \overline{b - c} = a - [b - c]$)

vin·di·cate \'vin-də-ˌkāt\ *vb* **1 a** : EXONERATE, ABSOLVE **b** : CONFIRM, SUBSTANTIATE ⟨later discoveries *vindicated* his claim⟩ **c** : to provide defense for : JUSTIFY **2** : to maintain a right to : ASSERT — **vin·di·ca·tion** \ˌvin-də-'kā-shən\ *n* — **vin·di·ca·tor** \-ˌkāt-ər\ *n*

vin·dic·tive \vin-'dik-tiv\ *adj* : disposed to seek revenge : VENGEFUL — **vin·dic·tive·ly** *adv* — **vin·dic·tive·ness** *n*

vine \'vīn\ *n* **1** : GRAPE 2 **2 a** : a plant whose stem requires support and which climbs by tendrils or twining or creeps along the ground **b** : the stem of a vine

vin·e·gar \'vin-i-gər\ *n* [from Old French *vinaigre*, from *vin* "wine" (from Latin *vinum*) and *aigre* "sour", from Latin *acer* "sharp"] : a sour liquid obtained by fermentation of cider, wine, or malt and used to flavor or preserve foods

vinegar eel *n* : a tiny roundworm often found in vinegar or other fermenting vegetable substances

vin·e·gary \'vin-i-g(ə-)rē\ *adj* **1** : resembling vinegar : SOUR **2** : disagreeable or bitter in character or manner ⟨a *vinegary* remark⟩

vine·yard \'vin-yərd\ *n* : a field of grapevines

vin·tage \'vint-ij\ *n* **1 a** : the grapes or wine produced during one season **b** : WINE; *esp* : a wine of a particular type, region, and year and usu. of superior quality **2** : the act or time of gathering grapes or making wine **3** : a period of origin or manufacture ⟨songs of the *vintage* of 1890⟩ — **vintage** *adj*

vint·ner \'vint-nər\ *n* : a wine merchant

viny \'vī-nē\ *adj* **vin·i·er**; **-est 1** : of, relating to, or resembling vines ⟨*viny* plants⟩ **2** : covered with or abounding in vines ⟨*viny* hillsides⟩

vi·nyl resin \ˌvīn-əl-\ *n* : any of a group of elastic resins that are resistant to chemical agents and are used for protective coatings and molded articles — called also *vinyl plastic*

vi·ol \'vī(-ə)l\ *n* : a bowed stringed instrument like the violin usu. with six strings

1vi·o·la \vē-'ō-lə\ *n* : a stringed musical instrument like a violin but slightly larger and lower in pitch — **vi·o·list** \-ləst\ *n*

2vi·o·la \vī-'ō-lə, vē-\ *n* : VIOLET 1a; *esp* : any of various garden hybrids with solitary white, yellow, or purple often variegated flowers resembling but smaller than typical pansies

viola

vi·o·late \'vī-ə-ˌlāt\ *vb* **1** : to fail to keep : BREAK, DISREGARD ⟨*violate* the law⟩ **2** : to do harm esp. to the chastity of; *esp* : RAPE **3** : PROFANE, DESECRATE **4** : INTERRUPT, DISTURB — **vi·o·la·tion** \ˌvī-ə-'lā-shən\ *n* — **vi·o·la·tor** \'vī-ə-ˌlāt-ər\ *n*

vi·o·lence \'vī-ə-lən(t)s\ *n* **1 a** : the use of physical force in a way that harms a person or his property **b** : injury esp. to something that merits respect or reverence : OUTRAGE ⟨does *violence* to our principles⟩ **c** : alteration of the wording or sense of a text **2 a** : ENERGY; *esp* : destructive energy ⟨the *violence* of the storm⟩ **b** : ARDOR, PASSION ⟨denied the charge with *violence*⟩

vi·o·lent \-lənt\ *adj* **1** : marked by extreme force or sudden intense activity ⟨a *violent* attack⟩ **2 a** : notably furious or vehement ⟨a *violent* denunciation⟩ **b** : EXTREME, INTENSE ⟨*violent* pain⟩ **3** : caused by force ⟨a *violent* death⟩ — **vi·o·lent·ly** *adv*

vi·o·let \'vī-ə-lət\ *n* **1 a** : any of a genus of herbs or woody-stemmed plants with alternate leaves having stipules and with both aerial and underground flowers **b** : any of several plants of other genera — compare DOGTOOTH VIOLET **2** : a reddish blue

vi·o·lin \ˌvī-ə-'lin\ *n* **1** : a bowed stringed instrument with four strings that has a shallower body and a more curved bridge than a viola **2** : VIOLINIST

vi·o·lin·ist \-'lin-əst\ *n* : a violin player

vi·o·lon·cel·lo \ˌvī-ə-lən-'chel-ō, ˌvē-\ *n* : CELLO — **vi·o·lon·cel·list** \-'chel-əst\ *n*

VIP \ˌvē-ˌī-'pē\ *n* [from the abbreviation for *very important person*] : a person of great influence or prestige

vi·per *n* \'vī-pər\ *n* **1** : any of a family of sluggish heavy-bodied broad-headed Old World venomous snakes with hollow tubular fangs **2** : PIT VIPER **3** : any venomous or reputedly venomous snake — **vi·per·ine** \-pə-ˌrīn\ *adj*

vi·ra·go \və-'räg-ō, -'rāg-; 'vir-ə-ˌgō\ *n, pl* **-goes** *or* **-gos** : a scolding quarrelsome woman

vi·ral \'vī-rəl\ *adj* : of, relating to, or caused by a virus

vir·eo \'vir-ē-ˌō\ *n, pl* **-e·os** : any of a family of small insect-eating songbirds that are chiefly olive-green or grayish in color

1vir·gin \'vər-jən\ *n* **1** *cap* : VIRGIN MARY **2** : a girl or woman who has not had sexual intercourse — **vir·gin·al** \-əl\ *adj* — **vir·gin·al·ly** \-ə-lē\ *adv*

2virgin *adj* **1** : being a virgin : CHASTE, MODEST **2** : PURE, FRESH, UNSOILED ⟨*virgin* snow⟩; *esp* : not altered by human activity ⟨*virgin* soil⟩ **3** : being used or worked for the first time or produced by a simple extractive process ⟨*virgin* wool⟩ ⟨*virgin* oil⟩

vir·gin·al \'vər-jən-əl\ *n* : a small rectangular spinet having no legs

Vir·gin·ia creeper \vər-ˌjin-yə-\ *n* : a common No. American tendril-climbing vine related to the grapes and having leaves with five leaflets and bluish black berries — called also *woodbine*

Virginia deer *n* : WHITE-TAILED DEER

Virginia reel *n* : a country-dance in which all couples in turn participate in a series of figures

vir·gin·i·ty \(ˌ)vər-'jin-ət-ē\ *n, pl* **-ties** : the quality or state of being virgin : CHASTITY; *esp* : MAIDENHOOD

Virgin Mary *n* : the mother of Jesus

Vir·go \'vər-gō\ *n* — see ZODIAC table

vir·ile \'vir-əl\ *adj* **1** : having the nature, powers, or qualities of a man **2 a** : ENERGETIC, VIGOROUS **b** : MASTERFUL, FORCEFUL

vi·ril·i·ty \və-'ril-ət-ē\ *n* : the quality or state of being virile; *esp* : manly vigor : MASCULINITY

vi·rol·o·gist \vī-'räl-ə-jəst\ *n* : a specialist in the study of viruses

vir·tu·al \'vər-ch(ə-w)əl\ *adj* : being in effect but not in fact or name ⟨the *virtual* ruler of the country⟩ — **vir·tu·al·ly** \-ē\ *adv*

vir·tue \'vər-chü\ *n* **1** : moral action or excellence : MORALITY; *esp* : CHASTITY **2** : a particular moral excellence ⟨justice and charity are *virtues*⟩ **3 a** : an active beneficial power ⟨quinine has *virtue* in the treatment of malaria⟩ **b** : a desirable quality or trait ⟨the *virtues* of country life⟩ — **by virtue of** *or* **in virtue of** : through the force of : by authority of

vir·tu·os·i·ty \ˌvər-chə-'wäs-ət-ē\ *n, pl* **-ties** : great technical skill in the fine arts

vir·tu·o·so \ˌvər-chə-'wō-sō, -zō\ *n, pl* **-sos** *or* **-si** \-(ˌ)sē, -(ˌ)zē\ **1** : one skilled in or having a taste for the fine arts **2** : one who excels in the technique of an art; *esp* : a skilled instrumentalist — **virtuoso** *adj*

vir·tu·ous \'vər-chə-wəs\ *adj* : having moral virtue; *esp* : CHASTE — **vir·tu·ous·ly** *adv* — **vir·tu·ous·ness** *n*

vir·u·lent \'vir-(y)ə-lənt\ *adj* **1 a** : marked by a rapid, severe, and malignant course ⟨a *virulent* infection⟩ **b** : able to overcome or break down the defenses of the body ⟨a *virulent* pathogen⟩ **2** : extremely poisonous : NOXIOUS **3** : SPITEFUL, MALIGNANT — **vir·u·lence** \-lən(t)s\ *n* — **vir·u·lent·ly** *adv*

vi·rus \'vī-rəs\ *n* [from Latin, "slime", "liquid poison"] **1** : any of a large group of tiny disease-causing agents that are smaller than bacteria **2** : a disease caused by a virus

vis *abbr* visual

[1]**vi·sa** \'vē-zə\ *n* : an official endorsement on a passport denoting that it has been examined and that the bearer may proceed

[2]**visa** *vb* **vi·saed** \-zəd\; **vi·sa·ing** \-zə-ing\ : to give a visa to

vis·age \'viz-ij\ *n* : FACE

viscera *pl of* VISCUS

vis·cer·al \'vis-ə-rəl\ *adj* : of, relating to, or being the viscera — **vis·cer·al·ly** \-rə-lē\ *adv*

vis·cid \'vis-əd\ *adj* : STICKY, VISCOUS

ə abut	ər further	a back	ā bake
ä cot, cart	aů out	ch chin	e less	ē easy
g gift	i trip	ī life	j joke	ng sing	ō flow
ȯ flaw	ȯi coin	th thin	th this	ü loot
ů foot	y yet	yü few	yů furious	zh vision

vis·cose \'vis-ˌkōs\ *n* **1** : a viscous golden-brown solution used in making rayon **2** : viscose rayon — **viscose** *adj*

vis·cos·i·ty \vis-'käs-ət-ē\ *n, pl* **-ties** : the quality of being viscous; *esp* : a tendency of a liquid to flow slowly resulting from friction of its molecules

vis·count \'vī-ˌkaůnt\ *n* : a member of the British peerage ranking below an earl and above a baron — **vis·count·cy** \-sē\ *n* — **vis·count·ess** \-əs\ *n*

vis·cous \'vis-kəs\ *adj* **1** : somewhat sticky or glutinous **2** : having or characterized by viscosity

vis·cus \'vis-kəs\ *n, pl* **vis·cera** \'vis-ə-rə\ : an internal organ of the body; *esp* : one (as the heart, liver, or intestine) located in the great cavity of the trunk proper

vise \'vīs\ *n* : a tool with two jaws for holding work that operates usu. by a screw, lever, or cam

vise

vis·i·bil·i·ty \ˌviz-ə-'bil-ət-ē\ *n* **1** : the quality or state of being visible **2** : the degree of clearness of the atmosphere

vis·i·ble \'viz-ə-bəl\ *adj* **1** : capable of being seen ⟨stars *visible* to the naked eye⟩ **2** : APPARENT, DISCOVERABLE ⟨no *visible* means of support⟩ — **vis·i·bly** \-blē\ *adv*

[1]**vi·sion** \'vizh-ən\ *n* **1 a** : something seen in a dream, trance, or ecstasy **b** : an object of imagination **c** : APPARITION, GHOST **2 a** : the act or power of imagination **b** : unusual discernment or foresight **3 a** : the act or power of seeing : SIGHT **b** : the sense by which the appearances of an object (as color, luminosity, or shape and size) are perceived **4** : something seen; *esp* : a lovely or charming sight

[2]**vision** *vb* : IMAGINE, ENVISION

[1]**vi·sion·ary** \'vizh-ə-ˌner-ē\ *adj* **1** : given to dreaming or imagining **2** : resembling a vision esp. in fanciful or impractical quality ⟨*visionary* schemes⟩ — **vi·sion·ar·i·ness** *n*

[2]**visionary** *n, pl* **-ar·ies** **1** : a person who sees visions : SEER **2** : a person whose ideas or projects are impractical : DREAMER

[1]**vis·it** \'viz-ət\ *vb* **1** : to go to see in order to comfort or help **2 a** : to pay a call upon as an act of friendship or courtesy **b** : to go or come to see in an official or professional capacity **c** : to dwell with temporarily as a guest **3 a** : to come to as a reward, affliction, or punishment **b** : INFLICT **4** : to make a visit or frequent or regular visits **5** : CHAT, CONVERSE — **vis·i·tor** \-ət-ər\ *n*

[2]**visit** *n* **1** : a brief stay : CALL **2** : a stay as a guest or nonresident ⟨a weekend *visit*⟩ ⟨made a *visit* to the city⟩ **3** : an official or professional call

vis·it·a·ble \'viz-ət-ə-bəl\ *adj* **1** : subject to or allowing visitation or inspection **2** : socially eligible to receive visits

vis·i·tant \'viz-ət-ənt\ *n* **1** : one that visits; *esp* : a supernatural visitor **2** : a migratory bird that appears at intervals for a limited period

vis·i·ta·tion \ˌviz-ə-'tā-shən\ *n* **1** : VISIT; *esp* : an official visit **2 a** : an instance of divine favor or wrath **b** : a severe trial : AFFLICTION

vi·sor \'vī-zər\ *n* **1** : the front piece of a helmet; *esp* : a movable upper piece **2** : a projecting part (as on a cap) to protect or shade the eyes — **vi·sored** \-zərd\ *adj*

vis·ta \'vis-tə\ *n* **1** : a distant view through an opening or along an avenue : PROSPECT **2** : a mental view over a stretch of time

vi·su·al \'vizh-(ə-w)əl\ *adj* **1** : of, relating to, or used in vision ⟨*visual* organs⟩ **2** : attained or maintained by sight ⟨maintaining *visual* contact⟩ ⟨*visual* impressions⟩ **3** : VISIBLE — **vi·su·al·ly** \-ē\ *adv*

visual aid *n* : an instructional device (as a chart, map, or model) that appeals chiefly to vision; *esp* : an educational motion picture or filmstrip

visual area *n* : a sensory area of the cerebral cortex concerned with the sense of sight

vi·su·al·ize \'vizh-ə-(wə-),līz\ *vb* : to make visible; *esp* : to form a mental image of : ENVISAGE — **vi·su·al·i·za·tion** \,vizh-ə-(wə-)lə-'zā-shən\ *n* — **vi·su·al·iz·er** \'vizh-ə-(wə-),lī-zər\ *n*

visual purple *n* : a red or purple pigment in the retina of man and various other vertebrates that is sensitive to dim light and functions in night vision

vi·tal \'vīt-əl\ *adj* **1** : of, relating to, or characteristic of life ⟨*vital* activities⟩ **2** : concerned with or necessary to the maintenance of life ⟨*vital* organs⟩ **3** : full of vitality : ANIMATED **4** : FATAL, MORTAL **5** : of first importance : BASIC ⟨matters *vital* to national security⟩ — **vi·tal·ly** \-ə-lē\ *adv*

vital capacity *n* : the breathing capacity of the lungs expressed as the number of cubic inches or cubic centimeters of air that can be forcibly exhaled after a full inspiration

vi·tal·i·ty \vī-'tal-ət-ē\ *n, pl* **-ties** **1 a** : the property distinguishing the living from the nonliving : LIFE **b** : capacity to live and develop **2** : physical or mental vigor **3 a** : the power of enduring or continuing ⟨the *vitality* of bad habits⟩ **b** : lively and animated character

vi·tal·ize \'vīt-ə-,līz\ *vb* : to give vitality to : ANIMATE — **vi·tal·i·za·tion** \,vīt-ə-lə-'zā-shən\ *n*

vi·tals \'vīt-əlz\ *n pl* **1** : vital organs **2** : essential parts

vital statistics *n pl* : statistics relating to births, deaths, marriages, health, and disease

vi·ta·min \'vīt-ə-mən\ *n* : any of various organic substances that are essential in minute quantities to the nutrition of human beings and animals and some plants and are present in natural foodstuffs or sometimes produced within the body

vitamin A *n* : a vitamin or vitamin mixture found esp. in animal products (as egg yolk, milk, or fish-liver oils) whose lack causes injury to certain tissues (as in the eye with resulting visual defects)

vitamin B *n* **1** : VITAMIN B COMPLEX **2** : THIAMINE

vitamin B complex *n* : a group of vitamins found widely in foods that are essential for normal function of certain enzymes and for growth — called also *B complex*

vitamin B_1 \-'bē-'wən\ *n* : THIAMINE

vitamin B_6 \-'bē-'siks\ *n* : PYRIDOXINE; *also* : a closely related compound

vitamin B_{12} \-'bē-'twelv\ *n* : a complex cobalt-containing member of the vitamin B complex that occurs esp. in liver and is essential to normal blood formation, nerve function, and growth

vitamin B_2 \-'bē-'tü\ *n* : RIBOFLAVIN

vitamin C *n* : a vitamin that is present esp. in fruits and leafy vegetables, apparently functions as an enzyme in certain bodily oxidations and syntheses, and is used medicinally in the prevention and treatment of scurvy

vitamin D *n* : any or all of several vitamins that are essential for normal bone and tooth structure, and are found esp. in fish-liver oils, egg yolk, and milk or produced in response to ultraviolet irradiation

vitamin E *n* : any of several tocopherols of which the lack in various mammals and birds is associated with infertility, muscular dystrophy, or vascular disorders and which occur esp. in leaves and in seed-germ oils

vitamin K *n* : any of several vitamins essential for the clotting of blood

vi·ti·ate \'vish-ē-,āt\ *vb* **1** : to injure the quality of : SPOIL, DEBASE **2** : to destroy the validity of ⟨fraud *vitiates* a contract⟩ — **vi·ti·a·tion** \,vish-ē-'ā-shən\ *n* — **vi·ti·a·tor** \'vish-ē-,āt-ər\ *n*

vit·re·ous \'vi-trē-əs\ *adj* : of, relating to, derived from, or resembling glass : GLASSY ⟨*vitreous* rocks⟩ ⟨*vitreous* luster⟩

vitreous humor *n* : the clear colorless transparent jelly that fills the eyeball posterior to the lens

vit·ri·fy \'vi-trə-,fī\ *vb* **-fied**; **-fy·ing** : to change into glass or a glassy substance by heat and fusion — **vit·ri·fi·a·ble** \-,fī-ə-bəl\ *adj* — **vit·ri·fi·ca·tion** \,vi-trə-fə-'kā-shən\ *n*

vit·ri·ol \'vi-trē-əl\ *n* **1 a** : a sulfate of any of various metals (as copper, iron, or zinc) **b** : SULFURIC ACID **2** : something like vitriol in caustic quality; *esp* : bitterness of feeling or speech

vit·tle \'vit-əl\ *n* : VICTUAL

vi·tu·per·ate \vī-'t(y)ü-pə-,rāt, və-\ *vb* : to abuse severely : BERATE — **vi·tu·per·a·tion** \-,t(y)ü-pə-'rā-shən\ *n* — **vi·tu·per·a·tive** \-'t(y)ü-p(ə-)rət-iv, -pə-,rāt-\ *adj* — **vi·tu·per·a·tive·ly** *adv*

vi·va·ce \vē-'väch-ā\ *adv or adj* : in a brisk spirited manner — used as a direction in music

vi·va·cious \və-'vā-shəs, vī-\ *adj* : lively in temper or conduct : SPRIGHTLY — **vi·va·cious·ly** *adv* — **vi·va·cious·ness** *n* — **vi·vac·i·ty** \-'vas-ət-ē\ *n*

vi·var·i·um \vī-'ver-ē-əm\ *n, pl* **-ia** \-ē-ə\ *or* **-i·ums** : an enclosure for keeping or raising and observing animals or plants indoors; *esp* : one for land-dwelling animals

viv·id \'viv-əd\ *adj* **1** : having the appearance of vigorous life ⟨a *vivid* sketch⟩ **2** : very strong or intense ⟨a *vivid* red⟩ **3** : producing a strong or clear impression : SHARP; *esp* : producing distinct mental images ⟨a *vivid* description⟩ **4** : acting clearly and vigorously ⟨a *vivid* imagination⟩ — **viv·id·ly** *adv* — **viv·id·ness** *n*

viv·i·fy \'viv-ə-,fī\ *vb* **-fied**; **-fy·ing** **1** : to put life into : ANIMATE **2** : to make vivid — **viv·i·fi·ca·tion** \,viv-ə-fə-'kā-shən\ *n* — **viv·i·fi·er** \'viv-ə-,fī(-ə)r\ *n*

vi·vip·a·rous \vī-'vip-(ə-)rəs\ *adj* : producing living young from within the body rather than from eggs — **vi·vi·par·i·ty** \,vī-və-'par-ət-ē\ *n*

vivi·sec·tion \,viv-ə-'sek-shən\ *n* : the cutting of or operation on a living animal usu. for scientific investigation — **vivi·sect** \'viv-ə-,sekt\ *vb* — **vivi·sec·tion·ist** \-'sek-sh(ə-)nəst\ *n* — **vivi·sec·tor** \'viv-ə-,sek-tər\ *n*

vix·en \'vik-sən\ *n* **1** : a female fox **2** : an ill-tempered woman

viz \'nām-lē, 'viz\ *abbr* [for Latin *videlicet* (*z* being a substitute for the medieval symbol of abbreviation ʒ), contraction for *vidēre licet*, literally "it is possible to see"] namely

viz·ard \'viz-ərd\ *n* : MASK, DISGUISE

vi·zier \və-'zi(ə)r\ *n* : a high officer of various Muslim countries and esp. of the former Ottoman Empire

vi·zor *var of* VISOR

vocab *abbr* vocabulary

vo·cab·u·lary \vō-'kab-yə-,ler-ē\ *n, pl* **-lar·ies** **1** : a list or collection of words or of words and phrases usu. alphabetically arranged and explained or defined **2** : a stock of words used by a language, group, individual, work, or field of knowledge

[1]**vo·cal** \'vō-kəl\ *adj* **1** : uttered by the voice : ORAL

2 : composed or arranged for or sung by the human voice ⟨*vocal* music⟩ 3 : VOCALIC 4 : having the power of speech 5 : expressing oneself freely or insistently : OUTSPOKEN 6 : of, relating to, or resembling the voice — **vo·cal·ly** \-kə-lē\ *adv*

2**vocal** *n* 1 : a vocal sound 2 : a vocal musical number

vocal cords *n pl* : either of two pairs of elastic folds of mucous membrane that project into the cavity of the larynx and function in the production of vocal sounds — called also *vocal folds*; see LARYNX illustration

vo·cal·ic \vō-'kal-ik\ *adj* 1 : marked by or consisting of vowels 2 : of, relating to, or functioning as a vowel

vo·cal·ist \'vō-kə-ləst\ *n* : SINGER

vo·cal·ize \'vō-kə-ˌlīz\ *vb* 1 : to give vocal expression to 2 : SING — **vo·cal·i·za·tion** \ˌvō-kə-lə-'zā-shən\ *n* — **vo·cal·iz·er** \'vō-kə-ˌlī-zər\ *n*

vo·ca·tion \vō-'kā-shən\ *n* 1 : a summons to a particular course of action; *esp* : a divine call to the religious life 2 a : the work in which a person is regularly employed : OCCUPATION b : the persons engaged in a particular occupation

vo·ca·tion·al \-sh(ə-)nəl\ *adj* 1 : of, relating to, or concerned with a vocation 2 : concerned with choice of or training in a skill or trade to be pursued as a career ⟨*vocational* guidance⟩ ⟨*vocational* school⟩ — **vo·ca·tion·al·ly** \-ē\ *adv*

vo·cif·er·ate \vō-'sif-ə-ˌrāt\ *vb* : to cry out or utter loudly : CLAMOR, SHOUT — **vo·cif·er·a·tion** \-ˌsif-ə-'rā-shən\ *n*

vo·cif·er·ous \vō-'sif(ə-)rəs\ *adj* : making a loud outcry : NOISY, CLAMOROUS — **vo·cif·er·ous·ly** *adv* — **vo·cif·er·ous·ness** *n*

vod·ka \'väd-kə\ *n* [from Russian, diminutive of *voda* "water", from the same prehistoric source as English *water*] : a colorless alcoholic liquor distilled from a mash (as of rye or wheat)

vogue \'vōg\ *n* 1 : the leading place in popularity or acceptance 2 a : popular favor : POPULARITY b : a period of popularity 3 : something or someone in fashion at a particular time — **vogue** *adj*

1**voice** \'vȯis\ *n* 1 a : sound produced by vertebrates by means of vocal organs; *esp* : sound so produced by human beings b : the power of speaking ⟨lost his *voice*⟩ 2 a : musical sound produced by the vocal cords b : the ability to sing c : SINGER d : one of the melodic parts in a vocal or instrumental composition e : condition of the vocal organs for singing ⟨in good *voice*⟩ 3 : a sound like or suggesting vocal utterance 4 : a medium of expression 5 a : wish, choice, or opinion openly or formally expressed b : right of expression : SUFFRAGE 6 : distinction of form or a system of inflections of a verb to indicate the relation of the subject of the verb to the action which the verb expresses — **with one voice** : UNANIMOUSLY

2**voice** *vb* 1 : UTTER 2 : to regulate the tone of (as organ pipes) 3 : to vibrate the vocal cords in pronouncing ⟨*voice* a consonant⟩

voice box *n* : LARYNX

voice·less \'vȯis-ləs\ *adj* 1 : having no voice : MUTE 2 : not voiced ⟨a *voiceless* consonant⟩ — **voice·less·ness** *n*

ə abut	ər further		a back	ā bake
ä cot, cart	au̇ out	ch chin	e less	ē easy
g gift	i trip	ī life	j joke	ng sing	ō flow
ȯ flaw	ȯi coin	th thin	th this	ü loot
u̇ foot	y yet	yü few	yu̇ furious	zh vision

1**void** \'vȯid\ *adj* 1 : containing nothing : EMPTY ⟨*void* space⟩ 2 : WANTING, DEVOID 3 : of no legal force or effect : NULL

2**void** *n* 1 : empty space 2 : a feeling of want or hollowness

3**void** *vb* 1 : to make empty or vacant : CLEAR 2 : DISCHARGE, EMIT ⟨*void* excrement⟩ 3 : NULLIFY, ANNUL ⟨*void* a contract⟩ — **void·a·ble** \'vȯid-ə-bəl\ *adj*

voile \'vȯil\ *n* : a soft sheer fabric of silk, cotton, rayon, or wool

vol *abbr* volume

vol·a·tile \'väl-ət-əl\ *adj* 1 : readily becoming a vapor ⟨a *volatile* solvent⟩ 2 a : LIGHTHEARTED, LIVELY b : easily aroused 3 : CHANGEABLE, FICKLE — **vol·a·til·i·ty** \ˌväl-ə-'til-ət-ē\ *n*

vol·can·ic \väl-'kan-ik\ *adj* 1 : of or relating to a volcano ⟨a *volcanic* eruption⟩ 2 : having volcanoes ⟨a *volcanic* region⟩ 3 : made of materials from volcanoes ⟨*volcanic* dust⟩

volcanic glass *n* : natural glass produced by the cooling of molten lava too rapidly to permit crystallization

vol·ca·nism \'väl-kə-ˌniz-əm\ *n* : volcanic power or action

vol·ca·no \väl-'kā-nō\ *n, pl* **-noes** *or* **-nos** : a vent in the earth's crust from which molten or hot rock and steam issue; *also* : a hill or mountain composed wholly or in part of the ejected material

vol·ca·nol·o·gy \ˌväl-kə-'näl-ə-jē\ *n* : a branch of science that deals with volcanic phenomena

vole \'vōl\ *n* : any of various small rodents closely related to the lemmings and muskrats but in general resembling stocky mice or rats

vole (up to 7 in. long)

vo·li·tion \vō-'lish-ən\ *n* 1 : the act or power of making one's choices or decisions : WILL 2 : the choice made or decision reached — **vo·li·tion·al** \-'lish-(ə-)nəl\ *adj*

1**vol·ley** \'väl-ē\ *n, pl* **volleys** 1 a : a flight of missiles (as arrows or bullets) b : simultaneous discharge of a number of weapons 2 : the act of volleying 3 : a bursting forth of many things at once ⟨a *volley* of curses⟩

2**volley** *vb* **vol·leyed**; **vol·ley·ing** 1 : to discharge in a volley 2 : to propel an object while in the air and before touching the ground; *esp* : to hit a tennis ball on the volley

vol·ley·ball \'väl-ē-ˌbȯl\ *n* : a game played by volleying a large inflated ball over a net

volt \'vōlt\ *n* : a unit of electromotive force equal to a force that when steadily applied to a conductor whose resistance is one ohm will produce a current of one ampere

volt·age \'vōl-tij\ *n* : electromotive force measured in volts

vol·ta·ic cell \väl-ˌtā-ik-\ *n* : an apparatus for generating electricity through chemical action on two unlike metals in an electrolyte

voltaic pile *n* : 3PILE 3a

vol·tam·e·ter \vōl-'tam-ət-ər, 'vōl-tə-ˌmēt-\ *n* : an apparatus for measuring the quantity of electricity passed through a conductor by the amount of electrolysis produced (as by measuring the gases generated or by weighing the metal deposited)

volt·me·ter \'vōlt-ˌmēt-ər\ *n* : an instrument for measuring in volts the differences of potential between different points of an electrical circuit

vol·u·ble \'väl-yə-bəl\ *adj* : speaking readily or rapidly : GLIB, FLUENT ***syn*** see TALKATIVE ***ant*** curt — **vol·u·bil·i·ty** \ˌväl-yə-'bil-ət-ē\ *n* — **vol·u·bly** \'väl-yə-blē\ *adv*

vol·ume \'väl-yəm\ *n* [from Latin *volumen*, literally "roll", applied to a book in the form of a roll of papyrus, from *volvere* "to roll", the source of English *revolve*] **1** : BOOK ⟨a dozen *volumes* on the shelf⟩ **2** : one of a series of books forming a complete work or collection ⟨the 5th *volume* of an encyclopedia⟩ **3** : space occupied : bounded space as measured in cubic units ⟨the *volume* of a cylinder⟩ **4** : a large amount : MASS ⟨*volumes* of smoke⟩ **5** : intensity or quantity of tone : LOUDNESS ⟨turn up the *volume* on the radio⟩

vol·u·met·ric \ˌväl-yə-'me-trik\ *adj* : of or relating to the measurement of volume

vo·lu·mi·nous \və-'lü-mə-nəs\ *adj* **1** : BULKY, LARGE; *esp* : AMPLE, FULL ⟨*voluminous* skirts⟩ **2** : NUMEROUS **3** : containing or writing many words : LENGTHY ⟨*voluminous* prose⟩ — **vo·lu·mi·nous·ly** *adv* — **vo·lu·mi·nous·ness** *n*

vol·un·tar·i·ly \ˌväl-ən-'ter-ə-lē\ *adv* : of one's own free will

[1]**vol·un·tary** \'väl-ən-ˌter-ē\ *adj* **1** : done, given, or made in accordance with one's own free will ⟨*voluntary* assistance⟩ **2** : not accidental ⟨*voluntary* manslaughter⟩ **3** : of or relating to the will : controlled by the will ⟨*voluntary* behavior⟩

syn VOLUNTARY, INTENTIONAL, DELIBERATE can mean done or brought about in accordance with one's own will. VOLUNTARY may imply free choice ⟨*voluntary* manslaughter⟩ or control of the will ⟨*voluntary* eye movements⟩; INTENTIONAL implies a conscious purpose following on thought taken ⟨an *intentional* oversight⟩; DELIBERATE implies full awareness of the nature and probable consequences of one's action ⟨*deliberate* vandalism⟩ ***ant*** involuntary

[2]**voluntary** *n, pl* **-tar·ies** : a musical piece played esp. on the organ before, during, or after a religious service

voluntary muscle *n* : muscle (as most striated muscle) under voluntary control

[1]**vol·un·teer** \ˌväl-ən-'ti(ə)r\ *n* : one who enters into or offers himself for any service of his own free will; *esp* : one who enters into military service voluntarily

[2]**volunteer** *adj* : of, relating to, or consisting of volunteers : VOLUNTARY ⟨a *volunteer* army⟩

[3]**volunteer** *vb* **1** : to offer voluntarily ⟨*volunteered* his services⟩ **2** : to offer oneself as a volunteer

vo·lup·tu·ary \və-'ləp-chə-ˌwer-ē\ *n, pl* **-ar·ies** : a person whose chief interest is luxury and sensual pleasures — **voluptuary** *adj*

vo·lup·tu·ous \və-'ləp-chə-wəs\ *adj* **1** : giving pleasure to the senses **2** : being a voluptuary — **vo·lup·tu·ous·ly** *adv* — **vo·lup·tu·ous·ness** *n*

vol·vox \'väl-ˌväks\ *n* : any of a genus of green flagellates that form sphere-shaped colonies

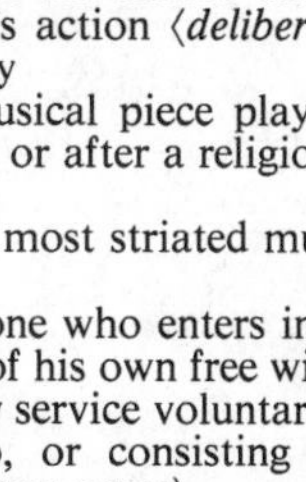

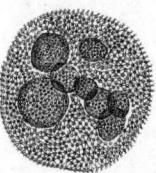

volvox colony (magnified 100 times)

[1]**vom·it** \'väm-ət\ *n* : an act or instance of throwing up the contents of the stomach through the mouth; *also* : the matter thrown up

[2]**vomit** *vb* **1** : to throw up the contents of the stomach through the mouth **2** : to spew forth : BELCH ⟨lava *vomited* from the volcano⟩ — **vom·it·er** *n*

voo·doo \'vüd-ü\ *n, pl* **voodoos** **1** : VOODOOISM **2** : one who deals in spells and necromancy — **voodoo** *adj*

voo·doo·ism \'vüd-ü-ˌiz-əm\ *n* **1** : a religion derived from African ancestor worship, practiced chiefly by Negroes of Haiti, and consisting largely of magic and sorcery **2** : WITCHCRAFT — **voo·doo·ist** \'vüd-ˌü-əst\ *n*

vo·ra·cious \vȯ-'rā-shəs, və-\ *adj* **1** : consuming food with vigor : RAVENOUS ⟨a *voracious* animal⟩ **2** : INSATIABLE ⟨a *voracious* reader⟩ — **vo·ra·cious·ly** *adv* — **vo·rac·i·ty** \-'ras-ət-ē\ *n*

vor·tex \'vȯr-ˌteks\ *n, pl* **vor·ti·ces** \'vȯrt-ə-ˌsēz\ *also* **vor·tex·es** **1** : a mass of whirling fluid forming a cavity in the center toward which things are drawn : WHIRLPOOL **2** : a whirling mass (as a whirlwind, tornado, or waterspout) **3** : the eye of a cyclone

vo·ta·ry \'vōt-ə-rē\ *n, pl* **-ries** : a devoted adherent; *esp* : a devout or zealous worshiper

[1]**vote** \'vōt\ *n* **1 a** : a formal expression of opinion or will; *esp* : one that indicates approval or disapproval of a proposal or a candidate for office **b** : the number of such expressions of opinion made at a single time (as at an election) **c** : BALLOT 1 **2** : the collective opinion of a body of persons expressed by voting **3** : the right to cast a vote : SUFFRAGE **4 a** : the act or process of voting ⟨bring the issue to a *vote*⟩ **b** : a method of voting ⟨a voice *vote*⟩ **5 a** : VOTER **b** : a group of voters with common characteristics ⟨the farm *vote*⟩

[2]**vote** *vb* **1** : to express one's wish or choice by a vote : cast a vote **2** : to make into law by a vote ⟨*vote* an income tax⟩ **3** : ELECT ⟨*voted* him into office⟩ **4** : to declare by common consent **5** : PROPOSE, SUGGEST

vote·less \'vōt-ləs\ *adj* : having no vote; *esp* : denied the political franchise

vot·er \'vōt-ər\ *n* : one that votes or has the legal right to vote

vo·tive \'vōt-iv\ *adj* : offered or performed in fulfillment of a vow or in gratitude or devotion

vouch \'vau̇ch\ *vb* **1** : PROVE, SUBSTANTIATE **2** : to give a guarantee ⟨I'll *vouch* for his honesty⟩ ⟨*vouch* for the truth of a story⟩ **3** : to supply supporting evidence or testimony

vouch·er \'vau̇-chər\ *n* **1** : one who vouches for another **2** : a document that serves to establish the truth of someting; *esp* : a paper (as a receipt) showing payment of a bill or debt

vouch·safe \vau̇ch-'sāf\ *vb* : to grant in the manner of one doing a favor

[1]**vow** \'vau̇\ *n* : a solemn promise or assertion

[2]**vow** *vb* **1** : to make a vow or as a vow **2** : to bind or consecrate by a vow

vow·el \'vau̇(-ə)l\ *n* **1** : a speech sound produced without obstruction or audible friction in the mouth **2** : a letter (as *a, e, i, o, u,* and sometimes *y*) representing a vowel

[1]**voy·age** \'vȯi-ij\ *n* **1** : a journey by water : CRUISE **2** : a journey through air or space

[2]**voyage** *vb* **1** : to take a trip : TRAVEL **2** : SAIL, TRAVERSE — **voy·ag·er** *n*

VP *abbr* **1** verb phrase **2** vice-president

vs *abbr* versus

V-shaped \'vē-ˌshāpt\ *adj* : shaped like the letter V

vt *abbr* verb transitive

Vt *or* **VT** *abbr* Vermont

VTOL *abbr* vertical takeoff and landing

vul·can·ite \'vəl-kə-ˌnīt\ *n* : a hard vulcanized rubber

vul·can·ize \'vəl-kə-ˌnīz\ *vb* : to treat rubber or similar plastic material chemically in order to give it useful properties (as elasticity, strength, or stability) — **vul·can·i·za·tion** \\,vəl-kə-nə-'zā-shən\\ *n* — **vul·can·iz·er** \\'vəl-kə-,nī-zər\\ *n*

Vulg *abbr* Vulgate

vul·gar \\'vəl-gər\\ *adj* **1** : generally used, applied, or accepted **2** : VERNACULAR **3** : of or relating to the common people : ORDINARY **4 a** : lacking in cultivation, perception, or taste : COARSE **b** : morally crude : GROSS **c** : excessively showy : PRETENTIOUS **5** : OBSCENE, PROFANE — **vul·gar·ly** *adv*

vul·gar·ism \\'vəl-gə-,riz-əm\\ *n* : a vulgar expression or action

vul·gar·i·ty \\,vəl-'gar-ət-ē\\ *n, pl* **-ties** **1** : the quality or state of being vulgar **2** : something vulgar

vul·gar·ize \\'vəl-gə-,rīz\\ *vb* : to make vulgar

Vul·gate \\'vəl-,gāt\\ *n* : a Latin version of the Bible authorized and used by the Roman Catholic Church

vul·ner·a·ble \\'vəln-(ə-)rə-bəl, 'vəl-nər-bəl\\ *adj* **1** : capable of being wounded **2** : open to attack or damage : ASSAILABLE ⟨a *vulnerable* fort⟩ — **vul·ner·a·bil·i·ty** \\,vəln-(ə-)rə-'bil-ət-ē\\ *n* — **vul·ner·a·bly** \\'vəln-(ə-)rə-blē, 'vəl-nər-blē\\ *adv*

vulture 1 (about 41 in. long)

vul·ture \\'vəl-chər\\ *n* **1** : any of various large carrion-eating birds that are related to the hawks and eagles but have weaker claws and the head usu. naked **2** : a greedy or predatory person

vul·va \\'vəl-və\\ *n* : the external parts of the female genital organs; *also* : the opening between their projecting parts

vv *abbr* verses

vying *pres part of* VIE

ə abut	ər further	a back	ā bake	
ä cot, cart	aü out	ch chin	e less	ē easy
g gift	i trip	ī life	j joke	ng sing
ō flow	ȯ flaw	ȯi coin	th thin	th this
ü loot	u̇ foot	y yet	yü few	yu̇ furious
zh vision				

W w W w W

w \'dəb-əl-(ˌ)yü, -yə\ *n, often cap* : the 23d letter of the English alphabet

w *abbr* **1** water **2** watt **3** week **4** weight **5** wide **6** width

W *abbr* **1** walk **2** west **3** western **4** wins

WA *abbr* Washington

wab·ble \'wäb-əl\ *var of* WOBBLE

Wac \'wak\ *n* : a member of the Women's Army Corps

wacky \'wak-ē\ *adj* **wack·i·er**; **-est** : ODD, CRAZY — **wack·i·ly** \'wak-ə-lē\ *adv* — **wack·i·ness** \'wak-ē-nəs\ *n*

[1]**wad** \'wäd\ *n* **1** : a small mass, bundle, or tuft ⟨plugged the hole with *wads* of clay⟩ ⟨a *wad* of cotton⟩ **2** : a soft pad or plug used to hold a powder charge in a gun or cartridge **3** : a roll of paper money

[2]**wad** *vb* **wad·ded**; **wad·ding** **1** : to form into a wad ⟨*wad* up a handkerchief⟩ **2** : to push a wad into ⟨*wad* a gun⟩ **3** : to hold in by a wad ⟨*wad* a bullet in a gun⟩ **4** : to stuff or line with a wad or padding

wad·ding \'wäd-ing\ *n* **1** : wads or material for wads **2** : a soft mass or sheet of fibers used for stuffing or padding

wad·dle \'wäd-əl\ *vb* **wad·dled**; **wad·dling** \-(ə-)ling\ : to walk with short steps swaying from side to side like a duck — **waddle** *n* — **wad·dler** \-(ə-)lər\ *n*

[1]**wade** \'wād\ *vb* **1** : to step in or through a substance (as water, mud, or sand) offering more resistance than air **2** : to struggle slowly or determinedly ⟨*wade* through a dull book⟩ ⟨*wade* into a task⟩ **3** : to cross by wading

[2]**wade** *n* : an act of wading ⟨a *wade* in the brook⟩

wad·er \'wād-ər\ *n* **1** : one that wades **2** : WADING BIRD **3** *pl* : high waterproof boots or trousers for wading

wading bird *n* : any of many long-legged birds including the shorebirds and various inland water birds (as cranes and herons) that wade in water in search of food

Waf \'waf\ *n* : a member of the women's branch of the U.S. Air Force

wa·fer \'wā-fər\ *n* **1 a** : a thin crisp cake or cracker **b** : a round thin piece of bread used in the Eucharist **2** : something (as a piece of candy) resembling a wafer

waf·fle \'wäf-əl\ *n* [from Dutch *wafel*, from the same source as English *weave*] : a crisp cake of pancake batter baked in a waffle iron

waffle iron *n* : a hinged metal cooking utensil that impresses indentations on a waffle

[1]**waft** \'wäft, 'waft\ *vb* : to move lightly by or as if by the impulse of wind or waves — **waft·er** *n*

[2]**waft** *n* : a slight breeze : PUFF

[1]**wag** \'wag\ *vb* **wagged**; **wag·ging** : to swing to and fro or from side to side ⟨the dog *wagged* his tail⟩ — **wag·ger** *n*

[2]**wag** *n* **1** : WIT, JOKER **2** : a wagging movement

[1]**wage** \'wāj\ *vb* : to engage in : carry on ⟨*wage* war⟩ ⟨*wage* a campaign⟩

[2]**wage** *n* : payment for work or services usu. on an hourly, daily, or piecework basis — often used in pl.

[1]**wa·ger** \'wā-jər\ *n* **1** : something risked on an uncertain event : BET **2** : an act of betting : GAMBLE

[2]**wager** *vb* **wa·gered**; **wa·ger·ing** \'wāj-(ə-)ring\ : RISK, VENTURE; *esp* : GAMBLE, BET — **wa·ger·er** \'wā-jər-ər\ *n*

wag·gery \'wag-ə-rē\ *n, pl* **-ger·ies** **1** : mischievous fun **2** : JEST, JOKE

wag·gle \'wag-əl\ *vb* **wag·gled**; **wag·gling** \-(ə-)ling\ : WAG — **waggle** *n*

wag·on \'wag-ən\ *n* **1** : a four-wheeled vehicle; *esp* : one drawn by animals and used for carrying goods **2** : a child's four-wheeled cart **3** : STATION WAGON **4** : PATROL WAGON — **wag·on·er** \'wag-ə-nər\ *n* — **on the wagon** : abstaining from alcoholic beverages

waif \'wāf\ *n* : a stray person or animal; *esp* : a homeless child

[1]**wail** \'wāl\ *vb* **1** : to express sorrow : LAMENT **2** : to make a sound suggestive of a mournful cry **3** : to express dissatisfaction : COMPLAIN — **wail·er** *n*

[2]**wail** *n* **1** : a cry or sound expressing grief or pain **2** : a sound suggestive of a wail ⟨the *wail* of an air-raid siren⟩

[1]**wain·scot** \'wān-skət, -ˌskōt, -ˌskät\ *n* **1** : a usu. paneled wooden lining of the wall of a room **2** : the lower three or four feet of an interior wall when finished differently from the rest

[2]**wainscot** *vb* **-scot·ed** *or* **-scot·ted**; **-scot·ing** *or* **-scot·ting** : to line with wainscot

wain·scot·ing \-ˌskōt-ing, -ˌskät-, -skət-\ *or* **wain·scot·ting** \-ˌskät-, -skət-\ *n* : WAINSCOT

waist \'wāst\ *n* **1 a** : the part of the body between the chest and hips **b** : the narrow front part of the abdomen of some insects (as a wasp) **2** : a part likened to the human waist ⟨the *waist* of a ship⟩ ⟨the *waist* of a violin⟩ **3** : a garment or the part of a garment that covers the body from the neck to the waist — **waist·like** \-ˌlīk\ *adj*

waist·band \'wās(t)-ˌband\ *n* : a band (as of trousers) fitting around the waist

waist·coat \'wās(t)-ˌkōt, 'wes-kət\ *n, chiefly Brit* : VEST

waist·line \'wāst-ˌlīn\ *n* **1 a** : a line surrounding the waist at its narrowest part **b** : the length of this line **2** : the line at which the waist and skirt of a dress meet

[1]**wait** \'wāt\ *vb* **1 a** : to remain in readiness : AWAIT ⟨*wait* for sunrise⟩ ⟨*wait* your turn⟩ ⟨*wait* for orders⟩ **b** : to pause to let someone catch up ⟨hey, *wait* for me⟩ **2** : POSTPONE, DELAY ⟨*wait* dinner for a guest⟩ **3** : to attend as a waiter : SERVE ⟨*wait* tables⟩ ⟨*wait* at a luncheon⟩ — **wait on** *or* **wait upon** **1 a** : to attend as a servant **b** : to supply the wants of : SERVE ⟨*wait on* a customer⟩ **2** : to make a formal call on — **wait up** : to delay going to bed ⟨I'll be late; don't *wait up*⟩

[2]**wait** *n* **1** : a hidden position : AMBUSH — used chiefly in the expression *lie in wait* **2** : an act or period of waiting

wait·er \'wāt-ər\ *n* : one that waits; *esp* : a man who waits on table (as in a restaurant)

waiting room *n* : a room (as at a bus station) for the use of persons waiting

wait·ress \'wā-trəs\ *n* : a woman who waits on table (as in a restaurant)

waive \'wāv\ *vb* : to give up claim to ⟨*waive* his right to answer⟩

waiv·er \'wā-vər\ *n* **1** : the act of waiving a right, claim, or privilege **2** : a document containing a declaration of a waiver

[1]**wake** \'wāk\ *vb* **waked** \'wākt\ *or* **woke** \'wōk\; **waked** *or* **wo·ken** \'wō-kən\; **wak·ing** **1** : to be or remain awake **2** : AWAKE — often used with *up* — **wak·er** *n*

[2]**wake** *n* : a watch held over the body of a dead person prior to burial

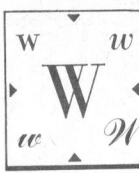

[3]**wake** *n* : a track or path left by a moving body esp. in water

wake·ful \'wāk-fəl\ *adj* : not sleeping or able to sleep — **wake·ful·ly** \-fə-lē\ *adv* — **wake·ful·ness** *n*

wak·en \'wā-kən\ *vb* **wak·ened**; **wak·en·ing** \'wāk-(ə-)ning\ : AWAKE

wake–rob·in \'wāk-ˌräb-ən\ *n* **1** : TRILLIUM **2** : JACK-IN-THE-PULPIT

wale \'wāl\ *n* **1 a** : a streak or ridge made on the skin usu. by a rod or whip : WHEAL **b** : a raised surface or ridge (as on cloth like corduroy) **2** : one of the strakes on the sides of a wooden ship just above the waterline

[1]**walk** \'wȯk\ *vb* [from Old English *wealcan* "to roll", "toss about"] **1** : to move or cause to move along on foot at a natural slow gait ⟨*walk* to town⟩ ⟨*walk* a horse up a hill⟩ **2** : to pass over, through, or along by walking ⟨*walk* the streets⟩ **3** : to perform or affect by walking ⟨*walk* guard⟩ **4** : to take or cause to take first base with a base on balls — **walk off with 1** : STEAL **2** : to win or gain esp. without difficulty ⟨*walked off with* the state championship⟩ — **walk over** : to disregard the wishes or feelings of

[2]**walk** *n* **1** : a going on foot ⟨go for a *walk*⟩ **2** : a place, path, or course for walking **3** : distance to be walked ⟨it's a long *walk*⟩ **4 a** : manner of living : CONDUCT, BEHAVIOR **b** : social or economic status ⟨various *walks* of life⟩ **5 a** : manner of walking **b** : a gait of a four-footed animal in which there are always at least two feet on the ground; *esp* : a slow 4-beat gait of a horse in which the feet strike the ground in the sequence left hind, left fore, right hind, right fore **6** : BASE ON BALLS

walk·er \'wȯ-kər\ *n* **1** : one that walks **2** : something used in walking; *esp* : a framework that supports a baby learning to walk or a crippled or handicapped person learning to walk again

walk·ie–talk·ie \ˌwȯ-kē-'tȯ-kē\ *n* : a small portable radio set for receiving and sending messages

walking leaf *n* : any of several insects of southern Asia and the East Indies that are related to grasshoppers and have wings and legs resembling leaves in color and form

walking leg *n* : an appendage of an arthropod adapted for walking

walking stick *n* **1** : a stick used in walking **2** *usu* **walk·ing·stick** : STICK INSECT

walk·out \'wȯk-ˌau̇t\ *n* **1** : STRIKE 2a **2** : the leaving of a meeting or organization as an expression of disapproval

walk out \-'au̇t\ *vb* **1** : to go on strike **2** : to leave suddenly often as an expression of disapproval — **walk out on** : ABANDON, DESERT

walk–up \'wȯk-ˌəp\ *n* : a building or apartment house without an elevator — **walk–up** *adj*

walk·way \-ˌwā\ *n* : a passage for walking : WALK

[1]**wall** \'wȯl\ *n* **1** : a structure (as of brick or stone) meant to enclose or shut off a space; *esp* : a side of a room or building **2** : something resembling a wall; *esp* : something that acts as a barrier or defense ⟨a tariff *wall*⟩ **3** : a layer of material that encloses space ⟨the heart *wall*⟩ ⟨the *walls* of a boiler⟩ — **walled** \'wȯld\ *adj*

[2]**wall** *vb* **1** : to provide, separate, or surround with or as if with a wall ⟨*wall* in the garden⟩ **2** : to close off an opening with a wall ⟨*wall* up a door⟩

wal·la·by \'wäl-ə-bē\ *n, pl* **-bies** *also* **-by** : any of various small or medium-sized kangaroos

wallaby
(about 50 in. long)

wall·board \'wȯl-ˌbōrd, -ˌbȯrd\ *n* : a structural material (as of wood pulp, gypsum, or plastic) made in large rigid sheets and used esp. for inside walls and ceilings

wal·let \'wäl-ət\ *n* **1** : a bag or sack for carrying things on a journey **2** : BILLFOLD

wall·eye \'wȯl-ˌī\ *n* **1 a** : an eye with a whitish iris or an opaque white cornea **b** : an eye that turns outward showing more than a normal amount of white; *also* : the condition of having such eyes **2** : a large vigorous American freshwater food and sport fish that has prominent eyes and is related to the perches but resembles the true pike — called also *walleyed pike* — **wall·eyed** \-'īd\ *adj*

wall·flow·er \'wȯl-ˌflau̇(-ə)r\ *n* **1** : a common Old World herb widely grown for its showy fragrant flowers **2** : a person who from shyness or unpopularity remains alone (as at a dance)

wallflower 1

[1]**wal·lop** \'wäl-əp\ *n* **1** : a powerful blow or impact **2** : the ability to hit hard

[2]**wallop** *vb* **1** : to beat soundly : TROUNCE **2** : to hit with force : SOCK — **wal·lop·er** *n*

[1]**wal·low** \'wäl-ō\ *vb* **1** : to roll oneself about in or as if in deep mud ⟨elephants *wallowing* in the river⟩ **2** : to immerse oneself **3** : to become or remain helpless — **wal·low·er** \'wäl-ə-wər\ *n*

[2]**wallow** *n* **1** : an act or instance of wallowing **2** : an area used by animals for wallowing

wall·pa·per \'wȯl-ˌpā-pər\ *n* : decorative paper for the walls of a room — **wallpaper** *vb*

wal·nut \'wȯl-(ˌ)nət\ *n* [from Old English *wealhhnutu*, literally "foreign nut", from *wealh* "Celt", "Welshman", "foreigner", and *hnutu* "nut"] **1 a** : an edible nut with a furrowed usu. rough shell; *also* : any of a genus of trees related to the hickories that produce such nuts **b** : the usu. reddish to dark brown wood of a walnut widely used for cabinetwork and veneers **c** : a hickory nut or tree **2** : a moderate reddish brown

Wal·pur·gis Night \väl-'pu̇r-gəs-\ *n* : the eve of May Day on which witches are held to ride to a satanic rendezvous

wal·rus \'wȯl-rəs, 'wäl-\ *n, pl* **walrus** *or* **wal·rus·es** : either of two large mammals of northern seas related to the seals and hunted esp. for the hide, the ivory tusks of the males, and oil

walrus
(up to 11 ft. long)

waltz \'wȯl(t)s\ *n* : a round dance in $\frac{3}{4}$ time with strong accent on the first beat — **waltz** *vb*

ə abut	ər further	a back	ā bake
ä cot, cart	au̇ out	ch chin	e less	ē easy
g gift	i trip	ī life	j joke	ng sing	ō flow
ȯ flaw	ȯi coin	th thin	t͟h this	ü loot
u̇ foot	y yet	yü few	yu̇ furious	zh vision

wam·pum \'wäm-pəm\ *n* **1** : beads of shells strung in strands, belts, or sashes and used by No. American Indians as money and ornaments **2** *slang* : MONEY

wan \'wän\ *adj* **1** : SICKLY, PALE **2** : LANGUID ⟨a *wan* smile⟩ — **wan·ly** *adv* — **wan·ness** \'wän-nəs\ *n*

wand \'wänd\ *n* **1** : a fairy's, diviner's, or magician's staff **2** : a light rod or tube

wan·der \'wän-dər\ *vb* **wan·dered**; **wan·der·ing** \-d(ə-)riŋ\ **1** : to move about aimlessly : RAMBLE **2 a** : to deviate from a course : STRAY **b** : to become delirious or mentally disoriented — **wander** *n* — **wan·der·er** \-dər-ər\ *n*

wandering Jew *n* : any of several creeping or trailing plants

wan·der·lust \'wän-dər-ˌləst\ *n* : strong longing to travel

1**wane** \'wān\ *vb* **1** : to grow gradually smaller or less ⟨the moon *wanes*⟩ **2** : to lose power, prosperity, or influence ⟨the nation *waned* as its commerce declined⟩ **3** : to draw toward an end ⟨summer is *waning*⟩

2**wane** *n* **1** : the act or process of waning **2** : a period of waning

1**want** \'wȯnt, 'wänt\ *vb* **1** : to be without : LACK ⟨this coat is *wanting* a button⟩ **2** : to fall short by ⟨he *wants* one year of being of full age⟩ **3** : to feel or suffer the need of ⟨cannot get the rest he *wants*⟩ **4** : NEED, REQUIRE ⟨our house *wants* painting⟩ **5** : to desire earnestly : WISH ⟨*wants* to go to college⟩

2**want** *n* **1 a** : a lack of a required or usual amount **b** : great need : DESTITUTION **2** : something wanted : NEED, DESIRE

1**want·ing** *adj* **1** : ABSENT, LACKING **2 a** : falling below standards or expectations **b** : lacking in ability or capacity : DEFICIENT

2**wanting** *prep* **1** : WITHOUT ⟨a book *wanting* a cover⟩ **2** : LESS, MINUS ⟨a month *wanting* two days⟩

wan·ton \'wȯnt-ən, 'wänt-\ *adj* **1** : PLAYFUL **2** : INDECENT, LEWD **3 a** : MERCILESS, INHUMANE ⟨*wanton* cruelty⟩ **b** : MALICIOUS ⟨a *wanton* attack⟩ **4** : UNRESTRAINED, EXTRAVAGANT — **wan·ton·ly** *adv* — **wan·ton·ness** \-ən-nəs\ *n*

wa·pi·ti \'wäp-ət-ē\ *n, pl* **-tis** *or* **-ti** : ELK 2

1**war** \'wȯ(ə)r\ *n* **1 a** : a state or period of armed hostile conflict between states or nations **b** : the science of warfare **2 a** : a state of hostility or conflict **b** : a struggle between opposing forces or for a particular end ⟨a *war* on disease⟩

2**war** *vb* **warred**; **war·ring** **1** : to engage in warfare ⟨*warring* nations⟩ **2** : to be in conflict ⟨his desire for life *warring* with his fear of it⟩

1**war·ble** \'wȯr-bəl\ *n* **1** : a melodious succession of low pleasing sounds **2** : the action of warbling : TRILL

2**warble** *vb* **war·bled**; **war·bling** \-b(ə-)liŋ\ **1** : to sing with trills **2** : to express by warbling

war·bler \'wȯr-blər\ *n* **1** : one that warbles **2 a** : any of numerous small Old World singing birds many of which are noted songsters and are closely related to the thrushes **b** : any of numerous small brightly colored American songbirds with a usu. weak and unmusical song

war·bon·net \'wȯr-ˌbän-ət\ *n* : a long feathered ceremonial Indian headdress

1**ward** \'wȯrd\ *n* **1** : a guarding or being under guard; *esp* : CUSTODY **2** : a division in a hospital **3** : an electoral or administrative division of a city **4** : a person (as a child or lunatic) under the protection of a court or guardian

2**ward** *vb* **1** : to keep watch over : GUARD **2** : to turn aside : DEFLECT — usu. used with *off* ⟨*ward* off a cold⟩

1**-ward** \wərd\ *also* **-wards** \wərdz\ *adj suffix* [from Old English *-weard* meaning literally "turned", from the same Indo-European root as Latin *vertere* "to turn", the source of English *invert*, *convert*, *revert*] **1** : that moves, tends, faces, or is directed toward ⟨wind*ward*⟩ **2** : that occurs or is situated in the direction of ⟨left*ward*⟩

2**-ward** *or* **-wards** *adv suffix* **1** : in a (specified) direction ⟨up*wards*⟩ ⟨after*ward*⟩ **2** : toward a (specified) point, position, or area ⟨earth*ward*⟩

war·den \'wȯrd-ən\ *n* **1** : GUARDIAN, KEEPER **2** : the governor of a town, district, or fortress **3** : an official charged with special duties or with the enforcement of specified laws ⟨game *warden*⟩ ⟨air-raid *warden*⟩ **4** : an official in charge of a prison **5 a** : a lay officer of an Episcopal parish **b** : any of various British college officials

ward·er \'wȯrd-ər\ *n* : WATCHMAN, WARDEN

ward·robe \'wȯrd-ˌrōb\ *n* **1** : a room, closet, or chest where clothes are kept **2** : a collection of clothes (as of one person or for one activity)

ward·room \-ˌrüm, -ˌru̇m\ *n* : the space in a warship allotted to the officers excepting the captain; *esp* : the messroom assigned to them

ware \'wa(ə)r, 'we(ə)r\ *n* **1 a** : manufactured articles or products of art or craft : GOODS ⟨*ware* whittled from wood⟩ ⟨tin*ware*⟩ **b** : an article of merchandise ⟨a peddler hawking his *wares*⟩ **2** : POTTERY

ware·house \-ˌhau̇s\ *n* : a place for the storage of goods — **ware·house·man** \-mən\ *n*

war·fare \'wȯr-ˌfa(ə)r, -ˌfe(ə)r\ *n* **1 a** : military operations between enemies : WAR **b** : activity undertaken by one country to weaken or destroy another ⟨economic *warfare*⟩ **2** : STRUGGLE, CONFLICT ⟨industrial *warfare*⟩

war·fa·rin \'wȯr-fə-rən\ *n* : a compound that deters blood clotting and is used as a rodent poison and in medicine

war·head \'wȯr-ˌhed\ *n* : the section of a missile containing the charge

war·like \-ˌlīk\ *adj* **1** : fond of war ⟨*warlike* people⟩ **2** : of or relating to war **3** : threatening war : HOSTILE ⟨*warlike* attitudes⟩ ***syn*** see MARTIAL

war·lock \'wȯr-ˌläk\ *n* : SORCERER, WIZARD

1**warm** \'wȯrm\ *adj* **1 a** : having or giving out heat to a moderate or adequate degree ⟨*warm* food⟩ ⟨a *warm* stove⟩ **b** : serving to retain heat (as of the body) ⟨*warm* clothes⟩ **c** : feeling or inducing sensations of heat ⟨*warm* from exertion⟩ ⟨a long *warm* walk⟩ **2 a** : showing or marked by strong feeling : ARDENT ⟨a *warm* advocate of temperance⟩ **b** : marked by tense excitement or anger ⟨a *warm* political campaign⟩ **3** : marked by or tending toward injury, distress, or pain ⟨gave the enemy a *warm* reception⟩ **4 a** : newly made : FRESH ⟨a *warm* scent⟩ **b** : near to a goal or answer **5** : giving a pleasant impression of warmth, cheerfulness, or friendliness ⟨*warm* colors⟩ — **warm·ly** *adv* — **warm·ness** *n*

2**warm** *vb* **1** : to make or become warm **2 a** : to give a feeling of warmth or vitality to **b** : to experience feelings of affection or pleasure ⟨*warmed* to her young guests⟩ **3** : to reheat for eating ⟨*warm* over some potatoes⟩ **4 a** : to make or become ready for operation or performance by preliminary exercise or operation — usu. used with *up* ⟨tell a relief pitcher to *warm* up⟩ **b** : to become ardent, interested, or competent ⟨a speaker *warming* to his topic⟩

warm–blood·ed \'wȯrm-'bləd-əd\ *adj* **1** : able to maintain a relatively high and constant body temperature that is essentially independent of the environment **2 :** FERVENT, ARDENT

warm·er \'wȯr-mər\ *n* : one that warms; *esp* : a device for keeping something warm ⟨foot *warmer*⟩

warm front *n* : an advancing edge of a warm air mass

warm·heart·ed \'wȯrm-'härt-əd\ *adj* : marked by warmth of feeling — **warm·heart·ed·ness** *n*

warming pan *n* : a long-handled covered pan filled with live coals and formerly used to warm a bed

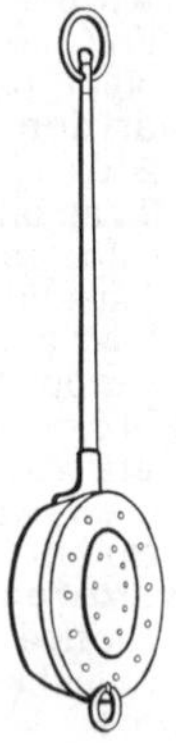

warming pan

war·mon·ger \'wȯr-ˌməng-gər, -ˌmäng-\ *n* : one who urges or attempts to stir up war — **war·mon·ger·ing** \-g(ə-)ring\ *n*

warmth \'wȯrm(p)th\ *n* **1 :** the quality or state of being warm **2 a :** emotional intensity (as of enthusiasm, anger, or love) **b :** a glowing effect such as is produced by the use of warm colors

warm–up \'wȯrm-ˌəp\ *n* **1 :** the act or an instance of warming up **2 :** a procedure (as a set of exercises) used in warming up

warn \'wȯrn\ *vb* **1 a :** to give notice to beforehand esp. of danger or evil **b :** ADMONISH, COUNSEL ⟨*warned* her not to go⟩ **2 :** to order to go or stay away — **warn·er** *n*

warn·ing \'wȯr-ning\ *n* **1 :** the act of warning : the state of being warned ⟨he had *warning* of his illness⟩ **2 :** something that warns — **warning** *adj* — **warn·ing·ly** \-ning-lē\ *adv*

[1]**warp** \'wȯrp\ *n* **1 :** a series of yarns extended lengthwise in a loom and crossed by the woof **2 :** a twist or curve in something once flat or straight ⟨a *warp* in a door⟩

warp 1

[2]**warp** *vb* **1 a :** to turn or twist out of shape **b :** to cause to judge, choose, or act wrongly : PERVERT **2 :** to arrange so as to form a warp ⟨*warp* yarns⟩ **3 :** to move by a line attached to a fixed object ⟨*warp* a ship through a lock⟩ — **warp·er** *n*

war·path \'wȯr-ˌpath, -ˌpȧth\ *n* **1 :** the route taken by a party of American Indians going on a warlike expedition **2 :** a hostile course of action or frame of mind

war·plane \-ˌplān\ *n* : a military airplane

[1]**war·rant** \'wȯr-ənt, 'wär-\ *n* **1 a :** AUTHORIZATION **b :** JUSTIFICATION, GROUND **2 :** evidence of authorization (as a document); *esp* : a legal writ authorizing an officer to make an arrest, seizure, or search **3 :** a certificate of appointment issued to an officer of lower rank than a commissioned officer

[2]**warrant** *vb* **1 a :** to declare or maintain positively **b :** to assure of the truth of what is said **2 :** to guarantee something to be as it appears or is represented to be **3 :** SANCTION, AUTHORIZE **4 :** JUSTIFY — **war·rant·a·ble** \-ə-bəl\ *adj* — **war·rant·er** \-ər\ *or* **war·ran·tor** \ˌwȯr-ən-'tȯ(ə)r, ˌwär-\ *n*

ə abut	ər further	a back	ā bake
ä cot, cart	aù out	ch chin	e less
ē easy	g gift	i trip	ī life
j joke	ng sing	ō flow	ȯ flaw
ȯi coin	th thin	th this	ü loot
ù foot	y yet	yü few	yù furious
zh vision			

warrant officer *n* : an officer ranking below a commissioned officer

war·ran·ty \'wȯr-ənt-ē, 'wär-\ *n, pl* **-ties** : a usu. written statement that some situation or thing is as it appears or is represented to be

war·ren \'wȯr-ən, 'wär-\ *n* **1 :** a place for keeping small game (as hare or pheasant) **2 :** an area where rabbits breed or are kept

war·rior \'wȯr-yər; 'wȯr-ē-ər, 'wär-ē-\ *n* : a man engaged or experienced in warfare

war·ship \'wȯr-ˌship\ *n* : a ship for use in war; *esp* : one armed for combat

wart \'wȯrt\ *n* **1 :** an irregular projection on the skin often caused by a virus **2 :** a protuberance (as on a plant) resembling a wart — **warty** \-ē\ *adj*

wart·hog \-ˌhȯg, -ˌhäg\ *n* : any of a genus of African wild hogs with two pairs of rough warty protuberances on the face and large protruding tusks

warthog (about 2½ ft. at shoulder)

war·time \'wȯr-ˌtīm\ *n* : a period during which a war is in progress

wary \'wa(ə)r-ē, 'we(ə)r-\ *adj* **war·i·er**; **-est** : very cautious; *esp* : being on guard against danger or deception ***syn*** see CAREFUL ***ant*** daring — **war·i·ly** \'war-ə-lē, 'wer-\ *adv* — **war·i·ness** \'war-ē-nəs, 'wer-\ *n*

was *past 1st & 3d sing of* BE

[1]**wash** \'wȯsh, 'wäsh\ *vb* **1 :** to cleanse with or as if with water ⟨*wash* clothes⟩ **2 :** to wet thoroughly with liquid **3 :** to flow along the border of ⟨waves *wash* the shore⟩ **4 :** to pour or flow in a stream or current ⟨the river *washes* against its banks⟩ **5 :** to move or carry by the action of water ⟨a man *washed* overboard⟩ **6 :** to cover or daub lightly with a liquid (as whitewash or varnish) **7 :** to run water over in order to separate out valuable matter ⟨*wash* sand for gold⟩ **8 :** to bear washing ⟨this dress *washes* well⟩ **9 :** to stand a test for truthfulness ⟨that story won't *wash*⟩ **10 :** to be worn away by washing ⟨the heavy rain caused the bridge to *wash* out⟩

[2]**wash** *n* **1 a :** the act or process or an instance of washing **b :** articles to be or being washed **2 :** WASHING **3 a :** a piece of ground washed by the sea or river **b** *West* : the dry bed of a stream **4 :** worthless esp. liquid waste : REFUSE **5 a :** a thin coat of paint (as watercolor) **b :** a liquid used for coating a surface (as a wall) or for washing **6 a :** BACKWASH 1 **b :** a disturbance in the air produced by the passage of an airfoil or propeller

[3]**wash** *adj* : WASHABLE

Wash *abbr* Washington

wash·a·ble \'wȯsh-ə-bəl, 'wäsh-\ *adj* : capable of being washed without damage ⟨a *washable* silk⟩

wash and wear *adj* : of, relating to, or being a fabric or garment not needing to be ironed after washing

wash·ba·sin \'wȯsh-ˌbā-sən, 'wäsh-\ *n* : WASHBOWL

wash·board \-ˌbōrd, -ˌbȯrd\ *n* : a grooved board to scrub clothes on

wash·bowl \-ˌbōl\ *n* : a large bowl or a sink for water esp. to wash one's hands and face

wash·cloth \-ˌklȯth\ *n* : a cloth for washing one's face and body

washed–up \'wȯsht-'əp, 'wäsht-\ *adj* : left with no

power and no capacity or opportunity for recovery : FINISHED

wash·er \'wȯsh-ər, 'wäsh-\ *n* **1** : one that washes; *esp* : WASHING MACHINE **2** : a ring (as of metal or leather) used to make something fit tightly or to prevent rubbing

wash·er·wom·an \-ˌwu̇m-ən\ *n* : a woman who works at washing clothes

wash·ing \'wȯsh-ing, 'wäsh-\ *n* : articles washed or to be washed

washing machine *n* : a machine for washing clothes and household linen

washing soda *n* : SAL SODA

Washington's Birthday *n* **1** : February 22 formerly observed as a legal holiday in most states of the U.S. **2** : the third Monday in February observed as a legal holiday in most states of the U.S.

wash·out \'wȯsh-ˌau̇t, 'wäsh-\ *n* **1 a** : the washing away of earth esp. in a roadbed by a freshet **b** : a place where earth is washed away **2** : one that fails to measure up : FAILURE

wash out \-'au̇t\ *vb* **1 a** : to drain the color from in laundering **b** : to become faded **2** : to deplete the strength or vitality of **3** : to eliminate or be eliminated as useless or unsatisfactory

wash·room \'wȯsh-ˌrüm, 'wäsh-, -ˌru̇m\ *n* : a room equipped with washing and toilet facilities : LAVATORY

wash·stand \-ˌstand\ *n* **1** : a stand holding articles for washing one's face and hands **2** : WASHBOWL

wash·tub \-ˌtəb\ *n* : a tub for washing or soaking clothes

wash up *vb* : ELIMINATE, FINISH ⟨the scandal *washed* him *up* as a politician⟩

wasn't \'wəz-ənt, 'wäz-\ : was not

1**wasp** \'wäsp, 'wȯsp\ *n* : a winged insect related to the bees and ants that has a slender body with the abdomen attached by a narrow stalk and in females and workers a powerful sting

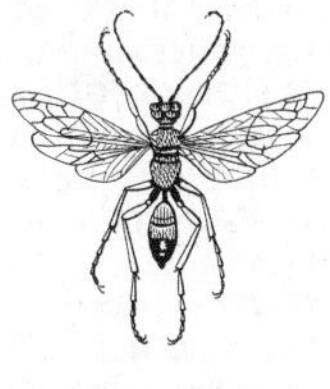

wasp (about one inch long)

2**wasp** *n, often cap W or all cap* [from the initial letters of *white Anglo-Saxon protestant*] : an American of English Protestant ancestry

wasp·ish \'wäs-pish, 'wȯs-\ *adj* **1** : IRRITABLE, SNAPPISH **2** : like a wasp in form; *esp* : slightly built — **wasp·ish·ly** *adv* — **wasp·ish·ness** *n*

wasp waist *n* : a very slender waist

1**was·sail** \'wäs-əl, wä-'sāl\ *n* [from Middle English *washail*, from Old Norse *ves heill* "be in good health!", from the same sources as English *was* and *hale* respectively] **1** : an early English toast to someone's health **2** : riotous drinking : REVELRY

2**wassail** *vb* : CAROUSE — **was·sail·er** *n*

wast \wəst, (ˈ)wäst\ *archaic past 2d sing of* BE

wast·age \'wā-stij\ *n* : loss by use, decay, erosion, or leakage or through wastefulness

1**waste** \'wāst\ *n* **1 a** : a sparsely settled or barren region : DESERT **b** : uncultivated land **2 a** : the act or an instance of wasting **b** : the state of being wasted **3 a** : material left over, rejected, or discarded **b** : material rejected during a textile manufacturing process and used for wiping away dirt and oil **c** : REFUSE **d** : material (as excrement) produced by a living body and of no value to the organism that produces it

2**waste** *vb* **1** : DEVASTATE **2** : to wear away or diminish gradually **3** : to spend carelessly : SQUANDER **4** : to lose or cause to lose weight, strength, or vitality — often used with *away*

3**waste** *adj* **1** : being wild and uninhabited : DESOLATE, BARREN **2** : RUINED, DEVASTATED **3** : thrown away as worthless after being used **4** : of no further use to a person, animal, or plant ⟨means by which the body throws off *waste* matter⟩

waste·bas·ket \'wās(t)-ˌbas-kət\ *n* : an open receptacle for wastepaper

waste·ful \'wāst-fəl\ *adj* : given to or marked by waste : LAVISH, PRODIGAL — **waste·ful·ly** \-fə-lē\ *adv* — **waste·ful·ness** *n*

waste·land \'wāst-ˌland\ *n* : barren or uncultivated land

waste·pa·per \'wās(t)-'pā-pər\ *n* : paper discarded as used, superfluous, or not fit for use

waste product *n* : material resulting from a process (as of metabolism or manufacture) that is of no further use to the system producing it

wast·er \'wā-stər\ *n* : one that wastes or squanders

wast·rel \'wā-strəl\ *n* : WASTER, SPENDTHRIFT

1**watch** \'wäch\ *vb* [from Old English *wæccan*, from the same root as *wake*] **1** : to stay awake intentionally (as at the bedside of a sick person) **2** : to be on the alert or on the lookout **3** : to keep guard ⟨*watch* outside the door⟩ **4** : to keep one's eyes on : keep in view ⟨*watch* a game⟩ **5** : to keep in view so as to prevent harm or warn of danger ⟨*watch* a brush fire carefully⟩ **6** : to keep oneself informed about ⟨*watch* his career⟩ **7** : to be on the alert for the chance to make use of ⟨*watched* his opportunity⟩ — **watch·er** *n*

2**watch** *n* **1 a** : the act of keeping awake to guard, protect, or attend **b** : a state of alert and continuous attention **c** : close observation **2 a** : LOOKOUT, WATCHMAN **b** : a body of sentinels or watchmen **3 a** : a period during which a part of a ship's company is on duty **b** : the part of a ship's company on duty during a watch **4** : a portable timepiece designed to be worn (as on the wrist) or carried in the pocket

watch·dog \'wäch-ˌdȯg\ *n* **1** : a dog kept to guard property **2** : a watchful guardian

watch·ful \-fəl\ *adj* : steadily attentive and alert esp. to danger — **watch·ful·ly** \-fə-lē\ *adv* — **watch·ful·ness** *n*

watch·mak·er \-ˌmā-kər\ *n* : one that makes or repairs watches or clocks — **watch·mak·ing** \-king\ *n*

watch·man \-mən\ *n* : a person assigned to watch : GUARD

watch out *vb* : to be vigilant ⟨*watch out* for cars⟩

watch·tow·er \'wäch-ˌtau̇(-ə)r\ *n* : a tower for a lookout

watch·word \-ˌwərd\ *n* **1** : a secret word used as a signal or sign of recognition **2** : a motto used as a slogan or rallying cry

1**wa·ter** \'wȯt-ər, 'wät-\ *n* **1 a** : the liquid that descends from the clouds as rain, forms streams, lakes, and seas, and is a major constituent of all living matter and that is an odorless, tasteless, very slightly compressible oxide of hydrogen **b** : a natural mineral water — usu. used in pl. **2** *pl* : a band of seawater bordering on and under the control of a country ⟨sailing Canadian *waters*⟩ **3** : travel or transportation on water ⟨came by *water*⟩ **4** : the level of water at a particular state of the tide : TIDE **5** : a liquid containing or resembling water; *esp* : a watery fluid (as tears, urine, or sap) formed or circulating in a living body **6 a** : the clearness and luster of a precious stone and esp. a diamond **b** : a wavy lustrous pattern (as of a textile) — **wa·ter·less** \-ləs\ *adj*

2**water** *vb* **1 :** to supply with or get or take water ⟨*water* horses⟩ ⟨the ship *watered* at each port⟩ **2 :** to treat with or as if with water; *esp* : to impart a wavy pattern to cloth **3 :** to dilute by or as if by the addition of water **4 :** to form or secrete water or watery matter (as tears or saliva) — **wa·ter·er** \-ər-ər\ *n*

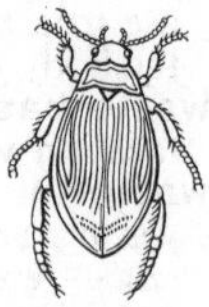

water beetle (about one inch long)

water beetle *n* **:** any of numerous oval flattened aquatic beetles that swim by means of their fringed hind legs which act together as oars

wa·ter·buck \'wȯt-ər-ˌbək, 'wät-\ *n, pl* **waterbuck** *or* **waterbucks :** any of various Old World antelopes that commonly frequent streams or wet lands

water buffalo *n* **:** an often domesticated Asiatic buffalo somewhat resembling a large ox

water clock *n* **:** a device or machine for measuring time by the fall or flow of water

water closet *n* **1 :** a compartment or room for defecation and excretion into a hopper **2 :** a hopper with its accessories

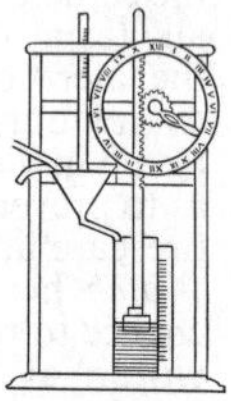

water clock

wa·ter·col·or \'wȯt-ər-ˌkəl-ər, 'wät-\ *n* **1 :** a paint whose liquid part is water **2 :** a picture painted with watercolor **3 :** the art of painting with watercolor — **wa·ter·col·or·ist** \-ˌkəl-ə-rəst\ *n*

wa·ter·course \-ˌkōrs, -ˌkȯrs\ *n* **1 :** a bed or channel in which water flows **2 :** a stream of water (as a river)

wa·ter·craft \-ˌkraft\ *n* **1 :** skill in water activities (as managing boats) **2 :** craft for water transport

wa·ter·cress \-ˌkres\ *n* **1 :** a plant with leaves that are crisp and peppery to the taste growing usu. in clear running water **2 :** the leaves of watercress used in salad or as a garnish

water cycle *n* **:** HYDROLOGIC CYCLE

wa·ter·fall \-ˌfȯl\ *n* **:** a perpendicular or steep descent of the water of a stream

water flea *n* **:** any of various small active dark or brightly colored freshwater crustaceans

wa·ter·fowl \'wȯt-ər-ˌfau̇l, 'wät-\ *n* **1 :** a bird that frequents water; *esp* : a swimming bird **2 waterfowl** *pl* **:** swimming game birds as distinguished from upland game birds and shorebirds

wa·ter·front \-ˌfrənt\ *n* **:** land or a section of a town bordering on a body of water

water gas *n* **:** a poisonous flammable gaseous mixture that consists chiefly of carbon monoxide and hydrogen, that is usu. made by blowing air and then steam over red-hot coke or coal, and that is used as a fuel

water glass *n* **1 :** a glass vessel (as a drinking glass) for holding water **2 :** a water-soluble substance consisting usu. of a silicate of sodium of varying composition, found in commerce as a glassy mass, a stony powder, or dissolved in water as a syrupy liquid, and used as a protective coating and in preserving eggs

ə abut　ər further　a back　ā bake
ä cot, cart　au̇ out　ch chin　e less　ē easy
g gift　i trip　ī life　j joke　ng sing　ō flow
ȯ flaw　ȯi coin　th thin　t͟h this　ü loot
u̇ foot　y yet　yü few　yu̇ furious　zh vision

water hyacinth *n* **:** a floating aquatic plant often clogging waterways in the southern U.S.

water lily *n* **:** any of a family of aquatic plants with rounded floating leaves and usu. showy flowers

water lily

wa·ter·line \'wȯt-ər-ˌlīn, 'wät-\ *n* **:** any of several lines that are marked on the outside of a ship and correspond with the surface of the water when it is afloat on an even keel

wa·ter·logged \-ˌlȯgd, -ˌlägd\ *adj* **:** so filled or soaked with water as to be heavy or hard to manage ⟨a *waterlogged* boat⟩

1**wa·ter·mark** \-ˌmärk\ *n* **1 :** a mark that indicates a line to which water has risen **2 :** a mark (as the maker's name or trademark) made in paper during manufacture and visible when the paper is held up to the light

2**watermark** *vb* **:** to mark with a watermark

wa·ter·mel·on \-ˌmel-ən\ *n* **1 :** a large oblong or rounded fruit with a hard green or white rind often striped or variegated, a sweet watery pink, yellowish, or red pulp, and many seeds **2 :** a widely grown African vine related to the squashes and bearing watermelons

watermelon begonia *n* **:** a tropical plant often cultivated for its silvery striped foliage

water moccasin *n* **:** a venomous pit viper of the southern U.S. closely related to the copperhead

water pipe *n* **:** HOOKAH

water pistol *n* **:** a toy pistol designed to throw a jet of water — called also *water gun*

water polo *n* **:** a goal game played in water by teams of swimmers with a ball resembling a soccer ball

wa·ter·pow·er \'wȯt-ər-ˌpau̇(-ə)r, 'wät-\ *n* **:** the power of moving water used to run machinery (as for generating electricity)

1**wa·ter·proof** \ˌwȯt-ər-'prüf, ˌwät-\ *adj* **:** not letting water through; *esp* **:** covered or treated with a material to prevent permeation by water

2**wa·ter·proof** \'wȯt-ər-ˌ, 'wät-\ *n, chiefly Brit* **:** RAINCOAT

wa·ter–re·pel·lent \ˌwȯt-ə(r)-ri-'pel-ənt, ˌwät-\ *adj* **:** treated with a finish that is resistant but not impervious to penetration by water

wa·ter–re·sist·ant \-ri-'zis-tənt\ *adj* **:** resistant to but not wholly proof against the action or entry of water

wa·ter·shed \'wȯt-ər-ˌshed, 'wät-\ *n* **1 :** a dividing ridge (as a mountain range) separating one drainage area from others **2 :** the area that drains into a river or lake

water–ski *vb* **:** to ski on water while towed by a speedboat — **wa·ter·ski·er** *n*

water ski *n* **:** a ski used in water-skiing

water snake *n* **:** any of numerous snakes frequenting or inhabiting fresh waters and feeding largely on aquatic animals

water spaniel *n* **:** a rather large spaniel with a heavy curly coat used esp. for retrieving waterfowl

water spider *n* **:** an aquatic European spider that constructs beneath the surface of the water a bell-shaped structure of silk which is open beneath and filled with air carried down by the spider in the form of small bubbles

wa·ter·spout \'wȯt-ər-ˌspau̇t, 'wät-\ *n* **1 :** a pipe for carrying off water from a roof **2 :** a slender funnel-shaped cloud that extends down to a cloud of spray torn up from water by a whirlwind

water strider *n* : any of various long-legged bugs that move about on the surface of the water

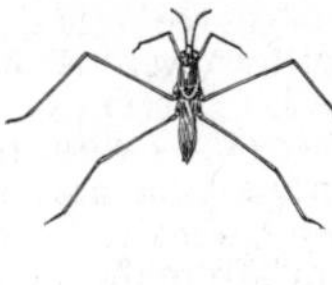

water strider (less than one inch long)

water table *n* : the upper limit of the ground wholly saturated with water

wa·ter·tight \ˌwȯt-ər-ˈtīt, ˌwät-\ *adj* **1** : so tight as to be waterproof **2** : leaving no possibility of misconstruction or evasion ⟨a *watertight* case against the accused⟩

water vapor *n* : the vapor of water esp. when below the boiling temperature and in diffused form (as in the atmosphere)

water–vascular system *n* : a system of vessels in echinoderms containing a circulating water fluid that is used for the movement of tentacles and tube feet and may also function in excretion and respiration

wa·ter·way \ˈwȯt-ər-ˌwā, ˈwät-\ *n* : a channel by which ships can travel

wa·ter·weed \-ˌwēd\ *n* : a weedy aquatic plant usu. with inconspicuous flowers — compare WATER LILY

wa·ter·wheel \-ˌhwēl\ *n* : a wheel made to turn by a flow of water against it

water wings *n pl* : an air-filled device to give support to the body of a swimmer

waterwheel

wa·ter·works \-ˌwərks\ *n pl* : a system of reservoirs, channels, mains, and pumping and purifying equipment for supplying water (as to a city)

wa·tery \ˈwȯt-ə-rē, ˈwät-\ *adj* **1** : of or having to do with water ⟨a *watery* grave⟩ **2** : containing, full of, or giving out water ⟨*watery* clouds⟩ **3** : being like water : THIN, WEAK ⟨*watery* lemonade⟩ **4** : being soft and soggy ⟨*watery* turnips⟩

watt \ˈwät\ *n* [named in honor of James *Watt* (1736–1819), Scottish engineer] : the unit of power equal to the work done by a current of one ampere under a pressure of one volt

watt·age \-ij\ *n* : amount of power expressed in watts

watt–hour \ˈwät-ˈau̇(ə)r\ *n* : a unit of work or energy equivalent to the power of one watt operating for one hour

1**wat·tle** \ˈwät-əl\ *n* **1 a** : a framework of poles interwoven with slender branches or reeds and used in building **b** : material for such a framework **2** : a fleshy process hanging usu. about the head or neck (as of a bird) — **wat·tled** \-əld\ *adj*

2**wattle** *vb* **wat·tled**; **wat·tling** \ˈwät-(ə-)liŋ\ **1** : to form or build of or with wattle **2 a** : to interlace to form wattle **b** : to unite or make solid by interweaving light flexible material

W. Aust *abbr* Western Australia

1**wave** \ˈwāv\ *vb* **1** : to float or shake in an air current : FLUTTER **2** : to signal or salute with the hand or with something held in it **3** : BRANDISH, FLOURISH ⟨*waved* a pistol menacingly⟩ **4** : to move before the wind with a wavelike motion ⟨a field of *waving* grain⟩ **5** : to follow or cause to follow a curving line or take a wavy form

2**wave** *n* **1** : a moving swell or crest on the surface of water **2** : a wavelike formation or shape ⟨a *wave* in the hair⟩ **3** : the action or process of making wavy or curly **4** : a waving motion ⟨a *wave* of his hand⟩ **5** : FLOW, GUSH ⟨a *wave* of color swept the girl's face⟩ **6** : a surge or rapid increase ⟨a *wave* of buying⟩ ⟨a heat *wave*⟩ **7** : a disturbance similar to a wave in water that transfers energy progressively from point to point ⟨a light *wave*⟩ ⟨radio *waves*⟩ — **wave·like** \-ˌlīk\ *adj*

Wave \ˈwāv\ *n* : a woman serving in the U.S. Navy

wave·length \ˈwāv-ˌleŋ(k)th\ *n* : the distance (as from crest to crest) in the line of advance of a wave from any one point to the next corresponding point

wave·let \-lət\ *n* : a little wave : RIPPLE

wave mechanics *n* : a theory of matter that states that elementary particles (as electrons, protons, or neutrons) have wave properties

wa·ver \ˈwā-vər\ *vb* **wa·vered**; **wa·ver·ing** \ˈwāv-(ə-)riŋ\ **1** : to fluctuate between choices **2** : to weave or sway to and fro **3** : FALTER — **wa·ver·er** \ˈwā-vər-ər\ *n* — **wa·ver·ing·ly** \ˈwāv-(ə-)riŋ-lē\ *adv*

wavy \ˈwā-vē\ *adj* **wav·i·er**; **wav·i·est** : having or moving in waves — **wav·i·ly** \-və-lē\ *adv* — **wav·i·ness** \-vē-nəs\ *n*

1**wax** \ˈwaks\ *n* **1** : a yellowish plastic substance secreted by bees and used by them for constructing the honeycomb **2** : any of various substances resembling beeswax in physical or chemical properties — **wax·like** \-ˌlīk\ *adj*

2**wax** *vb* : to treat or rub with wax

3**wax** *vb* **1** : to grow larger or greater; *esp* : to increase in apparent size and brightness ⟨the moon *waxes* toward the full⟩ **2** : BECOME ⟨the party *waxed* merry⟩

wax bean *n* : a kidney bean with pods that are yellow when fit for use as snap beans

wax·en \ˈwak-sən\ *adj* : resembling or made of wax

wax gland *n* : a gland (as in the honeybee) that secretes wax

wax myrtle *n* : an American shrub having small hard berries with a thick coating of white wax used for candles

wax·wing \ˈwaks-ˌwiŋ\ *n* : any of several American and Eurasian birds that are mostly brown with a showy crest and velvety plumage

waxy \ˈwak-sē\ *adj* **wax·i·er**; **-est** **1** : full of or covered with wax ⟨a *waxy* surface⟩ ⟨*waxy* berries⟩ **2** : WAXEN — **wax·i·ness** *n*

1**way** \ˈwā\ *n* **1 a** : a track for travel : PATH, ROAD, STREET **b** : an opening for passage (as through a crowd or a gate) **2 a** : a course traveled : ROUTE **b** : DIRECTION ⟨come this *way*⟩ ⟨the wrong *way*⟩ **3 a** : a course of action ⟨chose the easy *way*⟩ **b** : PREFERENCE, CHOICE ⟨determined to have his *way*⟩ **c** : POSSIBILITY ⟨there are no two *ways* about it⟩ **4 a** : MANNER, METHOD ⟨this *way* of thinking⟩ ⟨a new *way* of painting⟩ **b** : FEATURE, RESPECT ⟨a good worker in many *ways*⟩ **c** : STATE, CONDITION ⟨the *way* things are⟩ ⟨in a bad *way* with rheumatism⟩ **5** : a particular or characteristic mode or trick of behavior ⟨it's just his *way*⟩ ⟨a nice *way* with her pets⟩ **6 a** : DISTANCE ⟨a short *way* down the road⟩ **b** : progress along a course ⟨earning his *way* through school⟩ ⟨made their *way* with difficulty⟩ **7** : NEIGHBORHOOD, LOCALITY ⟨out our *way*⟩ **8** : room or chance to progress or advance ⟨make *way* for the queen⟩ **9 a** : a guiding track **b** *pl* : an inclined support on which a ship is built and from which it is launched **10** : CATEGORY, KIND ⟨get what you need in the *way* of supplies⟩ **11** : motion or speed through the water ⟨making slow *way* down the harbor⟩ — **by way of 1** : for the purpose of ⟨*by way of* illustration⟩ **2** : by the route through : VIA — **out of the**

way **1** : WRONG, IMPROPER **2** : SECLUDED, REMOTE — **under way** **1** : in motion through the water **2** : in progress

[2]**way** *adv* : [1]AWAY 7

way·far·er \'wā-ˌfar-ər, -ˌfer-\ *n* : a traveler esp. on foot — **way·far·ing** \-ˌfar-ing, -ˌfer-\ *adj*

way·lay \'wā-ˌlā\ *vb* **-laid** \-ˌlād\; **-lay·ing** : to lie in wait for esp. to seize, rob, or kill

way–out \-'au̇t\ *adj* : marked by great departure from the conventional or traditional ⟨*way-out* ideas⟩

-ways \ˌwāz\ *adv suffix* : in such a way, course, direction, or manner ⟨side*ways*⟩ ⟨flat*ways*⟩

way·side \'wā-ˌsīd\ *n* : the side or border of a road or path — **wayside** *adj*

way station *n* : an intermediate station on a line of travel (as a railroad)

way·ward \'wā-wərd\ *adj* **1** : taking one's own usu. improper way : DISOBEDIENT ⟨*wayward* children⟩ **2** : opposite to what is desired or expected : CONTRARY ⟨*wayward* weather⟩ **3** : UNSTEADY, IRREGULAR — **way·ward·ly** *adv* — **way·ward·ness** *n*

WBC *abbr* white blood cells; white blood count

we \(')wē\ *pron* **1** : I and one or more others **2** : I — used by a sovereign or an editor or writer

weak \'wēk\ *adj* **1** : lacking physical strength **2** : not able to bear or exert much weight, pressure, or strain **3 a** : lacking strength of mind or character **b** : resulting from or indicative of such deficiency ⟨a *weak* policy⟩ **4** : DILUTE ⟨*weak* tea⟩ **5** : not well grounded or argued ⟨a *weak* argument⟩ **6** : lacking skill or proficiency **7** : wanting in vigor of expression or effect **8** : not having or exerting authority ⟨*weak* government⟩ **9** : of, relating to, or being a verb or verb conjugation that forms the past tense and past participle by adding the suffix *-ed* or *-d* or *-t* **10** : bearing the least degree of stress ⟨a *weak* syllable⟩ **11** : ionizing only slightly in solution ⟨*weak* acids⟩ — **weak·ly** *adv*

syn WEAK, INFIRM, FEEBLE can mean lacking resources of strength. WEAK, a term of general application, may imply deficiency or inferiority of strength, whether of body, will, mind, or spirit ⟨a character too *weak* to resist temptation⟩; INFIRM implies a loss of strength or resolution with consequent instability, unsoundness, or vacillation ⟨left *infirm* by the crippling disease⟩ ⟨*infirm* judgment⟩; FEEBLE suggests extreme and pitiable weakness esp. of human beings or their actions ⟨managed only a *feeble* cry⟩ *ant* strong

weak·en \'wē-kən\ *vb* **weak·ened**; **weak·en·ing** \'wēk-(ə-)ning\ : to make or become weak or weaker

weak·fish \'wēk-ˌfish\ *n* : a common sport and market fish of the eastern coast of the U.S. that is related to the perches

weak·ling \'wēk-ling\ *n* : one that is weak in body, character, or mind — **weakling** *adj*

weak·ly \'wēk-lē\ *adj* **weak·li·er**; **-est** : FEEBLE, WEAK

weak–mind·ed \-'mīn-dəd\ *adj* **1** : lacking in judgment or good sense **2** : FEEBLE-MINDED

weak·ness \-nəs\ *n* **1** : the quality or state of being weak **2** : a weak point : FAULT, DEFECT **3** : an object of special desire or fondness

[1]**weal** \'wēl\ *n* : WELL-BEING, PROSPERITY

ə abut	ər further	a back	ā bake	
ä cot, cart	au̇ out	ch chin	e less	ē easy
g gift	i trip	ī life	j joke	ng sing	ō flow
ȯ flaw	ȯi coin	th thin	<u>th</u> this	ü loot
u̇ foot	y yet	yü few	yu̇ furious	zh vision

[2]**weal** *n* : WELT

wealth \'welth\ *n* **1** : abundance of possessions or resources : AFFLUENCE **2** : abundant supply : PROFUSION ⟨a *wealth* of detail⟩

wealthy \'wel-thē\ *adj* **wealth·i·er**; **-est** **1** : having wealth : AFFLUENT **2** : characterized by abundance : AMPLE — **wealth·i·ly** \-thə-lē\ *adv* — **wealth·i·ness** \-thē-nəs\ *n*

wean \'wēn\ *vb* [from Old English *wenian* "to accustom", from the same root as English *wont*] **1** : to accustom a child or young animal to take food otherwise than by nursing **2** : to turn one away from something long desired or followed ⟨*wean* a boy from a bad habit⟩ — **wean·er** *n*

weap·on \'wep-ən\ *n* **1** : something (as a gun, knife, or club) that may be used to fight with **2** : a means by which one contends against another

weap·on·ry \-rē\ *n* **1** : WEAPONS **2** : the science of designing and making weapons

[1]**wear** \'wa(ə)r, 'we(ə)r\ *vb* **wore** \'wō(ə)r, 'wȯ(ə)r\; **worn** \'wōrn, 'wȯrn\; **wear·ing** **1 a** : to bear on the person or use habitually for clothing or adornment ⟨*wears* a toupee⟩ ⟨*wore* a jacket⟩ **b** : to carry on the person ⟨*wear* a sword⟩ **2** : to have or show an appearance of ⟨*wore* a happy smile⟩ **3 a** : to impair, diminish, or decay by use or by scraping or rubbing ⟨the dress *wore* to bits⟩ **b** : to produce gradually by wearing ⟨*wear* a hole in the rug⟩ **c** : to exhaust or lessen the strength of : TIRE, FATIGUE ⟨*worn* by care and toil⟩ **4** : to endure use ⟨a silk that *wears* well⟩ **5 a** : to diminish or fail with the passage of time ⟨her nagging *wore* his patience away⟩ ⟨the day *wore* on⟩ **b** : to grow or become by or as if by wearing ⟨hair *worn* thin about the temples⟩ — **wear·a·ble** \'war-ə-bəl, 'wer-\ *adj* — **wear·er** \-ər\ *n*

[2]**wear** *n* **1 a** : the act of wearing : USE **b** : the state of being worn **2** : clothing or an article of clothing usu. of a particular kind or for a special occasion or use **3** : wearing quality : durability under use **4** : diminution or impairment due to use ⟨a *wear*-resistant surface⟩

wea·ri·some \'wir-ē-səm\ *adj* : causing weariness : TIRESOME — **wea·ri·some·ly** *adv* — **wea·ri·some·ness** *n*

wear off *vb* : to diminish gradually (as in effect)

wear out *vb* **1** : to make or become useless by wear **2** : TIRE, WEARY **3** : EXHAUST ⟨*wore out* his welcome by bad jokes⟩

[1]**wea·ry** \'wi(ə)r-ē\ *adj* **wea·ri·er**; **-est** **1** : worn out in strength, endurance, vigor, or freshness **2** : expressing or characteristic of weariness **3** : having one's patience, tolerance, or pleasure exhausted ⟨*weary* of his attacks⟩ **4** : TIRESOME — **wea·ri·ly** \'wir-ə-lē\ *adv* — **wea·ri·ness** \'wir-ē-nəs\ *n*

[2]**weary** *vb* **wea·ried**; **wea·ry·ing** : to become or make weary *syn* see TIRE

wea·sel \'wē-zəl\ *n, pl* **weasel** *or* **weasels** : any of various small slender active flesh-eating mammals related to the minks

weasel
(up to 12 in. long)

[1]**weath·er** \'we<u>th</u>-ər\ *n* **1** : the state of the atmosphere with respect to heat or cold, wetness or dryness, calm or storm, clearness or cloudiness : meteorological condition **2** : a particular and esp. a disa-

greeable atmospheric state ⟨it looks like we are going to have *weather*⟩ ⟨good *weather*⟩ ⟨stormy *weather*⟩ — **under the weather** : somewhat ill or drunk

[2]**weather** *adj* : WINDWARD

[3]**weather** *vb* **weath·ered**; **weath·er·ing** \'weth-(ə-)ring\ **1 a** : to expose to the weather **b** : to alter (as in color or texture) by exposure **2** : to sail or pass to the windward of **3** : to bear up against and come safely through ⟨*weather* a storm⟩

weath·er–beat·en \'weth-ər-ˌbēt-ən\ *adj* : worn or altered by exposure to weather

weath·er·board \-ˌbōrd, -ˌbȯrd\ *n* : CLAPBOARD

weath·er·cock \-ˌkäk\ *n* : VANE 1

weath·er·man \-ˌman\ *n* : one who reports and forecasts the weather : METEOROLOGIST

weath·er·proof \ˌweth-ər-'prüf\ *adj* : able to withstand exposure to weather — **weatherproof** *vb*

weather strip *n* : a strip of material used to seal a door or window at the sill or casing

weather vane *n* : VANE 1

[1]**weave** \'wēv\ *vb* **wove** \'wōv\; **wo·ven** \'wō-vən\; **weav·ing** **1 a** : to form by interlacing strands of material; *esp* : to make on a loom by interlacing warp and filling threads ⟨*weave* cloth⟩ **b** : to interlace into a fabric and esp. cloth **2** : SPIN 2b **3 a** : to produce by elaborately combining elements : CONTRIVE **b** : to unite in a coherent whole **c** : to introduce as an appropriate element : work in ⟨*wove* the episodes into a story⟩ ⟨*weave* a moral into a tale⟩ **4** : to move in a winding or zigzag course ⟨*weaving* his way through a crowd of holiday shoppers⟩ — **weav·er** *n*

[2]**weave** *n* : a pattern or method of weaving ⟨a coarse *weave*⟩

[1]**web** \'web\ *n* **1** : a fabric on a loom or in process of being removed from a loom **2 a** : SPIDERWEB **b** : SNARE, TRAP **3** : a membrane of an animal or plant; *esp* : one uniting toes (as of many birds) **4** : NETWORK

[2]**web** *vb* **webbed**; **web·bing** **1** : to cover or provide with webs or a web **2** : ENTANGLE, ENSNARE **3** : to make a web

web·bing \'web-ing\ *n* : a strong closely woven tape used esp. for straps, harness, or upholstery

web·foot \'web-'fu̇t\ *n* : a foot having webbed toes — **web–foot·ed** \-əd\ *adj*

wed \'wed\ *vb* **wed·ded** *also* **wed**; **wed·ding** [from Old English *weddian*, from *wedd* "pledge"] **1** : to take, give, or join in marriage : MARRY **2** : to unite firmly

we'd \(ˌ)wēd\ : we had : we should : we would

Wed *abbr* Wednesday

wed·ding \'wed-ing\ *n* **1** : a marriage ceremony usu. with accompanying festivities : NUPTIALS **2** : a wedding anniversary or its celebration — usu. used in combination ⟨golden *wedding*⟩

[1]**wedge** \'wej\ *n* **1** : a tapered piece of wood or metal used esp. to split wood or rocks and to lift heavy weights **2** : something (as a piece of pie or land or a flight of wild geese) shaped like a wedge **3** : a thing that serves to make a gradual opening or cause a change in something ⟨use a concession as a *wedge* to gain further concessions⟩

[2]**wedge** *vb* **1** : to fasten or tighten by or as if by driving in a wedge **2** : to press or force into a narrow space ⟨*wedged* a stick into the crack⟩ **3** : to separate or split with or as if with a wedge

wed·lock \'wed-ˌläk\ *n* : the state of being married : MARRIAGE

Wednes·day \'wenz-dē\ *n* [from Old English *wōdnesdæg*, meaning "day of Odin", from *Wōden* "Odin", the chief god of Germanic mythology] : the 4th day of the week

wee \'wē\ *adj* **1** : very small : TINY **2** : very early ⟨the *wee* hours of the morning⟩

[1]**weed** \'wēd\ *n* : a wild and often useless plant that is unattractive or tends to crowd out more desirable plants

[2]**weed** *vb* **1** : to free from weeds or something harmful, inferior, or superfluous ⟨*weed* a garden⟩ **2** : to get rid of weeds or unwanted items ⟨*weed* out the loafers from the crew⟩ — **weed·er** *n*

weeds \'wēdz\ *n pl* : mourning clothes

weedy \'wēd-ē\ *adj* **weed·i·er**; **-est** **1** : full or consisting of weeds ⟨a *weedy* field⟩ **2** : like a weed esp. in rapid growth **3** : LEAN, LANKY

week \'wēk\ *n* **1 a** : seven successive days ⟨was sick for a *week*⟩ **b** : a period of seven days beginning with Sunday and ending with Saturday ⟨the last *week* of the month⟩ **2** : the working or school days of the calendar week

week·day \-ˌdā\ *n* : a day of the week except Sunday or except Saturday and Sunday

[1]**week·end** \-ˌend\ *n* : the end of the week; *esp* : the period between the close of one working or school week and the beginning of the next

[2]**weekend** *vb* : to spend the weekend

[1]**week·ly** \'wē-klē\ *adj* **1** : occurring, done, produced, or issued every week **2** : computed in terms of one week ⟨a *weekly* wage⟩ — **weekly** *adv*

[2]**weekly** *n, pl* **weeklies** : a weekly publication

ween \'wēn\ *vb, archaic* : IMAGINE, SUPPOSE

weep \'wēp\ *vb* **wept** \'wept\; **weep·ing** **1** : to express emotion and esp. sorrow by shedding tears : CRY **2** : to give off liquid slowly or in drops : OOZE — **weep·er** *n*

weep·ing \'wē-ping\ *adj* **1** : TEARFUL **2** : having slender pendent branches

weeping willow *n* : an Asiatic willow with weeping branches

wee·vil \'wē-vəl\ *n* : any of a large group of mostly small beetles having the head long and usu. curved downward to form a snout bearing the jaws at the tip and including many very injurious to plants or plant products — **wee·vily** *or* **wee·vil·ly** \'wēv-(ə-)lē\ *adj*

weevil (less than one inch long)

weft \'weft\ *n* **1 a** : WOOF 1 **b** : yarn used for the woof **2 a** : FABRIC **b** : an article of woven fabric

weigh \'wā\ *vb* **1 a** : to determine the heaviness of **b** : to have weight or a specified weight **2 a** : to consider carefully : PONDER **b** : to be important : COUNT ⟨the evidence will *weigh* heavily against him⟩ **3** : to heave up preparatory to sailing ⟨*weigh* anchor⟩ **4** : to measure or apportion on or as if on a scales ⟨*weigh* out several pounds of rice⟩ **5** : to press down with or as if with a weight ⟨his worries *weigh* heavily on him⟩ — **weigh·er** *n*

[1]**weight** \'wāt\ *n* **1 a** : quantity as determined by weighing ⟨sold by *weight*⟩ **b** : the property of a body that is measurable by weighing and that depends on the interaction of its mass with a gravitational field **c** : the standard amount that something should weigh ⟨coin of full *weight*⟩ **2 a** : a quantity or portion weighing a usu. specified amount ⟨equal *weights* of flour and butter⟩ ⟨100 lbs. *weight* of iron⟩ **b** : the amount that something weighs ⟨worth his *weight* in gold⟩ **3** : a unit (as a pound or kilogram) of weight or mass — see MEASURE table, METRIC SYSTEM table **4 a** : an object (as a piece of metal) of known weight

for balancing a scale in weighing other objects **b :** a heavy object used to hold, press down, or counterbalance something else ⟨clock *weights*⟩ **c :** a heavy object (as a metal ball) used in athletic exercises **5 a :** something heavy : LOAD **b :** a mental or emotional burden ⟨had a *weight* on his conscience⟩ **6 a :** relative importance : NOTE ⟨opinions that carry *weight*⟩ ⟨a man of *weight* in the community⟩ **b :** the greater or more impressive part ⟨the *weight* of the evidence⟩

2**weight** *vb* **1 :** to load or make heavy with a weight **2 :** to oppress with a burden ⟨*weighted* down with cares⟩

weight·less \'wāt-ləs\ *adj* **:** having little weight **:** lacking apparent gravitational pull — **weight·less·ness** *n*

weighty \'wāt-ē\ *adj* **weight·i·er; -est 1 :** having much weight : HEAVY **2 a :** of much importance or consequence : SERIOUS ⟨*weighty* problems⟩ **b :** expressing seriousness : SOLEMN ⟨a *weighty* manner⟩ **3 :** exerting authority or influence ⟨*weighty* arguments⟩ — **weight·i·ness** *n*

wei·ma·ra·ner \ˌvī-mə-'rän-ər, 'wī-mə-ˌ\ *n* **:** any of a German breed of large gray short-haired sporting dogs

weimaraner

weir \'wa(ə)r, 'we(ə)r, 'wi(ə)r\ *n* **1 :** a fence set in a stream to catch fish **2 :** a dam in a stream to raise the water level or divert its flow

weird \'wi(ə)rd\ *adj* **1 a :** of, relating to, or caused by witchcraft or the supernatural **:** MAGICAL **b :** UNEARTHLY, MYSTERIOUS **2 :** ODD, FANTASTIC — **weird·ly** *adv* — **weird·ness** *n*

1**wel·come** \'wel-kəm\ *interj* — used to express a greeting to a guest or newcomer upon his arrival

2**welcome** *vb* **1 :** to greet hospitably and with courteous cordiality **2 :** to meet or face gladly ⟨*welcomed* criticism of his report⟩ — **wel·com·er** *n*

3**welcome** *adj* **1 :** received gladly ⟨a *welcome* visitor⟩ **2 :** giving pleasure : PLEASING ⟨a *welcome* rainfall⟩ ⟨*welcome* news⟩ **3 :** willingly permitted to do, have, or enjoy something ⟨anyone is *welcome* to use the swimming pool⟩

4**welcome** *n* **:** a cordial greeting or reception

1**weld** \'weld\ *vb* **1 :** to join pieces of metal or plastic by heating and allowing the edges to flow together or by hammering or pressing together **2 :** to join as if by welding ⟨*welded* together in friendship⟩ **3 :** to become or be capable of being welded ⟨certain metals *weld* easily⟩ — **weld·er** *n*

2**weld** *n* **1 :** a welded joint **2 :** union by welding

wel·fare \'wel-ˌfa(ə)r, -ˌfe(ə)r\ *n* **1 :** the state of doing well esp. in respect to happiness, well-being, or prosperity **2 :** WELFARE WORK **3 :** RELIEF 1b — **welfare** *adj*

welfare work *n* **:** organized efforts for the social betterment of a group in society — **welfare worker** *n*

wel·kin \'wel-kən\ *n* **:** SKY

1**well** \'wel\ *n* **1 a :** a spring or a pool fed by a spring **b :** a source of supply ⟨was a *well* of information⟩ **2 :** a hole sunk into the earth to reach a natural deposit (as of water, oil, or gas) **3 :** an open space extending vertically through floors of a structure (as for a staircase) **4 :** something (as a container or space) suggesting a well for water

2**well** *vb* **:** to rise to the surface and flow forth : RUN, GUSH ⟨tears *welled* from her eyes⟩

3**well** *adv* **bet·ter** \'bet-ər\; **best** \'best\ **1 a :** in a pleasing or desirable manner ⟨the party turned out *well*⟩ **b :** in a good or proper manner : EXCELLENTLY ⟨did his work *well*⟩ **2 :** ABUNDANTLY, FULLY ⟨eat *well*⟩ ⟨the orchard bore *well*⟩ **3 :** with reason or courtesy : PROPERLY ⟨she could not very *well* refuse⟩ **4 :** COMPLETELY, THOROUGHLY ⟨received a *well*-deserved ovation⟩ **5 :** INTIMATELY, CLOSELY ⟨know a person *well*⟩ **6 :** CONSIDERABLY, FAR ⟨*well* ahead⟩ ⟨*well* over his quota⟩ **7 :** without trouble or difficulty ⟨he could *well* have gone⟩ **8 :** EXACTLY, DEFINITELY ⟨remember it *well*⟩ — **as well 1 :** in addition : ALSO ⟨other features *as well*⟩ **2 :** without real loss or gain : EQUALLY ⟨might *as well* stop here⟩ — **as well as :** and not only : and in addition ⟨skillful *as well as* strong⟩ ⟨students *as well as* faculty are invited⟩

4**well** *interj* **1** — used to express surprise or indignation **2** — used to begin a discourse or to resume one that was interrupted

5**well** *adj* **1 :** SATISFACTORY, PLEASING ⟨all's *well* that ends well⟩ **2 :** being in satisfactory or prosperous condition or circumstances ⟨he lives *well*⟩ **3 :** ADVISABLE, DESIRABLE ⟨not *well* to anger him⟩ **4 a :** HEALTHY **b :** CURED, HEALED ⟨the wound is nearly *well*⟩ **5 :** FORTUNATE ⟨it is *well* that this has happened⟩

we'll \(ˌ)wēl\ **:** we shall : we will

well–be·ing \'wel-'bē-ing\ *n* **:** the state of being happy, healthy, or prosperous : WELFARE

well·born \-'bórn\ *adj* **:** born of good stock either socially or genetically

well–bred \-'bred\ *adj* **:** having or displaying good breeding : REFINED

well–de·fined \ˌwel-di-'fīnd\ *adj* **1 :** having clearly distinguishable limits or boundaries ⟨a *well-defined* scar⟩ **2 :** described precisely enough that any object can be included or excluded as a member ⟨a *well-defined* collection is a mathematical set⟩

well–dis·posed \-dis-'pōzd\ *adj* **:** disposed to be friendly, favorable, or sympathetic ⟨*well-disposed* to our plan⟩

well–done \'wel-'dən\ *adj* **1 :** rightly or properly performed **2 :** cooked thoroughly

well–found·ed \-'faùn-dəd\ *adj* **:** based on sound reasoning, information, judgment, or grounds

well–known \-'nōn\ *adj* **:** fully or widely known

well–mean·ing \-'mē-ning\ *adj* **:** having or based on good intentions

well–nigh \-'nī\ *adv* **:** ALMOST, NEARLY

well–off \-'óf\ *adj* **:** being in good condition or circumstances; *esp* : WELL-TO-DO

well–read \-'red\ *adj* **:** well informed or deeply versed through reading ⟨*well-read* in history⟩

well–spoken \-'spō-kən\ *adj* **1 :** having a good command of language : speaking well and esp. courteously ⟨a *well-spoken* man⟩ **2 :** spoken with propriety ⟨*well-spoken* words⟩

well·spring \'wel-ˌspring\ *n* **1 :** SPRING, FOUNTAINHEAD **2 :** a source of continual supply

well–to–do \ˌwel-tə-'dü\ *adj* **:** having more than adequate material resources : PROSPEROUS

Welsh \'welsh\ *n* **1 Welsh** *pl* **:** the natives or inhabitants of Wales **2 :** the Celtic language of the Welsh people — **Welsh** *adj*

Welsh cor·gi \-'kȯr-gē\ *n* : a short-legged long-backed Welsh dog with foxy head occurring in two varieties: **a** : CARDIGAN **b** : PEMBROKE

Welsh corgi

Welsh·man \'welsh-mən\ *n* : one of the Welsh — **Welsh·wom·an** \-,wu̇m-ən\ *n*

Welsh rabbit *n* : melted cheese poured over toast or crackers

Welsh rare·bit \-'ra(ə)r-bət, -'re(ə)r-\ *n* : WELSH RABBIT

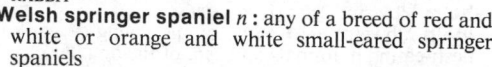

Welsh springer spaniel *n* : any of a breed of red and white or orange and white small-eared springer spaniels

welt \'welt\ *n* **1** : the narrow strip of leather between a shoe upper and sole to which other parts are stitched **2 a** : a ridge or lump raised on the skin usu. by a blow **b** : a heavy blow

1**wel·ter** \'wel-tər\ *vb* **wel·tered**; **wel·ter·ing** \-t(ə-)riŋ\ **1** : to tumble about : WALLOW **2** : to toss about in or with waves

2**welter** *n* **1** : a state of wild disorder : TURMOIL **2** : a chaotic mass or jumble

wen \'wen\ *n* : a cyst formed by obstruction of a skin gland and filled with fatty material

wench \'wench\ *n* **1** : GIRL **2** : a female servant

wend \'wend\ *vb* : to direct one's course : proceed on ⟨*wending* his way home⟩

went *past of* GO

wept *past of* WEEP

were *past 2d sing, past pl, or past subjunctive of* BE

we're \(,)wi(ə)r, (,)wər\ : we are

weren't \(')wərnt, 'wər-ənt\ : were not

were·wolf \'wi(ə)r-,wu̇lf, 'wər-, 'we(ə)r-\ *n, pl* **were·wolves** \-,wu̇lvz\ [from Old English *werwulf*, from *wer* "man" (from the same source as Latin *vir* "man", seen in English *virile*) and *wulf* "wolf"] : a person changed or able to change into a wolf

wert \(')wərt\ *archaic past 2d sing of* BE

1**west** \'west\ *adv* [from Old English, probably from the same prehistoric root as Latin *vesper* "evening", the source of English *vespers*] : to or toward the west

2**west** *adj* **1** : situated toward or at the west **2** : coming from the west

3**west** *n* **1 a** : the general direction of sunset **b** : the compass point directly opposite to east **2** *cap* : regions or countries west of a specified or implied point

1**west·er·ly** \'wes-tər-lē\ *adv or adj* **1** : from the west **2** : toward the west

2**westerly** *n, pl* **-lies** : a wind blowing from the west

1**west·ern** \'wes-tərn\ *adj* **1** *often cap* : of, relating to, or characteristic of the West **2** : lying toward or coming from the west

2**western** *n* : a novel, story, motion picture, or broadcast dealing with life in the western U.S. during the latter half of the 19th century

West·ern·er \'wes-tə(r)-nər\ *n* : a native or inhabitant of the West (as of the U.S.)

western hemlock *n* : a commercially important hemlock ranging from Alaska to California and having leaves without pale lines on the underside

west·ern·ize \'wes-tər-,nīz\ *vb* : to give western characteristics to — **west·ern·i·za·tion** \,wes-tər-nə-'zā-shən\ *n*

western larch *n* : an important timber tree of western North America with pale green sharply pointed leaves and oblong cones; *also* : its wood

western pine beetle *n* : a bark beetle destructive to various pines of the western U.S.

western wheatgrass *n* : a valuable forage grass of the western U.S.

West Highland white terrier *n* : a small white long-coated dog of a breed developed in Scotland

West Indian *adj* : of, relating to, or characteristic of the West Indies or the people of the West Indies — **West Indian** *n*

1**west·ward** \'wes-twərd\ *adv or adj* : toward the west — **west·wards** \-twərdz\ *adv*

2**westward** *n* : westward direction or part

1**wet** \'wet\ *adj* **wet·ter**; **wet·test** **1** : consisting of, containing, covered with, or soaked with liquid (as water) **2** : RAINY **3** : still moist enough to smudge or smear ⟨*wet* paint⟩ **4** : WRONG, MISTAKEN ⟨you're all *wet*⟩ — **wet·ly** *adv* — **wet·ness** *n*

2**wet** *n* **1** : WATER **2** : WETNESS, MOISTURE **3** : rainy weather : RAIN

3**wet** *vb* **wet** *or* **wet·ted**; **wet·ting** **1** : to make or become wet **2** : URINATE

weth·er \'weth-ər\ *n* : a male sheep castrated before sexual maturity

wet·land \'wet-,land\ *n* : swampy or boggy land

wetting agent *n* : a substance that when adsorbed on a surface reduces its tendency to repel a liquid

we've \(,)wēv\ : we have

wh *abbr* which

WH *abbr* watt-hour

1**whack** \'hwak\ *vb* : to strike or cut with a whack — **whack·er** *n*

2**whack** *n* **1 a** : a smart or ringing blow **b** : the sound of such a blow **2** : proper working order ⟨the car is out of *whack*⟩ **3** : TRY, ATTEMPT ⟨take a *whack* at it⟩

1**whale** \'hwāl\ *n, pl* **whale** *or* **whales** **1** : any of a

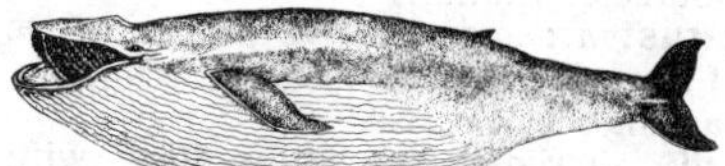

whale 1
(about 100 ft. long)

group of aquatic mammals valued for their oil, flesh, and sometimes whalebone; *esp* : one of the larger members of this group **2** : a person or thing impressive in size or qualities

2**whale** *vb* : to hunt whales

3**whale** *vb* : THRASH

whale·boat \'hwāl-,bōt\ *n* : a long narrow rowboat orig. used by whalers for hunting whales

whale·bone \-,bōn\ *n* : a horny substance found in two rows of long plates attached along the upper jaw of whalebone whales

whalebone whale *n* : any of various usu. large whales having whalebone instead of teeth

whale oil *n* : an oil obtained from whales that is used in tempering steel, in dressing leather, in making margarine and soap, and as a lubricant

whal·er \'hwā-lər\ *n* : a person or ship engaged in whale fishing

whale shark *n* : a very large harmless shark of tropical seas

wharf \'hwȯrf\ *n, pl* **wharves** \'hwȯrvz\ *also* **wharfs** : a structure built on the shore to enable ships to receive and discharge cargo and passengers

1**what** \(')hwät, (')hwət\ *pron* **1** — used in asking about the identity or nature of a thing or person

⟨*what* are those things on the table⟩ ⟨*what* is honor⟩ ⟨*what* do you think I am⟩ **2** : that which : the one or ones that ⟨no income but *what* he gets from his writings⟩ **3** : WHATEVER 1 ⟨do *what* you want⟩

[2]**what** *adv* **1 a** : in what way : HOW ⟨*what* does it matter⟩ **b** : how much ⟨*what* does he care⟩ **2** : in part ⟨kept busy *what* with studies and extracurricular activities⟩

[3]**what** *adj* **1 a** — used to inquire about the identity or nature of a person, object, or matter ⟨*what* minerals do we export⟩ **b** : how remarkable or surprising ⟨*what* a charming girl⟩ **2** : WHATEVER 1a

[1]**what·ev·er** \hwät-'ev-ər, (ˌ)hwət-\ *pron* **1** : anything or everything that ⟨take *whatever* is needed⟩ **2** : no matter what ⟨obey orders, *whatever* happens⟩

[2]**whatever** *adj* **1 a** : any ... that : all ... that ⟨take *whatever* action is needed⟩ **b** : no matter what **2** : of any kind at all ⟨no food *whatever*⟩

what·not \'hwät-ˌnät, 'hwət-\ *n* : a light open set of shelves for bric-a-brac

what·so·ev·er \ˌhwät-sə-'wev-ər, ˌhwət-\ *pron or adj* : WHATEVER

wheal \'hwēl\ *n* : WELT, WALE

wheat \'hwēt\ *n* [from Old English *hwǣte*, from the same root as English *white*] **1** : a cereal grain that yields a fine white flour, is the chief breadstuff of temperate climates, and is important in animal feeds **2** : any of a genus of grasses grown in most temperate areas for the wheat they yield; *esp* : an annual grass with long dense flower spikes and white to dark red grains that is the chief source of wheat and is known only in cultivation

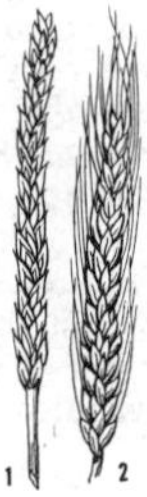

wheat 2: *1*, beardless; *2*, bearded

wheat·en \'hwēt-ən\ *adj* : made of wheat

wheat germ *n* : the embryo of the wheat kernel separated in milling and used esp. as a source of vitamins

wheat rust *n* : a destructive disease of wheat caused by rust fungi; *also* : a fungus causing a wheat rust

whee·dle \'hwēd-əl\ *vb* **whee·dled**; **whee·dling** \-(ə-)liŋ\ **1** : to coax or entice by soft words or flattery **2** : to gain or get by wheedling

[1]**wheel** \'hwēl\ *n* [from Old English *hwēol*, from the same prehistoric noun as Greek *kyklos* "circle", the source of English *cycle*] **1** : a disk or circular frame turning on a central axis **2** : something resembling a wheel (as in being round or in turning on an axis) **3** : a device the main part of which is a wheel **4** : BICYCLE **5** : a circular frame which when turned controls some apparatus ⟨a steering *wheel*⟩ **6** : a curving or circular movement **7 a** : a moving power : MECHANISM ⟨the *wheels* of government⟩ **b** : an important person — **wheeled** \'hwēld\ *adj*

[2]**wheel** *vb* **1** : to carry or move on wheels or in a vehicle with wheels ⟨*wheel* a load into the barn⟩ **2** : ROTATE, REVOLVE ⟨the earth *wheels* about the sun⟩ **3** : to change or reverse direction ⟨*wheeled* about⟩

wheel·bar·row \'hwēl-ˌbar-ō\ *n* : a small vehicle with handles and one or more wheels for carrying loads

wheel·base \-ˌbās\ *n* : the distance between the front and rear axles of an automotive vehicle

ə abut	ər further	a back	ā bake	
ä cot, cart	aù out	ch chin	e less	ē easy
g gift	i trip	ī life	j joke	ng sing	ō flow
ȯ flaw	ȯi coin	th thin	th this	ü loot
ù foot	y yet	yü few	yù furious	zh vision

wheel·chair \-ˌche(ə)r, -ˌcha(ə)r\ *n* : a chair on wheels used esp. by invalids

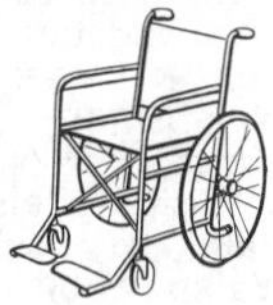
wheelchair

wheel·house \-ˌhau̇s\ *n* : PILOTHOUSE

wheel·wright \-ˌrīt\ *n* : a person who makes or repairs wheels and wheeled vehicles

wheeze \'hwēz\ *vb* **1** : to breathe with difficulty usu. with a whistling sound **2** : to make a sound like wheezing — **wheeze** *n* — **wheez·i·ness** \'hwē-zē-nəs\ *n* — **wheezy** \-zē\ *adj*

whelk \'hwelk, 'wilk\ *n* : any of numerous large marine snails; *esp* : one much used as food in Europe

whelm \'hwelm\ *vb* : OVERWHELM

[1]**whelp** \'hwelp\ *n* **1** : one of the young of various flesh-eating mammals and esp. of the dog **2** : CUR 2

[2]**whelp** *vb* : to give birth to whelps

[1]**when** \(')hwen, hwən\ *adv* **1** : at what time ⟨*when* will he return⟩ **2** : at or during which time ⟨a time *when* things were upset⟩

[2]**when** *conj* **1 a** : at or during the time that : WHILE ⟨went fishing *when* he was a boy⟩ **b** : just after the time that ⟨left *when* the bell rang⟩ **c** : every time that ⟨*when* she hears that tune, she cries⟩ **2** : in the event that : IF ⟨the batter is out *when* he bunts foul with two strikes⟩ **3** : THOUGH ⟨teases her *when* he knows she gets upset⟩

[3]**when** \ˌhwen\ *pron* : what or which time ⟨since *when* have you known that⟩

whence \(')hwen(t)s\ *adv* **1** : from what place, source, or cause ⟨*whence* come all these doubts⟩ **2** : from or out of which ⟨the stock *whence* he sprang⟩

[1]**when·ev·er** \hwen-'ev-ər, hwən-\ *conj* : at any or every time that ⟨stop *whenever* you wish⟩

[2]**whenever** *adv* : at whatever time ⟨available *whenever* desired⟩

when·so·ev·er \'hwen(t)-sə-ˌwev-ər\ *conj* : WHENEVER

[1]**where** \(')hwe(ə)r, (')hwa(ə)r, (ˌ)hwər\ *adv* **1** : at, in, or to which place, circumstances, or respect ⟨*where* are we going⟩ ⟨*where* is he wrong⟩ **2** : in, at, or to which ⟨the house *where* he was born⟩ **3** : from what place or source ⟨*where* did you get that idea⟩

[2]**where** *conj* **1 a** : at or in the place at or in which ⟨stay *where* you are⟩ **b** : to the place at, in, or to which ⟨went *where* he had promised to go⟩ **2** : WHEREVER ⟨sits *where* he pleases⟩ **3** : in a case, situation, or respect in which ⟨outstanding *where* endurance is called for⟩

[3]**where** \'hwe(ə)r, 'hwa(ə)r\ *pron* : what place, source, or cause ⟨*where* is he from⟩

[1]**where·abouts** \'hwer-ə-ˌbau̇ts, 'hwar-\ *also* **whereabout** \-ˌbau̇t\ *adv* : about where ⟨*whereabouts* is the house⟩

[2]**whereabouts** *n sing or pl* : the place where a person or thing is

where·as \hwer-'az, hwar-, (ˌ)hwər-\ *conj* **1** : in view of the fact that : SINCE **2** : while on the contrary ⟨water puts out fire, *whereas* alcohol burns⟩

where·at \-'at\ *conj* **1** : at or toward which **2** : in consequence of which

where·by \-'bī\ *conj* : by, through, or in accordance with which

[1]**where·fore** \'hwe(ə)r-ˌfōr, 'hwa(ə)r-, -ˌfȯr\ *adv* **1** : for what reason or purpose : WHY **2** : THEREFORE

[2]**wherefore** *n* : REASON, CAUSE

where·from \-ˌfrəm, -ˌfräm\ *conj* : from which

[1]**where·in** \hwer-'in, hwar-, (ˌ)hwər-\ *adv* : in what : in what respect ⟨*wherein* was he wrong⟩

[2]**wherein** *conj* : in which ⟨the city *wherein* he lives⟩
where·of \-'əv, -'äv\ *conj* **1** : of what ⟨knows *whereof* she speaks⟩ **2** : of which or whom ⟨books *whereof* the best are lost⟩
where·on \-'ȯn, -'än\ *adv* : on which ⟨the base *whereon* it rests⟩
where·so·ev·er \'hwer-sə-ˌwev-ər, 'hwar-\ *conj, archaic* : WHEREVER
where·up·on \'hwer-ə-ˌpȯn, 'hwar-, -ˌpän\ *conj* **1** : on which **2** : and then : at which time
[1]**wher·ev·er** \hwer-'ev-ər, hwar-, (ˌ)hwər-\ *adv* : where in the world ⟨*wherever* did she get that hat⟩
[2]**wherever** *conj* **1** : at, in, or to whatever place ⟨thrives *wherever* he goes⟩ **2** : in any circumstance in which ⟨*wherever* it is possible, he tries to help⟩
where·with \'hwe(ə)r-ˌwit͟h, 'hwa(ə)r-, -ˌwith\ *adv* : with or by means of which
where·with·al \'hwe(ə)r-wit͟h-ˌȯl, 'hwa(ə)r-, -with-\ *n* : MEANS, RESOURCES; *esp* : MONEY
wher·ry \'hwer-ē\ *n, pl* **wherries** : a long light rowboat pointed at both ends
whet \'hwet\ *vb* **whet·ted**; **whet·ting** **1** : to sharpen by rubbing on or with something (as a stone) ⟨*whet* a knife⟩ **2** : to make keen : STIMULATE ⟨*whet* the appetite⟩
wheth·er \'hwet͟h-ər, (ˌ)hwət͟h-ər\ *conj* **1 a** : if it is or was true that ⟨ask *whether* he is going⟩ **b** : if it is or was better ⟨uncertain *whether* to go or stay⟩ **2** : whichever is or was the case, namely, that ⟨*whether* we succeed or fail, we must try⟩ **3** : EITHER ⟨seated him next to her *whether* by accident or design⟩
whet·stone \'hwet-ˌstōn\ *n* : a stone for whetting sharp-edged tools
whew *often read as* 'hwü, 'hyü\ *n* : a sound like a half-formed whistle used chiefly to express amazement, discomfort, or relief
whey \'hwā\ *n* : the watery part of soured milk that separates from the thickened curd esp. in the process of making cheese
[1]**which** \(')hwich\ *adj* **1** : being what one or ones ⟨*which* tie should I wear⟩ ⟨knew *which* men were outsiders⟩ **2** : WHICHEVER ⟨it will not fit, turn it *which* way you like⟩
[2]**which** *pron* **1** : what one or ones out of a group ⟨*which* of those houses do you live in⟩ ⟨he is swimming or canoeing, I don't know *which*⟩ **2** : WHICHEVER ⟨take *which* you like⟩ **3** — used to introduce a relative clause which refers to other than human beings ⟨the records *which* he bought⟩
[1]**which·ev·er** \hwich-'ev-ər\ *pron* : whatever one or ones out of a group
[2]**whichever** *adj* : being whatever one or ones out of a group : no matter which ⟨*whichever* way you go⟩
[1]**whiff** \'hwif\ *n* **1** : a quick puff or slight gust ⟨a *whiff* of air⟩ **2** : an inhalation of odor, gas, or smoke
[2]**whiff** *vb* **1** : to expel, puff out, or blow away in or as if in whiffs **2** : to inhale an odor
whif·fle·tree \'hwif-əl-(ˌ)trē\ *n* : the pivoted swinging bar to which the traces of a harness are fastened and by which a vehicle or implement is drawn

whiffletree

Whig \'hwig\ *n* **1** : a member or supporter of a British political group of the 18th and early 19th centuries seeking to limit royal authority and increase parliamentary power **2** : an American favoring independence from Great Britain during the American Revolution **3** : a member or supporter of a 19th century American political party formed to oppose the Democrats
[1]**while** \'hwīl\ *n* **1** : a period of time ⟨stay here for a *while*⟩ **2** : time and effort used ⟨worth your *while*⟩
[2]**while** *conj* **1 a** : during the time that ⟨take a nap *while* I'm out⟩ **b** : as long as ⟨enjoy life *while* we can⟩ **2** : THOUGH ⟨*while* respected, he is not liked⟩
[3]**while** *vb* : to cause to pass pleasantly or without boredom ⟨*while* away the time⟩
[1]**whi·lom** \'hwī-ləm\ *adv, archaic* : FORMERLY
[2]**whilom** *adj* : FORMER ⟨his *whilom* friends⟩
whilst \'hwīlst\ *conj, chiefly Brit* : WHILE
whim \'hwim\ *n* : a sudden wish, desire, or change of mind
whim·per \'hwim-pər\ *vb* **whim·pered**; **whim·per·ing** \-p(ə-)ring\ : to make a low whining plaintive or broken sound — **whimper** *n*
whim·si·cal \'hwim-zi-kəl\ *adj* **1** : full of whims : CAPRICIOUS ⟨a *whimsical* person⟩ **2** : resulting from or characterized by whim : ERRATIC ⟨*whimsical* behavior⟩ — **whim·si·cal·i·ty** \ˌhwim-zə-'kal-ət-ē\ *n* — **whim·si·cal·ly** \'hwim-zi-k(ə-)lē\ *adv*
whim·sy *or* **whim·sey** \'hwim-zē\ *n, pl* **whimsies** *or* **whimseys** **1** : WHIM, CAPRICE **2** : FANTASY, IMAGINATION **3** : a fanciful or fantastic object or creation
whine \'hwīn\ *vb* **1** : to utter a high plaintive or distressed cry or a similar sound **2** : to complain with or as if with a whine — **whine** *n* — **whin·er** *n* — **whin·ing·ly** \'hwī-ning-lē\ *adv*
whin·ny \'hwin-ē\ *vb* **whin·nied**; **whin·ny·ing** : to neigh esp. in a low gentle manner — **whinny** *n*
[1]**whip** \'hwip\ *vb* **whipped**; **whip·ping** **1** : to move, snatch, or jerk quickly and forcefully ⟨*whip* out a gun⟩ **2** : to strike (as with a lash or rod) esp. as a punishment **3** : to thoroughly overcome : DEFEAT **4** : to stir up : INCITE ⟨*whip* up enthusiasm⟩ **5** : to beat into a froth ⟨*whip* cream⟩ **6** : to thrash about — **whip·per** *n*
[2]**whip** *n* **1** : a flexible instrument for whipping **2** : a dessert made by whipping eggs or cream **3** : a whipping motion
whip·cord \-ˌkȯrd\ *n* **1** : a thin tough braided cord **2** : a hard-woven cloth with fine diagonal ribs
whip·lash \'hwip-ˌlash\ *n* **1** : the lash of a whip **2** : WHIPLASH INJURY
whiplash injury *n* : injury to the spine often with concussion that is caused by violent flexing of the head and neck in an automobile accident
whip·per·snap·per \'hwip-ər-ˌsnap-ər\ *n* : a small, unimportant, or presumptuous person
whip·pet \'hwip-ət\ *n* : a small swift slender dog of greyhound type that is often used for racing
whip·ple·tree \'hwip-əl-(ˌ)trē\ *var of* WHIFFLETREE
whip·poor·will \ˌhwip-ər-'wil, 'hwip-ər-ˌ\ *n* : an insect-eating bird of the eastern U.S. and Canada that is active at night and is often heard at nightfall and just before dawn

whippoorwill
(about 10 in. long)

whip·tail \'hwip-ˌtāl\ *n* : any of a genus of slim-bodied long-tailed New World lizards that have granular scales on the back, large 4-sided scales on the belly, and scales on the tail differing from those on the body

[1]**whir** *also* **whirr** \'hwər\ *vb* **whirred**; **whir·ring** : to fly, revolve, or move rapidly with a buzzing whizzing sound

[2]**whir** *also* **whirr** *n* : a whirring sound

[1]**whirl** \'hwərl\ *vb* **1** : to move or drive in a circle or curve esp. with force or speed **2 a** : to turn rapidly in circles : SPIN **b** : to turn abruptly : WHEEL **3** : to move or go quickly **4** : to become giddy or dizzy : REEL — **whirl·er** *n*

[2]**whirl** *n* **1 a** : a rapid whirling movement **b** : something whirling ⟨a *whirl* of dust⟩ **2 a** : a confused tumult **b** : a confused or giddy mental state

whirl·i·gig \'hwər-li-ˌgig\ *n* **1** : a toy that has a whirling motion **2** : something that continuously whirls or changes

whirligig beetle *n* : any of a family of swift-moving beetles

whirl·pool \'hwərl-ˌpül\ *n* : water moving rapidly in a circle with a depression in the center into which floating objects are drawn : EDDY

whirl·wind \-ˌwind\ *n* : a windstorm with an upward whirling of the air

whish \'hwish\ *vb* : to move with a whizzing or swishing sound — **whish** *n*

[1]**whisk** \'hwisk\ *n* **1** : a quick brush or sweep ⟨a *whisk* of the hand⟩ **2** : a small kitchen implement used for beating food **3** : WHISK BROOM

[2]**whisk** *vb* **1** : to move nimbly and quickly ⟨squirrels *whisked* up the trees⟩ **2** : to move or convey briskly ⟨*whisked* the children off to bed⟩ **3** : to mix or fluff up by or as if by beating with a whisk ⟨*whisk* eggs⟩ **4** : to brush or wipe off lightly

whisk broom *n* : a small broom with a short handle used esp. as a clothes brush

whis·ker \'hwis-kər\ *n* **1 a** : a hair of the beard **b** *pl* : the part of the beard growing on the sides of the face or on the chin **2** : one of the long projecting hairs or bristles growing near the mouth of an animal (as a cat or bird) — **whis·kered** \-kərd\ *adj*

whis·key *or* **whis·ky** \'hwis-kē\ *n, pl* **whiskeys** *or* **whis·kies** [from Irish Gaelic *uisce beathadh* and Scotch Gaelic *uisge beatha*, meaning literally "water of life"] : a distilled alcoholic liquor made from fermented mash of grain (as rye, corn, or barley)

[1]**whis·per** \'hwis-pər\ *vb* **whis·pered**; **whis·per·ing** \-p(ə-)ring\ **1** : to speak very low or under the breath **2** : to tell or utter by whispering ⟨*whisper* a secret⟩ **3** : to make a low rustling sound ⟨*whispering* leaves⟩ — **whis·per·er** \-pər-ər\ *n*

[2]**whisper** *n* **1 a** : an act or instance of whispering **b** : a sibilant sound that resembles whispered speech **2** : HINT, RUMOR ⟨*whispers* of a scandal⟩

whist \'hwist\ *n* : a card game for four players in two partnerships

[1]**whis·tle** \'hwis-əl\ *n* **1** : a device by which a shrill sound is produced ⟨tin *whistle*⟩ ⟨steam *whistle*⟩ **2 a** : a shrill clear sound produced by forcing breath out or air in through puckered lips **b** : a sound or signal produced by a whistle or as if by whistling

[2]**whistle** *vb* **whis·tled**; **whis·tling** \'hwis-(ə-)ling\ **1** : to make a whistle through puckered lips **2** : to make a shrill clear sound esp. by rapid movement ⟨bullets *whistled* by⟩ **3** : to blow or sound a whistle **4** : to utter by whistling ⟨*whistle* a tune⟩ — **whis·tler** \-(ə-)lər\ *n*

ə abut	ər further		a back	ā bake
ä cot, cart	aù out	ch chin	e less	ē easy
g gift	i trip	ī life	j joke	ng sing	ō flow
ȯ flaw	ȯi coin	th thin	t͟h this	ü loot
u̇ foot	y yet	yü few	yu̇ furious	zh vision

whit \'hwit\ *n* : the smallest part or particle : BIT ⟨cared not a *whit*⟩

[1]**white** \'hwīt\ *adj* **1 a** : free from color **b** : of the color of new snow or milk **c** : light or pale in color ⟨*white* wine⟩ ⟨lips *white* with fear⟩ **d** : lustrous pale gray : SILVERY **2** : of, relating to, or being a member of a group or race characterized by relatively light pigmentation **3** *slang* : FAIR, HONEST ⟨that was *white* of him⟩ **4 a** : INNOCENT, PURE **b** : unmarked by writing or printing **c** : not intended to cause harm ⟨a *white* lie⟩ ⟨*white* magic⟩ **5** : SNOWY ⟨a *white* Christmas⟩ — **white·ness** *n*

[2]**white** *n* **1** : the color of fresh snow **2** : a white or light-colored thing or part (as the albuminous material around the yolk of an egg or the white part of the ball of the eye) **3** : a person belonging to a light-skinned race

white ant *n* : TERMITE

white blood cell *n* : a blood cell that does not contain hemoglobin : LEUKOCYTE — called also *white cell, white blood corpuscle, white corpuscle*

white·cap \'hwīt-ˌkap\ *n* : a wave crest breaking into white foam

white cedar *n* : any of various No. American timber trees including true cedars, junipers, and cypress

white clover *n* : any of various tall or low-growing clovers with white flowers

white crappie *n* : an edible silvery No. American sunfish

white dwarf *n* : a small, very dense whitish star of high surface temperature and low luminosity — compare RED GIANT

white elephant *n* [so called from the fact that in parts of India pale-colored elephants are held sacred and are maintained without being required to work] : something requiring much care and expense and yielding little profit or enjoyment

white·fish \'hwīt-ˌfish\ *n* : any of various freshwater food fishes related to the salmons and trouts and mostly greenish above and silvery white below

white flag *n* : a flag of plain white used as a flag of truce or as a sign of surrender

white gold *n* : a pale alloy of gold resembling platinum in appearance

white goods *n pl* **1** : cotton or linen fabrics or articles (as sheets or towels) **2** : major household appliances (as stoves)

white·head \'hwīt-ˌhed\ *n* : a small whitish elevation of the skin caused by accumulation of oil gland secretion when the duct of the gland is blocked by a thin layer of skin cells

white heat *n* **1** : a temperature at which a metallic body becomes brightly incandescent so as to appear white **2** : a state of intense strain, emotion, or activity — **white–hot** *adj*

white lead *n* : a heavy white poisonous carbonate of lead chiefly used as a pigment

white matter *n* : whitish nerve tissue that consists largely of nerve fibers sheathed in a fatty material and that underlies the gray matter of the brain and spinal cord or forms nerves

whit·en \'hwīt-ən\ *vb* **whit·ened**; **whit·en·ing** \-(ə-)ning\ : to make or become white or whiter — **whit·en·er** \-(ə-)nər\ *n*

white oak *n* : any of various oaks with acorns that mature in one year and leaf veins that never extend beyond the margin of the leaf; *also* : the hard, strong, durable, and moisture-resistant wood of a white oak

white pepper *n* : a pungent seasoning that is prepared by grinding the fruit of the East Indian pepper after the outer husk is removed

white pine *n* : a tall-growing pine of eastern No. America with leaves in clusters of five; *also* : its wood which is much used in construction

white–pine blister rust *n* : a destructive disease of white pine caused by a rust fungus that passes part of its life on currant or gooseberry bushes; *also* : this fungus

white potato *n* : POTATO 2b

white sturgeon *n* : a sturgeon of the pacific coast of No. America that is the largest freshwater fish of No. America

white·tail \'hwīt-ˌtāl\ *n* : a No. American deer with forward-arching antlers and a long tail white on the underside — called also *white-tailed deer* \ˌhwīt-ˌtāl(d)-'di(ə)r\

1**white·wash** \-ˌwȯsh, -ˌwäsh\ *vb* **1** : to whiten with whitewash **2** : to clear of a charge of wrongdoing by offering excuses, hiding facts, or conducting a careless investigation **3** : to hold an opponent scoreless — **white·wash·er** *n*

2**whitewash** *n* **1** : a composition (as of lime and water) for whitening walls **2** : a clearing by whitewashing

whith·er \'hwit͟h-ər\ *adv* **1** : to what place or situation ⟨*whither* will they go⟩ **2** : to which place ⟨the village *whither* we had brought our horses⟩

1**whit·ing** \'hwīt-ing\ *n, pl* **whiting** *or* **whitings** : any of several edible fishes (as the hake) found mostly near seacoasts

2**whiting** *n* : calcium carbonate prepared as fine powder and used esp. as a pigment, in putty, and in rubber compounding

whit·ish \'hwīt-ish\ *adj* : somewhat white

whit·low \'hwit-ˌlō\ *n* : an inflammation of a finger or toe esp. near the nail and usu. with pus

Whit·sun·day \'hwit-'sən-dē, -sən-ˌdā\ *n* [from Old English *hwīta sunnandæg* "white Sunday"; so called from the ancient custom of wearing white robes by the newly baptized, who were numerous at this season] : PENTECOST 2

Whit·sun·tide \'hwit-sən-ˌtīd\ *n* : the week beginning with Whitsunday; *esp* : the first three days of this week

whit·tle \'hwit-əl\ *vb* **whit·tled**; **whit·tling** \-(ə-)ling\ **1 a** : to pare or cut off chips from the surface of wood with a knife **b** : to shape or form by so paring or cutting **2** : to reduce gradually : PARE ⟨*whittle* down expenses⟩ — **whit·tler** \-(ə-)lər\ *n*

1**whiz** *or* **whizz** \'hwiz\ *vb* **whizzed**; **whiz·zing** **1** : to hum, whir, or hiss like a speeding object (as an arrow) passing through air **2** : to fly or move swiftly with a whiz — **whiz·zer** *n*

2**whiz** *or* **whizz** *n, pl* **whiz·zes** : a whizzing sound

3**whiz** *n, pl* **whiz·zes** : WIZARD 2

who *pron* **1** \(')hü\ : what or which person or persons ⟨*who* was elected president⟩ ⟨find out *who* they are⟩ **2** \(ˌ)hü, ü\ — used to introduce a relative in reference to persons ⟨my father, *who* was a lawyer⟩

WHO *abbr* World Health Organization

whoa \'wō, 'hō, 'hwō\ *imperative verb* — used as a command to a draft animal to stand still

who·dun·it \hü-'dən-ət\ *n* : a detective or mystery novel, play, or motion picture

who·ev·er \hü-'ev-ər\ *pron* : whatever person

1**whole** \'hōl\ *adj* [from Old English *hāl*, the source also of English *health*] **1** : being in healthy or sound condition : free from defect or damage : WELL, INTACT ⟨careful nursing made him *whole*⟩ ⟨every egg was *whole*⟩ **2** : having all its proper parts or elements ⟨*whole* milk⟩ **3** : made up of all its parts ⟨the *whole* family⟩ **4** : not divided or scattered ⟨a *whole* roast pig⟩ ⟨his *whole* attention⟩ **5** : COMPLETE, TOTAL ⟨the *whole* sky was red⟩ **6** : each or all of the ⟨the *whole* 10 days⟩

2**whole** *n* **1** : a complete amount or sum **2** : something whole or entire ⟨the *whole* of an apple⟩ — **on the whole** **1** : in view of all the circumstances : all things considered **2** : in general : in most instances : TYPICALLY

whole gale *n* : wind having a speed of 55 to 63 miles per hour

whole·heart·ed \'hōl-'härt-əd\ *adj* : undivided in purpose, enthusiasm, or will : HEARTY ⟨*wholehearted* effort⟩ — **whole·heart·ed·ly** *adv* — **wholeheart·ed·ness** *n*

whole note *n* : a musical note equal to one measure of four beats

whole number *n* **1** : one of the set of natural numbers together with zero **2** : INTEGER

1**whole·sale** \'hōl-ˌsāl\ *n* : the sale of goods in large quantity usu. for resale by a retail merchant

2**wholesale** *adj* **1** : of, relating to, or engaged in wholesaling ⟨a *wholesale* grocer⟩ ⟨*wholesale* prices⟩ **2** : done on a large scale : GENERAL ⟨*wholesale* slaughter⟩ — **wholesale** *adv*

3**wholesale** *vb* : to sell at wholesale — **whole·sal·er** *n*

whole·some \'hōl-səm\ *adj* **1** : promoting health or well-being ⟨*wholesome* advice⟩ ⟨a *wholesome* environment⟩ **2** : sound in body, mind, or morals : HEALTHY ***syn*** see HEALTHFUL ***ant*** noxious — **whole·some·ly** *adv* — **whole·some·ness** *n*

whole step *n* : a musical interval comprising two half steps — called also *whole tone*

whole wheat *adj* : made of ground entire wheat kernels

whol·ly \'hōl-(l)ē\ *adv* **1** : to the full or entire extent : COMPLETELY, TOTALLY **2** : EXCLUSIVELY, SOLELY

whom \(')hüm; (ˌ)hüm, üm\ *pron, objective case of* WHO

whom·ev·er \hü-'mev-ər\ *objective case of* WHOEVER

whom·so·ev·er \ˌhüm-sə-'wev-ər\ *objective case of* WHOSOEVER

1**whoop** \'h(w)üp, 'h(w)u̇p\ *vb* **1** : to shout or call loudly and vigorously esp. in enthusiasm or enjoyment ⟨the boys *whooped* with joy⟩ **2** : to make the sound that follows an attack of coughing in whooping cough — **whoop it up** **1** : to celebrate loudly : CAROUSE **2** : to stir up enthusiasm

2**whoop** *n* **1** : a whooping sound or utterance **2** : a loud booming call of a bird (as an owl or crane) : HOOT **3** : a crowing sound accompanying the intake of breath after a coughing attack in whooping cough

whooping cough *n* : an infectious bacterial disease esp. of children marked by a spasmodic cough sometimes followed by a crowing intake of breath

whooping crane *n* : a large white nearly extinct No. American crane

whop·per \'hwäp-ər\ *n* **1** : something unusually large **2** : a monstrous lie

whop·ping \'hwäp-ing\ *adj* : extremely large

whore \'hō(ə)r, 'hȯ(ə)r\ *n* : PROSTITUTE

whorl \'hwȯrl, 'hwərl\ *n* **1** : a row of parts (as leaves or petals) encircling an axis and esp. a stem **2** : something that whirls, coils, or spirals ⟨the *whorl* of a fingerprint⟩

whooping crane
(about 50 in. long)

W

3 : one of the turns of a univalve shell — **whorled** \'hwȯrld, 'hwərld\ *adj*

1**whose** \(')hüz, üz\ *adj* **:** of or relating to whom or which ⟨*whose* bag is it⟩ ⟨the book *whose* cover is torn⟩

2**whose** \(')hüz\ *pron* **:** whose one **:** whose ones

who·so \'hü-ˌsō\ *pron* **:** WHOEVER

who·so·ev·er \ˌhü-sə-'wev-ər\ *pron* **:** WHOEVER

wh–question \ˌdəb-əl-yü-'ăch-\ *n* **:** a question headed by one of a small group of interrogative words (as *who, where,* or *how*)

whr *abbr* watt-hour

1**why** \(')hwī\ *adv* **:** for what cause, reason, or purpose ⟨*why* did you do it⟩

2**why** *conj* **1 :** the cause, reason, or purpose for which ⟨know *why* you did it⟩ **2 :** for which **:** on account of which ⟨the reason *why* he did it⟩

3**why** \'hwī\ *n, pl* **whys :** REASON, CAUSE ⟨the *why* of race prejudice⟩

4**why** \(ˌ)wī, (ˌ)hwī\ *interj* — used to express surprise, hesitation, approval, disapproval, or impatience

WI *abbr* Wisconsin

wick \'wik\ *n* **:** a cord, strip, or ring of loosely woven material through which a liquid (as wax or oil) is drawn to the top in a candle, lamp, or oil stove for burning

wick·ed \'wik-əd\ *adj* **1 :** morally bad **:** EVIL **2 :** HARMFUL, DANGEROUS ⟨a *wicked* cough⟩ **3 :** UNPLEASANT, VILE ⟨a *wicked* odor⟩ ⟨*wicked* weather⟩ **4 :** disposed to mischief **:** ROGUISH — **wick·ed·ly** *adv* — **wick·ed·ness** *n*

wick·er \'wik-ər\ *n* **1 :** a flexible twig or osier **2 :** WICKERWORK — **wicker** *adj*

wick·er·work \-ˌwərk\ *n* **:** work of osiers, twigs, or rods **:** BASKETRY

wick·et \'wik-ət\ *n* **1 :** a small gate or door; *esp* **:** one in or near a larger one **2 :** a small window with a grille or grate (as at a ticket office) **3 :** either of the 2 sets of 3 rods topped by 2 crosspieces at which the ball is bowled in cricket **4 :** an arch or hoop in croquet

wick·i·up \'wik-ē-ˌəp\ *n* **:** a cone-shaped Indian hut consisting of a rough frame covered with reed mats, grass, or brushwood

1**wide** \'wīd\ *adj* **1 :** covering a vast area ⟨the *wide* world⟩ **2 :** measured across or at right angles to length ⟨cloth 54 inches *wide*⟩ **3 :** having a generous measure across **:** BROAD **4 :** opened as far as possible ⟨eyes *wide* with wonder⟩ **5 :** not limited **:** EXTENSIVE ⟨*wide* experience⟩ **6 :** far from the goal, mark, or truth ⟨a *wide* guess⟩ — **wide·ly** *adv* — **wide·ness** *n*

2**wide** *adv* **1 :** over a great distance or extent **:** WIDELY ⟨searched far and *wide*⟩ **2 a :** so as to leave much space between ⟨*wide* apart⟩ **b :** so as to clear by a wide distance ⟨ran *wide* around left end⟩ **3 :** COMPLETELY, FULLY ⟨opened her eyes *wide*⟩ **4 :** so as to diverge or miss **:** ASTRAY ⟨the bullet went *wide*⟩

wide–awake \ˌwīd-ə-'wāk\ *adj* **1 :** fully awake **2 :** KEEN, ALERT

wide–eyed \'wīd-'īd\ *adj* **1 :** having the eyes wide open **2 :** struck with wonder or astonishment **3 :** INNOCENT, NAÏVE ⟨a *wide-eyed* belief in the goodness of everybody⟩

wide·mouthed \-'mau̇t͟hd, -'mau̇tht\ *adj* **1 :** having a wide mouth ⟨*widemouthed* jars⟩ **2 :** having one's mouth opened wide (as in awe)

wid·en \'wīd-ən\ *vb* **wid·ened; wid·en·ing** \-(ə-)ning\ **:** to make or become wide or wider **:** BROADEN — **wid·en·er** \-(ə-)nər\ *n*

wide·spread \'wīd-'spred\ *adj* **1 :** widely spread out ⟨*widespread* wings⟩ **2 :** widely scattered or prevalent ⟨*widespread* dissatisfaction⟩

wid·geon *also* **wi·geon** \'wij-ən\ *n, pl* **widgeon** *or* **wid·geons :** any of several freshwater ducks between the teal and the mallard in size

1**wid·ow** \'wid-ō\ *n* [from Old English *widuwe*, from a prehistoric root meaning "to separate", the source of English *divide*] **:** a woman who has lost her husband by death — **wid·ow·hood** \-ˌhu̇d\ *n*

2**widow** *vb* **:** to cause to become a widow ⟨*widowed* by war⟩

wid·ow·er \'wid-ə-wər\ *n* **:** a man who has lost his wife by death

width \'width\ *n* **1 a :** a distance from side to side **b :** BREADTH, WIDENESS **2 :** largeness of extent or scope **3 :** a measured piece of material ⟨a *width* of calico⟩ ⟨a *width* of lumber⟩

wield \'wēld\ *vb* **1 :** to handle effectively ⟨*wield* a broom⟩ **2 :** to exert one's authority by means of ⟨*wield* influence⟩ — **wield·er** *n*

wie·ner \'wē-nər, -nē\ *n* [short for German *wienerwurst* "Vienna sausage"] **:** FRANKFURTER

wife \'wīf\ *n, pl* **wives** \'wīvz\ **1** *dial* **:** WOMAN **2 :** a married woman

wife·ly \'wīf-lē\ *adj* **wife·li·er; -est :** of, relating to, or befitting a wife

wig \'wig\ *n* **:** a manufactured covering of natural or artificial hair for the head

wig·gle \'wig-əl\ *vb* **wig·gled; wig·gling** \-(ə-)ling\ **1 :** to move to and fro with quick jerky or shaking motions **:** JIGGLE ⟨*wiggled* his toes⟩ **2 :** WRIGGLE — **wiggle** *n*

wig·gler \'wig-(ə-)lər\ *n* **1 :** one that wiggles **2 :** a larval or pupal mosquito — called also *wriggler*

wig·gly \'wig-(ə-)lē\ *adj* **wig·gli·er; -est 1 :** tending to wiggle ⟨a *wiggly* worm⟩ **2 :** WAVY ⟨*wiggly* lines⟩

wight \'wīt\ *n* **:** a living being **:** CREATURE

1**wig·wag** \'wig-ˌwag\ *vb* **wig·wagged; -wag·ging :** to signal esp. by a flag or light waved according to a code

2**wigwag** *n* **1 :** the art or practice of wigwagging **2 :** a wigwagged message

wig·wam \'wig-ˌwäm\ *n* [from an American Indian word *wīkwām*, meaning literally "their dwelling"] **:** a domed hut made of poles overlaid with bark, rush mats, or hides

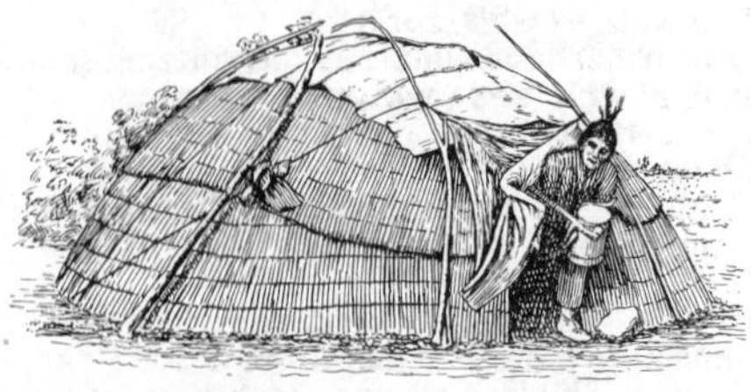

wigwam

1**wild** \'wīld\ *adj* **1 a :** living in a state of nature and not ordinarily tame or domesticated ⟨*wild* duck⟩ **b :** growing or produced without the aid and care of man ⟨*wild* honey⟩ **c :** of or relating to wild organisms ⟨the *wild* state⟩ **2 :** not inhabited or cultivated

ə abut	ər further	a back	ā bake
ä cot, cart	au̇ out	ch chin	e less
ē easy	g gift	i trip	ī life
j joke	ng sing	ō flow	ȯ flaw
ȯi coin	th thin	t͟h this	ü loot
u̇ foot	y yet	yü few	yu̇ furious
zh vision			

⟨*wild* land⟩ **3 a :** UNCONTROLLED, UNRULY ⟨*wild* rage⟩ ⟨a *wild* young stallion⟩ **b :** TURBULENT, STORMY ⟨a *wild* night⟩ **c :** EXTRAVAGANT, FANTASTIC ⟨*wild* colors⟩ ⟨*wild* ideas⟩ **4 :** UNCIVILIZED, SAVAGE **5 :** deviating from the proper course ⟨a *wild* pitch⟩ — **wild·ly** *adv* — **wild·ness** \'wīl(d)-nəs\ *n*

2**wild** *n* : WILDERNESS

3**wild** *adv* **1 :** WILDLY **2 :** without regulation or control ⟨running *wild*⟩

wild bee *n* : any of numerous undomesticated social bees; *also* : the honeybee when escaped from domestication

wild boar *n* : an Old World wild hog that has contributed to the ancestry of most domestic swine

wild carrot *n* : a widely naturalized white-flowered Eurasian weed that is prob. the original of the cultivated carrot — called also *Queen Anne's lace*

1**wild·cat** \'wīl(d)-,kat\ *n, pl* **wildcats** *or* **wildcat** **1 :** any of various small or medium-sized cats (as the lynx or ocelot) **2 :** a savage quick-tempered person

2**wildcat** *adj* **1 :** operating or produced outside the bounds of standard or legitimate business practices **2 :** of, relating to, or being an oil or gas well drilled in territory not known to be productive **3 :** begun without union approval or in violation of a contract ⟨a *wildcat* strike⟩

3**wildcat** *vb* **-cat·ted; -cat·ting :** to drill a wildcat oil or gas well — **wild·cat·ter** *n*

wil·der·ness \'wil-dər-nəs\ *n* : an uncultivated and uninhabited region : wild or waste land

wild·fire \'wīl(d)-,fī(ə)r\ *n* : a sweeping and destructive fire

wild flower *n* : the flower of a wild or uncultivated plant or the plant bearing it

wild·fowl \'wīl(d)-,faůl\ *n* : a game bird; *esp* : a game waterfowl (as a wild duck or goose)

wild geranium *n* : a geranium of the eastern U.S. with rosy purple or white flowers

wild·life \'wīl-,(d)līf\ *n* : creatures that are neither human nor domesticated; *esp* : mammals, birds, and fishes hunted by man — **wildlife** *adj*

wild rice *n* : a tall aquatic No. American grass yielding an edible grain

wild·wood \'wīl-,(d)wůd\ *n* : a wood unaltered or unfrequented by man

1**wile** \'wīl\ *n* **1 :** a trick or stratagem intended to deceive or tempt **2 :** TRICKERY, GUILE

2**wile** *vb* : LURE, ENTICE

1**will** \wəl, (ə)l, (')wil\ *vb, past* **would** \wəd, (ə)d, (')wůd\; *pres sing & pl* **will** **1 :** DESIRE, WISH ⟨call it what you *will*⟩ **2** — used as an auxiliary verb to express (1) desire, willingness, or in negative constructions refusal ⟨*will* you have another⟩ ⟨no one *would* do it⟩ ⟨he *won't* stop⟩, (2) customary or habitual action ⟨*will* get angry over nothing⟩, (3) simple futurity ⟨tomorrow we *will* go shopping⟩, (4) capability or sufficiency ⟨the back seat *will* hold three⟩, (5) determination or willfulness ⟨I *will* go despite them⟩, or (6) a command ⟨you *will* do as I say⟩

2**will** \'wil\ *n* **1 :** wish or desire often combined with determination ⟨the *will* to win⟩ **2 :** something desired; *esp* : a choice or determination of one having authority or power ⟨the king's *will*⟩ **3 :** the process or power of wishing, choosing, desiring, or intending **4 :** SELF-CONTROL ⟨a man of iron *will*⟩ **5 :** a legal declaration in which a person states how he wishes his property to be disposed of after his death

3**will** \'wil\ *vb* **1 :** to dispose of by or as if by a will **:** BEQUEATH **2 :** to determine by an act of choice ⟨his conformity was *willed*, not forced on him⟩ **3 :** DECREE, ORDAIN ⟨Providence *wills* it⟩ **4 :** INTEND, PURPOSE ⟨he *willed* it so⟩ **5 :** CHOOSE ⟨went wherever they *willed*⟩

willed \'wild\ *adj* : having a will esp. of a specified kind ⟨strong-*willed*⟩

will·ful *or* **wil·ful** \'wil-fəl\ *adj* **1 :** governed by will without regard to reason : OBSTINATE **2 :** done deliberately : INTENTIONAL ⟨*willful* murder⟩ — **will·ful·ly** \-fə-lē\ *adv* — **will·ful·ness** *n*

will·ing \'wil-ing\ *adj* **1 :** inclined or favorably disposed in mind : READY ⟨*willing* to go⟩ **2 :** prompt to act or respond ⟨*willing* workers⟩ **3 :** done, borne, or accepted by choice : VOLUNTARY ⟨*willing* obedience⟩ — **will·ing·ly** \-ing-lē\ *adv* — **will·ing·ness** *n*

wil·li·waw \'wil-i-,wȯ\ *n* : a sudden violent gust of cold land air common along mountainous coasts of high latitudes

will-o'-the-wisp \,wil-ə-t͟hə-'wisp\ *n* **1 :** a light that sometimes appears in the night over marshy ground and is often attributable to the combustion of gas from decomposed organic matter **2 :** a goal or hope that lures or misleads

wil·low \'wil-ō\ *n* **1 :** any of a large genus of trees and shrubs bearing catkins of flowers without petals and including forms of value for wood, osiers, or tanbark and a few ornamentals **2 :** an object made of willow wood — **willow** *adj* — **wil·low·like** \-,līk\ *adj*

wil·lowy \'wil-ə-wē\ *adj* **1 :** abounding with willows **2 a :** resembling a willow : PLIANT **b :** gracefully tall and slender ⟨a *willowy* young woman⟩

wil·ly-nil·ly \,wil-ē-'nil-ē\ *adv or adj* [alteration of *will I nill I* and *will ye nill ye*, using *nill*, archaic negative of *will*, from Old English *nyllan*, from *ne* "not" and *wyllan* "to wish", "will"] : whether one wants to or not ⟨rushed us along *willy-nilly*⟩

1**wilt** \wəlt, (')wilt\ *archaic pres 2d sing of* WILL

2**wilt** \'wilt\ *vb* **1 :** to lose or cause to lose freshness and become limp : DROOP ⟨*wilting* roses⟩ **2 :** to grow weak or faint

3**wilt** \'wilt\ *n* : a plant disorder (as various fungus diseases) in which the soft tissues become limp and often shrivel

wily \'wī-lē\ *adj* **wil·i·er; -est :** full of guile : TRICKY *syn* see CUNNING — **wil·i·ness** *n*

wim·ple \'wim-pəl\ *n* : a cloth covering worn over the head and around the neck and chin by women in late medieval times and by some nuns

1**win** \'win\ *vb* **won** \'wən\; **win·ning** **1 :** to gain the victory in a contest **2 :** to get esp. by effort : GAIN **3 a :** to gain in or as if in battle or contest **b :** to be the victor in ⟨*won* the war⟩ **4 :** PERSUADE; *esp* : to induce to accept oneself in marriage ⟨*won* the woman he loved⟩

2**win** *n* : VICTORY; *esp* : first place in a horse race

wince \'win(t)s\ *vb* : to shrink back (as from pain) : FLINCH — **wince** *n*

winch \'winch\ *n* : a machine that has a roller on which rope is coiled for hauling or hoisting

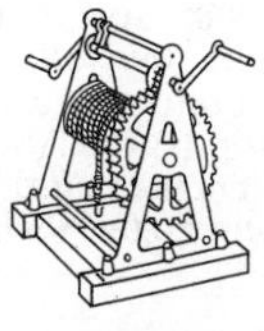
winch

1**wind** \'wind\ *n* **1 :** a movement of air **2 :** TENDENCY, TREND **3 :** BREATH 2a **4 :** gas generated in the stomach or the intestines **5 :** something insubstantial; *esp* : idle words **6 a :** air carrying a scent (as of a hunter or game) **b :** slight information esp. about something secret ⟨got *wind* of our plans⟩ **7** *pl* : the wind instruments of a band or orchestra **8 :** the direction from which the wind is blowing — **in the wind :** about to happen : ASTIR, AFOOT

W

2**wind** *vb* **1 :** to get a scent of ⟨the dogs *winded* game⟩ **2 :** to cause to be out of breath **3 :** to allow to rest so as to recover breath ⟨*wind* a horse⟩

3**wind** \'wīnd, 'wind\ *vb* **wound** \'wau̇nd\; **wind·ing :** to sound by blowing ⟨*wind* a horn⟩

4**wind** \'wīnd\ *vb* **wound** \'wau̇nd\ *also* **wind·ed**; **wind·ing 1 :** to move in a curving course ⟨a river *winding* through the valley⟩ **2 :** ENTANGLE, INVOLVE **3 a :** to encircle or cover with something pliable **b :** to coil completely or repeatedly about an object **:** TWINE ⟨*wind* thread on a spool⟩ **4 a :** to hoist or haul by means of a rope or chain and a windlass ⟨*wind* up a pail⟩ **b :** to move a ship by hauling on a capstan **5 a :** to tighten the spring of ⟨*wind* a clock⟩ ⟨*wind* up a toy train⟩ **b :** CRANK ⟨*wound* down the car window⟩ — **wind·er** *n*

5**wind** \'wīnd\ *n* **:** COIL, TURN

wind·age \'win-dij\ *n* **1 :** the influence of the wind in turning the course of a projectile **2 :** the amount of deflection caused by the wind

wind·blown \'win(d)-ˌblōn\ *adj* **:** blown by the wind ⟨*windblown* pollen⟩; *also* **:** having the appearance of being blown by the wind

wind·break \-ˌbrāk\ *n* **:** something (as a growth of trees) that serves as a shelter from the wind

wind·burn \-ˌbərn\ *n* **:** skin irritation caused by wind — **wind·burned** \-ˌbərnd\ *adj*

wind erosion *n* **:** erosion and dispersal of topsoil by the action of wind

wind·fall \'win(d)-ˌfȯl\ *n* **1 :** something (as a tree or fruit) blown down by the wind **2 :** an unexpected gift, gain, or advantage

wind·flow·er \-ˌflau̇(-ə)r\ *n* **:** ANEMONE

wind·ing \'wīn-ding\ *n* **1 :** material (as wire) wound or coiled about an object (as an armature) **2 :** a single turn of wound material

wind·ing–sheet \-ˌshēt\ *n* **:** a sheet used to wrap a corpse for burial **:** SHROUD

wind instrument *n* **:** a musical instrument (as a flute or horn) sounded by wind and esp. by the breath

wind·jam·mer \'win(d)-ˌjam-ər\ *n* **:** a sailing ship or one of its crew

wind·lass \'win-dləs\ *n* **:** a winch esp. on a ship

wind·mill \'win(d)-ˌmil\ *n* **:** a mill or a machine (as a pump) worked by the wind turning sails or vanes at the top of a tower

windmill

win·dow \'win-dō\ *n* [from Old Norse *vindauga*, literally "wind eye"] **1 :** an opening esp. in a wall to admit light or air or to permit viewing **2 :** WINDOWPANE

window box *n* **:** a box designed to hold soil for growing plants on a windowsill

win·dow·pane \'win-dō-ˌpān\ *n* **:** a pane in a window

window shade *n* **:** a shade or curtain for a window

win·dow–shop \-ˌshäp\ *vb* **:** to look at the displays in store windows without going inside to buy — **win·dow–shop·per** *n*

win·dow·sill \-ˌsil\ *n* **:** the horizontal piece at the bottom of a window

wind·pipe \'win(d)-ˌpīp\ *n* **:** a firm tubular passage connecting the pharynx and lungs **:** TRACHEA

wind·row \'win-ˌ(d)rō\ *n* **1 :** hay raked up into a row to dry **2 :** a row of something (as sand or dry leaves) heaped up by or as if by the wind

wind·shield \'win(d)-ˌshēld\ *n* **:** a transparent screen (as of glass) in front of the occupants of a vehicle

wind·storm \-ˌstȯrm\ *n* **:** a storm marked by high wind with little or no rain

wind tunnel *n* **:** an enclosed passage through which air is blown against structures (as airplanes) to test the effect of wind pressure on them

1**wind·up** \'wīn-ˌdəp\ *n* **1 a :** the act of bringing to an end **b :** a concluding act or part **:** FINISH **2 :** movement of the arms and legs preliminary to pitching a baseball

2**windup** *adj* **:** having a spring wound by hand ⟨*windup* toy⟩

wind up \'wīn-'dəp\ *vb* **1 :** to bring or come to a conclusion **:** END **2 :** to put in order **:** SETTLE **3 :** to arrive in a place, situation, or state ⟨*wound up* as millionaires⟩ **4 :** to make preliminary motions with the arms and legs (as before pitching a baseball)

1**wind·ward** \'win-(d)wərd\ *adj* **:** moving or situated toward the direction from which the wind is blowing

2**windward** *n* **:** the side or direction from which the wind is blowing ⟨sail to *windward*⟩

windy \'win-dē\ *adj* **wind·i·er**; **-est 1 :** having wind **:** exposed to winds ⟨a *windy* day⟩ ⟨a *windy* prairie⟩ **2 :** indulging in or characterized by useless talk ⟨a *windy* speaker⟩ — **wind·i·ness** *n*

1**wine** \'wīn\ *n* **1 :** fermented grape juice containing alcohol **2 :** the usu. fermented juice of a plant product (as a fruit) used as a beverage **3 :** a dark red color

2**wine** *vb* **1 :** to treat to wine ⟨*wined* and dined his friends⟩ **2 :** to drink wine

1**wing** \'wing\ *n* **1 :** one of the movable feathered or membranous paired appendages by means of which a bird, bat, or insect is able to fly **2 :** a flat or broadly expanded plant or animal part likened to a wing in shape, appearance, or position ⟨a stem with woody *wings*⟩ **3 :** a sidepiece at the top of an armchair **4 :** an airfoil that supports a heavier-than-air aircraft **5 :** the act or manner of flying **:** FLIGHT **6 :** ARM; *esp* **:** a throwing or pitching arm **7 :** a part projecting from a main element ⟨the rear *wing* of the house⟩ **8** *pl* **:** the area at the side of the stage out of sight **9 a :** a section of an army, fleet, or air division **b :** one of the positions or players on each side of a center position or line **10 :** either of two opposing groups in an organization **:** FACTION — **winged** \'wingd, 'wing-əd\ *adj* — **on the wing :** in flight **:** FLYING — **under one's wing :** under one's protection **:** in one's care

2**wing** *vb* **1 :** to pass through in flight **:** FLY **2 :** to wound in the wing; *also* **:** to wound without killing

wing case *n* **:** ELYTRON

wing·less \'wing-ləs\ *adj* **:** having no wings or very rudimentary wings

wing·span \-ˌspan\ *n* **:** WINGSPREAD; *esp* **:** the distance between the tips of an airplane's wings

wing·spread \-ˌspred\ *n* **:** the spread of the wings; *esp* **:** the distance between the tips of the fully extended wings of a bird, bat, or insect

1**wink** \'wingk\ *vb* **1 :** to close and open the eyes quickly **:** BLINK **2 :** to avoid seeing; pretend not to look ⟨*wink* at a violation of the law⟩ **3 :** FLICKER, TWINKLE **4 :** to close and open one eye quickly as a signal

2**wink** *n* **1 :** a brief period of sleep **:** NAP **2 a :** a hint or sign given by winking **b :** an act of winking **3 :** the time of a wink **:** INSTANT

win·ner \'win-ər\ *n* **:** one that wins

1**win·ning** \'win-ing\ *n* **1 :** the act of one that wins

: VICTORY **2** : something won; *esp* : money won at gambling — often used in pl.
²winning *adj* : ATTRACTIVE, CHARMING — **win·ning·ly** \-ing-lē\ *adv*
win·now \'win-ō\ *vb* **1 a** : to remove chaff from grain by a current of air **b** : to subject grain to a current of air to remove waste **2** : to sort or separate as if by winnowing — **win·now·er** \'win-ə-wər\ *n*
win·some \'win(t)-səm\ *adj* **1** : causing joy or pleasure : WINNING, CHARMING **2** : CHEERFUL, GAY — **win·some·ly** *adv* — **win·some·ness** *n*
¹win·ter \'wint-ər\ *n* **1** : the season between autumn and spring comprising in the northern hemisphere usu. the months of December, January, and February or extending from the December solstice to the March equinox **2** : YEAR ⟨a man of 70 *winters*⟩ **3** : a time or season of inactivity or decay
²winter *vb* **win·tered**; **win·ter·ing** \'wint-ə-ring, 'win-tring\ **1** : to pass or live through the winter ⟨the cattle *wintered* on the range⟩ **2** : to keep, feed, or manage during the winter ⟨*winter* livestock⟩
³winter *adj* : occurring in or surviving the winter; *esp* : sown in autumn for harvesting in the following spring or summer ⟨*winter* wheat⟩
winter bud *n* : the dormant shoot of a woody plant that is enclosed by overlapping scales
win·ter·green \'wint-ər-ˌgrēn\ *n* **1** : any of several low-growing evergreen plants related to the heaths; *esp* : one with white bell-shaped flowers followed by spicy red berries **2** : an oil from the common wintergreen or its flavor; *also* : something flavored with wintergreen

wintergreen 1

win·ter·ize \'wint-ə-ˌrīz\ *vb* : to make ready for winter ⟨*winterize* the car⟩
win·ter–kill \'wint-ər-ˌkil\ *vb* : to kill (as a plant) by exposure to winter conditions; *also* : to die as a result of such exposure — **winterkill** *n*
winter squash *n* : any of various squashes or pumpkins that keep well in storage
win·ter·time \'wint-ər-ˌtīm\ *n* : the winter season
win through *vb* : to survive difficulties and reach a desired or satisfactory end
win·try \'win-trē\ *adj* **win·tri·er**; **-est** **1** : of, relating to, or characteristic of winter **2** : CHILLING, CHEERLESS ⟨a *wintry* welcome⟩ — **win·tri·ness** *n*
¹wipe \'wīp\ *vb* **1** : to clean or dry by rubbing ⟨*wipe* dishes⟩ **2** : to remove by or as if by rubbing ⟨*wipe* away tears⟩ **3** : to pass or draw over a surface ⟨*wiped* his hand across his face⟩ — **wip·er** *n*
²wipe *n* : an act or instance of wiping
wipe out *vb* : to erase completely : DESTROY ⟨the platoon was *wiped out*⟩
¹wire \'wī(ə)r\ *n* **1 a** : metal in the form of a usu. flexible thread or slender rod **b** : a thread or rod of metal **2** *usu pl* : hidden or secret influences on a person or organization **3 a** : a line of wire for conducting electrical current **b** : a telephone or telegraph wire or system **c** : TELEGRAM, CABLEGRAM — **wire-like** \-ˌlīk\ *adj* — **under the wire** **1** : at the finish line **2** : at the last moment
²wire *vb* **1** : to provide with wire **2** : to provide with electricity ⟨*wire* a farm⟩ **3** : to send or send word to by telegraph
wire cloth *n* : a fabric of woven metallic wire (as for strainers)
wire·haired \'wī(ə)r-'ha(ə)rd, -'he(ə)rd\ *adj* : having a stiff wiry outer coat of hair
¹wire·less \-ləs\ *adj* **1** : having no wire or wires **2** *chiefly Brit* : of or relating to radiotelegraphy, radiotelephony, or radio
²wireless *n* **1** : WIRELESS TELEGRAPHY **2** : RADIOTELEPHONY **3** *chiefly Brit* : RADIO — **wireless** *vb*
wireless telegraphy *n* : telegraphy carried on by radio waves and without connecting wires
wire recorder *n* : a magnetic recorder using magnetic wire
wire recording *n* : magnetic recording on magnetic wire or the recording made by this process
wire service *n* : a news agency that sends out syndicated news copy by wire to subscribers
¹wire·tap \'wī(ə)r-ˌtap\ *vb* : to tap a telephone or telegraph wire to get information — **wire·tap·per** *n*
²wiretap *n* : the act or an instance of wiretapping
wire·worm \-ˌwərm\ *n* : the slender hard-coated larva of various beetles that is often destructive to roots
wiry \'wī(ə)r-ē\ *adj* **wir·i·er**; **wir·i·est** **1** : of, relating to, or resembling wire **2** : being slender yet strong and sinewy
Wis *or* **Wisc** *abbr* Wisconsin
wis·dom \'wiz-dəm\ *n* **1 a** : accumulated learning : KNOWLEDGE **b** : ability to discern inner qualities and relationships **c** : good sense : JUDGMENT **2** : a wise attitude or course of action
wisdom tooth *n* : the last tooth of the full set on each half of each jaw in man
¹wise \'wīz\ *n* : WAY, MANNER, FASHION — used in such phrases as *in any wise, in no wise, in this wise*
²wise *adj* **1** : having or showing wisdom : SENSIBLE **2** : aware of what is going on : INFORMED — **wise-ly** *adv*
³wise *vb* : to make or become informed or knowledgeable — used with *up*
-wise \ˌwīz\ *adv comb form* **1 a** : in the manner of ⟨crab*wise*⟩ ⟨fan*wise*⟩ **b** : in the position or direction of ⟨slant*wise*⟩ ⟨clock*wise*⟩ **2** : with regard to : in respect of ⟨dollar*wise*⟩
wise·acre \'wī-ˌzā-kər\ *n* : one who pretends to knowledge or cleverness : SMART ALECK
wise·crack \'wīz-ˌkrak\ *n* : a clever, smart, or flippant remark — **wisecrack** *vb* — **wise·crack·er** *n*
wise guy \'wīz-ˌgī\ *n* : WISEACRE
¹wish \'wish\ *vb* **1** : to have a desire : long for : WANT ⟨*wish* you were here⟩ ⟨*wish* for a puppy⟩ **2** : to form or express a desire concerning ⟨*wished* him a merry Christmas⟩ **3** : REQUEST ⟨I *wish* you to go now⟩ — **wish·er** *n*
²wish *n* **1 a** : an act or instance of wishing or desire **b** : an object of desire : GOAL **2** : a wishing of good or evil fortune on someone ⟨sends his best *wishes*⟩
wish·bone \'wish-ˌbōn\ *n* : a forked bone in front of the breastbone of a bird consisting chiefly of the fused clavicles
wish·ful \'wish-fəl\ *adj* **1** : having a wish : DESIROUS **2** : according with wishes rather than fact ⟨*wishful* thinking⟩ — **wish·ful·ly** \-fə-lē\ *adv* — **wish·ful-ness** *n*
wishy–washy \'wish-ē-ˌwȯsh-ē, -ˌwäsh-\ *adj* **1** : WEAK, INSIPID **2** : morally weak
wisp \'wisp\ *n* **1** : a small bunch of hay or straw **2 a** : a thin piece or strand **b** : a thready streak ⟨a *wisp* of smoke⟩ **c** : something frail, slight, or fleeting ⟨a *wisp* of a girl⟩ — **wispy** \'wis-pē\ *adj*
wis·tar·ia \wis-'tir-ē-ə, -'ter-\ *n* : WISTERIA
wis·te·ria \wis-'tir-ē-ə\ *n* [from scientific Latin, named after Caspar *Wistar* (1761–1818), American physician] : any of a genus of chiefly Asiatic mostly woody vines related to the pea and having compound leaves and showy blue, white, purple, or rose flowers in long hanging clusters

wist·ful \'wist-fəl\ *adj* : full of longing : YEARNING — **wist·ful·ly** \-fə-lē\ *adv* — **wist·ful·ness** *n*

[1]**wit** \'wit\ *vb* **wist** \'wist\; **wit·ting**; *pres 1st & 3d sing* **wot** \'wät\ *archaic* : KNOW, LEARN

[2]**wit** *n* **1** : reasoning power : INTELLIGENCE **2 a** : mental soundness : SANITY — usu. used in pl. **b** : practical good judgment **3 a** : a talent for making clever remarks **b** : clever remarks **c** : one noted for making witty remarks — **at one's wit's end** *or* **at one's wits' end** : at a loss for a means of solving a problem

witch \'wich\ *n* **1** : a person believed to have magic powers **2** : an ugly old woman : HAG **3** : a charming girl or woman

witch·craft \-ˌkraft\ *n* : the power or practices of a witch : SORCERY

witch doctor *n* : a professional worker of magic in a primitive society resembling a medicine man

witch·ery \'wich-(ə-)rē\ *n, pl* **-er·ies 1** : WITCHCRAFT **2** : an irresistible fascination : CHARM

witch·grass \'wich-ˌgras\ *n* : any of several weedy grasses most of which spread aggressively by underground rhizomes

witch ha·zel \'wich-ˌhā-zəl\ *n* **1** : any of a genus of shrubs with slender-petaled yellow flowers borne in late fall or early spring; *esp* : one of eastern No. America that blooms in the fall **2** : an alcoholic solution of material from the bark of the common witch hazel that is sometimes used as a remedy for bruises and sprains

witch hazel 1

witch–hunt \-ˌhənt\ *n* **1** : a searching out and persecution of persons accused of witchcraft **2** : the searching out and deliberate harassment of those (as political opponents) with unpopular views — **witch–hunt·er** *n*

witch·ing \'wich-ing\ *adj* : BEWITCHING, FASCINATING

with \(ˈ)with, (ˈ)with\ *prep* **1 a** : in opposition to : AGAINST ⟨fought *with* his brother⟩ **b** : FROM ⟨parting *with* his friends⟩ **2** : in mutual relation to ⟨talking *with* a friend⟩ ⟨trade *with* other countries⟩ **3** : as regards : TOWARD ⟨angry *with* her⟩ ⟨on friendly terms *with* all nations⟩ **4 a** : compared to : equal to ⟨on equal terms *with* the others⟩ ⟨a dress identical *with* hers⟩ **b** : on the side of : FAVORING ⟨voted *with* the majority⟩ **c** : as well as ⟨can pitch *with* the best of them⟩ **5 a** : in the judgment or estimation of ⟨in good standing *with* his classmates⟩ **b** : in the experience or practice of ⟨*with* him a promise is a real obligation⟩ **6 a** : by means of ⟨write *with* a pen⟩ **b** : because of ⟨danced *with* joy⟩ **7** : having or showing as manner of action or attendant circumstance ⟨spoke *with* ease⟩ ⟨stood there *with* his hat on⟩ **8 a** : in possession of : HAVING ⟨animals *with* horns⟩ **b** : characterized or distinguished by ⟨a person *with* a hot temper⟩ **9 a** : in the company of ⟨went to the movies *with* her⟩ : in addition to ⟨his money, *with* his wife's, comes to a million⟩ **b** : inclusive of : CONTAINING ⟨costs $5 *with* the tax⟩ ⟨tea *with* sugar⟩ **10 a** : at the same time as ⟨rose *with* the sun⟩ **b** : in proportion to ⟨the pressure varies *with* the depth⟩ **11** : in spite of ⟨*with* all his cleverness, he failed⟩ **12** : in the direction of ⟨drift *with* the current⟩

with·al \with-'ȯl, with-\ *adv* **1** : together with this : BESIDES **2** : on the other hand : NEVERTHELESS

with·draw \with-'drȯ, with-\ *vb* **-drew** \-'drü\; **-drawn** \-'drȯn\; **-draw·ing 1** : to take back or away : draw away : REMOVE ⟨*withdrew* his money from the bank⟩ ⟨*withdrawing* a knife from his pocket⟩ ⟨*withdraw* troops⟩ **2 a** : to call back : RECALL, RESCIND ⟨*withdrew* the nomination⟩ ⟨*withdrew* his opposition to a plan⟩ **b** : RETRACT, RECANT ⟨*withdrew* his remarks and apologized⟩ **3** : to go away : RETREAT, LEAVE ⟨*withdrew* to the country⟩

with·draw·al \-'drȯ(-ə)l\ *n* : an act or instance of withdrawing (as a removal, a retreat, or a retraction)

with·drawn \-'drȯn\ *adj* **1** : ISOLATED, SECLUDED **2** : socially detached and unresponsive

withe \'with\ *n* : a slender flexible branch or twig; *esp* : one used as a band or rope

with·er \'with-ər\ *vb* **with·ered**; **with·er·ing** \-(ə-)ring\ **1** : to become dry and destitute of sap; *esp* : to shrivel from or as if from loss of bodily moisture **2** : to lose vitality, force, or freshness **3** : to cause to wither or feel withered ⟨*withered* him with a glance⟩

with·ers \'with-ərz\ *n pl* : the ridge between the shoulder bones of a horse; *also* : the corresponding part in other four-footed animals

with·hold \with-'hōld, with-\ *vb* **-held** \-'held\; **-hold·ing 1** : to hold back : RETAIN **2** : to refrain from granting, giving, or allowing ⟨*withhold* permission⟩ — **with·hold·er** *n*

[1]**with·in** \with-'in, with-\ *adv* **1** : in or into the interior : INSIDE **2** : inside oneself : INWARDLY ⟨calm without but furious *within*⟩

[2]**within** *prep* **1** : in or into the inner part of ⟨*within* the house⟩ **2** : not beyond the bounds or limits of ⟨lives *within* his income⟩ ⟨*within* sight⟩

[3]**within** *n* : an inner place or area ⟨revolt from *within*⟩

[1]**with·out** \with-'au̇t, with-\ *prep* **1** : OUTSIDE 1, 2 **2 a** : not having : LACKING ⟨*without* food⟩ **b** : with absence or omission of ⟨listened *without* answering⟩

[2]**without** *adv* **1** : on the outside : EXTERNALLY **2** : with something lacking or absent ⟨learn to do *without*⟩

[3]**without** *n* : an outer place or area ⟨came from *without*⟩

with·stand \with-'stand, with-\ *vb* **-stood** \-'stu̇d\; **-stand·ing** : to stand against : RESIST; *esp* : to oppose (as an attack or bad influence) successfully

wit·less \'wit-ləs\ *adj* : lacking wit : FOOLISH — **wit·less·ly** *adv* — **wit·less·ness** *n*

[1]**wit·ness** \'wit-nəs\ *n* **1** : TESTIMONY ⟨bear false *witness*⟩ **2** : one that gives evidence; *esp* : one who testifies in a cause or before a court **3 a** : one present at a transaction so as to be able to testify to its having taken place **b** : one who has personal knowledge or experience of something **4** : EVIDENCE, PROOF

[2]**witness** *vb* **1** : to bear witness : TESTIFY **2** : to act as legal witness of ⟨*witness* a document⟩ **3** : to serve as proof of **4** : to be a witness of

wit·ted \'wit-əd\ *adj* : having wit or understanding — used in combination ⟨dull-*witted*⟩

wit·ti·cism \'wit-ə-ˌsiz-əm\ *n* : a witty saying

wit·ting·ly \'wit-ing-lē\ *adv* : with knowledge or awareness of what one is doing : CONSCIOUSLY

wit·ty \'wit-ē\ *adj* **wit·ti·er**; **-est** : marked by or full of wit : AMUSING ⟨a *witty* writer⟩ ⟨a *witty* remark⟩ — **wit·ti·ly** \'wit-ə-lē\ *adv* — **wit·ti·ness** \'wit-ē-nəs\ *n*

ə abut	ər further	a back	ā bake	
ä cot, cart	au̇ out	ch chin	e less	ē easy
g gift	i trip	ī life	j joke	ng sing	ō flow
ȯ flaw	ȯi coin	th thin	th this	ü loot
u̇ foot	y yet	yü few	yu̇ furious	zh vision

wives *pl of* WIFE

wiz·ard \'wiz-ərd\ *n* [from Middle English *wysard* "wise man", "sage", from *wys* "wise"] **1 :** MAGICIAN, SORCERER **2 :** a very clever or skillful person ⟨a *wizard* at chess⟩

wiz·ard·ry \'wiz-ər-drē\ *n, pl* **-ries 1 :** the art or practices of a wizard **:** SORCERY **2 :** a seemingly magical power or influence

wiz·en \'wiz-ən\ *vb* **:** WITHER, SHRIVEL

wk *abbr* week

wob·ble \'wäb-əl\ *vb* **wob·bled; wob·bling** \-(ə-)ling\ **1 a :** to move or cause to move with an irregular rocking or side-to-side motion **b :** TREMBLE, QUAVER **2 :** WAVER, VACILLATE — **wobble** *n* — **wob·bler** \-(ə-)lər\ *n* — **wob·bly** \-(ə-)lē\ *adj*

woe \'wō\ *n* **1 :** deep suffering from misfortune, affliction, or grief **2 :** CALAMITY, MISFORTUNE ⟨economic *woes*⟩

woe·be·gone \'wō-bi-ˌgȯn, -ˌgän\ *adj* **1 :** exhibiting great woe, sorrow, or misery ⟨*woebegone* faces⟩ **2 :** DISMAL, DESOLATE ⟨a *woebegone* village⟩

woe·ful *also* **wo·ful** \'wō-fəl\ *adj* **1 :** full of woe **:** AFFLICTED **2 :** involving or bringing woe **3 :** PALTRY, DEPLORABLE — **woe·ful·ly** \-f(ə-)lē\ *adv* — **woe·ful·ness** \-fəl-nəs\ *n*

woke *past of* WAKE

woken *past part of* WAKE

wold \'wōld\ *n* **:** an upland plain or rolling country without woods

[1]**wolf** \'wu̇lf\ *n, pl* **wolves** \'wu̇lvz\ *also* **wolf 1 :** any of several large erect-eared bushy-tailed predatory mammals that resemble the related dogs and that often hunt in packs — compare COYOTE, JACKAL **2 :** a person who resembles a wolf (as in ferocity or guile) — **wolf·ish** \'wu̇l-fish\ *adj*

[2]**wolf** *vb* **:** to eat greedily **:** DEVOUR

wolf·hound \'wu̇lf-ˌhau̇nd\ *n* **:** any of several large dogs used in hunting large animals (as wolves)

wol·fram \'wu̇l-frəm\ *n* **:** TUNGSTEN

wolfs·bane \'wu̇lfs-ˌbān\ *n* **:** ACONITE 1; *esp* **:** a highly variable yellow-flowered Eurasian herb

wolf spider *n* **:** any of various active wandering ground spiders

wol·ver·ine \ˌwu̇l-və-'rēn\ *n* **:** a blackish shaggy-furred flesh-eating mammal of northern No. America that is related to the martens and sables and is noted for its thievishness, strength, and cunning

wolverine
(about 40 in. long)

wom·an \'wu̇m-ən\ *n, pl* **wom·en** \'wim-ən\ [from Middle English *wimman, wumman,* from Old English *wīfman,* from *wīf* "wife", "woman" and *man* "man", "person"] **1 :** an adult female person **2 :** WOMANKIND **3 :** a female servant or attendant — **woman** *adj*

wom·an·hood \'wu̇m-ən-ˌhu̇d\ *n* **1 :** the state of being a woman **2 :** womanly qualities **3 :** WOMEN

wom·an·ish \'wu̇m-ə-nish\ *adj* **1 :** characteristic of a woman **2 :** suitable to a woman rather than to a man

wom·an·kind \'wu̇m-ən-ˌkīnd\ *n* **:** female human beings **:** WOMEN

wom·an·like \-ˌlīk\ *adj* **:** resembling or characteristic of a woman **:** WOMANLY

wom·an·ly \-lē\ *adj* **:** marked by qualities characteristic of a woman

womb \'wüm\ *n* **1 :** UTERUS **2 :** a place where something is generated or developed

wom·bat \'wäm-ˌbat\ *n* **:** any of several stocky burrowing Australian marsupials resembling small bears

wom·en·folk \'wim-ən-ˌfōk\ *or* **wom·en·folks** \-ˌfōks\ *n pl* **:** WOMEN

won *past of* WIN

[1]**won·der** \'wən-dər\ *n* **1 :** a cause of astonishment or surprise **:** MARVEL **2 a :** a feeling (as awe or astonishment) aroused by something extraordinary **b :** the quality of exciting wonder

[2]**wonder** *vb* **won·dered; won·der·ing** \-d(ə-)ring\ **1 :** to feel surprise or amazement **2 :** to feel curiosity or doubt — **won·der·er** \-dər-ər\ *n*

wonder drug *n* **:** a medicinal substance of outstanding effectiveness

won·der·ful \'wən-dər-fəl\ *adj* **1 :** exciting wonder **:** MARVELOUS **2 :** unusually good **:** ADMIRABLE — **won·der·ful·ly** \-f(ə-)lē\ *adv*

won·der·land \-ˌland, -lənd\ *n* **1 :** a fairylike imaginary realm **2 :** a place that excites admiration or wonder

won·der·ment \-mənt\ *n* **1 :** ASTONISHMENT, SURPRISE **2 :** curiosity about something

won·drous \'wən-drəs\ *adj* **:** WONDERFUL — **wondrous** *adv, archaic* — **won·drous·ly** *adv* — **won·drous·ness** *n*

[1]**wont** \'wȯnt, 'wōnt\ *adj* **:** ACCUSTOMED, USED ⟨as he is *wont* to do⟩

[2]**wont** *n* **:** CUSTOM, USAGE ⟨she was far more serious than was her *wont*⟩

won't \(')wōnt, 'wənt\ **:** will not

wont·ed \'wȯnt-əd, 'wōnt-\ *adj* **:** ACCUSTOMED, USUAL ⟨took his *wonted* rest⟩ — **wont·ed·ly** *adv* — **wont·ed·ness** *n*

woo \'wü\ *vb* **1 :** to try to gain the love of **:** make love **:** COURT **2 :** to seek to gain or bring about ⟨a clever auctioneer *wooing* dollars from his audience⟩

[1]**wood** \'wu̇d\ *n* **1 :** a dense growth of trees usu. smaller than a forest — often used in pl. ⟨a thick *woods* runs along the ridge⟩ **2 :** a hard fibrous substance that is basically xylem and makes up the greater part of the stems and branches of trees or shrubs beneath the bark; *also* **:** this material prepared for some use (as burning or building) **3 :** something made of wood; *esp* **:** a golf club having a wooden head — **out of the woods :** escaped from peril or difficulty

[2]**wood** *adj* **1 :** WOODEN **2 :** suitable for cutting or working wood ⟨*wood* chisels⟩ **3** *or* **woods** \'wu̇dz\ **:** living or growing in woods

[3]**wood** *vb* **1 :** to supply with or take on wood esp. for fuel ⟨*wood* up the stove⟩ ⟨the boat *wooded* up at night⟩ **2 :** to cover with or plant with trees

wood·bine \'wu̇d-ˌbīn\ *n* **:** any of several climbing vines (as a honeysuckle or the Virginia creeper) of Europe and America

wood block *n* **1 :** a solid block of wood (as for paving) **2 :** WOODCUT

wood–carv·er \'wu̇d-ˌkär-vər\ *n* **:** a person who carves ornamental objects of wood — **wood carv·ing** \-ving\ *n*

wood·chop·per \-ˌchäp-ər\ *n* **:** WOODCUTTER

wood·chuck \-ˌchək\ *n* [from Ojibwa *otchig* "fisher", "marten", or Cree *otcheck* "fisher"] **:** a grizzled thickset marmot of the northeastern U.S. and Canada; *also* **:** a related rodent of mountainous western No. America

woodchuck
(up to 2 ft. long)

W

wood·cock \\-ˌkäk\\ *n, pl* **woodcocks** *or* **woodcock** : either of two long-billed mottled and usu. brown birds related to the snipe; *esp* : an American upland bird prized as a game bird

wood·craft \\-ˌkraft\\ *n* : knowledge about the woods and how to take care of oneself in them

wood·cut \\-ˌkət\\ *n* **1** : a printing surface consisting of a wooden block with a design cut with the grain **2** : a print from a woodcut

wood·cut·ter \\-ˌkət-ər\\ *n* : one that cuts wood esp. as an occupation

wood duck *n* : a showy American duck the male of which has a large crest and plumage varied with green, black, purple, white, and chestnut

wood·ed \\ˈwu̇d-əd\\ *adj* : covered with trees

wood·en \\ˈwu̇d-ən\\ *adj* **1** : made of wood **2** : STIFF, AWKWARD ⟨written in a *wooden* style⟩ — **wood·en·ly** *adv* — **wood·en·ness** \\-ən-(n)əs\\ *n*

wood engraving *n* **1** : a printing surface consisting of a design on wood and esp. on the end grain of wood **2** : a print from a wood engraving

1**wood·land** \\ˈwu̇d-lənd, -ˌland\\ *n* : land covered with woody vegetation : FOREST

2**woodland** *adj* **1** : of, relating to, or being woodland **2** : growing or living in woodland

wood·lot \\ˈwu̇d-ˌlät\\ *n* : a relatively small area of trees kept usu. to meet fuel and timber needs

wood louse *n* : a small flat grayish crustacean that lives esp. under stones and bark — called also *pill bug, sow bug*

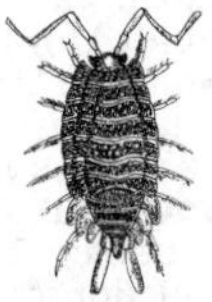

wood louse (less than 1 in. long)

wood·man \\ˈwu̇d-mən\\ *n* : WOODSMAN

wood·peck·er \\-ˌpek-ər\\ *n* : any of numerous usu. brightly marked birds with specialized feet and stiff spiny tail feathers used in climbing or resting on tree trunks and a very hard bill used to drill into trees for insect food or to excavate nesting cavities

wood pewee *n* : a flycatcher of eastern No. America that is grayish olive with a yellowish white belly and has a note resembling the syllables *pee-a-wee*

wood·pile \\ˈwu̇d-ˌpīl\\ *n* : a pile of wood and esp. firewood

wood·shed \\-ˌshed\\ *n* : a shed for storing wood and esp. firewood

woods·man \\ˈwu̇dz-mən\\ *n* : one who frequents or works in the woods; *esp* : one skilled in woodcraft

wood sorrel *n* : any of a genus of herbs with acid sap, compound leaves, and regular 5-petaled flowers; *esp* : a stemless herb having leaves with three leaflets that is considered to be the original shamrock

wood thrush *n* : a large thrush of eastern No. America noted for its loud clear song

wood·wind \\ˈwu̇d-ˌwind\\ *n* **1** : one of a group of wind instruments including flutes, clarinets, oboes, bassoons, and sometimes saxophones **2** : the woodwind section of a band or orchestra — **woodwind** *adj*

wood·work \\-ˌwərk\\ *n* : work made of wood; *esp* : interior fittings (as moldings or stairways) of wood

wood·work·ing \\-ˌwər-kiŋ\\ *n* : the act, process, or occupation of working with wood — **wood·work·er** \\-kər\\ *n*

woody \\ˈwu̇d-ē\\ *adj* **wood·i·er**; **-est** **1** : abounding or overgrown with trees **2** : of or containing wood or wood fibers **3** : characteristic of or resembling wood ⟨a *woody* texture⟩

woo·er \\ˈwü-ər\\ *n* : one that woos : SUITOR

woof \\ˈwu̇f, ˈwüf\\ *n* **1** : the threads that cross the warp in a woven fabric **2** : a woven fabric or its texture

woof 1

wool \\ˈwu̇l\\ *n* **1** : the heavy soft wavy or curly undercoat of various mammals and esp. the sheep **2** : a product of wool; *esp* : a woven fabric or garment of such fabric **3 a** : a filamentous mass (as of glass or metal) ⟨steel *wool*⟩ **b** : short thick often crisp curly hair on a human head — **wooled** \\ˈwu̇ld\\ *adj*

1**wool·en** *or* **wool·len** \\ˈwu̇l-ən\\ *adj* **1** : made of wool **2** : of or relating to the manufacture or sale of woolen products

2**woolen** *or* **woollen** *n* **1** : a fabric made of wool **2** : garments of woolen fabric — usu. used in pl.

wool·gath·er·ing \\ˈwu̇l-ˌgath-(ə-)riŋ\\ *n* : the act of daydreaming

1**wool·ly** *also* **wooly** \\ˈwu̇l-ē\\ *adj* **wool·li·er**; **-est** **1 a** : of, relating to, or bearing wool **b** : resembling wool **2** : CONFUSED, BLURRY ⟨*woolly* thinking⟩ **3** : marked by a lack of order or restraint ⟨the wild and *woolly* West⟩ — **wool·li·ness** *n*

2**wool·ly** *also* **wool·ie** *or* **wooly** \\ˈwu̇l-ē\\ *n, pl* **wool·lies** : a woolen garment; *esp* : underclothing of knitted wool — usu. used in pl.

woolly aphid *n* : any of several plant lice that secrete a dense coating of woolly wax filaments

woolly bear *n* : any of various rather large very hairy moth caterpillars

woolly mammoth *n* : a heavy-coated extinct mammoth known from fossil remains, from the drawings of prehistoric men, and from entire corpses dug from the frozen Siberian ground

woo·zy \\ˈwü-zē\\ *adj* **woo·zi·er**; **-est** : affected with dizziness, mild nausea, or weakness

1**word** \\ˈwərd\\ *n* **1 a** : something that is said **b** *pl* : TALK, DISCOURSE **c** : a brief remark or conversation **2 a** : a speech sound or series of speech sounds that symbolizes and communicates a meaning without being divisible into smaller units capable of independent use **b** : a written or printed character or group of characters representing a spoken word **3** : ORDER, COMMAND **4** : GOSPEL 1a **5** : NEWS **6** : PROMISE ⟨I give you my *word*⟩ **7** : a quarrelsome statement or conversation — usu. used in pl. — **word for word** : in the exact words : VERBATIM — **word·less** \\ˈwərd-ləs\\ *adj*

2**word** *vb* : to express in words : PHRASE ⟨*worded* his request with great care⟩

word·age \\ˈwərd-ij\\ *n* : WORDS

word·book \\ˈwərd-ˌbu̇k\\ *n* : VOCABULARY, DICTIONARY

word·ing \\ˈwərd-iŋ\\ *n* : expression in words : PHRASING

word order *n* : the order of arrangement of words in a phrase, clause, or sentence

wordy \\ˈwərd-ē\\ *adj* **word·i·er**; **-est** : using or containing too many words — **word·i·ly** \\ˈwərd-ə-lē\\ *adv* — **word·i·ness** \\ˈwərd-ē-nəs\\ *n*

wore *past of* WEAR

1**work** \\ˈwərk\\ *n* **1** : the use of one's strength or ability to get something done or to achieve a result : LABOR, TOIL; *esp* : such work undertaken as one's regular employment **2 :** something to be done : TASK, JOB ⟨have *work* to do⟩ **3 :** DEED, ACHIEVEMENT ⟨good *works*⟩ **4 :** the material on which effort is put in the process of making something **5 :** something produced by work **6** *pl* **:** a place where industrial labor is carried on : PLANT, FACTORY ⟨a locomotive *works*⟩ **7** *pl* **:** the working or moving parts of a mechanical device ⟨the *works* of a watch⟩ **8 :** manner of working : WORKMANSHIP ⟨careless *work*⟩ **9 :** a fortified structure **10 :** the transference of energy ⟨*work* is done when a force produces movement of a body⟩ **11** *pl* **a :** everything available ⟨a hamburger with the *works*⟩ **b :** subjection to drastic treatment ⟨gave him the *works*⟩ — **at work 1 :** engaged in working : BUSY; *esp* **:** engaged in one's regular occupation **2 :** having effect : OPERATING — **out of work :** without regular employment : JOBLESS

²**work** *adj* **1 :** suitable for wear while working ⟨*work* clothes⟩ **2 :** used for work ⟨*work* elephant⟩

³**work** *vb* **worked** \'wərkt\ *or* **wrought** \'rȯt\; **working 1 :** to bring about : EFFECT ⟨*work* a cure⟩ **2 :** MAKE, SHAPE ⟨*work* a vase⟩ **3 a :** to prepare by stirring or kneading **b :** to bring into a desired form by a manufacturing process ⟨*work* cold steel⟩ **4 :** to set or keep in motion or operation ⟨a pump *worked* by hand⟩ **5 :** to solve by reasoning or calculation ⟨*work* an arithmetic puzzle⟩ **6 a :** to cause to toil or labor ⟨*worked* the crew hard⟩ **b :** to make use of : EXPLOIT ⟨*work* a mine⟩ **c :** to control or guide the operation of ⟨*work* a lever⟩ **7 :** to pay for with labor ⟨*work* off a debt⟩ **8 a :** to get into or out of a state or position by stages ⟨*worked* himself free⟩ ⟨*worked* the boat loose⟩ **b :** CONTRIVE, ARRANGE ⟨if we can *work* it⟩ **9 a :** to exert oneself esp. in sustained effort **b :** to perform a task requiring sustained effort or repeated operations **c :** to perform work regularly for wages ⟨*works* on the railroad⟩ **10 :** to function or operate properly ⟨hinges *work* better with oil⟩ **11 :** to produce a desired effect : SUCCEED ⟨his plan *worked*⟩ **12 :** to react in a specified way to being worked ⟨this wood *works* easily⟩ **13 a :** FERMENT **b :** to move slightly in relation to another part **c :** to get gradually into a specified state ⟨the knot *worked* loose⟩

syn WORK, LABOR, TOIL can mean to exert oneself at a physical or mental task. WORK, a general term, implies no more than an effort, enjoyable or not, toward an end; LABOR suggests greater physical exertion that is often hard, unpleasant, and done of necessity; TOIL implies extremely hard, fatiguing, and prolonged work ⟨*toiled* all day in the hot sun⟩

— **work on :** to strive to influence or persuade

work·a·ble \'wər-kə-bəl\ *adj* **1 :** capable of being worked **2 :** PRACTICABLE, FEASIBLE

work·a·day \'wər-kə-ˌdā\ *adj* **1 :** relating to or suited for working days **2 :** PROSAIC, ORDINARY

work·bench \'wərk-ˌbench\ *n* **:** a bench on which work esp. of mechanics, machinists, and carpenters is performed

work·book \-ˌbu̇k\ *n* **:** a student's book of problems to be solved directly on the pages

work·day \-ˌdā\ *n* **1 :** a day on which work is performed **2 :** the period of time in a day during which work is performed — **workday** *adj*

worked up *adj* **:** emotionally aroused : EXCITED ⟨all *worked up* over the coming wedding⟩

work·er \'wər-kər\ *n* **1 a :** one that works **b :** a member of the working class **2 :** one of the sexually undeveloped members of a colony of social ants, bees, wasps, or termites that perform most of the labor and protective duties of the colony

work·house \'wərk-ˌhau̇s\ *n* **1** *Brit* **:** POORHOUSE **2 :** an institution where persons who have committed minor offenses are confined

¹**work·ing** \'wər-king\ *adj* **1 a :** doing work esp. for a living ⟨*working* girl⟩ **b :** FUNCTIONING ⟨a *working* model⟩ **2 :** relating to work **3 :** good enough to allow work to be done ⟨a *working* majority⟩ ⟨a *working* arrangement⟩

²**working** *n* **:** an excavation or excavations made in mining, quarrying, or tunneling — usu. used in pl.

working class *n* **:** the class of people who are employed for wages usu. in manual labor — **working–class** *adj*

work·ing·man \'wər-king-ˌman\ *n* **:** one who works for wages usu. at manual labor or in industry

work·man \'wərk-mən\ *n* **1 :** WORKINGMAN **2 :** ARTISAN, CRAFTSMAN

work·man·like \-ˌlīk\ *or* **work·man·ly** \-lē\ *adj* **:** worthy of a good workman : SKILLFUL

work·man·ship \-ˌship\ *n* **1 :** the art or skill of a workman : CRAFTSMANSHIP **2 :** the quality or character of a piece of work ⟨the excellent *workmanship* of the desk⟩

work out \'wərk-'au̇t\ *vb* **1 :** to bring about by effort or by resolving difficulties **2 a :** SOLVE **b :** DEVELOP ⟨*work out* a plan⟩ **3 :** to discharge (as a debt) by labor **4 :** to exhaust (as a mine) by working **5 :** to prove effective, practicable, or suitable ⟨his scheme *worked out*⟩ **6 :** to engage in athletic practice ⟨*working out* in the gym⟩

work·out \-ˌau̇t\ *n* **:** a practice or exercise to test or improve one's fitness esp. in athletics

work·room \'wərk-ˌrüm, -ˌru̇m\ *n* **:** a room used esp. for manual work

work·shop \-ˌshäp\ *n* **:** a shop where manufacturing or handicrafts are carried on

world \'wərld\ *n* **1 :** UNIVERSE, CREATION **2 :** the earth with its inhabitants and all things upon it **3 :** people in general : MANKIND **4 :** a state of existence : scene of life and action ⟨the *world* of the future⟩ **5 :** a great number or quantity ⟨a *world* of troubles⟩ **6 :** a part or section of the earth or its inhabitants by itself ⟨the Old *World*⟩ ⟨the musical *world*⟩ **7 :** the affairs of men ⟨withdraw from the *world*⟩ **8 :** a celestial body esp. if inhabited — **in the world :** among innumerable possibilities : EVER — used as an intensive ⟨what *in the world* is it⟩ — **out of this world :** of extraordinary excellence : SUPERB

world·ling \'wərl-(d)ling\ *n* **:** a worldly person

world·ly \'wərl-(d)lē\ *adj* **world·li·er; -est 1 :** of, relating to, or devoted to this world and its pursuits rather than to spiritual affairs **2 :** WORLDLY-WISE — **world·li·ness** *n*

world·ly–wise \'wərl-(d)lē-ˌwīz\ *adj* **:** wise as to things and ways of this world

world series *n, often cap W & S* **:** a series of baseball games played each fall between the pennant winners of the major leagues to decide the professional championship of the U.S.

world war *n* **:** a war involving all or most of the chief nations of the world; *esp, cap both Ws* **:** either of two such wars of the 20th century

world·wide \'wərl-'dwīd\ *adj* **:** extended throughout the world ⟨*worldwide* fame⟩

¹**worm** \'wərm\ *n* **1 :** any of various small long usu. naked and soft-bodied creeping animals (as a maggot or planarian); *esp* **:** EARTHWORM **2 :** a contemptible or pitiful person : WRETCH **3** *pl* **:** infestation with or disease caused by parasitic worms **4 :** something spiral in form; *esp* **:** a short revolving screw whose threads mesh with the teeth of another mechanical part — **worm·like** \-ˌlīk\ *adj*

2**worm** *vb* **1 :** to move, go, or work slowly in the manner of a worm ⟨*wormed* out of the trap⟩ ⟨*wormed* his way into a job⟩ **2 :** to free from worms ⟨*worm* a puppy⟩ **3 :** to obtain by artful questioning or by pleading or persuading ⟨*wormed* the truth out of him⟩ — **worm·er** *n*
worm cast *n* **:** a cylindrical mass of earth voided by an earthworm
worm gear *n* **1 :** WORM WHEEL **2 :** a gear of a worm and a worm wheel working together
worm·hole \'wərm-ˌhōl\ *n* **:** a hole or passage burrowed by a worm
worm wheel *n* **:** a toothed wheel meshing with the thread of a worm

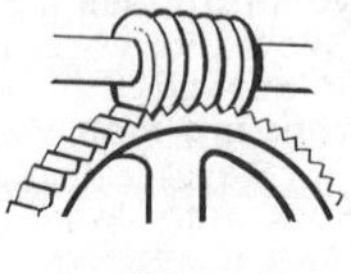
worm gear 2

worm·wood \'wərm-ˌwu̇d\ *n* **1 :** any of a genus of woody herbs related to the daisies; *esp* **:** a European plant yielding a bitter slightly aromatic dark green oil used in the manufacture of certain alcoholic liquors **2 :** something bitter or painful
wormy \'wər-mē\ *adj* **worm·i·er; -est 1 :** containing, infested with, or damaged by worms **2 :** resembling or suggestive of a worm
worn *past part of* WEAR
worn–out \'wōrn-'au̇t, 'wȯrn-\ *adj* **:** exhausted or used up by or as if by wear
wor·ri·some \'wər-ē-səm, 'wə-rē-\ *adj* **1 :** causing worry **2 :** inclined to worry
1**wor·ry** \'wər-ē, 'wə-rē\ *vb* **wor·ried; wor·ry·ing 1 :** to shake and tear or mangle with the teeth ⟨a puppy *worrying* an old shoe⟩ **2 :** to torment with anxiety **:** FRET, TROUBLE ⟨his late hours *worried* his parents⟩ **3 :** to feel or express great anxiety — **wor·ri·er** *n*
2**worry** *n, pl* **worries 1 :** ANXIETY **2 :** a cause of anxiety **:** TROUBLE
1**worse** \'wərs\ *adj, comparative of* BAD *or of* ILL **1 :** of poorer quality, value, or condition **2 :** more unfavorable, unpleasant, or painful; *esp* **:** more unwell **:** SICKER ⟨the boy was *worse* the next day⟩ **3 :** bad, evil, or corrupt in a greater degree
2**worse** *n* **1 :** something worse **2 :** a greater degree of ill or badness ⟨a turn for the *worse*⟩
3**worse** *adv, comparative of* BAD *or of* ILL **:** in a worse manner **:** to a worse extent or degree
wors·en \'wər-sən\ *vb* **wors·ened; wors·en·ing** \-s(ə-)ning\ **:** to make or become worse
1**wor·ship** \'wər-shəp\ *n* [from Old English *weorthscipe* "worthiness" "respect", "reverence", from *weorth* "worthy" and *-scipe* "-ship"] **1** *chiefly Brit* — used as a title for some officials **2 a :** reverence toward God, a god, or a sacred object **b :** the expression of such reverence **3 :** extravagant admiration or devotion ⟨*worship* of the dollar⟩
2**worship** *vb* **-shiped** *or* **-shipped; -ship·ing** *or* **-ship·ping 1 :** to honor or reverence as a divine being or supernatural power **2 :** to regard with extravagant respect, honor, or devotion **:** IDOLIZE **3 :** to perform or take part in worship — **wor·ship·er** *or* **wor·ship·per** *n*
wor·ship·ful \'wər-shəp-fəl\ *adj* **:** VENERATING, WORSHIPING

ə abut	ər further	a back	ā bake
ä cot, cart	au̇ out	ch chin	e less
ē easy	g gift	i trip	ī life
j joke	ng sing	ō flow	ȯ flaw
ȯi coin	th thin	t͟h this	ü loot
u̇ foot	y yet	yü few	yu̇ furious
zh vision			

1**worst** \'wərst\ *adj, superlative of* BAD *or of* ILL **:** most bad, evil, or ill **:** POOREST
2**worst** *n* **1 :** one that is worst **2 :** the greatest degree of ill or badness
3**worst** *adv, superlative of* ILL *or of* BAD *or* BADLY **:** to the extreme degree of badness
4**worst** *vb* **:** to get the better of **:** DEFEAT
wor·sted \'wu̇s-təd, 'wərs-\ *n* **1 :** a smooth compact yarn from long wool fibers **2 :** a fabric made from worsted yarns — **worsted** *adj*
wort \'wərt, 'wȯrt\ *n* **:** a dilute solution of sugars obtained by steeping malt and fermented to form beer
1**worth** \'wərth\ *prep* **1 a :** equal in value to **b :** having possessions or income equal to **2 :** deserving of ⟨well *worth* the effort⟩ **3 :** capable of ⟨ran for all he was *worth*⟩
2**worth** *n* **1 a :** monetary value **b :** the equivalent of a specified amount or figure ⟨10 cents *worth*⟩ **2 :** the value of something measured by its qualities **3 :** MERIT, EXCELLENCE
worth·less \'wərth-ləs\ *adj* **1 a :** lacking worth **:** VALUELESS **b :** USELESS **2 :** LOW, DESPICABLE — **worth·less·ly** *adv* — **worth·less·ness** *n*
worth·while \'wərth-'hwīl\ *adj* **:** being worth the time or effort spent
1**wor·thy** \'wər-t͟hē\ *adj* **wor·thi·er; -est 1 a :** having worth or value **b :** HONORABLE **2 :** having sufficient worth ⟨a man *worthy* of the honor⟩ — **wor·thi·ly** \-t͟hə-lē\ *adv* — **wor·thi·ness** \-t͟hē-nəs\ *n*
2**worthy** *n, pl* **worthies :** a worthy person
wot *pres 1st & 3d sing of* WIT
would \wəd, (ə)d, (')wu̇d\ *past of* WILL **1 :** strongly desire **:** WISH ⟨I *would* I were young again⟩ **2** — used as an auxiliary verb to express (1) preference or willingness ⟨he *would* sooner die than face them⟩, (2) wish or intent ⟨those who *would* forbid gambling⟩, (3) custom or habitual action ⟨we *would* meet often for lunch⟩, (4) possibility ⟨if he were coming, he *would* be here now⟩, (5) completion of a statement of desire, request, or advice ⟨we wish that he *would* go⟩, or (6) probability or presumption in past or present time ⟨*would* have won if he had not tripped⟩ **3 :** COULD ⟨the barrel *would* hold 20 gallons⟩ **4** — used as an auxiliary verb to express a request or doubt or uncertainty ⟨*would* you please help us⟩ ⟨the explanation *would* seem satisfactory⟩ **5 :** SHOULD ⟨knew I *would* enjoy the trip⟩ ⟨*would* be glad to know the answer⟩
would–be \ˌwu̇d-ˌbē\ *adj* **:** desiring or pretending to be ⟨a *would-be* poet⟩
wouldn't \'wu̇d-ənt\ **:** would not
wouldst \(')wu̇dst\ *archaic past 2d sing of* WILL
1**wound** \'wünd\ *n* **1 :** an injury involving cutting or breaking of bodily tissue (as by violence, accident, or surgery) **2 :** an injury or hurt to feelings or reputation
2**wound** *vb* **1 :** to cause a wound to or in **2 :** to inflict a wound
3**wound** \'wau̇nd\ *past of* WIND
wove *past of* WEAVE
woven *past part of* WEAVE
wrack \'rak\ *n* **1 :** WRECKAGE, WRECK **2 a :** marine vegetation; *esp* **:** KELP **b :** dried seaweeds
wraith \'rāth\ *n* **1 a :** an apparition of a living person seen just before his death **b :** GHOST, SPECTER **2 :** an insubstantial appearance **:** SHADOW
1**wran·gle** \'rang-gəl\ *vb* **wran·gled; wran·gling** \-g(ə-)ling\ **1 :** to dispute angrily or peevishly **:** BICKER **2 :** ARGUE **3 :** to herd and care for livestock and esp. horses on the range
2**wrangle** *n* **1 :** an angry, noisy, or prolonged dispute or quarrel **2 :** CONTROVERSY

wran·gler \-g(ə-)lər\ *n* **1** : one that bickers **2** : a ranch hand who takes care of the saddle horses

[1]**wrap** \'rap\ *vb* **wrapped; wrap·ping 1 a** : to cover esp. by winding or folding ⟨*wrap* a baby in a blanket⟩ **b** : to enclose and secure for transportation or storage : BUNDLE ⟨*wrap* groceries⟩ **c** : ENFOLD, EMBRACE **d** : to coil, fold, or draw about something **2 a** : SURROUND, ENVELOP ⟨*wrapped* in mist⟩ **b** : to involve completely : ENGROSS ⟨*wrapped* up in a hobby⟩

[2]**wrap** *n* **1** : WRAPPER **2** : a warm loose outer garment (as a coat or shawl)

wrap·per \'rap-ər\ *n* **1** : that in which something is wrapped (as the paper cover of a book or a paper wrapped around a newspaper in the mail) **2** : one that wraps **3** : an article of clothing worn wrapped around the body

wrap·ping \'rap-ing\ *n* : WRAPPER

wrap–up \'rap-,əp\ *n* : a summarizing news report

wrap up \-'əp\ *vb* : END, CONCLUDE

wrath \'rath\ *n* **1** : violent anger : RAGE **2** : punishment for sin or crime

wrath·ful \-fəl\ *adj* **1** : filled with wrath : very angry **2** : showing wrath ⟨a *wrathful* expression⟩ — **wrath·ful·ly** \-fə-lē\ *adv* — **wrath·ful·ness** *n*

wreak \'rēk\ *vb* **1** : to exact as a punishment : INFLICT ⟨*wreak* vengeance⟩ **2** : to give free scope or rein to ⟨*wreaked* his wrath⟩

wreath \'rēth\ *n, pl* **wreaths** \'rēthz, 'rēths\ [from Old English *writha*, from the root of *wrīthan* "to twist", the source of English *writhe*] : something intertwined into a circular shape; *esp* : GARLAND ⟨a *wreath* of flowers⟩

wreathe \'rēth\ *vb* **1** : to twist or become twisted so as to show folds, coils, or creases ⟨a face *wreathed* in smiles⟩ **2** : to form into a wreath **3** : to encircle or adorn with or as if with a wreath ⟨ivy *wreathed* the pole⟩

[1]**wreck** \'rek\ *n* **1** : goods cast upon the land by the sea after a shipwreck **2** : broken remains (as of a ship or vehicle after heavy damage by storm, collision, or fire) **3** : a disabled, ruined, or dilapidated person or thing **4** : SHIPWRECK **5** : the action of wrecking

[2]**wreck** *vb* **1** : SHIPWRECK **2** : to damage or ruin by breaking up ⟨*wreck* a building⟩ ⟨*wreck* a friendship⟩

wreck·age \'rek-ij\ *n* **1 a** : the act of wrecking **b** : the state of being wrecked **2** : the remains of a wreck

wreck·er \'rek-ər\ *n* **1** : one that wrecks **2** : a person who searches for or works upon wrecks of vessels **3** : a ship used in salvaging wrecks **4** : a truck equipped to remove wrecked or disabled cars

wren \'ren\ *n* **1** : any of a large family of small mostly brown singing birds with short rounded wings and short erect tail **2** : any of various small singing birds resembling the true wrens in size and habits

[1]**wrench** \'rench\ *vb* **1** : to move with a violent twist **2** : to pull, strain, or tighten with violent twisting or force **3** : to injure by a violent twisting or straining **4** : to distort the meaning of a word **5** : to snatch forcibly : WREST

[2]**wrench** *n* **1 a** : a violent twisting or pull **b** : a sharp twist or sudden jerk straining muscles or ligaments or the resultant injury (as of a joint) **2** : a hand or power tool for holding, twisting, or turning an object (as a bolt or nut)

[1]**wrest** \'rest\ *vb* **1** : to pull, force, or move by violent wringing or twisting movements **2** : to gain by or as if by force or violence ⟨*wrest* a living⟩ ⟨*wrest* power from the king⟩ — **wrest·er** *n*

[2]**wrest** *n* : a forcible twist : WRENCH

[1]**wres·tle** \'res-əl\ *vb* **wres·tled; wres·tling** \-(ə-)ling\ **1** : to grapple with an opponent to trip him or throw him down **2** : to contend against in wrestling **3** : to struggle for mastery (as with something difficult) ⟨*wrestle* with a problem⟩ ⟨*wrestle* with a heavy suitcase⟩ — **wres·tler** \'res-lər\ *n*

[2]**wrestle** *n* : the action or an instance of wrestling : STRUGGLE

wres·tling \'res-ling\ *n* : the sport in which two contestants seek to throw each other

wretch \'rech\ *n* **1** : a miserable unhappy person **2** : a base, degraded, or vile person

wretch·ed \'rech-əd\ *adj* **1** : very miserable or unhappy **2** : causing misery or distress ⟨a *wretched* accident⟩ **3** : CONTEMPTIBLE, DESPICABLE ⟨a *wretched* trick⟩ **4** : very poor in quality or ability : INFERIOR ⟨*wretched* workmanship⟩ — **wretch·ed·ly** *adv* — **wretch·ed·ness** *n*

wrig·gle \'rig-əl\ *vb* **wrig·gled; wrig·gling** \-(ə-)ling\ **1** : to twist or move to and fro like a worm : SQUIRM ⟨*wriggled* in his chair⟩ ⟨*wriggled* her toes⟩ **2** : to progress by such movements ⟨a snake *wriggled* along the path⟩ — **wriggle** *n* — **wrig·gly** \-(ə-)lē\ *adj*

wrig·gler \'rig-(ə-)lər\ *n* : one that wriggles; *esp* : WIGGLER 2

wright \'rīt\ *n* [from Old English *wyrhta, wryhta*, from the same root as *wyrcan* "to work"] : a workman in wood : CARPENTER — usu. used in combination ⟨ship*wright*⟩ ⟨wheel*wright*⟩

wring \'ring\ *vb* **wrung** \'rəng\; **wring·ing** \'ring-ing\ **1** : to squeeze or twist esp. so as to make dry or to extract moisture or liquid ⟨*wring* wet clothes⟩ **2** : to get by or as if by twisting or pressing ⟨*wring* the truth out of him⟩ **3** : to twist so as to strain, sprain, or strangle ⟨*wring* a chicken's neck⟩ : CONTORT **4** : to affect painfully as if by wringing : TORMENT ⟨her plight *wrung* our hearts⟩

wring·er \'ring-ər\ *n* : one that wrings; *esp* : a device for pressing out liquid or moisture ⟨clothes *wringer*⟩

[1]**wrin·kle** \'ring-kəl\ *n* **1** : a crease or small fold on a surface (as in the skin or in cloth) **2 a** : information about a method : HINT **b** : a new method, technique, or device : NOVELTY ⟨the latest *wrinkle* in hairdos⟩ — **wrin·kly** \-k(ə-)lē\ *adj*

[2]**wrinkle** *vb* **wrin·kled; wrin·kling** \-k(ə-)ling\ : to develop or cause to develop wrinkles — **wrin·kled·ness** \-kəl(d)-nəs\ *n*

wrist \'rist\ *n* : the joint or the region of the joint between the human hand and the arm; *also* : a corresponding part on a lower animal

wrist·band \'ris(t)-,band\ *n* : a band or a part of a sleeve encircling the wrist

wrist·let \'ris(t)-lət\ *n* : WRISTBAND; *esp* : a close-fitting knitted band worn for warmth

wrist·watch \'rist-,wäch\ *n* : a small watch attached to a bracelet or strap to fasten about the wrist

writ \'rit\ *n* **1** : something written : WRITING ⟨Holy *Writ*⟩ **2** : a legal order in writing signed by a court or judicial officer

write \'rīt\ *vb* **wrote** \'rōt\; **writ·ten** \'rit-ən\ *also* **writ** \'rit\; **writ·ing** \'rīt-ing\ [from Old English *wrītan*, meaning literally "to scratch"] **1** : to form letters or words with pen or pencil ⟨learn to read and *write*⟩ **2** : to form the letters or the words of (as on paper) ⟨*write* his name⟩ ⟨*write* a check⟩ **3** : to put down on paper : express in writing ⟨*wrote* his impressions of the circus⟩ **4** : to make up and set down for others to read : COMPOSE ⟨*write* a book⟩ ⟨*wrote* music⟩ **5** : to pen, dictate, or typewrite a letter to ⟨*write* the president⟩ **6** : to communicate by

W

letter : CORRESPOND **7** : to be fitted for writing ⟨this pen *writes* easily⟩

write off *vb* **1** : to reduce the estimated value of : DEPRECIATE **2** : to take off the books : CANCEL ⟨*write off* a bad debt⟩

writ·er \'rīt-ər\ *n* : one that writes esp. as a business or occupation : AUTHOR

writer's cramp *n* : a painful spasmodic cramp of muscles of the hand or fingers brought on by excessive use (as in writing)

write–up \'rīt-,əp\ *n* : a written account (as in a newspaper); *esp* : a flattering article

write up \'rīt-'əp\ *vb* **1** : to write an account of : DESCRIBE **2** : to put into finished written form ⟨*write up* a set of notes⟩

writhe \'rī<u>th</u>\ *vb* **1** : to twist and turn this way and that ⟨*writhe* in pain⟩ **2** : to suffer with shame or confusion : SQUIRM

writ·ing \'rīt-ing\ *n* **1 a** : the act or process of one that writes : the formation of letters to express words and ideas **b** : HANDWRITING **2** : something (as a letter, book, or document) that is written or printed **3** : a style or form of composition **4** : the occupation of a writer

[1]**wrong** \'ro̊ng\ *n* **1** : an injurious, unfair, or unjust act **2** : something that is wrong : wrong principles, practices, or conduct ⟨know right from *wrong*⟩ **3 a** : the state, position, or fact of being or doing wrong ⟨he is in the *wrong*⟩ **b** : the state of being guilty **4** : a violation of the legal rights of another

[2]**wrong** *adj* [of Scandinavian origin, perhaps from Danish *vrang*, from the same Germanic root as Old English *wringan* "to twist", the source of English *wring*] **1** : not according to the moral standard : SINFUL, IMMORAL **2** : not according to a code, standard, or convention : IMPROPER **3** : not suitable or appropriate **4** : not true or correct : FALSE **5** : not satisfactory (as in condition, results, health, or temper) **6** : being a side or part of something turned down, inward, or away, or least finished or polished ⟨the *wrong* side of a fabric⟩ — **wrong** *adv* — **wrong·ly** \'ro̊ng-lē\ *adv* — **wrong·ness** *n*

[3]**wrong** *vb* **wronged**; **wrong·ing** \'ro̊ng-ing\ **1** : to do wrong to : INJURE, HARM **2** : to make unjust remarks about

wrong·do·er \'ro̊ng-'dü-ər\ *n* : a person who does wrong and esp. moral wrong — **wrong·do·ing** \-'dü-ing\ *n*

wrong·ful \'ro̊ng-fəl\ *adj* **1** : WRONG, UNJUST **2** : UNLAWFUL — **wrong·ful·ly** \-fə-lē\ *adv* — **wrong·ful·ness** *n*

wrong·head·ed \'ro̊ng-'hed-əd\ *adj* : stubborn in adherence to wrong opinion or principles : PERVERSE — **wrong·head·ed·ly** *adv* — **wrong·head·ed·ness** *n*

wroth \'ro̊th, 'rōth\ *adj* : filled with wrath : ANGRY

wrought \'ro̊t\ *adj* **1** : FASHIONED, FORMED **2** : ORNAMENTED **3** : beaten into shape by tools : HAMMERED ⟨*wrought* metals⟩ **4** : deeply stirred : EXCITED ⟨gets *wrought* up over nothing⟩

wrought iron *n* : a commercial form of iron that is tough, malleable, and relatively soft

wrung *past of* WRING

wry \'rī\ *adj* **wri·er** \'rī(-ə)r\; **wri·est** \'rī-əst\ **1** : twisted to one side : CONTORTED **2** : made by twisting facial muscles ⟨a *wry* smile⟩ **3** : cleverly and often ironically humorous — **wry·ly** *adv* — **wry·ness** *n*

wry·neck \'rī-,nek\ *n* **1** : a disorder marked by a twisting of the neck and an unnatural position of the head **2** : any of a genus of unusual woodpeckers with soft tail feathers and a peculiar way of twisting the neck

wt *abbr* weight

W. Va. *or* **WV** *abbr* West Virginia

WW *abbr* World War

wy·an·dotte \'wī-ən-,dät\ *n* : any of an American breed of medium-sized domestic fowls

Wyo *or* **WY** *abbr* Wyoming

ə abut	ər further		a back	ā bake
ä cot, cart	au̇ out	ch chin	e less	ē easy
g gift	i trip	ī life	j joke	ng sing	ō flow
ȯ flaw	ȯi coin	th thin	<u>th</u> this	ü loot
u̇ foot	y yet	yü few	yu̇ furious	zh vision

X x X x X

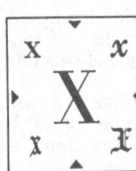

¹x \'eks\ *n, often cap* **1** : the 24th letter of the English alphabet **2** : the roman numeral 10 **3** : an unknown quantity

²x *vb* **x–ed** *also* **x'd** *or* **xed** \'ekst\; **x–ing** *or* **x'ing** \'ek-sing\ **1** : to mark with an *x* **2** : to cancel with a series of *x*'s

x–ax·is \'eks-\ *n* : the horizontal axis of a graph

X chromosome *n* : a sex chromosome that carries factors for femaleness and usu. occurs paired in each female zygote and cell and single in each male zygote and cell — compare Y CHROMOSOME

xe·bec \'zē-ˌbek\ *n* : a usu. 3-masted Mediterranean sailing ship with long overhanging bow and stern

xebec

xe·non \'zē-ˌnän\ *n* : a heavy gaseous element occurring in air in minute quantities and used esp. in specialized electric lamps — see ELEMENT table

xenon tri·ox·ide \-trī-'äk-ˌsīd\ *n* : a highly explosive compound of oxygen and xenon

xeno·pho·bia \ˌzen-ə-'fō-bē-ə, ˌzēn-\ *n* : fear of foreigners or things foreign — **xeno·phobe** \'zen-ə-ˌfōb\ *n* — **xeno·pho·bic** \ˌzen-ə-'fō-bik, ˌzēn-\ *adj*

xe·ric \'zi(ə)r-ik\ *adj* **1** : low or deficient in available moisture for the support of life **2** : adapted for growth in drought or under desert conditions : XEROPHYTIC

xe·ro·phyte \'zir-ə-ˌfīt\ *n* : a plant (as an agave, cactus, sagebrush, or yucca) adapted for growth in drought or desert conditions — **xe·ro·phyt·ic** \ˌzir-ə-'fit-ik\ *adj*

xi \'zī\ *n* : the 14th letter of the Greek alphabet — Ξ or ξ

XL *abbr* extra large

Xmas \'kris-məs, 'eks-məs\ *n* [from *X*, symbol for Christ, from the Greek letter chi (X), initial of *Christos* "Christ"] : CHRISTMAS

X–ra·di·a·tion \ˌeks-\ *n* **1** : exposure to X rays **2** : radiation consisting of X rays

X ray \'eks-ˌrā\ *n* **1** : any of the electromagnetic radiations of the same nature as light rays but of very short wavelength that are generated by a stream of electrons striking against a metal surface in vacuum and that are able to penetrate various thicknesses of solids and act on photographic film like light and to cause a fluorescent screen to emit light **2** : a photograph esp. of conditions inside the surface of a body taken by the use of X rays — **X–ray** *adj*

x–ray *vb, often cap X* : to examine, treat, or photograph with X rays

X–ray photograph *n* : a shadow picture made with X rays

X–ray tube *n* : a vacuum tube in which a concentrated stream of electrons strikes a metal target and produces X rays

xy·lem \'zī-ləm\ *n* : a complex tissue of higher plants that transports water and dissolved materials upward, functions also in support and storage, lies internal to the phloem, and typically constitutes the woody element (as of a plant stem)

xy·lo·phone \'zī-lə-ˌfōn\ *n* [from Greek *xylon* "wood" and *phōnē* "sound"] : a musical instrument consisting of a series of wooden bars varying in length and sounded by striking with two wooden hammers — **xy·lo·phon·ist** \-ˌfō-nəst\ *n*

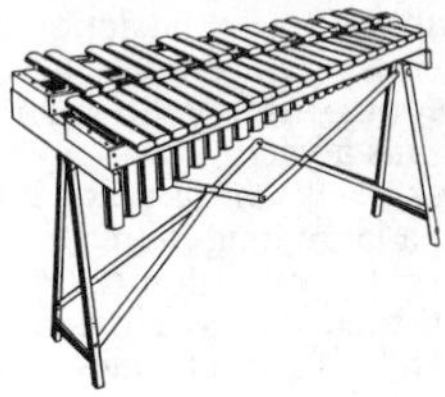
xylophone

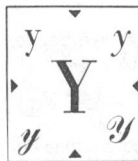

y \'wī\ *n, often cap* : the 25th letter of the English alphabet
1**-y** *also* **-ey** \ē\ *adj suffix* **-i·er**; **-i·est** **1 a** : characterized by : full of ⟨blossom*y*⟩ ⟨dirt*y*⟩ ⟨mudd*y*⟩ ⟨clay*ey*⟩ **b** : composed of ⟨ic*y*⟩ ⟨wax*y*⟩ **c** : like : like that of ⟨hom*ey*⟩ ⟨wintr*y*⟩ ⟨stag*y*⟩ **d** : devoted to : enthusiastic over ⟨hors*y*⟩ **2 a** : tending or inclined to ⟨sleep*y*⟩ ⟨chatt*y*⟩ **b** : giving occasion for or performing (specified) action ⟨tear*y*⟩ **3 a** : somewhat : rather : -ISH ⟨chill*y*⟩ **b** : having (such) characteristics to a marked degree or in an affected or superficial way ⟨French*y*⟩
2**-y** \ē\ *n suffix, pl* **-ies** **1** : state : condition : quality ⟨beggar*y*⟩ **2** : activity, place of business, or goods dealt with ⟨grocer*y*⟩ ⟨laundr*y*⟩ **3** : whole body or group ⟨soldier*y*⟩
3**-y** *n suffix, pl* **-ies** : instance of a (specified) action ⟨entreat*y*⟩ ⟨inquir*y*⟩
4**-y** — see -IE
Y *abbr* YMCA
1**yacht** \'yät\ *n* [from obsolete Dutch *jaght*, from medieval Low German *jachtschiff*, literally "hunting ship"] : any of various small ships that usu. have a sharp prow and graceful lines and are used esp. for pleasure cruising or racing
2**yacht** *vb* : to race or cruise in a yacht
yacht·ing *n* : the action, fact, or pastime of racing or cruising in a yacht
yachts·man \'yäts-mən\ *n* : a person who owns or sails a yacht
yak \'yak\ *n, pl* **yaks** *also* **yak** [from Tibetan *gyak*] : a large long-haired wild or domesticated ox of Tibet and adjacent elevated parts of central Asia

yak
(about 6 ft. at shoulder)

yam \'yam\ *n* **1** : an edible starchy tuberous root that is a staple food in tropical areas; *also* : a plant distantly related to the lilies that produces these **2** : a moist-fleshed and usu. orange-fleshed sweet potato
yank \'yangk\ *n* : a strong sudden pull : JERK — **yank** *vb*
Yank \'yangk\ *n* : YANKEE
Yan·kee \'yang-kē\ *n* : a native or inhabitant of New England, of the northern U.S., or of the U.S. — **Yankee** *adj*
yap \'yap\ *n* : a quick sharp bark : YELP — **yap** *vb*
1**yard** \'yärd\ *n* **1** : any of various units of measure; *esp* : a unit of length equal in the U.S. to 0.9144 meter — see MEASURE table **2** : a long spar tapered toward the ends that supports and spreads the head of a sail
2**yard** *n* **1 a** : a small often enclosed area open to the sky and adjacent to a building **b** : the grounds of a building **2 a** : an enclosure for livestock **b** : an area with its buildings and facilities set aside for a particular activity ⟨a navy *yard*⟩ **c** : a system of railroad tracks for storage and maintenance of cars and making up trains
3**yard** *vb* : to drive into or gather or confine in a yard
yard·age \'yärd-ij\ *n* **1** : a total number of yards **2** : the length, extent, or volume of something as measured in yards
yard·arm \'yärd-,ärm\ *n* : either end of the yard of a square-rigged ship
yard·mas·ter \-,mas-tər\ *n* : the person in charge of a railroad yard
yard·stick \-,stik\ *n* **1** : a measuring stick a yard long **2** : a rule or standard by which something is measured : CRITERION
1**yarn** \'yärn\ *n* **1 a** : textile fiber (as spun wool, cotton, flax, or silk) for use in weaving, knitting, or the manufacture of thread **b** : a strand of material (as metal, glass, or asbestos) for uses comparable to those of a textile yarn **2** : an interesting or exciting often fictitious story
2**yarn** *vb* : to tell a yarn
yar·row \'yar-ō\ *n* : a strong-scented herb related to the daisies that has finely divided leaves and white or rarely pink flowers in flat clusters
yaw \'yȯ\ *vb* : to turn abruptly from a straight course : SWERVE, VEER — **yaw** *n*
yawl \'yȯl\ *n* **1** : a ship's small boat **2** : a fore-and-aft rigged sailboat carrying a mainmast and a mizzenmast far aft

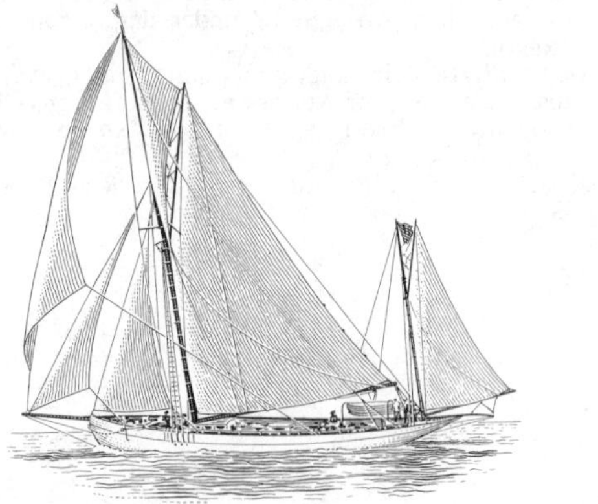

yawl 2

yawn \'yȯn, 'yän\ *vb* **1** : to open wide : GAPE **2** : to open the mouth wide usu. as an involuntary reaction to fatigue or boredom — **yawn** *n* — **yawn·er** *n*
yaws \'yȯz\ *n sing or pl* : a tropical contagious skin disease caused by a spirochete
y–ax·is \'wī-\ *n* : the vertical axis on a graph
Y chromosome *n* : a sex chromosome usu. occurring only in male zygotes and cells — compare X CHROMOSOME
yclept \i-'klept\ *or* **ycleped** \-'klēpt, -'klept\ *adj* [from Middle English, from Old English *geclipod*, past participle of *clipian* "to cry out", "call"] *archaic* : NAMED, CALLED
yd *abbr* yard
1**ye** \(')yē\ *pron, archaic* : YOU 1
2**ye** \yē, yə, *or like* THE\ *definite article, archaic* : THE ⟨*Ye* Olde Gifte Shoppe⟩
1**yea** \'yā\ *adv* **1** : YES — used in oral voting

ə abut	ər further	a back	ā bake	
ä cot, cart	au̇ out	ch chin	e less	ē easy
g gift	i trip	ī life	j joke	ng sing	ō flow
ȯ flaw	ȯi coin	th thin	th this	ü loot
u̇ foot	y yet	yü few	yu̇ furious	zh vision

2 — used to introduce a more explicit or emphatic phrase
[2]**yea** *n* **1 :** an affirmative vote **2 :** a person casting a yea vote
year \'yi(ə)r\ *n* **1 :** the period of one apparent revolution of the sun around the ecliptic or of the earth's revolution around the sun amounting to approximately 365¼ days **2 a :** a period of 365 days or in leap year 366 days beginning January 1 **b :** a period of time equal to this but beginning at a different time ⟨a fiscal *year*⟩ **3 :** a period of time greater or less than the calendar year ⟨a school *year* of nine months⟩
year·book \-ˌbu̇k\ *n* **1 :** a book published yearly **:** ANNUAL **2 :** a school publication recording the history and activities of a graduating class
year·ling \-ling\ *n* **1 :** one that is a year old or in the second year after birth **2 :** a racehorse between January 1st of the year after the year in which it was foaled and the next January 1st — **yearling** *adj*
year·ly \-lē\ *adj* **1 :** occurring, made, done, or produced every year **:** ANNUAL **2 :** computed in terms of one year — **yearly** *adv*
yearn \'yərn\ *vb* **1 :** to feel a longing or craving **2 :** to feel tenderness or sympathy — **yearn·er** *n*
yearn·ing *n* **:** a tender or urgent longing
yeast \'yēst\ *n* **1 a :** a surface froth or a sediment that occurs esp. in sweet liquids in which it promotes alcoholic fermentation and consists largely of cells of a tiny fungus **b :** a commercial product containing yeast plants in a moist or dry medium **c :** any of various tiny fungi that are usu. one-celled and reproduce by budding; *esp* **:** one present and active in a yeast froth or sediment **2 :** foam or spume esp. of waves **3 :** something that causes ferment or activity — **yeasty** \'yē-stē\ *adj*
[1]**yell** \'yel\ *vb* **1 :** to utter a loud cry, scream, or shout **2 :** to give a cheer usu. in unison — **yell·er** *n*
[2]**yell** *n* **1 :** SCREAM, SHOUT **2 :** a usu. rhythmic cheer used esp. in schools or colleges to encourage athletic teams
[1]**yel·low** \'yel-ō\ *adj* **1 a :** of the color yellow **b :** yellowish from age, disease, or discoloration **c :** having a yellow complexion or skin **2 :** COWARDLY — **yellow** *vb* — **yel·low·ness** *n*
[2]**yellow** *n* **1 :** a color like that of ripe lemons **2 :** something yellow or yellowish
yellow fever *n* **:** an acute destructive infectious disease of warm regions marked by yellowness of the skin, intestinal bleeding, and vomiting and caused by a virus transmitted by a mosquito — called also *yellow jack*
yellow–green alga *n* **:** any of a division of algae (as diatoms) with the chlorophyll masked by brown or yellow pigment
yel·low·ham·mer \'yel-ō-ˌham-ər\ *n* **1 :** a common European finch having the male largely bright yellow **2 :** YELLOW-SHAFTED FLICKER
yel·low·ish \'yel-ə-wish\ *adj* **:** somewhat yellow
yellow jack *n* **1 :** YELLOW FEVER **2 :** a flag raised on ships in quarantine
yellow jacket *n* **:** any of various small yellow-marked social wasps that commonly nest in the ground
yel·low·legs \'yel-ō-ˌlegz\ *n sing or pl* **:** either of two American shorebirds with long yellow legs

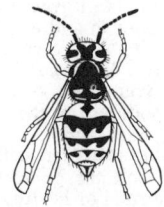

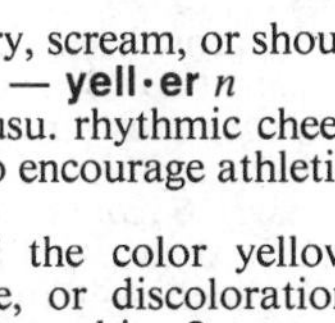
yellow jacket (less than one inch long)

yel·low–shaft·ed flicker \ˌyel-ō-ˌshaf-təd-\ *n* **:** a common large woodpecker of eastern No. America with bright markings including a black crescent on the breast, red nape, white rump, and yellow shafts to the tail and wing feathers — called also *yellowhammer*
yellow warbler *n* **:** a small No. American warbler that is in the male bright yellow with brown streaks on the underparts
yelp \'yelp\ *vb* **:** to utter a sharp quick shrill cry ⟨*yelping* dogs⟩ — **yelp** *n* — **yelp·er** *n*
[1]**yen** \'yen\ *n, pl* **yen** **1 :** the basic monetary unit of Japan **2 :** a coin or note representing one yen
[2]**yen** *n* **:** an intense desire **:** LONGING
yeo·man \'yō-mən\ *n* **1 a :** an attendant in a royal or noble household **b :** a naval petty officer who performs clerical duties **2 :** a small landowning farmer
yeo·man·ly \-lē\ *adj* **:** becoming to a yeoman **:** STURDY, LOYAL
yeo·man·ry \-rē\ *n* **:** a body of yeomen
-yer — see -ER
yer·ba ma·té \ˌyer-bə-'mä-ˌtā, ˌyər-\ *n* **:** MATÉ
[1]**yes** \'yes\ *adv* **1** — used to express assent or agreement ⟨are you ready? *Yes*, I am⟩ **2** — used to introduce correction or contradiction of a negative assertion, direction, or request ⟨don't say that! *Yes*, I will⟩ **3** — used to introduce a more emphatic or explicit phrase ⟨we are glad, *yes*, very glad to see you⟩ **4** — used to indicate interest or attentiveness ⟨*yes*, what is it you want⟩
[2]**yes** *n* **:** an affirmative reply
ye·shi·va *or* **ye·shi·vah** \yə-'shē-və\ *n, pl* **-shivas** *or* **-shivahs** *or* **-shi·voth** \-ˌshē-'vōt(h)\ **1 :** a school for study of the Talmud **2 :** an Orthodox Jewish rabbinical seminary **3 :** a Jewish day school
yes–man \'yes-ˌman\ *n* **:** a person who endorses without criticism every opinion or proposal of a superior
yes/no question *n* **:** a question that requires an answer of either *yes* or *no*
[1]**yes·ter·day** \'yes-tərd-ē\ *adv* **1 :** on the day preceding today **2 :** at a time not long past
[2]**yesterday** *n* **1 :** the day next before the present **2 :** recent time **:** time not long past ⟨fashions of *yesterday*⟩
yes·ter·year \'yes-tər-ˌyi(ə)r\ *n* **1 :** last year **2 :** the recent past
[1]**yet** \(')yet\ *adv* **1 a :** in addition **:** BESIDES ⟨gives *yet* another reason⟩ **b :** EVEN 2b ⟨a *yet* higher speed⟩ **2 a :** up to now **:** so far ⟨hasn't done much *yet*⟩ **b :** at this time **:** so soon as now ⟨not time to go *yet*⟩ **c :** STILL ⟨is *yet* a new country⟩ **d :** EVENTUALLY ⟨may *yet* see the light⟩ **3 :** NEVERTHELESS ⟨strong, *yet* not strong enough⟩
[2]**yet** *conj* **:** despite that fact **:** BUT
yew \'yü\ *n* **1 :** any of a genus of evergreen trees and shrubs with stiff poisonous needles and fleshy fruits **2 :** the wood of a yew; *esp* **:** the heavy fine-grained wood of an Old World yew that is used for bows and small articles
Yid·dish \'yid-ish\ *n* [from Yiddish *yidish*, short for *yidish daytsh*, literally Jewish German, from medieval German *jüdisch diutsch*, from *Jüde* "Jew"] **:** a Germanic language that is spoken by Jews chiefly in eastern Europe and areas to which Jews from eastern Europe have migrated and that is commonly written in Hebrew characters — **Yiddish** *adj*

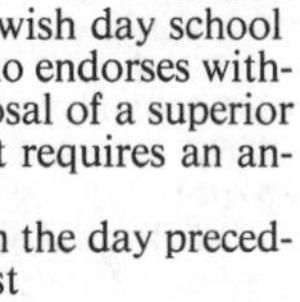
yew 1

[1]**yield** \'yēld\ *vb* **1 :** to give up possession of on claim or demand : SURRENDER **2 :** to give oneself up to an inclination, temptation, or habit **3 a :** to bear as a natural product ⟨trees that *yield* much fruit⟩ **b :** to produce as a result **c :** to furnish as profit or interest ⟨investments that *yield* a good profit⟩ **4 :** to be fruitful or productive **5 :** to give up and cease resistance or contention ⟨the fortress *yielded*⟩ **6 :** to submit to urging, persuasion, or entreaty **7 :** to give way under physical force so as to bend, stretch, or break ⟨the bridge *yielded* under pressure⟩ **8 :** to give place or precedence ⟨*yielded* to the car coming from the right⟩ — **yield·er** *n*

syn YIELD, SUBMIT, SURRENDER can mean to give up or fail to offer resistance to the besetting force that someone or something presents. YIELD applies to any sort or degree of giving way or giving in (as before raw force, argument, persuasion, or entreaty); SUBMIT implies more strongly a conflicting will that overrides one's own wishes or preference ⟨*submitted* to the indignity of arrest⟩; SURRENDER applies to the total yielding of one who by not resisting places himself entirely in the power or at the mercy of another ⟨*surrendered* without a fight⟩

[2]**yield** *n* **:** something yielded : PRODUCT; *esp* **:** the amount or quantity produced or returned ⟨the *yield* of wheat per acre⟩

yield·ing *adj* **1 :** not rigid or stiff : FLEXIBLE ⟨a *yielding* mass⟩ **2 :** inclined to submit : COMPLIANT ⟨a cheerful *yielding* nature⟩

yip \'yip\ *vb* **yipped**; **yip·ping :** YELP — used chiefly of a dog — **yip** *n*

yip·pee \'yip-ē\ *interj* — used to express delight or triumph

-yl \əl, (,)il\ *n comb form* **:** chemical and usu. univalent radical ⟨eth*yl*⟩ ⟨hydrox*yl*⟩

YMCA *abbr* Young Men's Christian Association

YMHA *abbr* Young Men's Hebrew Association

yo·del \'yōd-əl\ *vb* **-deled** *or* **-delled**; **-del·ing** *or* **-del·ling** \-(ə-)liŋ\ **:** to sing by suddenly changing from the natural voice to falsetto and the reverse; *also* **:** to shout or call in this manner — **yodel** *n* — **yo·del·er** \-(ə-)lər\ *n*

yo·ga \'yō-gə\ *n* **1** *cap* **:** a Hindu philosophy teaching the suppression of all activity of body, mind, and will so as to attain liberation from them **2 :** a system of exercises for attaining bodily or mental control and well-being

yo·gi \'yō-gē\ *or* **yo·gin** \-gən\ *n* **1 :** a person who practices yoga **2** *cap* **:** an adherent of Yoga

yo·gurt *or* **yo·ghurt** \'yō-gərt\ *n* **:** a fermented slightly acid semifluid milk food made of skimmed cow's milk and milk solids to which cultures of bacteria have been added

[1]**yoke** \'yōk\ *n, pl* **yokes 1 a :** a wooden bar or frame by which two draft animals (as oxen) are coupled at their necks **b :** a frame fitted to a person's shoulders to carry a load in two equal portions **c :** a clamp or brace that holds or unites two parts **2** *pl usu* **yoke :** two animals yoked together **3 a :** an oppressive force or power **b :** SERVITUDE, BONDAGE **c :** TIE, LINK ⟨the *yoke* of matrimony⟩ **4 :** a fitted or shaped piece at the top of a skirt or at the shoulder

ə abut	ər further	a back	ā bake	
ä cot, cart	au̇ out	ch chin	e less	ē easy
g gift	i trip	ī life	j joke	ŋ sing	ō flow
ȯ flaw	ȯi coin	th thin	t͟h this	ü loot
u̇ foot	y yet	yü few	yu̇ furious	zh vision

[2]**yoke** *vb* **1 a :** to put a yoke on **b :** to couple with a yoke **2 :** to attach (a draft animal) to something **3 :** to join as if by a yoke **4 :** to put to work

yoke·fellow \'yōk-,fel-ō\ *n* **:** a close companion : MATE

yo·kel \'yō-kəl\ *n* **:** RUSTIC, BUMPKIN

yolk \'yōk, 'yōlk\ *n* [from Old English *geoloca*, from *geolu* "yellow"] **1 a :** the yellow inner mass of the egg of a bird or reptile **b :** the material stored in an ovum that supplies food material to the developing embryo **2 :** oily material in raw sheep wool — **yolk** *adj*

Yom Kip·pur \,yōm-'kip-ər, ,yəm-, ,yōm-, -ki-'pu̇(ə)r\ *n* **:** a Jewish holiday observed in September or October with fasting and prayer as a day of atonement

[1]**yon** \'yän\ *adj* **:** YONDER

[2]**yon** *adv* **1 :** YONDER **2 :** THITHER ⟨ran hither and *yon*⟩

yond \'yänd\ *adv, archaic* **:** YONDER

[1]**yon·der** \'yän-dər\ *adv* **:** at or to that place : over there

[2]**yonder** *adj* **1 :** more distant ⟨the *yonder* side of the river⟩ **2 :** being at a distance within view ⟨*yonder* hills⟩

yore \'yō(ə)r, 'yȯ(ə)r\ *n* **:** time long past — usu. used in the phrase *of yore*

you \(')yü, yə, yē\ *pron* **1 :** the one or ones spoken to ⟨can I pour *you* a cup of tea⟩ ⟨*you* are my friends⟩ **2 :** [2]ONE 2 ⟨*you* never know what will happen⟩

you–all \(')yü-'ȯl, 'yȯl\ *pron* **:** YOU — usu. used in addressing two or more persons or sometimes one person as representing also another or others

you'd \(,)yüd, (,)yu̇d, yəd\ **:** you had : you would

you'll \(,)yül, (,)yu̇l, yəl\ **:** you shall : you will

[1]**young** \'yəŋ\ *adj* **young·er** \'yəŋ-gər\; **young·est** \'yəŋ-gəst\ **1 a :** being in the early stage of life, growth, or development **b :** JUNIOR 1 **2 :** INEXPERIENCED **3 :** recently come into being : NEW ⟨*young* rock strata⟩ **4 :** of, relating to, or having the characteristics of youth or a young person ⟨*young* at heart⟩ **5** *cap* **:** belonging to or representing a new or revived usu. political group or movement ⟨*Young* England⟩ — **young·ness** \'yəŋ-nəs\ *n*

[2]**young** *n pl* **1 :** young persons : YOUTH **2 :** immature offspring esp. of lower animals — **with young** : PREGNANT — used of animals

young·est \'yəŋ-gəst\ *n* **:** the least old member esp. of a family

young·ish \'yəŋ-ish\ *adj* **:** somewhat young

young·ling \'yəŋ-liŋ\ *n* **:** a young person or animal — **youngling** *adj*

young·ster \'yəŋ-stər\ *n* **1 :** a young person : YOUTH **2 :** CHILD

youn·ker \'yəŋ-kər\ *n* **:** YOUNGSTER

your \yər, (')yu̇(ə)r, (')yō(ə)r, (')yȯ(ə)r\ *adj* **1 :** of or relating to you or yourself or yourselves ⟨*your* house⟩ ⟨*your* contributions⟩ ⟨*your* discharge⟩ **2 :** of or relating to one ⟨when you face the north, east is at *your* right⟩ **3** — used before a title of honor in address ⟨*your* Majesty⟩ ⟨*your* Honor⟩

you're \yər, (,)yu̇(ə)r, (,)yō(ə)r, (,)yȯ(ə)r\ **:** you are

yours \'yu̇(ə)rz, 'yō(ə)rz, 'yȯ(ə)rz\ *pron* **:** your one : your ones — often used esp. with an adverbial modifier in the complimentary close of a letter ⟨*yours* truly⟩

your·self \yər-'self\ *pron* **1 a :** that one that is you ⟨don't hurt *yourself*⟩ ⟨carry them *yourself*⟩ **b :** your normal or healthy self **2 :** ONESELF

your·selves \-'selvz\ *pron* **1 :** those identical ones that are you **2 :** your normal or healthy selves

youth \'yüth\ *n, pl* **youths** \'yüt͟hz, 'yüths\ **1 :** the time of life marked by growth and development;

esp : the period between childhood and maturity **2 a** : a young man **b** : young persons — usu. pl. in constr. **3** : YOUTHFULNESS

youth·ful \'yüth-fəl\ *adj* **1** : of, relating to, or appropriate to youth **2** : being young and not yet mature **3** : FRESH, VIGOROUS — **youth·ful·ly** \-fə-lē\ *adv* — **youth·ful·ness** *n*

youth hostel *n* : HOSTEL 2

you've \(,)yüv, yəv\ : you have

yowl \'yaůl\ *vb* : to utter a loud long often mournful cry or howl : WAIL — **yowl** *n*

yo-yo \'yō-,yō\ *n, pl* **yo-yos** *also* **yo-yoes** : a thick divided disk that is made to fall and rise to the hand by unwinding and rewinding on a string

yr *abbr* year

yt·ter·bi·um \i-'tər-bē-əm, ə-\ *n* : a metallic element that occurs in several minerals — see ELEMENT table

yt·tri·um \'i-trē-əm\ *n* : a metallic element usu. included among the rare-earth metals with which it occurs in minerals — see ELEMENT table

yu·an \'yü-ən, yů-'än\ *n, pl* **yuan 1** : the basic monetary unit of China **2** : a coin or note representing one yuan

yuc·ca \'yək-ə\ *n* : any of a genus of plants related to the lily and growing in dry regions and having stiff sharp-pointed fibrous leaves at the base and whitish flowers usu. in erect clusters

Yu·go·sla·vi·an \,yü-gō-'släv-ē-ən\ *adj* [from Serbian *Jugoslavija* "Yugoslavia", literally "land of the South Slavs, from *jug* "south"] : of, relating to, or characteristic of Yugoslavia or its people — **Yugoslavian** *n*

yule \'yül\ *n, often cap* : CHRISTMAS

yule log *n, often cap Y* : a large log formerly put on the hearth on Christmas Eve as the foundation of the fire

yule·tide \'yül-,tīd\ *n, often cap* : the Christmas season

yum·my \'yəm-ē\ *adj* : highly attractive or pleasing esp. in taste

yurt \'yů(ə)rt\ *n* : a light round tent of skins or felt used by nomadic tribes in Siberia

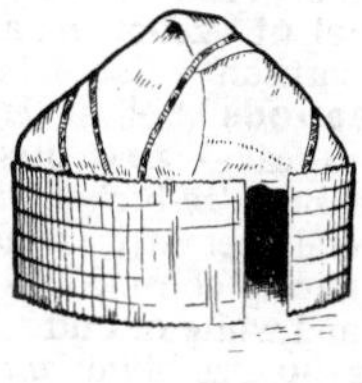
yurt

YWCA *or* **YW** *abbr* Young Women's Christian Association

Y

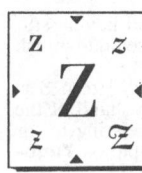

z \'zē\ *n, often cap* : the 26th letter of the English alphabet
z *abbr* zero
[1]**za·ny** \'zā-nē\ *n, pl* **zanies** [from Italian *zanni*, from *Zanni* "Johnny", a dialect form of nickname for Italian *Giovanni* "John"] **1** : CLOWN, BUFFOON **2** : SIMPLETON
[2]**zany** *adj* **za·ni·er**; **-est** : resembling, being, or characteristic of a zany — **za·ni·ly** \-nə-lē\ *adv* — **za·ni·ness** \-nē-nəs\ *n*
zap *vb, slang* : HIT; *esp* : SHOOT
zeal \'zēl\ *n* : ardent eagerness in pursuit of something : FERVOR
zeal·ot \'zel-ət\ *n* : a zealous person; *esp* : a fanatical partisan
zeal·ous \'zel-əs\ *adj* : filled with, marked by, or due to zeal — **zeal·ous·ly** *adv* — **zeal·ous·ness** *n*
ze·bra \'zē-brə\ *n, pl* **zebras** *also* **zebra** : any of several fleet African mammals related to the horse and having conspicuous stripes of black or dark brown and white or buff
ze·bu \'zē-b(y)ü\ *n* : an Asiatic domesticated ox distinguished from European cattle with which it crosses freely by a large fleshy hump over the shoulders and a loose skin prolonged into dewlap and folds

zebu
(about 6 ft. at shoulder)

Zech·a·ri·ah \ˌzek-ə-'rī-ə\ *n* — see BIBLE table
zed \'zed\ *n, chiefly Brit* : the letter *z*
ze·nith \'zē-nəth\ *n* **1** : the point in the heavens directly overhead **2** : the highest point : SUMMIT ⟨the *zenith* of a hero's glory⟩
ze·o·lite \'zē-ə-ˌlīt\ *n* : any of various silicates chemically related to the feldspars that are used esp. in water softening — **ze·o·lit·ic** \ˌzē-ə-'lit-ik\ *adj*
Zeph·a·ni·ah \ˌzef-ə-'nī-ə\ *n* — see BIBLE table
zeph·yr \'zef-ər\ *n* **1 a** : a breeze from the west **b** : a gentle breeze **2** : a fine soft yarn or fabric
zep·pe·lin \'zep-(ə-)lən\ *n* : a rigid airship consisting of a cylindrical covered framework supported by internal gas cells
[1]**ze·ro** \'zē-rō, 'zi(ə)r-ō\ *n, pl* **zeros** *also* **zeroes** [from Italian, from medieval Latin *zephirum* (the source also of English *cipher*), from Arabic *ṣifr*, from *ṣifr* "empty"] **1 a** : the numerical symbol 0 **b** : the number represented by the symbol 0 — see NUMBER table **2 a** : a point (as on a graduated scale) from which reckonings are made **b** : a value or reading of zero; *esp* : the temperature represented by the zero mark on a thermometer **3** : something of no importance : NONENTITY **4** : the lowest point : NADIR
[2]**zero** *adj* **1 a** : of, relating to, or being a zero **b** : having no modified inflectional form ⟨*zero* plural⟩ **2 a** : limiting vision to 50 feet or less ⟨*zero* cloud ceiling⟩ **b** : limited to 165 feet or less ⟨*zero* visibility⟩
[3]**zero** *vb* : to aim or adjust fire on a target — usu. used with *in*
zero hour *n* **1** : the hour at which a military operation is scheduled to start **2** : a moment of crisis
zest \'zest\ *n* **1** : a quality of enhancing enjoyment **2** : keen enjoyment : RELISH — **zest·ful** \-fəl\ *adj* — **zest·ful·ly** \-fə-lē\ *adv* — **zest·ful·ness** *n* — **zesty** \'zes-tē\ *adj*
ze·ta \'zāt-ə\ *n* : the 6th letter of the Greek alphabet — Z or ζ
[1]**zig·zag** \'zig-ˌzag\ *n* **1** : a line or course made up of frequent sharp angles or turns **2** : a road, path, or line that takes a zigzag course **3** : one of the units making up a zigzag ⟨the road followed a *zigzag* around the obstruction⟩
[2]**zigzag** *adv* : in or by a zigzag path or course
[3]**zigzag** *adj* : having short sharp turns or angles
[4]**zigzag** *vb* **zig·zagged**; **zig·zag·ging** : to lie in, proceed along, or consist of a zigzag course
zil·lion \'zil-yən\ *n* : a large indeterminate number
zinc \'zingk\ *n* : a bluish white metallic element that tarnishes only slightly in moist air at ordinary temperatures and is used esp. as a protective coating for iron — see ELEMENT table
zinc chloride *n* : a poisonous caustic deliquescent salt used esp. in fireproofing and preserving wood
zinc·ite \'zing-ˌkīt\ *n* : a brittle deep-red to orange-yellow mineral consisting of zinc oxide that occurs in massive or granular form
zinc ointment *n* : an ointment containing about 20 percent of zinc oxide and used in treating skin diseases
zinc oxide *n* : a white substance used esp. as a pigment, in compounding rubber, and in medicinal and cosmetic preparations
zinc sulfide *n* : a fluorescent compound used as a white pigment and as the light-producing substance in fluorescent lamps and television tubes
zinc white *n* : a white pigment used esp. in house paints and glazes that consists of zinc oxide
zinj·an·thro·pus \zin-'jan(t)-thrə-pəs, ˌzin-ˌjan-'thrō-\ *n, pl* **-pi** \-ˌpī, -ˌpē\ *or* **-pus·es** : any of a genus of fossil relatives of man based on a skull found in eastern Africa, characterized by very low brow and large molars, and tentatively assigned to the Lower Pleistocene
zin·nia \'zin-ē-ə\ *n* : any of a small genus of tropical American herbs related to the daisies and having showy flower heads with long-lasting ray flowers
[1]**zip** \'zip\ *vb* **zipped**; **zip·ping** **1** : to move or act with speed and vigor **2** : to travel with a sharp hissing or humming sound **3** : to add zest, interest, or life to — often used with *up*
[2]**zip** *n* **1** : a sudden sharp hissing or sibilant sound **2** : ENERGY, VIM
[3]**zip** *vb* **zipped**; **zip·ping** : to close or open with a zipper
zip code *n* : a 5-digit number that identifies each postal delivery area in the U.S.
zip gun *n* : a homemade gun powered by a rubber band
zipped \'zipt\ *adj* : bearing a zip code ⟨*zipped* mail⟩
zip·per \'zip-ər\ *n* : a fastener consisting of two rows of metal or plastic teeth on strips of tape and a sliding piece that closes an opening by drawing the teeth together — **zip·pered** \-ərd\ *adj*
zip·py \'zip-ē\ *adj* **zip·pi·er**; **-est** : full of zip : BRISK, SNAPPY
zir·con \'zər-ˌkän\ *n* **1** : a crystalline mineral which is a silicate of zirconium and of which several trans-

parent varieties are used as gemstones **2 :** a gem cut from zircon

zir·co·ni·um \ˌzər-ˈkō-nē-əm\ *n* **:** a steel-gray strong ductile metallic element with a high melting point that is highly resistant to corrosion and is used in alloys and ceramics — see ELEMENT table

zith·er \ˈzith-ər, ˈzith-\ *n* **:** a many-stringed musical instrument played with the tips of the fingers and a plectrum

zither

zlo·ty \zə-ˈlȯt-ē\ *n, pl* **zlo·tys** \-ēz\ *also* **zloty 1 :** the basic monetary unit of Poland **2 :** a coin representing one zloty

zo·di·ac \ˈzōd-ē-ˌak\ *n* [from Greek *zōidiakos*, from *zōidion* "carved figure", "sign of the zodiac", diminutive of *zōion* "animal"] **1 :** an imaginary belt in the heavens that includes the apparent paths of all the principal planets except Pluto, that has as its central line the apparent path of the sun, and that is divided into 12 constellations or signs **2 :** a figure representing the signs of the zodiac — **zo·di·a·cal** \zō-ˈdī-ə-kəl\ *adj*

THE SIGNS OF THE ZODIAC

NUMBER	NAME	SYMBOL	SUN ENTERS
1	Aries the Ram	♈	March 21
2	Taurus the Bull	♉	April 20
3	Gemini the Twins	♊	May 21
4	Cancer the Crab	♋	June 22
5	Leo the Lion	♌	July 23
6	Virgo the Virgin	♍	August 23
7	Libra the Balance	♎	September 23
8	Scorpio the Scorpion	♏	October 24
9	Sagittarius the Archer	♐	November 22
10	Capricorn the Goat	♑	December 22
11	Aquarius the Water Bearer	♒	January 20
12	Pisces the Fishes	♓	February 19

zom·bi *or* **zom·bie** \ˈzäm-bē\ *n* **:** a will-less and speechless human being capable only of automatic movement who is held to have died and been brought back to life

zon·al \ˈzōn-əl\ *adj* **:** of, relating to, or having the form of a zone

[1]**zone** \ˈzōn\ *n* [from Greek *zōnē*, literally "belt", "girdle"] **1 :** any of five great divisions of the earth's surface with respect to latitude and temperature **2 a :** an encircling anatomical structure **b :** a distinctive belt, layer, or series of layers of earth materials (as rock) **3 :** a region or area set off from surrounding or adjoining parts; *esp* **:** any of the eight bands of territory centered on a U.S. parcel-post shipment point to which mail is charged at a single rate

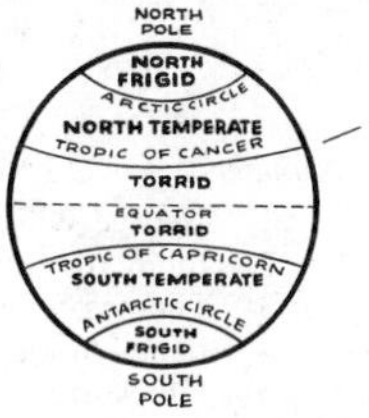

zones 1

[2]**zone** *vb* **:** to divide into zones; *esp* **:** to divide (as a city) into sections reserved for different purposes

zoo \ˈzü\ *n, pl* **zoos :** ZOOLOGICAL GARDEN

zool *abbr* **1** zoological **2** zoology

zoological garden *n* **:** a garden or park where wild animals are kept for exhibition

zo·ol·o·gy \zō-ˈäl-ə-jē\ *n* **1 :** a branch of biology concerned with the animal kingdom and animal life **2 a :** animal life **:** FAUNA **b :** the biological properties of an animal, animal type, or group — **zo·o·log·i·cal** \ˌzō-ə-ˈläj-i-kəl\ *adj* — **zo·o·log·i·cal·ly** \-i-k(ə-)lē\ *adv* — **zo·ol·o·gist** \-jəst\ *n*

[1]**zoom** \ˈzüm\ *vb* **1 :** to move with a loud low hum or buzz **2 :** to climb for a short time at a steep angle **3 a :** to photograph or televise using a special lens that permits the apparent distance of the object to be varied ⟨the camera *zoomed* closer and closer⟩ **b :** to cause to zoom

[2]**zoom** *n* **1 :** an act or process of zooming **2 :** a zooming sound

zoo·phyte \ˈzō-ə-ˌfīt\ *n* **:** any of numerous invertebrate animals (as a coral, sea anemone, or sponge) suggesting plants in appearance or mode of growth — **zoo·phyt·ic** \ˌzō-ə-ˈfit-ik\ *adj*

zoo·plank·ton \ˌzō-ə-ˈplang(k)-tən, -ˌtän\ *n* **:** animal life of the plankton — **zoo·plank·ton·ic** \-ˌplang(k)-ˈtän-ik\ *adj*

Zo·ro·as·tri·an \ˌzōr-ə-ˈwas-trē-ən, ˌzȯr-\ *adj* **:** of or relating to the Persian prophet Zoroaster or the religion founded by him and marked by belief in a cosmic war between good and evil — **Zoroastrian** *n* — **Zo·ro·as·tri·an·ism** \-trē-ə-ˌniz-əm\ *n*

zounds \ˈzau̇n(d)z\ *interj* — used as a mild oath

zuc·chi·ni \zü-ˈkē-nē\ *n, pl* **-ni** *or* **-nis :** a summer squash of bushy growth with smooth slender cylindrical dark green fruits

zwie·back \ˈswē-ˌbak, ˈswī-\ *n* **:** a usu. sweet bread enriched with eggs that is baked and then sliced and toasted until dry and crisp

zy·gote \ˈzī-ˌgōt\ *n* **:** a cell formed by the union of two sex cells; *also* **:** the developing individual produced from such a cell — **zy·got·ic** \zī-ˈgät-ik\ *adj*

PRESIDENTS OF THE U.S.A.

Number	*Name and Pronunciation of Surname*	*Life Dates*	*Birthplace*	*Term*
1	George Washington \'wȯsh-ing-tən, 'wäsh-\	1732–1799	Virginia	1789–1797
2	John Adams \'ad-əmz\	1735–1826	Massachusetts	1797–1801
3	Thomas Jefferson \'jef-ər-sən\	1743–1826	Virginia	1801–1809
4	James Madison \'mad-ə-sən\	1751–1836	Virginia	1809–1817
5	James Monroe \mən-'rō\	1758–1831	Virginia	1817–1825
6	John Quincy Adams \'ad-əmz\	1767–1848	Massachusetts	1825–1829
7	Andrew Jackson \'jak-sən\	1767–1845	South Carolina	1829–1837
8	Martin Van Buren \van-'byu̇r-ən\	1782–1862	New York	1837–1841
9	William Henry Harrison \'har-ə-sən\	1773–1841	Virginia	1841
10	John Tyler \'tī-lər\	1790–1862	Virginia	1841–1845
11	James Knox Polk \'pōk\	1795–1849	North Carolina	1845–1849
12	Zachary Taylor \'tā-lər\	1784–1850	Virginia	1849–1850
13	Millard Fillmore \'fil-ˌmō(ə)r, -ˌmȯ(ə)r\	1800–1874	New York	1850–1853
14	Franklin Pierce \'pi(ə)rs\	1804–1869	New Hampshire	1853–1857
15	James Buchanan \byu̇-'kan-ən, bə-\	1791–1868	Pennsylvania	1857–1861
16	Abraham Lincoln \'ling-kən\	1809–1865	Kentucky	1861–1865
17	Andrew Johnson \'jän(t)-sən\	1808–1875	North Carolina	1865–1869
18	Ulysses Simpson Grant \'grant\	1822–1885	Ohio	1869–1877
19	Rutherford Birchard Hayes \'hāz\	1822–1893	Ohio	1877–1881
20	James Abram Garfield \'gär-ˌfēld\	1831–1881	Ohio	1881
21	Chester Alan Arthur \'är-thər\	1830–1886	Vermont	1881–1885
22	Grover Cleveland \'klēv-lənd\	1837–1908	New Jersey	1885–1889
23	Benjamin Harrison \'har-ə-sən\	1833–1901	Ohio	1889–1893
24	Grover Cleveland \'klēv-lənd\	1837–1908	New Jersey	1893–1897
25	William McKinley \mə-'kin-lē\	1843–1901	Ohio	1897–1901
26	Theodore Roosevelt \'rō-zə-ˌvelt, -vəlt\	1858–1919	New York	1901–1909
27	William Howard Taft \'taft\	1857–1930	Ohio	1909–1913
28	Woodrow Wilson \'wil-sən\	1856–1924	Virginia	1913–1921
29	Warren Gamaliel Harding \'härd-ing\	1865–1923	Ohio	1921–1923
30	Calvin Coolidge \'kü-lij\	1872–1933	Vermont	1923–1929
31	Herbert Clark Hoover \'hü-vər\	1874–1964	Iowa	1929–1933
32	Franklin Delano Roosevelt \'rō-zə-ˌvelt, -vəlt\	1882–1945	New York	1933–1945
33	Harry S Truman \'trü-mən\	1884–	Missouri	1945–1953
34	Dwight David Eisenhower \'ī-zən-ˌhau̇(-ə)r\	1890–1969	Texas	1953–1961
35	John Fitzgerald Kennedy \'ken-əd-ē\	1917–1963	Massachusetts	1961–1963
36	Lyndon Baines Johnson \'jän(t)-sən\	1908–	Texas	1963–1969
37	Richard Milhous Nixon \'nik-sən\	1913–	California	1969–

VICE-PRESIDENTS OF THE U.S.A.

Number	*Name and Pronunciation of Surname*	*Life Dates*	*Birthplace*	*Term*
1	John Adams \'ad-əmz\	1735–1826	Massachusetts	1789–1797
2	Thomas Jefferson \'jef-ər-sən\	1743–1826	Virginia	1797–1801
3	Aaron Burr \'bər\	1756–1836	New Jersey	1801–1805
4	George Clinton \'klint-ən\	1739–1812	New York	1805–1812
5	Elbridge Gerry \'ger-ē\	1744–1814	Massachusetts	1813–1814
6	Daniel D. Tompkins \'täm(p)-kənz\	1774–1825	New York	1817–1825
7	John C. Calhoun \kal-'hün\	1782–1850	South Carolina	1825–1832
8	Martin Van Buren \van-'byu̇r-ən\	1782–1862	New York	1833–1837
9	Richard M. Johnson \'jän(t)-sən\	1780–1850	Kentucky	1837–1841
10	John Tyler \'tī-lər\	1790–1862	Virginia	1841
11	George M. Dallas \'dal-əs\	1792–1864	Pennsylvania	1845–1849
12	Millard Fillmore \'fil-,mō(ə)r, -,mȯ(ə)r\	1800–1874	New York	1849–1850
13	William R. King \'king\	1786–1853	North Carolina	1853
14	John C. Breckinridge \'brek-ən-(,)rij\	1821–1875	Kentucky	1857–1861
15	Hannibal Hamlin \'ham-lən\	1809–1891	Maine	1861–1865
16	Andrew Johnson \'jän(t)-sən\	1808–1875	North Carolina	1865
17	Schuyler Colfax \'kōl-,faks\	1823–1885	New York	1869–1873
18	Henry Wilson \'wil-sən\	1812–1875	New Hampshire	1873–1875
19	William A. Wheeler \'hwē-lər\	1819–1887	New York	1877–1881
20	Chester A. Arthur \'är-thər\	1830–1886	Vermont	1881
21	Thomas A. Hendricks \'hen-driks\	1819–1885	Ohio	1885
22	Levi P. Morton \'mȯrt-ən\	1824–1920	Vermont	1889–1893
23	Adlai E. Stevenson \'stē-vən-sən\	1835–1914	Kentucky	1893–1897
24	Garret A. Hobart \'hō-,bärt\	1844–1899	New Jersey	1897–1899
25	Theodore Roosevelt \'rō-zə-,velt, -vəlt\	1858–1919	New York	1901
26	Charles W. Fairbanks \'fa(ə)r-,bang(k)s, 'fe(ə)r-\	1852–1918	Ohio	1905–1909
27	James S. Sherman \'shər-mən\	1855–1912	New York	1909–1912
28	Thomas R. Marshall \'mär-shəl\	1854–1925	Indiana	1913–1921
29	Calvin Coolidge \'kü-lij\	1872–1933	Vermont	1921–1923
30	Charles G. Dawes \'dȯz\	1865–1951	Ohio	1925–1929
31	Charles Curtis \'kərt-əs\	1860–1936	Kansas	1929–1933
32	John N. Garner \'gär-nər\	1868–1967	Texas	1933–1941
33	Henry A. Wallace \'wäl-əs\	1888–1965	Iowa	1941–1945
34	Harry S Truman \'trü-mən\	1884–	Missouri	1945
35	Alben W. Barkley \'bär-klē\	1877–1956	Kentucky	1949–1953
36	Richard M. Nixon \'nik-sən\	1913–	California	1953–1961
37	Lyndon B. Johnson \'jän(t)-sən\	1908–	Texas	1961–1963
38	Hubert H. Humphrey \'həm(p)-frē\	1911–	South Dakota	1965–1969
39	Spiro T. Agnew \'ag-n(y)ü\	1918–	Maryland	1969–

THE STATES OF THE U.S.A.

Name and Pronunciation	*State Capital and Pronunciation*
Alabama \ˌal-ə-ˈbam-ə\	Montgomery \mənt-ˈgəm-(ə-)rē\
Alaska \ə-ˈlas-kə\	Juneau əˈjü-nō\
Arizona \ˌar-ə-ˈzō-nə\	Phoenix \ˈfē-niks\
Arkansas \ˈär-kən-ˌsȯ\	Little Rock \ˈlit-əl-ˌräk\
California \ˌkal-ə-ˈfȯr-nyə\	Sacramento \ˌsak-rə-ˈment-ō\
Colorado \ˌkäl-ə-ˈrad-ō, -ˈräd-\	Denver \ˈden-vər\
Connecticut \kə-ˈnet-i-kət\	Hartford \ˈhärt-fərd\
Delaware \ˈdel-ə-ˌwa(ə)r, -ˌwe(ə)r\	Dover \dō-vər\
Florida \ˈflȯr-əd-ə, ˈflär-\	Tallahassee \ˌtal-ə-ˈhas-ē\
Georgia \ˈjȯr-jə\	Atlanta \ət-ˈlant-ə\
Hawaii \hə-ˈwä-(y)ē, -ˈwī-(y)ē, -ˈwȯ-(y)ē\	Honolulu \ˌhän-ə-ˈlü-lü, ˌhōn-\
Idaho \ˈīd-ə-ˌhō\	Boise \ˈbȯi-sē, -zē\
Illinois \ˌil-ə-ˈnȯi\	Springfield \ˈspring-ˌfēld\
Indiana \ˌin-dē-ˈan-ə\	Indianapolis \ˌin-dē-ə-ˈnap-(ə-)les\
Iowa \ˈī-ə-wə\	Des Moines \di-ˈmȯin\
Kansas \ˈkan-zəs\	Topeka \tə-ˈpē-kə\
Kentucky \kən-ˈtək-ē\	Frankfort \ˈfrangk-fərt\
Louisiana \lu̇-ˌē-zē-ˈan-ə, ˌlü-ə-zē-\	Baton Rouge \ˌbat-ən-ˈrüzh\
Maine \ˈmān\	Augusta \ȯ-ˈgəs-tə, ə-\
Maryland \ˈmer-ə-lənd\	Annapolis \ə-ˈnap-(ə-)ləs\
Massachusetts \ˌmas-ə-ˈchü-səts\	Boston \ˈbȯ-stən\
Michigan \ˈmish-i-gən\	Lansing \ˈlan(t)-sing\
Minnesota \ˌmin-ə-ˈsōt-ə\	St. Paul \sānt-ˈpȯl\
Mississippi \ˌmis-ə-ˈsip-ē\	Jackson \ˈjak-sən\
Missouri \mə-ˈzu̇r-ē, -ə\	Jefferson City \ˌjef-ər-sən-\
Montana \män-ˈtan-ə\	Helena \ˈhel-ə-nə\
Nebraska \nə-ˈbras-kə\	Lincoln \ˈling-kən\
Nevada \nə-ˈvad-ə, -ˈväd-\	Carson City \ˌkär-sən-\
New Hampshire \-ˈham(p)-shər, -ˌshi(ə)r\	Concord \ˈkäng-kərd\
New Jersey \-ˈjər-zē\	Trenton \ˈtrent-ən\
New Mexico \-ˈmek-si-ˌkō\	Santa Fe \ˌsant-ə-ˈfā\
New York \-ˈyȯrk\	Albany \ˈȯl-bə-nē\
North Carolina \-ˌkar-ə-ˈlī-nə\	Raleigh \ˈrȯl-ē, ˈräl-ē\
North Dakota \-də-ˈkōt-ə\	Bismarck \ˈbiz-ˌmärk\
Ohio \ō-ˈhī-ō\	Columbus \kə-ˈləm-bəs\
Oklahoma \ˌō-klə-ˈhō-mə\	Oklahoma City
Oregon \ˈȯr-i-gən, ˈär-\	Salem \ˈsā-ləm\
Pennsylvania \ˌpen(t)-səl-ˈvā-nyə\	Harrisburg \ˈhar-əs-ˌbərg\
Rhode Island \rō-ˈdī-lənd\	Providence \ˈpräv-əd-ən(t)s, -ə-ˌden(t)s\
South Carolina \-ˌkar-ə-ˈlī-nə\	Columbia \kə-ˈləm-bē-ə\
South Dakota \-də-ˈkōt-ə\	Pierre \ˈpi(ə)r\
Tennessee \ˌten-ə-ˈsē\	Nashville \ˈnash-ˌvil, -vəl\
Texas \ˈtek-səs, -siz\	Austin \ˈȯs-tən, ˈäs-\
Utah \ˈyü-tȯ, -tä\	Salt Lake City \ˌsȯlt-ˌlāk-ˈsit-ē\
Vermont \vər-ˈmänt\	Montpelier \mänt-ˈpēl-yər\
Virginia \vər-ˈjin-yə\	Richmond \ˈrich-mənd\
Washington \ˈwȯsh-ing-tən, ˈwäsh-\	Olympia \ə-ˈlimp-ē-ə, ō-\
West Virginia \-vər-ˈjin-yə\	Charleston \ˈchärl-stən\
Wisconsin \wis-ˈkän(t)-sən\	Madison \ˈmad-ə-sən\
Wyoming \wī-ˈō-ming\	Cheyenne \shī-ˈan, -ˈen\

THE PROVINCES OF CANADA

Name and Pronunciation	*Provincial Capital and Pronunciation*
Alberta \al-ˈbərt-ə\	Edmonton \ˈed-mən-tən\
British Columbia \-kə-ˈləm-bē-ə\	Victoria \vik-ˈtōr-ē-ə, -ˈtȯr-\
Manitoba \ˌman-ə-ˈtō-bə\	Winnipeg \ˈwin-ə-ˌpeg\
New Brunswick \-ˈbrenz-(ˌ)wik\	Fredericton \ˈfred-(ə-)rik-tən\
Newfoundland \ˈn(y)ü-fən-lənd, -ˌland\	St. John's \sānt-ˈjänz\
Nova Scotia \ˌnō-və-ˈskō-shə\	Halifax \ˈhal-ə-ˌfaks\
Ontario \än-ˈter-ē-ˌō\	Toronto \tə-ˈränt-ō\
Prince Edward Island \-ˌed-wərd-\	Charlottetown \ˈshär-lət-ˌtau̇n\
Quebec \kwi-ˈbek\	Quebec
Saskatchewan \sə-ˈskach-ə-wən\	Regina \ti-ˈjī-nə\

NATIONS OF THE WORLD

Name and Pronunciation	*Location*
Afghanistan \af-'gan-ə-ˌstan\	Asia
Albania \al-'bā-nē-ə\	Europe
Algeria \al-'jir-ē-ə\	Africa
Andorra \an-'dȯr-ə, -'där-ə\	Europe
Argentina \ˌär-jən-'tē-nə\	South America
Australia \ȯ-'strāl-yə, ä-\	Between Indian and Pacific Oceans
Austria \'ȯs-trē-ə, 'äs-\	Europe
Bahrein \bä-'rān\	Asia
Barbados \bär-'bād-əs, -äs\	West Indies
Belgium \'bel-jəm\	Europe
Bhutan \bü-'tan, -'tän\	Asia
Bolivia \bə-'liv-ē-ə\	South America
Botswana \bät-'swän-ə\	Africa
Brazil \brə-'zil\	South America
Bulgaria \ˌbəl-'gar-ē-ə, bu̇l-, -'ger-\	Europe
Burma \'bər-mə\	Asia
Burundi \bu̇-'rün-dē\	Africa
Cambodia \kam-'bōd-ē-ə\	Asia
Cameroon \ˌkam-ə-'rün\	Africa
Canada \'kan-əd-ə\	North America
Central African Republic \-'af-ri-kən-\	Africa
Ceylon \si-'län, sā-\	Asia
Chad \'chad\	Africa
Chile \'chil-ē\	South America
China \'chī-nə\	Asia
Colombia \kə-'ləm-bē-ə\	South America
Congo Republic (formerly Middle Congo) \'käng-go-\	Africa
Costa Rica \ˌkäs-tə-'rē-kə, ˌkȯs-, ˌkōs-\	Central America
Cuba \'kyü-bə\	West Indies
Cyprus \'sī-prəs\	Eastern Mediterranean
Czechoslovakia \ˌchek-ə-slō-'väk-ē-ə, -'vak-\	Europe
Dahomey \də-'hō-mē\	Africa
Denmark \'den-ˌmärk\	Europe
Dominican Republic \də-ˌmin-i-kən-\	West Indies
Ecuador \'ek-wə-ˌdȯr\	South America
Egypt, Arab Republic of \-'ē-jəpt\	Africa and Asia
El Salvador \el-'sal-və-ˌdȯr\	Central America
Equatorial Guinea \-'gin-ē\	Africa
Ethiopia (Abyssinia) \ˌē-thē-'ō-pē-ə (ˌab-ə-'sin-ē-ə, -'sin-yə)\	Africa
Fiji \'fē-(ˌ)je\	Southwest Pacific
Finland \'fin-lənd\	Europe
France \'fran(t)s\	Europe
Gabon \ga-ˌbōn\	Africa
Gambia \'gam-bē-ə\	Africa
Germany \'jər-mə-nē\	Europe
Ghana \'gän-ə\	Africa
Greece \'grēs\	Europe
Guatemala \ˌgwät-ə-'mäl-ə\	Central America
Guinea \'gin-ē\	Africa
Guyana \gī-'an-ə\	South America
Haiti \'hāt-ē\	West Indies
Honduras \hän-'d(y)u̇r-əs\	Central America
Hungary \'həng-gə-rē\	Europe
Iceland \'īs-lənd, -ˌland\	North Atlantic Ocean
India \'in-dē-ə\	Asia
Indonesia \ˌin-də-'nē-zhə\	Asia
Iran (Persia) \i-'ran, -'rän ('pər-zhə)\	Asia
Iraq \i-'rak, -'räk\	Asia
Ireland, Republic of \-'ī(ə)r-lənd\	Europe
Israel \'iz-rē-əl\	Asia
Italy \'it-ə-lē\	Europe
Ivory Coast \'īv-(ə-)rē-\	Africa
Jamaica \jə-'mā-kə\	West Indies
Japan \jə-'pan\	Asia
Jordan \'jȯrd-ən\	Asia
Kenya \'ken-yə, 'kēn-\	Africa
Korea \kə-'rē-ə\	Asia
Kuwait \kə-'wāt\	Asia
Laos \'lau̇s, 'lä-ōs\	Asia
Lebanon \'leb-ə-nən\	Asia
Lesotho \lə-'sō-tō\	Africa
Liberia \lī-'bir-ē-ə\	Africa
Libya \'lib-ē-ə\	Africa
Liechtenstein \'lik-tən-ˌs(h)tīn\	Europe
Luxembourg \'lu̇k-səm-ˌbu̇rg, 'lək-səm-ˌbərg\	Europe
Malagasy Republic \ˌmal-ə-ˌgas-ē-\	Africa
Malawi \mə-'lä-wē\	Africa
Malaysia \mə-'lā-zh(ē-)ə\	Asia
Maldive Islands \'mal-ˌdīv-, 'mȯl-\	Indian Ocean
Mali \'mäl-ē\	Africa
Malta \'mȯl-tə\	Central Mediterranean
Mauritania \ˌmȯr-ə-'tā-nē-ə, ˌmär-\	Africa
Mauritius \mȯ-'rish-(ē-)əs\	Indian Ocean
Mexico \'mek-si-ˌkō\	North America
Monaco \'män-ə-ˌkō\	Europe
Mongolian People's Republic \män(g)-'gōl-yən-\	Asia
Morocco \mə-'räk-ō\	Africa
Nauru \nä-'ü-(ˌ)rü\	South Pacific
Nepal \nə-'pȯl\	Asia
Netherlands \'neth-ər-lən(d)z\	Europe
New Zealand \-'zē-lənd\	Southwest Pacific
Nicaragua \ˌnik-ə-'räg-wə\	Central America
Niger \'nī-jər\	Africa
Nigeria \nī-'jir-ē-ə\	Africa
Norway \'nȯr-ˌwā\	Europe
Oman \ō-'män\	Asia
Pakistan \ˌpak-i-'stan, ˌpäk-i-'stän\	Asia
Panama \'pan-ə-ˌmä, -ˌmȯ\	Central America

Nations of the World

Name and Pronunciation	*Location*
Paraguay \'par-ə-ˌgwī, -ˌgwā\	South America
Peru \pə-'rü\	South America
Philippines \'fil-ə-ˌpēnz, ˌfil-ə-'\	Asia
Poland \'po-lənd\	Europe
Portugal \'pōr-chi-gəl, 'pór-\	Europe
Qatar \'kät-ər\	Asia
Romania \rú-'mā-nē-ə, rō-\	Europe
Rwanda \rú-'än-də\	Africa
San Marino \ˌsan-mə-'rē-nō\	Europe
Saudi Arabia \ˌsaùd-ē-ə-'rā-bē-ə, sä-ˌùd-ē-\	Asia
Senegal \ˌsen-i-'gól\	Africa
Sierra Leone \sē-ˌer-ə-lē-'ōn\	Africa
Singapore \'sing-(g)ə-ˌpō(ə)r, -ˌpó(ə)r\	Asia
Somalia \sō-'mäl-ē-ə\	Africa
South Africa, Republic of	Africa
Southern Yemen \-'yem-ən\	Asia
Spain \'spān\	Europe
Sudan \sü-'dan\	Africa
Swaziland \'swäz-ē-ˌland\	Africa
Sweden \'swēd-ən	Europe
Switzerland \'swit-sər-lənd\	Europe
Syria \'sir-ē-ə\	Asia
Tanzania \ˌtan-zə-'nē-ə\	Africa
Thailand (Siam) \'tī-ˌland, -lənd (sī-'am)\	Asia

Name and Pronunciation	*Location*
Togo \'tō-gō\	Africa
Trinidad and Tobago \'trin-ə-ˌdad-ən-tə-'bā-gō\	West Indies
Tunisia \t(y)ü-'nē-zhə, -'nizh-ə\	Africa
Turkey \'tər-kē\	Asia and Europe
Uganda \(y)ü-'gan-də\	Africa
Union of Soviet Socialist Republics (U.S.S.R.) \-'sō-vē-ˌet-, -ət-, 'säv-ē- (ˌyü-ˌes-ˌes-ˌär)\	Asia and Europe
United Kingdom of Great Britain and Northern Ireland \-'brit-ən . . . 'ī(ə)r-lənd\	Europe
England \'ing-glənd\	
Northern Ireland	
Scotland \'skät-lənd\	
Wales \'wālz\	
United States of America \-ə-'mer-ə-kə\	North America
Upper Volta \-'väl-tə, -'vōl-\	Africa
Uruguay \'(y)ùr-ə-ˌgwī, 'yùr-ə-ˌgwā\	South America
Vatican City State \'vat-i-kən-\	Europe
Venezuela \ˌven-ə-zə-'wā-lə, -'wē-\	South America
Vietnam \vē-'et-'näm, -'nam\	Asia
Western Samoa \-sə-'mō-ə\	South Pacific
Yemen \'yem-ən\	Asia
Yugoslavia \ˌyü-gō-'släv-ē-ə\	Europe
Zaïre \zä-i(ə)r\	Africa
Zambia \'zam-bē-ə\	Africa

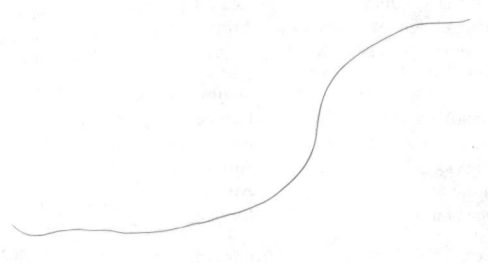

ARBITRARY SIGNS AND SYMBOLS

ASTRONOMY

● new moon

☽, ◐, ☽, ☽ first quarter

○ *or* ☺ full moon

☾, ◑, ☾, ☾ last quarter

BIOLOGY

① *or* ⊙ annual plant

② *or* ⊙ biennial plant

♃ perennial herb

♄ tree or shrub

♀ female

♂ male

× crossed with; hybrid; magnified by

= equals

BUSINESS

@ at; each ⟨4 apples @ 5¢ = 20¢⟩

℔ per ⟨sheep $4 ℔ head⟩

number if it precedes a numeral ⟨track #3⟩; pounds if it follows ⟨a 5# sack of sugar⟩

lb pound; pounds

% percent

‰ per thousand

$ *or* $ dollars

¢ cents

£ pounds

/ shillings

© copyrighted

® registered trademark

MATHEMATICS

+ plus; positive ⟨a + b = c⟩

− minus; negative

± plus or minus ⟨the square root of $4a^2$ is ±2a⟩; more or less than ⟨an error of ±2⟩

× multiplied by; times ⟨6 × 4 = 24⟩ —also indicated by placing a dot between the numbers ⟨6 · 4 = 24⟩

÷ *or* : divided by ⟨24 ÷ 6 = 4⟩ —also indicated by writing the divisor under the dividend with a line between ⟨$\frac{24}{6} = 4$⟩ or by writing the divisor after the dividend with a diagonal between ⟨3/8⟩

⊕ plus—used to indicate addition with a base other than 10 and esp. a base of 12

⊖ minus—used to indicate subtraction with a base other than 10 and esp. a base of 12

⊗ multiplied by—used to indicate multiplication with a base other than 10 and esp. a base of 12

= equals ⟨6 + 2 = 8⟩

≠ *or* ≠ is not equal to

> is greater than ⟨6 > 5⟩

< is less than ⟨3 < 4⟩

≧ *or* ≥ is greater than or equal to

≦ *or* ≤ is less than or equal to

≯ is not greater than

≮ is not less than

≈ is approximately equal to

: is to; the ratio of

0 zero

∠ angle; the angle ⟨∠ABC⟩

∟ right angle ⟨∟ABC⟩

⊥ the perpendicular; is perpendicular to ⟨AB ⊥ CD⟩

∥ parallel; is parallel to ⟨AB ∥ CD⟩

√ *or* √ square root ⟨as in √4 = 2⟩

( ) parentheses, [ ] brackets, { } braces — indicate that the quantities enclosed by them are to be taken together

π pi; the number 3.14159265+; the ratio of the circumference of a circle to its diameter

° degree ⟨60°⟩

′ minute; foot ⟨30′⟩

″ second, inch ⟨30″⟩

^{2}, ^{3}, etc.—used as exponents placed above and at the right of an expression to indicate that it is raised to a power indicated by the figure ⟨a^2, the square of a⟩

n —used as an unspecified number

∪ union of two sets

∩ intersection of two sets

⊂ is included in, is a subset of

⊃ contains as a subset

∈ *or* ϵ is an element of

∉ is not an element of

Λ *or* o *or* ∅ *or* { } empty set

⊙ *or* ○ circle

△ triangle

□ square

▭ rectangle

MISCELLANEOUS

& and

&c et cetera; and so forth

† died—used esp. in genealogies

☧ monogram from Greek XP signifying Jesus

LXX Septuagint

✡ Star of David

✻ —used in Roman Catholic and Anglican service books to divide each verse of a psalm indicating where the response begins

✠ *or* + —used in some service books to indicate where the sign of the cross is to be made: also used by certain Roman Catholic and Anglican prelates as a sign of the cross preceding their signatures

fl or f: relative aperture of a photographic lens

☠ poison

℞ take—used on prescriptions

 civil defense

☢ radioactive

MUSIC

staff with notes—whole note, half note, quarter, eighth, sixteenth; a dot after a note adds to it half the length of the note without the dot

𝄞 G clef; treble clef—used to indicate that the second line represents the first G above middle C

𝄢 F clef; bass clef—used to indicate that the fourth line represents the first F below middle C

♯ sharp

♭ flat

♮ natural—used to annul the effect of a previous ♯ or ♭; the *sharps* or *flats* placed at the beginning of a composition or section are called collectively the *key signature*

𝄪 *or* ※ double sharp—used to raise a note two half steps

𝄫 double flat—used to lower a note two half steps

 repeat—used to indicate the beginning and end respectively of a passage to be played or sung twice

 crescendo

 decrescendo: diminuendo

 swell

 rests—whole, half, quarter, eighth, & sixteenth

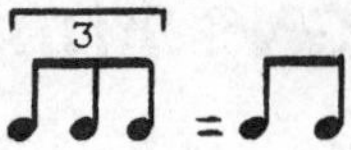

Triplet—three notes grouped together under a curved line or bracket. The three notes have a total duration that two of those notes would ordinarily receive.

$\frac{2}{4}$ two counts per measure

$\frac{3}{4}$ three counts per measure

$\frac{4}{4}$ four counts per measure

$\frac{5}{4}$ five counts per measure

$\frac{6}{8}$ six counts per measure

$\frac{12}{8}$ twelve counts per measure

common time: four counts per measure

cut time: two counts per measure

Dal Segno (D.S.)—repeat from the sign

Fermata—hold, pause

Sforzato—strong accent

Staccato—shorten value of note and substitute a rest

Tenuto—give full value to note

< *Marcato*—accent, marked

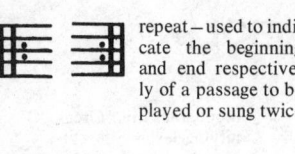